SUPERFORM

Races &

Racehorses

Flat Edition

**Results, Ratings and Commentaries
for Flat Racing, Turf and All Weather
from Nov 10th 2003 - Nov 6th 2004**

Sixtieth Annual

www.superform.com

Foreword

Welcome to the 60th and largest ever Superform Annual. The ever expanding fixture list means that we have covered over three hundred races more than last season and have reached the maximum size of annual that is practical to print. As a consequence the first 917 races (up to the start of the turf season) are covered in a results only fashion. We appreciate that this is not ideal, but feel this is the only way to produce the annual without moving to two editions.

2004 was no more than an average season on most fronts. Champion middle-distance accolade goes to Doyen (130) thanks to a highly impressive three length King George win. Sulamani (126) ran with credit all season and ended his career on a high with wins in the Group 1 Juddmonte and the Canadian International. Bago (128) finally lived up to connections expectations when sweeping to victory in the Arc, from the arguably unlucky Ouija Board. Dual Oaks winner Ouija Board (123) had a fantastic season and went on to land the Fillies and Mares race at the Breeders' Cup, she will make her presence felt in all the top middle-distance races next year. Derby winner North Light (123) failed to fire in two subsequent starts before returning to form in the Arc.

The sprint division was particularly lacking in any depth. Former American sprinter and Abbaye winner Var (121), and Haydock Sprint Cup second Somnus (121), shared top honours. The Tatling (120) kept his form all summer and posted fine weight carrying wins in Group 2 and 3 company before a second successive placed run in the Abbaye. Evergreen nine year old Bahamian Pirate (119) landed his first Group 1 success in the Nunthorpe - a fine effort, but proof of the dearth of top-class sprinters.

2000 Guineas winner Haafhd (126) returned to form in late season to land the Champion Stakes, and take the 1m/10f honours. Rakti (125) can race too freely, but is top-class and won a couple of Group 1's at Ascot. Attraction (121) confirmed her top-class juvenile form when landing the 1000 Guineas. She went on to win three further Group 1 contests, but had to give best both times she faced the equally tough and top-class Soviet Song (122).

Westerner (122) won four staying Group races on his favoured soft ground at Longchamp (including two Group 1's). He is clearly high-class on fast ground too, as shown when runner-up in the Ascot Gold Cup, but had to give best that day to Papineau (123) who shares the staying crown with Irish St Leger winner and Melbourne Cup runner-up Vinnie Roe (123). Tribute must also be made to Persian Punch who paid the ultimate price after entertaining us most gallantly for nearly a decade.

Several highly promising juveniles came to the fore this year, notably Shamardal (122), Ad Valorem (121), Dubawi (121), Motivator (120) and Divine Proportions (119). Shamardal destroyed the field in the Champagne Stakes/Dewhurst and is a Champion juvenile of immense potential. Ad Valorem won the Middle Park and looks the best of Aidan O'Brien's typically strong team, while the filly Divine Proportions won a brace of Group 1's and is the pick of the French juveniles. Dubawi is from the first crop of Dubai Millennium and should be at his best next season over middle-distances, while Motivator justified stable confidence when landing the Racing Post Trophy on only his second start and looks a serious Derby prospect.

Godolphin stepped up their operation in the UK this year and as a consequence Saeed bin Suroor topped the trainers title (based on prize money) and Frankie Dettori regained his jockey title from Kieren Fallon, who has had several off track problems. Many of the big yards struggled for consistency this year - Mick Channon, Barry Hills and John Dunlop all posted significantly smaller totals than last season. However, Richard Fahey, David Evans and Kevin Ryan all had excellent seasons and once again Sir Mark Prescott topped the winning percentage list. The excellent Seb Sanders recorded his highest win total to date, while R Moore and N Callan confirmed themselves near the top of their profession - both recording well in excess of one hundred winners.

Best of luck for the new season from all at Superform.

Contents

Publisher Kevin Gilroy thanks the following for their
tremendous help in the compilation of this annual.

D Caiels	D Mitchell
A Clouder	T Mummery
J Craven	M Olley
M Green	D Scholey
J Jenkins	P Towning
R Johnson	V Gilroy
J Limb	C Woods

Photographs by Alec Russell, Huttons Ambo, York.

Front cover (paperback only)
Lord Derby's top-class filly, Ouija Board (K Fallon) winning the Vodafone Oaks at Epsom.

Printed In Finland
Published by Furlong Press, High St, Shoreham, West Sussex.
Copyright Furlong Press 2004

Superform Champions Of 2004

5f	*Var 5 h*	*Mohammed Rashid, C E Brittain*	**121**
6f	*Tante Rose 4 f*	*Mr B E Nielsen, R Charlton*	**120**
7f	*Somnus 4 g*	*Legard Sidebottom, T D Easterby*	**121**
8f	*Haafhd 4 c*	*Mr Hamdan Al Maktoum, B W Hills*	**126**
10f	*Sulamani 5 h*	*Godolphin, Saeed Bin Suroor*	**126**
11f	*Ouija Board 3 f*	*Lord Derby, E A L Dunlop*	**123**
12f	*Doyen 4 c*	*Godolphin, Saeed Bin Suroor*	**130**
13f	*Mubtaker 7 h*	*Mr Hamdan Al Maktoum, M P Tregoning*	**123**
14f	*Rule Of Law 4 c*	*Godolphin, Saeed Bin Suroor*	**122**
16f	*Vinnie Roe*	*S Sheridan, P J Smullen*	**123**
20f	*Papineau 4 c*	*Godolphin, Saeed Bin Suroor*	**123**
2yo	*Shamardal 2 c*	*Gainsborough Stud, M Johnston*	**122**

Introduction

The race results in this book include every horse in each race in Britain. The principal foreign races are also included. The results and commentaries are published in weekly parts throughout the season under the title of "Superform".

WHY IS SUPERFORM DIFFERENT?

Our mission at Superform is not simply to report the results but to interpret them. Race results/form have little meaning unless the reader can grasp the value or worth of the form. Why is the form of one handicap, maiden or stakes race likely to prove better than another? Superform performance ratings, calculated on at least the first ten in every race, pin-point the likely worth of the form. Superform performance ratings are printed horse by horse, race by race. **These ratings are revised daily throughout the season** by six professional handicappers who strive to provide the most accurate ratings possible.

There are other vital aspects of form study which the bare results do not reveal. If a horse runs badly, our comment writers search for the likely cause, when it runs well they pin-point the conditions which favour success. Without a lot of page thumbing (sometimes through more than one book) race results give no indication of where or when a horse has won in the past. Superform now lists any wins and second placings in the past two years for each horse within each detailed commentary. The optimum going, distance and track preferences for each horse are written up in full and we make particular note of long absences from the track. Trainer changes are pin-pointed, along with all-weather debuts. The bare results do not indicate whether a horse is likely to be suited by a longer distance or whether a newcomer is closely related to high class performers. Only a study of breeding can reveal this potential. Such research is time consuming and the tools of reference are costly. Superform comment writers do all this to save you valuable time!

CHARACTER COMMENTARIES

To obtain a character summary simply refer to the horse's last race. This race will either provide the summary or point out where the latest summary is printed with the reference "see ---". Our aim is to give each horse a full commentary plus breeding, then on further runs add any new information with a reference back to the full commentary.

Example full commentary:

1407+ **KRIS KIN 30** [4] Sir Michael Stoute 3-9-0 K Fallon 6/1: 01-11: ch c Kris S - Angel In My Heart (Rainbow Quest) Mid-div, prog 3f out, switched dist, drvn & strong run to lead cl home: supplemented for 90,000, fast time, massive gamble from 12/1: stays 12f well on firm & soft, any trk: fast improving, top-class colt & given a fine ride here: open to further improvement & can win more Gr 1 races: see 1407.
1 May'03 Ches 10.3g/f 110-86 A: 1 Oct'02 Donc 7sft 89– D:

RACE TIMES AND THE GOING

A single race time reveals little. It's meaningful only when compared with some standard or average. Consistent methods must then be used to evaluate the condition of the track. Superform produces **pace and going figures** which pin-point fast run races and reflect the condition of the track, on the day. Often our "going" figures differ from the official going report supplied by the racecourse. More information on pace and going figures appear on page 1951.

STARTING PRICES

Starting prices are included not for the purpose of settling bets, but as a **guide** to the relative chance of each horse, expressed by the bookmakers at the track, on the day.

RATINGS

The Superform ratings published here reflect the judgement of our own handicappers, and the ratings are presented on the international 0-140 scale, as used by the official BHB handicappers. In the A-Z style index at the back of the book, you can see at a glance the Superform performance rating, race by race for each horse, for the whole of last season. For future races we normally base our calculations on the best rating the horse achieved in it's last three races. Often you discover a higher rating when searching back through a horse's form. The successful use of ratings often involves pin-pointing just which rating to use for your calculations. For example, with a seasoned handicapper, it may be prudent to use an earlier, higher rating, if the ground suddenly alters in the horse's favour or the horse returns to form. However, ratings achieved within the previous 40 days are the most reliable. Full information on how to use Superform ratings appears on page 1950.

OFFICIAL RATINGS

In handicaps and non-handicaps, the official BHB rating of each horse is printed in brackets after the horse's weight. In the race title in handicap races, in the right hand margin, the figure in brackets represents the official rating of a horse set to carry 10-0. If the figure is 70, the horse carrying 10-0 is rated officially 70. A horse carrying 8-8 is rated 50 officially.

FAST TIME HORSES "+ -"

Horses which win in a fast time of **10 Fast** or more are marked with a **+ sign** instead of the usual asterisk. Second placed horses, beaten 2 lengths or less in a similarly fast time are marked --. These symbols are placed after the race reference number. Fuller explanation of the pace and going figures can be found on page 1951.

COURSE REQUIREMENTS

In the race results we describe the type of race and note the prize money for the winner. The distance of each race, the prevailing going and the pace of the race are also noted. At the beginning of each race meeting there is a brief comment on the course characteristics. Many sharp tracks like Chester and Epsom produce real course specialists.

WEIGHTS__"ex__ow__oh" AND APPRENTICE ALLOWANCES

Regarding the weights shown in the results, these are the weights (plus overweights) allotted to the horse by the race conditions or the handicapper. We do not subtract riders' allowances. The rider's allowance is however, noted in brackets. Penalties are marked **ex: ow** signifies overweight and **oh** notes that the horse was carrying more than the long handicap weight originally set by the handicapper.

LONG HANDICAP WEIGHTS__"oh"

Handicaps are compiled from the highest rated horse downwards. The top-weight is usually set to carry 10-0. As the minimum weight in a Flat handicap is normally 7-12, any horse rated more than 30 pounds below the top-weight must still carry the minimum weight of 7-12 - not the weight originally allotted by the handicapper. It is the originally allotted weight which is known as the **long handicap weight**. A horse may originally be set 7-0 by the handicapper, but on the day must carry the minimum weight of 7-12 and is therefore said to be **12lbs out of the handicap.**

DRAW

The draw for stall position is in [ ] after the horses name. When facing a set of starting stalls, draw position one is on the right-hand side and progresses from right to left. In many races under 1m in distance we make note of any particular draw advantages alongside the prize money at the start of a race.

Reading Superform

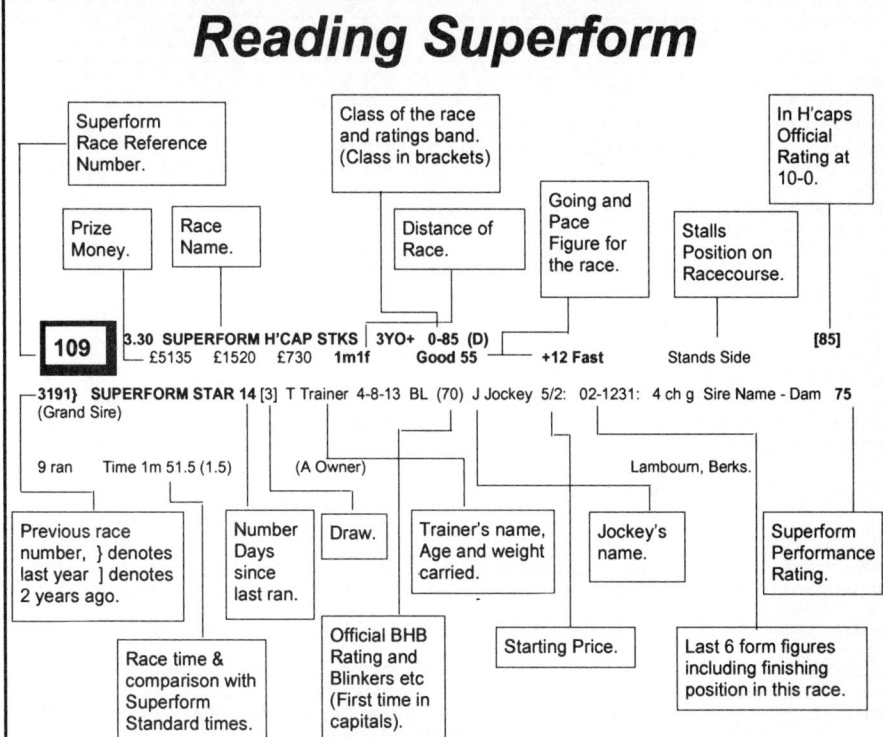

Superform Race Reference Number.

Class of the race and ratings band. (Class in brackets)

In H'caps Official Rating at 10-0.

Prize Money.

Race Name.

Distance of Race.

Going and Pace Figure for the race.

Stalls Position on Racecourse.

109   3.30 SUPERFORM H'CAP STKS | 3YO+ 0-85 (D)   [85]
         £5135   £1520   £730   **1m1f**   **Good 55**   **+12 Fast**   Stands Side

3191} SUPERFORM STAR 14 [3] T Trainer 4-8-13 BL (70) J Jockey 5/2: 02-1231: 4 ch g Sire Name - Dam 75
(Grand Sire)

9 ran   Time 1m 51.5 (1.5)   (A Owner)   Lambourn, Berks.

Previous race number, } denotes last year] denotes 2 years ago.

Number Days since last ran.

Draw.

Trainer's name, Age and weight carried.

Jockey's name.

Superform Performance Rating.

Race time & comparison with Superform Standard times.

Official BHB Rating and Blinkers etc (First time in capitals).

Starting Price.

Last 6 form figures including finishing position in this race.

Notes:

GOING FIGURES And PACE FIGURES:

For each race meeting, from the race times we calculate a "going allowance" which gives a fairly accurate picture of what the ground was like - this sometimes differs from the official going description! A pace figure is also calculated which indicates the pace at which each race was run. Fast and slow run races can be seen at a glance. There is a full explanation of the going and pace calculations at the back of the annual.

PREVIOUS RACE REFERENCE:

If the horse is running for the first time in the current season, the race reference in Superform is printed with a } after the number for last season and a] for two seasons ago.

NUMBER OF DAYS SINCE RAN:

We believe this feature is very important. You are immediately aware how long the horse has been off the track since it's last run. Any period over 40 days usually needs some explanation. The horse might have had a problem in training or the going might have been unsuitable.

FORM FIGURES:

The last six form figures are shown for each runner, the right-hand figure being the finishing position in the current race. When assessing form you can see quickly whether the winner beat consistent, improving types, previous winners, or horses with strings of "duck eggs".

OFFICIAL BHB RATING:

This is the official rating awarded by the BHB handicapper going into the race. It is usually referred to as the mark the horse "runs off". The higher the rating, the better the horse. 140 is the top of the ratings range and 40 and below, the bottom.

Index To Flat Race Meetings By Race Number

Continued on page 1936

Official Going STANDARD.

1

12.45 Littlewoods Bet Direct Aw Jockeys Championship Nursery Handicap Stakes 2yo 0-75 (E) [82]

£2093 £598 £299   6f f/sand rnd   Going 36   -21 Slow   Stalls Inside

4618} MAUNBY RAVER 35 [6] P C Haslam 2-8-1 (55) Rory Moore (7) 12/1: 06641: Held up, hdwy inner halfway, led over 1f out, drvn out:		69a
4487} BRIDGEWATER BOYS 44 [8] K A Ryan 2-8-4 bl (58) G Duffield 10/1: 2302562: Sn prom, ev ch fnl 2f, rider drpd whip over 1f out, kept on well ins last:	½	69a
4594} EMARADIA 37 [4] P D Evans 2-8-0 (54) Joanna Badger 14/1: 4205623: Led 1f, rem prom, onepce.	4	53a
4610} LITTLE EYE 35 [5] J R Best 2-8-11 (65) N Pollard 16/1: 0640004: Stumbled start & bhd, kept on wide, nrst fin:	nk	63a
4959} PICCLEYES 10 [7] R Hannon 2-8-11 (65) P Dobbs 9/1: 0526035: Prom, outpcd fnl 2f.	shd	63a
4973} GREEN RIDGE 9 [9] P W D'Arcy 2-9-3 (71) J F Egan 9/2-FAV: 2506: Handy, btn/edged left over 1f out:	hd	68a
4636} EMBASSY LORD 34 [10] J O'Reilly 2-8-6 bl (60) J D O'Reilly 16/1: 6221507: Led after 1f, hdd over 1f out when hung left, sn btn:	shd	57a
4578} CREWES MISS ISLE 38 [12] A G Newcombe 2-9-7 (75) S Whitworth 14/1: 2156428: Bhd, eff wide, no impress, eased.	1	69a
4874} BIRIKINA 17 [11] A Berry 2-8-3 (57) P Mathers (3) 25/1: 6000009: Slow away & al outpcd.	1	48a
4822} BAJAN STORM 20 [3] M Blanshard 2-8-7 BL (61) F Norton 20/1: 2603200: Sn rdn & struggling:	3	43a
4892} TREGARRON 16 [2] R Hannon 2-8-8 (62) Dane O'Neill 5/1: 2426000: Sn bhd.	nk	43a
4941} EASILY AVERTED 12 [1] J A Osborne 2-9-6 (74) S W Kelly 13/2: 0241300: Prom, btn 2f out:	2	49a
4997} COMPASSION 6 [13] Miss L A Perratt 2-8-9 (63) S Hitchcott (3) 10/1: 0254450: Chsd ldrs, strugg hway:	6	22a
13 Ran 1m 16.21 (3.41) Owner Maunby Investment Management		Trained at Middleham

2

1.15 Betdirect Co Uk Handicap Stakes Div 1 3yo+ 0-85 (D) [85]

£3318 £948 £474   1m100y f/sand rnd   Going 36   +11 Fast   Stalls Inside

4977} CARDINAL VENTURE 9 [6] K A Ryan 5-9-9 (80) R Winston 7/2-FAV: 5322001: Made all, rdn clr 2f out, eased cl-home,		91a
4818*} SPARK UP 21 [10] J W Unett 3-8-5 bl (64) M Henry 6/1: 0040612: Chsd wnr, rdn & no impress fnl 2f:	7	64a
4673} COUNTYKAT 30 [2] K R Burke 3-9-4 vis (77) Darren Williams 11/2: 22-55363: Chsd ldrs trav well, rdn & onepace fnl 2f:	hd	76a
4778} CHERISHED NUMBER 24 [3] I Semple 4-8-10 (67) G Duffield 5/1: 1634004: Held up, no prog fnl 2f.	4	58a
4593} GLORY QUEST 37 [7] Miss Gay Kelleway 6-9-1 (72) L Enstone (3) 6/1: 2106545: Rear, not pace to chall:	1	61a
3138} MIDDLETON GREY 108 [8] A G Newcombe 5-10-0 (85) S Whitworth 12/1: 5203606: Rear, btn 2f out:	12	54a
4818} YMLAEN 21 [9] B Palling 3-9-0 (73) M Fenton 50/1: 0-066007: Well bhd, tkn wide & little prog.	1½	39a
4967} BELLA BEGUINE 9 [4] A Bailey 4-8-12 bl (69) C Catlin 8/1: 3010028: Chsd ldr 3f, btn over 2f out:	2	31a
2685} SURDOUE 128 [5] P Howling 3-9-8 (81) Lisa Jones (3) 20/1: 0-005009: Keen/prom 4f:	17	14a
9 Ran 1m 48.32 (2.12) Owner Mr Tony Fawcett		Trained at Hambleton

3

1.50 Littlewoods Bet Direct Aw Trainers Championship Maiden Stakes 2yo (D)

£3021 £863 £432   6f f/sand rnd   Going 36   -06 Slow   Stalls Inside

4941} POMPEY BLUE 12 [10] P J McBride 2-8-9 (71) N Callan 5/2-FAV: 23551: Handy & led 2f out, edged left & styd on well, rdn		69a
COLOUR CODE [2] M P Tregoning 2-9-0 A Daly 10/1: 2: Dwelt, rear, hdwy halfway & styd on for press, not pace to chall:	1¾	68a
4923} BOND BROOKLYN 13 [13] B Smart 2-9-0 VIS (67) R Ffrench 6/1: 0552353: Sn handy, kept on onepace for press in first time visor.	nk	67a
4636} BLUE POWER 34 [4] K R Burke 2-9-0 (59) Darren Williams 33/1: 0044: Led till 2f out, no extra.	1½	62a
4823} PICK OF THE CROP 20 [11] J R Jenkins 2-9-0 (73) S W Kelly 7/1: 40525: Mid-div, not pace to chall ldrs.	hd	61a
DOCKLANDS BLUE [9] N P Littmoden 2-8-9 I Mongan 13/2: 6: Prom till over 2f out on debut.	6	40a
VITTORIOSO [6] Miss Gay Kelleway 2-9-0 P M Fenton 33/1: 7: Held up, nvr pace to threaten:	2½	37a
4559} KING OF MUSIC 39 [3] G Prodromou 2-9-0 Dane O'Neill 9/2: 358: Slow away, switched wide & nvr dngr:	½	35a
5014} INTIKRAFT 4 [1] Mrs S A Liddiard 2-9-0 vis (68) C Catlin 25/1: 0006209: Prom 4f:	½	33a
4965} MASAFI 9 [5] Sir Mark Prescott 2-9-0 G Duffield 25/1: 000: Prom early, sn outpcd:	¾	31a
4937} DIAL SQUARE 12 [8] P Howling 2-9-0 S Drowne 16/1: 00: Sn outpcd & bhd.	2½	23a
2439} BRAVE CHIEF 137 [12] J A Pickering 2-9-0 S Whitworth 50/1: 00: Hung badly right, sn well bhd.	10	0
5013} SONNE DE LOUP 4 [7] Mrs S A Liddiard 2-8-9 F Norton 100/1: 00: Prom till halfway, qck reapp.	dht	0
13 Ran 1m 15.31 (2.51) Owner Mrs Joan Langmead		Trained at Newmarket

4

2.25 Littlewoods Bet Direct Maiden Stakes Div 1 3yo (D)

£2310 £660 £330   7f f/sand rnd   Going 36   +01 Fast   Stalls Outside

4913} PERFECT NIGHT 14 [7] R Charlton 3-8-9 (67) S Drowne 8/11-FAV: 0220221: Led/dsptd lead, went on halfway & asserted dist, rdn out:		72a
4460} ZAGALA 45 [9] S L Keightley 3-8-9 T (55) R Winston 9/1: 44-63002: Chsd ldrs, rdn & chsd wnr over 2f out, kept on but held	5	61a
4136} DANGER BIRD 62 [10] R Hollinshead 3-8-9 (53) A Culhane 16/1: 5-320053: Held up, eff to chase ldr over 2f out, sn no impress:	4	51a
4849} SHAMWARI FIRE 19 [6] I W McInnes 3-9-0 (52) Natalia Gemelova (7) 6/1: 0005244: In tch, btn 1f out.	5	48a
4712} BAHAMIAN BELLE 28 [3] J Balding 3-8-9 bl (52) J Edmunds 20/1: 6523405: Keen & prom, btn over 1f out:	1¾	40a
NICHOLAS NICKELBY [4] N P Littmoden 3-9-0 I Mongan 11/1: 6: Dwelt, sn rdn & al bhd:	4	37a
4901} ABANINETOES 14 [2] P D Evans 3-8-9 (44) N Callan 100/1: 0-000007: Led 3f, btn 2f out.	3	26a
HARRY TU [5] Miss Gay Kelleway 3-9-0 B Fayos Martin (7) 20/1: 8: Dwelt & al bhd on debut.	¾	30a
2680} SWEET TALKING GIRL 128 [1] J M Bradley 3-8-9 P Fitzsimons 50/1: 659: Chsd ldrs, struggling halfway:	23	0a
EASY BREEZE [8] J M Bradley 3-9-0 L Keniry (3) 100/1: 0: Sn bhd, t.o. on debut.	2½	0a
10 Ran 1m 28.66 (2.46) Owner Perfect Night Partnership		Trained at Beckhampton

5

3.00 Betdirect Co Uk Handicap Stakes Div 2 3yo+ 0-85 (D) [84]

£3308 £945 £473   1m100y f/sand rnd   Going 36   -04 Slow   Stalls Inside

4591} LAKOTA BRAVE 37 [8] Mrs S A Liddiard 9-9-10 (80) S Drowne 8/1: 2104331: Held up, hdwy 2f out, styd on for press to lead		87a

cl-home, gamely:

5017}	**SHATIN HERO 4** [2] Miss L A Perratt 3-7-13 p (57) R Ffrench 7/1: 5341442: Trkd ldrs, led 3f out, drvn & hdd cl-home:	nk	63a
4735}	**JUST WIZ 27** [5] N P Littmoden 7-9-1 bl (71) J P Guillambert (3) 8/1: 1045053: Held up, drvn & kept on.	1½	74a
4767*}	**SHOTACROSS THE BOW 25** [10] M Blanshard 6-8-10 (66) F Norton 5/1: 2600414: Held up, smooth hdwy to chall 3f out, sn rdn & onepace:	1¼	66a
3150}	**CRUSOE 108** [6] A Sadik 6-8-11 (67) Lisa Jones (3) 7/1: 3010535: Cl-up, rdn & no extra over 1f out:	¾	66a
4597}	**ULYSEES 32** [4] I Semple 4-9-1 (71) G Duffield 12/1: 5000066: Prom, btn over 2f out:	5	61a
4919}	**ZILCH 13** [9] M L W Bell 5-9-9 (79) I Mongan 8/1: 0403-007: Held up, eff 3f out, sn btn:	½	68a
4950}	**SWIFT ALCHEMIST 11** [7] K R Burke 3-9-1 (73) G Baker 8/1: 4052008: Led till 3f out, sn btn.	2½	57a
5021}	**BRESSBEE 4** [3] J W Unett 5-9-8 vis (78) Dane O'Neill 9/2: 1100039: Held up, btn 2f out:	9	45a
4591}	**ZARIN 37** [1] D W Chapman 5-9-5 (75) A Culhane 25/1: 2030060: Prom, struggling fnl 3f.	1¾	39a

10 Ran 1m 49.61 (3.41) Owner Valley Fencing — Trained at Hungerford

---

6 3.35 Bet Direct Freephone 0800 32 93 93 Classified Stakes 3yo+ 0-60 (F)
£2100 £600 £300 1m4f f/sand Going 36 -14 Slow Stalls Inside

5019}	**SMOOTHIE 4** [1] Ian Williams 5-9-4 (60) C Catlin 4/1 JT FAV: 0001661: Held up, rdn to chase ldr over 2f out, led ins last, all out, gamely:		64a
5010}	**EASIBET DOT NET 5** [4] I Semple 3-8-12 p (58) G Duffield 5/1: 0443232: Dwelt, sn trkd ldrs, pushed along early, hdwy to lead 4f out, drvn & hdd ins last, kept on:	½	62a
4855}	**GERI ROULETTE 19** [3] E J Alston 5-9-1 (51) J Carroll 14/1: 3166003: Trkd ldrs, briefly led 4f out, btn when no room over 2f out:	14	44a
4724*}	**PARADISE VALLEY 28** [5] Mrs S A Liddiard 3-8-12 t (54) S Drowne 14/1: 6302514: Held up, hdwy 5f out, no threat to front pair.	2	44a
4828}	**IPLEDGEALLEGIANCE 20** [9] D W Chapman 7-9-4 (50) A Culhane 13/2: 6050045: Held up, nvr land blow:	2½	40a
5010}	**PEARSON GLEN 5** [2] G A Swinbank 4-9-4 (58) R Winston 7/1: 52-00546: Prom, btn 3f out:	nk	39a
4817}	**QUEENSBERRY 21** [7] J O'Reilly 4-9-4 vis (55) J D O'Reilly (7) 7/1: 3033027: Al bhd.	½	38a
4918}	**NIMBUS TWOTHOUSAND 13** [12] P R Wood 3-8-9 bl (48) D Corby (3) 33/1: 4560508: Handy & chsd ldr over 4f out, wknd qckly over 2f out.	¾	34a
4828}	**AMANPURI 20** [8] Miss Gay Kelleway 5-9-4 e (52) B Fayos Martin (7) 33/1: 023-0009: Al bhd in eye-shield.	3	33a
4318}	**INTERSTICE 53** [11] A G Newcombe 6-9-4 (58) S Whitworth 4/1 JT FAV: 2003000: Rear, brief eff 4f out.	13	18a
4970}	**EUROLINK ARTEMIS 9** [10] Miss Gay Kelleway 6-9-1 bl e T (52) M Fenton 25/1: 0620000: Led till 4f out.	9	4a

11 Ran 2m 39.55 (5.95) Owner Miss S Howell — Trained at Alvechurch

---

7 4.10 Littlewoodscasino Com Handicap Stakes 3yo+ 0-70 (E) [66]
£2065 £590 £295 2m46y f/sand Going 36 -32 Slow Stalls Inside

4817*}	**VIN DU PAYS 21** [7] M Blanshard 3-9-5 (66) N Callan 11/2: 0005511: Held up, hdwy halfway & led 3f out, styd on gamely, drvn out:		73a
3405}	**DIGGER 96** [12] Miss Gay Kelleway 4-9-13 t (65) L Enstone (3) 14/1: 3132002: In tch, keen early, smooth hdwy to chall over 2f out, no extra ins last:	1½	70a
4620}	**MYSTERIUM 35** [9] N P Littmoden 9-8-2 vis (40) G Gibbons 9/1: 0-505003: Bhd, styd on for press fnl 2f.	5	40a
4740}	**PRINCE OF THE WOOD 27** [11] A Bailey 3-7-13 (46) C Catlin 20/1: 0200064: In tch, no impress fnl 3f.	7	39a
4819*}	**HIGH POLICY 21** [2] R Hollinshead 7-10-0 p (66) Stephanie Hollinshead (7) 4/1 FAV: 0613015: Held up, no impress.	2	57a
4918}	**MELOGRANO 13** [3] R M Beckett 3-7-13 (46) J Mackay 14/1: 0006036: Cl-up, led 5f out, hdd 3f out, no extra.	1½	36a
5001}	**SPITTING IMAGE 6** [4] Mrs M Reveley 3-9-3 (64) A Culhane 5/2: 2420247: In tch, btn 4f out:	6	48a
4931}	**WORLABY DALE 13** [5] Mrs S Lamyman 7-8-8 (46) R Thomas (5) 9/2: 0233348: Dwelt, sn bhd, mod prog:	3	27a
4938}	**GOLDEN FIELDS 12** [8] A P Jones 3-8-4 6ow vis (45) G Hannon 66/1: 4010029: Led halfway till 5f out, wknd.	dist	0a
4461}	**KEBREYA 45** [10] R Ford 4-9-13 VIS (65) S Hitchcott (3) 33/1: 5/6604-00: Led 1m, sn wknd, t.o. in visor.	12	0a
2039}	**GROUNDSWELL 153** [6] Ferdy Murphy 7-8-4 (42) J Fanning 14/1: 000-0030: In tch, wknd from halfway, t.o., abs.	3	0a
4581}	**LITTLE SKY 38** [1] D Mullarkey 6-8-8 (46) J P Guillambert (3) 66/1: 2000: Mid-div, struggling halfway, t.o.	1½	0a

12 Ran 3m 40.14 (10.94) Owner JOliver WGarrett CJWard & Anne — Trained at Upper Lambourn

---

8 4.40 Littlewoods Bet Direct Maiden Stakes Div 2 3yo (D)
£2310 £660 £330 7f f/sand rnd Going 36 -20 Slow Stalls Outside

4540}	**REZZAGO 392** [3] P W Harris 3-9-0 N Callan 7/4 FAV: 5-1: Held up, hdwy tp lead dist, drvn to hold on:		66a
4883}	**KINGSTON TOWN 16** [1] N P Littmoden 3-9-0 P J P Guillambert (3) 7/1: 402: Handy & rdn/led over 2f out, hdd over 1f out, rallied gamely, just held:	hd	65a
4590}	**VICTORY FLIP 37** [10] R Hollinshead 3-8-9 p (55) A Culhane 7/2: 2020003: Held up, rdn to press ldr over 1f out, onepace:	1¼	55a
4427}	**BRANDYWINE BAY 47** [8] A P Jones 3-8-9 (41) G Hannon 14/1: 4353504: Dwelt, bhd, late gains.	3½	50a
4968}	**DECO LADY 9** [6] P D Evans 3-8-9 vis (50) S W Kelly 14/1: 0-050005: Led till over 3f out, sn btn.	12	30a
3370}	**RICH DANCER 98** [5] J D Bethell 3-8-9 (55) J Fanning 16/1: 6-03006: Led/dsptd lead till 2f out, sn btn:	2	26a
4929}	**SHOW ME THE LOLLY 13** [2] P J McBride 3-8-9 S Whitworth 5/1: 057: Hmpd start, eff wide, no impress.	5	16a
4785}	**GUARD 24** [7] N P Littmoden 3-9-0 (44) I Mongan 33/1: 0-00008: Prom, btn over 2f out.	shd	21a
4623}	**EDDIES JEWEL 35** [4] J S Wainwright 3-9-0 VIS (36) P Mathers (7) 50/1: 0-000309: Outpcd, nvr a factor:	5	11a
4260}	**SADIE JANE 55** [9] J M Bradley 3-8-9 C Catlin 66/1: 500: Prom, btn 4f out:	4	0a

10 Ran 1m 30.13 (3.93) Owner Mrs P W Harris — Trained at Berkhamsted

---

SAINT CLOUD Saturday 10.11.03 Lefthand, Galloping Track

Official Going GOOD/SOFT.

9 2.15 Gr 1 Criterium de Saint Cloud 2yo ()
£55656 £22266 £11133 £5562 1m2f Good/Soft

SAINT CLOUD Saturday 10.11.03 Lefthand, Galloping Track

4836} **VOIX DU NORD 20** [4] D Smaga 2-9-0 D Boeuf 51/10: 212421: Mid-div, rdn to lead over 1f out, drvn out:		**115**
SIMPLEX [11] C Laffon Parias 2-9-0 O Peslier 18/10 FAV: 212: Mid-div, rdn & led ins last, sn hdd & not pace of wnr:	1½	112
DAY OR NIGHT [3] J E Pease 2-9-0 bl T Gillet 57/10: 143: Rear, styd on to take 3rd ins last, no dngr to front pair:	4	106
5003} **TOP SEED 7** [6] M R Channon 2-9-0 A Culhane 76/10: 45373624: Led, rdn & hdd ins last, no extra.	2	103
4400} **HAPPY CRUSADER 49** [5] P F I Cole 2-9-0 T Thulliez 17/2: 3331136: Trkd ldrs, rdn & btn over 1f out:	2	100
4866} **SGT PEPPER 15** [7] R Hannon 2-9-0 R Hughes 159/10: 31149-: Rear, no prog 2f out.	4	94
4975} **COHN BLUE 7** [1] C Soumillon 2-9-0 Mrs A J Perrett 49/10: 21120: Rear, btn & eased over 1f out.	10	80
Ran 2m 16.00 Owner Baron T de Zuylen de Nyevelt		Trained at France

LEOPARDSTOWN Saturday 10.11.03 Lefthand, Galloping Track

Official Going GOOD.

10 | **3.05 Listed Eyrefield Stakes 2yo ()**
£21775 £6365 £3015 **1m1f** **Good**

MIKADO 51 [8] M J Kinane 2-9-0 A P O'Brien 4/5 FAV: 211: Trkd ldrs, led over 2f out, sn rdn clr, readily:		**112**
TARAKALA 24 [2] F M Berry 2-8-11 J M Oxx 7/2: 312: Mid-div, chall over 2f out, kept on, not pace of wnr:	1½	103
LISS ARD 21 [5] J J Murphy 2-9-0 D M Grant 33/1: 33: Held up, rdn & kept on, not able to chall:	4	100
Ran Not Taken Owner Mrs John Magnier		Trained at Ballydoyle

LINGFIELD Wednesday 12.11.03 Lefthand, V Sharp Track

Official Going Standard

11 | **12.05 Littlewoodscasino Com Apprentice Handicap Stakes Div 1 3yo+ 0-75 (F)** [75]
£2258 £645 £323 `.m5f p/track` **Going 41** -00 Slow Stalls Inside

4755} **MAYSTOCK 28** [8] G A Butler 3-8-8 vis (62) L Treadwell 3/1: 5036041: Trkd ldr, rdn to lead over 1f out, styd on strongly to assert ins last:		**72a**
4457} **ASTROMANCER 47** [7] M H Tompkins 3-7-12 2oh (50) D Fentiman (7) 20/1: 0-00P502: Led/dsptd lead, went on after 3f, pulled clr with wnr over 2f out, hdd over 1f out & no extra ins last:	2	57a
4828} **MACARONI GOLD 22** [5] W Jarvis 3-8-3 (57) D Tudhope 25/1: 50303: Slow away & rear, eff wide 4f out, no threat.	4	56a
4963} **FINAL DIVIDEND 12** [6] J M P Eustace 7-8-1 (48) Ashleigh Horton (7) 8/1: 1655064: Mid-div, outpcd 3f out, no danger.	1½	45a
4687} **TWO OF A KIND 31** [10] J W Hills 3-8-10 (64) H Gemberlu (5) 20/1: 05555: Rear, eff wide, only mod prog.	5	54a
4622} **HELLO HOLLY 37** [4] Mrs A L M King 6-7-12 (45) Kristin Stubbs 25/1: 35310/-06: Rear, outpcd 3f out, sn no impress.	1	34a
4985} **ESPERANCE 10** [1] J Akehurst 3-8-7 (61) M Coombe (4) 11/2: 0002047: Mid-div, lost place 3f out, nvr factor.	nk	49a
4655} **BEYOND THE POLE 35** [2] B R Johnson 5-8-13 (60) W Hogg (3) 9/1: 2240008: Trkd ldrs till 3f out, sn btn.	2½	44a
4859} **AVEIRO 20** [9] B G Powell 7-7-12 11oh bl (34) Liam Jones (5) 16/1: 3006039: Trkd ldrs, lost tch fnl 3f.	3½	24a
4957} **SEA PLUME 12** [3] Lady Herries 4-10-0 (75) P Gallagher 9/4 FAV: 35-43020: Led 3f, wknd qckly 4f out on AW bow.	8	44a
10 Ran 2m 47.57 (5.27) Owner Stock Hill Racing		Trained at Blewbury

12 | **12.35 Betdirect Co Uk Handicap Stakes Div 1 3yo+ 0-75 (E)** [73]
£2300 £657 £329 **1m p/track rnd** **Going 41** +05 Fast Stalls Outside

5017} **DIDNT TELL MY WIFE 6** [8] C F Wall 4-9-1 (60) Lisa Jones (3) 4/1: 2041021: Rear, hdwy over 1f out & rdn to lead well ins last:		**66a**
4861*} **DEEPER IN DEBT 20** [11] J Akehurst 5-9-12 (71) G Carter 7/2 FAV: 0003112: Sn handy wide, drvn to lead narrowly dist, hdd ins last & no extra:	1¼	74a
4910} **COLLEGE DELINQUENT 16** [1] K Bell 4-9-7 t (66) Dane O'Neill 8/1: 0450033: Trkd ldrs, rdn & outpcd over 2f out, rallied well for press fnl 1f, not pace of wnr.	nk	68a
4958} **MISS ISSY 12** [5] J Gallagher 3-8-10 (57) N Callan 50/1: 0623404: Held up, hdwy wide to chase ldrs 2f out, onepace dist:	1¼	56a
4920} **EMBER DAYS 15** [7] J L Spearing 4-8-12 (57) A Daly 20/1: 011160-05: Rear, short of room over 1f out, drvn & onepace.	1	54a
3569} **DHAKHIRAH 91** [12] A C Stewart 3-9-9 (70) L Dettori 12/1: 002326: Mid-div, wide, drvn halfway, only mod prog.	1	65a
4907} **FOOLISH THOUGHT 16** [4] R A Fahey 3-9-2 (63) S Hitchcott (3) 12/1: 36-00047: Led/dsptd lead till dist, wknd.	½	57a
4949} **MAGIC WARRIOR 13** [10] J C Fox 3-8-13 (60) P Dobbs 14/1: 36-50058: Rear, eff 2f out, only onepace.	¾	53a
4897} **PANGO 18** [3] H Morrison 4-9-12 (71) S Drowne 5/1: 5210509: Trkd ldrs, poised to chall when badly hmpd over 1f out, no ch after:	½	63a
4919} **POLAR KINGDOM 15** [2] T D Barron 5-9-13 (72) D Mernagh 9/2: 00200-20: Dsptd lead, btn/hmpd dist.	½	63a
4949} **CHATEAU NICOL 13** [6] B G Powell 4-8-13 bl (58) L Keniry (3) 50/1: 0630000: Keen & trkd ldrs, rdn/chall when hung badly left & lost action over 1f out, wknd qckly.	6	39a
11 Ran 1m 39.09 (2.89) Owner Mr G D Newton		Trained at Newmarket

13 | **1.10 Littlewoods Bet Direct Aw Jockeys Championship Median Auction Maiden Stakes 2yo (E)**
£2300 £657 £329 **5f p/track rnd** **Going 41** -00 Slow Stalls Outside

4921} **DARTING 15** [6] G A Butler 2-8-9 L Dettori 13/8 FAV: 331: Dwelt, sn cl-up, rdn to lead on all out:		**76a**
4926} **DANDOUCE 15** [3] S L Keightley 2-8-9 vis A Culhane 7/1: 42: Led, narrowly hdd ins last, rallied well for press, just held:	shd	75a
4926} **APERITIF 15** [8] W J Haggas 2-9-0 M Hills 12/1: 663: Mid-div, wide, styd on for press ins last, nrst fin:	shd	80a
4959} **HELIBEL 12** [7] Mrs A J Perrett 2-8-9 (73) Dane O'Neill 2/1: 4424: Slow away & rear, kept on late for press, nrst fin:	1	72a
4926} **LACONIA 15** [5] J S Moore 2-8-9 (61) J F Egan 16/1: 0035: Trkd ldrs, hung & no extra over 1f out.	½	70a
5013} **AVERAMI 6** [4] A M Balding 2-8-9 S Drowne 25/1: 06: Trkd ldrs, outpcd fnl 2f.	2	64a
ASK THE CLERK 46 [1] H J Collingridge 2-9-0 G Bardwell 16/1: 2643037: Trkd ldrs, no impress dist:	½	67a
4959} **LIMIT DOWN 12** [9] M J Wallace 2-9-0 D Corby (3) 100/1: 008: Rear, al outpcd.	½	65a
4166} **BIG BAD BURT 62** [2] M J Wallace 2-9-0 N Callan 25/1: 609: Dwelt, rear, nvr able to chall:	¾	63a
4713} **YOUR JUST LOVELY 30** [10] A M Balding 2-8-9 L Keniry (3) 20/1: 060: Cl-up, btn over 1f out.	3	49a

LINGFIELD Wednesday 12.11.03 Lefthand, V Sharp Track

10 Ran   1m 0.62 (2.82)   Owner Mr Raymond Tooth   Trained at Blewbury

1.40 Littlewoods Bet Direct Aw Trainers Championship Maiden Stakes 3yo+ (D)

14   £2415 £690 £345   1m4f p/track   Going 41   -02 Slow   Stalls Inside

4989}	**SENTRY 9** [15] J H M Gosden 3-9-0 (87) L Dettori 13/8 FAV: 04-231: Trkd ldrs, rdn to chall fnl 2f:		**74a**
4931}	**BUCKS 15** [7] D K Ivory 6-9-6 (64) I Mongan 10/1: 0000-352: Trkd ldrs travelling well, hdwy to lead over 2f out, drvn & hdd cl-home:	hd	73a
4985}	**REMEMBRANCE 10** [6] J M P Eustace 3-9-0 t (66) J Tate 6/1: 4050203: Held up, hdwy over 3f out, drvn to press front pair ins last, no extra nr fin:	1¼	71a
1131}	**MAXILLA 205** [9] L M Cumani 3-8-9 (72) Dane O'Neill 11/2: 004-24: In tch, eff wide 4f out, no impress:	8	54a
4032}	**SCHOONER 70** [1] Lady Herries 3-9-0 M Tebbutt 20/1: 65: Rear, eff wide over 2f out, only mod prog:	2½	55a
4848}	**MOFEYDA 21** [13] A C Stewart 3-8-9 S Drowne 6/1: 546: Held up, eff wide 3f out, sn btn:	1¾	48a
111}	**LITTLE BUD 1085** [5] Miss A M Newton Smith 9-9-1 D Sweeney 66/1: 0//-7: Rear, no impress fnl 3f, long abs.	7	38a
4848}	**DAISYCUTTER 21** [4] G Wragg 3-8-9 (60) J F Egan 20/1: 40-558: Sn rdn, no impress fnl 3f.	1¼	36a
4968}	**LADIES DAY 11** [14] T G Mills 3-8-9 (70) J Paulielo 20/1: 50509: Hmpd start, sn prom, btn 2f out.	3	32a
	GLESNI [8] S C Williams 4-9-1 B Reilly (5) 33/1: 0: Dwelt & al bhd.	2	29a
4567}	**BYINCHKA 41** [10] S L Keightley 3-9-0 (50) A Culhane 50/1: 0006040: Prom, rdn & lost place after 4f, abs.	1¾	32a
3579}	**SEEJAY 91** [12] M A Allen 3-8-9 S Carson 100/1: 60: Trkd ldr, led over 3f out till over 2f out, wknd qckly.	4	21a
786}	**MUSICAL GIFT 242** [3] C N Allen 3-9-0 G Carter 9/1: 2240: Led till over 3f out, sn btn:	11	12a
2723}	**REPETOIRE 128** [11] K O Cunningham Brown 3-8-9 L Keniry (3) 40/1: 00-40B0: Al bhd, t.o. fnl 3f, abs.	shd	7a

14 Ran   2m 34.39 (5.19)   Owner Highclere Thoroughbred Racing   Trained at Manton

2.10 Littlewoods Bet Direct On 0800 329393 Nursery Handicap Stakes 2yo (C)

15   £5133 £1947 £974 £443   7f p/track rnd   Going 41   +01 Fast   Stalls Inside   [94]

4948*}	**BRAVO MAESTRO 13** [13] D W P Arbuthnot 2-9-6 (86) S Whitworth 9/4 FAV: 011: Sn trkd ldrs trav well, led over 1f out, styd on strongly under hands & heels:		**100a**
4903}	**PREGNANT PAUSE 16** [11] S Kirk 2-7-12 2oh (62) D Fox (5) 10/1: 5453002: Chsd ldrs, styd on for press fnl 2f, not able to chall wnr:	2½	66a
4886*}	**ROWAN PURSUIT 18** [8] M H Tompkins 2-7-12 11oh bl (53) F P Ferris (3) 50/1: 4P40013: Pushed along & bhd, styd on wide for press, nrst fin:	1	64a
4869}	**CELTIC HEROINE 19** [10] M A Jarvis 2-8-8 (74) M Henry 1/1: 5154: Chsd ldrs halfway, onepace.	½	73a
4956}	**ANUVASTEEL 12** [6] N A Callaghan 2-8-13 (79) W Ryan 25/1: 0515005: Bmpd start, rear, kept on late, nvr dngrs.	1	76a
5034*}	**CARTRONAGEERAGHLAD 4** [7] J A Osborne 2-8-9 6ex 1ow bl (74) L Dettori 5/2: 0106416: Sn led till over 1f out.	1	70a
4997*}	**KNIGHT ONTHE TILES 8** [12] J R Best 2-8-13 6ex bl (79) N Pollard 16/1: 1051417: Dwelt, rear, eff wide, no dngr.	1¾	74a
4956}	**BINNION BAY 12** [3] R Hannon 2-9-4 (84) P Dobbs 20/1: 3108: Mid-div, btn over 1f out:	2	72a
4233}	**TARANAI 58** [1] B W Duke 2-7-12 7oh (57) Lisa Jones (3) 100/1: 060009: Dwelt, al outpcd rear:	3½	45a
5028}	**WAVERTREE DREAM 5** [9] N P Littmoden 2-9-6 (86) I Mongan 12/1: 0216200: Rdn towards rear, no impress.	½	66a
4911}	**BIG BRADFORD 16** [4] E L James 2-9-7 bl (87) S Drowne 11/2: 6432420: Sn struggling, no ch halfway.	9	52a
3931*}	**RISE 76** [2] Andrew Reid 2-9-6 bl (86) S Carson 20/1: 4352310: Prom, wknd qckly over 2f out, abs.	3	45a
4911}	**SCARLET EMPRESS 16** [5] R Hannon 2-8-12 bl (78) Dane O'Neill 20/1: 0060140: Chsd ldrs early, sn bhd.	13	16a

13 Ran   1m 25.59 (2.79)   Owner Mr Derrick C Broomfield   Trained at Upper Lambourn

2.45 Littlewoods Bet Direct E B F Handicap Stakes Fillies 3yo 0-100 (C)

16   £7482 £2838 £1419 £645   1m2f p/track   Going 41   -01 Slow   Stalls Inside   [85]

4909}	**DANCE IN THE SUN 16** [6] Mrs A J Perrett 3-9-7 (78) Dane O'Neill 3/1: 2-215241: Rear, smooth hdwy wide over 2f out, led over 1f out & sn rdn clr, rdly:		**86a**
4940}	**BRAVO DANCER 14** [5] M R Channon 3-9-6 (77) A Culhane 3/1: 0260102: In tch, smooth prog to chall 2f out, kept on, not pace of wnr:	2	79a
4958*}	**ESTIMATION 12** [7] R M H Cowell 3-8-11 (68) L Dettori 5/2 FAV: 2442113: Rear, smooth hdwy over 3f out, rdn & no extra over 1f out:	3	66a
4588}	**ESTIMATE 39** [4] C E Brittain 3-8-7 vis (64) J F Egan 33/1: 0026264: Cl-up, led 3f out till over 1f out.	5	55a
4783}	**WASTED TALENT 26** [3] J G Portman 3-9-2 p (73) S Drowne 9/1: 2442625: Handy & led over 7f out till 3f out, sn btn.	2½	60a
4985}	**NUZZLE 10** [1] M Quinn 3-8-5 (62) S Carson 16/1: 0233606: Led till over 7f out, btn 2f out.	7	40a
4950}	**MISS PEBBLES 13** [2] B R Johnson 3-9-0 (71) I Mongan 5/1: 232107: Keen & prom, btn 2f out.	14	30a

7 Ran   2m 07.03 (4.23)   Owner Hesmonds Stud   Trained at Pulborough

3.15 Betdirect Co Uk Handicap Stakes Div 2 3yo+ 0-75 (E)

17   £2289 £654 £327   1m p/track rnd   Going 41   -25 Slow   Stalls Outside   [73]

4897}	**LABRETT 18** [10] Miss Gay Kelleway 6-9-12 p (71) M Fenton 100/30 FAV: 2343651: Trkd ldrs wide, drvn to lead ins last, styd on strongly:		**78a**
3305}	**PRIORS DALE 103** [8] K Bell 3-9-11 (72) Dane O'Neill 66/1: 5-0402: Drvn to chall dist, kept on but not pace of wnr:	1¼	74a
4951}	**MY MAITE 13** [2] R Ingram 4-8-9 t (54) N Day 10/1: 6005003: Led till outpcd over 2f out, rallied late for press to retake 3rd:	¾	56a
4910}	**QUANTUM LEAP 16** [6] S Dow 6-9-1 (60) Paul Eddery 20/1: 2004004: Rear, short of room fnl 1f, nrst fin:	nk	61a
4910}	**HADATH 16** [5] B G Powell 6-9-7 P (66) L Keniry (3) 25/1: 0026005: Cl up, led over 2f out, hdd ins last, no extra.	hd	66a
4999}	**QUALITAIR WINGS 8** [9] J Hetherton 4-9-3 (62) S Hitchcott (3) 4/1: 6021026: Trkd ldrs, drvn & onepace dist.	hd	61a
4297}	**AMORAS 56** [1] J W Hills 6-9-13 (72) M Hills 14/1: 1052007: Trkd ldrs, hung left & no extra dist, abs.	shd	71a
4985}	**FEATHER BOA 10** [12] M Blanshard 3-9-6 (67) N Callan 16/1: 5300008: Held up, drvn over 1f out, onepace.	½	65a
4944}	**RESONATE 14** [3] A G Newcombe 5-9-0 (59) F P Ferris 9/1: 0315209: Rear, eff 2f out, no room fnl 1f, closer with clr run.	½	56a
4950}	**COPPINGTON FLYER 13** [4] B W Duke 4-9-11 (58) Lisa Jones (3) 20/1: 0560000: Trkd ldrs, short of room over 1f out, no ch after, closer with a clr run.	hd	54a
4986}	**OASES 10** [7] D Shaw 4-8-12 (57) S Whitworth 8/1: 6000040: Dwelt, keen rear, no prog dist.	shd	53a
4949}	**NIGHT KISS 13** [11] R Hannon 3-8-13 (60) R Smith 4/1: 0300220: Rear, drvn & btn over 1f out:	1	54a

12

12 Ran 1m 41.49 (5.29) Owner Mr A P Griffin Trained at Newmarket

18 **3.50 Littlewoodscasino Com Apprentice Handicap Stakes Div 2 3yo+ 0-75 (F)** **[65]**
£2258 £645 £323 **1m5f p/track** **Going 41** **-01 Slow** Stalls Inside

4951*} **COLD TURKEY 13** [5] G L Moore 3-9-10 (68) H Poulton (3) 11/4: 2200111: Rear, gd hdwy over 3f out & led over 1f out, rdly pulled clr: **80a**
4951} **DANEHILL LAD 13** [8] T Keddy 3-9-9 (67) L Treadwell 3/1: 0002222: Trkd ldrs, led 3f out, hdd over 1f out, kept on, no ch with wnr: *6* **67a**
4646} **DAME MARGARET 36** [7] M L W Bell 3-7-13 (43) Liam Jones (5) 25/1: 0-402063: Keen & trkd ldrs, outpcd over 2f out, kept on ins last. *1¼* **41a**
4546} **FOREVER MY LORD 42** [3] J R Best 5-9-5 (56) D Fentiman (7) 8/1: 4212004: Slow away, rear, hdwy 3f out, onepace bef *3½* **49a**
4876} **CLASSIC MILLENNIUM 19** [9] W J Musson 5-8-12 (49) Laura Pike (5) 5/2 FAV: 2540155: Trkd ldrs, not able to chall. *4* **36a**
3477] **CHARMANTE FEMME 35** [6] P D Evans 5-8-13 (50) P Gallagher 14/1: 1-541036: Led till over 2f out, btn 2f out. *1½* **35a**
2552} **ZOEANNA 134** [4] R Guest 3-8-6 (50) W Hogg (3) 33/1: 0005067: Trkd ldr, led over 4f out till 3f out, wknd qckly. *18* **12a**
4581} **HEKTIKOS 40** [1] S Dow 3-9-4 (62) J Coffill Brown (7) 100/1: 040-08: Rear, btn 4f out, t.o., abs. *7* **15a**
4782} **PERSEPHONE HEIGHTS 26** [2] D J Coakley 3-8-8 (52) D Stamp 11/1: 0210069: Trkd ldrs, btn/eased 2f out *1¼* **3a**
9 Ran 2m 47.42 (5.42) Owner Mr A Grinter Trained at Brighton

19 **12.20 E B F Bet Direct On 0800 32 93 93 Maiden Stakes Div 1 2yo (D)**
£3094 £884 £442 **1m p/track rnd** **Going 39** **-11 Slow** Stalls Outside

RENDEZVOUS POINT [8] J H M Gosden 2-8-9 L Dettori 5/2 FAV: 1: Trkd ldrs wide, pushed along over 2f out, rdn & styd on to lead cl-home: **79a**
4987} **PERGOLACHA 10** [11] L M Cumani 2-8-9 Dane O'Neill 8/1: 032: Sn handy & led over 2f out, drvn & kept on well, hdd cl-home: *hd* **78a**
4987} **PUKKA 10** [5] L M Cumani 2-9-0 K Dalgleish 10/1: 043: Dwelt, sn trkd ldrs, kept on, not pace to chall: *1* **81a**
4945} **RESONANCE 14** [1] Mrs A J Perrett 2-8-9 W Ryan 33/1: 04: Slow away, rear, late gains under hands & heels, nrst fin: *1¾* **73a**
4580} **LA LANDONNE 41** [6] P M Phelan 2-8-9 J P Guillambert (3) 7/1: 35: Keen in mid-div, onepace bef dist, op 4/1. *1¼* **70a**
4948} **EVALUATOR 14** [9] T G Mills 2-9-0 A Clark 3/1: 36: Keen & led till over 2f out, no extra: *2½* **70a**
4895} **LAND OF NOD 19** [4] G A Butler 2-8-9 S W Kelly 4/1: 07: Trkd ldrs, ch over 2f out, sn lost place: *1¼* **62a**
JUST FILLY [3] A P Jones 2-8-9 G Hannon 100/1: 8: Slowly away, sn mid-div, outpcd fnl 2f on debut. *1½* **59a**
DONASTRELA [10] A M Balding 2-8-9 M Fenton 33/1: 9: Slow away & al bhd on debut. *1* **57a**
5024} **WAKE UP HENRY 6** [7] R Charlton 2-9-0 S Drowne 20/1: 00: Sn pshd along rear, no prog 3f out, qck reapp. *1½* **59a**
4387} **BURLINGTON PLACE 52** [12] S Kirk 2-9-0 J F Egan 25/1: 040: Mid-div, struggling fnl 3f, abs. *2* **55a**
SKELTHWAITE [2] M H Tompkins 2-9-0 J Fanning 33/1: 0: Slowly away & sn well bhd, t.o. on debut. *17* **26a**
12 Ran 1m 40.19 (3.99) Owner Mr George Strawbridge Trained at Manton

20 **12.50 Betdirect Co Uk New Site Handicap Stakes Div 1 3yo+ 0-75 (E)** **[74]**
£2405 £687 £344 **7f p/track rnd** **Going 39** **+04 Fast** Stalls Inside

4753} **COMPTON BANKER 29** [5] G A Butler 6-9-10 vis (70) S W Kelly 12/1: 0050041: Rear, drvn & strong run wide to lead well ins last, going away: **74a**
1573} **SIR LAUGHALOT 180** [6] Miss E C Lavelle 3-9-7 (68) A Culhane 50/1: 00-0002: Mid-div, hdwy wide to chall ins last, not pace of wnr fnl 50y: *½* **70a**
4979} **DORCHESTER 12** [3] W J Musson 6-10-0 (74) L Dettori 13/2: 4013053: Rear, hdwy 2f out, ch ins last, no extra nr fin: *½* **75a**
12 **FOOLISH THOUGHT 1** [7] R A Fahey 3-9-2 (63) S Hitchcott (3) 10/1: 36-000404: Handy & led 3f out, rdn clr 2f out, wknd & hdd well ins last: *1* **62a**
4826} **ZAK FACTA 23** [2] Miss D A McHale 3-8-10 vis (57) C Cogan 16/1: 3200425: Trkd ldrs, onepce: *2* **52a**
4986} **JAGGED 11** [16] K R Burke 3-8-12 (59) Darren Williams 6/1: 0504026: Prom, drvn & no extra dist. *nk* **53a**
4564} **DUO LEONI 42** [11] R M Beckett 3-8-13 (60) M Tebbutt 33/1: 3302157: Rear, styd on well fnl 2f under kind ride: *nk* **53a**
4753*} **MAJHOOL 29** [9] G L Moore 4-9-12 (72) I Mongan 4/1 FAV: 145-0018: Trkd ldrs, short of room 2f out & again ins last: *nk* **64a**
4949*} **MISTRAL SKY 14** [1] Mrs S A Liddiard 4-9-10 vis (70) S Drowne 5/1: 2304119: Mid-div, swtchd & onepace dist. *nk* **61a**
4485} **PEYTO PRINCESS 47** [12] M A Buckley 5-9-1 (61) Lisa Jones (3) 20/1: 3440000: Rear, eff 2f out, no impress. *shd* **52a**
4908*} **TEYAAR 17** [4] Mrs N Macauley 7-9-5 (65) P McCabe 12/1: 4003510: Held up, hdwy halfway, btn dist: *hd* **55a**
4286} **RIPPLE EFFECT 57** [8] C A Dwyer 3-9-12 t (73) B Reilly (5) 12/1: 6341530: Prom 5f, abs, new yard. *1¼* **60a**
4925} **ITS ECCO BOY 16** [14] P Howling 5-8-9 (55) D Kinsella 25/1: 6413500: Sn handy, hmpd/wknd over 1f out. *4* **34a**
3333} **AZREME 103** [10] P W D'Arcy 3-9-10 vis (71) M Fenton 25/1: 5-261000: Dwelt, rear, no prog 2f out, abs. *2* **46a**
4719} **TOPPLING 31** [13] J M Bradley 5-8-11 (57) P Fitzsimons 20/1: 5200000: Led till 3f out, wknd qckly. *½* **31a**
3251} **FIRE DOME 106** [15] Andrew Reid 11-9-0 (60) J P Guillambert (3) 25/1: 3500-340: Al bhd & no ch fnl 2f, abs. *7* **22a**
16 Ran 1m 25.28 (2.48) Owner Mr Erik Penser Trained at Blewbury

21 **1.20 E B F Bet Direct On 0800 32 93 93 Maiden Stakes Div 2 2yo (D)**
£3080 £880 £440 **1m p/track rnd** **Going 39** **-15 Slow** Stalls Outside

RED SPELL [7] R Hannon 2-9-0 Dane O'Neill 7/1: 1: Handy, rdn & led over 1f out, held on well ins last: **80a**
BIENVENUE [8] M P Tregoning 2-8-9 A Daly 5/1: 2: Held up, short of room over 2f out, styd on well from over 1f out, nrst fin: *2* **70a**
IMPARTIAL [5] P F I Cole 2-9-0 J Fanning 5/1: 3: Trkd ldrs, rdn & kept on from over 1f out: *nk* **74a**
4981} **WAZIRI 11** [2] H Morrison 2-9-0 M Fenton 11/4 FAV: 464: Cl-up & led over 2f out, hdd over 1f out. *nk* **73a**
5022} **INCHPAST 6** [3] M H Tompkins 2-9-0 L Dettori 25/1: 05: Chsd ldrs, drvn & onepace fnl 2f, qck reapp. *2* **69a**
4906} **POLAR DANCER 17** [4] Mrs A J Perrett 2-8-9 W Ryan 20/1: 06: Led till over 2f out, no extra. *2* **60a**
4898} **AMEYRAH 19** [1] M R Channon 2-8-9 A Culhane 6/1: 07: Dwelt, rear, only mod gains under hands & heels: *½* **59a**
4942} **CORA 15** [10] L M Cumani 2-8-9 S W Kelly 20/1: 08: Mid-div, no impress fnl 2f. *2½* **54a**
4972} **NUTS FOR YOU 12** [6] R Charlton 2-8-9 S Drowne 10/1: 09: Keen & prom, no impress fnl 2f: *shd* **54a**
CRACKLEANDO [11] N P Littmoden 2-9-0 J P Guillambert (3) 14/1: 0: Al rear. *5* **50a**
SOLO SOLE 11 [12] L M Cumani 2-9-0 K Dalgleish 14/1: 60: Slowly away, struggling fnl 2f. *1½* **47a**
11 Ran 1m 40.54 (4.34) Owner Mrs John Lee Trained at Marlborough

LINGFIELD Thursday 13.11.03 Lefthand, V Sharp Track

22 **1.50 Betdirect Co Uk New Site Handicap Stakes Div 2 3yo+ 0-75 (E)** **[74]**
£2405 £687 £344 **7f p/track rnd** **Going 39** **-02 Slow** Stalls Inside

4807} **MR BOUNTIFUL 26** [5] M Dods 5-8-9 (55) S W Kelly 7/1: 3020641: Trkd ldrs, drvn to lead cl-home: **58a**
4925} **JUST ONE SMILE 16** [6] T D Easterby 3-9-1 (62) J F Egan 5/1: 0332142: Trkd ldrs, drvn to chall ins last, styd on well for press, just held: *nk* **64a**
4658*} **TROUSERS 36** [3] Andrew Reid 4-9-12 (72) L Dettori 3/1 FAV: 00-03213: Trkd ldrs trav well, rdn & led ins last, hdd cl-home: *shd* **74a**
4908} **BLAKESHALL BOY 17** [4] R Lee 5-8-12 (58) Dean McKeown 14/1: 6000044: Mid-div, hdwy & poised to chall when no run fnl 1f, prob unlucky: *1* **58a**
4810} **GEORGE STUBBS 24** [10] N P Littmoden 5-9-10 bl (70) J P Guillambert (3) 10/1: 6032305: Mid-div, swtchd & kept on. *shd* **70a**
4864} **HEIDELBURG 20** [14] S Kirk 3-9-2 (63) A Culhane 20/1: 0040606: Rear, rdn & styd on well ins last, nrst fin: *½* **62a**
2001] **KILMEENA LAD 520** [1] J C Fox 7-9-12 (72) L Keniry (3) 50/1: 6611/00-7: Trkd ldrs trav well, badly hmpd over 1f out, no *nk* **69a**
4925} **GOODENOUGH MOVER 16** [12] J S King 7-9-8 (68) Dane O'Neill 8/1: 6030008: Led till hdd ins last, wknd. *nk* **65a**
4616} **FEARBY CROSS 38** [2] W J Musson 7-9-7 (67) Lisa Jones (3) 11/1: 1514409: Dwelt & held up, hdwy 2f out & keeping on when badly hmpd ins last, closer with a clr run. *1¼* **61a**
4901} **INISTRAHULL ISLAND 17** [9] M H Tompkins 3-8-9 (56) J Fanning 20/1: 2050260: Rear, late gains, needs 1m. *nk* **49a**
4986} **KING DAVID 11** [11] D Burchell 4-8-11 (57) R Price 10/1: 3630030: Cl-up till 2f out, sn no extra. *½* **49a**
4999} **JONNY EBENEEZER 9** [16] R M H Cowell 4-9-10 (70) S Drowne 7/1: 4224640: Prom, btn/hmpd over 1f out. *2½* **57a**
4907} **SESTINA 17** [7] S Dow 3-9-4 (65) P Doe 100/1: 340000: Al bhd. *7* **40a**
4964} **TUSCAN TREATY 13** [13] T T Clement 3-8-13 (60) J F McDonald (5) 40/1: 0010000: Dwelt, wide, in tch 5f. *hd* **34a**
4287} **DUNEDIN RASCAL 57** [8] E A Wheeler 6-9-12 bl (72) S Carson 25/1: 0000000: Al bhd, abs. *3½* **39a**
3087} **FULVIO 113** [15] Jamie Poulton 3-9-11 (72) I Mongan 25/1: 0366500: Held up, btn 2f out, abs. *2* **35a**
16 Ran 1m 25.67 (2.87) Owner Denton Hall Racing Ltd Trained at Darlington

23 **2.20 Bet Direct On Attheraces Interactive Maiden Stakes 3yo+ (D)**
£2300 £657 £329 **6f p/track rnd** **Going 39** **+01 Fast** Stalls Inside

4913} **PHRENOLOGIST 17** [6] J R Fanshawe 3-9-0 Dane O'Neill 7/1: 561: Trkd ldrs, drvn to lead cl-home: **67a**
4913} **SALON PRIVE 17** [9] C A Cyzer 3-9-0 (68) L Dettori 5/2 FAV: 0232: Led, rdn & hdd cl-home: *nk* **66a**
4815} **MONTE MAYOR LAD 24** [1] D Haydn Jones 3-9-0 BL (62) S Drowne 14/1: 20-43303: Held up, rdn & kept on, not pace to chall front pair: *1½* **61a**
5000} **MYND 9** [10] R M Whitaker 3-9-0 (56) Dean McKeown 14/1: 5-050034: Cl-up till over 1f out, no extra: *nk* **60a**
5037} **TATWEER 5** [2] D Shaw 3-9-0 vis Darren Williams 50/1: 5-005: *2* **54a**
4654} **INCHING 36** [3] R M H Cowell 3-8-9 (60) M Henry 14/1: 3604006: Dwelt, in tch, onepace & held dist. *shd* **49a**
4719} **CALUSA LADY 31** [7] G B Balding 3-8-9 VIS (59) A Clark 14/1: 30-44607: Dwelt, sn in tch, not pace to chall: *shd* **48a**
4519} **MONTANA 45** [13] R Hannon 3-9-0 (68) R Smith 8/1: 36-22308: Slow away, mid-div, hanging & btn dist. *1¼* **49a**
4691} **GO GO GIRL 32** [14] L G Cottrell 3-8-9 (63) L Keniry (3) 4/1: 6565339: Held up wide, nvr pace to threaten. *nk* **43a**
4913} **ARRAN 17** [5] H J Collingridge 3-9-0 M Tebbutt 100/1: U000: Dwelt & sn bhd, mod late prog. *½* **46a**
4949} **BENEKING 14** [8] J Gallagher 3-9-0 (62) N Callan 6/1: 5260400: Chsd ldrs 5f. *2½* **38a**
4913} **NATHAN DETROIT 17** [11] P J Makin 3-9-0 D Sweeney 20/1: 000: Sn prom, btn 2f out, qual for h'caps. *nk* **37a**
4 **EASY BREEZE 3** [4] J M Bradley 3-9-0 P Fitzsimons 200/1: 00: Struggling from halfway, qck reapp. *7* **17a**
SARGENTS DREAM [12] J A Gilbert 3-8-9 A Daly 300/1: 0: Slowly away & sn well bhd on debut. *4* **1a**
14 Ran 1m 12.69 (2.29) Owner The Leonard Curtis Partnership Trained at Newmarket

24 **2.50 Bet Direct On Channel 4 Page 613 Claiming Stakes 3-5yo (E)**
£2065 £590 £295 **1m4f p/track** **Going 39** **-03 Slow** Stalls Inside

4951} **COMPTON ECLAIRE 14** [6] G A Butler 3-8-1 VIS (57) J F McDonald (5) 9/4: 2126401: Dwelt, rear, eff wide from over 2f out, styd on for press to lead line, all out: **50a**
4984} **LANDESCENT 11** [10] M Quinn 3-8-5 vis (52) M Fenton 8/1: 5540042: Held up, hdwy 3f out, drvn & led narrowly cl-home, hdd line: *hd* **53a**
4939} **RASID 15** [7] C A Dwyer 5-9-3 (79) Dane O'Neill 7/1: 6-040003: Dwelt, rear, eff wide 3f out, drvn to dispute lead well ins last, just held: *shd* **59a**
5010} **KHUZDAR 8** [2] M R Channon 4-8-13 (39) S Hitchcott (3) 7/1: 3414064: Dwelt & held up, hdwy to press ldr over 1f out, not pace of front trio well ins last. *¾* **54a**
4831} **WATER OF LIFE 23** [1] J R Boyle 4-8-6 (49) R Miles (4) 20/1: 0000005: Trkd ldrs, led 2f out, hdd & no extra well ins last: *hd* **46a**
4859} **DARK DOLORES 21** [11] J R Boyle 5-8-6 (35) D Sweeney 25/1: 0620056: Led/dsptd lead 10f, sn btn. *7* **36a**
4582} **ROUTE BARREE 41** [8] S Dow 5-8-10 (46) P Doe 10/1: 3420067: Slow away, sn chsd ldrs, btn 2f out, abs. *1¼* **38a**
4817} **ELHEBA 24** [4] M Wigham 4-9-1 bl (55) Lisa Jones (3) 33/1: 0440008: Dwelt, rear, no ch fnl 2f. *¾* **42a**
4876} **APPLEACRE 20** [9] B R Johnson 4-9-0 (85) I Mongan 2/1 FAV: 10-15409: Dsptd lead 9f, sn btn: *1½* **39a**
2580} **ONYA 134** [5] J W Hills 3-8-5 (44) J F Egan 33/1: 00000: Keen, chsd ldrs 1m, t.o., abs. *18* **9a**
10 Ran 2m 34.18 (4.98) Owner Mr Erik Penser Trained at Blewbury

25 **3.20 Littlewoodscasino Com Selling Stakes 2yo (G)**
£2093 £598 £299 **6f p/track rnd** **Going 39** **-16 Slow** Stalls Inside

4903} **FOOLS ENTIRE 17** [6] M R Channon 2-8-11 (65) A Culhane 7/2: 2430001: Trkd ldrs halfway, drvn to lead well ins last: **62a**
4899} **LADY PREDOMINANT 17** [3] M R Channon 2-8-6 (55) D Corby (3) 14/1: 0400502: Held up, pushed along halfway, styd on for press, not reach wnr: *½* **54a**
4754} **PRINCESS KAI 29** [5] R Ingram 2-8-6 BL (60) N Day 5/1: 4640303: Handy & led over 2f out till well ins last, no extra: *¾* **52a**
1 **EMARADIA 3** [4] P D Evans 2-8-11 (54) N Callan 13/2: 2056234: Led till over 2f out, onepace dist. *nk* **54a**
4816} **CITY GENERAL 24** [2] J S Moore 2-9-2 p (58) L Keniry (3) 16/1: 3340625: Chsd ldrs, no extra dist. *1* **58a**
4947} **JAOLINS 14** [8] R Hannon 2-8-6 R Smith 13/2: 006: Keen & prom, found little over 1f out. *¾* **46a**
4578} **JOINT DESTINY 41** [9] G L Moore 2-8-6 (56) S Whitworth 5/2 FAV: 2502347: Prom, onepace over 1f out: *2½* **38a**
4959} **COSTA DEL SOL 13** [7] J J Bridger 2-8-11 (53) R Miles (5) 10/1: 3442068: Rear & outpcd, nvr on terms. *½* **41a**
5015} **STAMFORD BLUE 7** [1] J S Moore 2-9-2 p (53) J D Smith 50/1: 610009: Pushed along rear, nvr pace to chall. *nk* **45a**

LINGFIELD Thursday 13.11.03 Lefthand, V Sharp Track

4863} **LADY MO** 21 [10] Andrew Reid 2-8-11 (55) D Kinsella 16/1: 1436050: Reluctant to race & al bhd.   5   **26a**
     INTRODUCTION [12] W J Musson 2-8-11 M Fenton 20/1: 0: Slowly away & al bhd on debut, op 12/1.   hd   **25a**
4965} **HES A ROCKET** 12 [11] Mrs C A Dunnett 2-8-11 (50) N Chalmers (5) 50/1: 4560000: Prom wide 4f.   ½   **23a**
4917} **LA FONTEYNE** 16 [13] C B B Booth 2-8-6 J Fanning 25/1: 00: Sn bhd, t.o..   28   **0**
13 Ran   1m 13.69 (3.29)   Owner Village Racing   Trained at West Ilsley

---

26	**3.50 Littlewoods Bet Direct Apprentice Handicap Stakes** 3yo+ 0-85 (F)		[83]
	£3094 £884 £442 **1m2f p/track** Going 39 -00 Slow Stalls Inside		

4711} **DOWER HOUSE** 31 [2] Andrew Turnell 8-9-8 (77) D Corby 10/1: 5062031: Mid-div, swtchd & drvn to lead cl-home: **83a**
4342* **RETIREMENT** 55 [1] M H Tompkins 4-9-3 (72) Saleem Golam (7) 16/1: 0024212: Handy going well, drvn to lead ins last, hdd   hd   **77a**
     cl-home:
5029} **J R STEVENSON** 6 [9] M Wigham 7-9-7 (76) Lisa Jones 4/1 JT FAV: 0004263: Dictated pace & qcknd 2f out, hdd & no extra   2½   **77a**
     well ins last:
4897} **ALRAFID** 19 [7] G L Moore 4-10-0 (83) A Quinn (3) 4/1 JT FAV: 0106224: Mid-div, lost place over 2f out, kept on late, no dngr: hd   **83a**
4664} **MOST SAUCY** 35 [13] I A Wood 7-9-3 (72) D Nolan (3) 8/1: 4320035: Rear, styd on onepace, no dngr.   nk   **71a**
4820*} **OFARABY** 24 [3] M A Jarvis 3-9-7 (80) D Fox (3) 5/1: 010216: Trkd ldr, no extra over 1f out: ½   **78a**
4897} **LIBERTY ROYAL** 19 [14] P J Makin 4-9-9 (78) L McVicar (7) 20/1: 060-0407: Dwelt, rear, eff wide, kept on.   1   **75a**
4992} **CLASSIC ROLE** 10 [6] R Ingram 4-9-6 (75) S Hitchcott 16/1: 0410008: Trkd ldrs, outpcd fnl 2f.   1   **71a**
4894} **NIGHT WARRIOR** 19 [4] D Flood 3-9-2 (75) P Mathers (5) 20/1: 5212009: Bhd, only mod prog.   2½   **67a**
1232*} **CRUISE DIRECTOR** 199 [10] W J Musson 3-9-11 (84) A Rutter (7) 16/1: 5132210: Al rear, abs.   ½   **75a**
4614} **TROPICAL CORAL** 38 [8] A J Lidderdale 3-9-3 (76) J F McDonald (3) 20/1: 5501450: Chsd ldr halfway till 2f out, sn wknd,   5   **61a**
     1m poss ideal.
4897} **THE GAIKWAR** 19 [11] N E Berry 4-9-8 (77) M Savage (5) 40/1: 130-0000: Chsd ldrs, btn/hmpd over 1f out.   5   **56a**
5019} **INDIAN WELCOME** 7 [12] H Morrison 4-9-6 bl (75) L Keniry (5) 9/1: 0150100: Dwelt, rear, hdwy 3f out, btn/hmpd over 1f out.   1½   **52a**
13 Ran   2m 06.67 (3.87)   Owner Mrs Claire Hollowood   Trained at Malton

---

WOLVERHAMPTON Friday 14.11.03 Lefthand, V Sharp Track

Official Going   Standard

27	**12.30 Bet Direct No Q Handicap Stakes Div 1** 3yo+ 0-85 (D)		[83]
	£3360 £960 £480 **7f f/sand rnd** Going 41 -21 Slow Stalls Outside		

4982} **ASHTREE BELLE** 12 [1] D Haydn Jones 4-9-3 (72) R Thomas (5) 4/1: 1522401: Chsd ldrs, switched & rdn to lead ins last,   **79a**
     styd on strongly:
2   **BELLA BEGUINE** 4 [5] A Bailey 4-9-0 VIS (69) J Fanning 9/1: 0100202: Led/dsptd lead, went on after 3f till ins last, kept on: 1   **73a**
4883} **CLOUD DANCER** 20 [4] D J Coakley 4-9-5 (74) Dane O'Neill 9/2: 3062033: Held up, smooth hdwy to pres ldrs 2f out, rdn &   ½   **77a**
     no extra ins last:
4821} **JAN BRUEGHEL** 24 [7] T D Barron 4-8-11 (66) N Callan 9/4 FAV: 3311024: Chsd ldrs, rdn & onepace over 1f out: nk   **68a**
4540} **VINTAGE STYLE** 44 [8] H A McWilliams 4-8-7 (62) G Duffield 20/1: 0040405: Held up, hdwy halfway, btn 2f out: 9   **48a**
1046} **CAROLS CHOICE** 216 [3] A Sadik 6-7-12 8oh (45) Lisa Jones (3) 40/1: 4254006: Led 3f, btn 2f out, long abs.   3½   **33a**
4852} **COMPTON ARROW** 23 [9] D Nicholls 7-8-8 (63) Joanna Badger (5) 16/1: 6440107: Dwelt, struggling fnl 3f: 6   **33a**
4990} **MILLION PERCENT** 11 [2] K R Burke 4-10-0 (69) Darren Williams 6/1: 1215438: Sn struggling: 6   **43a**
4311} **MR STYLISH** 57 [6] J S Moore 7-7-12 vis t (53) D Kinsella 20/1: 4626609: Sn hanging right & lkd unsteerable: 16   **0a**
9 Ran   1m 30.57 (4.37)   Owner Mason Gill Racing   Trained at Pontypridd

---

28	**1.00 Bet Direct No Q Demo 08000 837 888 Claiming Stakes** 2yo (F)		
	£2086 £596 £298 **1m100y f/sand rnd** Going 41 -35 Slow Stalls Inside		

4930} **MYANNABANANA** 17 [9] P Howling 2-8-7 (52) S W Kelly 14/1: 6006601: Chsd ldrs, rdn early, drvn & led 2f out, all out: **60a**
5013} **JAKARMI** 8 [10] B Palling 2-8-9 D Kinsella 20/1: 02: Prom, rdn to chall fnl 2f, just held: shd   **61a**
4960} **ARMENTIERES** 14 [5] J L Spearing 2-8-4 bl (59) Lisa Jones (3) 6/4 FAV: 6300143: Held up, styd on for press fnl 3f, not pace   1   **54a**
     to chall:
3559} **TURKS AND CAICOS** 93 [7] P C Haslam 2-9-1 P Dineley (7) 40/1: 04: Dwelt, in tch, onepace fnl 2f, abs.   3   **59a**
3115} **DRUID** 113 [11] P C Haslam 2-8-13 L Enstone (3) 20/1: 065: Held up, eff over 3f out, btn ins last: 2   **53a**
4899} **YAMATO PINK** 18 [13] K R Burke 2-8-8 (53) Joanna Badger (5) 10/1: 50466: Dwelt, in tch, rdn/chall 2f out, wknd.   3   **42a**
4912} **MISTRESS HOLLIE** 18 [6] Mrs P N Dutfield 2-8-2 p R Thomas (5) 50/1: 007: Rear, eff halfway, btn 2f out.   5   **27a**
4139} **MAGGIES CHOICE** 66 [1] N P Littmoden 2-8-6 2ow (56) I Mongan 9/2: 4010008: Sn bhd & struggling, abs.   hd   **30a**
4578} **LITTLE FLUTE** 42 [3] C G Cox 2-8-11 (52) R Smith 8/1: 4000009: Prom, hmpd 3f out, sn btn: 4   **28a**
5015} **BE MY ALIBI** 8 [12] J S Moore 2-8-3 1ow (58) J F Egan 12/1: 5340500: Led, hdd 3f out, wknd.   27   **0a**
3297} **GIVEN A CHANCE** 105 [8] J G Given 2-8-10 (52) M Fenton 16/1: 0060: Cl-up, rdn 4f out, btn when hmpd 3f out, sn eased,   20   **0a**
     abs.
4751} **ROSIE MALONEY** 30 [4] N P Littmoden 2-8-8 J P Guillambert (3) 16/1: 00: Sn bhd, t.o, new stable.   9   **0a**
12 Ran   1m 52.66 (6.46)   Owner Mr Richard Berenson   Trained at Newmarket

---

29	**1.35 Bet Direct No Q Voice Automated Betting Nursery Handicap Stakes** 2yo 0-75 (E)		[82]
	£2086 £596 £298 **7f f/sand rnd** Going 41 -43 slow Stalls Outside		

4200} **ERMINE GREY** 63 [6] D Haydn Jones 2-9-7 vis (75) Paul Eddery 7/1: 065101: Trkd ldrs travelling well, led over 1f out, drvn   **80a**
     out:
3903} **COME WHAT JULY** 83 [10] R Guest 2-8-9 bl (63) A Culhane 12/1: 550202: Held up, drvn to press ldrs fnl 2f, not pace of   ¾   **66a**
4415} **AMONG DREAMS** 52 [4] J A Osborne 2-8-10 (64) S W Kelly 9/4 FAV: 153: Cl-up, rdn & led 2f out, hdd over 1f out & no extra: 1¼   **64a**
4709} **TWO OF CLUBS** 32 [9] P C Haslam 2-9-2 (70) L Enstone (3) 9/2: 43454: Prom, rdn/ch 2f out, no extra.   4   **63a**
3641} **NESSEN DORMA** 91 [12] J G Given 2-9-2 (70) M Fenton 14/1: 22505: Bhd, mod gains wide, abs, new yard.   2½   **58a**
4903} **PARK AVE PRINCESS** 18 [8] N P Littmoden 2-8-9 (63) I Mongan 7/1: 4100046: Prom, btn over 2f out.   1   **49a**

4611} **DESERT BEAU 39** [5] Mrs P N Dutfield 2-8-10 (64) R Havlin 50/1: 0507: Rear, mod hdwy, nvr a factor. ½ 49a
4377} **DESERT IMAGE 55** [11] A J Lidderdale 2-9-0 (68) S Drowne 8/1: 0338: Held up, rdn & btn 2f out, h'cap bow/abs. ¾ 52a
4923} **CHASE THE RAINBOW 17** [2] M Johnston 2-8-10 (64) J Fanning 8/1: 5109: Led till 2f out, sn btn: 7 37a
4827} **LORD GREYSTOKE 24** [7] C P Morlock 2-8-10 (64) S Whitworth 16/1: 005040: Prom 3f, sn bhd. 2½ 32a
4960} **CORYLUS 14** [1] Sir Mark Prescott 2-8-10 (64) G Duffield 20/1: 00000: Sn struggling & bhd, AW bow. 11 13a
11 Ran   1m 32.06 (5.86)   Owner Mr L M Baker   Trained at Pontypridd

---

30 2.10 Bet Direct No Q On 08000 93 66 93 Claiming Stakes Div 1 3-5yo (F)
£2093 £598 £299   6f f/sand rnd   Going 41   -11 Slow   Stalls Inside

4883} **QUEEN OF NIGHT 20** [2] T D Barron 3-8-10 (78) N Callan 2/1 FAV: 0300151: Dwelt, sn trkd ldrs, led over 1f out, drvn out: 55a
4728} **KOMENA 32** [11] J W Payne 5-8-8 (45) I Mongan 7/1: 2023052: Mid-div, drvn to chase wnr dist, al just held: ¾ 50a
3455} **CAUSTIC WIT 98** [3] M S Saunders 5-9-1 (52) R Miles (5) 33/1: 0-000303: Handy & led over 3f out till over 1f out, no extra: 3 48a
2028} **LEGALIS 158** [10] K A Ryan 5-9-5 (71) P Fessey 9/2: 601-0004: Mid-div, eff wide 2f out, onepace: 1½ 47a
3741} **FIENNES 86** [4] Mrs N Macauley 5-8-9 p (42) Lisa Jones (3) 33/1: 0260-005: Sn pushed along, not pace to chall, abs. hd 36a
4769} **PATIENTES VIRTIS 29** [13] Miss Gay Kelleway 4-8-10 vis (51) J P Guillambert (3) 6/1: 5110606: Prom wide, btn 2f out. 3 28a
5029} **LADY ALRUNA 7** [6] P T Midgley 4-7-12 VIS (53) D Fox (5) 33/1: 0005007: Dwelt, sn on terms with ldrs, tried visor. 4 5a
4901} **NICKEL SUNGIRL 18** [8] R Hollinshead 3-8-4 (45) Stephanie Hollinshead (7) 33/1: 3-002008: Struggling halfway. 1 8a
3572} **WESTMEAD TANGO 93** [1] J R Jenkins 3-8-10 vis (53) S W Kelly 7/1: 060-0129: Prom till over 1f out, abs. nk 13a
5000} **CLOUDLESS 10** [5] J W Unett 3-7-12 (64) M Henry 9/1: 6040300: Led over 2f, btn 2f out. 2½ 0
4826} **AVONDALE LAD 24** [9] M Dods 3-8-11 VIS (48) J F Egan 25/1: 2344600: Prom 3f, btn/eased 2f out: 9 0
4786} **LORD MERLIN 377** [7] D Nicholls 4-9-5 (78) Joanna Badger 16/1: 30/0060-0: Slow away & al bhd, long abs. 1¼ 0
4883} **BAYTOWN FLYER 20** [12] J Balding 3-8-4 P (37) J Edmunds 66/1: 6000000: Dwelt, al bhd, cheek pieces. 4 0
13 Ran   1m 15.89 (3.09)   Owner Mr Timothy Cox   Trained at Thirsk

---

31 2.45 Bet Direct No Q Handicap Stakes Div 2 3yo+ 0-85 (D)   [81]
£3360 £960 £480   7f f/sand rnd   Going 41   -04 Slow   Stalls Outside

4982} **FLINT RIVER 12** [4] H Morrison 5-9-7 (74) A Culhane 11/10 FAV: 0120021: Sn handy & led over 3f out, rdn over 1f out, al holding rivals ins last, hands & heels nr fin: 84a
4821+} **MUFREH 24** [5] A G Newcombe 5-9-10 (77) S Whitworth 9/2: 1102012: Dwelt & held up, eff to chase wnr 3f out, kept on, al 2 80a
4821} **DANIELLES LAD 24** [1] B Palling 7-9-5 bl (72) M Fenton 8/1: 2030003: Led early, rem handy, no extra dist: 3½ 68a
4986} **LOCKSTOCK 12** [8] M S Saunders 5-8-10 (63) R Miles (5) 20/1: 00-00004: Chsd ldrs, rdn/lost place & short of room 3f out, rallied for press ins last, no danger: 2 55a
4818} **BLONDE EN BLONDE 25** [2] N P Littmoden 3-9-1 (69) I Mongan 8/1: 1622035: Held up, eff 3f out, btn dist. ¾ 60a
4824} **CORONADO FOREST 24** [9] M R Hoad 4-8-10 (63) Dane O'Neill 8/1: 0022606: Led till 5f out, btn 2f out. 1½ 51a
4999} **LAGGAN MINSTREL 10** [3] P W D'Arcy 5-8-2 P (55) P Fessey 16/1: 0000007: Sn rear & al bhd, op 10/1, cheek pieces. 7 31a
4908} **ELLAMYTE 18** [7] D G Bridgwater 3-7-13 vis (53) B Swarbrick (7) 40/1: 0530308: Led/dsptd lead 4f, sn btn. 1½ 26a
3875} **SUGAR CUBE TREAT 798** [6] M Mullineaux 7-7-12 10oh (41) Lisa Jones (3) 66/1: 0/60060/-9: Al bhd, long abs. ½ 23a
9 Ran   1m 29.37 (3.17)   Owner The Firm   Trained at East Ilsley

---

32 3.20 Bet Direct On Attheraces Interactive Maiden Auction Stakes 2yo (F)
£2205 £630 £315   5f f/sand rnd   Going 41   +14 Fast   Stalls Inside

4850} **PETERS CHOICE 23** [9] I Semple 2-8-7 (67) N Callan 7/2 JT FAV: 4201: Made all & rdn clr from halfway, won rdly in a fast time: 90a
4761} **SCOTTISH EXILE 29** [8] K R Burke 2-8-8 (60) Darren Williams 6/1: 404402: Prom, rdn & kept on fnl 2f, no ch with easy wnr: 8 70a
3   **DOCKLANDS BLUE 4** [4] N P Littmoden 2-8-2 Lisa Jones (3) 6/1: 63: Outpcd, late gains for press wide, nvr danger: ½ 62a
4801} **SMART STARPRINCESS 27** [6] P A Blockley 2-8-2 bl (61) F P Ferris (3) 7/2 JT FAV: 053354: Cl-up 3f. 1 59a
4965} **FAYR FIRENZE 13** [11] M F Harris 2-8-7 bl (52) S Righton 25/1: 000065: Chsd ldrs till outpcd halfway. 1¼ 60a
4825} **MELAINA 24** [1] M S Saunders 2-8-2 (52) R Smith 33/1: 0546006: Chsd ldrs, btn halfway. 1¾ 50a
4822} **DESIGNER CITY 24** [10] A Berry 2-8-3 1ow (57) J Fanning 14/1: 0644667: Sn bhd/wide, mod late gains. 1¼ 47a
4899} **KUMARI 18** [7] W M Brisbourne 2-8-2 (50) J F McDonald (5) 9/1: 65008: Pushed along, nvr pace to threaten. ½ 44a
13   **LACONIA 17** [5] J S Moore 2-8-3 1ow (61) J F Egan 7/1: 0039: Chsd ldrs till 2f out: 2½ 37a
4454} **I WISH I KNEW 49** [3] P J Makin 2-8-7 D Sweeney 40/1: 00: Al outpcd, abs. nk 44a
4695} **INTITNICE 33** [13] A Berry 2-8-10 bl (52) G Duffield 25/1: 5204000: Chsd ldrs till 3f out. 3½ 33a
1458} **RECKLESS MOMENT 186** [12] W G M Turner 2-8-3 1ow (49) P Doe 33/1: 5000: Sn bhd, abs. 7 0a
12 Ran   1m 01.53 (1.33)   Owner Mr Peter Tsim   Trained at Carluke

---

33 3.50 Bet Direct No Q On 08000 93 66 93 Claiming Stakes Div 2 3-5yo (F)
£2086 £596 £298   6f f/sand rnd   Going 41   -20 Slow   Stalls Inside

4958} **ALLY MAKBUL 14** [8] J R Best 3-8-6 (55) D Fentiman (7) 8/1: 00-53001: Sn towards rear, short of room halfway, hdwy to lead dist, rdn clr: 52a
4769} **EMPRESS JOSEPHINE 29** [1] J R Jenkins 3-8-10 vis (55) S W Kelly 9/2: 0001242: Handy & led over 4f out, rdn clr 2f out, hdd dist & wknd. 3½ 50a
4311} **ATTORNEY 57** [13] D Shaw 5-8-10 e (45) Lisa Jones (3) 9/1: 3000003: Held up, sn pushed along, late gains for press ins 1st time eye-shield: 1 47a
4741} **TRAVELLING TIMES 31** [9] J S Wainwright 4-9-1 vis (52) L Enstone (3) 14/1: 4205004: Prom, outpcd halfway, kept on late for press. 2½ 44a
4769} **SOMETHINGABOUTHER 29** [5] P W Hiatt 3-8-4 (48) P Doe 10/1: 0502005: Prom, hit by whip over 1f out, no extra. 1½ 28a
3218} **AMELIA 109** [3] Andrew Reid 5-8-4 (51) D Kinsella 3/1 FAV: 605104&: Prom, btn dist: 2½ 20a
4519} **GIVERAND 46** [10] Miss Jacqueline S Doyle 4-8-10 (44) R Havlin 25/1: 0-0037: Outpcd, nvr on terms, abs. 2½ 18a
4986} **WARLINGHAM 12** [12] M Pitman 5-9-5 e (63) S Drowne 9/2: 43000-08: Outpcd, nvr factor. 2½ 19a
3477} **BELLS BOYS 98** [6] K A Ryan 4-8-9 (40) G Parkin 33/1: 0000-059: Bhd, nvr on terms with ldrs, new yard. ½ 7a
3299} **LAKE EYRE 105** [11] J Balding 4-8-6 (39) J Edmunds 16/1: 00-05460: Prom, btn 2f out, abs. 1¾ -1a

WOLVERHAMPTON Friday 14.11.03 Lefthand, V Sharp Track

2810} **STAR LAD 126** [7] R Brotherton 3-9-1 bl (57) G Gibbons 20/1: 2206000: Led over 1f, struggling halfway, abs.   3   0a

5006} **I T CONSULTANT 9** [2] Miss L A Perratt 5-8-7 bl (45) J Fanning 11/1: 0060000: Dwelt, chsd ldrs halfway, sn btn: ¾   0

12 Ran   1m 16.46 (3.66)   Owner Mr Malcolm Ward   Trained at Maidstone

---

34   4.20 Betdirect Co Uk Amateur Riders' Handicap Stakes 3yo+ 0-80 (G)   [44]
£2247 £642 £321   1m6f166y f/sand   Going 41   -37 Slow   Stalls Outside

4708} **MR MISCHIEF 32** [9] P C Haslam 3-11-12 (78) Mr B Haslam (4) 11/1: 1-005021: Held up, hdwy from halfway & rdn/led over 1f   84a
out, styd on for press to assert ins last:

2   **GLORY QUEST 4** [1] Miss Gay Kelleway 6-12-0 (72) Miss E J Jones 5/2 FAV: 1065452: Handy, led over 4f out, rdn & hdd   1¼   75a
over 1f out, no extra ins last:

7   **MYSTERIUM 4** [7] N P Littmoden 9-9-10 vis (40) Mrs Emma Littmoden (3) 9/2: 5050033: Keen & prom, no impress fnl 2f, quick   17   23a
reapp, clr of rem.

5010} **CHAKA ZULU 9** [11] A C Whillans 6-10-9 (53) Mr S Irving (7) 9/2: 3P20224: In tch wide, btn 3f out.   8   26a

3869} **ROYAL AXMINSTER 81** [6] Mrs P N Dutfield 8-9-11 (41) Miss A Wallace (5) 20/1: 2031605: Led after 5f till over 4f out: ½   13a

5010} **PARTY PLOY 9** [8] K R Burke 5-11-9 (67) Miss H A Clements (7) 12/1: 0042606: Led 5f, btn 3f out.   1¼   37a

4828} **DANCER POLISH 24** [3] A Sadik 5-9-12 (42) Miss S Brotherton 25/1: 136/35-07: Prom till 8f out, sn bhd.   10   0a

3750} **PROFILER 86** [5] Ferdy Murphy 8-9-10 (40) Miss Z Morgan Murphy (7) 20/1: 3050408: Al bhd, abs.   1½   0a

   INTENSITY 34 [10] P A Blockley 7-11-5 (63) Miss Faye Bramley (5) 7/1: 64-60209: Sn bhd.   1½   17a

704}   **HAJEER 260** [12] P W Hiatt 5-10-9 (53) Mrs Marie King (5) 7/2: 2321230: Prom 4f, sn dropped rear & t.o: dist   0a

10 Ran   3m 21.14 (11.54)   Owner Middleham Park Racing   Trained at Middleham

---

35   7.00 Candy Appliances At Waterline Handicap Stakes 3yo+ 0-75 (E)   [74]
£2051 £586 £293   5f f/sand rnd   Going 41   -09 Slow   Stalls Inside

4969} **GONENDUNNETT 14** [3] Mrs C A Dunnett 4-9-3 vis (63) Dane O'Neill 8/1: 0220041: Mid-div, hdwy/swtchd 2f out, rdn & led   70a
dist, styd on strongly:

4712} **FRASCATI 33** [8] A Berry 3-9-10 (70) S Donohoe (2) 14/1: 6260042: Twds rear, rdn & styd on well fnl 2f, not rch wnr: 1½   71a

4654} **SEA THE WORLD 38** [1] D Shaw 3-9-3 (63) N Callan 40/1: 1004003: Mid-div, rdn & kept on to take 3rd cl home, nvr dngr: 2½   57a

4654} **ROMAN QUINTET 38** [2] D W P Arbuthnot 3-9-8 (68) J F McDonald (5) 7/1: 0640344: Cl up, no extra dist.   1   60a

4991} **PARK STAR 12** [6] D Shaw 3-9-5 (65) I Mongan 20/1: 5110005: Mid-div, not pace to chall.   1¼   54a

3747} **ONLY ONE LEGEND 87** [7] K A Ryan 5-10-0 (74) G Parkin 25/1: 0524666: Chsd ldrs, no impress when hmpd over 1f out: 1¼   60a

4810} **ROXANNE MILL 26** [4] J M Bradley 5-9-10 (70) S Drowne 4/1 JT FAV: 2040027: Chsd ldrs 3f, new stable.   hd   55a

4670} **DAINTREE AFFAIR 36** [13] K R Burke 3-9-4 (64) Darren Williams 20/1: 6-033108: Sn led, hdd over 1f out, fdd.   1   47a

4969} **CASH 14** [9] Paul Johnson 5-9-2 (62) K Dalgleish 15/2: 0300009: Sn rdn & al bhd.   ½   43a

1046*} **PRIMA STELLA 217** [11] N P Littmoden 4-9-10 (70) J P Guillambert (3) 7/1: 1132410: Sn strugg rear: hd   50a

1878} **NEW OPTIONS 167** [10] W J Musson 6-9-9 (69) Paul Eddery 20/1: 4223000: Always bhd, abs.   2   44a

1073} **RIVER DAYS 214** [12] Miss Gay Kelleway 5-9-8 bl t (68) M Fenton 4/1 JT FAV: 1601440: Chsd dlrs till hway, abs: ½   41a

12 Ran   1m 02.69 (2.49)   Owner College Farm Thoroughbreds   Trained at Norwich

---

36   7.30 Stoves Cooking At Waterline Maiden Stakes 2yo (D)
£3063 £875 £438   7f f/sand rnd   Going 41   -05 Slow   Stalls Outside

4946} **DUMNONI 16** [6] Julian Poulton 2-8-9 (73) I Mongan 13/8 FAV: 3631: Chsd ldr, led over 2f out, rdn clr, easily: 83a

4786} **TITUS SALT 29** [5] T D Barron 2-9-0 N Callan 100/30: 442: Chsd ldrs, rdn to chse wnr over 1f out, no impress: 8   71a

4962} **REDBANK 15** [4] N A Callaghan 2-9-0 T (71) Dane O'Neill 3/1: 660043: Twds rear, hdwy wide hway, kept on for press to take   4   63a
3rd, nvr dngr:

   PAR INDIANA [1] I Semple 2-8-9 M Tebbutt 25/1: 4: Pshd along & /bhd, rdn & kept on well fnl 1f, nvr dngr: nk   57a

5013} **UNINTENTIONAL 9** [11] R Brotherton 2-8-9 G Gibbons 25/1: 065: Mid-div wide, drvn & onepace, AW bow.   ½   56a

   VAMPIRE QUEEN 52 [2] R P Elliott 2-8-9 Dean McKeown 33/1: 06: Led 5f, fdd.   1½   53a

5018} **ELUSIVE DREAM 9** [7] Sir Mark Prescott 2-9-0 G Duffield 12/1: 007: Rdn, al rear, wants h'caps/further.   hd   57a

   QUIRKIE [9] K R Burke 2-8-9 Darren Williams 33/1: 8: Dwelt, in tch 4f on debut.   3½   46a

4966} **ZONNEBEKE 14** [8] K R Burke 2-8-9 R Keogh (7) 20/1: 409: Prom till 3f out.   2½   41a

   FREDS FIRST [12] B Palling 2-9-0 D Kinsella 33/1: 0: Always rear on debut.   16   19a

10 Ran   1m 29.41 (3.21)   Owner Meddler Bloodstock   Trained at Newmarket

---

37   8.00 Belling Appliances At Waterline Maiden Stakes 2yo (D)
£3136 £896 £448   1m11f79y f/sand   Going 41   -05 Slow   Stalls Inside

4946} **CLOG DANCE 16** [13] J H M Gosden 2-8-9 (73) Dane O'Neill 11/8 FAV: 00021: Chsd ldrs, led over 4f out, rdn & held on well   76a
ins last:

4962} **BILL BENNETT 15** [10] J Jay 2-9-0 (71) K Dalgleish 10/1: 60332: Rdn rear, styd on well for press fnl 2f, not able to rch wnr: 1½   77a

4924} **BAAWRAH 18** [7] M R Channon 2-9-0 D Corby (3) 33/1: 063: Prom, rdn & chsd wnr over 2f out, kept on onepace: 1¾   74a

4847} **MAJESTIC VISION 24** [6] P W Harris 2-9-0 N Callan 7/2: 34: Chsd ldrs, hung right & onepace for press fnl 2f: 2   70a

4012} **DOLLY WOTNOT 74** [11] N P Littmoden 2-8-9 (67) J P Guillambert (3) 12/1: 0445: Mld div, btn 3f out, AW bow, abs.   14   40a

4164} **ILWADOD 46** [5] M R Channon 2-9-0 S Hitchcott (3) 20/1: 006: Al bhd, abs/AW bow.   3   39a

4532} **BRETTON 46** [4] R Hollinshead 2-9-0 P (45) Dean McKeown 66/1: 06507: Led till over 4f out, wknd, chkpcs, abs.   1   37a

4987} **VERASI 12** [2] R Charlton 2-9-0 S Drowne 10/1: 008: Chsd ldrs 7f, AW bow.   hd   36a

4635} **PLATINUM PIRATE 39** [8] K R Burke 2-9-0 BL (55) Darren Williams 50/1: 000609: Dsprd lead early, btn 3f out.   1¼   33a

2157} **QUARRY ISLAND 153** [12] P D Evans 2-8-9 VIS (45) S W Kelly 66/1: 6600: Al bhd, vis, abs.   12   8a

5024} **CAN CAN FLYER 8** [9] M Johnston 2-9-0 J Fanning 9/1: 00: Sn rdn & strugg, AW bow.   6   2a

4732} **SWEET FURY 32** [3] E A L Dunlop 2-9-0 (68) M Fenton 33/1: 0000: Mid-div, btn 3f out.   1¼   0a

   BEAUCHAMP SPARK [1] A P Jones 2-9-0 G Hannon 66/1: 0: Always outpcd & bhd on debut.   3   0a

13 Ran   2m 02.52 (4.32)   Owner Maktoum Al Maktoum   Trained at Manton

38	8.30 Waterline Uk's Number 1 Kitchen Distributor Handicap Stakes Fillies 3yo+ 0-75 (E)	[74]
	£2100 £600 £300 1m1f79y f/sand Going 41 +10 Fast Stalls Inside	

4768} **STRONG HAND** 30 [4] M W Easterby 3-9-11 (74) P Mulrennan (5) 4/1: 5313351: Trkd ldr, al trav well, shkn up to lead over 1f out, hands & heels, readily:			**88a**
5019*} **STAR OF NORMANDIE** 9 [5] G G Margarson 4-10-0 (74) B Reilly (5) 7/2 FAV: 4600312 Mid-div, styd on for press fnl 2f, nvr threatened wnr:		3½	**80a**
4024} **MISS GLORY BE** 74 [2] Miss Gay Kelleway 5-9-0 p (60) M Fenton 5/1: 0506323: Chsd ldrs, onepace.		1½	**63a**
4144} **JESSINCA** 67 [3] A P Jones 7-8-0 (46) D Kinsella 11/1: 6002464: Led till over 1f out, abs.		shd	**49a**
4809} **TOP OF THE CLASS** 26 [12] P D Evans 6-8-2 vis (48) Joanna Badger 12/1: 0615405: Slow away, bhd, mod prog.		3	**45a**
4788} **DENS JOY** 29 [7] Miss D A McHale 7-9-4 p (64) Darren Williams 13/2: 0000056: Dwelt, mid-div hway, no prog 2f out.		shd	**61a**
5021} **VERMILION CREEK** 9 [8] R Hollinshead 4-8-1 (47) Stephanie Hollinshead (7) 25/1: 1614007: Bhd, no impress 2f out.		¾	**43a**
4967} **MISS CHAMPERS** 14 [11] P D Evans 3-8-9 (66) N Callan 25/1: 0060308: In tch, efft wide 3f out, sn wknd.		6	**52a**
6 **EUROLINK ARTEMIS** 5 [13] Miss Gay Kelleway 6-8-6 p (52) Lisa Jones (3) 25/1: 6200009: Mid-div, no impress fnl 2f.		hd	**37a**
4640} **ZAHUNDA** 39 [10] W M Brisbourne 4-8-5 (51) B Swarbrick (7) 25/1: 0010000: Mid-div, btn 2f out.		1¼	**33a**
3703*} **TANGA DANCER** 88 [9] B Smart 3-8-1 (50) P M Quinn 25/1: 00-04610: Always bhd, 12 wk abs.		hd	**31a**
4929} **CHIASSO** 18 [6] H Morrison 3-8-8 (57) S Drowne 15/2: 40040: Chsd ldrs, btn 3f out.		12	**19a**
1003} **POOKAS DAUGHTER** 220 [1] J M Bradley 3-8-9 (58) P Fitzsimons 33/1: 1042000: Keen & cl up, btn 3f out.		18	**0a**
13 Ran 2m 01.07 (2.87) Owner Mrs Jean Turpin		Trained at Sheriff Hutton	

39	9.00 Franke Sinks And Taps At Waterline Maiden Stakes 3yo+ (D)	
	£2282 £652 £326 1m100y f/sand rnd Going 41 -12 Slow Stalls Inside	

5017} **MERDIFF** 9 [2] W M Brisbourne 4-9-2 T (64) S W Kelly 15/8 FAV: 0003201: Chsd ldrs, led over 6f out, rdn clr 2f out, held on all out close home:			**69a**
4689} **OVER RATING** 34 [12] J H M Gosden 3-8-9 (68) R Havlin 7/2: 42342: Held up, hdwy over 4f out & styd on well for press ins last, just failed:		nk	**61a**
1185} **REALISM** 205 [11] P W Hiatt 3-9-0 Darren Williams 100/1: 03: Mid div, hdwy to chall over 2f out, not pace of front pair:		5	**58a**
4720} **MAID FOR LIFE** 33 [4] M J Wallace 3-8-9 N Callan 8/1: 0464: Held up, hdwy 4f out, no prog fnl 2f, AW bow:		3	**47a**
4740} **FELIDAE** 32 [6] M Brittain 3-9-0 M Lawson (7) 100/1: 005: Dwelt, twds rear, only mod prog, AW bow.		5	**43a**
8 **DECO LADY** 5 [7] P D Evans 3-8-9 (50) Joanna Badger 50/1: 0500056: Mid-div, btn 2f out, qck reapp.		¾	**37a**
3372} **MARAKASH** 103 [13] M R Bosley 4-9-2 (60) D Sweeney 25/1: 2230-007: Bhd, nvr factor, abs.		¾	**41a**
4705} **BAR OF SILVER** 34 [10] R Brotherton 3-9-0 p (55) G Gibbons 40/1: 2025058: Chsd ldrs till hway.		4	**34a**
4531} **FOGGIELOAN** 46 [3] C G Cox 3-8-9 (48) R Smith 100/1: 0609: Chsd ldrs 4f, AW bow/abs.		17	**0a**
FULL ENGLISH [5] A P Jones 4-8-11 Lisa Jones (3) 50/1: 0: Al bhd on debut.		½	**0**
4815} **KALLISTAS PRIDE** 26 [9] J A Osborne 3-8-9 J Fanning 50/1: 00: Led 2f, sn bhd.		2	**0**
4848} **JUBILEE TIME** 24 [8] L M Cumani 3-9-0 Dane O'Neill 9/4: 03W: Refused to enter stalls, withdrawn.			**0**
4989} **CRYSTAL CHOIR** 12 [1] R Charlton 3-8-9 S Drowne 14/1: 0W: Unruly bef start & in stalls, withdrawn.			**0**
13 Ran 1m 50.67 (4.47) Owner Thats Racing Partnership		Trained at Baschurch	

40	9.30 Smeg Appliances At Waterline Handicap Stakes 3yo+ 0-65 (F)	[65]
	£2170 £620 £310 1m100y f/sand rnd Going 41 +01 Fast Stalls Inside	

4986} **PHAROAHS GOLD** 13 [2] D Shaw 5-9-9 e (60) Darren Williams 12/1: 0034201: Trkd ldrs 3f out, led dist, drvn out:			**67a**
4970} **ROCK CONCERT** 14 [12] I W McInnes 5-9-3 vis (54) P Mathers (7) 3/1 FAV: 0053232: Led after 2f, rdn & hdd dist, kept on for press:		1¾	**57a**
4985} **MCQUEEN** 13 [13] Mrs H Dalton 3-9-8 (61) D Sweeney 5/1: 0-332033: Trkd ldrs, rdn & onepace from dist, clr rem:		1¼	**61a**
4854} **GOLD GUEST** 24 [5] P D Evans 4-9-3 VIS (54) D Nolan (5) 10/1: 0046004: Trkd ldrs, no extra bef dist, fair run in vis:		5	**45a**
4699} **KIRKBYS TREASURE** 34 [7] A Berry 5-9-4 (54) S Donohoe (7) 25/1: 1226005: Held up, drvn & no imprss.		3	**40a**
3325} **ALLEGRINA** 105 [6] K A Ryan 3-9-12 (65) N Callan 13/2: 44-14056: Chsd ldrs till dist, abs.		nk	**49a**
RAS TAILTEANN 45 [1] D Wachman 3-9-7 (60) S Drowne 4/1: 0-067: Mid-div, efft 4f out, sn btn.		2½	**39a**
4374} **WHITE PARK BAY** 56 [3] J Gallagher 3-9-12 (65) Lisa Jones (3) 8/1: 3324038: Prom early, lost tch 4f out, new yard.		hd	**43a**
4862} **SCOTTISH RIVER** 23 [11] M D I Usher 4-10-0 (65) N Chalmers (5) 20/1: 0055009: V slow away, lost chance start.		7	**31a**
5017} **PHANTOM FLAME** 9 [9] M Johnston 3-9-2 (55) J Fanning 20/1: 0000000: Mid-div, abs.		2½	**16a**
4459} **OPEN HANDED** 50 [4] B Ellison 3-9-4 t (55) V Halliday 50/1: 0060000: Led 2f, sn strugg, abs.		hd	**17a**
4873} **THEORIST** 22 [8] J L Spearing 3-9-7 P (60) A Daly 25/1: 0650000: Al rear, new stable.		1½	**17a**
4722} **OUR PADDY** 33 [10] Mrs L C Jewell 4-9-4 (55) Dane O'Neill 33/1: 6503000: V slow away & al bhd for new yard.		9	**0a**
13 Ran 1m 49.8 (3.6) Owner The Whiteman Partnership		Trained at Newark	

41	12.40 Bet Direct No Q Handicap Stakes Div 1 3yo+ 0-85 (D)	[85]
	£3402 £972 £486 6f f/sand rnd Going 39 -04 Slow Stalls Inside	

4982} **CANTERLOUPE** 15 [8] P J Makin 5-9-5 (76) D Sweeney 11/2: 6533051: Trkd ldrs trav well, rdn & led over 1f out, rdn out:			**83a**
22 **HEIDELBURG** 4 [7] S Kirk 3-8-6 (63) J F Egan 15/2: 0406062: Rdn & towards rear, styd on strongly fnl 1f, nrst fin:		1¼	**66a**
4982} **LANDING STRIP** 15 [3] J M P Eustace 3-9-6 (77) F P Ferris (3) 7/2 FAV: 0011443: Cl-up & led after 1f till over 1f out, no extra:		1	**77a**
2529} **BOND ROYALE** 140 [11] B Smart 3-9-8 (79) I Mongan (5) 1-500004: Prom, rdn & kept on onepace.		shd	**79a**
5037} **LAW BREAKER** 9 [5] J A Gilbert 5-10-0 (85) A Daly 4/1: 0001005: Rear, rdn & nrst fin:		hd	**84a**
1305} **OUR CHELSEA BLUE** 198 [12] A W Carroll 5-8-3 (60) F Norton 25/1: 1560006: Cl-up, no extra dist.		2½	**52a**
4982} **INDIAN MAIDEN** 15 [10] M S Saunders 3-9-2 (73) S Whitworth 12/1: 1110607: Towards rear, nvr pace to threaten.		2½	**58a**
5025} **TURN AROUND** 10 [9] B W Hills 3-9-3 (74) Dane O'Neill 20/1: 3510-008: Rear, nvr able to chall.		1¼	**56a**
20 **TOPPLING** 4 [4] J M Bradley 5-8-0 (57) A Nicholls 33/1: 2000009: Prom, btn/eased ins last, qck reapp.		1	**37a**
4818} **BLAKESHALL QUEST** 28 [1] R Brotherton 3-9-3 (74) G Gibbons 33/1: 2610000: Chsd ldrs till halfway.		1½	**50a**
4991} **PRINCE OF BLUES** 14 [2] M Mullineaux 5-9-9 (80) T Williams 12/1: 0600000: Led 1f inner, struggling fnl 2f.		8	**36a**
35 **RIVER DAYS** 2 [13] Miss Gay Kelleway 5-8-11 bl t (68) B Fayos Martin (7) 14/1: 16014400: Al bhd, qck reapp.		3	**17a**
3456} **PIPS SONG** 101 [6] P W Hiatt 8-7-12 3oh (52) Joanna Badger 16/1: 0260030: Slow away al bhd, abs.		7	**0a**

WOLVERHAMPTON Monday 17.11.03 Lefthand, Sharp Track

13 Ran   1m 15.39 (2.59)   Owner R A Ballin & The Billinomas   Trained at Marlborough

42 | 1.10 Bet Direct On 0800 32 93 93 Median Auction Maiden Stakes 2yo (F)
£2289 £654 £327   6f f/sand rnd   Going 39   -24 Slow   Stalls Inside

1	BRIDGEWATER BOYS 7 [5] K A Ryan 2-9-0 bl (58) G Duffield 4/1: 3025621: Trkd ldrs, chall fnl 1f & drvn to lead well ins			73a
4965}	BOOKIESINDEXDOTCOM 16 [6] J R Jenkins 2-8-9 vis (65) S W Kelly 8/1: 0643222: Led/dsptd lead, went on halfway, hdd well ins last:		½	65a
3	BOND BROOKLYN 7 [10] B Smart 2-9-0 vis (67) Darren Williams 3/1 FAV: 5523533: In tch, eff wide to press ldrs fnl 1f, onepace:		1¼	67a
4766}	QUINCANNON 32 [9] T D Barron 2-9-0 S Drowne 5/1: 04: Pushed along mid-div, not able to chall:		1½	63a
3	VITTORIOSO 7 [7] Miss Gay Kelleway 2-9-0 p M Fenton 66/1: 05: Prom, no extra dist.		1	61a
	SABLE N SILK [1] D Haydn Jones 2-8-9 F Norton 25/1: 6: Pushed along, not pace to chall on debut.		3	49a
4575}	IPHIGENIA 45 [4] P W Hiatt 2-8-9 (63) Lisa Jones (3) 10/1: 02307: Chsd ldrs 4f, abs.		1¾	45a
4892}	GARRIGON 23 [12] N P Littmoden 2-9-0 (66) I Mongan 11/2: 2606208: Towards rear, no impress fnl 2f.		2	45a
4965}	FAITES VOS JEUX 16 [3] C N Kellett 2-8-9 (58) T Williams 33/1: 664439: Led 2f, btn over 1f out.		1¾	36a
2994}	SAFFRON RIVER 121 [2] R Hollinshead 2-9-0 A Culhane 25/1: 430: Dwelt & al bhd, abs.		3½	32a
	CALCULAITE [8] Mrs G S Rees 2-9-0 Angela Hartley 40/1: 0: Dwelt, sn outpcd on debut.		3	25a
3924}	ROYAL AWAKENING 82 [11] A P Jarvis 2-9-0 N Callan 9/1: 30: Chsd ldrs till halfway:		2½	18a

12 Ran   1m 16.56 (3.76)   Owner Bishopthorpe Racing   Trained at Hambleton

43 | 1.40 Bet Direct On Attheraces Interactive Maiden Auction Stakes 2yo (F)
£2282 £652 £326   1m100y f/sand rnd Going 39   -27 Slow   Stalls Inside

4988}	ALMOND WILLOW 14 [7] J Noseda 2-8-9 (66) S W Kelly 3/1: 060361: Trkd ldrs, rdn/flashed tail & briefly outpcd over 1f out, rallied well for press to lead well ins last:			71a
4966}	HAWKIT 16 [1] J A Osborne 2-9-0 (73) Dane O'Neill 6/4 FAV: 2322: Rear, smooth hdwy halfway & rdn/briefly led ins last, no extra cl-home:		1¼	72a
4966}	KELTIC RAINBOW 16 [4] D Haydn Jones 2-8-3 1ow (58) Paul Eddery 10/1: 0033: Trkd ldrs, styd on for press fnl 2f, not pace of front pair:		1½	58a
4912}	ROOD BOY 21 [10] J S King 2-8-7 D Kinsella 40/1: 004: Cl-up, led 3f out till hdd & no extra ins last:		½	61a
4912}	ELITISTA 21 [9] E J O'Neill 2-8-2 (58) J Tate 20/1: 0555: Held up, nvr able to chall ldrs.		7	44a
5018}	BEAU WEST 11 [6] S Kirk 2-8-3 1ow (47) J F Egan 8/1: 56: Led 5f, btn/eased ins last, AW bow.		1¾	42a
4635}	HOLD THE LINE 41 [12] W G M Turner 2-8-7 (70) L Treadwell (5) 11/2: 0627: Prom, hung left/btn over 1f out:		1¼	43a
4885}	BISCAR TWO 23 [3] R M Whitaker 2-8-7 Dean McKeown 66/1: 008: Al bhd, AW bow.		2½	38a
4966}	PATTERN MAN 16 [8] J R Norton 2-8-8 1ow Darren Williams 66/1: 009: Struggling fnl 4f.		1¾	36a
4942}	WINSLOW BOY 19 [5] C F Wall 2-8-10 M Fenton 16/1: 000: Bhd, short of room over 3f out, sn btn, AW bow.		5	28a
3093}	CASANTELLA 117 [2] M G Quinlan 2-8-2 (50) G Duffield 66/1: 60000: Prom, btn 3f out, abs/AW bow.		4	12a
3373}	SHALAMAK 105 [13] B R Millman 2-8-2 (57) M Henry 50/1: 5600: Bhd, no ch halfway, abs/AW bow.		21	0
4966}	WEET AN STORE 16 [11] R Hollinshead 2-8-10 T A Culhane 66/1: 00: Al bhd, t.o.:		2	0

13 Ran   1m 51.8 (5.6)   Owner Mr W L Armitage   Trained at Newmarket

44 | 2.10 Betdirect Co Uk Stakes Handicap 3yo+ 0-95 (C)   [95]
£5551 £1708 £854 £427   1m100y f/sand rnd Going 39   +05 Fast   Stalls Inside

2+*	CARDINAL VENTURE 7 [5] K A Ryan 5-9-5 6ex (86) N Callan 3/1 FAV: 3220011: Made all, rdn clr over 1f out, held on well for press ins last:			94a
5*	LAKOTA BRAVE 7 [1] Mrs S A Liddiard 9-9-5 6ex (86) F Norton 16/1: 1043312: Held up, hdwy halfway & rdn/chsd wnr over 1f out, kept on, not able to chall:		¾	92a
4992}	OVIGO 14 [2] P A Blockley 4-8-0 (67) F P Ferris (3) 33/1: 5-150003: Rear, swtchd & styd on for press fnl 1f, edged left & no extra fnl 100y:		2	69a
4977}	CERTAIN JUSTICE 16 [3] P F I Cole 5-9-4 (85) S Drowne 7/1: 2-050604: Chsd ldrs, no extra dist:		3½	80a
4939}	TE QUIERO GB 19 [6] Miss Gay Kelleway 5-9-12 t (93) S W Kelly 7/1: 11-20105: Prom, no extra 2f out:		nk	87a
5029}	BLUE TROJAN 10 [13] S Kirk 3-8-4 (73) J F Egan 8/1: 1030156: Held up, mod gains under hands & heels.		hd	66a
5030}	DIAMOND MAX 9 [10] P D Evans 5-9-4 (85) D Nolan (5) 9/1: 1010057: Rear, eff from halfway, no prog dist:		2	74a
4961*}	YORKER 17 [12] Ms Deborah J Evans 5-8-2 1ow (68) G Duffield 20/1: 6530018: Chsd ldrs, btn 3f out.		1¼	55a
4977}	NASHAAB 16 [4] P D Evans 6-9-8 (89) Dane O'Neill 6/1: 4020039: Slow away, lost ch start, forgive this.		hd	74a
4606}	LYGETON LAD 44 [11] Miss Gay Kelleway 5-9-1 t (95) M Fenton 20/1: 0055200: Slow away, al bhd, abs.		3½	73a
4890}	VICIOUS WARRIOR 23 [8] R M Whitaker 4-8-11 (78) Dean McKeown 12/1: 2004020: Chsd ldrs, btn 2f out.		3½	49a
5029}	DEL MAR SUNSET 10 [9] W J Haggas 4-9-8 (89) A Culhane 12/1: 0432200: Mid-div halfway, btn 2f out.		8	46a
5036}	NUIT SOMBRE 9 [7] M Johnston 3-9-1 bl (84) J Fanning 10/1: 5405600: Trkd ldrs, fdd fnl 3f, AW bow.		6	31a

13 Ran   1m 49.05 (2.85)   Owner Mr Tony Fawcett   Trained at Hambleton

45 | 2.40 Bet Direct No Q Handicap Stakes Div 2 3yo+ 0-85 (D)   [85]
£3388 £968 £484   6f f/sand rnd   Going 39   +06 Fast   Stalls Inside

4990}	BOND PLAYBOY 14 [4] B Smart 3-9-13 (84) I Mongan 25/1: 6200001: Led/dsptd lead, led after 2f, strongly prsd dist, gamely, all out:			89a
4969*}	QUIET TIMES 16 [7] K A Ryan 4-9-4 bl (75) N Callan 5/1: 6565012: Led/dsptd lead, ev ch fnl 1f, just held:		nk	79a
23	MONTE MAYOR LAD 4 [13] D Haydn Jones 3-8-5 bl (62) F Norton 9/1: 0-433033: Trkd ldrs, rdn & briefly outpcd over 1f out, styd on well for press cl-home, just held:		shd	66a
4591}	RAFTERS MUSIC 44 [3] Julian Poulton 8-9-1 (72) Lisa Jones (3) 7/1: 3552254: Chsd ldrs, not pace to chall.		2½	69a
4860}	ESATTO 25 [1] P A Blockley 4-8-10 (67) Dean McKeown 7/1: 2050635: Chsd ldrs, no extra over 1f out.		1½	60a
4478}	CASHEL MEAD 51 [2] J L Spearing 3-9-7 (78) A Daly 14/1: 011-0006: Bhd, only mod gains, abs.		¾	69a
4769}	GERONIMO 32 [6] Miss Gay Kelleway 6-7-12 (55) D Kinsella 7/1: 2566067: Towards rear, mod gains, nvr dngr:		nk	45a
4768}	EFFECTIVE 32 [12] A P Jarvis 3-8-11 (68) Darren Williams 25/1: 4002008: Prom, btn over 1f out.		hd	57a

19

WOLVERHAMPTON Monday 17.11.03 Lefthand, Sharp Track

4991} **SAFRANINE 14** [11] Miss A Stokell 6-8-3 p (60) Rory Moore (7) 14/1: 0060009: Chsd ldrs, struggling from halfway. 1½ 45a
5025} **CURRENCY 10** [9] J M Bradley 6-9-5 (76) P Fitzsimons 14/1: 3606600: Prom 2f, sn struggling. nk 60a
4477} **SIR DESMOND 51** [10] R Guest 5-9-9 p (80) A Culhane 11/4 FAV: 0401400: Al bhd: 5 53a
4949} **NEW FOUNDATION 18** [8] Mrs S A Liddiard 3-8-0 t (57) J F McDonald (5) 25/1: 5405000: Sn bhd. ¾ 28a
5025} **SEMENOVSKII 10** [5] P W D'Arcy 3-9-3 (74) J F Egan 14/1: 6000600: Al bhd. 1¾ 41a
13 Ran 1m 14.79 (1.99) Owner Mr R C Bond Trained at Thirsk

---

46 3.10 Bet Direct In Running Sky Text 293 Selling Stakes Div 1 3yo+ (G)
£2065 £590 £295 **1m100y f/sand rnd Going 39 -08 Slow** Stalls Inside

4961} **CONSIGNIA 17** [5] D Haydn Jones 4-9-0 VIS (48) Paul Eddery 7/1: 3031001: Held up, rdn & styd on for press to lead cl-home, 49a
all out:
2897} **CONCHONITA 126** [2] B Palling 3-8-7 (40) D Kinsella 25/1: 0-360662: Led/dpstd lead, drvn to lead over 1f out, hdd nr line: ½ 42a
1970} **GIVEMETHEMOONLIGHT 165** [11] L G Cottrell 4-8-9 (48) I Mongan 4/1: 3-405603: Held up, smooth hdwy wide to lead hd 41a
over 2f out, hdd over 1f out, just held cl-home:
4883} **SECOND VENTURE 23** [9] J R Weymes 5-9-0 (37) D Fentiman (7) 25/1: 0000504: Prom, no extra dist. 5 37a
4640} **AIR OF ESTEEM 41** [13] Ian Emmerson 7-9-5 (50) Dean McKeown 6/1: 0020045: Held up, eff wide 3f out, btn dist: 3 36a
4826} **NEUTRAL NIGHT 27** [1] R Brotherton 3-8-7 vis (45) G Gibbons 25/1: 5006066: Led/dpstd lead 5f, wknd. nk 25a
2244} **STORM SHOWER 151** [8] Mrs N Macauley 5-9-0 vis (41) Lisa Jones (3) 11/1: 2506037: Dwelt, rear, only mod hdwy, abs. 1¼ 27a
3934} **DISTINCTLYSPLENDID 81** [7] I A Wood 3-8-12 (36) G Duffield 25/1: 0006408: Led/dpstd lead 3f, btn 2f out: 1¾ 24a
4767} **NITE OWL FIZZ 32** [3] J O'Reilly 5-9-5 (55) J D O'Reilly (7) 10/1: 0056009: Al bhd. nk 28a
4859} **HIGH DIVA 25** [10] B R Johnson 4-8-10 1ow (48) Dane O'Neill 5/2 FAV: 5402000: Trkd ldrs, rdn & btn qckly 3f out. 1¾ 16a
4913} **GENEROUS SHARE 21** [12] M S Saunders 3-8-7 (50) S Whitworth 11/1: 40-00500: Held up, struggling halfway. 9 0a
3101} **THREAT 116** [6] J M Bradley 7-9-0 (43) P Fitzsimons 25/1: 4320000: Prom, btn 4f out, 4 mth abs. 2 1a
1873} **INDRAPURA STAR 169** [4] Miss J Feilden 3-8-12 (47) A Quinn (5) 25/1: 0-000: Bhd from halfway, t.o., abs/AW bow. dist 0a
13 Ran 1m 50.63 (4.43) Owner Mr I Jerrard Trained at Pontypridd

---

47 3.40 Bet Direct In Running Sky Text 293 Selling Stakes Div 2 3yo+ (G)
£2065 £590 £295 **1m100y f/sand rnd Going 39 -16 Slow** Stalls Inside

4093} **PUPS PRIDE 72** [5] Mrs N Macauley 6-9-5 vis (52) Lisa Jones (3) 10/1: 3516001: Mid-div, outpcd halfway, rallied wide for 56a
press fnl 2f to lead nr fin:
4591} **NOUL 44** [6] K A Ryan 4-9-5 (72) P Fessey 10/11 FAV: 6036042: Hld up, styd on wide for press fnl 2f, not pace of wnr cl-home: ¾ 54a
4093} **FEAST OF ROMANCE 72** [1] P Howling 6-9-0 (51) J P Guillambert (3) 5/1: 2002033: Led/dpstd lead, went on after 2f & rdn 1 47a
clr over 1f out, hdd nr fin:
4963} **SWYNFORD WELCOME 17** [12] I A Wood 7-9-0 (40) D Nolan (5) 10/1: 0000004: Prom, chsd wnr 2f out, no extra fnl 1f: ¾ 54a
4026} **MALMAND 76** [3] R Brotherton 4-9-5 vis (42) G Gibbons 25/1: 0050005: Dwelt, sn trkd ldrs, onepace fnl 3f, abs. 1 49a
4968} **SAMAR QAND 16** [11] Julian Poulton 4-8-9 p (49) J F Egan 6/1: 0300036: Rear, only mod prog, nvr dngr. 7 27a
3002} **MUTARAFAA 121** [2] D Shaw 4-9-0 e (44) I Mongan 16/1: 6300067: In tch, btn 2f out: ½ 31a
39 **DECO LADY 7** [4] P D Evans 3-8-7 (50) N Callan 20/1: 0500058: Led/dpstd lead 5f, sn btn. 3½ 19a
3119} **ACHILLES RAINBOW 116** [13] K R Burke 4-9-0 (39) Darren Williams 25/1: 040-0409: In tch, btn over 2f out. 1 22a
3004} **TEDZAR 121** [9] B R Johnson 3-8-12 bl (35) N Chalmers (5) 20/1: 000-0000: In tch, btn 3f out, abs. ½ 21a
2683} **BETTERGETGONE 135** [10] W Clay 4-8-9 (35) B Swarbrick (7) 66/1: 00000/-00: Al bhd, t.o., abs. dist 0a
PRESIDENTS LADY 1146 [7] P W Hiatt 6-8-9 (42) Joanna Badger 33/1: 0/0020//-0: Prom, lost place fnl 4f. 11 0a
12 Ran 1m 50.91 (4.71) Owner West Indies Capital Company Li Trained at Melton Mowbray

---

48 4.10 Littlewoodscasino Com Handicap Stakes 3yo+ 0-75 (E)
£2044 £584 £292 **2m46y f/sand Going 39 -21 Slow** Stalls Inside [72]

4957} **SNOWS RIDE 17** [6] W R Muir 3-9-5 (72) I Mongan 4/1: 6521501: Chsd ldr & led over 6f out, rdn clr over 2f out & eased ins 84a
last, val 10L+:
4538} **MADHAHIR 47** [3] C A Dwyer 3-8-8 p (61) N Callan 16/1: 6004062: Trkd ldrs, rdn & chsd wnr fnl 3f, no impress over 1f out but 5 64a
kept on:
4957} **RED SCORPION 17** [5] W M Brisbourne 4-9-11 (69) J F Egan 9/2: 0005203: Rear, onepace fnl 2f. 3 69a
4375*} **SASHAY 58** [4] R Hollinshead 5-9-3 (61) Stephanie Hollinshead (7) 9/1: 4040614: In tch, no impress fnl 2f. 3 58a
7 **DIGGER 7** [2] Miss Gay Kelleway 4-9-7 t (65) L Enstone (3) 15/8 FAV: 1320025: Held up racing v keenly, smooth hdwy halfway 3½ 59a
but rdn/btn 2f out:
4931} **E MINOR 20** [11] T Wall 4-9-8 (66) N Chalmers (5) 20/1: 5044006: Held up, btn 4f out. 6 54a
7 **MELOGRANO 7** [12] R M Beckett 3-7-12 5oh (46) Lisa Jones (3) 33/1: 0060367: Trkd ldrs, lost place from halfway. 3 36a
5009} **LAPADAR 12** [1] J R Weymes 4-9-7 p (65) D Fentiman (7) 66/1: 0-006058: Led till over 6f out, sn struggling. 17 37a
4422} **TONI ALCALA 54** [9] R F Fisher 4-9-8 (66) J Fanning 16/1: 3102049: Held up, eff halfway, btn 4f out, abs. shd 38a
2839} **FAST CINDY 128** [8] J W Unett 4-9-2 (60) Dane O'Neill 16/1: 5210-200: Al bhd, abs/new stable. ¾ 31a
3643} **ULSHAW 94** [10] B J Llewellyn 6-8-10 (54) P Mathers (7) 12/1: 3122000: Prom till lost place from halfway, t.o., abs. 24 7a
11 Ran 3m 38.92 (9.72) Owner The Parkside Partnership Trained at Lambourn

---

LINGFIELD Tuesday 18.11.03 Lefthand, V Sharp Track

Official Going Standard

49 12.20 Bet Direct Itv Page 367 Maiden Stakes Div 1 2yo (D)
£3080 £880 £440 **6f p/track rnd Going 46 -23 Slow** Stalls Inside

5014} **AESCULUS 12** [6] L M Cumani 2-8-9 W Ryan 13/2: 051: Made all, rdn & al holding rivals from dist: 75a
5013} **MUKTASB 12** [7] M P Tregoning 2-9-0 R Hills 4/1: 002: Keen trkg ldrs, prsd wnr over 1f out, no extra ins last: 1½ 74a
HALABALOO 2 [2] G Wragg 2-8-9 J F Egan 11/1: 3: Dwelt, hmpd start, swtchd wide & kept on late for press, not reach front pair: nk 68a
5013} **ROCKLEY BAY 12** [9] P J Makin 2-9-0 D Sweeney 8/1: 054: Chsd wnr, no extra over 1f out. 2½ 65a

5015}	**GET TO THE POINT** 12 [8] P W D'Arcy 2-9-0 (65) Paul Eddery 3/1 JT FAV: 540005: Held up in tch, btn dist:	3	56a
4926}	**BERESFORD BOY** 21 [10] D K Ivory 2-9-0 I Mongan 50/1: 06: In tch, outpcd from halfway:	1¼	52a
4462}	**EUGENIE** 53 [11] R Hannon 2-8-9 Dane O'Neill 10/1: 07: In tch wide, no impress fnl 2f, abs/AW bow.	5	32a
4898}	**RAGGED JACK** 24 [5] G A Butler 2-9-0 S W Kelly 3/1 JT FAV: 50U: Jinked right, stumbled & u.r. leaving stalls.		0
8 Ran	1m 14.54 (4.14) Owner Lord Hartington		Trained at Newmarket

---

50   **12.50 Bet Direct On Channel 4 Page 613 Stakes Handicap Div 1 3yo+ 0-70 (E)**   **[70]**

£2134 £610 £305   7f p/track rnd   Going 46   +02 Fast   Stalls Inside

4949}	**I WISH** 19 [10] M Madgwick 5-9-6 (62) L Keniry (3) 12/1: 0000061: Keen & prom, pushed along over 2f out, styd on well for press ins last to lead line, all out:		65a
22*	**MR BOUNTIFUL** 5 [15] M Dods 5-9-5 6ex (61) S W Kelly 11/2: 0206412: Keen, prom, led 3f out & rdn clr over 1f out, drvn & hdd line:	shd	63a
17	**HADATH** 6 [11] B G Powell 6-9-10 p (66) A Hindley (7) 14/1: 0260053: Prom, outpcd over 2f out, rallied well under inexperienced rider ins last, just held:	hd	67a
22	**INISTRAHULL ISLAND** 5 [9] M H Tompkins 3-8-13 (56) J Fanning 5/1: 0502604: Mid-div, styd on for press fnl 1f, nrst fin:	nk	56a
4564}	**ICECAP** 47 [2] P Butler 3-8-12 (55) A Daly 20/1: 0445665: Held up, styd on for press, nrst fin:	½	53a
22	**GEORGE STUBBS** 5 [5] N P Littmoden 5-10-0 bl (70) J P Guillambert (3) 9/2 FAV: 0323056: Mid-div, onepace:	nk	67a
4258}	**TAIYO** 63 [4] J W Payne 3-8-12 (55) I Mongan 25/1: 3-5057: Mid-div, rdn & kept on onepace, abs.	nk	51a
4986}	**TEMPER TANTRUM** 16 [7] Andrew Reid 5-9-6 p (62) S Carson 7/1: 1613058: Mid-div, onepace over 1f out for press.	hd	57a
2097}	**KINSMAN** 159 [1] T D McCarthy 6-8-12 p (54) P Doe 16/1: 6055509: Held up, eff 2f out, not pace to chall:	½	47a
17	**OASES** 6 [14] D Shaw 4-9-3 (59) S Whitworth 15/2: 0000400: Slow away, rear, nrst fin:	hd	51a
4860}	**BYO** 26 [3] M Quinn 5-9-12 (68) S Hitchcott (3) 16/1: 0122400: Prom, no extra over 1f out	1	57a
17	**COPPINGTON FLYER** 6 [12] B W Duke 3-9-1 (58) Lisa Jones (3) 14/1: 5600000: Held up, eff 2f out, no impress, qck reapp.	5	33a
4446}	**BEDAZZLED** 54 [16] J A Glover 3-8-13 (56) G Carter 50/1: 2440-00: U.r. bef start, al bhd, abs.	3	22a
4982}	**SHARPINCH** 16 [6] P R Chamings 5-10-0 (70) Dane O'Neill 66/1: 000-4000: Led 4f, btn dist.	7	17a
4516}	**BRILLIANT WATERS** 50 [8] D W P Arbuthnot 3-8-12 (55) S Drowne 50/1: 06000: Sn rdn, al rear, broke blood vessel, abs.	15	0
15 Ran	1m 25.86 (3.06) Owner Mrs Gail Gaisford		Trained at Denmead

---

51   **1.20 Bet Direct Itv Page 367 Maiden Stakes Div 2 2yo (D)**

£3066 £876 £438   6f p/track rnd   Going 46   -31 Slow   Stalls Inside

5031}	**KABREET** 10 [4] E A L Dunlop 2-9-0 (77) S Drowne 5/4 FAV: 5531: Chsd ldrs, shaken up to lead ins last & asserted under hands & heels, cosily:		74a
19	**BURLINGTON PLACE** 5 [11] S Kirk 2-9-0 J F Egan 10/1: 0402: Led, drvn & hdd ins last, not pace of wnr:	½	71a
4393}	**COMERAINCOMESHINE** 57 [5] T G Mills 2-8-9 R Miles (5) 8/1: 03: Chsd ldrs, rdn & kept on well cl-home, not pace of wnr:	½	64a
3530}	**FOOT FAULT** 99 [8] N A Callaghan 2-8-9 W Ryan 25/1: 004: Cl-up halfway, no extra dist:	1	61a
	LOCATOR [1] J M P Eustace 2-9-0 J Tate 12/1: 5: In tch, onepace over 1f out:	1¼	62a
4912}	**EMILYS DAWN** 22 [3] D K Ivory 2-8-9 A Nicholls 33/1: 006: Held up, rdn & only mod gains, no dngr:	½	55a
5014}	**SABRINA BROWN** 12 [7] G B Balding 2-8-9 S Carson 14/1: 07: Chsd ldrs, outpcd fnl 2f:	¾	53a
4822}	**CHARLIEISMYDARLING** 28 [9] J A Osborne 2-8-9 J Fanning 6/1: 48: Dwelt, chsd ldrs, outpcd from halfway:	2	52a
4652}	**SCIENCE ACADEMY** 41 [6] P F I Cole 2-8-9 Dane O'Neill 9/2: 509: Rear, eff from halfway, no impress, abs.	shd	47a
4952}	**MISS MILLIETANT** 18 [10] L Montague Hall 2-8-9 C Cogan 50/1: 00: Outpcd rear, nvr a factor.	14	9a
	EVENING FRAGRANCE [2] G C H Chung 2-9-0 M Fenton 16/1: 0: Dwelt, al rear:	2	8a
11 Ran	1m 13.4 (4.6) Owner Jumeirah Racing		Trained at Newmarket

---

52   **1.50 Betdirect Co Uk Claiming Stakes 2yo (F)**

£2244 £641 £321   7f p/track rnd   Going 46   -25 Slow   Stalls Inside

4948}	**STAR OF LIGHT** 19 [2] B J Meehan 2-9-2 (73) Paul Eddery 3/1 FAV: 0621: Dwelt, mid-div, pushed along over 2f out, drvn to lead well ins last:		75a
4870}	**STONOR LADY** 25 [1] B J Meehan 2-7-12 D Kinsella 20/1: 02: Dsptd lead, went on over 1f out, rdn & hdd well ins last:	¾	55a
4863}	**MUSTANG ALI** 26 [4] S Kirk 2-8-9 (65) J F Egan 5/1: 6522003: Mid-div, outpcd over 2f out, styd on well for press cl-home, nrst fin:	nk	65a
4822}	**EVER CHEERFUL** 28 [10] W G M Turner 2-8-11 (67) L Treadwell (7) 7/1: 2203434: Cl-up, led 2f out, hung right & hdd over 1f out, no extra:	1½	64a
4636}	**BLOFELD** 42 [11] W Jarvis 2-8-3 (55) F Norton 25/1: 060055: Keen & prom, no extra dist, abs.	2½	51a
15	**KNIGHT ONTHE TILES** 6 [13] J R Best 2-9-2 bl (77) D Fentiman (7) 4/1: 0514106: In tch wide, no prog dist:	1¾	61a
25	**INTRODUCTION** 5 [8] W J Musson 2-8-3 Lisa Jones (3) 50/1: 07: Bhd, late gains, nrst fin, qck reapp.	1	46a
3590}	**CZARS PRINCESS** 96 [12] G L Moore 2-8-6 (60) I Mongan 8/1: 0008: Mid-div, no impress fnl 2f, abs:	nk	48a
3	**SONNE DE LOUP** 8 [3] Mrs S A Liddiard 2-7-12 J F McDonald (3) 100/1: 009: Prom 2f, sn drpd rear, mod late rally.	½	39a
25	**JAOLINS** 5 [15] R Hannon 2-8-0 2ow A Nicholls 12/1: 0060: In tch wide 5f, qck reapp.	1¼	38a
4994}	**NORDIC DANCER** 14 [5] R M H Cowell 2-8-0 (60) M Henry 20/1: 0000: Dwelt, nvr pace of ldrs.	3½	31a
19	**SKELTHWAITE** 5 [6] M H Tompkins 2-8-8 J Fanning 66/1: 00: Rdn & bhd, no prog, qck reapp.	½	35a
4229}	**JOMUS** 66 [14] L Montague Hall 2-8-11 (65) C Cogan 20/1: 0400200: Bolted to start, chsd ldrs 4f, abs.	1	39a
	CICATRICE [9] A Charlton 2-9-0 P Gallagher (7) 40/1: 0: V slowly away & al bhd on debut.	½	41a
4787*}	**DEE DEE GIRL** 32 [7] R Hannon 2-8-1 (58) A Daly 12/1: 00010: Led 1f, sn btn, AW bow.	6	18a
15 Ran	1m 27.76 (4.96) Owner Mr J H Widdows		Trained at Upper Lambourn

---

53   **2.20 Bet Direct Freephone 0800 32 93 93 Maiden Stakes 3yo+ (D)**

£2331 £666 £333   1m2f p/track   Going 46   -12 Slow   Stalls Inside

4848}	**TETOU** 27 [8] B J Meehan 3-8-9 S W Kelly 6/1: 301: Chsd ldrs, short of room over 2f out, swtchd & styd on for press to lead line, all out:		67a
	SEVEN YEAR ITCH [4] M P Tregoning 3-9-0 A Daly 6/4 FAV: 2: Sn prom, rcd keenly, chsd ldr 2f out & led ins last, drvn/flashed tail & hdd cl-home:	hd	71a

4696}	**ROZANEE** 37 [6] J W Payne 3-8-9 I Mongan 5/1: 333: Handy & led 3f out, hdd ins last & no extra:	3½	61a
4929}	**SAADA ONE** 21 [11] L M Cumani 3-8-9 Dane O'Neill 11/4: 434: Chsd ldrs, outpcd from over 2f out:	5	54a
4848}	**TATA NAKA** 27 [12] Mrs C A Dunnett 3-8-9 N Chalmers (5) 50/1: 065: Mid-div, no impress fnl 2f.	¾	53a
551}	**SHAAMITS ALL OVER** 286 [2] B A Pearce 4-8-13 B Reilly (5) 100/1: 06: Mid-div, no impress fnl 2f, long abs.	nk	52a
	ELEGANT GRACIE [5] R Guest 3-8-9 S Drowne 20/1: 7: Slow away & rear, nvr on terms with ldrs, debut.	1¼	50a
1330}	**WAVET** 198 [1] Mrs Lydia Pearce 3-8-9 R Price 14/1: 0-68: Led till 3f out, sn btn, abs.	1¼	48a
14	**SEEJAY** 6 [14] M A Allen 3-8-9 S Carson 100/1: 609: Handy & briefly led over 3f out, sn btn, qck reapp.	nk	47a
4907}	**OSORNO** 22 [13] C F Wall 3-9-0 A Clark 33/1: 00: Slow away & wide, keen, btn 3f out.	11	39a
4615}	**MAXIMINUS** 43 [7] M Madgwick 3-9-0 L Keniry (3) 66/1: 0-00: Keen, chsd ldrs till halfway, abs/AW bow.	nk	38a
4565}	**MRS BOZ** 47 [9] A W Carroll 3-8-9 S Whitworth 50/1: 060: Dwelt, mid-div wide, btn 3f out, abs.	11	20a
4	**HARRY TU** 8 [10] Miss Gay Kelleway 3-9-0 B Fayos Martin (7) 33/1: 00: Al bhd.	7	15a
	SAWAH [3] D Shaw 3-9-0 N Callan 100/1: 0: Slowly away & sn well bhd on debut.	3½	10a

14 Ran   2m 08.58 (5.78)   Owner Mrs Susan Roy   Trained at Upper Lambourn

---

54

2.50 Littlewoods Bet Direct Nursery Stakes Handicap 2yo 0-85 (D)   [85]

£3206 £916 £458   **1m p/track rnd**   Going 46   -08 Slow   Stalls Outside

4988*}	**FREAK OCCURENCE** 15 [10] Miss E C Lavelle 2-9-6 VIS (77) S Drowne 5/2 FAV: 0000411: Chsd ldr, sn pushed along, styd on for press to lead well ins last, gamely:		85a
5034}	**CHUBBES** 10 [6] M C Pipe 2-9-3 vis (74) J Fanning 4/1: 5006142: Led, rdn & hdd ins last, no extra:	1½	77a
4906}	**KEEP ON MOVIN** 22 [9] T G Mills 2-9-4 (75) R Miles (5) 12/1: 0653: Bhd, late gains for press, nrst fin:	3	73a
4942}	**AMWELL BRAVE** 20 [11] J R Jenkins 2-9-0 (71) M Fenton 33/1: 050034: Bhd, late gains for press.	nk	68a
4962}	**BOLD JOE** 18 [1] P Mitchell 2-9-1 (72) G Gibbons 25/1: 0000025: Chsd ldrs, no impress fnl 2f.	1¾	66a
4814}	**WIZARD LOOKING** 29 [12] R Hannon 2-9-2 T (73) Dane O'Neill 16/1: 60526: Held up, eff wide, btn 2f out:	hd	66a
4750}	**ABINGTON ANGEL** 34 [8] B J Meehan 2-9-7 t (78) L Keniry (3) 20/1: 32667: Mid-div, btn 2f out, longer trip.	nk	70a
4994*}	**ST SAVARIN** 14 [4] J R Best 2-9-3 BL (74) N Pollard 7/2: 0002618: Sn pushed along chasing ldrs, btn 3f out:	shd	66a
4717}	**DARN GOOD** 36 [5] R Hannon 2-9-1 (72) P Gallagher (7) 20/1: 4536459: Rear, no room over 2f out till over 1f out, kept on late:	½	63a
4994}	**SACHIN** 14 [2] G A Butler 2-9-1 BL (72) S W Kelly 8/1: 04340: Chsd ldrs, drvn & btn 2f out:	2½	58a
4966*}	**UNCLE JOHN** 17 [3] S Kirk 2-8-12 (69) J F Egan 7/1: 0010: Mid-div, rdn halfway, sn btn:	7	41a

11 Ran   1m 40.48 (4.28)   Owner Lots of Luck Gentlemen Syndica   Trained at Andover

---

55

3.20 Bet Direct On Channel 4 Page 613 Stakes Handicap Div 2 3yo+ 0-70 (E)   [70]

£2125 £607 £304   **7f p/track rnd**   Going 46   +02 Fast   Stalls Inside

12	**CHATEAU NICOL** 6 [1] B G Powell 4-9-2 vis (58) J Fanning 40/1: 6300001: Mid-div rail, drvn & led cl-home:		62a
4986*}	**GALLERY BREEZE** 16 [7] J L Spearing 4-9-5 (61) A Daly 7/1: 0/-004112: Led/dpstd lead, went on over 2f out & arnd 3L clr trav well over 1f out, shaken up ins last, hdd cl-home:	nk	64a
4901}	**SMITH N ALLAN OILS** 22 [10] M Dods 4-8-13 p (55) J F Egan 12/1: 2000523: Towards rear, styd on for press ins last, nrst fin:	¾	57a
20	**PEYTO PRINCESS** 5 [3] M A Buckley 5-9-5 (61) S W Kelly 16/1: 4400004: Keen & chsd ldrs, kept on onepace:	¾	62a
3965}	**ACORAZADO** 81 [9] G L Moore 4-8-11 (53) G Carter 5/1: 0004055: Mid-div, kept on:	1¼	51a
4908}	**A WOMAN IN LOVE** 22 [5] Miss B Sanders 4-9-0 (56) S Drowne 13/2: 0354256: Slow away, nrst fin, imprve on this.	nk	53a
4944}	**LOOKING FOR LOVE** 20 [6] J G Portman 5-9-6 p (62) R Ffrench 13/2: 3450327: Prom, no extra dist.	shd	59a
4767}	**CASTAIGNE** 33 [12] B W Duke 4-8-12 t (54) S Carson 25/1: 0602408: Dwelt, rear, late prog, mdn.	½	50a
23	**CALUSA LADY** 5 [2] G B Balding 3-9-2 vis (59) A Clark 20/1: 0-446009: Chsd ldrs till over 1f out.	1¾	52a
22	**FEARBY CROSS** 5 [15] W J Musson 7-9-11 (67) Lisa Jones (3) 6/1: 5144000: Wide, held up, little prog.	shd	60a
20	**MISTRAL SKY** 5 [8] Mrs S A Liddiard 4-10-0 vis (70) M Fenton 5/2 FAV: 3041100: Keen, mid-div, no impress fnl 2f.	nk	52a
4908}	**ADANTINO** 22 [4] B R Millman 4-8-12 (54) M Henry 20/1: 0300560: Bhd, nvr a dngr to ldrs.	½	45a
5030}	**CONTRARY MARY** 10 [13] J Akehurst 8-9-8 (64) R Price 20/1: 3050000: Rear, drvn & no prog 2f out.	1¼	52a
31	**LAGGAN MINSTREL** 4 [10] P W D'Arcy 5-8-12 T (54) F Norton 25/1: 0000000: Mid-div, btn 2f out, t-strap.	1¾	39a
4785}	**BADOU** 32 [11] L Montague Hall 3-8-12 vis (55) C Cogan 25/1: 5000240: Chsd ldrs, btn 2f out.	¾	39a
5030}	**WARDEN WARREN** 10 [14] Mrs C A Dunnett 5-10-0 bl (70) Dane O'Neill 40/1: 0000000: Led/dsptd lead wide, btn 2f out:	3	48a

16 Ran   1m 25.9 (3.1)   Owner Basingstoke Commercials   Trained at Winchester

---

56

3.50 Bet Direct In Running Sky Text 372 Amateur Riders' Handicap Stakes 3yo+ 0-80 (F)   [52]

£3234 £924 £462   **1m4f p/track**   Going 46   +01 Fast   Stalls Inside

18*	**COLD TURKEY** 6 [15] G L Moore 3-10-9 (67) Mr E Dehdashti (5) 6/5 FAV: 2001111: Dwelt, rear, smooth hdwy 5f out & led over 3f out, rdn & held on well:		75a
4984*}	**MISSION TO MARS** 16 [7] P R Hedger 4-11-4 (70) Mr S Walker 3/1: 0211112: Dwelt, mid-div, hdwy to chase wnr 2f out, rdn & kept on, al held:	1½	75a
4582}	**REMINISCENT** 46 [16] R F Johnson Houghton 4-10-11 vis (63) Ms C Williams 20/1: 0503453: Dwelt, mid-div, rdn & outpcd 3f out, rallied well ins last:	1½	66a
4664}	**KING REVO** 40 [1] P C Haslam 3-11-7 (79) Mr B Haslam (5) 8/1: 3501604: Dwelt, cl up, onepace.	½	81a
26	**MOST SAUCY** 5 [13] I A Wood 7-11-6 (72) Mr G Bartley (7) 12/1: 3200355: Rear, chall wide 2f out, no extra.	3	70a
4951}	**GINGKO** 19 [2] P R Webber 6-10-13 (65) Mr J King (7) 12/1: 1006006: Led/dsptd lead 9f, fdd.	1¼	61a
4951}	**MANDOOB** 19 [6] B R Johnson 6-10-12 (64) Miss F Guillambert (7) 14/1: 112-5637: Mid-div, outpcd fnl 3f:	hd	59a
4167}	**SILVER PROPHET** 68 [3] M R Bosley 4-11-3 (69) Mr S Bosley 25/1: 0-004308: Chsd ldrs till outpcd from 3f out:	½	63a
4481}	**STARRY MARY** 52 [14] E L James 5-9-13 (51) Mrs S Moore (5) 25/1: 3-352009: Wide, held up, no impressf, abs.	5	38a
4909}	**CHEVRONNE** 22 [8] L G Cottrell 3-10-12 (70) Mr L Jefford (5) 12/1: 0-330350: Chsd ldrs, drvn & no impress 3f out.	8	47a
3072}	**PASO DOBLE** 118 [10] B R Millman 5-10-13 (65) Mr J Millman (7) 33/1: 0424000: Prom, btn 3f out:	5	36a
	PEPPERSHOT 96 [12] G P Enright 3-10-2 (60) Mr J Pemberton (7) 66/1: 540060: Slow away, chsd ldrs 1m, Brit bow.	15	11a

12 Ran   2m 34.64 (5.44)   Owner Mr A Grinter   Trained at Brighton

TOULOUSE TUESDAY 11.11.03

Official Going GOOD/SOFT.

57 | 2.15 Gr 3 Prix de l'Air (Fillies & Mares) 3yo+ ()
£21429 £8571 £6429 £4286 1m2f100y   Good/Soft

WALKAMIA 39 [11] A Fabre 3-8-8 C Soumillon : 1-5543: Rear, efft wide halfway, rdn to lead ins last, drvn out:		107
4841} MONTURANI 23 [7] G Wragg 4-8-11 D Bonilla : 10-6223422: Mid-div wide, rdn & led over 1f out, hdd ins last, no extra:	1½	102
HANDRIA 22 [10] F Rohaut 6-8-11 bl F X Bertras : 1231233: Rear, late gains into 3rd, no danger:	1½	100
4893} PLACE ROUGE 17 [4] J H M Gosden 4-9-4 T Thulliez : 11-102044: Cl up, onepace for press dist.	¾	106

Ran   2m 10.60   Owner Lagardere Family   Trained at France

MAISONS LAFFITTE FRIDAY 14.11.03 Left & Righthand, Sharpish Track

Official Going SOFT.

58 | 2.15 Listed Prix Isola Bella (Fillies) 3yo ()
£13312 £5325 £3994 £2662 7f   V Soft

GREAT NEWS FR 44 C Laffon Parias 3-8-12 M Blancpain : 2633751:		104
4749} BLAISE CASTLE 33 G A Butler 3-8-12 E Legrix : 31-00392: Led/dpstd lead till went on over 2f out, rdn & hdd dist, kept on:	4	95
COTE QUEST 32 Mme C Head Maarek 3-8-12 N Guesdon : 22313:	1	93

Ran   1m 26.80   Owner Mme C Morange   Trained at France

CAPANNELLE SUNDAY 16.11.03 Righthand, Flat, Galloping Track

Official Going GOOD/SOFT.

59 | 2.00 Gr 1 Premio Roma 3yo+ ()
£93377 £49903 £29805 £14901m2f   Good/Soft

4893+`IMPERIAL DANCER 22 [7] M R Channon 5-9-2 T E Durcan 53/10: 12316411: Held up, rdn to chall 2f out, led dist, rdn out:		116
1493} ALTIERI 189 [5] V Caruso 5-9-2 M Esposito 77/10: 41-11302: Rear, styd on for press to take 2nd ins last, no ch with wnr:	3	111
3711} SUNSTRACH 92 [6] E Borromeo 5-9-2 L Dettori 48/10: 1-243103: Trkd ldrs, led over 2f out, hdd over 1f out, wknd.	snk	110

Ran   2m 01.60   Owner Imperial Dancing   Trained at West Ilsley

SOUTHWELL Wednesday 19.11.03 Lefthand, Sharp, Oval Track

Official Going Standard

60 | 12.00 Press Red To Bet Direct Handicap Stakes Div 1 3yo+ 0-65 (F)   [65]
£2128 £608 £304   1m f/sand rnd   Going 57   +03 Fast   Stalls Inside

5030} BARZAK 11 [8] S R Bowring 3-9-12 t (65) A Culhane 16/1: 6000001: Prom, led over 2f out, drvn & held on well:		69a
4949} SECOND OF MAY 20 [12] P R Chamings 3-9-9 (62) F Norton 5/1 FAV: 6621542: Held up, styd on wide for press fnl 3f, not able to chall wnr:	1	63a
4824} MAGGIES PET 29 [11] K Bell 6-8-9 T (46) S Whitworth 25/1: 25-40003: Rear, kept on for press fnl 3f, not able to chall wnr:	nk	46a
4788} SHIFTY 33 [14] D Nicholls 4-9-3 bl (54) A Nicholls 8/1: 0406504: Held up, eff 2f out, onepace:	1¼	51a
1879} ROSTI 170 [1] P C Haslam 3-8-11 (50) Rory Moore (7) 12/1: 050005: Led till over 2f out, no extra:	3½	38a
4788} LORD OF METHLEY 33 [6] R M Whitaker 4-8-13 vis (50) V Halliday 12/1: 1340036: Chsd ldrs till dist.	¾	36a
4963"} DANGEROUS BEANS 19 [4] S Kirk 3-9-1 (54) A Daly 6/1: 6000217: Outpcd, late prog, nvr threat.	hd	39a
4890} BANUTAN 25 [3] K R Burke 3-9-11 (64) Darren Williams 20/1: 2306008: In tch, btn over 1f out.	3	42a
2179} SPY GUN 156 [5] T Wall 3-9-7 (60) N Chalmers (5) 25/1: 0-009: Prom till 2f out, new yard:	5	26a
5017} DUBAI DREAMS 13 [7] M J Polglase 3-9-4 vis (57) P Makin (7) 7/1: 5460000: Chsd ldrs 5f.	2	18a
4849} TITIAN LASS 28 [10] C E Brittain 4-8-11 bl (48) Dane O'Neill 13/2: 0002020: Al rear.	¾	7a
4967} LUCAYAN MONARCH 18 [9] P A Blockley 5-10-0 (65) Derek Nolan (7) 20/1: 3360000: Slowly away, in tch 6f.	3	17a
4854} WILDERBROOK LAHRI 28 [2] B Smart 4-8-8 bl (45) R Ffrench 12/1: 4200050: Dwelt & al bhd.	1¼	0
4699} THE LOOSE SCREW 38 [15] G M Moore 5-8-11 (48) N Pollard 16/1: 0-006200: Dwelt, chsd ldrs 5f:	6	0

14 Ran   1m 43.77 (4.34)   Owner Clark Industrial Services Part   Trained at Edwinstowe

61 | 12.30 Allweather-Racing Com Selling Stakes Div 1 3yo+ (G)
£2128 £608 £304   7f f/sand rnd   Going 57   -14 Slow   Stalls Inside

5029} HURRICANE COAST 12 [5] P A Blockley 4-9-5 (55) G Parkin 12/1: 5030201: Sn trkd ldrs, gd hdwy to chall when hung right/flashed tail ins last, rdn out:		59a
22 JONNY EBENEEZER 6 [8] R M H Cowell 4-9-5 P (70) M Fenton 10/11 FAV: 2246402: Led, sltly short of room when hdd over 1f out, onepace:	1¼	55a
4181} LEVANTINE 69 [9] A G Newcombe 6-9-5 P (41) S Whitworth 16/1: 000-3063: Handy, rdn & narrow lead when edged left over 1f out, hdd ins last, short of room & lost 2nd cl-home:	shd	55a
4958} PROUD VICTOR 19 [1] D Shaw 3-9-4 vis (45) Darren Williams 40/1: 0000604: Chsd ldrs, not able to chall.	2½	50a
4741} SPEEDFIT FREE 36 [16] I Semple 6-9-11 bl (58) N Callan 8/1: 0350105: Chsd ldrs 2f out, no extra dist.	nk	55a
4856} HEATHYARDSBLESSING 28 [10] R Hollinshead 6-9-5 (50) Dean McKeown 40/1: 00-00006: Towards rear, nrst fin.	1½	46a
47 SWYNFORD WELCOME 19 [11] I A Wood 7-9-6 (40) D Nolan (5) 9/1: 0000007: Mid-div, nvr pace to chall.	½	46a
2545} THAAYER 142 [3] I A Wood 8-9-5 (40) G Gibbons 25/1: 0000008: Mid-div, no prog over 1f out, abs.	1¾	42a
4150} TURKU 71 [15] D Shaw 5-9-5 vis (53) Lisa Jones (3) 10/1: 0006059: Mid-div wide, no prog fnl 2f, abs, new yard.	shd	42a
3287} A ONE 111 [7] B Palling 4-9-5 (45) D Sweeney 20/1: 0-300000: Chsd ldrs 4f, abs.	nk	41a

23

2676}	**EAGER ANGEL 137** [4] R F Marvin 5-9-0 (37) I Mongan 50/1: 2006000: Slow away & al rear, abs.	5	27a
18	**ZOEANNA 7** [14] R Guest 3-8-13 (50) A Culhane 20/1: 0050600: Hmpd start & al bhd.	3½	21a
4815}	**BLUE CIRCLE 30** [2] M Mullineaux 3-9-4 bl (34) T Williams 66/1: 0006000: Prom 5f.	1¼	23a
745}	**KUMAKAWA 260** [6] E A Wheeler 5-9-5 bl (42) S Carson 20/1: 0215000: Sn struggling, abs.	1¾	20a
2933}	**BETTER PAL 126** [13] P R Wood 4-9-5 (54) D Corby (3) 33/1: 6-600000: Al bhd, abs.	nk	19a
4690}	**MARGARETS WISH 38** [12] T Wall 3-8-13 (38) Stephanie Hollinshead (7) 40/1: 0000200: Dwelt & al bhd.	2	10a

16 Ran   1m 31.58 (4.98)   Owner Mrs Joanna Hughes   Trained at Southwell

---

62   **1.00 Press Red To Bet Direct Handicap Stakes Div 2 3yo+ 0-65 (F)**   [65]
     £2121 £606 £303   **1m f/sand rnd**   **Going 57**   **+02 Fast**   Stalls Inside

4767}	**SKY DOME 34** [12] M H Tompkins 10-9-6 vis (57) J Fanning 6/1: 0004051: In tch, hdwy halfway & led ins last, rdn & styd on strongly:		65a
47	**MUTARAFAA 123** [14] D Shaw 4-8-7 e (44) I Mongan 12/1: 6300062: Sn handy & rdn/led over 1f out, hdd ins last, onepace:	2½	46a
4854*}	**SCRAMBLE 28** [11] B Ellison 5-9-1 bl e t (52) Dane O'Neill 9/2 FAV: 2664413: Trkd ldrs, led trav well over 2f out, rdn & hdd over 1f out, onepace:	1	52a
2722}	**NOBLE PURSUIT 135** [13] P A Blockley 6-9-7 (58) Dean McKeown 7/1: 0006004: Chsd ldrs, no impress fnl 2f:	8	44a
5010}	**THESAURUS 14** [10] A Crook 4-9-11 (62) K Dalgleish 20/1: 0350005: Dwelt, rear, late gains for press, nrst fin.	1	46a
38	**JESSINCA 4** [1] A P Jones 7-8-9 (46) D Kinsella 15/2: 0024646: Sn pushed along towards rear, nvr factor:	1½	27a
4553}	**BALLARE 49** [3] Bob Jones 4-8-11 (48) F Norton 12/1: 25-40207: Dwelt & held up, btn over 1f out:	shd	29a
5029*}	**LOCOMBE HILL 12** [5] D Nicholls 7-9-13 (64) A Nicholls 5/1: 0600018: Trkd ldrs travelling well, rdn/btn 2f out.	nk	44a
4792}	**BLUNHAM 33** [2] M C Chapman 3-9-2 (55) Andrew Webb (7) 33/1: 0461009: Led 5f, fdd.	8	22a
3263}	**JESSIE 112** [6] Don Enrico Incisa 4-8-10 (47) Kim Tinkler 25/1: 040-0040: Mid-div, nvr land blow, abs.	nk	13a
3263}	**ALICE BRAND 112** [16] G M Moore 5-8-12 (49) N Pollard 16/1: 000-4030: Chsd ldrs 5f.	¾	14a
4824}	**RED DELIRIUM 29** [7] R Brotherton 7-9-3 bl (54) G Gibbons 16/1: 5554000: Dwelt & al outpcd.	3½	13a
4	**SHAMWARI FIRE 9** [4] I W McInnes 3-8-13 (52) P Mathers (7) 14/1: 0052440: Slowly away & sn struggling.	8	0a
3263}	**LANDOFHEARTSDESIRE 112** [15] J S Wainwright 4-8-11 vis (48) L Enstone (3) 40/1: 0606000: Chsd ldrs 5f, abs.	6	0a

14 Ran   1m 43.8 (4.4)   Owner Pollards Stables   Trained at Newmarket

---

63   **1.35 Tim & Kay Slater's Big Day Claiming Stakes 2yo (F)**
     £2058 £588 £294   **6f f/sand rnd**   **Going 57**   **-00 Slow**   Stalls Inside

5015}	**MUY BIEN 13** [4] J R Jenkins 2-9-2 VIS (75) S W Kelly 7/1: 5215001: Chsd ldr, led over 1f out, hung left but styd on well for press:		73a
1*	**MAUNBY RAVER 9** [9] P C Haslam 2-9-1 (55) Rory Moore (7) 3/1 FAV: 066412: Trkd ldrs, rdn to chall over 1f out, not pace of wnr:	1½	66a
4562}	**TICTACTOE 48** [10] D J Daly 2-8-7 (58) Lisa Jones (3) 6/1: 4250453: Bhd, styd on for press from halfway, nrst fin:	2½	51a
4892}	**ONLY IF I LAUGH 25** [7] B J Meehan 2-9-2 bl (76) L Keniry (3) 11/2: 2516504: Led till over 1f out, no extra:	nk	59a
4923}	**FOXIES FUTURE 22** [2] J R Weymes 2-8-9 P (67) Dane O'Neill 8/1: 066105: Dwelt, bhd, late gains:	2	47a
4766}	**SPARKLING CLEAR 34** [12] R M H Cowell 2-8-6 VIS (50) M Henry 50/1: 5066: Chsd ldrs, btn over 1f out:	4	35a
4503}	**WARES HOME 51** [8] K R Burke 2-9-2 (80) Darren Williams 9/2: 2321007: Dwelt, al towards rear:	6	31a
4463}	**SHAMROCK TEA 54** [5] M E Sowersby 2-9-0 (65) R Ffrench 33/1: 5155008: Chsd ldrs, 2f out, abs.	2½	22a
4875}	**ARE YOU THERE 26** [6] T D Barron 2-8-6 1ow (64) N Callan 7/1: 3110009: Chsd ldrs till halfway.	1¾	10a
4594}	**MISS JUDGED 46** [13] A P Jones 2-8-5 T (40) G Hannon 100/1: 6000: Al bhd, t-strap.	1¼	6a
4994}	**DARCIE MIA 15** [3] J R Weymes 2-8-3 BL (42) D Fentiman (7) 66/1: 00000: Al rear, blnks.	2	0a
4874}	**GAME FLORA 26** [11] M E Sowersby 2-8-5 (53) S Hitchcott 50/1: 445000: Bhd halfway.	5	0a
	DANDY JIM [14] D W Chapman 2-8-6 J Fanning 50/1: 0: Slow away & al bhd on debut.	30	0a

13 Ran   1m 16.72 (3.42)   Owner Mr Kevin Reddington   Trained at Royston

---

64   **2.05 Littlewoods Bet Direct Rated Stakes Handicap 3yo+ 0-95 (C)**   [102]
     £6906 £2125 £1062 £531   **5f f/sand str**   **Going 57**   **Inapplicab**   Stalls Stands Side

4884}	**TRINCULO 25** [7] N P Littmoden 6-9-0 p (88) J P Guillambert (3) 20/1: 6320001: Prom, led ins last, drvn out:		93a
4878}	**QUITO 25** [2] D W Chapman 6-9-7 bl (95) A Culhane 14/1: 4410052: Dwelt & held up, smooth hdwy halfway, drvn cl-home, just failed:	hd	99a
5025*}	**DANCING MYSTERY 12** [4] E A Wheeler 9-9-1 bl (89) S Carson 7/1: 0250013: Dwelt, sn chsd ldrs, led 2f out, hdd ins last, no extra.	1	90a
41	**LANDING STRIP 17** [9] J M P Eustace 3-8-4 1oh (77) F P Ferris (3) 8/1: 0011444: Dwelt, kept on for press.	½	77a
5000}	**ZARZU 15** [15] C R Dore 4-8-6 (80) R Thomas (5) 20/1: 0361025: Held up, styd on for press stands rail, not pace of ldrs towards centre:	shd	79a
5025}	**NOW LOOK HERE 12** [9] B A McMahon 7-8-5 (79) G Gibbons 12/1: 0504036: Led/dsptd lead 3f, hung left & no extra.	1¼	75a
5037}	**BOND BOY 11** [1] B Smart 6-9-5 (93) I Mongan 13/2: 0-362007: Rdn rear, mod gains for press:	¾	87a
5025}	**STEEL BLUE 12** [5] R M Whitaker 3-8-8 p (82) F Norton 9/1: 0500228: Chsd ldrs, no extra dist.	½	74a
4990}	**SUNDRIED TOMATO 16** [10] P W Hiatt 4-9-4 (92) Darren Williams 14/1: 2006009: Chsd ldrs, drvn & onepce dist.	hd	83a
4991*}	**MAKTAVISH 16** [14] J Semple 4-8-10 p (84) D McGaffin (3) 8/1: 0055010: Led/dsptd lead, btn/eased fnl 1f.	½	73a
41	**PRINCE OF BLUES 16** [8] M Mullineaux 5-8-6 (80) S W Kelly 33/1: 0600000: Led till over 3f out, sn btn.	2½	62a
1171}	**MASSEY 210** [16] T D Barron 7-9-7 (95) Dean McKeown 11/2 FAV: 02-11200: Outpcd, nvr factor:	½	75a
4810}	**KATHOLOGY 30** [13] D R C Elsworth 6-8-4 1oh (77) Lisa Jones (3) 10/1: 0600530: Dwelt & outpcd.	½	56a
5037}	**NO TIME 11** [11] M J Polglase 3-9-2 (90) Dane O'Neill 16/1: 1230000: Sn struggling.	2	63a
4990}	**CONSENSUS 16** [3] M Brittain 4-8-6 (80) T Williams 25/1: 1000060: In tch till halfway.	6	42a

15 Ran   58.42   Owner Miss Vanessa Church   Trained at Newmarket

---

65   **2.40 Betdirect Co Uk Maiden Stakes 3yo+ (D)**
     £2310 £660 £330   **6f f/sand rnd**   **Going 57**   **-06 Slow**   Stalls Inside

4967}	**JALOUHAR 18** [13] B P J Baugh 3-9-0 (60) J Fanning 14/1: 3225061: Rdn to go handy, chsd ldrs till led over 1f out, rdn out:		61a

SOUTHWELL Wednesday 19.11.03 Lefthand, Sharp, Oval Track

4460} **BEVELLER 54** [5] W M Brisbourne 4-9-0 (48) S W Kelly 13/2: 3042042: Dwelt, sn mid-div, rdn & hdwy to chall dist, hung left & no extra ins last: 1½ **56a**
3010} **SECOND MINISTER 123** [8] D Flood 4-9-0 BL (50) P Doe 8/1: 004-0003: Led, drvn & hdd over 1f out, no extra: 2 **51a**
4852} **DARK CHAMPION 28** [2] Jedd O'Keeffe 3-9-0 (61) I Mongan 5/1 FAV: 2332344: Mid-div, kept on. shd **51a**
23 **TATWEER 6** [6] D Shaw 3-9-0 vis (60) Darren Williams 8/1: 5-0055: Mid-div, outpcd halfway, nrst fin: shd **50a**
187} **SHADOWFAX 341** [12] Miss Gay Kelleway 3-9-0 A Culhane 7/1: 060426-6: Bhd, nrst fin: nk **49a**
4907} **FIRE CAT 23** [3] A P Jones 4-9-0 (48) D Sweeney 14/1: 00-22507: Hmpd & bhd start, hdwy halfway, sn onepace. hd **48a**
2692} **CLEVELAND WAY 136** [14] D Carroll 3-9-0 vis (52) R Fitzpatrick 50/1: 0520408: Chsd ldrs wide 5f: 1½ **44a**
4989} **BLUE MAEVE 16** [11] J Hetherton 3-9-0 G Parkin 100/1: 009: Held up, only mod gains. 3½ **35a**
4103} **LA CORUJERA 74** [4] T D Barron 3-8-9 (62) N Callan 13/2: 2055060: Chsd ldrs till halfway: 5 **17a**
4958} **SUBTLE MOVE 19** [10] D Shaw 3-8-9 vis (49) F Norton 66/1: 0300000: Al rear. nk **16a**
WHITE O MORN [7] B A McMahon 4-8-9 G Gibbons 50/1: 0: Prom till over 2f out, debut. 1¾ **12a**
4964} **ROAN RAIDER 19** [16] M J Polglase 3-9-0 vis t (44) K Ghunowa (7) 25/1: 0362460: Al bhd. 1¾ **13a**
NATURAL GRACE [15] D J Daly 3-8-9 M Fenton 33/1: 0: Dwelt & al rear on debut. 9 **0a**
4425} **DANCING RIDGE 56** [1] A Senior 6-9-0 p (45) Dean McKeown 66/1: 00436-00: Strugg hway, abs. nk **0a**
SIERRA NEVADA [9] M A Magnusson 3-8-9 Dane O'Neill 6/1: 0: Al bhd on debut. ¾ **0a**
16 Ran 1m 17.1 (3.8) Owner Miss S M Potts Trained at Stoke On Trent

66 3.10 Allweather-Racing Com Selling Stakes Div 2 3yo+ (G)
£2128 £608 £304 **7f f/sand rnd** **Going 57** **-10 Slow** Stalls Inside

4826} **REPEAT 29** [12] K A Ryan 3-9-4 (50) A Culhane 7/1: 5300031: Trkd ldrs, led over 1f out, drvn out: **55a**
4967} **BULAWAYO 18** [10] B A McMahon 6-9-11 (57) G Gibbons 3/1 FAV: 0103632: Trkd ldrs, rdn to chall dist, just held cl-home, nicely bckd: ½ **58a**
33 **TRAVELLING TIMES 5** [9] J S Wainwright 4-9-5 vis (52) L Enstone (3) 10/1: 2050043: Led 5f, no extra dist: 2 **49a**
27 **MR STYLISH 5** [2] J S Moore 7-9-5 vis t (53) J D Smith 12/1: 6266004: Dwelt & held up, kept on. ½ **48a**
4788} **BRILLIANTRIO 33** [14] M C Chapman 5-9-6 t (49) L Vickers 16/1: 501U065: Outpcd, hdwy 2f out, no prog dist. 2 **45a**
47 **ACHILLES RAINBOW 118** [5] K R Burke 4-9-5 (39) Darren Williams 40/1: 040-0406: Prom, rdn & no extra dist. ¾ **43a**
33 **ATTORNEY 5** [16] D Shaw 5-9-11 e (45) Lisa Jones (3) 11/2: 0000037: Held up, eff 2f out, onepace: 1½ **46a**
5020} **CHAMPAGNE RIDER 13** [11] D Shaw 7-9-5 vis (42) S Whitworth 25/1: 0000508: Prom 4f, btn over 1f out. 1¾ **37a**
5000} **TAYIF 15** [8] D Nicholls 7-9-5 (58) A Nicholls 11/2: 2060069: Dwelt, in tch, btn over 1f out: ¾ **36a**
46 **DISTINCTLYSPLENDID 83** [7] I A Wood 3-9-4 (36) D Nolan (5) 40/1: 0006400: Mid-div, lost pl hway: hd **35a**
3377} **BOLD EFFORT 106** [15] K O Cunningham Brown 11-9-5 bl (40) L Keniry (3) 50/1: 0060000: Dwelt & al towards rear, abs. 8 **21a**
3359} **CHESNUT CRACKER 107** [6] P C Haslam 3-8-13 T (40) P Dineley (7) 16/1: 0-4600: In tch till halfway: 1½ **13a**
4826} **BOND SOLITAIRE 29** [4] B Smart 3-8-13 (46) R Ffrench 33/1: 0-000000: Chsd ldrs, btn 2f out. ¾ **12a**
4024} **TAP 78** [3] Ian Emmerson 6-9-11 (53) L Treadwell (7) 9/1: 5114200: Bhd halfway, op 7/1: 3 **17a**
4330} **SALLY TRAFFIC 61** [13] R M Whitaker 4-9-0 p (35) F Norton 40/1: 0000000: Chsd ldrs 5f, abs. 5 **0**
4815} **PRECIOUS FREEDOM 30** [1] J Balding 3-9-4 p (48) J Fanning 40/1: 6400000: Dwelt, prom till halfway. 3½ **0**
16 Ran 1m 31.3 (4.7) Owner Crewe And Nantwich Racing Club Trained at Hambleton

67 3.40 Bet Direct On 0800 32 93 93 Handicap Stakes 3yo+ 0-60 (F) [59]
£2079 £594 £297 **2m f/sand rnd** **Going 57** **-67 Slow** Stalls Inside

11 **MACARONI GOLD 7** [9] W Jarvis 3-9-3 (57) M Tebbutt 6/1: 503031: Rear, sn hdwy to trk ldrs 6f out, led 2f out, rdly asserted, val for 7L: **66a**
3460*} **AMBITIOUS ANNIE 103** [13] R Hollinshead 4-8-8 (39) Stephanie Hollinshead (7) 10/1: 004-5012: Mid-div, wide, prog & led halfway, hdd 2f out, kept on: 3 **41a**
1446} **GREAT AS GOLD 193** [3] B Ellison 4-9-10 p (55) Dane O'Neill 3/1 FAV: 3356203: Rear, hdwy from halfway, kept on for press fnl 2f: 1¼ **56a**
2886} **FAIRMORNING 128** [8] J W Unett 4-8-10 (41) A Daly 25/1: 60-65544: Rear, styd on for press fnl 3f, nrst fin: 2 **40a**
4657} **HIGH JINKS 394** [6] R N Bevis 8-8-8 (39) Lisa Jones (3) 20/1: 004550-5: Chsd ldr till 3f out, abs. 12 **28a**
4951} **FIRST PRESSURE 20** [15] D R C Elsworth 3-9-4 (58) T Quinn 7/1: 50-00406: Led 3f, rem prom till 4f out: 2½ **45a**
4117} **KAGOSHIMA 72** [16] J R Norton 8-9-1 vis (46) V Halliday 33/1: 0/060-007: Bhd, hdwy halfway, btn 3f out, abs. 8 **26a**
4931*} **SPA LANE 22** [5] J F Coupland 10-9-11 (56) P Gallagher (7) 4/1: 5455618: Rear, eff wide 6f out, btn 3f out. nk **35a**
4819} **CHARNWOOD STREET 30** [4] D Shaw 4-8-11 e (42) Darren Williams 16/1: 0-446059: Mid-div, lost tch halfway. ¾ **20a**
4922} **KNOWN MANEUVER 22** [11] M C Chapman 5-10-0 (59) L Vickers 66/1: 00000-00: Bhd halfway. 7 **31a**
34 **HAJEER 5** [2] P W Hiatt 5-9-8 (53) A Culhane 13/2: 3212300: Al bhd, quick reapp. ¾ **24a**
1666} **KRISTAL FOREST 180** [7] Mrs S Lamyman 4-8-9 (40) I Mongan 14/1: 0300000: Prom, struggling fnl 4f, abs. 2 **9a**
4853} **SWEETSTOCK 28** [14] Mrs G S Rees 5-8-4 (35) L Keniry 50/1: 643-0000: Bhd halfway. 20 **0a**
1720} **A TWO 177** [10] B Palling 4-9-3 (48) M Fenton 50/1: 0/140-000: Led after 3f till halfway, sn struggling, t.o., abs. dist **0a**
4995} **ALL ON MY OWN 15** [12] I W McInnes 8-8-7 (38) P Mathers (5) 33/1: 0055000: In tch till halfway, t.o. ¾ **0a**
15 Ran 3m 45.78 (19.78) Owner Dr J Walker Trained at Newmarket

WOLVERHAMPTON Friday 21.11.03 Lefthand, V Sharp Track

Official Going STANDARD.

68 12.50 Bet Direct In Running Sky Text 293 Handicap Stakes Div 1 3yo+ 0-60 (F) [60]
£2107 £602 £301 **7f f/sand rnd** **Going 49** **-15 Slow** Stalls Outside

4 **ZAGALA 11** [10] S L Keightley 3-9-8 t (55) A Culhane 5/1 JT FAV: 4-630021: Cl-up, led 2f out, edged left ins fnl 1f, rdn out: **63a**
45 **GERONIMO 4** [6] Miss Gay Kelleway 6-9-9 p (55) D Kinsella 11/2: 5660602: Mid-div, prog 3f out, chsd wnr dist, kept on, all held: 1¾ **58a**
4967} **VICTORY VEE 20** [2] M Blanshard 3-9-12 (59) N Callan 8/1: 0413003: Handy, onepcd fnl 2f: 1½ **59a**
40 **GOLD GUEST 6** [5] P D Evans 4-9-8 vis (54) D Nolan (5) 5/1 JT FAV: 0460044: Slow away, prog 3f out, no impress fnl 1f: ¾ **52a**

971}	**PAWN IN LIFE 228** [1] T D Barron 5-10-0 (60) Laura Jayne Crawford (7) 16/1: 2422505: Cl-up, no extra 3f out.	2½	53a
62	**RED DELIRIUM 31** [7] R Brotherton 7-9-8 bl (54) G Gibbons 14/1: 5554006: Sn in rear, nvr nrr than mid-div.	5	37a
	TANGO STEP 21 [8] Bernard Lawlor 3-9-7 (54) P Mathers (7) 25/1: 2040607: Sn bhd, nvr nrr than mid-div.	2½	32a
4877}	**DASAR 28** [11] M Brittain 3-9-7 (54) Darren Williams 40/1: 6000008: Rear, prog 5f out, wknd 3f out.	1	30a
4634}	**ON THE TRAIL 45** [3] D W Chapman 6-9-10 (56) Lisa Jones (3) 11/1: 0332309: Handy, fdd 2f out:	½	31a
46*	**CONSIGNIA 4** [4] D Haydn Jones 4-9-8 6ex vis (54) Paul Eddery 6/1: 0310010: Handy, wknd 5f out:	1¾	25a
4969}	**BABY BARRY 20** [12] Mrs G S Rees 6-10-0 vis (60) Dane O'Neill 7/1: 3004230: Slow away, sn handy, fdd 4f out.	3	25a
50	**BEDAZZLED 3** [9] A A Glover 3-9-9 BL (56) G Carter 25/1: 2440-00F: Led 5f, wknd dist, sadly collapsed & died.		0a
12 Ran	1m 30.68 (4.48) Owner Mrs C C Regalado-Gonzalez	Trained at Newmarket	

---

69   **1.20 Bet Direct On 0800 32 93 93 Nursery Handicap Stakes 2yo 0-75 (E)**   **[77]**
£2233 £638 £319   **5f f/sand rnd**   Going 49   +07 Fast   Stalls Inside

32+*	**PETERS CHOICE 7** [4] I Semple 2-9-11 7ex (74) N Callan 4/9 FAV: 42011: Made all, pushed clr fnl 1f, val 4L+:		90a
3	**BLUE POWER 11** [8] K R Burke 2-8-10 (59) Darren Williams 15/2: 00442: Cl-up, kept on fnl 1f, no ch with easy wnr:	2½	63a
4965*}	**CHICKADO 20** [9] D Haydn Jones 2-9-5 (68) Paul Eddery 10/1: 00613: Handy, outpcd 3f out, rallied dist:	nk	71a
32	**SMART STARPRINCESS 7** [6] P A Blockley 2-8-12 bl (61) S Yourston (7) 25/1: 0533544: Cl-up, chsd wnr 3f out, no extra fnl 1f:	¾	62a
25	**EMARADIA 8** [7] P D Evans 2-8-5 (54) Joanna Badger 20/1: 0562345: In tch, no extra fnl 2f.	1½	51a
5015}	**BLUE MOON HITMAN 15** [10] A Berry 2-8-7 (56) A Daly 12/1: 2234546: Sn in rear, nvr nrr than mid-div.	nk	52a
4917}	**BOND ROMEO 24** [1] B Smart 2-9-7 (70) R Ffrench 12/1: 0555027: Cl-up, fdd 2f out.	9	40a
4094}	**KNIGHT TO REMEMBER 76** [3] K A Ryan 2-8-2 (51) P Fessey 100/1: 0068: Al bhd:	6	5a
3281}	**FINIANS GOLD 113** [2] J G M O'Shea 2-8-10 (59) D Sweeney 100/1: 54009: Al in rear:	1	10a
4822}	**DESERT LIGHT 31** [5] D Shaw 2-7-12 17oh VIS (30) Lisa Jones (3) 250/1: 0000: Al bhd:	5	0a
10 Ran	1m 02.32 (2.12) Owner Mr Peter Tsim	Trained at Carluke	

---

70   **1.50 Bet Direct Through Attheraces Red Button Claiming Stakes 3yo+ (F)**
£2100 £600 £300   **5f f/sand rnd**   Going 49   -01 Slow   Stalls Inside

5000*}	**SHARP HAT 17** [13] D W Chapman 9-9-2 (66) A Culhane 5/1: 0600011: Handy, styd on to lead ins fnl 1f, rdn out:		73a
35	**PRIMA STELLA 6** [4] N P Littmoden 4-9-1 (70) J P Guillambert (3) 4/1 FAV: 1324102: Mid-div, prog 2f out, kept on fnl 1f:	1	68a
4769}	**HENRY TUN 36** [7] J Balding 5-9-2 bl (56) J Edmunds 14/1: 0050003: Cl-up, led 3f out, hdd ins fnl 1f.	nk	68a
3455}	**BLUEBERRY RHYME 105** [10] P J Makin 4-8-12 vis (66) D Sweeney 9/2: 0620-04: Mid-div, hdwy 3f out, kept on fnl 1f:	1¾	59a
4776}	**MARABAR 35** [5] D W Chapman 5-8-11 (74) Dale Gibson (3) 12/1: 0255005: Sn bhd, kept on fnl 1f:	1½	54a
33	**STAR LAD 7** [6] R Brotherton 3-8-12 bl (57) G Gibbons 50/1: 2060006: Led 1f, styd in tch, fdd fnl 1f:	¾	53a
4432}	**CATCHTHEBATCH 58** [1] M J Wallace 7-9-0 (53) D Corby (3) 14/1: 6050207: Handy, wknd fnl 1f:	shd	54a
5000}	**MR SPLIFFY 17** [8] K R Burke 4-8-12 (54) Darren Williams 16/1: 0000208: Nvr nrr than mid-div.	nk	51a
4908}	**LADIES KNIGHT 25** [12] D Shaw 3-9-4 (56) N Callan 40/1: 5040009: Slow away, al in rear.	2	51a
3377}	**MONTE VERDE 108** [2] B Palling 3-8-7 p (50) D Kinsella 20/1: 0516040: Trkd ldrs, wknd 3f out:	1¼	36a
4477}	**ELLENS LAD 55** [3] W J Musson 9-9-8 bl (78) Paul Eddery 12/1: 62000-00: In tch, fdd 2f out:	2	45a
4805}	**VISION OF DREAMS 34** [9] B J Meehan 3-8-9 H bl (74) M Tebbutt 7/1: 5600000: Al bhd:	9	8a
12 Ran	1m 02.72 (2.52) Owner Miss N F Thesiger	Trained at York	

---

71   **2.25 Littlewoods Bet Direct Maiden Stakes 3yo (D)**
£2415 £690 £345   **7f f/sand rnd**   Going 49   -01 Slow   Stalls Outside

4968}	**ROMAN MAZE 20** [5] W M Brisbourne 3-9-0 S W Kelly 5/1: 0551: Cl-up, led over 1f out, pushed out, val 4L+:		71a
4	**NICHOLAS NICKELBY 11** [1] N P Littmoden 3-9-0 J P Guillambert (3) 25/1: 62: Cl-up, kept on fnl 1f, not pace wnr:	2½	63a
20	**JAGGED 8** [11] K R Burke 3-9-0 (61) Darren Williams 6/1: 5040263: Led, hdd over 1f out, no extra fnl 1f:	¾	61a
45	**MONTE MAYOR LAD 4** [12] D Haydn Jones 3-9-0 bl (62) F Norton 5/1: 4330334: Cl-up, onepcd fnl 1f.	½	60a
4964}	**WAINWRIGHT 21** [10] P A Blockley 3-9-0 p (60) Dean McKeown 4/1: 4205235: Rear, prog 3f out, no extra fnl 1f:	nk	59a
8	**VICTORY FLIP 11** [3] R Hollinshead 3-8-9 p (55) Stephanie Hollinshead (7) 16/1: 0200036: Rear, nvr nrr than mid-div.	1¼	52a
46	**NEUTRAL NIGHT 4** [4] R Brotherton 3-8-9 vis (45) G Gibbons 66/1: 0060667: Cl-up, fdd dist.	4	44a
4907}	**BUGLE CALL 25** [2] K O Cunningham Brown 3-9-0 (43) L Keniry (3) 80/1: 0050008: Slow away, al bhd.	12	29a
3512}	**MY GIRL PEARL 103** [9] M S Saunders 3-8-9 BL (48) J F McDonald (5) 66/1: 3000409: Al well bhd:	1½	21a
3972}	**BLAINA 83** [6] D R C Elsworth 3-8-9 (75) T Quinn 5/2 FAV: 032260: Cl-up, wknd 3f out:	2	17a
	MAGGIE MAQUETTE [8] W S Kittow 3-8-9 D Sweeney 66/1: 0: Rear, nvr a factor:	3	11a
4136}	**RUBY ANNIVERSARY 73** [7] J Balding 3-8-9 (43) J Edmunds 66/1: 04000: Al bhd:	5	1a
12 Ran	1m 29.86 (3.66) Owner The Jenko and Thomo Partnershi	Trained at Baschurch	

---

72   **3.00 Betdirect Co Uk Handicap Stakes Div 1 3yo+ 0-60 (F)**
£2051 £586 £293   **1m4f f/sand**   Going 49   -15 Slow   Stalls Inside   **[58]**

4828}	**FIGHT THE FEELING 31** [2] J W Unett 5-9-8 VIS (52) A Daly 7/1: 0135301: Mid-div, gd prog & ev ch dist, rdn out to lead cl-home:		58a
3632}	**KENTUCKY BULLET 98** [3] A G Newcombe 7-9-1 (45) S Whitworth 9/1: 1061042: Cl-up, led well over 1f out, hdd cl-home:	hd	49a
4931}	**ERSAAL 26** [6] J Jay 3-9-5 (55) K Dalgleish 50/1: 46-06503: Cl-up, ev ch 2f out, onepcd dist.	3½	53a
4970}	**SORBIESHARRY 20** [11] Mrs N Macauley 4-9-2 (46) Lisa Jones (3) 14/1: 0003504: Rear, prog 2f out, kept on fnl 1f.	½	43a
4144}	**SABRELINE 73** [8] B R Foster 4-9-1 (45) Dane O'Neill 33/1: 4400305: Led, hdd dist, no extra ins fnl 1f:	shd	41a
6	**IPLEDGEALLEGIANCE 11** [9] D W Chapman 7-9-6 (50) A Culhane 12/1: 0500456: Rear, nvr nrr than mid-div.	½	45a
4828}	**CLAPTRAP 31** [4] J A Osborne 3-9-4 (54) F P Ferris 9/1: 2334607: Held up, still last 3f out, kept on fnl 2f & a v kind ride:	½	48a
4259}	**PHANTOM STOCK 423** [10] W Jarvis 3-9-0 (50) T Quinn 10/1: 000-8: Al bhd:	2	41a
6*	**SMOOTHIE 11** [7] Ian Williams 5-10-6 6ex (60) D Nolan (5) 5/2 FAV: 0016619: Mid-div, wknd 2f out:	3	50a
4828}	**FAIRY WIND 31** [5] B J Curley 6-9-5 (49) S W Kelly 4/1: 6000020: Cl-up, wknd 4f out:	¾	33a
4120*}	**TOP TREES 74** [12] W S Kittow 3-9-7 (51) F Norton 12/1: 02-50010: Al well bhd:	shd	34a

26

WOLVERHAMPTON Friday 21.11.03 Lefthand, V Sharp Track

11 Ran   2m 41.38 (7.78)   Owner Mr T Morning   Trained at Wolverhampton

---

73
3.35 Bet Direct Rugby Prices Sky Page 372 Selling Stakes 2yo (G)
£2093 £598 £299   6f f/sand rnd   Going 49   -03 Slow   Stalls Inside

32	MELAINA 7 [1] M S Saunders 2-8-6 P (52) J F McDonald (5) 7/1: 5460061: Cl-up, led 4f out, edged left dist, drvn out:			56a
4594}	FISHERS DREAM 48 [13] J R Norton 2-8-11 vis (44) Darren Williams 16/1: 0000642: Led over 1f out, styd cl-up, edged ins fnl 1f, kept on, not pace wnr:	1¾	54a
4562}	PHILLY DEE 50 [2] J Jay 2-8-6 (47) Lisa Jones (3) 5/1: 5266043: Cl-up, ev ch dist, sn onepcd:	¾	47a
4917}	WHITTINGHAMVILLAGE 24 [7] A Berry 2-8-6 (59) F Norton 11/2: 3644604: Led early, styd cl-up, outpcd 3f out, rallied fnl 1f:	1¾	42a
25	CITY GENERAL 8 [8] J S Moore 2-9-2 p (58) L Keniry (3) 3/1 FAV: 3406255: Mid-div, outpcd 3f out, rallied 2f out.	nk	51a
32	FAYR FIRENZE 7 [6] M F Harris 2-8-11 bl (52) S Righton 10/1: 0000656: Cl-up, outpcd 3f out, rallied 1f out.	nk	45a
4463}	DRESS PEARL 56 [9] A Berry 2-8-6 (54) Dean McKeown 20/1: 0606007: Mid-div, wknd 3f out:	9	16a
25	HES A ROCKET 8 [10] Mrs C A Dunnett 2-8-11 (50) N Chalmers (5) 33/1: 5600008: Cl-up, fdd 3f out.	½	20a
4594}	ALMOST ROYAL 48 [11] R M Beckett 2-8-6 (47) N Callan 14/1: 00009: Cl-up, wknd 3f out:	1½	11a
4965}	MILLIETOM 20 [5] K A Ryan 2-8-11 P G Parkin 9/2: 00: Slow away, al bhd:	5	3a
4886}	CAPLAW SONG 27 [3] A Berry 2-8-6 (32) P Mathers (7) 50/1: 4000000: Slow away, al bhd.	5	0a

11 Ran   1m 15.97 (3.17)   Owner Bali Royal Racing   Trained at Wells

---

74
4.10 Bet Direct In Running Sky Text 293 Handicap Stakes Div 2 3yo+ 0-60 (F) [60]
£2100 £600 £300   7f f/sand rnd   Going 49   -18 Slow   Stalls Outside

4986}	SEMPER PARATUS 19 [6] H J Collingridge 4-9-7 bl (53) M Tebbutt 6/1: 0500001: Cl-up, chsd ldr 2f out, led ins fnl 1f, drvn out:		60a
4722*}	MON SECRET 39 [12] B Smart 5-9-9 (55) R Ffrench 5/1: 1000012: Rear, prog 2f out, ev ch fnl 1f, just denied:	hd	60a
971}	GAME GURU 228 [5] T D Barron 4-9-13 bl (59) Dean McKeown 14/1: 3306003D: Handy, onepcd ins fnl 1f:	1¼	62a
20	ITS ECCO BOY 8 [1] P Howling 5-9-9 (55) D Nolan (5) 12/1: 4135003: Led, hdd ins fnl 1f, no extra.	½	57a
66	MR STYLISH 7 [10] J S Moore 7-9-7 vis t (53) J D Smith 16/1: 6266004: Held up, prog 2f out, kept on fnl 1f:	1	53a
5017}	FABRIAN 15 [3] D W P Arbuthnot 5-9-9 e (55) Dane O'Neill 4/1: 0030055: Cl-up, outpcd 3f out, rallied fnl 1f:	½	54a
4540}	MUQARRAR 51 [7] T J Fitzgerald 4-9-8 e (54) K Dalgleish 20/1: 0650006: Rear, prog 2f out, nrst fin:	½	52a
4722}	GLENROCK 39 [9] A Berry 6-9-7 (53) P Bradley (5) 25/1: 0001007: Cl-up, wknd 2f out:	½	50a
5	SHATIN HERO 11 [11] G C H Chung 3-9-8 p (55) S Hitchcott (3) 9/4 FAV: 3414428: Rear, nvr able to chall.	½	51a
	VIJAY 55 [2] I Semple 4-10-0 BL (60) D McGaffin (3) 16/1: 5434369: Cl-up, fdd 2f out:	10	38a
4807}	THREE DAYS IN MAY 34 [4] M R Channon 4-10-0 (60) T O'Brien (4) 25/1: 0330000: Mid-div, fdd 2f out.	15	10a
	ANIMAL LOVER 21 [8] T Hogan 3-9-8 T (55) W M Lachance 33/1: 0100000: Al in rear.	1	3a

12 Ran   1m 30.92 (4.72)   Owner The Tin Man Partnership   Trained at Newmarket

---

75
4.40 Betdirect Co Uk Handicap Stakes Div 2 3yo+ 0-60 (F) [58]
£2044 £584 £292   1m4f f/sand   Going 49   -02 Slow   Stalls Inside

6	EASIBET DOT NET 11 [6] I Semple 3-9-7 p (57) D McGaffin (3) 9/4 FAV: 4432321: Cl-up, led 4f out, 3L clr dist, rdn out to hold on:		62a
4819}	AMBERSONG 32 [7] A W Carroll 5-9-3 (47) F Norton 7/2: 0001422: Held up, prog 3f out, kept on fnl 1f, nrst fin:	¾	49a
4970}	VANDENBERGHE 20 [4] J A Osborne 4-9-5 (49) Paul Eddery 10/1: 000-0063: Rear, prog 5f out, no impress fnl 1f:	2½	47a
4968*}	TO WIT TO WOO 20 [11] B W Hills 3-9-6 (56) M Hills 100/30: 040014: Mid-div, prog 6f out, chsd wnr 4f out, no extra fnl 1f:	nk	53a
4995}	CANTEMERLE 17 [10] W M Brisbourne 3-9-4 bl (54) S W Kelly 16/1: 2000035: Rear, nvr nrr than mid-div.	16	29a
4137}	MARGOLD 73 [9] R Hollinshead 3-9-5 (55) B Swarbrick (7) 50/1: 6033306: Al rear:	3½	25a
6	GERI ROULETTE 11 [3] E J Alston 5-9-7 (51) A Nicholls 14/1: 1660037: Cl-up, led briefly 4f out, sn fdd:	16	-1a
3920}	TARKWA 86 [12] R M H Cowell 4-9-0 (44) M Henry 25/1: 4053268: Rear, prog 5f out, fdd 3f out.	3½	0
4331}	LITTLE RICHARD 63 [5] M Wellings 4-9-0 vis (44) D Corby (7) 33/1: 2230009: Handy, fdd 4f out.	½	0
4209}	SPRING PURSUIT 70 [2] R J Price 7-9-2 (46) N Callan (5) 16/1: 0004-000: Sn well adrift:	18	0
6	INTERSTICE 11 [8] A G Newcombe 6-10-0 (58) S Whitworth 12/1: 0030000: Mid-div, fdd 4f out.	18	0
4184}	RIVELLI 71 [1] B R Foster 4-10-0 bl (58) L Keniry (3) 100/1: 000-0000: Led, hdd 4f out, sn fdd.	15	0

12 Ran   2m 39.76 (6.16)   Owner WWWEASIBET DOT NET   Trained at Carluke

---

LINGFIELD Saturday 22.11.03 Lefthand, V Sharp Track

Official Going STANDARD.

76
12.00 Big Al's 50th Birthday Maiden Stakes 2yo (D)
£3066 £876 £438   5f rnd   Going 42   -05 Slow   Stalls Outside

4868}	INTRIGUING GLIMPSE 29 [5] Miss B Sanders 2-8-9 S Drowne 5/1: 601: Handy, eff for press 2f out, styd on to lead ins last, drvn out:		66a
4926}	FIVE YEARS ON 25 [2] W J Haggas 2-9-0 P Robinson 6/1: 02: Handy, eff well over 1f out, kept on ins last, not btn far:	¾	69a
32	SCOTTISH EXILE 8 [3] K R Burke 2-8-9 (60) Darren Williams 3/1: 4044023: With ldr, went on over 3f out till ins last, onepace for press, not btn far:	shd	64a
4926}	DONT CALL ME DEREK 25 [7] S C Williams 2-9-0 B Reilly (5) 16/1: 04: Slow away, held up well off pace, kept on late, kind ride:	hd	66a
4917}	AFTER ALL 25 [6] G A Butler 2-8-9 (62) S W Kelly 5/2 FAV: 0235: Slow away, sn in tch, onepace dist:	1	60a
4926}	MISS JUDGEMENT 25 [1] W R Muir 2-8-9 (49) F Norton 20/1: 0006: Led till 3f out, ev ch till wknd fnl 1f.	½	58a
5015}	CRISPIN GIRL 16 [9] J L Spearing 2-8-9 (52) A Daly (3) 14/1: 0500007: In tch, no extra over 1f out.	¾	56a
4580}	CLEARING SKY 50 [4] Miss Z C Davison 2-8-9 I Mongan 25/1: 08: Slow away, sn bhd, some late gains.	½	54a
5015}	MAXIS PRINCESS 16 [10] P J Makin 2-8-9 T (60) D Sweeney 8/1: 44009: In tch wide, btn 2f out:	1½	50a

9 Ran   1m 0.14 (2.34)   Owner Mr Edward Hyde   Trained at Epsom

LINGFIELD Saturday 22.11.03 Lefthand, V Sharp Track

77 12.30 Betdirect Co Uk Selling Stakes Div 1 2yo (G)
£2037 £582 £291 1m rnd Going 42 -32 Slow Stalls Outside

4960} **THE JOB 22** [7] A D Smith 2-8-11 (65) W Ryan 7/1: 04001: Slow away, held up, hdwy 2f out, styd on well to lead ins last, going away: **62a**
4715} **DELCIENNE 40** [3] G G Margarson 2-8-6 (50) N Pollard 16/1: 04002: Led 2f, led again over 2f out & clr over 1f out, collared ins last: *1¼* **53a**
4892} **LYRICAL GIRL 28** [6] M R Channon 2-8-6 (64) S Hitchcott (3) 5/2 FAV: 2023003: Bhd, badly hmpd over 3f out, hdwy 2f out, late gains: *¾* **51a**
4930} **HUNTING PINK 25** [10] H Morrison 2-8-6 (48) J F Egan 12/1: 4463004: Handy, lost pl over 4f out but rallied over 3f out, wknd appr fnl 1f on AW bow. *1* **49a**
28 **ARMENTIERES 8** [2] J L Spearing 2-8-11 bl (55) A Daly 5/1: 3001435: In tch, eff 3f out, sn outpcd till rallied ins last. *1* **52a**
4988} **STANHOPE FORBES 19** [4] N P Littmoden 2-8-11 (69) N Callan 7/2: 063506: Cl-up, wknd over 1f out: *1* **50a**
4834} **LOOK NO MORE 32** [1] W G M Turner 2-8-11 (47) L Treadwell (7) 16/1: 04567: Handy, btn over 2f out. *1¾* **46a**
4577} **REEDSMAN 50** [9] M H Tompkins 2-8-11 bl (49) P Robinson 16/1: 00008: Dwelt, recovered to lead after 2f till 2f out. *¾* **44a**
4825} **ALLODARLIN 32** [11] P F I Cole 2-8-7 1ow (56) A Culhane 7/1: 50069: Al bhd: *1¼* **38a**
4816} **OH FRIGATE 33** [5] H Candy 2-8-11 Dane O'Neill 33/1: 00: Al bhd. *¾* **40a**
2096} **BOUNCER 163** [12] W R Muir 2-8-11 (46) S Drowne 50/1: 6060: In tch, wknd 3f out, t.o.: *12* **16a**
11 Ran 1m 42.13 (5.93) Owner Pertemps Group Limited Trained at Westward Ho

78 1.00 Betdirect Co Uk Selling Stakes Div 2 2yo (G)
£2037 £582 £291 1m rnd Going 42 -32 Slow Stalls Outside

15 **ROWAN PURSUIT 10** [8] M H Tompkins 2-8-11 bl (63) P Robinson 10/11 FAV: P400131: Held up, short of room over 3f out till over 1f out but styd on strongly to lead ins last, going away: **62a**
4578} **GOOD VIBRATIONS 50** [11] P F I Cole 2-8-7 1ow (42) A Culhane 20/1: 0002: Slow away, keen hld up, short of room 3f out, styd on well to lead over 1f out & clr till collared well *1½* **54a**
5015} **MUST BE SO 16** [12] D R C Elsworth 2-8-6 (60) N Pollard 7/1: 04003: Held up, hdwy appr 2f out, sn onepace: *1¾* **49a**
37 **QUARRY ISLAND 7** [4] P D Evans 2-8-6 (40) Joanna Badger 50/1: 66004: Led 3f out till dist. *4* **41a**
4960} **NOTHING MATTERS 22** [10] P R Chamings 2-8-6 (43) F Norton 33/1: 054005: Held up, plenty to do & short of room over 2f out, some late gains, nvr dngrs on AW bow. *1½* **38a**
29 **DESERT BEAU 8** [7] Mrs P N Dutfield 2-8-11 VIS (57) R Havlin 10/1: 05006: Handy, eff to chase ldr over 2f out, hung left & wknd over 1f out: *3* **37a**
4639} **YNYS 46** [1] B Palling 2-8-11 (42) D Kinsella 66/1: 05507: In tch, bhd over 2f out: *nk* **36a**
4034} **OUT OF MY WAY 80** [5] T M Jones 2-8-6 (35) R Brisland 50/1: 0408: Sn rdn & nvr a factor: *½* **30a**
25 **COSTA DEL SOL 9** [6] J J Bridger 2-8-11 (50) J F McDonald (5) 12/1: 4420609: Prom, wknd 2f out: *nk* **34a**
4578} **KINDA CUTE 50** [3] M Quinn 2-8-6 (40) Martin Dwyer 33/1: 00000: Led till 3f out, wknd qckly: *10* **28a**
28 **MAGGIES CHOICE 8** [2] N P Littmoden 2-8-11 (53) I Mongan 20/1: 0100000: Handy, wknd qckly over 2f out. *nk* **13a**
4930} **DAVIDS GIRL 25** [9] D Morris 2-8-6 (53) N Callan 7/1: 54060: In tch, hdwy over 2f out, sn wknd qckly. *1½* **5a**
12 Ran 1m 42.14 (5.94) Owner Rowan Stud Partnership Trained at Newmarket

79 1.35 Levy Board Conditions Stakes 2yo (C)
£4733 £1795 £898 £408 6f rnd Going 42 +02 Fast Stalls Inside

4754} **PETARDIAS MAGIC 22** [1] E J O'Neill 2-8-11 (82) R Ffrench 7/4 FAV: 612301: Handy, hdwy over 1f out, styd on well for press to lead ins last, all out: **87a**
4773} **MISTER SAIF 36** [3] R Hannon 2-9-0 (85) Dane O'Neill 11/4: 331062: With ldr, led over 2f out, styd on for press ins last & only gave best cl-home in a fine duel: *nk* **89a**
MR LAMBROS [5] A M Balding 2-8-8 Martin Dwyer 7/1: 3: Slow away, held up, rdn & hdwy dist, styd on ins last, nrst fin on debut: *nk* **82a**
787*} **WESTERN ROOTS 252** [4] P F I Cole 2-9-4 S Drowne 8/1: 14: In tch, rdn over 2f out, onepace. *3½* **82a**
4912} **ELUSIVE KITTY 26** [2] G A Butler 2-8-6 S W Kelly 5/2: 525: Handy, onepace well over 1f out: *hd* **69a**
4576} **ANATOM 50** [6] M Quinn 2-8-6 (40) F Norton 150/1: 00066: Led till 2f out, wknd qckly over 1f out: *14* **41a**
6 Ran 1m 12.8 (2.4) Owner Miss Sarah Diane Warren Trained at Newmarket

80 2.05 European Breeders Fund Littlewoods Bet Direct Rated Stakes Handicapfillies 3yo+ 0-90 (C [94]
£7179 £2723 £1362 £619 1m rnd Going 42 -03 Slow Stalls Outside

38 **STAR OF NORMANDIE 7** [4] G G Margarson 4-8-9 (75) B Reilly (5) 5/1: 6003121: Reluctant to post, handy, hdwy trav well 2f out, led ins last, hands-and-heels, readily: **83a**
17 **AMORAS 10** [7] J W Hills 6-8-4 (70) J F Egan 14/1: 0520002: Held up, plenty to do 2f out, styd on well dist, nvr get to wnr: *1½* **74a**
4055} **LOOKING DOWN 79** [10] R Hannon 3-8-4 (72) Martin Dwyer 10/1: 3400403: Led till 5f out, led again over 2f out till ins last, onepace: *1¼* **73a**
4985*} **ANNISHIRANI 20** [9] G A Butler 3-8-6 (74) S W Kelly 4/1 FAV: 322114: Keen, led 5f out till over 2f out, onepace: *hd* **74a**
4983} **DUTY PAID 20** [12] D R C Elsworth 3-9-7 (89) T Quinn 11/2: 0602045: Handy, onepace over 1f out. *¾* **87a**
4579} **CHETAK 50** [8] B W Hills 3-9-4 (86) M Hills 9/2: 1024326: Held up outer, eff 2f out, onepace: *hd* **83a**
4904} **SANDENISTA 26** [6] L M Cumani 3-8-4 (72) W Ryan 10/1: 4137: Dwelt, held up, hdwy over 2f out, sn onepace. *¾* **67a**
4999} **PERFECT LOVE 18** [2] G A Butler 3-8-12 (80) S Drowne 10/1: 1208: Held up, no impress fnl 2f: *5* **65a**
NO FRONTIER 22 [1] T Hogan 5-8-5 T (71) W M Lordan 20/1: 4535629: In tch, wknd qckly dist: *½* **55a**
4983} **ZITHER 20** [5] R Hannon 3-9-2 (84) Dane O'Neill 14/1: 2530560: In tch, bhd over 2f out. *1½* **65a**
4983} **JUST A GLIMMER 20** [3] L G Cottrell 3-9-0 (82) I Mongan 16/1: 56331-00: Al bhd. *8* **47a**
11 Ran 1m 39.84 (3.64) Owner Norcroft Park Stud Trained at Newmarket

81 2.40 Bet Direct On 0800 329393 Handicap Stakes 3yo+ 0-95 (C) [95]
£5150 £1954 £977 £444 7f rnd Going 42 +05 Fast Stalls Inside

44 **LYGETON LAD 5** [14] Miss Gay Kelleway 5-10-0 t (95) M Fenton 14/1: 0552001: Held up, plenty to do over 2f out but gd **103a**

hdwy wide appr fnl 1f to get up fnl strides, rdn out:

4999}	**INCLINE** 18 [6] T G Mills 4-8-10 (77) R Miles (5) 25/1: 113-0002: Slow away, sn in tch, eff 2f out, styd on to lead ins last till collared nr line:			shd	84a
4471}	**CAMP COMMANDER** 56 [12] C E Brittain 4-9-12 t (93) Dane O'Neill 20/1: 2000003: Slow away, held up, hdwy 2f out, styd on to chall ins last, not btn far:			½	99a
5030}	**MARSHMAN** 14 [10] M H Tompkins 4-9-8 (89) P Robinson 6/1: 4301534: Held up, eff & hung left over 1f out but kept on ins			1¼	92a
1995	**JUST FLY** 169 [8] S Kirk 3-8-13 (81) J F Egan 33/1: 1-500105: Chsd ldr, ev ch till wknd ins last:			hd	83a
64	**QUITO** 3 [15] D W Chapman 6-10-0 bl (95) A Culhane 8/1: 4100526: Held up, plenty to do 2f out, late gains, too much to do:			¾	95a
4500}	**WHAT A DANCER** 55 [11] G A Swinbank 6-8-11 (78) N Pollard 12/1: 0321547: In tch, onepace over 2f out, abs.			nk	77a
4977}	**BORDER EDGE** 21 [3] J J Bridger 5-9-5 vis (86) J F McDonald (5) 16/1: 0101208: Set gd pace till ins last, wknd.			hd	84a
4950}	**WATERSIDE** 23 [16] J W Hills 4-9-1 (82) M Hills 12/1: 0263149: Keen held up, eff 2f out, no impress.			½	79a
44	**CERTAIN JUSTICE** 5 [7] P F I Cole 5-9-4 (85) S Drowne 8/1: 0506040: In tch, btn over 1f out.			1	80a
4983}	**JUMMANA** 20 [2] G A Butler 3-9-10 (92) S W Kelly 8/1: 14-00: In tch, wknd over 1f out.			1¼	84a
5030}	**GOLDEN CHALICE** 14 [13] A M Balding 4-9-9 (90) Martin Dwyer 11/2: 3000520: In tch, wknd over 1f out.			shd	81a
4689}	**AGILIS** 41 [9] Jamie Poulton 3-9-1 (83) S Whitworth 25/1: 22-40500: In tch, bhd over 2f out.			5	64a
31*	**FLINT RIVER** 8 [1] H Morrison 5-9-0 (81) J Fanning 9/2 FAV: 1200210: Cl-up, wknd qckly over 1f out:			¾	60a
4928}	**GEM BIEN** 25 [4] Andrew Turnell 5-9-1 (82) D Corby (3) 25/1: 30-01640: In tch, wknd 2f out on AW bow.			4	53a
15 Ran	1m 25.38 (2.58)	Owner Mr J McGonagle & Mr B J McGona			Trained at Newmarket

82

3.15 Listed Littlewoods Bet Direct Churchill Stakes 3yo+ (A)
£14500 £5500 £2750 £1250 **1m2f** **Going 42** **+02 Fast** Stalls Inside

4893}	**COMPTON BOLTER** 28 [1] G A Butler 6-9-2 (103) Martin Dwyer 7/2 JT FAV: 5112201: Held up, gd hdwy 2f out, staying on strongly for press ins last to get up last stride, gamely, drvn out:				106a
4976}	**GRAND PASSION** 21 [2] G Wragg 3-8-10 (103) J F Egan 8/1: 0412032: In tch, gd hdwy to lead over 1f out, hard prsd ins last & just gave best nr fin:			shd	103a
4735*	**WINDY BRITAIN** 39 [6] L M Cumani 4-8-9 (82) S W Kelly 14/1: 1331313: Dwelt, held up rear, hdwy wide 2f out, styd on strongly ins last, nrst fin:			1½	95a
5020}	**BLUE SKY THINKING** 16 [5] K R Burke 4-9-0 (90) Darren Williams 50/1: 1-016334: Held up, hdwy & short of room over 2f out, styd on late, nvr dngrs:			½	99a
5027}	**PERSIAN LASS** 15 [13] P W Harris 4-8-9 (94) S Drowne 12/1: 4303355: With ldrs, chall over 2f out, onepace fnl 1f:			¾	93a
5036}	**EASTERN BREEZE** 14 [4] P W D'Arcy 5-9-0 (96) Paul Eddery 4/1: 0331666: Held up, hdwy over 2f out, onepace.			shd	98a
4225}	**RAPSCALLION** 70 [8] J M P Eustace 4-9-0 BL (85) J Tate 50/1: 64-00007: Keen in tch, wknd 2f out:			1½	96a
4983*}	**TADRIS** 20 [14] M P Tregoning 3-8-7 (103) R Hills 7/2 JT FAV: 1341218: Held up, btn 2f out:			2½	89a
4976*}	**BABODANA** 21 [12] M H Tompkins 3-8-12 (107) P Robinson 14/1: 4004219: Led 2f, lost pl over 3f out, eff when badly hmpd over 1f out, not recover:			1¼	92a
4800}	**LUNDYS LANE** 35 [3] C E Brittain 3-8-10 (107) I Mongan 8/1: 0213460: Slow away, held up, hdwy to lead over 3f out till over 1f out, wknd qckly.			1¼	88a
4955}	**TIZZY MAY** 22 [10] R Hannon 3-8-10 (96) Dane O'Neill 14/1: 4223240: Led 7f till 3f out, wknd.			1¼	86a
4939}	**CZARINA WALTZ** 24 [7] C F Wall 4-8-9 (86) R Mullen 20/1: 1351040: Held up, btn over 2f out.			1¼	79a
5020*	**CORNELIUS** 16 [9] P F I Cole 6-9-0 (100) A Culhane 20/1: 0300410: Held up, wknd over 2f out:			6	74a
4955}	**SUNNY GLENN** 22 [11] Mrs P N Dutfield 5-9-0 (85) P McCabe 200/1: 00-25000: Handy, wknd over 3f out.			13	56a
14 Ran	2m 06.83 (4.03)	Owner Mr Erik Penser			Trained at Blewbury

83

3.45 Bet Direct In Running Sky Text 293 Handicap Stakes 3yo+ 0-95 (C)
£5785 £1780 £890 £445 **1m4f** **Going 42** **-10 Slow** Stalls Inside [93]

4796}	**HIGH POINT** 35 [10] G P Enright 5-8-11 (76) Dane O'Neill 16/1: 2150001: Cl-up, led over 2f out, styd on well ins last, rdn out:				82a
4894}	**GIG HARBOR** 28 [8] Miss E C Lavelle 4-9-5 (84) A Culhane 5/1: 0000062: Handy, hdwy trav well over 2f out, chall over 1f out, kept on:			1	88a
4677}	**TYPHOON TILLY** 42 [7] C R Egerton 6-8-10 (75) S Drowne 14/1: 3-133033: Keen cl-up, lost pl over 2f out, rallied over 1f out, onepcd:			¾	77a
11*	**MAYSTOCK** 10 [9] G A Butler 3-7-12 1oh vis (68) J F McDonald (5) 12/1: 0360414: Slow away, held up, lost pl 2f out, styd on well fnl 1f:			½	70a
5036}	**GALLANT BOY** 14 [16] P D Evans 4-9-1 t (80) N Callan 14/1: 4410005: Held up, late gains, nvr dngrs.			1½	79a
4909}	**NAWOW** 26 [14] P D Cundell 3-8-9 (80) Martin Dwyer 13/2: 3650326: Set pace till over 1f out, wknd.			shd	79a
4879}	**SIENA STAR** 28 [2] P F I Cole 5-8-12 (77) M Hills 10/1: 5610257: Held up, hdwy trav well over 2f out, sn rdn & not find as much as expected.			¾	74a
5019}	**COMPLETE CIRCLE** 16 [5] P W D'Arcy 3-8-13 vis (84) Paul Eddery 20/1: 0004558: Held up, btn over 2f out.			½	80a
3649}	**BRILLIANT RED** 98 [4] Jamie Poulton 10-9-12 t (91) I Mongan 16/1: 0432449: Slow away, held up, some late gains.			hd	86a
4909*}	**GOLANO** 26 [11] C F Wall 3-8-4 (75) R Mullen 7/2 FAV: 3343110: In tch, wknd over 1f out.			1	68a
4612}	**HIGH HOPE** 47 [12] G L Moore 5-9-1 (80) S Whitworth 14/1: 1-250000: Held up, btn 2f out.			hd	73a
1699}	**BACK IN ACTION** 182 [1] M A Magnusson 3-8-8 t (79) R Hills 8/1: 53-500: Dwelt, held up, btn over 2f out.			3	68a
4339}	**LINNING WINE** 64 [13] B G Powell 7-10-0 (93) L Keniry (3) 10/1: 3020000: In tch, wknd qckly 2f out:			½	81a
4954}	**ASTROCHARM** 22 [6] M H Tompkins 4-8-10 bl (75) J Fanning 16/1: 0300400: Handy, wknd qckly over 2f out.			nk	63a
14 Ran	2m 35.48 (6.28)	Owner The Aedean Partnership			Trained at Lewes

Official Going STANDARD.

84

12.05 Bet Direct Through Attheraces Amateur Riders' Handicap Stakes Div 1 3yo+ 0-60 (G)
£2114 £604 £302 **1m f/sand rnd** **Going 49** **-21 Slow** Stalls Inside [36]

40	**ROCK CONCERT** 9 [11] I W McInnes 5-11-5 (55) Miss E J Jones 9/2: 0533221: Cl-up, chsd ldr 3f out, led ins fnl 1f, drvn out:				60a
62	**MUTARAFAA** 5 [9] D Shaw 4-10-8 e (44) Ms C Williams 6/1: 0006022: Chsd ldrs, kept on well fnl 1f, just held by wnr:			shd	48a

62*	SKY DOME 5 [10] M H Tompkins 10-11-13 6ex vis (63) Mr S Warren (7) 6/1: 0040513: Bhd, prog wide 3f out, kept on fnl 1f, nrst fin:	1¾	63a
62	SCRAMBLE 5 [15] B Ellison 5-11-2 bl t (52) Miss L Ellison (3) 4/1 FAV: 6644134: Led after 2f, clr 2f out, wknd & hdd ins fnl 1f:	2	48a
4582}	OUR GLENARD 52 [16] S L Keightley 4-10-11 (47) Miss A L Turner (5) 25/1: 1005005: Slow away, sn handy, onepcd fnl 2f:	nk	42a
4391}	DISABUSE 63 [14] S C Williams 3-10-12 (50) Mr A Duarte (7) 9/1: 000266: Bhd, prog wide 4f out, no impress fnl 2f.	3½	38a
38	TOP OF THE CLASS 9 [6] P D Evans 6-10-10 vis (46) Miss Hayley Bryan (5) 20/1: 6154057: Nvr nrr than mid-div.	3½	27a
46	STORM SHOWER 7 [8] Mrs N Macauley 5-10-5 vis (41) Mrs M Morris 28/1: 5060308: Chsd ldrs, wknd 2f out:	3	16a
62	JESSINCA 5 [3] A P Jones 7-10-9 (45) Mr Wayne Lewis (5) 20/1: 0246469: Chsd ldrs, fdd 3f out:	¾	19a
4944}	HALCYON MAGIC 26 [2] Miss J Feilden 5-10-3 bl (39) Mr S Rees (5) 16/1: 0005060: Led 2f, prom, fdd 2f out.	11	0a
4769}	STAND BY 39 [1] T D McCarthy 6-11-0 vis (50) Mr W Rich (7) 33/1: 2250000: Prom, fdd 3f out.	6	0a
3607}	LARKYS LOB 102 [5] Paul Johnson 4-11-0 e (50) Mr P Evans (7) 40/1: 0400000: Mid-div, wknd 3f out:	shd	0a
47	PRESIDENTS LADY 7 [4] P W Hiatt 6-10-6 (42) Mrs Marie King (5) 100/1: 0/0020//-0: Handy, wknd when hmpd 4f out:	6	0a
61	BETTER PAL 5 [12] P R Wood 4-11-4 (54) Miss A Wallace (5) 50/1: 6000000: Slow away, sn in tch wide, fdd 4f out:	3	0a
66	ACHILLES RAINBOW 5 [7] K R Burke 4-10-3 (39) Mr S Dobson (3) 33/1: 0-040060: Al in rear:	27	0a

15 Ran 1m 45.01 (5.61) Owner Ivy House Racing Trained at Catwick

---

85 **12.35 Bet Direct Red To Bet Handicap Stakes Div 1 Fillies 3yo+ 0-70 (E)** **[68]**
£2051 £586 £293 6f f/sand rnd Going 49 -04 Slow Stalls Inside

3725}	GRANDMA LILY 97 [1] M C Chapman 5-9-13 (67) I Mongan 7/2: 0000001: Handy, styd on to lead ins fnl 1f, rdn out:		77a
5006}	CHISPA 19 [10] K R Burke 5-9-4 (58) Darren Williams 5/2 FAV: 0005302: Led till ins fnl 1f, not pace wnr:	¾	66a
27	CAROLS CHOICE 10 [12] A Sadik 6-8-5 (45) N Chalmers (3) 10/1: 2540063: Cl-up, ev ch dist, sn no extra.	4	41a
4689}	NAJAABA 43 [5] Miss J Feilden 3-9-3 (57) A Quinn (5) 20/1: 660-04: Sn bhd, prog 2f out, nrst fin.	1¾	48a
4330}	BIJAN 66 [2] R Hollinshead 5-7-12 1oh (37) B Swarbrick (7) 8/1: 0360405: Nvr nrr than mid-div.	1¾	24a
4791}	LADYSTGEORGE 38 [11] M Mullineaux 4-7-12 3oh (35) Liam Jones (7) 66/1: 0-000046: Handy, wknd 2f out:	2½	17a
4642}	SWEET CORAL 48 [4] B S Rothwell 3-8-3 (43) Joanna Badger 33/1: 5007: Nvr nrr than mid-div:	½	21a
5017}	LADY NATILDA 18 [6] D Haydn Jones 3-8-13 BL (53) Paul Eddery 9/1: 0304508: Nvr nr ldrs:	1	28a
4821}	CERTA CITO 34 [7] T D Easterby 3-9-8 (62) K Dalgleish 10/1: 1309: Hmpd start, al rear.	¾	35a
4550}	PENNY VALENTINE 54 [8] J R Best 3-7-12 (38) D Fentiman (7) 14/1: 6-600050: Al in rear:	nk	10a
4949}	MABEL RILEY 25 [3] M A Buckley 3-8-9 (49) Lisa Jones (3) 17/2: 6035000: In tch, short of rm & wknd 3f out.	4	9a
4446}	AUNT DORIS 415 [9] Paul Johnson 6-7-13 e (39) Sarah Mitchell 66/1: 0/40500-0: Cl-up, wknd 4f out:	5	0a

12 Ran 1m 16.51 (3.21) Owner David Fravigar Alan Mann David Trained at Market Rasen

---

86 **1.05 Bet Direct Through Attheraces Amateur Riders' Handicap Stakes Div 2 3yo+ 0-60 (G)** **[39]**
£2107 £602 £301 1m f/sand rnd Going 49 -21 Slow Stalls Inside

4769}	MISTER BENJI 39 [14] B P J Baugh 4-10-12 p (51) Mr E Dehdashti (5) 33/1: 3540001: Prom, led briefly bef 2f out, rallied well to lead ins fnl 1f, rdn out:		57a
60	SHIFTY 5 [13] D Nicholls 4-11-1 bl (54) Miss Kelly Harrison (5) 11/2: 4065042: Prom, led 2f out, sn hung badly left, hdd ins fnl 1f, no extra:	2	56a
61	LEVANTINE 5 [11] A G Newcombe 6-10-2 p (41) Miss C Hannaford 4/1 FAV: 00-30633: Led, hdd bef 2f out, sn onepcd:	2½	38a
2689}	FLAMBE 141 [5] P C Haslam 5-11-7 (60) Mr B Haslam (5) 13/2: 0300-004: Mid-div, wknd 3f out:	3½	50a
2104}	QOBTAAN 164 [9] M R Bosley 4-10-8 (47) Mrs S Bosley 16/1: 0024605: Bhd, prog 3f out, nrst fin:	shd	36a
60	MAGGIES PET 5 [15] K Bell 6-10-7 t (46) Miss J Ellis (5) 7/1: 5-400036: Chsd ldrs, no impress fnl 2f:	shd	34a
66	BRILLIANTRIO 5 [1] M C Chapman 5-10-10 t (49) Miss S Arnold (7) 14/1: 01U0657: Handy, ev ch 2f out, sn wknd.	hd	36a
61	PROUD VICTOR 5 [12] D Shaw 3-10-4 (45) Mr S Dobson (3) 11/1: 0006048: Bhd, prog 3f out, mod late gains.	1	30a
4817}	OUR DESTINY 35 [4] D Burchell 5-10-1 vis (40) Miss E Tucker (7) 14/1: 4100009: Handy, wknd fnl 3f.	5	15a
3646}	THE GAY FOX 91 [10] B G Powell 9-10-3 bl t (42) Mrs R Powell (7) 12/1: 6525350: Al bhd:	3½	10a
4	ABANINETOES 14 [6] P D Evans 3-10-0 (41) Miss Hayley Bryan (5) 100/1: 0000000: Chsd ldrs, wknd fnl 3f:	shd	8a
902}	SPANISH STAR 238 [2] Mrs N Macauley 6-10-6 (45) Mrs M Morris 14/1: 6534000: Al bhd:	2½	7a
1067}	TORZAL 223 [16] R F Marvin 3-9-13 (40) Miss A L Turner (5) 100/1: 540-000: Al in rear:	6	0a
4918}	SCURRA 27 [3] A C Whillans 4-11-0 (53) Mr E Whillans (7) 16/1: 0040320: Handy, fdd 4f out.	¾	2a
1750}	WATERLINE SPIRIT 181 [8] P D Evans 3-10-7 (48) Miss E Folkes (5) 100/1: 40000-000: Cl-up, wknd 3f out:	10	0a
3370}	THE GAMBLER 112 [7] Paul Johnson 3-11-2 e (57) Mr P Evans (5) 25/1: 6200500: Al bhd:	16	0a

16 Ran 1m 45.01 (5.61) Owner Mr JHChrimes and Mr & Mrs GWHa Trained at Stoke On Trent

---

87 **1.40 Bet Direct In Running Selling Stakes 2yo (G)**
£2135 £610 £305 7f f/sand rnd Going 49 -16 Slow Stalls Inside

4994}	COULD SHE BE MAGIC 20 [5] T D Easterby 2-8-6 (56) K Dalgleish 7/2 FAV: 003501: Cl-up, led 4f out, rdn clr dist:		58a
29	CHASE THE RAINBOW 10 [6] M Johnston 2-8-11 (59) J Fanning 13/2: 51002: Cl-up, chsd wnr 2f out, kept on fnl 1f, al held:	3	56a
4930}	RARE COINCIDENCE 27 [16] R F Fisher 2-8-11 P (54) S Righton 10/1: 0065053: Slow away, prog 5f out, hung left dist, sn onepcd:	¾	54a
4987}	SALUT SAINT CLOUD 21 [7] Miss V Haigh 2-8-11 vis (45) L Treadwell (7) 40/1: 0600004: Rear, outpcd 3f out, rallied fnl 1f.	2	50a
4844}	PARDON MOI 33 [15] Mrs C A Dunnett 2-8-11 (49) Dane O'Neill 12/1: 3026065: Handy, fdd dist.	shd	49a
4455}	COMIC GENIUS 59 [2] D Haydn Jones 2-8-6 (45) Paul Eddery 8/1: 4606: Rear, nvr nrr than mid-div:	3½	37a
28	YAMATO PINK 10 [4] K R Burke 2-8-6 (49) Joanna Badger 14/1: 504667: Slow away, hdwy 3f out, no impress fnl 2f.	shd	36a
4013}	SOLEIL DHIVER 83 [9] P C Haslam 2-8-6 (45) Rory Moore (7) 12/1: 040408: Led, hdd 4f out, wknd 3f out:	5	26a
43	CASANTELLA 7 [10] M G Quinlan 2-8-6 VIS (50) Saleem Golam (7) 50/1: 600009: Cl-up, fdd 3f out:	nk	25a
77	REEDSMAN 2 [3] M H Tompkins 2-8-11 bl (49) N Callan (5) 14/1: 00000: Handy, fdd 3f out:	3½	23a
77	DELCIENNE 2 [14] G G Margarson 2-8-6 (42) N Pollard 11/2: 040020: Handy, wknd 3f out:	nk	17a
4787}	JIMMY GEE 38 [13] D Nicholls 2-8-11 (49) A Nicholls 16/1: 2000: Al bhd:	2	18a
5014}	JOCKS BOY 18 [8] P R Wood 2-8-11 N Chalmers (5) 50/1: 000: Cl-up, fdd 3f out.	shd	17a
	POSH SHEELAGH [1] J G Given 2-8-7 1ow M Fenton 16/1: 0: Al bhd:	12	0a
4816}	SECRET BLOOM 35 [12] J R Norton 2-8-11 (43) V Halliday 100/1: 0050: Dwelt, al in rear.	nk	0a

15 Ran   1m 31.17 (4.57)   Owner Mr Malcolm Caine   Trained at Malton

88

2.10 Betdirect Co Uk Novice Stakes 2yo (D)
£3052 £872 £436   1m f/sand rnd   Going 49   +08 Fast   Stalls Inside

4770*} COUNTRYWIDE FLYER 39 [9] T D Barron 2-8-12 (82) N Callan 13/8 FAV: 2234211: Cl-up, ev ch 2f out, hung left, drvn out to lead cl-home:			85a
4857*} QUEENSTOWN 32 [12] B J Meehan 2-9-2 bl (88) L Keniry (3) 11/2: 2624412: Led, drvn 2f out, hdd & no extra cl-home:		nk	88a
4875} WEET A HEAD 31 [8] R Hollinshead 2-9-2 (85) A Culhane 7/2: 143263: Chsd ldrs, onepcd fnl 1f:		2½	83a
4898} BLUE JAVA 30 [4] H Morrison 2-8-12 K Dalgleish 20/1: 04: Rear, prog 3f out, late gains:		9	59a
4610} THEVENIS 49 [13] J S King 2-8-12 (59) R Ffrench 50/1: 050005: Chsd ldrs, no impress fnl 2f:		hd	58a
19 WAKE UP HENRY 11 [5] R Charlton 2-8-12 Dane O'Neill 25/1: 006: Handy, wknd 2f out:		1½	55a
5016} QUEENS FANTASY 18 [2] D Haydn Jones 2-8-7 Paul Eddery 100/1: 07: Nvr nrr than mid-div:		5	40a
4975} CARRIACOU 23 [3] P W D'Arcy 2-8-7 (80) B Reilly (5) 5/1: 52208: Bhd, hmpd 5f out, sn no impress:		¾	39a
4660} COTTINGHAM 46 [7] M C Chapman 2-8-12 (67) Andrew Webb (7) 50/1: 5424009: Al bhd:		2½	39a
4639} FIRST ACORN 48 [7] G M Moore 2-8-7 p (42) N Pollard 100/1: 0040060: Al in rear:		shd	33a
4827*} FREDDIE FRECCLES 34 [6] J G Given 2-9-0 M Fenton 12/1: 10: Bhd, hmpd 5f out, sn no impress.		1½	37a
4737} CEASAR 41 [10] P C Haslam 2-8-12 (58) P Dineley (7) 66/1: 620600: Bhd, wknd 5f out, sn btn:		3½	28a
5016} OVER THE YEARS 18 [14] T P Tate 2-8-12 Dale Gibson 100/1: 00: Slow away, al bhd.		2½	27a
4863} CITY AFFAIR 32 [11] Mrs L C Jewell 2-8-12 bl (62) D Corby (3) 25/1: 3050030: Cl-up, wknd 3f out:		17	0

14 Ran   1m 42.72 (3.32)   Owner Mr Nigel Shields   Trained at Thirsk

89

2.45 Littlewoods Bet Direct Maiden Stakes 3yo+ (D)
£2275 £650 £325   1m4f f/sand   Going 49   +03 Fast   Stalls Inside

14 BUCKS 12 [2] D K Ivory 6-9-4 (65) I Mongan 11/4 FAV: 000-3521: Handy, led 2f out, sn rdn clr, val 10L+:			76a
4846} SEA HOLLY 33 [15] G G Margarson 3-8-12 (74) K Dalgleish 7/2: 5-230602: Handy, kept on fnl 2f, al held by v easy wnr:		8	70a
16 WASTED TALENT 12 [11] J G Portman 3-8-7 p (68) R Havlin 4/1: 4426253: Handy, led 5f out, hdd 2f out, wknd:		1¾	62a
4998} FORTUNES FAVOURITE 20 [13] G M Moore 3-8-7 N Pollard 50/1: 04: Bhd, prog 3f out, sn onepcd:		6	53a
4998} CALCAR 20 [9] Mrs S Lamyman 3-8-12 (44) S Whitworth 50/1: 0205005: Mid-div, prog 7f out, ev ch 3f out, sn wknd:		5	51a
2738} BERKELEY HEIGHTS 139 [14] B Smart 3-8-7 (66) R Ffrench 16/1: 040-5006: Cl-up, wknd 6f out:		3½	41a
4238} T K O GYM 70 [12] D Nicholls 4-9-4 (42) Joanna Badger 14/1: 50B3627: Keen cl-up, sn lost pl, prog 6f out, fdd 3f out:		½	45a
4995} ASHTAROUTE 20 [5] M C Chapman 3-8-7 (46) Andrew Webb (7) 33/1: 4630058: Al bhd:		1¾	37a
4913} DESERT HEAT 28 [4] I Semple 5-9-4 (70) Dane O'Neill 8/1: 422-6409: Led 1f, in tch, fdd 3f out:		14	22a
4460} SWEET AROMA 59 [16] Mrs N Macauley 4-8-13 (26) Steven Harrison (7) 100/1: 006-000: Al bhd:		3	13a
5035} MY MATE HENRY 16 [7] T T Clement 4-9-4 (45) Dean McKeown 66/1: 0/-0600: Led after 1f, hdd 4f out, fdd.		5	11a
BRIAR 582 [1] M Pitman 4-9-4 D Corby (3) 13/2: 6/30-0: Al bhd:		15	0a
2711} MON PETIT DIAMANT 140 [6] M J Polglase 3-8-7 (40) M Nem (7) 50/1: 0005560: Slow away, sn cl-up 6f.		20	0a
39 FULL ENGLISH 9 [8] A P Jones 4-8-13 Lisa Jones (3) 100/1: 00: Handy, fdd 7f out.		6	0a
TADZIO [10] M J Gingell 4-9-4 B Reilly (5) 100/1: 0: Al well adrift:		20	0a

15 Ran   2m 39.83 (5.53)   Owner Mr M Murphy   Trained at Radlett

90

3.15 Bet Direct In Running Sky Text 293 Handicap Stakes 3yo+ 0-75 (E)   [75]
£2072 £592 £296   1m6f f/sand   Going 49   -05 Slow   Stalls Inside

67* MACARONI GOLD 5 [8] W Jarvis 3-8-8 6ex (63) M Tebbutt 15/8 FAV: 5030311: In tch, styd on to lead 2f out, sn wandered, rdn out to hold on:			68a
34 GLORY QUEST 10 [9] Miss Gay Kelleway 6-10-0 (75) A Culhane 3/1: 0654522: Held up, prog & ev ch 2f out, kept on ins fnl 1f, not pace wnr:		¾	78a
18 FOREVER MY LORD 12 [10] J R Best 5-8-7 (54) D Fentiman (7) 20/1: 2120043: Led, clr 6f out, hdd 2f out, no extra:		6	50a
4790} SIMPLE IDEALS 38 [6] Don Enrico Incisa 9-7-12 18oh (27) Kim Tinkler (3) 100/1: 5565004: In tch, fdd 7f out:		13	30a
48 LAPADAR 7 [2] J R Weymes 4-9-4 p (65) Dane O'Neill 100/1: 0060505: Cl-up, wknd 4f out:		6	44a
7* VIN DU PAYS 14 [3] M Blanshard 3-9-4 (73) N Callan 5/1: 0055116: Chsd ldrs, no extra 4f out:		2½	50a
4638} DASH OF MAGIC 48 [5] J Hetherton 5-7-12 2oh (43) Dale Gibson 33/1: 1410407: Bhd, nvr able to chall:		14	10a
4957} CROSSED WIRE 24 [4] Miss J Feilden 5-9-6 (67) A Quinn (5) 25/1: 604-0008: Handy, fdd 6f out:		11	23a
4998} IN LUCK 20 [7] B Smart 5-8-5 (52) R Ffrench 5/1: 4506039: Held up, prog 6f out, wknd fdd out:		1¼	7a
4020*} HUMDINGER 83 [1] D Shaw 3-8-8 (63) Lisa Jones (3) 16/1: 2213610: Handy, fdd 5f out:		9	10a

10 Ran   3m 7.39 (7.59)   Owner Dr J Walker   Trained at Newmarket

91

3.45 Bet Direct Red To Bet Handicap Stakes Div 2 Fillies 3yo+ 0-70 (E)   [68]
£2044 £584 £292   6f f/sand rnd   Going 49   -07 Slow   Stalls Inside

4* PERFECT NIGHT 14 [5] R Charlton 3-9-13 (67) Dane O'Neill 1/1 FAV: 2202211: Handy, led 2f out, edged left ins fnl 1f, rdn out:			74a
4728} EASTERN BLUE 42 [10] Mrs L Stubbs 4-8-8 p (48) I Mongan 8/1: 0450062: Chsd ldrs, outpcd 3f out, rallied well fnl 1f:		1¼	50a
33 LAKE EYRE 10 [4] J Balding 4-8-0 1oh 2ow (37) A Nicholls 16/1: 0-054603: Led 4f, in tch, onepcd fnl 1f:		½	41a
23 INCHING 11 [6] R M H Cowell 3-9-3 VIS (57) M Henry 14/1: 6040064: Dwelt, sn handy, onepcd fnl 1f.		1¼	54a
4728} SHAROURA 42 [7] R A Fahey 7-8-12 (52) D Swift 13/2: 1233505: Handy, kept on same pace fnl 1f:		¾	47a
61 EAGER ANGEL 5 [8] R F Marvin 5-7-12 1oh p (37) R Thomas 25/1: 0060006: Nvr nrr than mid-div:		1½	29a
33* ALLY MAKBUL 10 [11] J R Best 3-9-1 (55) D Fentiman (7) 5/1: 0-530017: Handy, onepcd when edged right dist.		nk	45a
4854} COURT MUSIC 33 [9] R E Barr 4-8-1 VIS (41) R Ffrench 20/1: 00-00008: Al bhd:		2½	24a
4958} PATS MIRACLE 24 [1] John Berry 3-8-4 (44) Joanna Badger 66/1: 004-09: Dwelt, al in rear.		3½	18a
31 SUGAR CUBE TREAT 10 [2] M Mullineaux 7-8-1 (41) Lisa Jones (3) 40/1: 60060/-00: Dwelt, al bhd.		¾	13a
4925} TAMARELLA 27 [3] G G Margarson 3-9-5 (59) N Pollard 14/1: 4500030: Handy, fdd 3f out.		8	10a

11 Ran   1m 16.7 (3.4)   Owner Perfect Night Partnership   Trained at Beckhampton

31

92	**12.10 Bet Direct No Q On 08000 93 66 93 Handicap Stakes Div 1** 3yo+ 0-65 (F)		[65]
	£2142 £612 £306	**6f f/sand rnd**	**Going 44**	**-09 Slow**	Stalls Inside	

4485} **FAR NOTE** 59 [2] S R Bowring 5-9-12 bl (63) A Culhane 8/1: 6410421: Handy, styd on to lead dist despite edging right, drvn out: **68a**

61* **HURRICANE COAST** 6 [5] P A Blockley 4-9-11 7ex (62) G Parkin 16/1: 0302012: Chsd ldrs, ev ch dist, kept on fnl 1f, just held by wnr: ½ **64a**

4634} **MAJIK** 49 [15] D J S ffrench Davis 4-9-9 (60) T Quinn 7/2 JT FAV: 3000423: Sn bhd, prog when short of room 2f out, styd on well fnl 1f: shd **61a**

4944} **DOCTOR DENNIS** 27 [3] Mrs Lydia Pearce 6-8-12 vis (49) N Pollard 11/1: 5040044: Sn in rear, prog 2f out, ev ch ins fnl 1f, onepcd cl-home: shd **49a**

5025} **CATCH THE CAT** 18 [6] J S Wainwright 4-9-1 vis (52) T Eaves (5) 10/1: 1005605: Cl-up, ev ch 2f out, no room dist, no extra. 3 **43a**

5000} **MALAHIDE EXPRESS** 21 [13] M J Polglase 3-10-0 bl (65) L Fletcher (3) 40/1: 6000056: Led, hdd & wknd dist. 1 **53a**

1071} **MR PERTEMPS** 224 [9] R A Fahey 5-9-5 (56) R Ffrench 7/2 JT FAV: 6-131107: Chsd ldrs, outpcd 3f out, rallied fnl 1f. hd **43a**

27 **VINTAGE STYLE** 11 [10] H A McWilliams 4-9-7 bl (58) I Mongan 33/1: 0404058: Handy wide, wknd fnl 2f. ¾ **43a**

4967} **SAVILES DELIGHT** 24 [8] R Brotherton 4-9-5 (56) G Gibbons 33/1: 2030209: In tch, edged left dist, sn wknd: 1¼ **37a**

4699} **XALOC BAY** 44 [1] B P J Baugh 5-9-3 bl (54) M Fenton 10/1: 0432360: Dwelt, al bhd: 2½ **28a**

5006} **BLESSINGINDISGUISE** 20 [4] M W Easterby 10-8-12 bl (49) Dale Gibson 12/1: 6022240: Handy, wknd 3f out. 1½ **19a**

4634} **BOISDALE** 49 [11] D Nicholls 5-9-4 (55) Joanna Badger 25/1: 6100600: Chsd ldrs, no extra 3f out: shd **24a**

23 **BENEKING** 12 [16] J Gallagher 3-9-8 (59) N Callan 25/1: 2604000: Al bhd. 1¼ **24a**

4634} **HIGH ESTEEM** 49 [7] M A Buckley 7-9-9 (60) J Fanning 18/1: 5-610000: Prom, wknd 3f out: 4 **13a**

3449} **VALUABLE GIFT** 110 [12] R C Guest 6-9-2 P (53) S Whitworth 40/1: 4632000: Al bhd: 1¼ **2a**

3802} **LEVELLED** 94 [14] D W Chapman 9-8-13 (50) K Dalgleish 66/1: 46/00-000: Al well adrift: 11 **0**

16 Ran 1m 16.50 (3.2) Owner APB Racing Trained at Edwinstowe

93	**12.40 Bet Direct In Running Sky Text 293 Handicap Stakes Div 1** 3yo+ 0-70 (E)		[70]
	£2086 £596 £298	**1m f/sand rnd**	**Going 44**	**-08 Slow**	Stalls Inside	

31 **LOCKSTOCK** 11 [11] M S Saunders 5-9-4 bl (60) J Fanning 8/1: 0-000041: Handy, led 1f out, rdn out: **68a**

4970+ **HOWS THINGS** 24 [7] D Haydn Jones 3-9-7 (65) R Thomas (5) 100/30 FAV: 6403112: Led, hdd 1f out, kept on fnl 1f, not pace of wnr: 1¼ **69a**

4824} **MAGIC MAMMAS TOO** 35 [4] T D Barron 3-8-9 (53) D Mernagh 16/1: 0640343: Prom, no extra dist. 1¼ **55a**

4540} **BRANDY COVE** 55 [14] B Smart 6-9-10 (66) R Ffrench 11/1: 3132104: Slow away, bhd, late gains: ½ **67a**

4922} **BOND MILLENNIUM** 28 [9] B Smart 5-9-13 (69) I Mongan 6/1: 5460245: Mid-div, nvr able to chall: 2½ **61a**

16 **ESTIMATION** 13 [2] R M H Cowell 3-9-10 (68) B Reilly (5) 5/1: 4421136: Held up, prog 4f out, no impress fnl 1f: 1 **62a**

3260} **SIMPLY THE GUEST** 118 [15] Don Enrico Incisa 4-7-12 6oh t (34) Kim Tinkler 66/1: 0000007: Cl-up, no extra 3f out. 1½ **31a**

4255} **CUMBRIAN PRINCESS** 70 [13] M Blanshard 6-7-12 2oh (38) Dale Gibson 66/1: 0-000008: Prom, no extra 3f out: ½ **30a**

66 **CHAMPAGNE RIDER** 6 [8] D Shaw 7-8-0 vis (42) Lisa Jones (3) 50/1: 0005009: In tch, wknd 2f out: shd **31a**

38 **VERMILION CREEK** 10 [12] R Hollinshead 4-8-5 (47) W Ryan 33/1: 6140000: Handy, wknd fnl 2f. 1¼ **34a**

38 **MISS GLORY BE** 10 [1] Miss Gay Kelleway 5-9-3 p (59) M Fenton 10/1: 5063230: Rear, prog 5f out, wknd 2f out. 6 **34a**

60* **BARZAK** 6 [5] S R Bowring 3-9-13 6ex t (71) A Culhane 11/2: 0000010: Chsd ldrs, wknd 4f out: 2 **42a**

5 **ULYSEES** 15 [14] J Semple 4-9-12 (68) D McGaffin (3) 25/1: 0000660: Al bhd. 7 **27a**

4184} **KANZ WOOD** 75 [10] A W Carroll 7-9-9 (65) S Whitworth 33/1: 3453000: Dwelt, al in rear: 2 **20a**

14 Ran 1m 43.56 (4.16) Owner Mr Chris Scott Trained at Wells

94	**1.10 Bet Direct No Q On 08000 93 66 93 Handicap Stakes Div 2** 3yo+ 0-65 (F)		[65]
	£2142 £612 £306	**6f f/sand rnd**	**Going 44**	**-18 Slow**	Stalls Inside	

55 **ACORAZADO** 7 [14] G L Moore 4-9-2 bl e (53) W Ryan 4/1 FAV: 0040551: Held up away, prog 2f out, rdn out to lead cl-home: **57a**

66 **TRAVELLING TIMES** 6 [11] J S Wainwright 4-8-13 vis (50) T Eaves (5) 14/1: 0500432: Handy, styd on to lead dist, hdd cl-home: hd **52a**

71 **WAINWRIGHT** 4 [16] P A Blockley 3-9-9 (60) Derek Nolan (7) 14/1: 2052353: Led 5f out, hdd dist, no extra ins fnl 1f: ¾ **60a**

74* **SEMPER PARATUS** 4 [1] H J Collingridge 4-9-9 7ex bl (60) Saleem Golam (7) 11/2: 5000014: Chsd ldrs, outpcd 5f out, rallied dist, nrst fin: ¾ **58a**

65 **TATWEER** 6 [10] D Shaw 3-9-7 vis (58) Darren Williams 14/1: 5-00555: Handy, onepcd dist: 2 **50a**

4330} **PILGRIM PRINCESS** 67 [7] E J Alston 5-8-10 (47) A Nicholls 9/1: 0356246: Handy, no extra 1f out: 1 **36a**

35 **CASH** 10 [12] Paul Johnson 5-9-8 (59) Lisa Jones (3) 16/1: 3000007: Rear, nvr nrr than mid-div: hd **47a**

4964} **POLAR FORCE** 25 [13] M R Channon 3-9-12 (65) T O'Brien (7) 16/1: 6500608: Mid-div wide, nvr a factor. 2½ **44a**

4022} **DIL** 84 [4] Mrs N Macauley 8-9-3 (54) K Dalgleish 20/1: 3600069: Al bhd: 1¼ **31a**

91 **ALLY MAKBUL** 1 [3] J R Best 3-9-4 (55) D Fentiman (7) 16/1: 0-5300100: Bhd, mod late gains: 1 **29a**

5017} **ROMAN EMPIRE** 19 [8] T J Etherington 3-9-8 (59) J F Egan 40/1: 00-15000: Al bhd. ¾ **31a**

62 **LOCOMBE HILL** 6 [6] D Nicholls 7-9-13 (64) L Treadwell (7) 9/1: 6000100: Slow away, al bhd: 2 **30a**

30 **CAUSTIC WIT** 11 [5] M S Saunders 5-9-1 (52) M Savage (5) 10/1: 0003030: Prom, wknd fnl 2f: 1 **15a**

68 **ON THE TRAIL** 4 [9] D W Chapman 6-9-5 (56) A Culhane 9/1: 3323000: Led 1f, styd prom, fdd fnl 2f: 1¼ **15a**

85 **MABEL RILEY** 1 [2] M A Buckley 3-8-12 (49) J Fanning 40/1: 60350000: Mid-div, fdd 3f out: 8 **0**

62 **BLUNHAM** 6 [13] M C Chapman 3-9-4 BL (55) I Mongan 25/1: 4610000: Prom, fdd fnl 3f out: 2 **0**

16 Ran 1m 17.03 (3.73) Owner D T L Limited Trained at Brighton

95	**1.40 Bet Direct No Q Claiming Stakes** 2yo (F)		
	£2107 £602 £301	**1m f/sand rnd**	**Going 44**	**-14 slow**	Stalls Inside	

28* **MYANNABANANA** 11 [11] Miss Gay Kelleway 2-9-1 VIS (60) M Fenton 5/1: 0066011: Mid-div, prog to lead ins fnl 1f, pushed out, val 4L+: **67a**

4886} **TURF PRINCESS** 31 [15] J R Best 2-9-0 (59) D Fentiman (7) 4/1: 0351022: Cl-up, led 2f out, hdd ins fnl 1f, no extra: 2½ **59a**

4996} **KATIES ROLE** 21 [14] Ian Emmerson 2-8-6 (57) A Nicholls 10/1: 630043: Cl-up, led 5f out, hdd 2f out, ev ch dist, wknd: 3½ **44a**

4139} **BROTHER CADFAEL** 77 [16] John A Harris 2-8-3 (47) R Ffrench 50/1: 530004: Rear, prog 4f out, btn 2f out. 3 **35a**

32

4455} **FRAMBO 60** [2] J G Portman 2-9-0 (57) Lisa Jones (3) 5/1: 00625: Handy, outpcd 3f out, modest late gains: *2½* **41a**
63 **TICTACTOE 6** [13] D J Daly 2-9-0 (58) A Culhane 7/2 FAV: 2504536: Slow away, prog 4f out, wknd fnl 2f. *nk* **40a**
87 **JIMMY GEE** [12] D Nicholls 2-8-5 (49) Joanna Badger 25/1: 20007: Slow away, prog 4f out, wknd 2f out: *6* **19a**
4455} **THE KING OF ROCK 60** [3] A G Newcombe 2-9-5 (63) S Whitworth 20/1: 0504208: Rear, nvr nrr than mid-div: *hd* **32a**
4804} **NOCATEE 38** [7] P C Haslam 2-9-2 (57) Rory Moore (7) 12/1: 00059: In tch, wknd 3f out. *½* **28a**
4139} **SUGARBABE 77** [4] M Blanshard 2-8-6 (48) R Thomas (5) 16/1: 003300: Handy, wknd 2f out: *nk* **17a**
28 **GIVEN A CHANCE 11** [10] J G Given 2-8-11 (47) A Daly 40/1: 00600: Led, hdd 2f out, sn wknd. *1* **20a**
4483} **TAMARINA 59** [1] N E Berry 2-8-8 M Savage (5) 14/1: 50: Cl-up, wknd 3f out: *¾* **15a**
52 **SKELTHWAITE 7** [8] M H Tompkins 2-8-13 J Fanning 50/1: 000: Al bhd: *hd* **19a**
4930} **CONFUZION 28** [5] A P Jones 2-8-4 P G Hannon 40/1: 000: Al well adrift: *15* **0a**
14 Ran 1m 44.11 (4.71) Owner Twilight Racing Trained at Newmarket

96 2.10 Littlewoods Bet Direct Maiden Stakes 3yo (D)

£2310 £660 £330 **1m f/sand rnd** **Going 44** **-19 Slow** Stalls Inside

8 **KINGSTON TOWN 15** [10] N P Littmoden 3-9-0 p (62) J P Guillambert (3) 11/4: 4021: Chsd ldrs, prog to lead dist, pushed clr fnl 1f, val 7L+: **70a**
4985} **SOPHRANO 23** [9] P W Harris 3-9-0 (68) N Callan 9/4 FAV: 53-60062: Cl-up, led 2f out, hdd dist, no extra: *5* **58a**
40 **WHITE PARK BAY 10** [13] J Gallagher 3-8-9 (62) Dane O'Neill 5/1: 3240303: Cl-up, onepcd fnl 1f: *½* **52a**
4929} **SILVER CRYSTAL 28** [8] Mrs N Macauley 3-8-9 (45) Lisa Jones (3) 33/1: 0003064: Handy, no extra 1f out. *½* **51a**
39 **REALISM 10** [14] P W Hiatt 3-9-0 Darren Williams 7/1: 035: Prom wide, ev ch 2f out, fdd 1f out: *3* **50a**
6 **NIMBUS TWOTHOUSAND 15** [4] P R Wood 3-8-9 bl (44) C Catlin 33/1: 5605006: Prom, wkng when no room 2f out. *3½* **38a**
2501} **DANUM 150** [1] R Hollinshead 3-9-0 (65) A Culhane 14/1: 46567: Nvr nrr than mid-div: *5* **33a**
TROFANA FALCON [15] H J Collingridge 3-9-0 M Tebbutt 20/1: 8: Mid-div, nvr able to chall: *3½* **26a**
4909} **COMPOS MENTIS 29** [6] D Morris 3-9-0 BL (67) D McGaffin (3) 16/1: 002-0009: Chsd ldrs, fdd 3f out: *4* **18a**
3952} **MATRIARCHAL 88** [11] Don Enrico Incisa 3-8-9 (38) Kim Tinkler 66/1: 0500040: Al bhd: *hd* **12a**
4531} **MOONGLADE 56** [16] Miss J Feilden 3-8-9 t A Quinn (5) 66/1: 0000: Led, hdd 2f out, fdd: *1½* **9a**
53 **SAWAH 7** [7] D Shaw 3-9-0 S Whitworth 100/1: 00: Slow away, al bhd: *10* **-4a**
4929} **RECALL 28** [3] J G Given 3-8-9 M Fenton 12/1: 00: Al in rear: *nk* **0**
4883} **SCRAPPY DOO 31** [12] Miss V Haigh 3-9-0 (26) L Treadwell (7) 100/1: 00-0P000: Mid-div, fdd 4f out. *3½* **0**
14 **REPETOIRE 13** [5] K O Cunningham Brown 3-8-9 (49) A Nicholls 50/1: 00-40B00: Slow away, al in rear: *18* **0**
15 Ran 1m 44.44 (5.04) Owner Friends of the Turf Racing Lim Trained at Newmarket

97 2.40 Betdirect Co Uk Handicap Stakes 3yo+ 0-75 (E) [75]

£2135 £610 £305 **1m3f f/sand** **Going 44** **+01 Fast** Stalls Inside

4638} **MI ODDS 49** [1] Mrs N Macauley 7-9-12 (73) A Culhane 3/1 FAV: 0650121: Held up, prog 4f out, led dist, drvn out: **81a**
48 **DIGGER 8** [15] Miss Gay Kelleway 4-9-9 t (70) N Callan 13/2: 3200252: Handy, hung left under press fnl 1f, al held by wnr: *¾* **75a**
26 **CLASSIC ROLE 12** [9] R Ingram 4-9-11 (72) I Mongan 16/1: 4100003: Cl-up, led 4f out, hdd dist, no extra: *1½* **74a**
4855} **STRAVMOUR 34** [14] R Hollinshead 7-7-12 2oh (43) Dale Gibson 66/1: 500604: Keen rear, prog 4f out, kept on fnl 1f. *1½* **44a**
4638} **EAST CAPE 49** [16] Don Enrico Incisa6-7-12 1oh (44) Kim Tinkler 14/1: 0663445: Bhd, prog 6f out, short of room & lost place 4f out, rallied fnl 1f: *½* **43a**
56 **GINGKO 7** [3] P R Webber 6-9-4 (65) Dean McKeown 11/2: 0060066: Handy, wknd fnl 1f: *hd* **62a**
4879} **TROUBLE MOUNTAIN 31** [11] M W Easterby 6-9-8 (69) P Mulrennan (5) 13/2: 0005447: Rear, prog 6f out, outpcd 3f out, modest late gains: *nk* **65a**
4984} **VANBRUGH 23** [13] Miss D A McHale 3-8-13 vis t (65) Darren Williams 66/1: 0000668: Dwelt, nvr nrr than mid-div. *8* **49a**
5 **CRUSOE 15** [7] A Sadik 6-9-5 (66) Dane O'Neill 16/1: 0105359: Cl-up, fdd 4f out. *8* **38a**
4931} **DUCS DREAM 28** [12] D Morris 5-9-0 (61) D McGaffin (3) 5/1: 2316300: Held up, nvr a factor. *3* **29a**
26 **NIGHT WARRIOR 12** [8] D Flood 3-9-4 (70) D Sweeney 14/1: 2120000: Al in rear. *2* **35a**
2 **SURDOUE 15** [2] P Howling 3-9-9 (75) Paul Eddery 66/1: 0050000: Led, hdd 4f out, wknd 3f out. *5* **33a**
4756} **TORO BRAVO 41** [4] R M Beckett 3-9-1 (67) M Tebbutt 66/1: 1-000000: Handy, wknd 4f out: *2* **22a**
4735} **GRACIOUS AIR 42** [6] J R Weymes 5-7-12 5oh P (40) D Fentiman (7) 50/1: 0-000060: Al in rear: *hd* **0a**
24 **KHUZDAR 12** [5] M R Channon 4-8-0 (47) T O'Brien (6) 10/1: 4140640: Al bhd. *8* **0a**
2008} **CRUNCHY 171** [10] B Ellison 5-9-6 t (67) T Hamilton (5) 20/1: 0-151300: Cl-up, fdd 4f out: *dist* **0a**
16 Ran 2m 26.09 (4.79) Owner Tic-Taccom Trained at Melton Mowbray

98 3.10 Bet Direct In Running Median Auction Maiden Stakes 2yo (F)

£2331 £666 £333 **7f f/sand rnd** **Going 44** **+00 Fast** Stalls Inside

4975} **BENNY THE BALL 24** [8] N P Littmoden 2-9-0 (88) I Mongan 10/11 FAV: 4261: Prom, led 3f out, rdn out fnl 1f: **82a**
4994} **FADEELA 21** [16] P W D'Arcy 2-8-9 e (67) B Reilly (5) 20/1: 40252: Cl-up, ev ch 2f out, kept on fnl 1f, not pace of wnr: *1* **74a**
5031} **BOOK MATCHED 17** [10] B Smart 2-9-0 R Ffrench 50/1: 003: Bhd, prog 3f out, nrst fin: *5* **69a**
4827} **BOLD BLADE 35** [12] B Smart 2-9-0 bl (48) C Catlin 66/1: 6004: Led, hdd 3f out, wknd fnl 2f. *½* **68a**
5023} **AFRICAN STAR 18** [14] Mrs A J Perrett 2-9-0 Dane O'Neill 25/1: 05: Chsd ldrs, wknd fnl 2f: *5* **67a**
5032} **CORNISH GOLD 17** [6] D Haydn Jones 2-8-9 (67) Paul Eddery 20/1: 0056: Handy, wknd 2f out. *nk* **61a**
5024} **JOLIZERO 18** [15] G G Margarson 2-9-0 N Pollard 50/1: 007: Al in mid-div. *3* **60a**
4726} **SMART BOY PRINCE 43** [11] P A Blockley 2-9-0 (55) S Yourston (7) 66/1: 00058: Chsd ldrs, no extra 3f out. *½* **59a**
5023} **DALIDA 18** [13] P C Haslam 2-8-9 Rory Moore (7) 33/1: 09: Mid-div, fdd 3f out. *½* **53a**
36 **VAMPIRE QUEEN 10** [4] R P Elliott 2-8-9 Dean McKeown 66/1: 060: Al bhd. *1* **51a**
3 **COLOUR CODE 15** [5] M P Tregoning 2-9-0 T Quinn 2/1: 20: Handy, fdd fnl 2f: *¾* **54a**
5007} **CELTIC SOLITUDE 20** [7] M Johnston 2-8-9 J Fanning 25/1: 60: Slow away, al in rear. *1* **47a**
21 **INCHPAST 12** [2] M H Tompkins 2-9-0 Saleem Golam (7) 20/1: 050: Slow away, al bhd. *2* **48a**
42 **IPHIGENIA 8** [3] P W Hiatt 2-8-9 (63) A Culhane 33/1: 023000: Al well adrift. *dist* **13a**
14 Ran 1m 29.68 (3.08) Owner Miss Vanessa Church Trained at Newmarket

99	**3.40 Bet Direct In Running Sky Text 293 Handicap Stakes Div 2 3yo+ 0-70 (E)**		**[70]**
	£2086 £596 £298	1m f/sand rnd Going 44 +05 Fast	Stalls Inside

40	MCQUEEN 10 [6] Mrs H Dalton 3-9-3 (61) J F Egan 7/1: 3320331: Cl-up, chsd ldr 3f out, led & edged left dist, rdn clr:		**75a**
4890}	NEVEN 31 [12] T D Barron 4-9-5 (61) D Mernagh 4/1: 01-13052: Handy, kept on fnl 2f, not pace easy wnr:	8	**62a**
44	OVIGO 8 [5] P A Blockley 4-9-11 (67) G Parkin 7/2 FAv: 1500033: Slow away, prog 3f out, onepcd fnl 2f:	2½	**63a**
20	ZAK FACTA 12 [14] Miss D A McHale 3-8-12 vis (56) C Cogan 20/1: 2004254: Led, hdd 6f out, led again 4f out, hdd & fdd dist:	4	**44a**
4756}	CAPTAIN DARLING 41 [14] R M H Cowell 3-9-8 (66) A Quinn (5) 20/1: 1545045: Rear, prog 4f out, wknd dist.	1½	**51a**
4999}	SUPREME SALUTATION 21 [10] D W Chapman 7-9-12 (68) A Culhane 10/1: 6000056: Nvr nrr than mid-div.	2	**49a**
4698}	HOHS BACK 44 [13] Paul Johnson 4-9-10 p (66) Lisa Jones (3) 8/1: 1430207: Handy, wknd 2f out:	1½	**51a**
40*	PHAROAHS GOLD 10 [2] D Shaw 5-9-9 e (65) Darren Williams 11/2: 0342018: Mid-div, wknd 3f out:	1	**41a**
4820}	GOODBYE MR BOND 36 [3] E J Alston 3-9-0 (58) Dean McKeown 14/1: 1005349: Cl-up, fdd 3f out.	nk	**33a**
364}	NEVINSTOWN 177 [8] Niall Moran 3-8-9 BL T (53) W M Lordan 66/1: 000-0000: Slow away, al bhd:	13	**3a**
5	SHOTACROSS THE BOW 15 [1] M Blanshard 6-9-9 (65) N Callan 7/1: 6004140: Al in rear.	½	**14a**
65	SUBTLE MOVE 6 [11] D Shaw 3-8-5 vis (49) T Hamilton 3/1: 3000000: Al bhd:	5	**0a**
2717}	FRIDAYS TAKINGS 141 [9] B Smart 4-10-0 bl (70) R Ffrench 16/1: 0-122000: Led 6f out, hdd 4f out, sn fdd.	10	**0a**
66	BOLD EFFORT 6 [7] K O Cunningham Brown 11-7-12 bl (40) C Catlin 100/1: 0600000: Handy, fdd 2f out:	25	**0a**
14 Ran	1m 42.54 (3.14) Owner Mr R Edwards and Mr W J Swinne		Trained at Shifnal

Official Going Standard

100	**11.45 Bet Direct On Attheraces Interactive Maiden Stakes Div 1 2yo (D)**		
	£3042 £869 £435	1m p/track rnd Going 48 -02 Slow	Stalls Outside

5023}	ASCERTAIN 19 [3] N P Littmoden 2-9-0 I Mongan 40/1: 01: Handy, styd on to lead 2f out, drvn out:		**85a**
	KALI [11] R Charlton 2-8-9 D Sweeney 20/1: 2: Hld up, trav well & hdwy over 2f out, styd on, wnr had first run:	1¼	**76a**
	BOXGROVE [6] C E Brittain 2-9-0 J F Egan 25/1: 3: Slow away, sn mid-div, chsd wnr dist, kept on fnl 1f, just held by front 2:	nk	**80a**
	MAGICAL GIFT [4] D W P Arbuthnot 2-8-9 S Whitworth 33/1: 4: Slow away, eff 3f out, no extra fnl 1f.	3½	**68a**
5023}	OKOBOJI 19 [7] M P Tregoning 2-9-0 Martin Dwyer 11/4 JT FAV: 45: Led, hdd 2f out, fdd dist.	4	**65a**
3295}	SOVIET SCEPTRE 117 [9] G A Butler 2-9-0 C Catlin 11/4 JT FAV: 56: Handy, fdd fnl 2f:	2½	**60a**
4973}	MAMBINA 25 [12] M R Channon 2-8-9 A Culhane 4/1: 57: Mid-div, outpcd 3f out, modest late gains:	¾	**53a**
	SECRET PLACE [10] E A L Dunlop 2-9-0 W Ryan 16/1: 8: Held up, nvr able to chall:	nk	**57a**
	IRISH BLADE [1] H Candy 2-9-0 Dane O'Neill 5/1: 9: Slow away, al bhd:	½	**56a**
4966}	GLIDING BY 25 [5] P R Chamings 2-8-9 M Fenton 33/1: 00: In tch, wknd 3f out.	½	**50a**
	SELF RAZIN [8] Mrs S A Liddiard 2-8-9 F P Ferris (3) 100/1: 0: Slow away, al bhd:	5	**40a**
4912}	RENDORO 30 [2] R Hannon 2-9-0 T Quinn 7/1: 630: Prom, fdd 2f out.	2	**41a**
12 Ran	1m 36.2 (4.01) Owner Mr Paul J Dixon		Trained at Newmarket

101	**12.15 Bet Direct On Itv Page 367 Handicap Stakes Div 1 3yo+ 0-60 (F)**		**[60]**
	£2086 £596 £298	1m2f p/trackd Going 48 -07 Slow	Stalls Inside

17	QUANTUM LEAP 14 [2] S Dow 6-10-0 (60) Paul Eddery 6/1: 0040041: Held up, hdwy wide 3f out, rdn out to lead cl-home:		**66a**
55	CASTAIGNE 8 [13] B W Duke 4-9-8 t (54) M Fenton 20/1: 6024002: Held up, plenty to do 3f out, prog 2f out, kept on fnl 1f, pace came too sn:	shd	**57a**
4992}	TRUE COMPANION 23 [8] N P Littmoden 4-9-13 (59) J P Guillambert (3) 3/1 FAV: 0046153: Bhd, hdwy 3f out, led dist, hdd cl-home:	½	**62a**
3648}	REGAL GALLERY 462 [6] C A Horgan 5-9-6 (52) T Quinn 20/1: 050040-4: Dwelt, bhd, prog 2f out, chsd wnr ins fnl 1f, not respond for press:	hd	**54a**
2583}	DICKIE DEADEYE 147 [5] G B Balding 6-10-0 (60) R Havlin 25/1: 52//00-005: Mid-div, prog 3f out, no impress fnl 1f.	2½	**58a**
3816}	SAMMYS SHUFFLE 454 [7] Jamie Poulton 8-9-12 bl (58) I Mongan 10/1: 400122-6: Mid-div, hdwy 3f out, wknd fnl 1f.	3	**51a**
5021}	ANOTHER SECRET 20 [3] G L Moore 5-9-10 (56) A Quinn (5) 16/1: 00006B7: Cl-up, no extra 2f out.	1¼	**47a**
4985}	HARLOT 24 [11] John Berry 3-9-9 (59) Lisa Jones (3) 25/1: 0-440008: Bhd, nvr nrr than mid-div.	nk	**49a**
4390}	KYLE OF LOCHALSH 65 [14] G G Margarson 3-9-9 (59) Dane O'Neill 12/1: 0510309: Slow away, nvr a factor:	2	**46a**
5001}	SQUEAKY 22 [1] Miss K M George 6-10-0 (60) J F Egan 14/1: 40: Cl-up, no extra 3f out.	½	**46a**
4855}	BALERNO 35 [12] R Ingram 4-9-7 (53) M Tebbutt 13/2: 5000530: Al bhd.	1½	**36a**
39	MARAKASH 11 [10] M R Bosley 4-9-6 P (52) G Baker 25/1: 230-0000: Chsd ldrs, fdd dist.	3	**30a**
4986}	PREMIER CHEVAL 24 [9] R Rowe 4-9-8 (54) Martin Dwyer 10/1: 004000: Cl-up, led 3f out, hdd & fdd dist.	3	**27a**
4861}	ANEMOS 34 [4] P W D'Arcy 8-9-11 (57) B Reilly (5) 10/1: 0205560: Led, hdd 3f out, fdd.	4	**24a**
14 Ran	2m 8.37 (5.57) Owner Mrs M E O'Shea		Trained at Epsom

102	**12.45 Bet Direct On Attheraces Interactive Maiden Stakes Div 2 2yo (D)**		
	£3042 £869 £435	1m p/track rnd Going 48 -32 Slow	Stalls Outside

4993}	MESSE DE MINUIT 23 [10] R Charlton 2-9-0 Dane O'Neill 7/2: 31: Handy, rdn 2f out, styd on well to lead cl-home:		**79a**
4906}	SUAVE QUARTET 30 [1] G A Butler 2-9-0 Martin Dwyer 5/2: 622: Led, drvn 1f out, hdd cl-home:	½	**77a**
21	BIENVENUE 13 [4] M P Tregoning 2-8-9 A Daly 7/4 FAV: 23: Handy, outpcd 2f out, rallied fnl 1f.	1	**70a**
	MUSIC MIX [2] E A L Dunlop 2-9-0 T Quinn 20/1: 4: Cl-up, onepcd fnl 1f.	¾	**73a**
5023}	DAGGERS CANYON 19 [6] Julian Poulton 2-9-0 N Callan 33/1: 05: Keen cl-up, no extra fnl 1f:	nk	**72a**
	SUNNY LADY [9] E A L Dunlop 2-8-9 W Ryan 20/1: 6: Bhd, outpcd 3f out, rallied dist, nrst fin:	1¼	**65a**
	DAY ONE [9] G Wragg 2-9-0 J F Egan 12/1: 7: Mid-div, prog 2f out, wknd fnl 1f.	½	**69a**
	PRINCE VALENTINE [7] D B Feek 2-9-0 M Tebbutt 100/1: 8: Bhd, outpcd 3f out, modest late gains:	¾	**67a**
	RED CONTACT [11] A Charlton 2-9-0 R Smith 50/1: 9: Held up, outpcd 3f out, modest late gains.	1¾	**63a**
	MONTE MAJOR [8] M A Jarvis 2-9-0 M Henry 20/1: 0: Cl-up, fdd 3f out.	19	**28a**
5022}	SILVER ISLAND 19 [3] G A Butler 2-9-0 C Catlin 20/1: 00: Slow away, sn mid-div, fdd 3f out.	nk	**27a**

BLESS EM ALL [12] M Blanshard 2-8-9 F Norton 50/1: 0: Al well adrift.   5   12a
12 Ran   1m 42.60 (6.4)   Owner Mountgrange Stud   Trained at Beckhampton

---

103   **1.15 Bet Direct On 0800 32 93 93 Claiming Stakes 3yo+ (F)**
£2128 £608 £304   1m4f p/track   Going 48   -38 Slow   Stalls Inside

997} **DECELERATE** 231 [2] I A Wood 3-8-11 (58) N Callan 10/1: 0-133331: Keen rear, hdwy 4f out, no room 2f out, switched wide & styd on well to lead cl-home, rdn out; long abs: 52a
4909} **RAHEEL** 30 [6] P Mitchell 3-9-5 t (54) Dane O'Neill 12/1: 4630002: Slow away, hdwy wide 3f out, ev ch dist, led ins fnl 1f, hdd cl-home: hd   58a
24 **WATER OF LIFE** 13 [9] J R Boyle 4-9-4 (49) I Mongan 9/1: 0000053: Keen mid-div, hdwy 3f out, led briefly dist, hdd ins fnl 1f & no extra: 1¼   49a
60 **DANGEROUS BEANS** 7 [11] S Kirk 3-9-5 (54) J F Egan 4/1: 0002104: Handy, outpcd 2f out, rallied fnl 1f: shd   55a
6 **PARADISE VALLEY** 16 [14] Mrs S A Liddiard 3-9-1 t (54) C Catlin 16/1: 3025145: Bhd, outpcd 3f out, rallied dist, nrst fin.   nk   50a
24 **LANDESCENT** 13 [10] M Quinn 3-9-3 vis (55) M Fenton 5/1: 5400426: Handy, ev ch 3f out, wknd fnl 1f: 2   49a
4517} **GEMMA** 58 [3] P J Makin 3-8-6 (40) D Sweeney 50/1: 0600007: Led 1f, rcd keenly, fdd dist: shd   37a
4359} **LEOPHIN DANCER** 67 [5] P W Hiatt 5-9-1 (38) Lisa Jones (3) 25/1: 0230508: Keen bhd, nvr nrr than mid-div.   nk   39a
24* **COMPTON ECLAIRE** 13 [4] G A Butler 3-8-10 vis (52) Martin Dwyer 5/2 FAV: 1264019: Held up, prog 3f out, no impress fnl 2f: ½   39a
4938} **RADIANT BRIDE** 28 [1] D W P Arbuthnot 3-8-0 (45) J F McDonald (5) 16/1: 5000500: Keen mid-div, prog 3f out, prom when badly hmpd dist, not recover: 1   27a
5021} **MAUREEN AN** 20 [8] Miss B Sanders 3-8-8 h (48) A Clark 25/1: 5010000: Dwelt, keen rear, nvr a factor.   5   28a
1363} **CADWALLADER** 205 [13] P Burgoyne 3-9-1 T (58) T Quinn 33/1: 03500: Led 11f out, hdd dist, fdd: shd   34a
4753} **TOP SON** 42 [16] A P Jones 4-9-7 Joanna Badger 100/1: 000: Cl-up, fdd 4f out   14   15a
2405} **COMANCHE WOMAN** 154 [7] K O Cunningham Brown 3-8-4 (39) S Whitworth 66/1: 0040: Dwelt, prog & ev ch 5f out, fdd 4f out: 2½   0a
14 Ran   2m 39.62 (10.4)   Owner Mr John Purcell   Trained at Upper Lambourn

---

104   **1.45 Bet Direct On Itv Page 367 Handicap Stakes Div 2 3yo+ 0-60 (F)**   [60]
£2079 £594 £297   1m2f p/track   Going 48   -03 Slow   Stalls Outside

5010*} **COMPTON DRAKE** 21 [10] G A Butler 4-9-6 (52) Martin Dwyer 11/10 FAV: 4050211: Cl-up, led 7f out, clr over 2f out, drvn out fnl 1f: 61a
4859} **LYRICAL WAY** 34 [7] P R Chamings 4-9-5 bl (51) F Norton 25/1: 0100022: Cl-up, chsd wnr 4f out, kept on fnl 1f, al held: 1½   55a
4864} **MAN THE GATE** 33 [3] P D Cundell 4-9-12 (58) T Quinn 11/1: 4100D53: Cl-up, outpcd by front 2 fnl 2f.   1¾   59a
4920} **WELSH WIND** 29 [8] M Wigham 7-9-10 t (56) I Mongan 16/1: 3400304: Dwelt, plenty to do 4f out, prog 2f out, nrst fin: 2   54a
12 **EMBER DAYS** 14 [11] J L Spearing 4-9-8 (54) A Daly 9/1: 1160-055: Bhd, hdwy 3f out, hung left & no impress fnl 2f.   1½   49a
17 **MY MAITE** 14 [1] R Ingram 4-9-7 t (53) N Day 7/1: 0050036: Mid-div, nvr a factor.   1¼   46a
11 **ESPERANCE** 14 [5] J Akehurst 3-9-10 (60) Dane O'Neill 16/1: 0020407: Sn hmpd, bhd, modest late gains.   2   50a
4587} **WELLINGTON HALL** 53 [4] Mrs S A Liddiard 2-9-8 (57) P Gallagher (7) 33/1: 0000508: Led till 7f out, styd cl-up, fdd 3f out.   nk   46a
4931} **COLOURFUL LADY** 29 [13] P W Harris 3-9-8 (58) N Callan 33/1: 3620009: Al bhd.   1¼   45a
4909} **TOLEDO SUN** 30 [12] H J Collingridge 3-9-9 (59) M Tebbutt 15/2: 0003000: Al in rear.   shd   45a
1701} **IN SPIRIT** 186 [9] B J Curley 5-10-0 (60) W M Lordan 50/1: 6/0-05530: Bhd, nvr a factor.   3½   41a
5021} **INDIAN BLAZE** 20 [2] Andrew Reid 9-9-9 (55) J P Guillambert (3) 16/1: 00340B0: Mid-div, fdd 4f out.   5   29a
4656} **FIFE AND DRUM** 49 [6] Miss J Feilden 6-9-13 p (59) A Quinn (5) 12/1: 134222U: Stumbled start & u.r.:   0a
13 Ran   2m 7.95 (5.15)   Owner Mr Erik Penser   Trained at Blewbury

---

105   **2.20 Littlewoods Bet Direct Nursery Handicap Stakes 2yo 0-85 (D)**   [78]
£2968 £848 £424   6f p/track rnd   Going 48   -08 Slow   Stalls Inside

63 **MAUNBY RAVER** 7 [7] P C Haslam 2-8-12 (62) Rory Moore (7) 9/2: 0664121: Handy, ev ch fnl 1f, drvn out to lead cl-home.   66a
76 **AFTER ALL** 4 [6] G A Butler 2-8-12 (62) Martin Dwyer 4/1: 02352: Slow away, held up, hdwy wide 3f out, led ins fnl 1f, hdd cl-home: nk   64a
25* **FOOLS ENTIRE** 13 [5] J A Gilbert 2-8-13 (63) B Reilly (5) 8/1: 4300013: Dwelt, bhd, hdwy 2f out, kept on fnl 1f, not btn far: hd   64a
51 **BURLINGTON PLACE** 8 [9] S Kirk 2-8-13 (63) J F Egan 11/4 FAV: 04024: Cl-up, led 2f out, hdd ins fnl 1f, no extra: ½   63a
3* **POMPEY BLUE** 16 [2] P McBride 2-9-7 (71) N Callan 7/2: 235515: In tch, short of room dist, onepcd well ins fnl 1f: nk   70a
15 **TARANAI** 14 [1] B W Duke 2-8-7 (57) Lisa Jones (3) 50/1: 0600006: Bhd, outpcd 2f out, rallied fnl 1f: ¾   54a
3 **INTIKRAFT** 14 [4] Mrs S A Liddiard 2-8-10 BL (60) F Norton 25/1: 0062007: Handy, ev ch 3f out, wknd fnl 1f: 3   48a
4997} **POWER TO BURN** 22 [8] K Bell 2-8-10 T (60) C Catlin 25/1: 40608: Bhd, nvr a factor.   4   36a
4700} **FORZENUFF** 45 [3] J R Boyle 2-9-6 (70) Dane O'Neill 12/1: 0545169: Led, hdd 2f out, sn fdd: 1   43a
9 Ran   1m 13.77 (3.37)   Owner Maunby Investment Management   Trained at Middleham

---

106   **2.55 Betdirect Co Uk Classified Stakes 3yo+ 0-80 (D)**
£3484 £1072 £536 £268   6f p/track rnd   Going 48   -02 Slow   Stalls Inside

4982*} **TEXAS GOLD** 24 [10] W R Muir 5-9-3 (85) Martin Dwyer 11/10 FAV: 0536011: Keen mid-div, hdwy 2f out, pushed out to lead well ins fnl 1f, val 2L+:   94a
41 **LAW BREAKER** 9 [6] J A Gilbert 5-9-3 (85) B Reilly (5) 14/1: 0010052: Cl-up, led 1f out, hdd well in fnl 1f, no extra: ¾   88a
45 **SIR DESMOND** 9 [5] R Guest 5-8-12 p (80) C Catlin 12/1: 4014003: Handy, outpcd 2f out, rallied dist, onepcd well ins fnl 1f: 1¼   79a
64 **ZARZU** 7 [8] C R Dore 4-8-12 (80) R Thomas (5) 10/1: 3610254: In tch, onepcd fnl 1f: 2½   72a
4990} **CRETAN GIFT** 23 [4] N P Littmoden 12-9-3 bl (85) J P Guillambert (3) 20/1: 40040/-05: Bhd, outpcd 3f out, rallied fnl 1f.   ½   76a
64 **PRINCE OF BLUES** 7 [13] M Mullineaux 5-8-12 P (80) J Bramhill 50/1: 0000006: Led, hdd 1f out & wknd: nk   70a
3735} **UNCLE BERNON** 98 [14] G B Balding 4-8-12 (78) R Havlin 50/1: 13-007: Slow away, nvr nrr than mid-div: 2   64a
 POWER BIRD 38 [2] D Flood 3-8-9 (78) P Doe 66/1: 6000058: Slow away, al in rear.   1¾   56a
64 **STEEL BLUE** 7 [7] R M Whitaker 3-9-0 p (82) Dean McKeown 13/2: 5002209: Slow away, nvr a factor.   shd   60a
4524} **MAGIC GLADE** 410 [12] C R Dore 4-9-3 (85) M Fenton 12/1: 31323-0: Bhd, prog 3f out, fdd dist: 1   60a

LINGFIELD Wednesday 26.11.03 Lefthand, V Sharp Track

4982}	**EMERALD FIRE** 24 [1] A M Balding 4-8-9 VIS (77) L Keniry (3) 14/1: 0603000: In tch, lost pl 3f out, wknd fnl 2f.				3 **43a**
41	**BOND ROYALE** 9 [3] B Smart 3-8-9 (79) I Mongan 10/1: 5000040: In tch, fdd 2f out, eased fnl 1f.				10 **18a**
12 Ran	1m 11.82 (3.02)	Owner Mr C L A Edginton			Trained at Lambourn

---

107   **3.30 Bet Direct In Running Sky Text 293 Handicap Stakes 3yo+ 0-75 (E)**   **[75]**

£2331 £666 £333   **2m p/track**   **Going 48**   **+06 Fast**   Stalls Inside

4755}	**HEFIN** 42 [12] I A Wood 6-8-12 (59) N Callan 4/1: 033131-: Cl-up, trav beat 3f out, led 2f out, rdn out fnl 1f:				**65a**
90*	**MACARONI GOLD** 2 [8] W Jarvis 3-8-7 6ex (63) M Tebbutt 11/4 FAv: 50303112: Held up, prog 4f out, chsd wnr dist, kept on fnl 1f, not pace wnr:				1 **67a**
11	**FINAL DIVIDEND** 14 [10] J M P Eustace 7-7-13 P (46) F P Ferris (3) 16/1: 6550643: Mid-div, outpcd 3f out, rallied fnl 1f:				3 **47a**
11	**ASTROMANCER** 14 [5] M H Tompkins 3-7-12 (54) M Henry 10/1: 00P5024: Cl-up, led 3f out, hdd 2f out, fdd fnl 1f:				1 **54a**
48	**RED SCORPION** 9 [2] W M Brisbourne 4-9-8 (69) J F Egan 5/1: 0052035: Mid-div, outpcd 6f out, modest late gains.				¾ **68a**
11	**HELLO HOLLY** 14 [6] Mrs A L M King 6-7-12 4oh (41) P M Quinn 25/1: 5310/-066: Mid-div, wknd 2f out.				4 **40a**
56	**STARRY MARY** 8 [1] E L James 5-8-4 (51) F Norton 66/1: 3520007: In tch, hmpd 3f out, sn onepcd.				3½ **43a**
4812}	**ACADEMY** 37 [11] Andrew Turnell 8-8-11 (58) C Catlin 14/1: 5220248: Dwelt, nvr nrr than mid-div.				1¼ **49a**
4581}	**ROME** 54 [4] G P Enright 4-9-11 (72) Dane O'Neill 14/1: 64539: Dwelt, bhd, nvr a factor.				hd **62a**
5009}	**DANCE LIGHT** 21 [7] T T Clement 4-9-4 (65) Dean McKeown 33/1: 1116-060: Al bhd.				1½ **54a**
11	**SEA PLUME** 14 [3] Lady Herries 4-10-0 (75) Martin Dwyer 8/1: 5-430200: Led, hdd 3f out, fdd.				½ **63a**
67	**HAJEER** 7 [13] P W Hiatt 5-8-4 (51) J Bramhill 25/1: 2123000: Handy, wknd 3f out.				shd **38a**
67	**FIRST PRESSURE** 7 [9] D R C Elsworth 3-8-2 P (58) Lisa Jones (3) 33/1: 0-004060: Keen mid-div, fdd 4f out.				hd **44a**
90	**FOREVER MY LORD** 14 [14] J R Best 5-8-7 (54) D Fentiman (7) 16/1: 2120040: Dwelt, al in rear.				3 **37a**
14 Ran	3m 26.81 (6.81)	Owner Mr Christopher Shankland			Trained at Upper Lambourn

---

SAINT CLOUD Friday 21.11.03 Lefthand, Galloping Track

Official Going V SOFT.

108   **1.45 Prix Tantleme Listed 3yo+**   ()

£13312 £5325 £3994   **1m**   **Soft**

4976}	**EXCELSIUS** 20 J L Dunlop 3-8-9 D Bonilla 136/10: 13-303301: Prom, switched stands rail str, led 2f out, drvn out:				**106**
2377}	**MAXWELL** 152 Mme C Head Maarek 3-8-12 S Pasquier : 193518:				2½ **104**
	LINDHOLM Werner Glanz 4-9-1 T Jarnet : 3:				hd **107**
Ran	1m 49.10	Owner V Schirone			Trained at Arundel, W Sussex

WOLVERHAMPTON Friday 28.11.03 Lefthand, Sharp Track

Official Going Standard

109   **12.50 Bet Direct On 0800 32 93 93 Handicap Stakes Div 1 3yo+ 0-75 (E)**   **[74]**

£2037 £582 £291   **5f rnd**   **Going 51**   **+00 Fast**   Stalls Inside

5025}	**POLISH EMPEROR** 21 [9] P W Harris 3-9-10 bl (70) F Janning 5/2 FAV: 0006641: Made all, rdn out fnl 1f to hold on:				**78a**
70	**BLUEBERRY RHYME** 7 [6] P J Makin 4-9-6 vis (66) D Sweeney 7/1: 6200-342: Cl-up, chsd wnr bef 1f out, just outpcd ins fnl 1f:				1½ **69a**
4964}	**KISS THE RAIN** 28 [8] R Brotherton 3-8-4 (50) G Gibbons 16/1: 0265103: Cl-up, outpcd 3f out, rallied dist:				2 **48a**
4446}	**CARK** 64 [10] J Balding 5-8-1 (47) A Nicholls 14/1: 0340004: Held up, prog 3f out, no impress fnl 1f.				½ **43a**
35	**FRASCATI** 13 [2] A Berry 3-9-13 (73) S Donohoe (7) 15/2: 2600425: Mid-div, nvr able to chall:				1¾ **64a**
4780}	**LONE PIPER** 42 [5] J M Bradley 8-8-0 1ow (45) C Catlin 14/1: 0000056: Cl-up, fdd fnl 1f:				2 **32a**
4925}	**INTELLIBET ONE** 31 [7] P D Evans 3-9-0 (60) Dane O'Neill 20/1: 2300007: Nvr nrr than mid-div.				¾ **44a**
35	**ONLY ONE LEGEND** 13 [12] K A Ryan 5-9-13 bl (73) N Callan 7/1: 5246668: Cl-up, fdd fnl 2f.				½ **56a**
438}	**VALAZAR** 311 [11] D W Chapman 4-9-4 (64) A Culhane 13/2: 401-5249: Cl-up, wknd fnl 2f:				hd **46a**
33	**SOMETHINGABOUTHER** 14 [13] P W Hiatt 3-7-12 (44) Lisa Jones (3) 25/1: 5020050: Slow away, al in rear.				1 **23a**
35	**SEA THE WORLD** 13 [1] D Shaw 3-9-2 (62) Darren Williams 12/1: 0040030: Al bhd.				5 **26a**
4908}	**BRIOSO** 32 [3] J M P Eustace 3-8-11 BL (57) J Tate 12/1: 1010000: Al in rear:				3½ **11a**
12 Ran	1m 02.77 (2.57)	Owner Mrs P W Harris			Trained at Berkhamsted

---

110   **1.20 Bet Direct On 0800 32 93 93 Handicap Stakes Div 2 3yo+ 0-75 (E)**   **[74]**

£2037 £582 £291   **5f rnd**   **Going 51**   **+01 Fast**   Stalls Inside

1878}	**WOODLAND BLAZE** 180 [6] P R Chamings 4-9-13 (73) I Mongan 6/1: 0021001: Handy, chsd ldr 3f out, drvn out to lead cl-home:				**79a**
4432}	**RELLIM** 65 [2] P A Blockley 4-8-4 (50) F P Ferris (3) 10/1: 0406442: Led, rdn dist, hdd cl-home:				hd **56a**
92	**MALAHIDE EXPRESS** 3 [5] M J Polglase 3-9-5 bl (65) L Fletcher (3) 10/1: 0000563: Mid-div, prog 3f out, onepcd fnl 1f:				2 **65a**
4969}	**TIME N TIME AGAIN** 27 [10] E J Alston 5-9-7 (67) D Allan (3) 5/1 FAV: 1034054: Mid-div, prog 2f out, short of room dist till well ins fnl 1f, not recover:				¾ **65a**
70	**HENRY TUN** 7 [11] J Balding 3-8-10 bl (56) J Edmunds (3) 13/2: 0500035: Cl-up, no extra fnl 1f:				½ **52a**
4712}	**SANDGATE CYGNET** 46 [4] J Semple 3-9-1 (61) D McGaffin (3) 5/1 FAV: 6-500026: Slow away, nvr nrr than mid-div.				½ **56a**
70	**CATCHTHEBATCH** 7 [9] M J Wallace 7-8-7 (53) D Corby (3) 20/1: 0502007: Held up, prog 2f out, nrst fin:				¾ **46a**
85	**CAROLS CHOICE** 4 [8] A Sadik 6-7-13 (45) R Ffrench 9/1: 5400638: Cl-up, fdd fnl 1f.				hd **37a**
4791}	**ENJOY THE BUZZ** 42 [12] J M Bradley 4-7-13 (45) Lisa Jones (3) 16/1: 006-0029: Al bhd:				2½ **30a**
35*	**GONENDUNNETT** 13 [13] Mrs C A Dunnett 4-9-10 vis (70) Dane O'Neill 4/1: 2200410: Al bhd.				2 **50a**
4184}	**SABANA** 78 [3] J M Bradley 5-8-1 (47) P Fitzsimons 25/1: 0-003000: Slow away, al in rear:				¾ **25a**
1046}	**HAGLEY PARK** 230 [1] M Quinn 4-8-4 (50) A Clark 25/1: 0201640: Handy, fdd 2f out.				6 **12a**
4670}	**FLOPPIE DISK** 49 [7] J A Pickering 3-9-3 (63) C Catlin 25/1: 6030000: Cl-up, wknd 4f out.				3½ **15a**

WOLVERHAMPTON Friday 28.11.03 Lefthand, Sharp Track

13 Ran   1m 02.72 (2.52)   Owner Patrick Chamings Sprint Club   Trained at Basingstoke

111

1.50 Bet Direct On Attheraces Interactive Median Auction Maiden Stakes 2yo (F)
£2317 £662 £331   1m100y rnd   Going 51   -24 Slow   Stalls Inside

4592}	LASTING DELIGHT 55 [6] Sir Mark Prescott 2-8-9 G Duffield 9/2: 051: Mid-div, prog 3f out, led dist, drvn out:	67a
5022}	RUSSALKA 21 [11] Julian Poulton 2-8-9 (63) N Callan 20/1: 4602: Slow away, bhd, prog 3f out, kept on fnl 1f, not pace of wnr: ¾	65a
1	PICCLEYES 18 [4] R Hannon 2-9-0 (63) Dane O'Neill 10/1: 5260353: Cl-up, led 5f out, hdd dist, no extra: 2½	64a
5005}	NEW YORK 23 [5] W J Haggas 2-8-9 A Culhane 2/1 FAV: 324: Cl-up, wknd fnl 1f: 1½	56a
4980}	PETITE COLLEEN 26 [9] D Haydn Jones 2-8-9 (72) F Norton 9/2: 0235: Mid-div, outpcd 2f out, rallied cl-home. ¾	54a
28	JAKARMI 14 [12] B Palling 2-9-0 D Kinsella 7/1: 026: Bhd, prog 5f out, wknd 2f out: 2	55a
4945}	IVORY COAST 29 [3] W R Muir 2-8-9 I Mongan 16/1: 07: Cl-up, fdd 3f out. 12	26a
5024}	VESTA FLAME 21 [7] M Johnston 2-8-9 J Fanning 33/1: 08: Al in rear. nk	25a
4786}	DRIZZLE 42 [13] J W Unett 2-9-0 M Henry 10/1: 39: Slow away, al bhd: nk	30a
	KILMINCHY LADY 86 [8] W R Muir 2-8-9 K Dalgleish 50/1: 00: Slow away, al in rear: nk	24a
42	CALCULAITE 11 [2] Mrs G S Rees 2-9-0 M Fenton 100/1: 00: Led 3f, fdd 3f out. 8	13a
	WHAT A SPREE [10] W R Muir 2-8-9 L Keniry (3) 66/1: 0: Al in rear. 2½	3a
5032}	BEAUCHAMP SURPRISE 20 [1] G A Butler 2-8-9 C Catlin 33/1: 000: Mid-div, fdd 4f out. 1	1a

13 Ran   1m 52.59 (6.39)   Owner Miss K Rausing   Trained at Newmarket

112

2.20 Littlewoods Bet Direct Nursery Handicap Stakes 2yo 0-85 (E)   [88]
£3402 £972 £486   7f rnd   Going 51   +02 Fast   Stalls Outside

98	FADEELA 3 [8] P W D'Arcy 2-8-7 e (67) B Reilly (5) 6/1: 402521: Rear, prog 3f out, led ins fnl 1f, rdn out:	77a
1	LITTLE EYE 18 [6] J R Best 2-8-3 (63) N Pollard 7/1: 6400042: Cl-up, led 2f out, hdd ins fnl 1f, just outpcd by wnr: 1	70a
54	CHUBBES 10 [3] M C Pipe 2-9-0 vis (74) J Fanning 6/4 FAV: 0061423: Led, hdd 2f out, sn fdd: 8	67a
4923}	SWEET CANDO 31 [5] Miss L A Perratt 2-8-5 (65) G Duffield 12/1: 3610334: Handy, wknd 2f out: nk	57a
4988}	BETHANYS BOY 25 [4] B Ellison 2-9-2 (76) C Catlin 9/1: 6404025: Cl-up, ev ch 2f out, sn fdd. hd	67a
29*	ERMINE GREY 14 [9] D Haydn Jones 2-9-7 vis (81) Paul Eddery 8/1: 0651016: Rear, nvr nrr than mid-div: 2	68a
4578}	LADY PISTE 56 [7] P D Evans 2-8-8 1ow T (67) N Callan 25/1: 3145537: Al bhd: 3	49a
4514}	BAKER OF OZ 60 [2] R Hannon 2-8-12 (72) Dane O'Neill 7/1: 22468: Al bhd: ¾	51a
4903}	GARNOCK VENTURE 32 [11] A Berry 2-8-0 (60) Dale Gibson 66/1: 66509: Al in rear. 8	27a
42	BOND BROOKLYN 11 [1] B Smart 2-8-10 bl (70) R Ffrench 14/1: 5235330: Cl-up, fdd 4f out. 6	27a

10 Ran   1m 29.63 (3.43)   Owner Mr M Al Salem   Trained at Newmarket

113

2.50 Betdirect Co Uk Handicap Stakes 3yo+ 0-80 (D)   [80]
£3052 £872 £436   6f rnd   Going 51   -01 Slow   Stalls Inside

2549}	PORT ST CHARLES 151 [13] P R Chamings 6-9-8 (74) I Mongan 10/1: 4002301: Cl-up, led dist, all out to hold on:	78a
45	CASHEL MEAD 11 [7] J L Spearing 3-9-12 (78) A Daly 8/1: 11-00062: Slow away, prog 2f out, styd on well fnl 1f, just failed: nk	81a
45	RAFTERS MUSIC 11 [4] Julian Poulton 5-9-11 (77) Lisa Jones (3) 9/2: 5522543: Bhd, styd on well fnl 1f, nrst fin: hd	74a
22	DUNEDIN RASCAL 15 [6] E A Wheeler 6-9-4 bl (70) S Whitworth 20/1: 0000004: Hld up, prog 2f out, late gains. 1¼	68a
4925}	IF BY CHANCE 31 [12] R Craggs 5-9-4 bl (70) S Hitchcott (3) 11/1: 1500105: Led, hdd dist, sn no extra. 1¼	64a
5030}	PADDYWACK 20 [9] D W Chapman 4-9-8 bl (72) A Culhane 9/4 FAV: 0360566: Rear, prog 3f out, ev ch dist, wknd fnl 1f. ½	64a
4925}	WINNING PLEASURE 15 [1] J Balding 5-9-8 (74) J Edmunds 12/1: 0600007: Cl-up, outpcd 4f out, rallied fnl 1f. ¾	64a
4805}	AFRICAN SPUR 41 [8] P A Blockley 3-9-9 (75) Derek Nolan (7) 20/1: 0420008: Nvr nrr than mid-div: shd	64a
5025}	RONNIE FROM DONNY 21 [5] B Ellison 3-9-8 (74) Dane O'Neill 10/1: 0500009: Cl-up, outpcd 3f out, mod gains. hd	62a
30	LEGALIS 14 [3] K A Ryan 5-9-3 (69) N Callan 6/1: 01-00040: Al bhd. 1¾	53a
2271}	WHIPPASNAPPER 161 [10] J R Best 3-9-7 (73) D Fentiman (7) 33/1: 0006000: Al in rear: ½	56a
55	WARDEN WARREN 10 [2] Mrs C A Dunnett 5-9-4 p (70) B Reilly (5) 25/1: 0000000: Handy, fdd 4f out. hd	52a
41	BLAKESHALL QUEST 11 [11] R Brotherton 3-9-8 (74) G Gibbons 50/1: 6100000: Cl-up, fdd fnl 2f. 2	50a

13 Ran   1m 15.92 (3.11)   Owner Twenty Twenty Research   Trained at Basingstoke

114

3.20 Bet Direct On Itv Page 367 Selling Stakes 3yo+ (G)
£2093 £598 £299   1m4f   Going 51   -12 Slow   Stalls Inside

2461}	ROYAL PRODIGY 154 [1] R J Hodges 4-9-11 (63) Dane O'Neill 10/11 FAV: 5130131: Handy, led 1f out, rdn out:	65a
4984}	ALS ALIBI 26 [2] W R Muir 10-9-6 (41) F Norton 6/1: 6304002: Mid-div, prog 5f out, ev ch dist, kept on fnl 1f, not pace of wnr: 1¼	58a
4567}	BELLA PAVLINA 409 [8] W M Brisbourne 5-9-1 (39) K Dalgleish 6/1: 540345-3: Handy, led 5f out, hdd 1f out, fdd: 9	39a
11	AVEIRO 16 [12] B G Powell 7-9-6 bl (34) L Keniry (3) 10/1: 0060304: Mid-div, wknd 2f out. 3½	39a
47	SAMAR QAND 11 [6] Julian Poulton 4-9-1 p (49) N Callan 10/1: 3000365: Cl-up, fdd 2f out. 5	27a
3819}	GIUST IN TEMP 97 [10] P W Hiatt 4-9-6 (37) L Fletcher (3) 12/1: 0005006: Held up, nvr nrr than mid-div. 15	10a
71	BUGLE CALL 7 [4] K O Cunningham Brown 9-9-0 (43) S Whitworth 25/1: 0500007: Slow away, prog 5f out, fdd 3f out: 5	3a
4938}	FELIX HOLT 30 [5] J R Best 3-9-0 bl (32) N Pollard 66/1: 050-48: Dwelt, al bhd. 1½	1a
3461}	FINAL VIEW 112 [9] N P Littmoden 4-9-6 BL J P Guillambert (3) 25/1: 40-059: Slow away, al well adrift: dist	0a
4944}	LOOK EAST 30 [7] Mrs C A Dunnett 4-9-6 p (35) C Catlin 66/1: 0-060000: Al well adrift. dist	0a
1973}	BATHWICK DREAM 895 [3] B R Millman 6-9-1 G Baker 16/1: 230106/-0: Led 6f, fdd 4f out, broke blood vessel. 4	0a
47	MALMAND 11 [11] R Brotherton 4-9-11 (42) G Gibbons 16/1: 0500050: Slow away, al well adrift. dist	0a

12 Ran   2m 41.13 (7.53)   Owner Mr D Charlesworth   Trained at Somerton

115

3.50 Bet Direct In Running Sky Text 293 Maiden Stakes 3yo (D)
£2300 £657 £329   1m1f79y rnd   Going 51   -04 Slow   Stalls Inside

	VALERIAN 34 [11] Charles O'Brien 3-9-0 M Fenton 10/1: 40-0051: Slow away, sn cl-up, led ins fnl 1f, sn carried hd high, drvn out:	72a
71	NICHOLAS NICKELBY 7 [6] N P Littmoden 3-9-0 J P Guillambert (3) 3/1 FAV: 622: Cl-up, led 3f out, hdd ins fnl 1f, not pace of wnr: 2½	65a

16	**NUZZLE 16** [9] M Quinn 3-8-9 vis (58) F Norton 12/1: 2336063: Cl-up, kept on fnl 1f, not pace front 2:	½	58a
4989}	**SUERTE 25** [8] J G Given 3-8-9 (62) J Fanning 6/1: 00-04: Rear, prog 5f out, no impress fnl 2f.	3	49a
96	**SILVER CRYSTAL 3** [4] Mrs N Macauley 3-8-9 (45) Lisa Jones (3) 20/1: 0030645: Rear, nvr nrr than mid-div:	2	43a
39	**OVER RATING 13** [2] J H M Gosden 3-8-9 (64) Dane O'Neill 6/5 FAV: 423426: Led, hdd 3f out, sn fdd:	¾	41a
53	**TATA NAKA 10** [10] Mrs C A Dunnett 3-8-9 N Chalmers (5) 40/1: 0657: Rear, nvr a factor.	¾	39a
4958}	**RED MOOR 28** [3] R Hollinshead 3-9-0 (45) A Culhane 25/1: 00-65008: Chsd ldrs, wkng when short of room 2f out.	1¼	40a
3451}	**LOVELLIAN 113** [12] B R Millman 3-8-9 (52) G Baker 20/1: 00549: Slow away, sn cl-up, fdd 3f out.	nk	34a
96	**REALISM 3** [1] P W Hiatt 3-9-0 Darren Williams 20/1: 0350: Led early, styd cl-up, fdd 3f out.	12	3a
4488}	**GALLEY LAW 62** [5] R Craggs 3-9-0 S Hitchcott (3) 100/1: 000: Slow away, al adrift:	6	0a

11 Ran   2m 03.46 (5.26)   Owner Mr L V Pearson   Trained at Ireland

Official Going Standard

---

116   11.55 Bet Direct No Q Maiden Stakes Div 1 2yo (D)
£3559 £1095 £548 £274   1m2f p/track   Going 41   -61 Slow   Stalls Inside

54	**KEEP ON MOVIN 11** [3] T G Mills 2-8-9 (74) R Miles (5) 7/2: 06531: Chsd ldrs, lost pl over 4f out, rallied for press to lead ins last, drvn out:		71a
4808}	**TROMPE LOEIL 40** [12] E A L Dunlop 2-8-9 (60) M Fenton 25/1: 40502: Mid-div, hdwy & led 5f out, rdn clr over 2f out, hdd ins last, kept on, just held:	shd	69a
19	**RESONANCE 16** [4] Mrs A J Perrett 2-8-9 W Ryan 5/1: 043: Hld up last, hdwy trav well 2f out, 'flew home' under kind ride ins last, nvr plcd to chall/too much to do:	1½	68a
4514}	**ABSOLUTELYTHEBEST 61** [10] E A L Dunlop 2-9-0 T Quinn 25/1: 004: Rear, eff wide over 3f out, kept on for press:	¾	72a
4757}	**MASTER THEO 45** [8] H J Collingridge 2-9-0 I Mongan 5/2 FAV: 335: Chsd ldrs, no extra fnl 1f:	nk	71a
4945}	**SEMELLE DE VENT 30** [9] J H M Gosden 2-8-9 R Havlin 7/1: 056: Trkd ldrs, onepace fnl 2f.	nk	65a
21	**CRACKLEANDO 16** [13] N P Littmoden 2-9-0 J P Guillambert (3) 33/1: 07: Rear, eff 3f out, no prog dist.	2	67a
	WINGS OF MORNING 34 [5] N A Callaghan 2-9-0 S Whitworth 40/1: 008: Keen, rear, eff wide, mod prog:	¾	64a
37	**BILL BENNETT 14** [7] J Jay 2-9-0 (74) K Dalgleish 5/1: 603329: Wide, led 5f, btn/hmpd 2f out.	1	65a
3991}	**ALMOST WELCOME 89** [11] S Dow 2-9-0 (39) P Doe 100/1: 0000: Al bhd, abs/AW bow.	½	64a
4730}	**WARIF 46** [6] E J O'Neill 2-9-0 R Ffrench 8/1: 000: Chsd ldrs till 2f out:	hd	63a
4942}	**SPORTULA 31** [2] Mrs A J Perrett 2-8-9 Dane O'Neill 50/1: 000: Sn struggling, no ch 2f out:	2½	54a

12 Ran   2m 13.00 (10.2)   Owner Mr J E Harley   Trained at Epsom

---

117   12.25 Bet Direct No Q Voice Automated Betting Classified Stakes Div 1 3yo+ 0-60 (F)
£2114 £604 £302   7f p/track rnd   Going 41   -22 Slow   Stalls Inside

4907}	**PANTS 33** [15] Andrew Reid 4-8-10 (52) A Nicholls 16/1: 2040031: Rear, switched wide & over 1f out, strong run for press to lead cl-home:		58a
50	**INISTRAHULL ISLAND 11** [13] M H Tompkins 3-8-12 (57) J Fanning 5/1: 5026042: Sn handy, led 2f out & rdn clr, hdd cl-home:	nk	60a
68*	**ZAGALA 8** [10] S L Keightley 3-8-9 t (61) A Culhane 100/30 FAV: 6300213: Mid-div, eff wide to chall over 2f out, kept on onepace for press:	½	56a
55	**A WOMAN IN LOVE 11** [12] Miss B Sanders 4-8-10 (55) T Quinn 9/2: 3542564: Rear, styd on wide for press, not pace to chall:	nk	55a
1671}	**PANCAKEHILL 190** [7] D K Ivory 4-8-10 (56) I Mongan 16/1: 2023655: Keen & prom, no extra ins last, abs.	½	54a
50	**KINSMAN 11** [9] T D McCarthy 6-8-13 p (53) P Doe 14/1: 0555006: Slow away, rear, eff 2f out:	1	55a
4519}	**MAD MICK MEESON 61** [16] G B Balding 3-8-12 T (58) A Clark 25/1: 4505047: Rear/wide, mod prog:	nk	54a
12	**MISS ISSY 17** [11] J Gallagher 3-8-9 VIS (55) N Callan 9/1: 6234048: Rear, mod hdwy from halfway:	shd	51a
94	**ROMAN EMPIRE 4** [5] T J Etherington 3-8-12 (59) J McAuley 20/1: 0-150009: Chsd ldrs, hung left/btn dist, qck reapp.	1	52a
4986}	**A TEEN 27** [2] P Howling 5-8-13 (55) D Kinsella 25/1: 0656100: Prom, btn over 1f out:	nk	51a
55	**SMITH N ALLAN OILS 11** [8] M Dods 4-8-13 p (56) M Fenton 11/2: 0005230: Mid-div, hmpd & lost pl 2f out, keeping on when hmpd again ins last, forget this:	hd	49a
22	**TUSCAN TREATY 16** [6] T T Clement 3-8-9 (56) J Mackay 33/1: 0100000: Briefly chsd ldr over 1f out, sn wknd.	6	37a
23	**MONTANA 16** [3] R Hannon 3-8-12 (60) Dane O'Neill 20/1: 6-223000: Led/dsptd lead 5f, wknd qckly.	2½	35a
4183}	**SANDRONE 79** [4] P M Phelan 3-8-9 BL (53) C Catlin 50/1: 2003-000: Cl-up 3f, wknd qckly fnl 3f:	13	11a
4590}	**GINGER ICE 56** [1] G G Margarson 3-8-12 (55) N Pollard 66/1: 60-00000: Led/dsptd lead till halfway, sn bhd, abs.	3½	7a

15 Ran   1m 27.2 (4.4)   Owner Mr A S Reid   Trained at Mill Hill London

---

118   12.55 Press Red To Bet Direct Maiden Stakes 3yo (D)
£2310 £660 £330   1m4f p/track   Going 41   -05 Slow   Stalls Inside

89	**SEA HOLLY 5** [12] G G Margarson 3-9-0 (74) K Dalgleish 11/2: 2306021: Trkd ldrs, hdwy to lead over 3f out, drvn & held on well ins last:		73a
4989}	**SO VITAL 26** [9] Mrs Lydia Pearce 3-9-0 R Price 12/1: 62: Mid-div, hdwy to chase wnr 3f out, no extra well ins last:	¾	71a
14	**SCHOONER 17** [11] Lady Herries 3-9-0 M Tebbutt 10/1: 653: Rear, styd on strongly over 1f out, nrst fin:	hd	70a
4614}	**GRAND FOLLY 54** [2] A M Hales 3-8-9 (65) I Mongan 14/1: 5200304: Trkd ldrs, outpcd/short of room over 2f out, kept on ins last, nrst fin:	nk	64a
3466}	**HOH VISS 113** [6] S Kirk 3-9-0 (72) J F Egan 10/1: 4452255: Trkd ldrs, short of room 3f out, onepce, abs.	1	68a
14	**REMEMBRANCE 17** [8] J M P Eustace 3-9-0 t P (63) J Tate 5/2 FAV: 0502036: Mid-div, chall 2f out, no extra dist.	1	67a
4998}	**NAMASTE 25** [13] H R A Cecil 3-8-9 T Quinn 7/2: 327: Led/dsptd lead 9f, btn/hmpd dist.	5	55a
	SPLENDID TOUCH 98 [4] J R Jenkins 3-8-9 (38) S Whitworth 66/1: 5400008: Held up, little hdwy, Brit abs, abs.	6	46a
66	**DISTINCTLYSPLENDID 10** [10] I A Wood 3-9-0 (34) D Nolan (4) 100/1: 0640009: Al towards rear.	1½	49a
4968}	**NASSAU STREET 28** [5] D J S ffrench Davis 3-9-0 M Fenton 50/1: 040: Al bhd, t.o.	16	29a
		4	23a

LINGFIELD Saturday 29.11.03 Lefthand, V Sharp Track

DUB DASH [1] S C Williams 3-9-0 B Reilly (5) 16/1: 0: Slow away & al bhd on debut.
83 BACK IN ACTION 7 [7] M A Magnusson 3-9-0 BL t (75) C Catlin 7/1: 53-5000: Keen & disptg lead till 4f out, blnks. 7 14a
4985} ELLAS WISH 27 [16] J H M Gosden 3-8-9 BL (60) R Havlin 25/1: 04000: Prom, wknd qckly over 2f out, blnks. 5 3a
4121} PRINCE IVOR 82 [3] J C Fox 3-9-0 (40) R Smith 66/1: 0005000: Al bhd, abs. 24 0a
4929} CAROLINA MORNING 32 [14] H J Collingridge 3-8-9 N Callan 33/1: 00: Rear, no ch from halfway. dist 0a
15 Ran 2m 34.76 (5.56) Owner Mr P E Axon Trained at Newmarket

119 1.25 Betdirect Co Uk Novice Stakes 2yo (D)
£3248 £928 £464 7f p/track rnd Going 41 -24 Slow Stalls Inside

4971} CALEDONIAN 28 [1] D R C Elsworth 2-8-12 T Quinn 16/1: 01: Rear, shkn up over 2f out & strong run ins last to lead cl-home, 83a
shade cheekily:
79 MISTER SAIF 7 [11] R Hannon 2-9-5 (84) Dane O'Neill 2/1: 3310622: Trkd ldrs, rdn & outpcd over 2f out, kept on for press till hd 89a
well ins last, just hdd cl-home:
SKIDMARK [13] D R C Elsworth 2-8-8 P Fitzsimons 50/1: 3: Slow away & bhd, smooth hdwy over 2f out, 'flew home' under kind ½ 77a
ride ins last, too much to do:
15 RISE 17 [4] Andrew Reid 2-8-11 bl (84) I Mongan 10/1: 3523104: Led, rdn clr over 2f out, hdd ins last & no extra: nk 79a
4866} CROCODILE DUNDEE 36 [5] Jamie Poulton 2-9-5 S Whitworth 6/4 FAV: 105: Trkd ldrs, rdn & outpcd over 2f out, kept on. nk 86a
52 EVER CHEERFUL 11 [2] W G M Turner 2-8-12 (66) L Treadwell (7) 20/1: 2034346: Chsd ldr 3f out, no extra ins last. nk 78a
4972} SCARLETT ROSE 28 [14] Dr J D Scargill 2-8-7 C Lowther 11/1: 367: Chsd ldr 4f out, btn over 1f out. 3 67a
51 COMERAINCOMESHINE 11 [6] T G Mills 2-8-7 R Miles (5) 10/1: 038: Trkd ldrs, outpcd fnl 2f. nk 66a
32 I WISH I KNEW 15 [3] P J Makin 2-8-12 D Sweeney 100/1: 009: Mid-div, outpcd from halfway. 1¼ 68a
4568} MOSCOW TIMES 57 [9] D R C Elsworth 2-8-12 N Pollard 11/1: 600: Rear, nvr pace to threaten: hd 67a
GOLDEN DRIFT [8] G Wragg 2-8-5 2ow J F Egan 25/1: 0: Dwelt & al rear on debut. 5 51a
52 STONOR LADY 11 [12] P W D'Arcy 2-8-7 B Reilly (5) 33/1: 020: Al bhd: 3 47a
4034} FOX HOLLOW 87 [7] M J Haynes 2-8-12 (35) C Catlin 200/1: 66500: Chsd ldr till 4f out, abs. 4 45a
13 Ran 1m 27.37 (4.57) Owner The Caledonian Racing Society Trained at Whitsbury

120 1.55 Bet Direct No Q Maiden Stakes Div 2 2yo (D)
£3543 £1090 £545 £273 1m2f p/track Going 41 -29 Slow Stalls Inside

19 PUKKA 16 [5] L M Cumani 2-9-0 (79) L Dettori 8/15 FAV: 0431: Mid-div, qcknd to lead over 1f out, hands-and-heels, readily: 79a
37 BAAWRAH 14 [10] M R Channon 2-9-0 (71) A Culhane 8/1: 0632: Chsd ldrs, eff to chase ldr over 4f out, not pace of wnr: 2 74a
21 POLAR DANCER 16 [12] Mrs A J Perrett 2-8-9 W Ryan 16/1: 063: Dwelt, rear, eff wide 3f out, kept on onepace fnl 2f: nk 68a
4973} CHARA 28 [2] J R Jenkins 2-8-9 S Whitworth 10/1: 404: Rear, kept on wide for press fnl 2f: 1 67a
43 HOLD THE LINE 12 [3] W G M Turner 2-9-0 (67) L Treadwell (7) 16/1: 06205: Keen, led/dsptd lead till halfway. 3 68a
4975} ABBEYGATE 28 [11] T Keddy 2-9-0 M Tebbutt 14/1: 006: Dwelt, hung right thr'out, mod gains: nk 67a
4962} JANGO MALFOY 29 [7] B W Duke 2-9-0 M Fenton 100/1: 007: Cl-up, led over 4f out till over 1f out, wknd. ½ 66a
36 ELUSIVE DREAM 14 [6] Sir Mark Prescott 2-9-0 J Mackay 10/1: 0008: Rear, no ch over 2f out: 2½ 62a
54 DARN GOOD 11 [4] R Hannon 2-9-0 (69) Dane O'Neill 8/1: 5364509: Chsd ldr till 2f out. nk 61a
5023} SPRING WHISPER 29 [9] E A L Dunlop 2-8-9 VIS T Quinn 20/1: 00: Mid-div, wknd qckly 2f out, visor. ½ 55a
4962} FLYING PATRIARCH 29 [1] G L Moore 2-9-0 bl R Brisland 100/1: 000: Chsd ldrs till 6f out. 8 49a
4827} MYSTIC PROMISE 39 [8] Mrs N Macauley 2-9-0 BL (30) K Dalgleish 100/1: 00000: Dwelt, keen & led after 2f, sn clr, hdd dist 0a
over 4f out, to toe.:
12 Ran 2m 09.84 (7.04) Owner Fittocks Stud Trained at Newmarket

121 2.30 Bet Direct No Q Demo 08000 837 888 Handicap Stakes 3yo+ 0-70 (E) [70]
£2149 £614 £307 6f p/track rnd Going 41 -01 Slow Stalls Inside

55 MISTRAL SKY 11 [5] Mrs S A Liddiard 4-9-12 vis (68) M Fenton 9/1: 0411001: Trkd ldrs, eff wide over 1f out, styd on for press 71a
to lead well ins last:
4949} SIRAJ 30 [3] N A Graham 4-9-5 BL (61) L Dettori 5/1 FAV: 6-041002: Rear, rdn & hdwy to lead over 1f out, hdd well ins last, just nk 63a
held:
94 POLAR FORCE 4 [8] M R Channon 3-9-7 (63) D Corby (3) 10/1: 5006003: Rear, smooth hdwy when no room over 1f out, 2 59a
onepace for press from dist:
22 FULVIO 16 [1] Jamie Poulton 3-10-0 vis (70) I Mongan 25/1: 3665004: Trkd ldrs, kept on onepace. ½ 64a
55 PEYTO PRINCESS 11 [4] M A Buckley 5-9-4 (60) Lisa Jones (3) 7/1: 4000045: Rear, prog/no room over 1f out, not able to nk 53a
recover:
35 PARK STAR 14 [7] D Shaw 3-9-7 (63) Darren Williams 20/1: 1100056: Rear, late gains, not pcd to chall. 1 53a
4925} WOODBURY 32 [2] K R Burke 4-9-2 (58) G Baker 7/1: 225D267: Trkd ldrs over 2f out, short of room over 1f out, wknd. ½ 46a
35 ROMAN QUINTET 14 [12] D W P Arbuthnot 3-9-10 T (66) Dane O'Neill 8/1: 6403448: Held up, not pace to chall: 1¼ 50a
4964} CAPTAIN CLOUDY 29 [6] M Madgwick 3-9-4 (60) L Keniry (3) 25/1: 0004009: Led/dsptd lead 5f, wknd. 3 35a
20 TEYAAR 16 [14] Mrs N Macauley 7-9-8 (64) P McCabe 8/1: 0035100: Prom till 2f out, wknd. 2½ 31a
4753} LEGAL SET 45 [10] J R Best 7-9-10 (66) F Norton 11/2: 0300060: Led/dsptd lead till over 1f out, fdd. shd 33a
22 KILMEENA LAD 16 [13] J C Fox 7-10-0 (70) J F Egan 13/2: 611/00-00: Dwelt, wide, in tch 4f: 2½ 29a
91 TAMARELLA 5 [11] G G Margarson 3-9-3 (59) N Pollard 20/1: 5000500: Prom, wknd qckly over 1f out, qck reapp. 1 15a
4689} GOODWOOD PRINCE 48 [9] S Dow 3-10-0 (70) T Quinn 20/1: 2000600: Held up, al bhd. 15 0
14 Ran 1m 12.93 (2.53) Owner Shefford Valley Stud Trained at Hungerford

122 3.05 Bet Direct No Q On 08000 93 66 93 Handicap Stakes 3yo+ 0-75 (E) [75]
£2405 £687 £344 1m2f p/track Going 41 -34 Slow Stalls Inside

886} PARAGON OF VIRTUE 246 [12] P Mitchell 6-9-13 (74) J Fanning 12/1: 01-16331: Trkd ldr halfway, led over 2f out, held on 81a
well ins last:
4963} MAD CAREW 29 [6] G L Moore 4-9-9 bl e (70) S Whitworth 6/1: 0041322: Trkd ldrs trav well, rdn & chsd wnr over 1f out, kept 1 75a
on for press:

39

LINGFIELD Saturday 29.11.03 Lefthand, V Sharp Track

4711} **HIP HOP HARRY 47** [5] E A L Dunlop 3-9-7 (72) T Quinn 20/1: 3103: Mid-div, lost pl over 3f out & drpd rear: *2* **74a**
4849*} **RYANS FUTURE 38** [13] J Akehurst 3-9-10 (75) C Catlin 8/1: 1340514: Keen & led till over 2f out. *shd* **77a**
101* **QUANTUM LEAP 3** [14] S Dow 6-9-5 6ex (66) Paul Eddery 10/1: 0400415: Held up, chsd ldrs 4f out, onepace. *nk* **67a**
4167} **ANALYZE 79** [7] B G Powell 5-9-11 (72) L Keniry (3) 12/1: 3331506: Keen & trkd ldrs, onepace over 1f out *hd* **72a**
17 **PRIORS DALE 17** [4] K Bell 3-9-7 (72) A Culhane 14/1: 5-04027: Chsd ldr halfway, no extra over 1f out. *1¾* **70a**
4716} **CLIMATE 47** [11] J R Boyle 4-10-0 (75) D Sweeney 10/1: 0050S38: Rear, hung & no impress over 1f out, abs. *¾* **72a**
12 **COLLEGE DELINQUENT 17** [9] K Bell 4-9-5 t (66) Dean McKeown 14/1: 4500339: Mid-div trav well, btn 1f out. *nk* **62a**
4985} **CARROWDORE 27** [2] R Hannon 3-9-6 (71) Dane O'Neill 9/2 FAV: 3345220: Rear, eff 3f out, no prog fnl 2f. *hd* **66a**
4984} **BURGUNDY 27** [3] P Mitchell 6-9-6 vis (67) I Mongan 8/1: 3030150: Reluctant to race, sn drvn & al rear. *½* **61a**
24 **RASID 16** [1] C A Dwyer 5-9-9 (70) N Callan 14/1: 0400030: Rear, no prog fnl 2f: *shd* **64a**
4689} **FOUR JAYS 48** [8] N P Littmoden 3-9-7 (72) J P Guillambert (3) 20/1: 5300260: Al rear: *nk* **65a**
4752} **FREE OPTION 45** [10] B Hanbury 8-9-13 (74) L Dettori 11/2: 0530030: Al bhd, abs. *nk* **66a**
14 Ran 2m 10.27 (7.47) Owner Debbie & Marc Thornton Trained at Epsom

123 **3.40 Bet Direct No Q Voice Automated Betting Classified Stakes Div 2 3yo+ 0-60 (F)**
£2114 £604 £302 **7f p/track rnd** **Going 41** **+06 Fast** Stalls Inside

55* **CHATEAU NICOL 11** [10] B G Powell 4-8-13 vis (62) J Fanning 5/1: 3000011: Trkd ldrs, led & qcknd clr over 1f out, eased cl-home, val for 8L+: **75a**
4944} **COLD CLIMATE 31** [5] Bob Jones 8-8-13 (56) F Norton 10/1: 0405152: Dwelt, sn trk ldrs, drvn & kept on, no ch with wnr: *5* **56a**
50 **MR BOUNTIFUL 11** [4] M Dods 5-8-13 (63) J F Egan 9/4 FAV: 2064123: Led till over 1f out, onepace. *nk* **55a**
4691} **PIROUETTES 48** [13] Miss Gay Kelleway 3-8-9 (58) M Fenton 12/1: 040-4304: Dwelt, mid-div, styd on onepace for press: *2* **46a**
4901} **BALMACARA 33** [7] Miss K B Boutflower 4-8-10 p (50) A Culhane 33/1: 2000055: Rear, drvn & mod prog. *1* **44a**
74 **ITS ECCO BOY 8** [12] P Howling 5-8-13 (54) D Kinsella 14/1: 1350036: Rear, short of room over 1f out, nrst fin. *hd* **46a**
4986} **TENDER 27** [11] D J Daly 3-8-9 (60) Lisa Jones (3) 7/1: 6640067: Mid-div, not pcd to chall. *½* **42a**
4907} **GUN SALUTE 33** [2] G L Moore 3-8-12 (53) R Brisland 16/1: 0000058: Dwelt, trkd ldrs 3f out, sn no room & wknd. *½* **44a**
50 **ICECAP 11** [15] P Butler 3-8-9 (55) A Daly 14/1: 4456659: Rear, only mod prog. *1* **39a**
71 **JAGGED 8** [1] K R Burke 3-8-12 (60) G Baker 7/1: 0402630: Trkd ldrs till over 1f out. *½* **41a**
23 **NATHAN DETROIT 16** [16] P J Makin 3-8-12 BL (60) D Sweeney 20/1: 0000: Mid-div, btn 2f out: *1¾* **38a**
33 **WARLINGHAM 15** [8] M Pitman 5-8-13 (57) I Mongan 25/1: 3000-000: Cl-up, wknd 2f out. *2½* **33a**
4171} **CRAFTY POLITICIAN 79** [9] G L Moore 6-8-13 (50) W Ryan 25/1: 1040000: Chsd ldrs till over 2f out, abs. *2½* **28a**
4389} **UNSUITED 68** [6] J E Long 4-8-10 (60) S Whitworth 25/1: 500-0650: Slowly away & al bhd, abs. *3½* **18a**
4542} **SUNSET KING 59** [14] J C Fox 3-8-12 (59) R Smith 25/1: 0022000: Mid-div, struggling from halfway: *2* **17a**
66 **BULAWAYO 10** [3] Andrew Reid 6-8-13 (57) J P Guillambert (3) 9/1: 1036320: Chsd ldrs, no ch fnl 4f. *10* **2a**
16 Ran 1m 25.27 (2.47) Owner Basingstoke Commercials Trained at Winchester

WOLVERHAMPTON Saturday 29.11.03 Lefthand, Sharp Track

Official Going STANDARD

124 **7.00 Bet Direct Freephone 0800 32 93 93 Handicap Stakes 3yo+ 0-60 (F)** **[60]**
£2100 £600 £300 **5f f/sand rnd** **Going 44** **-20 Slow** Stalls Inside

4908} **LADY PEKAN 33** [6] P S McEntee 4-9-7 BL (53) F P Ferris (3) 28/1: 0500001: Trkd ldr, rdn & led ins last, drvn out **60a**
4991} **STRENSALL 26** [7] R E Barr 6-9-10 (56) R Fitzpatrick 11/4 FAV: 0600142: Al prom, drvn & kept on ins last, not pace of wnr: *½* **60a**
4780} **ERRACHT 43** [8] K R Burke 5-9-8 (54) G Baker 8/1: 3136203: Mid-div, prog/short of room & switched ins last, kept on: *1* **55a**
4969} **LAUREL DAWN 28** [3] I W McInnes 5-9-12 (58) L Fletcher (3) 7/1: 6500204: Led till ins last, no extra. *shd* **58a**
94 **CASH 4** [10] Paul Johnson 5-9-13 (59) Lisa Jones (3) 7/1: 0000005: Pushed along mid-div, not able to chall. *1¼* **56a**
41 **OUR CHELSEA BLUE 12** [9] A W Carroll 5-9-13 (59) S Righton 9/1: 5600066: Slow away & well bhd, nrst fin. *nk* **55a**
4856} **KINGS BALLET 38** [2] P R Chamings 5-9-10 (56) Dane O'Neill 9/2: 0000037: Slow away/outpcd, not pace to threaten. *nk* **51a**
70 **STAR LAD 8** [5] R Brotherton 3-9-6 bl (52) G Gibbons 33/1: 0600068: Prom, btn over 1f out. *1* **44a**
110 **CATCHTHEBATCH 1** [11] M J Wallace 7-9-7 (53) D Corby (3) 12/1: 05020079: Prom wide till halfway. *2½* **42a**
75 **RIVELLI 8** [1] B R Foster 4-9-9 bl (55) N Chalmers (5) 66/1: 00-00000: Sn outpcd. *½* **43a**
1046} **SALERNO 231** [4] Miss Gay Kelleway 4-9-9 (55) M Fenton 12/1: 0000400: Mid-div, btn/eased ins last, abs. *2* **41a**
109 **INTELLIBET ONE 1** [13] P D Evans 3-10-0 (60) D Nolan (5) 25/1: 23000070: Sn struggling rear, unplcd yesterday. *7* **39a**
12 Ran 1m 3.41 (3.21) Owner Mr P S J Croft Trained at Newmarket

125 **7.30 Bet Direct On Attheraces Interactive Claiming Stakes 3yo+ (E)**
£2065 £590 £295 **1m6f166y f/sand** **Going 44** **-43 Slow** Stalls Outside

72 **CLAPTRAP 8** [8] J A Osborne 3-8-8 (54) I Mongan 7/4 FAV: 3346001: Slow away & settled rear, smooth hdwy to lead 2f out, easily: **60a**
103 **PARADISE VALLEY 3** [6] Mrs S A Liddiard 3-8-10 t (54) C Catlin 17/2: 0251452: Mid-div, rdn & kept on fnl 2f, no ch with wnr: *10* **47a**
34 **MYSTERIUM 15** [1] N P Littmoden 9-9-4 vis (40) J P Guillambert (3) 5/1: 0500333: Held up, hdwy 4f out, no impress fnl 2f. *5* **39a**
6 **QUEENSBERRY 19** [5] J O'Reilly 4-9-6 (52) J D O'Reilly (7) 8/1: 0330204: Keen & trkd ldr, led 7f out till 2f out, wknd. *2* **38a**
11 **TWO OF A KIND 17** [7] J W Hills 3-9-2 (61) M Henry 12/1: 055555: Chsd ldr 7f out, btn 2f out: *2½* **39a**
67 **SPA LANE 10** [11] J F Coupland 10-8-12 (55) P Gallagher (7) 5/1: 4556106: Held up, btn 2f out. *3* **23a**
4295} **ROPPONGI DANCER 73** [9] Mrs N Macauley 4-8-11 t (30) A Culhane 20/1: 300-0647: Al towards rear, abs. *9* **11a**
4546} **PEGGY LOU 59** [10] B J Llewellyn 3-8-1 (47) Joanna Badger 12/1: 4143368: Slow away, mid-div, struggling fnl 3f: *16* **0a**
90 **LAPADAR 5** [4] J R Weymes 4-9-9 BL (60) D Fentiman (7) 20/1: 0605059: Led till 7f out, quick reapp in blnks. *17* **0a**
1029] **SHEARWATER 591** [3] A Senior 6-8-11 (22) S Righton 80/1: 0/66/000-0: Prom 5f, sn well bhd, long abs. *dist* **0a**
10 Ran 3m 22.7 (13.1) Owner Mountgrange Stud Trained at Upper Lambourn

126 **8.00 Bet Direct Live Football In Running Maiden Stakes 2yo (D)**
£3010 £860 £430 **6f f/sand rnd** **Going 44** **-38 Slow** Stalls Inside

WOLVERHAMPTON Saturday 29.11.03 Lefthand, Sharp Track

42	**SABLE N SILK** 12 [3] D Haydn Jones 2-8-9 F Norton 10/1: 61: Dwelt, pushed along towards rear, hdwy for press to lead cl-home, all out:		**59a**
	ANISETTE [8] Julian Poulton 2-8-9 N Callan 14/1: 2: Sn handy & led over 1f out, drvn & hdd line:	shd	59a
3696}	**TURKISH DELIGHT** 103 [12] D Morris 2-8-9 (70) M Tebbutt 9/2: 4443: Chsd ldrs wide, ch dist, no extra nr fin:	½	58a
5031}	**UNITED SPIRIT** 21 [13] M A Magnusson 2-8-9 C Catlin 10/1: 504: Wide, styd on for press fnl 2f, nrst fin:	¾	56a
51	**CHARLIEISMYDARLING** 11 [7] J A Osborne 2-9-0 J Fanning 8/1: 405: Led 2f out till over 1f out, wknd:	2½	54a
4822}	**SIR JASPER** 39 [4] T D Barron 2-9-0 VIS D Mernagh 16/1: 556: Chsd ldr, outpcd from halfway:	nk	53a
4903}	**LOVE IN THE MIST USA** 33 [10] E A L Dunlop 2-8-9 (67) Dane O'Neill 9/2: 46507: Mid-div, nvr pace to chall:	nk	47a
63	**MISS JUDGED** 10 [9] A P Jones 2-8-9 (33) G Hannon 8/1: 60008: Chsd ldrs till halfway.	shd	46a
	ROVING VIXEN [1] J L Spearing 2-8-9 A Daly 33/1: 9: Bhd, al outpcd on debut.	½	45a
	CORNWALLIS [11] R Guest 2-9-0 A Culhane 14/1: 0: Sn outpcd on debut.	2½	43a
	MONKEY OR ME [6] P T Midgley 2-9-0 G Parkin 66/1: 0: Sn bhd on debut.	7	22a
	SHAYMEES GIRL [5] Ms Deborah J Evans 2-8-9 G Gibbons 66/1: 0: Led 4f, wknd qckly on debut.	1	14a
4072}	**CELADON** 85 [2] N P Littmoden 2-9-0 (73) I Mongan 100/30 FAV: 4350: Slow away & sn bhd, abs/AW bow.	5	4a
13 Ran	1m 17.72 (4.92) Owner Mrs M L Parry		Trained at Pontypridd

---

127

8.30 Bet Direct In Running Sky Text 293 Handicap Stakes 3yo+ 0-85 (D)   [79]
£3500 £1000 £500   **1m1f79y f/sand**   **Going 44**   **+14 Fast**   Stalls Inside

38+*	**STRONG HAND** 14 [7] M W Easterby 3-10-0 (82) P Mulrennan (5) 11/8 FAV: 3133511: Hld up, smooth hdwy to lead over 1f out, shaken up to assert, eased cl-home:		**90a**
97*	**MI ODDS** 4 [5] Mrs N Macaulay 7-10-0 6ex (79) A Culhane 13/2: 6501212: Mid-div, drvn & kept on to take 2nd ins last, no ch with wnr:	½	86a
4992}	**INTRICATE WEB** 26 [11] E J Alston 7-9-7 (72) D Allan (3) 12/1: 2445043: Rear, styd on for press fnl 2f, nrst fin:	2	75a
26	**OFARABY** 16 [6] M A Jarvis 3-9-12 (80) N Callan 15/2: 0102164: Handy & led over 3f out till over 1f out:	1½	80a
	HENRY AFRIKA 21 [8] Gerard McArdle 5-9-11 P (76) Dean McKeown 40/1: 30/00-005: Prom, no extra dist:	1	72a
4738*}	**NOWELL HOUSE** 46 [3] M W Easterby 7-9-12 (77) Dale Gibson 33/1: 33-51416: Mid-div, struggling fnl 3f, abs.	6	63a
17*	**LABRETT** 17 [13] Miss Gay Kelleway 6-9-11 p (76) M Fenton 7/1: 3436517: Held up, eff wide, no prog 2f out:	4	54a
5029}	**MISTER ARJAY** 22 [10] B Ellison 3-9-10 bl e (78) C Catlin 33/1: 4535208: Al rear, nvr factor.	7	42a
2840}	**OLDENWAY** 140 [2] R A Fahey 4-9-5 (70) D Swift (7) 25/1: 1250209: Prom, btn 3f out, abs.	½	33a
5	**BRESSBEE** 19 [1] J W Unett 5-9-11 bl (76) Dane O'Neill 12/1: 1000300: Led till 6f out, sn struggling.	2½	34a
26	**THE GAIKWAR** 16 [4] N E Berry 4-9-10 (75) M Savage (5) 66/1: 30-00000: Led after 3f till over 3f out, sn btn.	1½	30a
4992}	**HIAWATHA** 23 [12] I Semple 4-9-6 (71) D McGaffin (3) 10/1: 4002020: Chsd ldrs, btn 4f out.	17	0a
2249}	**TODLEA** 163 [9] J A Osborne 3-9-11 (79) I Mongan 14/1: 41000: Al bhd, breathing prob reported, abs.	dist	0a
13 Ran	2m 1.07 (2.87) Owner Mrs Jean Turpin		Trained at Sheriff Hutton

---

128

9.00 Allweather-Racing Com Selling Stakes 3yo+ (G)
£2107 £602 £301   **1m100y f/sand rnd**   **Going 44**   **-34 Slow**   Stalls Inside

47*	**PUPS PRIDE** 12 [10] Mrs N Macaulay 6-9-4 vis (55) Lisa Jones (3) 100/30: 5160011: Rear, hdwy to lead ins last, drvn out:		**60a**
2307}	**FORTY FORTE** 16 [9] Miss S J Wilton 7-9-4 (58) N Callan 9/1: 4000002: Led till ins last, hung right & onepace:	1½	56a
92	**HURRICANE COAST** 4 [1] P A Blockley 4-9-4 (55) G Parkin 11/4 FAV: 3020123: Held up, rdn & hdwy to chall dist, no extra ins last:	hd	55a
66*	**REPEAT** 10 [7] Miss Gay Kelleway 3-9-2 (52) A Culhane 5/1: 3000314: Mid-div, kept on wide for press, not able to chall:	1	53a
46	**NITE OWL FIZZ** 12 [13] J O'Reilly 5-9-4 (55) J D O'Reilly (7) 12/1: 0560005: Chsd ldr 7f out, no extra when hmpd ins last:	½	52a
4731}	**JOUVERT** 46 [4] R Hannon 3-8-11 (49) P Gallagher (7) 22/1: 0-000056: Prom, wknd qckly fnl 1f, abs.	7	33a
5021}	**MEHMAAS** 23 [6] R E Barr 7-8-13 vis (51) Dean McKeown 13/2: 0535007: Mid-div, strugg fnl 2f:	2	29a
23	**EASY BREEZE** 19 [2] J M Bradley 3-8-11 P Fitzsimons 100/1: 008: Al bhd.	14	1a
1540}	**HARRY THE HOOVER** 197 [3] M J Gingell 3-8-11 (78) Dane O'Neill 10/1: 01-09: Slow away & al bhd, saddle slipped.	2	0
4938}	**BONTADINI** 31 [8] D Morris 4-8-13 (60) M Tebbutt 16/1: 2000000: Sn bhd.	shd	0
89	**TADZIO** 5 [5] M J Gingell 4-8-13 VIS B Reilly (5) 50/1: 00: V slowly away & t.o. halfway:	dist	0
11 Ran	1m 52.9 (6.7) Owner West Indies Capital Company Li		Trained at Melton Mowbray

---

129

9.30 Bet Direct Football Cashbacks Handicap Stakes Fillies 3yo+ 0-65 (F)   [64]
£2072 £592 £296   **7f f/sand rnd**   **Going 44**   **-14 Slow**   Stalls Outside

4692}	**BINT MAKBUL** 48 [7] R Hannon 4-9-3 (53) Dane O'Neill 9/4 FAV: 4603231: Trkd ldrs, led over 2f out, rdn out:		**52a**
20	**DUO LEONI** 16 [6] R M Beckett 3-9-9 (60) M Tebbutt 9/1: 3021502: Mid-div, rdn & chsd wnr 2f out, no extra ins last, op 6/1:	2	54a
85	**NAJAABA** 5 [8] Miss J Feilden 3-9-6 (57) Lisa Jones (3) 12/1: 660-043: Held up, rdn & kept on fnl 2f, not able to chall:	¾	49a
30	**KOMENA** 15 [3] J W Payne 5-9-0 (50) N Callan 9/2: 0230524: Mid-div, kept on onepace.	1¾	38a
38	**MISS CHAMPERS** 14 [2] P D Evans 3-9-11 (62) K D Maher (7) 12/1: 0603005: Led after 2f till over 2f out, no extra.	1½	47a
2	**SPARK UP** 19 [9] J W Unett 3-9-13 bl (64) M Henry 7/2: 0406102: Held up, only mod late prog:	2½	44a
85	**LADY NATILDA** 5 [4] D Haydn Jones 3-9-2 (53) Paul Eddery 16/1: 3045007: Led 2f, btn dist, quick reapp.	6	21a
4901}	**IVY MOON** 33 [11] B J Llewellyn 3-9-1 (52) R Havlin 14/1: 6103038: Prom wide till halfway.	3	14a
4342}	**LUNAR LEADER** 71 [5] M J Gingell 3-10-0 p (65) B Reilly (5) 20/1: 2120009: Slow away & al bhd, abs.	2	13a
1253}	**HISPANIOLA** 574 [10] M W Easterby 5-9-10 (60) Dale Gibson 40/1: 03230/0-0: Al bhd, long abs.	3	12a
4985}	**GUNNHILDR** 27 [12] P J Makin 3-9-9 vis (60) D Sweeney 22/1: 504000: Slowly away & sn struggling.	9	-6a
38	**POOKAS DAUGHTER** 14 [1] J M Bradley 3-9-3 (54) P Fitzsimons 33/1: 0420000: Prom early, sn bhd.	4	0
12 Ran	1m 30.27 (4.07) Owner Mr Malih L Al Basti		Trained at Marlborough

LINGFIELD Tuesday 02.12.03 Lefthand, V Sharp Track

Official Going STANDARD.

130
12.00 Chris Weatherly Retirement Classified Stakes Div 1 3yo+ 0-70 (E)
£2016 £576 £288   6f p/track rnd   Going 31   +06 Fast   Stalls Inside

4776}	**TARANAKI** 46 [1] P D Cundell 5-8-12 (70) S Whitworth 3/1: 1506101: Trk ldr, led dist, pushed clr, rdly:		75a
65	**SECOND MINISTER** 13 [2] D Flood 4-8-12 bl (50) P Doe 16/1: 04-00032: Led, rdn & hdd dist, kept on:	5	58a
23*	**PHRENOLOGIST** 19 [5] J R Fanshawe 3-8-12 (69) Dane O'Neill 3/1: 5613: Trkd ldrs, outpcd 2f out, kept on late for press:	¾	56a
50	**BYO** 14 [6] M Quinn 5-8-12 (67) F Norton 11/1: 1224004: Chsd ldr, no extra dist:	nk	55a
86	**THE GAY FOX** 8 [4] B G Powell 9-8-12 bl t (42) L Keniry (3) 100/1: 5253505: Dwelt, rear, not pace to chall.	1¼	51a
4949}	**TICKLE** 33 [3] P J Makin 5-8-9 VIS T (50) D Sweeney 66/1: 6-200506: Trkd ldrs, outpcd halfway:	shd	48a
50	**GEORGE STUBBS** 14 [9] N P Littmoden 5-8-12 bl (69) J P Guillambert (3) 6/1: 3230567: Sn pushed along & al outpcd.	1¾	46a
4701}	**TRIPTI** 51 [7] J J Bridger 3-8-9 (57) J F McDonald (5) 25/1: 0606048: Dwelt, al rear & outpcd:	shd	43a
121*	**MISTRAL SKY** 3 [8] Mrs S A Liddiard 4-9-4 vis (68) M Fenton 11/4 FAV: 4110019: Rear, struggling halfway:	hd	51a
	RICHIE RICH 98 [11] Jarlath Fahey 8-8-12 (55) W M Lordan 50/1: 03000P0: Al bhd:	5	30a
4691}	**WALKER BAY** 51 [10] J C Fox 5-8-9 BL (48) R Smith 66/1: 000-0240: Dwelt, wide, al rear:	1¼	23a
11 Ran	1m 11.89 (1.49) Owner Mr Eric Evers		Trained at Compton

131
12.30 Allweather-Racing Com Handicap Stakes Div 1 3yo+ 0-75 (E)   [75]
£2331 £666 £333   1m p/track rnd   Going 31   -01 Slow   Stalls Outside

5017}	**LOBOS** 26 [8] G L Moore 4-9-1 (62) I Mongan 4/1: 0000101: Rear, hdwy wide 3f out, rdn & chall dist, drvn & narrow lead ins last, all out:		67a
4467}	**SEWMORE CHARACTER** 67 [1] M Blanshard 3-9-10 (72) D Sweeney 25/1: 02-40462: Held up, hdwy 3f out, drvn & narrow lead dist, hdd ins last, just held:	hd	76a
122	**COLLEGE DELINQUENT** 3 [5] K Bell 4-9-5 t (66) S Whitworth 7/1: 5003303: Rear, hdwy when short of room over 1f out, keeping on onepace when short of room cl-home:	1¼	67a
44	**BLUE TROJAN** 15 [12] S Kirk 3-9-8 (70) J F Egan 11/2: 0301564: Trkd ldrs wide, kept on onepace:	1¾	67a
99	**CAPTAIN DARLING** 7 [10] R M H Cowell 3-9-4 (66) B Reilly (5) 8/1: 5450455: Keen & cl-up, ch dist, no extra.	1	61a
22	**TROUSERS** 19 [2] Andrew Reid 4-9-13 (74) Dane O'Neill 100/30 FAV: 0-032136: Led, hdd dist, no extra:	1	67a
3839}	**CAPTAIN GINGER** 100 [7] H Morrison 3-9-10 (72) L Fletcher (5) 8/1: 0-003407: Keen early, held up, no impress fnl 2f:	1¾	62a
4910}	**SUPERCHIEF** 36 [6] Miss B Sanders 8-9-4 bl t (65) E Ahern 14/1: 4020008: Keen & trkd ldrs, eff 2f out, sn no extra.	shd	55a
60	**BANUTAN** 13 [4] K R Burke 3-8-12 (60) J Fanning 25/1: 3060009: Trkd ldrs trav well, wknd qckly dist.	1½	47a
50	**HADATH** 14 [3] B G Powell 6-9-7 (68) L Keniry (3) 10/1: 2600530: Rear, no ch fnl 3f:	5	46a
3404}	**LEONOR DE SOTO** 118 [11] J R Best 3-8-11 (59) N Pollard 40/1: 1146600: Prom 4f:	½	36a
11 Ran	1m 38.75 (2.55) Owner The Winning Hand		Trained at Brighton

132
1.00 Bet Direct No Q On 08000 93 66 93 Nursery Handicap Stakes 2yo 0-85 (E)   [91]
£2342 £669 £335   1m p/track rnd   Going 31   -01 Slow   Stalls Outside

15	**ANUVASTEEL** 20 [8] N A Callaghan 2-8-13 (76) W Ryan 2/1 FAV: 5150051: Held up, hdwy when briefly no room over 2f out, rdn to lead ins, styd on strongly:		85a
112	**LITTLE EYE** 4 [5] J R Best 2-8-2 2ow (63) N Pollard 5/1: 4000422: Trkd ldrs, rdn & chall dist, not pace of wnr:	1½	70a
3841*}	**MOUNTCHARGE** 100 [11] C N Allen 2-9-2 (79) G Carter 9/2: 0613: Rear, drvn & kept on fnl 2f, not pace of wnr:	1	82a
54*	**FREAK OCCURENCE** 14 [1] Miss E C Lavelle 2-9-7 (84) J F McDonald (5) 3/1: 0004114: Led, rdn & hdd ins last, no extra:	nk	86a
52	**JOMUS** 14 [2] L Montague Hall 2-8-1 1oh 3ow (60) C Cogan 16/1: 4002005: Dwelt & rear, only mod prog:	6	55a
63	**WARES HOME** 13 [9] K R Burke 2-8-7 (70) D Sweeney 40/1: 3210006: Rear, only mod prog, no danger.	½	60a
4863}	**TURNBERRY** 40 [6] J W Hills 2-8-2 BL (65) S Whitworth 40/1: 00007: Trkd ldrs, no impress fnl 2f:	shd	55a
112	**CHUBBES** 4 [3] M C Pipe 2-9-1 vis (78) Dane O'Neill 7/1: 0614238: Cl-up till 2f out, sn btn/eased, qck reapp.	nk	67a
29	**PARK AVE PRINCESS** 18 [4] N P Littmoden 2-7-12 3oh (58) J Bramhill 16/1: 1000469: Held up wide, no ch fnl 2f.	¾	49a
4651}	**RUMOUR MILL** 55 [7] N E Berry 2-8-5 (68) M Savage (5) 33/1: 0000: Chsd ldrs 5f:	3	50a
10 Ran	1m 38.79 (2.59) Owner Tipp-Ex Rapid Racing		Trained at Newmarket

133
1.30 Chris Weatherly Retirement Classified Stakes Div 2 3yo+ 0-70 (E)
£2016 £576 £288   6f p/track rnd   Going 31   -04 Slow   Stalls Inside

20	**RIPPLE EFFECT** 19 [4] C A Dwyer 3-8-9 t (70) B Reilly (5) 4/1: 3415301: Chsd ldr halfway, led dist & rdly asserted for press:		67a
1122}	**ROYAL FASHION** 227 [5] Miss S West 3-8-9 (65) N Chalmers (5) 9/1: 0360-302: Dwelt, sn chsd ldrs, styd on wide for press, no ch with wnr:	2½	57a
3005}	**NIGHT CAP** 136 [6] T D McCarthy 4-8-12 (47) J P Guillambert (3) 16/1: 0-005003: Keen & led, hung right & hdd dist, no extra:	¾	58a
50*	**I WISH** 14 [3] M Madgwick 5-8-9 (65) L Keniry (3) 7/2: 0000614: Chsd ldr, onepace dist:	¾	53a
4780}	**AINTNECESSARILYSO** 46 [8] N E Berry 5-8-12 (42) M Savage (5) 66/1: 0003005: Chsd ldrs 4f:	1½	51a
3050}	**KILMEENA STAR** 134 [10] J C Fox 5-8-12 (39) Dane O'Neill 66/1: 0030306: Bhd, switched & rdn/late prog.	shd	51a
113	**DUNEDIN RASCAL** 4 [2] E A Wheeler 6-8-12 bl (70) S Whitworth 7/2: 0000047: Rear, drvn & no prog dist.	½	49a
4692}	**ONEFORTHEBOYS** 51 [7] D Flood 4-8-12 (36) P Doe 33/1: 0-000608: Dwelt, al outpcd:	shd	49a
121	**FULVIO** 3 [9] Jamie Poulton 3-8-12 vis (70) I Mongan 11/4 FAV: 6650049: Trkd ldrs wide, btn dist:	½	47a
4815}	**CALENDAR GIRL** 43 [1] P J Makin 3-8-9 (48) D Sweeney 20/1: 3500: Chsd ldrs till 2f out.	nk	40a
10 Ran	1m 12.48 (2.08) Owner Miss Lilo Blum		Trained at Newmarket

134
2.00 Littlewoods Bet Direct Rated Stakes Showcase Handicap 3yo+ 0-95 (C)   [97]
£6287 £2385 £1192 £542   1m2f p/track   Going 31   -42 Slow   Stalls Inside

80*	**STAR OF NORMANDIE** 10 [5] G G Margarson 4-8-12 (81) B Reilly (5) 9/1: 0031211: Trkd ldrs, rdn to lead well in last:		85a
26	**ALRAFID** 19 [4] G L Moore 4-9-0 (83) S Whitworth 5/1 JT FAV: 1062242: Keen, trkd ldrs over 3f out, rdn & narrow lead 2f out, hdd ins last, kept on:	nk	85a
4977	**ZONERGEM** 31 [1] Lady Herries 5-9-7 bl (90) M Tebbutt 16/1: 4003603: Mid-div, switched & styd on for press cl-home, nrst	hd	91a
4666}	**NORTHSIDE LODGE** 53 [2] P W Harris 5-9-0 (83) J Fanning 11/2: 0220404: Dictated pace 2f, remained handy, styd on for press:	nk	83a

26	J R STEVENSON 19 [14] M Wigham 7-8-7 (76) S W Kelly 8/1: 0042635: Held up, kept on late for press.		¾	75a
83	GIG HARBOR 10 [6] Miss E C Lavelle 4-9-2 (85) C Catlin 7/1: 0000626: Handy, dsptd lead 3f out, no extra ins last.		shd	84a
83	BRILLIANT RED 10 [11] Jamie Poulton 10-9-6 t (89) I Mongan 16/1: 4324407: Dwelt, held up, mod prog for press.		½	87a
83	LINNING WINE 10 [10] B G Powell 7-9-7 (90) L Keniry (3) 20/1: 0200008: Held up, eff wide, not able to chall.		hd	87a
4897}	REJUVENATE 38 [12] Mrs A J Perrett 3-8-13 (85) Dane O'Neill 5/1 JT FAV: 4-139: Led after 2f, hdd dist & wknd.		nk	81a
26*	DOWER HOUSE 19 [8] Andrew Turnell 8-8-13 (82) D Corby (3) 12/1: 0620310: Keen & cl-up, no impress dist.		shd	78a
83	GALLANT BOY 10 [9] P D Evans 4-8-10 t (79) E Ahern 10/1: 4100050: Keen & held up, eff wide, no impress.		½	74a
3945}	BLUE PATRICK 96 [13] J M P Eustace 3-9-2 (88) J Tate 40/1: 05-40160: Dwelt, rear, no impress, abs, gldd.		nk	82a
26	LIBERTY ROYAL 19 [3] P J Makin 4-8-7 (76) D Sweeney 16/1: 60-04000: Keen mid-div, no impress fnl 2f.		¾	69a
13 Ran	2m 10.12 (7.32) Owner Norcroft Park Stud			Trained at Newmarket

2.30 Betdirect Co Uk Novice Stakes 2yo **(D)**
£3178 £908 £454   6f p/track rnd   Going 31   -15 Slow   Stalls Inside

	MISSUS LINKS [13] R Hannon 2-8-3 R Smith 11/4 FAV: 1: Led/dsptd lead, narrowly asserted fnl 1f:			72a
4947}	SWEETEST REVENGE 33 [9] M D I Usher 2-9-0 (78) A Daly 4/1: 3201042: Led/dsptd lead, narrowly hdd dist, kept on for press:		¾	80a
13	DANDOUCE 20 [2] S L Keightley 2-8-7 A Culhane 5/1: 423: Trkd ldrs, outpcd over 2f out, kept on for press ins last:		nk	72a
4558}	IMPERIUM 61 [3] B J Meehan 2-8-12 (79) J F Egan 7/1: 3462004: Trkd ldrs when hmpd after 1f, switched for eff when hung dist, not pace to chall:		hd	76a
63*	MUY BIEN 13 [14] J R Jenkins 2-9-2 vis (75) S W Kelly 10/1: 2150015: Mid-div, not pace to chall:		1½	75a
3932}	BETTALATEHANNEVER 96 [6] S Dow 2-8-12 Dane O'Neill 33/1: 06: Rear, wide, late gains:		½	69a
4754}	ORO VERDE 48 [4] R Hannon 2-9-5 (91) P Gallagher (7) 7/2: 4203347: Cl-up, btn dist:		hd	75a
5013}	PRENUP 26 [7] L M Cumani 2-8-7 D Corby (3) 33/1: 508: Mid-div, outpcd fnl 2f.		1¼	59a
21	SOLO SOLE 19 [8] L M Cumani 2-8-12 C Catlin 40/1: 609: Mid-div, outpcd halfway:		1¼	60a
	EMBASSY SWEETS [5] P F I Cole 2-8-3 J F McDonald (5) 14/1: 0: Rear, al outpcd:		1	48a
	BACKLASH [1] A W Carroll 2-8-3 S Whitworth 50/1: 0: Slowly away on debut, al rear.		1	45a
11 Ran	1m 13.15 (2.75) Owner Coriolan Partnership II			Trained at Marlborough

3.00 Allweather-Racing Com Handicap Stakes Div 2 3yo+ 0-75 **(E)**   **[75]**
£2331 £666 £333   1m p/track rnd   Going 31   -15 Slow   Stalls Outside

5030}	TOPTON 24 [1] P Howling 9-9-5 bl (66) R Winston 10/1: 4050601: Dwelt, sn mid-div, rdn to lead well in last:			72a
4944}	TOURMALET 34 [8] M R Channon 3-9-10 (72) A Culhane 9/2: 3506202: Handy, led over 1f out, no extra when hdd well ins		1	74a
41	HEIDELBURG 15 [11] S Kirk 3-9-3 (65) J F Egan 11/2: 4060623: Rear, drvn & kept on late, not reach front pair:		¾	65a
26	TROPICAL CORAL 19 [2] C Tinkler 3-9-12 (74) T Quinn 8/1: 5014504: Trkd ldrs, outpcd 2f out, kept on onepace:		1	73a
4207}	LEARNED LAD 81 [6] Jamie Poulton 5-9-4 (65) I Mongan 7/1: 4020005: Led till over 1f out, no extra:		1	62a
17	RESONATE 20 [10] A G Newcombe 5-8-10 (57) Dane O'Neill 7/2 FAV: 3152006: Dwelt & rear, switched & kept on late under hands & heels, nrst fin:		nk	58a
40	SCOTTISH RIVER 17 [3] M D I Usher 4-9-1 (62) A Daly 20/1: 0550007: Keen & cl-up, btn dist.		shd	58a
93	KANZ WOOD 7 [12] A W Carroll 7-9-4 (65) S Whitworth 40/1: 4530008: Rear, mod prog under hands & heels.		1	59a
5029}	OH SO ROSIE 25 [9] J S Moore 3-8-12 p (60) L Keniry (3) 10/1: 2064029: Chsd ldrs, btn over 1f out.		1¾	51a
2325}	SNUKI 164 [5] G L Moore 4-9-7 (68) R Brisland 9/1: 0620000: Mid-div, outpcd fnl 3f, abs.		½	58a
4969}	MADDIES A JEM 31 [7] J R Jenkins 3-9-6 (68) S W Kelly 12/1: 0203460: Prom, wknd qckly 2f out:		2½	53a
11 Ran	1m 39.91 (3.71) Owner Mr Liam Sheridan			Trained at Newmarket

3.30 Fred Gibson Memorial Amateur Riders' Handicap Stakes 3yo+ 0-65 **(F)**   **[44]**
£2093 £598 £299   2m p/track   Going 31   -24 Slow   Stalls Inside

4439}	WAVERLEY ROAD 68 [5] M Madgwick 6-9-11 (41) Mr B King (5) 10/1: 0006051: Trkd ldrs, led dist, rdn out:			44a
89*	BUCKS 8 [13] D K Ivory 6-11-12 5ex (70) Mr Michael Murphy (3) 9/4 FAV: 00-35212: Held up, short of room 6f out & again 4f out, kept on, not rch wnr:		1½	71a
125	MYSTERIUM 3 [9] N P Littmoden 9-9-10 vis (40) Mrs Emma Littmoden (3) 8/1: 5003333: Held up, hdwy & led 6f out, sn qcknd clr, hdd dist, no extra:		nk	40a
107	ASTROMANCER 6 [6] M H Tompkins 3-10-2 (54) Mr S Warren 5/1: 0P50244: Chsd ldr, rdn & kept on onepace fnl 2f:		1¾	52a
810}	TOMMY CARSON 617 [8] Jamie Poulton 8-9-8 (38) Miss Kelly Harrison (5) 33/1: 0/020/26-5: Rear, mod gains, abs.		11	27a
103	LANDESCENT 6 [11] M Quinn 3-10-3 vis (55) Mr G Bartley (7) 16/1: 4004266: Rear, only mod prog, qck reapp.		1	43a
67	HIGH JINKS 13 [10] R N Bevis 8-9-9 2ow (37) Mr S Dobson 8/1: 04550-57: Chsd ldrs, btn 3f out.		½	26a
103	RAHEEL 6 [1] P Mitchell 3-10-2 t (54) Mr S Walker 4/1: 6300028: Dwelt, hdwy to chase ldr 3f out, sn wknd.		½	40a
56	PEPPERSHOT 14 [2] G P Enright 3-10-4 (56) Mr J Pemberton (7) 50/1: 5400609: Dwelt & al bhd.		¾	41a
897}	ALKA INTERNATIONAL 964 [3] Mrs P Townsley 11-9-10 (40) Mrs C Thompson (5) 25/1: 5/////5/-: Chsd ldr 3f, sn wknd.		2½	23a
18	CHARMANTE FEMME 20 [7] P D Evans 5-10-2 (46) Miss E Folkes (3) 10/1: 5410360: Led & sn clr, hdd 6f out.		12	20a
3049}	COCTAIL LADY 134 [14] B W Duke 3-9-7 t (45) Mr Ashlee Price (5) 25/1: 0000000: Chsd ldrs 10f:		1	18a
4515}	PRINCE DU SOLEIL 64 [12] J R Jenkins 7-9-12 (42) Mr N Soares (7) 25/1: 63-00000: Al bhd, t.o.:		dist	0
13 Ran	3m 28.84 (8.84) Owner All Four Corners			Trained at Denmead

Official Going Standard

1.00 Littlewoodspoker Com Apprentice Handicap Stakes 3yo+ 0-75 **(E)**   **[71]**
£2023 £578 £289   1m4f f/sand   Going 32   -09 Slow   Stalls Inside

60	DUBAI DREAMS 14 [8] M J Polglase 3-8-6 vis (54) K Ghunowa (10) 16/1: 4600001: Made all, rdn clr over 1f out, held on all out cl-home:			60a
2795}	MAJLIS 146 [2] R M H Cowell 6-9-1 (58) P Makin 10/1: 34//-05002: Rear, rdn & hdwy wide over 3f out, styd on well for press,		nk	63a

just failed:
97 **DIGGER 8** [10] Miss Gay Kelleway 4-9-13 t (70) P Mathers 6/5 FAV: 2002523: In tch travelling well, shaken up & onepace for press over 1f out: ¾ **74a**
5001} **COURT OF APPEAL 29** [1] B Ellison 6-9-13 t (70) Rory Moore 9/2: 0464024: Trkd ldrs, no impress fnl 2f. *5* **67a**
56 **MOST SAUCY 15** [5] I A Wood 7-10-0 (71) Saleem Golam (5) 7/1: 2003555: Held up, rdn & no impress over 1f out. *nk* **67a**
72 **PHANTOM STOCK 12** [4] W Jarvis 3-8-1 (49) D Tudhope 8/1: 000-06: Trkd ldrs, btn 2f out. *1¼* **43a**
56 **SILVER PROPHET 15** [9] M R Bosley 4-9-9 (66) L Treadwell 16/1: 0043007: Dwelt, held up wide, no dngr. *1½* **58a**
304} **BID SPOTTER 335** [6] Mrs Lucinda Featherstone 4-8-2 (45) S Yourston (5) 20/1: 06204-08: Chsd wnr, btn over 2f out: ¾ **36a**
34 **INTENSITY 19** [3] P A Blockley 7-9-3 (60) Derek Nolan (10) 33/1: 4-602009: Trkd ldrs, btn over 2f out. *10* **39a**
8 **SHOW ME THE LOLLY 23** [7] P J McBride 3-8-6 (54) Dean Williams (5) 40/1: 0500: Chsd ldrs, strugg halfway. *19* **0**
10 Ran 2m 39.22 (4.92) Owner APB Racing Trained at Newark

139 1.30 Free #25 Bonus @ Littlewoodspoker Com Selling Stakes 2yo (G)
£2016 £576 £288 **5f f/sand str** **Going 32** **Inapplicab** Stalls Stands Side

4636} **ALIZAR 57** [7] M J Polglase 2-8-7 (45) L Fletcher (3) 8/1: 4406361: Handy & led over 1f out, rdn clr from dist: **58a**
73 **PHILLY DEE 12** [8] J Jay 2-8-8 1ow (47) A Culhane 7/2: 2660432: Trkd ldrs, outpcd halfway, rdn & kept on ins last: *3* **49a**
69 **BLUE MOON HITMAN 12** [9] A Berry 2-8-12 (53) F Norton 100/30: 2345463: Chsd ldrs, onepace dist. *1½* **48a**
69 **EMARADIA 12** [6] P D Evans 2-8-12 (54) Joanna Badger 5/1: 5623454: Chsd ldrs, no extra fnl 1f. *1* **45a**
87 **JOCKS BOY 9** [10] P R Wood 2-8-12 A Nicholls 66/1: 0005: Dwelt, outpcd, nrst fin: *1¾* **40a**
63 **ARE YOU THERE 14** [2] T D Barron 2-8-12 VIS (57) P Makin (7) 9/4 FAV: 1100006: Sn pushed along, btn dist, vis. *shd* **40a**
3486} **COLEORTON PRINCE 116** [5] K A Ryan 2-8-12 R Winston 20/1: 00007: Led till over 1f out, fdd, 4 month abs. *1½* **35a**
69 **DESERT LIGHT 12** [4] D Shaw 2-8-12 (23) M Fenton 66/1: 00008: Prom till halfway, sn struggling. *shd* **35a**
4887} **KATZ PYJAMAS 39** [3] Mrs A Duffield 2-8-7 (42) G Duffield 20/1: 6000009: Al outpcd. *½* **28a**
4917} **SHAMONE 36** [1] H A McWilliams 2-8-12 P (38) J Fanning 66/1: 00P00: Went left start, chsd ldrs till halfway. *8* **13a**
10 Ran 59.98 Owner Mr Paul J Dixon Trained at Newark

140 2.00 Littlewoodspoker Com Handicap Stakes 3yo+ 0-85 (D) [80]
£3290 £940 £470 **2m f/sand** **Going 32** **-45 Slow** Stalls Inside

48* **SNOWS RIDE 16** [7] W R Muir 3-9-9 (83) I Mongan 7/4 FAV: 5215011: Cl up, led over 2f out, rdn & duelled with rnr-up, narrowly asserted for press: **93a**
3502} **BID FOR FAME 116** [2] N J Henderson 6-10-0 (80) T Quinn 7/2: 11-20062: Al prom & duelled with wnr from over 2f out, just held cl-home: *nk* **89a**
90 **GLORY QUEST 9** [5] Miss Gay Kelleway 6-9-9 (75) A Culhane 9/2: 6545223: In tch, rdn & no impress on front pair fnl 3f: *12* **74a**
83 **COMPLETE CIRCLE 11** [8] P W D'Arcy 3-9-8 e (82) Paul Eddery 14/1: 0045504: Chsd ldrs till 3f out. *6* **75a**
127 **NOWELL HOUSE 4** [4] M W Easterby 7-9-11 (77) Dale Gibson 14/1: 3-514165: Held up, rdn & btn 3f out: *7* **63a**
67 **KAGOSHIMA 14** [3] J R Norton 8-7-12 7oh vis (43) J F McDonald (5) 50/1: 060-0006: Chsd ldrs 5f out, sn struggling. *3½* **33a**
89 **CALCAR 9** [6] Mrs S Lamyman 3-7-12 14oh (44) C Catlin 80/1: 2050057: Led till over 5f out, sn btn. *¾* **40a**
357} **REBELLE 327** [1] P Bowen 4-8-11 (63) S Whitworth 7/2: 5132-128: Trkd ldrs, drvn & btn 3f out: *3* **42a**
8 Ran 3m 38.36 (12.36) Owner The Parkside Partnership Trained at Lambourn

141 2.30 Littlewoods Bet Direct Stakes Handicap 3yo+ 0-95 (C) [92]
£5532 £1702 £851 £426 **1m f/sand rnd** **Going 32** **+06 Fast** Stalls Inside

44* **CARDINAL VENTURE 16** [5] K A Ryan 5-10-0 (92) R Winston 11/4 FAV: 2200111: Made all & rdn clr over 1f out, held on well for press: **97a**
44 **TE QUIERO GB 16** [8] Miss Gay Kelleway 5-10-0 t (92) M Fenton 8/1: 1-201052: Trkd ldrs, eff 2f out, kept on: *½* **95a**
5029} **COOL TEMPER 26** [9] P F I Cole 7-8-13 t (77) J Fanning 8/1: 1101403: Rdn rear, switched wide & styd on well for press ins last, nrst fin: *½* **79a**
97 **CRUSOE 8** [10] A Sadik 6-8-2 bl (66) J F McDonald (5) 16/1: 1053504: Chsd ldrs, rdn & onepace fnl 2f: *2* **64a**
93 **BRANDY COVE 8** [3] B Smart 6-8-2 (66) R Ffrench 5/1: 1321045: Held up, eff 3f out, no prog dist. *2* **60a**
705} **PENWELL HILL 279** [4] T D Barron 4-8-5 (69) D Mernagh 7/1: 2111346: Chsd ldrs, btn over 2f out: *2* **59a**
44 **DEL MAR SUNSET 16** [1] W J Haggas 4-9-8 (86) A Culhane 14/1: 4322007: Prom, drvn & btn 2f out. *¾* **75a**
93 **BARZAK 8** [12] S R Bowring 3-8-3 P (68) J Bramhill 7/1: 0000108: Chsd ldrs wide 6f: *5* **47a**
60 **LUCAYAN MONARCH 14** [7] P A Blockley 5-7-12 p (62) S Yourston (7) 50/1: 3600009: Dwelt & al bhd. *½* **40a**
106 **POWER BIRD 7** [11] D Flood 3-8-13 (78) P Doe 14/1: 0000500: Al bhd. *8* **42a**
2 **COUNTYKAT 23** [6] K R Burke 3-8-12 (77) I Mongan 11/1: 2-553630: Sn struggling: *2½* **36a**
2255} **PRIDE OF KINLOCH 167** [2] J Hetherton 3-8-0 1oh 2ow (62) C Catlin 40/1: 6340500: Chsd ldrs, struggalfway, abs. *9* **9a**
12 Ran 1m 41.5 (2.1) Owner Mr Tony Fawcett Trained at Hambleton

142 3.00 Royal Flush Jackpot @ Littlewoodspoker Com Claiming Stakes 3yo+ (F)
£2044 £584 £292 **1m3f f/sand** **Going 32** **-14 Slow** Stalls Inside

34* **MR MISCHIEF 19** [2] P C Haslam 3-9-9 (84) Rory Moore (7) 8/13 FAV: 0050211: Trkd ldrs, hdwy halfway, rdn clr fnl 2f: **83a**
114 **ALS ALIBI 5** [3] W R Muir 10-8-7 (41) F Norton 7/2: 3040022: In tch, rdn to chase wnr fnl 2f, onepace: *3* **57a**
MOON SHOT 398 [4] A G Juckes 7-9-13 (64) V Slattery 16/1: 004251-3: Trkd ldrs, ch 3f out, sn rdn & no impress: *4* **70a**
86 **SPANISH STAR 9** [5] Mrs N Macauley 6-8-13 (45) Joanna Badger 20/1: 5340004: Held up, rdn & no impress fnl 3f: *4* **50a**
4802} **TURFTANZER 46** [6] Don Enrico Incisa 4-9-7 (41) Kim Tinkler 66/1: 21600-05: Led till halfway, btn 3f out, abs. *3½* **54a**
4678] **BROUGHTON MELODY 754** [1] W J Musson 4-8-10 M Fenton 33/1: 00/-6: Mid-div, struggling fnl 4f, long abs. *nk* **42a**
4802} **BEHAN 46** [7] A Crook 4-8-7 bl (27) V Halliday 50/1: 4030067: Prom, rdn & struggling halfway, jumps fit. *16* **17a**
3127} **PORT MORENO 132** [10] J G M O'Shea 3-8-6 1ow vis (48) R Havlin 14/1: 2140068: Chsd ldrs till halfway: *¾* **19a**
413} **BY ALL MEN 319** [8] P A Blockley 3-9-5 Derek Nolan (7) 10/1: 0-09: Held up, struggling fnl 3f, long abs. *1½* **30a**
4828} **MAWHOOB 43** [9] Mrs N Macauley 5-8-9 vis (47) Steven Harrison (7) 66/1: 6-100000: In tch, btn 5f out, abs. *4* **10a**
10 Ran 2m 26.35 (5.05) Owner Middleham Park Racing Trained at Middleham

SOUTHWELL Wednesday 03.12.03 Lefthand, Sharp, Oval Track

143 **3.30 Littlewoodscasino Com Maiden Stakes 3yo+ (D)**
£2240 £640 £320 **1m f/sand rnd** **Going 32** **+02 Fast** Stalls Inside

	TRANCE 147 [10] T D Barron 3-9-0 (75) D Mernagh 11/8 FAV: 00-02001: Trkd ldrs, hdwy wide to lead over 2f out & sn rdn clr:		**75a**
3360}	**CHESNUT RIPPLE 121** [6] D Shaw 4-8-10 (53) R Havlin 4/1: 6040662: Trkd ldrs, rdn & chsd wnr fnl 2f, sn held:	6	**51a**
4456}	**PACIFIC OCEAN 68** [2] Mrs S A Liddiard 4-9-1 T (46) F Norton 9/1: 0-566653: Trkd ldrs, hmpd after 2f, switched & kept on onepace fnl 2f:	2½	**51a**
4460}	**PETROLERO 68** [4] Mrs S A Liddiard 4-9-1 t (41) C Catlin 33/1: 00-00004: Keen & chsd ldrs, no impress fnl 2f:	1	**49a**
	DEVIOUS PADDY 49 [1] N Tinkler 3-9-0 (76) Kim Tinkler 11/1: 206305: Outpcd, al bhd, 7 wk abs, ex-Irish.	13	**28a**
3365}	**MIDDLEHAM PARK 121** [12] P C Haslam 3-9-0 (65) L Enstone (3) 4/1: 32006: Handy & led over 3f out, hdd over 2f out, sn btn, abs.	2½	**23a**
3090}	**QUIDDITCH 133** [11] P Bowen 3-8-9 S Whitworth 50/1: 007: Led till over 3f out, sn wknd, 4 month abs.	1½	**15a**
96	**MOONGLADE 8** [3] Miss J Feilden 3-8-9 t Paul Eddery 100/1: 00008: Prom, btn 2f out.	2½	**10a**
38	**CHIASSO 18** [7] H Morrison 3-8-9 (52) L Fletcher (3) 13/2: 400409: Mid-div, struggling from halfway:	4	**3a**
96	**SAWAH 8** [5] D Shaw 3-9-0 J Fanning 66/1: 000: Dwelt & al bhd.	3½	**2a**

10 Ran 1m 41.83 (2.43) Owner Mr Nigel Shields Trained at Thirsk

LINGFIELD Saturday 06.12.03 Lefthand, V Sharp Track

Official Going Standard

144 **11.55 Bet Direct In Running Sky Text 293 Handicap Stakes Div 1 3yo+ 0-65 (F)** **[65]**
£2100 £600 £300 **7f p/track rnd** **Going 44** **-13 Slow** Stalls Inside

123	**COLD CLIMATE 7** [10] Bob Jones 8-9-7 (58) F Norton 10/1: 4051521: Chsd ldrs, led ins last & pulled clr under hands & heels:		**67a**
5021*}	**HE WHO DARES 30** [9] A W Carroll 5-9-4 (55) M Fenton 10/1: 0-401012: Dwelt, rear, no room over 1f out, styd on well ins last, not threaten wnr:	1½	**59a**
117	**INISTRAHULL ISLAND 7** [14] M H Tompkins 3-9-8 (59) J Fanning 7/1: 0260423: Prom, rdn & chsd wnr ins last, no impress nr fin:	¾	**62a**
123	**ITS ECCO BOY 7** [16] P Howling 5-9-3 (54) R Winston 14/1: 3500364: Mid-div, kept on for press fnl 2f, no dngr:	1¼	**54a**
5029}	**WALTZING WIZARD 29** [1] A Berry 4-9-1 (52) P Bradley (5) 50/1: 0-000605: Led, rdn & hdd ins last, no extra.	¾	**51a**
4427}	**SOCIAL CONTRACT 73** [2] S Dow 6-9-3 (54) Paul Eddery 25/1: 6602006: Prom, no extra dist:	shd	**52a**
123*	**CHATEAU NICOL 7** [15] B G Powell 4-10-9 vis (74) A Hindley (7) 5/1 FAV: 0000117: Chsd ldrs wide, not able to chall.	½	**72a**
123	**MR BOUNTIFUL 7** [6] M Dods 5-9-12 (63) S W Kelly 8/1: 0641238: Dwelt, chsd ldrs, btn dist:	nk	**60a**
117	**KINSMAN 7** [8] T D McCarthy 6-9-2 p (53) J P Guillambert (3) 20/1: 5550069: Mid-div, no impress dist.	½	**49a**
136	**HEIDELBURG 4** [3] S Kirk 3-10-0 (65) J F McDonald (5) 13/2: 0606230: Rear, nvr able to chall:	nk	**60a**
117	**A WOMAN IN LOVE 7** [7] Miss B Sanders 4-9-4 (55) I Mongan 9/1: 5425640: Dwelt & keen rear, nvr a factor.	¾	**49a**
121	**PARK STAR 7** [11] D Shaw 3-9-10 (61) R Havlin 33/1: 1000560: Chsd ldrs 5f.	½	**54a**
117*	**PANTS 7** [13] Andrew Reid 4-9-8 (59) A Nicholls 16/1: 0400310: Wide, rear, nvr a factor:	1¾	**49a**
4910}	**ROY MCAVOY 40** [4] Mrs G Harvey 5-10-0 (65) E Ahern 50/1: 0600000: Dwelt, al rear:	1	**53a**
50	**TAIYO 18** [12] J W Payne 3-9-3 (54) T Quinn 16/1: 3-50560: Prom 5f.	¾	**41a**
20	**FOOLISH THOUGHT 23** [5] R A Fahey 3-9-11 (62) D Swift (7) 12/1: 0004040: Rear, no ch fnl 2f:	nk	**48a**

16 Ran 1m 26.8 (4.0) Owner The Cold Climate Partnership Trained at Newmarket

145 **12.25 Bet Direct On Channel 4 Page 613 Claiming Stakes Div 1 3yo+ (F)**
£2058 £588 £294 **1m p/track rnd** **Going 44** **-02 Slow** Stalls Outside

122	**BURGUNDY 7** [1] P Mitchell 6-8-12 (65) K Dalgleish 2/1 FAV: 0301501: Slow away, pushed along rear, swtchd wide & strong run for press to lead well ins last, going away:		**62a**
46	**GIVEMETHEMOONLIGHT 19** [3] L G Cottrell 4-8-5 (46) J F Egan 8/1: 4056032: Trkd ldrs, drvn to chall ins last, not pace of wnr:	1¼	**48a**
1657}	**SENOR MIRO 197** [5] J Akehurst 5-8-6 (50) C Catlin 11/1: 2/03-0043: In tch, hdwy to lead over 1f out, drvn & hdd well ins last, no extra:	1	**47a**
74	**FABRIAN 15** [12] D W P Arbuthnot 5-9-2 e (53) Dane O'Neill 6/1: 0300554: Cl-up, led 2f out till over 1f out, no extra:	½	**56a**
4815}	**ESTRELLA LEVANTE 47** [2] G L Moore 3-8-13 BL e (52) R Brisland 12/1: 504U055: Dwelt, rear, hmpd over 2f out, rallied late for press, no dngr:	2½	**49a**
5017}	**JAMESTOWN 30** [4] C Smith 6-9-0 (50) J Fanning 12/1: 5435406: Mid-div, no impress, clmd by M Polglase.	¾	**48a**
117	**GINGER ICE 7** [6] G G Margarson 3-8-3 P (47) N Pollard 66/1: 0-000007: Rear, eff 2f out, no impress on ldrs:	hd	**37a**
4767}	**ZHITOMIR 51** [8] M Dods 5-9-4 (52) S W Kelly 16/1: 6000008: Mid-div, rdn & no impress fnl 3f, abs.	½	**50a**
1410}	**ESPADA 212** [11] J A Osborne 7-9-8 (81) E Ahern 9/2: 40-61009: Led till 2f out, sn btn:	nk	**53a**
1279}	**SENOR TORAN 219** [7] P Burgoyne 3-8-13 (52) T Quinn 33/1: 40-5500: Chsd ldrs 5f, sn btn, abs/new yard.	1½	**42a**
5021}	**EUROLINK ZANTE 30** [10] T D McCarthy 7-9-4 P (49) J P Guillambert (3) 12/1: 6006060: Chsd ldrs 6f.	shd	**46a**

11 Ran 1m 39.88 (3.68) Owner Mr Nigel Shields Trained at Epsom

146 **12.55 Bet Direct No Q Demo 08000 837 888 Maiden Auction Stakes 2yo (E)**
£2258 £645 £323 **6f p/track rnd** **Going 44** **-39 Slow** Stalls Inside

19	**LA LANDONNE 23** [6] P M Phelan 2-8-2 F Norton 2/1: 351: Trkd ldr, led over 1f out, drvn out:		**65a**
4996}	**LADY KORRIANDA 32** [9] M J Wallace 2-8-4 2ow J Fanning 14/1: 002: Mid-div, eff wide from over 1f out, kept on well for press, just held:	nk	**66a**
	STARCROSS VENTURE [12] R A Fahey 2-8-2 T Hamilton 100/1: 3: Dwelt, rdn rear, kept on fnl 2f for press:	½	**62a**
4814}	**LYRICAL LADY 47** [5] Mrs A J Bowlby 2-8-5 E Ahern 20/1: 054: Prom, onepace dist, abs.	1	**62a**
	EX MILL LADY [1] John Berry 2-8-2 J F McDonald (5) 100/1: 5: Mid-div, not able to chall, debut.	1½	**54a**
2332}	**RED ROCKY 167** [4] J Gallagher 2-8-2 C Catlin 8/1: 56: Slow away, keen, eff wide, no impress:	½	**52a**
2038}	**VRISAKI 179** [13] Miss D Mountain 2-8-13 Dane O'Neill 25/1: 07: Prom till over 1f out, abs.	½	**61a**
5014}	**VELVET TOUCH 30** [2] J R Jenkins 2-8-2 J Mackay 6/1: 30638: Led till over 1f out, sn btn.	¾	**48a**

	MUGEBA [7] W J Musson 2-8-3 1ow Paul Eddery 50/1: 9: Slow away & rear, nvr a factor on debut.	nk	48a
4094}	MARKSGOLD 91 [8] K Bell 2-8-7 L Keniry (3) 33/1: 000: Chsd ldrs till halfway, abs.	½	50a
52	INTRODUCTION 18 [11] W J Musson 2-8-7 M Fenton 40/1: 000: Outpcd rear, no impress.	1	47a
	CHORUS BEAUTY [3] G Wragg 2-8-8 J F Egan 15/8 FAV: 0: Mid-div, no impress when hung left dist.	nk	47a
	MYSTIC MOON [14] J R Jenkins 2-8-2 A Mackay 50/1: 0: Dwelt, wide, nvr a factor on debut.	1½	36a
	CAPE TIA [10] R A Fahey 2-8-5 A Nicholls 25/1: 0: Dwelt & sn bhd on debut:	6	23a

14 Ran   1m 15.38 (4.98)   Owner Wood Hall Stud Limited   Trained at Shenley

---

147   1.25 Bet Direct No Q On 08000 93 66 93 Handicap Stakes 3yo+ 0-75 (E)   [75]
£2331 £666 £333   1m5f p/track   Going 44   -03 Slow   Stalls Inside

4951}	WESTERN 37 [7] J Akehurst 3-9-1 (68) T Quinn 16/1: 0005641: Mid-div, drpd towards rear & swtchd 3f out, rdn & styd on fnl 1f to lead line:		76a
56*	COLD TURKEY 18 [11] G L Moore 3-9-8 (75) H Poulton (7) 100/30 FAV: 0011112: Slow away, keen & held up, hdwy to lead ins last, shaken up nr fin & hdd line:	hd	82a
4984}	BIG BERTHA 34 [4] John Berry 5-9-4 (65) J F Egan 12/1: 0416623: Rear, styd on for press fnl 2f, nrst fin:	1	69a
118*	SEA HOLLY 7 [5] G G Margarson 3-9-6 (73) K Dalgleish 7/1: 3060214: Handy & led over 2f out, sn rdn clr, hdd ins last & no extra:	nk	77a
56	REMINISCENT 18 [2] R F Johnson Houghton 4-9-2 vis (63) Dane O'Neill 7/1: 5034535: Wide & rear, smooth prog 3f out, onepace for press over 1f out:	1	66a
2161}	EASTER OGIL 174 [9] Jane Southcombe 8-9-2 (63) V Slattery 40/1: 0414306: Mid-div, chsd wnr 1f out, no extra, abs.	2½	62a
83	MAYSTOCK 14 [6] G A Butler 3-9-0 vis (69) E Ahern 4/1: 3604147: In tch, chsd ldr 2f out till over 1f out, fdd:	1	67a
138	MOST SAUCY 3 [10] I A Wood 7-9-10 (71) S W Kelly 20/1: 0035558: Mid-div, btn 2f out:	1¼	67a
4876}	MUMBLING 43 [8] B G Powell 5-9-8 (69) L Keniry (3) 14/1: 0660339: Chsd ldrs, btn 2f out, abs.	1¾	63a
56	MANDOOB 18 [1] B R Johnson 6-9-1 (62) J P Guillambert 16/1: 12-56300: Chsd ldrs bill over 3f out.	¾	55a
4448}	DANAKIL 71 [13] S Dow 8-9-12 (73) J Coffill Brown (7) 20/1: 4500430: Rear, nvr a factor, abs.	¾	65a
4909}	KRISTOFFERSEN 40 [14] R M Stronge 3-9-8 (75) I Mongan 8/1: 1035430: Mid-div wide, btn 3f out, abs/new yard.	½	66a
4806}	LAZZAZ 49 [3] P W Hiatt 5-9-4 (65) R Winston 25/1: 2201330: Led till 2f out, fdd, abs.	½	55a
2547}	GO CLASSIC 159 [12] A M Hales 3-9-2 (69) M Fenton 100/1: 00400: Chsd ldr, struggling fnl 3f, abs/new yard.	10	47a

14 Ran   2m 48.38 (6.08)   Owner Mr H R Hunt   Trained at Epsom

---

148   1.55 Bet Direct No Q Maiden Stakes 3yo+ (D)
£2300 £657 £329   1m2f p/track   Going 44   -35 Slow   Stalls Inside

14	MAXILLA 24 [8] L M Cumani 3-8-9 (63) E Ahern 3/1: 004-241: Cl-up & led after 2f, drvn & held on well nr fin:		66a
4720}	MARGERY DAW 54 [13] M P Tregoning 3-8-9 Dane O'Neill 5/2 FAV: 3-22: Handy & rdn/strong chall over 1f out, just held cl-home:	nk	64a
4542}	BLUEGRASS BOY 66 [12] G B Balding 3-9-0 (63) R Havlin 16/1: 400-0253: In tch, hdwy to chase ldrs 2f out, kept on onepace ins last:	1	67a
4658}	STATE OF BALANCE 59 [3] K Bell 5-8-12 L Keniry (3) 100/1: 004: Rear, hdwy when no room & swtchd over 1f out, nrst fin:	1¼	60a
2734}	BETTERWARE BOY 151 [7] P M Phelan 3-9-0 F Norton 14/1: 545: Keen, mid-div, outpcd fnl 2f, abs/new yard.	¾	64a
4929}	CAYMAN SUNRISE 39 [6] E A L Dunlop 3-8-9 (65) T Quinn 9/2: 34426: Keen, led 2f, btn over 1f out.	hd	58a
1363}	BLUE RONDO 215 [9] Ian Williams 3-9-0 (65) C Catlin 20/1: 00-4007: Cl-up, btn 2f out:	5	56a
	BOLD RIDGE [4] S Kirk 3-9-0 J F Egan 33/1: 8: Held up, no impress fnl 3f on debut.	1¼	54a
1501}	WOOD FERN 206 [1] M R Channon 3-9-0 R Lappin 6/1: 339: Held up, btn 2f out:	1¾	52a
53	SHAAMITS ALL OVER 18 [10] B A Pearce 4-8-12 B Reilly (5) 33/1: 060: Chsd ldrs, btn 2f out.	¾	46a
96	RECALL 11 [5] J G Given 3-8-9 M Fenton 50/1: 000: Held up, no ch fnl 3f.	5	39a
53	ELEGANT GRACIE 18 [14] R Guest 3-8-9 J Mackay 25/1: 00: Slow away, eff wide halfway, sn btn.	5	32a
4984}	SILISTRA 34 [11] Mrs L C Jewell 4-9-3 p (65) I Mongan 50/1: 20064-00: Prom, wknd qckly 2f out.	1¼	35a

13 Ran   2m 02.8 (7.91)   Owner Mr L Marinopoulos   Trained at Newmarket

---

149   2.30 Betdirect Co Uk New Site Handicap Stakes 3yo+ 0-80 (D)   [80]
£3178 £908 £454   6f p/track rnd   Going 44   -09 Slow   Stalls Inside

20*	COMPTON BANKER 23 [6] G A Butler 6-9-8 vis (74) E Ahern 7/2 FAV: 0500411: Dwelt & held up, hdwy 2f out, styd on to lead on line, rdn out:		79a
4982}	JAYANJAY 34 [4] Miss B Sanders 4-9-7 (73) T Quinn 9/1: 2006602: Prom, rdn & led ins last, hdd line:	shd	77a
109	ONLY ONE LEGEND 8 [10] K A Ryan 5-9-6 bl (72) R Winston 7/1: 2466603: Mid-div, hmpd over 2f out, rallied well for press ins last:	1½	71a
106	SIR DESMOND 10 [3] R Guest 5-9-12 p (78) C Catlin 5/1: 0140034: Prom, kept on onepace for press.	nk	76a
106	EMERALD FIRE 10 [7] A M Balding 4-9-7 vis (73) N Chalmers (5) 20/1: 6030005: Mid-div, rdn & kept on, nrst fin.	1	68a
1906}	OVERRIDE 186 [9] J M P Eustace 3-9-7 (73) J Tate 8/1: 16-22006: Held up, rdn & styd on, not able to chall, abs.	½	66a
81	JUST FLY 14 [5] S Kirk 3-10-0 (80) J F McDonald (5) 6/1: 5001057: Handy, no extra dist.	nk	72a
121	GOODWOOD PRINCE 7 [2] S Dow 3-9-2 (68) P Doe 50/1: 0060008: Led & sn clr, hdd ins last, wknd.	1	57a
3584}	AWARDING 114 [8] R F Johnson Houghton 3-10-0 (80) Dane O'Neill 12/1: 4045509: Keen mid-div, onepace when hmpd ins last.	nk	68a
41	TURN AROUND 19 [11] B W Hills 3-9-3 (69) F Norton 40/1: 510-0000: Rear, no impress over 1f out.	2	51a
70	PRIMA STELLA 15 [14] J A R Toller 4-9-2 (68) S W Kelly 12/1: 3241020: Slow away, nvr factor, new yard.	½	48a
5025}	THE FISIO 29 [13] A M Balding 3-9-6 (72) R J Killoran (7) 33/1: 3-000000: Slow away & bhd, nvr a factor.	3	43a
4810}	TELEPATHIC 47 [1] A Berry 3-9-3 (69) G Carter 50/1: 5600000: Slow away, chsd ldrs, btn/hmpd ins last, abs.	4	30a
64	CONSENSUS 17 [12] M Brittain 4-9-9 (75) T Williams 25/1: 0000600: Keen mid-div, wide, nvr a factor.	11	6a

14 Ran   1m 13.55 (3.15)   Owner Mr Erik Penser   Trained at Blewbury

---

150   3.05 Bet Direct On Channel 4 Page 613 Claiming Stakes Div 2 3yo+ (F)
£2051 £586 £293   1m p/track rnd   Going 44   +04 Fast   Stalls Outside

117	**SMITH N ALLAN OILS 7** [1] M Dods 4-9-4 p (56) J F Egan 11/4 FAV: 0052301: Chsd ldrs & led over 1f out, drvn out:			56a
4150}	**DISPOL EVITA 88** [2] Jamie Poulton 4-9-3 (47) H Poulton (7) 16/1: 0653502: Slow away, mid-div, drvn & kept on well in last, just held:		hd	55a
4433}	**ZINGING 73** [7] J J Bridger 4-8-12 (48) F Norton 16/1: 0000003: Trkd ldrs, ch dist, kept on well:		hd	49a
123	**BALMACARA 7** [11] Miss K B Boutflower 4-8-13 p (50) I Mongan 12/1: 0000554: Mid-div, late gains.		½	49a
122	**FOUR JAYS 7** [4] N P Littmoden 3-9-7 p (70) J P Guillambert (3) 9/2: 3002605: Cl-up, led after 2f till over 1f out, no extra.		1½	55a
68	**CONSIGNIA 15** [12] D Haydn Jones 4-8-5 vis (49) Paul Eddery 8/1: 3100106: Held up, rdn & kept on, no dngr:		shd	38a
86	**MAGGIES PET 12** [8] K Bell 6-8-5 t (46) C Catlin 10/1: 4000367: Chsd ldrs, btn over 1f out.		½	37a
3781}	**PAINTBRUSH 106** [10] Mrs L Stubbs 3-8-8 (47) S W Kelly 50/1: 00-3568: Rear, drvn & kept on ins last, abs.		½	40a
4918}	**COMPTON EMERALD 39** [5] G A Butler 3-7-12 bl (65) J F McDonald (5) 4/1: 0-003469: Held up, no impress:		½	29a
141	**POWER BIRD 3** [6] D Flood 3-9-2 (72) P Doe 9/1: 0005000: Led 2f, btn over 1f out.		4	40a
55	**BADOU 18** [3] L Montague Hall 3-8-13 vis (51) E Ahern 11/1: 0002400: Cl-up, wknd qckly over 1f out.		6	27a
4594}	**CHOCOLATE BOY 416** [9] G L Moore 4-9-0 (48) J Fanning 25/1: 000/000-0: Al rear:		8	13a

12 Ran 1m 39.43 (3.23) Owner Smith & Allan Racing Trained at Darlington

---

151 3.40 Bet Direct In Running Sky Text 293 Handicap Stakes Div 2 3yo+ 0-65 (F) **[65]**
£2093 £598 £299 7f p/track rnd Going 44 -12 Slow Stalls Inside

117	**MISS ISSY 7** [8] J Gallagher 3-9-2 vis (53) I Mongan 10/1: 2340401: Mid-div, led over 1f out, drvn out:			58a
50	**TEMPER TANTRUM 18** [11] Andrew Reid 5-9-10 p (61) Rory Moore (7) 5/1: 6130502: Held up, hdwy to chall 1f out, drvn & not pace of wnr:		¾	65a
4944}	**CAYMAN BREEZE 38** [10] S Dow 3-10-0 (65) P Doe 40/1: 2210003: Rear, hdwy when wide over 1f out, kept on for press:		1¼	66a
129*	**BINT MAKBUL 7** [2] R Hannon 4-9-7 (58) Dane O'Neill 5/1: 6032314: Chsd ldrs, onepace for press dist.		nk	58a
55	**CALUSA LADY 18** [14] G B Balding 3-9-4 (55) A Clark 33/1: 4460005: Rear, hdwy 2f out, onepace for press dist.		1	53a
121	**PEYTO PRINCESS 7** [6] M A Buckley 5-9-8 (59) J Bramhill 8/1: 0000456: Rear, rdn & kept on, nrst fin.		1¼	54a
99	**ZAK FACTA 11** [16] Miss D A McHale 3-9-3 vis (54) C Cogan 20/1: 0042547: Prom, no extra over 1f out.		1½	46a
94	**SEMPER PARATUS 11** [7] H J Collingridge 4-9-8 bl (59) M Tebbutt 10/1: 0000148: Led briefly early, no impress fnl 2f.		½	50a
4922}	**PENNY PIE 39** [5] P W Harris 3-9-12 (63) T Quinn 8/1: 353009: Pushed along mid-div, no prog 2f out.		¾	53a
55	**GALLERY BREEZE 18** [12] J L Spearing 4-9-13 (64) A Daly 7/2 FAV: 0041120: Mid-div, btn 2f out:		1	52a
130	**RICHIE RICH 4** [3] Jarlath Fahey 8-9-4 (55) W M Lordan 66/1: 3000P00: Chsd ldrs till over 1f out, qck reapp.		1¼	40a
4967}	**SPINDOR 35** [13] J A Osborne 4-9-10 bl (61) S W Kelly 14/1: 0100050: Led till over 1f out, sn btn.		hd	45a
94	**TATWEER 11** [4] D Shaw 3-9-4 vis (55) R Winston 20/1: 5-005550: Rear & lost tch fnl 3f, nvr a factor.		2½	34a
30	**WESTMEAD TANGO 22** [1] J R Jenkins 3-9-1 (52) A Mackay 50/1: 60-01200: Al bhd.		¾	30a
50	**COPPINGTON FLYER 18** [15] B W Duke 4-9-3 BL (54) M Fenton 16/1: 6000000: Chsd ldrs till 2f out, tried blnks.		2½	27a

15 Ran 1m 26.72 (3.92) Owner C R Marks (Banbury) Trained at Moreton-In-Marsh

---

Official Going SLOW

152 7.00 Bet Direct On Sky Active Classified Stakes 3yo+ 0-70 (E)
£2079 £594 £297 7f f/sand rnd Going 66 -24 Slow Stalls Outside

1785}	**ARC EL CIEL 192** [9] Mrs S A Liddiard 5-9-0 (66) C Catlin 20/1: 1323001: Rdn rear, hdwy halfway, led 2f out, rdn out:			74a
5	**ZARIN 26** [3] D W Chapman 5-9-0 (69) A Culhane 50/1: 0300602: Rdn rear, styd on well for press fnl 2f, not pace of wnr:		2	69a
31	**BLONDE EN BLONDE 22** [1] N P Littmoden 3-8-11 (69) I Mongan 8/1: 6220353: Mid-div, rdn & kept on fnl 2f, not pace of front pair.		2	62a
71*	**ROMAN MAZE 15** [4] W M Brisbourne 3-9-0 (68) S W Kelly 5/2: 05514: Dwelt, sn trkd ldrs trav well, onepace for press over 1f out:		hd	64a
4967*}	**TEEHEE 35** [8] B Palling 5-9-0 bl (70) M Fenton 8/1: 4502015: Handy trav well, hung left & no extra ins last.		½	63a
91*	**PERFECT NIGHT 12** [11] R Charlton 3-8-11 (72) Dane O'Neill 2/1 FAV: 2022116: Trkd ldrs going well, rdn & led over 2f out, hdd dist & wknd:		1½	57a
113	**WARDEN WARREN 8** [7] Mrs C A Dunnett 5-9-0 (67) B Reilly (5) 16/1: 0000007: Mid-div, btn 2f out.		2	56a
31	**DANIELLES LAD 22** [5] B Palling 7-9-0 bl (70) F Norton 9/1: 0300038: Trkd ldr, led halfway till 2f out, wknd.		4	48a
93	**ULYSEES 11** [6] I Semple 4-9-0 (63) R Winston 25/1: 0006609: Sn struggling & bhd.		11	28a
41	**PIPS SONG 19** [2] P W Hiatt 8-9-0 (50) P Doe 50/1: 2600300: Led till hdd halfway, btn/eased dist.		17	0a

10 Ran 1m 32.5 (6.3) Owner Shefford Valley Stud Trained at Hungerford

---

153 7.30 Bet Direct Press Red To Bet Claiming Stakes 3yo+ (F)
£2079 £594 £297 6f f/sand rnd Going 66 -15 Slow Stalls Inside

70	**ELLENS LAD 15** [9] W J Musson 9-9-6 bl (70) Paul Eddery 25/1: 2000-001: Al handy & drvn/kept on to prevail line, all out:			73a
113	**RAFTERS MUSIC 8** [3] Julian Poulton 8-9-6 (74) I Mongan 2/1 FAV: 5225432: Rdn rear, swtchd & styd on well in last, chall cl-home, just held:		hd	72a
70*	**SHARP HAT 15** [5] D Nicholls 9-9-6 bl (69) A Nicholls 11/2: 6000113: Al handy & led over 1f out, just hdd cl-home.		nk	71a
61	**SPEEDFIT FREE 17** [13] I Semple 6-8-10 bl (56) M Tebbutt 9/1: 3501054: Rdn mid-div wide, onepce.		3½	51a
30*	**QUEEN OF NIGHT 22** [2] T D Barron 3-8-11 (78) D Mernagh 3/1: 3001515: Hmpd/slow away, rdn & only mod prog:		shd	51a
124	**CATCHTHEBATCH 7** [7] M J Wallace 7-8-12 (50) D Corby (3) 20/1: 0200006: Chsd ldr, no extra dist.		3	43a
124	**SALERNO 7** [12] Miss Gay Kelleway 4-9-0 p (53) T Eaves 25/1: 0004007: Led till over 1f out, fdd.		1¼	41a
92	**VALUABLE GIFT 11** [6] R C Guest 6-8-8 e (49) A Cooper (7) 33/1: 6320008: Al rear:		nk	34a
113	**LEGALIS 8** [8] K A Ryan 5-9-10 P (65) R Winston 11/1: 1-000409: Outpcd, nvr a factor.		shd	49a
2021}	**QUEEN LOUISA 180** [4] F Watson 3-8-5 t R Ffrench 100/1: 00: Al outpcd in rear.		6	12a
109	**VALAZAR 8** [1] D W Chapman 4-8-10 (62) A Culhane 11/1: 01-52400: Sn struggling rear.		7	-3a

11 Ran 1m 17.7 (4.9) Owner Mrs Rita Brown Trained at Newmarket

154

8.00 Littlewoods Bet Direct Maiden Stakes 3yo+ (D)
£2247 £642 £321   1m4f f/sand   Going 66   -54 Slow   Stalls Inside

	ALEXANDER ANAPOLIS 42 [7] N A Callaghan 3-8-9 (80) F Norton 4/5 FAV: 6020661: Dwelt, keen & sn trkd ldrs, led 3f out, drvn out:		66a
4658}	EXIT TO HEAVEN 59 [6] Miss Gay Kelleway 3-8-9 (57) M Fenton 16/1: 0060002: Keen, mid-div, outpcd 3f out, rallied late for press, not reach wnr:	2	58a
96	WHITE PARK BAY 11 [9] J Gallagher 3-8-9 (59) C Catlin 9/2: 2403033: Trkd ldrs, kept on:	1	56a
89	DESERT HEAT 12 [5] I Semple 5-9-5 P (60) R Winston 10/1: 22-64004: Trkd ldr, no extra dist.	3	57a
72	SABRELINE 15 [3] B R Foster 4-9-0 (45) N Chalmers (5) 12/1: 4003055: Led till 3f out, fdd under press.	4	46a
96	DANUM 11 [11] R Hollinshead 3-9-0 (60) A Culhane 12/1: 465606: Bhd, only mod late prog:	2½	47a
5020}	SIMON THE POACHER 30 [2] L P Grassick 4-9-5 (42) V Slattery 50/1: 0-000007: Mid-div, struggling halfway.	dist	-3a
4995}	BRIDEWELL 32 [12] F Watson 4-9-5 (38) D Mernagh 50/1: 00-00008: Al bhd.	6	0
666}	KAMALA 288 [10] R Brotherton 4-9-0 I Mongan 16/1: 65203-09: Mid-div, struggling fnl 5f:	18	0
23	SARGENTS DREAM 23 [8] J A Gilbert 3-8-9 Dean Williams (7) 50/1: 00: In tch, saddle slipped, bhd hway.	dist	0

10 Ran   2m 48.0 (14.4)   Owner Mrs N O'Callaghan   Trained at Newmarket

155

8.30 Bet Direct No Q On 08000 93 66 93 Handicap Stakes 3yo+ 0-85 (D)
£3388 £968 £484   5f f/sand rnd   Going 66   +08 Fast   Stalls Inside   [85]

113	PADDYWACK 8 [6] D W Chapman 6-8-13 bl (70) A Culhane 4/1: 3605661: Pushed along rear, strong run wide for press ins last, led nr fin, going away:		77a
110	TIME N TIME AGAIN 8 [3] E J Alston 5-8-10 (67) D Allan (3) 3/1 FAV: 0340542 Trkd ldrs, rdn & led dist, hdd cl-home:	1½	70a
110	GONENDUNNETT 8 [1] Mrs C A Dunnett 4-8-12 vis (69) B Reilly (5) 16/1: 2004103: Pushed along rear, strong run fnl 1f, nrst fin:	nk	70a
124*	LADY PEKAN 7 [8] P S McEntee 4-8-0 bl (57) J F McDonald (5) 12/1: 5000014: Chsd ldrs, no extra.	hd	58a
35	DAINTREE AFFAIR 21 [2] K R Burke 3-8-6 (63) Joanna Badger 33/1: 0331005: Rear, kept on late for press.	1¼	60a
110	RELLIM 8 [10] P A Blockley 4-7-13 1oh 1ow 7 [54] C Catlin 8/1: 4064426: Led till dist, fdd fnl 1f:	½	51a
64	MAKTAVISH 17 [7] I Semple 4-9-11 p (82) I Mongan 6/1: 0550107: Prom, fdd fnl 1f.	1¼	73a
5025}	RAYMONDS PRIDE 29 [4] K A Ryan 3-9-0 bl (71) R Winston 25/1: 04501F8: Mid-div, outpcd bef dist.	hd	61a
106	PRINCE OF BLUES 10 [11] M Mullineaux 5-9-2 p (73) J Bramhill 10/1: 0000069: Prom wide 3f, sn struggling.	2	57a
2999*}	GILDED COVE 140 [9] R Hollinshead 3-8-12 (69) J Mackay 15/2: 3121310: Slow away, al bhd & wide:	2½	45a
834}	TIGRESS 257 [5] J W Unett 4-8-6 bl (63) S W Kelly 14/1: 1132660: Al bhd, t.o.:	20	0a

11 Ran   1m 3.1 (2.9)   Owner Mr T S Redman   Trained at York

156

9.00 Bet Direct Through Attheraces Handicap Stakes 3yo+ 0-65 (F)
£2065 £590 £295   2m46y f/sand   Going 66   -22 Slow   Stalls Inside   [64]

5001}	KILLING JOKE 32 [2] J G Given 3-9-5 (63) M Fenton 12/1: 30-0601: Trkd ldr, led 6f out, rdn clr 3f out, styd on strongly:		75a
103	RADIANT BRIDE 10 [5] K R Burke 3-8-1 (45) A Reilly (6) 33/1: 0005002: Rear, rdn & kept on fnl 2f for press, nr ch with wnr:	11	45a
48	SASHAY 19 [9] R Hollinshead 5-9-10 (60) Stephanie Hollinshead (7) 13/2: 0406143: Chsd ldrs, chsd wnr 5f out, no impress fnl 2f.	2½	57a
3806}	COTTAM GRANGE 105 [4] M W Easterby 3-8-2 (46) Dale Gibson 33/1: 6000654: Chsd ldrs 13f, jmps fit.	5	38a
125	PARADISE VALLEY 7 [7] Mrs S A Liddiard 3-8-6 t (50) C Catlin 8/1: 2514525: Rear, only mod prog:	6	36a
1592}	BROUGHTON KNOWS 201 [11] W J Musson 6-7-13 (35) J Mackay 13/2: 0140436: Held up, rdn & no ch fnl 4f:	3½	17a
2771}	ELLA FALLS 149 [12] Mrs H Dalton 8-8-0 (36) F Norton 9/1: 20/5-4557: Trkd ldrs, btn 4f out:	shd	17a
75	CANTEMERLE 15 [8] W M Brisbourne 3-8-7 (51) S W Kelly 33/1: 0000358: Al bhd.	9	23a
48	MADHAHIR 19 [6] C A Dwyer 3-9-4 p (62) B Reilly (5) 15/8 FAV: 0040629: Sn struggling rear:	9	25a
124	RIVELLI 7 [3] B R Foster 4-9-0 (50) N Chalmers (5) 80/1: 0-000000: Al bhd & no ch 4f out.	11	2a
48	FAST CINDY 19 [1] J W Unett 4-9-7 (57) R Winston 12/1: 210-2000: Mid-div, strugg fnl 4f:	shd	8a
453}	WELCOME BACK 317 [13] K A Ryan 6-7-13 1oh 1ow (33) R Ffrench 10/1: 30//616-20: Led till 6f out.	dist	0a

12 Ran   3m 43.29 (14.09)   Owner Mr A Clarke   Trained at Gainsborough

157

9.30 Bet Direct Red To Bet Handicap Stakes 3yo+ 0-70 (E)
£2135 £610 £305   1m1f79y   Going 66   +08 Fast   Stalls Inside   [68]

4595}	BUSCADOR 63 [1] W M Brisbourne 4-9-11 (65) Mark Flynn (5) 100/30 J FAV: 3611061: Made all, rdn & held on well from over 1f out:		71a
4506}	HUGH THE MAN 68 [9] N P Littmoden 4-9-13 (67) I Mongan 5/1: 1250002: Mid-div, rdn to chase wnr fnl 2f, no extra fnl 100y:	1¼	69a
86	SHIFTY 12 [12] D Nicholls 4-9-1 bl (55) A Nicholls 4/1: 0650423: Chsd ldrs, no extra over 1f out.	3½	50a
141	CRUSOE 3 [10] A Sadik 6-9-11 bl (65) L Vickers 100/30 J FAV: 0535044: Chsd wnr, rdn & btn 2f out.	7	46a
4244}	YENALED 82 [5] K A Ryan 6-9-11 (65) R Winston 15/2: 3542545: Mid-div, rdn & btn 3f out:	6	34a
20	AZREME 23 [8] P W D'Arcy 3-9-12 e (68) Paul Eddery 20/1: 2610006: Chsd wnr, btn 3f out:	¾	35a
629}	LEONORA TRUCE 118 [13] R P Elliott 4-8-9 (49) A Elliott (7) 20/1: 2203267: Slow away & al bhd:	7	2a
850}	PRIDEWAY 256 [2] W M Brisbourne 7-9-11 bl (65) N Chalmers (5) 11/1: 4011568: Slow away & al bhd:	5	8a

8 Ran   2m 3.75 (+08 Fast)   Owner Real Soda   Trained at Baschurch

---

Official Going Standard

158

12.10 Bet Direct On 0800 32 93 93 Nursery Handicap Stakes 2yo 0-75 (E)
£2324 £664 £332   7f f/sand rnd   Going 69   -13 Slow   Stalls Inside   [74]

4825}	WEET AN HAUL 48 [6] P A Blockley 2-7-12 8oh (44) J Bramhill 66/1: 060001: Handy, led 2f out, rdn out:		56a
135	MUY BIEN 6 [13] J R Jenkins 2-9-6 vis (74) S W Kelly 7/1: 1500152: Led, hdd 5f out, ev ch 2f out, kept on fnl 1f, not pace of	1	77a
3960}	PHLUKE 101 [2] R F Johnson Houghton 2-9-7 (75) Dane O'Neill 8/1: 62243: Mid-div, eff 1f out, kept on fnl 1f:	1½	75a

112	**GARNOCK VENTURE** 10 [14] A Berry 2-7-13 BL (53) Dale Gibson 50/1: 665004: Led 5f out, hdd 2f out, no extra fnl 1f:		1	51a
105*	**MAUNBY RAVER** 12 [15] P C Haslam 2-8-13 (67) Rory Moore (7) 11/4: 6641215: Handy, edged left & onepcd fnl 1f:		1¾	62a
4993}	**DUNCANBIL** 35 [7] R F Fisher 2-8-2 (56) S Righton 25/1: 6050066: Mid-div, nvr able to chall:		2	47a
63	**FOXIES FUTURE** 19 [1] J R Weymes 2-8-11 (65) D Fentiman (7) 14/1: 0661057: Rear, prog 4f out, short of room 2f out, sn wknd.		nk	55a
87	**CASANTELLA** 14 [12] M J Polglase 2-7-12 14oh (38) J F McDonald (5) 66/1: 6000008: Nvr nrr than mid-div.		1	40a
4981}	**DR CERULLO** 36 [11] C Tinkler 2-9-7 (75) A Culhane 2/1 FAV: 2639: Slow away, al bhd:		hd	62a
13	**LIMIT DOWN** 26 [9] M J Wallace 2-8-10 (64) D Corby (3) 25/1: 0000: Al bhd.		2½	46a
77	**STANHOPE FORBES** 16 [8] N P Littmoden 2-8-4 P (58) G Gibbons 14/1: 0635060: In tch, wknd fnl 3f.		1	38a
95	**THE KING OF ROCK** 13 [5] A G Newcombe 2-8-3 (57) C Catlin 25/1: 5042000: Al bhd.		nk	36a
4496}	**SIR FRANK GIBSON** 71 [3] M Johnston 2-8-2 (56) J Fanning 12/1: 003040: Al in rear.		4	27a
4056}	**ZOLUSHKA** 95 [4] B W Duke 2-7-13 (53) J Mackay 66/1: 0000: Slow away, al in rear.		8	10a
14 Ran	1m 32.37 (5.77) Owner Ed Weetman (Haulage & Storage)			Trained at Southwell

---

159 **12.40 Littlewoods Bet Direct Median Auction Maiden Stakes Div 1 2yo (F)**
£2219 £634 £317   **1m f/sand rnd**   Going 69   -29 Slow   Stalls Inside

4823}	**ATLANTIC BREEZE** 48 [2] Mrs N Macauley 2-8-9 L Enstone (3) 7/1: 41: Handy, prog 2f out, led ins fnl 1f, rdn out:			67a
4482}	**MRS GEE** 72 [3] R Hollinshead 2-8-9 (63) R Winston 7/2: 5542: Cl-up, outpcd 5f out, short of room 4f out, prog when not clr run dist, swtchd & kept on well fnl 1f,		1	64a
29	**COME WHAT JULY** 24 [6] R Guest 2-9-0 bl (67) A Culhane 13/8 FAV: 5502023: Keen bhd, hmpd 4f out, prog 2f out, kept on fnl 1f:		shd	68a
116	**TROMPE LOEIL** 9 [10] E A L Dunlop 2-8-9 (71) M Fenton 7/2: 405024: In tch, led 2f out, hdd & no extra ins fnl 1f:		1½	60a
4927}	**DANTES DEVINE** 41 [5] A Bailey 2-9-0 (65) C Catlin 16/1: 0055: Slow away, prog 4f out, fdd dist:		5	55a
102	**MONTE MAJOR** 12 [7] M A Jarvis 2-9-0 M Henry 25/1: 06: In tch, fdd fnl 1f.		1½	52a
111	**CALCULAITE** 10 [9] Mrs G S Rees 2-9-0 J Fanning 100/1: 007: Mid-div, wknd fnl 1f.		1	50a
95	**TAMARINA** 13 [1] N E Berry 2-8-9 Dane O'Neill 50/1: 508: Led 5f, fdd dist:		nk	44a
	OKTIS MORILIOUS [4] J A Osborne 2-9-0 S W Kelly 16/1: 9: Slow away, prog 4f out, wknd fnl 2f:		2	40a
5013}	**TIMBUKTU** 32 [8] C W Thornton 2-9-0 M Tebbutt 50/1: 00: Slow away, al bhd.		14	17a
51	**EVENING FRAGRANCE** 20 [11] G C H Chung 2-9-0 BL J Mackay 50/1: 00: Slow away, sn cl-up, fdd 3f out.		24	0
11 Ran	1m 47.26 (7.86) Owner Mr Richard Underwood			Trained at Melton Mowbray

---

160 **1.10 Littlewoodspoker Com Handicap Stakes Div 1 3yo+ 0-60 (F)**   [58]
£2072 £592 £296   **1m f/sand rnd**   Going 69   -06 Slow   Stalls Inside

125	**QUEENSBERRY** 9 [10] J O'Reilly 4-9-5 (49) J D O'Reilly (7) 9/1: 3302041: Held up, prog 3f out, hung left dist, led ins fnl 1f, rdn out:			53a
84	**MUTARAFAA** 14 [11] D Shaw 4-9-2 e (46) T Hamilton (5) 2/1 FAV: 0060222: Cl-up, ev ch fnl 1f, just held by wnr:		½	49a
86	**QOBTAAN** 14 [1] M R Bosley 4-9-1 (45) G Baker 14/1: 0246053: Held up, prog 4f out, kept on fnl 1f:		½	47a
99	**GOODBYE MR BOND** 13 [3] E J Alston 3-9-10 (56) D Allan (3) 10/1: 0053404: In tch, led dist, hdd ins fnl 1f, no extra.		shd	56a
74	**SHATIN HERO** 17 [12] G C H Chung 3-9-13 p (59) R Ffrench 11/2: 4144205: Handy, onepace dist:		3½	52a
636}	**PRINCESS GRACE** 294 [4] M L W Bell 4-8-9 (39) Rory Moore 11/1: 0630-026: Cl-up, led 4f, hdd dist, sn wknd.		1¾	29a
114	**MALMAND** 10 [9] R Brotherton 4-9-0 BL (40) G Gibbons 40/1: 5000507: Slow away, sn cl-up, outpcd 3f out:		2	30a
38	**EUROLINK ARTEMIS** 23 [7] Miss Gay Kelleway 6-9-3 p (47) M Fenton 25/1: 2000008: Held up, nvr nrr than mid-div:		½	32a
72	**ERSAAL** 17 [14] J Jay 3-9-8 (54) K Dalgleish 12/1: 6-065039: In tch, wknd dist.		½	37a
4883}	**CHICKASAW TRAIL** 44 [8] R Hollinshead 5-8-4 (34) Dale Gibson 50/1: 20-00000: Al bhd:		4	10a
4890}	**SARN** 44 [5] A Bailey 4-8-13 (43) J Fanning 66/1: 1140000: Cl-up, fdd 4f out:		½	18a
4708}	**MAUNBY ROCKER** 56 [13] P C Haslam 3-10-0 (60) L Enstone (3) 11/1: 04-01260: In tch, wknd 3f out:		5	24a
4638}	**MARENGO** 62 [6] Paul Johnson 9-8-7 (37) Joanna Badger 22/1: 0040600: Slow away, al bhd:		1	0a
4691}	**GOODWOOD PROMISE** 57 [2] N E Berry 4-8-10 (40) M Savage (3) 66/1: 0-000000: Led 3f, fdd 3f out.		28	0
14 Ran	1m 45.45 (6.05) Owner Mr J Saul			Trained at Barnsley

---

161 **1.40 Bet Direct Press Red To Bet Claiming Stakes 3yo+ (F)**
£2121 £606 £303   **7f f/sand rnd**   Going 69   +02 Fast   Stalls Inside

27	**CLOUD DANCER** 24 [15] D J Coakley 4-9-0 (74) Dane O'Neill 2/1 FAV: 0620331: Slow away, prog 3f out, led trav west dist, rdn out to assert:			76a
4093*}	**NIMELLO** 93 [12] A G Newcombe 7-9-5 (78) L Keniry (3) 10/1: 4110612: In tch, styd on to chase wnr 1f out, kept on fnl 1f, just held by wnr:		nk	79a
123	**BULAWAYO** 9 [16] Andrew Reid 6-8-12 (57) A Nicholls 16/1: 0363203: Handy, onepcd fnl 1f:		5	62a
74	**MR STYLISH** 17 [6] J S Moore 7-8-10 vis t (50) J D Smith 25/1: 6600444: Bhd, prog 2f out, kept on late.		1¼	58a
4448}	**TINIAN** 43 [5] K R Burke 5-8-13 (65) Darren Williams 25/1: 3211615: Held up, prog 3f out, edged left & onepcd dist:		½	60a
130	**GEORGE STUBBS** 6 [4] N P Littmoden 5-9-5 P (69) J Fanning 9/2: 2305606: Handy, led 2f out, hdd dist, sn wknd.		hd	65a
27	**JAN BRUEGHEL** 24 [2] T D Barron 4-9-1 (66) Laura Jayne Crawford (7) 100/30: 3110247: Dwelt, nvr nrr than mid-div.		3½	54a
68	**RED DELIRIUM** 17 [11] R Brotherton 7-8-12 bl (50) G Gibbons 33/1: 5400068: Dwelt, nvr able to chall.		1½	48a
38	**ZAHUNDA** 23 [7] W M Brisbourne 4-8-6 (49) K Dalgleish 66/1: 0100009: Cl-up, fdd 2f out.		½	41a
3741}	**WATERLINE DANCER** 110 [4] P D Evans 3-8-6 vis t (48) S W Kelly 66/1: 3040000: Al bhd.		nk	40a
3748}	**LIONS DOMANE** 110 [13] A Berry 5-8-11 (47) R Winston 50/1: 0110000: Led, hdd 2f out, sn wknd.		2½	40a
128	**REPEAT** 9 [10] Miss Gay Kelleway 3-8-13 (55) A Culhane 9/2: 0003140: Al bhd.		1	40a
4777}	**COOLFORE JADE** 52 [14] N E Berry 3-8-11 M Savage (4) 33/1: 01400: Cl-up, fdd fnl 2f:		1	36a
62	**SHAMWARI FIRE** 19 [3] W McInnes 3-9-1 (47) Natalia Gemelova (7) 50/1: 0524400: Cl-up, wknd fnl 3f.		7	28a
22	**KING DAVID** 25 [9] D Burchell 4-8-11 (56) R Price 20/1: 6300300: Handy, wknd 3f out.		2½	19a
4591}	**BETTER OFF** 65 [1] Mrs N Macauley 5-8-13 p (73) L Fletcher (5) 20/1: 5110000: Al bhd:		3	15a
16 Ran	1m 31.30 (4.7) Owner Cloud Dancer Racing			Trained at West Ilsley

162 — 2.10 Littlewoods Bet Direct Median Auction Maiden Stakes Div 2 2yo (F)
£2212 £632 £316 1m f/sand rnd Going 69 -09 Slow Stalls Inside

29	**NESSEN DORMA** 24 [5] J G Given 2-9-0 (66) A Culhane 6/5 FAV: 225051: Chsd ldrs, hdwy to lead ins fnl 1f, rdn out:			**72a**
21	**NUTS FOR YOU** 25 [2] R Charlton 2-8-10 1ow Dane O'Neill 11/2: 002: Mid-div, hdwy to lead dist, hdd & not pace of wnr ins fnl 1f:		1½	**62a**
111	**DRIZZLE** 10 [8] J W Unett 2-9-0 M Henry 14/1: 303: Handy, rdn 3f out, onepace fnl 1f.		5	**56a**
98	**SMART BOY PRINCE** 13 [4] P A Blockley 2-9-0 (50) Derek Nolan (7) 14/1: 000504: Led till dist, wknd.		hd	**55a**
111	**JAKARMI** 10 [7] B Palling 2-9-0 (62) D Kinsella 9/1: 0265: Midfield, onepace fnl 2f:		1¾	**51a**
37	**CAN CAN FLYER** 23 [1] M Johnston 2-9-0 J Fanning 15/2: 006: Chsd ldrs, rdn halfway & wknd after.		6	**39a**
28	**TURKS AND CAICOS** 24 [10] P C Haslam 2-9-0 L Enstone 7/1: 047: Al in rear.		½	**38a**
120	**SPRING WHISPER** 9 [3] E A L Dunlop 2-8-9 M Fenton 16/1: 008: Midfield, rdn & btn 3f out:		shd	**32a**
3007}	**BELT AND BRACES** 142 [6] C Smith 2-9-0 (30) A Nicholls 100/1: 0009: Nvr on terms		dist	**7a**
52	**SONNE DE LOUP** 20 [9] Mrs S A Liddiard 2-8-9 (42) J F McDonald (5) 33/1: 000R: Mid-div, rdn halfway, very wide & spectacularly ran off crse 3f out:			**0a**

10 Ran 1m 45.65 (6.25) Owner Hokey Cokey Partnership Trained at Gainsborough

163 — 2.40 Betdirect Co Uk Handicap Stakes Fillies 3yo+ 0-75 (E) [71]
£2121 £606 £303 1m f/sand rnd Going 69 +06 Fast Stalls Inside

129	**MISS CHAMPERS** 9 [3] P D Evans 3-9-1 (59) Joanna Badger 14/1: 6030051: In tch, hdwy to lead dist, rdn out:			**68a**
5029}	**ELLEN MOONEY** 31 [2] B Smart 4-9-12 p (69) R Ffrench 15/8 JT FAV: 0021502: Prsd ldr, rdn to chall 1f out, no extra cl home:		2½	**71a**
84*	**ROCK CONCERT** 14 [4] I W McInnes 5-9-1 (58) L Fletcher (3) 15/8 JT FAV: 5332213: Midfield, rdn & onepace 2f out:		1¾	**56a**
71	**VICTORY FLIP** 17 [7] R Hollinshead 3-8-10 p (54) A Culhane 10/1: 2000364: Rear, hdwy 2f out, onepcd.		1½	**49a**
93	**ESTIMATION** 13 [1] R M H Cowell 3-9-9 (67) B Reilly (5) 3/1: 4211365: Keen, dsptd lead until 2f out, wknd last.		3	**56a**
4849}	**ORIENTAL MOON** 47 [9] G C H Chung 4-7-12 10h P (40) Dean Williams (7) 50/1: 0-000006: Chsd ldrs 4f:		8	**16a**
94	**MABEL RILEY** 13 [8] M A Buckley 3-8-2 P (46) J Bramhill 25/1: 3500007: Midfield, rdn btn 2f out:		2	**17a**
3249}	**CHANTEUSE** 131 [5] D W Chapman 3-8-10 (54) R Brisland 66/1: 6420008: Nvr a factor on AW bow:		5	**15a**
91	**SUGAR CUBE TREAT** 14 [6] M Mullineaux 7-7-12 6oh (35) S Righton 80/1: 0060/-009: Al rear, t.o.		12	**0a**

9 Ran 1m 44.49 (5.09) Owner Mrs S J Lawrence Trained at Abergavenny

164 — 3.10 Bet Direct On Itv Page 367 Selling Stakes 2yo (G)
£2100 £600 £300 1m f/sand rnd Going 69 -14 Slow Stalls Inside

77	**LYRICAL GIRL** 16 [2] M R Channon 2-8-6 (57) C Catlin 7/4 FAV: 0230031: Rear, hdwy 3f out, styd on to lead cl home, rdn out:			**53a**
87	**RARE COINCIDENCE** 14 [10] R F Fisher 2-8-11 p (54) S Righton 7/1: 0650532: With ldr, led 2f out, edged left & hdd nr fin:		½	**56a**
77	**ARMENTIERES** 16 [1] J L Spearing 2-8-11 bl (54) A Daly 6/1: 0014353: In tch, chall 1f out, onepace.		2	**52a**
77	**HUNTING PINK** 16 [6] H Morrison 2-8-6 (49) L Fletcher (3) 4/1: 4630044: Dsptd lead over 5f, wknd.		4	**39a**
87	**SALUT SAINT CLOUD** 14 [11] Miss V Haigh 2-8-11 vis (50) M Fenton 16/1: 6000045: Rear, rdn 4f out, nvr on terms.		1¾	**41a**
1862}	**RED ACER** 191 [15] P D Evans 2-8-11 (49) S W Kelly 33/1: 0006: Slowly away, late gains but nvr dngrs:		7	**27a**
78	**DAVIDS GIRL** 16 [7] D Morris 2-8-6 (49) J Fanning 25/1: 540607: Handy, wknd 2f out.		shd	**21a**
73	**CITY GENERAL** 17 [12] J S Moore 2-9-2 p (58) L Keniry (3) 14/1: 4062558: Nvr on terms.		¾	**29a**
32	**INTITNICE** 24 [3] Miss K M George 2-8-11 (45) B Reilly (5) 20/1: 2040009: Handy until 3f out:		1	**22a**
78	**YNYS** 16 [4] B Palling 2-8-11 (42) D Kinsella 80/1: 055000: Nvr on terms.		3	**16a**
28	**BE MY ALIBI** 24 [9] J S Moore 2-8-6 (51) K Dalgleish 33/1: 3405000: In tch until halfway.		3	**5a**
	BLUES OVER [5] W J Musson 2-8-6 Paul Eddery 33/1: 0: Nvr dngrs on racecourse bow.		5	**0a**
25	**STAMFORD BLUE** 25 [8] J S Moore 2-9-2 (49) J D Smith 50/1: 6100003: In tch until 3f out.		3½	**0a**
2035}	**THE LAVERTON LAD** 181 [13] C W Thornton 2-8-11 (41) M Tebbutt 100/1: 0000: Al struggling on AW bow.		1¾	**0a**
4930}	**PLATINUM CHIEF** 41 [14] A Berry 2-8-11 bl (53) Darren Williams 33/1: 6020400: In tch until 3f out, eased.		17	**0a**
73	**MILLIETOM** 17 [16] K A Ryan 2-8-11 BL R Winston 20/1: 000: Nvr dngrs:		25	**0a**

16 Ran 1m 46.08 (6.68) Owner C S G Limited Trained at West Ilsley

165 — 3.35 Littlewoodspoker Com Handicap Stakes Div 2 3yo+ 0-60 (F) [59]
£2072 £592 £296 1m f/sand rnd going 69 -02 Slow Stalls Inside

60	**SPY GUN** 19 [5] T Wall 3-9-9 (55) N Chalmers 2/1: 0-0001: In tch, hdwy to lead 2f out, rdn out:			**62a**
72	**SORBIESHARRY** 17 [4] Mrs N Macauley 4-9-0 (44) L Enstone (3) 7/2: 0035042: Rear, hdwy after 5f, rdn appr last, not clr run ins last, kept on:		1	**49a**
907}	**KALOU** 252 [14] B J Curley 5-9-4 (48) S W Kelly 4/1: 250-6503: Held up, hdwy halfway, hard rdn appr last, kept on despite hanging right:		1½	**50a**
62	**NOBLE PURSUIT** 19 [12] P A Blockley 6-9-12 (56) G Parkin 3/1 FAV: 0060044: Dsptd lead, rdn to chall 2f out, onepcd ins:		½	**57a**
114	**GIUST IN TEMP** 10 [2] P W Hiatt 4-8-3 (33) Joanna Badger 25/1: 0050065: Hdwy but not clr run 3f out, no dngr:		3	**28a**
114	**BELLA PAVLINA** 10 [6] M W Brisbourne 5-8-5 (35) B Swarbrick (7) 9/1: 40345-36: In tch, nvr dngrs.		½	**29a**
68	**DASAR** 17 [10] M Brittain 3-9-3 (49) Darren Williams 40/1: 0000007: Dsptd lead until 2f out, wknd last.		½	**41a**
5021}	**SINJAREE** 32 [9] Mrs S Lamyman 5-9-8 (52) C Catlin 16/1: 0000008: In tch, lost place after halfway & nvr dngrs:		5	**35a**
93	**MISS GLORY BE** 13 [11] Miss Gay Kelleway 5-10-0 p (58) T Eaves (5) 15/2: 0632309: In tch, rdn after 5f, wknd next.		2	**37a**
4970}	**EL PEDRO** 37 [13] N E Berry 4-9-6 (50) M Savage (5) 25/1: 5605400: Slowly away, in tch, btn 2f out.		shd	**28a**
93	**VERMILION CREEK** 13 [1] R Hollinshead 4-8-12 (42) Stephanie Hollinshead (7) 16/1: 1400000: Nvr on terms.		½	**19a**
38	**TANGA DANCER** 23 [7] B Smart 3-9-1 (47) R Ffrench 14/1: 0-046100: Nvr dngrs.		4	**15a**
4724}	**LITTLETON VALAR** 56 [3] J R Weymes 3-8-8 p (40) D Fentiman (3) 50/1: 0020060: Nvr dngrs:		4	**0a**
99	**SUBTLE MOVE** 13 [8] D Shaw 3-8-8 vis (40) G Gibbons 66/1: 0000000: Bhd after halfway.		9	**0a**

14 Ran 1m 45.15 (5.75) Owner Mr Derek & Mrs Marie Dean Trained at Church Stretton

166	12.00 Bet Direct On Attheraces Interactive Handicap Stakes Div 1 3yo+ 0-60 (F)		[60]
	£2121 £606 £303	6f f/sand rnd Going 72 -22 Slow	Stalls Inside

85	CHISPA 15 [3] K R Burke 5-10-0 (60) Darren Williams 11/2: 0053021: Handy, led 2f out, drvn & held on well:		65a
91	EASTERN BLUE 15 [4] Mrs L Stubbs 4-9-2 p (48) I Mongan 7/1: 4500622: Trkd ldrs, drvn to chall fnl 1f, just held cl-home:	½	50a
74	GAME GURU 18 [7] T D Barron 4-9-13 bl (59) Laura Jayne Crawford (7) 9/1: 30600D3: Prom, kept on for press, btn under 1L:	shd	61a
157	SHIFTY 3 [11] D Nicholls 4-9-9 bl (55) A Nicholls 9/2 FAV: 6504234: Mid-div wide, styd on for press, nrst fin:	1¼	53a
65*	JALOUHAR 20 [6] B P J Baugh 3-10-0 p (60) J Fanning 12/1: 2250615: Held up, kept on for press, no dngr.	2½	51a
2934}	BEST LEAD 146 [5] Ian Emmerson 4-9-10 VIS (56) C Catlin 66/1: 0-000006: Led 4f, wknd:	½	45a
94	DIL 14 [10] Mrs N Macauley 8-9-5 (51) Steven Harrison (7) 14/1: 6000607: Outpcd & bhd, mod gains wide.	nk	39a
4023}	SILVER MASCOT 98 [2] R Hollinshead 4-8-13 (45) A Culhane 10/1: 660-0608: Held up, nvr pace to chall:	¾	31a
65	CLEVELAND WAY 20 [1] D Carroll 3-9-3 vis (49) R Fitzpatrick 25/1: 5204009: Chsd ldrs 4f.	1¾	31a
117	MAD MICK MEESON 10 [15] G B Balding 3-9-9 t (55) A Clark 12/1: 5050400: Hmpd & bhd start, mod late prog.	1¾	33a
4791}	AMANDAS LAD 53 [16] M C Chapman 3-8-11 (43) G Duffield 25/1: 0000030: Chsd ldrs wide 4f, abs.	nk	20a
4701}	EVANGELIST 58 [9] A Berry 3-8-8 (40) P Bradley (3) 50/1: 4000000: Al rear, abs.	1½	13a
2712}	YOB 155 [13] P D Evans 4-8-8 t (40) S W Kelly 66/1: 00-00000: Sn bhd, abs.	1	11a
110	CAROLS CHOICE 11 [14] A Sadik 6-8-11 (43) N Chalmers (5) 16/1: 4006300: Chsd ldrs 3f out, wknd.	shd	14a
3329}	FESTIVE AFFAIR 129 [12] B Smart 5-9-7 (53) R Ffrench 12/1: 0-164300: Struggling halfway, abs.	hd	23a
124	CASH 10 [8] Paul Johnson 5-9-11 (57) Lisa Jones (3) 10/1: 0000050: Mid-div, struggling from 2f out.	5	15a
16 Ran	1m 18.94 (5.64)	Owner Mrs Elaine M Burke	Trained at Leyburn

167	12.30 Bet Direct In Running Sky Text 293 Selling Stakes Div 1 3yo+ (G)		
	£2086 £596 £298	6f f/sand rnd Going 72 -05 Slow	Stalls Inside

4360}	PLAYFUL SPIRIT 80 [1] J Balding 4-8-7 vis (46) J Edmunds 20/1: 0030001: Cl-up trav well, led halfway, rdn out ins last:		47a
61	HEATHYARDSBLESSING 20 [2] R Hollinshead 6-8-12 (46) A Culhane 12/1: 00-00062: Chsd ldrs, kept on for press, not rch wnr:	1¾	46a
91	EAGER ANGEL 15 [4] R F Marvin 5-8-7 p (35) L Fletcher (3) 33/1: 0600063: Held up, kept on late for press.	hd	40a
133	AINTNECESSARILYSO 7 [5] N E Berry 5-8-12 (42) M Savage 25/1: 0030054: Rear, late gains.	1	43a
4432}	BALI STAR 76 [6] R J Hodges 8-8-12 (43) C Catlin 16/1: 0405005: Prom, no extra dist.	2	38a
30	FIENNES 25 [8] Mrs N Macauley 5-8-12 (43) Lisa Jones (3) 13/2: 260-0056: Led till halfway, wknd dist.	shd	38a
93	CHAMPAGNE RIDER 14 [14] D Shaw 7-8-12 e (36) Darren Williams 40/1: 0050007: In tch, not pace to chall.	nk	37a
55	LAGGAN MINSTREL 21 [16] P W D'Arcy 5-8-12 (48) B Reilly (5) 11/1: 0000008: Chsd ldrs, outpcd fnl 2f.	3½	28a
30	PATIENTES VIRTIS 25 [7] Miss Gay Kelleway 4-9-0 vis (49) J P Guillambert (3) 11/2: 1106069: Rdn in rear, mod prog.	1¾	26a
30	RECADERO 123 [10] Trond Hansen 7-9-5 M Fenton 11/8 FAV: 02010-10: Chsd ldrs, eff wide, drvn & btn dist.	nk	30a
130	THE GAY FOX 7 [12] B G Powell 9-8-12 bl t (40) L Keniry (3) 14/1: 2535050: Sn struggling.	2	18a
4608}	ATTILA THE HUN 66 [9] F Watson 4-8-12 (38) D Mernagh 66/1: 0-000000: Chsd ldrs till halfway, abs.	½	16a
3748}	LIONS DOMANE 11 [11] A Berry 6-9-5 (47) R Winston 25/1: 0110000: Slowly away, al rear, eased, abs.	6	8a
5020}	FINNINGLEY CONNOR 33 [15] Ronald Thompson 3-8-12 (65) D Sweeney 33/1: 1435-000: Prom, btn 2f out.	9	0a
30	LORD MERLIN 25 [13] D Nicholls 4-8-12 (70) Joanna Badger 50/1: 0/0060-00: Slowly away & sn bhd.	16	0a
15 Ran	1m 18.68 (5.38)	Owner Simon Mapletoft Racing II	Trained at Doncaster

168	1.00 Bet Direct On Attheraces Interactive Handicap Stakes Div 2 3yo+ 0-60 (F)		[60]
	£2114 £604 £302	6f f/sand rnd Going 72 -05 Slow	Stalls Inside

92	MAJIK 14 [7] D J S ffrench Davis 4-10-0 (60) I Mongan 7/2 FAV: 0004231: Mid-div, swtchd rail & hdwy to lead dist, rdn out:		71a
4929}	NEVER WITHOUT ME 42 [12] P J McBride 3-8-12 VIS (44) Paul Scallan 9/1: 5002: Trkd ldrs trav well, ev ch fnl 2f, rdn & not pace of wnr:	2	48a
	MISS WONG ONE 52 [8] Frederick John Bowles 3-9-9 (55) S W Kelly 25/1: 0000203: Led/dsptd lead till dist, kept on for	1	56a
92	DOCTOR DENNIS 14 [11] Mrs Lydia Pearce 6-9-3 vis (49) N Pollard 10/1: 0400444: Held up, kept on for press, nrst fin:	1¼	47a
94*	ACORAZADO 14 [15] G L Moore 4-9-10 bl e (56) G Carter 9/2: 0405515: Rear/wide, late gains, nvr dngr.	5	42a
65	BLUE MAEVE 20 [14] J Hetherton 3-8-11 (43) G Parkin 80/1: 0006: Held up, late gains for press, no dngr.	nk	28a
94	TRAVELLING TIMES 14 [13] J S Wainwright 4-9-5 vis (52) T Eaves (5) 12/1: 5004327: In tch wide, outpcd fnl 2f:	¾	35a
68	BABY BARRY 18 [5] Mrs G S Rees 6-9-13 vis (59) G Duffield 11/1: 0042308: Prom, no extra bef dist.	nk	41a
68	GERONIMO 18 [1] Miss Gay Kelleway 6-9-11 p (57) Lisa Jones (3) 6/1: 6606029: Mid-div, no impress fnl 2f.	hd	38a
94	ON THE TRAIL 14 [3] D W Chapman 6-9-7 (53) A Culhane 8/1: 3230000: Led/dsptd lead 4f, wknd.	1¾	30a
66	ATTORNEY 20 [4] D Shaw 5-9-1 e (47) R Winston 14/1: 0000300: Chsd ldrs till 2f out.	½	22a
4922}	KENNY THE TRUTH 42 [16] Mrs J Candlish 4-8-8 T (40) P M Quinn 50/1: 2450000: Wide & al bhd, abs/t-strap.	6	0a
129	DUO LEONI 10 [10] R M Beckett 3-10-0 (60) M Tebbutt 12/1: 0215020: Chsd ldrs wide till halfway.	shd	21a
4722}	FITZ THE BILL 57 [9] N B King 3-8-9 (41) L Fletcher (3) 66/1: 06000: Sn bhd, abs.	12	0a
3782}	FORMERIC 109 [6] Miss L C Siddall 7-8-8 (40) J McAuley 66/1: 1-000000: Al bhd, abs.	8	0a
15 Ran	1m 17.9 (4.6)	Owner Mr Andrew Stimpson	Trained at Lambourn

169	1.30 Bet Direct Press Red To Bet Nursery Handicap Stakes 2yo 0-85 (E)		[86]
	£2016 £576 £288	5f f/sand str Going 72 Inapplicab	Stalls Stands Side

69	BLUE POWER 18 [5] K R Burke 2-8-3 (61) A Reilly (7) 5/2 FAV: 004421: Trkd ldrs, led over 1f out, rdn & styd on well:		68a
5015}	HELLO ROBERTO 33 [7] M J Polglase 2-9-5 (77) K Ghunowa (7) 9/2: 1030432: Chsd ldrs, swtchd & kept on for press, not pace of wnr:	1½	78a
3450*}	FISSION 124 [4] J A Osborne 2-9-7 bl (79) S W Kelly 7/2: 4414513: Bmpd start, sn led till over 1f out, rallied for press:	1	78a
3766}	DEMOLITION MOLLY 110 [8] R F Marvin 2-9-5 (77) L Fletcher (3) 8/1: 0515054: Led/dsptd lead 3f.	3	69a
3242*}	BACK AT DE FRONT 132 [1] N E Berry 2-9-4 (76) M Savage (5) 11/1: 0115: Chsd ldrs, outpcd fnl 2f:	1	66a
126	CHARLIEISMYDARLING 10 [3] J A Osborne 2-8-7 (65) J Fanning 11/2: 4056: Chsd ldrs till outpcd from halfway.	1½	51a
5015}	SIEGFRIEDS NIGHT 33 [6] M C Chapman 2-7-12 4oh (52) Lisa Jones (3) 25/1: 5540007: Sn struggling & outpcd.	2	37a
3209}	CIACOLE 134 [2] S C Williams 2-8-12 (70) Joanna Badger 14/1: 6548: Al outpcd:	2	46a

SOUTHWELL Tuesday 09.12.03 Lefthand, Sharp, Oval Track

8 Ran 1m 02.30 Owner Mr F Jeffers	Trained at Leyburn

170

2.00 Betdirect Co Uk Maiden Stakes 3yo (D)
£2212 £632 £316   1m f/sand rnd   Going 72   -06 Slow   Stalls Inside

129	NAJAABA 10 [3] Miss J Feilden 3-8-9 (56) B Reilly (5) 3/1 FAV: 660-0431: Mid-div, hdwy to chase ldr 2f out, styd on to lead well ins last:		62a
93	MAGIC MAMMAS TOO 14 [8] T D Barron 3-9-0 (53) D Mernagh 9/2: 6403432: Handy, led 2f out, drvn & hdd well ins last:	1¾	63a
123	PIROUETTES 10 [12] Miss Gay Kelleway 3-8-9 (55) M Fenton 8/1: 40-43043: Chsd ldrs wide, no impress 2f out:	6	47a
4590}	JARRAAF 66 [14] J W Unett 3-9-0 (62) R Winston 5/1: 2652424: Chsd ldrs, no impress dist:	2½	47a
4	DANGER BIRD 29 [7] R Hollinshead 3-8-9 (50) A Culhane 20/1: 3200535: Rear, bmpd after 2f, only mod late prog.	3	36a
	HAVE SOME FUN [11] P R Chamings 3-9-0 I Mongan 10/1: 6: Chsd ldrs 6f on debut.	1½	38a
115	SILVER CRYSTAL 11 [13] Mrs N Macauley 3-8-9 P (50) Lisa Jones (3) 25/1: 0306457: Mid-div, btn 2f out, cheek pieces.	3½	27a
3032]	BLUE MARINER 503 [4] P W Harris 3-9-0 K Dalgleish 4/1: 2-8: Dwelt, somehdwy when hmpd after 2f, no impress after.	2	28a
3248}	GWAZI 132 [1] Miss D A McHale 3-9-0 t S W Kelly 66/1: 09: Al outpcd & rear:	3	22a
3308}	FANTASMIC RIVER 130 [9] B Smart 3-8-9 R Ffrench 50/1: 060: Bhd halfway, abs.	1¾	14a
96	TROFANA FALCON 14 [6] H J Collingridge 3-9-0 M Tebbutt 40/1: 00: Al bhd.	1	17a
2015	KUSTOM KIT FOR HER 183 [5] S R Bowring 3-8-9 BL (53) J Bramhill 25/1: 5054020: Led till 2f out, blnks, abs.	1¼	9a
96	MATRIARCHAL 14 [2] Don Enrico Incisa 3-8-9 (38) Kim Tinkler 100/1: 5000400: Sn bhd.	8	0a
86	TORZAL 15 [10] R F Marvin 3-9-0 (35) L Fletcher (3) 100/1: 540-0000: Al bhd.	17	0a

14 Ran 1m 45.6 (6.2) Owner Mr A K Sparks	Trained at Newmarket

171

2.30 Littlewoods Bet Direct Handicap Stakes 3yo+ 0-100 (C)   [98]
£6929 £2132 £1066 £533   5f f/sand str   Going 72   Inapplicab   Stalls Stands Side

106	ZARZU 13 [16] C R Dore 4-8-9 (79) R Thomas (5) 14/1: 6102541: Held up, strong run for press 1f to lead well ins last, going away:		88a
45*	BOND PLAYBOY 22 [5] B Smart 3-9-3 (87) I Mongan 14/1: 2000012: Chsd ldrs, drvn & kept on well, not pace of wnr:	1¼	90a
64	DANCING MYSTERY 20 [11] E A Wheeler 9-9-5 (89) S Carson 10/1: 2500133: Led/dsptd lead, went on halfway, hdd & no extra well ins last:	½	90a
81	QUITO 17 [1] D W Chapman 6-10-0 bl (98) A Culhane 11/2 FAV: 1005264: Rdn towards rear, nrst fin.	nk	98a
85*	GRANDMA LILY 15 [3] M C Chapman 5-8-2 (72) G Duffield 14/1: 0000015: Chsd ldrs, onepace dist.	shd	72a
64*	TRINCULO 20 [4] N P Littmoden 6-9-8 p (92) J P Guillambert (3) 13/2: 3200016: Chsd ldrs, ch dist, no extra:	hd	91a
106	MAGIC GLADE 13 [14] C R Dore 4-8-10 (80) M Fenton 66/1: 31323-07: Chsd ldrs, onepace dist.	2	74a
64	LANDING STRIP 20 [6] J M P Eustace 3-8-7 (77) J Tate 9/1: 1144348: Mid-div, no impress fnl 1f:	nk	70a
45	QUIET TIMES 22 [9] K A Ryan 4-8-7 bl (77) R Winston 12/1: 5650129: Outpcd, nrst fin:	hd	77a
109*	POLISH EMPEROR 11 [7] P W Harris 3-8-7 bl (77) J Fanning 7/1: 0066410: Led/dpstd lead till halfway.	1¼	66a
64	SUNDRIED TOMATO 20 [12] P W Hiatt 4-9-6 (90) L Fletcher (3) 16/1: 0060000: Chsd ldrs 3.5f.	½	77a
4867}	FROMSONG 46 [8] B R Millman 5-9-6 (90) G Baker 20/1: 0010000: In tch till halfway.	1	75a
64	NOW LOOK HERE 20 [10] B A McMahon 7-8-7 bl (77) G Gibbons 12/1: 5040360: Chsd ldrs till halfway.	hd	61a
64	MASSEY 20 [13] T D Barron 7-9-11 (95) P Makin (7) 25/1: 2-112000: Al outpcd.	1¼	76a
110*	WOODLAND BLAZE 11 [15] P R Chamings 4-8-8 (78) L Keniry (3) 20/1: 0210010: Sn struggling:	2½	52a
4990}	LINCOLN DANCER 36 [2] D Nicholls 6-9-1 (85) A Nicholls 25/1: 0-060000: Al outpcd.	3	51a

16 Ran 1m 0.05 Owner Page Pickering Taylor Ward	Trained at Spalding

172

3.00 Bet Direct In Running Sky Text 293 Selling Stakes Div 2 3yo+ (G)
£2079 £594 £297   6f f/sand rnd   Going 72   -18 Slow   Stalls Inside

3456}	POLAR HAZE 123 [15] Mrs Lydia Pearce 6-8-12 vis (46) R Price 14/1: 0000041: Mid-div, styd on for press to lead well ins		54a
3535}	LAY DOWN SALLY 119 [13] J White 5-8-7 (47) L Fletcher (3) 8/1: 0030302: Held up, hdwy wide for press fnl 2f, not rch wnr:	1	45a
153	CATCHTHEBATCH 3 [16] M J Wallace 7-8-12 (50) D Corby (7) 7/1: 2000063: Handy, rdn/led over 1f out, hdd ins last & no extra:	½	48a
4821}	HEADLAND 49 [11] D W Chapman 5-9-5 bl (71) A Culhane 9/2 FAV: 0400004: Rear/wide, kept on for press, not able to chall:	1¼	52a
33	BELLS BOYS 25 [2] K A Ryan 4-8-12 P (38) G Parkin 33/1: 000-0505: Held up, not able to chall, cheek pieces.	1	43a
4913}	EJAY 43 [10] Julian Poulton 4-8-7 (45) Lisa Jones (3) 33/1: 0/-006: Held up, mod late gains for press.	½	36a
3329}	BOND DOMINGO 129 [5] B Smart 4-8-12 bl (40) M Stainton (2) 25/1: 6000007: Chsd ldrs till dist.	½	39a
70	MR SPLIFFY 18 [3] K R Burke 4-8-12 (52) A Reilly (5) 6/1: 0002008: Chsd ldrs, no impress fnl 1f.	1	37a
92	BOISDALE 14 [8] D Nicholls 5-9-5 (52) N Nicholls 7/1: 1006009: Led, hdd 2f out, wknd.	2	39a
505}	ABOVE BOARD 312 [9] R F Marvin 8-8-12 (43) K Ghunowa (2) 50/1: 60-50000: Al bhd:	8	14a
2394}	TEFI 167 [12] J Balding 5-8-12 bl (43) J Edmunds 12/1: 0026060: Prom, struggling hway.	nk	13a
4691}	GOODWOOD PROMISE 58 [6] N E Berry 4-8-12 (40) M Savage (5) 66/1: 0-000000: Prom, btn 2f out:	shd	13a
4561}	KATALI 773 [1] A Bailey 6-8-7 (35) J Fanning 11/1: 600/-0: Al bhd:	1	6a
1097}	SECOND GENERATION 950 [4] R J Hodges 6-8-12 (37) C Catlin 50/1: 00006/0/-0: Sn struggling, long abs.	1	9a
	ROYAL OVATION 141 [7] N P Littmoden 4-8-12 (30) I Mongan 5/1: 00-00000: Sn bhd:	1½	5a

15 Ran 1m 18.71 (5.41) Owner Mr M M Foulger	Trained at Newmarket

173

3.30 Littlewoodspoker Com Handicap Stakes 3yo+ 0-80 (D)   [80]
£3052 £872 £436   1m6f f/sand   Going 72   +10 Fast   Stalls Inside

140	BID FOR FAME 6 [6] N Tinkler 6-10-0 (80) P Mulrennan (5) 4/5 FAV: 1-200621: Chsd ldrs trav well, led over 1f out, pulled clr ins last, eased cl-home:		93a
3692}	VICTORY QUEST 113 [10] Mrs S Lamyman 3-8-4 vis (63) C Catlin 100/1: 0001252: Prom & keen, led 10f out till over 2f out, styd on well for press, no ch with wnr:	5	67a
138	COURT OF APPEAL 6 [9] B Ellison 6-9-4 t (70) T Hamilton (5) 12/1: 4640243: Prom, chsd ldr over 4f out, led going well over 2f out, sn hdd & no extra:	4	70a
3599}	NORTHERN NYMPH 477 [12] R Hollinshead 4-9-11 (77) Stephanie Hollinshead (7) 66/1: 406235-4: Held up, eff to chase	1½	76a

52

Idrs halfway, no impress fnl 2f:

140	**GLORY QUEST 6** [5] Miss Gay Kelleway 6-9-11 (77) A Culhane 12/1: 5452235: In tch, no impress fnl 3f:	12	67a
138	**DIGGER 6** [1] Miss Gay Kelleway 4-9-6 p (72) I Mongan 8/1: 0025236: Keen early, trkd ldrs, btn 3f out.	7	55a
107	**SEA PLUME 13** [3] Lady Herries 4-9-4 (70) G Duffield 14/1: 4302007: Chsd ldrs, struggling fnl 4f.	8	46a
138	**MAJLIS 6** [8] R M H Cowell 6-8-6 (58) P Makin (7) 13/2: 4//-050028: Al bhd:	3	31a
2543}	**PAULA LANE 162** [7] R Curtis 3-8-13 (72) J F McDonald (5) 50/1: 2405329: In tch halfway, strugg fnl 3f:	hd	44a
67	**KNOWN MANEUVER 20** [11] M C Chapman 5-8-1 (53) Rory Moore (7) 150/1: 0000-000: Prom, btn 4f out.	¾	24a
90	**SIMPLE IDEALS 15** [2] Don Enrico Incisa 9-7-12 23oh (27) Kim Tinkler 100/1: 5650040: Chsd ldrs, strugg hway.	¾	20a
4461*}	**SUDDEN FLIGHT 74** [4] R Ingram 6-10-0 (80) R Havlin 9/1: 0660010: Led 4f, sn bhd:	dist	0a

12 Ran   3m 08.51 (8.71)   Owner Elite Racing Club   Trained at Malton

Official Going STANDARD.

174	11.50 Lynhurst Press Handicap Stakes Div 1 3yo+ 0-75 (E)		[73]
	£2300 £657 £329 **1m2f** p/track **Going 40** **-13 Slow** Stalls Inside		

122	**RYANS FUTURE 11** [6] J Akehurst 3-9-13 (75) N Chalmers (5) 11/2: 3405141: Keen & held up, hdwy 2f out, drvn to lead cl-home:		83a
104	**LYRICAL WAY 14** [12] P R Chamings 4-8-9 bl (54) E Ahern 9/2: 1000222: Mid-div wide, hdwy & led 2f out, rdn & hdd	¾	60a
101	**TRUE COMPANION 14** [9] N P Littmoden 4-9-1 (60) J P Guillambert (3) 3/1 FAV: 0461533: Held up, hdwy wide over 2f out, kept on for press, not able to chall:	nk	65a
147	**EASTER OGIL 4** [14] Jane Southcombe 8-9-4 (63) V Slattery 10/1: 4143064: Wide/rear, kept on for press, nrst fin:	2	65a
122	**RASID 11** [10] C A Dwyer 5-9-6 (65) Dane O'Neill 11/1: 4000305: Keen, rear, rdn & late gains, nvr dngr.	½	66a
1036}	**STREET LIFE 242** [11] W J Musson 5-9-8 (67) M Fenton 14/1: 6300006: Held up, hdwy inner 2f out, no extra dist.	¾	67a
101	**SAMMYS SHUFFLE 14** [5] Jamie Poulton 8-8-12 bl (57) I Mongan 8/1: 00122-67: In tch, rdn & no impress fnl 2f.	nk	56a
104	**INDIAN BLAZE 14** [3] Andrew Reid 9-8-7 (52) Rory Moore (7) 16/1: 0340B08: Prom, btn over 1f out.	1	50a
31	**CORONADO FOREST 26** [13] M R Hoad 4-9-2 (61) A Culhane 16/1: 0226069: Rear, no prog over 1f out.	1¼	57a
101	**ANEMOS 14** [8] P W D'Arcy 8-8-10 bl e (55) B Reilly 16/1: 2055600: Held up, rdn 2f out, no impress.	¾	50a
127	**TODLEA 11** [1] J A Osborne 3-9-13 (75) S W Kelly 25/1: 410000: Led 1m, sn btn.	1	69a
3586}	**ICANNSHIFT 118** [4] S Dow 3-9-8 (70) P Doe 33/1: 0004060: Chsd ldrs, wknd 2f out:	8	53a
1203}	**FRANKSKIPS 228** [7] Miss B Sanders 4-9-10 (69) A Clark 33/1: 20-10500: Trkd ldrs, btn 2f out:	11	38a
148	**SILISTRA 4** [2] Mrs L C Jewell 4-9-6 H bl (65) C Catlin 50/1: 0064-000: Trkd ldr, btn over 2f out:	1	33a

14 Ran   2m 08.11 (5.31)   Owner Mr Vimal Khosla   Trained at Epsom

---

175	12.20 Bet Direct No Q Maiden Stakes 2yo (D)		
	£3147 £899 £450 **1m** p/track **Going 40** **-06 Slow** Stalls Outside		

	JAKE THE SNAKE [6] C N Allen 2-9-0 I Mongan 2/1 JT FAV: 1: Trkd ldrs, led over 2f out, rdn & styd on strongly ins last:		83a
100	**SECRET PLACE 14** [4] E A L Dunlop 2-9-0 E Ahern 25/1: 02: Trkd ldrs, rdn & chsd wnr ins last, no impress:	3	75a
5016}	**ALBINUS 34** [11] A M Balding 2-9-0 Dane O'Neill 20/1: 03: Slow away, hdwy wide halfway, outpcd 2f out, late rally:	1	73a
4927}	**NANTUCKET SOUND 634** [7] M C Pipe 2-9-0 Paul Eddery 20/1: 534: Led 2f out, kept on:	nk	72a
102	**BIENVENUE 14** [10] M P Tregoning 2-8-9 A Daly 4/1: 235: Held up, late gains for press.	shd	67a
100	**BOXGROVE 14** [8] C E Brittain 2-9-0 J F Egan 2/1 JT FAV: 36: Mid-div, sn pushed, nrst fin:	shd	71a
102	**PRINCE VALENTINE 14** [3] D B Feek 2-9-0 M Tebbutt 25/1: 07: Rear, eff/hmpd ins last, no impress.	½	70a
88	**BLUE JAVA 16** [12] H Morrison 2-9-0 L Fletcher (3) 14/1: 048: Trkd ldrs, btn over 1f out.	hd	69a
100	**OKOBOJI 14** [1] M P Tregoning 2-9-0 P Fitzsimons 14/1: 459: Dwelt & held up, nvr a dngr.	½	68a
	SEPARATED [2] E A L Dunlop 2-8-9 M Fenton 25/1: 0: Slow away, al rear on debut.	3½	56a
135	**EMBASSY SWEETS 8** [5] P F I Cole 2-8-9 A Culhane 20/1: 00: Rear & nvr a factor.	shd	56a
4927}	**SKATER BOY 43** [9] Miss S West 2-9-0 D Corby (3) 100/1: 000: Sn struggling, t.o.:	dist	0a

12 Ran   1m 39.88 (3.68)   Owner Mr T P Ramsden   Trained at Newmarket

---

176	12.50 Bet Direct On Attheraces Interactive Novice Stakes 2yo (D)		
	£3136 £896 £448 **5f** p/track rnd **Going 40** **-09 Slow** Stalls Outside		

	TREASURE CAY [1] P W D'Arcy 2-8-8 e Paul Eddery 20/1: 1: Dwelt, sn mid-div, hdwy to lead ins last, rdn out:		78a
135	**ORO VERDE 8** [8] R Hannon 2-9-5 (91) Dane O'Neill 7/2: 2033402: Trkd ldr, rdn & briefly led dist, not pace of wnr nr fin:	½	87a
	PASS GO [6] G A Butler 2-8-8 E Ahern 4/1: 3: Trkd ldrs, shaken up & onepace from dist:	1	73a
49	**RAGGED JACK 22** [3] G A Butler 2-8-12 C Catlin 12/1: 50U4: Slow away, rdn rear, styd on strongly ins last, nrst fin:	hd	76a
13	**AVERAMI 28** [4] A M Balding 2-8-7 L Keniry (3) 25/1: 065: Rear, mod late gains.	1	66a
4947}	**TROTTERS BOTTOM 41** [10] Andrew Reid 2-9-2 (87) J P Guillambert (3) 5/2 FAV: 0206329: In tch wide 4f, abs.	½	75a
119	**RISE 11** [2] Andrew Reid 2-8-11 bl (81) I Mongan 7/2: 5231047: Led till dist, wknd.	nk	69a
	MIDMAAR 54 [5] M Wigham 2-9-2 N Forton 12/1: 5318: Trkd ldrs, btn over 1f out.	4	62a
	PATS NEMISIS 87 [7] B R Johnson 2-8-7 N Chalmers (5) 66/1: 09: Al rear on Brit bow:	¾	51a
	DONT LET GO [9] C R Dore 2-8-3 J Bramhill 100/1: 0: Mid-div wide, struggling fnl 2f on debut.	3	38a

10 Ran   1m 0.25 (2.45)   Owner Bigwigs Bloodstock IV   Trained at Newmarket

---

177	1.25 Bet Direct Press Red To Bet Nursery Handicap Stakes 2yo 0-85 (D)		[87]
	£3150 £900 £450 **7f** p/track rnd **Going 40** **-10 Slow** Stalls Inside		

4892}	**OFF BEAT 46** [8] R F Johnson Houghton 2-9-0 bl (73) S Carson 33/1: 0061061: Rear, smooth prog over 2f out, led ins last, rdn out:		77a
105	**FOOLS ENTIRE 14** [6] J A Gilbert 2-8-5 (64) F Norton 14/1: 3000132: Prom, rdn & kept on fnl 1f, not pace of wnr:	1	65a
132*	**ANUVASTEEL 8** [5] N A Callaghan 2-9-9 6ex (82) Rory Moore (7) 15/8 FAV: 1500513: Chsd ldrs, sltly hmpd after 2f, rdn & kept on ins last, not able to chall:	½	82a

15	**PREGNANT PAUSE 28** [13] S Kirk 2-8-6 (65) J F Egan 7/1: 4530024: Led, rdn & hdd ins last, no extra:		½	64a
4751}	**LORD OF THE SEA 56** [12] Jamie Poulton 2-9-0 (73) I Mongan 33/1: 0655: Rear, rdn & styd on fnl 2f, nrst fin:		nk	71a
135	**IMPERIUM 8** [7] B J Meehan 2-9-6 (79) R Winston 16/1: 4620046: Chsd ldr, no extra dist:		hd	76a
5005*}	**DISENGAGE 35** [9] G A Butler2-9-4 (77) E Ahern 5/1: 4317: Prom, ch dist, no extra:		½	73a
126	**TURKISH DELIGHT 11** [10] D Morris 2-8-9 (68) M Tebbutt 25/1: 44438: Mid-div wide, no prog dist.		5	55a
51*	**KABREET 22** [4] E A L Dunlop 2-9-1 (74) M Fenton 11/2: 55319: Hmpd after 2f, chsd ldrs, btn dist:		shd	61a
3942}	**MISS JULIE JAY 104** [3] Noel T Chance 2-7-13 (58) J F McDonald (5) 100/1: 0000: Slow away, al rear:		1	43a
112*	**FADEELA 12** [11] P W D'Arcy 2-9-1 e (74) B Reilly (5) 8/1: 4025210: Prom, btn dist:		1¼	56a
25	**LADY PREDOMINANT 27** [15] Andrew Reid 2-7-12 2oh (55) D Kinsella 20/1: 4005020: Al rear, new yard.		nk	38a
29	**LORD GREYSTOKE 26** [14] C P Morlock 2-8-2 (61) J Mackay 40/1: 0050400: Mid-div, sn struggling.		9	26a
4761}	**MAGICO 55** [16] A M Balding 2-8-1 (60) C Catlin 50/1: 0000: Slow away & al bhd:		1¼	22a
79	**WESTERN ROOTS 18** [1] P F I Cole 2-9-7 (80) A Culhane 14/1: 140: Chsd ldrs, hmpd after 2f, drpd rear & virtually p.u. halfway.		dist	0

15 Ran   1m 26.29 (3.49)   Owner Eden Racing (II)   Trained at Didcot

---

178   **1.55 Lynhurst Press Handicap Stakes Div 2 3yo+ 0-75 (E)**   [73]
£2300 £657 £329   1m2f p/track   Going 40   -12 Slow   Stalls Inside

122	**HIP HOP HARRY 11** [6] E A L Dunlop 3-9-10 (72) E Ahern 5/1: 31031: Chsd ldrs, hdwy wide to lead dist, duelled with rnr-up, just prevailed, all out:			76a
104	**EMBER DAYS 14** [3] J L Spearing 4-8-7 (52) S W Kelly 10/1: 160-0552: In tch, rdn & hdwy to chall ins last, just held in a driving fin:		shd	55a
122	**QUANTUM LEAP 11** [14] S Dow 6-9-4 (63) Paul Eddery 8/1: 4004153: Rear, styd on for press, no threat to front pair:		2	63a
5017}	**WAR OWL 34** [12] Ian Williams 6-8-8 (53) C Catlin 14/1: 04550-04: Keen, rear, smooth hdwy wider over 2f out & chall dist, no extra for press:		nk	52a
16	**MISS PEBBLES 28** [8] B R Johnson 3-9-9 P (71) Dane O'Neill 10/1: 2321005: Rear, hdwy 2f out, onepace for press dist:		hd	69a
4428}	**LONDONER 77** [11] S Dow 5-9-6 (65) P Doe 25/1: 0000006: Mid-div, rdn & no prog dist:		1	62a
4207}	**MISTER CLINTON 89** [10] D K Ivory 6-8-11 (56) G Carter 33/1: 2041007: Mid-div, no impress fnl 2f:		nk	52a
97	**CLASSIC ROLE 15** [9] R Ingram 4-9-13 (72) D Sweeney 10/1: 1000038: Led till dist, btn extra:		½	67a
104	**ESPERANCE 14** [5] J Akehurst 3-8-9 P (57) J Mackay 14/1: 0204009: Al bhd in cheek pieces.		1½	50a
136	**LEARNED LAD 8** [1] Jamie Poulton 5-9-6 (65) I Mongan 13/2: 0200050: Prom, btn dist.		nk	57a
4862}	**GABOR 48** [4] G L Moore 4-9-2 bl e (61) H Poulton (7) 14/1: 3210450: Chsd ldrs till 2f out, abs.		shd	53a
104	**MAN THE GATE 14** [2] P D Cundell 4-8-13 (58) S Carson 7/2 FAV: 100D530: Keen & chsd ldr, btn dist.		4	44a
96	**SOPHRANO 15** [7] P W Harris 3-9-3 VIS (65) A Culhane 14/1: 3-600620: Al bhd:		1	50a

13 Ran   2m 07.98 (5.18)   Owner Lucayan Stud   Trained at Newmarket

---

179   **2.25 Littlewoods Bet Direct Conditions Stakes 3yo+ (D)**
£3419 £1052 £526 £263   1m2f p/track   Going 40   -91 Slow   Stalls Inside

82	**WINDY BRITAIN 18** [9] L M Cumani 4-8-12 (92) E Ahern 5/6 FAV: 3313131: In tch, shaken up over 1f out & rdn to lead cl-home, going away:			88a
134	**LINNING WINE 8** [6] B G Powell 7-9-1 (90) S Carson 7/1: 2000002: Trkd ldrs, rdn & led dist, hdd nr fin & no extra:		½	89a
134	**BRILLIANT RED 8** [2] Jamie Poulton 10-9-1 t (89) I Mongan 6/1: 3244003: Styd on wide for press fnl 2f, not rch front pair:		¾	88a
2515*}	**INVADER 164** [8] C E Brittain 7-9-1 (86) M Fenton 12/1: 0602014: Trkd ldr, onepace fnl 1f:		1¾	86a
4390}	**JACK OF TRUMPS 79** [7] G Wragg 3-8-12 (62) J F Egan 33/1: 006-35: Dictated v slow pace, qcknd over 3f out, hdd dist, no extra:		hd	85a
134	**ALRAFID 8** [1] G L Moore 4-9-1 (83) H Poulton (7) 9/2: 0622426: Keen rear, late prog, too much to do off this slow gallop:		½	84a
4491}	**BARRANTES 73** [5] Miss S West 6-8-10 (83) N Chalmers (5) 33/1: 4236007: Mid-div, no impress fnl 2f, abs.		2½	75a
4939}	**SAHAAT 42** [3] J A Osborne 5-9-1 (97) Dane O'Neill 14/1: 6450008: Al bhd:		1¾	78a
1231}	**BRIGHT GREEN 226** [10] J A B Old 4-9-1 (76) C Catlin 66/1: 00150-09: Keen rear, no impress fnl 2f:		5	71a
2200}	**WELSH BORDER 538** [4] C R Dore 5-9-1 (82) J Bramhill 50/1: 0/00000-0: Slow away & al bhd:		dist	0

10 Ran   2m 15.94 (13.14)   Owner Scuderia Giocri   Trained at Newmarket

---

180   **2.55 Bet Direct In Running Sky Text 371 Selling Stakes 3yo+ (G)**
£2170 £620 £310   7f p/track rnd   Going 40   -01 Slow   Stalls Inside

122	**FREE OPTION 11** [2] B Hanbury 8-9-4 BL (73) Dane O'Neill 3/1 FAV: 5300301: Held up, hdwy 2f out, styd on for press to lead line, al out:			62a
123	**WARLINGHAM 11** [14] M Pitman 5-8-12 (54) V Slattery 14/1: 000-0002: Trkd ldrs trav well, rdn & led dist, hdd cl-home:		hd	55a
145	**SENOR MIRO 4** [5] J Akehurst 5-8-12 (50) C Catlin 7/2: 03-00433: Trkd ldrs, rdn to chall ins last, no extra nr fin:		nk	54a
131	**HADATH 8** [1] B G Powell6-8-12 p (68) L Keniry (3) 4/1: 6005304: Mid-div, hmpd & lost place over 2f out, late rally, no dngr:		6	43a
691}	**DOLPHINELLE 288** [7] Jamie Poulton 7-8-12 vis (49) J F Egan 33/1: 0005005: Mid-div, only mod prog:		¾	42a
161	**REPEAT 11** [4] Miss Gay Kelleway 3-9-4 (55) A Culhane 14/1: 0003146: Mid-div, no impress fnl 2f:		shd	48a
3077}	**CARGO 140** [12] H J Collingridge 4-8-12 (48) E Ahern 14/1: 0500007: Mid-div, no prog fnl 2f:		shd	41a
130	**WALKER BAY 8** [6] J C Fox 5-8-7 (48) R Smith 33/1: 00-02408: Slow away, nvr on terms.		1¾	33a
4311}	**AL MUALLIM 83** [13] Andrew Reid 4-9-4 t (50) J P Guillambert (3) 25/1: 0000009: Held up, no impress fnl 2f:		shd	44a
4134}	**XSYNNA 92** [3] P S McEntee 7-8-12 (47) L Fletcher (3) 33/1: 0003000: Led after 1f till dist:		1¾	35a
123	**CRAFTY POLITICIAN 11** [8] G L Moore 6-9-4 BL e (47) I Mongan 8/1: 0400000: Strugg hway:		nk	40a
4826}	**MEELUP 50** [15] A G Newcombe 3-9-4 P (64) N Chalmers (5) 20/1: 0060100: Chsd ldrs 5f:		nk	39a
94	**ALLY MAKBUL 15** [9] J R Best 3-8-13 (53) D Fentiman (7) 12/1: 3001000: Al bhd.		½	33a
4907}	**BUCKENHAM STONE 44** [10] Mrs Lydia Pearce 4-8-8 1ow R Price 33/1: 00: Mid-div, struggling halfway:		½	27a
70	**MONTE VERDE 19** [16] B Palling 3-8-13 p (48) D Kinsella 25/1: 5160400: Led 1f, struggling fnl 2f.		¾	31a
4961}	**PRINCE DOMINO 40** [11] G L Moore 4-9-4 BL e t (49) S W Kelly 14/1: 1620040: Prom, btn 2f out:		1	34a

16 Ran   1m 25.70 (2.9)   Owner Mr B Hanbury   Trained at Newmarket

	181	**3.30 Betdirect Co Uk Handicap Stakes 3yo+ 0-80 (D)**				**[80]**
		£2331 £666 £333	7f p/track rnd	Going 40	+15 Fast	Stalls Inside

81	**WHAT A DANCER** 18 [1] G A Swinbank 6-9-11 (77) R Winston 11/2: 3215401: Held up, smooth hdwy halfway & led dist, rdn & sn asserted:			85a
81	**INCLINE** 18 [4] T G Mills 4-10-0 (80) R Miles (5) 6/4 FAV: 13-00022: Trkd ldrs, rdn to chase wnr dist, al held:		1½	84a
5	**ZILCH** 30 [2] M L W Bell 5-9-9 (75) M Fenton 33/1: 403-0003: Prom, cht dist, kept on onepace:		¾	78a
127	**THE GAIKWAR** 11 [10] N E Berry 4-9-4 bl (70) M Savage 100/1: 0-000004: Slow away, sn in tch, styd on for press fnl 2f, no dngr:		1½	70a
3244}	**GREY PEARL** 133 [3] Miss Gay Kelleway 4-9-7 (73) I Mongan 25/1: 36-00405: Trkd ldr, hdd dist, wknd:		1¾	70a
1660}	**PHECKLESS** 201 [5] R F Johnson Houghton 4-9-4 (70) S Carson 10/1: 00-10056: Rear, eff over 1f out, onepace:		nk	66a
152	**DANIELLES LAD** 4 [6] B Palling 7-9-4 bl (70) D Kinsella 25/1: 3000307: Led 5f, hdd dist, qck reapp.		½	65a
81	**AGILIS** 18 [15] Jamie Poulton 3-10-0 (80) H Poulton (7) 14/1: 2-405008: Rear, mod prog, no dngr.		¾	74a
133	**ROYAL FASHION** 8 [12] Miss S West 3-8-13 (65) N Chalmers (5) 16/1: 360-3029: Slow away, only mod prog:		1¼	56a
133	**FULVIO** 8 [7] Jamie Poulton 3-9-2 (68) J F Egan 16/1: 6500400: Chsd ldrs, btn 2f out.		1½	56a
121	**KILMEENA LAD** 11 [8] J C Fox 7-9-3 (69) Dane O'Neill 20/1: 11/00-000: Trkd ldrs wide, btn 2f out.		nk	56a
151	**CAYMAN BREEZE** 4 [11] S Dow 3-8-13 (65) P Doe 12/1: 2100030: Sn bhd:		nk	51a
2441}	**SPANISH GOLD** 167 [16] A M Balding 3-9-9 (75) L Keniry (3) 16/1: 0-2160: Al bhd:		hd	60a
106	**UNCLE BERNON** 14 [13] G B Balding 4-9-6 (72) R Havlin 20/1: 13-0000: Al towards rear.		½	56a
133*	**RIPPLE EFFECT** 8 [9] C A Dwyer 3-9-10 6ex t (76) B Reilly (5) 12/1: 4153010: Mid-div, struggling fnl 2f.		hd	59a
20	**SIR LAUGHALOT** 27 [14] Miss E C Lavelle 3-9-4 (70) E Ahern 5/1: 00-00020: Handy wide, btn 2f out:		6	42a
16 Ran	1m 24.57 (1.77)	Owner Mr A Barnes			Trained at Richmond

Official Going STANDARD.

	182	**12.15 Bet Direct On Attheraces Interactive Nursery Handicap Stakes 2yo 0-85 (D)**				**[80]**
		£3360 £960 £480	6f f/sand rnd	Going 59	-02 Slow	Stalls Inside

52	**BLOFELD** 24 [2] W Jarvis 2-8-3 (55) Lisa Jones (3) 13/2: 0600551: Trkd ldrs trav well, led dist & rdn clr:			70a
5014}	**SMOKIN JOE** 36 [7] J R Best 2-9-1 (67) N Pollard 7/2: 0662: Trkd ldrs, rdn & outpcd 2f out, kept on for press ins last:		4	70a
4997}	**LIZHAR** 38 [3] M J Polglase 2-9-7 (73) L Fletcher (3) 3/1: 0223143: Led till over 1f out, no extra		¾	73a
42	**SAFFRON RIVER** 25 [6] R Hollinshead 2-8-7 (59) R Ffrench 20/1: 4304: Chsd ldrs, onepce for press.		¾	58a
42*	**BRIDGEWATER BOYS** 25 [4] K A Ryan 2-9-3 bl (69) R Winston 5/2 FAV: 0256215: Sn pshd along, nvr on terms.		2	63a
105	**BURLINGTON PLACE** 16 [1] S Kirk 2-9-2 (68) J D Smith 4/1: 040246: Dwelt, sn strugg:		8	45a
6 Ran	1m 16.97 (3.67)	Owner Byculla Thoroughbreds			Trained at Newmarket

	183	**12.50 Bet Direct No Q Demo 08000 837 888 Handicap Stakes Div 1 3yo+ 0-60 (F)**				**[60]**
		£2086 £596 £288	5f f/sand str	Going 59	Inapplicab	Stalls Stands Side

166	**CASH** 3 [8] Paul Johnson 5-9-11 P (57) R Fitzpatrick 12/1: 0000501: Chsd ldrs, led dist, drvn & held on well:			63a
4116}	**ABRAXAS** 95 [2] J Akehurst 5-9-4 p (50) C Catlin 40/1: 0000002: Mid-div, drvn & styd on well ins last, not reach wnr:		½	53a
109	**KISS THE RAIN** 14 [4] R Brotherton 3-9-3 vis (49) L Fletcher (3) 12/1: 2651033: Chsd ldrs, outpcd halfway, rallied well ins		nk	51a
110	**SANDGATE CYGNET** 14 [7] I Semple 3-9-13 p (59) D McGaffin (3) 7/1: 5000264: Swerved left start, chsd ldrs, kept on onepace for pressure.		1	59a
155	**RELLIM** 6 [1] P A Blockley 4-9-8 (54) D Nolan (5) 7/1: 0644265: Led till dist, no extra:		¾	52a
91	**INCHING** 18 [14] R M H Cowell 3-9-9 vis (55) M Henry 10/1: 0400646: Stands side, in tch, not able to chall.		1¾	49a
4856}	**SOAKED** 51 [3] D W Chapman 10-9-11 bl (57) A Culhane 10/1: 2500357: Chsd ldrs, btn dist:		shd	51a
110	**HENRY TUN** 14 [9] J Balding 5-9-12 bl (58) J Edmunds 7/1: 5000358: Rdn & chsd ldrs, btn dist:		1¼	49a
124	**KINGS BALLET** 13 [6] P R Chamings 5-9-8 (54) I Mongan 11/2 FAV: 0000309: Hmpd start, chsd ldrs, nvr able to chall.		shd	45a
166*	**CHISPA** 3 [12] K R Burke 5-10-7 7ex (67) Darren Williams 13/2: 0530210: Rdn chasing ldrs, no impress.		shd	57a
124	**OUR CHELSEA BLUE** 13 [15] A W Carroll 5-9-8 (54) S Righton 16/1: 6000660: Dwelt, sn rear.		2	43a
65	**FIRE CAT** 23 [5] A P Jones 4-9-3 (49) D Sweeney 33/1: 0-225000: Mid-div, al outpcd.		½	32a
172	**CATCHTHEBATCH** 3 [11] M J Wallace 7-9-4 (50) D Corby (3) 7/1: 0000630: Struggling early, nvr a factor		1	31a
2124}	**SO SOBER** 182 [16] D Shaw 5-9-0 (46) T Hamilton (5) 25/1: 3020000: Stands side, al outpcd, abs.		5	15a
4908}	**FIAMMA ROYALE** 46 [13] M S Saunders 5-9-7 p (53) J Fanning 20/1: 5205000: Sn struggling, abs, chkpcs.		1½	18a
70	**LADIES KNIGHT** 21 [10] D Shaw 3-9-8 (54) R Winston 50/1: 040000: Reared start, v slowly away, t.o.		17	0a
16 Ran	1m 01.37	Owner Insull White Pritchard & Joh			Trained at Stanley

	184	**1.20 Bet Direct Maiden Stakes 2yo (D)**				
		£3126 £893 £447	7f f/sand rnd	Going 59	-00 Slow	Stalls Inside

36	**TITUS SALT** 27 [6] T D Barron 2-9-0 BL (71) D Mernagh 7/2: 4421: Broke well & made all, rdn & styd on strongly ins last:			78a
4917}	**KINGSMAITE** 45 [5] S R Bowring 2-9-0 (66) J Bramhill 9/1: 603642: Chsd ldrs, rdn & chsd wnr dist, kept on but al held:		3½	68a
36	**REDBANK** 27 [4] N A Callaghan 2-9-0 BL (67) Dane O'Neill 4/1: 6600433: Chsd ldrs, kept on onepace for press, no dngr:		3	62a
102	**DAGGERS CANYON** 16 [16] Julian Poulton 2-9-0 J Mongan 9/1: 054: Chsd ldrs, not able to chall.		5	52a
37	**BRETTON** 27 [10] R Hollinshead 2-9-0 p (45) A Culhane 33/1: 065005: Sn struggling rear, nrst fin:		2½	47a
102	**MUSIC MIX** 16 [2] E A L Dunlop 2-9-0 W Ryan 11/4 FAV: 46: Sltly hmpd start & bhd, late gains under hands-and-heels:		¾	46a
98	**VAMPIRE QUEEN** 17 [11] R P Elliott 2-8-9 Dean McKeown 33/1: 0607: Mid-div, nvr threat to ldrs.		shd	41a
42	**VITTORIOSO** 25 [3] Miss Gay Kelleway 2-9-0 p M Fenton 4/1: 058: Chsd ldrs, wknd fnl 2f:		nk	45a
	CHIMES EIGHT [7] R A Fahey 2-8-9 T Hamilton (5) 14/1: 9: Outpcd/bhd, little hdwy on debut.		nk	39a
126	**MONKEY OR ME** 13 [15] P T Midgley 2-9-0 G Parkin 66/1: 00: Chsd ldrs till over 1f out.		6	38a
	KILLING ME SOFTLY [14] J Gallagher 2-9-0 D Sweeney 66/1: 0: Slow away & sn bhd on debut.		1¾	29a
4973}	**BATTLE BACK** 41 [8] S C Williams 2-8-9 B Reilly (5) 33/1: 00: Sn well bhd, abs/AW bow.		3	18a
51	**EMILYS DAWN** 24 [13] D K Ivory 2-8-9 (57) A Nicholls 12/1: 0060: Chsd ldrs, rdn & btn 2f out.		2½	13a

	MARIA MARIA [12] Mrs N Macauley 2-8-9 L Enstone (3) 50/1: 0: Dwelt, al well bhd on debut.	½	12a
159	EVENING FRAGRANCE 4 [3] G C H Chung 2-9-0 bl J Mackay 66/1: 000: Went left start, sn well bhd, qck reapp.	10	0a
15 Ran	1m 30.76 (4.16) Owner Sporting Occasions Racing No 5	Trained at Thirsk	

185

1.55 Littlewoods Bet Direct Handicap Stakes 3yo+ 0-65 (F)   [63]
£2149 £614 £307   1m6f f/sand   Going 59   -17 Slow   Stalls Inside

4644}	VINCENT 66 [8] John A Harris 8-7-12 2oh (33) J Mackay 10/1: 6245061: Rear/wide, styd on for press fnl 3f to lead nr line:		42a
97	VANBRUGH 17 [4] Miss D A McHale 3-9-2 vis t (60) Darren Williams 16/1: 0006602: Cl-up & led 8f out, rdn & hdd cl-home:	hd	66a
4457}	MERCURIOUS 77 [5] J Mackie 3-7-12 1oh (41) Dale Gibson 7/1: 000-0633: Chsd ldrs, rdn & not able to chall fnl 2f:	5	42a
65}	DAUNTED 387 [10] P A Blockley 7-9-8 (59) D Nolan (5) 8/1: 421526-4: Chsd ldrs 12f:	6	52a
125*	CLAPTRAP 13 [2] R Brotherton 3-8-3 (61) I Mongan 11/10 FAV: 3460015: Trkd ldrs, rdn & no impress over 1f out, eased nr fin:	7	46a
7	HIGH POLICY 32 [9] R Hollinshead 7-10-0 p (65) Stephanie Hollinshead (7) 5/1: 6130156: Mid-div, eff 3f out, no impress.	3½	46a
4587}	UNLEADED 69 [13] J Akehurst 3-7-12 12oh (30) Lisa Jones (3) 40/1: 0-0007: Chsd ldrs, struggling halfway:	11	10a
90	DASH OF MAGIC 18 [14] J Hetherton 5-8-3 (40) C Catlin 20/1: 4104008: Held up, eff halfway, no impress.	2½	5a
138	BID SPOTTER 9 [7] Mrs Lucinda Featherstone 4-8-8 (45) L Keniry (2) 25/1: 6204-009: Led till 8f out, sn bhd.	2	7a
2170}	FAYRAY RHYTHM 180 [11] Ian Emmerson 6-8-3 (40) A Nicholls 33/1: 3//-000050: Chsd ldrs 12f, abs.	23	0a
103	TOP SON 16 [1] A P Jones 4-7-12 10oh (25) Joanna Badger 50/1: 0000: Bhd halfway, h'cap bow.	15	0a
107	DANCE LIGHT 16 [3] T T Clement 4-9-9 (60) Dean McKeown 12/1: 116-0600: Chsd ldrs 9f.	¾	0a
90	HUMDINGER 18 [12] D Shaw 3-9-4 e (62) T Hamilton (5) 16/1: 2136100: Sn struggling, eye-shield.	½	0a
142	MAWHOOB 9 [15] Mrs N Macauley 5-8-10 vis (47) Steven Harrison (7) 50/1: 1000000: Dwelt, al bhd, t.o.	17	0a
14 Ran	3m 10.43 (10.63) Owner Mrs A E Harris	Trained at Melton Mowbray	

186

2.30 Bet Direct No Q On 08000 93 66 93 Handicap Stakes 3yo+ 0-85 (D)   [79]
£3430 £980 £490   1m f/sand rnd   Going 59   +02 Fast   Stalls Inside

47	NOUL 25 [6] K A Ryan 4-9-4 bl (69) R Winston 14/1: 0360421: Trkd ldrs, drvn to lead cl-home, all out:		73a
93	HOWS THINGS 17 [7] D Haydn Jones 3-9-1 (67) Paul Eddery 6/1: 4031122: Chsd ldrs, drvn & led over 1f out, hdd cl-home:	hd	70a
141	COOL TEMPER 9 [10] P F I Cole 7-9-12 t (77) A Culhane 7/4 FAV: 1014033: Wide, pushed along halfway, styd on well for press ins last against stands rail, nrst fin:	1¾	77a
93*	LOCKSTOCK 17 [3] M S Saunders 5-9-0 bl (65) J Fanning 5/1: 0000414: Trkd ldrs, onepace for press ins last:	nk	64a
5019}	CRITICAL STAGE 36 [2] John Berry 4-8-10 e (61) Lisa Jones (3) 10/1: 5000335: Trkd ldrs, led over 2f out till dist, kept on for press:	shd	60a
127	LABRETT 13 [8] Miss Gay Kelleway 6-9-11 p (76) M Fenton 12/1: 4365106: Pushed along towards rear, kept on late wide, no dngr:	1¼	72a
4855}	FIRST MAITE 51 [5] S R Bowring 10-9-6 (71) J Bramhill 20/1: 4053067: Led wide overall till 4f out, no impress fnl 2f:	1½	64a
157	CRUSOE 6 [11] A Sadik 6-9-0 bl (65) Dane O'Neill 12/1: 5350448: Chsd ldr, no impress fnl 2f:	½	57a
99	PHAROAHS GOLD 17 [9] D Shaw 5-9-0 e (65) Darren Williams 20/1: 3420109: Dwelt, sn rdn & nvr on terms.	1¾	54a
127	OLDENWAY 13 [12] R A Fahey 4-9-2 (67) D Swift (6) 25/1: 2502000: Chsd ldrs till 4f out.	3½	49a
113	WHIPPASNAPPER 14 [4] J R Best 3-9-3 (69) D Fentiman (7) 33/1: 0060000: Dsptd lead inner 6f.	8	37a
11 Ran	1m 43.94 (4.54) Owner Mr John Duddy	Trained at Hambleton	

187

3.05 Bet Direct No Q Demo 08000 837 888 Handicap Stakes Div 2 3yo+ 0-60 (F)   [60]
£2086 £596 £298   5f f/sand str   Going 59   Inapplicab   Stalls Stands Side

124	LAUREL DAWN 13 [14] I W McInnes 5-9-12 (58) L Fletcher (3) 11/2: 5002041: Sn prom, drvn to lead well ins last:		64a
4023}	THE LEATHER WEDGE 101 [3] A Berry 4-9-1 (47) P Bradley (5) 25/1: 3000402: Led overall far rail, hdd well ins last:	1	50a
94	WAINWRIGHT 17 [12] P A Blockley 3-10-0 (60) Dean McKeown 7/1: 0523533: Sn prom, styd on onepace for press:	¾	61a
33	EMPRESS JOSEPHINE 28 [6] J R Jenkins 3-9-8 vis (54) S W Kelly 10/1: 0012424: Chsd ldrs, styd on:	1½	51a
3741}	SERGEANT SLIPPER 114 [10] C Smith 6-9-0 vis (46) P Makin (7) 33/1: 5100005: Bhd, late gains for press, abs.	nk	42a
5006}	COLLEGE HIPPIE 37 [7] J F Coupland 4-9-3 (49) P Gallagher (7) 16/1: 0000046: Dwelt, late prog for press, no dngr.	1¼	42a
124	STRENSALL 13 [4] R E Barr 6-9-12 (58) R Fitzpatrick 9/2: 6001427: Chsd ldr, no extra dist:	hd	50a
92	CATCH THE CAT 17 [1] J S Wainwright 4-9-4 vis (50) T Eaves 4/1 FAV: 0056058: Dwelt, nvr on terms:	hd	41a
172*	POLAR HAZE 3 [9] Mrs Lydia Pearce 6-9-7 7ex vis (53) R Price 8/1: 0000419: Mid-div, nvr pcd to chall:	½	42a
45	SAFRANINE 25 [2] Miss A Stokell 6-9-11 p (57) L Treadwell (7) 16/1: 0600000: Chsd ldrs 4f.	hd	45a
109	SEA THE WORLD 14 [11] D Shaw 3-10-0 (60) Darren Williams 33/1: 0400300: Al outpcd, nvr factor.	2½	41a
110	HAGLEY PARK 14 [15] M Quinn 4-9-2 (48) R Winston 8/1: 2016400: Chsd ldrs stands side till halfway.	5	17a
952}	IVORY VENTURE 252 [16] D K Ivory 3-9-11 (57) D Sweeney 25/1: 0646-540: Outpcd, nvr factor.	3½	17a
2692}	STAR APPLAUSE 159 [5] J Balding 3-9-0 (46) J Edmunds 25/1: 5206000: Sn bhd, eased dist:	2½	0a
4022}	CRESSEX KATIE 101 [13] J R Best 4-9-12 (58) N Pollard 8/1: 1106400: Slow away, al bhd:	30	0a
15 Ran	1m 0.76 Owner Ivy House Racing	Trained at Catwick	

188

3.35 Littlewoodspoker Com Apprentice Classified Stakes 3yo+ 0-60 (G)   [ ]
£2142 £612 £306   1m f/sand rnd   Going 59   Inapplicab   Stalls Inside

163*	MISS CHAMPERS 4 [9] P D Evans 3-8-11 (59) S Donohoe (7) 2/1 FAV: 0300511: Rear, hdwy halfway, rdn/led over 1f out, asserted under hands-and-heels ins last:		69a
163	ROCK CONCERT 4 [11] I W McInnes 5-8-6 vis (58) Natalia Gemelova (5) 11/4: 3322132: Al prom, styd on for press, no ch with wnr:	1½	59a
160	SHATIN HERO 4 [7] G C H Chung 3-8-8 p (59) Dean Williams (7) 7/1: 1442053: Trkd ldrs, led over 3f out, edged left & hdd over 1f out, no extra:	1¾	59a
308}	CHABIBI 198 [4] Trond Hansen 4-8-6 (40) B Reilly (3) 4/1: 0600-014: Chsd ldrs, styd on onepace for press:	½	55a
46	AIR OF ESTEEM 25 [13] Ian Emmerson 3-8-9 (48) L Keniry 33/1: 0200455: Chsd ldrs, not able to chall:	nk	57a
131	LEONOR DE SOTO 10 [14] J R Best 3-8-5 (53) D Fentiman (7) 20/1: 1466006: Bhd, eff wide, no impress on ldrs.	¾	53a
736}	JUNGLE LION 284 [2] John A Harris 5-8-9 t (55) Derek Nolan (3) 33/1: 030-6067: Chsd ldrs till dist.	5	47a
128*	PUPS PRIDE 13 [10] Mrs N Macauley 6-8-9 vis (60) Lisa Jones 5/1: 1600118: Bhd, only mod prog:	4	40a

SOUTHWELL Friday 12.12.03 Lefthand, Sharp, Oval Track

4552} COLLEGE STAR 72 [6] J F Coupland 5-8-9 bl (29) L Treadwell (4) 50/1: 0000009: Chsd ldrs till over 2f out, abs. 3½ 30a
4967} ROBIN SHARP 41 [1] J Akehurst 5-8-9 p (55) N Chalmers (3) 16/1: 4210P00: Led 5f till 3f out, wknd. 5 24a
66 TAP 23 [5] Ian Emmerson 6-8-9 (51) D Corby 25/1: 1142000: Chsd ldrs till 3f out: 10 7a
4102} ANSWERED PROMISE 97 [3] A W Carroll 4-8-9 (58) P Gallagher (3) 20/1: 0010100: Led 3f, new stable. 1¼ 4a
91 COURT MUSIC 18 [12] R E Barr 4-8-6 vis (36) T Eaves 50/1: 0-000000: Sn pushed along & al bhd. 9 0a
13 Ran 1m 44.18 (4.78) Owner Mrs S J Lawrence Trained at Abergavenny

189 12.00 Bet Direct No Q On 08000 93 66 93 Nursery Handicap Stakes Div 1 2yo 0-75 (E) [81]
£2576 £736 £368 1m f/sand rnd Going 64 -21 Slow Stalls Inside

15 CELTIC HEROINE 31 [11] M A Jarvis 2-9-5 (72) M Henry 9/4 FAV: 51541: Chsd ldrs, led 3f out, rdn & hdd over 1f out, rallied 78a
for press to lead again line, all out:
4988} BLUE EMPIRE 40 [4] P C Haslam 2-8-12 (65) Rory Moore (7) 7/2: 0102: Chsd ldrs, rdn & led over 1f out, hung left ins last & shd 70a
hdd line:
4532} ABROGATE 74 [8] P C Haslam 2-7-13 (52) D Fentiman (7) 20/1: 0503003: Chsd ldrs, hung left & no impress. 5 49a
77* THE JOB 21 [7] A D Smith 2-8-9 (62) W Ryan 13/2: 040014: Led 2f, btn 2f out: 3½ 53a
54 UNCLE JOHN 25 [2] S Kirk 2-9-1 (68) J D Smith 11/1: 00105: Pushed along rear, mod prog: 2 55a
3246} BUCHANAN STREET 136 [5] N A Callaghan 2-8-7 BL T (60) F Norton 14/1: 0206: Mid-div, struggling fnl 3f: 3 42a
69 KNIGHT TO REMEMBER 22 [3] K A Ryan 2-7-13 4oh 1ow (47) R Ffrench 25/1: 00607: Chsd ldrs, btn 2f out. 8 21a
4723} TRY THE AIR 61 [10] C Tinkler 2-8-6 (59) C Catlin 25/1: 0008: Prom, btn 3f out: 9 13a
15 CARTRONAGEERAGHLAD 31 [6] J A Osborne 2-9-7 bl (74) S W Kelly 7/2: 1064169: Led after 2f till 3f out, wknd, lame. 8 15a
139 DESERT LIGHT 10 [9] D Shaw 2-7-12 28oh e (23) Lisa Jones (2) 50/1: 000000: Al outpcd rear: 2½ 0
10 Ran 1m 46.22 (6.82) Owner Mr P D Savill Trained at Newmarket

190 12.30 Bet Direct No Q On 08000 93 66 93 Nursery Handicap Stakes Div 2 2yo 0-75 (E) [79]
£2576 £736 £368 1m f/sand rnd Going 64 -27 Slow Stalls Inside

98 BOLD BLADE 18 [9] B Smart 2-8-9 bl (60) R Ffrench 8/1: 60041: Led after 2f, hung right over 2f out, drvn out: 73a
4834} CHARIOT 53 [10] M R Bosley 2-8-13 (64) G Baker 9/1: 064032: Held up, rdn & kept on fnl 2f, no impress on wnr: 6 65a
95* MYANNABANANA 18 [5] J R Weymes 2-9-2 vis (67) M Fenton 5/1: 0660113: Chsd ldrs, hung right & onepace over 1f out: ½ 67a
4808} YANKEEDOODLEDANDY 54 [4] P C Haslam 2-7-13 (50) D Fentiman (7) 16/1: 04004: Pushed along rear, nrst fin: 3 44a
54 ST SAVARIN 25 [2] J R Best 2-9-7 (72) N Pollard 8/1: 0026105: Chsd ldrs, no extra dist: nk 65a
95 TURF PRINCESS 18 [1] Ian Emmerson 2-8-10 (61) A Nicholls 12/1: 3510226: Led 2f, btn dist: shd 54a
4827} RESTART 53 [7] P C Haslam 2-9-3 (68) Rory Moore (7) 11/2: 6037: Al outpcd: 8 48a
111* LASTING DELIGHT 15 [8] Sir Mark Prescott 2-9-5 (70) J Mackay 5/2 FAV: 0518: Chsd ldrs, btn 3f out: 8 37a
4974} ALTARES 42 [6] P Howling 2-8-3 (54) F Norton 16/1: 0009: Slowly away & sn struggling: 18 0a
5024} SAMOLIS 36 [3] R Curtis 2-7-13 14oh 1ow BL (35) R Thomas 66/1: 0000: Chsd ldrs 4f: 10 0a
10 Ran 1m 46.68 (7.28) Owner Mr Paul J Dixon Trained at Thirsk

191 1.00 Stephanie Smith Birthday Claiming Stakes 3-4yo (E)
£2086 £596 £298 1m3f f/sand Going 64 -28 Slow Stalls Inside

5001} THEATRE TINKA 39 [4] R Hollinshead 4-9-1 p (62) A Culhane 5/1: 5003201: Trkd ldrs, led over 4f out & rdn clr from 3f out, 70a
held on well for press:
3198} CAROUBIER 139 [5] Ian Williams 3-8-13 (83) C Catlin 8/11 FAV: 0015022: Pushed along towards rear, hdwy to chase wnr 3f 2 69a
out, onepace:
114 SAMAR QAND 15 [1] Julian Poulton 4-8-4 p (41) J Jeffrey (7) 25/1: 0003653: Led 4f, btn 3f out. 18 34a
5001} PLATINUM CHARMER 39 [12] K A Ryan 3-8-13 (65) R Winston 10/1: 4300004: Bhd & wide, mod gains. 5 41a
156 RADIANT BRIDE 7 [9] K R Burke 3-8-0 (45) A Reilly (5) 14/1: 0050025: Pushed along towards rear, nvr a factor: 1¾ 26a
1444} PERTEMPS BIANCA 217 [8] A D Smith 3-7-12 BL (45) F P Ferris (3) 33/1: 50-54006: Chsd ldrs 7f: 15 5a
BONJOUR DIRECTA 41 [11] Trond Hansen 3-8-3 J Mackay 10/1: 0606507: Held up, nvr a factor: 3 6a
97 TORO BRAVO 18 [6] R M Beckett 3-8-8 BL (64) W Ryan 16/1: 0000008: Led/dsptd lead 7f, sn btn: 2½ 7a
142 TURFTANZER 10 [7] Don Enrico Incisa 4-9-7 T (40) Kim Tinkler 66/1: 1600-059: Chsd ldrs, btn 3f out, t-strap. 4 11a
67 A TWO 24 [10] B Palling 4-8-4 (44) J Fanning 33/1: 140-0000: Prom, btn 4f out. 1¼ 0a
1882} TWO STEPS TO GO 194 [3] Ian Emmerson 4-8-9 (40) A Nicholls 33/1: 5004040: Struggling halfway, abs. dist 0a
11 Ran 2m 31.37 (10.07) Owner Mr Tim Leadbeater Trained at Upper Longdon

192 1.35 Littlewoods Bet Direct Maiden Stakes 2yo (D)
£2142 £612 £306 1m f/sand rnd Going 64 -33 Slow Stalls Inside

112 BETHANYS BOY 15 [15] B Ellison 2-9-0 (73) R Winston 7/1: 4040251: Prom & led over 3f out, rdn & styd on strongly: 82a
88 CARRIACOU 19 [2] P W D'Arcy 2-8-9 e (72) B Reilly (5) 9/2: 522002: In tch, styd on for press fnl 2f, not able to chall: 3½ 71a
43 HAWKIT 26 [4] J A Osborne 2-9-0 (72) Dane O'Neill 3/1 FAV: 23223: Chsd ldrs, kept on for press, nvr able to chall: 1½ 74a
VICTORY LAP [7] M R Channon 2-8-9 C Catlin 20/1: 3: Dwelt, bhd, styd on under hands & heels fnl 2f, nrst fin: dht 68a
54 AMWELL BRAVE 25 [16] J R Jenkins 2-9-0 (69) S W Kelly 12/1: 0500345: Prom, wide, no extra fnl 2f: ½ 72a
162 SMART BOY PRINCE 5 [13] P A Blockley 2-9-0 (50) D Nolan (2) 25/1: 0005046: Led 4f, btn 2f out, qck reapp. 7 61a
MY PARIS [3] K A Ryan 2-9-0 G Parkin 40/1: 7: Dwelt, sn chsd ldrs, btn 3f out, debut. ¾ 60a
4825} CASSANOS 53 [11] Miss Gay Kelleway 2-9-0 (60) M Fenton 50/1: 0008: Chsd ldrs till halfway, abs. hd 59a
102 SUNNY LADY 17 [10] E A L Dunlop 2-8-9 W Ryan 7/1: 69: Dwelt, prom 5f. 6 45a
FRANKIES WINGS [5] T G Mills 2-9-0 R Miles (5) 9/2: 0: Dwelt & al bhd: 7 39a
PATRICIA RAY [6] C Drew 2-8-9 M Halford (7) 66/1: 0: Dwelt, sn outpcd on debut. nk 33a
4223} KNICKYKNACKIENOO 91 [14] T T Clement 2-9-0 (56) M Henry 50/1: 6040060: Keen & prom 4f, abs. 1 36a
5018} MAID THE CUT 37 [8] A D Smith 2-8-9 J Bramhill 66/1: 00: Slow away & al bhd. 5 24a
THARAA [12] E A L Dunlop 2-8-9 J Fanning 20/1: 0: Dwelt, keen & prom 5f on debut. 3½ 17a
5024} FUBOS 36 [9] Julian Poulton 2-9-0 (75) I Mongan 12/1: 0000: Prom, btn 3f out: 8 9a
MIKES MATE [1] C J Teague 2-9-0 T Eaves (5) 66/1: 0: Slowly away & sn bhd on debut. dist 0a

57

16 Ran   1m 47.19 (7.79)   Owner Mr Graeme Redpath   Trained at Malton

	193	2.05 Betdirect Co Uk Handicap Stakes 3yo+ 0-85 (D)			[79]
		£2212 £632 £316 7f f/sand rnd Going 64 -09 Slow Stalls Inside			

74   MON SECRET 22 [6] B Smart 5-8-7 (58) R Ffrench 7/2: 0000121: Chsd ldrs, rdn to chall fnl 2f, narrow lead ins last, held on all out: **64a**

152   WARDEN WARREN 7 [5] Mrs C A Dunnett 5-8-13 bl (64) B Reilly (5) 16/1: 0000002: Dwelt, sn chsd ldrs, swtchd wide to chall fnl 2f, hung left dist, styd on well for press, just held: *hd* **69a**

168*   MAJIK 4 [1] D J S ffrench Davis 4-9-2 7ex (67) I Mongan 100/30 FAV: 0042313: Trkd ldrs, smooth hdwy to chall fnl 2f, drvn & just held: *shd* **71a**

27*   ASHTREE BELLE 29 [4] D Haydn Jones 4-9-11 (76) R Thomas (5) 13/2: 5224014: Trkd ldrs, short of room over 1f out, kept on for press ins last: 1¼ **78a**

113   WINNING PLEASURE 15 [8] J Balding 5-9-7 (72) J Edmunds 12/1: 6000005: Trkd ldrs, rdn & led 2f out, sn hdd & no extra dist: 3 **68a**

84   SCRAMBLE 19 [7] B Ellison 5-8-0 bl e t (51) F P Ferris (3) 5/1: 6441346: Chsd ldrs, ch 2f out, hung left & no extra over 1f out: 3½ **40a**

92*   FAR NOTE 18 [3] S R Bowring 5-9-0 bl (65) Darren Williams 8/1: 4104217: Led till 2f out, fdd: 7 **42a**

99   SUPREME SALUTATION 18 [2] D W Chapman 7-9-1 (66) A Culhane 11/1: 0000568: Chsd ldrs till halfway, joc reported gelding nvr moving well.   1½ **40a**

113   AFRICAN SPUR 15 [9] P A Blockley 3-9-7 (72) Derek Nolan (7) 20/1: 4200009: In tch, hmpd halfway, sn strugg rear.   2 **42a**

9 Ran   1m 31.72 (5.12)   Owner Pinnacle Monash Partnership   Trained at Thirsk

	194	2.40 Littlewoodspoker Com Maiden Stakes 3-4yo (E)			
		£2254 £644 £322 1m4f f/sand Going 64 -47 Slow Stalls Inside			

118   DUB DASH 14 [8] S C Williams 3-9-0 B Reilly (5) 33/1: 01: Chsd ldrs, led 4f out, rdn clr 2f out, styd on strongly & eased   **75a**

154   EXIT TO HEAVEN 7 [7] Miss Gay Kelleway 3-8-9 (60) M Fenton 4/1: 0600022: Chsd ldrs, rdn & outpcd 4f out, rallied late for press, nvr threatened wnr: 5 **62a**

951}   NEWTONIAN 253 [11] J Parkes 4-9-5 Dean McKeown 13/2: 6-23: Chsd ldrs, smooth hdwy to press wnr 3f out, no extra for press fnl 1f: ½ **66a**

HEATHYARDS PRIDE [4] R Hollinshead 3-9-0 Dale Gibson 33/1: 4: Dwelt, bhd, little hdwy on debut.   18 **43a**

89   FORTUNES FAVOURITE 19 [14] G M Moore 3-8-9 T Eaves (5) 7/1: 045: Bhd, nvr a factor.   4 **32a**

118   REMEMBRANCE 14 [6] J M P Eustace 3-9-0 BL t (65) J Tate 11/4 FAV: 5020366: Trkd ldrs & keen, led over 6f out till 4f out, sn btn: 4 **31a**

115   GALLEY LAW 15 [10] R Craggs 3-9-0 (25) R Ffrench 66/1: 0007: Chsd ldrs till 4f out.   2½ **27a**

4995}   DR JULIAN 39 [5] Miss A Stokell 3-9-0 p (43) P Makin (7) 25/1: 0005008: In tch till halfway, 'lost action'.   14 **9a**

SEANS MEMORY [12] Mrs C A Dunnett 3-9-0 C Catlin 20/1: 9: Slowly away & nvr a factor on debut.   6 **1a**

154   SIMON THE POACHER 7 [13] L P Grassick 4-9-5 (42) L Keniry (3) 66/1: 0000000: Slow away, al bhd.   9 **0a**

142   BY ALL MEN 10 [2] P A Blockley 3-9-0 (50) S Yourston (7) 25/1: 0-000: Sn bhd, broke blood vessel.   11 **0a**

2718}   SENZA SCRUPOLI 159 [16] M D Hammond 3-9-0 A Culhane 11/1: 0-0050: Dwelt, al bhd, new yard.   ¾ **0a**

4961}   PERTEMPS CONECTION 43 [3] A D Smith 3-8-9 W Ryan 33/1: 00: Prom 6f, abs, 'lost action'.   11 **0a**

2693}   HARTSHEAD 160 [16] G A Swinbank 4-9-5 (65) R Winston 7/2: 304460: Led till over 6f out, sn btn: 27 **0a**

14 Ran   2m 47.59 (13.29)   Owner Mr Stuart C Williams   Trained at Newmarket

	195	3.15 Bet Direct In Running Sky Text 293 Handicap Stakes 3yo+ 0-75 (E)			[73]
		£2163 £618 £309 1m f/sand rnd Going 64 +10 Fast Stalls Inside			

4949}   SANGIOVESE 44 [3] H Morrison 4-9-4 (63) L Fletcher (3) 5/1: 0622-301: Made all & readily pulled clr fnl 3f, won easily in a fast time: **79a**

141   BRANDY COVE 10 [6] B Smart 6-9-6 (65) R Ffrench 9/2: 3210452: Chsd ldrs, onepace fnl 2f: 13 **64a**

152   ZARIN 7 [16] D W Chapman 5-9-11 (70) A Culhane 8/1: 3006023: Held up, mod gains for press, nvr a dngr: 2 **65a**

2241}   FARAWAY LOOK 177 [15] J G M O'Shea 6-9-2 (61) R Havlin 25/1: 4635534: Held up, only mod gains: 1¾ **53a**

136   TROPICAL CORAL 11 [10] C Tinkler 3-9-13 (73) J Fanning 12/1: 0145045: In tch, no impress fnl 3f.   1½ **62a**

141   LUCAYAN MONARCH 10 [5] P A Blockley 5-8-13 p (58) Dean McKeown 10/1: 6000006: In tch, btn 2f out.   2½ **42a**

99*   MCQUEEN 18 [14] Mrs H Dalton 3-10-0 (74) P Mulrennan (5) 11/8 FAV: 3203317: Chsd ldrs wide, hung left & btn 2f out: ¾ **57a**

4740}   TROPICAL SON 60 [12] D Shaw 4-7-12 2oh vis (41) R Thomas 50/1: 2030008: Towards rear, nvr a factor, abs.   hd **25a**

40   ALLEGRINA 28 [9] K A Ryan 3-9-2 BL (62) R Winston 14/1: 4-140569: Chsd wnr halfway, btn 2f out: 3½ **37a**

62   JESSIE 24 [7] Don Enrico Incisa 4-7-13 (44) Kim Tinkler 50/1: 40-00400: Chsd ldrs till halfway,   shd **19a**

86   PROUD VICTOR 19 [1] D Shaw 3-7-12 2oh vis (42) D Kinsella 25/1: 0060400: Prom, no ch fnl 3f.   shd **18a**

3150}   QUIET READING 141 [11] M R Bosley 6-9-10 vis (69) G Baker 14/1: 0613460: In tch till over 2f out.   6 **33a**

97   SURDOUE 18 [4] P Howling 3-9-12 (72) Paul Eddery 50/1: 0500000: Prom till halfway.   12 **16a**

4944}   LADY OF GDANSK 45 [8] H J Collingridge 4-8-0 (45) C Catlin 50/1: 0004000: Cl-up, wknd qckly halfway, abs.   25 **0**

14 Ran   1m 43.69 (4.29)   Owner Kentisbeare Quartet   Trained at East Ilsley

	196	1.00 Bet Direct On Attheraces Interactive Handicap Stakes 3yo+ 0-70 (E)			[69]
		£2058 £588 £294 1m3f f/sand Going 44 -14 Slow Stalls Inside			

142   SPANISH STAR 12 [13] Mrs N Macauley 6-8-0 (41) Lisa Jones (3) 15/2: 3400041: Hld up, hdwy 2f out, styd on to lead well ins last: **47a**

97   TROUBLE MOUNTAIN 20 [5] M W Easterby 6-10-0 (69) P Mulrennan (5) 85/40 FAV: 0054402: Mid-div, drvn & styd on well fnl 2f, nrst fin: ½ **74a**

161   GEORGE STUBBS 7 [1] M J Polglase 5-9-12 (67) S W Kelly 10/1: 3056063: Led after 1f & clr after 3f out, rdn & hdd well ins last, no extra: 1½ **70a**

72   SMOOTHIE 24 [4] Ian Williams 5-9-9 (64) D Nolan (5) 8/1: 0166104: Dwelt & held up, hdwy to chase wnr 2f out, sn rdn & no extra: 5 **60a**

141   PENWELL HILL 12 [15] T D Barron 4-9-13 (68) P Makin (7) 8/1: 1113465: Mid-div, no impress fnl 2f: 3 **60a**

154	**DANUM 9** [2] R Hollinshead 3-8-9 P (54) A Culhane 20/1: 4656066: Chsd ldrs, no extra fnl 2f:		3½	41a
97	**NIGHT WARRIOR 20** [10] D Flood 3-9-8 (67) P Doe 20/1: 1200007: Mid-div, no impress fnl 3f.		3½	49a
44	**YORKER 28** [7] Ms Deborah J Evans 5-9-11 (66) I Mongan 14/1: 5300108: Held up, rdn 4f out, no hdwy.		¾	47a
140	**CALCAR 12** [11] Mrs S Lamyman 3-8-3 VIS (48) R Thomas (4) 33/1: 0500509: Al bhd:		8	19a
165	**SINJAREE 7** [14] Mrs S Lamyman 5-8-11 VIS (52) Dane O'Neill 25/1: 0000000: Led 1f, cl-up till 2f out, visor.		2½	19a
160	**ERSAAL 7** [3] J Jay 3-8-9 (54) K Dalgleish 16/1: 0650300: Chsd ldrs, btn 3f out:		2½	17a
131	**CAPTAIN GINGER 13** [6] H Morrison 3-9-10 (69) L Fletcher (3) 12/1: 0034000: Trkd ldrs 7f.		8	22a
165	**GIUST IN TEMP 7** [8] P W Hiatt 4-7-12 6oh (33) Joanna Badger 14/1: 0500650:		5	0a
39	**FELIDAE 30** [12] M Brittain 3-8-1 (46) T Williams 33/1: 0050: Struggling halfway, h'cap bow.		8	0a
2687}	**MORNING SUN 163** [9] K O Cunningham Brown 3-7-12 3oh (40) F P Ferris (3) 66/1: 6650000: Sn well bhd, t.o., abs.		dist	0a

15 Ran   2m 27.65 (6.35)   Owner Mrs N Macauley   Trained at Melton Mowbray

197   1.30 Bet Direct On 0800 32 93 93 Maiden Auction Stakes 2yo   (F)
£2205 £630 £315   5f f/sand str   Going 44   Inapplicab   Stalls Stands Side

76	**SCOTTISH EXILE 23** [7] K R Burke 2-8-6 VIS (64) Darren Williams 11/8 FAV: 0440231: Broke well & made all, in command dist, readily.			71a
146	**VELVET TOUCH 9** [5] J R Jenkins 2-8-2 J Bramhill 9/2: 302: Chsd ldrs, kept on fnl 2f, nvr any ch with wnr:		5	56a
2357}	**FAYRZ PLEASE 175** [3] M C Chapman 2-8-9 Andrew Webb (7) 50/1: 03: Hmpd start, sn chsd wnr, no impress over 1f out:		½	61a
	ELVINA [10] A G Newcombe 2-8-4 F P Ferris (3) 6/1: 4: Dwelt, some hdwy halfway, nvr threat to ldrs.		3	48a
146	**RED ROCKY 9** [4] J Gallagher 2-8-2 P Doe 6/1: 565: Dwelt & al outpcd.		2	41a
146	**LYRICAL LADY 9** [11] Mrs A J Bowlby 2-8-6 (65) D Corby (3) 8/1: 0546: Dwelt, sn struggling.		5	32a
169	**CHARLIEISMYDARLING 6** [2] J A Osborne 2-8-7 (65) J Fanning 11/2: 40567: Dwelt, nvr a factor.		½	31a
79	**ANATOM 23** [1] M Quinn 2-8-2 (40) F Norton 40/1: 000668: Slowly away, prom till halfway.		10	1a

8 Ran   59.74   Owner Mrs Melba Bryce   Trained at Leyburn

198   2.00 Littlewoods Bet Direct Handicap Stakes 3yo+ 0-85 (D)   [82]
£3402 £972 £486   6f f/sand rnd   Going 44   +05 Fast   Stalls Inside

4485}	**BLAKESET 79** [3] T D Barron 8-9-0 VIS (68) D Mernagh 8/1: 6211101: Trkd ldr, rdn & led over 1f out, held on well for press:			75a
193	**WINNING PLEASURE 2** [8] J Balding 5-9-4 bl (72) J Edmunds 6/1: 60000052: Held up wide, styd on for press ins last, nrst fin:		1¼	73a
113	**CASHEL MEAD 17** [1] J L Spearing 3-9-12 (80) S W Kelly 6/1: 1-000623: Trkd ldrs, kept on fnl 2f, rider eased nr line & lost 2nd:		hd	81a
128	**HURRICANE COAST 16** [12] P A Blockley 4-8-8 (62) Dean McKeown 16/1: 0201234: Trkd ldrs, onepace fnl 2f:		½	61a
110	**MALAHIDE EXPRESS 17** [5] M J Polglase 3-8-10 bl (64) L Fletcher (3) 12/1: 0005635: Led till over 1f out, no extra dist:		¾	61a
41*	**CANTERLOUPE 28** [10] P J Makin 5-10-0 (82) D Sweeney 5/1: 5330516: Trkd ldr, onepace fnl 2f:		nk	78a
161*	**CLOUD DANCER 7** [2] K A Ryan 4-9-12 6ex (80) R Winston 5/1: 6203317: Mid-div, no impress & eased in last.		3	68a
183	**CHISPA 3** [11] K R Burke 5-8-12 6ex (66) Darren Williams 12/1: 5302108: Chsd ldrs till dist:		shd	54a
171	**GRANDMA LILY 6** [7] M C Chapman 5-9-4 (72) I Mongan 4/1 FAV: 0000159: Al rear:		2	55a
155+*	**PADDYWACK 9** [9] D W Chapman 6-9-7 bl (75) A Culhane 9/1: 6056610: Al rear:		nk	57a
61	**BLUE CIRCLE 26** [4] M Mullineaux 3-7-12 18oh P (34) Lisa Jones 150/1: 0060000: Chsd ldrs 3f, chkpcs.		15	0

11 Ran   1m 15.62 (2.32)   Owner Mr Nigel Shields   Trained at Thirsk

199   2.30 Betdirect Co Uk Maiden Stakes 3yo+   (D)
£2258 £645 £323   1m f/sand rnd   Going 44   -17 Slow   Stalls Inside

115	**NUZZLE 17** [10] M Quinn 3-8-9 vis (58) R Winston 5/1: 3360631: Broke well & led after 1f, drvn & held on well fnl 2f:			51a
170	**MAGIC MAMMAS TOO 6** [9] T D Barron 3-9-0 (53) D Mernagh 11/10 FAV: 4034322: Led 1f, remained handy & styd on for press fnl 2f, al just held by wnr:		1	53a
3493}	**SANTA CATALINA 128** [3] Miss Gay Kelleway 4-8-10 t (35) T Eaves (5) 25/1: 30-00603: Mid-div, styd on for press fnl 2f, not able to chall:		1¾	45a
143	**PACIFIC OCEAN 12** [11] Mrs S A Liddiard 4-9-1 t (46) F Norton 7/1: 5666534: Held up wide, eff 3f out, not able to chall:		¾	49a
143	**CHESNUT RIPPLE 12** [2] D Shaw 4-8-10 (53) R Havlin 5/1: 0406625: Chsd ldrs, no impress dist.		½	43a
115	**RED MOOR 17** [6] R Hollinshead 3-9-0 P (45) A Culhane 20/1: 6-650006: Held up, eff 2f out, nvr a dngr.		1	46a
1929}	**DESIRES DESTINY 194** [1] M Brittain 5-8-10 (48) M Lawson (6) 66/1: 6607: Dwelt, sn handy, btn 2f out, abs.		2½	36a
4677]	**HELLBENT 419** [4] J A Osborne 4-9-1 (50) S W Kelly 8/1: 530-8: Dwelt, nvr on terms:		1¾	38a
170	**GWAZI 6** [8] Miss D A McHale 3-9-0 t Darren Williams 66/1: 009: Held up, nvr a factor.		nk	37a
143	**PETROLERO 12** [7] Mrs S A Liddiard 4-9-1 t (44) M Fenton 25/1: 0-000040: Chsd ldrs till 2f out:		13	14a
	MOUNT LOGAN 1172 [5] R Curtis 8-9-1 Dale Gibson 66/1: 0//-0: Slowly away & sn bhd, long abs.		1¼	11a
71	**RUBY ANNIVERSARY 24** [12] J Balding 3-8-9 (38) J Edmunds 50/1: 040000: Cl-up 3f, sn btn.		3	0a
84	**PRESIDENTS LADY 21** [13] P W Hiatt 6-8-10 (30) Joanna Badger 66/1: 0020//-000: Al rear.		13	0

13 Ran   1m 44.46 (5.06)   Owner Mr A Newby   Trained at Wantage

200   3.00 Allweather-Racing Com Selling Stakes 2yo   (G)
£2044 £584 £292   6f f/sand rnd   Going 44   -07 Slow   Stalls Inside

139*	**ALIZAR 12** [7] M J Polglase 2-8-12 (54) L Fletcher (3) 6/4 FAV: 4063611: Sn led, readily asserted from dist, val for 8L+:			59a
139	**EMARADIA 12** [2] P D Evans 2-8-12 (52) S W Kelly 13/2: 6234542: Chsd ldrs, chall over 2f out, sn outpcd by easy wnr.		6	47a
73	**HES A ROCKET 24** [11] Mrs C A Dunnett 2-8-12 VIS (40) N Chalmers (5) 40/1: 6000003: In tch wide, styd on for press, nvr threat to wnr:		2½	40a
87	**PARDON MOI 21** [13] Mrs C A Dunnett 2-8-12 (49) Dane O'Neill 14/1: 0260654: Dwelt, sn chsd ldrs wide, onepace for press fnl 2f:		1½	36a
139	**PHILLY DEE 12** [3] J Jay 2-8-8 1ow (47) A Culhane 5/2: 6604325: Cl-up, no extra dist:		hd	31a
73	**FISHERS DREAM 24** [12] J R Norton 2-8-12 vis (54) Darren Williams 10/1: 0006426: Dwelt, prom wide 4f:		½	33a
139	**ARE YOU THERE 12** [10] T D Barron 2-8-12 BL (52) Gemma Anderson (7) 12/1: 1000067: Chsd ldrs 4f, blnks.		2½	26a

59

SOUTHWELL Monday 15.12.03 Lefthand, Sharp, Oval Track

73	WHITTINGHAMVILLAGE 24 [6] A Berry 2-8-7 (50) F Norton 9/1: 6446048: Pushed along rear, nvr on terms.		*shd*	**21a**
126	MISS JUDGED 16 [9] A P Jones 2-8-7 e t (50) G Hannon 25/1: 600009: Dwelt, nvr a factor.		½	**19a**
4454}	TICKLEPENNY LOCK 80 [1] C Smith 2-8-12 (40) Dean McKeown 50/1: 6066000: Al outpcd rear, abs.		1¾	**20a**
139	COLEORTON PRINCE 12 [5] K A Ryan 2-8-12 (40) R Winston 33/1: 000000: Held up, btn 2f out.		8	**2a**
63	DANDY JIM 26 [4] D W Chapman 2-8-12 R Brisland 66/1: 00: Slow away, nvr factor.		10	**0a**
12 Ran	1m 16.33 (3.03) Owner Mr Paul J Dixon		Trained at Newark	

201   **3.30 Free #25 Bonus @ Littlewoodspoker Com Handicap Stakes 3yo+ 0-75 (E)**   **[75]**
£2044 £584 £292   **1m6f f/sand**   **Going 44**   **-07 Slow**   Stalls Inside

173	VICTORY QUEST 6 [4] Mrs S Lamyman 3-8-9 vis (63) Dane O'Neill 11/2: 0012521: Cl-up, led 3f out, drvn & held on well ins last:			**72a**
147	REMINISCENT 9 [5] R F Johnson Houghton 4-9-1 vis (62) S Carson 100/30: 0345352: Trkd front pair, eff to press wnr over 1f out, edged left & no extra nr fin:		¾	**69a**
97	STRAVMOUR 20 [1] R Hollinshead 7-7-12 2oh (43) Dale Gibson 12/1: 5006043: Chsd ldrs, styd on onepace for press fnl 3f:		4	**46a**
138*	DUBAI DREAMS 12 [3] M J Polglase 3-8-5 vis (59) P Makin (6) 14/1: 6000014: Led & keen early, hdd 3f out, no extra bef dist:		2	**57a**
137	BUCKS 13 [2] D K Ivory 6-10-0 (75) I Mongan 8/11 FAV: 0-352125: Held up, rdn 4f out, no impress over 2f out:		1¾	**71a**
5 Ran	1m 16.33 (3.03) Owner Mr P Lamyman		Trained at Louth	

202   **12.25 Bet Direct In Vision Sky Page 293 Handicap Stakes Div 1 3yo+ 0-60 (F)**   **[60]**
£2079 £594 £297   **7f f/sand rnd**   **Going 62**   **-03 Slow**   Stalls Inside

68	PAWN IN LIFE 25 [5] T D Barron 5-9-12 (58) D Mernagh 11/2: 4225051: Sn prom, led over 2f out, drvn out:			**62a**
166	SHIFTY 7 [1] D Nicholls 4-9-8 bl (54) A Nicholls 5/1: 5042342: Missed break, hdwy to trk ldrs 3f out, drvn & kept on, al held by wnr:		1½	**54a**
188*	MISS CHAMPERS 4 [10] P D Evans 3-10-5 6ex (65) S Donohoe (7) 7/2 FAV: 3005113: Dwelt, rdn towards rear, styd on for press, not reach front pair:		nk	**64a**
60	ROSTI 27 [9] P C Haslam 3-9-1 (47) Rory Moore (7) 11/1: 0500054: Trkd ldrs, hung left but kept on onepace for press:		¾	**44a**
86	BRILLIANTRIO 22 [3] M C Chapman 5-9-0 (46) Andrew Webb (7) 33/1: 1U06505: Dwelt, chsd ldrs, no room dist, onepce.		2	**39a**
165	DASAR 8 [8] M Brittain 3-9-3 (49) Darren Williams 50/1: 0000006: Led/dsptd lead 2f, btn over 1f out:		1¼	**39a**
150*	SMITH N ALLAN OILS 10 [2] M Dods 4-9-10 p (56) S W Kelly 10/1: 0523017: Chsd ldrs 5f:		3	**40a**
161	BULAWAYO 8 [15] Andrew Reid 6-9-11 (57) Dane O'Neill 10/1: 3632038: Mid-div, no impress fnl 2f:		3½	**35a**
74	GLENROCK 25 [4] A Berry 6-9-4 (50) P Bradley (5) 25/1: 0010009: Led/dsptd lead 5f, wknd.		¾	**27a**
40	OPEN HANDED 31 [12] B Ellison 3-9-5 t (51) R Winston 40/1: 0600000: Dsptd lead 2f, struggling halfway.		nk	**27a**
168	TRAVELLING TIMES 7 [6] J S Wainwright 4-9-6 vis (52) T Eaves (5) 20/1: 0043200: In tch 4f.		3	**22a**
4958}	NEWCLOSE 46 [13] N Tinkler 3-9-0 (46) J Fanning 16/1: 00500: Slow away & al bhd:		6	**6a**
161	RED DELIRIUM 8 [16] R Brotherton 7-9-4 bl (50) L Fletcher (3) 20/1: 4000600: Dwelt, al bhd:		¾	**9a**
117	PANCAKEHILL 17 [11] D K Ivory 4-9-9 (55) I Mongan 10/1: 0236550: Al towards rear.		1¼	**11a**
141	PRIDE OF KINLOCH 13 [7] J Hetherton 3-10-0 (60) Dean McKeown 33/1: 3405000: Prom 4f.		2½	**11a**
4499}	BALALAIKA TUNE 79 [14] W Storey 4-9-2 (48) J Bramhill 50/1: 44-0550: Chsd ldrs 4f:		6	**0**
16 Ran	1m 31.16 (4.56) Owner Mr Laurence O'Kane		Trained at Thirsk	

203   **12.55 Bet Direct On Sky Active Nursery Handicap Stakes 2yo 0-75 (E)**   **[75]**
£2457 £702 £351   **7f f/sand rnd**   **Going 62**   **-03 Slow**   Stalls Inside

189	BLUE EMPIRE 3 [7] P C Haslam 2-9-4 (65) L Enstone (3) 10/11 FAV: 01021: Handy & led going well over 2f out, hung left under press dist but sn asserted, eased nr fin:			**76a**
158*	WEET AN HAUL 8 [2] P A Blockley 2-8-3 6ex (50) J Bramhill 7/2: 0600012: Dwelt, hdwy to chase wnr over 1f out, sn no impress but kept on:		5	**50a**
158	GARNOCK VENTURE 8 [6] A Berry 2-8-6 bl (53) Dale Gibson 25/1: 6650043: Led till over 2f out, kept on onepace for press:		1½	**50a**
88	CEASAR 22 [9] P C Haslam 2-8-5 (52) Rory Moore (7) 33/1: 6206004: Chsd ldrs, nvr able to chall:		5	**40a**
4132}	JASMINE PEARL 98 [1] B J Meehan 2-9-7 (68) L Keniry (3) 16/1: 52055: Chsd ldrs, no impress fnl 2f:		1½	**53a**
4761}	SONDERBORG 61 [3] G L Moore 2-9-1 (62) G Carter 14/1: 63006: Outpcd, nvr a factor.		½	**46a**
4610}	ROMANTIC DRAMA 71 [8] B J Meehan 2-9-4 bl (65) R Winston 13/2: 00467: Prom 4f, sn btn:		8	**36a**
4946}	ONE ALONE 47 [10] J G Given 2-8-8 (55) Joanna Badger 33/1: 0008: Al rear:		3	**20a**
2018}	GENTLEMAN GEORGE 190 [5] D K Ivory 2-8-3 (50) F P Ferris 40/1: 0509: In tch 5f:		nk	**14a**
4903}	SAVERNAKE BRAVE 50 [4] K R Burke 2-8-5 (52) Lisa Jones (3) 40/1: 0266500: Slowly away & al bhd:		4	**9a**
10 Ran	1m 31.03 (4.53) Owner Blue Lion Racing II		Trained at Middleham	

204   **1.25 Press Interactive To Bet Direct Classified Claiming Stakes 3yo+ 0-60 (F)**   **[60]**
£2079 £594 £297   **1m3f f/sand**   **Going 62**   **-00 Slow**   Stalls Inside

114	AVEIRO 18 [6] B G Powell 7-8-9 bl (31) K Dalgleish 8/1: 0603041: Held up, rdn & outpcd 4f out, styd on for press fnl 2f to lead line, all out:			**42a**
160*	QUEENSBERRY 8 [10] J O'Reilly 4-9-0 (49) J D O'Reilly (7) 3/1 JT FAV: 3020412: Trkd ldrs, led 3f out, rdn & hdd line:		*shd*	**46a**
2457}	DELTA FORCE 172 [9] P A Blockley 4-8-12 (41) Derek Nolan (7) 25/1: 0635603: Held up & keen, hdwy wide 3f out, onepace for press dist:		2	**41a**
4096}	MISTY MAN 101 [5] Miss J Feilden 5-8-11 (30) B Reilly (5) 33/1: 0000044: Chsd ldrs 9f, wknd:		10	**29a**
89	BERKELEY HEIGHTS 22 [8] B Smart 3-8-9 bl (45) R Ffrench 14/1: 40-50065: Cl-up, hmpd 3f out, wknd, blnks.		¾	**30a**
4918}	GRAND LASS 49 [4] T D Barron 4-8-11 (55) D Mernagh 7/2: 4002046: Led 1m, btn 2f out:		*shd*	**28a**
165	NOBLE PURSUIT 8 [1] P A Blockley 6-8-12 p (56) Dean McKeown 3/1 JT FAV: 0600447: In tch 7f:		1¾	**27a**
4970}	PRINCE PROSPECT 45 [3] Mrs L Stubbs 7-9-0 (48) Kristin Stubbs (7) 15/2: 053-4648: Al bhd:		7	**20a**
3159}	GINNER MORRIS 144 [2] J Hetherton 8-8-11 (27) G Parkin 25/1: 030-0009: Struggling halfway:		28	**0a**
9 Ran	2m 28.07 (6.77) Owner The Dream Connection		Trained at Winchester	

60

	1.55 Littlewoods Bet Direct Handicap Stakes 3yo+ 0-85 (D)		[80]
205	£3500 £1000 £500　　5f f/sand str　　Going 62　　Inapplicab	Stalls Outside	

109	FRASCATI 18 [7] A Berry 3-9-6 (72) F Norton 9/1: 6004251: Chsd ldrs, rdn to chall fnl 2f, prevailed nr line, all out:		77a
4491}	PALAWAN 79 [5] A M Balding 7-9-13 (79) Amy Parsons (7) 10/1: 0110102: Sn prom & led 2f out, just hdd line:	hd	84a
155	DAINTREE AFFAIR 10 [2] K R Burke 3-8-10 (62) G Baker 11/1: 3310053: Chsd ldrs, ch over 1f out, not pace of front pair:	1¾	62a
35	NEW OPTIONS 31 [4] W J Musson 6-9-1 (67) Paul Eddery (3) 25/1: 2230004: Rdn towards rear, nrst fin.	½	65a
4969}	ST IVIAN 45 [14] Mrs N Macauley 3-8-11 vis (63) L Enstone (3) 25/1: 6060005: Prom, onepace dist:	½	59a
153	RAFTERS MUSIC 10 [3] Julian Poulton 8-9-7 (73) N Callan 10/1: 2254326: Outpcd, late gains:	nk	68a
187	SEA THE WORLD 4 [8] D Shaw 3-8-8 VIS (60) Darren Williams 40/1: 4003007: Dwelt, nvr pace to chall:	½	53a
4287}	RIDICULE 90 [1] J G Portman 4-9-2 bl (68) R Havlin 25/1: 4630548: Dwelt, chsd ldrs, no impress dist:	1	59a
198	MALAHIDE EXPRESS 1 [15] M J Polglase 3-8-12 bl (64) L Fletcher (3) 7/1: 00056359: Cl-up 3f:	nk	54a
113	RONNIE FROM DONNY 18 [6] B Ellison 3-9-4 P (70) Dane O'Neill 10/1: 5000000: Chsd ldrs, no impress fnl 2f:	shd	60a
171	NOW LOOK HERE 7 [9] B A McMahon 7-9-11 (77) K Dalgleish 11/2 FAV: 0403600: Dwelt, sn outpcd by ldrs.	shd	66a
4769*}	COUNT COUGAR 61 [16] S P Griffiths 3-8-9 (61) J McAuley 12/1: U060010: Al outpcd:	1½	46a
183	HENRY TUN 4 [11] J Balding 5-8-6 vis (58) J Edmunds 10/1: 0003500: Dwelt, sn strugg:	1¾	39a
5025}	PRIME RECREATION 39 [10] P S Felgate 6-9-5 (71) Dale Gibson 10/1: 0002400: Keen & led 3f, sn btn.	1½	48a
144	PARK STAR 10 [13] D Shaw 3-8-6 vis (58) J F McDonald (5) 10/1: 0005600: Struggling halfway.	1	33a
106	CRETAN GIFT 20 [12] N P Littmoden 12-10-0 vis (80) J P Guillambert (3) 10/1: 0040/-050: Slow away & al rear.	1¾	51a

16 Ran　　1m 0.18　　　　Owner Lord Crawshaw　　　　　　　　　　Trained at Cockerham

	2.25 Betdirect Co Uk Handicap Stakes 3yo+ 0-60 (F)		[60]
206	£2065 £590 £295　　2m f/sand　　Going 62　　-40 Slow	Stalls Inside	

185*	VINCENT 4 [1] John A Harris 8-8-7 6ex (39) J Mackay 5/1 JT FAV: 2450611: Chsd ldrs, hdwy to chase ldr 4f out & led 2f out, drvn out:		48a
185	VANBRUGH 4 [6] Miss D A McHale 3-9-6 vis t (60) Darren Williams 8/1: 0066022: Led after 1f, trav well, hdd 2f out, no extra:	1¾	66a
2241}	PIPSSALIO 180 [7] Jamie Poulton 6-8-10 bl t (42) F Norton 25/1: 2/-000043: Held up, hdwy to chase front pair 3f out, no impress nr last:	10	39a
67	AMBITIOUS ANNIE 27 [11] R Hollinshead 4-8-8 (40) Stephanie Hollinshead (7) 5/1 JT FAV: 04-50124: Keen & prom, btn 2f out:	8	30a
75	VANDENBERGHE 25 [9] J A Osborne 4-9-3 (49) Paul Eddery 17/2: 00-00635: Held up, only mod prog:	11	30a
	KYALAMI 477 [12] M J Polglase 4-7-12 5oh (25) D Kinsella 10/1: 000/0-6: Led 1f, prom till 4f out:	2½	9a
107	HAJEER 20 [4] P W Hiatt 5-9-2 (48) R Winston 12/1: 1230007: Dwelt, sn prom, outpcd fnl 4f.	2½	25a
140	KAGOSHIMA 13 [8] J R Norton 8-8-11 vis (43) J F McDonald (5) 16/1: 60-00068: Chsd ldrs till 3f out.	1¼	19a
125	ROPPONGI DANCER 17 [3] Mrs N Macauley 4-7-12 5oh VIS t (25) Lisa Jones (5) 33/1: 00-06409: Held up, no dngr, vis.	4	2a
4331}	JONALTON 88 [13] C R Dore 4-7-13 (31) J Bramhill 14/1: 66-00000: Mid-div, no impress:	6	0
137	HIGH JINKS 14 [5] R N Bevis 8-8-5 P (37) L Keniry 20/1: 4550-500: Held up, no ch 6f out:	2	2a
4644}	ILOVETURTLE 70 [16] M C Chapman 3-8-5 (45) Andrew Webb (5) 14/1: 4200000: Chsd ldrs till 4f out.	1	9a
4582}	TEMPLE OF ARTEMIS 74 [10] P A Blockley 4-10-0 (60) D Nolan (5) 33/1: 6-000000: Sn bhd:	7	18a
154	SABRELINE 10 [15] B R Foster 4-9-2 (48) N Chalmers (5) 33/1: 0030550: Lost tch from halfway.	1½	5a
103*	DECELERATE 20 [16] A Charlton 3-9-4 (68) Dane O'Neill 6/1: 1333310: Well bhd 6f out:	4	11a
4359}	LEAHSTAR 87 [2] Miss L C Siddall 4-7-12 1oh (29) J McAuley 66/1: 0-006050: Chsd ldrs till halfway.	dist	0

16 Ran　　3m 42.26 (16.26)　　Owner Mrs A E Harris　　　　　　　　Trained at Melton Mowbray

	2.55 Bet Direct Football Cashbacks Selling Stakes 2yo (G)		
207	£2044 £584 £292　　7f f/sand rnd　　Going 62　　-09 Slow	Stalls Inside	

126	SIR JASPER 17 [10] T D Barron 2-8-11 vis (65) D Mernagh 4/1: 5561: Led/dsptd lead, went on halfway, duelled with rnr-up from dist, drvn to lead cl home:		58a
116	WINGS OF MORNING 17 [8] N A Callaghan 2-8-11 Rory Moore (7) 2/1 FAV: 0002: Led/dsptd lead, chall dist, hung right & hdd cl home under a kind ride:	shd	56a
158	CASANTELLA 8 [4] M J Polglase 2-8-7 1ow (38) L Fletcher 40/1: 0000003: Chsd ldrs, hmpd halfway, kept on onepace for press:	3½	45a
164	PLATINUM CHIEF 8 [6] A Berry 2-8-11 (53) Darren Williams 25/1: 0204004: Chsd ldrs, no room over 2f out, onepace bef dist.	½	48a
95	BROTHER CADFAEL 21 [13] John A Harris 2-8-11 (42) R Ffrench 18/1: 5300045: Pushed rear, eff wide, no dngr.	nk	47a
189	DESERT LIGHT 3 [7] D Shaw 2-8-11 e (23) Lisa Jones (3) 66/1: 0000006: Prom, no impress fnl 2f:	½	46a
78	QUARRY ISLAND 24 [2] P D Evans 2-8-6 (40) Joanna Badger 25/1: 660047: Dwelt & al towards rear.	4	33a
164	RARE COINCIDENCE 8 [9] R F Fisher 2-8-11 p (54) S Righton 9/4: 6505328: Dwelt, sn prom till dist:	½	37a
88	FIRST ACORN 22 [1] G M Moore 2-8-6 p (42) N Pollard 25/1: 0400609: Dwelt & al rear.	18	2a
73	DRESS PEARL 25 [12] A Berry 2-8-6 (47) Dean McKeown 25/1: 6060000: Prom 4f.	1	0a
3210}	BURKEES GRAW 141 [11] D Nicholls 2-9-2 (60) A Nicholls 10/1: 2100530: Chsd ldrs 4f:	10	-6a

11 Ran　　1m 31.59 (4.99)　　Owner Mrs Liz Jones　　　　　　　　　Trained at Thirsk

	3.25 Bet Direct In Vision Sky Page 293 Handicap Stakes Div 2 3yo+ 0-60 (F)		[60]
208	£2072 £592 £296　　7f f/sand rnd　　Going 62　　-05 Slow	Stalls Inside	

715}	SHAHM 291 [10] B J Curley 4-9-1 (47) S W Kelly 10/1: 00000-51: Held up wide, styd on for press to lead well in last:		54a
144	WALTZING WIZARD 10 [2] A Berry 4-9-4 (50) F Norton 16/1: 0006052: Mid-div, rdn & hdwy to lead over 1f out, hdd well ins last:	1¼	52a
168	ACORAZADO 7 [16] G L Moore 4-9-10 (56) G Carter 13/2: 4055153: Rear/wide, styd on for press fnl 2f, not reach front pair:	1½	55a
165*	SPY GUN 8 [8] T Wall 3-10-1 6ex (61) N Chalmers (5) 5/1: 0-00014: Mid-div, drvn & kept on fnl 2f, not able to chall:	nk	59a
4767}	MISTER MAL 61 [3] B Ellison 7-9-12 bl e (58) T Hamilton (5) 14/1: 2624005: Led/dsptd lead till dist:	1	54a
168	DOCTOR DENNIS 7 [15] Mrs Lydia Pearce 6-9-3 vis (49) N Pollard 25/1: 4004446: Rear, swtchd & mod hdwy 2f out.	1¼	42a
86*	MISTER BENJI 22 [7] B P J Baugh 4-9-10 p (56) J Fanning 11/1: 5400017: Cl-up, btn dist:	½	48a
4824}	SUDRA 56 [4] J O'Reilly 6-9-9 (55) J D O'Reilly (7) 25/1: 2050000: Dwelt & held up, mod gains for press, abs.	nk	46a

SOUTHWELL Tuesday 16.12.03 Lefthand, Sharp, Oval Track

161	**MR STYLISH** 8 [13] J S Moore 7-9-4 vis t (50) J D Smith 10/1: 6004449: Rear, only mod prog:		1¾	38a
166	**GAME GURU** 7 [6] T D Barron 4-9-13 bl (59) D Mernagh 3/1 FAV: 0600D30: Dwelt, sn pushed along & chsd ldrs, btn 2f out:		nk	46a
168	**ATTORNEY** 7 [5] D Shaw 5-9-1 e (47) Lisa Jones (3) 20/1: 0003000: Chsd ldrs till halfway, needs 5/6f.		2½	29a
166	**DIL** 7 [11] Mrs N Macauley 8-9-5 (51) Steven Harrison (7) 25/1: 060000: Dwelt, al bhd.		1¼	30a
156	**RIVELLI** 10 [1] B R Foster 4-8-13 bl (45) A Nicholls 100/1: 0000000: Chsd ldrs till 2f out.		3	18a
143	**MIDDLEHAM PARK** 13 [12] P C Haslam 3-9-11 (57) L Enstone (3) 25/1: 320060: Sn struggling.		nk	29a
151	**ZAK FACTA** 10 [14] Miss D A McHale 3-9-6 vis (52) Darren Williams 11/1: 0425400: Led/dsptd lead 3f, wknd qckly.		1½	21a
62	**ALICE BRAND** 27 [9] G M Moore 5-9-0 (46) T Eaves (5) 33/1: 00-40300: Dwelt, chsd ldrs till halfway.		6	5a
16 Ran	1m 30.61 (4.01) Owner Mrs B J Curley			Trained at Newmarket

SHA TIN Sunday 14.12.03 Righthand Track

Official Going GOOD/FIRM.

209 5.45 Gr 1 Hong Kong Vase 3yo+ ()
£640000 £240000 £120000 **1m4f** **Good/Firm**

4837*} **VALLEE ENCHANTEE** [3] E Lellouche 3-8-5 D Boeuf 11/2: -6371411: Held up, hdwy 2f out, drvn to lead wll ins last.			116
4007*} **POLISH SUMMER** 105 [7] A Fabre 6-9-0 C Soumillon 8/1: 4622512: Mid-div, hdwy to lead over 1f out, hdd & no extra wll ins last.		¾	118
4840} **WARRSAN** 56 [1] C E Brittain 5-9-0 P Robinson 12/1: 12126333: Trkd ldr, styd on for press fnl 2f, not pace of wnr nr fin.		shd	118
59* **IMPERIAL DANCER** 28 [14] M R Channon 5-9-0 T E Durcan 4/1 FAV: 23164117: Rear, short of room/swtchd over 1f out, kept on, no dngr, fin 7th.		1½	116
4798} **INDIAN CREEK** 57 [8] D R C Elsworth 5-9-0 T Quinn 8/1: 13153339: Rear, eff wide, little prog.		½	115
14 Ran	2m 28.20 Owner Ecurie Wildenstein		Trained at France

210 6.50 Gr 1 Hong Kong Sprint 3yo+ ()
£456000 £176000 £80000 **£55f** **Good/Firm**

SILENT WITNESS [11] A Cruz 4-9-0 F Coetzee 10/11 FAV: -1111111: Chsd ldr, rdn to lead ins last, styd on strongly.			124
NATIONAL CURRENCY [6] M Azzie 4-9-0 W Mawing 8/1: -3121112: Led, rdn & hdd ins last.		1	121
3985} **CAPE OF GOOD HOPE** [14] D Oughton 5-9-0 M J Kinane 33/1: 2805443: Mid-div, kept on press.		½	120
4629} **ACCLAMATION** 70 [7] L G Cottrell 4-9-0 L Dettori 11/1: 20131145: Rear, kept on for press in 5th.		2½	113
4629} **THE TRADER** 70 [13] M Blanshard 5-9-0 bl K Fallon 20/1: 51661426: Dwelt, rear, late gains into 6th.		¾	111
4775} **THE TATLING** 58 [12] J M Bradley 6-9-0 R Moore 16/1: 12655347: Missed break, rear, mod prog into 7th.		¾	109
4011*} **DEPORTIVO** 105 [9] R Charlton 3-9-0 R Hughes 10/1: 8-611810: Chsd wnr, btn dist, fin last of 14.		8	88
14 Ran	56.50 Owner Arthur Antonio Da Silva & Bett		Trained at Hong Kong

211 7.55 Gr 1 Hong Kong Mile 3yo+ ()
£640000 £240000 £120000 **£61m** **Good/Firm**

LUCKY OWNERS [7] A Cruz 4-9-0 F Coetzee 12/1: 5112111: Mid-div, hdwy to lead ins last, drvn out.			120
BOWMANS CROSSING [13] D Oughton 4-9-0 M J Kinane 25/1: 1120-372: Rear, styd on for press, nrst fin.		½	118
3712} **LOHENGRIN** 119 [12] M Ito 4-9-0 K Desormeaux 9/2 FAV: 1130203: Trkd ldr, no extra wll ins last.		½	117
3230} **FIREBREAK** 138 [10] Saeed bin Suroor 4-9-0 L Dettori 14/1: 12-21005: Mid-div, kept on onepace, fin 5th.		¾	116
4747} **PASSING GLANCE** 63 [11] A M Balding 4-9-0 Martin Dwyer 16/1: 01212160: Mid-div wide, eff over 2f out, sn no impress, fin 11th.		8½	99
14 Ran	1m 34.30 Owner Mr & Mrs Leung Kai Fai		Trained at Hong Kong

212 8.35 Gr 1 Hong Kong Cup 3yo+ ()
£816000 £320000 £144000 **1m2f** **Good/Firm**

4916} **FALBRAV** 50 [5] L M Cumani 5-9-0 L Dettori 5/4 FAV: 51512131: Mid-div, qcknd to lead over 1f out, powered clr, readily:			128
4798*} **RAKTI** 57 [4] M A Jarvis 4-9-0 P Robinson 4/1: 630-1212: Rear, rdn & styd on to take 2nd ins last.		2	123
ELEGANT FASHION [7] D Hayes 5-8-10 G Mosse 10/1: 1223213: Mid-div, styd on onepace fnl 2f.		1¼	117
14 Ran	2m 00.90 Owner Scuderia Rencati & T Yoshida		Trained at Newmarket

LINGFIELD Wednesday 17.12.03 Lefthand, V Sharp Track

Official Going Standard

213 12.00 Littlewoods Bet Direct Novice Stakes Div 1 2yo (D)
£3024 £864 £432 **7f p/track rnd** **Going 47** **-05 Slow** Stalls Inside

135	**BETTALATETHANNEVER** 15 [2] S Dow 2-8-12 Dane O'Neill 11/4: 061: Keen, trkd ldrs, drvn to lead narrowly ins last, all out:		84a
88	**QUEENSTOWN** 23 [1] B J Meehan 2-9-2 bl (85) R Winston 4/6 FAV: 6244122: Dwelt, sn led, drvn & hdd ins last, just held:	hd	87a
135	**SOLO SOLE** 15 [5] L M Cumani 2-8-12 E Ahern 14/1: 6003: Mid-div, eff over 2f out, sn no impress:	5	71a
	HILLTOP FANTASY [11] D J Daly 2-8-5 2ow W Ryan 16/1: 4: Mid-div, outpcd fnl 2f on debut, op 12/1.	5	54a
158	**LIMIT DOWN** 9 [7] M J Wallace 2-8-12 (64) D Corby (3) 50/1: 00005: Pushed along towards rear, only mod prog.	2½	56a
100	**MAGICAL GIFT** 21 [9] D W P Arbuthnot 2-8-7 J F McDonald (5) 20/1: 46: Prom, wide, btn 2f out, op 8/1.	nk	50a
	ITS BLUE CHIP [6] P W D'Arcy 2-8-8 e Paul Eddery 20/1: 7: Dwelt, mid-div, no impress on debut, eyeshield.	¾	50a
	GROUND PATROL [3] A M Balding 2-8-8 L Keniry (3) 25/1: 8: Slow away & bhd, little hdwy on debut.	¾	49a
164	**INTITNICE** 9 [4] Miss K M George 2-8-12 (45) Joanna Badger 100/1: 0400009: Chsd ldrs 4f.	shd	53a
	OPERA STAR [10] B W Hills 2-8-3 A Daly 14/1: 0: Dwelt, held up wide, no impress on debut, op 10/1.	3	38a
	MR STROWGER 178 [8] A Charlton 2-8-12 R Smith 100/1: 00000: Led 1f, btn halfway, abs, Brit bow.	21	7a
11 Ran	1m 26.43 (3.63) Owner Mr J R May		Trained at Epsom

214 12.30 Greenacre Homes Claiming Stakes Div 1 3yo+ (F)
£2086 £596 £298   7f p/track rnd   Going 47   +01 Fast   Stalls Inside

180	WARLINGHAM 7 [12] M Pitman 5-8-11 (54) V Slattery 5/1: 00-00021: Keen chsg ldrs, led ins last, drvn out:			54a
4961}	HARBOUR HOUSE 47 [3] J J Bridger 4-8-5 (39) F Norton 20/1: 3000002: Keen & led 2f, not pace of wnr ins last:	1¾	44a
180*	FREE OPTION 7 [8] G L Moore 8-9-3 bl (73) N Callan 13/8 FAV: 3003013: Chsd ldrs, keeping on for press when hmpd ins	nk	55a
	last, nrst fin, wld have gone v close with a clr run:			
92	SAVILES DELIGHT 22 [13] R Brotherton 4-9-5 p (52) I Mongan 20/1: 0302004: Handy & led over 1f out till ins last, no extra:	½	56a
4963}	MAYZIN 47 [14] R M Flower 3-9-7 P (45) S Whitworth 100/1: 6000005: Led/dsptd lead till over 1f out:	2	54a
3465}	LADYWELL BLAISE 131 [1] J J Bridger 6-8-0 (41) J F McDonald (5) 25/1: 4300006: Mid-div, not able to chall, abs.	3	27a
4753}	DANCING FOREST 63 [5] D K Ivory 3-9-1 (68) Dane O'Neill 9/1: 0020007: Slow away, nrst fin, lost ch start.	3	36a
180	HADATH 7 [9] B G Powell 6-8-9 p (67) L Keniry (3) 11/2: 0053048: Sn pushed along towards rear, only mod gains.	shd	30a
	THAI HI 51 [11] S Kirk 3-8-12 J F Egan 20/1: 0-646009: Chsd ldrs 5f, abs, Brit bow.	shd	32a
129	KOMENA 18 [15] J W Payne 5-8-8 (49) E Ahern 8/1: 2305240: Mid-div, no impress fnl 2f.	1¼	25a
128	JOUVERT 18 [10] R Hannon 3-8-3 (45) R Smith 20/1: 0000560: Mid-div, outpcd from halfway.	2	16a
180	WALKER BAY 7 [4] J C Fox 5-8-2 bl (44) J Tate 33/1: 0-024000: Dwelt & al bhd.	5	6a
154	SARGENTS DREAM 11 [2] J A Gilbert 3-8-8 B Reilly (5) 100/1: 000: Mid-div, sn struggling.	2½	7a
150	BADOU 11 [6] L Montague Hall 3-8-13 vis (47) C Cogan 33/1: 0024000: Dwelt, sn rdn & bhd.	nk	11a
165	SUBTLE MOVE 9 [16] D Shaw 3-8-10 (40) Darren Williams 66/1: 0000000: Mid-div, struggling halfway.	22	0a
4258}	RECYCLING RITA 92 [7] P R Hedger 4-8-8 D Corby (3) 100/1: 00: Sn well bhd, t.o., abs.	dist	0a
16 Ran	1m 26.03 (3.23) Owner Mr Martin Butler		Trained at Upper Lambourn	

215 1.00 Bet Direct On Attheraces Interactive Handicap Stakes Fillies 3yo+ 0-70 (E) [65]
£2065 £590 £295   1m2f p/track   Going 47   -18 Slow   Stalls Inside

101	REGAL GALLERY 21 [2] C A Horgan 5-9-2 (53) Paul Eddery 9/1: 50040-41: Held up, hdwy 2f out & rdn & led ins last:		60a
178	EMBER DAYS 7 [13] J L Spearing 4-9-1 (52) E Ahern 100/30 FAV: 60-05522: Chsd ldrs wide, hdwy to chall ins last, not pace	1¾	54a
	of wnr:			
101	HARLOT 21 [5] John Berry 3-9-2 P (56) Lisa Jones (3) 40/1: 4400003: Led till ins last, no extra nr fin:	nk	57a
170	PIROUETTES 8 [7] Miss Gay Kelleway 3-9-1 (55) N Callan 20/1: 0-430434: Handy, chall over 2f out, no extra dist:	1¼	53a
148	MARGERY DAW 11 [9] M P Tregonning 3-9-10 (64) Dane O'Neill 9/2: 3-225: Mid-div, not able to chall, h'cap bow.	hd	61a
188	LEONOR DE SOTO 5 [14] J R Best 3-9-1 (55) D Fentiman (7) 25/1: 4660066: Held up wide, nrst fin, quick reapp.	2	48a
148	STATE OF BALANCE 11 [10] K Bell 5-9-11 (62) L Keniry (3) 9/1: 0047: Keen rear, eff/hmpd over 1f out, no impress after:	hd	54a
150	POWER BIRD 11 [1] D Flood 3-9-11 (65) P Doe 20/1: 0050008: Prom, drvn/btn 2f out.	1½	54a
53	WAVET 29 [8] Mrs Lydia Pearce 3-9-1 (55) A Culhane 20/1: 0-609: Mid-div inner, no impress dist, h'cap bow.	½	43a
101	CASTAIGNE 21 [12] B W Duke 4-9-5 t (56) I Mongan 7/1: 0240020: Slow away & wide, nvr factor, lost ch start.	1½	41a
150	DISPOL EVITA 11 [4] Jamie Poulton 4-9-2 (53) H Poulton (7) 9/1: 6535020: Slow away, no impress, `struck into'.	½	37a
3310}	BOOGIE MAGIC 138 [6] C N Allen 3-10-0 (68) G Carter 13/2: 00400: Prom till 2f out, eased :	9	36a
115	SUERTE 19 [11] J G Given 3-9-3 (57) M Fenton 10/1: 00-040: In tch till 3f out.	½	24a
13 Ran	2m 09.25 (6.45) Owner Mrs B Sumner		Trained at Marlborough	

216 1.30 Greenacre Homes Claiming Stakes Div 2 3yo+ (F)
£2079 £594 £297   7f p/track rnd   Going 47   -07 Slow   Stalls Inside

150	ZINGING 11 [9] J J Bridger 4-8-13 (48) F Norton 6/1: 0000031: Held up, strong run for press ins last to lead cl-home:		54a
145	ESPADA 11 [2] J A Osborne 5-9-0 (74) S W Kelly 10/1: 0-610002: Led, rdn & hdd cl-home:	¾	59a
180	DOLPHINELLE 7 [10] Jamie Poulton vis (49) J F Egan 16/1: 0050053: Rear, strong fin, nrst line.	shd	47a
3456}	DILYS 131 [7] W S Kittow 4-8-6 (48) E Ahern 33/1: 0-000004: Held up, kept on for press fnl 2f:	shd	45a
55	ADANTINO 29 [5] B R Millman 4-8-11 (51) G Baker 14/1: 3005605: In tch, ch dist, no extra cl-home:	nk	49a
47	FEAST OF ROMANCE 30 [14] P Howling 6-8-9 p (51) J P Guillambert (3) 16/1: 0020336: Chsd ldrs wide, onepce.	1½	48a
4427}	DEFINITELY SPECIAL 84 [1] N E Berry 5-8-10 (40) L Keniry (3) 40/1: 3060007: Prom 5f, abs, new yard.	¾	44a
150	FOUR JAYS 11 [6] N P Littmoden 3-9-7 p (64) I Mongan 11/2: 0026058: Mid-div, not able to chall fnl 1f.	shd	55a
180	XSYNNA 7 [12] P S McEntee 7-8-3 (47) J Tate 25/1: 0030009: Held up wide, no impress fnl 1f.	nk	36a
167	THE GAY FOX 8 [16] B G Powell 9-8-5 bl t (44) Karen Peippo (7) 25/1: 5350500: Prom wide 5f.	2	34a
1508}	RATHMULLAN 217 [8] E A Wheeler 4-8-7 (38) S Carson 66/1: 65-00000: Rear, little hdwy, abs.	2	32a
118	PRINCE IVOR 18 [3] J C Fox 3-8-3 (40) R Smith 66/1: 0050000: Mid-div, btn when no room ins last.	½	27a
80	LOOKING DOWN 25 [15] R Hannon 3-8-8 (72) Dane O'Neill 1/1 FAV: 4004030: Prom wide, btn 2f out:	shd	40a
3787}	GOOD FORM 117 [4] Miss K M George 3-8-3 (41) J F McDonald (5) 50/1: 5030000: Prom, btn 3f out, abs.	1¼	24a
68}	PICATRIP 390 [13] P R Hedger 3-7-12 (40) F P Ferris (3) 100/1: 00000-0: Slow away & al bhd, long abs.	5	10a
15 Ran	1m 26.57 (3.77) Owner Mr J Jenner		Trained at Liphook	

217 2.00 Bet Direct On 0800 32 93 93 Nursery Handicap Stakes 2yo 0-85 (D) [85]
£2937 £839 £420   5f p/track rnd   Going 47   -01 Slow   Stalls Outside

76*	INTRIGUING GLIMPSE 25 [3] Miss B Sanders 2-8-9 (66) N Callan 2/1 FAV: 6011: Handy, led dist, drvn out:		70a
182	SMOKIN JOE 5 [4] J R Best 2-8-10 (67) N Pollard 9/1: 06622: In tch, styd on for press ins last, nrst fin:	¾	68a
105	FORZENUFF 21 [5] J R Boyle 2-8-8 (65) E Ahern 14/1: 5451603: Sn handy, styd on onepace for press:	¾	64a
169	HELLO ROBERTO 8 [2] M J Polglase 2-9-6 (77) L Fletcher (3) 7/1: 0304324: Chsd ldrs, keeping on for press when short of	hd	75a
	room ins last, prob gone close with a clr run:			
135	SWEETEST REVENGE 15 [10] M D I Usher 2-9-7 (78) A Daly 13/2: 2010425: Trkd ldrs wide, onepcd dist.	nk	75a
1	EASILY AVERTED 37 [6] J A Osborne 2-9-0 (71) S W Kelly 13/2: 2413006: Led till dist, no extra:	hd	67a
177	PREGNANT PAUSE 7 [8] S Kirk 2-8-6 (65) J F Egan 9/2: 5300247: Pushed along, not able to chall:	shd	61a
2347}	IVORY LACE 177 [9] D K Ivory 2-8-9 (66) Dane O'Neill 40/1: 3361508: Hmpd early, held up wide, no impress:	4	51a
169	BACK AT DE FRONT 8 [7] N E Berry 2-9-5 (76) M Savage (5) 25/1: 01159: Prom but, btn/eased ins last.	1	58a
52	KNIGHT ONTHE TILES 29 [1] J R Best 2-8-13 (70) I Mongan 8/1: 5141060: Dwelt, outpcd	1¾	47a

LINGFIELD Wednesday 17.12.03 Lefthand, V Sharp Track

10 Ran   1m 0.02 (2.4)   Owner Mr Edward Hyde   Trained at Epsom

---

218 **2.30 Betdirect Co Uk Handicap Stakes** 3yo+ 0-80 (D)   [79]
£3073 £878 £439   **1m4f p/track**   **Going 47**   **-01 Slow**   Stalls Inside

4607*}	**TIGHT SQUEEZE** 74 [10] P W Hiatt 6-9-11 (76) A Culhane 12/1: 6155011: Rear, hdwy 2f out & strong run for press ins last to lead cl-home:		81a
174	**EASTER OGIL** 7 [13] Jane Southcombe 8-8-11 (62) V Slattery 10/1: 1430642: In tch, hdwy & rdn/led ins last, hdd cl-home:	¾	65a
83	**HIGH HOPE** 25 [2] G L Moore 5-9-13 BL e (78) S Whitworth 12/1: 2500003: In tch, hdwy to lead dist till well in last, kept on:	½	80a
196	**NIGHT WARRIOR** 22 [12] D Flood 3-8-11 (67) P Doe 33/1: 1200004: Rear, styd on for press fnl 2f.	nk	68a
134	**GALLANT BOY** 15 [6] P D Evans 4-9-12 t (77) S Donohoe (7) 7/1: 1000505: Held up, short of room over 2f out & again over 1f out, drvn & kept on ins last, nrst fin:	¾	77a
18	**DANEHILL LAD** 35 [8] T Keddy 3-8-10 (66) Dane O'Neill 13/2: 0022226: Mid-div, smooth hdwy inner when no room over 1f out, switched & kept on late, ch had gone:	½	65a
122*	**PARAGON OF VIRTUE** 18 [16] P Mitchell 6-10-0 (79) J Fanning 5/2 FAV: 1-163317: Trkd ldrs, led over 2f out till dist, no extra:	2	75a
148	**BLUEGRASS BOY** 11 [1] G B Balding 3-8-11 (67) R Thomas (5) 16/1: 00-02538: Prom, no extra fnl 1f.	shd	63a
147	**MOST SAUCY** 11 [4] A Wood 7-9-3 (68) D Nolan (5) 14/1: 0355509: Chsd ldrs, onepace fnl 2f.	1	63a
118	**HOH VISS** 18 [5] S Kirk 3-9-0 (70) J F Egan 16/1: 4522550: Led 2f, btn 2f out.	5	58a
134	**LIBERTY ROYAL** 15 [3] P J Makin 4-9-9 (74) D Sweeney 20/1: 0-040000: Led after 2f till over 2f out, sn btn.	1½	60a
80	**PERFECT LOVE** 25 [15] G A Butler 3-9-7 BL (77) E Ahern 12/1: 12000: No impress fnl 2f, blnks.	1	62a
178	**GABOR** 7 [11] G L Moore 4-8-10 bl e (61) J Mongan 14/1: 2104500: Pushed along early, chsd ldrs 10f.	shd	46a
148	**WOOD FERN** 11 [7] M R Channon 3-9-0 (70) R Lappin 25/1: 3300: Rear, eff wide, btn 3f out, h'cap bow.	1¾	53a
1962}	**AFADAN** 195 [14] J R Jenkins 5-10-0 (79) S W Kelly 33/1: 4300000: Slow away, mid-div, btn 2f out, jumps fit.	3	58a
97	**DUCS DREAM** 22 [9] D Morris 5-8-8 (59) N Callan 20/1: 3163000: Prom, btn 3f out.	4	32a

16 Ran   2m 34.98 (5.78)   Owner Mr Anthony Harrison   Trained at Banbury

---

219 **3.00 Bet Direct On Channel 4 Page 613 Maiden Stakes** 3yo+ (D)
£2321 £663 £332   **6f p/track rnd**   **Going 47**   **-18 Slow**   Stalls Inside

123	**GUN SALUTE** 18 [2] G L Moore 3-9-0 P (52) R Brisland 8/1: 0000501: Keen & trkd ldrs, led ins last, drvn & prevailed all out:		57a
3898}	**PRINCE AARON** 113 [12] C N Allen 3-9-0 (47) G Carter 8/1: 60P0062: Chsd ldrs, drvn & briefly led dist, styd on gamely, just held:	nk	56a
4116}	**LUCIUS VERRUS** 100 [3] D Shaw 3-9-0 Darren Williams 16/1: 043: Prom, ch over 1f out, not pace of front pair ins last:	2	50a
166	**MAD MICK MEESON** 8 [7] G B Balding 3-9-0 t (55) A Clark 11/2: 0504004: Trkd ldrs, onepace dist.	1¼	46a
673}	**A BEETOO** 298 [1] J R Best 3-8-9 (63) N Pollard 7/1: 0-246265: Dwelt, drvn & not able to chall ldrs, abs.	hd	44a
4459}	**ISLAND STAR** 82 [10] S Dow 3-9-0 (57) P Doe 25/1: 4640006: Led till dist, no extra, abs.	nk	44a
65	**DARK CHAMPION** 28 [9] Jedd O'Keeffe 3-9-0 (56) Dane O'Neill 7/2: 3323447: Mid-div, nvr pace to chall.	1	41a
71	**MAGGIE MAQUETTE** 26 [14] W S Kittow 3-8-9 D Sweeney 50/1: 08: Went right start, keen rear, no impress.	1	33a
	BANDINI [5] P D Evans 3-9-0 S Donohoe (7) 20/1: 9: Prom 4f on debut.	1¾	33a
	MIDNIGHT MAMBO [11] R Guest 3-8-9 E Ahern 3/1 FAV: 0: Bhd, eff wide, no impress on debut.	½	26a
151	**TATWEER** 11 [13] D Shaw 3-9-0 vis (52) R Winston 8/1: 0055500: Wide, in tch, hung left & wknd fnl 2f:	1¼	27a
	WODHILL BE [8] D Morris 3-8-9 N Callan 40/1: 0: Mid-div, btn 2f out, debut.	½	20a
4913}	**PREVEZA** 51 [4] J White 4-8-9 N Chalmers (5) 100/1: 000: Slow away & well bhd, nvr on terms, abs.	9	0a

13 Ran   1m 14.31 (3.91)   Owner Mr R Henderson   Trained at Brighton

---

220 **3.30 Littlewoods Bet Direct Novice Stakes Div 2** 2yo (D)
£3024 £864 £432   **7f p/track rnd**   **Going 47**   **-25 Slow**   Stalls Inside

4166}	**WHITGIFT ROCK** 97 [11] S Dow 2-8-12 (71) P Doe 7/2: 0405631: Held up in tch, eff wide fnl 2f & drvn to prevail cl-home:		71a
177	**FOOLS ENTIRE** 7 [3] J A Gilbert 2-8-12 P (64) B Reilly (5) 2/1: 0001322: Trkd ldrs travelling well, narrow lead dist, drvn & hdd cl-home:	½	69a
	JUMEIRAH SCARER [6] M R Channon 2-8-8 A Culhane 7/4 FAV: 3: Chsd ldrs, short of room 2f out, drvn & onepace dist:	1¼	62a
	STAR FERN [7] J Akehurst 2-8-8 G Carter 33/1: 4: Slow away, held up & pulled hard early, shaken up & styd on fnl 2f, nrst fin on debut:	nk	61a
120	**JANGO MALFOY** 18 [2] B W Duke 2-8-12 M Fenton 20/1: 0005: Led till dist, wknd.	2½	60a
51	**SABRINA BROWN** 29 [1] G B Balding 2-8-7 S Carson 16/1: 006: Keen & trkd ldrs, onepace from dist.	hd	54a
102	**RED CONTACT** 21 [4] A Charlton 2-8-12 R Smith 20/1: 07: Prom, btn over 1f out.	nk	58a
	SAUCY PICKLE [10] Miss Z C Davison 2-8-4 1ow N Pollard 66/1: 8: Mid-div, no impress fnl 2f on debut.	3½	43a
	PICK A BERRY [9] G Wragg 2-8-4 1ow J F Egan 14/1: 9: Dwelt, al bhd on debut.	6	32a
	LAKESIDE GUY [5] P S McEntee 2-8-8 F P Ferris (3) 33/1: 0: Slow away & keen, btn 2f out on debut.	1½	33a
176	**MIDMAAR** 7 [8] M Wigham 2-9-2 F Norton 10/1: 53100: Held up, no ch halfway.	2	37a

11 Ran   1m 27.84 (5.04)   Owner Whitgift Racing   Trained at Epsom

---

SOUTHWELL Friday 19.12.03 Lefthand, Sharp, Oval Track

Official Going STANDARD.

---

221 **11.40 Bet Direct On Sky Text Page 371 Handicap Stakes Div 1** 3yo+ 0-60 (F)   [59]
£2107 £602 £301   **1m f/sand rnd**   **Going 57**   **-24 Slow**   Stalls Inside

160	**MUTARAFAA** 11 [5] D Shaw 4-9-1 e (46) T Hamilton (5) 5/1: 0602221: Chsd ldrs, drvn to lead cl-home, all out:		58a
188	**CHABIBI** 7 [6] Trond Hansen 4-8-9 (40) A Starke 4/1: 600-0142: Led, drvn/hung right & hdd cl-home:	shd	51a
145	**JAMESTOWN** 13 [10] M J Polglase 6-9-3 (48) L Fletcher (3) 9/1: 4354063: Chsd ldrs, kept on onepace for press, no dngr to front pair:	5	48a
195	**LUCAYAN MONARCH** 6 [2] P A Blockley 5-9-13 p (58) D Nolan (5) 8/1: 0000064: Rear, switched & late gains for press, nvr	3½	54a

64

threatened:

202	MISS CHAMPERS 3 [9] P D Evans 3-10-5 6ex (65) S Donohoe (7) 100/30 FAV: 0051135: Rdn towards rear, late gains for press:	½	60a
199	MAGIC MAMMAS TOO 4 [1] T D Barron 3-9-7 (53) P Makin (7) 5/1: 0343226: Dwelt, sn trkd ldrs, no extra dist.	hd	47a
195	TROPICAL SON 6 [8] D Shaw 4-8-10 vis (41) Darren Williams 66/1: 0300007: Mid-div at best:	½	34a
3949}	ROUTE SIXTY SIX 112 [4] Jedd O'Keeffe 7-9-0 (45) Leanne Kershaw (7) 25/1: 0003508: Al rear:	2½	33a
150	CONSIGNIA 13 [3] D Haydn Jones 4-9-4 vis (49) Paul Eddery 14/1: 1001069: Trkd wnr, wknd dist:	5	28a
4321}	DANCING KING 92 [11] P W Hiatt 7-8-0 (31) Joanna Badger 25/1: 5040000: Prom wide 6f:	1½	7a
4427}	SENNEN COVE 86 [7] R Bastiman 4-8-5 t (36) J Mackay 33/1: 0045000: Al bhd:	11	0a
4792}	RELATIVE HERO 63 [13] Miss S J Wilton 3-9-10 P (56) N Callan 25/1: 0011650: Sn struggling, abs/cheek pieces, new	2½	8a
61	THAAYER 30 [12] I A Wood 8-8-7 (38) G Gibbons 33/1: 0000000: Chsd ldrs wide till halfway.	7	0a

13 Ran   1m 45.84 (6.44)   Owner Mr J C Fretwell   Trained at Newark

---

222 — 12.10 Bet Direct No Q Maiden Stakes 2yo (D)
£2898 £828 £414   5f f/sand rnd   Going 57   Inapplicab   Stalls Stands Side

69	SMART STARPRINCESS 28 [1] P A Blockley 2-8-9 bl (58) F P Ferris (3) 100/30: 5335441: Broke well & sn clr, in command dist, eased cl-home:		65a
197	VELVET TOUCH 4 [2] J R Jenkins 2-8-9 S W Kelly 5/2: 3063022: Rdn & chsd wnr, nvr pace to chall:	1¼	58a
169	SIEGFRIEDS NIGHT 10 [4] M C Chapman 2-9-0 (52) Andrew Webb 25/1: 5400003: Rdn & outpcd, nvr a factor:	4	52a
76	FIVE YEARS ON 27 [3] W J Haggas 2-9-0 C Lowther 5/6 FAV: 024: Slow into stride & lkd reluctant, sn rdn & nvr threatened ldrs:	shd	52a

4 Ran   1m 01.16   Owner Brooklands Racing   Trained at Southwell

---

223 — 12.40 Bet Direct On 0800 32 93 93 Nursery Handicap Stakes 2yo 0-75 (E) [72]
£3444 £984 £492   6f f/sand rnd   Going 57   -17 Slow   Stalls Inside

182*	BLOFELD 7 [3] W Jarvis 2-9-4 7ex (62) Lisa Jones (3) 11/10 FAV: 6005511: Made all & al trav well, shkn up & in command from dist, readily:		72a
3641}	DARING AFFAIR 126 [2] K R Burke 2-9-4 (62) N Callan 14/1: 00452: Trkd ldr, outpcd halfway, rallied ins last, no dngr:	1½	65a
43	ROOD BOY 32 [1] J S King 2-9-3 (61) I Mongan 13/2: 0043: Rdn chasing ldrs halfway, kept on onepace:	2½	57a
158	FOXIES FUTURE 11 [4] J R Weymes 2-9-7 (65) Dane O'Neill 20/1: 6610504: Dwelt, sn rdn rear, mod late gains for pressure:	2	56a
200*	ALIZAR 4 [8] M J Polglase 2-9-3 7ex (61) L Fletcher (3) 5/2: 0636115: Chsd ldrs wide, no impress dist:	1½	48a
51	FOOT FAULT 31 [7] N A Callaghan 2-9-3 (61) Rory Moore (7) 10/1: 0046: Chsd ldrs till over 1f out:	2	43a
32	KUMARI 35 [5] W M Brisbourne 2-8-4 (48) J F McDonald (5) 25/1: 650007: Prom, struggling from halfway.	3	23a
4770}	PEACE TREATY 64 [6] S R Bowring 2-8-5 (49) J Bramhill 50/1: 05008: Sn rdn & outpcd:	5	12a

8 Ran   1m 17.76 (4.46)   Owner Byculla Thoroughbreds   Trained at Newmarket

---

224 — 1.10 Bet Direct On Attheraces Interactive Median Auction Maiden Stakes 3-4yo (F)
£2205 £630 £315   1m3f f/sand   Going 57   -29 Slow   Stalls Inside

89	WASTED TALENT 25 [3] J G Portman 3-8-9 P (60) R Havlin 10/11 FAV: 4262531: Made all, drvn & held on gamely:		44a
4567}	MAKE MY HAY 78 [7] J White 4-9-4 BL (30) L Fletcher (3) 10/1: 3334002: Trkd ldrs, rdn to chase wnr dist, styd on well, al just held:	½	47a
1503}	NEXT FLIGHT 219 [10] R E Barr 4-9-4 (44) R Fitzpatrick 25/1: 0-000003: Trkd ldrs, drvn & kept on fnl 2f, al just held:	½	46a
145	GIVEMETHEMOONLIGHT 13 [11] Mrs S A Liddiard 4-8-13 (46) I Mongan 4/1: 0560324: Rear, hdwy to chase ldrs 3f out, rdn & not able to chall:	1½	39a
199	RED MOOR 4 [2] R Hollinshead 3-9-0 (45) A Culhane 7/1: 6500065: Trkd ldrs trav well 3f out, no extra dist.	shd	44a
46	CONCHONITA 32 [6] B Palling 3-8-9 (43) Dane O'Neill 8/1: 3606626: Dwelt, rear, kept on for press fnl 2f.	¾	38a
4241}	ALJOMAR 95 [4] R E Barr 4-9-4 P (41) T Eaves (5) 50/1: 000407: Chsd wnr, btn 2f out:	5	36a
199	RUBY ANNIVERSARY 4 [5] J Balding 3-8-9 (38) Lisa Jones (3) 20/1: 0400008: Reared start & sn bhd, qck reapp.	28	0a
	VELVET RHYTHM [8] K R Burke 3-8-9 R Keogh (5) 25/1: 9: Al bhd on debut.	21	0a

9 Ran   2m 30.77 (9.47)   Owner Wasted Talent Partnership   Trained at Compton

---

225 — 1.40 Littlewoods Bet Direct Handicap Stakes 3yo+ 0-95 (C) [94]
£5379 £1655 £828 £414   1m4f f/sand   Going 57   +12 Fast   Stalls Inside

127	MI ODDS 20 [1] Mrs N Macauley 7-9-3 (83) A Culhane 11/4 FAV: 5012121: Held up, rdn & styd on to lead cl-home:		89a
196	GEORGE STUBBS 4 [8] M J Polglase 5-8-1 (67) J F McDonald (5) 11/1: 0560632: Handy & led 2f out, rdn around 3L clr over 1f out, hdd cl-home:	½	71a
141	TE QUIERO GB 16 [3] Miss Gay Kelleway 5-10-0 t (94) N Callan 6/1: 2010523: Led, rdn & hdd 2f out, kept on:	2½	94a
5036}	KYLKENNY 41 [5] H Morrison 8-9-5 (85) L Fletcher (3) 7/2: 2405004: Trkd ldrs, rdn & onepace fnl 2f:	1	84a
173	GLORY QUEST 10 [7] Miss Gay Kelleway 6-8-11 p (77) Lisa Jones (3) 8/1: 4522355: Rear, rdn & mod late gains, nvr dngr.	4	70a
5036}	ROYAL CAVALIER 41 [4] R Hollinshead 6-9-7 (87) I Mongan 5/1: 4420206: Chsd ldrs, btn 2f out:	9	69a
99	OVIGO 24 [2] P A Blockley 4-8-1 (67) W M Lorden 12/1: 5000337: In tch, btn 2f out:	6	41a
147	SEA HOLLY 13 [6] G G Margarson 3-8-3 (74) J Mackay 8/1: 0602148: Chsd ldrs till out 4f out	13	0

8 Ran   2m 39.65 (5.35)   Owner Tic-Taccom   Trained at Melton Mowbray

---

226 — 2.15 Betdirect Co Uk Maiden Stakes 2yo (D)
£3126 £893 £447   1m f/sand rnd   Going 57   -06 Slow   Stalls Inside

184	KINGSMAITE 7 [4] S R Bowring 2-9-0 (66) J Bramhill 100/30 FAV: 6036421: Handy & led over 1f out, in command dist, rdn out:		78a
	DENVER 75 [5] B J Meehan 2-9-0 L Keniry (3) 6/1: 4252: Trkd ldrs, short of room over 3f out, drvn & styd on wide fnl 2f, nrst fin:	3	71a
192	HAWKIT 6 [11] J A Osborne 2-9-0 (72) L Fletcher (3) 4/1: 232233: Trkd ldrs, eff to lead 2f out, hdd over 1f out, no extra ins last:	hd	70a
88	COTTINGHAM 25 [10] M C Chapman 2-9-0 (60) I Mongan 33/1: 4240004: Handy & led over 4f out till 2f out, no extra:	5	61a
120	CHARA 20 [1] J R Jenkins 2-8-9 (66) S W Kelly 11/1: 4045: Mid-div when hmpd/lost pl halfway, rallied late on, nvr dngr:	3	50a
184	MUSIC MIX 7 [13] E A L Dunlop 2-9-0 W Ryan 8/1: 466: Mid-div wide, no impress fnl 2f:	1½	52a

88 **THEVENIS 25** [3] J S King 2-9-0 (60) N Callan 12/1: 0500057: Chsd ldrs, btn 2f out. *1¼* **49a**
159 **TROMPE LOEIL 11** [2] E A L Dunlop 2-8-9 (71) Dane O'Neill 13/2: 4050248: Mid-div, no impress fnl 2f: *3* **38a**
49 **GET TO THE POINT 31** [12] P W D'Arcy 2-9-0 e (63) B Reilly (5) 8/1: 5400059: Mid-div, eff wide, no impress 2f out. *hd* **42a**
95 **NOCATEE 24** [14] P C Haslam 2-9-0 (49) Rory Moore (7) 100/1: 000500: Wide & al bhd. *½* **41a**
126 **ROVING VIXEN 20** [9] J L Spearing 2-8-9 A Daly 50/1: 00: Led till 4f out, sn btn. *6* **26a**
ARCTIC QUEEN [8] A M Balding 2-8-9 R J Killoran (7) 20/1: 0: Dwelt, mid-div, strugg halfway on debut. *2* **22a**
164 **RED ACER 11** [7] P D Evans 2-9-0 (49) Joanna Badger 100/1: 00060: Dwelt & sn bhd. *21* **0a**
MIND THE TIME [6] J Hetherton 2-9-0 T Hamilton (5) 50/1: 0: Dwelt & al bhd on debut. *14* **0a**
14 Ran 1m 44.43 (5.03) Owner Mr S R Bowring Trained at Edwinstowe

227 **2.50 Free #25 Bonus @ Littlewoodspoker Com Selling Stakes 3yo+ (G)**
£2142 £612 £306 **6f f/sand rnd** **Going 57** **-14 Slow** Stalls Inside

172 **HEADLAND 10** [2] D W Chapman 5-9-5 bl (71) A Culhane 6/1: 4000041: Mid-div, drvn to chall dist, prevailed line, all out: **65a**
187 **POLAR HAZE 7** [5] Mrs Lydia Pearce 6-9-5 vis (46) J F McDonald (5) 7/1: 0004102: Pushed along towards rear, hdwy halfway & styd on well for press cl-home, just held: *nk* **64a**
167 **HEATHYARDSBLESSING 10** [3] R Hollinshead 6-8-12 (46) N Callan 10/1: 0000623: Handy & rdn/led over 1f out, drvn & hdd cl-home: *shd* **57a**
198 **HURRICANE COAST 4** [6] P A Blockley 4-9-5 (62) D Nolan (5) 15/8 FAV: 2012344: Pushed along towards rear, tkn wide over 2f out, hung left but styd on strongly cl-home, nrst fin: *hd* **63a**
MAGIC GREY 96 [1] Trond Hansen 8-8-12 A Starke 7/1: 4222565: Rear, switched wide from halfway & styd on well for press, nrst fin: *½* **54a**
124 **STAR LAD 20** [16] R Brotherton 3-8-12 bl (49) I Mongan 16/1: 6000606: Prom, no extra dist. *1¾* **50a**
208 **ATTORNEY 3** [4] D Shaw 5-9-5 e (47) Lisa Jones (3) 20/1: 0030007: Rear, nvr able to threaten: *½* **55a**
172 **LAY DOWN SALLY 10** [12] J White 5-8-7 (47) L Fletcher (3) 6/1: 0303028: Rrd start, late gains: *½* **41a**
166 **CAROLS CHOICE 10** [10] A Sadik 6-8-7 (43) N Chalmers (5) 25/1: 0063009: Led 5f, wknd: *½* **39a**
152 **PIPS SONG 13** [9] P W Hiatt 8-8-12 (48) J Tate 25/1: 6003000: Mid-div, no impress when hmpd dist. *nk* **43a**
33 **AMELIA 35** [14] W M Brisbourne 5-9-0 (50) S W Kelly 16/1: 0510460: Mid-div wide, btn 2f out. *1* **43a**
109 **CARK 21** [13] J Balding 5-9-5 (45) J Bramhill 25/1: 3400040: Keen & handy, btn over 1f out. *1¾* **44a**
167 **ATTILA THE HUN 10** [15] F Watson 4-8-12 (38) L Keniry (3) 66/1: 0000000: Prom 4f. *3* **30a**
153 **VALAZAR 13** [7] D W Chapman 4-8-12 (59) Dale Gibson 14/1: 1-524000: Chsd ldrs inner 4f. *½* **28a**
172 **BOISDALE 10** [11] D Nicholls 5-9-5 t (52) A Nicholls 16/1: 0060000: Chsd ldrs till over 2f out. *nk* **34a**
959} **ST CASSIEN 259** [8] T M Jones 3-8-12 (40) R Brisland 100/1: 060-00: Sn bhd, abs/AW bow. *1¾* **23a**
16 Ran 1m 17.56 (4.26) Owner Mr Harold D White Trained at York

228 **3.20 Bet Direct On Sky Text Page 371 Handicap Stakes Div 2 3yo+ 0-60 (F)** **[59]**
£2107 £602 £301 **1m f/sand rnd** **Going 57** **-06 Slow** Stalls Inside

208 **GAME GURU 3** [3] T D Barron 4-10-0 (59) Laura Jayne Crawford (7) 4/1: 600D301: Sn handy, drvn dist, led cl-home, all out: **63a**
165 **SORBIESHARRY 11** [6] Mrs N Macauley 4-8-13 (44) P McCabe 3/1 FAV: 0350422: Mid-div, smooth hdwy from halfway, rdn & narrow lead over 1f out, drvn & hdd well ins last: *shd* **47a**
188 **AIR OF ESTEEM 7** [2] Ian Emmerson 7-9-3 (48) A Nicholls 6/1: 2004553: Mid-div, rdn to chall dist, no extra well ins last: *2½* **46a**
160 **QOBTAAN 11** [4] M R Bosley 4-9-0 (45) G Baker 5/1: 2460534: Rear, hdwy to chase ldrs 3f out, onepace. *3½* **36a**
93 **CUMBRIAN PRINCESS 24** [11] M Blanshard 6-8-3 (34) Dale Gibson 14/1: 0000005: Chsd ldrs, no extra fnl 2f: *1¼* **22a**
195 **PROUD VICTOR 6** [5] D Shaw 3-8-10 vis (42) Darren Williams 16/1: 0604006: Rear, eff halfway, only mod prog: *shd* **30a**
208 **SUDRA 3** [13] J O'Reilly 6-9-10 p (55) J D O'Reilly (7) 9/1: 0500007: Trkd ldr, led 3f out, hdd 2f out, wknd. *¾* **42a**
188 **COLLEGE STAR 7** [12] J F Coupland 5-7-12 bl (29) Dean Williams (7) 66/1: 0000008: Chsd ldrs wide, btn 2f out. *2½* **11a**
161 **ZAHUNDA 11** [1] W M Brisbourne 4-9-4 (49) S W Kelly 25/1: 1000009: Mid-div, no ch fnl 2f. *6* **21a**
168 **FORMERIC 10** [8] Miss L C Siddall 7-8-9 vis (40) W M Lordan 50/1: 0000000: Al bhd. *8* **0**
128 **FORTY FORTE 20** [10] Miss S J Wilton 7-9-12 p (57) N Callan 6/1: 0000020: Rdn to lead early, hdd 3f out, sn btn. *¾* **14a**
91 **PATS MIRACLE 25** [9] John Berry 3-8-6 (38) Joanna Badger 33/1: 004-000: Dwelt, al bhd. *4* **0**
94 **BLUNHAM 24** [7] M C Chapman 3-9-2 (48) I Mongan 25/1: 6100000: Prom, btn 2f out. *dist* **0**
13 Ran 1m 44.46 (5.06) Owner Mr Kevin Shaw Trained at Thirsk

LINGFIELD Saturday 20.12.03 Lefthand, Sharp, Oval Track

Official Going STANDARD.

229 **11.50 Bet Direct On Attheraces Interactive Novice Stakes Div 1 2yo (D)**
£3052 £872 £436 **1m p/track rnd** **Going 26** **-49 Slow** Stalls Outside

119 **SKIDMARK 21** [4] D R C Elsworth 2-8-12 P Fitzsimons 7/4: 31: Dwelt, keen rear, hdwy 3f out & shkn up to lead well ins last **82a**
177 **ANUVASTEEL 10** [1] N A Callaghan 2-9-6 (83) W Ryan 10/11 FAV: 5005132: Led, drvn & hdd well ins last, no extra when bmpd cl-home: *1¼* **86a**
3855} **MARCUS EILE 117** [6] K R Burke 2-9-9 (86) Darren Williams 16/1: 1044263: Trkd ldr, drvn to chall dist, no extra well ins last: *1½* **85a**
220 **RED CONTACT 3** [3] A Charlton 2-8-12 R Smith 25/1: 004: Mid-div, hdwy to trk ldr trav well 2f out, hung right & no extra dist: *nk* **74a**
PURE EMOTION [10] W R Muir 2-8-8 1ow I Mongan 40/1: 5: Slow away, sn trk ldrs, btn 2f out on debut. *10* **52a**
111 **KILMINCHY LADY 22** [9] W R Muir 2-8-7 P Doe 66/1: 006: Chsd ldr, no impress when hmpd 2f out. *½* **42a**
4786*} **COMPETITOR 64** [8] J Akehurst 2-9-2 C Catlin 8/1: 17: Chsd ldrs, btn 3f out: *1½* **56a**
WALTZING BEAU [7] I A Wood 2-8-12 J Fanning 25/1: 8: Slow away, chsd ldrs 6f on debut. *1¾* **49a**
5018} **ATLANTIC TERN 44** [5] N M Babbage 2-8-12 S Righton 66/1: 09: Keen & held up, btn 3f out: *1¾* **46a**
CORTON DENHAM [2] G P Enright 2-8-12 Dane O'Neill 50/1: 0: Slow away & sn bhd on debut. *8* **32a**
10 Ran 1m 42.19 (5.99) Owner Mr Raymond Tooth Trained at Whitsbury

---

230	**12.20 Bet Direct On Itv Page 367 Handicap Stakes Div 1 3yo+ 0-60 (F)**		[60]
	£2079 £594 £297	**1m2f p/track** Going 26 **-31 Slow**	Stalls Inside

68	GOLD GUEST 29 [6] P D Evans 4-9-6 (52) S Donohoe (7) 11/2: 4600441: Rear, hdwy over 3f out, led dist, rdn clr, readily:		60a
104	WELSH WIND 24 [8] M Wigham 7-9-10 t (56) I Mongan 100/30 FAV: 4003042: Mid-div, rdn & kept on fnl 2f, no impress on	3	58a
136	SCOTTISH RIVER 18 [11] M D I Usher 4-9-13 (59) A Daly 14/1: 5500003: Slow away, switched & styd on for press fnl 1f, not able to chall:	½	60a
161	COOLFORE JADE 12 [7] N E Berry 3-9-11 (60) M Savage (5) 50/1: 014004: Trkd ldrs, no extra 1f out.	2½	57a
12	MAGIC WARRIOR 38 [10] J C Fox 3-9-9 (58) R Smith 12/1: 6-500505: Keen & prom, led briefly dist, fdd.	½	54a
137	RAHEEL 18 [5] P Mitchell 3-9-4 t (53) J Fanning 7/1: 3000206: Rear, eff when no room over 2f out, sn onepace.	½	48a
104	TOLEDO SUN 24 [3] H J Collingridge 3-9-8 (57) M Tebbutt 5/1: 0030007: Led, hdd/wknd over 1f out.	1¼	50a
123	ICECAP 21 [12] P Butler 3-9-5 (54) B Reilly (5) 20/1: 4566508: Trkd ldrs, btn over 1f out.	2	44a
101	DICKIE DEADEYE 24 [2] G B Balding 6-10-0 (60) S Carson 8/1: 2//00-0059: Trkd ldr, btn 2f out.	7	41a
145	FABRIAN 14 [1] D W P Arbuthnot 9-9-7 e (53) Dane O'Neill 14/1: 3005540: Dwelt, keen & sn trkd ldr, btn 3f out.	2½	30a
3864}	YELLOW RIVER 117 [14] R Curtis 3-9-11 (60) S W Kelly 33/1: 2600000: Al rear:	1¾	35a
4294}	SUNGIO 450 [9] B G Powell 5-10-0 (60) A Hindley (7) 33/1: 500005-0: Mid-div, outpcd fnl 3f:	¾	34a
178	MISTER CLINTON 10 [4] D K Ivory 6-9-10 (56) G Carter 10/1: 0410000: Held up, struggling fnl 2f.	1	29a
101	PREMIER CHEVAL [13] R Rowe 4-9-5 (51) P Doe 20/1: 0040000: Held up, hdwy wide halfway, btn 3f out.	6	16a
14 Ran	2m 08.53 (5.73) Owner Diamond Racing Ltd		Trained at Abergavenny

---

231	**12.50 Bet Direct No Q On 0800 32 93 93 Handicap Stakes 3yo+ 0-70 (E)**		[69]
	£2058 £588 £294	**5f p/track rnd** Going 26 **-15 Slow**	Stalls Outside

4969}	PANJANDRUM 49 [5] N E Berry 5-9-10 (65) M Savage (5) 16/1: 1/03-3001: Mid-div, drvn to lead cl-home, all out:		66a
121	ROMAN QUINTET 21 [7] D W P Arbuthnot 3-9-8 t (63) Dane O'Neill 4/1: 4034402: Wide, led, went on over 1f out, drvn & hdd well ins last:	hd	63a
121	TEYAAR 21 [4] Mrs N Macauley 7-9-7 VIS (62) P McCabe 10/1: 0351003: Cl-up, drvn & chall dist, no extra cl-home:	nk	61a
130	BYO 18 [3] M Quinn 5-9-10 (65) R Winston 11/2: 2240044: Cl-up, outpcd over 2f out, late rally.	nk	63a
121	SIRAJ 21 [8] N A Graham 4-9-9 bl (64) A Culhane 7/2 JT FAV: 0405005: Held up, drvn & kept on, nrst fin:	½	60a
149	GOODWOOD PRINCE 14 [10] S Dow 3-9-10 (65) P Doe 8/1: 0060006: Wide, rear, late gains.	hd	60a
205	PARK STAR 4 [1] D Shaw 3-9-3 (58) Darren Williams 12/1: 0056007: Cl-up, outpcd/hmpd halfway, sn btn.	1	50a
3965}	PLAYTIME BLUE 113 [9] K R Burke 3-9-6 (61) G Baker 20/1: 1014408: Chsd ldrs, no extra over 1f out.	½	51a
133	DUNEDIN RASCAL 18 [2] E A Wheeler 6-9-13 bl (68) S Carson 14/1: 0000409: Sn rdn rear, al outpcd:	1½	53a
187*	LAUREL DAWN 8 [6] I W McInnes 5-9-8 (63) L Fletcher (3) 7/2 JT FAV: 0020410: Drvn & struggling halfway.	21	0
10 Ran	59.87 (2.07) Owner Leeway Group Limited		Trained at Earlswood

---

232	**1.20 Bet Direct On Attheraces Interactive Novice Stakes Div 2 2yo (D)**		
	£3052 £872 £436	**1m p/track rnd** Going 26 **-46 Slow**	Stalls Outside

175	BOXGROVE 10 [4] C E Brittain 2-8-12 A Culhane 11/2: 361: Mid-div, pushed along from halfway:		80a
132	FREAK OCCURENCE 18 [5] Miss E C Lavelle 2-9-9 (84) J F McDonald (5) 9/4: 0041142: Trkd ldrs, led 3f out, drvn clr over 1f out, hdd line:	shd	90a
4906}	ANOTHER CON 54 [10] Mrs P N Dutfield 2-8-7 R Havlin 20/1: 63: Cl-up, outpcd over 3f out, rallied late:	6	64a
111	IVORY COAST 22 [9] W R Muir 2-8-7 E Ahern 33/1: 004: Chsd ldrs till 2f out.	4	56a
1230}	DUBAIAN MIST 236 [7] A M Balding 2-8-7 N Chalmers (5) 14/1: 05: Mid-div, no impress fnl 3f:	¾	55a
4639}	LA DANSEUSE 74 [3] G C Bravery 2-8-7 (53) S Whitworth 33/1: 0636: Mid-div, struggling fnl 3f:	1¼	52a
4575}	VENDORS MISTAKE 78 [6] Andrew Reid 2-8-7 A Nicholls 14/1: 607: Led till 3f out, wknd.	nk	51a
220	MIDMAAR 3 [2] M Wigham 2-9-2 I Mongan 33/1: 531008: Al bhd, qck reapp.	1	58a
119*	CALEDONIAN 21 [8] D R C Elsworth 2-9-5 (82) Dane O'Neill 11/8 FAV: 019: Stumbled start, rear, btn/eased 2f out:	8	48a
	THE STAFFORD [1] L Wells 2-8-12 C Catlin 33/1: 0: Slow away & sn bhd, t.o. on debut.	23	0a
10 Ran	1m 41.92 (5.72) Owner Mr A J Richards		Trained at Newmarket

---

233	**1.50 Bet Direct No Q Selling Stakes 2yo (G)**		
	£2037 £582 £291	**6f p/track rnd** Going 26 **-35 Slow**	Stalls Inside

78	MUST BE SO 28 [2] D R C Elsworth 2-8-6 (50) N Pollard 5/2 FAV: 040031: Trkd ldrs, styd on for press to lead well ins last, all out:		49a
158	STANHOPE FORBES 12 [11] N P Littmoden 2-8-11 (53) E Ahern 9/2: 6350602: Rdn rdn, hdwy wide halfway, drvn & styd on, just failed:	shd	53a
164	STAMFORD BLUE 12 [10] J S Moore 2-8-11 BL (45) J D Smith 25/1: 1000003: Rear, hdwy wide to lead 2f out, rdn clr, hdd well ins last & no extra:	1¼	49a
112	LADY PISTE 22 [1] P D Evans 2-8-11 t (63) S Donohoe (7) 11/4: 1455304: Trkd ldrs, ch over 1f out, not pace of front pair cl-home:	hd	48a
78	COSTA DEL SOL 28 [4] J J Bridger 2-8-11 VIS (47) J F McDonald (5) 8/1: 4206005: Cl-up, wknd dist.	5	34a
4966}	LADY ELLENDUNE 49 [5] D J S ffrench Davis 2-8-8 2ow bl (42) I Mongan 25/1: 0000006: Nvr pace to chall:	1¾	26a
4816}	TIMELY TWIST 61 [8] S Kirk 2-8-6 (47) J Fanning 10/1: 0460537: Sn rdn & struggling rear:	8	3a
176	DONT LET GO 10 [3] C R Dore 2-8-6 J Bramhill 20/1: 08: Led 4f, wknd qckly.	nk	2a
76	CRISPIN GIRL 28 [6] J L Spearing 2-8-6 (54) C Catlin 9/2: 5000009: Sn rdn & cl-up, btn 2f out.	1½	0
164	BLUES OVER 12 [7] W J Musson 2-8-6 Laura Pike (7) 33/1: 00: Chsd ldr till halfway.	1¼	0
4307}	RUE DE VERTBOIS 93 [9] J C Fox 2-8-6 (49) R Smith 33/1: 00000: Al bhd, t.o.:	24	0
11 Ran	1m 14.04 (3.64) Owner Mrs Irene Clifford		Trained at Whitsbury

---

234	**2.25 Betdirect Co Uk Conditions Stakes 3yo+ (D)**		
	£3478 £1070 £535 £268	**1m p/track rnd** Going 26 **+04 Fast**	Stalls Outside

| 179 | LINNING WINE 10 [12] B G Powell 7-8-12 (88) S Carson 11/2: 0000021: Rear, smooth hdwy halfway, led over 1f out, readily | | 94a |

asserted, hands-&-heels:
44 **LAKOTA BRAVE 33** [6] Mrs S A Liddiard 9-8-12 (90) C Catlin 5/2 FAV: 0433122 Rear, hdwy wide halfway, chall 2f out, sn no impress on wnr: 2½ **88a**
179 **INVADER 10** [10] C E Brittain 7-8-12 bl (86) Dane O'Neill 9/2 6020143: Rear, hdwy wide 2f out, kept on onepace: ¾ **86a**
181 **AGILIS 10** [1] Jamie Poulton 3-8-11 (80) I Mongan 16/1: 4050004: Rear, drvn & styd on fnl 2f, not able to chall: nk **86a**
44 **NASHAAB 33** [4] P D Evans 6-8-12 vis (86) N Callan 13/2: 2000305: Chsd ldrs, wknd over 1f out. 5 **76a**
4306] **EASTBOROUGH 449** [3] B G Powell 4-8-12 (80) L Keniry (3) 33/1: 054000-6: Mid-div, no impress fnl 2f: nk **75a**
144 **CHATEAU NICOL 14** [7] B G Powell 4-8-12 bl (72) J Fanning 10/1: 0001107: Mid-div, hdwy trav well & led 2f out, sn hdd & wknd qckly: 6 **64a**
167 **RECADERO 11** [8] Trond Hansen 7-9-1 J Mackay 14/1: 2010-108: Chsd ldr, led over 2f out, sn hdd & wknd qckly. 7 **54a**
MARGALITA 186 [2] P Mitchell 3-8-6 E Ahern 10/1: 1131309: Chsd ldr, btn 2f out, abs. ¾ **45a**
134 **BLUE PATRICK 18** [9] J M P Eustace 3-9-2 (86) J Tate 14/1: 5-401600: Led till 2f out, wknd qckly. 3½ **48a**
ROAR BLIZZARD 42 [11] Trond Hansen 5-8-12 t (59) G Carter 66/1: 5000550: Rdn rear, no ch fnl 2f, abs. 1½ **40a**
179 **SAHAAT 10** [5] J A Osborne 5-8-12 (97) L Fletcher (3) 14/1: 4500000: Chsd ldrs, btn 3f out. **0**
12 Ran 1m 37.94 (1.74) Owner Favourites Racing Trained at Winchester

235 **3.00 Bet Direct On 0800 329393 Rated Stakes Handicap 3yo+ 0-100 (C)** **[107]**
£7430 £2818 £1409 £641 **6f p/track rnd** **Going 26** **+09 Fast** Stalls Inside

106 **LAW BREAKER 24** [5] J A Gilbert 5-8-6 (85) B Reilly (5) 8/1: 0100521: Mid-div, hdwy to lead dist, rdn out **92a**
4088} **DUSTY DAZZLER 105** [1] W G M Turner 3-9-1 (94) A Quinn (5) 16/1: 0004202 Chsd ldrs, styd on for press, not able to chall wnr ins last: 1¼ **96a**
106* **TEXAS GOLD 24** [10] W R Muir 5-8-9 (88) E Ahern 9/4 FAV: 5360113: Mid-div, drvn & kept on, not able to chall: shd **90a**
81 **WATERSIDE 28** [13] J W Hills 4-8-4 2oh (81) S Whitworth 16/1: 2631404: Rear, hdwy halfway, styd on onepace ins last ¾ **83a**
171 **QUITO 11** [4] D W Chapman 6-9-5 bl (98) A Culhane 4/1: 0052645: Dwelt, rear, late gains, nvr dngr: shd **98a**
4608} **JUSTALORD 77** [2] J Balding 5-8-4 1oh p (82) J Mackay 25/1: 5215206: Led, hung right on bend over 1f out, sn hdd & no extra: hd **82a**
81* **LYGETON LAD 28** [12] Miss Gay Kelleway 5-9-7 t (100) I Mongan 7/1: 5520017: Dwelt, rear, nrst fin: shd **99a**
64 **NO TIME 31** [11] M J Polglase 3-8-6 (85) L Fletcher 10/1: 2300008: Mid-div wide, no impress fnl 1f. 2 **78a**
205 **CRETAN GIFT 4** [14] N P Littmoden 12-8-4 3oh vis (80) J Bramhill 40/1: 040/-0509: Rear, nvr factor: ½ **74a**
171 **TRINCULO 11** [7] N P Littmoden 6-8-13 p (92) Lisa Jones (3) 12/1: 2000160: Cl-up, wknd over 1f out: ¾ **81a**
171 **SUNDRIED TOMATO 11** [8] P W Hiatt 4-8-9 (88) G Baker 20/1: 0600000: Chsd ldrs, btn 2f out. 4 **66a**
171 **MASSEY 11** [9] T D Barron 7-9-0 (93) P Makin (7) 25/1: 1120000: Chsd ldrs 4f. 1¼ **67a**
5037} **ACTION FIGHTER 42** [6] N P Littmoden 3-9-5 (98) J P Guillambert (3) 20/1: 0025100: Dwelt & al bhd, abs. 2½ **64a**
13 Ran 1m 11.4 (1.0) Owner Mr Terry Connors Trained at Bury St Edmunds

236 **3.30 Bet Direct On Itv Page 367 Handicap Stakes Div 2 3yo+ 0-60 (F)** **[60]**
£2072 £592 £296 **1m2f p/track** **Going 26** **-41 Slow** Stalls Inside

174 **LYRICAL WAY 10** [11] P R Chamings 4-9-11 vis (57) I Mongan 11/4 FAV: 0002221: Rear, rdn & hdwy 3f out, styd on for press to lead well ins last: **62a**
5017} **DOUBLE RANSOM 44** [8] Mrs L Stubbs 4-9-4 bl (50) S W Kelly 10/1: 0-000032: Sn trkd ldrs trav well, led over 1f out, drvn & hdd well ins last: ½ **53a**
4422} **ZAWRAK 87** [3] I W McInnes 4-10-0 (60) Natalia Gemelova (7) 4/1: 6000003: Mid-div, rdn & hdwy to chall over 1f out, no extra nr fin: 1¼ **60a**
101 **ANOTHER SECRET 24** [4] G L Moore 5-9-7 BL e (53) A Culhane 14/1: 0006B04: Mid-div, onepace fnl 2f: 4 **48a**
174 **SAMMYS SHUFFLE 10** [6] Jamie Poulton 8-9-10 bl (56) H Poulton (7) 8/1: 0122-605: Chsd ldrs, no extra dist. 1 **50a**
4767} **LEGALITY 65** [9] Julian Poulton 3-9-5 (54) N Callan 25/1: 0500006: Held up, eff 3f out, wknd dist: nk **47a**
188 **ANSWERED PROMISE 8** [13] A W Carroll 4-9-9 (55) S Whitworth 33/1: 0101007: Held up, no impress fnl 2f. nk **47a**
178 **MAN THE GATE 10** [1] P D Cundell 4-9-12 (58) S Carson 7/1: 00D5308: Led till over 1f out. 1¾ **48a**
104 **FIFE AND DRUM 24** [10] Miss J Feilden 6-9-13 p (59) B Reilly (5) 8/1: 34222U9: Towards rear, no ch fnl 2f. 1¼ **47a**
101 **KYLE OF LOCHALSH 24** [14] G G Margarson 3-9-9 (58) J Mackay 10/1: 5103000: Wide, rear, btn 3f out. hd **45a**
4753} **TRAVEL TARDIA 66** [5] I A Wood 5-9-8 (54) J Fanning 66/1: 0000-000: Chsd ldr, btn 2f out, abs. 3½ **36a**
4970} **ESCALADE 49** [2] W M Brisbourne 6-9-4 (50) P Mulrennan (5) 4/1: 4240450: Keen & prom till 3f out, abs. 5 **25a**
104 **IN SPIRIT 24** [7] B J Curley 5-9-10 (56) W M Lordan 10/1: 0-055300: Chsd ldrs, no ch fnl 3f. 5 **24a**
4332} **PLATINUM BOY 92** [12] M Wellings 3-9-6 p (55) L Fletcher (3) 50/1: 3315000: Mid-div, btn 3f out, abs. 2½ **19a**
14 Ran 2m 09.45 (6.65) Owner Mrs Alexandra J Chandris Trained at Basingstoke

WOLVERHAMPTON Monday 22.12.03 Lefthand, Sharp, Oval Track

Official Going Slow

237 **12.40 Merry Christmas From Bet Direct Nursery Handicap Stakes 2yo 0-75 (E)** **[70]**
£2002 £572 £286 **5f f/sand rnd** **Going 86** **-10 Slow** Stalls Inside

4594} **HEAD OF STATE 79** [5] R M Beckett 2-7-12 10oh (40) J Mackay 8/1: 0061: Cl-up, led 3f out, rdn out to hold on fnl 2f: **55a**
28 **LITTLE FLUTE 38** [6] T Keddy 2-7-12 2oh (48) Lisa Jones (3) 20/1: 0000002 Mid-div, prog 2f out, chsd wnr fnl 1f, just held by wnr: ½ **52a**
169* **BLUE POWER 13** [7] K R Burke 2-9-3 (69) Darren Williams 4/7 FAV: 0044213: Slow away, prog & ev ch 3f out, fdd fnl 1f: 6 **59a**
4917} **SUITCASE MURPHY 55** [3] Ms Deborah J Evans 2-7-12 (50) P M Quinn 25/1: 00004: Cl-up, wknd 2f out. 2 **35a**
182 **LIZHAR 10** [1] M J Polglase 2-9-6 (72) L Fletcher (3) 11/4: 2231435: Led, hdd 3f out, sn wknd: nk **56a**
5 Ran 1m 04.98 (4.78) Owner Mr Pedro Rosas Trained at Lambourn

238 **1.10 Littlewoods Bet Direct Maiden Stakes Div 1 2yo (D)**
£2926 £836 £418 **1m1f79y f/sand rnd** **Going 86** **-15 Slow** Stalls Inside

158	**DR CERULLO** 14 [5] C Tinkler 2-9-0 (75) Dane O'Neill 7/4 FAV: 26301: Cl-up, led 6f out, clr dist, rdn out:				**75a**
36	**UNINTENTIONAL** 37 [6] R Brotherton 2-8-9 (57) I Mongan 5/1: 0652: Chsd ldrs, chsd wnr 4f out, no extra dist:			6	**58a**
4993}	**CTESIPHON** 49 [2] J G Given 2-8-9 K Dalgleish 5/1: 03: Handy, wknd 3f out:			8	**45a**
184	**BRETTON** 10 [7] R Hollinshead 2-9-0 p (45) N Callan 10/1: 0650054: Held up, prog 5f out, fdd 3f out.			7	**38a**
164	**DAVIDS GIRL** 14 [1] D Morris 2-8-9 (42) J Fanning 33/1: 5406005: Ledf 1f, styd cl-up, fdd 4f out.			6	**23a**
207	**CASANTELLA** 6 [3] M J Polglase 2-8-9 (38) L Fletcher (3) 20/1: 0000036: Led 1m out, hdd 6f out, grad wknd:			1	**21a**
	ONCE AROUND [9] T G Mills 2-9-0 J Paulielo 6/1: 7: Dwelt, al bhd:			8	**13a**
37	**PLATINUM PIRATE** 37 [8] K R Burke 2-9-0 (48) Lisa Jones (3) 20/1: 0006008: Al in rear:			¾	**12a**
4002}	**IT MUST BE SPEECH** 112 [4] S L Keightley 2-9-0 (63) C Catlin 9/1: 0009: Al in rear:			17	**0a**
9 Ran	2m 07.68 (9.48) Owner Doubleprint			Trained at Compton	

---

239 **1.40 Bet Direct Claiming Stakes 3yo+ (F)**
£2065 £590 £295 1m1f79y f/sand rnd Going 86 -15 Slow Stalls Inside

127	**HIAWATHA** 23 [9] I Semple 4-9-3 (66) N Callan 2/1 FAV: 0020201: Held up, smooth hdwy to trk ldrs going well 2f out, led over 1f out, sn rdn clr, rdly:				**67a**
86	**OUR DESTINY** 28 [10] D Burchell 5-8-5 vis (37) J Tate 7/1: 1000002: Led, rdn & hdd over 1f out, no extra in last:			7	**45a**
161	**TINIAN** 14 [7] K R Burke 5-9-7 (62) Darren Williams 4/1: 2116153: Trkd ldrs travelling well, rdn & ch 2f out, no extra fnl 1f:			1½	**58a**
180	**REPEAT** 12 [11] Miss Gay Kelleway 3-8-13 (53) I Mongan 6/1: 0314064: Trkd ldrs, ch 2f out, wknd fnl 1f.			nk	**51a**
163	**ORIENTAL MOON** 14 [6] G C H Chung 4-8-0 p (36) Dean Williams (7) 33/1: 0000065: Rear, nvr danger to ldrs.			3½	**30a**
165	**VERMILION CREEK** 14 [3] R Hollinshead 4-8-9 (39) Stephanie Hollinshead (7) 7/1: 4000006: Held up, nvr pace to chall.			5	**31a**
161	**BETTER OFF** 14 [4] Mrs N Macauley 5-8-13 VIS (70) Joanna Badger 33/1: 1100007: Keen & chsd ldrs, btn 3f out.			8	**22a**
4968}	**ZIGGY DAN** 51 [5] Ms Deborah J Evans 3-8-11 E Ahern 33/1: 08: Chsd ldr, btn 4f out, abs.			1¾	**19a**
	BACHELORS TONIC [8] K A Morgan 5-8-5 P Makin (5) 14/1: 9: Dwelt & sn bhd, t.o. halfway, sadly died.			dist	**0a**
9 Ran	2m 07.72 (9.52) Owner Mr D Irvine			Trained at Carluke	

---

240 **2.10 Littlewoods Bet Direct Maiden Stakes Div 2 2yo (D)**
£2926 £836 £418 1m1f79y f/sand rnd Going 86 -10 Slow Stalls Inside

116	**BILL BENNETT** 23 [6] J Jay 2-9-0 (73) I Mongan 2/1 FAV: 6033201: Held up, hdwy & led over 3f out, sn rdn clr, styd on strongly:				**72a**
111	**RUSSALKA** 24 [5] Julian Poulton 2-8-9 (66) N Callan 3/1: 46202: Handy, rdn to chase wnr 3f out, hung left & no impress ins last:			4	**60a**
36	**PAR INDIANA** 37 [3] I Semple 2-8-9 M Tebbutt 9/2: 43: Rear, hdwy wide 3f out, onepace & no impress ins last:			¾	**59a**
159	**TAMARINA** 14 [8] N E Berry 2-8-9 (50) C Catlin 33/1: 5004: Handy & led over 5f out, rdn & hdd over 3f out, sn no extra:			3½	**52a**
175	**SEPARATED** 12 [2] E A L Dunlop 2-8-9 E Ahern 6/1: 05: Held up, eff 3f out, no impress on ldrs.			2	**48a**
159	**TIMBUKTU** 14 [9] C W Thornton 2-9-0 Dean McKeown 50/1: 006: Dwelt & held up, rdn & no impress fnl 2f.			9	**37a**
116	**CRACKLEANDO** 23 [1] N P Littmoden 2-9-0 J P Guillambert (3) 15/2: 007: Led early, sn struggling & no ch 3f out.			14	**9a**
111	**VESTA FLAME** 24 [4] M Johnston 2-8-9 J Fanning 40/1: 008: Sn rdn & al bhd.			2½	**-1a**
4823}	**SKY COVE** 63 [7] M W Easterby 2-9-0 P Mulrennan (5) 33/1: 009: Led till over 5f out, wknd qckly, abs.			2	**0a**
9 Ran	2m 07.19 (8.99) Owner Mr & Mrs Jonathan Jay			Trained at Newmarket	

---

241 **2.40 Betdirect Co Uk Handicap Stakes 3yo+ 0-75 (E)** [74]
£2086 £596 £298 7f f/sand rnd Going 86 -01 Slow Stalls Outside

205	**RONNIE FROM DONNY** 6 [7] B Ellison 3-9-10 (70) Dane O'Neill 9/2: 0000001: Cl-up, styd on to lead ins last, drvn out:				**74a**
196	**YORKER** 7 [3] Ms Deborah J Evans 5-9-6 (66) Lisa Jones (3) 10/1: 3001002: Cl-up, eff to chall fnl 1f, styd on, just held:			hd	**69a**
181	**GREY PEARL** 12 [4] Miss Gay Kelleway 4-9-11 (71) N Callan 8/1: 6-004053: Set pace, clr over 3f out, rdn & hdd ins last, no extra:			½	**73a**
131	**CAPTAIN DARLING** 20 [10] R M H Cowell 3-9-4 (64) E Ahern 13/2: 4504554: Held up, sltly outpcd well over 2f out, kept on late.			1	**65a**
4821}	**NOBLE LOCKS** 62 [5] J W Unett 5-9-5 (65) Carlo Bandiera (7) 14/1: 1401005: Held up, mod late gains:			6	**58a**
152*	**ARC EL CIEL** 16 [9] Mrs Stef Liddiard 5-10-0 (74) C Catlin 7/2 FAV: 3230016: Nvr a factor.			3	**63a**
136	**KANZ WOOD** 20 [12] A W Carroll 7-9-2 (62) S Whitworth 20/1: 5300007: Slow away, nvr a factor.			¾	**50a**
181	**THE GAIKWAR** 12 [8] N E Berry 4-9-9 bl (69) M Savage (5) 7/1: 0000048: Slow away held up, eff over 2f out, sn btn.			¾	**56a**
144	**HEIDELBURG** 16 [6] S Kirk 3-9-4 BL (64) J Fanning 9/2: 6062309: Handy, wkng when short of room 3f out.			5	**45a**
	REX ROMELIO 436 [2] K R Burke 4-9-5 (65) A Reilly (7) 33/1: 051505-0: Al bhd.			11	**33a**
3459}	**WEET WATCHERS** 136 [11] R Hollinshead 3-10-0 (74) D Sweeney 33/1: 4-1030P0: Prom, wknd over 2f out.			1¾	**40a**
11 Ran	1m 32.3 (6.1) Owner Mr Keith Middleton			Trained at Malton	

---

242 **3.10 Bet Direct On 0800 32 93 93 Maiden Stakes 3yo+ (D)**
£2258 £645 £323 5f f/sand rnd Going 86 +21 Fast Stalls Inside

30	**CLOUDLESS** 38 [8] J W Unett 3-8-9 (55) S Whitworth 16/1: 0403001: In tch, hdwy to lead just ins last, edged left but rdn clr:				**61a**
183	**INCHING** 10 [12] R M H Cowell 3-8-9 (53) E Ahern 11/2: 4006462: Cl-up, eff to chall appr fnl 1f, onepace:			5	**50a**
109	**BLUEBERRY RHYME** 24 [4] P J Makin 4-9-0 vis (68) D Sweeney 11/8 FAV: 200-3423: Held up, eff over 2f out, onepace:			1¼	**51a**
3419}	**DIAPHANOUS** 138 [9] E A Wheeler 5-8-9 bl (37) S Carson 16/1: 0300644: Led till ins last, wknd.			shd	**46a**
913}	**MULTAHAB** 266 [5] Miss Gay Kelleway 4-9-0 (55) I Mongan 4/1: 20555: Held up, eff 2f out, sn no extra:			½	**49a**
163	**VICTORY FLIP** 14 [1] R Hollinshead 3-8-9 p (52) N Callan 11/1: 0003646: Sn bhd, some late gains:			½	**43a**
167	**EAGER ANGEL** 13 [13] R F Marvin 5-8-9 p (41) Dean McKeown 25/1: 6000637: Bhd, mod late gains.			nk	**42a**
4116}	**LADY PROTECTOR** 105 [6] J Balding 4-8-9 (42) J Bramhill 16/1: 2000068: Handy, wknd over 1f out.			2	**37a**
91	**LAKE EYRE** 28 [10] J Balding 4-8-9 (39) J Edmunds 16/1: 0546039: Handy, wknd well over 1f out.			1	**34a**
219	**TATWEER** 5 [7] D Shaw 3-9-0 vis (52) Darren Williams 25/1: 0555000: Slow away & al bhd.			¾	**37a**
198	**BLUE CIRCLE** 7 [2] M Mullineaux 3-9-0 p (34) T Williams 100/1: 0600000: Al bhd.			7	**23a**
65	**WHITE O MORN** 33 [3] B A McMahon 4-8-9 P M Quinn 33/1: 00: Nvr a factor.			¾	**16a**
12 Ran	1m 3.47 (3.27) Owner Mr James Unett			Trained at Wolverhampton	

243 | **3.40 Seasons Greetings From Bet Direct Handicap Stakes Div 1 3yo+ 0-60 (F)** [60]
£2044 £584 £292   1m4f f/sand   Going 86   -19 Slow   Stalls Inside

907}	**ADALPOUR** 266 [3] D Burchell 5-9-4 (50) J Tate 20/1: 1613301: Keen chsd ldrs, hdwy to lead over 1f out, rdn out:		**54a**
156	**BROUGHTON KNOWS** 16 [6] W J Musson 6-8-0 (32) Lisa Jones (3) 5/1: 1404362: Held up, eff over 2f out, kept on ins last, not btn far:	½	**35a**
103	**COMPTON ECLAIRE** 26 [10] G A Butler 3-9-1 bl (52) E Ahern 6/1: 2640103: Held up, eff over 3f out, onepace:	1¾	**52a**
185	**MERCURIOUS** 10 [7] J Mackie 3-8-4 (41) Dale Gibson 5/1: 00-06334: In tch, eff to go 2nd halfway, led over 2f out till over 1f out, onepace.	½	**40a**
194	**EXIT TO HEAVEN** 9 [2] Miss Gay Kelleway 3-9-9 (60) T Eaves (5) 12/1: 6000225: Led after 1f till over 2f out, wknd:	3	**55a**
4951}	**MAKARIM** 53 [1] M R Bosley 7-10-0 VIS (60) G Baker 10/1: 3604006: Prom, outpcd over 1f out, rallied over 1f out, no impress:	3½	**50a**
4995}	**SHATIN SPECIAL** 48 [5] G C H Chung 3-8-12 p (49) Dean Williams (7) 25/1: 0504047: Led early, saddle sn slipped & bhd:	23	**9a**
75	**AMBERSONG** 31 [11] A W Carroll 5-9-5 (51) I Mongan 11/8 FAV: 0014228: Slow away & al bhd:	hd	**11a**
464}	**FLAMENCA** 332 [9] Mrs L B Normile 4-8-8 (40) P Mulrennan (3) 50/1: 0/6406-59: In tch, btn over 6f out, prev with R Allan.	½	**-1a**
2103}	**FINAL LAP** 192 [12] S T Lewis 7-7-12 8oh (22) F P Ferris (3) 100/1: 000/0-000: Al bhd.	5	**0**

10 Ran   2m 46.26 (12.66)   Owner Lewis Racing   Trained at Ebbw Vale

244 | **4.10 Seasons Greetings From Bet Direct Handicap Stakes Div 2 3yo+ 0-60 (F)** [59]
£2037 £582 £291   1m4f f/sand   Going 86   -14 Slow   Stalls Inside

1896}	**ONLY FOR SUE** 203 [2] W S Kittow 4-9-0 (45) I Mongan 10/1: 5/045-061: Prom, hdwy to lead over 2f out, clr & edged right over 1f out, styd on rdn out:		**54a**
206	**AMBITIOUS ANNIE** 6 [6] R Hollinshead 4-8-9 (40) Stephanie Hollinshead (7) 6/1: 4-501242: Held up, plenty to do over 3f out, styd on late, nvr getting to wnr:	5	**43a**
4809}	**NAKWA** 63 [3] E J Alston 5-8-12 (43) D Allan (3) 11/4 FAV: 5401043: Keen cl-up, onepace over 2f out:	hd	**46a**
204*	**AVEIRO** 6 [12] B G Powell 7-8-7 7ex bl (38) K Dalgleish 4/1: 6030414: Led after 4f, hdd over 2f out, no extra:	2	**38a**
72	**KENTUCKY BULLET** 31 [9] A G Newcombe 7-9-4 (49) S Whitworth 4/1: 0610425: Held up, no impress fnl 2f:	2½	**45a**
185	**HUMDINGER** 10 [7] D Shaw 3-9-10 (60) T Hamilton (5) 25/1: 1361006: In tch, btn over 4f out.	dist	**0a**
4828}	**ANNAKITA** 62 [1] W J Musson 3-9-3 (53) Lisa Jones (3) 22/1: 000067: In tch, wknd over 4f out:	2½	**0a**
206	**KYALAMI** 6 [4] M J Polglase 4-7-12 4oh (25) R Thomas (5) 8/1: 000/0-68: Keen, sn well bhd.	2	**0a**
3764}	**BRIOS BOY** 123 [5] G A Harker 3-8-3 p (39) J Fanning 50/1: 00-0609: Led 4f, wknd over 4f out, changed stable.	17	**0a**
129	**HISPANIOLA** 23 [10] M W Easterby 5-9-10 (55) P Mulrennan (3) 16/1: 3230/0-00: Al bhd.	shd	**0a**
4181}	**NOMINATE** 102 [11] S T Lewis 3-9-10 T (60) Dane O'Neill 50/1: 0350000: Slow & al bhd, t.o.:	dist	**0a**
154	**KAMALA** 16 [8] R Brotherton 4-9-5 VIS (50) N Callan 33/1: 5203-00P: In tch, wknd over 6f out, t.o./p.u. over 5f out.		**0a**

12 Ran   2m 45.65 (12.05)   Owner Ms Susan Arnesen   Trained at Cullompton

245 | **1.05 Bet Direct No Q On 08000 93 66 93 Amateur Riders' Handicap Stakes Div 1 3yo+ 0-75 (E)** [47]
£2044 £584 £292   6f f/sand rnd   Going 67   -19 Slow   Stalls Inside

205	**ST IVIAN** 10 [4] Mrs N Macauley 3-11-2 vis (63) Mrs M Morris 8/1: 0600051: Trkd ldr, drvn to lead cl-home:		**70a**
84	**LARKYS LOB** 32 [6] Paul Johnson 4-9-12 (45) Mr P Evans (5) 11/1: 4000002: Led, rdn/hdd cl home:	½	**50a**
208	**MISTER MAL** 10 [2] B Ellison 7-10-11 bl e (58) Miss L Ellison (5) 7/2: 6240053: Slow away, sn rdn chasing ldrs, hung right & not able to chall fnl 2f.	3	**54a**
152	**BLONDE EN BLONDE** 20 [3] N P Littmoden 3-11-6 (67) Mrs Emma Littmoden (3) 2/1 FAV: 2203534: Mid-div, not pace to chall front pair:	1¾	**58a**
216	**THE GAY FOX** 9 [7] B G Powell 9-9-10 1oh bl t (42) Mrs R Powell (7) 14/1: 3505005: Mid-div, nvr pace to chall.	shd	**34a**
143	**SAWAH** 23 [5] D Shaw 3-9-10 23oh (20) Miss Kelly Harrison (5) 80/1: 0006: Slow away, nvr on terms.	3	**27a**
208	**MR STYLISH** 10 [8] J S Moore 7-10-3 vis t (36) Mrs S Moore (5) 9/1: 0044407: Pulled hard wide, nvr a factor.	hd	**33a**
113	**BLAKESHALL QUEST** 28 [10] R Brotherton 3-11-9 (70) Miss C Hannaford (5) 25/1: 1000008: Sn rdn & struggling halfway.	¾	**51a**
198	**PADDYWACK** 11 [9] D W Chapman 6-12-0 bl (75) Mr R Clark (5) 100/30: 0566109: Mid-div, btn 2f out, struck into early & saddle slipped, best forgiven:	10	**31a**
242	**BLUE CIRCLE** 4 [1] M Mullineaux 3-9-10 9oh (34) Miss M Mullineaux (7) 50/1: 6000000: Al bhd, t.o., qck reapp.	5	**0a**

10 Ran   1m 17.95 (5.15)   Owner Mr Godfrey Horsford   Trained at Melton Mowbray

246 | **1.40 Bet Direct No Q On 08000 93 66 93 Amateur Riders' Handicap Stakes Div 2 3yo+ 0-75 (E)** [44]
£2037 £582 £291   6f f/sand rnd   Going 67   -16 Slow   Stalls Inside

241	**NOBLE LOCKS** 4 [8] J W Unett 5-11-7 (65) Miss J C Williams (7) 4/1 FAV: 4010051: Mid-div, hdwy to lead over 1f out, rdn clr:		**74a**
227	**AMELIA** 7 [9] W M Brisbourne 5-10-6 (50) Mr C Davies (5) 8/1: 5104602: In tch, rdn & kept on fnl 2f, no ch with easy wnr:	6	**49a**
208	**DIL** 10 [10] Mrs N Macauley 8-10-4 (48) Mrs M Morris 13/2: 0060003: Wide, kept on late for press.	1	**45a**
227	**ATTORNEY** 7 [5] D Shaw 5-10-1 e (45) Miss Kelly Harrison (5) 10/1: 0300004: Mid-div, mod late prog.	1¾	**38a**
153	**SHARP HAT** 20 [6] D W Chapman 9-12-0 (72) Mr R Clark (5) 9/2: 0001135: Led/dsptd lead wide 4f, new stable.	4	**55a**
183*	**CASH** 14 [4] Paul Johnson 5-11-3 p (61) Mr P Evans (5) 5/1: 0005016: Cl-up, btn bef dist:	1	**42a**
5029}	**MUTARED** 49 [3] N P Littmoden 5-11-12 (70) Mrs Emma Littmoden (3) 40/1: 3000008: Sn struggling.	2½	**44a**
166	**YOB** 17 [7] P D Evans 4-9-10 7oh vis t (33) Miss E Folkes (5) 8/1: 0-000008: Al bhd & outpcd.	3½	**5a**
155	**PRINCE OF BLUES** 20 [1] M Mullineaux 5-11-12 (70) Miss M Mullineaux (7) 13/2: 0000609: Reared start, in tch till dist.	1	**33a**
227	**CAROLS CHOICE** 7 [3] A Sadik 6-9-10 1oh (39) Miss E J Jones (5) 16/1: 0630000: Led 4f, wknd qckly.	1	**14a**

10 Ran   1m 17.75 (4.95)   Owner Mr James Unett   Trained at Wolverhampton

247 | **2.15 Bet Direct No Q On 08000 93 66 93 Claiming Stakes 2yo (F)** [—]
£2037 £582 £291   6f f/sand rnd   Going 67   -21 Slow   Stalls Inside

95	**TICTACTOE** 31 [8] D J Daly 2-8-10 (54) C Catlin 9/2: 5045361: Chsd ldrs, swtchd wide & styd on for press to lead cl-home:		**59a**
200	**EMARADIA** 11 [9] P D Evans 2-8-2 bl (52) Joanna Badger 9/2: 2345422: Led, rdn & hdd cl-home:	nk	**50a**
223	**ALIZAR** 7 [1] M J Polglase 2-9-2 (54) K Ghunowa (7) 4/1 FAV: 6361153: Mid-div, not pace to chall fnl 1f:	2½	**57a**
217	**BACK AT DE FRONT** 9 [5] N E Berry 2-8-12 (74) M Savage (5) 5/1: 011504: Chsd ldrs, not able to chall fnl 1f:	½	**51a**

233	STAMFORD BLUE 6 [3] J S Moore 2-8-3 bl (45) Lisa Jones (3) 8/1: 0000035: Rdn rear, mod prog:				3½	33a
200	DANDY JIM 11 [6] D W Chapman 2-8-4 R Brisland 50/1: 006: Rear, eff wide, no impress.				5	22a
2242}	NANNA 190 [4] R Hollinshead 2-8-2 Paul Eddery 10/1: 07: Prom till halfway, abs.				5	8a
3888}	MOSCOW MARY 123 [2] A G Newcombe 2-8-8 (65) S Whitworth 5/1: 1203248: Sn struggling, abs.				1½	10a
2439}	ADRIATIC ADVENTURE 183 [7] J L Spearing 2-8-6 A Daly 20/1: 009: Al outpcd, abs/AW bow.				1¼	5a
9 Ran	1m 18.08 (5.28)	Owner Stormin Thoroughbreds			Trained at Newmarket	

248   2.50 Littlewoods Bet Direct Maiden Stakes 3yo+ (D)
£2237 £639 £320   1m100y f/sand rnd   Going 67   -01 Slow   Stalls Inside

3832}	FOREVER PHOENIX 125 [8] R M H Cowell 3-8-8 (74) E Ahern 2/1 FAV: 4201: Trkd ldr, led over 3f out, rdn clr, flashed tail & held on all out cl-home:			61a
224	GIVEMETHEMOONLIGHT 7 [2] Mrs Stef Liddiard 4-8-9 (46) C Catlin 7/1: 5603242: Chsd ldrs, rdn & chsd wnr fnl 2f, drvn & just failed:		shd	60a
170	DANGER BIRD 17 [7] R Hollinshead 3-8-8 (50) I Mongan 16/1: 2005353: Rear, kept on wide, no impress on front pair:		5	50a
170	JARRAAF 17 [3] J W Unett 3-8-13 (62) S Whitworth 11/4: 6524244: In tch, btn over 1f out:		9	40a
3734}	BEST BEFORE 128 [4] P D Evans 3-8-13 (68) S Donohoe (7) 9/2: 2242065: In tch 10f:		2	36a
1218}	IAMBACK 242 [5] Miss Gay Kelleway 3-8-8 P (44) T Eaves (4) 33/1: 330-0606: Led till over 3f out, new stble, abs/cheek		10	14a
239	ZIGGY DAN 4 [6] Ms Deborah J Evans 3-8-13 Joanna Badger 50/1: 007: Sn rear, al bhd, qck reapp.		5	11a
215	PIROUETTES 9 [1] Miss Gay Kelleway 3-8-9 1ow P (50) N Callan 6/1: 4304348: Prom 3f, sn bhd:		27	0a
8 Ran	1m 52.0 (5.8)	Owner Mr J M Greetham	Trained at Newmarket	

249   3.20 Betdirect Co Uk Handicap Stakes 3yo+ 0-85 (D)   [75]
£3346 £956 £478   1m1f79y f/sand rnd   Going 67   -02 Slow   Stalls Inside

104*	COMPTON DRAKE 30 [1] G A Butler 4-9-9 (59) E Ahern 15/8 FAV: 0502111: In tch, rdn & hdwy to lead dist, styd on			67a
5	JUST WIZ 46 [5] N P Littmoden 7-9-9 bl (70) J P Guillambert (3) 7/2: 0450532: Keen, in tch, drvn & kept on fnl 2f, not pace of wnr:		2½	71a
186	HOWS THINGS 14 [4] D Haydn Jones 3-9-7 (70) Paul Eddery 11/4: 0311223: Trkd ldrs, hdwy to lead 2f out, hdd dist & no extra:		1½	68a
4992}	TRAVELLERS TALE 53 [3] P G Murphy 4-9-10 (71) R Havlin 8/1: 52-43034: Led till over 3f out, no extra:		5	60a
93	BOND MILLENNIUM 31 [6] B Smart 5-9-6 (67) I Mongan 6/1: 4602455: Rear, no impress fnl 2f:		2½	51a
72*	FIGHT THE FEELING 35 [2] J W Unett 5-8-0 vis (57) A Daly 7/1: 1353016: Keen & trk ldr, outpcd fnl 4f:		5	32a
6 Ran	2m 04.72 (6.52)	Owner Mr Erik Penser	Trained at Blewbury	

250   3.50 Bet Direct On Attheraces Interactive Selling Stakes 3yo+ (G)
£2037 £582 £291   1m4f f/sand   Going 67   -20 Slow   Stalls Inside

204	DELTA FORCE 10 [4] P A Blockley 4-9-4 (41) Derek Nolan (7) 5/1: 6356031: Keen, mid-div, hdwy to lead over 2f out, drvn clr:			50a
243	SHATIN SPECIAL 4 [8] G C H Chung 3-8-8 p (49) Dean Williams (7) 11/1: 5040402: Held up, hdwy to chase ldr over 2f out, no extra ins last:		4	38a
67	FAIRMORNING 37 [5] J W Unett 4-9-4 (40) A Daly 16/1: 0-655443: Handy & led 5f till over 2f out, onepace:		2	40a
202	RED DELIRIUM 10 [9] R Brotherton 7-9-8 bl t (48) E Ahern 16/1: 0006004: In tch, onepace & held fnl 2f.		1¾	42a
165	EL PEDRO 18 [10] N E Berry 4-9-8 (47) M Savage (5) 5/1: 6054005: Held up, rdn & kept on onepce.		1½	40a
614}	FAILED TO HIT 315 [6] N P Littmoden 3-8-8 bl I Mongan 11/4 FAV: 012-1456: Led 7f, fdd under press:		7	31a
244	AVEIRO 4 [3] B G Powell 7-9-8 P (31) C Catlin 100/30: 0304147: Cl-up, fdd fnl 4f:		1½	29a
72	IPLEDGEALLEGIANCE 35 [2] D W Chapman 7-9-8 (48) R Brisland 5/1: 5004568: Sn struggling rear.		5	22a
3568}	LA ROSE 135 [7] J W Unett 3-8-8 (38) S Whitworth 20/1: 0566209: Dwelt & al bhd, t.o.:		14	0a
4550}	THINK QUICK 86 [1] R Hollinshead 3-8-8 t (40) Stephanie Hollinshead (7) 7/1: 3200040: Mid-div, btn 4f out:		11	0a
10 Ran	2m 44.07 (10.47)	Owner Miss Emma Shally	Trained at Southwell	

251   4.20 Littlewoodscasino Com Handicap Stakes 3yo+ 0-70 (E)   [70]
£2170 £620 £310   1m100y f/sand rnd   Going 67   +03 Fast   Stalls Inside

221*	MUTARAFAA 7 [6] D Shaw 4-8-11 6ex e (53) P Makin (7) 8/1: 6022211: Handy & led 5f out, styd on well in last, pushed out:			59a
221	MISS CHAMPERS 7 [2] P D Evans 3-9-9 (66) S Donohoe (7) 6/1: 0511352: Rdn chasing ldrs, kept on for press, not able to chall wnr:		1½	69a
195	QUIET READING 13 [11] M R Bosley 6-9-11 vis (67) G Baker 16/1: 6134603: Mid-div, rdn & kept on onepace fnl 2f:		1	68a
193	SCRAMBLE 13 [10] B Ellison 5-8-8 t p (50) T Hamilton (5) 7/1: 4413464: Held up, rdn & kept on onepce.		2½	46a
181	DANIELLES LAD 16 [4] B Palling 7-9-11 (67) N Callan 14/1: 0003005: Handy & ch one 1f out, no extra ins last:		½	62a
165	MISS GLORY BE 18 [7] Miss Gay Kelleway 5-9-0 p (56) T Eaves (5) 14/1: 6323006: Trkd ldrs, outpcd fnl 2f.		½	50a
99	HOHS BACK 31 [12] Paul Johnson 4-9-8 p (64) R Fitzpatrick 12/1: 4302007: Rear, eff wide, no impress fnl 2f.		8	45a
241	YORKER 4 [5] Ms Deborah J Evans 5-9-10 (66) E Ahern 11/4 FAV: 0010028: Led till 5f out, sn btn, qck reapp.		nk	46a
99	FRIDAYS TAKINGS 31 [8] B Smart 4-9-11 bl (67) R Ffrench 14/1: 1220009: In tch, btn 3f out:		hd	46a
188	PUPS PRIDE 14 [9] Mrs N Macauley 6-9-4 vis (60) Lisa Jones (3) 10/1: 6001100: Al bhd:		5	31a
186	PHAROAHS GOLD 14 [13] D Shaw 5-9-6 e (62) S Whitworth 8/1: 4201000: Sn bhd.		¾	32a
188	JUNGLE LION 14 [1] John A Harris 5-8-10 t (52) C Catlin 33/1: 30-60600: Sn struggling, t.o..		13	1a
157	HUGH THE MAN 20 [3] N P Littmoden 4-9-13 P (69) I Mongan 5/1: 2500020: In tch 2f, sn well bhd:		dist	0a
13 Ran	1m 51.64 (5.44)	Owner Mr J C Fretwell	Trained at Newark	

Official Going STANDARD.

252   12.55 Betdirect Co Uk Nursery Handicap Stakes 2yo 0-85 (D)   [91]
£3000 £857 £429   1m f/sand rnd   Going 63   -09 Slow   Stalls Inside

162* **NESSEN DORMA** 19 [10] J G Given 2-8-6 (69) I Mongan 7/1: 2250511: Pushed along rear/wide, hdwy 3f out, styd on for **75a**
press to lead well ins last:

226* **KINGSMAITE** 8 [3] S R Bowring 2-8-11 5ex (74) J Bramhill 3/1 FAV: 0364212: Sn handy trav well, led going easily over 1f out, 1 **77a**
rdn & hdd ins last, no extra:

190* **BOLD BLADE** 14 [9] B Smart 2-8-7 bl (70) R Ffrench 12/1: 600413: Led till dist, drvn & kept on. 2½ **68a**

88+* **COUNTRYWIDE FLYER** 33 [4] T D Barron 2-9-5 (82) N Callan 100/30: 2342114: Trkd ldr, rdn & no extra over 1f out: ½ **79a**

190 **MYANNABANANA** 14 [11] J R Weymes 2-8-4 vis (67) D Fentiman (7) 16/1: 6601135: Held up, kept on late for press. 1½ **61a**

119 **STONOR LADY** 28 [2] P W D'Arcy 2-7-12 5oh (56) Lisa Jones (3) 33/1: 0206: Dwelt, chsd ldrs, no impress fnl 2f: 3½ **48a**

159* **ATLANTIC BREEZE** 19 [8] Mrs N Macauley 2-8-5 (68) L Enstone 20/1: 417: Mid-div, no impress fnl 3f: 7 **43a**

226 **COTTINGHAM** 8 [6] M C Chapman 2-7-12 1oh (60) Joanna Badger 20/1: 2400048: Chsd ldrs wide 5f: 5 **27a**

232 **FREAK OCCURENCE** 7 [5] Miss E C Lavelle 2-9-7 (84) S Drowne 7/2: 0411429: Prom, struggling fnl 2f: nk **49a**

159 **MRS GEE** 19 [1] R Hollinshead 2-8-2 (65) C Catlin 11/1: 55420: Held up, strugg halfway: 2½ **25a**

203 **WEET AN HAUL** 11 [7] P A Blockley 2-7-12 6oh (55) R Thomas 25/1: 6000120: Chsd ldrs wide 5f: 1¾ **18a**

11 Ran   1m 45.15 (5.75)   Owner Hokey Cokey Partnership   Trained at Gainsborough

---

253

1.30 Bet Direct No Q On 08000 93 66 93 Claiming Stakes 3yo+ (F)
£2121 £606 £303   5f f/sand str   Going 63   Inapplicab   Stalls Stands Side

183 **LADIES KNIGHT** 15 [11] D Shaw 8-8-13 (54) T Hamilton (5) 20/1: 4000001: Chsd ldrs halfway, drvn to lead well ins last: **57a**

4446} **RIVER LARK** 93 [2] M A Buckley 4-8-8 (47) R Ffrench 11/1: 0-500102: Cl-up & led bef halfway, drvn & hdd ins last, no extra: 1 **48a**

167 **FIENNES** 18 [10] Mrs N Macauley 5-8-5 vis (42) Steven Harrison (7) 14/1: 60-00563: Rdn rear, nrst fin. ½ **43a**

172 **MR SPLIFFY** 18 [3] K R Burke 4-8-9 vis (49) A Reilly (7) 11/2: 0020004: Trkd ldr, no extra ins last. nk **46a**

166 **BEST LEAD** 18 [14] Ian Emmerson 4-9-3 BL (53) D Fentiman (7) 14/1: 0000065: Prom stands side, onepace: shd **54a**

167 **AINTNECESSARILYSO** 18 [7] N E Berry 5-9-3 (43) M Savage (5) 16/1: 0300546: Dwelt, bhd, nrst fin. 1½ **50a**

205 **MALAHIDE EXPRESS** 11 [1] M J Polglase 3-9-5 bl (64) M Nem (7) 7/2 FAV: 0563507: Dwelt, mid-div at best: 1¼ **49a**

227 **CARK** 8 [12] J Balding 5-8-9 (45) J Edmunds 5/1: 4000408: Chsd ldrs till over 1f out. ¾ **37a**

187 **COLLEGE HIPPIE** 15 [13] J F Coupland 4-8-12 (45) S Donohoe (7) 15/2: 0004069: Mid-div, nvr pace to chall. ¾ **38a**

4003} **AGUILA LOCO** 117 [9] M C Chapman 4-8-7 (36) Andrew Webb (7) 33/1: 0000000: Chsd ldrs 3f: shd **33a**

4150} **NEW PROSPECTIVE** 109 [4] D Nicholls 5-9-3 (45) L Treadwell (7) 11/1: 0630300: Outpcd: ½ **41a**

2299} **TUSCAN DREAM** 189 [5] A Berry 8-8-9 (41) P Bradley (2) 12/1: 0306060: Led early, prom till halfway, abs. 2 **28a**

172 **ABOVE BOARD** 18 [15] R F Marvin 8-8-9 P (38) Dean McKeown 50/1: 0-500000: Sn bhd. 1¾ **24a**

228 **BLUNHAM** 8 [6] M C Chapman 3-8-9 (48) J Mongan 33/1: 1000000: Mid-div, no ch fnl 2f. nk **23a**

172 **GOODWOOD PROMISE** 18 [8] N E Berry 4-8-13 BL (33) M Savage (5) 66/1: 0000000: Chsd ldrs 3f, blnks. 3 **20a**

15 Ran   1m 01.1   Owner Swann Racing Ltd   Trained at Newark

---

254

2.00 Bet Direct No Q On 08000 93 66 93 Maiden Stakes 3yo+ (D)
£2240 £640 £320   6f f/sand rnd   Going 63   -11 Slow   Stalls Inside

187 **WAINWRIGHT** 15 [9] P A Blockley 3-9-0 (60) G Parkin 11/4 FAV: 5235331: Rear/wide, styd on for press to lead well ins last, **64a**
going away:

65 **SHADOWFAX** 38 [3] Miss Gay Kelleway 3-9-0 (67) N Callan 3/1: 60426-62: Trkd ldrs, rdn & led over 1f out till held well ins last, no 1¾ **58a**
extra:

242 **LAKE EYRE** 5 [10] J Balding 4-8-9 (39) J Edmunds 20/1: 5460303: Prom, onepace fnl 2f: 1½ **47a**

219 **LUCIUS VERRUS** 10 [6] D Shaw 3-9-0 T Hamilton (5) 7/1: 0434: Held up, nrst fin: ¾ **52a**

219 **DARK CHAMPION** 10 [13] Jedd O'Keeffe 3-9-0 (56) I Mongan 10/1: 3234405: Chsd ldrs, onepace fnl 2f. 1 **50a**

242 **INCHING** 5 [2] R M H Cowell 3-8-9 (53) S Drowne 5/1: 0064626: Dwelt, mid-div, no impress dist: 1¾ **41a**

65 **ROAN RAIDER** 18 [1] M J Polglase 3-9-0 vis t (42) K Ghunowa (7) 40/1: 3624607: Chsd ldrs halfway, no extra dist. ½ **48a**

242 **VICTORY FLIP** 5 [4] R Hollinshead 3-8-9 p (52) Dane O'Neill 8/1: 0036468: Dwelt, wide, nvr on terms: ¾ **37a**

109 **SOMETHINGABOUTHER** 29 [7] P W Hiatt 3-8-9 (40) C Catlin 40/1: 0200509: Cl-up, wknd fnl 2f. ½ **35a**

170 **KUSTOM KIT FOR HER** 18 [8] S R Bowring 3-8-9 bl (50) J Bramhill 40/1: 0540200: Led till over 1f out, fdd. 2½ **28a**

214 **SUBTLE MOVE** 10 [5] D Shaw 3-8-9 (35) Lisa Jones (3) 80/1: 0000000: Al bhd. 1½ **24a**

4258} **GRANUAILE OMALLEY** 102 [12] P W D'Arcy 3-8-9 (50) Paul Eddery 20/1: 0060030: Sn bhd. 9 **5a**

4989} **WENTBRIDGE BOY** 54 [11] J O'Reilly 3-9-0 D R McCabe 50/1: 000: Al bhd: 7 **0a**

13 Ran   1m 17.72 (4.42)   Owner Mr David Wright   Trained at Southwell

---

255

2.35 Littlewoods Bet Direct Handicap Stakes 3yo+ 0-85 (D)   **[83]**
£3458 £988 £494   1m f/sand rnd   Going 63   -02 Slow   Stalls Inside

163 **ESTIMATION** 19 [12] R M H Cowell 3-8-10 (66) S Drowne 9/1: 2113651: Mid-div wide, led dist, rdn out: **73a**

186 **FIRST MAITE** 15 [8] S R Bowring 10-9-1 (70) Dane O'Neill 12/1: 0530602: Held up, swtchd wide & styd on for press, nrst fin: ¾ **75a**

195 **BRANDY COVE** 14 [6] B Smart 6-8-10 (65) R Ffrench 3/1 FAV: 2104523: Chsd ldrs, rdn & led 2f out, hdd dist, kept on: nk **69a**

2 **MIDDLETON GREY** 47 [6] R A G Newcombe 5-9-13 (82) S Whitworth 10/1: 2036064: Dwelt, mid-div, onepace fnl 2f: 3½ **79a**

141 **BARZAK** 24 [11] S R Bowring 3-8-12 p (68) J Bramhill 12/1: 0001005: Cl-up, no extra fnl 2f: 3 **59a**

202 **SHIFTY** 11 [2] D Nicholls 4-7-13 bl (54) Joanna Badger 4/1: 0423426: Led after 1f till 3f out, wknd: 3½ **38a**

12 **POLAR KINGDOM** 45 [10] T D Barron 5-9-3 (72) P Makin (7) 11/2: 0200-207: Handy & led 3f out till 2f out, wknd. 1 **54a**

3177} **RISKA KING** 154 [4] R A Fahey 3-9-5 (75) T Hamilton (5) 16/1: 4400108: Al bhd: 8 **44a**

4297} **HAITHEM** 101 [1] D Shaw 6-7-12 17oh e (36) Lisa Jones (3) 66/1: 0650009: Al rear: 2½ **17a**

5030} **LAKELANDS LADY** 49 [3] J Balding 3-9-7 (77) J Edmunds 25/1: 0600000: Led 1f, cl-up 5f: ¾ **40a**

4506} **NORTH BY NORTHEAST** 89 [7] J W Payne 5-8-9 2ow p (62) N Callan 8/1: 1665200: Al bhd: 10 **11a**

11 Ran   1m 44.58 (5.18)   Owner Bottisham Heath Stud   Trained at Newmarket

---

256

3.10 Bet Direct On Attheraces Interactive Selling Stakes 2yo (G)
£2002 £572 £286   5f f/sand str   Going 63   Inapplicab   Stalls Stands Side

222* **SMART STARPRINCESS** 8 [2] P A Blockley 2-8-12 bl (58) N Callan 4/5 FAV: 3354411: Made all, sn clr, rdn & al holding **61a**
rivals ins last:

3	BRAVE CHIEF 47 [6] J A Pickering 2-8-12 Dean McKeown 40/1: 002: Dwelt, chsd ldrs, rdn & kept on, all held by wnr:	1¾	55a
200	PHILLY DEE 12 [1] J Jay 2-8-7 (47) I Mongan 4/1: 6043253: Chsd wnr, hung left, drvn & kept on fnl 2f, nvr able to chall:	½	48a
200	FISHERS DREAM 12 [3] J R Norton 2-8-12 vis (54) J Bramhill 12/1: 0064264: Dwelt, chsd ldrs, no impress over 1f out:	1¾	49a
222	SIEGFRIEDS NIGHT 8 [5] M C Chapman 2-8-12 (48) Andrew Webb (7) 25/1: 4000035: Mid-div at best:	2	44a
139	BLUE MOON HITMAN 24 [7] A Berry 2-8-12 (49) S Drowne 9/2: 3454636: Chsd ldrs 4f:	shd	44a
207	BURKEES GRAW 11 [9] D Nicholls 2-9-3 BL (60) L Treadwell (7) 16/1: 1005307: Dwelt, went left start, sn bhd:	7	33a
139	SHAMONE 24 [4] H A McWilliams 2-8-12 p (28) Lisa Jones (3) 66/1: 00P008: Chsd ldrs till halfway:	hd	27a
4695}	QUIDNET 76 [8] Paul Johnson 2-8-7 P (46) R Fitzpatrick 33/1: 534009: AI outpcd & bhd:	8	4a

9 Ran   1m 01.51   Owner Brooklands Racing   Trained at Southwell

257
3.40 Littlewoodscasino Com Handicap Stakes 3yo+ 0-70 (E) [69]
£2114 £604 £302   1m4f f/sand   Going 63   +02 Fast   Stalls Inside

201	STRAVMOUR 12 [12] R Hollinshead 7-8-2 (43) Dale Gibson 14/1: 0060431: Trkd ldrs 4f out trav well, rdn/no room 2f out, swtchd & drvn to lead well ins last:		45a
201*	VICTORY QUEST 12 [9] Mrs S Lamyman 3-9-12 7ex vis (72) Dane O'Neill 6/1: 0125212: Handy, led over 4f out, drvn & hdd well ins last:	¾	73a
196	TROUBLE MOUNTAIN 12 [13] M W Easterby 6-10-0 (69) P Mulrennan (5) 5/2 FAV: 0544023: Well bhd, styd on well for press fnl 2f, too much to do:	¾	69a
173	COURT OF APPEAL 18 [7] B Ellison 6-9-12 t (67) T Hamilton (5) 4/1: 6402434: Rear, hdwy 5f out, rdn to chall over 1f out, no extra ins last:	nk	66a
195	SURDOUE 14 [6] P Howling 3-9-5 (65) Paul Eddery 66/1: 5000005: Trkd ldrs, ch 2f out, no extra for press dist:	1¼	62a
2864*]	MARMADUKE 528 [14] M Pitman 7-9-6 (61) S Drowne 8/1: 351631-6: Mid-div, smooth prog to trk ldrs over 3f out, sn no extra:	3	54a
3949}	KING PRIAM 120 [5] M J Polglase 8-7-12 50h bl (34) M Nem (7) 33/1: 0554007: Mid-div, rdn & kept on onepace, abs.	1½	30a
97	EAST CAPE 32 [8] Don Enrico Incisa 6-8-1 (42) Kim Tinkler (3) 12/1: 6634458: Chsd ldrs, drvn & onepace fnl 2f.	shd	33a
75	INTERSTICE 36 [15] A G Newcombe 6-8-13 (54) S Whitworth 12/1: 0300009: Trkd ldrs wide 4f out, wknd.	11	32a
196	ERSAAL 12 [1] J Jay 3-8-6 BL (52) Lisa Jones (3) 33/1: 6503000: Dwelt & al bhd:	11	17a
201	DUBAI DREAMS 12 [3] M J Polglase 3-8-12 vis (58) K Ghunowa (7) 7/1: 0000140: Led till over 4f out, sn wknd.	½	22a
206	ILOVETURTLE 11 [10] M C Chapman 3-7-13 (45) Joanna Badger 25/1: 2000000: Chsd ldrs, btn 5f out.	4	3a
2227}	MOYNE PLEASURE 192 [4] Paul Johnson 5-8-5 (46) R Fitzpatrick 25/1: 2024450: AI bhd:	dist	0
244	HUMDINGER 5 [2] D Shaw 3-9-0 (60) N Callan 40/1: 3610060: Chsd ldrs till halfway:	hd	0
148	BLUE RONDO 21 [11] Ian Williams 3-9-0 (60) C Catlin 25/1: 00-40000: Sn bhd.	5	0

15 Ran   2m 41.57 (7.27)   Owner Mr E Bennion   Trained at Upper Longdon

Official Going Standard

258
12.00 Bet Direct No Q On 08000 93 66 93 Maiden Stakes Div 1 2yo (D)
£2982 £852 £426   6f p/track rnd   Going 46   -23 Slow   Stalls Inside

217	SMOKIN JOE 12 [2] J R Best 2-9-0 (69) N Pollard 5/1: 066221: Chsd ldrs, styd on to lead ins last, rdn out:		75a
158	PHLUKE 21 [1] R F Johnson Houghton 2-9-0 (73) S Carson 6/1: 622432: Led/dsptd lead, rdn & led 3f out, hdd ins last:	1¼	71a
4952}	SAVIOURS SPIRIT 59 [6] T G Mills 2-9-0 (77) R Miles 4/1: 0053: Chsd ldrs, outpcd 2f out, kept on ins last:	hd	70a
	TONY THE TAP [9] N A Callaghan 2-9-0 W Ryan 25/1: 4: Hmpd start & bhd, eye-catching late hdwy under hands-and-heels, nrst fin:	½	68a
197	RED ROCKY 14 [5] J Gallagher 2-8-9 (52) P Doe 33/1: 5655: Led/dsptd lead 3f, flashed tail & no extra over 1f out:	1	60a
105	AFTER ALL 33 [8] G A Butler 2-8-9 BL (64) E Ahern 11/2: 023526: Mid-div, no impress over 1f out:	1	57a
32	DOCKLANDS BLUE 45 [4] N P Littmoden 2-8-9 J P Guillambert (3) 14/1: 637: Held up, outpcd fnl 3f, abs.	2½	49a
	NOBLE DESERT [3] R Guest 2-8-9 S Drowne 33/1: 8: Dwelt, al outpcd.	2½	41a
	NOSSENKO [7] J Noseda 2-8-9 Dane O'Neill 9/4 FAV: 9: Chsd ldrs wide early, sn strugg:	2½	33a
4580}	TOMOKIM 87 [10] M Quinn 2-9-0 R Winston 100/1: 000: Chsd ldrs wide, struggling halfway, abs.	20	0

10 Ran   1m 14.55 (4.15)   Owner Pennywise Racing Ltd   Trained at Maidstone

259
12.30 Littlewoods Bet Direct Aw Jockeys Championship Handicap Stakes Div 1 3yo+ 0-65 (F) [65]
£2058 £588 £294   1m5f p/track   Going 46   -23 Slow

114*	ROYAL PRODIGY 31 [10] R J Hodges 4-9-12 (63) Dane O'Neill 7/1: 1301311: Held up, pushed along halfway, drvn & styd on to lead cl-home, all out:		67a
201	REMINISCENT 14 [6] R F Johnson Houghton 4-10-0 bl (65) S Carson 11/2: 3453522: Trkd ldr halfway, led over 2f out & rdn clr, tired & hdd cl-home:	nk	67a
243	MAKARIM 7 [2] M R Bosley 7-9-9 p (60) Hayley Turner (5) 20/1: 6040063: Mid-div, short of room 3f out, rdn & kept on fnl 1f, not threaten front pair:	1¾	59a
243	COMPTON ECLAIRE 7 [3] G A Butler 3-8-9 (52) E Ahern 9/2 FAV: 6401034: Rear, pushed along over 3f out, kept on late for press, not dngr:	1¼	49a
230	COOLFORE JADE 9 [4] N E Berry 3-9-0 (57) M Savage (4) 14/1: 0140045: Keen, trkd ldrs, no impress fnl 1f:	2½	50a
2372}	KOMATI RIVER 188 [8] J Akehurst 4-9-1 (52) P Doe 8/1: 00-6256: Trkd ldr, lost pl halfway, no impress after:	2	42a
230	RAHEEL 9 [1] P Mitchell 3-8-10 t (53) W Ryan 9/1: 0002067: Rear, eff wide, no impress:	3	38a
4581}	MADIBA 87 [9] P Howling 4-9-6 BL (57) R Winston 20/1: 0050408: Cl-up, led halfway, hdd over 2f out, wknd.	nk	41a
147	LAZZAZ 23 [11] P W Hiatt 5-9-11 (62) Joanna Badger 10/1: 2013309: Led/dsptd lead till halfway, sn btn, op 14/1.	1¼	44a
4369}	COOL BATHWICK 100 [5] B R Millman 4-9-5 (56) G Baker 25/1: 0000-000: Rear, no impress, abs.	hd	38a
191	RADIANT BRIDE 16 [13] K R Burke 3-8-2 (45) A Reilly (7) 25/1: 0500250: AI bhd:	2½	24a
215	WAVET 12 [12] Mrs Lydia Pearce 3-8-8 1ow (50) N Callan 14/1: 0-6000: Keen, trkd ldrs 10f:	10	14a
4567}	VERY EXCLUSIVE 88 [7] G L Moore 4-8-10 (47) I Mongan 9/1: 5004300: Mid-div, btn 5f out:	7	0
	CHIRU 60 [14] B J Meehan 3-9-8 (65) L Keniry (3) 14/1: 4606440: Keen, chsd ldrs till 5f out, t.o., abs, Brit bow.	14	0

14 Ran   2m 51.27 (8.97)   Owner Mr D Charlesworth   Trained at Somerton

---

260

1.05 Bet Direct No Q On 08000 93 66 93 Maiden Stakes Div 2 2yo (D)
£2982 £852 £426   6f p/track rnd   Going 46   -25 Slow   Stalls Inside

146	**CHORUS BEAUTY** 23 [5] G Wragg 2-8-9 S Drowne 6/1: 01: Trkd ldrs, led over 1f out, rdn out:			66a
146	**MUGEBA** 23 [1] W J Musson 2-8-9 M Fenton 20/1: 02: Pushed along chasing ldrs inner, kept on for press, not pace of wnr:		1½	60a
	DEVIOUS AYERS [7] G A Butler 2-9-0 E Ahern 6/1: 3: Dwelt, bmpd start, rear, kept on late, no dngr:		1¼	61a
176	**AVERAMI** 19 [3] A M Balding 2-8-9 (68) N Callan 4/1: 0654: Chsd ldrs, onepace bef dist:		nk	55a
88	**CITY AFFAIR** 85 [6] Mrs L C Jewell 2-9-0 (57) I Mongan 12/1: 0500305: Keen, cl-up/dsptd lead till over 1f out, wknd.		½	58a
126	**CORNWALLIS** 30 [8] R Guest 2-9-0 J Mackay 8/1: 06: Pushed along mid-div, not pace to chall:		1¼	54a
4230}	**TONTO** 105 [4] Miss D Mountain 2-9-0 (76) Dane O'Neill 5/2 FAV: 0343027: Keen & led till over 3f out, wknd dist:		½	52a
4015}	**GENUINE JAY GEE** 118 [10] G G Margarson 2-9-0 N Pollard 14/1: 08: Pushed along rear, al outpcd, abs.		2½	44a
	SUSSEX STYLE [9] R M Flower 2-9-0 S Whitworth 50/1: 9: Dwelt, sn struggling rear on debut.		5	30a
176	**PATS NEMISIS** 19 [2] B R Johnson 2-8-9 R Smith 33/1: 000: Bmpd start, al bhd.		14	0

10 Ran   1m 14.64 (4.24)   Owner Mrs Claude Lilley   Trained at Newmarket

---

261

1.35 Betdirect Co Uk Nursery Handicap Stakes 2yo 0-85 (D)   [84]
£3066 £876 £438   7f p/track rnd   Going 46   -20 Slow   Stalls Inside

190	**ST SAVARIN** 16 [11] J R Best 2-8-12 (68) I Mongan 8/1: 0261051: Led after 1f, drvn & held on well ins last:			73a
42	**GARRIGON** 42 [9] N P Littmoden 2-8-4 (60) Lisa Jones (3) 14/1: 6062002: Sn trkd wnr, hdwy to chall cl-home, just held:		hd	64a
132	**LITTLE EYE** 27 [7] J R Best 2-8-12 (68) N Pollard 3/1 FAV: 0004223: Pushed along chasing front pair, kept on for press, not able to chall:		1¼	68a
132	**TURNBERRY** 27 [3] J W Hills 2-8-4 1ow bl (59) S Whitworth 12/1: 000004: Held up, eff 2f out, onepace:		½	58a
79	**ELUSIVE KITTY** 37 [2] G A Butler 2-9-0 (70) E Ahern 7/2: 5255: Mid-div, short of room/switched over 1f out, kept on:		½	66a
223	**DARING AFFAIR** 10 [4] K R Burke 2-8-8 (64) N Callan 9/1: 044526: Keen early, cl-up, onepace over 1f out.		nk	59a
184	**REDBANK** 17 [8] N A Callaghan 2-8-9 bl (65) Dane O'Neill 11/1: 6004337: Rear, switched wide & mod prog:		shd	60a
220	**JANGO MALFOY** 12 [6] B W Duke 2-8-7 2ow BL T (61) M Fenton 20/1: 00058: Mid-div, no impress, blnks & t-strap.		2½	50a
177*	**OFF BEAT** 19 [10] R F Johnson Houghton 2-9-7 bl (77) S Carson 5/1: 0610619: Keen, rear, no room over 2f out, sn btn:		2	58a
4159}	**MAN CRAZY** 110 [1] R M Beckett 2-9-0 (70) M Tebbutt 16/1: 2332300: Pulled hard & led 1f, prom 5f:		¾	49a
126*	**SABLE N SILK** 30 [5] D Haydn Jones 2-8-12 (68) S Drowne 16/1: 610: Keen, mid-div, btn 2f out:		1¼	43a

11 Ran   1m 27.43 (4.63)   Owner Mr D S Nevison   Trained at Maidstone

---

262

2.05 Bet Direct Football Cashbacks Handicap Stakes 3yo+ 0-100 (C)   [100]
£6078 £2306 £1153 £524   7f p/track rnd   Going 46   +07 Fast   Stalls Inside

235	**LYGETON LAD** 9 [10] Miss Gay Kelleway 5-10-0 t (100) M Fenton 9/2: 5200101: Rear, hdwy wide over 2f out, led ins last, drvn out:			106a
4950}	**THE BEST YET** 60 [9] A G Newcombe 5-8-0 (72) F P Ferris (3) 15/2: 2463022: Rear, hdwy inner 2f out, drvn & styd on well, just held:		hd	77a
4979}	**HAND CHIME** 58 [7] W J Haggas 6-9-1 (87) S Drowne 11/1: 3460003: Mid-div trav well, short of room 2f out, styd on well late/wide:		1¾	88a
81	**CAMP COMMANDER** 37 [6] C E Brittain 4-9-9 t (95) I Mongan 5/1: 0000034: Trkd ldrs, onepace.		1¾	94a
149*	**COMPTON BANKER** 23 [1] G A Butler 4-9-6 (78) E Ahern 7/2 FAV: 5004115: Trkd ldrs, onepace fnl 2f:		nk	76a
149	**AWARDING** 23 [2] R F Johnson Houghton 3-8-6 t (78) C Catlin 10/1: 0456506: Keen, rear, eff 3f out, no extra dist.		1¾	73a
4950*}	**HARIPUR** 60 [3] Andrew Reid 4-9-11 (97) S Carson 4/1: 1121117: Led/dsptd lead, went on halfway, hdd ins last, eased, fin lame.		½	91a
235	**SUNDRIED TOMATO** 9 [4] P W Hiatt 4-8-13 (85) G Baker 20/1: 6000008: Free to start, keen & led till over 3f out, wknd qckly over 1f out, eased.		5	70a
149	**OVERRIDE** 23 [8] J M P Eustace 3-7-13 (71) J Mackay 9/1: 6-220069: In tch early, struggling from halfway.		6	45a
235	**ACTION FIGHTER** 9 [5] N P Littmoden 3-9-7 (93) J P Guillambert (3) 33/1: 0251000: Chsd ldrs till halfway, t.o.		9	51a

10 Ran   1m 25.56 (2.76)   Owner Mr J McGonagle & Mr B J McGona   Trained at Newmarket

---

263

2.35 Cashbacks On Sky Text Page 372 Maiden Stakes 3yo+ (D)
£2352 £672 £336   7f p/track rnd   Going 46   -06 Slow   Stalls Inside

218	**WOOD FERN** 12 [4] M R Channon 3-9-0 (65) R Lappin 5/1: 33001: Trkd ldrs halfway trav well, led over 1f out, rdn out:			62a
248	**GIVEMETHEMOONLIGHT** 3 [1] Mrs Stef Liddiard 4-8-9 (44) C Catlin 7/1: 6032422: Trkd ldrs, rdn & outpcd over 2f out, rallied well late:		1¾	53a
216	**ADANTINO** 12 [13] B R Millman 4-9-0 (48) G Baker 14/1: 0056053: Held up, eff from halfway, onepace fnl 1f:		shd	58a
214	**MAYZIN** 12 [15] R M Flower 3-9-0 p (51) S Whitworth 14/1: 0000054: Led till over 1f out, wknd.		2	54a
219	**MIDNIGHT MAMBO** 12 [3] R Guest 3-8-9 E Ahern 4/1 FAV: 05: Held up, eff wide, no extra dist:		¾	48a
148	**CAYMAN SUNRISE** 23 [9] E A L Dunlop 3-8-9 (61) W Ryan 5/1: 344266: Held up, nvr pace to threaten:		2½	43a
219	**A BEETOO** 12 [7] J R Best 3-8-9 (60) N Pollard 11/2: 2462657: Rdn rear, only mod prog:		½	42a
219	**MAD MICK MEESON** 12 [10] G B Balding 3-9-0 VIS t (50) R Havlin 8/1: 5040048: Cl-up till 2f out, sn wknd:		¾	46a
216	**DEFINITELY SPECIAL** 12 [16] N E Berry 5-8-9 (40) L Keniry 25/1: 0600009: Keen, held up, no impress on ldrs.		1¾	38a
3358}	**STRIKE LUCKY** 148 [14] P J Makin 3-9-0 D Sweeney 25/1: 400: Chsd ldrs till halfway, abs/AW bow.		½	42a
123	**UNSUITED** 30 [2] J E Long 4-8-9 (53) R Miles (4) 40/1: 00-06500: Mid-div, btn over 1f out.		½	36a
219	**ISLAND STAR** 12 [12] S Dow 3-9-0 (52) P Doe 16/1: 6400060: Sn outpcd & struggling.		6	30a
174	**SILISTRA** 19 [11] Mrs L C Jewell 4-9-0 H bl (55) Dane O'Neill 50/1: 064-0000: Bmpd start & al bhd.		nk	29a
3158}	**LAW MAKER** 157 [5] M A Buckley 3-9-0 (40) R Winston 66/1: 0000000: Chsd ldrs till halfway:		4	22a
	DEVON MAID [8] R J Hodges 4-8-9 S Drowne 100/1: 0: Bhd halfway on debut.		1¼	14a

15 Ran   1m 26.42 (3.62)   Owner Mr M Channon   Trained at West Ilsley

LINGFIELD Monday 29.12.03 Lefthand, V Sharp Track

264 — 3.10 Littlewoods Bet Direct Aw Jockeys Championship Handicap Stakes Div 2 3yo+ 0-65 (F) [65]
£2051 £586 £293 1m5f p/track Going 46 -14 Slow Stalls Inside

173	MAJLIS 20 [12] R M H Cowell 6-9-10 bl (61) E Ahern 13/2: 0500201: Keen, rear, gd hdwy to lead on bit over 1f out, cmftbly:		69a
218	EASTER OGIL 12 [7] Jane Southcombe 8-9-12 (63) V Slattery 5/1 JT FAV: 4306422: Mid-div, lost pl inner halfway, styd on for press fnl 2f, wnr had flown:	2½	63a
1701}	GEMI BED 219 [10] G L Moore 8-8-4 bl (41) S Whitworth 6/1: 6651153: Hmpd early, held up, smooth hdwy wide to lead 2f out, hdd over 1f out & no extra:	¾	40a
1075}	LANOS 258 [5] R Ford 5-9-9 t (60) J P Guillambert (3) 7/1: 6166544: Slow away & rear, smooth hdwy 3f out, no extra dist:	3	55a
230	SUNGIO 9 [14] B G Powell 5-9-6 (57) A Hindley (7) 40/1: 00005-05: Rear, eff 3f out, onepace.	¾	51a
107	STARRY MARY 33 [1] E L James 5-8-10 (47) L Keniry (2) 20/1: 5200006: Handy, no extra over 1f out.	1¼	39a
137*	WAVERLEY ROAD 27 [4] M Madgwick 6-8-8 (45) I Mongan 5/1 JT FAV: 0060517: Trkd ldr 5f out, led 3f out till 2f out.	shd	37a
4481}	TREASURE TRAIL 93 [11] S Kirk 4-10-0 (65) C Catlin 7/1: 3206008: Mid-div, btn 2f out.	1¾	55a
236	FIFE AND DRUM 9 [6] Miss J Feilden 6-9-6 p (57) B Reilly (5) 14/1: 4222U09: Mid-div, btn 2f out:	½	46a
4263}	PROMOTE 104 [3] Ms A E Embiricos 7-8-13 (50) P McCabe 66/1: 60000-00: Trkd ldrs, lost pl 5f out, abs.	24	6a
178	ESPERANCE 28 [8] J Akehurst 3-8-12 (55) Dane O'Neill 10/1: 2040000: Prom wide till 3f out.	3	7a
154	WHITE PARK BAY 28 [13] J Gallagher 3-9-1 (58) N Callan 16/1: 4030330: Led 6f out till 3f out, wknd qckly.	3	6a
3862}	BEETLE BUG 126 [2] A M Hales 3-8-4 (47) J Mackay 50/1: 5000000: Led till 6f out, btn 5f out:	1½	0
3806}	CANTRIP 128 [9] Miss B Sanders 3-9-5 T (62) S Drowne 14/1: 1242660: Chsd ldrs, btn halfway, new stble, t-strap, abs.	16	0

14 Ran 2m 50.11 (7.81) Owner Mr Terry Warner Trained at Newmarket

265 — 3.40 Cashbacks On Itv Text Page 367 Apprentice Handicap Stakes 3yo+ 0-80 (F) [77]
£3000 £857 £429 1m2f p/track Going 46 -24 Slow Stalls Inside

134	J R STEVENSON 27 [5] M Wigham 7-9-12 (75) M Savage (3) 3/1 FAV: 0426351: Mid-div, smooth prog 2f out & led over 1f out, rdn & held on well:		81a
195	TROPICAL CORAL 16 [8] C Tinkler 3-9-5 (71) D Nolan 12/1: 1450452: Held up, hdwy inner 3f out, prsd wnr dist, no extra:	½	74a
174	RASID 19 [3] C A Dwyer 5-9-0 (63) B Reilly (4) 6/1: 0003053: Held up, short of room over 2f out, kept on to take 3rd, no dngr:	¾	66a
131	BLUE TROJAN 27 [1] S Kirk 3-9-2 (68) L Treadwell (5) 7/1: 3015644: Led 1f, cl-up, onepace:	½	70a
174*	RYANS FUTURE 19 [2] J Akehurst 3-10-0 (80) N Chalmers 5/1: 4051415: Held up, short of room over 2f out, onpce.	¾	81a
178	MISS PEBBLES 19 [7] B R Johnson 3-9-5 p (71) V Fdentiman (5) 7/1: 3210056: Keen & handy, led 2f out till over 1f out.	1¼	70a
145*	BURGUNDY 23 [9] P Mitchell 6-9-2 (65) R Miles 10/1: 3015017: Rear, eff wide, no impress dist:	2½	60a
218	BLUEGRASS BOY 12 [11] G B Balding 3-9-0 (66) R Thomas (2) 20/1: 0-025308: Dsptd lead till 2f out, wknd qckly.	hd	60a
4702}	MUYASSIR 78 [10] Miss B Sanders 8-8-7 (56) Hayley Turner (3) 16/1: 0300109: Prom till 2f out, wknd, abs.	1¾	48a
174	ANEMOS 19 [14] P W D'Arcy 8-8-2 h (51) B Swarbrick (5) 16/1: 0556000: Rear, no impress fnl 2f.	shd	43a
148	SHAAMITS ALL OVER 23 [4] B A Pearce 4-8-1 (50) Dean Williams (5) 40/1: 0600: Dwelt & al bhd:	3	38a
101	BALERNO 33 [12] R Ingram 4-8-1 (50) Stephanie Hollinshead (3) 20/1: 0005300: Cl-up, wknd over 1f out.	1¼	36a
136	SNUKI 21 [6] G L Moore 4-9-2 bl (65) A Quinn 12/1: 6200000: Led/dsptd lead till over 3f out, wknd qckly.	6	43a
2011]	ARC EN CIEL 565 [13] G L Moore 5-9-3 (66) H Poulton (5) 50/1: 1100/00-0: Mid-div, struggling fnl 4f:	1¾	42a

14 Ran 2m 09.76 (6.96) Owner Claret & Blue Army Trained at Newmarket

266 — 12.15 Littlewoods Bet Direct Aw Trainers Championship Handicap Stakes Div 1 3yo+ 0-70 (E) [69]
£2107 £602 £301 7f p/track rnd Going 33 -06 Slow Stalls Inside

202	SMITH N ALLAN OILS 14 [6] M Dods 4-9-0 p (55) R Winston 11/2: 5230101: Mid-div, smooth hdwy & squeezed through gap over 1f out, drvn out:		60a
131	SUPERCHIEF 28 [7] Miss B Sanders 8-9-7 bl t (62) S Drowne 12/1: 0200002: Held up, swtchd & drvn/kept on well ins last, not reach wnr:	½	65a
241	CAPTAIN DARLING 8 [10] R M H Cowell 3-9-9 (64) E Ahern 5/1 FAV: 5045543: Trkd ldrs, rdn & onepace dist:	2	63a
241	THE GAIKWAR 8 [2] N E Berry 4-10-0 bl (69) M Savage (5) 9/1: 0000404: Dwelt, rear, drvn & kept on inner fnl 2f, not able to chall.	nk	67a
216	FOUR JAYS 13 [14] N P Littmoden 3-9-5 p (60) Martin Dwyer 20/1: 0260505: Cl-up, no extra dist.	1¼	55a
133	I WISH 28 [9] M Madgwick 5-9-9 (64) L Keniry (3) 10/1: 0006146: Trkd ldrs, fdd fnl 1f.	nk	58a
214	HARBOUR HOUSE 13 [12] J J Bridger 4-8-2 (43) J Tate 11/1: 0000027: Led till over 1f out, fdd.	1¼	34a
144	ITS ECCO BOY 24 [4] P Howling 5-8-12 (53) Lisa Jones (3) 7/1: 5003648: Mid-div, eff dist, no extra.	shd	44a
151*	MISS ISSY 24 [16] J Gallagher 3-9-3 vis (58) N Callan 11/1: 3404019: Chsd ldrs wide, no prog/bmpd dist:	¾	48a
181	FULVIO 20 [3] Jamie Poulton 3-9-11 (66) Stephanie Hollinshead (7) 25/1: 5004000: Keen rear, eff 2f out, no impress.	2½	51a
214	DANCING FOREST 13 [8] D K Ivory 3-9-11 (66) C Catlin 20/1: 0200000: Rear, eff 2f out, no impress.	½	50a
219*	GUN SALUTE 13 [5] G L Moore 3-9-1 p (56) R Brisland 14/1: 0005010: Keen, rear, no room over 2f out, sn btn.	2	36a
174	ICANNSHIFT 20 [1] S Dow 3-9-11 (66) P Doe 25/1: 0040600: Rear, no room after 2f, nvr a factor.	½	45a
3528}	TREETOPS HOTEL 141 [11] B R Johnson 4-9-7 (62) Dane O'Neill 12/1: 0000000: Rear/wide, nvr a factor, abs.	½	40a
144	KINSMAN 24 [15] T D McCarthy 6-8-10 (51) J P Guillambert (3) 16/1: 5500600: Cl-up, btn 2f out.	¾	28a

15 Ran 1m 25.52 (2.72) Owner Smith & Allan Racing Trained at Darlington

267 — 12.45 Littlewoodscasino Com Selling Stakes Div 1 3yo+ (G)
£2051 £586 £293 1m2f p/track Going 33 -53 Slow Stalls Inside

4373}	ABSOLUTE UTOPIA 101 [3] J L Spearing 10-9-6 (63) J Mackay 2/1 FAV: 0232101: Dictated pace, hdd after 2f, chsd ldrs till led 2f out, drvn & held on well:		62a
230	ICECAP 10 [2] P Butler 3-8-6 (51) A Daly 7/1: 5665002: Keen, held up, smooth hdwy to trk ldrs 3f out, drvn to press wnr ins last, al just held:	½	49a
4690}	BLUE SAVANNA 79 [5] J G Portman 3-8-11 bl (48) E Ahern 8/1: 4002663: Trkd ldrs, onepce.	5	47a
214	LADYWELL BLAISE 13 [4] J J Bridger 6-8-9 (41) J Tate 14/1: 3000064: Held up, eff 2f out, no dngr.	¾	41a
216	DOLPHINELLE 13 [7] Jamie Poulton 7-9-0 vis (49) S Drowne 4/1: 0500535: Rear, rdn & late gains, no dngr-	¾	45a
46	HIGH DIVA 43 [1] B R Johnson 4-8-9 P (45) N Chalmers (5) 7/1: 4020006: Rear, chsd ldrs over 2f out, sn no extra.	1¼	38a
150	CHOCOLATE BOY 24 [4] G L Moore 4-9-0 (43) S Whitworth 25/1: 00/000-07: Held up, eff 2f out, no impress.	2	40a

191	**TORO BRAVO** 17 [9] R M Beckett 3-8-11 bl (60) M Tebbutt 14/1: 0000008: Chsd wnr over 2f out, sn wknd:	1¾	38a
234}	**CAROLINES ROSE** 375 [13] A P Jones 5-8-9 (20) Lisa Jones (3) 50/1: 000-9: Led, sn clr, hdd 2f out & wknd:	2½	29a
227	**ST CASSIEN** 11 [12] T M Jones 3-8-11 (35) R Brisland 66/1: 060-000: Mid-div, btn 2f out.	2	31a
118	**DISTINCTLYSPLENDID** 31 [10] I A Wood 3-8-11 BL (40) N Callan 25/1: 6400000: Dsptd 2nd, btn 3f out, blnks.	hd	30a
2711}	**KITTYLEE** 537 [11] M A Buckley 4-8-9 (25) R Ffrench 50/1: 00/0000-0: Dsptd 2nd, wknd qckly hway, long abs, new yard.	1½	23a
12 Ran	2m 11.36 (8.56) Owner Mr M T Lawrance	Trained at Kinnersley	

268

1.15 Betdirect Co Uk Nursery Handicap Stakes 2yo 0-85 (D)   [86]

£3094 £884 £442   **6f p/track rnd**   **Going 33   -11 Slow**   Stalls Inside

177	**KABREET** 20 [4] E A L Dunlop 2-9-1 (73) Dane O'Neill 6/1: 553101: Held up, swtchd & drvn to lead wll lns last:		81a
217	**PREGNANT PAUSE** 13 [3] S Kirk 2-8-7 (65) Martin Dwyer 100/30: 3002402: Mid-div, rdn to chall lns last, not pace of wnr cl-home:	nk	72a
217*	**INTRIGUING GLIMPSE** 13 [1] Miss B Sanders 2-8-13 (71) S Drowne 11/4 FAV: 60113: Trkd ldrs, drvn 2f out, kept on onepace ins last:	1½	73a
217	**SWEETEST REVENGE** 13 [6] M D I Usher 2-9-6 (78) A Daly 7/1: 0104254: Keen & cl-up, rdn & led over 1f out, hdd ins last, no extra:	1¼	76a
233	**STANHOPE FORBES** 10 [9] N P Littmoden 2-7-12 1oh p (55) Lisa Jones (3) 7/1: 3506025: Dwelt, rear, late prog, no dngr:	¾	52a
258	**SMOKIN JOE** 1 [7] J R Best 2-9-3 6ex (75) N Pollard 4/1: 0662216: Chsd ldrs, no extra when hmpd ins last.	¾	69a
176	**RISE ON** 8 [8] Andrew Reid 2-9-7 bl (79) S Donohoe (7) 25/1: 2310407: Held up, nvr pace to chall:	1¾	68a
4388}	**KURINGAI** 99 [2] B W Duke 2-9-0 (72) M Fenton 20/1: 0333028: Led till over 1f out, sn btn:	5	47a
8 Ran	1m 13.03 (2.63) Owner Jumeirah Racing	Trained at Newmarket	

269

1.45 Bet Direct On 0800 32 93 93 Maiden Stakes 3yo (D)

£2300 £657 £329   **1m2f p/track**   **Going 33   -36 Slow**   Stalls Inside

3090}	**GRAND WIZARD** 160 [1] W Jarvis 3-9-0 M Tebbutt 25/1: 001: Rear, hdwy 2f out, rdn & styd on to lead wll ins last:		71a
215	**MARGERY DAW** 13 [4] M P Tregoning 3-8-9 (64) Martin Dwyer 2/1: 3-2252: Keen, sn clr ldr, rdn 2f out, hdd wll ins last, no extra:	½	64a
148	**ELEGANT GRACIE** 24 [3] R Guest 3-8-9 S Drowne 25/1: 003: Mid-div, eff to chase ldr 2f out, onepace ins last:	1½	62a
4468}	**SPRINGALONG** 95 [6] P D Evans 3-9-0 (75) S Donohoe (7) 8/1: 43304: Prom, outpcd 3f out, kept on late under minimal	3	63a
3525}	**GOLDEN DUAL** 141 [8] S Dow 3-9-0 (73) P Doe 10/1: 4304365: Chsd ldr over 3f out, wknd qckly lns last:	1	62a
4820}	**RETAIL THERAPY** 71 [2] M A Buckley 3-8-9 (33) R Ffrench 50/1: 00-00006: Mid-div, outpcd 3f out:	3	53a
148	**BOLD RIDGE** 24 [7] S Kirk 3-9-0 Dane O'Neill 20/1: 07: Mid-div, no impress fnl 3f.	17	34a
115	**LOVELLIAN** 32 [9] B R Millman 3-8-9 (47) G Baker 25/1: 005408: Chsd ldr, wknd qckly fnl 3f.	1¾	27a
39	**JUBILEE TIME** 69 [5] L M Cumani 3-9-0 E Ahern 10/11 FAV: 03W: Withdrawn, ref to enter stalls.		0a
9 Ran	2m 09.66 (6.86) Owner Kelly Shenfield Slade & Stra	Trained at Newmarket	

270

2.15 Littlewoods Bet Direct Aw Trainers Championship Handicap Stakes Div 2 3yo+ 0-70 (E)   [69]

£2107 £602 £301   **7f p/track rnd**   **Going 33   -16 Slow**   Stalls Inside

4958}	**AND TOTO TOO** 60 [5] P D Evans 3-9-11 VIS (66) S Donohoe (7) 9/2 FAV: 0315351: Trkd ldrs, rdn & led over 1f out, styd on strongly for press:		70a
4184}	**LILY OF THE GUILD** 110 [8] W S Kittow 4-8-13 (54) N Callan 25/1: 0044462: Bmpd start, mid-div:	1¾	54a
151	**TEMPER TANTRUM** 24 [9] Andrew Reid 5-9-8 p (63) J P Guillambert (3) 6/1: 1305023: Held up, rdn & kept on onepace fnl 2f:	shd	63a
181	**PHECKLESS** 20 [14] R F Johnson Houghton 4-10-0 (69) S Carson 11/2: 0-100564: Keen, rear, late gains for press, too much to do:	½	68a
208	**ACORAZADO** 14 [13] G L Moore 4-9-1 (56) G Carter 7/1: 0551535: Rear, late gains for press, nrst fin:	shd	55a
181	**ROYAL FASHION** 20 [12] Miss S West 3-9-7 (62) N Chalmers (5) 20/1: 60-30206: Slow away, rear, drvn & late gains.	1½	58a
216*	**ZINGING** 13 [3] J J Bridger 4-8-11 (52) G Baker 10/1: 0000317: Cl-up, no extra fnl 1f:	shd	48a
180	**MEELUP** 20 [4] A G Newcombe 3-9-5 p (60) S Whitworth 50/1: 0601008: Led, hdd over 1f out, wknd.	1¼	53a
60	**TITIAN LASS** 41 [7] C E Brittain 4-8-4 bl (45) Dean Williams (7) 20/1: 0020209: Held up, nvr dngrs:	nk	37a
241	**HEIDELBURG** 8 [1] S Kirk 3-9-9 (64) Martin Dwyer 14/1: 0623000: Mid-div, no impress fnl 2f.	shd	56a
144	**MR BOUNTIFUL** 24 [11] M Dods 5-9-7 (62) C Catlin 10/1: 6412300: Chsd ldrs 5f, wknd:	nk	53a
4310}	**BLAKESEVEN** 103 [2] W J Musson 3-8-9 (50) Paul Eddery 16/1: 0000040: Chsd ldr 3f out, wknd qckly dist.	1¾	38a
181	**CAYMAN BREEZE** 20 [10] S Dow 3-9-10 (65) P Doe 16/1: 1000300: Rear, eff wide, no impress.	nk	52a
214*	**WARLINGHAM** 13 [15] P Howling 5-9-0 (55) R Winston 7/1: 0-000210: Held up, no impress 2f out:	nk	41a
1519}	**MASTER RATTLE** 229 [6] Jane Southcombe 4-9-1 (56) V Slattery 40/1: 1050000: Chsd ldr, btn 2f out, abs.	hd	41a
3941}	**PARKER** 124 [16] B Palling 6-9-11 bl (66) M Fenton 20/1: 4062150: Keen, wide, no impress fnl 2f:	2	47a
16 Ran	1m 26.22 (3.42) Owner Mrs S J Lawrence	Trained at Abergavenny	

271

2.45 Littlewoodspoker Com Claiming Stakes 3yo+ (F)

£2079 £594 £297   **6f p/track rnd**   **Going 33   -01 Slow**   Stalls Inside

4616}	**TYPE ONE** 85 [8] T G Mills 5-9-0 (78) R Miles (5) 10/11 FAV: 1214321: Made all, readily asserted dist, val for 3L+:		78a
181	**RIPPLE EFFECT** 20 [13] C A Dwyer 3-8-6 t (70) B Reilly (5) 5/1: 1530102: Held up wide, drvn & kept on fnl 1f, no threat to wnr:	2	60a
66	**TAYIF** 41 [6] Andrew Reid 7-8-7 t (52) S Carson 20/1: 0600603: Slow away, rear, hdwy halfway, short of room over 1f out, kept on ins last:	1¼	57a
231	**BYO** 10 [11] M Quinn 5-9-0 (65) R Winston 8/1: 2400444: Mid-div, styd on onepace for press.	1¼	60a
180	**CARGO** 10 [3] H J Collingridge 4-8-5 (47) E Ahern 25/1: 5000005: Dwelt, rear, eff from halfway, not able to chall.	shd	54a
130	**TRIPTI** 28 [1] J J Bridger 3-8-11 1ow (58) J Tate 25/1: 6060406: Mid-div, onepace.	2½	39a
130	**TICKLE** 28 [2] P J Makin 5-8-0 vis t (50) C Catlin 25/1: 2005067: Chsd wnr, wknd over 1f out.	1¼	34a
121	**LEGAL SET** 31 [5] J R Best 7-8-9 (64) Dean McKeown 7/1: 3000608: Prom, no extra over 1f out:	nk	42a
4753}	**JANES VALENTINE** 76 [7] J J Bridger 3-7-12 (52) Joanna Badger 50/1: 2000009: Al rear:	¾	29a

LINGFIELD Tuesday 30.12.03 Lefthand, V Sharp Track

4014}	NAUGHTY GIRL 119 [14] P D Evans 3-8-9 (74) S Donohoe (6) 14/1: 4126560: Al bhd:	2½	32a
117	A TEEN 31 [10] P Howling 5-8-11 (52) Lisa Jones (3) 16/1: 6561000: Chsd ldrs till halfway.	1½	29a
214	THAI HI 13 [9] S Kirk 3-8-4 (56) Martin Dwyer 33/1: 6460000: Prom, btn 2f out.	2	16a
187	IVORY VENTURE 18 [12] D K Ivory 3-8-0 (54) R Ffrench 40/1: 646-5400: Wide, nvr on terms.	6	0a
13 Ran	1m 12.42 (2.02) Owner Mrs A K Petersen		Trained at Epsom

272
3.15 Littlewoodscasino Com Selling Stakes Div 2 3yo+ (G)
£2044 £584 £292   1m2f p/track   Going 33   -31 Slow   Stalls Inside

4859}	PIQUET 68 [12] J J Bridger 5-8-9 (39) G Baker 16/1: 6000501: Dwelt, hdwy inner 3f out & squeezed through gap to lead ins last, drvn out:		48a
194	REMEMBRANCE 17 [2] J M P Eustace 3-8-11 t (63) J Tate 11/4 FAV: 0203662: Mid-div, rdn & outpcd 3f out, late rally for press:	1¼	50a
3698}	WILOM 134 [3] M R Hoad 5-9-0 (42) S Whitworth 20/1: 0053403: Keen & prom, led over 2f out till ins last, no extra:	¾	49a
139}	SIR NINJA 392 [5] S Kirk 6-9-0 (80) Martin Dwyer 6/1: 3/03000-4: Rear, kept on whole way, nrst fin:	¾	48a
4433}	PYRRHIC 97 [4] R M Flower 4-9-0 bl (31) E Ahern 33/1: 0004505: Keen, mid-div, onepace fnl 2f:	nk	47a
145	GINGER ICE 24 [11] G G Margarson 3-8-11 (38) N Pollard 14/1: 0000006: Slow away, hdwy 3f out, wknd ins last.	nk	46a
239	TINIAN 8 [7] K R Burke 5-9-6 (62) Darren Williams 5/1: 1161537: Led till over 2f out.	shd	52a
4859}	PRIVATE SEAL 68 [10] Julian Poulton 8-9-0 t (41) N Callan 10/1: 4030008: Chsd ldrs, outpcd fnl 2f:	1¼	44a
137	LANDESCENT 28 [6] M Quinn 3-8-11 vis (53) R Winston 4/1: 0042669: Trkd ldrs till dist:	7	35a
180	CRAFTY POLITICIAN 20 [1] G L Moore 6-9-6 bl (42) Dane O'Neill 20/1: 4000000: Cl-up, wknd qckly fnl 2f.	2½	37a
4735}	ORAKE PRINCE 428 [8] W G M Turner 4-9-0 (46) C Haddon (7) 50/1: 050206-0: Chsd ldr, lost place fnl 2f:	1½	29a
1135}	BADRINATH 253 [9] H J Collingridge 9-9-0 (48) G Carter 16/1: 306-0000: Mid-div, eff wide, btn 2f out:	14	10a
12 Ran	2m 09.23 (6.43) Owner Mr J J Bridger		Trained at Liphook

273
3.45 Littlewoods Bet Direct Classified Stakes 3yo+ 0-80 (D)
£3510 £1080 £540 £270   1m p/track rnd   Going 33   +08 Fast   Stalls Outside

186	LABRETT 18 [6] Miss Gay Kelleway 6-8-13 t (75) M Fenton 5/1: 3651061: Trkd ldrs, led dist, rdn & styd on strongly:		85a
134*	STAR OF NORMANDIE 28 [5] G G Margarson 4-8-13 (83) B Reilly (5) 15/8 FAV: 0312112: Trkd ldrs, short of room 2f out till ins last, winning ch had gone:	1¼	81a
1961}	SILKEN BRIEF 208 [4] D J Daly 4-8-10 t (78) W Ryan 12/1: 2/102-043: Mid-div, rdn & kept on fnl 2f, not pace to chall:	1	76a
2642}	SKYLARKER 179 [12] W S Kittow 5-8-13 (79) N Callan 33/1: 3604304: Keen, led/dsptd lead till dist, kept on:	nk	76a
149	JUST FLY 24 [10] S Kirk 3-8-12 (79) Martin Dwyer 8/1: 0010505: Prom, chsd ldr 3f out, no extra ins last.	hd	77a
234	AGILIS 10 [9] Jamie Poulton 3-8-12 (79) S Drowne 4/1: 0500046: Mid-div, onepace fnl 2f:	½	76a
214	FREE OPTION 13 [2] W J Musson 8-8-13 (73) Dean McKeown 14/1: 0030137: Held up, lost place over 2f out, mod late gains:	1¼	73a
3735}	AMMENAYR 132 [11] T G Mills 3-8-12 (80) Dane O'Neill 14/1: 61058: Mid-div, no impress fnl 2f.	½	72a
81	BORDER EDGE 38 [3] J J Bridger 5-9-3 vis (84) G Baker 5/1: 1012009: Held up, no impress fnl 2f.	4	68a
4434}	FELLOW SHIP 97 [8] P Butler 3-8-12 (73) L Keniry (3) 50/1: 5340350: Dwelt, rear, btn 2f out:	2½	59a
	ADALAR 443 [1] P D Evans 3-9-3 (85) S Donohoe (6) 25/1: 04210-0: Dwelt, drvn & led after 1f, hdd over 3f out, wknd:	7	52a
11 Ran	1m 38.19 (1.99) Owner Mr A P Griffin		Trained at Newmarket

WOLVERHAMPTON Wednesday 31.12.03 Lefthand, Sharp, Oval Track

Official Going SLOW.

274
12.40 Betdirect Co Uk Handicap Stakes Div 1 3yo+ 0-65 (F)   [63]
£2023 £578 £289   5f f/sand rnd   Going 59   -13 Slow   Stalls Inside

155	LADY PEKAN 25 [4] P S McEntee 4-9-8 bl (57) F P Ferris (3) 5/1: 0000141: Made all, pushed out fnl 1f, val 2L+:		66a
168	NEVER WITHOUT ME 22 [2] P J McBride 3-8-12 (47) Paul Scallan 9/2: 50022: Slow away, prog 2f out, kept on fnl 1f, not pace wnr:	1	50a
231	LAUREL DAWN 11 [3] I W McInnes 5-10-0 (63) D Allan (3) 8/1: 0204103: Cl-up, onepcd fnl 1f:	2½	59a
183	KISS THE RAIN 19 [9] R Brotherton 3-9-2 vis (51) L Fletcher (3) 12/1: 6510334: Cl-up wide, wknd fnl 1f.	1¼	43a
242+*	CLOUDLESS 9 [5] J W Unett 3-9-12 6ex (61) S Whitworth 9/4 FAV: 4030015: Quick away, sn lost place & nvr able to chall:	hd	52a
183	ABRAXAS 19 [6] J Akehurst 5-9-4 p (53) C Catlin 9/1: 0000026: Cl-up, wknd fnl 2f.	2½	37a
183	CATCHTHEBATCH 19 [8] E A Wheeler 7-9-1 (50) S Carson 20/1: 0006307: Al bhd.	¾	34a
124	ERRACHT 32 [1] K R Burke 5-9-5 (56) G Baker 11/2: 1362038: Cl-up, wknd 2 out.	3	27a
8 Ran	1m 3.80 (3.6) Owner Mr P S J Croft		Trained at Newmarket

275
1.15 Betdirect Co Uk Handicap Stakes Div 2 3yo+ 0-65 (F)   [63]
£2023 £578 £289   5f f/sand rnd   Going 59   -35 Slow   Stalls Inside

183	SANDGATE CYGNET 19 [6] I Semple 3-9-9 p (58) R Winston 7/2 FAV: 0002641: Keen in tch, led dist, rdn out:		65a
231	PLAYTIME BLUE 11 [9] K R Burke 3-9-10 (59) G Baker 12/1: 0144002: Handy wide, chsd wnr fnl 1f, just held:	½	63a
4856}	PERCY DOUGLAS 70 [8] Miss A Stokell 3-9-7 vis (56) Ann Stokell 16/1: 0003063: Bhd, prog 2f out, kept on fnl 1f:	¾	58a
246	CASH 5 [1] Paul Johnson 5-9-12 p (61) R Fitzpatrick 11/2: 0050164: Mid-div, prog when short of room dist, switched & kept on fnl 1f:	nk	62a
253	AINTNECESSARILYSO 4 [3] N E Berry 5-8-8 (43) C Catlin 8/1: 3005465: Sn bhd, hdwy dist, kept on late.	1½	40a
183	RELLIM 19 [7] P A Blockley 4-9-3 (52) Derek Nolan (7) 5/1: 6442656: Chsd ldr, wknd fnl 1f.	1	46a
153	SALERNO 25 [2] Miss Gay Kelleway 4-9-1 p (50) Lisa Jones (3) 9/2: 0040007: Al bhd:	½	43a
183	SO SOBER 19 [5] D Shaw 5-8-9 (44) T Hamilton (5) 16/1: 0200008: Mid-div, wknd 2f out.	¾	35a
187	THE LEATHER WEDGE 19 [4] A Berry 4-9-0 (49) P Bradley (5) 8/1: 0004029: Led, hdd dist, sn wknd & eased.	hd	39a
9 Ran	1m 4.92 (4.72) Owner Mrs A M Young		Trained at Carluke

WOLVERHAMPTON Wednesday 31.12.03 Lefthand, Sharp, Oval Track

276   1.45 Bet Direct On Channel 4 Page 613 Maiden Stakes   2yo   (D)
£3038 £868 £434   7f f/sand rnd   Going 59   -20 Slow   Stalls Outside

226	**DENVER** 12 [2] B J Meehan 2-9-0 BL R Winston 2/1: 42521: Cl-up, led 2f out, rdn out fnl 1f:			**82a**
5023}	**BAHIANO** 54 [4] C E Brittain 2-9-0 Dean Williams (7) 12/1: 62: Chsd ldrs, led 3f out, hdd 2f out, no extra fnl 1f:	2	76a
	ANNA PANNA [7] H Candy 2-8-9 D Sweeney 20/1: 3: Chsd ldrs wide, no impress fnl 1f:	6	59a
261	**LITTLE EYE** 29 [6] J R Best 2-9-0 (68) N Pollard 7/4 FAV: 0004224: Chsd ldrs, no extra fnl 2f:	1½	61a
	OBOE [9] R Charlton 2-8-9 S Drowne 10/1: 5: Cl-up wide, wknd 2f out:	6	44a
192	**SMART BOY PRINCE** 18 [5] P A Blockley 2-9-0 (55) Dean McKeown 6/1: 0050466: Led, hdd 3f out, sn wknd:	1	47a
184	**CHIMES EIGHT** 19 [3] R A Fahey 2-8-9 T Hamilton (5) 33/1: 07: Slow away, al bhd:	1	40a
184	**DAGGERS CANYON** 19 [1] Julian Poulton 2-9-0 (65) N Callan 16/1: 0548: Handy, fdd 3f out, eased fnl 1f.	25	10a

8 Ran   1m 31.75 (5.55)   Owner Gigginstown House Stud   Trained at Upper Lambourn

277   2.20 Littlewoods Bet Direct Handicap Stakes   3yo+ 0-75 (E)   [72]
£2009 £574 £287   1m6f166y f/sand   Going 59   -46 Slow   Stalls Outside

138	**PHANTOM STOCK** 28 [8] W Jarvis 3-7-12 3oh (49) D Mernagh 7/1: 000-061: Keen rear, prog to lead 3f out, sn pushed clr, eased cl-home, val 12L+:		**62a**
225	**GLORY QUEST** 12 [7] Miss Gay Kelleway 6-9-12 p (73) T Eaves (5) 4/1: 5223552: Held up, prog 4f out, chsd ldr 2f out, sn no impress with wnr:	8	75a
140	**NOWELL HOUSE** 28 [5] M W Easterby 7-10-0 (75) P Mulrennan (5) 10/1: 5141653: Chsd ldrs, no extra fnl 3f:	8	69a
156	**SASHAY** 25 [3] R Hollinshead 5-8-12 (59) Stephanie Hollinshead (7) 13/2: 4061434: Handy, no extra fnl 4f.	¾	52a
75*	**EASIBET DOT NET** 40 [1] I Semple 3-8-9 p (63) D McGaffin (3) 11/4 FAV: 4323215: Cl-up, led 4f out, hdd 2f out, sn fdd:	5	51a
206	**VANBRUGH** 15 [6] Miss D A McHale 3-8-11 vis t (65) Lisa Jones (3) 4/1: 0660226: Led, hdd 4f out, fdd:	7	46a
206	**HAJEER** 15 [2] P W Hiatt 5-7-12 1oh p (44) J Bramhill 12/1: 2300007: Al bhd.	19	10a
156	**FAST CINDY** 25 [4] J W Unett 4-8-8 (55) R Winston 20/1: 10-20008: Handy, fdd 5f out, eased to a walk fnl 2f.	dist	0a

8 Ran   3m 25.41 (15.81)   Owner The L E H Partnership   Trained at Newmarket

278   2.55 Bet Direct On 0800 32 93 93 Handicap Stakes   3yo+ 0-100 (C)   [98]
£6734 £2072 £1036 £518   1m1f79y f/sand   Going 59   +27 Fast   Stalls Inside

161	**NIMELLO** 23 [10] A G Newcombe 7-8-8 (78) S Whitworth 10/1: 1106121: Held up, prog 4f out, led dist, pushed out, val 4L+:		**89a**
225+*	**MI ODDS** 12 [3] Mrs N Macauley 7-9-5 (89) P McCabe 10/1: 0121212: Cl-up, chsd wnr fnl 1f, al held:	2½	92a
141	**DEL MAR SUNSET** 28 [6] W J Haggas 4-8-13 (83) Lisa Jones (3) 16/1: 3220003: Cl-up, led 3f out, hdd dist, no extra:	2½	81a
191	**CAROUBIER** 18 [7] T D Barron 3-8-8 (80) D Mernagh 25/1: 0150224: Bhd, nvr nrr than mid-div:	4	70a
234	**LAKOTA BRAVE** 11 [4] Mrs Stef Liddiard 9-8-6 (90) S Drowne 12/1: 4331225: Nvr nrr than mid-div:	2½	75a
186	**COOL TEMPER** 19 [8] P F I Cole 7-8-8 t (78) C Catlin 9/1: 0140336: Al bhd:	6	52a
82	**LUNDYS LANE** 39 [9] C E Brittain 3-10-0 (100) M Fenton 10/1: 2134607: Chsd ldrs, wknd 2f out:	shd	73a
127+*	**STRONG HAND** 32 [7] M W Easterby 3-9-2 (88) P Mulrennan (5) 2/1 FAV: 1335118: Mid-div, wknd 3f out:	1	59a
225	**TE QUIERO GB** 12 [1] Miss Gay Kelleway 5-9-10 t (94) N Callan 7/2: 0105239: Led, hdd 3f out, sn wknd:	6	54a
218	**GALLANT BOY** 14 [2] P D Evans 4-8-7 (77) K Dalgleish 11/1: 0005050: Al well adrift.	30	0a

10 Ran   2m 1.18 (2.98)   Owner Ms Gerardine P O'Reilly   Trained at Barnstaple

279   3.25 Bet Direct On Itv Page 367 Selling Stakes   2yo   (G)
£2009 £574 £287   1m100y f/sand rnd   Going 59   -41 Slow   Stalls Inside

184	**KILLING ME SOFTLY** 19 [11] J Gallagher 2-8-12 D Sweeney 25/1: 01: Handy, led 2f out, rdn out:		**52a**
87	**COMIC GENIUS** 37 [3] D Haydn Jones 2-8-7 vis (42) Paul Eddery 13/2: 46062: Held up, prog wide 3f out, edged left 2f out, chsd wnr fnl 1f, al held:	1¾	43a
4455}	**MARITA** 96 [5] J G Given 2-8-7 (51) M Fenton 8/1: 4020503: Led 1f, sltly outpcd 5f out, prog & kept on fnl 2f, no ch with front 2:	1½	40a
238	**BRETTON** 9 [10] R Hollinshead 2-8-12 BL (45) Dale Gibson 11/1: 6500544: Held up, prog when short of room 2f out, kept on fnl 1f:	nk	44a
207	**PLATINUM CHIEF** 15 [8] A Berry 2-8-12 (47) G Parkin 12/1: 2040045: Cl-up, wknd fnl 1f:	shd	43a
207	**BROTHER CADFAEL** 15 [9] John A Harris 2-8-12 (45) R Ffrench 10/1: 3000456: Led after 1f, hdd 2f out, no extra.	½	42a
162	**JAKARMI** 23 [2] B Palling 2-8-12 (60) N Callan 6/4 FAV: 02657: Cl-up, fdd 2f out:	3½	35a
77	**LOOK NO MORE** 39 [7] W G M Turner 2-8-12 (47) C Haddon (7) 20/1: 045608: Cl-up, fdd 3f out:	3	29a
164	**ARMENTIERES** 23 [1] J L Spearing 2-8-13 bl (53) A Daly 9/2: 0143539: Al in rear:	3	24a
207	**DESERT LIGHT** 15 [2] D Shaw 2-8-12 e (35) Lisa Jones 33/1: 0000060: Al bhd.	20	0
184	**EVENING FRAGRANCE** 19 [4] G C H Chung 2-8-12 bl (19) J Mackay 66/1: 0000: Slow away, al well adrift.	1¼	0

11 Ran   1m 55.56 (9.36)   Owner Mr Stuart Prior   Trained at Moreton-In-Marsh

280   3.55 Happy New Year From Bet Direct Handicap Stakes   3yo+ 0-80 (D)   [76]
£3024 £864 £432   7f f/sand rnd   Going 59   -14 slow   Stalls Outside

193	**WARDEN WARREN** 18 [8] Mrs C A Dunnett 5-9-4 bl (66) B Reilly (5) 6/1: 0000021: Chsd ldrs, chsd ldr 3f out, led dist, rdn out:		**73a**
241	**ARC EL CIEL** 9 [6] Mrs Stef Liddiard 5-9-12 vis (74) S Drowne 13/2: 2300162: Held up, prog 3f out, chsd ldr dist, kept on but just held cl-home:	½	78a
193*	**MON SECRET** 18 [4] B Smart 5-8-13 (61) R Ffrench 3/1 JT FAV: 0001213: Cl-up, wknd bef 1f out.	6	54a
241	**GREY PEARL** 9 [7] Miss Gay Kelleway 4-9-9 (71) N Callan 3/1 JT FAV: 0040534: Led, hdd dist, wknd:	1¾	61a
270	**AND TOTO TOO I** 2 [2] P D Evans 3-9-4 VIS (66) S Donohoe (7) 7/2: 03153515: Bhd, mod late gains:	¾	54a
129	**SPARK UP** 32 [3] J W Unett 3-9-2 bl (64) S Whitworth 12/1: 4061266: Al bhd:	hd	51a
152	**TEEHEE** 25 [5] B Palling 5-9-8 bl (70) M Fenton 14/1: 5020157: Chsd ldrs, wknd 3f out.	7	45a
188	**ROBIN SHARP** 19 [1] J Akehurst 5-8-4 VIS (52) P Doe 20/1: 210P008: Cl-up, wknd 4f out, t.o.:	dist	2a

8 Ran   1m 31.34 (5.14)   Owner Annwell Inn Syndicate   Trained at Norwich

281 — 12.50 Bet Direct No Q Voice Automated Betting Handicap Stakes Div 1 4yo+ 0-60 (F) [60]

£2926 £836 £418   1m1f79y   Going 36   -23 Slow   Stalls Inside

5019}	JAIR OHMSFORD 57 [2] W J Musson 5-9-11 (57) M Fenton 9/2 FAV: 40/0540-1: Held up, hdwy over 2f out, led over 1f out, rdn clr:		67a
248	DANGER BIRD 7 [8] R Hollinshead 4-9-3 (50) A Culhane 16/1: 005353-2: Keen, led after 1f till over 1f out, not pace of wnr:	4	52a
204	GRAND LASS 17 [12] T D Barron 5-9-6 BL (52) D Mernagh 16/1: 002046-3: Slow away, sn in tch, eff wide over 2f out, hung left over 1f out, onepace:	2	50a
195	FARAWAY LOOK 20 [7] J G M O'Shea 7-10-0 (60) R Havlin 6/1: 635534-4: Handy, rdn over 3f out, sn outpcd, late gains.	2	54a
160	GOODBYE MR BOND 25 [1] E J Alston 4-9-9 (56) D Allan (3) 7/1: 053404-5: Cl-up, eff to chall over 1f out, sn wknd.	¾	48a
228	QOBTAAN 14 [10] M R Bosley 5-8-13 (45) G Baker 6/1: 460534-6: Handy, wknd over 1f out:	nk	36a
115	OVER RATING 35 [5] K A Ryan 4-9-13 (60) N Callan 7/1: 423426-7: In tch, wknd over 1f out:	2	47a
84	JESSINCA 39 [9] A P Jones 8-8-11 (43) L Keniry (3) 20/1: 246460-8: Handy, chsd ldr over 5f out till over 3f out, wknd.	4	22a
236	ESCALADE 13 [6] W M Brisbourne 7-9-2 (48) P Mulrennan (5) 8/1: 240450-9: Keen held up, btn over 3f out.	2	23a
84	TOP OF THE CLASS 39 [4] P D Evans 7-8-12 vis (44) S Donohoe (7) 10/1: 154050-0: Dwelt, al bhd.	½	18a
221	CONSIGNIA 14 [3] D Haydn Jones 5-9-2 bl (48) Paul Eddery 14/1: 001060-0: Keen, al bhd.	8	6a
4968}	FIRST EAGLE 62 [13] Mrs N Macauley 5-9-4 vis (50) P McCabe 16/1: 40/0032-0: Held up, eff over 3f out, sn wknd.	13	0a
1463}	RED STORM 235 [11] J R Boyle 5-9-5 (51) J Mongan 9/1: 002105-0: Held up, btn over 3f out.	4	0a

13 Ran   2m 03.76 (5.56)   Owner Mr K A Cosby   Trained at Newmarket

282 — 1.20 Bet Direct No Q Handicap Stakes Fillies 4yo+ 0-75 (E) [71]

£3283 £938 £469   6f   Going 36   -21 Slow   Stalls Inside

275*	SANDGATE CYGNET 2 [8] I Semple 4-9-1 p (58) R Winston 9/2: 0002641-1: Made all, styd on well fnl 1f, rdn out:		66a
117	ZAGALA 34 [9] S L Keightley 4-9-4 t (61) A Culhane 9/2: 300213-2: Held up, eff 2f out, edged left ins last but kept on, not btn	1	64a
94	PILGRIM PRINCESS 38 [4] E J Alston 6-8-2 (45) A Nicholls 16/1: 356246-3: With ldr, ev ch till onepcd fnl 1f:	1	46a
149	PRIMA STELLA 27 [2] J A R Toller 5-9-10 (67) Lisa Jones (3) 100/30 FAV: 241020-4: Handy, eff well over 1f out, onepcd:	shd	68a
246	AMELIA 7 [1] W M Brisbourne 6-8-5 (48) B Swarbrick (7) 6/1: 104602-5: Held up, eff well over 1f out, onepace:	½	47a
155	TIGRESS 27 [7] J W Unett 5-9-4 bl (61) Martin Dwyer 16/1: 132660-6: Held up, eff over 2f out, sn btn:	1¾	55a
167*	PLAYFUL SPIRIT 24 [6] J Balding 5-8-3 vis (46) J Edmunds 10/1: 030001-7: Handy, wknd 2f out.	2½	33a
85	BIJAN 39 [3] R Hollinshead 6-7-12 6oh (35) Dale Gibson 25/1: 360405-8: In tch, wknd over 2f out.	1½	24a
5021}	INDIAN SHORES 57 [10] M Mullineaux 5-9-1 (58) Paul Scallan 25/1: 0/1006F-9: Handy, wknd over 3f out.	1¼	37a
163	CHANTEUSE 25 [11] D W Chapman 4-8-6 (49) R Brisland 40/1: 420000-0: Al bhd.	12	0a

10 Ran   1m 16.2 (3.4)   Owner Mrs A M Young   Trained at Carluke

283 — 1.50 Bet Direct No Q On 08000 93 66 93 Claiming Stakes 3yo (F)

£2877 £822 £411   7f   Going 36   -43 Slow   Stalls Outside

190	TURF PRINCESS 20 [4] Ian Emmerson 3-9-0 (61) D Fentiman (7) 9/4 JT FAV: 510226-1: Prom, hdwy over 2f out, styd on to lead ins last on for press despite joc becoming unbalanced.		63a
119	EVER CHEERFUL 34 [3] W G M Turner 3-9-5 (73) L Treadwell (7) 9/4 JT FAV: 034346-2: Keen, led & edged right over 1f out but kept on till collared well ins last, narrowly btn:	shd	68a
200	PARDON MOI 18 [5] Mrs C A Dunnett 3-8-4 (49) Hayley Turner (5) 4/1: 260654-3: Held up, hdwy 2f out, ev ch till no extra ins last:	1¼	50a
87	SECRET BLOOM 39 [2] J R Norton 3-8-7 VIS (38) Darren Williams 33/1: 0050-4: Slow away, held up, eff over 1f out, no:	nk	52a
203	SAVERNAKE BRAVE 17 [1] K R Burke 3-8-11 BL (48) G Baker 14/1: 266500-5: Handy, wknd well over 1f out:	5	46a
200	WHITTINGHAMVILLAGE 18 [6] A Berry 3-8-0 (44) Dale Gibson 9/2: 446040-6: In tch, wknd over 2f out.	2	31a

6 Ran   1m 31.76 (5.56)   Owner Mr Ian Emmerson   Trained at Chester-Le-Street

284 — 2.20 Betdirect Co Uk Maiden Stakes 3yo (D)

£3435 £1057 £529 £264   7f   Going 36   -33 Slow   Stalls Outside

175	SECRET PLACE 23 [6] E A L Dunlop 3-9-0 W Ryan 4/6 FAV: 02-1: Trav well, handy, led on bit over 2f out, pushed clr, easily:		76a
146	VRISAKI 27 [3] Miss D Mountain 3-9-0 C Catlin 9/1: 00-2: Led till over 2f out, no ch with wnr:	4	62a
95	KATIES ROLE 38 [2] Ian Emmerson 3-8-9 (52) A Nicholls 7/1: 630043-3: Prom, eff & short of room over 3f out, onepace over 1f out:	¾	55a
36	ZONNEBEKE 48 [5] K R Burke 3-8-9 (52) Darren Williams 25/1: 400-4: Held up, no impress:	3	48a
184	VITTORIOSO 21 [7] Miss Gay Kelleway 3-9-0 BL (57) M Fenton 8/1: 050-5: Keen, handy, wide str, wknd over 1f out:	½	52a
	ROYALTEA [1] Ms Deborah J Evans 3-8-9 I Mongan 20/1: 6: Slow away & al bhd.	2½	41a
	SILVER EMPEROR [4] P A Blockley 3-9-0 BL D Nolan (5) 16/1: 7: Slow away, bhd, no impress:	1½	42a

7 Ran   1m 31.02 (4.82)   Owner Mr Khalifa Sultan   Trained at Newmarket

285 — 2.50 Littlewoods Bet Direct Handicap Stakes 4yo+ 0-85 (D) [85]

£4076 £1254 £627 £314   7f   Going 36   -07 Slow   Stalls Outside

198*	BLAKESET 18 [4] T D Barron 9-9-1 vis (72) D Mernagh 5/2 FAV: 211101-1: Led till over 1f out, rallied gamely to lead again ins last, rdn out:		79a
193	ASHTREE BELLE 20 [3] D Haydn Jones 5-9-5 (76) Paul Eddery 9/2: 224014-2: Chsd ldrs, hdwy to lead over 1f out, collared ins last, onepace over 1f out:	1½	80a
80	JUST A GLIMMER 41 [9] L G Cottrell 4-9-8 (79) Martin Dwyer 12/1: 6331/00-3: With ldr, eff over 1f out, sn no extra:	1¾	78a
241*	RONNIE FROM DONNY 11 [7] B Ellison 4-9-2 6ex (73) R Winston 3/1: 000001-4: Prom, wknd over 1f out:	5	62a
235	CRETAN GIFT 13 [6] N P Littmoden 13-9-5 vis (76) J P Guillambert 8/1: 40//0500-5: Held up, eff over 2f out, sn no extra:	1	63a
245	BLONDE EN BLONDE 7 [2] N P Littmoden 4-8-10 (67) I Mongan 8/1: 203534-6: Slow away & sn bhd:	hd	53a
234	INVADER 13 [5] C E Brittain 8-10-0 bl (85) M Fenton 11/2: 020143-7: Slow away & al bhd:	1¾	67a
3872}	TALLY 130 [8] A Berry 4-9-1 (72) N Callan 40/1: 210646-8: In tch, btn over 2f out:	9	36a

8 Ran   1m 29.19 (2.99)   Owner Mr Nigel Shields   Trained at Thirsk

286		3.20 Bet Direct No Q Demo 08000 837 888 Claiming Stakes 4yo+ (F)			
		£2905 £830 £415	5f	Going 36	+03 Fast	Stalls Inside

253	BEST LEAD 6 [1] Ian Emmerson 5-9-3 bl (53) D Fentiman (7) 33/1: 000065-1: Handy, hdwy over 1f out, led ins last, rdn clr:		64a
187	HAGLEY PARK 21 [2] M Quinn 5-8-4 (46) Martin Dwyer 7/1: 016400-2: With ldrs, hdwy to lead over 1f out till ins last, not pace of wnr:	3½	44a
205	HENRY TUN 17 [5] J Balding 6-8-9 vis (55) J Edmunds 7/2: 003500-3: Handy, eff well over 1f out, onepace:	¾	47a
4432}	ALLERTON BOY 100 [3] R J Hodges 5-8-3 (37) Dale Gibson (3) 40/1: 000000-4: Held up, eff over 1f out, onepace:	½	39a
246	SHARP HAT 7 [6] D W Chapman 10-9-3 (72) A Culhane 13/8 FAV: 001135-5: Slow away, no dngr:	½	52a
275	THE LEATHER WEDGE 21 [12] A Berry 5-9-1 (49) P Bradley (5) 20/1: 000402-6: Led after 1f till over 1f out, wknd.	1	47a
253	MR SPLIFFY 6 [11] K R Burke 5-8-11 vis (49) Darren Williams 11/1: 020004-7: In tch, wknd over 2f out.	4	31a
275	SALERNO 27 [10] Miss Gay Kelleway 5-8-11 p (50) T Eaves (5) 12/1: 004000-8: In tch, wknd 2f out.	3	22a
253	FIENNES 6 [4] Mrs N Macauley 6-8-5 vis (42) Lisa Jones (3) 8/1: 0/00563-9: In tch, wknd over 2f out:	hd	15a
167	BALI STAR 24 [9] R J Hodges 9-8-3 (43) C Catlin 14/1: 405005-0: Al bhd.	1	10a

10 Ran   1m 01.88 (1.68)   Owner Mr Ian Emmerson   Trained at Chester-Le-Street

287		3.50 Bet Direct No Q Voice Automated Betting Handicap Stakes Div 2 4yo+ 0-60 (F)				[60]
		£2926 £836 £418	1m1f79y	Going 36	+05 Fast	Stalls Inside

188	ROCK CONCERT 21 [2] I W McInnes 6-9-10 (56) Natalia Gemelova (7) 5/1: 322132-1: Cl-up, led over 3f out, edged right ins last but styd on well, rdn out:		64a
263	GIVEMETHEMOONLIGHT 4 [6] Mrs Stef Liddiard 5-8-12 (44) C Catlin 5/1: 032422-2: Held up, eff to chall over 2f out, kept on till not pace of wnr cl-home:	1	49a
230	SCOTTISH RIVER 13 [4] M D I Usher 5-9-13 (59) A Daly 9/1: 500003-3: Held up, gd hdwy over 2f out, no extra ins last:	1¼	61a
270	TITIAN LASS 3 [12] C E Brittain 5-8-13 (45) Dean Williams (7) 6/1: 020200-4: Handy, wknd over 2f out:	9	29a
228	SORBIESHARRY 14 [1] Mrs N Macauley 5-9-3 p (49) L Enstone (3) 5/1: 350422-5: Handy, wknd over 2f out:	2	29a
	FREE STYLE 62 [10] K R Burke 4-9-3 (50) G Baker 25/1: 210020-6: Nvr a factor:	1	28a
204	PRINCE PROSPECT 17 [3] Mrs L Stubbs 8-9-0 (46) Kristin Stubbs 14/1: 53/4640-7: In tch, wknd over 2f out.	½	23a
221	ROUTE SIXTY SIX 14 [5] Jedd O'Keeffe 8-8-10 (42) Leanne Kershaw 20/1: 003500-8: Nvr a factor.	nk	18a
39	BAR OF SILVER 48 [11] R Brotherton 4-9-2 (49) I Mongan 16/1: 025050-9: Held up, btn over 2f out:	1¼	23a
4792}	PHOENIX NIGHTS 77 [8] A Berry 4-9-5 (52) P Mathers (7) 33/1: 401030-0: Al bhd:	hd	25a
228	FORTY FORTE 14 [9] Miss S J Wilton 8-9-9 p (55) N Callan 20/1: 000020-0: Sn clr ldr, hdd over 3f out, wknd:	4	20a
3877}	POLKA PRINCESS 130 [7] M Wellings 4-9-5 (52) L Treadwell 50/1: 060000-0: Al bhd.	5	7a
154	DESERT HEAT 27 [13] I Semple 6-10-0 p (60) R Winston 11/2: 2/64004-0: In tch, btn over 4f out, t.o.	23	0a

13 Ran   2m 01.12 (2.92)   Owner Ivy House Racing   Trained at Catwick

Official Going Standard

288		11.40 Bet All Weather: Bet Direct Apprentice Handicap Stakes 4yo+ 0-85 (F)				[78]
		£2891 £826 £413	2m p/track	Going 36	-31 Slow	Stalls Inside

107	RED SCORPION 38 [4] W M Brisbourne 5-9-3 (67) B Swarbrick (5) 9/4 FAV: 052035-1: Rear, smooth hdwy wide to lead over 2f out, held on well for press:		75a
147*	WESTERN 28 [3] J Akehurst 4-9-0 (71) N Chalmers (3) 11/4: 005641-2: Keen, held up, smooth hdwy to chase wnr over 2f out, drvn & styd on ins last, al just held:	nk	77a
4551}	REDSPIN 94 [7] J S Moore 4-9-4 (75) L Keniry 14/1: 042502-3: Trkd ldrs, no impress on front pair fnl 2f:	18	66a
265	ARC EN CIEL 5 [5] G L Moore 8-9-0 (71) A Quinn (3) 25/1: 100/00/0-4: Chsd ldr, led over 3f out till over 2f out, sn btn:	½	56a
264	TREASURE TRAIL 5 [8] S Kirk 5-9-1 (65) L Treadwell (5) 11/2: 206000-5: Mid-div, no impress fnl 3f:	2½	53a
2149}	HARIK 203 [1] G L Moore 10-9-12 (76) H Poulton (5) 10/1: 4/04206-6: Keen, held up, btn 3f out:	1½	63a
225	GEORGE STUBBS 15 [6] M J Polglase 6-9-7 (71) L Fletcher 7/1: 560632-7: Led till over 3f out, sn btn:	1½	57a
264	CANTRIP 5 [9] Miss B Sanders 4-8-5 t (62) Lisa Jones 25/1: 242660-8: Prom in chasing group till 6f out, sn bhd:	hd	48a

8 Ran   3m 30.77 (10.77)   Owner Mrs E M Coquelin   Trained at Baschurch

289		12.10 Bet Direct No Q On 08000 93 66 93 Maiden Stakes 3yo (D)			
		£3682 £1133 £567 £283	5f p/track rnd	Going 36	-32 Slow	Stalls Inside

25	PRINCESS KAI 51 [2] R Ingram 3-8-9 bl (55) F P Ferris (3) 12/1: 640303-1: Made all, drvn & held on gamely ins last:		61a
258	DOCKLANDS BLUE 5 [5] N P Littmoden 3-8-9 J P Guillambert (3) 25/1: 630-2: Rdn rear, styd on for press fnl 2f, nrst fin:	nk	60a
258	AFTER ALL 5 [1] G A Butler 3-8-9 (64) E Ahern 9/2: 023526-3: Trkd wnr, chall trav well over 1f out, rdn & found little:	¾	58a
268	PREGNANT PAUSE 4 [3] S Kirk 3-9-0 (65) Martin Dwyer 13/8: 002402-4: Chsd ldrs, rdn & outpcd fnl 2f:	1½	58a
76	DONT CALL ME DEREK 42 [4] S C Williams 3-9-0 M Fenton 6/4 FAV: 04-5: Hung right chasing ldrs, wide on bend 2f out, no impress when eased well ins last:	1½	53a

5 Ran   1m 01.18 (3.38)   Owner Brannigan Bros   Trained at Epsom

290		12.40 Bet Direct Interactive Maiden Stakes 3yo+ (D)			
		£3552 £1093 £547 £273	7f p/track rnd	Going 36	-10 Slow	Stalls Inside

79	MR LAMBROS 42 [8] A M Balding 3-8-7 Martin Dwyer 4/6 FAV: 3-1: Dwelt, sn handy & led after 2f, readily pulled clr fnl 2f, hands & heels:		79a
181	SIR LAUGHALOT 24 [12] Miss E C Lavelle 4-9-11 (70) L Keniry (3) 6/1: 0/00020-2: Keen early in mid-div, hdwy from halfway & chsd wnr dist, kept on, no impress:	4	68a
159	MONTE MAJOR 26 [13] M A Jarvis 3-8-7 N Callan 9/1: 06-3: Keen trkg ldrs, briefly chsd wnr over 1f out, sn no impress:	3½	61a
900}	DUSK DANCER 280 [1] B J Meehan 4-9-11 R Winston 9/1: 40-4: Pushed along towards rear, kept on late, no impress:	1¼	58a
192	FUBOS 21 [11] Julian Poulton 3-8-11 low VIS (61) I Mongan 25/1: 0000-5: Chsd ldrs, eff wide, no impress fnl 1f:	shd	59a
98	AFRICAN STAR 39 [14] Mrs A J Perrett 3-8-7 E Ahern 12/1: 05-6: Chsd wnr over 2f out, sn no impress.	nk	57a

4166}	JACKIE KIELY 114 [15] T G Mills 3-8-7 J Paulielo 16/1: 0-7: Led 2f, btn/no room 2f out:	5	47a
4961}	QUEEN EXCALIBUR 64 [4] J M Bradley 5-9-6 p (47) S Drowne 66/1: 000040-8: Rear, only mod late prog:	1¼	39a
	SOFISTICATION [10] T G Mills 3-8-2 C Catlin 16/1: 9: Dwelt, eff wide halfway, sn btn, debut.	¾	38a
24	ONYA 51 [7] J W Hills 4-9-6 T (39) S Whitworth 66/1: 00000-0: Rear, no ch fnl 3f, abs, t-strap.	2½	33a
254	ROAN RAIDER 7 [3] M J Polglase 4-9-11 BL t (42) L Fletcher (3) 66/1: 624600-0: Mid-div, btn 2f out:	nk	37a
184	BATTLE BACK 22 [5] S C Williams 3-8-2 R Ffrench 50/1: 00-0: Al bhd.	¾	31a
	THINK IT OVER [16] A P Jones 5-9-6 D Sweeney 66/1: 0: Chsd ldrs till halfway.	13	8a
	SPIDERS WEB 420 [9] T Keddy 4-9-11 M Fenton 50/1: 0/-0: Al bhd, long abs.	2½	8a
220	LAKESIDE GUY 17 [6] P S McEntee 3-8-7 F P Ferris (3) 66/1: 0-0: Sn bhd, t.o..	½	7a
3288}	VIVA ATLAS ESPANA 156 [2] Miss B Sanders 4-9-6 (52) A Clark 50/1: 00/0060-0: Al bhd, t.o., abs.	3	0
16 Ran	1m 26.0 (3.2) Owner Winterbeck Manor Stud		Trained at Kingsclere

---

291

1.15 Bet Direct On Itv Page 367 Claiming Stakes 3yo (F)
£2905 £830 £415   1m2f p/track rnd   Going 36   -48 Slow   Stalls Inside

164*	LYRICAL GIRL 26 [8] M R Channon 3-8-12 (55) S Hitchcott (3) 7/4 FAV: 230031-1: Rear, hdwy to chase ldr over 2f out, led over 1f out, drvn out:		60a
238	PLATINUM PIRATE 12 [9] K R Burke 3-8-11 bl (40) D Sweeney 12/1: 006000-2: Rear, hdwy to chase ldrs 2f out, kept on, al just held:	1	57a
240	CRACKLEANDO 12 [6] N P Littmoden 3-9-5 (62) J P Guillambert (3) 11/1: 000-3: Rear, hdwy to chase ldrs 2f out, not pace to threaten:	3½	60a
177	LADY PREDOMINANT 24 [7] Andrew Reid 3-8-4 (52) S Carson 5/1: 005020-4: Handy & led over 3f out, hdd over 1f out, no extra:	2	42a
207	QUARRY ISLAND 18 [5] P D Evans 3-8-0 (40) F P Ferris (3) 12/1: 660040-5: Handy & led over 7f out till over 3f out.	1½	36a
279	ARMENTIERES 3 [10] J L Spearing 3-8-2 bl (53) A Daly 4/1: 143530-6: Mid-div, eff 3f out, sn no extra:	6	30a
233	TIMELY TWIST 14 [2] S Kirk 3-8-4 (47) Martin Dwyer 12/1: 460530-7: Rcd freely, led 3f, btn 3f out.	4	26a
233	BLUES OVER 14 [4] W J Musson 3-8-4 Paul Eddery 25/1: 00-8: Bhd, nvr a factor.	8	15a
226	RED ACER 15 [1] P D Evans 3-8-5 (35) C Catlin 25/1: 00060-9: Chsd ldrs till 3f out.	5	10a
190	ALTARES 21 [3] P Howling 3-9-1 (48) R Winston 16/1: 0000-0: Sn handy, btn 3f out.	2	17a
10 Ran	2m 11.23 (8.43) Owner C S G Limited		Trained at West Ilsley

---

292

1.50 Bet Direct No Q Handicap Stakes 3yo+ 0-85 (D)   [83]
£4485 £1380 £690 £345   6f p/track rnd   Going 36   +05 Fast   Stalls Inside

234	CHATEAU NICOL 14 [6] B G Powell 5-9-3 vis (72) J Fanning 14/1: 001100-1: Held up, hdwy halfway, rdn to lead ins last, styd on strongly:		80a
273	JUST FLY 4 [10] S Kirk 4-9-10 (79) Martin Dwyer 14/1: 010505-2: Hmpd early & rear, no room over 2f out, styd on but wnr had first run:	1¼	83a
149	SIR DESMOND 28 [3] R Guest 6-9-8 p (77) C Catlin 10/1: 140034-3: Pushed along mid-div, styd on onepace for press:	nk	79a
171	POLISH EMPEROR 25 [11] P W Harris 4-9-7 bl (76) N Callan 16/1: 066410-4: Keen & cl-up, led over 3f out till ins last, no extra:	hd	78a
198	CASHEL MEAD 19 [2] J L Spearing 4-9-11 (80) A Daly 16/1: 000623-5: Chsd ldrs, hung left & onepace from dist:	½	81a
235	NO TIME 14 [4] M J Polglase 4-10-0 (83) L Fletcher (3) 8/1: 300000-6: Led till over 3f out, no extra dist.	1	82a
2418}	CORMORANT WHARF 192 [7] T E Powell 4-9-11 (80) A Quinn (5) 50/1: 16/0-7: Dwelt, hld up, hdwy & no run sev times fnl 3f, nrst fin, kind ride:	shd	79a
130*	TARANAKI 32 [1] P D Cundell 6-9-6 (75) S Whitworth 100/30 FAV: 506101-8: Chsd ldrs till over 1f out:	2	70a
149	ONLY ONE LEGEND 28 [9] K A Ryan 6-9-3 bl (72) R Winston 11/2: 466603-9: Mid-div, not able to chall:	nk	66a
4235}	JUWWI 110 [8] J M Bradley 10-9-3 (72) Lisa Jones (3) 33/1: 040040-0: Dwelt, outpcd, nrst fin, abs.	1¼	63a
271*	TYPE ONE 4 [5] T G Mills 6-10-1 6ex (84) R Miles (3) 3/1: 214321-0: Chsd ldrs till over 1f out.	1¾	72a
45	CURRENCY 47 [13] J M Bradley 7-9-4 (73) E Ahern 20/1: 606600-0: Wide, rear, nvr a factor, abs.	½	60a
149	JAYANJAY 28 [14] Miss B Sanders 5-9-7 (76) S Drowne 14/1: 006602-0: Al bhd:	1¼	60a
4753}	HAWK 80 [12] P R Chamings 6-9-3 (72) I Mongan 20/1: 001305-0: Mid-div, struggling halfway, abs.	9	40a
14 Ran	1m 12.25 (1.85) Owner Basingstoke Commercials		Trained at Winchester

---

293

2.25 Littlewoods Bet Direct Handicap Stakes 4yo+ 0-100 (C)   [95]
£12296 £4664 £2332 £1060   1m4f p/track   Going 36   +04 Fast   Stalls Inside

134	GIG HARBOR 32 [3] Miss E C Lavelle 5-9-4 (85) L Keniry (3) 7/1: 000626-1: Trkd ldrs, smooth hdwy to lead over 1f out, rdn clr, readily.		94a
4759}	FLIGHT OF ESTEEM 79 [1] P W Harris 4-9-6 (91) N Callan 12/1: 131430-2: Handy, briefly outpcd 2f out, styd on well for press ins last.	1¼	97a
26	CRUISE DIRECTOR 51 [4] W J Musson 4-8-12 (83) Lisa Jones (3) 7/1: 132210-3: Mid-div, rdn & outpcd out, styd on well for press ins last:	nk	88a
82	EASTERN BREEZE 42 [6] P W D'Arcy 6-10-0 e (95) Paul Eddery 13/2 JT FAV: 331666-4: Trkd ldr & led over 3f out, hdd over 1f out, no extra cl-home:	shd	100a
4227}	SANTANDO 112 [8] C E Brittain 4-9-13 vis (98) M Fenton 10/1: 042506-5: Slow away, rear, mod gains for press.	4	97a
218*	TIGHT SQUEEZE 17 [14] P W Hiatt 7-8-12 (79) R Winston 9/1: 155011-6: Rear, eff 2f out, mod prog:	1	77a
218	HIGH HOPE 17 [2] G L Moore 6-8-11 bl e (78) S Whitworth 12/1: 500003-7: Held up, eff 3f out, no impress dist.	¾	75a
278	GALLANT BOY 3 [7] P D Evans 5-8-10 t (77) S Donohoe (3) 14/1: 005050-8: Held up, eff 3f out, little hdwy, qck reapp.	nk	73a
173	SUDDEN FLIGHT 25 [5] R Ingram 7-8-13 (80) R Havlin (3) 50/1: 660010-9: Mid-div, no impress fnl 2f.	¾	75a
4091}	BRIAREUS 119 [12] A M Balding 4-8-9 (80) Martin Dwyer 10/1: 150324-0: Led till over 3f out, sn btn:	3	71a
5036}	INTERNATIONALGUEST 56 [11] G G Margarson 5-9-0 vis (81) B Reilly (5) 20/1: 000360-0: Mid-div, no impress dist.	¾	71a
225	ROYAL CAVALIER 15 [10] R Hollinshead 7-9-4 (85) E Ahern 16/1: 420206-0: Trkd ldrs, btn 2f out.	4	69a
4403}	DUSTY CARPET 810 [16] M J Weeden 6-8-9 (76) S Drowne 100/1: 233220//-0: Rear, no impress fnl 3f:	nk	59a
234	EASTBOROUGH 14 [9] B G Powell 5-8-11 (78) J Fanning 33/1: 54000/6-0: Keen, rear, no ch fnl 3f.	3	57a

LINGFIELD Saturday 03.01.04 Lefthand, V Sharp Track

83* **HIGH POINT 42** [13] G P Enright 6-8-13 (80) C Catlin 13/2 JT FAV: 150001-0: Chsd ldrs till 3f out. abs. *nk* **58a**
179 **BRILLIANT RED 24** [15] Jamie Poulton 11-9-6 t (87) I Mongan 10/1: 244003-0: Slow away, chsd ldrs till 2f out. *4* **59a**
16 Ran 2m 33.03 (3.83) Owner Fraser Miller Racing Trained at Andover

294 **3.00 Betdirect Co Uk Classified Stakes 4yo+ 0-70 (E)**
£3377 £1039 £520 £260 **1m2f p/track Going 36 -15 Slow** Stalls Inside

97 **GINGKO 39** [5] P R Webber 7-9-2 (62) W Ryan 7/1: 060066-1: Rear, rdn 3f out, strong run for press to lead well ins last: **72a**
265 **BLUE TROJAN 5** [6] S Kirk 4-9-0 (68) E Ahern 5/2 FAV: 015644-2: Mid-div, smooth hdwy to lead over 1f out, rdn & hdd ins last, no extra: *½* **71a**
4784*} **PERFIDIOUS 78** [2] J R Boyle 6-9-2 (70) I Mongan 100/30: 625201-3: Led, qcknd from 3f out, hdd over 1f out, styd on for *shd* **71a**
136* **TOPTON 32** [1] P Howling 10-9-2 bl (69) R Winston 8/1: 050601-4: Dwelt, rear, eff fnl 2f, not able to chall: *3½* **66a**
264 **EASTER OGIL 5** [8] Jane Southcombe 9-9-2 (63) V Slattery 4/1: 306422-5: In tch, no impress over 1f out, qck reapp. *½* **65a**
174 **TODLEA 24** [4] J A Osborne 4-9-0 t (70) Martin Dwyer 11/1: 410000-6: Chsd ldr till 6f out, no impress dist. *2* **62a**
178 **LONDONER 24** [7] S Dow 6-9-2 (65) P Doe 14/1: 000006-7: Chsd ldr 6f out, btn over 1f out. *nk* **61a**
4460} **STUNNING MAGIC 99** [3] Mrs Barbara Waring 4-9-0 (33) Lisa Jones (3) 100/1: 00/00-8: Mid-div, no ch fnl 3f, abs. *18* **38a**
8 Ran 2m 07.85 (5.05) Owner Olympic Group of Partners Trained at Banbury

295 **3.30 Bet Direct No Q Demo 08000 837 888 Handicap Stakes Fillies 3yo 0-65 (F)** **[70]**
£2968 £848 £424 **7f p/track rnd Going 36 -33 Slow** Stalls Inside

78* **ROWAN PURSUIT 42** [15] J Akehurst 3-9-7 bl (63) J Fanning 4/1 FAV: 400131-1: Mid-div, rdn & qcknd to lead dist, drvn out: **67a**
132 **PARK AVE PRINCESS 32** [2] N P Littmoden 3-8-10 (52) I Mongan 10/1: 000460-2: Held up, short of room after 2f, drvn & styd on fnl 2f, not pace to chall wnr: *1½* **52a**
78 **GOOD VIBRATIONS 42** [3] P F I Cole 3-8-10 (52) C Catlin 9/2: 0002-3: Keen in mid-div, eff wide 2f out, styd on for press: *½* **51a**
105 **TARANAI 38** [9] B W Duke 3-8-13 (55) Lisa Jones (3) 12/1: 600006-4: Cl-up & led 4f out till dist. *¾* **53a**
233* **MUST BE SO 14** [6] J J Bridger 3-8-8 (50) N Pollard 7/1: 040031-5: Cl-up, wknd ins last: *1¾* **45a**
203 **SONDERBORG 18** [12] G L Moore 3-9-1 p (57) G Carter 8/1: 63006-6: Dwelt & bhd, rdn & kept on fnl 2f, no dngr: *½* **51a**
184 **EMILYS DAWN 22** [13] D K Ivory 3-8-13 (55) D Sweeney 20/1: 0060-7: Rear, eff over 2f out, not able to chall. *½* **48a**
232 **VENDORS MISTAKE 14** [4] Andrew Reid 3-8-12 (54) S Carson 12/1: 600-8: Mid-div, hmpd over 2f out, sn no impress. *¾* **46a**
247 **ALIZAR 8** [14] M J Polglase 3-9-2 (58) L Fletcher (3) 9/1: 361153-9: Prom, btn over 1f out: *¾* **49a**
126 **LOVE IN THE MIST USA 35** [7] E A L Dunlop 3-9-6 (62) S Drowne 9/1: 46500-0: Chsd ldrs till 2f out: *2* **49a**
2695} **CHICA 181** [5] J A Osborne 3-8-3 (45) R Fitzpatrick 25/1: 000-0: Slow away, hmpd after 2f, no impress, AW bow. *1¼* **29a**
233 **LADY PISTE 14** [16] P D Evans 3-8-13 BL (55) S Donohoe (7) 10/1: 455304-0: Cl-up 4f out till 2f out, wknd, blnks. *1½* **36a**
200 **MISS JUDGED 19** [10] A P Jones 3-8-8 t (50) G Hannon 50/1: 600000-0: Prom 5f, sn btn. *2½* **26a**
78 **OUT OF MY WAY 42** [8] T M Jones 3-7-12 9oh (31) R Brisland 66/1: 0400-0: Al bhd: *3* **10a**
223 **FOOT FAULT 15** [11] N A Callaghan 3-9-4 (60) W Ryan 14/1: 0046-0: Led 3f, wknd qckly: *3½* **23a**
15 Ran 1m 27.65 (4.85) Owner Mr C C Clarke Trained at Epsom

WOLVERHAMPTON Saturday 03.01.04 Lefthand, Sharp Track

Official Going STANDARD

296 **12.55 Bet Direct On Sky Active Banded Stakes Div 1 3yo+ 0-45 (H)**
£1631 £466 £233 **6f f/sand rnd Going 55 -08 Slow** Stalls Inside

166 **CLEVELAND WAY 25** [12] D Carroll 4-9-8 vis (45) D Nolan (5) 6/1: 204000-1: Cl-up & led over 4f out, clr 2f out, drvn out: **49a**
4026} **LORD MELBOURNE 123** [3] J A Osborne 5-9-8 (44) S W Kelly 11/2: 006035-2: Held up, hdwy inner when no room over 2f out, styd on for press ins last: *1* **44a**
246 **ATTORNEY 8** [2] D Shaw 6-9-8 e (43) T Hamilton (5) 5/1 FAV: 300004-3: Rdn/bhd, kept on late, no dngr. *2* **38a**
110 **ENJOY THE BUZZ 36** [11] J M Bradley 5-9-8 (42) P Fitzsimons 12/1: 06/0020-4: Chsd ldrs, onepace. *½* **36a**
170} **MAGIC EAGLE 389** [5] P T Midgley 7-9-8 (45) G Parkin 14/1: 050000/-5: Led 1f, handy till over 1f out: *3* **27a**
246 **CAROLS CHOICE 8** [10] A Sadik 7-9-8 (36) G Baker 14/1: 630000-6: Led/dsptd lead 2f, sn no impression. *1¼* **23a**
227 **PIPS SONG 15** [6] P W Hiatt 9-9-8 (45) Darren Williams 11/2: 003000-7: Held up, nvr a threat to ldrs. *shd* **22a**
3088} **FLYING FAISAL 164** [8] J M Bradley 6-9-8 (44) Dean McKeown 8/1: 056000-8: Chsd ldrs till halfway, abs. *1½* **18a**
46 **THREAT 47** [4] J M Bradley 8-9-8 (40) L Enstone (3) 16/1: 320000-9: Mid-div, no ch fnl 2f, abs. *2½* **11a**
3477} **COUNTRYWIDE GIRL 148** [1] A Berry 5-9-8 (32) P Bradley (5) 33/1: 00/000U-0: Chsd ldrs 3f, abs. *14* **0**
85 **LADYSTGEORGE 40** [7] M Mullineaux 5-9-8 (34) J Bramhill 33/1: 000046-0: Dwelt, nvr a factor, abs. *2½* **0**
11 Ran 1m 16.6 (3.8) Owner The Boot & Shoe Ackworth Partn Trained at Warthilll

297 **1.30 Bet Direct On Sky Active Banded Stakes Div 2 3yo+ 0-45 (H)**
£1631 £466 £233 **6f f/sand rnd Going 55 -05 Slow** Stalls Inside

4258} **ITALIAN MIST 109** [9] Julian Poulton 5-9-8 e (39) G Faulkner 10/1: 620050-1: Led 1f, chsd ldr, rdn & outpcd over 2f out, rallied well for press till well ins last: **51a**
245 **LARKYS LOB 8** [11] Paul Johnson 5-9-8 (48) L Enstone (3) 6/4 FAV: 000002-2: Handy & led over 4f out, rdn/edged left & hdd well ins last: *1¾* **46a**
71 **NEUTRAL NIGHT 43** [5] R Brotherton 4-9-8 vis (44) A Culhane 11/2: 060660-3: Handy, onepace fnl 2f: *3½* **36a**
110 **SABANA 36** [8] J M Bradley 6-9-8 (44) P Fitzsimons 8/1: 003000-4: Chased ldrs, no impress dist. *3½* **26a**
245 **SAWAH 8** [10] D Shaw 4-9-8 (30) Darren Williams 25/1: 0006-5: Dwelt, mid-div, nvr pce to chall. *nk* **25a**
3416} **RIVENDELL 150** [1] M Wigham 8-9-8 t (20) D R McCabe 12/1: F50////00-: Bhd, only mod prog: *½* **24a**
4260} **VLASTA WEINER 109** [7] J M Bradley 4-9-8 bl (38) Dean McKeown 20/1: 000006-7: Dwelt, al outpcd, abs. *1¾* **19a**
5023} **PARIS DREAMER 57** [3] M W Easterby 3-8-1 1ow (42) P Mulrennan 14/1: 0000-8: Dwelt, sn struggling, abs. *1¾* **9a**
167 **LIONS DOMANE 25** [2] A Berry 7-9-8 (44) P Bradley (5) 10/1: 100000-9: Prom 4f. *½* **13a**
163 **SUGAR CUBE TREAT 26** [12] M Mullineaux 8-9-8 (35) J Bramhill 12/1: 060//000-0: Sn struggling. *¾* **11a**
245 **BLUE CIRCLE 8** [6] M Mullineaux 4-9-8 bl (30) S W Kelly 33/1: 000000-0: Chsd ldrs till 3f out. *6* **0**

4861} GEESPOT 72 [4] D J S ffrench Davis 5-9-8 (44) Paul Scallan 9/1: 6/00500-0: Al outpcd.   2½   0
12 Ran   1m 16.4 (3.6)   Owner Mr S P Shore   Trained at Newmarket

---

298
2.05 Bet Direct Interactive Selling Stakes 3yo+ (H)
£1320 £377 £189   7f f/sand rnd   Going 55   -25 Slow   Stalls Outside

239   REPEAT 12 [8] Miss Gay Kelleway 4-10-0 (51) T Eaves (5) 5/1: 314064-1: Chsd ldrs, led 2f out, rdn clr.   59a
221   LUCAYAN MONARCH 15 [9] P A Blockley 6-9-9 p (55) Dean McKeown 6/4 FAV: 000064-2: Slow away, sn chsd front trio,   3½   48a
     kept on for press, nvr threat to wnr:
227   STAR LAD 15 [10] R Brotherton 4-9-9 bl (47) A Culhane 9/1: 000606-3: Led 2f, remained prom, onepace fnl 2f: hd   47a
5000} AROGANT PRINCE 60 [7] I Semple 7-9-9 p (60) D McGaffin (3) 7/2: 560200-4: Led/dsptd lead, went on after 2f till 7f out, no   hd   46a
     extra:
239   BETTER OFF 12 [3] Mrs N Macauley 6-9-9 (65) Joanna Badger 11/1: 100000-5: Dwelt, nvr dngrs.   3   40a
2172} GLENVIEWS POLLY 202 [5] Ian Emmerson 4-9-4 (42) A Nicholls 14/1: 000600-6: Prom till 3f out, abs.   4   27a
3743} ALMOND BEACH 136 [4] B J Meehan 4-9-9 (65) D R McCabe 14/1: 30/5000-7: Chsd ldrs till 5f out, abs, op 9/1.   ½   31a
30   LADY ALRUNA 50 [2] P T Midgley 5-9-4 (40) G Parkin 25/1: 005000-8: Sn outpcd: 6   14a
3741} PRESENT N CORRECT 136 [6] J M Bradley 11-9-9 bl (30) Simon Jones (7) 25/1: 603006-9: Dwelt, al bhd, abs.   5   9a
3599} CHANTILLY GOLD 142 [1] J M Bradley 5-9-4 p (30) P Fitzsimons 40/1: 000000-0: Mid-div, no ch fnl 3f, abs.   3½   0
10 Ran   1m 31.8 (5.6)   Owner Mr J T Billson   Trained at Newmarket

---

299
2.40 Press Interactive To Bet Direct Median Auction Maiden Stakes 3-5yo (H)
£1439 £411 £206   1m1f79y f/sand   Going 55   +02 Fast   Stalls Inside

194   HEATHYARDS PRIDE 21 [4] R Hollinshead 4-9-10 Dean McKeown 7/1: 4-1: Prom, rdn & chsd ldr 3f out, drvn & prevailed   54a
     cl-home, all out:
248   IAMBACK 8 [7] Miss Gay Kelleway 4-9-5 p (44) T Hamilton (5) 9/1: 30/0606-2: Led after 1f, rdn & edged right in last, hdd   nk   48a
     cl-home:
4965} ANGELOS PRIDE 63 [1] J A Osborne 3-8-6 3ow S W Kelly 2/1 FAV: 0-3: Rdn chasing ldrs halfway, nvr plcd to chall: 1½   53a
161   SHAMWARI FIRE 26 [2] I W McInnes 4-9-10 (45) Natalia Gemelova (7) 9/2: 524400-4: Led 1f, cl-up 1m.   13   24a
216   GOOD FORM 17 [5] Miss K M George 4-9-10 (36) Derek Nolan (7) 14/1: 030000-5: Rear, mid-div, no ch fnl 3f.   5   14a
4724} LILIAN 82 [3] Miss Gay Kelleway 4-9-5 T P (46) T Eaves (5) 3/1: 246022-6: In tch, btn 4f out, t.o.:   15   0a
5000} CAYMAN MISCHIEF 60 [8] James Moffatt 4-9-5 A Nicholls 25/1: 00-7: Rear, no ch halfway, abs.   9   0a
     DANCES IN TIME [6] C N Kellett 4-9-5 T Williams 25/1: 8: Dwelt, hung right & sn bhd.   14   0a
8 Ran   2m 3.3 (5.1)   Owner Mr L A Morgan   Trained at Upper Longdon

---

300
3.15 #10 Free Bet @ Bet Direct Sky Active Banded Stakes 3yo+ 0-45 (H)
£1680 £480 £240   1m100y f/sand rnd   Going 55   -01 Slow   Stalls Inside

281   QOBTAAN 1 [3] M R Bosley 5-9-8 (45) G Baker 11/4 FAV: 460534-1: Rear, smooth hdwy 4f out & led over 2f out, sn clr, readily: 57a
150   MAGGIES PET 28 [2] K Bell 7-9-8 t (44) D R McCabe 6/1: 000360-2: Held up, styd on for press fnl 2f, no ch with easy wnr: 6   43a
202   NEWCLOSE 18 [10] N Tinkler 4-9-8 T (41) A Culhane 9/1: 00500-3: Dwelt, hdwy to lead over 3f out, hdd over 2f out & no   1¼   42a
228   PROUD VICTOR 15 [7] D Shaw 4-9-8 (39) Darren Williams 9/1: 604006-4: Held up, eff wide, no threat.   ¾   41a
163   MABEL RILEY 26 [6] M A Buckley 4-9-8 p (41) S W Kelly 14/1: 500000-5: Held up, no impress fnl 2f, 7f suits.   1¼   39a
3805} WILSON BLUEBOTTLE 133 [11] M W Easterby 5-9-8 bl (42) Dale Gibson 10/1: 014000-6: Prom till 3f out, abs.   1½   35a
4061} COURANT DAIR 121 [8] P C Haslam 3-8-2 (45) Rory Moore (7) 8/1: 4000-7: Prom 6f: 2   31a
157   LEONORA TRUCE 28 [9] R P Elliott 5-9-8 (44) Dean McKeown 10/1: 203260-8: Led till over 3f out, fdd.   ¾   30a
4722} SOPHOMORE 82 [5] John A Harris 10-9-8 (42) J Mackay 16/1: 550//00/0-: Al rear, jumps fit.   1¾   27a
4961} PAGEANT 64 [10] J M Bradley 7-9-8 (34) L Enstone (3) 14/1: 045300-0: Cl-up, btn 3f out: 14   0a
4089} KELTIC FLUTE 474 [4] Mrs Lucinda Featherstone 5-9-8 VIS (43) S Yourston (7) 40/1: 002000/-0: Keen, mid-div, sn strugg.   10   0a
213   INTITNICE 17 [12] Miss K M George 3-8-2 (39) Joanna Badger 16/1: 400000-0: Prom till 3f out.   2½   0a
160   EUROLINK ARTEMIS 26 [1] Miss Gay Kelleway 7-9-8 p (43) T Eaves (5) 11/1: 000000-0: In tch till 3f out, virtually p.u.   dist   0a
13 Ran   1m 51.0 (4.8)   Owner Inca Financial Services   Trained at Wantage

---

301
3.45 Littlewoods Bet Direct Banded Stakes 4yo+ 0-35 (H)
£1257 £359 £180   1m6f166y f/sand   Going 55   -39 Slow   Stalls Outside

765}   CITRUS MAGIC 298 [3] K Bell 7-9-4 P (33) Stephanie Hollinshead (7) 7/1: 3/04506-1: Made all, rdn clr from over 2f out: 47a
185   UNLEADED 22 [7] J Akehurst 4-8-12 (30) M Tebbutt 12/1: 0/0000-2: Held up, late gains for press to take 2nd, nvr threat to wnr: 7   33a
156   WELCOME BACK 28 [9] K A Ryan 7-9-4 (33) A Culhane 2/1 FAV: 0//616/20-: Chsd wnr 5f out, no impress fnl 2f: 2   30a
2886} THE LAST MOHICAN 173 [8] P Howling 5-9-4 P (31) D Nolan (5) 13/2: 5600/50-4: Prom, no prog fnl 2f, abs/cheek pieces,   4   24a
     jumps fit.
206   ROPPONGI DANCER 18 [5] Mrs N Macauley 5-9-4 BL t (25) Joanna Badger 10/1: 0/06400-5: Held up, rdn & no impress fnl   2   21a
     2f:
3460} GAELIC PROBE 148 [2] R M H Cowell 10-9-4 P (34) P Fitzsimons 6/1: 60//////6-: Bhd, no ch fnl 4f, jumps fit.   ½   20a
3061} INGLEWOOD 166 [4] C W Thornton 4-8-12 (35) Dean McKeown 7/1: 0/0040-7: Chsd wnr 1m, sn bhd: 8   8a
67   ALL ON MY OWN 45 [1] I W McInnes 9-9-4 bl (35) Natalia Gemelova (7) 10/1: 055000-8: Chsd wnr 7f out, btn 4f out.   27   0a
103   COMANCHE WOMAN 38 [6] K O Cunningham Brown 4-8-12 T (35) J Mackay 33/1: 0040-9: Sn bhd, t.o.:   28   0a
9 Ran   3m 23.8 (14.2)   Owner Mines A Double Club   Trained at Wantage

---

302
4.15 Bet Direct Football Cashbacks Banded Stakes 3yo+ 0-40 (H)
£1463 £418 £209   1m1f79y f/sand   Going 55   +01 Fast   Stalls Inside

4740} NDOLA 431 [12] B J Curley 5-9-9 (35) Paul Scallan 11/4 FAV: 000/00/-1: Trkd ldrs trav well, led 3f out, rdn out: 46a
221   TROPICAL SON 15 [6] D Shaw 5-9-9 vis (38) Darren Williams 8/1: 300000-2: Held up, rdn to chase wnr over 1f out, kept on,   1¼   42a
     al held:
4785} SERAPH 78 [1] John A Harris 4-9-8 (36) J Mackay 20/1: 030000-3: Rear, late gains, no dngr.   1¾   39a
4238} DANCING TILLY 110 [4] R A Fahey 6-9-9 p (38) T Hamilton (5) 10/1: 065306-4: Rear, eff wide, no dngr.   ½   38a

WOLVERHAMPTON Saturday 03.01.04 Lefthand, Sharp Track

191	**SAMAR QAND** 21 [13] Julian Poulton 5-9-9 p (38) M Tebbutt 3/1: 003653-5: Dwelt, sn handy, led over 4f out till 3f out.	1¾	36a
3460}	**FRATERNITY** 148 [3] J A Pickering 7-9-9 (38) Dean McKeown 8/1: 0/05064-6: In tch, no impress fnl 3f, op 13/2, abs.	4	28a
87	**SOLEIL DHIVER** 40 [5] P C Haslam 3-8-1 (40) Rory Moore (7) 10/1: 040400-7: Prom, btn 3f out, abs.	1¾	25a
160	**MALMAND** 26 [2] R Brotherton 5-9-9 vis (40) A Culhane 11/2: 000500-8: In tch till 2f out:	8	9a
160	**CHICKASAW TRAIL** 26 [9] R Hollinshead 6-9-9 P (30) Stephanie Hollinshead (7) 20/1: 0/000000-9: Led till over 4f out.	¾	7a
96	**REPETOIRE** 39 [7] K O Cunningham Brown 4-9-8 BL e (40) A Nicholls 40/1: 0/40B00-0: Dwelt & al bhd:	7	0a
164	**THE LAVERTON LAD** 26 [10] C W Thornton 3-8-1 (35) T Williams 25/1: 0000-0: Sn rdn & al bhd.	3	0a
63	**DARCIE MIA** 45 [11] J R Weymes 3-8-1 bl (38) D Fentiman (7) 25/1: 00000-0: Prom, rdn & struggling fnl 4f.	11	0a

12 Ran   2m 3.4 (5.2)   Owner Mrs B J Curley   Trained at Newmarket

SOUTHWELL Sunday 04.01.04 Lefthand, Sharp, Oval Track

Official Going STANDARD

303   12.30 Bet Direct On 0800 32 93 93 Apprentice Banded Stakes Div 1 3yo+ 0-45 (H)
£1642 £469 £235   7f f/sand rnd   Going 61   -16 Slow   Stalls Inside

202	**ROSTI** 19 [4] P C Haslam 4-9-8 (45) Rory Moore (5) 6/5 FAV: 500054-1: Handy, hung left under press 2f out, led 1f out, rdn out:		46a
202	**BRILLIANTRIO** 19 [7] M C Chapman 6-9-8 (44) Andrew Webb (5) 13/2: U06505-2: Cl-up, led 2f out, hdd 1f out, sn no extra:	2	41a
167	**CHAMPAGNE RIDER** 26 [2] D Shaw 8-9-8 e (36) T Hamilton 9/1: 050000-3: Prom, led 4f out, hdd 2f out, sn onepcd:	1¾	38a
84	**STORM SHOWER** 41 [1] Mrs N Macauley 6-9-8 vis (39) Steven Harrison (5) 14/1: 060300-4: Slow away, prog 4f out, no impress fnl 2f:	nk	37a
195	**JESSIE** 22 [3] Don Enrico Incisa 5-9-8 (41) Janice Webster (7) 22/1: 0/00400-5: Sn in rear, onepce/short of room well in fnl 1f.	shd	36a
202	**DASAR** 19 [9] M Brittain 4-9-8 (45) M Lawson (3) 8/1: 000006-6: In tch, hdd 4f out, no extra fnl 2f.	nk	35a
89	**T K O GYM** 41 [5] D Nicholls 5-9-8 VIS (42) L Treadwell (5) 6/1: 0B3620-7: Slow away, al bhd:	2	31a
202	**BALALAIKA TUNE** 19 [8] W Storey 5-9-8 (43) Stephanie Hollinshead (3) 25/1: 44/0550-8: Slow away, al in rear.	1¼	29a
224	**ALJOMAR** 16 [6] R E Barr 5-9-8 p (39) T Eaves 28/1: 000400-9: Handy, wknd 3f out.	2	25a

9 Ran   1m 32.0 (5.4)   Owner Exors of Late BM Hawkins/Lord   Trained at Middleham

304   1.00 Bet Direct On 0800 32 93 93 Apprentice Banded Stakes Div 2 3yo+ 0-45 (H)
£1642 £469 £235   7f f/sand rnd   Going 61   -13 Slow   Stalls Inside

297	**LARKYS LOB** 1 [4] Paul Johnson 5-9-8 (48) N Chalmers 6/5 FAV: 000002-21: Held up, prog 3f out, led dist, pushed clr, val 7L+:		50a
296	**CLEVELAND WAY** 1 [7] D Carroll 4-10-0 6ex vis (45) D Tudhope (5) 6/1: 204000-12: Cl-up, led 2f out, hdd dist, sn no extra:	5	45a
3263}	**SANDORRA** 158 [6] M Brittain 6-9-8 (43) M Lawson (3) 33/1: 00/5000-3: Handy, onepcd fnl 2f:	½	38a
282	**BIJAN** 2 [2] R Hollinshead 6-9-8 (35) Stephanie Hollinshead (3) 8/1: 360405-04: Held up, nvr dngrs.	½	37a
646}	**PROPRIUS** 320 [8] B Smart 4-9-8 (43) M Stainton (5) 16/1: 000/6-5: Dwelt, nvr nrr than mid-div.	4	29a
62	**LANDOFHEARTSDESIRE** 46 [9] J S Wainwright 5-9-8 vis (43) T Eaves 12/1: 606000-6: In tch, wknd 3f out.	5	19a
188	**COURT MUSIC** 23 [1] R E Barr 5-9-8 vis (32) T Hamilton 33/1: 000000-7: Cl-up, led 4f out, hdd 2f out, sn wknd.	6	7a
4417}	**MUJAGEM** 810 [3] M W Easterby 8-9-8 bl (45) P Mulrennan 11/1: 035/6P0//-: Al in rear.	5	-3a
172	**TEFI** 26 [5] J Balding 6-9-8 bl (41) P Makin (5) 11/2: 026060-9: Led, hdd 4f out, edged left & fdd 3f out.	3½	0

9 Ran   1m 31.8 (5.2)   Owner P and Mrs D M Johnson   Trained at Stanley

305   1.30 Bet Direct Press Red To Bet Banded Stakes 4yo+ 0-40 (H)
£1292 £369 £185   1m4f f/sand   Going 61   -9 Slow   Stalls Inside

185	**DASH OF MAGIC** 23 [6] J Hetherton 6-9-4 (36) C Catlin 5/1: 104000-1: In tch, led 2f out, pushed out, val 3L+:		40a
3896}	**PADDY MUL** 131 [4] W Storey 7-9-4 t (35) D R McCabe 11/1: 05/4626-2: Rear, prog 3f out, kept on well fnl 1f, no ch with wnr:	2	36a
204	**MISTY MAN** 19 [10] Miss J Feilden 6-9-4 BL (30) B Reilly (5) 12/1: 000044-3: Dwelt, sn keen in tch, chsd ldr dist, hung brght & onepcd fnl 1f:	¾	35a
191	**TWO STEPS TO GO** 22 [7] Ian Emmerson 5-9-4 vis (36) A Nicholls 14/1: 004040-4: Led, hdd 2f out.	2	32a
191	**TURFTANZER** 22 [11] Don Enrico Incisa 5-9-4 t (36) Kim Tinkler 20/1: 600/050-5: In tch, no extra fnl 2f.	hd	31a
103	**LEOPHIN DANCER** 39 [7] P W Hiatt 6-9-4 (38) Lisa Jones (3) 13/2: 230500-6: Held up, nvr nrr than mid-div.	hd	30a
3047}	**OULTON BROAD** 528 [9] R Ford 8-9-4 P (37) J P Guillambert (3) 10/1: 0/40016/-7: Mid-div, nvr able to chall.	nk	29a
257	**KING PRIAM** 8 [5] M J Polglase 9-9-4 bl (34) L Fletcher (5) 9/2 FAV: 554000-8: In tch, outpcd 5f out, mod late gains.	3	25a
142	**BEHAN** 32 [1] A Crook 5-9-4 (34) V Halliday 20/1: 000000-9: In tch, wknd 2f out.	2½	22a
4963}	**MAGIC CHARM** 65 [8] A G Newcombe 6-9-4 (39) S Whitworth 13/2: 561105-0: Mid-div, wknd 3f out.	9	8a
160	**MARENGO** 27 [2] Paul Johnson 10-9-4 (34) Joanna Badger 16/1: 040600-0: Keen rear, nvr able to chall.	4	2a
267	**KITTYLEE** 5 [13] M A Buckley 5-9-4 (25) R Ffrench 12/1: 0/0000/0-0: Al bhd.	13	0a
4106}	**TEN PAST SIX** 119 [12] R C Guest 12-9-4 bl e (23) A Cooper (7) 33/1: 40/00000-0: Al well adrift, new stable.	2½	0a
3564}	**SEA YA MAITE** 144 [14] S R Bowring 10-9-4 (30) J Bramhill 22/1: 003000-0: Slow away, prog 7f out, fdd 3f out.	11	0a

14 Ran   2m 42.7 (8.4)   Owner 21st Century Racing   Trained at Malton

306   2.00 Betdirect Co Uk Median Auction Maiden Stakes 4-6yo (H)
£1453 £415 £208   1m3f f/sand   Going 61   +2 Fast   Stalls Inside

259	**MADIBA** 6 [3] P Howling 5-9-3 bl (57) R Winston 4/1: 050400-1: Led, clr 2f out, eased cl-home, val 8L+:		60a
628}	**MR SMITHERS JONES** 323 [4] S C Williams 4-9-0 (50) B Reilly (5) 7/1: 00/5-2: In tch, ev ch 3f out, sn onepace:	6	51a
224	**MAKE MY HAY** 16 [1] J White 5-9-3 (45) L Fletcher (5) 5/2 FAV: 334002-3: Sn bhd, prog 6f out, no impress fnl 2f:	5	44a
196	**DANUM** 20 [2] R Hollinshead 4-9-0 p (49) A Culhane 3/1: 656066-4: Handy, wknd 3f out:	13	24a
264	**WHITE PARK BAY** 6 [5] J Gallagher 4-8-9 (58) N Callan 7/2: 030330-5: Bhd, prog 6f out, fdd 3f out:	23	0a
364}	**RED CRYSTAL** 1087 [1] C R Wilson 6-8-12 P L Enstone (3) 33/1: F0/0//-6: In tch, fdd 4f out:	4	0a

6 Ran   2m 27.85 (6.55)   Owner Eastwell Manor Racing Ltd   Trained at Newmarket

	307	**2.30 Littlewoods Bet Direct Banded Stakes 4yo+ 0-45 (H)**				
		£1645 £470 £235	**2m f/sand**	**Going 61**	**-64 Slow**	**Stalls Inside**

250*	DELTA FORCE 9 [6] P A Blockley 5-9-7 (51) Derek Nolan (7) 7/2: 356031-1: In tch, led 3f out, pushed clr fnl 1f, val 7L+:		**50a**
206	KAGOSHIMA 19 [9] J R Norton 9-9-7 vis (39) V Halliday 12/1: 0/00060-2: In tch, chsd ldr dist, al held fnl 1f:	5	**42a**
244	KYALAMI 13 [5] M J Polglase 5-9-7 (24) L Fletcher (3) 14/1: 000/00/60-3: Handy, hung left & no extra fnl 2f.	3½	**39a**
7	WORLABY DALE 55 [10] Mrs S Lamyman 8-9-7 (45) J Quinn 11/4 FAV: 233340-4: Held up, prog 4f out, short of room 3f out, sn onepcd:	1¾	**37a**
	MARAUD 1596 [7] R Hollinshead 10-9-7 (25) Stephanie Hollinshead (7) 10/1: /0030////-: Led, hdd 3f out, wknd.	½	**36a**
89	ASHTAROUTE 41 [2] M C Chapman 4-9-0 (40) Andrew Webb (7) 14/1: 430050-6: Chsd ldrs, outpcd 6f out & sn hung right, modest late gains:	1½	**35a**
97	KHUZDAR 40 [1] A Bailey 5-9-7 (43) B O'Neill (7) 4/1: 140640-7: Keen bhd, prog 7f out, hung left fnl 2f, sn wknd:	15	**20a**
821	NICIARA 649 [8] M C Chapman 7-9-7 (32) L Vickers (3) 33/1: 00/0/000/-: Mid-div, fdd 4f out.	7	**13a**
185	FAYRWAY RHYTHM 23 [3] Ian Emmerson 7-9-7 vis (39) A Nicholls 20/1: 000050-9: Held up, prog 9f out, wknd 4f out.	21	**0**
4802}	ROUSING THUNDER 78 [4] W Storey 7-9-7 p (41) D McGaffin (3) 15/2: 054463-0: Chsd ldrs, fdd 5f out.	nk	**0**
10 Ran	3m 46.1 (20.1) Owner Miss Emma Shally	Trained at Southwell	

	308	**3.00 Bet Direct On Itv Page 367 Selling Stakes 3yo+ (H)**				
		£1292 £369 £185	**6f f/sand rnd**	**Going 61**	**+7 Fast**	**Stalls Inside**

227	HURRICANE COAST 16 [1] P A Blockley 5-9-12 (61) D Nolan (5) 2/1 FAV: 012344-1: In tch, styd on lead ins fnl 1f, v easily, val 3L+:		**63a**
153	SPEEDFIT FREE 29 [2] J Semple 7-9-7 bl (55) R Winston 9/4: 501054-2: Mid-div, prog 3f out, styd on to chase ldr fnl 1f, al held:	¾	**55a**
253	AGUILA LOCO 8 [6] M C Chapman 5-9-7 (36) Andrew Webb (7) 40/1: 000000-3: Led, hdd ins fnl 1f, no extra:	¾	**53a**
4819}	DONEGAL SHORE 76 [3] Mrs J Candlish 5-9-7 t (66) N Chalmers (5) 20/1: 0/00600-4: Slow away, no dngr.	5	**38a**
202	TRAVELLING TIMES 19 [7] J S Wainwright 5-9-7 vis (51) T Eaves (5) 5/1: 043200-5: Cl-up, fdd dist.	½	**37a**
227	LAY DOWN SALLY 16 [8] J White 6-9-2 1ow (40) L Fletcher (3) 7/1: 303020-6: Handy, edged left & wknd 2f out.	2½	**27a**
256	FISHERS DREAM 8 [10] J R Norton 3-8-5 vis (48) J Bramhill 14/1: 064264-7: In tch wide, no extra 3f out.	1	**29a**
153	VALUABLE GIFT 29 [5] R C Guest 7-9-7 bl e (45) A Cooper (7) 16/1: 320000-8: Chsd ldrs, fdd dist.	½	**28a**
	THE BLOCK MONSTER 110 [4] P A Blockley 5-9-2 Derek Nolan (7) 14/1: 000000-9: Slow away, nvr a factor.	7	**2a**
66	PRECIOUS FREEDOM 46 [9] J Balding 4-9-7 VIS (43) J Edmunds 28/1: 400000-0: Handy, ev ch 2f out, sn fdd.	4	**0a**
10 Ran	1m 16.55 (3.25) Owner Mrs Joanna Hughes	Trained at Southwell	

	309	**3.30 Bet Direct In Vision Sky Page 293 Banded Stakes 3yo+ 0-40 (H)**				
		£1491 £426 £213	**1m f/sand rnd**	**Going 61**	**+00 Fast**	**Stalls Inside**

3263}	PRINTSMITH 158 [4] J R Norton 7-9-8 (32) J Bramhill 16/1: 0/00005-1: In tch, led 2f out, clr dist, rdn out to hold on:		**42a**
93	SIMPLY THE GUEST 40 [9] Don Enrico Incisa 5-9-8 t (34) Kim Tinkler (3) 13/2: 000000-2: In tch, outpcd 3f out, rallied fnl 1f, no ch with wnr:	1½	**38a**
168	KENNY THE TRUTH 26 [6] Mrs J Candlish 5-9-8 t (40) N Chalmers (5) 6/1: 450000-3: Chsd ldrs, outpcd 3f out, rallied dist.	1½	**35a**
95	GIVEN A CHANCE 40 [10] G Given 3-8-7 ow (30) J Fanning 6/1: 00600-4: In tch, fdd 2f out.	8	**19a**
221	DANCING KING 16 [2] P W Hiatt 8-9-8 (26) P Makin (7) 10/1: 040000-5: Led, hdd 2f out, sn wknd.	1	**17a**
255	HAITHEM 8 [8] D Shaw 7-9-8 e (36) Lisa Jones (3) 8/1: 650000-6: In tch, outpcd 4f out, modest late gains.	¾	**16a**
133	ONEFORTHEBOYS 33 [11] D Flood 5-9-8 (36) P Doe 9/2 FAV: 000600-7: In tch, wknd fnl 2f:	5	**6a**
228	FORMERIC 16 [3] Miss L C Siddall 8-9-8 vis (33) J McAuley 33/1: 000000-8: Slow away, al bhd.	1¾	**0a**
4621}	MISS WIZZ 90 [7] W Storey 4-9-8 (37) J Quinn 10/1: 000460-9: In tch, wknd dist.	¾	**0a**
4020}	WESTERN COMMAND 124 [5] Mrs N Macauley 9-9-8 (20) Joanna Badger 12/1: 005550-0: Slow away, al bhd.	5	**0a**
30	NICKEL SUNGIRL 51 [1] R Hollinshead 4-9-8 (40) N Callan 7/1: 002000-0: In tch, fdd 3f out.	3	**0a**
4918}	COUNTESS ELTON 68 [10] R E Barr 4-9-8 (35) T Eaves (5) 33/1: 0/00000-0: Handy, hung left & wknd 3f out.	5	**0a**
12 Ran	1m 44.3 (4.9) Owner Mrs Hazel Tattersall	Trained at Barnsley	

Official Going Standard

	310	**1.30 Bet Direct On Sky Active Banded Stakes 3yo+ 0-40 (H)**				
		£1470 £420 £210	**7f f/sand rnd**	**Going 49**	**-12 Slow**	**Stalls Outside**

3741}	INDIAN WARRIOR 138 [6] J Jay 8-9-7 (40) I Mongan 7/4 FAV: 010025-1: Sn handy & led after 2f, rdn & styd on strongly ins last:		**45a**
297	VLASTA WEINER 2 [7] J M Bradley 4-9-7 bl (40) L Fletcher (3) 14/1: 000006-02: Prom & chsd wnr after 2f, onepace fnl 2f:	2½	**41a**
3953}	LEMARATE 129 [8] D W Chapman 4-9-7 (40) R Brisland 16/1: 060000-3: Chsd ldrs, no extra dist:	4	**33a**
168	BLUE MAEVE 27 [10] J Hetherton 4-9-7 (40) G Parkin (7) 8/1: 0006-4: Held up, nvr pace to threaten:	½	**32a**
239	VERMILION CREEK 14 [3] R Hollinshead 5-9-7 (40) Stephanie Hollinshead (7) 9/2: 000006-5: Rdn, nvr pace to threaten.	1¾	**29a**
300	PAGEANT 2 [4] J M Bradley 7-9-7 (35) C Catlin 12/1: 045300-06: Led 1f, sn outpcd & no impress:	1¾	**26a**
3923}	MANIKATO 131 [2] K G Wingrove 10-9-7 (30) V Slattery 16/1: 000000-7: Sn rdn & al bhd, abs.	5	**17a**
298	PRESENT N CORRECT 2 [5] J M Bradley 11-9-7 bl (30) F P Ferris 16/1: 603006-08: Chsd ldrs 5f:	3½	**11a**
99	BOLD EFFORT 41 [11] K O Cunningham Brown 12-9-7 bl e (30) S Whitworth 20/1: 600000-9: Outpcd, nvr factor.	9	**0a**
9 Ran	1m 30.5 (4.3) Owner Mr & Mrs Jonathan Jay	Trained at Newmarket	

	311	**2.00 Press Interactive To Bet Direct Claiming Stakes 3yo+ (H)**				
		£1316 £376 £188	**1m100y f/sand rnd**	**Going 49**	**+06 Fast**	**Stalls Inside**

180	ALLY MAKBUL 26 [9] J R Best 4-9-9 (51) N Pollard 5/1: 001000-1: Briefly led early, sn trkd ldrs trav well, went on 2f out, readily asserted:		**55a**
4788}	LORD CHAMBERLAIN 80 [5] J M Bradley 11-10-0 bl (49) C J Davies (6) 12/1: 535450-2: Dwelt, hdwy to chase ldr ins last,	7	**49a**

	no impress:		
228	**SUDRA** 17 [12] J O'Reilly 7-10-0 p (53) D Allan (3) 7/2 JT FAV: 500000-3: Handy, led over 4f out, hdd 2f out, no extra:	2	45a
128	**NITE OWL FIZZ** 37 [6] J O'Reilly 6-10-0 (55) J D O'Reilly (7) 5/1: 560005-4: Cl-up, no extra fnl 2f.	shd	45a
228	**AIR OF ESTEEM** 17 [4] Ian Emmerson 8-10-0 (48) D Fentiman (7) 7/2 JT FAV: 004553-5: Chsd ldrs, not able to chall.	5	36a
250	**RED DELIRIUM** 10 [3] R Brotherton 8-10-0 bl t (45) I Mongan 11/2: 006004-6: Slow away, reluctant early, nvr factor.	3½	29a
4968}	**WELSH WHISPER** 65 [8] S A Brookshaw 5-9-9 L Keniry (3) 50/1: 0-7: Led 5f, sn btn, abs.	1¾	21a
3743}	**CRAIGMOR** 497 [1] M F Harris 4-10-0 (52) S Righton 33/1: 063600/-8: Chsd ldrs till halfway, jumps fit.	12	24a
290	**QUEEN EXCALIBUR** 2 [2] J M Bradley 5-9-9 p (47) P Fitzsimons 16/1: 000040-09: Sn bhd, breathing probs reported.	½	0
172	**ROYAL OVATION** 27 [10] N P Littmoden 5-10-0 (30) J P Guillambert (3) 25/1: 0/00000-0: Chsd ldrs till halfway.	26	0
10 Ran	1m 49.84 (3.64) Owner Mr Malcolm Ward	Trained at Maidstone	

---

312 | 2.30 Littlewoods Bet Direct Banded Stakes   3yo+ 0-45 (H)

£1638 £468 £234   **5f f/sand rnd**   Going 49   -04 Slow   Stalls Inside

275	**SO SOBER** 5 [8] D Shaw 6-9-7 (45) R Winston 13/2: 200000-1: Broke well, settled tracking ldrs, sqeezed thr' gap to lead over 1f out, drvn out:		48a
4741}	**TORRENT** 83 [11] D W Chapman 9-9-7 bl (45) R Brisland 8/1: 552060-2: Held up, smooth hdwy from halfway, kept on ins last, not btn far:	½	45a
3088}	**MANGUS** 166 [6] K O Cunningham Brown 10-9-7 BL e (40) S Whitworth 25/1: 000600-3: Rdn rear, nrst fin:	3	37a
296	**ENJOY THE BUZZ** 2 [2] J M Bradley 5-9-7 (45) P Fitzsimons 9/1: 06/0020-44: Rear, nrst fin.	nk	36a
296	**CAROLS CHOICE** 2 [13] A Sadik 7-9-7 (40) I Mongan 7/1: 630000-05: Prom wide, no extra dist, qck reapp.	½	34a
253	**CARK** 9 [3] J Balding 6-9-7 p (45) L Fletcher (3) 11/2: 000400-6: Chsd ldrs, no extra over 1f out.	½	32a
4124}	**MILLYS LASS** 119 [9] J M Bradley 6-9-7 BL (40) F P Ferris 33/1: 404000-7: Prom till over 1f out, blnks/abs.	3	25a
242	**DIAPHANOUS** 14 [7] E A Wheeler 6-9-7 bl (45) S Carson 5/1 FAV: 300644-8: Missed break, sn led till 2f out, fdd.	½	23a
4791}	**ON THE LEVEL** 80 [1] Mrs N Macauley 5-9-7 (45) P McCabe 12/1: 043255-9: Chsd ldrs till halfway, abs.	¾	21a
133	**CALENDAR GIRL** 34 [10] P J Makin 4-9-7 (45) D Sweeney 10/1: 3500-0: Nvr paced to chall ldrs:	¾	19a
187	**STAR APPLAUSE** 24 [12] J Balding 4-9-7 (45) D Allan (3) 14/1: 206000-0: Mid-div, no impress fnl 2f.	hd	18a
109	**LONE PIPER** 38 [5] J M Bradley 9-9-7 (45) C Catlin 14/1: 000056-0: Led/dsptd lead 4f, wknd qckly.	½	16a
4826}	**MESMERISED** 76 [4] Miss A Stokell 4-9-7 (45) Ann Stokell 25/1: 030000-0: Al bhd, abs.	2½	9a
13 Ran	1m 02.87 (2.67) Owner Averham Park Racing	Trained at Newark	

---

313 | 3.00 Betdirect Co Uk Median Auction Maiden Stakes   3-5yo (H)

£1439 £411 £206   **6f f/sand rnd**   Going 49   -01 Slow   Stalls Inside

263	**STRIKE LUCKY** 7 [2] P J Makin 4-9-7 D Sweeney 4/1: 400-1: Cl-up halfway, duelled with rnr-up fnl 2f, prevailed for press cl-home, all out:		55a
254	**DARK CHAMPION** 9 [5] Jedd O'Keeffe 4-9-7 (50) I Mongan 2/1: 234405-2: Led, strongly prsd by wnr fnl 2f, hdd ins last, just held:	nk	55a
126	**ANISETTE** 37 [7] Julian Poulton 3-8-0 J Tate 11/10 FAV: 2-3: In tch, outpcd by front pair halfway, kept on late:	3	42a
254	**SOMETHINGABOUTHER** 9 [1] P W Hiatt 4-9-2 (40) C Catlin 12/1: 200500-4: Led early, btn 2f out.	5	30a
298	**CHANTILLY GOLD** 2 [3] J M Bradley 5-9-2 p (30) P Fitzsimons 33/1: 000000-05: Held up & keen, btn 2f out.	2	25a
282	**CHANTEUSE** 3 [6] D W Chapman 4-9-2 BL (49) R Brisland 25/1: 20000-06: Held up & keen, no ch from hway:	4	15a
6 Ran	1m 15.78 (2.98) Owner Mrs P J Makin	Trained at Marlborough	

---

314 | 3.30 Bet Direct In Running Sky Text 293 Banded Stakes   3yo+ 0-45 (H)

£1474 £421 £211   **1m1f79y f/sand rnd**   Going 49   -13 Slow   Stalls Inside

302	**MALMAND** 2 [6] R Brotherton 5-9-9 vis (40) I Mongan 5/1: 000500-01: Slowly away, in tch, hdwy 2f out, edged left, led nr fin, all out:		45a
389}	**GOOD TIMING** 356 [9] J Hetherton 6-9-9 (45) G Parkin 20/1: 4/0000/0-2: Handy, hdwy to go 2nd 5f out, rdn sn after, ran on ins last	hd	44a
226	**NOCATEE** 17 [4] P C Haslam 3-8-1 VIS (45) Rory Moore (7) 9/2: 000500-3: Rear, sn rdn, hdwy 1f out, edged left ins last & styd on:	½	43a
196	**GIUST IN TEMP** 21 [5] P W Hiatt 5-9-9 (30) L Fletcher (3) 7/2: 500650-4: Handy, led 1f till nr fin.	¾	42a
3050}	**LUCKY ROMANCE** 168 [7] B J Meehan 5-9-9 (45) R Winston 6/1: 2600/00-5: Led till 1f out, wknd/eased.	2½	37a
75	**TARKWA** 45 [8] R M H Cowell 5-9-9 (45) M Henry 5/2 FAV: 053260-6: Al handy, rdn 4f out, wknd from 2f out.	hd	36a
240	**TIMBUKTU** 14 [1] C W Thornton 3-8-1 (45) T Williams 20/1: 006-7: Al bhd.	15	10a
165	**LITTLETON VALAR** 28 [3] J R Weymes 4-9-8 BL (40) D Fentiman (7) 20/1: 020060-8: Rcd keen, bhd from 5f out.	16	0a
196	**MORNING SUN** 21 [2] K O Cunningham Brown 4-9-8 BL e (40) C Catlin 33/1: 650000-9: Rear & t.o. 4f out:	5	0a
9 Ran	2m 04.01 (5.81) Owner Carpe Diem Racing	Trained at Pershore	

---

315 | 4.00 Littlewoodspoker Com Banded Stakes   4yo+ 0-45 (H)

£1442 £412 £206   **1m4f f/sand**   Going 49   -02 Slow   Stalls Inside

244	**NAKWA** 14 [8] E J Alston 6-9-4 (45) D Allan (3) 6/5 FAV: 401043-1: Handy, lost pl halfway, hdwy 5f out, led 2f out, rdn clr,		57a
250	**FAIRMORNING** 10 [3] J W Unett 5-9-4 (40) A Daly 6/1: 655443-2: Rear, hdwy when rdn 3f out, went 2nd ins fnl 1f but not pace of wnr:	8	42a
4538}	**LAMPOS** 96 [5] Miss J A Camacho 4-9-0 (45) R Winston 8/1: 040030-3: Rear, hdwy 3f out, onepace:	1½	40a
204	**BERKELEY HEIGHTS** 20 [4] B Smart 4-9-0 bl (45) C Catlin 25/1: 0/50065-4: Rear, hdwy to lead 3f out, hdd 2f out, wknd ins fnl 1f:	¾	39a
3923}	**HUSKY** 131 [7] R M H Cowell 6-9-4 p (45) I Mongan 8/1: 200000-5: Led till hdd 3f out, wknd fnl 2f:	½	38a
4457}	**XIXITA** 101 [6] Mr J D Scargill 4-9-0 (45) S W Kelly 33/1: 40450-6: Rear, hdwy 5f out, rdn 4f out & wknd:	10	26a
305	**LEOPHIN DANCER** 2 [1] P W Hiatt 6-9-4 (40) G Baker 8/1: 230500-07: Rear, hdwy 5f out, wknd 3f out.	2	23a
75	**LITTLE RICHARD** 45 [10] M Wellings 5-9-4 (40) V Slattery 25/1: 230000-8: Handy, wknd from 4f out.	hd	22a
196	**FELIDAE** 21 [2] M Brittain 4-9-0 (45) M Lawson (7) 33/1: 0050-9: Handy, wknd.	8	12a
156	**COTTAM GRANGE** 30 [9] M W Easterby 4-9-0 (45) Dale Gibson 11/2: 000654-0: Handy, lost pl after halfway.	2	9a

WOLVERHAMPTON Monday 05.01.04 Lefthand, Sharp, Oval Track

10 Ran 2m 39.7 (6.1) Owner Mr Alan Dick   Trained at Preston

SOUTHWELL Monday 05.01.04 Lefthand, Sharp, Oval Track

Official Going Standard

316 — 1.15 Bet Direct On Attheraces Interactive Handicap Stakes 3yo 0-70 (E)   [71]
£3290 £940 £470   **6f f/sand rnd**   Going 36   -19 slow   Stalls Inside

256	SIEGFRIEDS NIGHT 9 [1] M C Chapman 3-8-2 (45) Joanna Badger 12/1: 000035-1: Handy, styd on to lead ins fnl 1f, rdn out:	51a
73*	MELAINA 45 [2] M S Saunders 3-8-10 p (53) J Quinn 9/2: 460061-2: Led, hdd under press ins fnl 1f, no extra: 2	52a
261	DARING AFFAIR 7 [5] K R Burke 3-9-7 VIS (64) N Callan 13/8 FAV: 044526-3: In tch, ev ch dist, onepcd ins fnl 1f: nk	62a
203	GARNOCK VENTURE 20 [3] A Berry 3-8-7 bl (50) Dale Gibson 5/2: 650043-4: Dwelt, sn prom, fdd dist: 7	28a
4445}	NUMPTY 102 [4] N Tinkler 3-8-6 t (49) Kim Tinkler 10/1: 000-5: Al bhd: 1¾	22a
1	BIRIKINA 56 [6] A Berry 3-9-0 (57) P Bradley (5) 16/1: 000000-6: Chsd ldrs wide, fdd 2f out: 1¼	26a

6 Ran 1m 16.62 (3.32) Owner Mr K D Blanch   Trained at Market Rasen

317 — 1.45 Bet Direct Press Red To Bet Claiming Stakes 4yo+ (F)
£2891 £826 £413   **6f f/sand rnd**   Going 36   +01 Fast   Stalls Inside

308*	HURRICANE COAST 1 [4] P A Blockley 5-8-5 (61) Dean McKeown 7/4: 012344-11: Handy, ev ch & edged left dist, led ins fnl 1f, rdn out:	69a
286	SHARP HAT 3 [1] D W Chapman 10-9-1 (71) A Culhane 6/1: 01135-52: Prom, led 4f out, hdd ins fnl 1f, not pace wnr: 2	71a
153	LEGALIS 30 [3] K A Ryan 6-8-9 BL (60) N Callan 20/1: 000400-3: Cl-up, ev ch dist, wknd fnl 1f: 3	56a
92	HIGH ESTEEM 41 [2] M A Buckley 8-8-13 P (58) R Ffrench 28/1: 610000-4: Led 2f, styd prom, fdd fnl 2f: 5	45a
166	JALOUHAR 27 [7] B P J Baugh 4-8-9 p (59) J Fanning 9/1: 250615-5: Al bhd: 2	35a
308	TRAVELLING TIMES 1 [6] J S Wainwright 5-8-5 vis (51) D R McCabe 33/1: 043200-56: Handy, wknd fnl 2f: nk	30a
153	QUEEN OF NIGHT 30 [5] T D Barron 4-8-2 (76) D Mernagh 13/8 FAV: 001515-7: In tch, rcd wide turning in, sn bhd, eased fnl 1f: 7	7a

7 Ran 1m 15.41 (2.11) Owner Mrs Joanna Hughes   Trained at Southwell

318 — 2.15 Betdirect Co Uk Handicap Stakes 4yo+ 0-80 (D)   [77]
£4046 £1245 £623 £311   **1m f/sand rnd**   Going 36   -05 Slow   Stalls Inside

196	PENWELL HILL 21 [3] T D Barron 5-9-3 (66) D Mernagh 9/4 FAV: 113465-1: In tch, chsd ldr dist, rdn out to lead cl-home:	72a
251	PHAROAHS GOLD 10 [4] D Shaw 6-8-12 e (61) Darren Williams 16/1: 201000-2: Bhd, prog 3f out, kept on well fnl 1f, just held by wnr: ½	64a
251	QUIET READING 10 [6] M R Bosley 7-9-4 vis (67) Hayley Turner (5) 5/1: 134603-3: Mid-div, prog 3f out, kept on fnl 1f: 1	68a
86	FLAMBE 42 [2] P C Haslam 6-8-9 BL (58) L Enstone (3) 6/1: 300/004-4: Prom, led 4f out, clr 2f out, hung left dist, hdd & no extra cl-home: ½	58a
221	JAMESTOWN 17 [8] M J Polglase 7-7-12 (47) Joanna Badger (5) 7/1: 354063-5: In tch, outpcd 4f out, rallied dist. ½	46a
255	FIRST MAITE 9 [1] S R Bowring 11-9-8 bl (71) J Bramhill 9/1: 530602-6: In tch, wknd 2f out: 8	54a
255	RISKA KING 9 [11] R A Fahey 4-9-10 (73) T Hamilton (5) 25/1: 400100-7: Al in rear: 7	43a
3329}	MOUNT ROYALE 156 [9] N Tinkler 6-8-9 (58) Kim Tinkler 20/1: 334015-8: Handy, wknd 3f out: 1¼	25a
251	FRIDAYS TAKINGS 10 [10] B Smart 5-9-1 bl (64) R Ffrench 10/1: 220000-9: Led, hdd 4f out, fdd fnl 3f. nk	30a
196	SINJAREE 21 [5] Mrs S Lamyman 6-8-1 vis (50) J Quinn 28/1: 000000-0: Cl-up, fdd 3f out. 16	0a

10 Ran 1m 42.69 (3.29) Owner Mrs Liz Jones   Trained at Thirsk

319 — 2.45 Littlewoods Bet Direct Maiden Stakes 3yo+ (D)
£3426 £1054 £527 £264   **6f f/sand rnd**   Going 36   -18 Slow   Stalls Inside

2101}	CLASSIC VISION 206 [6] W J Haggas 4-9-5 A Culhane 3/1 FAV: 53-1: Dwelt, sn in tch, prog to lead dist, pushed out, val 2L+:	61a
	ILE FACILE 10 [10] N P Littmoden 3-8-8 N Callan 14/1: 2: Chsd ldrs, kept on fnl 1f, not pace wnr: ¾	61a
2746}	DISPOL VELETA 180 [11] T D Barron 3-8-3 J Fanning 33/1: 0- 3: Dwelt, prog wide 2f out, kept on fnl 1f: 1¼	52a
254	SHADOWFAX 9 [2] Miss Gay Kelleway 4-9-10 BL (60) M Fenton 7/2: 0426/62-4: Handy, onepcd fnl 1f. shd	56a
254	LAKE EYRE 9 [3] J Balding 5-9-5 (45) J Edmunds 11/1: 460303-5: Prom, led 3f out, hdd dist, sn no extra. shd	50a
42	QUINCANNON 49 [5] T D Barron 3-8-8 D Mernagh 100/30: 04-6: Slow away, prog 4f out, no impress fnl 2f: ½	54a
256	BRAVE CHIEF 9 [13] J A Pickering 3-8-8 (53) Dean McKeown 12/1: 002-7: Mid-div, prog 4f out, wknd fnl 2f: 1¾	49a
146	STARCROSS VENTURE 30 [1] R A Fahey 3-8-3 T Hamilton (2) 8/1: 3-8: In tch, wknd 2f out: 1¼	40a
	HARBOUR PRINCESS [14] M F Harris 3-8-3 A Nicholls 50/1: 9: Al bhd: 2½	33a
221	SENNEN COVE 17 [12] R Bastiman 5-9-10 t (35) K Dalgleish 50/1: 045000-0: Al in rear. 2	32a
263	LAW MAKER 7 [7] M A Buckley 4-9-10 (40) R Ffrench 66/1: 000000-0: Led, hdd 3f out, sn fdd: 1¼	28a
3790}	SVENSON 136 [9] A Berry 3-8-8 P Bradley (2) 33/1: 0-0: Al well bhd: 11	-2a
4823}	BISHOP TO ACTRESS 76 [8] M J Polglase 3-8-3 (52) Sarah Mitchell (7) 50/1: 453660-0: In tch, wknd 3f out: 4	0

13 Ran 1m 16.54 (3.24) Owner The Chosen Few Partnership   Trained at Newmarket

320 — 3.15 Littlewoodscasino Com Selling Stakes 3yo+ (G)
£2597 £742 £371   **7f f/sand rnd**   Going 36   -05 Slow   Stalls Inside

298	LUCAYAN MONARCH 2 [1] P A Blockley 6-9-7 p (55) Dean McKeown 9/2: 000064-21: Trkd ldrs, switched wide straight, hdwy to lead appr fnl 1f, rdn out:	56a
92	XALOC BAY 41 [3] B P J Baugh 6-9-7 (52) J Fanning 8/1: 432360-2: Handy, led 4f out, hdd appr 1f out, styd on same pace: ½	54a
161	JAN BRUEGHEL 28 [7] T D Barron 5-9-7 (65) D Mernagh 6/5 FAV: 110240-3: Handy, hdwy & ch 2f out, wknd qckly 1f out: 6	40a
227*	HEADLAND 17 [5] D W Chapman 8-9-7 A Culhane 5/1: 000041-4: Handy, wknd appr fnl 1f. 2	43a
202	BULAWAYO 20 [8] Andrew Reid 7-9-7 (55) A Nicholls 7/1: 632030-5: Chsd ldrs, rdn & wknd from 2f out. 4	30a
46	GENEROUS SHARE 49 [6] M S Saunders 4-9-2 (47) J Quinn 33/1: 0/00500-6: Al bhd. 5	15a
3623}	METICULOUS 143 [4] M C Chapman 6-9-7 (30) Andrew Webb (7) 100/1: 00000/0-7: Led till hdd 4f out, wknd: 2½	15a

SOUTHWELL Monday 05.01.04 Lefthand, Sharp, Oval Track

224 **VELVET RHYTHM 17** [2] K R Burke 4-9-2 R Keogh (7) 66/1: 0-8: Al bhd. 10 **0a**
8 Ran 1m 29.53 (2.93) Owner Mr A C Kirkham Trained at Southwell

321 3.45 Bet Direct In Running Sky Text 371 Handicap Stakes 4yo+ 0-65 (F) **[59]**
£2926 £836 £418 **1m4f f/sand** **Going 36** **+07 Fast** Stalls Inside

243 **BROUGHTON KNOWS 14** [1] W J Musson 7-8-4 bl (35) Lisa Jones (3) 5/1: 404362-1: Rear, hdwy 3f out, led dist, clr ins fnl 1f: **51a**
250 **AVEIRO 10** [5] B G Powell 8-9-0 bl (45) K Dalgleish 12/1: 304140-2: Trkd ldr, led 7f out & clr over 2f out, hdd dist, sn left bhnd by wnr: 8 **50a**
185 **DAUNTED 24** [10] P A Blockley 8-9-13 (58) D Nolan (5) 4/1 FAV: 21526/4-3: Bhd, hdwy 5f out, hung left & wknd dist: 5 **56a**
305 **KING PRIAM 1** [6] M J Polglase 9-8-4 bl (35) Dean McKeown 14/1: 554000-84: Rear, switched wide & mod late hdwy, nrst fin: hd **32a**
257 **EAST CAPE 9** [2] Don Enrico Incisa 7-8-9 (40) Kim Tinkler 6/1: 634450-5: Trkd ldrs, hdwy 3f out, wknd from 2f out. 2 **34a**
305* **DASH OF MAGIC 1** [3] J Hetherton 6-8-9 (40) T Hamilton (5) 9/2: 104000-16: Al mid-div: 7 **24a**
243 **EXIT TO HEAVEN 14** [4] Miss Gay Kelleway 4-9-9 (58) T Eaves (5) 14/1: 000225-7: Led to 7f out, wknd 4f out: 1½ **39a**
257 **SURDOUE 9** [8] P Howling 4-10-0 P (63) Paul Eddery 9/2: 000005-8: Trkd ldrs, wknd 2f out: 2 **41a**
196 **CALCAR 21** [7] Mrs S Lamyman 4-8-10 (45) J Quinn 50/1: 500500-9: Chsd ldrs, wknd 4f out, t.o. 23 **0a**
281 **OVER RATING 3** [9] K A Ryan 4-9-11 (60) N Callan 16/1: 23426-00: Chsd ldrs, wknd 4f out, t.o.: ¾ **7a**
10 Ran 2m 37.80 (3.5) Owner Broughton Thermal Insulation Trained at Newmarket

LINGFIELD Tuesday 06.01.04 Lefthand, V Sharp Track

Official Going Standard

322 12.00 Bet Direct On Sky Active Maiden Stakes 3yo (D)
£4115 £1266 £633 £317 **1m p/track rnd** **Going 45** **-32 Slow** Stalls Outside

CHASING THE DREAM [3] A M Balding 3-8-9 Martin Dwyer 7/1: 1: Mid-div, hdwy to lead dist, pushed out, cmtbly: **73a**
220 **JUMEIRAH SCARER 20** [5] M R Channon 3-9-0 C Catlin 7/4 FAV: 3-2: Sn cl-up & led over 2f out, drvn & hdd dist, not pace of wnr: 1¾ **71a**
WEBBSWOOD LAD [6] Mrs Stef Liddiard 3-9-0 M Fenton 25/1: 3: Dwelt, sn handy, outpcd 2f out, kept on ins last: 1¼ **68a**
4948} **ASHSTANZA 68** [9] M A Jarvis 3-9-0 M Henry 8/1: 04-4: Led till over 2f out, no extra: 2 **64a**
ON THE WATERFRONT [2] J W Hills 3-9-0 S Drowne 33/1: 5: Chsd ldrs, no extra dist, debut. 1½ **61a**
SUNSET DREAMER [1] P Mitchell 3-8-9 E Ahern 14/1: 6: Slow away, nvr able to chall on debut. 1¾ **53a**
OUR LITTLE ROSIE [8] M Blanshard 3-8-9 D Sweeney 33/1: 7: Al bhd, nvr a factor. hd **52a**
CHAMPAGNE SHADOW 91 [12] G L Moore 3-9-0 R Brisland 16/1: 04-8: Cl-up, btn 2f out: 1½ **54a**
DEVINE COMMAND [7] R Ingram 3-9-0 N Day 33/1: 9: Chsd ldrs till over 2f out on debut. ½ **53a**
SILVER CACHE [11] J Noseda 3-8-9 S W Kelly 7/1: 0: Slow away, sn in tch rear, btn 2f out: nk **47a**
ALFRIDINI [4] D R C Elsworth 3-9-0 BL Dane O'Neill 5/1: 0: Reluctant to race & sn bhd: 21 **15a**
11 Ran 1m 42.37 (6.17) Owner Mrs L R Lovell Trained at Kingsclere

323 12.30 Betdirect Co Uk Handicap Stakes 4yo+ 0-70 (E) **[70]**
£3465 £990 £495 **7f p/track rnd** **Going 45** **-12 Slow** Stalls Inside

266* **SMITH N ALLAN OILS 7** [2] M Dods 5-9-5 6ex p (61) E Ahern 4/1 FAV: 230101-1: Trkd ldrs trav well, drvn to lead cl-home, all out: **67a**
181 **KILMEENA LAD 27** [4] J C Fox 8-9-11 (67) P Dobbs 25/1: 1/00/000-2: Handy trav well & led 2f out, rdn clr over 1f out, hdd cl-home: hd **73a**
2491} **SPINNING DOVE 192** [6] N A Graham 4-9-6 (62) Martin Dwyer 25/1: 5/46423-3: Towards rear, hdwy 2f out & styd on well for press cl-home, nrst fin: hd **67a**
270 **PARKER 7** [5] B Palling 7-9-10 bl (66) M Fenton 20/1: 062150-4: Prom, kept on onepace for press. 1¾ **67a**
270 **TEMPER TANTRUM 7** [13] Andrew Reid 6-9-7 p (63) Rory Moore (7) 8/1: 305023-5: Rear, late gains for press. ¾ **62a**
266 **THE GAIKWAR 7** [9] N E Berry 5-9-11 bl (67) M Savage (5) 8/1: 000404-6: Dwelt, rear, eff wide, onepace. ¾ **64a**
290 **SIR LAUGHALOT 3** [12] Miss E C Lavelle 4-10-0 (70) L Keniry (3) 7/1: 00020-27: Trkd ldrs, no impress dist: ¾ **66a**
216 **ESPADA 20** [8] J A Osborne 8-9-13 (69) S W Kelly 11/1: 610002-8: Led 5f, fdd: 1¼ **62a**
266 **FOUR JAYS 7** [10] N P Littmoden 4-9-4 p (60) J Bramhill 25/1: 260505-9: Rear, only mod prog. shd **53a**
266 **ICANNSHIFT 7** [3] S Dow 4-9-10 (66) J Coffill Brown (7) 50/1: 040600-0: Towards rear, little hdwy. 1 **57a**
174 **FRANKSKIPS 27** [11] Miss B Sanders 5-9-10 (66) A Clark 40/1: 0/10500-0: Wide/bhd, nvr a factor. ½ **56a**
270 **CAYMAN BREEZE 7** [16] S Dow 4-9-9 (65) P Doe 33/1: 000300-0: Prom wide halfway, btn 2f out: 1 **53a**
130 **PHRENOLOGIST 35** [14] J R Fanshawe 4-9-11 (67) Dane O'Neill 13/2: 5613-0: Trkd ldrs, no extra over 1f out. 1¼ **52a**
266 **SUPERCHIEF 7** [7] Miss B Sanders 9-9-6 bl t (62) S Drowne 9/2: 200002-0: Keen trkg ldrs, btn over 1f out, eased. 1¼ **44a**
231 **DUNEDIN RASCAL 17** [15] E A Wheeler 7-9-10 bl (66) Liam Jones (7) 50/1: 000400-0: Chsd ldrs wide till halfway. 15 **22a**
50 **SHARPINCH 49** [1] P R Chamings 6-9-9 (65) I Mongan 50/1: 00/4000-0: Cl-up till 3f out, sn wknd, broke blood vessel, abs. dist **0**
16 Ran 1m 26.78 (3.98) Owner Smith & Allan Racing Trained at Darlington

324 1.00 Bet Direct All Weather On 0800 32 93 93 Median Auction Maiden Stakes 4-6yo (E)
£3266 £933 £467 **1m4f p/track** **Going 45** **-22 Slow** Stalls Inside

125 **TWO OF A KIND 38** [6] J W Hills 4-9-0 (56) E Ahern 9/2: 055555-1: Trkd ldrs trav well, led dist, drvn out: **57a**
993} **FLEETING MOON 272** [5] A M Balding 4-8-9 Martin Dwyer 7/2 JT FAV: 0-2: Rear, pushed along & hdwy from over 4f out, styd on for press ins last, not able to chall: 1½ **49a**
3927] **TROUBLE NEXT DOOR 848** [4] N P Littmoden 6-9-4 (35) J P Guillambert (3) 11/1: 664500//-3: Keen & cl-up, rdn & led over 3f out, hdd dist, onepace: hd **53a**
3756} **MORVERN 139** [9] J G Given 4-9-0 vis (51) M Fenton 10/1: 360004-4: Mid-div, styd on for press fnl 2f, not pace to chall: nk **52a**
4690} **VANILLA MOON 86** [3] J R Jenkins 4-8-9 vis (48) S W Kelly 8/1: 000405-5: Handy & ev ch fnl 2f, no extra well ins last: ½ **46a**
2358} **AITANA 197** [2] S C Williams 4-8-9 (58) S Drowne 7/1: 0060-6: Chsd ldrs, btn 3f out: 24 **15a**

265	**SHAAMITS ALL OVER** 8 [1] B A Pearce 5-8-13 P (50) G Baker 20/1: 0600-7: Slow away, rear, no ch fnl 3f, chkpcs.	4	9a
4849}	**AMNESTY** 76 [7] G L Moore 5-9-4 (60) I Mongan 7/2 JT FAV: 320030-8: Keen early chasing ldrs, btn 4f out, t.o.:	5	8a
1422}	**BOW SPRIT** 242 [8] B G Powell 4-9-0 (60) L Keniry (3) 20/1: 60300-9: Led till over 3f out, 6 mth abs, new yard.	18	0a
9 Ran	2m 37.29 (8.09) Owner Mr J W Hills	Trained at Lambourn	

325
1.35 Littlewoods Bet Direct Stakes Handicap 3yo 0-90 (C) **[95]**

£8093 £2490 £1245 £623 **1m2f p/track** **Going 45** **-56 Slow** Stalls Inside

4975}	**FORTHRIGHT** 66 [3] C E Brittain 3-9-7 (88) E Ahern 5/2 FAV: 216060-1: Trkd ldr & led over 3f out trav well, drvn to hold on well ins last:		93a
192	**AMWELL BRAVE** 24 [7] J R Jenkins 3-8-2 (69) J Bramhill 14/1: 500345-2: Rear, eff wide from 2f out, drvn & styd on well, not reach wnr:	1¼	71a
4960}	**MAYBE SOMEDAY** 67 [2] I A Wood 3-8-6 (73) D Sweeney 7/1: 60213-3: Handy & chsd wnr over 2f out, no extra well ins last:	½	74a
252*	**NESSEN DORMA** 10 [6] J G Given 3-8-9 (76) M Fenton 7/2: 250511-4: Trkd ldrs, onepace & held dist:	2½	73a
252	**MYANNABANANA** 10 [1] J R Weymes 3-7-13 vis (66) D Fentiman (7) 14/1: 601135-5: Held up in tch, not able to chall:	¾	62a
240*	**BILL BENNETT** 15 [5] J Jay 3-8-7 (74) Martin Dwyer 6/1: 033201-6: Led till over 3f out, sn btn:	6	61a
190	**LASTING DELIGHT** 24 [4] Sir Mark Prescott 3-8-1 (68) J Mackay 4/1: 0510-W: Ref to enter stalls, withdrawn.		0
7 Ran	2m 12.94 (10.14) Owner Wyck Hall Stud	Trained at Newmarket	

326
2.10 Bet Direct On 0800 32 93 93 Selling Stakes 3yo (G)

£2548 £728 £364 **1m p/track rnd** **Going 45** **-35 Slow** Stalls Outside

4960}	**PRINCESS ISMENE** 67 [5] J Jay 3-8-11 bl (54) I Mongan 7/2: 210405-1: Held up, smooth hdwy from halfway & rdn/led dist, held on well for press:		59a
261	**REDBANK** 8 [2] N A Callaghan 3-8-11 bl (65) Dane O'Neill 1/1 FAV: 004330-2: Dwelt, trkd ldrs trav well 3f out, ev ch dist, not pace of wnr:	¾	57a
158	**ZOLUSHKA** 29 [7] B W Duke 3-8-6 (45) E Ahern 20/1: 0000-3: Dwelt, mid-div, hung left & no extra dist:	4	42a
291	**LADY PREDOMINANT** 3 [3] Andrew Reid 3-8-6 (52) Rory Moore (7) 7/2: 05020-44: Trkd ldr, led over 2f out, hdd dist & wknd:	2½	37a
2670}	**DEFANA** 185 [6] M Dods 3-8-11 (54) S W Kelly 16/1: 0653-5: Rear, eff 3f out, not able to chall, abs.	1¼	39a
78	**NOTHING MATTERS** 45 [4] P R Chamings 3-8-6 (40) P Doe 20/1: 054005-6: Led till over 2f out, sn btn, abs.	1¾	31a
119	**FOX HOLLOW** 38 [8] M J Haynes 3-8-11 (35) C Catlin 33/1: 66500-7: Chsd ldrs, no ch fnl 2f.	16	6a
203	**GENTLEMAN GEORGE** 21 [1] D K Ivory 3-8-11 (45) R Miles (3) 25/1: 0500-8: Keen, chsd ldrs 2f, btn 3f out, t.o..	11	0
8 Ran	1m 42.57 (6.37) Owner Mr Aftab Ali	Trained at Newmarket	

327
2.45 Bet Direct In Running Sky Text 293 Classified Claiming Stakes 3yo 0-60 (F)

£2884 £824 £412 **6f p/track rnd** **Going 45** **-00 Slow** Stalls Inside

279	**DESERT LIGHT** 6 [4] D Shaw 3-8-4 vis (35) J F McDonald (5) 50/1: 000060-1: Prom & trk ldr 3f out, led over 2f out & rdn clr, readily.		59a
247	**STAMFORD BLUE** 11 [1] J S Moore 3-8-4 bl (50) Martin Dwyer 4/1: 000035-2: Pushed along rear, hdwy from halfway, kept on for press, no threat to wnr:	1½	50a
268	**STANHOPE FORBES** 7 [9] N P Littmoden 3-8-12 (55) E Ahern 6/4 FAV: 506025-3: Held up in tch wide, no impress fnl 2f:	5	43a
283	**PARDON MOI** 4 [3] Mrs C A Dunnett 3-8-5 (49) Hayley Turner (5) 11/2: 60654-34: Chsd ldrs, no extra.	3½	25a
25	**LADY MO** 54 [10] Andrew Reid 3-8-3 (50) Rory Moore (7) 11/1: 436050-5: Led after 1f till over 2f out, fdd, abs.	¾	21a
200	**HES A ROCKET** 22 [5] Mrs C A Dunnett 3-8-8 vis (40) N Chalmers (5) 25/1: 000003-6: In tch till outpcd fnl 2f:	6	10a
258	**RED ROCKY** 8 [7] J Gallagher 3-8-3 (52) P Doe 11/2: 5655-7: Held up & swtchd wide, nvr a factor.	½	3a
4154}	**ARAGON DANCER** 118 [2] T M Jones 3-8-10 (40) R Brisland 25/1: 006-8: Led 1f, btn 3f out, abs/AW bow.	2½	2a
233	**COSTA DEL SOL** 17 [8] J J Bridger 3-8-4 (45) J Tate 12/1: 206005-9: Sn rdn rear, nvr a factor.	½	0a
9 Ran	1m 13.12 (2.72) Owner Swann Racing Ltd	Trained at Newark	

328
3.20 Littlewoodspoker Com Handicap Stakes 3yo+ 46-55 (F) **[55]**

£2961 £846 £423 **6f p/track rnd** **Going 45** **-03 Slow** Stalls Inside

219	**PRINCE AARON** 20 [10] C N Allen 4-9-13 (54) G Carter 6/1: 0P0062-1: Chsd ldrs till best place halfway, hmpd over 2f out, hdwy & drvn to lead well ins last:		63a
271	**TAYIF** 7 [12] Andrew Reid 8-9-11 t (52) S Carson 7/1: 600603-2: Dwelt, rear, drvn & styd on well ins last, just failed:	nk	60a
214	**SAVILES DELIGHT** 20 [7] R Brotherton 5-9-13 p (54) I Mongan 6/1: 302004-3: Trkd ldrs & rdn to lead over 1f out, hdd well ins last:	¾	60a
266	**ITS ECCO BOY** 7 [8] P Howling 6-9-12 (53) R Winston 7/2 FAV: 003640-4: Held up, hdwy wide to chall 2f out, no extra ins last:	hd	58a
270	**ZINGING** 7 [4] J J Bridger 5-9-11 (52) G Baker 13/2: 000310-5: Rear, eff wide, not able to chall dist:	2	51a
133	**NIGHT CAP** 35 [13] T D McCarthy 5-9-10 (51) J P Guillambert (3) 10/1: 005003-6: Chsd ldr, led over 2f out till over 1f out, sn wknd:	½	48a
2852}	**LOCH LAIRD** 178 [1] M Madgwick 9-9-10 (51) L Keniry (3) 20/1: 045135-7: Held up inner, nvr able to chall:	1	45a
183	**KINGS BALLET** 25 [6] P R Chamings 6-9-11 p (52) S Drowne 12/1: 000300-8: Trkd ldrs, no extra dist:	1	43a
4964}	**PATANDON GIRL** 67 [2] A Bailey 4-9-10 (51) S Hitchcott (3) 20/1: 605300-9: Chsd ldrs 5f, abs, new yard.	¾	40a
4446}	**FLYING TACKLE** 103 [9] M Dods 6-9-10 p (51) S W Kelly 14/1: 325003-0: Dwelt, rear, little hdwy:	hd	39a
187	**SAFRANINE** 25 [5] Miss A Stokell 7-9-11 p (52) Ann Stokell 16/1: 600000-0: Chsd ldrs till over 3f out:	3½	30a
41	**TOPPLING** 50 [11] J M Bradley 6-9-11 (52) Dane O'Neill 25/1: 000000-0: Led till over 2f out, btn dist, wknd.	3	21a
271	**IVORY VENTURE** 7 [3] D K Ivory 4-9-13 (54) R Miles (3) 40/1: 46/5400-0: Al bhd.	3	14a
2451}	**WARAQA** 193 [14] T M Jones 5-9-11 (54) C Catlin 20/1: 00/0006-0: Chsd ldrs, wknd qckly 2f out, new yard/abs.	1¾	7a
14 Ran	1m 13.30 (2.9) Owner Black Star Racing	Trained at Newmarket	

329
3.55 Press Interactive To Bet Direct Handicap Stakes 3yo+ 0-75 (E) **[73]**

£3360 £960 £480 **5f p/track rnd** **Going 45** **+03 Fast** Stalls Outside

149	**THE FISIO** 31 [5] A M Balding 4-9-7 (66) Martin Dwyer 8/1: 000000-1: Cl-up, led 2f out, drvn & held on well:		72a
4860*}	**MADRASEE** 75 [1] L Montague Hall 6-9-8 (67) R Miles (3) 5/2 FAV: 231021-2: Chsd ldrs, kept on for press, al held:	1	69a
292	**CURRENCY** 3 [10] J M Bradley 7-10-0 (73) S Drowne 25/1: 66000-03: Pushed along rear, styd on for press, not able to chall,	nk	74a

LINGFIELD Tuesday 06.01.04 Lefthand, V Sharp Track

qck reapp.

292	JUWWI 3 [8] J M Bradley 10-9-13 (72) C J Davies (6) 16/1: 40040-04: Slow away/bhd, nrst fin:			1¼	69a
231	GOODWOOD PRINCE 17 [2] S Dow 4-9-5 (64) P Doe 9/1: 060006-5: Held up in tch, onepace dist.			½	59a
4432}	OUR FRED 104 [4] T G Mills 7-9-11 bl (70) J Paulielo 20/1: 000306-6: Led 3f, btn dist, abs.			hd	64a
271	BYO 7 [6] M Quinn 6-9-6 (65) R Winston 4/1: 400444-7: Chsd ldrs, not able to chall:			shd	59a
231*	PANJANDRUM 17 [3] N E Berry 6-9-9 (68) M Savage (5) 11/2: 03/3001-8: Dwelt, sn chsd ldrs, btn dist:			¾	60a
3077}	TABOOR 167 [9] J W Payne 6-9-10 h bl (69) I Mongan 14/1: 041000-9: Mid-div wide, no impress dist:			nk	60a
155	GONENDUNNETT 31 [7] Mrs C A Dunnett 5-9-10 vis (69) Dane O'Neill 8/1: 004103-0: Drpd rear early, sn strugg.			2	54a
10 Ran	59.92 (2.12)	Owner Mr D H Caslon		Trained at Kingsclere	

SOUTHWELL Tuesday 06.01.04 Lefthand, Sharp, Oval Track

Official Going Standard

330 | 12.20 Bet Direct On Attheraces Interactive Amateur Riders' Handicap Stakes Div 1 4yo+ 0-65 (G [44])

£2891 £826 £413   1m3f f/sand   Going 54   -35 Slow   Stalls Inside

321	DAUNTED 1 [4] P A Blockley 8-11-0 (58) Miss S Renwick (7) 7/2: 21526/4-31: Cl-up, led dist, rdn out:				63a
84	OUR GLENARD 43 [3] S L Keightley 5-10-1 (45) Miss A L Turner (5) 11/2: 005005-2: Slow away, bhd, prog 4f out, outpcd 2f out, rallied fnl 1f, no ch with wnr:			3	45a
257	INTERSTICE 10 [2] A G Newcombe 7-10-7 (51) Miss C Hannaford 3/1 FAV: 300000-3: Mid-div, prog & ev ch dist, sn onepcd:			hd	50a
259	LAZZAZ 8 [1] P W Hiatt 6-11-4 (62) Mrs Marie King (5) 11/2: 013300-4: Led, hdd under press dist, sn no extra:			hd	60a
250	SHATIN SPECIAL 11 [10] G C H Chung 4-9-7 p (40) Mr T Thomas (7) 6/1: 040402-5: Handy, ev ch dist, sn no extra.			1½	35a
3493}	NOBLE CYRANO 150 [7] Jedd O'Keeffe 9-9-5 (35) Miss J Waring (7) 12/1: 500600-6: Slow away, rear:			8	18a
34	ROYAL AXMINSTER 53 [5] Mrs P N Dutfield 9-9-10 (40) Miss A Wallace (5) 12/1: 031605-7: Bhd, nvr able to chall:			8	11a
309	WESTERN COMMAND 126 [6] Mrs N Macauley 8-9-3 3oh (30) Mrs M Morris 20/1: 005550-8: Nvr nr ldrs.			4	0
4701}	GOODENOUGH STAR 86 [9] A P Jones 4-9-7 (40) Mr Wayne Lewis (5) 50/1: 0600-9: In tch, fdd 4f out:			¾	4a
4582}	CHRISTMAS TRUCE 95 [8] Ian Williams 5-11-11 4ow p (65) Mr Michael Murphy 25/1: 000000-0: Mid-div, wknd 10f out:			24	3a
10 Ran	2m 31.1 (9.8)	Owner Mrs Joanna Hughes		Trained at Southwell	

331 | 12.50 Bet Direct On Attheraces Interactive Amateur Riders' Handicap Stakes Div 2 4yo+ 0-65 (G [41])

£2884 £824 £412   1m3f   Going 54   -48 Slow   Stalls Inside

4690}	SQUIRTLE TURTLE 86 [7] P F I Cole 4-11-7 bl (65) Mr O Cole (7) 11/1: 003503-1: Led, hdd dist, rallied well under press to regain lead cl-home:				69a
307*	DELTA FORCE 2 [3] P A Blockley 5-10-10 (51) Mr M Scales (5) 7/4 FAV: 356031-12: Chsd wnr, ev ch dist, hung left under press ins fnl 1f, just held:			nk	53a
244	KENTUCKY BULLET 15 [4] A G Newcombe 8-10-7 (48) Miss C Hannaford 4/1: 610425-3: Handy, styd on to lead dist, hdd cl-home:			hd	49a
196*	SPANISH STAR 22 [1] Mrs N Macauley 7-10-5 (46) Mrs S Moore (3) 7/2: 400041-4: Slow away, prog 5f out, outpcd 4f out, rallied fnl 1f:			1½	45a
56	PASO DOBLE 49 [8] B R Millman 6-11-7 (62) Mr J Millman (5) 14/1: 424000-5: In tch, no extra fnl 1f:			1	59a
4646}	NIGHT MAIL 91 [9] M W Easterby 4-9-10 (40) Mr C Collins (7) 16/1: 0044U0-6: Slow away, rear, nvr nrr than mid-div:			3½	32a
3056}	BRIERY MEC 169 [2] H J Collingridge 9-9-8 p (35) Miss A L Hutchinson 20/1: 00/0000-7: In tch, fdd 4f out:			6	18a
4567}	ABRACADABJAR 96 [6] Miss Z C Davison 6-9-12 9ow (30) Miss G D Gracey Davison 50/1: 000000-8: Cl-up, fdd 4f out:			9	9a
170	SILVER CRYSTAL 28 [5] Mrs N Macauley 4-10-3 VIS (47) Mr M Morris 16/1: 306450-9: Al bhd:			15	0
9 Ran	2m 32.54 (11.24)	Owner Mrs P F I Cole		Trained at Whatcombe	

332 | 1.25 Bet Direct Press Red To Bet Stakes Handicap Fillies 4yo+ 0-75 (E) [71]

£3367 £1036 £518 £259   1m f/sand rnd   Going 54   -01 Slow   Stalls Inside

170*	NAJAABA 28 [6] Miss J Feilden 4-8-12 (56) B Reilly (5) 2/1: 60/0431-1: Held up, prog 3f out, led dist, pushed clr fnl 1f, val 8L+:				70a
163	ELLEN MOONEY 29 [7] B Smart 5-9-12 p (70) R Ffrench 15/8 FAV: 021502-2: In tch, ev ch dist, sn no impress on wnr:			6	71a
255*	ESTIMATION 10 [1] R M H Cowell 4-9-11 (69) N Callan 5/1: 113651-3: Bhd, prog 4f out, ev ch dist, sn no extra:			nk	69a
967}	INCHCOONAN 276 [3] K R Burke 6-9-4 (62) Darren Williams 10/1: 454424-4: Chsd ldrs, fdd 2f out:			8	46a
129	POOKAS DAUGHTER 38 [2] J M Bradley 4-8-5 (49) S Whitworth (5) 33/1: 420000-5: Led 7f out, hdd & fdd dist:			2	30a
	SOFT MIST 114 [4] J J Quinn 4-9-3 (61) T Eaves (5) 20/1: 061200-6: Handy, fdd 3f out:			1	40a
199*	NUZZLE 22 [5] M Quinn 4-9-0 vis (58) A Culhane (5) 10/1: 360631-7: Led 1f, in tch, fdd 3f out:			5	27a
7 Ran	1m 43.83 (4.43)	Owner Mr A K Sparks		Trained at Newmarket	

333 | 2.00 Littlewoods Bet Direct Handicap Stakes 3yo 0-90 (C) [86]

£8028 £2470 £1235 £618   6f f/sand rnd   Going 54   +04 Fast   Stalls Inside

223*	BLOFELD 18 [6] W Jarvis 3-8-11 (69) Lisa Jones (3) 13/8 FAV: 005511-1: In tch, styd on to lead cl home, pushed out:				76a
158	MUY BIEN 29 [2] J R Jenkins 3-9-3 vis (75) B Reilly (5) 5/2: 500152-2: Trkd ldrs, led 2f out, sn hung left under press, hdd cl-home:			½	79a
223	FOXIES FUTURE 18 [1] J R Weymes 3-8-2 (60) J Quinn 18/1: 610504-3: Slow away, prog 3f out, onepcd fnl 1f:			5	49a
182	BRIDGEWATER BOYS 25 [4] K A Ryan 3-8-11 bl (69) N Callan 14/1: 256215-4: Ld fnl, sn fdd:			3	49a
105	POMPEY BLUE 41 [3] P J McBride 3-8-13 (71) Paul Scallan 5/1: 235515-5: Cl-up, fdd fnl 2f:			4	39a
197*	SCOTTISH EXILE 22 [7] K R Burke 3-8-12 vis (70) Darren Williams 7/1: 440231-6: Trkd ldrs, fdd 4f out:			17	3a
169	FISSION 28 [5] J A Osborne 3-9-7 bl (79) L Fletcher (3) 10/1: 414513-W: Ref to enter stalls & withdrawn start.				0
7 Ran	1m 16.35 (3.05)	Owner Byculla Thoroughbreds		Trained at Newmarket	

334 | 2.35 Betdirect Co Uk Maiden Stakes 4yo+ (D)

£3406 £1048 £524 £262   1m f/sand rnd   Going 54   -04 Slow   Stalls Inside

4989}	ALLIED VICTORY 64 [3] E J Alston 4-9-0 (73) J Quinn 4/6 FAV: 230324-1: Held up, short of room 3f out, swtched & prog 2f				66a

out, led ins fnl 1f, drvn out:

221	**MAGIC MAMMAS TOO** 18 [2] T D Barron 4-9-0 (53) D Mernagh 7/2: 343226-2: Led, clr 2f out, hdd cl-home:		nk	64a
	NOW AND AGAIN [6] M W Easterby 5-9-0 Dale Gibson 33/1: 3: Slow away, sn handy, outpcd 3f out, mod late gains:		8	48a
199	**CHESNUT RIPPLE** 22 [5] D Shaw 5-8-9 (48) R Havlin 9/1: 406625-4: In tch, hung left & wknd dist, lame.		hd	42a
1974}	**MING THE MERCILESS** 214 [1] J G Given 4-9-0 (63) A Culhane 14/1: 30/6000-5: Handy, fdd fnl 2f:		1½	45a
89	**BRIAR** 43 [4] M Pitman 5-9-0 p V Slattery 40/1: 6/30/0-6: Al bhd:		11	24a
75	**MARGOLD** 46 [7] R Hollinshead 4-8-9 (55) N Callan 20/1: 033306-7: Cl-up, fdd 3f out:		8	5a
7 Ran	1m 44.08 (4.68) Owner Honest Traders		Trained at Preston	

335

3.10 Bet Direct On 0800 32 93 93 Selling Stakes 3yo+   (G)

£2569 £734 £367   **5f f/sand str**   **Going 54**   **+01 Fast**   Stalls Outside

312	**CARK** 1 [9] J Balding 6-9-6 p (45) L Fletcher (3) 13/2: 000400-61: Handy, led dist, rdn out:			50a
183	**SOAKED** 25 [1] D W Chapman 11-9-6 bl (55) A Culhane 5/2 FAV: 500350-2: Cl-up, led 3f out, hdd dist, kept on fnl 1f, just held by wnr:		½	50a
166	**FESTIVE AFFAIR** 28 [6] B Smart 6-9-6 (51) R Ffrench 4/1: 164300-3: In tch, kept on fnl 1f, not extra far:		½	49a
242	**LADY PROTECTOR** 15 [8] J Balding 5-9-1 (40) P Makin (7) 20/1: 000060-4: Sn handy, no extra fnl 1f.		2	38a
286	**MR SPLIFFY** 4 [10] K R Burke 5-9-6 vis (47) A Reilly (7) 7/1: 20004-05: Cl-up, no extra dist:		1½	39a
253*	**LADIES KNIGHT** 10 [7] D Shaw 4-9-12 (56) T Hamilton (5) 9/2: 000001-6: Slow away, outpcd when stumbled 3f out, modest late gains:		½	44a
286	**FIENNES** 4 [4] Mrs N Macauley 6-9-6 vis (45) Steven Harrison (7) 14/1: 00563-07: Rear, nvr a factor:		½	37a
312	**LONE PIPER** 1 [5] J M Bradley 9-9-6 (45) B Reilly (5) 25/1: 000056-08: Slow away, prog 3f out, eased when no impress ins fnl 1f:		2½	30a
286	**SALERNO** 4 [2] Miss Gay Kelleway 5-9-6 bl (50) T Eaves (5) 14/1: 40000-09: Led, hdd 3f out, sn fdd:		5	16a
9 Ran	1m 0.46 (2.66) Owner Mr J E Abbey		Trained at Doncaster	

336

3.45 Littlewoodscasino Com Handicap Stakes 4yo+ 0-65 (F)   **[64]**

£2905 £830 £415   **2m f/sand**   **Going 54**   **-36 Slow**   Stalls Inside

277	**VANBRUGH** 6 [2] Miss D A McHale 4-9-8 vis t (65) Darren Williams 7/1: 660226-1: Slow away, sn in tch, led 6f out, rdn clr:			78a
277*	**PHANTOM STOCK** 6 [1] W Jarvis 4-8-12 6ex (55) M Tebbutt 4/6 FAV: 000/061-2: Rear, prog 1m out, chsd wnr 4f out, edged left & no impress on wnr fnl 1f:		7	61a
4620}	**JAMAICAN FLIGHT** 92 [3] Mrs S Lamyman 11-9-2 (52) J Quinn 22/1: 136450-3: Led 10f, fdd 3f out:		9	49a
206*	**VINCENT** 21 [10] John A Harris 9-8-10 (46) R Ffrench 9/2: 450611-4: Held up, nvr nrr than mid-div:		1	42a
277	**HAJEER** 6 [7] P W Hiatt 6-8-9 (45) Lisa Jones (3) 25/1: 300000-5: Cl-up, wknd 6f out:		12	29a
125	**LAPADAR** 38 [9] J R Weymes 5-9-4 bl (54) T Hamilton (5) 80/1: 605050-6: Al bhd:		26	20a
4359}	**MINIVET** 108 [5] T D Easterby 9-9-8 (58) D Allan (3) 33/1: 0//60054-7: Slow away, sn cl-up, fdd 6f out:		½	20a
156	**MADHAHIR** 31 [8] C A Dwyer 4-9-5 VIS (62) N Callan 20/1: 040620-8: Cl-up, fdd 4f out:		12	12a
194	**FORTUNES FAVOURITE** 24 [4] G M Moore 4-8-5 (48) N Pollard 18/1: 045-9: In tch, fdd 5f out:		dist	0a
9 Ran	3m 40.48 (14.48) Owner Mr N Bashir		Trained at Newmarket	

Official Going Standard

337

12.20 Littlewoods Bet Direct Handicap Stakes 3yo 0-75 (E)   **[80]**

£3474 £1069 £535 £267   **7f p/track rnd**   **Going 61**   **-07 Slow**   Stalls Inside

29	**DESERT IMAGE** 54 [4] C Tinkler 3-9-2 (68) E Ahern 14/1: 0330-1: Held up inner, hdwy over 2f out & rdn to lead well ins last:			72a
220	**FOOLS ENTIRE** 21 [5] J A Gilbert 3-9-2 (68) B Reilly (5) 7/1: 001322-2: Chsd ldrs, rdn & chsd ldr over 1f out, not pace of wnr cl-home:		¾	69a
4577}	**RESPLENDENT KING** 96 [1] T G Mills 3-9-5 (71) Dane O'Neill 8/1: 03040-3: Chsd ldrs, rdn & kept on fnl 2f, not pace of wnr:		nk	71a
4863}	**HEAD BOY** 76 [8] S Dow 3-8-7 (59) P Doe 25/1: 000510-4: Held up, hdwy over 2f out, nrst fin:		½	58a
258	**PHLUKE** 9 [6] R F Johnson Houghton 3-9-7 (73) S Carson 7/1: 622432-5: Cl-up & led halfway, drvn over 1f out, no extra when hdd well ins last:		1	70a
189	**THE JOB** 25 [11] A D Smith 3-8-10 (62) W Ryan 10/1: 040014-6: Dwelt, rear, late gains, no danger.		4	51a
158	**MAUNBY RAVER** 30 [13] P C Haslam 3-9-0 (66) Rory Moore (7) 8/1: 641215-7: Towards rear, mod late prog:		1	53a
4561}	**GAYLE STORM** 97 [14] C Tinkler 3-8-11 (63) J Quinn 33/1: 6536-8: Dwelt, rear, short of room over 1f out, kept on late:		1	48a
261	**JANGO MALFOY** 9 [15] B W Duke 3-8-9 (61) M Fenton 25/1: 00050-9: Rear, little hdwy for press.		nk	45a
289	**PREGNANT PAUSE** 4 [7] S Kirk 3-8-13 (65) A Culhane 9/2 FAV: 02402-40: Prom till over 1f out:		¾	47a
217	**KNIGHT ONTHE TILES** 21 [2] J R Best 3-9-3 bl (69) D Fentiman (7) 14/1: 141060-0: Keen & prom till dist.		hd	50a
13	**ASK THE CLERK** 56 [10] H J Collingridge 3-9-6 P (72) M Tebbutt 8/1: 643030-0: Keen, held up wide, btn 2f out.		¾	51a
3265}	**LORD BASKERVILLE** 160 [16] M G Quinlan 3-9-1 (67) V Slattery 50/1: 4030-0: Mid-div, no impress fnl 2f:		¾	44a
4411}	**TREVIAN** 106 [3] S C Williams 3-9-4 (70) Martin Dwyer 16/1: 056-0: Led till halfway, sn btn:		½	45a
29	**AMONG DREAMS** 54 [12] J A Osborne 3-9-0 (66) S W Kelly 8/1: 153-0: Al towards rear:		¾	39a
15 Ran	1m 27.54 (4.74) Owner Mr George Ward		Trained at Compton	

338

12.50 Bet Direct On 0800 32 93 93 Maiden Stakes 4yo+   (D)

£3523 £1084 £542 £271   **1m2f p/track**   **Going 61**   **-12 Slow**   Stalls Inside

179	**JACK OF TRUMPS** 28 [2] G Wragg 4-9-0 (80) S Drowne 6/4 FAV: 006/3-1: Mid-div inner, pushed along over 2f out, rdn to lead well ins last, shade cmftbly:			66a
174	**CORONADO FOREST** 28 [12] M R Hoad 5-9-2 (58) Dane O'Neill 14/1: 226060-2: Rear, styd on wide from over 2f out, drvn & narrow lead ins last, sn hdd & not pace of wnr:		1¼	60a
2931}	**MY LILLI** 175 [8] P Mitchell 4-8-9 (48) J Quinn 33/1: 430000-3: Chsd ldr halfway, rdn & led 3f out, hdd ins last, no extra:		1¼	52a
3314}	**BLAZING THE TRAIL** 159 [9] J W Hills 4-9-0 (70) S Whitworth 15/1: 0030-4: Mid-div, prog/chsd ldr 2f out, no extra dist:		1½	54a

287	GIVEMETHEMOONLIGHT 5	[7] Mrs Stef Liddiard 5-8-11 (51) C Catlin 9/2: 32422-25: Mid-div, onepc:	hd	48a
3943}	WIZARD OF EDGE 132	[3] G B Balding 4-9-0 (70) S Carson 6/1: 25/3-6: Held up, outpcd 3f out, late gains, abs.	½	52a
269	GOLDEN DUAL 8	[5] S Dow 4-9-0 (73) P Doe 14/1: 304365-7: Mid-div, eff wide, no extra dist.	shd	52a
1588}	OPERASHAAN 234	[10] G L Moore 4-9-0 (56) A Culhane 16/1: 0/600-8: Prom wide, btn 2f out:	2½	47a
1430}	CURZON LODGE 243	[1] C Tinkler 4-9-0 E Ahern 8/1: 0-9: Rear, no impress fnl 2f:	5	38a
263	UNSUITED 9	[4] J E Long 5-8-11 (53) R Miles (3) 66/1: 0/065500-0: Sn rear, no ch fnl 2f.	3	27a
199	MOUNT LOGAN 23	[6] R Curtis 9-9-2 Martin Dwyer 66/1: 0///0-0: Led 1f, chsd ldr till halfway.	7	20a
	SHOW ME HEAVEN 1628	[14] T T Clement 7-8-11 M Tebbutt 66/1: 06////0-0: Slow away, sn bhd, v long abs.	7	3a
	BENNANABAA 11	[11] S C Burrough 5-9-2 T W Ryan 20/1: 0: led/dsptd lead 7f, wknd, lame:	½	7a

13 Ran   2m 10.08 (7.28)   Owner Mollers Racing   Trained at Newmarket

---

339   1.20 Bet Direct Press Red To Bet Handicap Stakes 4yo+ 0-60 (F)   [60]
£3059 £874 £437   1m2f p/track   Going 61   -05 Slow   Stalls Inside

230*	GOLD GUEST 18	[10] P D Evans 5-10-0 (60) S Donohoe (7) 6/1 CO FAV: 600441-1: Held up, hdwy 3f out & rdn/led dist, sn in command:		67a
144	HE WHO DARES 32	[14] A W Carroll 6-9-11 (57) S Whitworth 15/2: 401012-2: Dwelt, keen rear, styd on wide for press fnl 2f, no threat to wnr:	2½	58a
230	WELSH WIND 18	[2] M Wigham 8-9-10 t (56) D R McCabe 6/1 CO FAV: 003042-3: Trkd ldrs, onepace dist.	hd	56a
4828}	STOLEN SONG 78	[6] M J Ryan 4-9-10 (58) Martin Dwyer 7/1: 403352-4: Chsd ldr, rdn & led 3f out, hdd & no extra dist:	shd	58a
215	EMBER DAYS 21	[5] J L Spearing 5-9-9 (55) E Ahern 8/1: 0/05522-5: Mid-div, onepace fnl 2f:	½	54a
4704}	ARCHIRONDEL 87	[3] M D Hammond 6-9-9 (55) A Culhane 11/1: 556030-6: Rear, late gains for press:	1	52a
215	CASTAIGNE 21	[13] B W Duke 5-9-8 t (54) M Fenton 14/1: 240020-7: Dwelt, rear, short of room 2f out, no dngr.	1½	50a
265	MUYASSIR 9	[4] Miss B Sanders 9-9-10 (56) S Drowne 16/1: 300100-8: Rear, hdwy to press ldrs over 1f out, sn no extra.	¾	51a
259	COOLFORE JADE 9	[12] N E Berry 4-9-9 (57) M Savage (5) 16/1: 140045-9: Cl-up 3f out, wknd dist:	¾	51a
287	SCOTTISH RIVER 5	[11] M D I Usher 5-9-13 (59) A Daly 14/1 CO FAV: 00003-30: Wide/rear, btn over 1f out:	nk	52a
251	MISS GLORY BE 12	[9] Miss Gay Kelleway 6-9-8 p (54) T Eaves (5) 12/1: 323006-0: Trkd ldrs, wknd over 1f out.	5	40a
215	HARLOT 21	[8] John Berry 4-9-10 p (58) Lisa Jones (5) 25/1: 400003-0: Keen & led till 3f out, sn btn:	1¾	42a
151	PENNY PIE 32	[7] P W Harris 4-9-12 VIS (60) N Callan 16/1: 353000-0: Held up, no ch when no room 2f out:	¾	43a
160	MAUNBY ROCKER 30	[1] P C Haslam 4-9-9 (57) Rory Moore (7) 33/1: 4/01260-0: Mid-div, btn 3f out.	3½	35a

14 Ran   2m 09.42 (6.62)   Owner Diamond Racing Ltd   Trained at Abergavenny

---

340   1.50 Bet On All Weather Classified Claiming Stakes 3yo+ 0-60 (F)
£2940 £840 £420   6f p/track rnd   Going 61   +11 Fast   Stalls Inside

328	TAYIF 1	[10] Andrew Reid 8-9-9 t (52) S Carson 2/1 FAV: 600603-21: Rear, hdwy halfway & led ins last, rdn clr:		64a
271	TRIPTI 8	[12] J J Bridger 4-9-2 (53) N Pollard 14/1: 060406-2: Cl-up & drvn/led over 2f out, hdd ins last & no extra:	3	47a
216	XSYNNA 21	[8] P S McEntee 8-9-3 vis (45) F P Ferris (3) 40/1: 030000-3: Led 4f, kept on onepace	1¼	44a
227	POLAR HAZE 19	[2] Mrs Lydia Pearce 7-9-7 vis (45) J F McDonald (5) 8/1: 004102-4: Chsd ldrs, onepace dist.	½	46a
271	A TEEN 8	[7] P Howling 6-9-11 (52) R Winston 16/1: 561000-5: Rear, some hdwy for press, no danger.	nk	49a
263	ADANTINO 9	[11] B R Millman 5-9-13 (48) G Baker 7/1: 056053-6: Rear/wide, only mod prog:	½	49a
266	HARBOUR HOUSE 8	[1] J J Bridger 5-9-7 (45) J Tate 6/1: 000020-7: Dwelt, nvr able to chall:	½	41a
263	DEFINITELY SPECIAL 9	[5] N E Berry 6-9-4 (40) M Savage (5) 20/1: 600000-8: Mid-div, outpcd from halfway.	hd	37a
296	FLYING FAISAL 4	[4] J M Bradley 6-9-3 (45) P Fitzsimons 25/1: 56000-09: Chsd ldrs 4f, quick reapp.	2½	28a
133	KILMEENA STAR 36	[13] J C Fox 6-9-3 (40) P Dobbs 25/1: 030306-0: Rear, no ch fnl 2f.	4	16a
271	CARGO 8	[9] H J Collingridge 5-9-5 (47) E Ahern 25/1: 000005-0: Mid-div wide, btn 2f out.	1	15a
216	RATHMULLAN 21	[3] E A Wheeler 5-9-3 p (40) Liam Jones (7) 11/2: 5/00000-0: Dwelt, sn bhd.	1	10a
4027}	GENTLE RESPONSE 127	[6] C A Dwyer 4-9-2 (45) S Whitworth 25/1: 520000-0: Prom, wknd qckly 2f out, abs.	nk	8a

13 Ran   1m 13.37 (2.97)   Owner Mr A S Reid   Trained at Mill Hill London

---

341   2.20 Betdirect Co Uk Handicap Stakes 3yo 0-85 (D)   [88]
£4433 £1364 £682 £341   1m p/track rnd   Going 61   -10 Slow   Stalls Outside

220*	WHITGIFT ROCK 21	[1] S Dow 3-8-11 (71) P Doe 5/1: 405631-1: Trkd ldrs, led over 1f out, drvn & held on all out:		77a
229*	SKIDMARK 18	[7] D R C Elsworth 3-9-5 (79) P Fitzsimons 6/4 FAV: 31-2: Dwelt, hld up, styd on well ins last, just failed:	hd	84a
4370}	ROYAL WARRANT 109	[3] A M Balding 3-9-6 (80) Martin Dwyer 7/1: 4310-3: Held up, rdn & kept on well cl-home, just held:	hd	84a
203*	BLUE EMPIRE 22	[5] P C Haslam 3-9-1 (75) L Enstone (3) 9/2: 01021-4: Keen, trkd ldrs, rdn to chall over 1f out, hung left & no extra cl-home:	nk	78a
252	COUNTRYWIDE FLYER 11	[4] T D Barron 3-9-7 BL (81) N Callan 8/1: 342114-5: Keen & cl-up, led over 3f out, hdd & wknd qckly over 1f out:	9	68a
88	FREDDIE FRECCLES 44	[2] J G Given 3-8-10 (70) M Fenton 40/1: 10-6: Led 5f, sn btn:	9	41a
232*	BOXGROVE 18	[6] C E Brittain 3-9-6 (80) A Culhane 9/1: 361-7: Cl-up, wknd qckly over 1f out:	¾	50a

7 Ran   1m 41.85 (5.65)   Owner Whitgift Racing   Trained at Epsom

---

342   2.50 Bet Direct Freephone 0800 32 93 93 Handicap Stakes 4yo+ 0-70 (E)   [70]
£3381 £966 £483   1m5f p/track   Going 61   -30 Slow   Stalls Inside

147	MAYSTOCK 32	[8] G A Butler 4-9-7 vis (68) L Treadwell (7) 8/1: D04140-1: Keen, hdwy to trk ldrs 3f out & led over 2f out, sn rdn clr, cmftbly:		79a
4755}	JADEERON 84	[4] Miss D A McHale 5-8-11 p (53) Lisa Jones (3) 11/1: 214400-2: Prom till pace 4f out, rallied for press fnl 2f, no ch with easy wnr:	5	57a
243	AMBERSONG 16	[14] A W Carroll 6-8-9 (51) A Culhane 8/1: 014220-3: Keen in mid-div, eff wide from 3f out, kept on onepace:	½	54a
147	BIG BERTHA 32	[3] John Berry 6-9-10 (66) G Baker 7/2 FAV: 416623-4: Mid-div, onepace fnl 2f.	1¼	67a
259	RAHEEL 9	[2] P Mitchell 4-8-6 t (53) W Ryan 20/1: 002060-5: Keen, rear, short of room over 1f out, nvr a threat.	5	47a
236	ZAWRAK 18	[12] I W McInnes 5-9-5 (61) Natalia Gemelova (7) 16/1: 00003-6: Prom wide, led 4f out till over 2f out, no extra:	1¼	53a
272	LANDESCENT 8	[5] M Quinn 4-8-6 (53) J Quinn 25/1: 042660-7: Dictated pace till 4f out, lost place qckly:	1	44a

LINGFIELD Wednesday 07.01.04 Lefthand, V Sharp Track

2858*}	BEECHY BANK 179 [6] Mrs Mary Hambro 6-10-0 (70) V Slattery 16/1: 6/01/431-8: Keen & cl-up, no impress fnl 2f:	nk	60a
259*	ROYAL PRODIGY 9 [11] R J Hodges 5-9-13 6ex (69) Dane O'Neill 5/1: 301311-9: Rear, no ch fnl 2f:	nk	58a
259	MAKARIM 9 [13] M R Bosley 8-9-1 p (57) Hayley Turner (5) 12/1: 040063-0: Cl-up 4f out, sn wknd:	hd	45a
259	RADIANT BRIDE 9 [9] K R Burke 4-7-13 1ow p (45) C Catlin 50/1: 500250-0: Rear, no ch fnl 4f:	1¼	32a
72	FAIRY WIND 47 [7] B J Curley 7-8-6 (48) W M Lordan 14/1: 000020-0: Cl-up, wknd qckly 4f out, abs.	4	28a
218	DANEHILL LAD 21 [1] T Keddy 4-9-5 (66) S Drowne 4/1: 022226-P: Rear when pulled up 4f out, lame.		0a
13 Ran	2m 54.12 (11.82) Owner Stock Hill Racing		Trained at Blewbury

343 3.20 Bet Direct In Running Sky Text 293 Selling Stakes 4yo+ (G)
£2639 £754 £377   1m p/track rnd   Going 61   -10 Slow   Stalls Outside

4944}	FRENCH HORN 70 [4] M J Ryan 7-9-0 p (50) Martin Dwyer 13/2: 630000-1: Rear, smooth hdwy from 2f out, rdn to lead well ins last:		52a
272	WILOM 8 [9] M R Hoad 6-9-0 (45) M Fenton 8/1: 053403-2: Rear, smooth hdwy from 2f out, led over 1f out, no extra when hdd well ins last:	¾	48a
216	FEAST OF ROMANCE 21 [10] P Howling 7-9-0 p (50) R Winston 6/1: 020336-3: Rear, rdn to chall over 1f out, no extra cl-home:	2	46a
4433}	DILIZA 105 [2] G B Balding 5-8-9 (49) R Thomas (5) 5/1: 532050-4: In tch, outpcd 3f out, late gains.	hd	40a
272	TINIAN 8 [5] K R Burke 6-9-5 P (57) Darren Williams 7/1: 161530-5: Keen & led/dsptd lead till over 1f out:	5	41a
191	PERTEMPS BIANCA 25 [7] A D Smith 4-8-9 bl (45) J Quinn 66/1: 0/54006-6: Dwelt, rear, eff 2f out, sn btn.	5	23a
267	LADYWELL BLAISE 8 [12] J J Bridger 7-8-9 (45) J Tate 14/1: 000064-7: Trkd ldrs, wknd qckly 3f out.	1¼	19a
263	ISLAND STAR 9 [3] S Dow 4-9-0 (52) P Doe 14/1: 400060-8: Keen/dsptd lead 5f, wknd qckly.	½	14a
266	DANCING FOREST 8 [6] D K Ivory 4-9-0 (66) Dane O'Neill 9/4 FAV: 200000-9: Slow away, mid-div wide, btn 3f out.	3½	17a
298	ALMOND BEACH 4 [8] B J Meehan 4-9-0 bl (65) D R McCabe 50/1: 0/5000-00: Led/dsptd lead 3f, btn 2f out.	3	11a
	NOD N A WINK [1] C A Dwyer 4-9-0 N Callan 40/1: 0: Slowly away, sn chsd ldrs, btn halfway.	21	0
11 Ran	1m 41.84 (5.64) Owner Mr M J Ryan		Trained at Newmarket

344 3.50 Bet Direct Football Cashbacks Handicap Stakes 3yo+ 46-55 (F) [55]
£3045 £870 £435   7f p/track rnd   Going 61   -00 Slow   Stalls Inside

45 :·}	NEARLY A FOOL 100 [1] G G Margarson 6-9-12 vis (53) N Pollard 4/1 JT FAV: 160353-1: Made all, prsd from over 1f out, held on all out, gamely:		61a
266	KINSMAN 8 [4] T D McCarthy 7-9-10 bl (51) J P Guillambert (3) 16/1: 500600-2: Dwelt, rear, strong run fnl 1f, just failed:	shd	58a
263	MAYZIN 9 [6] R M Flower 4-9-10 p (51) E Ahern 4/1 JT FAV: 000054-3: Keen, trkd ldrs, styd on well for press cl-home, just:	hd	57a
5029}	ALAFZAR 61 [15] P D Evans 6-9-11 vis (52) S Donohoe (7) 13/2: 400040-4: Rear, styd on for press fnl 2f, nrst fin:	nk	56a
4062}	LUCID DREAMS 125 [16] M Wigham 5-9-11 (52) D R McCabe 8/1: 501240-5: Cl-up, no extra well ins last, abs.	1	55a
144	TAIYO 32 [13] J W Payne 4-9-11 (52) Paul Eddery 12/1: 602006-0: Held up, eff 2f out, onepace.	1¼	52a
202	PANCAKEHILL 22 [10] D K Ivory 5-9-12 (53) R Miles (3) 10/1: 236550-7: Trkd ldrs, no extra over 1f out.	hd	52a
3947}	SCARROTTOO 132 [3] S C Williams 6-9-13 (54) B Reilly (5) 12/1: 645340-8: Trkd ldrs, no extra dist.	shd	53a
248	PIROUETTES 12 [12] Miss Gay Kelleway 4-10-0 (55) T Eaves (5) 14/1: 304340-9: Prom, fdd under press dist:	½	51a
4027}	ANGELICA GARNETT 127 [8] T E Powell 4-9-11 (52) J Quinn 8/1: 006/000-0: Held up, eff 2f out, no impress.	hd	49a
230	MISTER CLINTON 18 [7] D K Ivory 7-9-12 (53) Dane O'Neill 7/1: 410000-0: Rear, nvr a factor.	nk	49a
4181}	VIZULIZE 118 [11] A W Carroll 5-9-12 (53) S Whitworth 33/1: 405540-0: Keen, rear, no impress, jumps fit.	½	48a
144	SOCIAL CONTRACT 32 [14] S Dow 7-9-11 (52) Paul Eddery 12/1: 602006-0: Dwelt, mid-div, btn 2f out.	¾	45a
117	TUSCAN TREATY 39 [2] T T Clement 4-9-10 (51) J Mackay 40/1: 100000-0: Dwelt, no ch fnl 2f.	7	30a
14 Ran	1m 27.05 (4.25) Owner Mr J Burns		Trained at Newmarket

WOLVERHAMPTON Thursday 08.01.04 Lefthand, Sharp Track

Official Going SLOW.

345 1.10 Betdirect Co Uk Handicap Stakes Div 1 4yo+ 0-75 (E) [73]
£3387 £1042 £521 £261   6f f/sand rnd   Going 63   -37 Slow   Stalls Outside

254*	WAINWRIGHT 12 [5] P A Blockley 4-9-3 (62) D Nolan (5) 5/1: 235331-1: Cl-up, led dist, all out to hold on:		67a
168	GERONIMO 30 [6] Miss Gay Kelleway 7-8-12 p (57) J Quinn 8/1: 606020-2: Held up, prog 2f out, styd on well fnl 1f, just:	shd	60a
92	MR PERTEMPS 44 [4] R A Fahey 6-8-10 (55) T Hamilton (5) 9/2 JT FAV: 131100-3: Handy, led 3f out, hdd dist, kept on fnl 1f, just held:	nk	57a
245*	ST IVIAN 13 [3] Mrs N Macauley 4-9-9 vis (68) P McCabe 12/1: 600051-4: In tch, ev ch dist, no extra fnl 1f:	2½	63a
155	TIME N TIME AGAIN 33 [8] E J Alston 6-9-9 (68) D Allan (3) 5/1: 340542-5: Trkd ldrs, short of room & lost place 3f out, rallied dist:	½	62a
274	NEVER WITHOUT ME 8 [9] P J McBride 4-8-2 (47) Dale Gibson 9/2 JT FAV: 50022-6: Mid-div, prog 3f out, wknd fnl 1f:	¾	39a
149	TURN AROUND 33 [7] B W Hills 4-9-7 (66) E Ahern 7/1: 10/0000-7: Bhd, nvr nrr than mid-div:	1¼	54a
246*	NOBLE LOCKS 13 [2] J W Unett 6-10-0 (73) Carlo Bandiera (7) 9/1: 010051-8: Mid-div, wknd 2f out:	10	36a
246	PRINCE OF BLUES 13 [1] M Mullineaux 6-9-8 (67) Lisa Jones (5) 20/1: 000060-9: In tch, wknd 2f out:	½	29a
149	TELEPATHIC 33 [10] A Berry 4-9-7 (66) B P Bradley (5) 40/1: 600000-0: Led 3f out, fdd:	nk	27a
10 Ran	1m 18.80 (6.0) Owner Mr David Wright		Trained at Southwell

346 1.40 Bet Direct On Sky Active Apprentice Handicap Stakes 3yo+ 0-70 (G) [68]
£2604 £744 £372   1m100y f/sand rnd Going 63   -38 Slow   Stalls Outside

225	OVIGO 20 [3] P A Blockley 5-9-11 (65) Derek Nolan (5) 11/4: 000330-1: Held up, prog & hung left 2f out, led trav well ins fnl 1f, pushed out, val 3L+:		71a
287*	ROCK CONCERT 6 [4] I W McInnes 6-9-8 6ex (62) Natalia Gemelova (3) 2/1 FAV: 22132-12: Led, edged right under press dist, hdd ins fnl 1f, no extra:	1¼	62a
208	SPY GUN 23 [5] T Wall 4-9-6 (60) N Chalmers 4/1: 0/00014-3: Cl-up, hung left dist, onepcd fnl 1f.	2½	56a

WOLVERHAMPTON Thursday 08.01.04 Lefthand, Sharp Track

251* **MUTARAFAA 13** [2] D Shaw 5-9-4 e (58) T Hamilton 11/4: 022211-4: Cl-up, fdd dist: 5 **43a**
303 **T K O GYM 4** [1] D Nicholls 5-8-5 (45) J F McDonald 14/1: B3620-05: Handy, fdd 2f out: 10 **12a**
5 Ran 1m 54.74 (8.54) Owner The Dilum Partnership Trained at Southwell

347 **2.10 Bet Direct On 0800 32 93 93 Claiming Stakes 4yo+ (F)**
£2919 £834 £417 **1m4f f/sand** **Going 63** **-49 Slow** Stalls Outside

156 **PARADISE VALLEY 33** [7] Mrs Stef Liddiard 4-8-7 t (45) C Catlin 11/2: 514525-1: Held up, prog 3f out, led ins fnl 1f, rdn out: **52a**
185 **CLAPTRAP 27** [4] R Brotherton 4-8-9 (59) F P Ferris (3) 7/2: 460015-2: Held up, prog 5f out, led ins fnl 1f, sn hdd & no extra: 1 **51a**
4918*} **DANCING PHANTOM 72** [6] James Moffatt 9-9-7 (77) S Hitchcott (3) 9/4: 0/06521-3: Cl-up, led 6f out, hdd & no extra ins fnl 1f: 1½ **57a**
250 **EL PEDRO 13** [1] N E Berry 5-9-3 (45) M Savage (5) 40/1: 054005-4: Bhd, prog 6f out, ev ch dist, sn fdd: 6 **44a**
1882} **YOUNG OWEN 220** [3] Mrs L B Normile 6-8-7 (70) J Quinn 14/1: 54200-5: Cl-up, fdd 3f out: 8 **22a**
250 **LA ROSE 13** [8] J W Unett 4-7-12 vis (35) Lisa Jones (3) 66/1: 566200-6: Held up, nvr a factor. 1¾ **14a**
1975*} **INVER GOLD 216** [5] A G Newcombe 7-9-7 (74) S Whitworth 2/1 FAV: 5/52601-7: Led, hdd 5f out, sn fdd: 18 **8a**
1223} **LOVES DESIGN 255** [2] Miss S J Wilton 7-8-9 (52) J Tate 33/1: 013350-8: Keen cl-up, fdd 4f out: 23 **0**
8 Ran 2m 47.14 (13.54) Owner Valley Fencing Trained at Hungerford

348 **2.40 Littlewoods Bet Direct Maiden Stakes 4yo+ (D)**
£3227 £922 £461 **5f f/sand rnd** **Going 63** **+02 Fast** Stalls Outside

23 **MYND 56** [3] R M Whitaker 4-9-0 (58) Dean McKeown 3/1: 050034-1: Led, hdd bef 1f out, rallied well under press to lead again cl-home: **68a**
242 **BLUEBERRY RHYME 17** [6] P J Makin 5-9-0 vis (68) D Sweeney 1/1 FAV: 00/3423-2: Cl-up, led bef 1f out, edged right under press & hdd cl-home: *nk* **66a**
254 **LUCIUS VERRUS 12** [8] D Shaw 4-9-0 (50) T Hamilton (5) 8/1: 0434-3: Outpcd, prog 2f out, onepcd fnl 1f. 3½ **56a**
254 **INCHING 12** [2] R M H Cowell 4-8-9 (51) E Ahern 7/2: 064626-4: Handy, onepcd fnl 2f: *nk* **50a**
313 **SOMETHINGABOUTHER 3** [5] P W Hiatt 4-8-9 (40) C Catlin 20/1: 00500-45: In tch, fdd 2f out: 8 **28a**
4103} **ETERNAL BEAUTY 124** [1] M J Wallace 4-8-9 S Drowne 12/1: 060-6: Al bhd: 7 **8a**
4623} **VELOCITYS IMAGE 94** [4] E J Alston 4-8-9 (40) D Allan (3) 40/1: 060-7: Al in rear: *hd* **7a**
7 Ran 1m 3.27 (3.07) Owner Derek and Jean Clee Trained at Scarcroft

349 **3.10 Betdirect Co Uk Handicap Stakes Div 2 4yo+ 0-75 (E)** **[73]**
£3387 £1042 £521 £261 **6f f/sand rnd** **Going 63** **+01 Fast** Stalls Outside

4991} **SOBA JONES 66** [2] J Balding 7-9-7 (66) J Edmunds 6/1: 000052-1: Cl-up, led 2f out, pushed clr fnl 1f, val 7L+: **76a**
275 **PLAYTIME BLUE 8** [1] K R Burke 4-9-0 (59) G Baker 12/1: 144002-2: In tch, prog 2f out, no impress on wnr fnl 1f: 5 **60a**
205 **RAFTERS MUSIC 23** [5] Julian Poulton 9-9-13 (72) N Callan 7/1: 254326-3: Sn outpcd, prog 2f out, kept on fnl 1f, no ch with front 2: *nk* **72a**
129 **LADY NATILDA 40** [6] D Haydn Jones 4-8-3 (48) Paul Eddery 33/1: 045000-4: Sn bhd, prog 2f out, kept on late: ½ **47a**
205 **NEW OPTIONS 23** [4] W J Musson 7-9-8 bl (67) M Fenton 13/8 FAV: 230004-5: Handy, no extra when short of room ins fnl 1f: ¾ **64a**
274* **LADY PEKAN 8** [7] P S McEntee 5-9-4 6ex bl (63) F P Ferris (3) 8/1: 000141-6: Led 4f, wknd fnl 1f: *nk* **59a**
183 **OUR CHELSEA BLUE 27** [3] A W Carroll 6-8-11 (56) S Whitworth 10/1: 000660-7: Dwelt, prog & ev ch 2f out, fdd fnl 1f. 1¾ **47a**
329 **GONENDUNNETT 33** [10] Mrs C A Dunnett 5-9-10 vis (69) N Chalmers (5) 8/1: 004103-8: In tch, wknd 2f out: 1 **57a**
245 **BLAKESHALL QUEST 13** [8] R Brotherton 4-9-7 (66) C Catlin 33/1: 000000-9: In tch, fdd 2f out. 1¾ **49a**
113 **IF BY CHANCE 41** [9] R Craggs 6-9-9 (68) S Hitchcott (3) 7/1: 500105-0: In tch, wknd 2f out: 1 **48a**
10 Ran 1m 16.52 (3.72) Owner Mr R L Crowe Trained at Doncaster

350 **3.40 Allweather-Racing Com Selling Stakes 4yo+ (G)**
£2597 £742 £371 **7f f/sand rnd** **Going 63** **-30 Slow** Stalls Outside

298 **STAR LAD 5** [1] R Brotherton 4-8-11 vis (47) F P Ferris (3) 14/1: 00606-31: Made all, under press when left clr 1f out, rdn out: **48a**
298* **REPEAT 5** [2] Miss Gay Kelleway 4-8-11 (51) M Fenton 10/11 FAV: 14064-12: Handy, no impress in 3rd when left 2nd ins fnl 1f: 3½ **43a**
304 **TEFI 4** [4] J Balding 6-8-11 bl t (45) J Edmunds 33/1: 26060-03: Cl-up, fdd dist: 3 **37a**
180 **SENOR MIRO 29** [3] J Akehurst 6-8-11 (54) C Catlin 6/5: 3/00433-P: Chsd ldrs, ev ch & trav best dist, likely wnr but sn p.u., sadly died. **0**
4 Ran 1m 32.72 (6.52) Owner Mr R Austin & Mrs P Austin Trained at Pershore

351 **4.10 Free #25 Bonus @ Littlewoodspoker Com Handicap Stakes 3yo 0-65 (F)** **[71]**
£3290 £940 £470 **1m1f79y f/sand** **Going 63** **-04 Slow** Stalls Outside

190 **YANKEEDOODLEDANDY 26** [4] P C Haslam 3-8-2 (45) D Fentiman (7) 5/2 FAV: 04004-1: Handy, led 1f out, pushed clr fnl 1f: **60a**
279 **BRETTON 8** [9] R Hollinshead 3-8-2 bl (45) Dale Gibson 6/1: 500544-2: Led 7f out, hdd under press 1f out, sn no impress on wnr: 7 **49a**
192 **CASSANOS 26** [2] Miss Gay Kelleway 3-9-0 (57) M Fenton 4/1: 0000-3: Led 1f, sn drpd to mid-div, nvr able to chall: 8 **46a**
43 **KELTIC RAINBOW 52** [7] D Haydn Jones 3-9-1 (58) Paul Eddery 3/1: 0033-4: Held up, hdwy 4f out, wknd 3f out: 4 **39a**
132 **RUMOUR MILL 37** [5] N E Berry 3-9-5 P (62) M Savage (5) 33/1: 0000-5: In tch, hung left & fdd dist: 2½ **38a**
213 **LIMIT DOWN 22** [8] M J Wallace 3-9-0 (57) S Drowne 13/2: 00005-6: Cl-up, fdd 3f out: *shd* **32a**
4814} **LADY BAHIA 80** [6] R P Elliott 3-9-7 (64) T Woodley 14/1: 00240-7: Dwelt, led after 1f, sn hdd, fdd 3f out. 6 **28a**
203 **ONE ALONE 23** [3] J G Given 3-8-6 (49) Joanna Badger 20/1: 0000-8: Al bhd. 2½ **8a**
4960} **TORTUETTE 69** [1] Jean Rene Auvray 3-8-2 (45) Lisa Jones (3) 33/1: 03000-9: Al in rear: ½ **3a**
9 Ran 2m 4.51 (6.31) Owner Mr K Tyre Trained at Middleham

SOUTHWELL Thursday 08.01.04 Lefthand, Sharp, Oval Track

Official Going Standard

SOUTHWELL Thursday 08.01.04 Lefthand, Sharp, Oval Track

352 **1.20 Bet Direct On Sky Active Amateur Riders' Banded Stakes 4yo+ 0-40 (H)**
£1278 £365 £183 **6f f/sand rnd** **Going 74** **-40 Slow** Stalls Inside

3447} **MOUNT SUPERIOR 154** [1] P W D'Arcy 8-11-0 bl (40) Miss R D'Arcy (7) 10/1: 0/500/66-1: Rdn mid-div, hdwy under hands & heels over 1f out, led well ins last, going away: **42a**
308 **AGUILA LOCO 4** [4] M C Chapman 5-11-0 (40) Mr B King (5) 6/4 FAV: 00000-32: Trkd ldrs, led over 1f out, rdn & hdd ins last, no extra: *1¼* **39a**
310 **LEMARATE 3** [6] D W Chapman 7-11-0 bl (40) Miss Kelly Harrison (5) 8/1: 60000-33: Chsd ldrs, drvn & kept on onepace: *½* **37a**
296 **THREAT 5** [2] J M Bradley 8-11-0 (40) Miss E J Jones 9/1: 20000-04: Mid-div, not able to chall. *1¼* **34a**
253 **ABOVE BOARD 12** [5] R F Marvin 9-11-0 (35) Miss A L Turner (5) 20/1: 500000-5: Chsd ldrs, no impress fnl 2f. *1* **32a**
4456} **HOME COMING 104** [7] P S Felgate 6-11-0 VIS (35) Mr M Mackley (5) 20/1: 600000-6: Led, hung left under press & hit rail over 2f out, sn hdd & fdd: *1¾* **28a**
286 **ALLERTON BOY 6** [9] R J Hodges 5-11-0 (40) Mr James White (7) 9/2: 00000-47: Led over 2f out till over 1f out. *3* **21a**
4102} **MOON ROYALE 124** [10] Mrs N Macauley 6-11-0 (30) Mrs M Morris 9/1: 062500-8: Al bhd, abs. *1¾* **17a**
3101} **BATCHWORTH BREEZE 168** [11] E A Wheeler 6-11-0 (30) Mr C Witheford (7) 40/1: 0/60/000-9: Chsd ldrs wide 3f, abs. *nk* **16a**
85 **AUNT DORIS 45** [3] Paul Johnson 7-11-0 P (35) Mr P Evans (5) 25/1: 40500/0-0: Dwelt & al bhd: *5* **4a**
10 Ran 1m 20.11 (6.81) Owner Mr Paul D'Arcy Trained at Newmarket

353 **1.50 Press Interactive To Bet Direct Claiming Stakes 4yo+ (H)**
£1271 £363 £182 **1m4f f/sand** **Going 74** **-05 Slow** Stalls Inside

321 **KING PRIAM 3** [2] M J Polglase 9-9-7 bl (35) L Fletcher (3) 100/30: 4000-041: Made all, strongly prsd over 2f out, drvn & styd on strongly, in command ins last: **49a**
250 **IPLEDGEALLEGIANCE 13** [1] D W Chapman 8-9-3 (46) A Culhane 7/2: 004560-2: Trkd ldrs trav well, rdn to chall 2f out, no extra fnl 1f: *3½* **42a**
301 **ROPPONGI DANCER 5** [4] Mrs N Macauley 5-8-12 bl t (30) Stephanie Hollinshead (7) 14/1: 06400-53: Chsd ldrs, no impress on front pair fnl 3f: *16* **17a**
1580] **FIRST CLASS GIRL 595** [8] C B B Booth 5-9-2 M H Naughton 50/1: 0/-4: Held up, lost tch fnl 4f, abs. *9* **10a**
305 **SEA YA MAITE 4** [5] S R Bowring 10-9-3 t (30) L Enstone (3) 25/1: 03000-05: Trkd ldrs wide halfway, btn 3f out. *½* **10a**
4756] **POLISH BARON 435** [7] J White 7-9-7 (70) R Fitzpatrick 2/1 FAV: 312110/-6: V slowly away & well bhd, no ch after: *9* **4a**
4644} **COPPLESTONE 93** [6] W Storey 8-9-5 p (30) J Bramhill 6/1: 0/26565-7: Sn bhd, jumps fit. *11* **0**
4623} **OOS AND AHS 94** [3] C W Fairhurst 4-8-6 T Williams 25/1: 0-8: Cl-up till 5f out: *26* **0**
185 **MAWHOOB 27** [9] Mrs N Macauley 6-9-3 vis (45) Steven Harrison (7) 16/1: 000000-9: Sn rdn rear, no ch halfway. *dist* **0**
9 Ran 2m 43.72 (9.42) Owner Mr M J Polglase Trained at Newark

354 **2.20 Littlewoods Bet Direct Banded Stakes 3yo+ 0-45 (H)**
£1670 £477 £239 **1m f/sand rnd** **Going 74** **-03 Slow** Stalls Inside

303* **ROSTI 4** [6] P C Haslam 4-9-8 (45) Rory Moore (7) 5/4 FAV: 00054-11: Trkd ldrs, led 2f out, held on well for press: **50a**
309 **SIMPLY THE GUEST 4** [2] Don Enrico Incisa 5-9-8 t (35) Kim Tinkler 8/1: 00000-22: Towards rear, hdwy from halfway, styd on for press, not reach wnr: *¾* **47a**
4739} **DIAMOND ORCHID 86** [3] P D Evans 4-9-8 (45) S Donohoe (7) 11/2: 000062-3: Chsd ldrs, eff 2f out, onepace: *1¼* **45a**
309* **PRINTSMITH 4** [11] J R Norton 7-10-0 (35) J Bramhill 7/1: 00005-14: Mid-div, styd on onepace fnl 2f: *1¼* **47a**
302 **TROPICAL SON 5** [1] D Shaw 5-9-8 vis (40) Darren Williams 16/1: 00000-25: Trkd ldrs halfway, onepace. *1¼* **38a**
199 **DESIRES DESTINY 24** [10] M Brittain 6-9-8 (45) M Lawson (7) 25/1: 6600-6: Handy & led 3f out till 2f out, fdd: *1¼* **35a**
199 **SANTA CATALINA 24** [12] Miss Gay Kelleway 5-9-8 t (45) T Eaves (5) 12/1: 0/00603-7: Al bhd: *9* **20a**
4960} **REGENCY MALAYA 69** [13] M F Harris 3-8-2 BL t (45) S Righton 40/1: 000600-8: Sn rdn/wide, nvr a factor: *1¾* **17a**
14 **BYINCHKA 57** [5] S L Keightley 4-9-8 VIS (45) A Nicholls 33/1: 006040-9: Led, hdd 3f out, wknd: *hd* **17a**
223 **PEACE TREATY 20** [15] S R Bowring 3-8-4 2ow (45) N Pollard 50/1: 05000-0: Sn bhd. *6* **8a**
4854} **PEARTREE HOUSE 78** [7] D W Chapman 10-9-8 (45) A Culhane 14/1: 200000-0: Al bhd, abs. *9* **0a**
194 **DR JULIAN 26** [9] Miss A Stokell 4-9-8 vis (45) Ann Stokell 50/1: 005000-0: Dwelt & al bhd. *3* **0a**
309 **HAITHEM 4** [8] D Shaw 7-9-8 e (40) T Williams 25/1: 50000-60: Sn struggling, qck reapp. *8* **0a**
84 **BETTER PAL 45** [14] P R Wood 5-9-8 (45) L Keniry (3) 66/1: 000000-0: Chsd ldrs 4f, wknd qckly, abs. *20* **0a**
14 Ran 1m 45.53 (6.13) Owner Exors of Late BM Hawkins/Lord Trained at Middleham

355 **2.50 Betdirect Co Uk Median Auction Maiden Stakes 3-5yo (H)**
£1477 £422 £211 **1m f/sand rnd** **Going 74** **-00 Slow** Stalls Inside

252 **COTTINGHAM 12** [2] M C Chapman 3-8-5 (58) Stephanie Hollinshead (6) 11/4: 400040-1: Trkd ldrs, led 2f out, rdn clr over 1f out, styd on strongly: **69a**
162 **TURKS AND CAICOS 31** [8] P C Haslam 3-8-4 (58) Rory Moore (7) 9/4 FAV: 040-2: Trkd ldrs, smooth prog to lead briefly over 2f out, sn rdn & not pace of wnr: *4* **59a**
GALLOWAY MAC [5] W A O'Gorman 4-9-10 M Tebbutt 12/1: 3: Slow away & bhd, smooth hdwy wide to chase ldrs 3f out, no extra fnl 2f: *7* **48a**
4327} **PAPPY 111** [3] J G Given 3-7-13 (52) J Bramhill 5/1: 003500-4: Cl-up, wknd qckly 2f out: *15* **16a**
299 **LILIAN 5** [6] Miss Gay Kelleway 4-9-5 vis (46) T Eaves (5) 8/1: 46022-65: Led, hdd 3f out, fdd: *½* **16a**
166 **AMANDAS LAD 30** [1] M C Chapman 4-9-10 (40) Andrew Webb (7) 14/1: 000030-6: Trkd ldrs, no impress fnl 2f. *9* **6a**
3308} **MANASHIN 160** [4] B Smart 4-9-5 R Ffrench 33/1: 00-7: Chsd ldrs 5f, sn struggling. *2* **0a**
238 **CASANTELLA 17** [7] M J Polglase 3-8-1 2ow vis (47) A Nicholls 9/1: 000036-8: Chsd ldrs till 3f out. *5* **0a**
8 Ran 1m 45.32 (5.92) Owner Twinacre Nurseries Ltd Trained at Market Rasen

356 **3.20 Bet Direct Football Cashbacks Banded Stakes 3yo+ 0-45 (H)**
£1663 £475 £238 **7f f/sand rnd** **Going 74** **+08 Fast** Stalls Inside

304 **SANDORRA 4** [1] M Brittain 6-9-8 (45) M Lawson (7) 14/1: 0/5000-31: Made all, rdn clr over 1f out, held on well: **47a**
242 **EAGER ANGEL 17** [12] R F Marvin 6-9-8 p (45) Dean McKeown 16/1: 000630-2: Held up, kept on for press fnl 2f, not threaten wnr: *1¾* **44a**

300	**NEWCLOSE** 5 [5] N Tinkler 4-9-8 t (45) A Culhane 2/1 FAV: 00500-33: Held up, drvn to chase ldrs 2f out, sn no extra:		3½	37a
303	**BRILLIANTRIO** 4 [10] M C Chapman 6-9-8 (45) Andrew Webb (7) 100/30: 06505-24: Mid-div wide, onepace, no dngr:		¾	36a
303	**CHAMPAGNE RIDER** 4 [2] D Shaw 8-9-8 e (40) Darren Williams 13/2: 50000-35: Chsd wnr 3f out, sn no impress.		1½	33a
303	**JESSIE** 4 [3] Don Enrico Incisa 5-9-8 (45) Kim Tinkler 12/1: 00400-56: Slow away & bhd, eff halfway, sn no prog.		11	14a
304	**LANDOFHEARTSDESIRE** 4 [9] J S Wainwright 5-9-8 vis (45) T Eaves (5) 25/1: 06000-67: Chsd ldrs wide 5f, qck reapp.		6	4a
298	**GLENVIEWS POLLY** 5 [13] Ian Emmerson 4-9-8 (45) L Keniry (3) 20/1: 00600-68: Dwelt & al towards rear, qck reapp.		1¾	1a
309	**FORMERIC** 4 [8] Miss L C Siddall 8-9-8 vis (35) J McAuley 66/1: 00000-09: Mid-div, btn halfway, qck reapp.		½	0a
3847}	**CARONTE** 137 [4] S R Bowring 4-9-8 bl (40) J Bramhill 33/1: 600600-0: Prom till 2f out, abs.		13	0
4961}	**STARTLED** 69 [6] J Jay 5-9-8 (40) M Tebbutt 20/1: 6000/00-0: Sn bhd, abs.		8	0
253	**NEW PROSPECTIVE** 12 [7] D Nicholls 6-9-8 (45) A Nicholls 12/1: 630300-0: Cl-up 5f, eased, dismounted.		1½	0
254	**GRANUAILE OMALLEY** 12 [11] P W D'Arcy 4-9-8 (45) S W Kelly 10/1: 060030-0: Dwelt, sn struggling.		27	0
13 Ran	1m 31.2 (4.6) Owner Mr Mel Brittain			Trained at Warthill

---

357
3.50 Bet Direct In Vision Sky Page 293 Banded Stakes 4yo+ 0-40 (H)
£1453 £415 £208   1m6f f/sand   Going 74   -23 Slow   Stalls Inside

305	**PADDY MUL** 4 [4] W Storey 7-9-4 t (35) D R McCabe 9/4: 5/4626-21: Trkd ldrs, smooth hdwy from halfway & rdn/led over 1f out, just held on, all out:			41a
307	**KAGOSHIMA** 4 [3] J R Norton 9-9-4 vis (40) V Halliday 7/2: 00060-22: Handy & led halfway, drvn & hdd over 1f out, rallied gamely for press, just held:		hd	40a
1061}	**IRELANDS EYE** 269 [1] J R Norton 9-9-4 (30) J Bramhill 9/1: 60/460//0-: Chsd ldrs 4f out, no impress fnl 2f:		9	33a
307	**KYALAMI** 4 [7] M J Polglase 5-9-4 e (30) L Fletcher (3) 7/2: 00/0/60-34: Slowly away, sn lost tch:		17	19a
67	**CHARNWOOD STREET** 50 [5] D Shaw 5-9-4 vis (40) Darren Williams 7/2: 446050-5: Led 4f, prom till 5f out.		17	5a
305	**KITTYLEE** 4 [6] M A Buckley 5-9-4 P (30) R Ffrench 40/1: 0000/0-06: Sn bhd, qck reapp, cheek pieces.		3	2a
305	**MARENGO** 4 [8] Paul Johnson 10-9-4 (35) L Treadwell (7) 25/1: 40600-07: Keen & trkd ldrs, led after 4f till halfway.		18	0
7 Ran	3m 13.44 (13.64) Owner Gremlin Racing			Trained at Consett

---

WOLVERHAMPTON Friday 09.01.04 Lefthand, Sharp Track

Official Going STANDARD.

358
1.10 Bet Direct On Sky Active Amateur Riders' Handicap Stakes 4yo+ 0-65 (F)   [44]
£2919 £834 £417   2m46y f/sand   Going 35   -58 Slow   Stalls Inside

336	**PHANTOM STOCK** 3 [6] W Jarvis 4-10-4 6ex (55) Mr N Pearce (7) 6/4 FAV: 00/061-21: Held up, smooth hdwy 4f out, rdn & in command dist, hands & heels:			65a
257	**MARMADUKE** 13 [2] M Pitman 8-11-3 (61) Mr S Bosley 11/2: 51631/6-2: Led after 1f till over 2f out, kept on for press:		5	65a
336	**VINCENT** 3 [11] John A Harris 9-10-2 (46) Mrs M Morris 7/1: 50611-43: Held up, styd on for press fnl 4f, not pace of wnr:		2½	48a
2771}	**BUSTLING RIO** 183 [10] P C Haslam 8-11-5 (63) Ms C Williams 7/1: 031560-4: Held up, eff 3f out, not able to chall:		1½	64a
4071}	**JOELY GREEN** 126 [7] N P Littmoden 7-11-1 bl (59) Mrs Emma Littmoden (3) 14/1: 030435-5: Dwelt & held up, eff 6f out, no prog fnl 3f:		2½	58a
315	**FAIRMORNING** 4 [8] J W Unett 5-9-10 (40) Miss J C Williams 5/1: 55443-26: Chsd ldr 5f out, wknd:		19	24a
243*	**ADALPOUR** 18 [1] D Burchell 6-10-8 (52) Miss E Tucker (7) 13/2: 613301-7: Slowly away, sn mid-div, wknd 4f out.		12	27a
257	**MOYNE PLEASURE** 13 [3] Paul Johnson 6-10-1 (45) Mr P Evans (7) 20/1: 024450-8: Prom 1m, sn bhd.		26	0a
330	**CHRISTMAS TRUCE** 3 [5] Ian Williams 5-11-9 2ow p (65) Mr Michael Murphy (2) 33/1: 00000-09: Led/dsptd lead 11f.		3½	18a
3529}	**MIGHTY MAX** 511 [9] G A Ham 6-9-10 t (40) Mr G Denvir (5) 50/1: 000064-/0-: In tch till 6f out, t.o.:		26	0a
10 Ran	3m 44.09 (14.89) Owner The L E H Partnership			Trained at Newmarket

---

359
1.40 Press Interactive To Bet Direct Maiden Stakes 4yo+ (D)
£3426 £1054 £527 £264   1m4f f/sand   Going 35   -39 Slow   Stalls Inside

259	**COOL BATHWICK** 11 [3] B R Millman 5-9-4 (56) Martin Dwyer 11/1: 000/000-1: Led/dsptd lead, went on over 3f out, rdn & styd on strongly fnl 2f:			60a
269	**RETAIL THERAPY** 10 [8] M A Buckley 4-8-9 (35) R Ffrench 25/1: 0/00006-2: Bhd, styd on for press fnl 3f, nvr threatened wnr:		3½	50a
	MUNFARID 189 [7] P G Murphy 4-9-0 T (75) S Drowne 7/2: 004454-3: Held up, smooth hdwy 4f out, rdn & chsd wnr 2f out, no impress dist:		½	54a
2731}	**BESTSELLER** 185 [10] J G M O'Shea 4-8-9 R Havlin 20/1: 0-4: Prom, no extra dist.		2	46a
1009}	**LUXI RIVER** 95 [1] P A Blockley 4-9-0 (66) D Nolan (5) 3/1 FAV: 452/64-5: Cl-up 3f out, wknd.		2½	47a
321	**EXIT TO HEAVEN** 4 [4] Miss Gay Kelleway 4-8-9 (58) M Fenton 4/1: 00225-06: Keen rear, outpcd fnl 4f.		2	39a
16	**ESTIMATE** 58 [6] John A Harris 4-8-9 (60) S Whitworth 9/2: 026264-7: Held up, no impress fnl 3f:		3½	34a
194	**SEANS MEMORY** 27 [2] Mrs C A Dunnett 4-9-0 C Catlin 40/1: 0-8: Held up, no ch fnl 4f, t.o.		1½	37a
347	**YOUNG OWEN** 1 [9] Mrs L B Normile 6-9-4 (70) E Ahern 7/1: 54200-59: Slow away, sn led till 3f out, wknd qckly.		20	15a
4968}	**JUST RED** 69 [5] R Hollinshead 6-9-4 A Culhane 25/1: 50-0: Held up, no ch fnl 4f, t.o.		2	12a
10 Ran	2m 42.51 (8.91) Owner Mr W Clifford			Trained at Cullompton

---

360
2.10 Littlewoods Bet Direct Conditions Stakes 4yo+ (C)
£7186 £2726 £1363 £620   1m100y f/sand rnd   Going 35   -05 Slow   Stalls Inside

5030}	**HAIL THE CHIEF** 62 [7] D Nicholls 7-9-0 (100) A Nicholls 11/2: 110/650-1: Prom & led over 2f out, rdn clr over 1f out:			97a
278	**LAKOTA BRAVE** 9 [8] Mrs Stef Liddiard 10-9-0 (90) S Drowne 5/2: 331225-2: In tch, rdn & styd on fnl 2f, no threat to wnr:		4	87a
262	**ACTION FIGHTER** 11 [5] N P Littmoden 4-9-0 P (93) J P Guillambert (3) 20/1: 251000-3: Led till over 2f out, no extra fnl 1f:		1¾	85a
278	**LUNDYS LANE** 9 [1] C E Brittain 4-9-0 (90) E Ahern 5/1: 134600-4: Held up, eff 4f out, rdn & no impress fnl 2f.		3	89a
81	**GOLDEN CHALICE** 48 [1] A M Balding 4-9-0 (88) Martin Dwyer 15/8 FAV: 000520-5: Chsd ldr, btn 2f out:		2½	73a
318	**FIRST MAITE** 4 [4] S R Bowring 11-9-0 (71) J Bramhill 14/1: 30602-66: Rdn & struggling 4f out:		2½	68a
548}	**MIDSHIPMAN** 338 [6] A W Carroll 6-9-0 (92) Paul Scallan 12/1: 111/20/0-7: Sn rdn & al bhd:		7	56a
4515}	**MUQTADI** 102 [3] M Quinn 6-9-0 (51) R Winston 100/1: 214650-8: Bhd, lost tch halfway:		dist	0

96

WOLVERHAMPTON Friday 09.01.04 Lefthand, Sharp Track

8 Ran   1m 49.64 (3.44)   Owner Mr Peter M Crane   Trained at Thirsk

361 **2.40 Bet Direct On 0800 32 93 93 Stakes Handicap 3yo+ 0-100 (C)**   [98]
£10192 £3136 £1568 £784   **6f f/sand rnd**   **Going 35**   **+12 Fast**   Stalls Inside

235	**MASSEY** 20 [3] T D Barron 8-9-6 (90) D Mernagh 6/1: 120000-1: Made all, edged right & held on well for press fnl 1f:		96a
81	**FLINT RIVER** 48 [6] H Morrison 6-8-11 (81) L Fletcher (3) 5/2 FAV: 200210-2: Chsd ldrs, outpcd bef halfway, rdn & kept on fnl 2f, nvr threatened wnr:	1¼	83a
171*	**ZARZU** 31 [7] C R Dore 5-9-1 (85) R Thomas (5) 13/2: 102541-3: Rear, rdn & kept on onepace fnl 2f.	shd	87a
64	**BOND BOY** 51 [2] B Smart 7-9-6 (90) C Catlin 12/1: 362000-4: Trkd ldrs, rdn & onepace from dist:	nk	91a
171	**BOND PLAYBOY** 31 [12] B Smart 4-9-5 (89) R Ffrench 6/1: 000012-5: Prom, no extra dist:	2	85a
292	**NO TIME** 6 [13] M J Polglase 4-8-13 (83) E Ahern 7/1: 00000-66: Chsd ldrs, no impress fnl 1f:	3½	70a
235	**TRINCULO** 20 [8] N P Littmoden 7-9-8 p (92) J P Guillambert (3) 16/1: 000160-7: Bhd, eff wide, no prog dist:	1½	75a
198	**CANTERLOUPE** 25 [10] P J Makin 6-8-12 (82) D Sweeney 9/1: 330516-8: Prom till over 1f out:	½	63a
262	**HAND CHIME** 11 [5] W J Haggas 7-9-3 (87) Danielle Deverson (7) 12/1: 460003-9: Dwelt, nvr pace to chall:	shd	68a
262	**SUNDRIED TOMATO** 11 [4] P W Hiatt 5-9-1 (85) Lisa Jones (3) 11/1: 000000-0: Prom, lost place halfway:	1	64a
4667}	**FLYING TREATY** 91 [1] Miss A Stokell 7-9-4 (88) Ann Stokell 50/1: 030040-0: Chsd ldrs, struggling halfway, abs.	5	55a
2674}	**BEAUVRAI** 188 [9] J J Quinn 4-9-6 (90) R Winston 25/1: 1/00000-0: Well bhd 2f out:	11	33a

12 Ran   1m 13.87 (1.07)   Owner Mr J Edward Boynton   Trained at Thirsk

362 **3.10 Bet Direct On Sky Text Page 371 Selling Stakes 4yo+ (G)**
£2947 £842 £421   **1m100y f/sand rnd Going 35**   **-26 Slow**   Stalls Inside

4809}	**DAIMAJIN** 81 [3] Miss Gay Kelleway 5-9-0 T (55) M Fenton 5/1: 000000-1: Dwelt, sn in tch, drvn to lead cl-home:		58a
320	**HEADLAND** 4 [8] D W Chapman 6-9-5 bl (68) A Culhane 11/2: 00041-42: Keen & handy trav well, led over 4f out, rdn/hung left ins last & hdd nr fin:	1¼	59a
311	**SUDRA** 4 [10] J O'Reilly 7-9-0 BL (53) J D O'Reilly (7) 7/1: 00000-33: In tch, cl-up halfway, onepace & held fnl 2f:	2½	49a
311*	**ALLY MAKBUL** 4 [9] J R Best 4-9-0 (51) N Pollard 10/11 FAV: 01000-14: Chsd ldrs, rdn & no impress 3f out, mod late rally:	¾	49a
267	**TORO BRAVO** 10 [2] R M Beckett 4-9-0 bl (60) M Tebbutt 16/1: 000000-5: Bhd, little hdwy:	1¼	46a
251	**JUNGLE LION** 14 [7] John A Harris 6-9-0 t (47) S Whitworth 33/1: 0/60600-6: Bhd, hung left & lkd a difficult ride from 3f out:	hd	44a
300	**MABEL RILEY** 6 [1] M A Buckley 4-8-9 VIS (45) S W Kelly 20/1: 00000-57: Prom, btn 2f out:	shd	40a
287	**FORTY FORTE** 7 [6] Miss S J Wilton 8-9-0 p (55) J Tate 7/1: 00020-08: Led till over 4f out, sn btn:	6	32a

8 Ran   1m 51.35 (5.15)   Owner Simon Mapletoft Racing I   Trained at Newmarket

363 **3.40 Bet Direct In Vision Sky Page 293 Handicap Stakes 4yo+ 0-75 (E)**   [73]
£3455 £1063 £532 £266   **7f f/sand rnd**   **Going 35**   **-13 Slow**   Stalls Outside

280	**ARC EL CIEL** 9 [4] Mrs Stef Liddiard 6-10-0 vis (73) S Drowne 5/2 FAV: 300162-1: Chsd ldrs halfway, drvn to lead cl-home, all out:		77a
251	**YORKER** 14 [9] Ms Deborah J Evans 6-9-9 (68) N Callan 10/1: 010020-2: Chsd ldrs, short of room & lost place over 3f out, rallied well on inner fnl 2f, just failed:	hd	70a
280*	**WARDEN WARREN** 9 [1] Mrs C A Dunnett 6-9-13 6ex bl (72) B Reilly (5) 8/1: 000021-3: Keen & cl-up, narrow lead ins last, drvn & hdd cl-home:	shd	73a
251	**DANIELLES LAD** 14 [8] B Palling 8-9-6 bl (65) M Fenton 11/2: 003005-4: In tch, rdn to chall over 1f out, onepace fnl 100y:	1	65a
280	**GREY PEARL** 9 [3] Miss Gay Kelleway 5-9-13 (72) T Eaves (5) 11/2: 040534-5: Led till over 1f out, no extra nr fin:	nk	71a
285	**BLONDE EN BLONDE** 7 [5] N P Littmoden 4-9-6 (65) J P Guillambert (3) 8/1: 03534-66: Mid-div, drvn & not pace to chall:	3½	57a
280	**SPARK UP** 9 [7] J W Unett 4-9-5 bl (64) M Henry 16/1: 061266-7: Held up, short of room & drpd rear 3f out.	3	50a
255	**BARZAK** 13 [6] S R Bowring 4-9-7 BL (66) J Bramhill 16/1: 001005-8: Held up, eff wide 3f out, no prog dist:	shd	52a
202*	**PAWN IN LIFE** 24 [10] T D Barron 6-9-3 (62) D Mernagh 4/1: 225051-9: Cl-up halfway, btn 3f out:	¾	47a
186	**WHIPPASNAPPER** 28 [4] J R Best 4-9-6 (65) N Pollard 20/1: 060000-0: Keen & prom till 3f out:	¾	49a
70	**MARABAR** 49 [11] D W Chapman 6-9-11 (70) A Culhane 16/1: 255005-0: Sn rdn & al bhd:	14	29a

11 Ran   1m 29.55 (3.35)   Owner Shefford Valley Stud   Trained at Hungerford

---

LINGFIELD Saturday 10.01.04 Lefthand, V Sharp Track

Official Going Standard

364 **12.10 Bet Direct No Q Maiden Stakes 3yo (D)**
£3799 £1169 £585 £292   **6f p/track rnd**   **Going 39**   **-14 Slow**   Stalls Inside

283	**EVER CHEERFUL** 8 [6] W G M Turner 3-9-0 P (67) L Treadwell (7) 11/2: 34346-21: Keen & cl-up, led over 1f out, drvn out:		75a
258	**SAVIOURS SPIRIT** 12 [7] T G Mills 3-9-0 (72) I Mongan 6/4 FAV: 0053-2: Chsd ldrs, styd on for press, not pace of wnr:	1¾	71a
4758}	**ROYAL PAVILLION** 86 [10] W J Musson 3-9-0 Paul Eddery 5/1: 0-3: Led, hdd over 1f out, kept on for press:	nk	70a
	SIERA SPIRIT [5] M G Quinlan 3-8-9 Nicol Polli (7) 9/2: 4: Mid-div, kept on late for press, no threat to front trio:	2½	57a
	NOBLE MOUNT [2] R Guest 3-9-0 J Mackay 33/1: 5: Dwelt, mid-div, onepace on debut.	¾	60a
	LUCHI [3] A Charlton 3-8-9 R Smith 50/1: 6: Dwelt, sn mid-div, no impress fnl 2f on debut.	1¼	51a
260	**TONTO** 12 [14] Miss D Mountain 3-9-0 p (70) C Catlin 12/1: 343020-7: Rdn rear, nvr factor.	1¼	52a
135	**BACKLASH** 39 [9] A W Carroll 3-8-9 S Whitworth 50/1: 0-8: Dwelt, hmpd early & rear, mod late gains.	¾	45a
4576}	**SON OF REMBRANDT** 99 [12] D K Ivory 3-9-0 (66) J Quinn 16/1: 605063-9: Chsd ldrs 5f, abs.	¾	48a
260	**SUSSEX STYLE** 12 [8] R M Flower 3-9-0 E Ahern 50/1: 0-0: Prom 4f.	shd	48a
	JAYCEE STAR [13] D Flood 3-8-9 P Doe 40/1: 0: Dwelt, sn bhd, t.o. on debut.	18	0a
1124}	**TALE OF THE TIGER** 264 [11] Julian Poulton 3-9-0 VIS N Callan 100/1: 0-0: Drvn rear, nvr factor:	nk	1a
49	**EUGENIE** 53 [1] R Hannon 3-8-9 P Dobbs 50/1: 00-0: Mid-div, btn/hmpd 2f out, abs.	1¼	0a

13 Ran   1m 13.56 (3.16)   Owner Mr E Goody   Trained at Sherborne

---

365 **12.40 Betdirect Co Uk Handicap Stakes 3yo 0-75 (E)** [82]

£3413 £975 £488 **1m2f p/track** **Going 39** **-44 Slow** Stalls Inside

3955}	KEEPERS KNIGHT 134 [5] P F I Cole 3-8-7 1ow (60) I Mongan 8/1: 055-1: Cl-up, led over 3f out, rdn clr over 1f out, al holding rivals ins last:			67a
229	COMPETITOR 21 [2] J Akehurst 3-9-2 (70) C Catlin 12/1: 10-2: Led, hdd over 3f out, rdn & kept on fnl 2f, not pace of wnr:		1½	73a
238*	DR CERULLO 19 [7] C Tinkler 3-9-7 (75) Martin Dwyer 6/4 FAV: 26301-3: Trkd ldrs wide, styd on onepace for press:		1½	76a
232	IVORY COAST 21 [4] W R Muir 3-8-3 (57) P Doe 20/1: 004-4: Rear, short of room halfway, styd on for press fnl 2f, nrst fin:		½	57a
232	LA DANSEUSE 21 [1] G C Bravery 3-7-12 1oh (51) Lisa Jones (3) 25/1: 0636-5: Trkd ldrs, onepace & held fnl 2f.		¾	51a
261	ELUSIVE KITTY 12 [8] G A Butler 3-9-1 (69) E Ahern 5/2: 5255-6: Rear, eff wide 3f out, btn over 1f out:		2½	64a
162	SPRING WHISPER 33 [6] E A L Dunlop 3-8-1 vis (55) J Quinn 16/1: 000-7: Trkd ldrs, no impress/hung ins last.		3	46a
226	TROMPE LOEIL 22 [9] E A L Dunlop 3-8-12 (66) W Ryan 6/1: 050240-8: Keen & prom till 3f out, eased.		20	26a
177	LORD GREYSTOKE 31 [3] C P Morlock 3-8-2 (56) J Mackay 25/1: 050400-9: Prom till 4f out, sn bhd:		4	10a
9 Ran	2m 11.08 (8.28)	Owner P F I Cole Ltd		Trained at Whatcombe

---

366 **1.15 Bet Direct No Q On 08000 93 66 93 Classified Stakes 4yo+ 0-60 (F)**

£3003 £858 £429 **7f p/track rnd** **Going 39** **-06 Slow** Stalls Inside

5029}	ZAFARSHAH 64 [1] P D Evans 5-9-0 (58) S Donohoe (7) 11/2: 030050-1: Trkd ldrs, chsd ldr over 2f out, drvn to lead well ins last:			63a
344	MAYZIN 3 [16] R M Flower 4-9-0 p (51) J Quinn 8/1: 00054-32: Led, crossed to rail after 1f, hdd well ins last, just held:		nk	61a
266	MISS ISSY 11 [5] J Gallagher 4-8-11 vis (58) I Mongan 11/2: 404010-3: Mid-div, styd on for press, not pace to reach front pair:		½	58a
4780}	DOUBLE M 85 [8] Mrs L Richards 7-9-0 vis (49) N Callan 66/1: D40000-4: Rear, hdwy over 2f out, onepace for press dist.		¾	60a
121	CAPTAIN CLOUDY 42 [10] M Madgwick 4-9-0 (57) L Keniry (3) 50/1: 004000-5: Rear, short of room over 1f out, late gains, nvr dngr:		2½	55a
144	FOOLISH THOUGHT 35 [4] R A Fahey 4-9-0 VIS (60) E Ahern 9/2: 004000-6: Rdn mid-div, nvr pace to chall, vis.		2	51a
270	ACORAZADO 11 [7] G L Moore 5-9-0 (56) G Carter 7/2 FAV: 551535-7: Rear, mod gains for press:		hd	50a
144	PANTS 35 [6] Andrew Reid 5-8-11 (57) A Nicholls 8/1: 400310-8: Rear, mod prog, no dngr:		1½	44a
323	FOUR JAYS 4 [14] N P Littmoden 4-9-0 (58) Lisa Jones (3) 14/1: 60505-09: Chsd ldrs till over 1f out, qck reapp.		nk	46a
270	MASTER RATTLE 11 [2] Jane Southcombe 5-9-0 (53) V Slattery 33/1: 050000-0: Chsd ldrs till over 2f out.		2	42a
94	LOCOMBE HILL 46 [3] D Nicholls 8-9-0 (60) L Treadwell (7) 12/1: 000100-0: Dwelt, keen & cl-up, btn 2f out.		¾	41a
6	AMANPURI 61 [12] Miss Gay Kelleway 6-9-0 (46) M Fenton 33/1: 23/0000-0: Al bhd, abs.		3	35a
61	KUMAKAWA 52 [15] E A Wheeler 6-9-0 bl (45) Liam Jones (7) 100/1: 215000-0: Sn bhd, abs.		2	31a
966}	MAGIC STONE 280 [9] A Charlton 4-9-0 (45) R Smith 100/1: 000/0-0: Chsd ldrs till halfway, long abs.		3½	24a
241	KANZ WOOD 19 [11] A W Carroll 8-9-0 (59) S Whitworth 14/1: 300000-0: Mid-div wide, btn 2f out, eased right down.		2½	19a
15 Ran	1m 25.94 (3.14)	Owner Waterline Racing Club		Trained at Abergavenny

---

367 **1.45 Bet Direct No Q Demo 08000 837 888 Maiden Stakes 3yo (D)**

£4115 £1266 £633 £317 **1m2f p/track** **Going 39** **-34 Slow** Stalls Inside

116	ABSOLUTELYTHEBEST 42 [4] E A L Dunlop 3-9-0 (71) E Ahern 9/2: 004-1: Handy, trkd ldr over 2f out, drvn to lead well ins last, all out:			77a
120	BAAWRAH 42 [6] M R Channon 3-9-0 (72) C Catlin 7/2: 0632-2: Trkd ldr, rdn & led over 3f out, drvn & hdd cl-home:		nk	76a
3471}	FIDDLERS FORD 155 [10] J Noseda 3-9-0 S W Kelly 12/1: 0-3: Mid-div, hdwy 3f out, styd on for press, not able to chall:		1	75a
	ALEXANDER AMBITION 157 [9] S Kirk 3-8-9 (75) I Mongan 14/1: 020-4: Trkd ldrs, drvn & no extra over 1f out:		5	63a
3337}	NIGHT STORM 161 [12] S Dow 3-9-0 (72) P Doe 12/1: 025-5: Held up, eff wide, no impress dist.		1½	61a
229	ATLANTIC TERN 21 [8] N M Babbage 3-9-0 V Slattery 66/1: 00-6: Rear, no impress fnl 3f.		3	62a
238	ONCE AROUND 19 [2] T G Mills 3-9-0 J Paulielo 50/1: 0-7: Prom till over 1f out, longer trip.		1¼	60a
4945}	PRINCESS ALINA 72 [3] A M Balding 3-8-9 Martin Dwyer 5/2 FAV: 52-8: Led till over 3f out, btn 2f out.		1¼	53a
120	DARN GOOD 42 [13] R Hannon 3-9-0 p Dobbs 10/1: 364500-9: Chsd ldrs till halfway, btn 2f out, abs.		1½	56a
240	RUSSALKA 19 [14] Julian Poulton 3-8-9 P (65) N Callan 8/1: 46022-0: Mid-div wide, no ch fnl 2f:		nk	50a
4293}	DESERT TOMMY 115 [1] T G Mills 3-9-0 A Clark 33/1: 0-0: Dwelt, rear, t.o. 4f out, 4 month abs.		23	24a
5024}	ITS A BLESSING 64 [11] N P Littmoden 3-8-9 J P Guillambert (3) 66/1: 0-0: Sn rdn rear, t.o., abs.		5	12a
	CHARLIES PROFIT [7] J J Bridger 3-8-9 J Tate 66/1: 0: Slowly away sn bhd on debut.		dist	0a
	RED SILK [5] Mrs A J Perrett 3-8-9 M Hills 12/1: 0: Sn rear, t.o. halfway on debut.		1½	0a
14 Ran	2m 10.08 (7.28)	Owner Mr Saeed Suhail		Trained at Newmarket

---

368 **2.15 Betdirect Co Uk Handicap Stakes 3yo 0-100 (C)** [89]

£8932 £3388 £1694 £770 **7f p/track rnd** **Going 39** **-13 Slow** Stalls Inside

213*	BETTALATETHANNEVER 24 [6] S Dow 3-9-7 (82) P Fitzsimons 5/2: 061-1: Keen, held up, styd on strongly to lead well ins last, going away:			95a
261*	ST SAVARIN 12 [5] J R Best 3-8-10 (71) N Pollard 6/1: 261051-2: Led, hdd ins last, no extra:		2	76a
268*	KABREET 11 [3] E A L Dunlop 3-9-3 (78) E Ahern 7/2: 553101-3: Trkd ldrs, eff to chall dist, no extra ins last:		nk	82a
261	TURNBERRY 12 [2] J W Hills 3-7-13 1ow bl (59) J Quinn 14/1: 000004-4: Chsd ldrs, onepace fnl 2f:		¾	61a
341	BLUE EMPIRE 3 [1] P C Haslam 3-9-0 (75) L Enstone (3) 9/4 FAV: 01021-45: Trkd ldr, ch over 1f out, hung left & wknd ins		shd	77a
261	OFF BEAT 12 [4] R F Johnson Houghton 3-9-2 bl (77) S Carson 12/1: 610610-6: Keen & held up, no impress fnl 2f:		1	77a
217	HELLO ROBERTO 24 [7] M J Polglase 3-9-4 (79) J Fletcher (3) 12/1: 304324-7: Al bhd & no ch dist:		9	63a
7 Ran	1m 26.42 (3.62)	Owner Mr J R May		Trained at Epsom

---

369 **2.50 Littlewoods Bet Direct Handicap Stakes 4yo+ 0-85 (D)** [83]

£4784 £1472 £736 £368 **1m p/track rnd** **Going 39** **+06 Fast** Stalls Outside

4702}	DANCE ON THE TOP 90 [5] J R Boyle 6-9-11 t (80) Martin Dwyer 9/1: 004320-1: Cl-up & led over 3f out, rdn & in command dist:			91a
265*	J R STEVENSON 12 [6] M Wigham 8-9-10 (79) M Savage (5) 11/2: 426351-2: Trkd ldrs, eff to chase wnr 3f out, kept on, al		3½	81a

LINGFIELD Saturday 10.01.04 Lefthand, V Sharp Track

held:

273+*	**LABRETT** 11 [12] Miss Gay Kelleway 7-10-0 t (83) M Fenton 9/2: 651061-3: Mid-div wide, drvn & kept on fnl 2f, no dngr to wnr:	1¼	82a
131	**SEWMORE CHARACTER** 39 [4] M Blanshard 4-9-5 (74) N Callan 10/1: 2/40462-4: Keen in mid-div, styd on onepace for press:	hd	73a
273	**FREE OPTION** 11 [1] W J Musson 9-9-4 (73) Dean McKeown 4/1 FAV: 030130-5: Dwelt & rear, hdwy over 2f out, onepace ins last:	shd	71a
292	**CORMORANT WHARF** 7 [2] T E Powell 4-9-10 (79) A Quinn (5) 13/2: 16/0-06: Keen & trkd ldrs, outpcd fnl 2f:	1½	75a
3344}	**BOUNDLESS PROSPECT** 161 [3] J W Hills 5-9-6 (75) M Hills 33/1: 005500-7: Towards rear, little hdwy, abs.	1	68a
4291}	**MAMORE GAP** 115 [10] R Hannon 6-9-4 (73) P Dobbs 25/1: 511050-8: Held up, no impress fnl 3f, abs.	1¼	63a
273	**AMMENAYR** 11 [9] T G Mills 4-9-8 (77) I Mongan 8/1: 61050-9: Rear, little prog:	hd	67a
3654}	**TERRAQUIN** 147 [7] J J Bridger 4-9-10 (79) J Tate 33/1: 146416-0: Held up wide, btn 2f out, new stable/abs.	9	53a
3651}	**KINGHAM** 147 [11] Mrs Mary Hambro 4-9-9 (78) V Slattery 100/1: 1/00-0: Led till over 3f out, wknd, abs.	1	50a
80	**ANNISHIRANI** 49 [8] G A Butler 4-9-5 (74) E Ahern 6/1: 322114-0: Keen & trkd ldr, wknd qckly 3f out, abs.	9	30a
12 Ran	1m 38.8 (2.6)	Owner John Hopkins (T/A South Hatch)	Trained at Epsom

---

370

3.20 Bet All Weather On 0800 32 93 93 Selling Stakes 4yo+   (G)
£2639 £754 £377   1m2f p/track rnd   Going 39   -32 Slow   Stalls Inside

2631}	**BANK ON HIM** 190 [2] C Weedon 9-9-2 (56) J Quinn 6/1: 113000-1: Made all, drvn & held on gamely ins last:		57a
4587}	**STERLING GUARANTEE** 98 [7] D Nicholls 6-9-2 (69) A Nicholls 7/1: 4///0630-2: Held up, short of room over 1f out, styd on well for press cl-home, just failed:	nk	55a
272	**PYRRHIC** 11 [11] M R Flower 5-9-2 bl (40) E Ahern 8/1: 004505-3: Dwelt, mid-div, styd on onepace.	1	54a
4517}	**CHEROKEE BAY** 103 [1] G L Moore 4-8-9 (51) G Carter 7/2: 000003-4: Chsd wnr till over 1f out, fdd:	4	43a
214	**WALKER BAY** 24 [12] J C Fox 6-8-11 (40) R Smith 33/1: 024000-5: Rear, nvr pcd to threaten.	nk	42a
272	**PRIVATE SEAL** 11 [3] Julian Poulton 9-9-2 t (40) N Callan 12/1: 030000-6: Prom till over 1f out.	1	46a
267*	**ABSOLUTE UTOPIA** 11 [9] J L Spearing 11-9-7 (63) J Mackay 13/8 FAV: 232101-7: Trkd ldrs wide, btn over 1f out.	2½	47a
3444}	**BIRTH OF THE BLUES** 156 [14] A Charlton 8-9-2 (40) Donna Bashton (7) 25/1: 402560-8: Rear, no ch fnl 2f, abs.	1½	40a
4028}	**MR WHIZZ** 130 [10] A P Jones 7-9-2 (40) L Keniry (3) 33/1: 500000-9: Rear, no impress 2f out, abs.	5	33a
4767}	**ORIGINAL SIN** 86 [8] S Dow 4-9-0 (52) P Doe 25/1: 0560-0: Chsd ldrs till 2f out, abs/new stable.	4	27a
10 Ran	2m 09.9 (7.1)	Owner Vetlab Supplies Ltd	Trained at Pulborough

---

371

3.50 Bet Direct No Q Voice Automated Betting Handicap Stakes 3yo 0-65 (F)   [72]
£2905 £830 £415   5f p/track rnd   Going 39   -05 Slow   Stalls Inside

256*	**SMART STARPRINCESS** 14 [4] P A Blockley 3-9-0 bl (58) N Callan 3/1: 354411-1: Made all & clr halfway, drvn & held on well ins last:		66a
295	**ALIZAR** 7 [8] M J Polglase 3-8-12 (56) L Fletcher (3) 14/1: 61153-02: Towards rear/wide, styd on for press, nrst fin:	nk	63a
284	**VITTORIOSO** 8 [10] Miss Gay Kelleway 3-8-10 bl (54) T Eaves (5) 20/1: 050-53: Chsd ldr, drvn & hung left over 1f out, kept on for press:	1½	56a
237	**LITTLE FLUTE** 19 [3] T Keddy 3-8-8 (52) Lisa Jones (3) 11/2: 000002-4: Rdn rear, mod gains:	1½	49a
217	**FORZENUFF** 24 [2] J R Boyle 3-9-7 (65) E Ahern 5/2 FAV: 451603-5: Mid-div & rdn, not pace to chall:	dht	62a
217	**IVORY LACE** 24 [9] D K Ivory 3-9-2 (60) I Mongan 33/1: 361500-5: Chsd wnr halfway, wknd dist.	hd	56a
4513}	**REHIA** 103 [5] J W Hills 3-9-2 (60) M Hills 10/1: 013550-7: Rdn wide, nvr pace to threaten, abs.	½	54a
237*	**HEAD OF STATE** 19 [1] R M Beckett 3-8-10 (54) J Mackay 6/1: 0061-8: Sn outpcd rear:	1¼	44a
289*	**PRINCESS KAI** 7 [7] R Ingram 3-9-3 bl (61) F P Ferris (3) 7/1: 40303-19: Dwelt, hmpd early, nvr on terms:	nk	50a
260	**CITY AFFAIR** 12 [6] Mrs L C Jewell 3-9-4 P (62) L Keniry (3) 16/1: 500305-0: Chsd wnr 3f, sn wknd:	1½	46a
10 Ran	1m 0.49 (2.69)	Owner Brooklands Racing	Trained at Southwell

SOUTHWELL Monday 12.01.04 Lefthand, Sharp, Oval Track

Official Going Standard

372

1.20 Bet Direct On Sky Active Amateur Riders' Banded Stakes 4yo+ 0-35 (H)
£1376 £393 £197   1m f/sand rnd   Going 53   -53 Slow   Stalls Inside

3506}	**SMART SCOT** 155 [7] B P J Baugh 5-11-7 p (30) Mr E Dehdashti (5) 9/2 FAV: 000060-1: Cl-up, led 2f out, sn clr, edged left dist, rdn out to hold on:		34a
353	**SEA YA MAITE** 4 [6] S R Bowring 10-11-7 t (30) Miss Kelly Harrison (5) 5/1: 3000-052: Chsd ldrs, prog to chase wnr 2f out, styd on fnl 1f, just held:	1	31a
296	**COUNTRYWIDE GIRL** 9 [1] A Berry 5-11-7 (30) Mrs S Renwick (5) 25/1: 0/000U-03: Handy, onepcd dist:	5	21a
330	**WESTERN COMMAND** 6 [3] Mrs N Macauley 8-11-7 (30) Mrs M Morris 8/1: 5550-040: Bhd, prog 2f out, nrst fin:	¾	19a
310	**PAGEANT** 7 [8] J M Bradley 7-11-7 (35) Miss E J Jones 6/1: 5300-065: Handy, wknd 2f out:	6	7a
204	**GINNER MORRIS** 27 [9] J Hetherton 9-11-7 bl (30) Miss L Ellison (3) 9/1: 30/0000-6: Handy, wknd 2f out:	1½	4a
320	**METICULOUS** 7 [4] M C Chapman 6-11-7 (30) Mr M Scales (5) 25/1: 0000/0-07: Al bhd:	hd	3a
228	**COLLEGE STAR** 24 [5] J F Coupland 6-11-7 bl (30) Ms C Williams (5) 5/1: 000000-8: Prom, led 4f out, hdd 2f out, sn wknd:	1½	0a
2960}	**TOUCH OF SPIRIT** 132 [10] J R Jenkins 5-11-7 (35) Mr N Soares (7) 25/1: 210410-9: Mid-div wide, fdd 3f out:	14	0a
313	**CHANTILLY GOLD** 7 [11] J M Bradley 5-11-7 BL (30) Mr S Dobson (5) 20/1: 0000-050: Slow away, prog 4f out, fdd 2f out:	2½	0a
352	**AUNT DORIS** 4 [5] Paul Johnson 7-11-7 p (35) Mr P Evans (5) 8/1: 0500/0-00: Led, hdd 4f out, sn fdd:	¾	0a
11 Ran	1m 47.92 (8.52)	Owner Mr S Day	Trained at Stoke On Trent

---

373

1.50 Press Interactive To Bet Direct Claiming Stakes 3yo+   (H)
£1477 £422 £211   7f f/sand rnd   Going 53   -18 Slow   Stalls Inside

320*	**LUCAYAN MONARCH** 7 [4] P A Blockley 6-9-12 p (53) Dean McKeown 8/11 FAV: 0064-211: In tch, gd prog to lead dist, rdn out:		57a
308	**DONEGAL SHORE** 8 [5] Mrs J Candlish 5-9-12 VIS t (66) C Catlin 14/1: 00600-42: Prom, outpcd 3f out, rallied dist, no ch	2½	50a

with wnr:

166	**EVANGELIST 34** [3] A Berry 4-9-7 (40) F Lynch 40/1: 000000-3: In tch, outpcd 4f out, prog 2f out, chsd wnr dist, sn no extra:			2½	40a
362	**SUDRA 3** [6] J O'Reilly 7-9-12 bl (53) J D O'Reilly (7) 9/2: 0000-334: Cl-up, led 3f out, hdd over 1f out, sn wknd:			1	43a
350	**TEFI 4** [7] J Balding 6-9-9 bl t (45) P Makin (7) 20/1: 6060-035: Led, hdd 3f out, wknd:			3½	33a
245	**MR STYLISH 17** [2] J S Moore 8-9-10 vis t (47) J D Smith 9/1: 044400-6: Held up, nvr nrr than mid-div:			3	28a
3876}	**FRANKS QUEST 140** [8] John A Harris 4-9-12 (58) J Mackay 8/1: 420040-7: Al bhd:			7	16a
4904}	**THATS ALL JAZZ 77** [1] C R Dore 6-9-5 (45) J Bramhill 25/1: 060000-8: Al well in rear:			6	0a

8 Ran   1m 31.62 (5.02)   Owner Mr A C Kirkham   Trained at Southwell

---

374 2.20 Bet Direct On 0800 93 66 93 Banded Stakes 3yo+ 0-40 (H)

£1470 £420 £210   **5f f/sand str**   Going 53   +10 Fast   Stalls Outside

335	**LADY PROTECTOR 6** [9] J Balding 5-9-7 (40) P Makin (7) 5/1: 00060-41: Rcd centre, made all, clr 2f out, rdn out:				51a
286	**BALI STAR 10** [3] R J Hodges 9-9-7 (40) C Catlin 10/1: 05005-02: Cl-up far side, chsd wnr 2f out, no impress on wnr fnl 1f:			4	39a
172	**BELLS BOYS 34** [1] K A Ryan 5-9-7 p (40) G Parkin 7/1: 00/0505-3: In tch far side, outpcd 2f out, rallied fnl 1f:			3	30a
253	**BLUNHAM 16** [8] M C Chapman 4-9-7 (40) K Dalgleish 40/1: 000000-4: Sn in rear, switched to far side 2f out, kept on fnl 1f, nrst fin:			½	29a
4003}	**SOTONIAN 133** [5] P S Felgate 11-9-7 (40) Lisa Jones (3) 14/1: 505000-5: Mid-div centre, modest late gains, long abs.			shd	28a
352	**AGUILA LOCO 4** [16] M C Chapman 5-9-7 (40) Andrew Webb (7) 4/1 FAV: 00000-326: Cl-up stands side, no extra fnl 2f:			hd	27a
352	**THREAT 4** [14] J M Bradley 8-9-7 (40) Joanna Badger 9/1: 0000-047: Bhd, nvr nrr than mid-div:			¾	25a
4168}	**OUR OLD BOY 480** [2] J A Gilbert 4-9-7 (35) D R McCabe 33/1: 006/-8: Handy far side, wknd fnl 2f:			nk	24a
319	**LAW MAKER 4** [15] M A Buckley 4-9-7 (35) Dean McKeown 33/1: 00000-09: Cl-up stands side, wknd 2f out:			shd	23a
312	**CAROLS CHOICE 7** [4] A Sadik 7-9-7 (35) J P Guillambert 9/1: 00000-650: In tch centre, wknd fnl 2f:			1	20a
253	**TUSCAN DREAM 16** [12] A Berry 9-9-7 (40) P Bradley (5) 20/1: 306060-0: Cl-up, fdd fnl 2f.			½	19a
356	**CARONTE 4** [6] S R Bowring 4-9-7 bl (40) J Bramhill 20/1: 00600-00: In tch centre, wknd fnl 3f:			nk	18a
3800}	**WITTILY 143** [11] A Berry 4-9-7 (40) F Lynch 20/1: 000520-0: Chsd ldrs, wknd 3f out:			2½	11a
254	**SUBTLE MOVE 16** [10] D Shaw 4-9-7 (40) J Fanning 25/1: 000000-0: Hmpd start, al bhd:			2½	4a
4269}	**DIAMOND RACKET 118** [13] D W Chapman 4-9-7 bl (40) R Brisland 50/1: 000000-0: Al well adrift:			3	0a

16 Ran   59.95 (2.15)   Owner Simon Mapletoft Racing II   Trained at Doncaster

---

375 2.50 Bet Direct On Sky Text Page 372 Banded Stakes 4yo+ 0-40 (H)

£1624 £464 £232   **1m3f f/sand**   Going 53   -16 Slow   Stalls Inside

302	**SERAPH 9** [9] John A Harris 4-8-12 p (40) J Mackay 8/1: 30000-31: Mid-div, prog 5f out, chsd ldr dist, rdn out to lead cl-home:				43a
302	**DANCING TILLY 9** [3] R A Fahey 6-9-1 p (40) C Catlin 8/1: 65306-42: Sn outpcd, prog 5f out, styd onto lead 2f out, hdd under press cl-home:			hd	41a
321	**EAST CAPE 7** [1] Don Enrico Incisa 7-9-1 (40) Kim Tinkler 11/4 FAV: 34450-53: Held up, short of room bend after 2f & sn in rear, prog 3f out, staying on when short of room dist, switched & sn			6	32a
305	**TWO STEPS TO GO 8** [4] Ian Emmerson 5-9-1 bl (40) D Fentiman (7) 9/2: 04040-44: Prom, led 6f out, hdd 2f out, sn wknd:			1½	29a
3846}	**ANTONY EBENEEZER 141** [8] C R Dore 5-9-1 t (40) J Bramhill 4/1: 000400-5: In tch, prog trav well 3f out, ev ch 2f out, sn wknd:			1¾	26a
303	**ALJOMAR 8** [7] R E Barr 5-9-1 p (40) R Fitzpatrick 50/1: 00400-06: Prom, fdd 3f out.			shd	25a
302	**FRATERNITY 9** [5] J A Pickering 7-9-1 (40) Dean McKeown 8/1: 05064-67: Led, hdd 6f out, sn wknd:			7	15a
3596}	**THE RECRUITER 151** [10] J G M O'Shea 4-9-12 vis (40) Lisa Jones (3) 20/1: 500000-8: Mid-div, prog 4f out, sn wknd:			2½	11a
1261}	**MORRIS DANCING 257** [2] B P J Baugh 5-9-1 (40) J Fanning 50/1: 000/000-9: In tch, wknd 3f out:			3½	6a
118	**SPLENDID TOUCH 44** [6] J R Jenkins 4-8-12 (40) K Dalgleish 16/1: 400000-0: Slow away, al bhd:			1¾	3a

10 Ran   2m 28.95 (7.65)   Owner Mr M F Schofield   Trained at Melton Mowbray

---

376 3.20 Bet Direct Median Auction Maiden Stakes 4-6yo (H)

£1432 £409 £205   **1m6f f/sand**   Going 53   -45 Slow   Stalls Inside

306	**MR SMITHERS JONES 8** [4] S C Williams 4-9-0 (50) C Catlin 9/4 FAV: 00/5-21: Keen bhd, prog wide 3f out, led trav v easily for 1f out, pushed clr, val 8L+:				58a
4806}	**COLONNADE 86** [6] C Grant 5-9-1 (45) K Dalgleish 9/2: 0/36000-2: Chsd ldrs, outpcd 2f out, rallied fnl 1f, no ch with easy wnr:			5	45a
142	**BROUGHTON MELODY 40** [7] W J Musson 5-9-1 (46) Dean McKeown 5/1: 00//6-3: Held up, prog 3f out, onepcd fnl 1f:			1¼	44a
315	**XIXITA 7** [1] Dr J D Scargill 4-8-9 (45) J Bramhill 20/1: 40450-64: Cl-up, led 3f out, hdd bef 1f out, sn wknd:			1	43a
354	**DR JULIAN 4** [2] Miss A Stokell 4-9-0 p (45) Ann Stokell 25/1: 05000-05: Led, rcd keenly, hdd 3f out, sn fdd:			7	41a
2528}	**PENALTY CLAUSE 196** [5] K A Morgan 4-9-0 p (45) Lisa Jones (3) 9/2: 000064-5: In tch, wknd 3f out:			dht	41a
3378}	**THEME PARK 160** [3] John A Harris 4-9-0 (60) J Mackay 4/1: 63/0P60-7: Chsd ldrs, wknd 3f out:			11	31a

7 Ran   3m 13.52 (13.72)   Owner The Lager Khan   Trained at Newmarket

---

377 3.50 Littlewoodspoker Com Banded Stakes 3yo+ 0-35 (H)

£1379 £394 £197   **6f f/sand str**   Going 53   -05 Slow   Stalls Inside

1655}	**ETERNAL BLOOM 235** [2] M Brittain 6-9-7 (35) M Lawson (7) 9/2: 650/000-1: Prom, led 3f out, clr 1f out, rdn out:				46a
304	**COURT MUSIC 8** [9] R E Barr 5-9-7 vis (35) R Fitzpatrick 12/1: 00000-02: In tch, prog 2f out, edged left under press dist, sn no impress with wnr:			5	33a
327*	**DESERT LIGHT 6** [12] D Shaw 3-8-11 vis (35) Lisa Jones (3) 13/8 FAV: 00060-13: Mid-div, prog wide 3f out, chsd wnr & hung left dist, sn no extra:			1½	35a
4381}	**ZARA LOUISE 112** [7] R P Elliott 4-9-7 (30) A Elliott (3) 16/1: 300006-4: Bhd, prog 3f out, onepcd fnl 1f:			hd	28a
2020}	**MIMAS GIRL 217** [6] S R Bowring 5-9-7 t (35) J Bramhill 8/1: 305046-5: Chsd ldrs, hung left 2f out, short of room & no impress dist:			1¼	24a
3953}	**REDOUBTABLE 136** [11] D W Chapman 13-9-7 (35) R Brisland 7/1: 006600-6: Dwelt, prog 2f out, onepcd fnl 1f:			1¼	20a
66	**SALLY TRAFFIC 54** [4] R M Whitaker 5-9-7 (30) V Halliday 20/1: 00000-7: Prom, wknd fnl 2f:			¾	18a
352	**ABOVE BOARD 4** [10] R F Marvin 9-9-7 bl (35) Dean McKeown 6/1: 00000-58: Led, hdd 3f out, wknd fnl 2f:			shd	17a
297	**BLUE CIRCLE 9** [3] M Mullineaux 4-9-7 (30) K Dalgleish 40/1: 00000-09: Al bhd.			15	0a

SOUTHWELL Monday 12.01.04 Lefthand, Sharp, Oval Track

214	**SARGENTS DREAM 26** [1] J A Gilbert 4-9-7 (30) D R McCabe 40/1: 000-0: Al in rear.	1¼	0a
1380}	**COOL BART 251** [8] B P J Baugh 4-9-7 (30) J Fanning 40/1: 000/00-0: Chsd ldrs, wknd fnl 3f:	9	0a

12 Ran　1m 16.79 (3.49)　　Owner Mr Mel Brittain　　　　　　Trained at Warthill

WOLVERHAMPTON Monday 12.01.04 Lefthand, Sharp Track

Official Going　Standard

378 — 1.10 Bet Direct No Q 08000 93 66 93 Apprentice Handicap Stakes Div 1 3yo+ 0-60 (G) [60]
£2576 £736 £368　　7f f/sand rnd　　Going 32　　-28 Slow　　Stalls Outside

4769}	**MOUNT HILLABY 88** [8] M W Easterby 4-9-5 (51) P Mulrennan (3) 15/8 FAV: 006000-1: Sn handy & led 2f out, rdn & asserted ins last:		62a
151	**SPINDOR 37** [1] J A Osborne 5-9-12 bl (58) S Crawford (5) 16/1: 100050-2: Cl-up & led 3f out till 2f out, kept on, no ch with	3	61a
343	**FEAST OF ROMANCE 5** [9] P Howling 7-9-4 p (50) D Nolan (3) 4/1: 20336-33: In tch, eff 2f out, sn no extra:	4	45a
304*	**LARKYS LOB 8** [11] Paul Johnson 5-9-8 6ex (54) N Chalmers (3) 5/1: 0002-214: Held up, prog/ch 2f out, no extra:	1	47a
40	**PHANTOM FLAME 58** [5] M Johnston 4-9-3 (49) L Enstone 20/1: 000000-5: Prom, no extra fnl 2f:	2	38a
4986}	**KARAOKE KING 71** [3] J E Long 6-9-11 (57) R Miles (3) 16/1: 461600-6: Prom, lost pl halfway:	shd	46a
2093}	**LITTLETON ZEPHIR 214** [7] Mrs P Townsley 5-9-1 (47) Derek Nolan (7) 20/1: 123306-7: Prom till over 2f out:	1	34a
4807}	**BEAUTEOUS 86** [2] A Berry 5-9-2 (48) P Mathers (5) 5/1: 020400-8: Led 4f, wknd, abs.	½	34a
304	**BIJAN 8** [10] R Hollinshead 6-8-3 P (35) Stephanie Hollinshead (5) 16/1: 0405-049: Rdn/rear, nvr factor:	shd	21a
281	**JESSINCA 10** [4] A P Jones 8-8-8 vis (40) B Reilly (3) 14/1: 46460-00: Dwelt, nvr mount challenge.	½	25a
3631}	**MIZHAR 150** [6] J J Quinn 8-9-13 vis (59) L Keniry 33/1: 320300-0: Held up, sn struggling, eased, abs.	14	21a

11 Ran　1m 30.40 (4.2)　　Owner Mr D F Spence & Mr J Southway　　Trained at Sheriff Hutton

379 — 1.40 Bet Direct No Q 08000 93 66 93 Apprentice Handicap Stakes Div 2 3yo+ 0-60 (G) [60]
£2576 £736 £368　　7f f/sand rnd　　Going 32　　-31 Slow　　Stalls Outside

311	**LORD CHAMBERLAIN 7** [7] J M Bradley 11-9-3 bl (49) F P Ferris 10/1: 35450-21: Bhd/wide, hdway halfway & led over 1f out, rdn out:		56a
4485}	**UP TEMPO 107** [9] T D Easterby 6-9-13 p (59) A Mullen (7) 11/2: 000640-2: Mid-div, rdn & keeping on when short of room over 1f out, switched & kept on:	1¼	63a
208	**WALTZING WIZARD 27** [3] A Berry 5-9-6 (52) P Mathers (5) 7/2 FAV: 006052-3: Rdn/bhd, styd for press, nrst fin:	1½	53a
328	**ITS ECCO BOY 6** [5] P Howling 6-9-5 (51) D Nolan (3) 4/1: 03640-44: Handy & led 3f out, drvn & hdd over 1f out, wknd:	½	51a
275	**AINTNECESSARILYSO 12** [2] N E Berry 6-8-13 (45) M Savage (5) 12/1: 005465-5: Chsd ldrs, no extra dist:	nk	44a
74	**MUQARRAR 52** [10] T J Fitzgerald 5-9-6 e (52) S Donohoe (5) 10/1: 650006-6: Chasing ldrs trav well when stumbled badly over 3f out, sn recovered but rdn/no extra from dist:	½	50a
89]	**PORT NATAL 74** [8] P Morris 6-8-8 bl (40) R Miles 7/1: 600501-7: Led 4f out till 3f out, wknd, distressed:	2½	33a
199	**HELLBENT 28** [4] J A Osborne 5-9-2 (48) S Crawford (3) 14/1: 530/0-8: Led 3f, wknd over 1f out:	2	37a
4097}	**CHORUS 128** [6] B R Millman 7-9-9 (55) M Saunders (7) 11/1: 126406-9: Prom, btn 3f out, abs.	5	35a
350	**REPEAT 4** [1] Miss Gay Kelleway 4-9-12 P (58) T Eaves (3) 10/1: 4064-120: Led/dsptd lead till halfway, chkpcs.	1½	35a

10 Ran　1m 30.6 (4.4)　　Owner Mr W C Harries　　Trained at Chepstow

380 — 2.10 Bet Direct No Q Demo On 08000 837 888 Handicap Stakes 4yo+ 46-55 (F) [55]
£2933 £838 £419　　1m4f f/sand　　Going 32　　-01 Slow　　Stalls Inside

2955}	**SENDINTANK 179** [4] S C Williams 4-9-5 (50) B Reilly 4/1: 000/600-1: Mid-div, smooth hdwy wide over 2f out & led over 1f out, rdn clr, easily:		69a
359*	**COOL BATHWICK 3** [12] B R Millman 5-10-2 6ex (57) J Quinn 3/1 FAV: 00/000-12: Prom & led over 5f out, rdn & hdd over 1f out, no ch with easy wnr:	11	59a
342	**AMBERSONG 9** [9] A W Carroll 6-9-10 (51) A Culhane 4/1: 14220-33: Dwelt, drvn & styd on onepace:	2½	49a
249	**FIGHT THE FEELING 17** [10] J W Unett 6-10-0 vis (55) Martin Dwyer 7/1: 353016-4: Bhd, eff to chase ldr 3f out, no impress dist:	½	52a
104	**COLOURFUL LADY 47** [6] P W Harris 4-9-10 (55) N Callan 11/1: 620000-5: In tch, rdn & no impress fnl 3f:	15	32a
281	**RED STORM 10** [7] J R Boyle 5-9-7 (48) R Miles (3) 25/1: 02105-06: In tch till over 2f out.	3	21a
90	**IN LUCK 49** [3] B Smart 6-9-6 (47) R Ffrench 14/1: 506030-7: In tch, lost pl halfway, abs.	2½	16a
244*	**ONLY FOR SUE 21** [5] W S Kittow 5-9-12 (53) I Mongan 4/1: 045/061-8: Prom till over 2f out:	3	18a
236	**IN SPIRIT 23** [8] B J Curley 6-9-12 (53) W M Lordan 14/1: 055300-9: Sn bhd, t.o.:	14	0a
236	**PLATINUM BOY 23** [2] M Wellings 4-9-6 bl (51) V Slattery 50/1: 315000-0: Led till 5f out, t.o.	14	0a
257	**HUMDINGER 16** [11] D Shaw 4-9-5 VIS (50) T Hamilton (5) 33/1: 610060-0: Prom till 4f out, t.o., tried visor.	14	0a

11 Ran　2m 37.59 (3.99)　　Owner Steve Jones and Phil McGovern　　Trained at Newmarket

381 — 2.40 Littlewoods Bet Direct Maiden Stakes 3yo (D)
£3318 £948 £474　　7f f/sand rnd　　Going 32　　+03 Fast　　Stalls Outside

4987}	**HONEST INJUN 70** [4] B W Hills 3-9-0 Martin Dwyer 4/9 FAV: 02-1: Held up, pushed along halfway & hdwy to lead over 1f out, rdn out:		77a
	PLAY MASTER [8] D Haydn Jones 3-9-0 Paul Eddery 20/1: 2: Dwelt, rdn to chall over 1f out, no extra well ins last:	¾	75a
192	**MY PARIS 30** [7] K A Ryan 3-9-0 J Quinn 33/1: 0-3: Dwelt, eff from 4f out, styd on onepace for press:	3½	68a
	HEVERSHAM [2] W J Haggas 3-9-0 A Culhane 12/1: 4: In tch, rdn & onepace fnl 3f:	1½	65a
260	**MUGEBA 14** [3] W J Musson 3-8-9 M Fenton 11/2: 02-5: Led till over 1f out, fdd:	4	52a
284	**ROYALTEA 10** [6] Ms Deborah J Evans 3-8-9 I Mongan 20/1: 66: Prom, no extra fnl 2f.	1	50a
313	**ANISETTE 7** [9] Julian Poulton 3-8-9 N Callan 7/1: 2-37: Chsd ldrs till over 2f out:	6	39a
184	**MONKEY OR ME 31** [5] P T Midgley 3-9-0 D Mernagh 66/1: 00-8: Keen, chsd ldrs till halfway.	4	34a
87	**POSH SHEELAGH 49** [1] J G Given 3-8-9 S W Kelly 50/1: 0-9: Held up in tch, no ch fnl 3f, abs.	¾	31a

9 Ran　1m 29.67 (3.47)　　Owner Mr Guy Reed　　Trained at Lambourn

382 3.10 Betdirect Co Uk Handicap Stakes 4yo+ 0-85 (D) [83]
£4085 £1257 £629 £314 1m1f79y f/sand rnd Going 32 +06 Fast Stalls Inside

127	INTRICATE WEB 44 [3] E J Alston 8-9-3 (72) D Allan (3) 9/2: 445043-1: Chsd ldrs, styd on wide for press to lead ins last, rdn out:		80a
273	SKYLARKER 13 [6] W S Kittow 6-9-9 (78) I Mongan 9/2: 604304-2: Dsptd lead, rdn & went on 2f out, hdd ins last, no extra:	1	83a
186	CRITICAL STAGE 31 [1] John Berry 5-8-6 e (61) M Fenton 12/1: 000335-3: Bhd, styd on for press fnl 3f, not reach front pair:	1¾	63a
278	DEL MAR SUNSET 12 [9] W J Haggas 5-9-13 (82) A Culhane 7/2 FAV: 220003-4: Cl-up/dsptd lead trav well, hdd 2f out & sn no extra:	1¾	81a
278	CAROUBIER 12 [8] T D Barron 4-9-8 bl (78) D Mernagh 12/1: 150224-5: Dwelt, sn tracking ldrs, rcd keen early, rdn & no extra fnl 2f:	¾	76a
265	TROPICAL CORAL 14 [11] C Tinkler 4-9-2 (72) D Nolan (5) 9/1: 450452-6: Rear, eff 3f out, no impress:	2	66a
255	MIDDLETON GREY 16 [10] A G Newcombe 6-9-13 (82) S Whitworth 20/1: 036064-7: Held up, eff 3f out, no prog 2f out.	1¾	73a
157+*	BUSCADOR 37 [5] W M Brisbourne 5-9-1 (70) B Swarbrick (7) 6/1: 611061-8: Led/dsptd lead till 5f out, fdd fnl 3f:	5	52a
186*	NOUL 31 [4] K A Ryan 5-9-4 bl (73) N Callan 10/1: 360421-9: Held up, no ch fnl 4f:	1¼	52a
4725}	EAST FLARES 91 [12] J W Unett 4-8-11 (67) S W Kelly 33/1: 50/610-0: Bhd, nvr on terms with ldrs:	12	25a
4768}	HOV 88 [2] J J Quinn 4-10-0 (84) L Fletcher (3) 33/1: 112540-0: Led 1f, sn struggling:	7	30a
181	SPANISH GOLD 33 [7] A M Balding 4-9-2 (72) Martin Dwyer 8/1: 0/2160-0: Keen & prom, btn 3f out.	6	8a
12 Ran	2m 0.66 (2.46) Owner Morris Oliver Pierce		Trained at Preston

383 3.40 Littlewoodscasino Com Selling Stakes 3yo (G)
£2520 £720 £360 1m100y f/sand rnd Going 32 -28 Slow Stalls Inside

279	JAKARMI 12 [3] B Palling 3-8-11 (55) I Mongan 11/4 FAV: 02650-1: Led/dsptd lead, went on halfway, rdn & clr over 1f out, styd on well:		57a
279*	KILLING ME SOFTLY 12 [1] J Gallagher 3-8-11 (53) N Callan 7/2: 01-2: Led/dsptd lead till halfway, rdn & not pace of wnr fnl 2f:	3	49a
279	BROTHER CADFAEL 12 [8] John A Harris 3-8-11 (45) S Whitworth 4/1: 000456-3: Held up, styd on onepace for press, no dngr:	½	48a
283	SECRET BLOOM 10 [6] J R Norton 3-8-11 vis (47) Darren Williams 8/1: 0050-44: Dwelt, held up in tch, keen, no impress fnl 2f:	2	44a
279	MARITA 12 [7] J G Given 3-8-6 (45) M Fenton 4/1: 020503-5: Pushed along in tch, nvr pace to chall:	1¾	36a
279	PLATINUM CHIEF 12 [2] A Berry 3-8-11 (47) A Culhane 10/1: 040045-6: Prom till over 1f out:	nk	40a
295	MISS JUDGED 9 [4] A P Jones 3-8-6 BL e t (45) F P Ferris (3) 40/1: 00000-07: Keen & prom 6f:	9	19a
	REJOYCE [5] J Jay 3-8-6 J Quinn 20/1: 8: Sn bhd, debut:	13	0a
8 Ran	1m 51.31 (5.11) Owner Mrs M M Palling		Trained at Cowbridge

384 4.10 Bet Direct In Vision Sky Page 293 Handicap Stakes Div 1 3yo+ 0-60 (F) [60]
£2975 £850 £425 6f f/sand rnd Going 32 +01 Fast Stalls Inside

94	CAUSTIC WIT 48 [1] M S Saunders 6-9-4 (50) R Miles (3) 25/1: 003030-1: Chsd ldrs & rdn/led over 1f out, duelled with rnr-up & narrowly asserted cl-home:		59a
328	SAVILES DELIGHT 6 [2] R Brotherton 5-9-8 p (54) I Mongan 7/2: 02004-32: Led/dsptd lead, hdd over 1f out, duelled with wnr, just held cl-home:	hd	62a
297*	ITALIAN MIST 9 [11] Julian Poulton 5-9-4 e (50) G Faulkner 8/1: 20050-13: Led 2f, onepce dist.	4	47a
298	AROGANT PRINCE 9 [12] I Semple 7-9-9 VIS (55) P McGaffin (3) 10/1: 60200-44: Prom wide trav well, no extra dist:	hd	51a
282	TIGRESS 10 [3] J W Unett 5-9-13 bl (59) Martin Dwyer 20/1: 32660-65: Held up, not able to chall:	1½	50a
304	CLEVELAND WAY 8 [10] D Carroll 4-9-2 vis (48) D Nolan (5) 13/2: 4000-126: Prom, no extra over 1f out:	½	37a
296	ATTORNEY 9 [13] D Shaw 6-8-13 e (45) T Hamilton (5) 9/1: 00004-37: Chsd ldrs till 2f out:	1	31a
345	GERONIMO 4 [8] Miss Gay Kelleway 7-9-11 p (57) J Quinn 11/4 FAV: 06020-28: Towards rear, no impress:	shd	43a
319	LAKE EYRE 7 [4] J Balding 5-8-13 (45) J Edmunds 12/1: 60303-59: Bhd, nvr a factor:	nk	30a
270	WARLINGHAM 13 [6] P Howling 6-9-8 (54) V Slattery 9/1: 000210-0: Sn rdn & al bhd:	¾	37a
312	ENJOY THE BUZZ 7 [9] J M Bradley 5-8-8 (40) P Fitzsimons 20/1: 0020-440: Prom till halfway:	1½	18a
4792}	FLYING EDGE 87 [7] E J Alston 4-9-10 (56) A Nicholls 12/1: 215160-0: Mid-div, lost pl from halfway, abs.	¾	32a
254	VICTORY FLIP 16 [5] R Hollinshead 4-9-3 p (49) N Callan 28/1: 036460-0: Sn outpcd:	7	7a
13 Ran	1m 14.64 (1.84) Owner Mrs Sandra Jones		Trained at Wells

385 4.40 Bet Direct In Vision Sky Page 293 Handicap Stakes Div 2 3yo+ 0-60 (F) [60]
£2968 £848 £424 6f f/sand rnd Going 32 -10 Slow Stalls Inside

345	MR PERTEMPS 4 [10] R A Fahey 6-9-9 p (55) T Hamilton (5) 7/4 FAV: 31100-31: Handy & led dist, rdn out:		61a
282	AMELIA 10 [13] W M Brisbourne 6-9-2 (48) B Swarbrick (7) 9/1: 04602-52: Held up, styd on wide for press, not able to chall wnr:	1	50a
349	LADY NATILDA 4 [5] D Haydn Jones 4-9-2 (48) Paul Eddery 13/2: 45000-43: Mid-div, rdn & hdwy over 2f out, not pace of wnr:	1¼	46a
183	FIAMMA ROYALE 34 [6] M S Saunders 5-9-3 (49) R Miles (3) 11/1: 205000-4: Handy & led over 2f till dist, no extra:	nk	46a
308	SPEEDFIT FREE 8 [12] I Semple 7-9-9 bl (55) A Culhane 6/1: 01054-25: Held up, not pace to chall ldrs:	¾	50a
274	KISS THE RAIN 12 [7] R Brotherton 4-9-4 vis (50) I Mongan 11/2: 510334-6: Prom, lost pl from halfway:	3½	35a
202	PRIDE OF KINLOCH 27 [11] J Hetherton 4-9-8 (54) M Fenton 33/1: 405000-7: Mid-div, outpcd from halfway:	¾	37a
4139}	PICCOLO PRINCE 125 [9] E J Alston 3-8-10 (58) D Allan (3) 33/1: 003500-8: Led early, prom till 2f out, abs.	nk	40a
282	INDIAN SHORES 10 [3] M Mullineaux 5-9-7 (53) Paul Scallan 40/1: 1006F-09: Dwelt & al bhd.	¾	33a
3262}	BACK IN SPIRIT 166 [8] B A McMahon 4-8-13 t (45) P M Quinn 20/1: 6040/00-0: Keen, dsptd lead 4f, abs.	nk	24a
319	SHADOWFAX 7 [2] Miss Gay Kelleway 4-10-0 bl (60) T Eaves (5) 9/1: 426/62-40: Dwelt, nvr on terms:	1	36a
606}	DOCDUCKOUT 333 [4] J W Unett 4-9-11 (57) Martin Dwyer 20/1: 00/0160-P: P.u. lame halfway:		0
12 Ran	1m 15.32 (2.52) Owner Monohydrate Developments		Trained at Malton

Official Going STANDARD.

386 — 12.20 Littlewoods Bet Direct Handicap Stakes Div 1 4yo+ 0-80 (D) [80]
£4046 £1245 £623 £311   6f f/sand rnd   Going 23   +02 Fast   Stalls inside

282	PRIMA STELLA 11 [2] J A R Toller 5-9-1 (67) Lisa Jones (3) 10/1: 41020-41: Trkd ldrs, rdn & led ins last, styd on strongly:		78a
349*	SOBA JONES 5 [1] J Balding 7-9-6 6ex (72) J Edmunds 5/1: 00052-12: Led, hdd ins last, kept on for press:	1½	77a
255	POLAR KINGDOM 17 [9] T D Barron 6-9-4 (70) D Mernagh 5/2 FAV: 200/200-3: Sn cl-up, short of room & lost place halfway, styd on for press fnl 2f:	hd	74a
4671*}	ELLENS ACADEMY 95 [5] E J Alston 9-10-0 (80) Dean McKeown 8/1: Held up, rdn to press ldrs dist, no extra:	1½	79a
113*	PORT ST CHARLES 46 [3] P R Chamings 7-9-11 (77) S Donohoe (7) 10/1: 002301-5: Chsd ldrs, no extra dist:	½	74a
193	FAR NOTE 31 [4] S R Bowring 6-8-13 bl (65) J Bramhill 9/1: 104210-6: Prom & ch 2f out, wknd:	6	47a
193	MAJIK 31 [8] D J S ffrench Davis 5-9-3 (69) I Mongan 7/1: 042313-7: Mid-div wide, nvr land blow:	1¼	47a
171	MAGIC GLADE 35 [11] C R Dore 5-9-10 (76) R Thomas (5) 16/1: 1323/00-8: Cl-up wide till over 1f out.	hd	53a
292	CASHEL MEAD 10 [6] J L Spearing 4-10-0 (80) A Culhane 15/2: 00623-59: Unruly stalls, al rear:	6	42a
4674}	GREENWOOD 94 [7] P G Murphy 6-9-12 (78) S W Kelly 20/1: 062200-0: Cl-up till 2f out:	shd	40a
285	RONNIE FROM DONNY 11 [10] B Ellison 4-9-7 (73) N Callan 16/1: 00001-40: In tch till halfway:	20	0a

11 Ran   1m 14.58 (1.28)   Owner Mr John Drew   Trained at Newmarket

387 — 12.50 Bet Direct In Vision Sky Page 293 Handicap Stakes Div 1 4yo+ 0-65 (F) [65]
£2947 £842 £421   1m f/sand rnd   Going 23   -33 Slow   Stalls Inside

300*	QOBTAAN 10 [2] M R Bosley 5-9-0 (51) Joanna Badger 4/1: 0534-611: Fly-leapt start, hdwy halfway, led over 1f out, rdn & styd on strongly:		58a
287	SORBIESHARRY 11 [5] Mrs N Macauley 5-8-11 p (48) P McCabe 6/1: 50422-52: Mid-div, hdwy wide to press wnr over 1f out, not qckn ins last:	1¾	49a
270	BLAKESEVEN 14 [6] W J Musson 4-8-11 (48) Paul Eddery 10/1: 000040-3: Rear, styd on for press fnl 2f, not able to chall:	½	49a
255	BRANDY COVE 17 [1] B Smart 7-10-0 (65) M Stainton (7) 4/1: 104523-4: Trkd ldrs, no extra dist.	3	59a
281	FARAWAY LOOK 11 [7] D Shaw 7-9-7 (58) Dean McKeown 15/2: 35534-45: Rear, nvr pace to threaten:	2½	47a
281	GOODBYE MR BOND 11 [4] E J Alston 4-9-4 VIS (55) D Allan (3) 8/1: 53404-56: Keen & cl-up trav well, rdn & wknd qckly over 1f out:	½	44a
318	MOUNT ROYALE 8 [10] N Tinkler 6-9-7 vis (58) Kim Tinkler 25/1: 34015-07: Led till over 1f out, fdd.	2	42a
5017*}	DUELLING BANJOS 68 [3] J Akehurst 5-10-0 (65) I Mongan 9/4 FAV: 600001-8: Chsd ldrs, btn 3f out:	5	40a
251	HOHS BACK 18 [9] Paul Johnson 5-9-11 p (62) N Chalmers (5) 16/1: 302000-9: Chsd ldrs wide 5f.	2	33a
241	REX ROMELIO 22 [8] K R Burke 5-9-9 (60) Darren Williams 50/1: 51505/0-0: Sn struggling & bhd halfway.	25	0

10 Ran   1m 43.9 (4.5)   Owner Inca Financial Services   Trained at Wantage

388 — 1.20 Bet Direct No Q 08000 93 66 93 Apprentice Handicap Stakes 4yo+ 0-80 (F) [77]
£2884 £824 £412   1m4f f/sand   Going 23   -39 Slow   Stalls Inside

4984}	AMIR ZAMAN 72 [1] J R Jenkins 6-10-0 (77) B Reilly 11/4: 066113-1: Keen & chsd ldr, led 2f out, drvn & held on gamely:		80a
277	GLORY QUEST 13 [4] Miss Gay Kelleway 7-9-8 p (71) T Eaves 15/8 FAV: 223552-2: Held up, drvn & styd on well fnl 2f, just held:	nk	73a
194	NEWTONIAN 31 [6] J Parkes 5-9-7 (70) Derek Nolan (5) 14/1: 6/23-3: Trkd ldrs, rdn to chall when hung badly left over 1f out, no extra:	2½	68a
257	DUBAI DREAMS 17 [5] M J Polglase 4-8-3 (56) K Ghunowa (5) 9/1: 000140-4: Keen & led, hdd over 2f out, no extra bef dist:	shd	54a
264	LANOS 15 [2] R Ford 6-8-11 t (60) D Fentiman (5) 8/1: 166544-5: Dwelt, rear, hdwy halfway, rdn & btn 3f out:	9	47a
277	NOWELL HOUSE 13 [3] M W Easterby 8-9-7 (70) P Mulrennan (5) 7/2: 141653-6: Chsd ldrs, btn 2f out:	6	50a

6 Ran   2m 41.77 (7.47)   Owner The B C W Partnership   Trained at Royston

389 — 1.50 Bet Direct No Q Demo 08000 837 888 Claiming Stakes 3yo (F)
£2933 £838 £419   7f f/sand rnd   Going 23   -19 Slow   Stalls Inside

207*	SIR JASPER 28 [4] T D Barron 3-8-7 vis (59) D Mernagh 2/1 FAV: 5561-1: Made all, in command 2f out, eased down nr fin, easily:		73a
283*	TURF PRINCESS 11 [1] Ian Emmerson 3-9-0 (62) D Fentiman (7) 4/1: 10226-12: Mid-div, drvn & kept on fnl 2f, no ch with easy wnr:	10	60a
203	JASMINE PEARL 28 [8] B J Meehan 3-8-6 (62) L Keniry (2) 7/1: 52055-3: Chsd ldr over 2f out, drvn & no impress sn after:	2½	47a
355	CASANTELLA 5 [2] M J Polglase 3-8-0 (47) J Mackay 25/1: 00036-04: Rear, late gains for press, no dngr:	shd	41a
247	NANNA 18 [6] R Hollinshead 3-8-4 Dale Gibson 40/1: 00-5: Cl-up 5f, sn btn.	6	35a
247*	TICTACTOE 18 [7] D J Daly 3-8-8 (57) C Catlin 7/2: 045361-6: Chsd ldrs wide till 2f out:	5	30a
4726}	MRS CEE 92 [3] M G Quinlan 3-8-7 BL (76) S W Kelly 9/1: 10446-7: Slow away & al bhd:	12	8a
226	GET TO THE POINT 25 [5] P W D'Arcy 3-8-11 VIS (59) J Quinn 9/2: 400050-8: Chsd ldrs 3f:	1	10a

8 Ran   1m 29.56 (2.96)   Owner Mrs Liz Jones   Trained at Thirsk

390 — 2.20 Littlewoods Bet Direct Handicap Stakes Div 2 4yo+ 0-80 (D) [80]
£4046 £1245 £623 £311   6f f/sand rnd   Going 23   +01 Fast   Stalls Inside

171	QUIET TIMES 35 [9] K A Ryan 5-9-11 bl (77) N Callan 6/1: 650120-1: Broke well & sn prom, led 2f out, rdn clr, readily:		87a
106	BOND ROYALE 48 [3] B Smart 4-9-13 (79) M Stainton (7) 16/1: 000040-2: Hmpd start, trkd ldrs, kept on for press fnl 2f:	4	79a
1919}	ROYAL GRAND 223 [2] T D Barron 4-9-6 (72) P Makin (7) 8/1: 435312-3: Cl-up, styd on onepace for press:	1¼	68a
349	BLAKESHALL QUEST 5 [8] R Brotherton 4-9-0 VIS (66) F P Ferris (3) 33/1: 00000-04: Towards rear, styd on wide, nrst fin:	nk	61a
262	AWARDING 15 [5] R F Johnson Houghton 4-9-9 t (75) C Catlin 9/1: 456506-5: Hmpd start & rear, kept on onepace for press.	1½	65a
198	WINNING PLEASURE 29 [4] J Balding 6-9-6 (72) J Edmunds 7/2: 000052-6: Trkd ldrs, no impress dist.	nk	61a
155	GILDED COVE 38 [10] R Hollinshead 4-9-3 (69) A Culhane 9/1: 121310-7: Bhd/wide, little prog.	¾	56a

SOUTHWELL Tuesday 13.01.04 Lefthand, Sharp, Oval Track

4425*} JOHNSTONS DIAMOND 111 [6] E J Alston 6-9-11 (77) Dean McKeown 2/1 FAV: 244101-8: Trkd ldrs 4f: ½   62a
193   AFRICAN SPUR 31 [7] P A Blockley 4-9-3 (69) Derek Nolan (7) 12/1: 200000-9: Al bhd.   1¼   50a
3971} WINTHORPE 136 [1] J J Quinn 4-10-0 (80) L Fletcher (3) 25/1: 211100-0: Led till 2f out, sn btn: 2   55a
10 Ran   1m 14.59 (1.29)   Owner Yorkshire Racing Club and Fran   Trained at Hambleton

391
2.50 Betdirect Co Uk Handicap Stakes 4yo+ 0-80 (D)   [77]
£4076 £1254 £627 £314   **1m3f f/sand**   Going 23   -07 Slow   Stalls Inside

173   DIGGER 35 [9] Miss Gay Kelleway 5-9-8 (71) M Fenton 4/1: 025236-1: Prom wide, led dist, drvn & held on well: 75a
174   STREET LIFE 34 [8] W J Musson 6-9-4 (67) Lisa Jones (3) 7/2: 300006-2: Trkd ldrs wide, drvn to chall ins last, just held cl-home: ½   69a
257   TROUBLE MOUNTAIN 17 [7] M W Easterby 7-9-9 (72) Dale Gibson 3/1 FAV: 544023-3: Trkd ldrs wide, drvn & onepace fnl 2f: 1¼   72a
239*   HIAWATHA 22 [2] T D Barron 5-9-3 (66) D Mernagh 7/1: 020201-4: Trkd ldrs, no extra 1f out: 6   58a
191*   THEATRE TINKA 31 [4] R Hollinshead 5-9-7 p (70) N Callan 14/1: 003201-5: Trkd ldr, led 3f out, hdd & btn dist.   3   58a
5008} FIDDLERS CREEK 69 [5] R Allan 5-9-12 (75) A Culhane 7/1: 240360-6: Held up, btn 2f out: 2½   59a
577}   ENVIRONMENT AUDIT 339 [6] J R Jenkins 5-9-12 (75) S W Kelly 50/1: 32100/0-7: Al bhd: 5   53a
178*   HIP HOP HARRY 34 [3] E A L Dunlop 4-9-10 (76) W Ryan 13/2: 31031-8: Al rear: 3½   49a
318   JAMESTOWN 8 [1] M J Polglase 7-7-12 (47) J Mackay 20/1: 54063-59: Led till 3f out, sn btn: 13   4a
9 Ran   2m 24.57 (3.27)   Owner The Inside Rail   Trained at Newmarket

392
3.20 Littlewoodscasino Com Selling Stakes 4-6yo (G)
£2520 £720 £360   **1m4f f/sand**   Going 23   -14 Slow   Stalls Inside

339   COOLFORE JADE 6 [6] N E Berry 4-8-8 (55) C Catlin 7/1: 40045-01: Trkd ldrs, hdwy wide to lead over 1f out, drvn & just held on, al out: 60a
191   PLATINUM CHARMER 31 [2] K A Ryan 4-8-13 (65) N Callan 12/1: 300004-2: Held up, drvn to chall over 1f out, just held in a driving fin: hd   64a
727}   EIGHT WOODS 318 [3] T D Barron 6-9-3 (65) D Mernagh 5/4 FAV: 22/0/663-3: Held up, rdn & hung left over 1f out, not able to chal: 3   60a
281   GRAND LASS 11 [1] T D Barron 5-8-12 vis (50) P Makin (7) 4/1: 02046-34: Trkd ldrs, led over 4f out, hdd over 1f out, no: 2½   51a
359   LUXI RIVER 4 [5] P A Blockley 4-8-13 (66) G Parkin 2/1: 452/64-55: Cl-up 4f out, btn 2f out: 3   52a
244   KAMALA 22 [4] R Brotherton 5-8-12 (50) F P Ferris (3) 50/1: 203/00P-6: Led till over 4f out, sn bhd.   dist   0a
6 Ran   2m 38.73 (4.43)   Owner Leeway Group Limited   Trained at Earlswood

393
3.50 Bet Direct In Vision Sky Page 293 Handicap Stakes Div 2 4yo+ 0-65 (F)   [64]
£2947 £842 £421   **1m f/sand rnd**   Going 23   +02 Fast   Stalls Inside

332*   NAJAABA 7 [1] Miss J Feilden 4-9-11 6ex (62) B Reilly (5) 4/5 FAV: 0/0431-11: Dwelt, rear, hdwy/swtchd to lead over 1f out, shaken up to assert, cosily, prob val for 3L: 76a
178   WAR OWL 34 [7] Ian Williams 7-9-2 (53) Lisa Jones (3) 12/1: 4550/04-2: Handy & led over 2f out, rdn & hdd dist, kept on for press: ¾   58a
346   MUTARAFAA 5 [6] D Shaw 5-9-7 e (58) T Hamilton (5) 13/2: 22211-43: Held up, styd on onepace.   6   52a
280   MON SECRET 13 [2] B Smart 6-9-10 (61) R Ffrench 11/1: 001213-4: Chsd ldrs, no impress: nk   54a
346   SPY GUN 5 [4] T Wall 4-9-9 (60) N Chalmers (5) 6/1: 00014-35: Handy & led halfway, hdd over 2f out, wknd.   1½   51a
4257} GOLDBRICKER 119 [9] W M Brisbourne 4-9-0 (51) B Swarbrick (7) 20/1: 053302-6: Prom wide till over 2f out: 6   31a
228*   GAME GURU 25 [5] T D Barron 5-10-0 (65) Laura Jayne Crawford (7) 6/1: 000301-7: Led till halfway, sn btn: 2   40a
331   SILVER CRYSTAL 7 [8] Mrs N Macauley 4-8-11 1ow vis (47) P McCabe 80/1: 06450-08: Dwelt & al bhd.   15   0a
8 Ran   1m 41.1 (1.7)   Owner Mr A K Sparks   Trained at Newmarket

WOLVERHAMPTON Wednesday 14.01.04 Lefthand, Sharp, Oval Track

Official Going Standard

394
1.30 Bet Direct No Q 08000 93 66 93 Banded Stakes 3yo+ 0-35 (H)
£1425 £407 £204   **7f f/sand rnd**   Going 41   -34 Slow   Stalls Outside

4459} DAFA 464 [9] B J Curley 8-9-7 (30) Paul Scallan 9/4: 0005///0/-: Slow away, prog 4f out, rdn out to lead well ins fnl 1f: 41a
377*   ETERNAL BLOOM 237 [4] M Brittain 6-9-7 (35) M Lawson (7) 2/1 FAV: 650/000-2: Cl-up, edged left & ev ch dist, kept on, just held by wnr: ½   38a
2244} PACKIN EM IN 209 [12] J R Boyle 6-9-7 (35) M Henry 10/1: 00/000-3: Cl-up, edged left & dist, veered left under press & hdd well ins fnl 1f, no extra: 2½   33a
300   KELTIC FLUTE 11 [2] Mrs Lucinda Featherstone 5-9-7 vis (35) S Yourston (7) 50/1: 02000/-04: Prom, led 4f out, hdd dist, sn no extra.   hd   32a
372   COUNTRYWIDE GIRL 2 [1] A Berry 5-9-7 (30) Donna Caldwell (7) 16/1: 000U-035: Led 2f, no extra fnl 2f.   ¾   30a
299   GOOD FORM 11 [11] Miss K M George 4-9-7 (35) Derek Nolan (7) 10/1: 30000-56: Held up, nvr a factor.   7   16a
319   SENNEN COVE 9 [3] R Bastiman 5-9-7 t (35) K Dalgleish 4/1: 45000-07: Mid-div, wknd fnl 3f: 2   12a
352   HOME COMING 6 [6] P S Felgate 6-9-7 (35) Dean McKeown 10/1: 00000-68: Mid-div, hung left 3f out, sn fdd, lame.   10   0a
420]   DEAL IN FACTS 725 [8] C N Kellett 5-9-7 (35) Susannah Wileman (7) 50/1: 00000/00/-9: Slow away, al well adrift.   29   0a
2596} SINGLE TRACK MIND 196 [5] J R Boyle 6-9-7 (35) J Fanning 14/1: 0000/000-0: Slow away, bhd, 'lost action'.   2   0a
10 Ran   1m 31.46 (5.26)   Owner Mrs B J Curley   Trained at Newmarket

395
2.00 Bet Direct No Q Demo 08000 837 888 Banded Stakes 4yo+ 0-35 (H)
£1362 £389 £195   **2m46y f/sand**   Going 41   -41 Slow   Stalls Inside

301   UNLEADED 11 [7] J Akehurst 4-8-11 (35) J Mackay 9/4 FAV: 0/0000-21: Held up, prog 7f out, led 5f out, pushed out fnl 1f, val 3L+:   36a

301	THE LAST MOHICAN 11 [4] P Howling 5-9-4 p (30) K Dalgleish 3/1: 600/50-42: Held up, prog 6f out, chsd wnr 4f out, kept on fnl 1f, not pace wnr:	1½	33a
307	MARAUD 10 [6] R Hollinshead 10-9-4 (30) Stephanie Hollinshead (7) 3/1: 0030////-5: Led, hdd 5f out, fdd 3f out:	18	17a
357	IRELANDS EYE 6 [5] J R Norton 9-9-4 (30) J Bramhill 3/1: 0/460//0-3: Slow away, hmpd bef 1m out, prog 6f out, fdd 4f out:	8	9a
4331}	ALIABAD 117 [2] J G M O'Shea 9-9-4 vis (30) Dean McKeown 11/1: 00/0000-5: Held up, nvr a factor:	dist	0a
302	REPETOIRE 11 [1] K O Cunningham Brown 4-8-11 (30) D R McCabe 40/1: 40B00-06: Cl-up, fdd 5f out, eased fnl 3f.	27	0a

6 Ran 3m 42.39 (13.1) Owner Canisbay Bloodstock Trained at Epsom

---

396 2.35 Littlewoods Bet Direct Median Auction Maiden Stakes 3-5yo (H)
£1463 £418 £209 7f f/sand rnd Going 41 -11 Slow Stalls Outside

1241}	MODESTY BLAISE 260 [4] Miss Gay Kelleway 4-9-5 T Eaves (5) 9/1: 00-1: Hld up, prog 5f out, led 2f out, pushed clr, val		69a
5032}	WEAKEST LINK 67 [6] W Jarvis 3-8-6 D Allan (3) 16/1: 0-2: Cl-up, chsd ldr ins fnl 1f, al held:	6	62a
29	TWO OF CLUBS 61 [10] P C Haslam 3-8-6 (66) D Fentiman (7) 9/4: 43454-3: Bhd, onepcd fnl 1f.	1¼	60a
319	ILE FACILE 9 [7] N P Littmoden 3-8-6 K Dalgleish 11/8 FAV: 24: Slow away, sn outpcd, mod late stages:	shd	59a
299	DANCES IN TIME 11 [3] C N Kellett 4-9-5 T Williams 100/1: 05: Led 1f, styd cl-up, led briefly bef 2f out, wknd.	½	53a
299	IAMBACK 11 [1] Miss Gay Kelleway 4-9-5 bl (47) T Hamilton (5) 11/1: 0/0606-26: Led after 1f, hdd bef 2f out, sn wknd.	4	45a
299	ANGELOS PRIDE 11 [8] J A Osborne 3-8-6 Paul Eddery 10/1: 0-37: Dwelt, al in rear:	5	40a
4816}	ANOTHER EXPLETIVE 86 [2] J White 3-8-1 (47) R Thomas 41: 00004-8: Cl-up, fdd 4f out:	2½	30a
3	DIAL SQUARE 65 [5] P Howling 3-8-6 J Fanning 10/1: 00-9: Handy, fdd 4f out:	2	31a
319	SVENSON 9 [11] J S Wainwright 3-8-6 D R McCabe 66/1: 0-00: Al bhd.	3	25a
183	FIRE CAT 33 [9] A P Jones 5-9-10 P (45) A Nicholls 25/1: 225000-0: Al well adrift:	24	0a

11 Ran 1m 29.89 (3.69) Owner Twilight Racing Trained at Newmarket

---

397 3.10 Betdirect Co Uk Banded Stakes 3yo+ 0-45 (H)
£1652 £472 £236 6f f/sand rnd Going 41 -01 Slow Stalls Inside

384	ATTORNEY 2 [4] D Shaw 6-9-6 e (45) T Hamilton (5) 5/1: 00004-371: Sn outpcd, prog 3f out, led dist, all out to hold on:		46a
379	PORT NATAL 2 [3] P Morris 6-9-6 bl (40) L Treadwell (7) 5/1: 600501-72: Cl-up, chsd ldr 2f out, kept on well fnl 1f, only just denied:	nk	44a
297	SABANA 11 [5] J M Bradley 6-9-6 (45) P Fitzsimons 14/1: 03000-43: Sn outpcd, prog 2f out, onepcd.	3	35a
166	SILVER MASCOT 36 [8] R Hollinshead 5-9-6 (45) Dale Gibson 8/1: 60/0600-4: Handy, outpcd 2f out, rallied fnl 1f:	¾	33a
282	PILGRIM PRINCESS 12 [10] E J Alston 6-9-6 (45) A Nicholls 13/8 FAV: 56246-35: Cl-up, no extra fnl 2f:	nk	32a
282	PLAYFUL SPIRIT 12 [2] J Balding 5-9-6 vis (45) J Edmunds (7) 33/1: 000001-06: Cl-up, led 3f out, hdd dist, sn wknd.	nk	31a
3311}	LONG WEEKEND 166 [1] D Shaw 6-9-6 e (45) P Makin (7) 14/1: 001460-7: Slow away, nvr nrr than mid-div:	3½	22a
296	PIPS SONG 11 [13] P W Hiatt 9-9-6 (45) J Tate 12/1: 03000-08: Cl-up, lost place after 1f, nvr a danger.	1¼	19a
312	MESMERISED 9 [6] Miss A Stokell 4-9-6 (45) Ann Stokell 33/1: 30000-09: Nvr nrr than mid-div.	hd	18a
312	STAR APPLAUSE 9 [7] J Balding 4-9-6 VIS (45) D Allan (3) 25/1: 06000-00: Led, hdd 3f out, fdd fnl 2f.	5	4a
4243}	GARNOCK BELLE 121 [12] A Berry 3-8-4 (45) J Fanning 25/1: 500-0: Al in rear:	1½	0a
4695}	SALONIKA SKY 94 [9] C W Thornton 3-8-4 (45) J McAuley 40/1: 05000-0: Cl-up, wknd 3f out:	1¼	0a
233	LADY ELLENDUNE 25 [11] D J S ffrench Davis 3-8-4 (40) J Mackay 33/1: 000000-0: Al well adrift:	23	0a

13 Ran 1m 15.36 (2.56) Owner Mr K Nicholls Trained at Newark

---

398 3.40 Littlewoodscasino Com Selling Stakes 3yo+ (H)
£1491 £426 £213 1m100y f/sand rnd Going 41 +12 Fast Stalls Inside

	CONSONANT 1608 [11] D G Bridgwater 7-9-9 S Righton 9/2: 10////-1: Cl-up, led trav easily 2f out, pushed clr, eased cl-home, val 12L+:		69a
311	NITE OWL FIZZ 9 [1] J O'Reilly 6-9-9 (55) D Allan (3) 3/1 FAV: 60005-42: Handy, styd on to chase ldr ins fnl 1f, al held:	9	49a
129	IVY MOON 46 [9] B J Llewellyn 4-9-4 (47) R Thomas (5) 14/1: 103030-3: Keen rear, prog 5f out, chsd wnr dist, no extra ins fnl 1f:	¾	44a
343*	FRENCH HORN 7 [4] M Wigham 7-10-0 (50) J Mackay 7/2: 30000-14: Held up, prog 3f out, no impress fnl 1f:	1	51a
300	PROUD VICTOR 11 [10] D Shaw 4-9-9 vis (40) T Hamilton (5) 10/1: 04006-45: Held up, hdwy 5f out, onepcd fnl 2f.	1¼	45a
347	LOVES DESIGN 6 [6] Miss S J Wilton 7-9-9 (52) J Tate 9/1: 13350-06: Cl-up, led 5f out, hdd 2f out, sn wknd.	3½	37a
158	SIR FRANK GIBSON 37 [5] M Johnston 3-8-3 (50) J Fanning 7/1: 003040-7: Al bhd.	1½	31a
46	SECOND VENTURE 58 [3] P Howling 6-9-9 p (40) K Dalgleish 12/1: 000504-8: Cl-up, fdd 4f out:	1½	31a
314	LUCKY ROMANCE 9 [8] B J Meehan 5-9-4 BL (45) D R McCabe 9/1: 600/00-59: Led, hdd 3f out, sn wknd:	1¼	24a
354	HAITHEM 6 [2] D Shaw 7-9-9 e (40) R Fitzpatrick 40/1: 0000-600: Al in rear:	½	28a

10 Ran 1m 48.69 (2.49) Owner The Rule Racing Syndicate Trained at Winchcombe

---

399 4.10 Bet Direct In Vision Sky Page 293 Apprentice Banded Stakes 3yo+ 0-35 (H)
£1369 £391 £196 1m1f79y f/sand Going 41 -18 Slow Stalls Inside

165	BELLA PAVLINA 37 [4] W M Brisbourne 6-9-9 (35) B Swarbrick (5) 15/8 FAV: 0345/36-1: Cl-up, outpcd 4f out, rallied well to lead ins fnl 1f, rdn out:		38a
314	GIUST IN TEMP 9 [3] P W Hiatt 5-9-9 (30) P Makin (3) 9/2: 00650-42: Cl-up, led 6f out, hdd 5f out, led again 3f out, hdd ins fnl 1f, not pace wnr:	1½	34a
240	VESTA FLAME 23 [6] M Johnston 3-8-1 (35) R Thomas 20/1: 000-3: Led 2f, outpcd 4f out, rallied fnl 1f:	½	33a
301	ALL ON MY OWN 11 [7] I W McInnes 9-9-9 bl (35) Natalia Gemelova 33/1: 55000-04: Slow away, prog 4f out, no impress fnl 2f.	½	32a
305	MISTY MAN 10 [8] Miss J Feilden 6-9-9 bd (30) P Gallagher (3) 5/2: 00044-35: Slow away, strayed on to lead 5f out, hdd 3f out, no extra dist:	¾	31a
4787}	MIDDLEHAM ROSE 89 [1] P C Haslam 3-8-1 (35) D Fentiman (5) 9/2: 000-6: Rear, nvr nrr than mid-div.	1	29a
310	MANIKATO 9 [9] K G Wingrove 10-9-9 (30) L Treadwell 20/1: 00660-07: Cl-up, fdd 3f out.	5	22a
3599}	BY DEFINITION 153 [5] J C Tuck 6-9-9 (30) M Savage 50/1: 000/000-8: Prom, fdd 5f out:	14	2a
290	BATTLE BACK 11 [2] S C Williams 3-8-1 BL e (30) Derek Nolan 12/1: 00-09: Held up, nvr a factor:	8	0a

9 Ran   2m 3.72 (5.52)   Owner The Cartmel Syndicate   Trained at Baschurch

LINGFIELD Wednesday 14.01.04 Lefthand, V Sharp Track

Official Going Standard

400	**12.10 Bet Direct At Lingfield Park Apprentice Claiming Stakes 4yo+ (F)**			
	£2947 £842 £421	6f p/track rnd	Going 31	+14 Fast	Stalls Inside

317*	**HURRICANE COAST** 9 [2] D Flood 5-9-3 BL (61) R Miles (3) 5/1: 2344-111: Chsd ldr, led over 2f out & sn in command, rdly:		80a
271	**RIPPLE EFFECT** 15 [9] C A Dwyer 4-8-12 t (67) R Reilly (3) 7/4 FAV: 530102-2: Mid-div, hdwy to chase wnr over 1f out, kept on but no impress:	5	62a
360	**MUQTADI** 5 [1] M Quinn 6-8-9 (51) L Enstone 20/1: 14650-03: Dwelt, well bhd, late gains, nrst fin:	1¼	55a
285	**CRETAN GIFT** 12 [7] N P Littmoden 13-9-3 vis (73) J P Guillambert 5/1: 0//0500-54: Held up, late gains.	1¼	59a
214	**KOMENA** 28 [6] J W Payne 6-8-4 (47) Lisa Jones 25/1: 305240-5: Chsd ldrs, btn dist:	3	37a
151	**WESTMEAD TANGO** 39 [5] J R Jenkins 4-8-7 3ow (49) P Bradley 25/1: 0/01200-6: Chsd ldrs, keen, btn over 1f out.	3	31a
292	**HAWK** 11 [13] P R Chamings 6-8-9 (69) N Chalmers (3) 10/1: 01305-07: Led till over 2f out, sn btn.	1	30a
323	**DUNEDIN RASCAL** 8 [10] E A Wheeler 7-8-3 bl (66) Liam Jones (7) 10/1: 00400-08: Rear, nvr a factor.	nk	23a
290	**THINK IT OVER** 11 [8] A P Jones 5-7-12 Hayley Turner (4) 66/1: 09: Wide & sn bhd.	1¼	14a
343	**ISLAND STAR** 7 [11] S Dow 4-8-7 VIS (48) S Donohoe 25/1: 00060-00: Held up, nvr factor.	2	17a
4121}	**HAPPY CAMPER** 150 [12] C Von Der Recke 4-8-7 Rory Moore (5) 8/1: 630245-0: Chsd ldrs till halfway:	7	0a
4780}	**ZEITLOS** 89 [4] R M Flower 5-8-3 bl (40) F P Ferris 33/1: 000000-0: Rear, no ch 2f out, eased, abs.	4	0a
166	**EASTERN BLUE** 36 [3] Mrs L Stubbs 5-8-12 p (50) Kristin Stubbs (5) 8/1: 500622-W: Withdrawn, wearing undeclared head gear.		0a

13 Ran   1m 11.43 (1.03)   Owner Mrs Ruth M Serrell   Trained at Lingfield

401	**12.40 Bet Direct On Sky Active Maiden Stakes 4yo+ (D)**			
	£3513 £1081 £541 £270	1m p/track rnd	Going 31	-09 Slow	Stalls Outside

1367}	**DAWN PIPER** 254 [8] D R Loder 4-9-0 J P Spencer 1/3 FAV: 32-1: Trkd ldrs, smooth prog to lead over 1f out, rdly asserted, val for 8L+:		83a
4718}	**BALLINGER RIDGE** 93 [1] A M Balding 5-9-0 (65) Martin Dwyer 10/1: 200063-2: Led till over 1f out, kept on but no ch with easy wnr:	5	64a
170	**HAVE SOME FUN** 36 [2] P R Chamings 4-9-0 J Quinn 50/1: 6-3: Dwelt, sn handy, onepace fnl 2f:	nk	64a
	SKIP OF COLOUR 216 [4] P A Blockley 4-9-0 (83) D Nolan (5) 12/1: 340-4: Trkd ldr, no extra dist, abs.	1½	61a
269	**MARGERY DAW** 15 [6] M P Tregoning 4-8-9 E Ahern 11/2: 3/2252-5: Trkd ldrs, onepace fnl 2f:	shd	56a
344	**ANGELICA GARNETT** 7 [11] T E Powell 4-8-9 (52) M Fenton 40/1: 06/000-06: Keen, rear, only mod late prog.	5	46a
150	**BALMACARA** 39 [9] Miss K B Boutflower 5-8-9 p (48) I Mongan 16/1: 000554-7: Mid-div, no impress fnl 2f.	½	44a
	ALISA [3] B I Case 4-8-9 Hilda Jones 50/1: 8: Slow away & keen mid-div, btn 2f out.	¾	44a
1412}	**LUCRETIUS** 250 [7] D K Ivory 5-9-0 (47) N Callan 66/1: 0600-9: Sn drvn rear, nvr factor, abs.	1½	45a
	SALEEN [5] P D Cundell 4-8-9 S Whitworth 100/1: 0: Slow away & rear, no ch 2f out, debut.	10	23a
4519}	**MISS CELERITY** 107 [10] M J Haynes 4-8-9 (30) C Catlin 66/1: 060-0: Chsd ldrs, wknd qckly over 2f out, abs.	7	11a
290	**SPIDERS WEB** 11 [12] T Keddy 4-9-0 S Carson 50/1: 0/-00: Wide/rear, t.o. 3f out.	14	0

12 Ran   1m 39.41 (3.21)   Owner Jumeirah Racing   Trained at Newmarket

402	**1.10 Bet Direct On Sky Text Page 372 Handicap Stakes 3yo 0-60 (F)**				[66]
	£2961 £846 £423	1m p/track rnd	Going 31	-21 Slow	Stalls Outside

4580}	**DIAMOND WAY** 103 [9] D R Loder 3-9-7 VIS (59) J P Spencer 2/1 FAV: 000-1: Pushed along towards rear, rdn & hdwy to lead dist, drvn out:		68a
295	**PARK AVE PRINCESS** 11 [3] N P Littmoden 3-9-2 (54) I Mongan 9/1: 00460-22: Chsd ldrs, led over 2f out, hdd dist, kept on:	¾	59a
327	**LADY MO** 8 [6] Andrew Reid 3-8-12 (50) J P Guillambert (3) 50/1: 36050-53: Rear, hdwy/no room over 1f out, kept on well ins last:	1½	52a
295	**SONDERBORG** 11 [11] G L Moore 3-9-2 p (54) G Carter 9/2: 63006-64: Trkd ldr, ch 2f out, sn no extra.	3	50a
326*	**PRINCESS ISMENE** 8 [2] J Jay 3-9-8 6ex bl (60) N Callan 11/1: 10405-15: Rear, short of room over 2f out, onepace:	2½	51a
4765}	**EL MAGNIFICO** 90 [10] P D Cundell 3-9-4 (56) S Whitworth 20/1: 006-6: Mid-div, outpcd fnl 2f:	1½	44a
177	**MAGICO** 35 [8] A M Balding 3-9-1 VIS (53) Martin Dwyer 33/1: 0000-7: Led till over 2f out, sn wknd:	1½	38a
295	**MUST BE SO** 11 [5] J J Bridger 3-8-10 (48) N Pollard 14/1: 40031-58: Dwelt, mid-div, no ch over 1f out:	3½	26a
28	**DRUID** 61 [1] P C Haslam 3-9-0 (52) Rory Moore (7) 33/1: 065-9: Dwelt, sn cl-up, btn 2f out:	2½	25a
337	**HEAD BOY** 7 [4] S Dow 3-9-7 (59) P Doe 100/30: 00510-40: Mid-div, lost place 2f out, eased:	hd	31a
189	**TRY THE AIR** 32 [7] C Tinkler 3-9-2 (54) E Ahern 16/1: 0000-0: Chsd ldrs till over 3f out, wknd.	4	18a
189	**ABROGATE** 32 [12] P C Haslam 3-8-12 (50) L Enstone (3) 9/1: 503003-0: Chsd ldrs, wknd qckly 2f out.	1¼	11a

12 Ran   1m 40.38 (4.18)   Owner Jumeirah Racing   Trained at Newmarket

403	**1.40 Betdirect Co Uk Handicap Stakes 3yo 0-85 (D)**				[92]
	£4323 £1330 £665 £333	1m2f p/track	Going 31	-32 Slow	Stalls Inside

100*	**ASCERTAIN** 49 [6] N P Littmoden 3-9-7 (85) I Mongan 3/1: 01-1: Trkd ldrs, trav best & led over 1f out, pushed out:		94a
325	**AMWELL BRAVE** 8 [3] J R Jenkins 3-8-5 (69) S W Kelly 11/4: 00345-22: Trkd ldrs, rdn & narrow lead over 3f out, hdd over 1f out, kept on:	2	73a
365	**DR CERULLO** 4 [4] C Tinkler 3-8-11 (75) E Ahern 5/2 FAV: 26301-33: Led till over 3f out, no extra dist:	1	78a
229	**MARCUS EILE** 25 [5] K R Burke 3-9-5 (83) Darren Williams 7/1: 044263-4: Cl-up, btn 2f out:	13	56a
291*	**LYRICAL GIRL** 11 [1] H J Manners 3-8-0 3oh 2ow (59) C Catlin 6/1: 30031-15: Rear & pushed along halfway, no ch fnl 3f:	5	42a
351	**LADY BAHIA** 6 [2] R P Elliott 3-8-0 (64) J Quinn 25/1: 00240-06: Cl-up, btn 3f out:	6	34a

6 Ran   2m 09.05 (6.25)   Owner Mr Paul J Dixon   Trained at Newmarket

---

404	2.10 Bet Direct On 0800 32 93 93 Stakes Handicap 4yo+ 0-90 (C)	[89]

£7293 £2767 £1383 £629   1m4f p/track   Going 31   -20 Slow   Stalls Inside

147	**COLD TURKEY 39** [8] G L Moore 4-9-0 (79) S Whitworth 6/1 FAV: 011112-1: Rear, hdwy & not clr run over 1f out till ins last, styd on to lead home:		**86a**
293	**INTERNATIONALGUEST 11** [7] G G Margarson 5-9-3 vis (78) N Pollard 25/1: 00360-02: Trkd ldrs, rdn & led over 1f out, hdd cl-home:	nk	83a
142*	**MR MISCHIEF 42** [10] P C Haslam 4-9-6 (85) L Enstone (3) 14/1: 050211-3: Rear, styd on wide for press fnl 2f:	1	88a
178	**CLASSIC ROLE 35** [4] R Ingram 5-8-11 (72) I Mongan 16/1: 000030-4: Trkd ldrs, poised to chall when no room dist, kept on ins last:	¾	74a
293	**TIGHT SQUEEZE 11** [3] P W Hiatt 7-9-3 (78) A Culhane 13/2: 55011-65: Held up, eff when no room over 1f out, switched & kept on ins last, nrst fin:	¾	79a
83	**TYPHOON TILLY 53** [14] C R Egerton 7-9-0 (75) M Fenton 10/1: 133033-6: Keen in mid-div, hdwy to chall over 1f out, no extra:	nk	75a
293	**HIGH POINT 11** [5] G P Enright 6-9-5 (80) J P Spencer 8/1: 50001-07: Trkd ldrs, lost place over 2f out, kept on late.	nk	79a
3316}	**BORDER TALE 166** [15] C Weedon 4-9-1 (80) Hayley Turner (5) 33/1: 361254-8: Keen & held up, hdwy to chall 3f out, wknd dist:	hd	78a
294	**EASTER OGIL 11** [2] Jane Southcombe 9-8-3 (64) Lisa Jones (3) 10/1: 06422-59: Rear, eff over 2f out, no impress.	¾	61a
293	**BRIAREUS 11** [9] A M Balding 4-9-1 (80) Martin Dwyer 11/1: 50324-00: Keen, dsptd lead till over 1f out, wknd.	hd	76a
3502}	**MOON EMPEROR 158** [1] J R Jenkins 7-10-0 (89) E Ahern 7/1: 065500-0: Rear, no factor, btn dist:	½	84a
293	**DUSTY CARPET 11** [12] M J Weeden 6-9-0 (75) N Callan 66/1: 33220//-00: Mid-div, short of room over 2f out & again over 1f out, no impress.	nk	69a
293	**GALLANT BOY 11** [13] P D Evans 5-9-1 t (76) S Donohoe (7) 8/1: 05050-00: Chsd ldrs, btn 2f out:	¾	69a
288	**WESTERN 11** [11] J Akehurst 4-8-13 (78) C Catlin 10/1: 05641-20: Dwelt, rear, eff wide, no prog:	nk	70a
83	**NAWOW 53** [6] P D Cundell 4-9-0 (79) S Carson 16/1: 650326-0: Led/dsptd lead till 3f out, sn btn, jumps fit.	2½	67a
257	**VICTORY QUEST 18** [16] Mrs S Lamyman 4-8-8 vis (73) J Quinn 14/1: 125212-0: Keen, trkd ldrs, btn 3f out:	15	43a

16 Ran   2m 35.26 (6.06)   Owner Mr A Grinter   Trained at Brighton

---

405	2.45 Bet Direct Selling Stakes 3yo (G)	

£2562 £732 £366   5f p/track rnd   Going 31   -08 Slow   Stalls Outside

371*	**SMART STARPRINCESS 4** [5] P A Blockley 3-8-13 VIS (58) N Callan 1/1 FAV: 54411-11: Made all & sn well clr, al holding on ins last:		**67a**
371	**IVORY LACE 4** [2] D K Ivory 3-8-13 (60) I Mongan 6/1: 61500-52: Chsd wnr, kept on but nvr able to chall:	3	55a
247	**EMARADIA 19** [3] P D Evans 3-8-13 bl (48) Joanna Badger 14/1: 345422-3: Dsptd 2nd, kept on for press, nvr a threat to wnr:	1½	50a
327	**STAMFORD BLUE 8** [9] J S Moore 3-9-4 bl (50) Martin Dwyer 11/2: 00035-24: Rdn & bhd, kept on wide, nrst fin:	nk	54a
217	**EASILY AVERTED 28** [10] J A Osborne 3-9-4 (70) S W Kelly 7/2: 413006-5: Chsd ldrs wide, no impress 1f out.	hd	53a
319	**HARBOUR PRINCESS 9** [4] M F Harris 3-8-7 L Fletcher (3) 66/1: 06: Rdn rear, nrst fin:	¾	40a
4874}	**LAVISH TIMES 82** [6] A Berry 3-9-4 bl (52) F Lynch 20/1: 540030-7: Mid-div, outpcd, nvr factor:	1¾	46a
4941}	**A BID IN TIME 77** [7] D Shaw 3-8-13 (48) Darren Williams 33/1: 000000-8: Held up & wide, sn struggling:	1¾	36a
326	**GENTLEMAN GEORGE 8** [1] D K Ivory 3-8-12 (45) J Quinn 50/1: 0500-09: Sn outpcd rear.	5	20a

9 Ran   59.74 (1.94)   Owner Brooklands Racing   Trained at Southwell

---

406	3.20 Press Interactive To Bet Direct Handicap Stakes 3yo+ 46-55 (F)	[55]

£2982 £852 £426   1m p/track rnd   Going 31   -25 Slow   Stalls Outside

339	**MUYASSIR 7** [2] Miss B Sanders 9-9-12 (53) J Quinn 6/1 CO FAV: 00100-01: Trkd ldrs, drvn to lead well ins last:		**55a**
236	**DOUBLE RANSOM 25** [1] Mrs L Stubbs 5-9-12 bl (53) S W Kelly 6/1 CO FAV: 000032-2: Dwelt & held up, hdwy rail halfway & poised to chall from 2f out, drvn/styd on, nrst fin:	nk	54a
236	**KYLE OF LOCHALSH 25** [4] G G Margarson 4-10-0 P (55) N Pollard 8/1: 103000-3: Trkd ldrs, drvn to chall over 1f out, just held cl-home:	hd	56a
230	**MAGIC WARRIOR 25** [5] J C Fox 4-10-0 (55) R Smith 6/1 CO FAV: 500505-4: Chsd clr ldr, keen, rdn & led over 1f out, hdd ins last, no extra:	dht	56a
344	**TAIYO 7** [3] J W Payne 4-9-11 (52) N Callan 9/1: 50560-65: Held up, chsd ldrs 2f out, not able to chall.	1½	50a
344	**VIZULIZE 7** [8] A W Carroll 5-9-12 (53) A Culhane 25/1: 05540-06: Towards rear, eff 2f out, no impress.	1	48a
264	**FIFE AND DRUM 16** [12] Miss J Feilden 7-9-13 bl (54) B Reilly (5) 7/1: 222U00-7: Led & sn clr, hdd over 1f out, fdd.	1	47a
230	**FABRIAN 25** [10] D W P Arbuthnot 6-9-12 (53) G Carter 12/1: 005540-8: Held up wide, pulled hard, nvr factor.	shd	46a
236	**ANSWERED PROMISE 25** [7] A W Carroll 5-9-13 (54) S Whitworth 9/1: 101000-9: Mid-div, btn 2f out, op 20/1.	½	46a
344	**MISTER CLINTON 7** [6] D K Ivory 7-9-12 P (53) I Mongan 12/1: 10000-00: Rear, no impress fnl 2f, chkpcs.	1¼	42a
344	**PANCAKEHILL 7** [11] D K Ivory 5-9-12 p (53) E Ahern 13/2: 36550-00: Sn bhd, nvr factor.	3	36a
4615}	**SENNA 100** [9] P D Cundell 4-9-11 (52) S Carson 33/1: 0000-0: Prom till halfway, t.o., abs.	17	6a

12 Ran   1m 40.71 (4.51)   Owner Mr J M Quinn   Trained at Epsom

---

407	3.50 Littlewoodspoker Com Handicap Stakes 4yo+ 0-70 (E)	[70]

£3332 £952 £476   6f p/track rnd   Going 31   -05 Slow   Stalls Inside

340+*	**TAYIF 7** [3] Andrew Reid 8-9-5 6ex t (61) S Carson 4/1 FAV: 0603-211: Dwelt, rear, hdwy when no room over 2f out, squeezed thro' gap & drvn to lead line, all out:		**67a**
329	**CURRENCY 8** [1] J M Bradley 7-10-0 (70) E Ahern 5/1: 6600-032: Mid-div, drvn to lead ins last, just hdd line:	shd	75a
349	**PLAYTIME BLUE 6** [8] K R Burke 4-9-5 (61) Darren Williams 20/1: 44002-23: Led mid ins last:	1½	61a
121	**POLAR FORCE 46** [4] M R Channon 4-9-6 (62) T O'Brien (7) 8/1: 006003-4: Prom, ch dist, onepace.	½	60a
323	**KILMEENA LAD 8** [12] J C Fox 8-9-11 (67) P Dobbs 10/1: 00/000-25: Dwelt, rear, kept on onepace.	1½	60a
149	**EMERALD FIRE 39** [6] A M Balding 5-10-0 vis (70) N Chalmers (5) 5/1: 030005-6: Rear, late gains wide.	shd	63a
3921}	**HARD TO CATCH 140** [11] D K Ivory 6-10-0 (70) I Mongan 12/1: 300555-7: Led/dsptd lead till over 2f out, abs.	nk	62a
329	**TABOOR 8** [2] J W Payne 6-9-13 h bl (69) N Callan 33/1: 41000-08: Chsd ldr halfway, ch dist, wknd.	½	59a
345*	**WAINWRIGHT 6** [9] P A Blockley 4-9-12 6ex (68) D Nolan (5) 13/2: 35331-19: Cl-up till over 1f out:	¾	56a

107

LINGFIELD Wednesday 14.01.04 Lefthand, V Sharp Track

2462}	SOUNDS LUCKY 201 [10] N P Littmoden 8-9-12 bl (68) J P Guillambert (3) 16/1: 002540-0: Mid-div, btn dist:		1	53a
329	JUWWI 8 [7] J M Bradley 10-10-0 (70) C J Davies (7) 12/1: 0040-040: Slow away, sn drvn & nvr factor:		nk	54a
329	GOODWOOD PRINCE 8 [5] S Dow 4-9-8 (64) P Doe 12/1: 60006-50: Al bhd & no ch when hmpd over 2f out.		½	46a
285	TALLY 12 [11] A Berry 4-10-0 (70) F Lynch 50/1: 10646-00: Prom till over 1f out.		½	50a
231	TEYAAR 25 [13] Mrs N Macauley 8-9-7 bl (63) P McCabe 20/1: 351003-0: Mid-div wide, btn 2f out:		5	29a

14 Ran 1m 12.57 (2.17) Owner Mr A S Reid Trained at Mill Hill London

408 1.10 Press Interactive To Bet Direct Banded Stakes Div 1 3yo+ 0-45 (H)
£1645 £470 £235 1m p/track rnd Going 49 -11 Slow Stalls Outside

265	BALERNO 17 [2] R Ingram 5-9-8 (45) G Carter 11/4: 005300-1: Mid-div, prog 3f out, led dist, sn clr, pushed out, val 2L+:			50a
482}	MISS PEACHES 352 [5] G G Margarson 6-9-8 (45) Kristin Stubbs 20/1: 064/0/00-2: Prom, outpcd 3f out, rallied to chase wnr fnl 1f, kept on, al held by wnr:		¾	47a
354*	ROSTI 7 [8] P C Haslam 4-10-0 (45) Rory Moore 5/4 FAV: 0054-113: Mid-div, hdwy wide 3f out, no impress fnl 2f:		6	42a
372	PAGEANT 3 [10] J M Bradley 7-9-8 (35) C Catlin 14/1: 300-0654: Cl-up, led 4f out, hdd 3f out, no extra.		1¾	31a
310	VLASTA WEINER 10 [1] J M Bradley 4-9-8 bl (40) P Fitzsimons 12/1: 0006-025: Slow away, sn cl-up, led 3f out, hdd dist, fdd:		nk	31a
228	ZAHUNDA 27 [7] W M Brisbourne 5-9-8 (45) B Swarbrick (7) 10/1: 000000-6: Bhd, nvr a factor.		1½	27a
5010}	RO ERIDANI 71 [11] T J Etherington 4-9-8 (45) J McAuley 25/1: 602000-7: Bhd, nvr able to chall:		hd	27a
47	TEDZAR 59 [6] B R Johnson 4-9-8 (35) N Chalmers (5) 25/1: 00/0000-8: Al in rear.		1	25a
326	NOTHING MATTERS 9 [3] P R Chamings 3-8-4 2ow (40) P Doe 10/1: 54005-69: Trkd ldrs, rdn/stumbled 2f out, wknd.		nk	25a
351	TORTUETTE 7 [9] Jean Rene Auvray 3-8-2 VIS (45) Lisa Jones (3) 33/1: 03000-00: Al bhd:		6	11a
309	DANCING KING 11 [4] P W Hiatt 8-9-8 (30) Joanna Badger 20/1: 40000-50: Led, hdd 4f out, sn fdd.		10	0

11 Ran 1m 41.00 (4.8) Owner The Three Amigos Trained at Epsom

409 1.40 Bet Direct On Sky Text Page 372 Median Auction Maiden Stakes 4-6yo (H)
£1292 £369 £185 1m2f p/track Going 49 -33 Slow Stalls Inside

4518}	ITSONLYAGAME 108 [5] R Ingram 4-9-0 (60) I Mongan 6/4 FAV: 30/5406-1: Held up, prog 3f out, styd on to lead ins fnl 1f, rdn out:			51a
324	VANILLA MOON 9 [4] J R Jenkins 4-8-9 vis (48) S W Kelly 15/8: 00405-52: Led, hdd 7f out, styd cl-up, led 2f out, hdd dist, kept on, not pace of wnr:		¾	43a
272	GINGER ICE 16 [1] G G Margarson 4-9-0 p (40) N Pollard 5/1: 000006-3: Held up, prog 3f out, onepcd:		2½	44a
271	JANES VALENTINE 16 [6] J J Bridger 4-8-9 (47) N Callan 10/1: 000000-4: Held up, nvr nrr than mid div.		6	31a
	SOLMORIN 3 [3] R J Baker 6-8-11 V Slattery 20/1: 5: Rcd keenly, led 7f out, hdd & fdd 2f out:		1¾	28a
	GLOBE BEAUTY [2] A D W Pinder 6-8-11 C Catlin 20/1: 6: Handy, fdd 3f out:		11	13a

6 Ran 2m 11.01 (8.21) Owner Mrs Gina Brown Trained at Epsom

410 2.10 Press Interactive To Bet Direct Banded Stakes Div 2 3yo+ 0-45 (H)
£1642 £469 £235 1m p/track rnd Going 49 -13 Slow Stalls Outside

287	TITIAN LASS 13 [7] C E Brittain 5-9-8 bl (45) Dean Williams (7) 9/2: 20200-41: Cl-up, led & edged right dist, rdn out:			46a
351*	YANKEEDOODLEDANDY 7 [2] P C Haslam 3-8-8 (45) D Fentiman (7) 13/8 FAV: 04004-12: V slow away & lost arnd 10L, sn in rear group, hdwy 2f out, no room & swtchd right dist, styd on well fnl 1f,		2	50a
343	LADYWELL BLAISE 8 [9] J J Bridger 7-9-8 (45) N Pollard 14/1: 00064-03: Mid-div, hdwy 3f out, chsd wnr ins fnl 1f, no extra cl-home:		nk	43a
1659}	COLNE VALLEY AMY 237 [8] G L Moore 7-9-8 bl (40) A Quinn (5) 20/1: 422/060-4: Bhd, hdwy 3f out, onepcd fnl 1f:		¾	41a
343	WILOM 8 [10] M R Hoad 6-9-8 (45) C Catlin 7/2: 53403-25: Keen rear, hdwy wide 3f out, no impress 1f out.		1¼	39a
214	BADOU 29 [6] L Montague Hall 4-9-8 (45) R Miles (3) 10/1: 024000-6: Led, hdd dist, wknd.		nk	39a
311	QUEEN EXCALIBUR 10 [5] J M Bradley 5-9-8 (45) P Fitzsimons 25/1: 0040-007: Keen cl-up, fdd fnl 1f.		3	32a
168	FITZ THE BILL 37 [3] N B King 4-9-8 (35) Paul Scallan 33/1: 06000-8: Trkd ldrs, wknd 3f out.		hd	32a
3995}	WESTMEAD ETOILE 136 [1] J R Jenkins 4-9-8 (45) S W Kelly 16/1: 000300-9: Held up, nvr a factor:		nk	31a
297	NEUTRAL NIGHT [4] R Brotherton 4-9-8 vis (45) I Mongan 10/1: 60660-30: Keen cl-up, fdd 2f out:		9	14a

10 Ran 1m 41.20 (5.0) Owner Mr Michael Clarke Trained at Newmarket

411 2.40 Bet Direct On 0800 93 66 93 Banded Stakes 3yo+ 0-45 (H)
£1684 £481 £241 7f p/track rnd Going 49 -06 Slow Stalls Inside

296	LORD MELBOURNE 12 [8] J A Osborne 5-9-7 (45) S W Kelly 5/1 CO FAV: 06035-21: Mid-div, prog & trav v well 2f out, led 1f out, pushed out fnl 1f, val 4L+:			48a
245	THE GAY FOX 20 [15] B G Powell 10-9-7 bl t (40) L Keniry 16/1: 505005-2: Held up, hdwy wide 2f out, kept on ins fnl 1f, no ch with easy wnr:		2½	40a
4861}	ABUELOS 84 [7] S Dow 5-9-7 (40) P Doe 14/1: 000500-3: Held up, short of room 2f out, prog wide dist, nrst fin:		½	39a
297	GEESPOT 19 [7] D J S ffrench Davis 5-9-7 (40) R Miles 20/1: 00500-04: Cl-up, outpcd 2f out, rallied fnl 1f.		nk	38a
379	AINTNECESSARILYSO 3 [11] N E Berry 6-9-7 p (45) M Savage (5) 5/1 CO FAV: 05465-55: Chsd ldrs, chsd wnr briefly ins fnl 1f, sn no extra:		nk	37a
299	SHAMWARI FIRE 12 [6] I W McInnes 4-9-7 (45) Natalia Gemelova (7) 10/1: 24400-46: Prom, wknd fnl 1f:		2	33a
340	DEFINITELY SPECIAL 8 [10] N E Berry 6-9-7 (40) Rory Moore 16/1: 00000-07: In tch, no room 2f out & again dist, sn onepcd.		1	31a
216	DILYS 29 [5] W S Kittow 5-9-7 (40) I Mongan 5/1 CO FAV: 000004-8: Mid-div, outpcd when no room & snatched up 2f out, no impress when short of room ins fnl 1f:		nk	30a
310*	INDIAN WARRIOR 10 [13] J Jay 8-9-13 bl (40) N Callan 5/1 CO FAV: 10025-19: Cl-up, led 2f out, hdd/fdd 1f out.		nk	35a
373	THATS ALL JAZZ 3 [12] C R Dore 6-9-7 (45) R Thomas 33/1: 60000-00: Held up wide, nvr a factor.		½	28a
327	COSTA DEL SOL 9 [14] J J Bridger 3-8-3 (45) N Pollard 25/1: 06005-00: Rear, nvr a chsd.		hd	27a
4861}	SHIRLEY OAKS 84 [9] Miss Z C Davison 5-9-7 (40) Lisa Jones (3) 33/1: 404000-0: In tch, outpcd when short of room 2f out, eased ins fnl 1f, saddle slipped.		1½	24a
1576}	MISBEHAVIOUR 243 [4] P Butler 5-9-7 p (45) S Donohoe (7) 12/1: 40000/0-0: Sn outpcd, nvr a factor.		1	22a

108

340	**XSYNNA** 8 [2] T T Clement 8-9-7 vis (45) J Tate 10/1: 30000-30: Led, hdd 2f out, sn fdd:	3½	15a
4701}	**ALMARA** 95 [16] Miss K B Boutflower 4-9-7 T p (40) C Catlin 50/1: 60/0000-0: Bhd wide, nvr a factor:	½	14a
15 Ran	1m 26.67 (3.87) Owner Mr Paul J Dixon		Trained at Upper Lambourn

412 ### 3.10 Bet Direct On Sky Active Banded Stakes 4yo+ 0-45 (H)
£1663 £475 £238   **1m2f p/track**   **Going 49**   **-09 Slow**   Stalls Inside

354	**TROPICAL SON** 7 [10] D Shaw 5-9-0 vis (40) N Callan 11/2: 0000-251: Handy, outpcd 5f out, rallied 3f out, ev ch dist, rdn out to lead cl-home:		48a
330	**OUR GLENARD** 9 [4] S L Keightley 5-9-0 (45) L Keniry (3) 7/4 FAV: 05005-22: Dwelt, sn handy, led 2f out & sn clr, hdd under press cl-home:	shd	46a
272*	**PIQUET** 16 [14] J J Bridger 6-9-0 (45) N Pollard 10/1: 000501-3: Held up, hdwy 4f out, kept on fnl 1f, not pace front 2:	1¼	44a
4958}	**ESSAY BABY** 76 [5] P D Cundell 4-8-12 (45) C Catlin 20/1: 400050-4: In tch, onepcd bef 1f out:	1¾	41a
150	**PAINTBRUSH** 40 [7] Mrs L Stubbs 4-8-12 (45) S W Kelly 7/1: 00/3560-5: Slow away, prog 5f out, outpcd 3f out, modest late gains:	4	35a
267	**HIGH DIVA** 16 [13] B R Johnson 5-9-0 p (45) N Chalmers (5) 10/1: 020006-6: Held up, nvr nrr than mid-div.	hd	34a
370	**PYRRHIC** 5 [9] R M Flower 5-9-0 bl (40) P Doe 9/1: 04505-37: Keen cl-up, wknd fnl 2f:	7	24a
3416}	**MONDURU** 162 [2] G L Moore 7-9-0 bl (35) H Poulton (7) 33/1: 00/5000-8: Rcd keenly, dsptd lead till 2f out, sn fdd:	2	21a
62	**BALLARE** 57 [1] Bob Jones 5-9-0 (45) D Kinsella 7/1: 5/40200-9: Dsptd lead till 2f out, sn fdd:	hd	20a
314*	**MALMAND** 10 [8] R Brotherton 5-9-6 vis (40) I Mongan 12/1: 0500-010: Mid-div, wknd 3f out:	1¼	24a
103	**GEMMA** 50 [6] P J Makin 4-8-12 (40) W Ryan 25/1: 600000-0: Keen prom, fdd 4f out:	16	0a
2240}	**EMARATIS IMAGE** 210 [12] R M Stronge 6-9-0 (45) V Slattery 33/1: 304000-0: Keen cl-up, fdd 4f out.	11	0a
314	**TARKWA** 10 [11] R M H Cowell 5-9-0 (45) M Henry 9/1: 53260-60: Cl-up, wknd 4f out:	1	0a
13 Ran	2m 8.64 (5.84) Owner Swann Racing Ltd		Trained at Newark

413 ### 3.40 Littlewoodspoker Com Claiming Stakes 3yo+ (H)
£1281 £366 £183   **5f p/track rnd**   **Going 49**   **+10 Fast**   Stalls Outside

335	**MR SPLIFFY** 9 [7] K R Burke 5-9-8 vis (47) R Keogh (7) 12/1: 0004-051: Mid-div, hdwy 2f out, ev ch & just trav lead ins fnl 1f, pushed out to lead cl-home, v easily, val 2L+:		50a
335*	**CARK** 9 [4] J Balding 6-9-9 p (45) M Savage (5) 11/2: 0400-612: Prom, led dist, hdd under press cl-home:	nk	49a
256	**PHILLY DEE** 19 [8] J Jay 3-8-0 bl (47) Lisa Jones (3) 8/1: 043253-3: Held up, sn outpcd, hdwy despite hanging left dist, kept on cl-home:	3	32a
271	**TICKLE** 16 [9] P J Makin 6-9-4 vis t (48) C Catlin 11/4: 005060-4: In tch wide, outpcd dist, rallied late:	hd	34a
286	**HENRY TUN** 13 [2] J Balding 6-9-9 bl (52) I Mongan 5/2 FAV: 03500-35: Led, hdd 3f out, ev ch dist, sn wknd.	½	38a
400	**WESTMEAD TANGO** 1 [1] J R Jenkins 4-9-4 vis (49) S W Kelly 11/2: 0/01200-66: Slow away, sn in tch, short of room 2f out, wknd fnl 1f:	nk	32a
312	**DIAPHANOUS** 10 [3] E A Wheeler 6-9-4 bl (45) Liam Jones (7) 11/1: 00644-07: Sn cl-up, led 3f out, hdd dist, fdd.	2	26a
328	**IVORY VENTURE** 9 [5] D K Ivory 4-9-4 (50) R Miles (3) 16/1: 6/5400-08: Sn outpcd, nvr a factor.	1½	22a
340	**GENTLE RESPONSE** 8 [6] C A Dwyer 4-9-4 (45) Paul Scallan 50/1: 20000-09: Dwelt, al outpcd.	nk	21a
9 Ran	59.75 (1.95) Owner Mrs Elaine M Burke		Trained at Leyburn

414 ### 4.10 Littlewoods Bet Direct Banded Stakes 4yo+ 0-35 (H)
£1267 £362 £181   **1m4f p/track**   **Going 49**   **+03 Fast**   Stalls Inside

321*	**BROUGHTON KNOWS** 10 [2] W J Musson 7-9-10 bl (35) Lisa Jones (3) 11/10 FAV: 04362-11: Held up, hdwy trav well 4f out, styd on to lead ins fnl 1f, rdn out:		48a
324	**TROUBLE NEXT DOOR** 9 [3] N P Littmoden 6-9-4 (35) I Mongan 5/2: 64500//-32: Chsd ldr, led 4f out, hdd under press ins fnl 1f, no extra:	2	38a
4567}	**BUZ KIRI** 105 [5] A W Carroll 6-9-4 (35) N Callan 6/1: 030046-3: Mid-div, hdwy 3f out, kept on fnl 1f, no ch with front 2:	nk	37a
1871}	**DOCTOR JOHN** 948 [8] Andrew Turnell 7-9-4 (35) C Catlin 33/1: 44/00000//-: Handy, wknd 2f out.	8	25a
2287}	**RIPCORD** 209 [1] Lady Herries 6-9-4 (35) L Keniry 7/1: 00000//0-5: Cl-up, chsd ldrs, fdd fnl 2f:	1½	22a
331	**BRIERY MEC** 9 [9] H J Collingridge 9-9-4 p (35) G Carter 25/1: 0/0000-06: Held up, nvr nrr than mid-div.	¾	20a
2448}	**APRIL ACE** 923 [7] R J Baker 8-9-4 (35) V Slattery 50/1: 00000//0//-: Rear, nvr a factor:	14	0a
228	**PATS MIRACLE** 27 [10] John Berry 4-9-0 BL (35) W M Lordan 50/1: 004/000-8: Chsd ldrs, fdd 5f out:	29	0a
294	**STUNNING MAGIC** 12 [4] Mrs Barbara Waring 4-9-0 BL (35) D Kinsella 50/1: 00/00-09: Led & rcd v keen, wknd & hdd 4f out.	23	0a
9 Ran	2m 34.81 (5.61) Owner Broughton Thermal Insulation		Trained at Newmarket

Official Going Standard

415 ### 1.00 Betdirect Co Uk Handicap Stakes Div 1 3yo+ 0-85 (D)   [81]
£2645 £2645 £623 £311   **5f f/sand str**   **Going 27**   **Inapplicab**   Stalls Stands Side

4741}	**HOUT BAY** 93 [4] R A Fahey 7-7-12 1oh (51) F P Ferris (3) 11/1: 006500-1: Dwelt, sn chsd ldrs, rdn & kept on fnl 1f to join ldr line:	dht	54a
329*	**THE FISIO** 9 [6] A M Balding 4-9-4 6ex (72) Martin Dwyer 11/10 FAV: 00000-11: Chsd ldrs, sn pushed along, led over 1f out, rdn & joined on line:		74a
198	**GRANDMA LILY** 31 [3] M C Chapman 6-9-4 (72) T Hamilton (5) 10/1: 000150-3: Sn pushed along, rdn to chall ins last, not pace of front pair on line:	nk	73a
253	**MALAHIDE EXPRESS** 19 [8] M J Polglase 4-8-6 bl (60) L Fletcher 20/1: 563500-4: Chsd ldrs, rdn & ch over 1f out, no extra:	¾	59a
205	**SEA THE WORLD** 30 [9] D Shaw 4-8-4 vis (58) J Fanning 33/1: 003000-5: Dwelt, pushed long, not pace to chall:	1	54a
205	**PRIME RECREATION** 30 [2] P S Felgate 7-9-0 (68) Dale Gibson 16/1: 002400-6: Drvn chasing ldrs, not able to chall.	shd	64a
274	**LAUREL DAWN** 15 [10] I W McInnes 6-8-8 (62) D Allan (3) 10/1: 204103-7: Chsd ldrs, btn dist:	¾	56a
235	**JUSTALORD** 26 [5] J Balding 6-10-0 p (82) J Edmunds 100/30: 215206-8: Led 3f, no extra fnl 1f:	1	73a

286* **BEST LEAD** 13 [11] Ian Emmerson 5-8-11 bl (65) Dean McKeown 16/1: 00065-19: Cl-up 3f, wknd: ½ **54a**
9 Ran 1m 0.69 Owner Northumbria Leisure Ltd Trained at Malton

---

416 1.30 Bet Direct No Q 08000 93 66 93 Median Auction Maiden Stakes 4-6yo (F)
£2905 £830 £415 7f f/sand rnd Going 27 -19 Slow Stalls Inside

104} **KENNINGTON** 414 [13] Mrs C A Dunnett 4-9-0 Hayley Turner (5) 10/1: 0/-1: Led after 1f, edged left but held on gamely for **57a**
press fnl 1f:
84 **DISABUSE** 52 [3] S C Williams 4-9-0 (48) B Reilly (5) 5/2: 000266-2: Dwelt, pushed along chasing ldrs, drvn to chall over 1f nk **54a**
out, al just held:
340 **ADANTINO** 8 [8] B R Millman 5-9-0 (52) Martin Dwyer 9/2: 56053-63: Held up, drvn & kept on wide late: 2½ **51a**
334 **NOW AND AGAIN** 9 [5] M W Easterby 5-9-0 Dale Gibson 10/1: 34: Chsd ldrs, not pace to chall fnl 2f. ½ **50a**
334 **MAGIC MAMMAS TOO** 9 [6] T D Barron 4-9-0 (53) D Mernagh 7/4 FAV: 43226-25: Hmpd after 1f & sn pushed along nk **49a**
towards rear, late gains for press, no dngr:
254 **KUSTOM KIT FOR HER** 19 [2] S R Bowring 4-8-9 (50) J Bramhill 25/1: 540200-6: Dwelt, chsd ldrs, no impress dist. nk **43a**
85 **SWEET CORAL** 52 [4] B S Rothwell 4-8-9 (40) R Winston 50/1: 5000-7: Led 1f, wknd over 1f out, abs. 2 **37a**
4241} **ZANJEER** 122 [11] D Nicholls 4-9-0 (58) A Nicholls 16/1: 4/40-8: Chsd ldrs 5f, sn btn, abs/AW bow. 8 **30a**
172 **EJAY** 37 [7] Julian Poulton 5-8-9 (40) M Halford (7) 50/1: 0//006-9: Chsd ldrs till halfway. 6 **13a**
4408} **DALRIATH** 121 [12] M C Chapman 5-8-9 (45) Andrew Webb 7/ 40/1: 025000-0: Sn bhd, abs, new stable. nk **12a**
242 **WHITE O MORN** 24 [10] B A McMahon 5-8-9 G Gibbons 66/1: 00-0: Mid-div, no impress fnl 3f. shd **12a**
HEYWARD PLACE [9] T Keddy 4-8-9 J P Guillambert (2) 66/1: 0: Slowly away & sn bhd on debut. dist **0**
12 Ran 1m 29.83 (3.23) Owner Mr Andy Middleton Trained at Norwich

---

417 2.00 Bet Direct No Q Apprentice Claiming Stakes 4yo+ (F)
£2884 £824 £412 1m f/sand rnd Going 27 -26 Slow Stalls Inside

393 **GAME GURU** 2 [4] T D Barron 5-9-7 (65) Laura Jayne Crawford (5) 6/5 FAV: 00D301-01: Made all, rdn & held on well fnl 1f: **65a**
366 **LOCOMBE HILL** 5 [2] D Nicholls 8-9-4 (60) L Treadwell (5) 5/2: 00100-02: Chsd wnr after 2f, kept on ins last, al just held: ½ **60a**
343 **TINIAN** 8 [1] K R Burke 6-8-12 (54) A Reilly (5) 6/1: 61530-53: Chsd wnr 2f, not trkd front pair, not able to chall fnl 2f: 2 **50a**
353* **KING PRIAM** 7 [3] M J Polglase 9-8-6 bl (35) K Ghunowa (5) 5/1: 000-0414: Sn outpcd: 7 **30a**
4 Ran 1m 43.63 (4.23) Owner Mr Kevin Shaw Trained at Thirsk

---

418 2.30 Betdirect Co Uk Handicap Stakes Div 2 3yo+ 0-85 (D) [82]
£4037 £1242 £621 £311 5f f/sand str Going 27 Inapplicab Stalls Stands Side

345 **TIME N TIME AGAIN** 7 [11] E J Alston 6-9-0 P (68) A Nicholls 8/1: 40542-51: Sn pushed along but al prom, hung left & styd **72a**
on for press to lead cl-home, all out:
386 **FAR NOTE** 2 [2] S R Bowring 6-8-11 bl (65) J Bramhill 7/1: 104210-62: Prom, rdn & led over 1f out, hdd cl-home: nk **68a**
205 **COUNT COUGAR** 30 [3] S P Griffiths 4-8-7 (61) R Lappin 20/1: 060010-3: Prom & led 3f out till over 1f out, onepace: 2 **58a**
386 **SOBA JONES** 2 [5] J Balding 7-9-4 6ex (72) J Edmunds 2/1 FAV: 00052-124: Cl-up, ch over 1f out, wknd. nk **68a**
274 **ABRAXAS** 15 [1] J Akehurst 6-7-13 1ow p (52) J Quinn 11/1: 000026-5: Dwelt, chsd ldrs, no extra dist: nk **48a**
345 **ST IVIAN** 7 [10] Mrs N Macauley 4-9-0 vis (68) P McCabe 16/1: 000551-46: Chsd ldrs, hmpd dist, fdd. shd **63a**
153* **ELLENS LAD** 40 [7] W J Musson 10-9-5 bl (73) Paul Eddery 13/2: 000/001-7: Chsd ldrs till over 1f out: nk **67a**
205* **FRASCATI** 30 [6] A Berry 4-9-10 (78) F Lynch 7/2: 004251-8: Led 2f, btn dist: 2 **56a**
120} **IZZET MUZZY** 411 [9] D Shaw 6-8-11 (65) R Fitzpatrick 50/1: 060000/-9: Dwelt sn outpcd: 3 **44a**
4637} **SAHARA SILK** 100 [4] D Shaw 3-7-13 vis (68) Hayley Turner (5) 16/1: 210500-0: Chsd ldrs till halfway: 8 **26a**
2963} **SHEAPYS LASS** 181 [8] A Crook 3-7-12 7oh (60) J Mackay 25/1: 6526-0: Dwelt, hmpd start, sn bhd: nk **24a**
11 Ran 1m 0.73 Owner Spring Equestrian Ltd Trained at Preston

---

419 3.00 Littlewoods Bet Direct Handicap Stakes 4yo+ 0-95 (C) [93]
£8229 £2532 £1266 £633 7f f/sand rnd Going 27 +12 Fast Stalls Inside

31 **MUFREH** 62 [8] A G Newcombe 6-8-13 (78) S Whitworth 11/2 FAV: 102012-1: Held up in tch, smooth hdwy halfway & rdn/led **88a**
dist, styd on strongly:
292 **JUST FLY** 12 [2] S Kirk 4-9-1 (80) A Culhane 13/2: 10505-22: Trkd ldrs trav well, rdn & led over 1f out, sn hdd, not pace of wnr: ¾ **88a**
386 **MAJIK** 2 [1] D J S ffrench Davis 5-8-4 (69) J Quinn 16/1: 042313-03: Chsd ldrs, ch over 1f out, no extra: 3 **71a**
346* **OVIGO** 7 [5] P A Blockley 5-8-0 (65) F P Ferris (3) 6/1: 00330-14: Slow away & sn well bhd, taken wide & styd on for press, nrst 1¼ **64a**
fin:
248* **FOREVER PHOENIX** 20 [6] R M H Cowell 4-8-5 (70) E Ahern 16/1: 4201-5: Cl-up trav well, led 2f out, sn hdd & no extra: 3 **63a**
361 **SUNDRIED TOMATO** 6 [13] P W Hiatt 5-9-3 (82) L Fletcher (3) 25/1: 00000-06: Led till over 4f out, prom till dist: 1¼ **72a**
285 **JUST A GLIMMER** 13 [14] L G Cottrell 4-8-13 (78) Martin Dwyer 25/1: 331/00-37: Held up, not pace to chall: 1 **66a**
361 **FLYING TREATY** 6 [10] Miss A Stokell 7-9-3 (88) Ann Stokell 66/1: 30040-08: Chsd ldrs till 4f out: 1¼ **63a**
278 **TE QUIERO GB** 15 [15] Miss Gay Kelleway 6-10-0 t (93) M Fenton 12/1: 105230-9: Held up, nvr pace to chall: hd **77a**
171 **LINCOLN DANCER** 37 [9] D Nicholls 7-8-13 (78) A Nicholls 28/1: 060000-0: Held up, btn 2f out. shd **62a**
3178} **NO GROUSE** 173 [12] R A Fahey 4-8-11 (76) T Hamilton (5) 20/1: 110000-0: Hmpd & sn rear: ½ **59a**
4716} **YORK CLIFF** 94 [3] W M Brisbourne 6-9-1 (80) R Winston 25/1: 4//20200-0: Dwelt sn outpcd, abs. shd **63a**
361 **HAND CHIME** 6 [7] W J Haggas 7-9-8 (87) J Fanning 6/1: 60003-00: Chsd ldrs till halfway: 2 **66a**
360 **ACTION FIGHTER** 6 [4] N P Littmoden 4-9-9 p (88) J P Guillambert (3) 20/1: 51000-30: Sn led, hdd 2f out, wknd. 1¼ **64a**
270 **PHECKLESS** 16 [11] R F Johnson Houghton 5-8-9 (69) S Carson 11/1: 100564-0: Dwelt, al rear: shd **45a**
285* **BLAKESET** 13 [16] T D Barron 9-8-13 vis (78) D Mernagh 13/2: 11101-10: Chsd ldrs 4f, eased: 26 **7a**
16 Ran 1m 27.63 (1.03) Owner Mr M K F Seymour Trained at Barnstaple

---

420 3.30 Littlewoodscasino Com Selling Stakes 4yo+ (G)
£2548 £728 £364 1m3f f/sand Going 27 Inapplicab Stalls Inside

4481} **ORINOCOVSKY** 110 [7] C R Egerton 5-9-2 (64) Martin Dwyer 5/2: 205/004-1: Made all, readily pulled clr over 2f out, val for **62a**
10L+:

SOUTHWELL Thursday 15.01.04 Lefthand, Sharp, Oval Track

362	**JUNGLE LION** 6	[8] John A Harris 6-9-2 e (47) S Whitworth 20/1: 60600-62: Held up, late gains far rail under hands & heels, nvr any impress:	8	47a
287	**FREE STYLE** 13	[5] K R Burke 4-8-8 (47) Darren Williams 11/1: 10020-63: Chsd ldrs, no impress 2f out.	nk	41a
375	**DANCING TILLY** 3	[3] R A Fahey 6-8-11 (40) J Quinn 9/4 FAV: 5306-424: Chsd ldrs, btn over 1f out.	1½	39a
353	**IPLEDGEALLEGIANCE** 7	[2] D W Chapman 8-9-2 (46) A Culhane 7/2: 04560-25: Trkd ldr halfway, btn 2f out:	8	34a
334	**MING THE MERCILESS** 9	[1] J G Given 4-8-13 (63) M Fenton 11/1: 0/6000-56: Prom till halfway.	6	26a
330	**NOBLE CYRANO** 9	[4] Jedd O'Keeffe 9-9-2 (35) Dale Gibson 20/1: 00600-67: Lost tch 4f out.	11	12a
	DIAMOND DAZZLER 6	[6] D P Keane 6-9-2 bl E Ahern 16/1: 8: Dwelt, chsd ldrs till 4f out, debut.	16	0

8 Ran   2m 25.03 (3.73)   Owner Mr Andy J Smith   Trained at Chaddleworth

---

421 | 4.00 Bet Direct In Vision Sky Page 293 Handicap Stakes 4yo+ 0-75 (E) [72]
£3423 £978 £489   1m4f f/sand   Going 27   -05 Slow   Stalls Inside

380*	**SENDINTANK** 3	[8] S C Williams 4-8-8 6ex (56) B Reilly (5) 8/13 FAV: 00/600-11: Pushed along towards rear early & rems over 4f out, smooth hdwy to lead over 2f out, wandered after but		67a
315*	**NAKWA** 10	[5] E J Alston 6-8-7 6ex (51) D Allan (3) 11/2: 01043-12: Held up, rdn & chsd wnr over 1f out, kept on but no	1¾	57a
330	**LAZZAZ** 9	[2] P W Hiatt 6-9-2 (60) Martin Dwyer 22/1: 13300-43: Chsd ldrs, rdn & no impress fnl 2f.	6	57a
740}	**ELA RE** 317	[4] C R Dore 5-8-3 (47) J Bramhill 50/1: 40606/0-4: Prom & ch trav well over 2f out, sn no extra:	nk	43a
255	**SHIFTY** 19	[3] D Nicholls 5-8-10 (54) A Nicholls 40/1: 423426-5: In tch till over 2f out:	3½	45a
306*	**MADIBA** 11	[10] P Howling 5-9-2 6ex bl (60) R Winston 14/1: 50400-16: Chsd ldrs, btn over 2f out:	2	48a
257*	**STRAVMOUR** 19	[9] R Hollinshead 8-8-2 (46) Dale Gibson 7/1: 060431-7: Held up, rdn & struggling fnl 4f:	5	27a
3319}	**CALL OF THE WILD** 167	[7] R A Fahey 4-8-7 (55) T Hamilton (5) 33/1: 560346-8: Held up, rdn & lost tch fnl 4f:	2	33a
2507}	**FINGER OF FATE** 201	[11] M J Polglase 4-9-1 (63) L Fletcher (3) 50/1: 600060-9: Led till over 2f out, wknd qckly:	6	33a
4595}	**COTE SOLEIL** 103	[1] C R Egerton 7-8-5 (49) E Ahern 50/1: 50/6600-0: Chsd ldrs till halfway, abs.	dist	0

10 Ran   2m 38.09 (3.79)   Owner Steve Jones and Phil McGovern   Trained at Newmarket

---

WOLVERHAMPTON Friday 16.01.04 Lefthand, Sharp Track

Official Going   Standard

422 | 1.20 Press Interactive To Bet Direct Handicap Stakes 3yo 0-75 (E) [82]
£3290 £940 £470   6f rnd f/sand   Going 39   -01 Slow   Stalls Inside

247	**BACK AT DE FRONT** 21	[3] N E Berry 3-8-6 (60) C Catlin 20/1: 011504-1: Handy, led over 2f out, styd on well, drvn out:		65a
333	**MUY BIEN** 10	[8] J R Jenkins 3-9-7 vis (75) B Reilly (5) 13/8 FAV: 00152-22: Chsd ldrs, eff & hung left over 1f out, styd on ins last, just held:	½	78a
69	**CHICKADO** 56	[4] D Haydn Jones 3-8-13 (67) Paul Eddery 9/2: 00613-3: With ldr, hung left over 1f out & ins last, no extra cl-home:	1	67a
237	**LIZHAR** 25	[2] M J Polglase 3-9-4 (72) J P Spencer 11/1: 231435-4: Led till over 2f out, wknd ins last:	3	63a
4110}	**DIAMOND GEORGE** 131	[1] John Berry 3-8-7 (61) W M Lordan 40/1: 266-5: Bhd, some late gains, nvr dangerous:	shd	52a
333*	**BLOFELD** 10	[9] W Jarvis 3-9-7 6ex (75) Lisa Jones (3) 9/4: 05511-16: Sn bhd, no danger:	1¾	61a
316	**BIRIKINA** 11	[5] A Berry 3-8-3 (57) P Bradley (5) 10/1: 00000-67: Slow away & al bhd.	13	4a
2746*}	**BARRAS** 191	[7] Miss Gay Kelleway p (57) Martin Dwyer 16/1: 445321-8: In tch, btn 2f out ins.	1¾	-1a

8 Ran   1m 15.2 (2.4)   Owner Leeway Group Limited   Trained at Earlswood

---

423 | 1.50 Bet Direct Through Attheraces Claiming Stakes 4yo+ (F)
£2898 £828 £414   1m1f79y f/sand   Going 39   +07 Fast   Stalls Inside

391	**HIAWATHA** 3	[7] T D Barron 5-9-6 (66) E Ahern 4/7 FAV: 20201-41: Held up, gd hdwy to lead over 2f out, sn clr, pushed out:		78a
382	**NOUL** 4	[2] K A Ryan 5-9-8 bl (73) N Callan 4/1: 60421-02: Handy, eff over 1f out, kept on but wnr had flown:	5	73a
362	**TORO BRAVO** 7	[4] R M Beckett 4-8-7 bl (55) J Quinn 20/1: 00000-53: Held up, eff over 2f out, sn btn.	4	52a
392*	**COOLFORE JADE** 3	[6] N E Berry 4-8-6 (55) C Catlin 11/2: 0045-014: Led over 5f out till over 2f out, wknd:	nk	51a
287	**PHOENIX NIGHTS** 14	[5] A Berry 4-9-3 (47) F Lynch 50/1: 01030-05: Led till over 5f out, btn over 2f out:	16	38a
251	**PUPS PRIDE** 21	[1] Mrs N Macauley 7-8-10 vis (58) Lisa Jones (3) 16/1: 001100-6: In tch, btn over 3f out.	1	28a

6 Ran   2m 01.19 (2.99)   Owner Mr Nigel Shields   Trained at Thirsk

---

424 | 2.20 Littlewoods Bet Direct Handicap Stakes Fillies 4yo+ 0-70 (E) [67]
£3241 £926 £463   1m4f f/sand   Going 39   -09 Slow   Stalls Inside

4704}	**MOLLYS SECRET** 96	[4] C G Cox 6-8-6 p (45) J Quinn 16/1: 052300-1: Chsd ldrs, led over 2f out, sn rdn clr, pushed out:		52a
342	**BIG BERTHA** 9	[2] John Berry 6-10-0 e (67) J P Spencer 3/1: 16623-42: Hld up, hdwy 2f out, short of room 2f out, kept on ins last, wnr had flown:	3½	69a
259	**COMPTON ECLAIRE** 18	[1] G A Butler 4-8-9 vis (52) E Ahern 5/2 FAV: 401034-3: Held up, eff over 2f out, onepcd:	4	48a
228	**CUMBRIAN PRINCESS** 28	[9] M Blanshard 7-7-12 2oh (35) Dale Gibson 33/1: 000005-4: Hld up, eff 3f out, onepace:	2	30a
48	**E MINOR** 60	[8] T Wall 5-9-5 (62) A Culhane 9/1: 044006-5: Chsd ldrs, wknd 2f out:	1¾	52a
359	**RETAIL THERAPY** 7	[3] M A Buckley 4-7-13 6oh 1ow (35) R Ffrench 100/30: 00006-26: Nvr a factor:	½	31a
359	**EXIT TO HEAVEN** 7	[6] Miss Gay Kelleway 4-9-1 P (58) T Eaves (5) 20/1: 0225-067: Led till over 2f out, wknd:	½	46a
1598}	**ELA DARGENT** 242	[7] Miss K Marks 5-9-6 t (59) V Slattery 16/1: 240/205-8: In tch, bhd halfway on reapp.	15	25a
359	**ESTIMATE** 7	[5] John A Harris 4-9-3 vis (60) S Whitworth 20/1: 26264-09: Chsd ldrs till 3f out, wknd.	1¾	23a

9 Ran   2m 39.4 (5.8)   Owner The Two M'S Partnership   Trained at Hungerford

---

425 | 2.50 Betdirect Co Uk Maiden Stakes 3yo+ (D)
£3455 £1063 £532 £266   7f rnd f/sand   Going 39   -22 Slow   Stalls Outside

5031}	**RIO BRANCO** 69	[3] B W Hills 3-8-2 Martin Dwyer 7/4: 0-1: Made all, styd on well over 1f out, drvn out:		74a
	SABBAAG [5]	D R Loder 3-8-7 J P Spencer 4/7 FAV: 2: Rcd wide in tch, hdwy to chase wnr 2f out, kept on, al held:	1¾	74a
	MRS BROWN [1]	Sir Mark Prescott 3-8-2 J Mackay 25/1: 3: Slow away, sn in tch, btn 2f out.	3½	62a

2982}	SCORCH 182 [2] H J Collingridge 3-8-7 Saleem Golam (7) 40/1: 56-4: In tch, btn over 2f out:		11	45a
219	WODHILL BE 30 [4] D Morris 4-9-6 N Callan 66/1: 0-5: Keen, in tch till halfway, no extra:		3	34a
5 Ran	1m 30.44 (4.24) Owner Mr Guy Reed		Trained at Lambourn	

426
3.20 Littlewoodscasino Com Selling Stakes 4yo+ (G)
£2520 £720 £360 1m6f166y f/sand Going 39 -49 Slow Stalls Outside

358	VINCENT 7 [4] John A Harris 9-9-9 (46) J Mackay 11/8 FAV: 0611-431: With ldr, led over 2f out, pushed clr over 1f out, cmftbly, no bid:			49a
336	HAJEER 10 [2] P W Hiatt 6-9-3 (40) Lisa Jones (3) 5/1: 00000-52: Handy, lost place over 4f out, rallied over 1f out, kept on, no threat to wnr:		3	37a
137	MYSTERIUM 45 [1] N P Littmoden 10-9-3 vis (40) J P Guillambert (3) 5/2: 003333-3: In tch, eff to chase wnr appr fnl 1f, no extra ins last:		nk	37a
342	LANDESCENT 9 [3] M Quinn 4-8-11 (50) Martin Dwyer 4/1: 42660-04: Led till over 2f out, wknd & eased ins last:		7	27a
4 Ran	3m 22.44 (12.84) Owner Mrs A E Harris		Trained at Melton Mowbray	

427
3.50 Bet Direct In Vision Sky Page 293 Handicap Stakes Fillies 4yo+ 0-65 (F)
£2982 £852 £426 1m1f79y f/sand Going 39 +04 Fast Stalls Inside [61]

393*	NAJAABA 3 [11] Miss J Feilden 4-10-0 6ex (62) B Reilly (5) 4/7 FAV: 0431-111: Held up, hdwy 2f out, styd on to lead ins last, pushed out, shade cosily:			71a
338	GIVEMETHEMOONLIGHT 9 [12] Mrs Stef Liddiard 5-9-0 VIS (47) J Quinn 7/1: 2422-252: In tch, hdwy over 2f out, led briefly over 1f out, not pace wnr:		¾	52a
281	DANGER BIRD 14 [6] R Hollinshead 4-9-0 (48) A Culhane 20/1: 05353-23: Cl-up, led halfway, hdd over 1f out, onepace:		¾	51a
4809}	WODHILL FOLLY 88 [13] D Morris 7-8-12 vis (45) N Callan 50/1: 341500-4: Held up, hdwy over 2f out, onepcd fnl 2f:		½	47a
300	MAGGIES PET 13 [8] K Bell 7-8-12 t (45) D R McCabe 50/1: 00360-25: Keen in tch, onepace over 2f out:		½	46a
4396*}	MYTHICAL CHARM 116 [9] J J Bridger 5-9-3 (50) N Pollard 25/1: 006501-6: In tch, eff 2f out, no impress on reapp:		¾	47a
4542}	DEBBIE 107 [4] B D Leavy 5-8-12 (45) S Whitworth 8/1: 031133-7: In tch, lost place over 2f out, some late gains:		2½	39a
263	CAYMAN SUNRISE 18 [1] E A L Dunlop 4-9-10 (58) W Ryan 33/1: 344266-8: In tch, btn over 3f out:		nk	51a
281	CONSIGNIA 14 [7] D Haydn Jones 5-8-12 P (45) Paul Eddery 25/1: 01060-09: Keen in tch, wknd over 2f out:		2½	33a
215	SUERTE 30 [5] J G Given 4-9-9 (57) M Fenton 66/1: 00/040-0: Al bhd:		3½	38a
4512}	COODEN BEACH 109 [10] M L W Bell 4-9-0 (48) Hayley Turner (5) 10/1: 400032-0: Al bhd on reapp:		11	13a
332	NUZZLE 10 [3] M Quinn 4-9-10 vis (58) Martin Dwyer 33/1: 60631-00: Led till 6f out, wknd:		12	7a
12 Ran	2m 01.49 (3.29) Owner Mr A K Sparks		Trained at Newmarket	

Official Going Standard

428
12.15 Bet Direct No Q 08000 93 66 93 Median Auction Maiden Stakes 3yo (E)
£3339 £954 £477 1m p/track rnd Going 38 -28 Slow Stalls Outside

	GROUVILLE [4] B J Meehan 3-9-0 Paul Eddery 33/1: 1: Trkd ldr, styd on for press to lead well ins last:			74a
322	JUMEIRAH SCARER 11 [2] M R Channon 3-9-0 C Catlin 7/2: 3-22: Led, rdn & hdd well ins last, no extra:		1¼	70a
213	GROUND PATROL 31 [9] A M Balding 3-9-0 Martin Dwyer 12/1: 0-3: Slow away, held up in tch, styd on for press fnl 2f, not pace of wnr:		½	69a
5014}	FIZZY LADY 72 [3] B W Hills 3-8-9 M Hills 7/4 FAV: 54-4: Chsd ldrs over 2f out, onepace near dist:		shd	64a
220	STAR FERN 31 [5] J Akehurst 3-9-0 I Mongan 4/1: 4-5: Mid-div, no impress dist:		5	60a
	NEVER CRIED WOLF [8] D R C Elsworth 3-9-0 N Callan 25/1: 6: Slow away, mid-div at best on debut:		2½	55a
	FRESH CONNECTION [1] G G Margarson 3-8-9 M Fenton 66/1: 7: Dwelt, chsd ldrs 6f on debut:		¾	49a
	LA CONCHA [12] Mrs L C Jewell 3-9-0 K Dalgleish 50/1: 8: Al towards rear, debut:		2½	49a
	ELZEES [11] D R C Elsworth 3-9-0 Dane O'Neill 20/1: 9: Sn rdn rear, nvr a factor, debut:		1	47a
220	SAUCY PICKLE 31 [6] Miss Z C Davison 3-8-9 N Pollard 66/1: 0-0: Mid-div, btn 2f out:		4	34a
	SECOND USER [10] J R Jenkins 3-9-0 S W Kelly 33/1: 0: Sn bhd on debut:		11	17a
	TILL THERE WAS YOU [7] B J Meehan 3-8-9 R Winston 10/1: 0: Chsd ldrs 3f out, wknd qckly, debut:		hd	11a
12 Ran	1m 41.44 (5.24) Owner Mr F T Wilson		Trained at Upper Lambourn	

429
12.45 Bet Direct No Q Claiming Stakes 4yo+ (F)
£2954 £844 £422 1m2f p/track Going 38 -07 Slow Stalls Inside

4777}	BARRY ISLAND 92 [1] D R C Elsworth 5-9-9 (75) Dane O'Neill 100/30: 063604-1: Rear, strong run for press to lead well ins last, going away:			76a
412	PYRRHIC 7 [8] R M Flower 5-8-11 bl (48) E Ahern 14/1: 04505-32: Mid-div, styd on for press fnl 2f, not pace of wnr:		1¾	61a
293	EASTBOROUGH 14 [2] B G Powell 5-9-1 (75) J Fanning 3/1 FAV: 4000/6-03: Mid-div, hmpd early, rdn to chall ins last, not pace of wnr fnl 100y:		nk	64a
4207}	FORTUNE POINT 127 [12] A W Carroll 6-9-1 (63) L Treadwell (7) 14/1: 220640-4: Mid-div, rdn to chall dist, no extra:		hd	63a
128	BONTADINI 49 [6] D Morris 5-8-9 vis (48) R Winston 25/1: 000000-5: Trkd ldr 4f out, no extra dist, abs:		nk	56a
370*	BANK ON HIM 7 [5] C Weedon 9-8-11 (56) I Mongan 5/1: 13000-16: Handy & led 5f out till ins last, wknd:		¾	57a
103	WATER OF LIFE 52 [10] J R Boyle 5-8-10 (51) R Miles (3) 8/1: 000053-7: Dwelt, mid-div at best, abs:		5	49a
343	DILIZA 10 [3] G B Balding 5-8-4 (47) R Thomas (5) 16/1: 32050-48: Mid-div, hmpd early, no prog over 1f out:		½	42a
323	ICANNSHIFT 11 [4] S Dow 4-9-3 (60) J Coffill Brown (7) 33/1: 40600-09: Al rear:		3	36a
4719}	TWENTYTWOSILVER 96 [9] O Sherwood 4-8-9 (70) Martin Dwyer 20/1: 006000-0: Led 5f, btn 2f out, jumps fit:		6	36a
1659}	SUMMER STOCK 239 [11] J A Supple 6-8-9 t (52) T Eaves (5) 16/1: 004000-0: Al rear, eased dist, jumps fit:		8	23a
2822}	DON FAYRUZ 190 [13] B N Doran 12-8-6 low (54) W Ryan 33/1: 200/000-0: Wide & al rear, new stable:		10	6a
236	TRAVEL TARDIA 28 [14] I A Wood 8-8-6 low (51) S W Kelly 50/1: 000/000-0: Trkd ldrs, btn 3f out:		2½	2a
13 Ran	2m 07.25 (4.45) Owner Mr Matthew Green		Trained at Whitsbury	

430	1.20 Betdirect Co Uk Maiden Stakes 4yo+ (D)

£3829 £1178 £589 £295   **1m2f p/track**   Going 38   -14 Slow   Stalls Inside

	MILLVILLE [9] M A Jarvis 4-9-0 N Callan 6/1: 1: Held up, hdwy 2f out & led ins last, rdn & styd on strongly:	72a
122	PRIORS DALE 49 [5] K Bell 4-9-0 (72) I Mongan 9/2: 5/04020-2: Chsd ldr halfway, led 3f out, rdn & hdd ins last, no extra:	3½ 66a
2362}	ZALKANI 208 [3] B G Powell 4-9-0 (51) A Hindley (7) 50/1: 600-3: Rear, styd on for press fnl 2f, nrst fin:	1¼ 64a
338	CORONADO FOREST 10 [6] M R Hoad 5-9-2 (59) J Fanning 8/1: 26060-24: Held up, eff 3f out, onepace	4 58a
4203}	ANDAAD 483 [12] D J Daly 4-8-9 W Ryan 66/1: 0/-5: Slow away & rear, mod late prog:	1½ 51a
369	SEWMORE CHARACTER 7 [11] M Blanshard 4-9-0 (74) D Sweeney 2/1 FAV: 40462-46: Mid-div, eff 3f out, no extra:	1¼ 54a
269	SPRINGALONG 18 [14] P D Evans 4-9-0 (75) S Donohoe (6) 7/1: 43304-7: Mid-div, no impress fnl 2f:	¾ 53a
338	BLAZING THE TRAIL 10 [8] J W Hills 4-9-0 bl (63) S Whitworth 10/1: 0030-48: Chsd ldrs 3f out, no extra 1f out.	2½ 49a
	ALIMISTE [7] I A Wood 4-8-9 S W Kelly 66/1: 9: Rear, no ch fnl 3f on debut.	3 39a
338	GOLDEN DUAL 10 [13] S Dow 4-9-0 (65) P Doe 33/1: 04365-00: Trkd ldr, led after 3f till 3f out, wknd.	2½ 40a
1241}	PASSANDO 263 [10] A M Balding 4-8-9 Martin Dwyer 12/1: 0/4-0: Al rear, abs.	¾ 34a
835}	MYSTERLOVER 299 [1] N P Littmoden 4-9-0 J P Guillambert 25/1: 4P-0: Mid-div, hmpd halfway, sn btn, abs, 'lost action'.	12 23a
4398}	MURAQEB 117 [2] Mrs Barbara Waring Lisa Jones (3) 25/1: 55-0: Mid-div, hmpd 5f out, sn struggling, abs.	nk 22a
2511}	PRAGUE 563 [4] J R Boyle 6-9-2 (62) E Ahern 33/1: 60/4/0-1: Led 3f, btn 3f out, long abs.	5 15a
14 Ran	2m 07.99 (5.19)	Owner Mr T G Warner	Trained at Newmarket

431	1.55 Bet Direct On 0800 32 93 93 Conditions Stakes 3yo+ (C)

£7163 £2717 £1359 £618   **6f p/track rnd**   Going 38   +18 Fast   Stalls Inside

235	DUSTY DAZZLER 28 [4] W G M Turner 4-9-0 (95) A Quinn (5) 11/4: 004202-1: Chsd ldrs, led ins last, drvn out:	87a
4990}	QUEENS RHAPSODY 75 [6] A Bailey 4-9-5 (90) E Ahern 14/1: 44/1150-2: Dwelt & held up, hdwy & rdn/chsd wnr ins last, no extra cl home:	1 88a
292*	CHATEAU NICOL 14 [1] B G Powell 5-9-5 vis (77) J Fanning 9/2: 01100-13: Bmpd start, trkd ldrs trav well halfway, no extra dist.	2½ 80a
400+*	HURRICANE COAST 3 [2] D Flood 5-9-5 bl (61) P Doe 6/1: 344-1113: Led, rdn & hdd ins last, no extra:	dht 80a
235+*	LAW BREAKER 28 [8] J A Gilbert 6-9-5 (90) B Reilly (5) 9/4 FAV: 100521-5: Held up wide, in tch, rdn & btn over 1f out:	4 68a
360	GOLDEN CHALICE 8 [3] A M Balding 5-9-5 VIS (85) Martin Dwyer 9/2: 00520-56: Cl-up, btn 2f out:	7 47a
369	KINGHAM 7 [5] Mrs Mary Hambro 4-9-5 (73) V Slattery 66/1: 1/00-07: Rear, no ch fnl 3f.	½ 45a
7 Ran	1m 11.62 (1.22)	Owner TOCS Ltd	Trained at Sherborne

432	2.25 Bet Direct No Q Voice Automated Betting Handicap Stakes 3yo 0-85 (D)	[87]

£4391 £1351 £676 £338   **7f p/track rnd**   Going 38   -08 Slow   Stalls Inside

284*	SECRET PLACE 15 [4] E A L Dunlop 3-9-4 (77) E Ahern 4/1: 02-11: Keen, in tch, qcknd & led over 1f out, readily drew clr:	86a
177	WESTERN ROOTS 38 [8] P F I Cole 3-9-7 (80) S Drowne 4/1: 140-2: Held up, hdwy to chase wnr ins last, not able to chall:	2½ 81a
295*	ROWAN PURSUIT 14 [3] J Akehurst 3-8-11 bl (70) J Fanning 9/2: 00131-13: Mid-div, rdn/chall when short of room over 1f out, onepace.	1 69a
290	MONTE MAJOR 14 [5] M A Jarvis 3-8-4 (63) M Henry 11/2: 06-34: Led, hdd over 1f out, no extra:	1¼ 59a
261	GARRIGON 19 [2] N P Littmoden 3-8-3 (62) Lisa Jones (3) 10/1: 062002-5: Rear, hdwy inner when no room dist, no extra after:	1½ 55a
341	ROYAL WARRANT 10 [1] A M Balding 3-9-7 (80) Martin Dwyer 100/30 FAV: 4310-36: Trkd ldr, btn dist:	shd 73a
132	WARES HOME 46 [6] K R Burke 3-8-8 (67) Darren Williams 16/1: 210006-7: Mid-div, eff over 1f out, no extra.	1¾ 56a
2947}	EVEN EASIER 184 [9] G L Moore 3-8-3 (62) S Whitworth 50/1: 004126-8: Al bhd, 6 mth abs.	1¼ 48a
337	FOOLS ENTIRE 10 [10] J A Gilbert 3-8-11 (70) B Reilly (5) 11/1: 01322-29: Keen, mid-div, btn 2f out:	1½ 57a
364*	EVER CHEERFUL 7 [7] W G M Turner 3-9-2 (75) L Treadwell 20/1: 4346-210: Keen, in tch till over 1f out:	½ 57a
10 Ran	1m 25.99 (3.19)	Owner Mr Khalifa Sultan	Trained at Newmarket

433	3.00 Littlewoods Bet Direct Handicap Stakes 4yo+ 0-105 (B)	[105]

£12151 £4609 £2305 £1048   **1m2f p/track**   Going 38   -04 Slow   Stalls Inside

293	EASTERN BREEZE 14 [6] P W D'Arcy 6-9-4 (95) Paul Eddery 13/2: 31666-41: Trkd ldr, led & trav well over 2f out, styd on strongly fnl 1f:	105a
82	GRAND PASSION 56 [2] G Wragg 4-9-7 (100) S Drowne 6/4 FAV: 412003-2: Trkd ldr, hdwy 2f out, not pace of wnr ins last:	1½ 106a
293	SANTANDO 14 [5] C E Brittain 4-9-4 vis (97) E Ahern 12/1: 42506-53: Dwelt, mid-div, smooth hdwy over 2f out, onepace for press dist:	2½ 99a
360	LAKOTA BRAVE 8 [4] Mrs Stef Liddiard 10-8-11 (88) I Mongan 25/1: 31225-24: Keen mid-div, late gains.	1¼ 88a
262*	LYGETON LAD 19 [12] Miss Gay Kelleway 6-10-0 t (105) M Fenton 16/1: 200101-5: Hld up, mod late prog:	½ 104a
16*	DANCE IN THE SUN 53 [11] Mrs A J Perrett 4-8-6 (85) Martin Dwyer 11/1: 152410-6: Trkd ldrs, no extra dist.	½ 83a
134	ZONERGEM 46 [3] Lady Herries 6-9-0 p (91) M Tebbutt 10/1: 003603-7: Led dist, hdd over 2f out, no extra, abs:	2 86a
273	STAR OF NORMANDIE 18 [7] G G Margarson 5-8-6 (83) B Reilly (5) 13/2: 312112-8: Held up, eff 2f out, no impress.	½ 77a
278+*	NIMELLO 17 [10] A G Newcombe 8-8-8 (85) S Whitworth 16/1: 106121-9: Hld up, no impress fnl 2f:	hd 78a
2641}	ULUNDI 197 [8] P R Webber 9-10-0 (105) Dane O'Neill 16/1: 140/000-0: Rear, no impress:	¾ 97a
1377}	COMPTON COMMANDER 256 [9] Ian Williams 6-8-10 (87) Lisa Jones (3) 50/1: 55/1000-0: Al bhd, new stable.	1¼ 77a
234	NASHAAB 28 [14] P D Evans 7-8-6 (83) S W Kelly 20/1: 000305-0: Slow away & al rear.	¾ 72a
234*	LINNING WINE 28 [13] B G Powell 8-9-3 (94) S Carson 12/1: 000021-0: Mid-div wide, btn over 1f out:	½ 82a
13 Ran	2m 07.02 (4.22)	Owner Colin Cage and Peter Lupson	Trained at Newmarket

434	3.35 Bet Direct In Vision Sky Page 293 Handicap Stakes 4yo+ 0-70 (E)	[70]

£3465 £990 £495   **1m2f p/track**   Going 38   -27 Slow   Stalls Inside

265	RASID 19 [9] C A Dwyer 6-9-7 (63) N Callan 7/1: 003053-1: Trkd ldrs, chsd ldr 2f out, drvn to lead well ins last:	71a
294	BLUE TROJAN 14 [5] S Kirk 4-9-9 (67) Martin Dwyer 9/2: 15644-22: Led 4f out, rdn & hdd cl-home.	½ 73a
404	EASTER OGIL 3 [12] Jane Southcombe 9-9-8 (64) Lisa Jones (3) 14/1: 6422-503: Dwelt, rear, styd on for press, took 3rd ins last, nvr dngrs:	1½ 68a

LINGFIELD Saturday 17.01.04 Lefthand, V Sharp Track

236* **LYRICAL WAY 28** [6] P R Chamings 5-9-6 vis (62) I Mongan 14/1: 002221-4: Prom, onepace for press dist: 1¾ **64a**
294* **GINGKO 14** [4] P R Webber 7-10-0 (70) W Ryan 14/1: 60066-15: Led till 4f out, no extra dist: nk **71a**
265 **BURGUNDY 19** [13] P Mitchell 7-9-4 (60) K Dalgleish 33/1: 015010-6: Rear, eff over 1f out, no dngr: shd **61a**
339* **GOLD GUEST 10** [1] P D Evans 5-9-10 (66) S Donohoe (7) 5/2 FAV: 00441-17: Mid-div inner, no impress dist: nk **66a**
174 **TRUE COMPANION 38** [14] N P Littmoden 5-9-7 (63) E Ahern 12/1: 461533-8: Rear, mod late prog, no dngr: 2 **60a**
96* **KINGSTON TOWN 53** [2] N P Littmoden 4-9-12 p (70) J P Guillambert (3) 10/1: 4021-9: Al rear: shd **67a**
218 **NIGHT WARRIOR 31** [10] D Flood 4-9-9 (67) P Doe 20/1: 000004-0: Mid-div, eff 2f out, no impress: ¾ **63a**
178 **QUANTUM LEAP 38** [8] S Dow 7-9-7 (63) Paul Eddery 14/1: 004153-0: Al rear: ¾ **58a**
290 **DUSK DANCER 14** [3] B J Meehan 4-9-7 (65) R Winston 12/1: 40-40: Chsd ldrs, btn over 1f out: ¾ **59a**
249 **TRAVELLERS TALE 22** [7] P G Murphy 5-10-0 (70) D Kinsella 25/1: 2/43034-0: Keen & chsd ldrs, btn over 1f out: 3 **59a**
4158} **FIGURA 129** [11] R Ingram 6-9-8 (64) Dane O'Neill 16/1: 303000-0: Keen, held up, btn 2f out: 2½ **49a**
14 Ran 2m 09.3 (6.5) Owner Mr David L Bowkett Trained at Newmarket

435 **4.05 Plough Inn A420 Amateur Riders' Handicap Stakes 3yo+ 0-60 (F)** **[34]**
£2947 £842 £421 **5f p/track rnd** **Going 38** **-25 Slow** Stalls Outside

366 **DOUBLE M 7** [9] Mrs L Richards 7-11-3 vis (51) Mrs S Bosley 11/4 FAV: 40000-41: Towards rear, hdwy inner halfway & led over 1f out, held on gamely for press: **58a**
242 **MULTAHAB 26** [4] Miss Gay Kelleway 5-11-5 (53) Mr D Simms (7) 7/1: 20555-2: Mid-div, eff wide, styd on for press, just held: nk **58a**
335 **LADIES KNIGHT 11** [1] D Shaw 4-11-7 (55) Ms C Williams 8/1: 00001-63: Rdn rear, styd on from halfway, not pace to chall wnr: ½ **58a**
274 **CATCHTHEBATCH 17** [5] E A Wheeler 8-11-0 (48) Mr C Witheford (7) 25/1: 006300-4: Mid-div, onepace. 2½ **43a**
275 **RELLIM 17** [7] P A Blockley 5-11-2 (50) Mr M Scales (5) 8/1: 442656-5: Led till 2f out, btn dist. 1¾ **40a**
335 **SOAKED 11** [6] D W Chapman 11-11-5 bl (53) Miss Kelly Harrison (5) 4/1: 00350-26: Handy & led 2f out till over 1f out. 1¼ **39a**
328 **NIGHT CAP 11** [8] T D McCarthy 5-11-1 (49) Mr W Rich (7) 6/1: 05003-67: Chsd ldr, outpcd from halfway: ½ **33a**
3516} **BLESSED PLACE 160** [2] Jean Rene Auvray 4-11-7 (55) Mr S J Edwards (7) 8/1: 350050-8: Chsd ldrs, no impress dist: 1 **36a**
418 **ABRAXAS 17** [10] J Akehurst 6-11-4 p (52) Mr S Gascoyne (7) 7/1: 000026-9: Slow away & al rear: 4 **21a**
9 Ran 1m 0.95 (3.15) Owner Mr Bryan Mathieson Trained at Chichester

WOLVERHAMPTON Monday 19.01.04 Lefthand, Sharp Track

Official Going STANDARD.

436 **1.40 Bet Direct On Sky Active Handicap Stakes 3yo 46-55 (F)** **[65]**
£2947 £842 £421 **6f f/sand rnd** **Going 27** **-16 Slow** Stalls Inside

184 **VAMPIRE QUEEN 38** [7] R P Elliott 3-8-12 (49) Dean McKeown 12/1: 0600-1: Chsd ldrs, rdn/edged left & led ins last, styd on strongly: **55a**
222 **VELVET TOUCH 31** [8] J R Jenkins 3-9-3 (54) S W Kelly 7/2: 063022-2: Led after 1f, edged right & hdd ins last, no extra: 1½ **56a**
105 **POWER TO BURN 54** [5] K Bell 3-9-4 VIS (55) D R McCabe 20/1: 40600-3: Handy, ch over 1f out, kept on for press: 1½ **54a**
327 **PARDON MOI 13** [10] Mrs C A Dunnett 3-8-12 (49) Hayley Turner (5) 14/1: 0654-344: Chsd ldrs, onepace for press dist: ¾ **47a**
351 **LIMIT DOWN 11** [12] M J Wallace 3-9-4 VIS (55) J P Guillambert (3) 14/1: 00005-65: Sn handy, wknd fnl 1f: hd **52a**
295 **VENDORS MISTAKE 16** [4] Andrew Reid 3-9-0 (51) N Callan 16/1: 600-06: Prom, bmpd halfway, sn no impress. 2½ **43a**
316 **MELAINA 14** [13] M S Saunders 3-9-2 p (53) R Miles (3) 4/1: 60061-27: Led 1f, prom 4f: 1¾ **42a**
158 **THE KING OF ROCK 42** [9] A G Newcombe 3-8-13 BL (50) S Whitworth 14/1: 042000-8: Outpcd, nvr factor: ½ **38a**
389* **SIR JASPER 6** [11] M F Harris 3-9-10 6ex vis (61) S Righton 3/1 FAV: 5561-19: Sn outpcd: shd **49a**
237 **SUITCASE MURPHY 28** [2] Ms Deborah J Evans 3-8-10 (47) I Mongan 25/1: 00004-0: Dwelt & held up, al outpcd. 2 **31a**
223 **KUMARI 31** [6] W M Brisbourne 3-8-9 1oh (45) N Chalmers (5) 14/1: 650000-0: Sn bhd. hd **29a**
4454} **POACHERS PARADISE 115** [1] M W Easterby 3-8-12 (49) Dale Gibson 13/2: 000-0: Chasing ldrs when hmpd halfway, no impress after, abs/h'cap bow. 3 **26a**
4874} **INDRANI 87** [3] John A Harris 3-8-13 (50) J Mackay 33/1: 664560-0: Dwelt & sn bhd: 5 **18a**
13 Ran 1m 15.39 (2.59) Owner Mrs Sarah Grayson Trained at Formby

437 **2.15 Press Interactive To Bet Direct Claiming Stakes 4yo+ (F)**
£2898 £828 £414 **1m100y f/sand rnd** **Going 27** **-16 Slow** Stalls Inside

427 **GIVEMETHEMOONLIGHT 3** [2] Mrs Stef Liddiard 5-8-10 vis (48) I Mongan 2/1: 422-2521: Cl-up, went on over 3f out & al holding rival fnl 1f: **55a**
393 **MUTARAFAA 6** [5] D Shaw 5-9-1 e (58) T Hamilton (5) 13/8 FAV: 2211-432: Held up, hdwy to press wnr 3f out, hung left & no extra dist: 1¾ **56a**
239 **OUR DESTINY 28** [9] D Burchell 6-8-5 vis (45) J Bramhill 16/1: 000002-3: Cl-up/dsptd lead halfway, hdd over 3f out, sn no impress: 7 **33a**
408 **DANCING KING 4** [6] P W Hiatt 8-8-5 (30) Lisa Jones (3) 40/1: 0000-504: Led/dsptd lead 3f, btn 2f out: 1¾ **30a**
427 **CONSIGNIA 3** [4] D Haydn Jones 5-8-4 (45) Paul Eddery 11/1: 1060-005: Rear, eff halfway, no impress fnl 2f. 10 **11a**
125} **WEKIWA SPRINGS 415** [7] T Carberry 7-8-5 T R Ffrench 8/1: 05/0504/-6: Sn rdn & al bhd: ½ **11a**
311 **WELSH WHISPER 14** [1] S A Brookshaw 5-8-0 A Nicholls 66/1: 0-07: Went right start, held up, al rear. nk **5a**
311 **CRAIGMOR 14** [8] M F Harris 4-8-5 BL (45) S Righton 66/1: 63600/-08: Prom till 4f out: 1½ **8a**
362* **DAIMAJIN 10** [3] Miss Gay Kelleway 5-9-5 t (58) M Fenton 6/1: 00000-19: Sn rdn towards rear, nvr factor: 5 **11a**
9 Ran 1m 49.85 (3.65) Owner Valley Fencing Trained at Hungerford

438 **2.45 Bet Direct On 0800 93 66 93 Maiden Stakes 3yo (D)**
£3374 £1038 £519 £260 **1m1f79y f/sand rnd** **Going 27** **-17 Slow** Stalls Inside

4966} **ALWAYS FLYING 79** [6] M Johnston 3-9-0 (64) J Fanning 6/4 FAV: 250355-1: Made all, rdn clr over 2f out, styd on strongly: **70a**
229 **WALTZING BEAU 30** [11] I A Wood 3-9-0 N Callan 16/1: 0-2: Rear, rdn & hdwy halfway, kept on, no ch with wnr: 5 **59a**
213 **ITS BLUE CHIP 33** [2] P W D'Arcy 3-9-0 e I Mongan 5/1: 0-3: Dwelt, held up in tch, styd on onepace for press fnl 3f: ¾ **58a**

	VIVRE SA VIE [10] Sir Mark Prescott 3-8-9 J Mackay 13/2: 4: Chsd ldrs, chsd wnr 2f out, no impress dist on debut.	4	45a
3411}	**LOLAS DESTINY** 166 [7] P A Blockley 3-8-9 (52) Dean McKeown 11/1: 000-5: Chsd wnr, wknd dist:	3½	38a
4994}	**PEPE** 76 [1] R Hollinshead 3-8-9 p Dale Gibson 16/1: 06-6: Prom till 3f out:	hd	37a
240	**TAMARINA** 28 [8] N E Berry 3-8-9 P (55) C Catlin 10/1: 5004-7: Prom, fdd fnl 3f:	1¼	34a
276	**CHIMES EIGHT** 19 [5] R A Fahey 3-8-9 T Hamilton (5) 25/1: 00-8: Sn bhd, nvr factor:	½	33a
322	**SILVER CACHE** 13 [3] J Noseda 3-8-9 S W Kelly 8/1: 09: Slow away & al bhd:	shd	33a
88	**QUEENS FANTASY** 56 [6] D Haydn Jones 3-8-9 Paul Eddery 25/1: 00-0: Mid-div, struggling from halfway, abs.	8	19a
184	**MARIA MARIA** 38 [9] Mrs N Macauley 3-8-11 2ow P P McCabe 66/1: 0-0: Dwelt & sn bhd:	13	0a
11 Ran	2m 02.29 (4.09) Owner The Always Trying Partnership	Trained at Middleham	

<table>
<tr><td>439</td><td colspan="3">3.20 Bet Direct Handicap Stakes 3yo+ 0-80 (D)</td><td align="right">[78]</td></tr>
</table>

£4066 £1251 £626 £313   **1m100y f/sand rnd   Going 27   -04 Slow**   Stalls Inside

3839}	**VORTEX** 148 [12] Miss Gay Kelleway 5-9-9 e t (73) M Fenton 10/1: 6D1160-1: Held up, rdn & hdwy to chall 2f out, drvn & prevailed cl-home, all out:		77a
363	**DANIELLES LAD** 10 [13] B Palling 8-9-1 bl (65) R Miles (3) 20/1: 03005-42: Led, rdn & edged left/hdd cl-home:	nk	68a
363*	**ARC EL CIEL** 10 [11] Mrs Stef Liddiard 6-10-0 vis (78) I Mongan 9/1: 00162-13: Held up, eff wide to press ldrs 2f out, styd on well for press:	½	80a
318	**QUIET READING** 14 [8] M R Bosley 7-9-3 vis (67) Hayley Turner (5) 11/1: 34603-34: Trkd ldrs halfway, styd on onepace for press:	½	68a
363	**YORKER** 10 [1] Ms Deborah J Evans 6-9-5 (69) Lisa Jones (3) 13/2: 10020-25: Front rank, no extra ins fnl 1f.	½	69a
419	**OVIGO** 4 [6] P A Blockley 5-9-5 N Callan 9/4 FAV: 0330-146: Rear, wide & kept on fnl 2f, not able to chall.	nk	68a
127	**HENRY AFRIKA** 51 [5] Gerard McArdle 6-9-9 p (73) S W Kelly 11/2: 0/00/005-7: Mid-div, eff to press ldrs dist, no extra ins	nk	71a
127	**BRESSBEE** 51 [9] J W Unett 6-9-8 vis (72) R Winston 20/1: 000300-8: Chsd ldrs, btn 3f out:	3	64a
251	**MISS CHAMPERS** 24 [10] P D Evans 4-9-3 (67) S Donohoe (7) 8/1: 511352-9: Nvr a factor:	nk	59a
318	**PHAROAHS GOLD** 14 [2] D Shaw 6-8-13 e (63) Darren Williams 14/1: 01000-20: In tch, btn 2f out:	7	42a
334*	**ALLIED VICTORY** 13 [3] E J Alston 4-9-9 (73) Dean McKeown 16/1: 30324-10: Stumbled & nrly u.r. just after start, nvr on terms:	nk	52a
369	**FREE OPTION** 9 [4] W J Musson 9-9-9 (73) D Mernagh 20/1: 30130-50: Al bhd:	4	42a
3587}	**BOWING** 158 [7] P G Murphy 4-9-11 (75) D Kinsella 20/1: 320423-0: Chsd ldrs 4f:	9	29a
13 Ran	1m 48.81 (2.61) Owner Coriolis Partnership	Trained at Newmarket	

<table>
<tr><td>440</td><td colspan="3">3.50 Bet Direct On Sky Text Page 372 Selling Stakes 4yo+ (G)</td></tr>
</table>

£2618 £748 £374   **7f f/sand rnd   Going 27   -31 Slow**   Stalls Outside

378	**FEAST OF ROMANCE** 7 [6] P Howling 7-8-12 p (49) S W Kelly 7/1: 0336-331: Rear, switched wide & hdwy for press 3f out, led ins last, drvn out:		55a
373*	**LUCAYAN MONARCH** 7 [7] P A Blockley 6-9-3 p (56) Dean McKeown 11/4: 064-2112: Held up, eff to press ldrs over 1f out, not pace of wnr:	1¾	56a
320	**BULAWAYO** 14 [3] Andrew Reid 7-8-12 vis (53) A Nicholls 8/1: 32030-53: Led, rdn & hdd ins last, no extra:	¾	50a
320	**JAN BRUEGHEL** 14 [1] T D Barron 5-8-12 (63) P Makin (7) 9/4 FAV: 10240-34: Chsd ldrs hway, fdd dist.	4	42a
2404}	**CHANDELIER** 208 [8] M S Saunders 4-8-12 (58) R Miles (3) 25/1: 050060-5: Dwelt, eff wide halfway, hung left & no impress dist:	1	40a
202	**OPEN HANDED** 34 [2] B Ellison 4-8-12 t (45) T Hamilton (5) 33/1: 600000-6: Rear, eff 3f out, no prog dist:	1½	37a
332	**POOKAS DAUGHTER** 13 [4] J M Bradley 4-8-7 (45) C Catlin 16/1: 20000-57: Cl-up, btn over 1f out.	hd	31a
320	**XALOC BAY** 14 [10] B P J Baugh 6-8-12 p (55) J Fanning 9/2: 32360-28: Cl-up till 3f out:	7	24a
350*	**STAR LAD** 11 [11] R Brotherton 4-9-3 (47) I Mongan 14/1: 0606-319: Prom, no impress fnl 2f:	nk	28a
374	**THREAT** 7 [9] J M Bradley 8-8-12 p (40) P Fitzsimons 25/1: 000-0400: Prom, struggling halfway:	10	6a
356	**GLENVIEWS POLLY** 11 [5] Ian Emmerson 4-8-7 vis (35) J Bramhill 50/1: 0600-600: Dwelt & sn struggling.	10	0
11 Ran	1m 30.29 (4.09) Owner Mr D C Patrick	Trained at Newmarket	

<table>
<tr><td>441</td><td colspan="3">4.20 Littlewoodspoker Com Handicap Stakes 3yo 0-75 (E)</td><td align="right">[81]</td></tr>
</table>

£3269 £934 £467   **1m1f79y f/sand rnd   Going 27   +04 Fast**   Stalls Inside

3639}	**GAVROCHE** 157 [4] M J Wallace 3-8-10 (63) J P Guillambert (3) 7/2: 400-1: Mid-div, shkn up & hdwy to lead dist, drvn out:		73a
252	**BOLD BLADE** 23 [2] B Smart 3-9-3 bl (70) R Ffrench 3/1 FAV: 600413-2: Led, rdn & hdd dist, kept on:	2½	75a
325	**MYANNABANANA** 13 [6] J R Weymes 3-8-12 vis (65) D Fentiman (7) 12/1: 01135-53: Sn pushed along to go handy, styd on for press fnl 3f but no impress on front pair:	5	61a
325	**MAYBE SOMEDAY** 13 [9] I A Wood 3-9-7 (74) N Callan 6/1: 60213-34: Held up, rdn to chase ldrs 3f out, sn no extra:	3½	63a
25	**JOINT DESTINY** 67 [8] E J O'Neill 3-8-0 (53) Lisa Jones (3) 16/1: 502340-5: Mid-div, no impress fnl 3f:	9	27a
351	**BRETTON** 11 [3] R Hollinshead 3-7-12 4oh bl (47) Dale Gibson 12/1: 00544-26: Chsd ldr, btn 3f out:	3	19a
252	**ATLANTIC BREEZE** 23 [5] Mrs N Macauley 3-8-13 VIS (50) P McCabe 25/1: 410-7: Sn bhd, tried visor:	8	20a
159	**DANTES DEVINE** 42 [7] A Bailey 3-8-7 (60) C Catlin 12/1: 0055-8: Bhd, no ch 3f out:	13	0a
325	**BILL BENNETT** 13 [1] J Jay 3-9-7 (74) I Mongan 100/30: 33201-69: Chsd ldrs, wknd from halfway:	2½	1a
9 Ran	2m 0.36 (2.16) Owner Mr J L Guillambert	Trained at Newmarket	

Official Going Standard

<table>
<tr><td>442</td><td colspan="3">1.20 Press Interactive To Bet Direct Banded Stakes 3yo+ 0-40 (H)</td></tr>
</table>

£1481 £423 £212   **1m f/sand rnd   Going 53   -35 Slow**   Stalls Inside

370	**MR WHIZZ** 10 [12] A P Jones 7-9-8 BL e (35) Derek Nolan (7) 40/1: 00000-01: Prom, led over 2f out, drvn & held on gamely, all out:		39a
309	**KENNY THE TRUTH** 16 [2] Mrs J Candlish 5-9-8 t (40) N Chalmers (5) 9/2: 50000-32: Towards rear, drvn & styd on fnl 1f,	shd	38a

just failed:

398	SECOND VENTURE 6 [11] P Howling 6-9-8 BL T (40) R Winston 11/1: 00504-03: Chsd ldrs, no extra dist:	1½	35a
416	SWEET CORAL 5 [5] B S Rothwell 4-9-8 P (40) Joanna Badger 25/1: 5000-04: Chsd ldrs, onepace dist.	shd	36a
4883}	ABOUSTAR 87 [14] M Brittain 4-9-8 (40) M Lawson (7) 16/1: 6/00-5: Keen & led till over 2f out, no extra, abs.	¾	35a
398	PROUD VICTOR 6 [7] D Shaw 4-9-8 vis (40) Darren Williams 8/1: 4006-456: Held up, nrst fin, qck reapp.	3	29a
303	BALALAIKA TUNE 16 [3] W Storey 5-9-8 (40) D R McCabe 25/1: 4/0550-07: Mid-div, not pace to threaten.	3	22a
352	LEMARATE 12 [4] D W Chapman 7-9-8 bl (40) A Culhane 12/1: 0000-338: Slow away, rear, mod prog:	1¼	19a
356	BRILLIANTRIO 12 [6] M C Chapman 6-9-8 (40) I Mongan 7/4 FAV: 6505-249: Dwelt, chsd ldrs halfway, rdn & btn over 2f out:	nk	18a
408	VLASTA WEINER 5 [8] J M Bradley 4-9-8 bl (40) P Fitzsimons 25/1: 006-0250: Al bhd, qck reapp:	5	10a
61	MARGARETS WISH 62 [9] T Wall 4-9-8 (40) Stephanie Hollinshead (7) 33/1: 000200-0: Sn struggling, abs.	5	1a
164	YNYS 43 [10] B Palling 3-8-2 (40) D Kinsella 33/1: 055000-0: Wide, sn bhd, abs.	3	0
240	SKY COVE 29 [13] M W Easterby 3-8-2 (40) Dale Gibson 28/1: 000-0: Al bhd.	½	0
4793}	SHES A DIAMOND 95 [16] T T Clement 7-9-8 (40) V Slattery 66/1: 0/000-0: Chsd ldrs 4f, abs.	2½	0
4929}	DIVA DANCER 84 [15] J Hetherton 4-9-8 (40) C Catlin 50/1: 0/00-0: Sn bhd, abs.	2½	0
304	PROPRIUS 16 [1] B Smart 4-9-8 (40) R Ffrench 12/1: 000/6-50: Al rear.	5	0

16 Ran   1m 44.69 (5.29)   Owner The Milk Sheiks   Trained at Upper Lambourn

---

443   1.50 Bet Direct On Sky Active Banded Stakes 4yo+ 0-45 (H)
£1484 £424 £212   1m6f f/sand   Going 53   -10 Slow   Stalls Inside

315	LAMPOS 15 [8] Miss J A Camacho 4-9-0 (45) R Winston 11/2: 40030-31: Mid-div, smooth hdwy to lead over 1f out, rdn clr, readily:		52a
301*	CITRUS MAGIC 17 [7] K Bell 7-9-6 p (45) Joanna Badger 10/1: 04506-12: Led till over 1f out, onepce.	8	40a
357	KAGOSHIMA 12 [4] J R Norton 9-9-6 vis (40) V Halliday 9/2: 0060-223: Trkd ldrs, onepace.	hd	39a
307	WORLABY DALE 16 [5] Mrs S Lamyman 8-9-6 (35) J Fanning 7/2 JT FAV: 33340-44: Handy trav well, onepace fnl 2f:	2	36a
357	CHARNWOOD STREET 12 [2] D Shaw 5-9-6 e (35) Darren Williams 25/1: 46050-55: Held up, mod prog:	9	25a
4790}	MICHAELS DREAM 95 [3] J Hetherton 5-9-6 vis (40) C Catlin 7/2 JT FAV: 000300-6: Sn pushed along towards rear, btn 3f out:	1½	23a
305	TURFTANZER 16 [9] Don Enrico Incisa 5-9-6 t (35) Kim Tinkler 16/1: 00/050-57: Cl-up, wknd fnl 2f.	1½	21a
376	DR JULIAN 8 [10] Miss A Stokell 4-9-0 p (40) Ann Stokell 50/1: 5000-058: Mid-div, lost tch fnl 3f.	14	3a
315	LITTLE RICHARD 15 [11] M Wellings 5-9-6 p (35) V Slattery 50/1: 30000-09: Chsd ldrs till 4f out.	2	0a
4675*}	RODIAK 455 [12] P R Hedger 5-9-6 (45) I Mongan 8/1: 606401/-0: Strugg hway, jumps fit.	dist	0
334	MARGOLD 14 [13] R Hollinshead 4-9-0 (45) A Culhane 16/1: 33306-00: Mid-div, lost tch from halfway.	1	0
1455}	MILL EMERALD 615 [1] Mrs G Harvey 7-9-6 (40) M Henry 25/1: 64600//0/-: Sn bhd, virtually p.u., 2 mth jumps abs, new stable.	dist	0

12 Ran   3m 08.55 (8.75)   Owner Mr L A Bolingbroke   Trained at Malton

---

444   2.20 Littlewoods Bet Direct Median Auction Maiden Stakes 3-5yo (H)
£1474 £421 £211   6f f/sand rnd   Going 53   +05 Fast   Stalls Inside

3	PICK OF THE CROP 71 [2] J R Jenkins 3-8-7 (73) S W Kelly 11/4 FAV: 40525-1: Dwelt, rear, unbalanced after 1f, hdwy inner from halfway & drvn to lead well ins last:		67a
316	DARING AFFAIR 15 [11] K R Burke 3-8-2 (63) J Fanning 4/1: 44526-32: Mid-div, rdn & briefly led ins last, not pace of wnr nr fin:	½	59a
396	WEAKEST LINK 6 [12] W Jarvis 3-8-7 D Allan (3) 6/1: 0-23: Al handy, not pace of front pair:	1¾	59a
197	FAYRZ PLEASE 36 [4] M C Chapman 3-8-7 Andrew Webb (7) 14/1: 03-4: Went right start, rear, styd on for press fnl 2f, not able to chall:	nk	57a
208	ZAK FACTA 35 [7] Miss D A McHale 4-9-9 vis (50) C Cogan 11/2: 425400-5: Trkd ldrs trav well, onepace for press over 1f out:	½	56a
383	MISS JUDGED 8 [1] A P Jones 3-8-2 bl e (45) J F McDonald (5) 100/1: 0000-006: Led over 2f out, hdd ins last..	1½	46a
319	DISPOL VELETA 15 [13] T D Barron 3-8-2 D Mernagh 9/2: 0-37: Rear/wide, late gains, nrst fin:	½	44a
416	KUSTOM KIT FOR HER 5 [8] S R Bowring 4-9-4 (50) J Bramhill 33/1: 40200-68: Towards rear/wide, nrst fin.	nk	41a
226	MIND THE TIME 32 [10] J Hetherton 3-8-7 C Catlin 66/1: 0-9: Prom, btn 2f out.	9	25a
374	LAW MAKER 8 [3] M A Buckley 4-9-9 bl (35) R Ffrench 50/1: 00000-: Led till halfway, sn fdd.	hd	24a
418	SHEAPYS LASS 5 [9] A Crook 3-8-2 VIS (60) Dale Gibson 20/1: 6526-00: Dsptd lead 4f:	4	9a
396	DANCES IN TIME 6 [5] C N Kellett 4-9-4 T Williams 20/1: 050: Hmpd start, al bhd, qck reapp.	5	-4a
4668}	LIMITED MAGICIAN 102 [6] C Smith 3-8-2 R Fitzpatrick 100/1: 00-0: Hmpd start, sn bhd, abs/AW bow.	1¼	0

13 Ran   1m 16.19 (2.89)   Owner Buy and Sell Partnership   Trained at Royston

---

445   2.50 Bet Direct Interactive Banded Stakes 4yo+ 0-45 (H)
£1666 £476 £238   1m3f f/sand   Going 53   +06 Fast   Stalls Inside

321	AVEIRO 15 [1] B G Powell 8-9-3 bl (45) K Dalgleish 11/4 FAV: 04140-21: Made all, rdn clr over 3f out, styd on strongly:		51a
321	DASH OF MAGIC 15 [2] J Hetherton 6-9-3 (40) C Catlin 9/1: 4000-162: Prom, onepace fnl 2f.	13	39a
356	NEWCLOSE 12 [4] N Tinkler 4-9-0 t (40) A Culhane 6/1: 0500-333: Bhd, late gains for press, nrst fin:	¾	38a
311	RED DELIRIUM 15 [16] R Brotherton 8-9-3 bl (45) I Mongan 20/1: 06004-64: Chsd ldrs, drvn & styd on wide fnl 2f, nvr a dngr:	shd	38a
417	KING PRIAM 5 [7] M J Polglase 9-9-3 bl (45) Dean McKeown 10/1: 00-04145: Wide & bhd, late gains.	shd	37a
224	NEXT FLIGHT 32 [11] R E Barr 5-9-3 (45) T Eaves 25/1: 000003-6: Held up, late gains for press, nrst fin.	1¼	35a
354	DESIRES DESTINY 12 [8] R Hollinshead 8-9-3 (40) M Lawson (7) 20/1: 6600-67: Chsd wnr halfway, btn 2f out:	hd	34a
310	VERMILION CREEK 15 [10] R Hollinshead 5-9-3 P (35) Stephanie Hollinshead (7) 40/1: 00006-58: Mid-div, no impress fnl:	nk	33a
427	DEBBIE 4 [13] B D Leavy 5-9-3 (45) S Whitworth 7/2: 31133-09: In tch wide, btn fnl 2f:	½	32a
315	BERKELEY HEIGHTS 15 [15] B Smart 4-9-0 bl (40) R Ffrench 25/1: 50065-40: Bhd halfway.	3	28a
199	GWAZI 36 [12] Miss D A McHale 4-9-0 t P (45) Darren Williams 40/1: 0000-0: Al bhd, cheek pieces.	5	21a
302*	NDOLA 17 [14] B J Curley 5-9-3 (45) S W Kelly 11/2: 000/00/-10: Sn struggling rear.	1½	19a
287	POLKA PRINCESS 18 [3] M Wellings 4-9-0 (45) L Treadwell (7) 100/1: 60000-09: Chsd ldrs till 3f out.	nk	18a
250	THINK QUICK 25 [6] R Hollinshead 4-9-0 (40) Dale Gibson 66/1: 200040-0: Chsd ldrs, btn 3f out.	1½	16a

SOUTHWELL Tuesday 20.01.04 Lefthand, Sharp, Oval Track

314	GOOD TIMING 15 [9] J Hetherton 6-9-3 (45) G Parkin 33/1: 0000/0-20: Mid-div, struggling fnl 4f:	5	9a
307	ROUSING THUNDER 16 [5] W Storey 7-9-3 t p (45) D R McCabe 25/1: 54463-00: Sn bhd.	9	0
16 Ran	2m 26.48 (5.18) Owner The Dream Connection	Trained at Winchester	

446 3.20 Bet Direct Through Sky Active Selling Stakes 4yo+ (H)
£1264 £361 £181   1m4f f/sand   Going 53   -10 Slow   Stalls Inside

392	PLATINUM CHARMER 7 [3] K A Ryan 4-9-0 P (65) N Callan 4/9 FAV: 00004-21: Held up, smooth prog to chall over 2f out, rdn to assert ins last:		52a
330	SHATIN SPECIAL 14 [2] G C H Chung 4-8-9 p (40) R Ffrench 7/1: 40402-52: Cl-up & led over 4f out, drvn & hdd ins last, kept on:	½	45a
420	IPLEDGEALLEGIANCE 5 [5] D W Chapman 8-9-4 (45) A Culhane 9/2: 4560-253: Trkd ldrs trav well, rdn & no impress fnl 2f:	11	36a
336	LAPADAR 14 [1] J R Weymes 5-8-13 p (50) D Fentiman (7) 12/1: 05050-64: Led, rdn & hdd over 4f out, sn no impress:	6	23a
305	BEHAN 16 [4] A Crook 5-9-4 vis (30) V Halliday 40/1: 30060-05: Chsd ldrs, btn 4f out.	5	21a
5 Ran	2m 41.8 (7.5) Owner Platinum Racing Club Limited	Trained at Hambleton	

447 3.50 Littlewoodscasino Com Banded Stakes 3yo+ 0-40 (H)
£1481 £423 £212   6f f/sand rnd   Going 53   -13 Slow   Stalls Inside

356	CHAMPAGNE RIDER 12 [9] D Shaw 8-9-7 e (40) Darren Williams 13/2: 0000-351: Towards rear, rdn & hdwy from halfway, drvn & led well ins last:		45a
384	ENJOY THE BUZZ 8 [11] J M Bradley 5-9-7 (40) P Fitzsimons 16/1: 020-4402: Mid-div, drvn & kept on fnl 2f, not pace of wnr:	¾	42a
374	BELLS BOYS 8 [4] K A Ryan 5-9-7 p (40) G Parkin 5/1: 0/0505-33: Led & rdn clr over 1f out, drvn & hdd well ins last:	nk	41a
4332}	LIVELY FELIX 123 [6] D G Bridgwater 7-9-7 (40) B Swarbrick (7) 33/1: 600000-4: Chsd ldrs, outpcd over 2f out, kept on late, nrst fin, abs:	1	38a
374	BLUNHAM 8 [16] M C Chapman 4-9-7 (40) I Mongan 16/1: 00000-45: Chsd ldrs wide, styd on for press.	nk	37a
2700}	BELLS BEACH 198 [3] P Howling 6-9-7 (40) R Winston 13/2: 030040-6: Held up, short of room halfway, drvn & kept on, nrst fin:	hd	36a
296	MAGIC EAGLE 17 [15] P T Midgley 7-9-7 (40) D Nolan (5) 10/1: 50000/-57: Prom wide, no extra dist.	3	28a
294}	SPEEDY JAMES 384 [12] D Nicholls 8-9-7 (40) L Treadwell 7/1: 0/0000/-0: Dwelt & towards rear, mod hdwy.	½	26a
377	MIMAS GIRL 8 [10] S R Bowring 5-9-7 t (35) J Bramhill 20/1: 05046-59: Dwelt & al bhd.	shd	26a
340	FLYING FAISAL 13 [14] J M Bradley 6-9-7 bl (40) B Reilly (5) 14/1: 6000-000: Towards rear, eff wide, no impress.	shd	25a
300	LEONORA TRUCE 17 [2] R P Elliott 5-9-7 (40) V Slattery 9/1: 03260-00: Mid-div inner, nvr a factor.	2½	17a
3764}	MISTER RUSHBY 152 [8] D W Chapman 4-9-7 (40) A Culhane 33/1: 000000-0: Chsd ldrs, sn struggling, abs.	1½	12a
394	ETERNAL BLOOM 6 [13] M Brittain 6-9-13 (35) M Lawson (7) 7/2 FAV: 0/000-120: Dwelt & al rear:	1½	13a
397	MESMERISED 6 [7] Miss A Stokell 4-9-7 (40) Ann Stokell 66/1: 00000-000: Al bhd, qck reapp.	2	1a
308	PRECIOUS FREEDOM 16 [5] J Balding 4-9-7 BL (40) J Edmunds 28/1: 00000-00: Prom, wknd qckly dist:	2	0a
394	DEAL IN FACTS 6 [1] C N Kellett 5-9-7 (35) T Williams 50/1: 0000/00/-00: Chsd ldrs till halfway, qck reapp.	dist	0a
16 Ran	1m 17.27 (3.97) Owner The Whiteman Partnership	Trained at Newark	

LINGFIELD Wednesday 21.01.04 Lefthand, V Sharp Track

Official Going Standard

448 12.40 Littlewoods Bet Direct Handicap Stakes Div 1 3yo+ 0-60 (F) [60]
£2968 £848 £424   6f p/track rnd   Going 30   -06 Slow   Stalls Inside

344*	NEARLY A FOOL 14 [2] G G Margarson 6-9-9 vis (55) N Pollard 9/2: 60353-11: Chsd ldrs, led over 1f out, drvn out:		63a
407*	TAYIF 7 [10] Andrew Reid 8-10-5 6ex (65) S Donohoe 5/2 FAV: 603-2112: Mid-div, kept on for press.	1¼	68a
435*	DOUBLE M 4 [4] Mrs L Richards 7-9-11 6ex vis (57) N Callan 4/1: 00000-413: Hld up, kept on late.	¾	58a
366	MAYZIN 11 [7] R M Flower 4-9-8 p (54) E Ahern 4/1: 0054-324: Led/dsptd lead & sn clr with rival, hdd over 1f out, onepace:	1	52a
397	SABANA 7 [3] J M Bradley 6-8-13 bl (45) P Fitzsimons 12/1: 3000-435: Mid-div, styd on onepace for press:	½	41a
312	TORRENT 16 [13] D W Chapman 9-8-13 bl (45) A Culhane 16/1: 52060-26: Rear, late gains, no dngr:	2	35a
397	SILVER MASCOT 7 [9] R Hollinshead 5-8-13 (45) Dale Gibson 25/1: 0/0600-47: Mid-div, hung & btn over 1f out:	3½	24a
328	LOCH LAIRD 15 [11] M Madgwick 9-9-3 (49) L Keniry (3) 12/1: 01000-08: Rdn rear, little hdwy.	½	26a
400	KOMENA 7 [6] J W Payne 6-9-1 (47) Lisa Jones (3) 25/1: 05240-59: Sn outpcd:	1¾	19a
397*	ATTORNEY 7 [12] D Shaw 6-9-5 6ex vis (51) T Hamilton (5) 20/1: 004-3010: No dngr:	1½	18a
366	MASTER RATTLE 11 [1] Jane Southcombe 5-9-4 (50) V Slattery 50/1: 50000-00: Led/dsptd lead, wknd qckly over 1f out.	½	15a
31	ELLAMYTE 68 [8] D G Bridgwater 4-9-2 vis (48) S Righton 66/1: 530300-0: Chsd ldrs till halfway, abs.	2	7a
4991}	REGAL SONG 79 [14] T J Etherington 8-9-12 bl (58) J Fanning 20/1: 061005-0: Slow away & sn bhd, abs.	3	8a
13 Ran	1m 12.58 (2.18) Owner Mr J Burns	Trained at Newmarket	

449 1.10 Press Interactive To Bet Direct Maiden Stakes 3yo+ (D)
£3780 £1163 £582 £291   6f p/track rnd   Going 30   -29 Slow   Stalls Inside

	ALEUTIAN [3] D R Loder 4-9-10 J P Spencer 1/3 FAV: 1: Broke well & made all, rdly pulled clr from dist, easily:		81a
258	NOSSENKO 23 [8] J Noseda 3-8-3 E Ahern 8/1: 0-2: Trkd ldrs, styd on to take 2nd, nvr threat to easy wnr:	3½	59a
	PICKLE [11] S C Williams 3-8-3 R Ffrench 33/1: 3: Mid-div, late gains for press:	¾	57a
2542}	HEARTBEAT 205 [1] P J McBride 3-8-3 Dale Gibson 50/1: 06-4: Mid-div, onepce:	½	55a
219	MAGGIE MAQUETTE 35 [10] W S Kittow 4-9-5 D Sweeney 33/1: 00-5: Cl-up, wknd dist.	hd	54a
1863}	HORIZONTAL 235 [6] H J Collingridge 4-9-10 M Tebbutt 16/1: 5-6: Held up, mod late prog, fin lame:	2½	51a
	RECKLESS FRED [7] Miss K M George 5-9-10 Derek Nolan (7) 100/1: 7: Mid-div, mod late prog on debut.	¾	49a
319	STARCROSS VENTURE 16 [7] R A Fahey 3-8-3 T Hamilton 10/1: 3-08: Mid-div, outpcd from halfway.	hd	43a
276	OBOE 21 [13] R Charlton 3-8-3 J Fanning 12/1: 5-9: Chsd ldrs till over 1f out.	2½	35a
	IMPERIAL WIZARD [5] M D I Usher 3-8-8 A Daly 25/1: 0: Sn bhd on debut.	1	37a
4409}	HAZEWIND 120 [14] P D Evans 3-8-8 T Joanna Badger 33/1: 00-0: Wide & bhd halfway, abs/t-strap.	1	34a

117

3498}	**TANAFFUS** 165 [2] D W Chapman 4-9-10 (70) A Culhane 33/1: 04/56-0: Sn outpcd, new stable.	2½	26a
364	**BACKLASH** 11 [9] A W Carroll 3-8-4 1ow S Whitworth 20/1: 0-00: Slow away & sn bhd.	hd	21a
364	**JAYCEE STAR** 11 [12] D Flood 3-8-3 P Doe 50/1: 00: Keen & cl-up, btn over 2f out.	5	5a
14 Ran	1m 13.96 (3.56) Owner Jumeirah Racing	Trained at Newmarket	

450

1.40 Bet Direct On Sky Active Claiming Stakes 4yo+ (F)
£2982 £852 £426   **7f p/track rnd**   **Going 30**   -11 Slow   Stalls Inside

400	**RIPPLE EFFECT** 7 [5] C A Dwyer 4-8-12 t (67) B Reilly (5) 6/1: 30102-21: Handy travelling well, led ins last, rdly asserted:		73a
215	**POWER BIRD** 35 [2] D Flood 4-8-0 (62) J Mackay 14/1: 050000-2: Mid-div, styd on for press fnl 2f, no threat to wnr:	1¾	55a
419	**PHECKLESS** 6 [3] R F Johnson Houghton 5-8-13 (69) S Carson 7/2 FAV: 00564-03: Dwelt & towards rear, short of room 2f out, styd on onepace for press ins last:	1	66a
323	**THE GAIKWAR** 15 [6] N E Berry 5-8-9 bl (66) C Catlin 4/1: 00404-64: Held up, styd on fnl 2f.	½	61a
366	**FOOLISH THOUGHT** 11 [13] R A Fahey 4-8-3 (58) T Hamilton 8/1: 04040-65: Handy & led 3f out till ins last, wknd.	hd	54a
323	**SUPERCHIEF** 15 [15] Miss B Sanders 9-9-7 bl t (65) E Ahern 7/1: 00002-06: Held up, eff wide, no extra dist.	hd	71a
323	**ESPADA** 15 [1] J A Osborne 8-8-9 (65) S W Kelly 6/1: 10002-07: Led 4f, fdd:	nk	58a
384	**WARLINGHAM** 9 [9] P Howling 6-8-9 (54) V Slattery 14/1: 00210-08: Keen & prom till 2f out:	1¾	55a
400	**MUQTADI** 7 [16] M Quinn 6-8-9 (51) L Enstone (3) 20/1: 4650-039: Slow away, nvr nr ldrs:	hd	54a
400	**DUNEDIN RASCAL** 7 [4] E A Wheeler 7-8-5 bl (62) Liam Jones 7/1: 33/1: 0400-000: Al towards rear:	3	44a
271	**NAUGHTY GIRL** 22 [7] P D Evans 4-9-2 (70) S Donohoe (7) 33/1: 126560-0: Mid-div, btn 2f out.	¾	53a
370	**ORIGINAL SIN** 11 [12] S Dow 4-8-7 (46) Lisa Jones (3) 66/1: 0560-00: Mid-div, struggling fnl 2f.	½	43a
101	**SQUEAKY** 56 [14] Miss K M George 7-8-10 P (56) Derek Nolan (7) 100/1: 0/22000-0: Sn outpcd rear, abs/chkpcs.	¾	44a
400	**ISLAND STAR** 7 [8] S Dow 4-8-3 (45) P Doe 100/1: 0060-000: Chsd ldr, btn 2f out.	shd	37a
14 Ran	1m 25.65 (2.85) Owner Miss Lilo Blum	Trained at Newmarket	

451

2.10 Littlewoods Bet Direct Handicap Stakes Div 2 3yo+ 0-60 (F)   [60]
£2961 £846 £423   **6f p/track rnd**   **Going 30**   -19 Slow   Stalls Inside

328*	**PRINCE AARON** 15 [11] C N Allen 4-9-12 (58) G Carter 9/4 FAV: P0062-11: Rear, smooth hdwy wide to lead over 1f out, rdly asserted, val further:		70a
340	**A TEEN** 14 [13] P Howling 6-9-3 (49) J P Spencer 9/1: 61000-52: Rear, styd on wide for press, no threat to wnr:	2	50a
415*	**HOUT BAY** 6 [10] R A Fahey 7-9-11 6ex (57) T Hamilton (5) 11/2: 06500-13: Held up, rdn & styd on fnl 2f, not pace of wnr:	¾	56a
411*	**LORD MELBOURNE** 6 [1] J A Osborne 5-9-5 6ex (51) S W Kelly 7/2: 6035-214: Prom, ch dist, onepace:	1	47a
384	**ITALIAN MIST** 9 [9] Julian Poulton 5-9-4 e (50) G Faulkner 25/1: 0050-135: Trkd ldr & led over 2f out till over 1f out.	hd	45a
397	**LONG WEEKEND** 7 [2] D Shaw 6-8-13 vis (45) Darren Williams 20/1: 01460-06: Held up, keeping on for press when hmpd ins last, nvr danger:	¾	38a
435	**SOAKED** 4 [7] D W Chapman 11-9-7 bl (53) A Culhane 14/1: 0350-267: Held up, onepace for press:	nk	45a
227	**HEATHYARDSBLESSING** 33 [4] R Hollinshead 7-9-0 (46) N Callan 33/1: 000623-8: Mid-div, hmpd over 2f out, onepace.	hd	37a
121	**TAMARELLA** 53 [12] G G Margarson 4-9-8 (54) Martin Dwyer 16/1: 000500-9: Prom, no extra dist, abs.	1¼	41a
340	**TRIPTI** 14 [8] J J Bridger 4-9-2 (48) N Pollard 11/1: 60406-20: Mid-div, btn ins last:	¾	33a
328	**PATANDON GIRL** 15 [14] A Bailey 4-9-2 (48) R Lappin 25/1: 05300-00: Al rear.	hd	32a
3400}	**LYDIAS LOOK** 168 [3] T J Etherington 7-8-13 (45) J Fanning 20/1: 005000-0: Prom, btn over 1f out, abs.	1¼	25a
3644}	**ILLUSTRIOUS DUKE** 159 [5] M Mullineaux 6-9-3 (49) Lisa Jones (3) 25/1: 401200-0: Led till over 2f out, abs.	5	16a
13 Ran	1m 13.31 (2.91) Owner Black Star Racing	Trained at Newmarket	

452

2.40 Bet Direct Interactive Handicap Stakes 4yo+ 0-85 (D)   [83]
£4550 £1400 £700 £350   **1m2f p/track**   **Going 30**   +08 Fast   Stalls Inside

4846}	**SWIFT TANGO** 91 [8] E A L Dunlop 4-9-11 (82) E Ahern 14/1: 221623-1: Held up, al travelling well, drvn to lead well ins last:		87a
134	**NORTHSIDE LODGE** 50 [5] P W Harris 6-10-0 (83) P Doe 6/1 JT FAV: 220404-2: Handy & led over 2f out, rdn clr over 1f out, hdd well ins last:	nk	87a
218	**PARAGON OF VIRTUE** 35 [10] P Mitchell 7-9-10 (79) J Fanning 10/1: 163310-3: Chsd ldrs, styd on.	1½	81a
134	**DOWER HOUSE** 50 [6] Andrew Turnell 9-9-12 (81) F Lynch 16/1: 620310-4: Held up, hdwy when short of room & switched over 1f out, kept on ins last:	½	82a
265	**RYANS FUTURE** 23 [4] J Akehurst 4-9-9 (80) N Chalmers (5) 7/1: 051415-5: Slow away, styd on onepace fnl 2f.	hd	80a
273	**SILKEN BRIEF** 22 [1] D J Daly 5-9-8 t (77) W Ryan 10/1: 102/043-6: Trkd ldr, no extra dist.	1½	75a
4349}	**SCOTTYS FUTURE** 123 [12] D R Loder 6-10-0 (83) J P Spencer 15/2: 050000-7: Rear, late gains for press, no danger:	¾	80a
285	**INVADER** 19 [3] C E Brittain 8-9-13 bl (82) I Mongan 10/1: 20143-08: Led till over 2f out, no extra:	1	78a
369	**LABRETT** 11 [13] Miss Gay Kelleway 7-10-0 t (83) M Fenton 16/1: 51061-39: Mid-div, no impress fnl 2f:	2	76a
195+*	**SANGIOVESE** 39 [7] H Morrison 5-9-11 (80) L Fletcher (3) 6/1 JT FAV: 622/301-0: Trkd ldr, btn over 1f out.	2½	69a
338*	**JACK OF TRUMPS** 14 [11] G Wragg 4-9-7 (78) Martin Dwyer 7/1: 006/35-10: Prom, btn over 1f out:	1	66a
369	**J R STEVENSON** 11 [9] M Wigham 8-9-11 (80) M Savage (5) 7/1: 26351-20: Mid-div, btn 2f out:	shd	68a
2606}	**TRAVELLING BAND** 202 [14] A M Balding 6-9-9 (78) L Keniry (3) 33/1: 30/0024-0: Al rear, jumps fit.	½	65a
1782}	**TANAJI** 238 [2] P R Webber 5-9-9 (78) C Catlin 66/1: 3221/06-0: Sn struggling rear, 7 wk jumps abs.	7	56a
14 Ran	2m 06.38 (2.18) Owner Mr Khalifa Sultan	Trained at Newmarket	

453

3.10 Betdirect Co Uk Handicap Stakes 3yo+ 0-75 (E)   [73]
£3371 £963 £482   **5f p/track rnd**   **Going 30**   -02 Slow   Stalls Outside

431	**HURRICANE COAST** 4 [10] D Flood 5-9-6 bl (65) P Doe 15/8 FAV: 44-11131: Dwelt, sn in touch wide, smooth hdwy to lead ins last, rdn out:		72a
345	**PRINCE OF BLUES** 13 [1] M Mullineaux 6-9-5 p (64) S W Kelly 20/1: 00600-02: Led, rdn & hdd ins last, not pace of wnr:	1¾	62a
349	**LADY PEKAN** 13 [8] P S McEntee 5-9-4 bl (63) F P Ferris (3) 16/1: 00141-63: Trkd ldr, switched & kept on for press, not pace of wnr:	nk	61a
407	**CURRENCY** 7 [2] J M Bradley 7-10-0 (73) E Ahern 5/2: 600-0324: Dwelt, rear, staying on when no room twice over 1f out:	½	69a
415*	**THE FISIO** 6 [7] A M Balding 4-10-3 6ex (76) N Chalmers (5) 11/2: 0000-115: Mid-div, outpcd halfway, kept on.	hd	71a

118

407	PLAYTIME BLUE 7 [5] K R Burke 4-9-2 (61) G Baker 7/1: 4002-236: Trkd ldrs, no extra dist:	¾	54a
329	OUR FRED 15 [9] T G Mills 7-9-9 bl (68) I Mongan 16/1: 00306-67: Prom, wknd ins last:	¾	59a
407	TABOOR 7 [6] J W Payne 6-9-8 h bl (67) N Callan 14/1: 1000-008: Rear, eff wide, no impress.	hd	57a
407	TEYAAR 7 [1] Mrs N Macauley 8-9-4 bl (63) P McCabe 33/1: 51003-09: Rear, hmpd over 1f out, no danger.	shd	53a
418	COUNT COUGAR 6 [4] S P Griffiths 4-9-2 (61) R Lappin 25/1: 60010-30: Mid-div, btn ins last:	½	49a

10 Ran   59.42 (1.62)   Owner Mrs Ruth M Serrell   Trained at Lingfield

454 — 3.40 Bet Direct Through Sky Active Selling Stakes 4yo+ (G)
£2548 £728 £364   2m p/track   Going 30   -38 Slow   Stalls Inside

264	SUNGIO 23 [2] B G Powell 6-9-4 (53) Dale Gibson 4/1: 0005/05-1: Trkd ldrs, pushed along to lead over 2f out, in command dist under hands & heels:		42a
342	RADIANT BRIDE 14 [4] K R Burke 4-8-6 p (40) Darren Williams 11/1: 00250-02: Held up, rdn & styd on fnl 2f, nvr threatened wnr.	2	34a
307	KHUZDAR 17 [5] A Bailey 5-9-9 (40) B O'Neill (7) 7/1: 40640-03: Slow away & rear, kept on fnl 2f despite looking v awkward ride, no danger:	2½	42a
426	MYSTERIUM 5 [1] N P Littmoden 10-9-4 vis (40) I Mongan 3/1: 03333-34: Led till over 2f out, wknd ins last:	¾	36a
65}	NEPTUNE 427 [6] J C Fox 8-9-4 (40) R Smith 20/1: 640500/-5: Keen & held up, no danger.	shd	36a
267	BLUE SAVANNA 22 [10] J G Portman 4-8-11 (40) E Ahern 11/2: 002663-6: Trkd ldrs, btn 2f out:	11	27a
2864}	PHILOSOPHIC 553 [9] Mrs L C Jewell 10-9-4 (40) S Carson 50/1: 00///000/-: Dsptd lead early, trkd ldr, btn 4f out:	11	18a
353	ROPPONGI DANCER 13 [8] Mrs N Macauley 5-8-13 bl t (30) Stephanie Hollinshead (7) 50/1: 6400-538: Keen, bhd 6f out.	4	9a
4698}	BAMFORD CASTLE 453 [3] R Ford 9-9-4 p (75) J P Guillambert (3) 9/4 FAV: 20/060/0/-: Sn rdn rear, nvr factor.	½	13a

9 Ran   3m 30.89 (10.89)   Owner Mrs Rachel A Powell   Trained at Winchester

455 — 4.10 Free #25 Bonus @ Littlewoodscasino Com Apprentice Handicap Stakes 3yo 0-75 (E) [79]
£3262 £932 £466   1m p/track rnd   Going 30   -20 Slow   Stalls Outside

337	TREVIAN 14 [2] S C Williams 3-9-0 (65) S Donohoe (3) 8/1: 056-01: Mid-div, hdwy to lead over 1f out, rdn out:		69a
5005}	ARCHERFIELD 77 [5] J W Hills 3-9-2 (67) H Gemberlu (5) 20/1: 0055-2: Mid-div, forced wide to press ldrs 2f out, kept on for press:	½	69a
337	RESPLENDENT KING 14 [9] T G Mills 3-9-7 (72) M Savage 5/2 FAV: 03040-33: Mid-div, styd on onepace for press fnl 2f:	2	70a
13	BIG BAD BURT 70 [3] M J Wallace VIS (64) K Bowman (7) 7/2: 600-4: Slow away & rear, flashed tail for press, late gains, nrst fin:	3½	55a
368	ST SAVARIN 11 [4] J R Best 3-9-7 (72) D Fentiman (5) 3/1: 61051-25: Led aft 1f till over 1f out, wknd:	½	62a
290	FUBOS 18 [1] Julian Poulton 3-8-10 vis (61) M Halford (5) 10/1: 0000-56: Cl-up, hung right & bmpd 2f out, wknd.	1½	48a
4960}	MORNING HAWK 82 [6] J S Moore 3-8-1 (52) R Thomas 50/1: 05000-7: Rdn rear, nvr a factor, abs.	¾	38a
337	GAYLE STORM 14 [7] C Tinkler 3-8-7 (56) Rory Moore (3) 7/1: 6536-08: Slow away & held up wide, nvr danger.	3	38a
4561}	PARALLEL LINES 111 [10] P D Evans 3-8-5 (56) Hayley Turner (5) 25/1: 622000-9: Led 1f, btn 2f out, new stable, abs.	5	26a
1835}	RICKY MARTAN 236 [8] G C Bravery 3-9-5 (70) Derek Nolan (5) 25/1: 064-0: Chsd ldrs, wknd from halfway, virtually p.u.:	20	2a

10 Ran   1m 40.21 (4.01)   Owner The Little Trev Partnership   Trained at Newmarket

Official Going   Standard

456 — 12.40 Press Interactive To Bet Direct Amateur Riders' Handicap Stakes Div 1 4yo+ 0-60 (G) [37]
£2576 £736 £368   1m4f f/sand   Going 24   -39 Slow   Stalls Inside

331	DELTA FORCE 16 [2] P A Blockley 5-11-7 (58) Miss S Renwick (5) 100/30: 6031-121: Dwelt, keen & sn handy, led after 2f, styd on strongly for press fnl 2f:		62a
380	FIGHT THE FEELING 10 [6] J W Unett 6-11-4 vis (55) Miss J C Williams (5) 5/1: 53016-42: Pushed along chasing ldrs, styd on for press fnl 2f:	1¾	56a
376*	MR SMITHERS JONES 10 [9] S C Williams 4-11-0 5ex (55) Mr S Walker 11/4 FAV: 00/5-213: Held up, eff wide to chall over 2f out, drvn & kept on, a just held:	½	55a
3737}	JADE STAR 155 [8] Miss Gay Kelleway 4-10-7 (48) Miss E J Jones 20/1: 660325-4: Chsd ldrs, rdn & ch 2f out, no extra dist:	5	41a
372	WESTERN COMMAND 10 [7] Mrs N Macauley 8-9-7 (30) Mrs M Morris 20/1: 550-0045: Hld up, no impress fnl 3f:	3½	18a
330	INTERSTICE 16 [10] A G Newcombe 7-11-0 P (51) Miss C Hannaford 6/1: 00000-36: In tch, pulled hard, wknd 2f out.	1½	37a
443	CITRUS MAGIC 2 [11] K Bell 7-10-8 p (45) Miss J Ellis (5) 4/1: 04506-127: Chsd ldrs, btn 4f out:	5	24a
4929}	CRYPTOGAM 86 [5] M E Sowersby 4-10-11 (52) Mr N Pearce (5) 50/1: 000440-8: Lost tch 4f out, 7 wk jmps abs.	28	0
4820}	MAGENTA RISING 94 [4] D Burchell 4-11-5 VIS (60) Miss E Tucker (7) 50/1: 000200-9: In tch 7f:	5	0

9 Ran   2m 41.83 (7.53)   Owner Miss Emma Shally   Trained at Southwell

457 — 1.10 Betdirect Co Uk Handicap Stakes Div 1 4yo+ 0-65 (F) [65]
£2919 £834 £417   1m f/sand rnd   Going 24   +02 Fast   Stalls Inside

354	SIMPLY THE GUEST 14 [5] Don Enrico Incisa 5-8-8 t (45) Kim Tinkler 6/1: 0000-221: Pushed along chasing ldrs, rdn & led over 1f out, styd on strongly, rdn out:		55a
280	ROBIN SHARP 22 [10] J Akehurst 6-8-11 vis T (48) J Quinn 40/1: 10P000-2: Led, rdn & hdd over 1f out, no extra:	4	49a
157	YENALED 47 [11] K A Ryan 7-9-11 (62) N Callan 7/1: 542545-3: Held up, styd on for press fnl 2f, not pace of wnr:	1¾	60a
379*	LORD CHAMBERLAIN 10 [2] J M Bradley 11-8-12 bl (49) P Fitzsimons 10/1: 5450-214: Held up, swtchd wide & styd on for press, nrst fin:	nk	46a
363	BARZAK 13 [9] S R Bowring 4-9-13 bl t (64) R Winston 6/1: 01005-05: Cl-up, wknd ins last:	2½	57a
379	MUQARRAR 10 [7] T J Fitzgerald 5-9-1 BL e (52) D Mernagh 25/1: 50006-66: Dwelt, sn in tch, no impress dist:	2½	39a
387*	QOBTAAN 9 [6] M R Bosley 5-9-6 6ex (57) G Baker 13/8 FAV: 534-6117: Held up, eff fnl 3f, no impress dist:	nk	43a
318	FRIDAYS TAKINGS 17 [4] B Smart 5-9-8 VIS (59) Paul Scallan 20/1: 20000-08: Trkd ldrs, btn over 1f out:	nk	44a
406	PANCAKEHILL 8 [8] D K Ivory 5-9-0 p (51) I Mongan 14/1: 6550-009: Held up, btn 2f out.	4	28a

391	JAMESTOWN 9 [3] M J Polglase 7-8-9 (46) J Mackay 15/2: 4063-500: Chsd ldrs, lost place qckly bef halfway.	7	11a
3953}	CATERHAM COMMON 146 [12] D W Chapman 5-7-12 5oh (30) R Brisland 66/1: 600000-0: In tch 5f, 5 mth abs.	1¾	0

11 Ran   1m 41.19 (1.79)   Owner Don Enrico Incisa   Trained at Middleham

---

458   1.40 Press Interactive To Bet Direct Amateur Riders' Handicap Stakes Div 2 4yo+ 0-60 (G)   [37]

£2569 £734 £367   1m4f f/sand rnd   Going 24   -14 Slow   Stalls Inside

421*	SENDINTANK 7 [5] S C Williams 4-11-0 5ex (55) Mr S Walker 2/5 FAV: 0/600-111: Held up, hdwy to press ldrs over 2f out, hung left & led over 1f out, rdn out:		68a
399*	BELLA PAVLINA 8 [2] W M Brisbourne 6-9-12 (35) Mr C Davies (7) 14/1: 345/36-12: Held up, hdwy to chall over 1f out, styd on well for press:	1¼	45a
375	ANTONY EBENEEZER 10 [9] C R Dore 5-10-3 t (40) Miss E J Jones 22/1: 00400-53: Keen & handy, led over 2f out till over 1f out, no extra for press:	7	39a
412	HIGH DIVA 7 [8] J R Best 5-10-8 (45) Mrs K Hills (7) 50/1: 20006-64: Handy trav well & led over 3f out till over 2f out, wknd:	5	39a
4767}	DANNY LEAHY 98 [6] M D Hammond 4-11-5 (60) Mr O Nelmes (3) 25/1: 364053-5: Held up, no impress:	12	38a
331	SPANISH STAR 16 [3] Mrs N Macauley 7-10-9 (46) Mrs M Morris 14/1: 00041-46: Held up, hmpd over 4f out, sn btn.	4	18a
331	KENTUCKY BULLET 16 [11] A G Newcombe 8-10-13 (50) Miss C Hannaford 8/1: 10425-37: Dwelt, chsd ldrs till 3f out.	5	15a
259	KOMATI RIVER 24 [1] J Akehurst 5-11-0 (51) Mr S Gascoyne (7) 12/1: 00/6256-8: Prom 1m, wknd:	1	15a
372	METICULOUS 10 [7] M C Chapman 6-9-7 (30) Miss Kelly Harrison (5) 100/1: 000/0-009: Held up & keen, lost tch fnl 4f.	7	0a
387	FARAWAY LOOK 9 [4] D Shaw 7-11-7 (58) Ms C Williams 16/1: 5534-450: Hmpd 4f out, sn bhd.	5	6a
3572}	SUGAR SNAP 162 [10] C Drew 4-9-13 (40) Miss P Drew (7) 100/1: 260/000-0: Keen, led & sn clr, hdd over 3f out, wknd, abs.	6	0a

11 Ran   2m 38.91 (4.61)   Owner Steve Jones and Phil McGovern   Trained at Newmarket

---

459   2.10 Bet Direct On Sky Active Classified Stakes 4yo+ 0-60 (F)

£2912 £832 £416   6f f/sand rnd   Going 24   +02 Fast   Stalls Inside

379	UP TEMPO 10 [5] T D Easterby 6-8-11 p (59) A Mullen (7) 100/30: 00640-21: Held up, strong run from over 1f out under hands & heels, led nr fin, going away:		62a
317	LEGALIS 17 [10] K A Ryan 6-8-11 bl (58) N Callan 11/1: 00400-32: Trkd ldr & led over 2f out, drvn & hdd well ins last:	1	58a
397	PLAYFUL SPIRIT 8 [3] J Balding 5-8-8 vis (45) J Edmunds 33/1: 0001-063: Sn handy, styd on for press fnl 2f:	nk	54a
151	SEMPER PARATUS 47 [6] H J Collingridge 5-8-11 bl (59) M Tebbutt 10/1: 000140-4: Held up, late gains, nrst fin:	1¼	53a
378	SPINDOR 10 [4] J A Osborne 5-8-11 bl (58) S W Kelly 5/1: 00050-25: Dwelt, drvn/hung left & no impress dist:	1	50a
387	MOUNT ROYALE 9 [8] N Tinkler 6-8-11 vis (54) Kim Tinkler 20/1: 4015-006: Led 3f, btn dist:	nk	49a
362	HEADLAND 13 [2] D W Chapman 6-8-11 bl (60) A Culhane 15/2: 0041-427: Chsd ldrs, outpcd fnl 2f:	nk	48a
384	LAKE EYRE 10 [9] J Balding 5-8-8 (47) G Gibbons 33/1: 0303-508: Chsd ldrs, no impress from halfway:	5	31a
319*	CLASSIC VISION 17 [7] W J Haggas 4-8-8 (60) J Fanning 6/4 FAV: 53-19: Dwelt, mid-div wide, btn 2f out:	3½	21a

9 Ran   1m 14.64 (1.34)   Owner Mr T D Easterby   Trained at Malton

---

460   2.40 Bet Direct Interactive Maiden Stakes 3yo+ (D)

£3474 £1069 £535 £267   1m f/sand rnd   Going 24   -03 Slow   Stalls Inside

425	SABBAAG 6 [11] D R Loder 3-8-6 J P Spencer 2/5 FAV: 21: Chsd ldrs, rdn & led over 1f out, rdn out:		78a
	MARINAITE [2] S R Bowring 3-8-1 J Bramhill 12/1: 2: Chsd ldrs, led over 4f out, hung right & hdd over 1f out, no extra:	1¾	68a
367	ALEXANDER AMBITION 12 [8] S Kirk 3-8-1 (67) D Fox (5) 11/1: 020-43: Led 1f, trkd ldrs, styd on for press:	1	66a
	YLANG YLANG 75 [12] W Jarvis 3-8-1 J Quinn 9/2: 50-4: Held up in tch, styd on for press ins last, not pace to chall:	nk	66a
389	CASANTELLA 9 [10] M J Polglase 3-8-1 (35) J Mackay 50/1: 0036-045: In tch till 3f out.	10	47a
1168}	HOMERIC TROJAN 275 [9] M Brittain 4-9-12 (56) M Lawson (7) 100/1: 000-6: Prom 4f, abs.	4	45a
284	SILVER EMPEROR 20 [5] P A Blockley 3-8-6 bl Dean McKeown 33/1: 07: Dwelt & held up, struggling halfway.	2½	39a
4696}	ANACAPRI 102 [7] W S Cunningham 4-9-7 D Allan (3) 150/1: 0-8: Sn struggling, abs.	22	0
53	HARRY TU 65 [3] Miss Gay Kelleway 4-9-12 Paul Scallan 150/1: 00-9: Pushed along chasing ldrs, btn halfway, abs.	¾	1a
	MR LEHMAN [6] Mrs M Reveley 7-9-12 A Culhane 10/1: 0: Slow away & held up, no ch from halfway, debut.	3½	0
	CAMPBELLS TALE [4] T J Fitzgerald 5-9-12 D Mernagh 150/1: 0: Led after 1f till over 4f out, sn btn:	14	0
4985}	LOADED GUN 81 [1] Miss J Feilden 4-9-12 (62) M Tebbutt 66/1: 2205/00-0: Well bhd from halfway, abs.	5	0

12 Ran   1m 41.55 (2.15)   Owner Sheikh Ahmed Al Maktoum   Trained at Newmarket

---

461   3.10 Littlewoods Bet Direct Stakes Handicap 4yo+ 0-95 (C)   [90]

£8112 £2496 £1248 £624   5f f/sand str   Going 24   Inapplicab   Stalls Stands Side

171	DANCING MYSTERY 44 [10] E A Wheeler 10-10-0 bl (90) S Carson 14/1: 500133-1: Trkd ldrs, drvn & led cl-home, all out:		97a
415	JUSTALORD 7 [11] J Balding 6-9-6 p (82) J Edmunds 40/1: 15206-02: Sn prom & led over 1f out, drvn & hdd cl-home:	nk	88a
453*	HURRICANE COAST 1 [13] D Flood 5-8-9 6ex bl (71) P Doe 11/4 FAV: 44-111313: Held up, styd on well for press ins last, just held:	hd	76a
390*	QUIET TIMES 9 [5] K A Ryan 5-9-7 6ex bl (83) N Callan 8/1: 50120-14: Trkd ldrs, styd on well for press:	½	86a
361	ZARZU 13 [15] C R Dore 5-9-10 (86) R Thomas (5) 5/1: 02541-35: Trkd ldrs, onepace ins last:	1½	84a
361	BOND PLAYBOY 13 [6] B Smart 4-9-13 (89) F Lynch 10/1: 00012-56: Towards rear, late gains:	shd	87a
390	AFRICAN SPUR 9 [16] P A Blockley 4-8-7 (69) S Yourston (7) 50/1: 000000-07: Mid-div, not able to chall:	nk	66a
418*	TIME N TIME AGAIN 7 [8] E J Alston 6-8-12 6ex (74) A Nicholls 16/1: 0542-518: Dwelt, nvr on terms:	¾	69a
418	FAR NOTE 7 [14] S R Bowring 6-8-3 bl (65) J Bramhill 14/1: 4210-629: Hmpd & lost place after 1f, nvr on terms:	shd	60a
361	TRINCULO 13 [1] N P Littmoden 7-10-0 e (99) J P Guillambert (3) 12/1: 00160-00: Chsd ldrs, not able to chall.	hd	84a
205	PALAWAN 37 [3] A M Balding 8-9-8 (84) T Block (7) 10/1: 110102-0: Led 3f, btn dist:	hd	77a
292	ONLY ONE LEGEND 19 [12] K A Ryan 6-8-10 p (72) R Winston 40/1: 66603-00: Cl-up 2f, btn ins last.	1½	60a
415	GRANDMA LILY 7 [9] M C Chapman 6-8-10 (72) I Mongan 14/1: 00150-30: Hmpd start, sn outpcd:	1¼	56a
418	FRASCATI 7 [7] A Berry 4-9-2 (78) P Bradley (5) 33/1: 04251-00: Chsd ldrs till halfway:	1¼	58a
262	COMPTON BANKER 24 [4] G A Butler 7-9-2 vis (78) E Ahern 16/1: 0041115-0: Slowly away & sn struggling:	1¼	54a
415	PRIME RECREATION 7 [12] P S Felgate 7-8-6 (68) Dale Gibson 40/1: 02400-60: Dwelt & sn outpcd.	hd	43a

16 Ran   58.95   Owner Astrod TA Austin Stroud & Co   Trained at Pangbourne

	462	**3.40 Bet Direct Through Sky Active Selling Stakes** 3yo (G)				
		£2590 £740 £370	7f f/sand rnd	Going 24	-14 Slow	Stalls Inside

276	**SMART BOY PRINCE** 22 [6] P A Blockley 3-8-12 (55) Derek Nolan (7) 7/2: 050466-1: Sn handy & led over 4f out, styd on strongly under hands & heels ins last:		58a
164	**HUNTING PINK** 45 [3] H Morrison 3-8-7 (49) L Fletcher (3) 100/30 FAV: 630044-2: In tch, styd on for press, not able to chall wnr:	1½	49a
189	**KNIGHT TO REMEMBER** 40 [1] K A Ryan 3-8-12 (45) N Callan 25/1: 00600-3: Held up, styd on onepace for press:	2½	49a
284	**KATIES ROLE** 20 [4] Ian Emmerson 3-8-7 (53) A Nicholls 7/2: 30043-34: Chsd ldrs, no extra dist.	½	43a
284	**ZONNEBEKE** 20 [9] K R Burke 3-8-7 (47) Darren Williams 16/1: 400-45: Chsd ldrs, onepace.	3½	36a
402	**DRUID** 8 [10] P C Haslam 3-8-12 (52) D Wakenshaw (7) 25/1: 065-06: Led 3f, btn over 1f out.	nk	40a
4548}	**HEATHYARDS JOY** 113 [5] R Hollinshead 3-8-7 Dean McKeown 33/1: 0-7: In tch till 2f out, abs.	3	29a
159	**OKTIS MORILIOUS** 45 [13] J A Osborne 3-8-12 S W Kelly 16/1: 0-8: Sn outpcd, nrst fin, abs.	1¾	30a
200	**ARE YOU THERE** 38 [2] T D Barron 3-8-13 (47) Gemma Anderson (7) 20/1: 600000-9: Nvr on terms.	¾	29a
408	**NOTHING MATTERS** 7 [8] P R Chamings 3-8-7 (40) P Doe 25/1: 4005-600: Chsd ldrs till halfway.	¾	21a
316	**GARNOCK VENTURE** 17 [7] A Berry 3-8-12 bl (49) F Lynch 9/1: 50043-40: Trkd ldrs, taken wide, btn 2f out.	½	25a
200	**TICKLEPENNY LOCK** 38 [12] C Smith 3-8-12 (35) I Mongan 50/1: 066000-0: Prom, btn 3f out.	shd	25a
364	**EUGENIE** 12 [15] R Hannon 3-8-7 (47) R Smith 33/1: 00-00: Al struggling.	½	19a
3771}	**FAR FOR LULU** 154 [14] W R Muir 3-8-7 (40) J Quinn 50/1: 054500-0: Dwelt & sn bhd, abs.	1½	16a
438	**TAMARINA** 3 [11] N E Berry 3-8-7 BL (55) C Catlin 12/1: 5004-00: Dwelt & sn struggling:	13	0a
15 Ran	1m 29.27 (2.67) Owner Brooklands Racing	Trained at Southwell	

	463	**4.10 Betdirect Co Uk Handicap Stakes Div 2** 4yo+ 0-65 (F)				[64]
		£2919 £834 £417	1m f/sand rnd	Going 24	-08 Slow	Stalls Inside

416	**DISABUSE** 7 [10] S C Williams 4-8-11 (48) J P Spencer 5/2: 00266-21: Held up, pushed along & hdwy from over 2f out, staying on for press when left a cl-up 2nd ins last, sn led,		54a
388	**DUBAI DREAMS** 9 [1] M J Polglase 4-9-5 bl (56) L Fletcher (3) 20/1: 00140-42: Sn handy & led after 1f till over 1f out, left in lead again sn after, sn hdd, no extra:	1¾	58a
387	**SORBIESHARRY** 9 [2] Mrs N Macaulay 5-8-11 p (48) P McCabe 8/1: 0422-523: Chsd ldrs, onepace.	2	45a
115	**REALISM** 55 [7] P W Hiatt 4-9-4 (55) A Culhane 66/1: 0350-4: Held up, only mod prog for press:	3	47a
379	**WALTZING WIZARD** 10 [8] A Berry 5-9-1 (52) F Lynch 10/1: 06052-35: Chsd ldrs, no impress dist:	¾	42a
356+*	**SANDORRA** 14 [4] M Brittain 6-8-9 (46) M Lawson (6) 10/1: 5000-316: Led 1f, handy till over 1f out:	½	35a
363	**SPARK UP** 13 [5] J W Unett 4-9-11 b (62) M Henry 7/1: 61266-07: Chsd ldrs, btn 2f out:	1¾	49a
354	**PEARTREE HOUSE** 14 [11] D W Chapman 10-8-3 (40) R Brisland 66/1: 00000-08: Al rear:	6	16a
378*	**MOUNT HILLABY** 10 [9] M W Easterby 4-9-0 (51) Dale Gibson 5/4 FAV: 06000-19: Trkd ldrs, sn pushed along, hdwy to lead over 1f out, sn slipped & hdd, virtually p.u. 'knocked a stifle':	3½	21a
440	**POOKAS DAUGHTER** 3 [6] J M Bradley 4-8-8 BL (45) P Fitzsimons 66/1: 0000-500: Cl-up 5f, sn btn:	21	0
10 Ran	1m 41.97 (2.57) Owner J R and T J Allenby	Trained at Newmarket	

Official Going STANDARD.

	464	**12.50 Press Interactive To Bet Direct Amateur Riders' Handicap Div 1** 4yo+ 0-70 (G)				[48]
		£2569 £734 £367	1m1f79y f/sand rnd Going 38		-21 Slow	Stalls Inside

4855}	**STING LIKE A BEE** 93 [6] J S Goldie 5-10-1 (49) Miss Kelly Harrison (5) 8/1: 556060-1: Chsd ldrs, chsd ldr 2f out, led ins last, hands & heels, readily:		56a
378	**LITTLETON ZEPHIR** 11 [7] Mrs P Townsley 5-9-13 bl (47) Mrs C Thompson (5) 33/1: 23306-02: Led, clr 2f out, rdn & hdd ins last, no extra:	3½	46a
439	**OVIGO** 4 [5] P A Blockley 5-11-7 (69) Mr M Scales (5) 7/4 FAV: 330-1463: Slow away, hdwy halfway, kept on, no threat to front pair:	2	64a
230	**YELLOW RIVER** 34 [3] R Curtis 4-10-8 (57) Mr E Dehdashti (3) 33/1: 600000-4: Held up, kept on onepace.	1½	49a
391	**STREET LIFE** 10 [4] W J Musson 6-11-5 (67) Miss J Pledge (7) 5/2: 00006-25: Dwelt, mid-div, nvr mounted chall.	2½	54a
456	**WESTERN COMMAND** 1 [11] Mrs N Macaulay 8-9-3 7oh (30) Mr M Morris (5) 25/1: 550-00456: Bhd, eff wide, btn 2f out.	hd	23a
375	**MORRIS DANCING** 11 [10] B P J Baugh 5-9-10 4ow p (40) Mr J Pemberton (5) 66/1: 00/000-07: Chsd ldr till 3f out.	½	29a
331	**PASO DOBLE** 17 [12] B R Millman 6-11-0 (62) Mr J Millman (7) 11/1: 24000-58: Mid-div wide, btn 2f out.	1	45a
412*	**TROPICAL SON** 8 [2] D Shaw 5-9-11 5ex vis (45) Ms C Williams 11/2: 000-2519: Hmpd 3f out, no impress.	5	19a
4546}	**FLORENZAR** 114 [9] P D Evans 6-10-6 (54) Miss E Folkes (3) 25/1: 5/02620-0: Trkd ldrs 5f:	9	13a
4684}	**CLIQUEY** 457 [8] B J Llewellyn 5-11-0 (62) Miss A Frieze (7) 25/1: 100600/-0: Dwelt & sn struggling, 7 wk jumps abs.	1¼	18a
246	**MUTARED** 28 [1] N P Littmoden 6-11-3 (65) Mrs Emma Littmoden (3) 14/1: 000000-0: Prom 3f, sn bhd.	24	0
12 Ran	2m 03.75 (5.55) Owner Mrs C Brown	Trained at Glasgow	

	465	**1.25 Press Interactive To Bet Direct Amateur Riders' Handicap Div 2** 4yo+ 0-70 (G)				[48]
		£2569 £734 £367	1m1f79y f/sand rnd Going 38		-10 Slow	Stalls Inside

339	**SCOTTISH RIVER** 16 [8] M D I Usher 5-10-10 (58) Mr L Newnes (5) 5/1: 0003-301: Slow away, sn rcd keenly in tch, hdwy to lead over 1f out, drvn & just held on line, all out:		64a
437	**OUR DESTINY** 4 [1] D Burchell 6-9-11 vis (45) Miss E Tucker (3) 25/1: 00002-32: Led till over 1f out, rallied gamely for press, just held:	shd	50a
346	**ROCK CONCERT** 15 [6] I W McInnes 6-11-0 (62) Miss E J Jones 7/2: 2132-123: Chsd ldr, rdn & no impress dist.	4	59a
281*	**JAIR OHMSFORD** 21 [9] W J Musson 5-11-2 (64) Miss J Pledge (7) 6/1: 0/0540-14: Keen, drpd rear after 3f, kept on wide fnl 2f, no dngr:	1	59a
463	**SORBIESHARRY** 1 [5] Mrs N Macaulay 5-10-0 p (48) Mrs M Morris (5) 6/1: 0422-5235: Rear, some hdwy 2f out, no dngr.	3	37a
281	**TOP OF THE CLASS** 21 [2] P D Evans 7-9-11 vis (45) Miss E Folkes (3) 33/1: 54050-06: Prom, fdd fnl 3f:	¾	33a

434	KINGSTON TOWN 6	[4] N P Littmoden 4-11-7 p (70) Mrs Emma Littmoden (3) 10/1: 4021-07: Keen mid-div, no impress.	1¼	55a
398	LOVES DESIGN 9	[7] Miss S J Wilton 7-10-2 (50) Mr A Swinswood (7) 33/1: 3350-068: Keen, sn bhd:	1¾	32a
399	GIUST IN TEMP 9	[11] P W Hiatt 5-9-6 (40) Mrs Marie King (5) 12/1: 0650-429: Keen & prom, btn 2f out:	1½	19a
4319}	SPITFIRE BOB 127	[10] T D Barron 5-11-4 (66) Mr S Walker 15/8 FAV: 202100-0: Held up, btn 3f out, abs.	1½	42a
332	SOFT MIST 17	[3] J J Quinn 4-10-8 (57) Mr K Mercer (3) 50/1: 61200-60: Mid-div, wknd fnl 3f.	1½	30a

11 Ran   2m 02.74 (4.54)   Owner Mr M D I Usher   Trained at Lambourn

---

466   2.00 Bet Direct On Sky Active Claiming Stakes 3yo (F)
£2933 £838 £419   6f f/sand rnd   Going 38   -15 Slow   Stalls Inside

405	EMARADIA 9	[3] P D Evans 3-7-12 bl (48) Joanna Badger 8/1: 45422-31: Led, held on well for press ins last, drvn out:		56a
389	NANNA 10	[5] R Hollinshead 3-7-13 1ow J Quinn 25/1: 00-52: Prom, styd on for press, al just held by wnr:	1¾	51a
371	ALIZAR 13	[1] M J Polglase 3-8-8 (59) J P Spencer 5/2 FAV: 1153-023: Led/dsptd lead trav well, onepace for press from dist:	nk	59a
1	CREWES MISS ISLE 74	[7] A G Newcombe 3-8-8 (70) S Whitworth 6/1: 156420-4: Towards rear, hdwy from halfway, not able to chall:	½	57a
422*	BACK AT DE FRONT 7	[4] N E Berry 3-9-4 (60) M Savage (5) 11/4: 11504-15: Prom, no extra over 1f out:	3	58a
333	FISSION 45	[8] J A Osborne 3-9-4 bl (79) S W Kelly 7/2: 414513-6: Sn handy, lost pl 2f out:	2	52a
	FORA SMILE	[11] M D I Usher 3-8-9 A Daly 25/1: 7: Sn outpcd, nvr a factor:	1¼	39a
	FAIRLY GLORIOUS	[2] T H Caldwell 3-8-13 M Fenton 50/1: 8: Dwelt, al outpcd on debut.	1¼	39a
4814}	BISH BASH BOSH 95	[9] M F Harris 3-8-4 (45) S Righton 33/1: 006040-9: Sn rdn & outpcd:	2	24a
247	ADRIATIC ADVENTURE 28	[6] J L Spearing 3-8-0 (45) J Mackay 50/1: 000-0: Mid-div, outpcd halfway.	2½	12a
120	MYSTIC PROMISE 55	[10] Mrs N Macauley 3-8-13 bl (30) Steven Harrison (7) 100/1: 00000-0: Slow away, bhd.	3½	14a

11 Ran   1m 15.96 (3.16)   Owner Treble Chance Partnership   Trained at Abergavenny

---

467   2.35 Littlewoods Bet Direct Handicap Stakes 4yo+ 0-80 (D)   [77]
£4115 £1266 £633 £317   1m4f f/sand   Going 38   -02 Slow   Stalls Inside

458*	SENDINTANK 1	[5] S C Williams 4-8-3 6ex (56) R Ffrench 4/6 FAV: 0/600-1111: Held up, hdwy 3f out, qcknd for press to lead well ins last:		67a
342	JADEERON 1ὸ	[7] Miss D A McHale 5-8-5 p (54) Lisa Jones (3) 10/1: 14400-22: Sn handy & led inner over 2f out, drvn & hdd cl-home:	1	63a
5019}	DICK THE TAXI 78	[9] R J Smith 10-9-11 (74) R Miles (3) 8/1: 0/52132-3: Prom, onepace & held over 1f out:	6	74a
434	NIGHT WARRIOR 6	[1] D Flood 4-9-0 (67) P Doe 14/1: 00004-04: Held up, eff 2f out, no prog dist:	1	66a
421	LAZZAZ 8	[2] P W Hiatt 6-8-13 (62) A Culhane 20/1: 3300-435: Led till over 2f out, wknd ins last:	½	60a
141	COUNTYKAT 51	[6] K R Burke 4-9-9 p (76) Darren Williams 25/1: 553630-6: Rear, eff over 2f out, no impress:	½	73a
388	GLORY QUEST 10	[8] Miss Gay Kelleway 7-9-8 p (71) T Eaves (5) 4/1: 23552-27: Held up, eff 3f out, btn dist:	½	67a
173	PAULA LANE 45	[4] R Curtis 4-9-5 (72) J F McDonald (5) 50/1: 405320-8: Prom, wknd 3f out, t.o.:	17	47a
5008}	SPAINKRIS 79	[3] A Crook 5-9-7 (70) I Mongan 33/1: 65320/0-9: Cl-up, rdn & btn 4f out:	26	10a

9 Ran   2m 38.39 (4.79)   Owner Steve Jones and Phil McGovern   Trained at Newmarket

---

468   3.10 Bet Direct Interactive Maiden Stakes 3yo (D)
£3387 £1042 £521 £261   1m100y f/sand rnd Going 38   -17 Slow   Stalls Inside

381	PLAY MASTER 11	[7] D Haydn Jones 3-9-0 Paul Eddery 5/2: 21: Led/dsptd lead throughout, went on 2f out, edged right & held on all out cl-home:		80a
276	BAHIANO 23	[2] C E Brittain 3-9-0 A Culhane 11/8 FAV: 62-2: Sn prom, rdn to chall over 1f out, drvn & just held:	nk	79a
	GLOBAL ACHIEVER 6	[6] G C H Chung 3-9-0 R Ffrench 40/1: 3: Keen & led/dsptd lead till 2f out, no extra dist:	8	63a
381	ROYALTEA 11	[1] Ms Deborah J Evans 3-8-9 Joanna Badger 100/1: 664: Rear, no impress fnl 2f:	¾	57a
	NORWEGIAN	[3] D R Loder 3-9-0 J P Spencer 15/8: 5: Dwelt, sn in tch but rems halfway, btn 2f out:	½	61a
238	UNINTENTIONAL 32	[5] R Brotherton 3-8-9 (60) I Mongan 22/1: 0652-6: Led/dsptd lead early, btn 2f out.	10	40a

6 Ran   1m 50.86 (4.66)   Owner Mr Jason Weston   Trained at Pontypridd

---

469   3.45 Bet Direct Through Sky Active Selling Handicap Stakes 4yo+ 0-60 (G)   [56]
£2632 £752 £376   1m4f f/sand   Going 38   -20 Slow   Stalls Inside

399	MISTY MAN 9	[7] Miss J Feilden 6-8-7 bl (35) M Fenton 10/1: 0044-351: Keen & prom trav well, led 2f out, sn rdn & styd on well:		40a
454	KHUZDAR 2	[2] A Bailey 5-8-12 (40) B O'Neill (7) 4/1: 40640-032: Rear, hdwy 4f out, rdn to press wnr over 1f out, sn edged left & no extra:	1¾	42a
250	FAILED TO HIT 28	[6] N P Littmoden 11-9-10 vis (52) I Mongan 12/1: 12/1456-3: Led till 3f out, kept on for press:	3	50a
362	ALLY MAKBUL 14	[11] J R Best 4-9-9 (55) N Pollard 10/1: 1000-144: Chsd ldrs halfway & led 3f out, hdd 2f out, wknd:	2	50a
347	CLAPTRAP 15	[10] R Brotherton 4-9-7 (53) F P Ferris 3/1 FAV: 60015-25: Held up, rdn & no impress fnl 3f.	7	39a
442	PROUD VICTOR 3	[4] D Shaw 4-8-8 vis (40) Darren Williams 20/1: 00-4566: Mid-div, no impress:	1¾	24a
398	HAITHEM 9	[9] D Shaw 7-8-2 e (30) Lisa Jones (3) 28/1: 000-6007: Keen rear, nvr any impression.	3½	9a
358	ADALPOUR 14	[1] D Burchell 6-9-10 (52) A Quinn (5) 4/1: 13301-08: Mid-div inner, btn 3f out:	6	23a
443	DR JULIAN 3	[3] Miss A Stokell 4-8-8 p (40) Ann Stokell 66/1: 000-0509: Chsd ldrs 6f, wknd 3f out:	1¼	9a
3278}	KNOCKDOO 176	[8] J S Goldie 11-8-7 (35) R Fitzpatrick 14/1: 006203-0: Chsd ldr halfway, btn 4f out.	nk	3a
3996}	TOBEROE COMMOTION 144	[12] B J Llewellyn 6-9-4 (46) R Havlin 16/1: 040006-0: Nvr dngr, 8 wk jumps abs.	7	5a
343	PERTEMPS BIANCA 16	[5] A D Smith 4-8-8 bl (40) J Quinn 7/1: 54006-60: Keen & trkd ldrs, wknd qckly 3f out:	7	0

12 Ran   2m 40.6 (7.0)   Owner Mr R J Creese   Trained at Newmarket

---

470   4.15 Betdirect Co Uk Handicap Stakes 3yo 0-85 (D)   [90]
£4017 £1236 £618 £309   1m100y f/sand rnd Going 38   +10 Fast   Stalls Inside

| 341 | COUNTRYWIDE FLYER 16 | [5] T D Barron 3-9-4 (80) J P Spencer 9/2: 42114-51: In tch, smooth hdwy to lead over 2f out, rdn clr over 1f out, eased cl-home, readily: | | 92a |
| 441* | GAVROCHE 4 | [2] M J Wallace 3-8-7 6ex (69) J P Guillambert (8) 8/13 FAV: 400-12: Handy & led over 3f out, rdn & hdd over 2f | 5 | 69a |

WOLVERHAMPTON Friday 23.01.04 Lefthand, Sharp Track

out, sn no ch with wnr:

436	SIR JASPER 4 [1] M F Harris 3-7-13 6ex vis (61) S Righton 14/1: 5561-103: Led till over 3f out, sn no impress:		5	51a
403	MARCUS EILE 9 [7] K R Burke 3-9-7 (83) Darren Williams 25/1: 44263-44: Outpcd, rdn & no impress over 2f out:		2	69a
441	BOLD BLADE 4 [4] B Smart 3-8-8 bl (70) R Ffrench 7/2: 00413-25: Cl-up, lost tch qckly 3f out:		18	26a
341	BOXGROVE 16 [6] C E Brittain 3-9-3 (79) A Culhane 16/1: 361-06: Rear, lost tch hway:		21	-1a
6 Ran	1m 48.56 (2.36) Owner Mr Nigel Shields		Trained at Thirsk	

LINGFIELD Saturday 24.01.04 Lefthand, V Sharp Track

Official Going Standard

471

12.35 Bet Direct No Q 08000 93 66 93 Amateur Riders' Handicap Stakes 4yo+ 0-70 (F)   [47]

£2961 £846 £423   6f p/track rnd   Going 39   -03 Slow   Stalls Inside

363	WHIPPASNAPPER 15 [7] J R Best 4-10-13 (60) Mr E Dehdashti (3) 8/1: 60000-01: Dwelt, sn mid-div, hdwy 2f out & drvn to lead well in last:		68a
435	LADIES KNIGHT 7 [4] D Shaw 4-10-8 (55) Ms C Williams 7/1: 0001-632: Trkd ldrs, rdn to lead ins last, hdd well in last, no extra:	1¼	58a
144	INISTRAHULL ISLAND 49 [5] M H Tompkins 4-10-12 VIS (59) Mr S Warren (7) 6/1: 260423-3: Sn cl-up & led 3f out till ins last, onepace:	½	59a
450	SUPERCHIEF 3 [10] Miss B Sanders 9-11-4 bl t (65) Mr C Doran (7) 20/1: 0002-064: Dwelt, rear, short of room over 2f out, kept on late for press:	1¼	62a
407	SOUNDS LUCKY 10 [11] N P Littmoden 8-11-5 bl (66) Mrs Emma Littmoden (3) 8/1: 02540-05: Mid-div, not pace to chall:	3	54a
419	FOREVER PHOENIX 9 [6] R M H Cowell 4-11-7 (68) Mr S Dobson (3) 7/1: 4201-56: Cl-up, wknd from dist:	½	54a
248	BEST BEFORE 29 [1] P D Evans 4-10-13 (60) Miss E Folkes (3) 14/1: 242065-7: Led 3f, fdd.	1	43a
266	GUN SALUTE 25 [13] G L Moore 4-10-8 p (55) Mrs S Bosley 10/1: 005010-8: Dwelt, rear, little hdwy:	½	36a
3595}	STEELY DAN 163 [12] J R Best 5-10-10 (57) Mrs L A Best (7) 33/1: 000005-9: Bhd, nvr a factor, abs.	¾	36a
45	EFFECTIVE 68 [9] A P Jarvis 4-11-4 (65) Mr S Walker 14/1: 002000-0: Al rear, 2 mth abs.	2½	36a
418	ST IVIAN 9 [8] Mrs N Macauley 4-11-6 vis (67) Mrs M Morris 4/1: 0051-460: Wide/rear, nvr a factor:	¾	36a
624}	ILLUSIVE 343 [3] M Wigham 7-11-6 (67) Miss E J Jones 12/1: 530432-0: Chsd ldrs 4f, long abs.	½	34a
459	LEGALIS 2 [2] K A Ryan 6-10-11 bl (58) Mr M Seston (5) 9/2 FAV: 00400-320: Restless stalls, chsd ldrs 4f.	1½	20a
13 Ran	1m 12.9 (2.5) Owner Miss Vanessa Church	Trained at Maidstone	

472

1.05 Bet Direct No Q Demo 08000 837 888 Maiden Stakes 3yo (D)

£3838 £1181 £591 £295   7f p/track rnd   Going 39   -07 Slow   Stalls Inside

290	SOFISTICATION 21 [1] T G Mills 3-8-9 R Miles (3) 12/1: 01: Sn trkd ldrs trav well, rdn to lead well in last:		68a
396	ILE FACILE 10 [12] N P Littmoden 3-9-0 I Mongan 7/1: 242: Cl-up & led over 4f out, rdn clr over 2f out, hdd well in last, kept	½	71a
4972}	FIRST OF MAY 84 [2] M A Jarvis 3-8-9 M Henry 13/2: 0-3: Mid-div, kept on late for press, nvr threat to front pair:	6	54a
	STAGE RIGHT 16 [16] D R C Elsworth 3-9-0 N Pollard 16/1: 4: Slow away, rdn rear, closing well fnl 1f, nrst fin:	¾	58a
229	PURE EMOTION 35 [4] W R Muir 3-8-9 J Quinn 20/1: 5-5: Cl-up till 2f out, sn no impress.	¾	52a
	AIR OF GREENERY [6] J Noseda 3-9-0 S W Kelly 13/2: 7: Dwelt, towards rear, only mod prog on debut.	nk	55a
322	ALFRIDINI 18 [8] D R C Elsworth 3-8-9 L Keniry (3) 25/1: 08: Mid-div, no impress from halfway.	½	54a
146	MYSTIC MOON 49 [3] J R Jenkins 3-8-9 S Whitworth 66/1: 0-9: Led till over 4f out, sn btn, abs.	hd	48a
	LIVIA [9] J G Portman 3-8-9 M Havlin 66/1: 0: Dwelt, mid-div halfway, sn no impress on debut.	½	47a
322	SUNSET DREAMER 18 [11] P Mitchell 3-8-9 E Ahern 16/1: 60: Sn bhd.	1½	44a
232	DUBAIAN MIST 35 [14] A M Balding 3-8-9 W Ryan 20/1: 05-0: Chsd ldrs, no impress from halfway.	nk	43a
	GREEN FALCON [15] J W Hills 3-9-0 M Hills 8/1: 0: Dwelt, rear/wide, nvr a factor on debut.	hd	47a
	JOY AND PAIN [13] G L Moore 3-9-0 J P Spencer 33/1: 0: Al rear on debut.	5	38a
449	JAYCEE STAR 3 [10] D Flood 3-8-9 M Coumbe (3) 150/1: 000: Sn struggling, t.o., qck reapp.	15	6a
15 Ran	1m 26.04 (3.24) Owner Mrs L M Askew	Trained at Epsom	

473

1.40 Littlewoods Bet Direct Maiden Stakes 3yo (D)

£4134 £1272 £636 £318   1m2f p/track   Going 39   -23 Slow   Stalls Inside

367	BAAWRAH 14 [1] M R Channon 3-9-0 (71) C Catlin 7/2: 0632-21: Led, hard drvn & strongly prsd from dist, hdd when bmpd fnl strides.	shd	73a
367	FIDDLERS FORD 14 [12] J Noseda 3-9-0 J P Spencer 9/4 FAV: 0-32: Keen, towards rear, smooth hdwy & drvn to chall ins last, edged left & led fnl strides:		75a
403	AMWELL BRAVE 10 [3] J R Jenkins 3-9-0 (71) S W Kelly 7/2: 0345-223: Mid-div, smooth prog to press ldrs over 1f out, no extra for press dist:	2½	70a
232	ANOTHER CON 35 [5] Mrs P N Dutfield 3-8-9 R Havlin 25/1: 63-4: Chsd ldr, wide bend 2f out, no extra:	2½	61a
322	ON THE WATERFRONT 18 [4] J W Hills 3-9-0 M Hills 20/1: 55: Keen trkg ldrs, outpcd fnl 2f:	3	61a
290	JACKIE KIELY 21 [6] T G Mills 3-9-0 A Clark 25/1: 0-06: Mid-div, rdn & no impress on ldrs:	nk	60a
1694}	WILD PITCH 245 [13] P Mitchell 3-9-0 E Ahern 10/1: 6-7: Keen trkg ldrs, no impress fnl 2f, abs.	1¼	58a
	HERONS WING [10] Lady Herries 3-9-0 J Quinn 50/1: 8: Slow away & rear, mod late gains on debut, improve.	nk	57a
438	WALTZING BEAU 5 [11] I A Wood 3-9-0 I Mongan 6/1: 0-29: Reared start, rear, no impress:	shd	57a
175	PRINCE VALENTINE 45 [8] D B Feek 3-9-0 M Tebbutt 14/1: 0-0: Mid-div, btn 3f out, eased, abs.	19	29a
4635}	ATHBOY 109 [7] M J Wallace 3-9-0 N Callan 5/1: 60-0: Mid-div, no ch fnl 3f:	1	28a
229	CORTON DENHAM 35 [2] G P Enright 3-9-0 R Brisland 250/1: 0-0: Sn struggling rear.	3	23a
51	MISS MILLIETANT 67 [14] L Montague Hall 3-8-9 R Miles (3) 100/1: 00-0: Chsd ldrs, wknd qckly 3f out, abs.	nk	17a
322	DEVINE COMMAND 18 [9] R Ingram 3-9-0 N Day 100/1: 00: Chsd ldrs halfway, btn 3f out.	1½	20a
14 Ran	2m 08.97 (6.17) Owner Sheikh Ahmed Al Maktoum	Trained at West Ilsley	

LINGFIELD Saturday 24.01.04 Lefthand, V Sharp Track

---

474   **2.10 Charlie And Dan Handicap Stakes Fillies 3yo+ 0-75 (E)**   **[74]**
£3353 £958 £479   7f p/track rnd   Going 39   -04 Slow   Stalls Inside

363	GREY PEARL 15 [3] Miss Gay Kelleway 5-9-11 (71) M Fenton 9/1: 40534-51: Trkd ldrs, led over 1f out, drvn out:		78a
450*	RIPPLE EFFECT 3 [10] C A Dwyer 4-9-11 6ex (71) B Reilly (5) 7/2 FAV: 0102-212: Sn cl-up trav well, not pace of wnr from dist	1½	74a
198	CLOUD DANCER 40 [2] K A Ryan 5-10-0 (74) N Callan 10/1: 203310-3: Rear, hdwy inner from over 2f out, onepace for press ins last:	1	75a
151	COPPINGTON FLYER 49 [1] B W Duke 4-8-4 (50) Lisa Jones (3) 50/1: 000000-4: Mid-div, styd on onepace for press:	1¼	48a
432	ROWAN PURSUIT 7 [4] J Akehurst 3-8-6 bl (70) J Fanning 4/1: 0131-135: Dwelt, rdn towards rear, only mod prog.	½	67a
369	ANNISHIRANI 14 [12] G A Butler 4-10-0 (74) E Ahern 12/1: 22114-06: Keen, rear, mod prog:	shd	71a
366	PANTS 14 [11] Andrew Reid 5-8-9 (55) A Nicholls 25/1: 00310-07: Dwelt, rear, nvr able to chall:	½	51a
363	BLONDE EN BLONDE 15 [9] N P Littmoden 4-9-3 (63) I Mongan 25/1: 3534-668: Mid-div wide, no impress over 1f out.	¾	58a
266	I WISH 25 [7] M Madgwick 6-9-3 (63) L Keniry (3) 12/1: 006146-9: Chsd ldrs till over 1f out:	nk	57a
407	EMERALD FIRE 10 [6] A M Balding 5-9-9 (69) N Chalmers (5) 11/2: 30005-60: Rear, eff 2f out, wide & no impress.	hd	62a
270	LILY OF THE GUILD 25 [13] W S Kittow 5-8-8 (54) J Quinn 10/1: 044462-0: Keen, rear, short of room dist, nvr able to chall:	dht	46a
411	GEESPOT 9 [8] D J S ffrench Davis 5-7-13 (45) J F McDonald (5) 20/1: 0500-040: Prom, btn 2f out:	1¼	34a
169	CIACOLE 46 [5] S C Williams 3-8-6 (70) M Henry 40/1: 6540-0: Led till over 1f out, wknd qckly, eased, abs.	6	49a

13 Ran   1m 25.83 (3.03)   Owner Andrea Wilkinson Gay Kelleway   Trained at Newmarket

---

475   **2.45 Betdirect Co Uk Handicap Stakes 4yo+ 0-95 (C)**   **[92]**
£10637 £4035 £2017 £917   1m4f p/track   Going 39   +15 Fast   Stalls Inside

404*	COLD TURKEY 10 [4] G L Moore 4-9-2 (84) S Whitworth 6/1: 11112-11: Slow away & settled rear, smooth hdwy from halfway & rdn/led over 1f out, styd on strongly:		92a
293	FLIGHT OF ESTEEM 21 [7] P W Harris 4-9-10 (92) N Callan 5/1 FAV: 31430-22: Handy & led over 3f out, drvn & hdd over 1f out, kept on:	1½	97a
404	TIGHT SQUEEZE 10 [15] P W Hiatt 7-9-0 (78) A Culhane 12/1: 5011-653: Towards rear, hdwy to chase ldrs 2f out, styd on onepace for press:	nk	82a
433	DANCE IN THE SUN 7 [5] Mrs A J Perrett 4-9-3 (85) J P Spencer 12/1: 52410-64: Mid-div, hdwy & handy 2f out, drvn & kept on:	¾	88a
429*	BARRY ISLAND 7 [6] D R C Elsworth 5-8-11 (75) Lisa Jones (3) 11/2: 63604-15: Slow away, rear, hdwy 4f out, no extra over 1f out:	3	73a
404	MOON EMPEROR 10 [10] J R Jenkins 7-9-9 (87) E Ahern 20/1: 65500-06: Held up, only mod late prog, no impress:	11	71a
404	HIGH POINT 10 [14] G P Enright 6-9-1 (79) I Mongan 16/1: 0001-007: Rear, mod late prog:	½	62a
419	TE QUIERO GB 9 [2] Miss Gay Kelleway 6-10-0 t (92) M Fenton 40/1: 05230-08: Towards rear, hdwy 4f out, wknd 2f out:	5	68a
273	ADALAR 25 [1] P D Evans 4-8-12 (80) S Donohoe (3) 66/1: 04210/0-9: Cl-up, led over 5f out till over 3f out, sn btn.	1	55a
234	BLUE PATRICK 35 [16] J M P Eustace 4-9-0 (82) J Mackay 40/1: 401600-0: Rear, eff wide, btn 2f out.	7	48a
293*	GIG HARBOR 21 [9] Miss E C Lavelle 5-9-11 (89) L Keniry (3) 13/2: 00626-10: Chsd ldrs, wknd qckly from 4f out.	2½	51a
404	MR MISCHIEF 10 [8] P C Haslam 4-9-4 (86) Rory Moore (7) 8/1: 50211-30: Dwelt, rear, no ch fnl 3f:	4	42a
293	CRUISE DIRECTOR 21 [3] W J Musson 4-9-1 (83) Paul Eddery 7/1: 32210-30: Mid-div, efft 4f out, sn wknd.	2½	35a
404	INTERNATIONALGUEST 10 [13] G G Margarson 5-9-3 vis (81) N Pollard 20/1: 0360-020: Prom till 4f out, t.o.	10	22a
1537}	BLUE LEADER 253 [11] G Brown 5-8-13 p (77) Joanna Badger 100/1: 5160/00-0: Led over 5f out, abs.	23	0a
360	MIDSHIPMAN 15 [12] A W Carroll 6-9-8 (86) Paul Scallan 66/1: 11/20/0-00: Chsd ldrs till halfway, t.o..	18	0a

16 Ran   2m 32.11 (2.91)   Owner Mr A Grinter   Trained at Brighton

---

476   **3.15 Bet Direct Maiden Stakes 4yo+ (D)**
£3741 £1151 £576 £288   1m2f p/track   Going 39   -24 Slow   Stalls Inside

430	CORONADO FOREST 7 [6] M R Hoad 5-9-2 (59) A Culhane 5/1: 6060-241: Made all, went for home over 2f out, drvn/al holding rivals from dist:		65a
401	HAVE SOME FUN 10 [10] P R Chamings 4-9-0 J Quinn 7/1: 6-32: Trkd wnr, styd on for press fnl 2f, not able to chall wnr:	1¾	60a
430	ZALKANI 7 [11] B G Powell 4-9-0 (67) J P Spencer 5/2 FAV: 600-33: Rear, smooth hdwy 3f out, rdn & no impress from dist:	2	57a
342	RAHEEL 17 [3] P Mitchell 4-9-0 t (46) J Fanning 11/1: 02060-54: Mid-div, no room 2f out, kept on.	2½	53a
3600}	SKIBEREEN 163 [8] I W McInnes 4-9-0 (74) D Allan (3) 11/4: 0/24232-5: Mid-div, eff over 2f out, sn wknd:	2	50a
321	OVER RATING 19 [4] K A Ryan 4-8-9 P (56) N Callan 25/1: 3426-006: Chsd ldrs halfway, btn 2f out.	5	38a
14	GLESNI 73 [1] S C Williams 4-8-11 B Reilly (5) 11/2: 0-7: Bolted bef start, al rear & no ch 4f out, abs.	3	33a
4706}	PEDLERS PROFILES 456 [5] Miss K M George 4-9-0 Derek Nolan (7) 100/1: 00/-8: Keen, chsd ldrs, btn 4f out:	½	37a
	BRUZELLA [7] A J Lidderdale 5-8-11 E Ahern 25/1: 9: Sn bhd on debut.	¾	31a

9 Ran   2m 09.06 (6.26)   Owner Mr Ken Webb   Trained at Lewes

---

477   **3.45 Bet Direct Classified Stakes 4yo+ 0-60 (F)**
£3017 £862 £431   1m2f p/track   Going 39   -27 Slow   Stalls Inside

215*	REGAL GALLERY 38 [2] C A Horgan 6-8-13 (58) Paul Eddery 4/1 JT FAV: 0040/41-1: Mid-div, smooth hdwy 3f out & led over 1f out, asserted under hands & heels:		63a
339	WELSH WIND 17 [4] M Wigham 8-9-2 t (56) J Fanning 9/2: 03042-32: Trkd ldrs, ch when short of room over 1f out, swtchd & kept on, no threat to wnr:	2½	58a
342	ZAWRAK 17 [1] I W McInnes 5-9-2 (60) Natalia Gemelova (7) 7/1: 00003-63: Dwelt, rear/inner, styd on for press fnl 2f, no dngr:	1½	56a
324	AMNESTY 18 [6] G L Moore 5-9-2 BL e (60) S Whitworth 20/1: 20030-04: Towards rear, hdwy inner 2f out, not pace to chall:	¾	55a
343	DANCING FOREST 17 [5] D K Ivory 4-9-0 N Callan 20/1: 00000-05: Trkd ldrs, no extra fnl 1f:	1	54a
429	ICANNSHIFT 7 [12] S Dow 4-9-0 (57) C Catlin 50/1: 0600-006: Dwelt, sn handy, wknd over 1f out.	hd	53a
4390}	MEZEREON 124 [9] D Carroll 4-8-11 (58) R Fitzpatrick 6/1: 515010-7: Led till over 1f out, fdd, 12 wk jumps abs.	½	49a
409*	ITSONLYAGAME 9 [11] R Ingram 4-9-0 (58) I Mongan 14/1: 0/5406-18: Mid-div, no impress fnl 2f.	1	51a
5019}	ANYHOW 79 [13] Miss K M George 7-8-13 (60) J P Spencer 4/1 JT FAV: 161140-9: Towards rear, no prog 2f out, abs:	2½	44a
4542}	NOBLE CALLING 115 [3] R J Hodges 7-9-2 (60) E Ahern 16/1: 560006-0: Towards rear, btn 3f out, jumps fit.	1¾	45a

124

LINGFIELD Saturday 24.01.04 Lefthand, V Sharp Track

406	**MISTER CLINTON** 10 [8] D K Ivory 7-9-2 (50) R Miles (3) 25/1: 0000-000: Keen trkg ldrs, wknd 3f out.		3½	39a
1764}	**MASTER T** 241 [7] G L Moore 5-9-2 (60) A Quinn (5) 11/1: 24/4000-0: Al towards rear, 2 mth jumps abs.		6	30a
	SEKWANA 482 [10] Miss A M Newton Smith 5-8-13 p (60) D Sweeney 100/1: 202360/-0: Al bhd, jumps fit.		¾	26a
236	**LEGALITY** 35 [14] Julian Poulton 4-8-11 (51) B Reilly (5) 33/1: 500006-0: Al rear, nvr a factor.		3	21a
14 Ran	2m 09.38 (6.58) Owner Mrs B Sumner			Trained at Marlborough

---

478
4.20 Bet Direct On Sky Active Handicap Stakes 4yo+ 0-75 (E) **[75]**
£3402 £972 £486   **2m**   Going 39   -29 Slow   Stalls Inside

3408}	**LAND OF FANTASY** 171 [8] Lady Herries 5-8-9 (56) J Quinn 50/1: 00B500-1: Mid-div, lost place 4f out, hdwy 3f out & drvn to lead line, all out:			61a
4428}	**EZZ ELKHEIL** 122 [3] J R Jenkins 5-9-13 (74) E Ahern 14/1: 210050-2: Keen, trkd ldr early, remained handy & drvn to lead well ins last, hdd line:		hd	78a
4873}	**BOUMAHOU** 92 [6] A P Jarvis 4-9-2 (70) N Callan 40/1: 6440-3: Rear, hdwy to chall 3f out, rdn & led 2f out till well ins last:		½	73a
404	**TYPHOON TILLY** 10 [9] C R Egerton 7-9-13 (74) M Fenton 4/1: 33033-64: Keen, rear, smooth hdwy to trk ldr 3f out, drvn & ch ins last, no extra cl-home:		hd	77a
358	**MARMADUKE** 15 [1] M Pitman 8-9-2 (63) V Slattery 7/1: 1631/6-25: Led, increased tempo from 4f out, hdd 2f out, kept on for press:		½	65a
288*	**RED SCORPION** 21 [11] W M Brisbourne 5-10-0 (75) B Swarbrick (7) 7/1: 52035-16: Rear, eff wide, not able to chall.		2½	74a
358	**BUSTLING RIO** 15 [2] P C Haslam 8-9-0 (61) Rory Moore (7) 9/1: 31560-47: Trkd ldrs till 3f out.		2	58a
380	**AMBERSONG** 12 [13] A W Carroll 6-8-4 (51) Lisa Jones (3) 12/1: 4220-338: Keen, rear, eff 5f out, no impress:		6	42a
107	**MACARONI GOLD** 59 [7] W Jarvis 4-8-12 (66) M Tebbutt 2/1 FAV: 303112-9: Trkd ldrs till lost place 4f out:		½	56a
185	**DANCE LIGHT** 43 [5] T T Clement 5-8-8 (55) J Mackay 20/1: 16/0600-0: Towards rear, btn over 2f out, abs.		shd	45a
342	**MAKARIM** 17 [12] M R Bosley 8-8-10 p (57) Hayley Turner (5) 25/1: 40063-00: Chsd ldr, wknd qckly 3f out.		13	36a
4529}	**TOP TENOR** 116 [10] B R Johnson 4-9-5 (73) P Doe 6/1: 0/04123-0: Dwelt, sn handy, wknd qckly 4f out:		dist	0a
12 Ran	3m 30.85 (10.85) Owner Lady Herries			Trained at Littlehampton

WOLVERHAMPTON Monday 26.01.04 Lefthand, Sharp Track

Official Going Standard

479
1.45 Press Interactive To Bet Direct Amateur Riders' Handicap Stakes 4yo+ 0-75 (G) **[49]**
£2625 £750 £375   **1m100y f/sand rnd**   Going 35   -49 Slow   Stalls Inside

398+*	**CONSONANT** 12 [7] D G Bridgwater 7-11-7 (70) Mr L Newnes (5) 9/4 FAV: 10////-11: Trkd ldr, smooth hdwy to lead over 2f out, asserted under hands-and-heels, val 6L+:			82a
464	**PASO DOBLE** 3 [11] B R Millman 6-10-13 (62) Mr J Millman (7) 10/1: 4000-502: Chsd ldrs, rdn & kept on fnl 2f, no ch with wnr:		4	64a
4702}	**PAS DE SURPRISE** 106 [4] P D Evans 6-10-9 (58) Miss E Folkes (3) 12/1: 100364-3: Chsd wnr 2f out, rdn & no extra dist:		1¼	57a
442*	**MR WHIZZ** 6 [5] A P Jones 7-9-5 5ex bl e (40) Mr Ashlee Price 16/1: 0000-014: Rdn rear, kept on onepace:		1¾	36a
323	**FRANKSKIPS** 20 [6] Miss S Sanders 5-10-13 (62) Mr C Doran (7) 16/1: 10500-05: Hld up, kept on onepace wide:		½	57a
439	**QUIET READING** 7 [9] M R Bosley 7-11-4 vis (67) Mrs S Bosley 3/1: 4603-346: Mid-div, no extra dist:		2	58a
398	**NITE OWL FIZZ** 12 [10] J O'Reilly 6-10-1 (50) Miss T O'Brien (7) 14/1: 0005-427: Dwelt, rear, only mod prog:		1¼	38a
464	**LITTLETON ZEPHIR** 3 [8] Mrs P Townsley 5-9-11 bl (46) Mrs C Thompson (5) 12/1: 3306-028: Cl-up, led over 3f out till over 2f out, wknd qckly.		6	23a
208	**MISTER BENJI** 41 [3] B P J Baugh 5-10-7 p (56) Mr E Dehdashti (3) 12/1: 400010-9: Led over 4f out till over 3f out.		1¾	30a
417	**TINIAN** 11 [12] K R Burke 6-10-0 (49) Mr S Dobson (3) 12/1: 1530-530: Al rear.		2	19a
437	**DANCING KING** 7 [1] P W Hiatt 8-9-3 8oh (30) Mrs Marie King (2) 40/1: 000-5040: Cl-up 3f, wknd qckly, t.o.		20	0a
421	**FINGER OF FATE** 11 [2] M J Polglase 4-11-0 (63) Mr S Walker 20/1: 00060-00: Led 4f, sn struggling, t.o.		10	0a
12 Ran	1m 53.53 (7.1) Owner The Rule Racing Syndicate			Trained at Winchcombe

480
2.20 Bet Direct Through Sky Active Claiming Stakes 4yo+ (F)
£2912 £832 £416   **1m1f79y f/sand rnd**   Going 35   -11 Slow   Stalls Inside

429	**EASTBOROUGH** 9 [4] B G Powell 5-9-2 (67) J Quinn 11/2: 000/6-031: Chsd ldrs halfway, led over 1f out, drvn out:			68a
382	**CAROUBIER** 14 [9] T D Barron 4-9-11 VIS (75) N Callan 7/4 FAV: 50224-52: Held up, rdn to chall over 1f out, not pace of wnr ins last:		1½	74a
437*	**GIVEMETHEMOONLIGHT** 7 [6] Mrs Stef Liddiard 5-9-3 vis (48) I Mongan 5/2: 22-25213: In tch, rdn & led over 2f out till over 1f out, no extra:		½	64a
450	**FOOLISH THOUGHT** 5 [3] R A Fahey 4-3-5 P (58) T Hamilton (2) 13/2: 4040-654: Led/dsptd lead till over 2f out, wknd:		9	38a
375	**TWO STEPS TO GO** 14 [7] Ian Emmerson 5-8-6 bl (35) A Nicholls 50/1: 4040-445: Led/dsptd lead till 3f out, wknd.		4	30a
3320}	**CHAPEL ROYALE** 178 [8] Mrs N S Sharpe 7-8-8 t (47) Joanna Badger 40/1: 000066-6: Rear, nvr factor.		1¼	29a
406	**ANSWERED PROMISE** 12 [10] A W Carroll 5-8-12 (51) R Miles (3) 25/1: 01000-07: Prom 6f.		5	24a
427	**DANGER BIRD** 10 [8] R Hollinshead 4-8-12 (48) A Culhane 8/1: 5353-238: Prom, btn 2f out:		2	21a
224	**CONCHONITA** 38 [2] B Palling 4-8-2 (45) D Kinsella 20/1: 606626-9: Prom, lost pl from halfway:		10	0a
9 Ran	2m 02.49 (4.29) Owner Mr Christopher Shankland			Trained at Winchester

481
2.55 Betdirect Co Uk Maiden Stakes 3yo (D)
£3367 £1036 £518 £259   **6f f/sand rnd**   Going 35   -25 Slow   Stalls Inside

4926}	**MOUNT VETTORE** 90 [5] Mrs J R Ramsden 3-9-0 P Fitzsimons 14/1: 5-1: Held up, smooth hdwy under hands-and-heels to lead cl-home, v cosily, val further:			83a
4637}	**TORONTO HEIGHTS** 111 [8] P W Chapple Hyam 3-9-0 (76) J Quinn 2/1: 303206-2: Trkd ldrs, short of room 2f out, rdn to chall ins last, not pace of wnr nr fin:		¾	74a
337	**ASK THE CLERK** 19 [7] H J Collingridge 3-9-0 (67) M Tebbutt 16/1: 43030-03: Handy & led 2f out, rdn & hdd nr fin, no extra:		¾	71a
428	**FIZZY LADY** 9 [9] B W Hills 3-8-9 (67) M Hills 15/8 FAV: 54-44: Sn prom, rdn to chall 2f out, no extra dist:		1¼	63a
1965}	**SOUL PROVIDER** 235 [1] P A Blockley 3-8-9 (64) F P Ferris (3) 14/1: 525-5: Dwelt, kept on onepce, new yard:		1	60a

4464}	BROWN DRAGON 122 [12] D Haydn Jones 3-9-0 Paul Eddery 50/1: 00-6: Led early, wknd dist, abs/AW bow.		nk	64a
364	NOBLE MOUNT 16 [3] R Guest 3-9-0 J Mackay 16/1: 57: Prom, till dist.		½	62a
289	DOCKLANDS BLUE 23 [11] N P Littmoden 3-8-9 (60) J P Guillambert (3) 5/1: 630-28: Chsd ldrs, no extra over 1f out.		5	42a
371	CITY AFFAIR 16 [10] Mrs L C Jewell 3-9-0 p (60) S Donohoe (6) 33/1: 00305-09: Held up, sn outpcd.		hd	46a
	DANE RHAPSODY [2] B Palling 3-8-9 M Fenton 50/1: 0: Led till 2f out, sn btn on debut.		3	32a
466	FAIRLY GLORIOUS 3 [6] T H Caldwell 3-9-0 T Eaves (5) 66/1: 00: Sn outpcd, qck reapp.		½	35a
11 Ran	1m 16.38 (3.58) Owner Mr J David Abell		Trained at Thirsk	

482
3.30 Bet Direct On 0800 32 93 93 Stakes Handicap 3yo+ 0-95 (C) [95]
£8171 £2514 £1257 £629   6f f/sand rnd   Going 35   +08 Fast   Stalls Inside

4888}	CELTIC MILL 93 [1] D W Barker 6-9-4 (85) L Enstone (3) 20/1: 030140-1: Made all, rdn & clr over 1f out, held on well for press:			91a
461	HURRICANE COAST 4 [13] D Flood 5-9-0 6ex bl (81) P Doe 8/1: 1113132: In tch wide, styd on well for press cl-home, nrst fin:		¾	84a
418	SOBA JONES 11 [4] J Balding 7-8-8 (75) J Edmunds 16/1: 052-1243: Chsd wnr halfway, styd on.		hd	77a
292	JAYANJAY 33 [10] Miss B Sanders 5-8-9 (76) J Quinn 25/1: 06602-04: Chsd wnr 2f out, no extra dist:		dht	74a
419	SUNDRIED TOMATO 11 [7] P W Hiatt 5-8-12 (79) L Fletcher (3) 12/1: 0000-064: Chsd ldrs, rdn & kept on onepace, eased cl-home when short of room:		1¼	77a
386	ELLENS ACADEMY 13 [11] E J Alston 9-8-12 (79) D Allan (3) 10/1: 06131-46: Rear, mod late gains/hmpd ins last.		1	74a
361	FLINT RIVER 17 [12] H Morrison 6-9-1 (82) A Culhane 3/1 FAV: 00210-27: Chsd ldrs halfway, sn outpcd:		1¼	73a
292	SIR DESMOND 23 [5] R Guest 6-8-10 p (77) C Catlin 7/1: 40034-38: Drpd rear halfway, nvr threat:		1	65a
461	QUIET TIMES 4 [8] K A Ryan 5-9-5 bl (86) N Callan 5/1: 0120-149: Mid-div, nvr pace to chall:		1¾	69a
390	WINTHORPE 15 [9] J J Quinn 4-8-10 (72) Darren Williams 66/1: 11100-00: Al rear:		¾	58a
386	PORT ST CHARLES 13 [6] P R Chamings 7-8-10 (77) I Mongan 16/1: 02301-50: Chsd ldrs till over 1f out.		¾	56a
361+*	MASSEY 17 [2] T D Barron 8-10-0 (95) D Mernagh 5/1: 20000-10: Chsd ldrs, btn halfway:		2	68a
390	BOND ROYALE 13 [3] B Smart 4-8-12 (79) F Lynch 16/1: 00040-20: Chsd wnr 2f, sn btn:		2½	44a
13 Ran	1m 14.39 (1.59) Owner Mr P Asquith		Trained at Richmond	

483
4.05 Bet Direct In Running Sky Page 293 Selling Stakes 4yo+ (G)
£2590 £740 £370   6f f/sand rnd   Going 35   -14 Slow   Stalls Inside

397	PIPS SONG 12 [7] P W Hiatt 9-8-13 (40) A Culhane 33/1: 3000-001: Mid-div, hdwy for press 2f out & led ins last, styd on strongly:			47a
340	POLAR HAZE 19 [4] Mrs Lydia Pearce 7-9-5 vis (53) J Quinn 5/1: 04102-42: In tch, rdn to lead over 1f out, hdd ins last, not pace of wnr:		1½	47a
379	CHORUS 14 [9] B R Millman 7-8-9 1ow vis (54) G Baker 13/2: 26406-03: Dwelt & rear, styd on wide, nrst fin:		nk	36a
415	BEST LEAD 11 [3] Ian Emmerson 5-9-5 bl (62) D Fentiman (7) 8/1: 0065-104: Led till over 1f out, no extra.		hd	45a
378	MIZHAR 14 [6] J J Quinn 8-8-13 (55) R Winston 20/1: 20300-05: Outpcd, nrst fin.		shd	39a
451	HEATHYARDSBLESSING 5 [13] R Hollinshead 7-8-13 (46) N Callan 14/1: 00623-06: Led early, wknd fnl 1f, qck reapp.		3½	28a
384	AROGANT PRINCE 14 [2] A W Carroll 5-8-13 (53) Derek Nolan (7) 13/2: 0200-447: Prom, btn dist, new yard.		½	26a
4821}	CZAR WARS 97 [1] J Balding 9-8-13 bl (66) L Fletcher (3) 4/1 FAV: 512130-8: Chsd ldrs till halfway, abs.		1¼	22a
373	EVANGELIST 14 [10] Mrs Stef Liddiard 4-8-8 (40) M Fenton 16/1: 00000-30: Al outpcd, new stable.		hd	16a
400	HAWK 12 [8] P R Chamings 6-8-13 (65) I Mongan 7/1: 1305-000: Cl-up, wknd over 1f out.		5	8a
274	CLOUDLESS 26 [12] J W Unett 4-9-0 (60) S Whitworth 9/1: 030015-0: Al bhd:		nk	8a
2195}	BLAKESHALL GIRL 224 [5] J L Spearing 4-8-8 (53) Dean McKeown 50/1: 30000-0: Sn bhd, abs.		1¼	-2a
447	MESMERISED 6 [11] Miss A Stokell 4-8-8 (35) Ann Stokell 66/1: 000-0000: Al rear, qck reapp.		3½	-13a
13 Ran	1m 15.76 (2.96) Owner Mrs Lucia Stockley & Ken Read		Trained at Banbury	

484
4.35 Bet Direct Interactive Handicap Stakes 4yo+ 0-70 (E) [70]
£3283 £938 £469   1m4f f/sand   Going 35   +04 Fast   Stalls Inside

4458}	FALL IN LINE 122 [4] Sir Mark Prescott 4-9-0 (60) J Mackay 3/1: 343-1: Led/dsptd lead, rdn clr over 2f out, eased nr fin, val for 10L+:			78a
421	NAKWA 11 [11] E J Alston 6-8-12 (54) D Allan (3) 9/4 FAV: 1043-122: In tch, chsd wnr 4f out, rdn & no impress fnl 2f:		8	56a
467	LAZZAZ 3 [5] P W Hiatt 4-9-0 (60) A Culhane 11/1: 300-43533: Bhd, styd on for press fnl 3f, no dngr:		3½	57a
147	MANDOOB 51 [8] B R Johnson 7-9-4 p (60) J P Guillambert (3) 12/1: 2/56300-4: Bhd, hdwy halfway, no impress fnl 2f.		nk	56a
391	THEATRE TINKA 13 [9] R Hollinshead 5-9-12 p (68) N Callan 33/1: 03201-55: In tch, btn 4f out.		7	55a
380	COOL BATHWICK 14 [1] B R Millman 5-9-5 (61) J Quinn 7/1: 0/000-126: Prom till 3f out:		6	40a
420*	ORINOCOVSKY 11 [7] N P Littmoden 5-9-8 (64) I Mongan 7/1: 05/004-17: Held up, hdwy 5f out, no prog 3f out.		nk	42a
424*	MOLLYS SECRET 10 [3] C G Cox 6-8-9 p (51) Ashleigh Horton (7) 11/1: 52300-18: Rear, no ch fnl 3f:		1½	27a
380	ONLY FOR SUE 14 [10] W S Kittow 5-8-11 P (53) M Fenton 12/1: 45/061-09: Prom, btn 4f out:		½	28a
330*	DAUNTED 20 [6] P A Blockley 8-9-6 (62) Derek Nolan (7) 14/1: 526/4-310: Al bhd:		2½	33a
3788}	LORD GIZZMO 157 [12] P W Hiatt 7-8-3 (45) J Bramhill 50/1: 0//01355-0: Prom, struggling fnl 4f.		5	9a
160}	CHATER FLAIR 415 [2] D Burchell 7-8-9 1ow (50) V Halliday 100/1: 3640/05/-0: In tch, wknd qckly from 6f out, t.o., jumps fit.		dist	0
12 Ran	2m 37.34 (3.74) Owner Neil Greig - Osborne House II		Trained at Newmarket	

Official Going STANDARD.

485
1.20 Bet Direct No Q 08000 93 66 93 Handicap Stakes 3yo 0-75 (E) [80]
£3318 £948 £474   5f f/sand str   Going 60   Inapplicab   Stalls Stands Side

385	PICCOLO PRINCE 15 [4] E J Alston 3-8-1 (53) J Quinn 11/1: 03500-01: Chsd ldrs, rdn halfway, styd on for press to lead well ins last:			60a
405*	SMART STARPRINCESS 13 [6] P A Blockley 3-8-11 vis (63) N Callan 3/1 FAV: 4411-112: Sn led & showed fine pace, drvn		nk	69a

& hdd well ins last:

5015}	**BELLA BOY ZEE** 82 [2] P A Blockley 3-8-5 (57) F P Ferris (3) 33/1: 330000-3: Mid-div, drvn & kept on, nrst fin:	2½	54a
333	**SCOTTISH EXILE** 21 [13] K R Burke 3-9-2 vis (68) Darren Williams 8/1: 40231-64: Chsd ldrs, kept on onepace:	1	63a
316*	**SIEGFRIEDS NIGHT** 22 [1] M C Chapman 3-7-12 (50) Joanna Badger 16/1: 00035-14: Pushed along rear, nrst fin, ddhtd for 4th:	dht	45a
422	**LIZHAR** 11 [12] M J Polglase 3-9-3 (69) K Ghunowa (7) 20/1: 31435-46: Towards rear, drvn & kept on:	½	62a
371	**LITTLE FLUTE** 17 [8] T Keddy 3-8-0 2ow (50) C Catlin 8/1: 00002-47: Rdn rear, nrst fin:	nk	44a
422	**BARRAS** 11 [10] Miss Gay Kelleway 3-8-5 VIS (57) Lisa Jones (3) 20/1: 45321-08: Chsd ldrs till halfway:	1¼	45a
169	**DEMOLITION MOLLY** 49 [3] R F Marvin 3-9-7 P (73) Dean McKeown 10/1: 515054-9: Bmpd start, chsd ldr 4f:	½	59a
237	**BLUE POWER** 36 [11] K R Burke 3-9-0 (66) A Reilly (7) 7/1: 044213-0: In tch, outpcd halfway:	¾	50a
405	**IVORY LACE** 13 [9] D K Ivory 3-8-3 (55) R Ffrench 16/1: 1500-520: Sn outpcd:	1½	34a
371	**HEAD OF STATE** 17 [7] R M Beckett 3-8-0 (52) J Mackay 7/1: 0061-00: Al rear:	1¾	26a
364	**SON OF REMBRANDT** 17 [5] D K Ivory 3-8-10 BL (62) I Mongan 20/1: 05063-00: Hmpd start & sn bhd, blnks.	1¼	32a
418	**SAHARA SILK** 12 [14] D Shaw 3-8-13 vis (65) T Hamilton 16/1: 10500-00: Dwelt & sn struggling, reportedly slowly away after sitting down in the stalls.	25	0

14 Ran 1m 0.57   Owner The Burlington Partnership   Trained at Preston

---

486 1.50 Bet Direct No Q Voice Automated Betting Selling Handicap Stakes Div 1 3yo 0-60 (G)   [62]

£2548 £728 £364   **1m f/sand rnd**   Going 60   -10 Slow   Stalls Inside

462*	**SMART BOY PRINCE** 5 [2] P A Blockley 3-9-13 6ex (61) Derek Nolan (7) 13/8 FAV: 50466-11: Made all, drvn & held on gamely ins last:		68a
203	**CEASAR** 42 [7] P C Haslam 3-8-13 (47) G Faulkner 11/1: 206004-2: Chsd ldrs, drvn to chall dist, just held:	nk	53a
300	**COURANT DAIR** 24 [9] P C Haslam 3-8-6 (40) Rory Moore (7) 14/1: 4000-03: Sn handy & rdn/ch 2f out, no extra fnl 1f:	3	40a
398	**SIR FRANK GIBSON** 13 [3] M Johnston 3-8-11 (45) J Fanning 11/2: 03040-04: Pushed along mid-div, swtchd wide & kept on, nvr able to chall:	nk	44a
309	**GIVEN A CHANCE** 23 [4] J G Given 3-8-1 (35) J Quinn 15/2: 00600-45: Dwelt, no impress fnl 3f:	10	18a
399	**MIDDLEHAM ROSE** 13 [8] P C Haslam 3-8-1 (35) D Fentiman (7) 6/1: 000-66: Mid-div, struggling from 3f out.	2	14a
460	**CASANTELLA** 5 [5] M J Polglase 3-8-11 (45) J Mackay 12/1: 036-0457: Al rear:	nk	23a
383	**BROTHER CADFAEL** 15 [6] John A Harris 3-9-1 (49) S Whitworth 10/1: 00456-38: Slow away & sn struggling:	10	11a
462	**TICKLEPENNY LOCK** 5 [1] C Smith 3-8-2 1ow (35) A Nicholls 66/1: 66000-09: Prom till halfway, lost action.	½	0a

9 Ran 1m 44.97 (5.57)   Owner Brooklands Racing   Trained at Southwell

---

487 2.20 Bet Direct No Q Claiming Stakes 4yo+ (F)

£2919 £834 £417   **6f f/sand rnd**   Going 60   +04 Fast   Stalls Inside

419	**BLAKESET** 12 [4] T D Barron 9-9-1 vis (78) N Callan 5/6 FAV: 1101-101: Dwelt, sn clr-up, led after 3f out, clr dist, edged right & rdn out fnl 1f:		76a
377	**ABOVE BOARD** 15 [1] R F Marvin 9-8-5 t (35) Dean McKeown 100/1: 0000-502: Bhd, prog 3f out, chsd wnr ins fnl 1f, kept on but al held:	1¾	59a
355	**AMANDAS LAD** 19 [3] M C Chapman 4-8-7 (40) K Dalgleish 100/1: 00030-63: Handy, rdn bef 1f out, flashed tail & no impress ins fnl 1f:	¾	59a
349	**NEW OPTIONS** 19 [9] W J Musson 7-9-1 (66) Paul Eddery 6/1: 30004-54: Held up, prog 3f out, onepcd.	1	64a
27	**BELLA BEGUINE** 74 [8] A Bailey 5-8-7 1ow vis (70) M Fenton 11/4: 100202-5: Chsd ldrs, no extra fnl 1f:	2	50a
253	**RIVER LARK** 31 [2] M A Buckley 5-8-10 (47) R Ffrench 16/1: 500102-6: Led, hdd over 2f out, wknd:	2	47a
246	**DIL** 32 [7] Mrs N Macauley 9-8-5 vis (45) Joanna Badger 16/1: 060003-7: Slow away, al bhd:	4	31a
317	**HIGH ESTEEM** 22 [6] M A Buckley 8-8-9 p (56) J Fanning 20/1: 10000-48: Prom, fdd 3f out.	4	24a
447	**BLUNHAM** 7 [5] M C Chapman 4-8-5 (40) Andrew Webb (7) 40/1: 0000-459: Cl up, wknd 3f out:	1½	15a

9 Ran 1m 16.64 (3.34)   Owner Mr Nigel Shields   Trained at Thirsk

---

488 2.50 Littlewoods Bet Direct Median Auction Maiden Stakes 3-5yo (F)

£2989 £854 £427   **7f f/sand rnd**   Going 60   -05 Slow   Stalls Inside

207	**WINGS OF MORNING** 42 [5] P A Blockley 3-8-7 1ow N Callan 7/2 FAV: 0002-1: Led, styd on well fnl 2f to hold off rivals, rdn out:		69a
4863}	**REGULATED** 96 [11] J A Osborne 3-8-6 (73) R Winston 9/2: 520450-2: Chsd ldrs, chsd wnr ins fnl 1f, al held:	1¾	64a
355	**GALLOWAY MAC** 19 [1] W A O'Gorman 4-9-10 M Tebbutt 4/1: 33: Dwelt, sn rdn along, chsd wnr 2f out, onepcd fnl 1f:	½	62a
364	**TONTO** 17 [8] Miss D Mountain 3-8-6 (65) D Fox (5) 4/1: 43020-04: Bhd, prog wide 3f out, kept on late:	5	48a
406	**VIZULIZE** 13 [10] A W Carroll 5-9-5 (50) A Culhane (4) 5/1: 5340-065: Held up, prog wide 3f out, no impress fnl 1f.	¾	41a
385	**PRIDE OF KINLOCH** 15 [9] J Hetherton 4-9-5 (50) C Catlin 16/1: 05000-06: Trkd ldrs, wknd 2f out:	10	15a
	MIDNIGHT PROMISE [6] J A Glover 3-8-6 Dean McKeown 12/1: 7: Nvr nrr than mid-div:	1¼	16a
320	**VELVET RHYTHM** 22 [2] K R Burke 4-9-5 Darren Williams 100/1: 0-08: Al bhd.	2	5a
4861}	**COPPERFIELDS LASS** 96 [3] W G M Turner 5-9-5 BL (40) C Haddon (7) 40/1: 0/00600-9: In tch, wknd 2f out:	1	2a
4769}	**MIKASA** 103 [7] R F Fisher 4-9-10 (51) L Fletcher (3) 66/1: 006000-0: Al bhd:	nk	6a
1306]	**LADY DOUBLE U** 631 [12] T D Easterby 4-9-5 D Allan (3) 20/1: 0/-0: Cl-up, wknd 3f out:	2½	-7a

11 Ran 1m 31.16 (4.56)   Owner Ed Weetman (Haulage & Storage)   Trained at Southwell

---

489 3.20 Betdirect Co Uk Handicap Stakes Fillies 4yo+ 0-75 (E)   [70]

£3287 £939 £470   **1m f/sand rnd**   Going 60   +02 Fast   Stalls Inside

427*	**NAJAABA** 11 [1] Miss J Feilden 4-10-0 (71) R Billy (5) 5/4 FAV: 431-1111: Chsd ldrs, led 2f out, sn hung right under press, drvn out fnl 1f:		76a
427	**MAGGIES PET** 11 [6] K Bell 7-8-2 t (45) D R McCabe 11/1: 0360-252: Led, hdd 2f out, rallied ins fnl 1f, not pace wnr:	1	47a
332	**ELLEN MOONEY** 21 [5] B Smart 5-9-13 p (70) R Ffrench 100/30: 21502-23: In tch, kept on fnl 1f, not pace front 2:	¾	71a
356	**EAGER ANGEL** 19 [2] R F Marvin 6-8-2 p (45) J Quinn 14/1: 00630-24: Held up, prog 2f out, no impress fnl 1f:	½	45a
356	**JESSIE** 19 [7] Don Enrico Incisa 5-7-12 1oh T (40) Kim Tinkler 25/1: 0400-565: Handy wide, wknd dist:	4	33a

332	**ESTIMATION 21** [3] R M H Cowell 4-9-12 (69) I Mongan 6/1: 13651-36: Held up, hdwy wide 3f out, onepcd fnl 2f.	2 58a
396*	**MODESTY BLAISE 13** [8] Miss Gay Kelleway 4-9-13 (70) M Fenton 8/1: 00-17: Cl-up, fdd 2f out:	½ 58a
424	**ESTIMATE 11** [4] John A Harris 4-8-12 vis (55) S Whitworth 33/1: 6264-008: Cl-up, fdd 3f out:	9 27a
8 Ran	1m 44.07 (4.67) Owner Mr A K Sparks	Trained at Newmarket

490 3.50 Bet Direct No Q Voice Automated Betting Selling Handicap Stakes Div 2 3yo 0-60 (G)   **[63]**
£2541 £726 £363   1m f/sand rnd   Going 60   -13 Slow   Stalls Inside

207	**RARE COINCIDENCE 42** [7] R F Fisher 3-9-7 p (56) D Nolan (5) 11/4: 505320-1: Prom, led 3f out, edged left under press dist, rdn out:	62a
402	**ABROGATE 13** [4] P C Haslam 3-8-13 (48) Rory Moore (7) 100/30: 03003-02: In tch, chsd wnr 2f out, kept on but al held fnl 1f:	2 49a
462	**HUNTING PINK 5** [5] H Morrison 3-9-0 (49) L Fletcher (3) 5/2 FAV: 30044-23: Mid-div, prog 3f out, hung left & onepcd dist:	3 44a
43	**BISCAR TWO 71** [1] R M Whitaker 3-8-10 (45) Dean McKeown 12/1: 000-4: Slow away, prog 3f out, no impress & short of room dist:	½ 39a
302	**SOLEIL DHIVER 24** [8] P C Haslam 3-8-0 (35) D Fentiman (7) 16/1: 40400-05: Led, hdd 3f out, sn wknd:	5 20a
383	**PLATINUM CHIEF 15** [9] A Berry 3-8-12 (47) F Lynch (3) 44045-66: Handy wide, wknd fnl 3f.	hd 31a
383	**MARITA 15** [6] J G Given 3-8-10 VIS (45) M Fenton 8/1: 20503-57: Prom, wknd 3f out:	½ 28a
354	**PEACE TREATY 19** [3] S R Bowring 3-7-12 3oh (30) J Bramhill 33/1: 05000-08: Chsd ldrs, fdd 3f out.	8 2a
8 Ran	1m 45.25 (5.85) Owner Great Head House Estates Limit	Trained at Ulverston

491 4.20 Bet Direct In Vision Sky Page 293 Handicap Stakes 4yo+ 0-65 (F)   **[64]**
£2961 £846 £423   2m f/sand   Going 60   -39 Slow   Stalls Inside

339	**STOLEN SONG 20** [3] M J Ryan 4-9-1 e (58) S Whitworth 15/2: 03352-41: Held up, prog to lead dist, edged left & hdd ins fnl 1f, rallied to lead cl-home:	65a
443*	**LAMPOS 7** [6] Miss J A Camacho 4-8-8 6ex (51) R Winston 6/4 FAV: 0030-312: Mid-div, prog 5f out, led ins fnl 1f, hdd cl-home:	shd 57a
4538}	**ALTITUDE DANCER 118** [11] P A Blockley 4-9-2 (59) W M Lordan 14/1: 331053-3: Cl-up, led 3f out, hdd dist, sn no extra:	6 59a
336	**JAMAICAN FLIGHT 21** [10] Mrs S Lamyman 11-9-0 (50) J Quinn 8/1: 36450-34: Led, hdd 3f out, no extra fnl 2f:	1½ 49a
4331}	**ELA JAY 130** [1] H Morrison 5-8-9 (45) L Fletcher (3) 13/2: 5/26060-5: Chsd ldrs, onepcd fnl 2f:	½ 43a
426*	**VINCENT 11** [2] John A Harris 9-8-13 (49) J Mackay 13/2: 611-4316: Held up, nvr nrr than mid-div:	1 39a
443	**WORLABY DALE 7** [8] Mrs S Lamyman 8-7-13 (35) Lisa Jones (3) 7/1: 3340-447: Slow away, sn in tch, wknd 3f out.	1¾ 43a
484	**DAUNTED 1** [5] P A Blockley 8-9-12 (62) Derek Nolan (7) 14/1: 526/4-3108: Cl-up, fdd 4f out:	1 49a
445	**KING PRIAM 7** [9] M J Polglase 9-8-9 p (45) Dean McKeown 20/1: 0-041459: Al bhd.	14 21a
	TERDAD 1978 [4] J G Given 11-8-12 p (48) M Fenton 25/1: /610/////-: Chsd ldrs, wknd 7f out.	nk 23a
10 Ran	3m 41.77 (15.77) Owner The Aldora Partnership	Trained at Newmarket

Official Going Standard

492 1.00 Bet Direct No Q Claiming Stakes 3yo+ (F)
£2954 £844 £422   5f p/track rnd   Going 31   +09 Fast   Stalls Outside

292	**TYPE ONE 25** [5] T G Mills 6-9-13 (78) R Miles (3) 4/6 FAV: 14321-01: Led after 1f, hit rail halfway, shaken up & in command dist, rdly, val for 7L+:	82a
471*	**WHIPPASNAPPER 4** [9] J R Best 4-9-13 (60) N Pollard 8/1: 0000-012: Chsd ldrs, kept on fnl 1f, no ch with wnr:	5 67a
329	**PANJANDRUM 22** [10] N E Berry 6-9-9 (68) M Savage (5) 10/1: 3/3001-03: Mid-div, kept on over 1f out, no danger to wnr:	¾ 61a
485	**LIZHAR 1** [6] M J Polglase 3-8-6 (69) P Doe 25/1: 31435-464: Prom, drvn & onepace fnl 2f:	½ 57a
405	**EASILY AVERTED 14** [3] P Butler 3-8-8 T (66) L Keniry (4) 25/1: 13006-55: Missed break, towards rear, some late gains:	¾ 57a
4122*}	**SOMERSET WEST 142** [7] Mrs L Stubbs 4-9-6 (58) Kristin Stubbs (7) 33/1: 054001-6: Led 1f, wknd 2f out:	nk 53a
2176}	**DULCE DE LECHE 226** [4] S C Williams 3-8-12 BL e B Reilly (5) 14/1: 00-7: Dwelt, nvr pace to chall:	½ 58a
20	**MAJHOOL 76** [8] G L Moore 5-9-9 (72) I Mongan 7/1: 45/0010-8: Dwelt, chsd ldrs till outpcd from halfway:	hd 53a
407	**JUWWI 14** [2] J M Bradley 10-9-13 (69) C J Davies (7) 16/1: 040-0409: Slow away, sn reminders, broke blood vessel:	2 51a
9 Ran	58.88 (1.08) Owner Mrs A K Petersen	Trained at Epsom

493 1.30 Press Interactive To Bet Direct Handicap Stakes 4yo+ 0-75 (E)   **[75]**
£3413 £975 £488   1m4f p/track   Going 31   -11 Slow   Stalls Inside

56	**MISSION TO MARS 71** [4] P R Hedger 5-9-11 (72) J P Spencer 9/4 FAV: 211112-1: Mid-div, cruised thro' to lead in last, val for 5L+:	87a
294	**PERFIDIOUS 25** [9] J R Boyle 6-9-9 (70) R Miles (3) 16/1: 25201-32: Led after 1f till ins last, no ch with easy wnr:	2½ 74a
434	**EASTER OGIL 11** [6] Jane Southcombe 9-9-3 (64) V Slattery 12/1: 422-5033: In tch, hdwy to chall dist, not pace to threaten:	1¼ 66a
467	**NIGHT WARRIOR 5** [8] D Flood 4-9-1 (66) P Doe 11/1: 0004-044: Towards rear, styd on for press fnl 2f:	shd 68a
122	**MAD CAREW 60** [10] G L Moore 5-9-11 bl e (72) S Whitworth 16/1: 041322-5: Keen mid-div, eff wide, onepace:	1 73a
430	**GOLDEN DUAL 11** [2] S Dow 4-8-7 (58) Paul Eddery 50/1: 4365-006: Rear, hdwy 3f out, no extra dist:	nk 56a
404	**DUSTY CARPET 14** [3] M J Weeden 6-9-10 (71) C Catlin 33/1: 3220//-007: Mid-div, no impress dist:	nk 64a
424	**BIG BERTHA 12** [12] John Berry 6-9-7 (68) G Baker 11/1: 6623-428: Held up travelling well, rdn & onepace fnl 2f:	shd 67a
264*	**MAJLIS 30** [1] R M H Cowell 7-9-10 bl (71) E Ahern 14/1: 500201-9: In tch, ch over 1f out, sn no extra:	½ 69a
137	**ASTROMANCER 57** [5] M H Tompkins 4-8-2 (53) J Fanning 11/1: P50244-0: Led 1f, rdn & btn over 1f out:	¾ 50a
477	**ANYHOW 4** [13] Miss N K George 7-8-13 (60) Derek Nolan (7) 8/1: 61140-00: Al twds rear, nvr factor:	nk 56a
404	**CLASSIC ROLE 14** [15] R Ingram 5-9-11 (72) I Mongan 11/2: 00030-40: Chsd ldrs till over 1f out:	2½ 64a
293	**SUDDEN FLIGHT 25** [7] R Ingram 7-10-0 (75) R Havlin 25/1: 60010-00: Cl-up till over 1f out.	1 66a
201	**BUCKS 44** [14] D K Ivory 7-10-0 (75) M Tebbutt 20/1: 352125-0: Mid-div wide, btn 3f out, abs:	nk 65a
195	**MCQUEEN 46** [11] Mrs H Dalton 4-9-9 (74) D Sweeney 25/1: 203310-0: Prom, no ch fnl 3f, abs:	¾ 63a
434*	**RASID 11** [16] C A Dwyer 6-9-6 (67) N Callan 10/1: 03053-1P: Prom 9f, sn bhd, lame:	0a
16 Ran	2m 34.24 (5.04) Owner Mr Ian Hutchins	Trained at Chichester

---

494	**2.00 Littlewoods Bet Direct Handicap Stakes** 3yo 0-85 (D)			[85]
	£4693 £1444 £722 £361 **6f p/track rnd**	**Going 31**	**-05 Slow**	Stalls Inside

368	**KABREET** 18 [2] E A L Dunlop 3-9-7 (78) E Ahern 1/1 FAV: 53101-31: Cl-up, led 3f out, pushed out ins fnl 1f, val 3L+:		87a
368	**HELLO ROBERTO** 18 [3] M J Polglase 3-9-6 (77) J P Spencer 12/1: 04324-02: Keen rear, prog 3f out, ev ch dist, kept on fnl 1f, not pace wnr:	1¾	77a
455	**ST SAVARIN** 7 [7] J R Best 3-9-1 (72) R Miles (3) 7/1: 1051-253: Mid-div, outpcd 3f out, rallied dist, kept on cl-home:	¾	70a
268	**SMOKIN JOE** 29 [1] J R Best 3-9-3 (74) N Pollard 10/1: 662216-4: Dwelt, sn chsd ldrs, onepace fnl 1f:	1½	67a
333	**POMPEY BLUE** 22 [4] P J McBride 3-8-13 (70) N Callan 8/1: 35515-55: Keen cl-up, fdd dist:	1¼	59a
405	**STAMFORD BLUE** 14 [10] J S Moore 3-7-12 2oh bl (53) D Kinsella 12/1: 0035-246: Held up, nvr nrr than mid-div.	nk	43a
371	**FORZENUFF** 18 [8] J R Boyle 3-8-8 (65) D Sweeney 16/1: 51603-57: Chsd ldrs, no extra 2f out:	1¾	48a
371	**PRINCESS KAI** 18 [5] R Ingram 3-8-4 bl (61) J Quinn 16/1: 0303-108: Led 3f, fdd dist:	3	35a
268	**RISE** 29 [9] Andrew Reid 3-9-5 bl (76) I Mongan 40/1: 310400-9: Dwelt, sn mid-div, wknd 2f out:	1	47a
268	**KURINGAI** 29 [6] B W Duke 3-8-10 (67) M Fenton 14/1: 333020-0: Handy, fdd 3f out:	5	24a
10 Ran	1m 12.57 (2.17) Owner Jumeirah Racing		Trained at Newmarket

495	**2.30 Bet Direct Through Sky Active Selling Stakes** 3yo (G)			
	£2569 £734 £367 **6f p/track rnd**	**Going 31**	**-16 Slow**	Stalls Inside

466	**ALIZAR** 5 [8] M J Polglase 3-8-12 (59) J P Spencer 2/1 FAV: 153-0231: Cl-up, led dist, drvn out fnl 1f:		61a
87	**REEDSMAN** 65 [2] M H Tompkins 3-8-12 (45) N Callan 25/1: 000000-2: Cl-up, kept on same pace fnl 2f:	2	54a
436	**LIMIT DOWN** 9 [3] M J Wallace 3-8-12 vis (55) J P Guillambert (3) 7/1: 0005-653: Mid-div, prog 3f out, no impress fnl 1f:	nk	53a
295	**LADY PISTE** 25 [10] P D Evans 3-8-12 vis t (52) L Fletcher (3) 16/1: 55304-04: In tch, outpcd 3f out, carried wide turning in, kept on late:	½	51a
327	**STANHOPE FORBES** 22 [12] N P Littmoden 3-8-12 (53) E Ahern 7/2: 06025-35: Dwelt, sn outpcd, prog when carried left dist, mod late gains:	4	39a
371	**REHIA** 18 [14] J W Hills 3-8-12 (57) H Gemberlu (6) 12/1: 13550-06: Dwelt, in tch wide, fdd dist.	1½	34a
402	**MAGICO** 14 [5] A M Balding 3-8-12 vis (49) L Keniry (3) 25/1: 0000-07: Chsd ldrs, outpcd 3f out, no ch when hmpd dist.	¾	32a
449	**OBOE** 7 [6] R Charlton 3-8-7 J Fanning 20/1: 5-08: Reared start, al bhd:	hd	26a
326	**FOX HOLLOW** 22 [7] M J Haynes 3-8-12 (35) R Miles (3) 66/1: 66500-09: Nvr nrr than mid-div.	2½	23a
413	**PHILLY DEE** 13 [1] N E Berry 3-8-7 bl (47) C Catlin 14/1: 43253-30: Led, hdd & fdd dist:	½	16a
300	**INTITNICE** 25 [9] Miss K M George 3-8-12 bl (40) Derek Nolan (7) 66/1: 00000-00: Sn outpcd, nvr a factor:	nk	20a
337	**LORD BASKERVILLE** 21 [11] M G Quinlan 3-8-12 (60) Nicol Polli (7) 12/1: 4030-00: Cl-up fdd 2f out.	nk	19a
4966}	**IMPERIAL PRINCESS** 88 [4] D K Ivory 3-8-9 2ow (40) I Mongan 50/1: 00000-0: Al in rear.	1½	11a
428	**FRESH CONNECTION** 11 [13] G G Margarson 3-8-8 1ow M Fenton 10/1: 00: Dwelt, nvr a factor:	1	7a
14 Ran	1m 13.21 (2.81) Owner General Sir Geoffrey Howlett		Trained at Newark

496	**3.00 Betdirect Co Uk Maiden Stakes** 3yo (D)			
	£4193 £1290 £645 £323 **1m p/track rnd**	**Going 31**	**-29 Slow**	Stalls Outside

4603}	**SOMEWHERE MY LOVE** 116 [3] T G Mills 3-8-9 R Miles (3) 9/2: 50-1: In tch, hdwy to lead ins fnl 1f, rdn out:		69a
322	**WEBBSWOOD LAD** 22 [7] Mrs Stef Liddiard 3-9-0 M Fenton 5/1: 32: Keen cl-up, ev ch dist, kept on fnl 1f, just denied:	hd	74a
367	**NIGHT STORM** 18 [1] S Dow 3-8-9 (65) P Doe 9/1: 025-53: Keen in tch, prog 2f out, prom when short of room ins fnl 1f, kept on but just held by front 2:	½	67a
428	**GROUND PATROL** 11 [2] A M Balding 3-9-0 J P Spencer 5/2 FAV: 0-34: Dwelt, sn in tch, ev ch dist, onepcd well ins fnl 1f:	nk	71a
213	**OPERA STAR** 4 [5] B W Hills 3-8-9 M Hills 14/1: 0-5: Led, hdd dist, no extra fnl 1f:	3½	55a
2783}	**DANCING LYRA** 202 [11] J W Hills 3-9-0 E Ahern 3/1: 0300-6: Rear, nvr nrr than mid-div:	1¼	56a
	SHALATI PRINCESS [10] J C Fox 3-8-9 P Dobbs 100/1: 7: Nvr nrr than mid-div:	½	49a
	LOOKOUTHEREICOME [8] T T Clement 3-8-9 Lisa Jones (3) 66/1: 9: Nvr a factor:	1¼	45a
	GREATEST BY PHAR [4] J Akehurst 3-9-0 C Catlin 33/1: 9: Dwelt, al bhd:	3	41a
428	**NEVER CRIED WOLF** 11 [9] D R C Elsworth 3-9-0 N Pollard 20/1: 60: Al bhd.	½	39a
295	**EMILYS DAWN** 25 [6] D K Ivory 3-8-9 (51) D Sweeney 25/1: 0060-00: Keen cl-up, fdd 3f out.	18	0a
11 Ran	1m 40.98 (4.78) Owner Miss J A Leighs		Trained at Epsom

497	**3.30 Bet Direct In Running Sky Page 293 Handicap Stakes** 3yo 0-75 (E)			[82]
	£3392 £969 £485 **1m2f p/track**	**Going 31**	**-21 Slow**	Stalls Inside

365	**IVORY COAST** 18 [8] W R Muir 3-8-2 (56) J Quinn 12/1: 004-41: Handy, led 2f out, rdn out to hold on fnl 1f:		60a
337*	**DESERT IMAGE** 21 [3] C Tinkler 3-9-5 (73) E Ahern 6/1: 0330-12: Handy, ev ch ins fnl 1f, just denied:	nk	76a
365*	**KEEPERS KNIGHT** 18 [2] P F I Cole 3-8-13 (67) I Mongan 7/2: 055-13: Cl-up, hung left bef 2f out, ev ch fnl 1f, kept on, just held:	nk	69a
276	**LITTLE EYE** 28 [11] J R Best 3-9-0 (68) N Pollard 8/1: 042234-4: Bhd, prog 2f out, kept on fnl 1f:	½	69a
325	**NESSEN DORMA** 22 [10] J G Given 3-9-7 (75) M Fenton 14/1: 50511-45: Cl-up, ev ch 1f out, sn onepcd:	hd	75a
455*	**TREVIAN** 7 [7] S C Williams 3-8-11 (65) J P Spencer 5/2 FAV: 056-016: Held up, prog wide & hung right 2f out, onepcd fnl 1f:	nk	64a
402	**EL MAGNIFICO** 14 [4] P D Cundell 3-7-12 1oh P (51) F P Ferris (3) 33/1: 006-67: Mid-div, nvr a factor:	3	46a
367	**PRINCESS ALINA** 18 [6] A M Balding 3-8-13 (67) S Whitworth 16/1: 52-08: Held up, nvr able to chall.	shd	61a
291	**PLATINUM PIRATE** 25 [5] K R Burke 3-8-2 bl (56) C Catlin 20/1: 06000-29: Al bhd:	1¾	48a
325	**LASTING DELIGHT** 46 [1] Sir Mark Prescott 3-9-0 (68) J Mackay 11/1: 0510-0: Led, fdd 2f out:	5	53a
295	**TARANAI** 25 [13] B W Duke 3-8-0 (54) Lisa Jones (3) 25/1: 00006-40: Chsd ldrs wide, wknd 3f out:	12	23a
11 Ran	2m 08.03 (5.23) Owner Mrs J M Muir		Trained at Lambourn

498	**4.00 Bet Direct In Vision Sky Page 293 Handicap Stakes** 4yo+ 46-55 (F)			[61]
	£2989 £854 £427 **1m2f p/track**	**Going 31**	**-09 Slow**	Stalls Inside

429	**BANK ON HIM** 11 [4] C Weedon 9-9-6 (53) J Quinn 8/1: 3000-015: Mid-div, prog 3f out, led ins fnl 1f, drvn out:		62a
104	**MY MAITE** 63 [6] R Ingram 5-9-5 vis t (52) N Day 8/1: 050036-2: Led, rcd keenly, hdd ins fnl 1f, not btn far:	1	59a

406	**DOUBLE RANSOM** 14 [9] Mrs L Stubbs 5-9-6 bl (53) S W Kelly 11/2: 00032-23: Mid-div, eff 3f out, onepcd.	5	53a
406	**MAGIC WARRIOR** 14 [11] J C Fox 4-9-6 (55) P Dobbs 11/1: 00505-34: Rear, prog 2f out, kept on late:	2	52a
480	**GIVEMETHEMOONLIGHT** 9 [8] Mrs Stef Liddiard 5-9-7 6ex vis (54) J P Spencer 9/2 FAV: 22-25215: Handy, onepcd fnl 2f:	1½	49a
480	**ANSWERED PROMISE** 14 [14] A W Carroll 5-9-4 (51) R Miles (3) 50/1: 01000-06: Chsd ldr, no extra 2f out.	shd	46a
3666}	**WIND CHIME** 164 [1] A G Newcombe 7-9-4 (51) S Whitworth 10/1: 114000-7: In tch, no extra fnl 2f:	1¼	44a
4951}	**IN THE STARS** 90 [2] P R Webber 6-9-5 VIS (52) W Ryan 11/1: 4/04000-8: Nvr nrr than mid-div:	nk	44a
263	**A BEETOO** 30 [7] J R Best 4-9-6 (55) N Pollard 33/1: 462650-9: Nvr nrr than mid-div.	9	36a
427	**NUZZLE** 12 [10] M Quinn 4-9-4 (53) R Winston 66/1: 0631-000: Cl-up, fdd 4f out.	4	28a
406	**KYLE OF LOCHALSH** 14 [12] G G Margarson 4-9-6 p (55) E Ahern 7/1: 03000-30: Mid-div, wknd 3f out.	hd	29a
429	**WATER OF LIFE** 11 [5] J R Boyle 5-9-4 (51) I Mongan 12/1: 00053-00: Keen, nvr able to chall:	8	15a
339	**CASTAIGNE** 21 [13] B W Duke 5-9-7 (54) M Fenton 20/1: 40020-00: Dwelt, al in rear.	1½	16a
406	**FIFE AND DRUM** 14 [3] Miss J Feilden 7-9-5 p (52) P Doe 14/1: 22U00-00: In tch, wknd 4f out, eased fnl 2f.	3	10a

14 Ran   2m 06.75 (3.95)   Owner Vetlab Supplies Ltd   Trained at Pulborough

499	**4.30 Free #25 Bonus @ Littlewoodspoker Com Handicap Stakes 4yo+ 0-65 (F)**		[65]
	£2989 £854 £427 **7f p/track rnd** **Going 31** -03 Slow Stalls Inside		

474	**BLONDE EN BLONDE** 4 [2] N P Littmoden 4-9-12 BL (63) I Mongan 33/1: 534-6601: Handy, led 1f out, drvn out nr fin despite flashing tail:		70a
366	**ACORAZADO** 18 [4] G L Moore 5-9-4 e (55) G Carter 16/1: 51535-02: Rear, hdwy 2f out, ran on ins fnl 1f but not reach wnr:	½	60a
471	**SUPERCHIEF** 4 [9] Miss B Sanders 9-10-0 bl t (65) J Quinn 5/1: 002-0643: Rear, hdwy & not clr run 1f out, kept on:	1	58a
366*	**ZAFARSHAH** 18 [1] P D Evans 5-9-7 vis (58) Joanna Badger 12/1: 30050-14: Handy, led after 2f till hdd over 1f out, no extra:	1½	58a
323	**TEMPER TANTRUM** 22 [14] Andrew Reid 6-9-11 p (62) Rory Moore (7) 20/1: 05023-55: Bhd, hdwy 1f out, wknd fnl 1f.	1	60a
471	**INISTRAHULL ISLAND** 4 [5] M H Tompkins 4-9-8 (59) J Fanning 9/1: 60423-36: Trkd ldrs, wknd fnl 1f.	shd	57a
448	**DOUBLE M** 7 [15] Mrs L Richards 7-9-3 vis (54) N Callan 16/1: 000-4137: Keen, rear, hdwy 1f out, onepace:	hd	54a
270	**MR BOUNTIFUL** 29 [11] M Dods 6-9-9 p (60) S W Kelly 25/1: 412300-8: Keen, chsd ldrs, wknd 1f out:	1	55a
439	**DANIELLES LAD** 9 [16] B Palling 8-10-0 bl (65) R Miles (3) 20/1: 3005-429: Led to 5f out, wknd fnl 2f.	¾	59a
323*	**SMITH N ALLAN OILS** 22 [6] M Dods 5-10-0 p (65) R Winston 11/2: 30101-10: Mid-field, onepace.	½	58a
270	**MEELUP** 29 [10] A G Newcombe 4-9-6 p (57) S Whitworth 50/1: 601000-0: Mid-field, wknd 1f out:	5	41a
448*	**NEARLY A FOOL** 7 [7] G G Margarson 6-9-10 6ex vis (61) N Pollard 9/2 FAV: 0353-110: Chsd ldrs, rcd wide, wknd 2f out:	½	44a
263*	**WOOD FERN** 30 [12] M R Channon 4-10-0 (65) R Lappin 6/1: 33001-0: Nvr nr ldrs:	¾	47a
474	**PANTS** 4 [8] Andrew Reid 5-9-4 (55) A Nicholls 20/1: 0310-000: Slowly into stride, rcd wide, hdwy 4f out, wknd 2f out:	16	7a

14 Ran   1m 25.16 (2.36)   Owner Elliott and Brown Racing   Trained at Newmarket

Official Going Standard

500	**1.10 Press Interactive To Bet Direct Handicap Stakes Div 1 4yo+ 46-55 (F)**		[69]
	£2968 £848 £424 **6f f/sand rnd** **Going 58** -21 Slow Stalls Inside		

379	**ITS ECCO BOY** 17 [9] P Howling 6-8-11 (52) R Winston 5/1 JT FAV: 3640-441: Trkd ldrs, led over 1f out, drvn out:		57a
374	**AGUILA LOCO** 17 [1] M C Chapman 5-8-5 1oh (45) Joanna Badger 9/1: 000-3262: Sn handy trav v well, drvn & styd on fnl 1f, just held:	nk	50a
459	**PLAYFUL SPIRIT** 7 [4] J Balding 5-8-5 1oh vis (45) J Edmunds 5/1 JT FAV: 001-0633: In tch, rdn & kept on onepace fnl 2f:	3	41a
303	**DASAR** 25 [7] M Brittain 4-8-5 1oh ML (45) M Lawson (3) 25/1: 00006-64: Mid-div, kept on late:	¾	39a
384	**CLEVELAND WAY** 17 [10] D Carroll 4-8-6 vis (47) R Fitzpatrick 16/1: 000-1265: Led 4f, no extra dist:	1½	35a
400	**EASTERN BLUE** 51 [13] Mrs L Stubbs 5-8-9 p (50) S W Kelly 6/1: 500622-6: Mid-div wide, kept on onepace:	1¼	34a
448	**ATTORNEY** 8 [12] D Shaw 6-8-6 e (47) T Hamilton (5) 16/1: 04-30107: Nvr pace to chall:	3½	20a
168	**ON THE TRAIL** 51 [3] D W Chapman 7-8-9 (50) A Culhane 9/1: 230000-8: Led/dsptd lead till over 1f out, wknd:	1¾	18a
411	**DEFINITELY SPECIAL** 14 [6] N E Berry 6-8-5 6oh (40) C Catlin 20/1: 0000-009: Al outpcd rear.	3½	3a
444	**KUSTOM KIT FOR HER** 9 [11] S R Bowring 4-8-5 1oh bl (45) J Bramhill 33/1: 0200-600: Dwelt & al bhd.	½	1a
335	**FESTIVE AFFAIR** 23 [5] B Smart 6-8-8 (49) R Ffrench 13/2: 64300-30: Trkd ldrs, struggling from halfway.	¾	2a
440	**XALOC BAY** 10 [14] B P J Baugh 6-9-0 vis (55) Darren Williams 16/1: 2360-200: Sn pushed along to go handy, struggling from halfway:	4	0
187	**SERGEANT SLIPPER** 48 [2] C Smith 7-8-5 1oh vis (45) P Makin (4) 20/1: 100005-0: Slow away & nvr a factor:	¾	0

13 Ran   1m 18.05 (4.75)   Owner Mr J Hammond   Trained at Newmarket

501	**1.40 Press Interactive To Bet Direct Handicap Stakes Div 2 4yo+ 46-55 (F)**		[68]
	£2968 £848 £424 **6f f/sand rnd** **Going 58** -12 Slow Stalls Inside		

411	**AINTNECESSARILYSO** 14 [6] N E Berry 6-8-5 (45) C Catlin 8/1: 5465-551: Handy, styd on to lead ins fnl 1f, held narrow lead till joined & ddhtd on line:	dht	54a
451	**ITALIAN MIST** 8 [12] Julian Poulton 5-8-9 e (49) G Faulkner 20/1: 050-1351: In tch, led trav v well dist, hung left & just hdd ins fnl 1f, styd on well to force ddht on line:		58a
448	**TORRENT** 8 [10] D W Chapman 9-8-5 bl (45) R Brisland 16/1: 2060-263: Held up, rcd v keen, prog trav well 3f out, onepcd ins fnl 1f:	5	40a
345	**NEVER WITHOUT ME** 21 [14] P J McBride 4-8-10 vis (50) N Callan 6/1: 50022-64: Trkd ldrs, ev ch dist, sn wknd:	2	39a
385	**AMELIA** 17 [9] W M Brisbourne 6-8-10 (50) B Swarbrick (7) 11/2: 4602-525: Held up, prog 3f out, no impress fnl 1f.	½	37a
483	**POLAR HAZE** 3 [16] Mrs Lydia Pearce 7-8-13 vis (53) J Quinn 11/2: 4102-426: In tch, hung left 2f out, sn wknd:	¾	38a
109	**BRIOSO** 62 [2] J M P Eustace 4-9-0 (54) J Mackay 20/1: 010000-7: Led, hdd bef 1f out, fdd.	3	31a
208*	**SHAHM** 44 [8] B J Curley 5-8-13 (53) S W Kelly 9/2 FAV: 0000/51-8: Al bhd.	½	28a
3706}	**KATY OHARA** 163 [4] Miss S E Hall 5-8-5 (45) Dean McKeown 25/1: 600000-9: Slow away, nvr nrr than mid-div:	1	17a
385	**BACK IN SPIRIT** 17 [15] B A McMahon 4-8-5 5oh t (40) G Gibbons 40/1: 040/00-00: Trkd ldrs, ev ch 2 out, wknd.	1¾	12a
385	**LADY NATILDA** 17 [1] D Haydn Jones 4-8-7 (47) Paul Eddery 7/1: 5000-430: Held up, nvr a factor:	nk	13a

374	CARONTE 17 [7] S R Bowring 4-8-5 10oh bl (35) J Bramhill 50/1: 0600-000: Handy, fdd 2f out:	2	6a
447	ETERNAL BLOOM 9 [3] M Brittain 6-8-5 VIS (45) M Lawson (3) 10/1: 000-1200: Slow away, al bhd:	hd	5a
447	SPEEDY JAMES 9 [13] D Nicholls 8-8-5 5oh vis (40) A Nicholls 28/1: 0000/0-00: Al in rear:	dist	0a

14 Ran   1m 17.5 (4.2)   Owner Mrs Jan Adams   Trained at Earlswood

502 2.10 Bet Direct Through Sky Active Apprentice Claiming Stakes 4yo+   (F)
£2947 £842 £421   1m f/sand rnd   Going 58   -18 Slow   Stalls Inside

439	MISS CHAMPERS 10 [10] P D Evans 4-8-1 (67) B Swarbrick (5) 6/5 FAV: 11352-01: Handy, led 2f out, rdn out to hold on fnl 1f:		61a
204	NOBLE PURSUIT 44 [4] P A Blockley 7-8-3 (55) Derek Nolan 7/1: 600440-2: Cl-up, chsd wnr dist, kept on fnl 1f, just held by wnr:	½	60a
417*	GAME GURU 14 [2] T D Barron 5-8-12 (64) Laura Jayne Crawford (3) 11/4: D301-013: Led, hdd 2f out, wknd fnl 1f:	5	60a
379	REPEAT 17 [5] Miss Gay Kelleway 4-8-6 p (56) P Gallagher 20/1: 064-1204: Cl-up, ev ch 4f out, fdd fnl 1f.	3	50a
366	KUMAKAWA 19 [6] E A Wheeler 4-8-6 bl (45) Liam Jones (5) 33/1: 15000-05: Sn bhd, modest late gains:	2	45a
360	FIRST MAITE 20 [8] S R Bowring 11-9-4 t (70) B O'Neill (5) 15/2: 0602-666: Sn outpcd run wide, mod late gains.	1¼	54a
457	JAMESTOWN 7 [7] M J Polglase 7-9-4 (46) K Ghunowa (5) 40/1: 063-5007: Al in rear:	1¼	51a
442	SWEET CORAL 9 [12] B S Rothwell 4-7-12 (40) Kristin Stubbs 33/1: 5000-048: Rear, hung badly right, nvr a factor.	2½	27a
339	MAUNBY ROCKER 22 [3] P C Haslam 4-9-1 (54) D Wakenshaw (7) 14/1: 01260-09: Handy, fdd 2f out.	2	40a
308	THE BLOCK MONSTER 25 [1] P A Blockley 5-7-12 (45) S Yourston (5) 50/1: 00000-00: Cl-up, fdd 4f out.	14	0a

10 Ran   1m 45.44 (6.04)   Owner Mrs S J Lawrence   Trained at Abergavenny

503 2.40 Littlewoods Bet Direct Median Auction Maiden Stakes 3-4yo   (E)
£3248 £928 £464   1m f/sand rnd   Going 58   -35 Slow   Stalls Inside

468	NORWEGIAN 6 [7] D R Loder 3-8-6 N Pollard 11/4: 51: Handy, hard drvn 2f out, styd on to lead 1f out, rdn out:		69a
432	MONTE MAJOR 12 [1] M A Jarvis 3-8-6 (61) N Callan 4/6 FAV: 06-342: Led, still trav best bef 2f out, hdd 1f out, no extra fnl 1f:	2	64a
438	VIVRE SA VIE 10 [5] Sir Mark Prescott 3-8-1 J Mackay 15/2: 43: In tch, hard drvn 3f out, sn no extra:	6	49a
3882}	BUNDABERG 157 [4] P W Hiatt 4-9-12 A Culhane 33/1: 05-4: Cl-up, fdd 3f out.	20	19a
364	TALE OF THE TIGER 19 [2] Julian Poulton 3-8-6 vis I Mongan 50/1: 0-05: Al bhd:	8	5a
98	DALIDA 65 [6] P C Haslam 3-8-1 D Fentiman (7) 14/1: 00-U: U.r. 7f out:		0a

6 Ran   1m 46.87 (7.47)   Owner Jumeirah Racing   Trained at Newmarket

504 3.10 Betdirect Co Uk Handicap Stakes 4yo+ 0-75 (E)   [74]
£3350 £957 £479   1m4f f/sand   Going 58   +08 Fast   Stalls Inside

484*	FALL IN LINE 3 [5] Sir Mark Prescott 4-9-2 6ex (66) J Mackay 1/4 FAV: 343-11: Slowly away, chsd ldrs, led over 3f out, sn clr & eased nr fin, val 12L+:		86a
493	NIGHT WARRIOR 1 [3] D Flood 4-9-2 (66) P Doe 25/1: 0004-0442: Rear, hdwy over 4f out, outpcd by wnr 2f out:	8	67a
445*	AVEIRO 9 [1] B G Powell 8-8-6 6ex 1ow bl (51) K Dalgleish 9/1: 4140-213: Slowly away, rear, hdwy over 3f out, onepcd:	½	52a
391*	DIGGER 16 [8] Miss Gay Kelleway 5-10-0 (74) M Fenton 12/1: 25236-14: Chsd ldrs, no impress over 2f out:	8	64a
421	STRAVMOUR 14 [4] R Hollinshead 8-8-0 (46) Dale Gibson 50/1: 60431-05: Chsd ldrs, wknd 3f out:	6	28a
288	GEORGE STUBBS 26 [6] M J Polglase 6-9-10 (70) L Fletcher (3) 25/1: 60632-06: Led till over 3f out, no extra.	10	39a
404	VICTORY QUEST 15 [2] Mrs S Lamyman 4-9-9 vis (73) J Quinn 25/1: 25212-07: Chsd ldrs, wknd over 3f out:	dist	0a

7 Ran   2m 40.24 (5.94)   Owner Neil Greig - Osborne House II   Trained at Newmarket

505 3.40 Allweather-Racing Com Selling Stakes 4yo+   (G)
£2604 £744 £372   1m3f f/sand   Going 58   -07 Slow   Stalls Inside

423	COOLFORE JADE 13 [6] N E Berry 4-8-11 (57) C Catlin 11/8 FAV: 045-0141: Made most, drvn clr ins fnl furlong:		59a
387	REX ROMELIO 16 [7] K R Burke 5-9-0 VIS (50) G Faulkner 9/1: 1505/0-02: Handy, hdwy 2f out, onepace:	6	49a
372	SEA YA MAITE 17 [9] S R Bowring 10-9-0 t (35) J Bramhill 14/1: 000-0523: Chsd ldrs, asked for eff over 3f out, no extra:	5	42a
392	LUXI RIVER 16 [11] P A Blockley 4-8-11 (59) Dean McKeown 5/1: 52/64-554: Rear, hdwy 3f out, nvr dngrs:	1	41a
4826}	GLADYS AYLWARD 100 [5] A Crook 4-8-7 1ow (54) V Halliday 25/1: 310004-5: Chsd ldrs, wknd 3f out:	6	29a
446	IPLEDGEALLEGIANCE 9 [10] D W Chapman 8-9-0 (45) A Culhane 11/2: 560-2536: Rear, nvr nr ldrs:	hd	32a
460	MR LEHMAN 7 [12] Mrs M Reveley 7-9-0 M Fenton 8/1: 07: Rear, wknd over 3f out:	7	23a
389]	SPRING GIFT 744 [1] D W Thompson 7-8-9 (45) R Winston 33/1: 6460//40/-: Chsd ldrs, wknd 5f out:	dist	0a
1967}	DR RAJ 238 [4] B A McMahon 5-9-0 t G Gibbons 20/1: 0-9: Chsd ldrs, wknd after halfway:	20	0a

9 Ran   2m 28.5 (7.2)   Owner Leeway Group Limited   Trained at Earlswood

506 4.10 Bet Direct On Sky Active Handicap Stakes 3yo 0-70 (E)   [77]
£3255 £930 £465   1m f/sand rnd   Going 58   -10 Slow   Stalls Inside

410	YANKEEDOODLEDANDY 14 [5] P C Haslam 3-8-8 (57) Rory Moore (7) 8/15 FAV: 4004-121: Handy, rdn 3f out & outpcd, rallied to lead ent fnl 1f, drvn clr:		70a
87*	COULD SHE BE MAGIC 66 [6] T D Easterby 3-8-8 (57) K Dalgleish 7/2: 003501-2: Keen, with ldr, led over 1f out, hdd & no extra ins fnl 1f:	3½	62a
396	TWO OF CLUBS 15 [1] P C Haslam 3-8-13 (62) G Faulkner 12/1: 43454-33: With ldr, led over 3f out, hdd dist, wknd fnl 1f:	¾	66a
4773}	LA PUCE 104 [2] Miss Gay Kelleway 3-9-7 (70) M Fenton 20/1: 542300-4: Trkd ldrs, outpcd dist, rallied fnl 1f:	nk	73a
402	LADY MO 15 [3] Andrew Reid 3-8-4 2ow (51) J P Guillambert 20/1: 6050-535: Keen, nvr nr ldrs:	1¼	53a
432	WARES HOME 12 [4] K R Burke 3-8-13 (62) Darren Williams 12/1: 10006-06: Led 4f, wknd over 1f out.	11	44a

6 Ran   1m 44.83 (5.43)   Owner Mr K Tyre   Trained at Middleham

Official Going Standard

WOLVERHAMPTON Friday 30.01.04 Lefthand, Sharp Track

507 **1.20 Bet Direct No Q Demo 08000 837 888 Handicap Stakes Div 1 3yo+ 0-60 (F)** **[59]**
£2919 £834 £417 **5f rnd** **Going 45** **-20 Slow** Stalls Inside

187 **EMPRESS JOSEPHINE 49** [5] J R Jenkins 4-9-8 vis (53) D Corby (3) 6/1: 012424-1: Made all, kept on fnl 2f, drvn out: **59a**
384 **TIGRESS 18** [2] J W Unett 5-9-11 bl (56) J Quinn 9/2: 2660-652: Dwelt, held up, hdwy over 1f out, kept on, no threat to wnr: *1* **58a**
374 **SOTONIAN 18** [6] P S Felgate 11-8-9 (40) Lisa Jones (3) 25/1: 05000-53: Handy, rdn & sltly outpcd over 2f out, rallied over 1f out, kept on: *hd* **41a**
384 **SAVILES DELIGHT 18** [8] R Brotherton 5-10-0 bl (59) I Mongan 7/2 FAV: 2004-324: Cl-up, ev ch over 1f out, no extra: *hd* **59a**
312* **SO SOBER 25** [12] D Shaw 6-9-2 (47) R Winston 9/1: 00000-15: In tch, eff over 1f out, onepace: *1* **47a**
352 **ALLERTON BOY 22** [4] R J Hodges 5-8-9 (40) Dale Gibson 10/1: 0000-406: Dwelt, bhd, some late gains, nvr dngrs: *1* **37a**
374+* **LADY PROTECTOR 18** [9] J Balding 5-9-3 (48) P Makin (7) 10/1: 0060-417: Handy, btn over 1f out: *nk* **44a**
328 **KINGS BALLET 24** [1] P R Chamings 6-9-5 p (50) N Callan 8/1: 00300-08: In tch, wkng when short of room ins last. *1* **43a**
451 **SOAKED 9** [11] D W Chapman 11-9-6 bl (51) A Culhane 10/1: 350-2609: Handy, wknd well over 1f out *1¼* **40a**
328 **SAFRANINE 24** [7] Miss A Stokell 7-9-3 p (48) Ann Stokell 33/1: 00000-00: In tch, btn over 2f out. *hd* **36a**
286 **THE LEATHER WEDGE 28** [10] A Berry 5-9-3 (48) P Bradley (5) 20/1: 04020-60: Slow away, sn in tch, wknd over 2f out *4* **24a**
11 Ran 1m 03.47 (3.27) Owner Mrs Olive Meddle Trained at Royston

508 **1.50 Bet Direct No Q Demo 08000 837 888 Handicap Stakes Div 2 3yo+ 0-60 (F)** **[59]**
£2919 £834 £417 **5f rnd** **Going 45** **-14 Slow** Stalls Inside

348* **MYND 22** [12] R M Whitaker 4-10-0 (59) Dean McKeown 9/4 FAV: 50034-11: Cl-up, styd on to lead just ins last, pushed out: **67a**
4023} **OFF HIRE 150** [2] C Smith 8-9-3 vis (48) R Fitzpatrick 20/1: 005400-2: Cl-up, led over 2f out till just ins last, not pace of wnr: *2½* **48a**
349 **OUR CHELSEA BLUE 22** [4] A W Carroll 6-9-8 (53) A Quinn (5) 6/1: 00660-03: Slow away, held up, hdwy & swtchd right over 1f out, kept on, no threat: *1¾* **48a**
416 **WHITE O MORN 15** [3] B A McMahon 5-8-4 5ow T (30) G Gibbons 3/1: 00-04: In tch, onepace over 1f out. *½* **28a**
471 **LADIES KNIGHT 6** [6] D Shaw 4-9-10 (55) T Hamilton (5) 7/2: 001-6325: Slow away & bhd, some late gains: *¾* **46a**
385 **INDIAN SHORES 18** [9] M Mullineaux 5-9-3 P (48) Lisa Jones (3) 33/1: 006F-006: Sn bhd, modest late gains. *1¾* **34a**
413 **HENRY TUN 15** [5] J Balding 6-9-5 vis (50) J Edmunds 9/2: 3500-357: Handy, hung left & wknd over 1f out *2* **30a**
92 **LEVELLED 66** [1] D W Chapman 10-9-0 (45) A Culhane 50/1: 6/00/000-8: In tch, wknd appr fnl 1f. *shd* **25a**
374 **TUSCAN DREAM 18** [7] A Berry 9-8-9 (40) P Bradley (5) 33/1: 06060-09: Handy, wknd over 2f out. *2½* **13a**
4608} **FEELING BLUE 118** [10] B N Pollock 5-9-2 (47) J Fanning 20/1: 0102/60-0: Sn led, hdd over 2f out, wknd. *1½* **16a**
275 **PERCY DOUGLAS 30** [8] Miss A Stokell 4-9-11 vis (56) Ann Stokell 10/1: 003063-0: Slow away & al bhd. *hd* **24a**
11 Ran 1m 03.14 (2.94) Owner Derek and Jean Clee Trained at Scarcroft

509 **2.20 Bet Direct No Q Voice Automated Betting Maiden Stakes 4yo+ (D)**
£3341 £1028 £514 £257 **1m1f79y** **Going 45** **-14 Slow** Stalls Inside

14 **MUSICAL GIFT 79** [8] C N Allen 4-9-0 (70) I Mongan 15/8 FAV: 2240-1: Chsd ldrs, hdwy over 2f out, styd on to lead ins last, rdn out: **66a**
199 **PACIFIC OCEAN 46** [1] Mrs Stef Liddiard 5-9-1 t (48) J Quinn 4/1: 666534-2: Keen cl-up, led 6f out, kept on till collared ins last, not pace of wnr: *1* **63a**
416 **NOW AND AGAIN 15** [2] M W Easterby 5-9-1 Dale Gibson 12/1: 343: Led till 6f out, wknd over 2f out: *9* **46a**
416 **ADANTINO 15** [3] B R Millman 5-9-1 (52) G Baker 10/1: 6053-634: In tch, wknd over 2f out: *3* **42a**
401 **SKIP OF COLOUR 16** [5] P A Blockley 4-9-0 (75) W M Lordan 2/1: 340-45: Keen chsd ldrs, wknd over 2f out: *5* **34a**
ALBEE [7] Miss Gay Kelleway 4-9-0 M Fenton 25/1: 6: Dwelt, al bhd. *7* **24a**
MARINO MOU [4] Miss D Mountain 4-9-0 C Catlin 33/1: 7: Dwelt, al bhd on debut. *19* **0**
7 Ran 2m 0.79 (5.59) Owner Mr T P Ramsden Trained at Newmarket

510 **2.55 Bet Direct No Q 08000 93 66 93 Handicap Stakes 3yo 0-70 (E)** **[77]**
£3255 £930 £465 **7f rnd** **Going 45** **-29 Slow** Stalls Outside

333 **BRIDGEWATER BOYS 24** [12] K A Ryan 3-9-2 P (65) N Callan 9/2 JT FAV: 56215-41: Handy, hdwy to lead 2f out, kept on ins last, rdn out: **73a**
466* **EMARADIA 7** [9] A W Carroll 3-8-5 6ex bl (54) Joanna Badger 12/1: 5422-312: Led after 1f till 2f out, sn hung right but kept on ins last: *2* **57a**
368 **TURNBERRY 20** [10] J W Hills 3-8-10 bl (59) S Whitworth 5/1: 00004-43: Bhd, rdn over 2f out, onepace: *2* **57a**
389 **TURF PRINCESS 17** [11] Ian Emmerson 3-8-13 (62) D Fentiman (7) 9/1: 0226-124: Held up, hdwy over 3f out, wknd over 1f out: *1½* **57a**
295 **GOOD VIBRATIONS 27** [3] P F I Cole 3-8-4 (53) J Quinn 9/2 JT FAV: 0002-35: In tch, wknd well over 1f out: *5* **39a**
422 **DIAMOND GEORGE 14** [7] John Berry 3-8-8 (57) R Fitzpatrick 10/1: 266-56: Handy, lost place over 3f out: *6* **33a**
261 **SABLE N SILK 32** [1] D Haydn Jones 3-8-12 (61) A Culhane 10/1: 610-7: Handy, wknd over 2f out: *9* **21a**
284 **VRISAKI 28** [8] Miss D Mountain 3-8-11 (60) C Catlin 7/1: 00-28: Handy, btn over 2f out: *1½* **17a**
42 **BOOKIESINDEXDOTCOM 74** [4] J R Jenkins 3-9-0 vis (63) S W Kelly 9/1: 643222-9: Al bhd: *2* **16a**
9 Ran 1m 331.4 (5.2) Owner Bishopthorpe Racing Trained at Hambleton

511 **3.25 Littlewoods Bet Direct Conditions Stakes 3yo+ (C)**
£7186 £2726 £1363 £620 **1m100y rnd** **Going 45** **+05 Fast** Stalls Inside

278 **MI ODDS 30** [3] Mrs N Macauley 8-9-9 (90) A Culhane 7/1: 121212-1: Held up, rdn over 3f out, kept on well over 1f out, sn led, rdn clr, eased cl-home: **100a**
470+* **COUNTRYWIDE FLYER 7** [9] T D Barron 3-8-7 1ow (80) J P Spencer 2/1: 2114-512: Held up, hdwy over 2f out, kept on ins last, no threat to comfortable wnr: *4* **93a**
4095} **EPHESUS 146** [6] Miss Gay Kelleway 4-9-9 vis (85) M Fenton 50/1: 201330-3: Held up, gd hdwy over 2f out, swtchd right over 1f out, kept on same pace: *1½* **86a**
360* **HAIL THE CHIEF 21** [10] D Nicholls 7-10-0 (100) A Nicholls 6/5 FAV: 10/650-14: Cl-up, led 3f out till over 1f out, no extra: *2* **87a**
439 **ARC EL CIEL 11** [4] Mrs Stef Liddiard 6-9-9 vis (78) C Catlin 25/1: 0162-135: Held up, hdwy well over 1f out, no dngr: *2* **78a**
452 *2½* **73a**

WOLVERHAMPTON Friday 30.01.04 Lefthand, Sharp Track

	INVADER 9 [7] C E Brittain 8-9-9 bl (82) J Quinn 20/1: 0143-006: Handy, wknd over 2f out:		
433	LAKOTA BRAVE 13 [5] Mrs Stef Liddiard 10-9-9 (88) I Mongan 14/1: 1225-247: Al bhd:	shd	72a
1790}	CHAPPEL CRESENT 83 [8] D Nicholls 4-9-9 R Winston 50/1: 550540-8: Led after 1f till 3f out, wknd:	7	59a
419	FLYING TREATY 15 [1] Miss A Stokell 7-10-0 (84) C J Davies (7) 66/1: 0040-009: Cl-up, wknd over 2f out:	5	54a
423	PHOENIX NIGHTS 14 [2] A Berry 4-9-12 (45) P Bradley (5) 200/1: 1030-050: Al well bhd:	17	25a
10 Ran	1m 49.61 (3.41) Owner Tic-Taccom	Trained at Melton Mowbray	

512 4.00 Bet Direct No Q Selling Stakes 4yo+ (G)
£2604 £744 £372   7f rnd   Going 45   -21 Slow   Stalls Outside

450	WARLINGHAM 9 [12] P Howling 6-9-4 (52) J Fanning 14/1: 0210-001: Held up, hdwy over 2f out, led ins last, rdn out:		61a
483	MIZHAR 4 [10] J J Quinn 8-8-12 (55) R Winston 9/1: 0300-052: Held up, hdwy 2f out, kept on:	1¼	52a
440*	FEAST OF ROMANCE 11 [9] P Howling 7-9-4 p (48) S W Kelly 3/1: 336-3313: Held up, hdwy well over 1f out, kept on ins last:	1¼	58a
373	SUDRA 18 [1] J O'Reilly 7-8-12 bl (49) D Allan (7) 20/1: 000-3344: Sn bhd, eff over 2f out, onepace:	½	51a
440	LUCAYAN MONARCH 11 [6] P A Blockley 6-9-4 p (56) Dean McKeown 5/2 FAV: 64-21125: Handy, onepace over 1f out, reportedly fin lame:	¾	55a
483	AROGANT PRINCE 4 [5] A W Carroll 7-8-12 bl (53) A Culhane 16/1: 200-4406: Sn clr ldr, rdn & hdd ins last, wkng & hmpd ins last:	¾	47a
440	BULAWAYO 11 [2] Andrew Reid 7-8-12 vis (53) A Nicholls 7/1: 2030-537: Chsd ldr, wknd over 1f out:	2	43a
440	JAN BRUEGHEL 11 [4] T D Barron 5-8-12 (63) P Makin (7) 4/1: 0240-348: Sn bhd, reportedly broke a blood vessel:	10	25a
2152}	ALWAYS BELIEVE 230 [7] Mrs P Ford 8-8-12 t (48) R Ffrench 40/1: 030600-9: Al bhd:	2	21a
465	LOVES DESIGN 7 [11] Miss S J Wilton 7-8-12 p (48) A Quinn (5) 25/1: 350-0600: Keen in tch, wknd over 2f out:	½	20a
241}	HEATHERS GIRL 406 [3] D Haydn Jones 5-8-7 (46) Paul Eddery 40/1: 556040/-0: Handy, btn over 2f out:	5	5a
2322}	BLUE BIJOU 223 [8] T T Clement 4-8-12 D Fox (5) 20/1: 0-0: Al bhd.	5	0a
12 Ran	1m 30.8 (4.6) Owner Mr David Andrew Brown	Trained at Newmarket	

513 4.30 Bet Direct Through Sky Active Handicap Stakes 4yo+ 0-80 (D)   [79]
£4076 £1254 £627 £314   1m1f79y   Going 45   +08 Fast   Stalls Inside

382*	INTRICATE WEB 18 [10] E J Alston 8-9-11 (76) D Allan (3) 9/4 FAV: 45043-11: Held up, hdwy well over 1f out, styd on strongly ins last to get up cl-home, drvn out:		83a
75	TO WIT TO WOO 70 [8] B W Hills 4-8-4 (56) Dean McKeown 4/1: 040014-2: Cl-up, hdwy over 2f out, led ins last, collared last strides:	shd	62a
382	SKYLARKER 18 [1] W S Kittow 6-10-0 (79) I Mongan 5/1: 04304-23: With ldr, led over 2f out till ins last, no extra:	1	83a
755}	AIR MAIL 328 [5] Mrs N Macauley 7-10-0 (79) A Culhane 3/1: 000060-4: In tch, onepace fnl 2f on reapp:	1¾	80a
463	DUBAI DREAMS 8 [9] M J Polglase 4-8-4 vis (56) J P Spencer 7/1: 0140-425: Led till over 2f out, no extra ins last.	1½	54a
4897}	AFRICAN SAHARA 97 [12] Miss D Mountain 5-9-13 t (78) G Carter 4/1: 100226-6: Held up, btn well over 1f out.	4	69a
318*	PENWELL HILL 25 [3] T D Barron 5-9-4 (69) D Mernagh 11/2: 13465-17: Handy, wknd 2f out:	hd	59a
	BALLYRUSH 216 [11] K R Burke 4-9-2 (68) R Keogh (7) 33/1: 500/600-8: Hld up, eff 3f out, wknd 2f out:	4	51a
4614}	SAY WHAT YOU SEE 116 [7] J W Hills 4-9-3 (67) S Whitworth 25/1: 463200-9: Nvr a factor:	2½	51a
464	YELLOW RIVER 7 [4] R Curtis 4-8-5 (57) S W Kelly 33/1: 00000-40: In tch, wknd over 2f out.	1¾	3a
	HARRY POTTER 76 [6] K R Burke 5-9-5 (70) Darren Williams 33/1: 632213-0: Al bhd.	18	0a
	BOUGHT DIRECT 110 [2] R J Smith 5-8-12 (63) Joanna Badger 25/1: 200000-0: Slow away & al well bhd.	2½	0a
12 Ran	2m 01.7 (3.5) Owner Morris Oliver Pierce	Trained at Preston	

LINGFIELD Saturday 31.01.04 Lefthand, V Sharp Track

Official Going Standard

514 12.15 Bet Direct No Q 08000 93 66 93 Maiden Stakes 3yo+ (D)
£4199 £1292 £646 £323   1m p/track rnd   Going 37   -43 Slow   Stalls Outside

	QUICKSTYX [3] M R Channon 3-8-2 C Catlin 5/2: 1: Dwelt, mid-div, hdwy 2f out, styd on for press to lead cl-home:		68a
323	SPINNING DOVE 25 [11] N A Graham 4-9-8 (65) J P Spencer 5/2: 46423-32: Dwelt, rear, smooth hdwy from halfway, led over 1f out, rdn & hdd nr fin:	nk	68a
177	LORD OF THE SEA 52 [1] Jamie Poulton 3-8-8 1ow (73) I Mongan 4/1: 0655-3: Trkd ldrs, ch over 1f out, not pace of front pair:	4	65a
	THE KINGS BISHOP [5] S C Williams 3-8-7 G Carter 25/1: 4: Prom, rdn & chall over 1f out, no extra dist:	nk	63a
338	BENNANABAA 24 [4] S C Burrough 5-9-13 t A Nicholls 66/1: 05: Keen & led after 1f till over 1f out, wknd.	2	59a
430	PRIORS DALE 14 [12] K Bell 4-9-13 (72) D Sweeney 2/1 FAV: 40020-26: Sn handy wide, wknd over 1f out.	1¼	57a
	YOUNG DYNASTY [9] E A Wheeler 4-9-13 S Carson 50/1: 7: Dwelt, rear, nvr able to chall on debut.	¾	56a
322	OUR LITTLE ROSIE 25 [7] M Blanshard 3-8-2 J Quinn 25/1: 08: Al towards rear.	7	38a
425	SCORCH 15 [2] H J Collingridge 3-8-7 (53) Joanna Badger 50/1: 56-49: U.r. & bolted bef start, sn struggling.	¾	42a
449	RECKLESS FRED 10 [9] Miss K M George 5-9-13 Derek Nolan (7) 50/1: 00: Led 1f, chsd ldr 5f.	nk	41a
4945}	POLISH RHAPSODY 93 [8] J A Supple 3-8-4 2ow J Fanning 33/1: 0-0: Mid-div, btn 3f out, abs.	nk	37a
367	ONCE AROUND 21 [10] T G Mills 3-8-7 A Clark 14/1: 0-00: Keen, chsd ldrs wide till halfway.	2½	35a
12 Ran	1m 42.62 (6.42) Owner Mr John Breslin	Trained at West Ilsley	

515 12.45 Bet Direct No Q Classified Stakes 4yo+ 0-65 (E)
£3276 £936 £468   1m5f p/track   Going 37   -01 Slow   Stalls Inside

504+*	FALL IN LINE 2 [2] Sir Mark Prescott 4-9-6 (60) J Mackay 30/100 FAV: 343-111: Led/dsptd lead, rdn clr 4f out, eased down ins last, val for 10L+:		88a
493	EASTER OGIL 3 [5] Jane Southcombe 9-9-5 (64) I Mongan 8/1: 22-50332: Dwelt, rear, styd on for press fnl 2f, nvr threat to easy wnr:	7	66a

133

484 **LAZZAZ 5** [10] P W Hiatt 6-9-5 (58) A Culhane 20/1: 00-43533: Trkd ldrs halfway, rdn & chsd wnr 3f out, sn no impress: shd **66a**
358* **PHANTOM STOCK 22** [8] W Jarvis 4-9-0 (65) M Tebbutt 6/1: 0/061-214: Mid-div, drvn & onepace fnl 4f: nk **65a**
1350} **GRAND PRAIRIE 271** [4] G L Moore 8-9-5 (65) S Whitworth 33/1: 1140/00-5: Dwelt, rear, only mod prog: 5 **58a**
174 **INDIAN BLAZE 52** [7] Andrew Reid 10-9-5 (48) S Donohoe (7) 66/1: 340B00-6: Rear, hdwy to chase ldrs 3f out, sn no extra: 3 **54a**
359 **MUNFARID 22** [3] P G Murphy 4-9-0 t (62) P Doe 50/1: 04454-37: Cl-up till 4f out, sn wknd: 19 **33a**
288 **ARC EN CIEL 28** [12] G L Moore 6-9-5 (60) J Quinn 33/1: 00/00/0-48: Mid-div, no ch fnl 3f. 6 **25a**
477 **ITSONLYAGAME 7** [11] R Ingram 4-9-0 (55) N Callan 66/1: 5406-109: Sn rdn & al rear: ¾ **24a**
477 **SEKWANA 7** [6] Miss A M Newton Smith 5-9-2 p (48) D Sweeney 100/1: 02360/-00: Mid-div, struggling halfway. 16 **0a**
421 **MADIBA 16** [9] P Howling 5-9-5 bl (58) J P Spencer 25/1: 0400-160: Prom till wknd qckly 5f out: 7 **0a**
11 Ran 2m 47.18 (4.88) Owner Neil Greig - Osborne House II Trained at Newmarket

516 1.20 Betdirect Co Uk Classified Stakes 3yo+ 0-70 (E)

£3297 £942 £471 **6f p/track rnd** **Going 37** **-00 Slow** Stalls Inside

492 **WHIPPASNAPPER 3** [1] J R Best 4-9-7 (65) N Pollard 9/1: 000-0121: Made all, drvn & held on gamely cl-home: **70a**
499 **TEMPER TANTRUM 3** [8] Andrew Reid 6-9-7 p (62) S Donohoe (7) 16/1: 5023-552: Rear, drvn & styd on well ins last, nrst fin: nk **69a**
45 **SEMENOVSKII 75** [5] P W D'Arcy 4-9-7 (70) Paul Eddery 6/1: 000600-3: Rear, short of room halfway, styd on fnl 1f, nrst fin: 1½ **64a**
450 **PHECKLESS 10** [2] J M Bradley 5-9-7 (67) C Catlin 14/1: 0564-034: Chsd wnr halfway, onepace dist: ½ **62a**
492 **PANJANDRUM 3** [4] N E Berry 6-9-7 (67) M Savage (5) 12/1: 3001-035: Dwelt, sn mid-div, no extra fnl 1f: ½ **60a**
451* **PRINCE AARON 10** [11] C N Allen 4-9-7 (68) G Carter 11/8 FAV: 0062-116: Keen & held up, onepace. shd **60a**
407 **HARD TO CATCH 17** [12] D K Ivory 6-9-7 (69) I Mongan 20/1: 00555-07: Chsd ldrs, rdn & no extra dist: 1¼ **56a**
413 **TICKLE 16** [3] P J Makin 6-9-4 vis t (47) D Sweeney 100/1: 05060-48: Towards rear, only mod prog. ¾ **51a**
41 **RIVER DAYS 75** [10] Miss Gay Kelleway 6-9-4 bl t (65) M Fenton 50/1: 014400-9: Chsd wnr, btn over 1f out. 1½ **46a**
474 **RIPPLE EFFECT 7** [13] C A Dwyer 4-9-4 (73) N Callan 6/1: 102-2120: Chsd ldrs till over 1f out: nk **45a**
41 **INDIAN MAIDEN 75** [6] M S Saunders 4-9-4 (70) S Whitworth 20/1: 110600-0: Sn rdn & struggling, mod prog: 2 **39a**
329 **MADRASEE 25** [14] L Montague Hall 6-9-4 (68) R Miles (3) 9/1: 31021-20: Chsd ldrs till over 2f out: ¾ **37a**
4433} **MULAN PRINCESS 129** [7] S C Burrough 4-9-4 (52) A Nicholls 100/1: 046000-0: Sn rear & struggling, abs. 3 **28a**
487 **BELLA BEGUINE 4** [9] A Bailey 5-9-4 vis (70) T Hamilton (5) 25/1: 00202-50: Al outpcd, qck reapp: ¾ **26a**
14 Ran 1m 12.6 (2.2) Owner Miss Vanessa Church Trained at Maidstone

517 1.55 Bet Direct No Q Demo 08000 837 888 Handicap Stakes 3yo+ 0-80 (D) [78]

£4199 £1292 £646 £323 **1m p/track rnd** **Going 37** **-17 Slow** Stalls Outside

439* **VORTEX 12** [4] Miss Gay Kelleway 5-9-11 e t (75) M Fenton 7/2 FAV: D1160-11: Chsd ldr 3f out, drvn & led over 1f out, held on gamely for press: **79a**
12 **DEEPER IN DEBT 80** [10] J Akehurst 6-9-8 (72) G Carter 4/1: 003112-2: Chsd ldrs, rdn & hdwy to lead over 2f out, hdd over 1f out, kept on well for press, just held: nk **74a**
131 **COLLEGE DELINQUENT 60** [2] K Bell 5-9-2 t (66) S Whitworth 10/1: 003303-3: Rear, drvn & kept on fnl 1f, nrst fin: ½ **68a**
369 **TERRAQUIN 21** [8] J J Bridger 4-9-12 (76) G Baker 66/1: 46416-04: Rear, eff wide, not able to chall: 1 **77a**
4434} **RUDOOD 129** [6] Lady Herries 4-10-0 (78) J Quinn 10/1: 42/410-5: Rear, short of room over 2f out & again over 1f out, nrst fin: nk **78a**
218 **LIBERTY ROYAL 45** [9] P J Makin 5-9-7 (71) D Sweeney 12/1: 040000-6: Keen mid-div, no impress 1f out, abs. hd **69a**
433 **NASHAAB 14** [11] P D Evans 7-10-0 BL (78) S Donohoe (7) 16/1: 00305-07: Rear, only mod prog for press: 2½ **71a**
1642} **SUMMER RECLUSE 255** [3] B R Johnson 5-9-13 (77) N Chalmers (5) 9/2: 421013-8: Dwelt, sn mid-div, wknd dist, abs. 1¾ **67a**
3933} **SIR FRANCIS 156** [12] J Noseda 6-9-8 (72) S W Kelly 20/1: 504060-9: Chsd ldrs, wknd fnl 2f, abs. hd **61a**
369 **BOUNDLESS PROSPECT 21** [1] J W Hills 5-9-8 (72) M Hills 14/1: 05500-00: Chsd clr ldr halfway, btn 2f out. 1½ **58a**
273 **AGILIS 32** [5] Jamie Poulton 4-10-0 (78) I Mongan 11/1: 500046-0: Mid-div, btn 3f out: 3 **59a**
4396} **CONCER ETO 131** [7] S C Williams 5-9-9 BL (73) M Henry 14/1: 301200-0: Sn in clr lead, wknd & hdd over 2f out. 29 **0a**
12 Ran 1m 40.5 (4.3) Owner Coriolis Partnership Trained at Newmarket

518 2.30 Bet Direct On 0800 32 93 93 Handicap Stakes 4yo+ 0-90 (C) [90]

£7293 £2767 £1383 £629 **7f p/track rnd** **Going 37** **+05 Fast** Stalls Inside

474* **GREY PEARL 7** [8] Miss Gay Kelleway 5-9-1 (77) M Fenton 14/1: 0534-511: Chsd ldrs, led dist, rdn & styd on strongly: **85a**
419 **JUST FLY 16** [6] S Kirk 4-9-9 (85) A Culhane 7/1: 0505-222: Trkd ldrs, drvn to chall dist, not pace of wnr: 1¾ **88a**
386 **GREENWOOD 18** [1] P G Murphy 6-8-13 (75) D Kinsella 33/1: 62200-03: Rear, styd on for press fnl 2f, not able to chall: nk **77a**
262 **THE BEST YET 33** [3] A G Newcombe 6-9-0 (76) S Whitworth 7/1: 463022-4: Keen mid-div, hdwy to chase ldrs over 1f out, no extra ins last: ½ **77a**
369 **CORMORANT WHARF 21** [9] T E Powell 4-9-1 (77) A Quinn (5) 12/1: 16/0-065: Dwelt, rear, swtchd & styd on late, fin fast: ½ **77a**
361 **NO TIME 22** [5] M J Polglase 4-9-4 (80) I Mongan 20/1: 0000-666: Led till dist, wknd: shd **80a**
401* **DAWN PIPER 17** [10] D R Loder 4-9-9 (85) J P Spencer 6/5 FAV: 32-17: Mid-div, no impress fnl 1f: nk **84a**
474 **CLOUD DANCER 7** [15] K A Ryan 5-8-12 (74) N Callan 16/1: 03310-38: Rear, nvr able to chall: 1¼ **70a**
431 **QUEENS RHAPSODY 14** [14] A Bailey 4-10-0 (90) T Hamilton (5) 10/1: 4/1150-29: Keen, in tch wide, btn dist. nk **85a**
386* **PRIMA STELLA 18** [7] J A R Toller 5-8-11 (73) Lisa Jones (3) 33/1: 1020-410: Rear, nvr able to chall: nk **67a**
273 **BORDER EDGE 32** [11] J J Bridger 6-9-6 vis (82) G Baker 25/1: 012000-0: Sn cl-up till over 1f out. ½ **75a**
482 **HURRICANE COAST 5** [16] D Flood 5-8-13 bl (75) P Doe 11/2: 1131320: Wide/rear, nvr a threat: shd **68a**
431 **CHATEAU NICOL 14** [12] B G Powell 5-9-1 vis (77) J Fanning 10/1: 1100-130: Chsd ldr halfway, btn 1f out. 2 **66a**
4676] **PAIRING 69** [4] G L Moore 6-9-2 (78) R Brisland 66/1: 122366-0: Al bhd, abs: 6 **56a**
14 Ran 1m25.03 (2.23) Owner Andrea Wilkinson Gay Kelleway Trained at Newmarket

519 3.05 Littlewoods Bet Direct Handicap Stakes 4yo+ 0-100 (C) [100]

£14993 £5687 £2844 £1293 **1m2f p/track** **Going 37** **-03 Slow** Stalls Inside

82 **BLUE SKY THINKING 70** [1] K R Burke 5-9-10 (96) Darren Williams 16/1: 016334-1: In tch, hdwy over 3f out & led dist, rdn out: **102a**
452 **NORTHSIDE LODGE 10** [3] P W Harris 6-8-13 (85) P Doe 7/2 FAV: 20404-22: Trkd ldrs, drvn to chase wnr ins last, no extra: 1¾ **87a**

423*	**HIAWATHA** 15 [12] P A Blockley 5-8-4 (76) J Quinn 16/1: 0201-413: In tch, kept on onepace:		1¼	76a
452	**PARAGON OF VIRTUE** 10 [5] P Mitchell 7-8-7 (79) J Fanning 11/2: 63310-34: Handy & led over 3f out, drvn & hdd dist, fdd:		1	78a
419	**YORK CLIFF** 16 [14] W M Brisbourne 6-8-3 (75) B Swarbrick (7) 33/1: 20200-05: Drvn rear, lkd reluctant early, late gains for press, nrst fin:		hd	73a
452	**DOWER HOUSE** 10 [4] Andrew Turnell 9-8-9 (81) D Corby (3) 4/1: 20310-46: Prom wide, ch 2f out, sn no extra:		¾	78a
475	**TIGHT SQUEEZE** 7 [10] P W Hiatt 7-8-9 2ow (79) A Culhane 11/2: 011-6537: Mid-div, no impress fnl 2f:		3	74a
452	**RYANS FUTURE** 10 [7] J Akehurst 4-8-6 (80) C Catlin 10/1: 51415-58: Held up, no impress fnl 2f:		2	70a
293	**BRILLIANT RED** 28 [9] Jamie Poulton 11-8-13 t (85) S Whitworth 16/1: 44003-09: Slow away & nvr factor.		12	60a
262	**HARIPUR** 33 [6] Andrew Reid 5-9-11 (97) S Donohoe (7) 12/1: 121110-0: Trkd ldr, led 5f out till over 3f out, wknd.		6	64a
475	**TE QUIERO GB** 7 [2] Miss Gay Kelleway 6-9-4 t (90) M Fenton 25/1: 5230-000: Led till 5f out, sn btn.		1¾	55a
433	**STAR OF NORMANDIE** 14 [8] G G Margarson 5-8-11 (83) A McCarthy 10/1: 12112-00: Chsd ldrs till over 3f out.		6	40a
511	**LAKOTA BRAVE** 1 [13] Mrs Stef Liddiard 10-9-2 (88) I Mongan 20/1: 1225-2470: Mid-div wide, sn struggling.		1¼	43a

13 Ran   2m 06.83 (4.03)   Owner Triple Trio Partnership   Trained at Leyburn

---

520   3.40 Bet Direct In Vision Sky Page 293 Handicap Stakes 4yo+ 0-65 (F)   [65]
£3017 £862 £431   1m2f p/track   Going 37   -22 Slow   Stalls Inside

434	**TRUE COMPANION** 14 [11] N P Littmoden 5-9-11 (62) J P Guillambert (3) 7/1: 61533-01: Trkd ldrs, styd on to lead ins last, hands & heels:			68a
266	**TREETOPS HOTEL** 32 [7] B R Johnson 5-9-7 p (58) N Chalmers (5) 7/1: 000000-2: Towards rear, hdwy wide & drvn/led over 1f out, hdd ins last, no extra:		1¼	60a
434	**FIGURA** 14 [6] R Ingram 6-9-9 (60) N Callan 12/1: 03000-03: Rear, styd on for press fnl 2f, not pace of wnr:		1¼	60a
1021}	**CROSSWAYS** 188 [3] P D Evans 6-9-12 (63) S Donohoe (7) 14/1: 21/P034-4: Dsptd lead till went on over 3f out, hdd over 1f out, no extra:		½	62a
4037}	**INCHINNAN** 150 [5] C Weedon 7-9-7 (58) J Quinn 12/1: 4/46500-5: Trkd ldrs, no extra over 1f out:		½	56a
434	**QUANTUM LEAP** 14 [1] S Dow 7-9-11 (62) Paul Eddery 8/1: 04153-06: Keen rear, only mod prog:		nk	59a
3756}	**KAVI** 164 [4] Simon Earle 4-9-8 (61) G Baker 25/1: 2/43666-7: Mid-div, onepace fnl 2f, abs, new yard.		shd	58a
215	**STATE OF BALANCE** 45 [14] K Bell 6-9-11 (62) L Keniry (3) 8/1: 0040-8: Rear, only mod prog:		¾	58a
265	**SNUKI** 33 [12] G L Moore 5-9-11 (62) S Whitworth 33/1: 200000-9: Rear, rdn & no impress.		5	52a
476*	**CORONADO FOREST** 7 [2] M R Hoad 5-10-0 (65) A Culhane 7/1: 060-2410: Dsptd lead 7f, sn btn:		7	46a
477	**ZAWRAK** 7 [8] I W McInnes 5-9-7 (58) Natalia Gemelova (7) 7/1: 0003-630: Trkd ldrs wide, btn 3f out:		2	36a
434	**LYRICAL WAY** 14 [13] P R Chamings 5-9-11 vis (62) I Mongan 5/1 FAV: 02221-40: Mid-div, no ch fnl 3f:		3	36a
3089}	**PONT NEUF** 192 [10] J W Hills 4-9-8 (61) M Hills 33/1: 20/0200-0: Trkd ldrs till over 3f out, t.o., abs.		9	24a
2155*}	**KARAOKE** 231 [9] S Kirk 4-9-12 (65) J D Smith 8/1: 102331-0: Keen & prom wide 7f, abs.		½	27a

14 Ran   2m 08.74 (5.94)   Owner Novowel Racing   Trained at Newmarket

---

521   4.15 Betdirect Co Uk Maiden Stakes 3yo+ (D)
£3513 £1081 £541 £270   1m4f p/track   Going 37   -23 Slow   Stalls Inside

118	**SO VITAL** 63 [5] Mrs Lydia Pearce 4-9-10 J Quinn 7/4 FAV: 62-1: Prom & chsd ldr 4f out, led over 2f out till over 1f out, rallied gamely for press to narrowly assert cl-home:			73a
269	**ELEGANT GRACIE** 32 [9] R Guest 4-9-5 (61) J P Spencer 6/1: 003-2: Towards rear, short of room 4f out, rapid prog from 3f out & led over 1f out, hdd ins last, just held cl-home:		hd	67a
401	**ALISA** 17 [8] B I Case 4-9-5 T Lisa Jones (3) 66/1: 03: Towards rear, outpcd 4f out, late gains, no dngr:		6	59a
4486}	**IMPERATIVE** 126 [7] Ian Williams 4-9-10 (75) M Henry 14/1: 6/55000-4: Rear, eff wide 4f out, no dngr.		1¼	62a
439	**BOWING** 12 [3] P G Murphy 4-9-10 (70) D Kinsella 9/1: 20423-05: Rear, late gains, nvr dngr.		3	58a
476	**SKIBEREEN** 7 [13] I W McInnes 4-9-10 bl t (70) Natalia Gemelova (7) 10/1: 24232-56: Keen & prom, led over 5f out, pulled clr with wnr over 3f out, hdd over 2f out & wknd.		3	54a
430	**MYSTERLOVER** 14 [10] N P Littmoden 4-9-10 I Mongan 25/1: 4P-07: Mid-div, sn rdn, no impress fnl 3f.		½	53a
388	**NEWTONIAN** 18 [4] J Parkes 5-10-0 (69) Dean McKeown 5/1: 6/23-38: Pushed along mid-div, no impress 3f out.		9	42a
428	**LA CONCHA** 14 [14] Mrs L C Jewell 3-8-6 3ow S W Kelly 12/1: 09: Dwelt, chsd ldr, carried wide early & btn 3f out.		1¼	43a
429	**PYRRHIC** 14 [6] R M Flower 5-10-0 bl (50) S Donohoe (7) 9/1: 505-3020: Al bhd:		nk	39a
1575}	**KIRAT** 977 [12] G L Moore 6-10-0 S Whitworth 6/1: 0//-0: Dwelt, sn handy till 4f out, long abs, new yard.		½	38a
	LUTEUR DES PICTONS 353 [11] B G Powell 5-10-0 A Hindley (4) 40/1: 6-0: Prom till 4f out, jumps fit.		5	31a
367	**DESERT TOMMY** 21 [15] T G Mills 3-8-3 HBL R Miles (3) 20/1: 0-00: Slowly away, sn rdn to go handy, carried wide on bend after 3f & btn 4f out:		½	30a
462	**TAMARINA** 9 [1] N E Berry 3-7-12 p (55) Joanna Badger 66/1: 5004-000: Led, tried to run out on bend after 3f, sn struggling.		9	14a
	WILD WILD WES [2] R Ingram 4-9-10 N Day 40/1: 0: Slowly away & sn bhd on debut.		dist	0a

15 Ran   2m 36.34 (7.14)   Owner Mr Jim Furlong   Trained at Newmarket

---

Official Going Standard

522   1.30 Betdirect Co Uk Banded Stakes Div 1 3yo+ 0-45 (H)
£1635 £467 £234   1m1f79y f/sand rnd   Going 68   -23 Slow   Stalls Inside

380	**RED STORM** 21 [4] J R Boyle 5-9-8 VIS (45) R Miles (3) 4/1: 2105-061: Trkd ldrs, led over 2f out, rdn out:			50a
489	**MAGGIES PET** 6 [5] K Bell 7-9-8 t (45) D R McCabe 13/8 FAV: 360-2522: Cl-up & led over 6f out till over 2f out, not pace of wnr:		2½	45a
338	**UNSUITED** 26 [7] J E Long 5-9-8 (40) Natalia Gemelova (7) 50/1: 06500-03: Chsd ldrs halfway, not able to chall:		3½	38a
366	**AMANPURI** 23 [6] Miss Gay Kelleway 6-9-8 (45) M Fenton 4/1: 3/0000-04: Wide/rear, eff 3f out, onepce.		6	27a
2780}	**BEVIER** 207 [1] T Wall 10-9-8 (45) N Chalmers (5) 7/1: 100040-5: Rear, sn rdn, little hdwy, abs.		½	26a
465	**GIUST IN TEMP** 10 [3] P W Hiatt 5-9-8 (40) A Culhane 7/1: 650-4206: Trkd ldrs halfway, wknd qckly dist:		¾	25a
448	**ELLAMYTE** 12 [9] D G Bridgwater 4-9-8 (45) S Righton 33/1: 30300-07: Led 2f, btn 3f out.		1¼	22a
3979}			12	2a

135

	ARTE ET LABORE 156 [8] K A Ryan 4-9-8 (45) P Fessey 25/1: 620004-8: Al bhd:	
4918}	MARSHAL BOND 97 [2] B Smart 6-9-8 bl (45) F Lynch 12/1: 000000-8: Sn bhd, 2 month jumps abs.	1¾ -1a
9 Ran	2m 06.72 (8.52) Owner Mr Brian McAtavey	Trained at Epsom

---

523 | **2.00 Bet Direct No Q Demo 08000 837 888 Apprentice Banded Stakes 4yo+ 0-40 (H)**
£1288 £368 £184   **1m4f f/sand**   **Going 68**   **-04 Slow**   Stalls Inside

458	BELLA PAVLINA 11 [3] W M Brisbourne 6-9-3 (40) B Swarbrick (5) 1/1 FAV: 45/36-121: Mid-div, hdwy trav well to lead 4f out, rdn clr over 2f out, v easily:	63a
3999}	THE BEDUTH NAVI 154 [2] D G Bridgwater 4-9-0 (40) D Nolan 66/1: 0/000-2: Chsd ldrs, lost pl 4f out, rallied to take 2nd, no ch with wnr:	22 38a
194	GALLEY LAW 51 [7] R Craggs 4-9-0 (30) T Eaves 66/1: 0000-3: Mid-div, onepace fnl 2:	½ 37a
445	NEWCLOSE 13 [10] N Tinkler 4-9-0 t (40) T Hamilton 11/2: 500-3334: Chsd ldrs halfway, sn no impress.	1 36a
445	THINK QUICK 13 [8] R Hollinshead 4-9-0 (35) R Kennemore (7) 50/1: 00040-05: Held up, nvr a factor.	½ 35a
445	VERMILION CREEK 13 [11] R Hollinshead 5-9-3 p (30) Stephanie Hollinshead (3) 25/1: 0006-506: Chsd ldr 3f out, wknd.	2½ 31a
568}	GREENBOROUGH 360 [12] Mrs P Ford 6-9-3 P (30) Derek Nolan (5) 66/1: 00/50/00-7: Trkd ldr, briefly led over 4f out, sn btn:	7 22a
358	MOYNE PLEASURE 24 [4] Paul Johnson 6-9-3 (40) N Chalmers 9/1: 24450-08: Held up, rdn & btn 3f out:	9 11a
375	FRATERNITY 21 [6] J A Pickering 7-9-3 VIS (35) A Quinn 20/1: 5064-609: Keen, led 1m, sn btn:	5 0a
4918}	KINGSDON 97 [9] T J Fitzgerald 7-9-3 vis t (35) P Mulrennan 20/1: 404000-0: Sn rdn & al bhd:	20 0a
469	KHUZDAR 10 [5] A Bailey 5-9-3 P (40) B O'Neill (5) 100/30: 640-0320: Hld up & sn struggling:	2½ 0a
1626}	HABIBTI SARA 258 [1] A W Carroll 4-9-0 (35) M Savage (3) 40/1: 000-0: Trkd ldrs, lost pl from halfway:	dist 0a
12 Ran	2m 42.28 (8.68) Owner The Cartmel Syndicate	Trained at Baschurch

---

524 | **2.30 Bet Direct No Q On 08000 93 66 93 Claiming Stakes 3yo+ (H)**
£1330 £380 £190   **6f f/sand rnd**   **Going 68**   **-20 Slow**   Stalls Inside

480	FOOLISH THOUGHT 7 [5] R A Fahey 4-9-7 p (56) T Hamilton (5) 100/30 FAV: 040-6541: Chsd ldrs, sn pushed along, outpcd halfway but rallied from press to lead over 1f out, all out:	53a
447	BELLS BEACH 13 [9] P Howling 6-9-4 (40) S W Kelly 5/1: 30040-62: Mid-div, hdwy wide for press over 1f out, just held:	hd 50a
512	AROGANT PRINCE 3 [7] A W Carroll 7-9-10 bl (53) Rory Moore (7) 11/2: 00-44063: Trkd ldrs, led over 2f out till over 1f out, no extra:	2 50a
500	ATTORNEY 4 [1] D Shaw 6-9-10 e (47) Lisa Jones (3) 8/1: 4-301004: Mid-div, not able to chall:	1 47a
483	HEATHYARDSBLESSING 7 [8] R Hollinshead 7-9-10 P (45) Dean McKeown 20/1: 0623-065: Chsd ldrs till ins last.	2 41a
447	FLYING FAISAL 13 [6] J M Bradley 6-9-10 (35) C J Davies (3) 40/1: 000-0006: Mid-div, not able to chall:	shd 41a
410	NEUTRAL NIGHT 18 [4] R Brotherton 4-9-4 vis (45) Derek Nolan (7) 33/1: 0660-307: Rear, nrst fin:	½ 33a
448	KOMENA 12 [13] J W Payne 6-9-5 (45) I Mongan 8/1: 5240-508: Al rear:	3½ 24a
483*	PIPS SONG 7 [10] P W Hiatt 9-9-9 (40) J Fanning 7/1: 000-0019: Outpcd, nvr able to chall:	1¼ 24a
310	PRESENT N CORRECT 28 [2] J M Bradley 11-9-7 bl (30) Simon Jones (7) 66/1: 3006-000: Dwelt & al bhd.	5 9a
500	ON THE TRAIL 4 [3] D W Chapman 7-9-10 BL (50) A Culhane 11/2: 30000-00: Keen, led till over 2f out, wknd.	16 0a
460	CAMPBELLS TALE 11 [11] T J Fitzgerald 5-9-8 T D Mernagh 66/1: 00: Wide, al bhd, t-strap.	29 0a
12 Ran	1m 18.06 (5.26) Owner Northumbria Leisure Ltd	Trained at Malton

---

525 | **3.05 Betdirect Co Uk Ban 'ed Stakes Div 2 3yo+ 0-45 (H)**
£1631 £466 £233   **1m1f79y f/sand rnd Going 68**   **-06 Slow**   Stalls Inside

287	PRINCE PROSPECT 31 [8] Mrs L Stubbs 8-9-8 (45) Kristin Stubbs (7) 7/1: 3/4640-01: Slow away, sn pushed along, hdwy from halfway & led dist, rdn clr:	49a
378	PHANTOM FLAME 21 [3] M Johnston 4-9-8 (45) J Fanning 4/1: 00000-52: Led till 2f out, rallied & briefly led again over 1f out, no ch with wnr:	3½ 41a
469	HAITHEM 10 [7] D Shaw 7-9-8 e (30) Lisa Jones (3) 40/1: 00-60003: Mid-div, styd on for press late.	hd 40a
445	DEBBIE 13 [9] B D Leavy 5-9-8 (40) S Whitworth 4/1: 1133-004: Trkd ldrs, rdn & led 2f out till dist, kept on onepace	shd 40a
505	SEA YA MAITE 4 [4] S R Bowring 10-9-8 t (35) J Bramhill 14/1: 00-05235: Mid-div, no extra over 1f out:	5 31a
427	WODHILL FOLLY 17 [2] D Morris 7-9-8 vis (45) I Mongan 15/8 FAV: 41500-46: Mid-div, rdn & btn 2f out:	¾ 30a
297	PARIS DREAMER 30 [5] M W Easterby 3-8-1 (40) Dale Gibson 16/1: 0000-07: Mid-div, lost pl early, sn struggling:	1¼ 27a
378	BEAUTEOUS 21 [6] A Berry 5-9-8 (45) F Lynch 11/1: 20400-08: Led/dsptd lead 7f, sn btn.	5 18a
206	SABRELINE 48 [1] B R Foster 5-9-8 BL (45) C Catlin 14/1: 030550-9: Sn struggling, t.o.:	26 0a
9 Ran	2m 05.19 (6.99) Owner Mrs L Stubbs	Trained at Malton

---

526 | **3.35 Littlewoods Bet Direct Median Auction Maiden Stakes 3-5yo (H)**
£1449 £414 £207   **1m100y f/sand rnd Going 68**   **-01 Slow**   Stalls Inside

396	IAMBACK 19 [4] Miss Gay Kelleway 4-9-5 p (47) M Fenton 5/1: 0606-261: Handy & led over 4f out, hung right over 1f out, drvn out:_	52a
355	TURKS AND CAICOS 25 [5] P C Haslam 3-8-5 (58) Rory Moore (7) 4/9 FAV: 040-22: Chsd ldrs, rdn & outpcd 2f out, rallied well for press, just held:	nk 56a
	PADDY BOY [3] J R Boyle 3-8-5 R Miles (2) 16/1: 3: V slow away & bhd, hdwy to chase ldrs 2f out, kept on ins last under hands-and-heels riding:	6 44a
454	BLUE SAVANNA 12 [6] J G Portman 4-9-10 bl (46) I Mongan 13/2: 02663-64: Mid-div, rdn & btn 2f out:	nk 43a
447	MIMAS GIRL 13 [2] S R Bowring 5-9-5 t (30) J Bramhill 33/1: 5046-505: Keen & trkd ldrs, btn 2f out.	1 36a
3644]	DANZIG STAR 530 [1] P R Chamings 4-9-5 P Doe 25/1: 000/-6: Led till 4f out, sn lost pl & bhd:	25 0
6 Ran	1m 52.08 (5.88) Owner Twilight Racing	Trained at Newmarket

---

527 | **4.10 Bet Direct No Q Banded Stakes 3yo+ 0-45 (H)**
£1631 £466 £233   **5f f/sand rnd**   **Going 68**   **+11 Fast**   Stalls Inside

501	TORRENT 4 [5] D W Chapman 9-9-7 bl (45) A Culhane 5/2: 060-2631: Trkd ldrs trav well, squeezed through gap to lead ins	48a

WOLVERHAMPTON Monday 02.02.04 Lefthand, Sharp Track

286	**HAGLEY PARK 31** [2] M Quinn 5-9-7 (45) J Quinn 5/6 FAV: 16400-22: Chsd ldrs, drvn & briefly led dist, not pace of wnr:			1¼	43a
500	**SERGEANT SLIPPER 4** [3] C Smith 7-9-7 vis (45) J Fanning 10/1: 00005-03: Slow away, bhd, styd on for press, nrst fin:			1	40a
3329}	**STATOYORK 184** [4] D Shaw 11-9-7 (45) Dawn Watson (7) 14/1: 504000-4: Held up, kept on late, not able to chall:			1¾	35a
3304}	**PLEASURE TIME 185** [10] C Smith 11-9-7 vis (45) R Fitzpatrick 12/1: 000055-5: Handy & led over 3f out till dist, wknd qckly:			1¾	30a
3782}	**DANAKIM 164** [7] J R Weymes 7-9-7 (35) D Fentiman (7) 33/1: 005060-6: Wide, nvr a factor:			2	24a
508	**TUSCAN DREAM 3** [1] A Berry 9-9-7 (40) P Bradley (5) 20/1: 6060-007: Led 1f, btn dist:			3½	14a
4913}	**VIEW THE FACTS 98** [8] P L Gilligan 5-9-7 e (45) Lisa Jones (3) 25/1: 000/0/00-8: Slow away & al bhd, abs.			nk	13a
335	**LONE PIPER 27** [6] J M Bradley 9-9-7 BL (40) P Fitzsimons 25/1: 0056-009: Keen, al bhd:			hd	12a
4133}	**MILL END TEASER 146** [9] M W Easterby 3-8-7 (45) Dale Gibson 25/1: 006000-0: Sn outpcd:			1	9a
10 Ran	1m 03.05 (2.85) Owner Mr David W Chapman				Trained at York

---

528

4.40 Bet Direct On Sky Active Banded Stakes 3yo+ 0-40 (H)
£1463 £418 £209   7f f/sand rnd   Going 68   -12 Slow   Stalls Outside

410	**BADOU 18** [12] L Montague Hall 4-9-8 (40) R Miles (3) 4/1 FAV: 24000-61: Trkd ldrs, drvn to lead well ins last:				44a
448	**SILVER MASCOT 12** [8] R Hollinshead 5-9-8 (40) Dale Gibson 9/1: 0600-402: Trkd ldr, drvn to chall ins last, not pace of wnr cl-home:			½	42a
447	**ENJOY THE BUZZ 13** [7] J M Bradley 5-9-8 (40) P Fitzsimons 6/1: 20-44023: Mid-div, styd on wide for press, nrst fin:			½	41a
442	**VLASTA WEINER 13** [4] J M Bradley 4-9-8 bl (40) L Fletcher (3) 20/1: 06-02504: Rear, hdwy wide 2f out, nrst fin:			shd	41a
297	**LIONS DOMANE 30** [1] A Berry 7-9-8 (40) F Lynch 25/1: 00000-05: Led till dist, no extra:			nk	40a
451	**LONG WEEKEND 12** [6] D Shaw 6-9-8 e (40) Darren Williams 5/1: 1460-066: Held up, not able to chall.			2½	35a
408	**ZAHUNDA 18** [9] W M Brisbourne 5-9-8 P (40) B Swarbrick (7) 6/1: 00000-67: Chsd ldrs 5f.			2	31a
442	**SECOND VENTURE 13** [3] P Howling 6-9-8 bl t (40) S W Kelly 5/1: 0504-038: In tch, btn 2f out:			1½	28a
340	**KILMEENA STAR 26** [5] J C Fox 6-9-8 P (40) P Dobbs 16/1: 30306-09: Mid-div, btn 2f out:			4	20a
447	**LIVELY FELIX 13** [2] D G Bridgwater 7-9-8 (40) S Righton 8/1: 00000-40: Mid-div, bhd halfway:			1¾	17a
313	**CHANTEUSE 28** [10] D W Chapman 4-9-8 (40) R Brisland 50/1: 0000-060: Slow away al bhd.			2½	12a
442	**LEMARATE 13** [11] D W Chapman 7-9-8 (40) A Culhane 12/1: 000-3300: Sn rear, nvr factor:			1	10a
12 Ran	1m 31.78 (5.58) Owner Mr J Daniels				Trained at Epsom

SOUTHWELL Tuesday 03.02.04 Lefthand, Sharp, Oval Track

Official Going STANDARD

529

2.00 Bet Direct On Sky Active Amateur Riders' Handicap Stakes 4yo+ 0-80 (F)   [53]
£2884 £824 £412   2m f/sand   Going 40   -114 Slow   Stalls Inside

478	**BUSTLING RIO 10** [3] P C Haslam 8-10-7 (60) Ms C Williams 3/1: 1560-401: Rear, hdwy halfway, led 2f out, rdn clr:				71a
491	**ALTITUDE DANCER 7** [7] P A Blockley 4-10-0 (59) Miss S Renwick (5) 15/8 FAV: 31053-32: Chsd ldr, rdn halfway, hdwy to lead 3f out, hdd 2f out, onepace:			2½	66a
467	**GLORY QUEST 11** [8] Miss Gay Kelleway 7-11-6 (73) Miss E J Jones 5/1: 3552-203: Trkd ldrs, hdwy 3f out, wknd 2f out:			8	72a
259	**REMINISCENT 36** [5] R F Johnson Houghton 5-11-0 bl (67) Miss E Johnson Houghton 3/1: 453522-4: Midfield, hdwy to lead over 5f out, hdd 3f out & no extra:			¾	65a
467	**PAULA LANE 11** [6] R Curtis 4-10-11 (70) Mr Ashlee Price (5) 40/1: 05320-05: Handy, led halfway, hdd 5f out & wknd:			dist	28a
458	**HIGH DIVA 12** [2] J R Best 5-9-3 2oh (40) Mrs K Hills (4) 33/1: 0006-646: Keen, led to halfway, no extra.			1½	0a
4954}	**LA MUETTE 95** [1] M Appleby 4-11-7 (80) Mr O Nelmes (3) 25/1: 61/5300-7: Rear, t.o. fnl 6f:			dist	0a
7 Ran	3m 50.7 (24.7) Owner Rio Stainless Engineering Limi				Trained at Middleham

530

2.30 Bet Direct Interactive Handicap Stakes 3yo+ 0-70 (E)   [70]
£3283 £938 £469   1m f/sand rnd   Going 40   -27 Slow   Stalls Inside

457*	**SIMPLY THE GUEST 12** [3] Don Enrico Incisa 5-8-11 t (53) Kim Tinkler 13/2: 000-2211: Handy, rdn along aftr 3f, hdwy over 2f out, styd on ins fnl furlong & drvn to lead nr fin:				64a
513	**PENWELL HILL 4** [7] T D Barron 5-9-13 (69) P Makin (7) 5/2 FAV: 3465-102: Handy, led over 2f out, clr over 1f out, hung left ins fnl furlong & hdd nr fin:			1¼	76a
294	**TOPTON 31** [11] P Howling 10-9-13 bl (69) K Dalgleish 12/1: 50601-43: Slowly away, rear, hdwy over 2f out, sn short of room, styd on late, nrst fin:			5	66a
465	**KINGSTON TOWN 11** [10] N P Littmoden 4-9-11 p (67) J P Guillambert (3) 10/1: 4021-004: Midfield, hdwy over 2f out, edged left over 1f out, wknd:			1	62a
1417}	**BRAMANTINO 270** [9] R A Fahey 4-8-13 bl (55) Natalia Gemelova (7) 50/1: 003/000-5: Chsd ldrs, short of room & swtchd right over 1f out, onepace:			¾	48a
457	**ROBIN SHARP 12** [1] J Akehurst 6-8-6 vis t (48) J Quinn 14/1: 0P00-26: Led till wknd 2f out:			½	40a
186	**LOCKSTOCK 53** [12] M S Saunders 6-9-9 bl (65) S Carson 5/1: 000414-7: Handy, ch over 2f out, wknd over 1f out:			1½	54a
408	**ROSTI 19** [5] P C Haslam 4-9-4 (46) G Faulkner 8/1: 054-1138: Keen, handy, ch 3 out, wknd fnl 2f:			¾	33a
195	**ZARIN 52** [4] D W Chapman 6-9-13 (69) A Culhane 17/2: 006023-9: Midfield, nvr nr ldrs:			¾	54a
249	**BOND MILLENNIUM 39** [2] B Smart 6-9-8 (64) F Lynch 12/1: 602455-0: Al bhd:			nk	48a
513	**BOUGHT DIRECT 4** [6] R J Smith 5-9-7 (63) A Beech (3) 66/1: 00000-00: Midfield, wknd after 3f out.			6	35a
167	**LAGGAN MINSTREL 56** [8] P A Blockley 6-8-3 1ow (45) Dean McKeown 25/1: 000000-0: Al bhd:			12	0a
12 Ran	1m 44.8 (5.4) Owner Don Enrico Incisa				Trained at Middleham

531

3.00 #10 Free Bet @ Bet Direct Sky Active Maiden Stakes 3yo+ (D)
£3348 £1030 £515 £258   7f f/sand rnd   Going 40   -28 Slow   Stalls Inside

460	**MARINAITE 12** [7] S R Bowring 3-8-2 J Bramhill 11/8 FAV: 21: Handy, led over 2f out, clr over 1f out, hung left ins fnl furlong, rdn fnl:				79a
468	**GLOBAL ACHIEVER 11** [3] G C H Chung 3-8-7 R Ffrench 5/1: 32: Led till hdd over 2f out, onepace over 1f out:			3½	73a

SOUTHWELL Tuesday 03.02.04 Lefthand, Sharp, Oval Track

337	**PHLUKE** 27 [2] R F Johnson Houghton 3-8-7 (72) S Carson 9/2: 22432-53: Handy, onepace fnl 2f.	1	71a
472	**ILE FACILE** 10 [1] N P Littmoden 3-8-7 (70) I Mongan 2/1: 2424: Hmpd after 1f, midfield, hdwy 3f out, wknd:	nk	70a
	ZULOAGO [4] S L Keightley 3-8-2 A Nicholls 100/1: 5: Slowly away, in tch, wknd 2f out:	8	49a
460	**ANACAPRI** 12 [5] W S Cunningham 4-9-5 D Allan (3) 150/1: 0-06: Chsd ldrs, wknd after halfway:	8	33a
	UTAH FLATS [6] Mrs J R Ramsden 3-8-7 P P Fitzsimons 28/1: 7: Outpcd & al bhd:	dist	0

7 Ran   1m 31.4 (4.8)   Owner Mr S R Bowring   Trained at Edwinstowe

---

532   **3.30 Littlewoods Bet Direct Conditions Stakes 3yo+   (C)**
£9118 £3458 £1729 £786   6f f/sand rnd   Going 40   -05 Slow   Stalls Inside

482	**MASSEY** 8 [5] T D Barron 8-9-10 (95) P Makin (7) 4/1: 0000-101: Made all, styd on well ins fnl 1f, drvn out:		87a
482	**SOBA JONES** 8 [3] J Balding 7-9-4 (75) J Edmunds 11/1: 52-12432: Trkd ldrs, hdwy over 2f out, edged right over 1f out, styd on:	¾	77a
482	**ELLENS ACADEMY** 8 [9] E J Alston 9-9-8 (79) D Allan (3) 7/1: 6131-463: Slowly away in rear, hdwy 2f out, kept on ins last:	½	79a
482	**QUIET TIMES** 8 [1] K A Ryan 5-9-4 bl (85) G Parkin 9/1: 120-1404: Al handy, ch over 1f out, onepace.	nk	74a
4006}	**HAYDN** 142 [6] P W Chapple Hyam 3-8-9 (85) J Quinn 4/1: 10000-5: Bumped start, chsd ldrs, hdwy wide 2f out, styd on same pace ins fnl furlong.	nk	79a
1798}	**KENTUCKY KING** 250 [8] P W Hiatt 4-9-4 (89) A Culhane 25/1: 1/4-6: Rear, styd on fnl 2f but nvr dangerous:	4	61a
361	**BOND BOY** 25 [2] B Smart 7-9-4 (90) F Lynch 3/1 FAV: 62000-47: Handy, ch over 2f out, wknd over 1f out.	1	58a
494	**HELLO ROBERTO** 6 [10] M J Polglase 3-7-12 (77) J Mackay 22/1: 4324-028: Al bhd:	1	50a
	FULL PITCH 1676 [4] W Jenks 8-9-4 I Mongan 50/1: 1////-9: Mid-field, wknd after halfway:	10	25a
422	**MUY BIEN** 18 [7] J R Jenkins 3-8-3 vis (78) J Bramhill 14/1: 0152-220: Chsd ldrs, wknd over 2f out:	3	16a

10 Ran   1m 16.05 (2.75)   Owner Mr J Edward Boynton   Trained at Thirsk

---

533   **4.00 Press Interactive To Bet Direct Selling Stakes 3yo+   (G)**
£2618 £748 £374   6f f/sand rnd   Going 40   -25 Slow   Stalls Inside

501	**POLAR HAZE** 5 [2] J Pearce 7-9-13 vis (53) J Quinn 4/1: 102-4261: Mid-field, hdwy 2f out, led ins fnl furlong, drvn to hold on nr fin:		56a
461	**AFRICAN SPUR** 12 [7] P A Blockley 4-9-9 (66) Derek Nolan (7) 5/4 FAV: 0000-002: Handy, led over 1f out, hdd ins fnl furlong, rallied nr fin, just failed & jock stopped riding momentarily cl home:	hd	64a
471	**LEGALIS** 10 [1] K A Ryan 6-9-9 bl (57) P Fessey 15/2: 400-3203: Handy, led over 2f out, hdd over 1f out & styd on same pace ins fnl furlong:	2½	56a
317	**JALOUHAR** 29 [3] B P J Baugh 4-9-13 p (57) K Dalgleish 22/1: 50615-54: Chsd ldrs, outpcd over 2f out, styd on for press ins fnl furlong:	1¼	55a
4360}	**DUSTY WUGG** 136 [5] A Dickman 5-9-4 p (46) A Beech (3) 40/1: 020040-5: Chsd ldrs, wknd over 1f out:	3	38a
483	**CZAR WARS** 8 [6] J Balding 9-9-9 bl (66) M Savage (5) 11/1: 12130-06: Handy, ch over 2f out, wknd over 1f out.	5	28a
492	**LIZHAR** 6 [8] M J Polglase 3-8-7 (69) Dean McKeown 7/1: 435-4647: Al bhd:	½	25a
308	**VALUABLE GIFT** 30 [4] R C Guest 7-9-9 bl e (45) A Cooper (7) 66/1: 20000-08: Led, hdd over 2f out & wknd.	1½	21a
1086}	**MYSTERY MOUNTAIN** 293 [9] Mrs J R Ramsden 4-9-9 (60) D Egan (7) 10/1: 64300-9: Mid-field, wknd over 2f out:	8	0

9 Ran   1m 17.2 (3.9)   Owner Mr M M Foulger   Trained at Newmarket

---

534   **4.30 Bet Direct Football Cashbacks Handicap Stakes 4yo+ 0-70 (E)**   **[70]**
£3339 £954 £477   1m3f f/sand   Going 40   +05 Fast   Stalls Inside

515*	**FALL IN LINE** 3 [11] Sir Mark Prescott 4-9-8 6ex (66) J Mackay 1/4 FAV: 343-1111: Mid-field, hdwy to lead on bit over 2f out, sn well clr:		89a
439	**BRESSBEE** 15 [2] J W Unett 6-10-0 vis (70) D Nolan (5) 40/1: 00300-02: Chsd ldrs, lost place 4f out, styd on late, no ch with facile:	9	69a
321	**SURDOUE** 29 [12] P Howling 4-9-5 (63) Paul Eddery 25/1: 00005-02: Rear, hdwy halfway, chsd wnr fnl 2f, jnd for 2nd on line:	dht	61a
456*	**DELTA FORCE** 12 [7] P A Blockley 5-9-7 (63) Derek Nolan (7) 10/1: 031-1214: Led, hdd over 2f out & wknd:	2½	57a
4922}	**MELODIAN** 98 [5] M Brittain 9-8-9 bl (51) M Lawson (7) 33/1: 0/06156-5: Rear, hdwy 4f out, nvr dngrs:	6	36a
416	**DALRIATH** 19 [3] M C Chapman 5-7-12 (40) D Fox (5) 150/1: 25000-06: Chsd ldr, wknd 3f out:	nk	24a
375	**EAST CAPE** 22 [9] Don Enrico Incisa 7-7-12 (40) Kim Tinkler 33/1: 4450-537: Rear, nvr a factor:	2	21a
513	**DUBAI DREAMS** 4 [8] M J Polglase 4-8-12 (56) A Culhane 12/1: 140-4258: Chsd ldrs, wknd after halfway:	1	35a
439	**ALLIED VICTORY** 15 [6] E J Alston 4-9-11 (69) J Quinn 50/1: 0324-109: Trkd ldrs & hmpd after 1f, wknd 4f out.	7	37a
391	**ENVIRONMENT AUDIT** 21 [10] J R Jenkins 5-9-13 (69) S W Kelly 50/1: 2100/0-00: Chsd ldrs to halfway.	3	32a
4303}	**BANNINGHAM BLAZE** 139 [1] C R Dore 4-9-8 vis (66) J Bramhill 66/1: 210000-0: Al bhd, t.o. fnl 4f.	dist	0
446	**SHATIN SPECIAL** 14 [4] G C H Chung 4-8-1 p (45) R Ffrench 66/1: 0402-52F: Chsd ldrs, short of room & fell over 1f:		0

12 Ran   2m 25.2 (3.9)   Owner Neil Greig - Osborne House II   Trained at Newmarket

---

LINGFIELD Tuesday 03.02.04 Lefthand, V Sharp Track

Official Going   Standard

535   **1.40 Bet Direct No Q Banded Stakes Div 1 3yo+ 0-45 (H)**
£1642 £469 £235   1m p/track rnd   Going 51   -25 Slow   Stalls Outside

396	**DIAL SQUARE** 20 [11] P Howling 3-8-2 BL (40) C Catlin 5/1: 00-01: Keen & handy, led 3f out, sn rdn & joined over 1f out, held on all out:		47a
462	**ZONNEBEKE** 12 [3] K R Burke 3-8-2 (45) J Fanning 8/1: 400-452: Cl-up & briefly led 3f out, rdn & joined wnr over 1f out, edged right, just held:	shd	46a
370	**CHEROKEE BAY** 24 [8] G L Moore 4-9-7 e (45) G Carter 4/1: 00003-43: Trkd ldrs halfway, drvn & kept on, nrst fin:	nk	45a
411	**ABUELOS** 19 [9] S Dow 5-9-7 (45) P Doe 7/2 JT FAV: 00500-34: Held up, hdwy to press ldrs 2f out, no extra nr fin:	1½	42a
4832}	**FIRST CLASS LADY** 105 [5] P Mitchell 4-9-7 (45) Lisa Jones (3) 14/1: 060046-5: Pushed along, mod late gains:	3½	35a
429	**DILIZA** 17 [12] G B Balding 5-9-7 (45) R Thomas (5) 7/2 JT FAV: 2050-406: Held up wide, not able to chall:	¾	34a

138

1661] **EL GIZA 617** [10] J M Bradley 6-9-7 (45) S Whitworth 50/1: 0/500/00/-: Dwelt, rear, no impress, long abs. 1¼ **31a**
502 **KUMAKAWA 5** [1] E A Wheeler 6-9-7 bl (45) Liam Jones (7) 20/1: 5000-058: Chsd ldrs, btn over 1f out: nk **30a**
476 **PEDLERS PROFILES 10** [4] Miss K M George 4-9-7 (40) V Slattery 66/1: 00/-09: Chsd ldrs 6f. 2½ **25a**
4731} **LADY LIESEL 112** [7] J J Bridger 4-9-7 (45) G Baker 20/1: 645000-0: Cl-up trav well, wknd qckly 2f out: 2 **21a**
3859} **DREAMS UNITED 162** [2] A G Newcombe 3-8-2 (45) F P Ferris (3) 33/1: 050-0: Led till over 3f out, sn btn: 7 **9a**
11 Ran 1m 42.28 (6.08) Owner Mr Rory Murphy Trained at Newmarket

536 **2.10 Bet Direct No Q Demo 08000 837 888 Median Auction Maiden Stakes 3-5yo (H)**
£1470 £420 £210 **7f p/track rnd** **Going 51** **+02 Fast** Stalls Inside

509 **ADANTINO 4** [9] B R Millman 5-9-6 bl (52) J P Spencer 9/2: 053-6341: Swtchd & held up, smooth prog over 2f out, led dist, rdn clr: **59a**
473 **DEVINE COMMAND 10** [2] R Ingram 3-8-3 N Day 50/1: 002: Chsd ldrs, rdn & kept on ins last, not pace of wnr: 1¾ **54a**
401 **BALLINGER RIDGE 20** [6] A M Balding 5-9-6 (65) N Chalmers (5) 5/2 FAV: 00063-23: Led till dist. 1¼ **51a**
2620} **BOLD TRUMP 215** [4] Jean Rene Auvray 3-8-4 1ow S Whitworth 7/1: 0-4: Chsd ldrs, eff wide, kept on onepace: 1 **50a**
402 **SONDERBORG 20** [3] G L Moore 3-7-12 p (52) J F McDonald (4) 4/1: 3006-645: Handy & ch 2f out, onepace for press. shd **44a**
492 **DULCE DE LECHE 6** [12] S C Williams 3-8-3 bl e P Doe 7/2: 00-06: Cl-up halfway, wknd ins last: 2 **45a**
473 **PRINCE VALENTINE 10** [1] D B Feek 3-8-3 (65) C Catlin 10/1: 00-07: Trkd ldrs, eff wide, btn over 1f out: 2 **41a**
409 **JANES VALENTINE 19** [10] J J Bridger 4-9-1 (45) G Baker 20/1: 00000-48: Dwelt, rear, mod prog. hd **35a**
413 **IVORY VENTURE 19** [5] D K Ivory 4-9-1 (45) D Sweeney 50/1: 5400-009: Towards rear, nvr able to chall. 5 **26a**
428 **SAUCY PICKLE 17** [7] Miss Z C Davison 3-7-12 Joanna Badger 100/1: 0-00: Rear, no ch fnl 2f. 5 **17a**
4251} **THE FOOTBALLRESULT 140** [11] Mrs G Harvey 3-7-12 (63) M Henry 33/1: 060-0: Sn rdn towards rear, nvr a factor, abs/AW bow. 3 **11a**
462 **FAR FOR LULU 12** [8] W R Muir 3-7-12 (35) Lisa Jones (3) 66/1: 54500-00: Prom 3f, sn bhd. 7 **0a**
12 Ran 1m 26.22 (3.42) Owner Tarka Two Racing Trained at Cullompton

537 **2.40 Bet Direct No Q On 08000 93 66 93 Banded Stakes 4yo+ 0-40 (H)**
£1470 £420 £210 **1m5f p/track** **Going 51** **-02 Slow** Stalls Inside

2796} **MONTOSARI 208** [12] P Mitchell 5-9-2 (40) J Fanning 9/2: 004600-1: Handy trav well bef halfway, led over 1f out, rdn & in command ins last: **47a**
414 **BUZ KIRI 19** [10] A W Carroll 6-9-2 (35) P Doe 11/2: 30046-32: Trkd ldr halfway, rdn & led over 3f out, hdd over 1f out, not pace of wnr: 3 **42a**
395 **THE LAST MOHICAN 20** [9] P Howling 5-9-2 p (35) J P Spencer 4/1 FAV: 00/50-423: Chsd ldr 4f, remained handy, drvn & kept on onepace: 1 **41a**
443 **LITTLE RICHARD 14** [7] M Wellings 5-9-2 p (30) V Slattery 33/1: 0000-004: Chsd ldrs, drvn & outpcd 3f out, kept on ins last: ¾ **40a**
523 **KHUZDAR 1** [6] A Bailey 5-9-2 P (40) D Corby (3) 9/2: 640-03205: Dwelt, rear, eff 2f out, wknd: 1½ **38a**
454 **RADIANT BRIDE 13** [14] K R Burke 4-8-12 p (35) Darren Williams 8/1: 0250-026: Dwelt, rear, mod prog, op 11/2. 1 **37a**
445 **POLKA PRINCESS 14** [1] M Wellings 4-8-12 P (40) L Treadwell (5) 25/1: 0000-007: Keen mid-div, no impress: ½ **36a**
370 **BIRTH OF THE BLUES 24** [13] A Charlton 8-9-2 (40) R Smith 14/1: 02560-08: Held up wide, little hdwy. shd **36a**
370 **WALKER BAY 24** [2] J C Fox 6-9-2 (40) P Dobbs 16/1: 24000-59: Mid-div, outpcd fnl 3f. hd **35a**
305 **MAGIC CHARM 30** [5] A G Newcombe 6-9-2 (35) S Whitworth 10/1: 61105-00: Dwelt, rear, eff 4f out, no prog. 7 **26a**
4546} **GIKO 125** [11] Jane Southcombe 10-9-2 (40) C Catlin 12/1: 630200-0: Chsd ldrs, btn 2f out, abs. 1¼ **24a**
114 **BATHWICK DREAM 67** [3] B R Millman 7-9-2 (40) G Baker 50/1: 30106//0-0: Led till over 3f out, wknd, abs. 4 **18a**
412 **GEMMA 19** [8] P J Makin 4-8-12 P (35) D Sweeney 50/1: 00000-00: Mid-div, btn 3f out. 3 **14a**
454 **PHILOSOPHIC 13** [4] Mrs L C Jewell 10-9-2 P (35) S Donohoe (7) 50/1: 0///000/-0: Al bhd, cheek pieces. 3 **10a**
14 Ran 2m 49.17 (6.87) Owner Caterham Racing (jdrp) Trained at Epsom

538 **3.10 Bet Direct No Q Banded Stakes Div 2 3yo+ 0-45 (H)**
£1638 £468 £234 **1m p/track rnd** **Going 51** **-01 Slow** Stalls Outside

412 **PIQUET 19** [12] J J Bridger 6-9-7 (45) G Baker 11/2: 00501-31: Rear, hdwy inner over 2f out & led over 1f out, rdn clr: **51a**
3864} **WANNA SHOUT 162** [3] R Dickin 6-9-7 (45) R Miles (3) 12/1: 040004-2: Trkd ldrs halfway, rdn & poised to chall when no room over 1f out, kept on ins last, wnr had flown: 2 **47a**
2915} **LARAD 203** [4] J S Moore 3-8-2 BL (45) D Kinsella 25/1: 0504-3: Cl-up, ch 3f out, no extra dist: 2 **43a**
410 **WILOM 19** [1] M R Hoad 6-9-7 (45) M Fenton 7/2 JT FAV: 3403-254: Led till over 1f out, no extra. ½ **42a**
267 **CHOCOLATE BOY 35** [2] G L Moore 5-9-7 P (45) S Whitworth 16/1: 0/000/00-5: Mid-div, hmpd halfway, lost place, late shd **42a**
410 **LADYWELL BLAISE 19** [5] J J Bridger 7-9-7 (45) N Pollard 6/1: 0064-036: Held up, only mod prog: nk **41a**
474 **GEESPOT 10** [7] D J S ffrench Davis 5-9-7 P (45) J F McDonald (5) 8/1: 500-0407: Prom, no impress fnl 2f, cheek pieces. shd **41a**
408 **MISS PEACHES 19** [8] G G Margarson 6-9-7 (45) Kristin Stubbs (7) 7/2 JT FAV: 64/0/00-28: Prom, lost place over 2f out. ½ **40a**
309 **ONEFORTHEBOYS 30** [6] D Flood 5-9-7 (40) Rory Moore (7) 8/1: 00600-09: Prom, outpcd fnl 3f. 1¾ **37a**
326 **ZOLUSHKA 28** [11] B W Duke 3-8-2 (45) F P Ferris (3) 16/1: 0000-30: Wide, mid-div, btn 2f out: 10 **21a**
450 **ORIGINAL SIN 13** [10] S Dow 4-9-7 (45) P Doe 33/1: 0560-000: Al rear. nk **20a**
466 **ADRIATIC ADVENTURE 11** [9] J L Spearing 3-8-2 (40) A Daly 50/1: 000-00: Keen & held up, no ch fnl 2f. 19 **0a**
12 Ran 1m 40.34 (4.14) Owner Mr J J Bridger Trained at Liphook

539 **3.40 Littlewoods Bet Direct Banded Stakes 4yo+ 0-40 (H)**
£1502 £429 £215 **1m2f p/track** **Going 51** **-21 Slow** Stalls Inside

4788} **THEATRE LADY 109** [3] P D Evans 6-9-1 (30) S Donohoe (7) 5/1: 221300-1: Sn handy inner, drvn/styd on to lead cl-home, all out: **39a**
410 **COLNE VALLEY AMY 19** [4] G L Moore 7-9-1 bl (40) A Quinn (5) 5/1: 22/060-42: Sn handy, rdn & led over 1f out, just hdd cl-home: nk **38a**
370 **PRIVATE SEAL 24** [8] Julian Poulton 9-9-1 t p (40) M Halford (7) 20/1: 30000-63: Mid-div, styd on for press ins last, nrst fin: ½ **37a**
84 **ACHILLES RAINBOW 71** [5] K R Burke 5-9-1 (40) A Reilly (7) 33/1: 040060-4: Mid-div, styd on onpce: ¾ **36a**
409 **GINGER ICE 19** [12] G G Margarson 4-9-0 VIS (40) N Pollard 8/1: 00006-35: Keen, rear, hdwy 3f out, sn onepace: nk **42a**

420	DANCING TILLY 19 [10] R A Fahey 6-9-1 (40) T Hamilton (5) 4/1 FAV: 306-4246: Rear, eff wide, no extra over 1f out.	shd	35a
411	THATS ALL JAZZ 19 [6] C R Dore 6-9-1 (40) M Tebbutt 16/1: 0000-007: Dwelt, rear, late gains, nvr a dngr.	¾	34a
4331	BOOM OR BUST 137 [11] Miss K M George 5-9-1 p (40) V Slattery 14/1: 053200-8: Mid-div, no impress, jmps fit.	1½	32a
216	PRINCE IVOR 48 [1] J C Fox 4-9-0 (40) P Dobbs 66/1: 050000-9: Led till over 1f out, fdd, abs.	1½	30a
97	GRACIOUS AIR 70 [9] J R Weymes 6-9-1 VIS (40) J Fanning 20/1: 000060-0: Rear, eff wide 4f out, wknd qckly over 1f out.	3	26a
408	RO ERIDANI 19 [2] T J Etherington 4-9-0 (40) D Kinsella 33/1: 02000-00: Cl-up racing freely, wknd 3f out.	8	15a
4411	ITALIAN COUNSEL 488 [13] L A Dace 7-9-1 (30) L Treadwell (7) 5/1: 50000/0/0: Chsd ldrs 11f:	3½	10a
443	RODIAK 14 [7] P R Hedger 5-9-1 bl (40) G Carter 12/1: 06401/-00: Prom till 4f out, sn bhd.	dist	0

13 Ran 2m 10.01 (7.21)   Owner Waterline Racing Club   Trained at Abergavenny

---

540   **4.10 Betdirect Co Uk Selling Stakes 4yo+ (H)**

£1519 £434 £217   1m2f p/track   Going 51   -41 Slow   Stalls Inside

452	SCOTTYS FUTURE 13 [3] D R Loder 6-9-1 (81) J P Spencer 30/100 FAV: 50000-01: Trkd ldrs trav well over 2f out, short of room over 1f out, led ins last, shade cheekily:		59a
370	ABSOLUTE UTOPIA 24 [8] J L Spearing 11-9-6 (63) A Daly 6/1: 32101-02: Trkd ldrs, led over 1f out, hdd nr fin, flattered by narrow margin of defeat:	hd	59a
145	SENOR TORAN 59 [10] P Burgoyne 4-9-0 (46) L Keniry (3) 33/1: 40/5500-3: Trkd ldrs, led halfway till over 1f out, onepace:	2	51a
442	MARGARETS WISH 14 [5] T Wall 4-8-9 (30) N Chalmers (5) 33/1: 00200-04: Rear, rdn & styd on fnl 2f, nvr able to chall:	1½	44a
1503	BROUGHTONS MILL 265 [13] J A Supple 9-9-1 (30) P McCabe 40/1: 0346/00-5: Held up, eff wide 3f out, no extra.	¾	48a
315}	LADY AT LEISURE 395 [9] Julian Poulton 4-8-9 (50) M Tebbutt 33/1: 6300/5-6: Held up, hdwy/handy 2f out, no extra.	nk	42a
145	ESTRELLA LEVANTE 59 [6] G L Moore 4-9-0 e (52) Jemma Marshall (7) 12/1: 04U055-7: Held up, mod prog, abs.	¾	46a
161	WATERLINE DANCER 57 [7] P D Evans 4-8-9 t (45) S Donohoe (7) 14/1: 040000-8: Keen, cl-up till 2f out, wknd, abs.	shd	41a
430	ALIMISTE 17 [2] I A Wood 4-8-9 M Fenton 33/1: 09: Prom, lost place from 4f out.	5	34a
3825}	GEOGRAPHY 164 [4] P Butler 4-9-0 p (53) Rory Moore (7) 25/1: 300005-P: Rider lost irons start, led till 5f out, sn bhd/p.u., abs.		0a

10 Ran 2m 12.04 (9.24)   Owner Lucayan Stud   Trained at Newmarket

---

541   **4.40 Bet Direct Interactive Amateur Riders' Banded Stakes 4yo+ 0-35 (H)**

£1281 £366 £183   6f p/track rnd   Going 51   -17 Slow   Stalls Inside

377	REDOUBTABLE 22 [8] D W Chapman 13-11-0 (35) Mr S Walker 11/2: 06600-61: Chsd ldr halfway, led over 1f out, sn in command:		48a
394	PACKIN EM IN 20 [11] J R Boyle 6-11-0 (35) Mr E Dehdashti (3) 6/1: 0/0000-32: Mid-div, took 2nd well ins last, nvr threat to wnr:	3	38a
440	THREAT 15 [2] J M Bradley 8-11-0 (35) Miss A Wallace (5) 10/1: 00-04003: Led early, remained prom, kept on onepace:	1¼	34a
4358]	TINY TIM 491 [3] A M Balding 6-11-0 (35) Mr S Goswell (7) 10/1: 050050/-4: Sn bhd, kept on late:	¾	32a
3176}	MARON 192 [1] F Jordan 7-11-0 bl (35) Mr P Cowley 40/1: 40/0000-5: Slow away, sn led & clr, hdd over 1f out.	¾	30a
3953}	GRAND VIEW 158 [6] J R Weymes 8-11-0 P (35) Mr B King (5) 5/1 JT FAV: 050000-6: Bhd, mod prog:	1¼	26a
463	POOKAS DAUGHTER 12 [12] J M Bradley 4-11-0 (35) Mr S Dobson (3) 14/1: 000-5007: Rear, only mod gains.	nk	25a
524	FLYING FAISAL 1 [10] J M Bradley 6-11-0 (35) Miss M Sowerby (5) 5/1 JT FAV: 000-00068: Well bhd, mod late gains.	1	22a
3744}	BEENABOUTABIT 167 [7] Mrs L C Jewell 6-11-0 p (35) Mr J J Best (5) 25/1: 000/000-9: Chsd ldrs, btn 2f out, abs.	5	8a
401	MISS CELERITY 20 [9] M J Haynes 4-11-0 (30) Mr L Newnes (5) 10/1: 060-00: Chsd ldrs till halfway.	½	6a
172	KATALI 56 [13] A Bailey 7-11-0 (30) Mr G Bartley (7) 50/1: 600//0-0: Went right start, al bhd, abs.	2½	0a
394	GOOD FORM 20 [5] Miss K M George 4-11-0 BL (30) Mr R Stephens (7) 16/1: 000000-560: Mid-div, sn outpcd, blnks.	5	0a
2451}	KAFIL 221 [4] J J Bridger 10-11-0 vis (35) Miss Donna Handley (7) 20/1: 600/500-0: Squeezed out early, nrly u.r., sn bhd, abs.	1	0a

13 Ran 1m 14.5 (4.1)   Owner Mr David W Chapman   Trained at York

---

542   **1.10 Bet Direct On 0800 32 93 93 Handicap Stakes 4yo+ 46-52 (F)**   **[65]**

£3003 £858 £429   1m2f p/track   Going 26   -09 Slow   Stalls Inside

5029}	BRAVE DANE 89 [11] A W Carroll 6-9-0 (51) W Ryan 12/1: 0/53500-1: Rear, smooth hdwy 3f out, switched & qcknd to lead ins last, v cmftbly:		62a
498	ANSWERED PROMISE 7 [2] A W Carroll 5-9-0 (51) R Miles (3) 10/1: 000-0062: Led, drvn & hdd ins last, no ch with wnr fnl 100yds:	3	54a
236	ANOTHER SECRET 46 [13] G L Moore 6-8-13 bl (50) S Whitworth 11/1: 006B04-3: Rear, styd on for press fnl 2f, not pace of wnr, 6 wk abs.	½	52a
338	MY LILLI 28 [10] P Mitchell 4-9-0 (50) J Quinn 9/2: 30000-34: Rear, smooth hdwy wide 4f out, ch 2f out, no extra dist.	1½	52a
2520}	SHAMAN 220 [5] G L Moore 7-9-1 (52) I Mongan 4/1 FAV: 106600-5: Trkd ldrs, rdn to chall 2f out, no extra:	shd	52a
521	PYRRHIC 4 [9] R M Flower 5-8-13 bl (50) S W Kelly 12/1: 05-30206: Dwelt, rear, mod late gains:	1¼	48a
328	ZINGING 29 [1] J J Bridger 5-8-13 (50) J Tate 10/1: 00310-57: Chsd ldrs, no extra dist:	3½	43a
107	FOREVER MY LORD 70 [7] J R Best 6-8-13 (50) N Pollard 13.2: 200430-8: Chsd ldrs till halfway:	5	36a
464	FLORENZAR 12 [4] P D Evans 6-8-12 (49) S Donohoe (6) 33/1: 02620-09: Rear, no ch fnl 2f.	5	28a
336}	FOREST HEATH 392 [8] H J Collingridge 7-8-12 p (49) M Tebbutt 16/1: 53000/0-0: Chsd ldrs 7f, sn btn/eased dist.	2½	24a
264	ESPERANCE 37 [14] J Akehurst 4-8-13 (51) C Catlin 10/1: 040000-0: Rdn to go handy wide, btn 3f out.	3	22a
505	REX ROMELIO 6 [12] K R Burke 5-8-13 vis (50) G Faulkner 25/1: 505/0-020: In tch wide 7f, lost action.	dist	0a

12 Ran 2m 06.26 (3.46)   Owner Mrs E J Righton   Trained at Alcester

---

543   **1.40 Betdirect Co Uk Maiden Stakes 3yo (D)**

£4115 £1266 £633 £317   6f p/track rnd   Going 26   -16 Slow   Stalls Inside

481	TORONTO HEIGHTS 9 [4] P W Chapple Hyam 3-9-0 (76) J Quinn 9/4: 03206-21: Trkd ldrs, rdn & led over 1f out, all out to hold on cl-home:		76a
364	SAVIOURS SPIRIT 25 [5] T G Mills 3-9-0 (70) R Miles (3) 15/8 FAV: 0053-22: Led, joined halfway, rdn & hdd over 1f out, rallied well for press, just held, clr rem:	hd	75a
364	SIERA SPIRIT 25 [7] M G Quinlan 3-8-9 I Mongan 4/1: 43: Cl-up, rdn & no extra dist:	5	56a

LINGFIELD Wednesday 04.02.04 Lefthand, V Sharp Track

3552}	ORCHESTRATION 175 [3] J W Unett 3-9-0 S Whitworth 10/1: 26-4: Chsd ldrs, outpcd fnl 2f:		1	58a
4576}	DANCING PRINCE 124 [1] A P Jarvis 3-9-0 (46) N Callan 50/1: 005-5: Dwelt, sn mid-div, not pace to chall:		1	55a
436	VELVET TOUCH 16 [8] J R Jenkins 3-8-9 (57) S W Kelly 16/1: 63022-26: Dwelt, chsd ldrs till 2f out:		1¼	46a
449	PICKLE 14 [11] S C Williams 3-8-9 R Ffrench 12/1: 37: Bhd, nvr factor:		5	32a
472	PURE EMOTION 11 [6] W R Muir 3-8-9 Martin Dwyer 20/1: 5-58: Mid-div, sn outpcd.		1½	27a
	CLARE GALWAY [2] T D McCarthy 3-8-9 J P Guillambert (3) 100/1: 9: Slow away, sn well bhd, debut.		nk	26a
364	LUCHI 25 [10] A Charlton 3-8-9 R Smith 40/1: 60: Well bhd when hit rail after 2f, no ch after.		1	23a
260	CORNWALLIS 37 [9] R Guest 3-9-0 J Mackay 33/1: 06-0: Mid-div, sn struggling.		1¼	24a
11 Ran	1m 12.92 (2.52) Owner Mrs Jane Chapple-Hyam		Trained at Newmarket	

544   2.10 Bet Direct Interactive Classified Claiming Stakes 4yo+ 0-60 (F)
£2933 £838 £419   6f p/track rnd   Going 26   -14 Slow   Stalls Inside

471	GUN SALUTE 11 [3] G L Moore 4-8-9 p (53) S Whitworth 9/1: 05010-01: Chsd ldrs, hdwy to lead dist, drvn out:			55a
499	DOUBLE M 7 [2] Mrs L Richards 7-9-3 vis (56) N Callan 3/1 FAV: 00-41302: Chsd ldrs, rdn to lead over 1f out, hdd dist, no extra well ins last:		1¼	59a
344	SCARROTTOO 28 [13] S C Williams 6-8-13 BL e (52) B Reilly (5) 8/1: 45340-03: Chsd ldrs, drvn & kept on onepace, no danger:		2½	47a
340	CARGO 28 [7] H J Collingridge 5-8-3 (47) Rory Moore (7) 9/1: 00005-04: Chsd ldrs, drvn & onepace dist:		hd	36a
500	EASTERN BLUE 6 [5] Mrs L Stubbs 5-9-0 (50) M Fenton 8/1: 00622-65: Chsd ldrs, no extra dist, op 9/2:		½	45a
450	MUQTADI 14 [6] M Quinn 6-8-5 (51) Martin Dwyer 10/1: 650-0306: Well bhd, drvn & late prog:		½	34a
451	A TEEN 14 [10] P Howling 6-8-13 (50) S W Kelly 6/1: 1000-527: Rear, mod gains for press:		1½	37a
492	SOMERSET WEST 7 [14] Mrs L Stubbs 4-8-7 (58) Kristin Stubbs (7) 14/1: 54001-68: Held up, only mod prog.		1	28a
4793}	BOAVISTA 110 [11] P D Evans 4-9-0 (57) S Donohoe (5) 20/1: 032243-9: Reluctant bef start, at rear, abs/new stable.		½	33a
444	DANCES IN TIME 15 [4] C N Kellett 4-8-6 (55) T Williams 100/1: 0500: Chsd ldr, btn 2f out.		¾	23a
450	DUNEDIN RASCAL 14 [9] E A Wheeler 7-8-9 bl (57) S Carson 16/1: 400-0000: Sn struggling rear.		2½	18a
413+*	MR SPLIFFY 20 [1] K R Burke 5-8-7 vis (53) Darren Williams 15/2: 004-0510: Led, hdd over 1f out, wknd qckly.		1¾	11a
2605}	SPINNING JENNI 216 [12] J M Bradley 4-8-0 (54) C Catlin 66/1: 0/00000-0: Sn bhd, abs, new yard.		5	0
13 Ran	1m 12.8 (2.4) Owner Mr R Henderson		Trained at Brighton	

545   2.40 Bet Direct On Sky Active Handicap Stakes 3yo 0-75 (E)   [80]
£3413 £975 £488   7f p/track rnd   Going 26   -24 Slow   Stalls Inside

494	ST SAVARIN 7 [12] J R Boyle 3-9-6 (72) N Pollard 4/1: 051-2531: Sn led & rdn clr over 1f out, held on well for press:			79a
455	BIG BAD BURT 14 [7] M J Wallace 3-8-10 vis (62) K Fallon 100/30 FAV: 600-42: Dwelt, sn trkd ldrs, drvn & kept on ins last:		¾	66a
432	FOOLS ENTIRE 18 [13] J A Gilbert 3-9-3 VIS (69) B Reilly (5) 10/1: 1322-203: Cl-up, drvn & kept on onepace fnl 2f:		¾	71a
4926}	IFFY 99 [10] P D Cundell 3-8-8 (60) S Whitworth 5/1: 050-4: Rear, styd on for press fnl 2f, nrst fin:		1	60a
132	JOMUS 64 [5] L Montague Hall 3-8-5 (55) R Miles (3) 25/1: 002005-5: Slow away, rear, hdwy wide halfway, no extra dist.		½	56a
441	MAYBE SOMEDAY 16 [1] I A Wood 3-9-7 (73) N Callan 8/1: 0213-346: Prom, drvn & outpcd fnl 2f:		1¾	69a
432	GARRIGON 18 [9] N P Littmoden 3-8-10 (62) J Mongan 7/2: 62002-57: Handy when hmpd after 2f, btn over 1f out.		2½	53a
4613}	LADY STRIPES 121 [15] M J Wallace 3-8-10 (62) K Bowman (6) 66/1: 060-8: Al bhd:		6	42a
326	REDBANK 29 [14] S Dow 3-8-11 (63) Paul Eddery 12/1: 04330-09: Chsd ldrs wide till 2f out, eased:		nk	42a
4118}	TRISHAY 149 [11] A P Jarvis 3-8-7 (59) J Quinn 33/1: 04265-0: Rear, no ch halfway:		¾	36a
4532}	CHIQITITA 127 [3] T T Clement 3-8-9 (61) Saleem Golam (7) 66/1: 046600-0: Prom 2f, sn bhd:		1	36a
4900}	BLADES EDGE 100 [4] A Bailey 3-8-13 (65) C Catlin 50/1: 304-0: Al bhd, t.o:		8	26a
12 Ran	1m 26.28 (3.48) Owner Mr D S Nevison		Trained at Maidstone	

546   3.10 #10 Free Bet @ Bet Direct Sky Active Median Auction Maiden Stakes 4-6yo (F)
£2912 £832 £416   1m5f p/track   Going 26   -16 Slow   Stalls Inside

4033}	DOLZAGO 154 [3] G L Moore 4-9-0 BL (48) J Mongan 20/1: 0/000055-1: Cl-up & led over 4f out, rdn & hdd over 2f out, rallied gamely for press to prevail nr line, all out:			71a
324	FLEETING MOON 29 [7] A M Balding 4-8-9 Martin Dwyer 7/4: 0-22: Trkd ldrs, rdn & led over 2f out, drvn/just held line:		shd	65a
478	BOUMAHOU 11 [2] A P Jarvis 4-9-0 (71) N Callan 6/5 FAV: 6440-33: Trkd ldrs 3f out, drvn & no extra dist:		2	67a
409	VANILLA MOON 20 [6] J R Jenkins 4-8-9 vis (48) S W Kelly 12/1: 0405-524: Trkd ldrs, no impress fnl 3f:		4	56a
477	AMNESTY 11 [1] G L Moore 5-9-4 bl e (55) S Whitworth 50/1: 340020-36: Rear, eff 3f out, sn no impress:		3	57a
306	MAKE MY HAY 31 [4] J White 5-9-4 (45) L Fletcher (3) 33/1: 34002-36: Rear, no impress 5f out:		3	53a
4091}	JOEY THE SCHNOZE 865 [5] G G Margarson 6-9-4 N Pollard 66/1: 00//-7: Led till over 4f out, sn btn:		23	21a
7 Ran	2m 47.8 (5.5) Owner R Kiernan Paul Chapman		Trained at Brighton	

547   3.40 Littlewoods Bet Direct Stakes Handicap 4yo+ 0-95 (C)   [93]
£7273 £2759 £1379 £627   1m p/track rnd   Going 26   -02 Slow   Stalls Inside

369*	DANCE ON THE TOP 25 [1] J R Boyle 6-9-8 t (87) D Sweeney 9/4 FAV: 04320-11: With ldr, led over 3f out, clr 2f out, cmftbly:			96a
433	LINNING WINE 18 [9] B G Powell 8-10-0 (93) S Carson 8/1: 00021-02: Rear, hdwy 2f out,sn short of room, styd on well fnl 1f, no ch with wnr:		1¾	96a
520	QUANTUM LEAP 4 [8] S Dow 7-7-12 1oh (62) Lisa Jones (3) 20/1: 4153-063: Mid-field, wide & chsd ldrs over 2f out, onepace over 1f out:		1¼	62a
4201}	OUR TEDDY 145 [3] A M Balding 4-10-0 (93) Martin Dwyer 5/1: 100000-4: Trkd ldrs, slightly short of room on inner 2f out, onepace fnl 1f:		hd	91a
452	LABRETT 14 [4] Miss Gay Kelleway 7-9-3 p (82) M Fenton 8/1: 1061-305: Handy, chsd wnr over 1f out, onepace:		½	79a
517	AGILIS 4 [6] Jamie Poulton 4-8-13 BL (78) D Kinsella 25/1: 00046-06: Rear, hdwy & not clr run 2f out till over 1f out, onepace after:		3	69a
809}	JEWEL OF INDIA 320 [7] Mrs A L M King 5-9-6 (85) D Corby (3) 16/1: 511/350-7: Slowly away, rear, short of room over 2f out till over 1f out, onepace:		¾	75a

141

LINGFIELD Wednesday 04.02.04 Lefthand, V Sharp Track

475	INTERNATIONALGUEST 11 [10] G G Margarson 5-9-1 vis (80) N Pollard 20/1: 360-0208: Rear, nvr a factor:	½	69a
511	ARC EL CIEL 5 [2] Mrs Stef Liddiard 6-8-13 vis (78) I Mongan 9/1: 162-1359: Led, hdd over 3f out, chsd wnr over 1f out & no extra:	nk	66a
4156}	SERIEUX 147 [5] Mrs A J Perrett 5-9-13 (92) A Culhane 11/2: 504300-0: Keen, handy, rdn & found little 2f out, wknd & eased:	nk	79a
280	AND TOTO TOO 35 [11] P D Evans 4-8-5 vis (70) B Swarbrick (5) 16/1: 153515-0: Rcd wide in mid-div, wknd & bhd over 2f out:	7	45a

11 Ran   1m 38.45 (2.25)   Owner John Hopkins (T/A South Hatch   *Trained at Epsom*

548 | 4.10 Littlewoods Bet Direct Selling Stakes 3yo (G)

£2562 £732 £366   5f p/track rnd   Going 26   -10 Slow   Stalls Outside

485	IVORY LACE 8 [4] D K Ivory 3-9-0 (55) D Sweeney 8/1: 500-5201: Held up last pair, hdwy 3f out, led ins fnl 1f, pushed out:		57a
495	LADY PISTE 7 [1] P D Evans 3-9-0 vis t (52) S Donohoe (7) 7/1: 5304-042: Chsd ldrs, ch 2f out, kept on:	¾	54a
494	PRINCESS KAI 7 [6] R Ingram 3-9-0 bl (61) J Quinn 9/2: 303-1003: Prsd ldr, led over 1f out, hdd & no extra ins fnl furlong:	1	51a
533	LIZHAR 1 [2] M J Polglase 3-9-0 (69) I Mongan 4/1: 435-46404: Chsd ldrs, onepcd over 1f out.	1	48a
495	REHIA 7 [5] J W Hills 3-9-0 (57) H Gemberlu (7) 16/1: 3550-065: Rear, outpcd appr halfway, styd on fnl furlong but no ch with ldrs:	1¼	44a
495	LIMIT DOWN 7 [3] M J Wallace 3-8-12 (53) K Fallon 5/2 FAV: 005-6536: Chsd ldrs, asked for eff wide 2f out, fdd fnl 1f:	1½	37a
975}	TOP PLACE 303 [8] C A Dwyer 3-8-7 P B Reilly (5) 33/1: 0-7: Rear, outpcd halfway.	1¼	28a
4145]	INDIAN OAK 148 [7] M P Muggeridge 3-8-7 L Keniry (2) 66/1: 50-8: Led to over 1f out & no extra after:	1	25a
485	BLUE POWER 8 [9] K R Burke 3-9-5 (66) Darren Williams 11/2: 44213-09: Rcd wide, nvr nr ldrs:	2	31a
495	PHILLY DEE 7 [10] N E Berry 3-8-7 bl (47) C Catlin 20/1: 3253-300: Nvr dangerous:	1¼	15a

10 Ran   59.61 (1.81)   Owner Mr K T Ivory   *Trained at Radlett*

549 | 4.40 Bet Direct Football Cashbacks Handicap Stakes 4yo+ 0-80 (D)

£4134 £1272 £636 £318   1m4f p/track rnd   Going 26   +10 Fast   Stalls Inside   [80]

534*	FALL IN LINE 1 [13] Sir Mark Prescott 4-8-11 6ex (66) J Mackay 2/5 FAV: 343-11111: Trkd ldrs, led over 3f out, rdn clr 1f out, val 3L+ (rnr-up eased):		84a
391	HIP HOP HARRY 22 [11] E A L Dunlop 4-9-6 (75) K Fallon 6/1: 31031-02: Rear, hdwy over 4f out, ch 1f out, eased when btn ins fnl furlong, val 3L+ defeat:	5	84a
493	CLASSIC ROLE 7 [12] R Ingram 5-9-6 (72) I Mongan 25/1: 0030-403: Mid-field, hdwy 3f out, chsd leading pair over 1f out & kept on ins fnl furlong:	1	78a
404	GALLANT BOY 21 [14] P D Evans 5-9-7 t (73) S Donohoe (7) 16/1: 5050-004: Rear, styd on for press fnl 2f but not dangerous:	2½	75a
493	PERFIDIOUS 7 [15] J R Boyle 6-9-4 (70) R Miles (3) 14/1: 5201-325: Led, hdd over 3f out, no extra:	½	71a
249	JUST WIZ 40 [3] N P Littmoden 8-9-4 (70) J P Guillambert (3) 25/1: 450532-6: Chsd ldrs, no impress fnl 2f.	½	70a
504	NIGHT WARRIOR 6 [5] D Flood 4-8-10 (65) L Treadwell (7) 20/1: 04-04427: Held up last place, hdwy & short of room 2f out, kept on:	7	56a
493	SUDDEN FLIGHT 7 [6] R Ingram 7-9-9 (75) R Havlin (3) 50/1: 0010-008: With ldr to 7f out, wknd:	1½	64a
504	DIGGER 6 [9] Miss Gay Kelleway 5-9-8 p (74) M Fenton (5) 20/1: 5236-149: Handy, fdd over 1f out:	nk	62a
391	FIDDLERS CREEK 22 [4] R Allan 5-9-6 VIS (72) J Quinn 16/1: 40360-60: Keen, chsd ldrs, fdd over 1f out:	1¼	58a
478	TOP TENOR 11 [10] B R Johnson 4-9-3 (72) N Chalmers (5) 50/1: 04123-00: Al bhd:	1½	56a
424}	ROLEX FREE 382 [7] Mrs L C Taylor 6-10-0 p (80) S Whitworth 50/1: 1406/40-0: Al bhd:	6	55a
467	COUNTYKAT 12 [2] K R Burke 4-9-6 vis (75) Darren Williams 66/1: 53630-60: Handy, wknd 4f out:	6	41a
	TRUSTED INSTINCT 115 [1] C A Dwyer 4-9-8 (77) N Callan 33/1: 063610-0: Al bhd:	3	39a
3181]	REVIEWER 554 [16] M Meade 6-9-8 (74) D Sweeney 50/1: 660/116/-0: Rcd wide in mid-field, wknd after 5f out & t.o.:	11	21a

15 Ran   2m 31.14 (1.94)   Owner Neil Greig - Osborne House II   *Trained at Newmarket*

SOUTHWELL Thursday 05.02.04 Lefthand, Sharp, Oval Track

Official Going Standard

550 | 1.30 Bet Direct On Sky Active Handicap Stakes Div 1 3yo+ 0-75 (E)

£3283 £938 £469   6f f/sand rnd   Going 51   +02 Fast   Stalls Inside   [75]

386	POLAR KINGDOM 23 [9] T D Barron 6-9-11 (72) D Mernagh 2/1 FAV: 00/200-31: Sn cl-up & led over 2f out, rdn clr, readily:		85a
471	ST IVIAN 12 [5] Mrs N Macauley 4-9-5 vis (66) P McCabe 33/1: 051-4602: Handy, rdn & styd on fnl 2f, not pace of wnr:	2½	69a
471	EFFECTIVE 12 [1] A P Jarvis 4-9-1 (62) J Quinn 11/1: 02000-03: Dwelt, mid-div, drvn & kept on fnl 1f:	2	60a
390	BLAKESHALL QUEST 23 [14] R Brotherton 4-9-1 vis (62) I Mongan 14/1: 0000-044: Bhd, drvn & kept on fnl 2f:	½	58a
415	MALAHIDE EXPRESS 21 [6] M J Polglase 4-9-1 p (62) L Fletcher (3) 14/1: 63500-45: Led till halfway, sn no impress.	3	49a
451	HOUT BAY 15 [10] R A Fahey 7-8-9 (56) T Hamilton (5) 9/1: 6500-136: Mid-div wide, not able to chall:	nk	42a
390	GILDED COVE 23 [2] R Hollinshead 4-9-6 (67) Dale Gibson 12/1: 21310-07: Bhd, mod hdwy wide for press.	nk	52a
487	ABOVE BOARD 9 [7] R F Marvin 9-7-12 10oh t (35) R Brisland 50/1: 000-5028: Well bhd, mod late prog, nrst fin.	2	24a
461	FAR NOTE 14 [12] S R Bowring 6-9-7 bl (68) A Culhane 8/1: 210-6209: Wide/bhd, nvr a factor:	1¼	43a
461	GRANDMA LILY 14 [4] M C Chapman 6-9-2 (73) B Reilly (5) 12/1: 0150-300: Mid-div, no impress 2f out:	1	45a
461	ONLY ONE LEGEND 14 [3] K A Ryan 6-9-9 p (70) N Callan 12/1: 6603-000: Al bhd, prefers polytrack.	1	39a
390	JOHNSTONS DIAMOND 23 [15] E J Alston 6-10-0 (75) Dean McKeown 9/1: 44101-00: Cl-up wide 3f.	¾	42a
255	LAKELANDS LADY 40 [13] J Balding 4-9-11 (72) J Edmunds (3) 9/1: 600000-0: Prom till over 2f out, abs.	¾	37a
345	NOBLE LOCKS 28 [11] J W Unett 6-9-11 (72) D Nolan (5) 25/1: 10051-00: Sn outpcd:	shd	37a
471	ILLUSIVE 12 [8] M Wigham 7-9-3 (64) G Carter 33/1: 30432-00: Held up, btn 2f out.	1	26a

15 Ran   1m 16.21 (2.91)   Owner Millie and Poppy Squire   *Trained at Thirsk*

551 | 2.00 Bet Direct On Sky Active Handicap Stakes Div 2 3yo+ 0-75 (E)

£3283 £938 £469   6f f/sand rnd   Going 51   -08 Slow   Stalls Inside   [75]

461	**TIME N TIME AGAIN 14** [2] E J Alston6-9-12 p (73) J Quinn 8/1: 542-5101: Handy trav well, led over 2f out, drvn out:		**80a**
385*	**MR PERTEMPS 24** [9] R A Fahey 6-9-0 p (61) T Hamilton (5) 9/4 FAV: 1100-312: Mid-div wide, eff 2f out, kept on, not pace of wnr:	1	**64a**
457	**BARZAK 14** [6] S R Bowring 4-9-1 bl t (62) J Bramhill 6/1: 1005-053: Well bhd & outpcd, drvn & kept in late, nrst fin:	1½	**60a**
487	**AMANDAS LAD 9** [1] M C Chapman 4-7-12 5oh (40) D Fox (5) 33/1: 0030-634: Handy, onepace.	½	**41a**
418	**ELLENS LAD 21** [3] W J Musson 10-9-11 bl (72) Paul Eddery 9/1: 00/001-05: Trkd ldrs, no extra dist:	3½	**58a**
453	**TEYAAR 15** [10] Mrs N Macauley 8-9-1 bl (62) P McCabe 14/1: 1003-006: In tch/wide, nvr a dngr:	5	**35a**
275	**CASH 36** [7] Paul Johnson 6-9-0 p (61) L Fletcher (3) 12/1: 050164-7: Prom, fdd fnl 2f:	nk	**33a**
450	**NAUGHTY GIRL 15** [5] P D Evans 4-9-1 (62) S Donohoe (7) 28/1: 26560-08: Mid-div, no impress from halfway:	2	**28a**
155	**RAYMONDS PRIDE 61** [14] K A Ryan 4-9-7 bl (68) N Callan 20/1: 4501F0-9: Keen & held up, no impress, abs.	nk	**33a**
205	**RIDICULE 51** [4] J G Portman 5-9-5 bl (66) R Havlin 12/1: 630540-0: Led till halfway, wknd qckly, abs.	1¼	**27a**
390	**ROYAL GRAND 23** [13] T D Barron 4-9-10 (71) P Makin (7) 6/1: 35312-30: In tch wide, nvr a factor:	1	**29a**
2100}	**SCARY NIGHT 237** [12] J Balding 4-10-0 (75) J Edmunds 25/1: 122200-0: In tch 4f, abs.	11	**4a**
317	**SHARP HAT 31** [11] D W Chapman 10-9-9 (70) A Culhane 12/1: 1135-520: Sn struggling:	8	**0a**
13 Ran	1m 16.84 (3.54) Owner Springs Equestrian Ltd		Trained at Preston

---

552 — 2.30 Bet Direct Interactive Claiming Stakes 4yo+ (F)

£2905 £830 £415   **1m4f f/sand**   Going 51   -31 Slow   Stalls Inside

458	**SPANISH STAR 14** [4] Mrs N Macauley 7-8-12 (45) A Culhane 11/1: 0041-461: Bhd, hdwy for press from 4f out, drvn & led dist, rdn clr:		**56a**
347	**DANCING PHANTOM 28** [6] James Moffatt 9-9-0 (70) J Fanning 13/8 FAV: 06521-32: Trkd ldrs, smooth hdwy to lead 2f out, sn rdn/hung left & hdd dist, no extra, fin lame:	3	**52a**
484	**ORINOCOVSKY 10** [2] N P Littmoden 5-9-8 (64) I Mongan 7/2: 5/004-103: Led/dsptd lead till 3f out, drvn & kept on onepace:	hd	**59a**
505*	**COOLFORE JADE 7** [5] N E Berry 4-9-0 (57) M Savage (5) 6/1: 45-01414: Sn handy/dsptd lead, rdn & led over 2f out till 2f out, not pace of wnr:	1¼	**52a**
484	**THEATRE TINKA 10** [10] R Hollinshead 5-9-4 p (68) N Callan 5/1: 3201-555: In tch, outpcd 3f out, kept on late.	nk	**52a**
491	**KING PRIAM 9** [3] M J Polglase 9-8-10 vis (45) Dean McKeown 16/1: 0414506: Cl-up till 4f out.	8	**33a**
505	**GLADYS AYLWARD 7** [1] A Crook 4-8-0 P (54) J Quinn 50/1: 10004-57: Sn struggling rear.	26	**0**
4476}	**PURE SPECULATION 131** [8] M L W Bell 4-8-7 (71) Hayley Turner 5/2 12/1: 14/3000-8: Chsd ldrs halfway, btn 3f out, abs.	2½	**-5a**
380	**PLATINUM BOY 24** [9] M Wellings 4-9-1 vis (48) V Slattery 100/1: 15000-09: Sn bhd.	shd	**3a**
458	**METICULOUS 14** [7] M C Chapman 6-8-8 (30) D Fox (5) 100/1: 00/0-0000: Prom till halfway.	3	**0**
10 Ran	2m 44.19 (9.89) Owner Mrs N Macauley		Trained at Melton Mowbray

---

553 — 3.00 #10 Free Bet @ Bet Direct Sky Active Maiden Stakes 3yo (D)

£3387 £1042 £521 £261   **1m f/sand rnd**   Going 51   -27 Slow   Stalls Inside

4660}	**VENGEROV 119** [4] M L W Bell 3-9-0 (71) M Fenton 7/2: 50340-1: Led trav well, rdn clr from over 1f out:		**74a**
4737}	**KINGS ROCK 114** [7] K A Ryan 3-9-0 (69) N Callan 5/2: 53530-2: Keen & handy, not pace of wnr from 2f out:	5	**63a**
488	**TONTO 9** [12] Miss D Mountain 3-9-0 (65) D Fox (5) 8/1: 3020-043: Handy, styd on onepace for press fnl 2f:	1½	**60a**
192	**MAID THE CUT 54** [3] A D Smith 3-8-9 J Quinn 66/1: 00-4: Trkd ldrs, styd on onepace:	1	**48a**
425	**MRS BROWN 20** [13] Sir Mark Prescott 3-8-9 J Mackay 7/4 FAV: 35: Trkd ldrs wide, no impress fnl 2f.	2	**49a**
438	**LOLAS DESTINY 17** [1] P A Blockley 3-8-9 (52) Derek Nolan (7) 12/1: 000-56: Mid-div, no impress fnl 2f.	½	**48a**
5014}	**ALMANAC 91** [9] B P J Baugh 3-9-0 J Fanning 66/1: 0-7: Dwelt & al rear, abs.	2	**49a**
	GO GREEN [8] P D Evans 3-8-9 S Donohoe (4) 50/1: 8: Dwelt, bhd, only mod prog on debut.	1¼	**41a**
3891}	**BIENHEUREUX 163** [5] W J Musson 3-9-0 Paul Eddery 33/1: 00-9: Chsd ldrs till 2f out, abs.	1	**44a**
	THIS WAY THAT WAY [10] G C Bravery 3-9-0 S Whitworth 25/1: 0: Dwelt & al rear on debut.	10	**27a**
	DIVINA [2] S L Keightley 3-8-9 A Nicholls 20/1: 0: Slow away & sn bhd on debut.	17	**0**
444	**SHEAPYS LASS 16** [14] A Crook 3-8-9 (50) V Halliday 66/1: 6526-000: Chsd ldrs till halfway.	5	**0**
	CAPTAIN FEARLESS [11] Mrs C A Dunnett 3-9-0 G Faulkner 40/1: 0: Al outpcd & bhd on debut.	7	**0**
13 Ran	1m 45.66 (6.26) Owner Mr R A Pegum		Trained at Newmarket

---

554 — 3.30 Press Interactive To Bet Direct Handicap Stakes 4yo+ 0-70 (E)

£3255 £930 £465   **2m f/sand**   Going 51   -65 Slow   Stalls Inside   [64]

529	**ALTITUDE DANCER 2** [7] P A Blockley 4-9-3 (59) N Callan 9/4: 31053-31: Cl-up/dsptd lead, went on halfway & rdn clr over 2f out, styd on strongly:		**65a**
478*	**LAND OF FANTASY 12** [10] Lady Herries 5-9-9 (59) J Quinn 6/1: 0B500-12: Held up, hdwy 5f out, drvn & kept on fnl 2f, no threat to wnr:	3½	**62a**
137	**TOMMY CARSON 65** [9] Jamie Poulton 9-8-4 (40) C Catlin 66/1: 020/26/5-3: Trkd ldrs, drvn & styd on onepace fnl 2f, not pace of wnr:	shd	**43a**
185	**HIGH POLICY 55** [4] R Hollinshead 8-10-0 p (64) Stephanie Hollinshead (7) 14/1: 130156-4: Trkd ldrs halfway, onepace for press fnl 3f:	2	**65a**
491	**LAMPOS 9** [1] Miss J A Camacho 4-8-9 (51) A Culhane 1/1 FAV: 030-3125: Held up, rdn 6f out, no ch fnl 3f.	10	**44a**
206	**PIPSSALIO 51** [8] Jamie Poulton 7-8-9 bl (45) M Henry 12/1: 000043-6: Chsd ldrs till 5f out, abs.	13	**28a**
479	**FINGER OF FATE 10** [2] M J Polglase 4-9-7 (63) I Mongan 66/1: 0060-007: Keen & sn led till halfway, sn bhd.	dist	**0a**
456	**CRYPTOGAM 14** [6] M E Sowersby 4-8-6 1ow (47) T Eaves 66/1: 00440-08: Sn bhd & t.o. 4f out.	hd	**0a**
8 Ran	3m 44.54 (18.54) Owner Mr J D Cotterill		Trained at Southwell

---

555 — 4.00 Littlewoods Bet Direct Selling Stakes 3yo+ (G)

£2590 £740 £370   **7f f/sand rnd**   Going 51   -02 Slow   Stalls Inside

241	**WEET WATCHERS 45** [6] P A Blockley 4-9-8 (71) N Callan 6/1: 1030P0-1: Made all, styd on well fnl 1f, rdn out:		**59a**
512	**FEAST OF ROMANCE 6** [7] P Howling 7-9-13 bl (54) S W Kelly 5/1: 36-33132: Trkd ldrs, rdn to chase wnr 2f out, styd on but not rch wnr:	1¼	**60a**
512	**SUDRA 6** [3] J O'Reilly 7-9-8 bl (49) J D O'Reilly (7) 8/1: 00-33443: Rear, hdwy wide over 2f out, styd on well fnl 1f, nrst fin:	2½	**50a**

SOUTHWELL Thursday 05.02.04 Lefthand, Sharp, Oval Track

332	INCHCOONAN 30 [5] K R Burke 6-9-3 (60) Darren Williams 9/4 FAV: 54424-44: Trkd ldrs, onepcd fnl 2f.	5	36a
512	MIZHAR 6 [9] J J Quinn 8-9-8 (55) I Mongan 11/4: 300-0525: Chsd ldrs, btn 2f out:	2½	36a
363	MARABAR 27 [2] D W Chapman 6-9-3 (65) A Culhane 8/1: 55005-06: Nvr nr ldrs:	1	29a
256	BURKEES GRAW 40 [11] Mrs S Lamyman 3-8-5 (45) J Quinn 50/1: 005300-7: Chsd ldrs, wknd 3f out	5	25a
372	COLLEGE STAR 24 [12] J F Coupland 6-9-8 bl (30) M Fenton 66/1: 00000-08: Chsd wnr, wknd halfway.	2	21a
3122}	ILLUSIONIST 196 [1] Mrs N Macauley 6-9-8 vis (40) P McCabe 66/1: 000050-9: Al bhd:	5	12a

9 Ran   1m 30.33 (3.73)   Owner Ed Weetman (Haulage & Storage)   Trained at Southwell

556 4.30 Bet Direct Football Cashbacks Handicap Stakes 4yo+ 0-70 (E) [69]
£3283 £938 £469   7f f/sand rnd   Going 51   -00 Slow   Stalls Inside

502	GAME GURU 7 [2] P A Blockley 5-9-9 bl (64) Dean McKeown 11/2 301-0131: Handy, led over 2f out, styd on well fnl 1f, rdn out:		66a
387	BLAKESEVEN 23 [10] W J Musson 4-8-7 (48) Paul Eddery 9/1: 00040-32: Midfield, hdwy 2f out, chall fnl 1f, juts btn:	¾	50a
459	MOUNT ROYALE 14 [13] N Tinkler 6-8-11 vis t (52) Kim Tinkler 11/1: 015-0063: Handy wide, styd on under press fnl 1f, btn arnd 1L:	nk	53a
419	MAJIK 21 [8] D J S ffrench Davis 5-10-0 P (69) I Mongan 3/1 FAV: 2313-034: Midfield, hdwy over 2f out, onepcd & drifted left fnl 1f:	¾	69a
479	MISTER BENJI 10 [4] B P J Baugh 5-9-1 p (56) M Tebbutt 40/1: 00010-05: Rear, hdwy to chase ldrs over 1f out, onepace:	shd	56a
442	BRILLIANTRIO 16 [6] M C Chapman 6-7-13 (40) D Fox (5) 40/1: 505-2406: Slowly away, hdwy over 2f out, slightly hmpd over 1f out, nrst fin:	2½	35a
344	SOCIAL CONTRACT 29 [11] S Dow 7-8-9 (50) C Catlin 20/1: 02006-07: Rear, hdwy 2f out, no impress fnl 1f:	nk	44a
457	YENALED 14 [1] K A Ryan 7-9-5 p (60) N Callan 9/2: 42545-38: Trkd ldrs, wknd over 1f out:	nk	53a
489	EAGER ANGEL 9 [3] R F Marvin 6-8-4 v (45) J Quinn 16/1: 0630-249: Rear, hdwy trav well over 2f out, rdn when hmpd dist, not recover:	shd	38a
363	PAWN IN LIFE 27 [12] T D Barron 6-9-7 (62) D Mernagh 8/1: 25051-00: Slow away, al bhd:	4	48a
1505}	DISPOL PETO 267 [9] Ian Emmerson 4-9-7 (62) A Nicholls 50/1: 014500-0: Led till hdd over 2f out, wknd:	2	44a
193	SUPREME SALUTATION 54 [5] D W Chapman 8-9-8 (63) A Culhane 33/1: 000560-0: Nvr nr ldrs:	1	43a
416*	KENNINGTON 21 [7] Mrs C A Dunnett 4-9-4 (59) Hayley Turner (5) 13/2: 0/-10: Handy, ch over 2f out, wknd.	9	23a

13 Ran   1m 30.17 (3.57)   Owner Mr Carl Would   Trained at Southwell

WOLVERHAMPTON Friday 06.02.04 Lefthand, Sharp Track

Official Going Standard

557 1.30 Bet Direct On Sky Active Amateur Riders' Handicap Stakes 4yo+ 0-70 (G) [44]
£2618 £748 £374   1m4f f/sand   Going 52   -29 Slow   Stalls Inside

4567*}	ROBBIE CAN CAN 127 [6] A W Carroll 5-10-7 (51) Mrs S Bosley 7/2 FAV: 530261-1: Towards rear, hdwy from halfway & led over 1f out, styd on strongly:		61a
456	FIGHT THE FEELING 15 [4] J W Unett 6-10-13 vis (57) Miss J C Williams (5) 9/2: 3016-422: Al prom & led over 2f out till over 1f out, no ch with wnr ins last:	6	58a
465	TOP OF THE CLASS 14 [2] P D Evans 7-10-1 vis (45) Miss E Folkes (3) 12/1: 4050-063: Sn prom & led over 3f out till over 2f out, no extra fnl 1f:	1	45a
465	OUR DESTINY 14 [9] D Burchell 6-10-8 vis (52) Miss E Tucker (7) 14/1: 0002-324: Led after 1f till 3f out, fdd:	9	41a
465	ORO STREET 1404 [7] G F Bridgwater 8-11-7 (65) Mr Shaun Johnson (7) 33/1: 04/216///: Slow away, nvr on terms:	3½	49a
484	LORD GIZZMO 11 [1] P W Hiatt 7-10-1 (45) Mrs Marie King (5) 7/1: 01355-06: Led 1f, prom till 3f out.	1½	27a
424	E MINOR 21 [3] T Wall 5-11-0 (58) Mr M Howells (7) 11/1: 44006-57: Prom, fdd fnl 3f.	nk	39a
997}	PRINCE MINATA 303 [8] P W Hiatt 9-10-4 (48) Miss A Hockley (7) 20/1: 150006-8: In tch, no impress fnl 4f.	1¼	27a
331*	SQUIRTLE TURTLE 31 [11] P F I Cole 4-11-7 bl (68) Mr C Ogle (5) 6/1: 03503-19: Prom, no impress 3f out:	17	24a
4664}	GARGOYLE GIRL 120 [12] J S Goldie 7-10-11 p (55) Ms C Williams 11/2: 200640-0: Slow away, nvr on terms:	2	8a
464	CLIQUEY 14 [5] B J Llewellyn 5-10-11 bl (55) Miss A Frieze (7) 40/1: 00600/-00: Slow away & nvr a factor.	10	0a

11 Ran   2m 43.35 (9.75)   Owner Mr K F Coleman   Trained at Alcester

558 2.00 Press Interactive To Bet Direct Handicap Stakes Div 1 4yo+ 0-60 (F) [60]
£2968 £848 £424   7f f/sand rnd   Going 52   -11 Slow   Stalls Outside

3491}	ICED DIAMOND 181 [5] W M Brisbourne 5-9-6 (52) B Swarbrick (7) 5/1: 256200-1: Trkd ldrs & led over 1f out, edged left, drvn out:		60a
501*	ITALIAN MIST 8 [12] Julian Poulton 5-9-8 6ex e (54) G Faulkner 12/1: 50-13512: Chsd ldrs, styd on for press fnl 2f:	2	56a
459	SPINDOR 15 [11] J A Osborne 5-9-13 bl (59) S Crawford (7) 8/1: 0050-253: In tch, styd on for press over 1f out:	½	60a
463	WALTZING WIZARD 15 [10] A Berry 5-9-4 (50) F Lynch 5/1: 6052-354: Towards rear, late gains, nrst fin.	1¼	48a
378	LARKYS LOB 25 [1] Paul Johnson 5-9-2 (48) N Chalmers (5) 7/1: 002-2145: Chsd ldrs till dist:	nk	45a
501	LADY NATILDA 8 [2] D Haydn Jones 4-9-1 P (47) Paul Eddery 11/1: 000-4306: Handy travelling well & led over 2f out till over 1f out, no extra:	1	42a
344	LUCID DREAMS 30 [4] M Wigham 5-9-5 (51) G Carter 4/1 FAV: 01240-57: Held up, hmpd halfway, nvr a factor.	1½	43a
298	BETTER OFF 34 [8] Mrs N Macauley 6-10-0 p (60) Hayley Turner (5) 20/1: 150006-58: Slow away, sn in tch, btn dist:	2½	47a
524	PIPS SONG 4 [7] P W Hiatt 9-9-0 6ex (46) A Culhane 10/1: 00-00109: Led/dsptd lead till 2f out, wknd:	½	32a
3613}	YOUNGS FORTH 176 [3] A W Carroll 4-8-13 (45) S Whitworth 33/1: 3/05500-0: Slow away, nvr dngr.	nk	30a
482}	COMPTON BAY 374 [9] M Brittain 4-9-3 (49) M Lawson (7) 50/1: 00/0-0: Led/dsptd lead 2f, btn 2f out, abs.	3	28a

11 Ran   1m 30.59 (4.39)   Owner Mr P J Williams   Trained at Baschurch

559 2.30 Bet Direct Football Cashbacks Handicap Stakes Div 1 3yo+ 0-60 (F) [60]
£2954 £844 £422   1m100y f/sand rnd Going 52   -08 Slow   Stalls Inside

| 465 | SORBIESHARRY 14 [11] Mrs N Macauley 5-9-2 p (48) P McCabe 12/1: 22-52351: Chsd ldr halfway, rdn & outpcd 2f out, | | 51a |

rallied gamely & led line, all out:

4640}	FUTURISTIC 122 [13] J Pearce 4-9-11 (57) J Quinn 9/2: 126006-2: Prom & chsd ldr 2f out, rdn & led over 1f out, hung right & just hdd cl-home:	hd	60a
498	GIVEMETHEMOONLIGHT 9 [12] Mrs Stef Liddiard 5-9-4 vis (50) I Mongan 11/4 FAV: 2521353: Led till over 1f out, ev ch ins last, just held:	hd	52a
457	LORD CHAMBERLAIN 15 [3] J M Bradley 11-9-7 bl (53) C J Davies (3) 20/1: 450-2144: Dwelt & held up, hdwy wide to press ldrs dist, no extra fnl 100yds:	½	54a
393	GOLDBRICKER 24 [6] W M Brisbourne 4-9-0 (46) B Swarbrick (7) 12/1: 53302-65: Held up, styd on onepace for press fnl 2f:	¾	45a
4816}	RED LANCER 109 [10] R J Price 3-8-9 (60) R Miles (3) 80/1: 655010-6: Mid-div, outpcd 3f out, late gains, no danger:	½	58a
304)	POTSDAM 185 [9] Niall Moran 6-9-1 t (47) J Fanning 9/1: 000-024-7: Held up, smooth hdwy to press ldrs 3f out, no extra dist:	nk	44a
469	ALLY MAKBUL 14 [7] J R Best 4-9-9 (55) N Pollard 8/1: 000-1448: Chsd ldrs, no impress over 2f out:	1¾	48a
502	JAMESTOWN 8 [4] M J Polglase 7-8-13 (45) L Fletcher (3) 25/1: 63-50009: Chsd ldrs, btn 3f out:	nk	37a
429	FORTUNE POINT 20 [8] A W Carroll 6-9-13 (59) A Culhane 10/1: 20640-40: In tch, rdn & no impress fnl 2f.	¾	49a
315	FELIDAE 32 [5] M Brittain 4-8-8 BL T (40) M Lawson (7) 80/1: 0050-00: Slowly away & al bhd:	3½	23a
479	PAS DE SURPRISE 11 [2] P D Evans 6-9-12 (58) S Donohoe (7) 6/1: 00364-30: Trkd ldrs, btn 3f out:	1¾	38a
512	LUCAYAN MONARCH 7 [1] P S McEntee 6-9-9 BL (55) F P Ferris (3) 14/1: 4-211250: Struggling halfway:	19	0

13 Ran   1m 51.27 (5.07)   Owner Mrs Liz Nelson   Trained at Melton Mowbray

---

560   3.00 Bet Direct Interactive Claiming Stakes 3yo   (F)
£2933 £838 £419   7f f/sand rnd   Going 52   -12 Slow   Stalls Outside

368	BLUE EMPIRE 27 [6] P C Haslam 3-9-7 (75) G Faulkner 7/4 FAV: 1021-451: Chsd ldrs & led over 2f out, rdn & styd on strongly:		81a
4490}	HATCH 131 [12] R Charlton 3-8-13 (79) D Sweeney 9/4: 5420-2: In tch, hdwy wide to press wnr over 1f out, awkward head carriage & just held fnl 100yds:	1¼	69a
466	FISSION 14 [4] J A Osborne 3-9-2 bl (75) S W Kelly 11/1: 14513-63: Trkd ldr & led 4f out, hdd over 2f out, kept on for press:	1¾	69a
462	KATIES ROLE 15 [3] Ian Emmerson 3-8-2 (50) D Fox (5) 33/1: 0043-344: Chsd ldrs, outpcd inner halfway, switched wide & late gains, nvr dangerous:	2½	50a
510	TURF PRINCESS 7 [10] Ian Emmerson 3-8-10 (62) D Fentiman (7) 9/1: 226-1245: Chsd ldrs, no impress fnl 2f:	nk	57a
383*	JAKARMI 25 [8] B Palling 3-8-9 (56) N Callan 14/1: 02650-16: Chsd ldrs, rdn/outpcd when hmpd 2f out:	nk	55a
462	GARNOCK VENTURE 15 [5] A Berry 3-8-7 bl (47) J Fanning 50/1: 0043-407: Mid-div, no impress fnl 3f:	½	52a
510	EMARADIA 2 [2] A W Carroll 3-8-8 bl (54) Joanna Badger 10/1: 422-3128: Led 3f, btn 2f out:	2½	48a
337	KNIGHT ONTHE TILES 30 [1] J R Best 3-8-9 (65) N Pollard 14/1: 41060-09: Nvr on terms with ldrs:	4	41a
466	FORA SMILE 14 [7] M D I Usher 3-8-13 A Daly 66/1: 00: Al rear.	¾	44a
383	SECRET BLOOM 25 [9] J R Norton 3-8-7 vis (47) J Bramhill 66/1: 0050-440: Dwelt, nvr on terms.	7	26a
462	HEATHYARDS JOY 15 [11] R Hollinshead 3-8-2 Dale Gibson (7) 66/1: 0-00: In tch, btn halfway.	1	19a

12 Ran   1m 30.67 (4.47)   Owner Blue Lion Racing II   Trained at Middleham

---

561   3.30 #10 Free Bet @ Bet Direct Sky Active Maiden Stakes 4yo+   (D)
£3315 £1020 £510 £255   1m1f79y f/sand rnd Going 52   -19 Slow   Stalls Inside

2687}	CALL ME SUNSHINE 216 [6] P C Haslam 4-8-9 (70) G Faulkner 5/1: 52/5402-1: Trkd ldrs, drvn fnl 1f & led line, all out:		58a
	MASTER ROLE 104 [1] M A Jarvis 4-8-9 N Callan 9/2: 3/230-2: Led/dsptd lead & went on over 2f out, edged right & hdd line:	shd	62a
509	PACIFIC OCEAN 7 [4] Mrs Stef Liddiard 5-9-0 t (48) J Quinn 7/4 FAV: 66534-23: Dwelt & held up, pulled hard early, rapid prog to lead 4f out till over 2f out, no extra nr fin:	¾	61a
406	TAIYO 23 [5] J W Payne 4-8-9 (50) I Mongan 6/1: 0560-654: Trkd ldrs, ch over 2f out, no extra dist:	2½	51a
4848}	DORA CORBINO 107 [3] R Hollinshead 4-8-9 (48) A Culhane 33/1: 0/560-5: Prom 5f, sn no impress:	5	42a
509	ALBEE 7 [2] Miss Gay Kelleway 4-9-0 P M Fenton 14/1: 66: Dwelt, keen & led after 1f till 4f out, sn btn, cheek pieces.	9	31a
509	MARINO MOU 7 [7] Miss D Mountain 4-9-0 C Catlin 100/1: 07: Al outpcd.	18	-2a

7 Ran   2m 04.90 (6.7)   Owner Chelgate Public Relations Ltd   Trained at Middleham

---

562   4.00 Press Interactive To Bet Direct Handicap Stakes Div 2 4yo+ 0-60 (F)   [60]
£2968 £848 £424   7f f/sand rnd   Going 52   -07 Slow   Stalls Outside

512*	WARLINGHAM 7 [4] P Howling 6-9-12 6ex (58) J Fanning 6/1: 210-0011: In tch, led dist, rdn out:		62a
499*	BLONDE EN BLONDE 9 [12] N P Littmoden 4-10-6 6ex bl (66) I Mongan 7/1: 34-66012: Dwelt & held up, rdn & hdwy to press ldrs over 1f out, edged left & no extra nr fin:	½	68a
451	LORD MELBOURNE 16 [1] J A Osborne 5-9-4 (50) S W Kelly 7/2: 035-2143: Dwelt & held up, late gains for press, nrst fin:	¾	51a
397	PILGRIM PRINCESS 23 [8] E J Alston 6-8-13 (45) D Allan (3) 7/1: 6246-354: Led till dist, no extra.	¾	45a
544	SCARROTTOO 2 [10] S C Williams 9-9-6 BL e (52) B Reilly (5) 3/1 FAV: 45340-05: Slow away, not able to chall ldrs	2½	47a
398	IVY MOON 23 [11] B J Llewellyn 4-8-13 (45) R Thomas (5) 20/1: 03030-36: Prom, outpcd fnl 2f:	½	39a
459	HEADLAND 15 [7] D W Chapman 6-9-13 bl (59) A Culhane 11/1: 041-4207: Prom & ch over 1f out, wknd ins last.	hd	52a
4964}	LARGS 98 [3] J Balding 4-9-2 (48) J Edmunds 33/1: 520345-8: Chsd ldrs till outpcd 3f out:	1	39a
313	DARK CHAMPION 32 [6] Jedd O'Keeffe 4-9-4 P (50) M Fenton 16/1: 34405-29: Chsd ldrs till over 3f out, no impress.	hd	40a
451	ILLUSTRIOUS DUKE 16 [2] M Mullineaux 6-9-2 (48) Lisa Jones (7) 16/1: 01200-00: Prom 4f:	½	37a
448	MASTER RATTLE 16 [9] Jane Southcombe 5-9-1 (47) V Slattery 66/1: 0000-000: Cl-up till over 2f out.	hd	35a

11 Ran   1m 30.32 (4.12)   Owner Mr David Andrew Brown   Trained at Newmarket

---

563   4.30 Littlewoods Bet Direct Selling Handicap Stakes 4yo+ 0-60 (G)   [56]
£2534 £724 £362   2m46y f/sand   Going 52   -29 Slow   Stalls Inside

3988}	REFLEX BLUE 516 [5] R J Price 7-8-12 vis (40) R Miles (3) 9/2: 000U05-/-1: Held up, smooth prog to trk ldr 5f out, led over 2f out & rdn clr:		48a
537	THE LAST MOHICAN 3 [2] P Howling 5-8-7 p (35) S W Kelly 5/2 FAV: 0/50-4232: Led/dsptd lead till went on over 9f out, rdn & hdd over 2f out, no impress well ins last:	11	35a
469	KNOCKDOO 14 [1] J S Goldie 11-8-2 (30) C Catlin 9/1: 06203-03: Drvn rear, only mod prog, nvr dangerous:	17	17a

145

469	**FAILED TO HIT 14** [6] N P Littmoden 11-9-10 vis (52) I Mongan 4/1: 2/1456-34: Led after 2f, drvn & hdd 9f out, no impress fnl 4f:	3½	36a
454	**ROPPONGI DANCER 16** [8] Mrs N Macauley 5-8-2 bl t (30) Stephanie Hollinshead (5) 25/1: 400-5305: Chsd ldrs 12f.	4	10a
469	**CLAPTRAP 14** [7] R Brotherton 4-9-5 (53) A Culhane 11/4: 0015-256: Prom, no ch fnl 5f:	2½	31a
446	**BEHAN 17** [3] A Crook 5-8-2 bl (30) J Quinn 25/1: 0060-057: Held up, no ch from halfway	20	0a
	OLIMP 453 [4] Miss A M Newton Smith 8-9-7 (49) D Sweeney 20/1: 125224/-8: Sn wll bhd, jumps fit.	½	11a
8 Ran	3m 42.33 (13.13) Owner Fox and Cub Partnership		Trained at Hereford

564 **5.00 Bet Direct Football Cashbacks Handicap Stakes Div 2 3yo+ 0-60 (F)**   **[60]**
£2954 £844 £422   **1m100y f/sand rnd Going 52   +08 Fast**   Stalls Inside

490*	**RARE COINCIDENCE 10** [3] R F Fisher 3-8-11 6ex p (62) L Fletcher (3) 12/1: 05320-11: Led/dsptd lead, led over 5f out & rdn clr from 2f out, al holding rivals ins last:		71a
528	**ZAHUNDA 4** [1] W M Brisbourne 5-8-8 (40) B Swarbrick (7) 14/1: 0000-602: Prom & chsd wnr from 2f out, al held ins last:	2½	43a
339	**MISS GLORY BE 30** [6] Miss Gay Kelleway 6-9-5 p (51) J Quinn 5/1: 23006-03: Chsd ldrs, keen early, rdn & kept on onepace fnl 2f:	1¼	51a
437	**MUTARAFAA 18** [4] D Shaw 5-9-9 e (55) T Hamilton (5) 9/2 JT FAV: 211-4324: Chsd ldrs, lost place halfway, kept on for press ins last:	nk	54a
311	**AIR OF ESTEEM 32** [10] Ian Emmerson 8-9-1 (47) A Nicholls 16/1: 04553-55: Chsd ldrs, no extra dist.	3	40a
384	**VICTORY FLIP 25** [9] R Hollinshead 4-8-13 p (45) Stephanie Hollinshead (7) 33/1: 36460-06: Towards rear, mod prog.	1½	35a
464*	**STING LIKE A BEE 14** [11] J S Goldie 5-9-9 (55) T Eaves (5) 8/1: 56060-17: Dwelt & held up, no impress:	4	37a
393	**SPY GUN 24** [7] T Wall 4-9-12 (58) N Chalmers (5) 7/1: 0014-358: In tch till over 2f out:	1¼	37a
387	**HOHS BACK 24** [5] Paul Johnson 5-9-13 p (59) Lisa Jones (3) 12/1: 02000-09: Held up, rdn & no impress fnl 3f.	¾	37a
424	**CUMBRIAN PRINCESS 21** [12] M Blanshard 7-8-3 (35) Dale Gibson 12/1: 00005-40: Keen & prom wide 7f.	3	7a
463	**SANDORRA 15** [8] M Brittain 6-9-0 (46) M Lawson 25/1: 000-3160: Keen & sn led till over 5f out, btn 3f out:	1½	15a
477	**WELSH WIND 13** [2] M Wigham 8-9-10 t (56) J Fanning (3) 9/2 JT FAV: 3042-320: In tch 6f:	1	23a
12 Ran	1m 49.91 (3.71) Owner Great Head House Estates Limit		Trained at Ulverston

Official Going Standard

565 **12.45 Multiple Sclerosis Trust Apprentice Handicap Stakes 4yo+ 0-70 (F)**   **[70]**
£3087 £882 £441   **7f p/track rnd Going 48   -30 Slow**   Stalls Inside

499	**ZAFARSHAH 10** [7] P D Evans 5-9-1 (57) S Donohoe (5) 7/2 FAV: 0050-141: Trkd ldrs trav well, led dist, pushed clr, v cosily:		65a
516	**HARD TO CATCH 7** [5] D K Ivory 6-9-9 (65) M Savage (5) 12/1: 0555-002: Handy, rdn & lost place halfway, rallied for press fnl 1f, no threat to wnr:	1½	67a
516*	**WHIPPASNAPPER 7** [16] J R Best 4-10-0 (70) M Lawson (3) 15/2: 00-01213: Pulled hard, sn prom wide, ch dist, no extra:	nk	71a
509*	**MUSICAL GIFT 8** [14] C N Allen 4-10-0 (70) D Fox 7/1: 2240-14: Keen, sn led till rdn & hdd dist, no extra:	½	70a
4864}	**TIGER TOPS 106** [1] J A Supple 5-9-9 (65) P Gallagher (5) 14/1: 503006-5: Keen, towards rear, styd on late, nrst fin:	½	64a
538*	**PIQUET 4** [9] J J Bridger 6-8-9 6ex (51) Hayley Turner (3) 8/1: 0501-316: Hld up last, hdwy & no room over 1f out, kept on late, nrst fin:	hd	49a
499	**ACORAZADO 10** [8] G L Moore 5-9-2 e (58) A Quinn 9/2: 1535-027: Rear, swtchd wide & mod gains:	nk	55a
4698}	**CARLTON 118** [10] C R Dore 10-9-6 (62) R Thomas (3) 33/1: 055000-8: Cl-up, wknd over 1f out:	½	58a
471	**STEELY DAN 14** [15] J R Best 5-8-11 (53) Rory Moore (5) 16/1: 00005-09: Sn handy wide, no extra dist.	shd	49a
474	**LILY OF THE GUILD 14** [11] W S Kittow 5-8-12 (54) L Treadwell (7) 10/1: 44462-00: Rear/wide, no impress dist.	1	48a
450	**POWER BIRD 17** [3] B R Johnson 4-9-4 (60) N Chalmers 10/1: 50000-20: Rear, btn 2f out:	shd	54a
479	**FRANKSKIPS 12** [12] Miss B Sanders 5-9-4 (60) Karen Peippo (7) 20/1: 0500-050: Mid-div wide, btn dist.	4	46a
187	**CRESSEX KATIE 57** [6] J R Best 5-9-2 (58) D Fentiman (5) 33/1: 106400-0: Chsd ldr 3f, sn btn, abs.	8	30a
13 Ran	1m 26.19 (3.39) Owner Waterline Racing Club		Trained at Abergavenny

566 **1.15 M S Trust On 01462 476700 Maiden Stakes 3yo+ (D)**
£4115 £1266 £633 £317   **7f p/track rnd Going 18   -18 Slow**   Stalls Inside

448	**MAYZIN 17** [14] R M Flower 4-9-10 p (54) D Sweeney 7/4 FAV: 054-3241: Pulled hard early & sn led/clr, rdn & al holding rivals from dist:		67a
	LA PEREGRINA 6 [6] Sir Mark Prescott 3-8-2 J Mackay 8/1: 2: Mid-div, styd on for press, nrst fin & nvr threat to wnr:	1½	58a
472	**GREEN FALCON 14** [5] J W Hills 3-8-7 M Hills 11/2: 03: Dwelt, sn prom, onepace for press fnl 2f:	1¾	60a
460	**ALEXANDER AMBITION 16** [10] S Kirk 3-8-2 (65) D Fox 5/2: 020-434: Sn in tch wide, eff to chase wnr over 2f out, no extra dist:	1¾	52a
4692}	**DUE TO ME 118** [4] G L Moore 4-9-5 e (40) S Whitworth 33/1: 600/400-5: Chsd ldrs, no impress:	4	44a
4378}	**HINCHLEY WOOD 848** [3] J R Best 5-9-10 N Pollard 66/1: 00//-6: Chsd wnr halfway, btn 2f out, long abs.	nk	46a
4867}	**TIME FLYER 106** [2] W de Best Turner 4-9-10 (45) S Righton 66/1: 00007-7: Led 1f, prom till halfway:	2½	43a
449	**HEARTBEAT 17** [7] P J McBride 3-8-2 (59) Dale Gibson 14/1: 06-468: Bhd, little hdwy.	½	37a
472	**MYSTIC MOON 14** [13] J R Jenkins 3-8-2 J Bramhill 20/1: 0-09: Chsd ldrs wide 5f.	nk	36a
116	**ALMOST WELCOME 70** [12] S Dow 3-8-7 (50) P Doe 33/1: 0000-0: Al bhd, abs.	1½	38a
411	**COSTA DEL SOL 23** [1] J J Bridger 3-8-7 (40) R Miles (3) 33/1: 6005-000: In tch, struggling halfway.	2	34a
	MR DINGLAWI 11 [11] D B Feek 3-8-7 G Carter 33/1: 0: Dwelt & sn bhd, t.o.	11	14a
12 Ran	1m 25.3 (2.5) Owner Ms Z N Watkins		Trained at Jevington

567 **1.45 Bet Direct Handicap Stakes 3yo+ 0-95 (C)**   **[94]**
£7169 £2719 £1360 £618   **5f p/track rnd Going 18   +14 Fast**   Stalls Outside

461	**JUSTALORD 16** [6] J Balding 6-9-5 p (85) J Edmunds 7/2: 5206-021: Broke well & led 1f, trkd ldr after, styd on for press to lead well ins last:		92a

518	**NO TIME 7** [2] M J Polglase 4-8-12 (78) K Fallon 3/1 FAV: 000-6662: Pushed along chasing front pair, styd on for press, just failed:		hd	**84a**
461*	**DANCING MYSTERY 16** [1] E A Wheeler 10-10-0 bl (94) S Carson 7/1: 00133-13: Led after 1f, rdn clr over 1f out, wknd & hdd well ins last:		¾	**98a**
461	**ZARZU 16** [4] C R Dore 5-9-6 (86) R Thomas (5) 13/2: 2541-354: Rear, kept on for press, not reach ldrs.		hd	**89a**
431	**LAW BREAKER 21** [3] J A Gilbert 6-9-10 (90) D R McCabe 9/1: 00521-55: Pushed along mid-div, nrst fin:		nk	**92a**
4384*}	**TURIBIUS 138** [5] T E Powell 5-8-13 (79) S Whitworth 14/1: 134021-6: Bhd, nvr pace to threaten:		3	**72a**
461	**PALAWAN 16** [9] A M Balding 8-9-3 (83) N Chalmers (5) 14/1: 10102-07: Chsd ldrs wide, no impress dist:		shd	**76a**
461	**TRINCULO 16** [7] N P Littmoden 7-9-9 p (89) J P Guillambert (3) 11/1: 0160-008: Chsd ldrs till outpcd from halfway:		1¼	**78a**
361	**BEAUVRAI 29** [10] J J Quinn 4-9-6 (86) Martin Dwyer 25/1: 00000-09: Sn outpcd & no impress:		8	**53a**
4679}	**STRATHCLYDE 119** [8] J R Best 5-8-13 (79) N Pollard 13/2: 500000-0: Sn rdn & outpcd from halfway.		6	**30a**
10 Ran	58.02 (0.22)	Owner Mr T H Heckingbottom		Trained at Doncaster

568	**2.20 Betdirect Co Uk Handicap Stakes 3yo 0-95 (C)** [99]
	£8054 £2478 £1239 £620 **1m2f p/track** **Going 18** **-13 Slow** Stalls Inside

341	**SKIDMARK 31** [8] D R C Elsworth 3-8-8 (79) P Fitzsimons 6/4 FAV: 31-21: Rear, smooth hdwy inner to chase ldr over 2f out, rdn to narrowly assert cl-home:			**91a**
403*	**ASCERTAIN 24** [1] N P Littmoden 3-9-7 (92) I Mongan 7/1: 0-12: Trkd ldrs, led over 2f out & sn drvn around 3L clr, drvn/hdd cl-home:		hd	**102a**
514	**LORD OF THE SEA 7** [3] Jamie Poulton 3-8-0 (71) D Kinsella 50/1: 0655-33: In tch, chsd ldrs 2f out, no impress dist:		7	**71a**
473*	**BAAWRAH 14** [6] M R Channon 3-8-1 (72) C Catlin 9/1: 0632-214: Mid-div, rdn & no impress fnl 3f:		6	**64a**
438*	**ALWAYS FLYING 19** [9] M Johnston 3-7-12 (69) D Fox (5) 7/1: 50355-15: Led after 1f till over 2f out, fdd:		nk	**60a**
4988}	**INFIDELITY 96** [4] A Bailey 3-7-13 (70) Lisa Jones (3) 33/1: 455120-6: Mid-div, no impress fnl 2f, reapp.		½	**60a**
276*	**DENVER 38** [5] B J Meehan 3-8-6 (77) Paul Eddery 9/1: 42521-7: Led 1f, chsd ldr till 3f out:		6	**59a**
506	**LA PUCE 9** [7] Miss Gay Kelleway 3-7-12 1oh (68) J Mackay 33/1: 42300-48: Rear, no ch fnl 3f:		3	**47a**
497	**LITTLE EYE 10** [10] J R Best 3-7-7 (68) Dale Gibson 25/1: 42234-49: Prom, lost place from halfway.		hd	**46a**
460*	**SABBAAG 16** [2] D R Loder 3-8-5 T (76) D R McCabe 5/1: 210: Keen/trkd ldrs, wknd qckly 3f out:		22	**23a**
10 Ran	2m 05.86 (3.06)	Owner Mr Raymond Tooth		Trained at Whitsbury

569	**2.50 Bet Direct Football Cashbacks Classified Stakes 4yo+ 0-65 (E)**
	£3339 £954 £477 **1m2f p/track** **Going 18** **-06 Slow** Stalls Inside

549+*	**FALL IN LINE 3** [6] Sir Mark Prescott 4-9-6 (86) J Mackay 1/2 FAV: 3-111111: Made all, joined 4f out & sn rdn, styd on strongly for press to assert from dist:			**84a**
178	**LEARNED LAD 59** [1] Jamie Poulton 6-9-1 (62) I Mongan 16/1: 200050-2: Keen, trkd wnr, rdn to chall 4f out, no extra from		4	**67a**
4595}	**DANCE PARTY 126** [4] A M Balding 4-8-11 (62) Martin Dwyer 33/1: 043400-3: Mid-div, outpcd 4f out, kept on for press ins last:		1½	**62a**
3982}	**MUST BE MAGIC 161** [12] H J Collingridge 7-9-1 vis (63) N Callan 16/1: 043120-4: Chsd ldrs 3f out, no impress over 1f out:		1¾	**62a**
465*	**SCOTTISH RIVER 15** [9] I M J Usher 5-9-1 (62) A Daly 9/1: 003-3015: Slow away, keen rear, mod gains:		½	**62a**
270	**ROYAL FASHION 39** [8] Miss S West 4-8-11 (60) N Chalmers (5) 50/1: 0/30206-6: Slowly away, bhd, mod late prog.		6	**51a**
4920}	**REAP 102** [13] J Pearce 6-9-1 (65) Dean McKeown 6/1: 101112-7: Chsd wnr, btn 2f out:		1½	**52a**
4121}	**MY SHARP GREY 152** [7] J Gallagher 5-8-12 (54) D Sweeney 50/1: 602002-8: Rear, no ch fnl 4f, reapp.		6	**41a**
1309}	**PRINCE SLAYER 999** [3] T P McGovern 8-9-1 (65) M Fenton 66/1: 000/400//-: Mid-div, btn 3f out, `hung right'.		2	**41a**
4963}	**BELTANE 99** [10] W de Best Turner 6-9-1 (40) S Righton 100/1: 0100/0/P-0: Mid-div, no ch fnl 3f, reapp.		1	**40a**
429	**BONTADINI 21** [2] D Morris 5-9-1 vis (48) S Whitworth 33/1: 00000-50: Keen & prom till 4f out:		3½	**35a**
272	**REMEMBRANCE 39** [5] M J Gingell 4-9-0 t (57) S Donohoe (7) 50/1: 203662-0: Rear, no ch fnl 3f, new stable.		8	**24a**
427	**MYTHICAL CHARM 22** [11] J J Bridger 5-8-12 (48) Hayley Turner (5) 50/1: 06501-60: Keen & prom till 3f out.		nk	**20a**
13 Ran	2m 05.17 (2.37)	Owner Neil Greig - Osborne House II		Trained at Newmarket

570	**3.25 Bet Direct On 0800 32 93 93 Handicap Stakes 4yo+ 0-105 (B)** [104]
	£14964 £5676 £2838 £1290 **1m4f p/track** **Going 18** **-03 Slow** Stalls Inside

475	**GIG HARBOR 14** [6] Miss E C Lavelle 5-8-13 (89) L Keniry (3) 13/2: 0626-101: Handy & trkd ldr trav well 4f out, led over 2f out, al holding rivals for press ins last:			**97a**
475	**BARRY ISLAND 14** [5] D R C Elsworth 5-7-12 1oh (73) Lisa Jones (3) 6/1: 3604-152: Keen, rear, styd on for press, not able to chall.		¾	**80a**
475+*	**COLD TURKEY 14** [7] G L Moore 4-8-9 (88) S Whitworth 1/1 FAV: 1112-113: Dwelt, rear, eff wide over 2f out, onepace dist:		3	**90a**
478	**EZZ ELKHEIL 14** [2] J R Jenkins 5-8-0 (76) J Mackay 10/1: 10050-24: Led/dsptd lead till 5f out, no extra till over 1f out:		1½	**76a**
433	**LYGETON LAD 21** [4] Miss Gay Kelleway 6-10-0 (104) M Fenton 14/1: 00101-55: Mid-div, hdwy to press ldrs over 2f out, no extra over 1f out:		nk	**103a**
433	**ZONERGEN 21** [8] Lady Herries 6-9-0 bl (90) M Tebbutt 12/1: 03603-06: Rear, eff wide, no impress on ldrs:		1¾	**87a**
547	**INTERNATIONALGUEST 3** [3] G G Margarson 5-8-4 bl (80) Martin Dwyer 16/1: 60-02007: Trkd ldrs, no extra/eased ins		hd	**76a**
4612}	**TEAM MATE 124** [10] Miss J Feilden 6-8-2 (78) Dale Gibson 33/1: 061540-8: Mid-div, no impress fnl 3f:		3½	**69a**
549	**GALLANT BOY 3** [9] P D Evans 5-7-12 1oh vis t (73) Joanna Badger (5) 16/1: 050-0049: Held up, eff to go handy halfway, btn 2f out:		nk	**64a**
2523}	**DONT SIOUX ME 223** [1] C R Dore 6-9-0 t (90) J Bramhill 40/1: 240/00/4-0: Led after 1f till 5f out, jumps fit.		19	**54a**
10 Ran	2m 31.71 (2.51)	Owner Fraser Miller Racing		Trained at Andover

571	**4.00 Bet All Weather: Bet Direct Selling Stakes 4yo+ (G)**
	£2660 £760 £380 **1m p/track rnd** **Going 18** **-03 Slow** Stalls Outside

3933}	**MOAYED 163** [4] N P Littmoden 5-8-13 bl t (80) I Mongan 5/4 FAV: 111500-1: Rear, gd hdwy from halfway & led over 1f out, cmftbly:			**74a**
450	**THE GAIKWAR 17** [7] N E Berry 5-8-13 bl (65) M Savage (5) 2/1: 0404-642: Mid-div, chsd ldrs 3f out, onepace:		6	**61a**
440	**CHANDELIER 19** [3] M S Saunders 4-8-13 BL (54) R Miles (3) 16/1: 50060-53: Keen & handy, led 4f out till over 1f out, sn no		2½	**56a**

LINGFIELD Saturday 07.02.04 Lefthand, V Sharp Track

extra:

267	DOLPHINELLE 39 [1] Jamie Poulton 8-8-13 vis (47) D Kinsella 16/1: 500535-4: Rear, mod prog, no dngr.		1	54a
540	ESTRELLA LEVANTE 4 [5] G L Moore 4-8-13 (52) Jemma Marshall (7) 20/1: 4U055-05: Keen/dsptd lead till halfway.		2½	49a
555	FEAST OF ROMANCE 2 [10] P Howling 7-9-5 p (53) S W Kelly 8/1: 36-331326: Mid-div, rdn & no impress 2f out.		¾	54a
145	EUROLINK ZANTE 63 [12] T D McCarthy 8-8-13 BL (45) J P Guillambert (3) 20/1: 006060-7: Mid-div, no ch fnl 3f, abs/blnks.		1½	45a
540	WATERLINE DANCER 4 [2] P D Evans 4-8-8 vis t (45) N Callan 33/1: 40000-08: Keen & cl-up till over 3f out.		4	32a
85	PENNY VALENTINE 75 [9] J R Best 4-8-13 (35) N Pollard 50/1: 600050-9: Struggling halfway, nvr a factor, abs.		4	24a
457	PANCAKEHILL 16 [8] D K Ivory 5-8-8 bl (47) Martin Dwyer 11/1: 550-0000: Cl-up till 3f out.		1¼	21a
408	PAGEANT 23 [11] J M Bradley 7-8-8 (35) C Catlin 66/1: 00-06540: Led till 5f out, btn 3f out.		1½	18a
536	IVORY VENTURE 4 [6] D K Ivory 4-8-8 BL (45) D Sweeney 66/1: 400-0000: Mid-div, no ch fnl 3f, blnks.		1	16a
12 Ran	1m 37.88 (1.68) Owner Mr Nigel Shields		Trained at Newmarket	

---

572   4.30 Mstrust Org Uk Maiden Stakes 3yo+   (D)
£3721 £1145 £573 £286   5f p/track rnd   Going 18   -17 Slow   Stalls Inside

4250}	TAG TEAM 144 [10] A M Balding 3-8-10 Martin Dwyer 12/1: 0-1: Sn cl-up, rdn & led over 1f out, held on well:			71a
348	BLUEBERRY RHYME 30 [4] P J Makin 5-9-10 vis (66) D Sweeney 3/1: 0/3423-22: Chsd ldrs, rdn & kept on for press, not able to chall but nrst fin:		¾	68a
4765}	PURE FOLLY 114 [2] Sir Mark Prescott 3-8-5 J Mackay 10/1: 4-3: Led, & hdd over 1f out, onepace:		nk	63a
435	MULTAHAB 21 [7] Miss Gay Kelleway 5-9-10 (56) M Fenton 7/4 FAV: 20555-24: Chsd ldr, no extra dist.		shd	67a
481	ASK THE CLERK 12 [8] H J Collingridge 3-8-10 (70) M Tebbutt 5/1: 3030-035: Chsd ldrs, not able to chall:		1	64a
289	DONT CALL ME DEREK 35 [5] S C Williams 3-8-10 BL e M Henry 5/1: 04-56: Held up, rdn & no impress dist:		1¼	60a
481	DOCKLANDS BLUE 12 [9] N P Littmoden 3-8-5 (57) Lisa Jones (3) 12/1: 630-207: Rdn rear, nvr pace to chall:		1	52a
2597}	AVIT 220 [1] P L Gilligan 4-9-5 BL (45) Hayley Turner (5) 50/1: 050000-8: Sn outpcd & cl-up, blnks.		11	22a
	AKIRAMENAI [6] Mrs L Stubbs 4-9-5 Kristin Stubbs (5) 50/1: 9: U.r. bef start, v slow away & nvr a factor.		2½	14a
9 Ran	59.53 (1.73) Owner Magic Moments		Trained at Kingsclere	

SOUTHWELL Sunday 08.02.04 Lefthand, Sharp, Oval Track

Official Going Standard

573   2.00 Bet Direct On Attheraces Text Page 410 Apprentice Banded Stakes 3yo+ 0-35 (H)
£1306 £373 £187   7f f/sand rnd   Going 53   +07 Fast   Stalls Inside

372*	SMART SCOT 27 [5] B P J Baugh 5-9-7 p (35) M Savage 2/1 FAV: 00060-11: Trkd ldrs, led over 2f out, rdn & held on well, eased cl-home:			37a
794}	FRAAMTASTIC 325 [13] B A Pearce 7-9-7 (30) L Treadwell 28/1: 00/5040-2: Mid-div, styd on wide for press, not able to chall wnr:		1½	33a
1145}	GRUB STREET 652 [7] J Parkes 8-9-7 (35) M Lawson 50/1: 06/0000/-3: Chsd ldrs, onepace for press:		5	24a
309	MISS WIZZ 35 [12] W Storey 4-9-7 p (35) Rory Moore (3) 12/1: 00460-04: Chsd ldrs, no impress fnl 2f.		6	13a
479	DANCING KING 13 [14] P W Hiatt 3-9-7 (30) P Gallagher (3) 10/1: 00-50405: Prom till 3f out.		hd	12a
457	CATERHAM COMMON 17 [8] D W Chapman 5-9-7 (30) P Makin 16/1: 00000-06: Slow away, nvr on terms.		2	8a
348	VELOCITYS IMAGE 31 [2] E J Alston 9-9-7 (35) A Mullen (5) 16/1: 060-07: Mid-div, struggling halfway.		shd	8a
486	GIVEN A CHANCE 12 [4] J G Given 3-8-4 (30) B Swarbrick (5) 9/1: 0600-458: Chsd ldrs till halfway.		1¼	5a
297	RIVENDELL 36 [3] M Wigham 8-9-7 t (30) C Cavanagh (5) 11/1: 50///00-6: Dwelt, sn bhd.		¾	4a
377	ZARA LOUISE 27 [6] R P Elliott 4-9-7 (30) A Reilly (5) 8/1: 00006-40: Al outpcd.		3½	0
541	GRAND VIEW 5 [1] J R Weymes 3-8-4 (30) D Fentiman (5) 8/1: 50000-60: Rear, hmpd 4f out, sn bhd.		2½	0
552	METICULOUS 3 [10] M C Chapman 6-9-7 BL (30) Andrew Webb (5) 40/1: 0/0-00000: Al outpcd, blnks, qck reapp.		nk	0
501	CARONTE 10 [9] S R Bowring 4-9-7 bl (35) W Hogg (5) 16/1: 600-0000: Led till over 2f out, wknd qckly.		7	0
4163}	AMAR 151 [11] P A Blockley 3-8-4 (35) Derek Nolan (5) 9/1: 460-0: Slowly away & sn outpcd, reapp.		hd	0
14 Ran	1m 29.85 (3.25) Owner Mr S Day		Trained at Stoke On Trent	

---

574   2.30 Bet Direct On Attheraces Text Page 411 Claiming Stakes 4yo+   (H)
£1474 £421 £211   1m3f f/sand   Going 53   -14 Slow   Stalls Inside

491	DAUNTED 12 [6] P A Blockley 8-9-2 (60) Lisa Jones (3) 1/1 FAV: 6/4-31001: Chsd ldrs, rdn to lead over 1f out, styd on strongly:			59a
373	FRANKS QUEST 27 [4] John A Harris 4-8-10 (55) Rory Moore (7) 12/1: 20040-02: Trkd ldrs, led over 4f out till over 1f out, no extra:		5	47a
552*	SPANISH STAR 3 [7] Mrs N Macauley 7-9-2 (45) A Culhane 9/4: 041-4613: Held up, kept on for press, nvr able to chall:		hd	50a
525	SEA YA MAITE 6 [1] S R Bowring 10-8-12 t (40) J Bramhill 14/1: 0-052354: Chsd ldrs, no extra 2f out.		4	36a
445	RED DELIRIUM 19 [9] R Brotherton 8-9-2 bl (40) Dean McKeown 12/1: 6004-645: Trkd ldrs, btn 2f out:		1	43a
300	SOPHOMORE 36 [2] John A Harris 10-8-10 (40) J Mackay 25/1: 50//00/0-0: Held up, no ch fnl 2f:		3½	32a
2241}	TROJAN WOLF 234 [8] P Howling 9-8-10 (40) S W Kelly 16/1: 040000-7: Led till over 4f out, sn btn, reapp.		6	24a
3135}	STYLISH PRINCE 198 [3] J G M O'Shea 4-8-12 (45) D Sweeney 50/1: 4000/00-8: Held up, no ch from halfway, abs.		dist	0a
8 Ran	2m 29.12 (7.82) Owner Mrs Joanna Hughes		Trained at Southwell	

---

575   3.00 Bet Direct On Attheraces Text Page 412 Banded Stakes 4yo+ 0-45 (H)
£1684 £481 £241   1m4f f/sand   Going 53   -08 Slow   Stalls Inside

523*	BELLA PAVLINA 6 [6] W M Brisbourne 6-9-3 (40) B Swarbrick (7) 5/6 FAV: 5/36-1211: Held up, short of room over 3f out, switched & rdn/styd on to lead well in last:			50a
354	DIAMOND ORCHID 31 [3] P D Evans 4-9-0 P (45) R Fitzpatrick 12/1: 00062-32: Led/dsptd lead, went on after 4f & rdn clr 3f out, hdd well in last:		1	48a
347	EL PEDRO 31 [12] N E Berry 5-9-3 (45) M Savage (5) 33/1: 54005-43: Held up, rdn & kept on onepace.		2	45a
173	KNOWN MANEUVER 61 [8] M C Chapman 6-9-3 (45) D Fox (5) 100/1: 000/000-4: Chsd ldrs, no extra over 1f out:		6	37a
445	DASH OF MAGIC 19 [13] J Hetherton 6-9-3 (40) C Catlin 20/1: 000-1625: Chsd ldrs, btn over 1f out:		½	36a

552	KING PRIAM 3 [7] M J Polglase 9-9-3 bl (40) Dean McKeown 16/1: 4145066: Outpcd, nvr factor, qck reapp.		1½	34a
4638}	JAKE BLACK 124 [10] J J Quinn 4-9-0 (45) Darren Williams 20/1: 6/56500-7: Chsd ldrs till 2f out, 6 wk jumps abs.		nk	33a
375*	SERAPH 27 [4] John A Harris 4-9-0 p (45) J Mackay 16/1: 0000-318: Held up, nvr on terms:		1½	31a
342	FAIRY WIND 32 [9] B J Curley 7-9-3 (45) S W Kelly 5/1: 00020-09: Held up, no room 3f out, sn btn.		1	30a
973}	MODEM 307 [1] D Shaw 7-9-3 e (40) Dawn Watson (7) 33/1: 0/03050-0: Al outpcd, 3 month abs.		7	21a
412	OUR GLENARD 24 [2] S L Keightley 5-9-3 (45) A Culhane 9/2: 5005-220: Pushed along rear, btn 3f out:		hd	20a
3120}	EFFIE GRAY 199 [15] J W Unett 5-9-3 (45) D Sweeney 20/1: 0003/56-0: Chsd ldrs till 4f out, new stable.		1	19a
500	KUSTOM KIT FOR HER 10 [14] S R Bowring 4-9-0 (45) J Bramhill 100/1: 200-6000: Led 1m, sn struggling.		dist	0
13 Ran	2m 41.61 (7.31) Owner The Cartmel Syndicate			Trained at Baschurch

576 3.30 Bet Direct On Attheraces Text Page 413 Banded Stakes 4yo+ 0-45 (H)
£1631 £466 £233   2m f/sand   Going 53   -78 Slow   Stalls Inside

537	RADIANT BRIDE 5 [6] K R Burke 4-8-12 BL (35) Darren Williams 8/1: 250-0261: Trkd ldrs trav well, shkn up to lead well ins last, shade cosily :			43a
395*	UNLEADED 25 [8] J Akehurst 4-8-12 (40) J Mackay 4/1: 0000-212: Keen/dsptd lead, went on over 2f out, rdn & hdd ins last, kept on:		½	40a
443	KAGOSHIMA 19 [5] J R Norton 9-9-4 vis (40) V Halliday 100/30 FAV: 060-2233: Led/dsptd lead, outpcd fnl 2f:		6	34a
357*	PADDY MUL 31 [4] W Storey 7-9-4 t (40) D R McCabe 4/1: 4626-214: Held up, nvr able to chall ldrs:		6	28a
142	PORT MORENO 67 [1] J G M O'Shea 4-8-12 vis (45) D Sweeney 22/1: 140060-5: Held up, no impress fnl 3f:		¾	27a
995]	MARTHA REILLY 1021 [2] Mrs Barbara Waring 8-9-4 (35) Lisa Jones (3) 25/1: 155/005//-: Al rear:		½	26a
734}	BERGAMO 342 [7] B Ellison 8-9-4 bl (45) T Eaves (5) 7/2: 0/41220-7: Rear, drvn & no impress 4f out:		1¾	24a
376	XIXITA 27 [3] Dr J D Scargill 4-8-12 (40) J Quinn 16/1: 0450-648: Chsd ldrs, btn 3f out.		15	12a
307	NICIARA 35 [9] M C Chapman 7-9-4 (30) D Fox (5) 66/1: 0/0/000/-0: Dwelt, sn handy, btn 5f out.		nk	11a
9 Ran	3m 47.02 (21.02) Owner Mrs Y Goodwin			Trained at Leyburn

577 4.00 Bet Direct Daily Special Offers Selling Stakes 3yo+ (H)
£1516 £433 £217   1m f/sand   Going 53   -10 Slow   Stalls Inside

500	XALOC BAY 10 [7] B P J Baugh 6-9-8 (52) Darren Williams 8/1: 360-2001: Led after 1m, drvn & held on well, all out:			57a
502	NOBLE PURSUIT 10 [3] P A Blockley 7-9-8 (57) Dean McKeown 8/11 FAV: 00440-22: Held up, eff to chase wnr from halfway, carried head high, styd on for press, al just held:		nk	56a
535	KUMAKAWA 5 [9] E A Wheeler 6-9-8 bl (45) Liam Jones (7) 20/1: 000-0503: Outpcd, taken wide & styd on for press fnl 1f, not pace front 2:		¾	55a
490	HUNTING PINK 12 [8] H Morrison 3-7-12 (48) J Quinn 4/1: 0044-234: In tch, rdn & kept on onepace.		hd	49a
500	AGUILA LOCO 10 [6] M C Chapman 5-9-8 (50) Joanna Badger 10/1: 00-32625: Keen & led 1f, no extra over 1f out.		3½	47a
4373]	ACE MA VAHRA 495 [1] S R Bowring 6-9-3 (45) J Bramhill 33/1: 235/003/-6: Chsd ldrs till over 1f out:		3½	35a
4731}	LUKE AFTER ME 117 [5] G A Swinbank 4-9-8 (48) R Lappin 16/1: 0/64000-7: Prom till halfway:		1¾	37a
1899}	OVER TO YOU BERT 251 [4] R J Hodges 5-9-8 (49) C Catlin 22/1: 040500-8: In tch 5f, abs, new stable.		12	15a
8 Ran	1m 44.44 (5.04) Owner Miss S M Potts			Trained at Stoke On Trent

578 4.30 Bet Direct In Running Sky Text Page 293 Banded Stakes 3yo+ 0-35 (H)
£1267 £362 £181   5f f/sand rnd   Going 53   Inapplicab   Stalls Stands Side

527	DANAKIM 6 [1] J R Weymes 7-9-7 bl e (35) D Fentiman (7) 9/2: 05060-61: Chsd ldrs, briefly outpcd halfway, styd on for press to lead well ins last:			37a
508	WHITE O MORN 9 [2] B A McMahon 5-9-7 t (30) G Gibbons 6/4 FAV: 00-042: Chsd ldrs, rdn & led over 1f out, hdd well ins last:		½	34a
3706}	SPY MASTER 173 [8] J Parkes 6-9-7 bl t (35) M Lawson (7) 12/1: 0/00000-3: Slow away & outpcd, kept on, no threat to front pair:		2	28a
411	ALMARA 24 [7] Miss K B Boutflower 4-9-7 t p (35) J Quinn 20/1: 0/0000-04: Dwelt, outpcd, nvr on terms.		2	22a
172	SECOND GENERATION 61 [6] R J Hodges 7-9-7 (35) C Catlin 14/1: 0006/0//0-: Rdn towards rear, nrst fin.		¾	20a
397	SALONIKA SKY 25 [11] C W Thornton 3-8-7 (35) J McAuley 10/1: 05000-06: Chsd ldrs till 3f out.		1¼	16a
447	PRECIOUS FREEDOM 19 [5] J Balding 4-9-7 bl (35) J Edmunds 10/1: 00000-007: Cl-up 3f, wknd.		1	13a
374	OUR OLD BOY 27 [3] J A Gilbert 4-9-7 (35) D R McCabe 11/2: 006/-08: Dwelt & hmpd start, outpcd.		½	11a
164	MILLIETOM 62 [10] K A Ryan 3-8-7 bl (30) P Fessey 16/1: 000-9: Led 3f, wknd, abs.		1	8a
4304}	GRUFF 144 [9] P T Midgley 5-9-7 (35) G Parkin 14/1: 000000-0: Al outpcd, abs.		hd	7a
4267}	SILENT ANGEL 145 [4] Mrs Lucinda Featherstone 4-9-7 VIS (30) S Yourston (7) 66/1: 000-0: Hmpd start, sn outpcd, visor.		¾	5a
11 Ran	1m 0.86 Owner Miss K Buckle			Trained at Middleham

Official Going Standard To Slow

579 2.30 Bet Direct On Sky Active Banded Stakes 3yo+ 0-45 (H)
£1652 £472 £236   7f f/sand rnd   Going 78   -10 Slow   talls 7f - outside, rem - Insid

556	EAGER ANGEL 4 [6] R F Marvin 6-9-6 p (45) Dean McKeown 8/1: 630-2401: Hld up, prog 3f out, rdn out to lead ct home:			48a
559	POTSDAM 3 [7] Niall Moran 6-9-6 t (45) S W Kelly 7/2 JT FAV: 00/024-02: Bhd, hdwy 3f out, led dist, hdd under press cl-home:		shd	46a
86	LEVANTINE 77 [9] A G Newcombe 7-9-6 BL (45) S Whitworth 7/2 JT FAV: 0/30633-3: Led, hdd dist, no extra fnl 1f:		3	40a
354	PRINTSMITH 32 [3] J R Norton 7-9-6 (45) J Bramhill 5/1: 0005-144: Handy, outpcd 3f out, rallied late.		¾	38a
524	NEUTRAL NIGHT 7 [8] R Brotherton 4-9-6 vis (45) A Daly 50/1: 660-3005: Slow away, prog 2f out, kept on late.		1¼	36a
373	MR STYLISH 28 [12] J S Moore 8-9-6 vis t (45) J D Smith 20/1: 44400-66: Held up, nvr nrr than mid-div.		½	35a
500	DASAR 11 [4] M Brittain 4-9-6 bl (45) M Lawson (7) 25/1: 0006-647: Cl-up, fdd 2f out:		1¼	33a
508	INDIAN SHORES 10 [5] M Mullineaux 5-9-6 p (45) Lisa Jones (3) 33/1: 06F-0068: Al in rear.		½	32a
448	SABANA 19 [11] J M Bradley 6-9-6 bl (45) F P Ferris (3) 10/1: 000-4359: In tch, fdd 3f out:		2	28a

411	**INDIAN WARRIOR** 25 [10] J Jay 8-9-6 bl (45) I Mongan 6/1: 0025-100: Cl-up, fdd fnl 2f:			2	24a
525	**PHANTOM FLAME** 7 [2] M Johnston 4-9-6 (45) J Fanning 13/2: 0000-520: Prom, fdd 3f out:			6	13a
11 Ran	1m 32.39 (6.19)	Owner Mr J F Pitchford			Trained at Rolleston

580 3.00 Bet Direct No Q Demo 08000 837 888 Claiming Stakes 3yo+ (H)
£1470 £420 £210 1m1f79y f/sand Going 78 -02 Slow :talls 7f - outside, rem - Insid

392	**GRAND LASS** 27 [8] T D Barron 5-9-8 P (50) S W Kelly 11/4: 2046-341: Led, clr 2f out, rdn out to hold on fnl 1f:				50a
525*	**PRINCE PROSPECT** 7 [2] Mrs L Stubbs 8-9-13 (45) Kristin Stubbs (7) 4/1: 4640-012: Rear, prog fnl 3f out, chsd ldr ins fnl 1f, al held:			1½	51a
398	**FRENCH HORN** 26 [5] M Wigham 7-9-12 p (50) G Carter 9/4 FAV: 0000-143: Chsd ldrs, no extra fnl 2f:			6	41a
412	**MALMAND** 25 [9] R Brotherton 5-9-12 vis (46) I Mongan 9/1: 500-0104: Bhd, keen, no impress fnl 2f.			½	40a
512	**LOVES DESIGN** 10 [4] Miss S J Wilton 7-9-13 (45) A Quinn 20/1: 50-06005: Hld up, chsd wnr 3f out, wknd fnl 1f.			½	40a
523	**THINK QUICK** 7 [12] R Hollinshead 4-9-8 (35) H Fellows (7) 50/1: 0040-056: Held up wide, nvr nrr than mid-div:			1¼	33a
445	**GOOD TIMING** 20 [11] J Hetherton 6-9-13 (45) G Parkin 20/1: 000/0-207: Cl-up, fdd 2f out:			2½	34a
490	**PEACE TREATY** 13 [10] S R Bowring 3-8-1 T (30) J Bramhill 66/1: 5000-008: Mid-div, prog 4f out, fdd 2f out:			4	23a
462	**OKTIS MORILIOUS** 18 [1] J A Osborne 3-8-3 J Fanning 16/1: 0-09: Led early, sn lost pl, btn 3f out:			5	18a
525	**HAITHEM** 7 [6] D Shaw 7-9-13 e (30) Lisa Jones (3) 16/1: 0-600030: Cl-up, fdd 3f out:			1	19a
505	**DR RAJ** 11 [7] B A McMahon 5-9-11 t P G Gibbons 40/1: 0-00: Cl-up, fdd 4f out.			11	2a
11 Ran	2m 5.69 (7.49)	Owner Mr Nigel Shields			Trained at Thirsk

581 3.30 Bet Direct No Q Banded Stakes 4yo+ 0-35 (H)
£1278 £365 £183 1m4f f/sand Going 78 -03 Slow :talls 7f - outside, rem - Insid

537	**BUZ KIRI** 6 [3] A W Carroll 6-9-3 (35) P Doe 15/8 FAV: 0046-321: Held up, prog 5f out, styd on to lead ins fnl 1f, pushed out hands-and-heels:				43a
523	**GALLEY LAW** 7 [9] R Craggs 4-9-0 (30) T Eaves (4) 25/1: 0000-32: Cl-up, led 3f out, hdd ins fnl 1f, not pace wnr:			1¾	39a
537	**LITTLE RICHARD** 6 [6] M Wellings 5-9-3 p (30) V Slattery 14/1: 000-0043: Cl-up, wknd 2f out:			12	22a
563	**THE LAST MOHICAN** 3 [10] P Howling 5-9-3 (35) S W Kelly 11/4: 50-42324: Led, hdd 3f out, no extra.			2	19a
505	**IPLEDGEALLEGIANCE** 11 [1] D W Chapman 8-9-3 (35) R Brisland 14/1: 60-25365: Rear, nvr nrr than mid-div:			1¼	17a
464	**WESTERN COMMAND** 17 [2] Mrs N Macauley 8-9-3 (30) P McCabe 14/1: 0-004566: Held up, prog 6f out, wknd 4f out.			¾	16a
	KAID 1433 [5] R Lee 9-9-3 (35) I Mongan 10/1: 05/460///-: Held up, nvr a factor:			12	0a
537	**MAGIC CHARM** 6 [7] A G Newcombe 6-9-3 (35) S Whitworth 7/1: 1105-008: Cl-up, fdd 4f out:			15	0a
464	**MORRIS DANCING** 17 [4] B P J Baugh 5-9-3 p (30) J Fanning 25/1: 0/0000-009: Keen mid-div, fdd 4f out.			4	0a
114	**BUGLE CALL** 73 [8] K O Cunningham Brown 4-9-0 BL e T (35) L Keniry (3) 66/1: 500000-0: Keen mid-div, prog 6f out, fdd 4f out, t.o.:			3	0a
10 Ran	2m 43.38 (9.78)	Owner Mr Serafino Agodino			Trained at Alcester

582 4.00 Bet Direct No Q Demo 08000 837 888 Banded Stakes 3yo+ 0-45 (H)
£1645 £470 £235 6f f/sand rnd Going 78 +12 Fast :talls 7f - outside, rem - Insid

528	**ENJOY THE BUZZ** 7 [9] J M Bradley 5-9-7 (40) P Fitzsimons 15/2: 0-440231: Held up, prog 3f out, led ins fnl 1f, rdn out:				47a
501	**KATY OHARA** 11 [13] Miss S E Hall 5-9-7 (45) J Fanning 25/1: 00000-02: Slow away, sn mid-div, prog 2f out, ev ch ins fnl 1f, just held by wnr:			½	45a
550	**ABOVE BOARD** 4 [12] R F Marvin 9-9-7 t p (45) Dean McKeown 12/1: 00-50203: Cl-up, led dist, hdd ins fnl 1f, just held by front 2:			½	44a
411	**THE GAY FOX** 25 [11] B G Powell 10-9-7 bl t (45) L Keniry (3) 8/1: 05005-24: Rear, some late gains.			1	41a
352*	**MOUNT SUPERIOR** 32 [3] P W D'Arcy 8-9-7 bl (45) L Enstone (3) 7/1: 500/66-15: Cl-up, no extra fnl 2f:			1¼	37a
416	**EJAY** 25 [7] Julian Poulton 5-9-7 (40) Lisa Jones (3) 100/1: 0//006-06: Prom, no extra fnl 2f:			hd	36a
440	**STAR LAD** 21 [7] R Brotherton 4-9-7 vis (45) I Mongan 5/1: 606-3107: Led, hdd dist, fdd fnl 1f:			3½	27a
524	**BELLS BEACH** 1 [1] P Howling 6-9-7 (40) S W Kelly 9/2 FAV: 0040-628: Nvr nrr than mid-div:			1¼	24a
444	**MISS JUDGED** 20 [4] A P Jones 3-8-6 bl (45) J F McDonald 9/1: 000-0069: Keen in rear, nvr a factor:			3	15a
527	**SERGEANT SLIPPER** 7 [5] C Smith 7-9-7 vis (45) Re Fitzpatrick 8/1: 0005-030: Mid-div, prog & badly hmpd dist, not recover:			½	14a
527	**STATOYORK** 7 [3] D Shaw 11-9-7 e (45) Dawn Watson (7) 14/1: 04000-40: Slow away, al bhd:			2½	7a
379	**HELLBENT** 28 [10] J A Osborne 5-9-7 BL (45) S Crawford (7) 12/1: 530/0-00: Keen cl-up, fdd 2f out:			1½	3a
3796}	**ALIBONGO** 171 [6] P A Blockley 3-8-6 (40) J Bramhill 20/1: 660600-0: Cl-up, fdd 4f out.			28	0a
13 Ran	1m 16.79 (3.99)	Owner Miss F Fenley			Trained at Chepstow

583 4.30 Littlewoods Bet Direct Median Auction Maiden Stakes 4-6yo (H)
£1435 £410 £205 1m4f f/sand Going 78 -15 Slow :talls 7f - outside, rem - Insid

4951}	**EARLSFIELD RAIDER** 102 [2] G L Moore 4-9-0 e (58) I Mongan 6/4 FAV: 600400-1: Held up, prog 5f out, led 2f out, pushed clr fnl 1f, val 7L+:				62a
575	**KUSTOM KIT FOR HER** 1 [1] S R Bowring 4-8-9 (45) J Bramhill 14/1: 200-60002: Held up, prog 3f out, chsd wnr fnl 2f, al held:			5	45a
4883}	**RAHJEL SULTAN** 107 [3] B A McMahon 6-9-3 T (40) G Gibbons 16/1: 400540-3: Hld up, prog 3f out, wknd.			7	40a
324	**AITANA** 34 [5] S C Williams 4-8-9 (53) G Carter 2/1: 0060-64: Led, hdd 2f out, sn fdd:			shd	34a
18	**DAME MARGARET** 89 [4] J A B Old 4-8-9 (35) V Slattery 100/30: 402063-5: Cl-up, fdd 4f out:			20	4a
5 Ran	2m 44.82 (11.22)	Owner Mrs R J Doorgachurn			Trained at Brighton

584 5.00 Bet Direct Interactive Banded Stakes 3yo+ 0-35 (H)
£1295 £370 £185 1m100y f/sand rnd Going 78 -17 Slow :talls 7f - outside, rem - Insid

412	**MONDURU** 25 [1] G L Moore 7-9-6 bl e (35) S Whitworth 16/1: 0/5000-01: Rear, prog wide 2f out, led dist, drvn out:				38a
399	**ALL ON MY OWN** 26 [12] I W McInnes 9-9-6 bl (35) Natalia Gemelova (7) 14/1: 5000-042: Held up, prog 3f out, chsd wnr fnl 1f, kept on:			1	35a
399	**VESTA FLAME** 26 [11] M Johnston 3-8-1 (35) R Ffrench 5/2 FAV: 000-33: Bhd, hdwy 3f out, onepace.			1¼	33a

437	**WELSH WHISPER** 21 [5] S A Brookshaw 5-9-6 (30) L Keniry (3) 100/1: 0-004: Hld up, onepace fnl 2f.	½	32a
3980}	**A BIT OF FUN** 163 [6] J J Quinn 3-8-1 (35) J McAuley 33/1: 000-5: Nvr nrr than mid-div:	1¼	30a
445	**DESIRES DESTINY** 20 [10] M Brittain 6-9-6 (35) M Lawson (7) 7/2: 6600-606: Cl-up, outpcd 3f out, mod late gains.	hd	29a
463	**PEARTREE HOUSE** 18 [9] D W Chapman 10-9-6 (35) R Brisland 14/1: 0000-007: Rear, prog 4f out, fdd dist.	6	17a
541	**POOKAS DAUGHTER** 6 [3] J M Bradley 4-9-6 P (35) P Fitzsimons 9/1: 00-50008: Cl-up, led 2f out, hdd dist, sn fdd.	4	9a
571	**PAGEANT** 2 [4] J M Bradley 7-9-6 BL (35) I Mongan 25/1: 00-065409: Handy, hmpd dist, sn fdd.	2½	4a
394	**KELTIC FLUTE** 26 [13] Mrs Lucinda Featherstone 5-9-6 vis (35) Lisa Jones (3) 25/1: 2000/040: Cl-up, led 6f out, hdd 2f out.	5	0a
310	**BLUE MAEVE** 35 [2] J Hetherton 4-9-6 (35) G Parkin 6/1: 0006-40: Led 2f, styd cl-up, fdd 2f out.	¾	0a
502	**THE BLOCK MONSTER** 11 [8] P A Blockley 5-9-6 BL (35) Dean McKeown 20/1: 0000-000: Handy, fdd 2f out.	3	0a
12 Ran	1m 54.26 (8.06) Owner Pleasure Palace Racing	|	Trained at Brighton

Official Going Standard

585	**2.10 Bet Direct On Sky Active Handicap Stakes 4yo+ 0-75 (E)**		[75]
	£3262 £932 £466	7f f/sand rnd Going 58 -00 Slow Stalls Inside	

556	**MOUNT ROYALE** 4 [4] N Tinkler 6-8-5 vis t (52) Kim Tinkler 100/30 JT FA: 15-00631: Dwelt, sn trkd ldrs, short of room over 1f out, switched & rdn to lead in last:		61a
384	**FLYING EDGE** 28 [11] E J Alston 4-8-4 (51) A Nicholls 28/1: 15160-02: Al handy & led over 2f out, drvn & hdd over 1f out, led again in last, hdd & no extra fnl 100yds:	1¼	56a
439	**YORKER** 21 [5] Ms Deborah J Evans 6-9-7 (68) J P Spencer 100/30 JT FA: 0020-253: Chsd ldrs, rdn & outpcd 3f out, rallied late for press to snatch 3rd:	1¼	70a
363	**WARDEN WARREN** 31 [7] Mrs C A Dunnett 6-9-11 bl (72) Hayley Turner (5) 11/2: 00021-34: Chsd ldrs, prog & led over 2f out, sn rdn & hdd, no extra ins last:	shd	74a
556	**YENALED** 4 [8] K A Ryan 7-8-13 p (60) N Callan 8/1: 2545-305: Held up, short of room/switched 1f out, onpce.	½	61a
555*	**WEET WATCHERS** 4 [2] P A Blockley 4-9-2 6ex (77) D Nolan (5) 9/1: 030P0-16: Led till over 2f out, fdd:	4	71a
556	**SOCIAL CONTRACT** 4 [3] S Dow 7-8-3 (50) C Catlin 16/1: 2006-007: Prom, fdd over 2f out:	nk	43a
459	**SEMPER PARATUS** 18 [10] H J Collingridge 5-8-11 bl (58) M Tebbutt 8/1: 00140-48: Prom wide, btn 2f out:	2½	46a
556	**PAWN IN LIFE** 4 [9] T D Barron 6-9-1 bl (62) P Makin (7) 12/1: 5051-009: Dwelt, sn in trck wide, btn 2f out:	1¾	47a
4371}	**DRURY LANE** 142 [1] D W Chapman 4-10-0 (75) A Culhane 50/1: 503000-0: Sn well bhd, reapp:	11	42a
556	**BRILLIANTRIO** 4 [6] M C Chapman 6-7-12 5oh (40) D Fox (5) 25/1: 05-2406U: Reared start, u.r.:		0a
11 Ran	1m 30.69 (4.09) Owner Langton Partnership		Trained at Malton

586	**2.40 Press Interactive To Bet Direct Claiming Stakes 4yo+ (F)**		
	£2891 £826 £413	1m f/sand rnd Going 58 -07 Slow Stalls Inside	

480	**CAROUBIER** 14 [1] T D Barron 4-9-5 (73) J P Spencer 2/9 FAV: 0224-521: Dwelt, rems early rear, hdwy from halfway & led over 1f out, rdn clr:		75a
559	**FORTUNE POINT** 3 [3] A W Carroll 6-9-1 (59) A Culhane 7/1: 0640-402: Trkd ldrs, short of room 2f out, kept on ins last:	5	58a
479	**TINIAN** 14 [7] K R Burke 6-8-9 (45) Darren Williams 28/1: 530-5303: Handy, hung left/no extra fnl 2f.	1	50a
502	**REPEAT** 11 [2] Miss Gay Kelleway 4-8-7 p (53) D Allan (3) 14/1: 64-12044: Trkd ldrs, drvn/no impress dist.	shd	48a
469	**PROUD VICTOR** 17 [5] D Shaw 4-8-5 vis (40) N Callan 50/1: 06-45665: Trkd ldrs wide, btn over 1f out:	½	45a
538	**ONEFORTHEBOYS** 6 [6] D Flood 5-8-9 (40) Dean Williams (7) 50/1: 0600-006: Led, hdd 2f out, wknd:	3½	38a
6 Ran	1m 44.59 (5.19) Owner Mr Nigel Shields		Trained at Thirsk

587	**3.10 Littlewoods Bet Direct Classified Stakes 3yo+ 0-60 (F)**		
	£2898 £828 £414	5f f/sand str Going 58 Inapplicab Stalls Stands Side	

415	**SEA THE WORLD** 25 [7] D Shaw 4-9-5 vis (56) N Callan 7/1: 03000-51: Pushed along towards rear, styd on for press to lead cl-home, all out:		57a
508	**HENRY TUN** 10 [6] J Balding 6-9-5 hd (47) D Allan (3) 14/1: 500-3502: Al handy & led halfway, hung left under press from over 1f out, hdd cl-home:	hd	56a
507	**LADY PROTECTOR** 10 [1] J Balding 5-9-2 (48) P Makin (7) 16/1: 060-4103: Chsd ldrs, ch dist, no extra when short of room cl-home:	1	50a
495*	**ALIZAR** 12 [4] S Dow 3-8-2 (59) J Quinn 11/2: 53-02314: Chsd ldrs, styd on for press, nrst fin:	nk	49a
551	**MR PERTEMPS** 4 [10] R A Fahey 6-9-5 p (60) T Hamilton 5/6 FAV: 100-3125: Rdn towards rear & outpcd, hung left but late gains for press, nrst fin:	nk	51a
231	**PARK STAR** 51 [3] D Shaw 4-9-2 (56) Darren Williams 16/1: 056000-6: Bhd & outpcd, late gains, nrst fin:	2½	40a
500	**PLAYFUL SPIRIT** 11 [2] J Balding 5-9-2 vis (49) J Edmunds 20/1: 01-06337: Chsd ldrs, not able to chall ldrs.	1¾	35a
435	**RELLIM** 23 [12] P A Blockley 5-9-2 (48) S Yourston (7) 20/1: 42656-58: Led/dsptd lead till halfway, sn btn:	nk	34a
551	**AMANDAS LAD** 4 [11] M C Chapman 4-9-5 (45) D Fox (5) 66/1: 030-6349: Outpcd, only mod prog:	nk	36a
227	**VALAZAR** 52 [9] D W Chapman 5-9-5 (54) A Culhane 28/1: 524000-0: Chsd ldrs till halfway, abs:	½	34a
3455}	**MAROMITO** 185 [8] R Bastiman 7-9-5 (55) K Dalgleish 33/1: 5/00000-0: Chsd ldrs till halfway, abs, new yard.	1½	29a
3455}	**VANISHED** 185 [5] M J Polglase 4-9-2 p (60) V Halliday 25/1: 402440-0: Reluctant to go to start, cl-up till over 1f out, eased:	hd	25a
12 Ran	1m 0.95 Owner Swann Racing Ltd		Trained at Newark

588	**3.40 Betdirect Co Uk Maiden Stakes 4yo+ (D)**		
	£3328 £1024 £512 £256	1m4f f/sand Going 58 +04 Fast Stalls Inside	

3129}	**HARELDA** 199 [4] H Morrison 4-8-6 J Quinn 2/5 FAV: 42-1: Keen trkg ldrs, smooth prog to lead 3f out, readily pulled clr:		78a
359	**SEANS MEMORY** 31 [7] Mrs C A Dunnett 4-8-11 P C Catlin 80/1: 0-02: Pushed along rear, styd on for press fnl 2f, no ch with wnr:	14	52a
359	**BESTSELLER** 31 [6] J G M O'Shea 4-8-6 R Havlin 9/1: 0-43: Trkd ldrs, drvn & onepace fnl 2f:	¾	47a
505	**LUXI RIVER** 11 [2] P A Blockley 4-8-11 (55) Derek Nolan (7) 11/1: 2/64-5544: Chsd ldrs & led over 5f out, rdn/hdd 3f out, sn no	1½	50a

151

impress:

	DATAHILL 76 [5] P W D'Arcy 4-8-6 (72) Paul Eddery 9/2: 0440-5: Chsd ldr/dsptd lead, btn 4f out.		dist	0
1182}	LEYAALY 292 [1] B A Pearce 5-8-9 (30) P M Quinn 150/1: 00/00-6: Chsd ldrs, lost tch 4f out.		3	0
376	THEME PARK 28 [3] John A Harris 4-8-11 t (53) J Mackay 40/1: 3/0P60-07: Led till halfway, sn bhd.		28	0
7 Ran	2m 40.77 (6.47) Owner Sir Thomas Pilkington		Trained at East Ilsley	

589 4.10 Bet Direct Football Cashbacks Selling Stakes 3yo+ (G)
£2590 £740 £370   7f f/sand rnd   Going 58   -12 Slow   Stalls Inside

533	LEGALIS 6 [2] K A Ryan 6-9-8 b (57) N Callan 3/1: 00-32031: Trkd ldrs, smooth prog & led over 1f out, narrowly hdd well ins last, led again for press cl-home:			58a
571	FEAST OF ROMANCE 2 [6] P Howling 7-9-13 bl (53) J P Spencer 5/2 FAV: 6-3313262: In tch, smooth prog to press ldrs over 1f out, rdn & led well ins last, hdd cl-home:		hd	62a
562	HEADLAND 3 [3] D W Chapman 6-9-13 bl (59) A Culhane 5/1: 41-42003: Trkd ldrs, eff wide, ch dist, no extra:		2½	57a
4883}	EARLSTON 107 [4] Miss Gay Kelleway 4-9-8 e T (64) M Fenton 7/2: 224000-4: Led halfway till over 1f out, wknd.		1¾	49a
323	CAYMAN BREEZE 34 [5] S Dow 4-9-8 (62) Paul Eddery 7/1: 00300-05: Rear, eff 2f out, no impress dist:		1¼	46a
533	JALOUHAR 6 [1] B P J Baugh 4-9-13 p (57) K Dalgleish 10/1: 0615-546: In tch, wknd over 1f out:		3½	44a
409	GLOBE BEAUTY 25 [7] A D W Pinder 6-9-3 D Sweeney 100/1: 67: Led, hdd halfway, wknd.		9	18a
7 Ran	1m 31.51 (4.91) Owner Sunpak Potatoes		Trained at Hambleton	

590 4.40 Littlewoodspoker Com Handicap Stakes 4yo+ 0-65 (F)   [65]
£2954 £844 £422   1m6f f/sand   Going 58   -05 Slow   Stalls Inside

5017}	SUN HILL 95 [10] M Blanshard 4-8-10 (52) D Sweeney 66/1: 500/000-1: Trkd ldrs, chsd ldr 2f out & drvn to lead cl-home, all			59a
515	MADIBA 9 [9] P Howling 5-9-4 (55) K Dalgleish 25/1: 400-1602: Handy & led halfway, drvn & hdd well ins last:		shd	61a
515	LAZZAZ 9 [5] P W Hiatt 6-9-4 (57) A Culhane 7/1: 0-435333: Mid-div, drvn & onepace fnl 2f:		4	57a
534	DELTA FORCE 6 [11] P A Blockley 5-9-12 (63) D Nolan (5) 9/2: 31-12144: Chsd ldrs, drvn & no extra over 1f out:		5	56a
484	NAKWA 14 [3] E J Alston 6-9-5 (56) D Allan (3) 9/4 FAV: 043-1225: Chsd ldrs, rdn & no impress fnl 2f:		1¾	47a
478	AMBERSONG 16 [1] A W Carroll 6-8-13 (50) N Callan 7/1: 220-3306: Mid-div, btn 2f out		¾	40a
421	ELA RE 25 [13] C R Dore 5-8-9 low (45) M Tebbutt 11/2: 0606/0-47: Towards rear, eff wide, btn 2f out:		3½	31a
376	BROUGHTON MELODY 28 [12] W J Musson 5-8-8 (45) J P Spencer 12/1: 00//6-38: Al rear:		3	26a
458	ANTONY EBENEEZER 18 [2] C R Dore 5-8-3 t (40) C Catlin 10/1: 0400-539: Chsd ldrs till btn 3f out:		1	20a
420	JUNGLE LION 25 [4] John A Harris 6-8-10 t (47) J Mackay 40/1: 0600-620: Pulled hard towards rear, rapid prog wide to dispute lead 6f out, rdn & btn 4f out:		6	18a
3602}	SAN MARCO 179 [7] Mrs P Sly 6-8-8 p (45) M Fenton 33/1: 000404-0: Led till halfway, sn lost plc:		1½	14a
420	FREE STYLE 25 [6] K R Burke 4-8-3 (45) Joanna Badger 25/1: 0020-630: Chsd ldrs till halfway.		nk	13a
493	GOLDEN DUAL 8 [8] S Dow 4-8-7 (45) Paul Eddery 16/1: 365-0060: Dwelt & al bhd.		7	16a
13 Ran	3m 08.65 (8.85) Owner Mr Stanley Hinton		Trained at Upper Lambourn	

591 1.30 Bet Direct On Sky Active Handicap Stakes Div 1 3yo 0-60 (F)   [67]
£2912 £832 £416   6f f/sand rnd   Going 58   -28 Slow   Stalls Inside

485	HEAD OF STATE 14 [10] R M Beckett 3-8-11 VIS (50) J Mackay 14/1: 0061-001: Led/dsptd lead, went on over 2f out & rdn clr bef dist:			61a
485	BELLA BOY ZEE 14 [7] P A Blockley 3-9-2 (55) K Fallon 11/10 FAV: 30000-32: Chsd ldrs, styd on for press, no threat to wnr:		5	53a
485	BARRAS 14 [5] Miss Gay Kelleway 3-9-2 BL (55) M Fenton 12/1: 5321-003: Rdn towards rear, styd on wide for press:		nk	52a
436*	VAMPIRE QUEEN 22 [3] R P Elliott 3-9-3 (56) Dean McKeown 7/2: 0600-14: Chsd ldrs, nvr able to chall.		½	51a
316	NUMPTY 36 [4] N Tinkler 3-9-1 t (45) Kim Tinkler 14/1: 000-55: Prom till outpcd bef halfway, mod late gains.		1¾	36a
485	SAHARA SILK 14 [8] D Shaw 3-9-7 vis (60) Darren Williams 25/1: 0500-006: Led/dsptd lead 4f, fdd:		½	49a
449	BACKLASH 20 [9] A W Carroll 3-8-12 (51) S Whitworth 12/1: 0-007: Outpcd rear, late gains under hands & heels:		3	32a
455	PARALLEL LINES 20 [1] P D Evans 3-8-9 (48) S W Kelly 18/1: 22000-08: Chsd ldrs till over 1f out.		3	21a
466	MYSTIC PROMISE 18 [6] Mrs N Macauley 3-7-12 7oh bl (30) Joanna Badger 66/1: 00000-09: Dwelt, sn outpcd.		3	2a
4707}	JOE CHARLIE 120 [11] K A Ryan 3-9-0 BL (53) N Callan 9/1: 000-0: Dwelt, chsd ldrs 4f:		3½	9a
4060}	KATIES BATH TIME 159 [2] Ian Emmerson 3-8-6 (45) J Bramhill 50/1: 000-0: Prom early, sn bhd, abs:		23	0
11 Ran	1m 19.07 (5.77) Owner Mr Pedro Rosas		Trained at Lambourn	

592 2.00 Bet Direct On Sky Active Handicap Stakes Div 2 3yo 0-60 (F)   [67]
£2912 £832 £416   6f f/sand rnd   Going 58   -27 Slow   Stalls Inside

403	LADY BAHIA 27 [5] R P Elliott 3-9-1 (54) T Woodley 12/1: 0240-061: Sn led & rdn clr over 2f out, hung left but in command for press from dist:			67a
4803}	EMPEROR CAT 115 [8] P A Blockley 3-9-5 (58) D Nolan (5) 12/1: 160105-2: Hld up, drvn & styd on to chase wnr over 1f out, no threat:		5	58a
485	SIEGFRIEDS NIGHT 14 [6] M C Chapman 3-8-11 (50) Joanna Badger 4/1 JT FAV: 0035-143: Towards rear, styd on for press late, nvr a threat:		1¼	47a
536	DULCE DE LECHE 7 [7] S C Williams 3-9-7 bl e (60) B Reilly (5) 13/2: 00-064: Chsd ldrs, onpace for press.		1¾	53a
436	POWER TO BURN 22 [10] K Bell 3-9-1 vis (54) D R McCabe 7/1: 40600-35: Held up, nvr able to chall:		nk	46a
436	MELAINA 22 [4] M S Saunders 3-9-0 p (53) K Fallon 6/1: 0061-206: Chsd ldrs, btn 2f out:		3	37a
485	LITTLE FLUTE 14 [9] T Keddy 3-8-9 (48) J P Guillambert (3) 4/1 JT FAV: 0002-407: Prom early, sn lost place.		1	30a
247	DANDY JIM 46 [2] D W Chapman 3-7-12 7oh (30) R Brisland 7/1: 006-8: Slow away & al rear:		½	17a
466	NANNA 18 [3] R Hollinshead 3-8-12 (51) J Quinn 7/1: 00-529: Chsd ldrs, btn 3f out:		nk	30a
4942}	SAMARA SOUND 104 [1] A G Newcombe 3-8-6 (45) S Whitworth 10/1: 000-0: In tch till halfway:		12	7a
10 Ran	1m 18.98 (5.68) Owner Mrs Sarah Grayson		Trained at Formby	

593 2.30 Bet Direct No Q Demo 08000 837 888 Claiming Stakes 4yo+ (F)
£2905 £830 £415   7f f/sand rnd   Going 58   -05 Slow   Stalls Inside

487*	BLAKESET 14 [7] T D Barron 9-8-12 vis (78) J P Spencer 5/6 FAV: 101-1011: Trkd ldr, led 2f out, hung left, drvn out:			72a
518	CLOUD DANCER 10 [6] K A Ryan 5-9-4 (73) N Callan 9/4: 3310-302: Trkd ldrs, rdn to chase wnr over 1f out, kept on, al held:	1½	73a
544	BOAVISTA 6 [3] P D Evans 4-8-8 T (57) L Fletcher (2) 16/1: 32243-03: Led 5f, no extra dist:	5	54a
556*	GAME GURU 5 [2] P A Blockley 5-9-7 bl (62) Dean McKeown 7/2: 01-01314: Chsd ldrs, outpcd fnl 2f.	2	63a
556	DISPOL PETO 5 [4] Ian Emmerson 4-8-13 (62) J Bramhill 50/1: 14500-05: Chsd ldrs, btn 2f out:	4	48a
502	MAUNBY ROCKER 12 [1] P C Haslam 4-8-9 (48) D Wakenshaw (7) 50/1: 1260-006: Pushed along rear, sn outpcd:	2	40a
6 Ran	1m 31.02 (4.42) Owner Mr Nigel Shields			Trained at Thirsk

---

594   3.00 Bet Direct No Q Classified Stakes 4yo+ 0-65 (F)
£2877 £822 £411   1m4f f/sand   Going 58   +07 Fast   Stalls Inside

465	JAIR OHMSFORD 18 [3] W J Musson 5-9-0 (64) M Fenton 9/2: 0540-141: Held up, smooth hdwy to lead ins last, readily asserted, val for 5L+:			74a
504	GEORGE STUBBS 12 [6] M J Polglase 6-9-0 (65) L Fletcher (3) 11/2: 0632-062: Led/dsptd lead, went on over 3f out, rdn & hdd ins last, no extra:	2½	66a
552	COOLFORE JADE 5 [7] N E Berry 4-8-8 (57) C Catlin 16/1: 5-014143: Prom, ch 2f out, sn no extra:	2	60a
534	SURDOUE 7 [2] P Howling 4-8-11 (63) J P Spencer 9/4 FAV: 0005-024: Bhd, eff 3f out, no impress:	10	51a
590	DELTA FORCE 1 [5] P A Blockley 5-9-0 (63) Derek Nolan (7) 9/2: 31-121445: Led/dsptd lead till 3f out, sn btn.	5	45a
491*	STOLEN SONG 14 [4] M J Ryan 4-8-11 e (64) S Whitworth 7/2: 3352-416: Hld up, btn 4f out:	8	35a
2037}	SACSAYHUAMAN 245 [1] D W Thompson 5-8-11 (57) K Dalgleish 50/1: 304/000-7: Led after 1f till 5f out, sn lost place:	dist	0a
7 Ran	2m 40.47 (6.17) Owner Mr K A Cosby			Trained at Newmarket

---

595   3.30 Bet Direct No Q Demo 08000 837 888 Handicap Stakes 4yo+ 0-85 (D)   [80]
£4352 £1339 £670 £335   1m3f f/sand   Going 58   -01 Slow   Stalls Inside

382	CRITICAL STAGE 29 [8] John Berry 5-8-9 e (61) J P Spencer 7/4 FAV: 00335-31: Held up wide, smooth hdwy 3f out & led over 1f out, drvn out:			68a
513+*	INTRICATE WEB 11 [6] E J Alston 8-9-13 (79) D Allan (3) 6/1: 5043-112: Held up, pushed along over 3f out, styd on for press fnl 2f, al just held:	¾	85a
230	TOLEDO SUN 52 [7] H J Collingridge 4-8-1 (55) Joanna Badger 12/1: 030000-3: Cl-up & led 9f out, rdn & hdd over 1f out, not pace of front pair:	6	53a
534	BRESSBEE 7 [2] J W Unett 6-9-4 vis (70) D Nolan (5) 15/2: 0300-024: Chsd ldrs, onepace fnl 2f.	1	67a
519	DOWER HOUSE 10 [4] Andrew Turnell 9-10-0 (80) D Corby (3) 10/1: 0310-465: Hld up, eff fnl 3f, no impress:	1½	75a
388*	AMIR ZAMAN 28 [3] J R Jenkins 6-10-0 (80) K Fallon 3/1: 66113-16: Held up, eff to chase ldr 3f out, no impress.	2½	71a
530	KINGSTON TOWN 7 [1] N P Littmoden 4-8-13 p (67) J P Guillambert 14/1: 021-0047: Chsd ldrs, btn 3f out:	9	47a
382	HOV 29 [5] J J Quinn 4-9-12 (80) Darren Williams 40/1: 12540-08: Led 2f, prom till 3f out:	13	45a
8 Ran	2m 27.82 (6.52) Owner The 1997 Partnership			Trained at Newmarket

---

596   4.00 Littlewoods Bet Direct Selling Stakes Fillies 3yo (G)
£2555 £730 £365   1m f/sand rnd   Going 58   -41 Slow   Stalls Inside

506	LADY MO 12 [10] Andrew Reid 3-9-4 (51) J P Guillambert (3) 9/2: 050-5351: Sn prom & led 2f out, rdn & styd on well:			57a
291	QUARRY ISLAND 38 [5] P D Evans 3-8-12 vis (40) S Donohoe (6) 33/1: 60040-52: In tch, outpcd 3f out, styd on late for press, no threat to wnr:	1½	47a
279	COMIC GENIUS 41 [2] D Haydn Jones 3-8-12 (45) Paul Eddery 13/2: 46062-3: Trkd ldrs halfway, rdn & kept on onepace fnl	2	43a
474	CIACOLE 17 [1] S C Williams 3-8-12 (60) N Callan 9/4 FAV: 6540-04: Prom & led over 3f out till 2f out, no extra:	1¼	40a
486	CASANTELLA 14 [8] M J Polglase 3-8-12 (45) L Fletcher (3) 25/1: 36-04505: Chsd ldrs, no impress dist.	1	38a
4770}	MIND PLAY 117 [7] M E Sowersby 3-8-12 bl (40) T Eaves (5) 50/1: 0006-6: Dwelt, sn handy till over 2f out:	3½	31a
535	ZONNEBEKE 7 [3] K R Burke 3-8-12 P (45) J Fanning 7/2: 400-4527: Led/dsptd lead 5f:	½	30a
553	LOLAS DESTINY 5 [4] P A Blockley 3-8-12 (52) K Fallon 4/1: 000-568: Chsd ldrs 5f, sn btn:	23	0a
408	TORTUETTE 26 [6] Jean Rene Auvray 3-8-12 P (35) Lisa Jones (3) 50/1: 3000-009: Led 3f, sn btn:	nk	0a
9 Ran	1m 47.30 (7.9) Owner Mr A S Reid			Trained at Mill Hill London

---

597   4.30 Free #25 Bonus @ Littlewoodspoker Com Handicap Stakes Fillies 4yo+ 0-70 (E)   [70]
£3234 £924 £462   1m f/sand rnd   Going 58   -24 Slow   Stalls Inside

502*	MISS CHAMPERS 12 [2] P A Blockley 4-9-10 (66) N Callan 6/5 FAV: 1352-011: Chsd ldrs inner, hdwy to chase ldr halfway & led over 1f out, sn in command, rdn out:			73a
489	JESSIE 14 [7] Don Enrico Incisa 5-7-12 t (40) Kim Tinkler 14/1: 400-5652: Dwelt, rear, styd on for press fnl 2f, no threat:	3½	41a
410	WESTMEAD ETOILE 26 [5] J R Jenkins 4-7-12 VIS (40) J Mackay 25/1: 00300-03: Led till over 1f out, no extra:	1¼	38a
489	ELLEN MOONEY 14 [4] R P Elliott 5-10-0 (70) R Ffrench 4/1: 1502-234: Sn prom, rdn & outpcd over 2f out:	1¼	65a
564	MISS GLORY BE 4 [1] Miss Gay Kelleway 6-8-9 p (51) J Quinn 3/1: 3006-035: Chsd ldrs, no impress fnl 3f:	15	21a
378	JESSINCA 29 [3] A P Jones 8-7-12 (40) F P Ferris (3) 14/1: 6460-006: Prom early, sn lost place & struggling:	2½	5a
577	ACE MA VAHRA 2 [8] S R Bowring 6-8-3 (45) J Bramhill 50/1: 235/003/-6: Keen & prom 5f, long abs.	½	9a
551	NAUGHTY GIRL 5 [6] P D Evans 4-9-6 VIS (62) S Donohoe (7) 25/1: 6560-008: Chsd ldrs 4f:	dist	0a
8 Ran	1m 45.98 (6.58) Owner Mr J T Billson			Trained at Southwell

---

Official Going Fast

598   5.15 Gr 3 UAE 2000 Guineas 3yo ()
£90782 £27932 £13966 £6983 1m aw rnd   Standard   Stalls Inside

	LITTLE JIM T E Durcan 3-9-4 S Seemar 7/1: 1131-1: Chsd ldrs, led over 2f out, drvn out fnl 1f:			117a
4866}	JACK SULLIVAN 104 G A Butler 3-8-9 E Ahern 12/1: 532615-2: Slow away, plenty to do 3f out, styd on well fnl 2f, nrst fin:	2½	103a
	ROSENCRANS Saeed bin Suroor 3-8-9 TVIS L Dettori 7/2 FAV: 1-3: Led, hdd over 2f out, no extra ins fnl 1f.	½	102a

NAD AL SHEBA THURSDAY 05.02.04 Lefthand, Flat, Fair Track

4975}	**CARTE SAUVAGE 96** M Johnston 3-8-9 S Chin 12/1: 412336: Mid div, prog 2f out, kept on late.	3¾	93a
325*	**FORTHRIGHT 30** C E Brittain 3-8-9 S Sanders 16/1: 16050-18: Nvr nrr than mid div.	14	68a
4672}	**SUTTERS FORT 117** Saeed bin Suroor 3-8-9 t K McEvoy 10/1: 1315-0: Bhd, nvr a factor.	1	66a

14 Ran   1m 37.63   Owner H E Sheikh Rashid Bin Mohammed   Trained at Uae

599 | 5.10 UAE 1000 Guineas (Fillies) 3yo ()
£90782 £27932 £13966   **1m aw rnd**   **Standard**   Stalls Inside

2229}	**CATSTAR 234** Saeed bin Suroor 3-8-9 t L Dettori 6/4 FAV: 12-1: Made all, pushed out fnl 1f, val 2L+:		110a
4470}	**MENHOUBAH 133** C E Brittain 3-8-9 p E Ahern 15/8: 144434-2: Trkd ldrs, outpcd 3f out, rallied late, no ch with wnr:	1¼	107a
	FESTIVE STYLE S Seemar 3-9-4 R L Moore 14/1: 2212-3: In tch, outpcd 3f out, rallied ins fnl 1f.	1¾	113a

8 Ran   1m 40.46   Owner Godolphin   Trained at Uae

LINGFIELD Wednesday 11.02.04 Lefthand, V Sharp Track

Official Going Standard

600 | 12.50 Bet Direct On Sky Text Page 372 Handicap Stakes 3yo+ 46-55 (F)   [59]
£2989 £854 £427   **7f p/track rnd**   **Going 39**   **-05 Slow**   Stalls Inside

344	**KINSMAN 35** [4] T D McCarthy 7-9-7 bl (52) J P Guillambert (3) 14/1: 00600-21: Rear, hdwy over 1f out, forced thr' gaps ins last to lead line, joc given 2-day careless riding ban:		60a
566*	**MAYZIN 4** [5] R M Flower 4-10-1 6ex p (60) J Quinn 4/1 FAV: 54-32412: Keen & led, drvn & hdd line:	shd	67a
536*	**ADANTINO 8** [13] B R Millman 5-9-9 6ex bl (54) J P Spencer 9/1: 53-63413: Rear, swtchd wide/hmpd over 1f out, switched & strong run ins last, just held:	hd	60a
558	**LUCID DREAMS 5** [11] M Wigham 5-9-6 (51) G Carter 20/1: 1240-504: Towards rear, drvn & kept on well fnl 2f, not pace of front trio:	½	56a
444	**ZAK FACTA 22** [6] Miss D A McHale 4-9-5 vis T (50) S Whitworth 33/1: 25400-55: Keen & prom, chall dist, no extra cl-home:	nk	54a
542	**ZINGING 7** [3] J J Bridger 5-9-5 (50) G Baker 10/1: 0310-506: Trkd ldrs, kept on onepce:	1	52a
344	**ALAFZAR 35** [1] P D Evans 6-9-7 vis t (52) S Donohoe (7) 9/2: 00040-47: Towards rear, nvr able to chall.	nk	53a
559	**LUCAYAN MONARCH 5** [9] P S McEntee 6-9-9 p (54) K Fallon 16/1: 2112508: Chsd ldrs wide, no extra dist:	shd	55a
558	**ITALIAN MIST 5** [16] Julian Poulton 5-9-9 e (54) G Faulkner 25/1: 0-135129: Held up wide, nvr able to chall:	½	54a
544	**MUQTADI 7** [10] M Quinn 6-9-6 (51) Martin Dwyer 50/1: 50-03060: Slow away, rdn rear, little prog:	nk	50a
559	**LORD CHAMBERLAIN 5** [14] J M Bradley 11-9-8 bl (53) C J Davies (4) 25/1: 50-21440: Rear, little prog.	nk	51a
565	**STEELY DAN 4** [15] J R Best 5-9-8 (53) N Pollard 12/1: 0005-000: Sn handy wide, btn when hmpd ins last:	½	50a
562	**LORD MELBOURNE 5** [8] J A Osborne 5-9-5 (50) S W Kelly 13/2: 35-21430: Rear, nvr able to chall:	¾	45a
348	**LUCIUS VERRUS 34** [7] D Shaw 4-9-5 (50) Darren Williams 14/1: 0434-30: Went left start, rear, no prog.	hd	44a
378	**KARAOKE KING 30** [12] J E Long 6-9-10 (55) C Catlin 33/1: 61600-60: Cl-up, wkng/hmpd over 1f out.	nk	48a
562	**SCARROTTOO 5** [2] S C Williams 6-9-7 (52) B Reilly 9/1: 340-0350: Trkd ldrs, badly hmpd over 1f out, not able to recover:	5	36a

16 Ran   1m 25.90 (3.1)   Owner Mr James Etheridge   Trained at Godstone

601 | 1.20 Betdirect Co Uk Maiden Stakes 3yo (D)
£3848 £1184 £592 £296   **1m2f p/track**   **Going 39**   **-30 Slow**   Stalls Inside

159	**COME WHAT JULY 65** [3] R Guest 3-9-0 bl (67) K Fallon 2/1: 502023-1: Chsd ldrs, rdn to lead dist, sn in command:		75a
4509}	**LOOKS THE BUSINESS 135** [8] W G M Turner 3-9-0 t (68) C Haddon (7) 20/1: 445-2: Mid-div, eff wide to chall 2f out, not pace of wnr:	1¾	71a
473	**AMWELL BRAVE 18** [10] J R Jenkins 3-9-0 (70) S W Kelly 5/4 FAV: 345-2233: Held up, rapid prog to lead bef halfway, rdn & hdd dist, no extra:	½	70a
322	**CHAMPAGNE SHADOW 36** [5] G L Moore 3-9-0 R Brisland 25/1: 04-04: Hld up, late gains:	¾	69a
514	**OUR LITTLE ROSIE 11** [2] M Blanshard 3-8-9 D Sweeney 33/1: 005: Cl-up, no extra over 1f out.	1½	62a
472	**LIVIA 18** [7] J G Portman 3-8-9 R Havlin 33/1: 06: Handy over 2f out, no extra.	3½	57a
	PRESTON HALL [6] Mrs L C Jewell 3-9-0 K Dalgleish 66/1: 7: Dwelt, rear, eff 4f out, sn no impress on debut.	hd	61a
472	**JOY AND PAIN 18** [13] G L Moore 3-9-0 Dane O'Neill 50/1: 08: Rear, nvr able to chall.	¾	60a
438	**ITS BLUE CHIP 23** [4] P W D'Arcy 3-9-0 e Paul Eddery 15/2: 0-39: Led till over 6f out, btn 2f out:	1	59a
	ZAFFEU [12] N P Littmoden 3-9-0 J P Guillambert (3) 10/1: 0: Dwelt, rear, eff wide halfway, sn btn.	7	49a
521	**LA CONCHA 11** [11] Mrs L C Jewell 3-9-0 Darren Williams 50/1: 000: Chsd ldrs halfway, btn 3f out.	9	37a
496	**GREATEST BY PHAR 14** [1] J Akehurst 3-9-0 C Catlin 50/1: 00: Rear, no ch fnl 3f, gelded.	6	28a
428	**SECOND USER 25** [9] J R Jenkins 3-9-0 S Whitworth 66/1: 00: Slowly away & al bhd, t.o., gelded.	2½	24a

13 Ran   2m 09.72 (6.92)   Owner The Storm Again Syndicate   Trained at Newmarket

602 | 1.55 Bet Direct Through Sky Active Claiming Stakes 4yo+ (F)
£2919 £834 £417   **1m5f p/track**   **Going 39**   **-22 Slow**   Stalls Inside

11	**BEYOND THE POLE 91** [11] B R Johnson 6-9-1 (55) K Fallon 9/2 JT FAV: 240000-1: Sn trkd ldr, rdn & led over 3f out, al holding from dist:		59a
464	**TROPICAL SON 19** [2] D Shaw 5-9-3 vis (46) N Callan 50/1: 00-25102: Rear, styd on for press fnl 2f, not able to chall:	1½	60a
454*	**SUNGIO 21** [8] B G Powell 6-8-7 (53) Dale Gibson 8/1: 005/05-13: Pushed along chasing ldrs, styd on for press fnl 2f, not pace of wnr:	nk	49a
342	**ROYAL PRODIGY 35** [3] R J Hodges 5-9-7 (66) Dane O'Neill 9/2 JT FAV: 01311-04: Mid-div, styd on onepace for press fnl 3f:	¾	62a
426	**LANDESCENT 26** [12] M Quinn 4-8-3 (46) Martin Dwyer 20/1: 2660-045: Led till 3f out, no extra dist:	nk	47a
264	**GEMI BED 44** [4] G L Moore 9-8-11 bl (45) S Whitworth 11/2: 651153-6: Held up, eff 3f out, no impress dist:	3½	46a
477	**MASTER T 18** [7] G L Moore 5-9-1 (55) M Fenton 14/1: 4/4000-07: Rear, styd on fnl 2f:	hd	49a
957}	**SHOLAY 102** [5] P Mitchell 5-8-11 J Fanning 20/1: 065400-8: Cl-up, btn 2f out, jumps fit.	3	41a
4434}	**PRIVATE BENJAMIN 140** [1] Jamie Poulton 4-8-11 (56) D Kinsella 16/1: 643664-9: Keen, rear, little hdwy, abs.	2	42a
358	**JOELY GREEN 33** [6] N P Littmoden 7-8-13 bl (57) J P Guillambert (3) 6/1: 30435-50: Dwelt, rear, no impression.	1¼	38a

4819}	**FORTUNATE DAVE 114** [13] Ian Williams 5-8-11 (60) C Catlin 14/1: 4605/50-0: Chsd ldr, bhd hway:	¾	35a
4592}	**KNOCKTOPHER ABBEY 483** [9] B R Millman 7-9-3 (68) J P Spencer 7/1: 034050/0: Rear, bhd 4f out, jmps fit.	18	19a
537	**PHILOSOPHIC 8** [10] Mrs L C Jewell 10-8-9 2ow p (35) S Donohoe 20/1: ///000/-00: Keen & prom till 7f out.	8	0a

13 Ran 2m 50.24 (7.94) Owner Tann Racing Trained at Epsom

---

603 2.30 Bet Direct No Q On 08000 93 66 93 Handicap Stakes 3yo 0-70 (E) [77]

£3346 £956 £478 1m p/track rnd Going 39 -22 Slow Stalls Outside

473	**ATHBOY 18** [11] M J Wallace 3-8-6 VIS (55) J P Spencer 12/1: 60-01: Rear, hdwy/short of room 2f out, drvn & strong run to lead well ins last, shade cosy:		64a
455	**ARCHERFIELD 21** [2] J W Hills 3-9-6 (69) Dane O'Neill 4/1: 0055-22: Trkd ldr, led over 2f out till ove 1f out, kept on:	1¼	70a
496	**NIGHT STORM 14** [8] S Dow 3-9-3 (66) P Doe 13/2: 025-533: Dwelt, eff wide, drvn & led over 1f out, hdd well ins last:	nk	66a
545	**GARRIGON 7** [7] N P Littmoden 3-8-13 P (62) Lisa Jones (3) 11/2: 2002-504: Dwelt, held up, eff wide from over 2f out, no extra ins last:	1¼	59a
455	**RESPLENDENT KING 21** [3] T G Mills 3-9-7 (70) M Fenton 7/2 FAV: 3040-335: Bhd, outpcd 2f out, kept on late.	¾	66a
497	**TREVIAN 14** [12] S C Williams 3-9-5 (68) B Reilly (5) 7/1: 056-0166: Held up, short of room 2f out, not able to chall.	hd	63a
432	**EVEN EASIER 25** [10] G L Moore 3-8-6 p (55) S W Kelly 16/1: 04126-07: Mid-div, short of room 2f out, sn onepace:	nk	49a
455	**GAYLE STORM 21** [1] C Tinkler 3-8-3 (52) J Quinn 20/1: 6536-008: Dwelt, held up inner, no prog fnl 2f.	1½	43a
455	**RICKY MARTAN 21** [4] G C Bravery 3-9-0 BL (63) S Whitworth 66/1: 064-09: Keen & trkd ldrs, wknd qckly dist.	3	48a
252	**STONOR LADY 46** [9] P W D'Arcy 3-8-7 (56) Paul Eddery 33/1: 0206-0: Led till 2f out, sn btn, abs.	2	37a
337	**JANGO MALFOY 35** [5] B W Duke 3-8-8 (57) O Urbina 33/1: 00050-00: Cl-up, wknd over 1f out, lost action.	1¼	35a
402	**HEAD BOY 28** [6] S Dow 3-8-9 (58) C Catlin 12/1: 0510-400: Al bhd, hung badly over 1f out.	2	32a

12 Ran 1m 41.07 (4.87) Owner Mr D Mcgovern Trained at Newmarket

---

604 3.05 Littlewoods Bet Direct Handicap Stakes 4yo+ 0-80 (D) [78]

£4173 £1284 £642 £321 7f p/track rnd Going 39 -02 Slow Stalls Inside

518	**CHATEAU NICOL 11** [13] B G Powell 5-9-13 vis (77) J Fanning 14/1: 100-1301: Keen rear, switched wide & strong run for press to lead well ins last:		83a
130	**MISTRAL SKY 71** [7] Mrs Stef Liddiard 5-9-8 vis (72) J P Spencer 9/1: 110010-2: Cl-up, rdn & led over 1f out, edged right & hdd well ins last:	nk	77a
323	**SIR LAUGHALOT 36** [1] Miss E C Lavelle 4-9-4 (68) L Keniry (3) 8/1: 0020-203: Trkd ldrs, rdn & briefly outpcd 2f out, styd on well for press ins last, just held:	nk	72a
565	**HARD TO CATCH 4** [9] D K Ivory 6-9-1 (65) D Sweeney 16/1: 555-0024: Held up, styd on wide for press fnl 2f, nrst fin:	nk	68a
499	**SUPERCHIEF 14** [5] Miss B Sanders 9-9-1 bl t (65) J Quinn 8/1: 02-06435: Keen & cl-up, onepace for press dist.	nk	67a
547	**AND TOTO TOO 7** [2] P D Evans 4-9-6 bl (70) S Donohoe (7) 20/1: 53515-06: Dwelt, rear, kept on, not able to chall.	nk	71a
453	**CURRENCY 21** [3] J M Bradley 7-9-9 (73) S Drowne 16/1: 00-03247: Mid-div, onepace fnl 2f:	½	73a
518	**CORMORANT WHARF 11** [12] T E Powell 4-9-12 (76) S Whitworth 11/2: 16/0-0658: Dwelt, rear, nrst fin:	nk	75a
565	**WHIPPASNAPPER 4** [11] J R Best 4-9-6 (70) N Pollard 14/1: 0-012139: Led till over 1f out, btn ins last:	shd	69a
517	**SIR FRANCIS 11** [6] J Noseda 6-9-5 (69) Paul Scallan 10/1: 04060-00: Dwelt, rear, short of room over 1f out, nvr a threat:	nk	67a
518	**GREENWOOD 11** [10] P G Murphy 6-9-11 (75) D Kinsella 4/1: 2200-030: Cl-up, fdd dist:	nk	72a
339	**HE WHO DARES 35** [14] A W Carroll 6-8-7 (57) W Ryan 12/1: 01012-20: Keen, mid-div wide, btn over 1f out.	shd	54a
562	**BLONDE EN BLONDE 5** [8] N P Littmoden 4-9-4 (68) K Fallon 5/1 FAV: 4-660120: Chsd ldrs, btn/no room ins last, eased:	2	61a
550	**EFFECTIVE 6** [4] A P Jarvis 4-8-12 (62) N Callan 20/1: 2000-030: Mid-div, short of room 1f out, no impress.	3	49a

14 Ran 1m 25.65 (2.85) Owner Basingstoke Commercials Trained at Winchester

---

605 3.40 Bet Direct Through Atr Interactive Handicap Stakes 4yo+ 0-85 (D) [85]

£4823 £1484 £742 £371 2m p/track Going 39 +04 Fast Stalls Inside

546	**BOUMAHOU 7** [12] A P Jarvis 4-8-8 (71) N Callan 12/1: 6440-331: Mid-div, hdwy 3f out & drvn to lead over 1f out, styd on strongly:		78a
475	**HIGH POINT 18** [5] G P Enright 6-9-6 (77) Dane O'Neill 11/2: 001-0002: Handy & chsd ldr 3f out, kept on for press, not pace of wnr:	¾	82a
478	**TYPHOON TILLY 18** [2] C R Egerton 7-9-4 (75) S Drowne 7/1: 3033-643: Rear, styd on wide for press fnl 2f, not able to chall:	1¾	78a
4058}	**NAWAMEES 160** [8] G L Moore 6-9-11 (82) S Whitworth 3/1 FAV: 06/5236-4: Handy & led over 3f out, drvn & hdd over 1f out, no extra:	hd	84a
478	**RED SCORPION 18** [11] W M Brisbourne 5-9-2 (73) B Swarbrick (7) 4/1: 2035-165: Mid-div, eff 3f out, no impress:	5	70a
519	**BRILLIANT RED 11** [3] Jamie Poulton 11-9-11 t (82) H Poulton (6) 20/1: 4003-006: Dwelt, rear, only mod prog:	2½	77a
1652}	**LITZINSKY 265** [4] C B B Booth 6-8-2 (59) J McAuley 100/1: 40/0500-7: Chsd ldr, lost pl from 6f out:	3½	51a
2073}	**TURN OF PHRASE 244** [1] R A Fahey 5-7-13 bl (56) Dale Gibson 7/1: 13/5213-8: Rear, no ch 4f out:	8	41a
336*	**VANBROUGH 36** [14] Miss D A McHale 4-9-0 vis t (77) Darren Williams 14/1: 60226-19: Prom, led 5f out till 3f out, sn btn:	¾	61a
552	**ORINOCOVSKY 6** [6] N P Littmoden 5-8-5 (62) J Quinn 14/1: 004-1030: Led till 5f out, sn lost pl, eased, qck reapp:	¾	45a
493	**DUSTY CARPET 14** [10] M J Weeden 6-8-13 (70) C Catlin 25/1: 220//-0000: Rear, no ch fnl 3f, eased.	nk	52a

11 Ran 3m 25.54 (5.54) Owner Mrs B A Headon Trained at Twyford

---

606 4.15 Bet Direct @ Smartbet Com Selling Stakes 3yo (G)

£2569 £734 £367 6f p/track rnd Going 39 -09 Slow Stalls Inside

52	**JAOLINS 85** [10] R Hannon 3-8-6 (52) R Smith 14/1: 0060-1: Rear, hdwy 2f out & drvn to lead ins last, going away.		56a
494	**STAMFORD BLUE 14** [3] J S Moore 3-9-4 bl (53) Derek Nolan (7) 3/1: 035-2462: Led, rdn clr over 1f out, hdd well ins last:	1¼	61a
548*	**IVORY LACE 7** [7] D K Ivory 3-8-13 (52) D Sweeney 5/2 FAV: 00-52013: Chsd ldrs, outpcd halfway, kept on for press ins last:	¾	56a
548	**REHIA 7** [6] J W Hills 3-8-13 (54) K Fallon 5/1: 550-0654: Trkd ldr, no extra:	¾	52a
548	**LADY PISTE 7** [9] P D Evans 3-8-13 vis t (51) S Donohoe (6) 9/2: 304-0425: Trkd ldrs, short of room 1f out, onepace:	½	52a
462	**ARE YOU THERE 20** [1] P S McEntee 3-8-13 bl (45) F P Ferris (3) 16/1: 00060-06: Chsd ldrs, outpcd fnl 2f:	1¼	48a
436	**PARDON MOI 23** [2] Mrs C A Dunnett 3-8-13 (47) Hayley Turner (5) 20/1: 654-3447: Pushed along rear, only mod gains.	1¼	44a
42	**ROYAL AWAKENING 86** [5] A P Jarvis 3-8-11 J Quinn 11/1: 30-8: Rear, nvr factor, abs/gelded.	2	36a

155

	MASTER MAHOGANY [8] R J Hodges 3-8-11 S Drowne 25/1: 9: Mid-div, outpcd fnl 2f on debut.				shd 36a
200	COLEORTON PRINCE 58 [4] K A Ryan 3-8-11 (35) N Callan 100/1: 000000-0: Mid-div, no ch 2f out, eased.				13 2a
10 Ran	1m 13.27 (2.87) Owner Allen & Associates				Trained at Marlborough

607 4.50 Bet Direct On Attheraces Text Page 410 Handicap Stakes 4yo+ 0-65 (F) **[65]**
£2933 £838 £419 1m p/track rnd Going 39 +05 Fast Stalls Outside

565	ACORAZADO 4 [7] G L Moore 5-9-7 (58) G Carter 4/1 FAV: 535-0201: Trkd ldrs, rdn to lead ins last, sn asserted:		65a
498*	BANK ON HIM 14 [10] C Weedon 9-9-9 (60) J Quinn 7/1: 000-1612: Cl-up & led over 2f out, drvn & hdd ins last, no ch with	1¼	63a
434	BURGUNDY 25 [1] P Mitchell 7-9-8 (59) K Dalgleish 8/1: 15010-63: Rear, drvn & kept on fnl 2f, not able to chall:	2	58a
515	EASTER OGIL 11 [4] Jane Southcombe 9-9-13 (64) V Slattery 8/1: 2-503324: Rear, eff when short of room dist, kept on ins last:	¾	62a
5019}	FEN GYPSY 97 [9] P D Evans 6-9-11 (62) S Donohoe (7) 8/1: 016000-5: Trkd ldrs, outpcd halfway, kept on late, no threat:	hd	59a
366	CAPTAIN CLOUDY 32 [2] M Madgwick 4-9-6 (57) L Keniry (3) 12/1: 04000-56: Keen & trkd ldr, wknd over 1f out:	hd	53a
565	FRANKSKIPS 4 [12] Miss B Sanders 5-9-9 (60) S Drowne 33/1: 500-0507: Rear, mod late prog, no dngr.	½	55a
547	QUANTUM LEAP 7 [5] S Dow 7-9-10 (61) Paul Eddery 7/1: 153-0638: Held up wide, no impress over 1f out.	¾	55a
565	POWER BIRD 4 [8] B R Johnson 4-9-9 (60) N Pollard 20/1: 0000-209: Led till over 2f out, fdd, qck reapp:	shd	54a
294	LONDONER 39 [6] S Dow 6-9-11 (62) P Doe 25/1: 00006-00: Dwelt, rear, no impression.	1	54a
499	INISTRAHULL ISLAND 14 [3] M H Tompkins 4-9-7 (58) J Fanning 8/1: 0423-360: Mid-div, btn dist, lame:	1¼	47a
476	ZALKANI 18 [11] B G Powell 4-9-12 (63) K Fallon 8/1: 600-330: Trkd ldrs, btn dist, eased ins last:	2	48a
12 Ran	1m 38.88 (2.68) Owner D T L Limited		Trained at Brighton

Official Going Standard

608 1.40 Bet Direct In Running Sky Text Page 293 Handicap Stakes Div 1 3yo 0-65 (F) **[72]**
£2905 £830 £415 1m3f f/sand Going 50 -13 Slow Stalls Inside

559	RED LANCER 6 [8] R J Price 3-9-2 (60) R Miles (3) 9/2: 55010-61: Sn handy & led going well 3f out, rdn & asserted over 1f out, styd on strongly:		75a
506*	YANKEEDOODLEDANDY 14 [10] P C Haslam 3-9-7 (65) G Faulkner 4/6 FAV: 004-1212: Rear, rdn 3f out, kept on for press, nvr dngr to wnr:	5	72a
314	NOCATEE 38 [2] P C Haslam 3-8-1 (45) Rory Moore (7) 8/1: 00500-33: Prom, kept on onepace fnl 2f:	hd	51a
441	MYANNABANANA 24 [7] J R Weymes 3-9-5 vis (63) D Fentiman (7) 7/1: 1135-534: Rear & rdn early, nvr threatened ldrs:	15	49a
354	REGENCY MALAYA 35 [1] M F Harris 3-7-12 7oh bl t (35) S Righton 66/1: 00600-05: Led till 3f out, sn btn:	6	20a
438	PEPE 24 [9] R Hollinshead 3-8-7 p (51) J Quinn 25/1: 06-66: Sn bhd:	hd	28a
573	AMAR 4 [5] P A Blockley 3-7-13 7oh 1ow (35) J Bramhill 40/1: 460-07: Rdn & bhd halfway, qck reapp, longer trip.	hd	19a
525	PARIS DREAMER 10 [6] M W Easterby 3-7-12 2oh (40) Dale Gibson 66/1: 0000-008: Dwelt, chsd ldrs till halfway:	hd	17a
95	FRAMBO 79 [3] J G Portman 3-8-10 (54) B Reilly (5) 16/1: 00625-9: Chsd ldrs, lost place qckly halfway, abs.	7	20a
9 Ran	2m 28.25 (6.95) Owner Fox and Cub Partnership		Trained at Hereford

609 2.10 Bet Direct On Attheraces Text Page 410 Handicap Stakes 3yo 0-75 (E) **[79]**
£3248 £928 £464 5f f/sand str Going 50 Inapplicab Stalls Outside

591	SAHARA SILK 2 [7] D Shaw 3-8-9 vis (60) Darren Williams 20/1: 0500-0061: Broke well, dsptd lead, went on halfway, held on well despite edging left from dist:		69a
485*	PICCOLO PRINCE 8 [8] E J Alston 3-8-7 (58) J Quinn 85/40: 3500-012: Chsd ldrs, styd on for press, not able to chall wnr:	1¼	62a
485	SMART STARPRINCESS 16 [3] P A Blockley 3-9-2 vis (67) K Fallon 2/1 FAV: 411-1123: Led/dsptd lead till dist, no extra:	2½	63a
444	FAYRZ PLEASE 23 [2] M C Chapman 3-8-11 (62) Andrew Webb 20/1: 03-44: Chsd ldrs, outpcd halfway, kept on ins last:	shd	58a
466	BACK AT DE FRONT 20 [11] N E Berry 3-8-13 (64) M Savage (5) 14/1: 1504-155: Rdn rear, nrst fin:	1	57a
485	DEMOLITION MOLLY 16 [4] R F Marvin 3-9-3 T (68) Dean McKeown 16/1: 15054-06: Chsd ldrs till halfway:	1½	56a
592*	LADY BAHIA 2 [9] R P Elliott 3-8-9 6ex (60) T Hamilton 10/1: 0240-0617: Reared start, nvr on terms:	hd	47a
405	A BID IN TIME 29 [6] D Shaw 3-7-12 4oh (45) Hayley Turner (5) 50/1: 00000-008: Chsd ldrs till halfway:	3½	26a
582	MISS JUDGED 3 [1] A P Jones 3-7-12 4oh bl e (45) J F McDonald 33/1: 00-00609: Chsd ldrs, strugg hlfway.	½	24a
494	SMOKIN JOE 15 [5] J R Best 3-9-7 (72) N Pollard 4/1: 62216-40: Chsd ldrs early, sn bhd:	2	41a
572	ASK THE CLERK 15 [10] H J Collingridge 3-9-5 (70) M Tebbutt 14/1: 030-0350: Outpcd throughout, qck reapp	½	37a
11 Ran	1m 0.58 Owner Swann Racing Ltd		Trained at Newark

610 2.40 Bet Direct On Attheraces Text Page 411 Claiming Stakes 4yo+ (F)
£2954 £844 £422 6f f/sand rnd Going 50 -11 Slow Stalls Inside

516	PANJANDRUM 12 [14] N E Berry 6-9-1 (65) M Savage (5) 20/1: 001-0351: Chsd ldrs wide, styd on for press to lead ins last:		65a
593*	BLAKESET 2 [5] T D Barron 9-9-0 vis (78) S W Kelly 5/4 FAV: 101-10112: Rdn towards rear halfway, hdwy for press & led briefly dist, no extra nr fin:	¾	61a
550	GILDED COVE 7 [2] R Hollinshead 4-9-1 (67) M Fenton 12/1: 1310-003: Held up when badly hmpd after 2f, swtchd wide & styd on for press, not pace to chall:	¾	60a
501*	AINTNECESSARILYSO 14 [10] N E Berry 6-8-11 (50) C Catlin 20/1: 465-5514: Pushed along chasing ldrs, styd on for press fnl 2f, not able to chall:	nk	55a
533*	POLAR HAZE 9 [9] J Pearce 7-9-1 vis (52) J Quinn 5/1: 02-42615: Rdn rear, nrst fin:	1¾	54a
500	CLEVELAND WAY 14 [1] D Carroll 4-8-11 vis (46) D Tudhope (7) 80/1: 00-12656: Handy & led halfway, hung left & hdd over 1f out, wknd:	¾	48a
551	SHARP HAT 7 [7] D W Chapman 10-8-11 (70) A Culhane 14/1: 135-5207: Rdn towards rear, nvr a factor:	1¼	44a
487	NEW OPTIONS 16 [6] W J Musson 7-8-11 bl (64) Paul Eddery 14/1: 0004-548: Chsd ldrs, hmpd over 1f out, sn no extra:	½	42a
482	PORT ST CHARLES 17 [3] P R Chamings 7-9-9 (76) J F McDonald 5 100/30: 2301-509: Led 3f, btn/hmpd over 1f out.	3½	44a
550	ONLY ONE LEGEND 7 [8] K A Ryan 6-9-9 bl (70) N Callan 25/1: 603-0000: Prom till 2f out:	3	36a

| 551 | **SCARY NIGHT** 7 [13] J Balding 4-9-1 p (75) J Edmunds 25/1: 22200-00: Prom wide till 2f out. | 1¼ | 24a |
| 407 | **TALLY** 29 [11] A Berry 4-9-1 (67) F Lynch 66/1: 0646-000: Sn struggling. | 2 | 18a |

12 Ran 1m 16.96 (3.66) Owner Leeway Group Limited Trained at Earlswood

---

611 3.10 Littlewoods Bet Direct Stakes Handicap 3yo+ 0-95 (C) [93]
£8249 £2538 £1269 £635 7f f/sand rnd Going 50 +23 Fast Stalls Inside

550*	**POLAR KINGDOM** 7 [10] T D Barron 6-8-13 6ex (78) D Mernagh 7/1: 0/200-311: Trkd ldrs, rdn & led over 1f out, styd on strongly, shade readily.		88a
518	**PRIMA STELLA** 12 [4] J A R Toller 5-8-8 (73) Lisa Jones (3) 25/1: 020-4102: Led till over 1f out, kept on for press:	2½	75a
452	**SANGIOVESE** 22 [5] H Morrison 5-8-13 (78) L Fletcher (3) 3/1: 22/301-03: Handy & ch 2f out, not pace of wnr:	3	74a
532	**ELLENS ACADEMY** 9 [6] E J Alston 9-9-0 (79) D Allan (3) 8/1: 131-4634: Chsd ldrs, no extra dist.	1	73a
419+*	**MUFREH** 28 [3] A G Newcombe 6-9-7 (86) S Whitworth 11/4 FAV: 02012-15: Held up, rdn & no impress dist	3	74a
585	**WARDEN WARREN** 3 [8] Mrs C A Dunnett 6-8-7 bl (72) B Reilly (5) 12/1: 0021-346: Chsd ldrs till over 1f out:	6	50a
511	**EPHESUS** 13 [1] Miss Gay Kelleway 4-9-6 vis (85) M Fenton 16/1: 01330-37: Held up, no impress from halfway:	1¼	60a
513	**AIR MAIL** 13 [2] Mrs N Macauley 7-9-0 (79) A Culhane 14/1: 00060-48: Al bhd:	1½	51a
1990}	**MYSTIC MAN** 251 [7] K A Ryan 6-9-10 (89) N Callan 9/2: 311400-9: Rear, nvr a factor:	10	45a
419	**LINCOLN DANCER** 28 [9] D Nicholls 7-8-8 VIS (73) A Nicholls 25/1: 60000-00: Chsd ldrs wide till halfway, sn bhd:	6	20a

10 Ran 1m 28.5 (1.9) Owner Millie and Poppy Squire Trained at Thirsk

---

612 3.40 Bet Direct On Attheraces Text Page 412 Handicap Stakes 4yo+ 0-65 (F) [62]
£2919 £834 £417 2m f/sand Going 50 -72 Slow Stalls Inside

141}	**BOX BUILDER** 436 [9] H Morrison 7-9-10 (58) L Fletcher (3) 4/1: 000/006/-1: Held up, eff to chall 2f out, drvn & narrowly asserted ins last:		67a
414	**DOCTOR JOHN** 28 [7] Andrew Turnell 7-8-1 P (35) C Catlin 20/1: 4/0000//-4: Chsd ldrs, led over 3f out, rdn & hdd ins last, kept on:	1	42a
491	**VINCENT** 16 [1] John A Harris 9-8-12 (46) J Mackay 7/2: 11-43163: Prom, rdn & outpcd 5f out, onepace fnl 2f:	8	46a
563*	**REFLEX BLUE** 6 [3] R J Price 7-8-12 6ex vis (46) R Miles (3) 7/4 FAV: 00U05/-14: In tch, eff wide from 5f out, no impress fnl 2f:	1¾	44a
305	**OULTON BROAD** 39 [5] R Ford 8-8-1 p (35) Lisa Jones (3) 10/1: 40016/-05: Keen & held up, no impress fnl 3f:	4	29a
491	**WORLABY DALE** 16 [6] Mrs S Lamyman 8-8-1 (35) J Quinn 6/1: 340-4406: Rear, eff 3f out, no impress.	1¾	27a
376	**COLONNADE** 31 [8] C Grant 5-8-11 (45) K Dalgleish 16/1: 36000-27: Held up, led over 6f out till over 3f out.	17	23a
4375}	**AQUA PURA** 145 [4] B J Curley 5-9-4 (52) S W Kelly 12/1: 21300/5-8: Led till 6f out, sn bhd:	dist	0a
424	**EXIT TO HEAVEN** 27 [2] Mrs Lucinda Featherstone 4-8-13 (53) P Makin (7) 20/1: 225-0609: Chsd ldrs till 6f out, new yard, mdn.	20	0a

9 Ran 3m 45.46 (19.46) Owner Mr M Hutchinson Trained at East Ilsley

---

613 4.10 Bet Direct On Attheraces Text Page 413 Selling Stakes 3yo (G)
£2520 £720 £360 7f f/sand rnd Going 50 -36 Slow Stalls Inside

481	**FIZZY LADY** 17 [9] B W Hills 3-8-6 T (64) M Hills 8/13 FAV: 54-441: Chsd ldrs wide, sn pushed along, led over 1f out, drvn out:		54a
402	**PRINCESS ISMENE** 29 [2] J Jay 3-8-12 bl (59) K Fallon 9/2: 0405-152: Chsd ldrs, styd on for press, not able to chall:	2½	54a
495	**FOX HOLLOW** 15 [8] M J Haynes 3-8-11 (30) R Miles (3) 100/1: 6500-003: Mid-div, styd on for press, not able to chall:	1	51a
462	**KNIGHT TO REMEMBER** 21 [5] K A Ryan 3-8-11 P (48) N Callan 8/1: 00600-34: Dwelt, eff wide from halfway, not able to chall:	nk	50a
490	**PLATINUM CHIEF** 16 [1] A Berry 3-8-11 (45) F Lynch 25/1: 0045-665: Pushed along rear, only mod gains.	1½	47a
436	**INDRANI** 24 [6] John A Harris 3-8-6 (45) L Fletcher 33/1: 64560-06: Led till over 1f out, wknd.	5	34a
4479}	**KEDROSS** 138 [7] R P Elliott 3-8-6 (63) Dean McKeown 7/1: 643000-7: Cl-up, wknd 2f out, abs.	¾	33a
466	**BISH BASH BOSH** 20 [4] M F Harris 3-8-6 BL (40) S Righton 80/1: 60040-08: Chsd ldrs, struggling halfway:	5	25a
582	**ALIBONGO** 3 [10] P A Blockley 3-8-11 (40) Derek Nolan (7) 33/1: 60600-09: Sn struggling, qck reapp.	3	24a

9 Ran 1m 32.64 (6.04) Owner Baydon House Stud Trained at Lambourn

---

614 4.40 Bet Direct In Running Sky Text Page 293 Handicap Stakes Div 2 3yo 0-65 (F) [70]
£2898 £828 £414 1m3f f/sand Going 50 -38 Slow Stalls Inside

486	**CEASAR** 16 [4] P C Haslam 3-8-9 P (51) G Faulkner 5/2 FAV: 06004-21: Trkd ldrs trav well, led over 1f out, rdn out:		57a
486	**SIR FRANK GIBSON** 16 [8] M Johnston 3-8-3 (45) J Fanning 3/1: 3040-042: Led/dsptd lead, went on over 2f out till over 1f out, kept on for press:	1¼	48a
322	**ASHSTANZA** 37 [3] M A Jarvis 3-9-7 (63) N Callan 100/30: 04-43: Chsd ldrs, outpcd 3f out, kept on for press fnl 2f:	¾	65a
455	**MORNING HAWK** 22 [6] J S Moore 3-8-4 (46) D Kinsella 10/1: 05000-04: Held up, smooth hdwy to go handy 4f out, no extra over 1f out	¾	47a
238	**IT MUST BE SPEECH** 52 [2] S L Keightley 3-9-2 (58) A Nicholls 25/1: 0000-5: Rear, mod gains for press, no threat.	hd	58a
486	**COURANT DAIR** 16 [9] P C Haslam 3-7-12 (40) D Fentiman (7) 7/1: 4000-036: Handy & led after 2f till over 2f out, wknd.	4	32a
441	**ATLANTIC BREEZE** 24 [7] Mrs N Macauley 3-9-4 (60) A Culhane 6/1: 410-07: Mid-div, struggling from halfway.	19	19a
3450}	**DUGGANS DILEMMA** 189 [1] Ian Emmerson 3-8-10 (52) J Bramhill 80/1: 0500-8: Sn bhd & t.o./p.u. 3f out, reapp.	dist	0a

8 Ran 2m 30.94 (9.64) Owner Wilson Imports Trained at Middleham

---

Official Going Standard To Slow

615 2.20 Bet Direct No Q Demo 08000 837 888 Handicap Stakes 3yo 0-80 (D) [78]
£4037 £1242 £621 £311 7f f/sand rnd Going 53 -21 Slow Stalls Outside

| 506 | **COULD SHE BE MAGIC** 15 [1] T D Easterby 3-8-7 (57) Dale Gibson 9/2: 03501-21: Led/dsptd lead, went on 3f out, drvn & held on well: | | 61a |

444* **PICK OF THE CROP** 24 [5] J R Jenkins 3-9-7 (71) I Mongan 100/30: 40525-12: Held up in tch, trav well over 2f out, drvn & kept on well, just held: `nk` **74a**

510* **BRIDGEWATER BOYS** 14 [4] K A Ryan 3-9-7 p (71) N Callan 9/4 FAV: 6215-413: Held up, eff wide for 3f out, no extra dist: 4 **66a**

470 **SIR JASPER** 21 [3] M F Harris 3-8-12 vis (62) S Righton 10/1: 561-1034: Led/dsptd lead till 3f out, btn over 1f out: 4 **49a**

488* **WINGS OF MORNING** 17 [2] P A Blockley 3-9-6 (70) Derek Nolan (7) 7/2: 0002-15: Trkd ldrs, btn dist: `nk` **56a**

510 **SABLE N SILK** 14 [6] D Haydn Jones 3-8-7 BL (57) J Quinn 20/1: 610-06: Dwelt, bhd, lost tch from halfway, blnkd. 23 **2a**

6 Ran 1m 31.4 (5.2) Owner Mr Malcolm Caine Trained at Malton

---

616 2.55 Bet Direct No Q Claiming Stakes 4yo+ (F)
£2877 £822 £411 1m4f f/sand Going 53 -24 Slow Stalls Inside

484 **MANDOOB** 18 [6] B R Johnson 7-9-4 p (59) Dane O'Neill 13/8 FAV: 56300-41: Held up in tch, rdn & hdwy to lead over 2f out, in command at dist, styd on strongly: **65a**

602 **ROYAL PRODIGY** 37 [3] R J Hodges 5-9-8 (66) M Fenton 9/4: 01311-02: Rdn to go cl-up early, led over 4f out till over 2f out, btn dist: 3½ **63a**

549 **JUST WIZ** 9 [5] N P Littmoden 8-9-2 bl (70) J P Guillambert (3) 5/2: 50532-63: Rear, eff from 4f out, no impress fnl 2f: 4 **51a**

534 **SHATIN SPECIAL** 10 [2] G C H Chung 4-8-0 p (45) Dean Williams (7) 10/1: 402-52F4: Led, hdd over 4f out, btn over 1f out: 1¾ **36a**

480 **CHAPEL ROYALE** 18 [1] Mrs N S Sharpe 7-8-10 t P (45) Joanna Badger 40/1: 00066-65: Cl-up halfway, btn 4f out, t.o.: 23 **11a**

5 Ran 2m 42.85 (9.25) Owner Mr J L Guillambert Trained at Epsom

---

617 3.30 Betdirect Co Uk Maiden Stakes 3yo+ (D)
£3374 £1038 £519 £260 7f f/sand rnd Going 53 -25 Slow Stalls Outside

4952} **ALFONSO** 105 [1] B W Hills 3-8-7 M Hills 4/6 FAV: 04-1: Sn handy, shkn up to assert from dist, hands-and-heels, readily: **83a**

531 **GLOBAL ACHIEVER** 10 [7] G C H Chung 3-8-7 R Ffrench 7/2: 322: Keen & led after 1f till over 1f out, no ch with wnr from dist: 6 **69a**

510 **BOOKIESINDEXDOTCOM** 14 [6] J R Jenkins 3-8-2 vis (63) J Quinn 25/1: 43222-03: Held up, eff to chase front pair 3f out, no impress: 2½ **57a**

463 **REALISM** 22 [5] P W Hiatt 4-9-10 (53) A Culhane 40/1: 0350-44: Held up in tch, no impress over 2f out. `nk` **63a**

263 **MIDNIGHT MAMBO** 46 [3] R Guest 4-9-5 Martin Dwyer 7/1: 05-5: Chsd ldrs, outpcd halfway, no impress under tendering handling fnl 2f: 3 **52a**

553 **MRS BROWN** 8 [4] Sir Mark Prescott 3-8-2 J Mackay 11/1: 356: Hmpd start & slow away, al bhd: 1¼ **49a**

488 **LADY DOUBLE U** 17 [2] T D Easterby 4-9-5 D Allan (3) 100/1: 0-07: Led 1f, prom till 3f out. ¾ **11a**

7 Ran 1m 31.66 (5.46) Owner Mr Guy Reed Trained at Lambourn

---

618 4.05 Littlewoods Bet Direct Handicap Stakes 3yo+ 0-100 (C) [98]
£10140 £3120 £1560 £780 6f f/sand rnd Going 53 +18 Fast Stalls Inside

235 **QUITO** 55 [4] D W Chapman 7-10-0 bl (98) A Culhane 7/1: 052645-1: Mid-div trav well halfway, led ins last, hands-and-heels: **109a**

518 **QUEENS RHAPSODY** 13 [10] A Bailey 4-9-3 (87) J Fanning 15/2: 1150-202: Chsd ldrs wide, styd on for press, not pace of wnr: 3 **89a**

551* **TIME N TIME AGAIN** 8 [7] E J Alston 6-8-9 6ex p (79) J Quinn 3/1 FAV: 42-51013: Chsd ldrs, drvn & kept on, nvr able to chall: ¾ **79a**

482+* **CELTIC MILL** 18 [1] D W Barker 6-9-5 (89) L Enstone (3) 12/1: 30140-14: Led, rdn & hdd ins last, no extra. `nk` **88a**

532 **SOBA JONES** 10 [11] J Balding 7-8-6 (76) J Edmunds 13/2: 2-124325: Chsd ldrs wide, no impress dist. 1½ **70a**

482 **SUNDRIED TOMATO** 18 [3] P W Hiatt 5-8-8 (78) L Fletcher (3) 20/1: 000-0646: Prom, no extra fnl 1f: hd **71a**

461 **BOND PLAYBOY** 22 [12] B Smart 4-9-4 (88) F Lynch 25/1: 0012-567: Bhd, only mod prog: ½ **79a**

532 **BOND BOY** 10 [13] B Smart 7-9-6 (90) C Catlin 9/1: 2000-408: Rear, nvr a factor: `nk` **80a**

518 **HURRICANE COAST** 13 [8] D Flood 5-8-12 bl (82) Rory Moore (7) 4/1: 1313209: Trkd ldrs halfway, btn over 1f out. ½ **70a**

611* **POLAR KINGDOM** 1 [6] T D Barron 6-8-8 6ex (78) D Mernagh 25/1: 0/200-3110: Missed break, al bhd: `nk` **65a**

4674} **GAELIC PRINCESS** 125 [9] A G Newcombe 4-9-3 (87) Dane O'Neill 16/1: 524030-0: Sn drpd rear & outpcd: 10 **47a**

511 **CHAPPEL CRESENT** 14 [2] N Nicholls 4-9-6 (90) A Nicholls 33/1: 50540-00: Mid-div, struggling from halfway: 2 **44a**

492+* **TYPE ONE** 16 [5] J J Quinn 6-8-12 (82) R Miles 33/1: 4321-010: Prom early, sn lost pl: 3½ **26a**

13 Ran 1m 14.92 (2.12) Owner Mr Michael Hill Trained at York

---

619 4.40 Bet In Running @ Betdirect Co Uk Selling Stakes 3yo+ (G)
£2590 £740 £370 5f f/sand rnd Going 53 -07 Slow Stalls Inside

524 **AROGANT PRINCE** 11 [5] A W Carroll 7-9-7 bl (51) I Mongan 3/1: 0-440631: Led, drvn & held on well fnl 1f: **60a**

516 **RIVER DAYS** 13 [7] Miss Gay Kelleway 6-9-2 bl t (62) M Fenton 7/2: 14400-02: Trkd ldr, drvn & styd on fnl 1f, al held: 1 **51a**

435 **CATCHTHEBATCH** 27 [3] E A Wheeler 8-9-7 (47) Liam Jones (7) 8/1: 06300-43: Chsd ldrs, styd on onepace for press fnl 2f: ½ **54a**

507 **SOAKED** 14 [2] D W Chapman 11-9-7 bl (49) A Culhane 4/1: 50-26004: Held up, smooth hdwy wide halfway, no impress ins last: 3 **45a**

405 **LAVISH TIMES** 30 [4] A Berry 3-8-7 bl (47) P Bradley (3) 20/1: 40030-05: Chsd ldrs till over 1f out: 1¾ **40a**

527 **HAGLEY PARK** 11 [6] M Quinn 5-9-2 (45) Martin Dwyer 11/4 FAV: 6400-226: Prom, no impress fnl 2f: 3 **26a**

555 **BURKEES GRAW** 8 [8] Mrs S Lamyman 3-8-7 (45) J Quinn 40/1: 05300-07: Al outpcd & bhd: 3½ **20a**

348 **SOMETHINGABOUTHER** 36 [1] P W Hiatt 4-9-2 (40) C Catlin 40/1: 0500-458: Led early, sn bhd. 1¾ **10a**

8 Ran 1m 03.18 (2.98) Owner Mr Dennis Deacon Trained at Alcester

---

620 5.10 Press Interactive To Bet Direct Handicap Stakes Fillies 4yo+ 0-70 (E) [66]
£3248 £928 £464 1m1f79y f/sand rnd Going 53 -10 Slow Stalls Inside

456 **JADE STAR** 22 [7] Miss Gay Kelleway 4-8-10 (48) M Fenton 13/2: 60325-41: Led/dsptd lead & went on halfway, drvn & held on well ins last: **53a**

480 **DANGER BIRD** 18 [8] R Hollinshead 4-8-10 (48) A Culhane 12/1: 353-2302: Prom, chsd wnr 3f out, chall 2f out, just held well ins last: `nk` **53a**

557 **TOP OF THE CLASS** 7 [4] P D Evans 7-8-7 vis (45) Joanna Badger 12/1: 050-0633: Rear, kept on for press fnl 3f, no dngr: 1¼ **47a**

WOLVERHAMPTON Friday 13.02.04 Lefthand, Sharp, Oval Track

597*	**MISS CHAMPERS** 3 [5] P A Blockley 4-10-6 6ex (72) D Nolan (5) 3/1 FAV: 352-0114: Prom, btn 2f out:	5	65a
522*	**RED STORM** 11 [6] J R Boyle 5-8-13 6ex vis (51) R Miles (3) 9/1: 105-0615: Mid-div, no impress fnl 2f:	4	36a
559	**GIVEMETHEMOONLIGHT** 7 [9] Mrs Stef Liddiard 5-9-2 vis (54) I Mongan 7/2: 5213536: Held up, eff halfway, sn btn.	2½	34a
564	**ZAHUNDA** 7 [3] W M Brisbourne 5-8-2 (40) B Swarbrick (7) 7/2: 000-6027: Held up in tch, btn 3f out:	5	11a
525	**WODHILL FOLLY** 11 [2] D Morris 7-8-7 vis (45) N Callan 25/1: 1500-468: Mid-div, lost tch from 4f out:	1¼	13a
583	**AITANA** 4 [1] S C Williams 4-9-1 BL e (53) Martin Dwyer 14/1: 0060-649: Led/dsptd lead till 5f out, sn btn:	12	0a
9 Ran	2m 04.08 (5.88) Owner Mr Ian Frazer	Trained at Newmarket	

LINGFIELD Saturday 14.02.04 Lefthand, V Sharp Track

Official Going Standard

621

1.05 Miss Julie Andrews Will You Marry Me? Maiden Stakes 3yo (D)
£4043 £1244 £622 £311   **5f p/track rnd**   **Going 39**   **-12 Slow**   Stalls Outside

4487}	**CUT AND DRIED** 140 [5] D M Simcock 3-9-0 (57) Martin Dwyer 7/1: 46600-1: Keen chasing ldrs, sn pushed along & hdway to lead dist, styd on strongly:		68a
126	**CELADON** 77 [8] N P Littmoden 3-9-0 (66) J Quinn 3/1: 4350-2: Dwelt, pushed along chasing ldrs, took 2nd nr fin, no dngr to wnr:	3	58a
371	**VITTORIOSO** 35 [9] Miss Gay Kelleway 3-9-0 bl (53) M Fenton 9/2: 050-533: Chsd ldrs, chsd wnr dist, rdn & no impress ins last:	shd	58a
572	**PURE FOLLY** 7 [3] Sir Mark Prescott 3-8-9 J Mackay 5/2 FAV: 4-34: Led after 1f till dist, no extra:	1	50a
5015}	**BEAU JAZZ** 100 [7] W de Best Turner 3-9-0 (68) S Righton 8/1: 360056-5: Prom wide, no extra dist, abs.	shd	55a
	SIMPSONS MOUNT [2] R M Flower 3-9-0 e E Ahern 16/1: 6: Slow away, nvr pace to chall:	2	49a
548	**INDIAN OAK** 10 [4] M P Muggeridge 3-9-0 (35) L Keniry (2) 66/1: 50-07: Led 1f, chsd ldrs till dist.	5	30a
	COBALT RUNNER [10] G G Margarson 3-9-0 N Pollard 33/1: 9: Sn outpcd on debut.	9	10a
	HELLO SID [6] T E Powell 3-9-0 BL A Quinn 50/1: 0: Slow away & al bhd, blnks on debut.	30	0a
9 Ran	1m 0.33 (2.53) Owner Trillium Place Racing	Trained at Newmarket	

622

1.35 Bet Direct No Q Demo 08000 837 888 Handicap Stakes 3yo+ 0-65 (F)   **[65]**
£3360 £960 £480   **1m2f p/track**   **Going 39**   **-06 Slow**   Stalls Inside

542*	**BRAVE DANE** 10 [1] A W Carroll 6-9-7 (58) W Ryan 9/2 JT FAV: 53500-11: Rear, hdwy 2f out, switched & led ins last, qcknd clr, v cmftbly:		69a
430	**BLAZING THE TRAIL** 28 [10] J W Hills 4-9-5 (57) S Whitworth 50/1: 0030-402: Mid-div, hdwy to chall dist, not pace of wnr ins last:	2	60a
564	**WELSH WIND** 8 [11] M Wigham 8-9-5 t (56) J Fanning 9/1: 042-3203: Chsd ldrs, led 2f out, rdn & hdd ins last, no extra:	1¾	57a
498	**MY MAITE** 17 [9] R Ingram 5-9-6 t (57) N Day 7/1: 50036-24: Chsd ldrs, drvn & kept onepace:	½	57a
569	**LEARNED LAD** 7 [3] Jamie Poulton 6-10-3 (68) I Mongan 9/2 JT FAV: 00050-25: Handy, led 4f out till 2f out, wknd.	¾	67a
498	**MAGIC WARRIOR** 17 [2] J C Fox 4-9-2 (54) P McCabe 6/1: 0505-346: Trkd ldrs, no extra dist:	nk	52a
564	**MUTARAFAA** 8 [12] D Shaw 5-9-3 (54) N Callan 8/1: 11-43247: Rear, only mod prog for press:	¾	51a
520	**KAVI** 14 [8] Simon Earle 4-9-9 (61) G Baker 25/1: 43666-08: Held up, eff 3f out, no impress dist:	1	57a
236	**SAMMYS SHUFFLE** 56 [6] Jamie Poulton 9-9-2 bl (53) D Kinsella 14/1: 122/605-9: Mid-div, no impress over 1f out, abs.	2½	45a
520	**SNUKI** 14 [4] G L Moore 5-9-8 (59) Dane O'Neill 9/1: 00000-00: Mid-div wide, btn 2f out:	7	42a
382	**EAST FLARES** 33 [7] J W Unett 4-9-8 (60) U Orbina 66/1: 50/610-00: Trkd ldr, btn 2f out.	1½	41a
607	**EASTER OGIL** 3 [13] Jane Southcombe 9-9-13 (64) V Slattery 15/2: 5033240: Al bhd:	5	38a
4391}	**DARK CUT** 145 [5] H Alexander 4-9-3 (55) P Fitzsimons 66/1: 00/2100-0: Al bhd.	9	17a
554	**FINGER OF FATE** 9 [14] M J Polglase 4-9-4 BL (56) E Ahern 33/1: 050-0000: Led & sn clr till 4f out, sn bhd:	17	0
14 Ran	2m 07.34 (4.54) Owner Mrs E J Righton	Trained at Alcester	

623

2.05 Michael O'donovan Memorial Maiden Stakes 3yo (D)
£4115 £1266 £633 £317   **1m p/track rnd**   **Going 39**   **+03 Fast**   Stalls Outside

381	**HEVERSHAM** 33 [12] W J Haggas 3-9-0 M Hills 2/1 FAV: 41: Led after 2f & trav well in front, rdn clr over 1f out, eased		90a
	MYSTIC LAD [2] Jamie Poulton 3-9-0 I Mongan 14/1: 2: Slow away, rear, styd on for press to take 2nd nr fin, no dngr:	5	76a
	AFRICAN DREAM [8] P F I Cole 3-9-0 S Drowne 20/1: 3: In tch wide, hdwy to chase wnr bef halfway, no extra dist:	hd	75a
472	**FIRST OF MAY** 21 [4] M A Jarvis 3-8-9 M Henry 4/1: 0-34: Chsd ldrs, no extra over 1f out.	3½	63a
566	**LA PEREGRINA** 7 [11] Sir Mark Prescott 3-8-9 J Mackay 2/1 JT FAV: 25: In tch, eff wide over 2f out, no impress bef dist:	nk	62a
601	**JOY AND PAIN** 3 [1] G L Moore 3-9-0 Dane O'Neill 50/1: 006: Mid-div, no impress when hmpd over 1f out:	3	59a
	SAINT ZITA [9] B J Meehan 3-8-9 J F McDonald (5) 40/1: 7: Slow away, al rear on debut.	4	48a
	KING OF MEZE [7] G Prodromou 3-9-0 U Orbina 66/1: 8: Chsd ldrs till dist, btn dist.	2	49a
364	**SUSSEX STYLE** 35 [10] R M Flower 3-9-0 E Ahern 100/1: 0-09: Held up, rdn & btn 2f out:	3	43a
536	**THE FOOTBALLRESULT** 11 [5] Mrs G Harvey 3-8-9 (53) Martin Dwyer 66/1: 060-00: Al bhd.	4	30a
496	**SHALATI PRINCESS** 17 [3] J C Fox 3-8-9 P Dobbs 66/1: 00: Slow away & al bhd.	2½	25a
	SHANNKARAS QUEST [6] P F I Cole 3-9-0 J Quinn 14/1: 0: Keen, led 2f, sn btn on debut.	3	24a
12 Ran	1m 39.11 (2.91) Owner Mr & Mrs G Middlebrook	Trained at Newmarket	

624

2.40 Bet Direct In Running Sky Text Page 293 Handicap Stakes Fillies 4yo+ 0-75 (E)   **[62]**
£3297 £942 £471   **1m4f p/track**   **Going 39**   **-32 Slow**   Stalls Inside

477*	**REGAL GALLERY** 21 [5] C A Horgan 6-9-13 (61) Paul Eddery 9/4 FAV: 040/41-11: Held up, hdwy wide 3f out, styd on for press to lead ins last:		70a
493	**ANYHOW** 17 [6] Miss K M George 7-9-9 (57) J P Guillambert (3) 6/1: 1140-002: Mid-div, hdwy to chall dist, not pace of wnr:	1	64a
569	**DANCE PARTY** 7 [10] A M Balding 4-9-11 (62) Martin Dwyer 5/1: 43400-33: Mid-div, hdwy to lead over 1f out, hdd ins last, not pace of wnr:	¾	67a
624	**TOP OF THE CLASS** 1 [1] P D Evans 7-8-11 vis (45) E Ahern 15/2: 050-06334: Trkd ldrs, onepace for press fnl 2f:	1	50a

520	FIGURA 14	[12] R Ingram 6-9-12 (60) N Callan 6/1: 3000-035: Rear, styd on onepace for press:	1½	63a
53	ROZANEE 88	[7] J W Payne 4-9-11 (62) I Mongan 11/1: 333-6: Trkd ldr, led over 2f out till over 1f out, fdd:	½	64a
542	MY LILLI 10	[4] P Mitchell 4-8-13 (50) J Fanning 9/1: 0000-347: Mid-div, no room over 1f out, onepce.	shd	52a
520	PONT NEUF 14	[9] J W Hills 4-9-7 T (58) M Hills 33/1: 0/0200-08: Held up, rdn & btn 2f out, t-strap.	1	59a
215	DISPOL EVITA 59	[11] Jamie Poulton 5-9-5 (53) D Kinsella 20/1: 535020-9: Held up, no impress fnl 3f, abs.	1¼	52a
339	HARLOT 38	[3] John Berry 4-9-5 (56) Lisa Jones (3) 25/1: 00003-00: Led, hdd/hung right over 2f out, wknd.	nk	54a
4310}	BUSINESS MATTERS 149	[8] H Alexander 4-9-2 (53) R Lappin 100/1: 503000-0: Mid-div, lost tch from halfway.	22	21a

11 Ran   2m 37.7 (8.5)   Owner Mrs B Sumner   Trained at Marlborough

---

625 **3.10 Littlewoods Bet Direct Handicap Stakes 3yo+ 0-100 (C)**   [88]

£15103 £5729 £2864 £1302 **1m2f p/track**   **Going 39   -12 Slow**   Stalls Inside

513	AFRICAN SAHARA 15	[13] Miss D Mountain 5-9-2 t (76) G Carter 10/1: 00226-61: Rear, hdwy wide 3f out & drvn to lead ins last, all out:		80a
571*	MOAYED 7	[4] N P Littmoden 5-9-6 bl t (80) I Mongan 10/1: 11500-12: Slow away & rear, hdwy over 2f out, switched & styd on well for press, just held:	nk	83a
549	PERFIDIOUS 10	[2] J R Boyle 6-8-12 (72) R Miles (3) 7/1: 201-3253: Led, hdd bef dist, rallied well for press, just held cl-home:	nk	74a
595	DOWER HOUSE 4	[6] Andrew Turnell 9-9-6 t (80) D Corby (3) 12/1: 310-4654: Keen & held up, hdwy to chall over 1f out, no extra nr fin:	¾	81a
4904}	STATEROOM 110	[1] J A R Toller 6-8-11 bl (71) Lisa Jones (3) 33/1: 500154-5: Keen, mid-div rail, styd on for press ins last, not able to chall:	shd	72a
4894}	BROOKLYNS GOLD 112	[12] Ian Williams 9-9-5 (79) C Catlin 20/1: 2332///40-: Rear, styd on wide for press, not able to	½	79a
519	HIAWATHA 14	[11] P A Blockley 5-9-2 (76) N Callan 9/1: 201-4137: Chsd ldrs, hdwy to lead over 1f out, sn hdd & no extra when hmpd well ins last:	shd	76a
519	TIGHT SQUEEZE 14	[8] P W Hiatt 7-9-5 (79) Martin Dwyer 10/1: 11-65308: Mid-div, no impress 2f out:	½	78a
475	ADALAR 21	[5] P D Evans 4-9-0 (75) S Donohoe (7) 50/1: 4210/0-09: Mid-div, no impress fnl 3f.	½	72a
186	OLDENWAY 64	[10] R A Fahey 5-8-5 (65) T Hamilton (5) 8/1: 502000-0: Trkd ldrs till over 1f out, abs.	½	62a
547	JEWEL OF INDIA 10	[9] Mrs A L M King 5-9-9 (83) S Drowne 20/1: 11/350-00: Held up, no impress fnl 2f.	nk	79a
519	NORTHSIDE LODGE 14	[3] P W Harris 6-9-13 (87) E Ahern 100/30 FAV: 40-4220: Chsd ldrs, wknd qckly dist.	shd	83a
4459*]	LION HUNTER 495	[7] Miss E C Lavelle 5-10-0 (88) L Keniry (3) 6/1: 32251/-0: Keen & prom till over 2f out, abs.	1¼	82a
4768}	AVENTURA 121	[14] M J Polglase 4-9-10 (85) L Fletcher (3) 50/1: 635430-0: Chsd ldr, wknd qckly over 1f out, abs.	5	72a

14 Ran   2m 07.86 (5.06)   Owner Miss Debbie Mountain   Trained at Newmarket

---

626 **3.45 Betdirect Co Uk Claiming Stakes 3yo (D)**

£4134 £1272 £636 £318 **1m2f p/track**   **Going 39   -28 Slow**   Stalls Inside

3353}	VARUNI 195	[4] J G Portman 3-8-6 E Ahern 33/1: 0-1: Trkd ldrs trav well, led ins last, rdn out:		67a
5034}	ZAKFREE 98	[6] N P Littmoden 3-8-9 bl (66) J P Guillambert (3) 7/1: 304030-2: Rear, rdn & outpcd over 2f out, took 2nd well ins last, no threat:	¾	69a
545	MAYBE SOMEDAY 10	[2] I A Wood 3-8-11 (71) I Mongan 7/4: 213-3463: Held up, hdwy halfway & led over 1f out, rdn & hdd ins last, no extra:	2	68a
560*	BLUE EMPIRE 8	[5] P A Blockley 3-9-0 (78) N Callan 5/4 FAV: 021-4514: Keen & held up, eff to press ldrs over 2f out, no extra dist:	½	70a
538	LARAD 11	[3] J S Moore 3-8-7 bl (45) D Kinsella 12/1: 0504-35: Trkd ldr & led 3f out till over 1f out, wknd:	1	62a
120	HOLD THE LINE 77	[7] W G M Turner 3-9-0 P (67) C Haddon (7) 14/1: 06205-6: Keen & sn cl-up, btn 2f out, chkpcs.	5	62a
545	TRISHAY 10	[1] A P Jarvis 3-8-6 (56) J Quinn 25/1: 04265-07: Led till 3f out, wknd qckly.	20	27a
553	CAPTAIN FEARLESS 9	[8] Mrs C A Dunnett 3-8-8 Hayley Turner (5) 66/1: 08: Sn rdn & bhd 4f out, t.o.	26	0a

8 Ran   2m 09.47 (6.67)   Owner Mr J G B Portman   Trained at Compton

---

627 **4.20 Bet In Running @ Betdirect Co Uk Classified Stakes 3yo+ 0-80 (D)**

£4082 £1256 £628 £314 **7f p/track rnd**   **Going 39   +03 Fast**   Stalls Inside

449*	ALEUTIAN 24	[8] D R Loder 4-9-9 (85) J P Spencer 5/2 FAV: 11: Made all, rdn & styd on strongly fnl 1f, shade cosy:		96a
290*	MR LAMBROS 42	[9] A M Balding 3-8-1 (80) Martin Dwyer 3/1: 3-12: Dwelt, sn keen & cl-up, rdn & styd on well fnl 1f, not pace of wnr:	1	88a
518*	GREY PEARL 14	[4] Miss Gay Kelleway 5-9-3 (82) M Fenton 6/1: 534-5113: Mid-div, styd on for press, not able to chall front pair:	1¼	84a
181+*	WHAT A DANCER 66	[10] G A Swinbank 3-9-7 (83) E Ahern 9/2: 215401-4: Dwelt, sn in tch, styd on for press, no threat to front pair:	¾	87a
419	HAND CHIME 30	[1] W J Haggas 7-9-9 (85) Danielle Deverson (7) 20/1: 0003-005: Slow away, keen, in tch, kept on.	shd	89a
181	INCLINE 66	[2] T G Mills 5-9-9 (85) R Miles (3) 9/1: 3/00022-6: In tch, no impress over 1f out, abs:	½	85a
517	SUMMER RECLUSE 14	[3] B R Johnson 5-9-4 P (77) Dane O'Neill 16/1: 21013-07: Dwelt & held up, nvr able to chall:	½	82a
386	CASHEL MEAD 32	[6] J L Spearing 4-9-1 (79) A Daly 50/1: 0623-508: Chsd ldrs till over 1f out:	1½	76a
430*	MILLVILLE 28	[11] M A Jarvis 4-9-4 (80) N Callan 25/1: 19: Slow away, outpcd, no impress:	2	75a
518	BORDER EDGE 14	[7] J J Bridger 6-9-4 vis (79) G Baker 66/1: 12000-00: Keen, mid-div, btn over 1f out.	½	74a
547	AGILIS 10	[5] Jamie Poulton 4-9-4 bl (74) S Drowne 66/1: 0046-060: Trkd ldrs, wknd qckly over 1f out.	1	72a

11 Ran   1m 25.31 (2.51)   Owner Jumeirah Racing   Trained at Newmarket

---

628 **4.55 Bet Direct In Vision Sky Page 293 Apprentice Handicap Stakes 3yo+ 0-70 (F)**   [70]

£2940 £840 £420 **6f p/track rnd**   **Going 39   +01 Fast**   Stalls Inside

604	HARD TO CATCH 3	[6] D K Ivory 6-9-5 (65) M Savage (5) 11/2: 55-00241: Trkd ldrs, switched wide to lead dist, rdn out:		72a
516	PRINCE AARON 14	[3] C N Allen 4-9-12 (68) B Reilly 3/1 FAV: 062-1162: Mid-div, hdwy to chall dist, not pace of wnr:	½	72a
550	ILLUSIVE 9	[4] M Wigham 7-9-4 bl (60) T Eaves 20/1: 0432-003: Trkd ldr & led briefly over 1f out, onepace for press ins last:	1¼	60a
565	CARLTON 7	[5] C R Dore 10-9-4 (60) R Thomas (3) 20/1: 55000-04: Rear, kept on wide for press.	1	57a
604	SUPERCHIEF 3	[11] Miss B Sanders 9-9-9 bl t (65) N Chalmers 10/1: 2-064355: Slow away & rear, late gains, no dngr.	shd	62a

LINGFIELD Saturday 14.02.04 Lefthand, V Sharp Track

448	**TAYIF** 24 [7] Andrew Reid 8-9-10 t (66) S Donohoe (3) 100/30: 03-21126: Rear, keeping on for press when short of room ins last, no danger.		*1*	**60a**
551	**TEYAAR** 9 [12] Mrs N Macauley 8-9-4 (60) Hayley Turner (3) 20/1: 003-0067: Led till over 1f out, fdd:		*½*	**52a**
508	**LADIES KNIGHT** 15 [10] D Shaw 4-9-0 (56) T Hamilton 8/1: 01-63258: Slow away, only mod late gains:		*½*	**46a**
407	**POLAR FORCE** 31 [13] M R Channon 4-9-5 (61) T O'Brien (7) 7/1: 06003-49: Mid-div, nvr pace to chall:		*½*	**49a**
459	**CLASSIC VISION** 23 [2] W J Haggas 4-9-2 (58) J F McDonald 20/1: 53-100: Dwelt, mid-div, btn 2f out:		*nk*	**45a**
4616}	**FIREWORK** 131 [8] J Akehurst 6-9-10 p (66) M Coumbe (5) 25/1: 313420-0: Chsd ldrs till over 1f out, reapp:		*2½*	**45a**
471	**SOUNDS LUCKY** 21 [9] N P Littmoden 8-9-8 bl (64) A Quinn 16/1: 2540-050: Mid-div, no impress fnl 2f.		*1*	**40a**
12 Ran	1m 12.65 (2.25)	Owner Mrs Karen Graham		Trained at Radlett

WOLVERHAMPTON Saturday 14.02.04 Lefthand, Sharp Track

Official Going Standard

629	**7.00 Bet In Running On Sky Text Page 293 Handicap Stakes 4yo+ 0-70 (E)**		**[68]**
	£3346 £956 £478 7f f/sand rnd Going 60 -00 Slow Stalls Outside		

620	**GIVEMETHEMOONLIGHT** 1 [2] Mrs Stef Liddiard 5-8-10 vis (50) I Mongan 7/1: 2135361: Made alll, rdn clr over 1f out, styd on strongly:		**58a**
593	**DISPOL PETO** 4 [10] Ian Emmerson 4-9-5 p (59) J Bramhill 50/1: 4500-052: Chsd wnr, styd on for press, no impress bef dist:	*2½*	**61a**
384	**GERONIMO** 33 [5] Miss Gay Kelleway 7-9-5 p (59) M Fenton 7/1: 6020-203: Rear, hdwy 3f out, onepace.	*¾*	**60a**
280	**TEEHEE** 45 [4] B Palling 6-10-0 bl (68) J Quinn 11/1: 020150-4: Prom, chsd wnr 2f out, no extra dist.	*8*	**56a**
562*	**WARLINGHAM** 8 [8] P Howling 6-9-7 (61) J Fanning 4/1: 10-0015: Mid-div, no impress fnl 3f:	*1½*	**46a**
463	**SPARK UP** 23 [6] J W Unett 4-9-5 bl (59) M Henry 16/1: 1266-006: In tch, no impress wide 3f out:	*hd*	**43a**
585	**FLYING EDGE** 5 [7] E J Alston 4-8-11 (51) A Nicholls 7/1: 5160-027: Keen, cl up/dpstd lead 5f, sn btn:	*hd*	**34a**
564	**SPY GUN** 8 [1] T Wall 4-9-2 (56) D Corby (3) 14/1: 014-3508: Probs removing blindfold, v slow away & lost chance.	*½*	**38a**
558*	**ICED DIAMOND** 8 [3] W M Brisbourne 5-9-4 (58) B Swarbrick (7) 2/1 FAV: 56200-19: V slow away & lost all chance:	*10*	**25a**
9 Ran	1m 30.43 (4.23)	Owner Valley Fencing	Trained at Hungerford

630	**7.30 Bet Direct On Sky Active Classified Claiming Stakes 3yo+ 0-60 (F)**		
	£2926 £836 £418 1m100y f/sand rnd Going 60 -10 Slow Stalls Inside		

560	**JAKARMI** 8 [5] B Palling 3-8-5 (56) J Quinn 3/1: 2650-161: Held up, hdwy hway & wore down ldr for press, led ins last:		**62a**
483	**CLOUDLESS** 19 [7] J W Unett 4-9-6 (57) S Whitworth 8/1: 30015-02: Led, rdn clr from 3f out, hdd ins last, no extra:	*1¼*	**54a**
574	**FRANKS QUEST** 6 [3] P Burgoyne 4-9-10 (55) L Keniry (3) 6/1: 0040-023: Held up, late prog for press, no threat to front pair:	*1¾*	**55a**
479	**NITE OWL FIZZ** 19 [8] J O'Reilly 6-9-7 (48) I Mongan 11/4 FAV: 005-4204: Chsd ldr, no impress over 1f out:	*1¾*	**49a**
437	**DAIMAJIN** 26 [1] Mrs Lucinda Featherstone 5-9-10 (56) P Makin (7) 15/2: 0000-105: In tch, no impress fnl 3f, new yard:	*12*	**32a**
1598}	**MISS KOEN** 271 [6] D L Williams 9-9-6 (60) L Fletcher (3) 10/1: 10/6060-6: Sn rdn, nvr land blow:	*2*	**24a**
423	**PUPS PRIDE** 29 [2] Mrs N Macauley 7-9-8 vis (55) P McCabe 7/1: 01100-67: Rear & sn pushed along, no prog:	*8*	**13a**
483	**BLAKESHALL GIRL** 19 [4] J L Spearing 4-9-4 BL (45) Dean McKeown 66/1: 30000-08: Sn bhd, t.o:	*22*	**0a**
8 Ran	1m 52.15 (5.95)	Owner Mrs M M Palling	Trained at Cowbridge

631	**8.00 Tony Cowen Loss Of Independence Day Maiden Stakes 3yo (D)**		
	£3341 £1028 £514 £257 6f f/sand rnd Going 60 +02 Fast Stalls Inside		

364	**ROYAL PAVILLION** 35 [6] W J Musson 3-9-0 M Fenton 10/11 FAV: 0-31: Chsd ldr trav well, led halfway & asserted over 1f out, drvn out:		**74a**
481	**BROWN DRAGON** 19 [4] D Haydn Jones 3-9-0 (65) Paul Eddery 10/1: 00-62: Prom, drvn to chse wnr over 1f out, not pace to chall:	*2½*	**65a**
481	**SOUL PROVIDER** 19 [3] P A Blockley 3-8-9 (63) N Callan 9/2: 525-53: Rear, hdwy halfway, no impress from dist:	*5*	**47a**
543	**ORCHESTRATION** 10 [5] J W Unett 3-9-0 (67) S Whitworth 11/4: 26-44: Rear, outpcd from hway.	*6*	**36a**
126	**SHAYMEES GIRL** 77 [1] Ms Deborah J Evans 3-8-9 Joanna Badger 66/1: 0-06: Led 2f, btn 2f out, abs.	*1*	**28a**
444	**MIND THE TIME** 25 [2] J Hetherton 3-9-0 C Catlin 50/1: 0-06: Held up, swtchd wide & strugg hway.	*10*	**7a**
6 Ran	1m 16.27 (3.47)	Owner Mr Howard Spooner	Trained at Newmarket

632	**8.30 Betdirect Co Uk Handicap Stakes 3yo+ 0-85 (D)**		**[85]**
	£4085 £1257 £629 £314 1m100y f/sand rnd Going 60 +01 Fast Stalls Inside		

517*	**VORTEX** 14 [1] Miss Gay Kelleway 5-9-7 e t (78) M Fenton 6/1: 1160-111: Sn settled tracking ldrs, smooth prog & rdn/qcknd to lead ins last, asserted:		**86a**
530	**PENWELL HILL** 11 [7] T D Barron 5-9-2 (73) P Makin (7) 12/1: 465-1022: Mid-div, styd on wide for press fnl 2f, no threat to wnr:	*1¾*	**76a**
513	**SKYLARKER** 15 [4] W S Kittow 6-9-8 (79) M Savage (5) 11/2: 4304-233: Sn led/dsptd lead till ins last, kept on for press:	*shd*	**82a**
585	**YORKER** 5 [3] Ms Deborah J Evans 6-8-11 (68) Lisa Jones (3) 12/1: 020-2534: Rear, hdwy over 2f out, not pace of wnr from dist:	*½*	**70a**
419	**NO GROUSE** 30 [8] R A Fahey 4-9-2 (73) T Hamilton (5) 25/1: 10000-05: Held up, efft to press ldrs 3f out, no extra bef dist:	*2½*	**70a**
2689}	**MY BAYARD** 223 [9] J O'Reilly 5-8-12 (69) N Callan 50/1: 122020-6: Led/dsptd lead till over 1f out, no extra:	*nk*	**65a**
547	**ARC EL CIEL** 10 [5] Mrs Stef Liddiard 6-9-7 vis (78) I Mongan 14/1: 62-13507: Held up, efft over 2f out, no impress.	*½*	**73a**
482	**FLINT RIVER** 19 [6] H Morrison 6-9-11 (82) L Fletcher (3) 9/2 FAV: 0210-208: Trkd ldrs, wknd over 1f out:	*hd*	**76a**
611	**AIR MAIL** 2 [11] Mrs N Macauley 7-9-8 (79) A Culhane (3) 14/1: 00060-409: Held up, efft hway, btn 2f out, qck reapp.	*4*	**66a**
511	**INVADER** 15 [12] C E Brittain 8-9-7 bl (78) J Quinn 14/1: 143-0060: Cl up, short of room over 2f out, sn btn.	*7*	**53a**
540*	**SCOTTYS FUTURE** 11 [10] D R Loder 6-9-9 (80) J P Spencer 5/1: 0000-010: Bhd, btn 2f out:	*6*	**45a**
464	**OVIGO** 22 [2] P A Blockley 5-8-12 (69) Dean McKeown 10/1: 30-1463P: Led till p.u. lame after 2f, sadly died.		**0**
12 Ran	1m 51.22 (5.02)	Owner Coriolis Partnership	Trained at Newmarket

633 9.00 Bet Direct Interactive Selling Stakes 4-6yo (G)
£2534 £724 £362   1m1f79y f/sand rnd Going 60   -09 Slow   Stalls Inside

512	HEATHERS GIRL 15 [3] D Haydn Jones 5-8-8 (40) Paul Eddery 50/1: 56040/-01: Prom, chsd ldr over 2f out, led ins last, drvn out:		57a
287	DESERT HEAT 43 [1] I Semple 6-8-13 VIS (57) N Callan 14/1: 64004-02: Led/dpstd lead, went on over 2f out till ins last, no extra:	5	51a
445	GWAZI 25 [5] Miss D A McHale 4-8-13 vis t (40) A Culhane 66/1: 000-03: Bhd hway, mod late prog.	8	37a
392	EIGHT WOODS 32 [2] T D Barron 6-8-13 (60) J P Spencer 4/9 FAV: 2/0/663-34: Led/dpstd lead, lost action & hdd over 3f out, eased, fin lame:	15	11a
555	ILLUSIONIST 9 [4] Mrs N Macauley 6-8-13 vis (35) P McCabe 100/1: 00050-05: Sn rdn & always bhd.	2½	6a
3370}	DUNDONALD 194 [10] M Appleby 5-8-13 vis t (45) S Righton 50/1: 000040-6: Prom till 4f out, new yard.	7	0a
569	BONTADINI 7 [9] D Morris 5-8-13 vis (45) I Mongan 9/1: 0000-507: Led over 3f out, till over 2f out, sn btn.	¾	0a
540	GEOGRAPHY 11 [7] P Butler 4-8-13 p (53) J Quinn 50/1: 00005-P8: Sn bhd, t.o:	2	0a
580*	GRAND LASS 5 [8] A Sadik 5-9-0 (50) N Chalmers (5) 13/2: 046-341W: Refused to enter stalls:		0a

9 Ran   2m 04.65 (6.45)   Owner Trio Racing   Trained at Pontypridd

634 9.30 Bet In Running @ Betdirect Co Uk Handicap Stakes 4yo+ 0-60 (F)   [59]
£2968 £848 £424   1m4f f/sand   Going 60   -01 Slow   Stalls Inside

616*	MANDOOB 1 [9] B R Johnson 7-10-0 p (59) J P Guillambert (3) 11/2: 56300-411: Dwelt, rear, hdwy over 3f out & rdn/led over 1f out, styd on strongly:		68a
467	JADEERON 22 [11] Miss D A McHale 5-9-13 p (58) Lisa Jones (3) 5/1: 4400-222: Prom, rdn & kept on fnl 2f, not pace of wnr:	½	65a
557*	ROBBIE CAN CAN 8 [8] A W Carroll 5-9-13 (58) Hayley Turner (5) 5/1: 30261-13: Bhd, rdn & kept on fnl 2f, not trouble front pair:	4	59a
575*	BELLA PAVLINA 6 [7] W M Brisbourne 6-10-3 6ex (62) B Swarbrick (7) 8/1: 36-12114: Mid-div, hdwy to lead 3f out, hdd over 1f out & wknd:	2½	59a
594	COOLFORE JADE 4 [12] N E Berry 4-9-7 (55) C Catlin 11/1: 0141435: Prom, led over 5f out till 3f out, btn over 1f out:	5	45a
557	E MINOR 8 [4] T Wall 5-9-11 (56) N Chalmers (5) 40/1: 4006-506: Held up, no impress fnl 4f:	1	45a
590	LAZZAZ 5 [2] P W Hiatt 6-9-12 (57) A Culhane 7/2 FAV: 4353337: Prom till over 2f out:	nk	45a
557	FIGHT THE FEELING 8 [1] J W Unett 6-9-12 BL (57) D Nolan (5) 12/1: 016-4228: Mid-div, rdn/btn 3f out:	3	41a
484	MOLLYS SECRET 19 [3] C G Cox 6-9-5 p (50) J Quinn 15/2: 2300-109: Mid-div, btn over 2f out:	1½	32a
557	LORD GIZZMO 8 [5] P W Hiatt 7-8-9 (40) L Fletcher (3) 33/1: 1355-060: Led till over 5f out, sn btn:	12	7a
4121}	WIGMO PRINCESS 159 [10] S C Burrough 5-8-9 BL (40) A Nicholls (7) 66/1: 400000-0: Dwelt & always behind, blnks, jmps fit.	nk	6a
4130}	BRANSTON NELL 159 [6] C R Dore 5-9-1 BL (46) J Bramhill 50/1: 0/20100-0: Chsd ldr 4f, wknd qckly, t.o:	dist	0a

12 Ran   2m 40.89 (7.29)   Owner Mr J L Guillambert   Trained at Epsom

Official Going STANDARD.

635 2.00 Bet Direct On Sky Active Apprentice Banded Stakes 3yo+ 0-40 (H)
£1439 £411 £206   1m f/sand rnd   Going 39   -18 Slow   Stalls Inside.

539	GRACIOUS AIR 12 [2] J R Weymes 6-9-8 vis (35) D Fentiman (5) 10/1: 00060-01: Held up, hdwy 3 out & rdn/led dist, styd on strongly:		39a
573	DANCING KING 7 [5] P W Hiatt 8-9-8 (30) P Gallagher (5) 16/1: 0-504052: Led till dist, no extra:	4	31a
442	KENNY THE TRUTH 26 [1] Mrs J Candlish 5-9-8 t (40) N Chalmers (5) 5/4 FAV: 0000-323: Chsd ldrs, onepace for press bef dist:	1½	28a
528}	MATHMAGICIAN 379 [6] R F Marvin 5-9-8 P (35) K Ghunowa (5) 40/1: 300004-4: Chsd ldrs, styd on onepace for press:	¾	26a
528	LEMARATE 13 [7] D W Chapman 7-9-8 (40) Rory Moore (5) 8/1: 00-33005: Chsd ldr, btn over 1f out.	3	20a
580	HAITHEM 6 [4] D Shaw 7-9-8 e t (40) Dawn Watson (5) 12/1: 6000306: In tch, no impress fnl 3f:	5	10a
1422}	TE ANAU 643 [3] W J Musson 7-9-8 (30) Laura Pike (5) 33/1: 000/0/00/-: Held up, no impress fnl 3f:	½	9a
539	COLNE VALLEY AMY 12 [8] G L Moore 7-9-8 bl (40) A Quinn 5/2: 2/060-428: Slow away, chsd ldrs till over 2f out, sn btn:	6	0a

8 Ran   1m 44.03 (4.63)   Owner Sporting Occasions   Trained at Middleham

636 2.30 Press Interactive To Bet Direct Median Auction Maiden Stakes 3-5yo (H)
£1470 £420 £210   7f f/sand rnd   Going 39   -04 Slow   Stalls Inside.

444	DARING AFFAIR 26 [1] K R Burke 3-8-0 (63) Lisa Jones (3) 11/8 FAV: 4526-321: Sn cl-up, led 3f out, rdn clr over 1f out, styd on strongly:		65a
503	BUNDABERG 17 [6] P W Hiatt 4-9-0 (40) A Culhane 33/1: 05-42: Sn prom & rdn/ch over 2f out, not pace of wnr:	8	52a
444	WEAKEST LINK 26 [4] W Jarvis 3-8-5 (63) J Quinn 9/4: 0-233: In tch, rdn & no impress over 1f out:	1¾	49a
4901}	GILLYS GENERAL 111 [3] J W Unett 4-9-8 (46) M Fenton 14/1: 002050-4: Led 4f, btn over 1f out:	hd	49a
	MACPURSIE [5] T D Barron 3-8-0 D Mernagh 13/2: 5: Slow away, nvr on terms with ldrs:	1½	41a
1129}	FRIMLEYS MATTERRY 300 [2] R E Barr 4-9-8 (53) R Fitzpatrick 33/1: 4/56300-6: Rdn rear:	5	36a
4758}	STAR WELCOME 122 [7] W J Musson 3-8-0 Joanna Badger 8/1: 0-7: Slow away, nvr on terms with ldrs:	¾	29a

7 Ran   1m 29.61 (3.01)   Owner Mr Nigel Shields   Trained at Leyburn

637 3.00 Bet Direct Football Cashbacks Banded Stakes 3yo+ 0-35 (H)
£1358 £388 £194   6f f/sand rnd   Going 39   -21 Slow   Stalls Inside.

573	MISS WIZZ 7 [9] W Storey 4-9-7 (35) Rory Moore (7) 14/1: 0460-041: Sn prom, led over 2f out, held on all out:		37a
578	SPY MASTER 7 [10] J Parkes 6-9-7 bl t (35) M Lawson (7) 8/1: 00000-32: Dwelt & held up, rdn & hdwy when hmpd over 1f out, styd on for press, just denied:	shd	36a
526	MIMAS GIRL 13 [13] S R Bowring 5-9-7 bl (30) J Bramhill 16/1: 046-5053: Prom & chsd wnr 2f out, no extra ins last.	1	32a
541*	REDOUBTABLE 12 [11] D W Chapman 13-9-7 (45) A Culhane 7/2: 6600-614: Hmpd start, mid-div, not able to chall:	2	27a

592	**DANDY JIM 5** [5] D W Chapman 3-8-6 (30) R Brisland 50/1: 006-05: Dwelt, rdn rear, nrst fin:	nk	26a
377	**COURT MUSIC 34** [6] R E Barr 5-9-7 vis (35) R Fitzpatrick 13/2: 0000-026: Chsd ldrs, no impress/hmpd dist:	1½	22a
578*	**DANAKIM 7** [14] J R Weymes 7-9-13 bl e (35) D Fentiman (7) 8/1: 5060-617: Chsd ldrs till dist:	1¼	24a
573	**ZARA LOUISE 7** [1] R P Elliott 4-9-7 (30) Dean McKeown 16/1: 0006-408: Dwelt, chsd ldrs till hmpd over 1f out.	¾	15a
541	**PACKIN EM IN 12** [4] J R Boyle 6-9-7 (35) M Henry 3/1 FAV: 0000-329: Mid-div, drvn & no impress 2f out.	1½	11a
143	**MOONGLADE 74** [7] Miss J Feilden 4-9-7 t (30) A Quinn (5) 8/1: 00000-0: Slow away & nvr on terms:	hd	11a
578	**ALMARA 7** [12] Miss K B Boutflower 4-9-7 t p (35) J Quinn 16/1: 0000-040: Sn struggling, nvr factor.	¾	8a
578	**SALONIKA SKY 7** [3] C W Thornton 3-8-6 BL (35) J McAuley 33/1: 5000-060: Led 3f, btn over 1f out, blnks.	½	7a
578	**GRUFF 7** [2] P T Midgley 5-9-7 (35) G Parkin 33/1: 00000-00: Prom 3f, sn bhd.	4	0a
4850}	**IZZA 116** [8] W Storey 3-8-6 (30) D R McCabe 66/1: 00000-0: Sn outpcd, abs.	14	0a

14 Ran 1m 16.91 (3.61) Owner Mr Tony McCormick Trained at Consett

---

638 **3.30 Bet In Running @ Betdirect Co Uk Banded Stakes 4yo+ 0-45 (H)**
£1663 £475 £238 1m6f f/sand Going 39 -20 Slow Stalls Inside.

414*	**BROUGHTON KNOWS 31** [2] W J Musson 7-9-3 (45) Lisa Jones (3) 3/10 FAV: 4362-111: Rear, hdwy 4f out, rdn/led 2f out, sn hung left but in command, eased cl-home:		52a
445	**NEXT FLIGHT 26** [3] R E Barr 5-9-3 (45) R Fitzpatrick 12/1: 00003-62: Trkd ldr, led 10f out till 2f out, kept on for press but no impress on eased down wnr:	4	45a
336	**FORTUNES FAVOURITE 40** [7] G M Moore 4-8-12 (45) J Quinn 16/1: 045-03: Chsd ldrs till 2f out:	9	30a
575	**KING PRIAM 7** [4] M J Polglase 9-9-3 bl (40) L Fletcher (3) 8/1: 1450664: Drvn to lead, hdd aftr 4f & btn 3f out:	nk	29a
574	**SEA YA MAITE 7** [1] S R Bowring 10-9-3 t (35) J Bramhill 25/1: 0523545: Keen & prom till 2f out:	1¾	27a
1909}	**BLAZING SADDLES 257** [5] Mrs J Candlish 5-9-3 p (45) N Chalmers (5) 25/1: 6600/00-6: Mid-div, pushed along & no impress from 4f out:	7	17a
1529}	**LADY ARNICA 275** [6] A W Carroll 5-9-3 VIS (45) I Mongan 20/1: 0/0/0-7: Chsd ldrs, bhd 6f out:	dist	0a

7 Ran 3m 08.09 (8.29) Owner Broughton Thermal Insulation Trained at Newmarket

---

639 **4.00 Bet In Running On Sky Text Page 293 Selling Stakes 3yo+ (H)**
£1491 £426 £213 7f f/sand rnd Going 39 +10 Fast Stalls Inside.

555	**SUDRA 10** [6] J O'Reilly 7-9-7 bl (47) J D O'Reilly (7) 5/1: 0-334431: Trkd ldrs, led over 1f out, rdn & styd on strongly:		56a
373	**DONEGAL SHORE 34** [7] Mrs J Candlish 5-9-7 vis t (51) N Chalmers (5) 5/1: 0600-422: Held up, styd on for press, nvr threatened wnr:	5	46a
558	**LARKYS LOB 9** [4] Paul Johnson 5-9-7 (47) L Fletcher (3) 11/4 FAV: 02-21453: Led 5f, no extra dist.	¾	44a
272	**CRAFTY POLITICIAN 47** [5] G L Moore 7-9-7 (40) I Mongan 9/1: 000000-4: Trkd ldr, onepace for press fnl 2f:	1¼	41a
555	**MARABAR 10** [9] D W Chapman 6-9-2 (58) A Culhane 6/1: 5005-065: Chsd ldrs, no impress dist:	nk	35a
597	**ACE MA VAHRA 5** [2] S R Bowring 6-9-2 (45) J Bramhill 25/1: 5/003/-606: Prom, no extra fnl 2f:	3	29a
577	**NOBLE PURSUIT 7** [8] P A Blockley 7-9-7 (57) Dean McKeown 4/1: 0440-227: Slow away, no hdwy:	nk	33a
352	**MOON ROYALE 38** [10] Mrs N Macauley 6-9-2 vis (30) Saleem Golam (7) 28/1: 62500-08: Slow away & held up, bhd fnl 2f:	10	8a
2689}	**RIVER CANYON 224** [3] W Storey 8-9-7 (50) D R McCabe 16/1: 0/205//00-: Pushed rear, nvr factor:	3½	6a

9 Ran 1m 28.63 (2.03) Owner Mr J Morris Trained at Barnsley

---

640 **4.30 Bet Direct In Vision Sky Page 293 Banded Stakes 4yo+ 0-35 (H)**
£1393 £398 £199 1m3f f/sand Going 39 -08 Slow Stalls Inside.

581	**GALLEY LAW 6** [5] R Craggs 4-8-12 (30) J Quinn 13/2: 0000-321: Held up, prog to lead over 2f out & rdn clr over 1f out, rdn out:		41a
581*	**BUZ KIRI 6** [4] A W Carroll 6-9-6 (35) P Doe 3/1: 046-3212: Held up, tkn wide & styd on for press fnl 3f, nvr threatened wnr:	5	39a
302	**SAMAR QAND 43** [8] Julian Poulton 5-9-0 (35) M Tebbutt 6/1: 03653-53: Held up, kept on for press fnl 3f, no threat:	2	30a
573	**FRAAMTASTIC 7** [6] B A Pearce 7-9-0 (30) L Treadwell 12/1: 0/5040-24: Keen & trkd ldrs, led over 4f out till over 2f out, no extra:	1½	28a
4812}	**CUMWHITTON 118** [2] R A Fahey 5-9-0 (35) T Hamilton (5) 25/1: 056//60-5: Held up, badly hmpd 4f out & again 3f out, sn btn:	8	16a
357	**MARENGO 38** [10] Paul Johnson 10-9-0 (30) Joanna Badger 33/1: 0600-006: Dwelt, led after 2f till 4f out, sn btn.	2	13a
	TOP STYLE 543 [7] M J Wallace 6-9-0 (30) D Corby (3) 5/4 FAV: 000/004/-7: Held up & pushed along halfway, btn 3f out:	5	5a
581	**WESTERN COMMAND 6** [11] Mrs N Macauley 8-9-0 p (30) P McCabe 25/1: 0045668: Chsd ldrs till 3f out.	5	4a
442	**BALALAIKA TUNE 26** [3] W Storey 5-9-0 (35) D R McCabe 40/1: 0550-009: Keen mid-div, btn 3f out.	½	3a
442	**DIVA DANCER 26** [9] J Hetherton 4-8-12 (30) Dean McKeown 50/1: 0/00-00: Sn struggling, nvr factor.	1¾	1a
531	**ANACAPRI 12** [1] W S Cunningham 4-8-12 (35) L Enstone (3) 50/1: 0-060: Chsd ldr till 3f out, sn btn.	20	0a
488	**VELVET RHYTHM 19** [12] K R Burke 4-8-10 (30) Darren Williams 100/1: 0-000: Led till 9f out, lost tch fnl 4f.	dist	0a

12 Ran 2m 26.56 (5.26) Owner Mr Ray Craggs Trained at Sedgefield

---

Official Going Standard To Slow

641 **1.50 Bet Direct On Attheraces Text Page 411 Handicap Stakes Div 1 3yo+ 0-60 (F)** [60]
£2912 £832 £416 5f f/sand rnd Going 83 +01 Fast Stalls Inside

551	**CASH 11** [1] Paul Johnson 6-10-0 p (60) L Fletcher (3) 9/1: 50164-01: Trkd ldrs, led over 1f out, drvn out:		65a
507*	**EMPRESS JOSEPHINE 17** [5] J R Jenkins 4-9-10 vis (56) D Corby (3) 4/1 FAV: 12424-12: Led after 1f till over 1f out, drvn & kept on well, just held:	nk	60a
508	**OFF HIRE 17** [7] C Smith 8-9-2 vis (48) R Fitzpatrick 6/1: 05400-23: Led 1f, remained cl-up, no extra ins last:	1½	47a
507	**SO SOBER 17** [3] D Shaw 6-9-0 (46) Darren Williams 12/1: 0000-154: Mid-div, not pace to chall.	1¼	41a
501	**NEVER WITHOUT ME 18** [2] P J McBride 4-9-2 (48) Dale Gibson 6/1: 0022-645: Rdn mid-div, not able to chall.	½	41a
508	**OUR CHELSEA BLUE 17** [4] A W Carroll 6-9-7 (53) S Righton 9/1: 0660-036: Dwelt, hdwy halfway, onepace.	3	38a
274	**ERRACHT 47** [6] K R Burke 6-9-8 (54) G Baker 12/1: 362030-7: Mid-div, no impress fnl 2f:	2½	32a

413	CARK 32 [12] J Jay 6-9-6 (52) N Callan 6/1: 400-6128: Wide & prom till over 1f out:			3	22a
508	LEVELLED 17 [9] D W Chapman 10-8-8 (40) R Brisland 40/1: 00/000-09: Dwelt, al bhd:			¾	8a
508	PERCY DOUGLAS 17 [10] Miss A Stokell 4-9-9 p (55) Ann Stokell 25/1: 03063-00: Al bhd & outpcd:			nk	22a
483	HAWK 21 [8] P R Chamings 6-10-0 P (60) J Quinn 10/1: 305-0000: Prom, wknd qckly from halfway:			12	0
544	DANCES IN TIME 12 [11] C N Kellett 4-9-4 (50) T Williams 50/1: 05000: Sn bhd.			7	0
12 Ran	1m 04.31 (4.11) Owner Insull White Pritchard & Joh			Trained at Stanley	

---

642 2.20 Bet Direct On Attheraces Text Page 410 Apprentice Handicap Stakes 4yo+ 0-85 (F) [79]
£2877 £822 £411 1m4f f/sand Going 83 -64 Slow Stalls Inside

404	BORDER TALE 33 [4] C Weedon 4-9-10 (78) W Hogg 4/1: 61254-01: Prom & chsd ldr 3f out, led over 2f out, rdn out:				82a
549	DIGGER 12 [5] Miss Gay Kelleway 5-9-8 (73) P Gallagher 4/1: 236-1402: Handy & led after 4f till over 2f out, switched & onepace ins last:			1½	72a
475	CRUISE DIRECTOR 23 [6] W J Musson 4-10-0 (82) A Rutter (5) 4/1: 2210-303: Held up, hdwy to chase front pair 3f out, no prog fnl 2f:			4	77a
519	YORK CLIFF 16 [3] W M Brisbourne 6-9-10 (75) B Swarbrick 7/2 FAV: 0200-054: Dictated slow pace 4f, chsd ldr till btn over 2f out:			4	64a
602	TROPICAL SON 5 [1] D Shaw 5-7-12 3oh vis (46) Dawn Watson (3) 6/1: 0-251025: Rear, rdn & btn 3f out:			hd	37a
511	FLYING TREATY 17 [7] Miss A Stokell 7-10-0 (79) C J Davies 20/1: 040-0006: Chsd ldrs 3f out, sn btn.			13	49a
561*	CALL ME SUNSHINE 10 [2] P C Haslam 4-8-11 (65) Rory Moore 7/1: 2/5402-17: Prom, btn 3f out:			3	31a
7 Ran	2m 51.22 (17.62) Owner Chadwick Dyer & Flynn			Trained at Pulborough	

---

643 2.50 Bet Direct On Attheraces Text Page 411 Handicap Stakes Div 2 3yo+ 0-60 (F) [60]
£2905 £830 £415 5f f/sand rnd Going 83 +05 Fast Stalls Inside

453	PLAYTIME BLUE 26 [3] K R Burke 4-10-0 (60) G Baker 7/2 JT FAV: 002-2361: Made all, rdn & asserted from dist:				71a
507	KINGS BALLET 17 [5] P R Chamings 6-9-1 p (47) J Quinn 6/1: 0300-002: Chsd ldrs, kept on for press, no threat to wnr:			3	48a
582	SERGEANT SLIPPER 7 [11] C Smith 7-8-13 vis (45) R Fitzpatrick 16/1: 005-0303: Dwelt, rdn rear, nrst fin:			1¾	42a
483	BEST LEAD 21 [8] Ian Emmerson 5-10-0 bl (60) D Fentiman (7) 13/2: 065-1044: Prom, no extra dist.			½	55a
527+*	TORRENT 14 [10] D W Chapman 9-8-13 bl (45) A Culhane 13/2: 60-26315: Dwelt, towards rear, mod prog.			nk	39a
507	TIGRESS 17 [7] J W Unett 5-9-10 bl (56) M Hills 7/2 JT FAV: 660-6526: Chsd ldrs, not able to chall:			hd	49a
524	ATTORNEY 14 [1] D Shaw 6-9-0 e (46) T Hamilton (5) 16/1: 3010047: Rdn towards rear, little hdwy:			shd	39a
3814}	EXTEMPORISE 177 [9] P J McBride 4-9-2 (48) Dale Gibson 40/1: 050-8: Outpcd, nvr a factor:			1	38a
587	LADY PROTECTOR 7 [4] J Balding 5-9-2 (48) J Edmunds 12/1: 60-41039: Prom till over 1f out:			nk	37a
74	VIJAY 87 [2] I Semple 5-9-12 bl (58) F Lynch 16/1: 434360-0: Held up, nvr a threat, abs.			1½	42a
435	BLESSED PLACE 30 [6] Jean Rene Auvray 4-9-7 BL (53) E Ahern 14/1: 50050-00: Prom, btn 2f out:			13	1a
11 Ran	1m 04.11 (3.91) Owner Mr P Sweeting			Trained at Leyburn	

---

644 3.20 Bet Direct On Attheraces Text Page 412 Maiden Stakes 3yo+ (D)
£3309 £1018 £509 £255 1m4f f/sand Going 83 -42 Slow Stalls Inside

	ROYAL ATALZA 920 [6] C N Allen 7-9-13 P B Reilly (5) 7/2: 0/0/04//-1: Hld up in tch, rdn halfway, drvn & styd on for press fnl 2f, led line, all out:				62a
503	VIVRE SA VIE 18 [7] Sir Mark Prescott 3-7-12 J Mackay 7/2: 432: Led/dsptd lead & went on over 4f out, rdn clr over 1f out, hdd line:			shd	56a
561	PACIFIC OCEAN 10 [2] Mrs Stef Liddiard 5-9-13 t (60) J Quinn 4/1: 6534-233: Keen rear, eff 3f out, no impress on front pair bef dist:			5	54a
430	ANDAAD 30 [4] D J Daly 4-9-5 W Ryan 13/2: 0/-54: Held up in tch, eff over 2f out, no impress & eased ins last:			5	42a
4718}	MANY THANKS 126 [5] B S Rothwell 4-9-5 (70) M Fenton 8/1: 2444-5: Prom, btn 4f out, abs.			19	19a
521	IMPERATIVE 16 [1] Ian Williams 4-9-10 (70) M Henry 100/30 FAV: 55000-46: Led/dsptd lead till 4f out, sn btn.			6	16a
	FOXY TRIX [3] J W Unett 5-9-8 A Nicholls 66/1: 7: Dwelt & bhd, t.o. 5f out, 2 month jumps abs, Flat bow.			dist	0
2386}	GOTYA 237 [8] J R Weymes 4-9-5 D Fentiman (7) 50/1: 6-8: Keen in tch, lost pl 5f out, t.o.			dist	0
8 Ran	2m 48.57 (14.97) Owner Mr T P Ramsden			Trained at Newmarket	

---

645 3.50 Bet Direct On Attheraces Text Page 413 Handicap Stakes 3yo 0-80 (D) [84]
£3988 £1227 £614 £307 1m100y f/sand rnd Going 83 -20 Slow Stalls Inside

568	LA PUCE 9 [7] Miss Gay Kelleway 3-8-10 (66) F Lynch 12/1: 2300-401: Sn prom, rdn to chall 2f out, narrowly prevailed for press cl-home, all out:				74a
468*	PLAY MASTER 24 [1] D Haydn Jones 3-9-3 (73) Paul Eddery 100/30: 212: Led/dsptd lead, rdn & went on over 3f out, strongly prsd fnl 2f, edged right & hdd cl-home:			hd	80a
98	BOOK MATCHED 83 [6] B Smart 3-8-9 (65) R Ffrench 7/1: 003-3: Dwelt, held up in tch, drvn to chall 2f out, no extra cl-home:			hd	71a
608	MYANNABANANA 4 [5] J R Weymes 3-8-7 BL (63) J Quinn 7/1: 135-5344: Trkd ldrs, drvn & onepace over 2f out:			1¼	65a
226	HAWKIT 59 [3] J A Osborne 3-9-2 (72) E Ahern 6/1: 232233-5: Trkd ldrs halfway trav well, rdn & no extra ins last:			1½	69a
553*	VENGEROV 11 [4] M L W Bell 3-9-3 (73) M Fenton 9/4 FAV: 50340-16: Led till 3f out, sn btn:			11	42a
566	HEARTBEAT 9 [8] P J McBride 3-7-13 VIS (55) Dale Gibson 28/1: 06-407: Rear, eff 3f out, sn btn:			9	0a
470	MARCUS EILE 24 [2] K R Burke 3-9-7 (77) Darren Williams 10/1: 4263-448: Trkd ldrs, btn 3f out:			16	0a
8 Ran	1m 54.92 (8.72) Owner Wetherby Racing Bureau 52			Trained at Newmarket	

---

646 4.20 Bet Direct Daily Special Offers Selling Stakes 3yo+ (G)
£2611 £746 £373 6f f/sand rnd Going 83 -06 Slow Stalls Inside

579	SABANA 7 [10] J M Bradley 6-9-6 bl (45) P Fitzsimons 33/1: 00-43501: Mid-div, rdn & hdwy to lead ins last, drvn out:				54a
639	LARKYS LOB 1 [9] Paul Johnson 5-9-6 (47) L Fletcher 10/1: 02-214532: Led/dsptd lead, went on after 2f till hdd ins last, no extra:			3	45a
577	AGUILA LOCO 8 [7] Mrs Stef Liddiard 5-9-6 (50) M Fenton 5/1: 0-326253: Led/dsptd lead early, onepace fnl 2f:			nk	44a
492	JUWWI 19 [11] J M Bradley 10-9-6 (66) C J Davies (3) 9/1: 40-04004: Slow away & bhd, switched & late gains, nrst fin:			nk	43a

WOLVERHAMPTON Monday 16.02.04 Lefthand, Sharp Track

610	**NEW OPTIONS** 4 [12] W J Musson 7-9-6 bl (64) E Ahern 7/2 FAV: 004-5405: Trkd ldrs, onepace for press dist:	½	41a
385	**SPEEDFIT FREE** 35 [1] J Semple 7-9-6 bl (53) N Callan 5/1: 1054-256: Mid-div, nvr paced to chall:	hd	40a
610	**POLAR HAZE** 4 [5] J Pearce 7-9-11 vis (58) J Quinn 11/2: 2-426157: Rdn mid-div, no impress dist:	2	40a
555	**MIZHAR** 11 [2] J J Quinn 8-9-6 p (50) Darren Williams 12/1: 00-05258: Rdn towards rear, nvr a factor:	2	30a
585	**DRURY LANE** 7 [4] D W Chapman 4-9-6 bl (75) R Brisland 16/1: 03000-09: Sn outpcd:	½	28a
619*	**AROGANT PRINCE** 3 [8] A W Carroll 7-9-11 bl (49) Rory Moore (7) 9/1: 4406310: Led 2f, btn 1f out:	2½	26a
589	**HEADLAND** 7 [6] D W Chapman 6-9-11 bl (57) A Culhane 8/1: 1-420030: Bhd, nvr a factor, reported lost action.	½	24a
524	**HEATHYARDSBLESSING** 14 [3] R Hollinshead 7-9-6 p (45) Dean McKeown 33/1: 623-0650: Dwelt, & al bhd:	5	14a
12 Ran	1m 18.12 (5.32)	Owner Mr E A Hayward		Trained at Chepstow

647 — 4.50 Bet Direct In Running Sky Text Page 293 Handicap Stakes 4yo+ 0-60 (F) [60]
£2968 £848 £424   1m1f79y f/sand rnd   Going 83   -10 Slow   Stalls Inside

633	**DESERT HEAT** 2 [8] I Semple 6-9-11 VIS (57) A Culhane 20/1: 64004-021: Rear, hdwy 4f out & led over 2f out, sn rdn clr, drvn out:		66a
629*	**GIVEMETHEMOONLIGHT** 2 [2] Mrs Stef Liddiard 5-9-10 6ex vis (56) J Quinn 9/2: 21353612: Held up in tch, rdn to chase wnr over 1f out, kept on, al held:	1¾	61a
530	**BRAMANTINO** 13 [4] R A Fahey 4-9-7 (53) T Hamilton (5) 12/1: 03/000-53: Trkd ldrs, outpcd over 2f out, styd on for press to take 3rd late:	4	50a
561	**TAIYO** 10 [5] J W Payne 4-9-4 (50) N Callan 25/1: 560-6544: Led/dsptd lead till over 2f out:	hd	46a
456	**INTERSTICE** 25 [7] A G Newcombe 7-9-4 p (50) Dean McKeown 14/1: 0000-365: Pulled hard early, trkd ldrs, btn 2f out:	7	34a
564	**AIR OF ESTEEM** 10 [10] Ian Emmerson 8-8-13 (45) D Fentiman (7) 9/1: 4553-556: Dwelt, sn prom, btn 2f out:	5	20a
557	**OUR DESTINY** 10 [3] D Burchell 6-9-6 vis (52) J Tate 16/1: 002-3247: Led, hdd 6f out, btn 4f out:	8	13a
513	**TO WIT TO WOO** 17 [6] B W Hills 4-9-12 (58) M Hills 8/11 FAV: 40014-28: Prom, btn 3f out:	3	14a
4970}	**ROCINANTE** 107 [9] J J Quinn 4-9-8 (54) R Ffrench 25/1: 443010-9: Prom, struggling from halfway:	6	0a
9 Ran	2m 06.98 (8.78)	Owner Mr Gordon McDowall		Trained at Carluke

LINGFIELD Monday 16.02.04 Lefthand, V Sharp Track

Official Going STANDARD

648 — 1.40 Betdirect Co Uk Banded Stakes Div 1 3yo+ 0-45 (H)
£1638 £468 £234   1m p/track rnd   Going 48   +00 Fast   Stalls Outside

538	**MISS PEACHES** 13 [7] G G Margarson 6-9-8 (45) Kristin Stubbs (7) 10/1: 4/00/00-201: Rear, 5L 8th 2f out, hdwy over 1f out, led ins fnl 1f, pushed out cl-home:		50a
340	**HARBOUR HOUSE** 40 [3] J J Bridger 5-9-8 (45) N Pollard 10/1: 00020-02: Led 1f, remained handy, led again 1f out, hdd & onepace cl-home:	1¼	46a
4516}	**JAHANGIR** 140 [8] B R Johnson 5-9-8 (45) Dane O'Neill 7/1: 500030-3: Keen, led after 1f till hdd 1f out, no extra:	2	42a
522	**MAGGIES PET** 14 [11] K Bell 7-9-8 t (45) D R McCabe 5/1: 60-25224: Handy, rdn & ch over 1f out, no extra.	½	41a
538	**WILOM** 13 [2] M R Hoad 6-9-8 (45) S Drowne 9/1: 403-2545: Chsd ldrs, rdn & ch over 1f out, onepcd:	1	39a
571	**PANCAKEHILL** 9 [6] D K Ivory 5-9-8 T (45) Martin Dwyer 9/1: 50-00006: In tch, hdwy 3f out, onepace fnl 1f:	½	38a
562	**IVY MOON** 9 [4] B J Llewellyn 4-9-8 (45) D Sweeney 8/1: 3030-367: Rear, hdwy 3f out, no extra fnl 2f:	¾	36a
99	**NEVINSTOWN** 83 [1] Niall Moran 4-9-8 VIS t (45) W M Lordan 9/1: 00/00000-8: Slow away, sn in midfield, no extra 2f out.	¾	34a
291	**ALTARES** 44 [9] P Howling 3-8-3 (45) J Fanning 50/1: 0000-09: Rear, nvr nr ldrs:	nk	33a
354	**SANTA CATALINA** 39 [12] C A Dwyer 5-9-8 t (45) Lisa Jones (3) 10/1: 00603-00: Nvr nr ldrs:	1	31a
540	**LADY AT LEISURE** 13 [10] Julian Poulton 4-9-8 (45) R Havlin 16/1: 6300/5-60: With ldrs, wknd over 2f out.	1	29a
535	**CHEROKEE BAY** 13 [5] G L Moore 4-9-8 e (45) G Carter 5/2 FAV: 0003-430: Al bhd:	3	23a
12 Ran	1m 40.1 (3.9)	Owner Mr G G Margarson		Trained at Newmarket

649 — 2.10 Betdirect Co Uk Banded Stakes Div 2 3yo+ 0-45 (H)
£1635 £467 £234   1m p/track rnd   Going 48   -02 Slow   Stalls Outside

538	**WANNA SHOUT** 13 [11] R Dickin 6-9-8 (45) Lisa Jones (3) 7/1: 40004-21: Rcd wide in midfield, hdwy over 2f out, led ins fnl 1f, drvn out:		50a
538	**CHOCOLATE BOY** 13 [4] G L Moore 5-9-8 BL e (45) S Whitworth 5/1: 000/00-52: Slowly away in rear, bumped 2f out, styd on, rdn fnl 1f:	½	47a
412	**BALLARE** 32 [7] Bob Jones 5-9-8 (40) O Urbina 7/1: 40200-03: Rear, wide into straight, hdwy over 1f out, ran on for press cl-home:	nk	46a
528*	**BADOU** 14 [10] L Montague Hall 4-9-8 (45) R Miles (5) 3/1: 4000-614: Chsd ldrs, edged left & led over 1f out, hdd ins fnl 1f, onepace:	1½	43a
287	**BAR OF SILVER** 45 [9] R Brotherton 4-9-8 VIS (45) A Daly 25/1: 25050-05: Keen, hdwy 3f out, slt short of room when ch over 1f out, onepace ins fnl 1f:	½	42a
571	**EUROLINK ZANTE** 9 [12] T D McCarthy 8-9-8 bl (45) J P Guillambert (3) 14/1: 06060-06: Rear, hdwy 2f out, onepaced:	shd	41a
569	**MYTHICAL CHARM** 9 [3] J J Bridger 5-9-8 (45) N Pollard 100/30 FAV: 6501-607: Chsd ldrs, onepace 2f out.	hd	40a
3646}	**MALAAH** 184 [5] Julian Poulton 8-9-8 bl (45) M Halford (7) 20/1: 000/000-8: Led, hdd over 1f out, no extra:	1½	37a
566	**ALMOST WELCOME** 9 [1] S Dow 3-8-3 (45) P Doe 14/1: 0000-009: Chsd ldrs, squeezed out over 2f out, no extra.	½	36a
4720}	**ROYALE PEARL** 126 [2] R Ingram 4-9-8 (45) Dane O'Neill 10/1: 000340-0: Handy, wknd 2f out:	¾	34a
326	**LADY PREDOMINANT** 41 [6] Andrew Reid 3-8-3 (45) S Carson 12/1: 5020-440: Rear, hmpd 3f out, no dngr.	5	24a
539	**ACHILLES RAINBOW** 13 [8] K R Burke 5-9-8 (40) G Faulkner 20/1: 40060-40: Handy, wknd 3f out.	dist	0a
12 Ran	1m 40.2 (4.0)	Owner E R C Beech & B Wilkinson		Trained at Stratford-On-Avon

650 — 2.40 Bet Direct On 0800 32 93 93 Banded Stakes 4yo+ 0-40 (H)
£1463 £418 £209   2m p/track   Going 48   -17 Slow   Stalls Inside

581	**LITTLE RICHARD** 7 [9] M Wellings 5-9-6 p (35) A Daly 20/1: 00-00431: In tch, outpcd 4f out, rallied 2f out, drvn & styd on well		40a

523	**THE BEDUTH NAVI 14** [6] D G Bridgwater 4-9-0 (35) D Nolan (5) 20/1: 0/000-22: Led 3f, led again over 2f out till hdd ins fnl 1f, not btn far:		¾	38a
537	**POLKA PRINCESS 13** [1] M Wellings 4-9-0 p (40) L Treadwell (5) 40/1: 000-0003: Keen, hdwy 5f out, onepace fnl 2f:		1¼	36a
1125}	**SECOND PAIGE 301** [5] N A Graham 7-9-6 bl (40) O Urbina 5/4 FAV: 160450-4: Rear, hdwy 3f out, styd on ins fnl 1f:		hd	35a
576	**UNLEADED 8** [10] J Akehurst 4-9-0 (40) J Fanning 2/1: 000-2125: Handy, led 7f out till hdd over 2f out, no extra:		3½	31a
612	**OULTON BROAD 4** [8] R Ford 8-9-6 p (35) J P Guillambert 3-(3) 12/1: 0016/-056: Rear, hdwy 6f out, btn 2f out.		1¼	29a
734]	**SHARVIE 706** [4] M R Bosley 7-9-6 p (40) Joanna Badger 33/1: 0/64550/-7: Midfield, no impress on ldrs fnl 4f.		14	15a
4812}	**ANNIVERSARY GUEST 119** [3] Mrs Lucinda Featherstone 5-9-6 (35) R Miles (3) 25/1: 060305-8: Slowly away & lost 12L, keen in rear, modest hdwy 4f out, eased when btn over 2f out:		3	12a
576	**MARTHA REILLY 8** [7] Mrs Barbara Waring 8-9-6 (35) Lisa Jones (3) 33/1: 55/005//-6: Chsd ldrs, wknd after halfway.		1	11a
539	**GINGER ICE 13** [2] G G Margarson 4-9-0 vis (40) N Pollard 10/1: 0006-350: Slowly away, keen, led after 3f, hdd 7f out, no extra.		dist	0a

10 Ran   3m 30.55 (10.55)   Owner Mark Wellings Racing   Trained at Bridgnorth

---

651

3.10 Press Interactive To Bet Direct Median Auction Maiden Stakes 3-5yo (H)
£1463 £418 £209   1m p/track rnd   Going 48   -02 Slow   Stalls Outside

4988}	**GLENDALE 105** [2] C A Dwyer 3-8-5 (68) Lisa Jones (3) 7/4: 0000-1: Chsd ldrs, hdwy over 2f out, led ins fnl 1f & hung right, drvn out:			67a
536	**BALLINGER RIDGE 13** [4] A M Balding 5-9-10 P (60) Martin Dwyer 11/10 FAV: 0063-232: Led till hdd ins last, no extra:		1½	60a
571	**ESTRELLA LEVANTE 9** [6] G L Moore 4-9-10 (49) Jemma Marshall (7) 20/1: U055-053: Slow away, midfield, hdwy 3f out, no extra fnl 2f:		7	46a
566	**COSTA DEL SOL 9** [1] J J Bridger 3-8-5 1ow bl (35) N Pollard 33/1: 005-0004: Slow away, chsd ldr, wknd over 2f out, no extra.		1¾	42a
536	**DEVINE COMMAND 13** [5] R Ingram 3-8-5 (56) N Day 5/1: 0025: Chsd ldrs, wknd 2f out:		1¼	39a
396	**ANOTHER EXPLETIVE 33** [3] J White 3-8-0 (45) R Thomas (4) 33/1: 00004-06: In tch, rear from halfway.		16	2a

6 Ran   1m 40.25 (4.05)   Owner Mrs J A Cornwell   Trained at Newmarket

---

652

3.40 Free #10 Bet @ Bet Direct Interactive Selling Stakes 3yo+ (H)
£1516 £433 £217   6f p/track rnd   Going 48   +00 Fast   Stalls Inside

582	**BELLS BEACH 7** [12] P Howling 6-9-1 (45) J Fanning 7/1: 040-6201: Rear, hdwy 2f out, led ins fnl 1f, rdn clr:			51a
582	**THE GAY FOX 7** [10] B G Powell 10-9-6 bl t (45) L Keniry (3) 5/1: 5005-242: Rear, kept on late, nrst fin.		2½	45a
516	**TICKLE 16** [11] P J Makin 6-9-1 vis t (50) D Sweeney 5/1: 5060-403: Handy, onepace.		nk	39a
589	**CAYMAN BREEZE 7** [5] S Dow 4-9-6 VIS (62) Dane O'Neill 9/2 FAV: 0300-054: Handy, with ldrs halfway, onepace fnl 1f:		nk	43a
411	**SHIRLEY OAKS 32** [7] Miss Z C Davison 6-9-1 (40) N Chalmers (5) 50/1: 04000-05: Slowly away in rear, hdwy over 1f out, nrst fin:		½	36a
577	**OVER TO YOU BERT 8** [8] R J Hodges 5-9-6 (49) S Drowne 33/1: 40500-06: Chsd ldrs, onepace fnl 2f:		nk	40a
308	**LAY DOWN SALLY 43** [14] J White 6-9-1 (40) R Thomas (5) 7/1: 03020-67: Rear, late gain, nvr dngrs.		hd	34a
548	**TOP PLACE 12** [4] C A Dwyer 3-8-0 p Hayley Turner (5) 25/1: 0-08: Led, hdd ins fnl 1f, no extra.		1	31a
4258}	**CONFUZED 153** [2] Andrew Reid 4-9-6 Martin Dwyer 7/1: 0/0-9: Chsd ldrs, wknd over 1f out:		nk	35a
535	**ABUELOS 13** [3] S Dow 5-9-6 (45) P Doe 8/1: 0500-340: Rear, hdwy when hmpd in midfield over 1f out:		nk	34a
572	**AVIT 9** [9] P L Gilligan 4-9-1 (45) G Faulkner (5) 50000-00: Handy 4f, btn over 1f out.		2	23a
4929}	**ALBURY HEATH 111** [1] T M Jones 4-9-6 (40) A Daly 50/1: 0/05000-0: Rear, nvr nr ldrs:		2	22a
335	**FIENNES 41** [13] Mrs N Macauley 6-9-6 vis (45) Lisa Jones (3) 14/1: 0563-000: Rcd wide, chsd ldrs 2f, wknd.		5	7a
535	**LADY LIESEL 13** [6] J J Bridger 4-9-1 (40) N Pollard 12/1: 45000-00: In tch, btn when hmpd over 1f out.		¾	0a

14 Ran   1m 13.3 (2.9)   Owner Mr Richard Berenson   Trained at Newmarket

---

653

4.10 Free #25 Bonus @ Littlewoodspoker Com Banded Stakes 3yo+ 0-40 (H)
£1449 £414 £207   5f p/track rnd   Going 48   -14 Slow   Stalls Outside

571	**IVORY VENTURE 9** [7] D K Ivory 4-9-3 bl (35) R Miles (3) 25/1: 00-00001: Outpcd, plenty to do 2f out, switched left & styd on strongly to lead nr fin:			41a
586	**ONEFORTHEBOYS 7** [6] D Flood 5-9-3 (35) L Treadwell (7) 10/1: 600-0062: Outpcd, hdwy ins fnl 1f & ev ch, not pace to repel wnr cl home:		½	38a
619	**SOMETHINGABOUTHER 3** [5] P W Hiatt 4-9-3 (40) Lisa Jones (3) 14/1: 500-4503: Midfield, hdwy to chall dist, kept on & not btn far:		nk	37a
374	**BALI STAR 35** [8] R J Hodges 9-9-3 (40) J F McDonald (5) 5/1: 5005-024: Handy, led 1f out till cl home, btn under 1L in a bunched fin:		nk	36a
451	**LYDIAS LOOK 26** [4] T J Etherington 7-9-3 (40) J Fanning 3/1 FAV: 05000-05: Handy, kept on for press fnl 1f:		hd	35a
312	**CALENDAR GIRL 42** [3] P J Makin 4-9-3 BL (40) D Sweeney 10/1: 3500-06: Chsd ldrs, eff 2f out, not qckn ins fnl 1f, but only btn arnd 1L:		nk	34a
312	**MANGUS 42** [2] K O Cunningham Brown 10-9-3 bl e (40) S Whitworth 7/1: 00600-37: Led till dist:		1	31a
507	**ALLERTON BOY 17** [10] R J Hodges 5-9-3 (40) S Drowne 6/1: 000-4068: Chsd ldrs, onepace fnl 1f.		½	29a
522	**ELLAMYTE 14** [9] D G Bridgwater 4-9-3 T (40) D Nolan (5) 5/1: 0300-009: Midfield, btn over 1f out:		1¾	24a
312	**ON THE LEVEL 42** [1] Mrs N Macauley 5-9-3 BL (40) Hayley Turner (5) 14/1: 43255-00: With ldrs over 3f, wknd.		6	6a

10 Ran   1m 0.9 (3.1)   Owner Mr Dean Ivory   Trained at Radlett

---

654

4.40 Allweather-Racing Com Banded Stakes 4yo+ 0-35 (H)
£1302 £372 £186   1m2f p/track   Going 48   +01 Fast   Stalls Inside

523	**KINGSDON 14** [5] T J Fitzgerald 7-9-0 vis t (35) Martin Dwyer 12/1: 04000-01: Chsd ldrs, led over 2f out, drvn to hold on nr fin:			39a
584*	**MONDURU 7** [8] G L Moore 7-9-6 bl (35) S Whitworth 4/1: 5000-012: Slowly away, hdwy 3f out, ev ch fnl 1f, just btn in a thrill:		hd	39a
2410	**ADJIRAM 598** [1] A W Carroll 8-9-0 (30) G Carter 2/1 FAV: 0400/46/-3: Chsd ldrs, no extra fnl 1f:		7	23a
584	**ALL ON MY OWN 7** [3] I W McInnes 9-9-0 bl (35) Natalia Gemelova (7) 8/1: 000-0424: Midfield, chsd ldrs 4f out, onepace 2f out:		3½	18a

LINGFIELD Monday 16.02.04 Lefthand, V Sharp Track

out:

24	DARK DOLORES 95 [2] J R Boyle 6-9-0 (35) J P Guillambert (3) 5/1: 620056-5: Handy, led over 3f out till hdd over 2f out, no extra over 1f out:	5	11a
571	PENNY VALENTINE 9 [6] J R Best 4-8-13 (35) M Lawson (7) 12/1: 00050-06: Rear, nvr reach ldrs.	1¼	9a
540	MARGARETS WISH 13 [9] T Wall 4-8-13 (30) N Chalmers (5) 9/1: 0200-047: Rear, nvr dngrs:	1¼	7a
916}	LITTLE MISS TRICKY 321 [10] P Mitchell 5-9-0 (35) J Fanning 20/1: 00/0000-8: Al bhd:	7	0a
460	HARRY TU 25 [7] Miss Gay Kelleway 4-8-13 e T (35) S Drowne 14/1: 00-09: Al bhd:	1½	0a
527	VIEW THE FACTS 14 [12] P L Gilligan 5-9-0 e T (35) Lisa Jones (3) 33/1: 00/0/00-00: Chsd ldr, led 5f out till hdd over 3f out, no extra:	5	0a
1011}	STOPWATCH 312 [11] Mrs L C Jewell 9-9-0 p (35) Dane O'Neill 20/1: 0/3000/0-0: In tch, rear fnl 6f:	10	0a
539	RO ERIDANI 13 [4] T J Etherington 4-8-13 BL (35) D Kinsella 33/1: 2000-000: Led 5f, fdd:	11	0a

12 Ran   2m 7.5 (4.7)   Owner Mr Mike Browne   Trained at Malton

SOUTHWELL Tuesday 17.02.04 Lefthand, Sharp, Oval Track

Official Going Standard

655 1.10 Bet Direct On Atr Text Page 413 Handicap Stakes Div 1 3yo+ 0-80 (D)   [80]
£4027 £1239 £620 £310   5f f/sand str   Going 47   Inapplicab   Stalls Stands Side

155	MAKTAVISH 73 [7] I Semple 5-10-0 p (80) N Callan 7/2 JT FAV: 550100-1: Made all, clr halfway, hung right under press over 1f out, drvn & held on well:		86a
2801}	BLUE KNIGHT 222 [5] A P Jarvis 5-9-6 (72) J Quinn 16/1: 002600-2: Chsd ldrs, drvn & chsd wnr dist, kept on but al held:	¾	75a
587*	SEA THE WORLD 8 [6] D Shaw 4-8-10 6ex vis (62) Darren Williams 10/1: 3000-513: Pushed along towards rear, styd on for press, nrst fin:	nk	64a
487	RIVER LARK 21 [1] M A Buckley 5-7-12 3oh (47) J F McDonald (5) 14/1: 00102-64: Chsd ldrs, kept on.	¾	50a
453	TABOOR 27 [11] J W Payne 6-8-12 h bl (64) M Fenton 14/1: 000-0005: Chsd ldrs, not able to chall.	nk	63a
453	THE FISIO 27 [4] A M Balding 4-9-8 (74) Martin Dwyer 7/2 FAV: 000-1156: Dwelt, sn in tch, no impress dist:	2	67a
550	LAKELANDS LADY 12 [10] J Balding 4-9-7 (67) J Edmunds 40/1: 00000-07: Sn pushed along, nvr pace to threaten.	2	54a
461	FRASCATI 26 [8] A Berry 4-9-11 (77) F Lynch 12/1: 4251-008: Al outpcd:	½	62a
205	DAINTREE AFFAIR 63 [3] K R Burke 4-8-11 (63) G Baker 6/1: 310053-9: Prom till over 1f out, abs:	¾	46a
349	GONENDUNNETT 40 [2] Mrs C A Dunnett 5-9-1 vis (67) Dane O'Neill 12/1: 4103-000: Dwelt & sn outpcd, abs:	nk	49a
551	RAYMONDS PRIDE 12 [9] A A Ryan 4-8-13 bl (65) P Fessey 14/1: 501F0-00: Dwelt, sn struggling.	2½	39a

11 Ran   1m 00.06   Owner Mr D G Savala   Trained at Carluke

656 1.40 Littlewoods Bet Direct Maiden Handicap Stakes Div 1 3yo 0-60 (F)   [67]
£2933 £838 £419   1m f/sand rnd   Going 47   -23 Slow   Stalls Inside

4575}	POKER 137 [8] W J Haggas 3-8-6 (45) Martin Dwyer 6/4 FAV: 060-1: Pushed along mid-div & outpcd over 3f out, drvn & hdwy to lead well ins last, soon in command:		57a
545	JOMUS 13 [6] L Montague Hall 3-9-3 (56) F Lynch 13/2: 02005-52: Slow away, sn in tch, keen & rcd v wide, rdn & styd on fnl 2f, not pace of wnr:	1¾	61a
486	BROTHER CADFAEL 21 [4] John A Harris 3-8-8 (47) L Fletcher (3) 28/1: 0456-303: Trkd ldrs, rdn & led over 1f out, drvn/edged left & hdd ins last, onepace:	1¼	49a
490	ABROGATE 21 [12] P C Haslam 3-8-10 (49) G Faulkner 7/1: 3003-024: Held up, drvn & hdwy over 2f out, no extra dist:	2½	46a
603	GAYLE STORM 6 [5] C Tinkler 3-8-13 (52) E Ahern 9/1: 536-0005: Trkd ldrs halfway, rdn & no impress dist.	shd	49a
510	TURNBERRY 18 [2] J W Hills 3-9-4 bl (57) S Whitworth 13/2: 0004-436: Led/dsptd lead till over 1f out:	5	45a
553	TONTO 12 [10] Miss D Mountain 3-9-7 (60) D Fox (5) 8/1: 020-0437: Led/dsptd lead 5f, fdd under press:	nk	47a
591	MYSTIC PROMISE 7 [3] Mrs N Macauley 3-7-12 7oh VIS (30) Hayley Turner (5) 66/1: 0000-008: Chsd ldrs 6f, tried visor.	½	23a
596	QUARRY ISLAND 7 [9] P D Evans 3-8-1 vis (40) Joanna Badger 10/1: 0040-529: Dwelt & al bhd.	1	24a
3795}	PRINCE OF PERLES 179 [7] D Shaw 3-7-12 2oh VIS (35) J F McDonald (5) 20/1: 00000-0: Held up, pulled hard, nvr a factor:	½	20a
4250}	UNPRECEDENTED 154 [1] T T Clement 3-9-4 (57) Dean McKeown 50/1: 600-0: Chsd ldrs 5f, reapp/h'cap bow.	12	20a
397	GARNOCK BELLE 34 [11] A Berry 3-8-2 2oh 4ow (35) A Nicholls (5) 40/1: 500-00: Led, ran out on bend after 2f, sn bhd, reportedly difficult to steer.	18	0a

12 Ran   1m 45.03 (5.63)   Owner The Poker Partnership   Trained at Newmarket

657 2.10 Bet Direct On Atr Text Page 410 Handicap Stakes Fillies 3yo+ 0-75 (E)   [71]
£3262 £932 £466   6f f/sand rnd   Going 47   +02 Fast   Stalls Inside

471	FOREVER PHOENIX 24 [2] R M H Cowell 4-9-8 (65) E Ahern 4/1 FAV: 4201-561: Sn handy trav well, rdn to lead ins last, shade cosy:		74a
593	BOAVISTA 7 [1] P D Evans 4-8-10 t (53) L Fletcher (3) 8/1: 2243-032: Led, rdn & hdd ins last, kept on:	½	59a
587	PARK STAR 8 [5] D Shaw 4-8-13 (56) J F McDonald (5) 16/1: 56000-63: Chsd ldrs, drvn & kept on onepace:	1¾	57a
550	BLAKESHALL QUEST 12 [7] R Brotherton 4-9-3 vis (60) F P Ferris (3) 5/1: 000-0444: Pushed along wide, drvn & kept on fnl 2f, no threat:	½	59a
579*	EAGER ANGEL 8 [8] R F Marvin 6-8-8 6ex (51) Dean McKeown 16/1: 30-24015: Towards rear, mod late gains:	shd	50a
562	PILGRIM PRINCESS 11 [9] E J Alston 6-8-2 (45) J Quinn 11/2: 246-3546: Handy, rdn & no extra fnl 2f:	1¼	40a
587	PLAYFUL SPIRIT 8 [4] J Balding 5-8-6 vis (49) E J Edmunds 11/1: 1-063307: Chsd ldrs, no extra over 1f out.	2	38a
550	GRANDMA LILY 12 [10] M C Chapman 6-10-0 (71) B Reilly (5) 10/1: 150-3008: Rdn & al towards rear:	shd	60a
282	ZAGALA 46 [6] S L Keightley 4-9-6 t (63) A Nicholls 8/1: 00213-29: Dwelt & al rear:	1¾	47a
168	MISS WONG ONE 70 [3] Frederick John Bowles 4-8-13 (56) J P Spencer 8/1: 000203-0: Mid-div, wknd qckly over 1f out, eased:	17	0a

10 Ran   1m 16.01 (2.71)   Owner Mr J M Greetham   Trained at Newmarket

SOUTHWELL Tuesday 17.02.04 Lefthand, Sharp, Oval Track

658 **2.40 Bet Direct On Atr Text Page 411 Handicap Stakes 3yo 46-55 (F)** **[64]**
£2926 £836 £418 **1m3f f/sand** **Going 47** **-33 Slow** Stalls Inside

526 **TURKS AND CAICOS 15** [4] P C Haslam 3-9-4 (54) G Faulkner 9/2: 040-221: Chsd ldrs & led 2f out, drvn ins last, held on all out: **59a**
592 **SIEGFRIEDS NIGHT 7** [8] M C Chapman 3-9-0 (50) B Reilly (5) 11/1: 035-1432: Chsd ldrs & smooth prog to chall 2f out, sn hung left under press, drvn & styd on well, just held: *shd* **54a**
614 **SIR FRANK GIBSON 5** [3] M Johnston 3-8-9 (45) J Fanning 11/2: 040-0423: Led, hdd 2f out, kept on for press: *2½* **45a**
608 **NOCATEE 5** [2] P C Haslam 3-8-9 P (45) D Fentiman (7) 7/2 JT FAV: 0500-334: Held up in tch, kept on onepace for press, no threat: *2* **42a**
560 **SECRET BLOOM 11** [6] J R Norton 3-8-11 vis (47) Darren Williams 25/1: 050-4405: Mid-div, no impress fnl 3f. *5* **37a**
490 **BISCAR TWO 21** [10] R M Whitaker 3-8-9 (45) Dean McKeown 7/2 JT FAV: 000-46: Held up, rdn & no impress fnl 2f. *1* **34a**
608 **FRAMBO 5** [1] J G Portman 3-9-4 P (54) E Ahern 16/1: 00625-07: Trkd ldrs, wknd under press 2f out: *5* **36a**
383 **KILLING ME SOFTLY 36** [9] J Gallagher 3-9-1 (51) D Sweeney 15/2: 01-28: Trkd ldrs, btn 2f out: *1½* **31a**
596 **MIND PLAY 7** [7] M E Sowersby 3-8-9 bl (40) P Mulrennan (2) 66/1: 0006-69: Cl-up, wknd qckly over 2f out: *nk* **24a**
486 **TICKLEPENNY LOCK 21** [11] C Smith 3-8-9 (30) A Nicholls 100/1: 6000-000: Al bhd & no ch halfway. *12* **9a**
10 Ran 2m 30.15 (8.85) Owner Middleham Park Racing Trained at Middleham

659 **3.10 Bet Direct On Atr Text Page 412 Maiden Stakes 3yo+ (D)**
£3367 £1036 £518 £259 **6f f/sand rnd** **Going 47** **+05 Fast** Stalls Inside

509 **SKIP OF COLOUR 18** [12] P A Blockley 4-9-10 (65) D Nolan (5) 7/1: 340-451: Fine early speed from wide draw & sn clr ldr, in full command fnl 2f, eased down, val 6L+: **75a**
600 **ZAK FACTA 6** [8] Miss D A McHale 4-9-10 vis t (50) S Whitworth 5/1: 5400-552: Mid-div, styd on for press, nvr threatened wnr: *3½* **52a**
562 **LARGS 11** [2] J Balding 4-9-5 (46) J Edmunds 20/1: 20345-03: Mid-div, drvn & kept on fnl 2f, nvr a threat: *½* **45a**
562 **DARK CHAMPION 11** [6] Jedd O'Keeffe 4-9-10 (48) Dane O'Neill 12/1: 4405-204: Chsd wnr halfway, drvn & no impress fnl 2f: *shd* **50a**
4793} **OTYLIA 123** [11] A Berry 4-9-5 (52) F Lynch 28/1: 423544-5: Mid-div, little hdwy, nvr a threat: *1½* **40a**
587 **AMANDAS LAD 8** [5] M C Chapman 4-9-10 (45) B Reilly (5) 16/1: 30-63406: Chsd ldrs, not pace to chall: *hd* **44a**
1590} **BROOKLANDS TIME 274** [9] I W McInnes 3-8-4 (63) P Mathers (6) 10/1: 433-7: Chsd wnr, btn 2f out: *3* **31a**
385 **SHADOWFAX 36** [1] Miss Gay Kelleway 4-9-10 P (58) M Fenton 5/1: 26/62-408: Dwelt, nvr on terms, cheek pieces: *shd* **36a**
4921} **MISSION AFFIRMED 112** [10] T P Tate 3-8-9 D Mernagh 7/1: 55-9: Rear/wide, nvr factor, gelded, reapp. *nk* **35a**
531 **UTAH FLATS 14** [7] Mrs J R Ramsden 3-8-9 BL Martin Dwyer 16/1: 00: Mid-div, sn outpcd, tried blnks. *2½* **28a**
290 **ROAN RAIDER 45** [3] M J Polglase 4-9-10 bl t (45) L Fletcher (3) 40/1: 24600-00: Al outpcd rear, abs. *¾* **26a**
488 **GALLOWAY MAC 21** [4] W A O'Gorman 4-9-10 M Tebbutt 9/2 FAV: 330: Dwelt, settled rear & wide, nvr a factor: *nk* **25a**
ROYAL SHEPLEY [13] J Balding 3-8-4 A Nicholls 33/1: 0: Dwelt & sn outpcd & `hung left' on debut. *23* **0a**
13 Ran 1m 15.82 (2.52) Owner Mr Trevor Sleath Trained at Southwell

660 **3.40 Bet Direct On Atr Text Page 413 Handicap Stakes Div 2 3yo+ 0-80 (D)** **[80]**
£4017 £1236 £618 £309 **5f f/sand str** **Going 47** **Inapplicab** Stalls Stands Side

386 **MAGIC GLADE 35** [5] C R Dore 5-9-7 (73) R Thomas (5) 12/1: 323/00-01: Bmpd start, sn prom & led over 1f out, rdn out: **83a**
292 **POLISH EMPEROR 45** [2] P W Harris 4-9-10 bl (76) E Ahern 100/30 FAV: 66410-42: Al prom, drvn & kept on, not pace of wnr: *¾* **83a**
618 **TIME N TIME AGAIN 4** [10] E J Alston 6-9-12 p (78) J Quinn 4/1: 2-510133: Trkd ldrs stands side, drvn & kept on, not pace of wnr: *hd* **84a**
550 **FAR NOTE 12** [1] S R Bowring 6-9-1 bl (67) M Fenton 11/2: 10-62004: Mid-div, styd on for press, not able to chall: *½* **71a**
453 **LADY PEKAN 27** [3] P S McEntee 5-8-11 bl (63) Dane O'Neill 9/1: 0141-635: Led till over 1f out, no extra dist. *2½* **60a**
461 **PRIME RECREATION 26** [7] P S Felgate 7-8-12 (64) G Duffield 16/1: 2400-606: Prom, wknd over 1f out: *2½* **54a**
550 **ST IVIAN 12** [4] Mrs N Macauley 4-9-2 vis (68) P McCabe 10/1: 51-46027: Dwelt, mid-div, nvr able to chall: *2½* **51a**
587 **VANISHED 8** [6] M J Polglase 4-8-8 BL (60) L Fletcher (3) 66/1: 02440-08: Mid-div, btn over 1f out, tried blnks. *1* **40a**
231 **ROMAN QUINTET 59** [8] D W P Arbuthnot 4-8-11 t (63) S Whitworth 15/2: 034402-9: Dwelt & al outpcd, abs: *1¼* **39a**
453 **PRINCE OF BLUES 27** [9] M Mullineaux 6-8-13 p (65) J P Spencer 9/1: 0600-020: Chsd ldrs, sn outpcd, `struck head on the stalls'. *11* **12a**
10 Ran 1m 00.39 Owner Mr P O'Gorman Trained at Spalding

661 **4.10 Bet Direct On 0800 32 93 93 Selling Stakes 3yo+ (G)**
£2583 £738 £369 **7f f/sand rnd** **Going 47** **-04 Slow** Stalls Inside

589 **FEAST OF ROMANCE 8** [6] P Howling 7-10-0 bl (56) J P Spencer 6/4 FAV: 3132621: Held up, smooth prog from halfway & led ins last, rdn out: **61a**
528 **SILVER MASCOT 15** [9] R Hollinshead 5-9-9 (40) F Lynch 7/1: 600-4022: Led & sn clr, rcd towards centre fnl 2f, rdn & hdd ins last, no extra: *1¼* **52a**
592 **EMPEROR CAT 7** [4] P A Blockley 3-8-11 (58) D Nolan (4) 5/1: 60105-23: Chsd ldrs, rdn & chsd ldr over 1f out, sn no extra: *½* **56a**
646 **LARKYS LOB 1** [3] Paul Johnson 5-9-9 (47) L Fletcher (3) 11/2: 02-214524: Dwelt, rear, late gains, nvr a threat: *4* **43a**
533 **MYSTERY MOUNTAIN 14** [1] Mrs J R Ramsden 4-9-9 (53) Martin Dwyer 8/1: 64300-05: Chsd ldrs, no impress fnl 2f: *8* **29a**
3426} **BRILLYANT DANCER 195** [2] Mrs A Duffield 6-9-4 (40) G Duffield 14/1: 000004-6: Prom, struggling halfway: *1½* **21a**
4371} **JACKS DELIGHT 150** [7] B D Leavy 4-9-9 J Fanning 66/1: 00-7: Chsd ldrs 5f, abs, new yard. *9* **11a**
487 **DIL 21** [8] Mrs N Macauley 9-9-9 (45) Joanna Badger 16/1: 60003-08: Sn struggling rear. *2* **7a**
WILLYEVER 154 [5] Frederick John Bowles 10-9-9 vis T E Ahern 16/1: 005000-9: Mid-div, wknd 3f out, t-strap, Irish raider. *2½* **2a**
9 Ran 1m 30.19 (3.59) Owner Mr D C Patrick Trained at Newmarket

662 **4.40 Littlewoods Bet Direct Maiden Handicap Stakes Div 2 3yo 0-60 (F)** **[67]**
£2926 £836 £418 **1m f/sand rnd** **Going 47** **-01 Slow** Stalls Inside

444 **DISPOL VELETA 28** [11] T D Barron 3-9-0 (53) J Fanning 11/2: 0-301: Sn trkd ldrs & trav well, smooth prog 2f out & rdn/led over 1f out, sn in command, val for 7L+: **65a**
4639} *5* **60a**

SOUTHWELL Tuesday 17.02.04 Lefthand, Sharp, Oval Track

	BOND MOONLIGHT 133 [7] B Smart 3-9-7 (60) F Lynch 4/1 FAV: 404-2: Handy & led over 2f out, hdd over 1f out, no ch with wnr but kept on:			
536	**SONDERBORG** 14 [4] G L Moore 3-8-10 p (49) G Carter 5/1: 006-6453: Chsd ldrs, drvn & kept on, nvr a threat:	2½	44a
543	**DANCING PRINCE** 13 [2] A P Jarvis 3-8-12 (51) N Callan 8/1: 005-54: Held up, hdwy/eff to chase front pair over 1f out, sn rdn & no extra:	nk	45a
614	**COURANT DAIR** 5 [5] P C Haslam 3-8-1 (40) D Fentiman (7) 5/1: 000-0365: Led, hdd 3f out, fdd, qck reapp.	5	25a
351	**CASSANOS** 40 [9] Miss Gay Kelleway 3-9-4 P (57) M Fenton 9/2: 0000-36: Mid-div, nvr a factor:	1	40a
580	**PEACE TREATY** 8 [10] S R Bowring 3-7-13 7oh 1ow bl t (30) J Quinn 33/1: 000-0007: Towards rear, no impress.	2½	16a
553	**BIENHEUREUX** 12 [3] W J Musson 3-8-8 (47) D Mernagh 12/1: 00-08: Mid-div, eff 3f out, sn btn, h'cap bwn:	3½	19a
4770}	**MAJOR PROJECT** 124 [6] P C Haslam 3-7-12 2oh (35) Dean Williams (6) 33/1: 000-9: Dwelt & sn outpcd:	5	0a
596	**CASANTELLA** 7 [8] M J Polglase 3-8-6 (45) K Ghunowa (7) 20/1: 6-045050: Mid-div, struggling from halfway.	6	0a
10 Ran	1m 43.24 (3.84) Owner Mr W B Imison		Trained at Thirsk	

WOLVERHAMPTON Tuesday 17.02.04 Lefthand, Sharp Track

Official Going STANDARD TO SLOW

663 | **2.20 Bet Direct No Q 08000 93 66 93 Banded Stakes 3yo+ 0-35 (H)**
£1281 £366 £183   **7f f/sand rnd**   Going 92   -24 Slow   Stalls Outside

635	**DANCING KING** 9 [1] P W Hiatt 8-9-6 (30) P Makin (7) 4/1: 0-504051: Made all, shkn up over 2f out, rdn & 4L clr 1f out, easily:		42a
584	**POOKAS DAUGHTER** 8 [8] J M Bradley 4-9-6 p (35) A Culhane 100/30 FAV: 0-500002: Rear, hdwy to chase wnr fnl 2f, not pace of wnr:	8	28a
394	**COUNTRYWIDE GIRL** 34 [12] A Berry 5-9-6 (30) P Bradley (5) 11/1: 00U-0353: Handy, hdwy to chase wnr 5f out till 2f out, no extra:	1½	25a
584	**BLUE MAEVE** 8 [10] J Hetherton 4-9-6 BL (35) K Dalgleish 9/1: 0006-404: Slowly away, wide, hdwy 5f out, no impress:	shd	24a
584	**PAGEANT** 8 [11] J M Bradley 7-9-6 bl (35) C Catlin 9/1: 0654005: In tch, nvr a factor.	nk	23a
584	**KELTIC FLUTE** 8 [3] Mrs Lucinda Featherstone 5-9-6 vis (35) Lisa Jones (4) 14/1: 000/-0406: Handy, wknd appr fnl 1f.	3	17a
488	**COPPERFIELDS LASS** 21 [9] W G M Turner 5-9-6 P (35) L Treadwell (7) 12/1: 00600-07: Handy, sn lost tch, no dngr.	2	13a
447	**LEONORA TRUCE** 28 [5] R P Elliott 5-9-6 bl (35) J Tate 8/1: 3260-008: Nvr nr ldrs.	1	11a
4371}	**STAR WONDER** 150 [2] B N Doran 4-9-6 bl (35) D Corby (3) 40/1: 0040-9: Nvr nr ldrs:	2½	6a
	TYRRELLSPASS 559 [7] J D Frost 7-9-6 t (35) V Slattery 40/1: 000/000/-0: Nvr a factor:	shd	5a
4389}	**CULMINATE** 148 [4] J E Long 7-9-6 P (35) Natalia Gemelova (7) 33/1: 0/60000-0: Nvr nr ldrs:	5	0a
578	**OUR OLD BOY** 9 [6] J A Gilbert 4-9-6 (35) D R McCabe 8/1: 006/-000: Handy, wknd 3f out.	3	0a
12 Ran	1m 34.35 (8.15) Owner Mr P W Hiatt		Trained at Banbury

664 | **2.50 Bet Direct No Q Claiming Stakes 3yo+ (H)**
£1477 £422 £211   **1m100y f/sand rnd**   Going 92   -29 Slow   Stalls Inside

559	**ALLY MAKBUL** 11 [9] J R Best 4-9-7 (53) N Pollard 7/2 J FAV: 00-14401: Rear, hdwy to lead over 4f out, hdd 2f out, led again ins fnl furlong, drvn out:		51a
633	**GRAND LASS** 8 [2] A Sadik 5-9-7 p (50) N Chalmers (5) 9/2: 046-3412: Handy, styd on for press fnl 1f.	2	46a
512	**BULAWAYO** 18 [6] Andrew Reid 7-9-12 (48) S Donohoe (7) 12/1: 030-5303: Rear, hdwy 4f out, wknd fnl 1f.	½	49a
639+*	**SUDRA** 12 [1] J O'Reilly 7-9-11 bl (47) J D O'Reilly 7/2 J FAV: 0-334434: Led & keen early, remained with ldr, led & trav best over 2f out, rdn & hdd ins fnl furlong, no extra:	½	48a
580	**LOVES DESIGN** 8 [5] Miss J Wilton 7-9-12 (45) A Quinn 12/1: 0-060055: Slowly away rear, hdwy 4f out, wknd fnl 1f.	1½	46a
2702}	**INDIAN MUSIC** 225 [8] A Berry 7-9-12 p (35) P Bradley (5) 33/1: 530000-6: Rear, hdwy & wide straight, nvr dngrs:	¾	44a
589	**EARLSTON** 8 [7] Miss Gay Kelleway 4-9-12 t (64) S Drowne 5/1: 24000-47: Handy, no extra fnl furlong.	5	34a
573	**RIVENDELL** 9 [4] M Wigham 8-9-6 t (30) Dale Gibson 11/2: 0////00-60: Led, hdd over 4f out, wknd & eased when no ch 1f out:	17	0a
4787}	**HYMNS AND ARIAS** 123 [11] Ronald Thompson 3-8-2 (47) T Williams 25/1: 00010-9: Slowly away, wknd & eased 2f out.	18	0a
9 Ran	1m 56.55 (10.35) Owner Mr Malcolm Ward		Trained at Maidstone

665 | **3.20 Littlewoods Bet Direct Median Auction Maiden Stakes 3-5yo (H)**
£1449 £414 £207   **1m1f79y f/sand**   Going 92   +01 Fast   Stalls Inside

559	**GOLDBRICKER** 11 [6] W M Brisbourne 4-9-10 (46) B Swarbrick (7) 11/10 FAV: 3302-651: Handy, led over 4f out till hdd over 2f out, led again over 1f out, drvn out to hold on near fin:		54a
396	**ANGELOS PRIDE** 34 [9] J A Osborne 3-8-3 (57) C Catlin 13/2: 0-302: Handy, led over 2f out till hdd over 1f out, drvn to chall fnl 1f, al held:	hd	53a
583	**KUSTOM KIT FOR HER** 8 [3] S R Bowring 4-9-5 (45) J Bramhill 10/1: 0-600023: Keen, handy, wknd 2f out.	15	18a
	CERTIFIABLE [4] Andrew Reid 3-8-3 C Sarson 11/1: 4: Keen, handy, led 5f out, hdd sn after & no extra 3f out:	1	21a
306	**DANUM** 44 [7] R Hollinshead 4-9-10 p (47) A Culhane 9/1: 56006-45: Midfield, wknd 3f out:	2½	16a
355	**LILIAN** 40 [8] Miss Gay Kelleway 4-9-5 e (40) S Drowne 7/1: 6022-656: Rear, hdwy 5f out, wknd 3f out.	2½	6a
	SECRET CONNECTION [2] M Wigham 4-9-5 Dale Gibson 14/1: 7: Slowly away in rear, fin t.o. on racecourse bow.	dist	0a
	RADMORE SPIRIT [5] G A Ham 4-9-5 V Slattery 66/1: 8: Nvr nr ldrs on AW bow.	3½	0a
	LAURA LEA [1] Ronald Thompson 4-9-10 T Williams 33/1: P: Led till hdd 5f out, fdd & p.u. 4f out:		0a
9 Ran	2m 6.9 (8.7) Owner Mr K Bennett		Trained at Baschurch

666 | **3.50 Betdirect Co Uk Banded Stakes 4yo+ 0-45 (H)**
£1652 £472 £236   **1m4f f/sand**   Going 92   -19 Slow   Stalls Inside

616	**SHATIN SPECIAL** 4 [6] G C H Chung 4-9-0 p (49) R Ffrench 13/2: 02-52F41: Handy, led over 2f out, drvn out nr fin:		48a
554	**PIPSSALIO** 12 [2] Jamie Poulton 7-9-3 t (45) C Catlin 6/1: 00043-62: Rear, hdwy over 1f out, styd on well fnl furlong but not reach wnr:	¾	45a
522	**BEVIER** 15 [9] T Wall 10-9-3 (45) N Chalmers (5) 10/1: 00040-53: Rear, hdwy 3f out, styd on fnl furlong.	nk	44a
575	**DIAMOND ORCHID** 9 [8] P D Evans 4-9-0 (45) R Fitzpatrick 7/4 FAV: 0062-324: Led, hdd over 2f out, no extra fnl furlong:	1	42a

169

2886}	**VITELUCY** 218 [5] Miss S J Wilton 5-9-3 (45) A Quinn (5) 12/1: 00/2100-5: Midfield, outpcd 3f out, kept on ins last:		2½	38a
580	**THINK QUICK** 8 [3] R Hollinshead 4-9-0 (35) R Kennemore (7) 33/1: 040-0566: In tch, rear 3f out:		11	22a
590	**SAN MARCO** 8 [11] Mrs P Sly 6-9-3 bl (45) A Culhane 13/2: 00404-07: Slowly away in rear, nvr nr ldrs.		5	14a
4638}	**COOLING CASTLE** 486 [1] Ronald Thompson 8-9-3 (35) S Donohoe (7) 25/1: 00/00/0/-: Handy, wknd 3f out:		hd	13a
576	**PORT MORENO** 9 [10] J G M O'Shea 4-9-0 BL (45) R Havlin 12/1: 40060-59: Rear, hdwy 5f out, wknd 3f out:		nk	12a
552	**PLATINUM BOY** 12 [4] M Wellings 4-9-0 p (45) V Slattery 50/1: 5000-000: Handy, wknd 4f out, fin t.o..		25	0
	ANGIOLINI 556 [7] A E Jones 7-9-3 (35) S Drowne 11/1: 050300/-0: Slowly away, nvr dngrs on reapp.		11	0
11 Ran	2m 47.0 (13.4)	Owner Mr Peter Tsim		Trained at Newmarket

---

667

4.20 Bet Direct On Sky Text Page 372 Banded Stakes 3yo+ 0-40 (H)

£1460 £417 £209   **6f f/sand rnd**   **Going 92**   **+02 Fast**   Stalls Inside

483	**EVANGELIST** 22 [11] Mrs Stef Liddiard 4-9-7 VIS T (40) S Drowne 6/1: 0000-301: Midfield, hdwy wide 2f out, led ins fnl 1f, rdn out:			46a
582+*	**ENJOY THE BUZZ** 8 [2] J M Bradley 4-9-13 (40) C J Davies (7) 5/1: 4402312: Slowly away, hdwy 3f out, led over 1f out till ins fnl 1f, no extra:		1½	47a
507	**SOTONIAN** 18 [7] P S Felgate 11-9-7 (40) Lisa Jones (3) 9/2 FAV: 5000-533: Led early, remained handy, no extra fnl 1f:		1¼	37a
541	**FLYING FAISAL** 14 [10] J M Bradley 6-9-7 (40) C Catlin 11/1: 0-000604: Rear, styd on fnl 1f, not rch ldrs:		2½	29a
447	**BELLS BOYS** 28 [3] K A Ryan 5-9-7 BL (40) G Parkin 11/2: 0505-335: Handy, edged left over 1f out, wknd fnl 1f:		1¼	25a
528	**LIONS DOMANE** 15 [6] A Berry 7-9-7 (40) P Bradley (5) 2/1: 00000-056: Lled 4f out till 2f out, no extra.		1	22a
641	**LEVELLED** 1 [4] D W Chapman 10-9-7 (40) A Culhane 10/1: 00/000-07: Handy, slt lead 2f out, wknd fnl 1f:		nk	21a
502	**SWEET CORAL** 19 [8] S Rothwell 4-9-7 BL (40) K Dalgleish 8/1: 000-0408: Al bhd:		1½	16a
582	**EJAY** 8 [1] Julian Poulton 5-9-7 (40) M Halford (7) 16/1: 0/-0006-069: Slowly away, nvr nr ldrs:		2½	8a
447	**MAGIC EAGLE** 28 [5] P T Midgley 7-9-7 (40) L Enstone (3) 20/1: 0000/-500: Led till hdd over 2f out, wknd.		8	0a
10 Ran	1m 18.2 (5.4)	Owner Valley Fencing		Trained at Hungerford

---

668

4.50 Bet Direct In Vision Sky Page 293 Banded Stakes 3yo+ 0-40 (H)

£1453 £415 £208   **1m1f79y f/sand**   **Going 92**   **-05 Slow**   Stalls Inside

300	**WILSON BLUEBOTTLE** 45 [11] M W Easterby 5-9-9 bl (40) Dale Gibson 6/4 FAV: 14000-61: Keen, led after 1f, trav well, rdn clr fnl 1f:			47a
522	**UNSUITED** 15 [8] J E Long 5-9-9 (40) Natalia Gemelova (7) 14/1: 6500-032: In tch, hdwy to chase wnr 3f out, no impress fnl 1f:		3½	37a
118	**NASSAU STREET** 80 [13] D J S ffrench Davis 4-9-9 VIS (40) C Catlin 16/1: 040-3: Rear, hdwy 3f out, no impress fnl 2f:		2	33a
4238}	**TIME MARCHES ON** 155 [6] Mrs M Reveley 6-9-9 (40) A Culhane 9/1: 0036/20-4: Rear, styd on late, nvr dngrs:		3½	26a
529	**HIGH DIVA** 14 [5] J R Best 5-9-9 (40) N Pollard 7/1: 006-6465: Rear, hdwy 4f out, wknd 2f out:		1¼	23a
523	**VERMILION CREEK** 15 [12] R Hollinshead 5-9-9 p (30) Stephanie Hollinshead (7) 7/1: 006-5066: Rear, mod gains:		¾	21a
523	**GREENBOROUGH** 15 [3] Mrs P Ford 6-9-9 p (30) R Ffrench 33/1: 0/50/00-07: Handy, wknd 4f out:		9	3a
635	**HAITHEM** 8 [7] D Shaw 7-9-9 e (40) Lisa Jones (3) 10/1: 6000308: Nvr nr ldrs.		3½	0a
522	**AMANPURI** 15 [2] Miss Gay Kelleway 6-9-9 (40) S Drowne 10/1: 0000-049: Led 1f, handy till wknd 3f out.		3	0a
566	**HINCHLEY WOOD** 10 [9] J R Best 5-9-9 (40) L Enstone (3) 10/1: 000/-/60: Handy,wknd 2f out.		½	0a
442	**YNYS** 28 [1] B Palling 3-8-2 (35) D Kinsella 25/1: 55000-00: Nvr nr ldrs.		1½	0a
453}	**COUNTRYWIDE STAR** 390 [10] C N Kellett 6-9-9 (40) K Dalgleish 33/1: 000/000-0: Slowly away, handy, wknd 4f out & fin t.o. on reapp.		dist	0a
12 Ran	2m 7.5 (9.3)	Owner Mr and Mrs B Kelly		Trained at Sheriff Hutton

---

Official Going Standard

669

1.20 Littlewoods Bet Direct Handicap Stakes 4yo+ 46-52 (F)   [65]

£2947 £842 £421   **1m p/track rnd**   **Going 42**   **-14 Slow**   Stalls Outside

600	**ALAFZAR** 7 [2] P D Evans 6-9-1 BL t (52) K Fallon 3/1 FAV: 0040-401: Trkd ldrs, switched & rdn to lead ins last, styd on strongly:			59a
600	**STEELY DAN** 7 [10] J R Best 5-8-13 (50) N Pollard 7/1: 005-0002: Trkd ldrs, rdn & led over 1f out, hdd & no extra in last:		¾	55a
408*	**BALERNO** 34 [11] R Ingram 5-9-0 (51) G Carter 7/1: 05300-13: Rear, styd on wide for press, not able to chall:		nk	55a
4958}	**RANNY** 110 [9] Dr J D Scargill 4-8-13 (50) R Miles (3) 25/1: 504100-4: Keen trkg ldrs, styd on wide for press, not able to chall:		nk	53a
600*	**KINSMAN** 7 [6] T D McCarthy 7-9-7 6ex bl (58) J P Guillambert (3) 11/2: 0600-215: Held up rear, styd on for press.		shd	61a
565	**PIQUET** 11 [4] J J Bridger 6-8-13 (50) G Baker 11/2: 501-3166: Rear, late gains for press, no threat.		shd	52a
476	**RAHEEL** 25 [8] P Mitchell 4-8-12 t (49) J Fanning 10/1: 2060-547: Dwelt, trkd ldrs, briefly led 2f out, no extra dist.		1¾	48a
4396}	**GALEY RIVER** 149 [1] J J Sheehan 5-8-10 (47) N Callan 16/1: 000000-8: Led 1f, cl-up till lost place 2f out.		½	45a
401	**BALMACARA** 35 [7] Miss K B Boutflower 5-8-11 p (48) I Mongan 10/1: 00554-09: Led/dsptd lead 6f, fdd.		nk	45a
401	**ANGELICA GARNETT** 35 [3] T E Powell 4-8-12 e (49) A Quinn (5) 25/1: 6/000-060: Keen & led/dsptd lead 5f.		3	40a
477	**MISTER CLINTON** 25 [7] D K Ivory 7-8-13 T p (50) Dane O'Neill 14/1: 000-0000: Wide, no impress, t-strap.		4	33a
11 Ran	1m 40.65 (4.45)	Owner Waterline Racing Club		Trained at Abergavenny

---

670

1.50 Betdirect Co Uk Maiden Stakes 3yo (D)

£4105 £1263 £632 £316   **7f p/track rnd**   **Going 42**   **+06 Fast**   Stalls Inside

	SAINT ETIENNE [5] A M Balding 3-8-9 Martin Dwyer 5/2 FAV: 1: Made all, pulled clr under hands & heels over 1f out, rdn & styd on strongly ins last:			76a
472	**ALFRIDINI** 25 [12] D R C Elsworth 3-9-0 Dane O'Neill 16/1: 002: Dwelt, mid-div halfway, styd on for press fnl 2f, no threat:		3	71a
568	**LITTLE EYE** 11 [16] J R Best 3-9-0 (66) N Pollard 8/1: 2234-403: Chsd ldrs, carried badly right on bend over 1f out, onepace for press after:		nk	70a
449	**HAZEWIND** 28 [11] P D Evans 3-9-0 S Donohoe (9) 100/1: 00-04: Mid-div, late gains, nvr threat:		1¼	67a
3980}	**INSTINCT** 172 [2] R Hannon 3-9-0 P Dobbs 11/4: 0-5: Trkd ldrs travelling well, hung right from halfway & hung badly right on		3½	60a

3993}	LA PETITE CHINOISE 170 [7] R Guest 3-8-9 (69) K Fallon 13/2: 3406-6: Rdn to go handy, carried badly right over 1f out & wknd:		hd	54a
531	PHLUKE 15 [14] R F Johnson Houghton 3-9-0 (70) S Carson 6/1: 2432-537: Led/dsptd lead till 2f out, sn carried right & btn.		1¼	56a
545	REDBANK 14 [13] S Dow 3-9-0 (60) Paul Eddery 16/1: 4330-208: Mid-div, no impress fnl 2f:		4	48a
	FORGE LANE [3] C Weedon 3-9-0 J Quinn 33/1: 9: Slow away & bhd, mod late gains on debut.		1¾	45a
	FLY SO HIGH [15] D Shaw 3-8-9 Dawn Watson (7) 33/1: 0: Slow away, bhd, mod late prog, debut.		3	34a
4973}	GENUINELY 109 [4] W J Musson 3-8-9 M Fenton 40/1: 00-0: Sn bhd, nvr factor, abs.		1¼	31a
	ACCENDERE [1] R M Beckett 3-9-0 M Tebbutt 33/1: 0: Al bhd, debut.		3	30a
488	MIDNIGHT PROMISE 22 [9] J A Glover 3-9-0 Dean McKeown 66/1: 00: Keen & chsd ldrs 3f, fin lame.		2½	25a
3242}	THREE WELSHMEN 203 [6] B R Millman 3-9-0 (65) S Drowne 25/1: 200050-0: Mid-div, nvr a factor, reapp.		3	19a
4651}	EUNICE CHOICE 133 [10] M J Haynes 3-9-0 R Miles (3) 100/1: 00-0: Al bhd, reapp.		5	10a
15 Ran	1m 25.34 (2.54)	Owner Mr G W Chong		Trained at Kingsclere

---

671 2.20 Bet Direct Claiming Stakes 3yo (F)

£2968 £848 £424 7f p/track rnd Going 42 -12 Slow Stalls Inside

560	FISSION 12 [14] J A Osborne 3-8-10 bl (72) E Ahern 6/1: 4513-631: Handy & led over 1f out, rdn & styd on strongly:			67a
606*	JAOLINS 7 [5] R Hannon 3-8-6 (52) R Smith 11/2: 0060-12: Towards rear, hdwy for press 2f out, chall when rider dropped whip dist, no extra ins last:		1¼	59a
606	LADY PISTE 7 [15] P D Evans 3-8-2 vis t (55) B Swarbrick (2) 14/1: 04-04253: Wide, held up, kept on for press, nrst fin:		2	51a
481	CITY AFFAIR 23 [11] Mrs L C Jewell 3-8-13 p (55) S Donohoe (4) 33/1: 0305-004: Mid-div, kept on onepace fnl 2f:		¾	61a
432	EVER CHEERFUL 32 [6] W G M Turner 3-8-13 p (73) C Haddon (2) 8/1: 346-2105: Keen & cl-up, led 3f out till 1f out, fdd:		¾	60a
510	GOOD VIBRATIONS 19 [3] P F I Cole 3-8-6 (51) J Quinn 7/1: 0002-356: Dwelt, in tch, no impress fnl 2f:		1¼	50a
496	NEVER CRIED WOLF 21 [4] D R C Elsworth 3-9-5 Dane O'Neill 33/1: 607: Slow away & rear, mod prog, no danger:		2	59a
606	STAMFORD BLUE 7 [12] J S Moore 3-8-7 bl (53) Derek Nolan (7) 8/1: 35-24628: Keen, mid-div, no prog fnl 2f.		shd	47a
260	AVERAMI 51 [7] A M Balding 3-8-10 (68) Martin Dwyer 8/1: 0654-9: Held up, nvr danger, abs, op 5/1.		shd	49a
560	FORA SMILE 12 [13] M D I Usher 3-8-11 A Daly 100/1: 000: Keen, rear, drvn & no prog.		½	49a
603	STONOR LADY 7 [8] P W D'Arcy 3-8-4 VIS (56) Paul Eddery (5) 0206-00: Led till 3f out, wknd qckly:		½	41a
592	DULCE DE LECHE 8 [2] S C Williams 3-9-1 bl e (57) B Reilly (5) 14/1: 00-0640: Prom, btn 2f out:		1	50a
402	MUST BE SO 35 [1] J J Bridger 3-8-2 (48) N Pollard 25/1: 0031-500: Sn struggling:		1¼	34a
295	OUT OF MY WAY 46 [9] T M Jones 3-8-0 (35) R Brisland 100/1: 0400-00: Al bhd, abs.		nk	31a
603	GARRIGON 7 [10] N P Littmoden 3-9-1 BL (60) Lisa Jones (3) 5/1 FAV: 002-5040: Reluctant to race & v slow away in 1st time blnks, sn in tch, no impress fnl 3f:		½	45a
15 Ran	1m 26.57 (3.77)	Owner Mr Paul J Dixon		Trained at Upper Lambourn

---

672 2.50 Littlewoods Bet Direct Maiden Stakes 3yo+ (D)

£4124 £1269 £635 £317 1m4f p/track Going 42 -11 Slow Stalls Inside

602	PRIVATE BENJAMIN 7 [4] Jamie Poulton 4-9-10 (56) N Callan 50/1: 43664-01: Mid-div inner, hdwy to lead over 2f out, held on all out cl-home:			64a
116	RESONANCE 81 [6] N A Twiston Davies 3-7-12 (70) Joanna Badger 5/2 FAV: 042-3: Keen, rear, hdwy 3f out, drvn & styd on fnl 1f, just failed:		nk	58a
107	ROME 84 [5] G P Enright 5-9-13 (70) Dane O'Neill 7/1: 64530-3: Mid-div, drvn & chsd ldr over 1f out, no extra ins last:		2	60a
521	KIRAT 18 [9] G L Moore 6-9-13 S Whitworth 33/1: 0//-04: Cl-up 2f out, wknd, fin lame.		8	50a
521	ALISA 18 [10] B I Case 4-9-5 t Lisa Jones (3) 10/1: 035: Keen & prom till 4f out, fdd.		3	41a
521	ELEGANT GRACIE 18 [2] R Guest 4-9-5 (67) K Fallon 11/4: 003-26: Led/dsptd lead 10f, sn btn/eased:		5	34a
	CAPE CANAVERAL 623 [8] G L Moore 5-9-13 I Mongan 9/2: 2/-7: Drvn to go handy early, lost place from halfway.		nk	38a
263	SILISTRA 51 [7] Mrs L C Jewell 5-9-13 vis (50) V Slattery 66/1: 64/0000-8: Mid-div, btn 3f out, abs.		1¼	36a
401	SPIDERS WEB 35 [1] T Keddy 4-9-5 W G Carter 66/1: 0/-009: Keen, rear, no impress 3f out under minimal press, not given hard time & may do better in low grade h'caps.		6	28a
1749}	CROWN AGENT 267 [3] A M Balding 4-9-10 (75) Martin Dwyer 7/1: 6/0022U-0: Led till over 4f out, sn btn, abs.		nk	27a
18	HEKTIKOS 98 [11] S Dow 4-9-10 (57) J Coffill Brown (7) 50/1: 040/00-0: Mid-div, wide, no ch fnl 3f, abs.		22	-3a
11 Ran	2m 35.6 (7.4)	Owner Mrs J Wotherspoon		Trained at Lewes

---

673 3.20 Bet Direct On 0800 32 93 93 Handicap Stakes 3yo 0-80 (D)

£3998 £1230 £615 £308 6f p/track rnd Going 42 -03 Slow Stalls Inside [82]

543*	TORONTO HEIGHTS 14 [6] P W Chapple Hyam 3-9-5 (73) J Quinn 13/8 FAV: 3206-211: Trkd ldrs travelling well, led ins last, rdn & sn asserted, well bckd tho' op 11/8:			82a
532	HELLO ROBERTO 15 [2] M J Polglase 3-9-7 (75) J P Spencer 9/4: 324-0202: Rear, drvn & chsd wnr ins last, all held:		2	76a
609*	SAHARA SILK 6 [5] D Shaw 3-8-12 6ex vis (66) Darren Williams 8/1: 00-00613: Led, drvn & hdd over 1f out, kept on onepace:		shd	67a
494	KURINGAI 21 [3] B W Duke 3-8-13 (67) O Urbina 20/1: 33020-04: Cl-up & led over 1f out till ins last.		1¼	64a
545	BLADES EDGE 14 [1] A Bailey 3-8-4 (58) J Fanning 25/1: 304-05: Dwelt, rear, mod prog:		1½	50a
494	FORZENUFF 21 [4] J R Boyle 3-8-8 (62) D Sweeney 11/1: 1603-506: Keen & trkd ldr till 4f out, lost place 2f out.		nk	53a
592	LITTLE FLUTE 8 [8] T Keddy 3-7-12 4oh (48) Lisa Jones (3) 20/1: 002-4007: Dwelt, held up wide, nvr danger.		1	40a
591*	HEAD OF STATE 8 [7] R M Beckett 3-8-2 6ex vis (56) J Mackay 7/1: 061-0018: Chsd ldrs wide till halfway, sn btn/eased:		3	36a
8 Ran	1m 13.1 (2.7)	Owner Mrs Jane Chapple-Hyam		Trained at Newmarket

---

674 3.50 Bet In Running @ Betdirect Co Uk Handicap Stakes 4yo+ 0-75 (E)

£3402 £972 £486 1m2f p/track Going 42 -06 Slow Stalls Inside [72]

493	MAD CAREW 21 [3] G L Moore 5-10-0 bl e (72) S Whitworth 8/1: 41322-51: Sn handy & trkd ldrs 2f out, rdn to lead ins last, styd on strongly:			80a
607	BANK ON HIM 7 [7] C Weedon 9-9-2 (60) J Quinn 8/1: 00-16122: Dictated pace, qcknd from over 2f out, hdd ins last, not pace of wnr:		2	64a

520*	**TRUE COMPANION 18** [1] N P Littmoden 5-9-8 (66) J P Guillambert (3) 8/1: 1533-013: Mid-div, drvn & kept on onepace:	1¼	68a
513	**SAY WHAT YOU SEE 19** [13] J W Hills 4-9-9 (68) M Hills 20/1: 63200-04: Trkd ldr, onepace for press fnl 2f.	nk	69a
569	**MUST BE MAGIC 11** [12] H J Collingridge 7-9-5 vis (63) N Callan 14/1: 43120-45: Trkd ldrs, no extra over 1f out:	2½	60a
4655}	**SILVALINE 133** [6] T Keddy 5-9-8 (66) G Carter 4/1 FAV: 311033-6: Trkd ldrs, no extra over 1f out, reapp.	nk	62a
480*	**EASTBOROUGH 23** [11] B G Powell 5-9-9 (67) K Fallon 12/1: 00/6-0317: Held up, no impress fnl 2f:	hd	62a
393	**WAR OWL 36** [2] Ian Williams 7-8-13 (57) Lisa Jones (3) 9/1: 550/04-28: Dwelt, rear, only mod prog, no danger.	shd	52a
622	**LEARNED LAD 4** [14] Jamie Poulton 6-9-0 (68) I Mongan 14/1: 0050-259: Chsd ldrs, no impress fnl 2f:	hd	62a
434	**GINGKO 32** [10] P R Webber 7-9-12 (70) W Ryan 14/1: 0066-150: Rear, no impress fnl 2f:	hd	63a
3935}	**BALLY HALL 174** [4] G A Butler 4-10-0 (73) E Ahern 5/1: 011D54-0: Dwelt, rear, eff wide 2f out, sn btn, bckd.	½	65a
147	**DANAKIL 74** [5] S Dow 9-9-12 (70) C Catlin 25/1: 500430-0: Held up, outpcd fnl 3f, abs.	1	61a
369	**MAMORE GAP 39** [8] R Hannon 6-9-12 (70) P Dobbs 12/1: 11050-00: Mid-div, lost place from 2f out.	¾	60a
520	**CORONADO FOREST 18** [9] M R Hoad 5-9-5 (63) Dane O'Neill 66/1: 60-24100: Keen, rear, eff 3f out, sn btn:	7	44a
14 Ran	2m 07.56 (4.76) Owner Mr David Allen		Trained at Brighton

---

675   **4.20 Bet Direct On 0800 32 93 93 Selling Stakes 3yo+   (G)**
£2562 £732 £366   **1m p/track rnd   Going 42   +01 Fast**   Stalls Outside

577*	**XALOC BAY 10** [2] B P J Baugh 6-9-13 (52) Darren Williams 8/1: 60-20011: Made all, rdn & in command fnl 1f:		59a
101	**MARAKASH 84** [9] M R Bosley 5-9-8 T p (51) G Baker 14/1: 30/0000-2: Rear, styd on for press fnl 2f, no danger to wnr:	1	51a
571	**DOLPHINELLE 11** [5] Jamie Poulton 8-9-8 vis (47) I Mongan 7/1: 00535-43: Mid-div, styd on onepace for press fnl 2f:	nk	50a
600	**MUQTADI 7** [6] M Quinn 6-9-8 (49) Martin Dwyer 9/2 CO FAV: 0-030604: Rear, switched & late gains	1	48a
580	**FRENCH HORN 9** [7] M Wigham 7-9-13 p (50) G Carter 9/2 CO FAV: 000-1435: Trkd ldrs, no impress dist:	2	49a
585	**SOCIAL CONTRACT 9** [10] S Dow 7-9-8 vis (47) C Catlin 10/1: 006-0006: Prom, btn over 1f out.	1½	41a
602	**SHOLAY 7** [12] P Mitchell 5-9-8 J Fanning 10/1: 65400-07: Rear, no impress fnl 2f.	nk	40a
4207}	**RYANS BLISS 159** [3] T D McCarthy 4-9-3 (55) J P Guillambert (3) 25/1: 00/0000-8: Chsd wnr, btn dist, reapp.	nk	34a
569	**ROYAL FASHION 11** [1] Miss S West 4-9-3 (58) N Chalmers (5) 9/2 CO FAV: 30206-69: Trkd ldrs, btn over 1f out.	½	33a
566	**MR DINGLAWI 11** [11] D B Feek 3-8-5 BL Lisa Jones (3) 66/1: 00: Keen, rear, no impress, blnks.	5	28a
52	**DEE DEE GIRL 92** [4] R Hannon 3-8-3 (53) R Smith 20/1: 00010-0: Chsd ldrs 4f, sn btn, abs.	11	10a
400	**THINK IT OVER 35** [8] A P Jones 5-9-3 D Sweeney 66/1: 000: Rear, wknd qckly over 2f out.	1¾	2a
12 Ran	1m 39.46 (3.26) Owner Miss S M Potts		Trained at Stoke On Trent

---

676   **4.50 Bet Direct On Itv Page 367 Handicap Stakes 3yo 0-70 (E)**   [77]
£3325 £950 £475   **1m2f p/track   Going 42   -04 Slow**   Stalls Inside

473	**ANOTHER CON 25** [4] Mrs P N Dutfield 3-8-10 (59) R Havlin 8/1: 63-41: Made all & rdn clr from 2f out, styd on strongly for press in last:		67a
473	**JACKIE KIELY 25** [5] T G Mills 3-8-10 (59) R Miles (3) 8/1: 0-062: Mid-div, short of room over 2f out & again over 1f out, styd on for press, no threat:	5	60a
496	**GROUND PATROL 21** [8] A M Balding 3-9-7 (70) Martin Dwyer 9/2: 0-343: Rear, short of room over 2f out, kept on onepace for press:	1½	69a
503*	**NORWEGIAN 20** [2] D R Loder 3-9-2 (65) J P Spencer 7/2: 514: Trkd ldrs, drvn & no extra over 1f out:	shd	64a
497	**KEEPERS KNIGHT 21** [11] P F I Cole 3-9-5 BL (68) K Fallon 5/2 FAV: 055-135: Sn cl-up, drvn & no impress fnl 2f out:	1¼	65a
545	**LADY STRIPES 14** [1] M J Wallace 3-8-11 (60) N Callan 14/1: 060-06: Held up, short of room over 2f out, only mod late gains:	2	54a
365	**TROMPE LOEIL 39** [6] Andrew Reid 3-9-0 (63) S Donohoe (7) 33/1: 50240-07: Dwelt, rear, little prog, new yard.	3	53a
568	**INFIDELITY 11** [10] A Bailey 3-9-4 (67) E Ahern 8/1: 55120-68: Chsd ldrs wide, no impress fnl 2f.	1	56a
291	**CRACKLEANDO 46** [9] N P Littmoden 3-8-10 (59) J P Guillambert (3) 20/1: 000-39: Chsd wnr 3f, struggling from halfway:	4	42a
4213}	**STAGECOACH RUBY 158** [7] G L Moore 3-7-12 1oh c (46) R Brisland 33/1: 360650-0: Rear, eff wide, no impress:	shd	30a
10 Ran	2m 07.44 (4.6) Owner Mrs Jasmine B Chesters		Trained at Seaton

---

Official Going Standard

677   **1.40 Bet Direct On Sky Active Apprentice Maiden Handicap Stakes Div 1 4yo+ 0-60 (F)**   [60]
£2905 £830 £415   **1m f/sand rnd   Going 50   -13 Slow**   Stalls Inside

639	**ACE MA VAHRA 4** [1] S R Bowring 6-8-13 (45) C Haddon (5) 10/1: 003/-6061: Chsd ldrs till lost place halfway, hdwy for press 2f out & led well ins last:		49a
208	**MIDDLEHAM PARK 65** [6] P C Haslam 4-9-6 (52) D Wakenshaw (7) 11/2: 320060-2: Dwelt, rdn chasing ldrs halfway, hdwy to lead ins last, no extra when hdd well in last:	½	54a
416	**MAGIC MAMMAS TOO 35** [8] T D Barron 4-9-7 (53) Laura Jayne Crawford (3) 6/5 FAV: 3226-253: Trkd ldrs, rdn & led over 1f out, hdd ins last & no extra:	1	53a
4447}	**SHOTLEY DANCER 147** [5] N Bycroft 5-8-8 (40) Suzanne France (3) 8/1: 325060-4: Towards rear, styd on for press fnl 2f, nrst fin:	1¼	37a
635	**MATHMAGICIAN 4** [3] R F Marvin 5-8-3 bl (35) N Mem (7) 10/1: 00040-45: Led, hdd over 1f out, wknd:	½	31a
635	**TE ANAU 4** [4] W J Musson 7-7-12 (30) Laura Pike 40/1: 00/0/00/-0: Trkd ldrs, lost place from halfway, no dngr.	1½	23a
4699}	**CROWN CITY 130** [9] B P J Baugh 4-9-2 (48) B Swarbrick 11/1: 060600-7: In tch wide, btn 3f out, reapp.	5	32a
573	**METICULOUS 11** [7] M C Chapman 6-7-12 (30) Dean Williams (7) 6/1: 0-000008: Led 1f, btn halfway.	5	5a
640}	**PERTEMPS WIZARD 366** [7] A D Smith 4-9-1 (47) B O'Neill (5) 33/1: 6400/0-9: Trkd ldrs 4f:	27	0
449	**TANAFFUS 29** [10] D W Chapman 4-10-0 (60) D Fentiman (3) 25/1: 04/56-00: Unruly bef start, dwelt, al bhd.	1½	0
10 Ran	1m 44.4 (5.0) Owner Mr Stuart Burgan		Trained at Edwinstowe

---

678   **2.10 Bet Direct On Sky Active Apprentice Maiden Handicap Stakes Div 2 4yo+ 0-60 (F)**   [60]
£2898 £828 £414   **1m f/sand rnd   Going 50   +03 Fast**   Stalls Inside

617	**REALISM 6** [10] P W Hiatt 4-9-7 (53) P Gallagher 7/1: 0350-441: Trkd ldrs trav well, led 2f out & rdn clr, readily, fair time:		66a

556	BLAKESEVEN 14 [7] W J Musson 4-9-2 (48) A Rutter (5) 15/8 FAV: 0040-322: Chsd ldrs, styd on for press fnl 2f, no ch with easy wnr:	8	49a
635	KENNY THE TRUTH 4 [4] Mrs J Candlish 5-8-8 t (40) Dawn Watson (3) 11/2 000-3233: Rdn towards rear halfway, styd on for press, no threat to wnr:	hd	40a
659	AMANDAS LAD 10 [5] M C Chapman 4-8-13 (45) Andrew Webb (5) 25/1: 30-63404: Chsd ldrs 6f.	1	43a
248	JARRAAF 55 [8] J W Unett 4-9-12 (58) Derek Nolan 9/1: 524244-5: Rdn mid-div & wide halfway, nvr a dngr:	¾	55a
528	VLASTA WEINER 17 [9] J M Bradley 4-8-8 bl (40) B Swarbrick 10/1: 6-025046: Chsd ldrs wide, no extra over 1f out.	nk	36a
637	MIMAS GIRL 4 [6] S R Bowring 5-7-12 bl (30) C Haddon (5) 7/1: 46-50537: Led & clr halfway, hdd 2f out, wknd.	3	20a
579	PHANTOM FLAME 10 [3] M Johnston 4-8-8 (40) W Hogg (3) 7/1: 000-5208: Dwelt, in tch till over 2f out:	5	21a
554	CRYPTOGAM 14 [1] M E Sowersby 4-9-1 (47) A Mullen (5) 66/1: 0440-009: Slow away & al bhd:	14	4a
4093}	MIDGES PRIDE 166 [2] Mrs A Duffield 4-9-3 (49) Dean Williams (3) 40/1: 444000-0: Rear, drvn & bhd fnl 3f, reapp.	10	0a
10 Ran	1m 43.16 (3.76)	Owner Miss Maria McKinney	Trained at Banbury

<hr>

679

2.45 Press Interactive To Bet Direct Claiming Stakes 4yo+ (F)

£2870 £820 £410   1m4f f/sand   Going 50   -13 Slow   Stalls Inside

634	BELLA PAVLINA 5 [6] W M Brisbourne 6-9-5 (56) B Swarbrick (7) 85/40: 6-121141: Trkd ldrs, rdn & led 2f out, styd on strongly, in command dist:		67a
552	THEATRE TINKA 14 [3] R Hollinshead 5-9-2 p (62) A Culhane 5/2: 201-5552: Trkd ldr, led 7f out till 2f out, no extra bef dist	2½	58a
504	AVEIRO 21 [1] B G Powell 8-8-12 bl (51) K Dalgleish 2/1 FAV: 140-2133: Led till 7f out, onepace:	2½	49a
502	FIRST MAITE 21 [2] S R Bowring 11-9-2 (67) J Bramhill 8/1: 602-6664: Dwelt, eff wide 4f out, sn btn.	6	44a
638	KING PRIAM 4 [8] M J Polglase 9-8-6 bl (40) Dean McKeown 20/1: 4506645: Chsd ldrs, lost tch 4f out	nk	33a
644	MANY THANKS 3 [4] B S Rothwell 4-8-12 p (70) M Fenton 16/1: 2444-56: Chsd ldrs till 3f out	23	10a
	AGAIN JANE [7] J M Jefferson 4-8-0 P Fessey 66/1: 7: Lost place from halfway, t.o. on Flat debut, jumps fit (mod bumper form).	19	0
7 Ran	2m 41.86 (7.56)	Owner The Cartmel Syndicate	Trained at Baschurch

<hr>

680

3.20 Bet Direct On 0800 93 66 93 Handicap Stakes Fillies 3yo+ 0-70 (E)   [68]

£3241 £926 £463   7f f/sand rnd   Going 50   +10 Fast   Stalls Inside

657	EAGER ANGEL 10 [2] R F Marvin 6-8-11 6ex p (51) Dean McKeown 9/2: 30-24011: Trkd ldrs, rdn to lead over 1f out, styd on strongly:		59a
597	JESSIE 9 [1] Don Enrico Incisa 5-8-0 t (40) Kim Tinkler 100/30: 00-56522: Chsd ldrs, rdn & outpcd 3f out, styd on for press ins last, no threat:	3	41a
489	ESTIMATION 23 [7] R M H Cowell 4-10-0 (68) S Drowne 11/4 FAV: 3651-363: Reluctant to go to post, chsd ldrs, rdn 3f out, styd on onepace:	1¼	66a
630	CLOUDLESS 5 [3] J W Unett 4-9-3 (57) S Whitworth 4/1: 0015-024: Led till over 1f out, no extra:	¾	54a
564	VICTORY FLIP 13 [6] R Hollinshead 4-8-5 p (45) Stephanie Hollinshead (7) 9/1: 6460-065: Hld up in tch, eff wide halfway, no impress over 1f out:	½	41a
534	DALRIATH 16 [5] M C Chapman 5-8-0 (40) D Fox (5) 20/1: 5000-066: Chsd ldrs, outpcd frm 3f:	4	28a
469	PERTEMPS BIANCA 27 [4] A D Smith 4-8-0 bl (40) J Quinn 16/1: 4006-607: Slow away & lost tch from halfway.	17	0a
7 Ran	1m 29.43 (2.83)	Owner Mr J F Pitchford	Trained at Rolleston

<hr>

681

3.55 Bet Direct Handicap Stakes 4yo+ 0-80 (D)   [76]

£4046 £1245 £623 £311   1m6f f/sand   Going 50   -06 Slow   Stalls Inside

504	VICTORY QUEST 21 [3] Mrs S Lamyman 4-9-6 vis (73) Dane O'Neill 12/1: 5212-001: Trkd ldr & led over 5f out, strongly prsd fnl 3f, drvn out, gamely:		79a
612*	BOX BUILDER 7 [2] H Morrison 7-9-2 6ex (64) L Fletcher (3) 3/1 JT FAV: 00/006/-12: Chsd ldrs, rdn & outpcd 3f out, rallied gamely for press fnl 2f, not reach wnr:	½	68a
594	GEORGE STUBBS 9 [4] M J Polglase 6-9-3 (65) K Fallon 5/1: 632-0623: Cl-up & ch 3f out, rdn & no extra dist	1	67a
478	MACARONI GOLD 26 [6] W Jarvis 4-8-13 BL (66) M Tebbutt 3/1 JT FAV: 03112-04: Trkd ldrs from halfway, onepace for press fnl 2f:	1	68a
529	GLORY QUEST 16 [5] Miss Gay Kelleway 7-9-9 (71) M Fenton 6/1: 552-2035: Held up, eff wide fnl 2f, drvn/no impress.	3½	68a
605	VANBRUGH 8 [1] Miss D A McHale 4-9-10 vis t (77) Darren Williams 11/1: 0226-106: Led, rdn & hdd 6f out, sn bhd:	30	34a
521*	SO VITAL 19 [7] J Pearce 4-9-6 (73) J Quinn 5/1: 62-17: Chsd ldrs, lost place halfway, t.o.:	22	3a
7 Ran	3m 07.6 (7.8)	Owner Mr P Lamyman	Trained at Louth

<hr>

682

4.30 Bet Direct On Sky Text Page 372 Selling Stakes 3yo (G)

£2534 £724 £362   7f f/sand rnd   Going 50   -12 Slow   Stalls Inside

596*	LADY MO 9 [1] K A Ryan 3-8-12 (51) N Callan 6/4 FAV: 50-53511: Trkd ldrs & led over 2f out, rdn & in command ins last:		64a
613	PRINCESS ISMENE 7 [5] P A Blockley 3-8-12 bl (59) K Fallon 2/1: 405-1522: Trkd ldrs, ev ch over 2f out, rdn & not pace of wnr:	2	58a
577	HUNTING PINK 11 [3] H Morrison 3-8-6 BL (48) L Fletcher (3) 5/2: 044-2343: Rear, eff to press front pair over 2f out, edged left & no impress dist:	3	46a
606	ARE YOU THERE 8 [4] P S McEntee 3-8-12 (45) B Reilly (5) 20/1: 0060-064: Chsd ldrs, wknd over 1f out:	6	42a
4813}	AGGI MAC 122 [2] N Bycroft 3-8-6 (45) C Catlin 25/1: 303005-5: Led till over 2f out, sn btn:	3½	29a
5 Ran	1m 30.94 (4.34)	Owner Dr D H Wood	Trained at Hambleton

<hr>

683

5.00 Bet Direct Interactive Handicap Stakes 3yo+ 0-75 (E)   [73]

£3283 £938 £469   1m4f f/sand   Going 50   -08 Slow   Stalls Inside

594*	JAIR OHMSFORD 9 [2] W J Musson 5-9-11 6ex (70) M Fenton 6/5 FAV: 540-1411: Trkd ldrs, chsd ldr from 3f out & led over 1f out, rdn & in command ins last:		77a
594	SURDOUE 9 [6] P Howling 4-9-1 (63) K Fallon 6/1: 005-0242: Trkd ldr & led over 5f out till over 1f out, not pace of wnr:	1¾	66a
595*	CRITICAL STAGE 9 [5] John Berry 5-9-8 6ex e (67) J P Spencer 6/4: 0335-313: Held up, eff to press front pair 2f out, sn rdn & no extra:	3½	65a

173

SOUTHWELL Thursday 19.02.04 Lefthand, Sharp, Oval Track

575	**KNOWN MANEUVER 11** [1] M C Chapman 6-8-0 BL (45) D Fox (5) 66/1: 00/000-44: Chsd ldrs, edged left & no impress fnl 2f:	2½	39a
423	**NOUL 34** [3] K A Ryan 5-9-13 bl (72) N Callan 12/1: 0421-025: Rear, no impress 2f out:	3	62a
441	**BILL BENNETT 31** [4] J Jay 3-8-2 (71) C Catlin 33/1: 3201-606: Led till over 5f out, sn lost place:	1	60a

6 Ran   2m 41.31 (7.04)   Owner Mr K A Cosby   Trained at Newmarket

WOLVERHAMPTON Friday 20.02.04 Lefthand, Sharp track

Official Going SLOW.

684   1.50 Press Interactive To Bet Direct Handicap Stakes Div 1   3yo+ 0-65 (F)   [65]
£2926 £836 £418   7f f/sand rnd   Going 102   -15 Slow   Stalls Outside

585*	**MOUNT ROYALE 11** [5] N Tinkler 6-9-7 6ex vis t (58) Kim Tinkler 6/1: 5-006311: Made all, drvn out fnl 1f to hold on:		65a
585	**PAWN IN LIFE 11** [7] T D Barron 6-9-10 (61) J Fanning 9/1: 051-0002: Handy, chsd ldr dist, kept on fnl 1f, not pace wnr:	1½	64a
459*	**UP TEMPO 29** [8] K A Ryan 6-9-10 bl (61) N Callan 10/3 FAV: 0640-213: Rear, prog wide 3f out, onepcd ins fnl 1f:	½	63a
628	**CARLTON 6** [9] C R Dore 10-9-9 (60) R Thomas (5) 10/1: 5000-044: Bhd, prog 3f out, no impress fnl 1f:	2½	57a
558	**WALTZING WIZARD 14** [2] A Berry 5-8-12 (49) F Lynch 11/2: 052-3545: Cl-up, sn short of room & outpcd, rallying when short of room 3f out, kept on late:	shd	45a
661	**LARKYS LOB 3** [3] Paul Johnson 5-8-10 (47) L Fletcher (3) 7/1: 1453246: Trkd ldrs, ev ch 2f out, wknd fnl 1f:	3½	36a
500*	**ITS ECCO BOY 22** [10] P Howling 6-9-6 (57) K Fallon 5/1: 640-4417: Handy, fdd 2f out:	15	18a
629	**DISPOL PETO 6** [1] Ian Emmerson 4-9-8 bl (59) J Bramhill 11/1: 500-0528: Cl-up 5f, fdd:	½	19a
664	**EARLSTON 3** [6] Miss Gay Kelleway 4-9-3 BL t (64) M Fenton 16/1: 4000-40P: Slow away, al adrift, p.u. & dismounted ins fnl 1f:		0a

9 Ran   1m 34.41 (8.21)   Owner Langton Partnership   Trained at Malton

685   2.20 Press Interactive To Bet Direct Handicap Stakes Div 2   3yo+ 0-65 (F)   [65]
£2919 £834 £417   7f f/sand rnd   Going 102   -16 Slow   Stalls Outside

646	**AGUILA LOCO 4** [2] Mrs Stef Liddiard 5-8-13 p (50) M Fenton 11/1: 3262531: Led, hdd under press just ins fnl 1f, rallied well to lead cl-home, drvn out:		55a
600	**LORD CHAMBERLAIN 9** [9] J M Bradley 11-9-5 bl (56) C Catlin 9/1: 0-214402: Rear, prog 3f out, led ins fnl 1f, sn edged left under press, hdd cl-home:	1¼	58a
589*	**LEGALIS 11** [7] K A Ryan 6-9-9 6ex bl (60) N Callan 8/1: 0-320313: Cl-up, onepcd fnl 1f:	2½	57a
558	**SPINDOR 14** [5] J A Osborne 5-9-8 (59) S Crawford (7) 7/1: 050-2534: Mid-div, no impress fnl 2f.	3	50a
657	**BLAKESHALL QUEST 3** [3] R Brotherton 4-9-9 vis (60) I Mongan 5/1: 00-04445: Cl-up, ev ch 2f out, switched left & wknd dist:	3	45a
266	**CAPTAIN DARLING 52** [8] R M H Cowell 4-9-12 (63) S Drowne 3/1 FAV: 045543-6: Al in rear:	6	36a
629	**WARLINGHAM 6** [4] P Howling 6-9-10 (61) J Fanning 11/2: 0-001157: Mid-div, wknd 3f out:	1¼	31a
513	**YELLOW RIVER 21** [6] R Curtis 4-9-2 (53) Dane O'Neill 25/1: 0000-408: Mid-div, prog 4f out, wknd 2f out:	1¾	19a
68	**VICTORY VEE 91** [10] M Blanshard 4-9-7 (58) J Quinn 12/1: 413003-9: Al in rear:	19	0
657	**PILGRIM PRINCESS 3** [1] E J Alston 6-8-8 (45) D Allan (3) 12/1: 46-35460: V slow away & al bhd:	½	0

10 Ran   1m 34.49 (8.29)   Owner Valley Fencing   Trained at Hungerford

686   2.55 Bet Direct On Sky Active Maiden Stakes   3yo   (D)
£3374 £1038 £519 £260   1m1f79y f/sand   Going 102   -43 Slow   Stalls Inside.

460	**YLANG YLANG 29** [12] W Jarvis 3-8-9 M Tebbutt 7/2: 50-41: Slow away, held up wide, prog wide 3f out, led ins fnl 1f, pushed out, val 2L+:		72a
4834}	**HSI WANG MU 122** [11] R Brotherton 3-8-9 (50) I Mongan 33/1: 450300-2: Held up, prog 4f out, led dist, hdd & no extra ins fnl 1f:	1	69a
531	**ZULOAGO 17** [4] S L Keightley 3-8-9 A Nicholls 33/1: 53: Sn led, hdd after 2f out, fdd fnl 1f.	5	59a
601	**LOOKS THE BUSINESS 9** [3] W G M Turner 3-9-0 t (68) C Haddon (7) 11/2: 445-24: Cl-up, led after 2f out, hdd dist, wknd:	1¼	62a
	HARRY LAD [7] P D Evans 3-9-0 Joanna Badger 33/1: 5: Dwelt, sn adrift, modest late gains:	4	54a
553	**KINGS ROCK 15** [9] K A Ryan 3-9-0 (65) P Fessey 10/3: 53530-26: Cl-up, fdd 3f out:	3	48a
4926}	**STRANGELY BROWN 115** [10] S C Williams 3-9-0 J Mackay 25/1: 00-7: Rear, nvr a factor.	2½	43a
553	**DIVINA 15** [1] S L Keightley 3-8-9 R Havlin 50/1: 08: Led 1f, fdd 5f out.	16	8a
481	**FAIRLY GLORIOUS 25** [6] T H Caldwell 3-9-0 T Eaves (5) 100/1: 009: Cl-up, fdd 4f out.	6	0a
	VIAGRAH [2] M J Polglase 3-9-0 J Quinn 40/1: 0: Al in rear.	5	0a
488	**REGULATED 24** [5] J A Osborne 3-9-0 (67) K Fallon 3/1 FAV: 20450-20: Mid-div, fdd 4f out, t.o.:	14	0a
4927}	**ETERNAL DANCER 115** [8] M Johnston 3-9-0 J Fanning 8/1: 00-0: Cl-upl fdd 4f out:	11	0a

12 Ran   2m 11.72 (13.52)   Owner Mr R A Scarborough   Trained at Newmarket

687   3.30 Bet Direct Interactive Handicap Stakes   3yo+ 0-80 (D)   [78]
£4085 £1257 £629 £314   6f f/sand rnd   Going 102   +09 Fast   Stalls Inside.

550	**JOHNSTONS DIAMOND 15** [11] E J Alston 6-9-8 (72) K Fallon 8/1: 4101-001: Cl-up, styd on to lead fnl 1f, rdn out:		82a
643*	**PLAYTIME BLUE 4** [7] K R Burke 4-9-2 6ex (66) G Baker 8/1: 02-23612: Led, under press dist, hdd cl-home:	nk	73a
660	**TIME N TIME AGAIN 3** [6] E J Alston6-10-0 p (78) J Quinn 4/1 FAV: 5101333: Prom, styd on ins fnl 1f, not btn far:	¾	83a
4969}	**SUPER CANYON 111** [9] J Pearce 6-9-4 vis t (68) N Callan 9/1: 415532-4: Handy, onepcd fnl 1f:	3½	64a
5030}	**ROMANY NIGHTS 104** [13] J W Unett 4-9-11 (75) Dane O'Neill 14/1: 026000-5: Slow away, hdwy dist, nrst fin on reapp:	¾	69a
611	**PRIMA STELLA 8** [12] J A R Toller 5-9-9 (73) Lisa Jones (3) 9/2: 20-41026: In tch wide, wknd dist:	1½	63a
610*	**PANJANDRUM 8** [9] N E Berry 6-9-7 6ex (77) M Savage (5) 16/1: 01-03517: Handy, wknd dist:	½	60a
482	**BOND ROYALE 25** [1] B Smart 4-9-13 (77) M Stainton (5) 20/1: 0040-208: Mid-div, prog 3f out, wknd fnl 1f.	½	65a
551	**ELLENS LAD 15** [10] W J Musson 10-9-6 bl (70) Paul Eddery 20/1: 0/001-059: Cl-up, fdd dist:	2½	51a
618	**SUNDRIED TOMATO 7** [3] P W Hiatt 5-10-0 (78) L Fletcher (3) 5/1: 00-06460: Cl-up, fdd 1f out:	½	58a

WOLVERHAMPTON Friday 20.02.04 Lefthand, Sharp track

2621} **TIDY 232** [2] M D Hammond 4-10-0 (78) A Culhane 40/1: 1/13060-0: Al in rear. ¾ **56a**
532 **FULL PITCH 17** [4] W Jenks 8-9-6 (70) A Nicholls 50/1: 1////-00: Al bhd. 2 **42a**
660 **PRINCE OF BLUES 3** [8] M Mullineaux 6-9-1 (65) P Varley (7) 25/1: 600-0200: Cl-up, fdd 3f out: 4 **25a**
13 Ran 1m 18.41 (5.61) Owner Mollington Golf Club Boys Trained at Preston

688 **4.00 Betdirect Co Uk Handicap Stakes 3yo+ 0-100 (C)** **[92]**
£8515 £2620 £1310 £655 **1m100y f/sand rnd Going 102 +06 Fast** Stalls Inside.

479* **CONSONANT 25** [6] D G Bridgwater 7-9-2 (80) K Fallon 3/1 FAV: 10////-111: Cl-up, led 2f out, edged right under press ins fnl 1f, rdn out: **90a**
519 **TE QUIERO GB 20** [2] Miss Gay Kelleway 6-9-10 e t (88) F Lynch 8/1: 230-0002: Held up, prog wide 3f out, ev ch ins fnl 1f, just held: *nk* **96a**
611 **SANGIOVESE 8** [8] H Morrison 5-9-0 (78) L Fletcher (3) 100/30: 2/301-033: Led, hdd 2f out, wknd dist. 6 **74a**
4888} **THE BONUS KING 118** [10] M Johnston 4-9-7 (85) J Fanning 16/1: 006060-4: Cl-up, outpcd 3f out, rallied late: 3 **75a**
382 **DEL MAR SUNSET 39** [3] W J Haggas 5-9-2 (80) Lisa Jones (3) 100/30: 20003-45: Nvr nrr than mid-div, btr 278. 6 **58a**
532 **KENTUCKY KING 17** [12] P W Hiatt 4-9-7 (85) A Culhane 16/1: 1/4-66: Chsd ldrs, wknd 3f out: 1½ **60a**
611 **EPHESUS 8** [9] Miss Gay Kelleway 4-9-7 vis (85) M Fenton 11/1: 1330-307: Handy, fdd 3f out: *hd* **59a**
4471} **ILE MICHEL 146** [11] J G M O'Shea 7-9-8 (86) R Havlin 20/1: 663210-8: Al in rear: 16 **30a**
625 **AVENTURA 6** [7] M J Polglase 4-9-7 (85) J Quinn 20/1: 35430-09: Cl-up, fdd 3f out: 1½ **26a**
519 **LAKOTA BRAVE 20** [1] Mrs Stef Liddiard 10-9-8 (86) S Drowne 16/1: 25-24000: Held up, nvr a factor: 2 **23a**
RAINBOW WORLD 237 [4] Andrew Reid 4-9-3 (81) A Nicholls 50/1: 05160-0: Rear, prog 5f out, fdd 3f ouit: 8 **4a**
1823} **MADALYAR 266** [5] Jonjo O'Neill 5-9-1 (79) Dane O'Neill 40/1: 311/000-0: Al well adrift: 23 **0a**
12 Ran 1m 54.29 (8.09) Owner The Rule Racing Syndicate Trained at Winchcombe

689 **4.35 Betdirect Co Uk Selling Stakes 4yo+ (G)**
£2527 £722 £361 **1m4f f/sand Going 102 -52 Slow** Stalls Inside.

602 **SUNGIO 9** [7] B G Powell 6-9-10 (53) Dale Gibson 5/2 FAV: 05/05-131: Handy, styd on to lead ins fnl 1f, drvn out: **52a**
580 **PRINCE PROSPECT 11** [4] Mrs L Stubbs 8-9-10 (47) Kristin Stubbs (7) 7/2: 640-0122: Held up, prog 3f out, ev ch ins fnl 1f, just held by wnr: ½ **51a**
666 **THINK QUICK 3** [3] R Hollinshead 4-8-11 (35) H Fellows (7) 16/1: 40-05663: Held up, prog 4f out, no impress fnl 1f: 4 **35a**
630 **DAIMAJIN 6** [2] Mrs Lucinda Featherstone 5-9-10 (56) A Culhane 10/1: 000-1054: Rear, prog to lead 3f out, hdd ins fnl 1f, fdd: ½ **44a**
588 **BESTSELLER 11** [8] J G M O'Shea 4-8-11 R Havlin 7/2: 0-435: Cl-up, led 8f out, hdd 3f out, sn wknd: 9 **21a**
537 **BIRTH OF THE BLUES 17** [1] A Charlton 8-9-5 (35) Dane O'Neill 10/1: 2560-006: Held up, prog 5f out, fdd 2f out: 12 **10a**
3877} **BOJANGLES 179** [11] R Brotherton 5-9-5 (55) L Fletcher (3) 6/1: 004500-7: Nvr nrr than mid-div: 6 **1a**
633 **DUNDONALD 6** [10] M Appleby 5-9-5 BL t (45) S Righton 33/1: 00040-68: Al in rear: ¾ **0a**
939] **MR PERRY 1039** [6] Mrs P Ford 8-9-5 (30) R Ffrench 25/1: 0656/00//-: Rcd keenly, led 4f, fdd 4f out: 18 **0**
4181} **RIVAL 162** [9] S T Lewis 5-9-5 (45) C Catlin 66/1: 0/00000-0: Cl-up, fdd 5f out: *dist* **0**
243 **FINAL LAP 60** [5] S T Lewis 8-9-5 (30) A Nicholls 50/1: 00/0/000-0: Sn rear, nvr a factor: *dist* **0**
11 Ran 2m 52.13 (18.53) Owner Mrs Rachel A Powell Trained at Winchester

690 **5.10 Bet Direct Interactive Handicap Stakes 4yo+ 0-60 (F)** **[57]**
£2940 £840 £420 **2m46y f/sand Going 102 -35 Slow** Stalls Inside.

612 **DOCTOR JOHN 8** [8] Andrew Turnell 7-8-6 p (35) C Catlin 5/2: 0000//-421: Held up, prog 5f out, styd on to lead ins fnl 1f, rdn clr: **42a**
590 **MADIBA 11** [7] P Howling 5-9-12 (55) K Fallon 7/4 FAV: 00-16022: Cl-up, led 1m out, edged right & hdd ins fnl 1f, no extra: 3 **58a**
478 **MAKARIM 27** [4] M R Bosley 8-9-11 p (54) G Baker 7/1: 0063-003: Held up, prog 5f out, ev ch trav v well 2f out, onepcd fnl 1f: ¾ **56a**
304} **SPORTSMAN 414** [3] M W Easterby 5-8-11 bl (40) P Mulrennan (5) 10/1: 0500/3-4: Cl-up, wknd 5f out: 14 **30a**
277 **SASHAY 51** [1] R Hollinshead 6-10-0 (57) Stephanie Hollinshead (7) 5/1: 061434-5: Al in rear: 15 **34a**
576 **KAGOSHIMA 12** [2] J R Norton 9-8-11 vis (40) V Halliday 8/1: 60-22336: Prog to chase ldr 5f out, fdd 4f out. 6 **11a**
4038} **SARIBA 170** [6] A Charlton 5-8-11 (40) Dane O'Neill 14/1: 5/04410-7: Led 1m, fdd 5f out: *dist* **0a**
4901} **SPECTACULAR HOPE 116** [5] J W Mullins 4-8-11 (46) S Drowne 50/1: 055200-8: Mid-div, fdd 5f out: 25 **0a**
8 Ran 3m 51.44 (22.24) Owner Dr John Hollowood Trained at Malton

LINGFIELD Saturday 21.02.04 Lefthand, V Sharp Track

Official Going Standard

691 **1.00 Bet Direct No Q On 08000 93 66 93 Maiden Stakes 3yo (D)**
£4066 £1251 £626 £313 **6f p/track rnd Going 35 -27 Slow** Stalls Inside

543 **SAVIOURS SPIRIT 17** [3] T G Mills 3-9-0 (70) K Fallon 1/4 FAV: 0053-221: Made all, al holding rivals under hands-and-heels from dist: **74a**
4577} **MISTER COMPLETELY 141** [1] J R Best 3-9-0 (52) N Pollard 25/1: 03640-2: Sn chsd wnr, styd on for press, al held: 1¼ **65a**
572 **DOCKLANDS BLUE 14** [8] N P Littmoden 3-8-9 (55) J P Guillambert (3) 11/1: 630-2003: Pushed along rear, styd on for press to take 3rd, not threat to front pair: 1¼ **56a**
KRYSSA [2] G L Moore 3-8-9 I Mongan 16/1: 4: Chsd ldrs, onepace & held dist: 1¼ **52a**
JOANS JEWEL [5] G G Margarson 3-8-9 A McCarthy 33/1: 5: Chsd ldrs, outpcd fnl 2f on debut. 1¼ **48a**
623 **KING OF MEZE 7** [4] G Prodromou 3-9-0 O Urbina 40/1: 06: Chsd ldr, lost pl over 1f out. 6 **35a**
617 **BOOKIESINDEXDOTCOM 8** [7] J R Jenkins 3-8-9 vis (60) J Quinn 8/1: 3222-037: Sn rdn & bhd: ¾ **28a**
290 **LAKESIDE GUY 49** [6] P S McEntee 3-9-0 Dane O'Neill 100/1: 0-08: Slow away & nvr a factor, abs. 4 **21a**
8 Ran 1m 14.14 (3.74) Owner Mr J E Harley Trained at Epsom

692 **1.30 Bet Direct On 0800 32 93 93 Handicap Stakes 3yo+ 0-100 (C)** **[94]**
£8932 £3388 £1694 £770 **5f p/track rnd Going 35 -03 Slow** Stalls Outside

567	**NO TIME** 14 [2] M J Polglase 4-9-0 (80) K Fallon 7/4 FAV: 00-66621: Chsd ldr & led over 1f out, pushed out:			**91a**
567+*	**JUSTALORD** 14 [1] J Balding 6-9-8 p (88) J Edmunds 11/2: 206-0212: Trkd ldrs, hung right for press but styd on ins last:		1¼	**94a**
567	**ZARZU** 14 [8] C R Dore 5-9-6 (86) R Thomas (5) 7/1: 541-3543: Rear, styd on for press, nrst fin:		nk	**91a**
618	**HURRICANE COAST** 8 [7] D Flood 5-9-1 (81) J P Spencer 9/1: 3132004: Mid-div, onepce for press.		¾	**84a**
567	**DANCING MYSTERY** 14 [5] E A Wheeler 10-10-0 bl (94) S Carson 6/1: 0133-135: Prom, no extra ins last:		1½	**92a**
567	**PALAWAN** 14 [10] A M Balding 8-9-2 (82) L Keniry (3) 25/1: 0102-006: Broke well & led till dist, fdd:		½	**78a**
618	**TYPE ONE** 8 [9] J J Quinn 6-9-0 (80) R Winston 25/1: 321-0107: Sn nrn & al outpcd:		3½	**65a**
3826}	**CHICO GUAPO** 182 [6] J A Glover 4-8-13 (79) Dean McKeown 33/1: 441015-8: Slow away, in tch, outpcd fnl 2f:		nk	**63a**
567	**TRINCULO** 14 [3] N P Littmoden 7-9-8 e (88) J P Guillambert (3) 25/1: 160-000U: Rdn towards rear & no impress when badly hmpd ins last & u.r.:			**0a**
3970}	**OK PAL** 175 [4] T G Mills 4-9-12 (92) R Miles (3) 7/1: 610/04-U: Sn bhd, rdn & mod late prog when clipped heels ins last & u.r.:			**0a**
10 Ran	59.68 (1.88) Owner Mr Paul J Dixon		Trained at Newark	

693

2.05 Littlewoods Bet Direct Winter Derby Trial Conditions Stakes 4yo+   (B)
£15028 £5700 £2850 £1296   **1m2f p/track**   **Going 35**   **+08 Fast**   Stalls Inside

433	**GRAND PASSION** 35 [5] G Wragg 4-8-12 (104) K Fallon 13/8 FAV: 12032-21: Mid-div, hdwy 2f out & styd on strongly under hand riding to lead close home:			**106a**
433*	**EASTERN BREEZE** 35 [9] P W D'Arcy 6-8-13 (102) Paul Eddery 8/1: 1666-412: Handy & led over 1f out, rdn & hdd well ins last, no extra:		nk	**103a**
	CORRIOLANUS 216 [1] P Mitchell 4-8-12 J Quinn 66/1: 33/1263-3: Trkd ldrs, rdn & short of room over 1f out, styd on for		1	**102a**
4599}	**BONECRUSHER** 23 [3] D R Loder 5-9-2 vis J P Spencer 5/1: 64140-64: Rear, hdwy for press over 1f out, not able to chall front pair:		shd	**105a**
519*	**BLUE SKY THINKING** 21 [11] K R Burke 5-9-2 (102) Darren Williams 9/1: 16334-15: Switched start & rear on inner, short of room dist, late gains for press, no dngr:		1¾	**103a**
570	**LYGETON LAD** 14 [10] Miss Gay Kelleway 6-8-13 t (103) M Fenton 10/1: 0101-556: Held up wide, no impress fnl 2f:		2	**97a**
2659}	**VINTAGE PREMIUM** 231 [4] R A Fahey 7-8-13 (104) T Quinn 25/1: 624320-7: Led till 5f out, lost pl 2f out:		hd	**96a**
4042}	**BOURGAINVILLE** 171 [7] A M Balding 6-8-13 (109) Martin Dwyer 4/1: 455026-8: Mid-div wide, no extra dist:		nk	**95a**
622	**EASTER OGIL** 7 [2] Jane Southcombe 9-8-13 (64) V Slattery 200/1: 033240-9: Held up, no ch fnl 2f:		1	**94a**
511	**HAIL THE CHIEF** 22 [6] D Nicholls 7-9-2 (96) A Nicholls 20/1: 0/650-140: Trkd ldr & led 5f out till over 1f out.		shd	**97a**
569	**BELTANE** 14 [8] W de Best Turner 6-8-13 (40) S Righton 500/1: 100/0/P-00: Lost pl from 3f out, highly tried.		dist	**0**
11 Ran	2m 05.47 (2.67) Owner Mr H H Morriss		Trained at Newmarket	

694

2.40 Littlewoods Bet Direct Handicap Stakes 3yo 0-85   (D)   **[91]**
£4771 £1468 £734 £367   **1m p/track rnd**   **Going 35**   **-08 Slow**   Stalls Outside

432	**ROYAL WARRANT** 35 [5] A M Balding 3-9-2 (79) Martin Dwyer 5/1: 4310-361: Trkd ldrs, pushed along halfway & rdn over 2f out, drvn & led cl-home:			**87a**
623*	**HEVERSHAM** 7 [6] W J Haggas 3-9-2 (79) M Hills 5/4 FAV: 412: Led, rdn dist, drvn & hdd cl-home:		½	**85a**
432*	**SECRET PLACE** 35 [3] E A L Dunlop 3-9-7 (84) K Fallon 2/1: 02-113: Trkd ldr, rdn to chall over 1f out, no extra ins last:		2½	**85a**
432	**WESTERN ROOTS** 35 [2] P F I Cole 3-9-4 (81) S Drowne 40/1: 140-24: Held up, eff 2f out, not able to chall:		nk	**81a**
381	**MUGEBA** 40 [1] W J Musson 3-8-1 (64) Lisa Jones (3) 20/1: 02-55: Keen, rear, no impress fnl 2f:		5	**54a**
5 Ran	1m 39.6 (3.4) Owner The Queen		Trained at Kingsclere	

695

3.15 Betdirect Co Uk Handicap Stakes 4yo+ 0-95   (C)   **[90]**
£7279 £2761 £1381 £628   **1m4f p/track**   **Going 35**   **-24 Slow**   Stalls Inside

493*	**MISSION TO MARS** 24 [6] P R Hedger 5-9-9 (85) J P Spencer 1/1 FAV: 11112-11: Held up in tch, smooth hdwy 2f out & qcknd/led ins last, readily:			**97a**
605	**NAWAMEES** 10 [1] G L Moore 6-9-6 (82) I Mongan 9/4: 6/5236-42: Trkd ldrs, led 2f out, drvn & hdd ins last, not pace of wnr:		1¼	**88a**
4572}	**PAGAN DANCE** 141 [5] Mrs A J Perrett 5-10-0 p (90) Dane O'Neill 16/1: 501440-3: Held up, eff to chase ldr 2f out, no extra dist:		1½	**94a**
605	**BRILLIANT RED** 10 [4] Jamie Poulton 11-9-4 t (80) C Catlin 14/1: 003-0064: Held up, eff wide fnl 2f, not able to chall:		¾	**83a**
642	**YORK CLIFF** 5 [2] W M Brisbourne 6-8-13 (75) K Fallon 10/1: 200-0545: Keen & chsd ldr aft 3f, led 6f out till over 2f out, no extra:		3½	**73a**
605	**TYPHOON TILLY** 10 [3] C R Egerton 7-8-13 (75) S Drowne 7/1: 033-6436: Keen & chsd ldrs till over 2f out, sn btn.		2½	**69a**
4876}	**GRALMANO** 120 [8] K A Ryan 9-9-12 (88) F Lynch 25/1: 103102-7: Led till 6f out, sn bhd:		8	**71a**
7 Ran	2m 37.47 (8.27) Owner Mr Ian Hutchins		Trained at Chichester	

696

3.45 Betdirect Co Uk Claiming Stakes 3yo   (E)
£3494 £1075 £538 £269   **1m p/track rnd**   **Going 35**   **-06 Slow**   Stalls Outside

623	**AFRICAN DREAM** 7 [1] P F I Cole 3-9-5 K Fallon 3/1: 31: Trkd ldrs, led over 1f out, in command under hands & heels from			**84a**
626	**BLUE EMPIRE** 7 [3] P A Blockley 3-9-3 (78) J P Spencer 5/2 FAV: 21-45142: Dwelt & held up, smooth hdwy 2f out, onepace for press ins last:		1¾	**77a**
626	**MAYBE SOMEDAY** 7 [4] I A Wood 3-8-11 P (67) I Mongan 6/1: 13-34633: Mid-div, drvn & styd on onepace, not pace of front pair:		4	**64a**
4293}	**ECCENTRIC** 157 [2] Andrew Reid 3-9-5 J P Guillambert (3) 50/1: 0-4: Led till over 1f out, no extra:		1¼	**69a**
603	**EVEN EASIER** 10 [8] G L Moore 3-8-4 p (53) S Whitworth 8/1: 4126-005: V slow away, sn mid-div, btn over 1f out.		3	**48a**
4962}	**STEPPENWOLF** 113 [7] W de Best Turner 3-8-9 (47) S Righton 100/1: 0000-6: Held up, no impress fnl 2f:		3½	**46a**
474	**ROWAN PURSUIT** 28 [6] J Akehurst 3-9-0 bl (69) J Fanning 3/1: 131-1357: Held up, eff over 2f out, sn btn:		nk	**50a**
28	**MISTRESS HOLLIE** 99 [5] Mrs P N Dutfield 3-8-0 p (35) D Kinsella 66/1: 000-8: Prom, btn over 2f out, abs.		hd	**35a**
682	**ARE YOU THERE** 10 [11] P S McEntee 3-7-13 (45) J F McDonald (5) 33/1: 0060-069: Mid-div wide, no impress fnl 2f.		1½	**31a**
601	**LIVIA** 10 [10] J G Portman 3-9-0 R Havlin 40/1: 060: Keen & chsd ldr, wknd qckly 2f out.		shd	**46a**
623	**SHANNKARAS QUEST** 7 [9] P F I Cole 3-8-9 J Quinn 20/1: 00: Sn bhd.		15	**15a**
11 Ran	1m 39.46 (3.26) Owner P F I Cole Ltd		Trained at Whatcombe	

697	**4.20 Littlewoodscasino Com Maiden Stakes 3yo+ (D)**
	£3799 £1169 £585 £292 **1m p/track rnd** **Going 35** **-05 Slow** Stalls Inside

4981}	**TIGER TIGER 111** [2] Jamie Poulton 3-8-7 J Mongan 16/1: 0-1: Chsd ldrs, hmpd 3f out, styd on for press to lead well in last:		76a
430	**SEWMORE CHARACTER 35** [10] M Blanshard 4-9-12 (72) K Fallon 11/4: 0462-462: Settled mid-div, hdwy to lead ins last, drvn & hdd well in last, no extra:	¾	74a
566	**GREEN FALCON 14** [11] J W Hills 3-8-7 M Hills 8/1: 033: Chsd ldr, led 3f out, hdd ins last & no extra:	2	70a
781}	**LAWOOD 132** [8] K A Ryan 4-9-12 BL N Callan 9/1: 504530-4: Held up, eff fnl 2f, onepace for press:	1½	67a
438	**SILVER CACHE 33** [3] J Noseda 3-8-2 C Catlin 25/1: 005: Pushed along rear, mod late gains:	2	58a
514	**PRIORS DALE 21** [9] K Bell 4-9-12 (70) Dane O'Neill 10/1: 4020-266: Slow away, sn handy wide 7f.	1¼	60a
471	**BEST BEFORE 28** [1] P D Evans 4-9-12 (56) S Donohoe (5) 16/1: 42065-07: Led 1f, outpcd from halfway.	1	58a
	BALLINGER EXPRESS [4] A M Balding 4-9-7 Martin Dwyer 14/1: 8: Slow away & rear, nvr factor:	1½	50a
	MANDAHAR [6] A W Carroll 3-9-12 M Tebbutt 50/1: 9: Sn outpcd on debut.	shd	55a
566	**TIME FLYER 14** [5] W de Best Turner 4-9-12 (40) S Righton 100/1: 0000-00: Led after 1f till 3f out, wknd qckly.	3	47a
514	**SPINNING DOVE 21** [7] N A Graham 4-9-7 (67) J P Spencer 6/4 FAV: 6423-32R: Ref to race:		0a
11 Ran	1m 39.42 (3.22) Owner Mr R W Huggins	Trained at Lewes	

698	**4.55 Littlewoodspoker Com Handicap Stakes 3yo+ 0-75 (E)**		[74]
	£3465 £1066 £533 £267 **7f p/track rnd** **Going 35** **-11 Slow** Stalls Inside		

4619}	**HARRISON POINT 138** [14] P W Chapple Hyam 4-9-13 (73) J P Spencer 9/4 FAV: 610230-1: Switched start & held up mid-div, hdwy when short of room dist, drvn & narrow lead ins last, all out:		79a
628	**SUPERCHIEF 7** [8] Miss B Sanders 9-9-4 bl t (64) J Quinn 12/1: 0643552: Held up, prog when short of room dist, switched & drvn/styd on well, just denied:	hd	69a
600	**MAYZIN 10** [1] R M Flower 4-9-2 p (62) Dane O'Neill 8/1: 4-324123: Led, rdn & narrowly hdd in last, just held cl-home:	1	65a
565*	**ZAFARSHAM 14** [16] P D Evans 5-9-2 (62) K Fallon 7/1: 050-1414: Held up in tch wide, hdwy to lead briefly ins last, no extra nr fin:	hd	64a
571	**THE GAIKWAR 14** [5] N P Littmoden 5-9-3 bl (63) I Mongan 12/1: 404-6425: Held up in tch, short of room over 1f out, kept on, not pace to chall:	¾	64a
55	**FEARBY CROSS 95** [15] W J Musson 8-9-6 (66) Lisa Jones (3) 33/1: 144000-6: Held up, eff wide over 1f out, no extra ins	nk	66a
628	**TAYIF 7** [6] Andrew Reid 8-9-6 t (66) S Carson 20/1: 3-211267: Keen, eff wide, no extra dist:	shd	66a
604	**SIR FRANCIS 10** [7] J Noseda 6-9-8 (68) Paul Scallan 9/2: 4060-008: Trkd ldrs, no extra fnl 1f:	hd	67a
144*	**COLD CLIMATE 77** [11] Bob Jones 9-9-5 (65) O Urbina 14/1: 051521-9: Chsd ldrs wide, poised to chall when squeezed out dist, no ch after:	¾	63a
517	**CONCER ETO 21** [9] S C Williams 5-9-11 p (71) Martin Dwyer 33/1: 01200-00: Mid-div, eff wide 2f out, no extra.	½	68a
604	**MISTRAL SKY 10** [12] Mrs Stef Liddiard 5-10-0 vis (74) M Fenton 14/1: 10010-20: Trkd ldrs, wknd ins last:	nk	70a
604	**CURRENCY 10** [3] J M Bradley 7-9-12 (72) S Drowne 20/1: 0-032400: Chsd ldrs, btn dist:	hd	67a
516	**TEMPER TANTRUM 21** [10] Andrew Reid 6-9-3 p (63) J P Guillambert (3) 12/1: 023-5520: Rear, eff wide, no dngr.	shd	58a
513	**HARRY POTTER 22** [2] K R Burke 5-9-5 (65) Darren Williams 40/1: 32213-00: Trkd ldr, wknd over 1f out.	1¼	57a
4701}	**PAGAN STORM 132** [13] Mrs L Stubbs 4-9-11 (71) Kristin Stubbs (7) 100/1: 036146-0: Slow away & sn bhd, reapp.	5	54a
15 Ran	1m 26.04 (3.24) Owner R E Sangster M O'Donovan F C	Trained at Newmarket	

Official Going Slow

699	**2.05 Littlewoods Bet Direct Amateur Riders' Claiming Stakes 4yo+ (G)**
	£2940 £840 £420 **1m100y f/sand rnd** **Going 105** **-35 Slow** Stalls Inside

569	**SCOTTISH RIVER 16** [10] M D I Usher 5-11-5 (62) Mr L Newnes (5) 7/2: 03-30151: Slow away & rear, smooth hdwy from halfway & led over 1f out, edged left under press, pushed out:		74a
593	**CLOUD DANCER 13** [13] K A Ryan 5-11-0 (73) Mr M Seston (5) 7/4 FAV: 310-3022: Prom & smooth prog to chall 2f out, sn rdn & not pace of wnr:	3	62a
186	**CRUSOE 73** [2] A Sadik 7-11-1 bl (61) Miss E J Jones 10/1: 350440-3: Led till over 1f out, drvn & onepace:	1	61a
620	**ZAHUNDA 10** [6] W M Brisbourne 5-10-0 (40) Mr C Davies (7) 10/1: 00-60204: Dwelt & rdn/bhd halfway, late gains for press, nrst fin:	1	44a
661*	**FEAST OF ROMANCE 6** [8] P Howling 7-10-9 bl (58) Miss F Guillambert (7) 12/1: 1326215: Held up, eff from halfway, no extra fnl 2f:	1½	50a
479	**PASO DOBLE 28** [12] B R Millman 6-10-13 (61) Mr J Millman (7) 6/1: 000-5026: Chsd ldrs, lost pl after 3f, mod prog.	shd	54a
575	**EFFIE GRAY 15** [1] J W Unett 5-10-0 (45) Mr B King (5) 50/1: 003/56-07: Mid-div, lost pl bef halfway, nvr factor:	1¾	38a
689	**DUNDONALD 3** [3] M Appleby 5-10-5 bl t (40) Miss F Turner (7) 66/1: 0040-608: Sn hmpd & bhd, no dngr.	5	34a
362	**FORTY FORTE 45** [11] Miss S J Wilton 8-10-9 (50) Mr A Swinswood (7) 33/1: 0020-009: In tch halfway, btn 3f out:	5	29a
440	**OPEN HANDED 35** [9] B Ellison 4-11-1 t (40) Miss L Ellison (3) 50/1: 00000-60: Mid-div, eff 4f out, sn struggling.	5	26a
434	**DUSK DANCER 37** [4] B J Meehan 4-10-11 BL (61) Miss J Allison 14/1: 40-400: Keen & chsd ldr 7f:	dist	0a
143	**DEVIOUS PADDY 82** [5] N Tinkler 4-11-1 T (68) Miss A Rothery (7) 33/1: 206305-0: Sn bhd, t.o., abs, t-strap.	3	0a
397	**PORT NATAL 40** [7] P Morris 6-11-1 Mr I T Amond 14/1: 0501-02U: Chsd ldrs halfway, wknd 3f out, bhd/u.r. ins last.		0a
13 Ran	1m 58.08 (11.88) Owner Mr M D I Usher	Trained at Lambourn	

700	**2.40 Bet Direct No Q Demo 08000 837 888 Handicap Stakes 4yo+ 0-85 (D)**		[85]
	£4108 £1264 £632 £316 **1m100y f/sand rnd** **Going 105** **-05 Slow** Stalls Inside		

632*	**VORTEX 9** [6] Miss Gay Kelleway 5-9-12 e t (83) M Fenton 9/4 FAV: 160-1111: Hld up, smooth prog over 2f out, qcknd to lead over 1f out, drvn out:		91a
586*	**CAROUBIER 14** [1] J Gallagher 4-9-2 (73) J P Spencer 5/1: 224-5212: Dwelt, rear, hdwy wide over 2f out & drvn to press wnr ins last, no extra cl home:	½	79a
632	**ARC EL CIEL 9** [4] Mrs Stef Liddiard 6-9-6 vis (77) S Drowne 9/2: 2-135003: Led/dsptd lead, rdn & briefly led over 1f out, no	2½	78a

extra ins last:

565	**MUSICAL GIFT 16** [5] C N Allen 4-8-13 (70) I Mongan 3/1: 2240-144: In tch, rdn to chall over 1f out, no extra dist:	hd	70a
513	**BALLYRUSH 24** [2] K R Burke 4-8-10 (67) R Keogh (7) 40/1: 00/600-05: Trkd ldrs, rdn & no extra over 1f out:	3	61a
249	**HOWS THINGS 59** [7] D Haydn Jones 4-8-13 (70) Paul Eddery 9/2: 311223-6: Trkd ldrs, rdn & no impress over 1f out:	1	62a
386	**RONNIE FROM DONNY 41** [3] B Ellison 4-9-1 (72) T Eaves (5) 20/1: 0001-407: Keen & sn led, hdd over 1f out & fdd:	8	50a

7 Ran   1m 55.54 (9.34)   Owner Coriolis Partnership   Trained at Newmarket

---

701   3.15 Bet Direct No Q On 08000 93 66 93 Maiden Stakes 3yo+   (D)
£3315 £1020 £510 £255   **1m4f f/sand**   Going 105   -30 Slow   Stalls Inside

	JOMACOMI [6] M Johnston 3-8-3 J Fanning 3/1: 1: Went right start, sn led, rdn clr over 2f out, eased nr fin:		80a
3900	**CALVADOS 537** [1] John A Quinn 5-9-13 BL J Quinn 7/1: 4/036/-2: Held up, styd on for press to chase wnr 2f out, nvr any threat:	7	68a
644	**IMPERATIVE 7** [4] Miss Gay Kelleway 4-9-10 T (70) M Fenton 10/1: 5000-463: Chsd ldr after 4f, rdn & ch 3f out, sn no extra:	7	58a
624	**PONT NEUF 9** [2] J W Hills 4-9-5 t (55) M Hills 11/1: 0200-004: Handy, btn 3f out.	3	49a
644	**VIVRE SA VIE 7** [3] Sir Mark Prescott 3-7-12 J Mackay 8/11 FAV: 4325: Keen & led 1f, remained handy, rdn & lost pl from over 3f out:	9	37a

5 Ran   2m 49.74 (16.14)   Owner Mr T McDonagh   Trained at Middleham

---

702   3.50 Bet Direct On Atr Text Page 410 Handicap Stakes 3yo 0-85 (D)   [88]
£4007 £1233 £617 £308   **1m1f79y f/sand rnd** Going 105   +09 Fast   Stalls Inside

608*	**RED LANCER 11** [3] R J Price 3-8-8 (68) B Swarbrick (5) 14/1: 5010-611: Held up, hdwy wide over 2f out & led over 1f out, readily:		82a
601*	**COME WHAT JULY 12** [5] R Guest 3-8-13 w (73) J P Spencer 12/1: 02023-12: Held up in tch, styd on for press fnl 2f, not pace of wnr:	3½	77a
470	**GAVROCHE 31** [1] M J Wallace 3-8-11 (71) K Fallon 5/6 FAV: 400-123: Led after 2f, rdn & hdd over 1f out, onepace:	1	73a
662*	**DISPOL VELETA 6** [6] T D Barron 3-7-12 6ex 1oh (57) D Mernagh 3/1: 0-3014: Held up in tch, rdn & no impress 1f out:	1½	57a
88	**WEET A HEAD 91** [2] R Hollinshead 3-9-7 (81) A Culhane 6/1: 143265-3: Led early, remained handy, rdn & no extra over 2f out:	6	70a
497	**DESERT IMAGE 26** [7] C Tinkler 3-9-1 (75) J Quinn 20/1: 0330-126: Led 2f, trkd ldrs till over 2f out:	nk	63a

6 Ran   2m 07.22 (9.02)   Owner Fox and Cub Partnership   Trained at Hereford

---

703   4.25 Betdirect Co Uk Selling Stakes 3yo   (G)
£2520 £720 £360   **5f f/sand rnd**   Going 105   +04 Fast   Stalls Inside

560	**EMARADIA 17** [4] A W Carroll 3-8-13 bl (54) I Mongan 5/2: 22-31201: Led/dsptd led, rdn & outpcd halfway, styd on for press to lead well in last despite rider dropping whip:		61a
548	**LIZHAR 19** [1] M J Polglase 3-8-13 BL (60) J P Spencer 5/2: 5-464042: Led, rdn/edged left over 1f out, hdd well in last:	1	57a
619	**LAVISH TIMES 10** [3] A Berry 3-9-4 bl (45) F Lynch 20/1: 0030-053: Chsd ldrs, not pace to chall front pair:	2	57a
606	**REHIA 12** [5] J W Hills 3-8-13 (49) M Hills 6/1: 50-06544: Trkd ldrs wide halfway, outpcd over 1f out:	1¼	49a
591	**BELLA BOY ZEE 13** [6] P A Blockley 3-8-13 (54) D Nolan (5) 2/1 FAV: 0000-325: Chsd ldrs, no impress over 1f out:	5	37a
614	**DUGGANS DILEMMA 11** [2] Ian Emmerson 3-8-12 VIS (48) P Makin (7) 40/1: 0500-06: Sn outpcd in first time visor:	8	17a
197	**ANATOM 70** [7] M Quinn 3-8-7 (35) D R McCabe 66/1: 000660-7: Sn well outpcd:	2	7a

7 Ran   1m 05.25 (5.05)   Owner Mr Dennis Deacon   Trained at Alcester

---

704   5.00 Bet Direct In Running On Sky Text Page 293 Handicap Stakes 4yo+ 0-75 (E)   [74]
£3367 £1036 £518 £259   **7f f/sand rnd**   Going 105   -06 Slow   Stalls Outside

611	**WARDEN WARREN 11** [10] Mrs C A Dunnett 6-9-11 bl (71) B Reilly (5) 12/1: 021-3461: Held up, hdwy for press over 2f out & led dist, drvn out:		75a
632	**YORKER 9** [9] Ms Deborah J Evans 6-9-7 (67) S Drowne 7/1: 20-25342: Chsd ldrs, drvn & styd on well fnl 1f:	hd	71a
647	**GIVEMETHEMOONLIGHT 7** [8] Mrs Stef Liddiard 5-8-10 vis (56) I Mongan 3/1 FAV: 3536123: Held up, styd on for press fnl 2f, not pace of wnr cl-home:	½	59a
499	**DANIELLES LAD 26** [4] B Palling 8-9-6 bl (66) M Fenton 6/1: 005-4204: Chsd ldrs, short of room 2f & onepace when swtchd wide dist, styd on well close home:	¾	68a
	GRANT 135 [5] P Morris 4-9-4 P (64) J Quinn 25/1: 016004-5: Trkd ldrs trav well, rdn & led over 2f out, hdd dist & no extra:	4	58a
20	**DORCHESTER 102** [12] W J Musson 7-10-0 (74) Paul Eddery 12/1: 013053-6: Chsd ldrs till no extra dist:	½	67a
684	**PAWN IN LIFE 3** [7] T D Barron 6-9-0 (60) P Makin (7) 7/1: 51-00027: Dwelt, towards rear, nvr able to chall:	¾	52a
684*	**MOUNT ROYALE 3** [1] N Tinkler 6-9-3 6ex vis t (63) Kim Tinkler 8/1: 0063118: Led till over 2f out, fdd:	3	49a
4807}	**TANTRIC 128** [3] J O'Reilly 5-9-6 (66) J D O'Reilly (7) 33/1: 011000-9: Trkd ldrs, wknd qckly from dist:	3½	45a
245	**MISTER MAL 59** [11] B Ellison 4-8-10 bl e (56) T Eaves (5) 20/1: 240053-0: Slow away, lost chance start, abs.	4	27a
550	**NOBLE LOCKS 18** [6] J W Unett 6-9-10 (70) D Corby (3) 33/1: 0051-000: Held up, struggling halfway:	¾	40a
439	**HENRY AFRIKA 35** [7] Gerard McArdle 6-9-12 p (72) J P Spencer 100/30: 00/005-00: Sn rdn & bhd, eased over 1f out:	dist	0

12 Ran   1m 33.95 (7.7)   Owner Annwell Inn Syndicate   Trained at Norwich

---

Official Going STANDARD

705   1.55 Bet Direct No Q On 08000 93 66 93 Banded Stakes 4yo+ 0-45 (H)
£1656 £473 £237   **1m2f**   Going 44   -15 Slow   Stalls Inside

602	**LANDESCENT 12** [1] Miss K M George 4-8-13 (45) Derek Nolan (7) 12/1: 660-0451: Made all, clr 2f out, edged right ins fnl 1f, drvn to hold on nr fin:		49a
649*	**WANNA SHOUT 7** [6] R Dickin 6-9-6 (45) Lisa Jones (3) 9/1: 0004-212: Midfield, hdwy over 2f out, drvn & styd on fnl 1f but just held:	nk	54a

4864}	ON GUARD 122 [4] P G Murphy 6-9-0 vis (45) D Kinsella 8/1: 000650-3: Midfield, hdwy over 2f out, no extra nr fin:	½	47a
649	CHOCOLATE BOY 7 [13] G L Moore 5-9-0 bl e (45) S Whitworth 7/2: 00/00-524: Rear, hdwy over 1f out, onepcd fnl 1f:	½	46a
542	PYRRHIC 19 [7] R M Flower 5-9-0 bl (45) E Ahern 8/1: 5-302065: Rear, some late gains:	shd	45a
537*	MONTOSARI 20 [3] P Mitchell 5-9-0 (45) D Holland 9/4 FAV: 04600-16: Handy, onepcd over 1f out.	hd	44a
649	EUROLINK ZANTE 7 [2] T D McCarthy 8-9-0 bl (45) L Keniry (3) 21/1: 6060-067: Rear, hdwy wknd over 1f out:	2	41a
648	WILOM 7 [9] M R Hoad 6-9-0 (45) L Fletcher (3) 20/1: 03-25458: Keen, trkd wnr to 2f out, wknd:	1	39a
649	MYTHICAL CHARM 7 [8] J J Bridger 5-9-0 (45) G Baker 12/1: 501-6009: Rear, hdwy over 2f out, no extra fnl 1f.	1¼	37a
648	LADY AT LEISURE 7 [12] Julian Poulton 4-8-13 (45) M Tebbutt 33/1: 300/5-600: Rear, nvr dngrs.	6	28a
666	PLATINUM BOY 6 [14] M Wellings 4-8-13 p (45) V Slattery 50/1: 00000-: Rear, nvr nr ldrs:	hd	27a
648	CHEROKEE BAY 7 [10] G L Moore 4-8-13 e (45) P Dobbs 14/1: 003-4300: Chsd ldrs, wknd over 2f out.	1¼	25a
649	ROYALE PEARL 7 [11] R Ingram 4-8-13 (45) Dane O'Neill 20/1: 00340-00: Midfield, wknd 4f out.	7	15a
264	PROMOTE 56 [5] Ms A E Embiricos 8-9-0 (45) P McCabe 33/1: 0000/00-0: Rear, almost ran off crse bend over 1f out, t.o.	14	0a
14 Ran	2m 8.7 (5.9) Owner Stableline		Trained at Crediton

706   2.30 Bet Direct No Q Median Auction Maiden Stakes 3-5yo (H)
£1274 £364 £182   6f p/track rnd   Going 44   -06 Slow   Stalls Inside

531	ILE FACILE 20 [1] N P Littmoden 3-8-10 (70) D Holland 4/5 FAV: 24241: Midfield, 3/4L 4th 2f out, drvn & styd on to lead nr fin:		68a
	KNEAD THE DOUGH [2] D E Cantillon 3-8-10 J F Egan 10/1: 2: Midfield, chsd ldr 2f out, led over 1f out, collared nr fin:	nk	67a
4381}	FLAME PRINCESS 154 [5] J R Boyle 4-9-6 (60) N Callan 50/1: 005500-3: Rear, eff 2f out, onepace:	3½	51a
653	ONEFORTHEBOYS 7 [4] D Flood 5-9-11 (35) L Treadwell 20/1: 00-00624: Rear, mod late gains.	1¼	52a
289	AFTER ALL 51 [3] G A Butler 3-8-5 (61) E Ahern 9/4: 23526-35: Trkd ldr, led over 4f out till hdd over 1f out, no extra:	shd	46a
659	DARK CHAMPION 6 [7] Jedd O'Keeffe 4-9-11 (48) Dane O'Neill 9/1: 405-2046: Led till over 4f out, no extra:	2½	43a
653	SOMETHINGABOUTHER 7 [6] P W Hiatt 4-9-6 (35) Lisa Jones (3) 20/1: 00-45037: Chsd ldrs, wknd 2f out.	1½	33a
7 Ran	1m 13.4 (3.0) Owner Mr Paul J Dixon		Trained at Newmarket

707   3.05 Bet Direct No Q Demo 08000 837 888 Banded Stakes 4yo+ 0-40 (H)
£1463 £418 £209   1m4f p/track   Going 44   +08 Fast   Stalls Inside

590	FREE STYLE 14 [6] K R Burke 4-8-12 (40) G Baker 10/1: 020-6301: Rear, plenty to do over 4f out, gd hdwy under press to lead 3f out, 3L clr 2f out, drvn out ins fnl 1f:		43a
539	PRIVATE SEAL 20 [5] Julian Poulton 9-9-1 t (40) M Halford (7) 10/1: 0000-632: Midfield, hdwy from 2f out, went 2nd in fnl 1f but not reach wnr:	1¼	39a
537	GIKO 20 [1] Jane Southcombe 10-9-1 bl (35) E Ahern 20/1: 30200-03: Trkd ldrs, outpcd over 2f out, kept on for press:	1¾	35a
650*	LITTLE RICHARD 7 [15] M Wellings 5-9-7 p (30) V Slattery 8/1: 0-004314: Handy, led over 3f out, sn hdd & outpcd, no extra:	½	40a
654	ADJIRAM 7 [7] A W Carroll 8-9-1 (30) W Ryan 5/1 J FAV: 400/46/-35: Keen, in tch, onepcd 2f out:	2½	30a
540	BROUGHTONS MILL 20 [4] J A Supple 9-9-1 (35) Rory Moore (7) 25/1: 346/00-56: Rear, hdwy over 3f out, onepcd fnl 2f:	3	25a
539	BOOM OR BUST 20 [3] Miss K M George 5-9-1 p (40) Derek Nolan (7) 8/1: 53200-07: Keen, midfield, fdd 2f out.	4	19a
2897}	DONT WORRY BOUT ME 585 [12] T G Mills 7-9-1 vis (40) S Whitworth 5/1 J FAV: 1040/40/-8: Led till over 3f out.	5	11a
654	STOPWATCH 7 [2] Mrs L C Jewell 9-9-1 p (35) N Callan 50/1: 3000/0-09: Rear, outpcd over 3f out.	½	10a
4096}	TOJONESKI 170 [9] I W McInnes 5-9-1 VIS (40) P Mathers (7) 16/1: 003530-0: Handy, fdd 3f out.	5	2a
454	NEPTUNE 33 [11] J C Fox 8-9-1 (35) P Dobbs 10/1: 40500/-50: Rear, wknd 4f out, fin t.o.:	9	0
535	FIRST CLASS LADY 20 [10] P Mitchell 4-8-12 (40) Lisa Jones (3) 10/1: 60046-50: Midfield, wknd halfway.	½	0
650	POLKA PRINCESS 7 [8] M Wellings 4-8-12 (40) L Treadwell (2) 14/1: 00-00003: Midfield, wknd halfway, t.o.	21	0
583	DAME MARGARET 14 [13] J A B Old 4-8-12 (40) Dane O'Neill 12/1: 02063-50: Rear, wknd halfway & t.o.	2	0
654	PENNY VALENTINE 7 [14] J R Best 4-8-12 (35) N Pollard 33/1: 0050-060: Handy, fdd over 5f out, t.o.	13	0
15 Ran	2m 33.55 (4.35) Owner Mr P Sweeting		Trained at Leyburn

708   3.40 Bet Direct Interactive Claiming Stakes 3yo+ (H)
£1313 £375 £188   7f p/track rnd   Going 44   -03 Slow   Stalls Inside

652	CAYMAN BREEZE 7 [1] S Dow 4-9-10 (59) D Holland 4/1: 300-0541: Keen, trkd ldrs, eff 2f out, drvn to lead ins fnl 1f:		56a
394	SINGLE TRACK MIND 40 [3] J R Boyle 6-9-7 (30) Karen Peippo (5) 50/1: 000/00-02: Rear, gd hdwy over 1f out, chsd wnr ins fnl furlong, nrst fin:	1½	45a
648	JAHANGIR 7 [10] B R Johnson 5-9-10 (45) Dane O'Neill 9/2: 00030-33: Led after 1f, clr over 1f out, hdd & wknd ins last:	1¼	45a
536	JANES VALENTINE 20 [4] J J Bridger 4-9-4 (45) N Callan 16/1: 0000-404: Rear, hdwy 2f out, onepcd:	¾	37a
600	LORD MELBOURNE 12 [2] J A Osborne 5-9-10 (50) S Crawford (7) 7/2 FAV: 5-214305: Rear, trav well away slt short of room 2f out, hdwy, not clr run & switched to rail 1f out,	shd	42a
412	EMARATIS IMAGE 39 [8] R M Stronge 6-9-10 (45) A Daly 33/1: 04000-06: Handy, fdd over 1f out.	2	35a
668	HINCHLEY WOOD 6 [5] J R Best 5-9-10 (40) N Pollard 20/1: 00//-607: Chsd ldrs, wknd over 1f out.	shd	37a
675	SOCIAL CONTRACT 5 [15] S Dow 7-9-10 (47) J F Egan 7/1: 06-00068: Rear, hdwy over 1f out, no extra.	shd	36a
571	WATERLINE DANCER 16 [7] P D Evans 4-9-4 vis t (40) L Fletcher (3) 25/1: 0000-009: Mid-field, btn over 2f out.	hd	29a
652	SHIRLEY OAKS 7 [9] Miss Z C Davison 6-9-5 (40) N Chalmers (5) 16/1: 4000-050: Rear, nvr nr ldrs:	½	29a
582	HELLBENT 14 [6] J A Osborne 5-9-10 (40) V Slattery 25/1: 530/0-000: Rear, nvr nr ldrs.	1	32a
528	KILMEENA STAR 21 [11] J C Fox 4-9-6-8 (40) P Dobbs 25/1: 0306-000: Led 1st 1f, rem handy, fdd fnl 1f.	1	28a
653*	IVORY VENTURE 7 [12] D K Ivory 4-9-3 bl (35) M Savage (5) 12/1: 0-000010: Mid-field, wknd over 2f out.	8	7a
656	PRINCE OF PERLES 6 [14] D Shaw 3-8-5 vis (35) Lisa Jones (3) 33/1: 00000-00: Handy, rider lost iron bend 2f out, not recover.	1¼	9a
667	FLYING FAISAL 6 [13] J M Bradley 6-9-10 (40) C J Davies (4) 20/1: 0006040: Rear, hdwy over 2f out, wknd.	nk	10a
15 Ran	1m 26.1 (3.3) Owner The Cayman Breezers		Trained at Epsom

709   4.15 Bet In Running @ Betdirect Co Uk Banded Stakes 3yo+ 0-45 (H)
£1645 £470 £235   6f p/track rnd   Going 44   -01 Slow   Stalls Inside

649	BADOU 7 [2] L Montague Hall 4-9-6 (45) D Holland 9/4 FAV: 000-6141: In tch, led ins fnl 1f, edged left & drvn out:		48a
544	CARGO 19 [7] D Flood 5-9-6 BL T (45) Rory Moore (7) 11/2: 0005-042: Led after 1f, edged right & hdd ent fnl 1f, kept on & only	nk	47a

just btn:

652	**THE GAY FOX** 7 [4] B G Powell 10-9-6 bl t (45) L Keniry (3) 13/2: 005-2423: Rear, hdwy over 1f out, kept on fnl 1f & nrst fin:	1	**44a**
579	**INDIAN WARRIOR** 14 [1] J Jay 8-9-6 bl (45) N Callan 33/1: 025-1004: Chsd ldrs, onepcd over 1f out.	½	**42a**
562	**MASTER RATTLE** 17 [3] Jane Southcombe 5-9-6 (45) V Slattery 16/1: 000-0005: Chsd ldrs, onepcd over 1f out:	shd	**41a**
411	**XSYNNA** 39 [5] T T Clement 8-9-6 (45) Saleem Golam (7) 20/1: 0000-306: Led 1f, wknd 2f out:	3½	**30a**
648	**PANCAKEHILL** 7 [8] D K Ivory 5-9-6 bl (45) D O'Neill 16/1: 0-000067: Rear, eff 2f out, no impress.	1	**27a**
558	**YOUNGS FORTH** 17 [13] A W Carroll 4-9-6 (45) S Whitworth 33/1: 05500-08: Rear, hdwy over 2f out, onepcd:	1¼	**23a**
652*	**BELLS BEACH** 7 [9] P Howling 6-9-12 (45) D Kinsella 11/2: 40-62019: Rear, eff 2f out, wknd.	nk	**28a**
451	**TRIPTI** 33 [10] J J Bridger 4-9-6 (45) N Pollard 12/1: 0406-200: Chsd ldrs, wknd over 2f out:	½	**20a**
413	**WESTMEAD TANGO** 39 [14] J R Jenkins 4-9-6 (45) J F Egan 20/1: 1200-660: Al bhd:	nk	**19a**
591	**PARALLEL LINES** 13 [11] P D Evans 3-8-5 bl (45) E Ahern 20/1: 2000-000: Bmpd start, al bhd.	1	**16a**
401	**LUCRETIUS** 40 [6] D K Ivory 5-9-6 (45) M Savage (5) 14/1: 0600-00: Nvr nr ldrs:	nk	**15a**
649	**MALAAH** 7 [12] Julian Poulton 8-9-6 bl (45) M Tebbutt 10/1: 00/000-00: Handy to halfway, wknd after.	7	**0a**

14 Ran   1m 13.1 (2.7)   Owner Mr J Daniels   Trained at Epsom

---

710

4.50 Betdirect Co Uk Amateur Riders' Banded Stakes 4yo+ 0-40 (H)
£1463 £418 £209   1m p/track rnd   Going 44   -27 Slow   Stalls Outside

693	**BELTANE** 2 [12] W de Best Turner 6-11-7 (40) Mrs I de Best (7) 33/1: 100/00/P-01: Slow away, gd hdwy dist, styd on to lead cl-home:		**45a**
539*	**THEATRE LADY** 20 [9] P D Evans 6-11-7 (40) Miss E Folkes (3) 3/1: 21300-12: Dsptd lead, led over 2f out till caught	nk	**44a**
652	**LADY LIESEL** 7 [4] J J Bridger 4-11-7 (40) Miss Donna Handley (7) 25/1: 5000-003: Rear, styd on well fnl 1f, nrst fin:	1	**42a**
678	**VLASTA WEINER** 4 [11] J M Bradley 4-11-7 bl (40) Mr S Walker (3) 8/1: 0250464: In tch, ev ch 1f out, no extra.	1	**40a**
668	**HAITHEM** 6 [6] D Shaw 7-11-7 t (40) Mrs S Bosley 12/1: 0030605: Rear, hdwy over 1f out, onepcd:	nk	**39a**
137	**PRINCE DU SOLEIL** 83 [2] J R Jenkins 8-11-7 (40) Mr N Soares (7) 20/1: 3/00000-6: Keen, handy, wknd fnl 1f.	1¼	**36a**
411	**MISBEHAVIOUR** 39 [3] P Butler 5-11-7 (40) Miss G D Gracey Davison (7) 33/1: 0000/0-07: Chsd ldrs 6.5f.	1	**34a**
635	**COLNE VALLEY AMY** 8 [8] G L Moore 7-11-7 bl (40) Mr E Dehdashti (3) 11/4 FAV: 060-4208: Chsd ldrs, outpcd 3f out, no impress after:	1½	**31a**
538	**GEESPOT** 20 [1] D J S ffrench Davis 5-11-7 p (40) Mr J J Best (3) 7/1: 00-04009: Dsptd lead to 3f out, wknd.	1¼	**28a**
582	**MOUNT SUPERIOR** 14 [10] P W D'Arcy 8-11-7 (40) Miss R D'Arcy (5) 7/1: 00/66-150: Keen rear, nvr dngrs.	1	**26a**
652	**ALBURY HEATH** 7 [7] T M Jones 4-11-7 (40) Mr M Goldstein (5) 33/1: 05000-00: Nvr nr ldrs.	6	**14a**
668	**HIGH DIVA** 6 [5] J R Best 5-11-7 (40) Mrs K Hills (7) 7/1: 06-6465U: Keen, rear, stumbled & u.r. 5f out:		**0a**

12 Ran   1m 41.9 (5.7)   Owner Mrs Gillian Swanton   Trained at Calne

---

711

1.40 Bet Direct No Q On 08000 93 66 93 Amateur Riders' Handicap Stakes 4yo+ 0-60 (F)   [38]
£2996 £856 £428   1m4f p/track   Going 27   -28 Slow   Stalls Inside

634	**ROBBIE CAN CAN** 10 [4] A W Carroll 5-11-5 (57) Mrs S Bosley 4/1 FAV: 0261-131: Rear, hdwy halfway, short of room over 2f out, led dist, rdn out:		**64a**
634	**LAZZAZ** 10 [2] P W Hiatt 6-11-5 (57) Mrs Marie King (5) 13/2: 3533302: Led till 3f out, rdn & ev ch dist, not pace of wnr.	2	**60a**
138	**INTENSITY** 83 [3] P A Blockley 8-11-3 (55) Miss S Renwick (5) 7/1: 602000-3: Trkd ldrs, led 3f out till dist, no extra:	nk	**56a**
370	**STERLING GUARANTEE** 45 [9] Andrew Reid 6-11-1 (53) Mr J Gee (5) 10/1: 4///0630-2: Held up, eff to chase ldrs 2f out, onepace dist:	nk	**54a**
388	**LANOS** 42 [16] R Ford 6-11-7 t (59) Mr S Hughes (5) 10/1: 66544-55: V slow away & rear, hdwy wide to chall 2f out, no extra over 1f out:	nk	**51a**
602	**JOELY GREEN** 13 [5] N P Littmoden 7-11-3 (55) Mrs Emma Littmoden (3) 14/1: 0435-506: Nvr nr ldrs:	6	**43a**
590	**GOLDEN DUAL** 15 [15] S Dow 4-11-0 (52) Mr D Hutchison (7) 16/1: 65-00607: Held up wide, short of room over 2f out, sn no impress:	3	**39a**
624	**TOP OF THE CLASS** 10 [14] P D Evans 7-10-8 vis (46) Miss E Folkes (3) 10/1: 0-063348: Keen, rear, mod prog.	2½	**29a**
557	**CLIQUEY** 18 [13] B J Llewellyn 5-10-9 (47) Miss A Frieze (7) 100/1: 0600/-009: Rear, well bhd over 3f out, only mod prog:	½	**33a**
542	**FOREVER MY LORD** 20 [11] J R Best 6-10-9 (47) Mr E Dehdashti (3) 8/1: 00430-00: Cl-up till over 3f out.	1	**24a**
622	**KAVI** 10 [10] Simon Earle 4-11-5 (60) Mr J J Best (3) 20/1: 3666-000: Sn rear, nvr a factor.	3½	**28a**
602*	**BEYOND THE POLE** 13 [12] B R Johnson 6-11-3 (55) Mrs L A Best (3) 6/1: 40000-10: Cl-up, wknd qckly 3f out.	7	**18a**
	SECAM 128 [8] Mrs P Townsley 5-11-0 BL (52) Mrs C Thompson (5) 33/1: 331321-0: Cl-up, lost place 5f out:	3½	**10a**
288	**CANTRIP** 52 [6] Miss B Sanders 4-11-2 BL t (57) Mr C Doran (7) 40/1: 42660-00: Prom, lost place on ch 4f out:	5	**8a**

14 Ran   2m 35.76 (6.56)   Owner Mr K F Coleman   Trained at Alcester

---

712

2.10 Bet Direct No Q Handicap Stakes 3yo 0-70 (E)   [75]
£3262 £932 £466   5f p/track rnd   Going 27   -01 Slow   Stalls Outside

621*	**CUT AND DRIED** 10 [3] D M Simcock 3-9-5 (66) Martin Dwyer 4/1 JT FAV: 46600-11: Rdn rear, hdwy 2f out, led cl-home, all out:		**68a**
587	**ALIZAR** 15 [5] S Dow 3-8-11 (58) J F Egan 8/1: 3-023142: Chsd ldrs, styd on well for press, just held in a thrilling fin:	hd	**59a**
621	**BEAU JAZZ** 10 [1] W de Best Turner 3-9-4 (65) S Righton 33/1: 60056-53: Trkd ldrs, rdn & led ins last, hdd cl-home:	hd	**65a**
673	**SAHARA SILK** 6 [2] D Shaw 3-9-6 vis (67) Darren Williams 8/1: 0-006134: Trkd ldr, rdn/hung left & outpcd dist, kept on late:	1	**64a**
609	**SMART STARPRINCESS** 12 [4] P A Blockley 3-9-6 vis (67) N Callan 9/2: 11-11235: Led & rdn clr halfway, drvn & hdd ins last, wknd:	½	**62a**
671	**STAMFORD BLUE** 6 [9] J S Moore 3-8-11 bl (58) Derek Nolan (7) 12/1: 5-246206: Rdn rear, nrst fin:	nk	**52a**
494	**POMPEY BLUE** 27 [7] P J McBride 3-9-7 (68) K Fallon 4/1 JT FAV: 5515-557: Mid-div, no impress/eased ins last.	1¾	**57a**
609	**DEMOLITION MOLLY** 12 [6] R F Marvin 3-9-3 t (64) Dean McKeown 8/1: 5054-068: Chsd ldrs, hmpd halfway, sn btn.	2½	**45a**
4869}	**BARBILYRIFLE** 123 [10] H Morrison 3-9-6 (67) S Drowne 9/1: 310000-9: Sn outpcd & hung right, nvr a factor on reapp:	2	**42a**
492	**EASILY AVERTED** 27 [8] P Butler 3-9-2 t (63) I Mongan 20/1: 3006-550: Hmpd after 1f, nvr a factor.	shd	**38a**

10 Ran   59.22 (1.42)   Owner Trillium Place Racing   Trained at Newmarket

---

713 **2.40 Bet Direct No Q Demo 08000 837 888 Maiden Stakes 3yo+ (D)**
£4046 £1245 £623 £311 7f p/track rnd Going 27 -03 Slow Stalls Inside

468	**BAHIANO** 32 [2] C E Brittain 3-8-9 (72) K Fallon 5/4 FAV. 62-21: Made all, readily asserted under hands & heels dist, val for 4L+:		83a
560	**HATCH** 18 [5] R M H Cowell 3-8-9 (61) E Ahern 7/2: 5420-22: Dwelt, keen in rear, hdwy wide to chase wnr dist, sn no impress:	2	74a
603	**NIGHT STORM** 13 [1] S Dow 3-8-4 (66) P Doe 9/1: 025-5333: Trkd ldrs, styd one onepace for press, no threat to wnr:	1	67a
657	**BOAVISTA** 7 [8] P D Evans 4-9-7 t (54) N Callan 16/1: 243-0324: Keen & cl-up till over 1f out:	5	57a
603	**RESPLENDENT KING** 13 [7] T G Mills 3-8-9 BL (69) Dane O'Neill 5/1: 040-3355: Chsd ldrs, btn 2f out:	3	56a
2144}	**PENEL** 255 [3] B R Millman 3-8-10 1ow (64) S Drowne 33/1: 6540-6: Chsd ldrs, rdn & wknd halfway:	7	43a
514	**BENNANABAA** 24 [9] S C Burrough 5-9-12 t A Nicholls 50/1: 057: Dwelt, eff wide halfway, sn struggling:	1¾	39a
4149}	**DREAM OF DUBAI** 168 [6] P Mitchell 3-8-4 J Fanning 9/1: 05-8: Rear, struggling halfway, eased fnl 1f.	10	16a

8 Ran 1m 24.69 (2.09) Owner Mr C E Brittain Trained at Newmarket

---

714 **3.10 Bet Direct On Sky Active Handicap Stakes 3yo+ 0-75 (E)** [75]
£3445 £1060 £530 £265 1m p/track rnd Going 27 +10 Fast Stalls Outside

530	**TOPTON** 21 [10] P Howling 10-9-8 bl (69) J P Spencer 12/1: 0601-431: Dwelt, swtchd to race rail, hdwy over 2f out, drvn to lead well ins last:		74a
604	**SIR LAUGHALOT** 13 [3] Miss E C Lavelle 4-9-8 (69) L Keniry (3) 6/1: 020-2032: Trkd ldrs, drvn & styd on fnl 1f, not pace of wnr cl-home:	½	72a
674	**EASTBOROUGH** 6 [9] B G Powell 5-9-6 (67) S Whitworth 33/1: 0/6-03103: Mid-div, drvn & styd on, not able to chall:	¾	69a
517	**DEEPER IN DEBT** 24 [1] J Akehurst 6-9-12 (73) T Quinn 5/2 FAV: 03112-24: Led, rdn & hdd ins last, no extra:	nk	74a
698	**SUPERCHIEF** 5 [5] Miss B Sanders 9-9-3 bl t (64) S Drowne 7/1: 6435525: Dwelt, held up, eff 2f out, no extra dist.	3½	58a
607*	**ACORAZADO** 13 [12] G L Moore 5-9-3 (64) G Carter 7/1: 35-02016: Rear, not able to chall:	1¼	55a
4673}	**JOOLS** 136 [7] D K Ivory 6-9-11 (72) Martin Dwyer 20/1: 214100-7: Handy, wknd over 1f out, reapp:	6	52a
674	**TRUE COMPANION** 6 [6] N P Littmoden 5-9-5 (66) E Ahern 6/1: 533-0138: In tch, drpd rear halfway, nvr a factor.	4	38a
565	**TIGER TOPS** 17 [11] J A Supple 5-9-4 (65) J Fanning 7/1: 03006-59: In tch wide, btn 2f out:	5	28a
549	**TRUSTED INSTINCT** 20 [4] C A Dwyer 4-9-11 (72) N Callan 16/1: 63610-00: Cl-up, wknd qckly over 2f out:	5	26a
452	**SILKEN BRIEF** 34 [8] D J Daly 5-10-0 t (75) K Fallon 13/2: 02/043-60: Prom wide, btn 2f out & sn eased, virtually p.u.:	18	0

11 Ran 1m 37.57 (1.37) Owner Mr Liam Sheridan Trained at Newmarket

---

715 **3.40 Betdirect Co Uk Maiden Stakes 3yo+ (D)**
£3780 £1163 £582 £291 1m2f p/track Going 27 -39 Slow Stalls Inside

	BARATHEA DREAMS [10] J S Moore 3-8-3 Martin Dwyer 10/1: 1: Sn trkd ldr, led over 2f out, rdn clr dist, held on well:		70a
4694}	**JOROBADEN** 487 [6] C F Wall 4-9-10 G Baker 2/1 FAV: 4/-2: Trkd ldrs, rdn & chsd wnr ins last, al just held:	¾	68a
649	**ALMOST WELCOME** 8 [1] S Dow 3-8-3 (45) P Doe 20/1: 0000-003: Trkd ldrs, styd on for press:	¾	67a
430	**SPRINGALONG** 38 [3] P D Evans 4-9-10 (67) S Drowne 8/1: 43304-04: Trkd ldrs, onepace for press dist:	shd	67a
	ROLLSWOOD [14] P R Hedger 4-9-10 P S Whitworth 16/1: 5: Slow away, rear/inner, hdwy 3f out & poised to chall when no room dist till ins last, kept on:	½	66a
4907}	**BLUE QUIVER** 120 [2] C A Horgan 4-9-10 Paul Eddery 5/1: 06-6: Keen rear, eff over 2f out, not able to chall & eased cl-home:	2	59a
696	**STEPPENWOLF** 3 [4] W de Best Turner 3-8-3 (47) S Righton 20/1: 0000-67: Led till over 2f out, sn btn:	1¼	61a
367	**DARN GOOD** 45 [11] R Hannon 3-8-3 (62) R Smith 12/1: 64500-08: Al bhd, nvr a factor:	2½	57a
540	**ALIMISTE** 21 [8] I A Wood 4-9-5 J F McDonald (5) 33/1: 009: Mid-div, no impress fnl 2f.	1	51a
672	**SPIDERS WEB** 6 [9] T Keddy 4-9-10 G Carter 50/1: 0/-0000: Dwelt, rear, no prog 3f out:	4	50a
591	**NUMPTY** 14 [7] N Tinkler 3-8-3 t (40) Natalia Gemelova (7) 16/1: 000-550: Mid-div, well btn 3f out.	nk	49a
4718}	**HIGH CANE** 134 [12] M D Hammond 4-9-5 (67) K Fallon 9/2: 6036-0: Trkd ldrs, wknd 3f out, eased down.	27	9a
521	**WILD WILD WES** 24 [13] R Ingram 4-9-10 N Day 50/1: 00: Mid-div wide, btn 3f out, t.o.	9	3a

13 Ran 2m 09.44 (6.64) Owner Mrs Fitri Hay Trained at Hungerford

---

716 **4.10 Littlewoods Bet Direct Handicap Stakes 4yo+ 0-85 (D)** [85]
£4849 £1492 £746 £373 1m2f p/track Going 27 +07 Fast Stalls Inside

549	**HIP HOP HARRY** 20 [2] E A L Dunlop 4-9-5 VIS (77) K Fallon 2/1 FAV. 1031-021: Dwelt, rear, hdwy wide 3f out, led dist, asserted for press ins last:		86a
570	**INTERNATIONALGUEST** 17 [6] G G Margarson 5-9-7 vis (78) N Pollard 14/1: 0-020002: Trkd ldrs, drvn & kept on fnl 2f, not pace of wnr:	1¼	84a
127	**OFARABY** 87 [4] M A Jarvis 4-9-7 (79) M Henry 11/1: 102164-3: Trkd ldrs, rdn & chall over 1f out, no extra ins last:	shd	85a
570	**BARRY ISLAND** 17 [9] D R C Elsworth 5-9-7 (78) T Quinn 7/2: 604-1524: Rear, styd on late for press, not able to chall:	¾	82a
622*	**BRAVE DANE** 10 [11] A W Carroll 6-8-11 (68) W Ryan 7/1: 3500-115: Rear, hdwy wd no room over 2f out, no prog ins last:	¾	71a
625	**LION HUNTER** 10 [8] Miss E C Lavelle 5-10-0 (85) J P Spencer 7/1: 32251/-06: Led, hdd 2f out, no extra:	shd	88a
519	**PARAGON OF VIRTUE** 24 [5] P Mitchell 7-9-8 (79) J Fanning 7/1: 3310-347: Cl-up halfway, led over 2f out, hdd & no extra over 1f out:	1¼	79a
4396}	**REBATE** 155 [3] R Hannon 4-9-0 (72) P Dobbs 66/1: 314000-8: Mid-div, no impress fnl 2f:	hd	71a
4778}	**KRUGERRAND** 130 [1] W J Musson 5-9-11 (82) M Fenton 25/1: 054040-9: Slow away & sltly hmpd start, rear, eff wide 4f out, sn btn:	3½	76a
616	**JUST WIZ** 11 [7] N P Littmoden 8-8-11 bl (68) E Ahern 16/1: 0532-630: Mid-div, no prog fnl 3f:	9	50a
625	**ADALAR** 10 [10] P D Evans 4-9-1 VIS (73) S Drowne 50/1: 210/0-000: Keen & cl-up till halfway, wknd.	dist	0a

11 Ran 2m 04.82 (2.02) Owner Lucayan Stud Trained at Newmarket

---

717 **4.40 Bet In Running @ Betdirect Co Uk Selling Stakes 3yo+ (G)**
£2618 £748 £374 1m p/track rnd Going 27 -15 Slow Stalls Outside

675	**MUQTADI** 6 [2] M Quinn 6-9-8 (49) J P Spencer 11/2: 0306041: Sltly hmpd start, rear, hdwy 2f out, rdn to lead dist, rdn out:		54a
675*	**XALOC BAY** 6 [5] B P J Baugh 6-10-0 (53) Darren Williams 7/2: 0-200112: Led, rdn clr over 2f out, hdd dist & no extra:	1	58a
439			55a

	FREE OPTION 36 [9] W J Musson 9-10-0 bl (71) K Fallon 7/4 FAV: 0130-503: Rear, short of room 3f out, kept on wide for press, nvr threatened front pair:		
541	**MISS CELERITY 21** [4] M J Haynes 4-9-3 (30) S Drowne 100/1: 060-004: Chsd ldrs, no extra when short of room dist:	1¾	41a
4260}	**DARK SHAH 161** [3] D M Simcock 4-9-8 t (60) Martin Dwyer 7/2: 664000-5: Mid-div, hung right & no impress over 1f out:	1¾	43a
671	**NEVER CRIED WOLF 6** [1] D R C Elsworth 3-8-3 P R Thomas (5) 33/1: 6006: Chsd ldrs, outpcd fnl 2f, cheek pieces.	½	42a
117	**ROMAN EMPIRE 87** [7] T J Etherington 4-9-8 BL (56) J Fanning 20/1: 150000-7: Keen & chsd ldrs, wknd qckly dist.	11	22a
675	**MARAKASH 6** [6] M R Bosley 5-9-8 t p (51) G Baker 14/1: 0/0000-28: Keen, mid-div, btn 2f out, eased.	13	0
626	**LARAD 10** [8] J S Moore 4-9-8 bl (53) D Kinsella 20/1: 0504-359: Dwelt, keen & chsd ldrs till halfway.	6	0
9 Ran	1m 39.55 (3.35) Owner Mrs S G Davies	Trained at Wantage	

718

5.10 Bet Direct Football Cashbacks Handicap Stakes 4yo+ 46-55 (F) **[63]**
£3010 £860 £430   **1m2f p/track**   **Going 27**   **-44 Slow**   Stalls Inside

586	**FORTUNE POINT 15** [1] A W Carroll 6-9-5 (54) I Mongan 8/1: 640-4021: Led after 2f & rdn clr over 1f out, al holding on for press ins last:		61a
669	**STEELY DAN 6** [2] J R Best 5-9-1 (50) N Pollard 9/2: 05-00022: Rear, smooth hdwy over 2f out, shaken up ins last to chase wnr, closed to the line but al held:	nk	56a
630	**FRANKS QUEST 10** [11] P Burgoyne 4-9-4 (54) L Keniry (3) 20/1: 040-0233: Keen & prom, trav well 2f out, rdn & no extra	3½	55a
622	**SAMMYS SHUFFLE 10** [14] Jamie Poulton 9-9-1 bl (50) J F Egan 10/1: 22/605-04: Trkd ldrs, styd on wide for press, not pace of front pair:	¾	50a
542	**ANOTHER SECRET 20** [9] G L Moore 6-9-0 bl e (49) S Whitworth 7/2 FAV: 06B04-35: Chsd ldrs, onepace dist.	hd	48a
633	**GEOGRAPHY 10** [6] P Butler 4-9-3 p (53) C Haddon (7) 66/1: 0005-P06: Keen & cl-up, no extra fnl 2f:	2	49a
642	**TROPICAL SON 8** [13] D Shaw 5-9-4 vis (53) N Callan 16/1: 2510257: Chsd ldrs, eff wide, no extra dist.	nk	48a
546	**AMNESTY 20** [10] G L Moore 5-9-5 bl e (54) Dane O'Neill 25/1: 030-0458: Dwelt, rear, only mod prog.	nk	48a
669	**PIQUET 6** [8] J J Bridger 6-9-1 (50) G Baker 10/1: 01-31669: Rear & keen, eff wide, no impress:	hd	43a
339	**ARCHIRONDEL 48** [5] M D Hammond 6-9-6 (55) E Ahern 11/2: 56030-60: Mid-div, btn over 1f out:	3	44a
4963}	**TINTAWN GOLD 116** [7] S Woodman 4-9-3 (53) J P Spencer 12/1: 202500-0: Settled rear, no prog fnl 2f.	4	36a
421	**SHIFTY 40** [12] D Nicholls 5-9-5 (54) A Nicholls 12/1: 23426-50: Keen, held up, btn 2f out:	1	36a
430	**MURAQEB 38** [4] Mrs Barbara Waring 4-9-2 (52) S Drowne 33/1: 55-00: Al bhd on h'cap bow.	2½	30a
620	**RED STORM 11** [3] J R Boyle 5-9-1 (50) R Miles (3) 25/1: 05-06150: Led 2f, btn 3f out:	shd	28a
14 Ran	2m 09.87 (7.07) Owner The T J Racing Partnership	Trained at Alcester	

Official Going STANDARD TO SLOW

719

2.30 Betdirect Co Uk New Site Banded Stakes 3yo+ 0-35 (H)
£1302 £372 £186   **1m f/sand rnd**   **Going 80**   **-11 Slow**   Stalls Inside

640	**FRAAMTASTIC 9** [5] B A Pearce 7-9-8 p (35) B Reilly (5) 11/2: 5040-241: Chsd ldrs, hdwy over 1f out, drvn to lead fnl 1f:		37a
640*	**GALLEY LAW 9** [4] R Craggs 4-10-0 (30) J Quinn 9/4 FAV: 000-3212: Midfield, hdwy 3f out, ch ins fnl 1f, just held:	hd	41a
663*	**DANCING KING 7** [15] P W Hiatt 8-10-0 (30) P Makin (7) 7/1: 0405213: Handy, led over 1f out, hdd ins fnl 1f & no extra:	½	40a
573	**GRUB STREET 16** [14] J Parkes 8-9-8 (30) M Lawson (7) 12/1: 6-0000/-34: Rear, late gains.	1¼	31a
635*	**GRACIOUS AIR 9** [1] J R Weymes 6-9-8 vis (35) D Fentiman (7) 6/1: 0060-015: Rear, kept on late, nrst fin.	nk	30a
663	**COUNTRYWIDE GIRL 7** [13] A Berry 5-9-8 (30) P Mathers (7) 20/1: 0U-03536: Handy, led 3f out, hdd over 1f out.	4	22a
663	**PAGEANT 7** [8] J M Bradley 7-9-8 bl (30) Lisa Jones (3) 25/1: 6540057: Chsd ldrs, wknd over 2f out:	2	18a
573	**CATERHAM COMMON 16** [11] D W Chapman 3-8-9 (30) A Culhane 40/1: 0000-068: Nvr btr than mid-div:	3	12a
678	**MIMAS GIRL 5** [9] S R Bowring 5-9-8 t P (30) J Bramhill 20/1: 6-505309: Nvr btr than midfield:	3½	5a
375	**ALJOMAR 43** [3] R E Barr 5-9-8 (35) R Fitzpatrick 25/1: 0400-060: Nvr nr ldrs:	6	0a
523	**MOYNE PLEASURE 22** [2] Paul Johnson 6-9-8 p (35) L Fletcher (3) 12/1: 4450-000: Midfield, rear fnl 3f.	½	0a
381	**MONKEY OR ME 43** [6] P T Midgley 3-8-3 (30) J McAuley 40/1: 00-00: Led 1f, remained handy, wknd 2f out.	½	0a
663	**BLUE MAEVE 7** [7] J Hetherton 4-9-8 (30) K Dalgleish 25/1: 006-4040: Handy, led after 1f, hdd 3f out & no extra.	10	0a
581	**MORRIS DANCING 15** [16] B P J Baugh 5-9-8 p (30) M Tebbutt 25/1: 000-0000: Al bhd.	1¼	0a
399	**BY DEFINITION 41** [12] J C Tuck 6-9-8 VIS (30) M Savage (5) 66/1: 00/000-00: Al bhd.	7	0a
	HAVANA ROSE 132 [10] P Morris 4-9-8 P (30) D Mernagh 40/1: 0/00000-0: In tch, wknd & bhd fnl 3f.	2½	0a
16 Ran	1m 46.7 (7.3) Owner Mr Richard J Gray	Trained at Lingfield	

720

3.00 New Site @ Betdirect Co Uk Banded Stakes 3yo+ 0-45 (H)
£1652 £472 £236   **5f f/sand rnd**   **Going 80**   **+08 Fast**   Stalls Outside

643	**SERGEANT SLIPPER 8** [15] C Smith 7-9-5 vis (45) R Fitzpatrick 5/1: 05-03031: Slowly away, hdwy 2f out, plenty to do over 1f out, drvn & styd on well to lead nr fin:		48a
667	**EJAY 7** [14] Julian Poulton 5-9-5 (40) Lisa Jones (3) 12/1: 006-0602: Midfield, hdwy over 1f out, ch fnl furlong, held nr fin:	shd	47a
643	**TORRENT 8** [3] D W Chapman 9-9-5 bl (45) A Culhane 9/2 FAV: 0-263153: Midfield, hdwy over 1f out, led ins fnl furlong, hdd & no extra nr fin:	¾	45a
507	**THE LEATHER WEDGE 25** [5] A Berry 5-9-5 (45) P Bradley (5) 10/1: 4020-604: Led, hdd & no extra ins last.	1	42a
619	**HAGLEY PARK 11** [7] M Quinn 5-9-5 (45) P Gallagher (7) 9/2 FAV: 400-2265: Handy, ch when rider drpd whip 1f out, wknd:	1	39a
527	**LONE PIPER 22** [4] J M Bradley 9-9-5 (45) J Bramhill 25/1: 056-0006: Midfield, chsd ldrs 2f out, onepace fnl furlong:	1	36a
527	**PLEASURE TIME 22** [1] C Smith 11-9-5 vis (45) P Makin (7) 16/1: 00055-57: Chsd ldrs, wknd 1f out:	shd	35a
637	**DANAKIM 9** [11] J R Weymes 7-9-5 bl e (40) D Fentiman (7) 20/1: 060-6108: Chsd ldrs, wknd 1f out:	2½	27a
579	**INDIAN SHORES 15** [12] M Mullineaux 5-9-5 p (40) P Varley (7) 20/1: 6F-00609: Rear, modest late hdwy.	nk	26a
3329}	**ALASTAIR SMELLIE 206** [2] S L Keightley 8-9-5 (40) M McCabe 20/1: 50/0030-0: Nvr nr ldrs:	½	24a
524	**ON THE TRAIL 22** [10] D W Chapman 7-9-5 bl (40) K Dalgleish 16/1: 0000-000: Handy, wknd over 1f out.	1¼	20a
507	**SAFRANINE 25** [6] Miss A Stokell 7-9-5 p (45) Ann Stokell 14/1: 0000-000: Midfield, nvr dangerous.	hd	19a
2394}	**MR UPPITY 244** [13] Julian Poulton 5-9-5 (40) M Halford (7) 40/1: 250000-0: Nvr a factor.	1¼	15a

553	**SHEAPYS LASS 19** [8] A Crook 3-8-5 (45) Rory Moore (7) 50/1: 526-0000: Al bhd.	*shd*	**14a**
319	**BISHOP TO ACTRESS 50** [9] M J Polglase 3-8-5 (45) K Ghunowa (7) 50/1: 53660-00: Al bhd.	6	**0a**
508	**FEELING BLUE 25** [16] B N Pollock 5-9-5 (45) J Quinn 12/1: 102/60-00: Midfield, wknd 2f out.	1	**0a**
16 Ran	1m 1.4 (3.6) Owner Mr C Smith	Trained at Wellingore	

721   **3.30 Betdirect Co Uk Median Auction Maiden Stakes 3-5yo   (H)**
£1439 £411 £206   **1m f/sand rnd**   **Going 80**   **+02 Fast**   Stalls Inside

659	**GALLOWAY MAC 7** [4] W A O'Gorman 4-9-9 D Holland 2/1: 3301: Midfield, hdwy to chase ldrs 2f out, led over 1f out, drvn		**56a**
665	**KUSTOM KIT FOR HER 7** [5] S R Bowring 4-9-4 T (45) J Bramhill 12/1: 6000232: Led after 2f, hdd over 1f out, no extra:	2½	**45a**
665	**ANGELOS PRIDE 7** [1] J A Osborne 3-8-4 (57) J Quinn 1/1 FAV: 0-3023: Dwelt, in tch, wknd 2f out.	4	**42a**
636	**MACPURSIE 9** [2] T D Barron 3-7-13 D Mernagh 6/1: 54: Handy, wknd over 2f out:	7	**23a**
656	**MYSTIC PROMISE 7** [6] Mrs N Macauley 3-8-4 vis (30) Hayley Turner (5) 50/1: 000-0005: Chsd ldrs, wknd over 2f out:	18	**0a**
46	**INDRAPURA STAR 99** [8] Miss J Feilden 4-9-9 (40) B Reilly (5) 40/1: 0/000-6: Chsd ldrs, wknd over 3f out:	10	**0a**
636	**FRIMLEYS MATTERRY 9** [3] R E Barr 4-9-9 (53) R Fitzpatrick 28/1: 56300-67: Led, hdd after 2f, no extra 4f out:	7	**0a**
7 Ran	1m 45.7 (6.3) Owner Mr Michael McDonnell	Trained at Newmarket	

722   **4.00 Betdirect Co Uk Banded Stakes 4yo+ 0-45 (H)**
£1628 £465 £233   **1m3f f/sand**   **Going 80**   **-05 Slow**   Stalls Inside

638*	**BROUGHTON KNOWS 9** [2] W J Musson 7-9-6 bl (45) Lisa Jones (3) 11/10 FAV: 362-1111: Rear, hdwy over 3f out, drvn & styd on for press to lead ins fnl furlong:		**53a**
224	**RED MOOR 67** [5] R Hollinshead 4-8-12 (45) A Culhane 8/1: 500065-2: Midfield, hdwy 4f out, led over 1f out, hdd ins fnl furlong & no extra:	nk	**46a**
638	**NEXT FLIGHT 9** [4] R E Barr 5-9-0 (45) R Fitzpatrick 10/1: 0003-623: Chsd ldrs, onepace fnl 1f:	3	**41a**
443	**TURFTANZER 35** [6] Don Enrico Incisa 5-9-0 t (35) Kim Tinkler 16/1: 0/050-504: Led early, cl up, no extra ins fnl furlong:	1	**39a**
575	**OUR GLENARD 16** [7] S L Keightley 5-9-0 (45) P McCabe 4/1: 005-2205: Midfield, hdwy halfway, led over 2f out, hdd & no extra over 1f out:	11	**23a**
677*	**ACE MA VAHRA 3** [3] S R Bowring 6-9-0 (40) J Bramhill 12/1: 03/-60616: Rear, hdwy when hmpd bend over 4f out, wknd over 2f out:	3	**18a**
640	**MARENGO 9** [8] Paul Johnson 10-9-0 (30) Joanna Badger 33/1: 600-0067: Led after 2f, hdd/wknd over 2f out.	6	**9a**
559	**JAMESTOWN 18** [1] M J Polglase 7-9-0 (45) L Fletcher (3) 9/1: 3-500008: Rear, hdwy over 4f out, wknd.	21	**0a**
8 Ran	2m 30.75 (9.45) Owner Broughton Thermal Insulation	Trained at Newmarket	

723   **4.30 Daily Offers @ Betdirect Co Uk Selling Stakes 4yo+   (H)**
£1267 £362 £181   **1m4f f/sand**   **Going 80**   **-08 Slow**   Stalls Inside

574*	**DAUNTED 16** [3] P A Blockley 8-9-8 (60) Lisa Jones (3) 8/13 FAV: 4-310011: Midfield, gd hdwy to lead over 3f out, sn clr, kept on well, rdn out:		**59a**
576*	**RADIANT BRIDE 16** [5] K R Burke 4-9-0 bl (45) G Faulkner 5/1: 50-02612: Keen, rear, hdwy to chase wnr 2f out, not pace to chall:	3	**48a**
557	**ORO STREET 18** [2] G F Bridgwater 8-9-3 (61) D Holland 7/2: 4/216///-5: Trkd ldr, led over 4f out, hdd over 3f out, grad wknd:	5	**40a**
103	**CADWALLADER 90** [1] P Burgoyne 4-9-0 (58) D Sweeney 16/1: 03500-4: Led till over 4f out, wknd:	16	**16a**
633	**ILLUSIONIST 10** [4] Mrs N Macauley 6-9-3 vis (35) P McCabe 33/1: 0050-055: Al rear:	3½	**11a**
5 Ran	2m 44.9 (10.6) Owner Mrs Joanna Hughes	Trained at Southwell	

724   **5.00 Bet In Running @ Betdirect Co Uk Banded Stakes 4yo+ 0-40 (H)**
£1435 £410 £205   **1m6f f/sand**   **Going 80**   **-22 Slow**   Stalls Inside

534	**EAST CAPE 21** [3] Don Enrico Incisa 7-9-5 (35) Kim Tinkler 11/2: 450-5301: Midfield, hdwy to lead 1.5f out, sn clr, readily:		**46a**
640	**BUZ KIRI 9** [7] A W Carroll 6-9-5 (40) D Holland 4/6 FAV: 46-32122: Midfield, hdwy to chall 2f out, sn onepcd:	5	**37a**
576	**PADDY MUL 16** [1] W Storey 7-9-5 t (40) D R McCabe 9/2: 626-2143: Rear, hdwy when hmpd 4f out, chsd ldrs over 2f out, onepace fnl 1f:	1½	**34a**
574	**TROJAN WOLF 16** [6] P Howling 9-9-5 (35) A Culhane 25/1: 40000-04: Led till dist, wknd:	hd	**33a**
358	**FAIRMORNING 46** [5] J W Unett 5-9-5 (40) A Daly 10/1: 5443-265: Midfield, chsd ldrs 4f out, onepace fnl 2f.	5	**25a**
679	**KING PRIAM 5** [2] M J Polglase 9-9-5 bl (40) L Fletcher (3) 14/1: 5066456: Al bhd:	15	**2a**
925]	**SERGEANTS INN 1044** [4] T T Clement 7-9-5 (30) Saleem Golam (7) 50/1: 00600//-7: Chsd ldr, wknd 4f out & btn.	dist	**0a**
7 Ran	3m 14.15 (14.35) Owner Don Enrico Incisa	Trained at Middleham	

Official Going Standard

725   **1.30 Betdirect Co Uk New Site Maiden Stakes 3yo   (D)**
£3998 £1230 £615 £308   **5f p/track rnd**   **Going 39**   **-15 Slow**   Stalls Outside

258	**TONY THE TAP 58** [3] N A Callaghan 3-9-0 W Ryan 7/4: 4-1: Sn cl-up & led dist, drvn out:		**83a**
3777}	**SHRINK 187** [1] M L W Bell 3-8-9 K Fallon 4/5 FAV: 22-2: Slow away, keen in rear, hdwy to press wnr dist, no extra ins last:	1½	**71a**
119	**COMERAINCOMESHINE 88** [5] T G Mills 3-8-9 (64) I Mongan 8/1: 030-3: Pushed along in tch wide, outpcd over 1f out:	1½	**66a**
691	**LAKESIDE GUY 4** [4] P S McEntee 3-9-0 J P Spencer 80/1: 0-004: Cl-up, ch over 1f out, sn no extra.	hd	**70a**
485	**SON OF REMBRANDT 29** [2] D K Ivory 3-9-0 (56) M Savage (5) 25/1: 5063-005: Hung right, led till over 1f out.	1	**67a**
5 Ran	1m 0.51 (2.71) Owner Mr K J Mercer	Trained at Newmarket	

726   **2.00 New Site @ Betdirect Co Uk Handicap Stakes 3yo+ 0-65 (F)**   [65]
£2975 £850 £425   **1m2f p/track**   **Going 39**   **+15 Fast**   Stalls Inside

674	**WAR OWL 7** [6] Ian Williams 7-9-6 (57) Lisa Jones (3) 7/1: 50/04-201: Keen mid-div, hdwy 2f out & led in last, rdn clr:		**66a**
674	**BANK ON HIM 7** [8] C Weedon 9-9-11 (62) J Quinn 9/2 FAV: 0-161222: Chsd ldr & led over 3f out till ins last, no extra:	3	**65a**

604	**HE WHO DARES** 14 [11] A W Carroll 6-9-6 (57) I Mongan 11/2 1012-203: Slow away, keen rear, gd hdwy 2f out, onepace for press ins last:	1	59a
607	**FEN GYPSY** 14 [3] P D Evans 6-9-9 (60) K Fallon 7/1: 16000-54: Chsd ldrs, styd on onepace for press:	¾	61a
622	**BLAZING THE TRAIL** 11 [2] J W Hills 4-9-8 (60) S Whitworth 10/1: 030-4025: Dwelt, eff wide 2f out, onepace.	shd	61a
4586]	**HALLINGS OVERTURE** 497 [7] C A Horgan 5-10-0 (65) Paul Eddery 50/1: 0500/-6: Prom, no extra fnl 1f:	1¾	64a
520	**KARAOKE** 25 [14] S Kirk 4-9-13 (65) J F Egan 25/1: 02331-07: Mid-div wide, no prog dist:	1¼	62a
607	**LONDONER** 14 [4] S Dow 6-9-8 (59) P Doe 40/1: 0006-008: Mid-div, no prog over 1f out.	1½	54a
622	**SNUKI** 11 [10] G L Moore 5-9-2 bl e (53) J P Spencer 16/1: 0000-009: Keen & sn trkd ldrs, btn over 1f out.	2	45a
622	**MY MAITE** 11 [12] R Ingram 5-9-6 bl t (57) D Holland 11/2: 0036-240: Sn led till 3f out, wknd:	¾	48a
624	**DANCE PARTY** 11 [9] A M Balding 4-9-11 (63) Martin Dwyer 8/1: 3400-330: Mid-div wide, btn over 1f out:	5	47a
693	**EASTER OGIL** 4 [5] Jane Southcombe 9-9-12 (63) V Slattery 10/1: 3324000: Al towards rear, quick reapp:	4	41a
530	**LOCKSTOCK** 22 [13] M S Saunders 6-10-0 P (65) A Culhane 20/1: 00414-00: Reared start, wide/al bhd:	13	24a
	13 Ran 2m 06.64 (2.44) Owner Mrs Glennie Braune	Trained at Alvechurch	

---

727   2.30 Littlewoods Bet Direct Conditions Stakes 3yo (D)
£4017 £1236 £618 £309   1m2f p/track   Going 39   -35 Slow   Stalls Inside

568*	**SKIDMARK** 18 [1] D R C Elsworth 3-9-2 (86) K Fallon 8/15 FAV: 31-211: Keen cl up, hdwy to lead over 1f out, readily, val for 5L+:		99a
322*	**CHASING THE DREAM** 50 [4] A M Balding 3-8-11 Martin Dwyer 4/1: 12: Trkd ldr, led 2f out, sn rdn & hdd over 1f out, no ch with wnr:	2½	84a
511	**COUNTRYWIDE FLYER** 26 [2] T D Barron 3-9-2 (92) J P Spencer 100/30: 114-5123: Hung right thr'out, set steady pace, rdn & hdd 2f out, no extra:	1	88a
	3 Ran 2m 10.22 (7.42) Owner Mr Raymond Tooth	Trained at Whitsbury	

---

728   3.05 Daily Offers @ Betdirect Co Uk Selling Handicap Stakes 3yo+ 0-60 (G)   [60]
£2674 £764 £382   6f p/track rnd   Going 39   -07 Slow   Stalls Inside

709	**BELLS BEACH** 9 [14] P Howling 6-9-5 6ex (51) J Fanning 8/1: 40-62011: Trkd ldrs, led ins last, drvn out:		57a
709	**TRIPTI** 35 [3] J J Bridger 4-8-13 (45) N Pollard 14/1: 0406-202: Led & dictated pace, rdn & hdd ins last, kept on:	½	48a
4242}	**BANNISTER** 163 [7] D Nicholls 6-10-0 (60) L Treadwell (7) 12/1: 200100-3: Slow away & rear, switched & styd on well cl-home, nrst fin:	1	60a
271	**LEGAL SET** 57 [10] W J Musson 8-10-0 (60) K Fallon 13/2: 000600-4: Mid-div, rdn to press ldrs over 1f out, no extra nr fin:	nk	59a
589	**JALOUHAR** 16 [9] B P J Baugh 4-9-9 (55) Darren Williams 20/1: 615-5465: Prom, onepce dist:	½	52a
413	**GENTLE RESPONSE** 41 [11] B R Johnson 4-8-3 BL (35) S Whitworth 50/1: 0000-006: Slow away, rear, short of room ins last, nrst fin under kide ride:	nk	31a
671	**GOOD VIBRATIONS** 7 [2] P F I Cole 3-8-4 P (51) E Ahern 10/1: 002-3567: Chsd ldr 4f, no extra dist:	shd	47a
641	**SO SOBER** 9 [4] D Shaw 6-9-0 (46) N Callan 6/1: 000-1548: Mid-div, not pace to chall:	nk	41a
4330}	**TRUE HOLLY** 159 [12] S Kirk 4-8-8 (40) J F Egan 16/1: 06/0000-9: Hung left, al rear:	nk	34a
646	**NEW OPTIONS** 9 [8] W J Musson 7-10-0 (60) Lisa Jones (3) 5/1: 04-54050: Towards rear, eff wide 2f out, sn btn:	nk	53a
709	**CARGO** 2 [13] D Flood 5-8-13 BL T (45) J P Spencer 3/1 FAV: 0005-040: Slow away & rear, eff wide 2f out, sn btn:	1¼	34a
	11 Ran 1m 13.14 (2.74) Owner Mr Richard Berenson	Trained at Newmarket	

---

729   3.40 Bet All Weather: Bet Direct Handicap Stakes 3yo 0-75 (E)   [82]
£3465 £1066 £533 £267   7f p/track rnd   Going 39   -12 Slow   Stalls Inside

603*	**ATHBOY** 14 [1] M J Wallace 3-8-9 vis (63) J P Spencer 13/2: 60-011: Hld up, hdwy 2f out & styd on to lead well ins last, rdn		72a
670	**HAZEWIND** 7 [2] P D Evans 3-7-12 1oh t (51) Joanna Badger 6/1: 00-042: Cl-up & led over 2f out till well ins last:	¾	57a
368	**OFF BEAT** 46 [8] R F Johnson Houghton 3-9-7 bl (75) S Carson 12/1: 10610-63: Dwelt, mid-div, short of room & switched ins last, kept on for press:	1¼	77a
671	**GARRIGON** 7 [3] N P Littmoden 3-8-6 (60) I Mongan 12/1: 02-50404: Dwelt, rear, short of room over 1f out, late gains for press, no danger.	½	61a
402	**PARK AVE PRINCESS** 42 [13] N P Littmoden 3-8-4 (58) E Ahern 20/1: 0460-225: Sn trkd ldrs, no extra dist:	hd	58a
691	**MISTER COMPLETELY** 4 [9] J R Best 3-7-12 (52) J Quinn 10/1: 03640-26: Mid-div wide, no extra dist:	1	50a
623	**JOY AND PAIN** 11 [12j G L Moore 3-8-4 (58) J Mackay 40/1: 0067: Wide towards rear, nvr able to chall, h'cap bow:	1¼	53a
615	**PICK OF THE CROP** 12 [10] J R Jenkins 3-9-6 (74) D Holland 7/1: 0525-128: Rear, sn pushed along, nvr on terms:	nk	68a
673*	**TORONTO HEIGHTS** 7 [5] P W Chapple Hyam 3-9-11 6ex (79) D Nolan (5) 5/2 FAV: 206-2119: Trkd ldrs wide, drvn & btn over 1f out:	¾	72a
671	**JAOLINS** 7 [4] P G Murphy 3-7-12 (52) D Kinsella 14/1: 0060-120: Keen, led till over 2f out, wknd:	shd	45a
496*	**SOMEWHERE MY LOVE** 28 [7] T G Mills 3-9-0 (68) K Fallon 7/1: 50-10: Mid-div, hmpd over 2f out, sn btn.	¾	60a
497	**TARANAI** 28 [6] B W Duke 3-7-12 1oh (51) Lisa Jones (3) 66/1: 0006-400: Prom 4f, sn btn:	1½	41a
	12 Ran 1m 26.39 (3.59) Owner Mr D Mcgovern	Trained at Newmarket	

---

730   4.10 Bet In Running @ Betdirect Co Uk Claiming Stakes 4yo+ (F)
£2975 £850 £425   7f p/track rnd   Going 39   -05 Slow   Stalls Inside

262	**OVERRIDE** 58 [1] J M P Eustace 4-9-7 (68) J Tate 11/1: 220060-1: Trkd ldrs, led ins last, drvn out, all out:		73a
499	**MEELUP** 28 [5] A G Newcombe 4-8-3 p (53) S Whitworth 40/1: 01000-02: Led till ins last, styd on well for press, just held:	nk	54a
610	**BLAKESET** 13 [2] T D Barron 9-8-11 vis (76) D Holland 5/2: 1-101123: Cl-up, drvn & no extra ins last:	1¼	59a
492	**MAJHOOL** 28 [6] G L Moore 5-8-9 (70) I Mongan 15/8 FAV: 5/0010-04: Pulled hard, hld up, drvn & onepace dist:	nk	56a
516	**RIPPLE EFFECT** 25 [3] C A Dwyer 4-9-2 (72) B Reilly (5) 3/1: 02-21205: Chsd ldrs, prog to chall over 1f out, sn no extra & eased cl-home:	2½	58a
708	**SOCIAL CONTRACT** 7 [4] S Dow 7-8-3 (47) Paul Eddery 25/1: 06-00066: Held up, eff 2f out, not able to chall.	2½	40a
581	**BUGLE CALL** 16 [7] K O Cunningham Brown 4-8-9 bl e (35) C Catlin 66/1: 00000-07: Rear, outpcd from halfway.	hd	45a
709	**THE GAY FOX** 2 [8] B G Powell 10-8-3 bl t (45) Dale Gibson 10/1: 005-2428: Sn rdn rear, nvr factor, quick reapp.	2	35a
	8 Ran 1m 25.88 (3.08) Owner Mr Paul Kan	Trained at Newmarket	

731   4.45 Betdirect Co Uk Handicap Stakes   4yo+ 0-80 (D)   [79]

£4160 £1280 £640 £320   **1m4f p/track**   Going 39   -01 Slow   Stalls Inside

627	**MILLVILLE 11** [10] M A Jarvis 4-9-9 (77) N Callan 13/2: 101: Slow away & rear, rdn & hdwy over 2f out & styd on for press to lead well ins last:		86a
716*	**HIP HOP HARRY 1** [7] E A L Dunlop 4-10-1 6ex vis (83) K Fallon 11/10 FAV: 1031-0212: Chsd ldrs, rdn to lead ins last, hdd well ins last, not pace of wnr:	¾	89a
570	**EZZ ELKHEIL 18** [3] J R Jenkins 5-9-10 (75) D Holland 8/1: 0050-243: Led over 2f out till ins last, onepace:	2	78a
549	**CLASSIC ROLE 21** [8] R Ingram 5-9-6 (71) J Mongan 7/1: 030-4034: Chsd ldrs, drvn & kept on onepce.	½	73a
669	**KASHIMO 115** [5] G L Moore 5-8-7 (58) S Whitworth 40/1: 134000-5: Held up, eff wide over 2f out, not able to chall:	1½	58a
669	**RAHEEL 7** [6] P Mitchell 4-7-12 3oh t (49) J Quinn 33/1: 060-5406: Slow away & rear, eff wide 2f out, no impress.	nk	51a
672*	**PRIVATE BENJAMIN 7** [4] Jamie Poulton 4-8-4 6ex (58) J F Egan 20/1: 3664-017: Chsd ldrs, drvn & btn dist:	¾	56a
595	**BRESSBEE 15** [2] J W Unett 6-9-3 vis (68) D Nolan (5) 33/1: 300-0248: Mid-div, drvn & no prog fnl 2f:	nk	65a
147	**KRISTOFFERSEN 81** [14] R M Stronge 4-9-6 (74) D Sweeney 33/1: 035430-9: Rear, only mod prog:	1¼	69a
342*	**MAYSTOCK 49** [13] G A Butler 4-9-10 vis (78) L Treadwell (7) 10/1: 04140-10: Dwelt, held up, no prog, abs.	1½	71a
716	**ADALAR 5** [9] P D Evans 4-9-5 (73) S Donohoe (7) 100/1: 210/0-0000: Led till over 2f out, qck reapp.	7	57a
493	**MAJLIS 28** [11] R M H Cowell 7-9-4 bl (69) E Ahern 16/1: 00201-00: Slow away & al bhd:	2	50a
570	**GALLANT BOY 18** [12] P D Evans 5-9-6 t (71) S Drowne 14/1: 50-00400: Slow away, chsd ldrs wide till 4f out:	5	45a
674	**DANAKIL 7** [9] S Dow 9-9-5 (70) C Catlin 33/1: 00430-00: Wide & al rear, quick reapp.	¾	43a

14 Ran   2m 34.01 (4.81)   Owner Mr T G Warner   Trained at Newmarket

732   5.15 Bet Direct Football Cashbacks Handicap Stakes   3yo+ 46-55 (F)   [57]

£3003 £858 £429   **1m p/track rnd**   Going 39   -38 Slow   Stalls Outside

600	**LUCID DREAMS 14** [10] M Wigham 5-9-9 (52) J Fanning 7/1: 240-5041: Keen trkd ldrs, styd on for press to prevail cl-home:		57a
600	**LUCAYAN MONARCH 14** [8] P S McEntee 6-9-11 p (54) J P Spencer 10/1: 1125002: Prom, narrow lead ins last, drvn & hdd cl-home:	shd	58a
669*	**ALAFZAR 7** [12] P D Evans 6-10-1 6ex bl t (58) K Fallon 9/4 FAV: 040-4013: Led after 1f & dictated pace, qcknd over 2f out, drvn & hdd ins last, held nr fin:	½	61a
600	**ZINGING 14** [4] J J Bridger 5-9-7 (50) S Drowne 8/1: 310-5064: Led 1f, remained trkg ldrs, kept on.	¾	51a
559	**PAS DE SURPRISE 19** [2] P D Evans 6-9-12 (55) Joanna Badger 16/1: 0364-305: Shuffled towards rear after 2f, mod gains for press:	1	55a
571	**CHANDELIER 18** [1] M S Saunders 4-9-11 bl (54) A Culhane 8/1: 0060-536: Dwelt & keen early, hmpd after 1f, eff when hmpd 2f out, not able to chall:	shd	54a
622	**MUTARAFAA 11** [7] D Shaw 5-9-10 vis (53) N Callan 15/2: 1-432407: Pulled hard rear, mod gains for press when short of room dist:	1	51a
474	**COPPINGTON FLYER 32** [5] B W Duke 4-9-6 (49) J F McDonald (5) 16/1: 00000-48: In tch, short of room 2f out & hmpd over 1f out, no extra:	hd	46a
4427}	**MARNIE 154** [3] J Akehurst 7-9-6 (49) J Mackay 16/1: 204000-9: Dwelt & rear, eff wide, no impress:	hd	45a
651	**ESTRELLA LEVANTE 9** [6] G L Moore 4-9-6 bl e (49) Jemma Marshall (7) 40/1: 055-0530: Dwelt, in tch 6f.	2½	40a
669	**BALERNO 7** [9] R Ingram 5-9-8 (51) G Carter 6/1: 5300-130: Keen & chsd ldrs, btn dist:	1½	39a

11 Ran   1m 42.37 (6.17)   Owner Reds Bar Four Partnership II   Trained at Newmarket

733   1.40 Littlewoodscasino Com Handicap Stakes   4yo+ 0-65 (F)   [60]

£2975 £850 £425   **2m p/track**   Going 37   -17 Slow   Stalls Inside

602	**GEMI BED 15** [4] G L Moore 9-8-13 bl (45) S Whitworth 10/1: 51153-61: Rear, gd hdwy to lead over 1f out, pushed out:		52a
515	**PHANTOM STOCK 26** [2] W Jarvis 4-9-11 (63) M Tebbutt 11/4: 061-2142: Held up, hdwy & led 6f out, rdn clr over 2f out, hdd over 1f out & no extra:	2	66a
554	**LAND OF FANTASY 21** [7] Lady Herries 5-9-13 (59) J Quinn 2/1 FAV: B500-123: Chsd ldr 5f out, sn rdn & outpcd, kept on late for press, no threat:	1½	61a
493	**ASTROMANCER 29** [8] M H Tompkins 4-9-0 (52) D Holland 7/2: 50244-04: Chsd ldr 4f, in tch, no impress fnl 2f:	5	49a
707	**STOPWATCH 3** [1] Mrs L C Jewell 9-8-3 p (35) Joanna Badger 50/1: 000/0-005: Rear, eff from 5f out, nvr threatened ldrs:	2½	30a
588	**SEANS MEMORY 17** [5] Mrs C A Dunnett 4-9-3 (45) Dane O'Neill 16/1: 0-026: Mid-div, no impress fnl 3f:	nk	49a
1386}	**BROUGHTONS FLUSH 656** [3] W J Musson 6-9-1 (47) K Fallon 7/1: 211150/-7: Trkd ldr after 5f till 5f out, sn btn:	2½	39a
638	**LADY ARNICA 11** [6] A W Carroll 5-8-13 vis (45) I Mongan 50/1: 0/0/0-08: Led till 6f out, sn bhd, t.o..	dist	0a

8 Ran   3m 28.56 (8.56)   Owner Mr B Lennard   Trained at Brighton

734   2.10 Littlewoods Bet Direct Maiden Stakes   3yo   (D)

£4212 £1296 £648 £324   **1m p/track rnd**   Going 37   -00 Slow   Stalls Outside

665	**CERTIFIABLE 9** [2] Andrew Reid 3-9-0 S Carson 66/1: 41: Made all, rdn & pressed over 1f out, held on well for press ins last:		75a
112	**BAKER OF OZ 90** [3] R Hannon 3-9-0 (67) P Dobbs 9/2: 22460-2: Trkd ldrs trav well, drvn to chase wnr ins last, al just held:	½	73a
603	**ARCHERFIELD 15** [5] J W Hills 3-8-9 (70) Dane O'Neill 11/8 FAV: 0055-223: Cl-up & ch 2f out, no extra dist:	2½	63a
4980}	**KEELUNG 116** [6] M A Jarvis 3-9-0 M Henry 8/1: 0-4: Dwelt, keen in rear, kept on under hands & heels fnl 2f, nrst fin:	1½	65a
543	**CLARE GALWAY 22** [1] T D McCarthy 3-8-10 1ow D Holland 50/1: 05: Dwelt, mid-div, outcpd fnl 2f.	2½	56a
472	**AIR OF SUPREMACY 33** [11] J Noseda 3-9-0 E Ahern 7/2: 06: Mid-div wide, nvr able to threaten:	¾	59a
670	**REDBANK 8** [4] S Dow 3-9-0 (60) Paul Eddery 20/1: 330-2007: Mid-div, no impress fnl 2f:	1¼	56a
100	**MAMBINA 92** [10] M R Channon 3-8-9 D Corby (3) 10/1: 50-8: Towards rear/wide, nvr a factor:	1	49a
670	**FORGE LANE 8** [12] C Weedon 3-9-0 J Quinn 50/1: 09: Dwelt, rear, little hdwy.	hd	53a
4816}	**KILCULLEN LASS 129** [7] P D Evans 3-8-9 (50) S Drowne 100/1: 006-0: Held up, no ch fnl 3f, abs.	3½	41a
553	**ALMANAC 21** [8] B P J Baugh 3-9-0 Darren Williams 66/1: 0-00: Chsd ldrs, btn 3f out.	5	37a
496	**LOOKOUTHEREICOME 29** [9] T T Clement 3-8-9 V Slattery 33/1: 00: Dwelt & held up, nvr a factor.	3½	25a

12 Ran   1m 39.15 (2.95)   Owner Mr A S Reid   Trained at Mill Hill London

735 2.40 New Site @ Betdirect Co Uk Handicap Stakes 3yo 0-70 (E) [77]
£3444 £984 £492 6f p/track rnd Going 37 +03 Fast Stalls Inside

572*	TAG TEAM 19 [7] A M Balding 3-9-4 (67) Martin Dwyer 3/1 JT FAV: 0-11: Made all, pushed clr over 1f out, cmftbly:		81a
545	BIG BAD BURT 22 [8] M J Wallace 3-9-1 vis (64) K Fallon 100/30: 600-422: Dwelt, mid-div, styd on for press from over 1f out, nvr threatened wnr:	2½	66a
712	ALIZAR 17 [1] S Dow 3-8-9 (58) D Holland 3/1 JT FAV: 3-023143: Trkd ldrs, drvn & chsd wnr over 1f out, held dist:	½	58a
609	BACK AT DE FRONT 14 [3] N E Berry 3-9-0 (63) M Savage (5) 16/1: 504-1554: Chsd ldrs, no extra 1f out.	2	57a
609	SMOKIN JOE 14 [2] J R Best 3-9-7 (70) E Ahern 5/1: 2216-405: Dwelt, pushed along towards rear, late prog.	1¼	60a
389	JASMINE PEARL 44 [12] T M Jones 3-8-4 (53) J Quinn 50/1: 52055-36: Chsd ldrs, no impress fnl 2f, abs:	1¼	39a
54	SACHIN 100 [4] J R Boyle 3-9-4 (67) J Murtagh 14/1: 04340-7: Rdn & rear, mod late prog:	shd	53a
603	RICKY MARTAN 15 [9] G C Bravery 3-8-8 bl (57) S Whitworth 33/1: 064-008: Sn mid-div, no impress & hung over 1f out:	2½	35a
712	EASILY AVERTED 29 [10] P Butler 3-8-9 (63) I Mongan 12/1: 3006-559: Cl-up till over 1f out, no t-strap.	nk	40a
545	CHIQITITA 22 [5] T T Clement 3-8-6 (55) Saleem Golam (4) 66/1: 46600-00: Outpcd throughout.	shd	32a
671	MUST BE SO 8 [11] J J Bridger 3-7-13 (48) J F McDonald (5) 33/1: 031-5000: Sn struggling:	2½	17a

11 Ran 1m 12.44 (2.04) Owner Magic Moments Trained at Kingsclere

736 3.10 Bet In Running @ Betdirect Co Uk Handicap Stakes Fillies 3yo+ 0-80 (D) [78]
£4095 £1260 £630 £315 1m2f p/track Going 37 -21 Slow Stalls Inside

625	TIGHT SQUEEZE 12 [4] P W Hiatt 7-10-0 (78) K Fallon 9/4 FAV: 1-653001: Chsd ldrs, rdn to lead ins last, styd on strongly:		86a
4183}	DORIS SOUTER 168 [8] R Hannon 4-9-8 (73) Dane O'Neill 8/1: 123153-2: Led 2f, chsd ldr till led again 2f out, hdd ins last & no extra:	1½	78a
624*	REGAL GALLERY 12 [2] C A Horgan 6-9-2 (66) Paul Eddery 3/1: 40/41-113: Rear, hdwy when short of room over 1f out, styd on for press, winning ch had gone:	2	68a
624	DISPOL EVITA 12 [3] Jamie Poulton 5-8-0 (50) D Kinsella 16/1: 35020-04: Bhd, some late gains:	1¼	50a
489*	NAJAABA 30 [5] Miss J Feilden 4-9-10 (75) B Reilly (5) 5/1: 31-11115: In tch, eff wide to press ldrs over 2f out, no extra over 1f out, fdd:	1	74a
624	FIGURA 12 [6] R Ingram 6-8-9 (59) E Ahern 11/2: 000-0356: Dwelt, rear, eff wide over 2f out, no impress dist.	1	57a
711	TOP OF THE CLASS 2 [1] P D Evans 7-7-12 2oh vis (46) Joanna Badger 16/1: 0-063347: Keen & led after 2f, sn clr, wknd/hdd 2f out, qck reapp:	½	45a

7 Ran 2m 08.63 (5.83) Owner Mr Anthony Harrison Trained at Banbury

737 3.40 Betdirect Co Uk Claiming Stakes 3yo+ (F)
£2870 £820 £410 5f p/track rnd Going 37 -01 Slow Stalls Outside

628	SOUNDS LUCKY 12 [2] N P Littmoden 8-9-5 bl (60) D Holland 9/2: 540-0501: Chsd ldr, rdn & ch over 1f out, led ins fnl furlong, drvn out:		64a
671	EVER CHEERFUL 8 [9] W G M Turner 3-8-8 p (73) C Haddon (7) 7/2: 46-21052: Wide, chsd ldrs, styd on to ins fnl furlong to take 2nd nr fin:	1	63a
652	CONFUZED 10 [8] D Flood 4-9-7 e R Miles (3) 10/1: 0/0-03: Slowly away, keen, slt short of room 2f out, styd on ins fnl furlong to take 3rd nr fin:	½	60a
720	HAGLEY PARK 13 [5] M Quinn 5-9-0 VIS (45) P Gallagher (7) 10/1: 400-2264: Led, hdd ins last, no extra.	hd	52a
713	BOAVISTA 9 [1] P D Evans 4-9-4 t (54) S Drowne 5/1: 243-0325: Handy, wknd over 1f out:	1¾	51a
687	PANJANDRUM 6 [3] N E Berry 6-9-9 (66) M Savage (5) 3/1 FAV: 1-035106: Wide, chsd ldrs, lost place 2f out.	1½	51a
544	MR SPLIFFY 22 [6] K R Burke 5-9-5 vis (53) Darren Williams 7/1: 04-05107: Chsd ldrs, wknd 1f out:	¾	45a

7 Ran 59.69 (1.89) Owner Mr Paul J Dixon Trained at Newmarket

738 4.10 Betdirect Co Uk New Site Selling Stakes 4yo+ (G)
£2583 £738 £369 1m2f p/track Going 37 -22 Slow Stalls Inside

632	SCOTTYS FUTURE 12 [3] D R Loder 6-9-6 (78) J Murtagh 4/5 FAV: 000-0101: Rear, hdwy & 3L 6th 2f out, drvn to lead ins last:		66a
540	ABSOLUTE UTOPIA 23 [8] J L Spearing 11-9-6 (63) A Daly 10/1: 2101-022: Midfield, hdwy over 2f out, ch fnl furlong, just held nr fin:	nk	65a
717	FREE OPTION 38 [6] W J Musson 9-9-6 bl (71) K Fallon 5/2: 0130-503: Midfield, hdwy to chase ldr 2f out, ch fnl furlong, just held & fnl lame:	hd	64a
540	SENOR TORAN 23 [9] P Burgoyne 4-9-0 (45) L Keniry (3) 25/1: 0/5500-34: Trkd ldr, led 3f out, went clr over 1f out, hdd & no extra nr fin:	nk	58a
717*	MUQTADI 8 [10] M Quinn 4-9-1 (49) Martin Dwyer 8/1: 0306045: Rear, hdwy over 2f out, not clr run briefly over 1f out & switched to outer, kept on fnl furlong:	3	53a
649	ACHILLES RAINBOW 10 [1] K R Burke 5-9-1 (40) A Reilly (7) 66/1: 0060-406: Trkd ldrs, short of room & lost place over 2f out, no impress:	2	51a
577	KUMAKAWA 18 [2] E A Wheeler 6-9-1 bl (45) Liam Jones 7/1: 00-05037: Chsd ldrs, wknd over 2f out:	6	42a
677	CROWN CITY 7 [4] B P J Baugh 4-8-9 t (48) Darren Williams 66/1: 60600-08: Rear, btn over 2f out:	8	25a
2156}	VALDASHO 256 [5] Miss K M George 5-8-10 (30) J Quinn 66/1: 0100/00-9: Keen, led till hdd 3f out, fdd:	6	16a
514	RECKLESS FRED 26 [7] Miss K M George 5-9-1 Derek Nolan (7) 100/1: 000: Keen, chsd ldrs, wknd 3f out:	8	9a

10 Ran 2m 08.72 (5.92) Owner Lucayan Stud Trained at Newmarket

739 4.40 Betdirect Co Uk Handicap Stakes 3yo+ 46-55 (F) [58]
£3038 £868 £434 7f p/track rnd Going 37 -04 Slow Stalls Inside

718	STEELY DAN 8 [2] J R Best 5-9-6 (50) N Pollard 4/1 FAV: 05-00021: Midfield, gd hdwy over 2f out, pushed into lead ins fnl 1f, cmftbly:		59a
709	MASTER RATTLE 3 [9] Jane Southcombe 5-9-1 (45) V Slattery 12/1: 00-00052: Handy, led 3f out till hdd & no extra nr fin:	1½	48a
732	LUCAYAN MONARCH 1 [10] P S McEntee 6-9-10 p (54) J Murtagh 11/2: 11250023: Rear, hdwy over 2f out, styd on to take 3rd nr fin:	1¾	54a

186

685*	**AGUILA LOCO** 6 [3] Mrs Stef Liddiard 5-9-10 6ex p (54) S Drowne 8/1: 2625314: Handy, rdn in 4th when not clr run briefly 1f out, styd on:	¾	52a
410*	**TITIAN LASS** 42 [8] C E Brittain 5-9-2 bl (46) Dean Williams (7) 16/1: 0200-415: Handy, ch over 1f out, wknd:	1	43a
607	**CAPTAIN CLOUDY** 15 [4] M Madgwick 4-9-10 (54) Dane O'Neill 11/2: 4000-566: Keen, rear, styd on late.	1½	48a
543	**PURE EMOTION** 22 [1] W R Muir 3-8-1 14oh (48) J Quinn 20/1: 5-507: Rear, hdwy over 2f out, no impress on ldrs:	nk	41a
648	**HARBOUR HOUSE** 10 [6] J J Bridger 4-9-1 (45) J F McDonald (5) 6/1: 0020-028: Midfield, chsd ldrs 2f out, fdd.	½	37a
488	**VIZULIZE** 30 [7] A W Carroll 5-9-4 (48) D Holland 10/1: 540-0659: Keen, midfield, nvr nr ldrs:	hd	39a
669	**GALEY RIVER** 8 [11] J J Sheehan 5-9-3 e (47) I Mongan 50/1: 00000-00: Midfield, wknd 2f out.	nk	37a
600	**SCARROTTOO** 15 [12] S C Williams 6-9-6 (50) K Fallon 25/1: 40-03500: Rear, nvr nr ldrs.	6	28a
71	**MY GIRL PEARL** 97 [13] M S Saunders 4-9-1 bl (45) M Savage (5) 66/1: 000400-0: Wide in midfield, wknd 2f out.	9	7a
621	**INDIAN OAK** 12 [5] M P Muggeridge 3-7-12 27oh (35) D Kinsella 100/1: 50-000: Led till hdd 3f out, fdd.	6	0
13 Ran	1m 25.64 (2.84) Owner Mrs Louise Best	Trained at Maidstone	

740   5.10 Bet Direct Football Cashbacks Handicap Stakes 3yo+ 46-55 (F)   [61]

£2996 £856 £428   6f p/track rnd   Going 37   -00 Slow   Stalls Inside

544	**A TEEN** 22 [7] P Howling 6-9-3 (50) K Fallon 4/1 FAV: 000-5201: Midfield, switched wide over 1f out, drvn to lead last stride:		53a
657	**PARK STAR** 9 [8] D Shaw 4-9-6 (53) J F McDonald (5) 9/2: 6000-632: Trkd ldr, led ins fnl 1f, drvn & caught on line:	shd	55a
610	**AINTNECESSARILYSO** 14 [4] N E Berry 6-9-4 (51) M Savage (5) 12/1: 65-55143: In tch, short of room after 1f & lost place, hdwy & short of room 2f out, styd on fnl 1f, nrst fin:	1	51a
348	**INCHING** 49 [10] R M H Cowell 4-9-2 (49) E Ahern 10/1: 64626-44: Slowly away, hdwy to chase ldrs, onepcd fnl 1f:	hd	48a
208	**DOCTOR DENNIS** 72 [9] J Pearce 7-9-0 vis (47) N Pollard 12/1: 004446-5: Rear, styd on over 1f out but not dngrs:	nk	45a
628	**LADIES KNIGHT** 12 [14] D Shaw 4-9-8 (55) Darren Williams 12/1: 1-632506: Rear, hdwy wide over 1f out, styd on but not reach ldrs:	nk	52a
451	**TAMARELLA** 36 [13] G G Margarson 4-9-2 (49) A McCarthy 16/1: 00500-07: Handy, led over 1f out till ins fnl 1f, no extra:	nk	45a
544*	**GUN SALUTE** 22 [6] G L Moore 4-9-6 p (53) S Whitworth 5/1: 5010-018: Rear, not clr run over 2f out until ins fnl 1f, kept on but no ch:	½	48a
1740}	**LUCEBALL** 118 [1] P Morris 4-8-13 bl (46) J Murtagh 16/1: 604000-9: Midfield, hdwy over 1f out, onepcd.	¾	40a
448	**REGAL SONG** 34 [2] T J Etherington 8-9-6 bl (53) S Drowne 16/1: 61005-00: Chsd ldrs, lost place 2f out, fdd.	nk	46a
600	**KARAOKE KING** 15 [11] J E Long 6-9-7 (54) Dane O'Neill 16/1: 1600-600: Rear, nvr nr ldrs.	¾	46a
385	**FIAMMA ROYALE** 45 [5] M S Saunders 6-9-1 (48) J Quinn 6/1: 05000-40: In tch, short of room after 1f & drpd to rear, nvr dngrs:	¾	39a
643	**BLESSED PLACE** 10 [12] Jean Rene Auvray 4-9-6 T (53) I Mongan 50/1: 0050-000: Led till dist, fdd.	1¾	41a
13 Ran	1m 12.61 (2.21) Owner Mrs A K Petersen	Trained at Newmarket	

Official Going Standard To Slow

741   2.20 Betdirect Co Uk New Site Handicap Stakes 3yo+ 0-70 (E)   [70]

£3318 £948 £474   6f f/sand rnd   Going 100   -09 Slow   :alls 5f - Outside, Rem - Insi

684	**UP TEMPO** 6 [11] K A Ryan 6-9-5 (61) T Quinn 5/1: 640-2131: Rear, prog 2f out, styd on to lead well ins fnl 1f, pushed out, val 3L+:		73a
659*	**SKIP OF COLOUR** 9 [12] P A Blockley 4-10-1 6ex (71) D Nolan (5) 7/2 FAV: 340-4512: Sn prom, led after 3f out, sn 3L clr, tired & hdd well ins fnl 1f:	1¾	77a
610	**GILDED COVE** 14 [9] R Hollinshead 4-9-9 (65) M Fenton 4/1: 310-0033: Bhd, prog wide 2f out, nrst fin.	2	65a
556	**KENNINGTON** 21 [5] Mrs C A Dunnett 4-9-3 VIS (59) Hayley Turner (5) 14/1: 0/-104: Led, hdd after 3f out, sn no extra:	1	56a
610	**SHARP HAT** 14 [3] D W Chapman 10-9-10 (66) A Culhane 28/1: 35-52005: Handy, onepcd fnl 1f:	hd	62a
660	**FAR NOTE** 9 [7] S R Bowring 6-9-11 bl (67) N Callan 15/2: 0-620046: In tch, no extra fnl 2f:	½	62a
660	**ST IVIAN** 9 [10] Mrs N Macauley 4-9-12 p (68) P McCabe 14/1: 1-460207: Mid-div, modest late gains:	1¼	60a
704	**PAWN IN LIFE** 3 [2] T D Barron 6-9-4 P (60) D Mernagh 13/2: 1-000208: Slow away, nvr a factor:	2	46a
684	**ITS ECCO BOY** 6 [4] P Howling 5-9-1 (57) C Catlin 12/1: 40-44109: Al in rear:	1¼	40a
587	**MAROMITO** 17 [4] R Bastiman 7-8-8 (50) S Sweeney 50/1: 00000-00: Prom, wknd dist:	1¼	30a
643	**ATTORNEY** 10 [13] D Shaw 6-8-4 e (46) Lisa Jones (3) 33/1: 0100400: Al bhd:	½	25a
622	**FINGER OF FATE** 12 [1] M J Polglase 4-8-8 bl (50) K Ghunowa (7) 50/1: 60-00000: Sn in tch, wknd 3f out.	3½	20a
628	**TEYAAR** 12 [8] Mrs N Macauley 8-9-2 (58) J Mackay 25/1: 03-00600: Mid-div, wknd 3f out.	3	19a
13 Ran	1m 19.89 (6.59) Owner Yorkshire Racing Club and Fran	Trained at Hambleton	

742   2.50 New Site @ Betdirect Co Uk Maiden Stakes 3yo+ (D)

£3341 £1028 £514 £257   5f f/sand str   Going 100   Inapplicab   :alls 5f - Outside, Rem - Insi

572	**BLUEBERRY RHYME** 19 [2] P J Makin 5-9-11 vis (65) D Sweeney 8/11 FAV: 3423-221: In tch trav well, led on bit ins fnl 1f, pushed out to win cosily, val 3L+:		65a
621	**VITTORIOSO** 12 [4] Miss Gay Kelleway 3-8-11 bl (54) M Fenton 3/1: 050-5332: Led, hdd under press ins fnl 1f, no ch with easy wnr:	1¼	56a
	UHURU PEAK 1 [1] M W Easterby 3-8-11 P Mulrennan (5) 33/1: 3: Sn in rear, prog 2f out, kept on late:	4	44a
578	**WHITE O MORN** 18 [8] B A McMahon 5-9-6 P (35) G Gibbons 18/1: 00-0424: Prom, ev ch dist, sn wknd:	1	36a
4382}	**TABARKA** 157 [3] P A Blockley 3-8-6 (60) N Callan 4/1: 4530-5: Handy, outpcd 2f out, rallied late:	nk	35a
405	**HARBOUR PRINCESS** 43 [6] M F Harris 3-8-6 S Righton 50/1: 066: Al bhd:	3	26a
435	**ABRAXAS** 40 [5] J Akehurst 6-9-11 p (51) T Quinn 15/2: 0026-507: Prom, fdd 2f out:	6	13a
3359}	**MINIRINA** 206 [7] C Smith 4-9-6 (45) R Fitzpatrick 40/1: 230540-8: Prom, wknd 3f out:	2	2a
8 Ran	1m 02.43 (4.63) Owner Mrs P J Makin	Trained at Marlborough	

SOUTHWELL Thursday 26.02.04 Lefthand, Sharp, Oval Track

743	3.20 Littlewoods Bet Direct Handicap Stakes 4yo+ 0-85 (D)				[80]
	£4027 £1239 £620 £310 2m	Going 100	-60 Slow	alls 5f - Outside, Rem - Insic	

681*	**VICTORY QUEST** 7 [7] Mrs S Lamyman 4-9-7 6ex vis (79) C Catlin 8/1: 212-0011: In tch, prog trav well to lead 5f out, hard drvn 2f out, outstyd mr-up ins fnl 1f:		**84a**
173	**NORTHERN NYMPH** 79 [6] R Hollinshead 5-9-10 (76) A Culhane 16/1: 06235/4-2: Mid-div, prog 7f out, chsd wnr 4f out, ev ch 2f out, kept on fnl 1f, outstyd by wnr:	2	**78a**
598}	**OCEAN TIDE** 379 [9] R Ford 7-9-9 vis (75) B Swarbrick (7) 50/1: 36100/0-3: Held up, prog 1m out, no impress on front 2 fnl 4f:	18	**61a**
554*	**ALTITUDE DANCER** 21 [5] P A Blockley 4-8-6 (64) N Callan 7/4 FAV: 053-3214: Led 3f, styd prom, fdd 4f out:	15	**37a**
642	**DIGGER** 10 [3] Miss Gay Kelleway 5-9-7 (73) M Fenton 10/1: 36-14025: Mid-div, prog 5f out, wknd 3f out:	2	**44a**
549	**ROLEX FREE** 22 [1] Mrs L C Taylor 6-9-4 p (70) Dean McKeown 66/1: 406/40-06: Cl-up, fdd 6f out:	23	**23a**
3079]	**GRACILIS** 580 [4] G A Swinbank 7-10-0 (80) F Lynch 33/1: 2/30000/-7: Al in rear:	½	**32a**
644*	**ROYAL ATALZA** 10 [10] C N Allen 7-7-13 6ex bl (51) J Mackay 15/8: 0/0/04//-1: Prom, led 13f out, hdd 5f out, sn fdd:	3	**0a**
404	**WESTERN** 43 [8] J Akehurst 4-9-4 (76) T Quinn 7/1: 5641-209: Held up, prog 1m out, wknd 5f out:	2	**23a**
176}	**PERESTROIKA** 443 [2] B Ellison 6-8-13 (65) T Eaves (5) 66/1: 005050/-0: Al bhd:	dist	**0**
10 Ran	3m 51.67 (25.67) Owner Mr P Lamyman	Trained at Louth	

744	3.50 Betdirect Co Uk Classified Stakes 3yo+ 0-70 (E)			
	£3227 £922 £461 7f f/sand rnd	Going 100	+15 Fast	alls 5f - Outside, Rem - Insic

4919]	**UHOOMAGOO** 121 [5] K A Ryan 6-9-8 bl (67) N Callan 4/1: 033430-1: Held up, prog 3f out, ev ch dist, led ins fnl 1f, pushed out, val 4L+:		**78a**
632	**MY BAYARD** 12 [8] J O'Reilly 5-9-8 (69) J D O'Reilly (7) 4/1: 22020-62: Cl-up, ev ch 2f out, led bef 1f out, sn hdd, no ch with wnr fnl 1f:	2½	**70a**
530	**ZARIN** 23 [7] D W Chapman 4-9-8 (67) A Culhane 6/1: 06023-03: Held up, prog 3f out, no impress fnl 2f.	9	**54a**
585	**WEET WATCHERS** 17 [6] P A Blockley 4-9-8 (70) Dean McKeown 7/2 FAV: 3P0-164: Led till over 1f out.	½	**53a**
489	**MODESTY BLAISE** 30 [2] Miss Gay Kelleway 4-9-5 (68) M Fenton 10/1: 00-105: Handy, wknd 3f out:	1¾	**46a**
615	**WINGS OF MORNING** 13 [1] P A Blockley 3-8-5 (68) J Bramhill 14/1: 0002-156: Al in rear:	2	**45a**
318	**RISKA KING** 52 [4] R A Fahey 4-9-8 (69) T Hamilton (5) 12/1: 00100-07: Al in rear:	1	**43a**
551	**ROYAL GRAND** 21 [3] T D Barron 4-9-8 VIS (69) P Makin (7) 5/1: 5312-308: Prom, fdd fnl 2f:	3½	**36a**
8 Ran	1m 32.55 (5.95) Owner Mr John Duddy	Trained at Hambleton	

745	4.20 Daily Offers @ Betdirect Co Uk Selling Stakes 4yo+ (G)			
	£2534 £724 £362 1m4f	Going 100	-19 Slow	alls 5f - Outside, Rem - Insic

723*	**DAUNTED** 2 [6] P A Blockley 8-9-5 P (60) Lisa Jones (3) 4/6 FAV: 4-3100111: Led 1f, styd prom, led again 7f out, pushed clr fnl 2f, val 9L+:		**63a**
605	**ORINOCOVSKY** 15 [1] N P Littmoden 5-9-5 (58) N Callan 9/4: 04-10302: Prom, sn led, hdd 6f out, styd prom, outpcd 2f out, rallied late:	6	**52a**
574	**SPANISH STAR** 18 [4] Mrs N Macauley 7-9-5 (54) A Culhane 10/1: 41-46133: In tch, outpcd 6f out, rallied to chase wnr dist, edged left & sn no extra:	¾	**51a**
689	**THINK QUICK** 6 [5] R Hollinshead 4-8-6 (35) R Kennemore 33/1: 0-056634: Held up, prog 5f out, no impress fnl 2f:	1½	**39a**
463}	**STAR SEVENTEEN** 398 [2] Mrs N S Sharpe 6-8-9 B Swarbrick (7) 14/1: 30021/0-5: In tch, fdd 4f out:	5	**31a**
5 Ran	2m 48.58 (14.28) Owner Mrs Joanna Hughes	Trained at Southwell	

746	4.50 Bet In Running @ Betdirect Co Uk Handicap Stakes 4yo+ 46-55 (F)			[65]
	£2947 £842 £421 1m3f f/sand	Going 100	-06 Slow	alls 5f - Outside, Rem - Insic

647	**BRAMANTINO** 10 [11] R A Fahey 4-9-0 P (53) T Hamilton (5) 7/1: 3/000-531: Bhd, prog 2f out, ev ch & edged left dist, drvn out to lead cl-home:		**57a**
564	**STING LIKE A BEE** 20 [10] J S Goldie 5-9-4 (55) T Quinn 4/1 FAV: 6060-102: Held up, prog 4f out, switched twice to get a run bef 1f out, sn led, hung right & hdd cl-home:	hd	**58a**
463*	**DISABUSE** 35 [2] M W Easterby 4-9-1 (54) Dale Gibson 9/2: 0266-213: Chsd ldrs, prog 3f out, ev ch when short of room in fnl 1f, wknd:	5	**49a**
4550*}	**SO SURE** 148 [4] J G M O'Shea 4-8-13 (52) Dean McKeown 8/1: 00/5101-4: In tch, led 6f out, edged right dist, hdd ins fnl 1f, wknd:	3	**42a**
559}	**SORBIESHARRY** 20 [6] Mrs N Macauley 5-8-12 p (49) P McCabe 6/1: 2-523515: Held up, prog 5f out, no impress 1f out.	shd	**38a**
666*	**SHATIN SPECIAL** 9 [8] G C H Chung 4-8-7 6ex 2oh (46) R Ffrench 7/1: 2-52F416: Chsd ldrs wide, ev ch 2f out, sn wknd:	11	**20a**
689	**DAIMAJIN** 6 [9] Mrs Lucinda Featherstone 5-9-2 (53) A Culhane 14/1: 00-10547: Chsd ldrs, wknd 3f out:	5	**20a**
665	**DANUM** 9 [5] R Hollinshead 4-8-8 1oh (47) N Callan 40/1: 6066-458: Al bhd:	9	**2a**
711	**INTENSITY** 2 [7] P A Blockley 8-9-4 (55) G Parkin 11/2: 602000-39: Cl-up, fdd 3f out:	nk	**9a**
3247}	**ICE AND FIRE** 211 [1] B D Leavy 5-9-1 bl (52) J Fanning 20/1: 606005-0: Prom, led 1m out, hdd 5f out, sn wknd:	2	**3a**
460	**HOMERIC TROJAN** 35 [3] M Brittain 4-8-11 (50) M Lawson 40/1: 000-60: Led 3f, wknd 5f out.	1¼	**-1a**
11 Ran	2m 33.03 (11.73) Owner Mrs Kenyon A Rhodes Haulage	Trained at Malton	

WOLVERHAMPTON Friday 27.02.04 Lefthand, Sharp Track

Official Going Slow

747	1.00 Betdirect Co Uk New Site Amateur Riders' Handicap Stakes 4yo+ 0-65 (G)			[41]
	£2618 £748 £374 1m1f79y f/sand	Going 108	-49 Slow	Stalls Inside

699*	**SCOTTISH RIVER** 4 [13] M D I Usher 5-11-13 6ex (68) Mr L Newnes (5) 11/4: 3-301511: Slow away, held up, hdwy trav well to lead on bit over 2f out, pushed out, cmftbly:		**74a**
699	**PASO DOBLE** 4 [10] B R Millman 6-11-6 (61) Mr J Millman (7) 14/1: 00-50262: Bhd, hdwy to chall 2f out, kept on, not pace of wnr.	1	**62a**
421	**CALL OF THE WILD** 43 [6] R A Fahey 4-10-11 p (52) Mr R Stephens (5) 20/1: 60346-03: Chsd ldrs, eff to chall 2f out,	½	**52a**

188

onepace:

666	**BEVIER** 10 [8] T Wall 10-10-4 (45) Mr M Howells (7) 20/1: 0040-534: Bhd, kept on fnl 2f, nrst fin/weak ride.			hd	45a
318	**SINJAREE** 53 [7] Mrs S Lamyman 6-10-4 (45) Mrs M Morriss (7) 25/1: 00000-05: Bhd, hdwy over 3f out, onepace over 1f out:			½	44a
526*	**IAMBACK** 25 [5] Miss Gay Kelleway 4-10-9 e (50) Miss E J Jones 14/1: 606-2616: Handy, wknd over 1f out:			9	35a
639	**NOBLE PURSUIT** 12 [12] P A Blockley 7-11-0 (55) Miss S Renwick (5) 12/1: 440-2207: Slow away & bhd, no danger.			2	37a
683	**SURDOUE** 8 [4] P Howling 4-11-6 (61) Mr S Walker 9/4 FAV: 05-02428: Led 4f out till over 2f out:			2	40a
585	**YENALED** 18 [3] K A Ryan 7-11-3 (58) Mr M Seston (5) 7/1: 545-3059: Slow away & al bhd:			18	9a
562	**ILLUSTRIOUS DUKE** 21 [11] M Mullineaux 6-10-4 (45) Miss M Mullineaux (7) 50/1: 1200-000: In tch, wknd 2f out.			1¼	0
699	**CRUSOE** 4 [2] A Sadik 7-11-6 bl (61) Mr E Dehdashti (3) 12/1: 50440-30: In tch, wknd over 3f out:			1	9a
479	**LITTLETON ZEPHIR** 32 [1] Mrs C Thompson (5) 50/1: 306-0200: Led till over 4f out, wknd.			9	0

12 Ran   2m 12.98 (14.78)   Owner Mr M D I Usher   Trained at Lambourn

---

748 **1.35 New Site @ Betdirect Co Uk Handicap Stakes Div 1 3yo+ 0-70 (E)**   **[67]**
£3241 £926 £463   **5f f/sand rnd**   **Going 108   +06 Fast**   Stalls Inside

646	**AROGANT PRINCE** 11 [3] A W Carroll 7-8-12 bl (51) J Quinn 10/1: 4063101: Made all, trav well, clr over 1f out, rdn out:				60a
508*	**MYND** 28 [5] R M Whitaker 4-9-13 (66) Dean McKeown 6/5 FAV: 0034-112: Bmpd sltly start, sn rdn in tch, kept on over 1f out, nvr a threat to wnr:			3	66a
643	**VIJAY** 11 [2] I Semple 5-9-5 P (58) A Culhane 12/1: 34360-03: Bhd, eff 2f out, kept on ins last:			1	55a
610	**CLEVELAND WAY** 15 [4] D Carroll 4-8-7 vis (46) D Tudhope (5) 33/1: 0-126564: Chsd ldrs, onepace.			hd	42a
641	**ERRACHT** 11 [7] K R Burke 6-9-1 (54) G Baker 25/1: 62030-05: In tch, no extra over 1f out:			3	41a
660	**LADY PEKAN** 10 [10] P S McEntee 5-9-10 bl (63) N Callan 10/1: 141-6356: Chsd wnr, wknd over 1f out:			nk	49a
667	**SOTONIAN** 10 [11] P S Felgate 11-8-1 (40) Lisa Jones (3) 16/1: 000-5337: Bhd, nvr a factor.			½	24a
655	**GONENDUNNETT** 10 [8] Mrs C A Dunnett 5-10-0 p (67) Dane O'Neill 16/1: 103-0008: Al bhd:			shd	51a
550	**MALAHIDE EXPRESS** 22 [1] M J Polglase 4-9-7 bl (60) D Holland 12/1: 3500-459: In tch, wknd 2f out:			½	42a
619	**RIVER DAYS** 14 [9] Miss Gay Kelleway 6-9-3 bl t (56) M Fenton 12/1: 4400-020: Al bhd:			shd	38a
655	**TABOOR** 10 [6] J W Payne 6-9-11 h bl (64) I Mongan 10/1: 00-00050: Al bhd:			shd	45a

11 Ran   1m 05.33 (5.13)   Owner Mr Dennis Deacon   Trained at Alcester

---

749 **2.10 New Site @ Betdirect Co Uk Handicap Stakes Div 2 3yo+ 0-70 (E)**   **[67]**
£3241 £926 £463   **5f f/sand rnd**   **Going 108   -05 Slow**   Stalls Inside

687	**PLAYTIME BLUE** 7 [1] K R Burke 4-9-13 6ex (66) G Baker 6/5 FAV: 2-236121: Made all, travel well, drvn to hold on fnl 1f:				72a
643	**TIGRESS** 11 [4] J W Unett 5-9-3 bl (56) M Fenton 6/1: 60-65262: Cl-up, eff over 1f out, kept on for press ins last, not btn far:			½	60a
641*	**CASH** 11 [8] Paul Johnson 6-9-13 6ex p (66) L Fletcher (3) 8/1: 0164-013: Handy, onepace over 1f out.			2½	63a
4925}	**STOIC LEADER** 122 [5] R F Fisher 4-9-5 (58) S Righton 25/1: 420000-4: Sn rdn in tch, onepace over 1f out:			1	52a
641	**EMPRESS JOSEPHINE** 11 [9] J R Jenkins 4-9-3 vis (56) D Corby (3) 5/1: 2424-125: Handy, wknd over 1f out:			1¾	45a
653	**MANGUS** 11 [6] K O Cunningham Brown 10-8-1 bl e (40) J Mackay 40/1: 0600-306: Bhd, nvr a factor:			1	26a
345	**TELEPATHIC** 50 [2] A Berry 4-9-9 (62) F Lynch 66/1: 00000-07: Nvr a factor:			¾	46a
660	**PRIME RECREATION** 10 [7] P S Felgate 7-9-11 p (64) Dale Gibson 14/1: 400-6068: Chsd ldrs, wknd over 1f out:			1½	44a
4695}	**QUEEN OF BULGARIA** 138 [3] J Pearce 3-8-8 (61) J Quinn 20/1: 616202-9: Al bhd:			1¼	37a
687	**PRINCE OF BLUES** 7 [10] M Mullineaux 6-9-12 bl (65) S W Kelly 25/1: 00-02000: In tch, btn over 2f out.			5	26a

10 Ran   1m 05.87 (5.67)   Owner Mr P Sweeting   Trained at Leyburn

---

750 **2.45 Littlewoods Bet Direct Maiden Stakes 3yo+ (D)**
£3354 £1032 £516 £258   **6f f/sand rnd**   **Going 108   +08 Fast**   Stalls Inside

617	**GLOBAL ACHIEVER** 14 [10] G C H Chung 3-8-9 (67) R Ffrench 11/8 FAV: 3221: Made all, clr 2f out, kept on, rdn out:				74a
2567}	**FIT TO FLY** 245 [9] S Kirk 3-8-9 (81) J F Egan 5/2: 050-2: Cl-up, eff to chase wnr 2f out, kept on same pace:			1¾	67a
592	**NANNA** 17 [5] R Hollinshead 3-8-4 (50) J Quinn 14/1: 00-5203: In tch, rdn & outpcd over 2f out, some late gains:			6	47a
659	**OTYLIA** 10 [1] A Berry 4-9-5 (52) F Lynch 10/1: 23544-54: Prom, wknd well over 1f out:			nk	46a
3103}	**BRIGHT FIRE** 218 [7] W J Musson 3-8-4 (50) Lisa Jones (3) 8/1: 06-5: Slow away & al bhd on reapp:			8	30a
441	**DANTES DEVINE** 39 [3] A Bailey 3-8-9 (56) C Catlin 33/1: 0055-06: Al bhd.			2½	30a
659	**BROOKLANDS TIME** 10 [2] I W McInnes 3-8-4 (63) J Bramhill 20/1: 433-07: Slow away & nvr a factor.			nk	24a
4420}	**JILLY WH** 156 [4] Ms Deborah J Evans 3-8-4 (63) Joanna Badger 12/1: 6340-8: Al bhd.			5	14a

8 Ran   1m 18.81 (6.01)   Owner Dr Johnny Hon   Trained at Newmarket

---

751 **3.20 Betdirect Co Uk Median Auction Maiden Stakes 3-4yo (E)**
£3297 £942 £471   **1m100y f/sand rnd Going 108   -16 Slow**   Stalls Inside

645	**BOOK MATCHED** 11 [7] B Smart 3-8-6 (65) R Ffrench 5/4 FAV: 003-31: Handy, hdwy to lead over 1f out, sn pushed clr, cmftbtly:				76a
645	**HAWKIT** 11 [3] J A Osborne 3-8-9 3ow (72) D Holland 2/1: 32233-52: Led till over 1f out, kept on onepace:			1¾	72a
1717}	**WONKY DONKEY** 277 [5] S C Williams 3-8-9 J Tate 25/1: 0-3: In tch, wknd well over 1f out.			8	53a
700	**BALLYRUSH** 4 [6] K R Burke 4-9-11 (67) R Keogh (7) 7/1: 0/600-054: With ldrs, wknd over 2f out.			11	31a
	SUNSET BLUES [2] K O Cunningham Brown 4-9-11 BL e D Corby (3) 50/1: 5: Slow & al bhd.			1¾	27a
4737}	**SHOWTIME ANNIE** 136 [4] A Bailey 3-8-1 (65) C Catlin 12/1: 003300-6: In tch, wknd over 2f out.			¾	20a
671	**FORA SMILE** 9 [9] M D I Usher 3-8-6 D Kinsella 66/1: 0007: Al bhd.			½	18a
	BULBERRY HILL [8] M G Quinlan 3-8-6 D R McCabe 28/1: 8: V slow away & al bhd.			8	2a
	DIVERTED [1] M G Quinlan 3-8-1 Nicol Polli (7) 33/1: 9: Al bhd.			4	0a

9 Ran   1m 56.76 (10.56)   Owner Mr Paul Darling   Trained at Thirsk

---

752 **3.50 Daily Special Offers @ Betdirect Co Uk Classified Stakes 4yo+ 0-70 (E)**
£3213 £918 £459   **1m4f f/sand   Going 108   -55 Slow**   Stalls Inside

142	**MOON SHOT** 86 [3] A G Juckes 8-9-1 (67) V Slattery 14/1: 04251/3-1: Keen cl-up, led 2f out, kept on, rdn out:				74a
704	**YORKER** 4 [2] Ms Deborah J Evans 6-9-1 (67) N Callan 13/2: 0-253422: Cl-up, eff over 2f out, kept on same pace:			3½	68a

48	TONI ALCALA 102 [7] R F Fisher 5-9-1 (64) L Fletcher (3) 12/1: 102040-3: Sn bhd, eff over 3f out, kept on same pace:	1½	66a
277	EASIBET DOT NET 58 [4] I Semple 4-8-12 VIS (62) A Culhane 11/8 FAV: 323215-4: Led till over 2f out, wknd:	10	52a
679*	BELLA PAVLINA 8 [1] W M Brisbourne 6-9-4 (56) B Swarbrick (7) 11/4: 1211415: In tch, wknd over 3f out:	5	48a
347*	PARADISE VALLEY 50 [5] Mrs Stef Liddiard 4-8-12 (53) S Drowne 13/2: 14525-16: Al bhd:	23	5a
6 Ran	2m 50.14 (19.54) Owner Whistlejacket Partnership	Trained at Abberley	

753   **4.20 Bet In Running @ Betdirect Co Uk Handicap Stakes Div 1 3yo+ 0-60 (F)** [58]

£2968 £848 £424   **1m100y**   **Going 108   -34 Slow**   Stalls Inside

629	GERONIMO 13 [10] Miss Gay Kelleway 7-10-0 p (58) Dean Williams (7) 25/1: 020-2031: Bhd, hdwy over 2f out, led ins last, drvn out to hold on:		64a
647*	DESERT HEAT 11 [2] I Semple 6-10-3 6ex BL (61) N Callan 12/1: 004-0212: Held up, hdwy over 2f out, chall ins last, just held:	nk	66a
630*	JAKARMI 13 [4] B Palling 3-8-11 (60) D Kinsella 22/1: 650-1613: Led after 1f till ins last, just held:	nk	64a
620	DANGER BIRD 14 [7] R Hollinshead 4-9-7 (51) M Fenton 16/1: 53-23024: Led 1f, wknd fnl 1f:	1½	52a
664	GRAND LASS 10 [3] A Sadik 5-9-6 p (50) D Holland 10/1: 46-34125: Bhd halfway, kept on late:	nk	50a
704	GIVEMETHEMOONLIGHT 4 [5] Mrs Stef Liddiard 5-9-12 vis (56) I Mongan 5/1: 5361236: In tch, wknd 2f out:	nk	55a
4669]	INSIGNIFICANCE 149 [9] John A Quinn 4-9-2 (46) J Murtagh 9/1: 006002-7: In tch, wknd over 2f out:	3	39a
678*	REALISM 8 [6] P W Hiatt 4-9-9 (53) A Culhane 7/4 FAV: 350-4418: Al bhd:	hd	45a
559	FUTURISTIC 21 [1] J Pearce 4-9-13 VIS (57) J Quinn 5/1: 26006-29: Handy, wknd well over 1f out, reportedly unsuited by v slow surface:	1¼	46a
680+*	EAGER ANGEL 8 [11] R F Marvin 6-9-8 6ex p (52) Dean McKeown 12/1: 2401510: Keen in tch, wknd 2f out:	shd	41a
10 Ran	1m 58.27 (12.07) Owner Mr A P Griffin	Trained at Newmarket	

754   **4.50 Bet In Running @ Betdirect Co Uk Handicap Stakes Div 2 3yo+ 0-60 (F)** [58]

£2961 £846 £423   **1m100y f/sand rnd Going 108   -10 Slow**   Stalls Inside

719	DANCING KING 3 [6] P W Hiatt 8-8-6 6ex (36) B Swarbrick (7) 100/30: 4052131: Made all, kept on well fnl 1f, rdn out:		46a
685	LORD CHAMBERLAIN 7 [9] J M Bradley 3-8-12 (46) C Catlin (7) 9/1: 2144022: In tch, hdwy over 1f out, not pace of wnr:	3	39a
387	GOODBYE MR BOND 45 [4] E J Alston 4-9-9 (53) J Quinn 3/1 FAV: 3404-563: Chsd ldrs, btn over 1f out:	7	42a
639	DONEGAL SHORE 12 [7] Mrs J Candlish 5-9-7 vis t (51) N Chalmers (5) 16/1: 600-4224: In tch, btn 2f out:	1	38a
629	SPY GUN 13 [5] T Wall 4-9-12 (56) D Holland 13/2: 14-35005: Handy, wknd over 2f out:	2	39a
633*	HEATHERS GIRL 13 [2] D Haydn Jones 5-10-0 bl (56) Paul Eddery 16/1: 6040/016: In tch, wknd 2f out:	2	37a
659	SHADOWFAX 10 [8] Miss Gay Kelleway 4-9-12 e (56) M Fenton 16/1: 6/62-4007: Al bhd:	hd	34a
664	BULAWAYO 10 [1] Andrew Reid 7-9-4 (48) S Donohoe (5) 12/1: 30-53038: In tch, btn over 2f out:	¾	24a
647	TAIYO 11 [10] J W Payne 4-9-6 VIS (50) N Callan 10/1: 60-65449: Handy, wknd over 2f out:	4	18a
	TEMPTATION ISLAND 149 [3] John A Quinn 5-9-1 (45) J Murtagh 10/1: 410060-0: Al bhd on Brit debut:	nk	12a
10 Ran	1m 56.24 (10.04) Owner Mr P W Hiatt	Trained at Banbury	

Official Going Standard

755   **1.30 Daily Offers @ Betdirect Co Uk Handicap Stakes 3yo+ 0-80 (D)** [77]

£4095 £1260 £630 £315   **5f p/track rnd   Going 26   +01 Fast**   Stalls Outside

567	TURIBIUS 21 [10] T E Powell 5-10-0 (77) K Fallon 8/1: 34021-61: Handy, styd on well over 1f out to lead ins last, rdn out:		85a
660	POLISH EMPEROR 11 [1] P W Harris 4-10-0 bl (77) D Holland 5/4 FAV: 6410-422: Dwelt, bhd, hdwy over 1f out, styd on ins last, just held:	hd	84a
655	THE FISIO 11 [6] A M Balding 4-9-10 (73) Martin Dwyer 6/1: 00-11563: Set pace, rdn & hdd ins last, kept on, just held:	nk	79a
3077}	ANOTHER GLIMPSE 220 [4] Miss B Sanders 6-9-9 t (72) T Quinn 33/1: 550650-4: Chsd ldrs, eff over 1f out, onepace:	1¼	73a
692	CHICO GUAPO 7 [5] J A Glover 4-10-0 (77) Dean McKeown 16/1: 41015-05: Keen, in tch, onepace over 1f out:	¾	76a
704	GRANT 5 [9] P Morris 4-9-1 p (64) J Murtagh 25/1: 16004-56: Slow away, bhd, some late gains:	nk	62a
748	LADY PEKAN 1 [7] P S McEntee 5-8-13 bl (62) N Callan 20/1: 141-63567: Cl-up, wknd over 1f out:	½	58a
390	AWARDING 46 [2] R F Johnson Houghton 4-9-9 t (72) Dane O'Neill 7/1: 56506-58: Slow away, nvr a factor:	hd	67a
516	MADRASEE 28 [8] L Montague Hall 6-9-5 (68) F Lynch 14/1: 1021-209: Handy, wknd over 1f out:	2	57a
516	PHECKLESS 28 [3] J M Bradley 5-9-3 (66) R Hughes 9/1: 564-0340: Slow away & al bhd:	1¼	51a
10 Ran	59.06 (1.26) Owner Vogue Development Company (Ken	Trained at Reigate	

756   **2.00 Bet Direct On 0800 32 93 93 Conditions Stakes 3yo (B)**

£12035 £4565 £2283 £1038   **1m sw rnd   Going 26   +05 Fast**   Stalls Inside

568	ASCERTAIN 21 [4] N P Littmoden 3-8-11 (98) D Holland 10/11 FAV: 01-121: Handy, hdwy trav well & led 1f out, rdn clr:		103a
713*	BAHIANO 4 [9] C E Brittain 3-8-11 (72) K Fallon 7/2: 62-212: Trkd ldr, led over 2f out till 1f out, not pace of wnr:	2½	96a
694*	ROYAL WARRANT 7 [6] A M Balding 3-8-11 (79) Martin Dwyer 4/1: 310-3613: Held up, hdwy appr 2f out, onepcd over 1f out:	5	86a
79*	PETARDIAS MAGIC 77 [7] E J O'Neill 3-8-13 (84) R Ffrench 20/1: 123016-4: Keen, in tch wide, hdwy 2f out, no impress:	hd	87a
2745*}	FIREBELLY 237 [2] M J Wallace 3-8-12 VIS (95) S Drowne 16/1: 1311-5: Handy, no extra fnl 2f on reapp:	3½	79a
656	TONTO 11 [10] Miss D Mountain 3-8-11 p (60) G Carter 100/1: 20-04306: Nvr a factor:	½	77a
	WELL KNIT 167 [3] P W D'Arcy 3-8-6 J F Egan 100/1: 120-7: Al bhd:	1¼	69a
4770}	DOCTORED 135 [1] B A Pearce 3-8-11 p (54) C Catlin 100/1: 602023-8: Led till over 2f out, no extra on reapp:	4	66a
428*	GROUVILLE 42 [5] B J Meehan 3-8-11 Paul Eddery 20/1: 19: In tch, wknd over 2f out:	4	58a
9 Ran	1m 7.91 (1.71) Owner Mr Paul J Dixon	Trained at Newmarket	

757   **2.35 Betdirect Co Uk New Site Coming Soon Handicap Stakes 4yo+ 46-52 (F)** [65]

£2961 £846 £423   **1m2f p/track   Going 26   -09 Slow**   Stalls Inside

731	RAHEEL 3 [2] P Mitchell 4-8-11 t (49) D Holland 100/30 FAV: 60-54061: Chsd ldrs, hdwy to lead 2f out, rdn clr, cmftbly:		59a

515	**INDIAN BLAZE** 28 [1] Andrew Reid 10-8-9 1oh (45) T P Queally (3) 5/1: 40B00-62: Hld up, hdwy & no room 2f out, styd on strongly ins last:	4	48a
675	**FRENCH HORN** 10 [14] M Wigham 7-8-11 p (48) G Carter 14/1: 00-14353: Hld up & sn switched ins, eff & short of room 2f out, kept on ins last:	¾	48a
718	**ANOTHER SECRET** 4 [8] G L Moore 6-8-12 bl e (49) S Whitworth 9/2 6B04-354: Slow away, held up, hdwy to chase wnr over 1f out, no extra:	nk	49a
515	**ITSONLYAGAME** 28 [9] R Ingram 4-8-12 (50) I Mongan 16/1: 406-1005: Bhd, hdwy & short of room over 4f out, hdwy 2f out, onepace:	1	48a
746	**SO SURE** 2 [11] J G M O'Shea 4-9-0 (52) Dean McKeown 13/2 00/5101-46: In tch, wknd over 1f out:	5	42a
644	**ANDAAD** 12 [6] D J Daly 4-8-12 (50) C Catlin 16/1: 0/-547: Al bhd:	3½	34a
738	**KUMAKAWA** 2 [5] E A Wheeler 6-8-9 1oh bl (45) Liam Jones (7) 20/1: 00-050308: Al bhd:	nk	29a
115	**TATA NAKA** 92 [10] Mrs C A Dunnett 4-8-12 (50) Hayley Turner (5) 33/1: 0650-9: Cl-up, led over 2f out, sn hdd & no extra:	½	32a
257	**ERSAAL** 63 [4] J Jay 4-8-10 (48) N Callan 40/1: 503000-0: Handy, wknd over 2f out:	7	18a
620*	**JADE STAR** 15 [7] Miss Gay Kelleway 4-9-0 (52) M Fenton 4/1: 0325-410: Led till over 2f out, wknd qckly:	1	20a
3512}	**SILVER LOUIE** 202 [3] G B Balding 4-8-13 (51) S Carson 66/1: 00000R-0: In tch, wknd over 2f out:	½	18a
4459}	**TACA DOLI** 509 [13] E J O'Neill 5-9-1 (52) R Ffrench 40/1: 000/-0: In tch, wknd over 3f out.	17	0a
672	**SILISTRA** 10 [12] Mrs L C Jewell 5-8-13 vis (50) Dane O'Neill 100/1: 4/0000-00: In tch, wknd over 3f out.	dist	0a

14 Ran   2m 06.27 (3.47)   Owner Mrs S Sheldon   Trained at Epsom

---

758

3.10 Littlewoods Bet Direct Handicap Stakes 3yo+ 0-95 (C)   [95]
£12151 £4609 £2305 £1048 1m2f p/track   Going 26   -20 Slow   Stalls Inside

688*	**CONSONANT** 8 [3] D G Bridgwater 7-9-5 (86) K Fallon 5/1: 10////-111: In tch trav well, hdwy to lead 1f out, styd on well, drvn out:		94a
475	**DANCE IN THE SUN** 35 [1] Mrs A J Perrett 4-9-3 (85) Dane O'Neill 7/1: 2410-642: Led till 1f out, not pace of wnr but kept on:	¾	91a
625	**NORTHSIDE LODGE** 14 [6] P W Harris 6-9-6 (87) I Mongan 9/2 FAV: 404-2203: Held up, hdwy 2f out, styd on ins last, not btn far:	shd	92a
1190}	**ARRY DASH** 309 [5] M R Channon 4-9-5 (87) S Hitchcott (3) 14/1: 2/12015-4: Held up, hdwy over 1f out, kept on ins last:	¾	90a
570*	**GIG HARBOR** 21 [2] Miss E C Lavelle 5-10-0 (95) L Keniry (3) 10/1: 626-1015: Cl-up, no extra over 1f out:	¾	96a
625	**MOAYED** 14 [10] N P Littmoden 5-9-1 bl t (82) D Holland 5/1: 1500-126: Held up, hdwy 2f out, no extra in last.	½	82a
	QUDRAH 128 [4] E J O'Neill 4-9-3 BL (85) R Ffrench 66/1: 4/51650-7: In tch, onepcd over 1f out:	shd	84a
688	**KENTUCKY KING** 8 [8] P W Hiatt 4-8-12 (80) A Culhane 66/1: 1/4-668: In tch, no extra over 1f out:	1	77a
4894}	**DUMARAN** 126 [7] W J Musson 6-9-11 (92) M Fenton 20/1: 500403-9: Slow away & al bhd:	nk	89a
625	**DOWER HOUSE** 14 [9] Andrew Turnell 9-8-13 t (80) D Corby (3) 14/1: 10-46540: Keen, nvr a factor:	3	71a
625*	**AFRICAN SAHARA** 14 [13] Miss D Mountain 5-8-12 t (79) G Carter 10/1: 0226-610: Al bhd:	2	66a
632	**SKYLARKER** 14 [11] W S Kittow 6-8-12 VIS (79) M Savage (4) 20/1: 304-2330: Keen in tch, wknd dist:	1	64a
674*	**MAD CAREW** 10 [14] G L Moore 5-8-12 bl e (79) S Whitworth 16/1: 1322-510: In tch, wknd 2f out:	nk	63a
5036*}	**TURBO** 112 [12] G B Balding 5-9-13 p (74) R Havlin 9/1: 600021-0: Slow away & al bhd on reapp.	1½	75a

14 Ran   2m 05.41 (2.61)   Owner The Rule Racing Syndicate   Trained at Winchcombe

---

759

3.40 Betdirect Co Uk Maiden Stakes 3yo (D)
£5174 £1592 £796 £398   1m2f p/track   Going 26   -64 Slow   Stalls Inside

496	**DANCING LYRA** 31 [7] J W Hills 3-9-0 (73) M Hills 8/1: 0300-61: Trkd ldr, went on over 2f out, styd on strongly fnl 1f, rdn out:		82a
473	**FIDDLERS FORD** 35 [5] J Noseda 3-9-0 (72) J P Spencer 8/11 FAV: 0-322: Chsd ldrs, prog 2f out, chsd wnr fnl 1f, no impress cl-home:	1¼	78a
	SWAINSON [9] P Mitchell 3-9-0 D Holland 16/1: 3: Slow away, keen & chsd ldrs, not qckn fnl 1f on debut:	nk	77a
	ZANGEAL [14] C F Wall 3-9-0 G Baker 25/1: 4: Slow away, ran green till styd on nicely fnl 1f, nrst fin on debut:	1¼	75a
601	**AMWELL BRAVE** 17 [2] J R Jenkins 3-9-0 (68) K Fallon 15/2: 45-22335: Trkd ldrs, rdn & onepcd fnl 1f:	1½	72a
601	**ZAFFEU** 17 [4] N P Littmoden 3-9-0 T P Queally (3) 33/1: 06: Chsd ldrs, onepcd fnl 1f.	½	71a
21	**AMEYRAH** 107 [8] M R Channon 3-8-9 S Hitchcott (3) 16/1: 00-7: Held up, nvr nr ldrs on reapp/h'cap qual run.	4	58a
672	**RESONANCE** 10 [10] N A Twiston Davies 3-8-9 (70) Joanna Badger 6/1: 043-28: Slowly away, nvr nr ldrs on drop back in trip:	1¼	25a
4067}	**FOXILLA** 176 [12] D R C Elsworth 3-8-9 (63) Dane O'Neill 50/1: 000-9: Nvr btr than mid-div on reapp.	hd	24a
623	**SAINT ZITA** 14 [3] B J Meehan 3-8-9 J F McDonald 66/1: 00: Led till 2f out, wknd.	nk	23a
367	**ATLANTIC TERN** 49 [13] N M Babbage 3-9-0 (53) N Callan 100/1: 00-60: Al towards rear:	hd	27a
601	**CHAMPAGNE SHADOW** 17 [6] G L Moore 3-9-0 A Culhane 100/1: 04-040: Nvr nr ldrs:	5	19a
	HIGHFLUTING [1] R M Flower 3-8-9 D Sweeney 100/1: 0: Al towards rear on debut.	4	7a
	LAKAAM [11] G P Enright 3-8-9 R Brisland 100/1: 0: Rcd wide & al bhd, fin last on debut.	¾	6a

14 Ran   2m 11.86 (9.06)   Owner Mr N N Browne   Trained at Lambourn

---

760

4.15 New Site Coming Soon @ Betdirect Co Uk Handicap Stakes Fillies 3yo+ 0-75 (E)   [75]
£3387 £1042 £521 £261   6f p/track rnd   Going 26   -00 Slow   Stalls Inside

657*	**FOREVER PHOENIX** 11 [1] R M H Cowell 4-9-9 (70) J Murtagh 3/1 FAV: 201-5611: Chsd ldrs, prog to lead ent fnl 1f, sn clr, easily:		84a
604	**AND TOTO TOO** 17 [10] P D Evans 4-9-8 bl (69) K Fallon 9/2: 3515-062: Dwelt, hdwy over 1f out, fin well into 2nd but no ch with wnr:	3	71a
604	**BLONDE EN BLONDE** 17 [9] N P Littmoden 4-9-7 (68) I Mongan 8/1: 6601203: Outpcd, hdwy wide over 1f out, kept & nrst fin:	nk	69a
628	**CLASSIC VISION** 14 [8] W J Haggas 4-8-9 (56) A Culhane 25/1: 53-1004: Slowly away, styd on late:	1	54a
653	**LYDIAS LOOK** 12 [2] T J Etherington 7-7-12 5oh (40) D Kinsella 50/1: 5000-055: Chsd ldrs, onepcd fnl 2f:	½	41a
234	**MARGALITA** 70 [3] P Mitchell 4-10-0 (75) D Holland 16/1: 131300-6: Led till ent fnl 1f, no extra:	nk	70a
121	**WOODBURY** 91 [7] K R Burke 5-8-9 (56) G Baker 14/1: 25D260-7: Prom & wide, wknd fnl 1f:	¾	49a
261	**MAN CRAZY** 61 [4] R M Beckett 3-8-3 (65) J Mackay 20/1: 332300-8: Outpcd, nvr nr ldrs:	½	57a
4815+	**'MISS POPPETS** 131 [5] D R C Elsworth 4-9-6 (67) T Quinn 6/1: 030421-9: Mid-div, wkng when hmpd 1f out:	1	56a

740	PARK STAR 2	[6] D Shaw 4-8-8 (55) J F McDonald (5) 100/30: 6000-6320: Trkd ldr 4.5f, wknd:	¾	42a
740	LUCEBALL 2	[11] P Morris 4-7-13 bl (46) J Quinn 16/1: 604000-90: Chsd ldrs 4.5f, wknd:	3	23a
11 Ran	1m 11.99 (1.59)	Owner Mr J M Greetham	Trained at Newmarket	

---

761   **4.50 Bet Direct On 0800 32 93 93 Handicap Stakes**   3yo+ 46-52 (F)   [59]
£3073 £878 £439   **7f p/track**   Going 26   -07 Slow   Stalls Outside

732	ALAFZAR 3	[4] P D Evans 6-9-11 bl t (56) K Fallon 13/8 FAV: 40-40131: Held up, imprvd 2f out, led ins fnl 1f, rdn out:		64a
565	LILY OF THE GUILD 21	[11] W S Kittow 5-9-7 (52) N Callan 8/1: 4462-002: Held up, rapid hdwy 2f out, chsd wnr fnl 1f, no impress cl-home:	1¼	56a
678	BLAKESEVEN 9	[13] W J Musson 4-9-3 (48) Paul Eddery 11/1: 040-3223: Rear, hdwy wide late.	¾	51a
659	ZAK FACTA 11	[7] Miss D A McHale 4-9-5 vis t (50) S Whitworth 6/1: 400-5524: Keen & rear, late gains.	nk	52a
739	SCARROTTOO 2	[9] S C Williams 6-9-5 (50) Martin Dwyer 11/1: 40-035005: Trkd ldr, led 2f out till ins fnl 1f, no extra.	¾	50a
669	MISTER CLINTON 10	[1] D K Ivory 7-9-1 bl (46) R Miles (3) 20/1: 00-00006: Keen in rear, prog when no room 2f out, nrst fin:	2	42a
739	AGUILA LOCO 2	[8] Mrs Stef Liddiard 5-9-9 (52) M Fenton 7/1: 26253147: Led till 2f out, wknd:	¾	48a
441	JOINT DESTINY 40	[3] E J O'Neill 3-8-1 (49) R Ffrench 40/1: 02340-58: Slow away, nvr nr ldrs:	2	39a
662	DANCING PRINCE 11	[2] A P Jarvis 3-8-2 (50) C Catlin 16/1: 005-549: Chsd ldrs 5.5f, wknd.	hd	39a
673	LITTLE FLUTE 10	[12] T Keddy 3-7-12 1oh (45) Lisa Jones (3) 33/1: 02-40000: Slowly away, al bhd.	nk	34a
530	ROBIN SHARP 25	[10] J Akehurst 6-9-3 vis t (48) J Quinn 20/1: 00200-260: Chsd ldrs wide, btn halfway.	5	26a
3926}	TREE ROOFER 185	[5] N P Littmoden 5-9-3 (48) D Holland 16/1: 535040-0: Chsd ldrs, short of room 2f out, no ch after:	3½	19a
20	FIRE DOME 107	[6] Andrew Reid 12-9-7 t (52) I Mongan 40/1: 500/340-0: Chsd ldrs till halfway, sn bhd, fin last.	9	5a
13 Ran	1m 25.16 (2.36)	Owner Waterline Racing Club	Trained at Abergavenny	

---

762   **5.20 Maxie Fantoni 95th Anniversary Handicap Stakes**   4yo+ 0-65 (F)   [63]
£3038 £868 £434   **1m5f p/track**   Going 26   -09 Slow   Stalls Inside

520	CROSSWAYS 28	[1] P D Evans 6-10-0 (63) K Fallon 11/4 FAV: 1/P034-41: Prom, drvn to lead dist, held on gamely, all out:		70a
546*	DOLZAGO 24	[3] G L Moore 4-9-7 bl (60) I Mongan 13/2: 00055-12: Trkd ldr, imprvd to lead 2f out, hdd dist, rallied gamely & just btn in a tight fin:	hd	66a
634	JADEERON 14	[8] Miss D A McHale 5-9-13 p (62) Lisa Jones (3) 33/1: 400-2223: Bhd, late gains.	1¼	66a
515	MUNFARID 28	[6] P G Murphy t (60) S Drowne 25/1: 4454-304: Chsd ldrs, onepcd fnl 1.5f.	1¼	62a
4481}	TURTLE VALLEY 154	[5] S Dow 8-9-11 (60) J Coffill Brown (7) 25/1: 060310-5: Rear, prog 2f out, no impress fnl 1f:	1½	60a
711	JOELY GREEN 4	[4] N P Littmoden 7-9-6 (55) D Holland 12/1: 435-5066: Prom, wknd fnl 1f:	½	54a
521	MYSTERLOVER 28	[2] N P Littmoden 4-9-3 T (56) T P Queally (3) 33/1: 4P-007: Nvr btr than mid-div:	1	51a
723	RADIANT BRIDE 4	[7] K R Burke 4-8-6 bl (49) Darren Williams 8/1: 0-026128: Slow away, nvr nr ldrs:	2	42a
711	FOREVER MY LORD 4	[9] J R Best 6-8-12 (47) N Pollard 16/1: 0430-009: Led till 2f out, wknd:	¾	43a
590	ANTONY EBENEEZER 19	[11] C R Dore 5-8-0 t (35) J Bramhill 14/1: 400-5300: Al towards rear:	2	28a
1909}	ANGELS VENTURE 270	[12] J R Jenkins 8-9-1 (50) P Dobbs 14/1: 000/006-0: Chsd ldrs 10f, wknd:	16	25a
3436}	MURZIM 205	[10] J Gallagher 5-9-10 (59) J P Spencer 10/1: 500630-0: Slow away, chsd ldrs, wknd 2f out.	8	24a
12 Ran	2m 46.9 (4.6)	Owner Mr Trevor Gallienne	Trained at Abergavenny	

---

763   **1.35 Bet Direct In Vision Sky Page 293 Handicap Stakes Div 1**   3yo+ 0-60 (F)   [60]
£2940 £840 £420   **1m p/track rnd**   Going 32   -13 Slow   Stalls Outside

622	WELSH WIND 15	[6] M Wigham 8-9-10 t P (56) J Fanning 9/2: 42-32031: Trkd ldrs, led ins last, rdn out:		62a
730	MEELUP 4	[7] Jane Southcombe 4-9-7 p (53) V Slattery 16/1: 1000-022: Led, drvn & hdd well ins last, kept on:	¾	57a
607	FRANKSKIPS 18	[9] Miss B Sanders 5-9-10 (56) T Quinn 7/2: 00-05003: Sn prom, onepace for press.	1½	57a
726	HE WHO DARES 4	[2] A W Carroll 6-9-11 (57) S Whitworth 6/4 FAV: 012-2034: Slow away & bhd, kept on wide for press, nrst fin:	nk	57a
732	PAS DE SURPRISE 4	[5] P D Evans 6-9-9 (55) Joanna Badger 10/1: 364-3055: Trkd ldrs, no extra dist:	½	54a
4459}	EHAB 156	[4] G L Moore 5-9-11 (57) Dane O'Neill 12/1: 004000-6: Dwelt, sn trkd ldrs, no extra over 1f out:	5	47a
729	TARANAI 4	[10] B W Duke 3-8-0 (51) C Catlin 33/1: 006-4007: Mid-div, no impress when carried wide over 1f out, qck reapp.	nk	40a
647	ROCINANTE 13	[1] J J Quinn 4-9-8 (54) R Winston 7/1: 43010-08: In tch, btn over 1f out.	1	41a
2206}	THUMAMAH 257	[3] B P J Baugh 5-9-7 (53) I Mongan 25/1: 0/00600-0: Al towards rear on reapp.	2½	35a
9 Ran	1m 36.2 (3.61)	Owner Miss R M Spearing	Trained at Newmarket	

---

764   **2.05 Bet Direct In Running Sky Text Page 293 Maiden Stakes**   3yo   (D)
£3304 £944 £472   **7f p/track rnd**   Going 32   -13 Slow   Stalls Inside

696	ECCENTRIC 8	[4] Andrew Reid 3-9-0 A Nicholls 14/1: 0-41: Made all, rdn clr over 2f out, all out to hold on:		73a
670	ALFRIDINI 11	[1] D R C Elsworth 3-9-0 (65) Dane O'Neill 15/8 FAV: 0022 Slow away, chsd wnr from 3f out, drvn & closed, nrst fin:	nk	72a
3939}	WAVERTREE GIRL 185	[8] N P Littmoden 3-8-10 1ow (90) D Holland 5/2: 3404-3: In tch, drvn & kept on fnl 2f, nvr able to chall:	1¼	65a
177	IMPERIUM 81	[9] Mrs Stef Liddiard 3-9-0 t (77) S Drowne 7/1: 620046-4: In tch wide, btn 2f out:	8	57a
428	STAR FERN 43	[7] J Akehurst 3-9-0 G Carter 20/1: 4-55: Slow away, rear/wide, nvr on terms:	5	48a
649	LADY PREDOMINANT 13	[2] Andrew Reid 3-8-9 (45) S Carson 66/1: 020-4406: Chsd ldrs, btn 2f out.	1¼	40a
670	FLY SO HIGH 11	[6] D Shaw 3-8-9 R Winston 33/1: 07: Slow away & al bhd.	1	38a
1230}	LITTLETON LIBERTY 307	[5] Andrew Reid 3-8-9 BL I Mongan 33/1: 40-8: In tch, struggling halfway, blnks, abs.	19	6a
4875}	DEVILS BITE 128	[3] B W Hills 3-9-0 (77) M Hills 3/1: 65620-P: In tch, struggling 3f out & sn p.u., broke blood vessel.		0
9 Ran	1m 25.92 (3.12)	Owner Mr A S Reid	Trained at Mill Hill London	

---

765   **2.35 Bet Direct No Q 08000 93 66 93 Classified Stakes**   3yo+ 0-60 (F)
£2975 £850 £425   **7f p/track rnd**   Going 32   -04 Slow   Stalls Inside

| 729 | HAZEWIND 4 | [5] P D Evans 3-8-5 t (64) S Carson 6/1: 00-0421: Dwelt & rear, prog 2f out & drvn to lead well in last: | | 64a |
| 499 | NEARLY A FOOL 32 | [4] G G Margarson 6-9-8 vis (60) N Pollard 4/1: 353-1102: Trkd ldrs, drvn & ch fnl 1f, not pace of wnr | ¾ | 63a |

cl-home:

600	ADANTINO 18 [1] B R Millman 5-9-8 bl (57) S Drowne 9/2: 3-634133: Dwelt, mid-div, rdn & led over 1f out, hdd well ins last:		1¼	60a
544	DOUBLE M 25 [6] Mrs L Richards 7-9-8 vis (56) N Callan 14/1: 0-413024: Bhd, hdwy/short of room over 1f out, onepace ins last:		1	58a
628	ILLUSIVE 15 [3] M Wigham 7-9-8 (60) G Carter 8/1: 432-0035: Keen, in tch, hmpd when lost place over 1f out, kept on late, no dngr:		1¾	55a
168	DUO LEONI 82 [8] Mrs Stef Liddiard 4-9-5 (60) M Fenton 9/1: 215020-6: Held up, eff wide, no impress dist:		shd	52a
741	ITS ECCO BOY 3 [10] P Howling 6-9-8 (57) R Winston 14/1: 0-441007: Mid-div, eff 2f out, sn no impress:		1¼	52a
728	JALOUHAR 4 [2] B P J Baugh 4-9-8 (55) I Mongan 25/1: 15-54658: Chsd ldr, fdd under press fnl 2f:		2	48a
740	KARAOKE KING 3 [9] J E Long 6-9-9 (54) Dane O'Neill 33/1: 600-6009: Prom till over 1f out, qck reapp:		1	46a
728	LEGAL SET 4 [7] W J Musson 8-9-8 (60) K Fallon 11/4 FAV: 00600-40: Led till over 1f out, wknd qckly.		1¾	43a
10 Ran	1m 25.3 (2.5)	Owner Mr M W Lawrence		Trained at Abergavenny

---

766   **3.05 Betdirect Co Uk Handicap Stakes Div 1 4yo+ 46-52 (F)**   **[65]**

£2912 £832 £416   **1m p/track rnd**   **Going 32**   **-06 Slow**   Stalls Outside

757	INDIAN BLAZE 1 [3] Andrew Reid 10-8-8 (45) T P Queally (3) 6/1: 40B00-621: Mid-div, smooth hdwy to lead ins last, rdn out:			53a
498	WIND CHIME 32 [9] A G Newcombe 7-8-12 (49) S Whitworth 8/1: 14000-02: Cl-up & led over 2f out, hdd ins last, not pace of wnr:		1½	52a
739*	STEELY DAN 3 [8] J R Boyle 5-9-6 6ex (57) N Pollard 11/8 FAV: 0002213: Towards rear, hdwy over 1f out, not able to chall from dist:		½	59a
649	BALLARE 13 [10] Bob Jones 5-8-8 (45) O Urbina 20/1: 0200-034: Chsd ldrs, drvn & onepace over 1f out.		dht	44a
732	COPPINGTON FLYER 4 [5] B W Duke 4-8-12 (49) K Fallon 11/2: 0000-404: Chsd ldrs, onepace for press bef dist:		1¼	48a
710	HAITHEM 6 [4] D Shaw 7-8-9 10oh 1ow t (45) N Callan 50/1: 0306056: Rear, eff over 1f out, not able to chall:		nk	44a
718	PIQUET 5 [6] J J Bridger 6-8-13 (50) S Drowne 14/1: 1-316607: Held up, drvn & nvr able to chall:		½	47a
710	THEATRE LADY 6 [2] P Evans 6-8-8 5oh (45) L Fletcher (3) 10/1: 1300-128: Mid-div, rdn & no impress fnl 2f:		1½	39a
753	INSIGNIFICANCE 2 [7] John A Quinn 4-8-9 BL (45) M Fenton 16/1: 006002-09: Led till over 2f out:		5	31a
757	FRENCH HORN 1 [1] M Wigham 7-8-11 bl (48) G Carter 10/1: 00-14353P: Held up, lost action & p.u. over 2f out.			0a
10 Ran	1m 38.25 (2.05)	Owner Mrs Irene Clifford		Trained at Mill Hill London

---

767   **3.35 Littlewoods Bet Direct Handicap Stakes 3yo+ 46-52 (F)**   **[61]**

£3045 £870 £435   **6f p/track rnd**   **Going 32**   **-16 Slow**   Stalls Inside

740	DOCTOR DENNIS 3 [9] J Pearce 7-9-0 bl (47) N Pollard 9/1: 04446-51: Dwelt & rear, hdwy over 1f out & drvn to lead well ins last:			54a
528	LONG WEEKEND 27 [13] D Shaw 6-8-13 6oh vis (40) N Callan 16/1: 460-0662: Bhd, hdwy 2f out & ch ins last, not pace of wnr:		¾	50a
544	EASTERN BLUE 25 [3] Mrs L Stubbs 5-9-1 p (48) K Fallon 4/1: 0622-653: Trkd ldrs, drvn to chall over 1f out, not pace of front pair ins last:		1½	47a
709	PARALLEL LINES 6 [11] P D Evans 3-7-12 16oh bl (45) J F McDonald (4) 50/1: 000-0004: Chsd ldrs over 1f out, no extra for press:		½	43a
728*	BELLS BEACH 4 [14] P Howling 6-9-9 6ex (56) J Fanning 8/1: 6201015: Held up, eff when short of room over 1f out, nrst fin:		½	51a
759	AGUILA LOCO 1 [4] Mrs Stef Liddiard 5-9-7 p (54) M Fenton 13/2: 62531406: Chsd ldr, led over 1f out till ins last, no extra.		nk	48a
709*	BADOU 6 [5] L Montague Hall 4-9-4 6ex (51) D Holland 3/1 FAV: 00-61417: Bmpd sn after start, nvr a factor.		1¾	40a
740	TAMARELLA 3 [10] G G Margarson 4-9-2 (49) A McCarthy 8/1: 0500-008: Prom, drvn & btn dist:		1¼	34a
708	JAHANGIR 6 [1] B R Johnson 5-8-13 1oh (45) Dane O'Neill 7/1: 0030-339: Mid-div, hmpd after 1f, no dngr.		1½	26a
720	PLEASURE TEN 5 [8] C Smith 11-8-13 1oh vis (45) J F Egan 50/1: 0055-500: Held up, no impress.		5	12a
435	NIGHT CAP 43 [2] T D McCarthy 5-9-0 BL (47) C Catlin 16/1: 5003-600: Sn led & clr, hdd over 1f out.		¾	11a
740	FIAMMA ROYALE 3 [6] M S Saunders 6-9-1 (48) R Miles (3) 14/1: 5000-400: Keen, bmpd early, mid-div, btn 2f out, qck		nk	11a
444	LAW MAKER 40 [12] M A Buckley 4-8-13 11oh bl (35) S Carson 66/1: 000-0000: Mid-div wide, btn 2f out, abs.		½	7a
13 Ran	1m 13.25 (2.85)	Owner Mrs Lydia Pearce		Trained at Newmarket

---

768   **4.05 Bet In Running @ Betdirect Co Uk Handicap Stakes 4yo+ 46-55 (F)**   **[62]**

£3010 £860 £430   **1m4f**   **Going 32**   **-04 Slow**   Stalls Inside

711	BEYOND THE POLE 5 [4] B R Johnson 6-9-7 (55) K Fallon 9/2: 0000-101: Chsd ldrs, hdwy to lead ins last, drvn out:			62a
4739]	BELLE ROUGE 488 [12] C A Horgan 6-9-7 (55) Paul Eddery 20/1: 566022/-2: Chsd ldr, drvn to chall over 1f out, kept on, not pace of wnr:		¾	59a
718*	FORTUNE POINT 5 [13] A W Carroll 6-9-12 6ex (60) I Mongan 6/1: 40-40213: Led, drvn & hdd ins last, no extra:		¾	63a
412	ESSAY BABY 45 [9] P D Cundell 4-8-9 4oh (45) C Catlin 16/1: 00050-44: Chsd ldrs, drvn & kept on onepace fnl 2f:		¾	48a
718	TROPICAL SON 5 [8] D Shaw 5-9-1 vis (49) N Callan 20/1: 5102505: Towards rear, late gains for press, no dngr.		1	50a
624	MY LILLI 15 [7] P Mitchell 4-8-13 (50) J Murtagh 9/1: 00-3406: Prom, no extra over 1f out:		hd	50a
711	STERLING GUARANTEE 5 [1] Andrew Reid 6-9-5 (53) A Nicholls 4/1 FAV: 0630-247: Mid-div, onepace.		nk	52a
752	PARADISE VALLEY 15 [15] Mrs Stef Liddiard 4-9-2 t (53) S Drowne 12/1: 14525-168: Slow away & bhd, mod late gains:		2½	48a
711	GOLDEN DUAL 5 [3] S Dow 4-9-4 (45) C Haddon (7) 50/1: 5-006009: Slow away, swtchd rail/rear, nvr a factor.		1	49a
718	MURAQEB 5 [2] Mrs Barbara Waring 4-9-1 (52) J F Egan 33/1: 55-000: Sn rdn & nvr a factor, qck reapp.		3½	41a
718	GEOGRAPHY 5 [6] P Butler 4-9-2 p (53) C Haddon (7) 50/1: 005-P060: Mid-div, btn 3f out, qck reapp:		nk	41a
542	SHAMAN 5 [10] G L Moore 7-9-2 (50) Dane O'Neill 9/1: 06600-50: Chsd ldrs, btn 3f out.		½	37a
705	PYRRHIC 6 [5] R M Flower 5-8-12 1oh (45) S W Kelly 14/1: 3020650: Keen, hung right, in tch 10f, qck reapp.		1¼	31a
736	TOP OF THE CLASS 3 [11] P D Evans 7-8-12 vis (46) L Fletcher (3) 14/1: 6334000: Dwelt & keen mid-div, lost tch fnl 2f, qck reapp:		2	28a
14 Ran	2m 33.47 (4.27)	Owner Tann Racing		Trained at Epsom

---

769   **4.35 Bet Direct In Vision Sky Page 293 Handicap Stakes Div 2 3yo+ 0-60 (F)**   **[60]**

£2940 £840 £420   **1m p/track rnd**   **Going 32**   **+02 Fast**   Stalls Outside

697	**BEST BEFORE** 8 [4] P D Evans 4-9-10 (56) S Drowne 10/1: 2065-001: Prom, drvn to lead ins last, styd on strongly:		64a
739	**LUCAYAN MONARCH** 3 [3] P S McEntee 6-9-8 p (54) J Murtagh 7/2: 2500232: Mid-div, rdn & styd on fnl 2f, not pace of wnr:	1½	58a
717	**XALOC BAY** 5 [5] B P J Baugh 6-9-10 (56) I Mongan 7/1: 2001123: Led, drvn & hdd ins last, no extra:	¾	59a
607	**BURGUNDY** 18 [10] P Mitchell 7-9-11 (57) D Holland 11/4 FAV: 5010-634: Held up, eff wide over 2f out, no extra dist:	1½	57a
366	**KANZ WOOD** 50 [1] A W Carroll 8-9-9 (55) S Whitworth 12/1: 00000-05: Hld up, eff 2f out, not able to chall:	3	47a
710	**VLASTA WEINER** 6 [6] J M Bradley 4-8-8 bl (40) C Catlin 33/1: 2504646: Prom, no impress over 1f out, qck reapp.	2½	29a
732	**CHANDELIER** 4 [2] M S Saunders 4-9-8 bl (54) R Miles (3) 9/1: 060-5367: Dwelt, rdn & chsd ldrs till over 1f out.	½	42a
732	**MUTARAFAA** 4 [7] D Shaw 5-9-7 vis (53) N Callan 16/1: 4324008: Mid-div, lost place over 2f out, qck reapp.	4	33a
719	**BY DEFINITION** 5 [8] J C Tuck 6-7-12 (30) Kristin Stubbs (3) 66/1: 0/000-009: Prom, btn over 2f out, qck reapp.	12	0a
726	**FEN GYPSY** 4 [9] P D Evans 6-10-0 (60) K Fallon 3/1: 6000-540: Bhd, eff wide halfway, btn 2f out /eased.	3½	13a
10 Ran	1m 38.6 (2.4) Owner Mr M W Lawrence	Trained at Abergavenny	

770

5.05 Betdirect Co Uk Handicap Stakes Div 2 4yo+ 46-52 (F) [66]

£2905 £830 £415 1m p/track rnd Going 32 -02 Slow Stalls Outside

498	**DOUBLE RANSOM** 32 [8] Mrs L Stubbs 5-9-0 bl (52) K Fallon 6/4 FAV: 0032-231: Settled mid-div, hdwy 2f out & led dist, rdn clr:		61a
732*	**LUCID DREAMS** 4 [3] M Wigham 5-9-6 6ex (58) J Fanning 3/1: 40-50412: Prom, briefly led over 1f out, sn outpcd by wnr:	4	58a
648*	**MISS PEACHES** 13 [10] G G Margarson 6-8-9 (47) Kristin Stubbs (7) 6/1: 0/00-2013: Pushed along towards rear, late prog, no dngr:	2½	42a
732	**BALERNO** 4 [4] R Ingram 5-8-13 (51) G Carter 10/1: 300-1304: Pushed along rear, eff wide, not able to threaten:	hd	45a
739	**GALEY RIVER** 3 [7] J J Sheehan 5-8-8 (46) N Callan 25/1: 0000-005: Rdn & towards rear, late gains for press:	nk	39a
732	**ESTRELLA LEVANTE** 4 [5] G L Moore 4-8-11 bl e (49) A Quinn (5) 25/1: 55-05306: Mid-div, btn over 1f out, qck reapp.	1	40a
732	**ZINGING** 4 [1] J J Bridger 5-8-12 (50) S Drowne 11/2: 10-50647: Led 1f, remained prom, btn dist:	¾	40a
4859}	**GRAN CLICQUOT** 129 [9] G P Enright 9-8-8 1oh (45) R Brisland 20/1: 144500-8: Dwelt & bhd, nvr a factor:	½	35a
739	**VIZULIZE** 3 [6] A W Carroll 5-8-10 VIS (48) I Mongan 14/1: 40-06509: Led after 1f till over 1f out, sn btn, visor.	1½	34a
669	**ANGELICA GARNETT** 11 [2] T E Powell 4-8-8 1oh (45) J F Egan 33/1: 000-0600: Dwelt & keen, prom 6f.	½	31a
10 Ran	1m 38.89 (2.69) Owner Tyme Partnership	Trained at Malton	

Official Going Slow

771

2.25 New Site @ Betdirect Co Uk Banded Stakes 3yo+ 0-40 (H)

£1495 £427 £214 7f f/sand rnd Going 106 -03 Slow Stalls Inside

573*	**SMART SCOT** 21 [6] B P J Baugh 5-9-7 p (40) M Savage (5) 5/4 FAV: 0060-111: Chsd ldr & led 3f out, hung left under press but al holding rivals ins last:		45a
680	**JESSIE** 10 [12] Don Enrico Incisa 5-9-7 t (40) Kim Tinkler 6/1: 0-565222: Dwelt & sn rdn along, late gains.	1¼	41a
579	**NEUTRAL NIGHT** 20 [4] R Brotherton 4-9-7 vis (40) A Daly 25/1: 60-30053: Chsd lrs, styd on onepace.	¾	40a
677	**MATHMAGICIAN** 10 [3] R F Marvin 5-9-7 bl (35) Dean McKeown 20/1: 0040-454: In tch, kept on, not able to chall:	1¼	37a
661	**SILVER MASCOT** 12 [8] R Hollinshead 5-9-7 (45) A Culhane 11/4: 00-402025: Chsd ldrs, btn over 1f out:	5	28a
525	**BEAUTEOUS** 27 [1] A Berry 5-9-7 (40) F Lynch 16/1: 0400-006: Led 4f, btn 2f out	4	21a
667	**SWEET CORAL** 12 [10] B S Rothwell 4-9-7 bl (40) K Dalgleish 33/1: 00-04007: Prom, hung right & btn 2f out:	2½	16a
442	**ABOUSTAR** 40 [11] M Brittain 4-9-7 (40) M Lawson (7) 20/1: 6/00-58: Mid-div, btn 3f out:	½	15a
637	**DANDY JIM** 14 [2] D W Chapman 3-8-4 (30) J Quinn 20/1: 006-059: Dwelt & al outpcd rear.	1	13a
677	**SHOTLEY DANCER** 10 [9] N Bycroft 5-9-7 (40) J Bramhill 33/1: 25060-40: Sn struggling:	4	6a
661	**BRILLYANT DANCER** 12 [5] Mrs A Duffield 6-9-7 BL (35) G Duffield 50/1: 00004-60: Dwelt & al bhd:	13	0a
11 Ran	1m 34.24 (7.64) Owner Mr S Day	Trained at Stoke On Trent	

772

2.55 Betdirect Co Uk Median Auction Maiden Stakes 4-6yo (H)

£1446 £413 £207 1m3f f/sand Going 106 -13 Slow Stalls Inside

546	**FLEETING MOON** 25 [3] A M Balding 4-8-9 (55) L Keniry (3) 1/3 FAV: 0-221: Trkd ldrs, smooth prog to chase ldr 5f out, led over 2f out & readily assorted, eased nr fin, val for 6L+:		63a
721	**KUSTOM KIT FOR HER** 5 [6] S R Bowring 4-8-9 t (45) J Bramhill 9/2: 0002322: Led 1m, sn no ch with wnr from over 2f out:	4	43a
561	**DORA CORBINO** 23 [4] R Hollinshead 4-8-9 (45) A Culhane 12/1: 0/560-53: In tch, outpcd 5f out, mod late gains for press, nvr a dngr:	1¾	41a
93}	**BETTYS VALENTINE** 460 [1] D W Barker 4-8-9 T Eaves (4) 33/1: 000/-4: Chsd ldrs, lost tch from halfway:	dist	0
512	**BLUE BIJOU** 30 [5] T T Clement 4-9-0 Dean McKeown 50/1: 0-05: Chsd ldr, hung left & lost tch 5f out:	28	0
5 Ran	2m 34.38 (13.08) Owner Mr M E Wates	Trained at Kingsclere	

773

3.25 Bet In Running @ Betdirect Co Uk Banded Stakes 3yo+ 0-45 (H)

£1505 £430 £215 6f f/sand rnd Going 106 -00 Slow Stalls Inside

582	**STAR LAD** 20 [10] R Brotherton 4-9-6 (45) A Daly 25/1: 06-31001: Made all, held on all out cl-home:		49a
720+*	**SERGEANT SLIPPER** 5 [14] C Smith 7-9-12 vis (45) R Fitzpatrick 12/1: 5-030312: Dwelt, towards rear, styd on for press, just failed:	hd	54a
646*	**SABANA** 13 [5] J M Bradley 6-9-6 bl (52) B Reilly (3) 9/2 JT FAV: 0-435013: Held up in tch, lost pl halfway, styd on wide fnl 2f, not able to chall:	2½	41a
667	**ENJOY THE BUZZ** 12 [2] J M Bradley 5-9-6 (45) G Duffield 9/2 JT FAV: 4023124: Held up, hmpd after 2f, drvn & kept on fnl 2f, nvr able to chall:	hd	40a
637	**SPY MASTER** 14 [4] J Parkes 6-9-6 bl t (40) M Savage (5) 7/1: 0000-325: Dwelt, mod late gains for press:	3	32a
4104}	**WUB CUB** 176 [12] A Dickman 4-9-6 (45) A Beech (3) 40/1: 00400-6: Chsd wnr, edged left & btn dist:	½	30a
699	**PORT NATAL** 6 [8] P Morris 6-9-6 bl (45) L Treadwell 7/1: 501-02U7: Chsd ldrs till hmpd after 2f, btn 2f out.	4	20a
720	**TORRENT** 5 [7] D W Chapman 9-9-6 bl (45) A Culhane 6/1: 2631538: Held up, nvr able to chall:	1	18a

558	COMPTON BAY 23 [3] M Brittain 4-9-6 (45) T Eaves (5) 33/1: 00/0-09: Prom when hmpd after 2f, btn over 1f out:	nk	17a
720	ON THE TRAIL 5 [1] D W Chapman 7-9-6 (45) K Dalgleish 16/1: 000-0000: Held up, short of room 2f out, no dngr.	1½	13a
172	BOND DOMINGO 82 [11] B Smart 5-9-6 bl (40) M Stainton (7) 20/1: 000000-0: Chsd ldrs, btn over 1f out.	1½	9a
501	ETERNAL BLOOM 31 [15] M Brittain 6-9-6 (45) M Lawson (7) 20/1: 00-12000: Chsd ldrs, struggling fnl 2f.	3	1a
297	SUGAR CUBE TREAT 57 [13] M Mullineaux 8-9-6 (30) P Varley (7) 100/1: 60//000-00: Dwelt & sn struggling:	hd	0a
582	ABOVE BOARD 20 [9] R F Marvin 9-9-6 t (45) Dean McKeown 20/1: 0-502030: Chsd ldrs, hmpd after 2f, sn bhd.	1½	-4a
667	BELLS BOYS 12 [6] K A Ryan 5-9-6 bl (40) G Parkin 8/1: 505-3350: Prom early, hmpd after 2f & again 2f out.	¾	-6a
15 Ran	1m 19.67 (6.37) Owner Mr R Austin & Mrs P Austin	Trained at Pershore	

774

3.55 Betdirect Co Uk New Site Banded Stakes 4yo+ 0-45 (H)
£1635 £467 £234   1m4f f/sand rnd   Going 106   +04 Fast   Stalls Inside

590	JUNGLE LION 20 [3] John A Harris 6-9-1 (45) Dean McKeown 20/1: 600-6201: Cl-up & led after 4f, pushed clr:		57a
722*	BROUGHTON KNOWS 5 [6] W J Musson 7-9-7 bl (46) Lisa Jones (3) 8/11 FAV: 62-11112: Dwelt & held up, styd on wide for press, nvr threaten wnr:	7	53a
504	STRAVMOUR 31 [5] R Hollinshead 8-9-1 (45) Dale Gibson 7/2: 0431-053: Chsd wnr 4f out, rdn & no impress fnl 3f:	1½	45a
638	FORTUNES FAVOURITE 14 [8] G M Moore 4-8-12 (45) J Quinn 20/1: 045-034: Chsd ldrs, btn 2f out.	7	36a
593	MAUNBY ROCKER 19 [1] P C Haslam 4-8-12 (45) G Faulkner 14/1: 260-0065: Prom, no impress fnl 3f:	3	32a
746	SHATIN SPECIAL 3 [2] G C H Chung 4-8-12 p (45) Dean Williams (7): 52F4166: Held up, tkn wide, wknd 3f out.	7	23a
4467}	LAIRD DARA MAC 156 [9] N Bycroft 4-8-12 (40) Suzanne France (7) 100/1: 060-7: Led 3f, btn 3f out:	17	0a
	RISKY WAY 1721 [4] B S Rothwell 8-9-1 p (45) K Dalgleish 66/1: 60050////: Cl-up & led after 3f, sn hdd & no ch fnl 4f:	12	0a
511	PHOENIX NIGHTS 30 [7] A Berry 4-8-12 BL (45) P Bradley (5) 50/1: 030-0509: Held up, rdn & btn 4f out, blnks.	13	0a
9 Ran	2m 46.57 (12.27) Owner Mr Mick Rowley	Trained at Melton Mowbray	

775

4.25 Betdirect Co Uk Selling Stakes 3yo+ (H)
£1320 £377 £189   5f f/sand str   Going 106   Inapplicab   Stalls Outside

587	HENRY TUN 20 [3] J Balding 6-9-5 bl (51) D Allan (3) 11/4: 00-35021: Broke well & made all, rdn & in command fnl 1f & eased cl-home:		57a
533	AFRICAN SPUR 26 [4] S L Keightley 4-9-5 (64) Dean McKeown 15/8 FAV: 000-0022: Rdn chasing ldrs, outpcd halfway, drvn & kept on:	2	50a
646	HEATHYARDSBLESSING 13 [7] R Hollinshead 7-9-5 (45) Stephanie Hollinshead (7) 20/1: 23-06503: Pushed along rear, hdwy to chase wnr halfway, sn hung right & no impress dist:	½	48a
720	LONE PIPER 5 [8] J M Bradley 9-9-5 (35) B Reilly (3) 22/1: 56-00064: Held up, eff when hmpd 2f out, rider drpd whip ins last, nvr pace to chall:	nk	47a
737	MR SPLIFFY 3 [5] K R Burke 5-9-11 vis (51) A Reilly (7) 12/1: 4-051005: Chsd ldrs, not pace to chall:	nk	52a
741	ATTORNEY 3 [1] D Shaw 6-9-11 e (45) P Makin (7) 16/1: 1004006: Dwelt, nvr on terms with ldrs:	nk	51a
641	CARK 13 [2] J Jay 6-9-11 (50) J Quinn 9/1: 00-61207: Chsd ldrs, no impress fnl 2f:	5	39a
728	SO SOBER 4 [11] D Shaw 6-9-11 (45) Darren Williams 12/1: 00-15408: Rdn mid-div, no impress from halfway.	4	29a
587	VALAZAR 20 [6] D W Chapman 5-9-5 (50) A Culhane (7) 24000-09: Chsd ldrs, btn when hmpd over 1f out:	2	18a
720	THE LEATHER WEDGE 5 [10] A Berry 5-9-5 (45) P Bradley (5) 16/1: 020-6040: Dwelt, chsd ldrs till halfway.	nk	17a
3376}	SHADY DEAL 209 [9] J M Bradley 8-9-5 (30) G Duffield 16/1: 466235-0: Dwelt & sn outpcd/bhd:	9	0a
11 Ran	1m 03.44 Owner Mr J Bladen	Trained at Doncaster	

776

4.55 Littlewoods Bet Direct Banded Stakes 3yo+ 0-45 (H)
£1516 £433 £217   1m f/sand rnd   Going 106   -02 Slow   Stalls Inside

3084}	RUST EN VREDE 221 [14] D Carroll 5-9-8 (45) D Tudhope (7) 28/1: 003600-1: Chsd ldrs & led over 2f out, rdn & held on ins last:		57a
574	RED DELIRIUM 21 [5] P A Blockley 8-9-8 bl (40) D Nolan (5) 11/1: 004-6452: Dwelt, pushed along towards rear, styd on wide for press fnl 2f, not able to reach ldr:	1¼	53a
579	PRINTSMITH 20 [9] J R Norton 7-9-8 (45) J Bramhill 9/1: 005-1443: Mid-div, chsd wnr 2f out, no extra:	5	44a
479	MR WHIZZ 34 [12] A P Jones 7-9-8 bl e (45) Derek Nolan (7) 20/1: 000-0144: Chsd ldrs, styd on onepace.	½	43a
648	MAGGIES PET 13 [7] K Bell 7-9-8 t (45) D R McCabe 6/1: 0-252245: Trkd ldrs halfway, drvn & onepace fnl 2f.	1½	40a
530	ROSTI 26 [11] P C Haslam 4-9-8 (45) G Faulkner 5/1: 54-11306: Held up, short of room halfway, nvr a factor:	shd	40a
647	AIR OF ESTEEM 13 [3] Ian Emmerson 8-9-8 (45) D Fentiman (7) 8/1: 553-5567: Mid-div, no impress 2f out:	5	31a
668*	WILSON BLUEBOTTLE 12 [8] M W Easterby 5-9-8 (46) Dale Gibson 2/1 FAV: 4000-618: Led after 1f till over 2f out, wknd qckly:	½	30a
613	PLATINUM CHIEF 17 [1] A Berry 3-8-3 (45) P Mathers (4) 40/1: 045-6659: Mid-div, drpd rear halfway, nvr factor after:	1¼	27a
564	SANDORRA 23 [6] M Brittain 6-9-8 (45) M Lawson (7) 33/1: 00-31600: Led 1f, prom till 3f out:	5	18a
373}	SAMBA BEAT 414 [10] R F Marvin 5-9-8 (45) Dean McKeown 100/1: 000/050-0: Dwelt & sn struggling, long abs.	6	7a
586	TINIAN 20 [2] K R Burke 6-9-8 (45) Darren Williams 11/1: 30-53030: Sn prom till over 3f out:	18	0
754	TEMPTATION ISLAND 2 [4] John A Quinn 5-9-8 (45) J Quinn 28/1: 410060-00: Dwelt & sn bhd:	8	0
13 Ran	1m 48.00 (8.6) Owner Mr Alan Mann	Trained at Warthilll	

Official Going Slow

777

2.20 Bet Direct On Attheraces Text Page 410 Amateur Riders' Banded Stakes 4yo+ 0-40 (H)
£1449 £414 £207   1m100y f/sand rnd   Going 143   -63 Slow   Stalls Inside

575	JAKE BLACK 22 [6] J J Quinn 4-11-7 (40) Mr S Walker 9/4 FAV: 56500-01: Led 1f, led ins last, rdn out:		45a
3644}	SADLERS SWING 199 [8] J J Sheehan 8-11-7 (40) Mr E Dehdashti (3) 8/1: 0/00//605-: Slow away, sn in tch, hdwy to lead over 1f out, hdd ins last, no extra:	1¼	40a
699	DUNDONALD 7 [2] M Appleby 5-11-7 bl t (35) Mr L Newnes (5) 20/1: 040-6003: Led/dsptd lead till over 1f out, no extra:	¾	39a

678	**KENNY THE TRUTH** 11 [4] Mrs J Candlish 5-11-7 t (40) Mr D Weekes (7) 5/1: 00-32334: In tch, onepace.	**1**	**37a**
689	**MR PERRY** 10 [11] Mrs P Ford 8-11-7 (30) Mr K Ford (7) 20/1: 656/00//-0: Bhd, mod gains wide.	2½	32a
699	**ZAHUNDA** 7 [9] W M Brisbourne 5-11-7 (40) Mr C Davies (7) 4/1: 0-602046: Keen, mid-div, no prog dist, eased:	1½	29a
708	**WATERLINE DANCER** 7 [7] P D Evans 4-11-7 t (40) Miss Hayley Bryan (5) 16/1: 000-0007: Mid-div, not able to chall.	2½	24a
654	**ALL ON MY OWN** 14 [3] I W McInnes 9-11-7 bl (40) Miss E J Jones 8/1: 00-04248: Stumbled start, trkd ldrs, btn dist.	1¾	21a
399	**MANIKATO** 47 [5] K G Wingrove 10-11-7 T P (30) Mr S J Graham (7) 33/1: 0660-009: Al bhd, abs, t-strap & cheekpcs.	3½	14a
1701}	**TERN INTERN** 282 [1] Miss J Feilden 5-11-7 (35) Miss Fiona Brown (7) 22/1: 060/000-0: Sn bhd, reapp.	1½	11a
208	**RIVELLI** 76 [10] B R Foster 5-11-7 (40) Mr A Brooke (7) 25/1: 000000-0: Led/dsptd lead till 2f out, wknd qckly.	12	0a
719	**ALJOMAR** 6 [1] R E Barr 5-11-7 (35) Miss V Barr (7) 40/1: 400-0600: Prom, bhd fnl 3f.	11	0a
12 Ran	2m 03.72 (17.52) Owner Mr G A Lucas	Trained at Malton	

---

778   2.50 Bet Direct On Attheraces Text Page 411 Claiming Stakes 3yo+ (H)
£1477 £422 £211   6f f/sand rnd   Going 143   +02 Fast   Stalls Inside

708	**LORD MELBOURNE** 7 [3] A G Juckes 5-9-7 (50) D Holland 2/1 FAV: 2143051: Pushed along & bhd, hdwy from halfway & rdn to lead well ins last:		**53a**
555	**INCHCOONAN** 25 [8] K R Burke 6-9-2 p (55) Darren Williams 8/1: 4424-442: Prom & rdn/led over 1f out, edged right under press, hdd well ins last:	½	46a
684	**LARKYS LOB** 10 [13] Paul Johnson 5-9-7 (45) L Fletcher (3) 10/1: 4532463: Held up wide, hdwy to chall over 1f out, rdn & no extra well ins last:	½	49a
661	**MYSTERY MOUNTAIN** 13 [9] Mrs J R Ramsden 4-9-5 (47) I Mongan 20/1: 4300-054: Bhd, mod late prog.	5	35a
579	**LEVANTINE** 21 [12] A G Newcombe 7-9-7 bl (45) S Whitworth 7/1: 30633-35: Prom, btn over 1f out:	2½	30a
748	**RIVER DAYS** 3 [7] Miss Gay Kelleway 6-9-2 VIS t (56) M Fenton 9/2: 400-0206: Dwelt, sn rdn mid-div, no impress dist:	1	22a
619	**SOAKED** 17 [6] D W Chapman 11-9-7 bl (47) A Culhane 16/1: 0-260047: Led till over 1f out, no extra:	½	25a
708	**FLYING FAISAL** 7 [11] J M Bradley 8-9-7 p (40) C Catlin 16/1: 0060408: Led early, sn outpcd & no impress:	¾	23a
637	**COURT MUSIC** 15 [4] R E Barr 5-9-2 vis (45) R Fitzpatrick 33/1: 000-0269: Prom, btn 2f out:	8	0a
153	**QUEEN LOUISA** 86 [10] F Watson 4-9-1 T Eaves (5) 66/1: 00-0: Dwelt & al bhd:	3½	0a
649	**BAR OF SILVER** 14 [2] R Brotherton 4-9-7 vis (45) R Winston 9/1: 5050-050: No dngr:	10	0a
11 Ran	1m 21.26 (8.46) Owner Mrs K C Price	Trained at Abberley	

---

779   3.20 Bet Direct On Attheraces Text Page 412 Median Auction Maiden Stakes 3-5yo (H)
£1439 £411 £206   7f f/sand rnd   Going 143   -12 Slow   Stalls Outside

506	**TWO OF CLUBS** 32 [4] P C Haslam 3-8-5 P (61) G Faulkner 1/2 FAV: 3454-331: Dsptd led, led over 2f out trav well, rdn clr:		**64a**
662	**SONDERBORG** 13 [1] G L Moore 3-8-0 p (49) J Quinn 7/2: 06-64532: Chsd ldrs, onepace fnl 2f.	6	46a
641	**DANCES IN TIME** 14 [5] C N Kellett 4-9-2 BL (45) A Culhane 33/1: 050003: Dsptd lead till over 2f out, sn fdd:	5	36a
560	**HEATHYARDS JOY** 24 [3] R Hollinshead 3-8-0 (30) R Ffrench 50/1: 0-004: In tch, outpcd from halfway:	1½	33a
119	**MY LITTLE SOPHIA** [4] M Mullineaux 4-9-2 S W Kelly 40/1: 5: Sn bhd on debut.	5	23a
	I WISH I KNEW 93 [2] D J Coakley 3-8-5 (63) J F Egan 6/1: 000-6: In tch, btn 2f out:	2½	23a
6 Ran	1m 37.07 (10.87) Owner Blue Lion Racing II	Trained at Middleham	

---

780   3.50 Bet Direct On Attheraces Text Page 413 Banded Stakes 4yo+ 0-40 (H)
£1600 £457 £229   1m4f f/sand   Going 143   -27 Slow   Stalls Inside

724	**BUZ KIRI** 6 [3] A W Carroll 6-8-12 (40) P Doe 3/1: 6-321221: Held up, hdwy from halfway, rdn to lead ins last, rdn out:		**45a**
719	**GALLEY LAW** 6 [8] R Craggs 4-8-10 (40) T Eaves (5) 7/4 FAV: 00-32122: Prom & led over 3f out till ins last, drvn & kept on:	½	43a
575	**SERAPH** 22 [4] John A Harris 4-8-10 p (40) J Quinn 6/1: 000-3103: Prom, rdn & no impress fnl 2f.	10	31a
707+*	**FREE STYLE** 7 [9] K R Burke 4-9-2 (40) G Baker 15/2: 20-63014: Held up, eff 4f out, no impress:	3	33a
1806]	**BUYING A DREAM** 637 [5] Andrew Turnell 7-8-12 (30) C Catlin 50/1: 240/500/-0: Held up, lost pl halfway, nvr factor:	5	21a
719	**MOYNE PLEASURE** 6 [7] Paul Johnson 6-8-12 (35) L Fletcher (3) 33/1: 450-0006: Led/dsptd lead, went on halfway till 3f out, sn btn:	½	20a
745	**THINK QUICK** 4 [10] R Hollinshead 4-8-10 (35) H Fellows (7) 25/1: 0566347: Rear, hdwy 6f out, no prog 3f out.	nk	19a
581	**IPLEDGEALLEGIANCE** 21 [2] D W Chapman 8-8-12 (35) A Culhane 22/1: 0-253658: Al bhd, no threat.	8	9a
668	**TIME MARCHES ON** 13 [1] Mrs M Reveley 6-8-12 (40) J Fanning 8/1: 036/20-49: In tch 7f, reportedly hung:	dist	0a
3015}	**BLUE WATER** 226 [6] M Mullineaux 4-8-10 p (40) P Varley (7) 33/1: 063060-0: Led till halfway, sn bhd, abs.	dist	0a
10 Ran	2m 54.02 (20.42) Owner Mr Serafino Agodino	Trained at Alcester	

---

781   4.20 Bet Direct Daily Special Offers Banded Stakes 3yo+ 0-35 (H)
£1369 £391 £196   5f f/sand rnd   Going 143   -05 Slow   Stalls Inside

742	**WHITE O MORN** 4 [8] B A McMahon 5-9-4 t p (35) G Gibbons 11/4: 00-04241: Pushed along chasing ldrs, hdwy to lead over 1f out, drvn out:		**39a**
541	**MARON** 27 [4] F Jordan 7-9-4 bl (35) D Kinsella 7/1: 0/0000-52: Dwelt, towards rear, hdwy when forced wide over 1f out, styd on for press, just held:	nk	38a
775	**LONE PIPER** 1 [2] J M Bradley 9-9-4 (35) C Catlin 9/4 FAV: 56-000643: Held up, no room 3f out till 2f out, drvn & kept on, no extra fnl 50yds:	1¼	35a
227	**ATTILA THE HUN** 73 [10] F Watson 5-9-4 VIS (30) S Drowne 20/1: 000000-4: Led after 1f till over 1f out, sn btn:	3½	26a
3477}	**ONLY FOR GOLD** 206 [7] Dr P Pritchard 9-9-4 (35) S Whitworth 11/1: 500600-5: Late gains:	1	24a
374	**DIAMOND RACKET** 49 [5] D W Chapman 4-9-4 bl (35) A Culhane 20/1: 000006-6: In tch till over 1f out, abs.	nk	23a
527	**TUSCAN DREAM** 28 [3] A Berry 4-9-4 (35) F Lynch 12/1: 060-0007: Led 1f, btn 1f out.	nk	22a
719	**HAVANA ROSE** 6 [1] P Morris 4-9-4 p (30) D A McCormack (7) 33/1: 00000-08: Dwelt & sn outpcd, qck reapp.	1	20a
775	**SHADY DEAL** 9 [9] J M Bradley 8-9-4 (30) B Swarbrick (7) 9/2: 466235-09: Chsd ldrs, btn 1f out.	3½	11a
578	**SILENT ANGEL** 22 [6] Mrs Lucinda Featherstone 4-9-4 p (30) J Quinn 40/1: 000-00: Prom, strugg halfway, `breathing prob'.	27	0a
10 Ran	1m 07.61 (7.41) Owner Mrs A H Stokes	Trained at Tamworth	

WOLVERHAMPTON Monday 01.03.04 Lefthand, Sharp Track

782 4.50 Bet Direct In Running Sky Text Page 293 Banded Stakes 3yo+ 0-35 (H)

£1390 £397 £199   1m1f79y f/sand   Going 143   +03 Fast   Stalls Inside

4121}	MRS CUBE 175 [10] P Howling 5-9-8 (35) R Winston 9/2: 006060-1: Trkd ldrs trav well, led 3f out, rdn clr:		47a
584	A BIT OF FUN 21 [7] J J Quinn 3-8-2 (35) J Bramhill 6/1: 000-52: Keen, cl-up, onepace fnl 2f:	9	34a
574	SOPHOMORE 22 [4] John A Harris 10-9-8 (35) S Whitworth 8/1: 0/000-06: Mid-div, only mod prog.	1¾	31a
707	ADJIRAM 7 [12] A W Carroll 8-9-8 VIS (30) W Ryan 13/8 FAV: 00/46/-354: Trkd ldr, led 5f out till 3f out, sn rdn & wknd:	2½	26a
640	WESTERN COMMAND 15 [5] Mrs N Macauley 8-9-8 p (30) R Fitzpatrick 12/1: 0456605: Bhd, only mod prog for pressure.	3	20a
668	AMANPURI 13 [9] Miss Gay Kelleway 6-9-8 (35) M Fenton 9/1: 000-0406: Led till 5f out, sn btn:	½	19a
722	MARENGO 6 [3] Paul Johnson 10-9-8 P (30) Joanna Badger 20/1: 00-00607: Dwelt, nvr on terms with ldrs:	4	12a
584	WELSH WHISPER 21 [11] S A Brookshaw 5-9-8 (35) L Keniry (3) 9/1: 0-0048: Keen, bhd, no ch 3f out:	½	11a
291	RED ACER 58 [8] P D Evans 3-8-2 (35) J Tate 25/1: 00060-09: Dwelt, mid-div, bhd 3f out:	8	0a
302	CHICKASAW TRAIL 58 [2] R Hollinshead 4-9-8 (35) Stephanie Hollinshead (7) 33/1: 00000-00: Sn bhd, abs.	3	0a
4414}	RILEYS ROCKET 160 [1] J A Pickering 5-9-8 (35) Dean McKeown 11/1: 360005-0: Al rear:	3½	0a
3788}	UN AUTRE ESPERE 192 [6] T Wall 5-9-8 (35) L Vickers 33/1: 0/30500-0: Bhd from halfway, 4 month jumps abs.	1½	0a

12 Ran   2m 11.33 (13.13)   Owner Mrs J E Proctor   Trained at Newmarket

LINGFIELD Tuesday 02.03.04 Lefthand, V Sharp Track

Official Going   Standard

783 2.30 Bet Direct No Q Demo 08000 837 888 Banded Stakes 3yo+ 0-45 (H)

£1666 £476 £238   7f p/track rnd   Going 37   +04 Fast   Stalls Inside

637	REDOUBTABLE 16 [13] D W Chapman 13-9-7 (45) A Culhane 12/1: 600-6141: Dwelt, switched rail & held up rear, hdwy & led ins last, rdn out:		48a
730	SOCIAL CONTRACT 6 [1] S Dow 7-9-7 vis (45) J F Egan 7/1: 0006062: Mid-div, hdwy to chall dist, not pace of wnr:	1¾	43a
596	ZONNEBEKE 21 [7] K R Burke 3-8-5 (45) J Fanning 16/1: 00-45203: Trkd ldrs, chall dist, onepace.	1½	40a
709	MALAAH 8 [5] Julian Poulton 8-9-7 bl (45) M Halford (7) 50/1: 0/000-004: Led till ins last, fdd under press:	1	38a
709	YOUNGS FORTH 8 [6] A W Carroll 4-9-7 T (45) S Whitworth 16/1: 5500-005: Mid-div, onepace for press fnl 2f:	1	36a
737	CONFUZED 5 [2] D Flood 4-9-7 e (45) K Fallon 7/2: 0/0-036: Dwelt, keen in mid-div, eff 2f out, no extra dist:	1¼	33a
767	BADOU 2 [14] L Montague Hall 4-9-13 (45) D Holland 3/1 FAV: 00-614177: Mid-div, not able to chall:	2	35a
3535}	BALLYGRIFFIN KID 203 [12] T P McGovern 4-9-7 (45) Dane O'Neill 10/1: 0/00563-8: Cl-up, no extra dist.	nk	28a
730	THE GAY FOX 6 [15] B G Powell 10-9-7 t p (45) Dale Gibson 12/1: 5-242309: Rdn towards rear, nvr on terms.	¾	33a
636	GILLYS GENERAL 16 [4] J W Unett 4-9-7 BL (45) M Fenton 20/1: 02050-40: Chsd ldrs 4f:	hd	25a
739	MASTER RATTLE 5 [10] Jane Southcombe 5-9-7 (45) V Slattery 11/2: 0-000520: Chsd ldrs, eff wide, btn dist.	hd	24a
538	ZOLUSHKA 28 [8] B W Duke 3-8-5 (45) E Ahern 33/1: 00000-300: Dwelt & al rear.	2½	19a
662	BIENHEUREUX 14 [3] W J Musson 3-8-5 (45) Paul Eddery 40/1: 00-000: Dwelt & al bhd.	½	18a
709	LUCRETIUS 8 [16] D K Ivory 5-9-7 P (45) M Savage (5) 33/1: 0600-000: Wide, sn drvn, nvr a factor, cheek pieces.	9	1a

14 Ran   1m 25.14 (2.34)   Owner Mr David W Chapman   Trained at York

784 3.00 Bet Direct No Q On 08000 93 66 93 Banded Stakes 4yo+ 0-40 (H)

£1463 £418 £209   1m2f p/track   Going 37   -32 Slow   Stalls Inside

394*	DAFA 48 [8] B J Curley 8-8-12 (40) S W Kelly 11/4: 005///0/-1: Sn cl-up, led over 2f out, drvn/hung right & held on all out:		43a
707	PRIVATE SEAL 8 [14] Julian Poulton 9-8-12 t p (40) M Halford (7) 8/1: 000-6322: In tch wide, eff to chall dist, just held:	nk	42a
705	PLATINUM BOY 8 [5] M Wellings 4-8-12 p (40) V Slattery 40/1: 00-00003: Mid-div, kept on fnl 2f, not pace of front pair:	6	33a
412	PAINTBRUSH 47 [2] Mrs L Stubbs 4-8-12 (40) R Winston 7/2: 0/3560-54: Held up, hmpd over 2f out, kept on for press late, nvr dngr:	hd	32a
719	MORRIS DANCING 7 [6] B P J Baugh 5-8-12 (30) M Tebbutt 50/1: 00-00005: Led till over 2f out, no extra for press:	hd	31a
707	BROUGHTONS MILL 8 [1] J A Supple 9-8-12 (35) Rory Moore (7) 33/1: 46/00-566: Mid-div, not pace to chall.	nk	30a
851}	HONEYS GIFT 343 [3] G G Margarson 5-8-12 (40) A McCarthy 10/1: 6450/00-7: Chsd ldrs, no extra over 1f out.	1	29a
710	MISBEHAVIOUR 8 [9] P Butler 5-8-12 p (40) I Mongan 33/1: 00-000: Keen & prom, btn over 1f out.	6	20a
654*	KINGSDON 15 [4] T J Fitzgerald 7-8-12 vis t (40) K Fallon 9/4 FAV: 4000-019: Dwelt, held up, eff when hmpd over 2f out, position accepted:	9	9a
708	HINCHLEY WOOD 8 [12] J R Best 5-8-12 (40) N Pollard 33/1: 00//-6000: Wide/handy, btn when hmpd 2f out.	26	0
575	MODEM 23 [10] D Shaw 7-8-12 vis (40) N Callan 33/1: 03050-0B: Held up, b.d. over 2f out, sadly died.		0
539	THATS ALL JAZZ 28 [13] C R Dore 6-8-12 (40) R Thomas (5) 16/1: 000-000B: Dwelt, rear, b.d. over 2f out.		0
715	SPIDERS WEB 7 [11] T Keddy 4-8-12 BL (30) G Carter 40/1: 0/-0000B: Keen in rear, b.d. over 2f out, tried blnks.		0
738	ACHILLES RAINBOW 5 [7] K R Burke 4-8-12 (40) A Reilly (7) 25/1: 060-406S: Chsd ldrs 3f out, fell over 2f out, broke leg & sadly died.		0

14 Ran   2m 09.7 (6.9)   Owner Mrs B J Curley   Trained at Newmarket

785 3.30 Betdirect Co Uk Median Auction Maiden Stakes 3-5yo (H)

£1463 £418 £209   1m p/track rnd   Going 37   -11 Slow   Stalls Outside

2760}	RYE 237 [1] J A Osborne 3-7-12 C Catlin 8/11 FAV: 5-1: Chsd clr ldr, rdn halfway, styd on to catch eased wnr on line, all out:		57a
651	BALLINGER RIDGE 15 [5] A M Balding 5-9-7 BL (60) K Fallon 15/8: 063-2322: Led & snwell clr, briefly shaken up 2f out, joc lkd rnd & briefly eased dist, tried to get going	shd	63a
636	STAR WELCOME 16 [10] W J Musson 3-7-12 Lisa Jones (3) 25/1: 0-03: Mid-div, styd on for press fnl 2f, not able to chall:	2	54a
366	MAGIC STONE 52 [4] A Charlton 4-9-7 (40) R Smith 66/1: 000/0-04: Held up, nvr able to chall.	5	50a
514	YOUNG DYNASTY 31 [8] E A Wheeler 4-9-7 Liam Jones (7) 20/1: 05: Slow away, towards rear, nvr a dngr.	3	44a
623	SHALATI PRINCESS 17 [6] J C Fox 3-7-12 R Brisland 50/1: 05: Sn bhd, only mod prog.	2	35a
2046}	MR DIP 266 [7] A W Carroll 4-9-7 (65) A Culhane 9/1: 050-7: Chsd ldrs, btn 2f out:	2	36a
675	RYANS BLISS 13 [9] T D McCarthy 4-9-2 (50) J P Guillambert (3) 25/1: 0/0000-08: Chsd ldrs, btn 2f out.	1	29a
	MANTEL MINI [3] B A Pearce 5-9-2 BL B Reilly (3) 66/1: 9: V slow away, al bhd:	2½	24a

LINGFIELD Tuesday 02.03.04 Lefthand, V Sharp Track

LADY HECCLES [2] M R Hoad 5-9-2 S Whitworth 66/1: 0: Sn bhd: **27   0a**
10 Ran   1m 40.07 (3.87)   Owner Mr Danny Durkan   Trained at Upper Lambourn

---

786   **4.00** Littlewoods Bet Direct Banded Stakes   3yo+ 0-40 (H)
           £1467 £419 £210   **1m p/track rnd**   **Going 37**   **-10 Slow**   Stalls Outside

766	HAITHEM 2 [10] D Shaw 7-9-7 t (35) N Callan 7/1: 03060561: Dwelt, held up in tch, hdwy to lead ins last, hands & heels nr fin:	**45a**
566	DUE TO ME 24 [7] G L Moore 4-9-7 bl e (40) S Whitworth 11/2: 00/400-52: Keen & mid-div, switched wide to chall over 1f out, not pace of wnr nr fin:	¾ **43a**
766	THEATRE LADY 2 [1] P D Evans 6-9-7 (40) K Fallon 1/1 FAV: 1300-1283: Led, hdd ins last, kept on for press:	½ **42a**
541	TINY TIM 28 [2] A M Balding 6-9-7 (35) T Block (7) 14/1: 50050/-44: Cl-up, drvn & no extra ins last:	1¼ **39a**
710	HIGH DIVA 8 [5] J R Best 5-9-7 (35) N Pollard 15/2: 6-6465U5: Dwelt, trkd ldrs, found little dist.	nk **38a**
710	PRINCE DU SOLEIL 8 [4] J R Jenkins 8-9-7 P (40) E Ahern 12/1: 00000-66: Mid-div, eff wide, no extra dist.	hd **37a**
707	TOJONESKI 8 [8] I W McInnes 5-9-7 (40) Natalia Gemelova (7) 25/1: 03530-07: Rear, eff wide 3f out, btn dist.	3½ **30a**
429	TRAVEL TARDIA 45 [11] I A Wood 6-9-7 (40) I Mongan 25/1: 00/000-08: Sn cl-up, btn over 1f out:	3½ **23a**
410	QUEEN EXCALIBUR 47 [3] C Roberts 5-9-7 p (40) Dane O'Neill 20/1: 040-0009: Prom till halfway:	5 **14a**
717	MISS CELERITY 7 [6] M J Haynes 4-9-7 (30) R Miles (5) 16/1: 060-0040: Trkd ldrs, drvn & btn 2f out.	2 **10a**
258	TOMOKIM 64 [12] M Quinn 3-8-3 VIS (30) C Catlin 50/1: 000-0: Wide & al bhd:	6 **0a**

11 Ran   1m 39.99 (3.79)   Owner Century Racing   Trained at Newark

---

787   **4.30** Bet Direct On Sky Active Claiming Stakes 4yo+   (H)
           £1271 £363 £182   **1m5f p/track**   **Going 37**   **-11 Slow**   Stalls Inside

762	RADIANT BRIDE 3 [7] K R Burke 4-8-9 bl (45) Darren Williams 3/1: 0261201: Held up, smooth hdwy over 2f out & readily asserted well ins last, cheekily	**49a**
689*	SUNGIO 11 [4] B G Powell 6-9-3 bl (52) Dale Gibson 1/1 FAV: 5/05-1312 Trkd ldrs, rdn & led over 1f out, hdd well ins last, not pace of wnr:	nk **53a**
630	MISS KOEN 17 [6] D L Williams 5-8-12 T (53) Dane O'Neill 25/1: 0/6060-63: Rear/wide, smooth prog 3f out, kept on onepace for press from dist.	2 **45a**
581	THE LAST MOHICAN 22 [5] P Howling 5-9-3 (35) R Winston 8/1: 0-423244: Trkd ldrs, rdn & led over 2f out till over 1f out, no extra:	4 **44a**
634	BRANSTON NELL 17 [3] C R Dore 4-8-12 (45) R Thomas 16/1: 20100-05: Mid-div, btn 3f out:	5 **32a**
563	FAILED TO HIT 25 [8] N P Littmoden 11-9-1 vis (51) I Mongan 6/1: 1456-346: Led till 2f out, sn btn:	2 **32a**
257	BLUE RONDO 66 [1] Ian Williams 4-9-0 VIS (55) C Catlin 12/1: 0/40000-7: Chsd ldrs, btn 3f out:	16 **12a**
	LETANG BLEU 1203 [9] P Butler 6-9-3 t p C Haddon (7) 50/1: 0///-8: Dwelt, chsd ldrs till 4f out:	hd **11a**
644}	RAYWARE BOY 378 [2] D Shaw 8-8-13 vis Dawn Watson (7) 50/1: 5/00/600-9: Reluctant to race, sn t.o.	26 **0a**

9 Ran   2m 48.57 (6.27)   Owner Mrs Y Goodwin   Trained at Leyburn

---

788   **5.00** Bet Direct Interactive Banded Stakes 3yo+ 0-40 (H)
           £1456 £416 £208   **6f p/track rnd**   **Going 37**   **-03 Slow**   Stalls Inside

767	LONG WEEKEND 2 [13] D Shaw 9-9-6 vis (40) N Callan 13/8 FAV: 460-06621: Dwelt, switched rail & rear, switched wide & hdwy to lead ins last, held on all out:	**45a**
708	SHIRLEY OAKS 8 [7] Miss Z C Davison 6-9-6 (40) N Chalmers (5) 16/1: 000-0502: Chsd ldrs, drvn & styd on, just held:	shd **44a**
728	GENTLE RESPONSE 6 [11] B R Johnson 4-9-6 bl (35) S Whitworth 11/2: 000-0063: Dwelt, rear, switched rail, hdwy when short of room dist, styd on well cl-home:	½ **42a**
708	EMARATIS IMAGE 8 [8] R M Stronge 6-9-6 (40) A Daly 16/1: 4000-064: Keen & dsptd lead, led over 1f out, hdd ins last, kept on:	nk **41a**
748	SOTONIAN 4 [9] P S Felgate 11-9-6 (40) Lisa Jones (3) 4/1: 00-53305: In tch, ch dist, onepace for press:	shd **41a**
767	LAW MAKER 2 [6] M A Buckley 4-9-6 bl (35) J Fanning 50/1: 000-00006: Keen & prom, no extra ins last:	½ **39a**
728	TRUE HOLLY 6 [5] S Kirk 4-9-6 VIS (40) J F Egan 9/1: 6/0000-07: Dwelt, chsd ldrs, no extra fnl 1f:	1 **36a**
706	ONEFORTHEBOYS 8 [2] D Flood 5-9-6 (40) L Treadwell 15/2: 0-006248: Dwelt, mid-div, no impress fnl 1f.	nk **35a**
708	HELLBENT 8 [1] J A Osborne 5-9-6 (40) S Crawford (5) 20/1: 30/0-0009: Dwelt, rear, eff wide, no impress.	nk **34a**
667	LEVELLED 14 [4] D W Chapman 10-9-6 (35) A Culhane 16/1: 000-0000: Led till over 1f out:	6 **19a**
706	FLAME PRINCESS 8 [12] J R Boyle 4-9-6 (40) J Quinn 12/1: 05500-30: Mid-div, eff wide dist, no dngr.	¾ **17a**
720	INDIAN SHORES 7 [3] M Mullineaux 5-9-6 p (40) P Varley (7) 25/1: F-006000: Slow away & al bhd.	1 **14a**
637	MOONGLADE 16 [10] Miss J Feilden 4-9-6 t P (30) A Quinn (5) 66/1: 00000-00: Dwelt, mid-div wide, nvr a factor, cheek pieces.	1¾ **9a**

13 Ran   1m 12.81 (2.41)   Owner The Marlow Lewin Partnership   Trained at Newark

---

NAD AL SHEBA SATURDAY 28.02.04 Lefthand, Flat, Fair Track

Official Going Good/Firm

789   **4.45** Emirates Airline Stakes H'cap 3yo+   ()   **[238]**
           £32681 £10055 £5027   **1m2f**   **Good/Firm**   Stalls Inside

4684}	ADIEMUS 9 [ ] J Noseda 6-9-0 vis (98) L Dettori 3/1 FAV: 0620-431: Held up in tch, smooth hdwy & swtchd to lead over 1f out, rdn out:	**106**
452+*	SWIFT TANGO 16 [ ] E A L Dunlop 4-8-6 (90) P Hanagan 9/1: 1623-102: Mid-div, hdwy to press wnr dist, not pace of wnr:	3 **92**
5004}	ANANI 16 [ ] E A L Dunlop 4-9-6 (105) W Supple 9/2: 45102-03: Mid-div, styd on fnl 2f, not able to chall.	2¾ **102**

12 Ran   2m 03.90   Owner G Lansbury   Trained at Newmarket

790   **5.45** Emirates Airline Cup H'cap 3yo+   ()   **[230]**
           £36312 £11173 £5586   **6f110yds**   **Good/Firm**   Stalls Inside

3661} PIC UP STICKS 16 [ ] M R Channon 5-8-10 (90) T E Durcan 3/1: 0000P-31: Mid-div hdwy to lead over 1f out, drvn out ins last: **98**

NAD AL SHEBA SATURDAY 28.02.04 Lefthand, Flat, Fair Track

SUPER BRAND 202 M F de Kock 4-8-9 (90) W C Marwing 4/1: 1331-2: Held up in tch, rdn & kept on fnl 2f, not pace of wnr:		1	93
4621*} **BOSTON LODGE 16** G A Butler 4-9-0 (95) L Dettori 15/8 FAV: 3241-323: Held up in tch, rdn & prog 2f out, no extra in last:		½	96
9 Ran 1m 17.75 Owner A Ball & W Harrison Allan			Trained at West Ilsley

SOUTHWELL Wednesday 03.03.04 Lefthand, Sharp, Oval Track

Official Going Standard To Slow

791 1.50 Betdirect Co Uk Apprentice Handicap Stakes Div 1 4yo+ 0-60 (F) [60]
£2919 £834 £417 1m f/sand rnd Going 103 -19 Slow Stalls Inside

4864} **THUNDERCLAP 131** [5] J J Quinn 5-9-3 (49) A Mullen (4) 7/4 FAV: 004400-1: Hld up trav well, hdwy/hung left over 1f out, rdn & led well ins last:			56a
757 **KUMAKAWA 4** [8] E A Wheeler 6-8-13 bl (45) Liam Jones (4) 7/1: 0503002: Held up, hdwy & rdn to lead over 1f out, hdd well ins last:		¾	50a
680 **VICTORY FLIP 13** [2] R Hollinshead 4-8-8 (40) H Fellows (6) 8/1: 460-0653: Held up, short of room 2f out, took 3rd in last, no dngr:		5	36a
680 **DALRIATH 13** [1] M C Chapman 5-8-3 (35) C Haddon (4) 25/1: 000-0664: Cl-up & led over 3f out till over 2f out, wknd:		2	27a
754* **DANCING KING 5** [10] P W Hiatt 8-9-5 6ex (51) W Hogg 30/30: 0521315: Led/dsptd lead till over 1f out, fdd:		1¼	40a
530 **BOUGHT DIRECT 29** [6] R J Smith 5-9-11 (57) Dean Williams (4) 11/1: 0000-006: Chsd ldrs, btn 2f out:		6	36a
4024} **KING NICHOLAS 183** [4] J Parkes 5-9-10 t (56) D Fentiman 16/1: 2/10000-7: In tch till 3f out, reapp.		3½	28a
2270} **BLUE VENTURE 757** [3] P C Haslam 4-10-0 (60) D Wakenshaw (4) 14/1: 2/43300-8: Chsd ldrs, struggling fnl 3f.		¾	31a
776 **SAMBA BEAT 3** [7] R F Marvin 5-8-13 (45) M Nem (4) 50/1: 00/050-09: Slow away & sn bhd, quick reapp.		19	0a
380 **HUMDINGER 51** [9] D Shaw 4-9-1 (47) D Tudhope (4) 33/1: 10060-00: Chsd ldrs 4f, sn bhd, abs.		hd	0a
10 Ran 1m 49.15 (9.75) Owner The Wednesday Club			Trained at Malton

792 2.25 Betdirect Co Uk Apprentice Handicap Stakes Div 2 4yo+ 0-60 (F) [60]
£2919 £834 £417 1m f/sand rnd Going 103 -28 Slow Stalls Inside

719 **GRUB STREET 8** [9] J Parkes 8-7-12 (30) J D O'Reilly (4) 13/2: 0000/-341: Pushed along towards rear, hdwy for press 2f out & led well ins last:			34a
4970} **NODS NEPHEW 123** [5] D E Cantillon 7-9-2 (48) Derek Nolan 7/2 FAV: 403110-2: Trkd ldrs, rdn & led over 1f out, hdd well ins last:		nk	51a
719 **GRACIOUS AIR 8** [8] J R Weymes 6-8-13 vis (45) D Fentiman 9/1: 060-0153: Chsd ldrs, outpcd 2f out, kept on ins last:		2	44a
677 **MAGIC MAMMAS TOO 13** [1] T D Barron 4-9-7 p (53) Laura Jayne Crawford (4) 15/2: 226-2534: Led 5f, rdn & no extra dist:		1	50a
648 **SANTA CATALINA 16** [7] C A Dwyer 5-8-13 (45) Dean Williams (4) 40/1: 0603-005: Chsd ldrs, not able to chall.		½	41a
719* **FRAAMTASTIC 8** [3] B A Pearce 7-8-9 6ex (41) W Hogg 9/1: 040-2416: Cl-up & led over 2f out till over 1f out, fdd.		3	31a
754 **SPY GUN 5** [6] T Wall 4-9-10 (56) D Tudhope (4) 12/1: 4-350057: Dwelt & towards rear, keen, nvr mount chall.		1¾	43a
771 **MATHMAGICIAN 3** [2] R F Marvin 5-8-3 (35) K Ghunowa (4) 20/1: 040-4548: Sn twds rear & nvr factor:		nk	21a
754 **LORD CHAMBERLAIN 6** [4] Mrs N Macauley 11-9-11 bl (57) C J Davies (4) 6/1: 1440229: Held up, hung left & btn 2f out.		nk	42a
746 **SORBIESHARRY 6** [4] Mrs N Macauley 5-9-3 p (49) Saleem Golam (4) 4/1: 5235150: Mid-div, sn rdn & lost place.		1	32a
10 Ran 1m 49.87 (10.47) Owner Mrs B Sands			Trained at Malton

793 3.00 New Site @ Betdirect Co Uk Claiming Stakes 4yo+ (F)
£2912 £832 £416 5f f/sand str Going 103 Inapplicab Stalls Outside

610 **SCARY NIGHT 20** [5] J Balding 4-8-9 p (68) J Edmunds 20/1: 2200-001: Chsd ldrs, hung under press but styd on fnl 1f to lead cl-home:			65a
748 **MALAHIDE EXPRESS 5** [7] M J Polglase 4-9-5 bl (60) L Fletcher (3) 16/1: 500-4502: Led, hung left under press in last, hdd cl-home:		nk	74a
775* **HENRY TUN 3** [6] J Balding 6-8-5 bl (55) D Allan (3) 85/40 FAV: 0-350213: Prom, hung left & onepace dist:		2½	53a
646 **JUWWI 16** [8] J M Bradley 10-8-13 p (63) Darren Williams 8/1: 0-040044: Dwelt, not able to chall.		½	59a
741 **SHARP HAT 6** [2] D W Chapman 10-8-11 (66) A Culhane (4) 13/2: 5-520055: Chsd ldrs, no impress dist:		nk	56a
678 **AMANDAS LAD 13** [3] M C Chapman 4-8-7 (45) D Fox (5) 40/1: 0426406: Chsd ldrs, no impress from halfway:		nk	51a
749 **TIGRESS 5** [4] J W Unett 5-8-10 bl (56) J Quinn 7/2: 0-652627: In tch, nvr able to chall:		nk	53a
737 **PANJANDRUM 6** [1] N E Berry 6-9-1 (66) M Savage (5) 13/2: 0351068: Dwelt, nvr on terms with ldrs:		shd	58a
660 **VANISHED 15** [9] M J Polglase 4-8-0 bl (55) N Mackay (3) 11/1: 2440-009: Chsd ldrs, hung left & btn 2f out:		12	12a
9 Ran 1m 02.97 Owner Mr Derrick Moss			Trained at Doncaster

794 3.35 Bet In Running @ Betdirect Co Uk Handicap Stakes 3yo 0-85 (D) [84]
£4082 £1256 £628 £314 7f f/sand rnd Going 103 +09 Fast Stalls Inside

659 **MISSION AFFIRMED 15** [3] T P Tate 3-7-13 (55) D Mernagh 33/1: 55-01: Cl-up & led halfway, styd on strongly fnl 2f:			67a
568 **DENVER 25** [7] B J Meehan 3-9-7 (77) K Fallon 11/4: 42521-02: Pushed along chsg ldrs, rdn & chsd wnr over 1f out, no impress ins last:		3	82a
184* **TITUS SALT 82** [6] T D Barron 3-9-6 bl (76) E Ahern 9/4 FAV: 4421-3: Chsd ldrs, rdn & no extra dist:		1¼	78a
223 **ROOD BOY 75** [9] J S King 3-8-4 (60) C Catlin 25/1: 0043-4: Chsd ldrs, not able to chall fnl 2f:		3	56a
636* **DARING AFFAIR 17** [1] K R Burke 3-8-7 (63) Lisa Jones (3) 8/1: 526-3215: Slow into stride, nvr on terms with ldrs.		3	53a
696 **BLUE EMPIRE 11** [4] P A Blockley 3-9-7 (77) D Nolan (5) 40/1: 1-451426: Trkd ldrs trav well, wknd dist:		3½	60a
615* **COULD SHE BE MAGIC 19** [10] T D Easterby 3-8-5 (61) Dale Gibson 9/2: 3501-217: Rdn to go handy from wide draw, btn over 1f out:		6	34a
553 **MAID THE CUT 27** [8] A D Smith 3-7-12 1oh (53) J Quinn 40/1: 00-48: Dwelt, nvr on terms:		2½	22a
614 **ATLANTIC BREEZE 20** [5] Mrs N Macauley 3-8-0 (56) J Mackay 66/1: 410-009: Dwelt & sn outpcd:		14	0a
615 **SIR JASPER 19** [2] M F Harris 3-8-3 vis (59) S Righton 25/1: 61-10340: Led/dsptd lead till halfway:		¾	2a
10 Ran 1m 33.19 (6.59) Owner Mr T P Tate			Trained at Tadcaster

SOUTHWELL Wednesday 03.03.04 Lefthand, Sharp, Oval Track

795   4.10 Littlewoods Bet Direct Maiden Stakes 3yo (D)
£3439 £1058 £529 £265   6f f/sand rnd   Going 103   -14 Slow   Stalls Inside

4613}	GENEROUS GESTURE 149 [15] M L W Bell 3-8-9 (73) J Mackay 3/1JT FAV: 604-1: Gd speed to go handy from wide draw, led over 2f out, rdn & styd on strongly:		76a
5034}	TIME TO RELAX 116 [2] J J Quinn 3-8-9 (64) Darren Williams 3/1JT FAV: 43600-2: Chsd ldrs, rdn & chsd wnr fnl 2f, kept on but al held:	5	64a
631	SHAYMEES GIRL 18 [9] Ms Deborah J Evans 3-8-9 Joanna Badger 66/1: 0-53: Led/dsptd lead till halfway, no extra:	2½	57a
631	SOUL PROVIDER 18 [8] P A Blockley 3-8-9 (58) N Callan 7/2: 525-534: Mid-div, kept on onepace:	2½	50a
1656}	JACOB 285 [4] P A Blockley 3-9-0 (63) S Yourston 33/1: 355-5: Slow away & pushed along, nrst fin, reapp:	3½	46a
3265}	KILLERBY NICKO 216 [16] T D Easterby 3-9-0 D Allan (3) 25/1: 00-6: In tch, outpcd from halfway, reapp/AW bow.	¾	44a
3797}	SIR GALAHAD 194 [11] T D Easterby 3-9-0 A Mullen (7) 20/1: 6-7: Slow away, nvr on terms:	nk	43a
4789}	NITEOWL EXPRESS 138 [6] J O'Reilly 3-8-9 D R McCabe 66/1: 0-8: Mid-div, nvr a factor, reapp/AW bow.	nk	37a
	RED MONARCH [5] P A Blockley 3-9-0 Derek Nolan (7) 20/1: 9: Chsd ldrs till halfway, debut.	1	40a
	ADORATA [3] J Jay 3-8-9 C Catlin 25/1: 0: Slow away & sn outpcd, debut.	hd	34a
691	KING OF MEZE 11 [10] G Prodromou 3-8-9 O Urbina 40/1: 060: Al bhd.	1	37a
609	FAYRZ PLEASE 20 [13] M C Chapman 3-9-0 (60) Andrew Webb (7) 7/1: 03-440: Mid-div, hmpd/lost ch halfway.	1¼	34a
4993}	SMART DANNY 121 [1] J J Quinn 3-9-0 R Winston 33/1: 40-0: Sn prom, btn/eased over 1f out:	5	22a
1165}	BLUE EMPEROR 316 [12] P A Blockley 3-9-0 (70) D Nolan (5) 14/1: 346-0: Al bhd, reapp.	2½	15a
659	ROYAL SHEPLEY 15 [14] J Balding 3-8-9 J Edmunds 66/1: 00: Dwelt, sn prom till over 2f out.	18	0a

15 Ran   1m 20.34 (7.04)   Owner Mr & Mrs J & P Ransley   Trained at Newmarket

796   4.45 Bet Direct On Sky Active Handicap Stakes 3yo 0-75 (E)   [79]
£3350 £957 £479   1m4f f/sand   Going 103   +05 Fast   Stalls Inside

608	YANKEEDOODLEDANDY 20 [9] P C Haslam 3-9-0 (65) Rory Moore (7) 4/1: 04-12121: Cl-up & led over 3f out, drvn & held on well ins last:		75a
702+*	RED LANCER 9 [1] R J Price 3-9-9 6ex (74) B Swarbrick (7) 2/1 FAV: 010-6112: Chsd ldrs, rdn & chsd wnr 2f out, drvn & hung left, kept on well:	¾	82a
658	SIEGFRIEDS NIGHT 15 [6] M C Chapman 3-8-4 (55) D Fox (5) 18/1: 35-14323: Held up & keen, no dngr.	10	50a
614	ASHSTANZA 20 [10] M A Jarvis 3-8-12 P (63) N Callan 10/1: 04-434: Led till over 3f out, no extra.	1¼	56a
702	GAVROCHE 9 [2] M J Wallace 3-9-6 VIS (71) J P Guillambert 33/1: 11/2: 400-1235: Dwelt & held up, keen, hung left & btn over 2f out:	14	49a
686*	YLANG YLANG 12 [7] W Jarvis 3-9-7 (72) M Tebbutt 12/1: 50-416: Dwelt & held up, no impress fnl 3f:	9	39a
676	KEEPERS KNIGHT 14 [8] P F I Cole 3-9-3 (68) K Fallon 8/1: 055-1357: In tch, btn 3f out:	22	5a
658	SIR FRANK GIBSON 15 [5] M Johnston 3-7-12 3oh (46) J Quinn 20/1: 40-04238: Handy, wknd 4f out.	6	0a
226	THEVENIS 75 [5] J S King 3-8-9 (60) C Catlin 50/1: 500050-9: Chsd ldrs, no impress from halfway fnl 5f:	2½	0a
614*	CEASAR 20 [3] P C Haslam 3-8-4 p (55) G Faulkner 12/1: 6004-210: Chsd ldrs till 7f out, sn bhd:	½	0a

10 Ran   2m 46.09 (11.79)   Owner Mr K Tyre   Trained at Middleham

797   5.20 Bet Direct Interactive Handicap Stakes 3yo 0-60 (F)   [67]
£2982 £852 £426   6f f/sand rnd   Going 103   -19 Slow   Stalls Inside

609	PICCOLO PRINCE 20 [9] E J Alston 3-9-7 (60) J Quinn 7/4 FAV: 500-0121: Mid-div, smooth hdwy over 2f out, led & hung left over 1f out, drvn out:		66a
703*	EMARADIA 9 [1] A W Carroll 3-9-7 6ex bl (60) A Culhane 9/1: 2-312012: Cl-up & led 4f out, drvn & hdd over 1f out, kept on	1¼	61a
708	PRINCE OF PERLES 9 [8] D Shaw 3-7-12 2oh bl (35) Lisa Jones (3) 40/1: 0000-003: Held up, styd on for press fnl 2f, not reach front pair:	1	35a
613	INDRANI 20 [10] John A Harris 3-8-6 (45) L Fletcher (3) 80/1: 4560-064: Dwelt, rdn & styd on fnl 2f, no danger to front pair:	hd	42a
591	BARRAS 22 [5] Miss Gay Kelleway 3-9-0 vis (53) M Fenton 9/1: 321-0035: Led 2f, btn over 1f out:	4	40a
691	BOOKIESINDEXDOTCOM 11 [7] J R Jenkins 3-9-4 bl (57) S W Kelly 18/1: 222-0306: Chsd ldrs, short of room halfway, nvr able to chall:	¾	42a
591	VAMPIRE QUEEN 22 [12] R P Elliott 3-9-2 (55) N Mackay (5) 9/1: 0600-147: Held up, mod late prog:	3	33a
436	POACHERS PARADISE 44 [4] M W Easterby 3-8-8 (47) Dale Gibson 15/2: 000-08: Rdn to go handy, btn 2f out, abs.	¾	23a
771	DANDY JIM 3 [6] D W Chapman 3-7-12 7oh (30) D Fentiman (7) 25/1: 006-0509: Slow away, nvr on terms, quick reapp.	shd	13a
671	DULCE DE LECHE 14 [11] S C Williams 3-9-1 (54) B Reilly (3) 14/1: 00-06400: Sn outpcd.	3	23a
742	TABARKA 6 [13] P A Blockley 3-9-7 (60) N Callan 33/1: 4530-50: Dwelt & al bhd, quick reapp.	2½	22a
661	EMPEROR CAT 15 [3] P A Blockley 3-9-3 (56) D Nolan (5) 4/1: 0105-230: Dwelt, mid-div, btn 2f out:	6	4a
4965}	TIMES THE MASTER 123 [2] M F Harris 3-8-1 (40) S Righton 100/1: 604500-0: Keen & prom till over 2f out.	4	0

13 Ran   1m 20.66 (7.36)   Owner The Burlington Partnership   Trained at Preston

LINGFIELD Thursday 04.03.04 Lefthand, V Sharp Track

Official Going   Standard

798   1.40 Bet Direct On Sky Active Handicap Stakes 3yo 0-70 (E)   [77]
£3371 £963 £482   1m p/track rnd   Going 33   -09 Slow   Stalls Outside

656	JOMUS 16 [5] L Montague Hall 3-8-11 (60) F Lynch 8/1: 2005-521: Dwelt, mid-div wide, pushed along a hdwy over 2f out, led dist, drvn out:		67a
566	ALEXANDER AMBITION 26 [10] S Kirk 3-9-0 (63) J F Egan 20/1: 020-4342: Mid-div, rdn to press ldrs dist, drvn & not pace of wnr:	¾	68a
676	NORWEGIAN 15 [11] D R Loder 3-9-2 VIS (65) J Murtagh 6/1: 5143: Trkd ldrs, eff to chall wide 2f out, onepace ins last:	nk	69a
568	LORD OF THE SEA 26 [7] Jamie Poulton 3-9-7 (70) I Mongan 7/2 JT FAV: 0655-334: Trkd ldrs, onepace for press dist:	shd	74a
603	TREVIAN 22 [4] S C Williams 3-9-4 BL (67) B Reilly (3) 9/1: 56-01665: Keen & trkd ldrs, short of room 2f out & again over 1f out, onepace:	1¾	68a

713	**NIGHT STORM** 9 [9] S Dow 3-9-3 (66) D Holland 13/2: 25-53336: Dwelt, rear, late gains, not able to chall.	½	66a
486*	**SMART BOY PRINCE** 37 [1] P A Blockley 3-9-3 (66) Derek Nolan (7) 20/1: 0466-117: Keen & led till over 2f out, btn dist:	1½	63a
673	**FORZENUFF** 15 [3] J R Boyle 3-8-10 (59) S Dweeney 40/1: 603-5068: Cl-up, led over 2f out till dist:	½	55a
729°	**ATHBOY** 8 [6] M J Wallace 3-9-6 6ex vis (69) E Ahern 7/2 JT FAV: 60-0119: Mid-div inner, hmpd over 1f out, no prog.	½	64a
729	**SOMEWHERE MY LOVE** 8 [12] T G Mills 3-9-3 (68) K Fallon 8/1: 50-100: Dwelt, chsd ldrs, lost place 2f out.	¾	62a
4761}	**ELSINORA** 140 [8] H Morrison 3-8-11 (60) L Fletcher (3) 50/1: 0300-0: Al rear & no ch 2f out:	2½	49a
162	**DRIZZLE** 87 [2] Ian Williams 3-8-11 (60) M Henry 33/1: 303-0: Al rear, btn/hmpd 2f out:	5	40a
12 Ran	1m 39.56 (3.36) Owner Mr J Daniels	Trained at Epsom	

730	**RIPPLE EFFECT** 8 [5] C A Dwyer 4-9-10 t (72) B Reilly (3) 8/1: 2-212051: Trkd ldrs trav well, led dist, rdn clr:		81a
669	**RANNY** 15 [2] Dr J D Scargill 4-8-2 (50) J Quinn 10/1: 04100-42: Trkd ldr trav well, led over 2f out, hdd dist, no ch with wnr:	3	51a
760	**BLONDE EN BLONDE** 5 [7] N P Littmoden 4-9-6 bl (68) I Mongan 13/2: 6012033: Rear & inner, styd on for press fnl 2f, nrst fin:	hd	68a
760	**AND TOTO TOO** 5 [8] P D Evans 4-9-7 bl (69) K Fallon 2/1 FAV: 515-0624: Held up, switched wide over 2f out, onepace bef dist:	¾	68a
474	**I WISH** 40 [1] M Madgwick 6-9-0 (62) L Keniry (3) 10/1: 06146-05: Keen, chsd ldrs, hung & no impress dist:	nk	60a
687	**PRIMA STELLA** 13 [4] J A R Toller 5-9-11 (73) Lisa Jones (3) 4/1: 0-410266: Dwelt, keen in mid-div, no impress dist:	½	70a
4085}	**LARA FALANA** 180 [9] Miss B Sanders 6-8-12 (60) T Quinn 16/1: 100500-7: Trkd ldrs wide, outpcd fnl 2f:	1¼	54a
4689}	**MICHELLE MA BELLE** 144 [10] S Kirk 4-10-0 (76) J F Egan 12/1: 333655-8: Mid-div, eff 2f out, btn dist:	½	69a
620	**MISS CHAMPERS** 20 [6] P A Blockley 4-9-9 (71) N Callan 20/1: 52-01149: Slow away & rear:	¾	62a
680	**CLOUDLESS** 14 [11] J W Unett 4-8-9 (57) S Whitworth 20/1: 015-0240: Led till over 2f out, wknd:	5	39a
10 Ran	1m 25.46 (2.66) Owner Miss Lilo Blum	Trained at Newmarket	

758	**AFRICAN SAHARA** 5 [7] Miss D Mountain 5-9-9 t (79) O Urbina 7/1: 226-6101: Held up wide, hdwy to chall dist, drvn & led cl-home, joined line:	dht	83a
758	**KENTUCKY KING** 5 [9] P W Hiatt 4-9-10 (80) A Culhane 14/1: 1/4-6601: Rear, rdn & hdwy over 1f out, squeezed through gap to join ldr on line:		84a
4897}	**BRAZILIAN TERRACE** 131 [3] M L W Bell 4-9-3 (76) M Fenton 20/1: 536150-3: Trkd ldr inner, rdn & narrow lead ins last, hdd cl-home:	hd	76a
688	**AVENTURA** 13 [1] M J Polglase 4-9-10 (80) K Fallon 20/1: 5430-004: Mid-div, switched & drvn to chall dist, just held cl-home:	shd	83a
627	**SUMMER RECLUSE** 19 [6] B R Johnson 5-9-7 p (77) Dane O'Neill 4/1 JT FAV: 1013-005: Trkd ldr, rdn & led over 1f out, hdd dist & no extra cl-home:	½	79a
5030}	**KAREEB** 117 [5] W J Musson 7-9-8 (78) A Rutter (7) 20/1: 130000-6: Rear, styd on inner under hands & heels, nrst fin:	½	79a
625	**HIAWATHA** 19 [2] P A Blockley 5-9-6 (76) J Quinn 6/1: 01-41307: Chsd ldrs, rdn & no extra dist:	2½	72a
688	**DEL MAR SUNSET** 13 [10] W J Haggas 5-9-8 (78) D Holland 9/2: 0003-458: Sn led & clr early, hdd over 1f out, sn btn.	½	73a
5020}	**ZEIS** 119 [11] H Morrison 4-9-8 (78) S Drowne 20/1: 1/00-9: Rear, no ch fnl 2f, reapp.	5	64a
604	**CORMORANT WHARF** 22 [8] T E Powell 4-9-5 (75) I Mongan 4/1 JT FAV: 6/0-06500: Chsd ldrs, fdd under press fnl 2f:	¾	60a
700	**ARC EL CIEL** 10 [4] Mrs Stef Liddiard 5-9-5 vis (77) E Ahern 20/1: 1350030: Mid-div, drvn & btn 2f out:	1¼	59a
11 Ran	1m 38.31 (2.11) Owner Miss Debbie Mountain	Trained at Newmarket	

624	**ANYHOW** 19 [3] Miss K M George 7-9-8 (59) D Holland 5/1: 140-0021: Rear, short of room 3f out, sn hdwy & again short of room dist, rdn/strong run ins last to lead cl-home, shade		67a
736	**DISPOL EVITA** 7 [4] Jamie Poulton 5-8-13 (50) I Mongan 20/1: 5020-042: Dwelt, rear, hdwy wide over 2f out & drvn/led over 1f out, hdd nr fin:	½	55a
731	**KASHIMO** 8 [7] G L Moore 5-9-7 (58) R Brisland 2/1 FAV: 34000-53: Mid-div, eff wide from over 3f out & chall 2f out, onepace:	2½	59a
478	**MARMADUKE** 40 [1] M Pitman 8-9-12 (63) E Ahern 9/1: 631/6-254: Sn trkd ldr, styd on onepace:	shd	64a
672	**ALISA** 15 [9] B I Case 4-9-5 (58) Lisa Jones (3) 50/1: 0355: Keen, rear, eff wide 2f out, not able to chall:	½	58a
4922}	**AONINCH** 128 [6] Mrs P N Dutfield 4-9-9 (62) D Sweeney 10/1: 030113-6: Keen & rear, hdwy/short of room dist, sn no extra:	hd	61a
4488}	**MASJOOR** 159 [5] N A Graham 4-9-7 (60) J Murtagh 25/1: 030-7: Mid-div, onepace when short of room dist:	½	58a
634	**COOLFORE JADE** 19 [11] N E Berry 4-8-13 (52) C Catlin 20/1: 1414358: Led till over 1f out, fdd:	½	49a
763*	**WELSH WIND** 4 [2] M Wigham 8-9-11 6ex t p (62) J Fanning 12/1: 2-320319: Trkd ldrs, short of room over 2f out, wknd dist:	1	58a
446*	**PLATINUM CHARMER** 44 [10] K A Ryan 4-9-8 (61) N Callan 20/1: 0004-210: Mid-div, lost place bef halfway, nvr a factor:	½	56a
726	**LONDONER** 8 [12] S Dow 9-9-8 (59) P Doe 25/1: 006-0000: Held up, eff 5f out, sn btn.	3	50a
746*	**BRAMANTINO** 7 [8] R A Fahey 4-9-5 6ex p (58) T Hamilton (3) 13/2: 000-5310: Chsd ldrs, btn 2f out:	1½	47a
264	**WAVERLEY ROAD** 66 [13] M Madgwick 7-8-8 (45) L Keniry (2) 16/1: 060510-0: Trkd ldr, btn 2f out:	6	26a
634	**FIGHT THE FEELING** 19 [14] J W Unett 6-9-5 (56) K Fallon 14/1: 16-42200: Al bhd & eased 3f out:	9	26a
14 Ran	2m 32.93 (3.73) Owner Stableline	Trained at Crediton	

691	**KRYSSA** 12 [4] G L Moore 3-8-7 I Mongan 7/1: 41: Held up in tch, hdwy over 1f out & rdn to lead well ins last, styd on strongly:		62a
572	**MULTAHAB** 26 [8] Miss Gay Kelleway 5-9-11 (60) M Fenton 3/1: 0555-242: Cl-up & led 3f out, hung right 2f out, hdd well ins last:	1¼	62a
130	**SECOND MINISTER** 93 [2] D Flood 5-9-11 bl T (60) J Murtagh 11/4 FAV: 4/00032-3: Dwelt, sn trkd ldrs trav well, short of room dist, drvn & onepace:	½	60a
32	**LACONIA** 111 [1] J S Moore 3-8-7 (65) E Ahern 9/2: 00350-4: Cl-up & ch over 1f out, no extra dist:	1	52a

691	JOANS JEWEL 12 [6] G G Margarson 3-8-7 A McCarthy 25/1: 55: Dwelt, rear, outpcd halfway, late gains:	½	50a
449	MAGGIE MAQUETTE 43 [3] W S Kittow 4-9-6 (55) D Sweeney 20/1: 00-56: Chsd ldrs, no extra dist, abs.	hd	49a
742	VITTORIOSO 7 [10] Miss Gay Kelleway 3-8-12 VIS (54) D Holland 5/1: 50-53327: Chsd ldrs wide, btn dist:	hd	53a
3423}	VALENTIA 211 [7] M H Tompkins 3-8-7 Saleem Golam (5) 25/1: 05-8: Rear/wide, al outpcd.	2½	40a
761	TREE ROOFER 5 [5] N P Littmoden 5-9-11 (48) T P Queally (3) 20/1: 35040-09: Led till 3f out, sn btn, qck reapp.	nk	44a
	PARIS LATINO [9] C L Tizzard 5-9-11 V Slattery 66/1: 0: Dwelt, sn outpcd on Flat debut, jumps fit.	5	30a
10 Ran	1m 0.06 (2.8) Owner Mr D J Deer	Trained at Brighton	

---

803 4.10 Press Interactive To Bet Direct Handicap Stakes 3yo+ 0-70 (E) **[70]**
£3444 £984 £492   1m2f p/track   Going 33   -25 Slow   Stalls Inside

726	KARAOKE 8 [5] S Kirk 4-9-9 (65) J F Egan 20/1: 2331-001: Trkd ldrs inner, short of room 2f out, drvn to lead cl-home:		73a
674	SAY WHAT YOU SEE 15 [7] J W Hills 4-9-12 (68) M Hills 7/1: 3200-042: Led, qcknd clr over 2f out, drvn & hung right ins last, hdd cl-home:	hd	74a
738	ABSOLUTE UTOPIA 7 [3] J L Spearing 11-9-7 (63) A Daly 16/1: 101-0223: Short of room after 2f, sn rear, styd on for press fnl 2f, no threat:	2½	65a
736	REGAL GALLERY 7 [1] C A Horgan 6-9-10 (66) Paul Eddery 9/2: 0/41-1134: Rear, outpcd 3f out, styd on wide for press, nvr a threat:	nk	67a
715	SPRINGALONG 9 [4] P D Evans 4-9-11 (67) S Donohoe (7) 16/1: 3304-045: Mid-div, eff over 1f out, onepace.	½	67a
716	BRAVE DANE 9 [6] A W Carroll 6-9-12 (68) W Ryan 7/2 FAV: 500-1156: Rear, outpcd 3f out, nvr able to chall ldrs:	½	67a
4587}	KATIYPOUR 152 [2] Miss B Sanders 7-9-13 (69) Lisa Jones (3) 16/1: 061346-7: Keen in mid-div, outpcd fnl 2f:	½	67a
698	THE GAIKWAR 12 [11] N P Littmoden 5-9-7 bl (63) I Mongan 8/1: 04-64258: Dwelt, chsd ldrs wide, no extra over 1f out.	1	60a
625	OLDENWAY 19 [14] R A Fahey 5-9-7 D Hamilton (5) 10/1: 02000-09: Dwelt, rear, eff wide, no prog dist.	¾	59a
552	PURE SPECULATION 28 [10] M L W Bell 4-9-11 (67) K Fallon 14/1: 4/3000-00: Trkd ldr, btn over 1f out.	½	62a
674	SILVALINE 15 [13] T Keddy 5-9-10 (66) D Holland 4/1: 11033-60: Trkd ldrs, wknd 2f out:	½	60a
2532}	MURDINGA 248 [8] A M Hales 5-9-12 BL (68) Dane O'Neill 66/1: 020/03/4-0: Prom, lost place from 2f out:	1½	60a
521	BOWING 33 [9] P G Murphy 4-9-10 (66) S Drowne 25/1: 0423-050: Al rear:	1½	56a
1665}	LINBY LAD 286 [12] J A Glover 4-10-0 (70) M Fenton 100/1: 2312/00-0: Dwelt, sn rear, nvr a factor, reapp.	1¼	58a
14 Ran	2m 08.56 (5.76) Owner Speedlith Group	Trained at Upper Lambourn	

---

804 4.40 New Site @ Betdirect Co Uk Claiming Stakes 3yo (F)
£2954 £844 £422   7f p/track rnd   Going 33   -13 Slow   Stalls Inside

671	LADY PISTE 15 [5] P D Evans 3-8-1 vis t (53) B Swarbrick (7) 12/1: 4-042531: Al prom, led dist, drvn out:		55a
779	SONDERBORG 3 [4] G L Moore 3-7-13 BL e (49) Lisa Jones (3) 12/1: 6-645322: Trkd ldrs, eff to chall ins last, no extra cl-home:	nk	52a
735	BIG BAD BURT 7 [14] M J Wallace 3-9-0 (64) K Fallon 6/4 FAV: 600-4223: Mid-div, switched to inner halfway, drvn & kept on, not pace to chall:	1¾	64a
682	PRINCESS ISMENE 14 [8] P A Blockley 3-8-3 bl (57) J Quinn 20/1: 05-15224: Dwelt, rear, drvn & styd on wide, not able to chall:	½	52a
671	AVERAMI 15 [13] A M Balding 3-8-9 VIS (64) S Drowne 33/1: 0654-05: Led till dist, no extra:	½	57a
729	GARRIGON 8 [2] N P Littmoden 3-9-0 (60) D Holland 9/2: 2-504046: Slow away & rear, prog/no room 2f out, no threat:	hd	61a
4903}	FOLEY PRINCE 129 [11] D Flood 3-9-10 (67) J Murtagh 25/1: 305146-7: Chsd ldr, no extra over 1f out.	1½	68a
662	CASANTELLA 16 [3] M J Polglase 3-7-13 (40) J F McDonald (5) 66/1: 0450508: Rear, no impress on ldrs.	2½	38a
671*	FISSION 15 [10] J A Osborne 3-8-9 bl (72) E Ahern 5/1: 513-6319: Restless stalls, reared start, chsd ldrs 5f:	1¼	45a
783	ZOLUSHKA 2 [12] B W Duke 3-8-3 (45) C Catlin 66/1: 0000-3000: Chsd ldrs wide till 2f out:	1¾	36a
712	STAMFORD BLUE 9 [1] J S Moore 3-8-4 bl (58) D Kinsella 25/1: 2462060: Slow away & rear, nvr any impress.	nk	36a
682*	LADY MO 14 [9] K A Ryan 3-8-7 (62) N Callan 10/1: 0-535110: Dwelt & al bhd:	1	37a
226	ROVING VIXEN 76 [7] J L Spearing 3-8-2 1ow A Daly 100/1: 00-0: Dwelt, sn struggling, rear, abs.	2	28a
739	INDIAN OAK 7 [6] M P Muggeridge 3-8-3 (35) S Whitworth 66/1: 50-0000: Chsd ldrs till 3f out.	9	13a
14 Ran	1m 26.00 (3.2) Owner Mrs S J Lawrence	Trained at Abergavenny	

---

805 5.10 Bet Direct Daily Special Offers Handicap Stakes 4yo+ 46-55 (F) **[64]**
£2982 £852 £426   1m2f p/track   Going 33   -05 Slow   Stalls Inside

766	STEELY DAN 4 [14] J R Best 5-9-7 6ex (57) N Pollard 11/2: 0022131: Rear, smooth hdwy to inner 3f out, cruised into lead ins last, readily:		66a
766*	INDIAN BLAZE 4 [6] Andrew Reid 10-9-1 6ex (51) T P Queally (3) 11/2: B00-6212: Al prom, rdn to lead 2f out, hdd well ins last & no extra:	2	54a
165	KALOU 87 [4] B J Curley 6-8-12 (48) S W Kelly 4/1: 50/6503-3: Mid-div, drvn & styd on onepace fnl 2f:	nk	50a
757*	RAHEEL 5 [9] P Mitchell 4-9-5 6ex t (55) D Holland 13/8 FAV: 0-540614: Rear, styd on onepace, no threat to ldrs:	hd	56a
768	PARADISE VALLEY 4 [8] Mrs Stef Liddiard 4-9-3 t (53) S Drowne 25/1: 525-1605: Held up, eff 2f out, hung over 1f out, not able to chall:	¾	53a
786	THEATRE LADY 2 [13] P D Evans 6-8-9 5oh (40) K Fallon 10/1: 300-12036: Mid-div, no impress over 1f out.	½	48a
718	SAMMYS SHUFFLE 9 [2] Jamie Poulton 9-9-3 bl (50) I Mongan 10/1: 2605-047: In tch, no extra over 1f out:	¾	48a
4735}	GREAT VIEW 142 [10] Mrs A L M King 5-8-12 (48) D Corby (3) 14/1: 155432-8: Slow away & rear, eff wide 2f out, no impress on ldrs:	2½	42a
2270}	ARROW 258 [3] Mrs L B Normile 5-8-13 (49) G Faulkner 33/1: 4006/00-9: Led till 2f out, sn btn, reapp, new yard.	nk	42a
3701}	STORM CLEAR 199 [5] D J Wintle 5-9-1 (51) Dane O'Neill 66/1: 600050-0: Trkd ldr, btn 2f out, jumps fit.	1½	42a
718	AMNESTY 9 [11] G L Moore 5-9-4 bl e (54) S Whitworth 25/1: 30-04500: Dwelt, rear, no prog 2f out.	shd	45a
634	MOLLYS SECRET 19 [12] C G Cox 6-8-12 p (48) J Quinn 25/1: 300-1000: Prom, btn 2f out:	6	30a
557	PRINCE MINATA 27 [7] P W Hiatt 9-8-9 (45) C Catlin 66/1: 50006-00: Trkd ldr, btn 2f out.	½	26a
13 Ran	2m 06.55 (3.75) Owner Mr E A Condon	Trained at Maidstone	

Official Going Slow

	806		**1.50 Cashbacks @ Betdirect Co Uk Handicap Stakes Div 1 3yo+ 0-70 (E)**		**[70]**
			£3255 £930 £465 **1m100y f/sand rnd Going 116 -07 Slow**	Stalls Inside	

704	**DANIELLES LAD 11** [7] B Palling 8-9-10 (66) A Culhane 13/2: 05-42041: Sn led, made rest, kept on for press fnl 1f, drvn out:		**73a**
791*	**THUNDERCLAP 2** [1] J J Quinn 5-8-7 (49) A Mullen (6) 4/1: 004400-12: Cl-up, eff to chall over 1f out, kept on, just held:	½	**56a**
479	**QUIET READING 39** [10] M R Bosley 7-9-10 vis (66) Hayley Turner (5) 7/1: 603-3463: Held up, eff over 2f out, sn onepace:	9	**57a**
746	**STING LIKE A BEE 8** [5] J S Goldie 5-8-13 (55) T Quinn 7/2 FAV: 060-1024: Held up, eff over 2f out, sn no impress:	3	**40a**
744	**MY BAYARD 8** [9] J O'Reilly 5-9-13 (69) J D O'Reilly (7) 9/2: 2020-625: Handy, wknd over 1f out:	2	**50a**
685	**VICTORY VEE 14** [11] M Blanshard 4-9-1 (57) D Sweeney 33/1: 13003-06: Chsd wnr till wknd over 2f out:	3½	**32a**
752	**YORKER 7** [6] Ms Deborah J Evans 6-9-11 (67) N Callan 5/1: 2534227: In tch, wknd over 2f out:	hd	**41a**
730	**BUGLE CALL 9** [8] K O Cunningham Brown 4-8-0 5oh 2ow bl e (35) J Quinn 66/1: 0000-008: Slow away & al bhd:	hd	**15a**
753*	**GERONIMO 7** [3] Miss Gay Kelleway 7-9-8 6ex p (64) Dean Williams (7) 12/1: 20-20319: Dwelt, al bhd:	1	**35a**
144	**ROY MCAVOY 90** [2] Mrs G Harvey 6-9-4 (60) G Baker 66/1: 600000-0: In tch, wknd over 3f out:	3	**25a**
726	**EASTER OGIL 9** [4] Jane Southcombe 9-9-7 (63) V Slattery 25/1: 3240000: In tch, wknd over 4f out:	dist	**0a**
11 Ran	1m 56.69 (10.49) Owner Mrs M M Palling		Trained at Cowbridge

	807		**2.20 Cashbacks @ Bet Direct On Sky Active Handicap Stakes 3yo+ 0-80 (D)**		**[80]**
			£2664 £2664 £627 £314 **6f f/sand rnd Going 116 +06 Fast**	Stalls Inside	

692	**HURRICANE COAST 13** [5] D Flood 5-10-0 bl (80) J Murtagh 11/2: 1320041: Prom, hdwy & bmpd over 1f out, styd on well ins last to join ldr on line:		**85a**
687	**TIME N TIME AGAIN 14** [10] E J Alston 6-9-13 p (79) J Quinn 5/1 FAV: 1013331: Cl-up, hdwy to lead over 1f out, kept on well, joined on line:	dht	**84a**
382	**MIDDLETON GREY 53** [9] A G Newcombe 6-9-13 bl (79) S Whitworth 11/2: 36064-03: Held up, eff over 1f out, chall ins last, just held:	nk	**83a**
655	**BLUE KNIGHT 17** [7] A P Jarvis 5-9-7 (73) D Holland 7/1: 02600-24: Chsd ldr, hmpd over 1f out, eff to chall ins last, just held & carr left cl-home:	½	**75a**
741	**GILDED COVE 8** [13] R Hollinshead 4-8-13 (65) A Culhane 11/1: 10-00335: Sn bhd, hdwy dist, no extra ins last:	¾	**65a**
687	**SUNDRIED TOMATO 14** [4] P W Hiatt 5-9-9 (75) L Fletcher (3) 6/1: 0-064606: In tch, sltly outpcd well over 1f out, some late gains till no extra cl-home:	1	**72a**
748*	**AROGANT PRINCE 7** [12] A W Carroll 7-8-5 6ex bl (57) I Mongan 10/1: 0631017: Led till over 1f out:	2½	**47a**
349	**RAFTERS MUSIC 57** [6] Julian Poulton 9-9-5 (71) Lisa Jones (3) 14/1: 54326-38: Sn bhd, nvr a factor:	2	**55a**
728	**BANNISTER 9** [2] Mrs Stef Liddiard 6-8-9 (60) S Drowne 20/1: 00100-39: Held up, nvr a factor:	1¾	**40a**
748	**VIJAY 7** [3] I Semple 5-8-3 p (55) C Catlin 16/1: 4360-030: Slow away & al bhd:	shd	**34a**
687	**ROMANY NIGHTS 14** [8] J W Unett 4-9-8 (74) Dane O'Neill 7/1: 26000-50: Nvr a factor:	shd	**52a**
610	**PORT ST CHARLES 22** [11] P R Chamings 7-9-8 (74) R Winston 33/1: 301-5000: In tch, wknd well over 1f out.	½	**50a**
698	**MISTRAL SKY 13** [1] Mrs Stef Liddiard 5-9-7 vis (73) M Fenton 28/1: 0010-200: Al bhd:	2	**43a**
13 Ran	1m 19.41 (6.61) Owner Springs Equestrian Ltd		Trained at Preston

	808		**2.50 Bet Direct Fa Cup Cashbacks Maiden Stakes 3yo+ (D)**	
			£3387 £1042 £521 £261 **1m4f f/sand Going 116 -39 Slow**	Stalls Inside

4885}	**GOLDEN QUEST 132** [5] M Johnston 3-8-3 J Fanning 3/1: 0-1: Slow away, sn cl-up, led after 4f, styd on well to draw clr over 1f out, pushed out:		**76a**
662	**BOND MOONLIGHT 17** [8] B Smart 3-8-3 (63) R Ffrench 7/1: 404-22: Prom, chsd wnr after 4f, onepace over 1f out:	6	**63a**
701	**IMPERATIVE 11** [2] Miss Gay Kelleway 4-9-10 t (68) M Fenton 9/1: 000-4633: Held up, eff over 3f out, sn no impress:	5	**56a**
4552}	**COMMANDER FLIP 156** [7] R Hollinshead 4-9-10 (65) A Culhane 33/1: 0230-4: Held up, eff over 4f out, sn btn:	7	**44a**
686	**HARRY LAD 14** [9] P D Evans 3-8-3 Joanna Badger 25/1: 55: Handy, wknd 4f out:	1	**42a**
561	**MASTER ROLE 28** [3] M A Jarvis 4-9-10 D Holland 4/5 FAV: 3/230-26: Held up, wknd over 2f out:	27	**2a**
	SPOT IN TIME [4] J Pearce 4-9-5 J Quinn 20/1: 7: Nvr a factor on debut.	25	**0a**
	CLASSIC LIN [6] A Berry 4-9-5 F Lynch 100/1: 8: Led 4f, wknd over 4f out on debut.	dist	**0a**
8 Ran	2m 52.24 (18.64) Owner Syndicate 2002		Trained at Middleham

	809		**3.25 Cashbacks @ Betdirect Co Uk Handicap Stakes Div 2 3yo+ 0-70 (E)**		**[70]**
			£3255 £930 £465 **1m100y f/sand rnd Going 116 -23 Slow**	Stalls Inside	

645*	**LA PUCE 18** [1] Miss Gay Kelleway 3-8-8 (68) F Lynch 10/1: 300-4011: Led till over 3f out, led again 2f out, hung right but kept on for press:		**74a**
2257}	**ACTIVE ACCOUNT 260** [2] Mrs H Dalton 7-9-10 (66) I Mongan 14/1: 3/26233-2: Prom, hdwy & sltly hmpd over 1f out, kept on ins last on reapp:	1¼	**69a**
753	**GIVEMETHEMOONLIGHT 7** [5] Mrs Stef Liddiard 5-9-4 P (60) S Drowne 11/1: 3612363: Held up, hdwy over 2f out, kept on ins last, nrst fin:	½	**62a**
791	**DANCING KING 2** [6] P W Hiatt 8-8-9 6ex (51) P Makin (7) 14/1: 05203154: Slow away, held up, hdwy over 1f out, no extra ins last:	dht	**52a**
714	**EASTBOROUGH 10** [7] B G Powell 5-9-10 (66) S Whitworth 5/1: 6-031034: Handy, onepace over 1f out.	½	**67a**
593	**GAME GURU 24** [9] P A Blockley 5-9-10 bl (66) D Nolan (5) 20/1: 1-013146: Nvr a factor:	3½	**60a**
747*	**SCOTTISH RIVER 7** [8] M D I Usher 5-9-12 6ex (68) D Holland 8/11 FAV: 3015117: Nvr a factor.	2	**58a**
753	**DESERT HEAT 7** [4] I Semple 6-9-8 vis (64) R Winston 10/1: 04-02128: Handy, led 3f out till 2f out, no extra.	6	**42a**
747	**CRUSOE 7** [10] A Sadik 7-9-5 bl (61) B Reilly (3) 20/1: 0440-309: Al bhd:	9	**21a**
9 Ran	1m 58.08 (11.88) Owner Wetherby Racing Bureau 52		Trained at Newmarket

810	4.00 Littlewoods Bet Direct Stakes Handicap 3yo+ 0-100 (C)				[95]
	£8398 £2584 £1292 £646	1m4f f/sand	Going 116	+00 Fast	Stalls Inside

475	**MR MISCHIEF** 41 [7] P C Haslam 4-9-2 (85) Rory Moore (7) 15/2: 0211-301: Chsd ldrs, hdwy to lead 2f out, kept on well, rdn out:		93a
681	**GLORY QUEST** 15 [2] Miss Gay Kelleway 7-8-0 vis (67) Dean Williams (6) 12/1: 52-20352: Set pace till 2f out, rallied ins last, no threat to wnr:	2½	71a
695*	**MISSION TO MARS** 13 [3] P R Hedger 5-10-0 (95) J Quinn 11/4 FAV: 1112-113: Held up, eff to chase wnr fnl 1f, no extra cl-home:	½	98a
595	**INTRICATE WEB** 24 [1] E J Alston 8-9-4 (85) D Allan 3) 13/2: 043-1124: Cl-up, no extra over 1f out:	2½	84a
2846}	**RED WINE** 237 [5] J A Osborne 5-9-13 (94) D Holland 11/2: 1/53040-5: Held up, bhd, eff over 2f out, sn btn:	8	81a
681	**GEORGE STUBBS** 15 [4] M J Polglase 6-7-12 (65) J F McDonald (5) 9/1: 32-06236: Keen, in tch, lost tch halfway.	shd	52a
642*	**BORDER TALE** 18 [9] C Weedon 4-8-12 (81) Hayley Turner (5) 14/1: 1254-017: Handy, wknd over 2f out:	shd	52a
433	**COMPTON COMMANDER** 48 [10] Ian Williams 6-9-1 vis (82) Lisa Jones (4) 33/1: 5/1000-08: Nvr a factor:	15	47a
688	**EPHESUS** 14 [6] Miss Gay Kelleway 4-8-13 p (82) M Fenton 20/1: 330-3009: Al bhd:	nk	47a
634*	**MANDOOB** 20 [8] B R Johnson 7-8-4 p (71) C Catlin 4/1: 300-4110: Keen in tch, wknd 3f out:	1¼	34a
10 Ran	2m 47.52 (13.92) Owner Middleham Park Racing I & Mrs	Trained at Middleham	

811	4.35 Cashbacks @ Itv Teletext Page 367 Selling Stakes 4yo+ (G)				
	£2569 £734 £367	1m100y f/sand rnd	Going 116	-15 Slow	Stalls Inside

1622}	**GENERAL GB** 650 [9] Mrs N Smith 7-8-12 (65) C Catlin 14/1: 0642/0/-1: Slow away, held up, hdwy over 2f out, led ins last, drvn out:		68a
716	**JUST WIZ** 10 [8] N P Littmoden 8-8-12 bl (68) D Holland 4/7 FAV: 532-6302: Held up, eff to lead over 1f out, hdd ins last, no extra:	1¼	65a
747	**NOBLE PURSUIT** 7 [5] P A Blockley 7-8-12 (53) Dean McKeown 9/1: 40-22003: Cl-up, led over 2f out till over 1f out, no extra:	2½	60a
699	**EFFIE GRAY** 11 [1] J W Unett 5-8-7 BL (45) D Sweeney 50/1: 03/56-004: In tch, wknd 2f out:	7	43a
652	**OVER TO YOU BERT** 18 [6] R J Hodges 5-8-12 (45) S Drowne 40/1: 0500-065: In tch, lost pl 4f out, no impress.	8	34a
778*	**LORD MELBOURNE** 4 [3] A G Juckes 5-9-4 (50) V Slattery 6/1: 1430516: Al bhd:	1½	37a
747	**IAMBACK** 7 [4] Miss Gay Kelleway 4-8-13 e (50) M Fenton 8/1: 06-26167: Slow away & nvr a factor:	nk	31a
586	**REPEAT** 21 [7] Miss Gay Kelleway 4-9-4 p (47) F Lynch 16/1: 4-120448: Led till over 2f out, wknd:	5	28a
689	**RIVAL** 14 [2] S T Lewis 5-8-12 (40) G Gibbons 100/1: 00000-09: Handy, wknd over 4f out:	dist	0
9 Ran	1m 57.39 (11.19) Owner Mr Tony A Hayward	Trained at Pulborough	

812	5.10 Cashbacks @ Sky Text Page 372 Handicap Stakes 4yo+ 0-60 (F)				[60]
	£2961 £846 £423	2m46y f/sand	Going 116	-53 Slow	Stalls Inside

590*	**SUN HILL** 25 [7] M Blanshard 4-9-6 (57) D Sweeney 11/4 FAV: 00/000-11: Handy, trav well, led on bit 2f out, pushed clr, v cmftbly:		68a
690	**MADIBA** 14 [2] P Howling 5-10-0 (60) R Winston 7/2: 0-160222: Handy, hdwy to lead 4f out till 2f out, not pace of wnr:	7	61a
679	**AVEIRO** 15 [8] Miss Gay Kelleway 8-9-6 vis (52) M Fenton 3/1: 40-21333: Led after 1m till 4f out, onepace:	1	52a
590	**BROUGHTON MELODY** 25 [5] W J Musson 5-8-13 (45) Dean McKeown 10/1: 00//6-304: Held up, no impress:	10	37a
690	**MAKARIM** 14 [6] M R Bosley 8-9-12 p (58) G Baker 5/1: 063-0035: Held up, hung right 4f out, sn btn:	5	45a
	MANTLES PRINCE 640 [4] A G Juckes 10-10-0 (60) V Slattery 14/1: 1/130//4/-: Al bhd:	dist	0a
2296}	**PRINCE NASSEEM** 258 [10] A G Juckes 7-8-8 (40) J Quinn 33/1: 24253/0-7: Al bhd:	3½	0a
1056}	**PAARL ROCK** 1042 [1] S T Lewis 9-9-2 (48) G Gibbons 25/1: 51/1450//-: Led till 1m out, sn btn:	2½	0a
3999}	**PRIDEYEV** 186 [9] B J Llewellyn 4-9-6 (57) S Drowne 20/1: D34-9: In tch, bhd fnl 5f:	5	0a
2956}	**OUR PLACE** 594 [3] B N Doran 5-9-2 (48) L Keniry (7) 66/1: 040/-0: Handy, wknd 5f out:	dist	0a
10 Ran	3m 56.63 (27.43) Owner Mr Stanley Hinton	Trained at Upper Lambourn	

Official Going Standard

813	2.00 Bet Direct Apprentice Handicap Stakes 4yo+ 0-70 (E)				[68]
	£2919 £834 £417	2m p/track rnd	Going 33	-49 Slow	Stalls Outside

733	**PHANTOM STOCK** 11 [5] W Jarvis 4-9-5 (64) D Tudhope (3) 7/2 FAV: 61-21421: Trkd ldrs & keen, lost pl rear 5f & rear when stumbled & almost u.r. 5f out, hdwy wide 2f out, styd on		68a
690	**SASHAY** 17 [4] R Hollinshead 6-9-2 (56) Stephanie Hollinshead (5) 20/1: 61434-52: Led, strongly prsd fnl 2f, hdd well ins last:	1	58a
772*	**FLEETING MOON** 8 [9] A M Balding 4-9-3 6ex (62) L Keniry 7/1: 0-2213: Mid-div, smooth prog to press ldrs 2f out, onepace ins fnl 1f:	hd	63a
681	**MACARONI GOLD** 18 [10] W Jarvis 4-9-6 bl (65) Lisa Jones 11/2: 3112-044: Rear, eff wide from over 2f out, ch dist, no extra well ins last:	½	65a
733*	**GEMI BED** 11 [11] G L Moore 9-8-10 bl (50) A Quinn (3) 5/1: 1153-615: Rear, hdwy wide 3f out, ch over 1f out, no extra:	¾	49a
762	**JOELY GREEN** 9 [7] N P Littmoden 8-9-13 (53) T P Queally 12/1: 35-50666: Mid-div on onepace:	½	51a
147	**GO CLASSIC** 93 [3] A M Hales 4-9-6 (65) B Reilly 16/1: 00400-7: Keen, trkd ldr, no impress fnl 2f:	¾	62a
4475}	**KING FLYER** 163 [12] Miss J Feilden 8-9-12 (66) N Mackay (3) 7/1: 146036-8: Mid-div wide, chall 2f out, fdd:	¾	62a
762	**TURTLE VALLEY** 9 [1] S Dow 8-9-6 (60) J Coffill Brown (7) 12/1: 60310-59: Mid-div, no impress fnl 2f.	¾	54a
3038}	**OUR IMPERIAL BAY** 233 [2] R M Stronge 5-9-12 bl (66) Derek Nolan (5) 40/1: 0014/06-0: Keen rear, no impress.	hd	60a
336	**MADHAHIR** 62 [6] C A Dwyer 4-9-1 e (60) Hayley Turner (5) 33/1: 40620-00: Sn trkd ldr, btn 3f out, eye-shield, abs:	nk	53a
762	**MYSTERLOVER** 9 [8] N P Littmoden 4-8-6 t (51) J P Guillambert 16/1: 4P-0000: Chsd ldr 4f out, btn/eased 2f out.	6	38a
12 Ran	3m 33.11 (13.11) Owner The L E H Partnership	Trained at Newmarket	

814	2.30 Bet Direct No Q Demo 08000 837 888 Maiden Stakes 3yo+ (D)				
	£3819 £1175 £588 £294	7f p/track rnd	Going 33	+02 Fast	Stalls Inside

713	**HATCH 13** [2] R M H Cowell 3-8-8 1ow (74) D Holland 2/1 FAV: 5420-221: Reluctant to enter stalls, sn led, shkn up & pulled clr over 1f out, rdn out:			**83a**
4751}	**TRENCH COAT 145** [4] A M Balding 3-8-7 (73) Martin Dwyer 6/1: 253-2: Led 1f, sn chsd wnr, rdn & outpcd fnl 1f:		3½	74a
	EMSAM BALLOU [14] R Hannon 3-8-2 R Smith 14/1: 3: Dwelt, rear, shkn up & styd on well fnl 2f, nrst fin:		nk	68a
473	**ON THE WATERFRONT 44** [10] J W Hills 3-8-7 M Hills 25/1: 554: Keen, mid-div, eff wide over 1f out, styd on onepace:		nk	72a
750	**FIT TO FLY 10** [5] S Kirk 3-8-8 1ow (72) S Drowne 7/2: 050-25: Chsd ldrs, no impress dist:		2½	68a
425	**WODHILL BE 52** [8] D Morris 4-9-4 J Murtagh 100/1: 0-56: Rear, kept on under hands-and-heels fnl 2f, nrst fin:		2	58a
670	**INSTINCT 19** [9] R Hannon 3-8-7 P Dobbs 6/1: 0-57: Keen chasing ldrs, short of room over 2f out, fdd:		½	62a
2718}	**KARATHAENA 245** [3] J W Hills 4-9-4 (78) H Gemberli (7) 14/1: 02/503-8: Trkd ldrs, lost pl over 2f out, reapp.		2½	52a
	AVERTAINE [7] G L Moore 3-8-8 6ow I Mongan 50/1: 9: Dwelt, pushed along rear, mod prog on debut.		nk	57a
	SAINTLY SCHOLAR [15] E A L Dunlop 3-8-2 J Quinn 14/1: 0: Dwelt, held up wide, hmpd 2f out, no dngr.		½	50a
514	**POLISH RHAPSODY 37** [11] J A Supple 3-8-2 J Fanning 66/1: 0-00: Trkd ldrs till over 1f out.		hd	49a
	ALIANNA [6] S Dow 3-8-2 C Catlin 50/1: 0: Al towards rear on debut.		1½	46a
514	**THE KINGS BISHOP 37** [12] S C Williams 3-8-7 Dane O'Neill 12/1: 40: Keen, prom wide till over 1f out.		½	50a
1907}	**MISS TRINITY 279** [13] C N Allen 4-9-4 (64) B Reilly (3) 12/1: 350/050-0: Keen, held up wide, no impress, reapp.		nk	44a
697	**MANDAHAR 16** [16] A W Carroll 5-9-9 M Tebbutt 66/1: 00: Bhd, no dngr.		¾	48a
15 Ran	1m 24.94 (2.14) Owner Blue Metropolis			Trained at Newmarket

---

815 **3.00 Bet Direct No Q On 08000 93 66 93 Handicap Stakes 3yo 0-60 (F)** [67]

£3003 £858 £429   **7f p/track rnd**   Going 33   -20 Slow   Stalls Inside

729	**JOY AND PAIN 12** [13] G L Moore 3-9-2 (55) Dane O'Neill 6/1: 00601: Keen, chsd ldrs, rdn to lead ins last, held on all out:			**60a**
4357}	**JOSHUAS GOLD 170** [5] D Carroll 3-9-3 (56) R Fitzpatrick 25/1: 603555-2: Trkd ldrs, drvn to chall ins last, just held:		hd	60a
729	**PARK AVE PRINCESS 12** [12] N P Littmoden 3-9-5 (58) D Holland 5/2 FAV: 460-2253: Chsd ldrs, styd on for press, just		nk	61a
696	**LIVIA 16** [9] J G Portman 3-9-1 (54) R Havlin 25/1: 0604: Trkd ldrs, ch dist, onepace:		1	55a
729	**MISTER COMPLETELY 12** [16] J R Best 3-8-13 (52) N Pollard 13/2: 3640-265: Crossed from wide draw & sn cl-up, drvn/led 2f out, hdd ins last, no extra:		1¼	50a
691	**DOCKLANDS BLUE 16** [15] N P Littmoden 3-9-1 (54) J P Guillambert (3) 8/1: 30-20036: Slow away, switched rail & rear, no room 2f out, styd on for press late, nrst fin:		1	50a
636	**WEAKEST LINK 22** [1] W Jarvis 3-9-7 (60) Lisa Jones (3) 12/1: 0-2337: Cl-up till dist:		1	54a
797	**VAMPIRE QUEEN 5** [3] R P Elliott 3-9-2 (55) N Mackay (5) 10/1: 600-1408: Mid-div inner, nvr able to chall.		hd	48a
735	**RICKY MARTAN 11** [14] G C Bravery 3-8-13 bl (52) S Whitworth 33/1: 064-0009: Dwelt, switched rail/rear, no impress.		1	43a
671	**STONOR LADY 19** [8] P W D'Arcy 3-8-9 e (48) Paul Eddery (3) 50/1: 0206-000: Keen, rear, nvr mount chall.		nk	38a
735	**JASMINE PEARL 11** [10] T M Jones 3-8-10 (49) J Quinn 33/1: 2055-360: Led 5f, sn btn/eased ins last.		½	38a
4827}	**SHES OUR LASS 139** [7] D Carroll 3-9-4 (57) D Tudhope (7) 11/1: 25542-0: Sn wide mid-div, btn 2f out.		nk	45a
761	**DANCING PRINCE 9** [4] A P Jarvis 3-8-9 (48) S Drowne 10/1: 005-5400: Al bhd:		2½	31a
13	**YOUR JUST LOVELY 117** [2] A M Balding 3-9-7 (60) Martin Dwyer 12/1: 060-0: Rear, no prog 2f out:		1¼	40a
756	**DOCTORED 9** [6] B A Pearce 3-9-1 p (54) C Catlin 20/1: 02023-00: Sn towards rear & struggling:		3	28a
15 Ran	1m 26.54 (3.74) Owner E Farncombe T/A EWS Shavings			Trained at Brighton

---

816 **3.30 Avoid The Queues With Bet Direct No Q Claiming Stakes 4yo+ (F)**

£2884 £824 £412   **1m4f p/track**   Going 33   -14 Slow   Stalls Inside

787	**MISS KOEN 6** [3] D L Williams 3-8-6 t (53) D Corby (3) 33/1: 6060-631: Rear, hdwy 3f out, drvn & led ins last, held on well:			**56a**
122	**CARROWDORE 100** [9] R Hannon 4-9-3 (71) R Hughes 5/2: 345220-2: Trkd ldr, no room & drpd rear on inner over 2f out, switched & styd on well ins last, did well to fin so close		½	67a
688	**RAINBOW WORLD 17** [2] Andrew Reid 4-9-5 (77) T P Queally (3) 14/1: 05160-03: Keen in mid-div, rdn to chall dist, no extra cl-home:		nk	68a
758	**MAD CAREW 9** [8] G L Moore 5-9-7 bl e (79) S Whitworth 13/8 FAV: 322-5104: Keen in mid-div, hdwy to trk front pair 2f out, no room repeatedly from over 1f out, v unlucky:		½	67a
801	**COOLFORE JADE 4** [6] N E Berry 4-9-0 (52) M Savage (5) 16/1: 4143505: Keen & cl-up, led 3f out, drvn & hdd ins last, no extra:		½	61a
549	**TOP TENOR 33** [5] B R Johnson 4-8-11 BL (70) Dane O'Neill 15/2: 4123-006: Rear, hdwy to chall 2f out, no extra when short of room cl-home:		1¾	56a
218	**DUCS DREAM 82** [1] D Morris 6-9-1 (56) J Murtagh 14/1: 163000-7: Trkd ldrs, lost pl 4f out, no impress fnl 2f.		¾	57a
731	**KRISTOFFERSEN 12** [7] R M Stronge 4-9-0 BL (71) D Sweeney 6/1: 35430-08: Held up, eff 3f out, btn 1f out.		7	49a
745	**STAR SEVENTEEN 11** [4] Mrs N S Sharpe 6-8-2 (60) C Catlin 33/1: 0021/0-59: Led 3f out, sn fdd:		5	28a
	SINK OR SWIM [10] J J Bridger 6-8-0 J F McDonald 50/1: 0: Slow away & rear, eff wide, no impress:		nk	25a
476	**BRUZELLA 44** [11] A J Lidderdale 5-8-10 R Havlin 100/1: 00: Slow away, sn trkd ldr, btn 3f out.		1¼	33a
11 Ran	2m 34.88 (5.68) Owner Mr D L Williams			Trained at Chilton

---

817 **4.00 Bet Direct No Q Handicap Stakes 3yo 0-80 (D)** [87]

£4394 £1352 £676 £338   **1m2f p/track**   Going 33   -01 Slow   Stalls Inside

764	**ALFRIDINI 8** [1] D R C Elsworth 3-8-6 (65) Dane O'Neill 7/2: 00221: Sn pushed along & chsd ldrs, rdn to lead dist, drvn & held on all out:			**71a**
4175}	**VANTAGE 179** [3] N P Littmoden 3-9-4 (77) D Holland 10/1: 0330-2: Chsd ldrs, drvn & hdwy to chall dist, just held:		nk	82a
4175}	**CHARLIE TANGO 179** [7] M R Channon 3-8-11 (70) S Hitchcott (3) 25/1: 5030-3: Keen in rear, rdn & hdwy to chall dist, hung right & no extra cl-home:		1	74a
676*	**ANOTHER CON 19** [6] Mrs P N Dutfield 3-8-7 (66) R Havlin 4/1: 63-414: Led, rdn & hdd over 1f out, no extra:		1	69a
702	**COME WHAT JULY 14** [8] R Guest 3-9-0 bl (73) Martin Dwyer 7/1: 2023-125: Chsd ldrs, eff 2f out, onepcd dist.		½	75a
759	**FIDDLERS FORD 9** [10] J Noseda 3-8-13 (72) S W Kelly 3/1 FAV: 0-3226: Rear, outpcd 2f out, kept on late.		shd	74a
626*	**VARUNI 23** [4] J G Portman 3-8-7 (66) R Ffrench 20/1: 0-17: Held up, rdn 3f out, no impress:		4	62a
694	**WESTERN ROOTS 16** [5] P F I Cole 3-9-7 (80) S Drowne 8/1: 140-248: Rear, eff 3f out, no dngr:		2½	72a
686	**KINGS ROCK 17** [9] K A Ryan 3-8-4 (63) J Fanning 33/1: 3530-269: Chsd ldr, btn 2f out:		2	52a

696	**MAYBE SOMEDAY** 16 [2] I A Wood 3-8-8 p (67) I Mongan 25/1: 3-346330: Held up in tch, btn 3f out:				6 48a
10 Ran	2m06.2 (3.4) Owner Mr A Heaney				Trained at Whitsbury

---

818   **4.30 Betdirect Co Uk Handicap Stakes** 3yo 0-85 (D)   **[91]**

£4719 £1452 £726 £363   5f p/track rnd   Going 33   -05 Slow   Stalls Outside

3437*}	**PERUVIAN STYLE** 214 [2] N P Littmoden 3-8-13 (76) D Holland 14/1: 2401-1: Chsd ldrs, drvn to lead well ins last, all out:	85a
4653}	**TRICK CYCLIST** 152 [4] A M Balding 3-9-3 (80) T Block (7) 25/1: U00200-2: Mid-div, pushed along halfway, styd on well for press ins last, nrst fin:	nk 88a
735*	**TAG TEAM** 11 [1] A M Balding 3-9-0 (77) Martin Dwyer 4/5 FAV: 0-113: Led/dsptd lead, bmpd over 1f out, no extra ins last:	1 82a
4576*}	**GREEN MANALISHI** 157 [3] D W P Arbuthnot 3-9-0 (77) S Whitworth 4/1: 522551-4: Sn dsptd lead & narrow lead 2f out, bmpd over 1f out & hdd ins last, no extra:	hd 81a
673	**HELLO ROBERTO** 19 [9] M J Polglase 3-8-12 (75) Dean McKeown 8/1: 24-02025: Outpcd halfway, not able to chall:	½ 77a
712*	**CUT AND DRIED** 13 [10] D M Simcock 3-8-6 (69) Dane O'Neill 8/1: 6600-116: Rear, not rch ldrs:	1¼ 67a
712	**BEAU JAZZ** 13 [7] W de Best Turner 3-8-3 (66) S Righton 20/1: 0056-537: Chsd ldrs wide till halfway:	1½ 59a
4127}	**SHIELALIGH** 182 [5] Miss Gay Kelleway 3-9-7 (84) J Quinn 16/1: 1243-8: Mid-div, lost action down hill over 2f out, no ch after:	2 71a
8 Ran	59.7 (1.9) Owner M C S D Racing Ltd	Trained at Newmarket

---

819   **5.00 Bet Direct In Running Selling Stakes** 3yo+ (G)

£2646 £756 £378   6f p/track rnd   Going 33   -10 Slow   Stalls Inside

3815}	**YORKIE** 198 [13] D Carroll 5-9-7 (58) R Fitzpatrick 10/1: 406200-1: Rear, hdwy wide over 2f out, drvn to lead well ins last:	54a
737*	**SOUNDS LUCKY** 11 [11] N P Littmoden 8-9-12 bl (60) D Holland 6/1: 40-05012: Keen & trkd ldrs, drvn to chall ins last, just held:	nk 58a
558	**PIPS SONG** 31 [2] P W Hiatt 9-9-12 (48) Lisa Jones (3) 33/1: 0-001003: Led, hdd well ins last:	hd 57a
717	**ROMAN EMPIRE** 13 [12] T J Etherington 4-9-7 VIS (52) J Murtagh 20/1: 50000-04: Slow away, rear, styd on wide for press, not able to chall:	½ 50a
765	**LEGAL SET** 8 [14] W J Musson 8-9-7 (59) S Donohoe (7) 8/1: 0600-405: Rear, nrst fin:	shd 50a
767	**BELLS BEACH** 8 [10] P Howling 6-9-7 (55) J Fanning 5/1: 2010156: Chsd ldrs, onepcd dist:	¾ 48a
610	**ONLY ONE LEGEND** 25 [4] K A Ryan 6-9-7 bl (65) T Quinn 11/4 FAV: 03-00007: Trkd ldrs, no extra over 1f out.	hd 47a
802	**TREE ROOFER** 4 [3] N P Littmoden 5-9-7 (45) T P Queally (3) 40/1: 5040-008: Rear, only mod gains, qck reappr.	¾ 45a
788	**ONEFORTHEBOYS** 6 [7] D Flood 5-9-7 (45) R Hughes 25/1: 0062409: Rear, eff wide, no impress:	nk 42a
767	**JAHANGIR** 8 [8] B R Johnson 5-9-7 (45) Dane O'Neill 16/1: 030-3300: Cl-up 2f out, btn dist:	nk 43a
628	**FIREWORK** 23 [6] J Akehurst 6-9-7 p (63) J Quinn 7/1: 13420-00: Led/dsptd lead till over 1f out.	1¾ 38a
3100}	**ARABIAN KNIGHT** 228 [9] R J Hodges 4-9-7 (62) V Slattery 33/1: 401006-0: Chsd ldrs till lost pl halfway.	1 35a
544	**SOMERSET WEST** 33 [5] Mrs L Stubbs 4-9-7 (52) Kristin Stubbs (7) 20/1: 4001-600: Slow away, mid-div, hmpd halfway, sn btn.	hd 34a
783	**CONFUZED** 6 [1] D Flood 4-9-7 e (52) R Smith 14/1: 0/0-0360: Trkd ldr, lost pl qckly 2f out, qck reappr:	2½ 26a
14 Ran	1m 13.0 (2.6) Owner C H Stephenson & Partners	Trained at Warthilll

---

820   **5.30 New Site @ Betdirect Co Uk Handicap Stakes** 3yo+ 46-55 (F)   **[58]**

£3031 £866 £433   1m p/track rnd   Going 33   +06 Fast   Stalls Outside

763	**MEELUP** 8 [3] Jane Southcombe 4-9-11 p (55) V Slattery 14/1: 000-0221: Made all, strongly prsd over 1f out, held on gamely for press:	61a
715	**BLUE QUIVER** 13 [8] C A Horgan 4-9-9 (53) Paul Eddery 12/1: 06-62: Chsd wnr, drvn & chall over 1f out, no extra cl-home:	nk 59a
770	**LUCID DREAMS** 8 [7] M Wigham 5-9-10 P (54) J Fanning 11/2: 0-504123: Rear, drvn & styd on fnl 2f, not able to chall:	1¾ 56a
770*	**DOUBLE RANSOM** 8 [5] Mrs L Stubbs 5-10-0 6ex bl (58) D Holland 11/8 FAV: 032-2314: Trkd ldrs, onepace for press over 1f out:	½ 59a
770	**BALERNO** 8 [1] R Ingram 5-9-7 (51) K Darley 12/1: 00-13045: Trkd ldrs, switched & onepace dist:	nk 51a
718	**FRANKS QUEST** 13 [4] P Burgoyne 4-9-10 (54) L Keniry (3) 14/1: 40-02336: Trkd ldrs, outpcd fnl 2f:	4 46a
501	**SHAHM** 39 [6] B J Curley 5-9-9 (53) S W Kelly 8/1: 000/51-07: Dwelt, rear, hung right & little prog:	¾ 44a
738	**MUQTADI** 11 [10] M Quinn 6-9-8 (52) Martin Dwyer 14/1: 0604158: Rear, no prog 2f out:	hd 42a
769	**KANZ WOOD** 8 [2] A W Carroll 8-9-11 (55) R Hughes 12/1: 0000-059: Mid-div, wknd over 1f out, eased:	4 37a
805	**INDIAN BLAZE** 4 [11] Andrew Reid 10-9-9 6ex (53) T P Queally (3) 4/1: 00-62120: Wide & rear, btn 2f out:	1¾ 32a
763	**THUMAMAH** 8 [9] B P J Baugh 5-9-9 (53) I Mongan 50/1: 00600-00: Mid-div, struggling fnl 3f:	11 13a
11 Ran	1m 38.37 (2.17) Owner Mr Mark Savill	Trained at Chard

Official Going Slow

821   **2.20 Bet Direct On Sky Active Apprentice Banded Stakes** 3yo+ 0-45 (H)

£1463 £418 £209   1m1f79y f/sand   Going 112   -11 Slow   Stalls Inside

747	**SINJAREE** 10 [5] Mrs S Lamyman 6-9-8 (45) R Thomas (3) 11/4 FAV: 0000-051: Cl-up, styd on to lead 1f out, rdn out:	47a
747	**BEVIER** 10 [2] T Wall 10-9-8 (45) N Chalmers 4/1: 040-5342: Stumbled start, sn led, hdd 4f out, outpcd fnl 1f, rallied well ins fnl 1f, just held:	nk 46a
792	**GRACIOUS AIR** 5 [6] J R Weymes 6-9-8 BL (45) D Fentiman (5) 9/2: 60-01533: Keen cl-up, led 4f out, hdd 1f out, kept on, not btn far in 3rd:	shd 45a
777	**SADLERS SWING** 7 [7] J J Sheehan 8-9-8 (40) P Makin (3) 11/2: 00//605-24: Mid-div, kept on fnl 2f, no impress on front 3:	3½ 39a
777	**KENNY THE TRUTH** 7 [3] Mrs J Candlish 5-9-8 t (40) Dawn Watson (5) 10/1: 0-323345: Keen hld, nvr nrr than mid-div.	1 37a
668	**UNSUITED** 20 [1] J E Long 5-9-8 (40) Natalia Gemelova (5) 9/1: 500-0326: Nvr nrr than mid-div:	3½ 32a
580	**MALMAND** 28 [4] R Brotherton 5-9-8 vis (45) T Hamilton 10/1: 00-01047: Held up, nvr a factor:	2 29a
3613}	**DIAGON ALLEY** 207 [9] K W Hogg 4-9-8 (35) B Swarbrick 40/1: 00/0000-8: Cl-up, fdd 3f out:	3 25a
512	**ALWAYS BELIEVE** 38 [1] Mrs P Ford 8-9-8 (40) L Treadwell (3) 40/1: 30600-09: Led early, sn bhd, eased dist.	8 14a

9 Ran 2m 9.70 (11.5) Owner Mr P Lamyman Trained at Louth

822 **2.50 Bet Direct Interactive Banded Stakes 3yo+ 0-45 (H)**
£1635 £467 £234 **6f f/sand rnd** **Going 112** **+09 Fast** Stalls Inside

773 **ON THE TRAIL 8** [5] D W Chapman 7-9-6 (45) A Culhane 10/1: 00-00001: Prom, led 3f out, drvn out ins fnl 1f to hold on: **47a**
773 **ENJOY THE BUZZ 8** [4] J M Bradley 5-9-6 (45) P Fitzsimons 7/2 FAV: 0231242: Handy, chsd ldr 2f out, kept on ins fnl 1f, just held by wnr: *shd* **47a**
643 **EXTEMPORISE 21** [3] P J McBride 4-9-6 T (45) Dale Gibson 4/1: 050-03: In tch, outpcd 2f out, rallied ins fnl 1f: *3* **38a**
773* **STAR LAD 8** [2] R Brotherton 4-9-12 bl (45) A Daly 10/1: 6-310014: Led, hdd 3f out, in tch till no extra fnl 1f: *1* **41a**
775 **ATTORNEY 8** [6] D Shaw 6-9-6 e (45) T Hamilton (5) 8/1: 0040065: Chsd ldrs, outpcd 3f out, mod late gains. *4* **23a**
582 **KATY OHARA 28** [7] Miss S E Hall 5-9-6 (45) D Fentiman (7) 5/1: 0000-026: Slow away, nvr nrr than mid-div: *1* **20a**
667* **EVANGELIST 20** [1] Mrs Stef Liddiard 4-9-6 vis t (45) M Fenton 5/1: 000-3017: Handy, fdd dist: *1* **17a**
709 **INDIAN WARRIOR 14** [8] J Jay 8-9-6 bl (45) B Swarbrick (7) 15/2: 25-10048: Al rear: *1½* **13a**
65 **DANCING RIDGE 110** [9] A Senior 7-9-6 (40) D Kinsella 66/1: 0436/00-9: Cl-up, fdd 3f out: *12* **0a**
310 **BOLD EFFORT 63** [10] K O Cunningham Brown 12-9-6 bl e (30) J Mackay 66/1: 00000-00: V slow away, nvr a factor: *dist* **0a**
10 Ran 1m 19.01 (6.21) Owner Mr J M Chapman Trained at York

823 **3.20 #10 Free Bet @ Bet Direct Sky Active Median Auction Maiden Stakes 4-6yo (H)**
£1418 £405 £203 **1m4f f/sand** **Going 112** **-25 Slow** Stalls Inside

650 **THE BEDUTH NAVI 21** [4] D G Bridgwater 4-9-3 (35) B Swarbrick (7) 8/11 FAV: 0/000-221: Led 1f, led again 1m out, clr 4f out, eased fnl 1f, val 14L+: **51a**
772 **DORA CORBINO 8** [5] R Hollinshead 4-8-12 (45) A Culhane 7/2: 0/560-532: Held up, prog to chase wnr 6f out, no impress on wnr fnl 2f: *10* **35a**
780 **THINK QUICK 7** [1] R Hollinshead 4-8-12 (35) R Kennemore (7) 7/2: 5663403: Held up, prog 6f out, prog 4f out: *9* **22a**
355 **MANASHIN 60** [2] R P Elliott 4-8-12 (35) T Woodley 33/1: 00-04: Led 11f out, hdd 1m out, fdd 6f out: *27* **0a**
248 **ZIGGY DAN 73** [3] Ms Deborah J Evans 4-9-3 (30) Joanna Badger 20/1: 000-5: Keen cl-up, hung right 6f out, sn fdd: *18* **0a**
5 Ran 2m 50.15 (16.55) Owner Mr R W Neale Trained at Winchcombe

824 **3.50 Press Interactive To Bet Direct Banded Stakes 4yo+ 0-45 (H)**
£1621 £463 £232 **2m46y f/sand** **Going 112** **-41 Slow** Stalls Inside

454 **MYSTERIUM 47** [1] N P Littmoden 10-9-3 vis (40) G Gibbons 11/2: 3333-341: Held up, prog 4f out, edged left & led ins fnl 1f, rdn out: **43a**
780* **BUZ KIRI 7** [6] A W Carroll 6-9-9 (40) P Doe 9/4: 3212212: Held up, prog 7f out, led 5f out, hdd 3f out, led again over 1f out, hdd & no extra ins fnl 1f: *2½* **45a**
774 **STRAVMOUR 8** [3] R Hollinshead 8-9-3 (45) Dale Gibson 7/2: 431-0533: Cl-up, led 3f out, hdd over 1f out, no extra: *2½* **37a**
787* **RADIANT BRIDE 6** [5] K R Burke 4-9-4 bl (45) Darren Williams 2/1 FAV: 2612014: Held up, prog 5f out, fdd fnl 2f: *6* **37a**
650 **SHARVIE 21** [4] M R Bosley 7-9-3 VIS (35) Joanna Badger 25/1: 64550/-05: Cl-up, fdd 5f out: *dist* **6a**
3521} **TON CHEE 210** [2] K W Hogg 5-9-3 (30) J Bramhill 16/1: 50/0043-6: Led, hdd 5f out, sn wknd: *2* **4a**
6 Ran 3m 55.42 (26.22) Owner Alcester Associates Trained at Newmarket

825 **4.20 Littlewoods Bet Direct Selling Stakes 3yo+ (H)**
£1299 £371 £186 **7f f/sand rnd** **Going 112** **+01 Fast** Stalls Outside

771 **SILVER MASCOT 8** [9] R Hollinshead 5-9-7 (45) Dale Gibson 11/2: 0-402251: Made all, clr 2f out, pushed out, val 12L+: **56a**
778 **INCHCOONAN 7** [5] K R Burke 6-9-2 p (55) Darren Williams 7/2: 424-4422: Cl-up, styd on to go 2nd ins fnl 1f, no ch with easy wnr: *9* **36a**
783 **THE GAY FOX 6** [8] B G Powell 10-9-7 bl t (45) Karen Peippo (7) 11/1: 2423003: Sn outpcd, prog 2f out, kept on late: *1¼* **39a**
786 **TRAVEL TARDIA 6** [3] I A Wood 6-9-7 (40) T Hamilton (5) 12/1: 0/000-004: Handy, no extra fnl 2f: *1* **37a**
524* **FOOLISH THOUGHT 35** [1] I A Wood 4-9-12 (54) G Gibbons 6/1: 40-65415: Cl-up, wknd fnl 1f: *hd* **41a**
685 **LEGALIS 17** [2] K A Ryan 6-9-12 bl (56) P Fessey 3/1 FAV: 3203136: Slow away, nvr nrr than mid-div: *2* **37a**
811 **REPEAT 3** [7] Miss Gay Kelleway 4-9-12 p (47) M Fenton 8/1: 1204407: Cl-up, fdd dist: *2½* **32a**
667 **LIONS DOMANE 20** [4] A Berry 7-9-7 (40) F Lynch 16/1: 000-0568: Mid-div, wknd 2f out: *7* **15a**
2479] **LASTOFTHEWHALLEYS 616** [6] K W Hogg 6-9-2 (35) J Bramhill 66/1: 600//060/-: Al adrift: *29* **0a**
9 Ran 1m 34.01 (7.81) Owner Mr R Hollinshead Trained at Upper Longdon

826 **4.50 New Site @ Betdirect Co Uk Banded Stakes 3yo+ 0-35 (H)**
£1292 £369 £185 **1m100y f/sand rnd** **Going 112** **-29 Slow** Stalls Inside

782* **MRS CUBE 7** [1] P Howling 5-9-13 (35) R Winston 5/6 FAV: 06060-11: Cl-up, led dist, rdn clr: **44a**
784 **SPIDERS WEB 6** [13] T Keddy 4-9-7 bl (30) P Doe 80/1: 0/-0000B2: Mid-div, prog 3f out, kept on fnl 1f, not pace wnr: *3* **31a**
689 **FINAL LAP 17** [6] S T Lewis 8-9-7 (30) G Gibbons 100/1: 0/0/000-03: Handy, outpcd 4f out, rallied late: *2½* **26a**
777 **DUNDONALD 7** [5] M Appleby 5-9-7 bl t (35) D Fentiman (7) 13/2: 40-60034: Slow away, prog wide when bmpd 4f out, kept on fnl 1f: *hd* **25a**
656 **GARNOCK BELLE 20** [12] A Berry 3-8-3 (35) Dale Gibson 50/1: 500-005: Held up, nvr nrr than mid-div: *hd* **24a**
782 **UN AUTRE ESPERE 7** [8] T Wall 5-9-7 (35) L Vickers 80/1: 30500-06: Trkd ldrs, no extra fnl 2f: *½* **23a**
782 **WELSH WHISPER 7** [9] S A Brookshaw 5-9-7 (35) N Chalmers (5) 10/1: 0-00407: Slow away, prog 4f out, led 2f out, hdd dist, sn wknd: *½* **22a**
784 **BROUGHTONS MILL 6** [3] J A Supple 9-9-7 (35) Rory Moore (7) 14/1: 6/00-5668: Rear, prog 5f out, fdd 2f out. *4* **14a**
782 **CHICKASAW TRAIL 7** [10] R Hollinshead 6-9-7 (30) A Culhane 14/1: 0000-009: Nvr nrr than mid-div: *3* **8a**
719 **CATERHAM COMMON 13** [4] D W Chapman 5-9-7 bl (30) Darren Williams 16/1: 000-0600: Led, hdd 2f out, sn fdd. *½* **7a**
3854} **FOREST QUEEN 196** [2] K W Hogg 7-9-7 (30) J Bramhill 100/1: 000/0/00-0: Al in rear: *11* **0a**
654 **MARGARETS WISH 21** [7] T Wall 4-9-7 (30) M Fenton 14/1: 200-0400: Handy, fdd 4f out. *3½* **0a**
806 **BUGLE CALL 3** [11] K O Cunningham Brown 4-9-7 bl e (35) J Mackay 8/1: 000-0000: Slow away, prog wide when hung left 4f out, sn fdd: *26* **0a**

WOLVERHAMPTON Monday 08.03.04 Lefthand, Sharp Track

13 Ran   1m 58.07 (11.87)   Owner Mrs J E Proctor   Trained at Newmarket

LINGFIELD Tuesday 09.03.04 Lefthand, V Sharp Track

Official Going Standard

827

2.20 Cashbacks @ Bet Direct On Sky Active Banded Stakes 4yo+ 0-45 (H)
£1663 £475 £238   1m4f p/track   Going 47   +01 Fast   Stalls Inside

770	**ANGELICA GARNETT** 9 [1] T E Powell 4-8-12 (45) J F Egan 40/1: 00-06001: Slow away & bhd, strong run for press from 2f out, styd on wide to lead well ins last:		50a
666	**DIAMOND ORCHID** 21 [7] P D Evans 4-8-12 p (45) J Murtagh 5/1: 062-3242: Handy & led 5f out, drvn & hdd wns last:	½	48a
705	**MONTOSARI** 15 [14] P Mitchell 5-9-0 (45) D Holland 9/4 FAV: 4600-163: Dwelt, sn handy, onepace for press fnl 2f:	1	47a
705	**CHOCOLATE BOY** 15 [4] G L Moore 5-9-0 bl e (45) I Mongan 7/1: 0/00-5244: Rear, kept on for press, not able to chall:	½	46a
780	**FREE STYLE** 8 [2] K R Burke 4-8-12 (45) G Baker 7/1: 0-630145: Mid-div trav well, shaken up & onepace dist.	½	45a
705	**ON GUARD** 15 [15] P G Murphy 6-9-0 vis (45) D Kinsella 8/1: 00650-36: Mid-div wide, eff to chall 2f out, no extra dist:	1½	43a
780	**IPLEDGEALLEGIANCE** 8 [5] D W Chapman 8-9-0 (35) A Culhane 25/1: 2536507: Rear, kept on, no dngr:	½	42a
707	**LITTLE RICHARD** 15 [11] M Wellings 5-9-0 p (40) V Slattery 16/1: 0043148: Mid-div, outpcd 4f out, no impress.	1½	40a
784	**PRIVATE SEAL** 7 [12] Julian Poulton 9-9-0 t (40) M Halford (7) 10/1: 00-63229: Held up, eff 3f out, no impress.	4	34a
707	**POLKA PRINCESS** 15 [10] M Wellings 4-8-12 p (40) A Daly 40/1: 0-000300: Keen & prom, btn 2f out:	hd	33a
784	**MORRIS DANCING** 7 [13] B P J Baugh 5-9-0 (30) M Tebbutt 66/1: 0-000050: Chsd ldrs till dist:	6	25a
707	**GIKO** 15 [6] Jane Southcombe 10-9-0 bl (35) Dane O'Neill 25/1: 0200-030: Held up, btn 2f out:	3	21a
768	**ESSAY BABY** 9 [9] P D Cundell 4-8-12 (45) C Catlin 13/2: 0050-440: Chsd ldrs wide, btn 3f out:	nk	20a
542	**FOREST HEATH** 34 [8] H J Collingridge 7-9-0 p (45) J Quinn 20/1: 3000/0-00: Led till 5f out, sn btn:	14	1a

14 Ran   2m 34.69 (5.49)   Owner Three Lost Souls Partnership   Trained at Reigate

828

2.50 Bet Direct Champs League Cashbacks Banded Stakes 4yo+ 0-45 (H)
£1666 £476 £238   1m2f p/track   Going 47   -01 Slow   Stalls Inside

705*	**LANDESCENT** 15 [13] Miss K M George 4-8-12 (45) D Holland 4/1 FAV: 60-04511: Made all, rdn & in command dist:		51a
654	**MONDURU** 22 [12] G L Moore 7-8-12 bl e (45) S Whitworth 9/2: 000-0122: Slow away & rear, styd on for press ins last, nvr threatened wnr:	1½	48a
768	**TOP OF THE CLASS** 9 [3] P D Evans 7-8-12 vis (45) J F McDonald (5) 8/1: 3340003: Keen, trkd ldrs, drvn & kept on onepace:	2½	44a
427	**COODEN BEACH** 53 [7] M L W Bell 4-8-12 (45) Hayley Turner (5) 7/1: 00032-04: Slow away, sn mid-div, onepace & no impress dist:	¾	43a
617	**MIDNIGHT MAMBO** 25 [4] R Guest 4-8-12 (45) Martin Dwyer 9/2: 05-55: Trkd ldrs, onepace for press fnl 2f:	shd	43a
768	**PYRRHIC** 9 [8] R M Flower 5-8-12 bl (45) J Quinn 14/1: 0206506: Keen & held up, short of room over 1f out, late prog:	¾	42a
770	**GALEY RIVER** 9 [6] J J Sheehan 5-8-12 (45) I Mongan 14/1: 000-0057: Trkd ldrs, chsd wnr 2f out, btn dist:	1½	40a
770	**GRAN CLICQUOT** 9 [14] P Enright 9-8-12 (45) R Brisland 25/1: 44500-08: Wide, nvr on terms:	2	37a
3422}	**SWEET REFLECTION** 216 [2] W J Musson 4-8-12 T (45) Lisa Jones (3) 25/1: 0000-9: Slow away, nvr a factor:	hd	36a
784	**THATS ALL JAZZ** 7 [1] C R Dore 6-8-12 (40) R Thomas (5) 25/1: 00-000U0: Held up, btn 2f out.	1½	34a
1510}	**ELLE ROYAL** 300 [9] T P McGovern 5-8-12 (45) Dane O'Neill 40/1: 00000/0-0: Trkd wnr, btn 3f out, abs.	3½	29a
445	**NDOLA** 49 [5] B J Curley 5-8-12 (45) S W Kelly 10/1: 00/00/-100: Mid-div, no prog 3f out, abs:	1½	27a
2696}	**COUNT ON US** 247 [10] P Burgoyne 4-8-12 (45) L Keniry (3) 50/1: 600/06-0: Slow away & al bhd, reapp.	¾	26a
709	**PANCAKEHILL** 15 [11] D K Ivory 5-8-12 (45) C Catlin 14/1: 0000600: Mid-div, btn 2f out, op 10/1.	nk	25a

14 Ran   2m 07.62 (4.82)   Owner Stableline   Trained at Crediton

829

3.20 Cashbacks @ Bet Direct Interactive Median Auction Maiden Stakes 4-6yo (H)
£1439 £411 £206   1m2f p/track   Going 47   -02 Slow   Stalls Inside

785	**BALLINGER RIDGE** 7 [10] A M Balding 5-9-0 VIS (60) Martin Dwyer 4/5 FAV: 63-23221: Made all, rdn & al holding rivals from dist.		55a
526	**BLUE SAVANNA** 36 [8] J G Portman 4-9-0 bl (45) A Culhane 100/30: 2663-642: Sn chsd wnr, rdn & kept on, no impress dist:	3½	49a
4832}	**MR FLEMING** 140 [4] Dr J D Scargill 5-9-0 bl (45) J Quinn 12/1: 0/00044-3: Sn trkd ldrs, kept on fnl 2f, no impress on front	6	40a
772	**KUSTOM KIT FOR HER** 9 [5] S R Bowring 4-8-9 t (45) J Bramhill 7/1: 0023224: Chsd front pair, lost tch from halfway:	23	3a
785	**YOUNG DYNASTY** 7 [1] E A Wheeler 4-9-0 Liam Jones (7) 14/1: 055: V slow away & no ch halfway:	1¼	6a
468}	**PORTICHOL PRINCESS** 409 [3] R M Stronge 4-8-9 t D Sweeney 66/1: 0/00-6: Slow away & sn bhd:	5	0a
721	**INDRAPURA STAR** 14 [7] Miss J Feilden 4-9-0 (20) J McAuley 50/1: 0/000-67: Chsd wnr 2f, sn bhd:	nk	0a
393	**SILVER CRYSTAL** 56 [9] Mrs N Macauley 4-8-9 (45) Lisa Jones (3) 16/1: 6450-008: V slow away & sn bhd:	5	0a

8 Ran   2m 07.70 (4.9)   Owner Mrs Hazel Barber   Trained at Kingsclere

830

3.50 Cashbacks @ Betdirect Co Uk Banded Stakes 3yo+ 0-35 (H)
£1295 £370 £185   7f p/track rnd   Going 47   -03 Slow   Stalls Inside

788	**GENTLE RESPONSE** 7 [8] B R Johnson 4-9-7 bl (35) S Whitworth 6/4 FAV: 00-00631: Held up, switched & hdwy to lead over 1f out, rdn clr:		46a
786	**TINY TIM** 7 [15] A M Balding 6-9-7 (35) R J Killoran (7) 9/1: 0050/-442: Chsd ldrs wide, outpcd over 2f out, kept on for press ins last, no threat:	3½	37a
786	**TOJONESKI** 7 [6] I W McInnes 5-9-7 p (35) Natalia Gemelova (7) 8/1: 3530-003: Mid-div, switched wide 2f out & styd on for press to snatch 3rd line:	1	35a
708	**KILMEENA STAR** 15 [4] J C Fox 6-9-7 p (35) P Dobbs 16/1: 306-0004: Held up mid-div, onepace for press dist:	shd	35a
784	**HINCHLEY WOOD** 7 [9] J R Best 5-9-7 (35) N Pollard 6/1: 00//-60005: Chsd ldrs, lost pl halfway, no threat:	1¼	32a
473	**MISS MILLIETANT** 45 [13] L Montague Hall 3-8-5 VIS (30) J Quinn 66/1: 00-06: Chsd ldrs till dist:	1½	29a
663	**KELTIC FLUTE** 21 [2] Mrs Lucinda Featherstone 5-9-7 vis (30) S Yourston (7) 20/1: 00/-04067: Led till over 1f out, wknd qckly.	hd	28a

208

4822}	**LA VIGNA** 140 [5] Mrs Lucinda Featherstone 3-8-5 P (35) C Catlin 66/1: 0000-8: Trkd ldrs, btn over 1f out:	¾	27a
797	**PRINCE OF PERLES** 6 [3] D Shaw 3-8-5 bl (35) Lisa Jones (3) 7/1: 000-0039: Slow away, nvr on terms:	shd	27a
573	**CARONTE** 30 [11] S R Bowring 4-9-7 H (30) Joanna Badger 50/1: 00-00000: Al bhd:	hd	26a
777	**TERN INTERN** 8 [7] Miss J Feilden 5-9-7 (35) J McAuley 33/1: 60/000-00: Dwelt & sn bhd.	nk	25a
535	**PEDLERS PROFILES** 35 [14] Miss K M George 4-9-7 BL (35) Derek Nolan (7) 66/1: 00/-000: Al outpcd rear, blnks.	4	17a
719	**MIMAS GIRL** 14 [10] S R Bowring 5-9-7 bl t (35) J Bramhill 20/1: 5053000: Sn towards rear:	5	7a
663	**POOKAS DAUGHTER** 21 [12] J M Bradley 4-9-7 p (30) P Fitzsimons 10/1: 5000020: Chsd ldrs, btn 2f out:	3	1a
3517	**QUARTER TO** 572 [1] W de Best Turner 5-9-7 (35) S Righton 100/1: 000/-0: Sn bhd, long abs.	6	0

15 Ran   1m 26.28 (3.48)   Owner Coretech Systems Ltd   Trained at Epsom

---

831   4.20 Cashbacks @ Attheraces Text Page 410 Selling Stakes 3yo+ (H)

£1327 £379 £190   **1m p/track rnd**   **Going 47**   **+05 Fast**   Stalls Outside

811	**OVER TO YOU BERT** 4 [11] R J Hodges 5-9-7 (45) V Slattery 12/1: 500-0651: Keen & trkd ldr, led 3f out, rdn & held on well ins last:		47a
608	**REGENCY MALAYA** 26 [4] M F Harris 3-7-12 bl t (35) S Righton 20/1: 0600-052: Keen & trkd ldr, outpcd 3f out, styd on for press ins last, only just failed:	¾	40a
710	**GEESPOT** 15 [6] D J S ffrench Davis (40) J F McDonald (5) 11/2: 0-040003: Held up, eff to chase wnr over 1f out, no extra ins last:	1¼	38a
580	**OKTIS MORILIOUS** 29 [7] A W Carroll 3-8-3 (45) J Quinn 14/1: 0-004: Mid-div, outpcd 3f out, kept on ins last, no dngr:	½	42a
708	**SINGLE TRACK MIND** 15 [8] J R Boyle 6-9-7 (40) Karen Peippo (7) 6/1: 00/00-025: Rear, nvr able to chall.	1	41a
717	**MARAKASH** 14 [1] M R Bosley 5-9-7 t p (48) G Baker 7/2: 00000-206: Well bhd, rapid prog wide 2f out, btn dist.	1½	39a
819	**JAHANGIR** 1 [5] B R Johnson 5-9-7 (45) Dane O'Neill 3/1 FAV: 030-33007: Keen & led till 3f out:	nk	38a
788	**FLAME PRINCESS** 7 [9] J R Boyle 4-9-2 (45) D Sweeney 10/1: 5500-308: Mid-div, no impress 2f out:	1½	31a
4386}	**DIAMOND RIBBY** 169 [12] P D Evans 3-7-12 Joanna Badger 16/1: 0-9: Trkd ldrs, btn 2f out, reapp/AW bow.	3	27a
	GOLDEN OLDIE [2] D Flood 6-9-7 BL P Doe 25/1: 0: Slow away & t.o. halfway:	dist	0

10 Ran   1m 39.59 (3.39)   Owner Unity Farm Holiday Centre Ltd   Trained at Somerton

---

832   4.50 Cashbacks @ Sky Text Page 372 Banded Stakes 3yo+ 0-40 (H)

£1453 £415 £208   **5f p/track rnd**   **Going 47**   **-15 Slow**   Stalls Outside

788*	**LONG WEEKEND** 7 [10] D Shaw 4-9-12 vis (40) Darren Williams 5/1: 0-066211: Switched to rail & pushed along rear, prog halfway, led ins last, all out:		48a
652	**AVIT** 22 [6] P L Gilligan 4-9-6 (40) J F Egan 33/1: 0000-002: Chsd ldrs, briefly led dist, styd on, just held:	hd	41a
788	**SOTONIAN** 7 [9] P S Felgate 11-9-6 (40) Lisa Jones (3) 11/2: 0-533053: Held up, styd on onepace fnl 2f.	1¾	36a
788	**LEVELLED** 7 [2] D W Chapman 10-9-6 BL (35) A Culhane 16/1: 00-00004: Trkd ldrs, briefly short of room over 1f out, onepace ins last:	nk	35a
706	**SOMETHINGABOUTHER** 15 [8] P W Hiatt 4-9-6 (40) J Quinn 10/1: 0-450305: Rear, late gains, nrst fin:	nk	34a
788	**EMARATIS IMAGE** 7 [1] R M Stronge 6-9-6 (40) A Daly 7/2 FAV: 000-0646: Led till dist, wknd:	½	32a
653	**BALI STAR** 22 [3] R J Hodges 9-9-6 (40) C Catlin 6/1: 005-0247: Dsptd lead, btn dist:	shd	32a
767	**PARALLEL LINES** 9 [7] P D Evans 3-8-7 VIS (40) J F McDonald (5) 4/1: 00-00048: Pushed rear, al outpcd:	4	20a
413	**DIAPHANOUS** 54 [5] E A Wheeler 6-9-6 T (40) S Carson 14/1: 0644-009: Dsptd lead, btn 2f out:	6	3a
500	**DEFINITELY SPECIAL** 40 [4] N E Berry 6-9-6 (40) M Savage (5) 16/1: 000-0000: Slow away & sn outpcd.	1½	-2a

10 Ran   1m 0.90 (3.1)   Owner The Marlow Lewin Partnership   Trained at Newark

---

Official Going Good/Soft

833   2.50 Gr 3 Prix Exbury 4yo+ ()

£25704 £10282 £7711   **1m2f**   **Good/Soft**

4007*}	**POLISH SUMMER** 188 A Fabre 7-8-12 C Soumillon 22/10: 62251D2-1: Held up twds rear, pshd along & hdwy to chall ins last, stayed on for press to lead close home:		118
4916}	**BRIGHT SKY** 133 E Lellouche 5-8-13 D Boeuf 16/10 JT FAV: 213364-2: Held up hdwy to chall over 1f out, just denied:	shd	118
	SAMANDO F Doumen 4-8-6 C P Lemaire 30/1: 100131-3: Mid-div, hdwy to lead ins last, hdd nr fin.	¾	110
4624}	**NYSAEAN** 154 R Hannon 5-9-0 (114) R Hannon 48/10: /62110-5: Chsd ldrs, drvn & no extra over 1f out.	6	109

10 Ran   2m 10.70   Owner K Abdulla   Trained at France

Official Going Standard To Slow

834   1.50 Bet Direct On 0800 32 93 93 Handicap Stakes 3yo+ 0-100 (C)   [97]

£10244 £3152 £1576 £788   **6f f/sand rnd**   **Going 78**   **+08 Fast**   Stalls Inside

532	**QUIET TIMES** 39 [4] K A Ryan 5-9-0 bl (83) N Callan 10/1: 20-14041: Broke well & chsd ldrs, rdn to lead over 1f out, drvn out:		92a
611	**MUFREH** 30 [2] A G Newcombe 6-9-2 (85) S Whitworth 6/1: 2012-152: Dwelt, short of room halfway, styd on for press, not reach wnr:	1	90a
692	**OK PAL** 21 [6] T G Mills 4-9-7 (90) K Darley 14/1: 610/06-U3: Led 2f, rdn outpcd over 2f out, kept on ins last:	2	90a
618	**BOND BOY** 29 [3] B Smart 7-9-4 (87) C Catlin 11/1: 000-4004: Towards rear, styd on for press, nvr dngr.	1½	83a
807*	**TIME N TIME AGAIN** 8 [9] E J Alston 6-8-12 p (81) I Mongan 11/2: 0133315: Chsd ldrs, no impress over 1f out:	1	75a
618	**BOND PLAYBOY** 29 [7] B Smart 4-9-3 (86) F Lynch 10/1: 012-5606: Chsd ldrs, btn over 1f out:	1¾	76a
687*+	**JOHNSTONS DIAMOND** 22 [5] E J Alston 6-8-9 (78) E Ahern 4/1 JT FAV: 101-0017: Cl up, wknd bef 1f out:	nk	67a
4991}	**PICCLED** 131 [1] E J Alston 6-9-13 (96) D Holland 20/1: 606000-8: Chsd ldrs, prog to lead after 2f, rdn & hdd over 1f out, wknd qckly:	1¼	82a
807*	**HURRICANE COAST** 8 [10] D Flood 5-8-13 bl (82) R Hughes 4/1 JT FAV: 3200419: Chsd ldrs, fdd over 1f out.	4	58a

5037} ABBAJABBA 126 [11] C W Fairhurst 8-8-13 (82) J Bramhill 14/1: 000006-0: Sn struggling in rear: 9   37a
10 Ran   1m 16.97 (4.17)   Owner Yorkshire Racing Club and Fran   Trained at Hambleton

---

835   2.25 Bet Direct On Sky Active Claiming Stakes 3yo (F)
£2891 £826 £413   5f f/sand rnd   Going 78   -17 Slow   Stalls Inside

609   LADY BAHIA 30 [3] R P Elliott 3-8-12 (64) T Hamilton (5) 9/1: 40-06101: Broke well & led after 1f, drvn & held on well in last: 73a
797   EMARADIA 10 [1] A W Carroll 3-8-7 bl (60) I Mongan 3/1: 3120122: Led 1f, rdn & outpcd halfway, drvn & styd on ins last, not   1½   62a
     pace of wnr:
532   MUY BIEN 39 [5] J R Jenkins 3-9-3 BL (77) D Holland 13/8 FAV: 152-2203: Towards rear 1f, styd on for press halfway, not   shd   72a
     able to chall:
797   BARRAS 10 [2] Miss Gay Kelleway 3-9-3 vis (51) P Gallagher (7) 25/1: 21-00354: Prom, no extra dist.   1½   68a
735   BACK AT DE FRONT 16 [9] N E Berry 3-8-12 (60) M Savage (4) 14/1: 04-15545: Cl up, no extra ins last: 1¼   60a
737   EVER CHEERFUL 16 [6] W G M Turner 3-9-0 p (70) A Quinn (5) 6/1: 6-210526: Sn rdn & outpcd: 2½   55a
4503} WENDYS GIRL 166 [7] R P Elliott 3-8-7 (64) N Mackay (5) 20/1: 465330-7: Sn hld up.   1   46a
703   LIZHAR 19 [4] M J Polglase 3-8-9 bl (57) K Ghunowa (7) 14/1: 4640428: Slow away, nvr on terms with ldrs: 1   46a
4013} AMBER LEGEND 193 [8] Ms Deborah J Evans 3-8-5 (60) J F Egan 25/1: 226020-9: Chsd ldrs, btn halfway: 14   10a
9 Ran   1m 04.97 (4.77)   Owner Mrs Sarah Grayson   Trained at Formby

---

836   3.00 Littlewoods Bet Direct Lincoln Trial Stakes Handicap 4yo+ 0-105 (B)   [105]
£20300 £7700 £3850 £1750   1m100y f/sand rnd   Going 78   +15 Fast   Stalls Inside

700*   VORTEX 19 [13] Miss Gay Kelleway 5-8-12 e t (89) I Mongan 7/1: 60-11111: Held up, smooth hdwy to stalk wnr 3f out, led ins   100a
     last, all out:
688   TE QUIERO GB 22 [3] Miss Gay Kelleway 6-9-2 e t (93) S Drowne 7/2 FAV: 30-00022: Led, rdn & hdd ins last, rallied gamely   shd   103a
     & just held:
4999} CRESKELD 130 [4] B Smart 5-8-10 (87) F Lynch 16/1: 453100-3: Chsd ldr, no impress on front pair over 1f out but kept on: 6   87a
2864} DANELOR 245 [12] R A Fahey 6-8-10 (87) P Hanagan 16/1: 00/4220-4: Mid-div wide, drvn & kept on, nvr threat to front pair: hd   86a
511*   MI ODDS 43 [7] Mrs N Macauley 9-9-8 (99) D Holland 13/2: 21212-15: Bhd, styd on for press, nvr dngr: shd   98a
693   VINTAGE PREMIUM 21 [6] R A Fahey 7-9-9 (100) T Hamilton 25/1: 24320-06: Chsd ldrs till lost pl after 3f.   2½   94a
234   SAHAAT 84 [9] J A Osborne 6-8-12 (89) S W Kelly 25/1: 500000-7: Rear, mod prog for press: 1¾   80a
693   BONECRUSHER 21 [11] D R Loder 5-9-13 vis (104) R Hughes 6/1: 4140-648: In tch, rdn & btn 3f out: 2   91a
433   NIMELLO 56 [10] A G Newcombe 8-8-8 (85) S Whitworth 8/1: 06121-09: Bhd, brief eff 3f out, no dngr: hd   68a
618+* QUITO 29 [1] D W Chapman 7-10-0 bl (105) A Culhane 7/1: 52645-10: Chsd ldrs, wknd 3f out: 1¼   87a
611   MYSTIC MAN 30 [5] K A Ryan 6-8-10 (87) N Callan 14/1: 11400-00: Mid-div, no impress fnl 2f: 9   66a
82   CORNELIUS 112 [8] P F I Cole 7-9-9 (100) K Darley 16/1: 300410-0: Chsd ldrs, btn 3f out, abs.   5   71a
12 Ran   1m 51.55 (5.35)   Owner Coriolis Partnership   Trained at Newmarket

---

837   3.30 New Site @ Betdirect Co Uk Handicap Stakes 4yo+ 0-85 (D)   [84]
£5057 £1556 £778 £389   2m46y f/sand   Going 78   -48 Slow   Stalls Inside

812*   SUN HILL 8 [3] M Blanshard 4-8-5 (66) D Sweeney 11/4: 0/000-111: Trkd ldrs trav well, cruised up to join ldr 4f out, readily led   78a
     ins last, val for any amouth:
810   GLORY QUEST 8 [6] Miss Gay Kelleway 7-8-12 vis (68) I Mongan 10/1: 2-203522: Handy & led over 4f out, rdn & sn joined,   3½   70a
     hdd ins last & no ch with wnr:
743   NORTHERN NYMPH 16 [7] R Hollinshead 5-9-10 (80) A Culhane 16/1: 6235/4-23: Held up, styd on for press fnl 3f, no threat   7   76a
     to front pair:
743*   VICTORY QUEST 16 [5] Mrs S Lamyman 4-9-10 vis (85) Dane O'Neill 10/1: 12-00114: Led/dsptd lead till over 4f out, sn btn: 10   73a
813   MACARONI GOLD 5 [1] W Jarvis 4-8-4 bl (65) S Whitworth 8/1: 112-0445: Slowly to stride, in tch, btn 4f out.   2½   51a
1776} TEORBAN 290 [2] M Pitman 5-9-0 (70) E Ahern 15/2: 2/21010-6: Led 2f, rdn & lost pl halfway & no impress after: 12   46a
813*   PHANTOM STOCK 5 [4] W Jarvis 4-8-3 (64) D Mernagh 5/2 FAV: 1-214217: In tch, btn 3f out: 4   36a
     SZEROKI BOR 258 [8] M Pitman 5-8-11 (67) D Holland 13/2: 311/162-8: Bhd, sn tch from 3f out: 10   31a
8 Ran   3m 49.59 (20.39)   Owner Mr Stanley Hinton   Trained at Upper Lambourn

---

838   4.05 Betdirect Co Uk Conditions Stakes 4yo+ (C)
£7360 £2792 £1396 £635   7f f/sand rnd   Going 78   -11 Slow   Stalls Outside

627*   ALEUTIAN 28 [7] D R Loder 4-9-8 N Pollard 5/2 JT FAV: 111: Cl-up, rdn & outpcd briefly over 2f out, ev ch when bmpd over 1f   106a
     out, prevailed in a driving fin, all out:
141*   CARDINAL VENTURE 101 [3] K A Ryan 6-9-0 (95) N Callan 11/4: 200111-2: Led, rdn & edged right over 1f out, strongly   shd   97a
     prsd ins last & just hdd line:
1696} ROCKETS N ROLLERS 294 [6] R Hannon 4-9-0 (108) Dane O'Neill 6/1: 11/400-3: Dwelt, sn trk ldrs, eff to chall when edged   1   95a
     left over 1f out, just held nr fin:
618   QUEENS RHAPSODY 29 [5] A Bailey 4-9-0 (87) J Fanning 5/2 JT FAV: 150-2024: Held up trav well, eff to chall when short   ½   94a
     of room dist, no extra nr fin:
946}   SILVER SEEKER 345 [2] I Semple 4-9-0 P (96) R Winston 25/1: 310/0-5: Dwelt, sn in tch, outpcd fnl 2f: 4   86a
688   LAKOTA BRAVE 22 [4] Mrs Stef Liddiard 10-9-0 t (83) S Drowne 33/1: 5-240006: Rear, lost tch fnl 3f: 5   75a
773   SERGEANT SLIPPER 13 [8] C Smith 7-9-0 (47) R Fitzpatrick 100/1: 0303127: Slowly away, al in rear.   5   66a
4778} FIVEOCLOCK EXPRESS 148 [1] Miss Gay Kelleway 4-9-0 vis (90) D Holland 13/2: 021300-8: U.r. & bolted bef start,   0a
     withdrawn.
8 Ran   1m 32.45 (6.25)   Owner Jumeirah Racing   Trained at Newmarket

---

839   4.40 Bet Direct No Q On 08000 93 66 93 Maiden Stakes 3yo (D)
£3374 £1038 £519 £260   1m100y f/sand rnd   Going 78   -45 Slow   Stalls Inside

751   HAWKIT 15 [3] J A Osborne 3-9-0 (69) D Holland 2/1: 2233-521: In tch when short of room after 1f, hdwy to lead ins last, rdn clr: 70a
686   ZULOAGO 22 [10] S L Keightley 3-8-9 A Nicholls 33/1: 532: Chsd ldrs after 2f, rdn & led 2f out, hdd ins last & no extra: 2½   59a

808	BOND MOONLIGHT 8 [5] B Smart 3-9-0 (64) F Lynch 9/2: 404-223: Chsd ldrs till lost pl after 3f, kept on wide for press, no dngr:	5	55a
751	WONKY DONKEY 15 [6] S C Williams 3-9-0 Dane O'Neill 14/1: 0-34: Handy & led over 6f out till 2f out, fdd:	2½	50a
686	HSI WANG MU 22 [2] R Brotherton 3-8-9 (68) I Mongan 12/1: 50300-25: Chsd ldrs, btn over 1f out:	hd	44a
734	BAKER OF OZ 16 [1] R Hannon 3-9-0 (68) R Hughes 6/4 FAV: 22460-26: Sn led, hdd after 2f, remained cl-up, rdn & fdd 2f	9	34a
468	ROYALTEA 50 [7] Ms Deborah J Evans 3-8-9 (51) Joanna Badger 33/1: 6647: Sn bhd:	10	12a
4993}	ROYAL NITE OWL 131 [8] J O'Reilly 3-9-0 J D O'Reilly (7) 50/1: 00-8: Keen tracking ldrs wide, btn 3f out:	1¾	14a
	JUSTICE JONES [9] J L Spearing 3-9-0 Lisa Jones (3) 16/1: 9: Dwelt & al bhd on debut:	3	8a
	HARFORD BRIDGE [4] R J Baker 3-9-0 V Slattery 66/1: 0: Slowly away & sn bhd on debut.	27	0
10 Ran	1m 56.62 (10.42) Owner Mr Paul J Dixon	Trained at Upper Lambourn	

---

840   5.10 Press Interactive To Bet Direct Handicap Stakes 3yo+ 0-80 (D)   **[80]**
£4115 £1266 £633 £317   **7f f/sand rnd**   **Going 78**   **-11 Slow**   Stalls Outside

419	JUST A GLIMMER 58 [6] L G Cottrell 4-9-10 (76) R Hughes 11/1: 31/00-301: Handy & led going well 3f out, drvn ins last, held on all out:		85a
807	MIDDLETON GREY 8 [5] A G Newcombe 6-10-0 bl (80) S Whitworth 7/2 FAV: 6064-032: Dwelt & held up, hdwy from halfway, drvn & styd on well ins last, just failed:	shd	88a
323	PARKER 67 [7] B Palling 7-8-13 (65) K Darley 16/1: 62150-43: Chsd ldrs, kept on onepace fnl 2f:	5	64a
4807}	SARRAAF 147 [9] J Semple 8-9-2 (68) R Winston 20/1: 031042-4: Led till 3f out, btn dist:	¾	66a
4821}	BRANSTON TIGER 144 [2] J G Given 5-9-7 (73) D Holland 10/1: 610504-5: Mid-div, no impress dist:	¾	70a
800	ARC EL CIEL 9 [12] Mrs Stef Liddiard 6-9-10 vis (76) S Drowne 10/1: 3500306: Mid-div, no prog fnl 2f.	2	69a
704*	WARDEN WARREN 19 [11] Mrs C A Dunnett 6-9-8 bl (74) B Reilly (3) 10/1: 21-34617: In tch, no impress fnl 3f.	1	65a
697	LAWOOD 21 [4] K A Ryan 4-9-4 bl (70) N Callan 12/1: 04530-48: Dwelt & held up, eff 3f out, btn dist:	shd	61a
632	NO GROUSE 28 [8] R A Fahey 4-9-5 (71) P Hanagan 40/1: 0000-059: Mid-div wide, rdn & btn 2f out:	¾	61a
806	YORKER 8 [3] Ms Deborah J Evans 6-9-1 (67) I Mongan 9/1: 5342200: Al bhd:	1	55a
730	BLAKESET 17 [10] T D Barron 9-9-8 vis (74) E Ahern 7/1: 1011230: Chsd ldr, btn 2f out, eased:	5	53a
632	AIR MAIL 28 [1] Mrs N Macauley 7-9-10 p (76) A Culhane 16/1: 060-4000: Sn bhd:	6	45a
12 Ran	1m 32.4 (6.2) Owner Manor Farm Packers Ltd	Trained at Cullompton	

Official Going Standard

841   2.10 Littlewoods Bet Direct Maiden Stakes 3yo (D)
£3311 £946 £473   **1m p/track rnd**   **Going 43**   **-31 Slow**   Stalls Outside

4948}	COUNT DRACULA 136 [1] A M Balding 3-9-0 (72) Martin Dwyer 8/1: 020-1: Handy, rdn 3f out, led dist, drvn out:		69a
5022}	CATALINI 128 [8] M R Channon 3-9-0 (75) D Corby (3) 5/2: 55363-2: Rear, rdn & styd on fnl 2f, not rch wnr:	½	67a
795	SOUL PROVIDER 11 [4] P A Blockley 3-8-9 (56) Dean McKeown 20/1: 525-5343: Led, drvn & hdd dist, kept on:	1½	59a
815	DOCTORED 6 [6] B A Pearce 3-9-0 bl (54) B Reilly (3) 66/1: 2023-004: Prom, drvn & kept on:	shd	64a
	FARNBOROUGH 222 [3] D R C Elsworth 3-9-0 N Pollard 25/1: 0-5: Keen in mid-div, no impress dist:	1½	61a
4981}	MOMENTS I TREASURE 133 [5] E A L Dunlop 3-8-9 E Ahern 6/1: 00-6: Mid-div, no impress fnl 2f:	shd	56a
	APPOLONIOUS [2] D R C Elsworth 3-9-0 Dane O'Neill 25/1: 7: Slow away, shkn up & nrst fin:	1	59a
764	WAVERTREE GIRL 14 [10] N P Littmoden 3-8-9 (82) D Holland 5/4 FAV: 3404-38: Keen & chsd ldrs, rdn & btn over 2f out	7	42a
4216}	MUNAAWESH 183 [7] D W Chapman 3-9-0 A Culhane 20/1: 05-9: Chsd ldrs, hmpd after 2f & drpd rear, no impress.	nk	46a
4293}	ARTISTICIMPRESSION 179 [9] E A L Dunlop 3-9-0 S Drowne 14/1: 06-0: Dwelt, rapid hdwy to go handy wide halfway, btn over 2f out:	1	44a
	PRINCESS BANKES 168 [11] Miss Gay Kelleway 3-8-9 (68) M Fenton 20/1: 0605-0: Mid-div, strug halfway:	6	29a
11 Ran	1m 42.1 (5.9) Owner Kennet Valley Thoroughbreds IV	Trained at Kingsclere	

---

842   2.40 Bet Direct On Sky Active Handicap Stakes 4yo+ 46-55 (F)   **[63]**
£2870 £820 £410   **1m4f p/track**   **Going 43**   **+07 Fast**   Stalls Inside

827	CHOCOLATE BOY 5 [4] G L Moore 5-8-10 1oh bl e (45) R L Moore 7/2 JT FAV: 00-52441: In tch, led over 2f out, rdn clr over 1f out, readily:		56a
812	AVEIRO 9 [3] Miss Gay Kelleway 8-9-2 vis (52) M Fenton 5/1: 0-213332: Handy & led 5f out, short of room when hdd over 2f out, switched & kept on, no ch with wnr:	6	54a
745	ORINOCOVSKY 17 [5] N P Littmoden 5-9-5 (55) D Holland 7/2 JT FAV: 4-103023: Chsd ldrs, onepace.	1¾	55a
768	STERLING GUARANTEE 14 [6] Andrew Reid 6-9-3 VIS (53) A Nicholls 4/1: 630-24044: Mid-div, not able to chall:	4	47a
811	NOBLE PURSUIT 9 [1] P A Blockley 7-9-3 (53) Dean McKeown 12/1: 0-220035: Led till 5f out, sn btn:	5	40a
723	CADWALLADER 19 [2] P Burgoyne 4-9-0 (52) L Keniry (3) 25/1: 03500-46: Chsd ldrs, btn 3f out:	7	30a
757	ITSONLYAGAME 15 [8] R Ingram 4-8-10 VIS (48) J Quinn 11/2: 06-10057: Mid-div, drvn & btn 3f out:	1	25a
791	HUMDINGER 11 [7] D Shaw 4-8-8 8oh (40) Darren Williams 33/1: 0060-008: Sn bhd:	5	16a
675	SHOLAY 25 [9] P Mitchell 5-9-2 (52) K Darley 14/1: 5400-009: Sn bhd, eased 4f out:	dist	0a
9 Ran	2m 33.5 (4.3) Owner Sigma Estates	Trained at Brighton	

---

843   3.10 New Site @ Betdirect Co Uk Classified Stakes 3yo 0-60 (F)
£2898 £828 £414   **1m2f p/track**   **Going 43**   **-30 Slow**   Stalls Inside

715*	BARATHEA DREAMS 19 [1] J S Moore 3-8-12 (60) Martin Dwyer 5/1: 11: Made all, in command over 2f out, pushed out, readily:		74a
804	GARRIGON 10 [6] N P Littmoden 3-8-12 (60) D Holland 5/2: 5040462: Slow away & rear, kept on for press fnl 2f, no ch with easy wnr:	7	62a
804	PRINCESS ISMENE 10 [9] P A Blockley 3-8-9 bl (55) Dean McKeown 10/1: 5-152243: Chsd ldrs, chsd wnr 3f out, no impress over 1f out:	¾	58a

295	FOOT FAULT 71 [7] N A Callaghan 3-8-9 (57) W Ryan 25/1: 0046-04: Rear, kept on late, no dngr to ldrs:	¾	57a
715	ALMOST WELCOME 19 [5] S Dow 3-8-12 (50) P Doe 20/1: 000-0035: Chsd wnr, btn 2f out:	¾	59a
676	TROMPE LOEIL 25 [3] Andrew Reid 3-8-9 (60) T P Queally (3) 20/1: 0240-006: Mid-div, drvn/no impress fnl 3f.	½	55a
759	FOXILLA 15 [2] D R C Elsworth 3-8-9 (57) Dane O'Neill 16/1: 000-07: Chsd ldrs, btn 2f out:	7	46a
676	JACKIE KIELY 25 [10] T G Mills 3-8-12 (59) K Darley 7/4 FAV: 0-0628: Rdn & chsd ldrs wide 3f out, sn btn.	1¾	47a
804	CASANTELLA 10 [4] M J Polglase 3-8-9 (40) A Culhane 66/1: 4505009: Sn bhd.	1	43a
756	TONTO 15 [8] Miss D Mountain 3-8-12 p (58) O Urbina 12/1: 0-043060: Al rear, no ch 3f out:	5	39a
10 Ran	2m 10.13 (7.33) Owner Mrs Fitri Hay	Trained at Hungerford	

844

3.40 #10 Free Bet @ Bet Direct Handicap Stakes 3yo+ 46-52 (F)   **[49]**

£2926 £836 £418   6f p/track rnd   Going 43   +06 Fast   Stalls Inside

830	KILMEENA STAR 5 [10] J C Fox 6-9-0 11oh BL (35) R L Moore 25/1: 06-00041: Broke well, sn trckd ldrs, switched & led dist, drvn out:		50a
819	TREE ROOFER 6 [3] N P Littmoden 5-9-0 1oh (45) T P Queally (3) 14/1: 040-0002: Held up, styd on for press ins last, just failed:	hd	49a
822	ATTORNEY 6 [11] D Shaw 6-9-0 1oh vis (45) D Holland 11/1: 0400653: Mid-div, styd on for press ins last, not pace of wnr:	nk	47a
832*	LONG WEEKEND 5 [2] D Shaw 6-9-8 6ex vis (54) Darren Williams 5/1: 0662114: Slow away & rear, edged right & kept on for press, not able to chall:	1	53a
778	RIVER DAYS 13 [5] Miss Gay Kelleway 6-9-3 vis t (49) M Fenton 14/1: 00-02065: Led till dist, no extra:	2½	40a
767*	DOCTOR DENNIS 14 [8] J Pearce 7-9-5 bl (51) N Pollard 9/2 FAV: 4446-516: Bmpd, rear, hdwy wide/ hmpd over 2f out, no impress:	¾	40a
639	MARABAR 28 [4] D W Chapman 6-9-6 BL (52) A Culhane 12/1: 005-0657: Chsd ldrs till over 1f out:	1	38a
728	TRIPTI 18 [12] J J Bridger 4-9-1 (47) Martin Dwyer 8/1: 06-20028: Prom, btn over 1f out:	1¼	29a
740	INCHING 17 [7] R M H Cowell 4-9-3 p (49) E Ahern 5/1: 4626-449: Dwelt, held up, nvr a threat:	2	25a
819	PIPS SONG 6 [13] P W Hiatt 9-9-2 (48) Lisa Jones (3) 15/2: 0010030: Chsd ldrs till dist:	2	18a
773	SABANA 14 [6] J M Bradley 6-9-4 bl (50) P Fitzsimons (9) 9/1: 4350130: Mid-div, btn/bmpd 2f out:	3	11a
741	FINGER OF FATE 17 [9] M J Polglase 4-9-0 1oh bl (45) Dean McKeown 25/1: 0-000000: Dwelt & rear, eff wide, no impress:	2½	0a
12 Ran	1m 12.64 (2.24) Owner Mrs J A Cleary	Trained at Marlborough	

845

4.10 Press Interactive To Bet Direct Handicap Stakes 3yo+ 46-52 (F)   **[58]**

£2919 £834 £417   1m p/track rnd   Going 43   -24 Slow   Stalls Outside

732	MARNIE 18 [9] J Akehurst 7-9-3 (47) J Quinn 10/1: 04000-01: In tch, hdwy to chall dist, drvn & led line, all out:		54a
3	MASAFI 125 [10] Sir Mark Prescott 3-8-4 (52) J Mackay 7/4 FAV: 000-2: Sn prom wide, narrow lead dist, drvn & hdd line:	shd	60a
820	INDIAN BLAZE 6 [5] Andrew Reid 10-9-8 (52) T P Queally (3) 9/1: 0-621203: Chsd ldrs, poised to chall when short of room dist, swtchd & kept on:	¾	55a
768	MY LILLI 14 [6] P Mitchell 4-9-5 (49) D Holland 8/1: 00-34064: Led 1f, sn trckd ldrs, drvn & styd on onepace from dist:	hd	52a
770	MISS PEACHES 14 [3] G G Margarson 6-9-3 (47) Kristin Stubbs (7) 10/1: 00-20135: Mid-div, not pace to chall:	2½	42a
791	KUMAKAWA 11 [7] E A Wheeler 6-9-5 bl (49) Liam Jones (7) 20/1: 5030026: Bhd, nvr on terms:	5	31a
717	LARAD 19 [2] J S Moore 3-8-2 bl (50) D Kinsella 25/1: 504-3507: Dsptd lead 1f, led 2f out till over 1f out:	½	30a
809	DANCING KING 9 [1] P W Hiatt 8-9-5 (49) P Makin (7) 20/1: 2131548: Dsptd lead till 2f out, sn btn:	¾	27a
146	INTRODUCTION 99 [8] W J Musson 3-7-13 (47) Lisa Jones (3) 25/1: 000-9: Bhd, nvr on terms:	½	23a
766	COPPINGTON FLYER 14 [11] B W Duke 4-9-3 (47) O Urbina 12/1: 00-4040: Keen, wide, chsd ldrs 6f.	shd	23a
766	WIND CHIME 14 [12] A G Newcombe 7-9-7 (51) S Whitworth 3/1: 4000-020: Chsd ldrs wide, btn 2f out:	hd	26a
717	NEVER CRIED WOLF 19 [4] D R C Elsworth 3-8-4 p (52) Martin Dwyer 25/1: 60060: Sn bhd:	¾	25a
12 Ran	1m 41.56 (5.36) Owner The Grass is Greener Partnersh	Trained at Epsom	

846

4.40 Bet Direct Daily Special Offers Handicap Stakes 3yo+ 46-52 (F)   **[58]**

£2954 £844 £422   7f p/track rnd   Going 43   -14 Slow   Stalls Inside

448	LOCH LAIRD 53 [3] M Madgwick 9-9-3 (47) G Baker 14/1: 1000-001: Towards rear, drvn & styd on, led cl-home, all out:		51a
804	SONDERBORG 10 [11] G L Moore 3-8-5 bl e (51) Lisa Jones (3) 11/2: 6453222: Mid-div, drvn to chall ins last, just held:	shd	54a
535*	DIAL SQUARE 40 [10] P Howling 3-7-13 bl (45) C Catlin 10/1: 00-013: Chsd ldrs & led over 2f out, drvn & hdd cl-home:	nk	47a
831	SINGLE TRACK MIND 5 [2] J R Boyle 6-9-0 4oh (40) Martin Dwyer 10/1: 0/00-0254: Dwelt & bhd, no room over 1f out & ins last, nrst fin:	nk	45a
761	ROBIN SHARP 15 [8] J Akehurst 6-9-2 vis (46) J Quinn 25/1: 000-2605: Drvn to lead early, hdd over 2f out, no extra:	½	45a
766	BALLARE 14 [12] Bob Jones 5-9-1 VIS (45) O Urbina 12/1: 200-0346: Mid-div wide, hdwy to chall 2f out, onepace:	shd	44a
761	BLAKESEVEN 15 [4] W J Musson 4-9-4 (48) M Fenton 4/1 FAV: 40-32237: Rear/wide, not able to chall:	nk	46a
820	BALERNO 6 [1] R Ingram 5-9-6 (50) K Darley 7/1: 0-130458: Mid-div, badly hmpd after 2f & drpd towards rear, not able to chall after:	¾	46a
73	FAYR FIRENZE 114 [5] M F Harris 3-8-3 bl (49) S Righton 25/1: 000656-9: Keen, mid-div, btn 2f out:	nk	44a
783	SOCIAL CONTRACT 12 [13] S Dow 7-9-1 vis (45) J F Egan 7/1: 0060620: Chsd ldrs, btn 2f out:	1	38a
825	THE GAY FOX 6 [14] B G Powell 10-9-1 bl t (45) S Carson 6/1: 4230030: Dwelt, bhd, nvr on terms:	nk	37a
831	GEESPOT 5 [7] D J S ffrench Davis 5-9-0 4oh (40) J F McDonald (5) 16/1: 0040030: Mid-div, btn 2f out:	½	36a
783*	REDOUBTABLE 12 [9] D W Chapman 13-9-5 (49) A Culhane 8/1: 00-61410: Chsd ldrs, btn dist:	1	38a
831	FLAME PRINCESS 5 [15] J R Boyle 4-9-0 4oh (40) Karen Peippo (7) 50/1: 500-3000: Al rear:	¾	32a
792	FRAAMTASTIC 11 [6] B A Pearce 7-9-0 4oh BL (40) B Reilly (3) 20/1: 40-24160: Chsd ldrs, btn dist:	nk	31a
15 Ran	1m 26.76 (3.96) Owner Miss E M L Coller	Trained at Denmead	

SOUTHWELL Sunday 14.03.04 Lefthand, Sharp, Oval Track

Official Going STANDARD - SLOW.

SOUTHWELL Sunday 14.03.04 Lefthand, Sharp, Oval Track

847
2.20 New Site At Betdirect Co Uk Banded Stakes 3yo+ 0-40 (H)
£1460 £417 £209   **7f f/sand rnd**   **Going 95**   **-06 Slow**   Stalls Inside.

771*	**SMART SCOT** 14 [7] B P J Baugh 5-9-7 p (45) M Savage (5) 10/11 FAV: 060-1111: In tch, led 2f out, sn hung left, clr 1f out, eased cl-home, val 11L+:		**54a**
771	**NEUTRAL NIGHT** 14 [6] R Brotherton 4-9-7 vis (40) I Mongan 13/2 0-300532: Handy, kept on fnl 2f, no ch with easy wnr:	8	**40a**
585	**BRILLIANTRIO** 34 [1] M C Chapman 4-9-7 (40) L Vickers 14/1: 5-2406U3: Trkd ldrs, led 4f out, hdd 2f out, no extra:	1¼	**37a**
771	**JESSIE** 14 [8] Don Enrico Incisa 5-9-7 t (40) Kim Tinkler 7/2: 5652224: Slow away, prog wide 5f out, outpcd 3f out, modest late gains:	hd	**37a**
788	**TRUE HOLLY** 12 [4] S Kirk 4-9-7 (35) J D Smith 25/1: 0000-005: In tch, outpcd 3f out, modest late gains:	1¼	**34a**
528	**LIVELY FELIX** 41 [5] D G Bridgwater 7-9-7 (40) B Swarbrick (7) 25/1: 0000-406: Al in rear:	12	**9a**
709	**XSYNNA** 20 [3] T T Clement 8-9-7 P (40) J Tate 16/1: 000-3067: Led, hdd 4f out, wknd 3f out:	2	**5a**
720	**ALASTAIR SMELLIE** 19 [2] S L Keightley 8-9-7 (40) P McCabe 14/1: 0/0030-08: Sn in rear, nvr a factor:	½	**4a**

8 Ran   1m 33.70 (7.10)   Owner Mr S Day   Trained at Stoke On Trent

848
2.50 Betdirect Co Uk Median Auction Maiden Stakes 3-5yo (H)
£1463 £418 £209   **1m f/sand rnd**   **Going 95**   **-33 Slow**   Stalls Inside.

626	**HOLD THE LINE** 29 [5] W G M Turner 3-8-7 p (65) G Duffield 4/1: 06205-61: Handy, led 2f out, pushed clr fnl 1f, val 5L+:		**68a**
2369}	**CASPIAN DUSK** 264 [10] W G M Turner 3-8-7 (53) C Haddon (7) 33/1: 406-2: In tch, outpcd 4f out, rallied fnl 2f, no ch with wnr:	3	**60a**
721	**ANGELOS PRIDE** 19 [3] J A Osborne 3-8-7 (59) S W Kelly 7/2: 0-30233: Led 1f, styd in tch, hung left & led again 2f out, sn hdd & onepcd:	1½	**57a**
795	**JACOB** 11 [11] P A Blockley 3-8-7 (60) N Callan 4/1: 355-54: In tch, wknd 2f out:	11	**37a**
751	**BULBERRY HILL** 16 [1] M G Quinlan 3-8-7 D R McCabe 20/1: 05: Cl-up, led, hdd bef 2f out, sn fdd:	2½	**32a**
785	**MR DIP** 12 [4] A W Carroll 4-9-11 (57) I Mongan 16/1: 050-06: Slow away, al bhd:	9	**14a**
	MITZI CASPAR [7] P L Gilligan 3-8-2 A Mackay 33/1: 7: Slow away, nvr nrr than mid-div:	shd	**9a**
829	**KUSTOM KIT FOR HER** 5 [9] S R Bowring 4-9-6 (45) J Bramhill 14/1: 0232248: In tch, wknd 3f out.	5	**0a**
190	**CHARIOT** 92 [2] M R Bosley 3-8-7 (64) D Sweeney 33/1 FAV: 064032-9: Handy, under press & wknd 4f out:	3½	**0a**
	BAROQUE [12] C Smith 3-8-7 R Fitzpatrick 33/1: 0: Slow away, al adrift.	5	**0a**
	GOLNESSA [6] Mrs N Macauley 3-8-2 Joanna Badger 28/1: 0: Slow away, nvr a factor.	9	**0a**
4917}	**BILLY WHISTLER** 138 [8] J Balding 3-8-7 BL J Edmunds 50/1: 0-0: Sn adrift, t.o.:	2	**0a**

12 Ran   1m 49.64 (10.24)   Owner Mr Dermot Gascoyne and Mr Gary   Trained at Sherborne

849
3.20 Bet In Running @ Betdirect Co Uk Banded Stakes 4yo+ 0-45 (H)
£1645 £470 £235   **1m6f f/sand**   **Going 95**   **-06 Slow**   Stalls Inside.

824	**STRAVMOUR** 6 [8] R Hollinshead 8-9-2 (45) Dale Gibson 10/3: 31-05331: Keen mid-div, prog 8f out, led dist, rdn out:		**48a**
722	**NEXT FLIGHT** 19 [6] R E Barr 5-9-2 (40) R Fitzpatrick 9/1: 003-6232: Handy, styd on fnl 2f, just held by wnr:	1¼	**45a**
612	**COLONNADE** 31 [5] C Grant 5-9-2 (40) K Dalgleish 16/1: 6000-203: Slow away, prog 5f out, edged left dist, sn onepcd:	nk	**44a**
724	**PADDY MUL** 19 [7] W Storey 7-9-2 t (40) D R McCabe 10/1: 26-21434: In tch, led 3f out till dist, no extra:	4	**38a**
768	**MURAQEB** 14 [4] Mrs Barbara Waring 4-8-12 (45) I Mongan 28/1: 55-0005: Keen in tch, fdd dist:	9	**24a**
445	**BERKELEY HEIGHTS** 54 [3] Mrs J Candlish 4-8-12 (40) N Callan 16/1: 0065-406: Cl-up, led 5f out, hdd 3f out, wknd:	8	**12a**
576	**BERGAMO** 35 [2] B Ellison 8-9-2 bl (45) R Winston 9/1: 41220-07: Al rear:	5	**5a**
724*	**EAST CAPE** 19 [7] Don Enrico Incisa 7-9-2 (45) Kim Tinkler 13/8 FAV: 50-53018: Handy, wknd 5f out:	6	**0a**
683	**KNOWN MANEUVER** 24 [1] M C Chapman 6-9-2 (40) G Duffield 11/1: 0/000-449: Led, hdd 5f out, sn fdd & eased.	21	**0a**

9 Ran   3m 14.00 (14.20)   Owner Mr E Bennion   Trained at Upper Longdon

850
3.50 Betdirect Co Uk New Site Banded Stakes 3yo+ 0-45 (H)
£1645 £470 £235   **1m f/sand rnd**   **Going 95**   **+01 Fast**   Stalls Inside.

821	**KENNY THE TRUTH** 6 [9] Mrs J Candlish 5-9-7 t (40) I Mongan 10/1: 3233451: In tch wide, led bef 2f out, sn clr, eased cl-home, val 5L+:		**53a**
776	**PRINTSMITH** 14 [10] J R Norton 7-9-7 (45) J Bramhill 8/1: 05-14432: Handy, chsd ldr 2f out, kept on but no ch with easy wnr fnl 1f:	3½	**46a**
826*	**MRS CUBE** 6 [1] P Howling 5-9-13 (45) R Winston 5/2 FAV: 6060-113: Handy, edged left & no extra dist:	5	**42a**
792	**SANTA CATALINA** 11 [11] C A Dwyer 5-9-7 (45) T Eaves (5) 18/1: 603-0054: In tch, no extra fnl 2f.	1½	**33a**
776	**RED DELIRIUM** 14 [5] P A Blockley 8-9-7 bl (50) D Nolan (5) 3/1: 04-64525: Trkd ldrs, onepcd fnl 2f:	hd	**33a**
722	**TURFTANZER** 19 [6] Don Enrico Incisa 5-9-7 t (40) Kim Tinkler 10/1: 050-5046: Led, hdd bef 2f out, sn fdd:	8	**17a**
641}	**THE MOG** 390 [3] Miss M E Rowland 5-9-7 bl t (45) Joanna Badger 40/1: 20/0063-7: Slow away, nvr a factor:	7	**3a**
4887}	**WILHEHECKASLIKE** 141 [7] W Storey 3-8-4 1ow vis (45) D R McCabe 25/1: 000200-8: In tch, badly outpcd 4f out:	1½	**1a**
686	**ETERNAL DANCER** 23 [2] M Johnston 3-8-3 BL (45) J Fanning 16/1: 00-09: Slow away, nvr a factor:	dist	**0a**
821	**GRACIOUS AIR** 6 [8] J R Weymes 6-9-7 bl (45) D Fentiman (7) 6/1: 0-015330: In tch wide, fdd 4f out:	10	**0a**

10 Ran   1m 46.94 (7.54)   Owner S A Mace & A P Simmill   Trained at Leek

851
4.20 Betdirect Co Uk Selling Stakes 3yo+ (H)
£1306 £373 £187   **6f f/sand rnd**   **Going 95**   **+08 Fast**   Stalls Inside.

791	**KING NICHOLAS** 11 [7] J Parkes 5-9-5 t P (51) M Lawson (5) 20/1: 10000-01: Handy, outpcd 4f out, rallied 2f out, led ins fnl 1f, rdn out:		**61a**
646	**SPEEDFIT FREE** 27 [5] J Semple 7-9-5 vis (51) R Winston 2/1 FAV: 054-2562: In tch, led 2f out, edged left & hdd ins fnl 1f, no extra:	2	**54a**
533	**DUSTY WUGG** 40 [4] A Dickman 5-9-0 p (45) A Beech (3) 14/1: 20040-53: Bhd, prog 3f out, onepcd fnl 2f.	3½	**39a**
825	**LEGALIS** 6 [9] K A Ryan 6-9-10 bl (56) N Callan 5/2: 2031364: Handy, onepcd fnl 2f:	hd	**49a**
765	**JALOUHAR** 14 [8] B P J Baugh 4-9-10 (52) M Savage (5) 8/1: 5-546505: Cl-up, fdd dist:	6	**31a**
793	**AMANDAS LAD** 11 [3] M C Chapman 4-9-5 (45) Andrew Webb (7) 14/1: 3406466: Led, hdd 2f out, sn wknd:	2½	**19a**
773			1	**16a**

	SPY MASTER 14 [2] J Parkes 6-9-5 bl t (40) G Duffield 8/1: 000-3257: Slow away, sn in tch, wknd dist:		
797	EMPEROR CAT 11 [10] P A Blockley 3-8-10 VIS (54) D Nolan 7/1: 105-2308: Handy wide, wknd fnl 2f:	2	15a
548	PHILLY DEE 39 [1] N E Berry 3-8-0 (45) D Fox (5) 20/1: 253-3009: Al bhd:	6	0a
795	ROYAL SHEPLEY 11 [6] J Balding 3-8-0 J Bramhill 66/1: 000: Cl-up, fdd 2f out:	12	0a
10 Ran	1m 18.57 (5.27) Owner Mr M Wormald	Trained at Malton	

852   4.50 Littlewoods Bet Direct Banded Stakes 4yo+ 0-35 (H)

£1309 £374 £187   1m3f f/sand   Going 95   -10 Slow   Stalls Inside.

575	DASH OF MAGIC 35 [13] J Hetherton 6-9-1 (35) M Tebbutt 5/1: 00-16251: Mid-div, prog wide 6f out, styd on to lead dist, all out to hold on:		41a
823*	THE BEDUTH NAVI 6 [6] D G Bridgwater 4-9-6 (35) D Nolan (5) 11/4 FAV: 000-2212: Handy, led 4f out, hdd dist, rallied well fnl 1f, just denied:	hd	46a
640	SAMAR QAND 28 [7] Julian Poulton 5-9-1 T (35) M Halford (7) 8/1: 3653-533: Trkd ldrs, kept on fnl 1f, no ch with front 2:	2½	36a
792	MATHMAGICIAN 11 [2] R F Marvin 5-9-1 bl (35) L Fletcher (3) 22/1: 40-45404: Rear, drvn 5f out, kept on late:	¾	34a
724	KING PRIAM 19 [8] M J Polglase 9-9-1 bl (35) N Callan 10/1: 0664565: Bhd, prog wide 6f out, kept on late, see 353.	½	33a
640	BALALAIKA TUNE 28 [14] W Storey 5-9-1 (30) D R McCabe 28/1: 550-0006: In tch, hung left 2f out, wknd fnl 1f:	2	30a
792*	GRUB STREET 11 [4] J Parkes 8-9-1 (35) M Lawson (7) 6/1: 000/-3417: Bhd, nvr nrr than mid-div:	¾	28a
780	MOYNE PLEASURE 13 [15] Paul Johnson 6-9-1 (35) I Mongan 22/1: 50-00068: In tch, no extra fnl 2f:	¾	26a
640	CUMWHITTON 28 [5] R A Fahey 5-9-1 (30) T Hamilton 5/1: 056//60-59: Slow away, nvr nrr than mid-div.	1½	23a
638	SEA YA MAITE 28 [10] S R Bowring 10-9-1 t (35) J Bramhill 20/1: 5235450: Handy, fdd 1f out:	2	20a
782	WESTERN COMMAND 13 [1] Mrs N Macauley 8-9-1 p (30) R Fitzpatrick 40/1: 4566050: Al in rear.	3½	15a
823	THINK QUICK 6 [3] R Hollinshead 4-9-0 (35) H Fellows (7) 25/1: 6634030: Al adrift:	nk	14a
780	BUYING A DREAM 13 [11] Andrew Turnell 7-9-1 (35) D Mernagh 22/1: 40/500/-50: Handy, fdd 2f out	14	0a
782	SOPHOMORE 13 [9] John A Harris 10-9-1 (30) G Duffield 18/1: 00/0-0630: Handy, fdd 4f out:	7	0a
154	BRIDEWELL 99 [16] F Watson 5-9-1 (35) J Fanning 28/1: 0/00000-0: Al adrift:	dist	0a
724	TROJAN WOLF 19 [12] P Howling 9-9-1 (35) R Winston 12/1: 0000-040: Led, hdd 4f out, hung right & sn eased:	20	0a
16 Ran	2m 32.93 (11.63) Owner 21st Century Racing	Trained at Malton	

853   1.50 #10 Free Bet @ Betdirect Co Uk Handicap Stakes Div 1 3yo+ 0-70 (E)   [68]

£3248 £928 £464   5f f/sand str   Going 58   Inapplicab   Stalls Outside

600	ITALIAN MIST 34 [2] Julian Poulton 5-9-0 e (54) G Faulkner 8/1: 1351201: Trkd ldrs trav well, led dist & rdn clr, decisively:		67a
641	NEVER WITHOUT ME 29 [5] P J McBride 4-8-6 (46) K Jackson (7) 9/1: 022-6452: Led 3f, outpcd by wnr fnl 1f:	3	49a
740	LADIES KNIGHT 19 [4] D Shaw 4-9-1 (55) Darren Williams 9/1: 6325063: Dwelt, chsd ldrs, kept on.	1½	54a
641	OFF HIRE 29 [3] C Smith 8-8-8 vis (48) R Fitzpatrick 10/1: 5400-234: Dwelt, sn prom, no extra dist.	¾	45a
749	CASH 18 [7] Paul Johnson 5-9-1 p (65) L Fletcher (3) 5/1: 164-0135: Prom, drvn & onepace over 1f out:	1¼	59a
793*	SCARY NIGHT 13 [9] J Balding 4-10-0 p (68) J Edmunds 7/1: 200-0016: Chsd ldrs, btn dist, op 5/1.	2½	55a
793	HENRY TUN 13 [10] N E Berry 6-8-11 bl (51) M Savage (4) 9/2 FAV: 3502137: Chsd ldrs, btn dist:	2	33a
793	SHARP HAT 13 [6] D W Chapman 10-9-10 (64) A Culhane 10/1: 5200558: Sn rdn towards rear.	½	44a
2862}	PAYS DAMOUR 248 [11] D Nicholls 7-9-9 (63) A Nicholls 20/1: 114600-9: Outpcd throughout.	1	41a
814	MISS TRINITY 8 [12] C N Allen 4-9-10 (64) B Reilly (3) 25/1: 50/050-00: Outpcd, nvr a factor.	1½	38a
619	CATCHTHEBATCH 32 [8] E A Wheeler 8-8-7 (47) S Carson 7/1: 6300-430: Chsd ldrs, hmpd after 2f, sn strugg.	1	19a
4133}	CELLINO 189 [1] Andrew Turnell 3-8-2 (54) D Mernagh 50/1: 0050-0: Dwelt & sn outpcd:	6	12a
12 Ran	1m 0.35 Owner Mr S P Shore	Trained at Newmarket	

854   2.25 #10 Free Bet @ Bet Direct Sky Active Classified Claiming Stakes 4yo+ 0-60 (F)

£2877 £822 £411   1m6f f/sand   Going 58   -34 Slow   Stalls Inside

745*	DAUNTED 19 [2] P A Blockley 8-8-13 (60) Lisa Jones (3) 5/6 FAV: 1001111: Trkd ldr, went on over 4f out & rdn clr over 2f out, nvr in doubt after:		64a
842	ORINOCOVSKY 2 [4] N P Littmoden 5-9-1 (55) D Holland 100/30: 1030232: Led after 2f, rdn/hdd 4f out, sn no impress:	6	57a
456	MR SMITHERS JONES 54 [1] S C Williams 4-8-13 (56) C Catlin 9/4: 00/5-2133: Led, hdd after 2f, btn 5f out:	14	44a
852	KING PRIAM 2 [3] M J Polglase 9-8-9 bl (35) N Callan 25/1: 6645654: Sn rdn in tch, lost tch 5f out.	13	22a
4 Ran	3m 12.66 (12.86) Owner Mrs Joanna Hughes	Trained at Southwell	

855   3.00 Great Value Offers @ Betdirect Co Uk Handicap Stakes 3yo 0-80 (D)   [87]

£4069 £1252 £626 £313   1m f/sand rnd   Going 58   -23 Slow   Stalls Inside

794	DENVER 13 [6] B J Meehan 3-9-7 bl (80) J F McDonald (5) 9/2: 2521-021: Prom, led over 1f out, drvn & held on all out:		87a
798*	JOMUS 12 [2] L Montague Hall 3-8-4 (63) G Duffield 9/2: 005-5212: V slow away, held up, switched & drvn to chall ins last, just held:	shd	69a
564+*	RARE COINCIDENCE 39 [9] R F Fisher 3-8-9 p (68) L Fletcher 7/1: 5320-113: Chsd ldr, led 3f out, rdn/hdd over 1f out, no extra:	1½	71a
751*	BOOK MATCHED 18 [4] B Smart 3-8-11 (70) R Ffrench 9/2: 003-314: Chsd ldrs, no impress fnl 2f.	5	64a
794+*	MISSION AFFIRMED 13 [7] T P Tate 3-8-4 (63) D Mernagh 7/4 FAV: 55-015: Led till 3f out, btn over 1f out.	1¼	54a
5034}	SENOR BOND 129 [3] B Smart 3-9-0 (73) F Lynch 25/1: 100400-6: Dwelt, sn handy, hung left & btn over 1f out:	2½	59a
645	MYANNABANANA 29 [1] J R Weymes 3-8-3 bl (62) J Quinn 14/1: 35-53447: Chsd ldrs till halfway:	28	0a
7 Ran	1m 45.87 (6.47) Owner Gigginstown House Stud	Trained at Upper Lambourn	

856   3.40 Betdirect Co Uk Handicap Stakes 3yo+ 0-95 (C)   [95]

£8112 £2496 £1248 £624   1m4f f/sand   Going 58   +11 Fast   Stalls Inside

752	BELLA PAVLINA 18 [7] W M Brisbourne 6-7-13 (66) S Swarbrick (7) 14/1: 2114151: Prom & chsd ldr after 4f, led over 3f out, drvn & held on gamely:		72a
811	GENERAL GB 11 [10] N P Littmoden 7-7-13 low (65) C Catlin 16/1: 0642/0/-12: Dwelt & held up, rdn & styd on for press fnl 2f, not reach wnr:	¾	70a

214

SOUTHWELL Tuesday 16.03.04 Lefthand, Sharp, Oval Track

225	**KYLKENNY** 88	[3]	H Morrison 9-9-3 t (84)	S Drowne	9/4:	405004-3: In tch, rdn & onepace fnl 3f:	8	**77a**
810	**GEORGE STUBBS** 11	[6]	M J Polglase 6-7-12 (65)	Lisa Jones (3)	9/2	2-062364: Led till 3f out:	1½	**56a**
4593*}	**TEMPSFORD** 164	[1]	Sir Mark Prescott 4-9-6 (89)	G Duffield	2/1 FAV:	131511-5: Chsd ldrs, lost tch from 4f out:	16	**58a**
4717}	**MANIATIS** 507	[4]	Mrs J Candlish 7-10-0 (95)	L Vickers	40/1:	0/61465/-6: Chsd ldr 4f, btn 4f out:	nk	**63a**
642	**CRUISE DIRECTOR** 29	[8]	W J Musson 4-8-12 (81)	M Fenton	5/1:	210-3037: Held up, hmpd 5f out, sn btn:	6	**41a**
758	**QUDRAH** 17	[9]	E J O'Neill 4-9-1 bl (84)	R Ffrench	12/1:	51650-08: Mid-div, hung right & btn 5f out.	8	**34a**
475	**MIDSHIPMAN** 52	[5]	A W Carroll 6-9-6 1ow (86)	Paul Scallan	33/1:	1/20/0-009: Chsd ldrs till lost pl after 4f.	10	**25a**
9 Ran	2m 39.90 (5.6)		Owner The Cartmel Syndicate				Trained at Baschurch	

---

857 **4.20 Special Offers @ Betdirect Co Uk Selling Stakes 3-6yo (G)**
£2548 £728 £364   1m3f f/sand   Going 58   -45 Slow   Stalls Inside

809	**GAME GURU** 11	[6]	P A Blockley 5-10-0 P (66)	Dean McKeown	5/2:	0131461: Chsd ldrs, rdn & led over 1f out, all out		**67a**
672	**ELEGANT GRACIE** 27	[5]	R Guest 4-9-4 (67)	D Holland	7/4 FAV:	003-262: In tch, short of room when outpcd 3f out, rallied well for press cl-home, just held:	nk	**57a**
3027}	**CAPTAIN CRUSOE** 601	[7]	P Howling 6-9-10	R Winston	7/2:	240/023/-3: Held up, hdwy & led over 2f out, hdd over 1f out, no extra:	2½	**58a**
664	**HYMNS AND ARIAS** 28	[1]	Ronald Thompson 3-8-0 2ow (47)	J Quinn	16/1:	00010-04: Chsd ldrs, rdn & btn 2f out:	11	**42a**
751	**BALLYRUSH** 18	[3]	K R Burke 4-9-9 (60)	Darren Williams	13/2:	600-0545: Dwelt, keen & sn trkd ldrs, btn when hmpd over 1f out:	hd	**44a**
1750}	**GALAXY FALLON** 655	[4]	M Dods 6-9-5 (30)	L Enstone (3)	33/1:	0600/00/-6: Chsd ldr 1m, sn btn, jumps fit.	1¾	**37a**
699	**DEVIOUS PADDY** 22	[2]	N Tinkler 4-9-9 t (60)	Kim Tinkler	20/1:	06305-07: Led till 2f out, btn/hung dist.	hd	**41a**
639	**MOON ROYALE** 30	[8]	Mrs N Macauley 6-9-5 (30)	F Lynch	40/1:	2500-008: Lost tch from 5f out:	dist	**0**
8 Ran	2m 32.65 (11.35)		Owner Mr Carl Would				Trained at Southwell	

---

858 **5.00 New Site @ Betdirect Co Uk Classified Stakes 3yo+ 0-60 (F)**
£2940 £840 £420   7f f/sand rnd   Going 58   -10 Slow   Stalls Inside

765	**NEARLY A FOOL** 16	[12]	G G Margarson 6-9-6 vis (60)	N Pollard	4/1:	53-11021: Mid-div, sn rdn, hdwy to lead dist, rdn clr:		**67a**
721*	**GALLOWAY MAC** 21	[4]	W A O'Gorman 4-9-6 (60)	D Holland	7/2 JT FAV:	33012: Rdn rear, hmpd 2f out, styd on for press, no dngr:	3½	**60a**
659	**LARGS** 28	[7]	J Balding 4-9-3 (45)	J Edmunds	16/1:	0345-033: Chsd ldrs, rdn & led 2f out, sn hdd, no extra:	nk	**56a**
530*	**SIMPLY THE GUEST** 42	[11]	Don Enrico Incisa 5-9-6 t (60)	Kim Tinkler	7/1:	00-22114: Rdn towards rear, nrst fin:	1½	**56a**
604	**EFFECTIVE** 34	[3]	A P Jarvis 4-9-6 (60)	J Quinn	9/1:	000-0305: Handy, no extra dist:	¾	**55a**
769	**XALOC BAY** 16	[6]	B P J Baugh 6-9-6 (56)	Darren Williams	7/1:	0011236: Led 5f, fdd under press:	hd	**54a**
393	**MON SECRET** 63	[13]	B Smart 6-9-6 (60)	M Stainton (7)	7/2 JT FAV:	01213-47: Dwelt, chsd ldrs wide till over 1f out:	1¾	**51a**
749	**STOIC LEADER** 18	[1]	R F Fisher 4-9-6 (55)	L Fletcher (3)	16/1:	20000-48: Held up, eff 2f out, no prog/eased.	6	**41a**
741	**KENNINGTON** 19	[10]	Mrs C A Dunnett 4-9-6 vis (56)	Dane O'Neill	7/1:	0/-1049: Dwelt, chsd ldrs, btn/hung left 2f out.	10	**24a**
167	**FINNINGLEY CONNOR** 98	[8]	Ronald Thompson 4-9-6 (50)	Dean McKeown	100/1:	435/000-0: Al towards rear.	1½	**21a**
646	**DRURY LANE** 29	[5]	D W Chapman 4-9-6 (60)	A Culhane	33/1:	3000-000: Chsd ldrs 4f, sn btn & hmpd 2f out.	shd	**21a**
677	**TANAFFUS** 26	[9]	D W Chapman 4-9-6 (60)	K Dalgleish	66/1:	04/56-000: Chsd ldrs till lost place halfway.	nk	**20a**
1794}	**PRIME OFFER** 317	[2]	J Jay 8-9-6 (55)	N Callan	25/1:	600530-0: Sn drvn rear & bhd, abs, new yard.	10	**3a**
13 Ran	1m 31.33 (4.73)		Owner Mr J Burns				Trained at Newmarket	

---

859 **5.40 #10 Free Bet @ Betdirect Co Uk Handicap Stakes Div 2 3yo+ 0-70 (E)** [68]
£3248 £928 £464   5f f/sand str   Going 58   Inapplicab   Stalls Outside

741	**FAR NOTE** 19	[2]	S R Bowring 6-9-13 bl (67)	J Bramhill	13/2:	6200461: Led/dsptd lead throughout, narrow lead ins last, drvn out:		**74a**
655	**SEA THE WORLD** 28	[7]	D Shaw 4-9-7 vis (61)	Darren Williams	5/1:	000-5132: Dwelt, sn pushed along, styd on for press, not reach wnr:	½	**65a**
4222}	**DUNN DEAL** 185	[8]	W M Brisbourne 4-9-4 (58)	B Swarbrick (7)	20/1:	540660-3: Al prom & ev ch fnl 2f, no extra cl-home:	hd	**61a**
655	**RIVER LARK** 28	[6]	M A Buckley 5-8-8 (48)	R Ffrench	16/1:	0102-644: Al prom, ch dist, sn no extra:	1¼	**48a**
748	**CLEVELAND WAY** 18	[11]	D Carroll 4-8-6 vis (46)	R Fitzpatrick	12/1:	1265645: Pushed rear, not pace to chall.	¾	**44a**
740	**AINTNECESSARILYSO** 19	[5]	N E Berry 6-8-12 (52)	C Catlin	14/1:	5-551436: Pushed along & handy, outpcd hway.	nk	**49a**
773	**TORRENT** 16	[1]	D W Chapman 9-8-5 bl (45)	Lisa Jones (3)	16/1:	6315307: Led/dsptd lead till dist.	½	**49a**
742*	**BLUEBERRY RHYME** 19	[9]	P J Makin 5-9-11 (65)	D Sweeney	3/1 FAV:	423-2218: Held up, smooth prog halfway, btn when hmpd ins last:	nk	**59a**
643	**KINGS BALLET** 29	[3]	P R Chamings 6-8-7 p (47)	J Quinn	7/2:	300-0029: Chsd ldrs, btn over 1f out.	2	**36a**
819*	**YORKIE** 8	[10]	P A Blockley 5-9-10 6ex (64)	Dean McKeown	10/1:	06200-10: Outpcd:	1¾	**49a**
655	**LAKELANDS LADY** 28	[4]	J Balding 4-9-10 P (64)	J Edmunds	14/1:	0000-000: Chsd ldrs, btn/stumbled 2f out.	2½	**42a**
11 Ran	1m 01.54		Owner Mrs Ann Potts				Trained at Edwinstowe	

WOLVERHAMPTON Wednesday 17.03.04 Lefthand, Sharp Track

Official Going Standard To Slow

860 **1.40 Bet Direct No Q On 08000 93 66 93 Handicap Stakes Div 1 3yo+ 0-70 (E)** [68]
£4046 £1245 £623 £311   7f f/sand rnd   Going 97   -12 Slow   Stalls Outside

858	**STOIC LEADER** 1	[9]	R F Fisher 4-9-1 (55)	L Fletcher (3)	4/1:	20000-401: Cl-up, led over 2f out & sn rdn clr, eased cl-home:		**67a**
687	**SUPER CANYON** 26	[3]	J Pearce 6-10-0 (68)	N Callan	5/2 JT FAV:	15532-42: Pushed along & chsd ldrs, rdn & took 2nd ins last, no threat to easy wnr.	6	**69a**
741	**MAROMITO** 20	[10]	R Bastiman 7-8-5 (45)	J Fanning	16/1:	0000-003: Led/dsptd lead till over 2f out, sn btn:	3½	**40a**
806	**GERONIMO** 12	[5]	Miss Gay Kelleway 7-9-8 (62)	M Fenton	9/2:	0-203104: Held up, eff 3f out, no impress fnl 2f:	2	**53a**
857}	**EL HAMRA** 357	[11]	M J Haynes 6-9-0 (54)	A Culhane	16/1:	00000/0-5: Sn well bhd, mod late prog:	nk	**44a**

215

558	**BETTER OFF** 40 [4] Mrs N Macauley 6-9-3 (57) Joanna Badger 9/1: 0000-506: Slow away, al rear:	4	**40a**
61	**JONNY EBENEEZER** 119 [1] R M H Cowell 5-9-9 (63) E Ahern 5/2 JT FAV: 246402-7: Led 1f, handy till 2f out:	½	**45a**
7 Ran	1m 33.81 (7.61) Owner Great Head House Estates Limit	Trained at Ulverston	

861

2.15 Avoid The Queues With Bet Direct No Q Handicap Stakes Fillies 3yo+ 0-75 (E) [75]

£3248 £928 £464 **1m100y f/sand rnd Going 97 -04 Slow** Stalls Inside

736	**NAJAABA** 20 [5] Miss J Feilden 4-10-0 (75) B Reilly (3) 7/4 JT FAV: 1-111151: Held up, hdwy over 2f out, rdn & led ins last, pushed out fnl 100yds:		**80a**
629	**SPARK UP** 32 [4] J W Unett 4-8-10 (57) S W Kelly 14/1: 266-0062: Held up, pushed along bef halfway, styd on for press fnl 2f, not pace of wnr:	1½	**58a**
777	**ZAHUNDA** 16 [6] W M Brisbourne 5-7-12 5oh (40) B Swarbrick (7) 5/1: 6020463: Al prom, rdn & led over 2f out till ins last, no extra cl-home:	shd	**46a**
809*	**LA PUCE** 12 [3] Miss Gay Kelleway 3-8-7 (71) M Fenton 7/4 JT FAV: 00-40114: Led/dsptd lead, went on over 4f out till over 2f out, sn btn:	6	**62a**
680	**ESTIMATION** 27 [2] R M H Cowell 4-9-7 (68) E Ahern 4/1: 651-3635: Led/dsptd lead 4f, btn over 1f out:	1	**57a**
5 Ran	1m 54.81 (8.61) Owner Mr A K Sparks	Trained at Newmarket	

862

2.50 Bet Direct No Q Demo 08000 837 888 Claiming Stakes 4yo+ (F)

£2898 £828 £414 **1m1f79y f/sand rnd Going 97 +05 Fast** Stalls Inside

731	**BRESSBEE** 21 [7] J W Unett 6-9-7 vis (66) S W Kelly 5/2: 00-02401: Led after 1f, rdn/clr 3f out, drvn & al holding rivals from dist:		**71a**
754	**HEATHERS GIRL** 19 [2] D Haydn Jones 5-8-4 (58) Paul Eddery 11/1: 040/-0162: Chsd wnr, rdn & kept on fnl 3f, al held:	2	**49a**
811	**JUST WIZ** 12 [3] N P Littmoden 8-8-11 bl (62) C Catlin 4/5 FAV: 32-63023: In tch, rdn & outpcd 3f out, nvr able to chall:	5	**47a**
753	**GRAND LASS** 19 [5] A Sadik 5-8-8 2ow p (49) K Darley 4/1: 6-341254: Handy, lost cheek piece after 2f, rdn & btn over 1f out:	½	**43a**
4595}	**BLUSHING PRINCE** 165 [8] Mrs L Stubbs 6-9-7 t (61) R Winston 11/1: 563360-5: Bhd, eff wide 3f out, no impress:	13	**35a**
826	**CHICKASAW TRAIL** 9 [1] R Hollinshead 6-8-2 (30) Dale Gibson 7/1: 0000-006: Led 1f, btn 5f out:	2½	**12a**
826	**DUNDONALD** 9 [6] M Appleby 5-8-7 bl t (40) S Righton 33/1: 0-600347: Sn rdn & al bhd:	nk	**16a**
7 Ran	2m 06.88 (8.68) Owner Team Racing	Trained at Wolverhampton	

863

3.30 Bet Direct No Q Maiden Stakes 3yo (D)

£3367 £1036 £518 £259 **6f f/sand rnd Going 97 -02 Slow** Stalls Inside

751	**SHOWTIME ANNIE** 19 [4] A Bailey 3-8-9 (59) J Fanning 11/2: 03300-61: Prom, rdn & led ins last, held on well:		**63a**
631	**BROWN DRAGON** 32 [6] D Haydn Jones 3-9-0 (63) Paul Eddery 6/5 FAV: 00-622: Trkd ldr, rdn/hung left when chall 2f out, no extra cl-home:	¾	**65a**
795	**SHAYMEES GIRL** 14 [5] Ms Deborah J Evans 3-8-9 (58) Joanna Badger 9/1: 0-533: Led, rdn/edged right over 1f out, hdd ins last & no extra:	¾	**58a**
5005}	**GRACEFUL AIR** 133 [8] J R Weymes 3-8-9 (64) R Winston 3/1: 250303-4: Chsd ldrs, outpcd halfway, kept on late:	2½	**51a**
3639}	**FLYING SPUD** 215 [9] J L Spearing 3-9-0 A Daly 16/1: 00-5: Rear, nvr pace to chall:	2½	**49a**
795	**NITEOWL EXPRESS** 14 [3] J O'Reilly 3-8-9 D R McCabe 16/1: 0-06: Dwelt & sn outpcd:	1½	**40a**
676	**LADY STRIPES** 28 [2] M J Wallace 3-8-9 (58) D Corby (3) 6/1: 060-067: In tch, btn 2f out, eased:	4	**30a**
7 Ran	1m 18.73 (5.93) Owner Showtime Ice Cream Concessiona	Trained at Tarporley	

864

4.10 Bet Direct No Q On 08000 93 66 93 Handicap Stakes Div 2 3yo+ 0-70 (E) [68]

£4037 £1242 £621 £311 **7f f/sand rnd Going 97 -10 Slow** Stalls Outside

765	**DUO LEONI** 16 [6] Mrs Stef Liddiard 4-9-4 (58) M Fenton 5/1: 15020-61: Handy, led travelling well 3f out, strongly prsd dist, drvn & held on gamely:		**61a**
741	**ST IVIAN** 20 [3] Mrs N Macauley 4-9-12 vis (66) P McCabe 11/1: 4602002: Held up, eff halfway, rdn to chall dist, just held nr fin:	nk	**68a**
799	**CLOUDLESS** 13 [4] J W Unett 4-9-1 (55) S W Kelly 10/1: 15-02403: Held up, hdwy to chall 2f out, drvn & kept on:	¾	**55a**
792	**SPY GUN** 14 [8] T Wall 4-9-0 (54) R Ffrench 16/1: 3500504: Towards rear & rdn halfway, styd on for press, no danger:	1½	**51a**
822	**EXTEMPORISE** 9 [7] P J McBride 4-8-5 t (45) Dale Gibson 5/1: 050-035: Held up, eff 2f out, no extra dist:	1½	**39a**
840	**PARKER** 4 [9] B Palling 7-9-11 (65) K Darley 3/1 FAV: 2150-436: Held up, eff wide 3f out, btn dist:	¾	**58a**
704	**MOUNT ROYALE** 23 [10] N Tinkler 6-9-8 vis t (62) Kim Tinkler 7/2: 0631107: Keen, in tch, btn 2f out:	9	**39a**
845	**DANCING KING** 3 [1] P W Hiatt 8-8-9 (49) P Makin (7) 11/1: 1315408: Led till 4f out, sn btn:	1	**24a**
685	**PILGRIM PRINCESS** 26 [5] E J Alston 8-6-5 (45) J Quinn 11/1: 6-354609: Prom, btn 2f out:	1¼	**17a**
704	**TANTRIC** 23 [2] J O'Reilly 4-9-9 (63) J D O'Reilly (7) 10/1: 11000-00: Chsd ldrs, found little over 1f out, wknd:	10	**19a**
10 Ran	1m 33.72 (7.52) Owner Mrs Stef Liddiard	Trained at Hungerford	

865

4.45 Betdirect Co Uk Selling Stakes 3yo (G)

£2583 £738 £369 **1m100y f/sand rnd Going 97 -20 Slow** Stalls Inside

815	**STONOR LADY** 9 [8] P W D'Arcy 3-8-7 e (48) E Ahern 8/1: 206-0001: Handy & led over 3f out, drvn out:		**49a**
613	**FOX HOLLOW** 34 [2] M J Haynes 3-8-12 (48) R Winston 14/1: 500-0032: Led 1f, rem handy & ev ch dist, no extra nr fin:	1	**51a**
560	**KATIES ROLE** 41 [9] Ian Emmerson 3-8-7 (50) Dean McKeown 11/4 FAV: 043-3443: Prom, ev ch dist, onepcd fnl 1f:	1	**44a**
658	**SECRET BLOOM** 29 [12] J R Norton 3-8-12 vis (45) Darren Williams 20/1: 50-44054: Slow away, hdwy 3f out, onepcd fnl 2f:	½	**48a**
596	**COMIC GENIUS** 36 [1] D Haydn Jones 3-8-7 BL (45) Paul Eddery 4/1: 46062-35: Led after 1f till over 3f out, btn dist:	9	**28a**
441	**BRETTON** 58 [7] R Hollinshead 3-8-12 bl (47) A Culhane 9/2: 0544-266: In tch, btn/no room 3f out:	6	**23a**
739	**PURE EMOTION** 20 [11] W R Muir 3-8-7 (45) J Quinn 11/1: 5-5007: In tch till 2f out:	7	**7a**
670	**THREE WELSHMEN** 28 [3] B R Millman 3-8-12 (60) S Drowne 7/1: 00050-08: Sn bhd:	3	**6a**
613	**KNIGHT TO REMEMBER** 34 [5] K A Ryan 3-8-12 (48) N Callan 6/1: 0600-349: Lost tch from halfway:	14	**0a**
9 Ran	1m 56.16 (9.96) Owner Mrs J Harris	Trained at Newmarket	

866

5.20 New Site @ Betdirect Co Uk Handicap Stakes 4yo+ 0-65 (F) [64]

£2968 £848 £424 **2m46y f/sand Going 97 -37 Slow** Stalls Inside

WOLVERHAMPTON Wednesday 17.03.04 Lefthand, Sharp Track

842	**AVEIRO 3** [8] Miss Gay Kelleway 8-9-2 (52) M Fenton 15/8 FAV: 2133321: Made all & rdn clr over 2f out, styd on strongly:		**65a**
801	**PLATINUM CHARMER 13** [6] K A Ryan 4-9-5 (60) N Callan 6/1: 004-2102: Held up, hdwy to chase wnr 6f out, no impress over 1f out:	15	**62a**
787	**SUNGIO 15** [10] B G Powell 6-9-2 bl (52) Dale Gibson 9/2: 05-13123: Chsd ldr, rdn & outpcd fnl 4f.	10	**44a**
	SWING WEST 252 [3] A E Jones 10-7-12 4oh bl (30) S Righton 20/1: 0/0400/0-4: Held up, sn rdn along, lost tch fnl 3f:	1¼	**27a**
752	**TONI ALCALA 19** [1] R F Fisher 5-10-0 (64) L Fletcher (3) 5/1: 02040-35: In tch, lost place 5f out:	2	**55a**
634	**E MINOR 32** [9] T Wall 5-9-0 (50) R Ffrench 11/2: 006-5066: Chsd wnr, rdn & btn 4f out:	3	**38a**
805	**PARADISE VALLEY 13** [4] Mrs Stef Liddiard 4-8-11 t (52) S Drowne 9/2: 25-16057: In tch, btn 4f out, eased:	29	**17a**
7 Ran	3m 50.86 (21.66) Owner Mr J T Billson		Trained at Newmarket

SOUTHWELL Thursday 18.03.04 Lefthand, Sharp, Oval Track

Official Going   Standard

867
2.25 New Site @ Betdirect Co Uk Apprentice Handicap Stakes 3yo+ 0-60 (F)   [60]
£2996 £856 £428   1m4f f/sand   Going 67   +01 Fast   Stalls Inside

762	**ANTONY EBENEEZER 19** [16] C R Dore 5-8-3 t (35) R Thomas (3) 7/1: 00-53001: Chsd ldrs, rdn & led dist, drvn out:		**41a**
614	**IT MUST BE SPEECH 35** [13] S L Keightley 3-8-5 1ow (58) Derek Nolan 16/1: 0000-52: Mid-div, rdn & hdwy to lead 2f out, hdd dist, kept on:	1	**63a**
780	**SERAPH 17** [10] John A Harris 4-8-6 p (40) Rory Moore (3) 12/1: 00-31033: Mid-div, hdwy to press ldrs 2f out, onepace for press dist:	hd	**43a**
746	**DISABUSE 21** [12] M W Easterby 4-9-6 (54) P Makin (3) 4/1 FAV: 266-2134: Chsd ldrs & led 5f out, drvn & hdd 2f out, kept on onepace:	nk	**56a**
828	**TOP OF THE CLASS 9** [6] P D Evans 7-9-1 2ow vis (45) S Donohoe 20/1: 3400035: Chsd ldrs, no impress dist.	4	**43a**
458	**KENTUCKY BULLET 56** [7] A G Newcombe 8-9-3 (49) P Gallagher (3) 9/1: 0425-306: Prom, lost place early, nvr able to chall:	7	**36a**
	BERRYWHITE 144 [4] C Grant 6-8-13 (45) T Hamilton 50/1: 300200-7: Cl-up/dsptd lead, wknd 3f out:	4	**26a**
745	**SPANISH STAR 21** [1] Mrs N Macauley 7-9-5 (51) L Treadwell (3) 11/1: 1-461338: Rear, nvr able to chall:	3½	**27a**
852	**WESTERN COMMAND 4** [3] Mrs N Macauley 8-7-12 (30) C Haddon (5) 33/1: 5660509: Al bhd, qck reapp.	5	**0a**
827	**IPLEDGEALLEGIANCE 9** [5] D W Chapman 8-7-12 (30) D Fentiman (5) 14/1: 5365000: Sn strugg:	¾	**0a**
762	**MUNFARID 19** [14] P G Murphy 4-9-12 t (60) J F McDonald 10/1: 454-3040: Sn bhd:	½	**27a**
816	**COOLFORE JADE 10** [2] N E Berry 4-9-4 (52) M Savage 11/2: 1435050: Led 4f, rdn & btn 4f out.	2½	**15a**
774*	**JUNGLE LION 18** [11] John A Harris 6-9-10 t (56) N Mackay 15/2: 00-62010: Dsptd lead till 5f out, sn btn.	7	**10a**
3883}	**COURT ONE 206** [9] R J Price 6-8-3 (35) B Swarbrick (3) 10/1: 426000-0: Sn bhd, reapp.	24	**0a**
4369}	**PISTE BLEU 180** [8] R Ford 4-9-10 (58) D Tudhope (5) 25/1: 303165-0: Al rear, reapp.	20	**0a**
15 Ran	2m 42.16 (7.86) Owner Mr C L Weaver		Trained at Spalding

868
3.00 #10 Free Bet @ Betdirect Co Uk Classified Claiming Stakes 3yo+ 0-60 (F)
£2898 £828 £414   1m f/sand rnd   Going 67   -04 Slow   Stalls Inside

556	**SUPREME SALUTATION 42** [6] D W Chapman 8-9-7 (60) A Culhane 100/30: 00560-01: Rear, prog halfway & led over 1f out, rdn clr:		**64a**
769	**MUTARAFAA 18** [7] D Shaw 5-9-9 vis (51) N Callan 5/1: 3240002: Held up, hdwy to lead 2f out, rdn & hdd bef dist, no ch with wnr:	6	**53a**
747	**CALL OF THE WILD 20** [10] R A Fahey 4-9-7 p (51) P Hanagan 7/1: 0346-033: Led 3f, drvn & kept on.	1¼	**48a**
809	**CRUSOE 13** [5] A Sadik 7-9-10 (57) D Holland 9/2: 440-3004: Rdn towards rear, hmpd early, switched wide & kept on late for press, no dngr:	2	**47a**
842	**NOBLE PURSUIT 4** [4] P A Blockley 7-9-6 (53) Lisa Jones (3) 13/2: 2200355: Chsd ldrs, no impress fnl 2f:	3	**37a**
754	**BULAWAYO 20** [9] Andrew Reid 7-9-6 vis (49) A Nicholls 16/1: 0-530306: Wide, led after 3f till 2f out:	3	**31a**
792	**NODS NEPHEW 15** [2] D E Cantillon 7-9-11 (52) Derek Nolan (7) 3/1 FAV: 03110-27: Led/dsptd lead till 3f out, sn btn.	7	**25a**
763	**ROCINANTE 18** [8] J J Quinn 4-9-9 (51) R Ffrench 16/1: 3010-008: Chsd ldrs, no impress 2f out:	½	**22a**
776}	**HAVOC 371** [3] Ronald Thompson 5-9-11 (50) Dean McKeown 66/1: 3000/00-9: Sn bhd:	17	**0a**
828	**PANCAKEHILL 9** [1] D K Ivory 5-9-3 (45) M Savage (7) 25/1: 0006000: Chsd ldrs, struggling halfway.	½	**0a**
10 Ran	1m 45.05 (5.65) Owner Mr David W Chapman		Trained at York

869
3.40 Betdirect Co Uk Maiden Stakes 3yo+ (D)
£3328 £1024 £512 £256   6f f/sand rnd   Going 67   -28 Slow   Stalls Inside

814	**FIT TO FLY 10** [8] S Kirk 3-8-11 (72) D Holland 13/8 FAV: 050-251: Sn rdn towards rear, strong run for press from over 1f out, led well ins last, going away:		**69a**
754	**SHADOWFAX 20** [10] Miss Gay Kelleway 4-9-10 bl (52) M Fenton 20/1: 62-40002: Dwelt, sn handy wide, led dist, rdn & hdd well ins last, no extra:	1½	**63a**
737	**BOAVISTA 21** [11] P D Evans 4-9-5 (56) S J Donohoe (3) 9/1: 3-032453: Led/dsptd lead, drvn & hdd dist, kept on.	¾	**56a**
795	**TIME TO RELAX 15** [9] J J Quinn 3-8-6 (64) Darren Williams 7/2: 43600-24: Chsd ldrs, drvn & onepace.	½	**54a**
706	**DARK CHAMPION 24** [7] Jedd O'Keeffe 4-9-10 (48) I Mongan 25/1: 05-20465: Led/dsptd lead till 2f out:	¾	**57a**
761	**ZAK FACTA 19** [1] Miss D A McHale 4-9-10 vis t (50) S W Kelly 13/2: 00-55246: Chsd ldrs, no impress fnl 2f:	1¾	**53a**
795	**SIR GALAHAD 15** [4] T D Easterby 3-8-11 A Mullen (3) 50/1: 6-07: Mid-div, nvr pace to threaten:	2½	**46a**
802	**SECOND MINISTER 14** [6] D Flood 5-9-10 bl t (60) J Murtagh 4/1: 00032-38: Chsd ldrs halfway, sn btn:	1	**44a**
3198]	**MISS FLEURIE 596** [3] R Craggs 4-9-5 T Eaves (5) 50/1: 4/-9: Dwelt & al outpcd rear:	1¾	**35a**
742	**UHURU PEAK 21** [5] M W Easterby 3-8-11 Dale Gibson 16/1: 00: Nvr on terms:	nk	**39a**
750	**BROOKLANDS TIME 20** [2] I W McInnes 3-8-6 (52) G Edwards (7) 50/1: 433-000: Al rear.	1½	**30a**
11 Ran	1m 19.02 (5.72) Owner Mr M Magowan		Trained at Upper Lambourn

870	**4.20 New Site @ Betdirect Co Uk Handicap Stakes 3yo+ 0-85 (D)**		[83]
	£4046 £1245 £623 £311 **1m4f f/sand**	**Going 67** **+04 Fast**	Stalls Inside

837	**GLORY QUEST 5** [4] Miss Gay Kelleway 7-8-13 vis (68) I Mongan 7/4: 2035221: Handy & led after 5f, rdn over 2f out, drvn & styd on strongly to assert dist:		**77a**
752*	**MOON SHOT 20** [3] A G Juckes 8-9-3 (72) V Slattery 7/1: 4251/3-12: Held up in tch, smooth hdwy to join wnr 2f out, found little for press dist:	5	**74a**
549	**SUDDEN FLIGHT 43** [1] P D Evans 7-9-1 (70) R Havlin 7/1: 010-0003: Chsd ldrs, prog over 3f out, onepace fnl 2f:	¾	**71a**
491	**JAMAICAN FLIGHT 51** [6] Mrs S Lamyman 11-7-12 5oh (48) C Catlin 20/1: 6450-344: Led till 7f out, sn rdn & no impress fnl 4f:	18	**31a**
642	**CALL ME SUNSHINE 31** [2] P C Haslam 4-8-6 (63) G Faulkner 11/1: 5402-105: Cl-up, strugg fnl 5f:	25	**9a**
588*	**HARELDA 38** [5] H Morrison 4-9-10 (81) J Quinn 11/8 FAV: 42-16: Rear, rdn & btn 3f out:	16	**6a**
6 Ran	2m 41.85 (7.55) Owner Wetherby Racing Bureau 40		Trained at Newmarket

871	**4.55 Bet Direct On Sky Active Selling Stakes 3yo (G)**		
	£2604 £744 £372 **7f f/sand rnd**	**Going 67** **-23 Slow**	Stalls Inside

560	**GARNOCK VENTURE 41** [4] A Berry 3-8-12 bl (47) F Lynch 20/1: 043-4001: Handy, led 2f out, drvn out:		**56a**
817	**MAYBE SOMEDAY 10** [8] I A Wood 3-9-4 BL (67) D Holland 2/1: 3463302: Led till 2f out, rallied for press in last:	¾	**60a**
725	**SON OF REMBRANDT 22** [6] D K Ivory 3-8-12 (56) I Mongan 14/1: 063-0053: Bmpd start, chsd ldrs, eff to press front pair when bmpd dist, kept on for press:	shd	**54a**
192	**KNICKYKNACKIENOO 96** [7] A G Newcombe 3-8-12 (51) S Whitworth 14/1: 040060-4: Bmpd start, in tch & keen, no extra dist:	1¼	**51a**
798	**SMART BOY PRINCE 14** [3] P A Blockley 3-9-4 (66) G Duffield 6/4 FAV: 466-1105: Chsd ldrs, btn over 1f out:	1¾	**54a**
797	**BOOKIESINDEXDOTCOM 15** [9] J R Jenkins 3-8-7 bl (54) S W Kelly 13/2: 22-03066: Chsd ldrs, drvn & btn 2f out:	28	**0a**
656	**QUARRY ISLAND 30** [1] P D Evans 3-8-7 (45) Darren Williams 12/1: 040-5207: Sn well bhd, nvr a factor:	1½	**0a**
815	**DANCING PRINCE 10** [2] A P Jarvis 3-8-12 vis (48) J Quinn 9/1: 05-54008: Bhd, no hdwy:	2½	**0a**
1172}	**EMINENT AURA 330** [5] A Dickman 3-8-7 VIS R Fitzpatrick 50/1: 00-9: Chsd ldrs, strugg fnl 3f:	20	**0a**
9 Ran	1m 33.58 (6.98) Owner Mr Robert Aird		Trained at Cockerham

872	**5.30 #10 Free Bet @ Bet Direct Sky Active Handicap Stakes 3yo 0-75 (E)**		[74]
	£3416 £976 £488 **6f f/sand rnd**	**Going 67** **-17 Slow**	Stalls Inside

712	**SAHARA SILK 23** [5] D Shaw 3-9-6 vis (66) Darren Williams 5/1: 0061341: Dsptd lead trav well, drvn & hdd dist, rallied gamely to lead again well in last, all out:		**70a**
797*	**PICCOLO PRINCE 15** [8] E J Alston 3-9-4 (64) J Quinn 11/10 FAV: 00-01212: Held up, smooth hdwy to chall over 1f out, drvn & led dist, hdd in last, just held:	nk	**67a**
673	**HEAD OF STATE 29** [11] R M Beckett 3-9-0 vis (60) J Mackay 10/1: 61-00103: Mid-div, drvn & kept on, not pace of front pair:	½	**61a**
835	**LIZHAR 5** [10] M J Polglase 3-8-11 (57) G Duffield 12/1: 6404204: Sn handy wide, drvn & kept on fnl 2f:	hd	**57a**
5034}	**MEGABOND 131** [3] B Smart 3-9-2 (62) F Lynch 14/1: 05230-5: Rdn & bhd, keeping on when short of room in last, nrst fin:	1¾	**58a**
835	**BACK AT DE FRONT 5** [4] N E Berry 3-9-0 (60) M Savage (5) 10/1: 4-155456: Prom, ch 2f out, fdd:	1	**54a**
377	**DESERT LIGHT 66** [7] D Shaw 3-8-8 vis (54) Lisa Jones (3) 14/1: 0060-137: Chsd ldrs, fdd under press:	1	**46a**
797	**INDRANI 15** [2] John A Harris 3-7-13 (45) D Fentiman (7) 12/1: 560-0648: Bmpd start, rear, no hdwy:	2	**32a**
63	**SPARKLING CLEAR 120** [6] R M H Cowell 3-8-1 (47) M Henry 33/1: 5066-9: Mid-div, wknd 2f out:	7	**18a**
729	**JAOLINS 22** [9] P G Murphy 3-8-10 (56) R Havlin 14/1: 060-1200: Sn bhd, no impress:	2	**22a**
712	**BARBILYRIFLE 23** [1] H Morrison 3-9-7 BL (67) L Fletcher (3) 14/1: 10000-00: Led/dsptd lead till 3f out, blnks.	5	**22a**
11 Ran	1m 18.33 (5.03) Owner Swann Racing Ltd		Trained at Newark

Official Going Standard

873	**2.00 New Site @ Betdirect Co Uk Maiden Stakes 3yo (D)**		
	£4154 £1278 £639 £320 **1m4f p/track**	**Going 13** **-51 Slow**	Stalls Inside

4251}	**SETTLEMENT CRAIC 185** [12] T G Mills 3-9-0 K Darley 6/4 FAV: 2-1: Sn handy wide, led going well 3f out, in command dist, pushed out:		**84a**
	MUZIO SCEVOLA 2 [2] M R Channon 3-9-0 S Hitchcott (3) 10/1: 2: Trkd ldrs travelling well, rdn & kept on fnl 2f, not pace of wnr:	1¼	**78a**
	BORDER SAINT 4 [4] M L W Bell 3-9-0 I Mongan 12/1: 3: Mid-div, styd on wide for press fnl 2f, not able to chall:	1	**77a**
817	**FIDDLERS FORD 11** [3] J Noseda 3-9-0 (72) E Ahern 9/2: 0-32264: Trkd ldr, no extra over 1f out:	1½	**75a**
675	**MR DINGLAWI 30** [9] D B Feek 3-9-0 M Tebbutt 100/1: 005: Chsd wnr over 2f out, btn dist, longer trip:	1¼	**73a**
759	**ZAFFEU 20** [1] N P Littmoden 3-9-0 D Holland 20/1: 066: Chsd ldrs, outpcd fnl 2f, longer trip:	¾	**72a**
4971}	**OCEAN ROCK 139** [11] A C Horgan 3-9-0 Paul Eddery 50/1: 0-7: Rear, eff wide 3f out, btn/eased fnl 2f:	1¼	**70a**
759	**LAKAAM 20** [8] G P Enright 3-8-9 R Brisland 12/1: 08: Keen, rear, al bhd, longer trip:	3	**60a**
	STARMIX 10 [10] P F I Cole 3-9-0 S Drowne 10/1: 9: Mid-div, btn 3f out:	8	**53a**
	HARRY CAME HOME 13 [13] J C Fox 3-9-0 P Fitzsimons 100/1: 0: Slow away & al bhd on debut:	11	**38a**
686	**DIVINA 28** [5] S L Keightley 3-8-9 A Nicholls 66/1: 000: Led till 3f out, wknd qckly:	3	**28a**
	STAGE TWO 15 [15] M Johnston 3-9-0 K Dalgleish 12/1: 0: Green, chsd ldr halfway, btn 3f out, debut:	2½	**29a**
2088}	**PERTEMPS RED 281** [6] A D Smith 3-9-0 M Fenton 100/1: 0-0: Trkd ldrs, btn 2f out, t.o, reapp.	dist	**0a**
13 Ran	2m 36.83 (7.63) Owner Buxted Partnership		Trained at Epsom

874	**2.30 #10 Free Bet @ Betdirect Co Uk Handicap Stakes Div 1 3yo+ 0-80 (D)**		[80]
	£5083 £1564 £782 £391 **6f p/track rnd**	**Going 13** **+05 Fast**	Stalls Inside

| 628 | **PRINCE AARON 34** [2] C N Allen 4-9-5 (71) G Carter 11/2: 62-11621: Trkd ldrs travelling well, led ins last & pushed clr rdly: | | **86a** |
| 760* | **FOREVER PHOENIX 20** [1] R M H Cowell 4-10-0 (80) E Ahern 7/2 FAV: 01-56112: Trkd ldr & led 2f out, hdd ins last, kept on, no ch with wnr: | 2½ | **86a** |

859	**AINTNECESSARILYSO** 3 [4] N E Berry 6-8-0 (52) C Catlin 25/1: 5514363: Prom, styd on for press, not pace front pair:	1½ 53a
740	**GUN SALUTE** 22 [14] G L Moore 4-8-1 p (53) J Quinn 7/1: 010-0104: Mid-div wide, onepace for press dist:	¾ 52a
800	**CORMORANT WHARF** 15 [5] T E Powell 4-9-8 (74) J F Egan 8/1: 0-065005: Mid-div, onepcd dist:	hd 72a
819	**SOUNDS LUCKY** 11 [9] Andrew Reid 8-8-8 bl (60) A Nicholls 20/1: 0-050126: Keen, in tch, eff wide, no extra dist.	1¼ 54a
628	**POLAR FORCE** 34 [6] M R Channon 4-8-7 (59) D Corby (3) 10/1: 6003-407: Rear, only mod prog, no danger:	nk 52a
755	**THE FISIO** 20 [3] A M Balding 4-9-9 (75) Martin Dwyer 12/1: 0-115638: Led till 2f out, btn dist:	shd 68a
4768}	**SILVER CHIME** 155 [7] D M Simcock 4-9-2 (68) S Drowne 14/1: 231050-9: Mid-div, btn over 1f out:	1½ 56a
660	**ROMAN QUINTET** 31 [12] D W P Arbuthnot 4-8-10 t p (62) Dane O'Neill 16/1: 34402-00: Trkd ldrs, btn dist.	shd 50a
859	**YORKIE** 3 [10] P A Blockley 5-8-12 6ex (64) N Callan 33/1: 6200-100: Held up, eff 2f out, sn btn:	shd 51a
799	**PRIMA STELLA** 15 [13] J A R Toller 5-9-5 (71) Lisa Jones (3) 16/1: 4102660: Rear, no prog:	2 52a
844	**TRIPTI** 5 [11] J J Bridger 4-7-12 3oh (47) J F McDonald (4) 66/1: 6-200200: Mid-div, struggling fnl 2f:	1¼ 27a
755	**AWARDING** 20 [8] R F Johnson Houghton 4-9-4 t (70) K Darley 10/1: 6506-500: Slow away, keen & al rear:	5 33a
14 Ran	1m 10.9 (0.5) Owner Black Star Racing	Trained at Newmarket

<hr>

875 | **3.00 Bet Direct On Sky Active Maiden Stakes** 3yo (D)
£5200 £1600 £800 £400 7f p/track rnd Going 13 -16 Slow Stalls Inside

503	**MONTE MAJOR** 50 [4] M A Jarvis 3-9-0 (61) N Callan 9/1: 06-3421: Made all, rdn & styd on well fnl 1f:	81a
3731}	**FINDERS KEEPERS** 212 [6] E A L Dunlop 3-9-0 (87) J Murtagh 5/6 FAV: 320-2: Pulled v hard early & trkd ldrs, eff to chase wnr 2f out, edged right & no impress ins last:	1¼ 77a
	INSTANT RECALL [2] B J Meehan 3-9-0 M Hills 6/1: 3: Trkd ldrs, rdn/outpcd 3f out, styd on strongly cl-home:	shd 77a
	CHEEKY CHI [7] P S McEntee 3-8-9 B Reilly (3) 66/1: 4: Keen & trkd ldr, onepace for press fnl 2f.	2½ 67a
4772}	**DESERT REIGN** 154 [12] A P Jarvis 3-9-0 (67) J Quinn 33/1: 000-5: Chsd ldrs, btn dist, reapp/AW bow.	¾ 71a
	SUVARI [8] G C Bravery 3-8-9 D Holland 13/2: 6: Mid-div, rdn & no impress fnl 2f, debut.	3½ 59a
4981}	**SIMONOVSKI** 138 [5] J A Osborne 3-9-0 E Ahern 12/1: 55-7: Keen, mid-div, no impress fnl 2f.	1¼ 61a
543	**SIERA SPIRIT** 44 [3] M G Quinlan 3-8-9 Nicol Polli (7) 33/1: 438: Slow away, rear, not pace to threaten.	nk 55a
814	**SAINTLY SCHOLAR** 11 [13] E A L Dunlop 3-8-9 K Darley 25/1: 09: Rear, efft wide, btn over 1f out.	shd 55a
4851}	**HANA DEE** 149 [11] M R Channon 3-8-9 (72) C Catlin 16/1: 030-0: Rear, btn over 1f out, reapp.	hd 54a
	COOL CLEAR WATER [15] B J Meehan 3-8-9 J F McDonald (5) 33/1: 0: Slow away, always rear.	¾ 53a
814	**AVERTAINE** 11 [9] G L Moore 3-8-9 I Mongan 40/1: 00: Al bhd.	½ 52a
751	**DIVERTED** 21 [10] M G Quinlan 3-8-9 S W Kelly 50/1: 00: Mid-div, btn 2f out.	1¾ 49a
670	**ACCENDERE** 30 [16] R M Beckett 3-9-0 M Tebbutt 100/1: 00: Al rear.	2 50a
220	**PICK A BERRY** 93 [14] G Wragg 3-8-9 S Drowne 50/1: 0-0: Al bhd, abs.	2½ 40a
15 Ran	1m 26.25 (3.45) Owner The C H F Partnership	Trained at Newmarket

<hr>

876 | **3.30 Bet Direct On 0800 32 93 93 Handicap Stakes Fillies** 3yo+ 0-85 (D) [85]
£8398 £2584 £1292 £646 1m2f p/track Going 13 -17 Slow Stalls Inside

758	**DANCE IN THE SUN** 20 [2] Mrs A J Perrett 4-10-0 (85) Dane O'Neill 7/4 FAV: 410-6421: Trkd ldrs, chd ldr 3f out, rdn & led ins last, styd on well:	89a
799	**LARA FALANA** 15 [1] Miss B Sanders 6-8-3 (60) Lisa Jones (3) 15/2: 00500-02: Mid-div, hdwy for press fnl 2f, not able to chall wnr:	¾ 61a
731	**MAYSTOCK** 23 [8] G A Butler 4-9-6 (77) J Murtagh 11/1: 4140-103: Trkd ldr, led over 3f out, rdn & hdd ins last, no extra:	nk 77a
801*	**ANYHOW** 15 [9] Miss K M George 7-8-8 1ow (64) D Holland 4/1: 40-00214: Rear, drvn & hdwy wide from 2f out, not able to chall:	1 65a
856	**QUDRAH** 3 [7] E J O'Neill 4-9-13 (84) E Ahern 20/1: 1650-005: Held up, eff 2f out, onepce.	1 83a
736	**FIGURA** 22 [6] R Ingram 6-8-1 (58) J Quinn 10/1: 00-03566: Held up, short of room over 2f out, sn onepce.	shd 57a
4992}	**CUDDLES** 137 [5] C E Brittain 5-9-6 p (77) I Mongan 12/1: 433450-7: Mid-div, btn dist:	1¼ 74a
816*	**MISS KOEN** 11 [4] D L Williams 5-8-0 6ex 2oh 2ow t (53) C Catlin 20/1: 060-6318: Rear, eff 3f out, no impress.	¾ 53a
736	**DORIS SOUTER** 22 [3] R Hannon 4-9-2 (73) R Smith 7/1: 23153-29: Led till 3f out, wknd qckly, eased:	2 66a
9 Ran	2m 07.22 (3.02) Owner Hesmonds Stud	Trained at Pulborough

<hr>

877 | **4.00 Betdirect Co Uk Handicap Stakes** 4yo+ 0-95 (C) [95]
£12383 £4697 £2349 £1068 1m5f p/track Going 13 -17 Slow Stalls Inside

731*	**MILLVILLE** 23 [10] M A Jarvis 4-8-12 (82) N Callan 2/1 FAV: 1011: Mid-div, hdwy & squeezed thro' gap ins last, sn led & styd on strongly:	89a
570	**COLD TURKEY** 41 [12] G L Moore 4-9-4 (88) S Whitworth 4/1: 112-1132: Rear, hdwy wide to chall dist, outpcd by wnr ins last:	1¼ 92a
762	**DOLZAGO** 20 [6] G L Moore 4-7-12 4oh bl (64) Lisa Jones (3) 12/1: 0055-123: Towards rear, switched wide & styd on for press ins last, not able to chall:	shd 72a
5036}	**FLOTTA** 132 [2] M R Channon 5-9-3 (84) S Hitchcott (3) 16/1: 401210-4: Chsd ldrs trav well, squeezed out appr dist, kept on late:	nk 87a
731	**MAJLIS** 23 [3] R M H Cowell 7-8-1 (68) J Quinn 50/1: 0201-005: Mid-div, hdwy to chall when edged left dist, sn no extra:	¾ 70a
758	**GIG HARBOR** 20 [4] Miss E C Lavelle 5-10-0 (95) L Keniry (3) 11/1: 26-10156: Chsd ldrs wide, hdwy & led 2f out, hdd ins last & wknd:	hd 96a
695	**BRILLIANT RED** 27 [5] Jamie Poulton 11-8-12 t (79) I Mongan 20/1: 03-00647: Rear, mod prog:	nk 79a
736*	**TIGHT SQUEEZE** 22 [7] P W Hiatt 7-9-0 (81) J Murtagh 16/1: 6530018: Held up wide, no prog fnl 2f:	2 78a
4361}	**ANTICIPATING** 149 [9] A Newcombe 4-9-0 (84) Martin Dwyer 6/1: 221460-9: Keen, hdwy wide to lead 6f out, hdd 2f out &	1 80a
731	**EZZ ELKHEIL** 23 [8] J R Jenkins 5-8-8 (75) D Holland 10/1: 050-2430: Handy, btn 2f out:	¾ 70a
4862*}	**COUP DE CHANCE** 148 [11] P A Blockley 4-9-1 bl (85) Dean McKeown 20/1: 010411-0: Al rear, reapp.	11 64a
2581}	**SALFORD FLYER** 982 [1] Jane Southcombe 8-8-3 (70) A Nicholls 66/1: 045405//-0: Led till 6f out, 7 wk jmp abs.	7 39a
12 Ran	2m 46.23 (3.93) Owner Mr T G Warner	Trained at Newmarket

<hr>

878 | **4.30 Terry Smart's 60th Birthday Claiming Stakes** 4-6yo (D)
£4124 £1269 £635 £317 1m p/track rnd Going 13 -04 Slow Stalls Outside

803 **THE GAIKWAR 15** [6] N P Littmoden 5-8-12 bl (62) E Ahern 9/1: 4-642501: Sn trkd ldrs trav well, led over 1f out, edged right under press but in command from dist: **71a**
714 **ACORAZADO 24** [7] G L Moore 5-8-11 bl e (64) Lisa Jones (3) 8/1: 5-020162: Rear, hdwy 3f out, kept on for press, not able to chall: 2 **65a**
698 **HARRY POTTER 27** [5] K R Burke 5-9-2 VIS (61) Darren Williams 50/1: 2213-003: Chsd ldrs, eff to chase wnr dist, no extra: shd **70a**
800 **BRAZILIAN TERRACE 15** [3] M L W Bell 4-8-12 (74) Hayley Turner (5) 5/2 FAV: 36150-34: Trkd ldrs, rdn over 2f out, no impress dist: 3½ **59a**
122 **CLIMATE 111** [9] J R Boyle 5-9-2 (72) D Sweeney 9/1: 050S30-5: Rear, eff wide, not able to chall: shd **63a**
829* **BALLINGER RIDGE 10** [11] A M Balding 5-9-0 vis (67) Martin Dwyer 10/1: 3-232216: Led after 1f till 2f out, wknd. ½ **60a**
769 **FEN GYPSY 19** [12] P D Evans 6-8-11 bl (59) S W Kelly 7/1: 000-5407: Led/dsptd lead 6f, fdd: ¾ **56a**
604 **GREENWOOD 37** [1] P G Murphy 6-9-7 (75) D Kinsella 12/1: 200-0308: Rear, no impress: 1½ **63a**
755 **PHECKLESS 20** [4] J M Bradley 5-9-3 (66) P Fitzsimons 20/1: 64-03409: Slow away, keen rear, no prog: 1¼ **56a**
799 **BLONDE EN BLONDE 15** [8] N P Littmoden 4-8-11 bl (68) D Holland 5/1: 0120330: Al rear: 1½ **47a**
816 **SINK OR SWIM 11** [2] J J Bridger 6-8-2 J F McDonald (5) 66/1: 00: Chsd ldrs till halfway. 10 **21a**
814 **KARATHAENA 11** [10] J W Hills 4-8-11 (78) M Hills 16/1: 02/503-00: Slow away, sn rdn & al bhd, reportedly lost action. 10 **13a**
12 Ran 1m 37.57 (1.37) Owner Mr Nigel Shields Trained at Newmarket

879 — 5.00 #10 Free Bet @ Bet Direct Sky Active Classified Stakes 3yo+ 0-80 (D)

£4401 £1354 £677 £339 **7f p/track rnd** **Going 13** **-14 Slow** Stalls Inside

3828} **MISS GEORGE 209** [3] D K Ivory 6-9-3 (83) Dane O'Neill 14/1: 005130-1: Rear, hdwy 2f out & styd on for press to lead well ins last: **87a**
518 **DAWN PIPER 48** [2] D R Loder 4-9-6 VIS (83) J Murtagh 2/1 FAV: 32-102: Led, rdn & hdd well ins last: nk **89a**
627 **WHAT A DANCER 34** [1] G A Swinbank 7-9-6 (83) R Winston 4/1: 15401-43: Trkd ldrs, styd on onepace. 1¼ **86a**
604* **CHATEAU NICOL 37** [4] B G Powell 5-9-3 bl (80) J Fanning 8/1: 00-13014: Keen, mid-div, rdn & no extra fnl 1f: ½ **82a**
688 **THE BONUS KING 28** [7] M Johnston 4-9-6 (83) K Dalgleish 12/1: 06060-45: Cl-up, wknd bef dist: ¾ **84a**
627 **GREY PEARL 34** [8] Miss Gay Kelleway 5-9-2 (82) M Fenton 4/1: 34-51136: Trkd ldrs, hdwy to chase wnr 2f out, wknd. nk **79a**
4980*} **BORDER MUSIC 138** [6] A M Balding 3-8-3 (81) Martin Dwyer 8/1: 361-7: Held up, eff wide, sn btn: ½ **80a**
4888} **COMPTON DRAGON 146** [5] D Nicholls 5-9-3 (80) A Nicholls 20/1: 500000-8: Dwelt & al bhd, reapp. 1 **77a**
8 Ran 1m 24.69 (1.89) Owner Mrs A Shone Trained at Radlett

880 — 5.30 #10 Free Bet @ Betdirect Co Uk Handicap Stakes Div 2 3yo+ 0-80 (D) [80]

£5083 £1564 £782 £391 **6f p/track rnd** **Going 13** **-02 Slow** Stalls Inside

755 **ANOTHER GLIMPSE 20** [7] Miss B Sanders 6-9-5 t (71) T Quinn 9/2 FAV: 50650-41: Rear, hdwy halfway, led ins last, held on all out: **77a**
765 **DOUBLE M 19** [9] Mrs L Richards 7-8-4 vis (56) A Daly 14/1: 4130242: Rear, strong run from dist, just failed: hd **61a**
698 **MAYZIN 27** [6] R M Flower 4-8-10 p (62) D Sweeney 8/1: 3241233: Sn handy wide & briefly led dist, styd on for press: nk **66a**
755 **MADRASEE 20** [1] L Montague Hall 6-8-13 (65) D Holland 10/1: 021-2004: Trkd ldrs, short of room & switched dist, kept on: ½ **67a**
799* **RIPPLE EFFECT 15** [5] C A Dwyer 4-9-13 t (79) B Reilly (3) 8/1: 2120515: Mid-div, ch dist, no extra: ½ **79a**
4 **BAHAMIAN BELLE 130** [2] P S McEntee 4-7-12 (50) Lisa Jones (3) 50/1: 523405-6: Dwelt, mid-div, hung right over 1f out, no extra: nk **49a**
807 **BLUE KNIGHT 14** [3] A P Jarvis 5-9-7 (73) J Quinn 11/2: 2600-247: Trkd ldrs, short of room when no extra ins last. ½ **70a**
572 **DONT CALL ME DEREK 41** [8] S C Williams 3-8-1 (66) R Ffrench 16/1: 04-568: Sn outpcd, nvr factor, abs: ¾ **61a**
628* **HARD TO CATCH 34** [11] D K Ivory 6-9-4 (70) R Miles (3) 15/2: 5-002419: Rear, eff wide, not able to chall: ¾ **63a**
741 **SKIP OF COLOUR 22** [4] P A Blockley 4-9-8 (74) Dean McKeown 11/2: 40-45120: Led till dist, wknd: 1 **64a**
765 **ILLUSIVE 19** [12] M Wigham 7-8-8 bl (60) G Carter 12/1: 32-00350: Rear, al outpcd: ½ **48a**
793 **PANJANDRUM 16** [13] N E Berry 6-8-11 (63) M Savage (5) 33/1: 3510600: Wide & al rear. 9 **26a**
12 Ran 1m 11.3 (0.9) Owner Mr Edward Hyde Trained at Epsom

881 — 1.05 Arena Leisure Maiden Stakes 3yo+ (D)

£5096 £1568 £784 £392 **1m p/track rnd** **Going 13** **-26 Slow** Stalls Outside

4620] **WAKE 519** [6] B J Meehan 4-9-11 P J Smullen 3/1: 2/-1: Sn hndy, rdn & led ins last, rdn out: **85a**
734 **KEELUNG 23** [8] M A Jarvis 3-8-8 P Robinson 11/4 FAV: 0-42: Led after 2f, rdn & hdd ins last, no extra: 1¼ **81a**
814 **EMSAM BALLOU 12** [1] R Hannon 3-8-3 R Smith 8/1: 33: Keen & led 2f, rdn & kept on fnl 2f, not able to chall: 3 **68a**
4868} **MISS ADELAIDE 148** [11] B W Hills 3-8-3 E Ahern 7/2: 43-4: Chsd ldrs, onepce over 1f out: ½ **69a**
697 **BALLINGER EXPRESS 28** [2] A M Balding 4-9-6 Martin Dwyer 20/1: 05: Trkd ldrs, onepace fnl 2f. ½ **68a**
LEBENSTANZ [4] L M Cumani 4-9-6 N Mackay (5) 20/1: 6: Dwelt, keen rear, late prog, nrst fin: hd **67a**
SUSPICIOUS MINDS [5] G C Bravery 3-8-4 1ow S Whitworth 33/1: 7: Dwelt, late gains for press, debut, improve. 3 **62a**
4872} **MUTASSEM 148** [9] E A L Dunlop 3-8-8 R Hills 10/1: 6-8: Mid-div wide, no prog fnl 2f, reapp/AW bow. ½ **65a**
IMPERIAL DRAGON [12] W A O'Gorman 4-9-11 D Holland 40/1: 9: Dwelt, sn in tch, btn over 2f out, debut. 7 **53a**
751 **SUNSET BLUES 22** [3] K O Cunningham Brown 4-9-11 bl e N Callan 100/1: 50: Chsd ldrs, no impress 3f out. 1½ **50a**
814 **ALIANNA 12** [10] S Dow 3-8-3 C Catlin 100/1: 00: Always bhd. 5 **36a**
802 **PARIS LATINO 16** [7] C L Tizzard 5-9-11 T V Slattery 100/1: 00: Always rear. shd **41a**
12 Ran 1m 39.35 (3.15) Owner Mr Joe L Allbritton Trained at Upper Lambourn

882 — 1.35 Axminster Carpets Juvenile Conditions Stakes 2yo (C)

£12180 £4620 £2310 £1050 **5f p/track rnd** **Going 13** **-26 Slow** Stalls Outside

BUNDITTEN [4] Andrew Reid 2-8-7 S Carson 9/2: 1: Broke well, hung right throughout but made all, drvn out: **80a**
IM AIMEE [6] P D Evans 2-8-7 S Drowne 33/1: 2: Sn pressed wnr, chall dist, rdn/always just held: ½ **77a**
WINDY PROSPECT [8] P A Blockley 2-8-12 Dean McKeown 4/1 JT FAV: 3: Dwelt, sn trkd wnr, kept on, not able to chall: 2½ **74a**
CUBIC CONFESSIONS [7] J A Osborne 2-8-7 S W Kelly 13/2: 4: Trkd ldrs, not able to chall fnl 1f. 3½ **58a**
JOE NINETY [2] J S Moore 2-8-12 J D Smith 14/1: 5: Mid-div, nvr able to threaten. 1¾ **58a**
BAMBOOZLED [3] P D Evans 2-8-7 N Callan 20/1: 6: Prom early, sn lost pl & outpcd. nk **52a**

	GRAND OPTION [9] B W Duke 2-8-12 R L Moore 9/2: 7: Sn bhd & no impress:	½	55a
	IM SPARTACUS [10] I A Wood 2-8-12 J Fanning 20/1: 8: Outpcd & sn bhd.	3	46a
	ITSA MONKEY [1] N P Littmoden 2-8-12 T P Queally (3) 25/1: 9: Always outpcd & bhd.	hd	45a
	HIS MAJESTY [5] N P Littmoden 2-9-12 D Holland 4/1 JT FAV: 0: Unruly stalls, slow away, sn bhd.	15	5a
10 Ran	59.61 (1.81) Owner Mr A S Reid	Trained at Mill Hill London	

883 2.05 Ladbrokes Com Sprint Conditions Stakes 4yo+ (B)
£17400 £6600 £3300 £1500 5f p/track rnd   Going 13   +21 Fast   Stalls Outside

692*	**NO TIME** 28 [2] M J Polglase 4-9-5 (85) L Dettori 12/1: 0-666211: Led after 1f, drvn & held on all out:		105a
4764}	**SPEED COP** 156 [7] A M Balding 4-8-7 (100) Martin Dwyer 9/2: 464410-2: Sn trkd ldrs wide, drvn to chall ins last, just held:	shd	92a
692	**JUSTALORD** 28 [8] J Balding 6-8-12 p (89) J Edmunds 12/1: 06-02123: Chsd ldrs wide, hung right on bend 2f out, styd on for press ins last:	¾	95a
4762}	**DRAGON FLYER** 156 [9] M Quinn 5-8-7 (95) S Drowne 14/1: 220300-4: Mid-div wide, outpcd halfway, kept on late for press, reapp.	¾	88a
4491}	**LITTLE EDWARD** 174 [6] B G Powell 6-9-4 (99) L Keniry 12/1: 010225-5: Led 1f, rem cl up till no extra ins last.	½	97a
431+*	**DUSTY DAZZLER** 63 [10] W G M Turner 4-8-10 (95) A Quinn 7/1: 04202-16: Held up, efft wide, not pace to chall.	½	87a
4350}	**FIRE UP THE BAND** 182 [5] D Nicholls 5-8-12 (106) A Nicholls 3/1 FAV: 112023-7: Held up, nvr pace to threaten:	hd	88a
4884}	**PERUVIAN CHIEF** 14 [4] N P Littmoden 7-9-10 vis E Ahern 12/1: 56-06008: Chsd ldrs till halfway, fit from Dubai.	1¼	96a
4629}	**STRIKING AMBITION** 167 [1] G C Bravery 4-9-10 (105) D Holland 11/2: 311000-9: Trkd ldrs inner early, sn lost pl.	nk	95a
4679}	**IKAN** 161 [3] N P Littmoden 4-8-7 (89) K Darley 33/1: 312400-0: Dwelt, always rear, reapp.	½	76a
10 Ran	57.39 (u0.41) Owner Mr Paul J Dixon	Trained at Newark	

884 2.35 Listed Littlewoods Bet Direct Winter Derby 4yo+ (A)
£43550 £16500 £8250 £3750 1m2f p/track   Going 13   -18 Slow   Stalls Inside

1452}	**CALUKI** 20 [2] Luigi Camici 7-9-1 L Dettori 14/1: 3201-141: Keen & sn trkd ldr, swtchd & drvn to lead line in a blanket fin, all out:		110a
789	**ANANI** 14 [3] E A L Dunlop 4-9-1 (104) E Ahern 12/1: 102-0342: Sn led & dictated pace, qcknd 3f out, drvn & narrowly hdd close home:	nk	108a
4955}	**BUSTAN** 141 [12] M P Tregoning 5-8-12 (107) R Hills 9/1: 543/442-3: Sn cl up, ev ch dist, styd on well, just held cl	hd	105a
693	**BOURGAINVILLE** 28 [1] A M Balding 4-8-12 (102) Martin Dwyer 14/1: 55026-04: Held up inner, swtch wide dist & styd on for press, just held.	nk	104a
4934}	**PUGIN** 146 [9] D R Loder 6-8-12 (105) J Murtagh 20/1: 200060-5: Rear, outpcd over 3f out, swtch wide & styd on strongly, nrst fin:	½	103a
693	**BLUE SKY THINKING** 28 [8] K R Burke 5-8-12 (102) Darren Williams 10/1: 6334-156: Dwelt, rear, effort wide over 1f out, kept on:	¾	102a
693	**EASTERN BREEZE** 28 [7] P W D'Arcy 6-8-12 (102) Paul Eddery 10/1: 666-4127: Trkd ldr, rdn & no extra dist.	½	101a
836	**VINTAGE PREMIUM** 7 [5] R A Fahey 7-8-12 (98) P Hanagan 66/1: 4320-068: Trkd ldrs, onepace fnl 2f.	1	100a
693+*	**GRAND PASSION** 28 [14] G Wragg 4-8-12 (104) D Holland 7/2 FAV: 2032-219: Mid-div wide, efft 2f out, not able to chall:	shd	100a
4955}	**PAWN BROKER** 141 [4] D R C Elsworth 7-8-12 (99) Dane O'Neill 14/1: 066025-0: Dwelt, rear, little hdwy, reapp.	1¼	98a
693	**CORRIOLANUS** 28 [6] P Mitchell 4-8-12 J Quinn 14/1: 3/1263-30: Dwelt, in tch, btn 2f out:	nk	97a
836+*	**VORTEX** 7 [10] Miss Gay Kelleway 5-8-12 e t (97) M Fenton 14/1: 0-111110: Held up, no impress:	2½	93a
3546}	**PRIVATE CHARTER** 223 [11] B W Hills 4-8-12 (110) M Hills 5/1: 132645-0: Mid-div & v wide, lost pl fnl 4f.	5	86a
836	**MI ODDS** 7 [13] Mrs N Macauley 8-8-12 (99) P McCabe 66/1: 1212-150: Rear/v wide, nvr factor:	18	59a
14 Ran	2m 05.85 (3.05) Owner Scuderia L 3 C di Lepori Anton	Trained at Italy	

885 3.10 Listed Ladbrokes Com Spring Cup 3yo (A)
£43500 £16500 £8250 £3750 7f p/track rnd   Going 13   +01 Fast   Stalls Inside

598	**ROSENCRANS** 21 [7] Saeed bin Suroor 3-8-11 VIS T L Dettori 6/4 FAV: 1-311: Always cl up, rdn & led ins last, drvn & held on well:		106a
4571}	**FOKINE** 169 [15] B W Hills 3-8-11 (114) M Hills 3/1: 1620-2: Mid-div, hdwy wide over 2f out & drvn to chall dist, kept on, al just held by wnr:	½	104a
756	**BAHIANO** 21 [14] C E Brittain 3-8-11 (92) D Holland 12/1: 62-2123: In tch, short of room dist, styd on well ins last:	1½	101a
368*	**BETTALATETHANNEVER** 70 [10] S Dow 3-8-11 (88) Dane O'Neill 14/1: 061-14: Mid-div, styd on for press fnl 2f:	hd	100a
3729}	**VENABLES** 213 [3] R Hannon 3-8-13 (106) R Hughes 14/1: 61140-5: Led/dspted lead, hdd ins last, no extra.	shd	102a
15*	**BRAVO MAESTRO** 129 [9] D W P Arbuthnot 3-8-11 (96) S Whitworth 6/1: 011-6: Held up, pshd along 3f out, not pace to threaten:	1	98a
119	**CROCODILE DUNDEE** 112 [1] Jamie Poulton 3-8-11 (88) I Mongan 50/1: 105-7: Held up, efft wide 2f out, no prog dist.	hd	97a
4335}	**TREASURE HOUSE** 183 [4] B J Meehan 3-8-11 (96) P J Smullen 66/1: 42210-8: Mid-div, btn over 1f out:	1	95a
4601*}	**VALJARV** 168 [6] N P Littmoden 3-8-6 (96) E Ahern 20/1: 344031-9: In tch, no room dist, sn btn:	3	84a
36*	**DUMNONI** 126 [2] Julian Poulton 3-8-7 1ow (81) N Callan 100/1: 3631-0: Prom, wknd fnl 2f:	1½	82a
4343}	**GLAMARAMA** 183 [8] A Bailey 3-8-11 BL (94) J Fanning 33/1: 013-0: Keen & held up, efft/hmpd over 1f out, no chance after:	shd	86a
5028}	**MAKFOOL** 134 [12] M R Channon 3-8-11 (96) C Catlin 50/1: 231243-0: Held up, no impress:	1¼	83a
5007*}	**RYDAL** 136 [16] G A Butler 3-8-11 bl (89) K Darley 50/1: 42221-0: Cl up wide 5f, wknd:	1½	80a
3253}	**SPANISH ACE** 234 [13] A M Balding 3-8-11 (103) Martin Dwyer 25/1: 216260-0: Dwelt, al rear:	5	71a
756	**WELL KNIT** 21 [5] P W D'Arcy 3-8-6 Paul Eddery 200/1: 120-00: Always bhd:	2½	61a
15 Ran	1m 23.64 (.84) Owner Godolphin	Trained at United Arab Emirates	

886 3.40 Lingfield Park Maiden Stakes 3yo (D)
£6939 £1601 £1601 £534 1m2f p/track   Going 13   -23 Slow   Stalls Inside

4469}	**OVER THE RAINBOW** 175 [2] B W Hills 3-9-0 (89) M Hills 5/2 JT FAV: 230-1: Trkd ldrs, rdn & squeezed through ins last to prevail close home:		82a
4216}	**GJOVIC** 189 [11] B J Meehan 3-9-0 (75) P J Smullen 4/1: 342-2: Sn led, drvn & kept on well, hdd nr fin:	nk	81a
817	**VANTAGE** 12 [8] N P Littmoden 3-9-0 (80) D Holland 5/2 JT FAV: 0330-22: Chsd ldrs, rdn to chall over 1f out, not pace of wnr	dht	81a

close home:
4981} **JUST TIM 139** [7] R Hannon 3-9-0 (78) Dane O'Neill 10/1: 0602-4: Cl up, drvn/chall over 1f out, no extra: 1½ 79a
686   **LOOKS THE BUSINESS 29** [6] W G M Turner 3-9-0 t (69) C Haddon (7) 25/1: 445-245: Held up, not able to chall.   2½ 75a
4943} **SCRIPTORIUM 143** [4] L M Cumani 3-9-0 N Mackay (5) 14/1: 0-6: Rear, nvr threatened ldrs, reapp/AW bow.   7 65a
526   **PADDY BOY 47** [1] J R Boyle 3-9-0 R Miles (3) 100/1: 37: Rear, rdn & no impress fnl 3f: 6 56a
601   **PRESTON HALL 38** [3] Mrs L C Jewell 3-9-0 S W Kelly 100/1: 08: Sn bhd, no impress.   1¾ 52a
734   **CLARE GALWAY 23** [10] T D McCarthy 3-8-9 E Ahern 50/1: 059: Hampered early, chsd ldrs wide 6f.   25 14a
798   **LORD OF THE SEA 16** [12] Jamie Poulton 3-9-0 (70) I Mongan 8/1: 655-3340: Trkd ldrs, wknd qckly 2f out, virtually p.u: dist   0
10 Ran   2m 06.37 (3.57)   Owner Harrison Jamieson Parker Sn   Trained at Lambourn

887 **4.15 New Site @ Betdirect Co Uk Handicap Stakes 3yo+ 0-105 (B)** [105]
£15080 £5720 £2860 £1300   **7f p/track rnd**   **Going 13**   **-09 Slow**   Stalls Inside

879   **WHAT A DANCER 1** [3] G A Swinbank 7-8-6 (83) R Winston 12/1: 15401-431: Dwelt, held up, hdwy wide 2f out & styd on for   91a
press to lead nr fin:
4867} **HIDDEN DRAGON 148** [5] P A Blockley 5-9-6 (97) Dean McKeown 33/1: 314000-2: Trkd ldrs inner, drvn & styd on well, just   shd 104a
failed:
758   **MOAYED 21** [7] N P Littmoden 8-8-5 bl t (82) E Ahern 10/1: 500-1263: Dwelt, held up, hdwy wide 2f out & led dist, hdd & no   ½ 88a
extra for press cl home:
838   **FIVEOCLOCK EXPRESS 155** [6] Miss Gay Kelleway 4-8-13 P (90) I Mongan 16/1: 021300-4: Mid-div, styd on onepace for   2 92a
press:
693   **LYGETON LAD 28** [15] Miss Gay Kelleway 6-9-11 t (102) M Fenton 6/1: 101-5565: Rear, efft wide over 1f out, onepce.   nk 103a
836   **QUITO 7** [2] D W Chapman 7-10-0 bl (105) T Quinn 14/1: 2645-106: Rear, late gains, nvr threat: shd 106a
838   **QUEENS RHAPSODY 7** [1] A Bailey 4-8-13 (90) J Fanning 10/1: 50-20247: Mid-div rail, forced to swtchd wide over 1f out,   hd 90a
not able to chall:
      FAST GATE 29 [10] L Pantuosco 5-9-1 BL T (92) L Dettori 4/1 FAV: 434-2118: Chsd ldrs, rdn/no impress dist.   nk 91a
547* **DANCE ON THE TOP 45** [13] J R Boyle 6-9-3 t (94) D Sweeney 7/1: 4320-119: Trkd ldrs, briefly led over 1f out, onepace.   hd 92a
4878} **DIGITAL 147** [8] M R Channon 7-9-2 (93) S Hitchcott (3) 33/1: 216002-0: Rear, short of room repeatedly fnl 1f under minimal shd 91a
press:
4106} **YAKIMOV 195** [14] D J Wintle 5-8-9 1ow (85) Dane O'Neill 33/1: 131023-0: Cl up, led 2f out till over 1f out, fdd: nk 83a
632   **FLINT RIVER 35** [12] H Morrison 6-8-3 (80) R L Moore 16/1: 210-2000: Keen & held up, btn dist: ¾ 76a
4675} **ARCTIC DESERT 161** [11] A M Balding 4-8-13 (90) Martin Dwyer 9/2: 004352-0: Keen, in tch wide, btn dist: ¾ 85a
618   **GAELIC PRINCESS 36** [4] A G Newcombe 4-8-8 (85) S Whitworth 16/1: 24030-00: Mid-div, btn 2f out.   shd 80a
3341} **ROYAL DIGNITARY 28** [9] D R Loder 4-9-5 vis (96) J Murtagh 16/1: 500-3650: Led till 2f out, wknd qckly.   5 82a
15 Ran   1m 24.31 (1.51)   Owner Mr A Barnes   Trained at Richmond

888 **4.50 Richard Gibbs Memorial Handicap Stakes 3yo+ 0-85 (D)** [83]
£5174 £1592 £796 £398   **1m p/track rnd**   **Going 13**   **-12 Slow**   Stalls Outside

698* **HARRISON POINT 28** [4] P W Chapple Hyam 4-9-7 (76) R Hughes 7/4 FAV: 10230-11: Held up trav well, smooth prog 2f out   80a
& drvn to lead close home, all out:
547   **LABRETT 45** [11] Miss Gay Kelleway 7-9-12 t p (81) M Fenton 14/1: 061-3052: Handy & led halfway, drvn & hdd cl home: hd 83a
716   **PARAGON OF VIRTUE 25** [3] P Mitchell 7-9-8 (77) J Fanning 10/1: 310-3403: Handy & joined ldr 2f out, drvn & kept on well: nk 78a
800   **SUMMER RECLUSE 16** [7] B R Johnson 5-9-8 p (77) Dane O'Neill 9/1: 013-0054: Dwelt, rear, styd on wide for press, not   ½ 77a
able to chall:
758   **DOWER HOUSE 21** [6] Andrew Turnell 9-9-10 (79) L Dettori 6/1: 0-465405: Held up, kept on wide for press, not able to chall: shd 79a
800* **AFRICAN SAHARA 16** [10] Miss D Mountain 5-9-11 t (80) G Carter 6/1: 26-61016: Held up wide, no impress fnl 2f: 2½ 75a
800* **KENTUCKY KING 16** [2] P W Hiatt 4-9-12 (81) K Darley 9/1: 1/4-66017: Mid-div, no impress dist: ¾ 75a
4350} **ONLYTIME WILL TELL 182** [9] D Nicholls 6-9-10 (79) J Murtagh 14/1: 002500-8: Dwelt, rear, efft 2f out, little hdwy on   1½ 70a
700   **CAROUBIER 26** [12] J Gallagher 4-9-7 vis (76) I Mongan 20/1: 24-52129: Dwelt, rear, no prog: 5 58a
3817} **ATAHUELPA 22** [5] M F Harris 4-9-13 (82) T Quinn 66/1: 4310-000: Chsd ldrs, btn 2f out: 1¾ 61a
4068} **RACING NIGHT 197** [1] J R Best 4-9-10 (79) E Ahern 40/1: 441450-0: Led 1f, btn 3f out, reapp, new yard.   nk 57a
3742*} **SUPER SONG 213** [8] P D Evans 4-9-8 (77) S Donohoe (7) 33/1: 00/201-0: Led after 1f till 4f out, btn 2f out: 13 33a
12 Ran   1m 38.18 (1.98)   Owner R E Sangster M O'Donovan F C   Trained at Newmarket

WOLVERHAMPTON Monday 22.03.04 Lefthand, Sharp Track

Official Going Standard To Slow

889 **2.15 New Site @ Betdirect Co Uk Banded Stakes 3yo+ 0-45 (H)**
£1446 £413 £207   **5f f/sand rnd**   **Going 82**   **+16 Fast**   Stalls Inside

859   **TORRENT 6** [5] D W Chapman 9-9-7 bl (45) A Culhane 11/2: 3153001: Rear, rdn & hdwy when bmpd dist, led ins last, rdn out: 54a
778   **SOAKED 21** [10] D W Chapman 11-9-7 bl (45) S Sanders 9/1: 2600402: Sn handy wide, rdn & led dist, no extra when hdd ins   1 50a
last:
737   **HAGLEY PARK 25** [6] M Quinn 5-9-7 vis (45) D Holland 11/4 FAV: 0-226543: Led early, rem prom, not pace of front pair over   3½ 41a
1f out:
775   **SO SOBER 22** [4] D Shaw 6-9-7 (45) R Winston 3/1: 0-154004: Mid-div, not pace to chall: 3 34a
775   **THE LEATHER WEDGE 22** [11] A Berry 5-9-7 (45) P Bradley (5) 16/1: 20-60405: Led/dsptd lead till dist, no extra.   1 32a
1741} **ABBIEJO 301** [8] G Fierro 7-9-7 P (40) V Slattery 50/1: 660/0-6: Dwelt & outpcd, nrst fin: 1¾ 28a
775   **VALAZAR 22** [9] D W Chapman 5-9-7 BL (45) G Duffield 10/1: 4000-007: Led/dsptd lead 3f, no extra: nk 27a
749   **MANGUS 24** [2] K O Cunningham Brown 10-9-7 bl e (45) N Callan 16/1: 600-3068: Rdn inner, mid-div, no impress fnl 2f: 1 25a
781* **WHITE O MORN 21** [12] B A McMahon 5-9-7 t p (40) G Gibbons 7/1: 0-042419: Al outpcd: hd 24a
830   **LA VIGNA 13** [7] Mrs Lucinda Featherstone 3-8-9 BL (45) C Catlin 50/1: 0000-00: Sn struggling: 1¼ 21a
587   **RELLIM 42** [1] P A Blockley 5-9-7 (45) Dean McKeown 11/2: 2656-500: Prom till over 1f out: 1½ 17a
773   **BOND DOMINGO 22** [3] B Smart 5-9-7 bl (40) F Lynch 14/1: 00000-00: Sn outpcd.   shd 17a

890 2.50 Betdirect Co Uk Claiming Stakes 3yo+ (H)
£1460 £417 £209   7f f/sand rnd   Going 82   -42 Slow   Stalls Outside

12 Ran   1m 03.51 (3.31)   Owner Mr David W Chapman   Trained at York

825	TRAVEL TARDIA 14 [8] I A Wood 6-9-12 T (35) T Hamilton (3) 10/1: 000-0041: Led/dsptd lead, went on after 2f, held on all out cl-home:		53a
851	LEGALIS 8 [6] K A Ryan 6-9-12 bl (55) N Callan 9/4 FAV: 0313642: Dwelt, in tch, drvn & styd on wide fnl 2f, just failed:	hd	52a
646	HEADLAND 35 [10] D W Chapman 6-9-12 bl (53) A Culhane 11/4: 4200303: Chsd ldrs & hdwy to chase wnr 4f out, rdn & found little over 1f out:	5	43a
777	WATERLINE DANCER 21 [9] P D Evans 4-9-5 t (35) R Winston 14/1: 00-00004: Held up, late gains for press, no threat:	nk	35a
826	WELSH WHISPER 14 [1] S A Brookshaw 5-9-3 (35) L Keniry (3) 25/1: 0-004005: In tch, no impress dist:	1¼	30a
864	DANCING KING 5 [2] P W Hiatt 8-9-10 (49) P Makin (7) 7/1: 3154006: Led 1f, remained prom till over 1f out:	½	36a
847	LIVELY FELIX 8 [4] D G Bridgwater 7-9-8 vis (40) B Swarbrick (7) 20/1: 000-4067: Prom, btn 3f out:	6	24a
1885}	LADY XANTHIA 294 [7] I A Wood 3-8-4 (40) G Duffield 20/1: 0066-8: Sn rdn & bhd, abs.	3½	15a
4093}	TODDEANO 198 [3] G Fierro 9-8-8 P V Slattery 50/1: 00-9: Dwelt, sn rdn & al bhd:	6	8a
820	MUQTADI 14 [5] M Quinn 6-9-12 (50) D Holland 7/2: 6041500: Sn bhd, reportedly not face kick-back.	1	10a

891 3.25 Special Offers @ Betdirect Co Uk Banded Stakes 4yo+ 0-45 (H)
£1446 £413 £207   1m4f f/sand   Going 82   -26 Slow   Stalls Inside

10 Ran   1m 34.88 (8.68)   Owner Neardown Stables   Trained at Upper Lambourn

4268}	ISAAF 188 [11] P W Hiatt 5-9-0 (45) P Makin (7) 11/2: 006602-1: Held up, smooth hdwy & led over 3f out, sn clr, val for 10L+:		57a
824	BUZ KIRI 14 [3] A W Carroll 6-9-0 (45) P Doe 5/4 FAV: 2122122: Rear, outpcd halfway, kept on late for press, no threat to wnr:	7	45a
757	ERSAAL 23 [1] J Jay 4-8-12 bl (45) N Callan 8/1: 03000-03: Led till over 3f out, no extra:	7	36a
185	BID SPOTTER 101 [12] Mrs Lucinda Featherstone 5-9-0 P (45) G Duffield 25/1: 204/000-4: In tch, rdn & no impress on ldrs fnl 3f:	1¼	34a
666	VITELUCY 34 [10] Miss S J Wilton 5-9-0 (45) A Quinn (5) 14/1: 0/2100-55: Rear, short of room 3f out, little hdwy.	½	33a
784*	DAFA 20 [7] B J Curley 8-9-0 (45) S W Kelly 4/1: 05///0/-11: Held up, rdn & btn 4f out:	4	27a
867	TOP OF THE CLASS 4 [2] P D Evans 7-9-0 vis (45) Joanna Badger 11/1: 4000357: Chsd ldrs, btn 3f out:	2½	23a
668	NASSAU STREET 34 [5] D J S ffrench Davis 4-8-12 vis (40) C Catlin 20/1: 040-38: Prom till over 2f out:	nk	22a
823	DORA CORBINO 14 [4] R Hollinshead 4-8-12 (40) A Culhane 20/1: 560-5329: In tch till halfway, t.o.:	18	0a
812	PAARL ROCK 17 [9] S T Lewis 9-9-0 vis (45) G Gibbons 20/1: 1/1450//-0: Cl-up, wknd qckly 4f out.	5	0a
4785}	SINGULARITY 157 [6] K F Clutterbuck 4-8-12 (45) M Tebbutt 33/1: 003055-0: Al towards rear, t.o.:	2	0a
2732}	SANDY BAY 258 [8] R Allan 5-9-0 (45) R Winston 25/1: 0/00000-0: Sn bhd & t.o./virtually p.u. fnl 1f:	dist	0a

892 4.00 Bet In Running @ Betdirect Co Uk Median Auction Maiden Stakes 3-5yo (H)
£1432 £409 £205   7f f/sand rnd   Going 82   -24 Slow   Stalls Outside

12 Ran   2m 46.53 (12.93)   Owner Miss Maria McKinney   Trained at Banbury

4988}	RILEY BOYS 140 [4] J G Given 3-8-9 (64) M Fenton 3/1: 033000-1: Made all, strongly prsd fnl 2f, drvn out, gamely:		66a
636	BUNDABERG 36 [7] P W Hiatt 4-9-10 (A) A Culhane 11/2: 05-422: Sn hdwy to chase wnr 4f out, drvn & al just held fnl 1f:	¾	64a
848	ANGELOS PRIDE 8 [2] J A Osborne 3-8-9 (59) S W Kelly 5/4 FAV: 0-302333: Chsd ldrs, rdn & not able to chall:	4	56a
846	FAYR FIRENZE 8 [5] M F Harris 3-8-9 bl (49) S Righton 12/1: 00656-04: Held up, lost tch halfway.	16	28a
	SYBILL [6] J W Unett 4-9-5 J Quinn 16/1: 5: Slow away & sn bhd, nvr factor on debut:	9	8a
1104}	VAUDEVIRE 340 [3] R P Elliott 3-8-9 T Hamilton (3) 20/1: 6-6: Sn rdn & al bhd:	1¾	10a
3475}	SPARTAN ODYSSEY 227 [8] A Senior 3-8-9 N Callan 100/1: 00-7: Cl-up 3f, sn bhd, reapp.	17	0a
848	JACOB 8 [1] P A Blockley 3-8-9 (60) Dean McKeown 9/2: 355-548: Chsd ldrs till 3f out, broke blood vessel:	8	0a

8 Ran   1m 33.65 (7.45)   Owner Mr Paul Riley   Trained at Gainsborough

893 4.35 Bet Direct On 0800 32 93 93 Banded Stakes 3yo+ 0-45 (H)
£1453 £415 £208   1m1f79y f/sand rnd   Going 82   -16 Slow   Stalls Inside

777*	JAKE BLACK 21 [6] J J Quinn 4-9-7 VIS (45) D Holland 9/4: 6500-011: Held up, rdn & outpcd halfway, styd on wide for press fnl 2f to lead well ins last, all out:		51a
776	WILSON BLUEBOTTLE 22 [5] M W Easterby 5-9-7 bl (45) Dale Gibson 9/1: 000-6102: Led after 1f, drvn & hdd ins last, just held:	nk	50a
850	MRS CUBE 8 [1] P Howling 5-9-7 (45) R Winston 5/4 FAV: 060-1133: Led 1f, remained handy, rdn & no extra dist:	6	40a
4809}	GOT TO BE CASH 154 [3] W M Brisbourne 5-9-7 (45) B Swarbrick (7) 4/1: 560260-4: Held up, eff when short of room over 2f out, sn no impress:	1½	37a
614	MORNING HAWK 39 [7] J S Moore 3-8-2 (45) D Kinsella 16/1: 5000-045: Held up, rdn & no impress fnl 3f:	1½	34a
722	RED MOOR 27 [2] R Hollinshead 4-9-7 (45) A Culhane 10/1: 00065-26: Held up in tch, no impress fnl 3f:	nk	33a
828	MIDNIGHT MAMBO 13 [4] R Guest 4-9-7 BL (45) S Sanders 16/1: 05-557: Cl-up halfway, wknd 2f out:	6	23a

7 Ran   2m 07.37 (9.17)   Owner Mr G A Lucas   Trained at Malton

894 5.10 Bet Direct On Sky Active Banded Stakes 3yo+ 0-40 (H)
£1470 £420 £210   1m100y f/sand rnd   Going 82   -18 Slow   Stalls Inside

846	FRAAMTASTIC 8 [13] B A Pearce 7-9-7 p (40) B Reilly (3) 8/1: 0-241601: Prom, rdn/led over 2f out, sn in command & eased nr fin:		50a
3695}	SIX PACK 217 [12] Andrew Turnell 6-9-7 (40) C Catlin 8/1: 000060-2: Mid-div, hdwy to chase wnr 2f out, kept on but al held:	1¼	44a
861	ZAHUNDA 5 [1] W M Brisbourne 5-9-7 (40) M Savage (5) 7/2: 0204633: Led till over 3f out, no extra:	6	34a
847	NEUTRAL NIGHT 8 [8] R Brotherton 4-9-7 vis (40) D Holland 4/1: 3005324: Handy & led over 4f out till over 2f out, no extra:	¾	33a
783	YOUNGS FORTH 20 [4] A W Carroll 4-9-7 (40) J Quinn 10/1: 500-0055: Held up, eff 4f out, no prog dist:	nk	32a
583	RAHJEL SULTAN 42 [2] B A McMahon 6-9-7 t P (40) G Gibbons 10/1: 00540-36: Chsd ldrs, btn dist, abs:	nk	31a
831	REGENCY MALAYA 13 [11] M F Harris 3-8-4 bl t (40) S Righton 10/1: 600-0527: Bhd, eff 3f out, no impress:	7	19a
564	CUMBRIAN PRINCESS 45 [9] M Blanshard 7-9-7 (30) D Sweeney 14/1: 0005-408: Held up, eff 4f out, no impress.	½	18a

WOLVERHAMPTON Monday 22.03.04 Lefthand, Sharp Track

160	**SARN** 105 [6] M Mullineaux 5-9-7 (40) S W Kelly 12/1: 140000-9: Bhd, eff 5f out, btn 2f out:		shd	**18a**
826	**UN AUTRE ESPERE** 14 [10] T Wall 5-9-7 (30) S Sanders 50/1: 0500-060: Sn rdn & al bhd.		¾	**17a**
747	**ILLUSTRIOUS DUKE** 24 [5] M Mullineaux 6-9-7 (40) Lisa Jones (3) 3/1 FAV: 200-0000: Led/dsptd lead till 4f out.		1	**15a**
826	**GARNOCK BELLE** 14 [3] A Berry 3-8-4 (30) Dale Gibson 50/1: 500-0050: Sn bhd.		8	**1a**
648	**ALTARES** 35 [7] P Howling 3-8-4 (40) S Whitworth 33/1: 0000-000: Al bhd, t.o.		16	**0a**
13 Ran	1m 54.74 (8.54) Owner Mr Richard J Gray		Trained at Lingfield	

CURRAGH SUNDAY 21.03.04 Righthand, Galloping Track

Official Going Heavy

895 | **3.45 Listed EBF Fillies Stakes (A)** | | | |
|---|---|---|---|
| | £32712 £9597 £4572 1m | Heavy | Inapplicab |

4933*}	**ALEXANDER GOLDRUN** 148 [2] J S Bolger 3-8-12 K J Manning 6/1: 301221-1: In tch, prog 3f out, led after 2f out & sn 3L clr, rdn out to hold on fnl 1f:			**107**
	BLUE REEMA 134 [10] M Halford 4-9-12 TP T P O'Shea 20/1: 104400-2: Hld up, prog bef 1f out, nrst fin.		1	**100**
	ROYAL TIGRESS 213 [6] A P O'Brien 3-8-9 J P Spencer 5/1: 2-3: Prom, led 2f out, sn hdd, no extra.		1½	**97**
10 Ran	1m 51.20 Owner Mrs N O'Callaghan		Trained at Coolcullen	

LINGFIELD Tuesday 23.03.04 Lefthand, V Sharp Track

Official Going Standard

896 | **2.00 Bet Direct Champs League Cashbacks Amateur Riders' Handicap Stakes 4yo+ 46-55 (F)** | | | **[40]** |
|---|---|---|---|
| | £2961 £846 £423 1m5f p/track Going 24 -20 Slow | Stalls Inside | |

805	**GREAT VIEW** 19 [14] Mrs A L M King 5-10-5 1oh vis (45) Mr S Walker 11/1: 55432-01: Rear, hdwy 4f out & led over 1f out, rdn out:			**54a**
768	**GOLDEN DUAL** 23 [4] S Dow 4-10-9 VIS (53) Mr D Hutchison (7) 20/1: 0060002: Mid-div inner, hdwy when no room over 1f out, styd on well:		1¼	**58a**
866	**SUNGIO** 6 [11] B G Powell 6-10-11 bl (52) Mrs R Powell (7) 16/1: 5-131233: Handy & dsptd lead after 4f, led 3f out till over 1f out, no extra for press:		3	**53a**
4352]	**FFIFFIFFER** 192 [6] C Tinkler 6-11-0 (55) Mr Nicky Tinkler 9/2: 005225-4: Led till 3f out, no extra dist:		2	**52a**
827	**FREE STYLE** 14 [1] K R Burke 4-10-2 4oh (45) Mr S Dobson (3) 14/1: 6301455: Mid-div, short of room & lost place 4f out, kept on wide fnl 2f, no dngr:		½	**42a**
722	**OUR GLENARD** 28 [9] S L Keightley 5-10-5 1oh (45) Miss A L Turner (5) 16/1: 05-22056: In tch wide, no impress fnl 2f.		nk	**41a**
18	**CLASSIC MILLENNIUM** 132 [3] W J Musson 6-10-5 (46) Miss J Pledge (7) 10/1: 540155-7: Slow away & rear, mod late prog:		hd	**40a**
812	**MAKARIM** 18 [5] M R Bosley 8-11-0 p (55) Mrs S Bosley 9/1: 63-00358: Rear/wide, only mod prog:		5	**42a**
4609}	**JENAVIVE** 171 [7] N J Hawke 4-10-5 (49) Mr L Newnes (5) 14/1: 002203-9: Mid-div, no impress fnl 3f:		2½	**32a**
842*	**CHOCOLATE BOY** 9 [8] G L Moore 5-10-9 sex bl e (50) Mr E Dehdashti 13/8 FAV: 0-524410: Mid-div, hmpd 5f out when sn btn:		2	**30a**
344]	**ESTUARY** 805 [12] Ms A E Embiricos 9-10-12 (53) Ms A Embiricos (3) 66/1: 32060/0/-0: Chsd ldrs 11f, sn btn, abs.		1½	**31a**
3539}	**FLETCHER** 224 [13] H Morrison 10-10-5 1oh (45) Miss G D Gracey Davison (7) 20/1: 006204-0: Chsd ldrs, btn 5f out, reapp.		nk	**23a**
827	**ESSAY BABY** 14 [10] P D Cundell 4-10-2 4oh (45) Miss C Nosworthy (7) 33/1: 050-4400: Keen & prom 3f, lost tch from halfway.		4	**17a**
13 Ran	2m 48.06 (5.76) Owner All The Kings Horses		Trained at Stratford-On-Avon	

897 | **2.30 Cashbacks @ Bet Direct On Sky Active Handicap Stakes Div 1 3yo+ 0-70 (E)** | | | **[70]** |
|---|---|---|---|
| | £3416 £1051 £526 £263 6f p/track rnd Going 24 -05 Slow | Stalls Inside | |

880	**MAYZIN** 4 [7] R M Flower 4-9-6 p (62) D Sweeney 5/1 FAV: 2412331: Cl-up & led over 2f out, drvn & held on well, gamely:			**69a**
685	**SPINDOR** 32 [11] J A Osborne 5-9-2 bl (58) D Holland 12/1: 50-25342: Rdn towards rear, switched wide & styd on well fnl 2f, took 2nd cl-home:		½	**62a**
874	**POLAR FORCE** 4 [2] M R Channon 4-9-3 (59) D Corby (3) 13/2: 003-4003: Trkd ldrs, kept on fnl 2f.		shd	**63a**
880	**HARD TO CATCH** 4 [6] D K Ivory 6-10-0 bl (70) L Treadwell (7) 6/1: 0024104: Hld up, eff 2f out, onepace.		½	**72a**
501	**AMELIA** 54 [4] W M Brisbourne 6-8-7 (49) B Swarbrick (7) 16/1: 602-5255: Trkd ldrs, onepace for press dist.		½	**49a**
740*	**A TEEN** 26 [13] P Howling 6-8-11 (53) R Winston 14/1: 00-520016: Dwelt, swtchd & mid-div, drvn & onepace dist.		nk	**52a**
853	**LADIES KNIGHT** 7 [3] D Shaw 4-8-13 (55) Darren Williams 10/1: 3250637: Dwelt, held up, not pace to chall.		½	**52a**
874	**SOUNDS LUCKY** 4 [12] Andrew Reid 8-9-1 (57) S Sanders 16/1: 0501268: Dwelt, switched inner, no dngr.		1	**51a**
788	**LAW MAKER** 21 [9] M A Buckley 4-7-12 5oh (35) Lisa Jones (7) 66/1: 0-000069: Trkd ldrs wide, no extra over 1f out:		shd	**34a**
4986}	**DAVIDS MARK** 142 [5] J R Jenkins 4-9-1 (57) W Ryan 9/1: 035030-0: Mid-div, eff wide from halfway, btn dist:		shd	**54a**
748	**MYND** 25 [1] R M Whitaker 4-9-10 (66) Dean McKeown 8/1: 034-1120: Led till 2f out, fdd under press:		nk	**58a**
819	**LEGAL SET** 15 [10] W J Musson 8-9-0 (56) R Hughes 10/1: 600-4050: In tch wide till halfway:		1	**45a**
123	**JAGGED** 115 [14] K R Burke 4-9-4 (60) G Baker 33/1: 402630-0: Rear/wide, no ch fnl 3f, abs.		2½	**41a**
806	**ROY MCAVOY** 18 [8] Mrs G Harvey 6-8-13 (55) Joanna Badger 50/1: 00000-00: Dwelt & sn bhd.		3	**27a**
14 Ran	1m 12.11 (1.71) Owner Ms Zoe Watkins		Trained at Jevington	

898 | **3.00 Cashbacks @ Betdirect Co Uk Maiden Stakes 3yo (D)** | | | |
|---|---|---|---|
| | £3731 £1148 £574 £287 6f p/track rnd Going 24 -21 Slow | Stalls Inside | |

4714}	**PRESTO SHINKO** 162 [3] R Hannon 3-9-0 (78) R Hughes 11/8 FAV: 033-1: Trkd ldr trav well, led over 2f out, qcknd clr under hands & heels, val 6L+:			**82a**
	KING OF DIAMONDS 6 [6] J R Best 3-9-0 N Pollard 20/1: 2: Rear, switched & shaken up over 1f out, styd on strongly, no ch with wnr:		3	**64a**
4412}	**TORQUEMADA** 182 [8] W Jarvis 3-9-0 P Doe 13/2: 60-3: Keen & sn cl-up, outpcd from dist:		¾	**62a**

4887}	**BOLD WOLF** 150 [2] J L Spearing 3-9-0 (54) A Daly 25/1: 000020-4: Led 2f, no extra dist	2½	54a
621	**SIMPSONS MOUNT** 38 [11] R M Flower 3-9-0 R L Moore 20/1: 65: Dwelt, rear, rdn & mod prog.	½	52a
623	**SUSSEX STYLE** 38 [7] R M Flower 3-9-0 D Sweeney 50/1: 0-006: Mid-div, no impress fnl 2f.	nk	51a
764	**IMPERIUM** 23 [1] Mrs Stef Liddiard 3-9-0 t (75) S Drowne 3/1: 20046-47: Trkd ldrs, btn over 1f out	nk	50a
3597}	**SWORN TO SECRECY** 222 [9] S Kirk 3-8-9 (69) D Holland 6/1: 0435-8: Handy, no room over 2f out, wknd.	1	42a
652	**TOP PLACE** 36 [4] C A Dwyer 3-8-9 p C Cogan 50/1: 0-009: Mid-div when short of room after 2f, no prog fnl 2f	½	40a
	MR HULLABALOU [5] R Ingram 3-9-0 S Sanders 33/1: 0: Slow away & al outpcd on debut.	1½	40a
751	**FORA SMILE** 25 [10] M D I Usher 3-9-0 (45) W Ryan 50/1: 00000: Handy & led 4f out till 2f out, `lost action'.	2	34a
11 Ran	1m 13.07 (2.67) Owner Major A M Everett	Trained at Marlborough	

---

899   **3.30** Cashbacks @ Bet Direct Interactive Claiming Stakes 3yo   (F)

£2884 £824 £412   **1m2f** p/track   Going 24   **-69 Slow**   Stalls Inside. Slow Time.

686	**REGULATED** 32 [7] J A Osborne 3-9-1 (65) D Holland 4/1: 0450-201: Mid-div outer, rdn & hdwy to lead over 1f out, drvn out		65a
497	**PLATINUM PIRATE** 55 [2] K R Burke 3-8-9 bl (55) G Faulkner 8/1: 6000-202: Keen & sn handy, led 3f out till over 1f out, hung right under press, no extra	1	57a
848	**CASPIAN DUSK** 9 [8] W G M Turner 3-8-13 (53) C Haddon (7) 11/2: 406-23: Held up in tch, drvn & styd on fnl 2f, not pace to chall	shd	61a
843	**FOOT FAULT** 9 [11] N A Callaghan 3-8-8 (57) W Ryan 5/2 FAV: 0046-044: Rear & switched inner, switched wide/chsd ldrs over 1f out, no extra	hd	55a
658	**FRAMBO** 35 [1] J G Portman 3-8-4 p (49) R L Moore 10/1: 0625-005: Led till 3f out, no extra	5	44a
841	**DOCTORED** 9 [5] B A Pearce 3-8-13 bl (50) B Reilly (3) 7/1: 023-0046: Prom, no impress fnl 3f:	¾	52a
871	**QUARRY ISLAND** 5 [10] P D Evans 3-7-12 BL (45) B Swarbrick (7) 20/1: 40-52007: Prom, rdn & btn 2f out	nk	36a
4611}	**BUNINO VEN** 169 [4] S C Williams 3-8-9 Paul Eddery 8/1: 000-8: Held up in tch, btn 3f out:	7	38a
721	**MYSTIC PROMISE** 28 [3] Mrs N Macauley 3-8-9 vis T (30) Hayley Turner (5) 50/1: 00-00059: Mid-div, short of room & drpd rear 5f out, sn btn:	2½	32a
9 Ran	2m 12.07 (9.27) Owner Mr Richard Leslie	Trained at Upper Lambourn	

---

900   **4.00** Cashbacks @ Attheraces Text Page 410 Handicap Stakes Div 1   3yo+ 0-75 (E)   [75]

£3377 £1039 £520 £260   **1m2f** p/track   Going 24   **-02 Slow**   Stalls Inside

803	**SAY WHAT YOU SEE** 19 [1] J W Hills 4-9-11 (72) M Hills 11/4 FAV: 200-0421: Made all, edged right under press, held on gamely for press:		78a
83	**SIENA STAR** 122 [6] P F I Cole 6-10-0 (75) R Hughes 100/30: 610250-2: Held up, drvn to chall ins last, just held cl-home:	nk	80a
803	**KATIYPOUR** 19 [3] Miss B Sanders 7-9-8 (69) S Sanders 13/2: 61346-03: Trkd ldrs inner, drvn & kept on fnl 2f, not btn far:	nk	73a
803	**SILVALINE** 19 [2] T Keddy 5-9-4 (65) G Carter 9/2: 1033-604: Trkd ldrs, drvn & onepace from dist:	1	67a
520	**LYRICAL WAY** 52 [9] P R Chamings 5-9-1 vis (62) S Drowne 12/1: 2221-405: Dwelt, rear, drvn & only mod prog, abs.	½	63a
4655}	**COMPTON AVIATOR** 167 [5] A W Carroll 8-8-9 t (56) D Holland 8/1: 530244-6: Held up in tch, not able to chall:	1½	54a
726	**HALLINGS OVERTURE** 27 [7] C A Horgan 5-9-2 (63) Paul Eddery 14/1: 0500/67: Mid-div outer, btn over 1f out.	3½	57a
786*	**HAITHEM** 21 [4] D Shaw 7-7-12 t (45) Lisa Jones (3) 20/1: 0605618: Keen, prom, btn 3f out:	7	30a
8 Ran	2m 05.39 (2.59) Owner Mr Richard Tufft & Mr Ken Wilk	Trained at Lambourn	

---

901   **4.30** Cashbacks @ Sky Text Page 372 Handicap Stakes Fillies 3yo 0-70 (E)   [76]

£3465 £1066 £533 £267   **7f** p/track rnd   Going 24   **-22 Slow**   Stalls Inside

798	**ALEXANDER AMBITION** 19 [3] S Kirk 3-9-2 (64) R Hughes 7/1: 20-43421: Cl-up & led over 1f out, drvn out:		69a
815	**PARK AVE PRINCESS** 15 [1] N P Littmoden 3-8-11 (59) D Holland 9/2: 60-22532: Led till over 1f out, drvn & kept on well, just held:	nk	63a
802*	**KRYSSA** 19 [9] G L Moore 3-8-12 (60) R L Moore 4/1 FAV: 413: Mid-div, short of room over 1f out, switched & styd on well for press cl-home, nrst fnl:	1½	61a
815	**DOCKLANDS BLUE** 15 [5] N P Littmoden 3-8-6 (54) C Catlin 10/1: 0-200364: Rear, styd on for press fnl 2f, not able to chall:	shd	55a
872	**JAOLINS** 5 [2] P G Murphy 3-8-8 (56) S Drowne 25/1: 60-12005: Trkd ldrs halfway, onepace for press:	1	55a
760	**MAN CRAZY** 24 [10] R M Beckett 3-8-12 (60) J Mackay 20/1: 32300-06: Held up wide, kept on onepace:	hd	58a
4885}	**THE STICK** 150 [4] M R Channon 3-9-1 (63) S Hitchcott (3) 16/1: 656-7: Mid-div, rdn & not pace to chall:	shd	61a
670	**LA PETITE CHINOISE** 34 [7] R Guest 3-9-7 BL (69) S Sanders 16/1: 3406-68: Chsd ldrs wide, no extra 2f out.	¾	66a
843	**TROMPE LOEIL** 9 [8] Andrew Reid 3-8-12 P (60) S Carson 33/1: 240-0069: Switched inner & rear, only mod prog.	nk	56a
846	**SONDERBORG** 9 [7] G L Moore 3-8-3 bl e (51) Lisa Jones (3) 11/2: 4532220: Chsd ldrs, btn over 1f out.	hd	46a
764	**LADY PREDOMINANT** 23 [11] Andrew Reid 3-7-12 1oh (45) B Swarbrick (7) 25/1: 20-44060: Hld up, no dngr.	1¼	38a
4700}	**DANIFAH** 163 [15] P D Evans 3-8-12 (60) S W Kelly 50/1: U00000-0: Dwelt, wide/rear, no impress, reapp.	2	48a
4669}	**SPRING DANCER** 165 [6] A P Jarvis 3-9-5 (67) J Quinn 12/1: 206600-0: Chsd ldrs, btn 2f out:	2½	50a
783	**ZONNEBEKE** 21 [13] K R Burke 3-7-12 1oh (45) Dale Gibson 20/1: 0-452030: Mid-div, btn 3f out:	1¾	26a
87	**YAMATO PINK** 120 [14] K R Burke 3-7-12 (46) Joanna Badger 50/1: 504660-0: Chsd ldrs 4f, abs.	1	24a
15 Ran	1m 26.04 (3.24) Owner Mrs N O'Callaghan	Trained at Upper Lambourn	

---

902   **5.00** Cashbacks @ Bet Direct On Sky Active Handicap Stakes Div 2   3yo+ 0-70 (E)   [70]

£3416 £1051 £526 £263   **6f** p/track rnd   Going 24   **+07 Fast**   Stalls Inside

880	**DOUBLE M** 4 [1] Mrs L Richards 7-9-0 vis (56) R Hughes 11/4 FAV: 1302421: Trkd ldrs, rdn & led ins last, sn clr, cmftbly:		66a
698	**TAYIF** 31 [9] Andrew Reid 8-9-9 t (65) S Carson 6/1: 2112602: Dwelt, switched inner & held up, styd on for press fnl 1f, no threat to wnr:	1¾	68a
728	**NEW OPTIONS** 27 [2] W J Musson 7-9-1 (57) Lisa Jones (3) 12/1: 4-540503: Mid-div inner, styd on for press, not pace to	½	58a
760	**WOODBURY** 24 [7] K R Burke 5-8-11 (53) G Baker 12/1: 5D260-04: Cl-up, rdn/no extra dist:	hd	53a
741	**TEYAAR** 26 [3] Mrs N Macauley 8-8-13 (55) Hayley Turner (5) 16/1: 3-006005: Led, drvn & hdd ins last, no extra:	¾	53a
844	**LONG WEEKEND** 9 [8] D Shaw 6-8-6 vis (48) Darren Williams (5) 16/1: 6621146: Mid-div, not pace to chall:	1½	41a
880	**ILLUSIVE** 4 [12] M Wigham 5-9-4 bl (60) G Carter 14/1: 2-003507: Rear/wide, no prog dist:	1	50a
878	**PHECKLESS** 4 [6] J M Bradley 5-9-10 (66) D Holland 12/1: 4-034008: Keen & trkd ldrs, btn over 1f out:	¾	54a

23	SALON PRIVE 131 [11] C A Cyzer 4-9-0 (65) S Sanders 15/2: 0232-9: Mid-div wide, no prog 2f out:		4	42a
684	CARLTON 32 [13] C R Dore 10-9-1 (57) R Thomas (5) 20/1: 000-0440: Rear & wide, no prog:		shd	34a
400	HAPPY CAMPER 69 [5] M R Hoad 4-9-4 (60) D Sweeney 50/1: 30245-00: Prom till halfway:		shd	36a
819	FIREWORK 15 [10] J Akehurst 6-9-2 (58) J Quinn 20/1: 3420-000: Chsd ldrs 4f.		3½	24a
641	OUR CHELSEA BLUE 36 [4] I A Wood 6-8-9 t (51) R Miles (3) 13/2: 660-0360: V slow away, switched wide & nvr a factor:		½	15a
13 Ran	1m 12.14 (1.74) Owner Mr Bryan Mathieson		Trained at Chichester	

903 5.30 Cashbacks @ Attheraces Text Page 410 Handicap Stakes Div 2 3yo+ 0-75 (E) [75]
£3377 £1039 £520 £260   1m2f p/track   Going 24   -14 Slow   Stalls Inside

805*	STEELY DAN 19 [2] J R Best 5-9-3 (64) N Pollard 9/4 FAV: 0221311: Rear, smooth hdwy under hands & heels to lead ins last, readily:		76a	
769	BURGUNDY 23 [9] P Mitchell 7-8-10 BL (57) R L Moore 10/1: 010-6342: Slow away & rear, hdwy to chall dist, not pace of wnr ins last:		¾	62a
714	TRUE COMPANION 28 [6] N P Littmoden 5-9-5 (66) D Holland 11/2: 33-01303: Mid-div, no room over 1f out till ins last, styd on:		nk	70a
803	ABSOLUTE UTOPIA 19 [4] J L Spearing 11-9-2 (63) A Daly 12/1: 01-02234: In tch, rdn & onepace fnl 2f.		½	65a
716	REBATE 28 [8] R Hannon 4-9-9 (70) P Dobbs 14/1: 14000-05: Keen in mid-div, onepace over 1f out.		nk	71a
731	ADALAR 27 [7] P D Evans 4-9-7 (68) S W Kelly 16/1: 0/0-00006: Chsd ldrs, onepace when sltly hmpd dist.		½	68a
685	CAPTAIN DARLING 32 [5] R M H Cowell 4-9-1 (62) R Hughes 9/1: 44543-67: Led/dsptd lead till ins last, no extra:		1	61a
738*	SCOTTYS FUTURE 26 [3] D R Loder 6-10-0 (75) J Murtagh 4/1: 00-01018: Dwelt, rear, eff wide, btn dist:		shd	74a
726	MY MAITE 27 [1] R Ingram 5-8-9 vis (56) S Sanders 9/1: 036-2409: Led after 5f till over 1f out, wknd:		1¼	53a
9 Ran	2m 06.6 (3.8) Owner Mr E A Condon		Trained at Maidstone	

Official Going STANDARD

904 2.10 New Site @ Betdirect Co Uk Banded Stakes 3yo+ 0-35 (H)
£1453 £415 £208   5f f/sand str   Going 87   +09 Fast   Stalls Outside

830	CARONTE 14 [10] S R Bowring 4-9-7 h bl (30) J Bramhill 33/1: 0-000001: Outpcd early, hdwy over 1f out, drvn to lead nr fin:		34a	
781	TUSCAN DREAM 22 [6] A Berry 9-9-7 (30) P Bradley (5) 20/1: 60-00002: Led till over 3f out, led again over 1f out, edged left & no extra when hdd nr fin:		¾	30a
778	FLYING FAISAL 22 [5] J M Bradley 6-9-7 (35) P Fitzsimons 5/1: 0604003: Chsd ldrs, styd on fnl 1f.		shd	29a
631	MIND THE TIME 38 [11] J Hetherton 3-8-9 (35) M Tebbutt 20/1: 0-064: Rear, kept on late.		1½	24a
832	LEVELLED 14 [9] D W Chapman 10-9-7 bl (35) A Culhane 9/4 FAV: 0-000045: Chsd ldrs, ch over 1f out, onepcd fnl 1f.		nk	23a
781	LONE PIPER 22 [4] J M Bradley 9-9-7 (35) S Whitworth 9/4 FAV: 0006436: Chsd ldrs, hdwy 2f out, no extra.		½	21a
720	MR UPPITY 28 [8] Julian Poulton 5-9-7 e (35) M Halford (7) 10/1: 50000-07: Outpcd, styd on fnl 1f, not reach ldrs.		hd	20a
667	MAGIC EAGLE 35 [2] P T Midgley 7-9-7 VIS (35) R Fitzpatrick 11/1: 0000/-5008: Rear, hdwy to lead over 3f out, hdd over 1f out, no extra:		hd	19a
619	BURKEES GRAW 39 [12] Mrs S Lamyman 3-8-9 (35) G Duffield 20/1: 5300-009: Midfield, nvr nr ldrs.		hd	18a
4516}	THE LADY WOULD 176 [3] D G Bridgwater 5-9-7 (35) Derek Nolan (7) 10/1: 0/50000-0: Al bhd.		¾	16a
781	DIAMOND RACKET 22 [7] D W Chapman 4-9-7 bl (30) K Dalgleish 16/1: 0000-060: Nvr a factor.		7	0a
637	GRUFF 37 [1] P T Midgley 5-9-7 (30) G Parkin 40/1: 0000-000: Rear, nvr nr ldrs.		nk	0a
12 Ran	1m 1.7 (3.9) Owner Mr D H Bowring		Trained at Edwinstowe	

905 2.40 Betdirect Co Uk Amateur Riders' Claiming Stakes 4yo+ (H)
£1460 £417 £209   1m f/sand rnd   Going 87   -26 Slow   Stalls Inside

647	OUR DESTINY 36 [6] D Burchell 6-10-10 vis (50) Miss E Tucker (7) 13/2: 02-32401: Al handy, chsd ldr over 4f out, led over 2f out, pushed out:		50a	
852	SEA YA MAITE 9 [7] S R Bowring 10-10-12 t (35) Mrs M Morris 11/1: 2354502: Chsd ldrs, styd on fnl 1f, not reach wnr:		3½	44a
805	PRINCE MINATA 19 [9] P W Hiatt 9-10-10 (40) Miss A Hockley (7) 12/1: 0006-003: Chsd ldrs, lost plc over 2f out, kept on fnl 1f:		2½	37a
811	IAMBACK 18 [5] Miss Gay Kelleway 4-10-7 p (48) Mr G Bartley (7) 10/1: 6-261604: Handy, onepace fnl 2f:		shd	33a
850	RED DELIRIUM 9 [3] P A Blockley 8-11-0 bl (50) Mr Shaun Johnson (7) 5/1: 4-645255: Rear, some late gains.		½	39a
778	LEVANTINE 22 [13] A G Newcombe 7-10-12 p (40) Miss C Hannaford (4) 11/1: 0633-356: Made most over 5f, no extra.		nk	36a
868	NOBLE PURSUIT 5 [10] P A Blockley 7-11-0 (53) Miss S Renwick (5) 3/1 FAV: 2003557: Chsd ldrs, wknd 2f out.		¾	36a
340	RATHMULLAN 76 [12] E A Wheeler 5-11-0 (35) Mr C Witheford (7) 50/1: 00000-08: With ldr, lost place 4f out, wknd & btn over 2f out:		3½	29a
738	CROWN CITY 26 [1] B P J Baugh 6-10-7 t (35) Miss Kelly Harrison (3) 28/1: 0600-009: Rear, nvr nr ldrs.		8	6a
777	MR PERRY 22 [4] Mrs P Ford 8-10-8 (30) Mr K Ford (7) 22/1: 56/00//-05: In tch, lost place & btn after 4f.		2	3a
830	TERN INTERN 14 [2] Miss J Feilden 5-10-8 (30) Miss Fiona Brown (7) 33/1: 0/000-000: Al bhd.		27	0
2402}	BETTERTHEDEVILUNO 993 [8] D McCain 5-10-12 Mr D F Williams (7) 40/1: 3/-0: Rear, hdwy 6f out, wknd.		14	0
12 Ran	1m 48.5 (9.1) Owner Three Acres Racing		Trained at Ebbw Vale	

906 3.10 Special Offers @ Betdirect Co Uk Banded Stakes 4yo+ 0-35 (H)
£1449 £414 £207   1m3f f/sand   Going 87   -13 Slow   Stalls Inside

852	CUMWHITTON 9 [4] R A Fahey 5-9-1 P (30) P Hanagan 8/1: 56//60-501: Chsd ldrs, led well over 1f out, rdn on fnl 1f:		40a	
4359}	THATS RACING 185 [8] J Hetherton 4-9-0 (35) G Duffield 7/1: 600000-2: Chsd ldr, led over 3f out till well over 1f out, no extra:		7	28a
826	SPIDERS WEB 15 [5] T Keddy 4-9-0 bl (35) N Callan 6/1: 0000B23: Chsd ldrs, wknd over 1f out.		8	16a
852	SAMAR QAND 9 [2] Julian Poulton 5-9-1 t (35) M Tebbutt 3/1 FAV: 653-5334: Chsd ldrs, wknd 3f out.		2½	12a
852	TROJAN WOLF 9 [3] P Howling 9-9-1 (35) A Culhane 7/1: 000-0405: Led till over 3f out, no extra.		2	9a
852	MATHMAGICIAN 9 [9] R F Marvin 5-9-1 bl (35) L Fletcher (3) 9/2: 0-454046: Rear, nvr nr ldrs:		1	7a

852	**THINK QUICK** 9 [7] R Hollinshead 4-9-0 (35) R Kennemore (7) 16/1: 6340307: Rear, wknd 3f out:	1½ 5a
1827}	**WETHAAB** 298 [6] Miss A Stokell 7-9-1 t p (35) Ann Stokell 12/1: 034000-8: Rear, wknd 3f out:	4 0a
791	**SAMBA BEAT** 20 [1] R F Marvin 5-9-1 bl (35) P McCabe 20/1: 0/050-009: Keen in rear, wknd 4f out.	13 0a
9 Ran	2m 32.35 (11.05) Owner Mr J Roundtree	Trained at Malton

907 3.40 Bet In Running @ Betdirect Co Uk Banded Stakes 3yo+ 0-45 (H)
£1439 £411 £206 6f f/sand rnd Going 87 -09 Slow Stalls Inside

773	**ABOVE BOARD** 23 [9] R F Marvin 9-9-7 t (45) L Fletcher (3) 16/1: 5020301: Chsd ldrs, led well ins fnl 1f, drvn out:	52a
858	**LARGS** 7 [6] J Balding 4-9-7 (45) J Edmunds 2/1 FAV: 345-0332: Midfield, hdwy over 1f out, styd on under press:	1¾ 46a
822+*	**ON THE TRAIL** 15 [4] D W Chapman 7-9-7 (45) A Culhane 5/1: 0-000013: Chsd ldrs, led dist till ins last, no extra:	hd 45a
773	**BELLS BOYS** 23 [8] K A Ryan 5-9-7 p (40) N Callan 12/1: 05-33504: Led to over 1f out, no extra:	2 39a
775	**HEATHYARDSBLESSING** 23 [7] R Hollinshead 7-9-7 (45) Stephanie Hollinshead (7) 17/2: 3-065035: Rear, late gains.	2 33a
822	**EVANGELIST** 15 [5] Mrs Stef Liddiard 4-9-7 t p (45) M Fenton 10/1: 00-30106: Outpcd, kept on fnl 1f but not rch ldrs:	nk 32a
851	**DUSTY WUGG** 9 [10] A Dickman 5-9-7 p (45) A Beech (3) 12/1: 0040-537: Rear, hdwy over 3f out, onepcd 2f out.	1 29a
783	**MALAAH** 21 [1] Julian Poulton 8-9-7 bl (40) M Halford (7) 11/1: 000-0048: Chsd ldrs, lost place 2f out & btn.	shd 28a
844	**ATTORNEY** 9 [3] D Shaw 6-9-7 vis (45) G Duffield 5/1: 4006539: In tch, wknd 3f out:	3 19a
773	**WUB CUB** 23 [2] A Dickman 4-9-7 (40) P Hanagan 33/1: 00400-00: In tch, sn outpcd & btn:	7 0a
10 Ran	1m 19.1 (5.8) Owner Mr W I Bloomfield	Trained at Rolleston

908 4.10 Bet Direct On 0800 32 93 93 Banded Stakes 3yo+ 0-45 (H)
£1449 £414 £207 1m f/sand rnd Going 87 -12 Slow Stalls Inside

850	**PRINTSMITH** 9 [6] J R Norton 7-9-8 (45) J Bramhill 8/1: 5-144321: Rear, hdwy over 2f out, led well ins fnl 1f, drvn out:	50a
847*	**SMART SCOT** 9 [5] B P J Baugh 5-10-0 p (45) M Savage (5) 11/10 FAV: 60-11112: Pressed ldr, led over 3f out till ins fnl 1f, no extra:	1 53a
776	**MR WHIZZ** 23 [7] A P Jones 7-9-8 bl e (45) Derek Nolan (7) 16/1: 00-01443: Prsd ldr, led after 2f till 3f out, wknd fnl 1f:	5 37a
850*	**KENNY THE TRUTH** 9 [1] Mrs J Candlish 5-10-0 t (40) N Callan 3/1: 2334514: Chsd ldrs, wknd dist.	3½ 36a
893	**JAKE BLACK** 1 [2] J J Quinn 4-9-8 vis (45) L Fletcher (3) 7/2: 6500-015: Led 2f, wknd halfway:	18 0a
5 Ran	1m 47.35 (7.95) Owner Mrs Hazel Tattersall	Trained at Barnsley

909 4.40 Bet Direct On Sky Active Banded Stakes 3yo+ 0-35 (H)
£1453 £415 £208 7f f/sand rnd Going 87 -22 Slow Stalls Inside

3126}	**TEE JAY KASSIDY** 243 [13] Julian Poulton 4-9-7 (35) M Halford (7) 16/1: 005004-1: Chsd ldrs, switched left 1f out, drvn & styd on well to lead nr fin:	38a
30	**BAYTOWN FLYER** 130 [12] P S McEntee 4-9-7 (35) P Makin (7) 8/1: 000000-2: Handy, bmpd over 1f out, sn led, hdd & no extra nr fin:	shd 37a
830	**MIMAS GIRL** 14 [9] S R Bowring 5-9-7 t p (35) J Bramhill 7/1: 0530003: Prsd ldr, ev ch entr fnl 1f, just btn in a tight fin:	nk 36a
719	**MONKEY OR ME** 28 [11] P T Midgley 3-8-6 (30) R Fitzpatrick 33/1: 00-004: Rear, hdwy over 2f out, styd on fnl 1f:	1¾ 32a
826	**CATERHAM COMMON** 15 [2] D W Chapman 5-9-7 bl (30) L Fletcher (3) 16/1: 00-06005: Made most till dist.	1 30a
394	**SENNEN COVE** 69 [4] R Bastiman 5-9-7 (35) K Dalgleish 7/1: 5000-006: Chsd ldrs, no extra fnl 1f:	½ 29a
781	**ONLY FOR GOLD** 22 [8] Dr P Pritchard 9-9-7 (30) S Whitworth 5/1: 00600-57: Chsd ldrs, lost pl halfway, kept on.	1 27a
830	**MISS MILLIETANT** 14 [1] L Montague Hall 3-8-6 (30) G Duffield 11/1: 00-068: Chsd ldrs, wknd over 1f out.	2½ 22a
857	**GALAXY FALLON** 7 [5] M Dods 6-9-7 (30) L Enstone (3) 20/1: 600/00/-69: In tch, sn outpcd & btn.	5 12a
297	**SAWAH** 80 [6] D Shaw 4-9-7 (30) N Callan 9/2 FAV: 0006-50: In tch, sn outpcd & btn:	1½ 9a
4550}	**MISS OCEAN MONARCH** 174 [3] D W Chapman 4-9-7 (30) A Culhane 7/1: 530440-0: Rear, nvr nr ldrs on reapp.	½ 8a
830	**POOKAS DAUGHTER** 14 [10] J M Bradley 4-9-7 p (30) P Fitzsimons 9/1: 0000200: Chsd ldrs, lost pl 3f out.	8 0a
12 Ran	1m 34.25 (7.65) Owner Meddler Bloodstock	Trained at Newmarket

Official Going Standard

910 1.25 Lenham Winners Cup Handicap Stakes Div 1 3yo+ 46-55 (F) [59]
£2940 £840 £420 1m p/track rnd Going 26 -17 Slow Stalls Outside

820	**LUCID DREAMS** 16 [9] M Wigham 5-9-10 p (55) J Fanning 3/1: 5041231: Held up trav well, short of room over 1f out, hands & heels to lead well ins last:	60a
710*	**BELTANE** 30 [4] W de Best Turner 6-9-1 1oh (45) S Righton 14/1: 0/0/P-0012: Rear, hdwy wide over 2f out, rdn & led ins last, sn hdd, just held:	nk 50a
769	**LUCAYAN MONARCH** 24 [10] P S McEntee 6-9-10 p (55) J Murtagh 9/4 FAV: 5002323: Handy wide, rdn & led over 1f out till ins last, no extra:	1¾ 56a
763	**PAS DE SURPRISE** 24 [5] P D Evans 6-9-8 (53) S W Kelly 7/1: 64-30554: Trkd ldrs, chall dist, no extra.	1¾ 51a
814	**WODHILL BE** 16 [6] D Morris 4-9-7 (52) D Holland 8/1: 0-565: Rear, switched wide for eff over 1f out, no impress:	1¾ 47a
623	**FIRST OF MAY** 39 [2] M A Jarvis 3-8-5 (53) M Henry 3/1: 0-346: Led till over 1f out, sn btn:	3 42a
710	**LADY LIESEL** 30 [3] J Bridger 4-9-1 6oh (40) J F McDonald 33/1: 000-0037: Cl-up till 2f out, wknd.	1 33a
7 Ran	1m 39.67 (3.47) Owner Reds Bar Four Partnership II	Trained at Newmarket

911 1.55 E E S Lightning Median Auction Maiden Stakes 3-4yo (F)
£2975 £850 £425 7f p/track rnd Going 26 -16 Slow Stalls Inside

	IFTERADH [10] B Hanbury 3-8-9 1ow D Holland 14/1: 1: Keen & cl-up after 1f, led ins last & asserted under hand riding, cmftbly:	91a
4751}	**INSTRUCTOR** 161 [2] R Hannon 3-8-8 (78) R Hughes 4/6 FAV: 042-2: Led, hdd on ins last, no extra:	¾ 84a
4002}	**WARDEN COMPLEX** 205 [4] J R Fanshawe 3-8-8 Dane O'Neill 7/2: 3-3: Keen mid-div, short of room over 1f out, took 3rd ins last, no threat to front pair:	3 75a
875	**CHEEKY CHI** 5 [8] P S McEntee 3-8-3 Lisa Jones (3) 20/1: 44: Reared start, chsd ldrs, onepace fnl 2f.	1 67a

4596} **DEIGN TO DANCE 172** [5] J G Portman 3-8-3 (75) R L Moore 10/1: 002620-5: Mid-div, outpcd fnl 2f: ½ **65a**
802 **JOANS JEWEL 20** [3] G G Margarson 3-8-3 A McCarthy 25/1: 556: Keen & cl-up, short of room over 1f out, sn no extra. 5 **50a**
785 **SHALATI PRINCESS 22** [1] J C Fox 3-8-3 (45) R Smith 100/1: 0067: Slow away & rear, only mod prog. 1¼ **46a**
4395} **BAHAMA REEF 184** [7] B Gubby 3-8-8 (67) C Catlin 33/1: 206400-8: Keen, chsd ldrs till 2f out, reapp. ¾ **49a**
5022} **BUNYAH 138** [2] E A L Dunlop 3-8-3 W Supple 16/1: 0-9: Keen, rear, sn outpcd, reapp/AW bow. nk **43a**
4652} **HABITUAL 168** [6] Sir Mark Prescott 3-8-8 S Sanders 50/1: 00-0: Wide & rear, no ch fnl 2f, reapp. 2½ **40a**
10 Ran 1m 25.75 (2.95) Owner Mr Hamdan Al Maktoum Trained at Newmarket

912 **2.25 L & M Body Repairs English Rose Classified Stakes 4yo+ 0-60 (F)**
£2933 £838 £419 **1m2f p/track** **Going 26** **-04 Slow** Stalls Inside

726 **BLAZING THE TRAIL 28** [7] J W Hills 4-9-0 (59) M Hills 11/2: 30-40251: Held up, hdwy wide over 2f out & drvn to lead well ins last: **65a**
768 **FORTUNE POINT 24** [12] A W Carroll 6-9-0 (60) D Holland 4/1 FAV: 0-402132: Led, drvn & hdd well ins last, just held cl-home: ½ **63a**
805 **RAHEEL 20** [3] P Mitchell 4-9-0 t (57) R L Moore 11/2: 5406143: Dwelt, hld up, chall over 2f out, onepace. ¾ **60a**
801 **WELSH WIND 20** [11] M Wigham 8-9-0 t p (60) J Fanning 12/1: 3203104: Trkd ldrs, kept on onepace. hd **61a**
876 **LARA FALANA 5** [8] Miss B Sanders 6-8-11 (60) Lisa Jones (3) 9/2: 0500-025: Dwelt, rear, styd on for press wide fnl 1f. hd **57a**
876 **FIGURA 5** [13] R Ingram 6-8-11 (58) J Quinn 10/1: 0-035666: Rear, smooth hdwy over 3f out, onepace dist. nk **56a**
820* **MEELUP 16** [6] Jane Southcombe 4-9-0 p (59) V Slattery 16/1: 00-02217: Cl-up, drvn & no extra over 1f out: 2 **56a**
206 **DECELERATE 99** [1] A Charlton 4-9-0 (55) R Hughes 33/1: 333310-8: Mid-div, outpcd fnl 2f: 1¼ **54a**
878 **FEN GYPSY 5** [10] P D Evans 6-9-0 bl (59) R Winston 20/1: 00-54009: Mid div wide, eff halfway, btn 2f out. 1¼ **52a**
674 **MUST BE MAGIC 35** [14] H J Collingridge 7-9-0 vis (60) W Supple 8/1: 3120-450: Mid-div wide, no impress fnl 2f. ½ **51a**
4566} **HALF INCH 174** [4] B I Case 4-8-11 (59) S Drowne 50/1: 400024-0: Rear, no prog fnl 2f: 1¼ **46a**
4849} **ARJAY 154** [5] Andrew Turnell 6-9-0 (59) C Catlin 50/1: 240000-0: Mid-div, btn over 2f out, reapp. 6 **40a**
803 **LINBY LAD 20** [2] J A Glover 4-9-0 BL (60) Dean McKeown 33/1: 312/00-00: Keen & chsd ldr till 3f out, wknd qckly: 17 **18a**
13 Ran 2m 05.82 (3.02) Owner Sir John Robb Trained at Lambourn

913 **3.00 Churchill Insurance Handicap Stakes 3yo+ 46-55 (F)** **[60]**
£3010 £860 £430 **7f p/track rnd** **Going 26** **-03 Slow** Stalls Inside

860* **STOIC LEADER 7** [8] R F Fisher 4-10-1 6ex (61) L Fletcher (3) 12/1: 000-4011: Trkd ldrs, rdn & led ins last, hung left under press & bmpd rnr-up, sn asserted: **71a**
799 **RANNY 20** [2] Dr J D Scargill 4-9-4 (50) J Quinn 6/1: 4100-422: Prom, rdn & led over 1f out, hdd & no extra when bmpd ins last, sn held: 2½ **55a**
763 **FRANKSKIPS 24** [7] Miss B Sanders 5-9-9 (55) T Quinn 8/1: 0-050033: Rear, styd on for press fnl 2f, nvr threatened front pair: ½ **59a**
761 **LILY OF THE GUILD 25** [13] W S Kittow 5-9-8 (54) N Callan 6/1: 462-0024: Rear, styd on wide for press. 1 **56a**
846 **BALERNO 10** [6] R Ingram 5-9-4 (50) G Carter 12/1: 1304505: Trkd ldrs, short of room 2f out, sn onepace: 1 **50a**
874 **GUN SALUTE 5** [12] G L Moore 4-9-7 p (53) R L Moore 4/1 FAV: 10-01046: Mid-div, eff 2f out, onepace: 1 **51a**
770 **ZINGING 24** [3] J J Bridger 5-9-2 (48) S Drowne 10/1: 0-506407: Trkd ldrs, rdn & no extra dist: 1¾ **43a**
783 **MASTER RATTLE 22** [4] Jane Southcombe 5-9-1 BL (47) V Slattery 14/1: 0005208: Cl-up/dsptd lead till over 1f out: shd **42a**
846* **LOCH LAIRD 10** [15] M Madgwick 9-9-7 6ex (53) G Baker 20/1: 000-0019: Rear, eff 2f out, no impress: ½ **47a**
4459} **JAKEAL 180** [1] R M Whitaker 5-9-8 (54) Dean McKeown 16/1: 00/0030-0: Led till over 2f out, sn btn: ½ **47a**
717 **DARK SHAH 29** [10] D M Simcock 4-9-9 P (55) Martin Dwyer 33/1: 64000-50: Rear, rdn & no prog fnl 2f: 1 **46a**
783 **BADOU 22** [14] L Montague Hall 4-9-1 (47) D Holland 14/1: 6141000: Cl-up till 2f out, sn btn: 1¾ **35a**
868 **MUTARAFAA 6** [16] D Shaw 5-9-5 vis (51) W Supple 20/1: 2400020: Mid-div wide, lost place from 2f out: shd **39a**
825 **FOOLISH THOUGHT 16** [11] I A Wood 4-9-6 p (52) T Eaves (5) 20/1: 0-654150: Chsd ldrs till 3f out: 4 **33a**
50 **BRILLIANT WATERS 127** [9] D W P Arbuthnot 4-9-6 (52) Dane O'Neill 33/1: 06000-0: Al rear, t.o., broke bloodvessel: 14 **10a**
15 Ran 1m 24.56 (2.06) Owner Great Head House Estates Limit Trained at Ulverston

914 **3.35 Scots Challenge Handicap Stakes 3yo 0-85 (D)** **[92]**
£5054 £1555 £778 £389 **5f p/track rnd** **Going 26** **+05 Fast** Stalls Outside

818* **PERUVIAN STYLE 16** [8] N P Littmoden 3-9-0 (78) D Holland 3/1: 2401-11: Sn chsd ldrs, styd on for press to lead line, all **85a**
818 **GREEN MANALISHI 16** [9] D W P Arbuthnot 3-8-12 (76) T Quinn 7/2: 22551-42: Led, rdn & hdd last stride: shd **82a**
63 **ONLY IF I LAUGH 126** [5] B J Meehan 3-8-6 (70) J F McDonald (5) 16/1: 516504-3: Chsd ldrs, kept on for press, not able to chall: ¾ **75a**
818 **TRICK CYCLIST 16** [3] A M Balding 3-9-3 (81) T Block (7) 11/2: 00200-24: Trkd ldrs, not pace to chall: nk **85a**
176* **TREASURE CAY 105** [4] P W D'Arcy 3-8-13 (77) Paul Eddery 5/2 FAV: 1-5: Towards rear, nvr pace to chall: 2½ **76a**
4761} **LA VIE EST BELLE 160** [1] B R Millman 3-8-12 (76) S Drowne 25/1: 016320-6: Cl-up till halfway, sn fdd, reapp. ¾ **74a**
176 **TROTTERS BOTTOM 105** [6] Andrew Reid 3-9-4 (82) J P Guillambert (3) 20/1: 206326-7: Dwelt, rear & outpcd, abs. 3½ **73a**
2198} **DELLAGIO 281** [2] C A Dwyer 3-9-7 (85) T P Queally (3) 33/1: 010-8: Dwelt, sn outpcd: 1¾ **73a**
818 **CUT AND DRIED 16** [10] D M Simcock 3-8-4 (68) Martin Dwyer 10/1: 600-1169: V slow away & nvr ch after: 3½ **49a**
9 Ran 58.83 (1.03) Owner M C S D Racing Ltd Trained at Newmarket

915 **4.10 Perfect Panes A Better Bet For A Warmer Home Handicap Stakes 3yo 0-85 (D)** **[86]**
£3968 £1221 £611 £305 **1m4f p/track** **Going 26** **-10 Slow** Stalls Inside

808* **GOLDEN QUEST 19** [2] M Johnston 3-9-7 (79) J Fanning 9/4: 0-11: Trkd ldrs, pushed along over 4f out, rdn to lead ins last & styd on strongly: **87a**
759 **CHAMPAGNE SHADOW 25** [5] G L Moore 3-8-7 bl (65) R L Moore 12/1: 04-0402: Rear, rdn & styd on to take 2nd ins last, nvr threatened wnr: 1¼ **69a**
715 **DARN GOOD 29** [4] R Hannon 3-7-12 4oh VIS (52) J F McDonald (5) 33/1: 4500-003: Held up, styd on for press cl-home, nvr a threat: nk **59a**
843* **BARATHEA DREAMS 10** [1] J S Moore 3-8-5 6ex (63) Martin Dwyer 5/4 FAV: 114: Led, rdn & hdd ins last, no extra: nk **65a**
817 **ANOTHER CON 16** [3] Mrs P N Dutfield 3-8-8 (66) R Havlin 9/2: 63-4145: Chsd ldr, wknd dist: 3½ **63a**

785° **RYE 22** [6] J A Osborne 3-8-12 (70) C Catlin 12/1: 5-16: Chsd ldrs, outpcd & dropped rear 5f out, no ch after: nk   **66a**
6 Ran   2m 33.53 (4.33)   Owner Syndicate 2002   Trained at Middleham

916   **4.45 Bet Direct Champs League Cashbacks Selling Stakes   4yo+   (G)**
           £2541 £726 £363   **1m4f p/track**   **Going 26**   **-61 Slow**   Stalls Inside

829   **BLUE SAVANNA 15** [10] J G Portman 4-9-2 p (47) R L Moore 10/1: 663-6421: Dictated pace, outpcd 4f out, rallied for   **47a**
       press to lead well ins last:
827   **PRIVATE SEAL 15** [2] Julian Poulton 9-9-4 t (40) D Holland 5/1: 0-632202: Rear, switched & styd on for press fnl 2f, no threat   1¼ **44a**
       to wnr:
689   **BIRTH OF THE BLUES 33** [8] A Charlton 8-9-4 (30) Donna Bashton (7) 40/1: 560-0063: Chsd ldrs, outpcd over 3f out, kept   nk **43a**
       on for press after:
816   **TOP TENOR 16** [7] B R Johnson 4-9-2 (65) S Whitworth 3/1: 123-0064: Keen mid-div, qcknd & hdwy wide to lead 4f out, sn   dht **43a**
       clr, drvn & hdd ins last, no extra:
107}   **MALARKEY 483** [3] A Crook 7-9-4 p Dane O'Neill 8/1: 101306/-5: Dwelt, rear, outpcd fnl 4f, no impress: 2 **40a**
877   **SALFORD FLYER 5** [4] Jane Southcombe 8-9-4 BL (70) V Slattery 7/1: 45405//-06: Keen & twds rear, outpcd fnl 4f: 2½ **36a**
488   **MIKASA 57** [5] R F Fisher 4-9-2 (45) L Fletcher (3) 50/1: 06000-07: Trkd ldrs, no impress fnl 3f: nk **35a**
715   **ALIMISTE 29** [9] I A Wood 4-8-11 N Callan 25/1: 0008: Trkd ldr, btn 3f out: 1¼ **28a**
707   **NEPTUNE 30** [6] J C Fox 8-9-4 (35) P Dobbs 25/1: 0500/-509: Rear, no impress fnl 4f: 1½ **31a**
857   **CAPTAIN CRUSOE 8** [1] P Howling 6-9-4 R Winston 11/4 FAV: 40/023/-30: Mid-div, struggling from 4f out, eased right down,   21   **1a**
       lame:
10 Ran   2m 39.67 (10.47)   Owner Mr A S B Portman   Trained at Compton

917   **5.20 Lenham Winners Cup Handicap Stakes Div 2   3yo+   46-55   (F)**   **[59]**
           £2933 £838 £419   **1m p/track rnd**   **Going 26**   **+04 Fast**   Stalls Outside

705   **WANNA SHOUT 30** [4] R Dickin 6-9-5 (50) Lisa Jones (3) 11/2: 004-2121: Sn trkd ldr, rdn to lead ins last, styd on strongly: **58a**
858   **PRIME OFFER 8** [9] J Jay 8-9-10 (55) N Callan 20/1: 00530-02: Led, rdn & hdd ins last, no extra: 1 **60a**
845°   **MARNIE 10** [1] J Akehurst 7-9-8 6ex (53) J Quinn 13/2: 4000-013: Held up, styd on for press fnl 2f, no threat to front pair: 4 **50a**
845   **COPPINGTON FLYER 10** [5] B W Duke 4-9-2 (47) R L Moore 8/1: 00-40400: Mid-div, rdn & no prog from dist: nk **39a**
845   **LARAD 10** [3] J S Moore 3-8-2 (50) D Kinsella 33/1: 04-35005: Chsd ldr, btn over 1f out: 2 **42a**
845   **INDIAN BLAZE 10** [7] Andrew Reid 10-9-7 (52) T P Queally (3) 100/30: 6212036: Trkd ldrs, wknd over 1f out: ¾ **43a**
900   **HAITHEM 1** [6] D Shaw 7-9-1 1oh t (45) D Holland 10/1: 06056107: Hanging right & rear, no ch fnl 2f: ½ **36a**
806   **THUNDERCLAP 19** [8] J J Quinn 5-9-10 (55) R Winston 2/1 FAV: 4400-128: Cl-up, drvn & wknd 2f out: 1¾ **42a**
4913}   **ARTZOLA 149** [2] C A Horgan 4-9-7 (52) Paul Eddery 50/1: 050-9: Dwelt & rear, eff wide 2f out, sn btn: ½ **38a**
       NEWCORR 271 [10] J J Bridger 5-9-1 6oh (40) J F McDonald (5) 50/1: 10U60/0-0: Al rear: 2½ **27a**
10 Ran   1m 37.99 (1.79)   Owner E R C Beech & B Wilkinson   Trained at Stratford-On-Avon

DONCASTER THURSDAY 25.03.04 Lefthand, Flat, Galloping Track

Official Going Good

918 1.50 Racing Schools Apprentice Handicap Stakes 4yo+ 0-80 (E) **[80]**
£3572 £1099 £550 1m4f Good 45 -00 Slow Inside

5001} **MIDDLETHORPE 142** [6] M W Easterby 7-8-10 bl (62) P Mulrennan(3) 4/1 FAV: 330055-1: b g Noble 66
Patriarch - Prime Property (Tirol) Mid-div, smooth hdwy to lead over 2f out, drvn out: well bckd: 2 mth jumps abs
(h'cap hdle wnr, rtd 125h, 2m, gd & hvy): dual h'cap plcd '03 (incl this race): won this race '02: eff at 10f, suited
by 12f on fast, likes gd & hvy, any trk, likes Doncaster: goes well fresh: suited by blnks. tough.
2 Mar'02 Catt 13.7g/s 69-65 D: 1 Mar'02 Donc 12sft 68-65 E: 1 Aug'01 Pont 12gd 68-62 C:
711* **ROBBIE CAN CAN 30** [14] A W Carroll 5-8-10 (62) Lisa Jones 12/1: 261-1312: Rear, styd on well for hd 65
press fnl 2f, just failed: likes to come late but too much to do here: in fine form.
4079} **INDIAN SOLITAIRE 201** [7] R A Fahey 5-9-5 VIS (71) T Hamilton(3) 14/1: 000200-3: b g Bigstone - 1 72
Terrama Sioux (Relkino) Mid-div, hdwy/no room over 3f out, drvn & styd on fnl 2f, just held cl-home: 6 wk jumps abs
(nov h'cap rnr-up, rtd 94h, 2m, soft): prob best around 12f, tried 2m: acts on firm, likes gd
& soft, any trk: eff in vis, tried blnks: well h'capped.
2 Jul'03 Leic 11.8fm 74-73 C: 2 Oct'02 Leic 11.8gd 85-81 C: 1 Oct'01 Bath 8g/s 88- E: 2 Aug'01 Folk 7g/f 69- E:
4802} **BLACKTHORN 159** [17] Mrs J R Ramsden 5-8-7 (59) A Beech 25/1: 152002-4: ch g Deploy - Ballasta 1 59
(Lyphard) Mid-div, styd on for press fnl 2f, not able to chall: reapp: clmr scorer '03 (R Fahey): unplcd '02 (rtd
80, h'cap): suited by 10/12f on firm & gd/soft, prob any trk: has tried cheek pieces: gd return.
2 Oct'03 Catt 12.0g/f 63-(61) F: 2 Aug'03 Catt 12.0fm 64-(62) F: 1 Jun'03 Beve 12.1fm 64-(60) F:
1 Aug'01 Newm 8g/s 84- E:
672 **CROWN AGENT 36** [21]4-9-7 (75) L Keniry 20/1: 0022U-05: b g Mukaddamah - Supreme Crown (Chief's 6 66
Crown) Switched start & held up inner, smooth hdwy 4f out, no prog bef dist: lightly rcd '03 (dual h'cap rnr-up):
unplcd '02 (rtd 70, mdn): eff around 12f on fast & gd/soft, easy trks.
2 May'03 Wind 11.6g/s 72-69 D: 2 May'03 Warw 12.6g/f 71-66 E:
1302 **BENBYAS 689** [5]7-8-13 (65) D Tudhope(7) 5/1: 22000/0-/6: b g Rambo Dancer - Light The Way 3½ 51
(Nicholas Bill) Led/dsptd lead till over 2f out, no extra: recent jumps rnr (Jan h'cap wnr, rtd 144h, 2m/2m4f, gd &
hvy, best dominating): last rcd on the level '02 (unplcd, rtd 62, h'cap, J L Eyre): stays 12f: acts on fast & hvy,
gall trks: eff with/without blnks or visor: improve for an uncontested lead.
2 Jun'01 Ayr 10g/f 69-68 C: 2 May'01 Donc 12g/f 72-68 D: 1 May'01 Redc 11hvy 69-56 E: 1 Apr'01 Pont 8hvy 65- F:
786 **QUEEN EXCALIBUR 23** [4]5-7-12 (5oh) (45) J F McDonald(3) 100/1: 40-00007: Dwelt, rear, mod gains. ½ 35
4346} **RAJAM 188** [8]6-9-8 (74) L Treadwell(5) 25/1: 302000-8: Chsd ldrs, no extra fnl 3f: jumps fit. 1¾ 57
731 **DANAKIL 29** [3]9-9-10 (76) J Coffill Brown(7) 40/1: 0430-009: Mid-div, led over 2f out, sn hdd & wknd. hd 58
4992} **ARCHIE BABE 143** [18]8-8-10 (62) S Hitchcott 9/1: 104000-0: 10th: Rear/wide, no prog: jumps abs. 7 35
3247} **INVITATION 239** [12]6-9-10 (76) B Reilly 25/1: 045500-0: 11th: Dwelt, rear, only mod prog: jumps fit. 2½ 45
743 **PERESTROIKA 28** [10]6-8-13 (65) T Eaves(3) 66/1: 05050/-00: 12th: Mid-div, no prog fnl 3f. 2 31
870* **GLORY QUEST 7** [22]7-9-3 (5ex)vis (69) P Gallagher(5) 12/1: 0352210: 13th: Dsptd lead, btn 3f out. 14 19
257 **ILOVETURTLE 89** [1]4-8-3 (57) Rory Moore(5) 33/1: 000000-0: 14th: Chsd ldrs, btn 3f out: jumps fit. ¾ 6
5036} **CHAMPION LION 138** [11]5-9-11 (77) T O'Brien(7) 20/1: 030050-0: 15th: Mid-div & hmpd early, wide, bhd. 1 25
3120} **KIDZPLAY 245** [23]8-8-13 (65) N Mackay(3) 20/1: 323564-0: 16th: Led/dsptd lead 6f, sn btn: reapp. 2 10
856+ **BELLA PAVLINA 9** [13]5-8-9 (5ex) (71) B Swarbrick(5) 14/1: 1141510: 17th: Mid-div wide, no prog 3f out. 4 10
3933} **TALK to MOJO 567** [20]7-10-0 (80) R Miles 12/1: 1//5/-0: 18th: Al rear: op 8/1, long abs. 3 15
806 **My Bayard 20** [16]5-8-6 (58) J D O'Reilly(4) 50/1:0
854 **King Priam 9** [9]9-7-12 (15oh)bl(35) Hayley Turner(5) 100/1:0
4659} **Every Note Counts 168** [15]4-9-7 (75) L Enstone 40/1:0718 **Archirondel 30** [2]6-8-0 (52) D Fentiman(5) 40/1:U
22 Ran Time 2m 35.17 (5.37) Owned: Mr J H Quickfall & Mr A G Black Trained: Sheriff Hutton

919 2.20 Badsworth Maiden Stakes 3yo (D)
£5590 £1720 £860 1m str Good 45 -04 Slow Stands Side

3691} **GATWICK 220** [6] M R Channon 3-9-0 T Quinn 4/1: 3-1: b c Ali Royal - Airport (Warpath) Pushed 91+
along rear early, hdwy halfway, drvn 2f out & led well ins last: op 3/1, reapp: promising 3rd sole '03 start (mdn):
related to wnrs at 7f/1m: eff at 1m, further looks sure: acts on fast & gd, gall trks: still green, expect progress.
MASTER MARVEL 0 [15] M Johnston 3-9-0 R Ffrench 20/1: 2: ch c Selkirk - Insijaam (Secretariat) hd 89+
Sn handy, narrow lead over 1f out, drvn & hdd last, just btn: lkd fit: eff at 1m, shld stay further: acts on gd &
a gall trk: promising debut, sure to win similar sn.
2819} **APPALACHIAN TRAIL 28** [3] I Semple 3-9-0 R Winston 33/1: 05-3: b c Indian Ridge - Karinski 3 83
(Palace Music) Trkd ldrs, rdn to chall over 1f out, onepace: reapp: unplcd tho' promise both '03 starts (mdn, rtd
80): half-brother to wnrs at 7f/1m: dam top-class over 1m/9f: should win a race.
5007} **MAN OF LETTERS 141** [11] M Johnston 3-9-0 K Dalgleish 33/1: 5-4: b c Belong To Me - Personal 1¼ 80
Business (Private Account) Led, rdn & hdd over 1f out, no extra: unruly paddock, reapp: unplcd sole '03 start
(mdn, rtd 66): dam top-class over 1m/9f: stablemate of 2nd: prob stays 1m.
4937} **PANSHIR 148** [16]3-9-0 G Baker 66/1: 0-05: ch g Unfuwain - Jalcamin (Jalmood) Mid-div & keen shd 80
early, switched to press ldrs over 1f out, onepace: unplcd '03 (rtd 54, mdn): eff at 1m, mid-dists h'caps suit.
2729} **GALVANISE 261** [14]3-9-0 R Hughes 7/2 FAV: 0-6: Chsd ldrs, shaken up & no impress fnl 2f: ndd race. 2 76
734 **AIR OF SUPREMACY 28** [12]3-9-0 S W Kelly 50/1: 067: Held up, eff 2f out, no impress. nk 75
5005} **TUDOR BELL 141** [13]3-9-0 D Sweeney 100/1: 4-8: Held up stands rail, no impress. 4 67
1862 **DOCTORATE 299** [5]3-9-0 K Darley 4/1: 4-9: Trkd ldrs, wknd fnl 2f: bckd, lngr trip. 1½ 64
759 **AMWELL BRAVE 26** [9]3-9-0 (68) Martin Dwyer 33/1: 5-223350: 10th: No dngr: see 601 (a/w). nk 63
5024} **BLAEBERRY 139** [10]3-8-9 J F Egan 100/1: 00-0: 11th: In tch till 3f out, reapp. 12 38
5022} **MUDAWIN 139** [8]3-9-0 W Supple 4/1: 5-0: 12th: Mid-div towards centre, no impress fnl 3f: scope. ¾ 42
4830} **TICERO 156** [2]3-9-0 D Holland 12/1: 04-0: 13th: Cl-up, btn 2f out: reapp. 1¼ 39
Byrd Island 0 [4]3-8-9 P Fitzsimons 100/1:0 848 **Mitzi Caspar 11** [7]3-8-9 A Mackay 150/1:0
Hoops And Blades 0 [1]3-9-0 J Murtagh 40/1:0 4357} **Kalush 187** [17]3-9-0 (66) Dean McKeown 66/1:0
17 Ran Time 1m 40.43 (3.93) Owned: Mr W H Ponsonby Trained: West Ilsley

DONCASTER   THURSDAY 25.03.04   Lefthand, Flat, Galloping Track

---

920

2.55 Mind Games Bearstone Stud Brocklesby Conditions Stakes 2yo (C)
£7398 £2806 £1403   **5f str**   **Good 45**   **-22 Slow**   Stands Side

NEXT TIME AROUND 0 [5] Mrs L Stubbs 2-8-11 R Winston 9/1: 1: b c Namid - In Due Course (A P Indy) Al prom, rdn dist & narrow lead ins last, rdn out: March foal: eff over a gall 5f, shld stay further: acts on gd & goes well fresh: fine start, this race usually works out well. **89**

DANCE NIGHT 0 [12] B A McMahon 2-8-11 G Gibbons 6/1: 2: b c Danehill Dancer - Tiger Wings (Thatching) Chsd ldrs, hdwy & chall dist, rdn & just held: March foal, cost 16,500gns: eff at 5f, shld stay further: acts on gd & a gall trk: win similar sn. **nk** **88**

WESTBROOK BLUE 0 [4] W G M Turner 2-8-11 A Daly 8/1: 3: b c Kingsinger - Gold And Blue (Bluebird) Led, rdn & hdd ins last, no extra: rcd on only 3 shoes after losing one bef start: Apr foal, cheaply bght: half-brother to 5 wnrs: eff at 5f on gd grnd/gall trk: fine run in circumstances, win sn. **1¼** **84**

MITCHELLAND 0 [13] James Moffatt 2-8-6 J Fanning 25/1: 4: b f Namaqualand - Precious Girl (Precious Metal) Keen early, mid-div, short of room halfway, shaken up & kept on fnl 2f, not pace to chall: May foal, half-sister to sprint wnrs: encouraging. **1¾** **74**

WINDY PROSPECT 5 [11]2-8-11 Dean McKeown 9/2 FAV: 35: ch c Intikhab - Yellow Ribbon (Hamas) Chsd ldrs & ch over 1f out, no extra ins last, qck reapp: Apr foal, £30,000 purchase: half-brother to a 6f juv wnr, dam a 7f juv wnr: eff at 5f, handles gd grnd & polytrack, gall or sharp/turning trk. **nk** **78**

GOGETTER GIRL 0 [9]2-8-6 N Callan 50/1: 6: Pushed along towards rear, styd on well ins last, nrst fin: encouraging, improve. **nk** **72+**

JUSTAQUESTION 0 [1]2-8-6 G Duffield 7/1: 7: Rdn bhd, late gains: improve. **shd** **72+**

YORKSHIRE LAD 0 [10]2-8-11 R Fitzpatrick 11/1: 8: Mid-div, nvr pace to threaten. **2½** **69**

KATHYS JOB 0 [16]2-8-6 D Fox(5) 17/2: 9: Prom, lost place 2f out. **hd** **63**

FLOSSYTOO 0 [15]2-8-6 D R McGuigan 33/1: 0: 10th: Dwelt, bhd, v green, mod late gains. **2** **57**

MISTY PRINCESS 0 [7]2-8-6 Martin Dwyer 14/1: 0: 11th: Sn outpcd & bhd. **2** **51**

Pennestamp 0 [14]2-8-11 R Havlin 12/1:0   **Hiats 0** [3]2-8-11 J D O'Reilly(7) 40/1:0
Sahara Mist 0 [6]2-8-6 P Hanagan 40/1:0   **Berham Maldu 0** [2]2-8-6 K Darley 11/1:0
15 Ran   Time 1m 01.57 (3.37)   Owned: Mr T Osborne   Trained: Malton

---

921

3.25 Lesley Garrett 'so Deep Is The Night' Stakes Handicap 3yo+ 0-90 (C)
£9946 £3060 £1530   **6f str**   **Good 45**   **-04 Slow**   Stands Side. Far Side Favoured.   **[90]**

106   **STEEL BLUE 120** [3] R M Whitaker 4-9-6 (82) M Hills 16/1: 002200-1: b g Atraf - Something Blue (Petong) Made all far side, drvn & held on all out cl-home: abs: dual h'cap rnr-up '03, dual nursery h'cap wnr '02: eff at 5/6f on fast & dirt, poss prefers gd & soft, stiff/gall trks, handles a sharp one: eff with/without cheek pieces & goes well fresh: enjoys dominating, fine return having been gelded. **87**
2 Nov'03 Donc 5gd 81-80 D: 2 Nov'03 Redc 6sft 83-80 C: 1 Oct'02 Newm 6g/f 87-85 C: 1 Aug'02 Newm 5gd 89-82 B: 2 Aug'02 Ayr 6sft 80- D:

567   **LAW BREAKER 47** [7] J A Gilbert 6-9-9 (85) B Reilly(3) 9/1: 0521-552: Pushed along mid-div far side, drvn & strong run ins last, just failed: abs: won this in '03 off a 5lb lower mark: v tough & useful, remains one to be with: see 235 & 106. **shd** **90**

5000} **ENDLESS SUMMER 142** [2] K A Ryan 6-9-2 (78) P Fessey 33/1: 004004-3: b g Zafonic - Well Away (Sadler's Wells) Rear far side, switched & styd on well ins last for press, not reach front pair: reapp: unplcd '03 (rtd 95, conn stks): plcd in US '02: nov & Gr 2 wnr back in '00 for J Gosden, rtd 113: eff at 6f on gd & fm, sharp or gall trk: has broken blood vessels: well h'capped on best form. **½** **80**

149   **CONSENSUS 110** [5] M Brittain 5-9-4 (80) T Williams 25/1: 000600-4: b f Common Grounds - Kilbride Lass (Lahib) Chsd ldrs far side, styd on onepace: abs: 5th in this race '03, also landed a turf h'cap: h'cap plcd '02 (rtd 88): eff at 5/6f on fast, gd/soft & any trk. **¾** **81**
1 Apr'03 Newc 5g/f 85-80 D: 1 Nov'01 Catt 6g/s 90-82 D: 1 Sep'01 Ayr 6gd 81-70 C: 2 Sep'01 Donc 6g/f 74-70 B: 1 Aug'01 Ripo 6g/f 72- E: 2 Aug'01 Hayd 6gd 68- E: 2 Jul'01 Beve 5g/f 69- F:

4341} **CD FLYER 188** [6]7-9-7 (83) T Eaves(5) 14/1: 034110-5: ch g Grand Lodge - Pretext (Grand Precedent) Held up stands side, styd on well from over 1f out, hung right: reapp: dual h'cap wnr '03 (M Channon): h'cap wnr '02: stays 7f, best at 6f, any trk: acts on fm & polytrack, likes gd & hvy: goes well fresh: excellent run (decisive wnr on the 'wrong' side), shld find compensation sn. **hd** **83+**
1 Aug'03 Good 6g/f 84-76 C: 1 Jul'03 Hayd 6gd 78-73 D: 2 Apr'03 Leic 6.0g/f 77-72 D: 2 Jun'02 Bath 5.7g/s 78-77 D: 1 Jun'02 Kemp 6fbn 78-72 C: 2 Jun'02 Newc 6hvy 77-76 C: 2 Sep'01 Kemp 6gd 77-73 C:

4341} **PLATEAU 188** [4]5-9-9 (85) Alex Greaves 33/1: 000000-6: b g Zamindar - Painted Desert (Green Desert) Chsd wnr far side, no extra ins last: reapp: unplcd '03 (rtd 85, h'cap): lightly rcd '02, rtd h'cap wnr: eff at 5/6f on fast & gd/soft, gall or sharp/easy trks: can go well fresh: on a handy mark. **1¼** **81**
1 Jul'02 Yarm 5.1g/f 95-95 C: 1 Jul'01 Ayr 6g/s 89- D:

517   **NASHAAB 54** [14]7-9-12 (88) S Drowne 25/1: 0305-007: Bhd stands side, late gains: needs 1m. **1¾** **79**

618   **CHAPPEL CRESENT 41** [17]4-10-0 (90) L Treadwell(7) 66/1: 0540-008: Handy stands side, onepace. **hd** **80**

879*   **MISS GEORGE 6** [1]6-9-13 (6ex) (89) Dane O'Neill 14/1: 05130-19: Bhd far side, mod prog. **¾** **77**

834   **ABBAJABBA 12** [6]8-9-9 (85) J Bramhill 16/1: 00006-00: 10th: Held up far side, nvr able to chall. **¾** **71**

840   **BRANSTON TIGER 12** [12]5-9-3 (79) M Fenton 7/1: 10504-50: 11th: Led stands side, hdd 2f out, sn btn. **shd** **65**

482   **WINTHORPE 59** [9]4-9-4 (80) K Dalgleish 50/1: 1100-000: 12th: Cl-up far side, fdd fnl 2f: abs, 5f suits. **¾** **64**

5025} **ARTIE 139** [11]5-9-3 (79) K Darley 8/1: 020630-0: 13th: Chsd ldrs stands side till over 1f out: reapp. **½** **61**

4477} **BLACKHEATH 180** [22]8-9-9 (85) J Fanning 12/1: 501023-0: 14th: Trkd ldrs stands side, btn dist: reapp. **hd** **66**

4768} **YOUNG MR GRACE 161** [8]4-9-2 (78) D Allan(3) 50/1: 0/20460-0: 15th: Mid-div far side, outpcd fnl 2f. **nk** **58**

1953   **RIDGEBACK 320** [19]4-9-4 (80) R Winston 14/1: 0/631-0: 16th: Chsd ldrs stands side till 2f out: new yard. **1** **57**

4471} **Loyal Tycoon 180** [21]6-9-10 (86) A Nicholls 16/1:0   692 **Type One 33** [10]6-9-2 (78) D Holland 14/1:0
2862} **Armagnac 257** [13]6-9-5 (81) R Ffrench 25/1:0   2329} **Namroud 280** [20]5-10-0 (90) P Hanagan 16/1:0
4286} **Musical Fair 190** [15]4-9-2 (78) R Hughes 20/1:0   3343} **Prince Cyrano 236** [18]5-10-0 (90) W Supple 16/1:0
22 Ran   Time 1m 13.74 (2.94)   Owned: Country Lane Partnership   Trained: Scarcroft

---

DONCASTER THURSDAY 25.03.04 Lefthand, Flat, Galloping Track

922 **4.00 Listed Freephone Stanleybet Doncaster Mile 4yo+ (A)**
£19500 £6000 £3000 **1m rnd** **Good 45** **+07 Fast** Outside

4976} **SUBLIMITY 145** [4] Sir Michael Stoute 4-8-12 t (102) J Murtagh 7/2: 41144-1: b c Selkirk - Fig Tree Drive (Miswaki) In tch, smooth hdwy over 2f out & led bef dist, rdn to assert: gd time, hvly bckd: impressive mdn & stks wnr '03: wng form at 1m, stays 10f on fm & gd, gall trks: eff in a t-strap & goes well fresh: lightly rcd, smart now & improved from three to four, keep on your side in a Gr 3. **114+**
1 May'03 Newm 8fm 100- C: 1 May'03 York 7.9fm 96- D:
4747} **GATEMAN 19** [7] M Johnston 7-9-3 K Dalgleish 100/30 FAV: 135-2602: b g Owington - Scandalette (Niniski) Chsd ldr, led over 2f out, rdn & hdd bef dist, not pace of wnr fnl 100y: fit from Dubai: Gr 3 & List wnr '03, also Gr 2 plcd: stks & Gr 3 wnr '02: eff at 7f/1m, stays 9f: acts on fm & hvy, any trk: can force the pace: v smart & tough, had the rest well covered, set for another productive campaign. *1¼* **115**
1 Sep'03 Hayd 8.1gd 115-(116) A: 1 Jun'03 Epso 8.5fm 114-(114) A: 2 Apr'03 Leic 7.0gd 114-(115) A:
2 Sep'02 Newb 7fm 117- A: 1 Jul'02 Curr 7sft 113- : 1 Jul'02 Yarm 7fm 109- C:
2 May'02 Good 6g/f 102- B:
838 **ROCKETS N ROLLERS 12** [6] R Hannon 4-8-12 (104) Dane O'Neill 25/1: 11/400-33: Trkd ldrs, ch over 1f out, not pace of front pair from dist: stays 1m: lightly raced, see 838. *3½* **103**
4626} **SUGGESTIVE 173** [10] W J Haggas 6-8-12 vis (109) A Culhane 7/1: 424415-4: b g Reprimand - Pleasuring (Good Times) Rear, hdwy over 3f out, no extra over 1f out: padd pick: cond stks wnr '03 (Gr 2 4th, rtd 111 at best): cond stks & List wnr '02, Gr 2 rnr-up: stays 1m, best at 6/7f on firm & soft grnd, any trk: eff in blnks/visor: useful gelding, prob sharper for this back at 7f. *2½* **98**
1 Sep'03 Muss 8g/f 96-(113) B: 2 Jul'03 Yarm 7.0gd 111-(115) C: 2 Oct'02 Long 8g/s 116- : 1 Aug'02 York 7g/f 114- A:
1 Jul'02 Hayd 6gd 106- C: 1 May'01 Yarm 7gd 105- C: 1 May'01 Ling 7g/f 92- D:
4710*}**MAKHLAB 164** [9]4-8-12 (108) W Supple 9/2: 131/001-5: b c Dixieland Band - Avasand (Avatar) In tch, rdn & no impress fnl 2f: ndd this: lightly rcd '03, stks wnr: mdn, h'cap & Gr 3 wnr '02: suited by 7f/1m on fast, likes soft grnd, any trk: can go well fresh: better than this. *1¼* **95**
1 Oct'03 Ayr 8g/s 112-(108) C: 1 Oct'02 Newb 7sft 109- A: 1 Aug'02 Ches 7g/f 97-85 C: 1 Aug'02 Pont 6g/s 100- D:
4838*}**LAGO DORTA 158** [1]4-9-1 (109) P Robinson 6/1: 110121-6: ch c Bahhare - Maelalong (Maelstrom Lake) Trkd ldrs, rdn & no impress over 1f out: reapp: landed 2 h'caps, 2 class stks a stks & List: eff btwn 7/9.3f on fm & soft, prob any trk: can go well fresh: most tough, smart & progressive last term, shld leave this bhd. *1¼* **95**
1 Oct'03 Long 9.3g/s 112- : 2 Sep'03 Newb 7g/f 108-(109) A: 1 Aug'03 Ches 7.6g/f 112-(100) B:
1 Jul'03 Ling 7.6gd 100-(93) C: 1 Jun'03 Newm 8fm 102-(92) C: 1 May'03 Ches 7.6fm 94-88 C:
1 Mar'03 Leic 7.0g/f 91-82 C: 2 Oct'02 Newb 6sft 85- D: 2 Oct'02 Wind 6g/f 85- D:
5035} **MIDDLEMARCH 138** [3]4-8-12 (109) T Quinn 25/1: 325016-7: Mid-div, drvn & outpcd fnl 3f: reapp. *3* **86**
360 **LUNDYS LANE 76** [2]4-8-12 bl (107) D Holland 25/1: 34600-48: Led till over 2f out, wknd qckly. *2½* **81**
108* **EXCELSIUS 125** [5]4-9-1 (106) K Darley 12/1: 303301-9: Rear, drvn & btn 3f out: 4 mth abs: btr 108. *2½* **79**
4604} **AUDIENCE 173** [8]4-8-12 (101) J Quinn 50/1: 000226-0: 10th: Sn bhd & rdn halfway, t.o.: new yard. *15* **51**
10 Ran Time 1m 39.13 (3.03) Owned: Mr Saeed Suhail Trained: Newmarket

923 **4.30 Balby Handicap Stakes 3yo 0-85 (D)** **[91]**
£5652 £1739 £870 **1m2f60y** **Good 45** **-23 Slow** Inside

4737*}**MUTAFANEN 163** [1] E A L Dunlop 3-9-7 (84) W Supple 9/2: 04331-1: gr c Linamix - Doomna (Machiavellian) Made all, qcknd tempo over 3f out & sn in command, easily, val 7L+: well bckd, op 6/1: reapp: h'cap wnr fnl '03 start: eff at 7f/1m, imprvd for step up to 10f, could get further: acts on fm, gd & any trk: goes well fresh: relished switch to front-rng & looks one to follow. 1 Oct'03 Ayr 8g/s 86-80 D: **101+**
568 **ALWAYS FLYING 47** [5] M Johnston 3-8-6 (69) J Fanning 9/1: 0355-152: Keen, chsd wnr, rdn & kept on fnl 2f, no ch with easy wnr: gd turf return, caught a tartar: stays 10f: see 438 (9f, AW mdn). *4* **71**
796 **SIEGFRIEDS NIGHT 22** [2] M C Chapman 3-7-12 (6oh) (55) D Fox(5) 25/1: 5-143233: In tch, rdn 3f out, styd on fnl 2f: encouraging turf return: acts on fibresand & gd grnd: drop in grade shld suit. *¾* **63**
4872} **LOCHBUIE 153** [10] G Wragg 3-8-9 (72) D Holland 8/1: 640-4: b c Definite Article - Uncertain Affair (Darshaan) Pushed along rear, styd on for press fnl 2f, nrst fin: reapp/h'cap bow, op 7/1: unplcd '03 (rtd 74): lkd in need of race, expect plenty of improvement & 12f will suit, v encouraging. *shd* **74+**
4975} **MRS PANKHURST 145** [11]3-8-10 (73) M Hills 7/1: 010-5: b f Selkirk - Melodist (The Minstrel) Dwelt, rear, hdwy 3f out, no prog dist: reapp, h'cap bow: lightly rcd '03, auct mdn wnr: winning form at 1m, mid-dists shld suit this term: acts on fast grnd, sharpish trk. 1 Sep'03 Ripo 8g/f 75- E: *1¼* **73**
4996*}**MR MIDASMAN 142** [3]3-8-9 (72) N Callan 16/1: 041-6: b c Entrepreneur - Sifaara (Caerleon) Mid-div, eff 3f out, no prog fnl 2f: reapp/h'cap bow: lightly rcd '03, auct mdn wnr fnl start: winning form at 7f, 1m could prove ideal: acts on gd & soft grnd, gall or sharp trk: has gone well fresh. 1 Nov'03 Catt 7sft 75- E: *2½* **68**
4717} **COVENTINA 164** [8]3-9-5 (82) K Darley 7/1: 5310-7: gr f Daylami - Lady of The Lake (Caerleon) Trkd ldrs, rdn & no impress over 2f out: reapp: mdn scorer '03: winning form at 1m, bred to stay mid-dists: acts on fast grnd, gall or sharp/undul trk. 1 Aug'03 Chep 8.1g/f 85- D: *1½* **76**
4543} **IN DEEP 176** [9]3-9-0 (77) R Havlin 12/1: 5562-8: Cl-up, btn over 2f out: reapp. *9* **60**
645 **PLAY MASTER 38** [6]3-8-11 (74) Paul Eddery 8/1: 2129: Held up, rdn & no impress fnl 3f: btr 645 (AW). *3½* **52**
676 **INFIDELITY 36** [7]3-8-7 (70) G Duffield 25/1: 5120-600: 10th: Mid-div, drvn & btn 3f out. *1¼* **46**
4874} **Indian Call 153** [4]3-8-3 (66) G Gibbons 20/1:0
4660} **Ace Coming 168** [12]3-7-12 (4oh)bl(57) Dale Gibson 50/1:0
568 **Baawrah 47** [14]3-8-7 (70) C Catlin 11/1:0
192* **Bethanys Boy 103** [13]3-8-13 (76) R Winston 16/1:0
14 Ran Time 2m 13.4 (7.0) Owned: Mr Hamdan Al Maktoum Trained: Newmarket

924 **5.00 David Scott & Co Pattern Makers Lady Riders' Handicap Stakes 4yo+ 0-75 (E)** **[61]**
£3660 £1126 £563 **1m2f60y** **Good 45** **-30 Slow** Inside

803 **BRAVE DANE 21** [10] A W Carroll 6-10-7 (68) Mrs S Bosley 7/1: 00-11561: Bhd, hdwy over 3f out, led ins last, rdn out: eff at 9/11f on fm, gd & likes polytrack/Lingfield: best held up off a strong pace, improving. **75**
803 **OLDENWAY 21** [17] R A Fahey 5-10-9 (70) Miss V Tunnicliffe(5) 12/1: 2000-002: Held up, short of room halfway, styd on for press fnl 2f, v weak ride: encouraging, see 803. *2* **73**
4039} **ETON 204** [9] D Nicholls 8-10-9 (70) Miss Kelly Harrison(3) 25/1: 053310-3: ch g Suave Dancer - Ermione (Surumu) Handy & smooth prog to lead 2f out, hdd ins last & no extra: reapp: val amat h'cap wnr '03: landed *1½* **71**

4 h'caps '02: suited by 10/12f on gd, loves fm & fast: goes well for appr/amat.
1 Aug'03 Epso 12.0g/f 70-63 C: 2 Jul'03 Carl 11.9g/f 65-(65) F: 2 Jun'03 Ayr 10g/f 69-65 D: 1 Oct'02 York 10.3fm 69-65 C:
1 Oct'02 Newm 10fm 75-68 E: 1 Sep'02 Beve 9.9g/f 67-52 F: 1 Sep'02 Pont 10fm 59-52 E: 2 Jun'02 Ripo 12.2fm 53-50 E:
806 **STING LIKE A BEE 20** [18] J S Goldie 5-9-3 (50) Miss Dawn Rankin(5) 8/1: 60-10244: Rear, styd on wide for press fnl 3f, nrst fin: stays gall 10f: see 464. ½ **50**
683 **NOUL 35** [20]5-9-13 bl (60) Miss S Brotherton 16/1: 421-0255: Mid-div, eff 3f out, kept on onepace fnl 2f: stays gall 10f, prob best around 1m: see 186 (1m). ½ **59**
230 **DICKIE DEADEYE 96** [12]7-9-11 (58) Miss J Hannaford(7) 14/1: 00/0050-6: b g Distant Relative - Accuracy (Gunner B) Chsd ldrs, kept on onepace: abs: unplcd '03 (lightly rcd, rtd 46, h'cap): unplcd '02 (rtd 66, lightly rcd, h'cap): eff at 10/12f on gd & soft grnd, stiff/gall trk. 1¾ **55**
713} **LUNAR LORD 391** [16]8-9-11 (58) Miss E Tucker(7) 25/1: 13100/5-7: b g Elmaamul - Cache (Bustino) Chsd ldrs 3f out, rdn & no extra fnl 2f: recent jumps rnr (unplcd, rtd 99h, h'cap hdle): unplcd '03 on the level (rtd 49a, class stks): dual h'cap wnr '02: eff btwn 10/14f, stays 2m: acts on gd, likes gd/soft & hvy. 1½ **53**
1 Jul'02 Epso 12gd 59-50 E: 1 May'02 Bath 10.2g/s 54-46 F: 1 Apr'01 Nott 14hvy 52-41 F:
726 **DANCE PARTY 29** [19]4-10-3 (64) Miss F Cumani(7) 25/1: 400-3308: Held up, hdwy 3f out, short of room 2f out, sn no extra: see 624 & 569. *nk* **58**
4419} **LIBRE 184** [5]4-10-9 t p (70) Miss C Metcalfe(5) 14/1: 040140-9: b g Bahamian Bounty - Premier Blues (Law Society) Held up, short of room halfway, eff 3f out, sn no extra: Flat reapp, jumps fit (mod form, nov): rating related mdn & h'cap wnr '03: dual h'cap rnr-up '02, also seller rnr-up: eff at 7f/1m on firm & soft grnd, sharp or stiff/gall trk: eff with/without cheek pieces or t-strap, tried blnks. 1¾ **62**
1 Sep'03 Bath 8.0fm 74-68 E: 1 May'03 Ayr 9.1g/s 71-(65) E: 2 Apr'03 Nott 8.2gd 71-67 E: 2 Oct'02 Donc 8sft 72-69 C:
2 Oct'02 Pont 8g/s 73-69 E: 2 Oct'02 Wind 8.3g/s 67- F:
884 **MI ODDS 5** [8]8-10-9 (70) Mrs M Morris 10/1: 212-1500: 10th: Held up, o prog fnl 2f: btr 511 (AW). ¾ **61**
747 **YENALED 27** [6]7-9-13 (60) Mrs S Owen(3) 33/1: 45-30500: 11th: Dwelt & bhd, only mod late prog. ½ **50**
288 **REDSPIN 82** [2]4-11-0 (75) Mrs S Moore(3) 33/1: 42502-30: 12th: Chsd ldrs 3f out, sn btn: abs: see 288. 1¾ **63**
97 **CRUNCHY 121** [7]6-9-7 t p (54) Miss L Ellison(3) 20/1: 151300-0: 13th: Bhd halfway, jumps fit. 2½ **38**
4593} **FOREST TUNE 173** [3]6-10-1 bl (62) Ms C Williams 11/2: 0/06106-0: 14th: Trkd ldrs, led over 2f out, sn hdd & wknd, jumps fit. 4 **40**
4824} **CRYFIELD 156** [1]7-10-4 (65) Miss A Rothery(7) 33/1: 630605-0: 15th: Led till 3f out, sn btn, reapp. 13 **25**
746 **INTENSITY 28** [13]8-9-13 (60) Miss Charmaine O'Neill 20/1: 2000-300: 16th: Mid-div wide, btn 3f out. 1¾ **18**
743 **DIGGER 28** [11]5-10-3 (64) Miss E J Jones 17/2: 6-140250: 17th: Chsd ldrs till 3f out: btr 642 (AW). 3½ **17**
868 **Crusoe 7** [4]7-9-10 bl(57) Mrs C Ford 40/1:0
2711] **Esher Common 623** [14]6-10-4 t(65) Miss Rachel Reynolds(7) 50/1:0
19 Ran Time 2m 14.16(7.76) Owned: Mr Gordon W Day Trained: Alcester

DONCASTER FRIDAY 26.03.04 Lefthand, Flat, Galloping Track

Official Going Good

925 1.15 Mexborough Maiden Stakes 3yo (D)
£5621 £1730 £865 7f Good 50 -27 Slow Stands Side

4870} **ZONUS 154** [10] B W Hills 3-9-0 Martin Dwyer 10/11 FAV: 2-1: b c Pivotal - Jade Mistress (Damister) In tch, hdwy halfway, led over 1f out, hands-and-heels ins last, shade cmftbly: well bckd on reapp: eye-catching 2nd sole '03 start: half-brother to a mid-dist wnr: stays a gall 7f well, 1m sure to suit: acts on fast, gd grnd & goes well fresh: useful, type to progress further & win again. 2 Oct'03 Newb 6.0g/f 87- D: **93**
SOUTH FACE 0 [7] R M Beckett 3-9-0 Darren Williams 33/1: 2: ch g Hector Protector - Crystal Cavern (Be My Guest) Dwelt, bhd, hdwy 2f out, kept on ins last, no threat to wnr on debut: cost 20,000gns: half-brother to wnrs at 7f: eff over a gall 7f, 1m will suit: acts on gd grnd: learn plenty from this v encouraging start & shld certainly be winning shortly. 2½ **86**
5023} **TABLEAU 140** [12] B W Hills 3-9-0 R Hughes 11/2: 5-3: ch c Marquetry - Model Bride (Blushing Groom) Cl-up, led 3f out till 1f out, no extra ins last: clr of rem on reapp, scope, ndd race, stablemate of wnr: 5th (rtd 70) sole juv start: eff at 7f on gd, bred to stay further: win a race. 1¾ **82**
4974} **MISSION MAN 146** [1] R Hannon 3-9-0 (84) K Darley 4/1: 024-4: b c Revoque - Opopmil (Pips Pride) Rcd alone far side, no impress: ndd race: rnr-up on 2nd of 3 juv starts (mdn): stays 1m on gd: ignore this. 5 **72**
2 Oct'03 Newb 8gd 82- D:
503 **DALIDA 57** [3]3-8-9 G Faulkner 66/1: 00-U5: In tch, eff over 2f out, sn no extra: 2 month abs. 3 **60$**
3797} **HABITUAL DANCER 217** [6]3-9-0 Leanne Kershaw(7) 100/1: 000-6: Nvr a threat to ldrs on reapp. 2½ **59**
3383} **STEPHANO 234** [2]3-9-0 K May(7) 20/1: 50-7: Nvr a factor. ½ **58**
5032} **COMPTON MICKY 139** [9]3-9-0 J Edmunds 100/1: 0-8: In tch, wknd over 2f out on reapp. 2½ **52**
3783} **SIMPLY RED 217** [11]3-9-0 (30) A Daly 100/1: 004-9: In tch, wknd over 2f out on reapp: lkd fit. *hd* **51$**
815 **SHES OUR LASS 18** [4]3-8-9 (56) R Fitzpatrick 66/1: 25542-00: 10th: Al bhd. ¾ **44**
INCHLOSS 0 [8]3-9-0 T Quinn 20/1: 0: 11th: Cl-up, wknd over 2f out on debut: burly. 5 **37**
795 **FAYRZ PLEASE 23** [13]3-9-0 (58) D Fox(5) 40/1: 03-4400: 12th: Al bhd: see 609 (5f, fibresand, 444). 4 **27**
1603} **PINK SUPREME 312** [5]3-8-9 G Duffield 14/1: 2-0: 13th: Led till 3f out, wknd: longer trip, reapp. 3½ **14**
13 Ran Time 1m 28.59 (5.39) Owned: Concord Racing Bonnycastle Grant Morton Trained: Lambourn

926 1.50 Lakeside Handicap Stakes 4yo+ 0-90 (C) [85]
£9755 £3002 £1501 2m2f Good 50 -01 Slow Inside

4677} **RAHWAAN 167** [10] C W Fairhurst 5-9-12 (83) J Murtagh 9/2: 555034-1: b g Darshaan - Fawaakeh (Lyphard) Made all, styd on strongly fnl 2f, drvn out: recent nov hdle wnr (2m, gd/firm, rtd 117h): plcd in h'caps '03: '02 mdn & h'cap wnr for J Dunlop: suited by 2m/2m2.5f on firm or soft grnd, any trk: best with an uncontested lead: game, shld run well in Chester Cup (2L 4th off 85 last term). 2 Jun'03 Hayd 16.2g/f 89-86 C: **88**
1 Aug'02 Newm 16.1sft 87-84 C: 1 Jun'02 Chep 12.1g/s 85- D: 2 May'02 Thir 12gd 84- D: 2 Apr'02 Bath 10.2gd 84- D:
4323} **VICARS DESTINY 190** [1] Mrs S Lamyman 6-8-8 (65) G Duffield 9/1: 65626-2: b f Sir Harry Lewis - Church Leap (Pollerton) Held up, short of room over 4f out & over 2f out, switched right & styd on well fnl 1f, nrst fin on reapp: fit from hdlg, earlier won 2 h'caps (stays 3m on gd, hvy): rnr-up in a h'cap in '03: stays 2m2f well, extreme trips will suit: acts on fm & gd: encouraging, marathon h'cap win well within her grasp. ¾ **68**
2 Aug'03 Ches 15.9fm 67-63 D:
743 **OCEAN TIDE 29** [6] R Ford 7-9-2 vis (73) K Darley 20/1: 6100/0-33: In tch, hdwy well over 2f out, *shd* **76**

hung left over 1f out but kept on, not btn far: stays 2m2f: on a wng mark & 5 wins from 23 Flat starts: see 743.
837   **PHANTOM STOCK** 13 [9] W Jarvis 4-8-4 (67) J Quinn 14/1: 2142104: Held up, hdwy well over 2f out, 3   67
kept on, no threat: encouraging: looks a thorough stayer & gets 2m2f, may apprec more positive tactics in 813.
2508} **SAHEM** 272 [8]7-9-9 (80) Dale Gibson 33/1: 231330-5: b g Sadler's Wells - Sumava (Sure Blade)   5   75
Held up, hdwy well over 2f out, sn no impress: lkd fit: '03 mdn wnr: prob stays at least 14f: handles
fast, likes gd/soft. 1 May'03 Hami 9.2g-s yr 79- D: 2 Apr'03 Newc 12.4g/f 72- D:
4796} **BOBSLEIGH** 160 [12]5-9-8 (79) S Drowne 10/1: 303040-6: b g Robellino - Do Run Run (Commanche Run)1   73
In tch, rdn over 3f out, no extra: reapp: fit from hdlg, nov wnr earlier (stays 2m4f on soft, rtd 116h): plcd in
h'caps in '03: won 3 h'caps in '02: all wins at 14f, stays 2m on firm & gd, handles gd/soft & stiff or easy trks,
likes Yarmouth. 2 May'03 Kemp 16fm 79-75 D: 1 Oct'02 Sali 14gd 76-69 E: 1 Sep'02 Yarm 14fm 69-67 E:
2 Aug'02 Yarm 14fm 68-67 E: 2 Aug'02 Sali 14g/f 68-65 E: 1 Jul'02 Yarm 14g/f 66-57 E:
856   **GEORGE STUBBS** 10 [7]6-8-8 (65) T Quinn 14/1: 0623647: Chsd ldrs, no extra fnl 2f: longer trip: see 196.3   56
743   **ALTITUDE DANCER** 29 [5]4-8-0 (63) J Bramhill 10/1: 53-32148: In tch, rdn over 3f out, no extra: btr 554.   2½   51
3252} **RIYADH** 240 [2]6-10-0 vis (85) J Fanning 10/1: 0/04060-9: In tch, btn over 2f out: changed stable.   11   63
837   **NORTHERN NYMPH** 13 [14]5-9-6 (77) W Supple 20/1: 235/4-230: 10th: Nvr a factor: see 743.   10   47
4931} **ALLEZ MOUSSON** 150 [3]6-8-1 P (58) P Hanagan 16/1: 00/6030-0: 11th: In tch, btn 3f out: cheekpieces.   19   12
4151} **RIDAPOUR** 199 [4]5-8-3 (60) Joanna Badger 100/1: 33300/0-0: 12th: Al bhd on reapp.   1   13
837* **SUN HILL** 13 [11]4-9-2 (79) D Sweeney 13/2: 000-1110: 13th: In tch, wknd over 4f out: needs fibresand?   4   29
140* **SNOWS RIDE** 114 [13]4-9-5 (82) Martin Dwyer 11/2: 215011-0: 14th: Handy, wknd over 4f out: long abs.   2½   30
14 Ran   Time 4m 01.78 (9.28)   Owned: Six Iron Partnership   Trained: Middleham

927   **2.20 Value Packed Yorkshire Season Ticket Stakes Handicap 3yo+ 0-105 (B)**   **[102]**
£14170 £4360 £2180   5f   Good 50   -01 Slow   Stands Side. 2 Groups - High Favoured.

655* **MAKTAVISH** 38 [18] J Semple 5-8-2 p (76) P Hanagan 16/1: 50100-11: Made all stands side, drvn out: 84
suited to 5f, tried 7f: acts on fast, loves gd, hvy & fibresand, any trk: best up with/forcing the pace in cheek
pieces: gd weight carrier who goes well fresh: in grand form, see 655.
692   **TRINCULO** 34 [21] N P Littmoden 7-8-12 p (86) J P Guillambert(3) 25/1: 60-000U2: Bhd stands side,   ¾   92
hdwy 2f out, kept on well fnl 1f, not btn far: v encouraging after mishap in 692: win a turf h'cap on this form.
834   **PICCLED** 13 [17] E J Alston 6-8-2 (76) D Allan(2) 13/2: 06000-03: Dwelt, in tch stands side, eff   ¾   80
over 1f out, kept on: won this race last term off a 4lb higher mark & h'capped to win.
692   **ZARZU** 34 [12] C R Dore 5-8-0 (74) J Bramhill 10/1: 41-35434: Bhd stands side, eff & hung right   nk   77
over 1f out, kept on despite short of room just ins last: in gd form: see 692.
4341} **RIVER FALCON** 189 [16]4-8-6 (80) W Supple 16/1: 420000-5: b g Pivotal - Pearly River (Elegant   2   77
Air) Bhd stands side, eff over 1f out, kept on ins last, no threat: '03 h'cap wnr: lightly rcd '02: eff at 5/6f
on firm or soft grnd, likes gall trks: encouraging rtn, sharper for this & shld win off current mark.
2 Jun'03 Ayr 5g/f 84-80 D: 1 May'03 Redc 5g/f 83-74 C:
4341} **PAX** 189 [20]7-8-8 (82) P M Quinn 66/1: 301640-6: ch g Brief Truce - Child's Play (Sharpen Up)   1¼   75
Bhd stands side, some late gains, nvr dngrs on reapp: won 2 h'caps in '03: won 3 h'caps in '02: eff over a stiff
5f & 6f on firm, gd/soft & any trk: enjoys a strong pace: sharper for this gd rtn.
1 Aug'03 Carl 5fm 84-77 D: 1 Jul'03 Newc 6g/f 82-70 E: 1 Jul'02 Pont 6gs 76-71 D: 2 Jun'02 Catt 6g/f 73-67 E:
1 Apr'02 Leic 6g/f 69-63 D: 2 Apr'02 Thir 7fm 64-58 E: 1 Apr'02 Sout 6g/f 67-55 F:
834   **BOND BOY** 13 [11]7-9-5 (93) F Lynch 16/1: 00-40047: Bhd far side, hdwy well over 1f out, styd on   1   83+
to lead that group ins last, no ch with stands side: won race on "wrong side" & looks one to keep in mind.
4764} **CARIBBEAN CORAL** 182 [15]5-9-2 (90) Darren Williams 16/1: 000012-8: ch g Brief Truce - Caribbean   ½   78
Star (Soviet Star) Dwelt, in tch stands side, no impress over 1f out: burly: '03 2 time h'cap scorer (with C Wall):
'02 auct mdn wnr: eff at 5/6f on fm & gd, any trk, likes a stiff one: has run well fresh & best held up, gd weight
carrier. 2 Oct'03 Newm 5g/f 91-88 B: 1 Oct'03 Newc 5gd 89-83 D: 1 Jun'03 Sand 5.0gd 86-82 D:
2 Jul'02 Hayd 6gd 90-86 C: 2 Apr'02 Sand 5gd 86-85 B: 1 Jul'01 Brig 6g/f 79- E:
3732} **CAPE ROYAL** 219 [1]4-8-9 (83) T Quinn 10/1: 210220-9: Slow away, sn handy far side, led that   ½   69
group trav well over 1f out, hdd & wknd ins last on reapp: much sharper for this.
4477+ **PTARMIGAN RIDGE** 181 [19]8-8-11 (85) N Mackay(5) 40/1: 005001-0: 10th: Chsd ldrs, btn 2f out..   ½   70
883+ ***NO TIME 6** [14]4-9-10 (6ex) (98) L Fletcher(3) 8/1: 6662110: 11th: In tch stands side, wknd over 1f out.   shd   82
4991} **AWAKE** 144 [9]7-8-2 (76) Martin Dwyer 40/1: 0/56500-0: 12th: Chsd ldrs, wknd 2f out on reapp.   hd   59
4014+ **WILLHEWIZ** 206 [2]4-9-0 vis (88) T P Queally(3) 20/1: 405101-0: 13th: Led far side till over 1f out, wknd.   1   68

4810} **SIERRA VISTA** 158 [4]4-8-5 (79) L Enstone(1) 16/1: 503604-0: 14th: In tch, wknd 2f out: swtg.   1   56
4884* **SMART HOSTESS** 153 [22]5-9-5 (93) R Winston 9/1: 511011-0: 15th: Nvr a factor stands side.   1½   60
755   **CHICO GUAPO** 27 [8]4-8-3 p (77) J Quinn 12/1: 1015-050: 16th: In tch far side, wknd over 1f out.   2   44
692   **DANCING MYSTERY** 34 [6]10-8-11 bl (85) S Carson 9/1: 133-1350: 17th: In tch far side, wknd 2f out.   ¾   50
1495} **KANGARILLA ROAD** 317 [10]5-8-1 (75) P Fitzsimons 33/1: 656/600-0: 18th: Slow away & al bhd far side.   5   26
4410} **POMFRET LAD** 185 [7]6-9-12 (100) Alex Greaves 50/1: 051052-0: 19th: In tch far side, wknd over 2f out.   3½   41
2203} **RECTANGLE** 283 [3]4-8-9 (83) A Nicholls 20/1: 1/02630-0: 20th: Cl-up far side, wknd 2f out on reapp.   1¾   19
20 Ran   Time 1m 00.75 (2.55)   Owned: Mr D G Savala   Trained: Carluke

928   **2.50 Freephone Stanleybet Spring Mile Handicap 4yo+   (B)**   **[94]**
£17420 £5360 £2680   1m   Good 50   +02 Fast   Stands Side. 2 Groups (High Fav).

4888} **AUTUMN GLORY** 153 [19] G Wragg 4-9-2 (82) S Drowne 20/1: 140-1: b c Charnwood Forest - Archipova   99+
(Ela Mana Mou) Cl-up stands side, hdwy to lead over 2f out, pushed clr, hands-and-heels on reapp: reportedly had
joint probs last term having won an early season mdn: stays 1m well on a gall trk, shld get further (dam 12/15f
wnr): acts on fast, gd & runs v well fresh: impressed here, looks useful, lightly rcd & can win again.
1 Mar'03 Leic 8.0g/f 84- D:
4950} **ST PETERSBURG** 148 [20] M H Tompkins 4-9-2 (82) G Duffield 33/1: 100315-2: ch g Polar Falcon -   1½   94
First Law (Primo Dominie) Cl-up stands side, eff to go 2nd 2f out, kept on but not wnr's pace on reapp: '03 dual
h'cap wnr: '02 mdn auct scorer: eff at 7f, stays 1m well, acts soft & polytrack, gall or sharp trk: in gd form.
1 Oct'03 Redc 8g/f 87-72 E: 1 Sep'03 Ling 7ap 75a-70 D: 2 Oct'02 Yarm 8sft 76-73 E: 1 Sep'02 Beve 7.4gd 73- E:
789   **SWIFT TANGO** 27 [21] E A L Dunlop 4-9-8 (88) W Supple 16/1: 623-1023: In tch stands side, eff   2½   95
over 1f out, kept on same pace: gd run: see 789, 452.
547   **LINNING WINE** 51 [15] B G Powell 8-9-3 (83) J Murtagh 16/1: 0021-024: Held up stands side, hdwy   1¾   85
2f out, kept on despite edging right fnl 1f, nrst fin: swtg, abs: all 3 wins on polytrack: see 547, 234.
836   **DANELOR** 13 [24]6-9-7 (87) P Hanagan 14/1: 0/4220-45: Cl-up stands side, led that group halfway   nk   88
till over 2f out, onepace: fair run: see 836.

278 **STRONG HAND 86** [22]4-9-2 T (82) P Mulrennan(5) 50/1: 335110-6: Dwelt, in tch stands side, some   *2*   **80**
late gains, no threat: 3 month abs, prob just sharper for this: see 127, 38.

4599} **EVEREST 174** [11]7-9-5 (85) R Winston 15/2: 023000-7: ch g Indian Ridge - Reine d'Beaute   nk   **82+**
(Caerleon) Held up far side, kept on fnl 2f, nrst fin, no ch with stands side group: dual h'cap wnr in '03: '02
ladies h'cap scorer: suited by 1m, stays a sharp 9f on firm or hvy: can run well fresh on any trk: tough, won race on
'wrong side here', v encouraging. 2 Jul'03 Newm 8g/f 85-83 C: 1 Apr'03 Asco 8gd 82-76 D:
1 Apr'03 Sand 8.1gd 82-71 E: 1 Nov'02 Donc 8hvy 74-65 E: 2 May'02 Ayr 8g/s 66-65 F:

888 **AFRICAN SAHARA 6** [7]5-9-6 (5ex)t (86) G Carter 16/1: 6-610168: Chsd ldrs far side, eff well over   ¾   **81**
1f out, kept on same pace: fine run on wrong side: see 800, 625.

758 **ARRY DASH 27** [3]4-9-6 (86) D Corby(3) 7/1: 12015-49: Held up far side, eff 2f out, onepace: gd run.   nk   **80**

4977+**THIHN 146** [10]9-9-10 (90) A Daly 11/1: 206011-0: 10th: ch g Machiavellian - Hasana (Private   nk   **83**
Account) Dwelt, held up far side, hdwy 2f out, onepace: lkd just btr for race: reapp: won fnl 2 h'cap starts in
'03: 3 time scorer back in '01: stays 10f, suited by 7f/1m & acts on fm or hvy: likes to come late in a big field.
1 Nov'03 Newm 8g/f 93-86 C: 1 Oct'03 Redc 7g/f 90-81 D: 2 Jun'03 Wind 8.3g/f 88-85 C: 2 Jun'02 Epso 8.5g/s 87-88 B:
2 Apr'02 Wind 8.3g/f 92- C: 2 Jun'01 Newm 8gd 98-93 C: 2 Oct'01 Newm 8g/s 90-85 C: 2 Jul'01 Sand 8gd 87-85 B:
1 Jun'01 Wind 8.3g/f 86- D: 2 Jun'01 Epso 8.5fm 81-77 B: 2 May'01 Beve 8.4fm 75-74 D: 1 Apr'01 Epso 8.5hvy 74- E:

838 **CARDINAL VENTURE 13** [2]6-9-7 (87) N Callan 6/1: 00111-20: 11th: Overall ldr far side, hdd over   shd   **79**
2f out, no extra fnl 1f: well bckd: far from disgraced on wrong side & a sharp 1m or 7f prob suits best: see 838.

879 **COMPTON DRAGON 7** [23]5-9-0 (80) A Nicholls 40/1: 00000-00: 12th: Held up stands side, rdn &   1½   **69**
short of room over 2f out, no impress.

716 **KRUGERRAND 31** [18]5-9-2 (82) Martin Dwyer(3) 33/1: 54040-00: 13th: In tch stands side, wknd 2f out.   1½   **68**
4939} **ACE OF HEARTS 149** [8]5-9-4 (84) J Quinn 14/1: 025362-0: 14th: In tch far side, btn over 1f out, reapp.   1¾   **66**
4486} **DUNASKIN 181** [17]4-9-7 (87) Dale Gibson 66/1: 105053-0: 15th: Led stands side group till halfway.   1   **67**
716 **INTERNATIONALGUEST 31** [4]5-9-1 bl (81) K Darley 14/1: 0200020: 16th: In tch far side, wknd 2f out.   nk   **60**
81 **MARSHMAN 125** [16]5-9-9 (89) P Robinson 33/1: 301534-0: 17th: In tch stands side, wknd 2f out.   ½   **60**
4928} **ATLANTIC ACE 150** [5]7-9-2 (82) F Lynch 16/1: 050105-0: 18th: Al bhd.   nk   **59**
800 **AVENTURA 22** [6]4-9-5 (85) L Fletcher(3) 20/1: 430-0040: 19th: Chsd ldr far side, wknd over 2f out.   2½   **57**
2139} **GO TECH 286** [12]4-9-5 (85) D Allan(3) 33/1: 5/50005-0: 20th: In tch far side, wknd over 2f out on reapp.   2   **53**
4226} **JABAAR 195** [9]6-9-9 (89) Alex Greaves 40/1: 500420-0: 21th: Al bhd far side on reapp.   6   **45**
836 **SAHAAT 13** [14]6-9-4 (84) S W Kelly 33/1: 00000-00: 22th: Al bhd stands side.   5   **30**
4492} **UNICORN REWARD 180** [1]4-9-4 (84) R Hughes 25/1: 111150-0: 23th: In tch far side, wknd 2f out.   nk   **29**
3344} **SAWWAAH 237** [13]7-9-2 (82) Joanna Badger 33/1: 501030-0: 24th: Al bhd far side on reapp.   20   **0**
24 Ran Time 1m 40.34 (3.84) Owned: Mollers Racing Trained: Newmarket

---

929 **3.25 Bawtry Maiden Selling Stakes 2yo (F)**
£2909 £831 £416   **5f**   **Good 50**   -73 Slow   Stands Side

      LISA MONA LISA 0 [6] V Smith 2-8-9 J Quinn 7/1: 1: b f Desert Style - Amneris (Alzao) Chsd   **66**
ldrs, styd on over 1f out to lead ins last, rdn out on debut: bght in for 6,000gns: Feb first foal: dam styd 12f:
eff over a gall 5f, shld get further: acts on gd grnd & runs well fresh in sell grade: gd start.

      GENERAL NUISANCE 0 [1] J S Moore 2-9-0 Martin Dwyer 7/1: 2: ch g General Monash - Baywood   ½   **69**
(Emarati) With ldrs, kept on fnl 1f, just held on debut: claimed for 6,000: Feb first foal, cost £3,500: speedily
bred & eff at 5f on gd grnd: should be suited by a seller.

      LITTLE WIZZY 0 [3] P D Evans 2-8-9 S W Kelly 11/1: 3: Slow away, sn in tch, hung left over 2f   1¼   **60**
out, kept on late: small.

      GREZIE 0 [8] A D Smith 2-8-9 D Fox(5) 10/1: 4: gr f Mark of Esteem - Lozzie (Siberian Express)   nk   **60**
Slow away & sn well bhd, plenty to do over 1f out, "flew home" fnl 1f on debut: Apr foal, cost 2,500gns: eff at 5f,
6f looks sure to suit: v green but impressed with finishing burst & can win at least a seller with this under
his belt (claimed by J Best for 6,000).

      EMMAS VENTURE 0 [2]2-8-9 P Mulrennan(5) 16/1: 5: Sn in tch, hdwy to lead over 1f out till ins last.   nk   **59**
      DOCKLANDS DUDE 0 [10]2-9-0 K Darley 11/4 JT FAV: 6: Slow away, hdwy to lead over 3f out till   1½   **60**
over 1f out, wknd & eased: bckd, claimed.

      CONCERT TIME 0 [5]2-8-9 R Fitzpatrick 16/1: 7: Al bhd: burly on debut.   1¾   **50**
      GOLDHILL PRINCE 0 [9]2-9-0 A Daly 11/4 JT FAV: 8: Led till over 3f out, sn hung left & wknd: bckd.   nk   **54**
      DIATONIC 0 [4]2-9-0 Lisa Jones(3) 12/1: 9: In tch, wknd 2f out on debut.   ½   **52**
9 Ran Time 1m 04.35 (6.15) Owned: Mr Stephen Dartnell Trained: Newmarket

---

930 **4.00 Maltby Maiden Stakes 3yo (D)**
£5538 £1704 £852   **1m2f60y**   **Good 50**   -19 Slow   Inside

4676} **KING OF DREAMS 167** [6] M Johnston 3-9-0 K Dalgleish 11/8 FAV: 42-1: b c Sadler's Wells - Koniya   **88**
(Doyoun) Trkd ldr, led 3f out, edged left over 1f out but styd on well, rdn out on reapp: bckd: rnr-up on 2nd of 2
'03 mdn starts: apprec step up to 10.3f, shld stay 12f: acts on fast, gd grnd & on a gall trk: remains open to further imp:
fine return, clrly going the right way & open to further improvement in h'caps. 2 Oct'03 York 7.9g/f 85- D:

881 **KEELUNG 25** [5] M A Jarvis 3-9-0 P Robinson 9/2: 0-422: In tch, hdwy over 3f out, short of room &   1½   **86**
switched right over 1f out, styd on ins last: bckd from 7/1: stays 10.3f & shapes like even further will suit:
acts on gd & polytrack: shade unfortunate here, shld be winning similar sn: see 734.

4937} **FLAMBOYANT LAD 149** [11] B W Hills 3-9-0 M Hills 15/8: 4-23: ch c Nashwan - Cheeky Charm   1½   **83**
(Nureyev) Cl-up, gd hdwy to chall 2f out, sn rdn & onepace: nicely bckd, scope on reapp: rnr-up on sole juv start:
stays 10.3f on gd & soft grnd: shown enough to win to race: well clr of rem. 2 Oct'03 Yarm 7.0sft 82- D:

4975} **DANCING BEAR 146** [2] Julian Poulton 3-9-0 N Callan 66/1: 0-4: b g Groom Dancer - Sickle Moon   12   **61**
(Shirley Heights) In tch, eff over 3f out, sn no extra: strong, ndd race on reapp: bred to apprec mid-dists.

4726} **NEGWA 165** [4]3-8-9 (74) D Corby(3) 10/1: 433-5: b f Bering - Ballet (Sharrood) Led till 3f out,   9   **46**
wknd: lkd fit on reapp: 3rd in a mdn & stks in '03 (rtd 76): half-sister to a 10f wnr: stays 10f on fast grnd.

4927} **SAAMEQ 150** [1]3-9-0 D McGaffin 66/1: 0-6: Al bhd: now with I Semple.   1   **49$**
865 **KATIES ROLE 9** [3]3-8-9 (57) Dean McKeown 100/1: 43-34437: In tch, wknd over 3f out: see 865.   5   **36**
4808} **DANEFONIQUE 158** [9]3-8-9 (53) R Fitzpatrick 100/1: 503050-8: Al bhd: swtg on reapp.   2   **33**
4483} **SIR BOND 181** [8]3-9-0 F Lynch 40/1: 0-9: Al bhd: lkd burly on reapp.   5   **30**
759 **ATLANTIC TERN 27** [1]3-9-0 A Daly 100/1: 00-600: 10th: Al bhd.   7   **18**
5018} **INCHCONNEL 141** [7]3-9-0 BL (67) J Quinn 50/1: 030-0: 11th: Dwelt, in tch, wknd 2f out: new stable, blnks.9   **4**

11 Ran Time 2m 13.55(7.15) Owned: Mr Saeed Buhaleeba Trained: Middleham

Official Going Standard

931

2.00 Bet Direct On Sky Active Maiden Auction Stakes 2yo (E)
£3387 £1042 £521 **5f aw rnd** **Going 22** **-43 Slow** Outside

KING AFTER 0 [7] J R Best 2-8-9 N Pollard 14/1: 1: b g Bahamian Bounty - Child Star (Bellypha) **78a**
In tch, staying on when switched wide dist, rdn out to lead cl-home: debut: Mar foal, cost 6,000gns: half-brothers to wnrs at 5/9f: dam won at 2m/hdles: sire high-class sprinter as a juv: eff at 5f, 6f will suit: acts on polytrack & a v sharp trk: goes well fresh: sure to rate higher for today.

EVANESCE 0 [9] M R Channon 2-8-4 S Hitchcott(2) 11/4 FAV: 2: b f Lujain - Search Party (Rainbow hd **71a**
Quest) Mid-div, hdwy 2f out, styd on to lead dist, hdd cl-home: op 2/1 on debut: Mar foal, cost E10,000gns: dam plcd at 1m/10f: eff at 5f, further shld suit: acts on polytrack: shld win similar.

TRANSACTION 0 [2] J M P Eustace 2-9-0 J Tate 7/2: 3: ch c Trans Island - Meranie Girl (Mujadil) nk **80a**
Dsptd lead, hung right thr'out, hdd dist, kept on & not btn far: op 9/4 on debut: Mar foal, cost 19,000gns: half-brother to a 6f wnr at 2: eff at 5f, bred to apprec 6/7f: acts on polytrack: lost little in defeat conceding weight all round: can rate higher.

AUNTY EURO 0 [1] E J O'Neill 2-8-9 M Fenton 10/1: 4: Dsptd lead, hdd bef 1f out, no extra ins last. 2 **69a**
ICENI WARRIOR 0 [3]2-8-10 (1ow) D Holland 12/1: 5: Held up, short room 3f out, onepcd. ½ **69a**
882 **JOE NINETY 6** [4]2-8-11 J D Smith 7/1: 56: Nvr nrr than mid-div: qck reapp. hd **69a**
WIZZSKILAD 0 [8]2-8-7 R Havlin 50/1: 7: Al bhd: debut. 3½ **55a**
TURTLE MAGIC 0 [5]2-8-2 C Haddon(7) 20/1: 8: Handy, under press & wknd fnl 2f: debut. ½ **49a**
DROOPYS JOEL 0 [6]2-8-7 T Hamilton(3) 4/1: 9: Slow away, al in rear: well bckd on debut. 7 **34a**
9 Ran Time 1m 1.06 (3.26) Owned: Mr D S Nevison Trained: Maidstone

---

932

2.30 Press Interactive To Bet Direct Handicap Stakes 4yo+ 0-75 (E) [75]
£3513 £1081 £541 **1m aw rnd** **Going 22** **+11 Fast** Outside

900 **KATIYPOUR 3** [2] Miss B Sanders 7-9-8 (69) R Miles(3) 11/2: 1346-031: Cl-up, led 2f out, clr 1f **77a**
out, rdn out to hold on: tchd 9/2 on qck reapp: eff btwn 1m/11f on firm, gd/soft & both AWs: in-form 7yo.
698 **CONCER ETO 34** [3] S C Williams 5-9-7 p (68) N Pollard 4/1: 1200-002: ch g Sabrehill - Drudwen 1½ **72a**
(Sayf El Arab) Held up, still trav well but plenty to do 2f out, styd on well to chase wnr ins fnl 1f, nrst fin: significant gamble from 14/1: h'cap win in '03 (also plcd twice): won 4 h'caps in '02: eff at 7f/10f & likes fast, acts on gd/soft & both AWs: can go well fresh: eff with cheek pieces, win similar on this evidence.
2 Aug'03 Ches 7.0g/f 72-70 E: 1 Aug'03 Yarm 8.0g/f 74-64 F: 1 Oct'02 Brig 9.9g/f 65-59 F: 1 Sep'02 Chep 8g/f 62-53 E: 1 Aug'02 Epso 8.5g/f 53-49 E: 1 Jul'02 Brig 9.9g/f 46-41 F: 2 Jun'02 Wolv 8.4af 52a-50 F:
714 **DEEPER IN DEBT 31** [9] J Akehurst 6-9-12 (73) J Mackay 3/1 FAV: 3112-243: Trkd ldrs, chsd wnr 1 **75a**
dist, sn onepcd: well bckd under top-weight: consistent performer: see 714 & 517.
714 **SIR LAUGHALOT 31** [4] Miss E C Lavelle 4-9-9 (70) L Keniry(3) 11/2: 20-20324: In tch, rdn dist, sn onepcd.dht **72a**
700 **MUSICAL GIFT 32** [11]4-9-8 P (69) B Reilly(3) 11/1: 240-1445: Bhd, trav well 2f out, short of room nk **70a**
dist till switched 1f out, kept on but ch had gone: op 7/1, cheek pieces: not get run of race, just btr 700.
1858} **NIGHT WOLF 300** [5]4-9-8 (69) S Hitchcott(3) 14/1: 334415-6: gr g Indian Ridge - Nicer (Pennine ¾ **68a**
Walk) Chsd ldrs, rdn 2f out, short of room dist, switched & kept on late: did not get run of race: h'cap wnr in '03: 4th on both '02 starts (rtd 68, mdn): eff at 6f/1m on firm, fast, prob handles polytrack.
1 May'03 Newc 8.0g/f 71-57 F:
131 **TROUSERS 115** [10]5-9-11 (72) D Holland 10/1: 032136-7: Handy, wknd 1f out: long abs: btr 22. 4 **63a**
26 **INDIAN WELCOME 134** [12]5-9-13 bl (74) M Fenton 12/1: 150100-8: Led, hdd 2f out, sn wknd: abs. ½ **64a**
4372} **LIFTED WAY 188** [7]5-9-13 (74) W Ryan 33/1: 135400-9: Held up, nvr a factor: long abs & top-weight. 4 **54a**
800 **ZEIS 22** [6]4-9-12 (73) A Culhane 50/1: 1/00-00: 10th: Held up, nvr a factor. nk **54a**
714 **Jools 31** [8]6-9-9 (70) Dane O'Neill 20/1:0 862* **Bressbee 9** [1]6-9-11 (6ex)bl(72) V Slattery 20/1:0
12 Ran Time 1m 37.10 (0.90) Owned: Mr Peter Crate Trained: Epsom

---

933

3.00 Bet Direct Interactive Handicap Stakes 3yo 0-75 (E) [82]
£3494 £1075 £538 **7f aw rnd** **Going 22** **-17 Slow** Inside

764* **ECCENTRIC 26** [1] Andrew Reid 3-9-3 (71) D Holland 7/4 FAV: 0-411: Made all, still trav well 2f **79a+**
out, sn clr, eased cl-home, val 3L+: h'cap bow: eff at 7f on polytrack/sharp trk: loves to force the pace & Lingfield: improving with ev run, land hat-trick: see 764.
337 **THE JOB 79** [6] A D Smith 3-8-5 (59) W Ryan 7/1: 40014-62: Keen in tch, styd on to chase wnr 1½ **59a**
dist, al held by wnr fnl 1f: tchd 9/1: 11 wk abs: gd run: eff at 7f/1m: see 77.
901 **DOCKLANDS BLUE 3** [4] N P Littmoden 3-8-0 (54) C Catlin 9/2: 2003643: Held up, hdwy 2f out, kept shd **53a**
on ins fnl 1f, not btn far: qck reapp: eff at 5/7f: lightly rcd in h'cap grade: see 691.
4997} **BLACK OVAL 143** [7] M R Channon 3-8-8 (62) S Hitchcott(3) 10/1: 000606-4: b f Royal Applause - ½ **60a**
Corniche Quest (Salt Dome) Cl-up, onepcd fnl 1f: op 7/1 on AW bow: fill mdn wnr first time out in '03: eff at 5/7f on firm grnd & polytrack: acts on a stiff trk & goes well fresh: encouraging eff after long lay-off.
1 Jun'03 Sali 5fm 81- D:
795* **GENEROUS GESTURE 23** [8]3-9-7 (75) J Mackay 5/2: 604-15: Keen cl-up, wknd dist: btr 795 (6f, fsnd). 3 **67a**
735 **SACHIN 29** [2]3-8-11 (65) R Miles(3) 16/1: 04340-06: Slow away, nvr a factor: btr 735. 7 **43a**
4903} **DISCO DIVA 151** [3]3-9-1 (69) Dane O'Neill 12/1: 360152-7: ch f Spectrum - Compact Disc (Royal 1 **45a**
Academy) Keen in tch, fdd 2f out: long abs: fill nurs wnr in '03: eff at 6/7f on firm & fast grnd.
2 Oct'03 Leic 7.0fm 69-65 E: 1 Sep'03 Leic 6.0g/f 66-60 E:
835 **WENDYS GIRL 13** [5]3-8-10 (64) T Woodley 33/1: 65330-08: In tch wide, fdd 2f out: op 20/1. 3½ **33a**
8 Ran Time 1m 25.59 (2.79) Owned: Mr A S Reid Trained: Mill Hill London

---

934	**3.35 Littlewoods Bet Direct Classified Stakes 3yo 0-70 (E)**
	£3465 £1066 £533 **1m aw rnd** **Going 22** -06 Slow Outside

734*   **CERTIFIABLE** 29 [8] Andrew Reid 3-9-0 (68) D Holland 6/1: 411: Made all, all out ins fnl 1f to   **76a**
hold on: eff at 1m on, further shld suit: acts on polytrack & suited by forcing tactics: genuine & progressive.
341*   **WHITGIFT ROCK** 79 [4] S Dow 3-9-2 (72) P Doe 5/2 FAV: 05631-12: Mid-div, hdwy 2f out, styd on to   ½   **76a**
chase wnr ins fnl 1f, just held': well bckd after 11 wk abs: lost little in defeat on hat-trick bid: see 241 & 220.
697*   **TIGER TIGER** 34 [1] Jamie Poulton 3-9-2 (72) P Dobbs 7/1: 0-13: Held up, hdwy 3f out, kept on ins   1½   **73a**
fnl 1f, nrst fin: op 11/2: eff at 1m, shapes as tho' 10f will suit: lightly raced: see 697.
817*   **ALFRIDINI** 18 [7] D R C Elsworth 3-9-0 (70) Dane O'Neill 3/1: 002214: Keen in tch, chsd wnr dist,   nk   **70a**
sn onepace: tchd 9/2: not disgraced & ran to form of win in 817 (10f).
841   **CATALINI** 12 [2]3-9-5 (75) A Culhane 4/1: 55363-25: Held up, rdn 4f out, kept on late: see 841.   nk   **74a**
4980} **ANDURIL** 145 [6]3-9-1 (71) J Tate 25/1: 045-6: ch c Kris - Attribute (Warning) Keen cl-up, fdd   3½   **63a**
1f out: long abs: unplcd in 3 '03 starts (rtd 76a & 49, mdns): dam plcd at 7f: with J M P Eustace.
839*   **HAWKIT** 13 [3]3-9-1 (71) V Slattery 14/1: 233-5217: Handy, wknd fnl 2f: polytrack bow, btr 839.   ¾   **61a**
5016] **STYLISH SUNRISE** 141 [5]3-9-0 (70) M Fenton 25/1: 036-8: b g Desert Style - Anita At Dawn   11   **39a**
(Anita's Prince) Prom, fdd 3f out: long abs & AW bow: plcd on 1 of 3 '03 starts (mdn, rtd 77): eff at 1m on fast.
8 Ran   Time 1m 38.47 (2.27)   Owned: Mr A S Reid   Trained: Mill Hill London

---

935	**4.10 Bet Rugby League @ Betdirect Co Uk Claiming Stakes 3yo+ (F)**
	£3017 £862 £431 **7f aw rnd** **Going 22** -17 Slow Inside

868*   **SUPREME SALUTATION** 8 [5] D W Chapman 8-9-7 (60) A Culhane 5/1: 0560-011: Mid-div, prog 2f out,   **64a**
styd on to lead cl-home, won going away: tchd 4/1: clmd for £8,000: eff at 7f, suited by 1m/9f: stays 11f well:
acts on firm, soft & both AWs: in gd form in claimers: see 868.
902   **ILLUSIVE** 3 [6] M Wigham 7-9-9 bl (60) M Tebbutt 14/1: 0035002: Keen cl-up, chsd ldr 2f out, styd   ¾   **62a**
on to lead ins fnl 1f, hdd cl-home: qck reapp: lost little in defeat & can find similar on this evidence: see 628.
804   **FOLEY PRINCE** 22 [4] D Flood 3-8-7 (67) J Mackay 5/1: 05146-03: Prom, led 2f out, hdd ins fnl 1f,   nk   **60a**
not btn far: claimed for £9,000: acts on firm, soft & both AW's: see 804.
669   **KINSMAN** 37 [13] T D McCarthy 7-9-5 bl (58) R Miles(3) 8/1: 600-2154: Held up, hdwy 2f out, nrst fin.   2½   **52a**
730   **MAJHOOL** 30 [2]5-9-6 (67) D Holland 7/2 FAV: 0010-045: Keen in rear, prog 2f out, nrst fin.   1   **51a**
910   **LUCAYAN MONARCH** 2 [12]6-9-7 p (55) B Reilly(3) 8/1: 0023236: Nvr nrr than mid-div: wknd 2f out.   1¾   **48a**
804*   **LADY PISTE** 22 [1]3-8-0 vis t (54) B Swarbrick(7) 8/1: 0425317: Cl-up, fdd dist: see 804.   nk   **41a**
846   **THE GAY FOX** 12 [9]10-9-4 bl t (45) L Keniry(3) 25/1: 2300308: Mid-div, nvr able to chall: btr 825.   1   **42a**
858   **EFFECTIVE** 10 [11]4-9-9 VIS (60) Dane O'Neill 25/1: 00-03059: Keen in tch, fdd dist: 1st time visor.   1¾   **43a**
4864} **EVA PERON** 154 [3]4-9-2 (59) C Haddon(7) 33/1: 066000-0: 10th: b f Alzao - High Flying Adored (In   1½   **33a**
The Wings) Mid-div, nvr a factor: long abs: unplcd in '03 (rtd 64 & 58a, h'caps, H Morrison): won fnl of 4 '02
starts (mdn auct): eff at 1m, middle dist bred: acts on gd, fast grnd & fibresand: with W Turner.
1 Oct'02 Sout 8af 78a- F: 2 Sep'02 Beve 7.4gd 72- E:
698   **PAGAN STORM** 34 [7]4-9-9 bl (67) Kristin Stubbs(7) 20/1: 36146-00: 11th: ch g Tabasco Cat -   1   **38a**
Melodeon (Alydar) Al in rear: mdn wnr in '03 (Mrs AJ Perrett): plcd on fnl '02 start (rtd 84): eff at 6f/sharp 1m
on firm & gd grnd: eff with/without blnks & goes well fresh: 1 Aug'03 Newm 6fm 74-(75) D:
846   **SOCIAL CONTRACT** 12 [14]7-9-5 vis (45) J F Egan 33/1: 0606200: 12th: Al bhd.   1½   **31a**
872   **BACK AT DE FRONT** 8 [10]3-8-3 (59) C Catlin 25/1: 1554560: 13th: Al adrift.   3½   **23a**
4692} **ORIONS BELT** 166 [8]4-9-4 (55) R Thomas(5) 50/1: 00500/0-0: 14th: Keen cl-up, fdd 2f out.   5   **13a**
541   **BEENABOUTABIT** 52 [15]6-8-13 p (30) V Slattery 66/1: 00/000-00: 15th: Led, hdd 2f out, sn fdd.   5   **0a**
15 Ran   Time 1m 25.59 (2.79)   Owned: Mr David W Chapman   Trained: York

---

936	**4.40 New Site @ Betdirect Co Uk Handicap Stakes 4yo+ 0-75 (E)**	**[72]**
	£3455 £1063 £532 **1m4f aw** **Going 22** -06 Slow Inside	

731   **CLASSIC ROLE** 30 [1] R Ingram 5-9-12 VIS (70) A Culhane 4/1: 30-40341: Mid-div, al trav well, hdwy   **79a**
2f out, led bef 1f out, rdn out: well bckd: eff at 10/12f on fast, soft & both AWs: sharpened by visor.
903*   **STEELY DAN** 3 [8] J R Best 5-9-12 (6ex) (70) N Pollard 5/2: 2213112: Held up, hdwy 2f out,   1½   **75a**
chsd wnr dist, kept on but not pace wnr: op 15/8 on qck reapp: eff at 7f/12f: v progressive, stays 12f.
681   **SO VITAL** 36 [3] J Pearce 4-9-13 (73) R Price 25/1: 62-103: Handy, under press 4f out, onepcd fnl 2f.   3½   **73a**
269*   **GRAND WIZARD** 87 [2] W Jarvis 4-9-12 (72) M Tebbutt 16/1: 001-4: Held up, short of room & lost pl   2½   **68a**
3f out, kept on late: 12 wk abs: btr 269 (10f).
876   **ANYHOW** 7 [7]7-9-6 (64) D Holland 3/1: 0-002145: Held up, prog 2f out, short of room till 1f out,   ½   **59a**
not recover: qck reapp: got no luck in running & can rate higher: see 801.
731   **PRIVATE BENJAMIN** 30 [4]4-9-0 (60) D Kinsella 25/1: 664-0106: Cl-up, led 2f out, hdd & fdd dist.   shd   **54a**
856   **GENERAL GB** 10 [10]7-9-7 (65) V Slattery 12/1: 642/0/-127: Cl-up, led 3f out, hdd 2f out, sn wknd.   3   **55a**
816   **RAINBOW WORLD** 18 [9]4-9-10 (70) M Fenton 25/1: 5160-038: Mid-div, fdd fnl 2f: btr 816.   3½   **55a**
762*   **CROSSWAYS** 27 [5]6-9-10 (68) Dane O'Neill 11/2: P034-419: In tch, fdd 3f out: btr 762 (K Fallon).   3   **49a**
597   **ELLEN MOONEY** 45 [6]5-9-12 (70) T Hamilton(3) 16/1: 502-2340: 10th: Led, hdd 3f out, sn fdd: 6 wk abs.   2½   **47a**
10 Ran   Time 1m 38.47(2.27)   Owned: Pillar To Post Racing   Trained: Epsom

Official Going Standard To Slow

---

937 7.00 Bet Direct On Sky Active Handicap Stakes 4yo+ 46-55 (F) [62]
£2954 £844 £422 1m4f aw Going 55 -21 Slow Inside

896	FFIFFIFFER 4 [5] C Tinkler 6-9-7 (55) A Culhane 7/2 FAV: 05225-41: Mid div, prog to lead 2f out, rdn out: qck reapp: eff at 10.5f/12f on both AW's: see 896.		61a
866*	AVEIRO 10 [11] Miss Gay Kelleway 8-10-0 (62) M Fenton 13/2: 1333212: Cl up, led 4f out, hdd 2f out, not pace wnr fnl 1f: gd run on drop back to 12f: see 866 (2m).	2½	63a
867	KENTUCKY BULLET 9 [4] A G Newcombe 8-8-13 (47) L Keniry(3) 7/1: 425-3063: Mid div, hdwy 2f out, kept on fnl 1f, just held for 2nd: just btr 331.	hd	47a
867	DISABUSE 9 [3] M W Easterby 4-9-5 (55) P Mulrennan(5) 5/1: 66-21344: Heldup, prog 3f out, styd on fnl 1f, nrst fin: shapes as though further will suit: see 867 & 746.	nk	54a
801	FIGHT THE FEELING 23 [2]6-9-7 vis (55) A Daly 11/1: 6-422005: Keen cl up, fdd fnl 1f: btr 557.	2½	50a
891	BUZ KIRI 5 [1]6-8-12 (1oh) (45) Hayley Turner(5) 9/2: 1221226: Nvr trav & nvr nrr than mid div.	7	31a
867	COOLFORE JADE 9 [6]4-9-2 (52) C Catlin 16/1: 4350507: Led, hdd 4f out, sn wknd: see 816.	6	28a
4131	MONSAL DALE 201 [8]5-8-12 (1oh) (45) V Slattery 10/1: 464235-8: ch g Desert King - Zanella (Nordico) Al in rear: new stable, 10 wk jumps abs, earlier sell h'cap hdle wnr (rtd 77h, stys 2m1.5f on soft, B J Llewellyn): AW sell wnr in early '03: unplcd in '02 (J Toller, rtd 58): eff at 12f/2m on firm, fast grnd & fibresand: likes to force the pace: with N E Berry. 2 Jun'03 Warw 16.2fm 52-52 F: 2 Apr'03 Sout 16g/f 55-54 F: 1 Jan'03 Sout 12af 59a- G:	6	13a
689	PRINCE PROSPECT 36 [7]8-9-2 (50) Kristin Stubbs(7) 14/1: 40-01229: Al in rear: btr 689 (seller).	1½	14a
850	SANTA CATALINA 13 [10]5-8-12 (6oh) (40) B Reilly(3) 50/1: 03-00540: 10th: Bhd, nvr a factor: btr 199.	4	4a
806	VICTORY VEE 22 [9]4-9-5 (55) R Havlin 40/1: 3003-060: 11th: Keen handy, fdd 4f out: btr 68.	23	0a

11 Ran Time 2m 42.74 (9.14) Owned: Mr George Ward Trained: Compton

---

938 7.30 Special Offers @ Betdirect Co Uk Selling Stakes 2yo (G)
£2506 £716 £358 5f aw rnd Going 55 -51 Slow Inside

	LITTLE BISCUIT 0 [1] K R Burke 2-8-6 G Faulkner 9/4: 1: br f Indian Lodge - Arjan (Paris House) Slow away, chsd ldr 3f out, led 1f out, rdn out: no bid, debut: Mar first foal, dam 5f wnr: sire Group 1 miler: eff at 5f on fibresand & a sharp trk, goes well fresh: bred for speed, gd start.		69a
	NUTTY TIMES 0 [6] W G M Turner 2-8-6 A Daly 2/1 FAV: 2: ch f Timeless Times - Nuthatch (Thatching) Led, hdd under press 1f out, not pace wnr: debut: April foal, cost 800 gns: sister won at 5f/8f: dam mdn: sire won numerous times at 2: eff at 5f on fibresand.	1¼	64a
	PETITE ELLE 0 [4] P J McBride 2-8-6 J Quinn 3/1: 3: b f Wolfhound - Start Again (Cyrano de Bergerac) Rear, prog 2f out, wknd fnl 1f: debut: Mar Foal, cost 1,200 gns: speedily bred.	3½	54a
	MARNE 0 [5] J M P Eustace 2-8-11 J Tate 4/1: 4: Cl up, fdd 2f out: debut.	11	29a

4 Ran Time 1m 5.50 (5.3) Owned: Mrs Elaine M Burke Trained: Leyburn

---

939 8.00 Press Interactive To Bet Direct Maiden Stakes 3yo+ (D)
£3396 £1045 £523 1m1f79y Going 55 -20 Slow Inside

4467}	SLALOM 183 [7] Miss Gay Kelleway 4-9-12 e M Fenton 5/1: 53-1: b g Royal Applause - Skisette (Malinowski) Slow away, sn rdn bhd, prog 3f out, led bef 1f out, sn edged right, drvn out: AW bow: plcd on last of only 2 '03 starts (rtd 80, mdn): eff at 1m/9.4f, further shld suit: acts on fibresand & gd/sft: eff on a sharp trk & goes well fresh: eff with eye-shield: open to further improvement.		80a
4015}	GOLDEN EMPIRE 207 [4] E A L Dunlop 3-8-7 W Supple 4/7 FAV: 32-2: br c Red Ransom - Golden Gorse (His Majesty) Sn led, hdd 2f out, kept on but not pace wnr ins fnl 1f: reapp & AW bow: plcd on both '03 starts (mdns, rtd 82): half brother to smart 10f wnr Lear Spear: eff at 6f/9.4f, 10f+ will suit: acts on firm, fast & fibresand: has done little wrong to date & can lose mdn tag. 2 Sep'03 Yarm 7.0g/f 82- D:	1½	77a
54}	PURE MISCHIEF 494 [6] W M Brisbourne 5-9-12 (45) B Swarbrick(7) 25/1: 200030/-3: Handy, led 2f out, edgd left & hdd bef 1f out, styd on: 2 yr absence: long jumps abs & new stable.	1¾	74a
561	ALBEE 50 [12] Miss Gay Kelleway 4-9-12 p Lisa Jones(3) 33/1: 664: Mid div, prog 2f out, onepcd fnl 1f.	3½	69a
678	JARRAAF 37 [10]4-9-12 (56) S W Kelly 6/1: 24244-55: In tch, no extra fnl 2f: see 678.	shd	68a
4924}	MENAI STRAIGHTS 151 [8]3-8-7 (66) J Fanning 16/1: 0553-6: Cl up, led 3f out, hdd 2f out, sn wknd.	6	59a
1044}	ALPHA ECHO 163 [11]5-9-12 S Righton 33/1: 5/0-7: Cl up, ev ch 3f out, sn fdd: reapp & new stable.	6	50a
1893}	SPARTAN PRINCIPLE 299 [1]4-9-7 C Lowther 80/1: 0-8: Nvr nrr than mid div.	5	38a
894	UN AUTRE ESPERE 5 [2]5-9-12 bl (30) L Vickers 100/1: 500-0609: Led 1f, fdd 5f out: qck reapp.	5	36a$
881	SUNSET BLUES 7 [3]4-9-12 bl e R Havlin 100/1: 500: 10th: Al adrift: qck reapp.	25	6a
	Learn The Lingo 0 [9]8-9-12 t P J F Egan 66/1:0	451}	Regal Ali 258 [5]5-9-12 (30) V Slattery 100/1:0

12 Ran Time 2m5.21 (7.01) Owned: Mr Hilton Guinle Trained: Newmarket

---

940 8.30 Betdirect Co Uk Handicap Stakes 3yo+ 0-85 (D) [85]
£4030 £1240 £620 7f aw rnd Going 55 +03 Fast Outside

887	FLINT RIVER 7 [9] H Morrison 6-9-7 (78) A Culhane 11/4: 10-20001: Held up, prog wide 3f out, led dist, rdn out: qck reapp: eff at 6f, appre return to 7f, stays sharp 10f: acts on firm, gd & both AW's, loves Wolverhampton: back to form at favourite crse: btr 361.		86a
840*	JUST A GLIMMER 14 [3] L G Cottrell 4-9-11 (82) D Holland 5/2 FAV: 1/00-3012: Cl up, ev ch dist, kept on but not pace wnr: gd eff under top weight, raised 6lbs since recent win here in 840.	1¼	86a
888	LABRETT 7 [8] Miss Gay Kelleway 7-9-11 p (82) M Fenton 4/1: 61-30523: Prom, rdn & onepcd ins fnl 1f: qck reapp: btr 888 (1m, Lingfield).	1½	83a
807	ROMANY NIGHTS 22 [6] J W Unett 4-9-1 vis (72) S W Kelly 14/1: 6000-504: Cl up, led 2f out, hdd dist, sn no extra: eff at 6f/7f on firm, gd grnd & fibresand: see 807.	½	72a
439	PHAROAHS GOLD 68 [7]6-8-5 e (62) W Supple 16/1: 1000-205: Held up, prog 3f out, no impress fnl 1f.	1	60a
880	RIPPLE EFFECT 8 [2]4-9-8 t (79) T P Queally(3) 16/1: 1205156: Al in rear: btr 799 (polytrack).	8	61a

WOLVERHAMPTON Fibresand SATURDAY 27.03.04 Lefthand, Sharp Track

935 **FOLEY PRINCE 1** [4]3-7-12 (3oh) (67) J Mackay 14/1: 05146-037: Led, hdd 2f out, sn wknd: fin 3rd   1   50a
yesterday in 935 (sell, Lingfield).
50 **OASES 130** [5]5-8-1 e (58) Lisa Jones(3) 25/1: 000400-8: ch g Zilzal - Markievicz (Doyoun) Slow   6   26a
away, nvr a factor: h'cap wnr in '03: unpicd in '02 (rtd 96 & 77a, B J Meehan): mdn wnr on sole '01 start: eff at
6f/7f on fast, hvy & polytrack: best without blnkd & visor, tried eye-shield: with D Shaw.
2 May'03 Ayr 6g/s 66-60 D: 1 May'03 Hami 6.0gd 65-54 E: 2 Dec'02 Ling 7ap 60a-58 E: 1 Oct'01 Newb 6hvy 94- D:
840 **WARDEN WARREN 14** [1]6-9-3 p (74) B Reilly(3) 12/1: 1-346109: Cl up, fdd 3f out: btr 704.   nk   41a
9 Ran   Time 1m 29.89 (3.69)   Owned: The Firm   Trained: East Ilsley

---

941 9.00 Free #10 Bet @ Bet Direct Interactive Claiming Stakes 4yo+   (F)
£2919 £834 £417   **6f aw rnd**   **Going 55**   **+05 Fast**   Inside

807 **GILDED COVE 22** [7] R Hollinshead 4-8-11 (64) A Culhane 5/4 FAV: 0-003351: Held up, prog 3f out,   64a
led after 2f out, drvn out: eff at 5f/6f on fibresand/sharp trk: likes claimers & Wolver, see 610.
807 **RAFTERS MUSIC 22** [3] Julian Poulton 9-8-13 (69) M Fenton 6/1: 4326-302: Bhd, prog 2f out, ev ch   ½   64a
ins fnl 1f, just held by wnr: see 349 & 153.
874 **AINTNECESSARILYSO 8** [2] N E Berry 6-8-11 (51) C Catlin 10/1: 5143633: Held up, hdwy 3f out, kept   ¾   60a
on ins fnl 1f, not btn far: see 874 & 501.
646 **POLAR HAZE 40** [5] J Pearce 7-8-13 vis (56) J Quinn 12/1: 4261504: Cl up, no extra ins fnl 1f: 6 wk abs.   2   56a
840 **BLAKESET 14** [1]9-8-10 (72) D Holland 2/1: 0112305: Prom, no extra ins fnl 1f: btr 730 & 610.   shd   52a
869 **SECOND MINISTER 9** [8]5-8-13 bl t (60) P Fitzsimons 8/1: 0032-306: Led, hdd after 2f out, sn fdd.   9   29a
6 Ran   Time 1m 15.82 (3.02)   Owned: Mr M Johnson   Trained: Upper Longdon

---

942 9.30 Cashbacks @ Betdirect Co Uk Handicap Stakes 3yo+ 0-75 (E)   [75]
£3283 £938 £469   **1m100y aw rnd**   **Going 55**   **-10 Slow**   Inside

800 **DEL MAR SUNSET 23** [3] W J Haggas 5-10-0 P (75) D Holland 15/8 FAV: 003-4501: Made all, drvn out   83a
fnl 1f to hold on: eff at 1m, stays a sharp 10f: acts on firm, hvy & both AW's: app fitting of cheek pieces: well
h'capped 5yo who gamely defied top weight: see 278.
809 **ACTIVE ACCOUNT 22** [4] Mrs H Dalton 7-9-5 (66) J F Egan 4/1: 26233-22: Mid div, prog & ev ch   1   71a
dist, not pace wnr ins fnl 1f: clr rem: another consistent eff, see 809.
806* **DANIELLES LAD 22** [6] B Palling 8-9-11 bl (72) A Culhane 5/1: 5-420413: Cl up, fdd dist: btr 806.   5   67a
861 **SPARK UP 10** [1] J W Unett 4-8-10 VIS (57) S W Kelly 8/1: 66-00624: Hld up, wknd 2f out: vis.   2   48a
809 **SCOTTISH RIVER 22** [2]5-9-12 (73) A Daly 12/1: 0151105: Rear, prog 3f out, hung left & wknd 1f out.   hd   63a
855 **RARE COINCIDENCE 11** [5]3-8-6 p (70) J Fanning 7/2: 320-1136: Slow away, rear & fdd 3f out: 16   30a
dismal run & surely something amiss, btr 564.
4001} **CLANN A COUGAR 208** [7]4-9-5 p (66) T Hamilton(3) 33/1: 064404-7: ch g Bahamian Bounty - Move   ½   25a
Darling (Rock City) Prom, fdd 3f out: reapp: plcd once in '03 (h'cap, rtd 73): mdn auct wnr in '02: eff at 6f/7f
on firm & soft grnd: has tried cheek pieces: with Ian Wood. 1 Jul'02 Chep 6gd 78- E: 2 Jun'02 Kemp 6g/s 76- E:
7 Ran   Time 1m 51.72(5.52)   Owned: Mr R A Dawson   Trained: Newmarket

---

KEMPTON SATURDAY 27.03.04 Righthand, Flat, Fair Track

Official Going Soft (Good/Soft places)

---

943 2.05 E B F Freephone Stanleybet 0808 100 1221 Maiden Stakes 2yo (D)
£5233 £1610 £805   **5f str**   **Soft 103**   **-27 Slow**   Far Side

LADY FILLY [1] W G M Turner 2-8-9 A Daly 20/1: 1: ch f Atraf - Just Lady (Emarati) Made all,   83
styd on well, hands & heels: Apr foal: half sister to useful sprint wnr Justalord: dam 5f juv scorer: eff at 5f on
soft: runs well fresh: fine start.
BIBURY FLYER [2] M R Channon 2-8-9 C Catlin 3/1: 2: br f Zafonic - Affair of State (Tate   1   80
Gallery) Handy, hmpd after 1f, bhd, kept on fnl 2f, nrst fin: op 2/1: Feb foal: sister to a mid-dist wnr: dam useful
sprint juv: eff at 5f, 6f will suit: acts on soft: got the hang of things late on & shld win sn.
882 **GRAND OPTION 7** [7] B W Duke 2-9-0 P Dobbs 10/1: 03: With wnr, onepace fnl 1f: Feb foal, cost   hd   84
8,000 gns: half brother to sev juv wnrs: dam 1m/10f wnr: eff at 5f on soft: improved from debut & shld find a race.
TREMAR [6] T G Mills 2-9-0 W Ryan 4/1: 4: b c Royal Applause - Sabina (Prince Sabo) Slow away   2½   79+
& sn well bhd, styd on nicely late, nrst fin: Mar foal, cost 26,000 gns: half brother to a mod 5f juv wnr: dam 6f juv
scorer: v green, shld come on plenty for this & one to keep in mind.
POLLY ALEXANDER [4]2-8-9 J Mackay 16/1: 5: With ldrs, wknd appr fnl 1f.   hd   73
CANTON [3]2-9-0 Dane O'Neill 9/4 FAV: 6: Slow away, sn in tch, wknd 2f out: bckd.   4   70
BRIDGE PLACE [5]2-9-0 S W Kelly 11/2: 7: Slow away, al bhd.   3½   63
7 Ran   Time 1m 04.8 (6.5)   Owned: Mrs M S Teversham   Trained: Sherborne

---

944 2.35 Stanleybet Com Handicap Stakes 3yo+ 0-80 (D)   [80]
£5590 £1720 £860   **5f str**   **Soft 103**   **+04 Fast**   Far Side. 2 Groups (Far side fav).

2002} **FURTHER OUTLOOK 294** [9] D K Ivory 10-9-9 (75) Dane O'Neill 25/1: 000200-1: gr g Zilzal - Future   88
Bright (Lyphard's Wish) Made all far side, clr 2f out, pushed out, cmftbly: rnr-up in a claim in '03 (rtd 73, with A
Reid): multiple wnr prev seasons: best at 5/6f, stays 1m on fm, hvy & any trk: gd weight carrier: formerly useful,
still has plenty of ability & on a handy mark for new stable, defy a pen.
2 May'03 Wind 6gd 73-(83) F: 2 Jun'02 Epso 6gd 94-87 C: 2 Jun'02 Kemp 6fm 88-83 C: 1 May'02 Wind 6g/f 82- F:
2 Apr'02 Ripo 5g/f 73- E: 2 Apr'01 Nott 5hvy 104- C:
4477} **SEVEN NO TRUMPS 182** [10] J M Bradley 7-10-0 (80) C J Davies(6) 20/1: 003000-2: ch g Pips Pride -   5   83
Classic Ring (Auction Ring) Cl up far side, kept on fnl 1f but not wnr's pace: plcd in a h'cap in '03 (rtd 85, with B
Hills): won reapp in '02 (h'cap): wng form at 5/6f on fm, hvy & any trk: best without blnks, eff in cheekpieces: runs
well fresh: gd start for new trainer, h'capped to win. 1 Mar'02 Donc 5sft 104-96 B: 1 Oct'01 Newb 6hvy 10-94 B:

---

2 Sep'01 Donc 5.6g/f 94-88 B: 1 May'01 Good 6fm 92-82 C: 1 May'01 Donc 6fm 88-75 D:
853* **ITALIAN MIST 11** [6] Julian Poulton 5-7-12 (5oh)e (45) M Halford(7) 12/1: 3512013: Bhd far side, kept on late, nrst fin: acts on fast, soft & loves fibresand: may do better on turf: see 853. *2* **49**
749* **PLAYTIME BLUE 29** [1] K R Burke 4-8-11 (63) G Baker 8/1: 2361214: Led stands side group, kept on, no ch with far side: acts on fast & fibresand, prob soft: gd run, see 749. *1¾* **58**
755 **POLISH EMPEROR 28** [7]4-9-7 (73) P Dobbs 5/1 FAV: 410-4225: In tch far side, onepace: see 292. *½* **67**
329 **BYO 81** [2]6-9-3 (69) S Hitchcott(3) 33/1: 00444-06: With ldr stands side, onepace: *shd* **63**
874 **THE FISIO 8** [15]4-9-9 (75) N Chalmers(5) 7/1: 1156307: In tch, no impress fnl 2f: see 415. *nk* **68**
807 **AROGANT PRINCE 22** [3]7-8-2 bl (54) J Quinn 12/1: 6310108: With ldrs stands side, onepace: see 748. *hd* **46**
749 **PRIME RECREATION 29** [5]7-9-2 (68) S Carson 16/1: 00-60609: Bhd far side, no impress: see 66. *1* **58**
834 **BOND PLAYBOY 14** [13]4-9-11 (77) C Catlin 12/1: 12-56060: 10th: Al bhd far side: see 45. *1½* **64**
687 **ELLENS LAD 36** [17]10-9-6 (72) A Rutter(7) 20/1: 001-0500: 11th: Hmpd after 1f far side, no impress. *½* **58**
4259} **WHISTLER 193** [8]7-10-0 p (80) P Fitzsimons 20/1: 214500-0: 12th: ch g Selkirk - French Gift (Cadeaux Genereux) Handy far side, wknd 2f out: won 3 h'caps in '03: eff at 5/6f on fm, soft & any trk: wears cheekpieces, best without blnks: tough, stable's rnrs tend to need a race or two before peaking. *1* **64**
1 Aug'03 Hayd 5fm 83-78 C: 2 Aug'03 Newb 5.2g/f 81-78 C: 2 Jul'03 Sand 5.0g/f 81-76 D: 1 Jul'03 Brig 5.3g/f 76-73 D:
2 May'03 Hayd 5sft 73-71 E: 1 May'03 Nott 5.1g/s 71-65 E: 2 Jul'02 Warw 5g/f 72-74 D: 1 Jun'02 Nott 5g/s 76-71 D:
2 Jun'02 Ches 5gd 71-66 D: 2 May'02 Bath 5.7g/s 71-70 D:
883 **JUSTALORD 7** [4]6-9-3 p (69) J Edmunds 6/1: 6-021230: 13th: Unruly stalls, no danger far side. *2* **49**
874 **Roman Quintet 8** [16]4-8-10 (62) S W Kelly 12/1:0   735 **Easily Averted 30** [14]3-8-7 (71) A Daly 40/1:0
742 **Abraxas 30** [12]6-7-12 (10oh)p(40) J Mackay 100/1:0   740 **Regal Song 30** [11]8-9-4 bl(70) G Carter 12/1:0
17 Ran Time 1m 03.24 (4.94) Owned: Mr K T Ivory Trained: Radlett

945

3.10 Freephone Stanleybet 0808 100 1221 Handicap Stakes 3yo+ 0-95 (C) **[94]**
£9805 £3017 £1509 **7f rnd** **Soft 103** **-17 Slow** Inside. Came stands side in str.

181 **ZILCH 108** [13] M L W Bell 6-8-9 (1ow) (75) Dane O'Neill 10/1: 03/0003-1: Cl up, led over 2f out, pushed clr: abs, bckd from 14/1: stays 7f on fm & polytrack, loves soft & hvy, any trk: runs well fresh: see 181. **88**
4539} **CAMBERLEY 178** [8] P F I Cole 7-9-9 (90) J Quinn 9/2 FAV: 020132-2: b g Sri Pekan - Nsx (Roi Danzig) Keen in tch, eff trav well over 2f out, kept on but not pace of wnr: class stks & h'cap wnr in '03: rtd 97 when 4th in '01: eff at 7/7.5f on fm & soft: runs well fresh on any trk, loves Goodwood: fine return, shld win again, prob at Goodwood (all 3 wins there). *2½* **96**
2 Oct'03 Newc 7gd 91-(90) C: 1 Aug'03 Good 7fm 91-87 B: 2 Jun'03 Newc 7gd 89-85 C: 1 Jun'03 Good 7g/f 88-(80) D:
887 **DIGITAL 7** [10] M R Channon 7-9-12 (93) C Catlin 11/2: 16002-03: ch g Safawan - Heavenly Goddess (Soviet Star) Hld up, eff 2f out, onepace: won a class stks & h'cap in '03: '02 h'cap wnr: eff at 1m, suited by 7f on fm or hvy: goes well fresh on any trk: tough & genuine. *4* **93**
2 Oct'03 Donc 7g/f 102-(94) B: 1 Sep'03 Good 7fm 93-87 B: 2 Aug'03 Ches 7.6fm 90-85 C: 2 Jul'03 Good 7gd 100-(86) B:
2 Jul'03 Hayd 7.1gd 90-86 C: 2 May'03 Donc 7gd 90-85 C: 1 May'03 Ling 7.6gd 88-(84) D: 1 May'02 Newb 7g/s 84-78 D:
1 Jul'01 York 7g/f 85-83 C: 2 May'01 Thir 8g/s 86-82 C: 2 Mar'01 Donc 8hvy 83-80 B:
292 **TARANAKI 84** [12] P D Cundell 6-8-12 (79) Lisa Jones(3) 16/1: 06101-04: Dwelt, with ldrs & rcd alone on far side in str, onepace: abs: uninspired ride, see 130. *½* **78**
688 **SANGIOVESE 36** [3]5-8-1 (68) J Mackay 11/2: 301-0335: With ldr, wknd 2f out: see 611, 195. *½* **66**
4471} **MARKER 182** [9]4-9-11 (92) S Carson 20/1: 461600-6: ch g Pivotal - Palace Street (Secreto) Handy, wknd over 2f out: '03 class stks wnr: '02 mdn wnr: eff at 6f on fm & gd/soft: eff with/without visor: has run well fresh on a gall or sharp trk. 1 Aug'03 Kemp 6fm 96-(90) C: 2 Sep'02 Ayr 6g/s 96-90 C: 1 Jul'02 Wind 6gd 91- D: *3½* **85**
3962} **IRONY 211** [7]5-9-8 (89) N Chalmers(5) 12/1: 660163-7: gr g Mujadil - Cidaris (Persian Bold) Made most to 2f out, wknd: '03 rtd h'cap wnr: plcd in List in '02 (rtd rtd 104): eff at 5/6f, stays 1m on fm & soft: likes to dominate on any trk. 1 Aug'03 Kemp 8fm 89-82 C: 2 Sep'01 Newb 6fm 104- A: 2 Aug'01 Good 5g/f 98- A: *¾* **81**
1 Jun'01 Asco 5g/f 99- B: 1 May'01 Hayd 5g/f 90- E:
369 **AMMENAYR 77** [11]4-8-10 (77) W Ryan 25/1: 61050-08: b g Entrepreneur - Katiyfa (Auction Ring) Cl up, wknd over 2f out: abs: '03 mdn wnr: eff over a gall 7f on fast & gd grnd: has run well fresh. *½* **68**
1 Apr'03 Newm 7gd 82- D:
627 **HAND CHIME 42** [1]7-8-11 (78) S W Kelly 13/2: 003-0059: Keen in tch, wknd 2f out: abs: see 262. *3* **65**
499 **WOOD FERN 59** [5]4-8-10 (77) R Lappin 50/1: 33001-00: 10th: Al bhd: abs, btr 263 (polytrack). *8* **52**
4474} **PENNY CROSS 182** [4]4-9-7 (88) N Mackay(5) 10/1: 221333-0: 11th: Keen with ldrs, wknd 3f out. *1* **62**
4888} **MASTER ROBBIE 154** [6]5-9-13 (94) S Hitchcott(3) 14/1: 012160-0: 12th: In tch, wknd 3f out: reapp. *½* **67**
517 **TERRAQUIN 56** [2]4-8-12 (79) N Pollard 16/1: 6416-040: 13th: Keen in tch, wknd 3f out: see 517. *7* **42**
13 Ran Time 1m 32.55 (8.44) Owned: Mary Mayall Linda Redmond Julie Martin Trained: Newmarket

946

3.45 Stanleybet Com Maiden Stakes 3yo+ (D)
£5434 £1672 £836 **6f str** **Soft 103** **-03 Slow** Far Side

4576} **BYGONE DAYS 176** [2] W J Haggas 3-8-12 S W Kelly 3/1: 02-1: ch g Desert King - May Light (Midyan) Led after 1f, pushed clr over 1f out: bckd: rnr-up in a mdn on 2nd of 2 juv starts: eff at 6f, 7f will suit (half brother to a 1m wnr): runs well fresh on fast grnd, improved here on soft & with positive tactics: looks useful. 2 Oct'03 Ling 5g/f 77- D: **86**
4952} **RANGOON 148** [1] Mrs A J Perrett 3-8-12 Dane O'Neill 1/1 FAV: 3-2: ch c Distant View - Rustic (Grand Lodge) Dwelt, hld up, plenty to do till kept on appr fnl 1f, nrst fin: well bckd: promising 3rd in a Newmarket mdn sole juv start (rtd 87+): dam styd 7f: eff at 6f, 7f sure to suit: acts on gd & soft, gall or easy trk: improve for this & with more positive tactics, shld win a mdn. *5* **75**
881 **EMSAM BALLOU 7** [10] R Hannon 3-8-7 R Smith 9/2: 333: Led 1f, chsd wnr, onepace fnl 2f: clr rem back at 6f, stayed 1m in 881 (polytrack). *1* **68**
4691} **POMPEY CHIMES 167** [6] G B Balding 4-9-11 S Carson 20/1: 5-4: b g Forzando - Silver Purse (Interrex) In tch, wknd 3f out: rtd 44 when 5th sole '03 start. *8* **57**
SILVER REIGN [3]3-8-12 R Thomas(5) 50/1: 5: Dwelt, nvr a factor on debut. *¾* **55**
SCRUNCH [8]3-8-7 P Fitzsimons 12/1: 6: Dwelt, keen & sn bhd on debut. *nk* **49**
814 **MANDAHAR 19** [9]5-9-11 J Quinn 100/1: 007: Al bhd: *10* **34**
TRIAGE [4]3-8-7 C Catlin 14/1: 8: In tch, wknd 3f out. *3* **23**
3525] **OUR SION 589** [7]4-9-11 A Daly 100/1: 00/-9: Sn bhd. *16* **2**
9 Ran Time 1m 17.47 (6.37) Owned: Mr J Hanson Trained: Newmarket

KEMPTON SATURDAY 27.03.04 Righthand, Flat, Fair Track

947 **4.20 Freephone Stanleybet 0808 100 1221 Classified Stakes 3yo 0-80 (D)**
£5408 £1664 £832 **1m1f** **Soft 103** **-36 Slow** Inside. Came stands side in str.

696* **AFRICAN DREAM 35** [8] P W Chapple Hyam 3-8-12 (81) J Quinn 11/4 FAV: 311: Cl up, led over 2f out, pushed clr, eased: bckd: prev with P Cole: stays 9f well, further sure to suit: acts on polytrack, relished this soft grnd: acts on easy trks: fast improving, can make a qk follow-up & looks one to follow: see 696, 623. **106**
796 **RED LANCER 24** [10] R J Price 3-8-11 (80) B Swarbrick(7) 6/1: 10-61122: Keen in tch, eff 2f out, kept on but no ch with wnr: acts on fibresand, prob soft: ran to form bhd a progressive sort: see 796 (12f), 702. *9* **89**
4757*}**CIMYLA 164** [4] C F Wall 3-9-0 (83) G Baker 5/1: 41-3: b c Lomitas - Coyaima (Night Shift) In tch, eff 3f out, onepace: won last of 2 juv starts (mdn): eff at 1m/9f on polytrack & prob fast & soft: clr of rem & a gd return. 1 Oct'03 Ling 8ap 85a- D: *¾* **91**
4834} **LE TISS 158** [6] M R Channon 3-8-13 (82) S Hitchcott(3) 10/1: 610162-4: b c Croco Rouge - Manarah (Marju) Bhd, mod late gains on reapp: '03 dual nursery h'cap wnr: stays 1m well on fast & gd grnd, prob any trk: poss needs faster grnd. 2 Oct'03 Yarm 8.0gd 82-81 E: 1 Sep'03 Muss 8gd 82-78 D: 1 Sep'03 Sali 8g/f 77-69 D: *6* **82**
4942} **SLAVONIC 150** [9]3-8-11 (79) P Dobbs 9/1: 554-5: ch c Royal Academy - Cyrillic (Irish River) Slow away, hld up, wknd over 2f out: 4th in a mdn on last of 3 juv starts (rtd 92 at best): dam 10f wnr: eff at 1m on fm & fast: apprec a return to a faster surface. *1½* **78**
229 **ANUVASTEEL 98** [7]3-8-13 (82) W Ryan 7/1: 005132-6: Handy, wknd 2f out: btr 229, 132 (polytrk). *1¼* **78**
694 **HEVERSHAM 35** [5]3-8-13 (82) S W Kelly 7/1: 4127: Led till 2f out, wknd: btr 623 (mdn, polytrk). *3* **74**
3131} **WINNERS DELIGHT 246** [3]3-9-0 (83) E Stack 33/1: 6165-8: Sn bhd on reapp. *3* **71**
5018} **SONG OF VALA 142** [2]3-8-12 (81) D Sweeney 10/1: 042-9: Chsd ldr to 3f out, wknd on reapp. *1¾* **66**
9 Ran Time 2m 02.51 (12.51) Owned: Franconson Partners Trained: Newmarket

948 **4.55 Freephone Stanleybet Handicap Stakes 4yo+ 0-75 (E)** **[73]**
£3406 £1048 £524 **1m6f92y** **Soft 103** **-92 Slow** Inside. Came stands side in str.

850} **LINENS FLAME 368** [1] B G Powell 5-8-9 (54) D Sweeney 33/1: 006/000-1: ch g Blushing Flame - Atlantic Air (Air Trooper) Led after 6f, hung left but pushed clr over 1f out: mod form prev: improved with positive tactics stepped up to 14.3f on soft grnd: runs well fresh. **69**
768 **BELLE ROUGE 27** [13] C A Horgan 6-8-7 (52) J Quinn 4/1 FAV: 66022/-22: Cl up, outpcd by wnr over 1f out: another gd run: see 768. *5* **60**
813 **TURTLE VALLEY 19** [2] S Dow 8-9-11 (70) P Doe 7/1: 0310-503: Hld up, eff over 2f out, onepace. *3½* **73**
695 **TYPHOON TILLY 35** [10] C R Egerton 7-10-0 (73) S Hitchcott(3) 8/1: 33-64364: In tch, onepace fnl 2f. *2½* **71**
711 **LANOS 32** [12]6-9-0 t (59) N Chalmers(5) 14/1: 6544-555: In tch, wknd 3f out: now with Miss S West. *1¼* **58**
4865} **SAN HERNANDO 155** [3]4-9-10 (73) R Thomas(5) 8/1: 216060-6: b g Hernando - Sandrella (Darshaan) Slow away, hld up, mod late gains: '03 mdn wnr, subs lkd difficult ride & tried cheekpieces & visor: stays 12f on fm & a gall or easy trk. 1 Jun'03 Donc 12fm 80-(77) D: 2 Jun'03 Yarm 11.5fm 74-75 E: *3* **69**
605* **BOUMAHOU 45** [6]4-9-6 (69) W Ryan 11/2: 440-3317: In tch, wknd 2f out: 6 wk abs, btr 605 (AW). *9* **56**
650 **UNLEADED 40** [9]4-7-12 (7oh) (40) J Mackay 20/1: 00-21258: Handy, bhd from halfway: btr 650 (a/w). *¾* **33**
867 **MUNFARID 9** [7]4-9-6 t (69) D Kinsella 25/1: 54-30409: In tch, wknd 3f out: see 359. *1½* **54**
813 **OUR IMPERIAL BAY 19** [5]5-9-5 bl (64) Derek Nolan(7) 16/1: 014/06-00: 10th: b g Smart Strike - Heat Lightning (Summer Squall) Sn bhd: well btn 2 '03 starts: '02 mdn & claim wnr: eff at 10/12f on fast & both a/w's: acts on any trk & eff with/without blnks. *2* **47**
1 Oct'02 Leic 11.8sft 71- F: 1 Mar'02 Sout 12af 81a- D: 2 Feb'02 Ling 10ap 69a- D:
801 **AONINCH 23** [4]4-8-13 (62) S Whitworth 7/1: 30113-60: 11th: Al bhd: btr 801 (polytrack). *nk* **45**
810 **MANDOOB 22** [11]7-10-0 (73) J P Guillambert(3) 16/1: 00-41100: 12th: Hld up, btn 3f out: btr 634 (12f). *6* **50**
813 **GO CLASSIC 19** [14]4-9-1 (64) S Carson 20/1: 00400-00: 13th: Cl up, wknd qckly 4f out. *dist* **0**
4439} **POLANSKI MILL 184** [8]5-9-3 (62) P Dobbs 20/1: 00/0000-P: Led 6f, wknd, t.o./p.u. 3f out. **0**
14 Ran Time 3m 30.87(28.07) Owned: D & J Newell Trained: Winchester

DONCASTER SATURDAY 27.03.04 Lefthand, Flat, Galloping Track

Official Going Good

949 **1.40 Mitsubishi Diamond Vision Conditions Stakes 3yo (C)**
£8412 £3191 £1595 **1m str** **Good 48** **-14 Slow** Inside

5022*}**DIVINE GIFT 141** [5] M A Jarvis 3-8-13 (87) P Robinson 9/2: 2021-1: b c Groom Dancer - Child's Play (Sharpen Up) Made all, styd on strongly & rdn clr fnl 1f on reapp: won last of 4 juv starts (mdn): dam 10f wnr: loves to front run & clearly stays 1m well, further shld suit: acts on gd, handles fast & gd/soft, gall trks, likes Doncaster: runs well fresh: progressed well over the winter, looks useful & can win another nice prize. **104**
1 Nov'03 Donc 7gd 90-(85) D: 2 Oct'03 Ayr 7.2g/s 83- D: 2 May'03 Newm 6g/f 90- D:
4557} **GOLD HISTORY 177** [1] M Johnston 3-9-3 (97) J Fanning 7/2: 110-2: b c Seeking The Gold - Battle Hymn (Danzig) Cl-up, ev ch over 1f out, kept on but not pace of wnr: reapp: won 1st 2 of 3 juv starts (mdn & stks): likes to dominate & eff over 7f/1m on fast & gd grnd, gall trks: useful, gd return & likely to go in again, esp with an uncontested lead. 1 Sep'03 Ayr 7.2g/f 94- C: 1 Sep'03 Leic 7.0g/f 87- D: *3½* **100**
885 **MAKFOOL 7** [7] M R Channon 3-8-13 (96) A Culhane 11/2: 31243-03: b c Spectrum - Abeyr (Unfuwain) In tch, hdwy 2f out, onepace: juv mdn wnr, plcd sev times: eff at 7f/1m on fast, gd/soft & on any trk: useful & tough. 2 Oct'03 Pont 8.0g/f 102-(80) A: 1 Oct'03 Ayr 7.2g/s 93-(80) D: 2 Sep'03 Epso 7gd 80- E: *¾* **94**
4811*}**NEW MEXICAN 159** [2] Mrs J R Ramsden 3-9-5 P (103) J P Spencer 3/1 FAV: 24121-4: ch g Dr Fong - Apache Star (Arazi) Prom, brief eff 2f out, no extra: nicely bckd, tried in cheek pieces, top-weight: won 2 of 5 juv starts, mdn auct & List: stays 1m well on fast & gd grnd, gall trks, likes Pontefract: may do better. *½* **99**
1 Oct'03 Pont 8.0g/f 104-(100) A: 2 Sep'03 Donc 7gd 101-(98) C: 1 Jul'03 Pont 6g/f 87- E: 2 May'03 Donc 6gd 88- D:
4978} **KELUCIA 147** [6]3-8-8 (104) R Ffrench 7/2: 121334-5: Keen in tch, wknd well over 1f out on reapp: busy as a juv, unruly in padd, lkd fit. *1¼* **86**
545 **FOOLS ENTIRE 52** [3]3-8-11 (69) B Reilly(3) 66/1: 322-2036: Keen in tch, wknd 2f out: see 545 (visor). *9* **71**
885 **WELL KNIT 7** [8]3-8-6 Paul Eddery 100/1: 120-007: Dwelt, al bhd. *5* **56**
7 Ran Time 1m 41.44 (4.94) Owned: Mr B E Nielsen Trained: Newmarket

DONCASTER SATURDAY 27.03.04 Lefthand, Flat, Galloping Track

950 **2.10 Konica East Doncaster Shield Conditions Stakes 4yo+ (B)**
£12540 £4807 £2404 **1m4f** **Good 48** **+14 Fast** Inside

293 **ROYAL CAVALIER 84** [2] R Hollinshead 7-8-12 (97) W Supple 33/1: 20206-01: Handy, gd hdwy to lead over 2f out, styd on well, rdn out: 3 mth abs, gd time: well btn on AW earlier: suited by 12f, prob stays 14f: acts on firm, hvy & handles f/sand: loves Doncaster: much imprvd & career best eff at fav trk: see 225. **102**
3032} **DUNHILL STAR 252** [1] B W Hills 4-8-10 (108) M Hills 3/1: 1/12305-2: b c Danehill - Sueboog (Darshaan) Held up, sltly short of room over 3f out, kept on over 1f out, no threat to wnr: joc received a 4-day careless riding ban: '03 class stks wnr, plcd in a Gr 2 (rtd 110): eff at 10f, clearly stays 12f well on firm & gd, handles polytrack, gall trks: has run well fresh: useful, poss more to come. *1* **100**
2 Apr'03 Newm 9gd 110-(89) A: 1 Mar'03 Kemp 9gd 92-(80) D: 1 Dec'02 Ling 6ap 81a- D:
4363} **SYSTEMATIC 189** [7] M Johnston 5-8-12 (111) K Darley 15/8 FAV: 511/255-3: b c Rainbow Quest - Sensation (Soviet Star) Chsd ldr, ev ch 2f out, sn onepace: hvly bckd on reapp: rnr-up in a Gr 2 on first of only 3 '03 starts: won 7 times in '02, incl a Gr 3: suited by 12f, poss stays 13.3f on firm or soft grnd, gall trks: loves to dominate: tried a vis: has had injury problems: formerly smart & tough, may do better. *1½* **98**
2 Aug'03 Newb 13.3fm 114-(113) A: 1 Sep'02 Asco 12g/f 115- A: 1 Sep'02 Donc 12fm 115- A: 1 Aug'02 Newb 12g/f 108- B: 1 Jun'02 Asco 12g/f 104-93 B: 2 Jun'02 Epso 10g/s 94-92 C: 1 May'02 York 10.3g/f 93-84 B: 1 Apr'02 Leic 10gd 85-76 D: 1 Mar'02 Donc 8sft 87- D: 2 Sep'01 Pont 8g/s 78- D:
4782*]**FOREST MAGIC 511** [5] P W D'Arcy 4-8-10 D Holland 11/1: 5211/-4: b c Charnwood Forest - Adultress (Ela Mana Mou) In tch, eff & sltly hmpd 2f out, onepace on reapp: missed '03, prev term won a mdn & List: eff at 10f, prob stays 12f on gd & soft grnd, gall trks: encouraging return, sharper for this. *2* **95**
1 Nov'02 Newm 10g/s 102- A: 1 Oct'02 Nott 9.9sft 92- D: 2 Oct'02 Ayr 7.2sft 85- D:
1791} **HEISSE 307** [3]4-8-10 J Murtagh 5/2: 120-5: b c Darshaan - Hedera (Woodman) Held up, rdn over 3f out, some late gains, nvr a factor on reapp: won 1st of 3 '03 starts (mdn): stays 12f on fast grnd & on a gall trk: has run well fresh: useful, prob ran to best. *1¾* **93**
2 May'03 Bath 10.2g/f 98-(85) B: 1 Apr'03 Newc 12.4g/f 89- D:
3975} **KINGS THOUGHT 210** [6]5-8-12 (98) R Hughes 33/1: 140310-6: Led till 2f out, no extra: wants 10f. *3½* **88**
5036} **PERFECT STORM 140** [4]5-9-2 (92) N Callan 14/1: 460012-7: Held up, hdwy over 2f out, sn no extra. *3* **87**
5008} **RAVENGLASS 143** [8]5-8-12 (83) R Havlin 125/1: 326100-8: Slow away, sn in tch, btn 3f out: ndd race. *2* **80**
8 Ran Time 2m 33.87 (4.07) Owned: The Three R's Trained: Upper Longdon

951 **2.45 Freephone Stanleybet Lincoln Heritage Handicap 4yo+ (B)** **[111]**
£65000 £20000 £10000 **1m str** **Good 48** **+03 Fast** Stands Side. 2 Groups.

82 **BABODANA 126** [23] M H Tompkins 4-9-10 (107) P Robinson 20/1: 004210-1: ch c Bahamian Bounty - Daanat Nawal (Machiavellian) Prom stands side, switched left & styd on strongly to lead over 1f out, drvn out, gamely: won last of 6 '03 starts (List): '02 mdn scorer: suited by a gall 1m & acts on fast, likes gd & soft: runs well fresh, outstanding weight carrying performance, v smart now & well up to Gr race success on this form. **113**
1 Nov'03 Newm 8g/f 110-(100) A: 2 Oct'03 Ayr 8g/s 104-(100) C: 2 Sep'02 Ayr 7.2gd 97- C: 2 Aug'02 Wind 6g/s 99- C: 1 Jun'02 Hami 6sft 82- D:
887 **QUITO 7** [16] D W Chapman 7-9-4 (5ex)bl (101) A Culhane 50/1: 645-1062: Held up stands side, hdwy well over 1f out, strong run ins last, not btn far: v tough, useful & still improving 7yo who relishes coming late through big fields & off a fast pace: eff over 6f/1m: shld continue to go well: see 618, 64. *¾* **105**
4867} **DARK CHARM 155** [12] R A Fahey 5-8-7 (90) P Hanagan 20/1: 520400-3: b g Anabaa - Wardara (Sharpo) Held up stands side, hdwy 2f out, kept on ins last: rnr-up in a rtd h'cap in '03, had some bad luck with draws: '02 mdn & h'cap wnr (with A Balding): eff at 7f, clearly stays 1m well on firm, soft & polytrack, any trk: excellent return, shld win a val prize soon. 2 Aug'03 Newb 7fm 93-93 C: 2 Oct'02 Sali 6gd 98-93 C: 2 Sep'02 Newb 7fm 94-89 C: 1 Jun'02 Ling 7ap 90a-82 D: 1 Jun'02 Newb 6sft 82- D: 2 May'02 Pont 6g/f 81- D: 2 May'02 Sali 6g/f 86- D: *hd* **93**
4684} **WING COMMANDER 168** [24] R A Fahey 5-8-9 (92) T Hamilton(3) 33/1: 540233-4: b g Royal Applause - Southern Psychic (Alwasmi) Held up stands side, hdwy 2f out, kept on ins last, not btn far on reapp: plcd twice for M Bell in '03: rnr-up in '02: eff at 1m, shld apprec a return to 10f: acts on firm, gd & on any trk: eff with/without visor: excellent return for new stable, spot on for this at 10f next time. *nk* **94+**
2 Sep'03 Epso 10.1gd 93-(90) C: 2 Apr'02 Ripo 9gd 95- C: 2 Sep'01 Newb 8fm 96- B: 1 Aug'01 Ayr 7.2gd 87- E:
3276*}**ALKAADHEM 240** [5]4-9-3 (100) W Supple 8/1: 121-5: b c Green Desert - Balalaika (Sadler's Wells) Handy far side, hdwy to lead that group over 1f out, styd on strongly, no ch with fav'd stands side group: won 2 of 3 '03 starts (mdn & class stks): v eff at 1m, shld stay further: acts on firm & gd grnd, any trk: lightly rcd, won race on "wrong" side & looks potentially smart, just the type to keep on your side, will be wng sn. *1½* **102+**
1 Jul'03 Good 7gd 106-(95) B: 2 Jul'03 Newb 7g/f 105- B: 1 Jul'03 Warw 8.1fm 93- D:
5020} **JAY GEES CHOICE 142** [14]4-8-10 (93) D Corby(3) 40/1: 402600-6: Overall ldr stands side till dist. *nk* **91**
4667} **BLUE SPINNAKER 169** [13]5-8-7 (90) Dale Gibson 66/1: 414004-7: Sltly hmpd start when switched right, in tch stands side, some late gains, nrst fin: fine return. *¾* **86**
4977} **UNSHAKABLE 147** [19]5-8-9 (92) J F Egan 12/1: 620000-8: Held up stands side, late gains. *shd* **88**
4977} **DESERT OPAL 147** [2]4-8-12 (95) R Hughes 11/1: 142110-9: ch c Cadeaux Genereux - Nullarbor (Green Desert) Dwelt, sn chsd ldrs far side, eff well over 1f out, kept on: v prog '03, won a mdn & 2 h'caps: suited by 1m on fast, gd & likes gall trks: has run well fresh: useful & progressive, fine return on wrong side here & shld have another profitable season. *shd* **91**
1 Sep'03 Hayd 8.1gd 96-90 C: 1 Jul'03 Newb 8g/f 91-85 D: 2 Jun'03 Sand 8.1gd 89-(81) D: 1 May'03 Sali 6g/f 86- D:
4599} **PENTECOST 175** [18]5-9-3 (100) L Keniry(3) 40/1: 013240-0: 10th: Held up stands side, hdwy over 1f out, kept on ins last, nvr dngrs: likes Ascot. *hd* **95**
547 **SERIEUX 52** [7]5-8-10 (1ow) (92) J Murtagh 33/1: 04300-00: 11th: Cl-up far side, hdwy to lead that group over 2f out till over 1f out, no extra. *nk* **87**
4471} **FREMEN 182** [10]4-8-10 (93) D Holland 8/1: 23110-0: 12th: Led far side till 2f out, wknd: bckd. *shd* **87**
884 **BLUE SKY THINKING 7** [4]5-9-0 (5ex) (97) Darren Williams 20/1: 334-1560: 13th: Hld up far, onepace. *1¾* **88**
758 **DUMARAN 28** [3]6-8-9 (92) M Fenton 66/1: 00403-00: 14th: Nvr a factor far side. *nk* **82**
4667} **FLIGHTY FELLOW 169** [8]4-8-9 bl (92) S Sanders 25/1: 014322-0: 15th: Bhd far side, mod late gains. *¾* **80**
4977} **CRAIOVA 147** [20]5-8-7 (90) S Drowne 25/1: 101250-0: 16th: Chsd ldrs stands side, wknd dist. *nk* **77**
4600} **EL COTO 175** [11]4-8-13 (96) T Quinn 20/1: 610304-0: 17th: Held up far side, eff 2f out, sn no extra. *1½* **80**
4599*}**CHIVALRY 175** [1]5-8-12 (95) G Duffield 16/1: 11304/1-0: 18th: Cl-up far side, wknd 2f out: jumps fit. *¾* **77**
4976} **PABLO 147** [21]5-9-8 (105) M Hills 7/1 FAV: 31/1455-0: 19th: In tch, wknd well over 1f out: nicely bckd: won this race last term off an 8lb lower mark. *3½* **80**
888 **ONLYTIME WILL TELL 7** [9]6-8-12 (95) J Fanning 80/1: 02500-00: 20th: Al bhd far side. *7* **56**
4225} **NORTON 196** [17]7-9-1 (98) K Darley 11/1: 320000-0: 21th: Stands side, wknd 2f out on reapp. *3* **53**

DONCASTER   SATURDAY 27.03.04   Lefthand, Flat, Galloping Track

3186} **TOUGH LOVE 245** [22]5-8-10 (93) K Dalgleish 14/1: 221330-0: 22th: Cl-up stands side, wknd 2f out.   3   42
4599} **CONVENT GIRL 175** [6]4-8-13 (96) R Havlin 25/1: 123126-0: 23th: In tch far side, wknd 2f out.   hd   44
547   **OUR TEDDY 52** [15]4-8-10 VIS (93) Martin Dwyer 14/1: 00000-40: 24th: Switched to race far side,   1   39
prom, wknd 2f out: 7 wk abs: visor, mod ride: see 547.
24 Ran   Time 1m 40.15 (3.65)   Owned: Mr M P Bowring   Trained: Newmarket

952 3.15 Listed Cammidge Trophy 3yo+ (A)
£19500 £6000 £3000   **6f str**   **Good 48**   -03 Slow   Stands Side

5037} **GOLDEVA 140** [16] R Hollinshead 5-8-11 (91) A Culhane 40/1: 065620-1: gr f Makbul - Gold Belt   100
(Bellypha) Chsd ldrs, hdwy 2f out, styd on to lead ins last, drvn out: rnr-up in a List race '03: '02 rtd h'cap wnr:
suited by 6f now on fm or hvy, prob any trk: runs well fresh: career best run, stable in fine form.
2 Oct'03 Newm 6g/f 93-(90) A: 1 Aug'02 Asco 6g/s 101-95 B: 2 Apr'02 Leic 6gd 95- C: 2 Sep'01 Beve 5gd 88- D:
2 Aug'01 Hayd 6gd 90- C: 2 Jul'01 Pont 6g/f 90- C: 2 Jun'01 Ripo 5g/f 90- D: 1 May'01 Ches 5fm 90- D:
4867} **ORIENTOR 155** [17] J S Goldie 6-9-7 (104) J Murtagh 4/1: 050006-2: b c Inchinor - Orient (Bay   nk   110
Express) Hld up, gd hdwy 2f out, short of room dist, styd on well ins last, just failed: '03 Gr 3 wnr, rnr-up in
this race: 4th in a Gr 1 in '02: best hld up over 6f, stays 7f: handles fm, loves gd or hvy & gall trks: runs well
fresh: tough, smart, excellent return under a big weight & a shade unlucky, win another gd prize.
1 Jun'03 Newc 6gd 110-(109) A: 2 May'03 Hayd 6sft 98-(113) C: 2 Mar'03 Donc 6gd 110-(113) A:
2 Oct'02 Newm 6g/f 110- A: 2 Oct'01 Newm 6g/s 113- A: 2 Sep'01 Asco 6g/s 114- A: 1 Aug'01 Asco 6gd 110- B:
1 Jun'01 York 6g/s 109-100 B: 1 May'01 Redc 7hvy 85- E: 2 Mar'01 Donc 6hvy 81- D:
3504} **THE KIDDYKID 231** [12] P D Evans 4-9-2 (96) J P Spencer 16/1: 115365-3: b g Danetime - Mezzanine   nk   104
(Sadler's Wells) With ldrs, led 2f out till ins last, just held: '03 class stks & List scorer: '02 mdn wnr: v eff
at 6f on firm or v soft grnd, sharp or gall trks: loves to dominate: tough & v useful, excellent return.
1 May'03 Hayd 6sft 104-98 A: 1 May'03 Nott 6.1g/s 100-(94) C: 2 May'03 Sali 6g/f 101-92 B: 2 Jul'02 Chep 5gd 87- D:
1 May'02 Nott 5gd 84- D: 2 May'02 Ches 5fm 80- D:
3653} **CHOOKIE HEITON 224** [3] I Semple 6-9-2 (106) R Winston 10/1: 0/00010-4: br g Fumo di Londra -   ¾   102
Royal Wolff (Prince Tenderfoot) Bhd, hdwy outer 2f out, kept on: ddhtd in a stks in '03: '02 dual rtd h'cap wnr:
all 5 wins at 6f on firm or gd, handles gd/soft: likes a gall trk & runs well fresh: smart, not easy to train but a
fine return & still retains ability.
1 Aug'03 Donc 6g/f 115-(101) C: 1 Jul'02 Newb 6g/f 106-97 B: 1 May'02 York 6fm 94-91 B: 2 May'02 Newm 6fm 93-91 B:
2 Oct'01 Newb 5gd 92-88 B: 1 Aug'01 Newc 6gd 94- D: 1 May'01 Redc 6g/f 77- E:
4436} **MONSIEUR BOND 148** [4]4-9-5 (110) F Lynch 11/1: 162125-5: ch c Danehill Dancer - Musical Essence   hd   105+
(Song) Held up, hdwy trav well & not clr run fnl 2f, fin on bridle still looking for room: '03 stks & List scorer:
'02 mdn & stks wnr: eff at 6f, suited by 7f & stays 1m on firm & gd/soft, any trk: has run well fresh: smart colt,
v eye-catching return & one to be with next time.
2 Sep'03 Good 7fm 111-(112) A: 1 Sep'03 Epso 7gd 112-(112) A: 2 Aug'03 York 7.0fm 110-(113) A:
1 Jul'02 Ches 7.0fm 109-(112) B: 2 Sep'02 Newb 6fm 107- A: 1 Aug'02 Wind 6g/s 106- C:
1 Jul'02 Pont 6g/f 102- D: 2 Jul'02 York 6g/f 85- E:
4555} **SMOKIN BEAU 177** [11]7-9-2 (98) M Henry 25/1: 605400-6: With ldrs, onepace fnl 1f on reapp.   nk   101
883   **FIRE UP THE BAND 7** [2]5-9-2 (106) A Nicholls 7/2 FAV: 12023-07: b c Prince Sabo - Green Supreme   hd   100
(Primo Dominie) Stumbled start, sn handy on outer, kept on same pace over 1f out: well bckd: '03 dual h'cap wnr,
plcd in Ayr Gold Cup & Stewards Cup: well suited by 6f, stays 7f on firm & gd, handles polytrack, gd/soft & any trk:
runs well fresh: tough, consistent & useful, gd return.
2 Sep'03 Donc 5gd 101-(104) A: 2 Aug'03 Good 6g/f 109-100 B: 1 May'03 Newm 6g/f 103-91 C:
1 Mar'03 Asco 6g/f 98-87 C: 2 Jun'02 Asco 5gd 90-84 B: 1 Apr'02 Newm 6fm 85-76 C: 1 Feb'02 Ling 7ap 73a- D:
5037} **CRIMSON SILK 140** [7]4-9-2 (102) Paul Eddery 20/1: 13/3063-8: Slow away, sn rdn bhd, mod gains.   nk   99
921   **LAW BREAKER 2** [5]6-9-2 (85) B Reilly 25/1: 521-5529: In tch, onepace fnl 2f: qck reapp.   ¾   95
5037} **HALMAHERA 129** [10]9-9-2 (102) N Callan 25/1: 001044-0: 10th: Chsd ldrs, onepace over 1f out.   hd   96
5037} **GOLDEN NUN 140** [8]4-8-11 p (99) K Darley 20/1: 002305-0: 11th: Bhd, modest late gains on reapp.   1¾   86
4905^}**WILL HE WISH 152** [15]8-9-2 bl (92) R Hughes 33/1: 451261-0: 12th: Held up, short of room 2f out,   shd   91
no dngr on reapp.
883   **STRIKING AMBITION 7** [14]4-9-2 (113) D Holland 5/1: 11000-00: 13th: Led till 2f out, no extra.   1   88
4451} **COCONUT PENANG 183** [9]4-9-2 (98) S Drowne 33/1: 236350-0: 14th: In tch, wknd over 1f out.   1½   84
4956} **FLASHING BLADE 148** [13]4-8-11 (85) W Supple 100/1: 005-0: 15th: In tch, btn 2f out on reapp.   2   73
834   **TIME N TIME AGAIN 14** [6]6-9-2 p (74) G Duffield 80/1: 1333150: 16th: In tch, wknd 2f out: see 551.   1   75
4749} **CAPRICHO 167** [1]7-9-7 (110) T Quinn 11/1: 014140-0: 17th: Held up, wknd 2f out on reapp.   1¾   75
17 Ran   Time 1m 13.89 (3.09)   Owned: Mr M Pyle & Mrs T Pyle   Trained: Upper Longdon

953 3.50 Polypipe Maiden Stakes 3yo (D)
£5450 £1677 £838   **6f str**   **Good 48**   -28 Slow   Stands Side

4881} **LOCAL POET 154** [2] B A McMahon 3-9-0 (98) G Gibbons 4/9 FAV: 6224-1: b c Robellino - Laugharne   73
(Known Fact) Trkd ldrs, prog to lead dist, rdn clr fnl 1f despite drifting right: hvly bckd, long abs: rnr-up on 2
of 4 '03 starts, incl hd 2nd in a val Redcar 2yo trophy, also 4th in List company: eff at 5/6f on gd & fast grnd, runs
well fresh: likes a gall trk: deserved win but made hard work of it, shld rate higher.
2 Oct'03 Redc 6g/f 104- B: 2 Aug'03 Pont 5g/f 82- D:
4316} **VOLATICUS 191** [1] D Nicholls 3-9-0 A Nicholls 25/1: 0-2: b c Desert Story - Haysel (Petorius)   2   63$
Tried to make all, hdd dist, kept on but no pace of wnr on reapp: just btr for race: May foal, cost E3,800: eff
over a gall 6f on gd grnd: sharper next time & could find a minor event.
673   **BLADES EDGE 38** [5] A Bailey 3-9-0 (59) J Fanning 2/1: 304-053: Chsd ldrs, kept on under press   ½   61
fnl 1f, not pace to chall: small: improved run, return to 7f+ will suit: see 673.
4750} **VELOCITAS 164** [3] H J Collingridge 3-9-0 T P Queally(3) 33/1: 0-4: b g Magic Ring - Folly   nk   60
Finnesse (Joligeneration) Chsd ldrs, onepcd fnl 1f on reapp: unplcd on sole '03 start (AW mdn): will apprec 7f.
       BOLLIN ARCHIE [7]3-9-0 K Darley 4/1: 5: b c First Trump - Bollin Joanne (Damister) Green in   2½   53
rear, styd on late, nvr dngrs on debut: bckd from 6/1 & ndd this race debut: scopey type, with T Easterby.
       ONYX [4]3-9-0 S Righton 33/1: 6: Dwelt, keen & chsd ldrs till halfway on debut.   7   32
4034} **DIAMOND SHANNON 206** [8]3-8-9 R Fitzpatrick 11/2: 2-7: Slowly away, al bhd on reapp.   2½   20
764   **FLY SO HIGH 27** [6]3-8-9 VIS N Callan 33/1: 008: Al outpcd, fin last in first time visor.   3½   10
8 Ran   Time 1m 15.39 (4.59)   Owned: Mr J C Fretwell   Trained: Tamworth

---

954

4.25 Orderit-Online Com Maiden Auction Stakes 2yo (E)
£3531 £1086 £543 **5f str** **Good 48** **-32 Slow** Stands Side

DARIO GEE GEE [6] K A Ryan 2-8-8 N Callan 14/1: 1: ch c Bold Fact - Magical Peace (Magical **93+**
Wonder) Dwelt, recovered to chase ldrs, went on ent fnl 1f, pushed clr on debut: March foal, cost £11,000: dam a
sprint wnr, sire a smart 7f performer: eff over a gall 5f on gd grnd, runs well fresh: plenty to like about this.
PERSIAN ROCK [11] J A Osborne 2-8-11 D Holland 7/2: 2: b c Namid - Cairo Lady (Persian Bold) **2½ 87**
Chsd ldrs, slightly outpcd halfway, styd on well into 2nd fnl 1f, not rch wnr: bckd from 9/2, debut: £10,000 March
foal: half-brother to a plcd bmpr performer: sire a high-class sprinter: eff at 5f on gd grnd, already looks to
need 6f: sure to learn from this & win sn.
TIVISKI [2] E J Alston 2-8-3 W Supple 25/1: 3: b f Desert Style - Mummys Best (Bustino) Front **hd 78**
rank, led briefly halfway, not qckn ins fnl 1f on debut: Feb foal, cost 9,000gns: half-sister to decent miler Rush
Brook: dam a 10f wnr, sire smart at 7f: eff at 5f, 6f sure to suit: will learn from this encouraging debut.
NEXT TIME [9] M J Polglase 2-8-4 Martin Dwyer 16/1: 4: b f Danetime - Muckross Park **2 73**
(Nomination) Slowly away, prog 2f out, kept on fnl 1f & nrst fin on debut: 20,000gns Apr foal: sister to sprint
wnr No Time & half-sister to a couple of wnrs abroad: sire a high-class sprinter: sure to learn from this.
THEATRE OF DREAMS [5]2-8-7 A Nicholls 8/1: 5: Dwelt, hdwy to chase ldrs after halfway, led **1 73**
dist till ins fnl 1f, wknd: ndd race, bckd from 25/1 & stable not renowned for its juv wnrs: scopey sort.
VON WESSEX [3]2-8-7 C Haddon(7) 18/1: 6: Led till after halfway, grad wknd: ndd race. **hd 72**
APOLOGIES [1]2-8-7 G Gibbons 6/1: 7: Dwelt & green, late prog, nvr dngrs: op 4/1, ndd race. **¾ 70**
LORD JOHN [14]2-8-7 Dale Gibson 33/1: 8: Chsd ldrs, wknd 1.5f out. **hd 69**
BEDTIME BLUES [10]2-8-3 G Duffield 25/1: 9: Dwelt, recovered to chase ldrs 3f on debut. **¾ 63**
BRUT [13]2-8-8 L Enstone(3) 10/1: 0: 10th: Slow away, nvr a factor on debut: bckd from 20/1. **3 59**
MINDFUL [12]2-8-7 J P Spencer 20/1: 0: 11th: Slowly away, al bhd on debut: scopey sort. **1½ 54**
CAMPEON [8]2-8-9 K Darley 5/2 FAV: 0: 12th: Chsd ldrs, lost place after halfway, no ch after: **1¼ 52**
hvly bckd from 4/1: scopey type, unruly in padd: with M Wallace & btr clearly expected.
CHAMPAGNE BRANDY [4]2-8-2 Joanna Badger 33/1: 0: 13th: Swerved start & al bhd, fin last. **1½ 41**
13 Ran Time 1m 02.22 (4.02) Owned: Crewe And Nantwich Racing Club Trained: Hambleton

---

955

5.00 March Handicap Stakes 3yo 0-85 (D)
£5746 £1768 £884 **7f str** **Good 48** **-26 Slow** Stands Side. 2 Groups. **[92]**

4869} **FREE TRIP** 155 [22] J H M Gosden 3-9-0 (78) R Hughes 3/1 FAV: 01120-1: ch c Cadeaux Genereux - **88**
Well Away (Sadler's Wells) Chsd ldrs stands side, led after halfway, held on well fnl 1f, pushed out despite
drifting left: well bckd from 9/2, reapp: dual '03 wnr (mdn & nursery h'cap): eff at 6/7f on fast & rain-softened
grnd: handles a gall trk, runs well fresh: continues on the upgrade, win again.
2 Oct'03 Newm 6g/f 79-78 B: 1 Sep'03 Nott 6.1g/f 79-71 E: 1 Sep'03 Hayd 6gd 75- D:
481* **MOUNT VETTORE** 61 [16] Mrs J R Ramsden 3-8-12 (76) J P Spencer 7/2: 5-12: Held up stands side, **nk 85+**
hdwy 2f out, fin well & only just btn: nicely bckd, 9 wk abs: just failed to get there over this longer 7f trip, 1m
sure to suit: improving, can win again sn: see 481 (AW mdn).
4803*}GRANSTON 161 [8] J D Bethell 3-8-8 (72) P Robinson 20/1: 055401-3: b g Revoque - Gracious **2½ 76+**
Gretclo (Common Grounds) Chsd ldr far side, led that group ins fnl 1f: nonapp: ended '03 with a nursery h'cap win:
eff at 7f, shld stay 1m: acts on fast & firm grnd, runs well fresh: likes to run up with/force the pace: fine run,
won race on prob unfav'ble far side, must sn go one better.
1 Oct'03 Catt 7g/f 75-69 D: 2 Jun'03 Carl 5fm 76- E:
4997} **IMPERIALISTIC** 144 [15] K R Burke 3-9-7 (85) Darren Williams 50/1: 043423-4: b f Imperial Ballet **¾ 87**
- Shefoog (Kefaah) Mid-div stands side, hdwy 2f out, styd on fnl 1f & nrst fin under top-weight on reapp: '03
fills' mdn wnr, subs plcd in h'cap company (incl in cheek pieces): eff at 6/7f, has tried 1m: acts on gd & soft
grnd: most encouraging reapp. 2 Sep'03 Ches 7.0g/s 85-79 C: 1 May'03 Hayd 6sft 85- D:
4112} **DISTANT TIMES** 201 [1]3-8-10 (74) K Darley 16/1: 43223-5: b c Orpen - Simply Times (Dodge) Tried **¾ 74**
to make all far side, worn down ins fnl 1f & no ch with stands side: bckd at long odds, reapp: plcd on 4 of 5 '03
starts (mdns, tried blnks on fnl outing): eff at 6f on gd & fast grnd, not quite stay this gall 7f on reapp: ran
well for a long way on prob wrong side.
2 Aug'03 Ripo 6g/f 77-(79) D: 2 Aug'03 Newc 6g/f 77- F:
4808} **ALPINE SPECIAL** 159 [20]3-8-8 (72) G Faulkner 33/1: 203210-6: Slowly away stands side, styd on late. **½ 71**
5034} **COTOSOL** 140 [4]3-8-12 (76) W Supple 40/1: 323026-7: Chsd ldrs far side, onepcd fnl 1.5f on reapp. **hd 74**
4482} **ANOTHER BOTTLE** 182 [5]3-8-8 (72) Dale Gibson 50/1: 033-8: Bhd far side, kept on late, nvr dngrs. **1 68**
4442} **RED BIRR** 184 [3]3-8-13 (77) Martin Dwyer 25/1: 043-9: Chsd ldrs far side, onepcd fnl 2f on reapp. **½ 72**
189 **CARTRONAGEERAGHLAD** 105 [11]3-9-4 bl (82) D Holland 25/1: 064160-0: 10th: Front rank stands side, **½ 76**
wknd fnl 1f on reapp.
252 **KINGSMAITE** 91 [14]3-8-13 (77) J Bramhill 20/1: 364212-0: 11th: In tch stands side, left bhd dist. **1 69**
5024} **GABANA** 141 [10]3-8-7 (71) S Sanders 20/1: 003-0: 12th: Switched stands side & rear, some late hdwy. **3 57**
794 **TITUS SALT** 24 [18]3-8-11 bl (75) D Mernagh 12/1: 4421-30: 13th: Nvr a factor stands side: see 794. **shd 61**
4660} **GO SOLO** 170 [6]3-9-0 (78) M Hills 10/1: 021516-0: 14th: Chsd ldrs far side, no ch fnl 2f: reapp. **nk 63**
4997 **LETS GET IT ON** 144 [2]3-9-0 (78) K Dalgleish 66/1: 13502-0: 15th: Held up far side, nvr a factor. **nk 62**
4413} **MORSE** 186 [17]3-9-3 (81) J Murtagh 14/1: 050336-0: 16th: Chsd ldrs stands side, btn 2f out on reapp. **3 59**
3916} **UNDER MY SPELL** 213 [19]3-8-11 (75) S Drowne 20/1: 033555-0: 17th: Nvr a factor stands side. **2½ 48**
4872} **WEST COUNTRY** 44 [21]3-9-1 (79) J Fanning 17/2: 232-430: 18th: Chsd ldrs till halfway stands side. **5 42**
4160} **Arfinnit** 199 [9]3-8-11 (75) A Culhane 40/1:0 4882} **Redwood Rocks** 154 [13]3-9-2 (80) F Lynch 40/1:0
4763} **Poppys Footprint** 163 [12]3-9-7 (85) N Callan 40/1:0 4669} **Rules For Jokers** 169 [7]3-9-4 (82) R Winston 28/1:0
22 Ran Time 1m 28.37(5.17) Owned: Mr K Abdulla Trained: Manton

WOLVERHAMPTON Fibresand MONDAY 29.03.04 Lefthand, Sharp Track

Official Going Standard To Slow

---

956 2.20 New & Improved Betdirect Co Uk Handicap Stakes 3yo+ 46-55 (F) [59]
£2933 £838 £419 7f aw rnd Going 48 -32 Slow Outside

868 **BULAWAYO 11** [3] Andrew Reid 7-9-1 BL (46) G Gibbons 8/1: 5303061: Rdn in tch, hdwy to lead over **51a**
1f out, drvn out: stays 1m, apprec return to 7f: acts on fast, gd & fibresand, loves W'hmpton: imprvd for blnks.
767 **AGUILA LOCO 29** [6] Mrs Stef Liddiard 5-9-8 p (53) M Fenton 4/1: 5314062: Led/dsptd lead till over nk **57a**
1f out, rallied gamely cl-home, just held: apprec rtn to W'hampton, win again: see 685 (C/D).
868 **ROCINANTE 11** [2] J J Quinn 4-9-4 (49) E Ahern 16/1: 010-0003: Hld up, kept on late: see 647. 1 **51a**
825* **SILVER MASCOT 21** [11] R Hollinshead 5-9-8 (53) D Holland 11/4 FAV: 4022514: Led/dsptd lead, no 1 **53a**
extra over 2f out: just btr 825 (seller, C/D, made all).
889 **ABBIEJO 7** [12]7-8-13 (4oh)p (40) R Miles(3) 33/1: 660/0-65: Wide & bhd, only mod prog: see 889. 5 **35a**
894 **ILLUSTRIOUS DUKE 7** [4]6-8-13 (4oh)BL (40) P Varley(7) 33/1: 00-00006: Dsptd lead 4f, sn btn: blnks. 2½ **30a**
935 **SOCIAL CONTRACT 3** [7]7-9-0 vis (45) D Sweeney 9/1: 6062007: Chsd ldrs, btn 2f out: btr 783. ½ **30a**
4727} **CHANTRY FALLS 168** [8]4-9-4 (49) G Duffield 14/1: 250463-8: br g Mukaddamah - Woodie Dancer nk **33a**
(Green Dancer) Held up, eff 3f out, no prog 2f out: AW bow: dual mdn rnr-up '03 (J Weymes): unplcd '02: eff
around 7f, tried 1m: fast grnd & a gall or easy trk: eff with/without t-strap.
2 Aug'03 Newc 7g/f 49-(48) D: 2 Jun'03 Thir 7g/f 47-(45) D:
4944} **PARISIAN PLAYBOY 152** [9]4-9-6 (51) Dane O'Neill 7/1: 0003-9: gr g Paris House - Exordium 9 **20a**
(Exorbitant) Sn bhd: reapp: op 5/1: h'cap plcd '03 (J O'Keeffe, rtd 52): eff around 7f on soft grnd & an easy trk.
4712] **PHARAOH HATSHEPSUT 520** [1]6-8-13 (40) K Dalgleish 25/1: 000400/-0: 10th: Sn bhd: new yard. 2½ **8a**
4181} **FRENCHMANS LODGE 200** [10]4-9-7 (52) A Culhane 12/1: 350000-0: 11th: Sn bhd, reapp, new yard. hd **15a**
846 **ROBIN SHARP 15** [5]6-9-0 vis (45) M Tebbutt 13/2: 00-26050: 12th: Sn struggling: likes to dominate. 27 **0a**
12 Ran Time 1m 31.83 (5.63) Owned: Mr A S Reid Trained: Mill Hill London

---

957 2.50 Betdirect Co Uk Apprentice Claiming Stakes 4yo+ (F)
£2870 £820 £410 1m100y aw rnd Going 48 -32 Slow Inside

905* **OUR DESTINY 6** [5] A W Carroll 6-8-7 (50) S Hitchcott 11/8 FAV: 2-324011: Led/dsptd lead till **54a**
over 4f out, led again over 1f out, rdn out: well bckd, new yard: won this race last year: suited by 1m/9.4f, stays
11f on fast, soft & loves fibresand/W'hampton/claimers: see 239.
890 **DANCING KING 7** [3] P W Hiatt 8-8-5 (47) B Swarbrick(5) 5/1: 1540062: Led/dsptd lead, not pace of 2 **47a**
wnr from dist: imprvd eff, likes to dominate as in 754.
905 **IAMBACK 6** [1] Miss Gay Kelleway 4-8-0 p (48) Dean Williams(6) 7/2: 2616043: Cl-up, rdn & not pace 1½ **39a**
of front pair fnl 2f: see 526 (auct mdn, C/D).
807 **PORT ST CHARLES 24** [6] P R Chamings 7-8-13 (72) J F McDonald(3) 4/1: 01-50004: Held up in tch, ¾ **51a**
smooth hdwy to lead over 4f out, sn rdn & hdd over 1f out, no extra: not btr, likes 6f as in 113.
4961} **PEREGIAN 150** [2]6-8-9 (49) M Coumbe(6) 11/1: 100005-5: b g Eagle Eyed - Mo Pheata (Petorius) Hld hd **46a**
up, eff over 2f out, no extra: amat h'cap wnr '03, AW seller rnr-up: turf unplcd '02 (rtd 46, AW seller plcd, rtd
52a, N Rossiter): all wins at 7f, stays an easy 10f: likes fast grnd, prob handles both AWs: best without headgear.
1 May'03 Yarm 7.0g/f 52-49 F: 2 May'03 Brig 8.0g/f 54-48 E: 2 Feb'03 Ling 8ap 51a-(52) G:
862 **DUNDONALD 12** [7]5-8-10 t (35) R Miles 20/1: 6003406: Prom, btn 3f out, eased: btr 777. 13 **19a**
6 Ran Time 1m 52.99 (6.79) Owned: Mr Dennis Deacon Trained: Alcester

---

958 3.20 New Site @ Betdirect Co Uk Handicap Stakes Fillies 3yo+ 0-75 (E) [75]
£3702 £1139 £570 5f aw rnd Going 48 +07 Fast Inside

685 **BLAKESHALL QUEST 38** [8] R Brotherton 4-8-11 vis (58) D Holland 8/1: 0-044451: Sn handy & led **68a**
dist, rdn to assert: best at 5/6f, stays 7f on fibresand, likes a sharp trk: trav better & closer to the pace today
for D Holland: well h'capped, win again if repeating this: see 550.
844 **RIVER DAYS 15** [4] Miss Gay Kelleway 6-7-12 vis t (45) Lisa Jones(3) 4/1 FAV: 0-020652: Led/dsptd 2½ **46a**
lead, short of room dist, sn no ch with wnr: well h'capped & likes W'hampton: see 619.
864 **CLOUDLESS 12** [7] J W Unett 4-8-8 (55) Dane O'Neill 6/1: 5-024033: Towards rear, styd on wide for 1½ **52a**
press, nvr dngrs: see 630 & 242 (C/D mdn).
655 **FRASCARA 41** [1] A Berry 4-10-0 (75) F Lynch 16/1: 251-0004: Led till dist, no extra: 6 wk abs. nk **71a**
897 **AMELIA 6** [10]6-8-2 (49) B Swarbrick(7) 5/1: 02-52555: Rdn/wide & bhd, short of room over 1f out, ½ **43a**
nrst fin: qck reapp: return to 6f shld suit: see 246 (6f).
835 **EMARADIA 16** [11]3-8-1 bl (60) G Duffield 7/1: 1201226: Prom, no extra over 1f out: btr 835 (claim). 1¼ **51a**
755 **LADY PEKAN 30** [3]5-8-13 bl (60) B Reilly(3) 7/1: 1-635607: In tch, btn dist: btr 274 (C/D). ½ **49a**
844 **INCHING 15** [5]4-8-2 (49) M Henry 16/1: 626-4408: Chsd ldrs, btn over 1f out: see 348 & 242. shd **38a**
793 **TIGRESS 26** [6]5-8-13 bl (60) S W Kelly 13/2: 6526209: Prom, outpcd over 1f out: op 5/1: btr 749. nk **48a**
844 **MARABAR 5** [2]6-8-2 p (49) S Carson 14/1: 05-06500: 10th: Al rear & outpcd: op 25/1: see 555. 3½ **28a**
MISS DANGEROUS 1302 [9]9-7-12 (45) D Kinsella 40/1: 500000///-0: 11th: Sn bhd: v long abs. 5 **12a**
11 Ran Time 1m 02.23 (2.03) Owned: Droitwich Jokers Trained: Pershore

---

959 3.50 Special Offers @ Betdirect Co Uk Maiden Stakes 3yo (D)
£3487 £1073 £537 1m4f aw Going 48 -49 Slow Inside

601 **OUR LITTLE ROSIE 47** [3] M Blanshard 3-8-9 (58) D Sweeney 8/1: 0051: b f Piccolo - Villella **59a**
(Sadler's Wells) Held up, chsd ldr 4f out, drvn to lead well ins last: abs: apprec step up to 12f & fibresand,
handles polytrack & a sharp trk: goes well fresh: lightly rcd, type to progress in low-grade h'caps:
839 **BOND MOONLIGHT 16** [2] B Smart 3-9-0 (63) F Lynch 5/4 FAV: 404-2232: Led/dsptd lead, rdn & hdd 1¼ **61a**
ins last, no extra: clr rem: bckd: consistent in defeat: see 839 & 808.
116 **SEMELLE DE VENT 121** [7] J H M Gosden 3-8-9 (63) Dane O'Neill 100/30: 056-3: b f Sadler's Wells - 15 **35a**
Heeremandi (Royal Academy) In tch, rdn & wknd fnl 3f: reapp: unplcd '03 (rtd 51 & 70a): half-sister to a 5f juv
wnr, dam a smart 6f juv wnr: prob stays 7f on polytrack.
4483} **VALIANT AIR 184** [5] J R Weymes 3-9-0 (57) D Holland 20/1: 040-4: b g Spectrum - Shining Desert 5 **33a**

245

WOLVERHAMPTON Fibresand MONDAY 29.03.04 Lefthand, Sharp Track

(Green Desert) Chsd ldr 5f out, sn btn: gelded, reapp, AW bow: lightly rcd & unplcd '03 (rtd 63, debut, mdn).

	KNIGHT OF HEARTS 0 [4]3-9-0 G Duffield 100/1: 5: Dwelt, sn trkd ldrs, btn 4f out.	5	26a
873	STAGE TWO 10 [1]3-9-0 K Dalgleish 11/2: 06: Led 4f, lost tch 5f out.	23	0a
3458}	ARGENT 234 [6]3-9-0 (62) R Fitzpatrick 10/1: 3550-P: Held up & bhd, lost action/p.u. 4f out, reapp.		0a

7 Ran   Time 2m 45.28 (11.68)   Owned: Mrs R G Wellman   Trained: Upper Lambourn

---

960   4.20 Cashbacks @ Betdirect Co Uk Selling Stakes 3yo+   (G)
£2555 £730 £365   **5f aw rnd**   **Going 48**   -06 Slow   Inside

859	BLUEBERRY RHYME 13 [7] P J Makin 5-9-12 vis (65) D Sweeney 7/2 JT FAV: 23-22101: Trkd ldrs trav well, rdn to lead well ins last: no bid: eff at 6f, suited by 5f on fast & both AWs, likes fibresand: gd weight carrier, apprec drop to sell grade: best delivered late & goes well for D Sweeney: see 742.		63a
889	THE LEATHER WEDGE 7 [8] A Berry 5-9-7 (45) P Bradley(5) 25/1: 0-604052: Led, rdn & hdd cl-home.	½	55a$
889	SOAKED 7 [3] D W Chapman 11-9-7 bl (45) A Culhane 9/2: 6004023: Chsd ldr, styd on for press, not pace of wnr: in gd form, best when dominating: 11yo, see 889 & 335.	1	53a
859	KINGS BALLET 13 [5] P R Chamings 6-9-7 p (47) Dane O'Neill 7/1: 00-00204: Dwelt, bhd, kept on late.	2½	46a
907	HEATHYARDSBLESSING 6 [9]7-9-7 (45) Stephanie Hollinshead(7) 40/1: 0650355: Mid-div, outpcd hway.	¾	44a
904	LONE PIPER 6 [2]9-9-7 (35) B Swarbrick(7) 25/1: 0064366: Mid-div, no impress dist: flattered 775.	1	42a
944	AROGANT PRINCE 2 [10]7-9-12 bl (59) D Holland 7/2 JT FAV: 3101007: Wknd 2f out: claimed.	nk	46a
819	ARABIAN KNIGHT 21 [6]4-9-7 (60) E Ahern 20/1: 01006-08: ch g Fayruz - Cheerful Knight (Mac's Imp) Bhd, nvr on terms with ldrs: AW mdn & turf clmr scorer '03 for A Berry: eff at 5/5.7f on firm, fast & both AWs, handles a sharp or stiffish trk: eff with/without visor or blnks.	1	39a

1 May'03 Bath 5.7g/f 61-(57) F: 2 Feb'03 Ling 5ap 63a-60 E: 1 Feb'03 Ling 5ap 62a- D: 2 Feb'03 Ling 5ap 57a- G:
2 Dec'02 Wolv 5af 56a- F: 2 Jul'02 Muss 5g/f 72- E:

889+	*TORRENT 0 [1]9-9-12 bl (45) G Duffield 8/1: 1530019: Chsd ldrs inner, btn 2f out: btr 889 (banded).	½	42a
904	FLYING FAISAL 6 [12]6-9-7 (35) P Fitzsimons 40/1: 6040030: 10th: Al outpcd rear, qck reapp.	shd	37a
889	HAGLEY PARK 7 [11]5-9-2 vis (45) S W Kelly 9/1: 2265430: 11th: Prom, btn 2f out:'lost action'.	4	21a
851	JALOUHAR 15 [4]4-9-12 vis (49) M Tebbutt 25/1: 5465050: 12th: Dwelt & sn outpcd: needs 6/7f.	2	26a

12 Ran   Time 1m 02.89 (2.69)   Owned: Mrs P J Makin   Trained: Marlborough

---

961   4.50 Bet Direct On Sky Active Handicap Stakes 3yo+ 46-55 (F)   [54]
£2919 £834 £417   **1m1f79y aw rnd**   **Going 48**   -38 Slow   Inside

792	SORBIESHARRY 26 [7] Mrs N Macauley 5-9-8 p (48) P McCabe 10/1: 2351501: Keen early, trkd ldr trav well 4f out, led over 1f out, drvn out: eff at 1m/9.4f, stays 12f: loves fibresand: see 559 & 165.		54a
757	JADE STAR 30 [5] Miss Gay Kelleway 4-9-12 (52) M Fenton 5/1: 325-4102: Trkd ldrs, rdn to chall over 1f out, kept on, al just held: back to form after latest: see 620 (C/D).	½	56a
868	CALL OF THE WILD 11 [6] R A Fahey 4-9-11 VIS (51) T Hamilton(3) 4/1: 346-0333: Rdn rear early, hdwy from halfway, not able to reach wnr: looked a hard ride in first time visor: see 747 & 421.	½	54a
753	DANGER BIRD 31 [1] R Hollinshead 4-9-11 P (51) A Culhane 6/1: 3-230244: Led after 2f till over 1f out.	1	52a
828*	LANDESCENT 20 [2]4-9-10 (50) D Holland 4/1: 0-045115: Led over 1f, btn 2f out: btr 828 (polytrack).	11	33a
718	RED STORM 34 [4]5-9-10 BL T (50) R Miles(3) 7/1: 5-061506: Trkd ldr, btn 2f out: blnks/t-strap: btr 522.	6	23a
821*	SINJAREE 21 [3]6-9-6 (46) G Duffield 7/2 FAV: 000-0517: Chsd ldrs till 3f out, easd: reportedly nvr trav.	9	3a

7 Ran   Time 2m 05.55(7.35)   Owned: Mrs Liz Nelson   Trained: Melton Mowbray

---

NEWCASTLE   MONDAY 29.03.04 Lefthand, Galloping, Stiff Track

Official Going Str Course - Good/Soft (Soft Places), Rnd - Soft

---

962   2.10 European Breeders Fund Maiden Stakes 2yo   (D)
£4362 £1342 £671   **5f str**   **Soft 94**   -62 Slow   Stands side

	TARA TARA 0 [4] J J Quinn 2-8-9 R Winston 10/1: 1: b f Fayruz - Gobolino (Don) Held up, prog when no room over 1f out till ld home, styd on strongly to get up, val 2L+: Apr foal, cost 20,000: sister to multiple wnr Don Fayruz: half-sister to a 1m/12f wnr: dam 7f wnr at 2: eff at 5f on soft, 6f shld suit: goes well fresh: showed a neat turn of foot & can follow up.		84+
	STANBURY 0 [7] M R Channon 2-9-0 T E Durcan 6/5 FAV: 2: ch c Zaminder - Staffin (Salse) Prom, led dist, hdd cl-home: well bckd on debut: Jan foal, cost 130,000gns: dam useful around 7f/1m: sire top-class as a juv: eff at 5f, 6f shld suit: acts on soft grnd: fine start, shld find similar.	nk	81
	WORD PERFECT 0 [6] M W Easterby 2-8-9 Dale Gibson 33/1: 3: b f Diktat - Better Still (Glenstal) Cl-up, kept on fnl 1f, hands & heel: Apr foal, half-sister to a 5/9f wnr: sire high-class at sprint dists: eff at 5f, shld stay 6f: acts on soft: encouraging: rate higher.	¾	74
	BOLD MARC 0 [9] K R Burke 2-9-0 Darren Williams 7/1: 4: Led, hdd dist, sn no extra: op 10/1 on debut: eff at 5f on soft grnd.	¾	77
	INDIBRAUN 0 [8]2-9-0 G Faulkner 5/1: 5: In tch, edged left & no extra ins fnl 1f: debut.	nk	76
	KILKENNY KITTEN 0 [5]2-8-9 T Kim Tinkler 50/1: 6: Cl-up, fdd 2f out: wore t-strap on debut.	8	51
	KRISTIKHAB 0 [5]2-9-0 K Darley 11/1: 7: Slow away, nvr a factor: debut.	3	48
	VERSTONE 0 [2]2-8-9 J Fanning 25/1: 8: Rear, nvr travelling: debut.	6	28
	NO COMMISSION 0 [1]2-9-0 L Fletcher(3) 16/1: 9: Veered badly start, ran green & nvr a factor.	6	18

9 Ran   Time 1m 06.0 (7.8)   Owned: Tara Leisure   Trained: Malton

963
2.40 Saltwell Signs Claiming Stakes 3yo+   (F)
£3059 £874 £437   **6f str**   **Soft 94**   **-73 Slow**   Stands side

4541} **AMERICAN COUSIN 180** [7] D Nicholls 9-9-7 (60) A Nicholls 10/1: 404140-1: b g Distant Relative - **65**
Zelda (Sharpen Up) Held up, prog to lead ins fnl 1f, rdn out: reapp: claim & h'cap wnr in '03: won 2 h'caps in
'02 & '01: suited by 5f, stays 6f: acts on firm, soft & fibresand: acts on any trk, likes a gall one: goes well
fresh: apprec return to claim grade. 1 Sep'03 Beve 5g/f 60-54 E: 1 Jun'03 Hami 5.0gd 57-(59) E:
1 Jul'02 Donc 5g/f 69-62 F: 1 Jul'02 Beve 5g/s 63-50 D: 1 Jul'01 York 5g/f 71-68 C: 2 Jun'01 Good 6g/f 70-66 E:
1 Jun'01 Muss 5g/f 71-59 E:
501 **SPEEDY JAMES 60** [6] D Nicholls 8-9-4 (40) L Treadwell(7) 25/1: 000/0-002: ch g Fayruz - Haraabah   ¾   **59**
(Topsider) Prom, led 3f out, edged left & hdd ins fnl 1f, not pace wnr: 9 wk abs: stablemate of wnr: unplcd sole
'03 start (h'cap): modest form in '02 (rtd 36a & 33, h'caps): last won back in 98 (mdn & stks, rtd 103, J Berry):
eff at 5/6f on fm & soft, eff with visor & can go well fresh: potentially well h'capped.
819 **ONLY ONE LEGEND 21** [1] K A Ryan 6-9-9 p (60) N Callan 5/2: 3-000003: Held up, prog 2f out, kept   2   **58**
on, no ch with front 2: acts on fast, soft & fibresand, loves polytrack: btr 149.
851 **SPEEDFIT FREE 15** [8] I Semple 7-9-4 bl (58) P Hanagan 9/4 FAV: 54-25624: Keen prom, onepcd fnl 1f.   hd   **52**
4793} **PAWAN 164** [3]4-9-9 (62) Kim Tinkler 10/1: 4/202-5: ch g Cadeaux Genereux - Born To Glamour   1   **54**
(Ajdal) Cl-up, no extra dist: reapp: rnr-up on 2 of 3 '03 starts (mdns): 4th on sole juv start (rtd 86, E A
Dunlop): eff at 6/7f on fast & gd grnd: below par run on today's first try on soft: with N Tinkler.
2 Oct'03 Redc 6g/f 63- D: 2 May'03 Ling 7gd 77- D:
637* **MISS WIZZ 43** [2]4-8-13 p (40) Rory Moore(7) 12/1: 460-0416: Prom, fdd 2f out: 6 wk abs: btr 637.   11   **19**
328 **FLYING TACKLE 83** [5]6-9-7 p (51) L Enstone(3) 7/2: 25003-07: Keen cl-up, hung left & fdd 2f out: abs.   1   **24**
850 **WILHEHECKASLIKE 15** [4]3-8-5 vis (45) D R McCabe 50/1: 00200-08: Led, hdd 3f out, fdd.   8   **1**
8 Ran   Time 1m 21.37 (10.07)   Owned: Middleham Park Racing XIV   Trained: Thirsk

964
3.10 Gary Robson Memorial Stakes Handicap 3yo+ 0-80 (D)
£5811 £1788 £894   **1m2f32y**   **Soft**   **Fair**   Far side   **[80]**

716 **OFARABY 34** [10] M A Jarvis 4-9-13 (79) P Robinson 9/2 FAV: 02164-31: In tch, led dist, sn edged   **89**
left, rdn & styd on, val further: op 7/2: eff at 9.4f/10f on both AWs: enjoyed this soft grnd: acts on a stiff/gall
& sharp trk: progressive 4yo who can rate higher: see 127.
2931} **SHARES 257** [5] P Monteith 4-8-4 (56) R Ffrench 9/1: 50/0330-2: b g Turtle Island - Glendora   2   **61**
(Glenstal) Handy, styd on to lead over 1f out, sn hdd, not pace wnr fnl 1f: recent hdles wnr (juv nov, rtd 115h,
2m, gd): plcd in 2 of only 4 '03 starts (rtd 56 & 52a, h'cap & class stks, G A Butler): eff at 1m/ 10f, poss stays
11f: acts on firm & soft grnd: eff with t-strap, tried blnks: shld find similar.
4167} **CAPTAIN CLIPPER 200** [11] D Nicholls 4-9-6 (72) A Nicholls 20/1: 335510-3: b g Royal Applause -   ¾   **76**
Collide (High Line) Mid-div, hdwy 2f out, onepcd ins fnl 1f: clr rem: reapp: mdn wnr in '03 (also plcd twice):
5th at best in 2 '02 starts (mdns, rtd 75, R M Whitaker): eff at 1m/10f, has tried further: acts on fast & soft
grnd: just sharper for today. 1 Aug'03 Beve 9.9gd 74-(69) D:
534 **MELODIAN 55** [6] M Brittain 9-8-8 bl (60) M Lawson(6) 13/2: 06156-54: Led, rcd keenly, hdd bef 1f out.   6   **56**
924 **LIBRE 4** [2]4-9-4 t p (70) Dean McKeown 12/1: 40140-05: Rear, prog 3f out, onepcd fnl 1f: qck reapp.   5   **59**
4711} **TONY TIE 168** [9]8-9-6 (72) W Supple 20/1: 430060-6: b g Ardkinglass - Queen of The Quorn   ¾   **60**
(Governor General) Held up, prog 3f out, onepcd dist: reapp: h'cap wnr in '03: '02 h'cap wnr, also plcd sev
times: dual h'cap wnr in '01: eff at 7f/10f, 1m/9f ideal: acts on firm & hvy grnd: loves a gall trk: has tried
visor & cheek pieces: can go well fresh tho' just sharper for today: v tough. 1 Jul'03 Beve 8.5g/f 76-72 D:
2 Jul'03 Hami 9.2gd 75-74 E: 2 Sep'02 Hami 8.2g/f 84-84 C: 1 Aug'02 Hami 9.1hvy 84-82 C:
2 Jun'02 York 8.9g/s 84-80 B: 1 Sep'01 Hami 8.2gd 84-78 C: 2 Aug'01 Sand 8sft 78-78 C:
2 Aug'01 Ches 7.5fm 82-75 C: 1 Jun'01 Newc 8g/f 78-73 C:
549 **FIDDLERS CREEK 54** [14]5-8-8 p (60) P Hanagan 14/1: 0360-607: Held up, prog 3f out, edged left &   6   **40**
onepcd ins fnl 1f: recent jumps unplcd (rtd 88h, mdn hdle): see 391.
METEORITE SUN 858 [13]6-9-9 (75) J F Egan 25/1: 5321//-8: Bhd & nvr trav, mod late gains: reapp.   1¾   **52**
50 **ROTUMA 144** [1]5-9-0 bl (66) L Enstone(3) 7/1: 224104-9: In tch, wknd fnl 2f: reapp.   3½   **38**
4453} **LUCKY LARGO 185** [12]4-9-2 bl (68) K Darley 33/1: 222020-0: 10th: Al bhd: jumps fit.   ¾   **39**
4992} **GRAFT 147** [7]5-8-13 (65) P Mulrennan(5) 14/1: 004000-0: 11th: Mid-div, wknd 3f out: reapp.   ½   **35**
2446+ **SILVERTOWN 277** [8]9-9-2 (68) D McGaffin 9/1: 0303/11-0: 12th: Chsd ldrs, fdd 3f out: jumps abs.   2   **35**
1069} **LOVE IN SEATTLE 349** [4]4-10-0 (80) J Fanning 7/1: 422-0: 13th: Prom, fdd 2f out: reapp.   25   **12**
809 **DESERT HEAT 24** [3]4-9-6 vis (72) R Winston 25/1: 4-021200: 14th: Chsd ldrs, wknd 3f out: btr 753.   23   **0**
14 Ran   Time 2m 16.14 (9.64)   Owned: Mr T G Warner   Trained: Newmarket

965
3.40 Putter And Flutter Handicap Stakes 4yo+ 0-70 (E)
£3614 £1112 £556   **2m19y**   **Soft**   **V Slow**   Far side   **[75]**

4812} **ACCELERATION IRE 161** [9] R Allan 4-8-13 vis (60) P Hanagan 25/1: 316040-1: b g Groom Dancer -   **67**
Overdrive (Shirley Heights) Handy, styd on to lead ins fnl 1f, rdn out: jumps fit (unplcd), earlier rtd 111h at
best (juv nov hdle, visor): h'cap wnr in '03 (also plcd 3 times, Sir M Prescott): eff at 12/14f, stays 2m1f:
acts on firm, fast grnd & soft, prob fibresand: eff in a visor.
1 Jun'03 Carl 17.2g/f 59-56 F: 2 May'03 Redc 14.1g/f 57-55 F:
4195} **MAGIC COMBINATION 556** [7] L Lungo 11-10-0 (70) P Mulrennan(5) 12/1: 00//0110/-2: b g Scenic -   2   **75**
Etage (Ile de Bourbon) Held up, prog to lead 2f out, edged left when hdd ins fnl 1f, not pace wnr: jumps fit,
earlier rtd 110h at best (h'cap hdle, stays 2m4f on fast & hvy): h'cap hdle wnr on fnl 2002-03 start (rtd 121h): won
2 of only 4 '02 Flat starts (h'caps): eff at 12f/2m on fast & soft grnd: likes a gall trk: 11yo.
1 Sep'02 Newc 16g/s 75-70 E: 1 Jul'02 Hayd 14g/s 72-66 D:
ZOLTANO 687 [11] M Todhunter 6-9-9 (65) R Winston 12/1: 64/2122/-3: b g In The Wings - Zarella   1   **69**
(Anatas) In tch, rdn & styd on well fnl 1f: recent jumps unplcd (nov h'cap hdle, rtd 95h at best, eff at 2m
on gd & prob hvy): ex German Flat wnr in early '02 (10f, gd, also plcd at 11f, soft): stays 2m on soft grnd.
866 **TONI ALCALA 12** [4] R F Fisher 5-9-7 (63) L Fletcher(3) 8/1: 2040-354: Held up, prog 2f out,   hd   **66**
onepcd: just btr 752 (fibresand).
849 **PADDY MUL 15** [1]7-7-12 t (40) J Bramhill 12/1: 6-214345: Rear, hdwy 2f out, kept on late: rdr   nk   **42**
received 1 day whip ban: hld up off slow pace, may do better: see 357 (banded stks).
690* **DOCTOR JOHN 38** [5]7-8-3 (45) C Catlin 7/1: 000//-4216: In tch, no room 2f out, sn no impress.   1   **46**

4609} **FLAME OF ZARA 177** [12]5-8-12 (54) T Eaves(5) 5/1: 0460-7: Cl-up, prog & ev ch 2f out, wknd dist. *1* **54**
852 **MOYNE PLEASURE 15** [2]6-7-12 p (40) D Fentiman(7) 20/1: 0-000608: Hld up, prog & ev ch 2f out, wknd. *2½* **38**
4639] **ALMNADIA 527** [3]5-8-9 (51) K Darley 5/1: 115005/-9: Chsd ldrs, no extra fnl 3f: jmps fit. *1½* **48**
458 **DANNY LEAHY 67** [10]4-9-4 (65) L Enstone(3) 33/1: 64053-50: 10th: Held up, nvr a factor: jumps fit & has been gelded since last term. *1½* **61**
926 **ALTITUDE DANCER 3** [8]4-9-2 (63) N Callan 4/1 FAV: 3-321400: 11th: Keen prom, fdd 2f out: qck reapp: rcd far too keenly & best form has come on faster grnd: btr 554. *3* **56**
746 **HOMERIC TROJAN 32** [6]4-7-13 (46) D Mernagh 50/1: 000-600: 12th: Led, hdd 2f out, sn wknd: see 460. *2* **37**
12 Ran Time 3m 59.57 (34.0) Owned: Kim Marshall Sue Rigby Susan Warren Trained: Cornhill-On-Tweed

966

4.10 Sharp Minds Betfair Maiden Stakes 3yo+ (D)
£3585 £1103 £552 **7f str** **Soft 94** **-09 Slow** Stands side. 2 Groups - Far Side fav.

4442} **ETMAAM 186** [4] M Johnston 3-8-11 R Hills 10/11 FAV: 4-1: b c Intikhab - Sudeley (Dancing Brave) **82**
Made all far side, rdn out: well bckd on reapp: promise when 4th sole '03 start (mdn): dam 11f wnr: eff at 7f, will apprec 1m+: acts on a soft, poss fast grnd: goes well fresh: open to plenty of improvement.
4868} **HENNDEY 157** [5] M A Jarvis 3-8-11 P Robinson 7/2: 0-2: b g Indian Ridge - Del Deya (Caerleon) *2* **76**
Prom far side, trav best over 1f out, onepace, not given hard time: unplcd sole '03 start: eff at 7f, shld get 1m: acts on soft: been gelded in winter & shld find similar.
715 **HIGH CANE 34** [16] M D Hammond 4-9-7 (65) Darren Williams 25/1: 6036-03: ch f Diesis - Aerleon Jane (Caerleon) Rcd stands side, led, kept on fnl 2f, no ch with far side: clr rem: plcd on 1 of 4 '03 starts (mdn, rtd 71, J Noseda): eff at 7f/1m on gd/soft & soft: tried blnks: won race on stands side, encouraging. *1¾* **67**
881 **IMPERIAL DRAGON 9** [6] W A O'Gorman 4-9-12 K Darley 20/1: 04: Cl-up far side, no extra dist. *5* **62**
LUCKY PISCEAN 0 [2]3-8-11 J Fanning 50/1: 5: b g River Falls - Celestine (Skyliner) Held up far, nvr nrr than mid-div: debut: half-brother to sprint wnr Prix Star & staying h'cap wnr Ringside Jack. *shd* **61**
INDI ANO STAR 0 [11]3-8-11 D Tudhope(7) 66/1: 6: Slow away, nvr nrr than mid-div: debut. *2½* **56**
NOUNOU 0 [3]3-8-11 C Catlin 25/1: 7: Al bhd far side: debut. *shd* **55**
BABA 0 [1]3-8-11 Dale Gibson 20/1: 8: Prom far side, fdd dist: debut. *½* **54**
4640} **SENOR EDUARDO 174** [14]7-9-12 (54) P Hanagan 16/1: 004305-9: Cl-up far side, fdd 2f out: jumps fit. *shd* **53**
4112} **NAFFERTON HEIGHTS 203** [7]3-8-11 P Mulrennan(5) 100/1: 000-0: 10th: Held up far side, nvr a factor. *shd* **52**
4707} **GLENCAIRN STAR 168** [13]3-8-11 W Supple 11/1: 05-0: 11th: Chsd ldrs stands side, wknd fnl 2f. *14* **26**
869 **MISS FLEURIE 11** [9]4-9-7 T Eaves(5) 100/1: 4/-00: 12th: Al bhd stands side. *1* **19**
Fast Lane 415 [12]5-9-12 L Vickers 100/1:0 4736} **Anicaflash 167** [10]3-8-6 L Enstone 100/1:0
Ice Planet 0 [8]3-8-11 R Winston 25/1:0 **Young Warrior 0** [15]3-8-11 A Nicholls 25/1:0
16 Ran Time 1m 31.36 (7.26) Owned: Mr Hamdan Al Maktoum Trained: Middleham

967

4.40 Ramside Event Catering Handicap Stakes 3yo+ 0-75 (E) **[75]**
£4173 £1284 £642 **6f str** **Soft 94** **+09 Fast** Stands side. 2 Groups - Far side fav.

741* **UP TEMPO 32** [5] K A Ryan 6-9-4 bl (65) N Callan 9/2 FAV: 40-21311: Mid-div far side, styd on under press dist, rdn out to lead cl-home: eff at 6/7f on firm, hvy & fibresand: eff with blnks & cheek pieces. **75**
349 **IF BY CHANCE 81** [4] R Craggs 6-9-3 bl (64) J Fanning 10/1: 00105-02: ch g Risk Me - Out of Harmony (Song) Rcd far side, led, clr 1f out, hdd under press cl-home: 11 wk abs: won 2 h'caps & 2 sellers in '03 (earlier with I W McInnes): sell wnr in '02 (M A Buckley, first time blnks): suited by 6f on fast, soft & fibresand: acts on any trk & eff with/without blnks, has tried visor: fine eff. *nk* **72**
1 Oct'03 Newc 6gd 63-59 E: 1 Apr'03 Wolv 6af 71a-64 E: 1 Apr'03 Sout 6af 66a-(50) G: 1 Jan'03 Sout 6af 54a- G:
1 Jul'02 Nott 6g/f 53- G: 2 Jan'02 Sout 6af 59a-58 E: 2 Jun'01 Folk 5g/f 60-59 D: 1 Jan'01 Ling 6ap 73a- D:
5006} **HIGHLAND WARRIOR 145** [2] J S Goldie 5-9-1 (62) W Supple 6/1: 000133-3: b c Makbul - Highland Rowena (Royben) Mid-div far side, prog 2f out, onepace well ins fnl 1f: clr rem: tchd 10/1 on reapp: h'cap wnr in '03 (also plcd 3 times): rtd mdn wnr in '02, also dual h'cap plcd: eff at 7/9f, best recent form has come at 6f: acts on firm & soft grnd: likes Ayr: sharper for this. *2* **64**
1 Oct'03 Ayr 6g/s 62-54 E: 2 Jul'03 Ayr 8gd 59-58 D: 1 May'02 Ayr 9g/s 74- E: 2 May'02 Newc 7g/f 70-67 E:
913* **STOIC LEADER 5** [17] R F Fisher 4-9-10 (6ex) (71) L Fletcher(3) 8/1: 00-40114: Led stands side, edged left under press dist, no with far side fnl 1f: qk reapp: won race on 'wrong' side, in fine form. *4* **62+**
655 **RAYMONDS PRIDE 41** [8]4-9-10 bl (71) P Fessey 33/1: 01F0-005: b g Mind Games - Northern Sal (Aragon) Cl-up far side, no extra fnl 1f: 6 wk abs: h'cap wnr in '03 (first time blnks): rnr-up on 4 of 7 juv starts: eff at 5f on firm, gd/soft & fibresand: handles gall or easy trk & can go well fresh. *hd* **61**
1 Oct'03 Ayr 5g/s 71-65 E: 2 Oct'02 Catt 5fm 75- D: 2 Aug'02 Thir 5g/s 74- D: 2 Jul'02 Wolv 5af 75a- E:
2 Jul'02 Warw 5gd 79- E:
618 **SOBA JONES 45** [12]7-9-11 6 (72) J Edmunds 12/1: 1243256: In tch far side, no extra dist: 6 wk abs. *2½* **55**
4999} **FAIR SHAKE 146** [6]4-9-6 (67) Dale Gibson 8/1: 010600-7: Bhd far side, nvr nrr than mid-div: reapp. *1½* **46**
4671} **QUICKS THE WORD 171** [1]4-9-9 (70) T Eaves(5) 14/1: 601600-8: Prom far side, fdd 2f out: reapp. *1* **46**
407 **WAINWRIGHT 75** [11]4-9-2 (63) Dean McKeown 12/1: 5331-109: Rcd far side, nvr nrr than mid-div. *1½* **35**
85 **CERTA CITO 126** [20]4-9-3 (64) D Allan(3) 25/1: 1300-0: 10th: Prom stands side, wknd fnl 2f: reapp. *4* **25**
4108} **BORDER ARTIST 204** [9]5-9-3 (64) A Nicholls 22/1: 160000-0: 11th: Cl-up far side, fdd 2f out: reapp. *2* **19**
3267} **TRE COLLINE 242** [7]5-10-0 (75) Kim Tinkler 50/1: 016320-0: 12th: Al in rear far side: reapp & top-weight. *nk* **29**
1153} **STORMVILLE 343** [13]7-9-1 (62) M Lawson(7) 40/1: 01500/0-0: 13th: Chsd ldrs far side, fdd 3f out. *8* **0**
4920} **THE WIZARD MUL 153** [19]4-9-3 (64) D R McCabe 50/1: 010104-0: 14th: Al in rear stands side. *½* **0**
775 **AFRICAN SPUR 29** [3]4-9-12 T (73) D Tudhope(7) 20/1: 00-00220: 15th: Al bhd far side. *10* **0**
4313} **GET STUCK IN 193** [16]8-9-12 (73) K Darley 50/1: 00250/0-0: 16th: Prom stands side, fdd dist. *1* **0**
4991} **NEMO FUGAT 147** [15]5-9-9 (70) Alex Greaves 25/1: 500400-0: 17th: Prom stands side, wknd 2f out. *½* **0**
4178} **EXTINGUISHER 200** [14]5-9-9 (70) L Treadwell(7) 66/1: 000000-0: 18th: Cl-up stands side, fdd 2f out. *5* **0**
700 **RONNIE FROM DONNY 35** [10]4-9-9 (70) R Winston 10/1: 001-400U: Jockey fell off leaving stalls: v disappointing for backers: see 241. **0**
19 Ran Time 1m 16.44(5.14) Owned: Yorkshire Racing Club & Derek Blackhurst Trained: Hambleton

LINGFIELD Polytrack MONDAY 29.03.04 Lefthand, V Sharp Track

Official Going STANDARD

968 **2.00 Bet Direct No Q 08000 93 66 93 Banded Stakes 4yo+ 0-40 (H)**
£1477 £422 £211 **1m4f aw** **Going 35** **-06 Slow** Inside

4051] **LISSAHANELODGE 563** [8] P R Hedger 5-9-2 (40) S Whitworth 20/1: 0060/-1: br g Grand Lodge - Lissahane Lass (Daring March) Rear, hdwy wide to lead well over 1f out, rdn out: reapp, first win: missed '03: unplcd all '02 mdn starts (rtd 53 at best): apprec first start at 12f & polytrack: runs well fresh on a sharp trk. **45a**
827 **LITTLE RICHARD 20** [3] M Wellings 5-9-2 p (40) V Slattery 9/2 CO FAV: 0431402: Trkd ldrs, went 2nd over 1f out but not pace of wnr: tchd 7/1: consistent: see 650, 537. *2½* **40a**
650 **ANNIVERSARY GUEST 42** [11] Mrs Lucinda Featherstone 5-9-2 (35) Derek Nolan(7) 20/1: 60305-03: b f Desert King - Polynesian Goddess (Salmon Leap) Keen in rear, hdwy over 2f out, onepcd fnl 1f: 6 wk abs: fin 3rd at best in a '03 h'cap (rtd 43): 3rd in a '02 h'cap (rtd 43): eff at 2m on firm grnd. *2* **37a**
705 **ROYALE PEARL 35** [9] R Ingram 4-9-0 (40) S Drowne 33/1: 0340-004: Rear, hdwy 3f out, no dngr. *shd* **36a**
867* **ANTONY EBENEEZER 11** [14]5-9-2 t (40) R Thomas(5) 5/1: 0-530015: Rear, hdwy 2f out, onepcd. *1½* **34a**
827 **GIKO 20** [6]10-9-2 bl (35) Martin Dwyer 14/1: 200-0306: Chsd ldrs, led over 3f out till over 1f out, wknd. *1½* **32a**
787 **THE LAST MOHICAN 27** [1]5-9-2 p (40) L Dettori 9/2 CO FAV: 4232447: Nvr btr than mid-div. *2* **29a**
410 **FITZ THE BILL 74** [2]4-9-0 (35) J Mackay 50/1: 06000-08: Rear, nvr nr ldrs: long abs. *7* **19a**
827 **POLKA PRINCESS 20** [12]4-9-0 p (35) J Quinn 20/1: 0003009: Nvr btr than mid-div. *1½* **17a**
697 **TIME FLYER 37** [5]4-9-0 (40) S Righton 50/1: 0000-000: 10th: Rear, keen & hdwy 6f out, wknd 2f out. *½* **16a**
3901} **AMETHYST ROCK 216** [10]6-9-2 (40) N Pollard 20/1: 00060-0: 11th: With ldr, led 6f to 4f out, no extra. *5* **9a**
916 **PRIVATE SEAL 5** [15]9-9-2 t (40) M Halford(7) 9/2 CO FAV: 6322020: 12th: Handy, fdd 3f out. *¾* **8a**
3602} **JEZADIL 228** [13]6-9-2 (40) Kristin Stubbs(7) 7/1: 060430-0: 13th: Keen & handy, led 4f out till over 3f out. *11* **0a**
917 **NEWCORR 5** [7]5-9-2 (40) G Baker 25/1: 0U60/0-00: 14th: Led to 6f, fdd 4f out, t.o.: qck reapp. *28* **0a**
14 Ran Time 2m 34.22 (5.02) Owned: Mr J J Whelan Trained: Chichester

969 **2.30 Bet Direct No Q Banded Stakes 3yo+ 0-45 (H)**
£1484 £424 £212 **7f aw rnd** **Going 35** **-17 Slow** Inside

637 **PACKIN EM IN 43** [7] J R Boyle 6-9-7 (35) D Corby(3) 25/1: 000-3201: b c Young Ern - Wendy's Way (Merdon Melody) Trkd ldr, led halfway, rdn ou: 6 wk abs: first win: modest in '03 & '02 (rtd 43): eff at 6/7f on soft & both AWs, acts on a sharp trk: tried blnks. 2 Feb'04 Ling 6ap 38a-(35) H: 2 Nov'00 Sout 6af 58a-57 E: **46a**
846 **DIAL SQUARE 15** [10] P Howling 3-8-6 bl (45) M Hills 5/1: 00-0132: Trkd ldrs, chsd wnr over 2f out, kept on ins last: consistent: see 846 & 535. *hd* **45a**
788 **SHIRLEY OAKS 27** [11] Miss Z C Davison 6-9-7 (40) N Chalmers(5) 16/1: 00-05023: Rear, hdwy wide over 2f out, kept on fnl 1f to go 3rd nr fin: see 788 & 652. *1½* **42a**
770 **VIZULIZE 29** [3] A W Carroll 5-9-7 (45) J Quinn 20/1: 0-065004: Trkd ldrs, onepcd fnl 1f: eff btwn 7f/10f on fast & polytrack: tried a visor 770, see 739. *hd* **41a**
846 **SINGLE TRACK MIND 15** [9]6-9-7 (45) L Dettori 11/4: 00-02545: Rear, hdwy over 2f out, sn onepcd. *½* **40a**
935 **THE GAY FOX 3** [8]10-9-7 t p (40) V Slattery 16/1: 3003006: Mid-div, hdwy 2f out, onepcd over 1f out. *¾* **38a**
846 **GEESPOT 15** [12]5-9-7 (40) Martin Dwyer 16/1: 4000307: Rear, hdwy 2f out, late gains fnl 1f. *½* **37a**
770 **ESTRELLA LEVANTE 29** [13]4-9-7 bl e (45) R L Moore 16/1: 5-053068: Rear, nvr nr ldrs: see 651. *1½* **34a**
830* **GENTLE RESPONSE 20** [4]4-9-7 bl (45) S Whitworth 5/2 FAV: 0-006319: Midfield, hdwy 3f out, sn wknd. *nk* **33a**
907 **MALAAH 6** [6]8-9-7 bl (40) M Halford(7) 20/1: 00-00400: 10th: Led to halfway, no extra over 1f out. *4* **25a**
910 **LADY LIESEL 5** [1]4-9-7 (40) G Baker 33/1: 00-00300: 11th: Rear, nvr a factor: see 710. *nk* **24a**
869 **BROOKLANDS TIME 11** [15]3-8-6 (45) G Edwards(3) 50/1: 433-0000: 12th: Rear, eff 3f out, sn wknd 2f out *5* **14a**
411 **SHAMWARI FIRE 74** [5]4-9-7 (45) Natalia Gemelova(7) 12/1: 4400-460: 13th: ch g Idris - Bobby's Dream (Reference Point) Chsd ldrs, wknd 2f out: long abs: rnr-up 1 of 9 '03 starts (class stks, earlier with M Tompkins): 3rd in a '02 mdn (rtd 67): eff around 7f/1m on firm & gd/soft: with I McInnes. *1½* **11a**
2 Oct'03 Newc 8.0fm 65-(50) F:
907 **EVANGELIST 6** [16]4-9-7 bl t (45) S Drowne 20/1: 0-301060: 14th: Al bhd: qck reapp: btr 667. *7* **0a**
708 **JANES VALENTINE 35** [2]4-9-7 (40) N Pollard 33/1: 000-4040: 15th: Rear, hmpd over 4f out, not recover. *12* **0a**
15 Ran Time 1m 26.5 (3.7) Owned: City Industrial Supplies Ltd Trained: Epsom

970 **3.00 Littlewoods Bet Direct Banded Stakes 3yo+ 0-45 (H)**
£1467 £419 £210 **1m2f aw** **Going 35** **-20 Slow** Inside

831 **OKTIS MORILIOUS 20** [7] A W Carroll 3-8-1 (45) J Quinn 10/1: 0-0041: Midfield, hdwy 3f out, led well over 1f out, drvn out: first win: stays 10f well on polytrack & a sharp trk. **47a**
785 **RYANS BLISS 27** [11] T D McCarthy 4-9-7 (40) J P Guillambert(3) 50/1: 0000-002: b f Danetime - Raja Moulana (Raja Baba) Rear, hdwy 3f out, chsd wnr fnl 1f but al held: unplcd all '03 starts (rtd 37): fin 4th in a mdn in '02 (rtd 78): improved stepped up to 10f on polytrack. *1* **45a**
805 **THEATRE LADY 25** [5] P D Evans 6-9-7 (45) L Dettori 9/4 FAV: 0-120363: Rear, onepcd fnl 2f. *2* **42a**
300 **EUROLINK ARTEMIS 86** [12] Julian Poulton 7-9-7 p (40) M Halford(7) 33/1: 00000-04: b f Common Grounds - Taiga (Northfields) Rear, hdwy 3f out, onepcd fnl 1f: long abs, rnr-up in 3 h'caps in '03 (part with Miss Kelleway): won a class stks in '02: eff at 1m/10f, has tried 12f, acts on firm, soft & fibresand, any trk: runs well in cheek pieces: has tried blnks, t-strap & an eye-sheild. *½* **41a**
2 Apr'03 Pont 10.0g/f 55-51 E: 2 Jan'03 Sout 8af 57a-55 F: 2 Jan'03 Wolv 9.3af 57a- F: 1 Dec'02 Wolv 8.4af 55a- G: 2 Nov'02 Sout 8af 59a-58 F: 1 Jun'01 Redc 10g/f 72-69 C: 2 Jun'01 Nott 10fm 65- F: 1 Jun'01 Newc 10.1g/f 70-67 E:
828 **GALEY RIVER 20** [2]5-9-7 (40) D Corby(3) 14/1: 00-00505: Led over 2f out till over 1f out, wknd. *¾* **40a**
705 **MYTHICAL CHARM 35** [10]5-9-7 (45) N Pollard 12/1: 01-60006: Rear, modest late gains. *3½* **35a**
715 **STEPPENWOLF 34** [4]3-8-1 P (45) S Righton 11/1: 0000-607: Midfield, wknd 2f out: cheekpieces. *2½* **31a**
828 **PYRRHIC 20** [8]5-9-7 bl (45) R L Moore 9/2: 2065068: Trkd ldrs, lost pl 3f out & btn. *3* **26a**
705 **WILOM 35** [1]6-9-7 (40) V Slattery 14/1: 3-254509: Led till joined after 2f, wknd over 2f out. *nk* **25a**
1457] **BARAKANA 127** [3]6-9-7 bl (45) J Mackay 8/1: 426060-0: 10th: Trkd ldrs, wknd 2f out: now with C Tinkler. *1¾* **22a**
891 **ERSAAL 7** [9]4-9-7 bl (45) S Drowne 9/1: 3000-030: 11th: Chsd ldrs, lost pl over 3f out & btn. *6* **13a**
11 Ran Time 2m 8.38 (5.58) Owned: Mr Dennis Deacon Trained: Alcester

971	**3.30 Betdirect Co Uk Banded Stakes 3yo+ 0-35 (H)**	
	£1456 £416 £208 **1m aw rnd** **Going 35** **-18 Slow** Outside	

894 **CUMBRIAN PRINCESS** 7 [5] M Blansharad 7-9-8 (30) R Thomas(5) 14/1: 005-4001: Chsd ldrs, drvn to **42a**
lead ins fnl 1f, decisively: eff at 1m/9f on fast, soft & both AWs, any trk: back to form: see 228.
909 **BAYTOWN FLYER** 6 [10] P S McEntee 4-9-8 (35) L Dettori 9/2: 00000-22: Led till jnd over 2f out, 1½ **38a**
led distt, hdd & no extra ins fnl 1f: qck reapp, tchd 13/2: eff at 6f/1m: see 909.
830 **TINY TIM** 20 [4] A M Balding 6-9-8 (35) R J Killoran(7) 100/30 FAV: 050:/-4423: Trkd ldrs, hdwy 1f 1½ **35a**
out, onepcd fnl 1f: nicely bckd: see 786.
830 **TOJONESKI** 20 [6] I W McInnes 5-9-8 p (35) Natalia Gemelova(7) 11/2: 530-0034: Midfield, onepcd fnl 2f. 1¼ **32a**
788 **HELLBENT** 27 [12]5-9-8 (35) S Crawford(6) 11/2: 0/0-00005: b g Selkirk - Loure (Lyphard) Keen in 1 **30a**
rear, hdwy 2f out, not pace to chall: missed '03: 3rd at best in '02 (mdn, rtd 62a): has tried blnks.
4730] **MAHLSTICK** 518 [3]6-9-8 (35) R L Moore 12/1: 400406/-6: b g Tagula - Guv's Joy (Thatching) Trkd 1½ **27a**
ldr, ev ch 2f out, wknd fnl 1f: missed '03: 4th at best in '02 (class stks, rtd 71): unplcd in '01 (rtd
40): prob stays a sharp 7f & handles polytrack: has been gelded: with D Arbuthnot.
784 **PLATINUM BOY** 27 [8]4-9-8 p (35) V Slattery 16/1: 0-000037: Chsd ldrs, wknd fnl 2f. 1 **25a**
671 **OUT OF MY WAY** 40 [2]3-8-5 (30) R Brisland 66/1: 0400-008: Mid-div, outpcd 2f out & btn. 1¾ **22a**
2107] **SUPERCLEAN** 290 [1]4-9-8 (30) J Quinn 20/1: 055-9: Al bhd: op 50/1, reapp. 3½ **15a**
4439] **DAPHNES DOLL** 186 [9]9-9-8 (30) Lucy Russell(7) 33/1: 0000U0-0: 10th: Chsd ldrs, wknd 3f out. nk **14a**
906 **SPIDERS WEB** 6 [7]4-9-8 bl (35) G Carter 11/2: 000B230: 11th: Nvr a factor: qck reapp. 1 **12a**
777 **ALL ON MY OWN** 28 [11]9-9-8 p (35) P Mathers(7) 10/1: 0-042400: 12th: Nvr a factor: btr 584. ½ **11a**
12 Ran Time 1m 40.46 (4.26) Owned: Mr David Sykes Trained: Upper Lambourn

972	**4.00 Bet Direct On Sky Active Claiming Stakes 3yo+ (H)**	
	£1460 £417 £209 **1m2f aw** **Going 35** **-48 Slow** Inside	

903 **ABSOLUTE UTOPIA** 6 [4] J L Spearing 11-9-11 (63) L Dettori 4/6 FAV: 1-022341: Chsd ldrs, led well **61a**
over 2f out, rdn out fnl 1f: nicely bckd, qck reapp, clmd for 4,000: eff at 10/12f on firm & gd/soft, loves
polytrack/Lingfield, handles any trk: now an 11yo but clrly retains some ability: see 267.
842 **ITSONLYAGAME** 15 [5] R Ingram 4-9-12 (45) S Drowne 12/1: 6-100502: Rear, hdwy over 3f out, kept 5 **50a**
on fnl 1f to go 2nd but no ch with wnr: see 409.
828 **MONDURU** 20 [6] G L Moore 7-9-12 bl e (47) R L Moore 3/1: 00-01223: Midfield, hdwy over 3f out, 1¾ **47a**
kept on into 3rd: see 654 & 584.
899 **FOOT FAULT** 6 [2] N A Callaghan 3-8-1 (57) D Fox(5) 5/1: 046-0444: Keen & trkd ldr, led over 3f ¾ **41a**
out till over 2f out, fdd fnl 1f: qck reapp, clmd for 5,000: needs to settle: see 899 & 843.
IVY HOUSE LAD 0 [3]4-9-9 P Mathers(7) 50/1: 5: b g Presidium - Nice Spice (Common Grounds) dist **0a**
Rear, wknd 4f out, t.o. on AW bow: fin last of 12 sole 03/04 bmpr start: with I McInnes.
SUDDEN 0 [1]9-9-12 N Pollard 50/1: 6: ch g Positive Statement - Tala 'a Ranee (Layal) Keen & 1½ **0a**
led, hdd over 3f out, fdd & t.o. on AW bow: rcd keenly on debut & ruined chances: with J Bridger.
6 Ran Time 2m 11.12 (8.32) Owned: Mr M T Lawrance Trained: Kinnersley

973	**4.30 Bet Direct No Q Demo 08000 837 888 Median Auction Maiden Stakes 3-5yo (H)**	
	£1467 £419 £210 **6f aw rnd** **Going 35** **+06 Fast** Inside	

3911] **KAMANDA LAUGH** 215 [6] B W Hills 3-8-8 M Hills 3/1 J FAV: 60-1: ch g Most Welcome - Kamada **77a**
(Blushing Groom) Handy, trkd ldr over 2f out, drvn to lead t-home: reapp, gd time: unplcd both '03 mdn starts
(rtd 72, with W Jarvis): eff at 6f on polytrack, acts on a sharp trk: gd start for new yard since gelded.
5032] **BUY ON THE RED** 142 [5] W R Muir 3-8-8 (72) J Quinn 3/1 J FAV: 424-2: b c Komaite - Red Rosein hd **76a**
(Red Sunset) Tried to make all, hdd under press t-home: reapp, clr of rem: rnr-up 1 of 3 '03 starts (mdn): eff at
5/6f, acts on gd/soft & polytrack: sure to find similar. 2 Oct'03 Nott 5.1g/s 69- D:
819 **ONEFORTHEBOYS** 21 [2] D Flood 5-9-7 (40) S Whitworth 25/1: 0624003: Rear, kept on for press fnl 13 **37a**
1f to go remote 3rd fnr: op 50/1: highly tried.
CEDRIC COVERWELL 0 [3] D K Ivory 4-9-7 S Drowne 25/1: 4: Rear, modest late gains on debut. ½ **35a**
76 **MISS JUDGEMENT** 128 [10]3-8-3 (58) J Mackay 5/1: 0006-5: Chsd ldrs, outpcd 2f out, wknd fnl 1f. 1½ **25a**
1807] **LADY ORIANDE** 305 [9]3-8-4 (1ow) R L Moore 11/2: 0-6: In tch, outpcd & btn 3f out on reapp. 1¼ **22a**
889 **LA VIGNA** 7 [8]3-8-8 p (30) Derek Nolan(5) 100/1: 0000-007: In tch, outpcd 3f out. 1¼ **22a**
4993] **QUINTILLION** 147 [4]3-8-8 G Carter 50/1: 00-8: Al bhd: reapp. 2½ **14a**
880 **BAHAMIAN BELLE** 10 [7]4-9-2 (48) L Dettori 11/2: 23405-69: Chsd ldr, lost pl over 2f out, btn fnl 1f. 1¼ **5a**
HALF A HANDFUL 0 [1]3-8-8 D Corby(3) 12/1: 0: 10th: Al bhd on debut. 3½ **0a**
10 Ran Time 1m 12.16 (1.76) Owned: Mr John Sillett Trained: Lambourn

Official Going Good/Soft (Soft Places)

974	**2.20 New Turf Season Median Auction Maiden Stakes 2yo (F)**	
	£2898 £828 £414 **5f str** **Soft 106** **-07 Slow** Stands side	

BRIGHT MOLL [4] M L W Bell 2-8-9 I Mongan 9/4: 1: b f Mind Games - Molly Brown (Rudimentary) **86+**
Handy, styd on to lead dist, sn rdn clr, val 6L+: op 5/4 on debut: March first foal, cost 37,000gns: dam wnr at
5/6f, sire top-class at sprint dists: eff at 5f, 6f shld suit: acts on soft grnd & a sharp/undul trk: goes well
fresh: decisive wnr who can impr with experience & find more races.
COLONEL BILKO [2] B R Millman 2-9-0 S Drowne 2/1 FAV: 2: b c General Monash - Mari Ela (River 4 **77**
Falls) Slow away, sn cl-up, ran green & ev ch dist, not pace of wnr fnl 1f: tchd 10/3 on debut: Feb foal, cost
19,000gns: dam 7f wnr as a juv, sire speedy juv: eff at 5f on soft: ran green here & sure to improve on today.
SMOKINCANON [1] W G M Turner 2-9-0 R Miles(3) 10/1: 3: ch c Fumo di Londra - Secret Miss shd **76**

(Beveled) Led till dist, sn no extra: clr rem on debut: April foal, half-brother to a mid-dist wnr: dam 5f wnr, sire Gr 3 wnr at 1m abroad: eff at 5f, shld stay further: acts on soft grnd.
VENEER [3] R Hannon 2-9-0 R Hughes 7/2: 4: Sn in rear, nvr able to chall: tchd 5/1 on debut. *11* **51**
KISSING A FOOL [5]2-9-0 C Haddon(7) 12/1: 5: Dwelt, al bhd: debut. *nk* **50**
JUSTENJOY YOURSELF [6]2-8-9 S Sanders 12/1: 6: In tch, wknd 3f out: debut. *7* **27**
6 Ran Time 1m 4.07 (5.67) Owned: Mr A Buxton Trained: Newmarket

975

2.50 Visit Port Lympne & Howletts Handicap Stakes 3yo 0-70 (E) **[77]**
£3445 £1060 £530 **6f str** **Soft 106** **-00 Slow** Stands side, field all rcd far side

609 **ASK THE CLERK 47** [11] V Smith 3-9-3 (66) M Tebbutt 9/1: 30-03501: b g Turtle Island - Some Fun (Wolverlife) In tch, chsd ldr 2f out, styd on to lead ins fnl 1f, rdn out: tchd 16/1: ex-Irish, plcd 3 times in '03 (mdns, P J Prendergast): earlier plcd here for H J Collingridge: stays 1m, eff at 6f on firm, fast grnd & f/sand, apprec return to soft grnd: acts on a sharp/undul trk & goes well fresh. **73**
875 **SIERA SPIRIT 11** [9] M G Quinlan 3-8-6 (55) Nicol Polli(7) 5/1: 4302: Chsd ldrs, hdwy when short of room dist, swtched & styd on well, post came too sn: op 3/1, h'cap bow: eff at 6f on polytrack, imprvd today on soft grnd: prob wnr with clr run & can find compensation: see 364. *nk* **61+**
814 **INSTINCT 22** [4] R Hannon 3-8-13 (62) R Hughes 5./1: 0-503: Dwelt, sn in tch, led 2f out, hdd ins fnl 1f, no extra: tchd 13/2 on h'cap bow: eff at 6f on soft grnd: gd eff from poor low draw, see 670. *1½* **64**
4869} **GOBLIN 158** [7] D E Cantillon 3-9-1 (64) S Sanders 10/1: 235000-4: b g Atraf - Forest Fantasy (Rambo Dancer) Held up, hdwy 3f out, onepcd fnl 1f: reapp: plcd on first 3 '03 starts (rtd 84, mdn, R Hannon): eff at 6f, has tried further but shld suit: acts on fast & gd grnd: just sharper for today. *4* **54**
2 Jun'03 Wind 6g/f 79- E:
670 **PHLUKE 41** [13]3-9-7 (70) S Carson 6/1: 432-5305: Cl-up, outpcd 3f out, rallied late: 6 wk abs. *¾* **58**
815* **JOY AND PAIN 22** [6]3-8-10 (1ow) (58) Dane O'Neill 10/1: 006016: In tch wide, no extra fnl 2f: turf bow: below form of win in 815 (7f, polytrack). *1½* **43**
815 **MISTER COMPLETELY 22** [8]3-8-2 (51) Martin Dwyer 4/1 FAV: 640-2657: Held up, nvr nrr than mid-div: op 8/1: return to further shld suit: btr 815 (7f). *1½* **31**
815 **JASMINE PEARL 22** [10]3-8-4 (53) C Catlin 25/1: 055-3608: Handy, fdd dist: btr 389 (fibresand). *½* **32**
543 **VELVET TOUCH 55** [5]3-8-11 (60) L Dettori 9/1: 3022-269: Led 5f out-2f out, sn wknd: 8 wk abs. *2½* **32**
872 **SPARKLING CLEAR 12** [3]3-7-12 (2oh)vis (45) J F McDonald(4) 50/1: 5066-00: 10th: Al bhd: see 872. *1* **16**
804 **AVERAMI 26** [12]3-8-10 vis (59) S Drowne 16/1: 0654-050: 11th: Led 1f, fdd 2f out: btr 804. *1¾* **23**
815 **LIVIA 22** [1]3-8-4 (53) R L Moore 20/1: 06040: 12th: Chsd ldrs wide, fdd 3f out: btr 815. *2* **11**
12 Ran Time 1m 17.38 (6.38) Owned: Mr R J Baines Trained: Newmarket

976

3.20 Folkestone-Racecourse Co Uk Handicap Stakes 3yo+ 0-80 (D) **[80]**
£5574 £1715 £858 **6f str** **Soft 106** **+07 Fast** Stands side, all bar one rcd far side

136 **MADDIES A JEM 119** [12] J R Jenkins 4-9-0 (66) S W Kelly 20/1: 203460-1: b f Emperor Jones - Royal Orchid (Shalford) Chsd ldrs, led dist, rdn out: reapp, gd time: fill mdn wnr in '03 (also plcd 4 times): eff at 6f on fast, soft & polytrack: acts on a gall or sharp/undul trk & goes well fresh: win more h'caps. **75**
2 Aug'03 Sand 5.0g/s 71-68 D: 1 Aug'03 Yarm 6.0g/f 68-(68) D: 2 Aug'03 Donc 5g/f 68-66 E: 2 Jul'03 Ling 5gd 58- F:
940 **OASES 3** [8] D Shaw 5-8-6 (58) S Whitworth 16/1: 00400-02: Held up, prog 3f out, chsd wnr fnl 1f, kept on but al held: qck reapp: back to form on return to turf & can find similar: see 940. *1½* **61**
902 **PHECKLESS 7** [16] J M Bradley 5-8-5 (57) S Carson 11/1: 0340003: Held up, gd hdwy wide 3f out & trav best, kept on fnl 1f, nrst fin: qck reapp: eff at 6f, crying out for a return to further: handles gd/soft & soft grnd, likes polytrack: set plenty to do & can find similar back at 7f: see 450. *nk* **60+**
4979} **KINGSCROSS 150** [10] M Blanshard 6-9-7 (73) D Sweeney 5/1 JT FAV: 043000-4: ch g King's Signet - Calamanco (Clantime) Mid-div, gd prog dist, no impress ins fnl 1f: reapp: plcd once in '03 (h'cap, rtd 75 at best): dual h'cap scorer in '02: h'cap wnr in '01: eff at 5f/sharp 6f on fast, likes gd & soft grnd: handles any trk: likes to come late off a strong pace: has slipped to a winning mark & can win similar granted easy surface. *1½* **72**
2 Aug'02 Newm 6sft 85-82 D: 1 Jul'02 Epso 6gd 83-77 C: 1 May'02 Good 6gd 77-71 C: 2 Apr'02 Warw 6g/s 70-68 E: 1 Oct'01 Newm 5g/f 68-64 D:
761 **SCARROTTOO 31** [9]6-8-2 (54) Martin Dwyer 14/1: 0350055: Handy, onepcd fnl 1f: btr 761. *¾* **51**
627 **CASHEL MEAD 45** [11]4-9-11 (77) L Dettori 5/1 JT FAV: 623-5006: Mid-div, hdwy 3f out, onepcd fnl 1f. *1½* **70**
4616} **KEW THE MUSIC 176** [4]4-9-1 (67) T E Durcan 33/1: 410000-7: b g Botanic - Harmonia (Glint of Gold) Handy, wknd fnl 1f: reapp: mdn wnr in '03: eff at 5/6f on fast grnd: with M R Channon. *hd* **59**
1 May'03 Newc 5g/f 74- F:
4616} **FORT MCHENRY 176** [2]4-9-8 (74) W Ryan 25/1: 041100-8: Cl-up, led 4f out till dist, wknd, reapp. *1½* **62**
4979} **ANTONIO CANOVA 150** [15]8-10-0 (80) O Urbina 8/1: 14/000/0-9: Bhd, onepcd when short of room ins fnl 1f: reapp & top-weight. *nk* **67**
235 **WATERSIDE 101** [3]5-9-5 (71) M Hills 6/1: 631404-0: 10th: Chsd ldrs, ev ch dist, fdd: btr 235. *1¾* **53**
2549} **PEDRO JACK 274** [14]7-9-9 (75) J F McDonald(5) 10/1: 030300-0: 11th: Al bhd: reapp. *1½* **53**
4979} **BEN LOMAND 150** [6]4-9-10 c (76) R L Moore 50/1: 412000-0: 12th: Al in rear: reapp. *1½* **50**
860 **JONNY EBENEEZER 13** [13]5-9-11 p (77) E Ahern 8/1: 46402-00: 13th: Led 2f, styd cl-up, wkng when short of room dist: op 10/1. *3½* **42**
793 **Juwwi 27** [5]10-8-13 p(65) C Catlin 25/1:0 3978} **Tappit 213** [1]5-9-3 (69) P Fitzsimons 40/1:0
15 Ran Time 1m 16.95 (5.95) Owned: Mrs Wendy Jenkins Trained: Royston

977

3.50 Sellinge Maiden Stakes Div 1 Fillies 3yo (D)
£3702 £1139 £570 **1m1f149y** **Soft** **Slow** Outside

2455} **GRETNA 277** [8] J L Dunlop 3-8-11 T Quinn 12/1: 6-1: ch f Groom Dancer - Llia (Shirley Heights) Made all, rdn along when left clr dist, styd on well: reapp: unplcd sole '03 start (mdn, rtd 71): eff at 9.6f, further shld suit: acts on soft & a sharp/undul trk: goes well fresh: only lightly rcd & can improve with racing. **74**
ON CLOUD NINE [1] M L W Bell 3-8-11 Hayley Turner(5) 33/1: 2: ro f Cloudings - Princess Moodyshoe (Jalmood) Slow away, hdwy wide & ev ch when veered away from whip dist, not recover: debut: eff at 9.6f, mid-dist bred: acts on soft grnd: in process of running a decent race & sure to learn from today: can rate higher. *5* **69**
226 **CHARA 102** [5] J R Jenkins 3-8-11 (64) Martin Dwyer 14/1: 4045-3: Mid-div, prog when short of room 2f out, sn onepcd: clr rem, long abs: see 226. *3½* **61**

5018} **CONCERT HALL** 145 [2] Mrs A J Perrett 3-8-11 (75) R Hughes 5/2 JT FAV: 333-4: b f Stravinsky -   11   49
Proflare (Mr Prospector) Cl-up, fdd fnl 2f: bckd on reapp: plcd on all 3 '03 mdn starts (rtd 74): eff at 7/8f on
firm & soft grnd: v disapp here on step up in trip.
875   **AVERTAINE** 11 [9]3-8-11   R L Moore 33/1: 005: Rear, nvr nrr than mid-div.   nk   48
3051} **SAUCY** 253 [4]3-8-11   L Dettori 8/1: 0-6: Cl-up, fdd 2f out: reapp.   5   41
4891} **NORTH SEA** 157 [3]3-8-11   T E Durcan 4/1: 0-7: Mid-div, fdd 3f out: reapp.   19   16
        OBSERVATION [7]3-8-11   P Robinson 5/2 JT FAV: 8: Cl-up, fdd 2f out: well bckd on debut.   5   9
        BOOT N TOOT [6]3-8-11   S Sanders 20/1: 9: Al in rear: debut.   1   7
        LOVE OF LIFE [10]3-8-11   D R McCabe 20/1: 0: 10th: Slow away, sn mid-div, fdd 4f out: debut.   10   0
10 Ran   Time 2m 12.43 (14.43)   Owned: Capt J Macdonald-Buchanan   Trained: Arundel

978   4.20 Wealden Advertiser Gets Results Classified Stakes 4yo+ 0-65 (E)
£3367 £1036 £518   1m1f149y   Soft   Slow   Outside

265   **MISS PEBBLES** 92 [7] B R Johnson 4-9-2 (70) N Pollard 5/1: 210056-1: ch f Lake Coniston - Sea of   72
Stone (Sanglamore) Cl-up, styd on to lead dist, rdn out: long abs: mdn wnr in '03 (also plcd 3 times): eff at
1m /9.6f on fast, soft grnd & polytrack: acts on a sharp/undul trk & can appr further: has tried cheek pieces.
1 Oct'03 Ling 8ap 72a-(73) D: 2 Aug'03 Sand 8.1g/f 73- D: 2 Jul'03 Wind 8.3g/f 70- D:
3591*}**DASH FOR COVER** 229 [5] R Hannon 4-9-4 (69) R Hughes 8/1: 0/33001-2: b g Sesaro - Raindancing   1½   71
(Tirol) Led, hdd dist, kept on but not pace of wnr: reapp: mdn wnr on fnl '03 start (also plcd twice): plcd on
first 2 of 3 '02 starts (rtd 86, mdn): eff at 5/7f, stays a slowly run 9.6f: acts on fast & soft grnd.
1 Aug'03 Ling 7.0g/f 77-(69) D: 2 May'02 Newb 5.1g/s 86- D: 2 May'02 Good 6g/s 85- D:
809   **EASTBOROUGH** 25 [4] B G Powell 5-9-0 (62) S Whitworth 9/2: 0310343: In tch, outpcd 2f out,   1¼   65
rallied ins fnl 1f: acts on fast, soft grnd & both AWs: app return to further: btr 714 & 480.
858   **GALLOWAY MAC** 14 [8] W A O'Gorman 4-9-0 (60) J Murtagh 5/2 FAV: 330124: Chsd ldrs, no extra fnl   1¾   62
1f: tchd 4/1 on turf bow: eff at 7f/1m, stays slowly run 9.6f: acts on soft grnd & fibresand: see 721.
876   **CUDDLES** 11 [3]5-8-11 p (65) T E Durcan 6/1: 33450-05: Mid-div, no impress fnl 2f: btr 876 (polytrk).   nk   58
803   **PURE SPECULATION** 26 [6]4-8-11 (65) I Mongan 9/1: 3000-006: Keen rear, nvr a factor: see 552.   hd   57
4253} **VOICE MAIL** 196 [1]5-9-5 (70) L Keniry(3) 10/1: 344550-7: b g So Factual - Wizardry (Shirley   nk   64
Heights) Held up, nvr able to chall: reapp: h'cap wnr in '03 (first time visor, also plcd numerous times): won 2
h'caps in '02: suited by 7f/1m on firm, gd grnd & polytrack: eff with a visor: tough 5yo who can rate higher on a
sound surface: with A M Balding.   2 Jul'03 Kemp 9g/f 72-71 E: 1 Aug'03 Bath 8.0fm 70-67 D:
1 Aug'03 Ling 7.6g/f 72-66 D: 1 Aug'03 Bath 8g/f 71-63 D: 2 Jul'02 Sali 8g/f 65-62 E:
806   **EASTER OGIL** 25 [2]9-9-0 (56) V Slattery 16/1: 2400008: Rear, no ch when no room dist: btr 515 (AW).   ¾   58
860   **EL HAMRA** 13 [9]6-9-0 (40) S Drowne 50/1: 0000/0-59: Mid-div, fdd 3f out: btr 860.   10   44
9 Ran   Time 2m 13.62 (15.62)   Owned: Mr A A Lyons   Trained: Epsom

979   4.50 Stowting Apprentice Handicap Stakes 3yo+ 0-70 (F)   [72]
£2898 £828 £414   1m4f   Soft   Slow   Outside

813   **MADHAHIR** 22 [9] C A Dwyer 4-9-0 (58) T P Queally 12/1: 0620-001: Led, chall 2f out, drvn out to   65
hold on: rider received a 2 day whip ban: stays 2m, now eff at 12f: acts on gd & fibresand, enjoyed today's switch
to soft: tough & game performer: see 48.
236   **MAN THE GATE** 101 [3] P D Cundell 5-8-13 (55) N Chalmers(3) 3/1 FAV: 0D5300-2: b g Elmaamul - Girl   hd   60
At The Gate (Formidable) Held up, hdwy & ev ch dist, kept on fnl 1f, just held: class stks wnr in '03: h'cap wnr
in '02: eff at 10/12f on firm, soft grnd & polytrack: runs well fresh: lost little in defeat & can find similar.
1 Jun'03 Leic 11.8g/f 64-(65) E: 2 May'03 Newm 12g/f 66-63 E: 1 Jul'02 Leic 8sft 64-58 E:
876   **MISS KOEN** 11 [1] D L Williams 5-8-13 t (55) D Corby 11/1: 60-63103: Slow away, smooth hdwy to   2½   55
chall 2f out, not find much for press & onepcd ins fnl 1f: needs to come v late: see 816.
813   **GEMI BED** 22 [2] G L Moore 9-8-7 bl (49) R Miles 9/2: 153-6154: Mid-div, onepcd fnl 1f: won this   3½   45
race 12 mths ago off a 10lb lower mark: best form now seems at further: btr 733 (2m).
4819} **GALANDORA** 162 [4]4-8-1 t (45) Lucy Russell(3) 20/1: 506300-5: b f Bijou d'Inde - Jelabna (Jalmood)   ¾   40
Keen mid-div, nvr a factor: reapp: plcd twice in '03 (h'caps, rtd 47 & 32a): unplcd in '02 (rtd 56 & 55a): eff at
13f, prob stays a slowly run 2m: acts on fast grnd & wears a t-strap.
4369} **VAL DE FLEURIE** 192 [5]9-9-2 (54) T Treadwell(5) 5/1: 003014-6: b f Mondrian - Valbonne (Master   shd   52
Willie) Led/dsptd lead, fdd dist: jumps fit, earlier prog over hdles, won 5 times (class & h'caps, rtd 122h, stays
2m5.5f on fast & soft): app h'cap wnr in '03: ex-German, former useful Flat wnr (10/12f): suited by 12f on fast &
soft grnd: can force the pace.   1 Jul'03 Chep 12.1g/f 57-55 F:
534   **ENVIRONMENT AUDIT** 56 [7]5-10-0 (70) J Jeffrey(10) 16/1: 100/0-007: ch g Kris - Bold And Beautiful   6   56
(Bold Lad) Held up, nvr a factor: recent hdles unplcd (rtd 44h, h'cap): unplcd sole '03 start (h'cap): mdn wnr in
'02: eff at 10/12f on firm & gd/soft grnd, likes a stiff/gall trk: reportedly lost both front shoes today.
1 Jul'02 Pont 10g/s 85- D: 2 Jul'02 Bath 10.2g/s 84- D: 2 May'02 Newm 12fm 84- D:
2133} **TRAGIC DANCER** 652 [8]8-8-5 (47) S Hitchcott 9/1: 0///0400/-8: Handy, wknd 2f out, eased.   ¾   32
896   **GOLDEN DUAL** 7 [6]4-9-2 vis (60) J Coffill Brown(10) 11/2: 0600029: Keen in tch, fdd 5f out: qck reapp.   dist   20
9 Ran   Time 2m 52.41 (20.91)   Owned: Mr M M Foulger Mr I Dodd Mr G Darrall   Trained: Newmarket

980   5.20 Sellinge Maiden Stakes Div 2 Fillies 3yo (D)
£3692 £1136 £568   1m1f149y   Soft   Slow   Outside

4479} **BOWSTRING** 185 [2] J H M Gosden 3-8-11 Dane O'Neill 9/1: 0-1: b f Sadler's Wells - Cantanta (Top   88+
Ville) Cl-up, led 4f out, sn clr, pushed out, val 14L+: reapp: unplcd sole '03 start (fills) mdn, rtd 54):
related to a smart 12f wnr: eff at 9.6f, shld apprec further: acts on soft grnd & a sharp/undul trk: goes well
fresh: lightly rcd performer who could not have been more impressive, can rate higher.
        HIGH SCHOOL [7] D R Loder 3-8-11 J Murtagh 8/11 FAV: 2: b f Sadler's Wells - High Hawk   10   70
(Shirley Heights) Slow away, sn in tch, outpcd 2f out, rallied late: well bckd on debut at odds-on: sister to 4
wnrs in Group company, incl In The Wings: shaped as tho' further will suit & can impr on today.
100   **KALI** 125 [4] R Charlton 3-8-11 D Sweeney 3/1: 2-3: gr f Linamix - Alkarida (Akarad) In tch, ev   1½   67
ch 2f out, sn wknd: reapp: rnr-up on sole '03 start (mdn): eff at 1m, shld apprec further: acts on polytrack.
2 Nov'03 Ling 8ap 76a- D:
3859} **ILLEANA** 218 [1] W R Muir 3-8-11 Martin Dwyer 20/1: 00-4: Keen mid-div, nvr able to chall: reapp.   1   65
        OLYMPIAS [3]3-8-11 S Drowne 10/1: 5: b f Kahyasi - Premier Amour (Salmon Leap) Mid-div,   ½   64

outpcd 3f out, rallied late: debut: related to an 11f Gr 3 wnr abroad: with H Morrison.

566	**MYSTIC MOON 52** [5]3-8-11 S Whitworth 66/1: 0-006: Held up, nvr a factor.	3½	59$
	PELLA [6]3-8-11 S Sanders 25/1: 7: Rear, nvr a factor.	4	53
875	**DIVERTED 11** [8]3-8-11 P McCabe 100/1: 008: Mid-div, wknd 3f out.	8	42
881	**ALIANNA 10** [9]3-8-11 C Catlin 100/1: 009: Led, hdd 4f out, sn fdd.	dist	17

9 Ran   Time 2m 12.68(14.68)   Owned: Mr R E Sangster & Mrs J Magnier   Trained: Manton

SOUTHWELL   Fibresand   TUESDAY 30.03.04   Lefthand, Sharp, Oval Track

Official Going Standard

---

981   2.10 New & Improved Betdirect Co Uk Banded Stakes 3yo+ 0-40 (H)
£1435   £410   £205   **5f aw str**   Going 93   **Inapplicable**   Stands Side

767	**PLEASURE TIME 30** [6] C Smith 11-9-7 vis (40) R Fitzpatrick 6/1: 055-5001: Made all, rdn & in		38a
	command dist, styd on strongly: best forcing the pace at 5f, stays 6f: acts on frm, gd/soft & fibresand: see 720.		
904	**TUSCAN DREAM 7** [8] A Berry 9-9-7 (30) P Bradley(5) 9/2: 0-000022: Al prom, kept on for press.	2½	30a
889	**BOND DOMINGO 8** [9] B Smart 5-9-7 vis (40) M Stainton(7) 9/1: 0000-003: b g Mind Games - Antonia's	¾	28a
	Folly (Music Boy) In tch, styd on for press, not able to chall: unplcd '03 (rtd 43a & 31, tried visor): late '01		
	h'cap wnr over C/D, turf unplcd '02 (rtd 53): eff at 5f on gd & fibresand, handles hvy, any trk: eff in blnks.		
	1 Nov'01 Sout 5af 79a-75 E: 1 Sep'01 Hami 5gd 77-69 E: 2 Apr'01 Nott 5hvy 82- D:		
720	**DANAKIM 35** [2] J R Weymes 7-9-7 bl e (40) D Fentiman(7) 11/2: 60-61004: Cl-up, no extra dist: see 578.	1	26a
904	**LEVELLED 7** [1]10-9-7 bl (35) A Culhane 4/1: 0000455: Dsptd lead, btn over 1f out: btr 832 (polytrack).	1¼	23a
851	**SPY MASTER 16** [5]6-9-7 t P (35) M Lawson(7) 3/1 FAV: 00-32506: Chsd ldrs, not able to chall: see 773.	hd	22a
207	**DRESS PEARL 105** [4]3-8-9 (40) M Fenton 12/1: 060000-7: b f Atraf - Dress Design (Brief Truce)	2	17a
	Dwelt, hmpd start & al rear: abs: fills mdn rnr-up '03 (flattered, A Berry): eff at 5f/6f, tried 7f: handles soft		
	grnd & a gall trk. 2 May'03 Hayd 6sft 81- D: 2 May'03 Hayd 5sft 73- D:		
677	**METICULOUS 40** [3]6-9-7 (30) L Vickers 40/1: 0000008: Sn outpcd & struggling, jumps fit.	1¼	14a
904	**DIAMOND RACKET 7** [7]4-9-7 bl (30) J Quinn 25/1: 000-0609: Chsd ldrs till halfway, eased.	8	0a

9 Ran   Time 1m 03.77 ()   Owned: Mr C Smith   Trained: Wellingore

---

982   2.40 Betdirect Co Uk Banded Stakes 3yo+ 0-40 (H)
£1456   £416   £208   **6f aw rnd**   Going 93   -08 Slow   Inside

664	**INDIAN MUSIC 42** [8] A Berry 7-9-7 (40) F Lynch 12/1: 30000-61: Wide & bhd, strong run for press		42a
	to lead line: 6 wk abs: eff at 5f/6f, stays up to 9.4f: acts on fast, hvy & fibresand, likes Southwell: see 664.		
904	**MR UPPITY 7** [11] Julian Poulton 5-9-7 e (35) Lisa Jones(3) 18/1: 0000-002: b g Shareef Dancer -	shd	41a
	Queenfisher (Scottish Reel) Mid-div, hdwy & led over 1f out, drvn & hdd line: AW mdn rnr-up '03, turf unplcd (rtd		
	26, h'cap): unplcd '02 (rtd 71 & 22a): eff at 5/6f on fibresand: fair runs in visor, cheek pieces & eye-shield,		
	also tried blnks. 2 Feb'03 Sout 5af 48a-(45) D:		
894	**NEUTRAL NIGHT 8** [12] R Brotherton 4-9-7 vis (40) D Holland 11/2: 0053243: Dwelt, in tch wide,	shd	41a
	hdwy to chall over 1f out, no extra cl-home: clr of rem: shown enough to find similar in this grade.		
832	**EMARATIS IMAGE 21** [10] R M Stronge 6-9-7 (40) K Darley 5/1: 00-06464: Handy & led over 2f till	6	27a
	over 1f out, fdd under press: btr 788 (polytrack).		
771	**ABOUSTAR 30** [5]4-9-7 (35) M Lawson(7) 25/1: 6/00-505: Chsd ldrs, bmpd early, not pace to chall.	½	25a
847	**BRILLIANTRIO 16** [7]6-9-7 (40) L Vickers 12/1: 2406U36: Dwelt & hmpd start, only mod prog from rear.	1½	21a
710	**MOUNT SUPERIOR 36** [4]8-9-7 bl (40) Paul Eddery 5/1: 0/66-1507: Bhd, mod late prog: btr 352 (C/D).	3½	12a
533	**VALUABLE GIFT 56** [3]7-9-7 bl e t (40) J F Egan 14/1: 0000-008: ch g Cadeaux Genereux - Valbra	¾	10a
	(Dancing Brave) Cl-up, wknd over 1f out: abs: AW mdn rnr-up '03 (l Semple, turf unplcd, rtd 31, current trainer):		
	rnr-up twice in '02 (h'caps): suited by 5/6f on fibresand, gd & soft grnd, any trk: eff in a visor/blnks, now wears		
	a t-strap. 2 Feb'03 Wolv 6af 54a- D: 2 Dec'02 Sout 6af 59a- D: 2 Dec'02 Sout 6af 53a- G:		
	2 May'02 Good 5gd 53-50 E: 2 May'02 Wolv 6af 56a-50 F:		
779	**DANCES IN TIME 29** [2]4-9-7 bl M Lawson(7) 33/1: 0500039: Dwelt & sn outpcd: btr 779.	nk	9a
971	**BAYTOWN FLYER 1** [9]4-9-7 (35) P Makin(7) 8/1: 00000-220: 10th: Al bhd: op 9/2: rnr-up yesterday.	2	4a
773	**COMPTON BAY 30** [6]4-9-7 bl (40) T Eaves(5) 33/1: 00-0000: 11th: Chsd ldrs, btn 2f out, blnks.	9	0a
907	**BELLS BOYS 7** [1]5-9-7 p (40) N Callan 7/2 FAV: 5-335040: 12th: Led till halfway, sn btn: 'nvr trav'.	8	0a

12 Ran   Time 1m 19.35 (6.05)   Owned: Mr Alan Berry   Trained: Cockerham

---

983   3.10 New Site @ Betdirect Co Uk Median Auction Maiden Stakes 3-5yo (H)
£1446   £413   £207   **1m aw rnd**   Going 93   +09 Fast   Inside

899	**CASPIAN DUSK 7** [8] W G M Turner 3-8-7 (58) A Culhane 5/2: 406-231: Cl-up & led halfway, readily		72a
	asserted fnl 2f, easily: nicely bckd: eff around 1m/sharp 10f on both AWs: see 899 & 848.		
5007}	**GOLD CARD 146** [6] J R Weymes 3-8-7 (71) K Darley 9/4 FAV: 634-2: Chsd ldrs, chsd wnr fnl 2f, nvr	14	48a
	any impress: gelded, reapp, AW bckn: auct mdn plcd '03 (rtd 77): eff around 1m on gd grnd, sharp trk.		
4635}	**BE WISE GIRL 175** [2] J G Given 3-8-2 G Duffield 5/1: 03-3: Cl-up, drvn & flashed tail over 2f	1	41a
	out, sn no impress: reapp: auct mdn plcd '03 (C/D, rtd 50a, turf unplcd earlier, rtd 51).		
5016}	**BONJOUR BOND 145** [4] B Smart 3-8-7 (67) F Lynch 5/1: 400-4: Led till halfway, sn btn, gelded.	7	35a
	PLATTOCRAT 0 [7]4-9-10 D Holland 8/1: 5: Dwelt, in tch 5f, debut.	11	17a
2038}	**AIREDALE LAD 294** [9]3-8-7 V Halliday 40/1: 0-6: Al bhd, reapp.	½	16a
438	**MARIA MARIA 71** [1]3-8-2 Joanna Badger 33/1: 0-07: Sn bhd.	6	1a
	HELLO TIGER 0 [3]3-8-7 G Faulkner 18/1: 8: Dwelt & al bhd, debut.	dist	0a
892	**VAUDEVIRE 8** [5]3-8-7 T Hamilton(3) 40/1: 6-69: Cl-up, rdn & struggling halfway.	1¼	0a

9 Ran   Time 1m 46.15 (6.75)   Owned: Mr P Nabavi   Trained: Sherborne

984 3.40 Special Offers @ Betdirect Co Uk Banded Stakes 4yo+ 0-45 (H)
£1442 £412 £206 2m aw Going 93 -63 Slow Inside

849* **STRAVMOUR 16** [1] R Hollinshead 8-9-3 (45) Dale Gibson 2/1 FAV: 1-053311: Rear, hdwy halfway to 48a
trk ldrs, drvn & led dist, styd on well to assert: eff at 12f/2m on fibresand: loves Southwell: see 849, 774 & 257.
849 **BERKELEY HEIGHTS 16** [9] Mrs J Candlish 4-8-12 (35) N Callan 16/1: 065-4062: Mid-div, prog to 1½ 46a
lead over 1f out, hdd dist, no extra: stays 2m in banded company: see 315.
891 **VITELUCY 8** [6] Miss S J Wilton 5-9-3 (45) A Quinn(5) 8/1: 2100-553: Mid-div, pushed along 5f out, 1¼ 45a
kept on onepace for press fnl 2f: stays 2m in banded company: clr of rem: see 666.
4819} **GOLFAGENT 162** [10] Miss K Marks 6-9-3 t (40) D Holland 4/1: P5020/0-4: b g Kris - Alusha (Soviet 6 39a
Star) Led 5f out till over 1f out, fdd: Flat reapp, jumps fit, recent sell hdle & h'cap hdle scorer (rtd 110h,
2m/3m, any grnd, sharp trk): unplcd sole '03 start: stays 2m1f on fm: eff in t-strap. 2 Oct'02 Pont 17.1fm 40-38 E:
867 **WESTERN COMMAND 12** [3]8-9-3 (30) R Fitzpatrick 33/1: 6605005: Chsd ldrs till 4f out: longer trip. 11 31a
906 **MATHMAGICIAN 7** [4]5-9-3 p (35) Dean McKeown 14/1: 4540466: In tch halfway, btn 3f out: up in trip. hd 30a
937 **MONSAL DALE 3** [8]5-9-3 (45) M Savage(5) 3/1: 64235-07: Cl-up, rdn & btn 4f out: qck reapp: see 937. 14 19a
528} **RHETORIC 423** [7]5-9-3 (40) B Swarbrick(7) 18/1: 000/005-8: b g Desert King - Squaw Talk (Gulch) 6 13a
Led till 5f out, sn strugg: gelded, long abs: unplcd '03 (rtd 26a, tried cheek pieces) & '02 (with J Gosden).
3384} **ERROL 238** [5]5-9-3 (30) A Culhane 33/1: 000000-9: Prom till halfway: 2 mth jumps abs. dist 0a
3061} **QUINN 253** [2]4-8-12 (45) Lisa Jones(3) 25/1: 005050-0: 10th: Al bhd, reapp. nk 0a
10 Ran Time 2m 50.94 (24.94) Owned: Mr E Bennion Trained: Upper Longdon

985 4.10 Cashbacks @ Betdirect Co Uk Selling Stakes 4yo+ (H)
£1446 £413 £207 1m3f aw Going 93 -21 Slow Inside

948 **OUR IMPERIAL BAY 3** [8] R M Stronge 5-9-1 P (58) G Duffield 7/1: 14/06-001: Chsd ldrs, drvn & styd 50a
on from over 2f out to lead well ins last: qck reapp in first time cheek pieces: eff at 10/12f on fast & both AWs:
apprec drop to sell grade & application of headgear: see 948.
905 **RED DELIRIUM 7** [3] P A Blockley 8-9-1 bl (50) N Callan 8/1: 6452552: Rear, hdwy wide 5f out & ev hd 49a
ch 2f out, drvn & not pace of wnr cl-home: now stays 11f in sell grade: see 445.
699 **FORTY FORTE 36** [5] Miss S J Wilton 8-9-1 (48) A Quinn(5) 20/1: 020-0003: Led, joined 2f out, drvn ½ 48a
& hdd well ins last: stays 11f in sell grade: see 128.
857 **ELEGANT GRACIE 14** [2] R Guest 4-8-9 (65) D Holland 4/6 FAV: 003-2624: Cl-up, drvn & chall 2f 3 39a
out, sn no extra: hvly bckd at odds-on: btr 857 & 521.
867 **IPLEDGEALLEGIANCE 12** [4]8-9-1 (35) A Culhane 18/1: 3650005: Chsd ldrs, btn 4f out: flattered 827. 17 23a
906 **THINK QUICK 7** [1]4-8-9 (30) H Fellows(7) 50/1: 3403006: Al bhd: see 823. 3½ 13a
890* **TRAVEL TARDIA 8** [6]6-9-6 t (35) Dean McKeown 20/1: 00-00417: Trkd ldrs trav well, wknd qckly 2f 10 12a
out: now with P Blockley: btr 890 (7f, Wolverhampton).
906 **WETHAAB 7** [7]7-9-1 t p (35) Ann Stokell 50/1: 34000-08: Mid-div, struggling from halfway: see 906. 5 0a
867 **SPANISH STAR 12** [9]7-9-6 vis (49) K Darley 13/2: 461330W9: Withdrawn on vet's advice: see 552. 0a
9 Ran Time 2m 33.83 (12.53) Owned: Mrs Bernice Stronge Trained: Newbury

986 4.40 Press Interactive To Bet Direct Tri-Banded Stakes 3yo 0-45 (H)
£1425 £407 £204 1m aw rnd Going 93 -31 Slow Inside

901 **LADY PREDOMINANT 7** [2] Andrew Reid 3-9-0 (45) B Swarbrick(7) 11/4: 0-440601: Cl-up, rdn & led 49a
dist, styd on well ins last: first win: eff at 6f/1m on fm, gd & both AWs: see 25.
865 **SECRET BLOOM 13** [3] J R Norton 3-9-0 vis (45) Darren Williams 2/1 FAV: 0-440542: Trkd ldrs & eff 2 44a
wide from over 2f out, drvn & no impress in last: op 5/2: eff around 1m on fibresand: see 283.
4996} **ROMAN THE PARK 147** [5] T D Easterby 3-8-9 (40) D Allan(3) 7/2: 600-3: b f Titus Livius - 1½ 36a
Missfortuna (Priolo) Led, drvn & hdd dist, no extra: reapp, AW bow: lightly rcd & unplcd '03 (rtd 45): poss stay
longer 1m trip in banded company, handles fibresand.
779 **HEATHYARDS JOY 29** [4] R Hollinshead 3-8-4 (30) Dean McKeown 8/1: 0-0044: Held up, nvr factor. 6 21a
797 **DANDY JIM 27** [1]3-8-4 (30) J Quinn 9/2: 06-05005: Trkd ldrs, struggling from halfway: longer trip. 21 0a
5 Ran Time 1m 49.31(9.91) Owned: Mr A S Reid Trained: Mill Hill London

MAISONS LAFFITTE MONDAY 29.03.04 Left & Righthand, Sharpish Track

Official Going SOFT.

987 2.50 Listed Prix Right Royal 4yo+ ()
£15845 £6338 £4754 1m7.5f Soft

5002* **)LE CARRE 151** A de Royer Dupre 6-9-2 C Soumillon 6/5 FAV: 11: gr g Miswaki - Dibs (Spectacular 116
Bid) Narrow wnr. 1 Thu'30 Sain 15.5sft 100- :
4627} **RISK SEEKER 177** E Lellouche 4-9-2 D Boeuf : 3-13321122: b c Elmaamul - Robertet (Roberto) snk 115
Narrow 2nd. 2 Sat'04 Long 15sft 112- A: 1 Thu'11 Long 15sft 112- : 1 Sun'13 Deau 15g/s 109- A:
4279* **)FOREIGN AFFAIRS 4** Sir M Prescott 6-9-2 (102) S Sanders : 46-4042813: ch h Hernando - Entente 2½ 112
Cordiale (Affirmed) Led till dist, no extra: won a 12f List contest at Longchamp 4 days ago: French List wnr last
term: cond stks wnr & List rnr-up '02: eff btwn 10f/2m on firm, soft & f/sand, any trk: goes well fresh: versatile
& v useful 6yo, sure to be well placed by master trainer.
1 Sun'14 La T 12.5gd 108- : : 2 Sat'16 Newm 12g/f 102-102 B: 2 Jul'02 Newb 12fm 109- A: 1 Jun'02 Donc 10.2g/f 109- C:
2 Aug'01 York 13.8gd 113-105 B: 1 Jul'01 York 10.3g/f 107-97 B: 1 Jun'01 Good 9.8g/f 101-91 C:
1 Jun '01 Sali 9.9g/f 94-C: 2 Jun'01 Epso 10fm 94-85 C: 1 Nov'00 Wolv 7af 87- F:
7 Ran Time 3m 25.20() Owned: J R Aragao Bozano Trained: France

NAD AL SHEBA   Fibresand   SATURDAY 27.03.04   Lefthand, Flat, Fair Track

Official Going Fast

988
1.40 Gr 2 Godolphin Mile 3yo+ ()
£335195 £111731 £55865   **1m aw rnd**   **Fast**   Inside

3230} **FIREBREAK** 222 Saeed bin Suroor 5-9-0 t (115) L Dettori 3/1: 1005-1: b c Charnwood Forest -   **118a**
Breakaway (Song) Mid-div, hdwy to lead 2f out, pushed clr, v readily: 3 mth abs: won this race in '03, subs: Gr 3
wnr '02: stays 1m well on fm, soft, dirt & any trk, likes Goodwood & Nad Al Sheba: smart, prob career best here.
1 Sat'29 Nad 8dirt 115- A: 2 Oct'02 Newm 7g/f 113- A: 1 Sep'02 Good 7fm 113- A: 1 Sep'01 Newb 6fm 111- A:
1 Aug'01 Deau 6sft 111- : 2 Jun'01 Asco 6gd 111- A: 1 Jun'01 Beve 5gd 100- B: 1 May'01 Good 5fm 92- D:
         TROPICAL STAR 21 A Al Raihe 4-9-0 tv R Mullen 14/1: -12322: Mid-div, short of room 2f out, kept on.   4½   108a
         EXCESSIVEPLEASURE 63 D O'Neill 4-9-0 tbl J K Court 12/1: 12-003: Dwelt, trkd ldrs, late gains.   2¾   103a
9 Ran   Time 1m 35.82 ()   Owned: Godolphin   Trained: Uae

989
2.20 Gr 2 UAE Derby 3yo ()
£670391 £223463 £111731   **1m1f aw rnd**   **Fast**   Inside

     LUNDYS LIABILITY 21 M F de Kock 3-9-4   W C Marwing 9/2: 11-421: - () Trkd ldrs, drvn to lead ins last.   **120a**

         PETIT PARIS 21 J Barton 3-9-4 t J D Bailey 4/1: 21-512: - () Led till over 2f out, kept on.   ¾   118a
59 **LITTLE JIM** 21 S Seemar 3-9-4   T E Durcan 7/2 FAV: 31-133: Trkd ldr, led over 2f out till well ins last.   ¾   117a
598 **ACK SULLIVAN** 51 G A Butler 3-8-9 (90) M J Kinane 13/2: 532615-24: Mid-div wide, styd on for   3¾   101a
press, not able to chall: abs: stays 9f: gd run, wld apprec drop in grade: see 598.
756* **ASCERTAIN** 28 3-8-9 (98) E Ahern 12/1: 01-1215: Mid-div, styd on for press late: useful.   ¾   100a
599 **MENHOUBAH** 16 3-8-5 (100) A Solis 20/1: 4434-237: Mid-div, rdn & no impress fnl 2f: see 599.   3½   89a
9 Ran   Time 1m 50.83()   Owned: Stud TNT & Mrs M Slack   Trained: South Africa

NAD AL SHEBA   SATURDAY 27.03.04   Lefthand, Flat, Fair Track

Official Going Good/Firm

990
3.10 G r 1 Dubai Sheema Classic 4yo+ ()
£670391 £223463 £111731   **1m4f**   **Good/Firm**   Inside

833* **POLISH SUMMER** 21 [6] A Fabre 7-8-11   G Stevens 100/30 JT FA: 512-11: Mid-div, smooth hdwy over   **116**
1f out & rdn/qcknd to lead well ins last, drvn out: suited by 10/12f on fast & soft ground, stays 2m4f: high class
entire with a fine turn of foot: reportedly heads for the Coronation Cup at Epsom: see 833 (Gr 3).
         HARD BUCK 34 [10] K McPeek 4-8-11   J R Velazquez 9/1: 11-412: Trkd ldr, led dist, drvn & hdd ins last.   ½   119
5035* **SCOTTS VIEW** 16 [7] M Johnston 5-8-11 (112) S Chin 20/1: 21-41013: b g Selkirk - Milly of The   ¾   113+
Vally (Caerleon) Held up, hdwy/no room & swtchd over 1f out, styd on strongly, not btn far: thrived in Dubai this
year, landing 2 val h'caps over this C/D: Listed wnr '03: won class stks & 7 h'caps '02: suited by 12f, stays 2m on
fm, gd/sft & polytrk, any trk: tough, shade unlucky here, keep an eye on: see 5035.
1 Sat'08 Donc 12gd 117-112 A: 2 Wed'05 Muss 16g/f 102-112 A: 2 Sun'12 Curr 12g/s 113- :
2 Thu'04 Sali 14.1fm 104-108 A: 2 Sat'23 Good 14fm 105-114 A: 1 Sep'02 Asco 12g/f 114-105 B:
1 Sep'02 York 11.8g/f 107-100 B: 1 Aug'02 Good 14fm 107-91 C: 1 Jul'02 Good 14fm 97-88 B:
3810} **RAZKALLA** 21 [2] D R Loder 6-8-11 (112) T E Durcan 16/1: 1124-144: b g Caerleon - Larrocha   ¾   112
(Sadler's Wells) Trkd ldrs, styd on onepace for press: earlier landed a 10f h'cap here at Nad Al Sheba: dual stks &
Listed wnr '03: missed '02: suited by 10/14f on fm, gd & fibresand: tough & smart.
2 Fri'01 Good 12g/f 111-110 A: 1 Sat'28 Newm 12fm 112-107 A: 1 Sun'15 Leic 11.8g/f 110-107 A:
1 Sat '22 Donc 12gd 110-0 B: 1 Jan'03 Wolv 8.4af 95a- C: 1 Sep'01 Redc 9g/f 84- D:
4840} **WARRSAN** 104 [9]6-8-11 (119) M J Kinane 12/1: 126333-5: Led, drvn & hdd dist, no extra cl home: abs.   ½   111
4196* **RAWYAAN** 21 [1]5-8-11 bl (108) R Hills 20/1: 7201-168: Mid-div, btn 2f out.   3½   106
3722} **DELSARTE** 21 [3]4-8-11 (112) K McKvoy 16/1: 2034-9: Mid-div, lost place 4f out, btn fnl 2f,   1¼   106
reapp.
82* **COMPTON BOLTER** 16 [5]7-8-11 bl (103) E Ahern 28/1: 271-4050: 10th: Al rear, no prog: see 82.   nk   103
4455} **LUNAR SOVEREIGN** 21 [4]5-8-11 t L Dettori 8/1: 176-30: 11th: Chsd ldrs, wknd dist, wants 1m.   1   102
13 Ran   Time 2m 31.09 ()   Owned: K Abdulla   Trained: France

991
4.30 Gr 1 Dubai Duty Free Stakes 4yo+ ()
£446927 £446927 £111731   **1m1f rnd**   **Good/Firm**   Inside

3714} **PAOLINI** 224 [4] A Wohler 7-9-0   E Pedroza 10/1: 2382-1: ch c Lando - Prairie Darling (Stanford)   **118**
Held up, strong run for press to join ldr on line: reapp: dual Gr 1 rnr up last term, incl this sect: Gr 1 rnr up
'02: suited by 9f/12f on fast & gd grnd, eff with/without blnks: goes well fresh: tough & v smart.
2 Sat'16 Arli 10gd 118- A: 2 Sat'29 Nad 8.9gd 118- A: 2 May'02 Kran 10gd 120- : 2 Sep'01 Wood 12gd 118- :
1 Jun'01 San 12gd 118- : 1 May'01 Capa 10gd 118- :
4800} **RIGHT APPROACH** 35 [7] M F de Kock 5-9-0 t (116) W C Marwing 12/1: 358-11: Rear, rdn & strong run   dht   118
from over 1f out to dispute lead nr line, dhtd: earlier prev with Sir M Stoute: set too much to do.
4795} **NAYYIR** 161 [6] G A Butler 6-9-0 (117) M J Kinane 16/1: 1/6182-3: ch g Indian Ridge - Pearl Kite   nk   117
(Silver Hawk) Mid-div, rdn & hdwy to lead well ins last, just hdd close home: reapp: lightly rcd '03, Gr 2 wnr: won
5 times '02, incl 2 Gr 3's & a Gr 2: suited by 7f/8.5f on fm, gd/sft & polytrk, any trk: can go well fresh: v smart,
has a fine turn of foot & more Group race success awaits.
2 Sat'18 Newm 7g/f 118-117 A: 1 Tue'29 Good 7gd 118-0 A: 1 Oct'02 Newm 7g/f 120- A: 1 Aug'02 Good 7fm 120- A:
1 Jun'02 Epso 8.5gd 116- A: 1 May'02 Beve 8.4gd 101-83 C: 1 Mar'02 Ling 7ap 83- D:
         CRIMSON PALACE 58 [2] Saeed bin Suroor 5-8-9   L Dettori 100/30: 014-14: Trkd ldrs, kept on.   ½   111
3712} **MARTILLO** 223 [9]4-9-0   W Mongil 20/1: 1317-5: Trkd ldr, led dist, hdd well ins last & no extra.   shd   116

NAD AL SHEBA   SATURDAY 27.03.04   Lefthand, Flat, Fair Track

3712} **MARTILLO** 223 [9]4-9-0 W Mongil 20/1: 1317-5: Trkd ldr, led dist, hdd well ins last & no extra. *shd* 116
4976} **CHECKIT** 16 [10]4-9-0 (113) T E Durcan 14/1: 329-4336: Held up, staying on when no run over 1f *nk* 115+
out till cl home, not recover: wld have gone close & fine run.
833 **BRIGHT SKY** 21 [11]5-8-9 D Beouf 11/4 FAV: 364-27: Held up wide, not pace to chall ldrs: see 833. *1¼* 107
4914} **REFUSE TO BEND** 154 [3]4-9-0 K McKvoy 11/1: 0100-8: Led till dist, wknd: reapp, prev with D Weld. *2¼* 107
3715} **EVOLVING TACTICS** 28 [1]4-9-0 P J Smullen 10/1: 19316-19: Mid-div, btn over 1f out. *2¼* 102
11 Ran Time 1m 49.36 () Owned: Frau C Ostermann Richter Trained: Germany

NAD AL SHEBA   Fibresand   SATURDAY 27.03.04   Lefthand, Flat, Fair Track

Official Going Fast

992
5.20 Gr 1 Dubai World Cup 4yo+ ()
£2011173 £670391 £335195   1m2f aw   **Fast**   Inside

PLEASANTLY PERFECT 56 [7] Richard E Mandella 6-9-0 t bl A Solis 5/2: 411-11: Trkd ldrs, hdwy to 126a
lead over 1f out, styd on strongly for press: top-class US dirt performer.
4752} **MEDAGLIA DORO** 49 [11] R J Frankel 5-9-0 t J D Bailey 2/1 FAV: 122-12: Trkd ldr, led over 2f out, *¾* 124a
rdn & hdd over 1f out, not pace of wnr: clr rem: top-class US dirt performer.
3187} **VICTORY MOON** 21 [9] M F de Kock 5-9-0 W C Marwing 4/1: 0-3113: Mid-div, styd on for press, not 5 117a
pace of front pair: well clr rem.
GRAND HOMBRE 175 [8] Saeed bin Suroor 4-9-0 t vis L Dettori 12/1: 1112-4: Trkd ldrs, no impress. *7¾* 106a
12 Ran Time 2m 0.24 () Owned: Diamond A Racing Corporation Trained: Usa

SAINT CLOUD   SUNDAY 28.03.04   Lefthand, Galloping Track

Official Going Soft

993
2.50 Gr 3 Prix Edmond Blanc 4yo+ ()
£25704 £10282 £7711   1m rnd   **Soft**

4626} **MY RISK** 176 J M Beguigne 5-9-0 C Soumillon 3/1: 161121-1: Twds rear, hdwy over 2f out, drvn to 116
lead ins last, all out:
1914} **ART MODERNE** 301 E Lellouche 4-8-12 BL D Boeuf 83/10: 21345-52: Held up, hdwy & led 2f out, rdn *hd* 113
& hdd ins last, rallied gamely, just held.
SARRE P Costes 4-8-8 C P Lemaire 125/10: 21437-23: Held up, styd on wide for press fnl 2f. *snk* 109
12 Ran Time 1m 43.00() Owned: R Monnier Trained: France

LEOPARDSTOWN   SUNDAY 28.03.04   Lefthand, Galloping Track

Official Going Yielding

994
5.00 Listed Alleged Stakes 4yo+ ()
£21808 £6399 £3049   1m2f   **Good/Soft**   Inside

4843} **BRIAN BORU** 161 A P O'Brien 4-9-7 t J P Spencer 1/2 FAV: 304213-1: b c Sadler's Wells - Eva Luna 118
(Alleged) Chsd ldrs, led 2f out, veered left dist, held on well for press: rider give 2-day whip ban: Gr 1 St Leger
wnr in '03: also Irish Derby 4th: '02 Gr 1 wnr: eff at 10f, suited by 12/14.6f: acts on firm & soft, loves a
stiff/gall trk: high-class, will apprec a return to 12f+ & a major force in top mid-dist/staying events.
1 Sat'13 Donc 14.6g/f 121-0 A: 2 Tue'19 York 11.9fm 119-0 A: 1 Oct'02 Donc 8sft 116- A: 2 Oct'02 Curr 8g/s 116- :
4406*}**NAPPER TANDY** 153 J S Bolger 4-9-3 bl K J Manning 7/1: 255414-2: ch c Spectrum - La Meillure *¾* 112
(Lord Gayle) Trkd ldrs, chall 2f out, hmpd & switched dist, kept on well nr fin: op 6/1: reapp: List wnr in '03,
prev term won a mdn: suited by 1m/10f on fast & soft, likes a stiff/gall trk: wears blnks: fine reapp against a
high-class rival: spot on next time & deserves Group success.
1 Sun'21 Curr 10g/f 112- A: 2 Oct'02 Leop 7g/s 101- :
4759*}**DAWN INVASION** 164 A Mullins 5-9-0 (100) D P McDonough 9/1: 14/041-3: Mid-div, styd on for 3 105
press, not pace of front pair: op 7/1: recent wng hdler (mdn hdle).
8 Ran Time 2m 10.80() Owned: Mrs John Magnier Trained: Ballydoyle

CATTERICK   WEDNESDAY 31.03.04   Lefthand, Undulating, Very Tight Track

Official Going Good

995
2.20 Tote Big Screen Is Here Classified Stakes 3yo 0-60 (F)
£2943 £841 £420   5f rnd   **Good 52**   -35 Slow   Inside

4454} **LINDA GREEN** 187 [8] P A Blockley 3-8-8 (58) Dean McKeown 10/1: 442030-1: b f Victory Note - Edge 63
of Darkness (Vaigly Great) Chsd ldrs, swtchd & qcknd to lead well ins last, hands & heels nr line: first win, small:
fills auct mdn rnr-up '03 (R Bastiman, AW h'cap plcd, rtd 58a): eff at 5f, acts on fast, gd & fibresand, sharp or
stiff trk: goes well fresh. 2 Jul'03 Beve 5g/f 64- F:
4709} **MR WOLF** 170 [9] D W Barker 3-8-13 (62) L Enstone(3) 16/1: 04500-2: b c Wolfhound - Madam Millie *¾* 65

(Milford) Chsd ldrs, rdn to chall & edged left dist, led well ins last, hdd cl-home: ndd reapp: unplcd '03 (rtd 71, mdn): half brother to 7f/1m wnr Celtic Mill: eff at 5f on fm & gd.
4695} **WILLJOJO 171** [5] R A Fahey 3-8-8 (54) T Hamilton(3) 15/2: 323503-3: b f Mind Games - Millie's Lady (Common Grounds) Handy & led ins last till well ins last cl-home: reapp: sell rnr-up for K Ryan '03, subs sell h'cap plcd for current yard (1st time visor, also rtd 60a, debut, mdn): eff at 5/6f on fm, gd/soft & fibresand, any trk. 2 Jun'03 Thir 6g/f 58- E: *hd* **59**
933 **BLACK OVAL 5** [11] M R Channon 3-8-10 (62) S Hitchcott(3) 7/2 FAV: 00606-44: Mid-div, keeping on for press when short of room ins last & cl-home: bckd: not btn far, shade closer with clr run: qk reapp. *1* **58**
802 **LACONIA 27** [7]3-8-13 (65) J D Smith 8/1: 00350-45: Chsd ldrs, keeping on when hmpd well ins last: op 10/1: wld have gone close with a clr run: see 802. *nk* **60+**
495 **LORD BASKERVILLE 63** [6]3-8-11 (60) D R McCabe 33/1: 4030-006: Pushed along rear, late gains. *shd* **58**
795 **KILLERBY NICKO 28** [3]3-8-11 (59) D Allan(3) 11/1: 00-67: Prom dsptd lead till ins last, fdd under press. *¾* **56**
2013} **REVERSIONARY 298** [10]3-8-11 (56) Dale Gibson 33/1: 0560-8: Dwelt, bhd, only mod prog: reapp. *¾* **54**
953 **BLADES EDGE 4** [1]3-8-11 (59) G Duffield 11/2: 304-0539: Prom & dsptd lead 3f, fdd, quick reapp. *2* **48**
3034} **LADY SUNSET 256** [4]3-8-13 BL (65) N Callan 6/1: 05200-0: 10th: Trkd ldrs, btn dist: op 7/2, blnks. *½* **48**
703 **LAVISH TIMES 37** [2]3-8-11 bl (51) R Winston 12/1: 030-0530: 11th: Led till 2f out, btn/eased ins last: reportedly hung left handed from halfway: btr 703 (AW). *½* **44**
591 **KATIES BATH TIME 50** [13]3-8-8 (40) J Bramhill 100/1: 000-00: 12th: Slow away & sn bhd, abs. *18* **0**
12 Ran Time 1m 01.64 (4.34) Owned: Mr Stephen Roots Trained: Southwell

996

2.50 Forcett Selling Stakes 3yo+ (G)
£2646 £756 £378 **7f rnd** **Good 52** **-19 Slow** Inside

145 **ZHITOMIR 116** [14] M Dods 6-9-6 (49) S W Kelly 10/1: 000000-1: ch g Lion Cavern - Treasure Trove (The Minstrel) Mid-div, led ins last, rdn out: no bid: 4 month abs: unplcd '03 (rtd 62, h'cap, mod sand form): '02 h'cap wnr (S Dow, AW unplcd, rtd 65a, h'cap): eff at 6/7f on any trk, likes a sharp one: acts on firm & soft grnd: goes well fresh: apprec drop to sell grade. **56**
1 Sep'02 Epso 7g/f 67-64 E: 1 Oct'01 Ling 7sft 74-68 E: 1 Sep'01 Epso 7gd 70-66 D: 2 Aug'01 Epso 7sft 67-66 E:
577 **LUKE AFTER ME 52** [2] G A Swinbank 4-9-6 (53) R Winston 20/1: 64000-02: Held up, styd on for press to chall ins last, just held: 8 wk abs: better run: see 577. *nk* **56**
164 **CITY GENERAL 114** [10] J S Moore 3-8-5 p (57) Dean McKeown 16/1: 062550-3: ch g General Monash - Astra (Glenstal) Mid-div, styd on for press, not pace to chall: 4 month abs: sell wnr '03, AW sell rnr-up: suited by 7f, tried 1m: acts on firm, gd/soft & fibresand, prob any trk: eff with/without cheek pieces & enjoys sell grade. 2 Oct'03 Wolv 7af 58a-(58) G: 1 Jun'03 Yarm 7.0fm 63- G: 2 Jun'03 Redc 7fm 64- G: *1* **54**
776 **TINIAN 31** [5] K R Burke 6-9-12 (56) G Faulkner 14/1: 0-530304: Dwelt, mid-div, onepace. *1¼* **57**
907 **DUSTY WUGG 8** [8]5-9-1 p (45) A Beech(3) 20/1: 040-5305: Mid-div, eff to chall dist, no extra: see 533. *hd* **45**
704 **MISTER MAL 37** [9]8-9-6 bl e (55) T Hamilton(3) 9/1: 40053-06: b g Scenic - Fashion Parade (Mount Hagen) Led after 2f till ins last, wknd: dual AW h'cap rnr-up '03, turf unplcd (rtd 61, class stks): h'cap plcd '02 (rtd 69): suited by 6/7f on firm & fibresand, likes gd & hvy: eff with/without cheekpieces/blnks & eye-shield. *½* **49**
2 Jul'03 Wolv 7af 61a-58 E: 2 Jun'03 Sout 7af 60a-55 F: 2 Jun'01 York 6gd 89-85 B: 2 May'01 Donc 6fm 86-80 D: 1 May'01 Brig 6g/s 83-73 D:
858 **XALOC BAY 15** [4]6-9-6 (56) Darren Williams 7/1 FAV: 0112367: Chsd ldrs, no extra: best dominating. *hd* **48**
4321} **ROYAL WINDMILL 195** [18]5-9-6 p (50) L Enstone(3) 14/1: 123206-8: Chsd ldrs, not able to chall. *1¼* **45**
963 **SPEEDFIT FREE 2** [13]7-9-12 bl (58) G Duffield 8/1: 4-256249: Mid-div, rdn & not pace to chall: op 13/2. *¾* **50**
851+***KING NICHOLAS 17** [6]5-9-12 t p (50) M Lawson(7) 15/2: 0000-010: 10th: Rear, eff wide, little prog. *1¼* **47**
699 **OPEN HANDED 37** [1]4-9-12 t (35) T Eaves(5) 33/1: 0000-600: 11th: Mid-div, at best. *shd* **47**
904 **MAGIC EAGLE 8** [17]7-9-6 (35) R Fitzpatrick 66/1: 00/-50000: 12th: Mid-div, no impress. *2½* **36**
3263} **TANCRED ARMS 245** [16]8-9-7 (45) T Williams 14/1: 501060-0: 13th: Al towards rear, reapp. *2* **33**
487 **BLUNHAM 64** [7]4-9-12 (53) L Vickers 14/1: 000-4500: 14th: Led 2f, prom till over 1f out, abs: see 374. *shd* **38**
985 **Travel Tardia 1** [11]6-9-12 t(30) D Nolan(5) 12/1:0
969 **Brooklands Time 2** [3]3-8-0 (45) Natalia Gemelova(7) 33/1:0
1419} **Miss Lyvennet 327** [15]3-8-0 (60) R Ffrench 50/1:0 825 **Lions Domane 23** [12]7-9-12 (57) N Callan 14/1:P
18 Ran Time 1m 27.95 (4.95) Owned: Mr M J K Dods Trained: Darlington

997

3.20 Catterickbridge Co Uk Handicap Stakes 4yo+ 0-80 (D) **[76]**
£5509 £1695 £848 **1m5f175y** **Good 52** **+04 Fast** Inside

257 **COURT OF APPEAL 95** [1] B Ellison 7-9-8 t (70) T Eaves(5) 13/2: 402434-1: Chsd ldrs, hdwy to lead over 1f out, shade readily: gd time, abs: eff at 10/14f on fast, soft & fibresand: goes well fresh. **84+**
4498} **TIYOUN 185** [4] Jedd O'Keeffe 6-9-11 (73) G Duffield 20/1: 342025-2: b g Kahyasi - Taysala (Akarad) Mid-div, drvn & kept on for clr 2nd: dual h'cap rnr-up '03, earlier with D W Barker, sand unplcd (rtd 18a): won 3 h'caps in '03: eff btwn 11f/2m on firm, soft & any trk: tried blnks: gd weight carrier: h'capped to win. *2½* **82**
2 Sep'03 Redc 14.1fm 75-74 C: 2 Aug'03 Thir 16g/f 75-71 D: 1 Sep'01 Thir 12g/f 88-85 C: 2 Sep'01 Ripo 12.2g/f 87-84 D: 2 Aug'01 Ripo 12.2g/f 89-84 C: 1 Jun'01 Ripo 12.2g/f 85-83 D: 1 May'01 Redc 11g/f 84-79 D:
4812] **CALATAGAN 511** [11] J M Jefferson 5-8-10 (58) R Winston 7/1: 032230/-3: ch g Danzig Connection - Calachuchi (Martinmas) Led till over 1f out, no extra: jumps fit, dual h'cap hdle wnr this term (rtd 126h, 2m, fast & soft): last rcd on the level '02, dual h'cap rnr-up: eff at 10/14f on fast & gd/soft grnd, stiff or easy trk: consistent. *2* **64**
2 Aug'02 Carl 11.9g/f 60-60 D: 2 Jul'02 Thir 12g/f 62-60 D:
679 **THEATRE TINKA 41** [13] R Hollinshead 5-8-12 p (60) Dale Gibson 12/1: 01-55524: Chsd ldr 4f out. *2½* **62**
918* **MIDDLETHORPE 6** [8]7-9-0 bl (62) P Mulrennan(5) 5/1: 30055-15: Slow away & held up, late gains, not able to chall: hmpd by slow start today, poss btr judged 918 (reapp). *1¼* **62**
918 **RAJAM 6** [14]6-9-12 (74) Alex Greaves 25/1: 02000-06: b g Sadler's Wells - Rafif (Riverman) Trkd ldrs, btn 2f out: quick reapp: dual nov hdle plcd for R Guest 03/04 (rtd 109h, 2m, soft & gd/soft): dual h'cap rnr-up '03 for current yard: unplcd '02 (A Stewart, rtd 71, h'cap, tried blnks & t-strap): suited by 12f/14f, tried 2m+: acts on firm, hvy & prob any trk: can go well fresh & likes to force the pace. *nk* **73**
2 Aug'03 Newc 14.4g/f 78-75 D: 2 Jul'03 Hayd 11.9gd 78-75 E: 2 Sep'01 Kemp 12g/f 97-93 C: 1 Aug'01 Newb 12fm 97- C: 1 Jun'01 Kemp 12g/f 85- D: 2 May'01 Ling 10gd 89- D:
816 **DUCS DREAM 23** [5]6-8-8 (56) D McGaffin 20/1: 63000-07: Bhd, mod gains for press, nvr threat. *2½* **51**
7 **SPITTING IMAGE 142** [9]4-8-10 (62) A Culhane 16/1: 420240-8: Held up, eff/stumbled 2f out & sn hmpd, sn btn, eased: jockey reported filly had not settled thro' the race, shld improve. *¾* **56**
534 **BANNINGHAM BLAZE 57** [6]4-8-2 BL (54) J Bramhill 25/1: 10000-09: Rear, eff 5f out, sn no impress. *3* **44**
4790} **BEST PORT 166** [7]8-8-6 (54) M Lawson(5) 20/1: 433054-0: 10th: Held up wide, btn 3f out, reapp. *2½* **40**

4819} **BOLSHOI BALLET 163** [10]6-8-8 BL (56) N Callan 8/1: 314/040-0: 11th: Prom 10f: 3 mth jmps abs, blnks. ½ 41
4992} **EDMO YEWKAY 149** [12]4-9-0 (66) D Allan(3) 11/1: 540060-0: 12th: Al rear, jumps fit. 2 48
4738} **THE PERSUADER 169** [3]4-10-0 (80) R Ffrench 100/30 FAV: 111210-0: 13th: Prom till halfway, sn 13 44
bhd: reapp: has been gldd, connections unable to offer explanation for poor run.
13 Ran Time 3m 02.03 (6.63) Owned: Spring Cottage Syndicate No 2 Trained: Malton

---

998	3.50 Gods Solution Handicap Stakes 3yo+ 0-85 (D)					[84]
	£5688 £1750 £875	**7f rnd**	**Good 52**	**-02 Slow**	Inside	

4541} **NATHAN BRITTLES 182** [16] T D Barron 4-9-2 (72) P Makin(7) 50/1: 121000-1: ch g Cat's Career - 80
Doc's Answer (Dr Schwartzman) Chsd ldrs, hdwy to lead ins last, rdn out: reapp: mdn & h'cap scorer '03: unplcd '02
(rtd 60, mdn): prev wins at 5f, apprec this first start at 7f: acts on fm & gd grnd, likes Catterick: goes v well fresh.
1 May'03 Catt 5fm 74-72 D: 2 Apr'03 Hami 5.0g/s 65-(72) C: 1 Apr'03 Thir 5fm 73- D:
840 **SARRAAF 18** [10] I Semple 8-8-12 (68) R Winston 6/1 FAV: 31042-42: Mid-div, styd on for press, ½ 74
not reach wnr: bckd: tricky ride but plenty of ability, can win similar: see 840.
5030} **WATCHING 144** [5] D Nicholls 7-9-13 (83) L Treadwell(7) 16/1: 400040-3: ch g Indian Ridge - 1½ 86
Sweeping (Indian King) Chsd ldrs, styd on for press fnl : reapp: twice h'cap plcd '03 (rtd 97, also rtd 83a, cond
stks): Listed rtd h'cap rnr-up '02: stays sharp 7f, suited by 5/6f on fast, likes soft & hvy, any trk: eff
with/without cheek pieces, tried visor: former v useful sprinter, well h'capped & this was encouraging.
2 Jun'02 Epso 5gd 91-96 A: 2 Oct'01 Donc 7hvy 100- B:
611 **LINCOLN DANCER 48** [1] D Nicholls 7-9-7 (77) Alex Greaves 12/1: 0000-004: Chsd ldrs, rdn & led ¾ 79
over 1f out, hdd ins last & no extra: stable-mate of 3rd: abs: likes soft: see 611.
967 **RONNIE FROM DONNY 2** [12]4-9-0 (70) T Eaves(5) 12/1: 01-400U5: Held up, styd on for press fnl 2f. nk 71
4919} **DISTANT COUNTRY 155** [9]5-9-5 (75) P Fitzsimons 14/1: 341014-6: b g Distant View - Memsahb hd 75+
(Restless Native) Held up, short of room dist, styd on in eyecatching style under hands & heels, nrst fin: lightly
rcd '03, mdn & clmr scorer: subs h'cap plcd: ex-French mdn: best at 7f, tried 1m: acts on firm & gd grnd, likes a
gall trk: both wins in chkpcs, not won today: one to note on a more gall trk, poss with headgear reapplied.
1 Oct'03 Donc 7g/f 81-(69) E: 1 Sep'03 Redc 7fm 68-(69) D:
840 **NO GROUSE 18** [18]4-9-5 (75) T Hamilton(3) 8/1: 000-0507: Held up, eff 2f out, onepace: see 632. 1 73
642 **FLYING TREATY 44** [2]7-8-10 (66) Ann Stokell 33/1: 40-00068: Chsd ldrs 5f, abs. ¾ 63
3610} **SIR DON 230** [6]5-8-11 vis (67) A Nicholls 16/1: 021530-9: Led till over 1f out, wknd qckly: reapp. 1¾ 61
4500} **BAILIEBOROUGH 185** [15]5-9-0 (70) P M Quinn 33/1: 010000-0: 10th: Slow away & bhd, only mod prog. 1¾ 61
4999} **RAPHAEL 148** [11]5-9-6 (76) D Allan(3) 13/2: 665223-0: 11th: Mid-div, no prog fnl 2f: ndd first reapp. nk 66
4792} **ACOMB 166** [13]4-8-9 (65) Dale Gibson 16/1: 314150-0: 12th: Prom, 5f, sharper for reapp. hd 54
744 **ROYAL GRAND 34** [3]4-8-10 (66) D Mernagh 10/1: 312-3000: 13th: Mid-div, btn 2f out: btr 390. 1½ 52
4890} **ATLANTIC QUEST 158** [14]5-9-13 (83) P Mulrennan(5) 14/1: 600410-0: 14th: Al towards rear, reapp. hd 68
4486} **Rifleman 186** [7]4-9-10 (80) G Duffield 14/1:0 4539} **Sea Storm 182** [8]6-10-0 (84) A Culhane 16/1:0
657 **Grandma Lily 43** [17]6-8-11 (67) D Fox(5) 25/1:0
4888} **H Harrison 158** [4]4-9-12 (82) Natalia Gemelova(7) 10/1:0
18 Ran Time 1m 26.75 (3.75) Owned: Mr Steve Vickers Trained: Thirsk

---

999	4.20 Toytop Maiden Stakes 3yo+ (D)				
	£3377 £1039 £520	**6f rnd**	**Good 52**	**-22 Slow**	Inside

2389} **PLACE COWBOY 280** [1] J A Osborne 3-8-11 S W Kelly 5/2 JT FAV: 2-1: b c Compton Place - Paris 75
Joelle (Fairy King) Dwelt, chsd ldrs trav well & led over 1f out rdn out: bckd, op 11/4, reapp: AW mdn rnr-up sole
'03 start: eff at 6f, 7f shld suit: acts on fibresand & gd, sharp trk: goes well fresh. 2 Jun'03 Sout 6af 68a- F:
EXTREMELY RARE 0 [10] T D Easterby 3-8-6 A Mullen(7) 20/1: 2: b f Mark of Esteem - Colourflash ¾ 67+
(College Chapel) Dwelt, mid-div, styd on well under hands & heels ins last, not reach wnr: debut: eff at 6f, 7f
shld suit: acts on gd grnd/sharp trk: likely improver with stronger handling.
851 **AMANDAS LAD 17** [11] M C Chapman 4-9-10 (45) L Vickers 50/1: 4064663: Trkd ldrs, onepace over 1f 1½ 67
out: acts on fast, gd & fibresand: much improved, fraced rating with caution: see 487.
3795} **TOP LINE DANCER 222** [5] M Johnston 3-8-11 R Ffrench 5/2 JT FAV: 54-4: b c Fasliyev - Twafeaj shd 67
(Topsider) Mid-div, styd on for press, not pace to chall: nicely bckd on reapp: lightly rcd '03 (unplcd, rtd 74,
mdn): half brother to wnrs at 7f/12f: eff at 6/7f, likely improver for 87+: acts on fast & gd grnd.
869 **UHURU PEAK 51** [7]3-8-11 P Mulrennan(5) 25/1: 305: Mid-div, styd on onepace. 1½ 62$
2968} **ORION EXPRESS 257** [6]3-8-11 Dale Gibson 33/1: 000-6: Bhd, mod late prog, nvr danger, reapp. hd 61
4709} **FOX COVERT 170** [8]3-8-11 (71) L Enstone(3) 4/1: 323230-7: Led 4f, wkng/stumbled ins last. 2 55
686 **STRANGELY BROWN 40** [9]3-8-11 J Bramhill 20/1: 00-08: Dwelt & sn outpcd, rear, abs. 3 46
4917} **LEOPARD CREEK 155** [3]3-8-6 A Culhane 10/1: 400-9: Dwelt, pulled hard early, nvr factor: jockey nk 40
reported fly hung badly RH'd thr'out, reapp.
1318} **SONG KOI 333** [2]3-8-6 G Duffield 10/1: 44-0: 10th: Led/dsptd lead, jinked over 2f out & sn hdd, fdd. 1¾ 35
STONEACRE 0 [4]4-9-5 A Nicholls 14/1: 0: 11th: Dwelt & sn bhd on debut: op 20/1. 29 0
11 Ran Time 1m 14.72 (4.42) Owned: Mountgrange Stud Trained: Upper Lambourn

---

1000	4.50 Yarm Handicap Stakes 3yo 0-75 (E)					[82]
	£3445 £1060 £530	**1m3f214y**	**Good 52**	**-03 Slow**	Inside	

4665} **LIQUIDATE 173** [10] H Morrison 3-8-8 (62) L Fletcher(3) 13/2: 006-1: b g Hector Protector - Cut 70
And Run (Slip Anchor) Trkd ldrs, rdn over 2f out & styd on for press to lead well ins last, all out: reapp/h'cap
bow: unplcd at up to 1m for J Hills '03 (mdns, rtd 65): half brother to a useful stayer, dam unplcd: has tried a
t-strap prev & been gldd: acts on gd grnd: ndd all of this 12f to prevail, improve again at 14f+.
796* **YANKEEDOODLEDANDY 28** [7] P C Haslam 3-9-4 (72) G Faulkner 4/1 FAV: 4-121212: Trkd ldrs, drvn to ½ 78
chall dist, narrow lead ins last, just hdd cl-home: nicely bckd: acts on fibresand & gd grnd: gd run.
923 **SIEGFRIEDS NIGHT 6** [2] M C Chapman 3-8-1 (55) D Fox(5) 6/1: 1432333: Led/dsptd lead & drvn/chall 1 60
fnl 2f, just held whn short of room nr line: quick reapp: stays a sharp 12f: see 923, 658 & 316.
4875} **WOODY VALENTINE 159** [6] M Johnston 3-9-7 (75) R Ffrench 5/1: 321400-4: ch g Woodman - 2 77
Mudslinger (El Gran Senor) Led after 1f till ins last, no extra: op 7/2, rest well covered: reapp, has been gldd:
mdn scorer '03, subs h'cap 4th (rtd 81): eff at 1m, stays sharp 12f today: acts on firm & gd grnd, stiff/undul
or sharp trk: likes to race with/force the pace. 1 Sep'03 Hami 8.3g/f 78- D: 2 Aug'03 Sand 8.1g/f 76- D:

258

CATTERICK WEDNESDAY 31.03.04 Lefthand, Undulating, Very Tight Track

683	**BILL BENNETT 41** [1]3-9-0 (68) N Callan 12/1: 201-6065: Held up, eff 3f out, no impress fnl 2f: 6 wk abs: yet to convince at 12f: see 240 (AW, 9f, mdn).	4	64
817	**COME WHAT JULY 23** [3]3-9-5 bl (73) R Winston 8/1: 023-1256: Mid-div inner, btn 2f out: btr 817 & 601.	2½	65
4988}	**CLASSIC EVENT 149** [4]3-8-11 (65) D Allan(3) 12/1: 0350-7: ch c Croco Rouge - Delta Town (Sanglamore) Rear, late gains, no danger: reapp: op 16/1: auct mdn plcd '03 (rtd 65): half brother to a 7f/10f wnr.	7	48
959	**ARGENT 2** [11]3-8-8 (62) R Fitzpatrick 33/1: 3550-P8: Chsd ldrs, btn 4f out, quick reapp.	11	30
	FRIENDS HOPE 187 [12]3-8-2 (56) G Duffield 25/1: 0501-9: Mid-div, no ch fnl 3f, abs, Brit bow.	1¼	22
901	**THE STICK 8** [5]3-8-9 (63) S Hitchcott(3) 5/1: 656-00: 10th: Held up, btn 3f out: up in trip.	1¼	27
584	Vesta Flame 51 [8]3-7-12 (17oh)(35) S Yourston(4) 40/1:0		
4693}	Northern Summit 171 [9]3-7-13 (1ow)(12oh)(40) J Bramhill 66/1:0		

12 Ran Time 2m 37.77(6.57) Owned: The Phantom Partnership Trained: East Ilsley

NOTTINGHAM WEDNESDAY 31.03.04 Lefthand, Galloping Track

Official Going Good (Good/Firm Places In Back Straight)

1001 2.10 E B F Maiden Stakes 2yo (D)
£4176 £1285 £643 5f13y str **Firm 14** -35 Slow Stands side

	ALVARINHO LADY [3] D Haydn Jones 2-8-9 Paul Eddery 11/2: 1: b f Royal Applause - Jugendliebe (Persian Bold) Cl-up, led dist, rdn out: tchd 7/1 on debut: Mar foal, cost E21,000: sister to a 6f juv wnr & half sister to a wnr at 2m: dam 10f wnr abroad, sire high-class at sprint dists: eff at 5f, shld apprec 6f: acts on firm grnd & a gall trk: goes well fresh: can improve with experience & rate higher.		76
	DANTES DIAMOND [4] F Jordan 2-9-0 J Murtagh 10/1: 2: b c Orpen - Flower From Heaven (Baptism) Slow away, sn outpcd, rallied well ins fnl 1f, nrst fin: debut: Mar foal, cost E20,000: half brother to a couple of wnrs at 6f: dam won numerous times at sprint dists: sire 6f Gr1 wnr as a juv: eff at 5f, 6f shld suit: acts on firm grnd: gd eff despite running green, can improve with experience.	1½	75
	EDGE FUND [2] B R Millman 2-9-0 S Drowne 4/5 FAV: 3: b c Bold Edge - Truly Madly Deeply (Most Welcome) Handy, hung left under press 2f out, ev ch dist, no extra ins fnl 1f: well bckd on debut: Apr foal, cost 32,000 gns: half brother to Forever Loved who won at 12/15f: dam unplcd, sire high-class sprinter: eff at 5f, further will suit: acts on firm grnd: just sharper for today.	shd	74
	WEET YER TERN [5] P A Blockley 2-9-0 K Darley 7/2: 4: Led, sn hung left, hdd dist, no extra: tchd 9/2 on debut: eff at 5f on firm grnd.	¾	72
	TOWN HOUSE [1]2-8-9 J Fanning 40/1: 5: In tch, wknd fnl 1f: debut.	3½	57

5 Ran Time 1m 0.99 (2.49) Owned: Mr Mick White Trained: Pontypridd

1002 2.40 Bottesford Handicap Stakes 3yo 0-75 (E) [82]
£3520 £1083 £542 5f13y str **Firm 14** -06 Slow Stands side

4558}	**JOHNNY PARKES 181** [2] Mrs J R Ramsden 3-9-7 (75) J Murtagh 6/4 FAV: 222215-1: b g Wolfhound - Lucky Parkes (Full Extent) Dwelt, prog 3f out, styd on to lead ins fnl 1f, pushed out, val 5L+: well bckd under top weight on reapp: consistent in '03, won a med auct mdn, also rnr-up on 4 of other 5 starts: eff at 5f on firm & gd grnd: poss acts on any trk & goes well fresh: won in style & more prizes await. 1 Aug'03 Carl 5fm 77-(76) F: 2 Aug'03 Hayd 5g/f 77-73 E: 2 Jul'03 Redc 5g/f 77- E: 2 Jul'03 Muss 5gd 77- E: 2 Jun'03 Redc 5g/f 72- D:		89+
712	**DEMOLITION MOLLY 36** [7] R F Marvin 3-9-2 t p (70) T P Queally(3) 17/2: 054-0602: Slow away, sn outpcd, rallied 2f out, kept on fnl 1f, no ch with wnr: back to form on return to turf, acts on firm & fast grnd.	3	72
673	**KURINGAI 42** [9] B W Duke 3-9-4 (72) T Quinn 7/1: 3020-043: Led, hdd 3f out, styd cl-up, kept on fnl 1f, just held for 2nd: 6 wk abs: see 268.	shd	73
485	**SCOTTISH EXILE 64** [4] K R Burke 3-9-0 vis (68) K Dalgleish 12/1: 0231-644: Led 3f out till ins fnl 1f, wknd: 9 wk abs: 1st try on firm grnd: btr 197 (fibresand, 1st time visor).	1¼	65
795	**SMART DANNY 28** [1]3-7-12 (52) P Hanagan 7/1: 40-05: gr g Danzero - She's Smart (Absalom) Trkd ldrs, hmpd 4f out & lost pl, rallied late: unplcd in both '03 starts (rtd 55, med auct mdn): half brother to useful sprint h'cappers Smart Predator & Rum Lad: did not get the run of today's race: with J J Quinn.	1	46
1567}	**FLASH RAM 319** [6]3-9-3 (71) K Darley 8/1: 333-6: b c Mind Games - Just A Gem (Superlative) Unruly stalls, in tch, wknd 3f out: reapp & h'cap bow: 3rd on all 3 '03 starts (mdns, rtd 75): eff at 5f, 6f shld suit: handles firm & gd/soft grnd: eff with/without blnks.	½	64
872	**DESERT LIGHT 13** [8]3-7-13 vis (53) J F McDonald(5) 8/1: 060-1307: In tch, fdd 2f out: btr 327 (AW).	hd	45
4450}	**SHORT CHORUS 187** [3]3-7-13 (53) C Catlin 14/1: 51000-8: Short of room start, al in rear: reapp.	5	31

8 Ran Time 59.53 (1.03) Owned: Mr Joseph Heler Trained: Thirsk

1003 3.10 Colston Bassett Stakes Handicap 3yo+ 0-80 (D) [80]
£5606 £1725 £863 2m9y **Firm 14** -26 Slow Inside

916	**MALARKEY 7** [9] Mrs Stef Liddiard 7-8-13 (65) S Drowne 16/1: 01306/-51: Held up, prog 3f out, led dist, rdn out: qck reapp: eff at 14f/2m1f on firm, gd grnd & fibresand: eff with/without cheek pieces: apprec today's switch to new stable: see 916 (A Crook).		69
813	**KING FLYER 23** [8] Miss J Feilden 8-9-12 (78) N Mackay(5) 13/2: 46036-02: Cl-up, ev ch dist, kept on, just denied: op 5/1: rnr-up in this race 12 months ago off a 3lb lower mark: fine run & can find similar.	nk	81
404	**NAWOW 77** [2] P D Cundell 4-9-5 (76) K Dalgleish 13/2: 50326-03: b g Blushing Flame - Fair Test (Fair Season) Held up, prog 2f out, kept on fnl 1f, not btn far: tchd 9/1: jumps fit, earlier juv nov hdle wnr at Sandown on hdles bow (rtd 114h, stays 2m on gd/soft grnd): plcd 5 times in '03 (rtd 82a & 81, h'caps & class stks): mdn wnr in late '02: eff at 1m/12f, imprvd on 1st try at 2m: acts on firm, gd grnd & polytrack: decent run. 2 Oct'03 Ling 12ap 80a-78 D: 2 Feb'03 Ling 10ap 81a-77 C: 1 Dec'02 Ling 8ap 77a- D:	½	78
762	**JADEERON 32** [7] Miss D A McHale 5-8-12 p (64) F Lynch 8/1: 00-22234: Held up, prog when wandered fnl 1.5f, nvr nrr: eff at 12/14f, now prob stays 2m: see 342.	nk	64
4529}	**SONOMA 183** [6]4-9-1 (72) J Mackay 11/2: 601225-5: ch f Dr Devious - Mazarine Blue (Chief's Crown) Led 2f, styd in tch, led 3f out, hdd dist, no extra: op 8/1 on reapp: med auct mdn wnr in '03: eff at 14f/2m on fast grnd & a sharp trk: with M L W Bell.	3	70

259

2 Aug'03 Folk 16.4g/f 71-67 F: 2 Aug'03 Nott 14.1g/f 71-67 D: 1 Jul'03 Catt 13.8g/f 71- F:
4865} **SIMONS SEAT 159** [5]5-9-1 (67) D Sweeney 20/1: 065030-6: Held up, prog 3f out, onepcd fnl 1f: 2   63
recent jumps unplcd (rtd 29h, nov hdle).
4538* **THE RING 182** [1]4-8-13 (70) K Darley 4/1 FAV: 344431-7: b g Definite Article - Renata's Ring   1½   65
(Auction Ring) Mid-div, prog & ev ch 2f out, wknd fnl 1f: op 11/4 on reapp: h'cap wnr on fnl '03 start (also plcd
3 times): mdn wnr in late '02 (M R Channon): eff at 11.5f, imprvd last term for step up to 2m: acts on fast, hvy &
fibresand, pass any trk: with Mrs M Reveley.   1 Oct'03 Newc 16.1gd 71-65 E: 1 Nov'02 Wolv 9.3af 72a- D:
4853* **GREENWICH MEANTIME 161** [3]4-9-9 (80) J Murtagh 9/2: 3221-8: Held up, hdwy 3f out, short of room   hd   74
dist, sn onepcd: tchd 11/1 on reapp, new stable, has been gelded since last year.
605   **LITZINSKY 49** [11]6-8-3 (55) J McAuley 16/1: 0/0500-09: Handy, fdd 2f out: jumps fit.   17   34
3460} **TERMONFECKIN 236** [4]6-8-6 (58) Joanna Badger 33/1: 3460-0: 10th: Keen cl-up, led 5f out-3f out, wknd 10   28
849   **MURAQEB 17** [10]4-7-13 (1ow)(5oh)bl (50) C Catlin 40/1: 55-00050: 11th: Rcd keenly, led 14f out,   10   17
hdd 5f out, sn wknd: stiffish task: btr 849.
11 Ran   Time 3m 30.65 (6.45)   Owned: Mr A Liddiard   Trained: Hungerford

---

1004   3.40 April Conditions Stakes 3yo+ (D)
£5379 £1655 £828   **5f13y str**   **Firm 14**   **+24 Fast**   Stands side

4629} **BAHAMIAN PIRATE 178** [2] D Nicholls 9-9-1 (114) J Murtagh 5/2 FAV: 454606-1: ch g Housebuster -   104+
Shining Through (Deputy Minister) Chsd ldrs, styd on to lead ins fnl 1f, rdn out, val 5/6f: well bckd, fast time:
rnr-up twice in '03 (Gr 3 & stks, also rtd 115 when 5th in Gr 1 July Cup): rnr-up in 02 (Gr 1 July Cup): eff at
5/6f & handles firm & fibresand, loves gd soft & hvy, any trk: goes well fresh: gd confidence boost.
2 May'03 Good 6g/f 88-(115) C: 2 May'03 Newm 5g/f 113-(116) A: 2 Aug'02 Curr 6sft 112- : 2 Jul'02 Newm 6g/s 119- A:
2 Oct'01 Long 5hvy 120- : 1 Aug'01 Leop 6g/s 112- : 2 Jun'01 Newc 6frm 109- A:
171   **FROMSONG 113** [3] B R Millman 6-9-10 (90) G Baker 16/1: 010000-2: b g Fayruz - Lindas Delight   1½   105$
(Batshoof) Cl-up, led dist, hdd ins fnl 1f, not pace easy wnr: reapp: class stks wnr in '03 (also 3rd in this
race): Listed & stks rnr-up in '02: won this race in '01: eff at 5/6f on firm, likes gd/soft & hvy grnd: has gone
well fresh: another gd effort here at Nottingham.
1 Jun'03 Wind 6g/f 95-(90) C: 2 Jun'02 Kemp 5fm 104- A: 1 Apr'01 Nott 5hvy 107- C:
4884} **HENRY HALL 158** [4] N Tinkler 8-9-1 (93) Kim Tinkler 8/1: 336513-3: b c Common Grounds -   1   93
Sovereign Grace (Standaan) Trkd ldrs, kept on ins fnl 1f, just held by front 2: reapp: won 2 h'caps in '03 (also
plcd 5 times): plcd twice in '02 (h'caps & stks, rtd 93): eff at 6f, all wins at 5f: handles soft, likes gd & firm
grnd 'ough & consistent 8yo who will apprec return to h'cap company.
1 Oct'03 Epso 5gd 94-89 C: 2 Jul'03 York 5.0fm 95-89 C: 2 Jun'03 Donc 5fm 92-89 B: 1 May'03 Thir 5gd 90-84 D:
2 Sep'02 Beve 5g/f 89- C: 1 Sep'01 Newm 5g/f 92-86 C: 2 Jun'01 Wind 5g/f 93-91 B:
5037} **INDIAN SPARK 144** [6] J S Goldie 10-9-1 (98) T Quinn 9/2: 400500-4: Sn bhd, prog 2f out, no   ½   92
impress fnl 1f: op 7/2 on reapp: 10yo now.
927   **TRINCULO 5** [5]7-9-1 p (86) J P Guillambert(3) 6/1: 0-000U25: In tch, no extra dist: qck reapp.   1¾   87
4953} **WITHORWITHOUTYOU 152** [7]3-7-12 (90) M Jackay 10/1: 201054-6: Led, hdd dist, sn wknd: reapp.   ¾   80
4762} **PROUD BOAST 167** [8]6-8-10 (95) K Darley 7/2: 240360-7: Slow away, sn in tch, wkng & short of   ¾   78
room ins fnl 1f: reapp & new stable.
7 Ran   Time 57.98 (u 0.52)   Owned: Lucayan Stud   Trained: Thirsk

---

1005   4.10 Listed Hblb 'further Flight' Stakes 4yo+ (A)
£17400 £6600 £3300   **1m6f15y**   **Firm 14**   **-20 Slow**   Inside

5035} **ALCAZAR 144** [2] H Morrison 9-9-0 (118) M Fenton 11/8 FAV: 1//11024-1: b g Alzao - Sahara Breeze   115+
(Ela Mana Mou) Handy, styd on to lead dist, pushed clr fnl 1f, val 6L+: well bckd on reapp: won this race 12
months ago, also a Gr 3 & 2.5L 2nd in a Gr 1: missed '02: h'cap wnr on sole '01 start: eff at 14f/2m on firm,
likes gd & soft grnd: acts on any trk & goes v well fresh: more Listed/Gr prizes await.
2 Oct'03 Long 15.5sft 115- : 2 Apr'03 Asco 16.2gd 110-(110) A: 1 Apr'03 Nott 14.1gd 109- A: 1 Sep'01 Newm 14g/f 101-95 B:
5026} **DUSKY WARBLER 145** [6] M L W Bell 5-9-0 (107) T Quinn 11/4: 533325-2: br g Ezzoud - Bronzewing   3½   108
(Beldale Flutter) Led, hung badly under press ins fnl 2f, hdd dist, no ch with easy wnr fnl 1f: tchd 4/1 on reapp:
plcd in 4 of 8 '03 starts (incl this race, rtd 108): stks wnr in '02, also Listed rnr-up: eff at 12f, 14f/2m, acts
on firm, loves soft & hvy grnd: fine eff & can return to wng ways back on easier surface.
2 Sep'03 Donc 18gd 108-(100) A: 2 Nov'02 Donc 12hvy 102- A: 1 Oct'02 Leic 11.8sft 102- D: 2 May'02 Newm 12fm 97- C:
2 Nov'01 Newm 10gd 99- : 1 Sep'01 Newm 7g/f 94- D:
4893} **HILBRE ISLAND 158** [4] B J Meehan 4-8-13 (111) M Hills 7/4: 660310-3: b c Halling - Faribole   ½   110
(Esprit du Nord) Held up, prog 3f out, led 2f out, hdd dist & no extra: reapp: Listed wnr in '03: mdn wnr on
reapp in '02: eff at 10/11f, imprvd for step up to 14f last term: likes firm & fast grnd, handles soft & stiff/gall
trk: just sharper for today & will apprec a stronger pace.
1 Oct'03 Newm 14g/f 112-(111) A: 2 Apr'03 Newb 10.0g/f 102-(102) C: 1 Jul'02 Newb 7g/f 91- D: 2 Jun'02 Newb 6sft 89- C:
876   **QUDRAH 12** [1] E J O'Neill 4-8-5 (81) J Carroll 50/1: 650-0054: Held up, outpcd 3f out, rallied   1¾   100$
late: stiff task & return to h'cap grade will suit: see 758.
4309} **TAFFRAIL 195** [3]6-9-0 p (86) R Price 40/1: 600505-5: Cl-up, under press when no room 2f out, sn   5   100$
wknd: stiff task: jumps fit & new stable.
CELTIC VISION [5]8-9-0 t S Righton 150/1: 6: Cl-up, fdd 4f out: Flat debut, jumps fit.   14   86
6 Ran   Time 3m 3.08 (4.78)   Owned: JRepard FMelrose OPawle MStokes RBlack   Trained: East Ilsley

---

1006   4.40 Roseland Group Classified Stakes 4yo+ 0-70 (E)
£3552 £1093 £546   **1m1f213y**   **Firm 14**   **-66 Slow**   Inside

840   **LAWOOD 18** [1] K A Ryan 4-9-0 (72) T Quinn 7/1: 4530-401: Held up, prog 2f out, styd on to lead   78
ins fnl 1f, rdn out: slow time: eff at 6/7f, improvd on today's 1st try at 10f: acts on firm, hvy grnd &
polytrack: has tried blnks, best without: 1st win: see 697.
924   **OLDENWAY 6** [12] R A Fahey 5-8-12 (70) P Hanagan 11/10 FAV: 000-0022: Held up, short of room 3f   ½   74
out, kept on well fnl 1f, not btn far: well bckd, qck reapp: won this race 12 months ago, see 924 & 803.
2561} **SIR HAYDN 274** [10] J R Jenkins 4-8-13 (71) W Ryan 16/1: 406033-3: ch g Definite Article -   1   73
Snowscape (Niniski) Held up, hdwy & ev ch fnl 1f, just held by front 2: reapp: plcd once in '03 (clmr, rtd 73, N P
Littmoden): won last of 2 juv starts (auct mdn): eff at 1m/10f on firm & soft grnd: acts on a gall trk, tried
blnks: has ben gelded since last term, encouraging effort.   1 Oct'02 Redc 8sft 79- E:

NOTTINGHAM WEDNESDAY 31.03.04 Lefthand, Galloping Track

521 **SKIBEREEN 60** [14] I W McInnes 4-9-0 (72) P Mathers(7) 33/1: 4232-564: Prom, led 2f out, hdd ins fnl 1f, no extra: 9 wk abs: acts on firm, gd/soft & polytrack: see 476. *nk* **73**
936 **GENERAL GB 5** [4]7-9-1 (73) T P Queally(3) 12/1: 42/0/-1205: Rear, prog 4f out, onepcd fnl 1f: quick reapp: btr 856 & 811 (fibresand). *2* **71**
4820} **MOUNT BENGER 163** [11]4-8-12 (65) K Darley 12/1: 63/000-6: ch g Selkirk - Vice Vixen (Vice Regent) Led, hdd 2f out, no extra when short of room ins fnl 1f: tchd 25/1 on reapp: unplcd on 3 '03 starts (rtd 45a & 61, h'cap & mdn): plcd in late '02 (mdn, rtd 70a): eff at 7f on fibresand. *1¾* **65**
434 **TRAVELLERS TALE 74** [3]5-8-13 (71) S Drowne 10/1: 43034-07: Keen rear, nvr nrr than mid-div. *½* **65**
4768} **PRINCE OF GOLD 167** [6]4-9-0 (72) W Supple 14/1: 413000-8: b c Polar Prince - Gold Belt (Bellypha) Held up, prog 5f out, wknd fnl 1f: reapp: won 2 h'caps & a class stks in '03: eff around 1m on firm, gd/soft & fibresand: with R Hollinshead. 1 Sep'03 Sout 8af 69a-64 F: 2 Jul'03 Beve 7.5g/f 75-73 D: 1 May'03 Nott 8.2g/s 77-(75) E: 1 May'03 Beve 8.5gd 74-70 D: 2 Oct'02 York 8fm 77- E: *1¼* **64**
674 **MAMORE GAP 42** [5]6-9-1 (73) P Gallagher(7) 12/1: 1050-009: Keen cl-up, wknd 5f out: 6 wk abs. *½* **64**
129 **LUNAR LEADER 123** [7]4-8-9 p (70) B Reilly(3) 33/1: 120000-0: 10th: Cl-up, wknd fnl 3f: 10 wk jmps abs. *nk* **57**
4533} **MARITIME BLUES 183** [2]4-8-12 (68) M Fenton 12/1: 113560-0: 11th: In tch 7f, wknd: been gelded. *nk* **59**
4979} **EASTERN HOPE 151** [9]5-8-12 (69) D Sweeney 33/1: 0/05060-0: 12th: Slow away, al bhd: long abs. *¾* **57**
4929} **ROCKY REPPIN 155** [13]4-8-12 BL (60) J Edmunds 66/1: 5640-0: 13th: Keen prom, fdd 2f out: blnks. *nk* **56**
5030} **EASTERN MAGENTA 144** [8]4-8-12 (70) Kristin Stubbs(7) 40/1: 23/0000-0: 14th: Slow away, al rear. *11* **41**
14 Ran Time 2m 10.32 (8.02) Owned: Mrs Norah M Kennedy Trained: Hambleton

1007 **5.10 Nottingham Racecourse Conference Centre Handicap Stakes 3yo 0-70 (E)** **[77]**
£3606 £1110 £555 **1m54y rnd** **Firm 14** **-49 Slow** Inside

702 **DISPOL VELETA 37** [3] T D Barron 3-9-1 (64) N Mackay(5) 9/1: 0-30141: Held up, prog 2f out, rdn out to lead cl-home: eff at 1m, further shld suit: acts on fibresand, imprvd here for firm grnd: unexposed in h'cap grade & can follow up: see 662. **70**
753 **JAKARMI 33** [4] B Palling 3-8-13 (62) P Hanagan 15/2: 50-16132: Trkd ldrs, led ins fnl 1f, hdd cl-home: tchd 12/1: acts on fibresand, imprvd eff here on firm grnd: see 630. *shd* **67**
5034} **ANOTHER CHOICE 144** [7] N P Littmoden 3-9-2 t (65) T P Queally(3) 14/1: 06000-3: ch c Be My Guest - Gipsy Rose Lee (Marju) Bhd, hdwy 3f out, ev ch fnl 1f, not btn far: reapp: unplcd in '03 (rtd 70, mdn): eff 1m, shaped as tho' further will suit: acts on firm grnd: eff with a t-strap. *½* **69**
514* **QUICKSTYX 60** [6] M R Channon 3-9-6 (69) T E Durcan 7/2 FAV: 14: Slow away, sn prom, led 1f out, sn hdd & no extra: 9 wk abs & h'cap bow: acts on polytrack & firm grnd: see 514. *1¼* **71**
933 **THE JOB 5** [5]3-8-10 (59) W Ryan 12/1: 0014-625: Cl-up, onepcd fnl 1f: qck reapp: btr 933 (AW). *1¾* **57**
4717} **BALEARIC STAR 170** [9]3-9-7 (70) G Baker 16/1: 60000-6: b c Night Shift - La Menorquina (Woodman) Slow away, hdwy 2f out, kept on late: reapp: unplcd in '03 (rtd 82, mdn): prob stays 1m on firm grnd: been gelded since last term, with B R Millman. *shd* **67**
817 **KINGS ROCK 23** [1]3-9-0 (63) P Fessey 12/1: 530-2607: Mid-div, outpcd 2f out, rallied fnl 1f. *nk* **59**
713 **PENEL 36** [12]3-8-11 BL (60) D Sweeney 33/1: 6540-68: In tch, led 2f out, hdd 1f out, sn wknd. *1¼* **54**
3066} **SATSU 253** [2]3-8-11 (60) M Fenton 33/1: 005-9: ch f Shinko Forest - Cap And Gown (Royal Academy) Rear, prog 3f out, hung left & wknd fnl 1f: reapp: unplcd in 3 '03 starts (rtd 55, mdn). *1¾* **50**
4368} **SUCHWOT 193** [16]3-8-10 (59) J Fanning 50/1: 600-0: 10th: Al in rear: reapp. *2½* **44**
5034} **MR BELVEDERE 144** [10]3-9-7 (70) P Dobbs 16/1: 205030-0: 11th: Prom, fdd 2f out: been gldd. *1¼* **53**
4610} **THADEA 177** [14]3-9-0 (63) J Murtagh 10/1: 30303-0: 12th: Led, hdd 2f out, sn wknd: reapp. *nk* **45**
949 **FOOLS ENTIRE 4** [18]3-9-6 (69) B Reilly(3) 20/1: 22-20360: 13th: Keen rear, nvr a factor: qck reapp. *2½* **46**
4994} **MILITARY TWO STEP 148** [15]3-9-4 (67) K Dalgleish 25/1: 235002-0: 14th: Al in rear: reapp. *1½* **41**
3998} **FARAWAY ECHO 212** [8]3-8-12 (61) T Quinn 10/1: 500-0: 15th: Nvr travelling, al bhd. *1* **33**
4923} **INSUBORDINATE 155** [17]3-8-10 (59) W Supple 20/1: 641006-0: 16th: Al in rear. *2* **27**
4480} **Perfect Balance 186** [13]3-8-11 (60) Kim Tinkler 50/1:0 855 **Book Matched 15** [11]3-9-7 (70) F Lynch 14/1:0
18 Ran Time 1m 44.63(5.23) Owned: Mr W B Imison Trained: Thirsk

LINGFIELD Polytrack WEDNESDAY 31.03.04 Lefthand, V Sharp Track

Official Going STANDARD

1008 **2.00 Bet Direct On Sky Active Maiden Stakes 3yo (D)**
£3751 £1154 £577 **7f aw rnd** **Going 34** **-16 Slow** Inside

875 **INSTANT RECALL 12** [3] B J Meehan 3-9-0 D Holland 5/4 FAV: 31: Keen & trkd ldr, led over 1f out, hdd ins fnl 1f, rallied to regain lead cl-home, drvn out: nicely bckd: eff at 7f on polytrack, sharp trk: imprvd from debut: game, shld relish 1m: see 875. **82a**
4758} **EMTILAAK 167** [5] B Hanbury 3-9-0 (79) R Hills 5/1: 023-2: b g Marju - Just A Mirage (Green Desert) Keen in tch, hdwy to lead ins fnl 1f, hdd cl-home: reapp: rnr-up one of 3 Flat '03 starts (mdn): eff at 6f/7f on fast & polytrack: has been gelded: shld find similar. 2 Sep'03 Newm 6g/f 81- E: *hd* **81a**
875 **FINDERS KEEPERS 12** [7] E A L Dunlop 3-9-0 (84) E Ahern 3/1: 320-23: Keen in tch, onepace. *2* **77a**
SYLVA ROYAL 0 [2] C E Brittain 3-8-9 Lisa Jones(3) 33/1: 4: gr f Royal Applause - Trim Star (Terimon) Rear early, sn trkd ldrs, outpcd 2f out, kept on fnl 1f: dam styd mid-dists, relish further. *¾* **70a**
875 **SAINTLY SCHOLAR 12** [6]3-8-9 R L Moore 40/1: 005: Rear, in tch 2f out, wknd fnl 1f. *2½* **65a**
898 **KING OF DIAMONDS 8** [10]3-9-0 N Pollard 7/1: 26: Keen & led, hdd over 1f out, fdd: see 898. *1¾* **66a**
841 **FARNBOROUGH 17** [11]3-9-0 Dane O'Neill 20/1: 0-57: Rear, hdwy 2f out, sn wknd. *2* **62a**
4651} **AIRGUSTA 175** [9]3-9-0 P Robinson 33/1: 000-8: Rear, nvr nr ldrs on reapp. *1½* **59a**
4948} **INDIAN EDGE 153** [12]3-9-0 (62) D Kinsella 40/1: 666-9: Keen & chsd ldrs, wknd 2f out on reapp. *¾* **57a**
PINS N NEEDLES 0 [1]3-8-9 S Whitworth 33/1: 0: 10th: Al bhd on debut. *½* **51a**
4618} **DR FOX 177** [8]3-9-0 (61) M Tebbutt 50/1: 000505-0: 11th: Nvr a factor: reapp, now with K Morgan. *4* **48a**
11 Ran Time 1m 26.34 (3.54) Owned: Mrs Susan Roy Trained: Upper Lambourn

LINGFIELD **Polytrack WEDNESDAY 31.03.04 Lefthand, V Sharp Track**

1009 **2.30 Press Interactive To Bet Direct Classified Stakes 4yo+ 0-70 (E)**
£3377 £1039 £520 **1m4f aw Going 34 -25 Slow** Inside

936 **STEELY DAN 5** [2] J R Best 5-9-6 (64) N Pollard 5/2 J FAV: 2131121: Rear, hdwy over 1f out, led cl-home, bit in hand: qck reapp: suited by 10/12f now on fm, soft & fibresand, loves polytrack/Lingfield: top weight: v progressive, unexposed at 12f: see 903. **80a**
493 **RASID 63** [1] C A Dwyer 6-9-0 (67) D Holland 8/1: 3053-102: Handy, hdwy & led ins fnl 1f, hdd & no extra cl-home: 9 wk abs: stays 12f: back to form after fin lame in 493, see 434. *nk* **72a**
918 **BELLA PAVLINA 6** [4] W M Brisbourne 6-9-1 (74) B Swarbrick(7) 7/1: 1415103: Trkd ldr, ch 1f out, onepcd: qck reapp: handles firm, fast & both AWs: shade btr 856 (fibresand). *¾* **72a**
870 **MOON SHOT 13** [5] A G Juckes 8-9-1 (71) V Slattery 10/1: 251/3-124: In tch, hdwy over 1f out, sn onepcd: handles firm, soft & both AWs: see 752 & 142. *hd* **71a**
876 **DORIS SOUTER 12** [3]4-8-11 (72) Dane O'Neill 7/1: 3153-205: Led till ins fnl 1f, no extra: see 736. *½* **68a**
1544*}**KINGKOHLER 320** [7]5-9-5 (75) R Miles(3) 5/2 J FAV: 630/11-6: b g King's Theatre - Legit (Runnett) Trkd ldrs, no extra over 1f out: reapp: recent jumps wnr (nov hdle, 2m, firm, rtd 110h): won both Flat '03 starts (class stks & mdn): eff around 1m4f on fibresand & gd/soft, stiff or sharp/undul trks. *1¼* **72a**
1 May'03 Hami 11.1g/s 79-(66) E: 1 Feb'03 Wolv 12af 70a-(65) D:
4876} **DISTANT COUSIN 159** [6]7-9-4 vis (74) S Sanders 12/1: 222256-7: b g Distant Relative - Tinaca (Manila) Rear, wknd 2f out, t.o.: reapp: rnr-up in 4 h'caps in '03: won 4 h'caps in '02: tried 2m, suited by 12/14f on firm, soft & both AWs: loves a sharp trk, esp Southwell, prob handles any: eff with/without a visor & a gd weight carrier: goes well fresh: tough. 2 Aug'03 Ripo 12.3g/f 65-62 D: 2 Aug'03 Ripo 12.3g/f 61-60 E: 2 Jul'03 Donc 12gd 61-59 D: 2 Jul'03 Nott 14.1fm 61-59 E: 1 Nov'02 Sout 14af 77a-72 E: 1 Oct'02 Ling 12ap 68a-62 E: 1 Oct'02 Sout 12af 70a-56 F: 2 Jul'02 Donc 12g/f 61-56 D: 2 Jul'02 Nott 14g/f 59-56 E: *15* **49a**
7 Ran Time 2m 36.33 (7.13) Owned: Mr E A Condon Trained: Maidstone

1010 **3.00 Alan Morgan Remembered By His Friends Handicap Stakes 3yo+ 0-70 (E)** **[70]**
£3533 £1087 £544 **7f aw rnd Going 34 -08 Slow** Inside

897 **SPINDOR 8** [10] J A Osborne 5-9-2 bl (58) D Holland 6/1: 0-253421: Rear, short of room 3f out, gd hdwy over 1f out, strong run to lead cl-home: eff at 6f/7f, tried 1m, acts on fast & both AWs, likes a sharp trk. **63a**
935 **ILLUSIVE 5** [2] M Wigham 7-9-2 bl (58) M Tebbutt 10/1: 0350022: In tch, hdwy & short of room 1f out, switched right & styd on ins fnl 1f, just held by wnr: qk reapp: well h'capped: see 628. *nk* **62a**
607 **QUANTUM LEAP 49** [8] S Dow 7-9-6 vis (62) R L Moore 25/1: 53-06303: Handy, led halfway till cl-home. *½* **65a**
698 **COLD CLIMATE 39** [6] Bob Jones 9-9-9 (65) O Urbina 10/1: 51521-04: Trkd ldrs, ch ins fnl 1f, onepcd cl-home: ran to form of 144, see 123. *shd* **67a**
897 **HARD TO CATCH 8** [13]6-10-0 (70) M Howard(7) 16/1: 0241045: In tch, hdwy & ch 1f out, no extra. *shd* **71a**
698 **ZAFARSHAH 39** [9]5-9-6 (62) S Sanders 8/1: 50-14146: In tch, stumbled over 2f out, styd on fnl 1f but not pace to reach ldrs: ran to form of 565, see 366. *1¼* **61a**
698 **FEARBY CROSS 39** [12]8-9-10 (66) Lisa Jones(3) 14/1: 44000-67: Rear, hdwy 2f out, nrst fin. *nk* **64a**
858* **NEARLY A FOOL 15** [11]6-9-6 vis (62) N Pollard 11/2 FAV: 3-110218: In tch, onepcd: btr 858. *¾* **58a**
969 **SINGLE TRACK MIND 2** [1]6-8-3 (45) Karen Peippo(7) 25/1: 0-025459: Rear, nvr nr ldrs: see 708. *1¼* **39a**
698 **SIR FRANCIS 39** [4]6-9-11 (67) E Ahern 7/1: 060-0000: 10th: Led till halfway, no extra 2f out. *2* **57a**
864 **PARKER 14** [5]7-9-7 bl (63) D Kinsella 14/1: 150-4360: 11th: Handy, wknd over 1f out & sn eased. *1¼* **51a**
699 **FEAST OF ROMANCE 37** [14]7-9-2 p (58) P Robinson 10/1: 3262150: 12th: Prsd ldrs, wknd 2f out. *1* **44a**
764 **STAR FERN 31** [3]3-8-3 (1ow) (59) S Whitworth 20/1: 4-550: 13th: Al bhd: see 220. *1¼* **44a**
860 **SUPER CANYON 14** [7]6-9-10 vis t (66) R Hills 9/1: 5532-420: 14th: Rear, t.o.: see 687. *19* **12a**
14 Ran Time 1m 25.74 (2.94) Owned: Mr Paul J Dixon Trained: Upper Lambourn

1011 **3.30 Cashbacks @ Betdirect Co Uk Rated Stakes Handicap 3yo+ 0-85 (D)** **[84]**
£4805 £1823 £911 **5f aw rnd Going 34 +09 Fast** Outside

874 **FOREVER PHOENIX 12** [4] R M H Cowell 4-9-13 (83) E Ahern 11/4 J FAV: 1-561121: Trkd ldr, led 2f out, rdn ins fnl 1f & flashed tail, held on cl-home: eff at 5f/1m on fast, gd/soft & both AWs, likes a sharp trk: gd run off top weight & thriving at present: versatile & can win more races: see 760 & 248. **90a**
660* **MAGIC GLADE 43** [3] C R Dore 5-9-7 (77) R Thomas(5) 4/1: 23/00-012: Trkd ldrs, hdwy 2f out, kept on fnl 1f but just failed: 6 wk abs, clr of rem: handles fast & both AWs: in gd form. *shd* **83a**
755* **TURIBIUS 32** [6] T E Powell 5-9-11 (81) J F Egan 11/4 J FAV: 4021-613: Rear, hdwy over 2f out, onepcd. *3½* **77a**
749 **PRINCE OF BLUES 33** [2] M Mullineaux 6-8-10 (5oh)p (61) P Varley(7) 20/1: 0-020004: Led to 2f out, wknd. *1* **59a**
4202} **ZARGUS 201** [7]5-8-13 (69) Dane O'Neill 8/1: 000040-5: b g Zamindar - My First Romance (Danehill) Bhd, eff 2f out, sn btn: reapp: unplcd all '03 starts (rtd 76): won val Balmoral h'cap at R Ascot in '02: eff at 5f, stays 6f on fast & gd/soft, prob any trk: tried cheek pieces: well h'capped on best form. *1¼* **58a**
1 Jun'02 Asco 5gd 88-82 B: 1 Oct'01 Catt 5g/s 75- D: 2 Oct'01 Bath 5.7g/f 83- D: 2 Sep'01 Good 6g/f 83- D:
859 **SEA THE WORLD 15** [5]4-8-10 (3oh)vis (63) Lisa Jones(3) 10/1: 00-51326: Al bhd: btr 587, see 415. *½* **53a**
4637} **MULTIPLE CHOICE 176** [8]3-9-1 (83) D Holland 8/1: 332004-7: ch c Woodborough - Cosmona (Dominion) Chsd ldrs, wknd over 1f out: reapp: won a mdn in '03: eff at 5/6f on gd, firm & fibresand, acts on a sharp/turning trk. 2 Aug'03 Ches 5.1g/f 84-79 D: 1 Jul'03 Wolv 5af 77a- E: *1* **67a**
7 Ran Time 59.05s (1.25) Owned: Mr J M Greetham Trained: Newmarket

1012 **4.00 Betdirect Co Uk Selling Stakes 3yo+ (G)**
£2590 £740 £370 **6f aw rnd Going 34 -19 Slow** Inside

819 **BELLS BEACH 23** [2] P Howling 6-9-8 (54) R Hills 7/2: 0101561: Trkd ldrs, hdwy over 1f out, led ins fnl 1f, drvn out: no bid: suited by 5/6f on fast, gd/soft & both AWs, likes Lingfield & sell grade. **55a**
844* **KILMEENA STAR 17** [1] J C Fox 6-9-13 bl (48) R L Moore 10/1: 6-000412: Made most, hdd ins fnl 1f, no extra: in form, imprvd in defeat: see 844 & 830. *1¼* **55a**
935 **ORIONS BELT 5** [5] G B Balding 4-9-8 (55) R Havlin 33/1: 0500/0-03: ch g Compton Place - Follow The Stars (Sparkler) Rear, gd hdwy 2f out, nrst fin: qck reapp: unplcd sole '03 mdn start: unplcd in '02 (rtd 67, mdn): eff at 6f on polytrack: imprvd here on drop to sell grade. *nk* **49a**

LINGFIELD Polytrack WEDNESDAY 31.03.04 Lefthand, V Sharp Track

897 **SOUNDS LUCKY 8** [6] Andrew Reid 8-9-13 bl (57) D Holland 15/8 FAV: 5012604: Rear, gd hdwy over 2f out, onepcd over 1f out: more expected: btr 737, see 471. *2½* **46a**
830 **HINCHLEY WOOD 22** [4]5-9-8 (35) N Pollard 16/1: 0//-600055: b g Fayruz - Audriano (Cyrano de Bergerac) Chsd ldrs, lost place halfway, short of room & dropped to rear over 2f out, kept on fnl 1f: missed '03 & '02: lightly rcd in '01 (unplcd both mdn starts, with K McAuliffe): with J Best. *½* **39a**
872 **LIZHAR 13** [8]3-8-9 (57) E Ahern 7/2: 4042046: Prom, wknd over 1f out: see 703 & 422. *¾* **37a**
907 **ATTORNEY 8** [9]6-9-13 vis (46) Lisa Jones(3) 14/1: 0065307: Rear, hdwy over 2f out, wknd 1f out. *2½* **34a**
2015} **MY WILD ROVER 296** [3]4-9-8 T p R Miles(3) 100/1: 0P-8: Prsd ldr, lost place over 2f out & wknd: t-strap. *6* **11a**
853 **MISS TRINITY 15** [7]4-9-3 p (57) P Robinson 8/1: 0/050-009: Prsd ldrs, wknd 2f out. *nk* **5a**
9 Ran Time 1m 13.58 (3.18) Owned: Mr Richard Berenson Trained: Newmarket

1013

4.30 New Site @ Betdirect Co Uk Handicap Stakes 3yo+ 46-55 (F) **[59]**
£2933 £838 £419 **1m aw rnd** **Going 34** **-03 Slow** Outside

4533} **SAMUEL CHARLES 183** [1] W M Brisbourne 6-9-10 (55) N Pollard 14/1: 44000-1: b g Green Desert - Hejraan (Alydar) Chsd ldrs, hdwy 2f out, led 1f out, rdn out: reapp: 4th at best '03 (mdn, rtd 71, with Mrs A King): eff at 1m on firm & polytrack, acts on a sharp trk: 1st win, improved for useful new trainer. **61a**
739 **TITIAN LASS 34** [12] C E Brittain 5-9-1 bl (46) R Hills 16/1: 200-4152: Wide in rear, gd hdwy over 2f out, chsd wnr ins fnl 1f but no impress: ran to form of wng 410, see 287. *1¼* **48a**
801 **LONDONER 27** [5] S Dow 6-9-8 (53) R L Moore 16/1: 06-00003: ch g Sky Classic - Love And Affection (Exclusive Era) Handy, dsptd lead 5f out to 1f out, no extra: unplcd all '03 starts (h'caps, rtd 73 at best): won a h'cap in '02: eff over 1m/10f on firm, gd & polytrack, stiff or easy trk: has worn a t-strap: v well h'capped. *½* **54a**
1 Oct'02 York 8fm 93-90 B:
917 **PRIME OFFER 7** [2] J Jay 8-9-7 (52) B Swarbrick(7) 7/2: 0530-024: Led till joined 5f out, dsptd lead till 1f out, no extra: see 917. *1* **51a**
910* **LUCID DREAMS 7** [7]5-10-2 (6ex)p (61) G Carter 5/1: 0412315: Keen in tch, hdwy over 2f out, fdd fnl 1f. *1¼* **58a**
805 **AMNESTY 27** [10]5-9-4 bl e (49) Lisa Jones(3) 16/1: 0-045006: Rear, mod late gains. *½* **45a**
917 **INDIAN BLAZE 7** [3]10-9-7 (52) S Sanders 10/1: 2120367: With ldrs, wknd fnl 1f: qck reapp. *1½* **45a**
913 **FRANKSKIPS 7** [9]5-9-10 (55) D Holland 5/2 FAV: 0500338: Keen in rear, short of room & snatched over 2f out, no ch after: qck reapp: rider reported mount was too free: see 479. *shd* **47a**
3902} **LUCEFER 218** [11]6-9-5 t (50) Dean Williams(7) 14/1: 043412-9: Keen in rear, nvr a factor on reapp. *1* **40a**
897 **ROY MCAVOY 8** [8]6-9-10 P (55) E Ahern 20/1: 0000-000: 10th: Keen in tch, wknd 2f out: cheekpieces. *2* **41a**
672 **HEKTIKOS 42** [4]4-9-5 (50) J Coffill Brown(7) 66/1: 040/00-00: 11th: Chsd ldrs, wknd 2f out: 6 wk abs. *5* **26a**
123 **SUNSET KING 123** [6]4-9-7 (52) Dane O'Neill 16/1: 022000-0: 12th: Chsd ldrs, wknd 3f out: long abs: reportedly hung left: recent jumps unplcd (nov hdle, 2m, rtd 66h). *4* **20a**
12 Ran Time 1m 39.22(3.02) Owned: Mr J F Thomas Trained: Baschurch

LEICESTER THURSDAY 01.04.04 Righthand, Stiff, Galloping Track

Official Going Good To Soft (Good Places)

1014

2.10 Levy Board Knighton Median Auction Maiden Stakes 2yo (F)
£3297 £942 £471 **5f str** **Good/Soft 88** **-21 Slow** Stands Side

BERKHAMSTED [1] J A Osborne 2-9-0 D Holland 13/8: 1: b c Desert Sun - Accounting (Sillery) Trkd ldrs & sn pushed along, hdwy to lead well ins last, just prevailed: nicely bckd: E50,000 March first foal, dam plcd at 12f abroad: sire smart 6f/1m performer: eff at 5f, shld get further: acts on gd/soft grnd & a stiff trk: goes well fresh: plenty of promise, type to rate higher & win more races. **80**
LACONICOS [3] D R Loder 2-9-0 J Murtagh 6/4 FAV: 2: ch c Foxhound - Thermopylae (Tenby) Led, rdn & hdd well ins last, kept on well, just held: nicely bckd tho' op 11/10, rest well covered: Jan first foal, cost E28,000: dam styd 10f: eff at 5f, breeding suggests mid-dists will suit in time: acts on gd/soft grnd & a stiff trk, most encouraging, can find similar. *shd* **79**
GEORGIE BELLE [4] C Tinkler 2-8-9 E Ahern 16/1: 3: ch f Southern Halo - Saabikah (Dayjur) Trkd ldr, outpcd fnl 1f: Jan first foal, cost 11,000gns: dam unrcd relative of a useful 7f/1m juv: handles gd/soft grnd, gave encouragement & well clr other pair. *3½* **64**
LANGSTON BOY [2] M L W Bell 2-9-0 L Dettori 100/30: 4: Swerved right start & sn outpcd: op 9/2. *5* **55**
EMERALD PENANG [5]2-9-0 S Drowne 33/1: 5: Sn outpcd & bhd halfway. *5* **41**
5 Ran Time 1m 03.75 (5.45) Owned: Mr Richard Leslie Trained: Upper Lambourn

1015

2.45 Burton Overy Selling Stakes 3yo (G)
£2618 £748 £374 **6f str** **Good/Soft 88** **-13 Slow** Stands Side

804 **STAMFORD BLUE 28** [6] J S Moore 3-9-5 bl (56) B Swarbrick(7) 11/1: 4620601: Held up, styd on for press despite being carried right to lead well ins last: no bid: eff at 5/6f on fast, gd/soft & polytrack: suited by blnks, sharp or stiff trk: enjoys sell grade: see 233. **66**
841 **SOUL PROVIDER 18** [5] P A Blockley 3-8-9 (56) Dean McKeown 100/30 FAV: 25-53432: Led after 1f, hung right under press & hdd well ins last: bckd tho' op 11/4: eff at 6f/sharp 1m on fast, gd/soft & both AWs. *½* **53**
872 **BARBILYRIFLE 14** [7] H Morrison 3-9-5 p (63) L Fletcher(3) 5/1: 0000-003: b g Indian Rocket - Age of Elegance (Troy) Chsd ldrs, ch dist, not pace of wnr cl-home: imprvd eff on drop to sell grade with cheek pieces reapplied: handles firm, gd/soft: see 712. 1 Jun'03 Bath 5.0fm 78- E: *shd* **63**
4463} **UNITED UNION 188** [1] D Haydn Jones 3-9-0 (65) Paul Eddery 9/2: 0300-4: b g Imperial Ballet - Madagascar (Puissance) Led 1f, outpcd over 1f out: reapp: C/D mdn plcd '03 (rtd 68, AW unplcd, rtd 61a, mdn): eff at 6f, handles gd & gd/soft grnd: clr rem. *3½* **48**
327 **HES A ROCKET 86** [9]3-9-0 vis (40) G Faulkner 25/1: 00003-65: Dwelt, chsd ldrs till dist: abs. *6* **32**
871 **SON OF REMBRANDT 14** [2]3-9-0 (64) M Howard(7) 7/1: 63-00536: Chsd ldrs, outpcd halfway: btr 871. *2* **26**
749 **QUEEN OF BULGARIA 34** [3]3-9-0 (61) R Price 11/2: 16202-07: b f Imperial Ballet - Sofia Aurora (Chief Honcho) Sn outpcd & struggling: op 9/2: '03 seller wnr for M Bell, AW unplcd (rtd 55a, auct fills mdn): suited by 6f on fast & gd grnd, handles fibresand, sharp/easy trk: enjoys claim/sell grade & can go well fresh. *½* **24**
2 Oct'03 Newc 6fm 61-60 G: 2 Aug'03 Yarm 6.0g/f 51-(60) F: 1 Jul'03 Yarm 6.0gd 59- G:

873 **DIVINA 13** [4]3-8-9 P Robinson 16/1: 0008: Sn outpcd & struggling: big drop in trip, mod form. **8** **0**
815 **YOUR JUST LOVELY 24** [8]3-8-9 (60) Martin Dwyer 8/1: 060-09: Sn struggling rear. **5** **0**
9 Ran Time 1m 15.83 (6.03) Owned: Miss Karen Theobald Trained: Hungerford

---

1016 **3.20 Rethink Severe Mental Illness Maiden Stakes 3-4yo** (D)
£4765 £1466 £733 **1m3f183y** **Good/Soft 88** **-09 Slow** Stands Side

4488} **ARRESTING 187** [4] J R Fanshawe 4-9-12 (85) J Murtagh 4/9 FAV: 3222-1: b g Hector Protector - **86**
Misbelief (Shirley Heights) Held up, hdwy halfway, rdn/styd on to lead well ins last, flashed tail: reapp: thrice
mdn plcd '03, plcd sole other start (debut): eff at 9/10f, best at 11/12f, further will suit: acts on fast & soft,
sharpish or stiff/gall trk: goes well fresh: gd weight-carrier: type to progress over further.
2 Sep'03 Ripo 11.1g/f 85-(85) D: 2 Jul'03 Newb 12.0g/f 86- D: 2 May'03 Ripo 10g/s 75- D:
      GRAN DANA [7] M Johnston 4-9-12 J Fanning 12/1: 2: b g Grand Lodge - Olean (Sadler's Wells) ¾ **84**
Handy & led over 3f out, hdd well ins last: clr of rem, op 9/1 on debut: IR 60,000gns purchase, brother to two
10f wnrs: styd stiff 12f well, may get further: acts on gd/soft grnd: encouraging, can be plcd to effect.
873 **LAKAAM 13** [1] G P Enright 3-8-1 R Brisland 100/1: 003: Keen, rear, mod late prog, no threat to **13** **59**
front pair: well held prev, now qual for h'caps.
438 **QUEENS FANTASY 73** [6] D Haydn Jones Paul Eddery 66/1: 00-04: Mid-div, no impress fnl 2½ **56**
3f: 10 wk abs, longer trip.
873 **MUZIO SCEVOLA 13** [8]3-8-6 T E Durcan 6/1: 25: Chsd ldrs, btn 2f out: op 9/2: btr 873. (AW). shd **60**
3129} **HASHID 251** [5]4-9-12 Dane O'Neill 11/1: 53-6: Slow away, eff wide halfway, sn no prog: new yard. 6 **52**
759 **AMEYRAH 33** [9]3-8-1 C Catlin 16/1: 00-07: Led till over 3f out, sn btn: longer trip: btr 759. 5 **41**
848 **BAROQUE 18** [3]3-8-6 R Fitzpatrick 100/1: 08: Al bhd. 19 **21**
      COURT EMPEROR [2]4-9-12 V Slattery 40/1: 9: Slow away, prom till halfway on debut: jumps fit. 20 **0**
9 Ran Time 2m 39.84 (11.54) Owned: Mrs Andrew Wates & Mr Tim Vestey Trained: Newmarket

---

1017 **3.55 Visit Jelsons' Showhome At The Furlongs Handicap Stakes 3yo 0-75** (E) **[82]**
£3611 £1111 £556 **1m2f rnd** **Good/Soft 88** **-09 Slow** Stands Side

4532} **SWAGGER STICK 184** [13] J L Dunlop 3-9-3 (71) K Darley 11/2: 00014-1: gr c Cozzene - Regal State **98**
(Affirmed) Handy, led over 3f out, rdn & styd on strongly ins last: op 7/2, reapp: nursery h'cap wnr '03: eff at
1m/10f, may get further: acts on fast & gd/soft grnd, stiff/undul or easy trk: goes well fresh: lightly rcd &
progressive type. 1 Sep'03 Yarm 8.0gd 72-67 E:
4960*}**HAZYVIEW 153** [10] N A Callaghan 3-8-13 (67) J Murtagh 5/2 FAV: 00031-2: b c Cape Cross - 1¼ **91**
Euridice (Woodman) Held up, hmpd after 3f, rdn & styd on to chase wnr ins last, al held: nicely bckd tho' op 7/2:
rest well covered: h'cap wnr fnl '03 start: winning form at 1m, styd longer 10f trip well, 12f could suit: acts on
fast & gd/soft grnd, sharp or stiff/undul trk: encouraging reapp, type to find similar. 1 Oct'03 Brig 8.0g/s 68-62 E:
5024} **BUMPTIOUS 146** [16] M H Tompkins 3-9-7 (75) G Duffield 11/1: 346-3: b c Mister Baileys - Gleam of 4 **90**
Light (Danehill) Mid-div, rdn & kept on, not pace of front pair: reapp: h'cap bow: promise tho' unplcd '03 (rtd
79, auct mdn): half-brother to wnrs at 7f: eff at 1m, stays 10f: handles gd & gd/soft, sharp or gall/undul trks.
4706} **LATE OPPOSITION 171** [5] E A L Dunlop 3-8-9 (1ow) (62) L Dettori 11/1: 006-4: Trkd ldrs, styd on nk **77**
onepace for press: reapp, h'cap bow: this longer 10f trip looks set to suit.
116* **KEEP ON MOVIN 124** [11]3-9-5 (73) R Miles 25/1: 06531-5: Held up, eff wide 3f out, nrst fin: abs. ¾ **86**
4175} **MISTER TRICKSTER 203** [12]3-8-9 (63) S Righton 33/1: 046650-6: Slow away, no gains, nvr a threat. shd **76**
817 **CHARLIE TANGO 24** [9]3-9-3 (71) T E Durcan 11/1: 5030-37: Mid-div, eff 3f out, sn no prog: btr 817. 4 **78**
112 **ERMINE GREY 125** [8]3-9-7 bl (75) Paul Eddery 33/1: 651016-8: Chsd ldr over 2f out, wknd: abs. 4 **76**
839 **HSI WANG MU 19** [1]3-7-12 (2oh) (50) Dale Gibson 33/1: 0300-259: Al bhd: btr 686 (9f). 3 **49**
702 **DESERT IMAGE 38** [2]3-9-7 (75) E Ahern 20/1: 330-1260: 10th: Al rear: btr 337 (7f). 3½ **67**
651* **GLENDALE 45** [18]3-9-0 (68) Lisa Jones 33/1: 0000-10: 11th: Mid-div, no prog fnl 3f: abs: btr 651. ½ **59**
4229} **KILLOCH PLACE 201** [15]3-8-2 (1ow) (55) Martin Dwyer 33/1: 0500-0: 12th: Al rear: reapp, longer trip. 15 **27**
796 **ASHSTANZA 29** [17]3-8-9 p (63) P Robinson 10/1: 04-4340: 13th: Chsd ldrs till 3f out: btr 614. 3½ **29**
4895} **NICK THE SILVER 159** [6]3-9-2 (70) S Drowne 25/1: 030-0: 14th: Slow away & al bhd: reapp/h'cap bow. 1 **35**
4610*}**HABANERO 198** [4]3-9-4 (72) D Holland 6/1: 060221-0: 15th: Al rear: reapp, longer trip. 12 **23**
756 **GROUVILLE 33** [7]3-9-4 BL (72) T Quinn 25/1: 100: 16th: Led till 3f out, sn eased/btn: blnkd. 6 **16**
3282} **Troubleinparadise 245** [14]3-8-7 (61) M Fenton 50/1:0923 **Indian Call 7** [3]3-8-12 (66) S Sanders 50/1:0
18 Ran Time 2m 12.18 (9.68) Owned: Mr Robin F Scully Trained: Arundel

---

1018 **4.30 Loddington Conditions Stakes 3yo** (D)
£7059 £2172 £1086 **6f str** **Good/Soft 88** **+23 Fast** Stands Side

3807} **SEVILLANO 222** [1] P D Cundell 3-8-12 (99) S Sanders 5/2: 2132-1: b g Nicolotte - Nashville Blues **108+**
(Try My Best) Made all, pulled well clr fnl 2f, easily in a v fast time: lightly rcd '03, auct mdn wnr & nov
rnr-up: suited by 6f, prob stays stiff 7f (bred to relish 7f+): acts on fast & polytrack, imprvd significantly on
gd/soft today: goes well fresh: most impressive, one to follow.
2 Aug'03 Wind 6g/f 98-(90) E: 1 Jul'03 Ling 5ap 78a- E:
4680} **HARRY UP 173** [2] J G Given 3-9-2 (93) M Fenton 8/1: 461040-2: ch c Piccolo - Faraway Lass 10 **86**
(Distant Relative) Pushed along rear, kept on late, no ch with easy wnr: reapp: auct mdn, h'cap & cond stks scorer
'03, List 4th & Gr 3 unplcd: all wins at 5f, first try at 6f today: acts on fast & gd grnd, prob any trk, loves a
sharp/turning one: caught a tartar today. 1 Aug'03 Ripo 5gd 94-(97) C: 2 Jul'03 Donc 5g/f 98-93 D:
1 Jul'03 Ches 5.1fm 95- E: 2 Jun'03 Ling 5g/f 85- F: 2 May'03 Beve 5gd 89- E:
814* **HATCH 24** [3] R M H Cowell 3-9-0 (79) D Holland 11/2: 420-2213: Pushed along rear, kept on late, 1½ **79**
nvr a threat: prob needs a return to 7f+: btr 814 (AW mdn).
4605} **VIENNAS BOY 180** [6] R Hannon 3-9-0 (92) Dane O'Neill 2/1 FAV: 342020-4: b c Victory Note - ¾ **77**
Shinkoh Rose (Warning) Chsd wnr after 2f, rdn & wknd fnl 1f: bckd from 7/2, reapp: auct mdn & nov auct scorer '03,
subs List rnr-up: best form at 5f, stays a stdly run 7f well: acts on firm & gd grnd, prob any trk: can go well
fresh: paid price for chasing this wnr & sharper next time. 2 Sep'03 Good 7g/f 86-(100) C: 2 Aug'03 Deau 5g/s 100- A:
1 Jun'03 Wind 5.0gd 95- E: 2 Jun'03 Asco 5fm 99- B: 1 May'03 Folk 5g/f 90- E:
4881} **MAC LOVE 173** [4]3-9-0 (106) T Quinn 7/2: 363232-5: Chsd wnr halfway, rdn & no impress dist: mkt 2 **72**
drifter on reapp, op 9/4: prev with M Channon.
818 **BEAU JAZZ 24** [5]3-8-10 (62) S Righton 66/1: 056-5306: Trkd wnr, btn 2f out: highly tried: btr 712. 11 **42**

6 Ran   Time 1m 13.68 (3.88)   Owned: Mr Pedro Rosas   Trained: Compton

1019   **5.05 Simon De Montfort Maiden Stakes 3yo+ (D)**
           £4862 £1496 £748   **1m2f rnd**   **Good/Soft 88**   **-07 Slow**   Stands Side

715   **JOROBADEN 37** [2] C F Wall 4-9-12 G Baker 16/1: 4/-21: Held up, hdwy when hmpd ins last, styd on   **87**
for press to lead cl home: confirmed reapp promise: eff at 10f, shaped like 12f will suit: acts on gd/soft, soft &
polytrack: gd weight-carrier: type to prog with racing: see 715.

4730} **GANYMEDE 170** [11] M L W Bell 3-8-7 D Holland 9/4 FAV: 63-2: gr c Daylami - Germane (Distant   *1*   **85**
Relative) Mid-div, hdwy 3f out, sltly hmpd when led dist, rdn & hdd well ins last: nicely bckd, op 11/4: reapp:
mdn plcd on 2nd of just 2 '03 starts (rtd 74): half-brother to a useful 1m wnr, dam a 7f juv wnr: eff at 7f, styd
longer 10f trip well: acts on fast & gd/soft grnd, stiff/undul trk.

4971} **BAYHIRR 152** [14] M A Jarvis 3-8-7 P Robinson 12/1: 0-3: b c Selkirk - Pass The Peace (Alzao)   *1*   **84+**
Held up, hdwy to press ldrs when badly hmpd over 1f out, styd on well cl-home: reapp: unplcd sole '03 start (rtd
56): stays 10f, may get further: acts on gd/soft & a stiff/gall trk: still green & poss unlucky here: can gain comp.

3321} **JUST A FLUKE 243** [16] M Johnston 3-8-7 K Dalgleish 5/1: 22-4: b c Darshaan - Star Profile   *4*   **78**
(Sadler's Wells) Led & clr over 3f out, ran away from whip & hdd dist, edged left again & no extra ins last: op 7/2,
reapp: nov stks & mdn rnr-up '03 (lightly rcd, well regarded & hvly bckd on both starts): sire high-class at
mid-dists: eff at 7f, stays 10f: acts on fast & gd/soft, stiff/gall trks: headgear may help.
2 Aug'03 Donc 7g/f 78- D: 2 Jul'03 Beve 7.5gd 76- D:

4043} **ABSOLUTELY SOAKED 211** [15]3-8-2 Lisa Jones(3) 50/1: 30-5: Prom & chsd ldr over 2f out, no extra.   *3*   **69**
        PANZER [6]3-8-7 S Drowne 50/1: 6: Rear, late gains, nvr a dngr, impr on this debut.   *3*   **70**
192   **FRANKIES WINGS 110** [10]3-8-7 R Miles(3) 22/1: 0-7: Mid-div, nvr pace to threaten: abs.   *2*   **67$**
5016} **RAREFIED 147** [12]3-8-7 R Hughes 8/1: 62-8: Trkd ldr, btn 2f out: reapp, longer trip.   *2½*   **63**
        AMANKILA [1]3-8-2 J Mackay 50/1: 9: Slowly away, rear, only mod prog on debut.   *¾*   **57**
489} **IPSA LOQUITUR 428** [4]4-9-7 Martin Dwyer 50/1: 4/5-0: 10th: Al towards rear: long abs.   *shd*   **57**
4972} **CALOMERIA 152** [5]3-8-2 G Duffield 66/1: 00-0: 11th: Sn bhd, reapp.   *7*   **48**
679} **DANCING PEARL 402** [17]6-9-7 V Slattery 33/1: 6/5-0: 12th: Dwelt & al bhd: jumps fit.   *1¼*   **46**
4544} **ENCHANTED OCEAN 888** [9]5-9-7 R Havlin 10/1: 40//-0: 13th: Slow away & sn bhd: long abs.   *5*   **40**
4407} **LITTLESTAR 191** [8]3-8-7 S Sanders 25/1: 000-0: 14th: Mid-div, struggling fnl 3f, reapp.   *2*   **42**
39   **CRYSTAL CHOIR 150** [7]4-9-7 J Murtagh 15/2: 0-0: 15th: Held up & al bhd: op 13/2, new yard.   *10*   **24**
4942} **SAINT LAZARE 155** [13]3-8-7 M Fenton 66/1: 60-0: 16th: Trkd ldrs, btn 3f out, reapp.   *5*   **23**
        MOONSHAFT [3]3-8-7 E Ahern 12/1: 0: 17th: Sn bhd & t.o., debut.   *dist*   **0**
17 Ran   Time 2m 12.03 (9.53)   Owned: The Storm Again Syndicate   Trained: Newmarket

1020   **5.40 Saffie Joseph & Sons Handicap Stakes 3yo+ 0-85 (D)**   **[82]**
           £5525 £1700 £850   **7f9y str**   **Good/Soft 88**   **-23 Slow**   Stands Side

945   **TARANAKI 5** [10] P D Cundell 6-9-11 (79) S Sanders 13/2: 6101-041: Sn prom, led over 1f out, drvn   **86**
out: qck reapp: suited by 6/7f, stays 1m: acts on firm, gd/soft & both AWs, any trk: gd weight-carrier: v tough,
with a progressive profile: see 130.

807   **MISTRAL SKY 27** [1] Mrs Stef Liddiard 5-8-12 vis (66) M Fenton 10/1: 010-2002: Mid-div, switched &   *¾*   **71**
drvn/styd on well ins last, not able to reach wnr: fine return to turf, keen: likes Leicester & Lingfield: see 121.

945   **AMMENAYR 5** [13] T G Mills 4-9-9 (77) K Darley 10/1: 1050-003: Prom & led over 1f out, hdd dist,   *shd*   **82**
styd on for press: op 14/1, qck reapp: acts on fast & gd/soft: lightly rcd & encouragement here: see 945.

136   **OH SO ROSIE 121** [9] J S Moore 4-8-6 (60) B Swarbrick(7) 25/1: 064020-4: b f Danehill Dancer -   *¾*   **64+**
Shinkoh Rose (Warning) Pushed along rear, hdwy wide 2f out, ch dist, no extra: 4 mth abs: thrice h'cap rnr-up in
'03: dual h'cap scorer '02, AW unplcd (rtd 54a, mdn, tried visor): eff at 7/9f on fast & gd/soft, disapp on both
AWs: acts on any trk: eff with/without cheek pieces: fine eff racing away from the best pace, keep in mind.
2 Nov'03 Donc 8gd 59-58 E: 2 Aug'03 Kemp 9g/f 58-56 E: 2 Aug'03 Wind 8.3g/f 59-56 E: 1 Aug'02 Wind 6gd 72-64 E:
1 Aug'02 Leic 6gd 67-57 G: 2 Jun'02 Wind 6g/f 52- G:

2697} **OAKLEY RAMBO 270** [2]5-9-12 (80) R Hughes 20/1: 0/00000-5: br g Muhtarram - Westminster Waltz   *1¾*   **81**
(Dance In Time) Led till halfway, trav well, not qckn under hand & heels from dist: reapp, has been gelded: unplcd
'03 (rtd 72a & 76, h'caps): h'cap wnr '02: eff at 7f/1m on firm & gd/soft, prob any trk: ran well for a long way
under a kind ride, can improve.
2 Oct'02 Nott 8.2hvy 90-86 C: 1 Sep'02 Newb 8fm 86-83 C: 2 Sep'02 Kemp 8fm 83-81 D: 2 Aug'02 Newm 7g/s 80-80 D:
1 Sep'01 Chep 7fm 79- F: 2 Sep'01 Hayd 7.1g/s 82- D: 2 Aug'01 Wind 6g/f 82- E:

885   **DUMNONI 12** [15]3-8-13 (81) N Callan 25/1: 3631-06: Trkd ldrs, rdn & onepace dist: acts on both   *nk*   **81**
AWs, handles fast & gd/soft: see 36 (AW mdn).

940   **PHAROAHS GOLD 5** [5]6-7-12 vis (52) Lisa Jones(3) 20/1: 000-2057: Held up, eff fnl 3f, not able to chall.   *½*   **51**
4722} **SNOW BUNTING 171** [16]6-8-0 (54) Leanne Kershaw(7) 25/1: 406560-8: ch g Polar Falcon - Marl   *nk*   **52**
(Lycius) Keen & held up, only mod prog: reapp: h'cap rnr-up '03: thrice h'cap wnr '02, sand unplcd (rtd 50a):
suited by 6/7f on firm & fast grnd, prob handles polytrack: likes a stiff/gall trk. 2 Jun'03 Donc 7fm 62-60 D:
1 Sep'02 Redc 6fm 62-57 D: 1 Aug'02 Newc 6g/f 58-50 E: 1 Jun'02 Donc 7fm 51-47 E: 1 Aug'01 Ayr 6gd 60- E:

5030} **GREY COSSACK 145** [11]7-9-9 (77) G Parkin 33/1: 110000-9: Sn cl-up/dsptd lead till over 1f out.   *½*   **74**
551   **BARZAK 56** [4]4-8-8 bl t (62) J Bramhill 10/1: 005-0530: 10th: Squeezed out & drpd rear early, rdn   *½*   **58+**
& late gains: 8 wk abs: on a handy mark & can improve on this in similar: see 551 & 60.
4768} **JACARANDA 168** [12]4-9-4 (72) S Drowne 25/1: D04024-0: 11th: Went left start, al rear for new yard.   *2½*   **63**
840   **MIDDLETON GREY 19** [3]6-8-10 bl (64) Martin Dwyer 7/1: 064-0320: 12th: Mid-div, no impress fnl 2f   *1*   **53**
on turf return: btr 840 (AW).
4854} **KELSEAS KOLBY 162** [8]4-8-3 (57) G Gibbons 33/1: 002120-0: 13th: Dwelt & al bhd: reapp.   *½*   **45**
800   **KAREEB 28** [6]7-9-10 (78) J Murtagh 9/2 FAV: 30000-60: 14th: Trkd ldrs, btn dist: see 800.   *2*   **62**
2668} **RED GALAXY 271** [14]4-9-12 t (80) L Dettori 20/1: 110/000-0: 15th: Sn bhd, reapp.   *hd*   **63**
2359} **FLEETWOOD BAY 283** [7]4-9-9 (77) G Baker 40/1: 000020-0: 16th: Chsd ldrs till 2f out, reapp.   *1¼*   **57**
3911*} **SOLINIKI 218** [17]3-8-12 (80) D Holland 5/1: 1-0: 17th: Chsd ldrs, strugg halfway: gelded.   *10*   **45**
17 Ran   Time 1m 29/77(7.77)   Owned: Mr Eric Evers   Trained: Compton

LINGFIELD Polytrack FRIDAY 02.04.04 Lefthand, V Sharp Track

Official Going Standard

1021
1.40 Betdirect Co Uk Median Auction Maiden Stakes Div 1 3-4yo (F)
£2905 £830 £415 **1m aw rnd** **Going 19** **+09 Fast** Outside

4980} **FANCY FOXTROT** 152 [1] B J Meehan 3-8-8 (1ow) (82) L Dettori 2/1 FAV: 252326-1: b c Danehill **92a+**
Dancer - Smooth Princess (Roi Danzig) Made all, pulled clr over 1f out & won easily in a fast time: hvly bckd,
reapp/AW bow: '03 sts & nov (2) rnr-up: eff at 6/7f, suited by forcing tactics at 1m: acts on firm, fast &
polytrack, sharp or gall trk: goes well fresh: well regarded, looks set for a productive 3yo campaign.
2 Oct'03 Nott 8.2g/f 87-(90) D: 2 Jul'03 Asco 7g/f 92- D: 2 May'03 Kemp 6fm 96- C:
5024} **EXTRA COVER** 147 [5] R Charlton 3-8-7 S Drowne 5/2: 5-2: b g Danehill Dancer - Ballycurrane 7 **73a**
(Elbio) Chsd wnr, no impress dist: nicely bckd tho' op 2/1, reapp/AW bow: promise sole '03 mdn start (rtd 75):
eff at 1m, mid-dists cld suit: handles polytrack & gd grnd, sharp/turning or gall trk: caught a tartar.
4789} **BEACH PARTY** 168 [10] M L W Bell 3-8-2 J Fanning 20/1: 05-3: b f Danzero - Shore Lark (Storm 1¼ **65a**
Bird) Chsd ldrs halfway, kept on, nvr a dngr: reapp/AW bow: unplcd '03 (lightly rcd, rtd 61, mdn): half-sister to
a 5/6f juv wnr: this longer 1m trip could suit, prob handles polytrack & fast grnd.
  TRIFTI [3] C A Cyzer 3-8-7 S Whitworth 50/1: 4: Mid-div, kept on fnl 3f under hands & heels, ½ **69a**
nvr threat to front pair: clr rem on debut.
697 **SEWMORE CHARACTER** 41 [6]4-9-8 (70) D Sweeney 7/2: 462-4625: Mid-div, eff 3f out, sn btn. 5 **60a**
19 **DONASTRELA** 141 [2]3-8-2 Martin Dwyer 33/1: 0-9: Prom, fdd fnl 3f: abs. 1¼ **52a**
841 **APPOLONIOUS** 19 [8]3-8-7 Dane O'Neill 9/1: 07: Dwelt & rar at rear: op 7/1. shd **57a**
  ANTIGIOTTO [9]3-8-7 N Mackay(5) 14/1: 8: Slow away & sn bhd on debut, op 10/1. 2½ **52a**
  LAURENS GIRL [7]3-8-7 (1ow) D R McCabe 66/1: 9: Dwelt & sn struggling, debut. 8 **34a**
911 **HABITUAL** 9 [4]3-8-7 S Sanders 50/1: 00-00: 10th: Chsd ldrs 4f, sn btn. 3 **32a**
10 Ran Time 1m 37.02 (.82) Owned: Mr Joe L Allbritton Trained: Upper Lambourn

1022
2.10 Betdirect Co Uk Median Auction Maiden Stakes Div 2 3-4yo (F)
£2898 £828 £414 **1m aw rnd** **Going 19** **-03 Slow** Outside

911 **INSTRUCTOR** 9 [4] R Hannon 3-8-8 (1ow) (78) R Hughes 4/5 FAV: 042-21: Made all, readily pulled clr **87a**
from dist: hvly bckd, confirmed reapp promise: eff at 7f/1m on fast grnd & polytrack: see 911.
4145} **SUNISA** 206 [2] B W Hills 3-8-2 (82) A Medeiros(5) 11/2: 624-2: b f Daggers Drawn - Winged Victory 2½ **74a**
(Dancing Brave) Chsd wnr, styd on for press, al held: op 4/1, AW bow: '03 fill mdn rnr-up: eff at 6f, stays 1m
well: handles fast, gd & polytrack, sharp/undul or stiff trk: now qual for h'caps & shld find a race.
2 Sep'03 Leic 6.0gd 82- D:
881 **BALLINGER EXPRESS** 13 [3] A M Balding 4-9-3 Martin Dwyer 5/1: 053: ch f Air Express - Branston ¾ **73a**
Ridge (Indian Ridge) Keen & trkd wnr, no extra dist: op 8/1: acts on polytrack & stays 1m: apprec h'caps.
  SOLOR [1] D J Coakley 3-8-9 (2ow) D Holland 12/1: 4: b c Spectrum - Bayadere (Green Dancer) 2 **76a**
Slow away & rear, styd on wide for press fnl 2f, nrst fin on debut: got the hang of things late on, expect
improvement, prob over 10f+ (mid-dist breeding).
4537} **STOP THE NONSENSE** 184 [8]3-8-7 J Fanning 50/1: 000-5: Chsd ldrs, no impress fnl 3f: AW bow. hd **73a$**
4180} **RAHEED** 204 [5]3-8-7 E Ahern 12/1: 46-6: Bhd halfway, mod prog: reapp, gelded. 4 **65a**
495 **FRESH CONNECTION** 65 [6]3-8-2 A McCarthy 66/1: 007: Chsd ldrs till 3f out, abs. 8 **45a**
  WITCHES BROOM [9]3-8-3 (1ow) S Whitworth 25/1: 8: Chsd ldrs halfway, strugg 3f out on debut. 8 **31a**
4034} **FIDDLES MUSIC** 212 [7]3-8-2 C Catlin 33/1: 0-9: Sn struggling: reapp/AW bow. 3 **24a**
9 Ran Time 1m 37.96 (1.76) Owned: Highclere Thoroughbred Racing IX Trained: Marlborough

1023
2.45 New Site @ Betdirect Co Uk Maiden Stakes 3yo+ (D)
£3692 £1136 £568 **5f aw rnd** **Going 19** **-08 Slow** Inside

725 **SHRINK** 37 [4] M L W Bell 3-8-8 (1ow) (68) D Holland 4/1: 22-21: Trkd ldrs, drvn to lead cl-home: **70a**
op 3/1: eff at 5f on fast grnd & polytrack: see 725.
898 **IMPERIUM** 10 [5] Mrs Stef Liddiard 3-8-12 (75) T Quinn 8/1: 0046-402: Trkd ldr & led 2f out, hdd shd **73a**
cl-home: imprvd eff with forcing tactics applied on drop to 5f: handles fast, gd/soft & polytrack: see 764.
898 **SIMPSONS MOUNT** 10 [9] R M Flower 3-8-12 R L Moore 33/1: 653: ch g Tagula - Brunswick (Warning) ¾ **71a**
Dwelt, rear, kept on for press, nrst fin: eff at 5f, tried 6f, shld suit: handles polytrack: h'caps will suit.
802 **MULTAHAB** 29 [6] Miss Gay Kelleway 5-9-9 (60) R Hughes 3/1 FAV: 555-2424: Trkd ldrs, hung right & 1 **68a$**
no extra dist: offic rtd 60, treat rating with caution: see 802 & 435.
  FOUR KINGS [8]3-8-12 J Tate 9/2: 5: b c Forzando - High Cut (Dashing Blade) Held up, rdn & 1¼ **64a**
only mod prog fnl 2f: bckd on debut: sprint bred, prob handles polytrack.
449 **HORIZONTAL** 72 [7]4-9-9 S Sanders 9/2: 5-66: Prom wide, v wide bend 2f out, sn btn: new yard. 2½ **56a**
2848} **POINT CALIMERE** 265 [10]3-8-12 (85) S Drowne 8/1: 0330-7: b g Fasliyev - Mountain Ash (Dominion) hd **55a**
Cl-up till over 1f out: op 9/2, reapp/gelded: auct mdn plcd '03 (rtd 76, AW unplcd, rtd 51a): eff over a
sharp/easy 5/6f on fast & gd grnd: rider reported gelding was unsuited by the track.
3772} **RYANS QUEST** 225 [1]5-9-4 (48) J P Guillambert(3) 25/1: 004405-8: Led 3f, fdd, reapp. 1 **47a**
819 **CONFUZED** 25 [2]4-9-9 e (45) P Fitzsimons 20/1: 0/0-03609: Rear, nvr a factor: see 737 (C/D clmr). nk **51a$**
9 Ran Time 59.15 (1.35) Owned: Mr Billy Maguire Trained: Newmarket

1024
3.20 Bet In Running @ Betdirect Co Uk Handicap Stakes Fillies 3yo+ 0-75 (E)
£3445 £1060 £530 **7f aw rnd** **Going 19** **-21 Slow** Inside **[75]**

4958} **ARTISTRY** 154 [12] B J Meehan 4-8-10 (57) D Holland 16/1: 534540-1: b f Night Shift - Arriving **63a+**
(Most Welcome) Sn trkd ldrs, led dist, rdn & styd on strongly: reapp: h'cap plcd '03 (rtd 55, P Howling): unplcd
'02 (rtd 66a & 66, mdns, J Hills): stays up to 10f, apprec drop to sharp 7f: acts on polytrack & fast grnd, likes a
sharp/turning trk: goes well fresh: overcame awkward wide draw, win again if repeating this.
799 **MICHELLE MA BELLE** 29 [10] S Kirk 4-10-0 (75) R Hughes 9/1: 33655-02: Held up, smooth prog wide 1½ **76a**
halfway, drvn & kept on from dist, not pace of wnr: well h'capped: acts on firm, soft & polytrack: see 799.
958 **AMELIA** 4 [5] W M Brisbourne 6-8-2 (49) B Swarbrick(7) 11/2: 2-525553: Mid-div & keen, styd on ½ **49a**

266

wide for press: qck reapp: stays a sharp 7f: see 246.

799   **AND TOTO TOO 29** [9] P D Evans 4-9-8 bl (69) S Donohoe(7) 6/1: 15-06244: Pushed along rear, late   *shd*   **69a**
gains, nrst fin: see 760 & 270.

4950} **DIXIE DANCING 155** [11]5-8-13 (60) S Sanders 25/1: 01/5030-5: ch f Greensmith - Daylight Dreams   ¾   **59a**
(Indian Ridge) Handy & led over 2f out till dist, no extra: reapp: '03 plcd (C/D, rtd 63a, clmr), no turf form:
late '02 h'cap wnr on sand, turf h'cap plcd (rtd 61): suited by 7f/sharp 1m on firm, fast & polytrack, stiff or
sharp trk: ran well for a long way from awkward wide draw.
1 Dec'02 Ling 8ap 67a-64 E: 2 Aug'02 Ling 8ap 67a-64 E: 2 Aug'02 Newm 7fm 70- E:

144   **A WOMAN IN LOVE 118** [1]5-8-7 (1ow) (53) S Drowne 8/1: 425640-6: gr f Muhtarram - Ma Lumiere   *hd*   **52a+**
(Niniski) Dwelt, keen rear, short of room over 1f out, kept on well under hands & heels cl-home: fills h'cap wnr
'03, AW h'cap unplcd (rtd 51a): class stks wnr '02 for J Hills, subs C/D h'cap wnr for current yard: eff around
7f/1m, tried 10f: acts on firm, gd & polytrack, loves a sharp trk, esp Lingfield: spot on next time.
2 Oct'03 Brig 8.0fm 62-(58) E: 1 Aug'03 Ling 7g/f 59-51 F: 1 Dec'02 Ling 7ap 60a-53 E: 1 Aug'02 Brig 8g/f 62- F:

4869} **JUST ONE LOOK 161** [4]3-8-12 (73) D Sweeney 20/1: 426500-7: Held up, eff 3f out, onepace, reapp.   ½   **70a**
799   **I WISH 29** [6]6-9-0 (61) G Baker 7/1: 6146-058: Rear, eff wide, no prog dist: btr 799.   ¾   **57a**
4824} **POPPYLINE 164** [8]4-8-11 (58) Martin Dwyer 25/1: 554440-9: Chsd ldrs, lost place 2f out, reapp.   1¾   **51a**
4903} **SAHARA STORM 158** [3]3-8-13 (74) L Dettori 3/1 FAV: 3340-0: 10th: Prom, rdn & btn over 2f out: 2   **63a**
well bckd: reapp, AW bow.
760   **MISS POPPETS 34** [7]4-9-6 (67) T Quinn 14/1: 30421-00: 11th: Led till over 2f out, sn btn.   *nk*   **55a**
861   **ESTIMATION 16** [2]4-9-6 (67) E Ahern 14/1: 51-36350: 12th: Mid-div innr, btn 2f out.   1   **53a**
12 Ran   Time 1m 25.62 (2.82)   Owned: Wyck Hall Stud   Trained: Upper Lambourn

---

1025   **3.55 Littlewoods Bet Direct Handicap Stakes 3yo+ 0-75 (E)**   **[74]**
        £3465 £1066 £533   **6f aw rnd**   **Going 19**   +02 Fast   Inside

935   **EFFECTIVE 7** [1] A P Jarvis 4-8-12 vis (58) D Holland 10/1: 0-030501: Led 1f, remained handy, styd   **65a**
on for press to lead cl-home: op 16/1, gd time: eff at 6f, tried 7f: acts on both AWs & gd grnd, sharp or stiff
trk: now suited by visor: well h'capped: see 550.

22   **GOODENOUGH MOVER 141** [3] J S King 8-9-5 (65) R Havlin 25/1: 030000-2: ch g Beveled - Rekindled   ½   **69a**
Flame (Kings Lake) Al prom, led well ins last, hdd cl-home: abs: h'cap plcd '03 (rtd 72): class stks & dual h'cap
wnr '02, AW class stks rnr-up: eff at 6f, suited by 7f & stays 1m: acts on firm, soft & polytrack, any trk, likes
Chepstow: loves to race with/force the pace.   2 Nov'02 Ling 7ap 84a- D: 2 Oct'02 Newm 7fm 85-80 C:
1 Sep'02 Ling 7fm 84-67 D: 1 Aug'02 Sali 7g/f 79-67 E: 1 Aug'02 Brig 7g/f 68- E: 2 Jul'02 Chep 7gd 67-65 E:
2 May'02 Ling 7gd 68-63 E: 2 Aug'01 Warw 8.1gd 72- D: 2 Jul'01 Bath 8fm 77-74 D:

944*   **FURTHER OUTLOOK 6** [6] D K Ivory 10-9-13 (7ex) (73) Dane O'Neill 7/1: 00200-13: Led after 1f, hung   1   **74a**
right over 1f out, hdd ins last, kept on: qck reapp: acts on firm, hvy & polytrack: see 944.

897*   **MAYZIN 10** [4] R M Flower 4-9-9 (7ex)p (69) D Sweeney 10/1: 4123314: Trkd ldr, drvn & chall dist,   *nk*   **69a**
no extra: tough & consistent: see 897 (C/D).

880   **MADRASEE 14** [2]6-9-5 (65) R L Moore 9/1: 21-20045: Trkd ldrs, ch dist, no extra: op 7/1: see 329.   *shd*   **65a**
1010   **ILLUSIVE 2** [7]7-8-12 bl (58) J Fanning 7/1: 3500226: Mid-div, drvn & not able to chall: qck reapp.   2½   **50a**
2761} **DONT TELL ROSEY 268** [5]4-10-0 (74) N Callan 40/1: 062210-7: b g Barathea - Patsy Western   2½   **58a**
(Precocious) Mid-div, no prog fnl 1f out: reapp, gelded: '03 mdn scorer, dual h'cap rnr-up: h'cap rnr-up '02:
eff at 5/6f on firm & soft grnd, any trk: entitled to be sharper for this. 1 Jun'03 Folk 5fm 76-(73) D:
2 Jun'03 Sand 5.0fm 76-69 D: 2 Jun'03 Chep 5.1g/f 73-67 E: 2 Sep'02 Nott 6g/f 71-68 E: 2 Jul'02 Leic 5sft 72- D:

874   **CORMORANT WHARF 14** [9]4-9-12 (72) J F Egan 12/1: 0650058: Rdn rear, nvr able to chall: btr 874.   *hd*   **55a**
880*   **ANOTHER GLIMPSE 14** [10]6-9-13 t (73) T Quinn 9/2 FAV: 0650-419: Rear, eff wide, no prog dist.   *shd*   **56a**
859   **DUNN DEAL 17** [11]4-8-13 (59) S W Kelly 25/1: 40660-30: 10th: Keen & rear, little prog: btr 859.   *shd*   **41a**
902*   **DOUBLE M 10** [12]7-9-4 (7ex)vis (64) R Hughes 11/2: 3024210: 11th: Bmpd start, switched rail &,   ½   **44a**
rear, no prog: btr 902.
853   **SHARP HAT 17** [13]10-9-2 bl (62) P Makin(7) 25/1: 2005500: 12th: Bmpd start & al rear: btr 70.   2½   **34a**
4999} **B A HIGHFLYER 150** [8]4-9-2 (62) C Catlin 20/1: 002216-0: 13th: b g Compton Place - Primulette   *hd*   **33a**
(Mummy's Pet) Rdn rear & al outpcd: h'cap scorer '03, AW h'cap rnr-up: auct mdn & dual h'cap scorer '02: eff at
6/7f on firm, soft & fibresand, any trk. 1 Oct'03 Brig 6.0g/s 65-59 F: 2 Oct'03 Donc 7g/f 64-59 E:
2 Oct'03 Sout 6af 63a-59 E: 2 Aug'03 Pont 6fm 71-(69) E: 2 Oct'02 York 6fm 85-83 C: 1 Sep'02 Hami 6fm 85-76 C:
1 Sep'02 Epso 6g/f 77-70 D: 1 Jul'02 Hami 6gd 70- E: 2 Jun'02 Yarm 6fm 78- E:

902   **TAYIF 10** [14]8-9-5 t (65) S Carson 10/1: 1126020: 14th: Held up, eff halfway, sn btn: btr 902.   ½   **35a**
14 Ran   Time 1m 11.41 (1.01)   Owned: Eurostrait Ltd   Trained: Twyford

---

1026   **4.30 Bet Direct On Sky Active Selling Stakes 3yo+ (G)**
        £2520 £720 £360   **1m2f aw**   **Going 19**   -30 Slow   Inside

        DISSIDENT 54 [8] D Flood 6-9-9 VIS (73) P Fitzsimons 11/2: 2002-4U1: b c Polish Precedent -   **55a**
Diasprina (Aspros) In tch, smooth hdwy over 2f out & led over 1f out, rdn clr: apprt h'cap wnr for 7,200gns: 8 wk abs:
ex-German, plcd form last term: last won in '01: prev winning form at 6.5f/7.5f, now stays easy 10f well: acts on
polytrack & hvy grnd: goes well fresh in sell grade & suited by visor.

866   **PARADISE VALLEY 16** [9] Mrs Stef Liddiard 4-9-13 t (52) S Drowne 7/2: 5-160502: Rear, eff to chase   3½   **53a**
front pair 2f out, not pace of wnr: op 4/1: see 347 & 125.

738   **SENOR TORAN 36** [4] P Burgoyne 4-9-9 (47) L Keniry(3) 8/1: 5500-343: Dwelt, led after 2f till over   *nk*   **48a**
1f out, no extra: jumps fit (p.u.): see 738 & 540.

890   **MUQTADI 11** [1] M Quinn 6-9-13 (50) S Sanders 8/1: 0415004: Mid-div, lost place & drpd rear   3½   **47a**
halfway, kept on late, no dngr: op 10/1: has ability for this grade but a tricky ride: see 717 (1m, seller).

985   **IPLEDGEALLEGIANCE 3** [2]8-9-9 (35) P Makin(7) 16/1: 6500055: Chsd ldrs, onepace fnl 3f, qck reapp.   *nk*   **42a$**
970   **PYRRHIC 4** [7]5-9-9 bl (45) E Ahern 10/1: 0650606: Mid-div, no impress fnl 2f, op 8/1, qck reapp.   5   **35a**
539   **PRINCE IVOR 59** [5]4-9-9 BL (35) P Dobbs 66/1: 50000-07: b g Polar Falcon - Mistook (Phone Trick)   18   **10a**
Led/dsptd lead 7f, wknd qckly: tried blnks, jumps fit (mod): unplcd '03 (rtd 52a & 44, tried visor, R Hannon):
unplcd '02 (rtd 79): tried blnks today, found to be coughing after the race.

912   **DECELERATE 9** [6]4-9-13 (55) R Hughes 7/4 FAV: 33310-08: Trkd ldrs, lost pl 2f out, eased, lame.   21   **0a**
8 Ran   Time 2m 07.67 (4.87)   Owned: Mrs Ruth M Serrell   Trained: Lingfield

LINGFIELD Polytrack FRIDAY 02.04.04 Lefthand, V Sharp Track

1027 5.05 Bet Direct Interactive Apprentice Handicap Stakes 3yo+ 0-80 (E) [80]
£4719 £1452 £726   1m2f aw   Going 19   -41 Slow   Inside

877	**TIGHT SQUEEZE 14** [1] P W Hiatt 7-10-0 (80) P Makin 13/2: 5300101: Dictated pace & sn well clr, given breather halfway, pulled clr over 2f out, readily: slow time, op 11/2: eff at 10/12f on fast, gd/soft & polytrack, handles fibresand & loves Lingfield: enjoyed forcing tactics under a well judged ride: see 736 & 218.		89a
726	**BANK ON HIM 37** [2] G L Moore 9-8-10 (62) Jemma Marshall(7) 9/2: 1612222: Keen, chsd clr ldr, kept on fnl 2f, no impress: most tough & consistent: see 498 (C/D).	3½	64a
4433}	**GIUNCHIGLIO 191** [5] W M Brisbourne 5-8-10 (62) B Swarbrick 6/1: 365600-3: ch g Millkom - Daffodil Fields (Try My Best) Trkd ldrs, onepace fnl 3f: op 7/1, reapp: h'cap rnr-up '03, subs tried visor, P Makin: class stks rnr-up '02: eff around 10f on fast & gd grnd, prob handles polytrack: AW bow today. 2 May'03 Sout 10g/f 70-69 E: 2 Jun'02 Nott 9.9gd 70- E:	1¼	62a
716	**BARRY ISLAND 38** [3] D R C Elsworth 5-9-12 (78) M Lawson 5/2 FAV: 04-15244: Keen in rear, only mod prog for press: bckd: btr 716 & 570.	1	77a
877	**BRILLIANT RED 14** [6]11-9-13 t [79] M Halford(5) 8/1: 3-006405: Slow away, no impress fnl 2f.	1½	76a
888	**PARAGON OF VIRTUE 13** [7]7-9-11 (77) S Donohoe 11/4: 10-34036: Held up, btn over 2f out: bckd.	¾	73a
6 Ran	Time 2m 08.76(5.96) Owned: Mr Anthony Harrison Trained: Banbury		

SOUTHWELL Fibresand FRIDAY 02.04.04 Lefthand, Sharp, Oval Track

Official Going Standard

1028 2.20 Bloor Homes Fiskerton Amateur Riders' Handicap Stakes 3yo+ 46-55 (F) [41]
£2954 £844 £422   1m aw rnd   Going 88   -05 Slow   Inside

776*	**RUST EN VREDE 33** [16] D Carroll 5-10-12 (53) Miss D Allman(7) 10/1: 03600-11: Chsd ldrs, styd on to lead dist, pushed clr, val 6L+: eff around a sharp or stiff/turning 1m, poss stays 10f: acts on firm grnd, likes fibresand: in fine form at present & can land hat-trick: see 776.		67a+
893	**WILSON BLUEBOTTLE 11** [10] M W Easterby 5-10-5 (1oh)bl (45) Miss S Brotherton 11/2: 00-61022: Cl-up, led 4f out bhd, not pace easy wnr: remains in form: see 893 (banded).	3½	50a
711	**SECAM 38** [14] Mrs P Townsley 5-10-6 (47) Mrs C Thompson(5) 33/1: 31321-03: gr g Alywar - Scytia (Euro Star) Cl-up, no extra fnl 1f: recent hdles unplcd (rtd 79h, nov hdle): ex-Polish, won twice on Flat in '03 (1m, gd): wnr in late '02 (1m, gd).	3½	44a
961*	**SORBIESHARRY 4** [3] Mrs N Macauley 5-10-13 (6ex)p (54) Mrs M Morris 7/1: 3515014: Held up, kept on fnl 2f, nrst fin: qck reapp: just btr 961.	nk	50a
96	**NIMBUS TWOTHOUSAND 129** [4]4-10-5 (1oh) (45) Mr E Dehdashti(3) 25/1: 605006-5: b f Cloudings - Blueberry Parkes (Pursuit of Love) Bhd, prog wide 3f out, onepcd ins fnl 2f: long abs: unplcd in '03 (rtd 55 & 43a, clmr & h'cap): modest form in '02: has tried blnks.	½	41a
957*	**OUR DESTINY 4** [15]6-11-1 (6ex)vis (56) Mrs S Bosley 9/2: 3240116: Chsd ldrs, no extra fnl 2f: qck reapp: btr 957 (clmr).	2½	46a
845	**KUMAKAWA 19** [11]6-10-8 bl (49) Mr C Witheford(7) 16/1: 0300267: Held up, nvr nrr than mid-div.	¾	38a
924	**CRUSOE 8** [12]7-11-0 bl (55) Mr L Newnes(5) 9/1: 0-300408: Chsd ldrs, wknd 2f out: btr 868.	2½	39a
913	**MUTARAFAA 9** [13]5-10-12 e (53) Ms C Williams 4/1 FAV: 4000209: Slow away, nvr nrr than mid-div.	nk	36a
905	**PRINCE MINATA 10** [9]9-10-5 (6oh) (40) Miss A Hockley(7) 14/1: 006-0030: 10th: Al bhd: btr 905.	2½	24a
956	**ILLUSTRIOUS DUKE 4** [7]6-10-5 (6oh)bl (40) Miss M Mullineaux(7) 20/1: 0-000060: 11th: Led, hdd 4f out, sn fdd: qck reapp.	¾	23a
564	**HOHS BACK 56** [5]5-11-0 p (55) Mr P Evans(5) 16/1: 2000-000: 12th: Cl-up, fdd 2f out: 8 wk abs.	5	22a
722	**ACE MA VAHRA 38** [2]6-10-7 P (48) Miss Kelly Harrison(3) 14/1: 3/-606160: 13th: Al in rear.	nk	14a
304}	**SUNRIDGE FAIRY 456** [8]5-10-10 (51) Miss J Foster(5) 25/1: 13060/0-0: 14th: Al bhd.	2	13a
905	**TERN INTERN 10** [6]5-10-5 (16oh)bl (30) Miss Fiona Brown(7) 50/1: 000-0000: 15th: Slow away, al rear.	14	0a
15 Ran	Time 1m 46.87 (7.47) Owned: Mr Alan Mann Trained: Warthilll		

1029 2.55 Esp Experience Challenge Maiden Auction Stakes Fillies 2yo (F)
£2863 £818 £409   5f aw str   Going 88   Inapplicable   Outside

	NOVA TOR [7] P C Haslam 2-8-2 Rory Moore(7) 4/1: 1: b f Trans Island - Nordic Living (Nordico) In tch, hung left, styd on to lead ins fnl 1f, pushed out hands & heels, val 2L+: debut: op 6/1: April foal, cost £5,000: half-sister to numerous wnrs at sprint dists: dam unplcd, sire high-class at 1m: eff at 5f, 6f shld suit: acts on fibresand & goes well fresh: gd first start.		68a+
	LADY ERICA [6] K R Burke 2-8-4 G Faulkner 7/2: 2: b f Komaite - Zamarra (Clantime) Led, hung badly left & hdd ins fnl 1f, not pace of wnr: op 5/2 on debut: April foal, cost 6,000gns: half-sister to a 5f juv wnr: sire 7f wnr: eff at 5f, 6f shld suit: acts on fibresand.	¾	65a
938	**NUTTY TIMES 6** [2] W G M Turner 2-8-2 A Daly 100/30 FAV: 23: Cl-up, outpcd 3f out, rallying when short of room dist, switched & kept on well fnl 1f: qck reapp: ran to form of 2nd in 938 (seller).	1¼	59a
	GLASSON LODGE [4] P D Evans 2-8-2 P Hanagan 10/1: 4: b f Primo Dominie - Petrikov (In The Wings) Sn in rear, kept on late: debut: op 7/1: April foal, cost 3,000gns: half-sister to a juv wnr abroad: dam unrcd: sire top-class juv: eff at 5f, bred to apprec further: acts on fibresand.	1¼	55a
	VOICE OF AN ANGEL [3]2-8-2 G Duffield 11/2: 5: Hmpd start, cl-up, hung left & fdd dist.	½	54a
920	**SAHARA MIST 8** [5]2-8-4 Lisa Jones(3) 16/1: 06: Keen cl-up, no extra fnl 2f: see 920.	1¾	51a
962	**KILKENNY KITTEN 4** [1]2-8-4 t Kim Tinkler 4/1: 67: Cl-up, fdd dist: well bckd from 12/1.	shd	50a
7 Ran	Time 1m 03.09 (5.29) Owned: Blue Lion Racing III Trained: Middleham		

268

1030   3.30 Betdirect Co Uk Maiden Stakes 3yo+   (D)
£3702 £1139 £570   **1m4f aw**   **Going 88**   **+07 Fast**   outside

DANCE WORLD 246 [6] Miss J Feilden 4-9-11 B Reilly(3) 4/1: 424-1: b g Spectrum - Dansara   **70a+**
(Dancing Brave) Chsd ldrs, styd on to lead dist, pushed clr, val 5L+: reapp & Brit bow, gd time: ex-French, plcd on
1 of 3 '03 starts: eff at 12/14f on gd & f/sand: goes well fresh: gd start & can rate higher.
801   **MASJOOR** 29 [2] N A Graham 4-9-11 (59) J Murtagh 9/4: 030-02: Cl-up, kept on fnl 1f, no ch with   2½   **63a**
easy wnr: stays 12f on fibresand: see 801.
608   **PEPE** 50 [7] R Hollinshead 3-8-0 (48) Dale Gibson 50/1: 06-663: b f Bahhare - Orange And Blue   3½   **53a**
(Prince Sabo) Led, hdd 2f out, wknd dist: clr rem: 7 wk abs: unplcd both '03 starts (rtd 55, auct mdn): eff at
12f on fibresand: has tried cheek pieces.
4871}   **PRAIRIE SUN** 161 [4] Mrs A Duffield 3-8-0 G Duffield 20/1: 000-4: In tch wide, wknd fnl 2f.   7   **43a**
867   **IT MUST BE SPEECH** 15 [1]3-8-5 (65) A Nicholls 4/1: 0000-525: Al bhd: tchd 7/1: btr 867.   13   **31a**
561   **MARINO MOU** 56 [5]4-9-11 BL G Carter 66/1: 006: Slow away, al in rear: 8 wk abs & tried blnks.   21   **6a**
873   **BORDER SAINT** 14 [3]3-8-5 J Mackay 15/8 FAV: 37: In tch, fdd 3f out: v disappointing effort &   13   **0a**
was found to be "tying up bhd": btr 873 (debut).
7 Ran   Time 2m 44.07 (9.77)   Owned: Stowstowquickquickstow Partnership   Trained: Newmarket

---

1031   4.05 Littlewoods Bet Direct Handicap Stakes 3yo 0-70   (E)
£3721 £1145 £573   **5f aw str**   **Going 88**   **Inapplicable**   Inside   [77]

1002   **DEMOLITION MOLLY** 2 [2] R F Marvin 3-8-13 t p (62) L Fletcher(3) 5/2: 54-06021: Made all, clr ins   **76a**
fnl 1f, drvn out: well bckd on qck reapp: eff at 5f on firm, fast grnd & fibresand: eff with t-strap & cheek
pieces: improving, can defy a pen: see 1002 & 712.
1002   **DESERT LIGHT** 2 [3] D Shaw 3-8-4 vis (53) Lisa Jones(3) 13/2: 60-13002: Cl-up, kept on fnl 1f, not   3   **57a**
pace of wnr: tchd 9/1 on qck reapp: betterr eff on return to fibresand: see 327 & 377.
548   **BLUE POWER** 58 [6] K R Burke 3-8-13 (62) Darren Williams 13/2: 4213-003: Mid-div, styd on under   1¼   **62a**
press 2f out, onepcd fnl 1f: tchd 8/1: 8 wk abs: btr 169 (C/D).
914   **ONLY IF I LAUGH** 9 [7] B J Meehan 3-9-7 (70) J F McDonald(5) 7/4 FAV: 16504-34: Handy, edged left   1   **67a**
& no extra dist: btr expected after promise in 3rd in 914 (polytrack).
4695}   **LOVEISDANGEROUS** 173 [1]3-8-6 (55) Kim Tinkler 16/1: 235206-5: b f Pursuit of Love - Brookhead   nk   **51a**
Lady (Petong) Handy, wknd bef 1f out: reapp: sell wnr in '03 (also plcd 4 times): eff at 5f, has tried 6f: acts
on fast & gd grnd, stiff/gall trk: suited by forcing tactics & cheek pieces: best form has come in sell grade.
2 Aug'03 Wind 5.0g/f 56-(58) F: 2 Jul'03 Folk 5g/f 59- F: 1 Jul'03 Leic 5.0g/f 63- G: 2 Jul'03 Leic 5.0gd 55- G:
995   **LAVISH TIMES** 2 [4]3-8-2 bl (51) G Duffield 10/1: 30-05306: Cl-up, wknd fnl 2f: qck reapp: see 703.   ¾   **45a**
872   **INDRANI** 15 [5]3-7-12 (2oh) (45) D Fentiman(7) 25/1: 60-06407: Mid-div, wknd 2f out: see 797.   2½   **34a**
725   **LAKESIDE GUY** 37 [8]3-8-8 T (57) O Urbina 14/1: 0-0048: b c Revoque - Glen of Imaal (Common   9   **20a**
Grounds) Al in rear: fitted with t-strap: modest form to date.
8 Ran   Time 1m 0.66 (2.86)   Owned: Mr D Blott   Trained: Rolleston

---

1032   4.40 #10 Free Bet @ Betdirect Co Uk Selling Stakes 3yo+   (G)
£2541 £726 £363   **6f aw rnd**   **Going 88**   **-05 Slow**   Outside

907   **ON THE TRAIL** 10 [5] D W Chapman 7-9-13 (45) A Culhane 7/2: 0000131: Cl-up, led dist, drvn out: **55a**
no bid: stays 7f, best up with/forcing the pace at 6f on both AWs: win again in this grade: see 907 & 822.
963   **PAWAN** 4 [2] N Tinkler 4-9-9 (62) Kim Tinkler 5/1: 4/202-52: Sn in rear, prog to chase wnr dist,   1¼   **46a**
kept on but al held ins fnl 1f: qck reapp: acts on fast, gd & fibresand: not disgraced on AW bow: btr 963.
905   **RATHMULLAN** 10 [7] E A Wheeler 5-9-9 bl (35) Liam Jones(7) 33/1: 0000-003: In tch wide, onepcd dist.   2   **40a**
500   **FESTIVE AFFAIR** 64 [3] B Smart 6-9-9 (47) F Lynch 9/2: 4300-304: b g Mujadil - Christmas Kiss   10   **15a**
(Taufan) Cl-up, led 2f out, hdd dist, sn fdd & eased: 9 wk abs: AW sell wnr in early '03: mdn wnr in '01: suited
by 6f on f/sand, has tried t-strap: can break blood vessels, had an irregular heartbeat today.
1 Jan'03 Sout 6af 57a- G: 2 Dec'02 Sout 6af 51a- G: 2 Mar'01 Nott 6hvy 66-60 E: 1 Feb'01 Sout 6af 66a- D:
941   **POLAR HAZE** 6 [1]7-9-13 bl (56) R Price 5/2 FAV: 2615045: Al in rear: tchd 7/2 on qck reapp: v   1   **16a**
disapp on return of blnks: btr 533 (visor).
830   **KELTIC FLUTE** 24 [6]5-9-9 vis (30) D Nolan(5) 20/1: 0/-040606: b g Piccolo - Nanny Doon (Dominion)   1¼   **8a**
Cl-up, wknd fnl 2f: unplcd sole 02/03 hdle start (rtd 65h): rnr-up once in '02 (seller, D Morris): eff at 7f on
fast grnd, acts on an easy trk: has tried blnks & visor: with Mrs Lucinda Featherstone.
2 Jul'02 Yarm 7g/f 43- G:
533   **CZAR WARS** 59 [4]9-9-0 bl (63) L Fletcher(3) 4/1: 2130-067: Led, hdd 2f out, sn fdd: 8 wk abs.   7   **0a**
7 Ran   Time 1m 18.91 (5.61)   Owned: Mr J M Chapman   Trained: York

---

1033   5.15 Sponsors Day Handicap Stakes 4yo+ 46-55   (F)
£2996 £856 £428   **1m6f**   **Going 88**   **+03 Fast**   Outside   [65]

867   **JUNGLE LION** 15 [9] John A Harris 6-8-8 (1oh) (45) Dean McKeown 18/1: 0-620101: In tch, led dist,   **51a**
drvn out fnl 1f: eff at 9f, stays 12/14f, acts on f/sand & hvy: eff with t-strap: back to form, see 774.
891*   **ISAAF** 11 [12] P W Hiatt 5-8-13 (6ex) (51) A Culhane 9/4 FAV: 06602-12: Cl-up, led 3f out, hdd   3½   **53a**
dist, sn no extra: tchd 3/1: ran to form of win in 891 (banded, 12f).
852   **THE BEDUTH NAVI** 19 [4] D G Bridgwater 4-8-6 (2oh) (47) Dale Gibson 11/1: 00-22123: Led, hdd 4f   ½   **48a**
out, rallied bef 1f out, kept on late: proving consistent: see 852 & 823.
774   **BROUGHTON KNOWS** 33 [6] W J Musson 7-9-2 bl (54) Lisa Jones(3) 17/2: 2-111124: Held up, hdwy 3f   nk   **54a**
out, kept on fnl 1f: see 774 & 722.
984   **WESTERN COMMAND** 3 [14]8-8-8 (16oh)p (30) Joanna Badger 50/1: 6050055: Held up, sn hung right,   shd   **45a**
prog 5f out, sn outpcd, rallied fnl 1f: clr rem: see 456.
4033}   **LIGHT BRIGADE** 212 [10]5-8-11 (49) J Mackay 16/1: 0506/03-6: b g Kris - Mafatin (Sadler's Wells)   9   **40a**
In tch, ev ch 2f out, sn fdd: reapp: plcd on last of only 3 '03 starts (mdn, rtd 72a): unplcd in '02 (rtd 49 &
34a, h'caps): eff at 12f on polytrack, has tried a visor.
554   **LAMPOS** 57 [16]4-9-0 (55) R Winston 4/1: 30-31257: Chsd ldrs, wknd fnl 3f: 8 wk abs: btr 491 (2m).   10   **37a**

SOUTHWELL Fibresand FRIDAY 02.04.04 Lefthand, Sharp, Oval Track

733	**BROUGHTONS FLUSH 36** [5]6-8-8 (1oh) (45) F Lynch 25/1: 11150/-08: Al in rear: see 733.		5	23a
866	**SWING WEST 16** [11]10-8-8 (16oh)P (30) S Righton 80/1: 0400/0-49: Al bhd: cheek pieces.		hd	22a
937*	**FFIFFIFFER 6** [7]6-9-9 (6ex) (61) S Hitchcott(3) 7/2: 5225-410: 10th: Cl-up, fdd 3f out: qck		3	34a

reapp: disapp run on step up to 14f: btr 937 (12f).

849	**EAST CAPE 19** [15]7-8-8 (1oh) (45) Kim Tinkler 22/1: 0-530100: 11th: Al in rear: btr 724.		2	17a
774	**FORTUNES FAVOURITE 33** [8]4-8-5 (9oh) (40) N Pollard 40/1: 045-0340: 12th: Cl-up, led 4f out, hdd		3½	14a

3f out, sn wknd: btr 638.

891	**Bid Spotter 11** [3]5-8-8 (1oh)p(45) G Duffield 50/1:0	324	**Morvern 87** [13]4-8-10 vis(51) M Fenton 20/1:0
816	**Star Seventeen 25** [1]6-8-12 (50) D Corby(3) 50/1:0	733	**Seans Memory 36** [2]4-8-9 p(50) G Faulkner 33/1:P

16 Ran   Time 3m 11.75(11.95)   Owned: Mr Mick Rowley   Trained: Melton Mowbray

NEWCASTLE SATURDAY 03.04.04 Lefthand, Galloping, Stiff Track

Official Going HEAVY.

1034   1.40 Cantorsport Co Uk Handicap Stakes 3yo+ 0-75 (E)   [74]
£5129 £1578 £789   **1m4f93y**   **Heavy 159**   -08 Slow   Inside.

918	**ARCHIE BABE 9** [9] J J Quinn 8-9-1 (61) K Darley 5/1: 04000-01: ch g Archway - Frensham Manor (Le		68

Johnstan: Prom trav well, hdwy to lead 3f out, pushed clr fnl 1f: nicely bckd: won a nov hdle in Nov '03 (eff at 2m on soft, rtd 122h): dual h'cap wnr in '03: eff at 10/12f, acts on firm & gd/soft, revels in soft & hvy: gd weight carrier, handles any trk, likes Pontefract: well h'capped, win again in the mud.
1 May'03 Pont 12.0g/s 70-64 E: 1 Mar'03 Donc 12g/s 65-59 E: 2 Jul'01 Hami 11gd 67-65 E:

801	**BRAMANTINO 30** [14] R A Fahey 4-8-12 bl (59) P Hanagan 12/1: 00-53102: Chsd ldrs, imprvd to chase	6	61

wnr dist, no impress ins fnl 1f: clr of 3rd: stays 12f on fm, hvy & fibresand: see 746.

590	**NAKWA 54** [10] E J Alston 6-8-10 (56) D Allan(3) 4/1: 43-12253: Keen & prom, led 4f out till 3f	5	51

out, left bhnd bef dist: clr of rem, 8 wk abs: prev in gd form on AW: see 484 & 315.

854]	**LUCKY JUDGE 737** [11] G A Swinbank 7-9-0 (60) R Winston 20/1: 25535/4/-4: b g Saddlers' Hall -	8	45

Lady Lydia (Ela Mana Mou) Rear, prog 3f out, sn no impress: comeback: missed '03, 4th on sole '02 start (h'cap, rtd 61): '01 mdn hdle wnr (rtd 108h, eff at 2m4f on gd): '01 h'cap wnr: eff at 13f/2m on fast & hvy: tried vis.
2 Jun'01 Muss 16g/f 66-65 E: 1 May'01 Hami 13gd 66-63 E:

924	**NOUL 9** [3]5-8-13 P (59) N Callan 10/1: 21-02555: Rear, nvr a factor: cheekpieces, longer trip.	13	29
86	**SCURRA 131** [1]5-8-7 (53) R Ffrench 33/1: 040320-6: b g Spectrum - Tamnia (Green Desert) Prom	1½	21

till after halfway, wknd: reapp: plcd in '03 (h'cap & claim): eff at 9/11f on fast, hvy & fibresand: still a mdn.
2 Oct'03 Redc 11g/f 52-(44) F: 2 Nov'01 Catt 7g/s 77- E:

965	**TONI ALCALA 5** [4]5-9-3 (63) L Fletcher(3) 10/1: 040-3547: Nvr nr ldrs: qck reapp.	2	29
4488}	**REGAL VINTAGE 189** [7]4-9-8 vis (69) T Hamilton(3) 66/1: 0/600-8: Rdn in rear, nvr dngrs: jumps fit.	nk	34
752	**EASIBET DOT NET 36** [2]4-9-0 p (61) D McGaffin 14/1: 23215-49: Chsd ldrs, wknd 3f out: see 752.	7	16
529	**LA MUETTE 60** [8]4-10-0 (75) D Fentiman(7) 33/1: 1/5300-00: 10th: Rdn in rear, nvr dngrs: jumps fit.	7	20
2858}	**WEAVER OF DREAMS 266** [12]4-8-1 (48) Dale Gibson 25/1: 0/00550-0: 11th: Rear wide, btn 4f out.	3	0
4832}	**STAFF NURSE 165** [6]4-7-12 (45) Kim Tinkler 20/1: 532353-0: 12th: Al bhnd, t.o.: reapp/new yard.	7	0
622	**DARK CAT 49** [13]4-8-3 (50) R Lappin 40/1: 0/2100-00: 13th: Held up, al bhnd, t.o.: 7 wk abs.	4	0
918	**ARCHIRONDEL 9** [15]6-8-6 (52) J Fanning 33/1: 030-60U0: 14th: Led halfway till 4f out, wknd, t.o.	6	0
4481*	}ALNAJA 189 [5]5-9-10 (70) M Hills 3/1 FAV: 603231-P: Led till halfway, sn wknd, t.o./p.u. fnl		0

1f: dismounted & reportedly swallowed tongue: nicely bckd, reapp: worth another chance.
15 Ran   Time 2m 58.70 (20.80)   Owned: Bowett Lamb & Kelly   Trained: Malton

1035   2.10 Betfred Sprint Series Handicap Stakes Qualifier 3yo+ 0-95 (C)   [94]
£13728 £4224 £2112   **7f str**   **Heavy 159**   +11 Fast   Stands Side.

687	**TIDY 43** [3] M D Hammond 4-8-8 (74) Darren Williams 66/1: 13060-01: b c Mujadil - Neat Shilling		83

(Bob Back) Nvr far away, led 2f out, styd on strongly fnl 1f, rdn out: 6 wk abs, gd time: p.u. on sole 03/04 jumps start: '03 h'cap wnr (J Osbourne, reapp): '02 mdn auct wnr: eff at 6/7f on fast, likes hvy & fibresand: handles a sharp or gall trk, runs well fresh: back on a wng mark & a surprise win.
1 May'03 Hayd 6sft 80-74 D: 1 Nov'02 Wolv 6af 78a- F: 2 Oct'02 Sout 6af 70a- F:

945*	**ZILCH 7** [5] M L W Bell 6-9-3 (83) S Sanders 9/4 FAV: 3/0003-12: Nvr far away, led 3f out till 2f	1	89

out, not pace of wnr ins fnl 1f: well bckd: remains in fine form & excels in testing conditions: see 945.

887	**MOAYED 14** [10] N P Littmoden 5-9-0 bl t (80) E Ahern 8/1: 00-12633: Rear, prog to chase ldrs 2f	2½	80

out, not qckn fnl 1f: not always find as much as expected, but consistent: see 887.

945	**DIGITAL 7** [14] M R Channon 7-9-2 (92) S Hitchcott(3) 13/2: 6002-034: Prom, ev ch halfway, onepcd	2½	86

& drifted left fnl 1.5f: qck reapp: again bhnd today's 2nd in 945.

921	**CHAPPEL CRESENT 9** [13]4-9-7 (87) L Treadwell(7) 20/1: 540-0005: Chsd ldrs, onepcd fnl 2f: acts	½	80

on gd & gd/soft, prob handles hvy grnd: see 511 (AW).

921	**NAMROUD 9** [8]5-9-8 (88) P Hanagan 33/1: 31210-06: b g Irish River - Top Line (Top Ville) Rear,	nk	80

switched & some hdwy dist, nvr nr ldrs: '03 mdn & h'cap wnr for Sir M Stoute: eff at 7f/1m on gd & fast, poss hvy: handles a fair or v tight trk: now with R Fahey & will apprec a return to faster grnd.
1 Jun'03 Ches 7.0g/f 91-87 C: 2 May'03 Good 8g/f 88-84 C: 1 Apr'03 Yarm 8.0gd 82- D:

951	**TOUGH LOVE 7** [6]5-9-11 (91) K Dalgleish 16/1: 21330-07: ch g Pursuit of Love - Food of Love	¾	81

(Music Boy) Held up, nvr nr ldrs: tough & prog in '03, dual h'cap wnr, also plcd sev times (val h'caps, incl reapp): suited by 7f/1m on gd & fast grnd, handles soft: 01 was a stiff/gall trk, runs well fresh: gd weight carrier, has a fine turn of foot & will relish a return to a faster surface.
1 Jun'03 Hayd 8.1g/f 93-82 C: 2 May'03 Muss 8gd 84-(82) D: 2 Nov'02 Muss 8.5gd 84-80 C: 1 Apr'03 Pont 8.0g/f 81-75 C:
1 Apr'02 Beve 7.4g/f 80-70 C: 2 Aug'01 Ripo 6gd 75- D: 1 Jul'01 Newc 6g/f 86- E:

4768+	**FLOWERDRUM 170** [11]4-8-11 (77) M Hills 11/4: 02/1101-8: Held up, nvr a factor: reapp, op 9/4.	1½	64
928	**GO TECH 8** [9]4-9-3 (83) D Allan(3) 25/1: 50005-09: Keen in rear, nvr dngrs.	½	69
967	**FAIR SHAKE 5** [7]4-8-1 (67) Dale Gibson 14/1: 10600-00: 10th: Chsd ldrs 5f, wknd: qck reapp.	5	41
4888}	**COLEMANSTOWN 161** [15]4-8-8 (74) T Eaves(5) 20/1: 400056-0: 11th: Al rear on reapp.	7	32
4539+	**FANTASY BELIEVER 185** [12]6-10-0 (94) K Darley 12/1: 102041-0: 12th: Keen & prom 5f, wknd, t.o.	24	2
838	**SILVER SEEKER 21** [1]4-9-9 p (89) R Winston 33/1: 310/0-50: 13th: Led till 3f out, wknd, t.o.	15	0

270

NEWCASTLE   SATURDAY 03.04.04   Lefthand, Galloping, Stiff Track

13 Ran   Time 1m 34.48 (10.38)   Owned: Mr P Davies and Mr L Crowther   Trained: Middleham

---

1036   2.40 Cantorodds Co Uk Handicap Stakes 3yo+ 0-80 (D)   **[80]**
£8304 £2555 £1278   **1m3y str   Heavy 159   -05 Slow**   Stands Side. 2 Groups.

932   **TROUSERS 8** [4] Andrew Reid 5-8-3 (55) G Duffield 15/2: 32136-01: b g Pivotal - Palo Blanco   64
(Precocious) Made all far side, led 1fr, rdn out: '03 AW mdn wnr, also plcd twice (incl turf h'cap): eff at
1m/9f on fast, hvy & polytrack: handles a gall or sharp trk, runs well fresh: likes to run up with or force the pace.
1 Oct'03 Ling 8ap 76a-(54) D: 2 Aug'03 Good 9g/f 54-46 D:
4920} **TOP DIRHAM 158** [17] M W Easterby 6-9-4 (70) Dale Gibson 20/1: 500000-2: ch g Night Shift -   3   73
Miller's Melody (Chief Singer) Trkd ldr stands side, led that gronp dist, no ch with far side wnr fnl 1f: reapp:
dual h'cap wnr in '03: h'cap plcd in '02 (Sir M Stoute): eff at 7f/1m on fm & hvy: handles a stiff/undul trk: runs
well fresh: on a wng mark, can sn go one better.
1 Jun'03 Carl 7.9g/f 75-72 D: 1 Jun'03 Thir 8g/f 78-65 E: 1 Jun'01 Epso 7fm 93-82 B: 1 May'01 Newc 7.4fm 90- D:
569   **REAP 8** [16] J Pearce 6-9-1 (67) P Robinson 7/1 JT FAV: 01112-03: b g Emperor Jones - Corn   nk   69
Futures (Nomination) Led till dist stands side, kept on well fnl 1f, but no ch with wnr far side: 8 wk abs: won 3
h'caps & a class stks in '03: suited by 1m/10f on firm, hvy & both AW's: loves to dominate & likes Newcastle.
2 Oct'03 Redc 8g/f 70-67 E: 1 Oct'03 Newc 8.0fm 71-(67) F: 1 Oct'03 Newc 8.0gd 68-60 E: 1 Aug'03 Newm 8g/s 63-56 D:
1 Jul'03 Ripo 8g/f 60-53 E: 1 Apr'02 Wolv 8.4af 71a-58 D: 1 Mar'02 Wolv 8.4af 59a-55 E: 1 Feb'02 Wolv 9.3af 57a-50 F:
754   **GOODBYE MR BOND 36** [5] E J Alston 4-7-13 (51) J Mackay 8/1: 404-5634: Prom far side, onepace.   1½   51
4708} **COMMITMENT LECTURE 173** [13]4-7-13 T (51) R Ffrench 33/1: 164200-5: Rear, far side, styd on fnl   ½   50
1f, nvr nrr: tried a t-strap, reapp: encouraging & sharper next time.
4958} **MEGANS MAGIC 155** [11]4-8-8 (60) D R McCabe 16/1: 401542-6: Rear far side, late prog, nvr dngrs.   6   49
4063} **TORRID KENTAVR 212** [6]7-8-8 (60) T Eaves(4) 10/1: 342305-7: Held up, nvr a factor: reapp.   1¼   47
595   **HOV 53** [12]4-9-9 (75) E Ahern 16/1: 2540-008: Prom 6f far side: 8 wk abs.   hd   62
4540} **HULA BALLEW 185** [8]4-8-9 (61) P Hanagan 16/1: 213366-9: Nvr dngrs far side: reapp.   11   28
5021} **APACHE POINT 149** [1]7-8-8 (60) Kim Tinkler 9/1: 000024-0: 10th: Chsd ldrs 6f far side: reapp.   1¼   25
878   **HARRY POTTER 15** [2]5-9-4 vis (70) Darren Williams 16/1: 213-0030: 11th: Chsd ldrs 6f far side, fdd.   7   23
836   **CRESKELD 21** [19]5-9-6 (72) F Lynch 7/1 JT FAV: 53100-30: 12th: Chsd ldrs 5f stands side: see 836.   4   18
718   **SHIFTY 39** [7]5-8-1 (1ow)bl (52) A Nicholls 25/1: 3426-500: 13th: Al rear far side.   8   0
2532} **CELTIC ROMANCE 278** [14]5-8-11 (63) J Carroll 33/1: 0/0/0000-0: 14th: Al rear far side: new stable.   1¼   0
932   **NIGHT WOLF 8** [10]4-9-3 (69) S Hitchcott(3) 8/1: 34415-60: 15th: Prom till halfway far side, wknd.   dist   0
4928} **TAGULA BLUE 158** [9]4-10-0 t (80) S Sanders 14/1: 621006-U: Dwelt, swereved & u.r. start: reapp.   0
16 Ran   Time 1m 50.18 (13.18)   Owned: Mr A S Reid   Trained: Mill Hill London

---

1037   3.15 E B F /Cantorindex Co Uk Novice Stakes 2yo (D)
£5021 £1545 £773   **5f str   Heavy 159   -27 Slow**   Stands Side.

920   **MITCHELLAND 9** [3] James Moffatt 2-8-7 J Fanning 9/4: 41: Keen & trkd ldr, went on dist, pushed   77
clr fnl 1f, readily: op 6/4: improved for debut on hvy grnd: eff at 5f: shld win a race: see 920 (debut).
943   **BIBURY FLYER 7** [4] M R Channon 2-8-7 S Hitchcott(3) 4/6 FAV: 22: Tried to make all, hdd dist &   5   67
no extra: well bckd: acts on soft & hvy grnd: shld win a race: see 943 (debut).
        PROCRASTINATE [5] R F Fisher 2-8-12 L Fletcher(3) 14/1: 3: ch g Rossini - May Hinton (Main   3½   64
Reef) Trkd ldrs till left bhnd fnl 1f on debut: April foal, cost E17,000: half brother to a 5f juv wnr, also a 1m
scorer: dam a sprint wng juv, also a 2yo performer: speedily bred, shld benefit from this & faster grnd.
        MOUNT EPHRAM [1] R F Fisher 2-8-12 S Righton 12/1: 4: b g Entrepreneur - Happy Dancer (Seattle   3½   56
Dancer) Prom till halfway on debut: Apr foal, cost E20,000: half brother to juv wnr Happy Camper: dam 1m juv wnr.
4 Ran   Time 1m 07.52 (9.32)   Owned: Mr R R Whitton   Trained: Cartmel

---

1038   4.05 Cantorsport Co Uk Maiden Stakes 3yo+ (D)
£3741 £1151 £576   **1m4f93y   Heavy 159   -61 Slow**   Inside.

4995} **OCTOBER MIST 151** [5] Mrs M Reveley 10-9-13 S Sanders 11/1: 3/2-1: gr g Roselier - Bonny Joe   75
(Derring Rose) Prom, went on 4f out, styd on strongly, drvn out: slow time: jumps fit, 4th in a h'cap chase (rtd
112c) & rnr-up over hdles (h'caps, rtd 138h, eff at 2m4f/3m on gd, likes soft & hvy): rnr-up on sole '03 start (mdn):
eff at 12f on soft & hvy grnd, will stay further: in form mudlark. 2 Nov'03 Catt 12.0sft 68- D:
4896} **TEMPLET 161** [6] I Semple 4-9-12 R Winston 8/1: 4-2: b c Souvenir Copy - Two Step Trudy (Capote)   2½   71
Chsd ldrs, went after wnr 2f out, kept on under press: clr of rem, reapp: 4th on sole '03 start (mdn, with J
Gosden, rtd 72): eff at 10/12f on gd & hvy grnd: sharper next time.
1534} **NOFAS MAGIC 323** [3] J L Dunlop 4-9-7 K Darley 9/4 FAV: 20-3: b f Rainbow Quest - Garah (Ajdal)   9   53
Chsd ldrs, rdn & outpcd fnl 2f: reapp, well bckd: rnr-up on 1st of 2 '03 starts (mdn): half sister to high-class
miler Olden Times: eff at 10f, 12f shld suit: acts on fast grnd: not handle hvy? 2 Apr'03 Newb 10.0g/f 79- D:
        SOUTHERN STAR 299 [8] R C Guest 4-9-12 N Callan 20/1: 24-4: Rear, nvr nr to chall: jumps fit.   4   52
2693} **TRANSIT 272** [1]5-9-13 p (65) T Eaves(5) 16/1: 00/0030-5: Held up, nvr dngrs: jumps fit.   3½   47
1005   **CELTIC VISION 3** [7]8-9-13 t S Righton 33/1: 66: Set pace t'll 4f out, wknd: qck reapp.   8   37
873   **FIDDLERS FORD 15** [2]3-8-6 (72) E Ahern 11/2: 0-322647: Chsd ldrs 1m, wknd, t.o.: btr 759 (AW).   dist   2
5007} **HATHLEN 150** [4]3-8-6 (77) S Hitchcott(3) 4/1: 223022-8: Chsd ldrs till halfway, t.o.: reapp.   ¾   1
8 Ran   Time 3m 05.20 (27.30)   Owned: Mrs E A Murray   Trained: Saltburn

---

1039   4.40 Cantorodds Co Uk Maiden Stakes Fillies 3yo+ (D)
£3838 £1181 £591   **1m3y str   Heavy 159   -78 Slow**   Stands Side.

        GLEN INNES [8] D R Loder 3-8-8 N Pollard 9/4: 1: b f Selkirk - Shinko Hermes (Sadler's Wells)   87+
Keen & chsd ldrs, imprvd to lead dist, sn well clr, easily on debut: slow time: drifted from 6/4: half sister to a
2m wnr in France: eff at 1m on hvy, runs well fresh: impressive debut, clearly revels in testing conditions.
        LYFORD LASS [3] I Semple 3-8-8 P Hanagan 10/1: 2: b f Bahamian Bounty - Ladykirk (Slip Anchor)   11   70
Keen & prom, outpcd 2f out, kept on for 2nd but no ch with wnr: debut, bckd from 25/1: related to wnrs: eff at 1m
on hvy grnd: not in same class as wnr, but likely to come on for this.
4505} **SHARDDA 187** [9] F Watson 4-9-9 (65) J Fanning 20/1: 430-3: b f Baratbea - Kronengold (Golden   1¼   68

NEWCASTLE   SATURDAY 03.04.04   Lefthand, Galloping, Stiff Track

Act) Prom till outpcd 2f out on reapp: encouraging fill mdn 4th on '03 debut (rtd 76$): eff at 1m on firm grnd, prob handles hvy: mid-dist bred.

881	**MISS ADELAIDE 14** [7] B W Hills 3-8-8 (80) M Hills 11/8 FAV: 43-44: Set pace till dist, no extra.		*hd*	**64**
4987}	**CHARMATIC 152** [1]3-8-8 S Sanders 14/1: 00-5: Wide in rear, nvr dngrs on reapp.		6	**58**
4993}	**SARATOGA SPLENDOUR 152** [5]3-8-8 Leanne Kershaw(7) 50/1: 00-6: Chsd ldrs till after halfway.		8	**44**
4305}	**BARTON FLOWER 199** [2]3-8-8 P Mulrennan(5) 25/1: 00-7: Prom till halfway, wknd on reapp.		5	**36**
4993}	**BABOUSHKA 152** [6]3-8-8 R Winston 13/2: 04-8: Prom 6f, wknd: reapp/new yard, tchd 12/1.		2	**33**

8 Ran   Time 1m 55.98(18.98)   Owned: Sheikh Mohammed   Trained: Newmarket

LINGFIELD   Polytrack   SATURDAY 03.04.04   Lefthand, V Sharp Track

Official Going Standard

1040 1.55 Listed Shadwell Stud International Trial Stakes 3yo (A)
£26000 £8000 £4000   1m aw rnd   Going 23   +11 Fast   Outside

4198} **LEITRIM HOUSE 204** [5] B J Meehan 3-8-11 S Drowne : 16-1: ch c Cadeaux Genereux - Lonely Heart **110a**
(Midyan) Trkd ldrs, rdn to lead ins last, styd on wll for press: best time of the day: reapp: lightly rcd '03, landing a mdn on debut bef Gr 2 6th (rtd 95): suited by step up to 1m: wng form on fm & polytrk: acts on a sharp or stiff & undul trk: goes well fresh: smart, progressed well from 2 to 3. 1 Aug'03 Newm 6fm 94- D:

4797*}**MILK IT MICK 168** [7] J A Osborne 3-9-0 (118) D Holland 20/1: 432511-2: b c Millkom - Lunar Music **109a**
(Komaite) Keen early rear, hdwy wide 2f out, styd on for press, not threaten wnr: hvly bckd on reapp: reapp: v tough juv, 5 wins, culminating in shock Gr 1 Dewhurst success: v eff at 7f, styd this sharp 1m well: acts on fm, gd/sft, polytrack & any trk: thrives on racing, v smart, set for another Guineas prep.
1 Oct'03 Newm 7g/f 117-(100) A: 1 Oct'03 Newm 7g/f 112-(100) A: 2 Aug'03 Sand 7.1g/s 110-(100) A:
1 Jun '03 Sali 6fm 96-B: 1 Jun'03 Wind 6g/f 92- E: 1 May'03 Beve 5gd 94- E:

727* **SKIDMARK 38** [9] D R C Elsworth 3-8-11 (92) J Murtagh 7/4 FAV: 31-2113: Rear, styd on wide for *1½* **106a**
press, nrst fin: op 7/1: eff at 1m, holds a Dante/Derby entry & a return to 10f+ will suit: up in grade & an imprvd effort in defeat, v useful & progressive, win again: see 727, 568.

885* **ROSENCRANS 14** [2] Saeed bin Suroor 3-8-11 vis t L Dettori 8/1: 1-3114: Led, rdn & hdd ins last, *shd* **104a**
no extra: bckd, tho' op 13/8: stays 1m, 7f prob suits this front runner best: just btr 885 (7f, Listed).

3253} **KINGS POINT 248** [6]3-8-11 (107) R Hughes 2/1: 24116-5: b c Fasliyev - Rahika Rose (Unfuwain) *1* **101a**
Rear, eff 2f out, no impress dist: op 8/1, reapp: mdn & Gr 3 scorer '03: winning form at 6/7f, dam 7f/1m wnr: this term: acts on firm & polytrk, handles gd & prob any trk: lightly & v useful.
1 Jul'03 Newm 7fm 105- A: 1 Jun'03 Good 6fm 93- D: 2 May'03 York 5.0fm 90- D:

885 **CROCODILE DUNDEE 14** [1]3-8-11 (90) J F Egan 10/1: 105-06: Trkd ldrs, btn dist. *1½* **100a**
885 **BRAVO MAESTRO 14** [3]3-8-11 (95) T Quinn 33/1: 011-67: Keen, mid div, eff over 2f out, no extra. *½* **99a**
3253} **PARKVIEW LOVE 248** [4]3-8-11 (104) S Chin 9/1: 12165-8: Prom, btn over 1f out, reapp. *½* **96a**
706* **ILE FACILE 40** [8]3-8-11 (67) S W Kelly 200/1: 242419: Dwelt, keen & sn cl up, btn 3f out: abs: *23* **51a**
supposed to act as pacemaker for Milk It Mick but could never get to the lead: see 706 (6f, mdn).

9 Ran   Time 1m 37.16 (0.96)   Owned: Gallagher Equine Ltd   Trained: Upper Lambourn

1041 2.30 Betdirect Co Uk Maiden Auction Stakes 2yo (E)
£3377 £1039 £520   5f aw rnd   Going 23   -06 Slow   Outside

943 **CANTON 7** [5] R Hannon 2-9-0 Dane O'Neill 3/1: 61: b c Desert Style - Thirlmere (Cadeaux **89a+**
Genereux) Slow away, sn trkd ldr, rdn to lead over 1f out & styd on strongly under hands & heels ins last: gd juv time: left soft ground debut bhd: Feb foal, cost 30,000gns: half brother to use 6/7f h'capper Banjo Bay: dam unraced: eff at 5f, shld get further: likes polytrk & sharp trk: wiin again.

931 **EVANESCE 8** [2] M R Channon 2-8-2 C Catlin 1/1 FAV: 22: Trkd ldr, went on over 2f out, hdd over *1½* **70a**
1f out & not pace of wnr: well clr of rem: see 931 (C/D).

MAJESTICAL 0 [1] W R Muir 2-9-0 Martin Dwyer 12/1: 3: b c Fayruz - Haraabah (Topsider) Slow *6* **65a**
away & pushed along, efft over 2f out, sn outpcd by front rapr: Apr foal, cost 30,000gns: brother to useful sprinter Speedy James & 2 juv wnrs: dam a 5/7f wnr.

882 **CUBIC CONFESSIONS 14** [3] J A Osborne 2-8-6 S W Kelly 9/2: 44: Chsd ldrs till over 1f out: hvly bckd. *1½* **52a**
954 **VON WESSEX 7** [4]2-8-7 C Haddon(7) 6/1: 65: Sn hanging badly right, led till halfway & proved *5* **39a**
unsteerable around bend over 1f out, sn rear.

5 Ran   Time 59.25 (1.45)   Owned: Mr Louis Stalder   Trained: Marlborough

1042 3.05 New Site @ Betdirect Co Uk Classified Stakes 3yo+ 0-70 (E)
£3474 £1069 £535   1m aw rnd   Going 23   +05 Fast   Outside

1009* **STEELY DAN 3** [10] J R Best 5-10-0 (75) L Dettori 100/30 JT FA: 1311211: Rear, smooth hdwy over **85a**
1f out & styd on under hand riding to lead line: op 5/2: qck reapp: eff at 1m/12f on firm, soft & fbsnd, thriving recently on polytrk at Lingfield: see 1009, 903.

932+***KATIYPOUR 8** [3] Miss B Sanders 7-9-8 (75) R Miles(3) 100/30 JT FA: 346-0312: Trkd ldr & led 3f *shd* **78a**
out, drvn & hdd line: well bckd, op 9/2: another gd run off a perfect passage: see 932.

932 **DEEPER IN DEBT 8** [8] J Akehurst 6-9-6 (73) G Carter 5/1: 112-2433: Sn handy, rdn & chall 2f out, *3* **70a**
no extra dist: not ideally drawn for one that likes to dominate but a gd run: see 12.

517 **COLLEGE DELINQUENT 63** [7] K Bell 5-9-3 t (66) Dane O'Neill 12/1: 03303-34: Mid-div, onepace: abs. *½* **66a**
697 **SPINNING DOVE 42** [5]4-9-0 (67) J Murtagh 14/1: 423-32R5: Reluctant to race & v slow away, rear, *shd* **63a**
efft wide, mod prog: abs: ref to race latest & tho' has ability she can't be trusted on this evidence: see 514 & 323.

878 **GREENWOOD 15** [2]6-9-6 (73) D Kinsella 20/1: 00-03006: Chsd ldrs, no extra over 1f out: wants 6/7f. *shd* **68a**
4781} **REDI 169** [4]3-8-2 (69) N Mackay(5) 14/1: 4054-7: b c Danehill Dancer - Rossella (Shareef Dancer) *shd* **65a**
Dwelt, chsd ldrs till over 1f out: reapp: mdn unplcd '03 (rtd 75): bred to appreciate this 1m trip, handles fast.

518 **THE BEST YET 63** [9]6-9-8 (75) S Whitworth 6/1: 63022-48: Dwelt, rear, eff 2f out, sn btn: wants 6/7f. *1* **68a**
627 **AGILIS 49** [12]4-9-3 (70) S Drowne 25/1: 046-0609: Rear, efft over 2f out, btn dist: abs: see 547, 234. *4* **55a**
4396} **OMAHA CITY 194** [11]10-9-8 (75) R Hughes 20/1: 005600-0: 10th: b g Night Shift - Be Discreet *7* **47a**
(Junius) Chsd ldrs 5f, eased: reapp: unplcd '03 (rtd 90, class stks): h'cap wnr '02: eff at 7f/sharp 1m: acts on

272

firm & gd/sft, any trk, Goodwood specialist: can go well fresh: eff in vis, best form without: 10yo.
1 May'02 Good 8g/f 99-96 C:

4890}	**DESERT DANCE 161** [1]4-9-3 (65) D Holland 20/1: 0/4300-0: 11th: Pulled hard chasing ldrs, btn 2f out: gelded, reapp, reportedly hung left throughout.	1¼	39a
912	**MEELUP 10** [6]4-9-3 p (59) V Slattery 28/1: 0-022100: 12th: Led till 3f out, sn btn: see 820 (C/D).	2	35a

12 Ran Time 1m 37.6 (1.4) Owned: Mr E A Condon Trained: Maidstone

---

1043 3.35 Littlewoods Bet Direct Conditions Stakes 4yo+ (C)
£9605 £3643 £1822 **7f aw rnd** **Going 23** -02 Slow Inside

887	**LYGETON LAD 14** [6] Miss Gay Kelleway 6-8-12 t (102) M Fenton 4/1: 01-55651: Keen early, dsptd lead till rdn clr over 1f out, always holding rivals for press after: stays 11f, best at 7f/1m on fast, gd & fibresand, Lingfield/Polytrack specialist: v useful & tough AW performer: see 262.		104a
887	**HIDDEN DRAGON 14** [1] P A Blockley 5-9-3 (100) Dean McKeown 7/1: 14000-22: Trkd ldrs, hung left/short of room over 1f out, always held: op 11/2: another gd run: see 887.	1	106a
4775}	**VANDERLIN 169** [4] A M Balding 5-9-7 (107) Martin Dwyer 8/1: 122040-3: ch g Halling - Massorah (Habitat) Dwelt, sn cl up, rdn & kept on onepace: reapp, Listed scorer '03, also rtd h'cap & Listed rnr up: mdn & rtd h'cap wnr '02: eff at 6f, prob best at 7f on fm, gd/sft & polytrk, any trk: best without vis: tough & useful.	nk	109a

2 Sep'03 Epso 7gd 110-(104) A:2 Aug'03 Ches 7.0gd 106-102 B:1 Aug'03 York 7.0fm 111-(99) A:2 Sep'02 Good 7fm 100-98 B:
2 Aug'02 Good 7fm 101- B: 2 Jul'02 Sand 7g/s 99-95 C: 2 May'02 Ling 6gd 100-92 B: 1 May'02 Sali 6g/f 97-88 B:
1 May'02 Pont 6gd 88- D: 2 Apr'02 Hayd 7.1g/f 88- D: 2 Jul'01 Pont 6g/f 97- E: 2 May'01 Newb 5.1gd 80- D:

879	**GREY PEARL 15** [2] Miss Gay Kelleway 5-8-7 (81) S Drowne 25/1: 4-511364: Dwelt, chsd ldrs, rdn & no extra dist: improved run if not flattered: see 518 (h'cap).	1¼	92a$
951	**QUITO 7** [3]7-8-12 bl (105) A Culhane 5/1: 45-10625: Rear, efft over 1f out, onepace: op 7/2: btr 951.	¾	96a
838*	**ALEUTIAN 21** [5]4-9-3 (104) J Murtagh 7/4 FAV: 1116: Dsptd lead till over 1f out, rdn wknd: hvy bckd.	shd	101a
921	**MISS GEORGE 9** [8]6-8-8 (1ow) (85) Dane O'Neill 16/1: 5130-107: Dwelt, rear, efft wide, not able to chall.	¾	91a
952	**WILL HE WISH 7** [7]8-9-3 bl (92) D Holland 16/1: 51261-08: b g Winning Gallery - More To Life (Northern Tempest) Chsd ldrs till over 1f out: op 10/1: v prog '03, landed a mdn, 3 h'caps & a stks event: suited by 6/7f on firm & gd/sft, in blnks: likes a stiff/gall trk: AW bow, shld leave this bhd on turf.	5	91a

1 Oct'03 Leic 7.0fm 99-(87) C: 2 Sep'03 Ayr 7.2fm 88-84 C: 1 Sep'03 Donc 7gd 86-79 C: 1 Jul'03 Kemp 7g/f 80-70 E:
1 Jul'03 Yarm 6.0g/f 70-62 E: 1 Jun'03 Redc 6g/f 69- D:

8 Ran Time 1m 24.53 (1.73) Owned: Mr J McGonagle & Mr B J McGonagle Trained: Newmarket

---

1044 4.20 Bet Direct On Sky Active Maiden Stakes 3yo (D)
£3760 £1157 £579 **6f aw rnd** **Going 23** -23 Slow Inside

5031}	**BOHOLA FLYER 147** [7] R Hannon 3-8-9 (74) R Hughes 7/1: 002-1: b f Barathea - Sharp Catch (Common Grounds) Made all, clr over 1f out, rdn & just held on: op 6/1: AW bow, reapp: mdn rnr up on fnl '03 start: eff at 6f, tried 7f: acts on good & polytrk, sharp/undul or gall trk: goes well fresh: suited by forcing tactics today under an enterprising ride. 2 Nov'03 Donc 6gd 76- D:		75a
1008	**KING OF DIAMONDS 3** [1] J R Best 3-9-0 J Murtagh 11/2: 262: Keen, rear, short of room over 2f out, swtchd & styd on strongly ins last, just failed: prob winner of this with an ideal passage throughout: op 9/2: imprvd for drop to 6f & return to waiting tactics: shld find compensation: see 1008 & 898.	shd	79a+
911	**CHEEKY CHI 10** [4] P S McEntee 3-8-9 L Dettori 8/1: 443: gr f Desert Style - Grey Patience (Common Grounds) Cl up, onepace over 1f out: eff at 6/7f on polytrk: 3 consistent runs.	2½	66a
	ANDALUZA 0 [9] P D Cundell 3-8-9 Martin Dwyer 16/1: 4: Held up, rdn & kept on fnl 2f, not pace to threaten: encouraging debut, get further, stable in great form.	1½	61a
4868}	**ALDERNEY RACE 162** [6]3-9-0 S Drowne 4/6 FAV: 4-5: Trkd ldrs, rdn & no impress over 1f out: bckd.	1	63a
592	**SAMARA SOUND 53** [2]3-9-0 (40) S Whitworth 20/1: 000-06: Keen chasing ldrs, onepace fnl 2f, abs.	1	60a$
898	**SUSSEX STYLE 11** [5]3-9-0 (53) D Sweeney 50/1: 0-0067: Mid-div, short of room/onepace 2f out.	¾	58a
	RADLETT LADY 0 [10]3-8-9 M Howard(6) 33/1: 8: Rear, efft wide, no prog over 1f out, debut.	½	51a
4870}	**HATCH A PLAN 162** [3]3-9-0 M Tebbutt 20/1: 000-9: Slow away & well bhd, mod prog, reapp, gelding reportedly struck jockey in the face leaving the stalls, resulting in a slow start.	4	44a
3911}	**NEBRASKA CITY 220** [8]3-9-0 (69) C Catlin 20/1: 55050-0: 10th: Cl up, btn over 2f out, reapp, gelded.	1¾	39a

795 **Adorata 31** [11]3-8-9 B Swarbrick(7) 100/1:0 **Sapphire Sky 0** [12]3-8-9 R Miles(3) 50/1:0

12 Ran Time 1m 13.16 (2.76) Owned: Mr William Durkan Trained: Marlborough

---

1045 4.55 Bill Revell 80th Birthday Handicap Stakes Fillies 3yo+ 46-55 (F)
£2947 £842 £421 **1m aw rnd** **Going 23** -06 Slow Outside [61]

845	**MY LILLI 20** [2] P Mitchell 4-9-2 (49) D Holland 4/1: 0-340641: Made all & rdn/clr over 2f out, always holding rivals after: bckd, 1st win: imprvd for switch to forcing tactics at 1m, stays 10f: acts on polytrk.		57a
917*	**WANNA SHOUT 10** [4] R Dickin 6-9-10 (57) Lisa Jones(3) 7/2 FAV: 04-21212: Chsd ldrs, efft to chse wnr 2f out, kept on, always held: remains in good form: see 917, 649.	2	60a
53	**SEEJAY 137** [3] M A Allen 4-9-1 (48) C Catlin 40/1: 600-3: b f Bahamian Bounty - Grand Splendour (Shirley Heights) Rear, styd on for press fnl 2f, nrst fin, encouraging h'cap bow after abs: unplcd '03: imprvd for drop to 1m, tried 12f: apprec switch to waiting tactics: acts on polytrk.	hd	50a
845	**MISS PEACHES 20** [9] G G Margarson 6-9-0 (47) A McCarthy 12/1: 0-201354: Held up, efft wide fnl 2f: kept on onepace: see 648 (banded).	1	47a
1013	**TITIAN LASS 3** [11]5-8-13 bl (46) R Hills 4/1: 00-41525: Held up, efft over 2f out, onepace: qck reapp.	½	45a
4785}	**KINDNESS 169** [12]4-9-5 (52) D Sweeney 33/1: 056003-6: ch f Indian Ridge - Kissing Gate (Easy Goer) Rear, efft 2f out, no impress dist, reapp: h'cap plcd final '03 start (rtd 53, AW unplaced, rtd 53, mdn, C/D): plcd '02 (rtd 65, h'cap): stays 1m on firm ground.	2½	46a
4636}	**SUMMERISE 179** [5]3-8-4 (2ow) (50) Dean McKeown 33/1: 0610-7: Dwelt, mid-div, no impress fnl 2f.	¾	45a
970	**THEATRE LADY 5** [1]6-8-13 (1oh) (45) R Havlin 14/1: 1203638: Chsd ldrs till over 1f out: qck reapp.	1¾	36a
917	**MARNIE 10** [8]4-9-4 (51) T Quinn 8/1: 000-0139: Chsd wnr, wknd 2f out, better when held up: see 845.	nk	40a
969	**VIZULIZE 5** [6]5-8-13 (1oh) (45) A Culhane 14/1: 0650040: 10th: Chsd ldrs, strugg halfway: qck reapp.	nk	34a
754	**TAIYO 36** [10]4-9-0 (47) J Murtagh 11/1: 0-654400: 11th: Chsd ldrs till 2f out, reapp, op 8/1.	1½	32a
4419}	**LARK IN THE PARK 193** [7]4-9-2 (49) B Swarbrick(7) 7/1: 031006-0: 12th: Wide, in tch till halfway: reapp.	12	14a

12 Ran Time 1m 38.55(2.35) Owned: Mr M Vickers Trained: Epsom

Official Going Good/Soft (Good Places)

1046   2.30 Festival Of Good Luck Handicap Stakes 3yo+ 46-55 (F)   [61]
£2961 £846 £423   **5f aw str**   **Standard**   **Inapplicable**   Stands Side

853   **NEVER WITHOUT ME** 20 [13] P J McBride 4-9-1 (48) K Jackson(7) 11/2 FAV: 22-64521: Sn cl-up & led   57a
over 1f out, rdn & in command ins last: first win: eff at 5f, stays 6f: likes fibresand.
853   **HENRY TUN** 20 [2] N E Berry 6-9-4 p (51) M Savage(5) 9/1: 5021302: Chsd ldrs, ch over 1f out, kept   1¾   53a
on, not pace of wnr: gd run, best when able to dominate as in 775 (C/D seller).
657   **PLAYFUL SPIRIT** 48 [12] J Balding 5-8-12 vis (45) D Allan(3) 20/1: 0633003: Dwelt, styd on for   hd   46a
press fnl 2f, not reach front pair: 7 wk abs: eff at 5f, all 3 wins at 6f: see 167 (seller).
960   **SOAKED** 7 [7] D W Chapman 11-9-0 bl (47) P Makin(7) 8/1: 0040234: Led, hdd over 1f out, no extra.   ½   46a
897   **LADIES KNIGHT** 13 [8]4-9-6 (53) N Callan 8/1: 2506305: Chsd ldrs, onepcd dist: just btr 853.   nk   51a
859   **RIVER LARK** 20 [6]5-9-1 (48) R Ffrench 8/1: 102-6446: Chsd ldrs, no extra dist: btr 859 & 655.   1   44a
750   **NANNA** 38 [11]3-8-6 (5oh) G Duffield 25/1: 00-52037: Prom, outpcd over 1f out: btr 750 & 466 (6f).   ½   44a
853   **OFF HIRE** 20 [14]8-9-1 vis (48) R Fitzpatrick 11/1: 400-2348: Pushed along, nvr on terms: op 14/1.   nk   41a
902   **OUR CHELSEA BLUE** 13 [5]6-9-1 t (48) S Righton 11/1: 60-03609: Slow away, only mod prog for press.   2   36a
720   **EJAY** 41 [10]5-8-13 (46) M Halford(7) 10/1: 06-06020: 10th: Outpcd, nvr dngr: abs: btr 720.   2½   27a
4115} **TANCRED TIMES** 210 [3]9-9-5 (52) L Enstone(3) 20/1: 031000-0: 11th: ch f Clantime - Mischievous   nk   32a
Miss (Niniski): Chsd ldrs, hung left & btn 2f out: reapp: h'cap & class stks scorer '03, mod sand form (rtd 18a,
C/D h'cap): AW unplcd '03 (rtd 60a, C/D h'cap): turf h'cap rnr-up): stays 7f, suited by forcing tactics at 5/6f:
likes firm & fast, handles hvy & fibresand, any trk: prob sharper for this.
1 Aug'03 Hami 5.0g/f 60-(60) F: 2 Jun'03 Hami 5.0g/f 64-62 D: 2 Jan'03 Catt 6.0g/f 63-59 E: 1 May'03 Thir 6g/f 59-56 E:
2 Aug'02 Catt 5g/f 58-55 F: 1 Sep'01 Hami 5gd 68-64 F: 1 Jul'01 Newc 5g/f 65-58 E: 2 Jul'01 Hami 5fm 66-60 D:
1 Jun'01 Sout 5af 62a-60 E: 1 Jun'01 Sout 5af 64a-54 F: 1 May'01 Newc 5g/f 60-54 E: 1 Apr'01 Sout 5af 56a-49 F:
802   **MAGGIE MAQUETTE** 32 [9]4-9-5 (52) E Ahern 14/1: 00-560: 12th: Dwelt & sn outpcd: btr 449 (ptrk).   1½   28a
775   **Cark** 36 [15]6-9-2 p(49) J Edmunds 16/1:0   907* **Above Board** 13 [4]9-9-3 t(50) Dean McKeown 16/1:0
669} **Mandys Collection** 409 [16]5-8-12 (45) S Whitworth 16/1:0
5006} **Grasslandik** 152 [1]8-8-12 vis(45) Ann Stokell 25/1:0
16 Ran   Time 58.67 ()   Owned: Mr P J McBride   Trained: Newmarket

---

Official Going Good/Soft (Good Places)

1047   3.00 St Juliana Of Liege's Amateur Riders' Claiming Stakes 4yo+ (G)
£2954 £844 £422   **1m4f rnd**   **Good/Soft 87**   **-38 Slow**   Inside

856   **MANIATIS** 20 [10] Mrs J Candlish 7-11-3 vis (90) Mr D Weekes(7) 3/1 FAV: 61465/-61: Led till ran   74
wide on bend after 4f, chsd ldr & led again 4f out, hung right under press but rdn clr: bckd: recent jumps unplcd
(rtd 112h, first time visor, nov): eff at 10/12f on fast, likes gd/soft & any trk: apprec drop to claim grade &
application of visor: see 856.
272   **SIR NINJA** 97 [7] S Kirk 7-10-11 (75) Miss M Gunstone(5) 11/2: 03000/4-2: b g Turtle Island - The   2½   63
Poachers Lady (Salmon Leap) Mid-div, styd on for press fnl 2f, not able to reach wnr: abs: 4th sole '03 start (rtd
48a, seller): plcd '02 (rtd 85, h'cap, subs rtd 80a, AW h'cap): eff at 1m/10f, now stays sharp 12f: acts on firm,
hvy & any trk. 2 Oct'01 York 8g/s 88-88 B:
862   **GRAND LASS** 19 [9] A Sadik 5-10-6 p (53) Miss E J Jones 6/1: 3412543: Held up, prog to chase wnr   1½   56
3f out, no extra dist: op 4/1: clr of rem: likes claimers: see 580.
1028 **PRINCE MINATA** 3 [12] P W Hiatt 9-10-7 (40) Miss A Hockley(7) 16/1: 06-00304: Handy & led over 8f   13   41
out till 4f out, sn fdd: qck reapp: see 905 (1m).
957   **DUNDONALD** 7 [3]5-10-7 bl t (35) Miss F Turner(7) 40/1: 0034065: Rear, no dngr: see 777.   2½   37
1099] **KILDARE CHILLER** 1068 [11]10-10-7 Miss E Kemp(7) 12/1: 01/0/46//-6: ch g Shahrastani -   1¼   35
Ballycuirke (Taufan) Dwelt, mod gains wide, no threat: long Flat abs, subs rtd 80a, AW unplcd '01: ex Irish Flat wnr at 9/11f, gd/soft & hvy.
3848] **LORD CONYERS** 583 [1]5-10-2 Miss L Ellison(3) 16/1: 042504/-7: b f Inzar - Primelta (Primo   3   26
Dominie) Mid-div, eff 3f out, no impress: long abs: missed '03: seller rnr-up '02, AW unplcd (rtd 41a, tried
visor & blnks): eff at 6/7f, handles gd/soft & fibresand. 2 Jul'02 Ayr 7.2g/s 51- F:
916   **MIKASA** 12 [14]4-10-6 (45) Mr K Mercer(2) 40/1: 6000-00: 10th: Went badly right start & al rear.   nk   30
      MISTER GRAHAM 0 [6]9-10-7 p Mr N Hyde(2) 40/1: 9: Dwelt & sn bhd, Flat debut, 6 wk jumps abs.   5   23
2549] **ROMAN KING** 641 [13]9-10-7 (70) Mr D R Cook(7) 16/1: 0/00055/-0: 10th: Al bhd: long abs, new yard.   hd   26
      MYSTERY SOLVED 264 [5]4-11-1 (50) Miss S Renwick(5) 14/1: 0/00000-0: 11th: Held up, struggling fnl 2f.   1¼   29
91**BLUE SAVANNA** 12 [8]4-10-10 p (47) Mr L Newnes(5) 8/1: 63-64210: Prom till 4f out: btr 916.   6   16
906   **Samar Qand** 13 [4]5-10-7 t(35) Mr Matthew Smith 12/1:0
896   **Estuary** 13 [2]9-11-7 (45) Ms A Embiricos(3) 20/1:0
14 Ran   Time 2m 49.33 (15.03)   Owned: Racing For You Limited   Trained: Leek

SOUTHWELL Fibresand MONDAY 05.04.04 Lefthand, Sharp, Oval Track

Official Going Good/Soft (Good Places)

1048 3.30 National Raisin And Spice Bar Day Maiden Auction Stakes 2yo (F)
£2919 £834 £417 **5f aw str** **Standard** **Inapplicable** Stands Side

920	**WESTBROOK BLUE 11** [5] W G M Turner 2-8-7 C Haddon(7) 4/7 FAV: 31: Made all, drvn out ins last: hvly bckd to confirm debut promise: eff at 5f on gd grnd & fibresand: likes to force the pace: speedy, win again.	**76a**
	UNLIMITED 0 [6] Mrs A Duffield 2-8-10 G Duffield 33/1: 2: b c Bold Edge - Cabcharge Blue (Midyan) Chsd wnr, rdn & kept on, al held ins last: Apr first foal, cost 7,000gns: dam multiple 5/6f juv wnr, subs a wnr at 1m/12f: eff at 5f, will get further: acts on fibresand: encouraging.	1½ 73a
	WHY HARRY 0 [1] J J Quinn 2-8-7 R Winston 11/2: 3: b g Cyrano de Bergerac - Golden Ciel (Septieme Ciel) Prom, outpcd by wnr over 1f out: op 9/2: Apr foal, cost 5,000gns: half-brother to a 1m AW 2yo wnr, dam multiple 7f wnr abroad: eff at 5f on fibresand: clr of rem here, gave encouragement.	nk 69a
	DANES ROCK 0 [3] P C Haslam 2-8-10 G Faulkner 8/1: 4: b c Indian Danehill - Cutting Ground (Common Grounds) Prom till over 1f out: Mar foal, cost 11,000 Euros: half-brother to a 6f wnr, dam 9f wnr.	6 58a
	RONNIES LAD 0 [4]2-8-7 V Halliday 33/1: 5: Nvr on terms.	2½ 48a
954	**MINDFUL 9** [8]2-8-10 E Ahern 20/1: 06: Chsd ldrs till over 1f out.	1 49a
	MARCELA ZABALA 0 [2]2-8-5 N Pollard 14/1: 7: Dwelt & sn outpcd rear.	5 32a
962	**VERSTONE 7** [7]2-8-8 S Righton 66/1: 08: Dwelt, sn outpcd, AW bow.	3 28a

8 Ran Time 59.88 () Owned: Mr Bob Chandler Trained: Sherborne

SOUTHWELL MONDAY 05.04.04 Lefthand, Sharp, Oval Track

Official Going Good/Soft (Good Places)

1049 4.00 Battle Of Nafels Handicap Stakes 3yo+ 0-75 (E) [73]
£4202 £1293 £647 **7f rnd** **Good/Soft 87** **+05 Fast** Inside

1010	**NEARLY A FOOL 5** [14] G G Margarson 6-9-6 vis (65) N Pollard 12/1: 1102101: Rear, hdwy wide for press from 2f out, led cl-home: best time of day, op 10/1: qck reapp: stays sharp 1m, suited by 6/7f on firm, soft & both AWs: still well treated on juv/3yo form, winning run may continue: see 858, 448 & 344.	73
903	**CAPTAIN DARLING 13** [7] R M H Cowell 4-9-2 p (61) E Ahern 10/1: 5543-602: Trkd ldrs, rdn & led 2f out, hdd cl-home: apprec drop to 7f, acts on fast, gd/soft & both AWs: imprvd for reapp of chkpcs: see 266.	¾ 67
2581	**SEA MARK 640** [12] B Ellison 8-9-1 (60) R Winston 50/1: 50/0000/-3: ro g Warning - Mettlesome (Lomond) Bhd, short of room over 1f out, styd on well in rear, nrst fin: long abs: missed '03: lightly rcd & unplcd '02 (rtd 51, h'cap, C Grant): thrice h'cap rnr-up '01: eff at 7/9f on fast, gd/soft & a gall or sharp trk: best without blnks: caught the eye, well h'capped, keep in mind for similar. 2 Jun'01 Ayr 9g/f 85-84 D: 2 Jun'01 Hayd 8.1gd 84-83 C: 2 May'01 Ripo 8g/f 85-80 D:	2 62+
834	**MUFREH 23** [5] A G Newcombe 6-9-1 (60) S Whitworth 4/1 FAV: 012-1524: Rear, styd on for press late, not able to chall: turf rtn, well h'capped: acts on gd/soft, fibresand specialist: see 419 & 31.	¾ 61
531*	**MARINAITE 62** [4]3-9-2 (75) K Dalgleish 7/1: 215: Led 1f, handy, no extra dist: 2 month abs: turf/h'cap bow, gd run against elders: acts on fibresand , poss gd/soft grnd: see 531.	2 72
4883}	**LUCAYAN DANCER 163** [1]4-9-6 (65) Alex Greaves 20/1: 640334-6: b g Zieten - Tittle Tattle (Soviet Lad) Prom, no extra over 1f out: reapp: has been gelded: h'cap rnr-up '03 (J S Goldie): '02 auct mdn wnr & val h'cap rnr-up, (E Dunlop): eff btwn 7f/10.5f, tried further: acts on firm & soft, any trk, with/without blnks or chkpcs: well h'capped on best form. 2 Aug'03 Hayd 10.5g/f 74-74 E: 2 Apr'03 Hayd 10.5g/f 83-(84) C: 2 Oct'02 Nott 8.2sft 88- D: 2 Sep'02 Ches 7.5fm 92- C: 2 Aug'02 Good 7fm 93-90 C: 1 May'02 Brig 6g/f 91- E:	shd 62
942	**DANIELLES LAD 9** [9]8-10-0 bl (73) S Donohoe(7) 12/1: 4204137: Led after 2f till 2f out, no extra.	1¾ 67
4485}	**SABALARA 191** [6]4-9-4 (63) N Callan 9/1: 5620-8: b f Mujadil - Sabaniya (Lashkari) Mid-div, no prog over 1f out: reapp: mdn rnr-up '03: eff over a stiff 6f, bred to apprec 7f/1m: handles gd/soft grnd & a stiff/undul trk. 2 Jul'03 Sali 6g/s 64- D:	hd 56
864	**ST IVIAN 19** [11]4-9-5 vis (64) P McCabe 20/1: 6020029: Mid-div, no prog fnl 2f: btr 864 (AW).	1 55
4883}	**LORD OF THE EAST 163** [10]5-9-6 (65) A Nicholls 33/1: 100502-0: 10th: Prom, btn dist, reapp.	1 54
	BRIGADIER MONTY 257 [3]6-9-2 (61) G Duffield 33/1: 006000-0: 11th: Keen, mid-div, eff 2f out, no extra dist: reapp, ex Irish.	½ 49
39*	**MERDIFF 142** [13]5-9-3 (62) S W Kelly 8/1: 003201-0: 12th: In tch till 2f out: abs: see 39.	6 40
967	**STOIC LEADER 7** [16]4-9-9 (68) L Fletcher(3) 5/1: 0-401140: 13th: Prom from awkward high draw 5f.	4 39
4752}	**ONE LAST TIME 173** [8]4-9-13 (72) H Bastiman 40/1: 000660-0: 14th: Dwelt & al bhd, reapp/new yard.	3 38
4619}	**Jimmy Byrne 182** [15]4-9-11 (70) T Eaves(5) 20/1:0 941 **Rafters Music 9** [2]9-9-7 (66) G Faulkner 14/1:0	

16 Ran Time 1m 32.77 (5.77) Owned: Mr J Burns Trained: Newmarket

1050 4.30 Booker T Washington Classified Stakes 3yo 0-65 (E)
£3367 £1036 £518 **6f rnd** **Good/Soft 87** **-25 Slow** Inside

872	**PICCOLO PRINCE 18** [6] E J Alston 3-8-12 (65) W Supple 85/40: 0-012121: Al handy & duelled with rnr-up fnl 2f, prevailed cl-home, all out: bckd on turf rtn: eff at 5/6f on fast, gd/soft & fibresand, loves Southwell.	71
875*	**MONTE MAJOR 17** [2] M A Jarvis 3-9-3 (70) N Callan 2/1 FAV: 06-34212: Led, strongly prsd fnl 2f, drvn & hdd cl-home: nicely bckd, op 9/4: confirmed improvement of 875: eff at 6/7f on both AWs & gd/soft.	nk 75
841	**MUNAAWESH 22** [7] D W Chapman 3-9-3 (70) P Makin(7) 12/1: 05-03: b c Bahri - Istikbal (Kingmambo) Dwelt, in tch, kept on late, not reach front pair: lightly rcd & unplcd '03 (M Tregoning, rtd 80, debut): dam related to a 1m scorer: eff at 6f, 7f in similar could suit, tried 1m: handles fm & gd/soft, sharp/undul trks.	1¾ 70
5031}	**IMPULSIVE BID 149** [1] Jedd O'Keeffe 3-8-10 (66) P Hanagan 6/1: 404-4: b f Orpen - Tamburello (Roi Danzig) Prom, onepace fnl 2f: op 12/1, reapp: lightly rcd & unplcd '03 (rtd 72, mdn): half-sister to 2 mdn performers: eff over a gall 6f on gd & gd/soft.	shd 63
933	**WENDYS GIRL 10** [4]3-8-9 (60) T Hamilton(3) 22/1: 5330-005: Dwelt & held up, nvr able to chall.	2½ 55
422	**CHICKADO 80** [3]3-8-9 (65) Paul Eddery 5/1: 00613-36: Keen & prom till 2f out: abs: btr 422 & 69.	6 41
795	**BLUE EMPEROR 33** [5]3-8-13 (66) D Nolan(3) 22/1: 346-07: b g Groom Dancer - Bague Bleue (Last	1 43

Tycoon) Prom, hung left & btn over 1f out: plcd debut '03 (rtd 78, AW unplcd, rtd 56a, subs disapp in a t-strap, lightly rcd): eff at 5f on gd grnd: mod form since debut.
7 Ran   Time 1m 19.99 (6.69)   Owned: The Burlington Partnership   Trained: Preston

---

1051   5.00 St Vincent Ferrer's Day Handicap Stakes 3yo 46-55 (F)   **[65]**
£2947   £842   £421   1m2f   Good/Soft 87   Inapplicable   Inside

925   **HABITUAL DANCER** 10 [8] Jedd O'Keeffe 3-9-1 (52) P Hanagan 7/1: 000-61: b g Groom Dancer -   **64**
Pomorie (Be My Guest) In tch, rdn & hdwy to lead over 1f out, drvn out: first win: unplcd '03 (rtd 59): dam hdles
wnr: relished step up to 10f, stay further: acts on gd/soft: unexposed at mid-dists.
276   **DAGGERS CANYON** 96 [7] Julian Poulton 3-9-4 (55) N Callan 10/1: 0540-2: ch g Daggers Drawn -   *1*   **65**
Chipewyas (Bering) Held up, drvn & styd on fnl 2f, not able to reach wnr: clr rem: unplcd '03 (rtd 72$): apprec step
up to 10f & handles gd/soft grnd & polytrack: shld win a race.
930   **DANEFONIQUE** 10 [5] D Carroll 3-9-2 (53) R Fitzpatrick 16/1: 03050-03: b f Danetime - Umlaut   *4*   **57**
(Zafonic) Towards rear, switched & kept on for press fnl 2f, no prog ins last: clr of rem: unplcd '03 (rtd 63,
auct mdn): stays a sharp 10f, acts on gd/soft grnd.
645   **HEARTBEAT** 49 [4] P J McBride 3-9-1 (52) K Jackson(7) 20/1: 06-4004: Chsd ldr halfway, led over 2f   *5*   **50**
out till over 1f out, fdd: 7 wk abs: not see out longer 10f trip under a positive ride.
855   **MYANNABANANA** 20 [6]3-9-4 P (55) R Winston 8/1: 5-534405: Held up, lost pl/hmpd halfway, mod gains.*3*   **49**
797   **POACHERS PARADISE** 33 [13]3-8-9 (1oh) (45) P Mulrennan(5) 11/2 FAV: 000-006: Led, hdd over 2f out,   *hd*   **39**
fdd: bckd: up in trip.
794   **ATLANTIC BREEZE** 33 [14]3-9-1 (52) Joanna Badger 22/1: 410-0007: Al rear, turf bow.   *8*   **34**
865*   **STONOR LADY** 19 [3]3-8-11 (48) E Ahern 13/2: 06-00018: Hld up, btn 2f out: btr 865 (seller, 1m).   *5*   **24**
314   **TIMBUKTU** 91 [12]3-8-9 (6oh) (40) T Eaves(5) 33/1: 006-09: Al rear: gelded, abs.   *¾*   **21**
899   **FRAMBO** 13 [9]3-8-9 (1oh)BL (45) B Reilly(3) 9/1: 625-0050: 10th: Sn bhd, blnks: btr 899 (polytrack).   *¾*   **20**
4532}   **LENWADE** 188 [11]3-9-2 (53) A McCarthy 9/1: 0.6000-0: 11th: Rear, eff halfway, no impress: reapp.   *8*   **16**
4930}   **ROYAL UPSTART** 160 [2]3-8-9 (46) S W Kelly 14/1: 035000-0: 12th: Chsd ldr 3f, nvr danger, reapp.   *5*   **3**
930   **KATIES ROLE** 10 [1]3-9-4 (55) Dean McKeown 10/1: 3-344300: 13th: Chsd ldr 3f, sn struggling.   *11*   **0**
857   **HYMNS AND ARIAS** 20 [10]3-8-10 (47) S Whitworth 16/1: 0010-040: 14th: In tch bhd 5f out, t.o.: btr 857.   *23*   **0**
14 Ran   Time 2m 20.80 (No Std Time)   Owned: The Country Stayers   Trained: Leyburn

---

1052   5.30 Happy Birthday Little Jimmy Osmond Handicap Stakes 3yo+ 46-55 (F)   **[64]**
£2961   £846   £423   6f rnd   Good/Soft 87   -05 Slow   Inside

4634}   **BALAKIREF** 181 [9] M Dods 5-9-3 (53) F Lynch 11/2: 000000-1: b g Royal Applause - Pluck (Never So   **67+**
Bold) Held up, strong run from over 2f out & rdn/led over 1f out, rdn clr: bckd from 8/1: reapp: h'cap rnr-up '03,
largely disapp, incl in visor: class stks scorer '02 for W Jarvis, AW unplcd, rtd 63a, h'cap): eff at 6f/sharp 7f on
fast, likes gd, soft & fibresand, any trk: goes well fresh: well h'capped, keep on side.
2 May'03 Thir 7gd 67-68 C: 2 Aug'02 Ling 6g/f 76-75 D: 1 Jul'02 Donc 6gd 77- D: 2 Jul'02 Kemp 7g/s 74-73 E:
2 Jun'02 Donc 7fm 77-72 D: 2 Jun'02 Newb 7sft 72-70 E: 1 Nov'01 Wolv 7af 77a- F: 2 Sep'01 Epso 7gd 76- E:
902   **CARLTON** 13 [4] C R Dore 10-9-4 (54) R Thomas(5) 11/2: 00-04402: Mid-div halfway, styd on for   *3*   **58**
press, no threat to wnr: well h'capped for similar: likes easy grnd: see 565.
858   **KENNINGTON** 20 [3] Mrs C A Dunnett 4-9-5 (55) Hayley Turner(5) 12/1: 0/-10403: Prom when   *2*   **54**
squeezed out halfway, rallied for press fnl 2f, not pace of front pair: eff at 6f, sole win at 7f: acts on fibresand
& gd/soft: encouraging turf bow: see 416.
869   **BOAVISTA** 18 [5] P D Evans 4-9-5 (55) S Donohoe(7) 8/1: 0324534: Handy & led over 4f out till over   *hd*   **53**
1f out, no extra: long standing mdn: see 713, 657 & 593.
4741}   **SUMMER SPECIAL** 174 [14]4-9-5 (55) L Enstone(3) 14/1: 000300-5: b g Mind Games - Summerhill   *2*   **48**
Special (Roi Danzig) Dwelt & held up, mod prog from halfway: reapp: h'cap & mdn rnr-up '03: seller & nurs h'cap
rnr-up '02: eff at 6/7f on fast & hvy grnd, prob any trk: eff with/without cheek pieces: mdn but has ability.
2 May'03 Hami 6.0g/s 70-67 C: 2 Mar'03 Catt 6.0g/f 66-(72) D: 2 Jul'02 Pont 6g/s 76-70 D: 2 Jun'02 York 6g/f 72- E:
864   **MOUNT ROYALE** 19 [13]6-9-3 vis t (53) Kim Tinkler 8/1: 6311006: Chsd ldrs wide, no prog dist: see 684.   *nk*   **45**
4856}   **THE OLD SOLDIER** 166 [8]6-9-5 (55) A Beech(3) 12/1: 305200-7: b g Magic Ring - Grecian Belle   *1¼*   **44**
(Ilium) Hmpd start, in tch till over 1f out: reapp: h'cap wnr '03, subs h'cap rnr-up: eff at 5/6f, tried 1m:
acts on fm & fast. 2 Sep'03 Newc 6g/f 74-74 F: 1 Aug'03 Catt 5fm 55-49 F: 2 Jul'02 Muss 5g/f 50-49 F:
4528}   **JAZZY MILLENNIUM** 188 [2]7-9-5 bl (55) G Baker 16/1: 001500-8: Bhd, mod hdwy, nvr dngr: reapp.   *1¾*   **40**
641   **PERCY DOUGLAS** 49 [10]4-9-3 p (53) Ann Stokell 33/1: 3063-009: Prom, btn over 1f out, 7 wk abs.   *3½*   **29**
956   **AGUILA LOCO** 7 [11]5-9-3 p (53) E Ahern 3/1 FAV: 3140620: 10th: Prom wide till over 1f out: 'too free'.   *¾*   **27**
859   **CLEVELAND WAY** 20 [6]4-9-2 vis (52) D Nolan(5) 10/1: 2656450: 11th: Led 1f, dsptd lead till over 1f out.   *3*   **19**
902   **Teyaar** 15 [12]8-9-3 (53) P McCabe 20/1:0   858   **Tanaffus** 20 [7]4-9-2 (52) P Makin(7) 33/1:0
13 Ran   Time 1m 19.62(5.52)   Owned: Septimus Racing Group   Trained: Darlington

---

Official Going Good/Soft (Soft places)

1053   2.10 French Brothers Median Auction Maiden Stakes 2yo (E)
£3455   £1063   £532   5f10y str   Good/Soft   Inapp   Inside

  CORNUS [4] R Hannon 2-9-0   R Hughes 8/1: 1: ch c Inchinor - Demerger (Distant View) Cl-up,   **90**
styd to lead over 1f out, pushed clr, cmftbly on debut: op 6/1: Apr first foal, cost 16,000gns: eff over an
easy 5f, 6f will suit: clrly enjoys gd/soft grnd & runs well fresh: potential useful, win again.
  GOODRICKE [5] D R Loder 2-9-0   J Murtagh 2/1 JT FAV: 2: b c Bahamian Bounty - Star (Most   *2½*   **83**
Welcome) Slow away, sn in tch, hdwy 2f out, chsd wnr ins last, no impress: bckd: Apr foal, cost 110,00gns: brother
to a useful 5f juv wnr: dam 5f juv scorer: eff for speed & clrly eff at 5f on gd/soft: win similar.
943   **TREMAR** 9 [8] T G Mills 2-9-0   R Miles(3) 7/2: 43: Reluctant start, slow away, sn rdn bhd, late   *½*   **82**
gains, nrst fin: ran similarly in 943, poss not straightforward.
931   **WIZZSKILAD** 10 [7] Mrs P N Dutfield 2-9-0   R Havlin 66/1: 04: b c Wizard King - Sure Babe (Sure   *3*   **76**

Blade) Set pace till over 1f out, no extra: Feb first foal, cheaply bght: speedily bred & imprvd for debut here.

CUMMISKEY [6]2-9-0 D Holland 2/1 JT FAV: 5: Handy, wknd over 1f out: nicely bckd. 2½ **71**

HIGH DAWN [3]2-9-0 S Sanders 20/1: 6: Dwelt, sn rdn in tch, wkng when hmpd dist on debut. 1¼ **69**

LEONALTO [2]2-9-0 J F McDonald(5) 33/1: 7: With ldrs, wknd & hung left over 1f out on debut. 5 **59**

BIG BAMBO [1]2-9-0 S Drowne 40/1: 8: Dwelt, al bhd on debut. 24 **11**

8 Ran Time 1m 04.53 () Owned: Mr David Mort Trained: Marlborough

1054

2.40 Welcome To Royal Windsor 2004 Handicap Stakes 3yo 0-75 (E) **[82]**
£3513 £1081 £541 **6f str** **Good/Soft** **Inapp** Inside. 2 Groups

835 **MUY BIEN 23** [4] J R Jenkins 3-9-1 bl (69) L Dettori 7/1: 52-22031: Made all far side, overall ldr over 2f out, held on for press ins last: eff over 5/7f on polytrack & gd, likes fibresand & gd/soft: eff with/without visor & blnks: in gd form & switched to forcing tactics up in class: see 835, 63. **80**

1015* **STAMFORD BLUE 4** [3] J S Moore 3-8-8 (6ex)bl (62) B Swarbrick(7) 12/1: 6206012: Handy far side, eff to chase wnr over 2f out, kept on, not btn far: clr rem: in gd form: up in class here, win another seller. 1 **71**

955 **ARFINNIT 9** [2] M R Channon 3-9-4 (72) T E Durcan 25/1: 63000-03: b g College Chapel - Tidal Reach (Kris S) Held up far side, well bhd halfway, late gains, nvr dngrs: juv nurs h'cap wnr: eff at 5/6f (dam 1m juv wnr): acts on fast & soft grnd, likes gall trks: slipped down the weights & worth another try over 7f now. 6 **69**
1 Jul'03 Ayr 6gd 84-80 D:

631* **ROYAL PAVILLION 51** [15] W J Musson 3-9-2 (70) M Fenton 7/2 FAV: 0-314: Bhd stands side, eff 2f out, led that group ins last, no ch on far side: encouraging after 7 wk abs, won race on "wrong" side: acts on both AWs & prob gd/soft: keep in mind, lightly rcd: see 631, 364. ¾ **65+**

603 **HEAD BOY 54** [8]3-8-4 (58) R L Moore 40/1: 510-4005: ch g Forzando - Don't Jump (Entitled) Held up stands side, hdwy & short of room appr fnl 1f, kept on, no ch with far side: encouraging on wrong side after 8 wk abs: won 1 of 6 '03 starts, nurs h'cap: stays a sharp/undul 7f on fast grnd, poss gd/soft. nk **52**
1 Oct'03 Ling 7g/f 62-55 E:

4761} **NIGHT WORKER 172** [12]3-8-11 (65) P Dobbs 12/1: 43040-6: b c Dracula - Crystal Magic (Mazilier) With ldr stands side, wknd ins last: plcd on 1 of 5 '03 starts (mdn, rdn 72$ at best): prob eff at 6f on fast grnd. 2½ **54**

2644} **PERFECT HINDSIGHT 276** [11]3-8-8 (62) R Smith 20/1: 005-7: In tch stands side, wknd over 1f out. hd **50**

901 **SPRING DANCER 13** [1]3-8-9 (63) E Stack 20/1: 06600-08: Chsd wnr far side till wknd 2f out. 2½ **46**

975 **INSTINCT 6** [6]3-8-8 (62) R Hughes 6/1: 0-5039: Led stands side group till dist, wknd: qk reapp. 1¾ **41**

872 **HEAD OF STATE 18** [5]3-8-6 vis (60) J Mackay 16/1: 1-001030: 10th: In tch far side, wknd 2f out. 2 **35**

898 **TORQUEMADA 13** [9]3-9-0 (68) P Doe 12/1: 60-30: 11th: In tch stands side, wknd 2f out: btr 898. shd **43**

4641} **PARTY PRINCESS 181** [13]3-8-9 (63) D Holland 7/1: 253-0: 12th: In tch stands side, wknd 2f out. shd **38**

729 **OFF BEAT 40** [7]3-9-7 bl (75) S Carson 20/1: 0610-630: 13th: In tch 4f stands side: btr 729 (aw). shd **49**

5032} **MY MICHELLE 149** [14]3-9-6 (74) K Darley 8/1: 553-0: 14th: Al bhd stands side: softer grnd. 7 **34**

3957} **MELODY KING 220** [10]3-9-1 bl (69) R Havlin 40/1: 003140-0: 15th: Nvr a factor stands side. 1¼ **27**

15 Ran Time 1m 17.53 () Owned: Mr Kevin Reddington Trained: Royston

1055

3.10 Sweet & Maxwell Archbold Maiden Stakes 3yo (D)
£4173 £1284 £642 **1m2f7y** **Good/Soft** **Inapp** Inside. Rcd Far Side.

BULL RUN [3] D R Loder 3-9-0 J Murtagh 9/4 JT FAV: 1: ro c Daylami - Bulaxie (Bustino) Cl-up, led 3f out, sn clr, v easily: half-brother to a smart 10f wnr: dam useful over 7/10f: stays an easy 10f well, 12f shld suit: acts on gd/soft & runs well fresh: bred to be smart & looks potentially so, win in btr grade. **100**

4937} **LARKWING 159** [11] G Wragg 3-9-0 D Holland 9/4 JT FAV: 4-2: b c Ela Mana Mou - The Dawn Trader (Naskra) Held up, eff well over 2f out, sn chsd wnr, no impress: nicely bckd: some promise when 4th sole juv start (rtd 71+): brother to a 12f wnr: dam 7f scorer: eff at 10f, 12f sure to suit: acts on gd/soft, clr of rem & prob caught a useful type, keep in mind for a mdn. 9 **83**

SPRINGTIME ROMANCE [6] E A L Dunlop 3-8-9 L Dettori 10/1: 3: br f Kris S - Khamsin (Mr Prospector) In tch, eff well over 3f out, no extra fnl 2f: bred to apprec mid-dists & shld learn plenty from this. 7 **70**

4568} **OBAY 185** [5] E A L Dunlop 3-9-0 S Drowne 11/2: 0-4: ch c Kingmambo - Parade Queen (A P Indy) In tch, outpcd over 2f out, some late gains: promise when 7f in a mdn sole '03 starts (rtd 88+): dam high-class miler in US: 10f shld suit & looks sure to do btr back on a sounder surface. 5 **70**

4943} **MAGIC STING 159** [7]3-9-0 I Mongan 25/1: 5-5: In tch, no impress over 2f out on reapp. nk **70**

676 **GROUND PATROL 47** [9]3-9-0 (70) Martin Dwyer 20/1: 0-3436: In tch, outpcd 3f out, mod gains. 1¼ **68**

4942} **PATRIXTOO 159** [1]3-9-0 P Robinson 16/1: 00-7: Led till over 3f out, wknd: longer trip. 1 **66$**

5018} **GRIST MIST 151** [4]3-8-9 R Havlin 66/1: 00-8: Al bhd on reapp. 7 **53**

886 **LOOKS THE BUSINESS 16** [8]3-9-0 t (69) A Culhane 16/1: 445-2459: Handy, wknd over 2f out: see 886. ¾ **57**

886 **SCRIPTORIUM 16** [14]3-9-0 T E Durcan 33/1: 0-60: 10th: Al bhd on h'cap qual run. 1½ **55**

875 **Cool Clear Water 17** [10]3-8-9 M Hills 25/1:0 4895} **Persian Dagger 163** [12]3-9-0 T Quinn 33/1:0
5018} **No Dilemma 151** [2]3-9-0 K Darley 50/1:0 367 **Red Silk 86** [13]3-8-9 S Sanders 66/1:0

14 Ran Time 2m 15.78 () Owned: Sheikh Mohammed Trained: Newmarket

1056

3.40 Hblb Charlton Athletic Fc Handicap Stakes 3yo+ 0-85 (D) **[85]**
£5623 £1730 £865 **1m3f135y** **Good/Soft** **Inapp** Inside. Rcd far side.

856 **CRUISE DIRECTOR 20** [4] W J Musson 4-9-9 (80) M Fenton 12/1: 10-30301: Held up, hdwy over 2f out, styd on to lead ins last, rdn out: eff at 10/12f on gd/soft & polytrack, any trk, likes sharp ones, esp Windsor. **87**

936* **CLASSIC ROLE 10** [12] R Ingram 5-9-5 vis (75) A Culhane 5/1 FAV: 0-403412: Prom, led 3f out, sn clr, rdn & collared ins last: clr of rem & in fine form: likes Windsor: see 936, 97. 1 **80**

493 **BUCKS 68** [3] D K Ivory 7-9-1 (71) M Howard(7) 33/1: 52125-03: Held up, hdwy 2f out, no dngr: abs. 5 **70**

4688} **LADY MCNAIR 176** [20] P D Cundell 4-9-7 (78) S Sanders 14/1: 004446-4: b f Sheikh Albadou - Bonita Bee (King of Spain) Handy, hdwy trav well over 2f out, sn no extra: 4th sev times in h'caps in '03 (rtd 79): won 2 h'caps & a stks in '02: eff at 7f, stays 10f on firm, gd/soft & handles polytrack, any trk, likes Brighton: much sharper for this back at around 10f & on a handy mark now. 1¼ **75**
1 Aug'02 Sand 8gd 93- C: 1 Aug'02 Newb 7g/f 93-82 D: 1 Jul'02 Brig 6.9g/f 86-73 E: 1 Jul'02 Brig 7g/s 74- E:

2623} **SKELLIGS ROCK 277** [9]4-9-7 (78) R L Moore 40/1: 44/20-5: b c Key of Luck - Drew (Double Schwartz) In tch, eff over 2f out, sn no extra: rnr-up on first of 2 '03 starts (mdn): eff at 10f on firm grnd & a 6 **69**

gall trk.   2 Jun'03 Sand 10.0fm 78- D:

918   **INVITATION 11** [5]6-9-4 (74) R Hughes 20/1: 45500-06: b g Bin Ajwaad - On Request (Be My Guest)   nk   64
In tch, brief eff over 2f out, sn btn: unplcd earlier over hdles (rtd 105h): 4th at best on the Flat in '03 (rtd
80): '02 dual h'cap wnr: suited by 10f & handles fast grnd, likes gd or hvy, any trk: can carry big weights & has
run well fresh: tried cheek pieces: back on a fair mark.
1 Oct'02 Leic 9.9sft 81-74 E: 1 Aug'02 Newm 10sft 76-71 C: 2 Jun'02 Chep 10.1hvy 75-76 D: 1 May'01 Wind 10gd 84- E:

856   **MIDSHIPMAN 20** [19]6-9-5 VIS (75) I Mongan 66/1: 20/0-0007: Sn handy, wknd 2f out: tried visor.   2   63
918   **CROWN AGENT 11** [13]4-9-2 (73) L Keniry(3) 10/1: 022U-058: In tch, gd hdwy 2f out, wknd: see 918.   1¼   60
        KIROV KING 119 [11]4-9-7 (78) J Murtagh 25/1: 110460-9: Held up, hdwy trav well 2f out, wknd.   3   62
928   **INTERNATIONALGUEST 10** [10]5-9-8 bl (78) P Robinson 11/2: 2000200: 10th: In tch, wknd 2f out.   2   60
856   **KYLKENNY 20** [18]9-9-6 (76) S Drowne 13/2: 05004-30: 11th: With ldrs, led halfway till 3f out,   2   56
wknd: remained on unfavourable centre of trk: btr 856, see 225 (fibresand).
3649} **PERSIAN KING 233** [7]7-10-0 (84) Dane O'Neill 33/1: 102/050-0: 12th: Nvr a factor on reapp.   2½   61
4983} **RIBBONS AND BOWS 155** [15]4-9-9 (80) Martin Dwyer 50/1: 0/05600-0: 13th: Handy, wknd 3f out.   9   48
928   **SAHAAT 10** [17]6-9-8 (78) S Crawford(7) 40/1: 0000-000: 14th: Dwelt, al bhd.   3   43
3277} **MAKULU 249** [14]4-9-6 (77) L Dettori 7/1: 102350-0: 15th: Dwelt, nvr a factor.   7   35
4465} **CLARADOTNET 192** [16]4-9-11 (82) T E Durcan 25/1: 210-0: 16th: Al bhd: prev with H Cecil.   1   39
803   **BOWING 32** [1]4-9-1 (72) D Kinsella 40/1: 423-0500: 17th: Dwelt, al bhd.   4   25
936   **RAINBOW WORLD 10** [6]4-9-4 (75) T P Queally(3) 50/1: 160-0300: 18th: Nvr nrr: btr 816 (aw).   12   16
912   **FORTUNE POINT 12** [2]6-8-8 (2ow) (62) D Holland 9/1: 4021320: 19th: Led to halfway, wknd: btr 912 (aw).   dist   0
3402} **ROYAL TRIGGER 243** [8]4-9-3 (74) C Catlin 33/1: 0/16020-0: 20th: Al bhd, t.o.: prev with B Hills.   dist   0
20 Ran   Time 2m 40.75 ()   Owned: Mr K A Cosby   Trained: Newmarket

---

1057   4.10 Colliers Cre Licence & Leisure Classified Stakes 3yo+ 0-80 (D)
£5541 £1705 £853   1m67y rnd   Good/Soft   Inapp   Inside. Rcd far side.

932   **JOOLS 10** [5] D K Ivory 6-9-4 (78) T Quinn 33/1: 4100-001: Mid-div, prog 2f out, styd on strongly   84
to lead cl-home, rdn out for a surprise win: eff btwn 6f & 10f on fm, soft & prob both AWs: 10 wins from 42.
4579} **SOYUZ 185** [12] M A Jarvis 4-9-6 (82) P Robinson 11/4 FAV: 323000-2: ch g Cadeaux Genereux -   nk   85
Welsh Mist (Damister). Keen & prom, led dist till worn down dying strides: nicely bckd, reapp: plcd on 3 of 6 '03
starts (h'caps): '02 mdn wnr: eff at 6f/1m on fast & soft: runs well fresh: tried blnks, been gelded.
2 May'03 Hayd 8.1sft 89-87 B: 1 Oct'02 Leic 6sft 89- D: 2 Oct'02 Wind 6g/s 87- D:
888   **KENTUCKY KING 16** [3] P W Hiatt 4-9-9 (85) A Culhane 16/1: 4-660103: Dwelt, rcd keenly & hdwy   1   86
from rear when short of room 2f out, styd on well & nrst fin: clr of rem: did not get the run of today's race.
878   **CLIMATE 17** [8] J R Boyle 5-9-4 VIS (77) D Sweeney 25/1: 50S30-54: Chsd ldrs, onepcd dist: vis.   3   76
928   **ACE OF HEARTS 10** [10]5-9-7 (83) S Sanders 11/2: 25362-05: b g Magic Ring - Lonely Heart (Midyan)   nk   79
Prom, ev ch 2f out, no extra ins fnl 1f: failed to win in '03, tho' plcd sev times (h'caps & class stks): dual '02
wnr (AW mdn & turf h'cap): eff at 7f, stays 10f well: acts on fast, soft & both AWs: handles any trk.
1 Jul'02 Yarm 10.1sft 86-(83) C: 2 Aug'03 Wind 8.3g/f 84-82 D: 2 May'03 Ripo 8g/s 85-81 C:
928   **AFRICAN SAHARA 10** [11]5-9-9 t (85) G Carter 9/1: 6101606: Held up, short of room halfway & again   1¼   79
2f out, nrst fin: 'not much luck today: see 800.
836   **TE QUIERO GB 23** [2]6-9-6 t P (82) S Drowne 11/2: 0-000227: Set pace till dist, wknd: cheek pieces.   ½   72
4619} **WELCOME STRANGER 182** [9]4-9-4 (78) J Tate 25/1: 011034-8: b g Most Welcome - Just Julia   2   70
(Natroun) Front rank 6.5f, wknd on reapp: won a h'cap & 2 class stks in '03: eff at 1m on firm, fast grnd &
polytrack: handles a stiff/gall or sharp trk: has run well fresh: with J Eustace & sharper next time.
1 Jun'03 Newc 8g/f 79-75 D: 1 Jun'03 Newb 8fm 77-(67) E: 1 May'03 Ling 8ag-7a-(60) F:
3028} **AIMEES DELIGHT 261** [13]4-9-1 (80) M Fenton 33/1: 010310-9: Chsd ldrs, no impress 2f out on reapp.   1   65
928   **KRUGERRAND 10** [4]5-9-4 (80) Lisa Jones(3) 16/1: 4040-000: 10th: Held up, nvr nr ldrs.   nk   68
3379*} **ANGLO SAXON 244** [14]4-9-8 (84) J Murtagh 9/2: 101-0: 11th: Nvr btr than mid-div from reapp.   ¾   71
21*   **RED SPELL 144** [7]3-8-3 (79) R L Moore 25/1: 1-0: 12th: Chsd ldrs 6f, sn wknd on reapp: btr 21 (aw, mdn).4   61
714+**TOPTON 41** [6]10-9-4 bl (80) K Darley 16/1: 601-4310: 13th: Al in rear: 6 wk abs: btr 714 (AW).   9   47
13 Ran   Time 1m 51.27 ()   Owned: Mr Anthony W Parsons   Trained: Radlett

---

1058   4.40 Come Racing At Royal Windsor Selling Stakes 3yo+ (G)
£2996 £856 £428   1m67y rnd   Good/Soft   Inapp   Inside. Rcd far side.

1013   **AMNESTY 5** [3] G L Moore 5-9-6 bl e (56) R L Moore 4/1: 0450061: Dwelt & rdn in rear, imprvd to   56
chase ldrs 2f out, forged ahd cl-home, drvn out: qck reapp, op 11/2, bght in for 3,600gns: first success, fit from
AW & apprec this drop into sell grade: eff at 7f/1m, prob stays 10f: acts on fast, gd/soft grnd & polytrack.
912   **FEN GYPSY 12** [6] P D Evans 6-9-12 (60) R Havlin 5/1: 0-540002: Front rank, led after halfway   1   60
till cl-home: clr of rem: apprec this rtn to 1m & sell grade: deserves similar, see 607 (AW).
1028   **OUR DESTINY 3** [11] A W Carroll 6-9-12 (40) S Hitchcott(3) 12/1: 2401163: Keen & led till after   7   50
halfway, wknd fnl 1f: qck reapp: fibresand specialist: see 957.
831*   **OVER TO YOU BERT 27** [12] R J Hodges 5-9-12 (45) V Slattery 20/1: 00-06514: Chsd ldrs, outpcd 2f out. 3   45
1026   **MUQTADI 3** [8]6-9-12 (50) S Sanders 12/1: 4150045: Rear, some hdwy, nvr dngrs: qck reapp.   2½   41
857   **BALLYRUSH 20** [1]4-9-6 (57) R Keogh(7) 14/1: 00-05456: Trkd ldrs, wide into str, sn no impress.   ¾   33
450   **ESPADA 75** [7]8-9-12 (77) D Holland 11/4 FAV: 0002-007: Front rank, switched to rail bef halfway,   nk   39
ev ch till wknd 1.5f out: well bckd, 11 wk abs: more expected on this drop to sell grade: see 216.
742}   **PRINCE ALBERT 398** [5]6-9-6 T J F Egan 20/1: 0035/05-8: ch g Rock City - Russell Creek (Sandy   27   0
Creek) Al bhd on reapp: tried a t-strap: lightly rcd & modest form in '03: hdles rnr-up in Oct '02 (nov,
rtd 90h): plcd in '02: eff at 7f, poss stays 10f: handles fast, soft grnd & polytrack.
1028   **KUMAKAWA 3** [10]6-9-6 bl (40) Liam Jones(2) 20/1: 3002609: Al bhd, t.o.: qck reapp.   ½   0
        JEMS LAW [9]5-9-1 VIS J Jeffrey(7) 66/1: 0: 10th: b f Contract Law - Alnasr Jewel (Al Nasr) Al   1½   0
well bhd, t.o. on Flat debut: tried a visor: modest bmpr form: with J Jenkins.
862   **JUST WIZ 19** [2]8-9-12 bl (40) T G McLaughlin 9/1: 2-630230: 11th: Mid-div till after halfway, t.o.   1¾   0
4610} **WHIPLASH 182** [4]3-8-5 (60) R Smith 12/1: 02000-0: 12th: b c Orpen - La Colombari (Lomond) Al   2   0
well bhd, t.o. on reapp: rnr-up once in '03 (mdn): eff at 5f on fast grnd, handles a sharp/undul trk: with R
Hannon.   2 May'03 Brig 5.3g/f 69- D:
786   **MISS CELERITY 34** [13]4-9-1 (35) S Drowne 40/1: 60-00400: 13th: Front rank till halfway, wknd, t.o.   11   0
13 Ran   Time 1m 51.29 ()   Owned: Mr GAJackman Mr JFJackman   Trained: Brighton

WINDSOR   MONDAY 05.04.04   Sharp, Fig 8 Track

1059
5.10 Canons Health Club Stoke Poges Handicap Stakes 3yo+ 0-75 (E)   [75]
£4355 £1340 £670   1m67y rnd   Good/Soft   Inapp   Inside. Most rcd Far Side.

888   **CAROUBIER** 16 [11] J Gallagher 4-9-7 (68) T E Durcan 16/1: 4-521201: Held up bhd, hdwy 2f out,   **75+**
led ins fnl 1f, sprinted clr: stays 11f, all wins at 1m: acts on firm, gd/soft grnd & fibresand: eff with/without
a visor & gd weight carrier: made most of a fair turf mark, shld follow-up. see 700.
4466} **SOLLER BAY** 192 [14] K R Burke 7-10-0 (75) Darren Williams 13/2: 000466-2: b g Contract Law -   5   77
Bichette (Lidhame) Front rank, led halfway & styd centre crse, collared dist, ev ch till swamped by wnr cl-home:
reapp: won 2 h'caps in '03: h'cap plcd in '02 & won a val h'cap in '01: eff at 1m/10f, loves gd & hvy grnd,
handles fibresand & any trk: runs well fresh: best with an uncontested lead, fine eff under top-weight today.
1 May'03 Hayd 8.1sft 79-76 C: 1 Apr'03 Wind 8.3g/s 75-67 E: 1 Nov'01 Newm 8gd 86-75 C: 2 Aug'01 Ayr 10sft 81- D:
1020   **OH SO ROSIE** 4 [13] J S Moore 4-8-13 (60) B Swarbrick(7) 7/1: 64020-43: Dwelt, hdwy in centre to   nk   62
lead dist, no extra ins fnl 1f: qck reapp & clr of rem: another gd run on prob the slowest grnd: see 1020.
4619} **TIBER TIGER** 182 [17] N P Littmoden 4-10-0 vis (75) Steven Harrison(7) 25/1: 160500-4: b g Titus   6   67
Livius - Genetta (Green Desert) Chsd ldrs, onepcd over 1f out: clr of rem, jt top-weight, reapp: won 3 h'caps in
'03, also plcd sev times: eff btwn 7f & 1m on firm, gd/soft grnd & stiff/gall trks: suited by blnks, has tried a
visor: back on a winning mark, sharper next time.
1 Jul'03 Newm 8g/f 83-76 C: 2 Jul'03 Newm 7fm 78-76 D: 1 Jun'03 Redc 7g/f 78-73 D: 2 Jun'03 Redc 7fm 77-74 E:
1 Jun'03 Beve 7.5g/f 75-68 D: 1 Jul'02 Newm 7g/f 78-66 D: 1 Jul'02 Chep 6gd 71- F:
753   **REALISM** 38 [6]4-9-4 (65) A Culhane 25/1: 50-44105: Rear, mod late hdwy, nvr dngrs: see 678 (AW).   8   45
4756} **PHRED** 173 [10]4-9-5 (66) S Carson 16/1: 060100-6: ch g Safawan - Phlirty (Pharly) Trkd ldrs,   1¼   44
wknd & eased over 1f out: reapp: jumps fit, mod hdle form: dual h'cap wnr in '03, subs tried blnks unsuccessfully:
best up with/forcing the pace arnd 1m on fast & gd/soft: handles a sharp or gall/undul trk.
1 Sep'03 Chep 8.1g/f 70-65 E: 1 Jun'03 Wind 8.3g/f 67-60 E: 2 May'03 Warw 8.1g/f 60-57 F:
932   **MUSICAL GIFT** 10 [18]4-9-8 p (69) P Robinson 5/1 FAV: 40-14457: Trkd ldrs, btn 2f out: bckd from   1¾   44
11/1: more expected on this switch back to turf: see 932.
878   **KARATHAENA** 17 [3]4-9-7 (68) T Quinn 33/1: 2/503-008: Held up, late progress, nvr dngrs.   1½   41
888   **SUPER SONG** 16 [2]4-9-12 T (73) R Havlin 25/1: 00/201-09: Set pace till halfway, sn wknd: t-strap.   2   43
517   **LIBERTY ROYAL** 65 [1]5-9-8 (69) S Sanders 14/1: 40000-60: 10th: Nvr btr than mid-div, 9 wk abs.   1½   37
5029} **GRACIA** 150 [8]5-9-6 (67) Martin Dwyer 10/1: 301003-0: 11th: Front rank 5f, wknd on reapp.   9   21
945   **WOOD FERN** 9 [16]4-9-9 (70) D Corby(3) 28/1: 3001-000: 12th: Chsd ldrs till halfway, sn btn.   5   17
3434} **BAKIRI** 603 [4]6-10-0 (75) L Dettori 12/1: 042/060/-0: 13th: Al bhd: jmps fit, been gldd, new stable.   5   15
345   **TURN AROUND** 88 [9]4-9-2 (63) K Darley 11/1: 0-/0000-00: 14th: Rdn in mid-div, btn halfway: abs.   12   0
3219*)**ENCHANTED PRINCESS** 252 [7]4-9-11 (72) M Hills 6/1: 01-0: 15th: Chsd ldrs till after halfway, sn   2½   0
wknd & eased, t.o.: bckd from 6/1, new stable, reapp.
714   **TRUSTED INSTINCT** 41 [12]4-9-11 T (72) T P Queally(3) 40/1: 3610-000: 16th: Al bhd, t.o.: abs.   7   0
2624} **OH BOY** 277 [5]4-9-7 (68) R Hughes 20/1: 0/040-0: 17th: Nvr trav, t.o.: abs.   22   0
4849} **BISHOPSTONE MAN** 166 [15]7-9-12 (73) C Cavanagh(7) 12/1: 242240-0: 18th: Mid-div till halfway, t.o.   30   0
18 Ran   Time 1m 51.63()   Owned: C R Marks (Banbury)   Trained: Moreton-In-Marsh

SAINT CLOUD   WEDNESDAY 31.03.04   Lefthand, Galloping Track

Official Going Good

1060
2.35 Listed Prix Omnium II (Colts & Geldings) 3yo ()
£15845 £6338 £4754   1m   Good

4880*)**AMERICAN POST** 157 Mme C Head Maarek 3-9-2 R Hughes : 2111-1: br c Bering - Wells Fargo   **119+**
(Sadler's Wells) Trkd ldr, led 5f out till dist, qcknd to lead again ins last, hands & heels: reapp: dual Gr 1 wnr
in '03, incl Racing Post Trophy: eff at 1m, mid-dist pedigree & will get 10f+: acts on fast & soft grnd, runs well
fresh: high-class colt with a fine turn of foot, excellent claims in the French 2000 Guineas.
1 Sat'25 Donc 8g/f 121-0 A: 1 Sun'05 Long 75ft 121- A:
       JOURSANVAULT A de Royer Dupre 3-9-2 C Soumillon : 2: gr c Verglas - Jane Brust (Brustolon)   4   108
       BLACKDOUN J L Pelletan 3-9-2 J B Eyquem : 3: gr c Verglas - Rade (Kaldoun)   ½   107
5 Ran   Time 1m 43.00()   Owned: K Abdulla   Trained: France

LONGCHAMP   SUNDAY 04.04.04   Righthand, Stiff, Galloping Track

Official Going Good

1061
2.45 Gr 2 Prix d'Harcourt 4yo+ ()
£42148 £16268 £7764   1m2f   Good

4837} **VANGELIS** A de Royer Dupre 5-8-12 C Soumillon 93/10: 517030-1: gr c Highest Honor - Capades   117
Dancer (Gate Dancer) Held up, swtchd wide 2f out, rdn & styd on to lead ins last: reapp: Gr 3 wnr in the Provinces
in '03, Gr 2 placed, also won 7th in the Arlington Million in Chicago: suited by 10f, stays 12f well: acts on good & soft
ground, reportedly prefers the former: goes well fresh: v smart colt, targeting the Arlington Million once again.
2 Sun'08 Chan 8gd 113- A:
4624} **EXECUTE** J E Hammond 7-8-12 T Jarnet 124/10: 625326-2: Trkd ldrs, short of room over 1f out,   ¾   115
swtchd & drvn to briefly lead ins last, not pace of wnr, reapp.
4624} **SHORT PAUSE** A Fabre 5-8-12 G Stevens 11/10: 34142-3: Rear, styd on for press fnl 3f.   1½   113
833   **NYSAEAN** R Hannon 5-8-12 (114) R Hughes 124/10: 62117-54: b c Sadler's Wells - Irish Arms   ½   112
(Irish River) Trkd ldr, led over 1f out, rdn & hdd ins last, no extra: dual Gr 3 wnr last term: '02 mdn, class stks
& Listed wnr: stays 12f well, suited by 10f: handles firm & gd, relishes gd/sft & soft grnd: acts on any trk & can go
well fresh: handles any trk, loves the Curragh & forcing tactics: smart colt.
1 Sun'08 Curr 10g/s 116- A: 1 Sun'27 Curr 10g/s 116- : 2 Mon'21 Kemp 10fm 114-114 A: 1 Aug'02 Deau 10sft 115- :

LONGCHAMP   SUNDAY 04.04.04   Righthand, Stiff, Galloping Track

1 Jun'02 Chep 10.1sft 110- C: 1 Apr'02 Wind 10gd 100- D:
8 Ran   Time 2m 02.60()   Owned: H Guy   Trained: France

CURRAGH   SUNDAY 04.04.04   Righthand, Galloping Track

Official Going Soft

1062   **3.45 Gr 3 Gladness Stakes 4yo+** ()
£30485 £8911 £4221   **7f str**   **Soft**

952   **MONSIEUR BOND 8** B Smart 4-9-0 (110) F Lynch 3/1 FAV: 162125-51: Handy trav well, led 2f out &   **119+**
rdn clr, impressive: op 7/2: apprec step up to 7f, eff at 6f/1m: acts on fm & gd/sft: v smart career best effort &
has improved over winter, keep on your side in Gr 2 class: v unlucky 952.
5037*}**STEENBERG 148** M H Tompkins 5-9-0 (109) P Robinson 8/1: 04434012: ch g Flying Spur - Kip's   7   **108**
Sister (Cawston's Clown) Held up, short of room 2f out, kept on fnl 2f, no chance with wnr: Listed wnr fnl '03
start, earlier Gr 1 4th: Gr 3 rnr up '02: suited by 6/7f, tried 9f: acts on firm & soft ground: best without blnks:
loves a stiff/gall trk: goes well fresh: tough & v useful, rate higher.
1 Sat'08 Donc 6gd 115-109 A: 2 Jun'02 Asco 7g/f 109- A: 1 Aug'01 Asco 7gd 101- B: 2 Jul'01 Yarm 6fm 87- D:
922   **ROCKETS N ROLLERS 10** R Hannon 4-9-0 (104) Dane O'Neill 12/1: 11/400-333: Chsd ldrs, chsd ldr 2f   ¾   **107**
out, kept on for press, no impress: op 10/1: up in grade, gd run: acts on fast, soft & fibresand: see 922, 838.
952   **ORIENTOR 8** J S Goldie 6-9-3 (104) J P Murtagh 5/1: 050006-24: Held up, hdwy 2f out, chsd wnr   shd   **110**
over 1f out, no impress ins last: not disgraced: see 952.
13 Ran   Time 1m 28.50 ()   Owned: R C Bond   Trained: Hambleton

---

1063   **4.45 Listed Loughbrown Stakes 3yo** ()
£21808 £6399 £3048   **7f str**   **Soft**

4935} **NEWTON 160** A P O'Brien 3-9-0 J P Spencer 5/2: 11053D2-1: b c Danehill - Elite Guest (Be My   **109**
Guest) Held up, rnd & styd on fnl 2f to lead close home: reapp: mdn & Listed wnr '03, subs Gr 1 plcd: suited by a
gall 7f on fast or soft: eff with/without blnks & goes well fresh: smart & progressive.
2 Mon'27 Leop 7gd 108- : 1 Sat'24 Curr 5sft 107- A:
       DABIROUN 14 J M Oxx 3-9-0 M J Kinane 7/2: 12: b c Desert Prince - Dabaya (In The Wings) Led,   ½   **107**
rdn & styd on strongly fnl 2f, just hdd close home: recent wnr of a 1m maiden here at The Curragh: eff at 7f/1m on
soft ground, may stay further: lightly raced colt who handled this step up in class well.
       AMARULA RIDGE 162 K Prendergast 3-9-0 D P McDonogh 7/1: 1-3: Chsd ldr halfway, chance 2f out,   ¾   **106**
not pace of wnr ins last: reapp.
4284} **WATHAB 203** D K Weld 3-9-0 P J Smullen 7/4 FAV: 026412-4: Held up, no impress fnl 2f.   4   **98**
7 Ran   Time 1m 31.00()   Owned: Mrs John Magnier   Trained: Ballydoyle

---

PONTEFRACT   TUESDAY 06.04.04   Lefthand, Undulating Track, Stiff Uphill Finish

Official Going Soft

1064   **2.20 Betfair Com Apprentice Series Round One Handicap Stakes 3yo+ 0-70 (E)**   **[70]**
£4222 £1299 £650   **1m4f8y**   **Heavy**   **Inapp**   **Inside**

918   **BENBYAS 12** [3] D Carroll 7-9-9 (65) D Tudhope(5) 5/1: 2000/0/-61: Made all, clr over 3f out, styd   **76**
on well, rdn out: stays 12f well & acts on fast, relishes soft & hvy, gall trks: loves an uncontested lead & took
advantage of ideal conds here, shld follow up qckly on similar grnd: see 918.
4806} **TOM BELL 171** [11] J G M O'Shea 4-8-2 (45) C Haddon(3) 50/1: 00/0005-2: b g King's Theatre -   3½   **51**
Nordic Display (Nordico) In tch, rdn 3f out, kept on to go 2nd ins last, no threat to wnr: 5th at best in '03
(class stks, rtd 48): unplcd prev: has tried a visor: imprvd on reapp at 12f & clearly enjoys hvy.
467*   **SENDINTANK 74** [8] S C Williams 4-9-3 (60) Dean Williams(3) 7/2: 00-11113: Chsd ldrs, eff 2f out,   nk   **66**
no extra ins last: clr rem: joc rec 1-day whip ban, abs: acts on fibresand & hvy: in fine heart.
683*   **JAIR OHMSFORD 47** [15] M J Musson 5-9-10 (66) A Rutter(5) 6/1: 40-14114: Held up, late gains, nvr   4   **67**
dngrs: padd pick after 7 wk abs: prob handles hvy, likes fibresand: in gd heart, see 683.
1034* **ARCHIE BABE 3** [5]8-9-11 (6ex) (67) D Fentiman 100/30 FAV: 4000-015: Chsd ldrs, wknd over 1f out: ¾   **67**
6lb penalty & too sn after 1034?
906   **THATS RACING 14** [1]4-7-12 (6oh) (35) A Reilly(1) 16/1: 00000-26: Held up, no impress fnl 2f: btr 906.   4   **36**
4319} **PROTOCOL 201** [14]10-7-12 (10oh)t (30) S Yourston(5) 33/1: 000040-7: b g Taufan - Ukraine's Affair   1½   **33**
(The Minstrel) Nvr a factor on reapp: jumps fit, recent sell h'cap hdle wnr (rtd 104h, 2m1f, likes gd/soft & hvy):
4th at best in '03 (h'cap): eff btwn 10f/2m1f on firm, gd & fibresand, loves soft & hvy: best in a t-strap, tried
visor.   2 May'01 Nott 14hvy 43-42 E:
821   **BEVIER 29** [2]10-7-13 (1ow) (40) K Ghunowa 25/1: 40-53428: No dngr: btr 821 (10f, f/sand), 666.   15   **16**
244   **ANNAKITA 106** [10]4-8-5 (48) Laura Pike(5) 50/1: 000060-9: b f Unfuwain - Cuban Reef (Dowsing) Al   6   **17**
bhd: unplcd in '03 (rtd 72$, tried up to 12f).
924   **ETON 12** [6]8-10-0 (70) M Howard(7) 33/1: 53310-30: 10th: in tch, wknd 2f out: needs faster grnd.   ½   **38**
866}   **FATEHALKHAIR 377** [13]12-9-6 (62) D Swift(5) 25/1: 0304/60-0: 11th: Al bhd.   11   **19**
1612} **Niagara 323** [16]7-9-13 (69) Saleem Golam(5) 18/1:0   867   **Piste Bleu 19** [4]4-8-12 (55) Liam Jones(5) 33/1:0
808   **Commander Flip 32** [17]4-9-1 (58) H Fellows(7) 33/1:0
4918} **Washington Pink 161** [9]5-8-8 (50) R Keogh(5) 66/1:0
850   **Turftanzer 23** [12]5-7-12 (5oh)t(35) Janice Webster(2) 66/1:0
870   **Call Me Sunshine 19** [7]4-9-8 (65) D Wakenshaw(7) 20/1:0
17 Ran   Time 2m 51.73 (17.63)   Owned: C H Stephenson & Partners   Trained: Warthilll

1065 **2.50 Jason & Rachel Joint 30th Birthday Selling Stakes 3yo+ (E)**
£3858 £1187 £594 **6f rnd** **Heavy** **Inapp** Inside. Rcd Stands Side.

958 **MARABAR 8** [17] D W Chapman 6-9-2 bl (70) A Culhane 7/1 CO FAV: 5-065001: Held up, hdwy over 2f out, led ins last, rdn clr: both wins at 6f, prob stays 7f: acts on firm, clearly enjoyed this hvy grnd & handles any trk: relished drop into the lowest grade: see 555. **50**
847 **ALASTAIR SMELLIE 23** [11] S L Keightley 8-9-7 vis (45) P McCabe 33/1: 0030-002: Dwelt, held up, gd hdwy to lead over 1f out, edged right & hdd ins last, no extra: likes easy grnd & sellers now: see 847. *3* **48**
4531} **COMPTON PRINCESS 189** [10] Mrs A Duffield 4-9-2 (45) G Duffield 33/1: 400000-3: b f Compton Place - Curlew Calling (Pennine Walk) In tch, eff well over 1f out, kept on: plcd twice in '03 (seller & mdn, rtd 47): eff over 6/7f on firm, prob handles hvy: tried a visor: sell h'caps will suit. *1½* **39**
573 **GRAND VIEW 58** [1] J R Weymes 8-9-7 p (35) D Holland 40/1: 0000-604: ch g Grand Lodge - Hemline (Sharpo) Handy, eff over 1f out, sn no extra: unplcd in '03 (rtd 40): plcd in '02 (rtd 44): stays 7f, best at 5/6f on firm, soft & both AWs: best without blnks, tried cheek pieces. *1¾* **39**
1 Jul'01 Muss 5g/f 59- F: 1 Jul'01 Nott 6g/f 59- G: 2 Jun'01 Newc 5g/f 52- F: 1 May'01 Muss 5g/f 58- F:
982* **INDIAN MUSIC 7** [5]7-9-12 (40) F Lynch 16/1: 0000-615: Chsd ldrs, no extra appr fnl 1f: btr 982 (AW). *1* **42**
652 **TICKLE 50** [4]6-9-2 vis t (57) S Sanders 15/2: 060-4036: Led till dist, no extra: abs, see 413. *1¾* **27**
996 **DUSTY WUGG 6** [6]5-9-2 p (40) A Beech(3) 25/1: 40-53057: Dwelt, in tch, btn 2f out. *8* **11**
5021} **RILEYS DREAM 152** [7]5-9-2 (52) S Drowne 14/1: 030000-8: Chsd ldrs, wknd 2f out. *1¼* **8**
902 **NEW OPTIONS 14** [16]7-9-7 p (57) M Fenton 7/1 CO FAV: 5405039: Handy, wknd over 1f out: btr 902. *2½* **8**
996 **SPEEDFIT FREE 6** [9]7-9-7 bl (58) P Hanagan 9/1: 2562400: 10th: Nvr a factor: see 646, 308. *½* **7**
646 **MIZHAR 50** [8]8-9-7 (55) R Winston 10/1: 0-052500: 11th: Nvr a factor: abs, see 512 (fibresand). *1¼* **5**
904 **GRUFF 14** [14]5-9-7 (30) R Fitzpatrick 100/1: 000-0000: 12th: Al bhd. *¾* **3**
982 **VALUABLE GIFT 7** [13]7-9-7 t p (40) J F Egan 33/1: 000-0000: 13th: Nvr a factor. *4* **0**
773 **SUGAR CUBE TREAT 37** [18]8-9-2 (30) K Dalgleish 50/1: 0//000-000: 14th: Dwelt, al bhd. *4* **0**
822 **DANCING RIDGE 29** [12]7-9-7 (35) T Williams 100/1: 436/00-00: 15th: Al bhd. *4* **0**
963 **SPEEDY JAMES 8** [3]8-9-7 (40) L Treadwell(7) 14/1: 00/0-0020: 16th: In tch, wknd 2f out: btr 963. *3½* **0**
963* **AMERICAN COUSIN 8** [15]9-9-12 (60) A Nicholls 7/1 CO FAV: 04140-10: 17th: In tch, wknd qckly over 2f out, virtually p.u.: this is not his form: soft grnd wnr in 963. *15* **0**
17 Ran Time 1m 26.13 (12.13) Owned: Miss N F Thesiger Trained: York

1066 **3.20 Pontefract Park Stakes Handicap 3yo+ 0-95 (C)** **[94]**
£9442 £3582 £1791 **1m4y rnd** **Heavy** **Inapp** Inside

928 **ST PETERSBURG 11** [12] M H Tompkins 4-9-6 (86) P Robinson 7/2 FAV: 00315-21: Cl-up trav well, led over 1f out, pushed clr fnl 1f, readily: hvly bckd: stays 1m well on fast, gd & polytrack, clearly enjoys hvy & any trk: v progressive, stable in grand heart & likely to make a qck follow up: useful, see 928. **94**
879 **THE BONUS KING 18** [9] M Johnston 4-9-4 (84) J Fanning 11/1: 6060-452: Led early, cl-up, led again halfway till over 1f out, kept on but not pace of wnr: padd pick: caught a fast improving type: styd this stiff/undul 1m & clearly enjoyed hvy grnd, acts on fast: clr of rem, h'capped to win: see 688. *4* **85**
928 **STRONG HAND 11** [6] M W Easterby 4-9-0 (80) K Darley 6/1: 35110-63: Handy, eff over 1f out, sn onepace: not disgraced, may have more to come on a sounder surface, see 928, 127. *5* **74**
928 **UNICORN REWARD 11** [4] M D Hammond 4-9-0 (80) A Culhane 20/1: 11150-04: b c Turtle Island - Kingdom Pearl (Statoblest) Held up, sn hmpd, hdwy 2f out, no dngr: landed 4 consecutive h'caps in '03: plcd in '02: best up with/forcing the pace at around 1m/8.3f & likes fast & gd grnd, handles polytrack & prob any trk, likes Chepstow: v progressive last term, back on a fair mark now & likely to apprec a sounder surface. *5* **67**
1 Aug'03 Chep 8.1gd 86-82 D: 1 Jul'03 Chep 8.1g/f 84-74 D: 1 Jul'03 Leic 8.0gd 84-74 D: 1 Jun'03 Wind 8.3gd 73-68 E:
4976} **SHOT TO FAME 157** [10]5-10-0 (94) S Drowne 9/1: 056300-5: b g Quest For Fame - Exocet (Deposit Ticket) Held up, some late gains, nvr dngrs on reapp: plcd on 1 of 8 '03 starts (rtd h'cap): plcd in a val h'cap in '02: v eff at 1m on firm & gd/soft, has disapp on hvy: has run well fresh on gall trks: needs a sounder surface. 1 Oct'01 York 8g/s 96- E: *3* **77**
951 **FLIGHTY FELLOW 10** [8]4-9-12 (92) S Sanders 5/1: 14322-06: ch g Flying Spur - Al Theraab (Roberto) In tch, eff over 3f out, no impress: '03 dual h'cap scorer: '02 auct mdn & nursery h'cap wnr: suited by 1m/8.5f on fast & soft, any trk: imprvd last term in blnks & will do btr shortly back in headgear. *2* **72**
2 Oct'03 York 7.9g/f 92-90 B: 2 Sep'03 Hayd 8.1gd 93-90 C: 1 Aug'03 Pont 8.0g/f 90-87 C: 1 Jul'03 Beve 8.5g/s 89-77 D:
2 Jun'03 Beve 8.5g/f 77-75 D: 1 Oct'02 Catt 7g/s 81-74 D: 1 Aug'02 Thir 7gd 74- E: 2 Jun'02 Hami 6sft 77- F:
4684} **BROADWAY SCORE 178** [1]6-9-10 (90) Dale Gibson 20/1: 100000-7: b g Theatrical - Brocaro (Mr Prospector) Led after 2f till halfway, wknd dist: ndd race: won 1 of 8 '03 starts (val h'cap, J Hills): '02 class stks & rtd h'cap wnr: eff over 1m/10.6f & likes fm & fast, any trk: has run well fresh: best up with/forcing the pace: slipped to a handy mark for new trainer (been gelded), keep an eye on on faster grnd. *1½* **68**
1 Apr'03 Kemp 10fm 96-95 B: 2 Apr'03 Pont 10.0g/f 102-(95) C: 1 Aug'02 Wind 8.3g/f 98-92 C:
2 Jun'02 Sand 8g/f 94-92 B: 1 Apr'02 Hayd 10.5g/f 96- C: 1 Sep'01 Sand 9gd 88- D:
4846} **MEZUZAH 167** [2]4-9-6 (86) D Holland 4/1: 630406-8: Held up, no impress fnl 2f: been gelded. *2½* **60**
2 **CHERISHED NUMBER 148** [7]5-9-1 (81) R Winston 14/1: 634004-9: Keen in tch, eff 2f out, no extra. *2½* **51**
4165} **LES ARCS 209** [5]4-9-5 (85) J F Egan 25/1: 210-0: 10th: Nvr a factor on reapp: new yard, gelded. *13* **37**
JAHIA 451 [11]5-8-9 (75) N Callan 80/1: 110/6-0: 11th: Al bhd. *¾* **26**
HUXLEY 164 [3]5-9-5 (85) P McCabe 25/1: 321010-0: 12th: Keen, in tch till wknd over 2f out. *1¾* **33**
12 Ran Time 1m 54.21 (12.41) Owned: Mr P Heath Trained: Newmarket

1067 **3.50 Yorkshire Racing Club Median Auction Maiden Stakes 3yo (E)**
£4076 £1254 £627 **1m2f6y** **Heavy** **Inapp** Inside. Rcd Stands Side.

WINGED DARGENT [8] M Johnston 3-9-0 J Fanning 11/2: 1: b c In The Wings - Petite D Argent (Noalto) Dsptd lead till went on over 1f out, kept on gamely for press to hold on ins last: half-brother to tough/useful stayers Mana D'Argent & Greta D'Argent: eff at 10f, sure to relish further: acts on hvy grnd & runs well fresh: learn plenty from this & there will be plenty more to come, esp over further & in time. **77**
919 **TUDOR BELL 12** [2] J G M O'Shea 3-9-0 D Sweeney 25/1: 4-02: b c Definite Article - Late Night Lady (Mujadil) In tch, eff to chase wnr well over 1f out, kept on ins last, just held: 4th in an auct mdn sole '03 start: apprec step up to 10f & acts on hvy grnd: shld find a modest race. *hd* **76**
AT YOUR REQUEST [1] E A L Dunlop 3-9-0 W Supple 14/1: 3: gr g Bering - Requesting (Rainbow *1¼* **74**

Quest) Held up, eff 2f out, kept on ins last, not btn far: clr rem, scope: mid-dist bred & clearly eff at 10f, shld get further: handles hvy grnd: open to improvement & fin clr of rem here, shld win a race.

4974} **CROCIERA** 157 [3] M H Tompkins 3-9-0   P Robinson 8/1: 00-4: b c Croco Rouge - Ombry Girl   11   58
(Distinctly North) Keen, dsptd lead till over 1f out, no extra: lkd in need of race: some promise when unplcd in 2 '03 mdns: bred to stay at least 1m.

4996} **HERNANDOS BOY** 154 [6]3-9-0   A Culhane 14/1: 000-5: Keen, handy, wknd 2f out: longer trip.   5   51

814   **POLISH RHAPSODY** 29 [5]3-8-9 (48) G Faulkner 66/1: 0-006: Held up, btn over 2f out.   dist   0

930   **SAAMEQ** 11 [7]3-9-0   D McGaffin 33/1: 0-067: Keen cl-up, wknd over 2f out: small.   18   0

      SERENGETI SKY [4]3-9-0   L Dettori 4/7 FAV: 8: Sn rdn along in tch, wknd 4f out, eased: hvly   dist   0
bckd: clearly btr expected, not handle hvy?
8 Ran   Time 2m 29.25 (21.15)   Owned: Mr Daniel A Couper   Trained: Middleham

---

1068   4.20 High-Rise Classified Stakes 3yo+ 0-90 (C)
£9210 £3494 £1747   **1m2f6y**   **Heavy**   **Inapp**   Inside. Rcd stands side.

      AKASH 205 [2] M Johnston 4-9-8 (90) J Fanning 9/1: 4/05220-1: b g Dr Devious - Akilara (Kahyasi)   95
 Made just about all, held on gamely cl-home, all out on reapp: lkd superb, bckd from 14/1: prev trained in Ireland, rnr-up twice in '03 (h'caps): dual '02 wnr: eff at 10/12f on fm & hvy: likes to force the pace & runs v well fresh: looks a typically game recruit to yard.

4504} **BOURGEOIS** 190 [5] T D Easterby 7-9-13 (95) K Darley 12/1: 030350-2: ch g Sanglamore - Bourbon   shd   99
Girl (Ile de Bourbon) Chsd ldrs, prog to chall 2f out, just btn in a thrilling fin: clr 3rd: jumps fit, Jan '04 nov hdle wnr (rtd 117h), eff at 2m on gd): '03 reapp wnr (h'cap), plcd sev times subs incl visor: eff at 10/12f, stays 14f: acts on firm & hvy, eff with/without blnks/visor: gd weight-carrier, runs v well fresh: excellent reapp.
2 May'03 Hami 12.1g/s 103-101 A: 1 Apr'03 Hayd 14g/f 102-94 C: 1 Jul'02 York 11.8g/f 97-90 B:

951   **WING COMMANDER** 10 [8] R A Fahey 5-9-11 (93) P Hanagan 4/1 JT FAV: 40233-43: Rdn in rear, hdwy   15   79
into 3rd 1.5f out, sn no impress: btr expected on this return to 10f, not handle this hvy grnd? worth another ch on a sounder surface after 951.

928   **SWIFT TANGO** 11 [9] E A L Dunlop 4-9-8 vis (90) W Supple 9/2: 23-10234: Held up, eff 3f out, sn   11   63
btn: not handle hvy? much btr 928 & 452.

3834} **PRINCE HOLING** 226 [7]4-9-8 (89) A Culhane 12/1: 32/4122-5: ch g Halling - Ella Mon Amour (Ela   3½   58
Mana Mou) Rear, prog to chase ldrs 3f out, sn wknd on reapp: p.u. recently over hdles: '02 mdn wnr, also rnr-up twice (class stks & h'cap): eff at 10/12f on gd & firm grnd: will apprec a return to a faster surface.
2 Aug'03 Good 12g/f 89-85 D: 2 Jun'03 Bath 11.7fm 86-(85) C: 1 Jun'03 Sali 9.9fm 88-(85) D:
2 Sep'02 Ches 7fm 87- D: 2 Aug'02 Yarm 8fm 87- E:

2135*}**ARGONAUT** 297 [10]4-9-8 (88) F Lynch 4/1 JT FAV: 31-6: b g Rainbow Quest - Chief Bee (Chief's   1¾   56
Crown) Rdn in rear, nvr dngrs on reapp: has been gelded: won fnl of two '03 starts (Sandown mdn): eff at 10f, will relish 12f: acts on fast & firm grnd & on a stiff/gall trk: much btr than this & sure to apprec a return to faster grnd.   1 Jun'03 Sand 10.0fm 89- D:

3293} **WAHCHI** 249 [3]5-9-8 (90) Dale Gibson 80/1: 01/23/40-7: Slowly away, al bhd, t.o.: reapp, gelded.   29   26

4334} **LOVE YOU ALWAYS** 555 [6]4-9-13 (95) L Dettori 11/2: 13/-8: Prom 7f, wknd qckly, t.o.: comeback,   9   21
tchd 13/2, has been gelded: unsuited by this soft grnd.

3835} **AMANDUS** 226 [1]4-9-13 (95) D Holland 7/1: 24/0214-9: Prom 7f, wknd qckly, t.o. in last on reapp.   dist   0
9 Ran   Time 2m 24.61 (16.51)   Owned: Mr Markus Graff   Trained: Middleham

---

1069   4.50 Jamaican Flight Handicap Stakes 4yo+ 0-75 (E)
£4144 £1275 £638   **2m1f216y**   **Heavy**   **Inapp**   Inside. Rcd stands side.   **[79]**

2411} **GREEN N GOLD** 286 [1] M D Hammond 4-7-12 (1oh) (49) P Hanagan 25/1: 000400-1: b f Cloudings -   57
Fishki (Niniski) Held up, smooth hdwy to lead 2f out, styd on strongly, rdn out: plcd in a nov hdle 7 days ago (eff at 2m6f on gd, rtd 99h): plcd once in '03 (h'cap): stays 2m2f well, handles fast, likes gd/soft & hvy grnd: has tried cheek pieces: thorough stayer, clearly revelled in these testing conds & gained first success.
2 Jul'02 Beve 7.4g/s 54- F:

926   **VICARS DESTINY** 11 [9] Mrs S Lamyman 6-9-6 (67) G Duffield 11/4: 65626-22: Chsd ldrs, imprvd to   3½   69
lead briefly over 2f out, kept on but not pace of wnr: well bckd, padd pick: acts on firm & hvy, deserves similar.

5008} **RINGSIDE JACK** 153 [4] C W Fairhurst 8-8-5 (52) J Fanning 12/1: 600344-3: b g Batshoof -   5   49
Celestine (Skyliner) Chsd ldrs, ev ch 2f out, sn no extra: jumps fit (nov hdle 4th, eff at 2m1f on gd/soft, rtd 104h): h'cap plcd in '03: '02 appr h'cap wnr: eff at 13f, stays 2m, acts on fast, likes hvy grnd: handles any trk, runs well fresh: eff with/without a visor: thorough stayer: return to 2m shld prove ideal.
1 Jun'02 Hami 13sft 61-57 F: 2 Jun'02 Newc 12.4g/s 56- F: 2 Apr'02 Beve 10g/f 63-62 D:
2 Sep'01 Ches 10.3g/s 66-67 E: 2 Jun'01 Ripo 10g/f 68-67 D: 2 May'01 Donc 10.2fm 66-63 C:

870   **JAMAICAN FLIGHT** 8 [8] Mrs S Lamyman 11-8-5 (52) J F Egan 14/1: 450-3444: Led till over 2f out,   12   39
wknd: longer priced s/mate of rnr-up: far from disgraced in race named in his honour on grnd softer than ideal.

4812} **ACCEPTING** 169 [2]7-8-6 BL (53) R Winston 16/1: 60/0010-5: b g Mtoto - D'Azy (Persian Bold)   ½   39
Mid-div, rdn along halfway, nvr nr to chall in first time blnks: jumps fit, May '03 h'cap hdle wnr (rtd 103h, eff at 2m4f/3m2f on fast & soft, also tried cheek pieces): '03 wnr here at Pontefract (h'cap): eff at 2m on firm & gd/soft, prob any trk: runs well fresh: often wears cheek pieces, blnkd today.
1 Oct'03 Pont 17.1g/f 55-50 E: 2 Sep'01 Ches 15.8gd 79-83 D: 1 Jun'01 Muss 16g/f 82-80 D:

1776} **CHARMING ADMIRAL** 314 [15]11-8-3 (50) J Mackay 33/1: 30/510//0-6: Al bhd, t.o.: jumps fit.   28   10

997   **RAJAM** 6 [12]6-9-11 (72) Alex Greaves 20/1: 2000-067: Prom, wknd qckly 3f out, t.o.: qck reapp.   17   16

529* **BUSTLING RIO** 63 [6]8-9-4 (65) Rory Moore(7) 12/1: 560-4018: Al bhd, t.o.: jumps unplcd since 529 (AW).19   0

965   **DANNY LEAHY** 8 [3]4-8-13 (65) K Dalgleish 50/1: 4053-509: Chsd ldr, wknd over 3f out, t.o..   8   0

4461} **MY LINE** 193 [10]7-9-0 bl (61) D Holland 9/4 FAV: 1450/62-0: 10th: Al bhd, t.o. halfway: well bckd.   dist   0

156* **KILLING JOKE** 122 [14]4-9-8 (74) M Fenton 14/1: 30/0601-0: 11th: Prom, wknd qckly 5f out, t.o.   ¾   0

      ONTOS 1256 [13]8-9-9 (70) L Dettori 14/1: 214103///-0: 12th: Chsd ldrs, wknd over 4f out, t.o.   22   0

926   **ALLEZ MOUSSON** 11 [7]6-8-9 (56) S Sanders 11/1: 0/6030-00: 13th: Rdn in rear, t.o. halfway.   28   0
13 Ran   Time 4m 22.11 (41.81)   Owned: Mr E Whalley   Trained: Middleham

PONTEFRACT TUESDAY 06.04.04 Lefthand, Undulating Track, Stiff Uphill Finish

1070 **5.20 Pontefract-Races Co Uk Maiden Stakes Fillies 3yo (D)**
£5473 £1684 £842 **6f rnd** **Heavy** **Inapp** Inside. Field split in str.

4827} **CAPETOWN GIRL 168** [1] K R Burke 3-8-11 (67) G Faulkner 9/2: 302025-1: b f Danzero - Cavernista (Lion Cavern) Prom & rcd alone on ins, led halfway, clr fnl 2f, unchall: op 7/1, lkd fit for reapp: rcd on 3 of 6 '02 starts (mdns): eff at 6/7f, handles fast, likes gd & hvy grnd: runs v well fresh, likes a gall trk: much imprvd on reapp & in these testing conditions. 2 Oct'03 Newc 7gd 71-(68) F: 2 Jul'03 Thir 6g/s 71- D: **71**
CRATHES [6] J G Given 3-8-11 M Fenton 10/1: 2: ch f Zilzal - Sweet Dreams (Selkirk) Dwelt, hdwy from rear over 2f out, took 2nd cl-home but no ch with wnr on debut: sire a top-class miler: bred to apprec 7f/1m, prob handles hvy grnd: sure to learn from this. *8* **59**
2793} **CEFIRA 271** [8] M H Tompkins 3-8-11 P Robinson 100/30 FAV: 0-3: b f Distant View - Bold Jessie (Never So Bold) Trkd ldrs, went after wnr 2f out, sn left bhd & caught for 2nd cl-home: nicely bckd, just btr for reapp: unplcd on sole '03 start: scopey sort, shld benefit from a return to faster grnd. *nk* **58**
543 **PICKLE 62** [5] S C Williams 3-8-11 K Darley 7/1: 304: Led till halfway, wknd 2f out: abs. *18* **22**
863 **GRACEFUL AIR 20** [7]3-8-11 (64) R Winston 9/2: 50303-45: b f Danzero - Samsung Spirit (Statoblest) Chsd ldrs, lost place halfway: tchd 6/1: plcd several times in '03 (incl h'caps & in cheek pieces): eff at 6f on gd & fast grnd: has tried cheek pieces: with J Weymes. 2 Jul'03 Pont 6g/f 64-64 D: *2* **18**
4301} **BLADES DAUGHTER 202** [10]3-8-11 N Callan 25/1: 000-6: Prom, wknd qckly halfway, t.o. on reapp. *19* **0**
5013} **ESTIHLAL 152** [3]3-8-11 R Hills 9/2: 60-7: Chsd ldrs till halfway, sn wknd & t.o.: mkt drifter, reapp. *4* **0**
2608} **SAVANNAH RIVER 278** [2]3-8-11 T D Mernagh 50/1: 000-8: Slow away, al bhd, t.o. on reapp: t-strap. *15* **0**
875 **PICK A BERRY 18** [4]3-8-11 D Holland 14/1: 0-09: Al well bhd, t.o.. *23* **0**
32 **DESIGNER CITY 144** [11]3-8-11 (57) J Carroll 20/1: 644660-0: 10th: Slowly away, al bhd, t.o. on reapp. *26* **0**
10 Ran Time 1m 24.53(10.43) Owned: Danum Racing Trained: Leyburn

LINGFIELD Polytrack TUESDAY 06.04.04 Lefthand, V Sharp Track

Official Going Standard

1071 **2.30 Betdirect Co Uk Maiden Auction Stakes 2yo (H)**
£1285 £367 £184 **5f aw rnd** **Going 49** **-08 Slow** Outside

974 **SMOKINCANON 7** [8] W G M Turner 2-9-0 R Miles(3) 4/1: 31: Made all, in command dist, hands & heels, readily: op 3/1, confirmed debut promise: eff at 5f, shld get further: acts on soft grnd & polytrack, sharp/undul trk: likes to force the pace: progressing, can win again: see 974. **82a**
LATERAL THINKER [6] J A Osborne 2-8-9 S W Kelly 11/1: 2: b f Desert Sun - Miss Margate (Don't Forget Me) Chsd ldrs, hdwy tho' wide on bend 2f out, kept on, al held: op 8/1: April foal, half-sister to a 1m wnr, dam styd 11f: eff at 5f, looks sure to get further: acts on polytrack: good start, expect improvement. *1½* **72a**
GAUDALPIN [5] M J Wallace 2-8-9 T E Durcan 7/2 FAV: 3: b f Danetime - Lila Pedigo (Classic Secret) Chsd ldrs, sn pushed along, kept on fnl 2f: nicely bckd: cheaply bght May foal, half-sister to a 6f plcd juv: dam a dual 6f juv wnr, subs won at 10f: eff at 5f, stay further: handles polytrack: encouraging. *1¾* **67a**
929 **GREZIE 11** [10] J R Best 2-8-9 N Pollard 4/1: 44: Chsd wnr, no extra dist: bckd tho' op 3/1: changed stable since eye-catching 929 (turf). *½* **65a**
SPEED DIAL HARRY [4]2-9-0 Darren Williams 10/1: 5: Chsd ldrs, led onepace over 1f out. *½* **68a**
ZACHY BOY [9]2-9-0 Martin Dwyer 12/1: 6: Dwelt & rear, eff wide, mod hdwy. *1¾* **63a**
COMINTRUE [3]2-8-9 T P Queally(3) 16/1: 7: Chsd ldr, no extra fnl 1f. *¾* **56a**
IL PRANZO [2]2-9-0 R Hughes 4/1: 8: Mid-div & sn outpcd: op 6/1. *4* **49a**
FAITHFULL GIRL [7]2-8-9 N Chalmers(5) 25/1: 9: Dwelt, al outpcd. *2½* **36a**
SHES MY DREAM [1]2-8-9 J D Smith 50/1: 0: 10th: Slow away & sn outpcd. *1¼* **32a**
10 Ran Time 1m 0.67 (2.87) Owned: Mr D A Drake Trained: Sherborne

1072 **3.00 New Site @ Betdirect Co Uk Banded Stakes 4yo+ 0-40 (H)**
£1453 £415 £208 **1m2f aw** **Going 49** **-09 Slow** Inside

970 **GALEY RIVER 8** [6] J J Sheehan 5-9-0 (40) D Corby(3) 5/1 JT FAV: 0-005051: Mid-div, styd on for press to lead well ins last: bckd from 11/1: eff at 1m, now stays 10f: acts on fast & polytrack: see 770. **43a**
2467} **CANDY ANCHOR 284** [4] R E Peacock 5-9-0 bl (35) I Mongan 33/1: 0/00306-2: b f Slip Anchor - Kandavu (Safawan) Keen in mid-div, hdwy to chall dist, not pace of wnr nr fin: reapp: sell plcd in '03 (rtd 33, with A Reid): fill h'cap rnr-up '02: eff arnd 10/12f, tried 2m: handles fast, gd/soft & polytrack, sharp/undul or stiff trk: eff with/without blnks/t-strap. 2 Jul'02 Beve 9.9g/s 47-45 E: *¾* **41a**
828 **NDOLA 28** [2] B J Curley 5-9-0 (40) S W Kelly 5/1 JT FAV: 0/00/-1003: Sn cl-up, ev ch going well 2f out, onepace for press dist: op 8/1: found less than lkd likely, eff at 9/10f on both AWs: see 302. *hd* **40a**
784 **KINGSDON 35** [13] T J Fitzgerald 7-9-0 vis t (40) Martin Dwyer 6/1: 000-0104: Led after 1f till hdd well ins last: op 9/2: back to form after 784, see 654. *½* **39a**
970 **RYANS BLISS 8** [8]4-9-0 (40) J P Guillambert(3) 13/2: 000-0025: Chsd ldrs, no extra dist: op 5/1. *1¾* **37a**
971 **HELLBENT 8** [12]5-9-0 (35) L Fletcher(3) 10/1: 0-000056: Slow away, rear, eff 3f out, no extra dist: return to 1m in similar could suit: see 971. *1* **36a**
971 **PLATINUM BOY 8** [14]4-9-0 p (35) V Slattery 25/1: 0000307: Rear, only mod prog: see 784. *¾* **35a**
786 **PRINCE DU SOLEIL 35** [5]8-9-0 H (35) R Hughes 7/1: 0000-668: b g Cardoun - Revelry (Blakeney) Trkd ldrs, found little over 1f out: tried hood: lightly rcd & unplcd '03 (rtd 39, h'caps): dual h'cap plcd '02 (rtd 53): suited by 1m on gd/soft & hvy, handles fast: best form without visor, eff in a t-strap. 2 Apr'01 Nott 8.2hvy 65-63 E: *¾* **34a**
828 **SWEET REFLECTION 28** [3]4-9-0 t (40) Lisa Jones(3) 20/1: 0000-09: Dwelt, rear, no impress on ldrs. *4* **28a**
970 **EUROLINK ARTEMIS 8** [10]7-9-0 p (40) M Halford(7) 10/1: 0000-040: 10th: Chsd ldrs 1m: btr 970. *¾* **27a**
3756} **DANCES WITH ANGELS 230** [1]4-9-0 (35) P M Quinn 12/1: 044400-0: 11th: Rear, no impress: op 8/1. *1½* **25a**
968 **TIME FLYER 8** [11]4-9-0 (40) S Righton 33/1: 000-0000: 12th: Dwelt, keen & rear, no prog. *shd* **25a**
937 **SANTA CATALINA 10** [9]5-9-0 p (40) T P Queally(3) 12/1: 3-005400: 13th: Led 1f, prom till 2f out. *5* **18a**
324 **SHAAMITS ALL OVER 91** [7]5-9-0 (40) B Reilly(3) 20/1: 0600-00: 14th: Dwelt & al rear, reportedly resented kick-back: 3 month abs. *5* **11a**

14 Ran Time 2m 08.62 (5.82) Owned: Mr D J Dowling Trained: Findon

---

1073 | 3.30 Bet In Running @ Betdirect Co Uk Banded Stakes 3yo+ 0-45 (H)
£1645 £470 £235 **1m aw rnd** **Going 49** **+05 Fast** Outside

846 **BALLARE** 23 [2] Bob Jones 5-9-7 vis (45) O Urbina 3/1 FAV: 00-03461: Keen, sn trkd ldrs, led over **53a**
1f out & rdn clr, decisively: best time of day, tchd 9/2, first win: eff at 7/10f on fast & polytrack, prob any
trk: now suited by visor: see 846 & 649.
1010 **SINGLE TRACK MIND** 6 [9] J R Boyle 6-9-7 (45) Martin Dwyer 11/2: 0254502: Pushed along rear, styd 3½ **45a**
on for press, nvr threatened wnr: op 6/1: stays a sharp 1m, prob best at 7f: see 846 & 708 (7f).
969 **DIAL SQUARE** 8 [8] P Howling 3-8-6 bl (45) C Catlin 4/1: 00-01323: Keen & cl-up, ch 2f out, sn 1 **43a**
hung right & no extra: just btr 969 & 535.
828 **COODEN BEACH** 28 [11] M L W Bell 4-9-7 (45) Hayley Turner(5) 9/1: 0032-044: Handy, onepace dist. ¾ **42a**
917 **LARAD** 13 [3]3-8-6 bl (45) D Kinsella 12/1: 4-350055: Mid-div, short of rm & lost pl 2f out, no ch after. ¾ **41a**
739 **HARBOUR HOUSE** 40 [10]5-9-7 (45) N Pollard 13/2: 020-0206: Keen & led/dsptd lead till dist. ¾ **40a**
894 **REGENCY MALAYA** 15 [12]3-8-6 bl t (40) S Righton 16/1: 00-05207: Rdn rear, little prog: btr 831. 1¼ **37a**
8 **BRANDYWINE BAY** 148 [6]4-9-7 p (45) G Hannon 16/1: 353504-8: b f Mujadil - Ned's Contessa (Persian ½ **36a**
Heights) Rear, hdwy over 2f out, sn no prog: 5 mth abs: dual turf h'cap plcd '03 (rtd 42 & 45a, W Muir): eff btwn
6f/1m on fast & f/sand, gall or sharp/undul trk: eff in blnks/cheek pieces, has tried t-strap: breathing probs today.
676 **STAGECOACH RUBY** 48 [1]3-8-6 e (45) R L Moore 16/1: 60650-09: b f Bijou d'Inde - Forum Girl 3½ **29a**
(Sheikh Albadou) Al rear: op 9/2, abs, eye-shield: sell & clmr wnr for M Johnston in '03, subs unplcd for J Best:
both wins at 7f, eff at 6f: acts on firm & fast grnd, gall or sharp/undul trk.
1 Jun'03 Brig 7.0g/f 61- F: 1 Jun'03 Redc 7fm 65- G:
597 **WESTMEAD ETOILE** 56 [4]4-9-7 vis (40) R Hughes 12/1: 0300-030: 10th: Mid-div, no prog 2f out, abs. 1 **27a**
757 **SILVER LOUIE** 38 [5]4-9-7 (45) S Carson 33/1: 0000R-00: 11th: V slow away, al t.o. 25 **0a**
970 **WILOM** 8 [7]6-9-7 BL (40) Dane O'Neill 16/1: 2545000: 12th: Led/dsptd lead 5f, sn btn: blnks. 2 **0a**
12 Ran Time 1m 39.7 (3.5) Owned: The Ballare Partnership Trained: Newmarket

---

1074 | 4.00 Littlewoods Bet Direct Selling Stakes 3yo+ (H)
£1288 £368 £184 **7f aw rnd** **Going 49** **-09 Slow** Inside

819 **SOMERSET WEST** 29 [12] Mrs L Stubbs 4-9-7 (50) Dane O'Neill 16/1: 001-6001: Handy wide, led 3f **54a**
out till dist, rallied to regain lead cl-home: op 12/1, sold to J Best for 4,000gns: eff at 5.7f/7f, tried 1m:
acts on fast & polytrack: apprec drop to sell grade: see 492.
897 **LEGAL SET** 14 [10] W J Musson 8-9-7 (53) R Hughes 3/1: 00-40502: Led/dsptd lead, led dist, rdn & hd **53a**
hdd cl-home: clmd by A Stokell for 4,000: reportedly went down with colic after race: see 728.
957 **PEREGIAN** 8 [1] J Akehurst 6-9-7 (49) M Coumbe(7) 7/1: 00005-53: Dwelt, keen rear, shaken up & nk **52a**
styd on fnl 1f, not reach front pair: may have done btr under more experienced rider: clmd by A Reid for 4,000.
1012 **HINCHLEY WOOD** 6 [8] J R Best 5-9-7 BL (35) N Pollard 14/1: 6000554: Dwelt, rear, drvn & styd on 1¾ **49a$**
fnl 2f, not able to chall: imprvd eff in first time blnks: stays sharp 7f on polytrack: see 1012.
935 **LUCAYAN MONARCH** 11 [11]6-9-12 p (54) S W Kelly 11/4 FAV: 0232365: Pushed along rear, only mod nk **53a**
prog: op 7/2: btr 910 & 769 (1m).
902 **HAPPY CAMPER** 14 [4]4-9-7 (55) I Mongan 14/1: 0245-006: Keen & trkd ldrs, lost place over 2f out. nk **47a**
973 **ONEFORTHEBOYS** 8 [9]5-9-7 (40) S Whitworth 12/1: 6240037: Dwelt, rear, eff 2f out, no impress. 2 **43a**
832 **DEFINITELY SPECIAL** 28 [5]6-9-2 P (35) M Savage(5) 33/1: 00-00008: Chsd ldrs 5f, chkpcs. 1¾ **35a**
3701} **OUT OF TUNE** 232 [3]4-9-7 (45) D Corby(3) 66/1: 00/500-9: ch g Elmaamul - Strawberry Song (Final 3½ **33a**
Straw) Keen, in tch till 2f out: reapp: lightly rcd '03, unplcd (rtd 50, tried blnks): mod prev.
890 **LIVELY FELIX** 15 [6]7-9-7 BL (35) D Nolan(5) 50/1: 00-40600: 10th: Led after 1f till 3f out, wknd: blnks. 8 **18a**
913 **FOOLISH THOUGHT** 13 [7]4-9-12 T p (49) T Eaves(5) 12/1: 6541500: 11th: Chsd ldrs till 3f out, wknd. 6 **12a**
652 **ABUELOS** 50 [2]5-9-7 (45) D Fox(5) 6/1: 500-3400: 12th: V slow away, al t.o.: new yard, tchd 11/1. 1 **5a**
12 Ran Time 1m 26.83 (4.03) Owned: Mrs L Stubbs Trained: Malton

---

1075 | 4.30 Bet Direct On Sky Active Banded Stakes 3yo+ 0-45 (H)
£1631 £466 £233 **6f aw rnd** **Going 49** **-01 Slow** Inside

969 **SHIRLEY OAKS** 8 [1] Miss Z C Davison 6-9-7 (40) N Chalmers(5) 5/1: 0-050231: Rdn rear, hdwy & **49a**
switched wide 2f out, styd on for press to lead well ins last: eff at 6f/1m on firm, gd/soft & polytrack: see 788.
767 **NIGHT CAP** 37 [2] T D McCarthy 5-9-7 (45) J P Guillambert(3) 11/2: 003-6002: Dwelt, chsd ldrs & ¾ **46a**
rdn/led ins last, hdd well ins last: see 328.
783 **BALLYGRIFFIN KID** 35 [5] T P McGovern 4-9-7 (45) D Fox(5) 6/1: 00563-03: Mid-div, short of room 2 **40a**
halfway, styd on for press, nrst fin: shade closer with a clr run: acts on firm grnd & polytrack: see 783.
897 **LAW MAKER** 14 [9] M A Buckley 4-9-7 VIS (40) Martin Dwyer 14/1: 0000604: Keen & cl-up, led over 1f ½ **38a**
out till ins last, no extra: tried visor, fair run: acts on polytrack: see 897.
898 **TOP PLACE** 14 [4]3-8-9 p (45) Helen Smith(7) 33/1: 0-0005: b f Compton Place - Double Top 1 **35a**
(Thatching) Trkd ldr, onepace fnl 1f: unplcd sole '03 start (rtd 55): weras cheek pieces.
892 **FAYR FIRENZE** 15 [3]3-8-9 VIS (45) S Righton 20/1: 0656-046: Rear, mod prog: visor: see 846. shd **35a**
709 **WESTMEAD TANGO** 43 [8]4-9-7 (40) R Hughes 10/1: 200-6607: Led till dist, sn btn: abs: see 400. 2½ **27a**
904 **THE LADY WOULD** 14 [6]5-9-7 (35) D Nolan(5) 50/1: 50000-08: ch f Woodborough - Kealbra Lady hd **26a**
(Petong) Chsd ldrs till over 1f out: unplcd '03 (rtd 36a & 27, cheek pieces): fills h'cap rnr-up '02: eff around
a sharp/turning 6f on gd grnd. 2 Jun'02 Warw 6gd 48-47 F:
3741} **TRAVELLERS JOY** 230 [7]4-9-7 (45) V Slattery 33/1: 005660-9: Chsd ldrs, btn over 1f out, reapp. 1 **23a**
874 **TRIPTI** 18 [10]4-9-7 (45) N Pollard 10/1: 2002000: 10th: Cl-up, wknd over 1f out. 1½ **18a**
1023 **CONFUZED** 4 [11]4-9-7 e (45) O Urbina 7/1: 0-036000: 11th: Al rear: acts well polytrack: flattered 1023. 5 **4a**
969* **PACKIN EM IN** 8 [12]6-9-13 (35) D Corby(3) 4/1 FAV: 00-32010: 12th: Al rear: btr 969 (7f). 6 **0a**
12 Ran Time 1m 13.37 (2.97) Owned: The Secret Circle Trained: East Grinstead

LINGFIELD Polytrack TUESDAY 06.04.04 Lefthand, V Sharp Track

1076 5.00 Bet Direct Interactive Apprentice Banded Stakes 4yo+ 0-40 (H)
£1477 £422 £211 **1m5f aw** **Going 49** -04 Slow Inside

916	**BIRTH OF THE BLUES 13** [12] A Charlton 8-9-2 (40) Donna Bashton(5) 25/1: 60-00631: Rear, hdwy wide to led over 1f out, styd on strongly: eff at 1m, suited by 12/13f on firm, hvy & polytrack: see 916 & 689.			**44a**
968*	**LISSAHANELODGE 8** [6] P R Hedger 5-9-8 (40) N Chalmers 15/8 FAV: 0060/-12: Dwelt, rear, hdwy wide to chall fnl 2f, not pace of wnr from dist: hvly bckd from 5/2: stays 13f: see 968.		1¼	**47a**
968	**LITTLE RICHARD 8** [1] M Wellings 5-9-2 p (40) M Savage 9/2: 4314023: Cl-up & drvn/led over 3f out till over 1f out, no extra: consistent in this grade: see 968, 650 & 537.		nk	**40a**
243	**MERCURIOUS 106** [2] J Mackie 4-9-0 (40) D Nolan 8/1: 0/06334-4: ch f Grand Lodge - Rousinette (Rousillon) Chsd ldrs, styd on onepace for press: 3 mth abs: AW h'cap plcd '03 (rtd 42a, turf unplcd, rtd 41, h'cap): unplcd '02 (rtd 46): eff btwn 11/14f on both AWs, sharp trk.		1¼	**38a**
4755}	**RESSOURCE 174** [11]5-9-2 bl e (40) A Quinn 25/1: 00/000/0-5: b g Broadway Flyer - Rayonne (Sadler's Wells) Rear, outpcd 3f out, late gains: gelded: 7 wk jumps abs (plcd, rtd 94h, sell hdle, 2m, gd & soft grnd, blnks): no form sole start on the level '03: looks likely to apprec 2m.		nk	**37a**
690	**SARIBA 46** [3]5-9-2 (35) Hayley Turner(3) 33/1: 04410-06: Led till 5f out, onepcd fnl 3f, abs.		1¼	**35a**
709}	**MANTILLA 403** [10]7-9-2 vis (30) S Crawford(3) 9/1: 30000//0-7: In tch, outpcd fnl 3f, 5 mth jmps abs.		1¾	**33a**
968	**THE LAST MOHICAN 8** [5]5-9-2 p (40) S Donohoe(3) 12/1: 2324408: Led/dsptd lead till 3f out, sn btn.		5	**26a**
3163}	**DASH FOR GLORY 256** [13]5-9-2 (40) J F McDonald 20/1: 000000-9: Prom till halfway, reapp.		hd	**25a**
916	**ALIMISTE 13** [8]4-9-0 (40) T Eaves 50/1: 00000: 10th: Mid-div, no impress fnl 3f.		2½	**21a**
968	**ANTONY EBENEEZER 8** [4]5-9-2 t (40) R Thomas 7/1: 5300150: 11th: In tch till 3f out: btr 867 (fbrsd).		2	**18a**

828 **Elle Royal 28** [7]5-9-2 (40) D Fox 66/1:0 968 **Jezadil 8** [9]6-9-2 p(40) Kristin Stubbs(3) 20/1:0
13 Ran Time 2m 49.22(6.92) Owned: Mr J M Sancaster Trained: Marlborough

---

FOLKESTONE WEDNESDAY 07.04.04 Righthand, Sharpish, Undulating Track

Official Going Good/Soft (Soft Places)

1077 2.10 European Breeders Fund Tenterden Maiden Stakes 2yo (D)
£4069 £1252 £626 **5f str** **Good/Soft 88** -25 Slow Stands Side

	OBSERVER 0 [2] D R Loder 2-9-0 L Dettori 4/7 FAV: 1: b c Distant View - Virgin Stanza (Opening Verse) U.r bef start, made all, rdn & held on well from dist: hvly bckd at odds-on: Feb foal, 95,000 gns purchase: dam US wnr: eff at 5f, 6f will suit: acts on gd/soft & goes well fresh: rate higher.		**83**
	NORCROFT 0 [3] N A Callaghan 2-9-0 E Ahern 2/1: 2: b c Fasliyev - Norcroft Joy (Rock Hopper) Sn chsd wnr, chall dist, kept on but al just held: well clr of other pair: nicely bckd: Feb 1st foal: dam styd 14f: eff at 5f, 6f sure to suit: acts on gd/soft: v encouraging start, win sn.	½	**80+**
	DUSTINI 0 [1] W G M Turner 2-9-0 A Daly 12/1: 3: ch c Rossini - Truly Modest (Imp Society) Chsd wnr, hung right & outpcd from halfway, op 10/1: 21,000 gns Mar foal, half brother to a 1m wnr.	12	**48**
	GRYSKIRK 0 [4] P W D'Arcy 2-9-0 Paul Eddery 33/1: 4: Dwelt, in tch, wknd 2f out.	6	**33**

4 Ran Time 1m 04.03 (5.63) Owned: Sheikh Mohammed Trained: Newmarket

---

1078 2.40 Barham Median Auction Maiden Stakes 3yo (F)
£2968 £848 £424 **6f str** **Good/Soft 88** +17 Fast Stands Side

	PETITE ROSE 0 [13] J H M Gosden 3-8-9 L Dettori 11/4: 1: b f Turtle Island - Double Grange (Double Schwartz) Made all against far rail & in command dist, wd 6L+: gd time: sister to useful soft grnd sprinter Lincoln Dancer: eff at 6f on gd/soft, shld get further: goes well fresh: useful, win more races.		**91+**
911	**WARDEN COMPLEX 14** [12] J R Fanshawe 3-9-0 Dane O'Neill 5/2 FAV: 3-32: Chsd wnr far side halfway, kept on but all held: clr rem: bckd: acts on gd/soft & handles polytrack: win similar.	4	**81**
	WUNDERBRA 0 [8] M L W Bell 3-8-9 I Mongan 16/1: 3: b f Second Empire - Supportive (Nashamaa) Dwelt & bhd far side, rdn/short of room & switched over 2f out, late prog, nvr threat: debut, op 14/1: sprint bred.	8	**58**
3297}	**NAFFERTON GIRL 250** [7] J A Osborne 3-8-9 S W Kelly 33/1: 03-4: b f Orpen - Petomi (Presidium) Pushed along towards centre, no impress over 2f out, reapp: clmr plcd '03 (rtd 55, M W Easterby): eff over an easy 7f in claiming grade: acts on fast ground.	3	**51**
	INDIAN LILY 0 [10]3-8-9 G Baker 25/1: 5: Dwelt & bhd far side, mod prog from halfway, debut.	shd	**51**
946	**SILVER REIGN 11** [11]3-9-0 R Thomas(5) 33/1: 56: Mid-div far side, no impress over 1f out.	6	**42**
2987}	**DELIGHTFULLY 264** [6]3-8-9 E Ahern 9/1: 0-7: Chsd ldrs stands side, led group ins last, no ch with ldrs far side, op 12/1, reapp: 1st home from unfav stands side group, prob worth another chance.	1¼	**34**
973	**LADY ORIANDE 9** [15]3-8-9 Martin Dwyer 16/1: 0-68: Slow away, al bhd far side.	½	**32**
592	**POWER TO BURN 57** [9]3-9-0 vis (52) D R McCabe 33/1: 0600-359: Chsd ldrs far side till halfway: abs.	¾	**35**
2765}	**TURTLE PATRIARCH 273** [2]3-9-0 S Sanders 10/1: 60-0: 10th: Dwelt, prom stand side 3f, reapp.	shd	**35**
4869}	**EIGHT ELLINGTON 166** [1]3-9-0 (59) P Robinson 33/1: 340000-0: 11th: Dwelt, led stands side till ins last, sn btn, reapp.	½	**33**
973	**HALF A HANDFUL 9** [14]3-9-0 D Corby(3) 33/1: 00: 12th: Chsd wnr far side 3f, sn bhd.	¾	**31**
260	**PATS NEMISIS 100** [4]3-8-9 N Chalmers(5) 100/1: 000-0: 13th: Stands side, prom 2f, abs.	¾	**24**
2701}	**SEGUIDILLA 275** [3]3-8-9 (84) T Quinn 8/1: 204-0: 14th: Keen & prom stands side till dist, jockey reported saddle slipped: reapp, prob best forgiven.	½	**22**
898	**MR HULLABALOU 15** [5]3-9-0 G Carter 66/1: 00: 15th: U.r bef start, v slow away & al bhd stands side.	3	**19**

15 Ran Time 1m 15.25 (4.25) Owned: Mr Salem Suhail Trained: Manton

---

1079   3.10 Visit Port Lympne Wild Animal Park Classified Stakes 3yo+ 0-70 (E)
£3416 £1051 £526   7f str   Good/Soft 88   -11 Slow   Stands Side

879 **CHATEAU NICOL** 19 [1] B G Powell 5-9-3 vis (68) S Sanders 7/1: 0-130141: b g Distant Relative -   78
Glensara (Petoski) Keen, held up against fav far rail, no room over 1f out, gap appeared & hands & heels to lead
well ins last: op 5/1: suited by 6/7f, stays 1m: acts on fast, gd/soft & fibresand, Lingfield/polytrack
specialist: well treated on this turf return, likely to win again: see 604, 292 & 123.
1 Feb'04 Ling 7ap 83a-77 D: 1 Jan'04 Ling 6ap 80a-72 D: 1 Nov'03 Ling 7ap 75a-(62) F: 1 Nov'03 Ling 7ap 62a-58 E:
1 Aug'01 Wolv 6af 80a- B: 1 Aug'01 Warw 6gd 77- E:
1024 **MICHELLE MA BELLE** 5 [2] S Kirk 4-9-5 (75) R Hughes 5/1: 3655-022: Led, hdd & 4f out, rdn & led   1½ 76
again over 1f out till well ins last: op 7/2: quick reapp: turn prob not far away: see 1024.
4727*}**PERFECT PORTRAIT** 177 [3] D R Loder 4-9-7 (74) L Dettori 11/8 FAV: 1-3: ch g Selkirk - Flawless   1¾ 75
Image (The Minstrel) Cl-up/dsptd lead till over 1f out, no extra ins last: hvly bckd, op 7/4: reapp: mdn win on
sole start '03: half brother to a Gr2 wnr: eff at 7f, shld get 1m: acts on fast & gd/soft grnd, stiff/gall or
sharp/undul trk: open to improvement. 1 Oct'03 Leic 7.0g/f 76- D:
839 **BAKER OF OZ** 25 [6] R Hannon 3-8-5 (72) R L Moore 16/1: 2460-264: Keen & handy, outpcd over 1f   ¾ 72
out: op 12/1: mdn: acts on firm, gd/soft & polytrack: see 734.
1020 **AMMENAYR** 6 [5]4-9-8 (75) I Mongan 5/2: 050-0035: Chsd ldrs, drvn & no extra over 1f out: qk reapp.   nk 74
3289}**AMONG FRIENDS** 251 [4]4-9-5 (72) T Quinn 33/1: 000/036-6: b g Among Men - Anita's Contessa   13 49
(Anita's Prince) Keen & handy, led 3f out till over 2f out, sn btn & eased dist: reapp: h'cap plcd '03 (rtd 63):
mdn wnr '02: wng form at 5f: acts on fast grnd, has gone well fresh.
1 May'02 Kemp 5g/f 88- D:
6 Ran   Time 1m 31.16 (6.96)   Owned: Basingstoke Commercials   Trained: Winchester

---

1080   3.40 Folkestone-Racecourse Co Uk Maiden Stakes 3yo+ (D)
£3848 £1184 £592   7f str   Good/Soft 88   -22 Slow   Stands Side

    WISTMAN 0 [1] D R Loder 3-8-7 L Dettori 10/1: 1: br c Woodman - Saik (Riverman) Dwelt, rear,   80
switched towards centre & kept on to lead well ins last: op 7/1: eff at 7f, lks sure to apprec 1m+: acts on gd/soft &
a sharp/undul trk: goes well fresh: gd start, rate higher.
946 **RANGOON** 11 [7] Mrs A J Perrett 3-8-7 R Hughes 9/4 FAV: 3-22: Mid-div & pushed along halfway,   hd 79
hdwy & rdn/led cl-home, hdd line: stays 7f: shld wein a mdn: see 946.
814 **THE KINGS BISHOP** 30 [11] S C Williams 3-8-7 G Carter 33/1: 403: Trkd ldrs far rail, switched &   nk 78
hdwy to lead dist, hdd & hdd cl-home: improved on gd/soft at 7f here: see 514.
4293}**ROYAL PRINCE** 203 [2] J R Fanshawe 3-8-7 Martin Dwyer 11/4: 34-4: gr c Royal Applause -   1 76
Onefortheditch (With Approval) Dwelt, mid-div, hdwy to chall dist, no extra nr fin: reapp: promise both '03 mdn
starts (rtd 73a & 77): eff at 7f, 1m shld suit: handles fast, gd/soft grnd.
4727}**ISAZ** 177 [10]4-9-7 (75) Dane O'Neill 8/1: 025/4-5: b c Elmaamul - Pretty Poppy (Song) Prom, no   1½ 73
extra when short of room well ins last: reapp: 4th on sole '03 start (mdn, rtd 70): mdn rnr-up '02: eff at 6/7f,
has shaped as if 1m will suit: handles firm & gd/soft grnd, gall or sharp trk. 2 Sep'02 Newb 6fm 81- D:
3219}**PHOTOFIT** 254 [13]4-9-7 T Quinn 11/2: 62-6: Led/dsptd lead till dist, no extra: gldd, reapp.   1 71
881 **MUTASSEM** 18 [12]3-8-7 R Hills 20/1: 6-07: Led/dsptd lead till over 1f out, wknd.   ¾ 70
    GENEROUS SPIRIT 0 [9]3-8-7 S W Kelly 50/1: 8: Prom, rdn & no extra over 1f out, debut.   1 68
    BEAUCHAMP STAR 0 [4]3-8-2 R L Moore 66/1: 9: Pushed along rear, only mod hdwy on debut.   3 57
3733}**RUSSIAN SYMPHONY** 231 [5]3-8-7 P Robinson 16/1: 05-0: 10th: Rear, hdd halfway, mod hdwy.   1¾ 59
2083}**COMPTON EAGLE** 300 [6]4-9-7 T E Durcan 50/1: 0-0: 11th: Chsd ldrs 5f, reapp.   1¼ 56
4861}**GRUMPYINTMORNING** 167 [8]5-9-7 (53) P Dobbs 66/1: 042054-0: 12th: Mid-div, rdn & btn 2f out: reapp.   ¾ 55
946 **POMPEY CHIMES** 11 [3]4-9-7 S Carson 40/1: 5-40: 13th: Sn bhd & struggling.   6 45
977 **LOVE OF LIFE** 8 [14]3-8-3 (1ow) D R McCabe 100/1: 00: 14th: Chsd ldrs till halfway, t.o.   17 0
14 Ran   Time 1m 31.92 (7.72)   Owned: Sheikh Mohammed   Trained: Newmarket

---

1081   4.10 Come Racing In Kent Selling Handicap Stakes 3yo 0-60 (F)   [67]
£2513 £718 £359   7f str   Good/Soft 88   -36 Slow   Stands Side

899 **DOCTORED** 15 [5] B A Pearce 3-9-4 p (57) L Dettori 11/2: 23-00461: Made all, drvn out: nicely   64
bckd: bt in for 3,600 gns: 1st win: eff at 7f/1m on fast, gd/soft & fibresand: eff in blnks, t-strap or cheek
pieces: apprec return to forcing tactics in seller.
656 **BROTHER CADFAEL** 50 [4] John A Harris 3-8-1 (40) J F McDonald(5) 13/2: 456-3032: Chsd ldr, onepace   2 41
fnl 2f: op 5/1, 7 wk abs: handles fibresand & gd/soft grnd: see 383.
996 **CITY GENERAL** 7 [6] J S Moore 3-9-4 p (59) Martin Dwyer 2/1 FAV: 62550-33: Chsd wnr, wknd 1f out.   nk 57
1058 **WHIPLASH** 2 [7] R Hannon 3-9-7 (60) Dane O'Neill 12/1: 02000-04: Held up, eff & hung left 2f out,   hd 59
sn no impress: quick reapp: prob styd longer 7f trip in sell company: see 1058.
898 **FORA SMILE** 15 [3]3-8-6 (45) A Daly 14/1: 000005: Chsd ldrs, onepace & no impress 1f out: mod form.   2½ 40
865 **FOX HOLLOW** 21 [1]3-8-1 (40) R Miles(2) 3/1: 00-00326: Chsd ldrs till halfway, sn bhd: op 9/2: btr 865.   28 0
797 **DULCE DE LECHE** 35 [2]3-8-11 bl e (50) B Reilly(3) 10/1: 0-064007: Keen in mid-div, rdn & btn over   2½ 0
1f out, eased: op 8/1: btr 671 & 592.
7 Ran   Time 1m 32.86 (8.66)   Owned: Mr T M J Keep   Trained: Lingfield

---

1082   4.40 Hblb Lunch In The Lookout Restaurant Handicap Stakes Fillies 3yo+ 0-70 (E)   [69]
£3416 £1051 £526   1m4f   Good/Soft 88   -86 Slow   Centre

948 **BELLE ROUGE** 11 [5] C A Horgan 6-8-13 (54) L Dettori 5/4 FAV: 6022/-221: Made all, qcknd 3f out,   60
held on all out under typically well judged L Dettori ride: hvly bckd, slow time: eff btwn 12f/2m on both AWs, gd &
hvy grnd, prob any trk: see 948 & 768.
264 **STARRY MARY** 100 [1] R M Beckett 6-8-12 (53) S Sanders 8/1: 200006-2: b f Deploy - Darling   hd 58
Splodge (Elegant Air) Trkd ldrs & pushed along halfway, rallied well for press ins last, just held: h'cap rnr-up '03
(E James): h'cap rnr-up '02: eff at 10/12f on fast & soft, prob any trk.
2 May'03 Bath 13.1g/s 56-54 E: 2 Mar'02 Leic 11.8sft 58-53 E: 1 Sep'01 Brig 10sft 55-51 E:

FOLKESTONE   WEDNESDAY 07.04.04   Righthand, Sharpish, Undulating Track

759   **RESONANCE 39** [2] N A Twiston Davies 3-8-2 (64) Joanna Badger 12/1: 043-203: Mid-div wide, hdwy   1¼   66
to press wnr 3f out, edged left under press & no extra from dist: acts on polytrack & gd/soft grnd: see 672 & 116.
924   **DANCE PARTY 13** [9] A M Balding 4-9-8 (64) P Robinson 8/1: 00-33004: Trkd wnr, styd on onepace   ½   64
for press fnl 2f: clr of rem: handles fast, gd/soft & polytrack: see 624 & 569.
948   **AONINCH 11** [7]4-9-5 (61) R Havlin 11/1: 0113-605: Keen, held up wide, hdwy 3f out, not able to chall.   5   57
979   **GALANDORA 8** [8]4-8-3 t (45) Lucy Russell(7) 25/1: 06300-56: Keen & trkd wnr, btn 2f out: see 979.   2½   37
915   **RYE 14** [4]3-8-8 (70) S W Kelly 14/1: 5-167: Pushed along rear, no ch fnl 2f: op 12/1: see 915 & 785.   1¾   60
979   **MISS KOEN 8** [3]5-9-0 t (55) D Corby(3) 9/1: 0-631038: Dwelt, mid-div, btn 2f out: see 979 & 816.   4   40
978   **CUDDLES 8** [6]5-9-10 p (65) T E Durcan 10/1: 3450-059: Trkd ldrs, btn 3f out, op 8/1: see 876.   2   47
827*   **ANGELICA GARNETT 29** [10]4-8-5 (47) J F Egan 12/1: 0-060010: 10th: Dwelt, rear, bhd 3f out, t.o.,   28   0
reportedly hung left: much btr 827 (fibresand, banded).
10 Ran   Time 2m 52.43 (20.93)   Owned: Mrs B Woodford   Trained: Ogbourne Maizey

1083	5.10 Click On Howletts Net Handicap Stakes 4yo+ 0-70 (E)				[70]
	£3523 £1084 £542	1m1f149y rnd	Good/Soft 88	-83 Slow Inside	

4655}   **ROYAL RACER 182** [9] J R Best 6-8-5 (47) N Pollard 33/1: 60350/0-1: b g Danehill - Green Rosy   52
(Green Dancer): Led/dsptd lead, went on over 3f out & rdn clr sn after, held on all out: well btn sole '03 start: AW
h'cap plcd '02 (rtd 56a): eff around 9f/sharp 10f on polytrack, gd/soft & soft grnd: goes well fresh: improved for
switch to front running tactics.
978   **EASTER OGIL 8** [11] Jane Southcombe 9-9-0 (56) R Hughes 25/1: 4000002: Rear & pushed along over   nk   60
3f out, styd on for press fnl 2f, nrst fin: back to form, nicely treated on turf for similar: see 218.
912*   **BLAZING THE TRAIL 14** [5] J W Hills 4-9-9 (65) R Hills 8/1: 0-402513: Dwelt, rear, drvn & styd on   hd   68
fnl 2f, nrst fin: acts on polytrack & gd/soft grnd: worth another try at 10f+: see 912 & 622.
912   **HALF INCH 14** [1] B I Case 4-9-3 p (59) D Corby(3) 25/1: 00024-04: Trkd ldrs 3f out, styd on for   nk   61
press, not reach wnr: acts on fast & gd/soft grnd: see 912.
924   **DICKIE DEADEYE 13** [7]7-9-1 (57) R Thomas(5) 7/1: 0/0050-65: Bhd, kept on late, set too much to   2   55
do: could improve under more enterprising tactics: see 924.
978   **GALLOWAY MAC 8** [3]4-9-4 (60) T E Durcan 10/1: 3301246: Handy travelling well, rdn & found little   nk   57
from 2f out: styd this trip latest but a drop to 7f/1m would appeal in similar: see 978, 858 & 721.
452   **JACK OF TRUMPS 77** [6]4-9-11 (67) S Sanders 14/1: 06/35-107: Mid-div, outpcd 3f out, no threat: abs.   1¾   61
477   **ICANNSHIFT 74** [4]4-8-12 (54) R L Moore 25/1: 600-0068: Rear, eff 4f out, sn no impress: 11 wk abs.   3   43
647   **TO WIT TO WOO 51** [10]4-9-2 P (58) E Ahern 7/1: 0014-209: Chsd ldrs, btn 2f out: abs: chkpieces.   9   32
924   **FOREST TUNE 13** [15]6-9-5 (61) P Robinson 5/1 JT FAV: 06106-00: 10th: b g Charnwood Forest -   3   30
Swift Chorus (Music Boy): Trkd ldrs till 3f out: plcd over hdles this winter (rtd 111h, 2m, h'cap hdle): h'cap
scorer on the Level '03, AW unplcd (rtd 68a, h'cap): dual AW h'cap wnr '02, turf unplcd (rtd 63, h'cap): eff at
1m/10f: handles fast, likes gd/soft, hvy & both AWs. 1 May'03 Brig 9.9g/s 62-58 F: 2 Jul'02 Sout 8af 78a-73 E:
1 Jun'02 Sout 8af 77a-66 E: 1 Apr'02 Wolv 8.4af 66a-62 E: 1 Apr'01 Pont 10hvy 82- E:
2453}   **MADAME MARIE 285** [13]4-8-12 (54) Paul Eddery 50/1: 5/40003-0: 11th: b f Desert King - Les Trois   1   21
Lamas (Machiavellian): Slow away & bhd, little hdwy: reapp: unplcd '03 (lightly rcd, rtd 63, C/D fills mdn):
unplcd '02 (rtd 71, fills mdn): dam an 11f wnr.
903   **REBATE 15** [14]4-10-0 (70) P Dobbs 12/1: 4000-050: 12th: Prom till 3f out: btr 903.   6   28
607   **ZALKANI 56** [2]4-9-0 (56) L Dettori 5/1 JT FAV: 600-3300: 13th: Led after 1f till over 3f out,   dist   14
wknd qckly, eased: hvly bckd, abs: btr 476 & 430.
932   **BRESSBEE 12** [8]6-8-11 vis (53) S W Kelly 7/1: 024010P: P.u. after 3f, dismounted: lame, see 862.   0
14 Ran   Time 2m 14.60(16.6)   Owned: Mr & Mrs R Dawbarn   Trained: Maidstone

---

WARWICK   WEDNESDAY 07.04.04   Lefthand, Sharp Track

Official Going Soft (Good/Soft places)

1084	2.30 European Breeders Fund Maiden Stakes Fillies 2yo (D)			
	£4362 £1342 £671	5f rnd	Soft	Inapp Inside

943   **POLLY ALEXANDER 11** [3] M J Wallace 2-8-11 K Darley 100/30: 51: ch f Foxhound - Fiveofive (Fairy   69
King): With ldr, hdwy & switched left over 1f out, styd on to lead ins last, rdn out: nicely bckd: Apr foal, cost
9,000 gns: half sister to wnrs over 7/12f: dam 5f/1m scorer: eff at 5f on soft grnd, 6f looks sure to suit.
920   **GOGETTER GIRL 13** [1] J Gallagher 2-8-11 N Callan 5/2 FAV: 62: b f Wolfhound - Square Mile Miss   ½   67
(Last Tycoon): Led, edged right over 2f out & over 1f out but kept on ins last, not btn far: nicely bckd: Apr foal,
cheaply bought: eff at 5f on soft grnd: imprvd from debut & shld find similar, clr of rem.
931   **AUNTY EURO 12** [6] E J O'Neill 2-8-11 M Fenton 12/1: 43: br f Cape Cross - Alexander Goddess   2½   62
(Alzao): In tch, eff & hung left over 1f out, kept on ins last: Mar foal, cost £25,000: half sister to a 7f juv
wnr: bred to appreciate 6f, win a sell.
    SEASONS ESTATES [8] B R Millman 2-8-11 S Drowne 12/1: 4: Wide & went right start, in tch, some   ¾   60
late gains, nvr dangerous on debut.
    IAM FOREVERBLOWING [5]2-8-11 A Nicholls 33/1: 5: In tch, wknd over 1f out.   2½   55
    RIBBONS OF GOLD [4]2-8-11 D Holland 11/4: 6: Handy, wknd appr fnl 1f: nicely bckd on debut.   1¾   52
    ARTADI [2]2-8-11 T P Queally(3) 20/1: 7: Dwelt, al bhd.   2   48
    KINDLELIGHT DREAM [7]2-8-11 D Sweeney 25/1: 8: Dwelt, al bhd.   13   22
    ELVINA HILLS [9]2-8-11 A Culhane 10/1: 9: Carried right start, nvr a factor on debut.   5   12
9 Ran   Time 1m 06.73 ()   Owned: Mrs T A Foreman   Trained: Newmarket

1085	3.00 Wardington Handicap Stakes 3yo 46-55 (F)				[65]
	£3206 £916 £458	7f26y rnd	Soft	Inapp Inside	

925   **SHES OUR LASS 12** [2] D Carroll 3-9-3 (54) R Fitzpatrick 15/2: 5542-001: b f Orpen - Sharadja   61
(Doyoun): Cl-up, switched left & styd on to lead over 1f out, styd on well, rdn out: rnr-up on 2 of 5 '03 starts
(mdns): eff at 7f on firm, fibresand & clrly enjoys soft, sharp trks: gd confidence boost.
2 Oct'03 Sout 7af 59a-(58) F: 2 May'03 Catt 5fm 63- F:

871 **KNICKYKNACKIENOO 20** [11] A G Newcombe 3-9-0 (51) S Whitworth 10/1: 40060-42: Slow away, held up & short of room 2f out, kept on ins last, nrst fin: imprvd eff on this soft grnd & stays a sharp 7f well, 1m suit. *1½* **55**

975 **SIERA SPIRIT 8** [6] M G Quinlan 3-9-4 (55) S Drowne 15/8 FAV: 43023: Cl-up, eff over 1f out, onepace: well bckd: stays 7f: consistent, see 975. *1¼* **57**

898 **BOLD WOLF 15** [4] J L Spearing 3-9-3 (54) K Darley 16/1: 00020-44: b g Wolfhound - Rambold (Rambo Dancer) Led till over 1f out, no extra: rnr-up once in '03 (nurs h'cap, with P Harris): eff at 5f on firm grnd: wore a t-strap last term. 2 Oct'03 Bath 5.0fm 52-46 E: *2½* **52**

591 **BACKLASH 57** [1]3-8-9 (1oh) (45) S Righton 11/1: 0-0005: b f Fraam - Mezza Luna (Distant Relative) In tch, eff 2f out, sn no impress: 2 month abs prob best eff to date over this sharp 7f on soft. *shd* **44**

975 **LIVIA 8** [9]3-9-3 (54) A Culhane 20/1: 060406: Chsd ldr, wknd appr fnl 1f: btr 815 (polytrack). *¾* **50**

4996} **UPTHEDALE 155** [13]3-8-11 (48) P Hanagan 33/1: 0500-7: In tch, btn over 2f out on reapp. *1¾* **41**

933 **DOCKLANDS BLUE 12** [7]3-9-3 (54) D Holland 9/2: 0036438: Held up, btn 2f out: btr 933 (polytrk). *nk* **46**

901 **JAOLINS 15** [3]3-9-3 (54) D Kinsella 20/1: 0-120059: Keen, slow away & nvr a factor btr 671 (polytrk). *1½* **43**

832 **PARALLEL LINES 29** [8]3-8-12 vis (49) R Winston 12/1: 0-000400: 10th: Keen, slow away, al bhd. *1½* **35**

779 **I WISH I KNEW 37** [12]3-9-4 (55) W Supple 28/1: 000-60: 11th: Keen cl-up, wknd over 1f out. *½* **40**

763 **TARANAI 38** [5]3-8-11 BL (48) M Fenton 33/1: 06-40000: 12th: Slow away, al bhd. *shd* **33**

4146} **SCENIC FLIGHT 211** [10]3-9-4 (55) C Catlin 33/1: 04000-0: 13th: Cl-up, wknd over 1f out. *6* **31**

4766} **JESSE SAMUEL 174** [14]3-8-13 (50) J Jeffrey(7) 40/1: 660000-0: 14th: Al bhd. *5* **18**

14 Ran Time 1m 29.28 () Owned: We-Know Partnership Trained: Warthilll

1086

3.30 Warwick Courier Maiden Stakes Div 1 3yo (D)
£3673 £1130 £565 **1m22y rnd** **Soft** **Inapp** Inside

4868} **HASAYIS 166** [6] J L Dunlop 3-8-9 W Supple 9/4 FAV: 00-1: b f Danehill - Intizaa (Mr Prospector) Held up, hdwy to lead over 1f out, wandered left but kept on for press: nicely bckd: well btn in 2 6f juv starts: much imprvd for step up to 1m & clrly acts on soft grnd & a sharp trk: runs well fresh: more to come in h'caps. **70**

CESARE [4] J R Fanshawe 3-9-0 K Darley 11/4: 2: b c Machiavellian - Tromond (Lomond) Hld up, hdwy 2f out, kept on ins last, not pace of wnr: half brother to useful wnrs over 1m/mid-dists: dam 9f scorer: eff at 1m, sure to relish 10f: acts on soft: clr rem, will learn plenty from this, rate higher over further. *¾* **73**

536 **PRINCE VALENTINE 64** [3] D B Feek 3-9-0 (57) M Tebbutt 12/1: 00-003: b g My Best Valentine - Affaire de Coeur (Imperial Fling) Cl-up, onepace well over 1f out: 2 month abs: imprvd eff at 1m on soft. *5* **61**

606 **MASTER MAHOGANY 56** [7] R J Hodges 3-9-0 V Slattery 33/1: 04: Hld up, eff 2f out, no impress. *1¼* **61**

750 **DANTES DEVINE 40** [5]3-9-0 (56) J Bramhill 20/1: 0055-065: Led till over 1f out, wknd. *2* **58$**

PREMIER DREAM [2]3-9-0 J Fanning 3/1: 6: Held up, brief eff over 2f out, no impress on debut. *nk* **58**

PURPLE RAIN [1]3-8-9 J Mackay 8/1: 7: Cl-up, hung right & wide over 2f out, sn wknd. *7* **43**

4942} **HILLY BE 161** [9]3-8-9 S Whitworth 20/1: 0-8: Al bhd. *28* **3**

8 Ran Time 1m 46.79 () Owned: Mr Hamdan Al Maktoum Trained: Arundel

1087

4.00 Scottish Equitable / Jockeys Association Handicap Stakes 3yo+ 0-80 (D) **[80]**
£5824 £1792 £896 **1m6f213y** **Soft** **Inapp** Inside

948 **TURTLE VALLEY 11** [4] S Dow 8-9-3 (69) P Doe 9/2: 310-5031: In tch, hdwy over 2f out, led dist, sn hung left & kept on, rdn out: suited by 14/15f, stays 2m on gd & polytrack & loves gd/soft & hvy: tough 8yo. **77**

1003* **MALARKEY 7** [1] Mrs Stef Liddiard 7-9-0 (6ex) (66) S Drowne 11/2: 1306/-512: Hld up, hdwy & short of room over 2f out, kept on ins last, just held: clr rem: lkd a shade unlucky: acts on fm, soft & fibresand. *shd* **73**

926 **GEORGE STUBBS 12** [9] M J Polglase 6-8-10 (62) L Fletcher(3) 7/1: 6236403: Led after 6f till over 1f out, no extra ins last: prob btr at shorter now: acts on firm, gd/soft & both AWs, prob soft: see 681, 196. *4* **65**

3679} **MOONSHINE BEACH 234** [12] P W Hiatt 6-8-11 (63) A Culhane 14/1: 20/6105-4: b g Lugana Beach - Monongelia (Welsh Pageant) Held up, eff 2f out, sn no extra: won 1 of 4 '03 starts (mdn h'cap): stays 2m2f well on fast, gd grnd & polytrack. 1 Jul'03 Chep 18gd 63-61 E: 2 Oct'02 Ling 13ap 76a- D: *5* **61**

3252} **HEIR TO BE 252** [13]5-9-8 (74) K Darley 9/2: 001006-5: b g Elmaamul - Princess Genista (Ile de Bourbon) In tch, hdwy to go 2nd 3f out, wkng when sltly hmpd appr fnl 1f on reapp: won 1 of 6 '03 starts (h'caps): '02 h'cap wnr: suited by 2m, tried 2m5f: acts on gd, likes gd/soft or hvy, prob any trk. 1 May'03 Newc 16.1g/s 75-73 D: 1 Oct'02 Nott 16hvy 76-65 F: *1* **71**

2114} **WHIST DRIVE 299** [3]4-8-11 (66) C Catlin 16/1: 00/500-6: ch g First Trump - Fine Quill (Unfuwain) Held up, nvr a factor on reapp: fit from hdlg, earlier plcd in a nov (rtd 107h, 2m2.5f, soft): rtd 68 when unplcd on 3 '03 Flat starts for J Dunlop (tried up to 14f & in blnks). *3* **60**

4796} **DON FERNANDO 172** [8]5-10-0 (80) D Holland 4/1 FAV: 60/0000-7: Cl-up, wknd over 2f out. *¾* **73**

5033} **MUSKATSTURM 151** [11]5-10-0 (80) T P Queally(3) 25/1: 014/000-8: Al bhd. *¾* **72**

90 **VIN DU PAYS 135** [10]4-8-6 (2ow) (59) N Callan 25/1: 055116-9: In tch, wknd 3f out: long abs. *dist* **0**

926 **SUN HILL 12** [5]4-9-11 (80) D Sweeney 9/1: 00-11100: 10th: Chsd ldr, wknd over 2f out, t.o.: not enjoy turf? much btr 837 (fibresand). *2½* **0**

948 **MUNFARID 11** [2]4-8-11 t (66) D Kinsella 50/1: 4-304000: 11th: Led 6f, wknd over 3f out: see 359. *2* **0**

11 Ran Time 3m 31.26 () Owned: Cazanove Clear Height Racing Trained: Epsom

1088

4.30 Dunchurch Classified Stakes 3yo 0-70 (E)
£3656 £1125 £563 **6f21y rnd** **Soft** **Inapp** Inside

955 **DISTANT TIMES 11** [1] T D Easterby 3-9-0 (73) K Darley 5/4 FAV: 43223-51: Front rank, led halfway, styd on strongly fnl 1f, rdn out: hvly bckd: apprec this return to 6f, acts on fast & soft grnd: likes to run-up with/force the pace: speedy sort, confirmed promising reapp in 955. **81**

1054* **MUY BIEN 2** [3] J R Jenkins 3-9-3 bl (69) D Holland 9/4: 2-220312: Nvr far away, chsd wnr fnl 1f but no impress: qck reapp & not disgraced conceding wnr 3lbs: acts on gd, soft & f/sand: see 1054 (h'cap). *2½* **78**

855 **SENOR BOND 22** [5] B Smart 3-8-13 (72) F Lynch 18/1: 00400-63: Held up, prog & short of room dist, switched & kept on fnl 1f: op 14/1: some promise on grnd prob softer than ideal: see 855 (AW, reapp). *2* **70**

146* **LA LANDONNE 123** [4] P M Phelan 3-8-8 (70) T P Queally(3) 11/1: 351-4: Led till halfway, wknd fnl 1f: long abs: see 146 (AW). *1¾* **61**

4994} **TYZACK 155** [2]3-8-12 (71) M Fenton 7/1: 25240-5: b g Fasliyev - Rabea (Devil's Bag) Held up, nvr nr ldrs on reapp: has been gldd: rnr-up on 2 of 5 '03 starts (mdns): eff at 7f/1m on gd & fast grnd, has run well fresh: sure to apprec a return to further. 2 Oct'03 Newc 8gd 78- D: 2 Jun'03 Ayr 7.2g/f 80- D: *2½* **60**

466   **CREWES MISS ISLE 75** [6]3-8-10 (72) S Whitworth 11/1: 56420-46: Prom 4.5f, wknd: 11 wk abs.   1½   55
6 Ran   Time 1m 14.5 ()   Owned: Times of Wigan   Trained: Malton

---

1089   5.00 Warwick Courier Maiden Stakes Div 2 3yo   (D)
£3656 £1125 £563   **1m22y rnd**   **Soft**   **Inapp**   Inside

4870} **CITY PALACE 166** [2] B W Hills 3-9-0   A Culhane 6/4: 6-1: ch c Grand Lodge - Ajuga (The Minstrel)   81
Nvr far away, went on ins fnl 1f, held on drvn out: nicely bckd, reapp: 6th in a Newbury mdn on sole juv start
(rtd 74): half brother to sev wnrs, incl decent stayer Bangalore: dam a 6f juv wnr, sire a top class miler: apprec
this step up to 1m, acts on soft grnd & runs well fresh: gd start, can improve.
4980} **OH GOLLY GOSH 157** [8] N P Littmoden 3-9-0   K Darley 14/1: 30-2: ch g Exit To Nowhere - Guerre de   1   79
Troie (Risk Me)   Slowly away, hdwy from rear to lead dist, hdd ins fnl 1f, kept on & not btn far: tchd 20/1, reapp:
plcd on 1st of 2 '03 starts (AW mdn, rtd 69a): cost E28,000 & half brother to sev wnrs: eff over an easy 1m on soft
grnd, runs well fresh: could find similar.
919   **MAN OF LETTERS 13** [6] M Johnston 3-9-0   K Dalgleish 11/10 FAV: 5-43: Nvr far away, led 2f out   1¼   77
till dist, not qckn ins fnl 1f: nicely bckd, well clr rem: stays 1m, acts on gd & soft grnd: see 919.
19   **LAND OF NOD 146** [3] G A Butler 3-8-9   T P Queally(3) 14/1: 00-4: b f Barathea - Rafif (Riverman)   10   55
Held up, nvr nr ldrs on reapp/h'cap qual run: some mdn promise in 2 '03 starts: sire a top class miler: sharper
next time & may do btr now h'capped.
4948} **REBEL ROUSER 160** [7]3-9-0   S Drowne 66/1: 000-5: Nvr nr ldrs on reapp: has been gldd.   9   46
977   **SAUCY 8** [1]3-8-9   L Keniry(3) 20/1: 0-66: Led till 2f out, wknd.   ½   40
ALEXEI [9]3-9-0   J D Smith 20/1: 7: Slowly away, al bhd on debut.   6   36
925   **SIMPLY RED 12** [4]3-9-0 VIS (40) G Duffield 66/1: 000-08: Chsd ldr till halfway, wknd qckly, t.o.   24   0
SUMMER JOY [5]3-8-9   M Howard(6) 66/1: 9: V slowly away, al t.o. on debut.   dist   0
9 Ran   Time 1m 46.78 ()   Owned: Mr K Abdulla   Trained: Lambourn

---

1090   5.30 Draycote Handicap Stakes 3yo+ 46-55   (F)
£3500 £1000 £500   **1m2f188y**   **Soft**   **Inapp**   Inside   [56]

267*} **CRISTOFORO 466** [7] B J Curley 7-9-6 (48) T P Queally(3) 11/4 FAV: 042111/-1: b g Perugino - Red   55
Barons Lady (Electric)   Held up, stdy hdwy & wide into str, led ent fnl 1f, styd on strongly, pushed out: bckd from
9/2, reapp: won a nov h'cap hdle in Oct '03 (eff at 2m on fast grnd, rtd 83h): missed '03, prev term won all 3
starts (mdn & 2 h'caps): eff at 9/13f on soft grnd & both AWs: runs well fresh: prog & h'capped to win again.
1 Dec'02 Ling 13ap 56a-42 F: 1 Dec'02 Sout 12af 60a-43 E: 1 Dec'02 Wolv 9.3af 71a- D:
896* **GREAT VIEW 15** [8] Mrs A L M King 5-9-11 vis (53) G Duffield 9/1: 5432-012: Chsd ldrs, imprvd to   2   57
lead 2f out, collared ent fnl 1f, kept on but not pace of wnr: gd run back on turf, met a prog rival: see 896.
4622} **MOONSHINE BILL 184** [16] P W Hiatt 5-9-10 (52) A Culhane 16/1: 001520-3: ch g Master Willie -   1¼   54
Monongela (Welsh Pageant)   Held up, gd hdwy to chall 1.5f out, onepcd ins fnl 1f on reapp: '03 ladies h'cap wnr:
eff at 10f on fast & soft grnd, stiff/undul or sharp trk: runs v well fresh.
2 Sep'03 Pont 10.0g/f 55-52 E: 1 Jul'03 Pont 10.0g/f 53-41 F:
1045   **THEATRE LADY 4** [18] P D Evans 6-9-8 (50) K Darley 20/1: 2036304: Rear, styd on fnl 1.5f, nrst fin.   2½   49
4922} **RUTLAND CHANTRY 162** [20]10-9-5 (47) K Dalgleish 40/1: 00/0000-5: b g Dixieland Band -   4   42
Christchurch (So Blessed)   Held up, nvr nrr on reapp: mod hdle form this winter: lightly rcd &
little '03 form: '02 ladies h'cap & class stks wnr: eff at 10/12f on firm, likes gd & hvy, handles fibresand:
handles any trk, best without blnks: well h'capped if returning to form.
1 Aug'02 Leic 11.8gd 68- E: 1 Jul'02 Beve 10gd 73-62 E: 2 Jul'02 Beve 10g/s 67-65 E: 2 Sep'01 Hayd 10.5sft 67-70 E:
1 Aug'01 Epso 12g/f 72-65 C: 1 Aug'01 Newm 10gd 69-60 E: 2 Aug'01 Pont 10gd 64-60 E: 2 May'01 Newb 10sft 64-60 D:
961   **CALL OF THE WILD 9** [11]4-9-12 vis (54) P Hanagan 14/1: 46-03336: Prom till wknd dist: see 961.   1¼   47
4685} **IMTIHAN 178** [3]5-9-9 (51) A Nicholls 11/2: 5/00000-7: ch c Unfuwain - Azyaa (Kris)   Rdn in rear,   1   43
late hdwy, nvr dngrs: jumps fit, completed qck hat-trick of h'cap hdle wins (2m6f on fm & soft, rtd 116h): mod '03
Flat form, incl in blnks & cheek pieces: dual h'cap wnr for B Hills in '02: eff at 10/12f on fm & hvy: well
h'capped now.   1 Jul'02 Ripo 12.2g/f 77-73 D: 2 Jun'02 Sali 12fm 76-71 C: 1 May'02 Beve 9.9gd 71-62 D:
689   **BOJANGLES 47** [15]5-9-8 (50) L Fletcher(3) 33/1: 04500-08: Led 5f out till 2f out, wknd: 7 wk abs.   7   35
985   **FORTY FORTE 8** [19]8-9-6 (48) A Quinn(5) 50/1: 20-00039: Prom 9f, wknd: see 985.   1½   31
60   **THE LOOSE SCREW 140** [4]6-9-6 (48) M Fenton 28/1: 006200-0: 10th: Early ldr, wknd 2f out on reapp.   2½   28
956   **ROCINANTE 9** [1]4-9-7 (49) R Winston 28/1: 10-00030: 11th: Held up, nvr nr ldrs: see 956 (AW).   1¼   27
529   **PAULA LANE 64** [14]4-9-13 (55) S Hitchcott(3) 33/1: 5320-050: 12th: Led till 5f out, wknd dist: 9 wk abs.   ¾   32
1047   **GRAND LASS 2** [9]5-9-11 p (53) D Holland 15/2: 4125430: 13th: Al bhd: quick reapp.   2½   27
1026   **PARADISE VALLEY 5** [5]4-9-10 t (52) S Drowne 11/1: 1605020: 14th: Al bhd: qck reapp: btr 1026 (AW).   nk   26
864   **SPY GUN 21** [2]4-9-10 (52) R Ffrench 50/1: 5005040: 15th: Chsd ldrs 9f, sn wknd.   nk   26
4512} **DREAM FALCON 191** [17]4-9-8 (50) V Slattery 16/1: 000/00-0: 16th: Al bhd: jumps fit.   9   14
854   **ORINOCOVSKY 22** [6]5-9-13 (55) N Callan 15/2: 0302320: 17th: Prom 9f, wknd: bckd from 14/1.   2½   16
827   **ON GUARD 29** [13]6-9-13 vis (55) D Kinsella 14/1: 0650-360: 18th: Al bhd: see 705.   7   9
299* **HEATHYARDS PRIDE 95** [12]4-9-11 (53) W Supple 4/1: 4-10: 19th: Al bhd, t.o. in last: 3 mnth abs.   dist   0
19 Ran   Time 2m 29.41()   Owned: Mr P Byrne   Trained: Newmarket

---

MUSSELBURGH   THURSDAY 08.04.04   Righthand, Sharp Track

Official Going GOOD/FIRM (GOOD places Str Crse; FIRM places Rnd Cⁱse). All Times Slow.

1091   2.40 Kathleen And Kevin Devine Pre-Birthday Maiden Auction Stakes 2yo   (F)
£3348 £1030 £515   **5f str**   **Good/Firm**   **Slow**   Stands Side

962   **BOLD MARC 10** [8] K R Burke 2-8-11   Darren Williams 11/4: 41: b c Bold Fact - Zara's Birthday   88+
(Waajib)   Nvr far away, led trav strongly halfway, clr fnl 1f, easily, val 6L+: April foal, cost 11,500gns:
half-brother to several mid-dist wnrs: dam scored over 2m, sire a high-class sprinter: eff at 5f, apprec today's
fast grnd: impressive wnr, clearly benefitted from recent debut & looks the type to win more races.
FORFEITER [3] T D Barron 2-8-11   K Darley 11/2: 2: ch c Petionville - Picabo (Wild Again)   2   68
Swerved start, outpcd till switched & styd on strongly fnl 1f, no ch with wnr: nicely bckd, clr rem on debut:

MUSSELBURGH   THURSDAY 08.04.04   Righthand, Sharp Track

13,000gns March foal: half-brother to wnrs abroad: dam unrcd, sire a high-class 6/9f performer in the US: eff at 5f on fast grnd: got the hang of things too late today & prob met an above average rival.

| | **RIGHTPRICE PREMIER** [6] K A Ryan 2-8-4   P Fessey 11/2: 3: b f Cape Cross - Machudi (Bluebird) | 5 | 46 |

Led till after halfway, no extra on debut: tchd 7/1: Feb first foal, cost 8,000gns: sire a high-class miler.

| | **FAVOURING** [2] R A Fahey 2-8-9 P Hanagan 5/2 FAV: 4: ch c Fayruz - Peace Dividend (Alzao) | 3½ | 42 |

Dwelt & green in rear, some late hdwy, nvr dngrs on debut: nicely bckd: April foal, cost 6,500gns: half-brother to 1m wnr Badger Kennedy: sire a decent juv performer: sure to learn from this.

	BEVERLEY BEAU [1]2-8-7 R Winston 16/1: 5: Prom till after halfway, wknd on debut.	¾	37
954	**BRUT** 12 [7]2-8-9 L Enstone(3) 33/1: 06: Dwelt, recovered to chase ldrs 3f, wknd.	1¾	35
	ETERNALLY [4]2-8-8 (1ow) D Holland 16/1: 7: Swerved start, al outpcd on debut.	11	4
	STEAL THE THUNDER [5]2-8-10 (3ow) F Lynch 14/1: 8: Slowly away, al well bhd on debut.	6	0

8 Ran   Time 1m 02.29 (4.79)   Owned: Market Avenue Racing Club 1   Trained: Leyburn

---

1092   3.10 Dm Hall Handicap Stakes 3yo+ 0-80 (D)   [76]
£5395 £1660 £830   1m rnd   **Good/Firm**   **Slow**   Outside

| 4391} | **BRIEF GOODBYE** 199 [6] John Berry 4-9-10 (72) M Fenton 11/1: 401663-1: b g Slip Anchor - Queen of | | 78 |

Silk (Brief Truce). Trkd ldrs, went on entering fnl 1f, styd on strongly, rdn out: op 8/1, top-weight, reapp: '03 h'cap wnr: suited by 1m on fast & firm grnd, runs well fresh: gd weight-carrier, fairly lightly rcd & can win again. 1 Jun'03 Sali 8fm 74-69 E:

| 4466} | **QUEEN CHARLOTTE** 195 [2] Mrs K Walton 5-9-6 (68) J Fanning 7/2: 0106/10-2: ch f Tagula - Tisima | 1¾ | 69 |

(Selkirk). Tried to make all, collared entering fnl 1f, not pace of wnr cl-home: bckd from 9/2, reapp: won first of 2 '03 starts (h'cap, reapp): '02 mdn wnr for A Crook: eff at 6f/1m on fast grnd & on a sharp or gall trk: runs well fresh. 1 Sep'03 York 7.9g/f 70-63 D: 1 Aug'02 Catt 6g/f 66- D: 2 Jul'02 Catt 7g/f 64- F:

| 998 | **SARRAAF** 8 [5] I Semple 8-9-6 (68) R Winston 5/2: 1042-423: Held up, hdwy when short of room | 1¾ | 65 |

dist, kept on fnl 1f & not btn far: nicely bckd tho' op 15/8: rtd sltly higher in 998 (7f).

| 4711} | **REGENTS SECRET** 178 [4] J S Goldie 4-9-5 (67) R Ffrench 14/1: 300040-4: br c Cryptoclearance - | hd | 64 |

Misty Regent (Vice Regent). Trkd ldrs, onepcd fnl 1f: reapp: plcd sev times in '03 (2 mdns & a h'cap, R Hannon, incl in first time cheek pieces): eff at 7/9f on fast & firm: has worn a visor & cheek pieces. 2 Nov'02 Brig 6g/s 85- D: 2 Aug'02 Epso 7g/f 84- E: 2 Aug'02 Epso 7gd 86- D: 2 Jun'02 Ling 5ap 86a- D: 2 Jun'02 Hayd 5sft 86- D:

| 278 | **COOL TEMPER** 99 [3]8-9-8 t (70) K Darley 15/8 FAV: 140336-5: Trkd ldr, ev ch till wknd fnl 1f: | shd | 67 |

bckd from 9/4, 3 mth abs: see 186 (AW).

| 4607} | **REPULSE BAY** 187 [1]6-8-9 (57) C Catlin 25/1: 003500-6: Al bhd, fin last on reapp. | 12 | 29 |

6 Ran   Time 1m 43.55 (6.05)   Owned: Mr J McCarthy   Trained: Newmarket

---

1093   3.40 Musselburgh Town Handicap Stakes 4yo+ 0-85 (D)   [85]
£6708 £2064 £1024   2m   **Good/Firm**   **Slow**   Stands Side

| 965 | **ZOLTANO** 10 [10] M Todhunter 6-8-8 (65) R Winston 20/1: 4/2122//-31: Made all, clr over 2f out, | | 70 |

kept on strongly, decisively: op 14/1: eff at 2m on fast & soft: given a well judged ride from the front, see 965.

| | **PLUTOCRAT GB** 1422 [1] L Lungo 8-8-13 (70) K Dalgleish 8/1: 231/10///-2: b g Polar Falcon - | 2 | 70 |

Choire Mhor (Dominion). Chsd ldrs, went after wnr 2f out, kept on but nvr going to get there: op 6/1, rider given a 2-day careless riding ban: last rcd over hdles 12 wks ago, '02 wnr here at Musselburgh (h'caps, rtd 120h, eff at 2m/3m on fast, soft): '99 Flat wnr here at Musselburgh for J Noseda (clmr): stays 2m on fast, runs well fresh.

| 1630 | **MIRJAN** 1630 [7] L Lungo 8-10-0 (85) K Renwick 66/1: 32404////-3: b g Tenby - Mirana (Ela Mana | shd | 85 |

Mou). Held up, hdwy 3f out, styd on fnl 1f & nrst fin: longer priced s/mate of rnr-up, jumps fit tho' lightly rcd this winter: '03 h'cap hdle wnr at Ayr (rtd 127h, eff at 2m/2m6f on firm & soft, eff in blnks/visor): '99 Flat wnr at Newmarket (mdn): eff at 10/12f, stays 2m: acts on fast & soft: btr with headgear & fine return to Flat.

| 926 | **OCEAN TIDE** 13 [4] R Ford 7-9-4 vis (75) L Enstone(3) 3/1: 100-0334: Trkd wnr, onepace fnl 1.5f. | 1 | 74 |
| 5008} | **OVERSTRAND** 155 [3]5-9-7 (78) K Darley 11/4 FAV: 6330/02-5: b g In The Wings - Vaison La Romaine | 5 | 72 |

(Arctic Tern). Chsd ldrs, onepace fnl 2f: nicely bckd: jumps fit, won 4 times this winter, notably val h'cap at Sandown (rtd 138h, eff at 2m/2m4f on gd & hvy): '03 h'cap rnr-up: eff at 12f/2m on firm, gd/soft & polytrack: 2 Nov'03 Muss 16g/f 80-78 C: 1 Jun'02 Bath 11.6g/f 83- D: 2 Jun'02 Ling 12ap 82a- D: 2 May'02 Bath 10.2g/s 84- E:

| 965* | **ACCELERATION IRE** 10 [9]4-8-5 (6ex)vis (66) P Hanagan 6/1: 16040-16: Chsd ldrs, onepace fnl 2f: | hd | 60 |

tchd 9/1: just btr 965 (soft grnd).

837	**MACARONI GOLD** 26 [6]4-8-3 (64) C Catlin 12/1: 12-04457: Held up, nvr nr to chall.	2	56
926	**RIYADH** 13 [5]6-9-12 vis (83) J Fanning 6/1: 04060-08: Chsd ldrs, wknd 2f out: nicely bckd.	6	69
4738}	**SONO** 177 [11]7-9-4 (75) A Culhane 33/1: 020000-9: Chsd ldrs, hmpd 4f out & lost pl, no ch after.	11	51
956	**PHARAOH HATSHEPSUT** 10 [8]6-7-12 (15oh) (40) D Fentiman(7) 100/1: 00400//-00: 10th: Al bhd, t.o.	9	21

10 Ran   Time 3m 27.95 (15.45)   Owned: Leeds Plywood and Doors Ltd   Trained: Penrith

---

1094   4.10 Robin Cook And Uia Classified Stakes 3yo+ 0-75 (D)
£5343 £1644 £822   7f3oy rnd   **Good/Firm**   **Slow**   Outside

| 1018 | **HATCH** 7 [1] R M H Cowell 3-8-8 (79) D Holland 3/1: 20-22131: Made all, clr fnl 1f, cmftbly: | | 90 |

nicely bckd: eff at 7f on fast, firm grnd & both AWs: likes a sharp trk: enjoys forcing tactics & in fine heart.

| 940* | **FLINT RIVER** 12 [7] H Morrison 6-9-4 (74) A Culhane 11/4 FAV: 0-200012: Trkd ldrs, went after wnr | 5 | 76 |

dist, sn no impress: well bckd: gd run back on turf, met an improving rival: see 940 (fav'd W'hampton).

998	**NO GROUSE** 8 [4] R A Fahey 4-9-4 (75) T Hamilton(3) 7/1: 00-05003: Chsd ldrs, onepace fnl 1.5f.	nk	75
887*	**WHAT A DANCER** 19 [3]7-9-8 (79) R Winston 3/1: 401-4315: Chsd ldrs wide, btn over 1f out: btr 887.	5	69
4289}	**HIGH FINANCE** 204 [6]4-9-5 (79) K Darley 6/1: 510455-5: b f Entrepreneur - Phylella (Persian	4	58

Bold). Rdn in rear, hdwy when hmpd dist, no ch after: tchd 8/1, reapp: '03 mdn, class stks & h'cap wnr: stays 1m, suited by 7f: acts on gd, firm & polytrack: has a decent turn of foot, no luck today & must be given another chance. 1 Jun'03 Newb 7fm 80-72 D: 1 May'03 Yarm 7.0gd 75-(65) E: 1 Apr'03 Ling 8ap 66a- F:

| 3507} | **COUSTOU** 242 [2]4-9-4 p (75) P Fessey 66/1: 21/0005-6: b g In Command - Carranza (Lead On Time) | 6 | 45 |

Chsd wnr, wknd dist: rider given a 1-day careless riding ban: u.r. on sole hdles start 9 wks prev: trained by M Jarvis on the Flat in '03, failed to sparkle (incl in cheek pieces & blnks): '02 mdn auct wnr: eff at 6f/1m on gd & fast grnd, sharp or gall trk: now with A Dicken. 1 Oct'02 Brig 7gd 83- E: 2 Oct'02 Ling 6gd 85- D:

| 935 | **PAGAN STORM** 13 [5]4-9-4 bl (70) Kristin Stubbs(7) 66/1: 6146-007: Keen in rear, nvr dngrs. | 3 | 39 |

7 Ran   Time 1m 30.72 (5.82)   Owned: Blue Metropolis   Trained: Newmarket

MUSSELBURGH   THURSDAY 08.04.04   Righthand, Sharp Track

1095
4.40 John Richard Memorial Maiden Stakes 3yo+   (D)
£4735 £1457 £729   **1m1f**   **Good/Firm**   **Slow**   Outside

919   **MASTER MARVEL 14** [6] M Johnston 3-8-7   R Ffrench 8/13 FAV: 21: Prom, led bef halfway till 2f **84**
out, wandered & rallied to regain lead entering fnl 1f, drvn out: hvly bckd: eff at 1m/9f on gd & fast grnd, sharp
or gall trk: nrly threw this away but proved too gd for today's rivals: see 919 (debut).
1739} **KHANJAR 318** [9] D R Loder 4-9-10 VIS (82) D Holland 7/4: 24/22-2: ch g Kris S - Alyssum (Storm   3   **78**
Cat) Led till bef halfway, regained lead 2f out till entering fnl 1f, kept on but not pace of wnr: well bckd, tried
a visor, reapp: rnr-up on both '03 starts (mdns): '02 mdn rnr-up: cost $1,200,000 & eff at 7/9f on fast grnd: has
been gelded, clearly has ability but his share of temperament.
2 May'03 Chep 8.1g/s 74-(90) D: 2 Sep'02 Leic 7g/f 90- D:
240   **PAR INDIANA 108** [3] I Semple 3-8-2   P Hanagan 25/1: 43-3: Chsd ldrs, styd on under press fnl 1f,   1¾ **69$**
nrst fin: reapp: acts on fast grnd & fibresand: see 240 (AW).
4318} **KINGS ENVOY 203** [1] Mrs J C McGregor 5-9-10 (50) D McGaffin 200/1: 06/000/0-4: b g Royal Academy   1   **72$**
- Island of Silver (Forty Niner) Held up, hdwy when switched outside 2f out, in 3rd when eased down cl-home & caught
nr line: p.u. over halfway in Dec '03: modest Flat form in recent seasons: eff at 9f on fast
grnd: shld have been 3rd today, rider reportedly suffered from cramp!
1006 **SKIBEREEN 8** [5]4-9-10 (72) P Mathers(7) 18/1: 232-5645: Chsd ldrs, onepcd fnl 2f: clr of rem.   1   **70**
      MY ACE [11]6-9-5 bl t J Fanning 50/1: 6: b f Definite Article - Miss Springtime (Bluebird)   12   **45**
Chsd ldrs, btn over 2f out on Flat debut: trained by Mrs H Dalton to win a nov hdle in Nov '03 (eff arnd 2m1f on
firm & gd/soft, rtd 88h, eff in blnks/visor/t-strap): now with J Moffatt.
4791} **ISLANDS FAREWELL 174** [2]4-9-10 M Fenton 100/1: 000-7: Al towards rear on reapp.   nk   **49**
891   **SANDY BAY 17** [8]5-9-10 P (40) L Enstone(3) 200/1: 00000-08: Nvr nr ldrs in 1st time cheek pieces.   6   **37**
4885} **LAPDANCING 166** [7]3-8-2   P Fessey 100/1: 00-9: Slowly away, al bhd on reapp/h'cap qual run.   1   **31**
1168} **OPTIMUM NIGHT 352** [4]5-9-10   R Winston 150/1: 000-0: 10th: Chsd ldrs till halfway on reapp.   nk   **35**
2157} **QUEENSLANDER 298** [10]3-8-2   D Mernagh 66/1: P-0: 11th: Chsd ldrs till halfway: new stable.   1½ **28**
11 Ran   Time 1m 55.50 (4.80)   Owned: Maktoum Al Maktoum   Trained: Middleham

1096
5.10 Honest Toun Handicap Stakes Fillies 3yo+ 0-75 (E)   [71]
£4017 £1236 £618   **5f str**   **Good/Firm**   **Slow**   Stands Side

958   **FRASCATI 10** [4] A Berry 4-9-10 (67) F Lynch 5/1: 51-00041: Prom, led after halfway, held on well   **74**
fnl 1f, rdn out: top-weight: eff at 5f on firm, gd/soft & fibresand: likes to run up with the pace: see 205 & 35.
958   **LADY PEKAN 10** [1] P S McEntee 5-9-3 P (60) D Holland 3/1 JT FAV: 6356002: Led till after halfway,   1¼ **61**
kept on but not pace of wnr fnl 1f: back to form on turf & in first time cheek pieces: see 274 (AW h'cap).
123   **TENDER 131** [6] D J Daly 4-9-1 (58) C Catlin 7/2: 640060-3: b f Zieten - Jayess Elle (Sabrehill)   ¾   **56**
Chsd ldrs, onepcd fnl 1f on reapp: failed to win in '03, class stks plcd: '02 mdn auct & h'cap wnr: eff at 5/6f on
firm, fast grnd & polytrack: likes a sharp trk: prev with D Cosgrove.
2 Oct'02 Newm 5fm 76-73 C: 1 Aug'02 Ches 6fm 74-67 D: 1 Jul'02 Ling 5ap 70a- E:
5006} **COLLEGE MAID 155** [3] J S Goldie 7-8-10 bl (53) R Ffrench 5/1: 303006-4: b f College Chapel - Maid   3½ **41**
of Mourne (Fairy King) Outpcd, late hdwy, nvr dngrs on reapp: dual h'cap wnr in '03: won a class stks in '02: eff
at 5/6f on fast, likes gd & hvy: tried cheek pieces, best in blnks: handles a gall or sharp trk: on a wng mark.
1 Jun'03 Muss 5g/f 63-60 E: 1 May'03 Ayr 5g/s 62-54 E: 1 Aug'02 Redc 6g/s 57- F: 2 Jul'02 Hami 5g/s 59-58 D:
2 Jul'01 Ayr 6g/s 77-76 D: 1 Jul'01 Ayr 5g/s 72-67 C: 2 Jun'01 York 6g/s 69-66 D:
767   **TAMARELLA 39** [2]4-9-2 (59) A McCarthy 3/1 JT FAV: 500-0005: Prom, wknd dist.   10   **17**
5 Ran   Time 1m 01.87(4.37)   Owned: Lord Crawshaw   Trained: Cockerham

BATH   THURSDAY 08.04.04   Lefthand Turning Track with Uphill Finish

Official Going Good

1097
2.20 Severn Valley Catering Claiming Stakes 2yo (F)
£3066 £876 £438   **5f11y rnd**   **Good/Soft 87**   **-32 Slow**   Far Side

      TREAT ME WILD [9] R Hannon 2-8-6   R L Moore 5/2 FAV: 1: ch f Loup Sauvage - Goes A Treat   **71**
(Common Grounds) Sn bhd, hdwy for press 2f out, styd on well ins last to lead cl-home, rdn out on debut: April
foal, cost 2,000gns: half-sister to a modest 5f juv wnr: dam 7f scorer: eff at 5f, 6f will suit: acts on gd/soft
grnd: green here, shld learn plenty from this & rate higher.
882   **IM SPARTACUS 19** [8] I A Wood 2-8-9 G Duffield 20/1: 02: b c Namaqualand - Captivating   nk   **73**
(Wolfhound) Sn rdn bhd, hdwy 2f out, styd on strongly ins last, just failed: April foal, half-brother to a 12f wnr:
eff at 5f, bred to relish 6f+: acts on gd/soft: imprvd from debut down in class & shld certainly win one of these.
1029 **NUTTY TIMES 6** [6] W G M Turner 2-8-0 C Haddon(7) 8/1: 233: With ldr, hung right over 3f out, led   1½ **60**
2f out till ins last, no extra: acts on fibresand & gd/soft: consistent, see 938.
929   **GOLDHILL PRINCE 13** [3] W G M Turner 2-8-4 P A Daly 16/1: 61: b c Prince Sabo - Lady Mabel   1   **61**
(Inchinor) Made most till 2f out, no extra ins last: April foal, cost only 500gns: shade better here & eff at 5f
on gd/soft tried in cheek pieces.
      ZIMBALI [5]2-8-1   J Bramhill 40/1: 5: With ldrs, wknd over 1f out on debut.   3   **49**
929   **GENERAL NUISANCE 13** [7]2-8-9 D Kinsella 5/1: 26: Dwelt, sn in tch, wknd 2f out: changed   ¾   **55**
stable, clmd for 10,000: btr 929 (gd).
929   **LITTLE WIZZY 13** [10]2-8-4 S W Kelly 7/1: 37: With ldrs, carried right 3f out, wknd over 1f out.   2   **44**
929   **DOCKLANDS DUDE 13** [2]2-8-7 V Slattery 5/1: 68: Slow away, nvr a factor: now with M Meade.   6   **29**
      PETITE NOIRE [1]2-8-6 E Ahern 11/1: 9: Dwelt, nvr a factor on debut.   9   **10**
920   **BERHAM MALDU 14** [4]2-8-9 T Quinn 16/1: 00: 10th: In tch, wknd over 2f out.   2½ **6**
10 Ran   Time 1m 06.26 (5.96)   Owned: The Old Downton Partnership   Trained: Marlborough

BATH THURSDAY 08.04.04 Lefthand Turning Track with Uphill Finish

1098

2.50 Totetrifecta Handicap Stakes 3yo+ 0-75 (E) [75]
£4193 £1290 £645 **1m2f46y** **Good/Soft 87** **+11 Fast** Inside

726+***WAR OWL 43** [12] Ian Williams 7-8-13 (60) Lisa Jones(3) 4/1 FAV: 0/04-2011: Slow away, held up, gd hdwy to lead over 1f out, pushed clr, v cmftbly: abs, gd time: suited by 10f now & likes gd, gd/soft & both AWs: runs well fresh: thriving at present, shld land hat-trick: see 726, 393. **71**

4533} **CASTAWAY QUEEN 191** [11] W R Muir 5-9-0 (61) L Dettori 10/1: 205620-2: ch f Selkirk - Surfing (Grundy) Held up, hdwy appr 2f out, chsd wnr ins last, no impress: rnr-up in a h'cap & class stks in '03: rnr-up 4 times in '02: eff at 1m, stays 10f & likes firm & fast grnd, handles gd/soft & any trk: tried cheek pieces: mdn. *7* **62**

2 Sep'03 Nott 10.0g/f 62-(62) E: 2 Jul'03 Bath 10.2g/f 63-62 E: 2 Sep'02 Bath 8fm 70-70 D: 2 Sep'02 Epso 8.5g/f 71- D: 2 Jul'02 Epso 72-(70) : 2 Jun'02 Nott 8.2g/s 72-67 D: 2 Aug'01 Wind 6gd 73- D:

265 **BLUEGRASS BOY 101** [18] G B Balding 4-9-2 (63) S Carson 25/1: 025300-3: b g Bluegrass Prince - Honey Mill (Milford) Held up, hdwy over 2f out, onepace over 1f out: rnr-up in a h'cap in '03: stays 10f on fast, polytrack & gd/soft: fair run after absence. 2 Aug'03 Kemp 10g/f 66-65 E: *¾* **63**

978 **EASTBOROUGH 9** [14] B G Powell 5-9-1 (62) S Whitworth 8/1: 3103434: Held up, short of room 4f out & 2f out, late gains: may have fin 2nd with a clr run: see 978. *3* **58**

900* **SAY WHAT YOU SEE 16** [8]4-9-12 (73) R Hills 5/1: 00-04215: Led early, led again over 2f out till over 1f out, no extra: prob best with an uncontested lead as in 900 (polytrack). *nk* **69**

1006 **TRAVELLERS TALE 8** [10]5-9-10 (71) S Drowne 14/1: 3034-006: Keen bhd, eff 2f out, no impress. *1¾* **65**

916 **SALFORD FLYER 15** [2]8-8-13 bl (60) S Sanders 50/1: 5405//-067: b g Pharly - Edge of Darkness (Vaigly Great) Led after 2f till over 2f out, wknd: missed '03 & '02, unplcd in '01 (with D Elsworth, rtd 78): suited by 14.4f on firm or gd/soft, any trk: 8yo now & wears blnks. *2½* **50**

4963} **KERNEL DOWERY 160** [9]4-8-13 p (60) T Quinn 10/1: 320043-8: In tch, wknd over 2f out on reapp. *7* **40**

3310} **DEXILEOS 251** [4]5-9-4 (65) D Sweeney 50/1: 4/04000-9: Keen in tch, wknd over 2f out: mdn. *1¾* **42**

4704} **SNINFIA 179** [17]4-9-4 (65) G Duffield 33/1: 040200-0: 10th: Keen in tch, wknd over 2f out: mdn. *3* **38**

978 **DASH FOR COVER 9** [6]4-9-8 (69) R Hughes 10/1: 33001-20: 11th: In tch, wknd 2f out: btr 978. *nk* **42**

610 **TALLY 56** [16]4-8-11 (58) L Fletcher(3) 66/1: 646-0000: 12th: In tch, wknd 2f out: new stable. *1¼* **29**

803 **SPRINGALONG 35** [13]4-9-6 (67) R Havlin 16/1: 304-0450: 13th: Nvr a factor. *2½* **34**

394} **IN TUNE 449** [5]4-8-8 (55) A Nicholls 50/1: 0000/55-0: 14th: Al bhd. *½* **21**

803* **KARAOKE 35** [3]4-9-13 (74) Dane O'Neill 16/1: 331-0010: 15th: In tch, wknd over 2f out. *5* **33**

4984} **DESERT ISLAND DISC 158** [15]7-10-0 (75) J Tate 18/1: 366030-0: 16th: Chsd ldrs, wknd over 2f out. *2½* **30**

4506} **JACK DURRANCE 192** [1]4-9-13 (74) J Quinn 40/1: 0/50100-0: 17th: Slow away & al bhd. *5* **22**

4201] **AMONG EQUALS 922** [7]7-10-0 (75) V Slattery 12/1: 2215/60//-0: 18th: Virtually ref to race & sn t.o. *dist* **0**

18 Ran Time 2m 13.62 (7.62) Owned: Mrs Glennie Braune Trained: Alvechurch

1099

3.20 Bathwick Tyres Handicap Stakes Fillies 3yo 0-75 (E) [80]
£3624 £1115 £558 **1m5y rnd** **Good/Soft 87** **-04 Slow** Inside

869 **TIME TO RELAX 21** [7] J J Quinn 3-8-12 (64) T Quinn 7/1: 3600-241: Handy, hdwy 2f out, styd on well ins last to lead cl-home, rdn out: eff at 6f, clearly stays 1m: acts on fast, fibresand & gd/soft, any trk. **68**

4803} **RABITATIT 173** [9] J G M O'Shea 3-8-10 (62) R Miles(3) 16/1: 321150-2: b f Robellino - Coupled (Wolfhound) Sn chsd ldr, styd on to lead ins last, collared cl-home: sell & h'cap wnr in '03: stays 1m on fast & gd/soft, prob any trk, likes Bath: runs well fresh: gd return. *hd* **65**

1 Sep'03 Bath 8.0g/f 65-59 D: 1 Aug'03 Folk 7g/f 61-(60) F: 2 Aug'03 Sali 7.0g/f 61-(61) E:

4871} **MYSTICAL GIRL 167** [15] M Johnston 3-9-7 (73) S Chin 9/1: 230-3: ch f Rahy - Miss Twinkletoes (Zafonic) In tch, hdwy 2f out, styd on to chall ins last, just held in a 4-way photo: reapp: plcd in 2 of 3 '03 starts (mdns): eff at 7f, clearly stays 1m & acts on fast & gd/soft grnd: consistent, likely to be plcd to win for top stable. 2 Oct'03 Redc 7g/f 73- D: *nk* **75**

4960} **KESHYA 160** [2] D J Coakley 3-8-11 (63) W Supple 11/2 FAV: 0062-3: b f Mtoto - Liberatrice (Assert) Chsd ldrs, sltly outpcd 2f out, rallied ins last, styd on well, just held on reapp: rnr-up in a nursery h'cap last of 4 '03 starts: stays 1m well, looks sure to relish further: acts on gd/soft grnd: likely type for similar over 10f. 2 Oct'03 Brig 8.0g/s 64-59 E: *dht* **65+**

4988} **CARTE NOIRE 157** [1]3-8-10 (62) E Ahern 25/1: 6030-5: Led, rdn & collared ins last, no extra. *1¼* **62**

955 **GABANA 12** [13]3-9-3 (69) S Sanders 6/1: 003-06: Held up, hdwy 2f out, sn onepace. *¾* **68**

696 **EVEN EASIER 47** [5]3-8-8 p (60) R L Moore 14/1: 126-0057: Slow away, held up, some late gains. *2½* **55**

901 **TROMPE LOEIL 16** [8]3-8-0 p (52) J F McDonald(5) 12/1: 40-00608: Slow away & bhd, eff & short of room over 2f out, no dngr: see 901, 116. *1* **45**

4923} **DESERT DAISY 163** [10]3-8-13 (65) S W Kelly 33/1: 2260-9: In tch, wknd 2f out. *¾* **57**

734 **KILCULLEN LASS 42** [3]3-7-12 (3oh) (47) Joanna Badger 66/1: 006-00: 10th: Slow away, no dngr. *2* **39**

734 **ARCHERFIELD 42** [12]3-9-3 (69) Dane O'Neill 7/1: 055-2230: 11th: In tch 6f, wknd: abs, see 603. *¾* **57**

4435} **BARABELLA 196** [11]3-9-0 (66) J Murtagh 8/1: 4440-0: 12th: In tch, wknd over 2f out. *3* **50**

4959} **MISKINA 160** [4]3-8-7 (59) B Swarbrick(7) 10/1: 024-0: 13th: In tch, wknd over 2f out. *1¼* **41**

875 **HANA DEE 20** [14]3-9-4 (70) T E Durcan 20/1: 030-00: 14th: Slow away & al bhd. *hd* **52**

367 **RUSSALKA 89** [6]3-8-11 (63) N Callan 20/1: 46022-00: 15th: In tch, wknd 2f out: btr 240 (aw). *nk* **45**

15 Ran Time 1m 45.55 (7.25) Owned: Mr Grahame Liles Trained: Malton

1100

3.50 Letheby & Christopher Maiden Stakes Div 1 3yo+ (D)
£3556 £1094 £547 **1m5y rnd** **Good/Soft 87** **-09 Slow** Far Side

894 **RAHJEL SULTAN 17** [7] B A McMahon 6-9-11 t (40) G Gibbons 100/1: 0540-361: In tch, lost place over 2f out, rallied over 1f out to lead ins last, rdn out: btn in banded earlier: much imprvd today on gd/soft at 1m. **63**

5024} **CAPTAIN MARRYAT 153** [3] P W Harris 3-8-10 E Ahern 33/1: 0-2: ch g Inchinor - Finlaggan (Be My Chief) Held up, hdwy to lead over 1f out, kept on till collared well ins last: unplcd sole '03 start: imprvd here on gd/soft grnd & clearly stays 1m: gelded since last term & shld find a modest race. *1* **61**

CREDIT [8] R Hannon 3-8-10 Dane O'Neill 8/1: 3: b c Intikhab - Tycooness (Last Tycoon) Slow away, held up, hdwy over 2f out, no extra ins last on debut: cost 100,000gns: eff at 1m on gd/soft: encouraging. *hd* **60**

4972} **ALYOUSUFEYA 159** [11] J L Dunlop 3-8-5 R Hills 7/2: 04-4: ch f Kingmambo - Musicale (The Minstrel) Cl-up, led over 2f out till over 1f out, no extra: 4th in a Newmarket mdn last of 2 '03 starts: dam smart 7f/1m wnr: eff at 7f, shld stay at least 1m: acts on gd grnd. *2* **52**

3108} **ZONIC BOOM 259** [1]4-9-11 J Murtagh 9/2: 00-5: Held up, short of room 2f out till over 1f out, *shd* **57**

kept on ins last, nrst fin: gelded, improve.
644   **PACIFIC OCEAN 52** [5]5-9-11 t (60) S Drowne 10/1: 534-2336: Chsd ldrs, no extra over 1f out: abs.   3½   51
919   **PANSHIR 14** [9]3-8-10 G Baker 100/30: 0-57: Keen in tch, wknd well over 1f out: btr 919.   ¾   49
        MISS LIBRATE [10]6-9-6 R L Moore 100/1: 8: Cl-up, wknd 2f out on debut.   ¾   42
713   **BENNANABAA 44** [2]5-9-11 t (57) A Nicholls 100/1: 0509: In tch, wknd over 2f out.   nk   46
4757} **MIX IT UP 176** [6]3-8-5 G Duffield 66/1: 0-0: 10th: Led till over 2f out, wknd.   6   31
10 Ran   Time 1m 46.01 (7.71)   Owned: Mrs J McMahon   Trained: Tamworth

---

1101   4.20 Letheby & Christopher Maiden Stakes Div 2 3yo+ (D)
            £3556 £1094 £547   1m5y rnd   Good/Soft 87   -02 Slow   Inside

886   **JUST TIM 19** [11] R Hannon 3-8-10 (78) Dane O'Neill 11/2: 0602-41: ch c Inchinor - Simply Sooty   78
(Absalom) Led till over 3f out, led again over 1f out, rdn out to hold on: rnr-up on last of 4 '03 starts (mdn):
stays 10f, apprec return to 1m: acts on fast, gd/soft & polytrack, prob any trk: gd confidence boost.
2 Nov'03 Ling 8ap 79a-(78) D:
5018} **SAILMAKER 154** [10] R Charlton 3-8-10 S Drowne 16/1: 6-2: ch g Peintre Celebre - Princess Amalie   nk   77
(Rahy) Led over 3f out till over 1f out, kept on for press ins last, just hld: rtd 67 when 6th sole '03 start:
stays 1m on gd/soft: gelded since last term & looks to have imprvd for it, can win similar shortly.
4126} **BRINDISI 213** [6] B W Hills 3-8-5 R Hills 2/1: 2-3: b f Dr Fong - Genoa (Zafonic) Held up, hdwy   nk   71
well over 1f out, hung ins last but styd on, just held: promise when rnr-up sole mdn start in '03: dam 11f
wnr: stays 1m, further shld suit: acts on firm & gd/soft: can win a race, prob over further.
2 Sep'03 Warw 7.1fm 80- D:
947   **SLAVONIC 12** [2] J H M Gosden 3-8-10 BL (79) R Hughes 6/1: 554-54: In tch, onepace fnl 2f: acts   3   71
on firm & gd/soft, fair run in blnks: see 947.
794   **ROOD BOY 36** [3]3-8-10 (57) I Mongan 33/1: 0043-45: In tch, onepace fnl 2f: longer trip but   ½   70$
seemingly imprvd here at 1m on gd/soft: see 223.
        FIRE FINCH [5]3-8-5 T E Durcan 25/1: 6: Bhd, nvr a factor: debut.   3   60
        LOGGER RHYTHM [1]4-9-11 G Duffield 66/1: 7: Bhd, nvr a factor on debut.   3½   59
3859} **CHAMBRAY 227** [7]3-8-5 Martin Dwyer 20/1: 5-8: Al bhd.   nk   53
1002} **STAKHANOVITE 365** [8]4-9-11 J Murtagh 7/4 FAV: 3-9: Keen, chsd ldrs, wknd over 2f out: 2   55
reportedly lost action on reapp.
269   **BOLD RIDGE 100** [4]4-9-11 P Dobbs 66/1: 00-0: 10th: Al bhd.   10   37
        ZAMBEZI RIVER [9]5-9-11 R L Moore 100/1: 0: 11th: Al bhd.   3   33
11 Ran   Time 1m 45.47 (7.17)   Owned: Mr D J Walker   Trained: Marlborough

---

1102   4.50 Bbc Radio Bristol Handicap Stakes 3yo 0-70 (E)   [72]
            £3517 £1082 £541   5f11y rnd   Good/Soft 87   -16 Slow   Far Side

606   **IVORY LACE 57** [1] S Woodman 3-9-2 (60) D Sweeney 20/1: 0-520131: Chsd ldrs, hdwy 2f out, styd on   70
strongly to lead cl-home, rdn out: 2 mth abs: impr for new stable stepped up in class: eff at 5f, stays 6f: acts
on firm, gd/soft & polytrack, prob any trk: see 548, 371.
995   **LACONIA 8** [3] J S Moore 3-9-7 (65) Martin Dwyer 14/1: 0350-452: Cl-up, hdwy to lead over 1f out,   nk   73
collared cl-home, just held: deserves a win & imprvd here: see 995, 802.
901   **KRYSSA 16** [9] G L Moore 3-9-2 (60) R L Moore 5/4 FAV: 4133: Carried right start, sn bhd, hdwy   2   64+
over 1f out, kept on ins last: hvly bckd: hung run drpd in trip back to 5f, styd 7f well last time: acts on
polytrack & gd/soft: prob unlucky here, can win again over 6/7f shortly: see 901, 802.
548   **PRINCESS KAI 64** [4] R Ingram 3-8-12 bl (66) T Quinn 20/1: 03-10034: Led till over 1f out, no   nk   59
extra: handles firm, gd/soft & polytrack: see 289.
995   **BLACK OVAL 8** [5]3-9-3 (61) S Hitchcott(3) 7/2: 0606-445: Bhd, late gains, nvr a factor: see 995.   1   62
725   **COMERAINCOMESHINE 43** [8]3-9-4 (62) L Dettori 4/1: 030-36: Carried right start, in tch, wknd over   nk   62
1f out: 6 wk abs, see 725, 51.
901   **DANIFAH 16** [2]3-8-11 (55) S W Kelly 16/1: 00000-07: In tch, wknd over 1f out.   ¾   53
1012   **LIZHAR 8** [6]3-8-10 (54) G Duffield 20/1: 0420468: Went right start, in tch, wknd over 1f out: 3½   45
reportedly hung right: see 703, 422.
1015   **UNITED UNION 7** [7]3-9-7 BL (65) Paul Eddery 22/1: 0300-49: Carried right start, keen, al bhd: 7   42
reportedly lost action: blnks, see 1015.
9 Ran   Time 1m 05.47 (5.17)   Owned: Mr Christopher J Halpin   Trained: Chichester

---

1103   5.20 Screenchina Classified Stakes 3yo+ 0-70 (E)
            £3624 £1115 £558   5f161y rnd   Good/Soft 87   +02 Fast   Inside

3296} **DEVISE 251** [13] M S Saunders 5-9-7 (72) T G McLaughlin 25/1: 103600-1: b g Hamas - Soreze   79
(Gallic League) Slow away, held up, gd hdwy to lead appr fnl 1f, hung left but styd on well, drvn out on reapp: joc
received a 3-day careless riding ban: '03 h'cap wnr: eff at 5/5.7f on firm & gd/soft: clearly goes well fresh.
1 Jun'03 Wind 5.0g/f 75-68 E: 1 May'01 Warw 5gd 80- D:
944   **THE FISIO 12** [7] A M Balding 4-9-5 vis (70) Martin Dwyer 9/1: 1563002: Led till appr fnl 1f,   1½   73
carried left & switched ins last, kept on: gd run: see 415, 329.
927   **ZARZU 13** [14] C R Dore 5-9-9 (74) R Thomas(5) 3/1 FAV: 1-354343: Held up, hdwy 2f out, onepace   ¾   75
when carried left ins last: acts on firm, gd/soft & both AWs: see 171.
957   **PORT ST CHARLES 10** [8] P R Chamings 7-9-5 (70) R Hughes 16/1: 1-500044: Held up, hdwy & short of 1¼   68
room just ins last, onepace: see 957, 113.
1010   **HARD TO CATCH 8** [3]6-9-5 (70) M Howard(7) 10/1: 2410455: In tch, onepace over 1f out: best 628.   shd   68
4719*}**FULL SPATE 178** [9]9-9-5 (69) S Hitchcott(3) 14/1: 606061-6: ch g Unfuwain - Double River (Irish   nk   67
River) Bhd, some late gains on reapp: won fnl '03 start (h'cap): won 3 h'caps & a class stks in '02: stays 1m,
suited by 6f fast grnd, handles hvy & any trk: likes to come late: tough, sharper for this fair reapp.
1 Oct'03 Wind 6g/f 71-66 E: 2 Jul'03 Kemp 6g/f 72-69 D: 2 Apr'03 Ripo 6g/f 74-72 C: 1 Oct'02 Wind 6g/f 73-68 E:
1 Jul'02 Leic 6gd 72-66 E: 1 Jul'02 Hami 6sft 66- F: 1 Jun'02 Donc 6g/f 68-60 D: 1 Aug'01 Folk 7gd 74- E:
2 Jul'01 Folk 7g/f 73-69 D: 1 Jun'01 Warw 6gd 71-69 D: 1 Apr'01 Folk 6g/f 70-66 D:
960   **ARABIAN KNIGHT 10** [6]4-9-5 (57) V Slattery 66/1: 1006-007: Held up, kept on late, nvr dngrs.   nk   66$
551   **RIDICULE 63** [11]5-9-5 bl (66) R Havlin 33/1: 30540-08: b g Piccolo - Mockingbird (Sharpo) Bhd,   2½   61
hdwy & short of room 2f out, kept on ins last: plcd in a class stks in '03: won 2 h'caps & a class stks in '02:

BATH THURSDAY 08.04.04 Lefthand Turning Track with Uphill Finish

eff over 5/6f on firm or soft grnd, prob any trk: tried blnks, prob best in a visor: slipped down the weights.
1 Aug'02 Pont 6sft 77- E: 2 Jun'02 Redc 6fm 68-66 D: 1 Jun'02 Muss 5g/s 65-59 E: 1 Jun'02 Redc 6fm 56-52 G:
807 **SUNDRIED TOMATO 34** [4]5-9-8 (73) L Fletcher(3) 15/2: 0646069: In tch, outpcd over 2f out. *1½* **61**
1011 **ZARGUS 8** [5]5-9-5 (69) J Quinn 20/1: 00040-50: 10th: In tch, wknd over 1f out: see 1011. *hd* **57**
1023 **IMPERIUM 6** [16]3-8-9 (72) S Drowne 16/1: 046-4020: 11th: Al bhd: btr 1023, 764. *¾* **57**
976 **WATERSIDE 9** [1]5-9-6 (71) R Hills 12/1: 31404-00: 12th: Slow away, nvr a factor. *1* **54**
1018 **BEAU JAZZ 7** [15]3-8-7 (62) S Righton 100/1: 56-53060: 13th: In tch, wknd over 2f out. *2½* **48**
4805} **BRANTWOOD 173** [10]4-9-5 T (70) W Supple 8/1: 005000-0: 14th: In tch, wknd over 2f out: gelded. *2½* **43**
976 **TAPPIT 9** [12]5-9-5 (69) R L Moore 25/1: 30000-00: 15th: Slow away & al bhd. *6* **31**
944 **POLISH EMPEROR 12** [2]4-9-7 bl (72) T Quinn 9/2: 10-42250: 16th: Prom, wknd over 2f out: btr 755. *1¾* **29**
16 Ran Time 1m 13.88(4.78) Owned: Mr D Naylor Trained: Wells

HAYDOCK SATURDAY 10.04.04 Lefthand, Flat, Galloping Track

Official Going Soft (Heavy Places)

1104

2.00 Bet365 Call 08000 322 365 Classified Stakes 3yo+ 0-80 (D)
£5606 £1725 £863 **1m2f120y** **Soft 99** **-24 Slow** Outside

4873} **ZERO TOLERANCE 169** [3] T D Barron 4-10-1 (85) M Fenton 7/2 FAV: 101304-1: ch g Nashwan - Place de L'Opera (Sadler's Wells) Handy & led 4f out, rdn clr over 2f out, styd on well ins last: bckd: '03 AW mdn & turf h'cap scorer: eff at 1m, suited by 10f, tried 12f: acts on fast & fibresand, likes soft & gall or sharp trks: goes well fresh: useful on easy grnd, win again. **90**
2 May'03 Sand 10.0g/f 82-77 C: 1 May'03 Beve 9.9gd 85-72 D: 1 Feb'03 Sout 8af 79a- D: 2 Jan'03 Sout 8af 69a- D:
928 **ARRY DASH 15** [9] M R Channon 4-10-1 (85) T E Durcan 11/2: 2015-402: Held up, styd on for press fnl 2f, not able to chall wnr: clr rem: back to form, shld win similar: see 758. *1¼* **87**
702 **WEET A HEAD 47** [7] R Hollinshead 3-8-8 (84) W Supple 25/1: 43263-53: Trkd ldrs, no impress over 1f out: 7 wk abs: not disgraced on & poss stays 10f on fast, soft & fibresand: see 702. *5* **81**
2531*}**FERNERY 285** [5] L M Cumani 4-9-10 (83) T Quinn 5/1: 031-4: b f Danehill - Fern (Shirley Heights) Trkd ldrs, onepace fnl 2f: reapp: lightly rcd '03, mdn scorer fnl start: eff over 10f on gd/soft & any trk: goes well fresh. 1 Jun'03 Pont 10.0g/s 82- D: *¾* **76**
3290} **TAWNY WAY 253** [6]4-9-11 (84) A Culhane 9/1: 401220-5: b f Polar Falcon - Ma Petite Anglaise (Reprimand) Held up, no impress fnl 2f: op 11/1, reapp: fills h'cap scorer '03, dual h'cap rnr-up: eff at 7f, suited by 9/10f on fast & gd, poss handles soft: handles a stiff/gall or easy trk. *¾* **76**
2 Jul'03 Newc 10.1gd 85-(82) D: 2 Jul'03 Newb 10.0g/f 81-80 D: 1 Jul'03 Kemp 9g/f 80-74 D:
810 **INTRICATE WEB 36** [8]8-9-10 (78) D Allan(3) 16/1: 43-11246: Rear & rdn early, nvr on terms: btr 513. *5* **70**
4226} **CATS WHISKERS 210** [11]5-10-0 (84) Dale Gibson 12/1: 220000-7: Keen tracking ldrs, btn 2f out, reapp. *hd* **73**
1066 **THE BONUS KING 4** [1]4-10-0 (84) J Fanning 4/1: 060-4528: Led till 4f out, sn lost plc, eased: bckd: qck reapp: longer trip: btr 1066 (1m). *5* **68**
4873} **LEIGHTON 169** [10]4-9-11 (81) B Doyle 14/1: 043403-9: Keen in rear, btn 2f out, eased: reapp. *¾* **64**
928 **AVENTURA 15** [2]4-9-13 (83) K Ghunowa(7) 33/1: 30-00400: 10th: Keen & trkd ldrs, lost place 3f out. *8* **58**
10 Ran Time 2m 23.05 (13.05) Owned: The Hornsey Warriors Racing Syndicate Trained: Thirsk

1105

2.30 Bigwigs Bloodstock Racing Club Rated Stakes Handicap 3yo 0-90 (C) **[94]**
£10010 £3080 £1540 **1m30y** **Soft 99** **+01 Fast** Inside

955 **IMPERIALISTIC 14** [3] K R Burke 3-9-4 p (84) Darren Williams 7/2: 43423-41: Chsd ldrs & led far side 2f out, led overall dist, rdn out: nicely bckd, fair time: eff at 6/7f, improved at 1m here back in cheekpieces: acts on gd, relishes soft & loves Haydock: see 955. **95**
947 **RED LANCER 14** [7] R J Price 3-9-0 (80) B Swarbrick(7) 8/1: 0-611222: Held up, rdn & hdwy to chall 2f out, short of room ins last, no extra cl-home: most tough & consistent, win more races: see 947, 796 & 702 (AW). *1¼* **88**
4903} **ODDSMAKER 166** [6] P D Evans 3-8-7 (1oh) (72) S W Kelly 25/1: 000015-3: b g Barathea - Archipova (Ela Mana Mou) Trkd ldrs & v keen early, led & came towards centre over 4f out, edged left & hdd dist, no extra: clr of rem: reapp: h'cap scorer '03, earlier unplcd for A Berry, tried cheek pieces & blnks: eff at 1m on fast & soft grnd, gall or easy trk: gd eff racing alone, can impr on this & win a h'cap. 1 Oct'03 Yarm 8.0gd 74-61 E: *1½* **79**
4978} **SAFFRON FOX 161** [9] J G Portman 3-9-7 (87) A Culhane 13/2: 40120-4: ch f Safawan - Fox Oa (French Friend) Mid-div, not able to chall ldrs: reapp: auct mdn scorer '03, subs cond stks rnr-up: well suited by 1m on gd/soft & soft grnd: likes a stiff/gall trk: h'cap bow today. *5* **86**
2 Aug'03 Sand 8.1sft 86-(84) C: 1 Aug'03 Newm 8g/s 82- E:
886 **GJOVIC 21** [4]3-9-0 (80) K Darley 7/1: 342-25: Led/dsptd lead till halfway, no extra over 1f out: h'cap bow: btr 886 (polytrack,10f mdn). *nk* **78**
4737} **ROYAL DISTANT 179** [8]3-8-13 (79) Dale Gibson 20/1: 63124-6: ch f Distant View - Encorenous (Diesis) Pushed along rear, mod late gains: reapp: auct mdn wnr '03, subs h'cap rnr-up: best around 1m on fast & gd grnd, stiff/gall & undul trks: prev with J Gosden, now with M W Easterby. *1¼* **75**
2 Sep'03 Pont 8.0g/f 79-76 D: 1 Sep'03 Chep 8.1gd 77- E:
817 **WESTERN ROOTS 33** [5]3-8-13 (79) T Quinn 16/1: 140-2407: Trkd ldrs & keen, btn 2f out: btr 432 (AW). *1* **74**
955 **MOUNT VETTORE 14** [1]3-9-2 (82) E Ahern 15/8 FAV: 5-128: Trkd ldrs, rdn 4f out, sn btn: hvly bckd: prob not handle testing conds over further: btr 955 & 481 (6/7f). *1¾* **75**
4729} **THE VIOLIN PLAYER 179** [2]3-9-0 (80) M Tebbutt 20/1: 0313-9: Keen rear, carried hd high & struggling over 2f out, eased: reapp. *14* **55**
9 Ran Time 1m 48.5 (8.0) Owned: Bigwigs Bloodstock II Trained: Leyburn

1106

3.00 Listed Field Marshal Rated Stakes Handicap 3yo 0-110 (A) **[111]**
£17850 £6600 £3300 **5f** **Soft 99** **+09 Fast** Centre

4315} **IF PARADISE 205** [1] R Hannon 3-9-3 (100) R L Moore 7/1: 416205-1: b c Compton Place - Sunley Stars (Sallust) Trkd ldr & led over 1f out, pushed out: best time of day: reapp: auct mdn scorer bef landing val Newbury super sprint contest '03, subs List rnr-up: best at 5f, tried 6f: acts on firm & soft grnd, goes well fresh: loves a stiff/gall trk: career best encountering soft grnd for the first time today, v useful. **106**

HAYDOCK SATURDAY 10.04.04 Lefthand, Flat, Galloping Track

2 Aug'03 York 5.0fm 97-(100) A: 1 Jul'03 Newb 5.2fm 100- B: 1 May'03 Leic 5.0gd 91- E:

4953} **CRAFTY FANCY 162** [5] D J S ffrench Davis 3-8-7 (5oh) (85) T Quinn 4/1: 065655-2: ch f Intikhab - **2½** **90**
Idle Fancy (Mujtahid) Pushed along in tch, kept on to take 2nd, nvr threat to wnr: op 3/1, reapp: fills auct mdn &
cond stks scorer '03: both wins at 5f, 6f shld suit this term: acts on gd/soft & soft grnd, prob fm: acts on any
trk, likes Windsor: encouraging reapp, spot on at 6f in similar.

1 May'03 Wind 5.0g/s 91- B: 1 Apr'03 Wind 5.0g/s 86- F:

1018 **HARRY UP 9** [2] J G Given 3-8-9 (92) M Fenton 3/1: 61040-23: Led till over 1f out, not pace of *shd* **92**
front pair: op 4/1: acts on firm & soft grnd: see 1018.

4680} **NIGHTS CROSS 182** [4] M R Channon 3-9-7 (104) T E Durcan 2/1 FAV: 303212-4: b c Cape Cross - **1¼** **101**
Cathy Garcia (Be My Guest) Trkd ldrs, rdn & no extra over 1f out: nicely bckd w/ op 7/4: v tough & progressive
'03, kept v busy, mdn, nov & List scorer, Gr 3 rnr-up on fnl start: suited by 5/5.7f on firm & gd/soft grnd, prob
handles soft & any trk: v tough, likely to impr on this, poss on faster grnd.

2 Oct'03 Asco 5gd 103-(100) A: 1 Oct'03 Tipp 5g/f 105- : 2 Sep'03 Ayr 5g/f 101-(100) A: 2 Jul'03 Good 5gd 103-(97) A:
2 Jul'03 Ches 5.1fm 97- B: 1 Jul'03 Beve 5g/s 94- D: 1 May'03 Bath 5.7g/f 85- D:

4264*}**LAKE GARDA 207** [3]3-8-7 (5oh) (85) G Gibbons 11/2: 22001-5: Cl-up, switched to race alone stands **2½** **82**
rail after 1f, no impress on ldrs far side fnl 1f, eased: bckd on reapp.

5 Ran Time 1m 03.32 (4.52) Owned: Mrs J Wood Trained: Marlborough

---

1107 3.35 Haydock Park Annual Badgeholders Maiden Auction Stakes 2yo (E)
£3770 £1160 £580 **5f** **Soft 99** **-20 Slow** Centre

954 **APOLOGIES 14** [3] B A McMahon 2-8-7 G Gibbons 13/2: 01: b c Robellino - Mistook (Phone Trick) **80**
Dsptd lead, went on 2f out, edged right under press, held on well: op 8/1: jock given 7-day careless riding ban:
Feb foal, cost 5,000gns: eff at 5f, shld stay further: imprvd today on soft grnd: going the right way.

MYSTICAL LAND 0 [7] J H M Gosden 2-8-11 R Havlin 5/1 JT FAV: 2: b c Xaar - Samsung Spirit *1* **80**
(Statoblest) Sn rdn in tch, styd on for press ins last, not pace of wnr: bckd tho' op 7/2: 20,000gns Feb foal,
half-brother to useful 6f juv wnr: dam 6f wnr: eff at 5f on soft, 6f suit: win a race.

CAMMIES FUTURE 0 [6] P W Chapple Hyam 2-8-11 A McCarthy 11/2: 3: gr c Efisio - Impulsive *¾* **78**
Decision (Nomination) Trkd ldrs & ch dist, struck by whip of winning rider & no extra well ins last: nicely bckd on
debut: 22,000gns March foal, half-brother to 7f/1m AW wnr Ermine Grey: dam a 6f/1m wnr: eff at 5f, get further:
did well to fin so close despite trouble in running, expect improvement on this in similar.

CHISELLED 0 [1] K R Burke 2-8-11 Darren Williams 6/1: 4: Went left start, chsd ldrs, hmpd 2f *2* **74**
out, no extra from dist: closer without trouble in running, expect improvement.

SPECIAL GOLD 0 [9]2-9-0 K Darley 6/1: 5: Dwelt, trkd ldrs, outpcd fnl 2f: well bckd on debut, op 11/1. *¾* **76**
88**BM AIMEE 21** [10]2-8-2 S Carson 5/1 JT FAV: 26: Led till 2f out, btn dist, eased: bckd: btr 882 (AW). *1¼* **61**
GIFTED GAMBLE 0 [5]2-8-7 N Callan 10/1: 7: Slow away & bhd, mod late prog, impr in time. *2½* **61**
974 **VENEER 11** [2]2-8-9 R L Moore 14/1: 48: Sn struggling rear: see 974. *1¾* **60**
FANTASY DEFENDER 0 [4]2-8-7 R Winston 25/1: 9: Al outpcd & rear, debut. *1* **56**
931 **DROOPYS JOEL 15** [8]2-8-7 J Fanning 16/1: 00: 10th: Chsd ldrs till halfway, sn btn. *17* **20**
10 Ran Time 1m 04.74 (5.94) Owned: Mr J C Fretwell Trained: Tamworth

---

1108 4.10 Runcorn Maiden Stakes 3yo (D)
£5902 £1816 £908 **1m30y** **Soft 99** **-06 Slow** Inside

4302} **BAFFLE 206** [12] J L Dunlop 3-8-9 (77) T Quinn 9/4 FAV: 026-1: b f Selkirk - Elude (Slip Anchor) **74**
Made all, rdn & asserted from dist, styd on strongly: hvly bckd tho' op 7/4: reapp: fills mdn rnr-up '03 (lightly
rcd): eff at 7f, apprec step up to 1m, further shld suit: acts on firm, enjoyed soft here: likes a stiff/gall trk
& goes well fresh; shld improve again on easy grnd in h'caps. 2 Aug'03 Newm 7fm 78- D:

4885} **TYTHEKNOT 168** [6] Jedd O'Keeffe 3-9-0 T E Durcan 13/2: 02-2: b g Pursuit of Love - Bundled Up *3* **73**
(Sharpen Up) Trkd wnr, styd on for press, al held from dist: op 8/1, reapp: auct mdn rnr-up 2nd of just 2 '03
starts: eff at 1m, 10f could suit: handles gd & soft grnd, sharp or gall trk: shld find a race.

2 Oct'03 Muss 8gd 80- E:

FOOLISH GROOM 0 [1] R Hollinshead 3-9-0 A Culhane 20/1: 3: ch g Groom Dancer - Scared (Royal *2* **70**
Academy) Dwelt, chsd ldrs, no extra over 1f out on debut: half-brother to a useful 7f/1m performer: stays 1m on
soft grnd & a gall trk: pleasing debut.

925 **INCHLOSS 15** [10] B A McMahon 3-9-0 W Supple 20/1: 04: Rear, styd on from over 2f out, nvr *1¾* **68**
threatened wnr: this longer 1m trip is likely to suit, imprvd today on soft ground.

4067} **BURNING MOON 218** [8]3-9-0 E Ahern 3/1: 50-5: Pushed along rear, mod late prog, nvr dngr: *2½* **64**
nicely bckd on reapp, impr on faster surface.

966 **INDI ANO STAR 12** [5]3-9-0 R Fitzpatrick 10/1: 56: Slow away, mod late prog: bckd, op 12/1. *nk* **63**
2982} **TOP ACHIEVER 267** [2]3-9-0 R Winston 25/1: 5-7: Chsd ldrs till over 1f out, reapp. *1¼* **61**
553 **GO GREEN 65** [7]3-8-9 S W Kelly 33/1: 08: Chsd ldrs, struggling 2f out, abs. *8* **44**
5024} **ZABADOU 155** [11]3-9-0 T Eaves(5) 100/1: 00-9: Mid-div till lost place 3f out, reapp. *5* **42**
4825} **TRUE TO YOURSELF 172** [4]3-9-0 J Mackay 50/1: 0: 10th: Slow away & al bhd, reapp. *5* **35**
839 **Royal Nite Owl 28** [3]3-9-0 J D O'Reilly(7) 50/1:0: 4450} **Grande Terre 197** [9]3-8-9 M Fenton 6/1:P
12 Ran Time 1m 49.12 (8.62) Owned: Plantation Stud Trained: Arundel

---

1109 4.45 Rectangle Group Handicap Stakes 4yo+ 0-85 (D)
£5753 £1770 £885 **1m6f** **Soft 99** **-04 Slow** Inside [82]

1064* **BENBYAS 4** [1] D Carroll 7-8-11 (65) D Tudhope(7) 7/2 FAV: 000/0/-611: Led & clr after 6f, styd on **79+**
strongly & in full command fnl 3f, readily: well bckd, qck reapp: eff at 12/14f: acts on fast, loves soft & hvy,
gall trks: best with an uncontested lead & currently exploiting fav'ble Flat mark (talented hdler): see 1064, 918.

1034 **NAKWA 7** [7] E J Alston 6-8-1 (55) D Allan 9/1: 3-122532: Chsd wnr, styd on fnl 2f, nvr any *7* **61**
threat to wnr: stays 14f on soft & fibresand: see 1034, 315 (12f).

4475} **THEWHIRLINGDERVISH 196** [3] T D Easterby 6-9-0 (78) A Mullen(7) 50/1: 402000-3: ch g Definite *1½* **82**
Article - Nomadic Dancer (Nabeel Dancer) Held up, hdwy from halfway, onepace: reapp: h'cap rnr-up '03: dual h'cap
scorer '02: eff at 12/14f, stays by stiff 2m/2m2f: prob handles soft, loves gd & firm, reportedly prefers the
latter: encouraging return & a likely improver on a faster surface. 2 Jul'03 Asco 16.2g/f 82-78 B:
1 Jul'02 Asco 16.2g/f 82-75 D: 1 Jun'02 Pont 17.9fm 75-68 D: 2 Jul'01 Hayd 14g/f 70-67 D:

HAYDOCK SATURDAY 10.04.04 Lefthand, Flat, Galloping Track

2 Jun'01 Redc 11g/f 65- F: 2 Jun'01 Beve 12g/f 68-66 E:

2686* }CARA FANTASY 280 [11] J L Dunlop 4-9-9 (80) T Quinn 9/1: 43/1661-4: b f Sadler's Wells - Gay Fantasy (Troy) Chsd ldrs, no impress fnl 3f: reapp: mdn & fills h'cap scorer '03 (lightly rcd): plcd '02 (lightly rcd, rtd 75): both wins at 11.8f, longre trip here: handles firm & soft grnd, stiff/undul trk, loves Leicester: can go well fresh. 1 Jul'03 Leic 11.8gd 81-75 D: 1 Apr'03 Leic 11.8g/f 73- D: **2½ 82**

1019 **DANCING PEARL 9** [6]6-7-12 (12oh) (40) B Swarbrick(7) 20/1: 6/5-05: ch f Dancing Spree - Elegant Rose (Noalto) Bhd, eff wide over 2f out, mod late prog: landed a mares' h'cap hdle last month (rtd 127h, 2m/2m1f, gd & soft, sharp or gall trk): again shaped as a thorough stayer on the level: see 679. **¾ 53$**

997 **MIDDLETHORPE 10** [2]7-8-13 bl (67) P Mulrennan(5) 14/1: 0055-156: Mid-div, no impress fnl 3f: see 918. **¾ 67**

1069 **RINGSIDE JACK 4** [12]8-7-12 (52) J Mackay 13/2: 00344-37: Mid-div, no impress 2f out: qck reapp. **1 51**

926 **NORTHERN NYMPH 15** [13]5-9-7 T (75) A Culhane 20/1: 35/4-2308: Bhd, eff 3f out, no impress: t-strap. **½ 73**

1087* **TURTLE VALLEY 3** [10]8-9-7 (6ex) (75) P Doe 4/1: 10-50319: Bhd, hdwy to chase ldrs from halfway, wknd qckly 2f out: nicely bckd under a pen, poss too sn after 1087 (all out). **1¾ 72**

918 **CHAMPION LION 16** [5]5-9-7 (75) T E Durcan 14/1: 30050-00: 10th: Rear, hdwy 3f out, wknd, eased. **6 66**

997 **EDMO YEWKAY 10** [9]4-8-8 bl (65) W Supple 16/1: 40060-00: 11th: Chsd ldrs till 3f out. **4 52**

4422} **LILLEBROR 199** [8]6-8-11 (65) S W Kelly 40/1: 540000-0: 12th: Trkd ldrs till 6f out, sn bhd: jumps abs. **6 46**

1955} **NOBRATINETTA 310** [4]5-9-9 (77) K Darley 8/1: 410-0: 13th: Trkd ldrs till lost place 5f out, eased, t.o. **dist 0**

13 Ran   Time 3m 12.45(14.45)   Owned: C H Stephenson & Partners   Trained: Warthilll

KEMPTON SATURDAY 10.04.04 Righthand, Flat, Fair Track

Official Going Good/Soft (Good places)

1110   1.35 Listed Turftours Com Masaka Stakes Fillies 3yo (A)
£17400 £6600 £3300   1m Jub   Good/Soft 76   +05 Fast   Inside

4891} HATHRAH 168 [4] J L Dunlop 3-8-8 (103) R Hills 10/11 FAV: 4122-1: gr f Linamix - Zivania (Shernazar) Cl-up, trav best, led over 2f out, pushed clr, v cmftbly: well bckd, gd time: juv mdn wnr, Gr 2 rnr-up: stays 1m, 10f lks sure to suit: acts on gd, relished this gd/soft & goes well fresh: progressed well from 2 to 3, looks smart & up to wng in Gr class under similar conditions. **117+**
2 Oct'03 Newb 7gd 93-(100) A: 2 Sep'03 Donc 8gd 101- A: 1 Aug'03 Newm 7gd 99- D:

4869* }COQUETERIA 169 [3] G Wragg 3-8-8 (80) S Drowne 25/1: 0441-2: b f Cozzene - Miss Waikiki (Miswaki) Chsd ldrs, rdn & outpcd by wnr 2f out, kept on same pace on reapp: won last of 4 juv starts (nursery h'cap): eff at 7f, stays 1m on fast, prob imprvd here on gd/soft: handles a gall or fair trk: progressive & open to further improvement, caught a useful sort. 1 Oct'03 Newb 7g/f 81-74 D: **9 104**

3763* }HALICARDIA 233 [7] P W Harris 3-8-8 (97) D Holland 9/2: 311-3: br f Halling - Pericardia (Petong) Chsd ldrs, hard rdn 2f out, onepace on reapp: won fnl 2 of 3 juv starts (auct mdn & nursery h'cap): eff at 7f, stays 1m & could get further: acts on firm & gd/soft: gd return & going the right way. 1 Aug'03 York 7.0fm 96-90 C: 1 Jul'03 Folk 7g/f 82- E: **½ 103**

4932} DOCTRINE 172 [8] J H M Gosden 3-8-8 (99) L Dettori 8/1: 62116-4: b f Barathea - Auspicious (Shirley Heights) Slow away, keen in tch, eff over 2f out, no impress on reapp: won 2 of 5 juv starts (mdn & nursery h'cap): eff at 1m, bred to stay 10f: acts on fast grnd, poss gd/soft: useful, consistent. 1 Oct'03 Catt 7g/f 93-82 D: 1 Sep'03 Yarm 8.0g/f 91- D: 2 Aug'03 Not. 8.2g/f 80- D: **1½ 101**

177 FADEELA 122 [1]3-8-8 (69) Paul Eddery 66/1: 025210-5: Led till over 2f out, no extra: 4 mth abs: see 112 (7f, fibresand, nursery h'cap). **6 91$**

5023* }SPRING SURPRISE 155 [9]3-8-8 K Fallon 12/1: 01-6: Al bhd on reapp: up in class/trip. **5 83**

4946* }ZERLINA 163 [2]3-8-8 (86) Dane O'Neill 20/1: 201-7: Slow away & al bhd on reapp: up in class/trip. **6 73**

4596} WHY DUBAI 189 [6]3-8-8 (89) R Hughes 9/1: 0102-8: In tch, wknd qckly over 2f out: reportedly stumbled & knocked herself on reapp: up in trip/different grnd. **2 70**

4891} BETTY STOGS 168 [5]3-8-8 (84) S Sanders 20/1: 0610-9: Al bhd: changed stable, up in class. **11 54**

9 Ran   Time 1m 42.47 (5.67)   Owned: Mr Hamdan Al Maktoum   Trained: Arundel

1111   2.10 Coral Rosebery Stakes Heritage Handicap 4yo+ 0-105 (B)
£23200 £8800 £4400   1m2f Jub   Good/Soft 76   -05 Slow   Inside   **[105]**

4760} SILENCE IS GOLDEN 177 [19] B J Meehan 5-9-4 (95) J F McDonald(5) 11/1: 022325-1: ch f Danehill Dancer - Silent Girl (Krayyan) Held up, hdwy well over 2f out, styd on to lead ins last, styd on well, rdn out on reapp: plcd on 6 of 9 '03 starts (h'caps & List): '02 dual h'cap wnr: suited by 10f, stays a slowly run 12f on fm & soft, any trk: best without blnks: clearly runs well fresh: tough & useful, returned with a career best effort. **103**
2 Sep'03 Yarm 10.1g/f 98-(93) A: 2 Aug'03 Hayd 10.5fm 97-83 B: 2 Jul'03 Asco 10gd 98-88 B:
2 May'03 Sali 12fm 90-87 C: 1 Jul'03 Asco 10g/f 88-81 C: 1 Jun'03 Good 10g/s 83-78 C: 2 Jun'02 Newb 8sft 81- D:
2 Apr'02 Kemp 9fm 78- D: 1 Aug'01 Newm 8fm 79-71 C: 1 Jul'01 Ling 7g/f 73- F:

951 DUMARAN 14 [5] W J Musson 6-8-13 (90) K Fallon 8/1: 0403-002: b g Be My Chief - Pine Needle (Kris) Hld up, hdwy 3f out, switched right & kept on fnl 1f, not btn far: plcd on 1 of 8 '03 starts (rtd h'cap, with A Balding, rtd 95): former nov hdle wnr (rtd 115h, 2m, soft): 3 time h'cap wnr in '02: suited by around 9/10f & handles fm, likes gd/soft & soft: tried vis: tough, on a fair mark, freshened up by new stable. **¾ 96**
1 Oct'02 Newb 9sft 97-91 B: 2 Aug'02 Asco 9.5g 95-91 B: 1 Jun'02 Epso 8.5g/s 90-87 B: 1 May'02 Good 7gd 90-84 C:
1 Aug'01 Good 9g/s 84-77 C: 1 Jul'01 Chep 7gd 83- D:

4955} COUNSELS OPINION 162 [20] C F Wall 7-9-12 (103) S Sanders 14/1: 300110-3: ch g Rudimentary - Fairy Fortune (Rainbow Quest) Dwelt, held up, hdwy over 2f out, kept on to chase wnr ins last, not btn far on reapp: won 3 of 10 '03 starts (2 h'caps & class stks): '02 class stks wnr: suited by 10/12f now on firm & gd/soft, handles hvy & both AWs: has run well fresh under big weights: v tough, useful & genuine, fine return. **nk 108**
1 Oct'03 Asco 10gd 104-97 B: 1 Sep'03 Asco 10g/f 102-(95) B: 1 May'03 Newb 12.0gd 96-89 C:
1 Apr'01 Sout 12gd 77a- D: 1 Mar'01 Ling 12ap 81a- D:

4364} BLYTHE KNIGHT 203 [7] E A L Dunlop 4-9-7 (98) L Dettori 5/1 FAV: 150430-4: ch c Selkirk - Blushing Barada (Blushing Groom) Handy, hdwy trav best to lead over 1f out, rdn & hdd ins last, no extra: won 2 of 8 '03 starts (mdn & class stks): suited by 10f, poss just stays 12f: acts on gd/soft, prob fm: runs well fresh: useful, travels well, gd return. 1 Jun'03 Pont 10.0g/f 98-(92) C: 1 Mar'03 Donc 10.3gd 95- D: **nk 103**
2 Aug'02 Kemp 8fm 80- D:

836 BONECRUSHER 28 [3]5-10-0 vis (105) J Murtagh 12/1: 140-6405: Chsd ldrs, onepace fnl 2f: ran to best. **1¼ 108**

296

4684} **PUTRA KUANTAN 182** [9]4-9-2 (93) P Robinson 10/1: 601200-6: Handy, hdwy to lead over 2f out, edged left & hdd over 1f out, onepace on reapp: prob wants faster grnd. 1¼ **95**
3914} **VENGEANCE 227** [6]4-9-0 (91) G Duffield 25/1: 112105-7: Hmpd & drpd rear sn after start, eff & hmpd again 2f out, not recover: forgive this. 4 **88**
950 **KINGS THOUGHT 14** [2]5-9-7 (98) D Holland 9/1: 40310-68: Led after 2f till over 2f out, no extra. 1¾ **92**
4493} **PRINCE NUREYEV 195** [17]4-9-6 (97) S Drowne 14/1: 102440-9: Bhd, modest late gains: gelded. 1¼ **89**
758 **TURBO 42** [14]5-9-3 p (94) Martin Dwyer 12/1: 00021-00: 10th: Al bhd: btr expected. 2½ **82**
951 **UNSHAKABLE 14** [18]5-8-13 (90) J F Egan 8/1: 20000-00: 11th: In tch, wknd 2f out: frustrating. 3 **74**
4759} **TRUST RULE 177** [8]4-9-7 (98) R Hills 10/1: 032102-0: 12th: Sn bhd: prefers faster grnd? ½ **81**
82 **TIZZY MAY 140** [16]4-9-5 (96) Dane O'Neill 16/1: 223240-0: 13th: In tch, wknd over 3f out: abs. ½ **78**
951 **SERIEUX 14** [10]5-8-13 (90) R Hughes 16/1: 4300-000: 14th: In tch, wknd over 2f out. 9 **60**
4684} **GALLERY GOD 182** [13]8-9-9 (100) Paul Eddery 40/1: 610030-0: 15th: Al bhd. 1¼ **69**
3823} **TYCOON HALL 231** [12]4-8-13 (90) P Dobbs 33/1: 153/550-0: 16th: Led 2f, wknd 3f out on reapp. 10 **45**
2514} **ARABIE 42** [1]6-9-1 (92) K Dalgleish 25/1: 3/05-0000: 17th: In tch, wknd 2f out: gelded. 11 **31**
17 Ran Time 2m 10.38 (8.08) Owned: Miss J Semple Trained: Upper Lambourn

1112 **2.40 Alanbrazilracing Com Queen's Prize Handicap 4yo+ 0-100 (C)** **[104]**
£9874 £3038 £1519 **2m** **Good/Soft 76** **-18 Slow** Inside

5033} **ANAK PEKAN 154** [17] M A Jarvis 4-8-4 (80) P Robinson 9/4 FAV: 221222-1: ch g In The Wings - Trefoil (Blakeney) Made all, drew clr fnl 2f, pushed out, readily: hvly bck: mdn h'cap wnr in '03, rnr-up sev times: stays 2m, further shld suit: acts on fast & gd, imprvd here on first try on gd/soft & relished switch to forcing tactics: runs well fresh on a gall or fair trk: progressed well through winter, more to come, one to follow. **94+**
2 Nov'03 Donc 16.5gd 82-77 C: 2 Oct'03 Newb 16g/f 81-75 C: 2 Sep'03 Kemp 14.4g/f 81-74 D:
1 Aug'03 Yarm 14.1g/f 76-70 E: 2 Aug'03 Sand 14g/f 70-67 D: 2 Aug'03 Newm 12gd 68-65 E:
4957} **TERESA 162** [4] J L Dunlop 4-8-0 (76) J Quinn 16/1: 033133-2: b f Darshaan - Morina (Lyphard) Handy, eff to chase wnr appr 2f out, kept on: '03 mdn wnr, plcd several times (rtd 82): stays 2m well on fast & gd/soft, any trk: consistent, gd return bhd a useful sort & still unexposed at 2m, win again. 5 **81**
1 Aug'03 Ling 14g/f 76-(78) D:
605 **HIGH POINT 59** [5] G P Enright 6-8-8 (1ow) (79) Dane O'Neill 20/1: 01-00023: In tch, hdwy over 3f out, no impress till kept on well fnl 1f: encouraging after 2 mth abs: acts on fast, gd/soft & likes polytrack. 1½ **84**
877 **COLD TURKEY 22** [16] G L Moore 4-8-3 (79) S Whitworth 16/1: 12-11324: Keen held up rear, gd hdwy over 3f out, no extra fnl 1f: made up gd grnd from well bhd & prob just stays 2m: h'capped to win on turf, interesting back around 14f, poss on a sounder surface: see 877, 475. ¾ **82**
HAWADETH 1059 [6]9-8-8 p (80) R Hughes 8/1: 4//06/0//-5: ch g Machiavellian - Ghzaalh (Northern Dancer) Chsd ldrs, rdn 3f out, some late gains: fit from hurdling, earlier fine rnr-up in val Count h'cap at Cheltenham (rtd 145h, 2m, acts on gd & hvy): plcd in several val h'caps in 02/03: v lightly rcd on Flat in recent yrs: stays 2m well on gd/soft & in cheek pieces, has worn blnks: clr of rem. ½ **82**
4572} **REVEILLEZ 190** [13]5-9-7 (93) L Dettori 12/1: 243613-6: gr g First Trump - Amalancher (Alleged) Handy, wknd 2f out on reapp: won 2 of 10 '03 starts (h'cap & class stks): dual h'cap wnr in '02: all 4 wins at 12f, stays 14f & likes firm & gd grnd, gall or fair trks: can front run or come from bhd: has run well fresh: tough, apprec a sounder surface & return to 12f. 1 Sep'03 Kemp 12gd 94-(87) C: 2 Jul'03 Newm 12fm 87-86 C: 7 **88**
1 Jun'03 Newm 12g/f 90-83 D: 2 Jun'03 Hayd 14g/f 84-80 D: 2 May'03 Sand 14g/f 86-80 D:
1 Jul'02 Asco 12g/f 79-77 D: 1 Jun'02 Yarm 11.4fm 81-67 E: 2 May'02 Yarm 11.4g/f 71-67 E:
810 **RED WINE 36** [9]5-9-8 (94) D Holland 14/1: 53040-57: In tch, outpcd over 4f out, some late gains. 1 **88**
5033*}**PONDERON 154** [12]4-9-1 (91) G Duffield 15/2: 330131-8: Chsd wnr, wknd 2f out: gelded. 1 **84**
475 **MOON EMPEROR 77** [18]7-9-1 VIS (87) S Drowne 33/1: 5500-069: Nvr a factor, abs, visor: see 475. 6 **75**
948 **TYPHOON TILLY 14** [10]7-7-13 (71) C Catlin 20/1: 3-643640: 10th: In tch, nvr a factor: see 478, 404. 4 **55**
5033} **ESTABLISHMENT 154** [7]7-8-7 (79) S Sanders 33/1: 502015-0: 11th: Chsd ldrs, wknd 3f out: likes fast. 1½ **62**
4685} **MOSTARSIL 181** [11]6-8-0 p (71) Lisa Jones(2) 33/1: 415206-0: 12th: Al bhd. 1 **54**
926 **BOBSLEIGH 15** [14]5-8-4 (76) P Hanagan 25/1: 03040-60: 13th: Al bhd: see 926. ¾ **57**
950 **HEISSE 14** [8]4-9-7 (97) J Murtagh 12/1: 120-50: 14th: Al bhd: longer trip, see 950 (12f). 11 **68**
173+***BID FOR FAME 123** [15]7-9-0 (86) W Ryan 25/1: 200621-0: 15th: Al bhd: long abs, see 173. 1¼ **56**
926 **SNOWS RIDE 15** [2]4-8-5 (81) Martin Dwyer 33/1: 15011-00: 16th: In tch, wknd 3f out: something amiss? 3½ **48**
1056 **MIDSHIPMAN 5** [1]6-8-3 vis (75) Paul Eddery 100/1: 0/0-00000: 17th: Keen, al bhd: see 1056. 3 **41**
5026} **GULF 155** [3]5-9-13 (99) K Fallon 12/1: 360606-0: 18th: Held up, btn 4f out: likes fast grnd. ½ **64**
18 Ran Time 3m 39.22 (15.02) Owned: HRH Sultan Ahmad Shah Trained: Newmarket

KEMPTON SATURDAY 10.04.04 Righthand, Flat, Fair Track

Official Going Good/Soft (Good places)

1113 **3.10 Listed Alanbrazilracing Com Easter Stakes Colts & Geldings 3yo (A)**
£17400 £6600 £3300 **1m Jub** **Good/Soft 76** **+01 Fast** Inside

4469} **PRIVY SEAL 196** [3] J H M Gosden 3-8-11 (105) L Dettori 9/1: 613155-1: b c Cape Cross - Lady Joshua (Royal Academy) Held up, hdwy to chase wnr 2f out, lkd held till strong run ins last, led cl-home, going away: juv auct mdn & List wnr: stays 1m well on fm/fast, imprvd here on gd/soft, stay further (dam 12f wnr): clearly runs v well fresh: v useful, front 2 well clr here, looks up to Gr 3 class. **110**
1 Jul'03 Leop 7g/f 104- A: 1 Jun'03 Wind 6g/f 93- F:
4205} **MUTAHAYYA 211** [7] J L Dunlop 3-8-8 (104) R Hills 3/1 FAV: 14212-2: b c Peintre Celebre - Winsa (Riverman) Prom, hdwy to lead over 2f out, sn rdn clr & lkd in command till rdn & hdd well ins last: well bckd on reapp: juv mdn & stks wnr: stays 1m, shld get further (dam 12f scorer): acts on firm & gd/soft, any trk: can force the pace: consistent & useful, well clr of rem here & can find similar. 1 **104**
2 Sep'03 Good 8g/f 106-(99) A: 1 Aug'03 Ches 7.6g/f 100-(97) D: 2 Aug'03 Sand 7.1g/f 100- C: 1 Jun'03 Sali 7.0fm 94- D:
4160} **PSYCHIATRIST 213** [6] R Hannon 3-8-8 (105) R Hughes 4/1: 221412-3: ch g Dr Devious - Zahwa (Cadeaux Genereux) Set pace till over 2f out, onepace: reapp: juv mdn & stks wnr: eff at 6f, stays 1m on fast & soft grnd, any trk: best up with/forcing the pace: tough & progressive last term, shld do btr. 7 **94**
2 Sep'03 Donc 6gd 105- B: 1 Aug'03 Sand 8.1sft 100-(97) C: 1 Aug'03 Good 7g/f 99- D: 2 Jul'03 Newm 6g/f 91- D:
2 Jun'03 Good 6g/f 90- E:

949* **DIVINE GIFT** 14 [1] M A Jarvis 3-8-8 (104) P Robinson 100/30: 2021-14: With ldrs, no extra 2f   *1*   **92**
out: bckd tho' op 11/4: would prob appr an uncontested lead as in 949 (ready stks wnr, gd).
4839} **BARBAJUAN** 174 [2]3-8-13 (110) J Murtagh 11/2: 145143-5: b c Danehill Dancer - Courtier   *1¼*   **95**
(Saddlers' Hall) Chsd ldrs, wknd 2f out on reapp: juv mdn, stks & Gr 3 wnr (rtd 114 at best): eff at 7f/1m & acts
on firm, gd/soft & any trk: has run well fresh up with/forcing the pace: smart & tough last term, may do btr with a
return to positive tactics. 1 Aug'03 Sand 7.1g/s 112-(100) A: 1 May'03 Kemp 6fm 101-: C: 1 May'03 Ling 5gd 91- D:
4881*}**NEROS RETURN** 168 [5]3-8-11 K Dalgleish 12/1: 11-6: b c Mujadil - Snappy Dresser (Nishapour)   *2*   **90**
Cl-up, wknd over 2f out: won both juv starts, mdn & List: eff at 6f, shld stay at least 7f: acts on fast grnd & a
gall trk: may do btr back at 7f on a sounder surface. 1 Oct'03 Donc 6g/f 109- A: 1 Oct'03 York 6.0g/f 100- D:
4568} **GRAVARDLAX** 190 [4]3-8-8 K Fallon 10/1: 42-7: Sn rdn bhd, nvr a factor.   *1¾*   **84**
7 Ran   Time 1m 42.8 (6.0)   Owned: Sheikh Mohammed   Trained: Manton

---

KEMPTON   SATURDAY 10.04.04   Righthand, Flat, Fair Track

Official Going Good/Soft (Good places)

1114   3.45 Turftours Com E B F Maiden Stakes 2yo (D)
£5246 £1614 £807   **5f str**   **Good/Soft**   Inapp   Far Side

     PRINCE CHARMING [2] J H M Gosden 2-9-0 L Dettori 4/6 FAV: 1: b c Royal Applause - Miss Primula   **90+**
(Dominion) Dwelt, recovered to chase ldrs, qcknd to lead well fnl 1f, readily: hvly bckd from 11/10:
110,000gns Mar foal: half-brother to numerous wnrs: dam a fair sprinter, sire a top-class sprinter: eff at 5f on
gd/soft, shld stay 6f: runs well fresh: fine start, plenty of speed in pedigree, win more races.
943   **GRAND OPTION** 14 [1] B W Duke 2-9-0 P Dobbs 6/1: 032: Led/dsptd lead, went on after halfway, not   *¾*   **84**
pace to repel wnr cl-home: op 9/2: acts on gd/soft & soft grnd: prob met an above average rival, deserves similar.
     EARL OF LINKS [3] R Hannon 2-9-0 R Hughes 9/2: 3: ch c Raise A Grand - Metroella (Entitled)   *1¾*   **80**
Dwelt, recovered to chase ldrs, onepcd fnl 1f on debut: drifted from 3/1: cost £30,000: April foal, half-brother
to a couple of mid-dist wnrs: dam a winning hdler, sire a 7f winning juv: bred to apprec further given time,
handles gd/soft grnd: sure to learn from this.
     ART LEGEND [5] D R C Elsworth 2-9-0 S Sanders 7/1: 4: b g Indian Ridge - Solo Performance   *4*   **70**
(Sadler's Wells) Keen in rear, wandered 2f out, not pace to chall on debut: well bckd from 10/1: £22,000 March 1st
foal: dam a high-class sprinter: likely to apprec 6/7f given time: sure to learn from this.
1053   **LEONALTO** 5 [4]2-9-0 K Fallon 14/1: 05: ch c Raise A Grand - Chrismas Carol (Common Grounds)   *1*   **68**
Dsptd lead till after halfway, wknd: qck reapp: 14,000gns March foal: sire a high-class juv: with B Meehan.
5 Ran   Time 1m 03.68 (5.38)   Owned: Sheikh Mohammed   Trained: Manton

1115   4.20 Listed Surrey Herald Snowdrop Stakes Fillies 4yo+ (A)
£17400 £6600 £3300   **1m Jub**   **Good/Soft 76**   -03 Slow   Inside

4760} **BENEVENTA** 177 [7] J L Dunlop 4-8-9 (95) S Sanders 14/1: 111340-1: b f Most Welcome - Dara Dee   **110**
(Dara Monarch) Led till ent fnl 1f, rallied gamely to regain lead cl-home, drvn out: reapp: won 4 successive races
in '03 (mdn, 2 h'caps & a class wnr): eff at 1m, stays 10f well: acts on firm & gd/soft grnd, easy or gall trk:
clearly runs well fresh: v game here, imprvd effort & clearly v progressive.
1 Aug'03 Yarm 10.1g/f 95-(94) C: 1 Jul'03 Asco 10gd 90-81 D:
1 Jul'03 Kemp 10g/f 88- D: 2 Jun'03 Sali 8fm 81- D:
4473} **SOVIET SONG** 196 [5] J R Fanshawe 4-8-9 (114) J Murtagh 4/11 FAV: 11/4245-2: b f Marju - Kalinka   *hd*   **109**
(Soviet Star) Held up, stdy hdwy to lead ent fnl 1f, worn down cl-home: hvly bckd, reapp: lightly rcd in '03, 4th
in 1,000 Guineas (reapp) & rnr-up in Gr1 Coronation stks: unbtn in '02, notably Gr1 Fillies Mile: eff at 7f/1m on
fast & soft, any trk: has run well fresh, capable of better.
2 Jun'03 Asco 8g/f 115-(114) A: 1 Sep'02 Asco 8g/f 116- A: 1 Aug'02 Newm 7sft 111- A: 1 Jul'02 Kemp 6g/f 97- E:
57   **MONTURANI** 151 [3] G Wragg 5-8-9 (104) D Holland 6/1: 223422-3: Nvr far away, kept on fnl 1f but   *2*   **106**
not pace of front 2 on reapp: sound eff, plenty of plcd form: see 57.
58   **COTE QUEST** 148 [8] S C Williams 4-8-9 Martin Dwyer 33/1: 2/63013-4: b f Green Desert - West   *2½*   **101**
Brooklyn (Gone West) Trkd wnr till no extra fnl 1f on reapp: prev trained in France by Mme C Head, '03 Longchamp
wnr: eff at 7f/1m on gd/soft & v soft grnd: sharper next time.
861* **NAJAABA** 24 [4]4-8-9 (78) B Reilly 33/1: 1111515: Held up, nvr nr ldrs: not disgraced up in   *6*   **89**
grade & on return to turf: v progressive on the AW in h'caps: see 861 (fills h'cap).
4888} **DAME DE NOCHE** 168 [2]4-8-9 (92) L Dettori 14/1: 110300-6: b f Lion Cavern - Goodnight Kiss   *3*   **83**
(Night Shift) Chsd ldrs, btn 2f out: op 20/1, reapp: won a mdn, class stks & val h'cap in '03, also plcd several
times: best from over 7f/1m on gd & firm grnd, any trk, likes Ascot: can find similar in grade today, will apprec a
return to faster grnd & front running tactics..
1 Jul'03 Good 7gd 92-87 C: 1 Jul'03 Ayr 7.2gd 85-(81) D: 1 Apr'03 Nott 8.2gd 82-(81) D: 2 Aug'02 Nott 6g/f 80- E:
3356} **ALMAVIVA** 251 [1]4-8-9 (92) R Hughes 33/1: 1/65-7: Al towards rear on reapp.   *5*   **73**
1034   **LA MUETTE** 7 [6]4-8-9 (75) S Righton 150/1: 5300-008: Al bhd, fin last: highly tried.   *5*   **63**
8 Ran   Time 1m 43.11 (6.31)   Owned: Mr R N Khan   Trained: Arundel

1116   4.55 Turftours Com Handicap Stakes 3yo 0-85 (D)   **[92]**
£5642 £1736 £868   **6f str**   **Good/Soft**   Inapp   Far Side. High No's Fav.

756   **PETARDIAS MAGIC** 42 [11] E J O'Neill 3-8-13 (77) K Fallon 5/1: 23016-41: Trkd ldrs far side, led   **85**
2f out, styd on strongly fnl 1f, drvn out: 6 wk abs, well bckd & made most of fav'ble high draw: prob stays a sharp
1m, apprec this return to 6f: acts on fast, gd/soft & polytrack, prob any trk: runs well fresh, on a fav'ble turf mark.
955   **MORSE** 14 [14] J A Osborne 3-9-1 (79) J Murtagh 11/1: 50336-02: b c Shinko Forest - Auriga   *1½*   **83**
(Belmez) Chsd ldrs far side, styd on fnl 1f & not btn far: '03 mdn & nov wnr, also plcd in nursery h'cap: eff at
6/7f on fast, gd/soft grnd & polytrack: apprec fav'ble high draw: can find similar.
1 Jun'03 Wind 6g/f 82- E: 1 May'03 Nott 6.1g/s 83- E:
3265} **STORMY NATURE** 254 [15] P W Harris 3-8-12 (90) P Robinson 16/1: 420-3: b f Mujadil - Ossana   *1¾*   **79**
(Tejano) Led after 2f till 1f out on far side, not qckn fnl 1f on reapp: h'cap bow: rnr-up in a mdn auct on middle
of 3 '03 starts: eff at 5/6f on fast & gd/soft grnd, 7f shld suit: runs well fresh: spot on next time.

298

KEMPTON   SATURDAY 10.04.04 Righthand, Flat, Fair Track

2 Jun'03 Pont 5g/s 74- E:
1044* **BOHOLA FLYER 7** [10] R Hannon 3-8-9 (73) R Hughes 12/1: 002-14: Chsd ldrs far side, hung to   ¾   71
stands side halfway & led that group dist, kept on but no ch with far side: bckd from 20/1: threw away winning
chance by racing on unfav'ble stands side: see 1044 (AW).
5015} **FOUR AMIGOS 156** [13]3-8-13 (77) L Dettori 8/1: 050102-5: b c Southern Halo - Larentia (Salse)   ½   74
Chsd ldrs far side, onepace fnl 1f: nicely bckd, reapp: '03 mdn auct & nursery h'cap wnr: eff at 5/6f on gd & soft
grnd: handles a sharp trk: sharper for this.
2 Nov'03 Nott 5.1g/s 77-74 E: 1 Oct'03 Epso 5gd 77-68 D: 1 May'03 Ling 5sft 76- F:
4941***AFTER THE SHOW 164** [16]3-8-5 (69) Martin Dwyer 16/1: 604051-6: b c Royal Applause - Tango Teaser   1½   63
(Shareef Dancer) Early ldr far side, hung to stands side halfway, no ch fnl 1f on reapp: ended '03 with a nursery
h'cap win: stays 6f, suited by 5f: handles fast grnd, likes soft grnd & an easy trk: fav'ble high draw but hung away
winning chance: capable of btr. 1 Oct'03 Yarm 5.2sft 70-64 D:
4892} **MOTU 168** [12]3-8-13 (77) S Sanders 9/1: 410-7: Chsd ldrs far side, onepace fnl 1.5f: gelded.   ½   70
1002   **KURINGAI 10** [2]3-8-8 (72) O Urbina 33/1: 020-0438: Front rank stands side, no ch with far side: ½   64
poor low draw, forget this: see 1002.
4160} **BATHWICK BILL 213** [3]3-9-7 (85) S Drowne 40/1: 411530-9: Chsd ldrs stands side, short of room   1¼   74
dist, switched & no ch after: top-weight, has been gelded: on the wrong side & this must be forgiven.
1054   **ROYAL PAVILLION 5** [4]3-8-6 (70) Paul Eddery 10/1: 0-3140: 10th: Chsd ldrs till 2f out stands   ½   58
side, wknd: qck reapp, poor draw.
933*   **ECCENTRIC 15** [5]3-8-12 (76) D Holland 10/1: 0-4110: 11th: Chsd ldrs stands side, led that group   hd   63
2f out till dist, wknd: on hat-trick, on the wrong side, ignore this: see 933 (AW h'cap, 7f).
955   **CARTRONAGEERAGHLAD 14** [8]3-9-2 (80) R Keogh(7) 33/1: 64160-00: 12th: Bhd halfway stands side.   ½   66
4605} **ALCHERA 189** [1]3-8-11 bl (75) J Quinn 50/1: 650210-0: 13th: Led till 2f out stands side, wknd.   5   51
532   **HAYDN 67** [9]3-9-2 (80) J F Egan 4/1 FAV: 10000-50: 14th: Chsd ldrs 4.5f far side, wknd: well   5   46
bckd tho' op 5/2, 3 mth abs: btr expected after 532 (AW).
4200} **PINK SAPPHIRE 211** [7]3-8-8 (72) Dane O'Neill 25/1: 510-0: 15th: Al bhd far side on reapp.   1¾   34
750+* **GLOBAL ACHIEVER 43** [6]3-8-8 (72) R Ffrench 20/1: 32210: 16th: Chsd ldrs 4f stands side.   4   26
16 Ran   Time 1m 14.46(3.36) Owned: Miss Sarah Diane Warren Trained: Newmarket

MUSSELBURGH   SUNDAY 11.04.04 Righthand, Sharp Track

Official Going GOOD/FIRM (GOOD places Str Crse; FIRM places Rnd Crse). All Times Slow.

1117   2.40 Sharp Minds Betfair Maiden Stakes 2yo (D)
£4745 £1460 £730   **5f str**   **Good/Firm**   **Slow**   Stands Side.

    JOSEPH HENRY [7] M Johnston 2-9-0 J Fanning 4/1: 1: b c Mujadil - Iris May (Brief Truce) Trkd   85+
ldrs, prog to lead over 1f out, asserted under hands-and-heels, readily: nicely bckd tho' op 9/4: Mar foal: dam a
5f juv wnr & subs sprint performer: eff over a sharp 5f, 6f shld suit: acts on fast grnd & goes well fresh: plenty
to like about this intro, potentially useful & one to keep on side.
    NEE LEMON LEFT [6] A Berry 2-8-9 P Mathers(7) 50/1: 2: b f Puissance - Via Dolorosa   4   68
(Chaddleworth) Chsd ldrs, switched & kept on ins last, nvr threat to wnr: Apr foal, dam unrcd: sire a smart sprint
performer: handles fast grnd: gave encouragement.
    MONSIEUR MIRASOL [4] K A Ryan 2-9-0 N Callan 10/1: 3: b c Mind Games - Nom Francais (First   ½   72
Trump) Dwelt & pushed in rear, kept on late, nrst fin: op 12/1: Mar first foal, cost 21,000gns: dam plcd at
12f/2m as a 3yo: sire a v useful sprinter: might need much further in time.
954   **TIVISKI 15** [5] E J Alston 2-8-9 W Supple 2/1 FAV: 34: Handy, no extra dist: nicely bckd.   shd   67
954   **NEXT TIME 15** [1]2-8-9 D Holland 10/3: 45: Led till over 1f out: bckd from 5/1.   1   64
    CITY TORQUE [3]2-8-9 P Makin(7) 16/1: 6: Prom, btn over 1f out.   nk   63
1037 **PROCRASTINATE 8** [8]2-9-0 L Dettori 6/1: 37: Dwelt & sn outpcd: op 7/2: see 1037.   6   53
7 Ran   Time 1m 02.21 (4.71) Owned: John Brown & Megan Dennis Trained: Middleham

1118   3.10 Sharp Minds Winners Welcome Handicap Stakes 3yo+ 0-70 (E)
£4066 £1251 £626   **1m6f**   **Good/Firm**   **Slow**   Inside.   [70]

5033} **TANDAVA 155** [4] I Semple 6-10-0 (70) G Duffield 10/1: 020400-1: ch g Indian Ridge - Kashka (The   72
Minstrel) Dictated pace, qcknd 4f out, held on well for press fnl 2f under a well judged ride: reapp: h'cap & class
stks rnr-up '03, disapp in a visor: class stks wnr '02: eff at 10f, suited by 12/15f on firm & gd grnd, likes a
stiff/undul or sharp trk: goes well fresh: gd weight carrier who apprec forcing tactics today.
2 Aug'03 Hami 13.0gd 77-(78) D: 2 Sep'02 Hami 13fm 81-79 C: 1 Jul'02 Pont 12g/f 81- D:
2 Jul'02 Ches 12.3fm 78- D: 1 Jul'01 Pont 10gd 90- D:
1034   **TONI ALCALA 8** [6] R F Fisher 5-9-7 (63) L Fletcher(3) 7/1: 40-35402: Trkd ldrs, briefly lost pl   ½   63
over 4f out, rdn & styd on fnl 2f, not pace to rch wnr: back to form on faster surface, still on a fair mark.
997   **SPITTING IMAGE 11** [9] Mrs M Reveley 4-9-3 (62) A Culhane 10/1: 20240-03: ch f Spectrum -   1   61
Decrescendo (Polish Precedent) Trkd wnr, drvn & onepace fnl 3f: h'cap, class stks & clmr rnr-up '03: dual auct mdn
rnr-up '02: best arnd 12f on firm & gd, stiff or sharp/turning trk: remains a mdn, shown enough to find a race.
2 Oct'03 Leic 11.8g/f 61-(64) D: 2 May'03 Carl 11.9fm 65-(64) E: 2 Mar'03 Catt 12.0g/f 63-63 E:
2 Sep'02 Beve 7.4gd 65- E: 2 Jun'02 Beve 7.4g/f 70- E:
1003   **JADEERON 11** [1] Miss D A McHale 5-9-9 p (65) D Holland 10/3 FAV: 0-222344: Trkd ldrs, lost pl 5f   nk   63
out, short of room 2f out, switched & kept on late: nicely bckd: best coming late off a strong pace.
557   **GARGOYLE GIRL 65** [3]7-8-10 p (52) W Supple 11/2: 00640-05: b f Be My Chief - May Hills Legacy (Be   hd   49
My Guest) Chsd wnr 4f out, no extra for press bef dist: recent jumps rnr (unplcd, rtd 92h, h'cap): fill h'cap wnr
'03 on the level, landed 4 h'caps in '02: eff btwn 11/14f on firm & gd/soft grnd, stiff or sharp trk, loves
Musselburgh: eff with/without visor or cheek pieces.
2 Jul'03 Hami 12g/f 61-61 D: 1 Jul'03 Muss 12gd 60-55 F: 2 Jun'03 Muss 12g/f 57-55 E: 1 Sep'02 York 11.8g/f 59-55 D:
1 Aug'02 Muss 14fm 54-47 E: 2 Aug'02 Pont 12g/s 47-44 E: 2 Aug'02 Catt 13.7g/f 47-44 E: 1 Jul'02 Muss 12g/s 44-38 F:
2 Jul'02 Muss 12g/f 38-37 F: 1 May'02 Hami 11gd 42-40 F:
4664} **TBM CAN 185** [7]5-9-9 (65) B Swarbrick(7) 6/1: 331506-6: Bhd, rdn & late gains, nst fin: op 9/2.   1¾   60
964   **FIDDLERS CREEK 13** [5]5-9-1 T (57) R Winston 7/1: 360-6007: Held up, nvr nr ldrs: t-strap.   5   47
852   **BRIDEWELL 28** [8]5-7-12 (40) R Ffrench 66/1: 00000-08: Chsd ldrs till 4f out.   6   23
877   **MAJLIS 23** [2]7-9-12 (68) E Ahern 6/1: 201-0059: Held up, struggling fnl 3f: btr 877.   5   45

4504} **HOWARDS DREAM 195** [10]6-7-12 t (40) P Fessey 33/1: 550060-0: 10th: Al bhd: reapp. *21* **0**
10 Ran Time 3m 08.06 (11.56) Owned: Woodspeen Sport & Leisure Trained: Carluke

1119 **3.40 Sharp Minds Betfair: Bet In Running Maiden Stakes 3yo+ (D)**
£4862 £1496 £748 **7f30y rnd** **Good/Firm** **Slow** Outside.

1008 **FINDERS KEEPERS 11** [6] E A L Dunlop 3-8-8 (80) L Dettori 1/1 FAV: 320-231: Keen & sn led, al holding rivals for press fnl 2f: well bckd: eff at 6f/sharp 7f: acts on fast, gd/soft & polytrack: appeared suited by forcing tactics today: see 1008 & 875. **78**
4668} **NEVER WILL 184** [12] M Johnston 3-8-8 K Dalgleish 7/1: 5-2: b c Cadeaux Genereux - Answered Prayer (Green Desert) Chsd ldrs & rcd wide 3f out, ch 2f out, no extra dist: clr of rem, reapp: unplcd sole '03 start (mdn, rtd 56): half-sister to 1m/10f 3yo wnrs: eff at 7f, 1m+ shld suit: handles fast grnd. *2* **72**
996 **LUKE AFTER ME 11** [4] G A Swinbank 4-9-8 (51) R Winston 10/1: 4000-023: Slow away & rear, styd on late for press, nrst fin, nvr threat: bckd, op 16/1: seller rnr-up in 996, see 577. *6* **53**
4803} **ONE N ONLY 176** [10] Miss L A Perratt 3-8-3 (57) P Hanagan 40/1: 045450-4: b f Desert Story - Alpina (El Prado) Mid-div, styd on for press, nvr in dngr: reapp: unplcd '03 (rtd 59, h'cap): eff around 6/7f, sharp or gall trk: handles fast grnd: mdn h'caps would be ideal. *1* **49**
3764} **EAST RIDING 234** [11]4-9-3 (50) Ann Stokell 33/1: 602005-5: b f Gothenberg - Bettynouche (Midyan) Mid-div, no impress fnl 2f on reapp: appr mdn h'cap rnr-up '03 (M Johnston): debut plcd '02 (mdn, rtd 66, AW unplcd, rtd 29a): eff at 6/7f on fast & hvy grnd, gall or easy trk. 2 Aug'03 Thir 7g/f 49-48 E: *¾* **47**
721 **FRIMLEYS MATTERRY 47** [3]4-9-8 (45) P Mulrennan(5) 100/1: 6300-606: Chsd ldrs till 2f out, abs. *1½* **45**
5005} **COLLOSEUM 158** [9]3-8-8 D Holland 40/1: 56-7: Rear, mod late gains, nvr threat, reapp. *2½* **43**
176 **PASS GO 123** [5]3-8-8 E Ahern 3/1: 3-8: Chsd wnr, btn 3f out: gelded, bckd tho' op 7/4, turf bow. *1* **41**
4850} **CONSTABLE BURTON 172** [1]3-8-8 G Duffield 66/1: 000-9: Al rear, reapp. *shd* **41**
CLOUDS OF GOLD [13]3-8-3 D R McCabe 100/1: 0: 10th: V slow away & sn bhd on debut. *½* **35**
4385} **ENVIRONMENTALIST 202** [2]5-9-8 t (58) D Allan(3) 66/1: 520/006-0: 11th: Chsd ldrs 4f: reapp/new yard. *8* **24**
Caseys House [7]4-9-3 T Eaves(5) 100/1:0 4316} **Musiotal 206** [8]3-8-8 W Supple 100/1:0
13 Ran Time 1m 30.66 (5.76) Owned: Maktoum Al Maktoum Trained: Newmarket

1120 **4.10 Sharp Minds Betfair Handicap Stakes 3yo+ 0-100 (C)** **[95]**
£13754 £4232 £2116 **5f str** **Good/Firm** **Fair** Stands Side.

1011 **MAGIC GLADE 11** [2] C R Dore 5-8-11 (78) R Thomas(5) 4/1 JT FAV: 3/00-0121: Trkd ldrs stands side trav well, rdn to lead well ins last: eff at 5/6f on fast grnd & fibresand, stiff/gall or sharp/turning trk: in great heart, could continue to progress: see 660. **90**
927* **MAKTAVISH 16** [11] I Semple 5-9-0 p (81) P Hanagan 7/1: 0100-112: Overall ldr far side, hdd well ins last: op 9/1, ran to form of 927 & 655. *1½* **86**
927 **SIERRA VISTA 16** [4] D W Barker 4-8-10 P (77) L Enstone(3) 12/1: 03604-03: ch f Atraf - Park Vista (Taufan) Al handy stands side & ch dist, no extra cl-home: fine run in first time cheek pieces: class stks & thrice h'cap plcd '03 (rtd 85 at best): auct mdn & h'cap wnr '02: eff at 5/6f on firm & gd/soft grnd, prob any trk: well h'capped & this was encouraging in headgear, win sn if repeating. *1¼* **78**
2 Aug'02 Ches 6fm 95-89 D: 1 Aug'02 Thir 5g/s 90-75 C: 1 Jul'02 Carl 5gd 81- E: 2 Jul'02 Catt 5fm 63- G:
4990} **VIEWFORTH 160** [5] I Semple 6-8-11 bl (78) R Winston 20/1: 254600-4: b g Emarati - Miriam (Forzando) Chsd ldrs stands side, rdn & kept on, not able to chall: reapp: dual h'cap wnr '03, prog profile: dual h'cap & also a clmr wnr '02 for Miss L A Perratt: eff at 5/6f on firm & hvy grnd, any trk, suited by blnks: in gd form for majority of '03 campaign, this was a promising rtn. *nk* **78**
2 Sep'03 Hayd 5gd 81-79 C: 1 Aug'03 Beve 5g/f 81-71 E: 1 Aug'03 Hayd 6g/f 72-66 C: 2 Jun'03 Hami 5.0g/f 68-64 D:
2 May'03 Ayr 5g/s 65-61 E: 2 May'03 Hami 6.0g/s 63-60 E: 1 Jun'02 Hami 6sft 64-59 E: 1 Jun'02 Hami 5sft 64- E:
1 Jun'02 Hami 5hvy 57-44 F: 1 Jun'01 Muss 5g/f 65- D:
4670} **CHAIRMAN BOBBY 184** [7]6-8-3 (70) Rory Moore(7) 20/1: 233062-5: ch g Clantime - Formidable Liz (Formidable) Al handy stands side, drvn & no extra nr fin: reapp, s/mate of 3rd: '03 mdn h'cap & h'cap wnr, plcd sev times: AW h'cap rnr-up '02, turf clmr plcd: suited by 5/6f on firm, gd & f/sand, prob any trk, loves a stiff/undul one: loves to race with/force the pace: proved v consistent last term & most promising reapp. *nk* **69**
2 Oct'03 York 5.0g/f 72-68 D: 2 Aug'03 Carl 5fm 69-64 D: 2 Aug'03 Pont 5fm 67-64 E: 2 Jul'03 Hami 6.0gd 62-(62) E:
2 Jun'03 Redc 6g/f 64-61 C: 1 Jun'03 Carl 5.9fm 58-50 E: 1 Jun'03 Hami 5.0gd 58-44 F: 2 Oct'02 Sout 5af 55a-52 F:
2 Jun'01 Muss 5g/f 63- D: 2 Apr'01 Sout 6af 67a-65 D:
927 **CAPE ROYAL 16** [8]4-9-1 (82) D Holland 4/1 JT FAV: 10220-06: Trkd ldrs, switched & onepace for press dist: joc gvn 1 day careless riding ban. *nk* **80**
927 **RIVER FALCON 16** [12]4-8-12 (79) W Supple 16/1: 20000-57: Chsd ldrs far side, btn over 1f out. *nk* **76**
927 **PTARMIGAN RIDGE 16** [3]8-9-3 (84) J Carroll 33/1: 05001-08: Mid-div stands side, no impress when carr right over 1f out. *2½* **74**
4991} **OBE ONE 160** [16]4-8-10 (77) P Mathers(7) 50/1: 010000-9: Chsd ldrs far side till 2f out, reapp. *1¾* **62**
927 **NO TIME 16** [9]4-10-0 (95) L Dettori 10/1: 6621100: 10th: Led stands side 3f, sn btn: bckd. *shd* **80**
4884} **INTER VISION 169** [1]4-9-7 (88) A Beech(3) 20/1: 012054-0: 11th: Stands side, nvr on terms, reapp. *1½* **69**
4884} **BEYOND THE CLOUDS 169** [6]8-9-1 (82) D R McCabe 33/1: 003000-0: 12th: Nvr on terms centre. *1* **60**
69* **PETERS CHOICE 142** [13]3-8-1 (79) P Fessey 25/1: 42011-0: 13th: Chsd ldrs far side 3f: long abs. *1¼* **53**
967 **GET STUCK IN 13** [10]8-8-2 (69) R Ffrench 100/1: 0250/0-00: 14th: Chsd ldrs stands side till halfway. *1¼* **39**
4341} **SEAFIELD TOWERS 205** [14]4-8-11 p (78) K Dalgleish 50/1: 213160-0: 15th: Al strugg far side. *hd* **48**
927 **PICCLED 16** [15]6-8-11 (78) E Ahern 8/1: 6000-030: 16th: Chsd ldr far side, btn dist: see 927. *1¼* **44**
16 Ran Time 59.56 (2.06) Owned: Mr P O'Gorman Trained: Spalding

1121 **4.40 Sharp Minds Phone 0870 90 80 121 Maiden Stakes 3yo+ (D)**
£4735 £1457 £729 **1m4f** **Good/Firm** **Slow** Inside.

1016 **GRAN DANA 10** [7] M Johnston 4-9-12 J Fanning 8/11 FAV: 21: Led/dsptd lead till over 4f out, led again 3f out, asserted for press ins last: hvly bckd: eff arnd a stiff or sharp 12f, shld get further: acts on fast & gd/soft, gd weight carrier: could prove typical of this yard & type to improve with racing/over further: see 1016. **81**
939 **GOLDEN EMPIRE 15** [4] E A L Dunlop 3-8-6 VIS (78) W Supple 9/4: 32-22: Handy, led over 4f out till 3f out, no extra ins last: hvly bckd in first time visor: not btn far, but carr head high & lkd a tricky ride: stays 12f, rtn to shorter could suit: see 939. *¾* **79**

MUSSELBURGH   SUNDAY 11.04.04   Righthand, Sharp Track

849   **NEXT FLIGHT 28** [2] R E Barr 5-9-13   (45) D Holland 16/1: 03-62323: Chsd front pair, nvr able to   5   **71$**
chall fnl 3f: offic rtd 45, treat rating with caution: see 638 & 224.
959   **STAGE TWO 13** [1] M Johnston 3-8-6   K Dalgleish 16/1: 064: b c Sadler's Wells - Meteor Stage   5   **61$**
(Stage Door Johnny) Chsd ldrs, btn 2f out: now quals for h'caps, may improve with racing.
959   **VALIANT AIR 13** [5]3-8-6 VIS (55) P Hanagan 50/1: 040-45: Mid-div, no impress fnl 2f, visor: see 959.   3   **55**
ILLICIUM [9]5-9-8   A Culhane 20/1: 6: b f Fourstars Allstar - Sweet Mignonette (Tina's Pet)   ½   **49**
Dwelt & al bhd on debut: jumps fit (bmpr plcd, 2m, gd): with Mrs M Reveley.
STRAVONIAN [10]4-9-12   D McGaffin 33/1: 7: Dwelt & al near on debut.   13   **34**
ARCHENKO [3]4-9-12   P Mathers(7) 66/1: 8: Mid-div, struggling halfway on Flat debut: jumps fit.   1   **32**
3990}   **EYES DONT LIE 223** [6]6-9-13 (35) P Fessey 66/1: 005620-9: Bhd halfway, reapp.   16   **8**
9 Ran   Time 2m 40.16 (9.56)   Owned: Mrs I Bird   Trained: Middleham

---

1122   5.10 Sharp Minds Betfair: Back And Lay Handicap Stakes 3yo+ 0-85 (D)   [84]
£6825 £2100 £1050   **7f30y rnd**   **Good/Firm**   **Slow**   Outside.

40   **KIRKBYS TREASURE 148** [3] A Berry 6-7-13   (55) P Hanagan 33/1: 226005-1: ro g Mind Games - Gem of   **62**
Gold (Jellaby) Bhd, rdn & hdwy to lead over 1f out, hung right & drvn out: reapp: nicely bckd, 5 month abs: clmr
scorer '03: h'cap & class stks wnr '02, AW unplcd (rtd 58a, clmr): btn 6f/1m on firm, hvy & any trk: best
delivered late: eff with/without cheek pieces, tried blnks: goes well fresh.
2 Aug'03 Carl 6.9fm 59-(59) E: 2 Aug'03 Carl 6.9g/f 58-(46) F: 1 Jul'03 Carl 5.9gd 61-(46) F: 1 Jun'02 Carl 8g/s 77- D:
1 Mar'02 Catt 7g/s 74-70 D: 1 Oct'01 Catt 6g/s 62- D: 2 Sep'01 Catt 7g/f 74- D: 2 Sep'01 Beve 5gd 68- D:
2 Sep'01 Thir 6g/f 71- D: 2 Aug'01 Catt 6fm 68- D: 2 Aug'01 Beve 5g/f 62- D: 2 Jul'01 Hami 6hvy 55- D:
1092   **SARRAAF 3** [5] I Semple 8-9-1 (71) N Callan 5/1: 042-4232: In tch, rdn & staying on when hmpd ins   ¾   **76**
last: quirky type who likes to find trouble in running, a likely type for similar: see 998 & 840.
967   **HIGHLAND WARRIOR 13** [10] J S Goldie 5-8-7 (63) W Supple 7/2 FAV: 00133-33: Rear, hdwy to chall   shd   **68**
over 1f out, not pace of wnr: bckd, op 9/2: eff at 6/7f, likes Ayr: see 967.
771   **BEAUTEOUS 42** [8] M J Polglase 5-8-9 (65) L Dettori 4/1: 400-0064: Handy & ch over 2f out, no   4   **62**
extra for press dist: nicely bckd, 6 wk abs: prev with A Berry: see 771.
998   **SEA STORM 11** [2]6-9-13 p (83) D Holland 10/1: 00205-05: b g Dolphin Street - Prime Interest   1   **78**
(Kings Lake) Rear, styd on for press fnl 2f, nrst fin: h'cap & class stks wnr for R Fisher in '03: plcd numerous
times '02, subs late '02 AW h'cap & class stks wnr: suited by 7/7.5f on firm, gd & polytrack, any trk, loves a
sharp/easy one: eff with/without cheek pieces, tried blnks: can go well fresh.
2 Sep'03 Muss 8g/f 85-(88) B: 1 Jul'03 Warw 7.1g/f 91-(86) C: 1 Jun'03 Newc 7gd 88-83 C: 1 Dec'02 Ling 7ap 93a-85 C:
1 Nov'02 Ling 7ap 87a- D: 2 Oct'02 Newc 7fm 85- C: 2 Sep'02 Ayr 7.2gd 84-81 C: 2 Jul'01 Newc 7g/f 88-83 D:
1 Jul'01 Beve 7.4fm 82-78 D: 1 Jul'01 Sout 7fm 79-72 E: 1 May'01 Sout 7g/f 76- F:
998   **H HARRISON 11** [11]3-9-12 (82) P Mathers(7) 11/1: 11103-06: b g Eagle Eyed - Penrose (Wolfhound)   ½   **76**
Chsd ldrs, hdwy to chall wide over 1f out, no extra ins last: rattled off a h'cap hat-trick '03, mdn wnr '02: eff at
5/6f, suited by sharp/easy 7f on firm & gd/soft: goes well for an inexperienced rider.
1 Sep'03 Muss 7.1gd 84-75 D: 1 Sep'03 Yarm 7.0g/f 78-72 F: 1 Sep'03 Catt 7g/f 72-66 D: 2 Aug'03 Newc 6g/f 67-62 F:
1 Oct'02 Catt 5fm 76- D: 2 May'02 Muss 5gd 69- F:
998   **FLYING TREATY 11** [7]7-8-7 (63) Ann Stokell 25/1: 0-000607: Chsd ldrs, no impress fnl 2f: well   ½   **56**
h'capped, needs professional handling.
793   **MALAHIDE EXPRESS 86** [6]4-8-1 (57) D Allan 20/1: 00-45028: Led till dist: new stable.   shd   **50**
86   **THE GAMBLER 139** [14]4-7-13 p (55) D Fentiman(7) 50/1: 200500-9: Al bhd, abs.   3   **42**
4246}   **ANTHEMION 209** [9]7-8-6 (62) D McGaffin 40/1: 200025-0: 10th: Sn bhd & struggling, reapp.   3   **43**
4888}   **BALLYHURRY 169** [12]7-9-4 (74) J Currie(7) 10/1: 130154-0: 11th: Rear, little prog on reapp.   1½   **52**
4852}   **DESERT ARC 172** [11]6-8-2 (1ow) (57) G Duffield 16/1: 46600-0: 12th: Trkd ldrs 6f, reapp, new yard.   1¾   **33**
4349}   **TRUE NIGHT 204** [4]7-9-10 (80) A Nicholls 10/1: 634215-0: 13th: Al bhd, reapp.   5   **45**
13 Ran   Time 1m 30.78(5.88)   Owned: Kirkby Lonsdale Racing   Trained: Cockerham

---

WARWICK   MONDAY 12.04.04   Lefthand, Sharp, Turning Track

Official Going Good/Soft

1123   2.15 Sunrise Median Auction Maiden Stakes Fillies 2yo (E)
£3819 £1175 £588   **5f rnd**   **Good 5a**   -63 Slow   Inside

920   **JUSTAQUESTION 18** [5] I A Wood 2-8-11   G Duffield 6/4 FAV: 01: b f Pursuit of Love - Queenbird   **78**
(Warning) Al prom & led over 1f out, drvn out: nicely bckd: caught the eye on debut earlier: Feb foal, cost
6,800gns: sister to a multiple 7f/1m wnr: dam a multiple 5/7f juv scorer: eff at 5f, shld stay 6f: acts on gd grnd &
a sharp/turning trk: going the right way.
CHILLY CRACKER 0 [11] R Hollinshead 2-8-11   D Sweeney 25/1: 2: ch f Largesse - Polar Storm (Law   1¼   **72**
Society) Dwelt, switched & pushed along rear, hdwy 2f out, kept on: 5,000gns March foal: half-sister to wnrs at
6f/hdles: dam 1m wnr: eff at 5f, sure to apprec 6f+: encouraging start.
WITHERING LADY 0 [7] Mrs P N Dutfield 2-8-11   B Havlin 12/1: 3: b f Tagula - Princess Oberon   1½   **67**
(Fairy King) In tch, kept on 1f out, not pace of wnr: Jan foal, cost 8,000gns: half-sister to a 5f juv wnr: dam a
multiple 5f wnr: acts on gd grnd: bred to be a sharp juvenile, fitter for this.
1097   **ZIMBALI 4** [4] J M Bradley 2-8-11   S Carson 22/1: 54: Prom, no extra dist, qck reapp.   1½   **62**
LADY MISHA 0 [6]2-8-11   K Dalgleish 40/1: 5: Held up, not pace to chall ldrs.   nk   **61**
STRAFFAN 0 [9]2-8-11   Dane O'Neill 16/1: 6: Held up wide, no prog over 1f out.   1   **58**
1001   **TOWN HOUSE 12** [2]2-8-11   A Culhane 20/1: 57: Led till over 1f out, fdd: see 1001.   ½   **56**
STANS GIRL 0 [8]2-8-11   T E Durcan 9/2: 8: Dwelt, sn outpcd, nvr on terms: op 7/2.   2½   **48**
FANTASTIC STAR 0 [3]2-8-11   M Fenton 8/1: 9: Cl-up 2f, btn over 1f out.   4   **36**
BLADE RUNNER 0 [10]2-8-11   Paul Eddery 8/1: 0: 10th: Dwelt & al outpcd rear: op 6/1.   5   **22**
CHAMPAGNE IN PARIS 0 [1]2-8-11   G Gibbons 16/1: 0: 11th: Prom till over 1f out.   1¼   **18**
11 Ran   Time 1m 03.37 (6.07)   Owned: Mr Christopher Shankland   Trained: Upper Lambourn

1124 2.50 Shrewley Handicap Stakes 3yo 0-70 (E) [77]
£3998 £1230 £615 1m2f188y Good 58 -21 Slow Inside

1000 **BILL BENNETT 12** [6] J Jay 3-9-2 (65) G Baker 9/1: 01-60651: Rear, hdwy 3f out & styd on for press to lead cl-home: eff at 9/11f: acts on firm, gd/soft & fibresand: see 1000 & 240. **70**
873 **ZAFFEU 24** [3] N P Littmoden 3-9-6 (69) J P Guillambert(3) 25/1: 0662: ch g Zafonic - Leaping ½ **72**
Flame (Trempolino) Held up, hdwy short of room over 2f out, sn rdn & chall dist, not pace of wnr: fine h'cap/turf bow: eff around a sharp 11f, prob handles polytrack & gd grnd: unplcd at up to 12f prev.
4732} **GLIDE 181** [1] R Charlton 3-9-7 (70) S Drowne 7/1: 045-3: ch g In The Wings - Ash Glade (Nashwan) nk **72**
Trkd ldrs, hdwy to lead over 2f out, sn rdn & hdd ins last, kept on: op 7/2, reapp/h'cap bow: unplcd at up to 1m '03 (rtd 70, lightly rcd): apprec step up to 11f, acts on gd grnd: find a race on this evidence.
734 **MAMBINA 46** [5] M R Channon 3-9-2 (65) T E Durcan 14/1: 50-04: ch f Kingmambo - Sonata (Polish shd **67**
Precedent) Mid-div, hdwy 4f out & rdn/led ins last, hdd nr fin, no extra: btn less than 1L in a v tight fin: 6 wk abs: turf/h'cap bow: promise sole turf start '03 (rtd 72, mdn): apprec step up to 11f on gd: encouraging.
436 **THE KING OF ROCK 84** [16]3-8-8 (57) S Whitworth 50/1: 42000-05: Dwelt, rear, hdwy 4f out, ch/hmpd 1 **56**
dist, no extra: shade closer without interference, 12 wk abs: styd longer 11f trip well.
1007 **SUCHWOT 12** [8]3-8-7 (56) S W Kelly 20/1: 600-06: Dwelt & rear, drvn to chall dist, sn no extra: clr rem. 1½ **54**
4906} **SPECTESTED 168** [7]3-9-2 (65) L Keniry(3) 14/1: 550-7: Dwelt, hdwy/short of room 3f out, sn no impress. 8 **52**
1017 **DESERT IMAGE 11** [19]3-9-7 (70) D Corby(3) 40/1: 30-12608: Held up, eff wide 3f out, sn no prog. nk **56**
871 **SMART BOY PRINCE 25** [2]3-9-2 (65) D Nolan(5) 22/1: 66-11059: Led after 2f till over 2f out, wknd. 2½ **47**
4713} **CHARLIE BEAR 182** [9]3-9-6 (69) M Hills 7/2 FAV: 500-0: 10th: Mid-div at best: reapp/h'cap bow. 3 **47**
915 **ANOTHER CON 19** [12]3-9-3 (66) R Havlin 14/1: 63-41450: 11th: Mid-div, no impress: btr 676. ¾ **43**
1030 **PEPE 10** [11]3-8-0 (49) Stephanie Hollinshead(1) 25/1: 06-6630: 12th: Prom, btn 2f out: btr 1030 (AW). 5 **19**
1017 **MISTER TRICKSTER 11** [13]3-9-0 (63) S Righton 8/1: 46650-60: 13th: Prom till over 2f out: btr 1017. 4 **27**
915 **DARN GOOD 19** [18]3-9-6 vis (69) Dane O'Neill 12/1: 500-0030: 14th: AI rear: see 915. 1 **32**
796 **KEEPERS KNIGHT 40** [4]3-9-3 (66) A Culhane 11/1: 55-13500: 15th: Prom, btn 2f out: abs: btr 497. 3 **25**
111 **PETITE COLLEEN 136** [14]3-9-6 (68) Paul Eddery 40/1: 0235-0: 16th: Prom, btn 4f out: abs, longer trip. ¾ **26**
1017 **KILLOCH PLACE 11** [10]3-8-2 BL (51) S Carson 40/1: 0500-00: 17th: Led 2f, prom till 3f out: blnks. 22 **0**
1017 **TROUBLEINPARADISE 11** [17]3-8-9 BL (58) M Fenton 40/1: 035-00: 18th: Bhd halfway, t.o.: blnks. 6 **0**
959* **OUR LITTLE ROSIE 14** [15]3-8-11 (60) D Sweeney 12/1: 00510: 19th: Sn well bhd & virtually p.u. dist **0**
fnl 2f: something amiss?: btr 959 (AW).
19 Ran Time 2m 24.83 (8.63) Owned: Mr & Mrs Jonathan Jay Trained: Newmarket

1125 3.20 Geoff Woodward 'lifetime in Racing' Maiden Stakes Div 1 3yo (D)
£3705 £1140 £570 7f26y rnd Good 58 -01 Slow Inside

4668} **RIVER TREAT 185** [4] G Wragg 3-9-0 (85) S Drowne 10/11 FAV: 524-1: ch c Irish River - Dance Treat **82**
(Nureyev) Keen & handy, led ins last & duelled with rnr-up, just prevailed for press: hvly bckd on reapp: mdn rnr-up '03, subs disapp when btn at odds-on in similar: eff at 6f, apprec step up to sharp 7f, return to sprint trips may well suit on this evidence: acts on fast & gd grnd, sharp/turning or stiff/undul trk: goes well fresh.
2 Sep'03 Pont 6g/f 88- D:
4948} **CELLO 165** [3] R Hannon 3-9-0 (78) P Dobbs 5/1: 6355-2: gr c Pivotal - Raffelina (Carson City) hd **81**
Led/dsptd lead & went on 4f out, narrowly hdd ins last, kept on well, just held: well clr rem on reapp: mdn plcd '03 (rtd 74, AW unplcd, rtd 59a): eff at 6/7f: prob handles firm, gd & any trk: shld win a race.
146 **MARKSGOLD 128** [7] P F I Cole 3-9-0 M Hills 28/1: 000-3: b g Goldmark - Lady of Shalott (Kings 10 **61**
Lake) Led/dsptd lead, no extra over 1f out: gelded, abs: unplcd prev at up to 1m (rtd 44 & 53a, K Bell).
1015 **SOUL PROVIDER 11** [9] P A Blockley 3-8-9 (52) D Nolan(1) 9/1: 5-534324: Prom, btn over 1f out. 1½ **53**
875 **ACCENDERE 24** [2]3-9-0 D Sweeney 100/1: 005: Rear, kept on late in eyecatching fashion, never ½ **57+**
dangerous: stewards noted explanations that gelding was big & backward: interesting for h'caps.
4527} **VERKHOTINA 195** [13]3-8-9 (75) Dane O'Neill 9/2: 550-6: Held up, rdn & btn 2f out: reapp. 2 **48**
2627} **SNOW JOKE 283** [12]3-8-9 R Havlin 25/1: 000-7: Mid-div, no prog fnl 2f: reapp. shd **48**
5032} **DORINGO 156** [5]3-9-0 A Daly 33/1: 0-8: Sn outpcd & al bhd, reapp. 1 **51**
4386} **DON ARGENTO 203** [6]3-9-0 D Corby(3) 100/1: 000-9: Slow away & nvr on terms, reapp. 1½ **48**
839 **JUSTICE JONES 30** [8]3-9-0 Lisa Jones(3) 50/1: 00: 10th: Sn struggling. 1¾ **45**
1017 **Indian Call 11** [11]3-9-0 (60) G Gibbons 14/1:0   848 **Golnessa 29** [10]3-8-9 Paul Eddery 150/1:0
12 Ran Time 1m 26.57 (4.17) Owned: Mr Peter R Pritchard Trained: Newmarket

1126 3.55 'west Midlands' Conditions Stakes 4yo+ (C)
£10115 £3837 £1918 7f26y rnd Good 58 +11 Fast Inside

951 **PABLO 16** [1] B W Hills 5-8-8 P (103) M Hills 2/1 FAV: 1/1455-01: b c Efisio - Winnebago (Kris) **102**
Led after 1f, hdd over 1f out, rallied to lead again ins last, drvn out: fast time: hvly bckd, op 9/4: lightly rcd '03, landed Lincoln h'cap on reapp, subs Gr 3 4th (rtd 109): mdn & dual h'cap scorer '02: eff at 7f/1m, poss stays 9f: acts on fast, loves gd & gd/soft, any trk: goes well fresh: suited by chkpcs today: useful.
1 Mar'03 Donc 8gd 109-97 B: 1 Nov'02 Newm 8g/s 99-89 C: 1 Jul'02 Sand 7g/s 89-83 C: 1 May'02 Good 7g/s 91- B:
2 Apr'02 Warw 7.1g/s 81- D:
1062 **ROCKETS N ROLLERS 8** [2] R Hannon 4-8-8 (104) Dane O'Neill 5/2: 400-3332: AI handy & rdn/narrow nk **101**
lead dist, hdd well ins last: nicely bckd: running well in defeat: see 1062, 922.
4329} **KOOL 562** [3] P F I Cole 5-8-8 S Drowne 16/1: 011120/-3: b g Danehill Dancer - New Rochelle 1 **99**
(Lafontaine) Held up, styd on for press fnl 2f, not pace of front pair: op 12/1, long abs, gelded: missed '03: clmr & dual h'cap scorer '02: eff at 6/7f on fm & gd/soft grnd, any trk: gd weight-carrier: excellent reapp after such a long break, shld be plcd to effect if repeating this.
2 Sep'02 Kemp 8fm 92- D: 1 Aug'02 Leic 7g/s 100-92 B: 1 Jul'02 Kemp 7g/s 91-85 D: 1 Jul'02 Warw 6g/f 89- D:
2 Sep'01 Donc 6gd 89- B: 1 Aug'01 Pont 5gd 79- D: 2 Aug'01 Leic 5g/f 88- D: 2 Jul'01 Wind 5g/f 97- E:
2 Jul'01 Bath 5gd 75- D:
887 **QUEENS RHAPSODY 23** [7] A Bailey 4-8-8 (85) T E Durcan 16/1: 0-202404: Held up, eff 2f out, 2 **95$**
onepace: acts on gd, gd/soft & both AWs: see 431.
1043 **QUITO 9** [8]7-9-6 bl (103) A Culhane 6/1: 5-106255: In tch, eff to chase ldr over 2f out, no extra 1¾ **104**
dist: stiffish task under top-weight, far from disgraced: see 951 & 618.

957 **DANCING KING 14** [6]8-8-12 (46) Lisa Jones(3) 100/1: 5400626: Led/dsptd lead till over 1f out. *nk* **95$**
940 **JUST A GLIMMER 16** [10]4-8-3 (84) A Daly 20/1: 00-30127: Prom, btn 2f out: see 940, 840. *3* **80**
4350} **HITS ONLY MONEY 205** [5]4-8-8 (98) D Nolan(2) 4/1: 411130-8: br g Hamas - Toordillon (Contract Law) Handy, btn 2f out: reapp: lightly rcd & progressive '03, landed a seller, subs dual h'cap wnr: all wins at 6f: acts on firm & gd grnd, stiff or sharp/undul trk. *2* **81**
1 Apr'03 Ripo 6gd 100-83 C: 1 Apr'03 Kemp 6fm 90-76 D: 1 Apr'03 Leic 6.0g/f 82- G:
3560} **TAKES TUTU 243** [9]5-8-8 (83) K Dalgleish 40/1: 400065-9: Al rear, nvr a factor: reapp, new yard. *1½* **78**
1038 **CELTIC VISION 9** [4]8-8-8 S Righton 150/1: 660: 10th: Dwelt & sn outpcd. *½* **77$**
10 Ran Time 1m 25.67 (3.27) Owned: Mr Guy Reed Trained: Lambourn

1127

4.30 Pearse Handicap Stakes 3yo+ 0-70 (E) **[70]**
£4014 £1235 £618 **5f rnd** **Good 58** **-49 Slow** Inside

1025 **DUNN DEAL 10** [4] W M Brisbourne 4-9-3 (59) T E Durcan 20/1: 0660-301: Held up, hdwy when short of room over 1f out, styd on for press to lead cl-home: suited by 5f on firm, soft & fibresand: see 859. **64**
897 **MYND 20** [8] R M Whitaker 4-9-6 (62) M Hills 9/2 JT FAV: 34-11202: Led/dpstd lead & went on dist, rdn & hdd cl-home: excellent turf return, find similar: acts on fibresand, gd & soft grnd: see 748 & 508. *nk* **66**
944 **PLAYTIME BLUE 16** [7] K R Burke 4-9-7 (63) G Baker 9/2 JT FAV: 3612143: Led 2f, ch dist, not pace of wnr cl-home: gd run: see 944, 749. *1½* **63**
1052 **BOAVISTA 7** [13] P D Evans 4-8-13 (55) R Havlin 20/1: 3245344: Held up, styd on for press, not able to chall: gd run but a longstanding mdn: see 593. *shd* **55**
4722} **ASTRAC 182** [6]13-8-9 (51) P M Quinn 33/1: 530115-5: b g Nordico - Shirleen (Daring Display) Held up, eff to chall dist, no extra: reapp: seller & h'cap wnr '03, AW unplcd (rtd 44, h'cap): turf h'cap & AW clmr wnr '02: eff at 5/7f on firm, hvy & fibresand: v tough & genuine 13yo. *¾* **49**
1 Sep'03 Bath 5.7fm 51-48 D: 1 Sep'03 Brig 7.0g/f 52-(43) G: 1 Sep'02 Wolv 7af 53a- F: 1 May'02 Yarm 7g/f 55-50 F: 1 Jul'01 Warw 7.1g/s 51-40 G:
1025 **DOUBLE M 10** [12]7-8-7 vis (49) A Daly 10/1: 0242106: Rear, styd on for press, not reach ldrs: see 902. *nk* **46**
748 **TABOOR 45** [16]6-9-1 h bl (57) K Dalgleish 12/1: 0-000507: Keen rear, styd on late, no dngr, abs. *shd* **54**
1046 **RIVER LARK 7** [9]5-8-6 (48) Lisa Jones(3) 25/1: 02-64468: Rear, mod hdwy for press, no dngr: see 655. *½* **43**
958* **BLAKESHALL QUEST 14** [5]4-9-2 vis (58) A Culhane 11/2: 0444519: Chsd ldrs, onepace dist: btr 958. *hd* **52**
1011 **PRINCE OF BLUES 12** [3]6-9-2 p (58) S W Kelly 16/1: 0200040: 10th: Led/dpstd lead till over 1f out, wknd. *hd* **51**
960 **KINGS BALLET 14** [10]6-9-0 p (56) S Drowne 16/1: 0-002040: 11th: Hld up, eff 2f out, btn/eased ins last. *2* **43**
4964} **STOKESIES WISH 164** [14]4-9-10 (66) G Carter 25/1: 330102-0: 12th: ch f Fumo di Londra - Jess Rebec (Kala Shikari) Mid-div, nvr pace to chall: mdn scorer '03, subs h'cap rnr-up: eff at 5/6f on firm & gd/soft grnd, likes a sharp/undul trk. 2 Oct'03 Brig 6.0g/s 64-63 F: 1 Oct'03 Good 6fm 64-(49) D: *2½* **45**
781 **SHADY DEAL 42** [2]8-8-10 (52) S Carson 25/1: 6235-000: 13th: Chsd ldrs till dist, abs: see 775. *hd* **30**
3880} **Pulse 231** [20]6-9-5 p(61) M Fenton 25/1:0
944 **Prime Recreation 16** [15]7-9-9 (65) Dane O'Neill 33/1:0
1103 **Brantwood 4** [19]4-10-0 (70) G Gibbons 16/1:0
832 **Bali Star 34** [11]9-8-3 (45) Paul Eddery 33/1:0
3140} **Boanerges 262** [17]7-9-6 (62) G Duffield 16/1:0
1049 **St Ivian 7** [18]4-9-8 vis(64) Joanna Badger 16/1:0
19 Ran Time 1m 02.65 (5.35) Owned: Mr Raymond McNeill Trained: Baschurch

1128

5.05 'isle Of Inisfree' Handicap Stakes 4yo+ 0-75 (E) **[75]**
£4339 £1335 £668 **1m2f188y** **Good 58** **-12 Slow** Inside

903 **TRUE COMPANION 20** [2] N P Littmoden 5-9-4 (65) J P Guillambert(3) 10/1: 3-013031: Rear, hdwy 3f out & rdn to lead well ins last: eff at 1m/11f on fast, gd/soft & polytrack: see 520, 174. **71**
1056 **CLASSIC ROLE 7** [14] R Ingram 5-10-0 vis (75) A Culhane 7/2: 4034122: Held up, smooth hdwy & rdn/led over 1f out, hdd well ins last: remains in fine form: see 936. *1* **78**
1098+ **WAR OWL 4** [19] Ian Williams 7-9-5 (6ex) (66) Lisa Jones(3) 2/1 FAV: 04-20113: Rear, hmpd over 3f out, styd on wide for press, not reach front pair: qck reapp, remains in gd heart: see 1098. *½* **68**
891 **TOP OF THE CLASS 21** [1] P D Evans 7-8-11 vis (58) S Drowne 33/1: 0003504: Mid-div, eff to chase ldrs 2f out, kept on onepace: encouraging turf return: see 557 & 465. *½* **59**
3617} **LENNEL 241** [7]6-9-7 (68) T E Durcan 16/1: 160114-5: b g Presidium - Ladykirk (Slip Anchor) Dwelt, rear, kept on late, not able to chall: reapp: seller & dual h'cap scorer '03: unplcd '02 (rtd 64, h'cap): suited by 10/11f on fast & gd/soft grnd, gall/stiff trk: loves to come late & eff with/without blnks. *2½* **65**
1 Aug'03 Beve 9.9g/f 66-65 C: 1 Aug'03 Hayd 10.5g/f 67-59 E: 1 Jul'03 Ayr 10.9gd 58-(59) F: 1 May'01 Muss 8gd 77- E: 1 Apr'01 Muss 8hvy 76- D: 2 Mar'01 Muss 8hvy 72-69 E:
918 **QUEEN EXCALIBUR 18** [16]5-7-12 (45) D Fox(5) 50/1: 0-000006: ch f Sabrehill - Blue Room (Gorytus) Mid-div, styd on onepace, no threat to ldrs: h'cap plcd '03 (J M Bradley, rtd 47, sell h'cap, earlier fills mdn rnr-up, prob flattered): mdn plcd '02 for H Cecil (rtd 70, mod sand form, h'cap): eff btwn 7/10f, tried 12f: handles fast & gd grnd: tried cheek pieces & blnks & has had breathing problems reported prev. *1¾* **40**
2 May'03 Warw 8.1g/f 70-(60) D:
903 **BURGUNDY 20** [20]7-8-11 (58) K Dalgleish 12/1: 10-63427: Held up, eff 2f out, onepace dist: see 903. *shd* **53**
1026* **DISSIDENT 10** [9]6-9-9 vis (70) Dane O'Neill 9/1: 002-4U18: Prom & led 2f out till over 1f out, wknd. *shd* **64**
857* **GAME GURU 27** [10]5-9-1 bl (62) S Yourston(7) 33/1: 1314619: Prom, btn dist: see 857. *nk* **55**
484 **COOL BATHWICK 77** [13]5-8-12 (59) G Baker 12/1: 000-1260: 10th: Handy till lost place 3f out: abs. *5* **45**
4951} **PAY THE SILVER 165** [8]6-9-12 p (73) G Duffield 40/1: 640230-0: 11th: Mid-div, no prog fnl 2f: reapp. *1½* **57**
4533} **SUMMER BOUNTY 195** [6]8-9-3 (64) S W Kelly 33/1: 222450-0: 12th: Slow away, hdwy halfway, no prog 2f out, 4 mth jumps abs. *7* **39**
624 **ROZANEE 58** [11]4-9-1 (62) M Hills 25/1: 333-60: 13th: Led/dsptd lead till 2f out, wknd: abs. *2½* **33**
3247} **NAUTICAL 257** [5]6-9-1 (62) D Sweeney 66/1: 24310/0-0: 14th: In tch till 2f out: jumps fit: gelded. *¾* **32**
4517} **LEITRIM ROCK 196** [3]4-8-8 (55) S Whitworth 25/1: 203000-0: 15th: Slow away & al bhd on reapp. *1½* **23**
1034 **LA MUETTE 2** [17]4-9-9 (70) S Righton 50/1: 300-0000: 16th: Dwelt & al bhd, qck reapp. *shd* **38**
339 **EMBER DAYS 96** [4]5-9-3 BL (64) G Carter 33/1: 05522-50: 17th: Keen, in tch till over 1f out: blnks. *2½* **28**
3017} **KINGS MOUNTAIN 268** [12]4-8-13 (60) P M Quinn 66/1: 00/0600-0: 18th: Al bhd, reapp. *¾* **23**
4457} **BURLEY FIREBRAND 199** [18]4-8-13 (60) M Fenton 33/1: 312020-0: 19th: Sn bhd, t.o., reapp, gelded. *dist* **0**
1531} **ACE IN THE HOLE 332** [15]4-7-13 P (46) Joanna Badger 66/1: 3000/00-0: 20th: Led after 1f till over 5f out, wknd qckly, t.o.: cheek pieces, reapp. *12* **0**
20 Ran Time 2m 23.86 (7.66) Owned: Novowel Racing Trained: Newmarket

WARWICK   MONDAY 12.04.04   Lefthand, Sharp, Turning Track

1129   5.35 Geoff Woodward 'lifetime in Racing' Maiden Stakes Div 2 3yo   (D)
£3689   £1135   £568   7f26y rnd   Good 58   -17 Slow   Inside

4668} **KEY PARTNERS 185** [1] P A Blockley 3-9-0   D Nolan(5) 9/2: 52-1: Handy & led 3f out, drvn & held on   **76**
all out: op 11/2, reapp: mdn rnr-up '03: apprec step up to 7f, 1m+ could suit: handles fast & gd grnd, gall or
sharp/turning trk: goes well fresh.
4942} **RIVER OF BABYLON 166** [3] M L W Bell 3-8-9   A Culhane 5/2 FAV: 50-2: Handy & rdn/chall dist, just   nk   **70**
held: bckd on reapp: unplcd both '03 starts (mdns, rtd 64, debut): half-sister to a smart 9/10f wnr: eff at 7f,
return to 1m+ could suit: handles gd grnd: now qual for h'caps.
1080 **BEAUCHAMP STAR 5** [9] G A Butler 3-8-9   S Carson 25/1: 03: Held up, switched & hdwy from halfway,   2½   **65**
no extra dist: qck reapp: imprvd from intro, stays a sharp 7f on gd.
5016} **BURLEY FLAME 158** [5] J G Given 3-9-0   M Fenton 14/1: 0-4: Prom, no extra over 1f out: reapp, gelded. 2   **66**
4527} **DAYDREAM DANCER 195** [7]3-8-9   R Smith 28/1: 000-5: Mid-div, no prog fnl 2f, reapp.   1   **59$**
4906} **GENERAL FLUMPA 168** [10]3-9-0   G Baker 12/1: 0-6: In tch, not pace to chall fnl 2f, reapp.   1   **62**
2439} **THE FUN MERCHANT 291** [12]3-9-0   G Duffield 10/1: 60-7: Bhd, mod hdwy, no dngr, reapp, gelded.   shd   **62**
804 **ROVING VIXEN 39** [11]3-8-9   A Daly 50/1: 00-08: Al bhd.   6   **47**
ROCKET 0 [8]3-9-0   P Dobbs 7/1: 9: Prom till 2f out, debut.   5   **43**
3523} **THE BUTTERFLY BOY 245** [4]3-9-0   M Hills 11/4: 6-0: 10th: Led till 3f out, sn btn, reapp.   1   **41**
28   **Rosie Maloney 150** [2]3-8-9 J P Guillambert(3) 50/1:0   873   **Pertemps Red 24** [6]3-9-0 D Fox(5) 50/1:0
12 Ran   Time 1m 27.74(5.34)   Owned: Mr John Wardle   Trained: Southwell

YARMOUTH   MONDAY 12.04.04   Lefthand, Flat, Fair Track

Official Going GOOD/FIRM.

1130   2.05 Sharp Minds Betfair Maiden Stakes 3yo+   (D)
£3452   £1062   £531   1m str   Good/Firm   Slow   Stands Side

2729} **ANDEAN 279** [12] D R Loder 3-8-9   J Murtagh 11/4: 6-1: b c Singspiel - Anna Matrushka (Mill Reef)   **92+**
Made all, in command fnl 2f, impress: bckd tho' op 2/1, reapp: reportedly rtnd sore when 6th on sole '03 start
(mdn, rtd 87): half-brother to smart 12f+ performer Anna Of Saxony: apprec step up to 1m, will stay further: acts
on gd, handles fast, stiff/gall or easy trk: goes well fresh: highly regarded & one to follow.
3505} **MACLEAN 246** [3] Sir Michael Stoute 3-8-9   B Doyle 9/4 FAV: 2-2: b g Machiavellian - Celtic Cross   7   **76**
(Selkirk) Held up, eff to chase ldrs halfway, no impress on easy wnr fnl 2f: reapp: mdn rnr-up sole '03 start:
dam a 7f wnr, sire high-class at 1m: eff at 7f/1m, acts on gd grnd, stiff/undul or easy trk: caught a tartar.
2 Aug'03 Leic 7.0gd 76- D:
LEG SPINNER [4] M R Channon 3-8-9   S Hitchcott(3) 50/1: 3: b g Intikhab - Road Harbour (Rodrigo   1½   **73+**
de Triano) Dwelt, styd on well fnl 3f, no threat to wnr: encouraging intro, bred to apprec 1m/10f: acts on gd grnd:
will find easier races & expect improvement.
4942} **KING OF KNIGHT 166** [16] G Prodromou 3-8-9   O Urbina 100/1: 000-4: Held up, late hdwy, nvr dngrs.   nk   **72**
4721} **LA PERSIANA 182** [15]3-8-4   J Quinn 33/1: 40-5: Keen & prom, hmpd after 3f, kept on late, no   hd   **66**
impress: reapp, clr of rem: encouraging h'cap qual run.
COPPICE [7]3-8-9   R L Moore 25/1: 6: Dwelt, held up, only mod prog on debut.   6   **61**
SPECTOR [13]4-9-0   L Fletcher(3) 100/1: 7: Outpcd, mod late gains on debut.   1   **59**
IKTITAF [11]3-8-9   W Supple 8/1: 8: Trkd ldrs, btn 2f out, debut: op 16/1.   nk   **58**
4468} **HABSHAN 199** [20]4-9-10   A Beech(3) 9/1: 52-9: Chsd ldrs, hmpd early, btn over 1f out, reapp.   2½   **53**
CUNNING PURSUIT [8]3-8-9   J Mackay 50/1: 0: 10th: Sn pushed along, mid-div at best on debut.   1¼   **50**
STAR MAGNITUDE [9]3-8-9   R Hughes 5/1: 0: 11th: Prom 5f, fdd, debut.   ½   **49**
CELEBRE CITATION [19]3-8-9   J D Smith 33/1: 0: 12th: Dwelt, nvr on terms, debut.   1   **47**
875 **SUVARI 24** [5]3-8-4   C Catlin 50/1: 60: 13th: Prom 5f.   nk   **41**
4409} **Native Turk 202** [1]3-8-9 S Sanders 16/1:0   3992} **Tsarbuck 224** [10]3-8-9 M Henry 100/1:0
1072 **Time Flyer 6** [6]4-9-10 (40) J F Egan 100/1:0   919 **Byrd Island 18** [17]3-8-4 T P Queally(3) 100/1:0
416 **Heyward Place 88** [1]4-9-5 T B Reilly(3) 100/1:0   983 **Hello Tiger 13** [14]3-8-9 N Pollard 100/1:0
19 Ran   Time 1m 40.14 (5.04)   Owned: Sheikh Mohammed   Trained: Newmarket

1131   2.40 Custom Kitchens Handicap Stakes Fillies 3yo+ 0-85   (D)   **[83]**
£5512   £1696   £848   1m str   Good/Firm   Slow   Stands Side

1035 **FLOWERDRUM 9** [2] W J Haggas 4-9-7 (76) R Hughes 15/8 FAV: 2/1101-01: b f Mister Baileys -   **86**
Norelands (Irish River) Chsd ldrs, smooth hdwy to lead dist, cmftbly: hvly bckd: well bckd when disapp on hvy grnd
reapp: won 3 of 4 '03 starts, auct mdn, turf & AW h'cap: eff at 7f/1m on fast, gd & f/sand, sharp or stiff/undul
trk: can go well fresh: lightly rcd & progress filly, more to come.
1 Oct'03 Sout 7af 79a-71 D: 1 Jul'03 Pont 8.0g/f 74-70 E: 1 May'03 Leic 8.0gd 73- F:
4392*}**SOLAR POWER 203** [7] J R Fanshawe 3-8-10 (80) J D Smith 16/1: 1-2: b f Marju - Next Round (Common 1   **85**
Grounds) Trkd ldrs & keen, short of room dist, ev ch ins fnl 1f, not btn far: reapp/h'cap bow: won sole '03 start
(fill mdn): eff at 7f/1m on fast & gd grnd, easy trk: goes well fresh: only 2nd start, met a prog rival & can sn
regain wng thread.   1 Sep'03 Kemp 7g/f 82- D:
3983} **ODABELLA 226** [10] John Berry 4-9-0 (69) O Urbina 40/1: 232340-3: b f Selkirk - Circe's Isle (Be   1¼   **71**
My Guest) Dwelt, hdwy 2f out, not qckn fnl 1f on reapp: dual mdn rnr-up '03, subs AW h'cap plcd (J Gosden):
eff arnd 1m/10f on fast, gd & polytrack, gall or sharp/turning trk: encouraging rtn, can find a place.
2 Jun'03 Ches 10.3g/f 71- D: 2 May'03 Newb 8gd 77- D:
5036} **RICHEMAUR 135** [6] M H Tompkins 4-9-11 (80) M Henry 12/1: 1/00000-4: Led/dsptd lead, went on   ¾   **81**
halfway till over 1f out, no extra on reapp: acts on gd & soft grnd: well h'capped.
1024* **ARTISTRY 10** [1]4-8-7 (62) J F McDonald(5) 8/1: 34540-15: Chsd ldrs, rdn to chall dist, no extra.   3   **57**

1043 **GREY PEARL** 9 [3]5-10-0 t (83) S Sanders 14/1: 5113646: Chsd ldrs, no extra dist: prefer 7f. 1 76
1059 **GRACIA** 7 [4]5-8-12 (67) B Reilly(3) 12/1: 01003-07: In tch, hmpd over 1f out, sn no extra. ½ 59
1024 **ESTIMATION** 10 [11]4-8-13 (68) W Supple 33/1: 1-363508: Mid-div, no prog over 1f out. nk 59
1057 **AIMEES DELIGHT** 7 [12]4-9-11 (80) B Doyle 33/1: 10310-09: Chsd ldrs till dist, eased cl-home. 2½ 66
878 **BRAZILIAN TERRACE** 24 [8]4-9-6 (75) Hayley Turner(5) 10/1: 6150-340: 10th: Chsd ldrs till dist. ¾ 60
4950} **CHEESE N BISCUITS** 145 [13]4-9-13 (82) R L Moore 10/1: 033135-0: 11th: Al rear, reapp. 1¼ 64
4973 **VAS Y CARLA** 163 [5]3-9-0 (84) J Murtagh 9/1: 626-0: 12th: Prom 6f, wknd: reapp/h'cap bow. 4 59
4716} **JUBILEE TREAT** 182 [9]4-9-9 (78) J F Egan 20/1: 455120-0: 13th: Led 4f, btn/hmpd 2f out, reapp. 12 31
3003} **SISTER SOPHIA** 268 [14]4-8-13 (68) C Catlin 25/1: 320060-0: 14th: Held up, no ch fnl 3f, reapp. ½ 20
14 Ran   Time 1m 42.32 (7.22)   Owned: Mr J Caplan   Trained: Newmarket

---

1132   3.10 Saltwell Signs Handicap Stakes 3yo+ 46-55 (F)   [62]
£3374 £964 £482   7f str   Good/Firm   V Slow   Stands Side

976 **SCARROTTOO** 13 [5] C S Williams 6-9-3 (51) B Reilly(3) 8/1: 3500551: Held up, styd on for press to lead ins last, rdn out: suited by 6/7f on firm, & both AWs, any trk, likes a sharp/easy one: see 544. 57
913 **BALERNO** 19 [15] R Ingram 5-8-13 (47) R Hughes 9/1: 3045052: Trkd ldrs, rdn & kept on fnl 1f, only just btn: encouraging turf rtn, can find a race: see 408 (banded). ½ 52
1010 **FEAST OF ROMANCE** 12 [10] C N Allen 7-9-0 (48) S Sanders 25/1: 2621503: Led till halfway, again over 1f out till ins last, no extra: acts on fast, gd & polytrack: well treated on turf: see 661 (AW sell). 2 49
1052 **CARLTON** 7 [19] C R Dore 10-9-6 (54) J F McDonald(5) 15/2: 0-044024: Held up & short of room halfway, styd on for press, not rch ldrs: did not get run of race & a gd effort: see 1052 & 565. nk 54
84 **SKY DOME** 140 [16]11-9-5 bl (53) J Murtagh 12/1: 040513-5: Held up & short of room over 2f out, kept on late: 5 month abs: spot on in similar at 1m: see 62. shd 53
1045 **MISS PEACHES** 9 [4]6-8-13 (47) A McCarthy 16/1: 2013546: Mid-div, styd on onepace: fair run: sole win came at 1m: acts on gd, hvy & polytrack: see 648 (banded). ¾ 46
878 **ACORAZADO** 24 [9]5-9-7 bl e (55) R L Moore 13/2 FAV: 0201627: Trkd ldrs & ch 2f out, no extra. 1¾ 51
1013 **LUCEFER** 12 [11]6-8-13 (47) Dean Williams(7) 10/1: 43412-08: b g Lycius - Maharani (Red Ransom) Chsd ldrs till over 2f out: appr h'cap wnr '03: h'cap wnr '02: eff btwn 6f/sharp 1m on firm, soft & polytrack, likes a sharp/undul trk, prob handles any.   2 Aug'03 Yarm 8.0g/f 46-43 F: 1 Aug'03 Brig 8.0fm 49-43 F: 2 Dec'02 Ling 7ap 49a- G: 1 Sep'02 Yarm 6g/f 51-46 F: 1 Sep'01 Muss 7.1g/f 60- F: 1¼ 40
910 **WODHILL BE** 19 [7]4-9-2 (50) W Supple 40/1: 0-5659: Held up, eff when hmpd halfway, no ch after. hd 42
1073* **BALLARE** 6 [1]5-9-6 (6ex)vis (50) C Urbina 8/1: 0-034610: 10th: Trkd ldrs & keen, wknd dist. ½ 45
966 **SENOR EDUARDO** 14 [13]7-9-6 (54) N Pollard 33/1: 04305-00: 11th: gr g Terimon - Jasmin Path (Warpath) In tch till 2f out: unplcd over jumps this winter: h'cap plcd '03 (rtd 55, AW h'cap unplcd, rtd 34a): best eff around 7.5f, tried 12f: acts on fast grnd. shd 45
910 **BELTANE** 19 [8]6-9-0 (48) J F Egan 25/1: 0/P-00120: 12th: Mid-div, no prog over 1f out: btr 710. nk 38
722 **JAMESTOWN** 48 [2]7-9-2 (50) K Ghunowa(7) 50/1: 5000000: 13th: Prom, btn 2f out, 7 wk abs. ½ 39
1020 **SNOW BUNTING** 11 [3]6-9-5 (53) Leanne Kershaw(7) 17/2: 06560-00: 14th: Held up & keen, al bhnd. 1¾ 39
913 **RANNY** 19 [12]4-9-3 (51) J Quinn 15/2: 100-4220: 15th: Led/dsptd lead till dist, fdd: btr 913. 1¼ 34
4418} Fantasy Crusader 202 [18]5-9-1 (49) J Mackay 33/1:0 956   Parisian Playboy 14 [6]4-9-2 (50) C Catlin 12/1:0
659 Roan Raider 55 [14]4-9-1 vis(49) L Fletcher(3) 50/1:0   1012 Miss Trinity 12 [17]4-9-4 (52) T P Queally(3) 66/1:0
19 Ran   Time 1m 28.18 (5.58)   Owned: Mr Michael Peacock   Trained: Newmarket

---

1133   3.45 Racecourse Video Services Maiden Auction Stakes 2yo (F)
£2919 £834 £417   5f43y str   Good/Firm   V Slow   Stands Side

1041 **VON WESSEX** 9 [5] W G M Turner 2-8-7 C Haddon(7) 20/1: 651: b g Wizard King - Gay da Cheen (Tenby) Made all, rdn/edged left & held on for press in last: v slow time: cheaply bght Apr foal, half-brother to a hdles wnr: sire tough & smart at 7f/1m: eff with forcing tactics at 5f on gd grnd/easy trk. 76
MONASHEE PRINCE 2 [3] J R Best 2-8-11 N Pollard 10/1: 2: ch c Monashee Mountain - Lodema (Lycius) Chsd wnr, ch over 1f out, edged left & kept on, just held: op 8/1: Feb first foal, dam unrcd: sire high-class 7f performer: eff at 5f, get further in time: acts on gd grnd/easy trk. hd 80
RED AFFLECK 4 [4] P W Chapple Hyam 2-8-11 A McCarthy 10/11 FAV: 3: b c Nicholas - Lucie Mon Amour (Meadowlake) Dwelt, sn handy, ch over 1f out, no extra ins last: hvly bckd: Mar foal, 15,000gns purchase: dam a US wnr, half-sister to a 6f juv wnr: eff at 5f on gd grnd. 1¾ 77
1041 **EVANESCE** 9 [6] M R Channon 2-8-4 C Catlin 5/2: 224: Chsd ldrs, onepcd dist: bt this wnr in 1041. nk 69
SILVER VISAGE 7 [2]2-8-10 B Reilly(3) 50/1: 5: Mid-div, no impress ins last. 3 69
MISS TRUANT 8 [2]2-8-6 J Mackay 11/2: 6: Slow away, short of rm dist, hung left & no extra. hd 64
1071 **ZACHY BOY** 6 [9]2-8-7 S Hitchcott(3) 40/1: 67: Chsd ldrs till 2f out. 2½ 60
1071 **SHES MY DREAM** 6 [2]2-8-2 J F McDonald(5) 100/1: 08: Pushed along rear, nvr on terms. 1¼ 52
MISS GOOD TIME 1 [2]2-8-2 J Quinn 66/1:9: Prom & keen, wknd over 1f out. 1¾ 49
9 Ran   Time 1m 05.79 (5.69)   Owned: Mr Darren Coombes   Trained: Sherborne

---

1134   4.20 Bennetts Electrical Toshiba Selling Stakes 3yo (G)
£2520 £720 £360   1m2f21y   Good/Firm   V Slow   Inside

1022 **FIDDLES MUSIC** 10 [5] M R Channon 3-8-9 S Hitchcott(3) 9/1: 0-01: b f Fraam - Fiddles Delight (Colmore Row) Trkd ldr, led dist, styd on strongly fnl 1f, rdn out: bght in for 4,400gns: well btn sole '03 start (sell): apprec step up to 10f, may get further: acts on gd grnd & suited by sell grade. 49
514 **SCORCH** 72 [4] V Smith 3-9-0 (51) J Quinn 9/4: 56-402: b g Mark of Esteem - Red Hot Dancer (Seattle Dancer) Led till over 1f out, not pace of wnr: nicely bckd, 10 wk abs: unplcd '03 (lightly rcd, rtd 65, M Channon): stays an easy 10f in sell grade on gd grnd. 1½ 51
843 **PRINCESS ISMENE** 29 [2] P A Blockley 3-9-1 bl (55) J F Egan 10/11 FAV: 1522433: Keen & prom, rdn & onepace fnl 2f: hvly bckd: stays an easy 10f in sell grade, prob ideally suited by 7f/1m: see 843, 613 & 326. ½ 51
899 **BUNINO VEN** 20 [1] S C Williams 3-9-0 VIS B Reilly(3) 9/1: 000-04: gr g Silver Patriarch - Plaything (High Top) Dwelt & held up, not pace to chall: first time visor, only btn arnd 2L: prob stays a slowly run 10f in sell grade: handles gd grnd: mod form prev. shd 50$
1022 **FRESH CONNECTION** 10 [3]3-8-9 P A McCarthy 14/1: 0005: Prom, btn dist: cheek pieces. 4 39

626 **CAPTAIN FEARLESS 58** [1]3-9-0 Hayley Turner(5) 25/1: 006: Keen & prom, btn 3f out, turf bow. 23 14
6 Ran Time 2m 13.21 (9.01) Owned: Mr M Channon Trained: West Ilsley

1135	4.55 Saltwell Signs Great North Air Ambulance Handicap Stakes 3yo+ 0-70 (E)				[70]
	£3721 £1145 £573	1m3f101y	Good/Firm	Fair Inside	

104 **WELLINGTON HALL 138** [4] P W Chapple Hyam 6-8-11 (53) A McCarthy 4/1: 000500-1: b g Halling - 64
Wells Whisper (Sadler's Wells) Chsd ldrs, led 2f out, rdn out for a decisive win: reapp: unplcd '03 (rtd 53 & 73a,
h'caps, A Charlton, tried cheek pieces/blnks/visor): unplcd '02 (sole start, rtd 71, h'cap): ex German 11f wnr:
eff and 10f on gd & hvy grnd: type to follow up under a penalty.
4144} **TRANSCENDANTALE 216** [5] Mrs S Lamyman 6-8-0 (2ow) (40) C Catlin 28/1: 450000-2: b f Apple Tree - 5 45
Kataba (Shardari) Held up, rdn & styd on fnl 2f, no threat to wnr: reapp: fill h'cap rnr-up '03: h'cap scorer
'02: eff btwn 1m /10f, poss stays easy 11.5f: acts on fast, gd/soft & f/sand, prob any trk.
2 Apr'03 Beve 9.9g/f 49-44 E: 2 Jul'02 Kemp 9g/s 55-53 D: 1 Jul'02 Kemp 9g/s 53-48 C:
979* **MADHAHIR 13** [7] C A Dwyer 4-9-7 (63) T P Queally(3) 6/1: 620-0013: Led after 1f till over 1f out, ¾ 65
sn outpcd by wnr: see 979 (soft).
801 **KASHIMO 39** [2] G L Moore 5-9-2 (58) R L Moore 9/4 FAV: 4000-534: Chsd ldrs, onepace fnl 2f: ½ 59
jumps fit (unplcd, rtd 101h, nov): see 801 & 731.
595 **TOLEDO SUN 62** [1]4-8-3 (45) J Quinn 11/2: 30000-35: Led/dsptd lead till dist: jumps fit. 1½ 44
1042* **STEELY DAN 9** [6]5-10-0 (70) N Pollard 100/30: 3112116: Held up, nvr dngrs: op 9/4: btr 1042. hd 68
867 **COURT ONE 25** [8]6-7-12 (5oh) C Haddon(3) 28/1: 26000-07: Dwelt, handy, rdn & btn over 1f out. 2½ 34
1047 **DUNDONALD 7** [3]5-7-12 (5oh)bl t (35) Hayley Turner(5) 50/1: 0340658: Held up, btn 3f out. 10 20
8 Ran Time 2m 27.24(4.44) Owned: Allan Darke & Tom Matthews Trained: Newmarket

Official Going Good/Soft (Good places)

1136	2.10 Stpp Maiden Stakes 3yo+ (D)				
	£5590 £1720 £860	7f Jub	Good 58	-06 Slow Inside	

3373} **POULE DE LUXE 252** [14] J L Dunlop 3-8-6 T Quinn 6/1: 04-1: b f Cadeaux Genereux - Likely Story 73
(Night Shift) In tch, rdn & hdwy over 2f out, styd on well to lead ins last, drvn out: reapp: 4th on 2nd of only 2
juv starts: dam 6f wnr: apprec step up to a stiff 7f, 1m shld suit: acts on fast & gd grnd, runs well fresh:
typical 3yo improver for this stable, prob more to come in h'caps.
900 **HALLINGS OVERTURE 20** [4] C A Horgan 5-9-11 (60) R Hills 16/1: 0500/-602: Handy, led over 2f out nk 77
till ins last, kept on, just held: imprvd back at 7f & on gd grnd: 5yo: see 726.
KAURI FOREST [8] J R Fanshawe 3-8-11 L Dettori 100/30 FAV: 3: ch c Woodman - Kentucky Fall 1¼ 75
(Lead On Time) Chsd ldrs, onepace over 1f out: dam winning sprinter: stays a stiff 7f on gd grnd: encouraging.
19 **EVALUATOR 151** [5] T G Mills 3-8-11 K Darley 8/1: 36-4: b c Ela Mana Mou - Summerhill (Habitat) ½ 74
Keen in tch, onepace over 1f out: reapp: plcd on first of 2 '03 starts (rtd 68a): brother to a winning stayer: dam
sprint wnr: stays 7f on gd, prob polytrack: may be more to come if learning to settle.
4368} **DAY TO REMEMBER 205** [12]3-8-11 P McCabe 13/2: 43-5: gr c Daylami - Miss Universe (Warning) 1½ 71
Held up, brief eff over 1f out, no impress & eased cl-home: bckd tho' op 5/1 on reapp: plcd on second of only 2 juv
starts (mdn, rtd 78): stays 7f on fast & gd grnd: type to do btr in h'caps.
KEYAKI [11]3-8-6 R Mullen 40/1: 6: Slow away, bhd, some late gains on debut. 1¼ 63
4810} **EL CHAPARRAL 523** [17]4-9-11 M Howard(7) 25/1: 403/-7: In tch, wknd 1f out: new yard, gelded. 2½ 63
5031} **DR SYNN 156** [13]3-8-11 P Doe 14/1: 6-8: Bhd, modest late gains on reapp. ¾ 61
4898} **PLANTERS PUNCH 170** [9]3-8-11 K Fallon 8/1: 00-9: Bhd, modest late gains: reapp. ½ 60
966 **IMPERIAL DRAGON 14** [16]4-9-11 D Holland 20/1: 040: 10th: Slow away & nvr a factor. 2½ 55
472 **SUNSET DREAMER 79** [6]3-8-6 J Fanning 66/1: 600: 11th: Al bhd. 2½ 45
2955} **CATCH THE FOX 270** [7]4-9-11 (45) J Tate 100/1: 0/00050-0: 12th: In tch, wknd over 2f out. shd 49
4971} **ROYAL FLIGHT 163** [2]3-8-11 E Ahern 14/1: 5-0: 13th: Al bhd: changed stable. 3½ 42
98 **COLOUR CODE 139** [1]3-8-11 Martin Dwyer 14/1: 20-0: 14th: In tch, wknd over 2f out: see 3. shd 41
4035} **LADY FRANPALM 222** [3]4-9-6 (54) R Miles(3) 50/1: 00/54400-0: 15th: Slow away, in tch 5f, wknd. 1 34
946 **MANDAHAR 16** [10]5-9-11 M Tebbutt 66/1: 0000: 16th: In tch, wknd over 2f out. 10 19
973 **CEDRIC COVERWELL 14** [15]4-9-11 W Ryan 50/1: 40: 17th: Led till wknd over 2f out. 2½ 14
17 Ran Time 1m 28.57 (4.47) Owned: Mr D K Thorpe (Susan Abbott Racing) Trained: Arundel

1137	2.45 Quail Conditions Stakes 3yo+ (C)				
	£8343 £3165 £1582	6f str	Good	Inapp Stands Side	

4795} **BARONS PIT 177** [1] R Hannon 4-9-2 (114) K Fallon 15/8 FAV: 233000-1: b c Night Shift - Incendio 108
(Siberian Express) Chsd ldrs, hdwy 2f out, led dist, styd on strongly, drvn out: hvly bckd: plcd first 3 of 6 '03
starts (incl Gr 1 Jubilee, rtd 118): '02 stks & Gr 3 wnr: eff at 5f, suited by 6f & does stay 7f: acts on fast &
gd grnd, stiff or sharp trks: runs well fresh: smart, can rate more highly & win another List/Gr race.
2 Apr'03 Newm 7gd 108-105 A: 1 Jun'02 Asco 5g/f 105- A: 1 May'02 Wind 5g/f 101- B: 2 May'02 Kemp 5g/f 88- D:
952 **SMOKIN BEAU 16** [7] N P Littmoden 7-9-2 (98) T G McLaughlin 6/1: 05400-62: b g Cigar - Beau Dada 2 101
(Pine Circle) Rcd alone far side, cl-up, kept on fnl 1f, not pace of wnr: plcd on 2 of 10 '03 starts (Gr 3, rtd
112): '02 multiple wnr, incl List: eff at 5f, suited by 6f on any grnd/trk, likes Goodwood: tried vis & cheek
pieces: has run well fresh & loves to dominate: tough & smart at best, suffered bleeding/lameness probs last term.
1 Oct'02 Newb 6sft 115-110 B: 2 Oct'02 Newm 5fm 111- A: 2 Sep'02 Newb 5.1fm 113- A: 1 Sep'02 Good 6fm 111- A:
2 Aug'02 Ches 6g/f 102- A: 1 May'02 Good 6g/f 112- B: 2 May'02 Newm 6g/f 109-104 B: 1 Apr'02 Nott 5g/f 115-108 D:
2 Oct'01 Newm 5g/f 108- A: 1 Sep'01 Donc 5.6g/f 105-98 B: 2 Sep'01 Sand 5gd 101-95 B: 1 Aug'01 Good 6gd 95-91 C:
952 **FIRE UP THE BAND 16** [4] D Nicholls 5-9-2 (105) A Nicholls 9/4: 2023-003: Slow away, sn in tch, nk 100
hdwy over 1f out, kept on ins last, no threat to wnr: fair eff but shld rate even higher when stable starts to fire.
4867} **FRUIT OF GLORY 44** [2] J R Jenkins 5-8-11 D Holland 14/1: 335-0544: b f Glory of Dancer - Fresh nk 94
Fruit Daily (Reprimand) Trkd ldr, hdwy to lead over 1f out, sn hdd & onepace: unplcd in Dubai 6 wks ago: '03 4
time h'cap scorer: eff at 5f, suited by 6/7f & stays 1m on firm & gd, handles soft & polytrack, any trk, loves both

Newmarket courses: has run well fresh under big weights: tough & useful.
1 Aug'03 Newm 6fm 88-84 C: 1 Aug'03 Newm 7gd 86-80 C: 1 Aug'03 Newm 6g/f 83-77 D: 2 Jul'03 Wind 8.3g/f 79-76 D:
1 Jun'03 Good 7g/f 77-74 D: 1 Jul'02 Wind 8.3g/f 81-74 D: 2 Sep'01 Asco 7sft 84-74 B: 1 Sep'01 Epso 7gd 73- E:
2 Aug'01 Good 6g/s 79- D: 2 Aug'01 Folk 6g/f 77- F:

1043 **WILL HE WISH 9** [5]8-9-10 (92) I Mongan 50/1: 1261-005: Sn bhd, eff 2f out, onepace: stiff task.	2	100$
4867} **MAZEPA 171** [3]4-9-2 (96) L Dettori 8/1: 000100-6: b c Indian Ridge - Please Believe Me (Try My	2	86

Best) Set pace till over 1f out, no extra: won 1 of 7 '03 starts (h'cap): '02 mdn & stks wnr: eff over 5/6f, poss
stays 7f on gd/firm & gd/soft, poss polytrack, likes a gall trk.
1 Sep'03 Asco 6g/f 102-89 B: 2 May'02 Asco 5g/s 94- B: 1 Apr'02 Newm 5g/f 94- C: 1 Apr'02 Nott 5g/s 93- D:

1004 **INDIAN SPARK 12** [6]10-9-2 (96) T Quinn 10/1: 00500-47: Bhd, nvr a factor.	3	77

7 Ran   Time 1m 12.36 (1.26)   Owned: J T & K M Thomas   Trained: Marlborough

---

1138   3.15 Sharp Minds Betfair Stakes Handicap 4yo+ 0-95 (C)   [95]
£9760 £3003 £1502   **6f str**   **Good**   **Inapp**   Stands Side. Low No's favoured.

4979} **PERSARIO 163** [5] J R Fanshawe 5-8-11 (78) L Dettori 10/1: 1/62620-1: b f Bishop of Cashel -   89
Barford Lady (Stanford) Slow away stands side, held up, hdwy over 2f out, strong run ins last to lead cl-home, rdn
out: reapp: rnr-up twice in '03 (h'cap): mdn auct wnr in '02: wng form over 6/7f & acts on fast & gd, prob soft:
acts on any trk, likes a sharp one: runs well fresh: lightly rcd & improving.
2 Oct'03 Epso 7gd 78-(79) D: 2 Jul'03 Leic 7.0g/f 80-75 D: 1 Jun'02 Sout 7g/f 76- F:

1035 **ZILCH 9** [3] M L W Bell 6-9-6 (87) I Mongan 10/1: 0003-122: Handy stands side, hdwy to lead over	½	95

1f out, kept on till collared cl-home, just btn: clr of rem & continues in fine form: see 945, 181.

4674} **HIGH REACH 184** [13] T G Mills 4-9-8 (89) K Darley 7/1: 243144-3: b g Royal Applause -   4   87+
Lady of Limerick (Thatching) In tch far side, hdwy to lead that group 2f out, kept on, not pace of stands side
group: reapp: won 2 of 10 '03 starts (h'caps): unplcd sole '02 start: suited by 6/7f on fast or polytrack, sharp
or gall trks: gelded since last term, rtnd in fine heart & won race on wrong side, keep in mind.
1 Aug'03 Asco 6g/f 92-83 D: 2 Mar'03 Leic 7.0g/f 84-81 C: 2 Feb'03 Ling 8ap 83a-79 D: 1 Feb'03 Ling 7ap 81a-73 E:

1020* **TARANAKI 11** [15] P D Cundell 6-9-2 (83) K Fallon 7/1 CO FAV: 101-0414: Handy far side, eff well	½	79

over 1f out, kept on, no ch with stands side group: fine run: see 1020, 130.

944 **SEVEN NO TRUMPS 16** [18]7-9-1 (82) D Holland 7/1 CO FAV: 03000-25: Led far side till over 1f out,	¾	76

no extra: fair run, see 944.

4353} **WINNING VENTURE 205** [1]7-9-5 (86) W Ryan 40/1: 446305-6: b g Owington - Push A Button (Bold Lad) nk 79+
Bhd stands side, hdwy over 1f out, nrst fin: reapp: plcd twice in '03 (h'caps, rtd 88, with D Nicholls): rtd 96
for R Charlton in '02: wng form over 7f/1m & acts on firm grnd, likes soft & any trk: has run well fresh: tried
blnks & t-strap: h'capped to win on easy grnd, keep in mind over 7f/1m.
1 Sep'01 Good 8g/s 102- B: 2 Jul'01 Ches 7fm 103- B: 2 Jul'01 Yarm 7g/f 10- C: 2 May'01 Hayd 7.1sft 103- A:

921 **ARMAGNAC 18** [7]6-8-12 (79) J Fanning 33/1: 10460-07: b g Young Ern - Arianna Aldini (Habitat)	¾	70

Cl-up stands side, wknd over 1f out: won 1 of 9 '03 starts (h'cap): '02 h'cap scorer: suited by a gall 6f on firm
or soft grnd, likes Haydock: gd weight carrier: eff with/without cheek pieces on a fair mark.
1 Jun'03 Hayd 6g/f 83-78 D: 1 Jul'02 Hayd 6g/f 89-78 D: 1 Jun'01 Ripo 6g/f 90-83 C: 2 Jun'01 York 6g/s 91-83 B:

945 **MARKER 16** [17]4-9-9 (90) R Thomas(5) 12/1: 61600-68: Slow away far side, eff over 1f out, onepcd.	1	78
921 **NASHAAB 18** [16]7-9-6 (87) T G McLaughlin 16/1: 305-0009: Bhd far side, some late gains.	nk	74
1025 **FURTHER OUTLOOK 10** [8]10-9-6 (87) M Howard(7) 20/1: 0200-130: 10th: With ldrs, wknd over 1f out.	shd	74
921 **ABBAJABBA 18** [2]8-9-2 (83) J Bramhill 25/1: 0006-000: 11th: Nvr a factor stands side, reportedly	1	67

hung right thro'out.

618 **POLAR KINGDOM 59** [11]6-8-11 (78) E Ahern 12/1: 00-31100: 12th: Nvr a factor stands side: 2	shd	62

month abs, twice below 611 (fibresand).

3654} **MATERIAL WITNESS 240** [9]7-9-7 (88) Martin Dwyer 33/1: 002100-0: 13th: Slt lead stands side till	1	69

over 1f out, no extra.

4956} **FREE WHEELIN 164** [6]4-8-13 (80) M Tebbutt 33/1: 020000-0: 14th: Al bhd stands side.	2	55
921 **PRINCE CYRANO 18** [19]5-9-5 (86) R Mullen 14/1: 00200-00: 15th: Slow away, nvr a factor far side.	shd	61
4367} **LITTLE VENICE 205** [12]4-8-11 (78) S O'Hara(7) 33/1: 163240-0: 16th: Al bhd far side.	hd	53
921* **STEEL BLUE 18** [4]4-9-5 (86) R Hills 12/1: 02200-10: 17th: In tch 4f stands side: made all 921.	1	58
2329} **MITCHAM 296** [20]8-10-0 (95) R Miles(3) 12/1: 566100-0: 18th: Handy far side, wknd over 2f out.	nk	67
945 **TERRAQUIN 16** [10]4-8-11 (78) A Nicholls 33/1: 416-0400: 19th: Slow away, stands side, wknd 2f out.	3½	40
171 **LANDING STRIP 125** [14]4-8-10 (77) J Tate 33/1: 144340-0: 20th: Handy far side, wknd over 2f out.	12	3

20 Ran   Time 1m 12.36 (1.26)   Owned: Barford Bloodstock   Trained: Newmarket

---

1139   3.50 Listed Magnolia Stakes 4yo+ (A)
£17400 £6600 £3300   **1m2f**   **Good 58**   **+06 Fast**   Inside

990 **SCOTTS VIEW 16** [6] M Johnston 5-9-0 (115) S Chin 5/1: 1-410131: Held up, strong hdwy over 2f   117+
out, led over 1f out, rdn clr, readily: caught the eye in Dubai last time: eff over 10/12f, does stay 2m on firm,
gd/soft & polytrack: thriving at present, looks top-class & a typically tough & progressive M Johnston older horse,
must be followed in Group class at present: see 990.

884 **BUSTAN 23** [9] M P Tregoning 5-8-11 (107) R Hills 7/2 JT FAV: 43/442-32: b c Darshaan -   3   107
Dazzlingly Radiant (Try My Best) Handy, eff 2f out, styd on to chase wnr ins last, no impress: well bckd: rnr-up
on last of 3 '03 starts (List, rtd 107 at best): '02 mdn & List wnr: eff at 10/11f, prob stays 12f: handles firm &
gd, stiff or fair trks: smart, prob ran to best on reapp.
2 Oct'03 Newm 10gd 104-(110) A: 1 Jun'02 Newm 10g/f 109- A: 1 May'02 Kemp 8g/f 87- D:

4348} **ISLAND HOUSE 205** [5] G Wragg 8-8-11 (113) D Holland 13/2: 514432-3: ch c Grand Lodge - Fortitude   1¾   105
(Last Tycoon) Held up, hdwy 2f out, hung right appr fnl 1f, kept on ins last: won 1 of 6 '03 starts (List): won 3
List races in '02: eff over 10/12f on any gd/trk, likes gd or softer: has run well fresh: tough & smart, poised
for another big run in Festival stks at Goodwood.
2 Sep'03 Ayr 10.9fm 114-(114) A: 1 May'03 Good 9.9g/f 114-(113) A: 1 Nov'02 Newm 10gd 119- A:
1 Sep'02 Ayr 10.8gd 115- A: 1 Jun'02 Leic 11.8gd 113- A: 2 May'02 Good 10gd 109- A: 1 May'02 Ches 10.3fm 110- A:
2 Apr'02 Newm 9fm 115- A: 2 May'01 Ches 10.3fm 113- A: 1 Apr'01 Sand 10hvy 116- A:

5027} **LANDINIUM 157** [4] C F Wall 5-8-6 (104) R Mullen 50/1: 405440-4: b f Lando - Hollywood Girl   1   98
(Cagliostro) Held up, hdwy & wandered 3f out & over 1f out, some late gains on reapp: 4th in a List race in '03:
List wnr in Italy in '02: eff at 10f, prob stays 12f: acts on gd & hvy, prob fast grnd, tried a t-strap.

1061 **NYSAEAN 8** [1]5-9-2 (115) K Darley 11/2: 2110-545: Led early, led again over 3f out, hdd over 1f   ½   107
out, no extra conceding weight: likes easier grnd: see 1061.

1083 **EASTER OGIL 5** [7]9-8-11 (56) A Nicholls 100/1: 0000026: Hld up, some late gains: nvr dngrs: qck   2½   98$

reapp: remarkable run, offic rtd 56 & treat rating with caution: see 1083.
884 **CORRIOLANUS 23** [2]4-8-11 (104) J Fanning 50/1: 1263-307: Hld up, eff over 1f out, no impress. *1¾* **95**
4569} **PIANO STAR 192** [11]4-8-11 (103) K Fallon 11/2: 24103-8: b g Darshaan - De Stael (Nijinsky) In tch, wknd over 2f out: gelded: '03 mdn wnr (rtd 101 at best): eff at 10/11f on fast grnd & a sharp or gall trk. *2* **92**
1 Jul'03 Ayr 10g/f 89- D: 2 May'03 Ches 10.3g/f 100- D:
4624} **CHANCELLOR 191** [10]6-8-11 (110) L Dettori 7/2 JT FAV: 550/464-9: With ldrs, wknd dist, lame. *1¼* **90**
716 **LION HUNTER 48** [12]5-8-11 (84) Martin Dwyer 100/1: 2251/-060: 10th: Led after 2f till 3f out, wknd. *1* **88**
2290} **ROCKET FORCE 297** [8]4-8-11 (104) E Ahern 33/1: 41/320-0: 11th: In tch, wknd over 3f out. *5* **110**
4800} **TUNING FORK 177** [3]4-8-11 (100) T Quinn 33/1: 126650-0: 12th: In tch, wknd 2f out: new yard. *21* **43**
12 Ran Time 2m 07.53 (5.23) Owned: Great Escape Partnership Trained: Middleham

1140

4.25 Stpp Media Maiden Stakes 3yo (D)
£5434 £1672 £836 **1m3f30y** **Good 58** **-52 Slow** Inside

4067} **BUKIT FRASER 220** [4] P F I Cole 3-9-0 K Darley 5/4 FAV: 34-1: b c Sri Pekan - London Pride (Lear Fan) Keen, handy, hdwy to lead over 1f out, rdn clr fnl 1f on reapp: hvly bckd: 3rd & 4th both juv starts (rtd 84): dam 1m wnr: relished step up to 11f & acts on fast & gd grnd, gall or fair trks: runs well fresh: op to plenty of further improvement in h'caps. **87**
192 **SUNNY LADY 121** [1] E A L Dunlop 3-8-9 E Ahern 20/1: 60-2: ch f Nashwan - Like The Sun (Woodman) Held up, hdwy over 2f out, styd on fnl 1f, no threat to wnr: 4 month abs: imprvd for step up to 11f & acts on gd grnd: can win a race, poss over even further. *3* **75**
4943} **TANNOOR 166** [3] M A Jarvis 3-9-0 (80) P Robinson 2/1: 033-3: b c Miswaki - Iolani (Alzao) Led till over 1f out, onepcd: plcd on 2 of 3 '02 starts (rtd 81): stays 11f on fm & soft: consistent. *nk* **80**
4386} **SCARRABUS 203** [7] B G Powell 3-9-0 (67) T Quinn 20/1: 560-4: b c Charnwood Forest - Errazuriz (Classic Music) Held up, eff over 2f out, onepace & hmpd ins last: unplcd in '03 (rtd 70): prob stays 11f on gd. *1½* **77**
4937} **CLEAVER 166** [2]3-9-0 M Tebbutt 14/1: 0-5: In tch, wknd 2f out on reapp: longer trip. *6* **68**
1019 **FRANKIES WINGS 11** [5]3-9-0 R Miles(3) 15/2: 0-06: Held up, nvr a factor. *1½* **66**
843 **ALMOST WELCOME 29** [10]3-9-0 (45) P Doe 33/1: 00-00357: In tch, wknd 2f out: see 715. *½* **65$**
980 **PELLA 13** [9]3-8-9 K Fallon 16/1: 08: In tch, wknd 2f out. *½* **59**
4387} **NINA FONTENAIL 203** [6]3-8-9 I Mongan 100/1: 06-9: Slow away, keen in tch, wknd 2f out. *1½* **57$**
873 **HARRY CAME HOME 24** [8]3-9-0 P McCabe 100/1: 00: 10th: Al bhd. *18* **34**
10 Ran Time 2m 29.68 (12.28) Owned: HRH Sultan Ahmad Shah Trained: Whatcombe

1141

5.00 Sharp Minds Betfair Handicap Stakes 3yo 0-85 (D) **[89]**
£5681 £1748 £874 **1m1f** **Good 58** **-23 Slow** Inside

4924} **SHOW NO FEAR 167** [11] H R A Cecil 3-8-6 (67) W Ryan 10/1: 300552-1: b c Groom Dancer - La Piaf (Fabulous Dancer) Held up, hdwy 2f out, styd on to lead ins last, drvn out: rnr-up on last of 6 '03 starts (mdn, H Cyzer): stays 9f on gd & gd/soft: eff with/without a visor: clrly runs well fresh & sharpened up by new stable. **72**
2 Oct'03 Nott 8.2g/s 72-(65) D:
189* **CELTIC HEROINE 121** [13] M A Jarvis 3-9-3 (78) K Darley 5/2 FAV: 51541-2: Handy, hdwy to lead over 1f out, rdn & hdd cl-home well bckd: 4 month abs: stays 9f on fast, gd & both AWs: improving: see 189. *½* **81**
4714*}**MOMTIC 182** [6] W Jarvis 3-9-5 (80) M Tebbutt 33/1: 0321-3: ch c Shinko Forest - Uffizi (Royal Academy) Held up, hdwy over 2f out, kept on ins last, no dngr: won last of 4 '03 starts (mdn): eff at 5/6f, clrly stays this big step up to 9f well: acts on firm & gd grnd, easy trks: progressing well, unexposed at this trip. *1¼* **81**
1 Oct'03 Wind 6g/f 87-(75) D: 2 Sep'03 Thir 6fm 82- E:
MALIBU 169 [10] S Dow 3-9-1 (76) P Doe 33/1: 351500-4: b g Second Empire - Tootle (Main Reef) Held up, hdwy 2f out, kept on ins last, nvr dngrs: reapp: won a mdn auct in native Ireland in '03: eff at 7f, clrly stays 9f on fast & gd grnd: encouraging run. *½* **76**
4306} **PERUVIAN BREEZE 207** [7]3-7-13 (60) J Bramhill 66/1: 066-5: b g Foxhound - Quietly Impressive (Taufan) In tch, eff 2f out, sn no extra: unplcd in 3 '03 starts: gelded since last term & prob stays 9f on gd. *½* **59**
192 **CARRIACOU 121** [2]3-9-0 (75) P Robinson 9/1: 522002-6: Led till dist, no extra: btr 192 (1m, aw). *1¾* **70**
765* **HAZEWIND 43** [9]3-8-1 t (62) J Fanning 9/1: 00-04217: Bhd, late gains, nvr dngrs: longer trip. *nk* **56**
977* **GRETNA 13** [5]3-9-7 (82) T Quinn 13/2: 6-18: Chsd ldr, wknd 2f out: btr 977 (mdn fills soft). *2½* **71**
947 **WINNERS DELIGHT 16** [3]3-9-5 (80) E Stack 33/1: 6165-09: Held up rear, nvr plcd to chall: horse banned for 40 days, trainer fined & joc rec 9 day suspension for failing to obtain best poss placing: improve. *hd* **68**
5031*}**MISS LANGKAWI 156** [12]3-8-13 (74) D Holland 9/2: 31-0: 10th: Al bhd: reportedly nvr trav. *1* **60**
729 **PICK OF THE CROP 47** [8]3-8-13 (74) L Dettori 20/1: 525-1200: 11th: Held up, nvr a factor: see 615. *1¾* **56**
4537*}**ANOUSA 194** [4]3-9-4 (79) K Fallon 8/1: 2501-0: 12th: In tch, wknd 2f out: long trip. *1* **59**
841* **COUNT DRACULA 29** [1]3-8-9 (70) Martin Dwyer 14/1: 020-10: 13th: In tch, wknd over 2f out: gelded since winning 841 (mdn, 1m, polytrack). *8* **34**
13 Ran Time 1m 57.27(7.27) Owned: Mr Colin Davey Trained: Newmarket

REDCAR

MONDAY 12.04.04 **Lefthand, Flat, Galloping Track**

Official Going SOFT.

1142

2.20 Bank Holiday Classified Stakes 3yo+ 0-70 (E)
£3572 £1099 £550 **7f str** **Soft 122** **-04 Slow** Centre

967+***UP TEMPO 14** [13] K A Ryan 6-9-9 bl (71) N Callan 11/4 FAV: 0-213111: Trkd ldrs, hdwy to chall dist, led cl-home, drvn out: eff at 6/7f on firm, hvy & fibresand: eff in blnks & cheek pieces: has now won 4 of last 5 starts & clearly in fine heart: see 967 & 459 (AW). **73**
1036 **HOV 9** [6] J J Quinn 4-9-10 (72) R Winston 8/1: 540-0002: Nvr far away, ev ch fnl 1f, just btn in a close fin: back to form, acts on fast, soft & fibresand: see 595 (AW). *½* **72**
921 **YOUNG MR GRACE 18** [9] T D Easterby 4-9-13 (75) D Allan(3) 20/1: 20460-03: b c Danetime - Maid of Mourne (Fairy King) Tried to make all, collared ins fnl 1f & only just btn: jt top-weight, rider given a 2-day whip ban: rnr-up on reapp in '03 (h'cap): '02 nov wnr: eff at 5/7f, does stay 1m: acts on firm & soft grnd & on a stiff/gall or sharpish trk: runs well fresh: sound front running effort. *hd* **75**

2 Apr'03 Ripo 6gd 81-80 C: 1 May'02 Newc 5g/f 78- D:
4920} **HILLS OF GOLD** 167 [5] M W Easterby 5-9-8 (66) P Mulrennan(5) 20/1: 011400-4: b g Danehill -   2   **66**
Valley of Gold (Shirley Heights) Chsd ldrs, onepcd fnl 1f on reapp: dual h'cap wnr in '03: eff at 7/7.5f on firm &
soft, prefers the former: handles a stiff or tight trk: encouraging reapp, spot on next time & has won at Chester.
1 Aug'03 Ches 7.0g/f 70-61 E: 1 Aug'03 Beve 7.5g/f 61-55 E: 1 Sep'01 Donc 7g/f 103- D:
998   **RONNIE FROM DONNY** 12 [3]4-9-8 (70) T Eaves(5) 10/1: 1-400U55: Held up, styd on fnl 1.5f, nrst fin.   4   **58**
998   **BAILIEBOROUGH** 12 [11]5-9-8 (69) Alex Greaves 20/1: 10000-06: b g Charnwood Forest - Sherannda   2   **54**
(Trempolino) Slowly away, hdwy to chase ldrs after halfway, no impress fnl 1f: '03 class stks wnr, also h'cap
rnr-up: eff at 7/8.5f on firm & gd/soft: has tried a visor: handles a sharp or gall trk: with D Nicholls.
1 Aug'03 Folk 7g/f 73-(70) E: 2 Aug'03 Beve 8.5g/f 68-65 E: 2 Jul'03 Redc 7g/f 70-(63) G: 2 Aug'02 Hayd 7.1g/s 73-69 E:
1 Aug'01 Thir 6gd 79- D:
1006   **EASTERN HOPE** 12 [7]5-9-8 (67) Kristin Stubbs(7) 25/1: 05060-07: Rear, styd on late, nvr dngrs.   2½   **49**
1036   **CELTIC ROMANCE** 9 [8]5-9-5 (59) J Carroll 50/1: 0/0000-08: Slowly away, nvr nr ldrs.   ½   **45**
945   **HAND CHIME** 16 [2]7-9-13 (75) P Hanagan 7/2: 03-00509: Dwelt, recovered to chase ldrs, btn 2f out.   shd   **53**
967   **AFRICAN SPUR** 14 [1]4-9-8 t (70) D Tudhope(7) 33/1: 0-002200: 10th: Chsd ldrs wide, btn 2f out.   1¼   **45**
967   **TRE COLLINE** 14 [4]5-9-10 (72) Kim Tinkler 25/1: 16320-00: 11th: Al towards rear.   3½   **40**
999   **TOP LINE DANCER** 12 [12]3-8-8 (70) R Ffrench 7/1: 54-40: 12th: Chsd ldrs 5f, wknd: see 999 (6f).   hd   **38**
216   **LOOKING DOWN** 117 [10]4-9-5 (70) G Faulkner 12/1: 004030-0: 13th: Chsd ldrs, btn halfway, t.o.   13   **10**
13 Ran   Time 1m 30.68 (8.88)   Owned: Yorkshire Racing Club & Derek Blackhurst   Trained: Hambleton

---

1143   **2.55 Free Egg Give Away Maiden Stakes 2yo** **(D)**
           £3504 £1078 £539   **5f str**   **Soft 122**   **-40 Slow**   Centre

     BIGALOS BANDIT [3] J J Quinn 2-9-0 R Winston 2/1 JT FAV: 1: ch c Compton Place - Move Darling   **78**
(Rock City) Trkd ldrs, imprvd to lead ins fnl 1f, rdn clr: nicely bckd on debut: 13,500gns Mar foal: half-brother
to a couple of juv wnrs: sire a top-class sprinter: eff over a gall 5f on soft, runs well fresh: scopey sort.
1071 **SPEED DIAL HARRY** 6 [2] K R Burke 2-9-0 Darren Williams 2/1 JT FAV: 52: b c General Monash -   1½   **72**
Jacobina (Magic Ring) Tried to make all, collared ins fnl 1f & no extra cl-home: well bckd, rider given a 1-day ban
for failing to ride to draw: April 1st foal, cost 2,500gns: dam a 7f wnr: eff at 5f on soft.
     PARIS BELL [4] T D Easterby 2-9-0 A Mullen(7) 12/1: 3: b c Paris House - Warning Bell (Bustino)   nk   **71**
Dwelt, keen & prog when short of room after halfway, hmpd entering fnl 1f, fin well but too late: debut: March
foal, half-brother to several wnrs, incl 6f/1m performer Hand Chime: dam a 10f wnr, sire a v speedy juv: eff at 5f
on soft grnd: not much luck today, acts real juv.
     KEEPASHARPLOOKOUT [1] Mrs L Stubbs 2-9-0 P Hanagan 6/1: 4: b c Rossini - Zoyce (Zilzal) Prom,   1¾   **66**
rdn & onepcd fnl 1f: Mar foal, dam unrcd but from a decent family: sire a high-class juv.
     MISTY MILLER [6]2-9-0 D Allan(3) 9/2: 5: Held up, prog halfway, btn fnl 1f: s/mate of 3rd.   1½   **62**
920   **HIATS** 18 [5]2-9-0 J D O'Reilly(7) 16/1: 06: Keen & prom till after halfway, wknd.   5   **47**
6 Ran   Time 1m 04.61 (8.11)   Owned: Mr Ian Buckley   Trained: Malton

---

1144   **3.25 Easter Handicap Stakes 3yo 0-75 (E)**   **[80]**
           £4238 £1304 £652   **1m2f**   **Soft 122**   **-23 Slow**   Inside

899   **PLATINUM PIRATE** 20 [9] K R Burke 3-8-3 VIS (55) Rory Moore(7) 9/1: 000-2021: Chsd ldrs, led 2f   **64**
out, wandered but rdn well clr: bckd from 12/1, first time visor, rider given 5-day whip ban: eff at 10f on soft
grnd & polytrack: handles a gall or sharp trk: usually blnkd, apprec visor today: first win, see 899.
1000 **WOODY VALENTINE** 12 [7] M Johnston 3-9-7 (73) R Ffrench 5/2 FAV: 21400-42: Held up, hdwy to lead   5   **74**
3f out, hdd 2f out, kept on but no ch with wnr: jt top-weight: acts on firm & soft: met an imprvd rival, see 1000.
4808} **THIRD EMPIRE** 175 [6] C Grant 3-8-10 (62) R Winston 20/1: 4050-3: b g Second Empire - Tahnee   ¾   **62**
(Cadeaux Genereux) Held up, hdwy & ev ch 2f out, sn onepcd on reapp: lightly rcd in '03, some mdn promise (rtd 69
at best): 22,000gns Jan foal: eff at 10f on soft grnd, runs well fresh: encouraging reapp.
4099} **ATHOLLBROSE** 219 [2] T D Easterby 3-8-4 (56) G Faulkner 25/1: 400-4: b g Mister Baileys -   5   **48**
Knightly Cut Up (Gold Crest) Rear, switched & hdwy 2f out, nrst fin: reapp: 5th in an AW mdn on first of 3 juv
starts (rtd 67a): April foal, cost 8,000gns: prob handles fibresand.
869   **SIR GALAHAD** 25 [1]3-8-3 (55) D Allan(2) 6/1: 6-005: Rear, imprvd halfway, no impress fnl 2f.   3½   **42**
4532} **SPRING BREEZE** 195 [5]3-8-4 (56) P Fessey 16/1: 04030-6: ch g Dr Fong - Trading Aces (Be My   2½   **39**
Chief) Chsd ldrs, wknd 2f out: reapp: plcd once in '03 (clmr, with M Channon, rtd 50): eff at 1m at fast grnd.
4351} **ROCK LOBSTER** 205 [4]3-9-7 (73) D McGaffin 12/1: 14-7: b c Desert Sun - Distant Music (Darshaan)   6   **47**
Chsd ldrs, wknd 3f out on reapp: jt top-weight: won first of 2 juv starts (AW mdn): eff at 1m, mid-dist bred:
runs well fresh, acts on fibresand: with J Given. 1 Sep'03 Sout 8af 75a- D:
1007 **SATSU** 12 [10]3-8-6 (58) N Callan 20/1: 005-08: Prom, led 4f out till 3f out, wknd.   4   **26**
959   **BOND MOONLIGHT** 14 [11]3-8-11 (63) F Lynch 5/1: 04-22329: Trkd ldrs, wknd bef 3f out: btr 959 (AW).   18   **6**
4886} **BARGAIN HUNT** 170 [8]3-8-2 (1ow)vis (53) D R McCabe 20/1: 606403-0: 10th: Led till 4f out, wknd.   12   **0**
841   **ARTISTICIMPRESSION** 29 [3]3-9-2 (68) P Hanagan 7/1: 06-00: 11th: Chsd ldrs, btn halfway, t.o.   8   **0**
4709} **BEAMSLEY BEACON** 182 [12]3-8-5 (57) Dale Gibson 40/1: 56200-0: 12th: Al bhd, t.o. on reapp.   16   **0**
12 Ran   Time 2m 16.85 (14.55)   Owned: Platinum Racing Club Limited   Trained: Leyburn

---

1145   **4.00 Easter Bunny Handicap Stakes 3yo+ 0-80 (D)**   **[79]**
           £9074 £2792 £1396   **6f str**   **Soft 122**   **+04 Fast**   Centre

1020 **GREY COSSACK** 11 [6] P T Midgley 7-9-10 (75) G Parkin 10/1: 10000-01: gr g Kasakov - Royal Rebeka   **80**
(Grey Desire) Held up, gd hdwy halfway, switched & strong run to lead cl-home, narrowly: gd time: won a h'cap for
I McInnes & a class stks for J Wainwright in '03: dual h'cap wnr in '02 (D Barker): eff btwn 5 & 7f on firm & soft
grnd, handles a gall trk: best without a visor & gd weight-carrier: back on a fair mark.
1 May'03 Donc 6gd 81-(79) D: 1 May'03 Beve 5gd 81-74 D: 2 Jul'02 Newc 7g/f 84-82 D: 1 Apr'02 Pont 6fm 86-79 C:
1 Apr'02 Newc 7sft 83-71 D: 2 Oct'01 York 6g/s 73- D: 1 Jul'01 Ayr 6g/s 68-63 D:
1032 **PAWAN** 10 [8] Miss A Stokell 4-8-7 (58) Ann Stokell 50/1: 4/202-522: Chsd ldrs, led dist, not   ½   **64**
pace to repel wnr cl-home: gd run for new trainer: acts on fast, soft & fibresand.
998   **LINCOLN DANCER** 12 [12] D Nicholls 7-9-11 (76) Alex Greaves 10/1: 000-0043: Chsd ldrs, hdwy to   nk   **81**
chall dist, ev ch till no extra cl-home: gd run on fav'd soft grnd, well h'capped: see 998.
967   **IF BY CHANCE** 14 [9] R Craggs 6-9-3 bl (68) T Eaves(5) 12/1: 0105-024: Prom, ev ch 2f out, not qckn.   3   **64**
834+ ***QUIET TIMES** 30 [7]5-9-2 bl (67) N Callan 11/2: 0-140415: Chsd ldrs, lost pl halfway, rallied late.   nk   **62**

4856} **QUANTICA** 173 [11]5-9-1 (66) Kim Tinkler 7/1: 000002-6: b g Sri Pekan - Touche A Tout (Royal 1½ 57
Academy) Chsd ldrs, onepace fnl 1f on reapp: rnr-up on fnl '03 start (h'cap): '02 h'cap wnr: eff at 5/6f: acts
on gd, likes gd/soft & hvy grnd: eff with/without a t-strap: slipped down weights.
2 Oct'03 Newc 5gd 65-64 E: 1 Aug'02 Wind 5g/s 80-72 E: 2 Jul'02 Beve 5g/s 73-71 E: 2 Jun'02 Ayr 5hvy 72-71 D:
1 Nov'01 York 5g/s 71-63 E: 1 Oct'01 Redc 6sft 69-56 E:

921 **ARTIE** 18 [2]5-9-11 (76) D Allan(3) 15/2: 20630-07: b g Whittingham - Calamanco (Clantime) Set 3½ 57
pace till dist, wknd: plcd several times in '03 (h'caps): '02 val h'cap wnr, also rnr-up several times: eff at 5/6f
on firm & soft grnd, prefers the former: handles any trk: likes to dominate, well h'capped nowadays.
2 Aug'03 Ripo 6g/f 83-83 C: 2 Oct'02 Donc 5sft 93-91 B: 2 Oct'02 Newm 5g/f 92-90 B: 2 Oct'02 York 6g/f 91-87 B:
1 Jun'02 York 6g/s 87-80 B: 2 Sep'01 Muss 5g/f 83-80 C: 1 May'01 Ches 5fm 84- D: 2 Mar'01 Donc 5hvy 79- E:

2253*}**PALACE THEATRE** 298 [13]3-9-0 (77) P Makin(7) 16/1: 1-8: b g Imperial Ballet - Luminary (Kalaglow) ¾ 55
Dwelt, chsd ldrs stands side, edged left & btn fnl 1f: reapp: won sole '03 start (mdn): E48,000 half-brother to a
1m wnr abroad: eff at 6f on fast: has run well fresh: been gelded: shld do better. 1 Jun'03 Ripo 6g/f 79- D:

1052* **BALAKIREF** 7 [16]5-8-8 (6ex) (59) T Hamilton(3) 5/1 FAV: 00000-19: Chsd ldrs stands side, btn over ½ 36
1f out: nicely bckd & 6lb pen, prob on the slowest grnd: see 1052.

921 **WINTHORPE** 18 [5]4-9-13 (78) Dale Gibson 66/1: 100-0000: 10th: In tch, outpcd halfway, rallied late. 3½ 45
4671} **UNDETERRED** 185 [15]8-9-12 (77) P Fessey 33/1: 124000-0: 11th: Rear stands side, mod late prog. ½ 43
967 **QUICKS THE WORD** 14 [14]4-9-2 (67) P Mulrennan(5) 50/1: 01600-00: 12th: Chsd ldrs 4f, sn btn. 3 24
967 **CERTA CITO** 14 [1]4-8-10 (61) A Mullen(7) 33/1: 1300-00: 13th: Prom 4f, wknd. nk 17
921 **BRANSTON TIGER** 18 [20]5-9-12 (77) P Hanagan 8/1: 0500-500: 14th: Chsd ldrs 4f stands side. ½ 32
556 **MAJIK** 67 [4]5-8-9 (60) R Ffrench 10/1: 313-0340: 15th: Al rear after 9 wk abs: see 419 (AW). 1 12
944 **Bond Playboy** 16 [3]4-9-7 (72) F Lynch 25/1:0 921 **Type One** 18 [18]6-9-13 (78) R Winston 50/1:0
976 **Jonny Ebeneezer** 13 [19]5-9-10 p(75) L Enstone(3) 33/1:0
4852} **Dizzy In The Head** 173 [17]5-9-4 (69) J D O'Reilly(7) 14/1:0
19 Ran   Time 1m 16.00 (7.10)   Owned: Mr Robert E Cook   Trained: Westow

---

1146 4.35 Go Racing In Yorkshire Median Auction Maiden Stakes 3yo (D)
 £3357 £1033 £517 51 str **Soft 122** -27 Slow Centre

1044 **CHEEKY CHI** 9 [7] P S McEntee 3-8-9 (66) R Winston 5/1: 4431: Trkd ldrs, short of room dist, 66
switched & strong run to lead cl-home, rdn out: turf bow: eff at 5/7f on polytrack & soft grnd: see 1044.

995 **MR WOLF** 12 [5] D W Barker 3-9-0 (62) L Enstone(3) 4/1: 04500-22: Prom, led 1.5f out till ins fnl nk 68
1f, kept on & only just btn: acts on firm & soft grnd: deserves a small race, see 995.

3174} **BOND SHAKIRA** 261 [2] B Smart 3-8-9 (—) F Lynch 7/1: 5-3: ch f Daggers Drawn - Cinnamon Lady 3½ 53
(Emarati) Chsd ldrs, wandered dist, not qckn fnl 1f on reapp: last of 5 in a mdn auct on sole juv start: 44,000gns
Feb foal: half-sister to wnrs over sprint trips & 1m: handles soft grnd, success shld suit.

3924} **FISHLAKE FLYER** 229 [6] J G Given 3-8-9 VIS (71) P Hanagan 5/2 FAV: 220432-4: b f Desert Style - 1¼ 49
Millitrix (Doyoun) Prom, ev ch halfway, onepace fnl 1f: well bckd on reapp & in first time visor: plcd on 5 of 7
'03 starts (mdns): eff at 5f on firm & soft grnd, runs well fresh: has ability but often finds one too good.
2 Aug'03 Catt 5g/f 65-(74) F: 2 May'03 Ling 5sft 72- F: 2 Apr'03 Warw 5fm 76- E: 2 Mar'03 Donc 5gd 76- E:

4917} **SCOOBY DOOBY DO** 167 [9]3-8-9 V Halliday 12/1: 60-5: b f Atraf - Redgrave Design (Nebbiolo) 2 43
Dwelt, some late hdwy, nvr dngrs on reapp/h'cap qual run: twice rcd in '03, mdn 6th on debut (rtd 60): related to
several wnrs, incl a useful sprinter: with R Whitaker & shld do btr over further in h'caps.

4994} **TAPLEON** 160 [4]3-8-9 T Eaves(5) 66/1: 000-6: Slowly away, al bhd on reapp. 3 34
4693} **AGUILERA** 183 [3]3-8-9 R Ffrench 14/1: 00-7: Speed till halfway on reapp. 3½ 24
995 **LADY SUNSET** 12 [8]3-8-9 (62) N Callan 9/1: 05200-08: Led till dist, wknd. ½ 23
3609} **QUEENS SQUARE** 242 [1]3-8-9 (50) Kim Tinkler 9/1: 344200-9: Hmpd start, al bhd & fin last. hd 23
9 Ran   Time 1m 03.99 (7.49)   Owned: Mrs R L McEntee   Trained: Newmarket

---

1147 5.10 Redcarracing Co Uk Handicap Stakes 3yo 46-55 (F) [64]
 £3474 £1069 £535 1m str **Soft 122** -51 Slow Centre

1007 **PERFECT BALANCE** 12 [5] N Tinkler 3-9-5 (55) Kim Tinkler 33/1: 300-01: b g Shinko Forest - Tumble 63
(Mtoto) Mid-div, hdwy 2f out, forged ahd cl-home, drvn out: slow time: plcd on 1st of 3 juv starts (mdn auct, rtd
64): 21,000gns half-brother to a 7f juv wnr: eff at 1m on gd/soft & soft: open to more improvement.

658 **BISCAR TWO** 55 [1] R M Whitaker 3-8-10 (1oh) (45) V Halliday 25/1: 000-462: Slowly away, hdwy from 1½ 50
rear 2f out, ev ch ins fnl 1f, not btn far: 8 wk abs: eff over a gall 1m on soft: runs well fresh, see 490 (AW).

923 **ACE COMING** 18 [14] D Eddy 3-9-5 bl (55) P Mulrennan(5) 12/1: 42000-03: b g First Trump - Tarry 1¼ 56
(Salse) Prom, switched stands side & led 2f out, collared well ins fnl 1f, no extra: rnr-up in a sell & clmr for
Mrs L Stubbs in '03, subs jnd current stable & mdn rnr-up in 1st time blnks: eff at 7f/1m on gd & soft, has run well
fresh: wears blnks. 2 Jul'03 Redc 7gd 65- D: 2 May'03 Newc 6g/s 69- F: 2 Mar'03 Donc 5gd 72- F:

4443} **PAY ATTENTION** 200 [7] T D Easterby 3-9-2 (52) D Allan(3) 16/1: 065300-4: b f Revoque - Catch Me ½ 52
(Rudimentary) Hmpd start, hdwy to chall over 1f out, not qckn ins fnl 1f on reapp: plcd in a nov auct in '03 (rtd
62): eff at 7f/1m on firm & soft grnd: fair reapp.

925 **DALIDA** 17 [3]3-9-2 (52) G Faulkner 9/1: 00-U55: Trkd ldrs, ev ch 2f out till ins fnl 1f, wknd: clr rem. 3 46
164 **SALUT SAINT CLOUD** 126 [6]3-9-0 vis (50) Darren Williams 40/1: 000005-6: Prom 6f, grad wknd: 6 32
reapp & has been gelded.
4132} **PLAUSABELLE** 216 [16]3-9-1 (51) A Mullen(7) 50/1: 006-7: Chsd ldrs stands side, lost place 5 23
halfway, rallied late on reapp.
4312} **TANCRED IMP** 207 [13]3-8-10 (1oh) (45) T Eaves(5) 33/1: 003-8: Prom 6.5f, wknd on reapp. 1 16
4851} **TIZ WIZ** 173 [12]3-8-10 (46) D R McCabe 50/1: 060-9: Led till 2f out, wknd on reapp. 1¾ 12
1051 **POACHERS PARADISE** 7 [9]3-8-10 (1oh) (45) Dale Gibson 11/1: 000-0060: 10th: Chsd ldrs 5f, sn wknd. nk 11
4307} **HOLLY WALK** 207 [8]3-9-0 (50) L Enstone(3) 16/1: 0004-0: 11th: Nvr btr than mid-div: new stable. 2½ 10
1051 **MYANNABANANA** 7 [4]3-9-5 p (55) R Winston 11/1: 5344050: 12th: Chsd ldrs 6f, wknd: see 645. nk 14
495 **REEDSMAN** 75 [10]3-9-3 P (53) N Callan 9/1: 000000-20: 13th: Al bhd: 11 wk abs, tried cheek 5 2
pieces, tchd 16/1: prev with M Tompkins, now with R Guest: btr 495 (AW, 6f).
656* **POKER** 55 [2]3-9-5 (55) P Hanagan 6/4 FAV: 060-10: 14th: Trkd ldrs, ev ch 2f out, sn wknd & 2 0
eased: hvly bckd, 8 wk abs: much btr clearly expected, not handle this soft grnd? see 656 (fibresand).
4635} **SAROS** 188 [15]3-9-3 (53) F Lynch 33/1: 00606-0: 15th: Mid-div, btn halfway, t.o.: reapp, op 13/2. 13 0
4787} **DELTA LADY** 178 [11]3-8-10 (46) R Ffrench 33/1: 342600-0: 16th: Mid-div, btn halfway, t.o.: new yard. 7 0
16 Ran   Time 1m 48.67(13.87)   Owned: Alec & Pat Findlay   Trained: Malton

Official Going Good/Soft 62

1148

1.45 Giles Fox At Newmarket Racecourse Maiden Stakes 3yo   (D)
£5473 £1684 £842   **1m2f**   **Good 62**   **+06 Fast**   Far Side

ECOMIUM 0 [8] J Noseda 3-9-0   E Ahern 7/1: 1: b c Sadler's Wells - Encens (Common Grounds) Trkd   **95+**
ldrs & led over 1f out, rdn clr, readily: debut: brother to a useful mid-dist performer: eff at 10f, 12f sure to
suit: acts on gd/sft & a stiff trk: goes well fresh: impressive debut in a gd time, one to follow in Listed/Gr 3 class.
4772} **BUCKEYE WONDER 179** [5] M A Jarvis 3-9-0   P Robinson 7/1: 24-2: b c Silver Hawk - Ameriflora   5   **85**
(Danzig) Chsd ldr & led over 2f out, hdd over 1f out, kept on but not pace of wnr: reapp: mdn rnr-up on first of
just 2 '03 starts: full brother to a top-class mid-dist performer abroad: apprec step up to 10f, 12f will suit:
acts on fast & gd grnd: useful colt, sure to find similar. 2 Oct'03 Newm 8g/f 87- D:
PARLIAMENT SQUARE 0 [10] D R Loder 3-9-0   J Murtagh 13/8 FAV: 3: b c Sadler's Wells - Groom   1½   **83**
Order (Groom Dancer) Held up, rdn & styd on fnl 2f, not pace of wnr: hvly bckd on debut: cost 600,000gns: eff over
10f, 12f will suit: acts on gd/soft: plenty to like about this debut, can win similar sn.
5016} **GIRONDE 159** [6] Sir Michael Stoute 3-9-0   K Fallon 10/1: 5-4: b c Sadler's Wells - Sarah   3   **79**
Georgina (Persian Bold) Dwelt & hld up, eff 2f out, onepace: op 8/1: reapp: unplcd sole '03 start (mdn, rtd 66):
mid-dist pedigree (Derby entry): expected to relish 10f+ this term, open to improvement.
4868} **COMING AGAIN 172** [2]3-9-0   M Hills 3/1: 2-5: In tch, rdn/hung left & no impress over 1f out: bckd.   1¾   **77**
4480} **SHARAAB 199** [11]3-9-0   R Hills 14/1: 30-6: Led 7f, no extra fnl 2f: reapp, likely improver in h'caps.   4   **71**
1019   **MOONSHAFT 12** [7]3-9-0   S Drowne 100/1: 07: In tch, btn 2f out.   3½   **66**
4869} **DISTANT CONNECTION 172** [3]3-9-0   (75) D Holland 33/1: 04503-8: Al bhd, reapp.   ½   **65**
NIETZSCHE 0 [4]3-9-0   R Hughes 33/1: 9: Chsd ldrs till over 1f out on debut, stablemate of wnr.   3   **61**
4076} **YOUNG PATRIARCH 221** [9]3-9-0   L Keniry(3) 50/1: 44-0: 10th: Dwelt & held up, left bhd fnl 2f, reapp.   3½   **56**
1021   **TRIFTI 11** [1]3-9-0   S Sanders 66/1: 40: 11th: Keen & held up, struggling 3f out: see 1021.   20   **26**
11 Ran   Time 2m 07.70 (5.6)   Owned: Fieldspring Racing   Trained: Newmarket

1149

2.20 Federation Of Bloodstock Agents Conditions Stakes 2yo   (C)
£7186 £2726 £1363   **5f str**   **Good/Soft 62**   **-29 Slow**   Far Side

1053* **CORNUS 8** [8] R Hannon 2-9-2   R Hughes 11/10 FAV: 11: Trkd ldr & led over 1f out, asserted under   **98+**
hands & heels ins last, eased cl-home: eff over a stiff/sharp 5f on gd/soft: useful, win again.
954* **DARIO GEE GEE 17** [7] K A Ryan 2-9-2   N Callan 7/2: 12: Dwelt, sn trkd ldrs, rdn & styd on,   hd   **92**
flattered by margin of defeat: acts on gd & gd/soft grnd: useful, win again: see 954.
920* **NEXT TIME AROUND 19** [5] Mrs L Stubbs 2-9-4   R Winston 4/1: 13: Led 3f, hung left/no extra dist: 1¾   **89**
well bckd: acts on gd & gd/soft: prob ran to form of 920 (Brocklesby).
1084   **GOGETTER GIRL 6** [3] J Gallagher 2-8-7   T E Durcan 16/1: 624: Chsd ldrs, not pace to chall fnl   ½   **76**
1f: qck reapp: acts on gd/soft & soft grnd: shld find a race on the minor trks: see 1084.
954   **CAMPEON 17** [2]2-8-12   K Fallon 12/1: 05: b c Monashee Mountain - Arctic Lead (Arctic Tern) Chsd   1¼   **77$**
ldrs & pushed along halfway, no danger: Feb foal, half-brother to a 7f juv wnr: imprvd from debut on gd/soft.
931* **KING AFTER 18** [1]2-9-2   N Pollard 16/1: 16: Trkd ldrs, outpcd over 1f out: turf bow: see 931 (polytrack).   2   **75**
1071   **COMINTRUE 7** [6]2-8-7   J Quinn 66/1: 07: ch f Namid - Gute (Petardia) Keen & prom, no extra over   4   **54**
1f out: cheaply bght Feb foal: dam a 5f juv wnr: highly tried after intro.
OUR CHOICE 0 [4]2-8-9   D Holland 25/1: 8: b c Indian Danehill - Spring Daffodil (Pharly) Sn   3   **47**
struggling & outpcd on debut: 28,000gns March foal, half-brother to a useful 1m/10f wnr, dam plcd at 7f as a juv:
subs smart 7f/1m wnr: drop to mdn company likely to suit.
8 Ran   Time 1m 02.77 (4.57)   Owned: Mr David Mort   Trained: Marlborough

1150

2.55 David Oldrey Conditions Stakes 3yo   (C)
£8503 £3225 £1613   **7f str**   **Good/Soft 62**   **-15 Slow**   Far Side

4089} **IQTE SAAB 220** [4] J L Dunlop 3-9-1   R Hills 5/4 FAV: 12-1: b c Bahri - Shuhrah (Danzig) Trkd   **106+**
ldrs racing keenly, short of room over 2f out, qcknd to lead ins last, readily asserted: hvly bckd: mdn wnr & stks
rnr-up in '03: eff at 6/7f, 1m shld suit (dam 1m wnr): acts on fast & gd/sft, stiff or easy trk: goes v well fresh: v
useful & has a turn of foot, looks up to Group class. 2 Sep'03 Kemp 7g/f 92- C: 1 Aug'03 Sali 6g/f 92- D:
885   **GLARAMARA 24** [3] A Bailey 3-9-1   (94) K Fallon 16/1: 013-02: b c Nicolotte - Digamist Girl   3   **98**
(Digamist) Held up, hdwy to chall dist, not pace of wnr: lightly rcd '03, landed a mdn: eff at 6/7f on firm &
gd/soft grnd, stiff/gall trk: best without blnks: useful colt, shld win more races. 1 Aug'03 York 6.0fm 93- D:
4470} **ITHACA 199** [1] H R A Cecil 3-8-10   (102) R Hughes 7/2: 120-3: ch f Distant View - Reams of Verse   1¼   **90**
(Nureyev) In tch, kept on onepace: bckd on reapp: mdn scorer '03, stks Gr 3 rnr-up & Gr 1 unplcd (rtd 100): eff
at 7f, 1m shld suit this term: acts on fast & gd/soft grnd, sharp or stiff/undul trk: can go well fresh: useful,
type to improve at 1m. 2 Aug'03 Good 7g/f 96- A: 1 Jul'03 Good 7gd 94- D:
949   **MAKFOOL 17** [7] M R Channon 3-9-1   (95) T E Durcan 14/1: 1243-034: Led 4f, no extra dist: see 949.   ½   **94**
953* **LOCAL POET 17** [6]3-9-1   (98) G Gibbons 10/1: 6224-15: Keen & dsptd lead till led over 1f out, hdd   1   **92**
ins last & wknd: up in grade after 953 (6f, mdn, gd).
4911*}**TWO STEP KID 169** [5]3-9-1   E Ahern 7/2: 1-6: ch c Gone West - Marsha's Dancer (Northern Dancer)   1¼   **89**
Led/dsptd lead, went on over 2f out till over 1f out, no extra: reapp: turf bow: impressive sole start wnr in '03
(AW mdn, fast time): dam raced US mdn, sire top-class 1m/9f dirt performer: eff at 6f, shld get 7f/1m: acts on
polytrack & a sharp trk: can force the pace & go well fresh: may impr on this on a faster surface.
1 Oct'03 Ling 6ap 96a- D:
949   **WELL KNIT 17** [2]3-8-6   J F Egan 150/1: 120-0007: Chsd ldrs, btn 2f out: highly tried.   16   **50**
7 Ran   Time 1m 28.58 (5.38)   Owned: Mr Hamdan Al Maktoum   Trained: Arundel

1151   3.25 Grantchester Rated Stakes Handicap 4yo+ 0-105 (B)   [109]
£12441 £4719 £2360   **7f str**   Good/Soft 62   -05 Slow   Far Side

928   **THIHN 18** [12] J L Spearing 9-8-9 (90) A Daly 8/1: 06011-01: Hld up far side, strong run to lead   **97**
ins last, drvn out: stays 10f, suited by 7f/1m on fm or hvy, any trk: loves to come late in a big field: tough.
1035   **CHAPPEL CRESENT 10** [3] D Nicholls 4-8-4   (85) A Nicholls 25/1: 40-00052: Led stands side, rdn &   ½   **90**
styd on well, not pace of wnr far side cl-home: fine run, first home from smaller stands side group: win similar.
928   **MARSHMAN 18** [4] M H Tompkins 5-8-8   (89) P Robinson 14/1: 01534-03: ch g College Chapel - Gold   nk   **93**
Fly (Be My Guest) Chsd ldr stands side, ch over 1f out, kept on well for press: h'cap scorer '03, AW h'cap rnr-up:
turf h'cap & AW h'cap wnr '02: eff at 6f, suited by 7f on fast, soft & polytrack, prob any trk: can go well fresh:
tough & genuine, fine return. 1 Oct'03 Muss 7.1gd 89-82 C: 2 Feb'03 Ling 7ap 89a-86 C: 1 Nov'02 Ling 7ap 88a-81 C:
1 Jul'02 Hayd 6gd 83-78 C: 1 Oct'01 York 6g/s 81-75 C: 2 Jun'01 Beve 5g/f 80- D: 1 May'01 Hami 5g/f 72- E:
4217} **GREENSLADES 213** [10] P J Makin 5-8-8   (89) S Sanders 12/1: 11/0105-4: ch c Perugino - Woodfield   shd   **93**
Rose (Scottish Reel) Al prom far side & led over 2f out till ins last, kept on: bckd, reapp: lightly rcd '03,
h'cap scorer: auct mdn & h'cap wnr '02 (again lightly rcd): all wins at 6f, stays a stiff 7f & has tried 1m: acts
on fm & soft grnd, stiff or sharp trks: goes well fresh: v encouraging return.
1 Aug'03 Wind 6g/f 90-85 C: 1 Sep'02 Asco 6g/f 88-80 B: 1 Aug'02 Ayr 6sft 83- E: 2 Apr'02 Newm 6fm 83- D:
945   **CAMBERLEY 17** [13]7-8-11 (92) K Fallon 6/1 FAV: 20132-25: Held up far side, rdn & hdwy to chall   1   **94**
dist, onepace ins last: hvly bckd: remains in gd form, Goodwood specialist: see 945.
5030} **FLYING EXPRESS 157** [11]4-8-6 (87) M Hills 8/1: 1/60644-6: ch c Air Express - Royal Loft (Homing)   1¼   **86**
Mid-div far side, styd on onepace for press: reapp: lightly rcd & plcd fnl '03 start (appr h'cap, rtd 89): '02
auct mdn & stks wnr: eff at 6f, stays gall 7f well: acts on firm & gd grnd, likes to force the pace: prob handles
any trk. 1 Aug'02 Ches 6fm 97- C: 1 Aug'02 Ripo 6fm 90- E: 2 Jul'02 Good 6fm 81- D:
1035   **TOUGH LOVE 10** [9]5-8-8 (89) W Supple 16/1: 1330-007: Held up far side, prog when short of room   ½   **87+**
over 1f out, not able to chall: eff at 7f, 1m prob ideal: coming to hand, spot on at 1m on fast.
4555} **MANAAR 194** [15]4-8-5 (86) E Ahern 20/1: 312200-8: b g Titus Livius - Zurarah (Siberian Express)   nk   **83**
Handy far side till lost place 2f out, kept on late: reapp: auct mdn scorer '03, subs thrice rnr-up: eff at 5/6f,
prob stays 7f: acts on fast & firm grnd, stiff/undul or easy trk: can go well fresh: useful, been gelded.
2 Sep'03 Yarm 6.0g/f 88-(80) C: 2 Sep'03 Leic 5.0g/f 92-(80) C: 2 Aug'03 Newc 6g/f 82-(80) D: 1 Jul'03 Leic 5.0fm 82-(80)
2 Aug'02 Newc 6gd 82- F: 2 Jul'02 Newm 6gd 82- D:
4271*\MISS IVANHOE 179** [6]4-9-7 (102) D Holland 8/1: 422612-9: b f Selkirk - Robellino Miss   ½   **98**
(Robellino) Held up far side, nvr able to chall: reapp under top-weight: mdn & List scorer '03: eff at 7f/1m on
firm & soft grnd, latter reportedly suits best: loves a stiff/gall trk, can go well fresh: useful.
1 Sep'03 Mais 7sft 111- : 2 Jul'03 Asco 8gd 104-(101) A: 2 Jul'03 Sand 8.1g/f 106-(93) A: 1 Apr'03 Nott 8.2gd 90- D:
4778} **CALCUTTA 179** [19]8-9-5 (100) R Hills 25/1: 531314-0: 10th: Chsd ldrs far side, no prog dist on reapp.   ¾   **95**
4778} **HURRICANE FLOYD 179** [20]6-8-9 (1ow) (89) J Murtagh 10/1: 034003-0: 11th: Prom, outpcd fnl 1f.   ½   **84**
922   **AUDIENCE 19** [16]4-9-4 (99) T Quinn 25/1: 00226-00: 12th: Chsd ldrs far side till over 1f out.   nk   **92**
879   **DAWN PIPER 25** [18]4-8-4 (1oh)vis (84) D R McCabe 14/1: 32-1020: 13th: Chsd ldr far side & led   shd   **78**
over 4f out till over 2f out, wknd: see 879, 401 (AW).
4436} **ST PANCRAS 201** [7]4-9-0 (95) W Ryan 40/1: 42/5456-0: 14th: Pushed along stands side, nvr on terms.   nk   **87**
4950} **ROYAL STORM 166** [17]5-9-0 (95) R Hughes 12/1: 532126-0: 15th: Led far side, hdd 4f out & sn btn.   nk   **86**
3982} **TEDSTALE 227** [8]6-8-4 (85) J Quinn 33/1: 022604-0: 16th: Held up far side, nvr a factor on reapp.   shd   **76**
1035   **Fantasy Believer 10** [5]6-8-13 (94) K Darley 25/1:0   887   **Arctic Desert 24** [2]4-8-9 (90) Martin Dwyer 20/1:0
945   **Master Robbie 17** [1]5-8-13 (94) S Hitchcott(3) 25/1:0
4897} **Secret Formula 171** [14]4-8-4 (3oh)(82) Lisa Jones(3) 50/1:0
20 Ran   Time 1m 27.87 (4.67)   Owned: The Square Milers   Trained: Kinnersley

1152   4.00 Alex Scott Maiden Stakes Colts & Geldings 3yo (D)
£5473 £1684 £842   **7f str**   Good/Soft 62   -26 Slow   Far Side

DAVORIN 0** [6] D R Loder 3-8-11   J Murtagh 4/1: 1: br c Warning - Arvola (Sadler's Wells) Trkd   **81+**
ldrs, rdn hway & styd on for press to lead cl home: bckd: brother to top-class 6/7f performer Diktat, dam a 1m wnr &
half-sister to smart miler Cape Cross: eff at 7f, 1m sure to suit: acts on gd/soft & a stiff/gall trk: goes well
fresh: well bred colt who will learn plenty from this & improve.
925   **MISSION MAN 18** [2] R Hannon 3-8-11   (82) Dane O'Neill 9/2: 024-42: Trkd ldrs, rdn & led over 1f   hd   **80**
out, edged right & hdd well ins last: nicely bckd, left disapp reapp bhd: eff at 7f/1m on gd & gd/soft grnd: sure
to find a race on this evidence: see 925.
5022} **MOORS MYTH 158** [4] B W Hills 3-8-11   R Hughes 20/1: 0-3: b c Anabaa - West Devon (Gone West)   nk   **79**
Chsd ldrs, rdn to chall dist, just held cl-home: reapp: caught the eye when only mid-div sole '03 mdn start (rtd
67+): eff at 7f, 1m shld suit: acts on gd/soft grnd, stiff/gall trk, likely prob autumn, win races.
4971} **STAR PUPIL 164** [11] A M Balding 3-8-11   Martin Dwyer 8/1: 02-4: ch c Selkirk - Lochangel (Night   nk   **78**
Shift) Chsd ldrs & rdn/led 2f out till over 1f out, kept on well: btn less than 1L in a tight fin, reapp: rnr-up
2nd of just 2 '03 starts (mdn, C/D): eff at 7f, 1m willd suit: acts on gd & gd/soft grnd, stiff/gall trk.
2 Nov'03 Newm 7g/f 78- D:
MARSH ORCHID 0** [3]3-8-11 M Tebbutt 66/1: 5: b g Lahib - Majalis (Mujadil) Held up, outpcd 2f   2   **74**
out, kept on: dam a 5f wnr who styd 1m: eff over a stiff 7f on gd/soft grnd: not btn far, an encouraging intro.
3029} **GOLD MASK 269** [7]3-8-11   D Holland 4/1: 0-6: Led 5f, no extra ins last: reapp, bckd.   2½   **69**
IMTALKINGGIBBERISH 0 [5]3-8-11   S W Kelly 66/1: 7: Dwelt, sn handy till over 1f out, debut.   ¾   **68**
SUBMISSIVE 0 [10]3-8-11   R Hills 33/1: 8: Held up, outpcd fnl 3f on debut.   3   **62**
BLAKE HALL LAD 0 [12]3-8-11   B Reilly(3) 66/1: 9: Struggling from halfway on debut.   shd   **62**
2079} **SCIENTIST 306** [9]3-8-11   K Fallon 11/4 FAV: 65-0: 10th: Chsd ldrs, btn 2f out: hvly bckd on reapp.   shd   **61**
GUSTAVO 0 [8]3-8-11   M Hills 33/1: 0: 11th: Dwelt, sn outpcd & nvr a factor on debut.   nk   **60**
656   **UNPRECEDENTED 56** [1]3-8-11   S Drowne 100/1: 600-00: 12th: Held up & bhd from halfway, abs.   2   **56**
12 Ran   Time 1m 29.37 (6.17)   Owned: Sheikh Mohammed   Trained: Newmarket

---

1153 **4.35 Warren Hill Maiden Stakes 3yo** **(D)**
£5317 £1636 £818 **1m4f** **Good/Soft 62** **-32 Slow** Far Side

4942} **PERCUSSIONIST 167** [8] J H M Gosden 3-9-0 K Darley 4/6 FAV: 32-1: b c Sadler's Wells - **86**
Magnificient Style (Silver Hawk) Chsd ldrs, rdn over 3f out, hdwy to lead ins last, styd on strongly: hvly bckd at
odds-on, reapp: mdn rnr-up on 2nd of just 2 '03 starts: apprec step up to 12f, shaped as a thorough stayer: acts on
fast & soft grnd, stiff/gall or easy trk: goes well fresh: useful colt, more to come, esp over further.
2 Oct'03 Yarm 8.0sft 83- D:
4409} **CHAPLIN 203** [3] B W Hills 3-9-0 R Hughes 12/1: 0-2: b c Groom Dancer - Princess Borghese 1½ **83**
(Nijinsky) Held up, hdwy from halfway & led over 1f out, hdd ins last & not pace of wnr: rest well covered on
reapp: well held sole '03 mdn start (rtd 64): apprec step up to 12f, could get further: acts on gd/soft grnd,
stiff/gall trk: sharper for this, win sn.
886 **VANTAGE 24** [6] N P Littmoden 3-9-0 (80) D Holland 5/1: 0330-223: Led till over 1f out, no extra: 4 **77**
turf return, not quite convince over this longer 12f trip: see 886, 817.
1030 **BORDER SAINT 11** [2] M L W Bell 3-9-0 I Mongan 33/1: 304: Held up, switched for eff 2f out, hd **76**
onepace: turf debut: improved run: see 873.
  DALLOOL 0 [5]3-9-0 P Robinson 14/1: 5: b c Unfuwain - Sardonic (Kris) Chsd ldrs, outpcd fnl 2f ½ **75**
on debut: dam a 10f List wnr: mid-dists look sure to suit, gave encouragement.
1055 **SPRINGTIME ROMANCE 8** [7]3-8-9 J Murtagh 13/2: 36: Chsd ldrs, hung left & btn over 1f out. 4 **64**
4906} **TURN N BURN 169** [4]3-9-0 K Fallon 14/1: 53-7: Keen & trk ldr, rdn & wknd fnl 2f: reapp. 11 **53**
930 **INCHCONNEL 18** [1]3-9-0 bl (60) M Tebbutt 50/1: 030-08: Held up, left bhd fnl 5f, longer trip. 24 **20**
8 Ran Time 2m 40.11 (11.31) Owned: Exors of the late Mr R E Sangster Trained: Manton

---

1154 **5.10 Exning Stakes Handicap 3yo 0-100** **(C)** [107]
£9666 £2974 £1487 **6f str** **Good/Soft 62** **+02 Fast** Far Side

4801} **SARISTAR 178** [15] P F I Cole 3-8-1 (80) J Quinn 25/1: 51010-1: b f Starborough - Sari (Faustus) **86**
Trkd ldrs, hdwy 2f out, drvn to lead line: reapp, fair time: lightly rcd '03, fills mdn & AW nov stks scorer: eff
at 5/6f on fast, gd/soft & fibresand, stiff/undul or sharpish trk: goes v well fresh: lightly rcd & progressive
filly. 1 Oct'03 Sout 5af 85a-(84) D: 1 Aug'03 Chep 5.1g/f 82- F:
4669} **DANZIG RIVER 186** [18] B W Hills 3-9-0 (93) K May(7) 20/1: 046115-2: b c Green Desert - Sahara hd **97**
Breeze (Ela Mana Mou) Chsd ldrs & led over 1f out, hdd line: reapp: dual nursery h'cap wnr '03: eff at 5.7f/6f: acts
on fm & gd/soft, likes a stiff/gall trk: fine return, useful & progressive.
1 Oct'03 Newm 6g/f 86-83 B: 1 Sep'03 Bath 5.7fm 86-73 E:
1116* **PETARDIAS MAGIC 3** [11] E J O'Neill 3-8-5 (7ex) (84) E Ahern 4/1: 3016-413: Held up racing keenly, ¾ **86**
styd on for press ins last, not pace of front pair: well bckd under a pen: qck reapp: prog, see 1116.
4315} **MOSS VALE 208** [2] B W Hills 3-9-7 (100) M Hills 11/1: 5163-4: b c Shinko Forest - Wolf Cleugh 2 **96**
(Last Tycoon) Held up, went right start, styd on for press fnl 2f, not able to chall: reapp, stablemate of rnr-up:
lightly rcd '03, mdn scorer, subs List plcd (rtd 98): eff at 5/6f on fast & gd/soft grnd, sharp or stiff/undul trk:
encouraging return under top-weight: useful & shld win more races. 1 Aug'03 Wind 6gd 92- D:
4413} **MOLCON 203** [19]3-7-13 (78) D Fox(5) 12/1: 61150-5: b g Danetime - Wicken Wonder (Distant ½ **72**
Relative) Led/dsptd lead till over 2f out, hdd over 1f out & no extra: reapp: seller & nursery h'cap wnr
'03: stays a stiff 6f, both wins over a stiff 5f, return to that trip may suit: acts on firm & gd/soft grnd: been
gelded, sharper for this. 1 Aug'03 Newm 5g/f 79-72 C: 1 Aug'03 Bath 5.0fm 69- G:
4773} **BENTLEYS BALL 179** [10]3-8-13 (92) R Hughes 8/1: 311432-6: Slow away & held up, kept on: gelded. 3½ **76**
818 **SHIELALIGH 36** [9]3-8-5 (1ow)T (83) M Fenton 33/1: 1243-07: Chsd ldrs, btn dist: gelded. 1 **65**
4833} **COMPTONS ELEVEN 175** [13]3-8-11 (90) T E Durcan 25/1: 110033-8: Chsd ldrs 4f, sn wknd, reapp. 1 **68**
4833} **CONVINCE 175** [7]3-9-1 (94) S Drowne 25/1: 32104-9: Held up, short of room over 1f out, only mod 1¾ **67**
prog on reapp: gelded.
914* **PERUVIAN STYLE 20** [17]3-8-2 (81) Martin Dwyer 10/1: 2401-110: 10th: Led 3f, sn btn: btr 914 & 818. nk **53**
4442*}**GRANATO 201** [3]3-8-8 (87) K Fallon 11/4 FAV: 221-0: 11th: Hmpd start, chsd ldrs till over 1f out: bckd. shd **59**
4952} **Wyatt Earp 165** [5]3-7-12 (77) Lisa Jones(3) 25/1:0
975* **Ask The Clerk 14** [1]3-7-12 (6oh)(71) B Swarbrick(7) 25/1:0
818 **Tag Team 36** [16]3-7-12 (77) C Catlin 20/1:0 3939} **Dolce Piccata 229** [8]3-8-13 (92) T Quinn 16/1:0
1011 **Multiple Choice 13** [12]3-8-0 (79) J Bramhill 33/1:0 3034} **Mac The Knife 269** [4]3-8-7 (86) P Dobbs 33/1:0
4233} **Whos Winning 211** [14]3-7-12 (2oh)(75) J Mackay 50/1:0
914 **Dellagio 20** [6]3-8-3 (82) T P Queally(2) 50/1:0
19 Ran Time 1m 14.38(3.58) Owned: Mr R A Instone Trained: Whatcombe

---

Official Going HOLDING.

1155 **1.20 Listed 3YO Prix Djebel (Colts & Geldings)** **(A)**
£15845 £6338 £4754 **7f str** **Soft**

4571} **WHIPPER 186** Robert Collet 3-9-2 C Soumillon 3/10 FAV: 5341141-11: b c Miesque's Son - Myth To **116+**
Reality (Sadler's Wells) Cl up, led dist, sn pushed clr, val 12L+: reapp: v smart juv, won a Gr1 & Gr2 in native
France, also cl 4th in Gr1 Middle Park: eff, apprec step up to 7f: handles firm, likes soft grnd: goes well
fresh: v impressive today, heads for 2000 Guineas & sound claims if the grnd rides soft.
1 Sun'31 Deau 6fsft 114- A:
  RED MO Mme C Head-Maarek 3-9-2 O Peslier : 2: b c Red Ransom - Moiava (Bering) No chance 8 **95**
with easy wnr.
4835} **ALWAYS KING 175** J-C Rouget 3-9-2 I Mendizabal : 11123133: b c Desert King - Always On Time 4 **87**
(Lead On Time) Nvr able to live with wnr.
6 Ran Time 1m 28.8 () Owned: R C Strauss Trained: France

MAISONS LAFFITTE   TUESDAY 06.04.04   Righthand, Sharpish Track

1156   1.50 Listed 3YO Prix Imprudence (Fillies)   (A)
£15845   £6338   £4754   **7f str**   **Soft**

ONDA NOVA D Sepulchre 3-9-0   S Pasquier 5.3/1: 11: b f Keos - Northern Trick (D Sepulchre) In   **111**+
tch, styd on to lead ins fnl 1f, pushed out, val 3L+: eff at 7f, 1m will suit: acts on soft grnd & a sharpish trk:
won well & now reportedly heads for French 1000 Guineas.
    DOLMA N Clement 3-9-0   C-P Lemaire : 2: b f Marchand de Sabie - Young Manila (Manil) Not   2   **105**
disgraced, met a potentially smart rival.
4086} **PETIT CALVA** 213 R Gibson 3-9-0   T Jarnet : 164153: b f Desert King - Jimkana (Double Bed) Fair run.   2½   **100**
7 Ran   Time 1m 32.8()   Owned: Niarchos Family   Trained: France

SAINT CLOUD   FRIDAY 09.04.04   Lefthand, Galloping Track

Official Going GOOD/SOFT.

1157   1.50 Gr 3 3YO Prix Penelope (Fillies)   (A)
£25704   £10282   £7711   **1m2f110y**   **Good/Soft**

ASK FOR THE MOON J-C Rouget 3-9-0   I Mendizabal 1/2 JT FAV: 221-111: b f Dr Fong - Lune Rouge   **116**
(Unfuwain) In tch, styd on to lead dist, pushed out, val 5L+: earlier won here at St-Cloud: eff at 10.5f, further
shld suit: acts on gd/sft grnd & a gall trk: improving & smart, deserves her place in the French Oaks.
    SUPER LINA Y de Nicolay 3-9-0   C Soumillon 1/2 JT FAV: 21-22: gr f Linamix - Supergirl   2   **108**
(Woodman) Prom, outpcd 2f out, rallied for 2nd, but no ch with wnr: eff at 10f on gd/soft: useful.
    MISS FRANCE E Lellouche 3-9-0   D Boeuf 44/10: 1-33: ch f Sabrehill - Tonic Stream (Bering)   nk   **107**
Bhd, prog wide 2f out, no extra well ins fnl 1f: eff at 10f on gd/soft: useful.
6 Ran   Time 2m 17.2()   Owned: J-P Dubois   Trained: France

LONGCHAMP   SUNDAY 11.04.04   Righthand, Stiff, Galloping Track

Official Going SOFT.

1158   2.45 Gr 2 3YO Prix Noailles (Colts & Fillies)   (A)
£42148   £16268   £7764   **1m3f**   **Soft**

9*} **VOIX DU NORD** 155 D Smaga 3-9-2   C Soumilion 6/5 JT FAV: 212421-1: b c Valanour - Dame Edith   **115**+
(Top Ville) In tch, drvn to lead dist, sn clr, val 5L+: reapp: Gr 1 wnr at St-Cloud in '03, also cl Gr 1 2nd at
Longchamp: eff at 1m/11f, further will suit: acts on gd/sft & soft grnd, sharp & stiff/gall trk: goes well fresh:
improving & v smart 3yo who returns here for the Gr 1 Prix Du Lupin in May.
1 Sat'08 Sain 10g/s 115- : 2 Sun'19 Long 9g/s 106- : 2 Sat'23 Deau 8gd 96- A:
    CHERRY MIX A Fabre 3-9-2   Gary Stevens 17/2: 12-32: gr c Linamix - Cherry Moon (Quiet   3   **108**
American) Bhd, prog under press 2f out, kept on fnl 1f, not pace wnr: eff at 11f on soft grnd: v useful.
    FAST AND FURIOUS FR J-C Rouget 3-9-2   I Mendizabal 5/2: 11-13: b g Brief Truce - Zing Ping   snk   **107**
(Thatching) Held up, hdwy when no room dist, kept on ins fnl 1f, nrst fin: prev unbtn: eff at 11f on soft grnd.
9 Ran   Time 2m 17.47()   Owned: Baron T de Zuylen de Nyevelt   Trained: France

CORK   MONDAY 12.04.04   Righthand, Galloping Track, Long Run In

Official Going YIELDING.

1159   2.55 Listed Cork Stakes 3yo+   ()
£21808   £6399   £3048   **5f**   **Good/Soft**

1788} **MOON UNIT** 183 H Rogers 3-8-7   D M Grant 11/1: 2050-1: b f Intikhab - Chapka (Green Desert) Led   **107**
over 1f out, styd on strongly: subs List rnr-up: suited by a gall 5f, likes gd/soft & soft grnd: tried
6/7f last term, reportedly a 5f specialist: goes v well fresh: smart performance against older sprinters.
2 Sat'24 Curr 5sft 102- A:
883   **DRAGON FLYER** 23 M Quinn 5-9-4   (95) J A Heffernan 11/2: 300-42: Not pace of wnr fnl 1f: up in   1½   **101**
grade & a gd run: spot on next time at Bath: see 883.
4555} **PEACE OFFERING** 22 D Gillespie 4-9-7 p (102) P Cosgrave 14/1: 640-03: b c Victory Note - Amnesty   nk   **103**
Bay (Thatching) Btn under 2L wearing cheek pieces.
1 Oct'02 Asco 5g/f 109- A: 1 Sep'02 Sand 5g/f 88- D:
5037} **COLONEL COTTON** 156 S 5-9-11   (109) M J Kinane 11/4 FAV: 0130-6: b g Royal Applause - Cutpurse Moll   **0**
(Green Desert) Btn over 2L on reapp: '03 List wnr: mdn & val h'cap wnr in '02: suited by 5/6f on firm, soft
& polytrk: handles any trk: best delivered late: tough & v useful sprinter, likely to prove sharper for this.
1 Thu'02 Newm 5g/f 104-89 A: 2 Fri'04 Sand 5.0gd 91-87 C: 2 Wed'14 York 5.0fm 88-85 B: 1 Sep'02 Curr 5g/f 90-86 :
2 Aug'02 York 5g/f 84-82 C: 1 Jul'02 Newm 6g/f 86- D: 2 Jul'02 Beve 5g/s 70- D: 2 Jun'02 Newm 5fm 81-75 D:
2 Jun'02 Donc 5g/f 76- D: 2 May'02 Wind 6sft 77- D: 2 May'02 Beve 5gd 77- D: 2 May'02 Sali 6g/f 81- D:
8 Ran   Time 1m 01.10()   Owned: Mrs Paula Davison   Trained: Ardee

Official Going Good/Soft (Good Places)

1160   2.10 Start Of The Season Selling Stakes 3yo+   (G)
£2625 £750 £375   1m100y rnd   Good/Soft 82   +02 Fast   Inside

996   **OPEN HANDED 14** [13] B Ellison 4-9-12 t (35) T Eaves(5) 20/1: 000-6001: b g Cadeaux Genereux -   **59**
Peralta (Green Desert) Mid-div, prog 2f out, styd on well to lead cl-home, rdn out: no bid: mod form in 3 Brit '03
starts (rtd 35a & 47, h'caps): eff at 5f-1m, h'cap wnr in early '03 at Tipperary: eff at 7.4/8.4f on gd/soft grnd:
acts on a stiff/undul trk: eff with t-strap: gd weight carrier, eff in sell grade.

868   **NODS NEPHEW 27** [12] D E Cantillon 7-9-12 (58) J F Egan 11/2: 3110-202: In tch, styd on to lead   ½ **57**
dist, hdd cl-home: back to form on return to turf & can find similar: see 792.

744   **WEET WATCHERS 48** [17] P A Blockley 4-9-12 (67) N Callan 4/1 FAV: 0P0-1643: Handy, kept on fnl   nk **56**
1f, not btn far: 7 wk abs: eff at 6/7f, h'cap wnr: acts on gd/soft, soft grnd & fibresand: see 555.

1051   **HEARTBEAT 9** [10] P J McBride 3-8-0 (52) Dale Gibson 16/1: 06-40044: Sn rdn in rear, prog 3f out,   shd **44**
kept on fnl 1f: btn under 1L: eff at 8.4f, tried further but shld suit: acts on gd/soft grnd: see 1051.

964   **LUCKY LARGO 16** [6]4-9-6 bl (65) I Mongan 9/1: 22020-05: b g Key of Luck - Lingering Melody   ½ **48**
(Nordico) Mid-div, prog 2f out, styd on fnl 1f: mod jumps form in 03/04 (rtd 101h, juv nov): unplcd sole '03 Brit
start (h'cap, rtd 50), rnr-up on 4 of 5 starts in native Ireland: eff at 1m/9f on gd/soft & soft: wears blnks & not
disgraced from a mod draw.

668   **VERMILION CREEK 57** [7]5-9-1 (50) Stephanie Hollinshead(7) 25/1: 06-50666: Held up, prog 2f out,   2 **39**
nrst fin: 8 wk abs: mod low draw: see 445.

4731} **FINE FRENZY 183** [2]4-9-1 (47) A Quinn(5) 40/1: 203640-7: b f Great Commotion - Fine Project   ¾ **37**
(Project Manager) Led, hdd dist, sn wknd: 3rd at best in 3 03/04 jump starts (rtd 96h, sell hdle, stays 2m on
firm): plcd twice in '03 (sells, rtd 57 & 55a, J W Hills): mdn wnr in '02: stays 7f, ideally suited by 5/6f:
handles firm, gd/soft & prob polytrack, likes a sharp trk: tried visor & cheek pieces: with Miss S J Wilton.
2 Jul'03 Yarm 7.0g/f 47-(50) G: 1 May'02 Wind 5g/f 70- D:

935   **EVA PERON 19** [3]4-9-1 (55) A Daly 14/1: 66000-08: Cl-up, fdd dist: poor draw: see 935.   shd **36**
996   **TINIAN 14** [11]6-9-12 (54) Darren Williams 15/2: 5303049: Handy, no extra fnl 2f: btr 417.   nk **46**
820   **FRANKS QUEST 37** [4]4-9-12 (50) L Keniry(3) 20/1: 0-023360: 10th: Chsd ldrs, not pace chall: btr 718.   1 **44**
60   **LORD OF METHLEY 147** [15]5-9-12 vis (50) V Halliday 9/1: 340036-0: 11th: Nvr nrr than mid-div.   2½ **39**
771   **SHOTLEY DANCER 45** [1]5-9-1 (40) Suzanne France(7) 40/1: 5060-400: 12th: Al bhd: 6 wk abs.   shd **27**
996   **ROYAL WINDMILL 14** [9]5-9-12 p (48) D Fentiman(7) 14/1: 23206-00: 13th: Al in rear.   2 **34**
633   **GWAZI 60** [16]4-9-6 t (40) S Hitchcott(3) 25/1: 000-030: 14th: In tch, fdd dist: btr 633.   hd **27**
2090} **GOOD LOSER 307** [14]4-9-6 t (60) J Bramhill 8/1: 020244-0: 15th: Cl-up, fdd fnl 2f: reapp.   hd **26**
858   Finningley Connor 29 [5]4-9-6 (50) M Fenton 33/1:0   966   Fast Lane 16 [8]5-9-6 P(40) A Culhane 40/1:0
17 Ran   Time 1m 51.26 (7.46)   Owned: Mrs Andrea M Mallinson   Trained: Malton

1161   2.45 Beverley-Racecourse Co Uk Maiden Auction Stakes 2yo   (E)
£3653 £1124 £562   5f rnd   Good/Soft 82   -34 Slow   Inside

920   **DANCE NIGHT 20** [9] B A McMahon 2-8-11 G Gibbons 1/1 FAV: 21: Broke well sn cl-up, led dist,   **89+**
pushed clr fnl 1f, val 5L+: well bckd under top weight: eff at 5f, shld stay further: acts on gd & gd/soft grnd:
eff on stiff/undul & gall trk: confirmed debut promise & can win more races: see 920 (debut).

931   **TURTLE MAGIC 19** [15] W G M Turner 2-8-2 C Haddon(7) 20/1: 02: b f Turtle Island - Theda (Mummy's   3 **70**
Pet) Handy, chsd ldr dist, kept on but al held fnl 1f: clr rem: Apr foal, cost £4,000: half sister to numerous
sprint wnrs as juv: dam plcd at 7f: sire high-class 1m performer: eff at 5f, bred to apprec 6/7f in time: acts on
gd/soft grnd: improved on debut effort & can find a mdn.

1014   **GEORGIE BELLE 13** [12] C Tinkler 2-8-4 G Duffield 6/1: 33: Trkd ldrs, no extra ins fnl 2f: btr 1014.   5 **58**
954   **LORD JOHN 18** [11] M W Easterby 2-8-7 Dale Gibson 16/1: 04: b c Piccolo - Mahbob Dancer (Groom   1¾ **56**
Dancer) Veered left start, rear, mod late gains: May foal, cost 900gns: half brother to a 6f juv wnr: dam unrcd:
sire top class at sprint dists: stables rnrs usually improve with experience.
    TIFFIN DEANO [16]2-8-9 G Faulkner 8/1: 5: b c Mujadil - Xania (Mujtahid) Led, hdd dist, sn   shd **57**
fdd: debut: Mar first foal, cost 10,000gns: dam unplcd: sire speedy at 2: with P C Haslam.
    MIRAGE PRINCE [14]2-8-9 Darren Williams 33/1: 6: Chsd ldrs, no extra fnl 2f: debut.   nk **56**
    WELCOME DREAM [13]2-8-2 J Quinn 40/1: 7: Slow away, nvr nrr than mid-div: debut.   1¼ **45**
954   **BEDTIME BLUES 18** [5]2-8-6 T Hamilton(3) 20/1: 08: Al bhd: poor draw.   7 **31**
    VICTIMISED [7]2-8-9 L Keniry(3) 66/1: 9: Slow away, nvr a factor: poor draw.   6 **19**
    DRAMATIC REVIEW [10]2-8-9 Rory Moore(7) 33/1: 0: 10th: Bmpd after leaving stalls, al bhd.   ¾ **17**
    SILVER PHANTOM [8]2-9-0 N Pollard 9/1: 0: 11th: Handy, fdd 2f out: op 7/2 on debut.   3½ **13**
Frisby Ridge [2]2-8-2 D Allan(1) 66/1:0   Tartatartufata [6]2-8-4 P Hanagan 66/1:0
Brace Of Doves [4]2-8-9 P Makin(7) 33/1:0   Ruby Rebel [3]2-8-4 (2ow) R Fitzpatrick 100/1:0
15 Ran   Time 1m 7.13 (5.83)   Owned: Mr J C Fretwell   Trained: Tamworth

1162   3.20 Flying Five Classified Stakes 3yo+ 0-90 (C)
£9432 £2902 £1451   5f rnd   Good/Soft 82   -09 Slow   Inside

1004   **PROUD BOAST 14** [10] D Nicholls 6-9-2 (92) A Culhane 7/1: 40360-01: b f Komaite - Red Rosein (Red   **98**
Sunset) Handy, short of room dist, styd on well to lead cl-home, won going away: plcd 4 times in '03 (rtd 99, List
& class stks, Miss G S Rees): won 2 h'caps & a List event in '02: eff at 5/6f on firm & gd/soft: acts on any trk,
likes a stiff/gall one, has gone well fresh: rejuvenated by sprint king D Nicholls.
2 Sep'03 Hayd 6fm 95-(95) C: 1 Oct'02 Newm 5fm 102- A: 1 Jun'02 Newc 5g/f 93-89 B: 1 Jun'02 York 6g/f 89-86 B:
2 May'02 Hayd 5gd 87-80 B: 2 May'01 Ches 5fm 95-92 C:

927   **CARIBBEAN CORAL 19** [3] J J Quinn 5-9-3 (90) Darren Williams 9/2: 00012-02: Dwelt, sn in tch,   ¾ **94**
prog to lead trav well dist, edgd left under press & hdd cl-home: op 3/1: acts on firm & gd/ soft grnd: lost
little in defeat & can find similar this term: see 927 (reapp).

883   **IKAN 25** [5] N P Littmoden 4-9-1 (1ow) (89) T G McLaughlin 50/1: 12400-03: br f Sri Pekan -   ¾ **90+**
Iktidar (Green Desert) Held up, prog 2f out, short of room dist, kept on fnl 1f, nrst fin: won 2 h'caps in '03:

h'cap wnr & List 2nd in '02: suited by 5/6f on firm, hvy & gd/gall trk, likes Sandown: tough & prog 4yo who did not have much luck & a fine run from a poor low draw: keep in mind.
2 Aug'03 York 5.0fm 89-89 C: 1 Aug'03 Sand 5.0g/f 88-82 D: 1 Jul'03 Sand 5.0g/f 83-76 D: 2 Oct'02 Donc 6sft 92- A: 1 Sep'02 Newm 6g/f 80-72 D: 2 Sep'02 Bath 5fm 76-73 C:

834	**JOHNSTONS DIAMOND 32** [2] E J Alston 6-9-3 (85) J Quinn 33/1: 01-00104: Held up, prog wide 2f out, kept on fnl 1f: gd eff from poor low draw: see 687 (h'cap).		nk	91
4682}	**SIMIANNA 186** [7]5-9-0 (89) G Duffield 14/1: 436300-5: b f Bluegrass Prince - Lowrianna (Cyrano de Bergerac) Rear, prog wide 2f out, no impress ins fnl 1f: fills stks wnr in '03, also plcd sev times in h'caps: class stks rnr-up & val h'cap plcd in '02: eff at 5/6f on firm, hvy & polytrack: tried cheek pieces.		1¼	84
	1 Jun'03 Newm 6g/f 92-(88) C: 2 Jul'02 Wind 6g/f 90- C: 2 Jun'02 Yarm 6fm 91- B: 1 May'01 Ches 5fm 88- B: 1 Apr'01 Ripo 5hvy 79- E: 2 Apr'01 Muss 5hvy 74- D: 1 Mar'01 Muss 5hvy 76- D:			
927	**BOND BOY 19** [8]7-9-5 (92) F Lynch 4/1 FAV: 0-400406: Held up, prog when hmpd dist, switched & kept on well: fin full of running after getting hmpd & an eye-catching effort: see 927.		1¼	85+
952	**COCONUT PENANG 18** [12]4-9-8 (95) N Pollard 11/2: 36350-07: Led 1f, wkng when no room dist.		nk	87
4679}	**VITA SPERICOLATA 186** [4]7-9-0 (86) R Winston 28/1: 430000-8: Led 4f out, hdd dist, sn wknd.		1¼	75
5037}	**MATTY TUN 158** [6]5-9-3 (87) J Bramhill 20/1: 531100-9: Held up, prog 2f out, sn hmpd & eased.		hd	77
1004	**HENRY HALL 14** [3]8-9-6 (93) Kim Tinkler 14/1: 36513-30: 10th: Keen in tch, fdd dist: poor low draw.		1¾	75
1004	**TRINCULO 14** [11]7-9-3 p (89) J P Guillambert(3) 8/1: 000U250: 11th: In tch, fdd 1f out: btr 927.		3	63
2486}	**ARCTIC BURST 291** [1]4-9-3 t (90) P Hanagan 10/1: 424/10-0: 12th: Slow away, al in rear: poor low draw: reapp & new stable.		2½	56
834	**OK PAL 32** [9]4-9-3 (90) I Mongan 6/1: 10/04-U30: 13th: Handy, short of room 2f out & lost place.		nk	55

13 Ran   Time 1m 5.86 (4.56)   Owned: Mr P D Savill   Trained: Thirsk

---

1163	**3.55 New Minster Enclosure Stakes Handicap 3yo 0-75 (E)**		[82]
	£3718 £1144 £572 **7f100y rnd Good/Soft 82 +01 Fast** Inside		

975	**PHLUKE 15** [16] R F Johnson Houghton 3-8-13 (67) S Carson 12/1: 32-53051: Led till 2f out, rallied gamely to lead nr line, hung out: fair time: eff at 5/7.4f on fast, gd/soft & f/sand: game & tough 3yo who made gd use of favoured high draw: see 337 & 258.			72
892*	**RILEY BOYS 23** [11] J G Given 3-8-10 (64) M Fenton 14/1: 33000-12: Cl-up, led 2f out till collared dying strides: eff at 6/7.4f, has tried further: acts on firm, gd/soft & f/sand: gd run back in h'caps.		shd	67
744	**WINGS OF MORNING 48** [8] P A Blockley 3-8-12 (66) N Callan 20/1: 002-1563: Handy, kept on well fnl 1f, not btn far: eff at 7/7.4f, had tried further but shaped as tho' will suit: acts on gd/soft grnd & fibresand: decent eff from a mod middle draw: see 488.		½	68
4213}	**CHARNOCK BATES ONE 214** [13] T D Easterby 3-8-10 (64) J Quinn 9/1: 453354-4: b f Desert Sun - Fleetwood Fancy (Taufan) Chsd ldrs, under press fnl 1f, not btn far: tchd 14/1: reapp: plcd twice in '03 (h'caps & auct mdn, rtd 70): eff at 7/7.5f, tried 1m: acts on firm & gd/soft grnd: encouraging reapp.		nk	65
1007	**QUICKSTYX 14** [7]3-9-1 (69) A Culhane 11/4 FAV: 145: Slow away, prog 2f out, kept on fnl 1f: well bckd: eff 7.4f, return to 1m will suit: acts on firm, gd/soft & polytrack: not disgraced, btr 1007.		1	68
999	**ORION EXPRESS 14** [15]3-8-12 (66) Dale Gibson 14/1: 000-66: b c Bahhare - Kaprisky (Red Sunset) Mid-div, prog 2f out, styng on when no room well ins fnl 1f: unplcd in 3 '03 starts (rtd 59, mdn): eff at 7.4f, shaped as tho' further will suit: acts on gd/soft grnd: encouraging effort.		shd	64+
934	**ANDURIL 19** [14]3-9-2 (70) J Tate 16/1: 045-67: Keen bhd, sn in tch, hung right 2f out, no extra when short of room cl-home: see 934.		½	67
4293}	**AUROVILLE 210** [2]3-9-0 (68) I Mongan 22/1: 100-8: b c Cadeaux Genereux - Silent Tribute (Lion Cavern) Nvr nrr than mid-div: reapp: unplcd in 3 '03 starts (rtd 74, mdn): poor low draw: with M L W Bell.		1½	62
923	**MR MIDASMAN 20** [3]3-9-3 (71) D Sweeney 16/1: 041-69: Slow away, nvr nrr than mid-div: low draw.		½	64
5034}	**CHEVERAK FOREST 158** [10]3-8-12 (66) Kim Tinkler 20/1: 553150-0: 10th: Nvr nr ldrs.		1¾	55
3518}	**RIGONZA 247** [5]3-9-6 (74) D Allan(3) 33/1: 54346-0: 11th: Slow away, al bhd: reapp.		2½	58
1088	**SENOR BOND 7** [4]3-9-4 (72) F Lynch 16/1: 0400-630: 12th: Held up wide, nvr dngrs: poor draw.		1½	53
934	**WHITGIFT ROCK 19** [12]3-9-7 VIS (75) P Doe 9/2: 5631-120: 13th: In tch, hung 5f out, sn wknd: 1st time visor: disapp on switch to turf: btr 934 & 341 (polytrack).		3½	49
1055	**LOOKS THE BUSINESS 9** [1]3-9-1 t (69) C Haddon(7) 50/1: 45-24500: 14th: Rcd v wide in mid-div, wknd.		2½	38
939	**Menai Straights 18** [9]3-8-11 (65) G Duffield 12/1:o 470 **Bold Blade 82** [6]3-9-2 bl(70) M Stainton(7) 25/1:o			

16 Ran   Time 1m 36.80 (6.0)   Owned: Mrs R F Johnson Houghton   Trained: Didcot

---

1164	**4.30 New Course Enclosure Stakes Handicap 3yo+ 0-75 (E)**		[74]
	£3897 £1199 £600 **1m1f207y Good/Soft 82 +03 Fast** Inside		

997	**CALATAGAN 14** [13] J M Jefferson 5-8-12 (58) P Hanagan 6/1: 32230/-31: In tch, styd on to lead 1f out, drvn out: fair time: stays 14f, apprec drop back to 10f: acts on fast & gd/soft: see 997.			68
964	**TONY TIE 16** [12] J S Goldie 8-9-11 (71) N Callan 8/1: 30060-62: Chsd ldrs, slightly short of room dist, styd on well & only just btn: decent eff & is on a wng mark: see 964.		½	80
391	**TROUBLE MOUNTAIN 92** [16] M W Easterby 7-9-10 (70) P Mulrennan(5) 3/1 FAV: 44023-33: Bhd, hmpd early, styd on well fnl 2f: long abs: won this race from a 1lb higher mark last year: gd run in the circumstances, lost realistic chance when hmpd early on: see 164.		2	75+
4476}	**GREY CLOUDS 200** [16] T D Easterby 4-9-7 (67) D Allan(3) 10/1: 211430-4: gr f Cloudings - Khalsheva (Shirley Heights) Hmpd early & sn bhnd, kept on fnl 2f: reapp: won 2 h'caps in '03: nov stks rnr-up in '02 (A Berry): stays 13f, suited by 10f: acts on fast & gd/soft, gd/gall trk: promising reapp, expect improvement.		½	71
	1 Aug'03 Beve 9.9gd 68-62 E: 1 Jul'03 Newc 10.1g/s 63-57 E: 2 Jul'03 Beve 9.9gd 62-57 E: 2 Jul'02 Hayd 6g/s 73- D:			
964	**MELODIAN 16** [9]9-8-13 bl (59) T Williams 7/1: 6156-545: In tch, kept on fnl 2f: sn wknd.		1¾	60
964	**GRAFT 16** [11]5-9-0 (60) Dale Gibson 20/1: 04000-06: b g Entrepreneur - Mariakova (The Minstrel) Rear, nvr nrr than mid-div: unplcd in '03 (rtd 71, h'cap): plcd 3 times in '02 (h'caps, rtd 80, B W Hills): mdn wnr in late '01: eff at 1m/12f on firm, soft grnd & polytrack: has slipped to a decent mark.		¾	60
	2 Oct'02 Leic 9.9sft 78-74 E: 2 Oct'02 Newm 10fm 75-72 E: 1 Nov'01 Ling 8ap 78a- D:			
1006	**MARITIME BLUES 14** [6]4-9-5 (65) M Fenton 25/1: 13560-07: b g Fleetwood - Dixie d'Oats (Alhijaz) Bhd, prog wide 3f out, onepcd fnl 1f: won 3 times in '03 (h'caps): unplcd in '02 (rtd 59, G Bravery): suited by 8/10f on firm, gd & fibresand: likes Nottingham: not disgraced from poor draw.		1	63
	1 Jul'03 Nott 10.0gd 73-65 E: 1 Jul'03 Nott 10.0fm 67-60 E: 2 Jun'03 Wolv 9.4af 61a-61 F: 1 Jun'03 Wolv 8.5af 62a-51 F:			
1034	**ARCHIRONDEL 11** [1]6-8-4 (50) R Miles(3) 25/1: 30-60U08: Rear, prog & short of room 2f out, no ch after: poor draw & did not get the run of today's race.		5	40
4266}	**GIFTED FLAME 211** [15]5-9-6 (66) J Quinn 9/1: 604006-9: Slow away, prog & no room 2f out on reapp.		5	48

316

BEVERLEY   WEDNESDAY 14.04.04   Righthand, Undulating Track With Stiff, Uphill Fin

4486} **ROCKERFELLA LAD 200** [4]4-9-8 (68) G Duffield 40/1: 124530-0: 10th: Handy, fdd 2f out: jumps abs.	½	49	
4849} **ENCOUNTER 175** [2]8-8-3 (49) D R McCabe 16/1: 406500-0: 11th: Mid-div, prog wide 3f out, wknd fnl 2f.	3	26	
746 **DAIMAJIN 48** [14]5-9-2 (62) D Nolan(5) 40/1: 0-105400: 12th: Nvr nrr than mid-div: 7 wk abs.	¾	38	
1064 **WASHINGTON PINK 8** [3]5-8-4 (50) T Hamilton(1) 100/1: 5040/0-00: 13th: Al rear: poor draw.	½	25	
4809} **FACE THE LIMELIGHT 177** [8]5-9-6 (66) I Mongan 25/1: 155050-0: 14th: Al bhd: rider reported mount lost action: 12 wk jumps abs.	1¼	39	
918 **EVERY NOTE COUNTS 20** [7]4-9-10 (70) R Winston 28/1: 24520-00: 15th: Hmpd after 2f, al bhnd.	2	40	
1026 **SENOR TORAN 12** [19]4-8-10 (56) L Keniry(3) 25/1: 500-3430: 16th: Al bhd.	nk	25	
3950} **MOUNT PEKAN 229** [10]4-8-3 (49) R Ffrench 33/1: 405000-0: 17th: Led, hdd 6f out, sn wknd.	½	17	
5029} **BEN HUR 159** [5]5-8-12 (58) N Pollard 16/1: 210050-0: 18th: Cl-up, hdd 3f out: poor draw.	1½	23	
3302} **MEXICAN 257** [18]5-8-3 p (49) D Fentiman(7) 12/1: 000500-0: 19th: Led 6f out, hdd 2f out, fdd.	7	4	

19 Ran   Time 2m 10.13 (7.83)   Owned: Mr & Mrs J M Davenport   Trained: Malton

---

1165   5.05 Racing Here Again Next Thursday Stakes Handicap Fillies 3yo 0-75 (E)   [80]
£3575 £1100 £550   1m4f16y   Good/Soft 82   -64 Slow   Inside

977 **CHARA 15** [7] J R Jenkins 3-8-12 (64) I Mongan 9/2: 4045-31: ch f Deploy - Subtle One (Polish Patriot) Held up, rdn & prog 2f out, led ins final: drifting right, all-out: slow time: unplcd both '03 starts (rtd 71, mdn): eff at 10f, imprvd for step up to 12f: acts gd/soft & polytrack: see 977 & 120.		68	
817 **VARUNI 37** [2] J G Portman 3-8-12 (64) A Culhane 14/1: 0-102: Held up, styd on to lead well ins fnl 1f, hdd cl-home: eff at 10/12f on gd/soft grnd & polytrack: ran to form of win in 626.	nk	66	
959 **SEMELLE DE VENT 16** [10] J H M Gosden 3-8-6 (58) R Havlin 6/1: 056-33: Cl-up, led 5f out, clr 3f out, hdd under press well ins fnl 1f: imprvd for step up to 12f: acts on gd/soft grnd & polytrack: see 959.	nk	59	
1030 **PRAIRIE SUN 12** [1] Mrs A Duffield 3-8-4 (56) G Duffield 16/1: 000-44: b f Law Society - Prairie Flame (Marju) In tch, outpcd 2f out, rallied well ins fnl 1f, not btn far: unplcd in 3 '03 starts (rtd 61, mdn): eff at 12f, further shld suit: acts on gd/soft grnd.	hd	56	
37 **DOLLY WOTNOT 151** [8]3-9-1 (67) T G McLaughlin 25/1: 0445-5: b f Desert King - Riding School (Royal Academy) In tch, short of room dist, sn onepcd: reapp: unplcd in 3 '03 starts (rtd 67, fills mdn): stays 12f on gd/soft grnd: with NP Littmoden.	1¼	65	
4138} **SIGNORA PANETTIERA 218** [5]3-8-6 (58) S Hitchcott(3) 4/1: 640-6: Handy, bumped dist, sn no extra.	1	54	
4532} **MACCHIATO GB 197** [9]3-8-4 (56) S Carson 8/1: 00602-7: Led, hdd 5f out, hung left badly bend 4f out, sn wknd: rider reported mount lost action: reapp.	10	38	
1017 **KEEP ON MOVIN 13** [4]3-9-7 (73) R Miles(3) 15/8 FAV: 06531-58: In tch, hung right & no extra 2f out: top-weight: disappointing on step up to 12f: btr 1017 & 116 (10f).	nk	54	
841 **MOMENTS I TREASURE 31** [3]3-9-1 (67) P Hanagan 10/1: 00-69: In tch, wknd 2f out.	2	45	
596 **CIACOLE 64** [6]3-8-12 (62) J D O'Reilly(7) 33/1: 6540-040: 10th: Held up, nvr a factor: 9 wk abs.	nk	41	

10 Ran   Time 2m 48.89(17.5)   Owned: Mr M Ng   Trained: Royston

---

NEWMARKET   WEDNESDAY 14.04.04   Righthand, Stiff, Galloping Track

Official Going Good

1166   1.10 Turftours Com Wood Ditton Stakes 3yo   (D)
£6955 £2140 £1070   1m str   Good 43   -00 Slow   Far Side

UNITED NATIONS 0 [3] D R Loder 3-9-0 J Murtagh 11/2: 1: ch c Halling - Congress (Dancing Brave) Al prom, led 2f out, pushed out, bit in hand: well bckd: half brother to sev 3yo wnrs: eff at 1m, 10f will suit: acts on gd & a stiff: goes well fresh: already useful, win more races.		95+	
DENOUNCE 0 [4] H R A Cecil 3-9-0 R Hughes 4/1: 2: b c Selkirk - Didicoy (Danzig) Led till 2f out, kept on tho' op 3/1: well bred newcomer: eff at 1m, 10f expected to suit (Dante entry): acts on gd grnd & a stiff trk: promising start, win similar.	2½	88	
MARBUSH 0 [15] M A Jarvis 3-9-0 P Robinson 100/30 FAV: 3: ro c Linamix - Fig Tree Drive (Miswaki) Led pair far side, kept on for press, not pace of front pair towards centre: nicely bckd tho' op 11/4: eff at 1m, mid-dist pedigree (Dante/Derby entry): acts on gd grnd: fine run, win a mdn sn.	1¾	85	
DIAMOND LODGE 0 [5] J Noseda 3-8-9 S W Kelly 50/1: 4: ch f Grand Lodge - Movieland (Nureyev) Chsd ldrs, edged right & onepace: half sister to 10f wnrs: acts on gd grnd, likely improver over further.	1½	77	
MAHARAAT 0 [17]3-9-0 T W Supple 20/1: 5: Chsd ldr far side, kept on fnl 2f, not able to chall.	1½	79	
GRAND BUT ONE 0 [8]3-9-0 M Hills 16/1: 6: ch c Grand Lodge - Unscathed (Warning) Rdn bhd, eyecatching late prog, kind ride: will relish 10f & plenty to like about this, sure-fire improver, keep in mind.	1	77+	
KASKA 0 [12]3-8-9 D Holland 33/1: 7: Chsd ldrs till over 1f out.	½	71	
BALIMAYA 0 [13]3-8-9 E Ahern 33/1: 8: Held up, nvr pace to threaten ldrs.	2	67	
RAWDON 0 [6]3-9-0 L Dettori 15/2: 9: Dwelt, in tch till over 2f out.	1½	69	
HIGH FREQUENCY 0 [14]3-9-0 R Mullen 66/1: 0: 10th: Chsd ldrs 5f.	½	68	
MUSTAKHLAS 0 [12]3-9-0 R Hills 10/1: 0: 11th: Sn pushed along & al towards rear.	4	60	
KEY IN 0 [10]3-8-9 K Darley 40/1: 0: 12th: Chsd ldrs till over 2f out.	hd	54	
TUMBAGA 0 [9]3-9-0 S Drowne 10/1: 0: 13th: Held up, no impress fnl 2f.	½	58	
Hinode 0 [1]3-9-0 S Sanders 50/1:0	**Hilltop Rhapsody 0** [16]3-8-9 C Catlin 100/1:0		
Dorset 0 [2]3-8-9 Martin Dwyer 50/1:0	**Protecting Heights 0** [11]3-9-0 T Quinn 50/1:0		

17 Ran   Time 1m 40.06 (5.18)   Owned: Sheikh Mohammed   Trained: Newmarket

---

1167   1.45 Listed Victor Chandler European Free Handicap 3yo (A)   [120]
£17400 £6600 £3300   7f str   Good 43   -03 Slow   Far Side

4557} **BRUNEL 195** [4] W J Haggas 3-8-13 (105) D Holland 9/1: 2215-1: b c Marju - Castlerahan (Thatching) Made all far side, qcknd clr 2f out, pushed out, v readily: reapp: auct mdn scorer '03, subs Gr3 unplcd (rtd 104): suited by a stiff/undul 7f, 1m shld suit: acts on fast & gd, poss gd/soft: goes well fresh: likes to dominate: v smart/improved run, shld prove a major player in the German/Italian Guineas.		115+	

317

1 Sep'03 Sali 7.0g/f 95- E: 2 Aug'03 Newc 7g/f 74- D: 2 Jul'03 Asco 6g/s 93- D:
4881} **MOONLIGHT MAN 172** [6] R Hannon 3-8-13 (105) R L Moore 14/1: 341113-2: ch c Night Shift -   5   105
Fleeting Rainbow (Rainbow Quest) Prom far side, eff to chase wnr fnl 2f, kept on but no impress: most prog '03,
mdn, nurs h'cap & stks scorer, Listed plcd (rtd 106): eff at 6/7f, shld stay 1m: acts on fast & gd, poss gd/soft:
tough, useful & consistent. 1 Oct'03 York 7.0g/f 103-(89) B: 1 Sep'03 Newm 6g/f 93-83 D: 1 Aug'03 Kemp 6g/f 81- D:
1040   **PARKVIEW LOVE 11** [11] M Johnston 3-8-12 (104) J Fanning 14/1: 12165-03: b c Mister Baileys -   nk   103
Jerre Jo Glanville (Skywalker) Chsd wnr far side, kept on onepace frnl 2f: improved from reapp: mdn & Listed scorer
'03, subs dual Gr2 unplcd: wng form at 5/6f, stays a stiff 7f now & 1m could suit: acts on firm & soft grnd, sharp
or stiff/undul trk: can go well fresh: useful colt.
1 Jun'03 Epso 6fm 101- A: 2 May'03 Pont 6g/s 92- C: 1 May'03 Hami 5.0sft 80- E:
4880} **TAHREEB 172** [3] M P Tregoning 3-9-2 (108) Martin Dwyer 8/1: 221344-4: ch c Indian Ridge - Native   nk   106
Twine (Be My Native) Led centre, rdn & no extra over 1f out: mdn wnr '03, subs Gr2 plcd (rtd 107): wng form at 6f,
stays 7f & has tried 1m: acts on fast & gd/soft, gall or sharp/undul trk: useful.
1 Jul'03 Good 6g/s 103- D: 2 Jul'03 Kemp 6g/f 100- D: 2 Jun'03 Newb 6.0g/f 94- D:
4557} **AZAROLE 195** [9]3-9-2 (108) J Murtagh 6/1: 21144-5: Dwelt, in tch far side, outpcd 2f out, kept on late.   ½   105
4557} **MOKABRA 166** [10]3-9-1 (107) T E Durcan 20/1: 331165-6: Held up far side, nvr able to chall.   6   93
4006} **CARRIZO CREEK 227** [5]3-9-4 (110) K Fallon 4/1 FAV: 31115-7: Prom in centre, wknd qckly over 1f out.   ½   95
885   **SPANISH ACE 25** [2]3-9-0 (106) M Hills 40/1: 16260-08: Chsd ldrs till over 2f out.   nk   90
4672} **BLUE TOMATO 186** [7]3-8-12 (104) L Dettori 6/1: 111503-9: Dwelt, al rear, longer trip.   5   79
2246*}**RUSSIAN VALOUR 300** [1]3-9-7 (113) K Darley 7/1: 31211-0: 10th: Chsd ldr centre till over 2f out.   10   72
885   **VENABLES 25** [8]3-9-0 T (106) R Hughes 9/1: 61140-50: 11th: Chsd ldrs far side, btn 2f out: t-strap.   11   47
11 Ran   Time 1m 26.45 (3.25)   Owned: Highclere Thoroughbred Racing X   Trained: Newmarket

---

1168   **2.20 Gr3 Weatherbys Earl Of Sefton Stakes 4yo+ (A)**
       £29000 £11000 £5500   **1m1f str**   **Good 43**   +03 Fast   Far Side

922   **GATEMAN 20** [3] M Johnston 7-8-13 (112) K Dalgleish 3/1: 35-26021: Led 7f, rallied gamely for   118
press to lead again ins last, drvn out: eff at 7f/9f on firm & hvy, any trk: v smart & genuine, prob career best run.
4570} **KALAMAN 194** [6] Sir Michael Stoute 4-8-10 (119) K Fallon 4/5 FAV: 4/11202-2: b c Desert Prince -   1   112
Kalamba (Green Dancer) Trkd ldrs, led trav best over 1f out, hdd ins last & rdn/no extra nr fin: hvly bckd: mdn &
Listed scorer '03, subs unlucky in Gr 1: eff at 1m, stays a stiff 9f & has tried 10f: acts on fm & gd, stiff or easy
trks: smart & shld win a Gr race but yet to fulfil promise of early '03 form.
2 Oct'03 Newm 8fm 113-(122) A: 2 Jun'03 Asco 8g/f 120-(112) A: 1 May'03 Kemp 8fm 119- A: 1 Apr'03 Newb 8fm 96- D:
3822} **HURRICANE ALAN 235** [2] R Hannon 4-8-10 (110) R Hughes 7/1: 065205-3: b c Mukaddamah - Bint Al   3   106
Balad (Ahonoora) Trkd ldrs, keen early, chsd 2f out travelling well, rdn & no extra from dist: reapp: reapp wnr '03
(Gr 3), subs Listed rnr-up: mdn, dual val stks & Listed wnr '02: stays 9f, suited by 1m on firm, gd/soft & any trk:
can force the pace: smart at best, gd reapp.
2 Aug'03 Good 8g/f 112-(113) A: 1 Apr'03 Newm 8gd 112-(110) A: 1 Sep'02 Curr 6g/f 111- : 2 Sep'02 Kemp 6fm 104- A:
1 Jun'02 Curr 6.2g/s 104- : 1 May'02 Bath 5g/f 107- D: 1 May'02 Brig 5.2g/f 86- D:
922   **LAGO DORTA 20** [5] G Cox 4-8-10 (109) P Robinson 16/1: 10121-64: Dwelt & held up, rdn 2f out,   2½   101
no impress: yet to reach '03 best but left reapp behind today, shld do better: see 922.
884   **EASTERN BREEZE 25** [1]6-8-10 (102) Paul Eddery 25/1: 66-41205: Trkd wnr, btn over 1f out: see 433.   1½   98
881* **WAKE 25** [7]4-8-10 (90) L Dettori 16/1: 2/-16: Held up in tch, left bhd fnl 2f: much tougher than 881.   21   59
6 Ran   Time 1m 52.77 (3.57)   Owned: Kennet Valley Thoroughbreds V   Trained: Middleham

---

1169   **2.55 Gr3 Shadwell Stud Nell Gwyn Stakes Fillies 3yo (A)**
       £29000 £11000 £5500   **7f str**   **Good 43**   -09 Slow   Far Side

4605} **SILCAS GIFT 193** [2] M R Channon 3-8-9 (103) T E Durcan 25/1: 11000-1: b f Cadeaux Genereux -   109
Odette (Pursuit of Love) Trkd ldrs centre, smooth hdwy & led that group 2f out, overall ldr over 1f out, rdn clr,
readily: fillies mdn & Listed scorer '03: eff at 5/6f, imprvd over this stiff 7f today: acts on fast & gd, sharp or
stiff trk: goes v well fresh: lightly rcd: much improved through winter & can win more Gr races in this form.
1 Jun'03 Asco 6g/f 102- A: 1 May'03 Wind 5.0gd 87- D:
4945* }**INCHENI 167** [13] G Wragg 3-8-9 (75) S Drowne 50/1: 61-2: b f Nashwan - Inchmurrin (Lomond) Rear   3   102+
far side, gd hdwy to lead that group ins last, nrst fin: AW mdn wnr on 2nd of just 2 juv starts: eff at 7f, relish
1m+: acts gd, handles polytrack: eyecatching run, green here & a sure-fire improver, keep on your side over further.
1 Oct'03 Ling 7ap 69a- D:
4631} **ROSEANNA 162** [11] Mme C Head Maarek 3-8-9 K Darley 14/1: 1606-3: b f Anabaa - Dancing Rose   1   100
(Dancing Spree) Held up far side, styd on fnl 2f, nrst fin: French raider, '03 Listed wnr at Deauville, subs Gr1
unplcd: wng form at 6f, clrly stays a stiff 7f & 1m looks sure to suit: acts on gd & soft: v useful filly, Italian
1,000 Guineas is reportedly the aim.
5014*}**MALVERN LIGHT 160** [9] W J Haggas 3-8-9 D Holland 5/1: 41-4: b f Zieten - Michelle Hicks (Ballad   1¼   97
Rock) Chsd ldr far side, rdn & no extra dist: nicely bckd, op 7/1: lightly rcd juv, landed 2nd of just 2 '03
starts (mdn, easily), rtd 89+): eff at 6f, stays 7f: acts on gd & gd/soft grnd, stiff/gall trk: useful.
1 Nov'03 Nott 6.1g/s 89- D:
4172} **LUCKY PIPIT 216** [10]3-8-9 (103) M Hills 10/1: 01103-5: b f Key of Luck - Meadow Pipit   hd   96
(Meadowlake) Led/dsptd lead till over 1f out, no extra ins last: fills mdn & Listed fills scorer '03, subs Gr2
plcd: eff at 7f/1m on fast & gd grnd: handles a stiff/gall or easy trk: useful filly.
1 Jul'03 Sand 7.1g/f 98- A: 1 Jul'03 Kemp 7g/f 96- D:
4799} **BAY TREE 11** [12]3-8-9 (105) J Murtagh 33/2: 1100-6: Chsd ldrs far side, rdn/outpcd over 2f out,   1   94
kept on onepace: bckd: op 8/1: reapp & new yard, apprec return to 1m.
885   **VALJARV 25** [8]3-8-9 (95) T P Queally 50/1: 44031-07: Chsd ldrs far side till dist.   ½   93
4597*}**TOP ROMANCE 193** [1]3-8-9 K Fallon 5/1: 11-8: Held up, hung left & no impress fnl 2f: op 7/2.   3½   86
4556} **TOTALLY YOURS 195** [3]3-8-9 (93) Martin Dwyer 50/1: 02210-9: Chsd ldrs 5f.   1   84
4172} **QASIRAH 25** [5]3-8-9 (102) P Robinson 14/1: 120-0: 10th: Chsd ldrs till 2f out, sn btn.   1½   81
4799} **SNOW GOOSE 179** [7]3-8-9 (105) T Quinn 4/1 FAV: 41112-0: 11th: Held up, eff over 2f out, sn btn, lame.   nk   80
4631} **DANCLARE 192** [4]3-8-9 (84) L Dettori 20/1: 4210-0: 12th: Led in centre for 5f, sn btn.   2½   75
4978} **ST FRANCIS WOOD 165** [6]3-8-9 E Ahern 13/2: 2-0: 13th: Held up, rdn 2f out, sn btn: op 5/1, mdn.   1¾   72
13 Ran   Time 1m 26.81 (3.61)   Owned: Aldridge Racing Limited   Trained: West Ilsley

NEWMARKET WEDNESDAY 14.04.04 Righthand, Stiff, Galloping Track

---

1170 3.30 Interior Plc Maiden Stakes Fillies 2yo (D)
£4706 £1448 £724 5f Good 43 -45 Slow Far Side

SIENA GOLD 0 [7] B J Meehan 2-8-11 L Dettori 100/30 FAV: 1: br f Key of Luck - Corn Futures **94+**
(Nomination) Made all & rdly qcknd clr under hands & heels over 1f out: well bckd: Feb foal, 12,000 gns purchase:
half sister to wnrs over 5/9f: dam 6f juv wnr: eff over a stiff 5f, 6f will suit: acts on gd grnd & goes well fresh:
impressive here, juv to follow.
DANCE AWAY 0 [2] M L W Bell 2-8-11 J Mackay 4/1: 2: ch f Pivotal - Dance On (Caerleon) Sn 5 **81**
pushed along towards rear, styd on from halfway, nvr any threat to wnr: nicely bckd: Feb 1st foal, dam a dual
5f juv wnr: eff at 5f on gd: caught a useful sort, win a minor trk mdn.
MISS CASSIA 0 [3] R Hannon 2-8-11 P Dobbs 11/2: 3: b f Compton Place - Miller's Melody (Chief 1½ **76**
Singer) Dwelt, chsd ldrs, no impress on wnr over 1f out: op 4/1: Feb foal, cost 42,000 gns: half sister to wnrs
at 7f/10f, dam plcd at 6f as a juv: eff at 5f, sure to apprec further in time: handles gd grnd & a stiff trk.
1071 **GAUDALPIN 8** [8] M J Wallace 2-8-11 K Fallon 7/2: 34: Chsd ldrs, rdn & no impress over 1f out: 2 **70**
nicely bckd, op 4/1: turf bow: prob handles polytrack & gd grnd: see 1071.
920 **MISTY PRINCESS 20** [1]2-8-11 L Fletcher(3) 25/1: 05: gr f Paris House - Miss Whittingham (Fayruz) 1½ **65**
In tch, edged right & no impress over 1f out: Feb foal, sister to a dual 5f juv wnr, dam sprinter.
WATERLINE LOVER 0 [9]2-8-11 S Drowne 25/1: 6: Dwelt, chsd ldrs till halfway. 3 **56**
BEAUTIFUL MARIA 0 [4]2-8-11 T Quinn 6/1: 7: Chsd ldrs till over 1f out: op 5/1. ¾ **54**
CILLAS SMILE 0 [5]2-8-11 K Darley 20/1: 8: Dwelt, chsd ldrs, hung left & btn halfway. 2½ **46**
8 Ran Time 1m 02.6 (4.4) Owned: Mr N Attenborough & Mrs L Mann Trained: Upper Lambourn

---

1171 4.05 Geoffrey Barling Maiden Stakes Fillies 3yo (D)
£5486 £1688 £844 7f str Good 43 -38 Slow Far Side

4723} **RELAXED 184** [7] Sir Michael Stoute 3-8-11 K Fallon 7/1: 2-1: b f Royal Academy - Sleep Easy **86**
(Seattle Slew) Trkd ldrs stands side, rdn & led that group over 1f out, kept on to have led overall cl-home:
fills mdn rnr-up '03: eff at 7f, 1m will suit (dam smart over 7/9f): acts on fast & gd, stiff trks: goes well
fresh: gd return, can rate higher over further. 2 Oct'03 Leic 7.0g/f 80- D:
1481} **RED TOP 337** [14] R Hannon 3-8-11 Dane O'Neill 20/1: 3-2: b f Fasliyev - Petite Epaulette (Night ½ **84**
Shift) In tch far side, rdn & styd on, not pace of wnr stands side: plcd sole '03 start (rtd 83, fills nov): eff
at 6/7f on firm & gd grnd, stiff/gall trk: must find a mdn.
4601} **KIND 193** [16] R Charlton 3-8-11 R Hughes 12/1: 34-3: b f Danehill - Rainbow Lake (Rainbow shd **84**
Quest) Led far side, hdd cl-home: nicely bckd: plcd on 1st of just 2 '03 starts (mdn, rtd 83): half sister to a
smart mid-dist/staying performer, also a 1m 2yo wnr: eff at 6/7f, breeding suggests improvement at 1m+: acts on
firm & gd grnd, stiff/easy trk: has al been well regarded, shld find a race.
3942} **ATTUNE 230** [2] B J Meehan 3-8-11 S Drowne 50/1: 4-4: br f Singspiel - Arriving (Most Welcome) hd **83**
Chsd ldrs stands side, ch dist, just held cl-home: btn less than 1L in a tight fin: 4th on sole '03 start (mdn, rtd
74): half sister to a plcd 10f performer, dam useful at 10/11f: eff at 7f, 1m+ likely to suit: acts on fast & gd
grnd: encouraging return, improve over further.
49 **HALABALOO 148** [4]3-8-11 D Holland 14/1: 3-5: Held up stands side, styd on fnl 2f, nrst fin: 1 **81+**
bckd at long odds, shld relish 1m & improve.
CAPESTAR 0 [1]3-8-11 T Quinn 50/1: 6: Stands side, slow away, hdwy to chall over 1f out, no extra. nk **80**
146} **CARA BELLA 337** [3]3-8-11 J Murtagh 8/1: 4-7: Led stands side after 1f, hdd over 1f out & no nk **79$**
extra: bckd, op 10/1.
ARICIA 0 [10]3-8-11 L Dettori 10/1: 8: Chsd ldrs far side till dist. ½ **78**
SHARP NEEDLE 0 [13]3-8-11 E Ahern 66/1: 9: Chsd ldrs far side, no impress fnl 1f. nk **77**
2729} **ZAQRAH 281** [11]3-8-11 R Hills 4/5 FAV: 4-0: 10th: Chsd ldr far side, rdn & btn dist, fin lame: bckd. shd **77**
ANTIGUA BAY 0 [15]3-8-11 Lisa Jones(3) 100/1: 0: 11th: Prom far side, outpcd over 1f out. nk **76**
4972} **SPEEDBIRD 165** [17]3-8-11 T E Durcan 66/1: 20-0: 12th: Chsd ldrs far side till over 1f out. 1¾ **70**
STOCKING ISLAND 0 [8]3-8-11 P Robinson 66/1: 0: 13th: Led 1f stands side, no impress bef dist. 1 **71**
SEA OF GOLD 0 [5]3-8-11 Martin Dwyer 66/1: 0: 14th: Dwelt stands side, al rear. 7 **58**
KHAFAYIF 0 [6]3-8-11 W Supple 25/1: 0: 15th: Held up stands side, nvr a factor. 1½ **55**
MISS INKHA 0 [9]3-8-11 S Sanders 100/1: 0: 16th: Dwelt, al rear stands side. 1 **53**
4596} **SHEBAAN 312** [12]3-8-11 (58) S W Kelly 100/1: 02U050-0: 17th: In tch far side till over 1f out. 1¾ **47**
17 Ran Time 1m 28.89 (5.69) Owned: Mr K Abdulla Trained: Newmarket

---

1172 4.40 Babraham Handicap Stakes 4yo+ 0-95 (C) [95]
£9666 £2974 £1487 1m4f Good 43 -38 Slow Far Side

14* **SENTRY 154** [10] J H M Gosden 4-9-1 (82) L Dettori 10/1: 04/231-1: b c In Command - Keep Bobbin **87**
Up (Bob Back) Held up, rdn & hdwy over 2f out, hung left but styd on for press to lead cl-home, all out: 5 month
abs: eff at 11/12f, has shaped as if 14f+ will suit: acts on fast, soft & polytrack, stiff or sharp trk: goes well
fresh: lightly raced & v progressive. 1 Nov'03 Ling 12ap 69a-(87) D: 2 Apr'03 Newb 11.0g/f 87- D:
4957} **PRINS WILLEM 166** [16] J R Fanshawe 5-9-6 (86) K Fallon 10/1: 052610-2: b g Alzao - American hd **90**
Garden (Alleged) Mid-div, rdn to chall ins last, just held: hvly bckd on reapp: prog '03, landed 2 h'caps: dual
h'cap scorer '02: suited by 12/13.3f on firm, gd & handles gd/soft, prob any trk: eff with/without t-strap: best
held up (travels well in a race): tough. 1 Sep'03 Newb 13.3fm 86-82 C: 2 Aug'03 Newm 12gd 84-81 C:
1 May'03 Donc 12gd 84-76 D: 1 Jun'02 Beve 12gd 78-69 E: 1 Apr'02 Wind 11.6g/f 70-65 E:
4865} **PRAIRIE FALCON 173** [5] B W Hills 10-9-2 (82) A Medeiros(5) 33/1: 400010-3: b g Alzao - Sea hd **84**
Harrier (Grundy) Led till over 1f out, rallied gamely & narrow lead again ins last, hdd cl-home: fine reapp: dual
h'cap wnr '03: h'cap scorer '02: eff at 12f, suited by 14f/2m2.5f: acts on soft & gd, loves fm/fast, any trk, likes
Chester: loves to race with/force the pace: tough 10yo, returned in great heart.
1 Sep'03 Redc 14.1fm 84-82 C: 1 Apr'03 Ripo 16gd 89-82 C: 2 Apr'03 Kemp 16fm 82-80 C: 1 Aug'02 Ches 15.8fm 83-77 D:
2 Apr'02 Newb 16fm 82-79 C: 1 Sep'01 Ayr 13fg/f 82-77 C: 1 Jun'01 York 13.8g/f 85-80 C:
4228} **BAGAN 214** [7] H R A Cecil 5-9-5 (85) W Ryan 9/1: 5/20015-4: b c Rainbow Quest - Maid of Erin ¾ **87**
(Irish River) In tch, led over 1f out, hdd ins last & no extra nr fin: reapp: mdn rnr-up '03 bef landing val h'cap
(50/1): unplcd '02 (lightly rcd, rtd 82, mdn): eff at 10/12f on fast & soft grnd, likes a stiff/gall trk: gd
return. 1 Aug'03 York 11.9fm 84-80 C: 2 May'03 Sand 10.0g/f 82-(79) D:
877 **FLOTTA 26** [17]5-9-6 (86) T E Durcan 12/1: 01210-45: Towards rear, styd on stdly for press fnl ½ **86**

319

3f, not reach ldrs: go close over 14f next time: see 877.
1019* **JOROBADEN** 13 [6]4-9-2 (83) G Baker 16/1: 4/-216: Held up, short of room when hdwy over 1f out,   1½   82
kept on ins last: h'cap bow: styd longer 12f trip well, appears on the upgrade: see 1019 & 715.
5036] **GOLD RING** 158 [12]4-9-4 (85) S Drowne 12/1: 622413-7: ch g Groom Dancer - Indubitable (Sharpo)   1¾   82
Chsd ldrs, eff over 2f out, no extra ins last: reapp: mdn & val h'cap plcd '03, also dual h'cap rnr-up: unplcd '02
(rtd 79): eff at 10f, suited by 12/13.3f on firm & gd grnd, gall/easy trks: prove v consistent 2nd half of last
season, keep on side. 1 Sep'03 Kemp 12gd 85-(84) D: 2 Aug'03 Newb 13.3fm 81-82 C: 2 Jul'03 Asco 12g/s 83-80 D:
877* **MILLVILLE** 26 [15]4-9-6 (87) P Robinson 3/1 FAV: 10118: Held up, eff from over 2f out, no extra   3½   79
dist: hvly bckd on turf bow: btr 877 (AW).
5036] **WUNDERWOOD** 158 [20]5-9-10 (90) S Sanders 6/1: 222014-9: In tch, btn over 1f out: well bckd.   nk   81
4504] **MEPHISTO** 198 [13]5-9-8 (88) D Holland 25/1: 3216-0: 10th: Held up, short of room 2f out & hmpd   1   78
over 1f out, no impress, reapp.
3761] **ANNAMBO** 237 [11]4-9-4 vis (85) J Murtagh 14/1: 120100-0: 11th: Chsd ldrs till over 1f out, reapp.   nk   74
1030* **DANCE WORLD** 12 [14]4-8-13 (80) B Reilly(3) 14/1: 424-10: 12th: Prom, btn over 1f out: see 1030.   1¾   67
1056* **CRUISE DIRECTOR** 9 [3]4-9-3 (4ex) (84) Lisa Jones(3) 12/1: 0-303010: 13th: Held up, btn 2f out.   ½   70
4361] **RING OF DESTINY** 207 [4]5-10-0 (94) T Quinn 33/1: 003010-0: 14th: Chsd ldrs, struggling fnl 2f, reapp.   3½   75
4275] **High Action** 213 [19]4-10-0 (95) C Catlin 66/1:0
4493] **Wait For The Will** 199 [2]8-9-10 bl(90) R L Moore 33/1:0
4879] **Dovedon Hero** 172 [18]4-8-13 (80) M Hills 25/1:0   870 **Harelda** 27 [8]4-9-0 (81) L Fletcher(3) 25/1:0
997 **The Persuader** 14 [1]4-8-11 (78) J Fanning 20/1:0   4573] **Island Light Usa** 217 [9]4-9-9 (90) K Darley 40/1:0
20 Ran Time 1m 28.89(5.69) Owned: Highclere Thoroughbred Racing IV Trained: Manton

---

Official Going Good (Good/Soft Places)

1173   **2.10 E B F Sharow Maiden Stakes 2yo (D)**
        £5395 £1660 £830   **5f str**   **Good 41**   **-15 Slow**   Stands Side

962 **WORD PERFECT** 17 [6] M W Easterby 2-8-9 Dale Gibson 4/1 CO FAV: 31: Rdn to lead/dspt lead early,   82
went on dist, rdn out: bckd tho' op 3/1: confirmed debut promise: eff at 5f, 6f shld suit: acts on gd & soft.
1001 **DANTES DIAMOND** 15 [5] F Jordan 2-9-0 S W Kelly 4/1 CO FAV: 22: Dwelt, sn cl-up & narrow lead 2f   1½   81
out till dist, not pace of wnr ins last: nicely bckd: acts on firm & gd grnd: likely type for similar after 1001.
        SMIDDY HILL 0 [8] R Bastiman 2-8-9 R Ffrench 33/1: 3: b f Factual - Hello Hobson's (Fayruz)   2   70
Chsd ldrs & ch over 1f out, no extra: cheaply retained April foal, half-sister to a 5f juv wnr, dam a 5/6f juv wnr:
eff at 5f on gd grnd/sharpish trk: fair debut from awkward stall, shld improve.
        PRINCE NAMID 0 [2] Mrs A Duffield 2-9-0 G Duffield 9/1: 4: b c Namid - Fen Princess (Trojan   3   66
Fen) Rdn in mid-div, kept on late: op 12/1, just ndd this: March foal, related to a 7f juv wnr, also half-brother
to 3 wnrs at 9f+, dam a winning stayer: relish further, likely improver.
        LINCOLNEUROCRUISER 0 [9]2-9-0 D R McCabe 33/1: 5: b c Spectrum - Rush Hour (Night Shift) Dwelt 1   63
& rear, rdn & hdwy halfway, nvr able to threaten: 4500 gns Feb first foal: dam unrcd.
        KINGS GAIT 0 [7]2-9-0 D Allan(3) 33/1: 6: Dwelt & towards rear, late gains: scopey type.   1½   58
1048 **WHY HARRY** 10 [11]2-9-0 R Winston 9/2: 37: Chsd ldrs, btn dist: op 6/1.   ½   56
        WONDERFUL MIND 0 [1]2-9-0 K Darley 4/1 CO FAV: 8: Led/dsptd lead till 2f out: padd pick.   5   42
        ICE RUBY 0 [4]2-8-9 P Hanagan 33/1: 9: Dwelt & al rear.   1½   32
        MORNING WORLD 0 [12]2-9-0 S Drowne 14/1: 0: 10th: Mid-div, sn outpcd.   1¾   32
        SERENE PEARL 0 [3]2-8-9 Nicola Topper 40/1: 0: 11th: Dwelt, al outpcd rear.   8   6
        URABANDE 0 [10]2-8-9 M Fenton 16/1: 0: 12th: Sn struggling & bhd, burly.   3½   0
12 Ran Time 1m 0.61 (2.81) Owned: Mrs Jean Turpin Trained: Sheriff Hutton

1174   **2.45 Mark Cocker Memorial Handicap Stakes 3yo 0-85 (D)**   **[92]**
        £5398 £1661 £830   **1m4f60y**   **Good 41**   **-14 Slow**   Inside

923 **LOCHBUIE** 21 [3] G Wragg 3-8-8 (72) J F Egan 9/2: 640-41: Held up, hdwy 3f out, styd on to lead   84+
ins last, all out: op 3/1: confirmed promise of latest: apprec step up to 12f, shld get further: acts on gd:
improving, more to come: see 923.
367* **ABSOLUTELYTHEBEST** 96 [9] E A L Dunlop 3-8-9 (73) W Supple 12/1: 004-12: Rear, hdwy & led over 6f ½   83
out, drvn & hdd dist, just held cl-home: rest well covered, 3 mth abs/h'cap bow: acts on gd & polytrack.
1017 **BUMPTIOUS** 14 [5] M H Tompkins 3-8-11 (75) G Duffield 7/1: 346-33: Handy, rdn/ch 2f out, no extra   3½   80
when short of room dist: op 10/1: prob styd longer 12f trip: see 1017 (10f).
873* **SETTLEMENT CRAIC** 27 [11] T G Mills 3-9-7 (85) K Darley 7/1: 2-14: Held up, short of room &   ½   89
switched 4f out, eff to chall 2f out, sn no extra: h'cap bow under top-weight: prob handles fast, gd & polytrack.
497 **NESSEN DORMA** 78 [8]3-8-11 (75) M Fenton 33/1: 0511-455: Led 1f, prom, no impress fnl 2f: 11 wk   2   76
abs: longer 12f trip: see 497 & 252 (1m, AW).
1038 **HÄTHLEN** 12 [6]3-8-13 (77) A Culhane 25/1: 23022-06: b c Singspiel - Kameez (Arazi) Held up,   nk   77
eff/short of room 3f out, nvr able to threaten ldrs: 4 times a mdn rnr-up in '03: eff at 1m/9f, mid-dists shld suit
this term: acts on firm & fast grnd, sharp/undul or gall trk.
2 Nov'03 Muss 8g/f 76-(75) D: 2 Oct'03 Brig 8.0fm 75-(76) D: 2 Sep'03 Redc 9fm 79- D: 2 Sep'03 Thir 8g/f 77- D:
915* **GOLDEN QUEST** 22 [10]3-9-4 (82) S Chin 4/1 FAV: 0-117: Sn rdn towards rear, only mod late prog: 6   74
nvr really trav from an early stage, poss best when able to race closer to the pace: btr 915 & 808 (AW).
923 **COVENTINA** 21 [7]3-9-3 (81) T Quinn 7/1: 5310-08: Mid-div, rdn/hmpd 4f out, sn btn: bckd: see 923.   3½   68
102* **MESSE DE MINUIT** 141 [4]3-8-13 (77) S Drowne 18/1: 31-9: Mid-div, drvn & struggling fnl 4f: 10   50
h'cap debut, 5 mth abs: longer trip & different grnd: btr 102 (1m, AW).
1000* **LIQUIDATE** 15 [1]3-8-3 (67) C Catlin 6/1: 006-10: 10th: Trkd ldrs, drvn & btn 4f out: much btr 1000.   12   25
4660] **WING COLLAR** 189 [2]3-8-2 (66) D Allan(3) 40/1: 4440-0: 11th: b c In The Wings - Riyoom (Vaguely   9   12
Noble) Keen, dwelt, sn led till over 6f out, wknd qckly: reapp: unplcd '03 (rtd 71, mdn): tried up to 1m prev.
11 Ran Time 2m 40.23 (6.73) Owned: Mollers Racing Trained: Newmarket

1175   3.20 Listed Ripon Silver Bowl Stakes Fillies 3yo (A)
£17850 £6600 £3300   6f str   Good 41   -03 Slow   Stands Side

4844} **BONNE DE FLEUR 176** [3] B Smart 3-8-11 (78) F Lynch 22/1: 311232-1: b f Whittingham - L'Estable   96
Fleurie (Common Grounds) Made all, held on well for press ins last: 6 mth abs, lkd superb on reapp: fills auct mdn
& h'cap scorer '03, subs dual h'cap plcd & nov auct rnr-up: eff at 5f, suited by 6f & likes to race with/force the
pace: acts on fast & gd grnd, stiff/gall or sharpish trk: goes well fresh: has thrived physically, useful filly.
2 Oct'03 Nott 6.1g/f 79-(80) F: 2 Sep'03 Leic 6.0g/f 79-74 E: 1 Aug'03 Nott 6.1g/f 74-70 E: 1 Jul'03 Beve 5g/f 70- F:
1078+**PETITE ROSE 8** [1] J H M Gosden 3-8-11 R Havlin 6/4 FAV: 12: Cl-up, rdn & ch dist, no extra   ½   93
cl-home: acts on gd & gd/soft: useful, fine run: see 1078 (mdn, easily, well drawn).
2727} **BIRTHDAY SUIT 282** [4] T D Easterby 3-8-11 (102) K Darley 7/2: 113-3: ch f Daylami - Wanton   2   87
(Kris) Chsd ldrs & ch over 1f out, sn no extra: reapp, ndd this: lightly rcd '03, fills mdn & nov stks wnr, subs
Gr 2 plcd (rtd 97): eff at 5/6f on firm & gd grnd, stiff/gall or sharpish trks: useful.
1 Jun'03 Beve 5g/f 94- D: 1 May'03 York 5.0fm 86- D:
4680} **NEEDLES AND PINS 187** [2] M L W Bell 3-9-1 (105) M Fenton 15/8: 126125-4: b f Fasliyev - Fairy   2   85
Contessa (Fairy King) Dwelt, pushed along chasing ldrs, no prog over 1f out: nicely bckd, op 5/2: progressive juv
'03, fills mdn & List scorer, subs Gr 3 rnr-up in France: eff at 5.5f: acts on firm & soft grnd, gall trks.
2 Sep'03 Mais 5.5sf 107- : 1 Aug'03 Newb 5.2fm 105-(94) A: 2 Jul'03 Donc 5gd 87- D: 1 May'03 Hayd 5sft 83- D:
1004 **WITHORWITHOUTYOU 15** [5]3-8-11 (87) W Supple 11/1: 01054-65: Pushed along in tch, no impress.   2   75
5 Ran Time 1m 12.61 (2.61) Owned: Miss N Jefford Trained: Thirsk

1176   3.55 Ripon 'cock O' The North' Handicap Stakes 3yo 0-90 (C)   [86]
£8542 £3240 £1620   1m rnd   Good 41   +04 Fast   Inside

955   **GRANSTON 19** [10] J D Bethell 3-9-1 (73) T Quinn 9/2: 55401-31: Trkd ldrs, keen early, led over   78
1f out, rdn out: best time of day: eff at 7f, imprvd for step up to 1m: acts on firm & gd: improving.
4535*}**LETS ROLL 197** [2] C W Thornton 3-8-15 (69) T Williams 25/1: 02251-2: b g Tamure - Miss   1½   70
Petronella (Petoski) Rear, styd on for press fnl 2f, no impress ins last: still ndd this on reapp: auct mdn wnr
fnl '03 start, earlier dual rnr-up in similar: eff at 7f/1m, half-sister to a multiple 10f/2m wnr & shld get
further: acts on fast & gd grnd, stiff or sharpish trks: remains in gd heart after 1007.
1 Oct'03 Newc 7gd 74-(72) F: 2 Aug'03 Ripo 6g/f 73- E: 2 Jul'03 Newc 7gd 69- F:
1007* **DISPOL VELETA 15** [6] T D Barron 3-8-9 (67) N Mackay 3/1: 0-301413: Mid-div, rdn/short of room   ½   67
2f out, styd on for press ins last: acts on firm, gd & fibresand: remains in gd heart after 1007.
1688*}**CATHERINE HOWARD 327** [8] M R Channon 3-9-2 (74) A Culhane 8/1: 1-4: b f Kingmambo - Darling   3   68
Flame (Capote) Trkd ldrs, eff to lead 2f out, sn rdn & hdd, btn dist: reapp/h'cap base: sole start wnr '03 (fills
mdn): half-sister to a 7f List wnr: eff at 6f, shld stay 1m: acts on fast grnd: has gone well fresh: clr of rem
here. 1 May'03 Ling 6g/f 79- D:
966* **ETMAAM 17** [7]3-9-5 (77) W Supple 9/4 FAV: 4-15: Rdn towards rear, only mod prog for press: padd   5   62
pick & well bckd on h'cap bow: nvr really trav & much more expected after 966 (mdn, soft).
4813*}**ATTACCA 178** [1]3-9-6 p (78) S Drowne 33/1: 0021-6: b c Piccolo - Jubilee Place (Prince Sabo) Led   ¾   62
till 2f out, wknd: ndd this on reapp: auct mdn scorer on fnl '03 start, earlier rnr-up in similar: winning form
over a stiff/undul 6f, sprint pedigree: acts on fast & gd grnd, eff in cheek pieces.
1 Oct'03 Pont 6g/f 75-(72) F: 2 Oct'03 Newc 6gd 76- D:
617* **ALFONSO 62** [11]3-9-7 (79) K Darley 5/1: 04-17: Mid-div, rdn & no impress over 2f out: nicely   ¾   62
bckd, 2 mth abs/h'cap bow: up in trip but much more expected after 617 (7f mdn, AW).
4869} **DARK DAY BLUES 174** [3]3-8-13 (71) Darren Williams 33/1: 206230-8: Dwelt, rear, mod gains for   nk   53
press, reapp/new yard.
5034} **TOPARUDI 159** [9]3-8-13 (71) G Duffield 11/1: 053330-9: Keen early, chsd ldrs till rdn & btn 2f out.   2½   48
923   **BETHANYS BOY 21** [5]3-9-3 (75) R Winston 16/1: 40251-00: 10th: Cl-up, btn 2f out.   3½   46
4891} **MAGICAL MIMI 173** [4]3-9-7 (79) M Fenton 25/1: 5130-0: 11th: Sn bhd: reapp, new yard.   8   36
11 Ran Time 1m 40.47 (2.97) Owned: The Four Players Partnership Trained: Middleham

1177   4.30 Skelton Maiden Stakes Div 1 3yo (D)
£4040 £1243 £622   1m rnd   Good 41   -08 Slow   Inside

4973} **ASHWAAQ 166** [3] J L Dunlop 3-8-9 W Supple 4/6 FAV: 4-1: b f Gone West - Wasnah (Nijinsky)   72
Dwelt, sn chsd ldrs, switched over 1f out & styd on for press to lead well ins last: hvly bckd on reapp: promise
when 4th on sole '03 start (mdn, rtd 80): half-sister to top-class 3yo 1m performer Bahri: apprec step up to 1m,
may get further: acts on fast & gd: goes well fresh: rate higher & win again.
192   **THARAA 124** [7] E A L Dunlop 3-8-9 S Drowne 100/1: 0-2: b f Desert Prince - Tycoon's Drama (Last   ½   69
Tycoon) Dwelt, chsd ldrs, qcknd & led 2f out, rdn & hdd cl-home: 4 mth abs, turf bow: left debut bhd: eff at 1m,
acts on gd grnd & a sharpish trk: shld find a race.
4845} **HOH NELSON 176** [4] H Morrison 3-9-0 L Fletcher(3) 22/1: 000-3: b c Halling - Birsay (Bustino)   1¾   71
Handy & led 3f out till 2f out, still ch dist, no extra: reapp: unplcd all 3 '03 starts (mdns, rtd 69):
half-brother to a 10/11f wnr: eff at 1m, 10f+ likely to suit: handles gd & a sharpish trk: may do btr.
5023} **LITTLE BOB 160** [9] J D Bethell 3-9-0 T Quinn 33/1: 0-4: Dwelt, rear, rdn & kept on fnl 2f, not   nk   70
able to chall: reapp, gelded, still ndd this: eff at 1m on gd grnd.
3790} **MOUFTARI 237** [2]3-9-0 K Darley 5/2: 0-5: Handy & ch 2f out, sn onepace under hands & heels: ½   69
not given hard time on reapp, stays longer 1m trip on gd grnd.
1086 **PREMIER DREAM 8** [6]3-9-0 S Chin 20/1: 66: Led till 3f out, rdn & no extra dist.   ½   68
      WEDOWANNAGIVEUTHAT 0 [11]3-8-9 G Faulkner 50/1: 7: Mid-div, rdn & no prog over 2f out, debut.   2½   58
4479} **THEATRE BELLE 201** [5]3-8-9 J F Egan 50/1: 00-8: Mid-div, drvn & struggling fnl 3f, reapp.   1¾   53
      TRYSTING GROVE 0 [8]3-8-9 G Parkin 50/1: 9: Dwelt, al towards rear on debut.   ¾   54
1086 **PURPLE RAIN 8** [10]3-8-9 F Lynch 25/1: 00: 10th: Rear, hung right & struggling fnl 3f.   2½   49
      GHANTOOT 0 [1]3-9-0 N Mackay(3) 20/1: 0: 11th: Dwelt & held up, no impress fnl 3f on debut.   7   42
11 Ran Time 1m 43.58 (6.08) Owned: Mr Hamdan Al Maktoum Trained: Arundel

321

1178   **5.00 Skelton Maiden Stakes Div 2 3yo** (D)
£4033 £1241 £620   **1m rnd**   **Good 41**   **-22 Slow**   Inside

919   **APPALACHIAN TRAIL 21** [5] I Semple 3-9-0 (76) R Winston 7/4 FAV: 05-31: Handy & led 2f out, rdn & **81**
styd on strongly ins last: hvly bckd, confirmed reapp promise: eff at 1m on firm & gd grnd, gall or sharpish trks.
4987} **FOSSGATE 164** [3] J D Bethell 3-9-0   C Catlin 8/1: 05-22: ch g Halling - Peryllys (Warning) Led,   2½   **75**
rdn & hdd 2f out, kept on but al held after: op 16/1, just ndd this on reapp: promise on 2nd of just 2 '03 starts
(mdn, rtd 77): eff at 1m, half-brother to a 7f h'cap wnr: handles gd & soft: win a race.
1008   **EMTILAAK 15** [7] B Hanbury 3-9-0 (79) W Supple 5/2: 023-23: Held up & pulled hard early, eff to   1¼   **72**
chall 2f out, no extra dist: bckd: not settle early stages, impr when learning restraint: prob just styd 1m on
fast, gd & polytrack: see 1008.
   QUEEN LUCIA 0 [6] J G Given 3-8-9   T Quinn 20/1: 4: b f Pursuit of Love - Inquirendo (Roberto)   1½   **64**
Held up, drvn & kept on fnl 2f, not able to chall on debut: ndd this: eff at 1m, dam a mid-dist wnr & shaped as if
10f+ will suit: handles gd grnd, likely improver over further.
4635} **PRINCESS KIOTTO 191** [2]3-8-9   A Mullen(7) 50/1: 000-5: b f Desert King - Ferghana Ma (Mtoto)   3   **58$**
Trkd ldrs, no impress fnl 2f: well clr of rem on reapp: unplcd all 3 '03 start (rtd 42 & 12a).
1539} **FOURSWAINBY 335** [2]3-8-9   T Eaves(5) 50/1: 00-6: Dwelt, rear, no impress fnl 3f on reapp.   10   **48**
4937} **SWEET REPOSE 169** [8]3-8-9   S Drowne 8/1: 5-7: Trkd ldrs & keen, drvn & btn 2f out, reapp.   1½   **40**
966   **ANICAFLASH 17** [10]3-8-9   L Enstone(3) 100/1: 00-08: Held up & keen, hmpd early, no impress fnl 3f.   4   **32**
   VIBE 0 [1]3-9-0   R Ffrench 11/2: U: Jinked left & u.r. leaving stalls, debut.   **0**
9 Ran   Time 1m 42.55 (5.05)   Owned: G L S Partnership   Trained: Carluke

---

1179   **5.30 Newby Apprentice Handicap Stakes 4yo+ 0-70** (E)   [70]
£4181 £1286 £643   **5f str**   **Good 41**   **-01 Slow**   Stands Side

1127   **MYND 3** [5] R M Whitaker 4-9-6 (62) D Tudhope 7/2 FAV: 4-112021: Al handy & led 2f out, in   **68**
command ins last, styd on well: bckd again, op 4/1: acts on fibresand, gd & soft grnd, handles polytrack: stays
sharp 6f, best at 5f on a sharp/turning trk: progressive sprinter: see 1127 & 508.
4810} **JOYCES CHOICE 178** [19] J S Wainwright 5-8-10 (52) K Ghunowa(5) 25/1: 050050-2: b g Mind Games -   1¼   **53**
Madrina (Waajib) Al prom far side, led that group well ins last, no dngr to wnr: reapp, first home on far side:
clmr rnr-up in '03 for A Berry: 4th at best '02 (h'cap, rtd 57): eff at 5f on firm & soft grnd, likes a sharp/easy
trk. 2 Jul'03 Catt 5fm 51-(50) F: 1 Aug'01 Thir 5gd 80- E:
187   **CATCH THE CAT 125** [2] J S Wainwright 5-9-12 bl (68) A Reilly(8) 20/1: 056050-3: b g Catrail -   nk   **68**
Tongabezi (Shernazar) Prom stands side & ch dist, no extra: 4 mth abs, stablemate of rnr-up: dual h'cap scorer
'03: h'cap wnr '02: suited by stiff/gall 5f, stays 6f: acts on fast, soft & any trk, loves Beverley: loves to
race with/force the pace in visor or blnks, eff in cheek pieces: gd reapp. 1 Sep'03 Donc 5gd 69-64 D:
1 Jul'03 Beve 5g/f 67-55 F: 2 Jul'03 Hayd 5g/f 57-51 E: 1 Jul'02 Beve 5g/s 57-50 E: 2 Apr'01 Newm 5g/s 71- C:
973   **BAHAMIAN BELLE 17** [20] P S McEntee 4-9-0 T (56) Dean Williams(3) 33/1: 3405-604: Al prom far side   ½   **54**
& led that group over 1f out, no extra nr fin: gd run in first time t-strap, apprec return to 5f: see 880.
4670} **VALIANT ROMEO 188** [6]4-8-12 (54) Saleem Golam(5) 33/1: 000000-5: Led stands side till 2f out.   nk   **51**
807   **VIJAY 41** [18]5-9-4 (60) W Hogg 9/1: 360-0306: Led far side till dist, no extra: abs: see 748.   nk   **56**
4062} **FAIRGAME MAN 224** [8]6-8-8 (50) Steven Harrison(5) 40/1: 300000-7: Prom, no extra over 1f out.   shd   **46**
1046* **NEVER WITHOUT ME 10** [14]4-8-13 (7ex) (55) K Jackson(8) 14/1: 2-645218: Mid-div, drvn & no prog dist.   1¼   **47**
960   **TORRENT 17** [4]9-8-7 bl (49) C Haddon 20/1: 5300109: Mid-div, no prog fnl 1f: btr 889.   hd   **40**
760   **PARK STAR 47** [1]4-9-4 (60) Dawn Watson(6) 11/1: 00-63200: 10th: Drvn mid-div stands side, no prog.   nk   **50**
4852} **YOMALO 176** [11]4-9-11 (67) R Mills(10) 25/1: 411220-0: 11th: Dwelt, rear stands side, mod prog, reapp.   ½   **55**
4856} **AAHGOWANGOWAN 176** [10]5-9-4 t (60) A Mullen(3) 20/1: 010230-0: 12th: Chsd ldrs 4f: reapp.   ½   **46**
1096   **COLLEGE MAID 7** [7]7-8-11 bl (53) J Currie(8) 11/1: 03006-40: 13th: Mid-div stand side, no impress.   nk   **38**
1103   **THE FISIO 7** [9]4-10-0 vis (70) T Block(8) 6/1: 5630020: 14th: Chsd ldrs stands side, btn over 1f out.   ¾   **53**
1046   **EJAY 10** [17]5-8-4 (46) M Halford(8) 40/1: 6-060200: 15th: Chsd ldrs far side till over 1f out: btr 720.   nk   **28**
897   **POLAR FORCE 23** [3]4-9-4 (60) T Dean(10) 13/2: 03-40030: 16th: Slow away & al rear stands side.   1½   **37**
998   Grandma Lily 15 [13]6-9-7 (63) Andrew Webb(8) 16/1:0 853   Cash 30 [15]6-9-0 VIS(56) D Fentiman 20/1:0
4446} Petongski 203 [16]6-8-8 bl e(50) R Keogh(5) 33/1:0   4608} Shirley Not 194 [12]8-8-4 (46) B O'Neill(5) 33/1:0
20 Ran   Time 59.89(2.09)   Owned: Derek and Jean Clee   Trained: Scarcroft

---

Official Going STANDARD.

1180   **5.05 Betdirect Co Uk Banded Stakes 4yo+ 0-35** (H)
£1474 £421 £211   **1m4f aw**   **Going 51**   **-00 Slow**   Inside

315   **LEOPHIN DANCER 101** [4] P W Hiatt 6-9-1 (35) B Doyle 7/1: 0500-601: b g Green Dancer - Happy Gal   **39a**
(Habitat) In tch, rdn & led over 1f out, sn joined, just prevailed, all out: abs: seller rnr-up '03, AW h'cap plcd
(rtd 35a): thrice plcd '02 in sellers & mdns: eff btwn 9f/sharp 2m on firm, gd & both AWs: best without t-strap &
goes well fresh: first win. 2 Aug'03 Catt 15.8fm 52-(34) G: 2 Sep'01 Pont 10fm 65- D: 2 Sep'01 Redc 9g/f 76- D:
916   **NEPTUNE 22** [3] J C Fox 8-9-1 (35) R Smith 10/1: 500/-5002: b g Dolphin Street - Seal Indigo   shd   **38a**
(Glenstal) Dwelt, rear, hdwy wide to chall over 1f out, just held: missed '03: early '02 C/D amat h'cap scorer,
subs appr h'cap plcd (rtd 44a, turf unplcd, rtd 31, h'cap): eff at 12/14.7f on both AWs, likes a sharp trk.
1 Jan'02 Ling 12ap 42a-43 E:
1072   **HELLBENT 9** [12] J A Osborne 5-9-1 (35) D Sweeney 4/1 FAV: 0000563: Dwelt, rear, smooth hdwy to   1½   **35a**
chall dist, no extra: rest well covered: styd longer 12f on polytrack: mdn.
752}   **FULL EGALITE 407** [2] B R Johnson 8-9-1 bl (30) N Pollard 7/1: 00/540/0-4: Trkd ldrs, no impress.   3   **30a**
2134} **SMARTER CHARTER 306** [11]11-9-1 (35) Kristin Stubbs(7) 14/1: 00/0000-5: Dwelt, sn keen & handy,   nk   **29a**
led over 3f out till over 1f out, wknd: long abs, has come out of retirement.
4704} **SHARP SPICE 186** [5]8-9-1 vis (35) S Whitworth 5/1: 050660-6: Dwelt, no impress fnl 3f: jumps abs.   5   **21a**

968	**GIKO** 17 [6]10-9-1 bl (35) D Corby(3) 9/2: 00-03067: Led/dsptd lead till over 3f out, sn btn: btr 707.	nk	20a
239	**ORIENTAL MOON** 115 [9]5-9-1 VIS (35) S Hitchcott(3) 12/1: 000065-8: Handy 3f out, sn wknd: jumps fit.	2	17a
588	**LEYAALY** 66 [1]5-9-1 (30) B Reilly(3) 33/1: 00/00-69: Al towards rear, jumps fit.	½	16a
971	**SUPERCLEAN** 17 [7]4-9-0 (30) M Lawson(7) 16/1: 055-00: 10th: Al bhd: op 20/1.	nk	15a
1072	**DANCES WITH ANGELS** 9 [10]4-9-0 p (35) P M Quinn 12/1: 44400-00: 11th: Wide, led till over 5f out.	7	5a
968	**POLKA PRINCESS** 17 [8]4-9-0 BL (35) V Slattery 20/1: 0030000: 12th: Keen & cl-up till over 5f out, blnks.	12	0a

12 Ran   Time 2m 35.33 (6.13)   Owned: Mr Clive Roberts   Trained: Banbury

---

1181

5.35 New Site @ Betdirect Co Uk Banded Stakes 3yo+ 0-35 (H)
£1267 £362 £181   **7f aw rnd**   **Going 51**   -07 Slow   Inside

982	**BAYTOWN FLYER** 16 [10] P S McEntee 4-9-0 (35) B Reilly(3) 7/1: 000-2201: Keen & chsd ldr, led over 2f out & sn rdn clr, al holding rivals from dist: nicely bckd, op 9/1: eff at 6/7f, has tried 1m: acts on firm, gd/soft & both AWs: enjoyed forcing tactics in banded company: see 909.		36a
640	**TOP STYLE** 60 [2] M J Wallace 6-9-0 (30) D Corby(3) 5/2: 00/004//-02: Dwelt & sn pushed along rear, styd on for press fnl 2f, nvr threatened wnr: 2 month abs: eff at 7f, crying out for 1m in similar: acts on polytrack.	1½	32a
971	**MAHLSTICK** 17 [6] D W P Arbuthnot 6-9-0 (35) S Hitchcott(3) 11/1: 00406/-63: Keen & held up, eff to chase wnr 2f out, no extra ins last: see 971.	nk	31a
1122	**BEAUTEOUS** 4 [7] M J Polglase 5-9-0 (35) C Lowther 6/4 FAV: 00-00644: Rdn to go handy when short of room after 1f, sn pulled hard & tkn wide, rdn & btn 2f out: qk reapp: well bckd, see 1122.	1	29a
971	**TINY TIM** 17 [8]6-9-0 (35) R J Killoran(7) 7/2: 50/-44235: Held up in tch, eff 2f out, not able to chall.	¾	27a
1074	**DEFINITELY SPECIAL** 9 [3]6-9-0 p (35) M Savage(5) 25/1: 0-000006: Chsd ldrs, wknd over 1f out.	2½	22a
541	**KAFIL** 72 [4]10-9-0 bl (35) N Chalmers(5) 50/1: 00/500-07: b g Housebuster - Alchaasibiyeh (Seattle Slew) Keen, short of room & drpd rear after 1f, nvr on terms: 10 wk abs: mod form.	1¾	18a
939	**UN AUTRE ESPERE** 19 [5]5-9-0 bl (30) B Swarbrick(7) 50/1: 00-06008: Drvn rear, no prog.	3	12a
4358}	**SUPERPRIDETWO** 208 [1]4-9-0 vis (35) S Whitworth 33/1: 005005-9: Led till over 2f out, wknd qckly.	1½	9a
1058	**MISS CELERITY** 10 [9]4-9-0 (35) R Miles(3) 33/1: 0-004000: 10th: Cl-up till halfway, sn bhd: flattered 717.	5	0a

10 Ran   Time 1m 26.86 (4.06)   Owned: Mr J Doxey   Trained: Newmarket

---

1182

6.05 Anne Gurney Birthday Banded Stakes 4yo+ 0-45 (H)
£1617 £462 £231   **1m2f aw**   **Going 51**   -05 Slow   Inside

315	**HUSKY** 101 [2] R M H Cowell 6-8-11 p (45) B Doyle 7/2: 00000-51: b g Special Power - Hallo Bambina (Neman) Trkd ldrs & led over 3f out, held on all out: 3 month abs: AW h'capped plcd '03 (rtd 42a, turf h'cap rnr-up, disapp in t-strap & visor): eff at 7f, best around 10f on fast & polytrack, eff in cheek pieces. 2 May'03 Folk 9.7g/f 47-47 G:		48a
1330}	**KINGS TOPIC** 347 [5] P Burgoyne 4-8-11 (45) R J Killoran(7) 14/1: 000/0-02: ch g Kingmambo - Topicount (Private Account) Keen, held up wide, chall trav well 2f out, rdn & just held line: reapp, may have won this with stronger handling: unplcd sole '03 starts (rtd 50, mdn, G Wragg): no form '02: eff around a sharp 10f, has tried 12f: acts on polytrack in banded company.	shd	47a
970	**MYTHICAL CHARM** 17 [6] J J Bridger 5-8-11 (40) N Chalmers 10/3: 1-600063: Chsd ldrs, onepace.	3	42a
575	**EL PEDRO** 67 [1] N E Berry 5-8-11 (45) M Savage(2) 9/4 FAV: 4005-434: Mid-div, rdn & btn 3f out: abs.	5	34a
752}	**SYLVAN TWISTER** 407 [7]5-8-11 (35) N Pollard 16/1: 000/00-5: Restless stalls, slow away & rear.	¾	32a
1026	**PYRRHIC** 13 [4]5-8-11 bl (40) D Sweeney 6/1: 6506066: Trkd ldrs, btn 2f out: op 7/2.	11	16a
165}	**COURTLEDGE** 859 [3]9-8-11 vis (35) S Hitchcott(3) 25/1: 000/0/0//-7: Led & sn clr, drvn/hdd over 3f out.	2	13a

7 Ran   Time 2m 08.46 (5.66)   Owned: Mrs J M Penney   Trained: Newmarket

---

1183

6.35 Littlewoods Bet Direct Banded Stakes 3yo 0-45 (H)
£1603 £458 £229   **1m2f aw**   **Going 51**   -10 Slow   Inside

1073	**LARAD** 9 [1] J S Moore 3-8-11 (45) B Swarbrick(7) 7/2: 3500551: Cl-up, led despite hanging right ins fnl 1f, drvn out: eff at 1m, apprec rtn to 10f: acts on polytrack & eff in blnks: first win: see 538.		49a
970*	**OKTIS MORILIOUS** 17 [3] A W Carroll 3-8-11 (45) J Quinn 5/4 FAV: 0-00412: Held up, hdwy 2f out, styd on well fnl 1f, just held by wnr: well bckd: ran to form of win here in 970 (banded).	½	47a
1073	**REGENCY MALAYA** 9 [6] M F Harris 3-8-11 bl t (40) S Righton 12/1: 0-052003: Keen cl-up, led trav well 3f out, sn clr, hdd under press ins fnl 1f, no extra: eff at 1m/10f on polytrack: see 831.	½	46a$
911	**SHALATI PRINCESS** 22 [8] J C Fox 3-8-11 (45) R Smith 8/1: 00604: Held up, hdwy 3f out, no impress ins fnl 1f: eff at 10f on polytrack: see 785.	¾	44a
1073	**STAGECOACH RUBY** 9 [7]3-8-11 e (45) R Brisland 8/1: 0650-005: Handy, no extra dist: see 1073.	3½	39a
893	**MORNING HAWK** 24 [5]3-8-11 (45) S Whitworth 6/1: 000-0456: Nvr nrr than mid-div: see 893.	1	37a
1081	**FORA SMILE** 8 [4]3-8-11 VIS (45) D Sweeney 14/1: 0000057: Led till 3f out, fdd: first time visor.	9	23a
4613}	**WEBBINGTON LASS** 192 [2]3-8-11 (45) S Carson 25/1: 00000-8: b f Petardia - Richardstown Lass (Muscatite) Handy, fdd 3f out: reapp: unplcd in '03 (rtd 52, mdn): with Dr J R Naylor.	22	0a

8 Ran   Time 2m 08.95 (6.15)   Owned: Mr A P Crook   Trained: Hungerford

---

1184

7.05 Bet Direct On Sky Active Banded Stakes 3yo+ 0-40 (H)
£1260 £360 £180   **6f aw rnd**   **Going 51**   +11 Fast   Inside

639	**CRAFTY POLITICIAN** 60 [4] G L Moore 7-9-0 bl (40) R L Moore 4/1: 00000-41: Prom, led 2f out, pushed out, val 4L: abs: improve for drop back to 6f & switch to banded grade: acts on fibresand & eff with blnks.		45a+
1074	**HINCHLEY WOOD** 9 [3] J R Best 5-9-0 bl (35) N Pollard 4/1: 0005542: Chsd ldrs, kept on fnl 1f, not pace wnr: op 11/4: eff at 6/7f: see 1074.	2½	36a
832	**SOTONIAN** 37 [1] P S Felgate 11-9-0 (40) S Hitchcott(3) 3/1: 5330533: Led till 2f out, no extra.	nk	35a
781	**MARON** 45 [2] R Jordan 7-9-0 bl (40) Dane O'Neill 11/4 FAV: 0000-524: Dwelt, nvr nrr than mid-div.	4	23a
4722}	**TECHNICIAN** 185 [5]9-9-0 bl (40) C Lowther 11/2: 400050-5: ch g Archway - How It Works (Commanche Run) Rear, nvr a factor: reapp: nvr won once in '03 (h'cap, E J Alston): mainly out of form in '02 & tumbled down h'cap: won 4 h'caps in '01: eff at 6f/sharp 7f on firm, soft & fibresand, blnks/visor, has tried cheek pieces. 2 Apr'03 Thir 7fm 63-60 E: 1 Aug'01 York 6gd 91-85 C: 2 Jul'01 Newc 6g/f 86-80 D: 2 Jun'01 Newc 6fm 83-77 C: 1 Jun'01 Pont 6fm 77-72 C: 2 May'01 Thir 6g/f 73-68 C: 1 May'01 Thir 6g/f 71-60 E: 1 Dec'00 Wolv 7af 63a-54 F:	4	11a

4104] **CHAKRA 577** [6]10-9-0 (30) R Miles(3) 20/1: 000000/-6: gr g Mystiko - Maracuja (Riverman) Handy,   ½   **10a**
wknd 3f out: earlier jumps unplcd (rtd 81h, nov hdle): missed '03: modest form in '02 (rtd 36, h'cap, M S
Saunders): h'cap wnr in '01: stays 7f, best over a sharp/undul 6f: acts on firm & gd grnd: with C J Gray.
1 May'01 Good 6g/f 53-49 D: 2 May'01 Brig 6fm 51-49 F: 2 May'01 Bath 5.7g/f 49-49 E:
6 Ran   Time 1m 12.81 (2.41)   Owned: Mr Raymond Gross Ms Adrienne Gross   Trained: Brighton

---

1185   **7.35 Bet Direct Interactive Banded Stakes 3yo+ 0-40 (H)**
£1449 £414 £207   **1m aw rnd**   **Going 51**   **-03 Slow**   Outside

971* **CUMBRIAN PRINCESS 17** [6] M Blanshard 7-9-7 (40) D Sweeney 9/4: 05-40011: .Handy, chsd ldr 2f   **45a**
out, rdn out to lead cl-home: well bckd: eff at 1m/9f in fast, soft grnd & both AWs: likes banded grade: see 971.
3788} **BENJAMIN 237** [1] Jane Southcombe 6-9-7 BL t (40) V Slattery 10/1: 003426-2: b g Night Shift -   1½   **41a**
Best Academy (Roberto) Cl-up, led 4f out, sn clr, tired & hdd cl-home: long jumps abs, earlier unplcd (rtd 36h,
sell h'cap): plcd twice in '03 (rtd 42, mdn & sell h'cap): modest form in '02 (rtd 30, P Mitchell): eff around 1m
on firm, fast grnd & polytrack: eff with t-strap & blnks.
939 **SUNSET BLUES 19** [9] K O Cunningham Brown 4-9-7 bl e (40) Dane O'Neill 20/1: 5003: Played up in   hd   **41a**
stalls, bhd, hdwy bef 1f out, nrst fin: eff at 1m, shapes as tho' further will suit: acts on polytrack: see 751.
783 **LUCRETIUS 44** [2] D K Ivory 5-9-7 (40) M Howard(7) 21/1: 600-0004: b g Mind Games - Eastern Ember   nk   **40a**
(Indian King) Bhd, hdwy 2f out, onepcd ins fnl 1f: 6 wk abs: cheek pieces left off: unplcd in '03 (rtd 50a & 54,
mdns): eff at 1m on polytrack.
786 **DUE TO ME 44** [8]4-9-7 e (40) R L Moore 7/4 FAV: 0/400-525: Bhd, nvr nrr than mid-div: abs, btr 782.   2½   **35a**
968 **NEWCORR 17** [4]5-9-7 (35) N Chalmers(5) 33/1: U60/0-006: Mid-div, fdd dist: see 968.   4   **27a**
782 **A BIT OF FUN 45** [5]3-8-6 (35) P M Quinn 7/1: 000-527: Handy, fdd 3f out: btr 782.   6   **15a**
1073} **TONG ICE 366** [3]5-9-7 P (40) R Brisland 25/1: 00400/0-8: Led, hdd 4f out, sn fdd: reapp.   5   **5a**
894 **YOUNGS FORTH 24** [7]4-9-7 VIS (40) J Quinn 5/1: 00-0055P: Trkd ldrs, fdd 3f out & sn p.u., broke   **0a**
blood vessel: first time visor: btr 783.
9 Ran   Time 1m 40.58(4.38)   Owned: Mr David Sykes   Trained: Upper Lambourn

---

Official Going Good

1186   **1.10 Bet365 Call 08000 322365 Handicap Stakes 3yo 0-95 (C)**   **[102]**
£9705 £2986 £1493   **7f str**   **Good/Firm 27**   **-22 Slow**   Stands Side

4899*]**OASIS STAR 171** [2] P W Harris 3-8-1 (75) Martin Dwyer 20/1: 1-1: b f Desert King - Sound Tap   **88+**
(Warning) Cl-up, styd on strongly over 1f out to lead ins last, drvn out, gamely: won sole juv start (mdn auct
fills): dam multiple 6/8f scorer: clearly stays 7f well, 1m sure to suit: acts on firm & fast grnd, stiff trks:
runs well fresh: improving, genuine & lightly rcd, type to go on again & land further success.
1 Oct'03 Leic 6.0fm 80- F:
911* **IFTERADH 22** [17] B Hanbury 3-8-9 (83) R Hills 10/1: 12: Handy, hdwy over 1f out, edged left but   nk   **94**
styd on to lead ins last, sn hdd, just held: acts on fast grnd & polytrack: 1m shld suit: lightly rcd, useful &
progressing well, shld win again: see 911.
3443*]**TARUSKIN 252** [8] N A Callaghan 3-8-8 (82) R L Moore 33/1: 3231-3: b g Danehill Dancer - Jungle   1¼   **90+**
Jezebel (Thatching) In tch, sltly outpcd over 2f out, kept on nicely fnl 1f, nrst fin: reapp: won last of 4 '03
starts (auct mdn): plcd other 3: stays 7f well, looks sure to relish 1m: acts on firm & gd/soft, any trk: plenty
to like about this, type to improve & win similar. 1 Aug'03 Brig 6.0fm 82- E: 2 Jul'03 Epso 7gd 82- E:
4368* }**IFFRAAJ 208** [1] M A Jarvis 3-8-12 (86) P Robinson 7/1: 12: b c Zafonic - Pastorale (Nureyev)   ½   **93**
Set pace, rdn & hdd ins last, no extra: won second of only 2 '03 starts (mdn): likes to force the pace at 7f & prob
handles any trk: acts on fast & soft: clr of rem on reapp, gd run. 1 Sep'03 Warw 7.1g/f 83- D:
4869} **LYCA BALLERINA 174** [5]3-7-13 (73) J Mackay 20/1: 564634-5: b f Marju - Lovely Lyca (Night Shift)   4   **72**
Held up, late gains, nvr dngrs on reapp: plcd on 3 of 8 juv starts (rtd 74): eff over 7f/1m on fast & gd grnd,
gall trks: encouraging return, will relish a return to 1m.
955* **FREE TRIP 19** [13]3-8-11 (85) R Hughes 7/2 JT FAV: 01120-16: In tch, brief eff 2f out, onepace: hd   **83**
well bckd: btr expected after 955 & reportedly run LH'd.
119 **MISTER SAIF 138** [3]3-8-13 (87) P Dobbs 33/1: 310622-7: Cl-up, no impress over 1f out: long abs.   1¼   **82**
1110 **FADEELA 5** [18]3-7-12 (3oh) (69) D Fox(5) 25/1: 25210-58: With ldr, wkng when hmpd over 1f out.   shd   **67**
694 **SECRET PLACE 54** [10]3-8-10 (84) E Ahern 25/1: 02-1139: Keen held up, short of room over 2f out,   hd   **78**
no dngr: 8 wk abs: see 694, 432 (polytrack).
1008* **INSTANT RECALL 15** [9]3-8-6 (80) D Holland 14/1: 310: 10th: In tch, wknd 2f out: reportedly rcd   2   **70**
too freely: btr 1008 (mdn, polytrack).
955 **POPPYS FOOTPRINT 19** [11]3-8-9 (83) N Callan 66/1: 01620-00: 11th: Slow away, sn rdn & bhd.   nk   **72**
4971*]**HEZAAM 166** [6]3-8-4 (78) I Mongan 14/1: 01-0: 12th: Slow away & al bhd on reapp.   ¾   **65**
4830} **GO YELLOW 177** [4]3-8-1 (75) J Fanning 50/1: 0626-0: 13th: In tch, wknd 2f out.   nk   **61**
3639*]**OUTER HEBRIDES 244** [16]3-8-9 vis (83) J Murtagh 12/1: 221-0: 14th: In tch, wknd 2f out: gelded.   1½   **65**
98* **BENNY THE BALL 142** [15]3-8-11 (85) J P Guillambert(3) 33/1: 4261-0: 15th: In tch, wknd 2f out: abs.   1¼   **65**
4484} **SWEET REPLY 201** [7]3-8-8 (2ow) (80) K Fallon 33/1: 045104-0: 16th: In tch, wknd 2f out: hung right.   2   **58**
4774*]**MAHMOOM 181** [14]3-9-4 (92) T E Durcan 7/2 JT FAV: 211-0: 17th: Held up, btn 2f out: well bckd.   2½   **63**
3345} **TRANQUIL SKY 257** [19]3-9-0 (88) W Ryan 66/1: 631310-0: 18th: Nvr a factor.   3   **53**
729 **TORONTO HEIGHTS 50** [12]3-8-5 (79) J Quinn 20/1: 06-21100: 19th: Keen in tch, wknd 3f out: abs.   1¼   **42**
885 **BETTALATETHANNEVER 26** [20]3-9-7 (95) Dane O'Neill 16/1: 061-140: 20th: Handy, wknd 2f out.   1   **56**
20 Ran   Time 1m 26.66 (3.46)   Owned: Mr R J Creese   Trained: Berkhamsted

---

1187

1.45 Listed Ngk Spark Plugs Abernant Stakes 3yo+ (A)
£17400 £6600 £3300 **6f str** **Good/Firm 27** **+01 Fast** Stands Side

4795} **ARAKAN 180** [5] Sir Michael Stoute 4-9-4 (111) K Fallon 5/2 JT FAV: 212263-1: br c Nureyev - Far **113**
Across (Common Grounds) Prom, led & edged left over 1f out, styd on strongly, bit in hand: hvly bckd on reapp: '03
mdn & h'cap wnr, subs plcd in Gr 2: v eff at 7f, stays 1m & clearly has plenty of speed for 6f: acts on firm &
fast, poss handles gd/soft: acts on gall or easy trks: smart, shld win a Gr race this term.
2 Jul'03 Good 7gd 113-(106) A: 2 Jun'03 Asco 7g/f 107-(101) A: 1 May'03 York 7.0fm 107-89 B:
2 May'03 Newm 8g/f 96-89 C: 1 Apr'03 Warw 8.1fm 95- D: 2 Sep'02 Newc 6g/s 83- D:
4762* }**FRIZZANTE 182** [1] J R Fanshawe 5-9-3 (99) L Dettori 3/1: 114611-2: b f Efisio - Juliet Bravo ½ **110**
(Glow) Held up, hdwy over 1f out, styd on well ins last, just held on reapp: won 4 of 6 '03 starts (3 h'caps & a
List): '02 mdn auct wnr: suited by 6f on a stiff trk, likes Newmarket: acts on firm & gd grnd: has a turn of
foot, still improving & a fine return, win more List/Gr races.
1 Oct'03 Newm 6g/f 101-(99) A: 1 Oct'03 Newm 6g/f 106-93 B: 1 Jun'03 Donc 6fm 90-80 D:
1 May'03 Leic 6.0gd 86-70 E: 1 Jun'02 Donc 5fm 74- E:
5037} **ASHDOWN EXPRESS 159** [4] C F Wall 5-9-10 (111) S Sanders 11/1: 135410-3: ch g Ashkalani - Indian 1½ **114**
Express (Indian Ridge) In tch, no room 2f out till just ins last, kept on: reapp: clr mem: '03 stks & Gr 3 wnr, 3rd
in this race: '02 List wnr: 6f ideal, stays 1m: likes firm & gd grnd, handles gd/soft: smart sprinter, fine return
conceding weight & would have fin closer with a clr run, set for another profitable season.
1 Oct'03 Newm 6g/f 111-(111) A: 1 Aug'03 Newm 6g/f 104-(111) C: 2 Jul'03 Newb 6.0fm 110-(111) A:
2 Jun'03 Sali 6fm 108-(111) A: 2 May'03 Wind 6g/f 110-(109) A: 2 Aug'02 Asco 6g/s 110- B: 1 Jul'02 Newb 6fm 112- A:
1 Nov'01 Newm 8gd 100- C: 2 Sep'01 Sali 8g/f 98- C: 1 Jul'01 Beve 7.4g/f 100- D: 1 Jul'01 Newc 7g/f 87- D:
1004 + **BAHAMIAN PIRATE 15** [2] D Nicholls 9-9-4 (112) J Murtagh 6/1: 54606-14: In tch, rdn 2f out, no 4 **96**
impress & hmpd ins last: btr expected after 1004.
922 **SUGGESTIVE 21** [8]6-9-4 BL (107) D Holland 8/1: 24415-45: Sn rdn in tch, btn 2f out: btr over further. 1¼ **92**
4011} **BONUS 228** [6]4-9-10 (108) R Hughes 9/1: 112515-6: b c Cadeaux Genereux - Khamseh (Thatching) ¾ **96**
With ldrs, trav well till wknd appr fnl 1f: '03 stks, dual h'cap & Gr 3 scorer: all 4 wins over 6f & acts on fast &
gd/soft, poss soft, not firm? prob handles any trk: tough, useful & progressive last term, shld be btr.
1 Aug'03 Curr 6gd 111- A: 2 Jun'03 Yarm 6.0fm 107-(105) C: 1 May'03 Ling 6gd 107-92 B: 1 May'03 Sali 6g/f 109-85 B:
1 Apr'03 Newm 6gd 97-(72) D: 2 Apr'03 Wind 6g/f 75-72 D: 2 Sep'02 Newb 6g/f 100- D: 1 Jul'01 Newc 7g/f 87- D:
952 **THE KIDDYKID 19** [7]4-9-4 (104) N Callan 15/2: 15365-37: Dsptd lead till wknd 2f out: btr 952. 3 **81**
952 **CRIMSON SILK 19** [3]4-9-4 (102) Paul Eddery 20/1: 3/3063-08: Led till 3f out, wkng & hmpd 1f out. 8 **57**
8 Ran Time 1m 12.37 (1.57) Owned: Niarchos Family Trained: Newmarket

1188

2.20 Gr3 Bet365 Craven Stakes Colts & Geldings 3yo (A)
£29000 £11000 £5500 **1m str** **Good/Firm 27** **+04 Fast** Stands Side

4797} **HAAFHD 180** [2] B W Hills 3-8-9 (115) R Hills 100/30: 1133-1: ch c Alhaarth - Al Bahathri **121**
(Blushing Groom) Made all, qcknd 2f out, pushed clr, readily: juv mdn & List wnr, subs unsuited by stdy pace in
Dewhurst (rtd 113): relished step up to 1m & forcing tactics: acts on fm & fast, handles gd/soft & stiff trks: goes
well fresh, v prog & looks high-class, gd tactical ride but shld not be underestimated in 2000 Guineas.
1 Aug'03 Newb 7fm 112- A: 1 Aug'03 Newm 6g/s 100- D:
4797} **THREE VALLEYS 180** [1] R Charlton 3-8-9 (118) R Hughes 2/1 FAV: 113D2-2: ch c Diesis - Skiable 5 **113**
(Niniski) Keen, handy, eff to chase wnr over 1f out, no impress under hands & heels: well bckd: juv stks, Gr 3 &
Gr 1 (subs disqual) wnr, rnr-up in Dewhurst: stays a stiff 7f, bred to get 1m but not conclusive here: acts on
firm, handles gd/soft & gall trks: smart, shld do btr, poss back at 7f.
2 Oct'03 Newm 7g/f 115-(111) A: 1 Oct'03 Redc 6g/f 110-(100) A: 1 Aug'03 Asco 6g/f 116- A: 1 May'03 Nott 6.1g/s 104- D:
4866* }**PEAK TO CREEK 174** [4] J Noseda 3-8-9 (111) E Ahern 6/1: 231111-3: b c Royal Applause - Rivers 1¼ **110**
Rhapsody (Dominion) Held up, hdwy 2f out, sn no impress: most tough juv, won a mdn, 2 h'caps, 2 stks, List & Gr 3:
eff over 6/7f, first try at 1m (dam sprinter): likes firm & fast grnd, handles soft & enjoys gall trks: v tough,
smart & progressive last term, may do btr back in trip.
1 Oct'03 Newb 7g/f 115-(100) A: 1 Oct'03 York 6.0g/f 110-(100) A: 1 Oct'03 Redc 6g/f 110-(100) B:
1 Sep'03 Yarm 6.0gd 105-(100) B: 2 Aug'03 Ripo 6g/f 102-(100) A: 2 Aug'03 Ripo 6g/f 100-(97) C:
1 Aug'03 Ches 6.1fm 102-97 D: 1 Jul'03 Redc 6g/f 102-86 D: 1 Jul'03 Hayd 6g/f 95- D:
4797} **IMPERIAL STRIDE 180** [5] Sir Michael Stoute 3-8-9 (113) K Fallon 7/1: 116-4: b c Indian Ridge - 2½ **105**
Place de L'Opera (Sadler's Wells) Keen in tch, rdn & btn 2f out on reapp: won first 2 of 3 juv starts (stks), subs
2.5L 6th in Dewhurst: stays a gall 7f, bred to stay at least 1m (dam 12f scorer): acts on fast grnd & has run well
fresh: shld be capable of better. 1 Jul'03 Donc 7g/f 110- C: 1 May'03 Yarm 6.0g/f 90- D:
4880} **FANTASTIC VIEW 173** [3]3-8-9 (113) P Dobbs 100/30: 12112-5: ch c Distant View - Promptly (Lead On 4 **97**
Time) Chsd wnr till over 6f out, wknd: won 3 of 5 juv starts, mdn, List & Gr 3, Gr 1 rnr-up: stays gall 1m on fast &
gd: has run well fresh: smart & progressive last term, connections confident this is not his form.
2 Oct'03 Donc 8g/f 116- A: 1 Oct'03 Asco 8gd 113-(100) A: 1 Sep'03 Good 8g/f 110- A: 2 Sep'03 Sali 8fm 101- D:
1 Jul'03 Asco 7gd 91- D:
5 Ran Time 1m 38.33 (1.83) Owned: Mr Hamdan Al Maktoum Trained: Lambourn

1189

2.55 Listed Bet365 Feilden Stakes 3yo (A)
£17400 £6600 £3300 **1m1f** **Good/Firm 27** **-25 Slow** Stands Side

949 **GOLD HISTORY 19** [3] M Johnston 3-8-11 (100) J Fanning 100/30: 110-21: Made all, styd on fnl 2f, **103**
drvn out, gamely: likes to dominate & apprec step up to 9f: acts on fast & gd grnd, gall trks: typically genuine,
useful & progressive M Johnston 3yo, more to come: see 949.
1113 **PSYCHIATRIST 5** [4] R Hannon 3-8-11 (105) R Hughes 3/1: 21412-32: Handy, keen, eff to chall over ¾ **101**
1f out, no extra cl-home: nicely bckd: much sharper for recent reapp & back to useful best: stays 9f: see 1113.
4678} **TEMPLE PLACE 187** [7] M L W Bell 3-8-11 (91) I Mongan 8/1: 513-3: b c Sadler's Wells - Puzzled ½ **100**
Look (Gulch) Keen held up, eff over 2f out, short of room 1f out, kept on: '03 mdn wnr: apprec step up to 9f,
10f sure to suit: acts on fast grnd: gd return, useful, sharper for this & can win a race over further.
1 Sep'03 Wind 8.3g/f 88- D:
3554} **ISIDORE BONHEUR 246** [6] B W Hills 3-8-11 BL M Hills 14/1: 14-4: b c Mtoto - Way O'Gold (Slew O' 1¼ **98**
Gold) Keen, trkd wnr, eff over 1f out, sn no extra on reapp: juv mdn wnr: eff at 7f, stays 9f on fast grnd & a
stiff trk: has run well fresh: bred to get even further & an encouraging return in first time blnks.

1 Jul'03 Newm 7g/f 95- D:
949   **NEW MEXICAN 19** [5]3-9-0 (102) L Dettori 7/1: 24121-45: Held up, no impress till some late gains,   nk   100
nvr dngrs: stays 9f: see 949.
4942*}**ROEHAMPTON 169** [1]3-8-11   K Fallon   11/4 FAV: 01-6: b c Machiavellian - Come On Rosi (Valiyar)   1   95
Slow away, sn handy, onepace fnl 2f: well bckd: juv mdn wnr: eff at 1m, prob stays 9f: acts on soft, prob fast
grnd: lightly rcd & poss more to come. 1 Oct'03 Yarm 8.0sft 89- D:
4830} **NAADDEY 177** [2]3-8-11 (92) T E Durcan 16/1: 254353-7: In tch, wknd over 2f out: reapp.   10   0
7 Ran   Time 1m 53.89 (4.69)   Owned: Mr Abdulla BuHaleeba   Trained: Middleham

---

1190   **3.30 Creature Comforts E B F Maiden Stakes Colts & Geldings 2yo (D)**
£4771 £1468 £734   **5f str**   **Good/Firm 27**   **-12 Slow**   Stands Side

   BLUE DAKOTA [9] J Noseda 2-8-11   E Ahern 10/11 FAV: 1: b c Namid - Touraya (Tap On Wood) Trkd   104+
ldrs, qcknd to lead dist, pushed clr, impressive: hvly bckd: Apr foal, cost £62,000: half-brother to high-class
miler Tarwiya: dam a 1m wnr abroad, sire a champion sprinter: eff at 5f, 6f will suit: acts on fast & on a
stiff/gall trk, runs well fresh: held in high regard & looks an ideal type for Royal Ascot.
   TURNKEY [2] M R Channon 2-8-11   T E Durcan 9/2: 2: br c Pivotal - Persian Air (Persian Bold)   5   89
Dwelt, recovered to chase ldrs, pushed clr on debut but no ch with impressive wnr: eff at 5f, 6f shld suit:
half-brother to wnts over 5f/1m:: eff at 5f, 6f shld suit: acts on fast grnd: gd start bhd a useful sort, win a race.
   ALPAGA LE JOMAGE [5] B J Meehan 2-8-11 L Dettori 14/1: 3: b c Orpen - Miss Bagatelle (Mummy's   ½   87
Pet) Chsd ldr, left bhd dist on debut: tchd 20/1: 24,000gns Feb foal: half-brother to several wnrs, incl a juv
scorer in France: dam 6f wnr: eff at 5f on fast grnd: sharper next time.
   CAVORTING [3] D R Loder 2-8-11   J Murtagh 9/2: 4: ch c Polar Falcon - Prancing (Prince Sabo)   ¾   85
Led till dist, wknd on debut: half-brother to a 6f wnr: dam a 5f juv wnr, sire a top-class miler: ran well for a
long way & stable shld place him to advantage.
   THE CROOKED RING [6]2-8-11   K Fallon 25/1: 5: Chsd ldrs, btn dist on debut.   3   76
1077 **GRYSKIRK 8** [7]2-8-11   Paul Eddery 50/1: 46: Slowly away, nvr a factor.   2   70
   DESTINATE [8]2-8-11   R Hughes 10/1: 7: Slowly away, recovered to chase ldrs 3.5f on debut.   2   64
   COUNTRYWIDE SUN [4]2-8-11   D Holland 33/1: 8: Chsd ldrs, btn halfway, fin last.   1¼   60
8 Ran   Time 1m 0.64 (2.44)   Owned: Mr A F Nolan Mrs J M Ryan Mrs P Duffin   Trained: Newmarket

---

1191   **4.05 Bet365 Call 08000 322365 Maiden Stakes 3yo (D)**
£5382 £1656 £828   **6f str**   **Good/Firm 27**   **+05 Fast**   Stands Side

4952} **FUN TO RIDE 167** [2] B W Hills 3-8-9   M Hills 8/1: 22-1: ch f Desert Prince - Zafaaf (Kris) Made   95
all, held on gamely cl-home on reapp: op 6/1: gd time: rnr-up on both juv starts (mdn): dam 7f/1m wnr: eff at 6f
on gd & fast grnd, handles a stiff/gall trk, runs well fresh: likes to force the pace: useful, shld hold her own in
h'cap company. 2 Oct'03 Newm 6gd 85- D: 2 Oct'03 Newc 6gd 85- D:
   SOLDIERS TALE [9] J Noseda 3-9-0   E Ahern 11/4 FAV: 2: ch c Stravinsky - Myrtle (Batshoof)   hd   99
Held up, hdwy to chase wnr fnl 1f, styd on well & only just failed on debut: hvly bckd tho' op 2/1, clr rem, rider
given 1-day whip ban: dam a useful miler: eff at 6f on fast: win at 7f sn.
4870} **MAJORCA 174** [4] J H M Gosden 3-9-0   L Dettori 5/1: 0-3: b c Green Desert - Majmu (Al Nasr)   7   79
Dwelt, switched & styd on late, no ch with front 2 on reapp: tchd 7/1: 7th in a mdn on sole juv start (rtd 76):
cost 400,000gns & half-brother to useful miler Muhtathir: needs further & will improve.
3160} **FAREWELL GIFT 265** [8] R Hannon 3-9-0 (92) Dane O'Neill 10/1: 200-4: b c Cadeaux Genereux -   ¾   79
Daring Ditty (Daring March) Chsd ldrs, rdn & btn 2f out on reapp: mdn rnr-up on first of 3 '03 starts, subs tried
in Gr company: 75,000gns half-brother to a couple of useful sprint performers: eff at 6f on gd grnd, has run well
fresh. 2 May'03 Newb 6.0gd 82- D:
4333} **PIZAZZ 209** [10]3-9-0   D Holland 11/1: 0-5: Prom, rdn & wknd 1.5f out: op 8/1.   2   73
4974} **MIDNIGHT BALLARD 166** [1]3-9-0 (84) S Carson 14/1: 536-6: Chsd wnr till after halfway, wknd on reapp.   1¼   69
3758} **THREE SECRETS 238** [7]3-8-9   J Murtagh 100/30: 20-7: Keen & prom 4.5f, wknd: well bckd, new yard.   ¾   62
1070   **CEFIRA 9** [3]3-8-9   P Robinson 33/1: 0-38: Chsd ldrs 4f, wknd: see 1070.   hd   61
4833} **SWINBROOK 197** [5]3-9-0   Lisa Jones(3) 14/1: 52-9: Nvr btr than mid-div on reapp.   ½   64
   EVOQUE [6]3-8-9   J Quinn 100/1: 0: 10th: Slowly away, al bhd on debut.   nk   58
10 Ran   Time 1m 12.15 (1.35)   Owned: Mr Abdulla BuHaleeba   Trained: Lambourn

---

1192   **4.40 Bet365 Call 08000 322365 Handicap Stakes 3yo 0-95 (C)**   [97]
£9646 £2968 £1484   **1m2f**   **Good/Firm 27**   **-09 Slow**   Stands Side

1017 **HAZYVIEW 14** [11] N A Callaghan 3-8-4 (73) D Fox(5) 9/2: 00031-21: Chsd ldr, led halfway, clr   88
dist, readily: nicely bckd: eff at 1m/10f, shld stay 12f: acts on fast & gd/soft grnd & on a sharp or stiff/gall
trk: made most of fitness advantage, clr cut wnr & shld follow up under a pen: see 1017.
5024*}**HELLO ITS ME 160** [3] H J Collingridge 3-9-0 (83) J Quinn 25/1: 331-2: ch g Deploy - Evening   5   89
Charm (Bering) Keen & prom, chsd wnr fnl 2f, sn no impress on reapp: ended '03 with a mdn auct win: eff at 1m,
stays 10f, acts on gd & fast grnd: handles a gall trk, likes to run up with the pace: rcd too keenly today, spot on
next time. 1 Nov'03 Donc 8gd 80- E:
4479*}**DAYTIME GIRL 201** [4] B W Hills 3-8-7 (76) M Hills 10/1: 51-3: gr f Daylami - Snoozeandyoulose   2   79
(Scenic) Chsd ldrs, kept on under press fnl 1f but not pace to chall on reapp: won fnl of 2 juv starts (fills mdn):
eff at 1m, prob stays 10f: acts on gd & fast grnd, handles a gall trk: only lightly rcd & shld improve.
1 Sep'03 Hayd 8.1gd 78- D:
4726} **MOCCA 185** [2] D J Coakley 3-8-7 (76) D Holland 25/1: 34152-4: b f Sri Pekan - Ewan (Indian   shd   79+
Ridge) Held up, prog when short of room dist, nrst fin on reapp: '03 mdn auct wnr, subs rnr-up in stks company: eff
at 1m, stays 10f & acts on fast grnd: handles an easy & gall trk: highly encouraging reapp, set plenty to do &
would have fin 2nd with a clr run: one to keep in mind.
2 Oct'03 Leic 10.0g/f 77-(76) C: 1 Aug'03 Wind 8.3g/f 75- F:
4583*}**PRIME POWERED 194** [10]3-9-0 (89) R L Moore 20/1: 021-5: b g Barathea - Caribbean Quest (Rainbow   1½   90
Quest) Dwelt, hdwy from rear 2f out, no impress in fnl 1f on reapp: won fnl of 3 '03 starts (stks): eff at 1m,
shld stay 10f: acts on gd, handles fast grnd, handles a sharp/undul trk, likes to run up with/force the pace.
1 Oct'03 Epso 8.5gd 95- C: 2 Sep'03 Epso 8.5gd 85- D:
4885*}**MR TAMBOURINE MAN 173** [12]3-9-0 (83) L Dettori 7/2 FAV: 261-6: b c Rainbow Quest - Girl From   6   75
Ipanema (Salse) Held up, prog to chase ldrs 2f out, btn dist: reapp, bckd from 5/1: won fnl juv start (mdn auct):

eff at 1m, bred to apprec mid-dists: acts on gd & firm grnd & on a sharp or stiff/gall trk: btr than this.
1 Oct'03 Muss 8gd 87- E: 2 Sep'03 Newm 7g/f 88- D:
3312} **SPIN KING 258** [7]3-8-13 (82) I Mongan 14/1: 5613-7: Held up, nvr nr ldrs on reapp. *5* **67**
4732*}**MUHAYMIN 184** [9]3-9-2 (85) T E Durcan 10/1: 031-8: Chsd ldrs, wkng when rider drpd whip dist. *nk* **69**
4974*}**GOLDEN GRACE 166** [5]3-9-7 (90) J Murtagh 16/1: 631-9: Nvr nr ldrs on reapp: top-weight. *3* **70**
4872} **SCREENPLAY 174** [6]3-8-8 (2ow) (75) K Fallon 11/1: 044-0: 10th: Chsd ldrs 1m, wknd: gelded. *hd* **57**
930* **KING OF DREAMS 20** [1]3-9-6 (89) K Dalgleish 5/1: 42-10: 11th: Led till halfway, grad wknd. *nk* **68**
947 **CIMYLA 19** [13]3-9-0 (83) R Hughes 12/1: 41-30: 12th: Held up, nvr nr ldrs: see 947. *hd* **62**
1017 **GLENDALE 14** [8]3-7-12 (2oh) (65) Lisa Jones(3) 33/1: 0000-100: 13th: Prom till halfway: see 651 (AW). *2½* **42**
4175*}**BREATHING SUN 217** [14]3-8-9 (78) E Ahern 16/1: 03011-0: 14th: Held up, al bhd on reapp. *½* **52**
14 Ran Time 2m 05.67(3.57) Owned: Mr T Mohan Trained: Newmarket

SOUTHWELL Fibresand THURSDAY 15.04.04 Lefthand, Sharp, Oval Track

Official Going STANDARD.

1193

5.20 New Site @ Betdirect Co Uk Classified Stakes 3yo 0-60 (F)
£2947 £842 £421 **1m aw rnd** **Going 55** **-01 Slow** Inside

975 **GOBLIN 16** [11] D E Cantillon 3-9-2 (62) S Sanders 3/1 FAV: 35000-41: Handy, hung left dist, styd on to lead cl-home, drvn out: tchd 7/1: rider received 2 day whip ban: eff at 6f, now stays 1m: acts on fast, gd grnd, handles fibresand but rider reported mount hated it: 1st win: see 975. **67a**
1007 **JAKARMI 15** [7] B Palling 3-9-4 (64) P Hanagan 7/2: 0-161322: Trkd ldrs, led 3f out, edged left under press ins fnl 1f, hdd cl-home: clr rem: remains in gd form: see 1007 & 630. *hd* **67a**
1124 **SMART BOY PRINCE 3** [10] P A Blockley 3-9-5 (65) D Nolan(5) 12/1: 6-110503: Led 6f out, hdd 3f out, no extra ins fnl 2f: qck reapp: btr 798 & 486. *7* **54a**
1134 **PRINCESS ISMENE 3** [2] P A Blockley 3-8-11 bl (55) N Callan 14/1: 5224334: Mid-div, prog 4f out, onepcd fnl 2f: qck reapp: has been running well & this was disapp: btr 1134 & 843. *4* **38a**
899* **REGULATED 23** [6]3-9-5 (65) S W Kelly 10/1: 450-2015: Slow away, prog fnl 2f, nrst fin: op 7/1: not apprec drop back to 1m & return to 10f will suit: btr 899 (claim, 10f). *1* **44a**
4668} **DANCE TO MY TUNE 188** [9]3-8-11 (57) P Mulrennan(5) 25/1: 340606-6: b f Halling - Stolen Melody (Robellino) In tch, no extra fnl 2f: reapp: plcd on first 2 '03 starts (rtd 68, med auct mdn, M E Sowersby): eff at 6f on fast & gd grnd: has tried visor: with M W Easterby. *shd* **35a**
4443} **IM DANCING 203** [4]3-8-11 e (60) D Allan(3) 20/1: 05360-7: b f Polish Precedent - Dancing Heights (High Estate) Led, hdd 6f out, fdd 3f out: reapp: AW bow: plcd once in '03 (rtd 67, auct mdn): eff at 7f, shld apprec further: acts on gd/soft grnd: with T D Easterby. *5* **25a**
4823} **CONSIDINE 177** [5]3-9-0 (60) J Tate 7/1: 045-8: Rear, nvr able to chall: reapp. *3½* **21a**
1050 **MUNAAWESH 10** [13]3-9-5 (65) P Makin(7) 12/1: 05-039: Bhd, nvr a factor: btr 1050 (6f, gd/soft). *½* **25a**
603 **JANGO MALFOY 64** [8]3-9-0 (57) O Urbina 66/1: 0050-000: 10th: Al in rear: 9 wk abs. *1½* **17a**
3993} **RAJAYOGA 227** [12]3-9-2 (62) M Henry 33/1: 440-0: 11th: Nvr a factor in rear: reapp & AW bow. *1¾* **15a**
839 **ZULOAGO 33** [14]3-8-11 (60) A Nicholls 9/1: 5320: 12th: Bhd, nvr a factor: btr 839. *nk* **9a**
4713} **APOLLO GEE 185** [3]3-9-4 (64) J F McDonald(5) 10/1: 030-0: 13th: In tch, fdd 3f out: AW bow. *4* **8a**
13 Ran Time 1m 43.95 (4.55) Owned: Mrs E M Clarke Trained: Newmarket

1194

5.50 Bet Direct No Q On 08000 93 66 93 Claiming Stakes 3yo+ (F)
£2891 £826 £413 **6f aw rnd** **Going 55** **-04 Slow** Inside

838 **SERGEANT SLIPPER 33** [9] C Smith 7-9-7 vis (51) R Fitzpatrick 10/1: 3031201: Rear, prog 3f out, rdn out to lead cl-home: eff at 5/6f, likes fibresand/Southwell, acts on fast & hvy: see 773 & 720. **59a**
956 **SILVER MASCOT 17** [4] R Hollinshead 5-9-5 (52) Dale Gibson 7/1: 0225142: Led, sn clr, hdd under press cl-home: clr rem: ran to form on drop back to 6f: can find similar: see 825 & 661. *nk* **55a**
941 **BLAKESET 19** [3] T D Barron 9-9-3 vis (68) S Sanders 6/5 FAV: 1123053: Trkd ldrs, no extra dist: below par eff: btr 610 & 593. *5* **38a**
317 **QUEEN OF NIGHT 101** [8] D W Chapman 4-8-11 (74) A Culhane 4/1: 01515-04: Chsd ldrs, onepcd fnl 2f. *3* **23a**
3428} **GIVE HIM CREDIT 253** [7]4-9-9 (68) G Duffield 16/1: 400400-5: b g Quiet American - Meniatarra (Zilzal) Handy, fdd 2f out: reapp: mdn wnr first time out in '03: showed promise on 2nd of 2 '02 starts (rtd 69, mdn, E Dunlop): eff at 7f on fast & soft grnd: acts on a stiff or sharp trk & has gone well fresh: eff in visor, has tried blnks: with Mrs A Duffield. 1 Apr'03 Catt 7g/f 72- D: *2½* **28a**
1046 **ABOVE BOARD 10** [1]9-9-2 t (50) T G McLaughlin 20/1: 2030106: Nvr nrr than mid-div: btr 907. *hd* **20a**
853 **SCARY NIGHT 30** [6]4-9-9 p (63) J Edmunds 7/1: 00-00167: Cl-up, fdd bef 1f out: btr 793 (5f). *3* **18a**
869 **ZAK FACTA 28** [2]4-9-4 vis (50) V Halliday 14/1: 0-552468: Prom, wknd 2f out: btr 659. *¾* **11a**
444 **LIMITED MAGICIAN 86** [5]3-8-4 J Bramhill 100/1: 00-09: b f Wizard King - Pretty Scarce (Handsome Sailor) Al in rear: 12 wk abs: unplcd both '03 starts (rtd 18): with C Smith. *20* **0a**
9 Ran Time 1m 16.89 (3.59) Owned: Mr C Smith Trained: Wellingore

1195

6.20 Betdirect Co Uk Handicap Stakes 3yo+ 0-80 (D) **[76]**
£5343 £1644 £822 **7f aw rnd** **Going 55** **-04 Slow** Inside

940 **WARDEN WARREN 19** [5] Mrs C A Dunnett 6-9-11 p (73) Hayley Turner(5) 7/1: 3461001: Cl-up, styd on to lead dist, held on despite hanging left ins fnl 1f: suited by 7f on firm, gd & fibresand: see 704. **80a**
1052 **MOUNT ROYALE 10** [8] N Tinkler 6-8-13 vis t (61) Kim Tinkler 11/4 FAV: 3110062: Led, hdd under press dist, kept on but not pace of wnr ins fnl 1f: bckd from 5/1: lost little in defeat: ran to form of win in 684. *¾* **65a**
753 **EAGER ANGEL 48** [4] R F Marvin 6-8-9 p (57) R Fitzpatrick(3) 11/2: 4015103: Trkd ldrs, no extra & edged left ins fnl 1f: 7 wk abs: btr 680. *6* **49a**
840 **AIR MAIL 33** [3] Mrs N Macauley 7-9-10 vis (72) P McCabe 10/1: 60-40004: Handy, no extra dist. *¾* **62a**
1132 **CARLTON 3** [6]10-8-6 (54) R Thomas(5) 7/2: 0440245: Nvr nrr than mid-div: qck reapp: btr 1052. *2½* **39a**
629 **TEEHEE 61** [1]6-9-4 bl (66) M Fenton 13/2: 20150-46: Keen in tch, fdd dist: 9 wk abs: see 280. *¾* **49a**
942 **CLANN A COUGAR 19** [7]4-8-12 (60) G Duffield 11/1: 64404-07: Handy, fdd 2f out: see 942. *1* **41a**
2501} **BANNERS FLYING 292** [2]4-9-12 (74) A Culhane 12/1: 245-8: ch c Zafonic - Banafsajee (Pleasant *3½* **48a**

Colony) Trkd ldrs, fdd 2f out: reapp: rnr-up on first of 3 '03 starts (rtd 80 at best, mdn, B W Hills): eff at 1m, shld apprec further: acts on gd grnd: with D W Chapman. 2 Mar'03 Nott 8.2gd 77- D: 8 Ran Time 1m 30.76 (4.16) Owned: Annwell Inn Syndicate Trained: Norwich

---

1196	6.50 Littlewoods Bet Direct Median Auction Maiden Stakes 3-4yo (F)						
	£2891 £826 £413	**7f aw rnd**	**Going 55**	-01 Slow	Inside		

1119 **CONSTABLE BURTON** 4 [7] Mrs A Duffield 3-8-12 G Duffield 14/1: 000-01: b g Foxhound - Actress **76a+**
(Known Fact) Made all, kept on well, val 4L+: qck reapp & AW bow: unplcd in 3 '03 starts (rtd 56, mdn): eff at 7f, shld apprec further: imprvd for switch to fibresand, can rate higher.
381 **MY PARIS** 94 [1] K A Ryan 3-8-12 N Callan 6/5 FAV: 0-32: Handy, chsd wnr 2f out, al held ins fnl 2½ **68a**
1f: well bckd: clr rem: ran to form of 3rd in 381.
892 **BUNDABERG** 24 [3] P W Hiatt 4-9-12 (55) A Culhane 2/1: 05-4223: Held up, prog & in tch 2f out, 5 **58a**
fdd dist: op 3/1: see 892 & 636.
983 **AIREDALE LAD** 16 [10] J R Norton 3-8-12 V Halliday 50/1: 0-64: b g Charnwood Forest - Tamarsiya 12 **36a**
(Shahrastani) Rcd wide, in tch, fdd 3f out: unplcd sole '03 start (med auct mdn).
1050 **BLUE EMPEROR** 10 [6]3-8-12 (60) D Nolan(3) 14/1: 346-005: Keen cl-up, fdd 2f out: btr 1050. 1¾ **32a**
4965} **MR MOON** 166 [4]3-8-12 P Hanagan 50/1: 000-6: Chsd ldrs, fdd 2f out: reapp. ¾ **31a**
892 **SYBILL** 24 [2]4-9-7 S W Kelly 40/1: 57: Rear, nvr a factor: see 892. 13 **2a**
7 Ran Time 1m 30.55 (3.95) Owned: Turf 2000 Limited Trained: Leyburn

---

1197	7.20 #10 Free Bet @ Betdirect Co Uk Handicap Stakes 4yo+ 46-55 (F)					[64]
	£2954 £844 £422	**1m4f aw**	**Going 55**	-09 Slow	Inside	

893 **RED MOOR** 24 [7] R Hollinshead 4-8-9 (2oh) (45) A Culhane 10/1: 0065-261: Handy, led trav well 3f **51a**
out, drvn out fnl 1f to hold on: eff at 11f, imprvd today at 12f: acts on fibresand, unexposed in h'caps, see 722.
896 **CLASSIC MILLENNIUM** 23 [3] W J Musson 6-8-10 (46) Lisa Jones(3) 2/1 FAV: 40155-02: Bhd, prog 4f 1 **48a**
out, kept on fnl 1f, just held by wnr: gd run & is on a winning mark: see 896.
4817} **RED FOREST** 178 [5] J Mackie 5-8-11 t (47) Dale Gibson 16/1: 054560-3: b g Charnwood Forest - High hd **48a**
Atlas (Shirley Heights) Keen rear, short of room & sltly outpcd 3f out, kept on fnl 2f, nrst fin: earlier jumps
p.u. (nov hdle): unplcd in '03 (rtd 54, h'cap): sell wnr in '02 (B W Hills), subs with W Clay: AW mdn wnr in '01:
eff at 1m, now stays 12f: acts on fast, gd grnd & fibresand: eff with t-strap: slipped to a winning mark.
1 Jul'02 Leic 8g/f 65- G: 1 Nov'01 Wolv 7af 80a- D: 2 Nov'01 Muss 7.1gd 75- E: 2 Oct'01 Sout 6af 74a- E:
4447} **SEA COVE** 203 [11] J M Jefferson 4-8-9 (12oh) (35) P Hanagan 28/1: 6500-4: b f Terimon - Regal ¾ **45a$**
Pursuit (Roi Danzig) Slow away, prog & ev ch dist, sn onepcd: earlier jumps unplcd (rtd 96h, nov hdle): unplcd in
4 '03 starts (rtd 33, appr class stks): left modest form bhd on switch to fibresand: stays 12f.
985 **RED DELIRIUM** 16 [8]8-8-13 bl (49) N Callan 8/1: 4525525: Held up, prog 3f out, onepace dist: btr 985. ½ **47a**
1033} **JUNGLE LION** 13 [6]6-9-3 t (53) S Sanders 7/2: 6201016: Chsd ldrs, ev ch dist, sn no impress: btr 1033. hd **50a**
1033 **LIGHT BRIGADE** 13 [10]5-8-10 (46) J Tate 7/1: 506/03-67: In tch, fdd dist: see 1033. 2 **40a**
985* **OUR IMPERIAL BAY** 16 [9]5-9-5 vis (55) G Duffield 8/1: 4/06-0018: Cl-up, fdd 3f out: see 985. 12 **33a**
1034 **STAFF NURSE** 12 [1]4-8-9 (7oh) (40) Kim Tinkler 9/2: 32353-09: Prom, fdd 4f out: see 1034. 3 **21a**
4724} **WELSH AND WYLDE** 185 [4]4-9-1 (52) M Fenton 20/1: 520600-0: 10th: Led till 3f out, fdd: jumps fit. 5 **20a**
985 **SPANISH STAR** 28 [2]7-8-13 vis (49) P McCabe 14/1: 4613300: 11th: Mid-div, fdd 4f out: btr 867 & 745. 9 **5a**
11 Ran Time 2m 42.01 (7.71) Owned: The C H F Partnership Trained: Upper Longdon

---

1198	7.50 Bet In Running @ Betdirect Co Uk Handicap Stakes 3yo+ 0-70 (E)					[83]
	£3474 £1069 £535	**1m aw rnd**	**Going 55**	+09 Fast	Inside	

855 **MISSION AFFIRMED** 30 [14] T P Tate 3-8-8 (63) Dale Gibson 12/1: 55-0151: Handy, styd on to lead **70a**
dist, drvn out: gd time: eff at 7f, now stays 1m: acts on fibresand: back to form after disapp here last time when
trying to make all, open to more improvement: see 794.
806 **QUIET READING** 41 [9] M R Bosley 7-9-11 vis (65) Hayley Turner(5) 8/1: 03-34632: Chsd ldrs, ev ch 1 **69a**
1f out, kept on but not pace of wnr: clr rem: 6 wk abs: imprvd again in defeat: see 806 & 318.
1020 **PHAROAHS GOLD** 14 [4] D Shaw 6-9-6 (60) Darren Williams 10/1: 00-20503: Held up, prog 3f out, 6 **52a**
kept on fnl 1f, no ch with front two: btr 318.
924 **YENALED** 21 [5] K A Ryan 7-9-1 (55) N Callan 12/1: 5-305004: Rear, prog 3f out, kept on late. ½ **46a**
1006 **PRINCE OF GOLD** 15 [3]4-9-11 (65) A Culhane 10/1: 13000-05: Chsd ldrs, no extra dist: btr 1006. 1¼ **54a**
848* **HOLD THE LINE** 32 [10]3-8-10 p (65) A Daly 16/1: 6205-616: Nvr nrr than mid-div: btr 848 (mdn). nk **53a**
1059 **REALISM** 10 [12]4-9-11 (65) P Makin(7) 14/1: 0-441057: Prom, led 2f out, hdd dist, wknd: btr 678. ½ **52a**
942 **RARE COINCIDENCE** 19 [13]3-9-1 p (70) L Fletcher(3) 14/1: 20-11368: Cl up 6f, sn fdd: btr 564. ½ **56a**
1083 **GALLOWAY MAC** 8 [7]4-9-6 (60) S Sanders 7/2 FAV: 3012469: Bhd, prog when no room 4f out, sn no 5 **36a**
impress: well bckd: btr 858 & 721.
457 **QOBTAAN** 84 [11]5-9-2 (56) G Baker 16/1: 34-61100: 10th: Rear, nvr a factor: 12 wk abs: btr 387. 6 **20a**
858 **SIMPLY THE GUEST** 30 [6]5-9-6 t (60) Kim Tinkler 12/1: 0-221140: 11th: Al in rear: btr 530. 1½ **21a**
908* **PRINTSMITH** 23 [8]7-8-10 (50) J Bramhill 16/1: 1443210: 12th: Handy, fdd 3f out: btr 908. 5 **1a**
387 **BRANDY COVE** 93 [2]7-9-10 (64) F Lynch 7/1: 04523-40: 13th: Led till 2f out, sn fdd: btr 195. 3 **9a**
908 **SMART SCOT** 23 [1]5-9-0 p (54) M Tebbutt 10/1: 0-111120: 14th: Rear, nvr a factor: btr 847 & 771. 15 **0a**
14 Ran Time 1m 43.12(3.72) Owned: Mr T P Tate Trained: Tadcaster

Official Going STANDARD.

1199 5.05 New Site @ Betdirect Co Uk Banded Stakes 3yo+ 0-45 (H)
£1446 £413 £207 **5f aw str** Going 61 Inapplicable Outside

1012 **ATTORNEY 16** [2] D Shaw 6-9-6 vis (45) G Duffield 9/2: 0653001: Prom & led dist, rdn out: suited — **48a**
by 5/6f on fast & hvy, likes fibresand: see 397.

889 **VALAZAR 25** [9] D W Chapman 5-9-6 (40) A Culhane 11/2: 000-0002: Chsd ldrs & led halfway till — 2 **41a**
dist, not pace of wnr: blnks omitted after 889, see 587.

960 **HAGLEY PARK 18** [5] M Quinn 5-9-6 (45) D Sweeney 13/2: 2654303: Cl-up & ch over 1f out, onepace — 3 **32a**
for press: visor omitted: see 286.

1075 **BALLYGRIFFIN KID 10** [1] T P McGovern 4-9-6 (45) J F McDonald(5) 7/2 FAV: 0563-034: Cl-up, rdn & — shd **32a**
kept on, not pace to chall: acts on firm & both AWs: see 1075.

981 **TUSCAN DREAM 17** [6]9-9-6 (35) P Bradley(5) 8/1: 0000225: Handy & ch over 1f out, no extra. — shd **32a**

981* **PLEASURE TIME 17** [4]11-9-6 vis (45) R Fitzpatrick 4/1: 55-50016: Led till halfway, btn dist: see 981. — ½ **31a**

981 **LEVELLED 17** [8]10-9-6 (35) C Haddon(7) 12/1: 0004557: Dwelt, nvr on terms with ldrs: see 832. — shd **31a**

981 **DANAKIM 17** [3]7-9-6 bl e (40) D Fentiman(7) 14/1: 0-610048: Cl-up, btn over 1f out: see 578. — 1 **28a**

8 Ran   Time 59.79 ()   Owned: Mr K Nicholls   Trained: Newark

1200 5.40 #10 Free Bet @ Betdirect Co Uk Banded Stakes 3yo+ 0-45 (H)
£1449 £414 £207 **1m aw rnd** Going 61 -03 Slow Inside

894* **FRAAMTASTIC 25** [6] B A Pearce 7-9-7 p (45) B Reilly(3) 9/4 FAV: 2416011: Trkd ldrs, chsd ldr over — **47a**
1f out, hand riding to lead well ins last: suited by 1m/8.5f on firm & fibresand: see 894 & 719.

776 **AIR OF ESTEEM 47** [8] Ian Emmerson 8-9-7 (40) D Fentiman(7) 9/2: 53-55602: Trkd ldrs & led 2f out, — 1¼ **43a**
rdn & hdd well ins last: 7 wk abs, clr of rem: see 228 & 188.

584 **DESIRES DESTINY 67** [3] M Brittain 6-9-7 (35) M Lawson(7) 8/1: 600-6063: Cl-up & led over 2f out, — 6 **31a**
sn hdd & btn over 1f out: 2 mth abs: see 354.

905 **SEA YA MAITE 24** [4] S R Bowring 10-9-7 t (40) J Bramhill 4/1: 3545024: Dwelt, in tch till outpcd fnl 2f. — 1¼ **28a**

4238} **CEZZARO 214** [5]6-9-7 (35) M Nem(7) 20/1: 261040-5: ch g Ashkalani - Sept Roses (Septieme Ciel) — ½ **27a**
Led after 2f till over 2f out, fdd: reapp: '03 sell wnr, AW unplcd: eff at 1m, suited by 9/11f: acts on firm or
hvy, best without visor/cheek pieces: suited by forcing tactics & sell grade, prob any trk.
1 Jul'03 Hami 9.2gd 46-(42) E: 2 Jul'03 Warw 12.6g/f 44-42 F: 2 Jun'03 Thir 8g/f 52-(37) E:
1 Jul'02 Wind 11.6g/f 40- G: 1 Oct'01 Wind 10hvy 63- G:

956 **ABBIEJO 18** [7]7-9-7 p (40) V Slattery 9/1: 660/0-656: Prom, btn 2f out: see 889. — 6 **15a**

966 **MISS FLEURIE 18** [1]4-9-7 (45) G Duffield 12/1: 4/-007: Led till 6f out, btn 3f out: see 869. — shd **15a**

4113} **DELAWARE TRAIL 221** [2]5-9-7 (45) A Culhane 9/1: 0/60006-8: b g Catrail - Dilwara (Lashkari) — dist **0a**
Prom till halfway, sn btn: reapp: AW bow: unplcd '03 (rtd 53, mdn): tried up to 12f prev.
8 Ran   Time 1m 44.56 (5.16)   Owned: Mr Richard J Gray   Trained: Lingfield

1201 6.10 Betdirect Co Uk Banded Stakes 3yo+ 0-45 (H)
£1435 £410 £205 **6f aw rnd** Going 61 +10 Fast Inside

1181 **BEAUTEOUS 1** [8] M J Polglase 5-9-0 (35) K Ghunowa(7) 11/2: 00-006441: Dsptd lead, went on over 3f — **64a**
out, rdn clr fnl 2f: gd time: unplcd when unable to race with/force the pace yesterday: suited by 6/7f, stays 1m:
acts on gd/soft & fibresand: best up with/forcing the pace: see 771.

1052 **CLEVELAND WAY 11** [3] D Carroll 4-9-0 vis (45) D Tudhope(7) 5/2: 6564502: Chsd ldrs, rdn & kept on, — 7 **44a**
no ch with wnr dist: see 304 & 296.

773 **ETERNAL BLOOM 47** [6] M Brittain 6-9-0 (45) M Lawson(7) 10/1: 0-120003: Dwelt, chsd ldrs, no — ¾ **41a**
impress over 1f out: 7 wk abs: see 394 & 377 (C/D).

1065 **INDIAN MUSIC 10** [7] A Berry 7-9-0 (45) F Lynch 9/4 FAV: 000-6154: Dwelt & held up, late gains, — 1¼ **37a**
nrst fin: btr 982 (C/D).

822 **INDIAN WARRIOR 39** [2]8-9-0 bl (45) G Duffield 15/2: 5-100405: Held up & outpcd, nvr able to — ¾ **34a**
threaten: btr 310 (7f).

981 **BOND DOMINGO 17** [5]5-9-0 bl (35) M Stainton(7) 14/1: 000-0036: Bmpd start, chsd ldrs till halfway. — 1¼ **30a**

396 **FIRE CAT 93** [4]5-9-0 (45) D Sweeney 14/1: 25000-07: ch g Beveled - Noble Soul (Sayf El Arab) — 10 **0a**
Led till over 3f out, sn btn: abs: cheek pieces omitted: turf & AW mdn rnr-up in '03: unplcd & no form '02: eff
at 7f on fast & fibresand, sharp/undul trks. 2 Sep'03 Sout 7af 50a-(45) D: 2 Sep'03 Ling 7g/f 49- D:

904 + *CARONTE 24** [1]4-9-0 h bl (40) J Bramhill 10/1: 0000018: Dwelt & al bhd: much btr 904 (5f). — 5 **0a**
8 Ran   Time 1m 16.41 (3.11)   Owned: Mr Paul J Dixon   Trained: Newark

1202 6.40 Bloor Homes Fiskerton Banded Stakes 3yo+ 0-40 (H)
£1481 £423 £212 **7f aw rnd** Going 61 -18 Slow Inside

660} **RED FLYER 421** [5] P C Haslam 5-9-7 (40) G Faulkner 7/2: 0300/40-1: br g Catrail - Marostica — **47a**
(Stone) Dwelt, styd on for press to lead well ins last, eased when in command nr line: Flat reapp: 6 mnth jumps
abs (sell hdle rnr-up, rtd 103h, 2m/2m2f, fast & gd/soft): AW h'cap plcd '03 (rtd 36a): seems suited by 7f/1m, prob
stays 9f & tried 12f: handles both AW's, sharp trks: goes well fresh.

1028 **ILLUSTRIOUS DUKE 14** [1] M Mullineaux 6-9-7 bl (40) P Varley(7) 6/1: 0000602: Chsd ldr & led over — 1¼ **40a**
4f out till over 1f out, led again ins last, sn hdd & not pace of wnr: see 562.

982 **NEUTRAL NIGHT 17** [3] R Brotherton 4-9-7 BL (40) A Culhane 2/1 FAV: 0532433: Chsd ldrs, drvn & ch — hd **40a**
2f out, no extra dist: clr of rem: first time blnks, fair run: see 982.

719 **COUNTRYWIDE GIRL 52** [2] A Berry 5-9-7 (30) F Lynch 13/2: U-035364: Led till over 4f out, btn — 5 **30a**
over 1f out: 7 wk abs: see 663.

982 **COMPTON BAY 17** [7]4-9-7 (35) M Lawson(7) 25/1: 00/0-0005: Held up & pulled hard, struggling fnl — 3 **24a**
2f: blnks omitted: see 773.

909 **MIMAS GIRL 24** [6]5-9-7 t p (35) J Bramhill 5/1: 5300036: Chsd ldrs, hung left & btn 2f out: see 909. — 3½ **17a**

1032 **KELTIC FLUTE 14** [4]5-9-7 vis (30) D Nolan(5) 12/1: 0406067: Chsd ldrs, strugg fnl 3f: see 1032. — 5 **7a**

SOUTHWELL Fibresand FRIDAY 16.04.04 Lefthand, Sharp, Oval Track

7 Ran   Time 1m 32.19 (5.59)   Owned: Mrs C Barclay   Trained: Middleham

1203   **7.10 Bet Direct No Q On 08000 93 66 93 Tri-Banded Stakes 3yo 0-45 (H)**
£1435 £410 £205   **1m aw rnd**   **Going 61**   **-25 Slow**   Inside

986   **ROMAN THE PARK** 17 [4] T D Easterby 3-8-9 (40) G Duffield 9/4 JT FAV: 600-31: Chsd ldrs, led over   **41a**
2f out, drvn & held on well: first win: eff around 1m on fibresand in banded company: see 986.

909   **MONKEY OR ME** 24 [5] P T Midgley 3-8-4 (30) R Fitzpatrick 5/1: 00-0042: b g Sri Pekan - Ecco Mi   1¼   **32a**
(Priolo) Held up, styd on for press fnl 3f, not able to reach wnr: styd longer 1m trip in banded company: unplcd &
only mod form prev: see 909.

899   **MYSTIC PROMISE** 24 [3] Mrs N Macauley 3-8-4 t (30) Hayley Turner(5) 25/1: 0-000503: Handy & led   hd   **32a**
over 4f out till over 2f out, not pace of wnr: prob eff around 1m in banded company on fibresand: see 899 & 721.

986   **SECRET BLOOM** 17 [1] J R Norton 3-9-0 BL (45) Darren Williams 7/2: 4405424: Trkd ldrs, drvn &   ½   **41a**
onepace fnl 2f: first time blnks: btr 986.

863   **NITEOWL EXPRESS** 30 [2]3-8-9 (40) D R McCabe 9/4 JT FAV: 0-065: b f Royal Applause - Nordan   5   **26a**
Raider (Domynsky) Led till over 4f out, struggling over 1f out: appeared not to stay longer 1m trip: no form sole
'03 start (rtd 38, mdn): dam a 6f wnr.

742   **HARBOUR PRINCESS** 50 [6]3-8-9 (40) S Righton 11/1: 0666: Prom, struggl fnl 2f: abs, longer trip.   9   **8a**
6 Ran   Time 1m 46.31 (6.91)   Owned: Middleham Park Racing II   Trained: Malton

1204   **7.40 Littlewoods Bet Direct Banded Stakes 4yo+ 0-45 (H)**
£1446 £413 £207   **1m4f aw**   **Going 61**   **-07 Slow**   Inside

984*   **STRAVMOUR** 17 [9] R Hollinshead 8-8-13 (45) Dale Gibson 5/2: 0533111: Dwelt & held up, keen, prog   **55a**
to lead over 2f out & pulled clr under hand riding, readily: completed hat-trick: suited by 12f/2m in banded
company, loves fibresand & Southwell: see 984, 849 & 257.

867   **SERAPH** 29 [3] John A Harris 4-8-12 p (45) Rory Moore(7) 11/2: 0-310332: Handy & led over 3f out   7   **41a**
till over 2f out, sn no ch with wnr: recent jumps runner: see 867 & 375.

1033   **WESTERN COMMAND** 14 [1] Mrs N Macauley 8-8-13 p (45) Joanna Badger 16/1: 0500553: Prom & led   1   **39a**
over 6f out till over 4f out, kept on onepace: see 456.

780   **GALLEY LAW** 46 [6] R Craggs 4-8-12 (45) J Quinn 11/8 FAV: 0-321224: Mid-div, rdn & no impress fnl   5   **31a**
2f: 6 wk abs: see 780, 719 & 640.

221}   **ZELEA** 486 [8]5-8-13 t (40) M Lawson(7) 33/1: 003500/-5: br f Be My Guest - Ebony And Ivory (Bob   9   **17a**
Back) Dwelt & pushed along rear, no impress fnl 3f: v long abs: missed '03: unplcd '02 (rtd 55, C Wall, subs no
sand form, rtd 42a, mdn, current yard): has tried up to 2m prev.

965   **HOMERIC TROJAN** 18 [7]4-8-12 (45) D Tudhope(7) 16/1: 000-6006: ch c Hector Protector - Housefull   6   **8a**
(Habitat) Handy & led over 8f out till over 6f out, btn 2f out: unplcd '03 (rtd 59, flattered).

918   **KING PRIAM** 22 [5]9-8-13 bl (35) A Culhane 12/1: 4565407: Sn struggling in rear: see 353.   1¾   **6a**

1076   **DASH FOR GLORY** 10 [4]5-8-13 (40) D Sweeney 16/1: 00000-08: ch g Bluegrass Prince - Rekindled   nk   **5a**
Flame (Kings Lake) Chsd ldrs, btn 3f out: unplcd '03 (rtd 48, tried t-strap): AW class stks plcd '02 (rtd 63a, mdn
unplcd, rtd 75$): tried up to 14f prev.

447   **MISTER RUSHBY** 87 [2]4-8-12 (35) Darren Williams 28/1: 00000-09: Led 3f, struggling fnl 5f, abs.   8   **0a**
9 Ran   Time 2m42.55(8.25)   Owned: Mr E Bennion   Trained: Upper Longdon

NEWBURY FRIDAY 16.04.04 Lefthand, Flat, Galloping Track

Official Going Good (Good/Soft places)

1205   **2.10 Pertemps European Breeders Fund Maiden Stakes 2yo (D)**
£5694 £1752 £876   **5f34y str**   **Good 40**   **-16 Slow**   Stands Side

TOURNEDOS [5] M R Channon 2-9-0 T E Durcan 10/1: 1: b c Rossini - Don't Care (Nordico) Handy,   **95+**
hdwy & short of room over 1f out, styd on well ins last, led cl-home, going away: Mar foal, cost £30,000: dam sprint
wnr: eff over a gall 5f on gd: runs well fresh: plenty to like about this, win again.

MOSCOW MUSIC [4] M G Quinlan 2-9-0 R L Moore 25/1: 2: ch c Piccolo - Anna Karietta   ¾   **91**
(Precocious) Dwelt, sn chsd ldr, styd on to lead over 1f out till ins last, not btn far, hand & heels: Mar foal,
cost 23,000gns: half-brother to sev wnrs: eff at 5f, 6f shld suit: acts on gd: sharper for this, win sn.

PLANET TOMATO [3] P F I Cole 2-9-0 K Fallon 11/4 FAV: 3: b c Soviet Star - Via Splendida   1   **88**
(Project Manager) Slow away, sn in tch, eff over 1f out, kept on same pace hands & heels: bckd on debut: Feb foal,
cost 58,000gns: half-brother to a 7f juv wnr: dam styd 1m: eff at 5f, sure to stay at least 6f: handles gd: clr of
rem, win similar on a minor trk.

SIMPLIFY [1] D R Loder 2-9-0 J Murtagh 3/1: 4: b c Fasliyev - Simplicity (Polish Precedent)   3   **80**
Switched to lead stands side rail, rdn & hdd over 1f out, no extra on debut: op 9/4: Feb first foal, cost 28,000
gns: dam 12f wnr: bred to apprec 6f+ in time.

MARCHING SONG [6]2-9-0 R Hughes 10/1: 5: Dwelt, sn in tch, wknd over 1f out.   ¾   **78**
DETONATE [8]2-9-0 D Holland 12/1: 6: In tch, wknd 2f out.   ½   **77**
PENINSULAR [2]2-9-0 L Dettori 3/1: 7: Dwelt, sn in tch, wknd over 1f out: bckd tho' op 9/4.   2½   **71**
CREE [7]2-9-0 Martin Dwyer 25/1: 8: Sn bhd.   9   **44**
8 Ran   Time 1m 03.22 (2.92)   Owned: Ridgeway Downs Racing   Trained: West Ilsley

1206   **2.45 Dubai Duty Free Finest Surprise Rated Stakes Handicap 3yo 0-95 (C)**   [101]
£10344 £3923 £1962   **1m str**   **Good 40**   **+06 Fast**   Stands Side

947*   **AFRICAN DREAM** 20 [14] P W Chapple Hyam (94) J Quinn 6/1: 3111: In tch, hdwy 2f out, trav   **116+**
well & led appr fnl 1f, rdn out: gd time: acts on gd, soft & polytrack: eff at 1m/9f, shld get further: thriving
at present, type to win in Listed, worth following: see 947.

1105   **RED LANCER** 6 [15] R J Price 3-8-7 (80) R Miles(3) 16/1: 6112222: Trkd ldr, led over 4f out till   2   **95**

330

over 1f out, kept on but not pace of wnr: continues in fine form & caught a well h'capped sort: see 947, 796.

919* **GATWICK** 22 [1] M R Channon 3-8-10 (83) T Quinn 4/1 FAV: 3-13: Slow away, sn handy, rdn over 2f out but kept on, no threat to front 2: gd run but clrly crying out for a step up to 10f: op to further improvement. 1¼ 94

925* **ZONUS** 21 [12] B W Hills 3-8-10 (83) M Hills 11/2: 2-14: Held up, eff 2f out, kept on ins last, no dngr: clr of rem & clrly stays 1m, shaped like even further may suit: op to further improvement: see 925 (mdn). ½ 93

1057 **RED SPELL** 11 [8]3-8-6 (79) R L Moore 40/1: 1-05: ch c Soviet Star - A To Z (Ahonoora) In tch, eff 2f out, onepace: won sole juv start (mdn): eff over a sharp 1m on polytrack: has run well fresh. 5 80
1 Nov'03 Ling 8ap 80a- D:

4975} **FRANK SONATA** 167 [6]3-9-3 (90) L Dettori 20/1: 01400-6: b c Opening Verse - Megdale (Waajib) 1¾ 87
Chsd ldrs, rdn over 2f out, some late gains, no dngr: won 1 of 5 '03 starts (mdn auct), subs highly tried: eff over a gall 7f, shld stay further (dam styd 2m): acts on rain softened grnd.   1 Jul'03 Newc 7gd 85- F:

252 **FREAK OCCURENCE** 111 [13]3-8-12 (85) S Drowne 40/1: 411420-7: In tch, no impress fnl 2f: abs. 1 80

879 **BORDER MUSIC** 28 [11]3-8-7 (70) D Harrison(5) 25/1: 361-08: Held up, eff 2f out, no impress: see 879. ¾ 73

4729* **JEDBURGH** 185 [10]3-9-6 (93) M J Kinane 5/1: 320111-9: b c Selkirk - Conspiracy (Rudimentary) ¾ 84
Chsd ldrs, hung left & wknd 2f out on reapp: won fnl 3 '03 starts (stks): suited by 7f on any trk, shld stay 1m: likes firm & fast grnd (unrcd on any other): poss best when dominating: shld do btr.
1 Oct'03 Leic 7.0g/f 94-(90) C: 1 Sep'03 Leic 7.0g/f 94-(90) D: 1 Aug'03 Epso 7g/f 93-85 D: 2 Jul'03 Sali 7.0g/f 93- D:

1051* **SENESCHAL** 368 [9]3-9-9 (94) T E Durcan 14/1: 21-0: 10th: b c Polar Falcon - Broughton Singer 5 75
(Common Grounds) Held up, eff & short of room over 2f out, no impress: reapp: won 2nd of only 2 juv starts (mdn): eff at 5f, shld stay further (dam 9f scorer): acts on fast grnd & imprvd last term for forcing tactics.
1 Apr'03 Wind 5.0g/f 91- D: 2 Apr'03 Folk 5g/f 78- D:

4365} **HORNER** 209 [3]3-8-10 (83) K Fallon 66/1: 446-0: 11th: Slow away, hdwy & short of room 4f out, no dngr. 1½ 61

885 **TREASURE HOUSE** 27 [2]3-9-7 (94) D Holland 20/1: 42210-00: 12th: Rcd alone centre, hdd 4f out. 11 50

4166* **WATAMU** 218 [7]3-8-8 (81) S Sanders 16/1: 01-0: 13th: Slow away, in tch, hmpd 2f out, no extra. 6 25

4160} **FLIP FLOP AND FLY** 219 [4]3-9-3 (90) R Hughes 20/1: 01300-0: 14th: In tch, wknd 2f out: gelded. 2 30

3930} **LOMMEL** 232 [5]3-9-6 (93) J Murtagh 12/1: 15-0: 15th: In tch, wknd over 2f out. 1¼ 31
15 Ran Time 1m 39.53 (2.73) Owned: Franconson Partners Trained: Newmarket

---

1207 3.15 Dubai Duty Free Full Of Surprises Rated Stakes Handicap 4yo+ 0-110 (B) [115]
£12095 £4588 £2294   5f34y str   Good 40   +07 Fast   Stands Side

4177} **BISHOPS COURT** 218 [4] Mrs J R Ramsden 10-9-7 (108) L Dettori 14/1: 464153-1: ch g Clantime - 112
Indigo (Primo Dominie) Held up, hdwy over 2f out, styd on to lead ins last, drvn & just held on: reapp: won 1 of 6 '03 starts (List): '02 dual stks wnr: stays 6f, best at 5f on firm or gd grnd, handles hvy & any trk, likes Epsom & Chester: eff with/without t-strap: most tough & smart 10yo with a nice turn of foot.
1 Jul'03 Ches 5.1fm 110-(109) A: 1 Sep'02 Donc 5fm 114- A: 1 Jul'02 Ches 5fm 107- A: 2 Jun'02 Sand 5g/s 106- C:
1 Jun'01 Epso 5fm 113-106 A:

883 **PERUVIAN CHIEF** 27 [6] N P Littmoden 7-8-8 vis (95) D Holland 13/2: 6-060002: b g Foxhound - shd 98
John's Ballad (Ballad Rock) Slow away, bhd, hdwy 2f out, styd on ins last, just failed: unplcd in Dubai earlier: '03 dual h'cap, stks & List wnr by end of May: '02 3-time h'cap wnr: best at 5f, stays 7f on fm, gd/soft & both AWs, any trk: eff with/without blnks/visor: v tough, consistent & useful, on a fair mark.
1 May'03 Kemp 5fm 111-(101) A: 1 May'03 Beve 5gd 109-(98) C: 1 Apr'03 Newb 5.2g/f 98-93 B:
1 Mar'03 Ling 5ap 104a-(97) B: 1 Mar'03 Wolv 6af 106a-94 C: 2 Feb'03 Ling 5ap 98a-95 C: 2 Feb'03 Ling 5ap 98a-95 C:
2 Jan'03 Wolv 6af 97a-95 C: 1 Sep'02 Asco 5fm 97 95-89 B: 2 Aug'02 Ches 7.5fm 90-86 C:

790* **PIC UP STICKS** 36 [11] M R Channon 5-8-9 (96) T E Durcan 15/2: 00P-3163: Held up, hdwy & no room 1 99+
2f out till ins last, styd on well, too late: Nd unlucky: been gelded & ready to score, prob at 6f: see 790.

1004 **FROMSONG** 16 [2] B R Millman 6-8-8 (95) S Drowne 7/1: 10000-24: In tch, eff over 1f out, onepace. hd 94

4142} **WHITBARROW** 220 [5]5-8-6 (93) R L Moore 33/1: 000/056-5: b g Royal Abjar - Danccini (Dancing shd 91+
Dissident) With ldr, led over 1f out, hdd & no extra ins last: unplcd all 3 '03 starts for B Millman: List h'cap wnr in '02: eff over 5/6f on firm & gd, any trk: has run well fresh with/without blnks: fine rtn for new stable, much fitter for this & h'capped to win sn, keep in mind.   1 May'02 Hayd 6gd 110-106 A: 1 Aug'01 Good 5g/f 103- A:
1 Jun'01 Epso 6fm 105- A: 1 May'01 Wind 5gd 100- B: 1 May'01 Ling 5g/f 93- D:

4867} **RINGMOOR DOWN** 175 [9]5-8-7 (1ow) [9]3 Dane O'Neill 7/1: 500243-6: b f Pivotal - Floppie (Law hd 91
Society) Slow away & bhd, hdwy & short of room over 1f out, styd on ins last, nrst fin: won 2 h'caps in '03 (rtd 94 at best): suited by 6f on firm or fast grnd: acts on gall or easy trks: has run well fresh: fine rtn over inadequate trip, has a turn of foot & can be winning again at 6f shortly.
2 Oct'03 Newm 6g/f 90-84 B: 1 Jul'03 Newb 6.0g/f 85-81 C: 1 May'03 Kemp 6fm 81-74 C: 1 Sep'01 Kemp 6g/f 86- D:

4762} **FANNYS FANCY** 183 [10]4-8-4 (91) J Quinn 7/2 FAV: 02/1143-7: Held up, hdwy & short of room over nk 87+
1f out, not recover: promising, 6f suits.

883 **LITTLE EDWARD** 27 [3]6-8-10 (97) L Keniry(3) 10/1: 10225-58: In tch, eff over 2f out, sn no extra. shd 92

4629} **REPERTORY** 194 [1]11-9-7 (108) T G McLaughlin 16/1: 364010-9: With ldrs, wkng when short of room 1¼ 99
over 1f out on reapp.

4362} **DUBAIAN GIFT** 209 [8]5-9-5 (106) Martin Dwyer 6/1: 002216-0: 10th: Rcd alone stands side, led 1¾ 92
till over 1f out, no extra on reapp.

1162 **TRINCULO** 2 [7]7-8-4 (2oh)bl (89) N Pollard 20/1: 00U2500: 11th: In tch, wknd 2f out: btr 927. 5 62
11 Ran Time 1m 02.01 (1.71) Owned: Mr D R Brotherson Trained: Thirsk

---

1208 3.45 Arabian International Raceday Conditions Stakes 3yo (C)
£8687 £3212 £1606   1m2f6y   Good 40   -14 Slow   Inside

4336} **LET THE LION ROAR** 210 [4] J L Dunlop 3-8-11 M J Kinane 6/4 FAV: 12-1: b c Sadler's Wells - 111
Ballerina (Dancing Brave) Handy, hdwy to lead over 2f out, drvn out to hold on: well bckd on reapp: won first of 2 juv starts (mdn): eff at 1m, clrly stays a gall 10f well & further will suit: acts on fast & gd grnd: runs well fresh: useful, more to come, esp over further.   2 Sep'03 Newb 8g/f 91- B: 1 Aug'03 Newm 8gd 90- D:

9} **TOP SEED** 160 [1] M R Channon 3-8-11 (108) T E Durcan 100/30: 303624-2: b c Cadeaux Genereux - ½ 109
Midnight Heights (Persian Heights) Led early, led again till over 2f out, kept on for press & chall again ins last, just held: reapp: '03 nov stks wnr, French Gr 1 rnr-up (rtd 109): stays 10f on firm, fast grnd & prob hvy: well clr of rem: useful.   2 Nov'03 Sain 8hvy 109-:   1 Jul'03 Beve 7.5gd 95- D: 2 Jul'03 Wolv 7fap 87/f 84- D:

MAC REGAL 177 [2] M G Quinlan 3-8-11 L Dettori 9/1: 1-3: b c King's Theatre - Shine Silently 17 79
(Bering) Held up, eff & switched over 2f out, sn no impress: won a stks race in Italy in '03: stays 9f on gd/soft.

3641} **WHITE HAWK** 245 [3] D R Loder 3-8-11 (100) J Murtagh 6/1: 1214-4: b c Silver Hawk - Polska 3½ 74
(Danzig) Keen, led after 1f till 3f out, no extra: '03 mdn & nurs h'cap wnr: eff at 7f, shld stay 1m+: acts on firm, fast & fibresand, gall or sharp trks: has run well fresh under big weights: too free here.

1 Aug'03 Wolv 7af 99a-90 E: 2 Jul'03 Donc 7g/f 95- C: 1 Jun'03 Warw 7.1fm 83- D:
3073*)**MANYANA** 268 [5]3-8-11   Martin Dwyer 7/2: 1-5: In tch, wknd 3f out: nicely bckd: breathing probs.   *1*   **72**
5 Ran   Time 2m 08.27 (5.47)   Owned: Mr L Neil Jones   Trained: Arundel

---

1209   4.20 Stan James Telebetting Maiden Stakes Fillies 3yo (D)
£5616 £1728 £864   **1m2f6y**   **Good 40**   **-36 Slow**   Inside

WINDS OF MARCH [5] J H M Gosden 3-8-11 L Dettori 9/4 FAV: 1: b f Sadler's Wells - Alidiva   **96+**
(Chief Singer) Slow away, held up, hdwy to lead over 1f out, drvn out to hold on: op 11/8: sister to a 10f wnr:
stays 10f well, 12f sure to suit: acts on gd grnd & goes well fresh on a gall trk: v useful & promising start, type
of filly to progress much further & win in List/Gr class.
4978} **CRYSTAL** 167 [4] B J Meehan 3-8-11 M Hills 5/1: 0-2: b f Danehill - Solar Crystal (Alzao) Set   *shd*   **95**
pace, kept on when chall & hdd appr fnl 1f, rallied gamely, just fld: rtd 89 when unplcd sole '03 start
(List): half-sister to a juv/hdles scorer: dam high-class 1m/10f wnr: clrly stays 10f well, 12f looks sure to
suit: goes well fresh on gd grnd & a gall trk, useful, well clr of rem here, win races.
4772} **KARAMEA** 182 [7] J L Dunlop 3-8-11 M J Kinane 5/1: 03-3: gr f Rainbow Quest - Karapucha   *7*   **84**
(Kaldoun) Held up, hdwy over 2f out, onepcd: op 9/1: plcd on 2nd of only 2 '03 starts (mdn, rtd 88): dam 1m juv
wnr: eff at 1m, bred to relish mid-dists: acts on fast grnd, prob caught 2 useful sorts & shld be wng sn.
MODESTA [1] H R A Cecil 3-8-11 R Hughes 8/1: 4: b f Sadler's Wells - Modena (Roberto) In tch,   *1½*   **81**
eff over 2f out, sn no impress: half-sister to top-class mid-dist performers: bred to be useful over 10f/12f & some
promise here, learn plenty from this.
2613} **CHERUBIM** 288 [6]3-8-11 J Murtagh 5/1: 32-5: Chsd ldr till over 3f out, no extra on reapp.   *4*   **75**
3859} **SERRAMANNA** 235 [3]3-8-11 W Ryan 13/2: 62-6: In tch, wknd 2f out on reapp.   *1*   **74**
4895} **WEE DINNS** 174 [10]3-8-11 T Quinn 40/1: 000-7: Slow away & al bhd: longer trip.   *1¼*   **72**
1019 **CALOMERIA** 15 [2]3-8-11 S Sanders 66/1: 00-08: In tch, hung badly left & wknd over 2f out.   *1¼*   **70**
APRON [8]3-8-11 S Drowne 20/1: 9: Nvr a factor on debut.   *nk*   **70**
4863} **CLOUDINGSWELL** 176 [9]3-8-11 (63) S Whitworth 66/1: 043006-0: 10th: Al bhd on debut: new yard.   *5*   **62**
10 Ran   Time 2m 10.47 (7.67)   Owned: Greenbay Stables Ltd   Trained: Manton

---

1210   4.50 Bridget Maiden Stakes Fillies 3yo (D)
£5850 £1800 £900   **7f str**   **Good 40**   **+02 Fast**   Stands Side

ILLUSTRIOUS MISS [9] D R Loder 3-8-11 J Murtagh 7/2 FAV: 1: b f Kingmambo - Our Wildirish Rose   **96+**
(Irish Tower) Handy, hdwy to lead over 1f out, sn pushed clr, readily: bckd: eff at 7f, sure to relish 1m: goes
well fresh on gd: v pleasing start, looks useful & the type to progress further & win more races.
LUCKY SPIN [8] R Hannon 3-8-11 P Dobbs 20/1: 2: b f Pivotal - Perioscope (Legend of France)   *3½*   **84**
In tch, eff & edged right over 2f out but styd on to chase wnr ins last, al held: half-sister to sev wnrs: stays a
gall 7f on gd grnd: fine start, can find a minor trk mdn.
DASHIKI [12] B W Hills 3-8-11 R Hughes 7/1: 3: ch f Distant View - Musicanti (Nijinsky) Chsd   *1*   **82**
ldr till led over 4f out till over 1f out, no extra: full sister to a smart 7f/10f scorer: eff at 7f, shld stay 1m:
acts on gd grnd: win a race on this from.
PINCHING [14] H R A Cecil 3-8-11 W Ryan 10/1: 4: ch f Inchinor - Input (Primo Dominie) Chsd   *1*   **80**
ldrs, eff & hmpd 2f out, hung well but kept on ins last, no dngr on debut: eff at 7f, looks sure to apprec 1m: acts
on gd grnd: mkt drifter, op to plenty of improvement.
TREE TOPS [4]3-8-11 L Dettori 4/1: 5: b f Grand Lodge - The Faraway Tree (Suave Dancer) Held   *3*   **73**
up, some late gains, nvr dngrs on debut: dam useful over 6f/14f: relished 1m & will learn plenty from this.
SHAZANA [11]3-8-11 M Hills 7/1: 6: Led till over 4f out, wknd 2f out: op 10/1.   *2*   **68**
VAMP [7]3-8-11 S Sanders 25/1: 7: Slow away & nvr bhd: modest late gains.   *1½*   **64**
WOMAN IN WHITE [13]3-8-11 K Fallon 8/1: 8: Slow away, bhd, modest late gains.   *¾*   **62**
SET ALIGHT [1]3-8-11 S Carson 33/1: 9: Sn rdn & no dngr on debut.   *1*   **60**
PRIVATE JESSICA [5]3-8-11 Dane O'Neill 12/1: 0: 10th: In tch, wknd over 2f out.   *1½*   **56**
MISS SHANGRI LA [3]3-8-11 D Holland 8/1: 0: 11th: Slow away & al bhd.   *1¾*   **51**
COTTON EASTER [2]3-8-11 C Catlin 33/1: 0: 12th: Chsd ldrs, wknd over 2f out.   *¾*   **49**
DULCIMER [6]3-8-11 S Drowne 25/1: 0: 13th: In tch, wknd over 2f out.   *3½*   **41**
13 Ran   Time 1m 26.96 (2.66)   Owned: Sheikh Mohammed   Trained: Newmarket

---

1211   5.20 Peter Smith Memorial Maiden Stakes 3yo (D)
£5486 £1688 £844   **1m3f5y**   **Good 40**   **-70 Slow**   Inside

4293} **GRAHAM ISLAND** 212 [4] G Wragg 3-9-0 D Holland 5/4 FAV: 05-1: b c Acatenango - Gryada (Shirley   **88**
Heights) Cl-up, hdwy & short of room over 3f out, styd on to lead appr fnl 1f, rdn to assert ins last: rtd 73 when unplcd on 2nd of only 2 juv starts: dam useful over 7f/1m: imprvd on big step up to 11f, further
looks sure to suit: acts on gd & runs well fresh: op to plenty of further improvement, unexposed.
STRIKE [1] J H M Gosden 3-9-0 L Dettori 9/2: 2: b c Silver Hawk - Shemozzle (Shirley Heights)   *2*   **82**
Slow away, sn handy, led over 3f out till dist, not pace of wnr on debut: dam useful mid-dist performer: stays 11f,
further will suit: acts on gd: v pleasing start, learn plenty from this & wins races over mid-dists.
YAAHOMM [5] D R Loder 3-9-0 J Murtagh 9/4: 3: ch c Unfuwain - Walesiana (Star Appeal) In tch,   *nk*   **80**
eff to chall well over 1f out, onepace ins last on debut: bckd: brother to a smart 10f wnr: stays 11f on gd grnd:
can win a mdn shortly.
5016} **TURNSTILE** 162 [2] R Hannon 3-9-0 R Hughes 7/1: 4-4: gr c Linamix - Kissing Gate (Easy Goer)   *4*   **76**
Led till over 3f out, no extra: 4th sole juv start (mdn, rtd 71): dam 1m wnr: bred to stay around 10f.
1016 **MUZIO SCEVOLA** 15 [1]3-9-0 T E Durcan 16/1: 255: Al bhd: see 873.   *10*   **60**
5 Ran   Time 2m 27.96(12.16)   Owned: Mollers Racing   Trained: Newmarket

Official Going GOOD/SOFT. All Times Slow due to Heavy Rain.

1212

2.30 E B F Alec Borrows 90th Birthday Novice Stakes Fillies 2yo (D)
£5486 £1688 £844 **5f str** **Good/Soft** **Slow** Stands Side

943* **LADY FILLY 20** [5] W G M Turner 2-9-1 A Quinn(5) 4/5 FAV: 11: Made all, clr fnl 1f, readily: 91
well bckd: eff at 5f on gd/soft & soft grnd: likes forcing tactics & a flat trk: fine run conceding weight & can
complete hat-trick: see 943.

WORLD AT MY FEET [6] N Bycroft 2-8-8 Suzanne France(7) 50/1: 2: b f Wolfhound - Rehaab (Mtoto) 3½ 72
Dwelt, styd on late into 2nd, no ch with wnr: gd debut from this rank outsider: cheaply bght Mar foal: dam a
mid-dist wnr: eff at 5f on gd/soft grnd, relish 6f: learn plenty from this & win a race.

1107 **IM AIMEE 6** [8] P D Evans 2-8-8 R Havlin 11/2: 263: Chsd ldrs, kept on fnl 1f, but not pace to hd 72
chall: op 4/1, qck reapp: not disgraced: debut in 882 (polytrack).

929* **LISA MONA LISA 21** [3] V Smith 2-8-10 G Duffield 11/1: 14: Chsd wnr till dist, no extra: op 1¾ 69
8/1: return to sell grade will suit: see 929.

1029 **LADY ERICA 14** [2]2-8-8 Darren Williams 12/1: 25: Chsd ldrs, onepcd fnl 1.5f: see 1029. 1 64

MIMI MOUSE [7]2-8-8 D Allan(3) 16/1: 6: br f Diktat - Shifty Mouse (Night Shift) Dwelt, hung ¾ 61
left, hdwy & ev ch after halfway, sn wknd: op 12/1 on debut: Mar foal, cost 14,000gns: half sister to a 12f wnr:
dam lightly rcd, but related to a host of wnrs with T Easterby.

GYPSY FAIR [1]2-8-8 K Darley 15/2: 7: b f Compton Place - Marjorie's Memory (Fairy King) 5 46
Front rank 4.5f, wknd on debut: 21,000gns Feb foal: half sister to 5f/1m: dam 5f wnr.

LUCY PARKES [4]2-8-8 W Supple 16/1: 8: ch f Piccolo - Janette Parkes (Pursuit of Love) Slowly ½ 45
away, al bhnd on debut: Feb 1st foal: dam once rcd, related to sev decent sprinters: sire a smart sprinter.
8 Ran Time 1m 04.31 (7.31) Owned: Mrs M S Teversham Trained: Sherborne

1213

3.05 Hygicare Maiden Stakes 3yo (D)
£5408 £1664 £832 **1m4f** **Good/Soft** **Slow** Inside

1055 **OBAY 11** [4] E A L Dunlop 3-9-0 W Supple 2/1: 0-41: Made all, came clr over 2f out, easily: 80
nicely bckd: apprec step up to 12f, acts on gd/soft grnd, handles firm: facile wnr today, useful.

4479} **BOLLIN ANNABEL 202** [5] T D Easterby 3-8-9 D Allan(3) 16/1: 0-2: b f King's Theatre - Bollin 11 60
Magdalene (Teenoso) Held up, hdwy to chase wnr fnl 1f, no ch on reapp: clr of rem: mid-div in a fill mdn on sole
juv start (rtd 54): bred to apprec mid-dists: prob caught a tartar here & will find easier races in the North.

1019 **GANYMEDE 15** [6] M L W Bell 3-9-0 (80) I Mongan 4/7 FAV: 63-23: Prom, wknd 3f out: well bckd: 8 53
longer 12f trip & reportedly not enjoy grnd: see 1019.

930 **SIR BOND 21** [1] B Smart 3-9-0 F Lynch 50/1: 0-04: ch g Desert Sun - In Tranquility (Shalford) 9 40
Swerved start, al bhnd, t.o.: longer 12f trip: mod form to date.

88 **OVER THE YEARS 144** [2]3-9-0 Dale Gibson 66/1: 00-5: b g Silver Hawk - Sporting Green (Green 16 18
Dancer) Chsd wnr, wknd over 3f out, t.o.: reapp: well btn on both '03 starts: modest.

808 **HARRY LAD 42** [3]3-9-0 R Havlin 40/1: 556: Chsd ldrs till halfway, t.o.: 6 wk abs. 11 3
6 Ran Time 2m 48.70 (18.90) Owned: Mr Abdulla BuHaleeba Trained: Newmarket

1214

3.35 Carpenters Arms Felixkirk Stakes Handicap 3yo+ 0-75 (E) [75]
£3692 £1136 £568 **1m rnd** **Good/Soft** **Slow** Inside

1036 **HARRY POTTER 13** [5] K R Burke 5-9-6 vis (67) Darren Williams 33/1: 13-00301: Trkd ldr, styd on 72
under press to lead cl-home despite drifting left, drvn out: rider given a 1-day careless riding ban: eff at 7f/1m
on gd & soft grnd, handles polytrack: wears a visor: battled well today, see 878 (AW).

1028 **HOHS BACK 14** [7] Paul Johnson 5-8-13 p (60) Lisa Jones(3) 33/1: 000-0002: b g Royal Applause - nk 63
Paris Joelle (Fairy King) Nvr far away, led over 2f out till worn down cl-home: back to form on this return to
turf: won 4 h'caps in '03: eff over 7/9.4f on fast, soft grnd & fibresand, prob any trk: wears cheek pieces:
tough, back on a winning mark & can go one better.
2 Oct'03 Sout 8af 66a-64 F: 1 Sep'03 Beve 8.5g/f 65-62 F: 1 Aug'03 Wolv 8.5af 56a-60 F: 1 Jul'03 Wolv 8.5af 62a-54 F:
1 Jul'03 Redc 8gd 59-54 E: 2 Jan'03 Wolv 8.4af 67a- F: 1 Nov'01 Wolv 8.4af 77a- E: 2 Oct'01 Brig 7sft 78- E:

1036 **TOP DIRHAM 13** [2] M W Easterby 6-9-10 (71) Dale Gibson 10/3 FAV: 00000-23: Chsd ldrs, ev ch 1½ 71
dist, no extra cl-home: nicely bckd: on a winning mark, knocking on the door & can sn find similar: see 1036.

913 **JAKEAL 23** [13] R M Whitaker 5-8-10 (57) M Tebbutt 40/1: 0/0030-04: Chsd ldrs, onepcd fnl 1f: 3 51
prob stays 1m: see 913.

1122 **SARRAAF 5** [18]8-9-10 (71) N Callan 8/1: 42-42325: Switched start, hdwy when switched wide 1.5f nk 64+
out, kept on & nrst fin: qck reapp: did not get the run of today's race: see 1122.

998 **DISTANT COUNTRY 16** [8]5-10-0 (75) J F Egan 11/2: 41014-66: Chsd ldrs, onepcd fnl 1f: 1¼ 65
top-weight: caught the eye in 998, not at home on this rain softened grnd?

1142 **BAILIEBOROUGH 4** [3]5-9-8 (69) L Treadwell(7) 16/1: 0000-067: Chsd ldrs, onepcd fnl 2f: qck reapp. ¾ 57

924 **CRYFIELD 22** [10]7-9-1 (62) Kim Tinkler 20/1: 30605-08: b g Efisio - Ciboure (Norwick) Rear, 1 48
late hdwy, nvr dngrs: won a h'cap in '03: dual '02 h'cap wnr: eff at 6f/1m, stays 10f: likes fm & gd, acts on soft &
fibresand, any trk: eff with/without a visor: on a wng mark.
1 Jun'03 Leic 8.0g/f 69-63 F: 1 Sep'02 Hami 8.2fm 68-64 E: 1 Sep'02 Beve 8.4gd 67-61 F:
1 Jul'01 Asco 7fm 66-63 C: 1 Jun'01 Sout 8af 62-55 G:

1049 **CAPTAIN DARLING 11** [14]4-9-0 p (61) E Ahern 15/2: 543-6029: Mid-div, hdwy & ev ch dist, wknd. 3½ 40

1059 **SUPER SONG 11** [12]4-9-12 t (73) R Havlin 50/1: 0/201-000: 10th: b g Desert Prince - Highland 2½ 47
Rhapsody (Kris) Chsd ldrs, outpcd 2f out: ended '03 with a mdn win (with Sir M Stoute), has since been gelded: eff
at 7f on fast grnd, handles a sharp trk: now with P Evans & wears a t-strap.
1 Aug'03 Ling 7g/f 75-(76) D: 2 Jul'03 Folk 7g/f 77- D:

967 **BORDER ARTIST 18** [15]5-9-0 (61) A Nicholls 25/1: 60000-00: 11th: Nvr nr ldrs. 3 29

585 **SEMPER PARATUS 67** [11]5-8-9 bl (56) M Fenton 33/1: 0140-400: 12th: Rear, hdwy wide 2f out, sn ½ 23
btn: 10 wk abs, changed stables.

1006 **ROCKY REPPIN 16** [4]4-8-10 bl (57) J Edmunds 50/1: 5640-00: 13th: Chsd ldrs 6f, wknd. hd 24

1036 **CRESKELD 13** [9]5-9-11 (72) F Lynch 12/1: 3100-300: 14th: Hit hd leav stalls, al rear: forgive this. 5 29

3305} **NEWCORP LAD 259** [6]4-9-12 (73) W Supple 33/1: 051126-0: 15th: Led till 2f out, wknd qckly: gelded. 3 24

632 **PENWELL HILL 62** [1]5-8-10 (57) K Darley 9/2: 65-10220: 16th: Prom 5f, wknd: op 13/2, 9 wk abs. ½ 7

966   **HIGH CANE** 18 [17]4-9-2 (63) K Dalgleish 20/1: 6036-030: 17th: Stdd start, al bhd: btr 966.   5   3
17 Ran   Time 1m 46.52 (11.12)   Owned: Mr F Jeffers   Trained: Leyburn

---

1215   4.10 Sinderby Stakes Handicap 3yo+ 0-75 (E)   [88]
£3751 £1154 £577   **7f rnd**   **Good/Soft**   **Slow**   Inside

955   **COTOSOL** 20 [12] B A McMahon 3-9-1 (75) W Supple 11/2: 23026-01: b g Forzando - Emerald Dream   81
(Vision) Chsd ldrs, styd on under press to lead cl-home, drvn out: op 9/2: '03 mdn auct wnr, also h'cap plcd sev
times: eff at 5/7f on fast, gd/soft & f/sand: handles a sharp or gall trk: likes to run up with the pace.
2 Oct'03 Catt 7g/f 78-76 D: 2 Aug'03 Hayd 6g/f 73-71 E: 1 May'03 Sout 5af 77a- F: 2 Apr'03 Ripo 5g/f 72- D:
4298} **EFIDIUM** 212 [3] N Bycroft 6-9-4 (65) Suzanne France(7) 14/1: 600046-2: b g Presidium - Efipetite   ¾   68
(Efisio) Keen in rear, short of room & hdwy wide 2f out, styd on fnl 1f & not btn far on reapp under a kind ride:
won 3 h'caps & a seller in '03 (for this jock): eff over 7f/1m on firm, gd/soft & fibresand: eff with/without blnks:
handles a sharp or gall trk, likes Redcar: shld prob have won this.
1 Jul'03 Carl 6.9g/f 70-63 E: 2 Jun'03 Redc 7g/f 65-(63) E: 1 May'03 Donc 7gd 64-60 E: 1 May'03 Redc 7g/f 62-(48) F:
1 Apr'03 Ripo 8gd 56-48 E: 2 Jun'02 Carl 6g/f 50- F: 2 Jun'02 Redc 7fm 50- F: 1 Aug'01 Redc 6g/f 55- F:
2 Jun'01 Redc 6g/f 51-51 E: 1 Dec'00 Sout 5af 64a- F:
1049   **LORD OF THE EAST** 11 [16] N Nicholls 5-9-4 (65) L Treadwell(7) 20/1: 00502-03: b g Emarati - Fairy   shd   68
Free (Rousillon) Tried to make all, collared cl-home: won 2 clmrs in '03 (one for P Howling & one for K Cunningham
Brown): eff at 6/7f on fast & gd/soft: handles any trk, all 4 wins at Epsom: has tried cheek pieces & a t-strap:
fine front running eff, keep in mind back at Epsom.
2 Oct'03 Donc 7g/f 67-(65) E: 1 Aug'03 Epso 6g/f 67-(63) E: 1 Jul'03 Epso 7g/f 65-(59) E: 1 Aug'02 Epso 6g/f 65- E:
1 Aug'02 Epso 6g/f 65-58 D: 2 Aug'02 Brig 6g/f 64-58 D: 2 Sep'01 Nott 5gd 65-65 D: 2 Jul'01 Folk 5g/f 68- F:
1142* **UP TEMPO** 4 [14] K A Ryan 6-10-2 (6ex)bl (77) N Callan 5/1 FAV: 2131114: Rear, prog 2f out, kept   shd   80
on fnl 1f & nrst fin: qck reapp & prob imprvd in defeat under big weight: see 1142.
1020   **JACARANDA** 15 [8]4-9-9 (70) E Ahern 11/1: 04024-05: Chsd ldrs, styd on under press fnl 1f: gd run.   1   69
998   **ACOMB** 16 [4]4-9-3 (64) P Mulrennan(5) 11/2: 14150-06: Chsd ldrs, wknd dist.   2½   60
1035   **COLEMANSTOWN** 13 [6]4-9-11 (72) T Eaves(5) 9/1: 00056-07: Chsd ldrs 5f, sn onepcd.   2½   63
4852} **BUNDY** 177 [9]8-9-5 (66) P Hanagan 10/1: 061450-8: Nvr nr ldrs on reapp.   3   51
488   **KIN KINLOCH** 80 [1]4-9-4 (65) T Hamilton(3) 25/1: 50000-069: Chsd ldrs 5f, wknd: 12 wk abs.   1½   47
998   **SIR DON** 16 [11]5-9-5 vis (66) A Nicholls 13/2: 21530-00: 10th: Chsd ldrs, wknd 2f out: s/mate 3rd.   ¾   46
853   **PAYS DAMOUR** 31 [13]7-9-4 (65) Alex Greaves 12/1: 14600-00: 11th: Al towards rear.   2½   40
3177} **WAHOO SAM** 265 [15]4-9-9 BL (70) P Makin(7) 16/1: 1/U0000-0: 12th: Slowly away, al bhd, t.o. in last.   22   5
12 Ran   Time 1m 32.51 (9.61)   Owned: J P Hames G Pickering RJH Limited   Trained: Tamworth

---

1216   4.40 Feversham Arms Median Auction Maiden Stakes 3-4yo (E)
£3682 £1133 £567   **6f str**   **Good/Soft**   **Slow**   Stands Side

4605} **COMMANDO SCOTT** 195 [12] A Berry 3-8-13 (80) F Lynch 7/1: 4340-1: b g Danetime - Faye (Monsanto)   80
Led 3f, regained lead ent fnl 1f, kept on well despite drifting right, drvn out: tchd 10/1, reapp: '03 mdn plcd:
eff at 6f, shld stay 7f: acts on fast & gd/soft grnd, runs well fresh: deserved victory.
CATHERINE WHEEL [13] J R Fanshawe 3-8-8   E Ahern 10/3: 2: b f Primo Dominie - Prancing (Prince   nk   74
Sabo) Dwelt, recovered to chase ldrs, short of room dist, kept on well fnl 1f & only just failed: sister to sprint
wnr Firework: eff at 6f on gd/soft, runs well fresh: speedily bred, sharper next time & shld find similar.
MISTER REGENT [4] K A Ryan 3-8-13   N Callan 50/1: 3: b c Mind Games - River of Fortune (Lahib)   3   70
Chsd ldrs, sltly short of room dist, switched & styd on well but not reach front 2 on debut: cost 4,000gns: dam a 7f
wnr: sire a high-class sprinter: eff at 6f on gd/soft grnd: can learn from this.
3265} **TROJAN FLIGHT** 260 [7] Mrs J R Ramsden 3-8-13   J F Egan 25/1: 000-4: ch g Hector Protector -   ½   69
Fairywings (Kris) Chsd ldrs, hmpd 1.5f out, kept on fnl 1f but ch had gone: caught the eye on fnl juv start (rtd
71+): cost 15,000gns: eff at 6f on gd/soft grnd, 7f looks sure to suit: qualified for h'caps & can leave this bhd.
999   **AMANDAS LAD** 16 [14]4-9-10 (49) L Vickers 33/1: 0646635: Prom 4.5f, grad wknd: flattered 999.   1¼   65
925   **COMPTON MICKY** 21 [3]3-8-13   J Edmunds 100/1: 0-06: Chsd ldrs, eff when hmpd 1.5f out.   shd   65
952   **FLASHING BLADE** 20 [11]4-9-5 (85) W Supple 5/2 FAV: 005-07: Prom, onepcd when sltly hmpd dist.   shd   60
4870} **RAYSOOT** 175 [10]3-8-13   P McCabe 11/1: 000-8: Outpcd, modest late hdwy on reapp.   4   51
4791} **STAVROS** 182 [1]4-9-10 (46) D R McCabe 20/1: 060006-9: Prom, led halfway till short of room & hdd   1½   46
entering fnl 1f, wknd: reapp.
RAGAZZI [6]3-8-13   K Darley 16/1: 0: 10th: Chsd ldrs wide 4f on debut.   1¼   42
953   **BOLLIN ARCHIE** 20 [8]3-8-13   K Dalgleish 16/1: 50: 11th: Al outpcd.   3   33
1585} **GASPARINI** 334 [5]3-8-13   D Allan(3) 18/1: 2-0: 12th: Nvr btr than mid-div on reapp.   5   18
4693} **DAME NOVA** 187 [9]3-8-8   D Wakenshaw(7) 66/1: 000-0: 13th: Al outpcd on reapp.   6   0
953   **VOLATICUS** 20 [2]3-8-13   A Nicholls 9/1: 0-20: 14th: Chsd ldrs, ev ch 2f out, sn wknd: op 13/2.   3   0
14 Ran   Time 1m 18.78 (9.28)   Owned: Mrs Ann Morris   Trained: Cockerham

---

1217   5.10 Hambleton Classified Stakes 3yo+ 0-80 (D)
£5460 £1680 £840   **5f str**   **Good/Soft**   **Fair**   Stands Side

1120   **MAKTAVISH** 5 [1] I Semple 5-9-4 p (81) P Hanagan 3/1 FAV: 100-1121: Broke well & crossed to stands   86
rail, made rest, styd on strongly, rdn out: qck reapp: continues in fine form, suited by 5f on fast, loves gd, hvy
& fibresand: handles any trk: loves to force the pace: tough & genuine.
4477} **HICCUPS** 202 [6] Mrs J R Ramsden 4-9-3 p (80) J F Egan 14/1: 010630-2: b g Polar Prince - Simmie's   1   83
Special (Precocious) Chsd ldrs, styd on under press fnl 1f, not quite get to wnr on reapp: dual '03 h'cap wnr: eff
at 5f on firm & gd/soft, likes a stiff trk: wears cheek pieces: best held up for a late chall & spot on next time.
1 Jul'03 Pont 5g/f 81-76 D: 1 Jun'03 Carl 5fm 77-70 E: 2 May'03 Donc 5gd 70-(73) E: 2 Apr'03 Nott 5.1g/f 73- F:
1011+ **FOREVER PHOENIX** 16 [9] R M H Cowell 4-9-3 (83) E Ahern 7/2: 5611213: Held up, hdwy wide 2f out,   ¾   80
nrst fin: has been in fine form on the AW: see 1011.
921   **BLACKHEATH** 22 [11] D Nicholls 8-9-7 (84) Alex Greaves 11/2: 01023-04: ch g Common Grounds -   2½   77
Queen Caroline (Chief's Crown) Chsd ldrs, onepcd when pushed along fnl 1f under top-weight: won 2 h'caps & a class stks in '03:
class stks & h'cap wnr in '02: eff at 6f, ideally suited by 5f: likes fast & firm grnd, handles gd/soft: gd
weight-carrier who shld again win his share of sprint h'caps this season.
2 Sep'03 Ayr 6g/f 85-81 B: 1 Sep'03 Hayd 5gd 81-76 C: 2 Jul'03 Ayr 6gd 80-75 D: 1 Jul'03 Carl 5g/f 76-70 E:
2 Jun'03 Hayd 6g/f 70-68 D: 2 May'03 Bath 5.7g/s 66-64 F: 2 Apr'03 Newc 6g/f 67-63 E: 1 Apr'03 Folk 5g/f 65-(56) E:

THIRSK FRIDAY 16.04.04 Lefthand, Flat, Oval Track

1 Jul'02 Pont 5g/f 63-60 E: 1 Apr'02 Catt 6g/f 65- G: 2 May'01 Ling 5g/f 84-80 D:
927 **WILLHEWIZ 21** [12]4-9-8 vis (85) T P Queally(3) 5/1: 05101-05: b c Wizard King - Leave It To Lib   ¾   75
(Tender King) Chsd wnr 4f, grad wknd: won 2 clmrs in '03: mdn auct, nov & val stks wnr in '02: suited by
dominating over 5/6f on firm, gd/soft & f/sand, any trk: wears a visor: suited by dominating in claim grade.
1 Sep'03 Yarm 6.0g/f 86-(89) D: 1 Jul'03 Warw 6.1g/f 86-(92) D: 2 May'03 Nott 6.1g/s 94-(90) C:
1 Jun'02 Beve 5gd 100- B: 1 May'02 Nott 6g/f 102- D: 1 Apr'02 Sout 5af 77a- F: 2 Apr'02 Leic 5gd 77- F:
927 **PAX 21** [7]7-9-4 (81) L Treadwell(7) 8/1: 01640-66: Blindfold left on & lost grnd start, styd on   shd   71
late but ch had gone: poor jockeyship & this must be forgiven: see 927.
2117} **JOHN OGROATS 308** [10]6-9-4 (81) S W Kelly 16/1: 040000-7: Chsd ldrs 3.5f, wknd on reapp.   12   36
927 **RECTANGLE 21** [2]4-9-3 (80) A Nicholls 16/1: 02630-08: Chsd ldrs wide, btn halfway.   9   10
4202} **TOMMY SMITH 217** [5]6-9-3 bl (77) R Winston 16/1: 652630-9: Cl-up 3f, sn wknd.   ¾   7
9 Ran Time 1m 02.70(5.70) Owned: Mr D G Savala Trained: Carluke

WOLVERHAMPTON Fibresand SATURDAY 17.04.04 Lefthand, Sharp Track

Official Going Standard

1218 6.00 Bet Direct No Q On 08000 93 66 93 Claiming Stakes 3yo+ (F)
£2877 £822 £411 **5f aw rnd** **Going 47** **-04 Slow** Inside

941* **GILDED COVE 21** [7] R Hollinshead 4-9-6 (64) A Culhane 10/11 FAV: 0033511: Handy, styd on despite   55a
edging left to lead cl home, rdn out: returned lame: eff at 5f/6f on fibresand/sharp trk: likes claim grade.
1052 **TEYAAR 12** [5] Mrs N Macauley 8-9-2 (53) Hayley Turner(5) 16/1: 0600502: Prom, led ins fnl 1f, hdd   nk   49a
cl home: lost little in defeat dropped in grade & can find similar: see 902 & 501.
643 **BEST LEAD 61** [6] Ian Emmerson 5-9-10 bl (57) Rory Moore(7) 5/1: 65-10443: Cl up, led 3f out, hung   1½   53a
right & hdd ins fnl 1f, no extra: 9 wk abs: see 643 & 286.
958 **RIVER DAYS 19** [1] Miss Gay Kelleway 6-9-1 vis t (46) Lisa Jones(3) 4/1: 0206524: Handy, onepcd fnl 1f.   ½   43a
822 **STAR LAD 40** [3]4-9-6 bl (46) A Daly 20/1: 3100145: Led till 3f out, no extra fnl 1f: 6 wk abs.   nk   47a
976 **JUWWI 18** [2]10-9-6 (60) S Carson 12/1: 4004406: Bhd, nvr a factor: see 646.   1½   43a
749 **TELEPATHIC 50** [8]4-9-10 (56) P Mathers(7) 25/1: 0000-007: b g Mind Games - Madrina (Waajib) In   4   35a
tch, wknd fnl 2f: 7 wk abs: rnr up once in '03 (h'cap): auct mdn wnr in '02: eff at 5f on firm & fast grnd.
2 Jun'03 Hayd 5g/f 80-82 D: 1 Sep'02 Pont 5fm 85- E: 2 Sep'02 Hayd 5fm 75- D:
247 **MOSCOW MARY 113** [4]3-8-5 (55) S Whitworth 20/1: 203240-8: b f Imperial Ballet - Baileys Firecat   5   11a
(Catrail) Al in rear: long abs: sell wnr in '03 (J G Portman, also plcd 5 times): eff at 5f/6f on fast & gd/soft
grnd: with A G Newcombe. 2 Aug'03 Wind 6g/f 64-57 E: 2 Jun'03 Chep 5.1g/f 62- G: 1 Jun'03 Wind 6g/f 66- G:
2 Jun'03 Thir 6g/f 59- E: 2 May'03 Chep 6.1g/s 60- G:
8 Ran Time 1m 2.78 (2.58) Owned: Mr M Johnson Trained: Upper Longdon

1219 6.30 Littlewoods Bet Direct Apprentice Handicap Stakes 3yo+ 0-85 (E)   [84]
£3539 £1089 £545 **1m100y aw rnd** **Going 47** **-04 Slow** Inside

836 **NIMELLO 35** [4] A G Newcombe 8-10-0 (84) N Chalmers 4/1: 6121-001: Bhd, prog to lead 1f out, rdn   91a
out: eff at 6f, suited by 7/9.3f on firm, prefers gd/soft, hvy & loves fibresand/Wolverhampton.
1013* **SAMUEL CHARLES 17** [1] W M Brisbourne 6-8-4 (60) B Swarbrick(3) 6/1: 44000-12: Prom, led 2f out,   1   64a
edgd left under press & hdd 1f out, sn short of room but not pace wnr: stays 8.5f on fm grnd & both AW's.
4486} **LAURO 203** [5] Miss J A Camacho 4-9-1 (71) P Mulrennan 6/1: 321214-3: b f Mukaddamah - Lapu Lapu   1½   72a
(Prince Sabo) Handy, kept on fnl 1f: won 2 h'caps in '03 (also plcd 3 times): mdn clmr wnr in '02: eff at
8f/8.4f, tried further: likes fast grnd, acts on fibresand: goes well fresh: sharper for this.
1 Aug'03 Ayr 8g/f 74-70 D: 2 Aug'03 Wolv 8.5af 69a-66 E: 1 Jun'03 Hayd 8.1g/f 71-65 E: 2 May'03 Wolv 8.5af 67a-65 E:
1 Jul'02 Hayd 6g/f 71- F:
942 **SPARK UP 21** [6] J W Unett 4-7-13 bl (55) J F McDonald 14/1: 6-006244: Rear, no room over 5f out,   1¾   52a
kept on fnl 2f, nrst fin: see 942 & 629.
1027 **BANK ON HIM 15** [8]9-8-6 (62) A Quinn 7/2 JT FAV: 6122225: Trkd ldrs, led 4f out till 2f out, sn wknd.   1¼   57a
1195 **AIR MAIL 2** [3]7-9-2 vis (72) Rory Moore(3) 10/1: 0-400046: Handy, fdd dist: qck reapp: btr 513.   1¼   65a
940 **LABRETT 21** [7]7-9-12 t p (82) D Nolan 7/2 JT FAV: 1-305237: Led till 4f out, fdd fnl 2f: btr 940.   1¾   71a
1095 **SKIBEREEN 9** [2]4-8-9 p (65) Natalia Gemelova(3) 20/1: 32-56458: Missed break, nvr nrr than mid div.   7   40a
8 Ran Time 1m 50.52 (4.32) Owned: Ms Gerardine P O'Reilly Trained: Barnstaple

1220 7.00 Betdirect Co Uk Maiden Stakes 3yo+ (D)
£3419 £1052 £526 **1m100y aw rnd** **Going 47** **-12 Slow** Inside

1022 **SUNISA 15** [2] B W Hills 3-8-6 (72) D Holland 4/5 FAV: 624-21: Cl up, led 3f out, drvn clr ins   80a+
fnl 2f, eased fnl 1f, val 10L+: eff at 6f, stays 8f/8.4f well: acts on fast, gd & both AW's: see 1022.
4568} **LANDUCCI 197** [8] J W Hills 3-8-11 S Whitworth 9/4: 00-2: b c Averti - Divina Luna (Dowsing)   7   71a
Bhd, prog & ev ch 2f out, no extra ins fnl 1f: reapp & AW bow: unplcd both '03 starts (rtd 80, mdn): prob stays
8.4f on fibresand: only lightly rcd & now qualifies for h'caps.
BANSHA BRU 0 [7] Miss E C Lavelle 4-9-11 A Culhane 25/1: 3: b g Fumo di Londra - Pride of   2½   66a
Duneane (Anita's Prince) Sn outpcd, rallied 3f out, fdd & hung left dist: Flat bow, hdles Fit, unplcd both 03/04
starts (bmpr & nov hdle).
1367} **PURI 348** [1] J G Given 5-9-11 M Fenton 12/1: 0-4: Led till 3f out, fdd 2f out: reapp & AW bow.   4   58a
1055 **MAGIC STING 12** [4]3-8-11 J Mackay 13/2: 5-55: Handy, fdd fnl 2f: AW bow: btr 1055.   3   52a
841 **PRINCESS BANKES 34** [6]3-8-6 (60) Lisa Jones(3) 25/1: 0605-06: Cl up, fdd 2f out.   6   36a
1101 **ZAMBEZI RIVER 9** [5]5-9-11 C J Davies(3) 100/1: 07: Trkd ldrs, fdd fnl 2f.   4   34a
1100 **MISS LIBRATE 9** [3]6-9-6 S Carson 33/1: 08: Bhd, nvr a factor: 'fin distressed'.   dist 4a
8 Ran Time 1m 51.19 (4.99) Owned: Mr Ray Richards Trained: Lambourn

1221   7.30 New Site @ Betdirect Co Uk Handicap Stakes 3yo+ 0-70 (E)   **[68]**
£3656 £1125 £563   **6f aw rnd**   **Going 47**   **-02 Slow**   Inside

944   **ITALIAN MIST 21** [12] Julian Poulton 5-9-9 e (63) G Faulkner 6/1: 5120131: In tch, led ins fnl 1f,   **68a**
drvn out to assert: suited by 5/6f, stays 7f on fast, soft & loves fibresand: continues in fine form.
657   **ZAGALA 60** [5] S L Keightley 4-9-9 t (63) A Culhane 13/2: 0213-202: Rear, prog 2f out, kept on fnl   ½   **66a**
1f, just held by wnr: 9 wk abs: reportedly in season in 657: return to 7f will suit: see 282.
1052   **AGUILA LOCO 12** [8] Mrs Stef Liddiard 5-9-1 p (55) M Fenton 12/1: 1406203: Prom, ev ch dist, kept   nk   **57a**
on & not btn far: apprec return to AW & lost little in defeat: just btr 956 (7f).
1052   **KENNINGTON 12** [11] Mrs C A Dunnett 4-9-0 vis (54) Hayley Turner(5) 16/1: 0/-104034: Led, hdd under   shd   **55a**
press ins fnl 1f, not btn far in 4th: ran to form of 3rd in 1052 (gd/soft).
1025*   **EFFECTIVE 15** [4]4-9-8 vis (62) E Stack 8/1: 0305015: Cl up, no room 3f out & sligtly outpcd, rallied dist.   2   **57a**
844   **SABANA 34** [10]6-8-8 bl (48) S Carson 16/1: 3501306: Nvr nrr than mid div: btr 773 & 646.   nk   **42a**
1010*   **SPINDOR 17** [9]5-9-7 bl (61) D Holland 4/1 FAV: 2534217: Sn mid div, outpcd half way, rallied ins   ¾   **53a**
fnl 1f: disappointing on drop back to 6f: btr 1010 (7f).
1145   **PAWAN 5** [2]4-9-1 (55) Ann Stokell 9/1: 202-5228: Bhd, nvr nvr than mid div: qck reapp: btr 1145.   1¾   **42a**
1127   **PULSE 5** [1]6-9-2 p (56) R L Moore 20/1: 11256-09: b g Salse - French Gift (Cadeaux Genereux) Al   shd   **42a**
bhd: qck reapp: won 2 hcaps & AW sell in '03: missed '02: plcd in '01 (h'cap, rtd 58a & 57, R Hannon): eff at
5f/6f, tried 1m: acts on both AW's, likes firm & fast grnd: eff within cheek pieces.
2 Jul'03 Wind 5.0g/f 63-58 E: 1 Jul'03 Bath 5.0g/f 65-58 G: 1 Jun'03 Brig 5.3g/f 59-54 F: 2 Jun'03 Bath 5.7fm 61-(53) G:
2 Jun'03 Newc 5fm 53-(50) F: 1 Feb'03 Wolv 5af 58a- G: 2 Jan'03 Wolv 5af 58a-54 F:
1024   **AMELIA 15** [13]6-8-8 (48) B Swarbrick(7) 15/2: 5255530: 10th: Cl up, fdd 2f out: btr 1024.   2½   **27a**
415   **LAUREL DAWN 93** [6]6-9-7 (61) P Mathers(7) 33/1: 04103-00: 11th: Al in rear: long abs: btr 187 (5f).   hd   **39a**
704   **NOBLE LOCKS 54** [7]6-10-0 (68) Lisa Jones(7) 16/1: 051-0000: 12th: Al bhd: 8 wk abs: btr 246.   8   **25a**
384*   **CAUSTIC WIT 96** [3]6-9-2 (56) R Miles(3) 7/1: 03030-10: 13th: Cl up, fdd 2f out, eased fnl 1f: 'lost action'.   5   **0a**
13 Ran   Time 1m 15.79 (2.99)   Owned: Mr S P Shore   Trained: Newmarket

1222   8.00 #10 Free Bet @ Betdirect Co Uk Selling Stakes 3yo (G)
£2527 £722 £361   **7f aw rnd**   **Going 47**   **-13 Slow**   Outside

804   **LADY MO 44** [8] K A Ryan 3-8-12 (60) N Callan 11/8 FAV: 5351101: Handy, led 2f out, sn clr, eased   **75a+**
fnl 1f, val 15L+: no bid: 6 wk abs: prev eff at 6f, now suited by 7f/1m on fm, fast & both AW's, poss gd/soft:
back to form today & loves sellers: see 682.
1050   **WENDYS GIRL 12** [3] R P Elliott 3-8-7 (57) T Hamilton(3) 12/1: 330-0052: Cl up, led 3f out, hdd 2f   12   **51a**
out, sn no extra: mdn after 16: see 835.
1015   **SON OF REMBRANDT 16** [5] D K Ivory 3-8-12 (53) M Howard(7) 12/1: 3-005363: Bhd, kept on ins fnl   3   **50a**
2f, well adrift of wnr: see 871.
863   **FLYING SPUD 31** [7] J L Spearing 3-8-12 (47) A Daly 9/1: 00-54: ch g Fraam - Lorcanjo (Hallgate)   nk   **49a**
Nvr nrr than mid div: unplcd both '03 starts (rtd 44a).
4786]   **VENETIAN ROMANCE 183** [2]3-8-7 (50) S Hitchcott(2) 16/1: 000305-5: ch f Desert Story - Cipriani   5   **34a**
(Habitat) Al bhd: reapp: plcd once in '03 (h'cap, rtd 57): eff at 7f, further shld suit: acts on gd/soft grnd.
955   **RULES FOR JOKERS 21** [4]3-9-3 (60) D Holland 2/1: 33110-06: Handy, fdd 3f out: shown little in '04.   5   **34a**
1196   **BLUE EMPEROR 2** [6]3-8-12 BL (60) D Nolan(5) 16/1: 346-0057: Al bhd: qck reapp & blnks.   9   **13a**
1193   **APOLLO GEE 2** [1]3-8-12 BL (64) J F McDonald(5) 11/1: 030-08: Led, hdd 3f out, sn fdd: 1st time blnks.   2   **9a**
8 Ran   Time 1m 30.41 (4.21)   Owned: Wooster Partnership   Trained: Hambleton

1223   8.30 Bet In Running @ Betdirect Co Uk Handicap Stakes 4yo+ 46-55 (F)   **[64]**
£2933 £838 £419   **1m1f79y aw**   **Going 47**   **+08 Fast**   Inside

961   **DANGER BIRD 19** [6] R Hollinshead 4-9-0 (50) A Culhane 13/2: 2302441: Trkd ldrs, led 2f out, drvn   **59a**
out to hold on: eff at 7.5f/9.4f on fast & fibresand: first win: see 620 & 248.
972   **MONDURU 19** [9] G L Moore 7-8-11 bl e (47) R L Moore 9/1: 0-012232: Held up, prog to chase wnr   2   **52a**
dist, sn hung left & al held: another gd run: see 972 & 654.
4832]   **CHAMPAIN SANDS 179** [7] W M Brisbourne 5-8-12 (48) B Swarbrick(7) 4/1 FAV: 000062-3: b g Green   2   **50a**
Desert - Grecian Bride (Groom Dancer) Cl up, no extra ins fnl 1f: reapp & new stable: plcd 3 times in '03 (h'caps,
rtd 64, J R Boyle): rnr up in late '02 (rtd 74. mdn): eff at 1m/9.4f, tried further: acts on gd, gd/soft &
fibresand: tried visor, blnks & cheek pieces: encouaging eff & is well h'capped.
2 Oct'03 Yarm 11.5gd 58-57 G: 2 Apr'03 Wind 8.3g/s 64-64 E: 2 Dec'02 Wolv 9.3af 57a- D:
1028   **CRUSOE 15** [4] A Sadik 7-9-1 bl (51) J F McDonald(5) 14/1: 3004004: Trkd ldrs, outpcd 3f out, rallied dist.   2   **50a**
791   **BOUGHT DIRECT 45** [13]5-9-2 (52) R Miles(3) 12/1: 00-000: Cl up, no room 2f out, sn no extra.   shd   **50a**
961   **JADE STAR 19** [5]4-9-3 p (53) M Fenton 13/2: 25-41026: In tch, led 3f out till 2f out, sn wknd.   nk   **50a**
477   **MEZEREON 84** [10]4-9-5 (50) D Tudhope(7) 10/1: 15010-07: Nvr nrr than mid div: jumps fit.   ¾   **50a**
937   **PRINCE PROSPECT 21** [12]8-8-13 (49) Kristin Stubbs(7) 20/1: 0-012208: Nvr nrr than mid div: btr 689.   nk   **43a**
4498]   **DOWN TO THE WOODS 202** [3]6-9-0 (50) R Ffrench 7/1: 060040-9: ch g Woodman - Riviera Wonder   shd   **43a**
(Batonnier) Cl up, fdd 4f out: reapp & new stable: plcd once in '03 (AW h'cap, rtd 66a, M J Polglase): app clmg
wnr in early '02: eff at 6f/10f on firm, soft grnd & fibresand: best in t-strap, has tried blnks & visor: sharper
for today: with R E Woodhouse. 1 Mar'02 Wolv 8.4af 88a- F: 2 Jun'01 Donc 10.2g/f 103- C:
1028   **WILSON BLUEBOTTLE 15** [2]5-8-13 bl (49) P Mulrennan(5) 13/2: 0-610220: 10th: Led till 3f out, sn fdd.   ¾   **40a**
1028   **SORBIESHARRY 15** [8]5-9-0 p (50) P McCabe 6/1: 5150140: 11th: Al bhd: btr 961.   nk   **40a**
2580]   **Maravedi 290** [1]4-8-11 (47) Lisa Jones(3) 28/1:0   860   **Better Off 31** [11]6-9-2 p(52) Joanna Badger 33/1:0
13 Ran   Time 2m 1.90(3.7)   Owned: The C H F Partnership   Trained: Upper Longdon

Official Going SOFT.

1224   2.30 Chris Bailey And Geoff Flavell 60th Birthday Claiming Stakes 2yo (E)
£3575 £1100 £550   **5f str**   **Soft 125**   -37 Slow   Stands Side

938* **LITTLE BISCUIT 21** [2] K R Burke 2-8-10 Darren Williams 3/1 FAV: 11: Prom, led after halfway,   **69+**
pushed clr fnl 1f, impressive: op 2/1, val 6/7L+: eff at 5f on soft grnd & fibresand: looks better than plating
grade judged on this: see 938 (AW seller).
929 **EMMAS VENTURE 22** [3] M W Easterby 2-8-10 P Mulrennan(5) 8/1: 52: b f Paris House - Emma Amour   2½   57
(Emarati) Sn prom, chsd wnr fnl 1.5f but sn left bhnd: March 1st foal: dam styd 6f: eff at 5f on soft grnd.
    MAUREENS LOUGH [1] T D Barron 2-9-0 N Callan 10/1: 3: b f Bachir - Tadjnama (Exceller) Dwelt,   3   52
recovered to chase ldrs, onepcd fnl 1f on debut: Apr foal, cost E3,200: half sister to wnrs over 5f/hdls.
    ALICE KING [6] W G M Turner 2-8-4 C Haddon(7) 9/2: 4: b f Key of Luck - Java Jive (Hotfoot)   1½   38
Dwelt, sn chsd ldrs, switched dist & styd on fnl 1f, nvr nrr: op 11/2, debut, clr of rem: E2,000 Mar foal: half
sister to a 6f juv wnr & a mid-dist scorer: dam a sprint wnr, sire high-class over 1m/10f.
    BOWLAND BRIDE [8]2-8-6 J Carroll 12/1: 5: Chsd ldrs till halfway on debut.   8   20
    OUR LOUIS [9]2-8-10 R Winston 14/1: 6: Led till after halfway, wknd on debut: op 20/1.   2   18
    FOLD WALK [5]2-8-2 Dale Gibson 25/1: 7: Slowly away, al bhnd on debut.   4   0
    JOSHAR [7]2-8-10 D Allan(3) 25/1: 8: Al outpcd on racecourse bow.   1¾   2
    KARITA [10]2-8-5 J Mackay 7/2: 9: V slowly away, al bhnd: op 11/4 & better clearly expected.   shd   0
    BORACAY BEAUTY [4]2-8-10 J Quinn 33/1: 0: 10th: Chsd ldrs 3f, wknd & eased on debut.   15   0
10 Ran   Time 1m 05.14 (8.14)   Owned: Mrs Elaine M Burke   Trained: Leyburn

1225   3.00 Harlequin Clear Air Conditions Stakes 4yo+ (C)
£8503 £3225 £1613   **1m rnd**   **Soft 125**   -07 Slow   Inside

5020} **HERETIC 163** [7] J R Fanshawe 6-9-1 (105) O Urbina 15/8: 6/41000-1: b g Bishop of Cashel -   **109**
Barford Lady (Stanford) Chsd ldrs, imprvd to lead 1.5f out trav well, sn clr, held on pushed out: bckd: '03 stks
wnr: in '02 won a val h'cap: v eff at 1m: acts on fast, likes gd & hvy grnd: handles any trk, runs well fresh:
has a decent turn of foot: smart & up to wng in List/Gr 3 company.
1 Jul'03 Donc 8gd 106-(107) C: 1 Jul'02 Sand 8g/s 103-93 B: 2 Jun'02 Hayd 7.1sft 93- C:
2 May'02 Kemp 8g/f 95-90 B: 1 Apr'01 Kemp 8hvy 91- C:
4976} **MINE 168** [4] J D Bethell 6-8-9 (99) R Winston 10/3: 203406-2: b c Primo Dominie - Ellebanna   ½   **102**
(Tina's Pet) Rear, hdwy when short of room dist & switched, styd on well but too late: nicely bckd, clr of rem,
reapp: '03 val h'cap wnr, also rnr-up in Bunbury Cup H'cap: dual '02 h'cap wnr (incl Bunbury Cup): eff at 7f/1m on
fm & soft, likes a gall trk, esp Newmarket: eff with/without a visor: v useful h'capper, enjoys big fields.
2 Jul'03 Newm 7fm 100-93 B: 1 May'03 Donc 7gd 95-88 C: 1 Jul'02 Newm 7g/s 92-87 B: 1 Jun'02 Sand 7g/s 89-80 C:
2 May'02 Thir 7g/s 80- D: 1 Aug'01 Thir 8gd 79-73 D: 2 Jul'01 Nott 8.2g/f 74-70 D: 1 Jul'01 Donc 8g/f 71-68 D:
720} **MYSTERINCH 413** [3] Jedd O'Keeffe 4-8-9 J F Egan 16/1: 44211/3-3: b g Inchinor - Hakone (Alzao)   5   **93**
Chsd ldrs, led 3f out till 1.5f out, no extra on reapp: plcd on sole '03 start (stks, with N Littmoden): '02 dual
dual '02 h'cap wnr: eff at 1m on fm & soft, likes a stiff trk: been gelded, fair reapp, sharper for this.
1 Sep'02 Donc 8fm 97-88 B: 1 Aug'02 Newc 8gd 93-81 B: 2 Aug'02 Newm 8g/s 82- E:
2231} **SELECTIVE 304** [6] A C Stewart 5-8-9 (104) T Quinn 7/4 FAV: 1/22230-4: Prog to chase ldrs over 2f   3   **87**
out, sn wknd & eased, awkward head carriage: nicely bckd, gelded, wants faster grnd.
1102} **LADY MYTTON 366** [2]4-8-4 (87) J Mackay 25/1: 02351/4-5: Led till 3f out, wkng when hmpd 1.5f out.   8   67
    CARIBE 217 [8]5-8-12 P Bradley(5) 50/1: 001046-6: Nvr nr bhnd: highly tried.   3   65
3817} **GALA SUNDAY 238** [1]4-9-1 (95) Dale Gibson 20/1: 125100-7: Chsd ldrs 5f, wknd: new yard, gelded.   23   32
7 Ran   Time 1m 45.99 (10.59)   Owned: Barford Bloodstock   Trained: Newmarket

1226   3.30 Gillamoor Classified Stakes 3yo+ 0-70 (E)
£3556 £1094 £547   **1m4f**   **Soft 125**   -73 Slow   Inside

964 **CAPTAIN CLIPPER 19** [4] D Nicholls 4-9-11 (75) A Nicholls 7/2: 35510-31: Waited with, hdwy to   **81**
lead dist, styd on strongly, drvn out: slow time: eff at 1m/10f, stays a slowly run 12f: acts on fast & soft.
1006* **LAWOOD 17** [5] K A Ryan 4-9-11 (75) N Callan 3/1 JT FAV: 530-4012: Chsd ldrs, imprvd to chall 2f   2   78
out, not pace of wnr ins fnl 1f: well bckd: eff at 6/7f, stays 12f: in gd form, see 1006.
1009 **RASID 17** [7] C A Dwyer 6-9-12 (75) T P Queally(3) 6/1: 053-1023: Chsd ldrs, slightly outpcd over   shd   78
2f out, kept on well fnl 1f & just failed to snatch 2nd: clr of rem: see 1009 & 434 (AW).
4738} **VICIOUS PRINCE 186** [1] R M Whitaker 5-9-12 (75) M Tebbutt 3/1 JT FAV: 000000-4: b g Sadler's   4   72
Wells - Sunny Flower (Dom Racine) Set slow pace, hdd dist, wknd: reapp, has been gelded: failed to win in '03,
subs dropped down the h'cap: won 2 h'caps in '02: eff at 10/12f on fast, prefers gd/soft & soft grnd: likes Ripon:
fairly h'capped now & sharper next time. 1 Aug'02 Ripo 10g/s 87-86 C: 1 Jun'02 Ripo 12.2sft 85-80 D:
4737} **RUTTERS REBEL 186** [2]3-8-6 (1ow) (74) R Winston 6/1: 400126-5: b g Entrepreneur - No Quest   5   64
(Rainbow Quest) Chsd ldrs, onepcd when slightly hmpd 1.5f out, eased: '03 nursery h'cap wnr: eff at 1m on gd &
fast grnd, handles a sharp trk: did not get run of race against elders today.
2 Sep'03 Muss 8gd 75-73 D: 1 Sep'03 Muss 8g/f 73-62 E:
2392} **SASPYS LAD 659** [6]7-9-7 (70) T G McLaughlin 16/1: 55506/-6: b g Faustus - Legendary Lady   1½   57
(Reprimand) Held up, hdwy wide 4f out, btn 2f out: won a h'cap hdle in Nov '03 (eff at 2m1f on fast & soft, rtd
119h): some mdn promise in '03: 01/02 sell hdle wnr: prob made grnd too qckly today & poss capable of better.
    ZAN LO 194 [3]4-9-3 (65) J F Egan 25/1: 52516-7: Prom 9f, wknd, t.o. on reapp.   17   19
7 Ran   Time 2m 53.67 (23.87)   Owned: Clipper Group Holdings   Trained: Thirsk

1227   4.05 Michael Foster Memorial Conditions Stakes 3yo+   (C)
£8364   £3172   £1586   **6f str**   **Soft 125**   **+17 Fast**   Stands Side

4502} **WELSH EMPEROR 150** [4] T P Tate 5-9-1 bl (109) Dale Gibson 11/2: 342426-1: b g Emperor Jones - 99
Simply Times (Dodge) Made all, styd on strongly fnl 1f, pushed out: op 9/2, reapp, gd time: '03 List wnr in
France, also Gr 3 plcd abroad: eff at 5/7f on fast, loves gd/soft & hvy: wears blnks, runs well fresh: useful, win
another List on easy grnd. 2 Jul'03 Hamb 6sft 102- A: 1 Nov'02 Mais 6hvy 102- : 2 Oct'02 Leic 7sft 95- C:
1 Aug'02 Hayd 6hvy 95- C: 2 Jul'02 Chep 5gd 90-89 C: 1 Oct'01 Catt 5sft 90- D: 2 Sep'01 Hami 6gd 79-75 D:
1 Jul'01 Hami 6gd 75- E: 2 Jul'01 Muss 7.1g/f 74- F: 2 Jun'01 Thir 7gd 76- F:

952   **HALMAHERA 21** [7] K A Ryan 9-9-1 bl (101) N Callan 5/1: 01044-02: b g Petardia - Champagne Girl   1   93
(Robellino) Mid-div, styd on well under press fnl 1f, not quite get there: clr of rem: dual h'cap wnr in '03, incl
Portland H'cap, also List 4th: won Portland again in '02, also Stewards Cup plcd: stays 7f, suited by 5/6f on fm &
hvy: eff with/without blnks/visor, runs well fresh: v tough & genuine, more races await.
1 Oct'03 Asco 5gd 106-99 B: 1 Sep'03 Donc 5.6gd 101-93 B: 2 Jul'03 Ches 7.0fm 103-(95) B:
2 May'03 Ches 5.1g/f 96-94 B: 1 Sep'02 Donc 5.6fm 95-91 B: 2 Aug'02 Good 6fm 93-87 B:
2 Aug'01 Good 6g/f 93-88 B: 2 May'01 Hayd 6sft 94- C:

4675} **CIRCUIT DANCER 189** [5] A Berry 4-9-1 (89) F Lynch 16/1: 122316-3: b g Mujadil - Trysinger (Try   4   81
My Best) Chsd ldrs, onepcd fnl 1f on reapp: dual '03 h'cap wnr, also plcd sev times: eff at 5/6f on firm &
gd/soft, poss handles soft: best up with/forcing the pace: handles a gall or tight trk & has won at Chester:
sharper for this on faster grnd. 1 Aug'03 Ches 6.1g/f 90-84 C: 2 Aug'03 Hayd 6g/f 89-(84) C:
1 Sep'02 Muss 5g/f 81- D: 2 Sep'02 Catt 6fm 79- D:

1137   **FIRE UP THE BAND 5** [2] D Nicholls 5-9-1 VIS (105) A Nicholls 3/1: 023-0034: Chsd ldrs, ev ch till   hd   81
wknd fnl 1f: tried a visor, qck reapp: prefers a faster surface: see 952.

1062   **ORIENTOR 13** [1]6-9-8 (109) T Quinn 7/4 FAV: 0006-245: Chsd ldrs till wknd dist: btr 952.   3   79

4502} **DAZZLING BAY 201** [8]4-9-1 (105) J F Egan 7/1: 110206-6: Chsd ldrs, rdn & wknd 2f out: reapp.   9   47

3725} **SMIRFYS SYSTEMS 242** [9]5-9-1 (80) T G McLaughlin 33/1: 0/50012-7: Al outpcd: reapp, highly tried.   4   35

7 Ran   Time 1m 16.01 (6.51)   Owned Mrs Sylvia Clegg   Trained: Doncaster

1228   4.35 Ken Durnin Memorial Maiden Stakes 3yo   (D)
£5395   £1660   £830   **5f str**   **Soft 125**   **-08 Slow**   Stands Side

4412} **TIZZYS LAW 207** [2] M A Buckley 3-8-9 J Bramhill 14/1: 0-1: b f Case Law - Bo' Babbity (Strong   73
Gale) Trkd ldrs, drvn to lead ins fnl 1f, drifted right & held on: op 10/1, reapp: unplcd sole '03 start
(Newmarket mdn): half sister to sprint h'capper Abbajabba: eff at 5f on soft grnd: runs well fresh.

973   **BUY ON THE RED 19** [7] W R Muir 3-9-0 (72) J Quinn 10/11 FAV: 424-22: Tried to make all, hdd ins   ¾   74
fnl 1f, only just btn: bckd from 11/8: acts on gd/soft, soft & polytrack: see 973 (AW).

966   **ICE PLANET 19** [9] D Nicholls 3-9-0 R Winston 28/1: 03: b c Polar Falcon - Preference (Efisio)   1   71
Slowly away, styd on well fnl 1f, nvr nrr: eff at 5f, 6f shld suit: acts on soft grnd, has a real soft grnd action.

       URBAN CALM [8] R M H Cowell 3-8-9 M Henry 14/1: 4: b f Cadeaux Genereux - Silver Sun (Green   ½   65
Desert) Chsd ldrs, onepcd fnl 1f on debut: dam a 1m wnr, sire a smart sprinter: eff at 5f on soft grnd.

4917} **TRUE MAGIC 172** [4]3-8-9 (65) D Allan(3) 7/1: 3306-5: Prom till wknd fnl 1f on reapp.   ¾   62

1102   **LACONIA 9** [5]3-8-9 (69) N Mackay(3) 11/4: 350-4526: Chsd ldrs, no impress fnl 1f: op 9/4: btr 1102.   1   59

953   **DIAMOND SHANNON 21** [6]3-8-9 D Tudhope(7) 20/1: 2-07: Slowly away, al bhnd.   5   44

4580} **RENOS MAGIC 197** [3]3-8-9 C Haddon(7) 25/1: 00: Al rear, fin last on reapp.   1¼   40

8 Ran   Time 1m 03.67 (6.67)   Owned: North Cheshire Trading & Storage Ltd   Trained: Stamford

1229   5.10 Thomas Lord Stakes Handicap 3yo 0-90 (C)
£9666   £2974   £1487   **5f str**   **Soft 125**   **-03 Slow**   Stands Side   [92]

1116   **FOUR AMIGOS 7** [2] J G Given 3-8-13 (77) T Quinn 10/3 FAV: 50102-51: Hld up, gd hdwy to lead ins   88
fnl 1f, rdn clr: bckd: v eff at 5f, poss stays 6f: acts on gd & soft: win again on similar grnd: see 1116.

4887} **BARON RHODES 175** [3] J S Wainwright 3-8-4 (68) P M Quinn 14/1: 316042-2: b f Presidium -   3½   72
Superstream (Superpower) Chsd ldrs, imprvd to lead dist, not pace to repel wnr ins fnl 1f: bckd at long odds,
reapp: '03 mdn auct wnr, also h'cap rnr-up: eff at 5f on gd & soft grnd, runs well fresh: likes Thirsk: met an
improving rival & can win similar. 2 Oct'03 Muss 5gd 70-67 E: 1 Aug'03 Thir 5g/s 69-(65) E:

2217} **A LITTLE BIT YARIE 304** [11] K R Burke 3-9-6 (84) Darren Williams 6/1: 3123-3: b g Paris House -   1½   85
Slipperose (Persepolis) Chsd ldrs, wandered & styd on under press fnl 1f: reapp: '03 mdn wnr, plcd on other 3
starts: eff at 5f on fast & soft grnd: encouraging reapp, has been gelded since last term.
2 May'03 Redc 5g/f 86- E: 1 May'03 Hami 5g/s 86- D:

2644} **ELLIOTS CHOICE 288** [12] D Carroll 3-8-7 (71) D Tudhope(6) 25/1: 03020-4: b c Foxhound - Indian   nk   71
City (Lahib) Rear, switched & styd on under press fnl 1.5f, nrst fin: reapp: plcd on 2 of 5 '03 starts (mdns): eff at 5f on
fast grnd, handles soft: plenty to like about this reapp & sharper next time.
2 Jun'03 Hayd 5g/f 73- D:

4713* }**FIDDLE ME BLUE 187** [15]3-8-13 (77) L Fletcher(3) 7/2: 31-5: Prom, led halfway, hung left & hdd   shd   77
dist, wknd: well bckd tho' op 11/4, reapp.

4941} **BAYLAW STAR 171** [13]3-8-12 (76) J Edmunds 14/1: 143003-6: Chsd ldrs, onepcd dist on reapp.   1¼   72

2867} **TYNE 280** [5]3-9-7 (85) N Mackay(3) 10/1: 216-7: Rear, late prog, nvr dngrs on reapp.   2   75

955   **LETS GET IT ON 21** [6]3-8-13 (77) R Winston 14/1: 13502-08: Slowly away, late prog.   nk   66

4641*}**JADAN 193** [8]3-8-10 (74) A Nicholls 25/1: 44501-9: Prom, wknd dist on reapp.   2½   56

4680} **EASTERN PEARL 189** [10]3-8-12 (76) T P Queally(3) 20/1: 022100-0: 10th: Chsd ldrs till after halfway. nk   57

4923} **LOUISIADE 172** [7]3-8-8 (72) D Allan(3) 12/1: 120000-0: 11th: Al bhnd on reapp: gelded.   3   44

1120   **PETERS CHOICE 6** [9]3-9-1 (79) N Callan 9/1: 42011-00: 12th: Cl-up till halfway: qck reapp.   ¾   48

3383} **MRS SPENCE 256** [16]3-8-4 (68) Dale Gibson 12/1: 025-0: 13th: Led till after halfway, wknd: 'lost action'. 14   7

13 Ran   Time 1m 03.40(6.40)   Owned: Bailey Booth Boorer Nelson   Trained: Gainsborough

Official Going Good (Good/Soft places)

1230 **1.40 Gr3 Dubai Irish Village Stakes Registered As The John Porter Stakes 4yo+ (A)**
£29000 £11000 £5500 **1m4f5y** **Good 53** **+01 Fast** Inside

4893} **DUBAI SUCCESS 175** [3] B W Hills 4-8-11 (110) M Hills 10/1: 105D3-1: b c Sadler's Wells - Crystal Spray (Beldale Flutter) Chsd ldrs, gd hdwy over 2f out, chall ins last, sn led, drvn out, gamely held on: reapp: won 2 of 5 '03 starts (mdn & List - subs disqual): v eff at 12f, shld stay further: acts on gd & gd/soft, sharp or gall trks: has run well fresh: smart & genuine, career best run: lightly rcd, win another Group race. **116**
1 Sep'03 Donc 12gd 115-(106) A: 1 May'03 Ripo 10g/s 90- D:
5035} **GAMUT 161** [15] Sir Michael Stoute 5-8-12 t (117) K Fallon 7/2 FAV: 4/13123-2: b c Spectrum - Greektown (Ela Mana Mou) Handy, hdwy to lead over 2f out, styd on well till collared ins last, rallied gamely, just held: nicely bckd on reapp: '03 List (this race) & stks scorer, Gr 1 rnr-up: eff over 11/14f on fast & gd grnd, sharp or gall trks: eff in a t-strap & can run well fresh: v smart & genuine, tough, fine return. *shd* **115**
2 Sep'03 Curr 14g/f 121- : 1 Aug'03 Wind 11.6g/f 118-(113) C: 1 May'03 Newb 13.3gd 115-(107) A:
2 Aug'02 Wind 11.6g/f 102- B: 1 Apr'02 Newb 11g/f 101- D: 2 Nov'01 Newm 7gd 84- D:
59* **IMPERIAL DANCER 125** [4] M R Channon 6-9-5 (117) T E Durcan 11/1: 164110-3: b c Primo Dominie - Gorgeous Dancer (Nordico) Held up, hdwy & no run over 2f out till dist, styd on, too late: reapp: v tough & smart performer, much closer with a clr run & an excellent run conceding weight all round, set for another fine season. *3* **118+**
1 Nov'03 Capa 10g/s 119f- : 1 Oct'03 Newb 12.0gd 117-(114) A: 1 Sep'03 Ayr 10.9fm 114-(114) A:
2 Aug'03 Curr 10g/f 116- A: 1 Jul'03 Good 9.9gd 114-109 B: 1 Jul'02 Curr 10gd 114- : 1 Jul'02 Ayr 10gd 113- A:
1 May'02 Good 10gd 115- A: 1 Apr'02 Kemp 10gd 105-96 B: 1 Oct'01 Ayr 8hvy 97- C:
1897* **SAYADAW 320** [6] H R A Cecil 4-8-11 T W Ryan 20/1: 21-4: b c Darshaan - Vingt Et Une (Sadler's Wells) Held up, hdwy over 2f out, hung left but kept on over 1f out, nrst fin on reapp: won 2nd of only 2 '03 starts (mdn): stays 12f well, further looks sure to suit: acts on fast & gd in a t-strap: lightly rcd, v pleasing rtn, looks smart & likely more to come, win a List/Gr 3 shortly. *½* **110**
1 Jun'03 Leic 11.8g/f 95- D: 2 May'03 Sali 12g/f 86- D:
884 **PUGIN 28** [13]6-8-12 (105) J Murtagh 10/1: 00060-55: b c Darshaan - Gothic Dream (Nashwan) Held up, eff but hung left over 2f out, no dngr: below best in '03 (rtd 103): Gr 1 rnr-up in '02, List wnr for J Oxx: suited by 12/14f on fast & soft grnd, gall trks: more encouraging but not straightforward now. *2½* **107**
2 Sep'02 Curr 14g/f 115- : 2 Aug'01 Curr 14gd 111- : 1 May'01 Curr 10gd 114- :
3728} **SALSALINO 241** [10]4-8-11 (107) A Culhane 10/1: 243243-6: Bhd, rdn 4f out, late gains: wants 14f. *2* **103**
5035} **THE WHISTLING TEAL 161** [5]8-8-12 (107) D Holland 11/1: 21/4452-7: Held up, some late gains. *¾* **102**
4227} **LET ME TRY AGAIN 217** [7]4-8-11 (107) K Darley 25/1: 120540-8: In tch, onepace: gelded. *1* **100**
950 **FOREST MAGIC 21** [11]4-8-11 (100) P Robinson 40/1: 5211/-49: Chsd ldrs, wknd 2f out: see 950. *2* **97**
4007} **DUTCH GOLD 42** [9]4-8-11 L Dettori 16/1: 006-0200: 10th: In tch, wknd 2f out: rnr-up in Dubai. *3* **93**
2728} **BANDARI 284** [17]5-8-12 (114) R Hills 11/2: 13/4442-0: 11th: Set pace till 2f out, wknd. *2* **90**
2865} **BAROLO 280** [12]5-8-12 (98) Martin Dwyer 33/1: 013114-0: 12th: In tch, hdwy to go 2nd after 5f till over 4f out, no extra on reapp. *2½* **86**
884 **ANANI 28** [16]4-8-11 (106) E Ahern 20/1: 02-03420: 13th: Chsd ldrs, hung left & wknd over 2f out. *1¼* **84**
4493} **DISTINCTION 202** [2]5-8-12 (107) S Drowne 25/1: 3/34015-0: 14th: In tch, wknd over 2f out. *nk* **83**
2814*]**JELANI 643** [14]5-8-12 F Lynch 25/1: 122/541/-0: 15th: In tch, wknd over 2f out. *3½* **78**
1005 **HILBRE ISLAND 17** [8]4-8-11 (111) R Hughes 20/1: 60310-30: 16th: In tch, wknd 2f out: btr 1005 (fm). *nk* **77**
950 **PERFECT STORM 21** [1]5-8-12 (92) S Sanders 66/1: 60012-00: 17th: Al bhd. *13* **59**
17 Ran Time 2m 35.54 (6.24) Owned: Maktoum Al Maktoum Trained: Lambourn

1231 **2.15 Stanjamesuk Com Spring Cup Handicap Stakes 4yo+ 0-105 (B)** **[105]**
£23200 £8800 £4400 **1m str** **Good 53** **+01 Fast** Centre. Raced Stands Side.

951 **EL COTO 21** [26] B A McMahon 4-9-3 (94) S Sanders 20/1: 10304-01: b c Forzando - Thatcherella (Thatching) Chsd ldrs, hdwy 2f out, led dist, rdn clr: '03 dual h'cap wnr: '02 mdn auct & h'cap scorer: eff at 7f/1m, prob stays 10.5f: acts on firm & gd, handles soft: runs v well fresh & enjoys big fields: v useful, career best run. 1 Aug'03 Leic 7.0gd 100-92 B: 2 Apr'03 Newb 8g/f 93-88 B: 1 Mar'03 Donc 7gd 89-83 D: **104**
1 Aug'02 Hayd 5g/s 87-81 E: 1 Apr'02 Leic 5gd 80- F: 2 Mar'02 Donc 5sft 77- E:
1111 **SERIEUX 7** [25] Mrs A J Perrett 5-8-11 (88) K Darley 25/1: 300-0002: b c Cadeaux Genereux - Seranda (Petoski) In tch, hdwy & sltly short of room over 2f out but styd on to lead over 1f out, sn hdd, not pace of wnr: early season stks wnr in '03: '02 h'cap wnr for B Hills: suited by 1m on a gall trk, does handle any: acts on firm & gd grnd: back to form, looks well h'capped & can win another nice prize. *1¾* **93**
1 Apr'03 Asco 8gd 105-(100) B: 1 May'02 York 6.9g/f 103-95 B: 1 Jul'01 Good 6fm 98- D: 2 Jul'01 Donc 6gd 98- D:
4977} **KINGS COUNTY 168** [8] L M Cumani 6-9-4 (95) D Holland 14/1: 00/5512-3: b g Fairy King - Kardelle (Kalaglow) Chsd ldrs, eff 2f out, kept on, not pace of front 2: '03 class stks wnr from 4 starts: former Cork wnr in '01 for A O'Brien: eff at 7f, stays 1m on firm & soft, has run well fresh on gall trks, tried blnks: useful rtn. *1¼* **99**
2 Nov'03 Newm 8g/f 98-92 C: 1 Oct'03 Newm 8fm 94-(90) C:
951 **ALKAADHEM 21** [24] M P Tregoning 4-9-9 (100) R Hills 7/4 FAV: 121-54: Held up in tch, hdwy & short of room sev times from 2 out, kept on late: hvly bckd: lkd a shade unfortunate again: useful colt, shld be winning shortly when things fall right: see 951 (won race on far side). *nk* **103**
951 **NORTON 21** [19]7-9-5 (96) R Miles(3) 33/1: 20000-05: ch g Barathea - Primrose Valley (Mill Reef) With ldrs, led 4f out till over 1f out, no extra: plcd in val h'caps (incl Lincoln) in '03: '02 Royal Hunt Cup h'cap wnr: poss stays 12f, suited by 7.5f/1m on firm & soft, any trk: has run well fresh: v useful & tough, clrly still retains plenty of ability & has slipped to a fair mark. 2 May'03 Kemp 8g/f 106-102 B: *2* **95**
1 Jun'02 Asco 8g/f 99-91 B: 1 May'02 Ling 7.6gd 96- C: 2 Apr'02 Newb 8fm 88-86 B: 1 Aug'01 Hayd 8.1g/f 88-83 C:
4667} **STAR SENSATION 190** [18]4-8-9 (86) R L Moore 33/1: 425400-6: b f Sri Pekan - Dancing Sensation (Faliraki) Held up, hdwy over 1f out, kept on, no threat: won 1 of 12 '03 starts (h'cap): eff at 7f/1m on fast, handles soft grnd & likes gall trks, esp Leicester: fine rtn, h'capped to win a less competitive h'cap soon. *nk* **84**
2 Aug'03 Wind 8.3gd 91-89 C: 1 Jun'03 Leic 8.0g/f 88-85 D: 2 May'03 Newm 8g/f 84-82 C: 1 Oct'02 Leic 7gd 87- D:
744+***UHOOMAGOO 51** [1]6-8-5 bl (82) P Hanagan 33/1: 33430-17: Held up, hdwy & no room 2f out till ins last, styd on, nrst fin: 7 wk abs: in fine form & would have gone much closer here with any sort of run: see 744. *¾* **78+**
951 **DESERT OPAL 21** [10]4-9-4 (95) R Hughes 10/1: 42110-08: Held up, eff 2f out, onepace: fair run. *shd* **90**
2871} **FISIO THERAPY 279** [23]4-8-6 (83) J Fanning 25/1: 614335-9: With ldrs, wknd over 1f out on reapp. *¾* **76**
4928} **IMPELLER 172** [22]5-8-10 (87) Martin Dwyer 33/1: 010022-0: 10th: Held up, hdwy when badly hmpd over 1f out, not recover: encouraging rtn. *hd* **79**
1151* **THIHN 4** [2]9-9-4 (5ex) (95) A Daly 14/1: 6011-010: 11th: Held up, eff 2f out, no extra: qk reapp. *½* **86**

431 **GOLDEN CHALICE 91** [4]5-8-13 (90) K Fallon 20/1: 0520-560: 12th: In tch, no impress fnl 2f: abs. *¾* **79**
4977} **FINISHED ARTICLE 168** [6]7-8-13 (90) Dane O'Neill 33/1: 152204-0: 13th: Held up, nvr a factor. *nk* **78**
4897*}**SPANISH DON 175** [9]6-8-9 (86) L Keniry(3) 16/1: 006141-0: 14th: In tch, wknd 2f out on reapp. *shd* **73**
836 **MYSTIC MAN 35** [11]6-8-10 (87) P Fessey 33/1: 1400-000: 15th: Nvr a factor: see 611. *shd* **74**
1035 **DIGITAL 14** [21]7-9-0 (91) T E Durcan 25/1: 002-0340: 16th: Held up, some late gains, nvr dngrs. *shd* **78**
884 **VORTEX 28** [17]5-9-6 t (97) M Fenton 33/1: 1111100: 17th: Held up, hdwy & hmpd 2f out, not recover. *1¾* **80**
1066 **SHOT TO FAME 11** [3]5-9-1 (92) S Drowne 33/1: 56300-50: 18th: In tch, wknd 2f out. *¾* **73**
2789} **CHINKARA 282** [14]4-9-1 (92) L Dettori 14/1: 414110-0: 19th: In tch, wknd 2f out. *1¾* **69**
1066 **HUXLEY 11** [16]5-8-6 (83) D R McCabe 100/1: 21010-00: 20th: Slow away & bhd, nvr dngrs. *1¾* **56**
1066* **ST PETERSBURG 11** [12]4-9-2 (93) P Robinson 12/1: 0315-210: 21th: Handy, wknd 2f out: btr 1066 (hvy). *1¾* **62**
951 **CRAIOVA 21** [7]5-8-13 P (90) M Hills 25/1: 01250-00: 22th: Nvr a factor. *hd* **59**
951 **JAY GEES CHOICE 21** [27]4-9-0 (91) D Corby(3) 16/1: 02600-60: 23th: Led 4f, wknd 2f out. *½* **59**
2559] **PRIZEMAN 1011** [15]6-9-4 (95) R Havlin 100/1: 2/05600//-0: 24th: In tch, wknd 2f out: new yard. *1* **61**
2482} **IBERUS 294** [13]6-8-8 (85) I Mongan 100/1: 0/60505-0: 25th: Al bhd: jumps rnr, prev with M Pipe. *8* **33**
887 **YAKIMOV 28** [20]5-9-1 (92) A Culhane 66/1: 31023-00: 26th: Nvr a factor. *4* **32**
922 **LUNDYS LANE 23** [5]4-10-0 (105) W Supple 66/1: 4600-400: 27th: In tch centre, wknd over 2f out. *1¼* **42**
27 Ran Time 1m 40.99 (4.19) Owned: R J H Ltd & J P Hames Trained: Tamworth

1232

2.45 Cantorsport Co Uk Handicap Stakes 4yo+ 0-90 (C) **[90]**
£9958 £3064 £1532 **2m** **Good 53** **-17 Slow** Inside

1087 **MALARKEY 10** [4] Mrs Stef Liddiard 7-8-8 (70) S Drowne 9/1: 306/-5121: In tch, gd hdwy 2f out, led on bit just ins last, pushed clr, v readily: val 5L+: eff over 14f/2m1f on firm, soft & fibresand, any trk: thriving since switched to new stable & this was thoroughly convincing, can follow up in this form: see 1003. **77+**
3107} **TOMINA 268** [8] N A Graham 4-8-9 (75) D Holland 9/1: 00/6143-2: b g Deploy - Cavina (Ardross) *2½* **76**
Held up, short of room over 2f out, switched & kept on over 1f out, no threat to cmftble wnr on reapp: '03 h'cap wnr: eff at 12f, imprvd here stepped up to 2m: acts on fast, gd grnd & prob any trk: lightly rcd, unexposed at this trip & shld find similar shortly. 1 May'03 Warw 12.6g/f 73-65 E:
1003 **KING FLYER 17** [16] Miss J Feilden 8-9-4 (80) S Whitworth 14/1: 6036-023: Held up, eff over 2f out, kept on, not pace of wnr: tough, another gd run: see 1003, 813. *hd* **81**
948 **SAN HERNANDO 21** [2] D R C Elsworth 4-8-7 (73) Dane O'Neill 16/1: 16060-64: Held up, hdwy to lead over 2f out, rdn & hdd just ins last, no extra: just stays 2m on firm & gd grnd: see 948. *¾* **73**
1003 **NAWOW 17** [14]4-8-11 (77) S Sanders 13/2: 0326-035: In tch, eff to chall 2f out, no extra fnl 1f. *3* **74**
950 **RAVENGLASS 21** [11]5-9-7 (83) R Havlin 25/1: 26100-06: b c Miswaki - Urus (Kris S) In tch, eff to chall 2f out, no extra ins last: '03 mdn & h'cap wnr: eff at 12f, stays 2m on firm & gd, handles soft & any trk. *1¾* **78**
1 Sep'03 Yarm 16gd 87-84 C: 2 Aug'03 Epso 12.0g/f 84-78 C: 1 Jun'03 Bath 11.7fm 79-(80) D:
2 Jun'03 Chep 10.2g/f 84-(80) D: 2 Oct'02 Nott 9.9sft 80- D:
4796} **RANDOM QUEST 182** [7]6-10-0 (90) R Hughes 16/1: 023250-7: b g Rainbow Quest - Anne Bonny (Ajdal) *¾* **84**
In tch, hdwy over 2f out, sn no impress: reapp: plcd in val h'caps in '03 for P Cole: '02 h'cap wnr: eff at 2m/2m5f on fast & hvy, any trk: can front run or come from bhd: has run well fresh: now with B J Llewellyn.
2 Aug'03 Asco 16.2g/f 92-89 B: 2 Jul'03 Newm 16.1g/f 89-85 C: 1 Aug'02 Ches 18.6g/f 97-91 B: 2 May'01 Sali 12sft 93- B:
1003 **SONOMA 17** [10]4-8-6 (72) M Fenton 16/1: 01225-58: Cl-up, led 4f out till over 2f out, no extra. *5* **61**
1093 **RIYADH 9** [9]6-9-2 vis (78) K Dalgleish 16/1: 4060-009: Slow away, sn in tch, wknd over 2f out. *5* **62**
4865} **PROMOTER 176** [18]4-9-8 (88) E Ahern 9/2 FAV: 521404-0: 10th: Bhd, some late gains. *shd* **72**
3352} **SPARKLING WATER 258** [1]5-8-13 (75) J Murtagh 50/1: 03/0050-0: 11th: In tch, btn 2f out on reapp. *5* **54**
812 **MADIBA 43** [13]5-7-12 (60) J F McDonald(5) 16/1: 1602220: 12th: In tch, wknd 2f out: 6 wk abs. *2* **37**
1112 **BID FOR FAME 7** [17]7-9-9 (85) W Ryan 25/1: 00621-00: 13th: Bhd, nvr a factor: see 173, 140. *4* **58**
1087 **HEIR TO BE 10** [3]5-8-12 (74) K Darley 9/1: 01006-50: 14th: In tch, wknd over 3f out: see 1087. *nk* **47**
924 **REDSPIN 23** [6]4-8-7 P (73) Martin Dwyer 50/1: 2502-300: 15th: Al bhd: see 288. *10* **36**
594 **STOLEN SONG 67** [5]4-7-12 (2oh) (62) Lisa Jones(3) 14/1: 352-4160: 16th: In tch, wknd 3f out: recent nov h'cap wnr (2m, rtd 106h): see 491 (fibresand). *6* **21**
4865} **MERSEY SOUND 176** [12]6-8-8 (70) J D Walsh(7) 25/1: 403210-0: 17th: Slow away & al bhd on reapp. *¾* **26**
1056 **MAKULU 12** [15]4-8-10 bl (76) L Dettori 20/1: 02350-00: 18th: Led till over 2f out, wknd: too keen. *17* **15**
18 Ran Time 3m 37.17 (11.17) Owned: Mr A Liddiard Trained: Hungerford

1233

3.15 Gr3 Dubai Duty Free Stakes Registered As The Fred Darling Stakesfillies 3yo (A)
£29000 £11000 £5500 **7f str** **Good 53** **-21 Slow** Centre

4556} **MAJESTIC DESERT 198** [6] M R Channon 3-9-0 (111) K Fallon 6/4 FAV: 12312-1: b f Fraam - Calcutta Queen (Night Shift) Handy, hdwy to lead dist, styd on strongly, rdn out: well bckd on reapp: '03 mdn & stks wnr, Gr 1 rnr-up: clrly stays 7f well, 1m shld suit: acts on firm & gd grnd, gall or easy trks: v smart filly, win more Group races & a leading 1,000 Guineas contender. **113**
2 Oct'03 Newm 6g/f 114-(93) A: 1 Aug'03 Curr 6g/f 102- : 2 May'03 York 6.0fm 90- D: 1 Apr'03 Warw 5fm 84- E:
4556} **NYRAMBA 198** [5] J H M Gosden 3-9-0 (109) L Dettori 6/1: 12110-2: b f Night Shift - Maramba (Rainbow Quest) Keen held up, hdwy over 1f out, styd on ins last, not pace of wnr on reapp: won 3 of 5 '03 starts (mdn, List & stks): eff at 6f, clrly styd this 7f well & 1m shld suit (dam 1m wnr): acts on firm & gd grnd, gall trks: smart filly, progressing with racing & can win a Group race shortly. *1* **109**
1 Sep'03 Asco 6.5g/f 108- B: 1 Sep'03 Sali 6fm 103- A: 2 Aug'03 Newb 5.2fm 97- A: 1 May'03 Sali 5fm 94- D:
3494} **NATALIYA 252** [9] J L Dunlop 3-9-0 S Sanders 12/1: 13-3: b f Green Desert - Ninotchka (Nijinsky) Held up, hdwy 2f out, onepace fnl 1f on reapp: '03 mdn & List 3rd in '03: stays 7f, 1m shld suit (dam mid-dist wnr): acts on firm & gd grnd, has run well fresh on gall trks: lightly rcd & useful. *1* **107**
1 Jul'03 Newb 6.0g/f 90- D:
4978*}**SPOTLIGHT 168** [7] J L Dunlop 3-9-0 (101) J Murtagh 100/30: 3121-4: ch f Dr Fong - Dust Dancer (Suave Dancer) Set stdy pace, rdn & hdd dist, no extra: nicely bckd on reapp: won 2 of 4 '03 starts, mdn & List: stays 1m & shld get further this term (dam 10f wnr): acts on firm & gd, any trk: v useful, do btr over further. *1¼* **104**
1 Nov'03 Newm 8g/f 108-(98) A: 2 Oct'03 Newm 7fm 104-(88) A: 1 Sep'03 Warw 7.1fm 84- D:
4556} **RUBY ROCKET 198** [1]3-9-0 (105) D Holland 12/1: 11314-5: In tch, wknd over 1f out: won 3 of 5 '03 starts, mdn, stks & List: v eff at 6f, shld stay at least 7f: acts on firm & fast grnd & has run well fresh on a gall or easy trk: useful, may do btr. *1* **102**
4758*}**PHANTOM WIND 184** [8]3-9-0 R Hughes 13/2: 01-6: Handy, wknd over 1f out: longer trip. *½* **101**
4597} **UNSHOODA 196** [3]3-9-0 (95) R Hills 20/1: 2126-7: Keen, in tch, wknd over 1f out. *¾* **97**
3335} **FRAGRANT STAR 259** [4]3-9-0 (81) T E Durcan 66/1: 040105-8: Al bhd. *11* **77**
8 Ran Time 1m 29.51 (5.21) Owned: Mr Jaber Abdullah Trained: West Ilsley

NEWBURY SATURDAY 17.04.04 Lefthand, Flat, Galloping Track

1234 **3.45 Gr3 Lane's End Greenham Stakes Colts & Geldings 3yo (A)**
£29000 £11000 £5500 **7f str** **Good 53** **+15 Fast** Centre

4898*}**SALFORD CITY 175** [11] D R C Elsworth 3-9-0 J Murtagh 100/30: 1-1: b c Desert Sun - Summer Fashion (Moorestyle) Slow away, rdn over 2f out, styd on strongly dist to lead ins last, going away: nicely bckd: won sole '03 start (mdn): dam 10f wnr: eff at 7f, relish a rtn to 1m: acts on gd & runs well fresh: likes Newbury: lightly rcd & smart, open to plenty of improvement, will relish extra furlong of the 2000 Guineas. **117+**
1 Oct'03 Newb 8gd 99- D:
885 **FOKINE 28** [5] B W Hills 3-9-0 (114) M Hills 11/2: 1620-22: Handy, hdwy to lead over 1f out, rdn & hdd ins last, not pace of wnr: useful: just the type for Italian Guineas: see 885. *1¾* **111**
4868*}**SO WILL I 176** [9] M P Tregoning 3-9-0 W Supple 14/1: 41-3: ch c Inchinor - Fur Will Fly (Petong) Held up, hdwy 2f out, chall & hung left ins last, not pace of wnr: won 2nd of 2 '03 starts (mdn): eff at 6f, stays 7f on fast & gd grnd, gall trks: has run well fresh: smart eff on step up in class: lightly rcd, shld win a List. 1 Oct'03 Newb 6.0g/f 90- D: *shd* **111**
3409*}**FORT DIGNITY 255** [10] Sir Michael Stoute 3-9-0 K Fallon 7/1: 1-4: b c Seeking The Gold - Kitza (Danehill) Held up, keen, hdwy 2f out, onepace fnl 1f: won a nov stks sole '03 start: eff at 7f, shld stay 1m+ (dam high-class/12f performer): acts on fast grnd & has run well fresh: useful, only 2nd start & more to come. *½* **110**
1 Aug'03 Yarm 7.0g/f 92- D:
1040 **MILK IT MICK 14** [1]3-9-0 (118) D Holland 3/1 FAV: 32511-25: Keen in tch, eff 2f out, no extra over 1f out: well bckd: yet to reproduce shock Dewhurst form this term: see 1040. *1¾* **106**
885 **BAHIANO 28** [8]3-9-0 (95) E Ahern 25/1: 62-21236: In tch, no extra dist: closer to this rnr-up in 885. *1* **104**
4163} **MUKAFEH 220** [2]3-9-0 R Hills 9/2: 13-7: b c Danzig - Bint Salsabil (Nashwan) Led till over 1f out, no extra: nicely bckd: won first of 2 juv starts (mdn): eff over a gall 7f, shld stay further (dam high-class 7f/1m wnr): acts on firm grnd & has run well fresh. 1 Aug'03 Newb 7fm 92- D: *nk* **103**
1113 **NEROS RETURN 7** [7]3-9-0 K Dalgleish 33/1: 11-68: In tch, wknd well over 1f out. *1½* **100**
4669} **JAZZ SCENE 190** [3]3-9-0 (88) T E Durcan 50/1: 0102-9: In tch, wknd 2f out: up in class & trip. *8* **84**
1040 **KINGS POINT 14** [4]3-9-0 (107) Dane O'Neill 16/1: 24116-50: 10th: In tch, wknd 2f out: see 1040. *1¼* **81**
10 Ran Time 1m 26.97 (2.67) Owned: Mr M Tabor Trained: Whitsbury

1235 **4.20 Dubai Duty Free Handicap Stakes 4yo+ 0-85 (D)** **[85]**
£6110 £1880 £940 **1m2f6y** **Good 53** **-34 Slow** Centre

4894} **IONIAN SPRING 175** [10] C G Cox 9-10-0 (85) P Robinson 12/1: 006530-1: b g Ela Mana Mou - Well Head (Sadler's Wells) Hld up, keen, hdwy over 2f out, led over 1f out, rdn clr: won 1 of 9 '03 starts, this v h'cap (6lb lower mark): h'cap wnr in '02: eff over 10/12f on firm, soft & fibresand, any trk, likes Newbury: loves to come late off a strong pace & clrly runs well fresh: tough & useful. 1 Apr'03 Newb 10.0fm 89-79 D: **94**
1 Mar'02 Nott 10sft 84-78 D: 1 Oct'01 York 10.3g/s 78-73 C: 1 Aug'01 Chep 10g/f 72-67 E:
1 Mar'01 Sout 12af 83a-79 D: 2 Mar'01 Wolv 12af 84a-79 C: 2 Nov'00 Sout 8af 81a-78 D:
464 **STREET LIFE 85** [12] W J Musson 6-9-0 (71) W Supple 20/1: 0006-252: Hld up, hdwy over 2f out, kept on ins last, not pace of wnr: abs: fine run: looks poised to strike, all 3 wins at Windsor on easy grnd: see 391. *1¼* **77**
1027 **BARRY ISLAND 15** [17] D R C Elsworth 5-9-7 (78) Dane O'Neill 16/1: 4-152443: Slow away, held up, hdwy 2f out, kept on, nrst fin: encouraging run but all 3 wins on polytrack at 10f: see 570, 429. *1¾* **80**
5020} **DREAM MAGIC 163** [19] M J Ryan 6-9-7 (78) E Ahern 14/1: 530044-4: b g Magic Ring - Pip's Dream (Glint of Gold) Handy, hdwy to lead over 1f out, sn hdd & onepace: reapp: '03 rtd h'cap wnr: '02 h'cap wnr: suited by 10f, stays a sharp 12f on fm, soft & polytrack, any trk: tough, likes a strong pace & back on a fair mark. *nk* **79**
1 Mar'03 Nott 10.0gd 85-80 D: 2 Feb'03 Ling 10ap 81a-80 C: 2 Oct'02 Yarm 10sft 82-78 D: 1 Aug'02 Sand 10g/f 79-74 C:
2 Aug'02 Newm 10sft 77-74 C: 2 Jun'02 Hayd 8.1sft 76-72 C: 2 May'02 Good 8g/s 73-71 D: 2 Sep'01 Asco 8gd 74-69 D:
1 Sep'01 Good 8g/f 69-64 E: 2 Sep'01 Hayd 8.1sft 69-64 E:
900 **SILVALINE 25** [16]5-9-4 (75) T E Durcan 20/1: 033-6045: Led early, cl-up, onepace fnl 2f: see 900. *nk* **76**
4291*}**BALKAN KNIGHT 213** [9]4-9-9 vis (80) J Murtagh 4/1 FAV: 01/1-6: b c Selkirk - Crown of Light (Mtoto) Chsd ldrs, sltly outpcd over 3f out, some late gains: nicely bckd: won sole '03 start (h'cap): nov stks '02 wnr: stays 10f well on fast & gd/soft, stiff/undul trks: goes well fresh & suited by a visor: lightly rcd, poss more to come. 1 Sep'03 Sand 10.0g/f 82-75 D: 1 Jul'02 Beve 7.4g/s 77- D: *nk* **80**
4873} **FREELOADER 176** [18]4-9-3 (74) R Hills 25/1: 311260-7: b g Revoque - Indian Sand (Indian King) In tch, hdwy to chall 2f out, no extra fnl 1f: '03 3-time h'cap wnr: suited by around 10f on fast, gd/soft & polytrack, handles any trk: progressive last term, been gelded & shld be much sharper for this next time. *¾* **72**
2 Sep'03 Chep 10.2gd 71-67 D: 1 Sep'03 York 10.4g/f 77-67 E: 1 Aug'03 Nott 10.0g/f 68-62 F: 1 May'03 Ling 10ap 59a-57 F:
4593} **GUILDED FLYER 196** [6]5-9-10 (81) L Keniry(3) 50/1: 216500-8: Led after 2f till dist, no extra. *3½* **74**
SHAMDIAN 229 [3]4-10-0 (85) K Fallon 8/1: 32262-9: Handy, wknd well over 1f out: ex French. *1½* **75**
404 **BRIAREUS 94** [13]4-9-9 (80) Martin Dwyer 20/1: 0324-000: 10th: In tch, wknd 2f out. *shd* **70**
1098 **KARAOKE 9** [4]4-9-1 (72) J D Smith 50/1: 31-00100: 11th: In tch, btn 3f out: btr 803 (polytrk). *½* **61**
1057 **KENTUCKY KING 12** [14]4-10-0 (85) R Hughes 16/1: 6601030: 12th: Handy, wknd 2f out: see 1057 (1m). *3½* **69**
1056 **KYLKENNY 12** [1]9-9-4 t (75) J Fanning 14/1: 5004-300: 13th: In tch, wknd 2f out: lost action. *hd* **58**
179 **ALRAFID 129** [8]5-9-13 (84) R L Moore 12/1: 622426-0: 14th: No danger: gelded: see 134 (polytrk). *1* **65**
1057 **AFRICAN SAHARA 12** [20]5-10-0 t (85) G Carter 16/1: 1016060: 15th: Al bhd: see 800. *¾* **64**
888 **DOWER HOUSE 28** [2]9-9-8 t (79) L Dettori 12/1: 4654050: 16th: Keen held up, btn 2f out: see 26. *1* **56**
4689+ **BEST BE GOING 188** [5]4-9-6 (77) D Holland 7/1: 3451-0: 17th: In tch, wknd 2f out: longer trip. *¾* **52**
138 **SILVER PROPHET 136** [15]5-9-8 t (79) G Baker 50/1: 043000-0: 18th: Slow away & al bhd. *6* **44**
939* **SLALOM 21** [7]4-9-5 (76) M Fenton 12/1: 53-10: 19th: Slow away & al bhd: btr 939 (fibresand). *4* **33**
4702} **COUNT WALEWSKI 188** [11]4-9-1 (72) W Ryan 66/1: 6/02210-0: 20th: Keen, al bhd: chngd stable. *13* **11**
20 Ran Time 2m 11.55 (8.75) Owned: Elite Racing Club Trained: Hungerford

1236 **4.55 Dubai International Airport Maiden Stakes 3yo (D)**
£6240 £1920 £960 **1m str** **Good 53** **-19 Slow** Centre

919 **MUDAWIN 23** [10] M P Tregoning 3-9-0 W Supple 20/1: 5-01: b g Intikhab - Fida (Persian Heights) Handy, led halfway, styd on strongly over 1f out, pushed out: rtd 76+ when unplcd sole juv start: half-brother to useful sprinter Maghaarb: enjoyed step up to 1m, shld stay further: acts on gd grnd & runs well fresh: useful eff here & looks capable of wng in stronger company. **97**
REHEARSAL [9] C G Cox 3-9-0 P Robinson 33/1: 2: b c Singspiel - Daralaka (The Minstrel) *2½* **89**

NEWBURY   SATURDAY 17.04.04   Lefthand, Flat, Galloping Track

Handy, hdwy to chase wnr over 1f out, kept on but not his pace: eff at 1m, bred to relish 10f: acts on gd grnd & a gall trk: learn plenty from this encouraging start, must win similar.

3652} **AKIMBO** 245 [15] H R A Cecil 3-9-0 R Hughes 8/11 FAV: 2-3: b c Kingmambo - All At Sea (Riverman)	¾	87
In tch, eff over 1f out, kept on same pace: hvly bckd on reapp: mdn rnr-up in '03: dam top-class mid-dist performer: eff at 7f/1m, shld get further: acts on firm & gd grnd: sharper for this & clrly held in some regard. 2 Aug'03 Newb 7fm 90- D:		
4409} **DR THONG** 207 [3] P F I Cole 3-9-0 L Dettori 9/1: 5-4: ch c Dr Fong - Always On My Mind (Distant Relative) Keen in tch, eff 2f out, no extra fnl 1f: 5th in a mdn sole '03 start: dam multiple 6f wnr: eff at 7f on fast grnd: minor trk mdn would suit.	2½	82
4974} **WHITSBURY CROSS** 168 [12]3-9-0 J Murtagh 16/1: 0-5: b c Cape Cross - Vallauris (Faustus) Slow away, held up, eff 2f out, kept on ins last on reapp: unplcd sole '03 start: stays 1m, further shld suit: acts on gd grnd, minor trk mdn would suit.	½	81
4898} **LAABBIJ** 175 [18]3-9-0 J Fanning 50/1: 0-6: Bhd, some late gains, nvr dngrs: apprec further.	½	79
HE JAA [13]3-8-9 T E Durcan 66/1: 7: Slow away & bhd, no dngr on debut.	nk	74
FUEL CELL [8]3-9-0 Dane O'Neill 50/1: 8: Bhd, some late gains, no dngr.	shd	77
5018} **ADMIRAL** 163 [2]3-9-0 K Fallon 14/1: 64-9: In tch, wknd well over 1f out.	1¾	75
175 **ALBINUS** 129 [7]3-9-0 Martin Dwyer 66/1: 03-0: 10th: Led to halfway, wknd well over 1f out.	½	74
DANDYGREY RUSSETT [19]3-8-9 R L Moore 66/1: 0: 11th: In tch, no extra over 1f out.	½	68
4651} **SAHARAN SONG** 192 [1]3-8-9 M Hills 50/1: 4-0: 12th: In tch, btn 2f out.	1½	63
PRINCIPAL WITNESS [4]3-9-0 M Fenton 100/1: 0: 13th: In tch, wknd 2f out.	¾	68
OGILVY [16]3-9-0 W Ryan 33/1: 0: 14th: Slow away & al bhd.	shd	67
NEWS SKY [6]3-9-0 E Ahern 25/1: 0: 15th: Slow away, in tch, wknd 2f out.	nk	66
2847} **LATIF** 280 [17]3-9-0 R Hills 9/2: 4-0: 16th: In tch, wknd 2f out: nicely bckd.	3½	59
LUCKY AGAIN [5]3-9-0 G Carter 66/1: 0: 17th: Slow away & al bhd.	5	49
ANNA PALLIDA [11]3-8-9 D Holland 16/1: 0: 18th: Sn rdn & al bhd.	½	43
623 **MYSTIC LAD** 63 [14]3-9-0 K Dalgleish 33/1: 20: 19th: Handy, btn halfway.	7	34

19 Ran   Time 1m 42.56(5.76)   Owned: Mr Hamdan Al Maktoum   Trained: Lambourn

---

NOTTINGHAM   SATURDAY 17.04.04   Lefthand, Galloping Track

Official Going Good

1237   5.15 Nottingham Racecourse Conference Centre Maiden Stakes 2yo   (D)
£3682 £1133 £567   **Good 60**   **-40 Slow**   Stands Side

1077 **NORCROFT** 10 [9] N A Callaghan 2-9-0 D Fox(5) 11/10 FAV: 21: Chsd ldrs, prog to lead ent fnl 1f, styd on strongly, rdn out: hvly bckd: eff at 5f on gd & gd/soft, shld stay 6f: made most of prev experience.		80
ON THE WATERLINE [5] P D Evans 2-8-9 G Duffield 25/1: 2: b f Compton Place - Miss Waterline (Rock City) Chsd ldrs, styd on under press fnl 1f, not quite reach wnr: debut: April foal, dam a 6f winning juv: sire a top-class sprinter: eff at 5f on gd grnd: sure to learn from this encouraging start.	2	66
1114 **GRAND OPTION** 7 [10] B W Duke 2-9-0 P Dobbs 16/1: 0323: Chsd ldrs, onepace: acts on gd & soft grnd: deserves a small race, see 1114.	1	68
SHARP N FROSTY [1] W M Brisbourne 2-9-0 S W Kelly 100/1: 4: b g Somayda - Wily Miss (Teenoso) Outpcd, styd on late, nrst fin on debut: March first foal: sire a decent 1m performer: looks sure to apprec 6f+.	hd	67
FIEFDOM [6]2-9-0 R Ffrench 5/2: 5: br c Singspiel - Chiquita Linda (Mujadil) Mid-div, sltly outpcd halfway, styd on fnl 1f & nrst fin on debut: Jan first foal, dam a juv wnr abroad, sire a top-class mid-dist performer: sure to need 6/7f given time: with M Johnston & sure to learn from this.	1	64
JOE JO STAR [3]2-9-0 P Hanagan 80/1: 6: Nvr btr than mid-div on racecourse bow.	½	62
SEA HUNTER [11]2-9-0 C Catlin 14/1: 7: Slowly away, late gains, nvr dngrs on debut.	hd	61
COLEORTON DANCER [8]2-9-0 G Parkin 40/1: 8: Led, drifted to far rail halfway, hdd ent fnl 1f, wknd.	3	52
RASA SAYANG [4]2-9-0 K Darley 9/1: 9: Chsd ldrs 3.5f, wknd: tchd 14/1.	1	49
974 **COLONEL BILKO** 18 [2]2-9-0 S Drowne 10/1: 20: 10th: Front rank, drifted to far rail halfway, wknd dist.	hd	48
HIAMOVI [7]2-9-0 B Doyle 100/1: 0: 11th: Slowly away, al bhd & fin last on debut.	2½	41

11 Ran   Time 1m 03.52 (5.02)   Owned: Norcroft Park Stud   Trained: Newmarket

1238   5.45 Richard Benson Final Fling Handicap Stakes 4yo+ 46-55 (F)   [65]
£3178 £908 £454   **1m6f15y**   **Good 60**   **+07 Fast**   Inside

997 **BEST PORT** 17 [12] J Parkes 8-9-2 (53) M Lawson(7) 8/1: 33054-01: b g Be My Guest - Portree (Slip Anchor) Held up, prog 2f out, switched dist & styd on to lead cl-home, rdn out: gd time: h'cap plcd in '03: dual '02 h'cap wnr: eff at 12f, suited by 14f/2m: acts on firm & soft, likes stiff/gall trks, esp Nottingham & Beverley: tough, on a decent mark. 1 Oct'02 Redc 14sft 62-57 E: 1 Sep'02 Nott 16g/f 57-54 F: 2 Sep'01 Muss 16g/f 54-55 C: 1 Aug'01 Redc 16fm 53-45 E: 1 Jul'01 Beve 16.1fm 45-40 F: 1 Jun'01 Nott 14fm 43-35 E:		59
924 **INTENSITY** 23 [6] P A Blockley 8-9-4 (55) S W Kelly 20/1: 00-3002: Trkd ldrs, imprvd to lead dist, collared cl-home: back to form, stays a gall 14f: well h'capped: see 711 (AW).	½	59
484 **ONLY FOR SUE** 82 [5] W S Kittow 5-9-0 BL (51) I Mongan 28/1: 5/061-003: Led till ent fnl 1f, kept on & only btn 1L: abs: eff at 12/14f on gd & f/sand: handles a sharp trk: improved in blnks.	½	54
965 **FLAME OF ZARA** 19 [1] Mrs M Reveley 5-9-2 (53) K Darley 8/1: 0460-04: ch f Blushing Flame - Sierra Madrona (Woodman) Rear, prog wide 2f out, kept on fnl 1f & nrst fin: '03 mdn 4th (rtd 65): bmpr plcd in 02/03, incl rnr-up in a List event (eff at 2m on firm & soft): eff at 14f on gd, will apprec a return to 2m.	1½	54
733 **ASTROMANCER** 51 [11]4-8-11 (50) Saleem Golam(7) 12/1: 0244-045: Chsd ldrs, onepcd fnl 1.5f: 7 wk abs, clr of rem: see 733 (2m, AW).	shd	51
4806} **FIELD SPARK** 182 [13]4-9-2 p (55) G Duffield 14/1: 046616-6: b g Sillery - On The Top (High Top) Rear, some prog halfway, no impress fnl 2f on reapp: won 2 h'caps in '03 (both at Catterick, incl reapp): eff around 12f on gd & fast grnd: wears cheek pieces, has tried a visor: handles any trk, likes a sharp one, esp Catterick. 1 Oct'03 Catt 12.0g/f 58-52 E: 2 May'03 Beve 12.1gd 60-54 E: 1 Mar'03 Catt 12.0g/f 61-59 E:	6	48
4481} **ROMIL STAR** 203 [4]7-9-3 (54) P Hanagan 11/1: 005560-7: Chsd ldrs, outpcd 1.5f out: new stable.	1¼	45
1197 **JUNGLE LION** 2 [9]6-8-13 t (50) S Drowne 7/1: 2010168: Chsd ldrs (2d, wknd: qck reapp.	shd	41
1064 **TOM BELL** 11 [16]4-8-8 (1oh) (47) D Sweeney 13/2: 0/0005-29: Nvr btr than mid-div: bckd from 11/1.	shd	37
1090 **RUTLAND CHANTRY** 10 [10]10-8-10 (47) B Reilly(3) 14/1: 0/0000-50: 10th: Chsd ldrs, outpcd 3f out.	shd	37
1082 **MISS KOEN** 10 [8]5-9-2 t (53) D Corby(3) 20/1: 6310300: 11th: Held up, nvr nr ldrs: btr 979.	4	37

342

424   **RETAIL THERAPY 92** [7]4-8-9 (48) R Ffrench 33/1: 0006-260: 12th: Nvr nrr than mid-div: 6 wk jumps abs. *3*   **28**
2316} **SUNNYSIDE ROYALE 301** [17]5-8-10 (1ow)(1oh)t (45) S Sanders 6/1 FAV: 006/346-0: 13th: Al bhnd.   4   **22**
984   **Monsal Dale 18** [15]5-8-13 P(50) M Savage(4) 28/1:0   1003 **Termonfeckin 17** [3]6-9-4 (55) Joanna Badger 40/1:0
979   **Golden Dual 18** [14]4-9-2 vis(55) Paul Eddery 20/1:0   1034 **Dark Cut 14** [18]4-8-9 (48) J Carroll 66/1:0
17 Ran   Time 3m 05.73 (7.43)   Owned: Mr M Wormald   Trained: Malton

---

1239   6.15 Sky Bet Press Red To Bet Handicap Stakes Fillies 3yo 0-75 (E)   [82]
£3630 £1117 £558   6f15y str   Good 60   -32 Slow   Stands Side. 2 Groups.

914*} **BEEJAY 382** [2] P F I Cole 3-9-3 (71) J Quinn 14/1: 31-1: b f Piccolo - Letluce (Aragon) Rear   **79+**
far side, prog halfway, strong run to lead cl-home, going away: tchd 20/1, reapp: won fnl of 2 '03 starts (AW,
fills mdn): eff at 6f, shld stay 7f: acts on gd grnd & polytrack, sharp or gall trk: clearly runs well fresh:
open to plenty more improvement & one to follow at this stage. 1 Apr'03 Ling 5ap 75a- D:
1049 **MARINAITE 12** [10] S R Bowring 3-9-5 (73) J Bramhill 9/1: 2152: Switched far rail start & tried   1¼   75
to make all, not pace to repel wnr cl-home: acts on gd grnd & fibresand, poss gd/soft: gd front running eff, caught
a lightly rcd & progressive rival: return to 7f shld suit, as in 1049.
4813} **WHISTFUL 180** [9] C F Wall 3-8-13 (67) S Sanders 16/1: 0542-3: b f First Trump - Atmospheric   shd   69
Blues (Double Schwartz) Held up far side, prog halfway, fin strongly but not quite get there: reapp: rnr-up on fnl
'03 start (mdn auct): eff at 6/7f on gd & fast: handles a gall trk, runs well fresh: decent reapp, deserves
similar. 2 Oct'03 Pont 6g/f 64-(60) F:
5014} **GOJO 163** [11] B Palling 3-8-13 (67) K Darley 20/1: 060-4: b f Danetime - Pretonic (Precocious)   nk   68+
Tried to make all stands side, kept on fnl 1f but just bhd trio on far side: reapp/h'cap bow: some mdn promise in
'03 (rtd 77): half-sister to a hdles wnr: eff at 6f, acts on gd, prob firm: decent reapp, first home on stands side.
135* **MISSUS LINKS 137** [8]3-9-2 (70) R Smith 9/2 FAV: 1-5: Chsd ldrs far side, onepcd fnl 1f on reapp: nk   70
well bckd: acts on soft & poltrack: see 135 (AW, debut).
933   **GENEROUS GESTURE 22** [7]3-9-6 (74) I Mongan 10/1: 604-156: Front rank far side, no extra fnl 1f.   ¾   72
4844} **URBAN ROSE 178** [17]3-8-13 (67) S W Kelly 22/1: 01044-7: Mid-div stands side, styd on well fnl 1f.   shd   64
1024 **JUST ONE LOOK 15** [20]3-9-3 (71) D Sweeney 7/1: 26500-08: Chsd ldrs stands side, onepcd fnl 1f.   hd   67
898   **SWORN TO SECRECY 25** [5]3-8-13 (67) P Dobbs 28/1: 0435-09: Chsd ldrs far side, onepcd fnl 1f.   nk   62
955   **UNDER MY SPELL 21** [6]3-9-4 (72) B Reilly(3) 20/1: 33555-00: 10th: Chsd ldrs far side, onepcd.   shd   67
1102 **BLACK OVAL 9** [1]3-8-5 (59) C Catlin 14/1: 606-4450: 11th: Outpcd far side, late hdwy: see 995.   hd   53
1050 **IMPULSIVE BID 12** [13]3-8-10 (64) P Hanagan 22/1: 404-40: 12th: Prom stands side, wknd fnl 1f.   2   52
735   **CHIQITITA 51** [3]3-8-5 (1ow)BL (58) R Price 66/1: 6600-000: 13th: Slow away, al bhd far side: 7 wk abs.   nk   46
260* **CHORUS BEAUTY 110** [4]3-8-12 (68) S Drowne 10/1: 01-0: 14th: Rear far side, nvr dngrs: long abs.   1¼   49
4997} **Alice Blackthorn 165** [18]3-9-1 (69) R Ffrench 20/1:0   863* **Showtime Annie 31** [15]3-8-10 (64) A Mackay 25/1:0
901   **Man Crazy 25** [16]3-9-0 (68) G Duffield 20/1:0   935 **Back At De Front 22** [19]3-9-2 (70) M Savage(5) 20/1:0
911   **Deign To Dance 24** [12]3-9-5 (73) J Carroll 28/1:0   5034} **Annie Harvey 161** [14]3-9-7 (75) M Stainton(7) 33/1:0
20 Ran   Time 1m 16.35 (5.55)   Owned: Mr A H Robinson   Trained: Whatcombe

---

1240   6.45 Colwick Park Handicap Stakes 3yo 46-55 (F)   [71]
£3129 £894 £447   1m1f213y   Good 60   -07 Slow   Inside

983   **BE WISE GIRL 18** [6] J G Given 3-8-4 (47) G Duffield 7/1: 03-31: Made all, clr fnl 1f, rdn out: 56
tchd 10/1, h'cap bow: apprec step up to gall 10f, acts on gd grnd: suited by forcing tactics & given a gd ride.
1051 **DANEFONIQUE 12** [1] D Carroll 3-8-9 (52) R Fitzpatrick 7/1: 3050-032: Chsd ldrs, took 2nd fnl 1f,   3   57
not reach wnr: acts on gd & gd/soft grnd: met an improving rival, see 1051.
1070 **SAVANNAH RIVER 11** [14] C W Thornton 3-8-3 (1oh)t (45) P Hanagan 33/1: 000-03: b f Desert King -   1¼   48
Hayward (Indian Ridge) Chsd ldrs, styd on under press fnl 1f: well btn in 3 '03 mdn starts: eff at 10f on gd.
4823} **CHEROKEE NATION 179** [11] P W D'Arcy 3-8-11 (54) Paul Eddery 9/2 FAV: 006-4: br c Emperor Jones -   ½   56
Me Cherokee (Persian Bold) Keen & trkd ldrs, found less than expected fnl 1f: op 11/2 on reapp: AW mdn 6th on fnl
'03 start: 12,000 gns half-brother to a 5f juv wnr: rcd too keenly for own gd today.
4563} **INCISOR 198** [12]3-8-8 (51) P Dobbs 14/1: 056-5: b g Dracula - Last Night's Fun (Law Society)   2   49
Mid-div, styd on late, nrst fin: seasonal/h'cap bow: rtd 60 at best in 3 '03 mdns starts: 12f may suit judged on
this: has been gelded since last term.
1147* **PERFECT BALANCE 5** [3]3-9-4 (6ex) (61) Kim Tinkler 6/1: 300-016: Rear, late hdwy, nvr dngrs: qck   1½   57
reapp: btr 1147 (1m, soft grnd).
1051 **TIMBUKTU 12** [9]3-8-3 (6oh) (40) J Quinn 50/1: 006-007: Rear, styd on fnl 2f, nvr nrr.   2½   38
1147 **MYANNABANANA 5** [2]3-8-9 p (52) D Fentiman(7) 14/1: 3440508: Slowly away, nvr nr ldrs: qck reapp.   3   39
4532} **NORTHERN SPIRIT 200** [4]3-8-12 (55) G Parkin 20/1: 0550-9: Rear, nvr nr ldrs on reapp.   1   40
1051 **LENWADE 12** [7]3-8-8 (51) A McCarthy 22/1: 06000-00: 10th: Slowly away, nvr a factor.   hd   35
4966} **CALARA HILLS 168** [10]3-8-9 (52) S W Kelly 28/1: 006-0: 11th: Nvr nrr than mid-div: reapp/h'cap bow.   shd   36
715   **NUMPTY 53** [8]3-8-3 (6oh)t (40) Joanna Badger 33/1: 000-5500: 12th: Chsd ldrs 1m, wknd: 8 wk abs.   5   22
1193 **PRINCESS ISMENE 2** [16]3-8-12 bl (55) J Bramhill 7/1: 2243340: 13th: Chsd ldrs 7f, wknd qckly: busy.   ¾   30
3648} **MISS HOOFBEATS 245** [5]3-8-8 (51) B Reilly(3) 14/1: 030-0: 14th: Chsd ldrs 1m, wknd qckly: reapp.   3   22
351   **RUMOUR MILL 100** [15]3-8-12 (55) C Catlin 33/1: 0000-50: 15th: Al bhd, t.o.: long abs.   30   0
1016 **QUEENS FANTASY 16** [13]3-8-12 BL (55) S Sanders 14/1: 00-040: 16th: Slowly away, t.o. halfway,   dist   0
virtually p.u.: tried blnks: see 1016.
16 Ran   Time 2m 08.97 (6.67)   Owned: Be Wise Racing   Trained: Gainsborough

---

1241   7.15 World Watch Departs Median Auction Maiden Stakes 3yo (F)
£3178 £908 £454   1m1f213y   Good 60   -06 Slow   Inside

4772} **WOODCRACKER 183** [10] M L W Bell 3-9-0 I Mongan 9/1: 0-1: ch g Docksider - Hen Harrier (Polar   93
Falcon) Chsd ldrs, hdwy to lead dist, pushed clr fnl 1f: tchd 12/1, reapp: unplcd sole '03 start: eff over a gall
10f, acts on gd grnd: runs well fresh: has reportedly done well over the winter & looks a progressive type.
4898} **MOUNTAIN MEADOW 175** [14] Mrs A J Perrett 3-9-0 K Darley 4/5 FAV: 2-2: ch g Deploy - Woodwardia   2½   86

(El Gran Senor) Chsd ldrs, ev ch entering fnl 1f, sn not pace of wnr: well bckd at odds-on, reapp: also rnr-up on sole '03 start (mdn): half-brother to a couple of mid-dist wnrs: eff at 10f on gd grnd, bred for mid-dists.
2 Oct'03 Newb 8gd 85- D:

1067	**TUDOR BELL** 11 [4] J G M O'Shea 3-9-0 (75) D Sweeney 15/2: 4-023: Front rank, led 4f out till dist, no extra: op 10/1: not disgraced bhd a couple of prob above average rivals: see 1067 (hvy grnd).	2½	82
	OUR JAFFA [12] D J Daly 3-8-10 (1ow) J Murtagh 13/2: 4: br f Bin Ajwaad - Griddle Cake (Be My Guest) Slow away, prog to chase ldrs halfway, onepcd fnl 2f on debut: prob eff at 10f on gd grnd: encouraging.	½	77
4981}	**PEAK OF PERFECTION** 167 [8]3-9-0 P Robinson 16/1: 00-5: b g Deploy - Nsx (Roi Danzig) Keen & led early, sn mid-div, kept on fnl 1f under a kind ride: reapp/h'cap qualifying run: well held on 2 '03 mdns starts, has since been gelded: half-brother to wnrs over 7/10f: sure to impr in h'cap company at 12f.	½	80
52	**MUSTANG ALI** 151 [13]3-9-0 (66) P Dobbs 33/1: 522003-6: Chsd ldrs, onepcd fnl 2f: reapp, gelded.	nk	79$
919	**BLAEBERRY** 23 [5]3-8-9 J F Egan 80/1: 00-07: Rear, modest late hdwy.	8	60
43	**WINSLOW BOY** 152 [7]3-9-0 J Quinn 100/1: 000-8: Nvr nr mid-div on reapp: has been gelded.	4	57
930	**DANCING BEAR** 22 [11]3-9-0 S Sanders 25/1: 0-49: Trkd ldrs 1m, wknd: see 930.	3	55
4750}	**PEARL OF YORK** 185 [6]3-8-9 G Duffield 80/1: 000-0: 10th: Al towards rear on reapp.	2½	46
	Muslin [3]3-8-9 J D Smith 11/1:0 **Miss St Albans** [1]3-8-9 R Price 100/1:0		
1016	**Baroque** 16 [2]3-9-0 R Fitzpatrick 200/1:0 1022 **Stop The Nonsense** 15 [9]3-9-0 (65) J Carroll 50/1:0		

14 Ran   Time 2m 08.88 (6.58)   Owned: Sir Thomas Pilkington   Trained: Newmarket

---

1242   7.45 Sky Vegas Live On Channel 295 Handicap Stakes 3yo 46-55 (F)   [67]
       £3143 £898 £449   1m54y rnd   Good 60   -28 Slow   Inside

4577}	**DAGOLA** 197 [9] C G Cox 3-9-2 (55) P Robinson 14/1: 0000-1: b g Daggers Drawn - Diabola (Devil's Bag) Trkd ldrs, imprvd to lead entering fnl 1f, pushed clr, readily: reapp, tchd 20/1: little mdn form in '03: cost £18,000: half-brother to wnrs over 7f/1m: apprec step up to gall 1m, acts on gd grnd: clearly runs well fresh: has been gelded since last yr & improved for it, win again.		64
4464}	**ASK THE DRIVER** 204 [5] D J S ffrench Davis 3-9-1 (54) K Darley 7/2 FAV: 050-2: b g Ashkalani - Tithcar (Cadeaux Genereux) Slowly away, prog when short of room after halfway, fin well into 2nd but no ch with wnr: well bckd, reapp: AW nov 5th on middle of 3 '03 starts: eff over a gall 1m, 10f shld suit: acts on gd grnd: met a potentially well h'capped rival here & spot on next time.	3	57
1085*	**SHES OUR LASS** 10 [3] D Carroll 3-9-7 (60) R Fitzpatrick 9/2: 542-0013: Chsd ldrs, sltly short of room 2f out, kept on fnl 1f: nicely bckd under top-weight: stays a gall 1m: see 1085 (7f, soft grnd).	nk	62
4618}	**BREEZIT** 194 [12] S R Bowring 3-9-1 (54) J Bramhill 16/1: 060300-4: b f Stravinsky - Sharka (Shareef Dancer) Rear, gd hdwy to lead 2f out, collared ent fnl 1f & no extra on reapp: '03 claim wnr, also h'cap plcd: eff at 5/6f, poss stays 1m: acts on gd & firm, has tried blnks & cheek pieces: sharper next time.	¾	54
	1 Jul'03 Brig 6.0g/f 63- F:		
865	**THREE WELSHMEN** 31 [2]3-9-1 BL (54) S Drowne 25/1: 0050-005: Rear, kept on fnl 1.5f: tried blnks.	½	53
1081	**BROTHER CADFAEL** 10 [10]3-8-7 (6oh) (40) R Thomas(5) 12/1: 56-30326: Led till 3f out, grad wknd.	3½	42
4930}	**WELSH EMPRESS** 172 [7]3-8-13 (52) J F Egan 7/1: 606603-7: Rear, nvr nr ldrs: bckd from 20/1.	1¼	42
980	**MYSTIC MOON** 18 [14]3-9-2 (55) S W Kelly 25/1: 0-0068: Slowly away, nvr nr ldrs.	½	44
1051	**DAGGERS CANYON** 12 [11]3-9-5 (58) S Sanders 7/1: 0540-29: Held up, nvr a factor: btr 1051.	¾	45
995	**REVERSIONARY** 17 [1]3-9-2 (55) Dale Gibson 145/1: 0560-00: 10th: Trkd ldrs 6f, sn bhd.	3	36
1008	**DR FOX** 17 [13]3-9-7 (55) P Makin(7) 25/1: 00505-00: 11th: Keen & prom, led briefly 3f out, wknd qckly.	nk	35
986*	**LADY PREDOMINANT** 18 [8]3-8-11 (50) G Duffield 8/1: 4406010: 12th: Trkd ldrs, sltly short of room halfway, btn qckly dist: see 986 (AW).	1¼	28
87	**DELCIENNE** 145 [6]3-8-13 T (52) A McCarthy 12/1: 040020-0: 13th: Chsd ldrs 6f, wknd qckly, fin last on reapp: tried a t-strap.	6	18

13 Ran   Time 1m 46.63(7.23)   Owned: The Originals   Trained: Hungerford

---

Official Going STANDARD

1243   2.20 Bet Direct On 0800 32 93 93 Banded Stakes 4yo+ 0-45 (H)
       £1617 £462 £231   1m4f   Going 39   +08 Fast   Inside

827	**MONTOSARI** 41 [3] P Mitchell 5-8-13 (45) D Holland 6/4 FAV: 600-1631: Handy, hdwy to lead over 3f out, pushed clr well over 1f out, eased: 6 wk abs: eff around 12/13f on fm, fast & polytrack, prob fibresand, acts on a gall or sharp trk: in gd form in banded company: see 537.		53a
3127}	**QUEST ON AIR** 270 [1] J R Jenkins 9-8-13 (45) L Dettori 4/1: 042103-2: b g Star Quest - Stormy Heights (Golden Heights) Trkd ldr till lost place 7f out, not pace of wnr from over 2f out: reapp: won a h'cap in '03: unplcd all '02 starts (rtd 42 at best, h'cap): likes to race with/force the pace at 10f/11.5f, acts on fast & gd grnd: likes Yarmouth. 1 May'03 Yarm 11.5g/f 45-42 E: 2 Apr'03 Yarm 11.5gd 43-38 E:	10	43a
4379}	**BOSPHORUS** 212 [7] D G Bridgwater 5-8-13 vis (45) D Nolan(5) 9/2: 432325-3: b g Polish Precedent - Ancara (Dancing Brave) Keen in rear, hdwy over 3f out, sn no impress: reapp: unplcd both 03/04 nov hdle starts (rtd 57h): rnr-up in a h'cap & mdn h'cap on the Flat in '03: eff around 14f/2m on fast & fibresand: eff in a vis. 2 Sep'03 Bath 13.1g/f 48-46 E: 2 Aug'03 Wolv 14.8af 47a-45 G:	1¾	40a
1076*	**BIRTH OF THE BLUES** 13 [4] A Charlton 8-8-13 (45) R Hughes 5/1: 0-006314: Bhd, outpcd 3f out, onepcd 2f out: well clr of rem: rtd higher in 1076, see 689.	1¼	38a
842	**CADWALLADER** 26 [6]4-8-12 P (45) R J Killoran(7) 33/1: 3500-465: Mid-field, btn 4f out: cheekpieces.	11	22a
1180	**FULL EGALITE** 4 [2]8-8-13 bl (30) K Fallon 10/1: 0/540/0-46: Chsd ldrs, wknd 3f out: see 1180.	1	20a
7	**LITTLE SKY** 161 [5]7-8-13 (45) Hayley Turner(5) 12/1: 2000-7: Led till over 3f out, no extra: abs.	1½	18a

7 Ran   Time 2m 32.95 (3.75)   Owned: Caterham Racing (jdrp)   Trained: Epsom

---

1244 2.50 #10 Free Bet @ Bet Direct Sky Active Banded Stakes 3yo+ 0-35 (H)
£1260 £360 £180 **1m2f** **Going 39** **-19 Slow** Inside

705 **LADY AT LEISURE 56** [2] M J Ryan 4-9-8 (35) S Whitworth 9/1: 00/5-6001: ch f Dolphin Street - In 37a
A Hurry (In Fijar) Trkd ldrs, led over 3f out, drvn fnl 1f, just held on: abs: p.u. both 03/04 nov hdle starts
(with J Poulton): 5th at best on the Flat '03 (clmr, rtd 38a, with W Turner): 4th in a mdn in '02 (rtd 59): 1st
win: eff at 10f on polytrack, acts on a sharp trk: lightly rcd 4yo: improved for new yard.
1181 **TOP STYLE 4** [3] M J Wallace 6-9-8 (30) K Fallon 4/9 FAV: 0/004/-022: Chsd ldrs, lost place 5f hd 36a
out, chsd wnr again fnl 1f, kept on well & nrst fin: op 4/6, quick reapp, clr of rem: eff bttwn 7/10f: see 1181.
909 **SENNEN COVE 27** [4] R Bastiman 5-9-8 t (30) S Sanders 14/1: 000-0063: ch g Bering - Dame Laura 5 28a
(Royal Academy) Bhd, hdwy 3f out, no impress over 1f out, eased fnl 1f: rnr-up in a clmr in '03 (with I Semple,
earlier with H Morrison): fin unplcd all '02 starts (rtd 67 at best, h'cap): eff bttwn 8/9f on fibresand & fast
grnd: has tried blnks, cheek pieces & a t-strap. 2 Mar'03 Muss 9g/f 59-(59) E:
890 **LADY XANTHIA 28** [1] I A Wood 3-8-5 (35) E Ahern 16/1: 0066-04: Led to over 3f out, sn no extra. 3½ 23a
1182 **SYLVAN TWISTER 4** [7]5-9-8 (35) N Pollard 11/1: 000/00-55: Chsd ldrs, wknd over 2f out. 1¾ 21a
677 **TE ANAU 60** [6]7-9-8 (30) Laura Pike(7) 33/1: 0/0/00/-066: Trkd ldr, lost place over 4f out, btn. ¾ 20a
971 **SPIDERS WEB 21** [5]4-9-8 bl (35) G Carter 9/1: 00B2307: Bhd, nvr nr ldrs: see 826. ½ 19a
7 Ran Time 2m 8.6 (5.8) Owned: The Aldora Partnership Trained: Newmarket

---

1245 3.20 Bet Direct Interactive Banded Stakes 3yo+ 0-40 (H)
£1267 £362 £181 **1m** **Going 39** **-17 Slow** Outside

1185 **DUE TO ME 4** [1] G L Moore 4-9-0 P (40) S Whitworth 9/4: 400-5251: In tch, trkd ldr over 2f out, 46a
led over 1f out, rdn clr: qck reapp: 1st win: stays 1m, acts on gd grnd & polytrack, sharp trks: imprvd for
fitting of cheek pieces, eye shield omitted: see 786.
1185 **BENJAMIN 4** [5] Jane Southcombe 6-9-0 bl t (40) V Slattery 11/4: 03426-22: Rcd keen with ldr, led 3 38a
5f out till over 1f out, no extra: qck reapp: mdn, fair run: see 1185.
1185* **CUMBRIAN PRINCESS 4** [2] M Blanshard 7-9-6 (40) D Sweeney 5/4 FAV: 5-400113: In tch, chsd ldr shd 43a
over 3f out till over 2f out, sn onepcd: qck reapp, top weight: ran to wng form of 971, see 228.
969 **LADY LIESEL 21** [4] J J Bridger 4-9-0 (40) J Tate 12/1: 0-003004: Bhd, nvr nr ldrs: see 710. 2½ 32a
1013 **HEKTIKOS 19** [3]4-9-0 (40) R L Moore 25/1: 40/00-005: ch g Hector Protector - Green Danube (Irish 19 0a
River) Led to 5f out, no extra over 3f out, t.o.: mod over hdles in 03/04 (rtd 49h, mdn): last of 14 sole Flat '03
start (mdn, rtd 1a): 4th in a mdn in '02 (rtd 73, with J Dunlop): lightly rcd 4yo.
5 Ran Time 1m 40.7 (4.5) Owned: Mrs Sheila Clarke Trained: Brighton

---

1246 3.50 Bet Direct On Sky Active Tri-Banded Stakes 3yo 0-45 (H)
£1603 £458 £229 **1m** **Going 39** **-08 Slow** Outside

1073 **DIAL SQUARE 13** [1] P Howling 3-9-0 (45) K Fallon 6/4 FAV: 0-013231: Rear, slt short of room over 53a
3f out, hdwy over 2f out, led over 1f out: eff brwn 7f/1m, likes Lingfield/polytrack: blnks discarded.
1183 **REGENCY MALAYA 4** [6] M F Harris 3-8-9 bl t (40) L Dettori 5/2: 0520032: Led to over 1f out, no 2 42a
extra fnl 1f: qck reapp: mdn: see 1183 & 608.
1183* **LARAD 4** [4] J S Moore 3-9-6 bl (45) L Keniry(3) 8/1: 5005513: Trkd ldr, lost place over 2f out, 2 49a
wknd qckly fnl 1f: qck reapp: not btn far under top weight: beat today's 2nd in race 1183, see 538.
1183 **STAGECOACH RUBY 4** [3] G L Moore 3-8-9 (40) R L Moore 12/1: 650-0054: Handy, chsd ldr over 2f out ¾ 36a
till lost place over 1f out, wknd fnl 1f: qck reapp: see 1073.
1085 **BACKLASH 12** [2]3-9-0 (45) D Holland 4/1: 0-00055: Mid-field, wknd fnl 1f: see 1085. 1 39a
495 **OBOE 82** [5]3-8-9 (40) J P Guillambert(3) 14/1: 5-006: ch f Piccolo - Bombay (Be My Chief) 27 0a
Mid-field, wknd 3f out, t.o.: op 20/1, long abs: 5th sole '03 start (mdn, rtd 44a, with R Charlton): now with T Keddy.
6 Ran Time 1m 40.0 (3.8) Owned: Mr Rory Murphy Trained: Newmarket

---

1247 4.20 New Site @ Betdirect Co Uk Claiming Stakes 3yo+ (H)
£1278 £365 £183 **7f** **Going 39** **-15 Slow** Inside

738 **FREE OPTION 53** [6] W J Musson 9-9-8 (65) Laura Pike(7) 5/1: 30-50331: Rear, hdwy over 2f out, rdn 64a
to lead ins fnl 1f, going away cl home: 8 wk abs: stays a sharp 10f, v eff at 7f, acts on firm, gd & on polytrack,
any trk: goes well fresh: likes Lingfield: see 180.
1074 **LUCAYAN MONARCH 13** [7] P S McEntee 6-9-8 p (52) L Dettori 2/1: 2323652: Made most, hdd ins fnl 1f 1¾ 59a
& no extra nr fin: clmd for £5,000: ran to wng form of 373, see 221.
1065 **NEW OPTIONS 13** [3] W J Musson 7-9-8 p (56) K Fallon 7/4 FAV: 4050303: Keen in tch, hdwy over 1f 1¼ 56a
out, sn wknd: op 3/1, clr of rem: shorter priced stable-mate of wnr: see 610.
1129 **ROCKET 7** [8] R Hannon 3-8-9 P Dobbs 14/1: 04: ch g Cadeaux Genereux - Prends Ca (Reprimand) 3 50a
Trkd ldrs, wknd fnl 1f: unplcd earlier mdn start.
1074 **HAPPY CAMPER 13** [2]4-9-8 (50) D Sweeney 20/1: 245-0065: Chsd ldr till over 1f out, wknd fnl 1f. 1¼ 47a
   LAST REBEL 666 [5]5-9-6 (79) E Ahern 10/1: 615/650/-6: b g Danehill - La Curamalal (Rainbow 2½ 40a
Quest) Trkd ldrs, wknd 2f out: reapp/jumps fit: mod over timber in 03/04 (rtd 37h, nov): fin unplcd all 3 '02
Flat starts in native Germany (incl 1 Gr3): won minor races in '01 (1m, gd): with R Phillips.
1012 **ORIONS BELT 19** [1]4-9-6 (49) R Havlin 10/1: 500/0-037: Keen & bhd, wknd over 2f out: see 1012. 1 38a
1085 **SCENIC FLIGHT 12** [4]3-7-13 (1ow)T (50) C Catlin 33/1: 04000-08: Keen in rear, wknd 2f out: t-strap. 2½ 25a
8 Ran Time 1m 26.61 (3.81) Owned: Mr W J Musson Trained: Newmarket

1248   4.50 Betdirect Co Uk Banded Stakes 3yo+ 0-45 (H)
£1610 £460 £230   6f   Going 39   -13 Slow   Inside

1199* **ATTORNEY 3** [2] D Shaw 6-9-13 vis (45) K Fallon 4/1: 6530011: Rear, hdwy ins fnl 2f, led ins fnl   **52a**
1f, rdn clr: landed double: quick reapp, top weight: suited by 5/6f on fast, hvy & both AWs, likes fibresand,
sharp trks: in fine form in banded company: see 1199 & 397.
913   **BADOU 26** [4] L Montague Hall 4-9-7 vis (45) D Holland 9/2: 1410002: Made most, slt hmpd over 1f   1½   **40a**
out, hdd ins fnl 1f, no extra: gd run: shade btr 709, see 528.
1073   **HARBOUR HOUSE 13** [1] J J Bridger 5-9-7 (45) J Tate 14/1: 20-02063: Keen & trkd ldrs, ch over 1f   ½   **38a**
out, onepcd fnl 1f: see 648 & 214.
760   **LYDIAS LOOK 51** [9] T J Etherington 7-9-7 (45) J Fanning 10/1: 000-0554: Trkd ldrs, lost place   nk   **37a**
over 2f out, late gains: 7 wk abs: see 653.
969   **GENTLE RESPONSE 21** [7]4-9-7 bl (45) S Whitworth 3/1 FAV: 0063105: Keen in rear, hdwy & ch over 1f   nk   **36a**
out, onepcd fnl 1f: rtd higher in 830 (7f), see 788.
1184   **HINCHLEY WOOD 4** [6]5-9-7 bl (45) N Pollard 12/1: 0055426: Bhd, some late gains: see 1184 & 1074.   ¾   **34a**
1075   **NIGHT CAP 13** [8]5-9-7 (45) J P Guillambert(3) 5/1: 03-60027: Keen & with ldr till over 1f out, sn wknd.   2   **28a**
1046   **OUR CHELSEA BLUE 14** [5]6-9-7 t (45) M Howard(7) 5/1: 0-036008: Hmpd start & bhd, gd hdwy halfway,   1   **25a**
wknd over 1f out: see 508.
1046   **MANDYS COLLECTION 14** [3]5-9-7 (45) C Catlin 33/1: 043/00-0U: ch f Forzando - Instinction (Never   **0a**
So Bold) Jinked left & u.r. start: unplcd both '03 starts (h'caps, rtd 29a): rnr-up in a h'cap in '02: eff at 5f,
yet to convince at 6f, likes fibresand & a sharp/turning trk: with A Newcombe.
2 Jan'02 Sout 5af 56a-50 E:
9 Ran   Time 1m 13.56(3.16)   Owned: Mr K Nicholls   Trained: Newark

Official Going SOFT (HEAVY places).

1249   2.40 Totesport Big Screen Median Auction Maiden Stakes Fillies 2yo (E)
£5447 £1676 £838   5f rnd   Heavy 142   -28 Slow   Inside

SOCIETY MUSIC [8] M Dods 2-8-11 L Enstone(3) 14/1: 1: b f Almutawakel - Society Fair (Always   **82**
Fair) Trkd ldrs, sltly outpcd halfway, styd on strongly to lead well ins fnl 1f, won going away on debut: Feb foal,
cost £16,000: dam a winning miler in France, sire a top-class mid-dist performer: eff at 5f, 6/7f will suit gvn
time: acts on hvy grnd, runs well fresh: ran geen today, sure to improve.
SAPPHIRE DREAM [1] A Bailey 2-8-11 R Winston 16/1: 2: b f Mind Games - Bombay Sapphire (Be My   1¼   **77**
Chief) Trkd ldrs, went on ent fnl 1f, not pace to repel wnr cl-home on debut: 14,000gns, sister to 6f juv
wnr Mind Alert: dam unrcd, sire a high-class sprinter: eff at 5f on hvy: sharper next time & shld find similar.
MARY READ [9] B Smart 2-8-11 F Lynch 8/1: 3: ch f Bahamian Bounty - Hill Welcome (Most   1½   **73**
Welcome) Prom, led halfway till ent fnl 1f, no extra cl-home on debut: 10,000gns Mar first foal: sire a top-class
juv: eff at 5f on hvy grnd: speedily bred: ran well for a long way.
ALTA PETENS [10] M L W Bell 2-8-11 I Mongan 3/1 FAV: 4: b f Mujadil - Be Exciting (Be My   1¼   **69**
Guest) Trkd ldrs, ev ch till green & outpcd dist, rallied cl-home: nicely bckd, clr of rem on debut: 4,000gns Apr
foal: dam 1m/12f wnr: sire a speedy juv: already needs 6f judged on this: can improve.
ROCKBURST [5]2-8-11 Darren Williams 8/1: 5: Rear, late gains, nvr dngrs on debut.   4   **59**
MEGELL [11]2-8-11 D R McCabe 9/2: 6: Chsd ldrs wide, no ch from halfway: op 3/1, debut.   3   **53**
DANEHILL FAIRY [4]2-8-11 G Duffield 25/1: 7: Al outpcd on racecourse bow.   7   **39**
1048   **VERSTONE 14** [2]2-8-11 L Fletcher(3) 50/1: 008: Led till after halfway, wknd.   3½   **32**
8 Ran   Time 1m 09.84 (8.54)   Owned: Mr M J K Dods   Trained: Darlington

1250   3.10 Friendly Service Selling Stakes 3yo (E)
£3692 £1136 £568   1m4f8y   Heavy 142   -15 Slow   Inside

796   **CEASAR 47** [1] P C Haslam 3-9-4 p (55) G Faulkner 5/1: 004-2101: Held up, hdwy to chall 2f out,   **60**
led ins fnl 1f, cleverly: 7 wk abs, sold to N Shields for 9,000gns: eff at 1m, suited by 12f: acts on gd, hvy grnd
& fibresand: suited by recent application of cheek pieces, runs well fresh: see 614 (AW h'cap).
1121   **VALIANT AIR 8** [6] J R Weymes 3-8-12 (55) R Winston 8/1: 040-452: Prom, led 4f out till ins fnl   ¾   **50**
1f, kept on & not btn far: clr of rem, flattered by proximity to wnr: eff at 12f on hvy: tried a visor in 1121.
1165   **CIACOLE 5** [7] Ronald Thompson 3-8-7 (64) Dean McKeown 12/1: 540-0403: Held up, imprvd to chase   8   **33**
ldrs over 2f out, sn onepcd: op 8/1, qck reapp, well clr rem: longer 12f trip: see 596 (Bw).
865   **BRETTON 33** [5] R Hollinshead 3-8-12 bl (45) Dale Gibson 11/1: 544-2664: Rear, prog to chase ldrs   25   **8**
4f out, sn wknd, t.o.: btr 351 (AW).
573   **GIVEN A CHANCE 71** [8]3-8-12 (40) R Thomas(5) 25/1: 600-4505: b g Defacto - Milly Molly Mango   6   **0**
(Mango Express) Chsd ldrs, wknd qckly 3f out, t.o.: 10 wk abs: lightly rcd & modest '03 form (rtd 52, clmr): prev
with J Given, now with Mrs S Lamyman.
1051   **FRAMBO 14** [2]3-8-7 (45) P Hanagan 8/1: 25-00506: Rear, nvr nr ldrs.   1   **0**
1134   **BUNINO VEN 7** [9]3-8-12 vis K Darley 5/1: 000-047: Led till 4f out, wknd: tchd 9/1: flattered 1134.   dist   **0**
1165   **SIGNORA PANETTIERA 5** [4]3-8-7 (58) S Hitchcott(2) 13/8 FAV: 640-68: ch f Lord of Men - Karaferya   11   **0**
(Green Dancer) Chsd ldrs, wknd qckly 4f out, t.o.: well bckd: lightly rcd in '03, some mdn promise (rtd 62):
half-sister to sev wnrs: btr clrly expected on this drop to sell grade, not handle hvy grnd &/or too sn after 1165.
8 Ran   Time 2m 53.00 (18.90)   Owned: Wilson Imports   Trained: Middleham

PONTEFRACT   MONDAY 19.04.04   Lefthand, Undulating Track, Stiff Uphill Finish

1251
3.40 Totepool Handicap Stakes 3yo+ 0-90 (C) [90]
£9350 £3546 £1773   **6f rnd**   **Heavy 142**   +07 Fast   Inside

1138 **ZILCH** 7 [4] M L W Bell 6-9-11   (87) I Mongan 9/4 FAV: 003-1221: Held up, gd hdwy to lead ent fnl 97
1f, styd on strongly, rdn out: well bckd, gd time: eff at 6/7f: acts on firm & polytrack, revels in soft & hvy
grnd: handles any trk, runs well fresh: gd weight carrier who remains in terrific form: see 1138 & 945.
921 **CD FLYER** 25 [7] B Ellison 7-9-7 (83) R Winston 9/1: 34110-52: Held up, hdwy & switched dist, 1¼ 89
styd on: closer with a clear & in gd form: won race on wrong side in 921.
1079* **CHATEAU NICOL** 12 [18] B G Powell 50-9-0 vis (76) G Duffield 7/1: 1301413: Held up, hdwy wide ½ 81
halfway, styd on fnl 1f & nrst fin: acts on fast, hvy & fibresand: win again at 7f: see 1079.
1145 **LINCOLN DANCER** 7 [1] D Nicholls 7-9-0   (76) Alex Greaves 9/1: 00-00434: Prom, led after halfway ½ 80
till ins fnl 1f, no extra: mudlark, see 1145.
1035+ **TIDY** 16 [14]4-9-4   (80) Darren Williams 5/1: 3060-015: Chsd ldrs, outpcd halfway, rallied fnl 1f: 2½ 78
will apprec a rtn to 7f & beat today wnr over that trip in 1035.
927 **AWAKE** 24 [12]7-8-10   (72) K Darley 16/1: 56500-06: ch g First Trump - Pluvial (Habat) Trkd ldrs, nk 69
ev ch dist, wknd cl-home: out of form in '03, incl in a visor: '02 h'cap wnr in Ireland, also plcd sev times: '00
h'cap wnr (M Johnston): wng form over 5/6f on firm & hvy: handles any trk, likes a sharp one: '00
1 Jul'02 Curr 5sft 85-78 : 2 Jul'02 Newm 5g/s 84-78 D: 2 Jul'02 Hami 5sft 81-78 D: 2 Jun'02 Ripo 5fm 79-77 D:
921 **LOYAL TYCOON** 25 [2]6-9-7   (83) L Treadwell(7) 40/1: 50000-07: br g Royal Abjar - Rosy Lydgate ¾ 77
(Last Tycoon) Chsd ldrs, sltly short of room dist, sn onepcd: won 2 h'caps, a stks & a clmr in '03: eff at 6/7f on
soft/hvy, loves fast & firm grnd & both AWs: handles any trk, likes a sharp one: gd weight carrier: eff
with/without a visor: on a winning mark, nk rnr-up in this race from a 5lb lower mark last term.
1 Jun'03 Epso 6fm 91-84 C: 2 May'03 Good 6g/f 85-82 C: 2 Apr'03 Pont 6g/f 84-78 C: 1 Jan'03 Ling 6ap 88a- C:
2 Jan'03 Sout 7af 87a-84 C: 1 Jan'03 Sout 6af 88a-84 C: 1 Jan'03 Sout 6af 85a- F: 2 Sep'02 York 7g/f 80-79 E:
1 Sep'02 Hami 5.9g/f 74- E: 1 Aug'02 Catt 6g/f 78- E: 1 Jun'01 Ling 6fm 85-77 D:
1145 **BOND PLAYBOY** 7 [11]4-8-10   (72) F Lynch 40/1: 5606008: Slow away, late gains, nrst fin: see 171 & 45. 3 59
4341} **GDANSK** 213 [13]7-8-11   (73) J Carroll 16/1: 502000-9: b g Pips Pride - Merry Twinkle (Martinmas) ½ 59
Chsd ldrs, btn fnl 1f on reapp: '03 h'cap rnr-up: plcd in h'caps in '02, won 3 times in '01 (class stks & 2
h'caps): eff at 6f, all wins at 5f: loves gd & softer grnd, any trk: on a fair mark.
2 Jul'03 Hayd 6gd 77-74 D: 2 Aug'02 Ripo 6g/s 80-84 D: 2 Jun'02 Hami 6sft 77-77 D: 2 Jun'02 Nott 5g/s 78-77 D:
1 Sep'01 Hayd 5hvy 81-75 C: 2 Sep'01 Hayd 5g/s 77-72 C: 2 Jul'01 Hami 6hvy 73-71 C: 1 May'01 Thir 5g/s 75-69 D:
1 Apr'01 Folk 5hvy 72- E:
976 **ANTONIO CANOVA** 20 [9]8-8-13   (75) F Norton 25/1: 4/000/0-00: 10th: Chsd ldrs, wknd 2f out. 1½ 57
4991} **BOLLIN JANET** 168 [5]4-9-0   (76) D Allan(3) 40/1: 041500-0: 11th: Prom 4.5f, wknd on reapp. 4 48
4810} **ONLINE INVESTOR** 182 [10]5-8-8   (70) A Nicholls 20/1: 006000-0: 12th: Slowly away, hdwy halfway, 15 12
btn dist, eased: reapp, new stable & has been gelded.
1138 **ABBAJABBA** 7 [16]8-9-7   (83) J Bramhill 9/1: 006-0000: 13th: Prom wide 4f, wknd. ¾ 23
1120 **Inter Vision** 8 [15]4-9-12   (88) A Beech(3) 50/1:0   1162 **Arctic Burst** 5 [17]4-10-0 t(90) M Fenton 50/1:0
15 Ran   Time 1m 22.21 (8.11)   Owned: Mary Mayall Linda Redmond Julie Martin   Trained: Newmarket

1252
4.10 Toteplacepot Marathon Handicap Stakes 4yo+ 0-70 (E) [63]
£6874 £2115 £1058   **2m5f122y**   **Heavy 142**   -39 Slow   Inside

67 **GREAT AS GOLD** 152 [14] B Ellison 5-9-6 p (55) R Winston 9/2: 356203-1: b g Goldmark - Great Land 66
(Friend's Choice) Bhd, hdwy to lead dist, drvn & kept on well: won 2 novs & a mdn hdle in 03/04 (eff at 2m/3m on
fast & soft, rtd 127h): 2nd in this race in '03 (1lb higher today): won 2 h'caps in '02: eff at 12f, thorough
stayer who apprec this 2m5.5f trip: acts on fast, hvy & both AW's: eff in blnks/cheek pieces: runs well fresh.
2 Apr'03 Pont 21.6g/f 56-54 E: 2 Jan'03 Sout 14af 56a-55 F: 1 Dec'02 Sout 16af 59a-49 F: 1 Mar'02 Wolv 12af 51a-46 E:
2 Feb'02 Sout 11af 46a- F:
1069 **CHARMING ADMIRAL** 13 [6] Mrs A Duffield 11-8-13 bl (48) G Duffield 10/1: 0/510//0-62: b g Shareef 2½ 56
Dancer - Lilac Charm (Bustino) Mid-field, hdwy to lead 3f out till dist, kept on but not pace of wnr: clr of rem:
jumps fit, h'cap chase plcd (eff at 2m4f/3m1.5f on gd/soft & hvy, rtd 93c wears blnks): unplcd sole '03 start
(h'cap): '01 h'cap wnr (this race): thorough stayer, acts on fast & f/sand, likes hvy & pontefract: eff in blnks.
1 Apr'01 Pont 21.5hvy 51-48 E:
1118 **TONI ALCALA** 8 [1] R F Fisher 5-10-0   (63) L Fletcher(3) 20/1: 0-354023: Handy, left bhnd by front 17 56
2 over 2f out: not stay 2m5.5f on unsuitably soft grnd: see 752.
1069 **JAMAICAN FLIGHT** 13 [3] Mrs S Lamyman 11-9-2 (51) J Quinn 12/1: 50-34444: Led to 3f out, wknd: 9 35
won this race off a 6lb lower mark last term & has won 4 times here at Pontefract: see 336.
1034 **REGAL VINTAGE** 16 [2]4-9-10 vis (65) T Hamilton(3) 50/1: 0/600-05: ch g Kingmambo - Grapevine 7 42
(Sadler's Wells) Rear, hdwy 6f out, sn no impress: unplcd all 03/04 hdle starts (rtd 77h): unplcd in '03 (rtd 70a,
earlier with B Meehan): has tried a t-strap, wears a visor: lightly rcd on the Flat & a return to 2m shld suit.
535} **MCCRACKEN** 804 [4]8-9-9 t (58) L Vickers 20/1: 202/6/60/-6: Nvr btr than mid-div: new yard, jmps fit. ½ 34
1087 **MOONSHINE BEACH** 12 [11]6-10-0 (63) P Makin(7) 10/1: 0/6105-47: Chsd ldrs, wknd 3f out: op 14/1. 5 34
937 **AVEIRO** 23 [5]8-9-3   (52) M Fenton 10/1: 3332128: Chsd ldrs, wknd over 2f out. 6 17
1064 **PROTOCOL** 13 [12]10-7-12 (3oh)t (30) R Thomas(2) 14/1: 00040-09: Handy, wknd over 4f out. dist 0
1069* **GREEN N GOLD** 13 [13]4-9-2   (57) P Hanagan 7/2 FAV: 00400-10: 10th: Nvr troubled ldrs: btr 1069. 3½ 0
48 **ULSHAW** 154 [10]7-9-8   (57) S Hitchcott(3) 25/1: 122000-0: 11th: Nvr a factor, t.o. fnl 2f: jmps fit. 24 0
1064 **THATS RACING** 13 [8]4-7-12 (4oh) (35) D Fentiman(7) 7/1: 0000-260: 12th: Chsd ldr, wknd 7f out, t.o. dist 0
1069 **ACCEPTING** 13 [7]7-9-2 bl (51) K Darley 11/1: 0/0010-50: 13th: Chsd ldrs halfway, wknd & t.o.: tchd 14/1. dist 0
13 Ran   Time 5m 18.81 (39.01)   Owned: Mr Keith Middleton   Trained: Malton

1253
4.40 Ladies In Red Classified Stakes 3yo+ 0-60 (F)
£4339 £1335 £668   **1m rnd**   **Heavy 142**   +07 Fast   Inside

1036 **TORRID KENTAVR** 16 [7] B Ellison 7-9-5   (59) R Winston 6/1 FAV: 42305-01: b g Trempolino - Torrid 70
Tango (Green Dancer) Bhd, hdwy & switched dist, led ins fnl 1f, drvn out: gd time, rider given 2-day careless
riding ban: won a h'cap hdle, h'cap & nov chase in 03/04 (eff by 2m on firm & gd/soft, rtd 120h & 105c): h'cap
rnr-up in '03: suited by 10/12f on firm, hvy & fibresand: best without blnks: v well h'capped.
2 Jul'03 Beve 8.5g/s 65-63 D: 1 Jul'01 Sand 11.4gd 86-81 D: 1 Jun'01 Kemp 12g/f 80-72 D: 2 Nov'00 Ling 12ap 85a- D:

347

PONTEFRACT   MONDAY 19.04.04   Lefthand, Undulating Track, Stiff Uphill Finish

1039 **CHARMATIC 16** [4] J A Glover 3-8-2 (60) G Duffield 20/1: 00-52: br f Charnwood Forest - Instamatic (Night Shift) Rear, hdwy 2f out, evch ins fnl 1f, not pace of wnr nr fin: unplcd both '03 mdn starts (rtd 59): eff at 1m on hvy grnd: has tried a t-strap: op to improvement & shld find similar. *1* **64**

763 **HE WHO DARES 50** [2] A W Carroll 6-9-5 (60) J Quinn 13/2: 12-20343: Rear, hdwy to chase ldrs over 1f out, briefly short of room ins fnl 1f, kept on: 7 wk abs, clr of rem: acts on fast, hvy & polytrack: see 339 & 144. *1* **65**

978 **PURE SPECULATION 20** [1] M L W Bell 4-9-4 (62) I Mongan 7/1: 000-0064: Trkd ldrs, led briefly dist, wknd fnl 1f: tchd 9/1: capable of better, stays 9f: see 552 (AW). *8* **49**

1049 **LUCAYAN DANCER 14** [12]4-9-8 (63) Alex Greaves 15/2: 40334-65: Chsd ldrs, wknd 1.5f out: see 1049. *2½* **49**

1100* **RAHJEL SULTAN 11** [11]6-9-7 t (62) G Gibbons 12/1: 540-3616: Chsd ldrs, wknd 2f out: btr 1100 (gd/soft). *4* **41**

5021} **PARNASSIAN 165** [13]4-9-5 (58) R Thomas(5) 11/1: 342500-7: ch g Sabrehill - Delphic Way (Warning) Trkd ldrs, led briefly 2f out, sn wknd: reapp: rnr-up in a mdn h'cap in '03: 4th at best in '02 (mdn, rtd 75): eff btwn 7f/1m, acts on gd & soft grnd, handles firm & fast: with G Balding. 2 Jul'03 Epso 8.5gd 63-62 E: *1½* **36**

1036 **APACHE POINT 16** [14]7-9-5 (60) Kim Tinkler 8/1: 00024-08: Rear, late gains. *½* **35**

1036 **SHIFTY 16** [8]5-9-5 VIS (51) A Nicholls 25/1: 426-5009: Keen in tch, wknd 2f out: tried a visor. *¾* **34**

417 **LOCOMBE HILL 95** [9]8-9-9 (64) L Treadwell(7) 11/1: 0100-020: 10th: Led to 2f out, fdd: abs, top weight. *22* **0**

747 **SURDOUE 52** [5]4-9-5 (56) K Darley 11/1: 5-024200: 11th: Handy, wknd 3f out, t.o.: 7 wk abs. *19* **0**

3858} **ESTEBAN 238** [17]4-9-5 (57) M Fenton 22/1: 0/00450-0: 12th: Mid-field, wknd after halfway on reapp. *11* **0**

4384} **General Smith 210** [16]5-9-5 (59) P Mulrennan(5) 20/1:0

4207} **Eastern Dagger 220** [6]4-9-5 (60) Dean McKeown 18/1:0

14 Ran Time 1m 52.63 (10.83) Owned: Mr Graeme Redpath Trained: Malton

1254

5.10 Punters Choice Handicap Stakes 4yo+ 0-75 (E) **[74]**
£4193 £1290 £645 **1m2f6y** **Heavy 142** **-44 Slow** Inside

1164 **MELODIAN 5** [2] M Brittain 9-8-13 bl (59) T Williams 5/1: 156-5451: Led till over 1f out, rallied gamely to regain lead cl home: qck reapp: eff at 7/10f on firm, loves gd/soft & hvy: likes Beverley. **67**

1083 **DICKIE DEADEYE 12** [6] G B Balding 7-8-10 (56) R Thomas(5) 7/2: 0050-652: Handy, kept on for press fnl 1f: acts on gd & hvy grnd: shld be plcd to find similar: see 924. *2* **60**

964 **METEORITE SUN 21** [5] Mrs J R Ramsden 6-9-10 (70) J F Egan 8/1: 5321//-03: b g Miesque's Son - Myth To Reality (Sadler's Wells) Mid-field, hdwy to lead well over 1f out, hdd ins fnl 1f & no extra: fair run under top weight: missed '03 & '02: won 1 of 4 '01 starts in native France (10f, hvy, with J Hammond): eff over 10f on hvy grnd: lightly rcd & running into form. *1½* **72**

1049 **JIMMY BYRNE 14** [12] B Ellison 4-9-8 (68) R Winston 20/1: 52300-04: ch g Red Sunset - Persian Sally (Persian Bold) Rear, hdwy 3f out, styd on ins fnl 1f & nrst fin: won a mdn in '03 (with M Channon): eff btwn 7f/10.4f on firm & gd grnd, handles hvy: acts on a gall trk. *1* **68**
2 Jul'03 Nott 8.2gd 73-(68) E: 1 Jul'03 Newm 7fm 74- D:

964 **ROTUMA 21** [10]5-9-5 bl (65) L Enstone(3) 8/1: 24104-05: b g Tagula - Cross Question (Alleged) Chsd ldrs, onepcd 2f out: op 13/2: won 2 h'caps in '03: won a clmr in '02: eff btwn 1m & 11f, acts on firm & hvy, prob any trk: suited by blnks, has tried a visor: can run well fresh: with M Dods. *nk* **64**
1 Oct'03 Ayr 10g/s 68-60 D: 2 Sep'03 Hayd 10.5fm 60-58 E: 2 Aug'03 Ayr 10g/f 62-58 E: 2 Aug'03 Newc 10.1g/f 60-56 E:
1 May'03 Hami 8.3gd 58-54 E: 2 Jun'02 Hami 11hvy 51- E: 1 Apr'02 Beve 9.9g/f 51- F:

961 **SINJAREE 21** [11]6-7-13 (45) J Quinn 8/1: 00-05106: Nvr troubled ldrs: see 821. *2½* **41**

1090 **MOONSHINE BILL 12** [9]5-8-6 (52) D Allan(3) 11/4 FAV: 01520-37: Trkd ldrs, wknd 2f out. *2* **45**

4466} **LIBERTY SEEKER 206** [4]5-9-4 (64) G Parkin 16/1: 33/0000-8: Chsd ldrs, wknd over 2f out, t.o. *14* **37**

1164 **DAIMAJIN 5** [8]5-9-2 (62) A Nicholls 33/1: 1054009: Bhd, hdwy & ch over 2f out, wknd & eased, t.o. *dist* **0**

9 Ran Time 2m 26.76(18.66) Owned: Mr Mel Brittain Trained: Warthill

WINDSOR   MONDAY 19.04.04   Sharp Fig 8 Track

Official Going Good/Soft (Soft places)

1255

5.20 Welcome To Monday Evenings At Windsor Apprentice Handicap Stakes 3yo+ 0-85 (E) **[85]**
£4329 £1332 £666 **6f rnd** **Good/Soft** **Inapp** Inside. Rcd across course.

4553} **MINE BEHIND 201** [20] J R Best 4-9-1 (72) M Savage 20/1: 032263-1: b c Sheikh Albadou - Arapi (Arazi) Made most stands side, hung left ins last but kept on gamely for press on reapp: '03 mdn wnr, plcd in h'caps: both wins at 6f, does stay 1m: acts on firm, gd/soft & polytrack, sharp or gall trks: runs well fresh: career best run on return. 2 Sep'03 Ling 7ap 73a-70 D: 2 Sep'03 Ling 7ap 73a-71 D: 1 Jun'03 Newb 6.0fm 76- D: **80**

604 **WHIPPASNAPPER 68** [4] J R Best 4-8-4 (61) Dean Williams(5) 8/1: 0121302: Slow away, sn in tch, hdwy over 2f out, led centre group over 1f out, kept on, not pace of wnr stands side: 10 wk abs, in gd form. *½* **68**

507 **SAVILES DELIGHT 80** [12] R Brotherton 5-8-7 (64) W Hogg(5) 22/1: 004-3243: In tch centre, led that group 2f out, sn hdd & onepace: gd run after 11 wk abs with no blnks or cheek pieces: see 384, 214. *2* **67**

1145 **MAJIK 7** [19] D J S ffrench Davis 5-8-3 p (60) Liam Jones(5) 20/1: 13-03404: In tch stands side, eff & edged left 2f out, onepace: fair run, see 193, 168 (AW). *hd* **62**

1025 **TAYIF 17** [14]8-8-5 t (62) B Swarbrick(3) 12/1: 1260205: In tch centre, onepace fnl 2f: see 407. *3½* **57**

897 **A TEEN 27** [15]6-8-6 (63) Hayley Turner 22/1: 0-520166: Bhd centre, modest late gains: best 740. *hd* **57**

914 **TRICK CYCLIST 26** [18]3-8-13 (81) T Block(5) 16/1: 0200-247: Chsd wnr stands side, no extra 2f out. *2* **71**

4950} **IDLE POWER 172** [3]6-9-3 (74) A Quinn 7/1 JT FAV: 004000-8: b g Common Grounds - Idle Fancy (Mujtahid) Chsd ldrs centre, no extra over 1f out on reapp: below best in '03 (rnr-up on reapp, h'cap): '02 h'cap wnr for P Harris: eff over 6/7f on firm, gd/soft & polytrack, any trk: has run well fresh: slipped to handy mark. *¾* **62**
2 Apr'03 Kemp 6fm 91-85 C: 1 Oct'02 Newm 7fm 87-81 C: 2 Jun'02 Ches 7gd 86-85 C: 1 Jul'01 Yarm 6fm 89-85 C:

1103 **ARABIAN KNIGHT 11** [5]4-8-3 (60) C Haddon(5) 25/1: 006-0009: Chsd ldrs far side, wknd over 1f out. *½* **47**

4492} **PRINCE HECTOR 204** [8]5-9-8 (79) Danielle Deverson(7) 16/1: 030010-0: 10th: ch g Hector Protector - Ceanothus (Bluebird) Sn bhd, modest late gains on reapp: won 1 of 9 '03 starts (h'cap): '02 h'cap wnr for Mrs A Perrett: best at 1m on fast or gd/soft: type to do btr. *1½* **63**
1 Sep'03 Yarm 8.0g/f 83-77 D: 1 Jun'02 Bath 8g/s 87-82 C: 1 Nov'01 Newm 7gd 88- D:

1127 **STOKESIES WISH 7** [16]4-8-9 (66) P Gallagher(3) 33/1: 30102-00: 11th: Led centre till 2f out, no extra. *1½* **47**

1138 **SEVEN NO TRUMPS 7** [13]7-9-11 (82) C J Davies(5) 8/1: 3000-250: 12th: In tch, wknd 2f out: see 944. *1* **61**

3526} **NIVERNAIS 252** [11]5-9-10 (81) C Cavanagh(5) 7/1 JT FAV: 00/1336-0: 13th: Nvr a factor. *nk* **59**

1020 **FLEETWOOD BAY 18** [1]4-9-4 (75) M Lawson(3) 20/1: 00020-00: 14th: Cl-up, wknd 2f out. *hd* **52**

1103 **PORT ST CHARLES 11** [7]7-8-11 (68) J F McDonald 8/1: 5000440: 15th: In tch, wknd over 2f out. *5* **35**

WINDSOR MONDAY 19.04.04 Sharp Fig 8 Track

494 **RISE 82** [10]3-8-2 bl (70) N Mackay 33/1: 10400-00: 16th: In tch, wknd 2f out: abs, see 494.   *nk*   **36**
760 **Margalita 51** [2]4-9-4 T(75) N Chalmers 20/1:0   775   **Mr Spliffy 50** [17]5-8-2 (59) D Fox 33/1:0
1020 **Kareeb 18** [6]7-9-7 (78) A Rutter(5) 14/1:0
1138 **Landing Strip 7** [9]4-9-6 (77) Saleem Golam(5) 33/1:0
20 Ran   Time 1m 18.89 ()   Owned: D Gorton M Folan R Crampton   Trained: Maidstone

1256   5.50 Windsor-Racecourse Co Uk Maiden Stakes 2yo (D)
£3426 £1054 £527   **5f10y**   **Good/Soft**   **Inapp**   Inside Rcd Far Side.

BEAVER PATROL 0 [8] R F Johnson Houghton 2-9-0 S Carson 9/2: 1: ch c Tagula - Erne Project   **89**
(Project Manager) Edged right start, held up, gd hdwy over 2f out, led dist, drvn out on debut: Apr foal, cost
E18,000: brother to a 1m wnr: dam 13f scorer: eff at 5f on gd/soft, bred to relish 6f+: runs well fresh: v
pleasing start, shld be more to come & landed a nice touch from 16/1 here, win again.
CHALISON 0 [2] R Hannon 2-9-0 R Hughes 3/1: 2: b c Anabaa - Raincloud (Rainbow Quest) Set pace   ½   **87**
till dist, not pace of wnr but kept on on debut: Feb foal, cost 42,000gns: dam 12f wnr: eff at 5f, bred to relish
6f+: acts on gd/soft grnd: plenty to like about this & can put his speed to gd use shortly, win soon.
1001 **EDGE FUND 19** [5] B R Millman 2-9-0 S Drowne 5/2 FAV: 33: With ldrs, rdn & onepace over 1f out: 2½   **81**
nicely bckd: prob handles firm & gd/soft: shown enough to win a minor race: see 1001.
CATWALK CLERIC 0 [9] M J Wallace 2-9-0 S Sanders 12/1: 4: b c Orpen - Ministerial Model   *nk*   **80**
(Shalford) Bhd, hdwy & hung left over 1f out, kept on, no threat on debut: op 9/1: Apr foal, cost 26,000gns: bred
to apprec 6/7f in time & showed promise here, learn plenty from the experience.
1029 **GLASSON LODGE 17** [6]2-8-9 R Havlin 16/1: 45: With ldrs, no extra appr fnl 1f: improved on debut.   *shd*   **75**
CHATEAU ISTANA 0 [7]2-9-0 E Ahern 6/1: 6: ch c Grand Lodge - Miss Queen (Miswaki) Short of   1¾   **76**
room start, sn bhd, nvr a threat on debut: Apr foal, cost E85,000: half-brother to a 7f juv wnr: bred to apprec
6/7f in time & this is worth forgiving: shld do btr.
FAIR ALONG 0 [1]2-9-0 T Quinn 14/1: 7: Slow away, sn in tch, wknd 2f out on debut.   7   **62**
WHISTLING ALONG 0 [4]2-9-0 R L Moore 33/1: 8: Slow away & al bhd on debut.   ¾   **60**
CALY DANCER 0 [3]2-9-0 Dane O'Neill 14/1: 9: Slow away, nvr a factor on debut.   ½   **59**
9 Ran   Time 1m 5.77 ()   Owned: Mr G C Stevens   Trained: Didcot

1257   6.20 Bugler Developments Handicap Stakes 3yo 0-85 (D)   [86]
£5688 £1750 £875   **1m67y rnd**   **Good/Soft**   **Inapp**   Inside. Rcd Far Side.

923 **PLAY MASTER 25** [1] D Haydn Jones 3-8-13 (71) Paul Eddery 8/1: 21201: Held up, rdn & lkd held   **73**
over 2f out, strong run appr fnl 1f to lead cl-home, drvn out: suited by 8.5f on fibresand or gd/soft, likes easy
trks: can come from bhd or force the pace: proving tough & back to form: see 468, 381.
4420} **RONDELET 208** [3] R M Beckett 3-9-4 (76) S Sanders 7/1: 064-2: b g Bering - Triomphale (Nureyev)   ¾   **76**
Chsd ldrs, eff over 2f out, led over 1f out, rdn & collared cl-home: reapp: 4th on last of 3 '03 starts (mdn, rtd
78): dam 6f juv wnr: stays 8.3f on gd/soft grnd: lightly rcd, shown enough to win a race.
1020 **DUMNONI 18** [4] Julian Poulton 3-9-7 (79) D Holland 13/2: 3631-063: Chsd ldr, short of room dist,   *nk*   **79**
switched right & kept on ins last: shade closer with clr run & stays 8.3f: see 1020, 36.
381* **HONEST INJUN 98** [6] B W Hills 3-9-7 (79) E Ahern 11/4 FAV: 02-14: Set pace, rdn & hdd ins last,   1   **77**
no extra: well bckd: clr run & stays 8.3f & may do btr with more waiting tactics as in 381.
1101 **ROOD BOY 11** [9]3-7-13 (57) J F McDonald(5) 13/2: 0043-455: In tch, lost pl bend 6f out, eff over   3   **50**
2f out, no extra: see 1101.
4912*}**THE WAY WE WERE 175** [5]3-9-5 (77) R Miles(3) 4/1: 31-6: ch c Vettori - Pandrop (Sharrood) In   *dist*   **0**
tch, wknd qckly over 2f out, t.o. on reapp: won 2nd of 2 '03 starts (mdn auct): stays 1m on polytrack, not enjoy
this easy grnd?: has run well fresh & shld do btr. 1 Oct'03 Ling 8ap 79a- E:
4943} **DESERT DIPLOMAT 173** [2]3-8-10 (68) K Fallon 8/1: 040-7: br g Machiavellian - Desert Beauty   4   **0**
(Green Desert) In tch, wknd qckly over 2f out, t.o.: reapp: 4th in mdn on 2nd of 3 '03 starts: bred to apprec 1m+
this term, been gelded & now twice disapp on easy grnd.
506 **WARES HOME 81** [7]3-8-12 (70) R Hughes 14/1: 0006-068: In tch, wknd 3f out, lost action.   3½   **0**
8 Ran   Time 1m 52.71 ()   Owned: Mr Jason Weston   Trained: Pontypridd

1258   6.50 Dine In The Castle Restaurant Maiden Stakes Fillies 3yo (D)
£4290 £1320 £660   **1m67y rnd**   **Good/Soft**   **Inapp**   Inside. Rcd Far Side.

3353} **CLASSICAL DANCER 260** [17] H Candy 3-8-11 Dane O'Neill 5/4 FAV: 3-1: ch f Dr Fong - Gorgeous   **84+**
Dancer (Nordico) Chsd ldrs, styd on to lead bef 1f out, pushed out, val 3L+: reapp: well bckd: 3rd of 13 on sole
'03 start (rtd 86, fill mdn): stays 8.3f well on fast & gd/soft: eff on a sharp, gall trk & goes well fresh: only
lightly rcd & looks sure to rate higher in h'caps.
4751} **HIDDEN HOPE 187** [4] G Wragg 3-8-11 D Holland 16/1: 00-2: ch f Daylami - Nuryana (Nureyev) In   1½   **80**
tch, eff 2f out, kept on: reapp: unplcd both '03 starts (rtd 63 & 67a, mdns): eff at 8.3f, will apprec 10f: acts
on gd/soft grnd: encouraging, win a mdn/h'cap sn.
4240} **NUKHBAH 217** [13] Lady Herries 3-8-11 S Sanders 14/1: 43-3: b f Bahri - El Nafis (Kingmambo)   1   **78$**
Slow away, sn in tch, rcd alone stands rail but prom with main bunch, onepcd ins fn 1f: reapp: 3rd of 6 on 1 of 2
'03 starts (rtd 75 at best, mdn, B W Hills): eff at 7f/8.3f on fast & gd/soft grnd: pleasing eff for new stable.
EMPRESS EUGENIE 0 [7] J M P Eustace 3-8-11 J Tate 50/1: 4: b f Second Empire - High Finish   ¾   **76**
(High Line) Rear, late gains: debut: eff at 8.3f, bred to apprec much further: acts on gd/soft grnd: encouraging.
5016} **PRINCIPESSA 165** [2]3-8-11 S Drowne 16/1: 3-5: Mid-div, prog 3f out, kept on late: reapp: eff   *shd*   **76**
around 8.3f on gd/soft & soft grnd: promising run & progressing.
4652} **LORIEN HILL 194** [5]3-8-11 (71) E Ahern 14/1: 034-6: Handy, fdd fnl 1f: reapp.   5   **68**
3487} **TRUE 254** [15]3-8-11 Martin Dwyer 9/2: 43-7: Sn led, hdd bef 1f out, hung left & wknd: reapp &   *nk*   **67**
new stable: prev with Sir Michael Stoute, now with M P Tregoning.
4043} **CASHEMA 229** [9]3-8-11 R Havlin 100/1: 000-8: Nvr nrr than mid-div: reapp.   4   **60**
4526} **ST TROPEZ 202** [10]3-8-11 S Whitworth 66/1: 00-9: Slow away, nvr nrr than mid-div: reapp.   ½   **59**
5024} **ELLINA 164** [11]3-8-11 R Price 100/1: 00-0: 10th: Rear, modest late gains: reapp.   *nk*   **59**
1021 **DONASTRELA 17** [6]3-8-11 N Chalmers(5) 66/1: 0-60: 11th: Rear, nvr a factor.   14   **39**
977 **OBSERVATION 20** [18]3-8-11 P Robinson 20/1: 0: 12th: Trkd ldrs, fdd 3f out.   ¾   **37**
4721} **PORTMANTEAU 189** [16]3-8-11 K Fallon 6/1: 0-0: 13th: Handy 5f, fdd: reapp.   6   **29**

WINDSOR   MONDAY 19.04.04   Sharp Fig 8 Track

4945} **REIGN OF FIRE** 172 [8]3-8-11   L Keniry(3) 33/1: 46-0: 14th: Chsd ldrs, fdd fnl 2f: reapp.   **2   25**
919   **Mitzi Caspar** 25 [1]3-8-11   A Mackay 100/1:0   670   **Genuinely** 61 [3]3-8-11 R Mullen 100/1:0
4636} **St Georges Girl** 195 [12]3-8-11   J Jeffrey(7) 100/1:0   **Collada** 0 [14]3-8-11 R Hughes 12/1:0
18 Ran   Time 1m 52.28 ()   Owned: Mr Jim Strange   Trained: Wantage

1259   7.20 Sponsors Evening Maiden Stakes 3yo   (D)
£4173   £1284   £642   1m2f7y   **Good/Soft**   **Inapp**   Inside. Rcd Far Side.

4974} **VINANDO** 170 [5] C R Egerton 3-9-0   S Drowne   11/2: 5-1: ch c Hernando - Sirena (Tejano)   Handy,   **83+**
chsd ldr 2f out, led ins fnl 1f, pushed out going away: reapp: 5th of 12 on sole '03 start (mdn, rtd 83): eff at
10f, shld apprec further: acts on gd/soft grnd & a sharp trk: goes well fresh: won well & can improve.
1021   **EXTRA COVER** 17 [12] R Charlton 3-9-0   R Hughes   9/2: 5-22: Led, clr over 3f out, under press &   **3½   77**
hdd ins fnl 1f, no extra: tchd 13/2: eff at 1m, stays 10f: acts on gd, gd/ soft & polytrack: see 1021.
4927} **MIDSHIPMAN EASY** 174 [3] P W Harris 3-9-0   D Holland   20/1: 0-3: ch g Irish River - Winger (In The   **2½   73**
Wings)   Chsd ldrs, sltly outpcd 4f out, rallied 2f out, no ch with front 2: reapp: unplcd '03 start (rtd 57,
mdn): eff at 10f, shld apprec further: acts on gd/soft grnd: encouraging eff & rate higher over further.
100   **IRISH BLADE** 145 [6] H Candy 3-9-0   Dane O'Neill   20/1: 0-4: b c Kris - Perle d'Irlande (Top   **1½   71+**
Ville)   Slow away, bhd, styd on late, nrst fin under kind ride: eff at 10f, crying out for 12f: acts on gd/soft
grnd: eye-catching eff, sure-fire improver.
4732} **NOTABLE GUEST** 188 [2]3-9-0   K Fallon   5/6 FAV: 22-5: b c Kingmambo - Yenda (Dancing Brave)   **shd   71**
tch, chsd ldr 4f out, wknd bef 1f out: well bckd on reapp: rnr-up on both '03 starts (rtd 84, mdn & nov stks): eff
at 7f/1m, bred to apprec mid-dists: acts on fast grnd: below par eff here but worth another ch on faster grnd.
2 Oct'03 Leic 8.0g/f 80- D: 2 Sep'03 Sand 7.1g/f 84- D:
5016} **FITTING GUEST** 165 [9]3-9-0   P Robinson   33/1: 40-6: Chsd ldrs, sltly outpcd 5f out, some late gains.   **2½   67**
1055   **PERSIAN DAGGER** 14 [11]3-9-0   G Carter   40/1: 0-07: Held up, nvr nrr than mid-div: see 1055.   **hd   66**
601   **LA CONCHA** 68 [10]3-9-0   J F McDonald(5) 100/1: 0008: Keen handy, no extra fnl 2f: 10 wk abs.   **3½   61$**
37   **MAJESTIC VISION** 156 [4]3-9-0   T Quinn   14/1: 34-9: Handy, wknd 2f out: reapp, gelded since '03.   **1½   58**
4898} **REGAL PERFORMER** 177 [1]3-9-0   P Dobbs   50/1: 00-0: 10th: Mid-div, prog 4f out, fdd fnl 2f: gelded.   **2   55**
   Singitta 0 [7]3-8-9 E Ahern 33/1:0   4895}   **Good Article** 177 [13]3-9-0 e D Sweeney 100/1:0
4307} **Kitley** 214 [8]3-9-0 (65) S Whitworth 33/1:0   **Jelly Baby** 0 [15]3-8-9 J Fanning 25/1:0
14 Ran   Time 2m 21.15 ()   Owned: Mrs Evelyn Hankinson   Trained: Chaddleworth

1260   7.50 Book Your Discounted Tickets On Line Handicap Stakes 3yo 0-75 (E)   **[80]**
£3523   £1084   £542   1m3f135y   **Good/Soft**   **Inapp**   Inside

601   **ITS BLUE CHIP** 68 [2] P W D'Arcy 3-8-6 e (58) Paul Eddery   33/1: 0-301: Held up, grad prog to lead   **67**
well ins fnl 1f, rdn out: 10 wk abs: eff at 9.4f, imprvd today for step up to 11.6f: handles fibresand, improved on
gd/soft grnd: eff with eye-shield: goes well fresh: see 438.
1017   **LATE OPPOSITION** 18 [14] E A L Dunlop 3-8-11   (63) L Dettori   3/1 FAV: 006-42: b c Unfuwain - Hawa   **nk   71**
(Woodman)   Mid-div, styd on to lead 2f out, hdd well ins fnl 1f, just held: unplcd 3 '03 starts (rtd 71, mdn): eff
at 11.6f on gd/soft grnd: drew well clr of 3rd & can find similar.
4981} **PANGLOSS** 169 [4] G L Moore 3-9-6   (72) R L Moore   16/1: 0300-3: ch g Croco Rouge - Kafayef   **7   71**
(Secreto)   Held up, prog & ev ch 2f out, sn carr head high under press & wknd fnl 1f: reapp: plcd once in '03 (mdn,
rtd 77): eff at 1m, poss stays 11.6f: handles firm & gd/soft grnd: worth a try in headgear.
4119} **CADEAUX ROUGE** 224 [11] Mrs P N Dutfield 3-8-13   (65) R Havlin   25/1: 5560-4: ch f Croco Rouge -   **5   59**
Gift of Glory (Niniski)   Chsd ldrs, no extra fnl 2f: reapp: unplcd in all 4 '03 starts (rtd 72, mdn): bred to
apprec mid-dists & just sharper for today.
843   **JACKIE KIELY** 36 [1]3-8-6   (58) R Miles(3) 16/1: 0-06205: Rear, nvr nrr than mid-div: btr 766 (10f).   **3   49**
1000   **SIEGFRIEDS NIGHT** 19 [9]3-8-5   (57) D Fox(5) 11/2: 4323336: Handy, led 3f out, hdd 2f out, sn wknd.   **¾   47**
4610} **WILFRED** 196 [7]3-9-6   (72) E Ahern   16/1: 0630-7: Led over 5f, styd prom, fdd 2f out: reapp.   **shd   62**
4993} **BAKHTYAR** 168 [5]3-8-11   (63) S Drowne   8/1: 005-8: Nvr nrr than mid-div on reapp: gelded since '03.   **1   52**
4781} **BOSCO** 185 [12]3-9-1   (67) P Dobbs   41/1: 605-9: Handy, fdd 3f out: reapp.   **hd   56**
1019   **LITTLESTAR** 18 [10]3-8-8   (60) S Sanders 16/1: 000-00: 10th: Cl-up, led 6f out, hdd 3f out, wknd.   **dist   0**
4501} **BLUE HILLS** 203 [3]3-9-7   (73) J Fanning   7/2: 052-0: 11th: Trkd ldrs, fdd 4f out, fin t.o.: bckd, gelded.   **21   0**
934   **ALFRIDINI** 24 [6]3-9-4   (70) Dane O'Neill   6/1: 0022140: 12th: Chsd ldrs, fdd 4f out: not handle soft?   **hd   0**
12 Ran   Time 2m 44.19()   Owned: Blue Chip Feed Ltd   Trained: Newmarket

WOLVERHAMPTON   Fibresand   MONDAY 19.04.04   Lefthand, Sharp Track

Official Going Standard

1261   5.35 New Site @ Betdirect Co Uk Amateur Riders' Banded Stakes 4yo+ 0-35 (H)
£1439   £411   £206   6f aw rnd   **Going 54**   **-33 Slow**   Inside

1181* **BAYTOWN FLYER** 4 [9] P S McEntee 4-11-6   (35) Miss J C Duncan(7) 7/1: 00-22011: Led till 5f out,   **47a**
styd cl-up, led again 2f out, rdn out: op 4/1 on qck reapp: eff at 6/7f, has tried 1m: acts on firm, gd/soft &
both AWs: likes forcing the pace in banded grade: see 1181 & 909.
1065   **ALASTAIR SMELLIE** 13 [2] S L Keightley 8-11-0 vis (35) Miss A L Turner(5) 7/2: 030-0022: Keen rear,   **1½   35a**
prog to chase wnr ins fnl 1f, al held: tchd 9/2: acts on fast, hvy grnd & fibresand: see 1065.
1202   **COUNTRYWIDE GIRL** 3 [10] A Berry 5-11-0   (30) Mr G Gibson(2) 12/1: 0353643: Handy, no extra fnl 1f.   **2½   28a**
960   **FLYING FAISAL** 21 [4] J M Bradley 6-11-0 bl (35) Mr S Walker   1/4 FAV: 0400304: Slow away, nvr nrr   **1½   24a**
than mid-div: tchd 2/1: blnks refitted: see 524.
981   **SPY MASTER** 20 [3]6-11-0 bl t (35) Miss Kelly Harrison(3) 7/2: 0-325065: Nvr nrr than mid-div: see 773.   **hd   23a**
890   **WELSH WHISPER** 28 [6]5-11-0   (35) Mr T J Malone   9/1: 0040056: Rear, late gains: mod form to date.   **2   17a**
1075   **THE LADY WOULD** 13 [11]5-11-0 BL (35) Mr L Newnes(5) 12/1: 0000-007: Led 5f out, hdd 2f out, wknd.   **shd   16a**

350

WOLVERHAMPTON Fibresand MONDAY 19.04.04 Lefthand, Sharp Track

4724} **POINT MAN 189** [5]4-11-0 BL (30) Miss J Wilmot Smith(7) 20/1: 00050-8: b g Pivotal - Pursuit of   **6**   **1a**
Truth (Irish River) Rear, nvr a factor: reapp & first time blnks: unplcd in '03 (rtd 39, mdn).
     REAL TING 1386 [7]8-11-0 (30) Dr H McCarthy(7) 33/1: 005/00///-9: br g Forzando - St Helena   **1¾**   **0a**
(Monsanto) Mid-div, wknd 3f out: reapp: off trk since 3 unplcd efforts in '00 (P D Evans, rtd 28a).
3158] **EXPECTEDTOFLI 630** [8]6-11-0 t (35) Mr M Howells(7) 50/1: 050000/-0: 10th: Cl-up, fdd 2f out.   **1¾**   **0a**
131} **TEA FOR TEXAS 504** [1]7-11-0 (30) Miss E J Jones 40/1: 000000/-0: 11th: Handy 4f, fdd, lame.   **8**   **0a**
11 Ran   Time 1m 18.03 (5.23)   Owned: Mr J Doxey   Trained: Newmarket

---

1262   6.05 Bet Direct No Q On 08000 93 66 93 Banded Stakes 3yo+ 0-40 (H)
£1435 £410 £205   **1m1f79y aw**   Going 54   +00 Fast   Inside

1072 **EUROLINK ARTEMIS 13** [2] Julian Poulton 7-9-0 p (40) N Callan 3/1: 000-0401: Rear, prog to lead 2f   **44a**
out, rdn out: op 2/1: eff at 1m/10f, has tried 12f: acts on firm, soft grnd & fibresand: eff with cheek pieces.
971 **TOJONESKI 21** [5] I W McInnes 5-9-0 p (35) R Ffrench 5/2 FAV: 30-00342: Cl-up, styd on under press   **1¾**   **40a**
but al held by wnr fnl 1f: not disgraced: see 830.
968 **AMETHYST ROCK 21** [6] P L Gilligan 6-9-0 (35) F Lynch 10/1: 00060-03: b g Rock Hopper - Kind Lady   **1½**   **37a**
(Kind of Hush) Led early, again 4f out till 2f out, no extra dist: unplcd in '03 (rtd 46, mdn): eff at 9.4f on f/sand.
1132 **JAMESTOWN 7** [3] M J Polglase 7-9-0 (40) K Ghunowa(7) 7/2: 0000004: Keen under restraint when   **3½**   **32a**
saddle slipped, prog 5f out, fdd fnl 1f: op 5/2: clr rem: this is best forgotten: btr 221.
985 **WETHAAB 20** [1] M J Polglase vis t (30) Ann Stokell 33/1: 4000-005: Led 6f, hdd 4f out, sn wknd: see 906.   **17**   **7a**
4859} **ALI PASHA 179** [1]5-9-0 (35) S W Kelly 3/1: 430000-6: b g Ali Royal - Edge of Darkness (Vaigly   **¾**   **6a**
Great) Sn in mid-div, fdd 2f out: tchd 7/1 on reapp: plcd once in '03 (seller, rtd 41 at best, M D I Usher):
unplcd in '02 (h'caps, rtd 46a & 45, D R Arbuthnot): eff at 10f, poss stays 12f: handles fast & gd grnd.
6 Ran   Time 2m 3.30 (5.1)   Owned: Mr Roberto Favarulo   Trained: Newmarket

---

1263   6.35 Betdirect Co Uk Banded Stakes 4yo+ 0-45 (H)
£1439 £411 £206   **2m46y aw**   Going 54   -10 Slow   Inside

1076 **MERCURIOUS 13** [3] J Mackie 4-8-10 (40) Dale Gibson 9/2: 06334-41: Bhd, prog to chase ldr 2f out,   **46a**
led ins fnl 1f, rdn out: eff at 11/14f, imprvd for step up to 2m: acts on both AWs, likes a sharp trk: see 1076.
965 **DOCTOR JOHN 21** [2] Andrew Turnell 7-9-0 p (45) D Corby(3) 10/11 FAV: 00//-42162: Rear, prog to   **2**   **44a**
lead 5f out, hdd under press ins fnl 1f, no extra: clr rem: see 690 (h'cap).
984 **BERKELEY HEIGHTS 20** [5] Mrs J Candlish 4-8-10 VIS (45) N Callan 8/1: 65-40623: Rear, hdwy over 1m   **12**   **32a**
out, fdd fnl 2f: below form in first time visor: btr 984.
948 **UNLEADED 23** [1] J Akehurst 4-8-10 (40) J Mackay 8/1: 0-212504: In tch, led 1m out-5f out, wknd.   **15**   **18a**
824* **MYSTERIUM 42** [7]10-9-0 vis (45) T P Queally(3) 9/2: 333-3415: Rear, nvr a factor: op 11/4, 6 wk abs.   **2½**   **16a**
1204 **HOMERIC TROJAN 3** [4]4-8-10 (45) D Tudhope(5) 33/1: 00-60066: Cl-up, fdd 6f out: qck reapp.   *dist*   **0a**
891 **PAARL ROCK 28** [6]9-9-0 vis (45) F Lynch 50/1: -007: ch g Common Grounds - Markievicz   *dist*   **0a**
(Doyoun) Led till halfway, sn fdd: recent hdles unplcd (rtd 80h, mdn hdle): missed '03 & '02: h'cap wnr on AW in
early '01 (G Barnett): won 3 h'caps in '00 (rtd 58a & 46a): stays 2m on fast, gd & fibresand, likes W'hampton: eff
in visor/blnks & has gone well fresh: with S T Lewis. 1 Jan'01 Wolv 16.2af 47a-45 E: 1 Dec'00 Wolv 16.2af 46a-40 F:
7 Ran   Time 3m 39.62 (10.42)   Owned: Gwen K DotCom   Trained: Church Broughton

---

1264   7.05 Littlewoods Bet Direct Banded Stakes 3yo+ 0-40 (H)
£1439 £411 £206   **1m100y aw rnd**   Going 54   +13 Fast   Inside

1201+**BEAUTEOUS 3** [5] M J Polglase 5-9-13 (35) K Ghunowa(7) 1/2 FAV: 0064411: Made all, clr & eased ins   **64a+**
fnl 1f, val 16L+: qck reapp, gd time: eff at 6f/8.4f on firm, gd/soft & fibresand: likes to force the pace:
thriving in banded grade & can land a quick-fire hat-trick: see 1201.
909* **TEE JAY KASSIDY 27** [4] Julian Poulton 4-9-7 (40) M Halford(7) 11/4: 05004-12: Rear, styd on wide   **13**   **36a**
to grab 2nd dist, no ch with v easy wnr: btr 909 (7f).
1135 **DUNDONALD 7** [1] M Appleby 5-9-7 bl t (35) S Righton 12/1: 3406503: Prom, fdd 3f out: qck reapp.   **2**   **32a**
605] **POWER AND DEMAND 1154** [2] K G Wingrove 7-9-7 (35) R Ffrench 66/1: 500/055//-4: b g Formidable -   **11**   **10a**
Mazurkanova (Song) Cl-up, fdd 3f out: unplcd over jumps in 02/03 (rtd 61h, sell hdle, Miss M Bragg): unplcd in all
3 '01 Flat starts (rtd 36a, h'cap, D Shaw): plcd in '00 (rtd 55a, seller): eff at 5f on both AWs: eff in blnks.
971 **ALL ON MY OWN 21** [6]9-9-7 bl (35) Natalia Gemelova(7) 12/1: 0424005: Slow away, al rear: btr 584.   **5**   **0a**
5 Ran   Time 1m 49.69 (3.49)   Owned: Mr Paul J Dixon   Trained: Newark

---

1265   7.35 #10 Free Bet @ Betdirect Co Uk Banded Stakes 4yo+ 0-40 (H)
£1435 £410 £205   **1m4f aw**   Going 54   -08 Slow   Inside

970 **ERSAAL 21** [4] J Jay 4-8-10 T (40) N Callan 11/4: 000-0301: Led 4f, styd cl-up, led dist, drvn out   **43a**
to hold on despite edging right: tchd 5/1: best around 12f on fibresand here at W'hampton: likes to force the
pace: app fitting of t-strap: first win: see 891.
724 **FAIRMORNING 55** [8] J W Unett 5-8-11 (40) Lisa Jones(3) 11/8 FAV: 443-2652: Rear, prog 2f out,   **¾**   **41a**
kept on but not pace wnr ins fnl 1f: see 315 & 250.
4644} **LADY LAKSHMI 195** [5] R Guest 4-8-10 (40) J Mackay 11/2: 035030-3: Held up, eff 3f out, onepcd   **hd**   **40a**
ins fnl 1f: op 3/1: reapp: plcd once in '03 (h'cap, rtd 49): eff at 12f on fast grnd & fibresand.
984 **RHETORIC 20** [3] D G Bridgwater 5-8-11 (35) D Nolan(3) 12/1: 00/005-04: Cl-up, led after 4f, hdd   **1**   **38a**
dist, no extra: clr rem: stays 12f on fibresand: see 984.
453} **KIMOE WARRIOR 452** [7]6-8-11 bl (35) S W Kelly 10/1: 06050//0-5: ch g Royal Abjar - Thewaari   **7**   **28a**
(Eskimo) Cl-up, ev ch 2f out, fdd dist: hdles fit, earlier h'cap wnr (rtd 83h, stays 2m1.5f on gd grnd, eff with
blnks): unplcd sole '03 Flat start (rtd 16a): plcd once in '01 (rtd 45, h'cap): eff at 1m on hvy grnd.
891 **DORA CORBINO 28** [2]4-8-10 (40) Stephanie Hollinshead(7) 9/1: 60-53206: Led briefly early on, styd   **7**   **18a**
in tch, fdd 3f out: op 7/1: twice below 2nd in 823.
826 **FINAL LAP 42** [6]8-8-11 (30) J G Gibbons 16/1: 0/000-037: Cl-up, fdd 5f out: 6 wk abs: btr 826.   *dist*   **0a**
4452] **MANNY 562** [1]4-8-10 (35) Ann Stokell 40/1: 005//8: Al in rear, hung badly right & sn adrift.   **12**   **0a**
8 Ran   Time 2m 41.12 (7.52)   Owned: Mr G Knight   Trained: Newmarket

WOLVERHAMPTON Fibresand MONDAY 19.04.04 Lefthand, Sharp Track

1266 8.05 Bet In Running @ Betdirect Co Uk Banded Stakes 3yo+ 0-45 (H)
£1446 £413 £207 **7f aw rnd** **Going 54** **-08 Slow** Outside

783 **GILLYS GENERAL 48** [9] J W Unett 4-9-7 (40) G Gibbons 25/1: 2050-401: Cl-up, led 4f out, all out 46a
cl-home to hold on: 7 wk abs: eff at 6/7f, has tried 1m: eff on fibresand: tried blnks: first win: see 636.
579 **DASAR 70** [10] M Brittain 4-9-7 VIS (45) D Tudhope(7) 9/1: 006-6402: Sn in mid-div, ev ch dist, shd 45a
kept on & just btn in a thrilling fin: 5L clr rem, 10 wk abs: swapped blnks for a visor: wng form at 5f, stays 6/7f.
1201 **ETERNAL BLOOM 3** [4] M Brittain 6-9-7 (45) M Lawson(7) 10/1: 1200033: Trkd ldrs, onepcd dist. 5 35a
982 **MR UPPITY 20** [8] Julian Poulton 5-9-7 e (40) Lisa Jones(3) 100/30: 000-0024: Rear, hung right 4f hd 34a
out, nvr nrr than mid-div: btr 982 (6f).
4136} **LIEUDAY 223** [6]5-9-7 p (45) S W Kelly 7/4 FAV: 0D5053-5: b g Atraf - Figment (Posse) Sn mid-div, 5 24a
short of room 3f out, wknd fnl 2f: reapp: plcd 3 times in '03 (rtd 50, h'caps & med auct mdn): plcd on reapp in
'02 (auct mdn, rtd 55, J L Eyre): eff at 6/7.5f on firm & soft grnd: eff with cheek pieces, tried visor.
2 Jul'03 Ches 7.6fm 50-48 E: 2 Aug'01 Ripo 6g/f 67- E:
1200 **ABBIEJO 3** [5]7-9-7 (40) D Corby(3) 25/1: 60/0-6566: Nvr nrr than mid-div: qck reapp: see 956. nk 23a
956 **ROBIN SHARP 21** [2]6-9-7 vis (45) P Doe 6/1: 0-260507: Cl-up, fdd 4f out: btr 457. 8 9a
996 **LIONS DOMANE 19** [1]7-9-7 (40) F Lynch 10/1: 0-0560P8: Led till 4f out, sn short of rm & wknd. 4 2a
913 **MASTER RATTLE 26** [7]5-9-7 bl (45) V Slattery 8/1: 0052009: Cl-up, led 4f out, sn hdd & wknd. 13 0a
9 Ran Time 1m 30.55(4.35) Owned: Gillian Rosano & Partners Trained: Wolverhampton

FOLKESTONE TUESDAY 20.04.04 Righthand, Sharp, Undulating Track

Official Going Soft (Good/Soft Places)

1267 2.10 Levy Board Apprentice Handicap Stakes 3yo+ 0-55 (G) [55]
£3059 £874 £437 **6f str** **Good/Soft 88** **-05 Slow** Stands side - 2 Groups

960 **AROGANT PRINCE 22** [2] J Pearce 7-9-11 (52) Saleem Golam 16/1: 1010001: Made all stands rail, 62+
pushed out fnl 1f, val 5L+: eff at 6/7f, prob best at 5f: loves fibresand/W'hampton, acts on firm & hvy: sharpened
up by switch to new stable & made gd use of stands rail: see 748.
84 **HALCYON MAGIC 148** [5] Miss J Feilden 6-9-8 bl (49) Laura Pike 33/1: 005060-2: b g Magic Ring - 3½ 50
Consistent Queen (Queen's Hussar) Held up stands side, kept on fnl 1f for 2nd, no ch with wnr: reapp: unplcd in
'03 (rtd 54, h'caps): mdn h'cap, appr h'cap & h'cap wnr in '02: suited by 6/7f on fast & gd/soft, handles firm:
acts on any trk, likes Yarmouth: eff with blnks: sharper next time.
1 Sep'02 Yarm 6g/f 66-56 F: 1 Sep'02 Yarm 7g/f 62-56 E: 1 Jul'02 Ripo 6gd 57-48 E:
897 **DAVIDS MARK 28** [1] J R Jenkins 4-10-0 (55) J Jeffrey(8) 25/1: 35030-03: Prom stands side, ev ch 1 53
dist, sn no extra: acts on firm, gd/soft grnd & polytrack: see 897.
1058 **MUQTADI 15** [3] M Quinn 6-9-6 (47) K May 33/1: 1500454: Dwelt stands side, kept on dist, nrst ½ 44
fin: not disgraced & will enjoy a return to further: btr 717 (1m).
242 **TATWEER 120** [15]4-9-8 vis (49) Liam Jones 14/1: 555000-5: Led far side, drifted centre 2f out, no ½ 45
extra dist: long abs: rcd on unfavoured far side: see 219.
907 **LARGS 28** [8]4-9-7 (48) K Pierrepont(8) 12/1: 45-03326: Prom far rail, drifted centre & fdd ins 5 30
fnl 1f: unsuited by racing on unfav'd far side: see 907.
1221* **ITALIAN MIST 3** [6]5-9-12 (7exe) (53) M Halford(3) 7/2 FAV: 1201317: Prom stands side 4f, sn wknd: 4 24
well bckd on qck reapp: btr 1221 (fibresand).
1127 **SHADY DEAL 8** [13]8-9-11 (52) K Ghunowa 20/1: 235-0008: Cl-up far side 4f, wknd: see 775. ½ 22
1012* **BELLS BEACH 20** [16]6-9-7 (48) K Jackson 8/1: 1015619: Cl-up 4f far side: btr 1012. ½ 17
4809} **HOLLY ROSE 183** [10]5-10-0 p (55) M Howard 33/1: 034100-0: 10th: b f Charnwood Forest - Divina shd 23
Luna (Dowsing) Sn in tch far side, wknd fnl 2f: reapp: fills h'cap & sell wnr in '03: '02 appr mdn h'cap scorer:
eff at 7/10f on firm & fast grnd: acts on a v sharp or gall trk: tried blnks: eff with cheek pieces.
1 Sep'03 Yarm 10.1g/f 60-(60) G: 1 Jul'03 Folk 9.7g/f 61-55 E: 2 Jul'03 Yarm 8.0g/f 71-(56) F: 1 Aug'02 Brig 7g/f 58-53 E:
902 **LONG WEEKEND 28** [14]6-9-7 (46) Dawn Watson(3) 7/1: 6211460: 11th: Bhd & no impress far side. 3½ 7
1132 **FEAST OF ROMANCE 8** [7]7-9-7 (48) S Archer(5) 12/1: 6215030: 12th: Bhd & nvr a factor stands side. 2 1
1221 **SABANA 3** [11]6-9-7 (1ow)bl (47) C J Davies 12/1: 5013060: 13th: Rcd far side, in tch, fdd 2f out. shd 0
913 **GUN SALUTE 27** [12]4-9-9 p (50) Jemma Marshall(8) 9/2: 0-010460: 14th: Dwelt far side, in tch 4f out. ½ 1
748 **GONENDUNNETT 53** [9]5-9-13 vis (54) Dean Williams 16/1: 03-00000: 15th: Al rear far side: 8 wk abs. 9 0
15 Ran Time 1m 16.62 (5.62) Owned: Mr Chris Marsh Trained: Newmarket

1268 2.40 Km Egg Cup Claiming Stakes 3yo (F)
£2905 £830 £415 **5f str** **Good/Soft 88** **-26 Slow** Stands side

1015 **HES A ROCKET 19** [5] Mrs C A Dunnett 3-8-11 BL (40) Lisa Jones(3) 50/1: 0003-651: Made all, drvn 56
out fnl 1f to hold on: clmd for 8,000: rider received 1-day ban for intereference: eff at 5f on good/soft, prob
fibresand: imprvd eff in first time blnks: see 200.
609 **A BID IN TIME 68** [6] D Shaw 3-8-7 (49) N Callan 16/1: 0000-002: Held up, prog & ev ch ins hd 50
fnl 1f, edged left under press & just held: 10 wk abs: acts on gd & gd/soft grnd: lost little in defeat but rider's
1lb overweight proved costly: see 609.
1239 **BLACK OVAL 3** [4] M R Channon 3-8-6 (59) S Hitchcott(3) 5/2 FAV: 06-44503: Prom, ev ch but just 1½ 45
getting worst of battle when hmpd well ins fnl 1f, not recover: clmd for 8,000: qck reapp: acts on firm, gd/soft &
polytrack: little closer with clr run but prob 3rd on merit: see 995. see 995.
1002 **SHORT CHORUS 20** [3] J Balding 3-8-4 P (50) S W Kelly 13/2: 51000-04: ch f Inchinor - Strawberry hd 42
Song (Final Straw) Bhd, prog 2f out, staying on when no room well ins fnl 1f, not recover: first time cheek pieces:
clmg wnr in '03: eff at 5f on firm & gd/soft grnd: spot on next time. 1 Jun'03 Beve 5g/f 61- F:
1031 **BLUE POWER 18** [1]3-9-5 (60) G Faulkner 6/1: 213-0035: Prom, ev ch when hmpd dist, sn lost place, 3 48+
kept on but not recover: worth another chance: btr 1031.
389 **TICTACTOE 98** [2]3-8-2 (57) C Catlin 11/2: 45361-66: Trkd ldrs, no extra when short of room dist. 2 25
606 **PARDON MOI 69** [8]3-8-2 (45) Hayley Turner(5) 16/1: 54-34407: In tch, wknd fnl 2f: 10 wk abs. hd 24
1031 **ONLY IF I LAUGH 18** [7]3-9-5 h bl (75) J F McDonald(5) 3/1: 6504-348: Cl-up, fdd 2f out: v disapp 13 11

352

FOLKESTONE   TUESDAY 20.04.04   Righthand, Sharp, Undulating Track

on return to turf: btr 1031 & 914.
8 Ran   Time 1m 4.19 (5.74)   Owned: Mrs Christine Dunnett   Trained: Norwich

---

1269   3.10 Folkestone-Racecourse Co Uk Classified Stakes 3yo+ 0-70 (E)
£3396 £1045 £523   **5f str**   **Good/Soft 88**   **+05 Fast**   Stands side

976*   **MADDIES A JEM 21** [3] J R Jenkins 4-9-2 (72) S W Kelly 5/2: 03460-11: In tch trav well, lead ins   **79+**
fnl 1f, pushed clr, val 4L+: op 7/4, gd time: eff at 5/6f on fast, soft & polytrack: likes Folkestone: continues
in fine form & can win again: see 976.
944   **BYO 24** [2] M Quinn 6-9-3 (67) S Drowne 6/1: 0444-062: gr g Paris House - Navan Royal (Dominion   2½   72
Royale) Dsptd lead 2f, outpcd dist, rallied well ins fnl 1f, no ch with wnr: class stks & h'cap wnr in '03: plcd
twice in '02 (rtd 70a, 55, h'cap, G M McCourt): eff at 5/5.7f on fast, hvy grnd & polytrack: has tried a visor.
2 Sep'03 Leic 5.0g/f 71-68 D: 2 Sep'03 Bath 5.7g/f 69-65 D: 1 Aug'03 Warw 5.5fm 66-62 E: 2 Jun'03 Bath 5.7fm 65-(64) E:
2 Apr'03 Folk 5.0g/f 65-(68) E: 1 Mar'03 Bath 5.7g/f 67-(57) E: 2 Jan'03 Ling 5ap 60a- F: 2 Jun'02 Ling 5ap 70a-68 E:
35   **ROXANNE MILL 157** [5] J M Bradley 6-9-5 (75) R L Moore 11/2: 040020-3: b f Cyrano de Bergerac -   ½   73
It Must Be Millie (Reprimand) Dsptd lead, led 3f out, hdd ins fnl 1f, no extra: reapp: plcd 3 times in '03 (h'caps
& class stks, M D I Usher, rtd 80): won 4 h'caps in '02: h'cap rnr-up in '01: eff at 5f on firm, soft & fibresand:
best when able to dominate: far from disgraced here on first start for new stable, sharper for today.
2 Oct'03 Pont 5g/f 77-75 D: 2 Aug'03 Kemp 5g/f 79-(75) D: 1 Aug'02 Yarm 5.1fm 88-79 C: 1 Jul'02 Hami 5g/s 85-72 D:
1 Jul'02 Nott 5g/f 73-66 D: 1 May'02 Nott 5g/s 67-62 E: 2 Aug'01 Yarm 5.1gd 64-64 C: 2 Jul'01 Sand 5fm 65-63 D:
2 Nov'00 Sout 5af 74a-71 E:
1179   **THE FISIO 5** [1] A M Balding 4-9-5 vis (72) Martin Dwyer 2/1 FAV: 6300204: In tch, outpcd 2f out,   1½   69
rallied late: qck reapp: twice below 2nd in 1103.
4544}   **TAPAU 202** [8]6-9-3 (73) S Carson 8/1: 032130-5: b f Nicolotte - Urtica (Cyrano de Bergerac)   5   54
Handy, fdd ins fnl 1f: tchd 11/1: h'cap wnr in '03 (I A Wood): class stks & h'cap wnr in '01 (D R C Elsworth): eff at 6/7f on firm, gd/soft & polytrack: entitled to come on for this.
1 Jun'03 Kemp 7fm 73-67 C: 2 Jun'03 Leic 6.0g/f 74-67 E: 2 Sep'02 Nott 6g/f 71-70 E: 1 Sep'01 Ling 6gd 73-68 D:
1 Aug'01 Brig 7gd 65- E: 1 Dec'00 Ling 7ap 67a- D:
1065   **TICKLE 14** [6]6-9-0 BL t (54) D Sweeney 25/1: 60-40366: Handy, outpcd 3f out, mod late gains.   nk   50
944   **ABRAXAS 24** [4]6-9-3 p (40) J Quinn 66/1: 26-50007: Slow away, al in rear: btr 183.   ¾   51
638}   **FOLEY MILLENNIUM 428** [7]6-9-3 (50) N Pollard 50/1: 000/0/6P-8: ch g Tagula - Inshirah (Caro)   13   21
Prom, fdd 2f out: reapp: unplcd & p.u. in both '03 starts (rtd 48a, h'cap): unplcd sole '02 start (h'cap, rtd 50a,
G M McCourt): mdn claim wnr & nov stks wnr in '00: eff at 5/6f on fast & gd grnd: with M Quinn.
8 Ran   Time 2.61 (4.16)   Owned: Mrs Wendy Jenkins   Trained: Royston

---

1270   3.40 Kentish Express Maiden Stakes 3yo+ (D)
£3858 £1187 £594   **7f str**   **Good/Soft 88**   **-02 Slow**   Stands side - All bar 3 far side

919   **DOCTORATE 26** [12] E A L Dunlop 3-8-10 E Ahern 9/2: 4-01: b c Dr Fong - Aunt Tate (Tate Gallery)   83
Prom far side, al trav well, led well ins fnl 1f, rdn out: 4th of 10 in sole '03 start (mdn, rtd 89): eff at 6/7f,
has tried 1m: acts on fast & gd/soft grnd: appreciate drop back in trip & is open to more improvement.
966   **HENNDEY 22** [9] M A Jarvis 3-8-10 N Callan 7/2: 0-22: Rcd far side, cl-up, led 3f out, hdd ins   1   78
fnl 1f, no extra: acts on gd/soft & gd grnd: again lost little in defeat & can finish similar: see 966.
4723}   **FLYING ADORED 190** [7] J L Dunlop 3-8-5 (74) T Quinn 7/1: 040-3: b f Polar Falcon - Shining High   ½   72
(Shirley Heights) Cl-up far side, owned clear ins fnl 2f, kept on fnl 1f, not btn far: reapp: unplcd in all
3 '03 starts (rtd 77, mdn): eff at 6/7f, 1m shld suit: acts on fast & gd/soft: only lightly rcd & can rate higher.
   NISTAKI 5 [5] Miss V Haigh 3-8-10 J F Egan 10/1: 4: ch c Miswaki - Brandywine Belle (Trempolino)   ¾   75
Rcd far side, bhd, hdwy & ev ch dist, sn no impress: clr rem: bckd from 33/1 on debut: cost 30,000 gns: eff at
7f, shld apprec further: acts on gd/soft grnd: gd eff on debut & can improve.
1080   **RANGOON 13** [2]3-8-10 (78) R Hughes 2/1 FAV: 3-225: Led stands side group, kept on but no ch with   6   63+
far side ins fnl 2f: lost all ch by racing away from main body of rnrs: worth another chance: btr 1080.
2330}   **KENSINGTON 270** [13]3-8-10 (77) Martin Dwyer 14/1: 33064-6: b c Cape Cross - March Star (Mac's   3½   56
Imp) Keen in tch far side, fdd fnl 2f: reapp: plcd once in '03 when trained in Ireland (rtd 82, mdn): with R Guest.
1136   **LADY FRANPALM 8** [8]4-9-4 (54) R L Moore 50/1: 0/5440-07: Nvr nrr than mid-div far side: see 1136.   1½   48
4974}   **RAWALPINDI 171** [3]3-8-10 J Lane Jones(3) 33/1: 0-8: Dwelt, nvr a factor on stands side: reapp.   3   47
1078   **INDIAN LILY 13** [10]3-8-5 J Quinn 25/1: 59: Al in rear far side: btr 1078.   nk   41
980   **DIVERTED 21** [6]3-8-5 S W Kelly 66/1: 0000: 10th: Al bhd far side.   8   27
180   **BUCKENHAM STONE 132** [1]5-9-4 R Price 100/1: 00-0: 11th: Rcd stands side, al in rear.   5   18
1078   **Pats Nemisis 13** [4]3-8-5 N Pollard 66/1:0   956   **Frenchmans Lodge 22** [11]4-9-9 (45) P Doe 66/1:0
13 Ran   Time 1m 30.51 (6.31)   Owned: Mr P G Goulandris   Trained: Newmarket

---

1271   4.10 Westenhanger Handicap Stakes 4yo+ 0-70 (E)   [70]
£3513 £1081 £541   **1m7f92y**   **Soft**   Slow   Inside

948*   **LINENS FLAME 24** [6] B G Powell 5-9-8 (64) D Sweeney 5/2 FAV: 06/000-11: Made all, clr trav well   72+
ins fnl 2f, pushed out fnl 1f, val 6L+: eff at 14.3f/15.4f on soft grnd: has imprvd for recent step up in trip &
switch to forcing tactics: open to more improvement & can land hat-trick: see 948.
1303}   **MISTER PUTT 353** [5] Mrs N Smith 4-9-4 bl (60) C Catlin 15/2: 3300//60-2: b g Mister Baileys -   3½   62
Theresita (Surumu) Held up, hdwy when short of room 4f out, chsd wnr ins fnl 1f, al held: 9 wk jumps abs, rtd 108c
in a nov chase (stays 2m2f on gd & hvy, eff in blnks & t-strap): unplcd both '03 starts (rtd 58, h'cap): hdles plcd
in 02/03 (rtd 104h, nov): eff at 14/15.5f on firm & soft grnd, can find similar.
1030   **MARINO MOU 18** [8] Miss D Mountain 4-7-12 (13oh) (30) D Fox(5) 66/1: 0063: b c Darshaan - Lia's   1   44
Dance (Lead On Time) Bhd, nvr trav, hdwy 2f out, no impress ins fnl 1f: clr rem: blnks left off: vastly imprvd
eff on step up to 15.4f on soft grnd: gd run from out of h'cap.
1059   **BAKIRI 15** [3] Andrew Reid 6-10-0 (70) S Carson 16/1: 42/060/-04: b g Doyoun - Bakiya   9   62
(Trempolino) Prom, fdd fnl 2f: earlier sell h'cap hdle wnr (R T Phillips, rtd 94h, stays 2m3.5f on firm & gd):
missed '03: unplcd on 3 '02 starts (rtd 81, class stks): mdn wnr in '01 (Sir M Stoute): eff at 1m/9f on gd & firm,
handles soft. 2 Aug'01 Ripo 9gd 90-87 C: 1 May'01 Kemp 8fm 86-72:
4812}   **HENRY ISLAND 183** [7]11-9-13 (69) E Ahern 7/1: 014443-5: Held up, nvr nrr than mid-div: reapp.   2   59
1090   **PAULA LANE 13** [2]4-8-7 (52) S Hitchcott(3) 20/1: 320-0506: Cl-up, fdd 4f out: see 529.   18   27

353

FOLKESTONE   TUESDAY 20.04.04   Righthand, Sharp, Undulating Track

WINDSOR BEAUTY 1009 [5]6-8-10 (52) P Doe 22/1: 6/00043//-7: Chsd ldrs, fdd 4f out: jumps abs.   *21*   **9**
1033 FFIFFIFFER 18 [10]6-9-3 (59) R Hughes 9/2: 225-4108: Handy, fdd 3f out, eased ins fnl 1f: btr 937.   *dist*   **0**
1034 ALNAJA 17 [1]5-10-0 VIS T (70) R Hills 7/2: 03231-P9: Cl-up, fdd 4f out, eased ins fnl 2f: 1st   *dist*   **0**
time visor & t-strap: another dismal effort & surely something amiss.
9 Ran   Time 3m 40.42 (23.22)   Owned: D & J Newell   Trained: Winchester

1272   4.40 Romney Marsh Maiden Stakes Fillies 3yo+ (D)
£3741 £1151 £576   **1m4f   Soft   Slow   Inside**

4973} MARINE CITY 171 [5] M A Jarvis 3-8-4   M Henry 20/1: 0-1: b f Carnegie - Marienbad (Darshaan)   **78+**
Rear, prog 3f out, led ins fnl 1f, pushed out, val 2L+: reapp: unplcd sole '03 start (rtd 41, mdn): app step up to
12f, further shld suit: acts on soft grnd & a sharp trk: goes well fresh: much to like on only 2 start.
LIGHT OF MORN [6] R Guest 3-8-4   Martin Dwyer 3/1: 2: gr f Daylami - My Emma (Marju) Chsd   *1*   **75**
ldrs, ev ch 2f out, sn hung left, kept on but not pace of wnr ins fnl 1f: debut: dam Group 1 wnr at 12f: eff at
12f, further will suit: acts on soft grnd: ran a little green & looks sure to impr for today.
4871} PORTRAIT OF A LADY 179 [7] H R A Cecil 3-8-4 (69) W Ryan 12/1: 540-3: ch f Peintre Celebre -   *hd*   **74**
Starlight Smile (Green Dancer) Mid-div, hdwy when switched wide dist, kept on & not btn far in 3rd: reapp: unplcd
in 3 '03 starts (rtd 72, mdn): app eff at 7f, stays 12f: acts on fast & soft grnd.
4526} AL BEEDAA 203 [8] J L Dunlop 3-8-4   R Hills 6/1: 03-4: ch f Swain - Histoire (Riverman) Dwelt,   *hd*   **73**
sn in tch, rdn & flashed tail ins fnl 2f, kept on, not btn far: reapp: plcd on last of only 2 '03 starts (rtd 63,
mdn): imprvd for step up to 12f: acts on soft grnd: still green & can rate higher.
173   SEA PLUME 133 [1]5-9-10 (75) R Hughes 6/1: 302000-5: Led, flashed tail under press bef 1f out,   *nk*   **70**
hdd well ins fnl 1f, no extra: tchd 8/1 on reapp.
980   HIGH SCHOOL 21 [4]3-8-4   N Pollard 2/1 FAV: 26: Cl-up, ev ch 2f out, found little under press 1f   *2½*   **68**
out, wknd: well bckd: below par on step up in trip: btr 980 (9.7f, debut).
3998} ROVELLA 232 [2]3-8-4   J F Egan 66/1: 000-7: Al in rear: reapp.   *23*   **38**
980   OLYMPIAS 21 [3]3-8-4   J Quinn 10/1: 58: Chsd ldrs, fdd 4f out.   *16*   **13**
8 Ran   Time 2m 49.57 (18.07)   Owned: Mr Saif Ali   Trained: Newmarket

1273   5.10 Saffie Joseph & Sons Handicap Stakes 4yo+ 0-70 (E)   [70]
£3582 £1102 £551   **1m1f149y   Soft   Slow   Inside**

1058* AMNESTY 15 [11] G L Moore 5-9-0 bl e (56) R L Moore 5/1: 4500611: Mid-div, styd on to lead dist,   **64**
rdn out: eff at 7f/9.6f, prob stays 10f: acts on fast, soft grnd & polytrack: eff with blnks & eye-shield: in fine
form since return to turf & can land hat-trick: see 1058.
1083 ICANNSHIFT 13 [5] S Dow 4-8-8 (50) W Ryan 9/1: 00-00602: b g Night Shift - Cannikin (Lahib)   *3*   **52**
Led, hdd dist, sn no extra: tchd 16/1: unplcd in '03 (rtd 94, h'cap, P W Harris): auct mdn & stks wnr in '02: eff
at 7f, now stays 9.6f: acts on firm & soft grnd: has gone well fresh: gd eff here & has slipped to a winning mark.
1 Aug'02 Yarm 7fm 94- D: 1 Jul'02 Pont 6g/f 90- E:
1083* ROYAL RACER 13 [7] J R Best 6-8-8 (50) N Pollard 6/1: 0350/0-13: Handy, ev ch dist, onepcd fnl   *hd*   **51**
1f: op 9/2: raised 3lb since recent win here in 1083.
978* MISS PEBBLES 21 [10] B R Johnson 4-10-0 (70) R Hughes 9/2 FAV: 10056-14: Held up, prog 2f out,   *1¾*   **68**
onepcd fnl 1f: top-weight: just btr 978 (class stks).
1139 EASTER OGIL 8 [1]9-9-1 (57) V Slattery 6/1: 0000265: Sn bhd, nvr nrr than mid-div: btr 1083.   *¾*   **53**
493   MCQUEEN 83 [4]4-9-4 (60) J F Egan 9/1: 03310-06: Nvr nrr than mid-div: 12 wk abs: btr 99.   *7*   **46**
4690} HAVANTADOUBT 191 [2]4-9-9 (65) G Baker 33/1: 533000-7: ch f Desert King - Batiba (Time For A   *5*   **44**
Change) Rear, nvr nrr than mid-div: earlier unplcd sole 03/04 jumps start (juv nov hdle, rtd 40h): h'cap wnr in
'03 (G J Portman): fills mdn wnr in '02: eff at 6/7.5f, stays 11f: acts on gd/soft grnd: eff with cheek
pieces, has tried a visor: with M R Bosley.
1 Jun'03 Good 11g/f 72-65 E: 1 Jun'02 Beve 7.4g/f 75- E: 2 Jun'02 Sali 6g/s 84- E:
1100 PACIFIC OCEAN 12 [6]5-8-13 t (55) S Drowne 14/1: 34-23368: Al in rear: btr 644.   *5*   **27**
674   CORONADO FOREST 62 [12]5-8-9 (51) J Quinn 12/1: 0-241009: Handy, fdd 3f out: btr 476.   *4*   **17**
1098 DEXILEOS 12 [9]5-9-4 (60) D Sweeney 33/1: 04000-00: 10th: b g Danehill - Theano (Thatching)   *hd*   **25**
Handy, fdd 3f out: plcd once in '03 (h'cap, rtd 69): ex-Irish, plcd on 6 starts in native country (mdns & h'caps,
6f/1m, firm & soft): eff at 6f/1m on firm & soft grnd: has tried a visor: with A D W Pinder.
1058 PRINCE ALBERT 15 [8]6-7-12 t (40) J Jeffrey(7) 33/1: 035/05-00: 11th: Reared stalls, no ch after.   *½*   **4**
942* DEL MAR SUNSET 24 [3]5-9-12 p (68) R Hills 11/2: 03-45010: 12th: Cl-up, fdd fnl 3f: v disapp on   *18*   **7**
return to turf: btr 942 (8.5f, fibresand).
12 Ran   Time 2m 11.74(13.74)   Owned: Mr GAJackman Mr JFJackman   Trained: Brighton

NEWCASTLE   TUESDAY 20.04.04   Lefthand, Galloping, Stiff Track

Official Going Heavy (Soft places)

1274   2.20 Benfield Alfa Romeo Maiden Stakes 2yo (D)
£4352 £1339 £670   **5f str   Soft 94   -63 Slow   Stands Side**

ELSIE HART [2] T D Easterby 2-8-9   W Supple 7/2: 1: b f Revoque - Family At War (Explodent)   **75**
Handy, hdwy to lead appr fnl 1f, hung left but rdn to assert: April foal, cost 18,000gns: full sister to a useful
sprint wnr & a 10f scorer: dam 5f juv wnr: eff at 5f, further shld suit: clearly enjoys soft grnd & runs well
fresh on a gall trk: more to come, win again.
SPIRIT OF FRANCE [6] M Johnston 2-9-0   R Ffrench 2/1 FAV: 2: b c Anabaa - Les Planches   *3*   **72**
(Tropular) Led, rdn & hung left over 1f out, sn hdd & not pace of wnr: debut: April foal, cost £60,000: dam
wnr abroad: eff at 5f, 6f will suit: prob handles soft grnd: likely to be sharper for this & can be plcd to win.
ALMATY EXPRESS [4] M Todhunter 2-9-0   R Winston 8/1: 3: b g Almaty - Express Girl (Sylvan   *½*   **71**
Express) Slow away & bhd, some late gains, nvr dngrs on debut: April foal: half-sister to a 5f juv wnr: dam 5f
2yo scorer: bred for speed & showed promise for the future here, learn plenty from this encouraging start.
VISION VICTORY [1] T P Tate 2-9-0   Dale Gibson 4/1: 4: b c Dashing Blade - Val d'Isere (Surumu)   *3½*   **64**
In tch, wknd over 1f out on debut: April foal, cost £16,000: bred to need 6f+ in time.

UREDALE [3]2-9-0   G Duffield 13/2: 5: With ldr, wknd over 1f out on debut.   1¾   60
LANE MARSHAL [5]2-9-0   T Eaves(5) 12/1: 6: Dwelt, al bhd on debut.   6   48
6 Ran   Time 1m 06.15 (7.95)   Owned: Mr C H Stevens   Trained: Malton

1275   2.50 James Fletcher Marquees And Pavilion Hire Maiden Stakes 3yo   (D)
£3478 £1070 £535   1m2f32y   Soft 94   -74 Slow   Far Side

930   **KEELUNG** 25 [5] M A Jarvis 3-9-0   (85) P Robinson 1/4 FAV: 0-4221: Keen, made virtually all,   91
pushed clr over 1f out, v easily at long odds-on: bckd: acts on gd, soft & polytrack: simple task here.
TWOFAN [3] M Johnston 3-9-0   J Fanning 11/2: 2: b c Lear Fan - Double Wedge (Northern Baby)   16   70
Handy, rdn & outpcd by wnr 3f out, kept on to go 2nd well over 1f out, no impress: cost 55,000gns: dam v smart in
US: bred to apprec 10f & shld be sharper for this next time.
4603}   **SILVER RHYTHM** 199 [6] K R Burke 3-8-9   V Halliday 20/1: 0-3: ch f Silver Patriarch - Party Treat   9   56
(Millfontaine) In tch, outpcd over 3f out: bred to apprec mid-dists.
1314}   **BEAVER DIVA** 353 [4] W M Brisbourne 3-8-9   B Swarbrick(7) 40/1: 0-4: b f Bishop of Cashel - Beaver   8   48$
Skin Hunter (Ballacashtal) Keen cl-up, wknd over 2f out: well btn sole juv start: bred to stay at least 1m.
BLUE NUN [1]3-8-9   G Duffield 20/1: 5: Slow away & al bhd, t.o. on debut.   dist   0
5 Ran   Time 2m 23.45 (16.95)   Owned: Mr Norman Cheng   Trained: Newmarket

1276   3.20 Weatherbys Insurance Handicap Stakes 3yo+ 0-80   (D)   [80]
£5902 £1816 £908   5f str   Soft 94   1m 02.38   Stands Side. 2 Groups - Far Side Fav.

967   **RAYMONDS PRIDE** 22 [2] K A Ryan 4-9-3 bl (69) P Fessey 14/1: 1F0-0051: Handy far side, styd on to   77
lead just ins last, rdn out: joc received a 2-day careless riding ban: both wins at 5f & likes gd/soft & soft, acts
on firm & fibresand: enjoys gall trks, handles any: see 967.
1122   **HIGHLAND WARRIOR** 9 [3] J S Goldie 5-8-11   (63) W Supple 4/1: 0133-332: Dwelt, held up far side,   1¾   66
slt lead appr fnl 1f, sn hdd & not pace of wnr: consistent, likes Ayr & easy grnd: see 1122, 967 (6f).
1221   **PAWAN** 3 [4] Miss A Stokell 4-8-6   (58) Ann Stokell 7/1: 02-52203: In tch far side, eff over 1f   1¼   59
out, kept on same pace: qck reapp: mdn: see 1145, 963.
1120   **VIEWFORTH** 9 [5] I Semple 6-9-12 bl (78) R Winston 100/30 FAV: 54600-44: In tch far side, rdn &   1¼   77
sltly short of room over 2f out, late gains: well bckd: again showed promise: prefers a stiffer 5f or 6f: see 1120.
1122   **MALAHIDE EXPRESS** 9 [6]4-8-5   (57) G Duffield 14/1: 0-450205: Led 1f far side, cl-up, no extra ins last.   hd   55
4810}   **KARMINSKEY PARK** 183 [13]5-8-10   (62) J Fanning 11/1: 300440-6: b f Sabrehill - Housefull   nk   59
(Habitat) Led stands side, clr of that group when hung badly left & joined far side over 1f out, no impress on
reapp: won 2 h'caps in '03 (rtd 67 at best): plcd several times in '02 (rtd 71): best at 5f, stays 6f: acts on
firm & both AWs, likes gd/soft & soft, prob any trk: has run well fresh: tough, returning to a fair mark.
2 Jul'03 Beve 5g/s 66-63 C: 1 May'03 Newc 5g/s 63-61 E: 2 Mar'03 Ling 5ap 61a-61 D: 1 Jan'03 Ling 5ap 62a-54 F:
2 Aug'02 Ayr 6sft 63- E: 2 May'02 Carl 5fm 71-65 E:
1179   **AAHGOWANGOWAN** 5 [8]5-8-8 t (60) R Ffrench 12/1: 10230-07: b f Tagula - Cabcharge Princess (Rambo   1¼   55
Dancer) Led after 1f far side, hdd over 1f out, no extra: '03 fills h'cap scorer: '02 rnr-up (with D Smith, rtd
73): best at 5f, stays a gall 7f on firm or soft, any trk: eff in a t-strap: likes to dominate.
2 Sep'03 Pont 5g/f 61-60 E: 1 Jul'03 Hami 5.0gd 61-55 D: 2 Aug'02 Catt 6g/f 67- E: 1 Nov'01 Muss 5gd 72- E:
2 Nov'01 Nott 5g/s 71-70 E: 1 Oct'01 Newm 5g/f 71-66 C: 1 Oct'01 Brig 6sft 69-59 D: 2 Sep'01 Hayd 6sft 63-59 D:
1 Aug'01 Ripo 6g/f 58- F:
1179   **PETONGSKI** 5 [1]6-7-12 bl e (50) P Hanagan 15/2: 05640-08: b g Petong - Madam Petoski (Petoski)   2½   40
Slow away far side, nvr a factor: rnr-up in 1 of 11 '03 starts (h'cap): rnr-up in '02: all 3 wins at 5f, eff at
5f: acts on fast grnd, likes gd/soft & hvy, any trk: best without blnks/visor, has run well in eye-shield: well
h'capped if showing signs of a return to form.
2 Jun'03 Newc 5gd 50-49 E: 2 Jun'02 Carl 6g/s 69-66 E: 1 Oct'01 Ayr 6hvy 72-64 E: 1 Oct'01 Nott 6sft 67- F:
4856}   **PROUD WESTERN** 181 [7]6-7-12   (50) D Fentiman(7) 25/1: 000140-9: Dwelt, al bhd far side.   2   36
4384}   **ROSIES RESULT** 211 [9]4-8-2   (54) R Thomas(5) 50/1: 600000-0: 10th: Chsd ldrs stands side, nvr a factor.   2   36
1179   **CASH** 5 [12]6-8-6 (2ow)p (56) L Fletcher 20/1: 4-013500: 11th: Handy stands side, wknd 2f out.   6   28
1120   **GET STUCK IN** 9 [10]8-9-3   (69) T Eaves(5) 31/1: 250/0-000: 12th: Handy stands side, wknd 2f out.   10   19
33   **I T CONSULTANT** 158 [11]6-7-12 (1oh)   (49) N Mackay(5) 14/1: 060000-0: 13th: Dwelt, al bhd.   8   0
13 Ran   Time 1m 02.38 (4.18)   Owned: Mr R E Robinson   Trained: Hambleton

1277   3.50 Sharp Minds Betfair Handicap Stakes 3yo+ 0-70   (E)   [70]
£3975 £1223 £612   6f str   Soft 94   -11 Slow   Stands Side. Rcd Far Side.

996   **MISTER MAL** 20 [14] B Ellison 8-8-8 bl e (50) P Hanagan 14/1: 0053-061: Dwelt, sn recovered & led,   56
clr entering fnl 1f, held on all out: eff at 5/7f on firm & fibresand, likes gd & hvy grnd: can miss the break,
likes to force the pace: v well h'capped now, see 996.
1195   **CARLTON** 5 [13] C R Dore 10-9-0   (56) R Thomas(5) 11/1: 4402452: Chsd ldrs, styd on well under   nk   61
press fnl 1f, just failed: qck reapp: revels in soft grnd & a sound eff: see 1052 & 565 (AW).
356   **FORMERIC** 103 [10] Miss L C Siddall 8-7-12 (5oh)vis (35) P Fessey 100/1: 0000-003: ch g Formidable   1¾   41
- Irish Limerick (Try My Best) Prog halfway, styd on fnl 1f & nrst fin: long abs: no form in '03 (h'caps):
won fnl '02 start (mdn): eff at 6f on soft grnd, handles a gall trk: has tried blnks, suited by a visor: runs well
fresh & gd run from out of the h'cap here.   1 Oct'02 Redc 6sft 58- D:
996   **KING NICHOLAS** 20 [5] J Parkes 5-8-8 t p (50) M Lawson(4) 7/1: 000-0104: Rear, switched & styd on   1½   48
fnl 1f, nrst fin: tchd 10/1: see 851 (AW seller).
1145   **QUIET TIMES** 8 [9]5-9-11 bl (67) R Winston 5/1 FAV: 1404155: Rear, styd on fnl 1f, nrst fin: well   nk   64
h'capped on turf: see 834 (loves fibresand).
4792}   **OLD BAILEY** 186 [6]4-8-7 bl (49) N Mackay(3) 8/1: 052626-6: gr g Lit de Justice - Olden Lek   nk   46
(Cozzene) Chsd ldrs, onepcd fnl 1f on reapp: dual h'cap rnr-up in '03: late '02 AW h'cap wnr, also turf mdn wnr:
eff at 5/7f on gd, fast grnd & fibresand, handles soft: acts on a sharp or gall trk: wears blnks now.
2 Aug'03 Folk 6g/f 51-46 F: 2 Aug'03 Carl 5.9g/f 49-44 F: 1 Dec'02 Wolv 7af 59a-58 E: 1 May'02 Newc 5gd 74- F:
864   **PILGRIM PRINCESS** 34 [15]6-8-3   (45) G Duffield 20/1: 3546007: Prom 4.5f, wknd: see 282.   shd   42
4944}   **DOWNLAND** 174 [11]8-8-10   (52) Kim Tinkler 12/1: 3/06000-8: b g Common Grounds - Boldabsa (Persian   1¼   47
Bold) Rear, late gains, nvr dngrs on reapp: out of form in '03: plcd once in '02 (h'cap, rtd 68, with R Beckett):
dual '01 h'cap wnr: eff at 6/7f, stays 1m: acts on firm, likes hvy grnd: eff with/without blnks: v well h'capped
when returning to form & v unenterprisingly rdn here.

NEWCASTLE TUESDAY 20.04.04 Lefthand, Galloping, Stiff Track

1 Oct'01 Newc 6hvy 90-77 C: 1 Sep'01 Asco 7g/s 81-72 B:

846	**REDOUBTABLE 37** [17]13-8-3 (45) J Fanning 25/1: 0-614109: Prom till wknd dist: btr 783 (AW).	8	24
4852}	**WILLIAMS WELL 181** [8]10-9-8 bl (44) Dale Gibson 9/1: 412020-0: 10th: Nvr btr than mid-div on reapp.	nk	42
1142	**RONNIE FROM DONNY 8** [12]4-10-0 (70) T Eaves(5) 12/1: 400U550: 11th: Nvr troubled ldrs: top-weight.	nk	48
995	**LORD BASKERVILLE 20** [16]3-8-7 (60) D R McCabe 33/1: 030-0060: 12th: Nvr nr ldrs.	1	36
1052	**THE OLD SOLDIER 15** [4]6-8-11 (53) A Beech(3) 16/1: 05200-00: 13th: Slowly away, nvr a factor.	1¼	27
1142	**AFRICAN SPUR 8** [7]4-10-0 t (70) D Tudhope(7) 33/1: 0022000: 14th: Al rear: jt top-weight: see 775.	¾	42
4856}	**FRIAR TUCK 181** [2]9-8-10 (52) R Ffrench 14/1: 003200-0: 15th: Nvr a factor on reapp.	shd	24
22	**JUST ONE SMILE 159** [3]4-9-7 (63) K Darley 6/1: 332142-0: 16th: Prom 4f, wknd & t.o. on reapp.	20	0

16 Ran Time 1m 17.62 (6.32) Owned: Mrs Andrea M Mallinson Trained: Malton

---

1278 4.20 Saltwell Signs Handicap Stakes 3yo+ 46-55 (F) [59]
£3416 £976 £488 1m2f32y Soft 94 -40 Slow Far Side

939	**PURE MISCHIEF 24** [14] W M Brisbourne 5-9-9 (54) B Swarbrick(7) 6/1: 00030/-31: b g Alhaarth -		57
	Bellissi (Bluebird) Chsd ldrs, went on 2f out trav well, drvn out ins last: drifted from 7/2: missed '03, March '03		
	juv nov claim hdle wnr (rtd 96h, eff at 2m on gd/soft & hvy): plcd on 3 of 6 '02 starts (with Miss Fielden, mdn &		
	seller): eff at 10f on gd/soft, soft & hvy: handles a sharp or gall trk: on a fair mark.		
	2 Mar'02 Wolv 9.3af 69a- D: 2 Oct'01 Nott 8.2hvy 79- D:		
820	**DOUBLE RANSOM 43** [1] Mrs L Stubbs 5-9-10 bl (55) P Hanagan 11/2 FAV: 32-23142: Chsd ldrs, ev ch	nk	57
	fnl 1f, just btn in a close fin: op 9/2, 6 wk abs, jt top-weight: remains in gd form on switch to turf: see 770.		
908	**JAKE BLACK 28** [6] J J Quinn 4-9-5 (50) R Winston 9/1: 00-01153: Chsd ldrs, kept on fnl 1f: clr	1¼	50
	rem: stays 10f on fibresand & soft: see 893.		
1072	**KINGSDON 14** [16] T J Fitzgerald 7-9-1 (6oh)vis t (40) G Duffield 10/1: 00-01044: Prom, ev ch till	5	39
	wknd fnl 1f: see 654 (banded stks).		
1052	**SUMMER SPECIAL 15** [3]4-9-6 (51) L Enstone(3) 16/1: 00300-55: Held up, prog 2f out, sn no extra.	3	40
3872}	**SPREE VISION 596** [12]8-9-7 (52) R Ffrench 8/1: 240360/-6: b g Suave Dancer - Regent's Folly	1¾	38
	(Touching Wood) Chsd ldrs, no impress: jumps fit, plcd in a sell h'cap hdle: missed '03 on the Flat, Nov '02 mdn		
	hdle wnr (rtd 102h, eff at 2m/2m4f on fast & soft): '02 h'cap wnr: eff at 9/12f on gd/soft & hvy grnd, handles		
	fast: acts on a gall or undul trk: gd weight-carrier, best without a visor.		
	2 Jul'02 Hami 11sft 59-57 E: 1 Jun'02 Ayr 10.8g/s 57-51 F: 2 Aug'01 Newc 9gd 51-52 E: 1 Aug'01 Hami 11g/s 51-46 D:		
	1 Aug'01 Ayr 9sft 50-41 E:		
4740}	**STELLITE 189** [15]4-9-1 (1oh) (45) W Supple 33/1: 0050-7: ch g Pivotal - Donation (Generous)	1¾	29
	Rear, some prog 3f out, sn no impress on reapp: lightly rcd & modest '03 mdn form (rtd 49 at best): with J Goldie.		
867	**BERRYWHITE 33** [7]6-9-1 (6oh) (45) T Hamilton(3) 20/1: 00200-08: Nvr btr than mid-div.	4	24
1090	**THE LOOSE SCREW 13** [13]6-9-1 (1oh) (45) J Fanning 20/1: 06200-09: Led 4f out till 2f out, wknd.	1¼	22
624	**BUSINESS MATTERS 66** [10]4-9-5 (50) R Lappin 33/1: 03000-00: 10th: Nvr btr than mid-div: 10 wk abs.	3	22
1033	**EAST CAPE 18** [9]7-9-1 (1oh) (45) Kim Tinkler 10/1: 5301000: 11th: Al rear: btr 724 (14f, AW).	3½	13
1047	**LORD CONYERS 15** [17]5-9-1 (6oh) (40) V Halliday 25/1: 42504/-00: 12th: Mid-div, btn 2f out.	1¼	11
1034	**SCURRA 17** [2]5-9-6 (51) T Eaves(5) 16/1: 40320-60: 13th: Al towards rear.	2½	12
1122	**THE GAMBLER 9** [11]4-9-10 p (55) L Fletcher(3) 33/1: 00500-00: 14th: Led after 1f till 4f out, wknd.	11	0
852	**BALALAIKA TUNE 37** [8]5-9-1 (6oh) (40) D R McCabe 33/1: 50-00060: 15th: Prom, led briefly 5f out, wknd.	12	0
5010}	**BORDER TERRIER 167** [5]6-9-10 (55) K Darley 7/1: 205010-0: 16th: Al bhd: long abs, jt top-weight.	5	0

16 Ran Time 2m 20.1 (13.6) Owned: The Cartmel Syndicate Trained: Baschurch

---

1279 4.50 Saltwell Signs Median Auction Maiden Stakes 3-4yo (F)
£3087 £882 £441 1m3y str Soft 94 -54 Slow Stands Side. Rcd Far Side.

1039	**LYFORD LASS 17** [5] I Semple 3-8-7 P Hanagan 9/2: 21: Tried to make all, collared ent fnl 1f,		71
	rallied gamely to regain lead cl-home: op 7/2: slow time: eff at 1m on soft & hvy: game, see 1039.		
1089	**OH GOLLY GOSH 13** [6] N P Littmoden 3-8-12 (76) K Darley 7/4 FAV: 30-22: Dwelt, recovered to	nk	75
	chase ldrs, led entering fnl 1f till worn down cl-home: well bckd from 11/4: deserves similar: see 1089.		
	INTO THE SHADOWS [8] Mrs M Reveley 4-9-7 T Eaves(5) 6/1: 3: ch f Safawan - Shadows of Silver	2	66
	(Carwhite) Chsd ldrs, onepcd fnl 1f on debut: op 9/2: rnr-up on 3 of 4 bmpr starts this spring (eff at 12f/2m on		
	gd & fast): eff at 1m on soft, crying out for a return to 12f+: encouraging run, needs further.		
	ALCAIDESA [8] Miss A Camacho 3-8-12 J Fanning 33/1: 4: b g Charnwood Forest - Calachuchi	nk	71+
	(Martinmas) Dwelt, hld up, late gains under v kind ride: clr rem: half-brother to wnrs over mid-dists/2m: dam 1m/12f		
	scorer: eff at 1m on soft, crying out for 10f+: plenty of promise, keep in mind over further with a more positive ride.		
	NODS STAR [4]3-8-7 R Winston 20/1: 5: ch f Starborough - Barsham (Be My Guest) Slowly away,	8	54
	some prog halfway, nvr nr ldrs on debut: half-sister to several wnrs: mid-dist bred.		
1108	**INDI ANO STAR 10** [7]3-8-12 D Tudhope(7) 9/1: 666: Dwelt, recovered to chase ldrs 6f, wknd.	2	56
1178	**VIBE 5** [2]3-8-12 R Ffrench 4/1: U7: Prom 6f, wknd: qck reapp.	1¾	53
1039	**BARTON FLOWER 17** [10]3-8-7 Dale Gibson 33/1: 00-08: Al towards rear, t.o..	12	30
4110}	**YORKSHIRE SPIRIT 226** [11]3-8-12 Kim Tinkler 33/1: 0-9: Al rear on reapp: has been gelded.	9	21
772	**BETTYS VALENTINE 51** [1]4-9-7 (30) L Enstone(3) 66/1: 000/-40: 10th: Chsd ldrs till halfway, t.o.	17	0
	PAULA [9]4-9-7 T Hamilton(3) 20/1: 0: 11th: Sn bhd, t.o. in last on debut.	9	0

11 Ran Time 1m 48.8(11.8) Owned: Evelyn Duchess of Sutherland Trained: Carluke

---

SOUTHWELL TUESDAY 20.04.04 Lefthand, Sharp, Oval Track

Official Going GOOD/SOFT (SOFT IN PLACES)

1280 2.00 La Dolce Vita Handicap Stakes 3yo 46-55 (F) [65]
£2961 £846 £423 1m2f Good 56 Inapplicable Inside

1000	**FRIENDS HOPE 20** [12] P A Blockley 3-9-1 (52) D Nolan(5) 14/1: 0501-01: ch f Docksider - Stygian		55
	(Irish River) Bhd, hdwy over 1f out, led ins fnl 1f & rdn out: won 1 of 4 '02 starts in native Ireland (clmr): eff		
	at 7f, stays 10f well on fm & gd, sharp trk: lightly raced, prob more to come.		
977	**AVERTAINE 21** [10] G L Moore 3-8-13 (50) I Mongan 16/1: 0052: b f Averti - Roufontaine	½	51

356

(Rousillon) Midfield, led over 1f out, hdd ins fnl 1f & no extra: unplcd all earlier mdn starts: eff at 10f on gd.
1144* **PLATINUM PIRATE 8** [5] K R Burke 3-9-10 (6ex)vis (61) Rory Moore(7) 7/4 FAV: 00-20213: Trkd ldrs, keen, kept on ins fnl 1f: rider received a 4-day ban for careless riding: top-weight: handles gd, soft & polytrack: ran to winning form of 1144, see 291. *nk* **61**
1242 **MYSTIC MOON 3** [7] J R Jenkins 3-9-4 (55) J P Murtagh 9/1: 0-00604: br f First Trump - Misty Moon (Polar Falcon) Rear, hdwy 3f out, no impress fnl 1f: qk reapp: unplcd prev: prob stays 10f on gd. *1½* **53**
1017 **HSI WANG MU 19** [2]3-8-12 (49) A Daly 7/1: 300-2505: Led over 4f, ch over 1f out, no extra fnl 1f. *1½* **45**
1045 **SUMMERISE 17** [8]3-9-4 (55) Dean McKeown 12/1: 0610-06: Chsd ldrs, onepcd over 1f out. *1* **49**
1051 **ATLANTIC BREEZE 15** [11]3-8-10 (47) Darren Williams 33/1: 10-00007: Rear, bhd, no dngr. *shd* **40**
1147 **PAY ATTENTION 8** [1]3-9-1 (52) D Allan(3) 5/1: 65300-48: Trkd ldrs, rdn when hmpd over 1f out. *1¾* **42**
865 **COMIC GENIUS 34** [9]3-8-9 (6oh) (40) Paul Eddery 50/1: 6062-359: Rear, nvr a factor: stiff ask. *1¾* **33**
1051 **HYMNS AND ARIAS 15** [6]3-8-9 (1oh) (45) M Fenton 50/1: 010-0400: 10th: Chsd ldrs, led over 5f out till over 1f out, no extra. *2½* **29**
1016 **AMEYRAH 19** [3]3-9-4 (55) T E Durcan 15/2: 00-000: 11th: Rear, nvr a factor. *5* **30**
11 Ran Time 2m 20.1 () Owned: Mr M J Wiley Trained: Southwell

1281

2.30 Festival Of Fabulous Wildwomen Maiden Stakes 3yo (D)
£3523 £1084 £542 **6f rnd** **Good 56** **+05 Fast** Inside

4200} **PRIMO WAY 221** [4] B W Hills 3-9-0 (80) M Hills 10/11 FAV: 435-1: b c Primo Dominie - Waypoint (Cadeaux Genereux) Chsd ldrs, led 2f out, rdn ins fnl 1f: nicely bckd on reapp: 5th at best in '03 (val yearling stks, rtd 81): eff over 6f on fast & gd, gall or sharp trk: runs v well fresh: rate higher, shld stay 7f. **81**
389 **GET TO THE POINT 98** [14] P W D'Arcy 3-9-0 (63) J Murtagh 25/1: 00050-02: ch g Daggers Drawn - Penny Mint (Mummy's Game) Bhd, hdwy over 1f out, styd on ins fnl 1f: long abs: fin unplcd all '03 starts (rtd 74): improved at 6f on gd: tried a visor & an eye-shield: worth another try over further. *1* **77**
4899} **ELA PAPAROUNA 176** [12] H Candy 3-8-9 (76) Dane O'Neill 9/2: 543-3: b f Vettori - Pretty Poppy (Song) Rear, short of room over 2f out, kept on well ins fnl 1f & nrst fin: reapp: 3rd 1 of 3 '03 starts (mdn, rtd 77): half sister to top-class sprinter Kyllachy: stays 6f on firm & gd: shld win a race, prob over further. *2½* **64**
1023 **POINT CALIMERE 18** [9] C R Egerton 3-9-0 (82) D Holland 8/1: 0330-04: Led to over 3f out, no extra fnl 1f: see 1023. *1* **66**
ARTIES LAD 0 [5]3-9-0 A Nicholls 33/1: 5: Handy, wknd ins fnl 1f on debut. *1* **63**
119 **SCARLETT ROSE 143** [1]3-8-9 (71) C Lowther 20/1: 360-6: Bhd, some late gains: long abs. *½* **56**
999 **EXTREMELY RARE 20** [8]3-8-9 D Allan(3) 16/1: 27: Chsd ldrs, wknd fnl 1f: btr 999. *1¾* **51**
1023 **FOUR KINGS 18** [2]3-9-0 J Tate 16/1: 58: Chsd ldrs, wknd fnl 1f: btr 1023. *1½* **52**
3265} **DAWN DUEL 264** [11]3-8-9 T E Durcan 50/1: 0-9: Nvr a factor on reapp. *½* **45**
953 **VELOCITAS 24** [3]3-9-0 T P Queally(3) 25/1: 0-40: 10th: Chsd ldr, led over 3f out till 2f out, no extra. *¾* **48**
1078 **HALF A HANDFUL 13** [6]3-9-0 R Havlin 100/1: 000: 11th: Rear, nvr a factor. *1* **45**
863 **BROWN DRAGON 34** [10]3-9-0 (63) Paul Eddery 16/1: 00-6220: 12th: In tch, wknd over 2f out. *2* **39**
4019} **PERERIN 231** [7]3-9-0 J Bramhill 100/1: 000-0: 13th: In tch, wknd over 2f out on reapp. *½* **37**
1146 **BOND SHAKIRA 8** [13]3-8-9 F Lynch 25/1: 5-30: 14th: In tch, wknd over 2f out: see 1146. *shd* **31**
14 Ran Time 1m 17.2 (3.1) Owned: Mr D M James Trained: Lambourn

1282

3.00 National Secretary Day Handicap Stakes 3yo+ 0-75 (E) **[75]**
£4394 £1352 £676 **7f rnd** **Good 56** **-06 Slow** Inside

834 **HURRICANE COAST 38** [12] D Flood 5-9-5 bl (66) Dane O'Neill 12/1: 2004101: Handy, led over 1f out, pushed clr ins fnl 1f, eased cl home: suited by 5/7f, stays 1m on firm, gd/soft & both AW's, likes a sharp trk: broke a blood vessel last time: well h'capped on turf, can follow-up: see 807 & 61. **75+**
1145 **BALAKIREF 8** [2] M Dods 5-9-1 (62) F Lynch 5/1: 0000-102: Rear, no room over 1f out, switched & styd on well ins fnl 1f, wnr had flown: much closer with clr run & shapes like another win sn: see 1052. *2* **67+**
807 **BANNISTER 46** [6] Mrs Stef Liddiard 6-8-13 (60) M Fenton 33/1: 0100-303: Bhd, hdwy over 1f out, kept on ins fnl 1f: 7 wk abs: see 728. *nk* **62**
1132 **BALLARE 8** [10] Bob Jones 5-8-1 (48) T Williams 12/1: 0346104: In tch, hdwy over 2f out, ch over 1f out, sn onepcd: shade btr 1073 (banded, polytrack), see 649. *1½* **47**
1025 **B A HIGHFLYER 18** [9]4-9-5 (66) T E Durcan 16/1: 02216-05: Chsd ldrs, kept on onepace. *¾* **63**
1090 **SPY GUN 13** [15]4-8-3 (50) N Chalmers(2) 40/1: 0050406: Chsd ldrs, led 2f out, sn hdd & no extra. *½* **46**
1079 **PERFECT PORTRAIT 13** [1]4-9-13 (74) J Murtagh 9/2: 1-37: Trkd ldrs, onepcd fnl 1f: see 1079. *hd* **69**
1023 **HORIZONTAL 18** [13]4-8-13 (60) M Tebbutt 11/1: 5-668: ch g Distant View - Proud Lou (Proud Clarion) Handy, wkng when short of room ins fnl 1f: 5th sole '03 start (mdn, rtd 64 with H Cecil): lightly rcd. *¾* **53**
1195 **EAGER ANGEL 5** [3]6-8-10 p (57) Dean McKeown 33/1: 0151039: Rear, nvr nr ldrs: see 680 & 356. *nk* **49**
1131 **ARTISTRY 8** [8]4-9-1 (62) D Holland 12/1: 4540-150: 10th: Handy & keen, lost place after 2f, hdwy 2f out, btn when hmpd ins fnl 1f: see 1024. *1* **52**
4184} **ZAMYATINA 222** [7]5-8-6 (53) D Allan(3) 66/1: 064000-0: 11th: br f Danehill Dancer - Miss Pickpocket (Petorius) Rear, nvr a factor: reapp: won a class stks in '03: eff at 7f on fast & soft. *¾* **41**
1 Jul'03 Catt 7g/f 62-(38) E: 1 Aug'01 Brig 6g/f 78- F: 2 Aug'01 Nott 5sft 78- E: 2 Jul'01 Wind 5g/f 68- D:
1049 **MUFREH 15** [5]6-8-13 (60) S Whitworth 7/2 FAV: 12-15240: 12th: Rear, short of room rail 3f out, nvr a factor: reportedly lost action early: see 1049 & 31. *shd* **47**
5034} **XPRES DIGITAL 164** [4]3-9-1 t (75) J Bramhill 50/1: 345610-0: 13th: b c Komaite - Kustom Kit Xpres (Absalom) Chsd ldrs, wkng when hmpd 1f out: reapp: won a nursery & a mdn in '03: stays 7f, suited by 6f on fast, gd & fibresand, stiff/gall or a sharp trk: eff with/without a t-strap: with S Bowring. *1¾* **59**
1 Oct'03 Redc 6g/f 78-72 E: 2 Jul'03 Leic 6.0g/f 74-73 E: 1 Jun'03 Sout 6af 75a- D:
1193 **MUNAAWESH 5** [14]3-8-9 (69) S Sanders 50/1: 05-0300: 14th: Rear, wknd 2f out: qck reapp. *1½* **50**
4107} **HOLLOW JO 226** [11]4-9-11 (72) I Mongan 6/1: 111120-0: 15th: Led 5f, fdd ins fnl 1f: reapp. *2½* **48**
15 Ran Time 1m 31.35 (4.35) Owned: Mrs Ruth M Serrell Trained: Lingfield

1283   3.30 Boston Marathon Median Auction Maiden Stakes 3yo (F)
£2940 £840 £420   1m2f   Good 56   Inapplicable   Inside

FLING 0 [8] J R Fanshawe 3-8-9 Dane O'Neill 13/2: 1: b f Pursuit of Love - Full Orchestra   **73+**
(Shirley Heights) Rear, gd hdwy to lead over 1f out, pushed clr, eased, val 10L+: debut: sister to a 1m/1m2f wnr:
eff at 10f on gd, shld apprec 12f: acts on a sharp trk & runs v well fresh: fine start & sure to rate higher.
4874} **JARVO 179** [9] N P Littmoden 3-9-0 (66) D Holland 9/2: 02230-2: b g Pursuit of Love - Pinkie Rose   7   66
(Kenmare) Chsd ldr, led after 2f till over 1f out, no extra: reapp: rnr-up 2 of 5 '03 starts (mdns): eff at 7f,
poss stays 10f on fast & gd. 2 Sep'03 Thir 7g/f 68- E: 2 Aug'03 Hami 6.0g/f 70- E:
1019 **AMANKILA 19** [3] M L W Bell 3-8-9 I Mongan 5/1: 03: b f Revoque - Steel Habit (Habitat) Handy,   nk   60
chsd ldr over 4f out, ch over 1f out, no impress fnl 1f: clr of rem: unplcd earlier mdn start: imprvd from debut.
4408} **MARIA BONITA 210** [6] R M Beckett 3-8-9 S Sanders 7/2: 03-4: Rear, hdwy over 6f out, wknd 2f out.   5   52
919 **AMWELL BRAVE 26** [4]3-9-0 vis (65) J P Murtagh 3/1 FAV: 2233505: Chsd ldrs, wknd over 1f out.   1½   55
351 **KELTIC RAINBOW 103** [7]3-8-9 (57) Paul Eddery 12/1: 0033-46: Rear, nvr nr ldrs: long abs.   2½   46
983 **BONJOUR BOND 21** [2]3-9-0 (64) F Lynch 16/1: 400-47: Led 2f, wknd 5f out.   22   18
4987} **LAWGIVER 169** [1]3-9-0 M Fenton 66/1: 000-8: Keen in rear, nvr a factor on reapp.   ½   17
919 **KALUSH 26** [5]3-9-0 Dean McKeown 20/1: 26336-09: Handy, lost place over 3f out & btn.   2   14
9 Ran   Time 2m 15.00 ()   Owned: Cheveley Park Stud   Trained: Newmarket

1284   4.00 St Peter Martyr's Day Selling Stakes 3yo+ (G)
£2667 £762 £381   7f rnd   Good 56   +01 Fast   Inside

1058 **FEN GYPSY 15** [6] P D Evans 6-9-7 (60) S J Donohoe(7) 7/4 FAV: 5400021: Al handy, chsd ldr 4f out,   62
led over 1f out, rdn out, eased cl home, val 3L: bght in for 4000 gns: eff btwn 7f/1m, tried 12f, acts on firm &
gd/soft, prob polytrack, gall or sharp trks: see 607.
1145 **JONNY EBENEEZER 8** [8] R M H Cowell 5-9-7 (75) B Doyle 6/1: 402-0002: Rear, hdwy 2f out, kept on   2   54
ins fnl 1f but not reach wnr: likes easy grnd, shld find a seller: see 61.
1194 **SILVER MASCOT 5** [2] R Hollinshead 5-9-12 (48) F Lynch 5/1: 2251423: Led till over 1f out, no   1¼   56
extra: top-weight: ran to winning form of 825, see 448.
ENNA 181 [10] A G Juckes 5-9-2 (51) N Chalmers(5) 25/1: 001013-4: ch f Don Corleone - Elba   2½   41
(Freedom's Choice) Rear, hdwy over 1f out, not reach ldrs: long abs, Brit bow: won 2 of 6 '03 starts in native
Poland (7f/1m, soft): won 2 of 7 '02 starts (1m, gd & soft): eff btwn 6f/1m on gd & soft: fair start.
1065 **RILEYS DREAM 14** [7]5-9-2 (49) R Havlin 25/1: 30000-05: b f Rudimentary - Dorazine (Kalaglow)   nk   40
Rear, modest late gains: won a h'cap in '03 (with M Channon): won a class stks & a mdn in '02: eff btwn 5/7f on
gd/soft, stiff/undul trks: can run well fresh: with B Llewellyn.
1 May'03 Brig 7.0g/s 62-59 E: 1 Jul'02 Pont 6g/s 69- E: 1 Jun'02 Nott 5g/s 67- E:
MY COUNTRY CLUB 188 [11]7-9-7 (53) Dane O'Neill 14/1: 122442-6: b c Alzao - Merry Rous   ¾   43
(Rousillon) Rear, some late gains: long abs, Brit bow: won 2 of 5 '03 starts in native Poland (6f, gd & soft):
won sole '02 start (7f, gd): eff btwn 5/7f on gd & soft: fair start.
1065* **MARABAR 14** [4]6-9-7 bl (65) S Sanders 9/2: 0650017: Rear, nvr a factor: btr 1065.   2   39
981 **METICULOUS 21** [13]6-9-7 (30) L Vickers 100/1: 0000008: Chsd ldrs, lost place halfway & btn.   10   19
362 **MABEL RILEY 102** [1]4-9-2 (45) J Bramhill 20/1: 00000-509: In tch, hdwy halfway, wknd 2f out.   1   12
463} **HOME BY SOCKS 817** [5]5-9-2 Andrew Webb(7) 50/1: 60060/0/-0: 10th: Nvr a factor on reapp.   ½   11
1160 **FINNINGLEY CONNOR 6** [9]4-9-7 (50) Dean McKeown 80/1: 5/000-000: 11th: Chsd ldrs, wknd 2f out.   hd   15
1179 **SHIRLEY NOT 5** [3]8-9-7 (46) A Nicholls 20/1: 00000-00: 12th: Rear, nvr nr ldrs: rep lost action.   1¾   11
12 Ran   Time 1m 30.9 (3.9)   Owned: Mr P D Evans   Trained: Abergavenny

1285   4.30 Harold Lloyd's Birthday Handicap Stakes 4yo+ 46-55 (F)
£3010 £860 £430   2m   Good 56   -58 Slow   Inside   [67]

1082 **GALANDORA 13** [7] Dr J R J Naylor 4-8-6 (1oh) (45) Lucy Russell(7) 33/1: 6300-561: Bhd & keen, hdwy   51
4f out, led over 1f out, kept on well under kind ride fnl 1f: first win: eff at 13f, stays 2m well: acts on fast &
gd grnd, sharp trks: see 979.
1082 **STARRY MARY 13** [4] R M Beckett 6-9-5 (55) S Sanders 6/1: 00006-22: Chsd ldrs, outpcd 3f out,   ½   58
rallied over 1f out, kept on ins fnl 1f: stays 2m: gd eff under top-weight: fin ahd of this wnr in 1082.
2073} **TOTALLY SCOTTISH 313** [6] Mrs M Reveley 8-8-10 (1oh) (45) D Holland 3/1 FAV: 0/00/4/42-3: b g   2   47
Mtoto - Glenfinlass (Lomond) Bhd, hdwy over 1f out, not pace of ldrs: reapp/jumps fit: rnr-up in a claim hdle in
03/04 (eff over 2m/2m4f on firm, hvy & any trk, rtd 114h): rnr-up 1 of 2 Flat '03 starts (h'cap): 4th sole '02
start (h'cap, rtd 44): eff at 13f, stays 2m on firm & gd/soft: needs further &/or softer grnd.
2 Jun'03 Hami 13.0gd 41-42 F:
1033 **THE BEDUTH NAVI 18** [2] D G Bridgwater 4-8-7 (3oh) (47) A Daly 11/2: 0-221234: Handy, led over 3f   2½   45
out till over 1f out, no extra: see 852 & 823.
149} **CASTANET 503** [5]5-8-10 (1oh) (45) R Miles(3) 20/1: 065043/-5: b f Pennekamp - Addaya (Persian   2½   41
Bold) Rear, hmpd over 5f out, hdwy 2f out, sn no impress: reapp/jumps fit: 3rd in a h'cap hdle in 03/04 (eff btwn
2m/2m5f on firm & hvy, rtd 84h): missed '03: 3rd at best in '02 (h'cap, rtd 47a): prev eff at 6f, stays at least
14f on gd/soft: has tried a visor: now with A Price. 2 Aug'01 Newm 6g/s 79- D:
4931} **LITTLE TOBIAS 175** [12]5-9-1 (51) D Corby(3) 12/1: 00/1010-6: ch g Millkom - Barbara Frietchie   ¾   45
(Try My Best) Chsd ldrs, wknd fnl 1f: reapp: won 2 of 4 '03 starts (h'caps): 6th at best in '02 (h'cap, rtd 59):
eff btwn 15/16f on gd & gd/soft grnd, acts on a sharp or gall trk: has run well fresh.
1 Sep'03 Catt 15.8g/s 53-47 F: 1 Jul'03 Ayr 15gd 49-42 F:
1033 **LAMPOS 18** [13]4-9-0 vis (54) F Lynch 8/1: 0-312507: Rear, hdwy over 5f out, wknd 2f out.   ½   47
1238 **ROMIL STAR 3** [3]7-9-4 VIS (54) Darren Williams 6/1: 05560-08: Trkd ldrs, lost place & hmpd over   3½   43
3f out, wknd: op 14/1, qck reapp: tried visor.
3015} **I GOT RHYTHM 276** [1]6-8-10 (1oh) (45) T E Durcan 11/1: 44/16/60-9: Rear, nvr a factor.   16   19
813 **SASHAY 43** [8]6-8-10 (1oh) (45) Stephanie Hollinshead(7) 15/2: 1434-520: 10th: Led 11f, no extra 2f out.   8   11
1003 **MURAQEB 20** [9]4-8-10 (50) I Mongan 50/1: 5-000500: 11th: Keen in rear, nvr a factor.   nk   14
4590} **EVIYRN 903** [11]8-8-10 (7oh)vis (35) M Fenton 33/1: 060/640//-0: 12th: Chsd ldr, led 5f out till   ¾   9
over 3f out, sn no extra.
12 Ran   Time 3m 45.1 (18.3)   Owned: Mr Michael Olpin   Trained: Shrewton

1286   5.00 Teletext Racing 'hands And Heels' Apprentice Handicap Stakes 4yo+ 0-70 (G)   [70]
£2940 £840 £420   1m3f   Good 56   -23 Slow   Inside

1033 **ISAAF** 18 [3] P W Hiatt 5-8-13 (55) P Makin(3) 7/2: 6602-121: Handy, led over 1f out, pushed out   63
ins fnl 1f: rider received a 1-day ban for careless riding: eff btwn 11/15.4f on firm, gd & fibresand, sharp or
stiff/undul trks: in fine form of late: see 891.

1128 **DISSIDENT** 8 [8] D Flood 6-10-0 vis (70) L Treadwell(3) 12/1: 02-4U102: Trkd ldrs & keen, ch over   1   76
1f out, styd on ins fnl 1f: jt top-weight: stays 10f/11f well, acts on gd, hvy & on polytrack: see 1026.

1164 **TROUBLE MOUNTAIN** 6 [4] M W Easterby 7-10-0 (70) P Mulrennan 5/2 FAV: 4023-333: Rear, hdwy over   2½   72
1f out, not pace to chall: jt top weight: see 196.

1047 **SIR NINJA** 15 [7] S Kirk 7-9-9 (65) J Daly(7) 14/1: 3000/4-24: Rear, hdwy 2f out, onepcd fnl 1f.   2½   63

1128 **GAME GURU** 8 [9]5-9-6 bl (62) D Nolan 15/1: 3146105: Led till over 8f out, led again over 2f out   1   57
till over 1f out, no extra ins fnl 1f: much btr 857 (seller), see 166.

218 **MOST SAUCY** 125 [5]8-9-9 (65) S Crawford(3) 10/1: 355500-6: br f Most Welcome - So Saucy (Teenoso)   4   54
Rear, kept on after 2f out, not pace to reach ldrs: abs: won 4 h'caps in '03 (rtd 75): won a h'cap & a class stks in
'02: eff over 10/12f on firm, hvy & both AWs: loves sharp trks, esp Lingfield: gd weight-carrier: v tough &
genuine. 2 Sep'03 Epso 10.1gd 74-70 D: 1 Jul'03 Epso 12.0gd 69-64 E: 2 Jul'03 Epso 12.0g/f 68-65 E:
2 Jun'03 Ling 10ap 68a-65 E: 1 Jun'03 Wind 11.6g/f 64-60 F: 1 Apr'03 Sout 11g/f 64-57 G: 1 Jan'03 Ling 10ap 72a-65 E:
1 Jul'02 Wind 8g/f 60-55 D: 2 Jul'02 Ling 8ap 71a- E: 1 Apr'02 Ling 8ap 73a- E: 2 Feb'02 Ling 7ap 64a- F:

1128 **TOP OF THE CLASS** 8 [12]7-9-2 vis (58) S Donohoe(2) 12/1: 0035047: Keen & led over 8f out, hdd over   1½   45
2f out, sn no extra: see 557 & 465.

1090 **GRAND LASS** 13 [1]5-8-11 bl (53) N Chalmers 25/1: 1254308: Midfield, wknd over 1f out: see 580.   ½   39

4077} **PARADISE GARDEN** 228 [6]7-7-12 (5oh) (35) R Kennemore(4) 40/1: 000050-9: b g Septieme Ciel - Water   2½   22
Course (Irish River): Rear, hdwy over 7f out, ch 2f out, wknd fnl 1f: reapp: unplcd all '03 starts (rtd 30):
rnr-up in a h'cap in '02: eff at 1m/11f on firm & gd/soft, handles soft: has tried blnks, cheek pieces & a visor.
2 Jun'02 Newc 10.1g/f 44-43 E: 1 Jul'01 Ayr 10g/s 44- F:

984 **MATHMAGICIAN** 21 [11]5-7-12 (10oh)bl (30) H Fellows 66/1: 5404660: 10th: Rear, hdwy 7f out, wknd   ½   21
2f out: stiff task at weights: see 771 & 635.

997 **THEATRE TINKA** 20 [2]5-9-1 p (57) Stephanie Hollinshead(3) 7/2: 1-555240: 11th: Chsd ldrs, wknd halfway6   29

1006 **LUNAR LEADER** 20 [10]4-9-9 p (35) A Quinn 33/1: 20000-00: 12th: b f Mujadil - Moon River (Groom   12   19
Dancer): Handy, wknd 3f out: won 3 times in '03 (h'cap, class stks, clmr, with Mrs L Stubbs, earlier with B Meehan):
eff btwn 7/9.3f on firm & gd grnd, likes Carlisle, acts on a gall trk: has tried blnks, wears cheek pieces.
2 Aug'03 Folk 9.7g/f 72-70 F: 1 Jul'03 Carl 9.3gd 72-(67) E: 2 Jul'03 Yarm 8.0fm 73-69 E: 1 Jul'03 Carl 9.3g/f 70-63 E:
1 Jun'03 Ayr 8g/f 58-(63) E: 2 May'03 Leic 8.0g/f 61-(62) F:
12 Ran   Time 2m 30.5(8.7)   Owned: Miss Maria McKinney   Trained: Banbury

Official Going STANDARD.

1287   5.15 New Site @ Betdirect Co Uk Banded Stakes 3yo+ 0-35 (H)
£1260 £360 £180   1m4f aw   Going 34   -36 Slow   Inside

852 **BUYING A DREAM** 38 [4] Andrew Turnell 7-9-9 (35) C Catlin 16/1: 0/500/-501: Chsd ldrs, styd on   40a
over 1f out, led ins fnl 1f, drvn clr: eff at 7f/12f on fast, gd/soft & polytrack, acts on a sharp trk: see 780.

1180* **LEOPHIN DANCER** 6 [3] P W Hiatt 6-10-1 (35) B Doyle 5/2: 500-6012: Handy, trkd ldr over 2f out,   1½   41a
onepcd over 1f out: qck reapp: not btn far under top-weight, ran to winning form of 1180.

1076 **THE LAST MOHICAN** 15 [1] P Howling 5-9-9 p (30) J Fanning 6/1: 3244003: Led 2f, led again over 5f   shd   35a
out till ins fnl 1f, no extra nr fin: mdn after 27: see 537 & 395.

1180 **NEPTUNE** 6 [6] J C Fox 8-9-9 (35) R Smith 9/4 FAV: 00/-50024: In tch, some late gains: see 1180.   1½   33a

330 **ROYAL AXMINSTER** 106 [2]9-9-9 (35) Amy Baker(7) 5/1: 31605-05: b g Alzao - Number One Spot   nk   32a
(Reference Point): Led after 2f till onepcd over 2f out: long abs: won a h'cap in '03:
3rd 3 times in '02 (h'caps, rtd 42a at best): eff around 12f on fast, firm & both AWs, stiff/gall trk: loves to
front-run, goes well for an amat: with Mrs P Dutfield.
1 Jul'03 Sali 12g/f 45-34 E: 2 Feb'03 Ling 12ap 43a-39 F: 2 Jun'01 Newm 12g/f 43-40 F:

826 **BROUGHTONS MILL** 44 [5]9-9-9 p (30) W Supple 12/1: 00-56606: Handy, wknd over 1f out: 6 wk abs.   3   27a

1180 **SMARTER CHARTER** 6 [7]11-9-9 (35) Kristin Stubbs(7) 11/2: 0/0000-57: br g Master Willie - Irene's   nk   26a
Charter (Persian Bold): Bhd, nvr a factor: qck reapp: unplcd all 3 '03 starts (h'caps, 1 class stks, rtd 35): won
a h'cap in '02: eff btwn 10/14f on any grnd, loves Bath, acts on any trk: best held up & has run well fresh.
2 Jul'02 Hayd 11.9g/s 52-54 E: 1 Jun'02 Leic 11.8g/f 42-40 F: 1 Sep'01 Redc 14g/f 46-41 E: 1 Jun'01 Yarm 10g/f 47-40 E:
2 May'01 Redc 11hvy 44-43 E:
7 Ran   Time 2m 37.62 (8.42)   Owned: Robinson Webster (Holdings) Ltd   Trained: Malton

1288   5.45 #10 Free Bet @ Betdirect Co Uk Banded Stakes 3yo+ 0-40 (H)
£1435 £410 £205   7f aw rnd   Going 34   -10 Slow   Inside

1261* **BAYTOWN FLYER** 2 [5] P S McEntee 4-9-6 (35) L Dettori 2/1: 0-220111: Made all, clr 2f out, pushed   49a
out fnl 1f: landed treble, qck reapp: eff at 6/7f, tried 1m, acts on firm, gd/soft & both AWs, likes a sharp trk.

1184+ **CRAFTY POLITICIAN** 6 [2] G L Moore 7-9-6 bl (40) R L Moore 11/8 FAV: 0000-412: Chsd wnr 2f, chsd   2½   42a
wnr again over 2f out, not pace to chall over 1f out: qck reapp: eff btwn 6/7f: shade btr 1184 (6f), see 639.

1203 **HARBOUR PRINCESS** 5 [3] M F Harris 3-8-1 (40) S Righton 33/1: 06663: Bhd, some late gains.   3   30a

1181 **MAHLSTICK** 6 [1] D W P Arbuthnot 6-9-0 T (35) S Hitchcott(3) 5/1: 0406/-634: Handy, chsd wnr   1¼   27a
briefly over 2f out, sn wknd: qck reapp: first time t-strap: see 971.

778 **BAR OF SILVER** 51 [4]4-9-0 vis (40) D Holland 11/2: 050-0505: ch g Bahhare - Shaping Up (Storm   7   12a
Bird): Bhd, hdwy & chsd wnr after 3f out, sn wknd: 7 wk abs: rnr-up in 2 sellers in '03 (with J
Osborne): 4th sole '02 mdn start (rtd 47a): eff btwn 7f/1m on fast, prob handles fibresand: has tried cheek pieces,
wears a visor. 2 Jul'03 Brig 8.0g/f 59-(62) G: 2 Apr'03 Folk 7g/f 62-59 G:
5 Ran   Time 1m 25.93 (3.13)   Owned: Mr J Doxey   Trained: Newmarket

1289   **6.15 Betdirect Co Uk Banded Stakes 3yo+ 0-45 (H)**
£1638 £468 £234   **1m2f aw**   **Going 34**   **-21 Slow**   Inside

1182 **KINGS TOPIC 6** [9] P Burgoyne 4-9-8 (45) L Keniry(3) 8/1: 000/0-21: Trkd ldrs, led over 2f out, **50a**
rdn clr: eff around a sharp 10f, has tried 12f, acts on polytrack in banded company: shaper from reapp: see 1182.
894 **SIX PACK 30** [7] Andrew Turnell 6-9-8 (45) C Catlin 4/1: 00060-22: Handy, went 2nd over 1f out, 1½ **46a**
kept on ins fnl 1f but not reach wnr: eff btwn 7f/10f, handles firm, soft & both AWs: shld win a banded.
1072 **RYANS BLISS 15** [5] T D McCarthy 4-9-8 (45) J P Guillambert(3) 16/1: 00-00253: In tch, hdwy 3f nk **45a**
out, edged right fnl 1f & onepcd: see 970.
896 **OUR GLENARD 29** [1] S L Keightley 5-9-8 (45) D Holland 7/2 JT FAV: 5-220564: In tch, outpcd & bhd ¾ **43a**
over 4f out, some late gains: see 330 & 84.
968 **PRIVATE SEAL 23** [8]9-9-8 t (45) N Callan 10/1: 3220205: Bhd, some late gains: see 707 & 539. 1½ **41a**
1072* **GALEY RIVER 15** [4]5-9-8 (45) D Corby(3) 9/2: 0050516: Handy, lost place over 4f out, sn btn. 4 **35a**
1072 **CANDY ANCHOR 15** [3]5-9-8 bl (45) L Dettori 7/2 JT FAV: 00306-27: Keen in rear, hdwy & led 5f out, 4 **29a**
hdd & no extra over 2f out: tchd 6/1: btr 1072.
891 **DAFA 30** [6]8-9-8 BL (40) S W Kelly 8/1: 5///0/-1168: Led to 5f out, no extra over 3f out: op 5/1, blnks. 2½ **25a**
1067 **POLISH RHAPSODY 15** [2]3-8-5 (45) W Supple 20/1: 0-0069: b f Charnwood Forest - Polish Rhythm 6 **16a**
(Polish Patriot) Rear, nvr a factor: last of 10 sole '03 mdn start (rtd 62a): seems modest: with J Supple.
9 Ran   Time 2m 08.37 (5.57)   Owned: Topics Tarts   Trained: Marlborough

1290   **6.45 Bet Direct Interactive Banded Stakes 3yo+ 0-40 (H)**
£1610 £460 £230   **5f aw rnd**   **Going 34**   **+10 Fast**   Outside

860 **MAROMITO 35** [5] R Bastiman 7-9-7 (40) S Sanders 4/5 FAV: 000-0031: Led, clr bef 1f out, rdn out: **49a**
bckd from 7/4: eff at 5f on firm, gd & both AW's, handles soft grnd: apprec drop to banded grade: see 860.
1075 **LAW MAKER 15** [7] M A Buckley 4-9-7 vis (40) D Holland 4/1: 0006042: Prom, led from fnl 2f, not 3 **40a**
pace wnr: eff at 5/6f on polytrack: see 1075 & 897.
832 **AVIT 43** [1] P L Gilligan 4-9-7 (40) J F Egan 5/1: 000-0023: Handy, outpcd 3f out, rallied fnl 1f. 2½ **33a**
1127 **BALI STAR 9** [2] R J Hodges 9-9-7 (40) S Drowne 10/1: 5-024004: Prom, no extra fnl 2f: see 374. 1 **30a**
578 **SECOND GENERATION 73** [6]7-9-7 (30) R L Moore 33/1: 006/0//-0-55: ch g Cadeaux Genereux - Title 3 **21a**
Roll (Tate Gallery) Slow away, nvr nrr than mid-div: 10 wk abs: missed '03 & '02: unplcd in sole '01 start
(h'cap, D R C Elsworth): unplcd in '00 (rtd 58, mdn, has tried blnks).
1074 **ONEFORTHEBOYS 15** [3]5-9-7 (40) S Whitworth 11/2: 2400306: Slow away, nvr a factor: tchd 8/1. 1½ **17a**
889 **MANGUS 30** [4]10-9-7 bl e (35) Dane O'Neill 25/1: 00-30607: Cl-up, fdd 2f out: see 749. 2½ **10a**
851 **PHILLY DEE 38** [8]3-8-11 bl (40) M Savage(3) 25/1: 53-30008: Slow away, nvr a factor: btr 413. 11 **0a**
8 Ran   Time 59.00 (1.20)   Owned: Mrs P Bastiman   Trained: Wetherby

1291   **7.15 Bet Direct On Sky Active Selling Stakes 4yo+ (H)**
£1456 £416 £208   **2m aw**   **Going 34**   **-22 Slow**   Inside

1076 **SARIBA 15** [6] A Charlton 5-8-11 (35) P Dobbs 8/1: 4410-061: Led, hdd 1m out, led again 3f out, **45a**
rdn out fnl 1f: bght in for 2,600gns: eff at 13f, suited by 2m/2m1f: acts on firm, gd/soft & polytrack: see 690.
INDIAN CHASE [2] Dr J R J Naylor 7-9-2 VIS Lucy Russell(7) 33/1: 2: b g Terimon - Icy Gunner 1¾ **47a**
(Gunner B) Held up, still plenty to do 4f out, kept on fnl 2f, no ch with wnr: Flat bow, 6 wk hdle abs, earlier
plcd twice in bmprs (styd 2m2.5f, acts on firm & fast): eff at 2m on polytrack: eff in a visor.
1197 **OUR IMPERIAL BAY 6** [5] R M Stronge 5-9-7 vis (55) A Daly 4/1: 06-00103: Rear, outpcd 4f out, ½ **51a**
rallied bef 1f out, nrst fin: qck reapp: dismounted after line: eff at 10f/12f, stays 2m: see 985.
1047 **MISTER GRAHAM 16** [4] K F Clutterbuck 9-9-2 B Reilly(3) 33/1: 04: b g Rock Hopper - Celestial Air ½ **45a**
(Rheingold) Slow away, prog & ev ch 3f out, onepcd dist: earlier unplcd over hdles (rtd 82h, seller, tried cheek
pieces, visor & t-strap): rnr-up once in 02/03 (rtd 72c, nov h'cap, stays 2m4f on fast & gd grnd, has gone well
fresh, Miss J Smith): eff at 2m on polytrack.
896 **SUNGIO 29** [7]6-9-7 bl (52) K Fallon 4/9 FAV: 1312335: In tch, styd on to chase wnr 2f out, wknd nk **49a**
ins fnl 1f: bckd at long odds on: btr expeceted after 896.
1238 **MONSAL DALE 4** [1]5-9-2 p (40) M Savage(5) 8/1: 235-0006: Cl-up, led 1m out, hdd 3f out, sn wknd. 9 **34a**
3640] **REGAL REPOSE 250** [3]4-8-7 (50) C Haddon(7) 16/1: 100200-7: Keen rear, nvr a factor: reapp. 10 **19a**
7 Ran   Time 3m 29.04 (9.04)   Owned: Woodhaven Racing Syndicate   Trained: Marlborough

1292   **7.45 #10 Free Bet @ Bet Direct Sky Active Banded Stakes 3yo+ 0-35 (H)**
£1257 £359 £180   **1m aw rnd**   **Going 34**   **-29 Slow**   Outside

1264+ **BEAUTEOUS 2** [5] M J Polglase 5-9-13 (35) L Dettori 1/4 FAV: 0644111: In tch, led after 3f, sn **64a+**
clr, pushed out to win v easily, val 8/9L+: quick reapp: top weight: eff at 6f/8.4f on firm, gd/soft & both AWs:
can force the pace: in gd form in bandit stakes: see 1264 & 1201.
1181 **TINY TIM 6** [6] A M Balding 6-9-7 (35) R J Killoran(7) 5/1: 0/-442352: Prom, kept on fnl 2f, no ch 5 **36a**
with v easy wnr: quick reapp: see 971 & 786.
1185 **NEWCORR 6** [3] J J Bridger 5-9-7 (35) N Chalmers(5) 33/1: 60/0-0063: b g Magical Wonder - Avionne nk **35a**
(Derrylin) Chsd ldrs, onepcd fnl 2f: qk reapp: ex-Irish, mdn wnr at Navan in '02: eff at 9f on hvy & polytrack.
1015 **DIVINA 20** [1] S L Keightley 3-8-7 VIS (30) D Holland 25/1: 00004: Led 1f, styd prom till fdd 3f out. 8 **19a**
3030] **MOOSE MALLOY 996** [4]7-9-7 p (30) S Whitworth 33/1: 00000/6//-5: ch g Formidable - Jolimo 7 **5a**
(Fortissimo) Led 7f out, hdd 5f out, sn fdd: v mod form in both hdles & Flat sphere.
1244 **SENNEN COVE 2** [2]5-9-7 bl t (30) S Sanders 10/1: 00-00636: Prom 5f, sn fdd: quick reapp: btr 1244. 6 **0a**
6 Ran   Time 1m 41.26(5.06)   Owned: Mr Paul J Dixon   Trained: Newark

Official Going SOFT.

1293　**1.50 Blue Square 0800 587 0200 Handicap Stakes 3yo+ 0-95 (C)**　　　　　[92]
　　　　　£9118　£3458　£1729　　**5f str**　　**Soft**　　**Fast**　Stands Side

1120　**CAPE ROYAL 10** [9] Mrs J R Ramsden 4-9-4　(82) L Dettori 5/1 CO FAV: 0220-061: Handy, gd hdwy to　　　**91**
lead 1f out, styd on well, drvn out: '03 auct mdn wnr, rnr-up 3 times: stays 6f, suited by 5f on firm & soft grnd,
any trk: useful, poss more to come: see 1120.
1096　**LADY PEKAN 13** [11] P S McEntee 5-7-12 (2oh)bl (60) Lisa Jones(3) 12/1: 3560022: Set pace, edged　　**2**　**66**
left & hdd 1f out, not pace of wnr: acts on firm, soft & fibresand, best at 5f: back in blnks, see 1096, 274.
1137　**FRUIT OF GLORY 9** [12] J R Jenkins 5-9-12　(90) D Holland 5/1 CO FAV: 35-05443: Slow away, held　　½　**93**+
up, hdwy & no room 2f out till ins last, styd on well, too late: acts on firm, soft & polytrack: would have gone
close with any sort of run & looks poised to win again: see 1137.
1127　**PRINCE OF BLUES 9** [6] M Mullineaux 6-7-12 (4oh)p (58) P Varley(6) 25/1: 2000404: Chsd ldrs, eff　　_shd_　**65**
over 1f out, onepcd: see 453.
1251　**AWAKE 2** [2] K Fallon 5/1 CO FAV: 6500-065: Bhd, eff & short of room over 1f out, late　　½　**74**
gains, no threat: qck reapp: another encouraging run & h'capped to win: see 1251.
880　**BLUE KNIGHT 33** [5]5-8-9 (73) R Hughes 10/1: 600-2406: Held up, eff & short of room over 1f out,　　**2**　**71**
some late gains: see 655.
1025　**MADRASEE 19** [4]6-9-0　(78) R L Moore 9/1: 1-200457: In tch, no impress fnl 2f: likes faster grnd.　　½　**75**
927　**CHICO GUAPO 26** [13]4-8-11 p (75) Dean McKeown 13/2: 015-0508: In tch, wknd over 1f out:　see 692.　½　**71**
1025　**ANOTHER GLIMPSE 19** [8]6-8-5 t (69) J Quinn 16/1: 650-4109: Slow away & al bhd: btr 880 (6f).　　½　**64**
692　**PALAWAN 60** [7]8-9-7　(85) L Keniry(3) 25/1: 102-0060: 10th: In tch, short of room dist, no extra.　　_hd_　**79**
1127　**KINGS BALLET 9** [10]6-7-12 (6oh)p (56) J Mackay 16/1: 0020400: 11th: Slow away & al bhd: see 643.　2½　**51**
927　**DANCING MYSTERY 26** [1]10-9-6 bl (84) S Carson 14/1: 33-13500: 12th: Slow away & al bhd: btr 461.　**5**　**63**
3699}　**IZMAIL 247** [3]5-8-10 (74) J Murtagh 50/1: 200015-0: 13th: b g Bluebird - My Lorraine (Mac's Imp)　3½　**46**
Cl-up, wknd over 1f out: '03 class stks wnr: 4th in '02 for E Dunlop (rtd 86): suited by 5f on fm & gd: tried vis.
1 Aug'03 Brig 5.3fm 76-(70) E:　2 Jul'03 Ayr 5g/f 73-70 C:　2 Aug'01 York 5gd 95- A:　1 Jun'01 Newc 5g/f 87- D:
13 Ran　Time 58.96 (4.66)　Owned: Mr D R Brotherton　Trained: Thirsk

---

1294　**2.20 Weatherbys Blue Riband Trial Stakes Conditions Race 3yo (B)**
　　　　　£12679　£4499　£2250　　**1m2f18y**　　**Heavy**　　**Fair**　Inside

1055*　**BULL RUN 16** [3] D R Loder 3-8-13　J Murtagh 13/8 FAV: 11: In tch, hdwy trav well & led over 2f　　**118**+
out, sn pushed clr, v easily, val further: hvly bckd: easy mdn wnr earlier: dam useful over 7/10f: stays a sharp
10f well, shld get further: relishes gd/soft & hvy: impressive here, looks well up to Gr race wng standard & must
be followed under similar conditions: see 1055.
980*　**BOWSTRING 22** [4] J H M Gosden 3-8-8　(95) L Dettori 7/1: 0-12: Led after 2f till 7f out, cl-up,　　**15**　**99**
lost place 2f out, some late gains: prob caught a high-class sort & ran to wng mdn form of 980.
923*　**MUTAFANEN 27** [1] E A L Dunlop 3-8-11　(100) R Hills 15/8: 04331-13: Led 2f, led again 7f out till　**1**　**101**
over 2f out, sn outpcd: bckd: prob caught a high-class sort & may prefer a sounder surface as in 923 (gd).
1040　**SKIDMARK 18** [2] D R C Elsworth 3-9-1　(102) K Fallon 7/2: 31-21134: Cl-up, rdn over 3f out, no　**5**　**100**
extra: v useful & prog earlier on polytrack, not enjoy this v testing grnd: worth another ch: see 1046, 727.
4 Ran　Time 2m 20.44 (16.44)　Owned: Sheikh Mohammed　Trained: Newmarket

---

1295　**2.55 Bet@Bluesq Com Great Metropolitan Stakes Handicap 3yo+ 0-95 (C)**　　　　　[95]
　　　　　£15892　£6028　£3014　　**1m4f10y**　　**Heavy**　　**Fair**　Centre

1112　**COLD TURKEY 11** [14] G L Moore 4-8-12　(79) S Whitworth 11/2 FAV: 2-113241: Held up, hdwy & short　**91**
of room 2f out, sn switched left & styd on well to lead over 1f out, rdn clr: eye-catching last time & most prog on
polytrack earlier: suited by 11/13f, not quite stay 2m: acts on firm soft & loves polytrack & sharp trks:
thriving, h'capped to win again on turf: see 1112, 475.
1006　**GENERAL GB 21** [18] N P Littmoden 7-8-3　(69) T P Queally(1) 20/1: 2/0/-12052: In tch, eff to lead　**3**　**75**
well over 1f out, sn hdd & not pace of wnr: acts on soft, hvy & fibresand: see 856, 811.
1111　**VENGEANCE 11** [13] Mrs A J Perrett 4-9-9　(90) Dane O'Neill 7/1: 12105-03: b c Fleetwood - Lady　1½　**95**
Isabell (Rambo Dancer) Chsd ldrs, eff over 2f out, kept on same pace: '03 auct mdn & dual h'cap scorer: suited by
12f on fast & hvy grnd, acts on any trk, likes a sharp one: useful, shld continue to give a gd account.
1 Jul'03 Wind 11.6g/f 90-83 D:　2 Jun'03 Newb 12.0g/f 87-79 D:　1 May'03 Good 12g/f 81-75 C:
1 May'03 Folk 9.7g/f 81- F:　2 Apr'03 Wind 10.0g/f 75- D:
695　**PAGAN DANCE 60** [11] Mrs A J Perrett 5-9-10 p (90) L Dettori 9/1: 01440-34: Held up, hdwy & badly　　½　**94**
bmpd over 2f out, sn hung left but kept on despite carrying head v awkwardly: 2 month abs: prob handles firm, hvy &
polytrack: talented but not easy ride: see 695.
1109　**CHAMPION LION 11** [6]5-8-4　(70) S Hitchcott(3) 14/1: 0050-005: b g Sadler's Wells - Honey Bun　**2**　**72**
(Unfuwain) Held up, eff well over 2f out, sn onepcd: plcd on 1 of 7 '03 starts (h'cap, rtd 81): '02 mdn wnr: eff
at 12/14f, poss stays 2m on fast & gd/soft, poss hvy: slipped down the weights.
1 Jul'02 Kemp 12g/s 86- D:　2 Jun'02 Kemp 12g/s 86- D:　2 May'02 Leic 11.8g/s 86- D:
964*　**OFARABY 23** [2]4-9-5　(86) P Robinson 13/2: 2164-316: Chsd ldrs, eff 2f out, no impress: longer trip.　½　**87**
1128　**LENNEL 9** [19]6-8-2 bl (68) F Norton 14/1: 60114-57: Held up, late gains, nvr a factor: see 1128.　1½　**67**
4954}　**INDIVIDUAL TALENTS 173** [8]4-8-2　(69) Martin Dwyer 10/1: 022513-8: ch f Distant View - Indigenous　**5**　**63**
(Lyphard) Bhd, mod late gains on reapp: '03 appr h'cap wnr, plcd sev times: eff at 10f, suited by 12f on gd grnd:
has run well fresh on any trk: no btr on a sounder surface.
1 Oct'03 Epso 12.0gd 68-60 E:　2 Jul'03 Yarm 10.1gd 61-57 E:　2 Jul'03 Nott 10.0gd 63-57 E:
918　**DANAKIL 27** [3]9-8-7　(73) R L Moore 20/1: 430-0009: b g Warning - Danilova (Lyphard) Bhd, nvr a　**1**　**66**
factor: plcd on last of 9 '03 starts (amat rider's h'cap, rtd 79 & 76a), also 4th in this race: '02 3 time h'cap
wnr: suited by 12f on fast or soft, both AWs & any trk, likes a sharp one: has run well fresh.
1 Sep'02 Asco 12g/f 86-80 D:　1 Sep'02 Epso 12gd 82-72 E:　1 Jul'02 Epso 12gd 73-67 E:
2 Jul'02 Sali 12gd 73-67 E:　2 Jan'02 Ling 12ap 73a-73 E:　1 Dec'01 Ling 12ap 70a-69 D:
1 Nov'01 Ling 12ap 70a-64 G:　2 Nov'01 Ling 10ap 66a-64 G:　2 Aug'01 Epso 10g/f 64-58 C:
1087　**MUSKATSTURM 14** [7]5-8-9　(75) S W Kelly 25/1: 14/000-00: 10th: Nvr a factor.　　　**4**　**63**
1056　**BUCKS 16** [16]7-8-5　(71) C Catlin 20/1: 2125-030: 11th: In tch, wknd 2f out: see 89 (mdn, f/sand).　**1**　**58**

877   **EZZ ELKHEIL 33** [9]5-8-8 (74) D Holland 16/1: 50-24300: 12th: Led 5f out till 2f out, wknd: best 478.   4   57
4939} **FOOTBALL CRAZY 175** [5]5-9-3 bl (83) K Fallon 14/1: 133200-0: 13th: In tch, btn 3f out: new yard.   7   59
1056   **PERSIAN KING 16** [15]7-9-1 (81) S Drowne 50/1: 02/050-00: 14th: Al bhd.   10   47
4356} **MEXICAN PETE 214** [12]4-8-9 (76) R Miles(3) 33/1: 421103-0: 15th: Nvr a factor: reapp.   10   32
4879} **JEEPSTAR 179** [17]4-8-10 (77) J Mackay 20/1: 121253-0: 16th: Led 7f, no extra: poss not handle hvy.   3   30
1112   **HEISSE 11** [10]4-10-0 VIS (95) J Murtagh 12/1: 120-500: 17th: Handy, wknd 4f out: visor, breathing probs.   2   46
4853} **STOLEN HOURS 182** [4]4-8-8 (75) T Quinn 33/1: 46434-0: 18th: Al bhd: jumps rnr, changed stable.   8   18
1286   **LUNAR LEADER 1** [20]4-7-12 p (65) Lisa Jones(3) 50/1: 20000-000: 19th: Al bhd: unplcd yesterday.   3½   4
4079} **SERGEANT CECIL 228** [1]5-9-8 (88) R Hughes 62/1: 121020-0: 20th: In tch, wknd over 4f out, t.o.   dist   0
20 Ran   Time 2m 53.93 (19.13)   Owned: Mr A Grinter   Trained: Brighton

---

1296   3.30 Blue Square City And Suburban Stakes Handicap 4yo+ 0-105 (B)   [104]
£17400 £6600 £3300   **1m2f18y**   **Heavy**   **Slow**   Inside

1111   **BLYTHE KNIGHT 11** [6] E A L Dunlop 4-9-9 (99) L Dettori 9/2 FAV: 50430-41: Held up, smooth hdwy   106
to trk ldrs 2f out, styd on strongly to lead fnl stride, drvn, gamely: well bckd: stays 12f, suited by 10f: acts on
firm & hvy, any trk: useful & improving, prob more to come, see 1111.
1111   **BONECRUSHER 11** [9] D R Loder 5-10-0 (104) J Murtagh 10/1: 40-64052: Held up, sltly short of room   shd   110
& switched 2f out, led ins fnl 1f, collared on line: bckd, top-weight: acts on fast, hvy, polytrack & any trk:
swished tail under press but a smart run under a big weight & well clr of rem.
4894} **SHAHZAN HOUSE 179** [5] M A Jarvis 5-9-4 (94) P Robinson 9/1: 2/60410-3: b c Sri Pekan - Nsx (Roi   5   94
Danzig) Prom, ev ch 2f out, left bhd by front 2 ins fnl 1f: reapp: '03 class stks wnr here at Epsom: '02 mdn wnr:
eff at 1m/10f on fast & hvy grnd, handles a sharp/undul or gall trk: decent reapp, spot on next time.
1 Sep'03 Epso 10.1gd 95-(91) C: 2 Jul'02 Newb 10g/f 95- C: 1 Jun'02 Sand 10g/s 92- D:
1111   **KINGS THOUGHT 11** [3] S Gollings 5-9-6 (96) D Holland 8/1: 0310-604: b c King's Theatre - Lora's   nk   96
Guest (Be My Guest) Led till ent fnl 1f, no extra: well clr rem: in fine form in '03, won 3 h'caps & a class stks:
eff at 1m/10f on firm, prefers gd, hvy grnd & polytrack: gd weight carrier who loves to dominate: tough but on
career h'cap mark. 1 Aug'03 Newm 10gd 97-88 C: 1 May'03 Ripo 10sft 88-82 D: 1 Mar'03 Ling 8ap 85a-(75) D:
1 Feb'03 Ling 8ap 80a-75 E: 1 Jun'02 Leic 8g/f 80- F:
1235   **SILVALINE 4** [1]5-7-13 (75) Dale Gibson 14/1: 33-60455: Chsd ldr, prom till wknd 2f out: quick   6   68
reapp: much softer grnd than prev encountered, see 900 (AW).
942   **SCOTTISH RIVER 25** [15]5-7-2 (1oh) (73) Hayley Turner(5) 50/1: 1511056: Rear, some late hdwy, nvr   1   66
dangerous: handles hvy grnd? btr 747 (AW).
1231   **NORTON 4** [10]7-9-6 (96) R Miles(3) 12/1: 0000-057: Chsd ldrs, nvr pace to chall: quick reapp: 2   85
btr dominating around 1m, fairly h'capped now: see 1231.
4684} **CROW WOOD 193** [12]5-9-2 (92) M Fenton 20/1: 101305-8: b g Halling - Play With Me (Alzao) Chsd   3   77
ldrs, btn 2f out on reapp: won 2 h'caps & a class stks in '03 (incl reapp): 10f specialist, likes to force the pace
on fast or gd/soft, handles f/sand: handles a sharp trk, loves a gall one: sharper next time back on faster grnd.
1 Aug'03 Ayr 10gd 93-(85) D: 1 Jun'03 Hayd 10.5g/f 89-79 C: 1 May'03 Donc 10.3gd 81-72 C:
1 Jul'02 Ches 10.3fm 76-71 D: 1 May'02 Leic 10g/s 72-66 D: 2 May'02 Newc 10.1g/f 67- E: 1 Aug'01 Wolv 7af 79a- D:
1804} **RECOUNT 328** [16]4-8-1 (1ow) (77) N Pollard 14/1: 101450-9: b g Sillery - Dear Countess (Fabulous   11   48
Dancer) Dsptd lead early, lost place halfway, no ch after on reapp: bckd at long odds: won a class stks & h'cap in
'03: suited by 12f, acts on gd & fast, sharp or gall trk: not handle hvy?
1 Apr'03 Leic 11.8gd 74-70 C: 1 Mar'03 Muss 12g/f 70-(60) F:
1128   **CLASSIC ROLE 9** [4]5-8-3 vis (79) J Quinn 8/1: 0341220: 10th: Nvr nrr than mid-div: btr 1128.   1½   48
816   **MAD CAREW 44** [14]5-8-3 bl e (79) R L Moore 25/1: 22-51040: 11th: Al bhd, t.o.: 6 wk abs.   11   34
5036} **HARCOURT 165** [2]4-8-12 (88) K Fallon 10/1: 52/310-0: 12th: b c Cozzene - Ballinamallard (Tom   5   37
Rolfe) Chsd ldrs, wknd 3f out, eased on reapp: won middle of 3 '03 starts (h'cap): eff at 10f on fast & gd/soft
grnd: lightly rcd & clrly had probs. 1 Apr'03 Newm 10gd 91-80 C: 2 Oct'02 Yarm 8g/s 83- D:
1104   **ARRY DASH 11** [13]4-8-11 (87) T E Durcan 6/1: 015-4020: 13th: Rear, short of rm ent str, nvr dngrs.   2   34
758   **NORTHSIDE LODGE 53** [11]6-8-7 (83) Martin Dwyer 12/1: 04-22030: 14th: Chsd ldrs till halfway,   28   0
wknd, eased & t.o.: 8 wk abs: consistent on a sound surface: see 758 & 519 (AW).
4939} **PRAIRIE WOLF 175** [8]8-8-10 (86) I Mongan 33/1: 032320-0: 15th: Al bhd, t.o. on reapp.   1½   0
1139   **CORRIOLANUS 9** [7]4-10-0 BL (104) J Fanning 25/1: 263-3000: 16th: Chsd ldr till halfway,   14   0
wknd qckly, eased & t.o.: top weight, tried blnks: reportedly lost action.
16 Ran   Time 2m 21.6 (17.8)   Owned: Maktoum Al Maktoum   Trained: Newmarket

---

1297   4.00 Drivers Jonas Maiden Stakes 3yo+ (D)
£5369 £1652 £826   **1m114y rnd**   **Heavy**   **Slow**   Inside

1125   **CELLO 9** [10] R Hannon 3-8-9 (78) P Dobbs 7/4 FAV: 6355-21: Trkd ldr, led halfway, styd on   86
strongly despiting drifting left fnl 1f, rdn out: bckd from 9/4: apprec step up to 1m: handles firm, acts on gd &
revels in hvy: handles any trk: ran green, but took advantage of race fitness: see 1125.
4056} **DESERT CRISTAL 230** [5] J R Boyle 3-8-4 Martin Dwyer 11/4: 25-2: ch f Desert King - Damiana   2   77
(Thatching) Trkd ldrs, chsd wnr 2f out, kept on but not pace of wnr, well clr of 3rd, reapp: eye-catching rnr-up
on 1st of 2 juv starts (mdn): stays a sharp 1m, acts on gd & hvy grnd: has shown enough to find similar.
2 Aug'03 Wind 6gd 78- D:
713   **RESPLENDENT KING 57** [7] T G Mills 3-8-9 (69) R Miles(3) 7/1: 40-33553: Led till halfway, wknd: 8   13   64
wk abs: ran as well as could be expected at today's weights: see 455 (AW).
175   **EMBASSY SWEETS 133** [2] P F I Cole 3-8-4 R L Moore 20/1: 00-4: b f Affirmed - Leaveemlaughing   ½   58
(Dynaformer) Rear, short of room & switched 2f out, mod late gains on reapp: mod AW mdn form on 2 '03 starts.
4750} **SECOND WARNING 189** [1]3-8-9 C Catlin 33/1: 000-5: ch c Piccolo - St Helena (Monsanto) Chsd   shd   63
ldrs, wknd qckly 2f out on reapp: mod '03 mdn form for D Daly.
3471} **MOSCOW BLUE 257** [3]3-8-9 R Hughes 3/1: 00-6: ch c Soviet Star - Aquamarine (Shardari) Chsd   2½   59
ldrs, rdn & wknd 2f out: nicely bckd, reapp: unplcd in a Newmarket mdn on sole juv start: bred to apprec 1m.
1130   **TSARBUCK 9** [6]3-8-9 Dale Gibson 50/1: 0-07: Al bhd, t.o.   19   35
333}   **BOOZY DOUZ 470** [4]4-9-5 S Drowne 50/1: 00/0-8: Al well bhd, t.o. on reapp.   21   4
8 Ran   Time 1m 56.63 (14.83)   Owned: Mr Louis Stalder   Trained: Marlborough

EPSOM   WEDNESDAY 21.04.04   Lefthand, Very Sharp, Undulating Track

1298   4.30 Philip Hall Memorial Classified Stakes 3yo+ 0-70 (E)
£4745 £1460 £730   1m114y rnd   **Heavy   Slow**   Inside

934   **TIGER TIGER 26** [2] Jamie Poulton 3-8-4 (72) J F Egan 7/1: 0-131: Held up, hdwy to lead after   **85**
halfway & styd far rail, rdn well clr fnl 1f: eff over a sharp 1m, 10f looks sure to suit: acts on polytrack,
revels in hvy grnd: likes a sharp trk: proved a class above today's rivals on turf bow.
878*   **THE GAIKWAR 33** [10] N E Berry 5-9-3 bl (68) M Savage(5) 14/1: 6425012: Chsd ldrs, came stands side   12   **69**
2f out, kept on but no ch with facile wnr on far side fnl 1f: prev trained by N Littmoden: handles hvy grnd, acts
on fast, gd & polytrack: met a fast imprvg rival, see 878 (AW clmr).
1092   **COOL TEMPER 13** [8] P F I Cole 8-9-3 (69) K Fallon 3/1 FAV: 40336-53: Chsd ldrs, styd far side &   ¾   **68**
left bhd by wnr over 1f out: well bckd: see 141 (AW).
1131   **GRACIA 9** [4] S C Williams 5-9-0 (66) Martin Dwyer 5/1: 1003-004: gr f Linamix - Francia (Legend   3½   **60**
of France) Chsd ldrs & styd far side, btn 2f out: won a fills h'cap here at Epsom in '03, also plcd sev times: eff
at 1m/10f on fast & soft grnd: likes to run up with/force the pace & any trk: btr than this.
1 Jul'03 Epso 8.5g/f 69-63 D: 1 Sep'02 Epso 10g/f 65-60 D: 1 Aug'02 Beve 9.9g/f 61-54 F:
1042   **DEEPER IN DEBT 18** [9]6-9-3 (70) G Carter 12/1: 12-24335: Chsd ldrs & wide into str, btn 2f out.   ½   **62**
1059   **LIBERTY ROYAL 16** [7]5-9-3 (66) S Sanders 20/1: 0000-606: b g Ali Royal - Hope Chest (Kris) Led   3   **58**
till after halfway, came stands side, sn wknd: 4th in a class stks in '03 (rtd 81): rnr-up in '02 (stks): '01 mdn
wnr: prob stays 10f & acts on polytrack, handles firm: can run well fresh: with P Makin.
2 Mar'02 Ling 8ap 93a- B: 1 Nov'01 Ling 8ap 78a- D:
1043* **LYGETON LAD 18** [5]6-9-7 t (74) M Fenton 5/1: 1-556517: Al bhd under top weight: prob not handle hvy.   7   **52**
1042   **KATIYPOUR 18** [6]7-9-5 (72) R Miles(3) 4/1: 46-03128: Trkd ldrs, led briefly after halfway & came   6   **40**
stands side, wknd qckly: not handle hvy? much btr 1042 & 932 (AW).
978   **VOICE MAIL 22** [1]5-9-3 (68) L Keniry(3) 12/1: 44550-09: Al bhd, styd far side, t.o.: see 978.   15   **0**
9 Ran   Time 1m 57.06(15.26)   Owned: Mr R W Huggins   Trained: Lewes

LEOPARDSTOWN   SUNDAY 18.04.04   Lefthand, Galloping Track

Official Going Soft

1299   2.30 Foxtrot 3yo Maiden ()
£7186 £1674 £7384   **7f   Soft**

LAST LOVE 28 A P O'Brien 3-8-11 J P Spencer 6/4 FAV: 21: b f Danehill - Summerosa (Woodman)   **99**
Led till hdd dist, rallied to lead cl home, rdn out: earlier rnr up on debut in Curragh mdn: eff at 7f/1m on soft &
hvy: lightly rcd, genuine & useful.
HAMAIRI 14 John M Oxx 3-9-2 M J Kinane 2/1: 42: ch c Spectrum - Haridaza (Be My Guest) Handy,   shd   **102**
styd on to lead dist, hdd cl home: clr rem: earlier 4th of 27 on debut at Curragh (mdn): eff at 7f/1m on soft
grnd: handled on a 6f baried course: useful, must win sn.
INDIAN PACE 183 D K Weld 3-9-2 P J Smullen 7/1: 2-3: ch c Indian Ridge - Blend Of Pace   5   **92**
(Sadler's Wells) In tch, kept on fnl 1f for clr 3rd, no ch with front two: reapp.
16 Ran   Time 1m 36.50 ()   Owned: Mrs John Magnier   Trained: Ballydoyle, Co Tipp

1300   3.00 Listed Fillies 1,000 Guineas Trial   (A)
£21157 £6207 £2957   **7f   Soft**

895   **ROYAL TIGRESS 28** A P O'Brien 3-8-11 J P Spencer 5/2 JT FAV: 2-31: b f Storm Cat - Warm Mood   **107**
(Alydar) Handy, chsd ldr dist, drvn out to lead cl home: rnr up on sole '03 start (mdn): eff at 7f/1m on gd & hvy
grnd: acts on a gall trk: improving & useful, now heads for Irish 1,000 Guineas.
4935} **TAKRICE 28** Kevin Prendergast 3-8-11 D P McDonogh 11/1: 143-02: b f Cadeaux Genereux - Hasanat   shd   **106**
(Night Shift) In tch, prog to lead dist, hdd cl home: Galway mdn wnr in '03 (also 4th of 13 in Gr 3): eff at 7f on
fast & soft grnd, 1m suit: only just denied & can find similar.
4404} **MISTY HEIGHTS 210** D K Weld 3-8-11 P J Smullen 3/1: 3142-3: b f Fasliyev - Mountains Of Mist   2   **102**
(Shirley Heights) Bhd, prog & ev ch dist, not pace front 2 ins fnl 1f.
2 Sun'21 Curr 7g/f 102- A:
7 Ran   Time 1m 39.20 ()   Owned: Mrs John Magnier   Trained: Ballydoyle, Co Tipp

1301   4.00 Listed Colt & Geldings 2,000 Guineas Trial   (A)
£21157 £6207 £2957   **1m   Soft**

4935*}**GREY SWALLOW 174** D K Weld 3-9-2 P J Smullen 4/9 FAV: 11-1: gr c Daylami - Style Of Life (The   **116+**
Minstrel) Mid div, prog to lead ins fnl 1f, rdn out, more in hand: won both '03 starts (mdn & Gr 3, easily): eff at
7f/1m, shld stay 10f: acts on gd & soft: goes well fresh: unbtn & high-class, will reportedly come on plenty for this
& looks poised for a v big run in the Newmarket 2,000 Guineas. 1 Mon'27 Leop 7gd 121- :
MEATH 183 A P O'Brien 3-8-11 J P Spencer 3/1: 31-2: b c Sadler's Wells - Twyla (Habitat) Led   hd   **108**
6f, styd on fnl 1f, just held: reapp: mdn wnr on 1 of 2 '03 starts: eff at 7f/1m on fast & soft, will stay
further: useful run bhd a high-class start, win a Listed race.
1063   **AMARULA RIDGE 14** Kevin Prendergast 3-8-11 D P McDonogh 8/1: 1-33: b c Indian Ridge - Mail Boat   3½   **101**
(Formidable) Prom, led 2f out, hdd ins fnl 1f, no extra.
5 Ran   Time 1m 51.70 ()   Owned: Mrs Rochelle Quinn   Trained: The Curragh, Co Kild

1302   **5.00 Group 3 P W McGrath Ballysax 3yo Stakes**   **(A)**
£31440 £8690 £4140   1m2f   **Soft**

4403*)YEATS 210 A P O'Brien 3-9-0 J P Spencer 1/3 FAV: 1-1: b c Sadler's Wells - Lyndonville (Top   120+
Ville) Led & al trav easily, pushed clr ins fnl 2f, canter, val further: mdn wnr sole '03 start: eff at 1m/10f, will
relish 12f (dam 14f wnr): acts on fast & soft: goes well fresh: v impressive here, unbtn & looks top-class,
justifiably Epsom Derby favourite. 1 Sun'21 Curr 8g/f 102- :
1063 **DABIROUN 14** John M Oxx 3-9-0 M J Kinane 5/2: 122: b c Desert Prince - Dabaya (In The Wings)   10   106
Chsd wnr, kept on but al held by v easy wnr fnl 2f: longer trip: see 1063.
2 Sun'04 Curr 7sft 110- :
       LORD ADMIRAL 239 Charles O'Brien 3-9-0 F M Berry 20/1: 510-3: b c El Prado - Lady Ilsley   14   86
(Trempolino) Bhd, eff 4f out, fdd fnl 3f.
3 Ran   Time 2m 23.5()   Owned: Mrs John Magnier   Trained: Ballydoyle, Co Tipp

---

Official Going Good/Soft (Soft places)

1303   **2.20 We Appreciate Our Wives Claiming Stakes 2yo**   **(F)**
£3045 £870 £435   5f rnd   **Soft 102**   -100 Slow   Inside

1173 **WHY HARRY 7** [5] J J Quinn 2-8-13 R Winston 15/8 FAV: 301: Handy, hdwy & short of room over 1f   67
out, styd on to lead ins last, hands & heels: eff at 5f on fibresand & soft: enjoyed drop into claim grade.
       STORY OF ONE [3] Ronald Thompson 2-9-1 Dean McKeown 25/1: 2: b g Desert Story - One O One   nk   67
(Wolfhound) Sn rdn bhd, hdwy 2f out, hung right but styd on ins last, just held: debut, clmd for 10,000: April
foal, cheaply bght: eff at 5f, sure to relish 6f: acts on soft grnd: learn plenty from this encouraging start.
1123 **STRAFFAN 10** [7] E J O'Neill 2-8-10 J Carroll 7/2: 63: b f Shinko Forest - Katherine Gorge   3½   55
(Hansel) Cl-up, led dist, hdd & no extra ins last: Jan foal: half-sister to a 6f/1m wnr: best kept to this grade.
1224 **FOLD WALK 5** [1] M W Easterby 2-8-6 P Mulrennan(3) 50/1: 04: ch f Paris House - Georgia (Missed   2   47
Flight) Slow away & bhd, late gains, nvr dngrs: April first foal: bred to apprec 6/7f & a hint of ability here.
1161 **FRISBY RIDGE 8** [4]2-8-10 D Allan(3) 10/1: 05: b f Monashee Mountain - Suave Lady (Suave Dancer)   2½   46
In tch, hmpd start, hdwy & hard drvn when no room over 1f out, not recover: Jan first foal, cost 3,000gns: btr than
finishing position indicates.
1133* **VON WESSEX 10** [2]2-9-1 A Quinn(5) 11/4: 6516: Prom, wknd dist: not enjoy soft? btr 1133 (fast).   2   47
       HUNIPOT [8]2-9-0 T Eaves(5) 14/1: 7: Al bhd.   nk   45
1224 **OUR LOUIS 5** [6]2-8-10 L Enstone(3) 20/1: 68: Led till over 1f out, wknd.   1   39
8 Ran   Time 1m 11.4 (10.1)   Owned: Mr Derrick Bloy   Trained: Malton

1304   **2.50 Constant Security Maiden Stakes 3yo+**   **(D)**
£4186 £1288 £644   1m100y rnd   **Soft 102**   -13 Slow   Inside

1086 **CESARE 15** [8] J R Fanshawe 3-8-11 J Murtagh 1/2 FAV: 21: Handy, gd hdwy over 2f out, led on bit   83+
ins last, v easily, val 4L+: eff at 1m, sure to relish 10f: acts on soft grnd & prob any trk: plenty more to come
& can win again: see 1086.
       CHANTELOUP [10] J R Fanshawe 3-8-6 K Darley 8/1: 2: ch f Grand Lodge - Nibbs Point (Sure   1¾   70
Blade) Held up, hdwy over 2f out, kept on fnl 1f, not pace of winning stablemate, hands & heels: op 4/1: half-sister
to a smart mid-dist performer: stays 8.5f on soft: gd start, likely plenty more to come.
1177 **PREMIER DREAM 7** [7] M Johnston 3-8-11 J Fanning 14/1: 663: ch c Woodman - Marina Duff   1   73
(Caerleon) Set pace, rdn & hdd ins last, no extra: stays a stiff/undul 8.5f on soft grnd.
       ESTEPONA [9] Miss J A Camacho 3-8-11 J Quinn 50/1: 4: ch g Polar Falcon - Kingdom Ruby   shd   73
(Bluebird) Slow away & bhd, hdwy 2f out, drvn & some late gains on debut: some promise here over this stiff/undul
8.5f on soft grnd: open to improvement.
5024} **SNOWED UNDER 167** [5]3-8-11 C Catlin 66/1: 0-5: Bhd, late gains, nvr dngrs under hands & heels.   1¼   71$
4002} **KALISHKA 234** [2]3-8-11 W Supple 33/1: 000-6: Chsd ldrs, onepace fnl 2f on reapp.   ½   70$
1108 **TOP ACHIEVER 12** [3]3-8-11 R Winston 25/1: 5-07: Chsd ldrs, wknd over 1f out.   ½   69$
966   **LUCKY PISCEAN 24** [12]3-8-11 K Dalgleish 20/1: 58: In tch, wknd over 2f out: see 966.   7   57
1121 **ILLICIUM 11** [1]5-9-6 J Carroll 50/1: 69: Slow away & al bhd: see 1121.   11   36
4851} **ADEES DANCER 183** [4]3-8-6 R Ffrench 8/1: 4-0: 10th: In tch, wknd over 2f out.   1   34
5017} **LETS PARTY 168** [6]4-9-6 t (52) D Allan(3) 66/1: 400400-0: 11th: Chsd ldr, wknd 2f out.   7   22
11 Ran   Time 1m 53.59 (9.79)   Owned: Cheveley Park Stud   Trained: Newmarket

1305   **3.20 Jaguar Centre Stakes Handicap 3yo+ 0-90**   **(C)**   [97]
£9487 £2919 £1460   7f100y rnd   **Soft 102**   +10 Fast   Inside

1105* **IMPERIALISTIC 12** [3] K R Burke 3-9-7 p (90) K Dalgleish 9/4 JT FAV: 3423-411: Chsd ldrs, hdwy to   96
chall appr fnl 1f, kept on to lead cl-home, hard drvn: gd time: v eff arnd 7.5f/1m & enjoys soft grnd, acts on gd:
handles any trk, likes Haydock & wears cheek pieces: useful, lightly rcd & progressive: see 1105.
1089 **MAN OF LETTERS 15** [5] M Johnston 3-8-4 (73) R Ffrench 7/2: 5-432: Chsd ldr, led 2f out, kept on   shd   78
till collared cl-home, drvn & just held: gd run, can win a mdn or h'cap: see 1089, 919.
1080* **WISTMAN 15** [6] D R Loder 3-8-11 (80) J Murtagh 9/4 JT FAV: 13: Handy, hdwy & switched left over   1¾   81
1f out, onepace: clr of rem on h'cap bow & stays 7.5f on gd/soft & soft: lightly rcd, see 1080.
955   **KINGSMAITE 26** [1] S R Bowring 3-8-5 (74) J Bramhill 8/1: 64212-04: In tch, no extra over 1f out: 8   63
btr 226 (fibresand), 184.
841   **WAVERTREE GIRL 39** [2]3-8-11 (80) K Darley 20/1: 3404-305: Al bhd: see 764 (polytrack).   1½   67
4845} **VADEMECUM 183** [7]3-8-13 (82) F Lynch 16/1: 0413-6: br g Shinko Forest - Sunshine Coast (Posse)   1½   67
Led till 2f out, wknd: '03 mdn auct wnr: eff at 7f on firm grnd & a gall trk: can front run: been gelded.

1 Oct'03 Newc 7fm 82- E:
1105 **ROYAL DISTANT 12** [4]3-8-10 (79) Dale Gibson 16/1: 63124-67: Al bhd: see 1105.   hd   64
7 Ran   Time 1m 37.69 (6.89)   Owned: Bigwigs Bloodstock II   Trained: Leyburn

1306	3.50 Birthday Celebration Handicap Stakes 3yo 0-75 (E)					**[82]**
	£4550 £1400 £700	1m1f207y	Soft 102	+ 03 Fast	Inside	

1007 **ANOTHER CHOICE 22** [1] N P Littmoden 3-8-12 t (66) K Darley 6/1: 06000-31: Qckly away & trkd ldrs,   78+
went on dist, rdn well clr: eff at 1m, apprec this step up to 10f: acts on firm & soft grnd, handles a stiff fin:
wears a t-strap: impressed here from a poor low draw: can defy a pen, see 1007.
1144 **ATHOLLBROSE 10** [10] T D Easterby 3-8-2 (56) J Quinn 12/1: 400-42: Chsd ldr, went on 2f out till   7   57
collared dist, sn left bhd by wnr: eff at 10f on soft grnd: met an improving rival, see 1144.
4808} **DUNLEA DANCER 185** [12] M Johnston 3-8-2 (56) R Ffrench 10/1: 50500-3: b g Groom Dancer - Be My 1½   55
Lass (Be My Guest) Chsd ldrs, onepcd fnl 2f: reapp: modest '03 form: 11,000gns half-brother to wnrs over 6/12f:
dam a mid-dist wnr: prob stays 10f on soft grnd: sharper next time.
1124 **THE KING OF ROCK 10** [7] A G Newcombe 3-8-3 (57) S Whitworth 9/2 CO FAV: 2000-054: b c Nicolotte 1¼ 54
- Lv Girl (Mukaddamah) Held up, prog to chase ldrs 2f out, sn no impress: tchd 7/1: rnr-up in '03 (clmr, first
time visor, with G Balding): eff at 7f, prob stays 11f, acts on gd grnd, prob soft: has tried blnks/visor.
2 Aug'03 Ches 7.0gd 65-(52) D:
966 **NAFFERTON HEIGHTS 24** [2]3-7-12 (52) Dale Gibson 20/1: 000-05: b c Peintre Celebre - Gold Mist   1½   47
(Darshaan) Led till 2f out, grad wknd: op 14/1: unplcd in 3 '03 mdn starts: rcd too keenly in this soft grnd.
1280 **PLATINUM PIRATE 2** [8]3-8-7 (6ex)vis (61) F Lynch 9/2 CO FAV: 0-202136: Keen in rear, nvr nr ldrs: 3   52
nicely bckd, qck reapp: btr 1280 & 1144.
3424} **OUR KID 260** [3]3-8-10 (64) D Allan(3) 40/1: 6640-7: Slowly away, late prog, nvr dngrs: stablemate of 2nd. ¾ 54
1099* **TIME TO RELAX 14** [9]3-8-12 (66) K Dalgleish 9/2 CO FAV: 600-2418: Rdn rear, nvr nr ldrs: btr 1099. 2 53
1067 **HERNANDOS BOY 16** [5]3-8-8 (62) J Carroll 12/1: 000-59: Rear, hdwy wide 2f out, btn dist: op 8/1.   6   41
1022 **RAHEED 20** [6]3-8-12 (66) W Supple 11/1: 46-60: 10th: Chsd ldrs, wknd 2f out on h'cap bow.   5   38
4845} **NAMED AT DINNER 183** [4]3-9-7 (75) G Duffield 25/1: 04224-0: 11th: Prom 7f, wknd on reapp: gelded. 5 40
1039 **BABOUSHKA 19** [11]3-8-5 (59) R Winston 14/1: 04-00: 12th: Nvr btr than mid-div, t.o. fnl 1f.   18   0
12 Ran   Time 2m 12.26 (9.96)   Owned: Mr A A Goodman   Trained: Newmarket

1307	4.20 Racing Again On Saturday 8th May Handicap Stakes Fillies 4yo+ 0-70 (E)					**[69]**
	£3679 £1132 £566	1m1f207y	Soft 102	-18 Slow	Inside	

1036 **MEGANS MAGIC 19** [8] W Storey 4-9-5 (60) J Bramhill 9/1: 01542-61: b f Blue Ocean - Hot Sunday   71
Sport (Star Appeal) Slowly away, gd hdwy when short of room 1.5f out, styd on strongly to lead cl-home, won going
away: '03 h'cap wnr, also plcd several times: eff at 7/10f, has tried 12f: acts on fast & soft grnd, likes
stiff/undul trks: showed a decent turn of foot to overcome trouble today.
2 Oct'03 Newm 8gd 59-59 E: 1 Oct'03 Pont 8.0g/f 58-50 D: 2 Jul'03 Newc 10.1g/s 52-49 E:
893 **GOT TO BE CASH 31** [6] W M Brisbourne 5-7-13 (40) B Swarbrick(7) 13/2 FAV: 60260-42: Mid-div, prog 3   46
& ev ch 2f out, led ins fnl 1f, not pace to repel wnr cl-home: op 11/2: acts on firm & soft grnd: see 893.
1135 **TRANSCENDANTALE 10** [7] Mrs S Lamyman 6-8-0 (1ow) (40) C Catlin 7/1: 50000-23: Chsd ldrs, styd on 1   46
under press fnl 1f, nrst fin: tchd 12/1: acts on fast, soft & f/sand: worth another try over 12f, see 1135.
1223 **JADE STAR 9** [9] Miss Gay Kelleway 4-8-12 (53) F Lynch 12/1: 5-410264: Led till ins fnl 1f, no   1¾   55
extra: qck reapp: see 961 (AW).
4855} **UNTIDY DAUGHTER 183** [13]5-9-0 BL (55) T Eaves(5) 7/1: 4050/00-5: b f Sabrehill - Branitska   ¾   57
(Mummy's Pet) Chsd ldrs, onepcd fnl 1.5f: tchd 12/1, first time blnks: jumps fit, h'cap hdle wnr, also plcd sev
times (eff at 2m/2m5f on fast & soft, rtd 110h): well btn in '03, incl in cheek pieces: prob eff at 10f on soft.
4622} **LIFE IS BEAUTIFUL 199** [1]5-8-5 (40) Dale Gibson 10/1: 062010-6: b f Septieme Ciel - Palombella   nk   46
(Groom Dancer) Chsd ldrs 1m, grad wknd: tchd 16/1, reapp: '03 sell wnr here at Beverley: '02 h'cap (2) & sell
wnr: eff at 12f on fast & gd/soft grnd, stiff/gall trk: suited by sell grade & Beverley.
1 Sep'03 Beve 12.1g/s 46-(43) G: 2 Aug'03 Redc 11g/f 45-41 E: 1 Sep'02 Beve 12g/f 55- G: 1 Jul'02 Beve 12gd 55-50 F:
1 May'02 Carl 9.2g/s 57-51 E:
5021} **OLIVIA ROSE 168** [4]5-9-5 (60) J Quinn 9/1: 000452-7: Held up, not pace to chall on reapp.   1¾   57
ACOLA 108 [15]4-9-5 (60) J Murtagh 20/1: 000-08: Chsd ldrs, onepcd over 2f out: long abs.   shd   57
1200 **DESIRES DESTINY 6** [3]6-8-4 (45) T Williams 33/1: 00-60639: Keen rear, nvr nr ldrs: qck reapp.   nk   41
4427} **UNO MENTE 211** [2]5-9-7 (62) Kim Tinkler 40/1: 301350-0: 10th: Al bhd on seasonal bow.   ¾   56
852* **DASH OF MAGIC 39** [5]6-8-4 (45) G Duffield 15/2: 0-162510: 11th: Nvr btr than mid-div: btr 852 (AW). 2½ 35
1083 **HALF INCH 15** [14]4-9-5 p (60) W Supple(3) 15/2: 0024-040: 12th: Chsd ldrs 1m, wknd: see 1083.   ½   49
4615} **DORMY TWO 199** [10]4-9-0 p (55) G Parkin 33/1: 340-0: 13th: Al bhd: jumps fit, new stable.   5   37
1059 **KARATHAENA 17** [11]4-9-10 (61) H Gemberlu(7) 16/1: 503-0000: 14th: Well bhd under top-weight.   1   46
3983} **GREEN OCEAN 236** [12]4-9-3 (58) R Winston 20/1: 556-0: 15th: Chsd ldrs till halfway, wknd: reapp.   hd   38
15 Ran   Time 2m 14.32 (12.02)   Owned: Steve Howard And Tony Peters   Trained: Consett

1308	4.50 Go Racing In Yorkshire Season Ticket Median Auction Maiden Stakes 3yo (E)					
	£3523 £1084 £542	1m4f16y	Soft 102	-67 Slow	Inside	

1153 **VANTAGE 9** [1] N P Littmoden 3-9-0 (80) K Darley 10/11 FAV: 330-2231: Trkd ldrs, went on 3f out,   80
rdn clr fnl 1f: bckd from 11/8, slow time: deserved win, eff at 10/12f on fast, soft & polytrack: see 1153 & 817 (AW).
1147 **HOLLY WALK 10** [2] M Dods 3-8-9 BL (50) L Enstone(3) 40/1: 0004-02: ch f Dr Fong - Holly Blue   7   65$
(Bluebird) Trkd ldrs, kept on fnl 1f but no ch with wnr: tried blnks: 4th on fnl '03 start (nursery, rtd 48, with
R Hannon): eff at 1m on gd grnd, prob handles soft: offic rtd 50.
1067 **AT YOUR REQUEST 16** [3] E A L Dunlop 3-9-0 W Supple 7/4: 33: Led after 4f till 3f out, wknd: op   14   56
11/8: much btr expected after 1067 (10f, debut).
1067 **SERENGETI SKY 16** [4] D R Loder 3-9-0 J Murtagh 5/1: 04: br c Southern Halo - Genovefa (Woodman)   18   38
Led early, remained prom till wknd 3f out, t.o. in last: clearly one of stable's lesser lights: see 1067.
4 Ran   Time 2m 51.63(20.33)   Owned: Mr Mark Harniman   Trained: Newmarket

Official Going STANDARD.

1309
5.45 #10 Free Bet @ Betdirect Co Uk Banded Stakes 3yo+ 0-35 (H)
£1425 £407 £204 **5f aw rnd** **Going 63** -05 Slow Inside

1199 **TUSCAN DREAM 6** [2] A Berry 9-9-7 (35) P Bradley(5) 5/2 JT FAV: 0002251: Led 2f, rallied to lead | | **40a**
again dist, rdn out: qck reapp: best dominating over a sharp 5f, likes firm, fast & fibresand: has run some gd
races in this grade & deserved this: see 981 & 904.
1199 **LEVELLED 6** [6] D W Chapman 10-9-7 (35) A Culhane 5/2 JT FAV: 0045502: In tch, led 3f out, hdd | 1¼ | **35a**
dist, kept on but not pace of wnr: clr rem, qck reapp: acts on firm, gd/soft & both AWs: see 832.
983 **VAUDEVIRE 23** [7] R P Elliott 3-8-11 BL (30) T Hamilton(3) 16/1: 6-603: b g Dancing Spree - | 5 | **20a**
Approved Quality (Persian Heights) Handy, no extra fnl 2f: unplcd sole '03 start (mdn, A Berry): gldd since '03.
1201 **BOND DOMINGO 6** [4] B Smart 5-9-7 vis (35) M Stainton(7) 3/1: 00-00364: In tch, no extra fnl 2f. | ½ | **19a**
1065 **DANCING RIDGE 16** [1]7-9-7 (30) P Hanagan 14/1: 36/00-005: Cl-up 2f, sn no extra: see 822. | 1¼ | **15a**
483 **MESMERISED 87** [5]4-9-7 p (30) Ann Stokell 12/1: 00-00006: b f Merdon Melody - Gracious Imp (Imp | 5 | **0a**
Society) Prom 3f, sn fdd: 12 wk abs: plcd 3 times in '03 (clmrs, rtd 51, A Berry): claim & sell wnr in '02: eff
at 5/6.9f on fast grnd: has tried cheek pieces: with Miss A Stokell.
2 Jun'03 Wolv 6af 57a-(40) F: 1 Jun'02 York 6mf 74- E: 2 Jun'02 Leic 5g/f 78- E: 1 May'02 Thir 5g/f 65- E:
764 **LITTLETON LIBERTY 53** [3]3-8-11 P (35) T P Queally(3) 7/1: 40-07: Mid-div, fdd 2f out: abs. | 7 | **0a**
7 Ran Time 1m 03.62 (3.42) Owned: Galaxy Moss Side Racing Clubs Limited Trained: Cockerham

---

1310
6.15 #10 Free Bet @ Betdirect Co Uk Claiming Stakes 3yo+ (H)
£1439 £411 £206 **6f aw rnd** **Going 63** +05 Fast Inside

976 **PEDRO JACK 23** [6] B J Meehan 7-9-8 (83) J F McDonald(5) 5/6 FAV: 30300-01: b g Mujadil - Festival | | **56a**
of Light (High Top) Cl-up, styd on well to lead cl home, rdn out: clmd for 5,000: AW h'cap wnr in '03 (also plcd
twice on turf, rtd 82): AW h'cap wnr in '02: stays 7f, all wins have come at 6f: acts on firm & gd, loves
fibresand/Wolverhampton: eff with/without blnks, best without visor & t-strap: apprec drop to claim grade.
1 Mar'03 Wolv 6af 86a-77 D: 2 Oct'02 York 6fm 81- D: 2 Sep'02 Redc 6fm 79-76 D: 1 Feb'02 Wolv 6af 86a-78 D:
1 Dec'01 Wolv 6af 82a-73 E: 2 Nov'01 Wolv 6af 76a- D: 1 Oct'01 Wolv 6af 72a-65 F: 2 Aug'01 Bath 5.7g/f 68- E:
1032* **ON THE TRAIL 20** [2] D W Chapman 7-9-8 (50) A Culhane 7/2: 0001312: Led, edged right under press | nk | **55a**
ins fnl 2f, hdd cl-home: lost little in defeat & imprvd on win in 1032.
1065 **SPEEDFIT FREE 16** [1] Mrs N Macauley 7-9-4 bl (52) P Hanagan 7/1: 5624003: Handy, outpcd after 2f, | nk | **50a**
rallied dist, kept on well fnl 1f, just btn in 3-way photo: clmd for 3,000: just btr 851 & 308.
1218 **TEYAAR 5** [4] Mrs N Macauley 8-9-8 (53) Hayley Turner(5) 7/1: 6005024: Cl-up, onepcd ins fnl 1f: | 1¼ | **50a**
qck reapp: clmd for 3,000: just btr 1218.
844 **PIPS SONG 39** [1]9-9-2 (50) R Miles(3) 14/1: 0100305: Handy, no extra dist: btr 819. | 3½ | **34a**
5 Ran Time 1m 16.32 (3.52) Owned: Mr Michael F B Peart Trained: Upper Lambourn

---

1311
6.45 Betdirect Co Uk Tri-Banded Stakes 3yo 0-45 (H)
£1421 £406 £203 **1m1f79y aw** **Going 63** -14 Slow Inside

1203 **SECRET BLOOM 6** [6] J R Norton 3-9-0 vis (45) J F Egan 11/10 FAV: 4054241: Cl-up, led 3f out, | | **51a+**
pushed out, val 5L+: well bckd, qck reapp: eff arnd 1m, stays 9.4f: acts on f/sand, eff with visor, see 986.
1108 **TRUE TO YOURSELF 12** [5] J G Given 3-9-0 (45) A Culhane 7/2: 000-02: b g Royal Academy - Romilly | 3 | **45a**
(Machiavellian) Cl-up, saddle slipped ins fnl 2f, sn onepcd: tchd 5/2: unplcd in all 3 '03 starts (rtd 41a & 13,
mdns): eff at 9.4f on fibresand: far run in circumstances.
1051 **ROYAL UPSTART 17** [3] W M Brisbourne 3-9-0 BL (45) S W Kelly 7/1: 35000-03: b g Up And At 'em - | 2½ | **41a**
Tycoon Tina (Tina's Pet) Led till 3f out, no extra fnl 2f: op 9/2 in first time blnks: plcd once in '03 (rtd 61,
seller): eff at 6f on fast grnd.
1085 **UPTHEDALE 15** [2] J R Weymes 3-9-0 (45) P Hanagan 7/1: 0500-04: Handy, no extra 4f out, btn when | 3 | **36a**
pilot drpd whip dist: see 1085.
776 **PLATINUM CHIEF 53** [4]3-9-0 (45) P Mathers(7) 6/1: 45-66505: Sn in rear & nvr a factor: tchd 9/1. | shd | **36a**
5 Ran Time 2m 05.42 (7.22) Owned: Reddal Racing Trained: Barnsley

---

1312
7.15 New Site @ Betdirect Co Uk Tri-Banded Stakes 3yo 0-45 (H)
£1432 £409 £205 **6f aw rnd** **Going 63** -05 Slow Inside

761 **LITTLE FLUTE 54** [3] T Keddy 3-9-0 (45) P Doe 3/1 JT FAV: 2-400001: Handy, styd on to lead dist, | | **52a**
rdn out to hold on despite edging left: tchd 9/2 after 8 wk abs: eff at 5/6f on fibresand: acts on a sharp trk:
enjoyed drop to banded grade: see 237.
1075 **FAYR FIRENZE 16** [7] M F Harris 3-9-0 vis (45) S Righton 3/1 JT FAV: 656-0462: Cl-up & led after | 2 | **45a**
2f, hdd 3f out, rallied to lead again 2f out, hdd dist, not pace of wnr: clr rem: eff at 6f on fibresand: see 846.
981 **DRESS PEARL 23** [1] R P Elliott 3-8-4 P (35) T Hamilton(3) 10/1: 60000-03: Cl-up, led 3f out, hdd | 5 | **20a**
2f out, grad wknd: tried cheek pieces: see 981.
1031 **INDRANI 20** [2] John A Harris 3-9-0 (45) D Fentiman(7) 5/1: 0-064004: Handy 3f, wknd fnl 2f: btr 797. | 2½ | **23a**
2608] **WEAVER SPELL 294** [6]3-8-9 (40) V Halliday 20/1: 0006-5: b g Wizard King - Impy Fox (Imp Society) | 6 | **0a**
Handy, wknd 3f out: reapp: unplcd in '03 (rtd 45 & 27a): with J R Norton.
975 **SPARKLING CLEAR 23** [4]3-9-0 (45) M Henry 7/1: 5066-006: Led, hdd 4f out, styd cl-up, short of | 3 | **0a**
room 2f out, sn fdd: see 872.
1089 **SIMPLY RED 15** [5]3-8-10 (1ow)vis (40) A Culhane 7/2: 004-007: Cl-up 3f, sn fdd: mod form to date. | 12 | **0a**
7 Ran Time 1m 16.93 (4.13) Owned: Mrs H Keddy Trained: Newmarket

1313 **7.45 Bet Direct On Sky Active Banded Stakes 3yo+ 0-45 (H)**
£1435 £410 £205 **1m4f aw** **Going 63** **+02 Fast** Inside

1243 **BOSPHORUS 3** [4] D G Bridgwater 5-9-5 vis (45) D Nolan(5) 11/4: 32325-31: Cl-up, led 4f out, sn **51a+**
clr, eased cl-home, val 4L+: qck reapp: eff at 12f/2m on fast grnd & fibresand: eff in a visor: can win again.
1197* **RED MOOR 7** [2] R Hollinshead 4-9-10 (45) A Culhane 5/2 JT FAV: 065-2612: Cl-up, kept on ins fnl 2½ **50a**
2f, no ch with easy wnr: clr rem: qck reapp: ran to form of win in 1197 (h'cap).
1204 **WESTERN COMMAND 6** [6] Mrs N Macauley 8-9-5 p (45) Joanna Badger 11/1: 5005533: Keen cl-up, rdn 9 **30a**
after 4f, hdd 4f out, sn wknd: qck reapp: btr 1204.
1064 **BEVIER 16** [1] T Wall 10-9-5 (45) N Chalmers(5) 5/2 JT FAV: 0-534204: Chsd ldrs, fdd 4f out: btr 821. 9 **16a**
984 **VITELUCY 23** [5]5-9-5 P (40) A Quinn(5) 5/1: 100-5535: Led, hdd 1m out, fdd 5f out: btr 984. 5 **9a**
1262 **WETHAAB 3** [3]7-9-5 t p (30) Ann Stokell 50/1: 000-0056: Al in rear: qck reapp: see 906. 20 **0a**
6 Ran Time 2m 40.95 (7.35) Owned: Led Astray Again Partnership Trained: Winchcombe

1314 **8.15 Bet In Running @ Betdirect Co Uk Banded Stakes 3yo+ 0-35 (H)**
£1435 £410 £205 **7f aw rnd** **Going 63** **-01 Slow** Outside

1292* **BEAUTEOUS 1** [2] M J Polglase 5-9-13 (35) K Ghunowa(7) 4/9 FAV: 06441111: Handy, led after 3f out, **59a+**
clr ins fnl 2f, val 8L+: bckd at odds-on: won similar contest here yesterday in 1292: eff at 6f/8.4f on firm,
gd/soft, acts on both AWs: thriving in banded grade & this was 4th success in row: see 1292 & 1264.
1288* **BAYTOWN FLYER 1** [7] P S McEntee 4-9-13 (35) B Reilly(3) 7/2: 0-2201112: Led till hdd 6f out, styd 5 **47a**
cl-up, kept on but no ch with wnr ins fnl 2f: won yesterday at Lingfield in 1288: another gd eff here.
1261 **COUNTRYWIDE GIRL 3** [8] A Berry 5-9-7 (30) P Bradley(5) 16/1: 3536433: Led after 1f, hdd 4f out, 1¼ **38a$**
no extra when hung left ins fnl 1f: qck reapp: see 1261.
1203 **MYSTIC PROMISE 6** [3] Mrs N Macauley 3-8-8 t (30) Hayley Turner(5) 50/1: 0005034: Rear, nvr nrr 3½ **30a**
than mid-div: qck reapp: btr 1203.
1181 **UN AUTRE ESPERE 7** [6]5-9-7 bl (30) L Vickers 100/1: 0-060005: Handy, outpcd 5f out, late gains. ½ **29a**
1261 **WELSH WHISPER 3** [4]5-9-7 (35) N Chalmers(5) 66/1: 0400566: Slow away, prog 4f out, wknd fnl 2f. shd **29a**
584 **PEARTREE HOUSE 73** [5]10-9-7 (30) A Culhane 20/1: 000-0007: Al in rear: 10 wk abs: see 463. 4 **21a**
1264 **POWER AND DEMAND 3** [1]7-9-7 T (35) R Ffrench 80/1: 00/055//-48: Al well bhd: btr 1264. 10 **1a**
8 Ran Time 1m 30.73(4.53) Owned: Mr Paul J Dixon Trained: Newark

Official Going GOOD/SOFT.

1315 **2.20 Jetair Esher Cup Handicap 3yo 0-100 (C)** [102]
£15674 £5946 £2973 **1m14y rnd** **Good/Soft 90** **+02 Fast** Inside

915 **BARATHEA DREAMS 30** [4] J S Moore 3-7-12 (1oh) (72) J Quinn 14/1: 1141: Keen cl-up, led over 2f **83**
out, hdd over 1f out & lkd held till rallied v gamely for press to get up again cl-home: op 10/1: eff back at 1m,
stays at least 10f: acts on gd/soft & polytrack, sharp or stiff trks: genuine, lightly rcd & progressive.
1178* **APPALACHIAN TRAIL 8** [8] I Semple 3-8-6 (5ex) (81) R Winston 100/30: 05-312: Cl-up, hdwy to lead nk **90**
over 1f out, styd on well but rdn & collared cl-home: clr of rem: useful: acts on firm & gd/soft: improving.
1141 **MOMTIC 11** [6] W Jarvis 3-8-5 (80) K Darley 3/1 FAV: 0321-33: Keen in tch, eff 2f out, onepace: 4 **82**
well bckd: easier grnd, shade btr 1141 (gd, 9f).
1101* **JUST TIM 15** [2] R Hannon 3-8-3 (78) R L Moore 10/1: 0602-414: Keen held up, eff 2f out, sn no 2 **77**
extra: shade btr expected after mdn win in 1101 (made most).
934* **CERTIFIABLE 28** [1]3-8-0 (1ow) (74) Martin Dwyer 8/1: 4115: With ldr, wknd 2f out: up in class & 1¾ **71**
first start on turf: btr 934 (class stks, polytrack).
4547} **COLOUR WHEEL 205** [3]3-9-1 (90) R Hughes 11/2: 0122-6: ch c Spectrum - Risanda (Kris) Held up, 8 **74**
pushed wide on bend over 4f out, wknd 2f out: '03 auct mdn wnr: stks rnr-up: eff at 7f, shld stay at least 1m:
acts on fast grnd & any trk.
2 Oct'03 Sali 7.0g/f 91-(90) D: 2 Sep'03 Ayr 7.2g/f 90-(84) C: 1 Sep'03 Folk 7g/f 84- C
5028} **OVERDRAWN 168** [5]3-9-7 (96) S W Kelly 16/1: 123415-7: b g Daggers Drawn - In Denial (Maelstrom nk **79**
Lake) Held up, eff over 2f out, sn wknd: '03 mdn & dual h'cap wnr: suited by 7f/1m on any trk, likes a gall one:
acts on fast, gd & fibresand: fully, useful & progressive last term on a sounder surface.
1 Oct'03 Donc 7g/f 97-91 C: 2 Sep'03 Donc 8gd 95-91 B: 1 Sep'03 York 7.0g/f 90-83 C:
1 Jun'03 Wolv 6af 83a- D: 2 Jun'03 Sand 5.0gd 88- E:
4978} **BAILEYS DANCER 174** [7]3-8-12 (87) J Fanning 7/1: 51140-8: b f Groom Dancer - Darshay (Darshaan) 6 **60**
Made most till over 2f out, wknd qckly: won 2 of 5 '03 starts (mdn & nurs h'cap): eff over a gall 1m on gd grnd:
dam 9f scorer. 1 Sep'03 Hayd 8.1gd 85-76 C: 1 Aug'03 Hami 8.3gd 76- D:
8 Ran Time 1m 46.04 (7.04) Owned: Mrs Fitri Hay Trained: Hungerford

1316 **2.55 Gr3 Betfred Classic Trial 3yo (A)**
£29750 £11000 £5500 **1m2f7y** **Good/Soft 90** **+02 Fast** Inside

1206* **AFRICAN DREAM 7** [5] P W Chapple Hyam 3-8-10 (94) J Quinn 7/2: 31111: Handy, hdwy trav well to **115+**
lead over 1f out, shied from path but rdn clr, readily: eff at 1m/10f on gd, soft & poltrack, any trk: thriving, most
progressive & potentially top-class, win more Gr races: see 1206.
1113* **PRIVY SEAL 13** [3] J H M Gosden 3-8-10 (110) L Dettori 8/11 FAV: 13155-12: Hld up, hdwy over 2f 3½ **108**
out, chsd wnr fnl 1f, onepace: clr of rem: hvly bckd: more ran to wng Listed form of 1113 & caught a smart sort.
1189* **GOLD HISTORY 8** [2] M Johnston 3-8-10 (98) J Fanning 7/1: 110-213: Led till over 1f out, no 5 **101**
extra: ran up in class & softer grnd: consistent: see 1189 (Listed, 9f, fast).
4164*}**MUTAWASSEL 226** [1] B W Hills 3-8-10 (90) R Hills 7/1: 01-4: b c Kingmambo - Danzig Darling 2½ **97**
(Danzig) Chsd ldrs, eff 3f out, wknd & flashed tail 2f out: won last of 2 juv starts (mdn, flashed tail): stays 1m,

SANDOWN   FRIDAY 23.04.04   Righthand, Galloping Track, Stiff Finish

shld get further: acts on gd grnd & a gall trk.   1 Sep'03 Donc 8gd 95- D:
598   **FORTHRIGHT 62** [4]3-8-10   (92) R Hughes 33/1: 060-1045: Chsd ldr, wknd 2f out: 9 wk abs, big step   *21*   **67**
up in class: see 325 (polytrack, h'cap).
5 Ran   Time 2m 12.93 (8.83)   Owned: Franconson Partners   Trained: Newmarket

---

1317   4.05 Sunderlands Conditions Stakes Colts & Geldings 3yo   (C)
£8928 £3168 £1584   **1m14y rnd**   **Good/Soft 90**   **-30 Slow**   Inside

3197*)**THAJJA 271** [3] J L Dunlop 3-9-0   R Hills 6/1: 1-1: b c Daylami - Jawlaat (Dayjur) Held up, hdwy   **105**
over 1f out, styd on to lead over 1f out, rdn clr: '03 mdn wnr: dam 6f scorer: apprec step up to 1m, could get
further: acts on fast & gd/soft, stiff trks: runs well fresh: imprvd & this was a v useful run, win more races.
1 Jul'03 Newm 7g/f 85- D:
4665*)**PUTRA SAS 196** [4] P F I Cole 3-8-10   (90) K Fallon 7/1: 21-2: b c Sri Pekan - Puteri Wentworth   *2*   **96**
(Sadler's Wells) Made most till over 1f out, not pace of wnr: clr of rem: op 5/1: reapp: won 2nd of 2 '03 starts
(auct mdn): stays 1m, shld get further (dam styd 2m4f): acts on firm & gd/soft, gall trks: useful, gd rtn.
1 Oct'03 York 7.9g/f 89- E: 2 Sep'03 Newb 7frm 89- D:
1166*   **UNITED NATIONS 9** [2] D R Loder 3-9-0   J Murtagh 10/11 FAV: 13: Unruly stalls, sn cl-up, wknd fnl   *4*   **92**
1f: hvly bckd up in class but city more expected after debut win in 1166 (gd grnd).
4870*)**WARRAD 182** [1] G A Butler 3-9-0   L Dettori 11/4: 1-4: b c Kingmambo - Shalimar Garden (Caerleon)   *5*   **86**
Handy, wknd over 1f out on reapp: '03 mdn wnr: eff at 6f, bred to stay at least 1m (dam styd mid-dists): acts on
fast grnd & a gall trk: has run well fresh: not enjoy easy grnd?   1 Oct'03 Newb 6.0g/f 91- D:
4 Ran   Time 1m 47.84 (8.84)   Owned: Mr Hamdan Al Maktoum   Trained: Arundel

---

1318   4.35 Betfred 'double Result On Singles And Multis' Handicap Stakes 3yo 0-90   (C)   **[94]**
£8700 £3300 £1650   **1m2f7y**   **Good/Soft 90**   **-05 Slow**   Inside

1192*   **HAZYVIEW 8** [4] N A Callaghan 3-8-13 (6ex)   (79) D Fox(5) 1/1 FAV: 0031-211: Cl-up, led over 2f out   **92**
till dist, rallied & lead again cl-home, drvn out, gamely: hvly bckd: stays 10f well, 12f looks sure to suit: acts
on fast & gd/soft, any trk: thriving at present, shld land quick-fire hat-trick: see 1192, 1017.
1206   **RED LANCER 7** [10] R J Price 3-9-4   (84) R Miles(3) 7/2: 1122222: In tch, gd hdwy to lead over 1f   *shd*   **96**
out, kept on till collared cl-home: clr of rem & proving v tough (2 wins & 5 rnr-up placings already this term).
4757)   **CUTTING CREW 191** [8] P W Harris 3-9-1   (81) Martin Dwyer 14/1: 402-3: ch c Diesis - Poppy Carew   *4*   **87**
(Danehill) In tch, onepace fnl 2f: rnr-up in a mdn in '03: stays 10f, shld get further (dam 12f scorer): acts on
fast, polytrack & prob gd/soft, prob any trk: sharper for this.   2 Oct'03 Ling 8ap 82a- D:
4154*)**CAMROSE 226** [1] J L Dunlop 3-9-3 (83) T Quinn 14/1: 4321-4: ch c Zafonic - Tularosa (In The   *¾*   **80**
Wings) Held up, eff 2f out, sn onepace: won last of 4 '03 starts (mdn): eff at 1m, prob stays 10f: acts on firm &
gd, prob gd/soft & any trk: consistent.   1 Sep'03 Epso 8.5gd 86-(85) D: 2 Aug'03 Kemp 8fm 85- D:
1067*   **WINGED DARGENT 17** [2]3-9-0   (80) J Fanning 10/1: 15: Cl-up, no extra 2f out: see 1067 (mdn, hvy).   *3½*   **80**
1176   **LETS ROLL 8** [9]3-8-3   (69) T Williams 8/1: 02251-26: Held up, btn 2f out: just btr 1176 (1m, gd).   *1*   **68**
1105   **SAFFRON FOX 13** [6]3-9-7   (87) T J Murphy 20/1: 40120-47: In tch, wknd 2f out: see 1105.   *4*   **80**
2205*)**LAAWARIS 311** [7]3-9-5   (85) J Murtagh 20/1: 1-8: b c Souvenir Copy - Seattle Kat (Seattle Song)   *7*   **68**
Slow away & bhd on reapp: sole start '03 wnr (auct mdn): eff at 7f, shld stay at least 1m: acts on fast grnd & has
run well fresh.   1 Jun'03 Thir 7g/f 79- E:
1017   **HABANERO 22** [5]3-8-5   (71) R L Moore 20/1: 60221-09: Led till over 2f out, wknd, t.o.   *23*   **20**
9 Ran   Time 2m 13.6(9.5)   Owned: Mr T Mohan   Trained: Newmarket

---

WOLVERHAMPTON   Fibresand   FRIDAY 23.04.04   Lefthand, Sharp Track

Official Going STANDARD.

1319   2.05 New Site @ Betdirect Co Uk Classified Stakes 3yo+ 0-60   (F)
£2947 £842 £421   **7f aw rnd**   **Going 46**   **-02 Slow**   Outside

918   **MY BAYARD 29** [1] J O'Reilly 5-9-12   (65) W Supple 8/1: 20-62501: Made all, styd on strongly fnl   **73a**
1f, drvn out: tchd 10/1, top-weight: eff 7f/1m, stays 11f: acts on gd, loves fibresand: likes to force the
pace & apprec return to AW: see 632 (1m here).
1195   **MOUNT ROYALE 8** [3] N Tinkler 6-9-8 vis t (61) Kim Tinkler 5/1: 1100622: Chsd ldrs, kept on well fnl 1f.   *1½*   **65a**
1221   **SPINDOR 6** [5] J A Osborne 5-9-8 bl (61) D Holland 4/1: 5342103: Chsd ldrs, onepcd fnl 1f: op 3/1.   *1¼*   **62a**
1132   **ACORAZADO 11** [8] G L Moore 5-9-11 bl e (64) S Whitworth 7/2 FAV: 2016204: Rear, hdwy 2f out, styd   *¾*   **63a**
on fnl 1f, nvr nrr: back to form on return to AW, see 878.
684   **DISPOL PETO 63** [7]4-9-7 p (59) J Bramhill 25/1: 00-05205: Held up wide, late hdwy, nvr nrr: abs.   *1¾*   **55a**
1010   **PARKER 23** [10]7-9-8 (61) I Mongan 7/1: 50-43606: Chsd ldrs 6f, wknd: see 840.   *shd*   **56a**
1221   **AGUILA LOCO 6** [2]5-9-7 p (55) M Fenton 9/1: 4062037: Front rank 6f, wknd: qck reapp.   *hd*   **55a**
231   **SIRAJ 125** [6]5-9-11   (64) A Culhane 11/2: 410025-8: Nvr nr ldrs: tchd 9/1, long abs: see 121 (6f).   *5*   **49a**
4242)   **JUBILEE STREET 221** [4]5-9-7   (51) G Duffield 33/1: 160005-9: b g Dr Devious - My Firebird   *3*   **39a**
(Rudimentary) Prom, wknd 2f out on reapp: '03 mdn wnr for D Nicholls (subs tried a visor): eff at 7f, poss stays
9f: acts on gd & fast grnd: now with Mrs A Duffield.   1 Jun'03 Catt 7g/f 49-(59) G:
937   **VICTORY VEE 27** [9]4-9-7   (52) D Sweeney 20/1: 003-0600: 10th: Prom till halfway, wknd: see 68.   *4*   **31a**
10 Ran   Time 1m 29.60 (3.40)   Owned: Burntwood Sports Ltd   Trained: Barnsley

---

1320   2.40 Littlewoods Bet Direct Maiden Claiming Stakes 3yo+   (F)
£2863 £818 £409   **5f aw rnd**   **Going 46**   **-02 Slow**   Inside

600   **LUCIUS VERRUS 72** [1] D Shaw 4-9-13   (48) W Supple 13/8 FAV: 0434-301: Chsd ldrs, drvn to lead cl   **55a**
home: 10 wk abs, gamble from 7/2: apprec this drop to claim grade & 5f, stays 6f: acts on both AW's: likes a
sharp trk & runs well fresh: first win, see 348 & 219.
1046   **NANNA 18** [2] R Hollinshead 3-8-12   (48) G Duffield 9/4: 0-520302: Tried to make all, caught cl   *nk*   **48a**

home: clr of rem: bold front running effort on this return to claim grade: eff at 5/6f: see 466 (6f here).

1129 **THE BUTTERFLY BOY 11** [4] P F I Cole 3-9-3 S Sanders 7/2: 6-03: ch c Inchinor - Crime of Passion   4   **41a**
(Dragonara Palace) Chsd ldrs, ev ch till wknd ins fnl 1f: op 2/1, AW bow: mdn 6th (rtd 69) on sole juv start:
half brother to numerous wnrs, incl sev sprinters: dropped in grade & better expected.

742 **MINIRINA 57** [5] C Smith 4-8-10 (45) R Fitzpatrick 16/1: 30540-04: b f Mistertopogigo - Fabulous   5   **9a**
Rina (Fabulous Dancer) Front rank 4f, wknd: 8 wk abs, bckd at long odds: plcd twice in '03 (class stks & clmr):
eff over a sharp/turning 5f on fast, gd/soft & f/sand: has tried blnks.
2 Apr'03 Folk 5g/f 55-(66) F: 2 Aug'02 Catt 5g/f 69- F:

4695} **CAMPBELLS LAD 194** [6]3-8-11 (45) F Lynch 16/1: 0540-5: b c Mind Games - T O O Mamma's (Classic   3   **11a**
Secret) Held up, nvr dngrs on reapp: lightly rcd & mod '03 mdn form: cheaply bought, dam a mid-dist/hdles wnr.

1119 **EAST RIDING 12** [7]4-9-8 (50) Ann Stokell 12/1: 02005-56: Swerved start, al bhnd: op 8/1.   ½   **11a**

1012 **MY WILD ROVER 23** [3]4-8-13 t p P Hanagan 25/1: 0P-07: Chsd ldrs 3f, wknd: poor.   15   **0a**
7 Ran   Time 1m 02.60 (2.40)   Owned: Swann Racing Ltd   Trained: Newark

---

1321   3.15 Betdirect Co Uk Median Auction Maiden Stakes 3yo   (F)
£2891 £826 £413   **7f aw rnd**   Going 46   **-13 Slow**   Outside

1044 **ANDALUZA 20** [5] P D Cundell 3-8-9 S Sanders 5/2: 41: b f Mujadil - Hierarchy (Sabrehill) Nvr   **72a**
far away, led ins fnl 1f, rdn out: nicely bckd: improved over a sharp 7f on fibresand: see 1044.

4229} **MAGIC AMIGO 223** [6] J R Jenkins 3-9-0 (75) D Holland 2/1 FAV: 05420-2: ch g Zilzal - Emaline   1   **74a**
(Empery) Prom, kept on fnl 1f but not pace of wnr: bckd from 7/2 on reapp: '03 fill mdn rnr-up: eff at 6/7f on
fast grnd & fibresand: runs well fresh: deserves similar. 2 Aug'03 Asco 6g/f 72- D:

4370} **CARRY ON DOC 216** [1] J W Hills 3-9-0 (75) S Whitworth 4/1: 5355-3: b c Dr Devious - Florentynna   nk   **73a**
Bay (Aragon) Chsd ldrs, ev ch ent fnl 1f, no extra cl home: tchd 11/2, reapp: '03 mdn auct plcd (rtd 79): half
brother to numerous wnrs: eff at 7f on gd, fast grnd & fibresand, 1m shld suit: sharper next time.

3259} **ALIBA 268** [4] B Smart 3-9-0 (66) F Lynch 14/1: 354-4: Led till ins fnl 1f, no extra on reapp: gelded.   2   **68a**

966 **NOUNOU 25** [2]3-9-0 C Catlin 16/1: 05: Nvr dngrs.   1½   **65a**

1125 **MARKSGOLD 11** [3]3-9-0 A Culhane 4/1: 000-36: Rear, rdn & btn 2f out: see 1125.   nk   **64a**
6 Ran   Time 1m 30.35 (4.15)   Owned: Mr Pedro Rosas   Trained: Compton

---

1322   3.50 New Site @ Betdirect Co Uk Handicap Stakes 3yo+ 0-75 (E)   [72]
£3712 £1142 £571   **1m100y aw rnd**   Going 46   **+10 Fast**   Inside

1219 **SPARK UP 6** [7] J W Unett 4-8-11 bl (55) S Sanders 16/1: 0062441: Made all, styd on well despite   **61a**
drifting right fnl 1f, drvn out: op 12/1, qck reapp, best time of day: eff at 7/8.5f on fast, gd/soft & fibresand.

1198 **QUIET READING 8** [9] M R Bosley 7-9-7 vis (65) Hayley Turner(5) 7/2: 3-346322: Held up, styd on fnl   1¼   **67a**
1.5f, not quite rch wnr: tchd 9/2: all 5 wins on fibresand: in gd form, see 1198.

1049 **DANIELLES LAD 18** [10] B Palling 8-10-0 (72) A Culhane 9/1: 2041303: Nvr far away, not qckn fnl 1f.   ½   **73a**

1160 **FRANKS QUEST 9** [8] P Burgoyne 4-8-9 (53) L Keniry(3) 25/1: 0233604: Chsd ldrs, onepcd fnl 1.5f.   2   **50a**

942 **ACTIVE ACCOUNT 27** [6]7-9-11 (69) I Mongan 3/1 FAV: 6233-225: Rear, late prog, nvr dngrs: btr 942.   2½   **61a**

3496} **SUMMER SHADES 258** [1]6-9-6 (64) R Swarbrick(7) 16/1: 121620-6: b f Green Desert - Sally Slade   1¼   **53a**
(Dowsing) Prom till wknd 3f out on reapp: dual '03 h'cap wnr, also plcd many times: won a mdn & 2 h'caps in '02:
eff at 1m/9f on firm, soft & f/sand: handles any trk, eff with/without blnks: tough & usually consistent.
2 Jul'03 Redc 8g/f 71-69 E: 1 Jul'03 Wind 8.3g/f 71-65 D: 2 Jul'03 Kemp 9g/f 67-65 D: 1 Jun'03 Pont 8.0g/f 67-60 E:
2 Jun'03 Thir 8g/f 61-58 C: 2 Jun'03 Redc 8fm 61-59 E: 2 Jun'03 Bath 8.0fm 60-(59) F: 2 May'03 Catt 7fm 57-(59) F:
2 Nov'02 Wolv 7af 67a-62 E: 2 Oct'02 Leic 8agd 62-56 E: 1 Sep'02 Wolv 7af 62a-55 F: 2 Aug'02 Beve 7.4g/f 54-55 E:

1198 **PHAROAHS GOLD 8** [4]6-9-2 e (60) W Supple 10/1: 0-205037: Held up, nvr a factor: see 1198.   ½   **48a**

1219 **AIR MAIL 6** [3]7-10-0 vis (72) P McCabe 16/1: 4000468: Prom till after halfway: top-weight.   9   **42a**

1214 **HOHS BACK 7** [2]5-8-7 p (51) Lisa Jones(3) 4/1: 00-00029: Stumbled start & al bhnd: nicely bckd: ½   **20a**
forgive this, see 1214 (turf).

917 **THUNDERCLAP 30** [5]5-8-11 (55) P Hanagan 11/2: 400-1200: 10th: Chsd ldrs, btn 2f out: tchd 8/1.   ½   **23a**
10 Ran   Time 1m 49.24 (3.04)   Owned: Mr Christopher Chell   Trained: Wolverhampton

---

1323   4.25 Bet Direct On Sky Active Apprentice Selling Stakes 4yo+   (G)
£2520 £720 £360   **1m4f aw**   Going 46   **-03 Slow**   Inside

1090 **ORINOCOVSKY 16** [1] N P Littmoden 5-9-5 (55) Steven Harrison(8) 8/15 FAV: 3023201: Made all, clr   **62a**
fnl 2f, easily: no bid: deserved win, eff at 10/14f, has tried 2m: acts on firm, gd grnd & both AWs: handles a
sharp or gall trk: suited by sell grade: see 854 & 420.

1058 **JUST WIZ 18** [4] N P Littmoden 8-8-13 bl (58) K Jackson(5) 7/4: 6302302: Rear, took 2nd 2f out, no   9   **41a**
ch with facile wnr: multiple course wnr, see 862 & 249.

4998} **MYRTUS 171** [3] J R Weymes 5-8-13 D Fentiman(3) 25/1: 0/0-3: ch g Double Eclipse - My Desire   12   **23a**
(Grey Desire) Chsd wnr, wknd qckly 2f out: reapp: no prev form (Mrs M Reveley): dropped in grade here.

155} **TOLAGA BAY 503** [2] T J Fitzgerald 6-8-8 D Tudhope 40/1: 00/-4: ch f Dr Devious - Swordlestown   19   **0a**
Miss (Apalachee) Held up, al bhnd, t.o. on come-back: well btn in 2 '03 AW mdns (with W Jarvis).
4 Ran   Time 2m 39.52 (5.92)   Owned: Mr Nigel Shields   Trained: Newmarket

---

1324   5.00 Bet In Running @ Betdirect Co Uk Handicap Stakes 3yo 46-55 (F)   [67]
£2870 £820 £410   **1m1f79y aw**   Going 46   **-07 Slow**   Inside

892 **ANGELOS PRIDE 32** [7] J A Osborne 3-9-2 (55) G Duffield 3/1: 3023331: Held up, hdwy to lead 2f   **63a**
out, styd on strongly, rdn out: bckd from 9/2: plcd sev times prev: eff at 7f, suited by 9.4f on fibresand: likes
a sharp trk: deserved 1st win, see 892 & 665.

1081 **FOX HOLLOW 16** [6] M J Haynes 3-8-12 (51) A Culhane 8/1: 0-003262: Prom, outpcd 3f out, rallied   2   **55a**
fnl 1f but not reach wnr: stays 9.3f: see 865 & 613.

1246 **LARAD 4** [4] J S Moore 3-8-12 (6ex)bl (51) J D Smith 5/1: 0055133: Prom, chall 2f out, onepcd dist.   2½   **51a**

1240 **CHEROKEE NATION 6** [2] P W D'Arcy 3-9-1 e (54) L Keniry(3) 7/4 FAV: 006-44: Keen & led till 2f out,   2   **50a**
grad wknd: quick reapp & tried an eye-shield: see 1240 (turf).

1089 **REBEL ROUSER 16** [1]3-8-8 (47) I Mongan 12/1: 000-55: b g Kris - Nanouche (Dayjur) Chsd ldrs,   3½   **38a**

WOLVERHAMPTON Fibresand FRIDAY 23.04.04 Lefthand, Sharp Track

wknd 2f out: well btn on 3 '03 mdn starts, has since been gldd: with W Muir.
4813} **SCORCHIO 186** [3]3-8-7 (46) S Righton 50/1: 60006-6: b g Desert Sun - White Wash (Final Straw)   1   35a
Prom early, sn bhd, no ch after on reapp: mod mdn form in '03: cost £7,000: dam scored over 1m/10f.
1078 **NAFFERTON GIRL 16** [5]3-8-11 (50) Dane O'Neill 11/2: 03-47: Al bhd, t.o. in last.   *dist* 0a
7 Ran   Time 2m 03.09(4.89)   Owned: Mr J A Osborne   Trained: Upper Lambourn

WARWICK FRIDAY 23.04.04 Lefthand, Sharp, Turning Track

Official Going GOOD

1325   5.25 Cubbington Maiden Auction Stakes 2yo (H)
£1666 £476 £238   5f rnd   Good/Soft 61   -38 Slow   Inside

1123 **ZIMBALI 11** [15] J M Bradley 2-8-2 S Carson 14/1: 541: ch f Lahib - Dawn (Owington) Made all,   67
rdn out fnl 1f: Mar first foal, cost 1,000gns: dam mdn: sire high-class 1m performer: eff at 5f, shld stay
further: acts on gd/soft grnd & a sharp trk.
1071 **LATERAL THINKER 17** [16] J A Osborne 2-8-6 S W Kelly 11/4 J FAV: 22: Cl-up, ev ch dist, kept on   2   64
but not pace wnr in fnl 1f: acts on gd/soft grnd & polytrack: can find similar: see 1071.
1161 **TURTLE MAGIC 9** [11] W G M Turner 2-8-4 C Haddon(7) 11/4 J FAV: 023: Handy 4f, no extra fnl 1f.   2   56
NINAHS INTUITION [9] J M Bradley 2-8-9 A Nicholls 50/1: 4: b c Piccolo - Gina of Hithermoor   nk   60
(Reprimand) Trkd ldrs, ev ch when jmpd path & lost action dist, not recover: debut: May foal, cost 3,000gns: dam
unrcd: sire top-class at sprint dists: eff at 5f on gd/soft grnd: ran well for a long way & will learn from this.
1133 **ZACHY BOY 11** [1]2-8-9 E Ahern 20/1: 605: Trkd ldrs 4f, no extra fnl 1f: see 1071.   nk   59
1053 **WIZZSKILAD 18** [14]2-8-7 R Havlin 7/1: 046: Keen in tch, onepace fnl 2f: btr 1053.   nk   56
PRINCELY VALE [10]2-8-9 A Daly 11/1: 7: Dwelt, nvr nrr than mid-div: debut.   1½   53
LADY CHEF [2]2-8-4 A McCarthy 33/1: 8: Rear, modest late gains on debut.   ¾   45
1173 **ICE RUBY 8** [3]2-8-3 P Hanagan 40/1: 09: Handy, wknd fnl 2f.   2   38
HIGGYS PRINCE [7]2-8-10 T P Queally(3) 16/1: 0: 10th: Al bhd.   2½   37
MUESTRA [5]2-8-5 F Norton 40/1: 0: 11th: Al in rear.   2½   24
LORD CHALFONT [13]2-8-11 BL S Whitworth 12/1: 0: 12th: Rear, nvr a factor: blnks on debut.   hd   29
FAITHISFLYING [12]2-8-11 S Sanders 20/1: 0: 13th: Al in rear.   1¼   25
Ryans Lil Ol Gal [6]2-8-3 J Mackay 40/1:0   **Mrs Willy Nilly** [8]2-8-2 C Catlin 50/1:0
15 Ran   Time 1m 2.25 (4.95)   Owned: Mr J M Bradley   Trained: Chepstow

1326   5.55 Mitie Sweep Selling Stakes 3yo+ (H)
£1582 £452 £226   1m2f188y   Good/Soft 61   -34 Slow   Inside

4426} **BARTON SANDS 212** [4] M C Pipe 7-9-10 vis t (61) N Mackay(3) 15/8 J FAV: 460100-1: b g Tenby -   63
Hetty Green (Bay Express) Held up, gd prog to lead 1f out, rdn out: bght for 2,000gns: 6 wk jumps abs, earlier mod
form (rtd 64h, mdn hdle): sn unplcd wnr in '02: rnr-up once in '02 (clmr, R Brotherton): auct mdn wnr in '00: eff at
1m/11f on firm & gd/soft grnd: likes Warwick: eff in visor & t-strap: win again in this grade.
1 Aug'03 Warw 10.9fm 62-(62) G: 2 Sep'02 York 9g/f 72- D:
1160 **NODS NEPHEW 9** [7] D E Cantillon 7-9-10 (58) T G McLaughlin 15/8 J FAV: 110-2022: Rear, prog to   2½   58
lead 2f out, hdd dist, sn no extra: see 1160 & 792.
1128 **QUEEN EXCALIBUR 11** [3] C Roberts 5-9-5 (45) E Ahern 5/1: 0000063: Handy, ev ch dist, sn onepcd: ¾   52
handles fast & gd/soft grnd: see 1128.
862 **HEATHERS GIRL 37** [5] D Haydn Jones 5-9-10 (45) Paul Eddery 8/1: 40/-01624: Cl-up, ev ch dist, sn   1½   55$
no extra: see 862 & 633.
922} **PRAYERFUL 388** [2]5-9-5 p (40) S Hitchcott(3) 33/1: 040/0-5: b f Syrtos - Pure Formality (Forzando)   nk   49$
Led, hdd 2f out, sn no extra: jumps fit, earlier plcd 4 times (mdns & h'caps, stays 2m3f on hvy, cheek pieces):
unplcd sole '03 start (rtd 32, class stks):   4th of 22 at best in 2 '02 starts (rtd 40).
4472} **YALLAMBIE 563** [1]5-9-5 T (57) P Hanagan 25/1: 6500/-6: Keen in tch, fdd fnl 2f: new stable.   7   39
1238 **TERMONFECKIN 6** [6]6-9-10 (55) B Doyle 10/1: 3460-007: Slow away, al well adrift.   7   34
7 Ran   Time 2m 26.7 (10.5)   Owned: Mr Stuart M Mercer   Trained: Wellington

1327   6.25 Harbury Banded Stakes 3yo+ 0-40 (H)
£1540 £440 £220   6f21y rnd   Good/Soft 61   +12 Fast   Inside

1314 **BAYTOWN FLYER 1** [2] P S McEntee 4-9-12 (35) T G McLaughlin 9/4: 22011121: Made all, rdn out fnl   53
1f to hold on: qck reapp, gd time: wnr at 6/7f, has tried 1m: acts on firm, gd/soft & both AWs: likes a sharp trk
in banded grade: 5th race in 9 days (4 wins) & clearly thriving: see 1314 & 1288.
1065 **GRAND VIEW 17** [9] J R Weymes 8-9-6 p (40) P Hanagan 2/1 FAV: 000-6042: Cl-up, styd on ins fnl 1f,   1¾   40
no ch with wnr: caught a tartar: just btr 1065.
847 **XSYNNA 40** [10] T T Clement 8-9-6 vis (40) C Lowther 10/1: 00-30603: Handy till dist, sn no extra: 1¾   34
6 wk abs: btr 340 (polytrack).
1185 **LUCRETIUS 8** [1] D K Ivory 5-9-6 (40) M Howard(7) 8/1: 00-00044: Sn bhd, kept on ins fnl 1f: see 1185.   ¾   32
1075 **TOP PLACE 17** [8]3-8-9 p (40) E Ahern 7/1: 0-00055: Cl-up, no extra fnl 1f: see 1075.   hd   31
1130 **TIME FLYER 11** [7]4-9-6 BL (35) A Daly 40/1: 0-00006: Slow away, nvr nrr than mid-div: blnks.   ¾   29
1266 **ABBIEJO 4** [6]7-9-6 (40) A Quinn(5) 16/1: 0/0-65667: Al in rear: qck reapp: see 889.   2½   21
788 **MOONGLADE 52** [5]4-9-6 t (30) J McAuley 66/1: 00000-008: ch f Carson City - Moonshine Girl   1¼   17
(Shadeed) Handy 4f, sn wknd: 7 wk abs: unplcd sole '03 start (mdn): earlier unplcd in Dubai: has tried a t-strap.
4 **SWEET TALKING GIRL 165** [3]4-9-6 (40) S Carson 28/1: 650-9: b f Bin Ajwaad - Arabellajill   2   11
(Aragon) Al in rear: reapp: unplcd both '03 starts (rtd 40, mdn).
46} **BOUND TO PLEASE 522** [4]9-9-6 vis (40) Ann Stokell 25/1: 050504/-0: 10th: Al adrift: chngd stables.   13   0
10 Ran   Time 1m 13.55 (2.95)   Owned: Mr J Doxey   Trained: Newmarket

1328

6.55 Claverdon Banded Stakes 3yo+ 0-40 (H)
£1540 £440 £220   1m22y rnd   Good/Soft 61   -24 Slow   Inside

864 **EXTEMPORISE** 37 [6] T T Clement 4-9-7 (40) T G McLaughlin 5/1: 050-0351: Cl-up, drvn out to lead cl-home: eff at 6f/1m on f/sand & gd/soft: gd start for new stable (prev with P McBride): see 822. **43**

1262 **TOJONESKI** 4 [7] I W McInnes 5-9-7 p (35) R Ffrench 6/1: 0-003422: Led, hdd under press cl-home: qck reapp: acts on fast, gd/soft & fibresand: see 1262. **shd 41**

1264 **ALL ON MY OWN** 4 [4] I W McInnes 9-9-7 bl (35) L Vickers 33/1: 4240053: Rear, prog 2f out, onepcd ins fnl 1f: qck reapp: btr 584. **2 37**

4360} **SEA JADE** 216 [11] J W Payne 5-9-7 (40) E Ahern 9/1: 026460-4: b f Mujadil - Mirabiraly (Crow) Prom, no extra dist: reapp: rnr-up once in '03 (h'cap): h'cap plcd 3 times in '02 (rtd 50): eff at 6f/1m on fast & gd/soft grnd: with J W Payne. 2 Jul'03 Kemp 7g/f 46-44 E: 2 Aug'02 Epso 8.5g/f 48-48 E: 2 Jul'02 Carl 7.9g/s 48-45 F: **1½ 34**

862 **CHICKASAW TRAIL** 37 [5]6-9-7 (40) Dale Gibson 20/1: 00-00065: Nvr nrr than mid-div: see 862. **3 28**

894 **ZAHUNDA** 32 [2]5-9-7 (40) S W Kelly 11/4 FAV: 2046336: Nvr nrr than mid-div: btr 894. **3 22**

523 **NEWCLOSE** 81 [8]4-9-7 t (40) Kim Tinkler 5/1: 00-33347: Rear, nvr a factor: 11 wk abs: btr 445 & 356. **½ 21**

4260} **DUNMIDOE** 220 [9]4-9-7 (40) G Carter 50/1: 000500-8: b f Case Law - Rion River (Taufan) Handy, wknd fnl 2f: reapp: modest form in '03 (rtd 45a & 49, sellers & mdns): has tried cheek pieces. **1½ 18**

821 **SADLERS SWING** 46 [10]8-9-7 (40) A Quinn(5) 7/1: 0//605-249: Al in rear: 7 wk abs. **1½ 15**

905 **CROWN CITY** 31 [3]4-9-7 t (40) M Tebbutt 25/1: 600-0000: 10th: Handy, fdd 2f out. **5 5**

10 Ran   Time 1m 43.65 (6.85)   Owned: Ms K Sadler   Trained: Newmarket

1329

7.25 Barford Banded Stakes 4yo+ 0-40 (H)
£1582 £452 £226   1m6f213y   Good/Soft 61   Inapplicable   Inside

1135 **COURT ONE** 11 [9] R J Price 6-9-0 (35) J F McDonald(5) 9/2: 6000-001: b g Shareef Dancer - Fairfields Cone (Celtic Cone) Dwelt, hdwy 2f out, led ins fnl 1f, rdn out: rnr-up once in '03 (h'cap, here at Warwick): unplcd in '02: eff arnd 2m on fast & gd/soft, likes a sharp trk, esp Warwick: has tried a visor. 2 Jul'03 Warw 16.2g/f 36-29 E: **40**

782 **AMANPURI** 53 [3] P A Blockley 6-9-0 (35) Dean McKeown 7/1: 00-04062: b g Fairy King - Aratika (Zino) Chsd ldrs, led 2f out till ins fnl 1f, kept on but not pace of wnr: clr of rem, 8 wk abs, new stable: ex German, won a h'cap at Munich in '02: stays an easy 2m, winning form on gd & hvy grnd: hdle rnr-up when trained by D Weld in Ireland in 03/04 (eff at 2m on soft, tried blnks): runs well fresh. **1 37**

1265 **DORA CORBINO** 4 [5] R Hollinshead 4-8-11 (40) P Hanagan 25/1: 0-532063: Led till 2f out, no extra: qck reapp. **6 28**

968 **ANNIVERSARY GUEST** 25 [8] Mrs Lucinda Featherstone 5-9-0 (40) C Catlin 20/1: 0305-034: Keen in rear, imprvd to chase ldrs 4f out, sn onepcd: see 968. **shd 27**

1263* **MERCURIOUS** 4 [1]4-9-3 (40) Dale Gibson 5/4 FAV: 6334-415: Chsd ldrs, btn 2f out: qck reapp. **5 25**

984 **GOLFAGENT** 24 [2]6-9-0 t (40) S Hitchcott(3) 8/1: 5020/0-46: Held up, nvr nr ldrs: p.u. in a h'cap hdle since 984. **5 11**

4755} **RIVER OF FIRE** 191 [4]6-9-0 vis (35) J Mackay 16/1: 410360-7: Chsd ldrs 14f, wknd on reapp. **30 0**

4020} **ROSE TEA** 234 [7]5-9-0 BL (40) S Sanders 8/1: 0/00000-8: Chsd ldrs 13f, wknd, t.o.: reapp, blnks. **¾ 0**

1313 **WETHAAB** 1 [6]7-9-0 t p (30) Ann Stokell 66/1: 000-00569: Prom till halfway, t.o.: ran yesterday. **12 0**

9 Ran   Time 3m 22.55 ()   Owned: Derek & Cheryl Holder   Trained: Hereford

1330

7.55 Haseley Tri-Banded Stakes 3yo 0-45 (H)
£1477 £422 £211   7f26y rnd   Good/Soft 61   -13 Slow   Inside

662 **COURANT DAIR** 66 [1] P C Haslam 3-8-9 (40) G Faulkner 5/2 J FAV: 00-03651: Made most, styd on gamely fnl 1f, drvn out: 10 wk abs, rider given a 4-day whip ban: apprec this rtn to turf, eff at 7f/1m on gd grnd & fibresand: runs well fresh, see 486. **40**

986 **HEATHYARDS JOY** 24 [2] R Hollinshead 3-8-4 (30) Dale Gibson 5/1: 0-00442: Chsd ldrs, ev ch fnl 1f, just btn in a close fin: eff over a sharp 7f on gd/soft grnd: handles a sharp trk: see 779. **hd 34**

1203 **MONKEY OR ME** 7 [3] P T Midgley 3-8-4 (30) R Fitzpatrick 7/2: 00-00423: Rear, hdwy to chall dist, no qckn ins fnl 1f: consistent, see 1203 (AW). **¾ 32**

1085 **JESSE SAMUEL** 16 [6] J R Jenkins 3-9-0 (45) S W Kelly 10/1: 60000-04: ch g First Trump - Miss Kellybell (Kirchner) Rear, late hdwy, nvr pace to chall: mod '03 form: poss stays a sharp 7f on gd/soft grnd. **1¼ 40**

1312 **FAYR FIRENZE** 1 [4]3-9-0 vis (45) Dean McKeown 5/1: 656-04625: Prom, wkng when short of room ins fnl 1f: rnr-up over 6f on AW yesterday in 1312. **1¼ 38**

1242 **BROTHER CADFAEL** 6 [5]3-8-9 (40) S Sanders 5/2 J FAV: 6-303266: Chsd ldrs 5f, wknd: qck reapp. **4 25**

6 Ran   Time 1m 27.6(5.2)   Owned: Mr M T Buckley   Trained: Middleham

---

CHEPSTOW   FRIDAY 23.04.04   Lefthand, Undulating, Galloping Track

Official Going GOOD/SOFT

1331

5.40 Saltwell Signs Claiming Stakes 3yo (H)
£1477 £422 £211   1m4f23y   Soft 130   -42 Slow   Inside

4847} **FLEETFOOT MAC** 184 [6] P D Evans 3-9-3 (59) N Callan 7/1: 0006-1: b g Fleetwood - Desert Flower (Green Desert) Handy, hdwy to lead over 3f out, rdn out fnl 1f: reapp: 1st win: unplcd all '03 mdn starts (rtd 63): eff over 12f on soft, acts on a gall/undul trk: runs well fresh: wide margin wnr, can rate higher. **68**

899 **QUARRY ISLAND** 31 [1] P D Evans 3-8-8 (40) Joanna Badger 14/1: 0-520002: Led till over 3f out, no extra: ran as well as cld be expected at today's weights: see 596. **13 38**

1183 **OKTIS MORILIOUS** 8 [3] A W Carroll 3-9-3 (45) M Fenton 7/2: 0-004123: Mid-field, onepcd over 2f out: well clr of rem: shade btr 970 (polytrack), see 831. **1¼ 45**

1082 **RYE 16** [2] J A Osborne 3-8-12 (65) D Holland 1/1 FAV: 5-1604: Reluctant to race, chsd ldr till   *dist* 0
6f out, wknd & t.o.: well bckd: showed signs of temperament here, see 785.
4378} **GRACE DARLING 216** [5]3-8-0 J F Egan 33/1: 0-5: b f Botanic - Light On The Waves (Greensmith)   *dist* 0
Rear, t.o.: reapp: unplcd sole '03 start (sell, rtd 0a): with Miss E Lavelle.
1280 **COMIC GENIUS 3** [4]3-8-6 (40) N Chalmers(5) 7/1: 062-3506: Rear, t.o.: qck reapp: see 279.   *dsit* 0
6 Ran Time 2m 51.75 (20.65) Owned: Mr M W Lawrence Trained: Abergavenny

---

1332   6.10 Premier Restaurant Opening Night Apprentice Banded Stakes 3yo+ 0-40 (H)
£1470 £420 £210 **1m2f36y** **Soft 130** -65 Slow Inside

1262* **EUROLINK ARTEMIS 4** [3] Julian Poulton 7-9-13 p (40) M Halford(5) 4/1: 00-04011: Rear, hdwy to lead   50
dist, rdn out: qck reapp: eff at 1m/10f, has tried 12f: acts on firm, soft & fibresand, any trk: fine eff under
top weight, in gd form in banded company: see 1262 & 970.
908   **MR WHIZZ 31** [5] A P Jones 7-9-7 p (40) L Treadwell 9/4 FAV: 0-014432: Handy, led 4f out till over   7 32
1f out, sn no extra: well clr of rem: recent hdles wnr (sell, 2m, gd, rtd 91h): see 442.
1076 **JEZADIL 17** [2] Mrs L Stubbs 6-9-7 (35) Kristin Stubbs 9/1: 0430-003: b f Mujadil - Tender Time   17 7
(Tender King) Led after 2f till 4f out, wknd 2f out: won a sell & a sell h'cap in '03: eff at 10/13.7f on fast,
soft & f/sand, any trk: likes forcing tactics: runs well fresh: has tried cheek pieces.
1 May'03 Catt 13.8fm 45-(45) G: 2 May'03 Newc 10.1g/f 46-44 G: 1 Apr'03 Ripo 12.3g/f 43-37 F:
2 Aug'02 Newc 12.4gd 33- G: 2 Oct'01 Brig 10sft 38-39 F: 1 Sep'01 Wolv 12af 55a-49 G:
2 Jun'01 Ling 11.4fm 47-47 E: 1 Jun'01 Brig 11.8g/f 49-44 E:
1180 **HELLBENT 8** [6] J A Osborne 5-9-7 (40) S Crawford 7/2: 0005634: Keen in rear, btn over 2f out.   9 0
3862} **JIM LAD 242** [7]4-9-7 vis (40) Lucy Russell(7) 11/1: 00/0000-5: b g Young Ern - Anne's Bank   5 0
(Burslem) Mid-field, fdd over 2f out: reapp/jumps fit: recent hdles unplcd (eff at 2m on gd/soft & soft, rtd 94h
at best): unplcd all '03 starts (h'caps, rtd 32): unplcd all '02 starts (rtd h'cap): has tried blnks, wears a visor.
4739} **FORTUNA MEA 192** [4]4-9-7 (40) S Swarbrick 15/2: 060000-6: Led till after 2f, fdd over 2f out.   4 0
3414} **MIDDLEMISS 261** [1]4-9-7 (40) M Lawson 25/1: 00/5554-7: Handy, sn lost place, t.o. fnl 4f.   *dist* 0
7 Ran Time 2m 23.65 (19.55) Owned: Mr Roberto Favarulo Trained: Newmarket

---

1333   6.40 Letheby & Christopher Banded Stakes 3yo+ 0-35 (H)
£1477 £422 £211 **1m2f36y** **Soft 130** -53 Slow Inside

826   **MARGARETS WISH 46** [5] T Wall 4-9-1 (35) D Holland 5/1: 00-04001: Mid-field, hdwy to lead 3f out,   43
pushed out: recent hdles unplcd (sell, rtd 78h): eff around 10f on fm, soft & polytrack.
937   **BUZ KIRI 27** [7] A W Carroll 6-9-1 (35) P Doe 4/5 FAV: 2212262: Bhd, hdwy 4f out, chsd wnr 2f   4 35
out, no impress & kept on for 2nd: clr of rem: acts on fast, soft & both AW's: see 824.
3804} **DANCING DOLPHIN 604** [3] Julian Poulton 5-9-1 (35) Lisa Jones(3) 12/1: 050646/-3: b f Dolphin   5 27
Street - Dance Model (Unfuwain) Chsd ldrs, lost place 5f out, some late gains: reapp: missed '03: unplcd all '02
starts (rtd 48): has tried a visor.
1198} **PHARLY REEF 364** [8] J Burchell 12-9-1 (30) R Price 11/1: 0//000//0-4: b g Pharly - Hay Reef   1¾ 24
(Mill Reef) Keen & trkd ldr after 2f, led 4 out till 3f out, fdd 2f out: reapp/jumps fit: recent hdles unplcd
(h'cap, rtd 80h): well beaten sole '03 start (sell, rtd 0a): missed '02: unplcd all 3 '01 starts (rtd 48): 12yo.
663   **TYRRELLSPASS 66** [4]7-9-1 t (30) V Slattery 11/1: 00/000/-5: Rear, mod late gains: 9 wk abs.   1½ 22
1180 **SUPERCLEAN 8** [1]4-9-1 VIS (30) M Lawson 33/1: 055-006: Led 1f & rem in tch, wknd over 2f out: vis.   ¾ 21
1180 **LEYAALY 8** [2]5-9-1 T P (30) B Reilly(3) 25/1: 00/00-607: Rear, t.o.: t-strap, cheek pieces.   *dist* 0
1076 **ALIMISTE 17** [6]4-9-1 (35) N Callan 14/1: 000008: Led after 1f till 4f out, fdd 3f out, t.o.   1¼ 0
8 Ran Time 2m 22.45 (18.35) Owned: Mr A H Bennett Trained: Church Stretton

---

1334   7.10 Betfair Sharp Minds Banded Stakes 3yo+ 0-45 (H)
£1512 £432 £216 **1m14y str** **Soft 130** +09 Fast Stands side

1090 **BOJANGLES 16** [8] R Brotherton 5-9-7 (45) D Holland 9/2: 4500-001: Veered right after start, made   49
most, rdn out ins fnl 1f: 1st win: gd time: eff at 1m/10f on gd/soft & soft grnd, prob acts on any trk.
1136 **CATCH THE FOX 11** [5] J J Bridger 4-9-7 (45) J Tate 25/1: 00050-02: b g Fraam -   1½ 45
Versaillesprincess (Legend of France) Rear, hdwy over 2f out, styd on ins fnl 1f to go 2nd nr fin: 5th at best in
'03 (h'cap, rtd 43): 4th in an auct mdn in '02 (rtd 87): eff over 1m on soft: shld be placed to win a banded race.
908   **KENNY THE TRUTH 31** [6] Mrs J Candlish 5-9-7 t (45) N Callan 3/1 FAV: 3345143: Keen & cl up, no   ½ 44
extra fnl 1f: clr of rem: handles soft & fibresand: see 850 & 442.
821   **UNSUITED 46** [4] J E Long 5-9-7 (45) Natalia Gemelova(7) 14/1: 00-03264: Chsd ldrs, wknd 2f out.   6 32
820   **KANZ WOOD 46** [9]8-9-7 (45) P Doe 9/2: 000-0505: Trkd ldrs, hdwy 3f out, wknd 2f out: 7 wk abs.   5 22
4615} **GRADY 200** [1]5-9-7 (45) B Swarbrick(7) 11/1: 000600-6: ch g Bluegrass Prince - Lady Sabina   nk 21
(Bairn) Mid-field, lost place halfway, some late gains: reapp: unplcd all '03 starts (rtd 50, with Miss J S
Doyle): rnr-up in a h'cap in '02: eff at 6f on polytrack: has tried blnks & cheek pieces: now with W Brisbourne.
1 Mar'02 Ling 6ap 58a-57 E:
1058 **OVER TO YOU BERT 18** [3]5-9-7 (45) V Slattery 11/2: 0-065147: Chsd ldrs, wknd over 2f out.   5 11
957   **IAMBACK 25** [10]4-9-7 p (45) M Fenton 15/2: 6160438: Keen & chsd ldrs, fdd 3f out.   7 0
4739} **MANTLES PRIDE 192** [7]9-9-7 (45) D Sweeney 25/1: 406450-9: Al bhd: now with Dr P Pritchard.   3 0
2349} **LADY DULCET 305** [2]4-9-7 (40) R Price 50/1: 0/004-0: 10th: Chsd ldrs, wknd over 3f out on reapp.   25 0
10 Ran Time 1m 41.65 (9.75) Owned: Mr Roy Brotherton Trained: Pershore

---

1335   7.40 Saltwell Signs Banded Stakes 3yo+ 0-40 (H)
£1477 £422 £211 **7f16y str** **Soft 130** -17 Slow Stands side

1314 **UN AUTRE ESPERE 1** [5] T Wall 5-9-7 bl (30) B Swarbrick(7) 25/1: 0-0600051: b g Golden Heights -   37
Drummer's Dream (Drumalis) Made all, styd on fnl 2f, drvn out: unplcd at W'hampton yesterday: 1st win & eff at 7f,
clrly enjoys gd/soft grnd: eff in blnks, tried cheek pieces: imprvd for front rng tactics.
1200* **FRAAMTASTIC 7** [3] B A Pearce 7-9-13 p (40) B Reilly(3) 9/4 J FAV: 4160112: Chsd ldrs, lost place   1¼ 40
halfway, some late gains: acts on firm, gd/soft & fibresand: in gd form in the lowest company: see 1200.
1264 **DUNDONALD 4** [2] M Appleby 5-9-7 t (35) S Righton 11/1: 4065033: ch g Magic Ring - Cal Norma's   3 28

CHEPSTOW FRIDAY 23.04.04 Lefthand, Undulating, Galloping Track

Lady (Lyphard's Special) Slow away & bhd, hdwy 2f out, onepace: quick reapp: eff at 7f/8.5f on fibresand, gd/soft & in banded class: tried blnks.
2 Feb'03 Wolv 8.5af 54a-62 G: 1 Nov'02 Wolv 7af 70a- D: 2 Aug'02 Carl 6.8g/f 63- F:
1181 **DEFINITELY SPECIAL 8** [7] N E Berry 6-9-7 p (35) M Savage(5) 9/1: 0000064: Keen in tch, wknd 2f out. *7* **14**
1264 **TEE JAY KASSIDY 4** [1]4-9-7 (40) J F Egan 7/2: 5004-125: Bhd, hdwy to chase wnr over 1f out, sn wknd qckly: not enjoy gd/soft? much btr 909 (fibresand). *shd* **13**
913 **ZINGING 30** [6]5-9-7 (40) J Tate 9/4 J FAV: 5064006: In tch, wknd qckly 2f out: best 216 (polytrack). *hd* **12**
4122} **MISS FAYE 228** [4]4-9-7 P (40) M Fenton 25/1: 00/466-7: Slow away & al bhd. *2½* **7**
7 Ran Time 1m 30.1 (10.3) Owned: Snax Catering Services Limited Trained: Church Stretton

1336

8.10 Letheby & Christopher Banded Stakes 3yo+ 0-45 (H)
£1547 £442 £221 **5f16y str** **Soft 130** **-09 Slow** Stands side

1290 **BALI STAR 2** [11] R J Hodges 9-9-7 (45) J F Egan 14/1: 0240041: Handy, rdn & sltly outpcd halfway, gd hdwy fnl 1f to get up cl-home, drvn out: stays 6f, both wins at 5f: acts on fast, gd/soft & both AWs: likes sharp trks & has tried blnks: see 374. **49**
1248* **ATTORNEY 4** [2] D Shaw 6-9-13 vis (45) K Fallon 5/2 FAV: 5300112: Held up, hdwy 2f out, styd on to chall ins last, just held: quick reapp & in gd heart in banded class: see 1248. *½* **52**
941 **AINTNECESSARILYSO 27** [3] N E Berry 6-9-7 (45) P Doe 9/2: 1436333: Chsd ldrs, hdwy to lead over 1f out, hdd & no extra ins last: in gd form & shld win a banded stks: see 501, 379. *shd* **45**
541 **THREAT 80** [9] J M Bradley 8-9-7 (45) C J Davies(7) 16/1: 0-040034: Held up, hdwy to chall over 1f out, no extra ins last: 11 wk abs: see 541. *2½* **37**
3880} **DIAMOND RING 242** [10]5-9-7 (45) N Chalmers(5) 14/1: 605360-5: b f Magic Ring - Reticent Bride (Shy Groom) Bhd, eff over 1f out, sn no extra on reapp: plcd in a sell & h'cap in '03 (rtd 46): eff over 5/6f on any trk: acts on fast & gd/soft: has tried a visor. *1* **34**
2 Jul'01 Donc 5g/s 81- D: 1 Jun'01 Sali 5g/f 81- D:
1261 **FLYING FAISAL 4** [6]6-9-7 bl (45) D Holland 7/1: 4003046: Led after 1f till over 1f out, wknd: see 1261. *1½* **30**
1046 **HENRY TUN 18** [5]6-9-7 p (40) M Savage(5) 9/2: 0213027: With ldrs, wknd fnl 1f: needs fibresand. *hd* **29**
1075 **TRAVELLERS JOY 17** [1]4-9-7 (40) M Fenton 40/1: 05660-08: b f The West - Persian Fortune (Forzando) With ldrs, wknd 2f out: rnr-up in a clmr in '03: eff over 5/5.5f on fast grnd. *2* **23**
2 May'03 Bath 5.0g/f 54-(45) F:
1179 **EJAY 8** [12]5-9-7 (45) Lisa Jones(3) 12/1: 0602009: Al bhd. *1½* **19**
1201 **FIRE CAT 7** [8]5-9-7 p (45) D Sweeney 33/1: 5000-000: 10th: With ldr till wknd 2f out. *1½* **15**
960 **Lone Piper 25** [4]9-9-7 P(45) Hazel Boyd(7) 33/1:0 2179] **Bright Mist 674** [7]5-9-7 (45) N Callan 33/1:0
12 Ran Time 1m 3.75(6.95) Owned: Mr E W Carnell Trained: Somerton

WOLVERHAMPTON Fibresand SATURDAY 24.04.04 Lefthand, Sharp Track

Official Going STANDARD

1337

6.00 New Site @ Betdirect Co Uk Amateur Riders' Handicap Stakes 4yo+ 0-70 (E) **[54]**
£3435 £1057 £529 **6f aw rnd** **Going 57** **-19 Slow** Inside

1127 **BLAKESHALL QUEST 12** [9] R Brotherton 4-10-11 vis (65) Mr L Newnes(5) 11/4 FAV: 4445101: Handy, led halfway, pushed out fnl 1f: best at 5/6f, stays 7f on fibresand, likes a sharp trk: see 958 & 550. **72a**
1127 **BOAVISTA 12** [3] P D Evans 4-10-1 (55) Miss E Folkes(3) 13/2: 2453442: Handy, chsd wnr dist, kept on & only just btn: clr of rem: acts on firm, gd/soft & fibresand: consistent: see 593. *½* **59a**
4544} **VAL DE MAAL 206** [5] G C H Chung 4-11-0 (68) Mr T Thomas(7) 10/1: 315240-3: ch c Eagle Eyed - Miss Bojangles (Gay Fandango) Cl up, one paced fnl 1f: reapp: class stks & h'cap wnr in '03: won a mdn in '02: eff at 5f, wng form at 6/7f: acts on firm, fast & f/sand, sharp/undul trk: has tried a visor. 2 Sep'03 Ling 6g/f 72-70 E: *3* **63a**
1 Aug'03 Pont 6fm 72-(70) E: 1 Jun'03 Wolv 7af 71a-65 E: 1 Oct'02 Sout 7af 74a- E: 2 Sep'02 Muss 5g/f 69- E:
1221 **NOBLE LOCKS 7** [8] J W Unett 6-10-12 (66) Miss J C Williams(5) 9/1: 51-00004: Rear, hdwy over 1f out, nrst fin: rcd wide: see 246. *shd* **60a**
4821} **BINT ROYAL 186** [12]6-10-13 p (67) Miss V Haigh(2) 12/1: 620010-5: ch f Royal Abjar - Living Legend (Septieme Ciel) Rear, hdwy over 2f out, no impress fnl 1f: reapp: won 2 h'caps in '03: won 5 h'caps in '02 (B Ellison): eff at 5f, suited by 6/7f on firm, soft & polytrack, loves fibresand/W'hampton: eff with/without blinks or cheek pieces, has tried a visor: on a high mark, but wins her share of h'caps. *hd* **60a**
1 Sep'03 Sout 7af 70a-61 F: 2 Aug'03 Yarm 7.0g/f 60-61 D: 1 Jul'03 Yarm 7.0gd 62-59 D: 2 May'03 Wolv 7af 58a-57 F:
2 May'03 Wolv 6af 58a-57 F: 2 May'03 Yarm 6.0gd 57-57 F: 2 Sep'02 Catt 7fm 60-59 F: 1 Jul'02 Wolv 6af 73a-64 E:
1 Jul'02 Pont 6g/f 63-55 D: 2 Jun'02 Donc 7g/f 62-55 E: 1 Jun'02 Wolv 6af 68a-55 E: 1 Jun'02 Wolv 7af 58a-52 G:
227 **BOISDALE 127** [10]6-9-7 (47) Miss A L Turner(5) 20/1: 060000-6: Handy, onepcd fnl 1f: long abs. *shd* **39a**
1202 **ILLUSTRIOUS DUKE 8** [4]6-9-0 bl (40) Miss M Mullineaux(7) 20/1: 0006027: Led till halfway, wknd fnl 1f. *nk* **31a**
1046 **LADIES KNIGHT 19** [6]4-9-13 (53) Mrs S Bosley 6/1: 5063058: Rear, nvr nr ldrs. *½* **42a**
1127 **ASTRAC 12** [2]13-9-10 (50) Ms C Williams 6/1: 30115-59: Bhd, hdwy over 1f out, sn onepcd. *hd* **38a**
1194 **SCARY NIGHT 9** [7]4-10-4 p (58) Mr S Dobson(3) 12/1: 0-001600: 10th: Handy, wknd over 1f out. *5* **31a**
1310 **PIPS SONG 2** [1]9-9-10 (50) Mrs Marie King(5) 10/1: 1003050: 11th: Rear, hmpd halfway, t.o. *15* **0a**
11 Ran Time 1m 17.4 (4.6) Owned: Droitwich Jokers Trained: Pershore

1338

6.30 Betdirect Co Uk Classified Stakes 3yo 0-65 (E)
£3338 £1027 £514 **5f aw rnd** **Going 57** **-07 Slow** Inside

1088 **CREWES MISS ISLE 17** [3] A G Newcombe 3-8-9 (65) S Whitworth 11/2: 6420-461: Chsd ldrs, hmpd halfway, led ins fnl 1f, drvn out: suited by 5/6f, tried 7f: acts on firm, gd & fibresand, sharp/undul trks: apprec return to fibresand: see 466. **70a**
872* **SAHARA SILK 37** [2] D Shaw 3-8-12 vis (68) D Holland 4/5 FAV: 0613412: Dsptd lead, led over 1f out, hdd ins fnl 1f & no extra: clr of rem, top weight: gd form continues: ran to wng form of 872, see 591. *½* **70a**
1002 **SCOTTISH EXILE 24** [1] K R Burke 3-8-10 vis (66) I Mongan 9/4: 231-6443: Led til over 1f out, sn no extra: btr 197 (mdn), see 32. *3½* **58a**

4923} **OBE BOLD 179** [4] A Berry 3-8-9 (65) P Bradley(5) 12/1: 533000-4: b f Orpen - Capable Kate (Alzao)   *1*   **54a**
Handy, left bhnd fnl 1f: reapp: '03 mdn wnr: eff at 5f on firm & fast, gall trk.
1 May'03 Redc 5g/f 72- E: 2 Apr'03 Thir 5fm 70- D:
4 Ran   Time 1m 3.4 (3.2)   Owned: Mr A McRoberts   Trained: Barnstaple

---

1339   7.00 Sweeney-Stevenson Handicap Stakes Fillies 3yo 0-75   (E)   [77]
£5031   £1548   £774   **1m100y aw rnd**   **Going 57**   **-13 Slow**   Inside

794   **DARING AFFAIR 52** [8] K R Burke 3-8-12 (61) G Faulkner 5/1: 26-32151: Mid-div, led over 2f out,   **70a**
drvn out ins fnl 1f: 7 wk abs: eff btwn 6/8.5f on fibresand & gd/soft, likes a sharp trk: back to wng form on
first try at this trip: runs well fresh: see 636 & 223.
1222* **LADY MO 7** [10] K A Ryan 3-9-7 (70) F Lynch 9/2: 3511012: Mid-div, smooth hdwy to chall 2f out,   *¾*   **76a**
just btn in a cl fin: gd eff under top weight: see 1222 & 402.
1099   **MISKINA 16** [11] W M Brisbourne 3-8-8 (57) B Swarbrick(7) 16/1: 024-03: b f Mark of Esteem -   *2*   **59a**
Najmat Alshemaal (Dancing Brave) Rear, imprvd halfway, onepcd fnl 1f: rnr-up 1 of 3 '03 starts (mdn, with M
Channon): eff btwn 7/8.5f on fast & fibresand, sharp trk: imprvd from reapp. 2 Oct'03 Catt 7g/f 56- E:
1141   **CARRIACOU 12** [5] P W D'Arcy 3-9-6 e (69) D Holland 3/1 FAV: 22002-64: Handy, onepcd 2f out.   *1½*   **68a**
1099   **RUSSALKA 16** [7]3-8-11 (60) Lisa Jones(3) 20/1: 6022-005: Bhd, mod late gains: see 240 & 111.   *9*   **40a**
87   **CHASE THE RAINBOW 152** [2]3-8-7 (56) R Ffrench 10/1: 51002-6: Led til over 2f out, wknd: long   *1¼*   **33a**
abs: now with A Berry: see 87.
1239   **SWORN TO SECRECY 7** [4]3-9-1 (64) S Whitworth 16/1: 0435-007: ch f Prince Sabo - Polly's Teahouse   *2*   **37a**
(Shack) Chsd ldrs till halfway: plcd 1 of 4 '03 starts (mdn, rtd 70): eff at 6f on fast: with S Kirk.
468   **UNINTENTIONAL 92** [1]3-8-9 (58) A Daly 20/1: 0652-68: Al bhd: long abs: see 238.   *1*   **29a**
1021   **BEACH PARTY 22** [6]3-9-0 (63) I Mongan 4/1: 05-39: Keen & handy, wknd 3f out: see 1021.   *7*   **20a**
1   **COMPASSION 166** [9]3-8-9 (58) Dean Williams(7) 25/1: 254450-0: 10th: b f Alhaarth - Titania (Fairy   *shd*   **14a**
King) Handy 2f, lost pl & no cls after: reapp: rnr-up for R Hannon in '03 (sell), later with Miss L Perratt: eff at
5f on gd/soft: now with G Chung. 2 Jun'03 Wind 6g/f 59- G:
1193   **ZULOAGO 9** [3]3-8-8 (57) A Nicholls 16/1: 53200: 11th: Rear, nvr a factor.   *6*   **0a**
11 Ran   Time 1m 52.2 (6.0)   Owned: Mr Nigel Shields   Trained: Leyburn

---

1340   7.30 Special Offers @ Betdirect Co Uk Maiden Stakes 3yo+   (D)
£3455   £1063   £532   **1m1f79y aw**   **Going 57**   **+09 Fast**   Inside

    FIRST DYNASTY 182 [5] Miss S J Wilton 4-9-10 (79) A Quinn(5) 9/2: 52/023-1: br c Danzig - Willow   **80a**
Runner (Alydar) Keen, chsd ldr, led 2f out, drvn out ins fnl 1f: gd time: long abs/jt top weight: rnr up in a mdn
in '03 in native Ireland (1m, firm): eff btwn 6/9.5f on firm, soft & fibresand: runs well fresh.
4872} **STRIDER 183** [3] Sir Michael Stoute 3-8-9   B Doyle 5/2 J FAV: 00-2: ch c Pivotal - Sahara Belle   *hd*   **79a**
(Sanglamore) Led til 2f out, kept on again nr fin, just held: clr of rem, reapp/AW bow: unplcd both '03 mdn starts
(rtd 67): eff at 9.5f on fibresand.
1129   **GENERAL FLUMPA 12** [4] C F Wall 3-8-9   G Baker 5/1: 0-63: b g Vettori - Macca Luna (Kahyasi)   *11*   **57a**
Rear, hdwy over 4f out, wknd 3f out: dam 12f wnr: unplcd sole '03 mdn start (rtd 70a).
520   **STATE OF BALANCE 84** [1] K Bell 6-9-5 (62) I Mongan 7/1: 0040-04: Rear, hdwy 6f out, wknd 3f out.   *7*   **38a**
959   **KNIGHT OF HEARTS 26** [8]3-8-9   A Nicholls 50/1: 55: Rear, hdwy over 5f out, wknd 3f out.   *2½*   **38a**
4851} **ADEEBA 185** [2]3-8-4   S Whitworth 25/1: 000-6: Handy, wknd 3f out: reapp.   *½*   **32a**
    DARENEUR   T G McLaughlin 50/1: 7: Rear, t.o.: Flat debut.   *15*   **0a**
4848} **SALFORD ROCKET 185** [6]4-9-10   R Ffrench 50/1: 0-8: Handy, wknd 5f out, t.o. on reapp.   *1*   **5a**
764   **DEVILS BITE 55** [7]3-8-9 (77) D Holland 5/2 J FAV: 65620-PP: Mid-div, fdd 5f out, p.u., broke   **0a**
blood vessel.
9 Ran   Time 2m 2.8 (4.6)   Owned: John Pointon and Sons   Trained: Stoke-On-Trent

---

1341   8.00 Bet Direct On 0800 32 93 93 Selling Stakes 3yo+   (G)
£2555   £730   £365   **1m100y aw rnd**   **Going 57**   **-05 Slow**   Inside

1058   **OUR DESTINY 19** [2] A W Carroll 6-9-13 (52) S Hitchcott(3) 7/2: 4011631: Mid-div, hdwy to lead   **60a**
over 1f out, drvn out: no bid: suited by 1m/9.4f, stays 11f on fast, soft, loves fibresand/ W'hampton.
1059   **TURN AROUND 19** [5] B W Hills 4-9-8 (58) D Holland 4/1: 0000-002: Handy, led over 2f out til over   *1½*   **51a**
1f out, onepaced ins fnl 1f: stays 8.5f on firm, gd/soft & fibresand: see 345.
996   **XALOC BAY 24** [6] B P J Baugh 6-9-13 (56) Lisa Jones(3) 11/2: 1123603: Led til over 2f out, sn no extra.   *¾*   **54a**
964   **DESERT HEAT 26** [4] I Semple 6-9-13 vis (64) I Mongan 3/1 FAV: 0212004: Rear, hdwy 2f out, onepcd.   *1¼*   **52a**
1323   **JUST WIZ 1** [7]8-9-8 (58) T G McLaughlin 7/2: 63023025: Rear, hdwy 3f out, wknd 2f out: too sn?   *2½*   **42a**
1090   **FORTY FORTE 17** [3]8-9-8 T p (45) A Quinn(5) 14/1: 0-000306: Handy, wknd 2f out: tried a t-strap.   *11*   **20a**
3151} **MUTABARI 274** [1]10-9-8 (45) Amy Myatt(7) 33/1: 550000-7: ch g Seeking The Gold - Cagey Exuberance   *8*   **4a**
(Exuberant) Rear, t.o.: reapp: won a h'cap in '03: won 2 clmrs in '02: all 7 wins at 7f, stays 12f, acts on fast
& soft, loves fibresand/W'hampton: eff with/without visor: has run well fresh. 1 Mar'03 Wolv 7af 50a-46 F:
2 Jul'02 Sout 7af 50a-49 F: 1 Jun'02 Muss 7.1gd 48- F: 1 Jun'02 Sali 7g/s 48- E: 1 Dec'00 Wolv 7af 52a-47 F:
7 Ran   Time 1m 51.5 (5.3)   Owned: Mr Dennis Deacon   Trained: Alcester

---

1342   8.30 Bet Direct On Sky Active Handicap Stakes 3yo+ 46-55   (F)   [53]
£2905   £830   £415   **1m4f aw**   **Going 57**   **+00 Fast**   Inside

1197   **RED FOREST 9** [8] J Mackie 5-9-8 t (47) A Culhane 5/2: 54560-31: Handy, hdwy to lead 3f out, drvn   **63a**
out fnl 1f: eff btwn 1m/12f on fast, gd & fibresand, likes W'hampton: on a fair mark: see 1197.
1197   **CLASSIC MILLENNIUM 9** [4] W J Musson 6-9-7 (46) Lisa Jones(3) 9/4 FAV: 0155-022: Handy, hdwy 2f   *6*   **48a**
out, no impress on wnr: clr of rem: fin ahead of today's wnr in 1197, see 896.
3846} **SHAPE UP 244** [6] T Keddy 4-9-13 bl (53) P Doe 20/1: 342640-3: b g Octagonal - Bint Kaldoun   *15*   **33a**
(Kaldoun) Led to 3f out, sn no extra: reapp: top weight: rnr up in a mdn & a h'cap in '03: eff around 12f on
fast, soft & polytrack: acts on stiff or sharp trk: wears blinks.
2 Jul'03 Thir 12sft 66-65 D: 2 Mar'03 Ling 12ap 71a- D:
590   **AMBERSONG 75** [3] A W Carroll 6-9-9 (48) I Mongan 4/1: 20-33064: Rear, some late gains: abs.   *1¾*   **25a**

374

WOLVERHAMPTON Fibresand SATURDAY 24.04.04 Lefthand, Sharp Track

1313 **WESTERN COMMAND 2** [5]8-9-4 (3oh)p (40) Joanna Badger 20/1: 0055335: Chsd ldr til 6f out, wknd   ½   **19a**
over 3f out: qck reapp: see 456.
937 **KENTUCKY BULLET 28** [7]8-9-8 (47) S Whitworth 9/2: 25-30636: Rear, nvr nr ldrs: see 72.   1¾   **20a**
866 **E MINOR 38** [2]5-9-8 (47) N Chalmers(5) 16/1: 06-50667: Handy, wknd over 3f out: see 424.   3   **15a**
2490} **FRENCH RISK 301** [1]4-9-8 (48) B Swarbrick(7) 14/1: 420355-8: b g Entrepreneur - Troyes (Troy)   15   **0a**
Rear, t.o. on reapp: rnr up in a h'cap in '03 (with N Graham): well btn sole '02 mdn start: eff at 10f on fast &
polytrack: tried blinks: now with W Brisbourne. 2 Feb'03 Ling 10ap 47a-45 E:
8 Ran Time 2m 40.5(6.9) Owned: Mr P Riley Trained: Church Broughton

HAYDOCK SATURDAY 24.04.04 Lefthand, Flat, Galloping Track

Official Going Soft (Good/Soft Places)

1343 5.45 European Breeders Fund Maiden Stakes Fillies 2yo (D)
£4719 £1452 £726 **5f str** **Good/Soft 63** -01 Slow Centre

920 **FLOSSYTOO 30** [5] J O'Reilly 2-8-11 J D O'Reilly(7) 4/1: 01: b f Royal Applause - Nite Owl Dancer   **72**
(Robellino) Prom, led 2f out, drvn out to hold on despite hanging left: Mar foal, dam wnr at 5f: sire high class
at sprint dists: eff at 5f, shld appreciate 6f: acts on gd/soft grnd & a gall trk: improved on debut eff here.
1091 **RIGHTPRICE PREMIER 16** [3] K A Ryan 2-8-11 N Callan 10/30 FAV: 32: In tch, short of room bef 2f   1½   **67**
out, styd on ins fnl 1f, not pace wnr: eff at 5f on gd/soft, shld enjoy further: better run, see 1091.
1123 **STANS GIRL 12** [7] M R Channon 2-8-11 S Hitchcock(3) 4/1: 03: b f Fraam - Gigetta (Brief Truce)   2½   **60**
Handy, no extra bef 1f out: Mar foal, cost 14,500 gns: dam unplcd: sire useful performer around 1m.
      MAKE US FLUSH 0 [1] A Berry 2-8-11 P Mathers(7) 10/1: 4: b f Mind Games - Pearls (Mon Tresor)   3½   **50**
Slow away, prog 2f out, nrst fin: debut: Feb foal, cost 900 gns: sister to Perle d'Azur & Prince Of Perles who
both won at 6f: dam unrcd: sire top class at sprint dists: improve for today's experience.
      TANTIEN 0 [6]2-8-11 R Winston 12/1: 5: Slow away, nvr nrr than mid div: debut.   1½   **46**
      MYTTONS DREAM 0 [8]2-8-11 B Reilly(3) 6/1: 6: Al in rear: debut.   3   **37**
      GLORIA NIMBUS 0 [4]2-8-11 S Righton 25/1: 7: Led 3f, fdd: debut.   11   **7**
      HOUDINI BAY 0 [2]2-8-11 T Hamilton(3) 12/1: 8: Al in rear: debut.   1½   **3**
8 Ran Time 1m 2.00 (3.2) Owned: Mr J Saul Trained: Barnsley

1344 6.15 Diane Organ 40th Birthday Handicap Stakes 3yo 0-85 (D) [92]
£5541 £1705 £853 **5f str** **Good/Soft 63** +12 Fast Centre

4941} **FOURSQUARE 178** [1] J Mackie 3-9-6 (84) N Callan 7/1: 5102-1: b g Fayruz - Waroonga (Brief Truce)   **93**
Made all, rdn out fnl 1f to assert: reapp: mdn wnr on 1 of 4 '03 starts (also h'cap rnr up): eff at 5f, 6f shld
suit: acts on firm & soft grnd: goes well fresh: likes to race with/force the pace: improved
for gelding op this winter, win again. 2 Oct'03 Yarm 5.2sft 80-80 D: 1 Oct'03 Nott 5.1fm 82- D:
1050* **PICCOLO PRINCE 19** [2] E J Alston 3-8-4 (68) W Supple 4/1 CO FAV: 0121212: Prom, kept on ins fnl   3   **68**
1f, not pace wnr: continues in gd form: seer 1050 & 872.
1106 **LAKE GARDA 14** [4] B A McMahon 3-9-7 (85) S W Kelly 6/1: 22001-53: b c Komaite - Malcesine   nk   **84**
(Auction Ring) Handy, onepcd from 1f out: med auct mdn wnr on fnl '03 start (also rnr up twice): eff at 5f/6f on
firm & gd/soft grnd: acts on a flat & stiff/gall trk: not disgraced under top weight.
1 Sep'03 Thir 6fm 83-(87) E: 2 Jun'03 Leic 6.0g/f 85- E: 2 May'03 Leic 5.0gd 85- E:
1229 **ELLIOTS CHOICE 7** [3] D Carroll 3-8-7 (71) D Tudhope(6) 4/1 CO FAV: 03020-44: Chsd ldrs, no extra   ¾   **68**
ins fnl 1f: qck reapp: just btr 1229 (reapp).
1281 **POINT CALIMERE 4** [6]3-9-4 (82) E Ahern 9/1: 0330-045: Handy 4f, sn wknd: qck reapp: see 1023.   4   **67**
1229 **MRS SPENCE 7** [5]3-8-4 (68) Dale Gibson 33/1: 025-06: b f Mind Games - Maid O'Cannie (Efisio)   1½   **49**
Slow away, nvr nrr than mid div: qck reapp: rnr up on 1 of 3 '03 starts (mdn): eff at 6f on firm grnd.
2 Jul'03 Catt 6.0fm 62- D:
1229 **A LITTLE BIT YARIE 7** [7]3-9-6 (84) Darren Williams 4/1 CO FAV: 3123-37: Handy till wknd 2f out: 5   **50**
qck reapp: btr expected after 3rd in 1229 (soft).
1229 **EASTERN PEARL 7** [8]3-8-9 (73) R Winston 25/1: 22100-08: In tch 4f, sn fdd: qck reapp.   ½   **38**
1154 **MULTIPLE CHOICE 11** [9]3-8-11 (75) J P Guillambert(3) 9/1: 2004-009: Al in rear: btr 1011 (AW).   15   **5**
9 Ran Time 1m 1.37 (2.57) Owned: Mr Tim Kelly Trained: Church Broughton

1345 6.45 Rednal Classified Stakes 3yo+ 0-75 (D)
£5655 £1740 £870 **6f str** **Good/Soft 63** -17 Slow Centre

4738*] **ZOOM ZOOM 543** [5] Mrs L Stubbs 4-9-3 (70) R Winston 4/1: 31/-1: b c Abou Zouz - Iltimas (Dayjur)   **77**
Led till 4f out, led again dist, drvn out ins fnl 1f: reapp: missed '03: mdn wnr on last of only 2 '02 starts:
eff at 5f/6f on gd/soft grnd: acts on a gall trk & goes well fresh: fine eff after such a long lay off with tibia &
pelvis fractures: only lightly raced & can rate higher. 1 Oct'02 Nott 5g/s 77- D:
1215 **UP TEMPO 8** [4] K A Ryan 6-9-5 bl (77) N Callan 1/1 FAV: 1311142: Lost footing bef 3f out, styd on   1   **76**
to chse wnr fnl 1f, kept on but al held: clr rem: gd run dropped back to 6f & can find similar: see 1215 & 1142.
1138 **FREE WHEELIN 12** [6] W Jarvis 4-9-3 (75) M Tebbutt 10/1: 20000-03: b g Polar Falcon - Farhana   6   **59**
(Fayruz) Keen in tch, no extra fnl 2f: mdn wnr once in '02: eff at 6f/7f on
gd/soft grnd, sharp or gall trk: has gone well fresh. 2 May'03 Hayd 6sft 88-85 D: 1 May'02 Wind 5g/s 90- D:
4616} **SEWMUCH CHARACTER 201** [2] M Blanshard 5-9-3 (72) D Sweeney 11/2: 050304-4: b g Magic Ring -   1½   **55**
Diplomatist (Dominion) Prom, led after 3f, hdd dist, sn fdd: reapp: h'cap wnr in '03 (also plcd 3 times): mdn wnr
in '02: eff at 6/7f, tried 1m: acts on fast & gd/soft, any trk: can force the pace.
1 Jun'03 Pont 6g/f 75-70 E: 2 Apr'03 Sout 7g/f 70-69 E: 1 Jul'02 Folk 7g/s 73- D: 2 Jun'02 Newb 6sft 71- D:
2 Sep'01 Ches 7g/s 75- D: 2 Sep'01 Ches 7gd 79- D: 2 Aug'01 Pont 6gd 78- D:
1065 **SUGAR CUBE TREAT 8** [1]8-9-0 P (30) S Righton 100/1: 000-0005: Sn in tch, wknd bef 2f out.   2½   **45**
687 **FULL PITCH 64** [7]8-9-3 (60) V Slattery 50/1: 1////-006: Handy 4f, sn wknd: 9 wk abs.   1¾   **43**
4178} **CROSS ASH 226** [8]4-9-4 (76) Dale Gibson 33/1: 05100-7: In tch 4f, sn fdd: reapp.   1¾   **39**
1251 **GDANSK 5** [3]7-9-3 (73) P Mathers(7) 7/1: 02000-0U: Veered right & u.r sn after start: qck reapp.   **0**
8 Ran Time 1m 16.14 (4.84) Owned: Mr Des Thurlby Trained: Malton

1346   7.15 Forton Rated Stakes Handicap 4yo+ 0-90 (C)   [95]
£9939 £3058 £1529   1m2f120y   Good/Soft 63   -12 Slow   Outside

4572} **RED FORT 204** [6] M A Jarvis 4-9-7 (88) P Robinson 11/2: 0140-1: b g Green Desert - Red Bouquet   96
(Reference Point) Handy, led despite hanging left bef 1f out, rdn out: reapp: mdn wnr in '03: eff at 10.5f/12f on
fast & gd/soft grnd: has been gelded since last term: useful, unexposed in h'cap
grade. 1 Jul'03 Newm 12g/f 90- D:
5036} **LA SYLPHIDE GB 168** [5] G M Moore 7-8-10 (77) S W Kelly 20/1: 211610-2: ch f Rudimentary -   nk   84
Primitive Gift (Primitive Rising) Led till bef 1f out, styd on & only just held by wnr: clr rem: reapp: in gd
form in '03 winning 3 h'caps: unplcd sole '02 start (h'cap): won 3 AW h'caps in '01 (Mrs A Duffield): eff btwn 7f &
10.5f on gd, rain softened grnd & fibresand: likes Hamilton & Southwell & goes well from the front.
1 Sep'03 Hayd 10.5gd 78-73 C: 1 Jul'03 Hami 9.2gd 74-63 E: 1 Jul'03 Hami 9.2gd 68-57 E: 2 Jun'03 Hami 9.2gd 55-53 E:
1 Jun'01 Sout 7af 64a-58 F: 1 May'01 Sout 8af 61a-55 E: 1 Apr'01 Sout 7af 60a-51 F:
5036} **KENTUCKY BLUE 168** [3] T D Easterby 4-9-4 (85) R Winston 6/1: 630550-3: b g Revoque - Delta Town   5   85
(Sanglamore) Chsd ldrs, outpcd 4f out, rallied over 2f out, onepace: 7 wk jumps abs, earlier won 2 juv nov hdles
(rtd 131?, eff at 2m on gd & soft): h'cap wnr in '03: med auct mdn & h'cap wnr in '02: eff at 7.4f/10.5f, poss
stays 12f: acts on fast, enjoys soft grnd: acts on any trk & can carry big weights. 1 May'03 Hayd 10.5sft 90-85 C:
2 Jul'02 Thir 7g/f 86- C: 1 Jul'02 Beve 7.4g/s 86-83 E: 1 Jun'02 Thir 7g/f 83- E: 2 Jun'02 Hayd 6sft 83- D:
1231 **FISIO THERAPY 7** [8] M Johnston 4-9-1 (82) J Fanning 9/2: 14335-04: ln tch, no extra ins fnl 2f.   ½   81
1128 **WAR OWL 12** [9]7-8-7 (74) N Callan 4/1 FAV: 4-201135: Slow away, nvr nrr than mid div: btr 1128.   1¼   71
5036} **TELEMACHUS 168** [1]4-9-7 (88) M Fenton 9/1: 135530-6: Prom, fdd dist: reapp.   9   73
1104 **INTRICATE WEB 14** [10]8-8-9 (76) W Supple 16/1: 3-112467: Bhd, prog 5f out, hung left & fdd 3f out.   7   51
1235 **DREAM MAGIC 7** [7]6-8-11 (78) E Ahern 11/2: 30044-48: Rear, nvr a factor: btr 1235 (reapp).   16   33
1066 **BROADWAY SCORE 18** [2]6-9-7 (88) Dale Gibson 25/1: 00000-09: Al in rear: btr 1066 (reapp).   hd   42
ARAWAN 224 [4]4-9-5 (86) P Mulrennan(5) 25/1: 232/104-0: 10th: Bhd, nvr a factor: reapp.   29   0
10 Ran   Time 2m 17.95 (17.95)   Owned: The Red Fort Partnership   Trained: Newmarket

1347   7.45 Sleap Maiden Stakes 3yo (D)
£5395 £1660 £830   1m3f200y   Good/Soft 63   -62 Slow   Outside

1153 **DALLOOL 11** [1] M A Jarvis 3-9-0 P Robinson 5/6 FAV: 51: Led till jinked on bend & hdd 4f out,   82+
led again 3f out, pushed out, val 4L+: eff at 12f, further shld suit: acts on gd/soft grnd & a gall trk: lightly
rcd & open to more improvement: see 1153 (debut).
WOOLLY BACK 0 [4] R Hollinshead 3-9-0 Dale Gibson 20/1: 2: b g Alzao - Hopping Higgins (Brief   2½   79
Truce) In tch, outpcd 3f out, rallied ins fnl 1f, no ch with wnr: debut: dam sprinter: eff at 10f, shapes as
though further will suit: acts on gd/soft grnd: encouraging effort.
CUMBRIA 0 [3] M Johnston 3-8-9 J Fanning 4/1: 3: b f Singspiel - Whitehaven (Top Ville) Cl up,   ½   73
left in lead 4f out, hdd 3f out, wkng when hung left ins fnl 1f: debut: half sister to useful hdles performer
Copeland: sire top class mid dist wnr: eff at 12f, shld stay further: acts on gd/soft grnd.
1121 **GOLDEN EMPIRE 13** [2] E A L Dunlop 3-9-0 vis (77) W Supple 11/4: 32-224: Rear, hung under press   18   53
ins fnl 3f, eased when btn fnl 1f: disappointing run on today's gd/soft grnd, btr 1121 (fast).
4 Ran   Time 2m 42.91 (15.1)   Owned: Sheikh Ahmed Al Maktoum   Trained: Newmarket

1348   8.15 High Ercall Handicap Stakes Fillies 3yo+ 0-75 (E)   [68]
£3809 £1172 £586   1m30y rnd   Good/Soft 63   -15 Slow   Inside

1036 **COMMITMENT LECTURE 21** [11] M Dods 4-8-11 t (51) W Supple 4/1 FAV: 64200-51: b f Komaite -   59
Hurtleberry (Tirol) Rear, prog to lead dist, rdn out: h'cap wnr in '03: unplcd in '02 (rtd 49, auct mdn): eff at
7f/1m on fast, enjoys gd/soft grnd: acts on a gall trk & enjoys a strong pace: eff with a t-strap.
2 Jul'03 Leic 8.0gd 53-53 E: 1 May'03 Newc 8g/s 53-49 E: 2 May'03 Newc 7g/f 49-49 E:
1160 **VERMILION CREEK 10** [6] R Hollinshead 5-8-8 (48) Stephanie Hollinshead(7) 16/1: 6-506662: Bhd,   ½   54+
prog when short of room 2f out, kept on ins fnl 1f, post came too sn: acts on fast, gd/soft & fibresand: did not
get best of runs here & would have won in a couple more strides: can find similar: see 1160 & 445.
1059 **OH SO ROSIE 19** [10] J S Moore 4-9-6 (60) J F McDonald(5) 13/2: 4020-433: Held up, prog ins fnl   7   54
2f, no ch with front two: btr 1059 & 1020.
1328 **ZAHUNDA 1** [4] W M Brisbourne 5-8-0 (40) D Fox(5) 10/1: 20463364: Led, hdd dist, wknd: qk reapp.   1   32
1198 **PRINTSMITH 9** [8]7-8-5 (45) J Bramhill 10/1: 4432001: Chsd ldrs, no extra fnl 2f: btr 908.   1¾   33
958 **CLOUDLESS 26** [7]4-9-1 (55) S W Kelly 11/1: 0240336: ln tch, chsd ldr bef 2f out, wknd fnl 1f.   1½   40
1049 **SABALARA 19** [1]4-9-7 (61) E Ahern 10/1: 5620-07: Handy 6f, sn wknd: btr 1049 (reapp).   3   40
1142 **CELTIC ROMANCE 12** [14]5-9-1 (55) J Carroll 25/1: 0000-008: b f Celtic Swing - Southern Sky   5   24
(Comedy Star) Bhd, nvr nrr than mid div: unplcd in all 4 '03 starts (rtd 61, h'cap, D Nicholls): unplcd sole '02
start (clmr): clmr & h'cap wnr in '01 (present stable): eff at 5f/7f on firm or hvy, likes gall trks.
1 Sep'01 Donc 7g/f 82-78 D: 2 Aug'01 Redc 7g/f 79- E: 2 Jul'01 Wind 6g/f 79- C: 1 Jun'01 Hami 5fm 63- E:
2 Apr'01 Ripo 5hvy 62- D:
936 **ELLEN MOONEY 29** [3]5-9-10 (64) T Hamilton(3) 8/1: 02-23409: Nvr nrr than mid div: see 597 & 489.   1½   30
4000} **SIENNA SUNSET 236** [12]5-9-6 (60) J F Egan 25/1: 420200-0: 10th: ch f Spectrum - Wasabi (Polar   shd   25
Falcon) Al in rear: 6 wk jumps abs, earlier rtd 84h at best (nov hdle): rnr up twice on Flat in '03 (h'caps):
class stks wnr in '02: eff at 10f on firm, handles soft grnd: acts on a sharp/undul trk.
1045 **LARK IN THE PARK 21** [2]4-8-7 (47) P M Quinn 10/1: 31006-00: 11th: Chsd ldrs, fdd 3f out.   1¾   8
1070* **CAPETOWN GIRL 18** [9]3-9-7 (75) Darren Williams 9/2: 02025-10: 12th: ln tch 5f, sn hung left &   6   24
wknd: disappointing on big step up in trip: btr 1070 (6f).
4391} **Milk And Sultana 215** [13]4-9-4 (58) P Mulrennan(5) 33/1:0
820 **Thumamah 47** [5]5-9-0 t(54) M Tebbutt 50/1:0
14 Ran   Time 1m 46.84(6.34)   Owned: Mrs B Riddell   Trained: Darlington

Official Going Good/Soft (Good places)

1349   2.55 Gr2 Betfred Com Mile 4yo+   (A)
£58000 £22000 £11000   **1m14y rnd**   **Good/Soft 69**   **+11 Fast**   Inside

1168 **HURRICANE ALAN** 10 [1] R Hannon 4-9-0 (110) P Dobbs 25/1: 65205-31: Keen in mid-div, prog 2f out,   **117**
styd on well to lead cl-home, drvn out: gd time, bckd at long odds: stays 9f, suited by 1m on firm, gd/soft grnd &
any trk: v smart, tough & game, career best run: see 1168.
1168* **GATEMAN** 10 [4] M Johnston 7-9-0 (112) K Dalgleish 8/1: 5-260212: Led till 2f out, rallied gamely   nk   **116**
to regain lead dist, collared cl-home: tough & v game, won the Diomed stks at Epsom last yr & an ideal target again.
1115 **SOVIET SONG** 14 [2] J R Fanshawe 4-8-11 (114) J Murtagh 5/2 FAV: 1/4245-23: Held up, short of   1   **111+**
room 2f out, switched dist, styd on fnl 1f, nrst fin: well bckd: btr run, worth a try over 10f now: see 1115.
4473} **NORSE DANCER** 210 [10] D R C Elsworth 4-9-0 (117) T Quinn 9/1: 340360-4: b c Halling - River   hd   **113**
Patrol (Rousillon) Keen in mid-div, prog to chall dist, no extra cl-home: reapp: 3rd in the 2,000 Guineas, 4th in
the Derby & 3rd in Gr 1 Sussex stks (first time visor) in '03 (rtd 119): juv mdn & nov stks wnr: stays 12f, poss
best arnd 1m: acts on fm & gd/soft, sharp/undul or gall trk: can run well fresh: smart but not straightforward.
1 Jul'02 Asco 7gd 104- D: 1 Jun'02 Sali 6.9g/f 96- D:
4798} **INDIAN HAVEN** 189 [8]4-9-0 (117) D Holland 11/2: 0/10100-5: ch c Indian Ridge - Madame Dubois   2   **109**
(Legend of France) Trkd ldrs, onepcd fnl 1f: nicely bckd, reapp: '03 List h'cap (reapp) & Irish 2,000 Guineas wnr:
'02 mdn wnr: suited by 1m, acts on fast grnd, revels in soft: high-class at best, apprec even softer grnd?
1 May'03 Curr 8sft 117- A: 1 Apr'03 Newm 7gd 111-102 A: 1 Jul'02 Yarm 6g/f 83- D:
951* **BABODANA** 28 [9]4-9-0 (111) G Duffield 7/1: 04210-16: Trkd ldrs, smooth hdwy to lead 2f out, hdd   1¼   **107**
dist & sn wknd: up in grade after 951 (Lincoln h'cap).
922* **SUBLIMITY** 30 [3]4-9-0 t (110) K Fallon 4/1: 41144-17: Dwelt, keen in rear, eff 2f out & sn no   shd   **107**
impress: well bckd: swtg & boiled over in the preliminaries & this shld be forgiven: impress in 922 (reapp).
991 **CHECKIT** 28 [5]4-9-0 (112) T E Durcan 12/1: 20-43368: br c Mukaddamah - Collected (Taufan) Held   nk   **106**
up, mod late gains: '03 stks wnr, also Gr 3 rnr-up: eff at 1m/9f on firm & soft grnd, any trk: has run well fresh:
btr than this & worth another ch after eye-catching run in 991.
2 Nov'03 Newm 8g/f 109-(113) A: 1 Sep'03 Donc 8gd 110-(105) C: 2 Oct'02 San 8sft 102- : 1 Aug'02 Bade 6sft 106- :
2 Jul'02 Newb 6fm 102- A: 1 May'02 Pont 6g/f 95- C: 1 May'02 Newm 6g/s 95- E: 2 May'02 Newm 5fm 93- D:
4747} **SALSELON** 160 [6]5-9-0 Martin Dwyer 16/1: 232310-9: b c Salse - Heady (Rousillon) Al towards   6   **96**
rear & nvr dngrs on reapp: trained in Italy prev, dual Gr 3 wnr in '03: winning form at 7f/1m on gd & hvy grnd:
smart entire, now with L Cumani. 2 May'03 San 8g/f 116- A:
1126+ **PABLO** 12 [7]5-9-0 p (103) M Hills 25/1: 1455-010: 10th: Stumbled start, recovered to trk ldrs 6f,   2½   **92**
wknd: up in grade after 1126.
10 Ran   Time 1m 43.67 (4.67)   Owned: Mr I A N Wight   Trained: Marlborough

1350   4.10 Gr3 Betfred Gordon Richards Stakes 4yo+   (A)
£29000 £11000 £5500   **1m2f7y**   **Good/Soft 69**   **-02 Slow**   Inside

1139 **CHANCELLOR** 12 [11] J L Dunlop 6-8-10 (110) K Fallon 13/2: 50/464-01: ch c Halling - Isticanna   **113**
(Far North) Nvr far away, challenged fnl 1f, forged ahd cl-home, drvn out: bckd from 10/1: trained by B Hills in
'03, lightly rcd & 4th in a Gr 1 on reapp (rtd 115): Gr 2 & Gr 3 wnr in '02: best up with/forcing the pace around
10f on gd or softer grnd: acts on a gall trk, runs well fresh: v game & smart entire who loves give in the grnd.
1 Aug'02 Curr 10sft 114- : 2 Jul'02 Curr 10gd 114- : 1 Apr'02 Sand 10g/s 115- A: 2 Oct'01 Long 9.7hvy 113- :
2 Aug'01 Deau 10sft 114- : 1 Apr'01 Sand 10hvy 112- A:
1139 **NYSAEAN** 12 [2] R Hannon 5-8-13 (112) P Dobbs 16/1: 110-5452: Mid-div, smooth prog to lead dist,   nk   **115**
worried out of it cl-home: bought right there too sn, prev suited -
59 **SUNSTRACH** 160 [4] L M Cumani 6-8-10 T Quinn 9/1: 243103-3: b c Polar Falcon - Lorne Lady (Local   1¾   **109**
Suitor) Keen & prom, led 2f out till dist, not pace of first two cl-home on reapp: trained in Italy in '03, won a
stks race: '02 Gr 1 wnr: winning form at 10f on gd/soft grnd: smart, sharper next time.
2 Mar'02 Long 10sft 114- :
2000} **FRANKLINS GARDENS** 322 [6] M H Tompkins 4-8-10 (108) G Duffield 12/1: 21/110-4: b c Halling -   shd   **109+**
Woodbeck (Terimon) Held up, gd prog 1.5f out, nrst fin on reapp: won first 2 of 3 '03 starts (incl Gr 3): eff at
10f, stays 12f well & a return to that trip will suit: acts on firm & gd/soft grnd, runs well fresh: most
encouraging reapp, one to keep in mind back over 12f.
1 May'03 Ling 11.8gd 108-(105) A: 1 Apr'03 Epso 10.1g/f 106-(89) B: 1 Sep'02 Ayr 7.2gd 90- D: 2 Sep'02 Yarm 7fm 82- D:
884 **BOURGAINVILLE** 35 [10]6-8-10 (113) Martin Dwyer 16/1: 5026-045: b g Pivotal - Petonica (Petoski)   2   **106**
Mid-div, wandered but styd on fnl 1f & nrst fin: failed to win in '03, tho' plcd several times, incl in Gr 3
company: eff at 1m/10f on firm, soft grnd & polytrack, prob any trk: can force the pace & run well fresh: v useful.
2 Aug'03 Wind 10.0g/f 110-(105) A: 2 Apr'03 Sand 10.0gd 111-(102) A: 2 Sep'02 York 8.9g/f 112- A:
2 Jul'01 Sali 8g/f 99- B: 2 Jun'01 Asco 8g/f 99- B: 2 May'01 Good 9fm 98-95 B:
2250*)**PERSIAN MAJESTY** 310 [3]4-8-10 J Murtagh 11/2: 1/1-6: b c Grand Lodge - Spa (Sadler's Wells)   2   **103**
Held up, some late hdwy, nvr dngrs on reapp: only 3rd race & prev unbeaten: won sole '03 start (List): eff at 10f
on fast grnd, shld stay further: runs well fresh, smart, sharper next time.
1 Jun'03 Asco 10g/f 109- A: 1 Oct'02 Newm 8g/f 98- D:
1139 **ISLAND HOUSE** 12 [7]8-8-10 (113) D Holland 11/2: 14432-37: Slow away, prog 2f out, sn no impress.   shd   **103**
4800} **MUQBIL** 189 [5]4-8-10 (113) T E Durcan 5/1: 2/10234-8: Led till 2f out, grad wknd: nicely bckd.   shd   **102**
1139 **BUSTAN** 12 [9]5-8-10 BL (107) R Hills 9/2 FAV: 3/442-329: Trkd ldrs 1m, wknd: tchd 11/2, first   ½   **101**
time blnks: reportedly unsuited by easy grnd: see 1139.
4066} **SIR GEORGE TURNER** 588 [1]5-8-10 K Dalgleish 20/1: 204632/-0: 10th: Prom till halfway, wknd 2f out.   15   **81**
3722} **YAWMI** 249 [8]4-8-10 (110) M Hills 16/1: 110-0: 11th: Chsd ldrs 1m, wknd & eased on reapp.   5   **74**
11 Ran   Time 2m 11.19 (7.09)   Owned: Mr M J Al-Qatami   Trained: Arundel

1351   4.45 Betfred 'treble Odds On Lucky's' Rated Stakes Handicap 4yo+ 0-95 (C)   [102]
£12586 £4774 £2387   1m14y rnd   Good/Soft 69   -10 Slow   Inside

1111 **UNSHAKABLE 14** [4] Bob Jones 5-9-0 (88) F Norton 7/1: 0000-001: b g Eagle Eyed - Pepper And Salt   95
(Double Schwartz) Held up, switched & hdwy to lead dist, rdn clr, val bit further: failed to win in '03, val h'cap
rnr-up: '02 mdn & h'cap wnr: eff at 7/10f on firm & soft grnd: likes a stiff/gall trk & runs well fresh: on a fair
mark & gd confidence booster, could follow up. 2 Jul'03 Newb 8fm 100-96 B: 2 Oct'02 Newb 9sft 99-91 B:
1 Aug'02 Sand 8gd 92-85 C: 1 Apr'02 Hayd 7.1g/f 90- D: 2 Nov'01 Donc 8sft 84- E:
4600} **ALWAYS ESTEEMED 203** [9] G Wragg 4-9-7 (95) Martin Dwyer 20/1: 340000-2: b g Mark of Esteem -   ¾   99
Always Far (Alydar) Held up, hdwy 2f out, chsd wnr fnl 1f, styd on: reapp, jt top-weight: '03 reapp wnr (mdn),
subs tried blnks: eff arnd 1m on fast & gd/soft: runs well fresh: has been gelded since last yr & this was a
useful run, win similar. 2 Apr'03 Sand 8gd 100- C: 1 Apr'03 Ripo 8g/f 91- D:
1057 **SOYUZ 19** [11] M A Jarvis 4-8-8 (82) K Fallon 7/2 FAV: 23000-23: Trkd ldrs, kept on under press fnl 1f.   1   84
3674} **DUBROVSKY 251** [13] J R Fanshawe 4-8-11 (85) R Hills 14/1: 01/030-4: ch g Hector Protector -   nk   86+
Reuval (Sharpen Up) Dwelt, hdwy from rear when no run 2f out till 1f out, fin well but too late: op 10/1, reapp:
lightly rcd in '03, plcd on middle of 3 starts (h'cap, rtd 87): mdn auct wnr in '02: eff at 1m on fast & gd/soft,
may stay 10f: gelded since last year, most eye-catching reapp & shld not be missed next time.
1 Aug'02 Warw 7.1g/f 87- F:
1057* **JOOLS 19** [1]6-8-7 (81) R Miles(3) 16/1: 100-0015: Wide in rear, prog 2f out, nrst fin: gd run in   nk   82
the circumstances, forced wide: see 1057.
5020} **JAZZ MESSENGER 170** [15]4-9-7 (95) T E Durcan 11/2: 311006-6: b g Acatenango - In The Saltmine   nk   96+
(Damister) Held up, hdwy when short of room dist, not recover on reapp: won a mdn (reapp) & 2 h'caps in '03: eff
at 1m, stays 10f on any trk: acts on fm & soft: v decent reapp, may have fin plcd with a clr run, keep in mind.
1 Jun'03 Epso 10.1fm 100-91 C: 1 May'03 Hayd 8.1sft 92-77 B: 1 Mar'03 Sout 7g/f 80- D:
1068 **AMANDUS 18** [14]4-9-7 (95) J Murtagh 20/1: 4/0214-07: Prom, led briefly dist, no extra.   ½   95
81 **CERTAIN JUSTICE 154** [17]6-8-8 (82) N Chalmers(5) 16/1: 506040-8: Rear, prog 2f out, onepcd fnl 1f.   2   79
945 **IRONY 28** [12]5-9-1 (89) L Keniry(3) 20/1: 60163-09: Led till dist, wknd.   ½   85
4979} **IMPERSONATOR 175** [2]4-8-6 (80) T Quinn 16/1: 000040-0: 10th: Nvr btr from mid-div on reapp.   1¼   74
4846} **ISLAND RAPTURE 185** [3]4-8-5 (79) A McCarthy 33/1: 223055-0: 11th: Rear, prog wide halfway,   hd   72
onepcd when short of room dist on reapp: new stable.
1151 **FLYING EXPRESS 11** [8]4-8-12 (86) M Hills 10/1: 60644-60: 12th: Front rank 6f, wknd: see 1151.   2   76
44 **NUIT SOMBRE 159** [10]4-8-9 (83) K Dalgleish 12/1: 405600-0: 13th: Trkd ldrs, trav well & ev ch 2f   hd   72
out, sn wknd.
1020 **OAKLEY RAMBO 23** [7]5-8-5 (79) R Smith 16/1: 000000-50: 14th: Wide in rear, nvr dngrs.   ¾   67
1057 **ACE OF HEARTS 19** [18]5-8-7 (81) J Mackay 9/1: 5362-050: 15th: Mid-div, hmpd 2f out, not recover.   shd 68
1131 **RICHEMAUR 12** [16]4-8-5 (79) G Duffield 20/1: 00000-40: 16th: Trkd ldrs 6f, wknd: see 1131.   ¾   65
1235 **AFRICAN SAHARA 7** [5]5-8-4 (82) G Carter 20/1: 0160600: 17th: Held up & reportedly nvr trav.   6   59
17 Ran   Time 1m 45.29 (6.29)   Owned: Unshakable Partnership   Trained: Newmarket

1352   5.20 Betfred 'the Bonus King' Flat V Jump Jockeys Handicap Stakes 4yo+ 0-75 (E)   [54]
£7036 £2165 £1083   1m14y rnd   Good/Soft 69   -19 Slow   Inside

932 **LIFTED WAY 29** [5] P R Chamings 5-11-4 (72) A P McCoy 11/1: 35400-01: b c In The Wings - Stack   80
Rock (Ballad Rock) Trkd ldr, went on 2f out, pushed clr fnl 1f, readily: '03 mdn wnr, also h'cap plcd:
eff at 7f/1m on firm & gd/soft grnd: acts on a sharp/turning or stiff/undul trk: gd weight-carrier.
1 Jul'03 Warw 8.1fm 78-(76) D: 2 Oct'02 Sand 9g/f 81- D: 2 Sep'02 Sand 10gd 79- D:
932 **SIR LAUGHALOT 29** [7] Miss E C Lavelle 4-11-2 (70) M A Fitzgerald 9/1: 0-203232: Chsd ldrs, went   4   72
after wnr fnl 1f, sn no impress: op 7/1: another consistent run: acts on polytrack & gd/soft.
5029} **MR VELOCITY 169** [10] A C Stewart 4-11-2 (70) Martin Dwyer 7/1: 633330-3: b g Tagula - Miss Rusty   nk   72
(Mukaddamah) Held up, prog 2f out, styd on under press fnl 1f on reapp: plcd numerous times in '03 (mdns & a
h'cap), has since been gelded: eff at 7f/1m on firm, gd/soft & polytrack: handles a sharp or stiff/gall trk.
294 **TODLEA 112** [12] J A Osborne 4-11-7 (75) B J Geraghty 14/1: 10000-64: b g Desert Prince - Imelda   1½   75
(Manila) Rear, styd on fnl 1.5f, nvr nrr: long abs: '03 mdn wnr (first time t-strap): eff at 1m on fast & fm.
1 May'03 Sand 8g/f 84- D:
1235 **KARAOKE 7** [11]4-11-2 (70) J Murtagh 6/1: 1-001005: Mid-div, short of room dist, sn no impress.   3½   65
3330} **MEDALLIST 266** [3]5-11-4 (72) C Llewellyn 12/1: 530330-6: Nvr btr than mid-div on reapp.   1   66
1059 **BISHOPSTONE MAN 19** [4]7-11-3 (71) T E Durcan 14/1: 42240-07: Rear, nvr a factor.   ¾   64
5 **SWIFT ALCHEMIST 166** [1]4-11-2 (70) T J Murphy 20/1: 052000-8: Sn in clr lead, hdd 2f out, wknd.   nk   62
888 **RACING NIGHT 35** [8]4-11-7 (75) R Johnson 14/1: 41450-09: Al towards rear.   2½   63
1135 **STEELY DAN 12** [7]5-10-12 (67) M Hills 4/1 FAV: 1121160: 10th: Held up, nvr nr ldrs: well bckd,   shd 54
reportedly lost action: prev in gd form, see 1042 (AW).
758 **SKYLARKER 56** [9]6-11-7 (75) G Duffield 9/1: 04-23300: 11th: Chsd ldrs 6f, wknd: 6 wk abs.   2½   58
1083 **REBATE 17** [6]4-10-13 (67) K Fallon 11/2: 000-0500: 12th: Keen & chsd ldrs 6f, wknd into last.   ¾   49
12 Ran   Time 1m 46.07(7.07)   Owned: Mrs Alexandra J Chandris   Trained: Basingstoke

Official Going GOOD/SOFT.

1353   2.10 'original' Median Auction Maiden Stakes 2yo (E)
£3543 £1090 £545   5f2y str   Good/Soft 67   -27 Slow   Stands Side

1053 **GOODRICKE 19** [3] D R Loder 2-9-0 L Dettori 1/5 FAV: 21: Slow away, sn recovered to lead, pushed   88+
clr over 1f out, easily: well bckd: eff over a stiff or sharp 5f, 6f will suit: goes well on gd/soft grnd:
potentially v useful, win more races: see 1053.
1014 **LANGSTON BOY 23** [2] M L W Bell 2-9-0 I Mongan 7/1: 42: Cl-up, eff to chase wnr over 1f out, not   5   70
his pace: sharper for debut, poss caught a useful sort: see 1014.
1071 **GREZIE 18** [4] J R Best 2-8-9 N Pollard 20/1: 443: Led early, prom, wknd dist: see 1071, 929 (gd).   2   59

MAURO [5] P M Phelan 2-8-9   T P Queally(3) 33/1: 4: b f Danehill Dancer - Stop The Traffic   5   51
(College Chapel) In tch, wknd 2f out on debut: March first foal, cost E12,000: dam stayed 7f.
LISTEN TO ME [1]2-9-0   Paul Eddery 33/1: 5: gr g Petong - Time Clash (Timeless Times) Al bhd   6   44
on debut: Feb foal: dam 6f juv wnr: bred for speed.
5 Ran   Time 1m 03.0 (4.7)   Owned: Sheikh Mohammed   Trained: Newmarket

---

1354   2.40 Tiger Best Bitter Handicap Stakes 3yo+ 0-80 (D)   [80]
£5772 £1776 £888   **5f21 8y str**   **Good/Soft 67**   -08 Slow   Stands Side

1255 **WHIPPASNAPPER 5** [15] J R Best 4-8-9   (61) N Pollard 5/1 FAV: 1213021: Held up stands side, hdwy   67
over 1f out, styd on strongly to lead ins last, rdn out: qck reapp: eff over 5/7f, suited by 6f: acts on fast,
gd/soft & likes polytrack, any trk, likes Lingfield: proving v tough & consistent: see 565, 516.
976 **KINGSCROSS 25** [11] M Blanshard 6-9-6   (72) D Sweeney 13/2: 43000-42: Held up stands side, hdwy 2f   ¾   76
out, styd on to lead ins last, collared cl-home: joc received a 2-day whip ban: loves easy grnd & h'capped to win.
940 **ROMANY NIGHTS 28** [7] J W Unett 4-9-9 vis (75) S W Kelly 20/1: 000-5043: Prom stands side, kept on   nk   78
fnl 1f, not btn far: acts on firm, gd/soft & fibresand: eff over 5/7f: see 807.
4394} **MR MALARKEY 215** [20] Mrs C A Dunnett 4-9-13 bl (79) A Nicholls 25/1: 304000-4: b g Pivotal - Girl   nk   81
Next Door (Local Suitor) Led far side pair, hung left but kept on till collared cl-home: '03 mdn auct, h'cap &
class stks wnr: v eff over a gall or easy 6f on firm, clearly handles gd/soft: best in blnks & can force the pace:
tough & genuine, spot on next time.
1 Jun'03 Kemp 6fm 85-(76) D: 2 May'03 Leic 6.0g/f 84-(76) D: 1 Apr'03 Nott 6.1g/f 78-70 E: 1 Apr'03 Thir 6fm 77-(55) E:
704 **DORCHESTER 61** [16]7-9-8   (74) Lisa Jones(3) 20/1: 13053-65: In tch stands side, some late gains,   ½   75
nvr dngrs, nrst fin: 2 mth abs: encouraging, likes Newmarket, see 704.
1282* **HURRICANE COAST 4** [19]5-9-7 (7ex)bl (73) Dane O'Neill 11/2: 0041016: Slow away, held up stands   nk   73
side, hdwy halfway, onepace: qck reapp, not disgraced: see 1282 (7f).
1103 **FULL SPATE 16** [2]9-9-2   (68) R L Moore 16/1: 06061-67: Slow away, bhd stands side, hdwy & not clr   ½   67+
run 2f out till 1f out, nrst fin: caught the eye here, h'capped to win again, poss on faster grnd at Windsor.
1145 **BRANSTON TIGER 12** [8]5-9-10   (76) L Dettori 8/1: 504-5008: b c Mark of Esteem - Tuxford Hideaway   2½   70
(Cawston's Clown) Chsd ldrs stands side, eff over 1f out, onepace: well btn sole jumps start: '03 h'cap wnr: '02
mdn scorer: eff over 6/7f on firm, soft & fibresand: acts on any trk.   1 May'03 Thir 6g/s 83-76 C:
1 Aug'02 Newm 6sft 78- D: 2 Jun'02 Thir 7g/f 79- D: 2 Jul'01 Redc 7fm 72- D: 2 Jul'01 Newc 7g/f 73- D:
1282 **HOLLOW JO 4** [3]4-9-6   (72) F Lynch 14/1: 11120-09: b g Most Welcome - Sir Hollow (Sir Ivor) Led   1¼   64
stand side group over 2f out till over 1f out, no extra: won 4 of 7 '03 starts, all h'caps: winning form over 6/7f
& acts on fast & gd grnd, any trk: v tough & progressive last term.
2 Aug'03 Good 5g/f 72-70 D: 1 Aug'03 Wind 6gd 72-63 F: 1 Aug'03 Carl 5.9g/f 68-56 F:
1 Jun'03 Muss 7.1g/f 59-51 F: 1 Jun'03 Thir 6g/f 56-42 E: 2 Jun'03 Ling 6g/f 43-40 F:
976 **KEW THE MUSIC 25** [12]4-8-13   (65) C Catlin 25/1: 10000-00: 10th: In tch stands side, no impress.   1¼   55
4367} **BOBS BUZZ 217** [13]4-9-4   (70) R Mullen 25/1: 0/3110-0: 11th: Al bhd stands side on reapp.   nk   59
1103 **RIDICULE 16** [14]5-8-11 vis (63) S Drowne 33/1: 0540-000: 12th: Nvr a factor stands side: see 1103.   1   50
4768} **ELIDORE 191** [18]4-9-12   (78) S Sanders 33/1: 40/3000-0: 13th: Chsd ldr far side, wknd dist.   hd   64
1122 **TRUE NIGHT 13** [5]7-9-13   (79) L Treadwell(7) 25/1: 34215-00: 14th: Nvr dngrs stands side.   ¾   64
976 **CASHEL MEAD 25** [10]4-9-7   (73) A Daly 16/1: 23-50060: 15th: Slow away & al bhd stands side.   ½   57
4925} **PINCHBECK 179** [6]5-9-10   (76) M Henry 14/1: 341033-0: 16th: Nvr a factor stands side on reapp.   3½   53
407 **GOODWOOD PRINCE 101** [1]4-9-2   (68) W Ryan 33/1: 0006-500: 17th: Led stands side till over 3f out.   3½   38
1251 **TIDY 5** [17]4-10-0   (80) R Hughes 8/1: 060-015U: Handy stands side, rdn but keeping on when saddle   82?
slipped & u.r. ins last: qck reapp: likely to have fin 3rd or 4th & an encouraging run: return to 7f shld suit.
1179 **PARK STAR 9** [9]4-8-6   (58) W Supple 33/1: 0-63200U: In tch stands side, wknd 3f out, hmpd & u.r.   0
19 Ran   Time 1m 14.28 (4.48)   Owned: Miss Vanessa Church   Trained: Maidstone

---

1355   3.15 Everards Popular Pubs Handicap Stakes 3yo 0-90 (C)   [87]
£9568 £2944 £1472   **1m3f1 83y**   **Good/Soft 67**   +01 Fast   Inside

1017* **SWAGGER STICK 23** [5] J L Dunlop 3-9-7   (80) S Sanders 8/11 FAV: 00014-11: Trkd ldr till led 2f   92
out, styd on well, pushed out: bckd: apprec first start at 12f, shaped like 14f sure to suit: acts on fast &
gd/soft, likes Leicester: useful, type to keep progressing as he steps up in trip, win again: see 1017.
1174 **NESSEN DORMA 9** [3] J G Given 3-9-1   (74) L Dettori 15/2: 511-4552: Set pace till 2f out, not pace   3   80
of wnr: prob stays 12f on gd/soft, acts on both AWs: see 252.
4240* **YOSHKA 222** [2] M Johnston 3-9-5   (78) R Ffrench 5/1: 1-3: ch c Grand Lodge - Greenvera (Riverman)   5   78
Slow away, held up, hdwy over 4f out, outpcd over 2f out, modest late gains on reapp: dam wnr sole '03 start:
half-brother to top-class stayer Royal Rebel: stays 9f, further shld suit this term: has run well fresh on firm
grnd & a gall trk: won till forcing tactics last term.   1 Sep'03 Redc 9fm 81- D:
1308* **VANTAGE 2** [1] N P Littmoden 3-9-12 (5ex) (85) T P Queally(3) 5/1: 30-22314: Keen cl-up, wknd 2f   1½   83
out: qck reapp, top-weight & penalty: too sn after 1308?
1144 **ROCK LOBSTER 12** [4]3-8-12   (71) B Doyle 25/1: 14-05: Handy, lost pl halfway, btn 3f out: lngr trip.   27   31
5 Ran   Time 2m 36.29 (7.99)   Owned: Mr Robin F Scully   Trained: Arundel

---

1356   3.50 Listed Totesport Leicestershire Stakes 4yo+ (A)
£17400 £6600 £3300   **7f9y str**   **Good/Soft 67**   +06 Fast   Stands Side

4626} **TOUT SEUL 146** [8] R F Johnson Houghton 4-8-12   (113) S Carson 7/2: 430605-1: b c Ali Royal -   114
Total Aloof (Groom Dancer) In tch, gd hdwy 2f out, styd on to lead ins last, styd on well, rdn out, bit more in
hand: not btn far when 4th in Newmarket '03 2,000 Guineas (rtd 115, subs pulled muscle): multiple '02 wnr incl Gr 1
Dewhurst: suited by a gall 7f/1m on fm or hvy: runs well fresh: v smart, win more Gr races in this form.
1 Oct'02 Newm 7g/f 118- A: 2 Oct'02 Redc 6fm 110- B: 1 Aug'02 Curr 6g/s 109- : 1 Aug'02 Asco 7g/s 108- B:
2 Jun'02 Sali 6g/f 102- B: 1 Jun'02 Chep 6hvy 105- D: 1 Jun'02 Chep 6sft 83- E:
4976} **POLAR BEN 175** [1] J R Fanshawe 5-9-3   (112) O Urbina 3/1: 653100-2: b g Polar Falcon -   1¾   115
Woodbeck (Terimon) Held up, hdwy over 1f out, kept on ins last, nrst fin: reapp: '03 Gr3 wnr: dual class stks
wnr in '02: stays a stiff 1m, suited by 7f: acts on fast, likes gd & soft, any trk: best held up: tough & smart,
fine return conceding weight & shld find another Gr 3 on similar grnd.
1 Sep'03 Donc 7gd 113-(103) A: 2 May'03 Hayd 7.1sft 103-(99) A: 1 Sep'02 Newm 7g/f 100- B:
1 Jun'02 Hayd 7.1sft 97- C: 1 Aug'01 Warw 7.1g/f 87- F:

LEICESTER SATURDAY 24.04.04 Righthand, Stiff, Galloping Track

1126 **ROCKETS N ROLLERS 12** [5] R Hannon 4-8-12 (104) Dane O'Neill 8/1: 00-33323: Handy, hdwy to lead over 1f out, hdd & no extra ins last: proving tough & consistent: see 1062, 922. *nk* **109**
1187 **BAHAMIAN PIRATE 9** [6] D Nicholls 9-8-12 (112) L Dettori 8/1: 4606-144: Handy, eff over 1f out, onepace: likes this grnd & prob stays 7f, best form has come around 5/6f as in 1004. *¾* **107**
922 **MAKHLAB 30** [3]4-8-12 (108) W Supple 9/2: 31/001-55: Handy, eff dist, sn no extra: see 922. *shd* **107**
1137 **WILL HE WISH 12** [9]8-8-12 (92) I Mongan 25/1: 261-0056: Chsd ldr, styd on to lead over 1f out, sn hdd & no extra: confirmed imprvd form of 1137, see 1043. *1¼* **105$**
1126 **KOOL 12** [4]5-8-12 S Drowne 12/1: 11120/-37: Keen in tch, no impress over 1f out: see 1126. *1* **103$**
4944*} **RIVA ROYALE 178** [11]4-8-7 (84) T P Queally 100/1: 035001-8: b f Royal Applause - Regatta (Mtoto) Led till over 1f out, wknd: won last of 9 '03 starts (h'cap): '02 mdn wnr: eff at 5f, stays 7f on firm or soft grnd: likes Yarmouth: can front run: stiff task, needs h'caps. *2½* **93$**
1 Oct'03 Yarm 7.0sft 85-79 D: 2 Jul'03 Chep 6.1g/f 82-(85) C: 1 Jul'02 Yarm 5.1g/f 83- D: 2 Jun'02 Sand 5g/s 83- D:
4776} **STARBECK 190** [10]6-8-9 (2ow) (84) P McCabe 66/1: 605520-9: Held up, no threat: with P Howling. *3½* **88**
1187 **CRIMSON SILK 9** [7]4-8-12 (102) Paul Eddery 28/1: 3063-000: 10th: Al bhd, stiff task. *½* **90**
1043 **ALEUTIAN 21** [2]4-8-12 (104) N Pollard 20/1: 11160: 11th: Slow away, held up, no dngr: btr 838 (aw). *1½* **87**
11 Ran Time 1m 26.31 (4.31) Owned: Eden Racing Trained: Didcot

1357

4.25 Pick Everard Handicap Stakes 3yo+ 0-75 (E) **[75]**
£3660 £1126 £563 **1m1f218y** **Good/Soft 67** **-00 Slow** Inside

1273 **ICANNSHIFT 4** [3] S Dow 4-8-3 (50) R L Moore 8/1: 0-006021: Made virtually all, styd on well fnl 2f, rdn out: stays 10f well & acts on firm & soft grnd: has run well fresh on gall & undul trks: well judged ride from the front here: see 1273. **55**
1286 **DISSIDENT 4** [7] D Flood 6-9-4 vis (65) Dane O'Neill 9/2: 2-4U1022: Chsd wnr, eff over 1f out, hung right & not wnr's pace ins last: qck reapp & another gd run: see 1286, 1026. *1¼* **69**
1235 **STREET LIFE 7** [6] W J Musson 6-10-0 (75) R Mullen 5/1: 006-2523: Held up, hdwy 2f out, nrst fin: h'capped to win & likes Windsor: see 1235, 391. *1½* **77**
1019 **IPSA LOQUITUR 23** [10] S C Williams 4-8-13 (60) S Drowne 20/1: 4/5-04: b f Unfuwain - Plaything (High Top) Held up, hdwy over 2f out, sn no impress: 5th in a mdn sole '03 start (rtd 67a): prob handles polytrack, acts on gd/soft & stays 10f: lightly rcd. *¾* **61**
979 **MAN THE GATE 25** [9]5-8-12 (59) S Sanders 7/2 FAV: D5300-25: In tch, hung left & onepace dist. *½* **59**
1006 **SIR HAYDN 24** [8]4-9-10 (71) W Ryan 22/1: 06033-36: Slow away, held up, eff & short of room over 1f out, eased when btn: see 1006. *1¼* **69**
1164 **MARITIME BLUES 10** [11]4-9-1 (62) B Doyle 8/1: 3560-007: In tch, no impress 2f out: see 1164. *1½* **58**
1098 **KERNEL DOWERY 16** [5]4-8-11 p (58) I Mongan 20/1: 20043-08: b g Sri Pekan - Lady Dowery (Manila) In tch, wknd 2f out: plcd several times in '03 (h'caps): stays 10f on firm & polytrack: prob handles any trk & eff with or without cheek pieces. 2 Sep'03 Brig 9.9g/f 65-64 E: 2 Nov'02 Ling 8ap 70a- D: *¾* **53**
4614} **LUCKY LEO 201** [4]4-9-7 (68) C Catlin 25/1: 400/300-9: b g Muhtarram - Wrong Bride (Reprimand) In tch, btn over 3f out: well btn sole hdle start last winter: plcd on first of only 3 '03 starts (clmr, with M Channon): eff over a stiff 1m on fast grnd. *1* **61**
1090* **CRISTOFORO 17** [2]7-8-9 (56) T P Queally(3) 4/1: 42111/-10: 10th: Dwelt, nvr a factor: btr expected after 1090 (well bckd), drifted from 9/4 here. *shd* **49**
901 **SONDERBORG 32** [1]3-7-12 (3oh) (59) D Fox(5) 50/1: 5322200: 11th: Al bhd: changed stable, see 804. *6* **45**
11 Ran Time 2m 09.23 (6.73) Owned: Mr R E Anderson Trained: Epsom

1358

5.00 Beacon Bitter Maiden Stakes 3yo+ (D)
£5746 £1768 £884 **1m1f218y** **Good/Soft 67** **+02 Fast** Inside

1019 **BAYHIRR 23** [2] M A Jarvis 3-8-8 (1ow) L Dettori 1/1 FAV: 0-31: Cl-up, led over 3f out, drew clr 2f out, eased down, val 7/8L+: hvly bckd: stays 10f well, further looks sure to suit: acts on gd/soft grnd & a stiff trk: bundles in hand here, useful, win races in stronger company: see 1019. **92+**
4408} **SUNSET MIRAGE 214** [8] E A L Dunlop 3-8-2 R L Moore 20/1: 0-2: br f Swain - Yafill (Nureyev) Held up, hdwy to go 2nd over 1f out, not pace of easy wnr: rtd 65 when unplcd sole '03 start: stays 10f on gd/soft grnd: prob caught a decent type, win a minor trk mdn. *2½* **76**
NUNKI [3] H R A Cecil 3-8-7 W Ryan 8/1: 3: ch g Kingmambo - Aqua Galinte (Kris S) Handy, eff 2f out, onepace on debut: stays 10f on gd/soft, encouraging start, learn from this. *1¼* **79**
RACE THE ACE [4] J L Dunlop 3-8-7 S Sanders 16/1: 4: b g First Trump - Princess Genista (Ile de Bourbon) Slow away & held up, brief eff over 2f out, onepace: debut: dam styd 2m: bred to apprec 10f+. *3½* **74**
1055 **PATRIXTOO 19** [1]3-8-7 Saleem Golam(7) 25/1: 00-05: Cl-up, wknd well over 1f out. *4* **68**
TALWANDI [12]3-8-7 B Doyle 11/1: 6: In tch, btn over 3f out on debut. *7* **58**
4488} **KALANISHA 210** [10]4-9-10 Paul Eddery 100/1: 000-7: Al bhd: gelded. *1½* **56$**
ILL FLY [11]4-9-10 O Urbina 12/1: 8: Held up, btn over 2f out on debut. *¾* **55**
1016 **COURT EMPEROR 23** [13]4-9-10 J Tate 150/1: 09: Slow away, al bhd. *¾* **54**
HELM [5]3-8-7 N Mackay(3) 12/1: 0: 10th: Sn rdn & nvr a factor on debut. *¾* **53**
15} **LAKE OF DREAMS 528** [14]5-9-10 Lucy Russell(7) 150/1: 00/-0: 11th: In tch, wknd over 2f out. *hd* **52**
1101 **LOGGER RHYTHM 16** [9]4-9-10 Dane O'Neill 66/1: 00: 12th: Al bhd. *½* **51**
CHOIR LEADER [6]3-8-7 R Mullen 11/1: 0: 13th: Slow away & nvr a factor on debut. *2½* **47**
BA CLUBMAN [7]4-9-10 BL S Drowne 40/1: 0: 14th: Sn clr ldr, hung left over 5f out, wknd & hdd over 3f out on debut: blnks. *dist* **0**
ATLANTIC WALTZ [15]4-9-10 T D Corby(3) 100/1: 0: 15th: Al bhd on debut. *dist* **0**
15 Ran Time 2m 09.0 (6.5) Owned: Sheikh Ahmed Al Maktoum Trained: Newmarket

1359

5.30 Perfick Handicap Stakes 3yo 0-75 (E) **[81]**
£3845 £1183 £592 **1m9y rnd** **Good/Soft 67** **-54 Slow** Inside

1176 **TOPARUDI 9** [14] M H Tompkins 3-9-2 (69) Saleem Golam(7) 12/1: 53330-01: b g Rudimentary - Topatori (Topanoora) Handy, hdwy 2f out, styd on well to lead nr line, rdn out: plcd on 3 of 6 '03 starts (nursery h'caps, rtd 72): stays 1m well & enjoys gd/soft, acts on fast & gall trks: stable having a fine start to the season. **74**
1163* **PHLUKE 10** [16] R F Johnson Houghton 3-9-3 (70) S Carson 4/1 FAV: 2-530512: Set pace, edged left over 1f out but kept on well for press, collared on line: fine run & improving: stays a stiff 1m: see 1163. *shd* **74**
5034} **LADY GEORGINA 168** [12] J R Fanshawe 3-9-4 (71) Dane O'Neill 8/1: 34300-3: gr f Linamix - Georgia *2½* **71**

LEICESTER SATURDAY 24.04.04 Righthand, Stiff, Galloping Track

Venture (Shirley Heights) In tch, eff to chall over 1f out, onepace: plcd on 2 of 5 '03 starts (fills mdns): eff at 7f, stays 1m on firm & gd/soft, gall or easy trks: eff with/without a t-strap: shld be plcd to win a race.
5034} **MORAG 168** [13] I A Wood 3-9-3 (70) T P Queally(3) 33/1: 110050-4: b f Aragon - Minnehaha (Be My Chief) In tch, hdwy 2f out, onepace: mdn auct & h'cap wnr in '03: stays 7f & likes firm & fast grnd: acts on a fair or gall trk: has rcd poorly in a t-strap. 1 Sep'03 Redc 7fm 67-68 E: 1 Aug'03 Thir 7g/f 70-(66) E: *1* **68**
1130 **KING OF KNIGHT 12** [5]3-9-3 (70) O Urbina 12/1: 000-45: Held up, eff 2f out, onepace. *½* **67**
1054 **HEAD BOY 19** [4]3-8-4 (57) P Doe 9/1: 10-40056: Held up, eff & edged right over 1f out, no extra. *2½* **50**
1017 **ERMINE GREY 23** [9]3-9-6 bl (73) Paul Eddery 10/1: 51016-07: Keen held up, hmpd 3f out, no dngr. *2* **63**
4987} **ABLAJ 173** [8]3-8-7 (60) S Drowne 14/1: 400-8: In tch, lost place over 3f out, no threat: reapp. *1* **48**
175 **NANTUCKET SOUND 136** [15]3-9-3 (70) N Mackay(3) 16/1: 634-9: Dwelt, held up, no impress fnl 2f. *shd* **58**
4610} **SUSIEDIL 201** [2]3-8-12 (65) B Doyle 33/1: 00140-0: 10th: In tch, wknd over 2f out: softer grnd. *½* **52**
4563} **DANISH MONARCH 205** [11]3-9-7 (74) D Corby(3) 20/1: 26224-0: 11th: Chsd ldr, wknd 2f out. *13* **43**
49* **AESCULUS 158** [10]3-9-5 (72) L Dettori 9/1: 051-0: 12th: In tch, wknd 2f out: abs, see 49 (6f). *6* **32**
4686} **ERTE 195** [1]3-8-11 (64) C Catlin 20/1: 403406-0: 13th: Al bhd: gelded, longer trip. *3* **18**
1163 **BOLD BLADE 10** [6]3-8-12 bl (65) F Lynch 20/1: 413-2500: 14th: Al bhd: see 441, 252. *dist* **0**
5034} **GROWLER 168** [7]3-8-8 (61) S Sanders 14/1: 0000-0: 15th: Al bhd: gelded. *20* **0**
1044 **HATCH A PLAN 21** [3]3-8-13 (66) R Mullen 20/1: 000-0U: In tch, stumbled & u.r. 3f out. **0**
16 Ran Time 1m 44.14(9.74) Owned: Mr M P Bowring Trained: Newmarket

RIPON SATURDAY 24.04.04 Righthand, Sharpish Track

Official Going Good/Soft

1360

2.00 Ripon Future Sprint Stars Handicap Stakes 3yo 0-95 (C) **[100]**
£8572 £3252 £1626 **6f str** **Good/Soft 63** **-06 Slow** Stands side, field rcd in 2 groups

4315} **HIGH VOLTAGE 219** [10] K R Burke 3-9-5 t (91) Darren Williams 40/1: 122020-1: ch g Wolfhound - Real Emotion (El Prado) Rcd far side, made all, rdn clr ins fnl 2f: defied burly appearance on reapp: med auct mdn wnr in '03 (also rnr-up 5 times): eff at 5/6f on fast & gd/soft grnd: acts on a sharp & gall trk, goes well fresh: eff with t-strap: improved for being gelded in the winter & this was a useful effort, win again. **99**
2 Aug'03 Ripo 5gd 93-(93) C: 2 Jul'03 Donc 6gd 91- C: 2 Jun'03 Donc 5g/f 93- D: 1 Jun'03 Ayr 5g/f 95- E:
2 May'03 Ayr 6g/s 85- E: 2 May'03 Muss 5g/f 88- E:
4344} **RED ROMEO 218** [4] G A Swinbank 3-8-2 (74) Dale Gibson 25/1: 2016-2: ch g Case Law - Enchanting Eve (Risk Me) Rcd nr side, led that group, kept on but not pace of wnr far side ins fnl 1f: well bckd despite looking burly on reapp: mdn wnr on 1 of 4 '03 starts: eff at 6/7f on fast & gd/soft grnd: handles a sharp & gall trk, has gone well fresh: likes to force the pace: gd eff on only 2nd h'cap start & shld just come on for today. *3* **74**
1 Aug'03 Newc 7g/f 75- D: 2 Jun'03 Ayr 6g/f 71- D:
1088* **DISTANT TIMES 17** [14] T D Easterby 3-8-7 (79) K Darley 7/4 FAV: 3223-513: Rcd far side, handy, kept on ins fnl 1f, just held for 2nd: well bckd: ran to form of recent win in 1088. *½* **78**
1282 **XPRES DIGITAL 4** [2] S R Bowring 3-8-3 t (75) J Bramhill 33/1: 45610-04: Rcd nr side, in tch, styd on ins fnl 1f, not btn far: qck reapp: see 1282. *1* **71**
1229 **LETS GET IT ON 7** [12]3-8-5 (77) R Winston 20/1: 3502-005: b f Perugino - Lets Clic Together (Don't Forget Me) Rcd far side, held up, prog ins fnl 2f, nrst fin: qck reapp: mdn wnr first time out in '03 (also h'cap rnr-up): dam wnr at 7/12f: eff at 5/6f on fast & gd/soft grnd: has gone well fresh: worth step up in trip. *1¼* **69**
2 Nov'03 Catt 6.0sft 79-77 D: 1 Jul'03 Ripo 5g/f 80- D:
4520} **ISKANDER 210** [13]3-9-7 bl (93) N Callan 25/1: 236154-6: Rcd far side, slow away, nvr nrr. *shd* **84**
1154 **PETARDIAS MAGIC 11** [11]3-8-13 (85) J Carroll 5/2: 016-4137: Rcd far side, handy, no extra bef 1f out: well bckd: below form of 1154 & 1116. *hd* **75**
4773} **BRIGHT SUN 190** [6]3-9-0 (86) Kim Tinkler 28/1: 52100-8: Rcd nr side, handy 4f, no extra: new stable. *hd* **75**
1229* **FOUR AMIGOS 7** [7]3-9-1 (87) J Fanning 6/1: 0102-519: Rcd far side, cl-up till dist fdd: btr 1229 (5f). *1* **73**
1186 **POPPYS FOOTPRINT 9** [9]3-8-8 (80) G Parkin 33/1: 1620-000: 10th: Rcd far side, al in rear: btr 1186. *1½* **62**
5034} **Mrs Moh 168** [5]3-8-11 (83) A Mullen(7) 14/1:0 4941} **Reidies Choice 178** [3]3-8-5 (77) M Fenton 33/1:0
4503} **George The Best 208** [1]3-8-10 (82) E Ahern 25/1:0 999 **Fox Covert 24** [8]3-7-12 (1oh)P(69) P Hanagan 25/1:0
14 Ran Time 1m 14.15 (4.15) Owned: Mrs K Halsall Trained: Leyburn

1361

2.35 C B Hutchinson Memorial Challenge Cup Handicap Stakes 4yo+ 0-90 (C) **[89]**
£8642 £3278 £1639 **2m** **Good/Soft 63** **-00 Slow** Stands side

1087 **GEORGE STUBBS 17** [17] M J Polglase 6-8-1 (62) J F McDonald(5) 14/1: 2364031: Keen rear, prog when short of room 2f out, switched wide & led dist, drvn out to just hold on: eff at 1m/12f, stays 2m well: acts on firm, gd/soft & both AWs, prob soft: unexposed around this trip: see 1087 & 681. **66**
1003 **THE RING 24** [12] Mrs M Reveley 4-8-5 (1ow) (69) K Darley 8/1: 44431-02: Cl-up, ev ch dist, styd on ins fnl 1f, only just denied: lost little in defeat here but rider's 1lb overweight proved costly, see 1003. *nk* **73**
1003 **GREENWICH MEANTIME 24** [7] Mrs J R Ramsden 4-9-0 (79) A Culhane 12/1: 3221-03: b g Royal Academy - Shirley Valentine (Shirley Heights) Held up, hdwy & short of room 3f out, styd on appr fnl 1f, nrst fin: mdn wnr on last of 4 '03 starts (with H Cecil): eff at 10/12f, now stays 2m: acts on fast & gd/soft grnd: has been gelded since last term & caught the eye, interesting next time with a more positive ride. *1¼* **81+**
1 Oct'03 Newc 12.4gd 82-(80) D: 2 Sep'03 Kemp 12gd 82- D: 2 Sep'03 York 10.4g/f 80- D:
1109 **THEWHIRLINGDERVISH 14** [16] T D Easterby 6-9-3 (78) A Mullen(7) 9/1: 02000-34: Bhd, prog 3f out, styd on cl-home, not btn far: padd pick: another creditable eff & can find similar, prob on a faster surface. *shd* **79**
5008} **KRISTENSEN 171** [8]5-9-8 p (83) J Quinn 16/1: 556233-5: ch g Kris S - Papaha (Green Desert) Bhd, prog ins last half mile, nrst fin: reapp: plcd numerous times in '03 (rtd 76a & 85, h'caps): won 2 h'caps in '02 (Mrs J R Ramsden): plcd in '02 (rtd 69, h'cap): prev eff at 12f, stays 2m/2m4f on firm, soft & fibresand, prob any trk: eff with cheek pieces: can rate higher with more of a stamina test. *1* **83**
2 Sep'03 Muss 16gd 80-77 C: 2 May'03 Muss 16gd 81-77 D: 2 May'03 Thir 16g/f 76-75 C: 2 Apr'03 Ripo 16gd 77-72 C:
2 Jan'03 Wolv 16.2af 76a-79 D: 2 Dec'02 Wolv 12af 81a- D: 1 Nov'02 Wolv 12af 82a-71 D: 2 Oct'02 Pont 10g/s 72-69 E:
2 Sep'02 Newc 10.1g/s 70-65 D: 1 Apr'02 Ripo 12.2g/f 75-67 D: 2 Mar'02 Nott 8.2sft 68-67 E:
1232 **HEIR TO BE 7** [3]5-8-11 (72) P Robinson 8/1: 1006-506: Rcd keenly, cl-up till dist, wknd: qck reapp. *3½* **69**
1118 **JADEERON 13** [9]5-8-4 p (65) S Hitchcott(3) 14/1: 2223447: Keen cl-up 14f, wknd: btr 634. *½* **61**

RIPON   SATURDAY 24.04.04   Righthand, Sharpish Track

2552} **DR SHARP** 298 [13]4-8-6 (71) Dale Gibson 15/2: 50/0114-8: ch g Dr Devious - Stoned Imaculate   ½   66
(Durgam) Led, hdd 3f out, sn wknd: jumps fit, earlier juv nov hdle wnr (rtd 113h, stays 2m2f on gd & hvy): h'cap &
class stks wnr on 2 of only 4 '03 starts: rnr-up in a 4-runner nov stks in '02: eff at 11f/12f, acts on gd & soft
grnd: likes to force the pace: appeared not to stay on first try at 2m but did get warm bef race.
1 Jun'03 Hami 11.1gd 71-(65) E: 1 May'03 Ripo 12.3sft 69-60 D: 2 Jul'02 Beve 7.4g/s 65- D:
4777} **FREEDOM NOW** 190 [11]6-9-1 (76) Darren Williams 33/1: 34/3660-9: Rear, hmpd over 3f out, nvr a   nk   70
factor: 11 wk jumps abs & new stable.
1232 **RIYADH 7** [1]6-8-11 vis (72) W Hogg(7) 25/1: 060-0000: 10th: Bhd, prog 4f out, fdd/hung right ins fnl 2f. 3½   63
4245} **MANA DARGENT** 222 [15]7-10-0 (89) J Fanning 16/1: 601433-0: 11th: Prom, led 3f out, hdd dist, fdd.   hd   79
4422} **MR FORTYWINKS** 213 [2]10-7-12 (3oh) (56) P Hanagan 16/1: 341406-0: 12th: Nvr nrr than mid-div.   3½   46
1069 **VICARS DESTINY** 18 [5]6-8-8 (69) E Ahern 7/1 FAV: 5626-220: 13th: Mid-div, wknd fnl 2f: recent   ½   55
jumps unplcd (rtd 111h, h'cap): btr 1069 & 926.
1126 **CELTIC VISION** 12 [14]8-7-13 t (60) S Righton 66/1: 6600: 14th: Bhd, nvr a factor: btr 1126.   1   45
1069 **KILLING JOKE** 18 [10]4-8-8 (73) M Fenton 33/1: 0/0601-00: 15th: Cl-up 12f, wknd: see 1069.   ½   57
4827} **ALWAYS RAINBOWS** 532 [4]6-9-0 vis (75) T Eaves(5) 50/1: 0/43000/-0: 16th: Prom 12f, fdd: jumps fit.   8   51
1093* **ZOLTANO** 16 [6]6-8-8 (69) R Winston 8/1: 2122/-310: 17th: Cl-up 12f, fdd: btr 1093.   8   37
17 Ran Time 3m 34.90 (10.1) Owned: Mr Paul J Dixon Trained: Newark

1362   3.10 Dishforth Novice Auction Stakes Fillies 2yo (E)
£4017 £1236 £618   5f str   Good/Soft 63   -31 Slow   Stands side

1084* **POLLY ALEXANDER** 17 [3] M J Wallace 2-8-10 K Darley 8/11 FAV: 511: Made all, drvn out to hold on   83
ins fnl 1f: well bckd at odds-on: top-wght: eff at 5f on gd/soft & soft grnd, shld be suited by 6f: improving
with every start & did well to concede weight all round here: see 1084.
1133 **EVANESCE** 12 [2] M R Channon 2-8-3 (1ow) S Hitchcott 3/1: 2242: Handy, ev ch dist, kept on but   ½   74
just denied cl-home: clr rem: acts on gd/soft grnd & polytrack: lost little in defeat but costly overweight.
ANGELOFTHENORTH 0 [4] J D Bethell 2-8-2 J Fanning 12/1: 3: b f Tomba - Dark Kristal (Gorytus)   5   58
Handy tll dist, wknd: debut: March foal, cost 5,000gns: half-sister to wnrs at 6f: dam wnr at 6f.
CHICAGO NIGHTS 0 [5] P C Haslam 2-8-2 P Hanagan 15/2: 4: ch f Night Shift - Enclave (Woodman)   2   52
Cl-up, wknd ins fnl 2f: debut: Feb first foal, cost 10,000gns: dam unplcd: sire speedily bred: just ndd race.
BALASHOVA 0 [1]2-8-2 Dale Gibson 25/1: 5: b f Imperial Ballet - Almasi (Petorius) Al in rear: ½   51
debut: Feb first foal, cost 800gns: dam won numerous times at 6f: sire decent h'capper around 1m: with K R Burke.
5 Ran Time 1m 2.52 (4.72) Owned: Mrs T A Foreman Trained: Newmarket

1363   3.45 Bandstand Selling Stakes 3-4yo (F)
£3241 £926 £463   1m2f   Good/Soft 63   -12 Slow   Inside

1033 **FORTUNES FAVOURITE** 22 [7] G M Moore 4-9-5 (40) E Ahern 7/2 FAV: 45-03401: Prom till outpcd after   50
6f, rallied to lead dist, pushed out, val 4L+: no bid: apprec drop back to 10f on gd/soft & a sharp trk.
4851} **LET IT BE** 185 [8] Mrs M Reveley 3-8-2 P Hanagan 11/2: 000-2: ch f Entrepreneur - Noble Dane   2   44
(Danehill) Chsd ldrs tll outpcd after 6f, rallied to chase wnr 1f out, kept on but al held: reapp: unplcd in 3
'03 starts (rtd 51, auct mdn): dam 1m juv wnr, subs styd 12f: eff at 10f, shld stay further: acts on gd/soft.
194 **SENZA SCRUPOLI** 133 [6] M D Hammond 4-9-10 bl (70) K Darley 9/2: 0/0050-3: ch g Inchinor -   1¼   47
Gravette (Kris) Mid-div, outpcd 5f out, rallied ins fnl 2f, not pace front 2: recently hdles rnr-up (sell h'cap,
rtd 74h, stays 2m on gd, 1st time blnks): unplcd all 3 '03 starts (rtd 70, L M Cumani): eff around 10f on gd/soft.
314 **LITTLETON VALAR** 110 [4] J R Weymes 4-9-10 (30) D Fentiman(7) 10/1: 20060-04: ch g Definite   3½   42$
Article - Fresh Look (Alzao) Led 4f out, styd cl-up till fdd dist, hdles fit, earlier rtd 84h at best (juv nov hdle):
rnr-up once in '03 (appr sell h'cap): eff around 10f on fast grnd: has tried cheek pieces.
2 Aug'03 Ripo 10g/f 44-44 F:
1058 **BALLYRUSH** 19 [3]4-9-10 P (53) R Keogh(7) 4/1: 0-054565: Prom, led 4f out, hdd dist, fdd & hung   7   32
right: disappointing with cheek pieces.
1108 **ZABADOU** 14 [2]3-8-7 T Eaves(4) 16/1: 00-06: Handy 5f, wknd: btr 1108.   23   2
LUCAYAN BELLE 0 [5]3-8-2 VIS Hayley Turner(5) 5/1: 7: Bhd, nvr a factor: debut: fitted with visor.   4   0
49**LORD WISHINGWELL** 175 [1]3-8-7 P A Reilly(7) 16/1: 000-8: Prom 6f, fdd: reapp & 1st time pieces.   6   0
8 Ran Time 2m 10.84 (7.54) Owned: Lucayan Stud Trained: Middleham

1364   4.20 Ripon-Races Co Uk Conditions Stakes 4yo+ (C)
£10332 £3666 £1833   1m4f60y   Good/Soft 63   -04 Slow   Inside

5035} **PUTRA SANDHURST** 168 [3] M A Jarvis 6-8-9 (104) P Robinson 7/4 FAV: 322025-1: b c Royal Academy -   106
Kharimata (Kahyasi) Made all, drvn out ins fnl 1f to hold on: well bckd on reapp: rnr-up twice in '03 (List &
stks): missed '02: mdn wnr & List rnr-up in '01: eff at 12/14f on firm & gd/soft grnd, acts on any trk: goes well
fresh: useful, sensibly held in a small field.
2 Jul'03 Newm 12g/f 106-(105) C: 2 Jun'03 Newm 12fm 107-(105) A: 2 Aug'01 Good 14g/f 102- A:
1 Jul'01 Newm 12g/f 92- D: 2 Jul'01 Newm 10g/f 102- D: 2 May'01 Ling 11.4gd 109- A:
4772} **GRAMPIAN** 540 [1] J G Given 5-8-9 (102) M Fenton 5/1: 311525/-2: b c Selkirk - Gryada (Shirley   1   103
Heights) Mid-div, prog to chase wnr ins fnl 2f, kept on & just held by wnr well fnl 1f: op 7/1 on reapp:
missed '03: won 2 class stks in '02 (also rnr-up in 3-runner List affair): mdn wnr in '01 (L Cumani): eff at
10/12.3f on fast, gd/soft & any trk: fine comeback after long abs: just sharper for today.
2 Jul'02 Hayd 12g/f 104- A: 1 May'02 Sali 12g/f 105- B: 1 May'02 Bath 10.2gd 97- B: 1 Aug'01 Newm 7g/s 89- D:
1483} **SILVER GILT** 352 [2] J H M Gosden 4-8-8 (102) K Darley 3/1: 212/34-3: b g Silver Hawk - Memory's   5   96
Gold (Java Gold) Handy, outpcd just ins fnl half-mile, modest late gains: reapp: 3rd of 4 in stks & last of 4 in
Gr 2 '03 starts (rtd 104): 12f wnr, subs Gr 3 rnr-up: eff at 9f, prob stays 12f: acts on firm & soft,
has gone well fresh: gelded since last term: just sharper for today.
2 Oct'02 Long 9sft 101- : 1 Sep'02 Donc 8fm 101- D: 2 Aug'02 Newm 7g/s 90- C:
4224*]**LEGAL APPROACH** 581 [4] M Johnston 5-8-9 J Fanning 5/2: 11/131/-4: b c Zafonic - Legaya (Shirley   ¾   95
Heights) Keen cl-up, fdd dist: well bckd on reapp: missed '03: lightly rcd in '02 winning 3 runner stks & a List
event: won both '01 starts (mdn & stks): eff at 10/11.6f: acts on firm or soft grnd: has gone well fresh.
1 Sep'02 Newb 11fm 112- A: 1 Jul'02 Hayd 10.5gd 106- C: 1 Sep'01 Asco 7sft 95- B: 1 Sep'01 Ayr 7.2gd 87- D:
4 Ran Time 2m 41.83 (8.33) Owned: HRH Sultan Ahmad Shah Trained: Newmarket

RIPON SATURDAY 24.04.04 Righthand, Sharpish Track

1365 4.55 Aldborough Maiden Stakes Fillies 3yo (D)
£4144 £1275 £638 **1m2f** **Good/Soft 63** **+01 Fast** Inside

4978} **MAGANDA 175** [7] M A Jarvis 3-8-11 P Robinson 4/6 FAV: 20-1: b f Sadler's Wells - Minnie Habit (Habitat) In tch, led 2f out, sn edged right under press & rdn out: reapp: well bckd: rnr-up on first of only 2 '03 starts: eff at 1m, stays 10f: acts on fast & gd/soft grnd, gall or sharp trks: goes well fresh: open to more improvement around mid-dists & can rate higher. 2 Sep'03 Yarm 8.0g/f 88- D: **84**
1171 **STOCKING ISLAND 10** [6] B Hanbury 3-8-11 J Carroll 16/1: 02: ch f Desert King - Rawya (Woodman) Led 1m, styd on but not pace of wnr ins fnl 1f: imprvd for today's step up to 10f, shld stay further: acts on gd/soft. *1½* **81**
4603} **TRULLITTI 203** [1] J L Dunlop 3-8-11 K Darley 6/1: 65-3: b f Bahri - Penza (Soviet Star) Mid-div, prog & ev ch bef 1f out, sn no impress: op 9/2 on reapp: unplcd both '03 starts (rtd 75, mdn): imprvd for today's step up to 10f: acts on gd/soft grnd: just ndd race. *3* **77**
4779} **BUBBLING FUN 190** [8] E A L Dunlop 3-8-11 P Hanagan 20/1: 02-4: Chsd ldrs, rcd keenly, outpcd just ins fnl half-mile, modest late gains: reapp. *3½* **72**
4851} **EXCLUSIVE DANIELLE 185** [5]3-8-11 A Culhane 9/2: 3-5: Prom 7f, sn no extra: tchd 6/1 on reapp. *1* **70**
4972} **CITRINE SPIRIT 175** [2]3-8-11 R Havlin 20/1: 0-6: Keen rear, prog & ev ch 2f out, sn wknd: ndd race. *1¼* **68**
JALOUSIE DREAM 0 [3]3-8-11 T Eaves(5) 100/1: 7: Mid-div 7f, sn fdd: debut. *5* **61**
238 **CTESIPHON 124** [4]3-8-11 M Fenton 33/1: 03-8: Al hung badly right, hmpd 7f out, sn wknd: long abs. *9* **49**
8 Ran Time 2m 9.55 (6.25) Owned: Mr N R A Springer Trained: Newmarket

1366 5.25 Bbc Radio York Sport Handicap Stakes 3yo+ 0-70 (E) **[70]**
£3936 £1211 £606 **1m rnd** **Good/Soft 63** **+09 Fast** Inside

1142 **HILLS OF GOLD 12** [20] M W Easterby 5-9-10 (66) K Darley 5/1 FAV: 11400-41: Cl-up, styd on to lead dist, rdn out: eff at 7f/1m on fm & soft, any trk: see 1142. **75**
1307* **MEGANS MAGIC 2** [14] W Storey 4-9-9 (5ex) (65) D R McCabe 6/1: 1542-612: Rear, prog 3f out, kept on well ins fnl 1f, nrst fin: qck reapp: ran to form of win in 1307, win again at 10f: see 1307. *¾* **71**
1036 **GOODBYE MR BOND 21** [4] E J Alston 4-8-9 (51) J F Egan 9/1: 04-56343: Bhd, hdwy 3f out, kept on well ins fnl 1f: fine run from poor low draw: see 387. *1* **55+**
1215 **PRIDE OF KINLOCH 8** [19] J Hetherton 4-9-4 (60) R Fitzpatrick 50/1: 000-0604: Chsd ldrs, onepcd fnl 1f. *2* **60**
1036 **HULA BALLEW 21** [17]4-9-3 (59) J Carroll 12/1: 13366-05: ch f Weldnaas - Ballon (Persian Bold) Led 6f, no extra fnl 1f: h'cap wnr in '03 (also plcd 3 times): mdn plcd in '02 (rtd 61): eff at 1m/10f on fast & gd, handles gd/soft grnd: acts on a stiff/gall or sharp trk: with M Dods. *shd* **58**
1 Jul'03 Carl 7.9gd 63-58 F: 2 Jul'03 Muss 9gd 59-54 E:
1214 **CRYFIELD 8** [10]7-9-4 (60) Kim Tinkler 16/1: 0605-006: Keen mid-div, onepace fnl 1f: btr 1214. *1¼* **57**
1198 **PRINCE OF GOLD 9** [13]4-9-13 (69) A Culhane 10/1: 3000-057: Prom, led 2f out, hdd dist, wknd. *1½* **63**
1020 **BARZAK 23** [18]4-9-4 t (60) J Bramhill 8/1: 05-05308: Handy till dist, wknd: btr 551. *1¾* **50**
1215 **EFIDIUM 8** [16]6-9-9 (65) Suzanne France(7) 7/1: 00046-29: Cl-up 6f, sn wknd: btr 1215. *5* **45**
967 **THE WIZARD MUL 26** [6]4-9-6 (62) D Fentiman(7) 33/1: 10104-00: 10th: br g Wizard King - Longden Pride (Superpower) Prom 6f, sn wknd: won 2 h'caps in '03: '02 nursery rnr-up: stays 1m, prob best at 6/7f: acts on fast, likes gd/soft, sharpish or stiff/gall trk: has gone well fresh. *1¾* **38**
1 Jul'03 Newc 7g/s 65-61 F: 1 May'03 Ripo 6g/s 61-57 E: 2 Sep'02 Muss 5g/f 59-58 D:
1214 **Jakeal 8** [9]5-8-13 (55) Dean McKeown 14/1:0
1160* **Open Handed 10** [8]4-9-3 t(59) T Eaves(5) 20/1:0
912 **Arjay 31** [1]6-9-0 bl(56) A Mullen(7) 40/1:0
388} **Late Arrival 466** [3]7-8-8 (50) L Enstone(3) 66/1:0
1049 **One Last Time 19** [11]4-9-13 (69) H Bastiman 50/1:0
5017} **Basinet 170** [5]6-9-2 (58) P Fessey 25/1:0
465 **Soft Mist 92** [15]4-9-4 (60) P Hanagan 66/1:0
753 **Futuristic 57** [12]4-8-12 (54) J Quinn 20/1:0
1164 **Rockerfella Lad 10** [7]4-9-9 (65) R Thomas(5) 40/1:0
5029} **Pepper Road 169** [2]5-8-10 (52) G Parkin 40/1:0
20 Ran Time 1m 41.86(4.36) Owned: Mr G Hart Mr D Scott & Mr G Sparkes Trained: Sheriff Hutton

BRIGHTON SUNDAY 25.04.04 Lefthand, V Sharp, Undulating Track

Official Going GOOD/FIRM

1367 2.10 European Breeders Fund Maiden Stakes 2yo (D)
£5041 £1551 £776 **5f59y rnd** **Good/Firm 31** **-37 Slow** Outside

1097 **IM SPARTACUS 17** [1] I A Wood 2-9-0 D Holland 9/4 J FAV: 021: Bhd, hdwy over 1f out, led ins fnl 1f, pushed out nr fin: eff arnd 5f, bred to relish 6f+: acts on fast & gd/soft grnd, sharp/undul trk: gd run, has imprvd with each start this term: see 1097. **72**
1001 **WEET YER TERN 25** [5] P A Blockley 2-9-0 Dean McKeown 9/4 J FAV: 42: b c Brave Act - Maxime (Mac's Imp) Handy, led over 2f out till ins fnl 1f, no extra nr fin: 4th sole prev mdn start: eff arnd 5f on fast & firm grnd: imprvd from debut & shown enough to find similar. *1¼* **67**
1114 **LEONALTO 15** [4] B J Meehan 2-9-0 BL K Fallon 7/1: 053: Keen & handy, ch 1f out, sn onepcd: eff around 5f on fast grnd: first time blnks: see 1114. *1¼* **63**
1041 **MAJESTICAL 22** [3] W R Muir 2-9-0 Martin Dwyer 4/1: 34: Led after 1f till over 2f out, no extra: see 1041. *1* **60**
1077 **DUSTINI 18** [2]2-9-0 A Daly 11/2: 35: Led over 1f, wknd 2f out: op 8/1: see 1077. *5* **45**
5 Ran Time 1m 3.78 (3.78) Owned: Mr John Purcell Trained: Upper Lambourn

---

1368
2.45 Broadwater Mailing Selling Stakes 3yo+ (G)
£2583 £738 £369 **5f213y rnd** **Good/Firm 31** -20 Slow Outside

1336 **FLYING FAISAL 2** [7] J M Bradley 6-9-6 bl (45) R L Moore 13/2: 40030461: Keen & chsd ldrs, led **49**
over 2f out, drvn out fnl 1f: no bid, qck reapp: stays 7f, best at 5/6f on fast, gd/soft & f/sand, any trk: see 524.
960 **JALOUHAR 27** [3] B P J Baugh 4-9-12 p (46) E Ahern 12/1: 4650502: Led till over 2f out, sn outpcd, **1¾ 49**
rallied fnl 1f to regain 2nd: not btn far under jt top-weight: handles fast, gd & fibresand: see 65.
1179 **POLAR FORCE 10** [1] M R Channon 4-9-6 (60) B O'Neill(7) 11/10 FAV: 3-400303: Mid-div, chsd wnr **nk 42**
over 1f out, sn onepcd & lost 2nd ins fnl 1f: nicely bckd: clmd for 6,000: see 407.
1032 **RATHMULLAN 23** [4] E A Wheeler 5-9-6 bl (40) Liam Jones(7) 16/1: 000-0034: Chsd ldr, onepcd fnl **1¾ 37**
1.5f: see 905.
1288 **CRAFTY POLITICIAN 4** [5]7-9-12 bl (47) A Quinn(5) 11/4: 000-4125: Rear, hdwy 3f out, onepcd fnl 1f: **¾ 41**
jt top-weight, qck reapp: see 1288 & 639.
1336 **LONE PIPER 2** [2]9-9-6 P (45) C Catlin 10/1: 06436606: Keen in tch, no impress over 1f out: op **1¼ 31**
14/1, qck reapp: first time cheek pieces: see 720.
 DALLINGTON BROOK [6]5-9-6 bl Lucy Russell(7) 50/1: 7: b g Bluegrass Prince - Valetta (Faustus) **20 0**
Bhd, nvr a factor on Flat debut: well btn both 03/04 bmpr starts (incl in first time blnks).
7 Ran Time 1m 10.9 (3.1) Owned: Mr Clifton Hunt Trained: Chepstow

---

1369
3.20 Brighton & Hove Albion Classified Stakes 3yo 0-70 (E)
£3445 £1060 £530 **1m1f209y** **Good/Firm 31** -06 Slow Inside

3884} **MEADAAF 244** [3] A C Stewart 3-9-3 (71) K Fallon 7/1: 045-1: b c Swain - Virgin Hawk (Silver **79**
Hawk) Keen & chsd ldrs, led ins fnl 1f, rdn out: reapp: first win: lightly rcd in '03, mdn 4th (rtd 81): eff at
10f on fast grnd, acts on a sharp/undul trk: runs well fresh: lightly rcd & op to improvement.
796 **GAVROCHE 53** [5] C A Dwyer 3-9-3 (71) J P Guillambert(3) 20/1: 00-12352: Rear, hdwy 2f out, kept **½ 77**
on for press fnl 1f but not pace of wnr: op 10/1, 8 wk abs: eff at 9.4/10f: prev with M Wallace & ran to
winning form of 441.
4808*}**KRISTALS DREAM 188** [4] J L Dunlop 3-9-3 (75) T Quinn 6/5 FAV: 56031-3: b f Night Shift - **1½ 75**
Kristal's Paradise (Bluebird) Led 2f, chsd ldr after, led again over 1f out, hdd ins fnl 1f & no extra: nicely bckd
on reapp: won fnl '03 start (nurs): eff at 7f/10f on fast grnd, sharp or stiff/undul trk.
1 Oct'03 Pont 8.0g/f 75-68 E:
1101 **SLAVONIC 17** [2] J H M Gosden 3-9-4 VIS (72) D Holland 5/1: 554-544: Chsd ldrs, hdwy dist, not clr **¾ 75**
run ins fnl 1f & sn onepcd: 5L clr of rem, tried a visor: see 1101 & 947.
4231*}**SOUND BLASTER 223** [7]3-9-7 (75) Martin Dwyer 15/2: 041-5: ch g Zafonic - Blasted Heath **5 70**
(Thatching) Led after 2f, hdd over 1f out, wkng when short of room ins fnl 1f: reapp, top-weight: won fnl '03
start (mdn): eff at 1m on fast & firm grnd, acts on a turning trk: with A M Balding.
1 Sep'03 Bath 8.0fm 79- D:
4532} **CANNI THINKAAR 208** [8]3-9-2 (70) R L Moore 20/1: 0406-6: Bhd, nvr a factor on reapp. **1¾ 62**
1129* **KEY PARTNERS 13** [6]3-9-2 (70) D Nolan(5) 15/2: 52-17: Rear, nvr nr ldrs: much btr 1129 (mdn). **8 50**
930 **NEGWA 30** [1]3-9-3 (74) T E Durcan 8/1: 433-58: Keen in tch, eff 3f out, eased when btn fnl 1f: **5 43**
op 12/1: reportedly spread a plate at the start & worth forgiving: see 930.
8 Ran Time 2m 1.58 (3.78) Owned: Sheikh Ahmed Al Maktoum Trained: Newmarket

---

1370
3.55 Totesport Com Handicap Stakes 3yo 0-85 (D) **[91]**
£5499 £1692 £846 **7f214y rnd** **Good/Firm 31** -04 Slow Outside

1186 **TARUSKIN 10** [1] N A Callaghan 3-9-7 (84) R L Moore 4/11 FAV: 3231-31: Trkd ldrs, not clr run **88**
over 2f out, led over 1f out, rdn out ins fnl 1f: nicely bckd at odds on: eff at 7f, relished this step up to 1m:
acts on firm & gd/soft, any trk: gd weight carrier: rate higher, see 1186.
814 **ON THE WATERFRONT 48** [3] J W Hills 3-8-3 (66) E Ahern 11/2: 5542: Bhd, hdwy & not clr run 2f **½ 68**
out, ch ins fnl 1f, kept on & not btn far: 7 wk abs: eff at 1m on fast & polytrack, worth a try over further.
1163 **ANDURIL 11** [5] J M P Eustace 3-8-6 (69) J Tate 10/1: 045-603: Midfield, hdwy over 2f out, kept **¾ 69**
on ins fnl 1f: clr of rem: eff at 1m on fast grnd: see 934.
3501} **VAMOSE 260** [2] Miss Gay Kelleway 3-8-9 (72) M Fenton 16/1: 0230-4: ro g Victory Note - Narrow **5 62**
Band (Standaan) Led till over 1f out, sn no extra: reapp: plcd on 2 of 4 '03 starts (mdn): eff at 7f on fast.
2 Jul'03 Newm 7g/f 71- D:
5028} **LIN IN GOLD 170** [4]3-9-4 (81) D Nolan(5) 16/1: 10-5: b g Second Empire - Wasmette (Wassl) Rear, **2½ 66**
prog halfway, wknd 1f out: reapp: won first of 2 '03 starts (mdn): eff at 1m, 10f shld suit, acts on firm & a
sharp/undul trk: has run well fresh. 1 Oct'03 Brig 8.0fm 81- E:
5 Ran Time 1m 34.81 (2.81) Owned: Mr M Tabor Trained: Newmarket

---

1371
4.30 Harry Bloom Memorial Handicap Stakes 3yo+ 0-75 (E) **[74]**
£3474 £1069 £535 **5f59y rnd** **Good/Firm 31** +08 Fast Outside

748 **ERRACHT 58** [11] Mrs H Sweeting 6-9-0 (60) G Baker 25/1: 2030-051: Led 1f, remained handy, led **68**
again ins fnl 1f, rdn out nr fin: 8 wk abs: suited by 5f: acts on firm, hvy & fibresand, prob any trk:
gd run on first start for new stable (prev with K Burke): see 641.
1221 **PULSE 8** [12] J M Bradley 6-9-0 p (60) R L Moore 16/1: 1256-002: In tch, hdwy & ch ins fnl 1f, **½ 65**
kept on but not pace of wnr: back to form & find similar: see 1221.
1103 **POLISH EMPEROR 17** [4] P W Harris 4-9-10 bl (70) D Holland 11/2: 0-422503: Chsd ldrs, onepcd ins **2 69**
fnl 1f: gd run under top-weight: rider reported his mount hung left: see 292 & 109.
880 **PANJANDRUM 37** [3] N E Berry 6-8-10 (56) P Doe 25/1: 5106004: Rear, short of rm over 2f out til **shd 54+**
ins fnl 1f, flew home: handles firm, fast & loves both AWs: eye-catching run, keep in mind: see 610 & 231.
1127 **TABOOR 13** [8]6-8-11 h bl (57) K Fallon 5/1: 0005005: In tch, hdwy 2f out, onepcd fnl 1f: rider **½ 53**
reported his mount hung left: see 748.
4964} **ELA FIGURA 177** [7]4-8-10 (56) S Sanders 25/1: 320020-6: ch f The West - Chili Bouchier (Stop The **1¾ 47**
Music) Bhd, hdwy over 1f out, sn onepcd: reapp: rnr-up in a mdn & a clmr in '03: 3rd at best at '02 (nurs, rtd

---

63): eff over a stiff/gall 5f on fast grnd: has tried a visor: long standing mdn.
2 Oct'03 Bath 5.7fm 47-(57) F: 2 Sep'03 Bath 5.7g/f 53-(61) D:

874   **YORKIE 37** [14]5-8-10 (56) Dean McKeown 20/1: 200-1007: Rear, staying on when not clr run 1f,   *shd*   46
kept on: closer with a clr run: see 819.

1354   **WHIPPASNAPPER 1** [9]4-9-1 (61) N Pollard 11/4 FAV: 12130218: In tch, nvr dngrs: won yesterday &   ½   49
rider reported that this race came too sn & also that mount found this trip too sharp: see 565, 516 & 471.

1293   **LADY PEKAN 4** [16]5-9-0 bl (60) Lisa Jones(3) 7/1: 5600229: Led after 1f, hdd ins fnl 1f, no extra.   *shd*   47

1103   **ZARGUS 17** [5]5-9-5 BL (65) Martin Dwyer 9/1: 0040-500: 10th: With ldr, hmpd over 1f out & sn btn: 1   49
rider reported his mount hung left: first time blnks: see 1011.

1103   **TAPPIT 17** [10]5-9-4 P (64) S Carson 25/1: 0000-000: 11th: Chsd ldrs 3f, wknd: cheek pieces.   ½   46

4319}   **LOUIS GEORGIO 182** [6]5-8-9 (55) J F Egan 20/1: 405400-0: 12th: b g Royal Applause - Swellegant   2   31
(Midyan) Al bhd: reapp: '03 wnr in Spain: '02 mdn wnr (J Noseda): eff btwn 5/6f on fast & polytrack, acts on a
sharp trk: runs well fresh: now with M Hoad.
2 Aug'02 Brig 5.2g/f 64-62 E: 1 Jan'02 Ling 5ap 65a- D:

1075   **TRIPTI 19** [13]4-8-8 (54) J Tate 50/1: 0020000: 13th: Handy, lost pl & btn over 2f out: see 340.   ½   28

739   **CAPTAIN CLOUDY 59** [1]4-9-2 (62) L Keniry(3) 20/1: 000-5660: 14th: Chsd ldrs, wkng when badly   *hd*   35
hmprd 1f out: 8 wk abs: see 607.

4810}   **GUNS BLAZING 188** [2]5-9-1 vis (61) M Howard(7) 14/1: 501000-0: 15th: b g Puissance - Queen of   2   28
Aragon (Aragon) Midfield, outpcd halfway, btn when hmpd over 1f out: reapp: won 4 h'caps in '03 (with Miss V
Haigh): 3rd at best in '02 (h'cap, rtd 77, with B McMahon): suited by around 5f on firm & soft grnd, prob acts on
any trk: has tried blnks, cheek pieces & a visor: on a fair mark: now with D K Ivory.
1 Sep'03 Pont 5g/f 64-60 E: 2 Aug'03 Hami 5.0g/f 61-(60) F: 1 Jul'03 Hayd 5g/f 62-55 D: 1 Jul'03 Brig 5.3g/f 55-49 E:
1 Jun'03 Leic 5.0g/f 49-43 E: 2 Jun'01 Wind 5gd 88- C: 1 May'01 Bath 5g/s 80- E:

15 Ran   Time 1m 1.28 (1.28)   Owned: Mr P Sweeting   Trained: Marlborough

---

1372   **5.05 Westows Play & Football In Hove Handicap Stakes 3yo 46-55 (F)**   [65]
£2898 £828 £414   **1m1f209y**   Good/Firm 31   -40 Slow   Inside

1240   **INCISOR 8** [3] S Kirk 3-8-13 (50) P Dobbs 5/2: 056-51: Midfield, not clr run 3f out, led ins fnl   56
1f, rdn out: first win: eff at 10f on fast grnd, acts on a sharp/undul trk: sharper from reapp: see 1240.

1240   **QUEENS FANTASY 8** [2] D Haydn Jones 3-9-4 VIS (55) Paul Eddery 14/1: 00-0402: ch f Grand Lodge -   *hd*   60
Alcalali (Septieme Ciel) Prsd ldr, outpcd over 1f out, rallied well ins fnl 1f, just failed: lightly rcd & unplcd
in '03 (rtd 46): eff at 10f on fast grnd: improvd in first time visor, has disapp in blnks.

4962}   **GARSTON STAR 177** [4] J S Moore 3-9-2 (53) Martin Dwyer 8/1: 650006-3: ch g Fleetwood - Conquista   1¾   55
(Aragon) Led till ins fnl 1f, no extra: op 16/1: unpcld all '03 starts (rtd 60, mdn): eff at 10f on fast grnd.

697   **SILVER CACHE 64** [5] J Noseda 3-9-3 (54) E Ahern 7/2: 0054: b f Silver Hawk - Nina Ashley   *nk*   55
(Criminal Type): Keen in midfield, hdwy over 2f out, onepcd fnl 1f: op 7/4, 9 wk abs: eff over 10f on fast.

1280*   **FRIENDS HOPE 5** [6]3-9-7 (6ex) (58) D Nolan(5) 5/4 FAV: 0501-015: Bhd, hdwy over 2f out, onepcd fnl   *shd*   58
1f: op 7/4, qck reapp, top-weight: just btr 1280.

5 Ran   Time 2m 4.91 (7.11)   Owned: Mr R Gander   Trained: Upper Lambourn

---

1373   **5.35 Pleasure Palace Racing Lady Riders' Series Handicap Stakes 3yo+ 46-55 (F)**   [41]
£2996 £856 £428   **1m3f196y**   Good/Firm 31   -11 Slow   Inside

1090   **GREAT VIEW 18** [3] Mrs A L M King 5-11-0 vis (55) Ms C Williams 11/4 FAV: 432-0121: Keen in   65
midfield, led over 3f out, pushed clr 2f out, readily: prev eff at 7f, now suited by 10/13f on firm, soft & both
AWs, any trk: in gd form: gd weight carrier: see 896 & 805.

896   **FREE STYLE 33** [4] Mrs H Sweeting 4-10-6 (48) Miss E Folkes(3) 16/1: 3014552: Led 6f, lost pl 4f   2½   52
out, rallied fnl 1f & took 2nd cl-home: acts on polytrack & fast: prev with K Burke & ran to winning form of 707.

594   **DELTA FORCE 75** [9] P A Blockley 5-10-8 (49) Miss Charmaine O'Neill 9/1: 1214453: In tch, hdwy 5f   1½   51
out, onepcd over 1f out & lost 2nd cl-home: long abs: see 456 & 204.

997   **BANNINGHAM BLAZE 25** [12] C R Dore 4-10-8 vis (50) Miss E J Jones 8/1: 0000-004: b f Averti - Ma   2   49
Pavlova (Irish River) Bhd, hdwy 4f out, onepcd 2f out: won 2 h'caps in '03 (earlier with D Shaw): 3rd in a seller
in '02 (rtd 49): eff around 12f on firm, fast & polytrack, stiff or sharp trk: wears a visor, has tried blnks.
1 Jul'03 Ling 12ap 67a-59 E: 2 Jun'03 Good 11g/f 60-59 E: 2 May'03 Ling 11.8g/f 60-56 F:
2 Apr'03 Pont 12.0g/f 60-54 D: 2 Apr'03 Warw 10.9fm 60-52 E: 1 Apr'03 Beve 12.1fm 54-46 E:

896   **FLETCHER 33** [2]10-10-5 (1oh) (45) Miss G D Gracey Davison(5) 16/1: 06204-05: b g Salse - Ballet   1½   43
Classique (Sadler's Wells) Chsd ldr, led 6f out till over 2f out, wknd: rnr-up in a clmr in '03: won a h'cap in
'02: stays 2m, suited by 12/14f, acts on firm & soft grnd, likes a gall trk: goes well for an amat & R Hughes: has
tried cheek pieces: well h'capped. 2 May'03 Brig 11.9fm 45-(44) E: 1 Jul'02 Sali 14g/f 55-52 E:
2 Sep'01 Good 16g/s 63-62 E: 1 Jul'01 Newb 13.2g/f 68-64 E: 1 Jun'01 Newm 12g/f 61-57 F:

1243   **BIRTH OF THE BLUES 6** [13]8-10-5 (1oh) (45) Miss Sarah Jane Durman(5) 11/1: 0063146: Bhd, some late   1   41
gains: qck reapp: see 1076 & 689.

1076   **LISSAHANELODGE 19** [11]5-10-5 (46) Miss E Kemp(7) 7/1: 0060/-127: Rear, late gains: see 1076.   ½   40

4862}   **SHORT CHANGE 185** [14]5-10-13 (54) Mrs S Bosley 10/1: 403222-8: b g Revoque - Maafi Esm (Polish   ¾   47
Precedent) Handy, outpcd over 2f out, sn wknd: reapp: won a h'cap in '03: won a h'cap earlier at 10/12f on
firm & gd/soft, likes Windsor, handles a sharp/undul or a gall trk: best without blnks, tried cheek pieces.
2 Oct'03 Brig 11.9fm 56-52 F: 2 Oct'03 Bath 11.7fm 55-52 E: 2 Sep'03 Beve 9.9g/s 55-52 F:
1 Aug'03 Wind 11.6g/f 56-52 E: 2 Jul'03 Wind 10.0g/f 52-50 E: 2 Aug'02 Brig 10g/f 56-55 F:
1 Jul'02 Wind 11.6g/f 55-52 E: 2 Jul'01 Chep 6g/f 71- E: 2 Jun'01 Nott 6g/f 77- D:

805   **SAMMYS SHUFFLE 52** [6]9-10-7 bl (48) Ms D Goad(5) 12/1: 605-0409: In tch, wknd 3f out: 7 wk abs.   3   36

813   **JOELY GREEN 48** [8]7-10-5 (1oh) (45) Mrs Emma Littmoden(3) 7/1: 5-506660: 10th: Rear, nvr a factor.   3½   29

1238   **INTENSITY 8** [5]8-11-3 (58) Miss Faye Bramley(5) 7/1: 00-30020: 11th: Chsd ldrs, outpcd 4f out & btn.   2½   37

768   **GEOGRAPHY 56** [7]4-10-4 (2oh)p (45) Miss S Cassidy(7) 50/1: 05-P0600: 12th: In tch, btn 5f out.   8   13

970   **STEPPENWOLF 27** [10]3-8-13 (21oh)p (45) Mrs I de Best(2) 33/1: 000-6000: 13th: Nvr nr ldrs.   *nk*   12

13 Ran   Time 2m 33.25(5.05)   Owned: All The Kings Horses   Trained: Stratford-On-Avon

Official Going STANDARD

1374

2.30 Bet Direct No Q Demo 08000 837 888 Handicap Stakes 3yo 46-55 (F)   [65]
£2961 £846 £423   **6f aw rnd**   **Going 52**   -05 Slow   Inside

592 **MELAINA 76** [4] M S Saunders 3-9-0 p (51) M Savage(5) 12/1: 061-2061: Led after 2f till dist,   57a
rallied well to regain lead well ins fnl 1f, drvn out: 11 wk abs: eff at 6f on fibresand: acts on a sharp trk,
likes W'hampton: eff with cheek pieces & goes well fresh: see 316 & 73.
283 **SAVERNAKE BRAVE 115** [3] Mrs H Sweeting 3-8-9 bl (46) G Baker 16/1: 66500-52: b g Charnwood Forest ½   50a
- Jordinda (Indian Ridge) Cl-up, led dist till edged right & hdd cl home: long abs: rnr-up once in '03 (auct mdn,
K R Burke): eff at 5.3f/6f on firm & f/sand: eff with blnks: back to best on first start for new stable.
2 Jun'03 Brig 5.3fm 63- F:
839 **WONKY DONKEY 44** [8] S C Williams 3-9-2 (53) M Fenton 3/1 FAV: 0-343: Handy, styd on ins fnl 1f,   hd   56a
not btn far in 3rd: tchd 4/1: 6 wk abs: imprvd eff on h'cap bow dropped back to 6f, 7f shld be ideal: see 751.
1085 **BOLD WOLF 19** [7] J L Spearing 3-9-3 (54) A Daly 6/1: 0020-444: Led early, styd cl-up, no extra   1   54a
ins fnl 1f: eff at 5f/6f on firm grnd & fibresand: see 1085.
1002 **SMART DANNY 26** [6]3-8-12 (49) R Winston 9/2: 40-055: Cl-up 5f, fdd: op 11/4: see 1002 (5f).   3   40a
381 **ANISETTE 105** [5]3-9-4 (55) I Mongan 10/1: 2-306: Bhd, nvr nrr than mid-div: long abs: btr 126.   nk   45a
613 **KEDROSS 74** [10]3-9-4 (55) M Tebbutt 10/1: 43000-07: ch f King of Kings - Nom de Plume (Nodouble)   1¾   40a
Rear, mod late gains: 11 wk abs: plcd in '03 (rtd 69, mdn, Mrs A Duffield): eff at 5/6f, handles gd & soft.
871* **GARNOCK VENTURE 39** [12]3-9-4 bl (55) D Holland 8/1: 43-40018: Al in rear: rider reported mount   1¼   36a
had become restless in stalls: btr 871 (7f).
1268 **SHORT CHORUS 6** [11]3-8-13 p (50) S W Kelly 8/1: 1000-049: Mid-div, wknd ins fnl 2f: qck reapp.   nk   30a
1218 **MOSCOW MARY 9** [1]3-8-13 (50) S Whitworth 20/1: 03240-00: 10th: Bhd, nvr a factor: see 1218.   1¼   26a
1070 **BLADES DAUGHTER 20** [9]3-8-9 (1oh)BL (45) S Hitchcott(3) 20/1: 000-60: 11th: Hmpd & al bhd.   ½   20a
1222 **WENDYS GIRL 9** [2]3-9-4 (55) T Hamilton(3) 9/1: 30-0052P: Cl-up when saddle slipped, p.u. 4f out.   0a
12 Ran   Time 1m 16.25 (3.45)   Owned: Bali Royal Racing   Trained: Wells

---

1375

3.00 Bet Direct No Q On 08000 93 66 93 Claiming Stakes 4yo+ (F)
£2870 £820 £410   **1m4f aw**   **Going 52**   +06 Fast   Inside

1047* **MANIATIS 21** [4] Mrs J Candlish 7-9-2 vis (75) N Chalmers(5) 7/4: 1465/-611: Rear, prog to lead 5f   77a
out, rdn out despite hanging right: clmd for 10,000: eff at 10/12f on fast & fibresand, likes gd/soft: has apprec
recent drop to claim grade & application of visor: see 1047 & 856.
948 **MANDOOB 30** [1] B R Johnson 7-8-10 p (71) J P Guillambert(3) 13/8 FAV: 0-411002: Dwelt, prog 3f   5   62a
out, styd on ins fnl 1f, not pace of wnr, saddle slipped: op 5/4: left prev 2 poor effs bhd here, btr 634.
1323* **ORINOCOVSKY 3** [2] N P Littmoden 8-8-13 (55) Steven Harrison(7) 7/2: 0232013: Led 7f, ev ch 2f   1¾   62a
out, fdd ins fnl 1f: qck reapp: just btr 1323 (seller).
1286 **GRAND LASS 6** [5] A Sadik 5-8-3 (49) T P Queally 14/1: 2543004: Cl-up till 1m out, wknd.   11   36a
1286 **THEATRE TINKA 6** [3]5-9-2 p (59) D Sweeney 7/1: 5552405: Cl-up when short of room after 4f, sn   1¾   46a
wknd, broke blood vessel: qck reapp: btr 997 & 679.
5 Ran   Time 2m 39.15 (5.55)   Owned: Racing For You Limited   Trained: Leek

---

1376

3.30 Avoid The Queues With Bet Direct No Q Handicap Stakes Fillies 3yo 0-70 (E)   [69]
£3435 £1057 £529   **7f aw rnd**   **Going 52**   -08 Slow   Outside

4857J **FARRIERS CHARM 186** [1] D J Coakley 3-9-4 (59) T P Queally(3) 14/1: 644-1: b f In Command - Carn   67a
Maire (Northern Prospect) Mid-div, prog to lead ins fnl 1f, rdn out: reapp & AW bow: unplcd on all 3 '03 starts
(mdns, rtd 57): eff at 7f, shaped as tho' further will suit: imprvd here for switch to fibresand: acts on a sharp
trk & goes well fresh: unexposed in h'cap grade & can follow up.
794 **COULD SHE BE MAGIC 54** [4] T D Easterby 3-9-6 BL (61) S W Kelly 9/4 FAV: 501-2102: Cl-up, ev ch   2½   63a
when edged left under press dist, kept on but not pace wnr fnl 1f: 8 wk abs & 1st time blnks: see 615.
4450J **MISS MADAME 213** [5] R Guest 3-9-7 (62) P Robinson 4/1: 060-3: b f Cape Cross - Cosmic Countess   1   62a
(Lahib) Led till hdd ins fnl 1f, no extra: tchd 6/1: reapp & AW bow: unplcd all 3 '03 starts (rtd 62, mdn, T P
McGovern): eff at 7f, bred to be suited by 1m: acts on fibresand: not disgraced on first start for new stable.
1239 **SHOWTIME ANNIE 9** [7] A Bailey 3-9-5 (60) G Carter 4/1: 300-6104: Nvr nrr than mid-div, btr 863 (6f).   2   56a
4766J **SHARPLAW DESTINY 193** [2]3-9-0 (55) D Holland 3/1: 004-5: b f Petardia - Coolrain Lady (Common   3½   44a
Grounds) Cl-up 5f, sn fdd: unplcd in 3 '03 starts (rtd 56 & 54a, mdns): with W Haggas.
1007 **FARAWAY ECHO 26** [3]3-9-2 (57) I Mongan 10/1: 500-06: Handy 4f, sn wknd: see 1007.   5   36a
4911J **TSHUKUDU 182** [6]3-8-6 (1ow) (46) D Sweeney 16/1: 05000-7: Rear, nvr a factor on reapp.   11   4a
7 Ran   Time 1m 30.4 (4.2)   Owned: Mr Alf Hall   Trained: West Ilsley

---

1377

4.00 Bet Direct No Q Median Auction Maiden Stakes 3yo (E)
£3367 £1036 £518   **1m100y aw**   **Going 52**   +05 Fast   Inside

1152 **SUBMISSIVE 13** [2] B W Hills 3-9-0 K May(7) 20/1: 01: ch c Young Ern - Sublime (Conquering Hero)   79a
Made all, rdn out ins fnl 1f to just hold on: imprvd on step up to 8.4f: acts on fibresand & a sharp trk: only
lightly rcd & open to more improvement.
1078 **DELIGHTFULLY 19** [1] B W Hills 3-8-9 M Hills 11/2: 0-02: b f Definite Article - Kingpin Delight   nk   73a
(Emarati) Cl-up, ev ch ins fnl 1f, just held by longer priced stablemate: tchd 7/1: unplcd sole '03 start (rtd 67,
fills mdn): eff at 8.4f on fibresand: can find similar.
1241 **PEAK OF PERFECTION 9** [6] M A Jarvis 3-9-0 (73) P Robinson 6/4 FAV: 00-53: Cl-up, edged left &   ¾   76a
just held by front 2 ins fnl 2f: bckd from 5/2: eff at 8.4f on fibresand: see 1241.
260 **DEVIOUS AYERS 119** [3] G A Butler 3-9-0 T P Queally(3) 3/1: 3-4: Mid-div, fdd dist: long abs.   3½   69a
1283 **JARVO 6** [5]3-9-0 (66) D Holland 9/4: 02230-25: Handy 6f, sn fdd: well bckd: disapp on qck   11   47a
reapp tho' rider reported mount hung LH'd: btr 1283 (gd).
1130 **CUNNING PURSUIT 14** [4]3-9-0 I Mongan 11/1: 06: Bhd, nvr a factor: with M L W Bell.   2½   42a
6 Ran   Time 1m 50.25 (4.05)   Owned: Mr Guy Reed   Trained: Lambourn

---

WOLVERHAMPTON **Fibresand MONDAY 26.04.04 Lefthand, Sharp Track**

1378 **4.30 Bet In Running @ Betdirect Co Uk Selling Stakes 3yo+ (G)**
£2520 £720 £360 **7f aw rnd Going 52 -13 Slow** Outside

1065 **MIZHAR 20** [3] J J Quinn 8-9-6 p (48) R Winston 6/1: 0525001: Rear, grad prog to lead ins fnl 1f, pushed out, val 4L+: op 9/2: no bid: eff at 5f/7f on firm, gd & both AWs, acts on any trk, likes W'hampton: eff in blnks/visor or cheek pieces: see 512. **59a+**
516 **BELLA BEGUINE 86** [1] A Bailey 5-9-1 vis (67) G Carter 4/6 FAV: 0202-502: Led till hdd ins fnl 1f, sn no extra: long abs: below form eff: btr 27 (first time visor). *2½* **48a**
769 **CHANDELIER 57** [2] M S Saunders 4-9-6 (51) M Savage(5) 3/1: 60-53603: Slow away, prog & ev ch 2f out, edged right & sn no extra: op 5/1 on 8 wk abs: btr 571. *1½* **50a**
1160 **FINE FRENZY 12** [4] Miss S J Wilton 4-9-1 (45) A Quinn(5) 5/1: 03640-04: Cl-up 5f, fdd: btr 1160. *6* **33a**
4 Ran Time 1m 30.75 (4.55) Owned: Mr Andrew Page Trained: Malton

1379 **5.00 Betdirect Co Uk Amateur Riders' Handicap Stakes 4yo+ 0-55 (G)** **[40]**
£2982 £852 £426 **1m100y aw rnd Going 52 -24 Slow** Inside

776 **MAGGIES PET 57** [11] K Bell 7-10-5 (1oh)t (45) Miss J Ellis(5) 9/1: 2522451: Cl-up till led 4f out, clr bef 1f out, pushed out, val 3L+: op 7/1 on 8 wk abs: eff around 1m/9.4f, has tried 11f: acts on fibresand & a sharp trk: eff in t-strap: deserved first win: see 522 & 489. **52a+**
1223 **CRUSOE 9** [9] A Sadik 7-10-9 bl (50) Miss E J Jones 7/2 FAV: 0040042: Led over 4f, styd cl-up, no extra ins fnl 1f: op 11/2: btr 699. *1½* **52a**
754 **DONEGAL SHORE 59** [10] Mrs J Candlish 5-10-7 vis t (48) Mr D Weekes(5) 8/1: 00-42243: Rear, prog ins fnl 2f, nrst fin: 8 wk abs: worth another try over further: see 639 & 373. *1* **48a**
1223 **BOUGHT DIRECT 9** [13] R J Smith 5-10-10 (51) Mr L Newnes(5) 9/2: 00-00654: Cl-up till dist, no extra. *1* **49a**
4817} **SAXE COBURG 189** [1]7-10-13 (54) Mr G Denvir(7) 16/1: 263540-5: b g Warning - Saxon Maid (Sadler's Wells) Slow away, prog 2f out, nvr nrr than mid-div: reapp: sell h'cap wnr in '03: lightly rcd in '02 (plcd, rtd 59a, AW h'cap): eff at 7f/10f, suited by around 11.5f: acts on both AWs & fast grnd, tried visor. *½* **51a**
2 Aug'03 Wind 10.0gd 56-(54) F: 2 Aug'03 Wind 11.6g/f 53-53 E: 1 Jul'03 Wind 11.6g/f 51-46 F:
4607} **RAINSTORM 205** [7]9-10-5 (1oh) (45) Mrs S Owen(3) 12/1: 211400-6: b g Rainbow Quest - Katsina (Cox's Ridge) Slow away, sn handy till dist, fdd: reapp: won 2 lady rider h'caps in '03: ladies h'cap wnr in '02: eff at 7f/11f on firm, gd & both AWs: goes well for an amateur. *4* **35a**
1 Aug'03 Carl 7.9g/f 47-44 E: 1 Jul'03 Beve 9.9g/f 45-38 E: 2 Jul'03 Newm 8g/f 41-38 E: 1 Aug'02 Chep 8gd 44-38 E:
2 Sep'01 Ayr 10.8gd 50-45 E: 2 Sep'01 Folk 9.6g/s 46-43 F: 1 Jul'01 Beve 10g/f 44-41 E: 1 Jan'01 Wolv 8.4af 54a-50 G:
4310} **ENCORE ROYALE 221** [12]4-10-9 (50) Mr T Thomas(7) 11/1: 025000-7: Slow away, nvr nrr than mid-div. *nk* **38a**
4944} **DESERT FURY 180** [6]7-10-11 (52) Miss R Bastiman(5) 14/1: 005000-8: Handy over 6f, wknd: reapp. *nk* **39a**
1198 **QOBTAAN 11** [3]5-11-0 (55) Mrs S Bosley 10/1: 4-611009: Slow away, nvr able to chall: btr 387. *shd* **41a**
910 **PAS DE SURPRISE 33** [2]6-10-11 (52) Miss E Folkes(3) 9/2: 4-305540: 10th: Nvr nrr than mid-div. *1½* **35a**
1047 **PRINCE MINATA 21** [4]9-10-5 (6oh) (40) Miss A Hockley(7) 12/1: 6-003040: 11th: Handy 4f, sn wknd. *5* **19a**
4824} **SMART MINISTER 188** [5]4-10-10 (51) Mr S Walker 8/1: 036420-0: 12th: Handy over 5f, fdd: reapp. *1½* **21a**
12 Ran Time 1m 52.7(6.5) Owned: Mr Len Purdy Trained: Wantage

WINDSOR **MONDAY 26.04.04 Sharp, Fig 8 Track**

Official Going Good (Good/Firm places)

1380 **5.35 Welcome To Monday Evenings At Windsor Maiden Auction Stakes Fillies 2yo (F)**
£3513 £1081 £541 **5f10y rnd Good Inapp** Inside

HIGH CHART [9] G G Margarson 2-8-4 A McCarthy 4/1 FAV: 1: b f Robellino - Bright Spells (Salse) In tch, hdwy 2f out, styd on ins last to lead cl-home, rdn out: bckd: April foal, cost 10,000gns: half-sister to a 7f juv wnr: dam 6f 2yo scorer: eff at 5f, 6f will suit: acts on gd & runs well fresh: v encouraging start, shld be more to come. **77**
AGENT KENSINGTON [7] R Hannon 2-8-2 R L Moore 7/1: 2: b f Mujahid - Monawara (Namaqualand) Dwelt, held up, hdwy & switched left well over 1f out, styd on strongly ins last, just failed on debut: March first foal, cost 2,500gns: dam plcd over 5f as a juv: eff at 5f, shaped like 6f sure to suit: acts on gd grnd: v pleasing but green, learn bundles from this & shld be winning similar shortly. *shd* **74+**
1325 **LATERAL THINKER 3** [4] J A Osborne 2-8-2 J F McDonald(3) 9/2: 223: With ldrs, hdwy to lead ins last, rdn & collared cl-home, hands & heels: acts on gd & polytrack: consistent: see 1071. *shd* **73**
ELISHA [8] D M Simcock 2-8-4 Martin Dwyer 33/1: 4: ch f Raise A Grand - Social Butterfly (Sir Ivor) With ldrs, led over 1f out till ins last, drvn & just held on debut: April foal, cost 5,200gns: half-sister to sev wnrs: eff at 5f on gd grnd: pleasing start, shld find a race. *nk* **75**
BAILEYS APPLAUSE [12]2-8-6 P J Fanning 25/1: 5: Slow away, sn cl-up, hung left & onepace fnl 1f, hands & heels: cheek pieces on debut. *1* **74**
1133 **MISS TRUANT 14** [14]2-8-6 J Mackay 9/2: 66: Dwelt, sn in tch, some late gains, nvr dangerous. *¾* **72**
CELTIC SPA [2]2-8-4 R Miles(3) 20/1: 7: In tch, eff over 2f out, wknd fnl 1f. *nk* **69**
CLINET [10]2-8-4 S Carson 33/1: 8: Dwelt, bhd, switched left & kept on over 1f out, nrst fin. *1½* **65**
ASPEN RIDGE [13]2-8-6 S Drowne 12/1: 9: With ldrs, short of room over 1f out, no extra. *1½* **63**
1170 **WATERLINE LOVER 12** [6]2-8-8 M Fenton 25/1: 60: 10th: In tch, wknd 2f out. *shd* **64**
ASHES [15]2-8-4 C Catlin 9/1: 0: 11th: In tch, wknd over 1f out. *2* **54**
CHUTNEY MARY [1]2-8-8 Dane O'Neill 50/1: 0: 12th: Dwelt, al bhd on debut. *¾* **56**
1097 **NUTTY TIMES 18** [11]2-8-2 A Daly 10/1: 2330: 13th: Led till over 1f out, wknd: consistent prev. *½* **48**
HEART OF ETERNITY [5]2-8-11 J Murtagh 14/1: 0: 14th: Dwelt, al bhd on debut. *nk* **56**
BE BOP ALOHA [3]2-8-2 W Supple 16/1: 0: 15th: Dwelt, nvr a factor on debut. *7* **26**
15 Ran Time 1m 01.74 () Owned: Mr Dennis Russell Trained: Newmarket

1381 **6.05 Gibbs And Dandy Classified Stakes 3yo+ 0-80 (D)**
£5639 £1735 £868 **1m2f7y** **Good** **Inapp** Inside

1104 **TAWNY WAY 16** [10] W Jarvis 4-9-5 (82) D Holland 7/1: 01220-51: Dwelt, in tch, hdwy 2f out, styd on to lead ins last, drvn out: suited by 9/10f on fast & gd, poss soft & a stiff or sharpish trk: genuine. **85**
4688} **DESERT ROYALTY 197** [7] E A L Dunlop 4-9-5 (82) L Dettori 9/2: 513123-2: b f Alhaarth - Buraida (Balidar) Handy, eff over 1f out, chall ins last, just held for press: '03 3-time h'cap scorer: winning form over 1m/12f: acts on firm & gd/soft, likes sharp trks, handles any: proving tough & consistent in this grade. *shd* **84**
2 Sep'03 Ayr 10g/f 82-80 C: 1 Sep'03 Epso 12.0gd 82-74 D: 1 Aug'03 Brig 9.9fm 78-70 E:
2 Jun'03 Nott 10.0g/f 71-(68) E: 1 May'03 Wind 8.3g/s 68-61 E:
1139 **LION HUNTER 14** [8] Miss E C Lavelle 5-9-10 (84) W Supple 10/1: 251/-0603: Cl-up, hdwy & short of room 2f out till over 1f out, sn led, rdn & hdd cl-home, just btn: another gd run here: see 716. *shd* **89**
1098 **DESERT ISLAND DISC 18** [1] J J Bridger 7-9-3 (73) J F McDonald(3) 50/1: 66030-04: b f Turtle Island - Distant Music (Darshaan) Held up, eff to chall over 1f out, sn onepace: won 2 h'caps in summer '03: won 3 h'caps in '02: best at 12f & acts on fast, hvy grnd, handles polytrack & any trk, likes Kempton: v tough mare. *2½* **77**
1 Aug'03 Sali 12g/f 76-66 D: 1 Jul'03 Kemp 12g/f 69-62 E: 2 Jul'03 Kemp 10g/f 64-57 C: 2 Jul'03 Kemp 9g/f 59-56 C:
2 Mar'03 Bath 10.2g/f 63-59 E: 2 Sep'02 Kemp 10fm 64-61 C: 2 Aug'02 Good 12g/f 63-59 D:
2 Jul'02 Kemp 12g/s 60-58 E: 1 Jul'02 Leic 11.8g/s 59-53 D: 2 Jun'02 Kemp 12g/f 53-52 D: 1 Jun'02 Sali 12gd 51-46 D:
2992*}**WIGGY SMITH 283** [13]5-9-6 (80) Dane O'Neill 7/2 FAV: 2615/41-5: ch g Master Willie - Monsoon (Royal Palace) In tch, lost place 3f out, some late gains: won 2nd of only 2 '03 starts (h'cap): '02 mdn wnr: eff at 1m/11f, stays a slowly run 12f on fast & soft, reportedly not firm: acts on a stiff or sharp trk. *shd* **80**
1 Jul'03 Newb 11.0g/f 81-73 D: 1 Oct'02 Wind 8.3g/s 75- D: 2 Aug'02 Sand 8g/s 75-73 E: 2 Jul'02 Chep 8sft 74-72 D:
4778} **BARKING MAD 192** [12]6-9-9 (83) M Fenton 10/1: 010350-6: Set pace, hdd & no extra over 1f out. *3½* **79**
1104 **FERNERY 16** [2]4-9-5 (82) T Quinn 8/1: 031-47: Handy, no extra over 1f out: see 1104. *1½* **73**
1038 **NOFAS MAGIC 23** [3]4-9-3 (80) J Murtagh 8/1: 20-38: Held up, eff 2f out, wknd over 1f out: mdn. *shd* **71**
1059* **CAROUBIER 21** [6]4-9-6 (76) R Miles(3) 16/1: 5212019: Held up, no impress dist: btr 1059 (1m). *shd* **74**
4378] **KENS DREAM 572** [9]5-9-6 (80) P McCabe 50/1: 511015/-0: 10th: Keen in tch, eff 2f out, fdd. *5* **66**
1257] **PARDISHAR 723** [11]6-9-11 (85) R L Moore 12/1: 134/00/-0: 11th: Sn well bhd: gelded, comeback. *shd* **71**
3514} **COLOPHONY 260** [5]4-9-6 t (79) Martin Dwyer 33/1: 3216-0: 12th: Al bhd: changed stable, gelded. *2* **63**
1104 **THE BONUS KING 16** [4]4-9-10 (84) J Fanning 12/1: 60-45200: 13th: Cl-up, wknd & eased 2f out. *9* **53**
13 Ran Time 2m 07.63 () Owned: Rams Racing Club Trained: Newmarket

1382 **6.35 Shorterm Engineers Handicap Stakes 3yo 0-85 (D)** **[88]**
£5509 £1695 £848 **1m3f135y** **Good** **Inapp** Inside

1019 **RAREFIED 25** [4] R Charlton 3-9-1 (75) S Drowne 12/1: 62-01: b c Danehill - Tenuous (Generous) Cl-up, led over 2f out, pushed out: first win: rnr-up on 2nd of 2 '03 mdn starts: imprvd here for step up to 11.5f & acts on gd & soft grnd, gall or sharp trks: lightly rcd & open to further improvement. **82**
2 Nov'03 Nott 8.2sft 77- D:
1260 **LATE OPPOSITION 7** [3] E A L Dunlop 3-8-3 (63) W Supple 5/2: 006-422: In tch, hdwy to chase wnr 2f out, onepace ins last: bckd: acts on gd & gd/soft: ran v similar race 1260 & shld find a race. *1½* **67**
701* **JOMACOMI 63** [6] M Johnston 3-9-6 (80) J Fanning 10/1: 13: Led after 4f, hung left 3f out & hdd 2f out, rallied ins last: 2 mth abs: acts on f/sand & gd grnd: shaped like even further will suit: see 701. *1½* **82**
4993*}**ZEITGEIST 175** [8] L M Cumani 3-9-3 (77) N Mackay(3) 12/1: 01-4: b c Singspiel - Diamond Quest (Rainbow Quest) Held up, rdn over 3f out, some late gains, nvr dngrs on reapp: won 2nd of 2 mdn starts in '03: eff at 7f, prob stays 11.5f: acts on gd & soft grnd: looks like more to come. 1 Nov'03 Redc 7sft 79- D: *1¼* **77**
4617*}**DUMFRIES 203** [10]3-9-7 (81) L Dettori 2/1 FAV: 031-5: ch g Selkirk - Pat Or Else (Alzao) In tch, wkng when stumbled over 1f out: nicely bckd on reapp: won last of 3 '03 mdn starts: eff at 10f on fast grnd & prob any trk: clearly btr expected. 1 Oct'03 Pont 10.0g/f 81- D: *hd* **80**
1220 **MAGIC STING 9** [7]3-8-5 (65) J Mackay 33/1: 5-556: Keen, held up, no impress fnl 2f. *½* **63**
1165* **CHARA 12** [2]3-8-6 (66) Martin Dwyer 16/1: 4045-317: Led 4f, lost place over 2f out: btr 1165. *3* **60**
915 **CHAMPAGNE SHADOW 33** [5]3-8-6 bl (66) R L Moore 16/1: 04-04028: Al bhd: btr 915 (polytrack), 601. *¾* **59**
1141 **MISS LANGKAWI 14** [1]3-9-0 (74) D Holland 13/2: 31-09: In tch, wknd over 2f out. *¾* **66**
1260 **BOSCO 7** [9]3-8-7 (67) P Dobbs 33/1: 605-00: 10th: In tch, wknd over 3f out. *3* **55**
10 Ran Time 2m 31.79 () Owned: Mr K Abdulla Trained: Beckhampton

1383 **7.05 Reed & Mackay Classified Stakes 3yo+ 0-80 (D)**
£5428 £1670 £835 **6f rnd** **Good** **Inapp** Inside

1251 **LINCOLN DANCER 7** [7] D Nicholls 7-9-3 (78) P Dobbs 9/1: 0-004341: In tch, hdwy 2f out, led appr fnl 1f, kept on, drvn out: suited by 6f, stays 7f on any trk: handles fast, prev much btr on gd/soft & hvy: formerly smart, has dropped to a v handy mark: see 611. **86**
1116 **MORSE 16** [10] J A Osborne 3-8-8 (82) L Dettori 9/4 FAV: 0336-022: Cl-up, lost place halfway, rallied over 1f out, chall ins last, just held: well bckd: proving tough: see 1116. *nk* **87**
1043 **MISS GEORGE 23** [8] D K Ivory 6-9-3 (83) Dane O'Neill 6/1: 130-1003: Dwelt, held up, hdwy & short of room 2f out till 1f out, styd on ins last & again short of room, nrst fin: big drifter from 11/4: lost a shoe beforehand & must have gone v close with any sort of run: loves Lingfield & Windsor: eye-catching here. *1* **82+**
1217 **BLACKHEATH 10** [3] D Nicholls 8-9-5 (82) Alex Greaves 10/1: 1023-044: Keen cl-up, no extra fnl 1f: best at 5f: stablemate of wnr, see 1217. *1½* **80**
921 **ENDLESS SUMMER 32** [1]6-9-3 (80) D Holland 7/2: 04004-35: Chsd ldrs, onepace over 1f out: nicely bckd: now with K Burke: see 921. *1¼* **74**
1103* **DEVISE 18** [6]5-9-3 (78) T G McLaughlin 12/1: 03600-16: Keen cl-up, wknd fnl 1f: shade btr 1103. *¾* **72**
1162 **OK PAL 12** [9]4-9-8 (85) R Miles(3) 16/1: 0/04-U307: Led till wknd just ins last: see 834, 692. *1½* **73**
4892} **MIRASOL PRINCESS 184** [4]3-8-5 (1ow) (81) T Quinn 16/1: 041100-8: ch f Ali Royal - Yanomami (Slew O' Gold) Dwelt, in tch, eff & short of room over 1f out, no extra on reapp: won a mdn auct, stks, clmr & h'cap in '03, first 3 wins for K Ryan: all 4 wins at 5f on fm or fast, prob any trk: has run well fresh: tough last term. *¾* **65**
1 Sep'03 Wind 5.0g/f 84-76 D: 1 Aug'03 Hayd 5g/f 71-(78) F: 1 May'03 Redc 5g/f 80- E: 2 May'03 Thir 5g/s 84- D:
1 Mar'03 Muss 5g/f 86- E:
3724} **BAHAMIAN BREEZE 251** [5]3-8-7 (81) S W Kelly 12/1: 216-9: b g Piccolo - Norgabie (Northfields) Slow away, al bhd on reapp: won middle of 3 '03 starts (mdn): eff at 5f on firm grnd: gelded since last term. *2½* **60**

1 Aug'03 Thir 5fm 77- D: 2 Jul'03 Yarm 5.2fm 82- D:
4544} **GOLDEN BOUNTY 208** [2]5-9-3 (80) P Gallagher(7) 25/1: 205000-0: 10th: In tch, wknd over 1f out.   2½   52
10 Ran   Time 1m 13.53 ()   Owned: The Gardening Partnership   Trained: Thirsk

---

1384   7.35 Windsor-Racecourse Co Uk Maiden Stakes 3yo (D)
             £4303 £1324 £662   1m2f7y   Good   Inapp   Inside

1209   **CRYSTAL 10** [5] B J Meehan 3-8-9   M Hills 1/1 FAV: 0-21: Cl-up, led trav well over 2f out, pushed   88
clr, more in hand: hvly bckd: stays 10f well, 12f lks sure to suit: acts on gd & a gall or sharp trk: useful filly,
more to come in stronger company: see 1209.
1148   **NIETZSCHE 13** [16] J Noseda 3-9-0   S W Kelly 25/1: 02: b c Sadler's Wells - Wannabe (Shirley   1¾   86
Heights) Handy trav well, hung left over 1f out & rdn, not pace of wnr: cost 300,000gns: imprvd from debut & eff
at 10f, bred to stay 12f: handles gd grnd: shld find similar.
1148   **GIRONDE 13** [10] Sir Michael Stoute 3-9-0   B Doyle 9/2: 5-43: Slow away, sn handy, hdwy to chase   1   84
wnr over 1f out, sn no impress: op 3/1: bred to apprec 12f & fin clr of rem.
2819} **SOUND OF FLEET 290** [12] P F I Cole 3-9-0   S Drowne 7/2: 2-4: ch c Cozzene - Tempo (Gone West)   5   76
Dwelt, keen, led after 3f out till over 2f out, no extra: well bckd on reapp: rnr-up on sole juv start (mdn): eff
at 7f, bred to stay at least 10f this term: handles firm grnd: clearly btr expected.
2 Jul'03 York 7.0fm 83- D:
5018} **BROUGH SUPREME 172** [8]3-9-0   P Dobbs 66/1: 0-5: b g Sayaarr - Loriner's Lady (Saddlers' Hall)   1¾   74
In tch, outpcd over 3f out, some late gains on reapp: unplcd (rtd 62) sole '03 start: bred to stay mid-dists.
1166   **PROTECTING HEIGHTS 12** [15]3-9-0   G Carter 100/1: 06: Held up, no impress fnl 2f.   ¾   73
       SILENCIO [7]3-9-0   V Slattery 66/1: 7: In tch, no impress fnl 2f on debut.   ¾   72
       MASKED [3]3-9-0   T Quinn 100/1: 8: Bhd, modest late gains on debut.   hd   71
4772} **LEVITATOR 192** [4]3-9-0   Dane O'Neill 66/1: 0-9: In tch, wknd over 2f out.   nk   70
       IDEALISTIC [13]3-8-9   N Mackay(3) 50/1: 0: 10th: Dwelt, al bhd on debut.   6   55
       TWELVE BAR BLUES [6]3-8-9   L Dettori 10/1: 0: 11th: Al bhd on debut.   ¾   54
1125   **DORINGO 14** [2]3-9-0   A Daly 100/1: 0-00: 12th: In tch, wknd over 2f out.   ¾   58
120   **Flying Patriarch 149** [9]3-9-0 R L Moore 100/1:0   **Oh So Hardy** [11]3-8-9 C Catlin 100/1:0
      Maidstone Midas [1]3-9-0 M Fenton 100/1:0   4943} **Seagold 180** [14]3-8-9 J Mackay 100/1:0
16 Ran   Time 2m 10.25 ()   Owned: Mr F C T Wilson   Trained: Upper Lambourn

---

1385   8.05 Come Racing At Royal Windsor Handicap Stakes 3yo+ 0-70 (E)   [70]
             £3650 £1123 £562   1m67y rnd   Good   Inapp   Inside

4075} **SALINOR 234** [10] A C Stewart 4-10-0 (70) L Dettori 7/2: 341323-1: ch g Inchinor - Salanka   79
(Persian Heights) In tch, hdwy over 2f out, styd on to lead ins last, drvn out on reapp: '03 appr h'cap wnr, lkd a
shade unlucky twice: eff around 8.5f on firm & gd grnd, prob any trk: clearly runs well fresh: gelding op this
winter appears to have helped.   2 Aug'03 Hayd 8.1g/f 77-66 E: 1 Jul'03 Beve 8.5g/f 64-61 F:
769* **BEST BEFORE 57** [17] P D Evans 4-9-5 (61) S Drowne 14/1: 065-0012: In tch, eff & short of room   hd   69
over 2f out, styd on to lead over 1f out, collared ins last, just held: 2 mth abs & continuing in fine heart.
1100   **ZONIC BOOM 18** [12] J R Fanshawe 4-9-6 (62) J Murtagh 2/1 FAV: 00-53: b g Zafonic - Rosi Zambotti   2½   63
(Law Society) Held up, hdwy & short of room over 2f out, kept on ins last, nrst fin: bckd: unplcd in 2 '03 starts:
dam useful mid-dist performer: eff at 1m on gd grnd, looks more to come when stepped up to 10f: win similar.
387   **DUELLING BANJOS 104** [8] J Akehurst 5-9-9 (65) T Quinn 25/1: 00001-04: ch g Most Welcome -   ½   65
Khadino (Relkino) In tch, eff over 2f out, kept on same pace fnl 1f: long abs: won first & last '03 starts
(h'caps): won 2 h'caps for T Barron in '02: suited by around 1m on both AWs & loves gd/soft & hvy: acts on any
trk, goes well fresh & can force the pace: gd weight-carrier: tough.
1 Nov'03 Nott 8.2sft 66-60 F: 1 Mar'03 Ling 8ap 67a-60 F: 1 Aug'02 Ayr 8hvy 73-63 D: 1 Jun'02 Hami 8.2hvy 67-55 F:
1273* **AMNESTY 6** [3]5-9-7 (7ex)bl e (63) R L Moore 15/2: 5006115: Slow away, held up, some late gains,   ½   64
nvr dngrs: qck reapp, likes even softer grnd: see 1273.
1098   **EASTBOROUGH 18** [13]5-9-4 (60) D Holland 9/1: 1034346: Held up, some late gains, nrst fin.   nk   60
1098   **DASH FOR COVER 18** [6]4-9-10 (66) P Dobbs 33/1: 3001-207: In tch, wknd appr fnl 1f: btr 978.   nk   65
1253   **PARNASSIAN 7** [5]4-9-2 (58) Martin Dwyer 20/1: 42500-08: Slowly away & al bhd: see 1253.   1½   54
4396} **MISS GRACE 217** [2]4-9-4 (60) D Corby(3) 50/1: 213360-9: Held up, nvr a factor: reapp.   1¾   52
4864} **SPIRITS AWAKENING 185** [11]5-9-2 (58) C Catlin 16/1: 060422-0: 10th: Handy, wknd 2f out on reapp.   ¾   48
935* **SUPREME SALUTATION 31** [1]8-9-12 (68) M Howard(7) 25/1: 560-0110: 11th: Slow away, eff over 2f   ¾   56
out, sn wknd: now with D Ivory: see 935.
2109} **BIJOU DANCER 318** [16]4-9-3 (59) G Baker 50/1: 0/00560-0: 12th: Slow away, nvr a factor: new yard.   hd   46
1042   **MEELUP 23** [15]4-9-4 p (60) V Slattery 66/1: 0221000: 13th: Cl-up, keen, led 3f out till 1f out.   1   45
1282   **BANNISTER 6** [4]6-9-4 (60) M Fenton 25/1: 100-3030: 14th: Keen hld up, eff 2f out, sn wknd.   2   41
1058   **ESPADA 21** [7]8-9-9 (65) S W Kelly 25/1: 002-0000: 15th: In tch, wknd over 2f out.   6   34
4949} **ONE WAY TICKET 179** [14]4-9-9 p (65) S Carson 50/1: 341020-0: 16th: Keen, led till 3f out, wknd.   9   16
4167} **SEAL OF OFFICE 228** [9]5-9-11 (67) Dane O'Neill 12/1: 360600-0: 17th: Slow away, al bhd: new yard.   9   0
1253   **SURDOUE 7** [18]4-9-0 (56) J Fanning 25/1: 0242000: 18th: In tch, btn over 2f out, t.o.: see 747.   19   0
18 Ran   Time 1m 44.76()   Owned: M J C Hawkes & A Goddard   Trained: Newmarket

---

Official Going Good (Good/Soft Places)

1386   2.20 Daily Record Maiden Auct Stakes   A Qualifier For Hamilton Park 2-Y-O Series Final 2yo   (E)
             £3461   £1065   £533   **5f4y str**   **Good 45**   **-25 Slow**   Far side

1133   **MONASHEE PRINCE 14** [6] J R Best 2-8-8   N Pollard   7/4: 21: Sn grabbed far rail & made all, pushed   **83+**
out ins fnl 1f, val 2L+: well bckd: eff at 5f, shld get further in time: acts on gd grnd & a stiff/undul & easy
trk: can rate higher: see 1133 (debut).
      EXIT SMILING 0 [4] M Johnston 2-8-9   K Dalgleish   13/8 FAV: 2: ch c Dr Fong - Away To Me (Exit To   *1*   **77**
Nowhere) Cl-up, edged right under press ins fnl 1f, not pace wnr: well bckd on debut: Mar foal, cost 24,000gns:
dam unrcd: eff at 5f, shld apprec further in time: acts on gd grnd: encouraging eff & can improve.
1107   **GIFTED GAMBLE 16** [1] K A Ryan 2-8-7   N Callan   8/1: 03: b c Mind Games - Its Another Gift (Primo   *1¼*   **71**
Dominie) Trkd ldrs, onepace: Jan foal, cost 8,000gns: dam plcd at 5f: sire top-class performer at sprint dists:
sprint bred: imprvd on debut eff.
1149   **OUR CHOICE 13** [5] N P Littmoden 2-8-10   T E Durcan   8/1: 04: Chsd ldrs, no extra ins fnl 1f: see 1149.   *2*   **68**
1091   **STEAL THE THUNDER 18** [3]2-8-8 (1ow)   F Lynch   100/1: 05: br c Timeless Times - Lavernock Lady   *hd*   **65**
(Don't Forget Me) Bhd, nvr able to chall: Feb foal, cost 2,200gns: brother to a couple of wnrs at 5f: dam unplcd.
      LERIDA 0 [2]2-8-7   K Darley   11/1: 6: Sn veered right, hdd till dist, fdd: debut.   *7*   **46**
6 Ran   Time 1m 1.62 (3.52)   Owned: Richmond Thoroughbreds   Trained: Maidstone

1387   2.50 Roa Scotland Conditions Stakes 3yo   (C)
             £8964   £3400   £1700   **5f4y str**   **Good 45**   **+09 Fast**   Far side

1018+ **SEVILLANO 25** [6] P D Cundell 3-8-12 (106)   T E Durcan   1/6 FAV: 2132-11: Made all, pushed out to   **95+**
assert, val 3L+: bckd at long odds on: eff at 5f, rtn to 6f will suit, prob stays stiff 7f: acts on fast, gd &
polytrack, best eff has come on gd/soft: useful, will rate higher: see 1018.
4669} **CELTIC THUNDER 199** [4] T J Etherington 3-8-9 (84)   R Havlin   14/1: 431246-2: b g Mind Games - Lake   *1¾*   **82**
Mistassiu (Tina's Pet) Cl-up, kept on but al held by wnr ins fnl 1f: reapp: auct mdn wnr in '03: eff at 5f,
suited by 6f: acts on fast & gd grnd: acts on a stiff trk: ran to best bhd a useful wnr.
2 Aug'03 Beve 5g/f 85-81 B: 1 Jul'03 Beve 5g/f 82- E:
1229   **BAYLAW STAR 9** [3] J Balding 3-8-9 (75)   J Edmunds   25/1: 43003-63: b c Case Law - Caisson (Shaadi)   *3*   **73**
Prom to 3f, no extra bef 1f out: auct mdn, claim & h'cap wnr in '03 (also plcd 4 times): eff at 5/6f on fast &
soft grnd: acts on a sharp & a stiff/undul trk, likes Hamilton: has tried visor: wants h'caps.
1 Jul'03 Muss 5gd 80-76 D: 1 Jun'03 Hami 5.0gd 78- E: 2 Jun'03 Catt 5g/f 77- D: 1 Apr'03 Hami 5.0gd 79- E:
2 Apr'03 Muss 5g/f 69- E:
1344   **A LITTLE BIT YARIE 2** [5] K R Burke 3-8-12 (84)   Darren Williams   14/1: 3123-304: Dwelt, in tch   *5*   **62**
till wknd fnl 2f: qck reapp: see 1344 & btr 1299.
1119   **ONE N ONLY 15** [2]3-8-4 (55)   P Hanagan   100/1: 45450-45: Al in rear: see 1119.   *1½*   **50**
4317} **BALWEARIE 221** [1]3-8-9 (66)   J Carroll   66/1: 044254-6: b g Sesaro - Eight Mile Rock (Dominion)   *7*   **37**
Slow away, nvr a factor: reapp: rnr-up once in '03 (auct mdn): eff at 6f, stays 7f: acts on fast & gd grnd: has
tried cheek pieces: with Miss L A Perratt.   2 Jul'03 Muss 7.1gd 68-(70) E:
6 Ran   Time 59.92 (1.82)   Owned: HESheikh Rashid Bin Mohammed   Trained: Compton

1388   3.20 Racegoers Club Racecourse Of The Year Handicap Stakes 3yo+ 0-75   (E)   **[71]**
             £3575   £1100   £550   **1m1f36y**   **Good 45**   **-09 Slow**   Inside

1322   **PHAROAHS GOLD 3** [D] D Shaw 6-8-7 vis (50)   T E Durcan   14/1: 2050301: Held up, led till prog wide   **53**
from 3f out, rdn out to lead cl-home: qck reapp: eff at 7f/9f: acts on firm, soft grnd, fibresand specialist: eff
with visor or eye-shield: unexposed around this trip: see 1198 & 318.
4194} **DISPOL FOXTROT 584** [15] Miss V Scott 6-9-8 (65)   D McGaffin   16/1: 512215/-2: ch f Alhijaz -   *nk*   **66**
Foxtrot Pie (Shernazar) Handy, styd on to lead dist, hdd under press cl-home: modest hdles form on both 02/03
starts (p.u. & rtd 68h, nov hdle): missed '02: progressive in '02, winning sell & 2 h'caps here (T D Barron): eff
at 1m/11f on fast, likes fibresand, soft & hvy, loves Hamilton: goes well fresh: tough 6yo, fine return.
1 Aug'02 Hami 9.1hvy 66-58 C: 2 Aug'02 Carl 8g/f 60-55 E: 2 Aug'02 Ayr 9sft 58-58 E: 1 Jul'02 Hami 9.1g/s 58- E:
1 Jun'02 Hami 9.1sft 52-47 E: 2 Jun'02 Hami 9.1hvy 50-47 E: 2 May'02 Hami 11gd 48-47 E: 1 Jul'01 Hami 9.1gd 50-45 E:
1 Jul'01 Hami 9.1hvy 50- F: 2 Feb'01 Ling 10ap 47a- E: 1 Feb'01 Sout 8af 47a- G:
1278   **SUMMER SPECIAL 6** [11] D W Barker 4-8-8 (51)   P Hanagan   10/1: 0300-553: Bhd, prog 3f out, kept on   *2½*   **48**
ins fnl 1f, no ch with front 2: qck reapp: stays 9f: mdn after 25: see 1052.
1295   **LENNEL 5** [9] A Bailey 6-9-0 bl (67)   F Norton   11/2: 0114-504: Held up, kept on ins fnl 2f, nrst   *1*   **62**
fin: qck reapp: eff at 9f, rtn to 10f/11f will suit: just btr 1128.
4920} **JORDANS ELECT 181** [12]4-9-9 (66)   N Pollard   12/1: 410500-5: ch g Fleetwood - Cal Norma's Lady   *½*   **60**
(Lyphard's Special) Prom till lead 3 out, hdd dist, wknd: reapp: med auct mdn wnr in '03: unplcd during both
'02 starts (rtd 64): eff at 1m/9.3f on firm & gd/soft grnd: has gone well fresh.
1 Sep'03 Carl 9.3fm 75-(74) E: 2 Mar'03 Donc 8g/s 76- D:
924   **STING LIKE A BEE 32** [4]5-8-7 (50)   J F Egan   5/1 FAV: 0-102446: Bhd, prog when short of room   *¾*   **42**
around 3f out, prog ins fnl 2f, nrst fin: tchd 7/1: needs further? just btr 924 & 806.
1164   **ENCOUNTER 12** [13]8-8-3 (46)   Dale Gibson   10/1: 06500-07: br g Primo Dominie - Dancing Spirit   *½*   **37**
(Ahonoora) Handy till dist, no extra: h'cap wnr in '03 (also plcd 4 times): h'cap wnr in '02: mulitple h'cap wnr
in prev seasons: best around 7f/9f, prob stays 10f: acts on firm, soft & any trk, likes Hamilton: back on a
winning mark.   2 Aug'03 Hami 9.2g/f 52-50 C: 2 Jul'03 Hami 9.2gd 52-51 E: 1 May'03 Redc 8g/f 54-50 F:
2 Oct'02 Brig 10gd 51-46 G: 1 May'02 Muss 7.1gd 56-49 F: 1 Aug'01 Epso 7sft 60-52 E: 1 Aug'01 Catt 7gd 55-47 F:
2 Jul'01 Sout 7fm 46-46 C: 1 Jun'01 Newm 7fm 49-46 E:
1254   **ROTUMA 7** [5]5-9-8 bl (65)   P Makin(7)   10/1: 4104-058: Handy 6f, sn no extra: qck reapp: btr 1254.   *1¼*   **54**
4890} **FOREST AIR 184** [8]4-8-6 (49)   P Fessey   50/1: 550300-9: Bhd, nvr nr than mid-div: reapp.   *5*   **31**
520   **INCHINNAN 86** [1]7-9-0 (57)   A Nicholls   20/1: 46500-50: 10th: Bhd, nvr a factor: 10 wk jumps abs.   *1½*   **36**
1093   **PHARAOH HATSHEPSUT 18** [6]6-7-12 (6oh) (35)   P M Quinn   100/1: 0400/-000: 11th: Led 6f.   *½*   **19**
1197   **RED DELIRIUM 11** [14]8-7-12 (1oh)bl (40)   B Swarbrick(7)   12/1: 5255250: 12th: Chsd ldrs till wknd fnl 2f.   *shd*   **18**
4461} **MILLENNIUM HALL 213** [7]5-9-0 (57)   R Ffrench   11/1: 510060-0: 13th: Cl-up 6f, sn fdd: reapp.   *nk*   **33**
1160   **LUCKY LARGO 12** [10]4-9-1 (58)   K Dalgleish   8/1: 2020-050: 14th: Bhd, nvr a factor: btr 1160.   *¾*   **33**
1034   **NOUL 23** [2]5-9-1 p (58)   N Callan   10/1: 1-025550: 15th: Bhd, nvr able to chall.   *3½*   **28**
15 Ran   Time 1m 58.99 (4.89)   Owned: The Whiteman Partnership   Trained: Newark

---

1389

3.50 Totetrifecta Stakes Handicap 4yo+ 0-90 (C)   [90]
£10387 £3196 £1598   **1m4f17y**   **Good 45**   -07 Slow   Stands side

56   **KING REVO 160** [8] P C Haslam 4-9-3 (79) G Faulkner 8/1: 501604-1: b g Revoque - Tycoon Aly (Last   88+
Tycoon) Bhd, grad prog ins fnl 4f, led well ins fnl 1f, going away, val 2L+: rider received 7 day ban: hdles fit,
earlier won first 4 of 5 03/04 starts (juv hdles, rtd 145h, eff 2m on gd & hvy): amat rdr h'cap wnr in '03: eff at
7f/10f , now stays 12f: acts on firm, gd/soft & polytrack: goes well fresh: improving & can follow up.
1 Sep'03 Hayd 10.5fm 79-73 E: 2 Jan'03 Ling 10ap 77a-73 C: 1 Aug'02 Redc 7g/s 77- E:
1172   **GOLD RING 12** [7] G B Balding 4-9-9 (85) R Havlin 7/1: 22413-02: Chsd ldrs, styd on ins fnl 1f,   ¾   90
not btn far: lost little in defeat here & can find similar: see 1172 (reapp).
918   **KIDZPLAY 32** [10] J S Goldie 8-8-2 (63) J F Egan 25/1: 23564-03: b g Rudimentary - Saka Saka   ½   67
(Camden Town) Led, hdd under press well ins fnl 1f, no extra: won this race last term off a 3lb lower mark: plcd
twice in 2 of 4 02/03 hdle starts (rtd 104h, nov hdle, eff at 2m on soft): amat h'cap wnr in '02: eff at 11/12f,
stays 13f: likes gd/soft & hvy, handles firm & any trk, likes Musselburgh & Ayr: best dominating.
2 May'03 Hami 11.1g/s 67-(65) E: 1 Apr'03 Hami 12.1g/s 66-60 C: 1 Sep'02 Ayr 10.8g/s 67-60 E:
1 Apr'01 Muss 12g/s 74-71 D: 1 Apr'01 Muss 9hvy 75-64 E: 1 Mar'01 Donc 10.2sft 66-57 E:
1172*   **SENTRY 12** [12] J H M Gosden 4-9-9 (85) K Darley 7/1 FAV: 04/231-14: Handy, ev ch dist, onepcd   hd   88
ins fnl 1f: well bckd: ran to form of recent win in 1172.
1164*   **CALATAGAN 12** [2]5-8-2 (63) P Hanagan 14/1: 2230/-315: Handy till dist, no extra: btr 1164 (9.9f).   2   63
4498}   **GOLDEN BOOT 211** [9]5-8-6 p (67) F Norton 16/1: 002343-6: ch g Unfuwain - Sports Delight (Star   1½   64
Appeal) Held up, eff when short of room 4f out, kept on late, nrst fin: reapp: plcd numerous times in '03 (h'caps,
class stks, rtd 74): missed '02: auct mdn wnr in '01 (R M Beckett): eff around 1m/12f, stays 2m: acts on firm &
gd/soft grnd: eff with cheek pieces, visor & first time blnks: encouraging eff & has slipped down h'cap.
2 Aug'03 Hami 12.1g/f 68-65 E: 2 Jun'03 Hami 13.0g/f 72-70 E: 2 Jun'03 Hami 11.1gd 71-(70) E:
1 Sept'01 Hayd 8.1g/s 83- E:
926   **SAHEM 31** [6]7-9-3 (78) B Swarbrick(7) 14/1: 31330-57: Bhd, prog when short of room 2f out,   nk   74
switched & kept on late: btr 926.
1278   **SPREE VISION 6** [14]8-7-12 (7oh) (52) R Ffrench 100/1: 40360/-68: Chsd ldrs, ev ch 3f out, wknd dist.   ½   54
1121*   **GRAN DANA 15** [11]4-9-6 (82) K Dalgleish 14/1: 219: Prom 11f, sn wknd: btr 1121 (fast).   ¾   75
1295   **GENERAL GB 5** [4]7-8-8 (69) N Callan 7/1: 0/-120520: 10th: Handy when no room 2f out, no extra.   3½   57
1172   **Cruise Director 12** [1]4-9-9 (85) F Lynch 20/1:0   1034   **Lucky Judge 23** [3]7-7-12 (59) Dale Gibson 33/1:0
1093   **Acceleration Ire 18** [5]4-8-1 vis(63) P M Quinn 50/1:0   4197}   **Spectrometer 227** [13]7-9-10 (85) A Culhane 16/1:0
14 Ran   Time 2m 38.06 (6.26)   Owned: Dick Renwick & Mrs C Barclay   Trained: Middleham

---

1390

4.20 Famous Grouse Maiden Stakes 3-4yo (D)
£6123 £1884 £942   **1m3f16y**   **Good 45**   -20 Slow   Stands side

1347   **GOLDEN EMPIRE 2** [4] E A L Dunlop 3-8-5 (77) T E Durcan 3/1: 32-2241: Led, hdd 7f out, styd prom   70
& lead again 2f out, drvn out to hold on ins fnl 1f despite edging right: well bckd: qck reapp: stays 12f: acts on
firm, gd grnd & fibresand: back to form without visor on a faster surface.
4488}   **SADLERS PRIDE 212** [8] Andrew Turnell 4-9-10   J Carroll 14/1: 30-2: b c Sadler's Wells - Gentle   nk   69
Thoughts (Darshaan) Held up, gd prog & ev ch dist, kept on, just held by wnr: reappd 25/1 on reapp: fin 3rd of 4 on
first of only 2 '03 starts (mdn, rtd 59): eff at 11f, shld apprec further: acts on gd grnd: lightly rcd performer
who vastly imprvd on last year's 2 efforts: can rate higher & find similar.
1038   **TEMPLET 23** [7] J Semple 4-9-10   P Hanagan 10/11 FAV: 4-23: Rear, prog on rail when hmpd 2f, sn   2½   63+
lost place, styd on again ins fnl 1f, but ch had gone: well bckd: looked sure to have gone close with a trouble free
passage: keep in mind for similar: see 1038.
2972}   **ACT OF THE PACE 283** [3] M Johnston 4-9-5   K Dalgleish 9/1: 5-4: b f King's Theatre - Lady In   2½   56
Pace (Burslem) Dwelt, prog 3f out, no impress fnl 1f: op 7/1 on reapp: fin last of 5 of sole '03 start (mdn, rtd
57): related to high-class & genuine stayer Yavanas Pace:@ shld improve for step up in trip.
            JORDANS SPARK 0 [5]3-8-7 (2ow) N Callan 20/1: 5: ch c Opening Verse - Ribot's Pearl (Indian   9   50
Ridge) Keen prom, led 7f out, hdd when left 2f out, fdd: debut: dam wnr at 7f/1m: with 1 length.
1141   **PERUVIAN BREEZE 14** [6]3-8-5 (59) N Pollard 10/1: 066-56: Handy frm, sn fdd: btr 1141.   1¾   45
1121   **ARCHENKO 15** [1]4-9-10 F Lynch 100/1: 07: Cl-up, ev ch bef 2f out, sn fdd: see 1121.   5   38
            FLYING RED 0 [2]3-8-0 B Swarbrick(7) 33/1: 8: Sn away, al well adrift on debut.   dist   3
8 Ran   Time 2m 26.04 (7.24)   Owned: Mr Ahmed BuHaleeba   Trained: Newmarket

---

1391

4.50 Rectangle Group Handicap Stakes 3yo+ 0-75 (E)   [72]
£3868 £1190 £595   **6f5y str**   **Good 45**   +05 Fast   Far side

152   **ULYSEES 142** [1] I Semple 5-9-6 (64) P Hanagan 33/1: 006600-1: b g Turtle Island - Tamasriya   76
(Doyoun) Chsd ldrs, gd prog to lead well ins fnl 1f, going away: long abs: ex Irish, modest form in '03: mdn wnr
at Galway in '02: eff at 6/7f, has tried further: acts on gd & soft grnd: goes well fresh: has had muscle probs
but won nicely on return to turf: more h'caps await.
1282   **BALAKIREF 6** [8] M Dods 4-9-4 (62) F Lynch 9/4: 000-1022: Chsd ldrs, gd hdwy when hmpd ins fnl   2½   66+
1f, kept on, nrst fin: well bckd on qck reapp: much closer to this wnr with a clr run & looks poised to win.
5006}   **PIRLIE HILL 173** [5] Miss L A Perratt 4-8-1 (45) R Ffrench 66/1: 446000-3: b f Sea Raven - Panayr   hd   48
(Faraway Times) Trkd ldrs, ev ch dist, kept on but not pace front 2: reapp: modest form in '03 (rtd 60, med auct
mdn): plcd sole '02 start (auct mdn): eff at 6f on fast & gd grnd.
1046   **TANCRED TIMES 21** [2] D W Barker 9-8-13 (57) N Callan 22/1: 31000-04: Led 3f, no extra ins fnl 1f.   hd   59
684   **WALTZING WIZARD 66** [7]5-8-11 (55) T E Durcan 12/1: 52-35455: Bhd, prog ins fnl 2f, nrst fin.   shd   56
1255*   **MINE BEHIND 7** [10]4-10-0 (72) N Pollard 7/4 FAV: 32263-16: Prom, led after 3f, hdd well ins fnl   ½   71
1f, no extra: well bckd: below par eff under top-weight after recent win in 1255.
1277   **FRIAR TUCK 6** [4]9-8-8 (52) K Dalgleish 25/1: 03200-07: ch g Inchinor - Jay Gee Ell (Vaigly   5   37
Great) Rear, nvr able to chall: qck reapp: plcd twice in '03 (h'caps, rtd 62 at best): '02 appr h'cap wnr: eff
at 5f, suited by 6f on a stiff/gall trk, likes Ayr & York: acts on firm & hvy grnd, has gone well fresh: v well
h'capped on old form but is on a long losing run.
2 Sep'03 Redc 6fm 53-51 E: 1 Sep'02 Redc 6g/f 72-67 E: 2 Sep'02 Ayr 5g/s 77-71 D: 2 Aug'02 Ayr 6sft 70-64 E:

HAMILTON MONDAY 26.04.04 Righthand, Undulating Track, Stiff Uphill Finish

2 Jul'02 Ayr 5gd 64-63 C: 2 Oct'01 Ayr 6hvy 72-69 E: 2 May'01 Hami 6fm 83-78 D:

976	**OASES 27** [6]5-9-2 (60) F Norton 11/2: 0400-028: Rear, nvr a factor, btr 976.	2	39
1179	**JOYCES CHOICE 11** [9]5-8-10 (54) D Tudhope(7) 9/1: 50050-29: Bhd & hung badly 5f out, nvr in hunt.	3	24
1094	**COUSTOU 18** [3]4-9-11 (69) P Fessey 50/1: 1/0005-60: 10th: Al in rear, btr 1094.	2½	32

10 Ran Time 1m 12.21(2.41) Owned: Mr John F Allan Trained: Carluke

NEWCASTLE MONDAY 26.04.04 Lefthand, Galloping, Stiff Track

Official Going SOFT.

1392 5.50 St James Security Median Auction Maiden Stakes 3yo (F)
£3234 £924 £462 **5f str** **Soft 93** **+01 Fast** Stands Side

1146 **MR WOLF 14** [5] D W Barker 3-9-0 (70) L Enstone(3) 9/4 JT FAV: 4500-221: Made all, rdn clr fnl 1f, **76**
decisively: fair time: improved with forcing tactics on soft, handles fm: see 995 (reapp).

FRABROFEN [6] James Moffatt 3-8-9 Dean McKeown 20/1: 2: b f Mind Games - Oh My Oh My **3½ 63**
(Ballacashtal) Chsd ldrs, outpcd 1.5f out, rallied fnl 1f but no ch with wnr on debut: half-sister to several
sprint wnrs: eff at 5f on soft grnd, 6f shld suit: can improve.

3368} **EL PALMAR 266** [2] T D Barron 3-9-0 K Darley 5/2: 62-3: b g Case Law - Aybeegirl (Mazilier) **½ 67**
Front rank, wknd ins fnl 1f on reapp: tchd 7/2: rnr-up on fnl of 2 juv starts (mdn auct): eff at 5f on fast grnd,
prob handles soft: now qual for h'caps. 2 Aug'03 Carl 5g/f 69- E:

4534} **LADY OF THE LINKS 208** [3] N Tinkler 3-8-9 (56) Kim Tinkler 10/1: 5400-4: b f Desert Style - **8 46**
Itkan (Marju) Rdn in rear, no ch halfway on reapp: £26,000 half-sister to 6/7f wnr Exceptional Paddy: some mdn
promise in '03 (rtd 64): handles fast grnd, shld apprec 6f+.

3265} **SEA FERN 270** [4]3-9-0 G Duffield 20/1: 000-5: Chsd ldrs till halfway, sn btn: too keen on reapp. **nk 50**

1078 **SEGUIDILLA 19** [1]3-8-9 (82) A Culhane 9/4 JT FAV: 204-06: Chsd ldrs wide, btn halfway: op 11/8. **4 37**

6 Ran Time 1m 02.84 (4.64) Owned: Mr P Asquith Trained: Richmond

---

1393 6.20 Cantorsport Co Uk Handicap Stakes 3yo+ 0-75 (E) [75]
£4261 £1311 £656 **6f str** **Soft 93** **-00 Slow** Stands Side. Far Side Favoured.

1276* **RAYMONDS PRIDE 6** [11] K A Ryan 4-10-0 (6ex)bl (75) T Eaves(5) 9/1: F0-00511: Chsd ldrs far side, **83**
led dist, styd on strongly, rdn out: qck reapp, top-weight: eff at 5/6f on gd/soft & soft grnd, acts on firm &
fibresand: handles any trk, likes a gall one, esp Newcastle: in fine form, see 1276 (5f here).

1277 **CARLTON 6** [6] C R Dore 10-8-8 (55) R Thomas(5) 8/1: 4024522: Mid-div far side, styd on strongly **½ 59**
fnl 1f, just failed: qck reapp, op 13/2: hdcd conds to suit, deserves to go one btr: see 1227 (C/D).

1035 **FAIR SHAKE 23** [15] D Eddy 4-9-4 P (65) G Duffield 16/1: 0600-003: b g Sheikh Albadou - Shamrock **1½ 65+**
Fair (Shavian) Made all stands side, kept on fnl 1f but no ch with front 2 on far side: back to form in first time
cheek pieces: dual '03 h'cap wnr: eff at 5/6f on gd/soft & soft grnd, prob handles firm: back on a winning mark,
first home on the wrong side & one to keep in mind on same grnd.
1 May'03 Hami 6.0g/s 73-68 C: 1 Mar'03 Newc 5g/s 70-65 D:

1145 **IF BY CHANCE 14** [9] R Craggs 6-9-7 bl (68) D Allan(3) 8/1: 105-0244: Prom far side, ev ch fnl 1f, **hd 68**
no extra cl-home: see 967.

1276 **PAWAN 6** [8]4-9-0 (61) Ann Stokell 10/1: 2-522035: Held up wide far side, styd on fnl 1f, nrst **shd 61**
fin: qck reapp & again bhd today's wnr in 1276 (5f here).

1142 **HOV 14** [3]4-9-11 P (72) P Mulrennan(5) 6/1 FAV: 40-00026: Outpcd far side, fin well but too late: **1¼ 68+**
fast finisher over this inadequate 6f in first time cheek pieces: return to 7f/1m will suit: see 1142 & 595.

1179 **CATCH THE CAT 11** [4]5-9-8 bl (69) A Reilly(7) 14/1: 56050-37: Led till dist far side, grad wknd. **shd 65**

4741} **TRINITY 195** [12]8-8-6 (53) T Williams 20/1: 0/00040-8: b c College Chapel - Kaskazi (Dancing **1¼ 46**
Brave) Prom far side, wknd fnl 1f on reapp: 4th at best in '03 (h'cap): '01 h'cap wnr: eff at 5/6f on fm & gd/soft
grnd: likes to race up with/force the pace, can run well fresh: likes a stiff/gall trk, has tried a t-strap: back
on a fair mark. 1 Aug'01 Newc 6gd 60-53 F:

1277 **OLD BAILEY 6** [10]4-8-2 bl (49) Dale Gibson 12/1: 52626-69: Trkd ldrs far side, onepcd when short **shd 42**
of room entering fnl 1f: qck reapp since 1277 (C/D).

1255 **MAJIK 7** [17]5-8-10 VIS (57) L Enstone(3) 14/1: 3-034040: 10th: Prom stands side, onepcd dist: **1 47**
tried a visor: 2nd home on unfav'ble stands side: see 1255 (cheek pieces).

1278 **THE GAMBLER 6** [20]4-8-5 p (52) Natalia Gemelova(7) 50/1: 0500-000: 11th: ch g First Trump - Future **2½ 36**
Options (Lomond) Chsd ldrs till halfway stands side: qck reapp: '03 claim wnr, also h'cap rnr-up: eff at 6f/1m on
firm & soft grnd: wears cheek pieces. 2 Jun'03 Hami 8.3gd 60-(65) E: 2 May'03 Catt 6.0fm 66-63 E:
1 May'03 Redc 6g/f 64-(63) F: 2 Apr'03 Catt 6.0g/f 65-(65) G: 2 Nov'02 Catt 7sft 68- E:

859* **FAR NOTE 41** [16]6-9-5 bl (66) J Bramhill 20/1: 2004610: 12th: Front rank stands side, wknd dist: abs. **1 48**

1215 **BUNDY 10** [18]8-9-4 (65) K Darley 12/1: 61450-00: 13th: Chsd ldrs till halfway stands side. **1 45**

1276 **CASH 6** [2]6-8-8 p (55) D Fentiman(7) 20/1: 0135000: 14th: Al bhd far side: qck reapp. **½ 34**

245 **PADDYWACK 122** [7]7-9-12 bl (73) P Makin(7) 22/1: 566100-0: 15th: Nvr btr than mid-div stands side. **¾ 50**

1142 **TRE COLLINE 14** [14]5-9-8 (69) Kim Tinkler 50/1: 6320-000: 16th: Al bhd stands side. **½ 45**

1247 New Options 7 [5]7-8-9 p(56) Lisa Jones(3) 20/1:0	858 Drury Lane 41 [1]4-9-4 bl(65) A Culhane 25/1:0	
1277 African Spur 6 [13]4-9-4 t(65) R Fitzpatrick 50/1:0	1214 High Cane 10 [19]4-8-13 (60) Darren Williams 20/1:0	

20 Ran Time 1m 16.93 (5.63) Owned: Mr R E Robinson Trained: Hambleton

---

1394 6.50 Cantorsport Co Uk Claiming Stakes 2yo (F)
£3010 £860 £430 **5f str** **Soft 93** **-93 Slow** Stands Side

974 **KISSING A FOOL 27** [4] W G M Turner 2-8-9 P Makin(7) 10/1: 51: b g Tipsy Creek - Amathus Glory **59**
(Mummy's Pet) Made all, styd on strongly fnl 1f, drvn out: April foal, half-brother to 7f juv wnr Rock From The Sun:
dam 5f juv wnr: eff over a gall 5f on soft: apprec drop in grade & forcing tactics.

1249 **DANEHILL FAIRY 7** [5] Mrs A Duffield 2-8-4 BL G Duffield 20/1: 02: b f Danehill Dancer - **1¼ 50**
Turntable (Dolphin Street) Nvr far away, kept on fnl 1f but not quite pace of wnr: £5,500 March first foal: sire a

top-class sprinter: eff at 5f on soft grnd: imprvd for first time blnks & drop to claim grade today.

1224   **JOSHAR 9** [3] M W Easterby 2-8-4   Dale Gibson 25/1: 03: b f Paris House - Penny Hasset   1¼   47
(Lochnager) Chsd ldrs & rdn throughout, onepcd fnl 1f: April foal, half-sister to juv wnr Happy Times: dam a
multiple sprint wnr, sire a speedy juv.

1224   **ALICE KING 9** [1] W G M Turner 2-8-0   C Haddon(7) 5/1: 44: Chsd ldrs wide, btn dist: op 7/2: see 1224.   2½   37
         BELLE LARGESSE [2]2-8-6 K Darley 9/1: 5: Prom, rdn halfway, btn dist on debut.   nk   42
1224   **EMMAS VENTURE 9** [7]2-8-8 P Mulrennan(5) 11/10 FAV: 526: Trkd ldrs, wknd dist: well bckd, btr 1124.   ¾   41
1362   **BALASHOVA 2** [6]2-8-8   Darren Williams 4/1: 5U: Dwelt, lost action & u.r. after 1f: qck reapp.   0
7 Ran   Time 1m 07.51 (9.31)   Owned: Mascalls Stud   Trained: Sherborne

---

1395   7.20 Cantor Sport Spread Betting Handicap Stakes 3yo 46-55 (F)   [64]
             £2919 £834   £417   1m3y str   Soft 93   -53 Slow   Stands Side

1147   **ACE COMING 14** [1] D Eddy 3-9-5 bl (55) G Duffield 11/2: 2000-031: Held up, smooth hdwy to lead   64
dist, rdn clr ins fnl 1f: tchd 8/1: first win: suited by blnks: see 1147.
1147   **BISCAR TWO 14** [10] R M Whitaker 3-8-12 (48) V Halliday 9/2: 000-4622: Outpcd, gd hdwy over 1f   3   50
out, fin well but not reach wnr: will apprec 10f judged on this: beat today's wnr in 1147.
1144   **SIR GALAHAD 14** [9] T D Easterby 3-9-3 (53) D Allan(3) 6/1: 6-0053: Chsd ldrs, led over 2f out   2   51
till dist, no extra: poss eff at 1m on soft grnd: see 869.
1242   **ASK THE DRIVER 9** [7] D J S ffrench Davis 3-9-4 (54) K Darley 4/1 FAV: 050-24: Rear, prog & ev ch   2   48
1.5f out, sn onepace: nicely bckd, clr of rem: btr 1242 (gd grnd).
1147   **TANCRED IMP 14** [11]3-8-10 (1oh) (45) L Enstone(3) 20/1: 003-05: b f Atraf - Tancred Mischief   7   29
(Northern State) Chsd ldrs 6f, grad wknd: op 14/1: plcd on fnl of 3 juv starts (seller, rtd 55): stays 1m, acts
on gd grnd, mid-dist bred: with D Barker.
1144   **SATSU 14** [8]3-9-5 (55) A Culhane 7/1: 0-005-006: Prom, led briefly 2f out, wknd: tchd 11/1: see 1007.   8   26
1124   **KILLOCH PLACE 14** [3]3-8-11 VIS (47) Dean McKeown 16/1: 0500-007: b g Compton Place - Hibernica   6   8
(Law Society) Prom 6f, wknd in 1st time visor: mod '03 mdn form: has tried blnks.
4808} **EGO TRIP 189** [12]3-9-4 (54) P Mulrennan(5) 10/1: 360000-8: b c Deploy - Boulevard Rouge (Red   5   7
Ransom) Rdn in rear, nvr dngrs on reapp: plcd early in '03 (mdn, rtd 67): eff at 6f on firm grnd.
1144   **BEAMSLEY BEACON 14** [6]3-9-3 BL (53) T Eaves(5) 16/1: 56200-09: Keen & led 6f, wknd: tried blnks.   7   0
1240   **NUMPTY 9** [2]3-8-10 (6oh)†(40) Kim Tinkler 25/1: 00-55000: 10th: Prom 5f, wknd: stiff task.   1¼   0
4119} **JOHNNY ALLJAYS 231** [4]3-9-0 (50) Derek Nolan(7) 20/1: 0000-0: 11th: Prom till halfway, wknd, t.o.   25   0
11 Ran   Time 1m 48.73 (11.73)   Owned: Mr I R Clements   Trained: Newcastle Upon Tyne

---

1396   7.50 Cantor Sport Good Luck Paul Hunter Handicap Stakes 4yo+ 46-55 (F)   [64]
             £2975 £850   £425   1m6f97y   Soft 93   No Standard Time   Far Side

1121   **NEXT FLIGHT 15** [12] R E Barr 5-8-12 (48) R Fitzpatrick 7/1: 3-623231: Keen & prom, led after 1m,   55
held on gamely fnl 1f: deserved win, consistent in mdns/banded class prev: eff at 11/14.7f on fast, soft grnd &
fibresand: handles a sharp or gall trk: see 1121 & 224 (AW).
4538} **CUSP 208** [11] C W Thornton 4-8-8 (1oh) (45) Dean McKeown 16/1: 0030-2: b f Pivotal - Bambolona   ½   52
(Bustino) Prom, ev ch fnl 1f, only just btn: well clr rem: jumps fit, disputing 3rd in a juv now when u.r. run-in
(rtd 102h?, eff at 2m on gd): distant mdn 3rd in '03 (rtd 47): eff at 14f on soft grnd, handles a gall trk.
1278   **BERRYWHITE 6** [9] C Grant 6-8-10 (6oh) (40) G Duffield 14/1: 0200-003: Rear, prog to chase ldrs 3f   8   40
out, outpcd 2f out: qck reapp: see 867.
1164   **WASHINGTON PINK 12** [5] C Grant 5-8-10 (45) T Hamilton(3) 20/1: 040/0-004: b g Tagula - Little Red   1¼   38
Rose (Precocious) Rear, imprvd to chase ldrs 2f out, sn outpcd: '03 juv mdn hdle wnr (eff arnd 2m on fast &
gd/soft, rtd 101h): lightly rcd & mod Flat form in recent seasons: '02 sell wnr (M Channon), also plcd sev times,
incl in h'cap company: eff at 1m/10f on fast & soft grnd, any trk: with C Grant.
2 Jun'02 Newc 10.1g/s 65-63 E: 2 May'02 Ripo 8g/s 66- F: 1 May'02 Beve 10gd 57- F: 2 Jul'01 Epso 7g/s 72- E:
4117} **EXALTED 231** [10]11-9-5 (55) Dale Gibson 13/2: 142200-5: b g High Estate - Heavenward   1¾   45
(Conquistador Cielo) Prom, wknd over 1f out on reapp: '03 class stks wnr, dual h'cap rnr-up: '02 & '01 amat h'cap
wnr: eff at 12/15f on fast, loves gd or softer grnd: handles any trk, loves Hamilton.
2 Jul'03 Carl 14.1gd 59-57 F: 2 Jul'03 Ayr 15gd 61-57 F: 1 May'03 Ayr 13.1g/s 58-(55) F: 1 Jun'02 Hami 13sft 63-55 E:
2 May'02 Ayr 13g/s 60- F: 1 Jun'01 Hami 13gd 61-57 F: 2 Jun'01 Ayr 13g/f 57- F: 2 May'01 Hami 12fm 56- F:
2 May'01 Hami 13gd 60-59 E:
1033   **BROUGHTON KNOWS 24** [6]7-9-4 bl (54) Lisa Jones(3) 6/1: 1111246: Rear, nvr nr ldrs: btr 774.   6   34
2935} **BULGARIA MOON 285** [3]4-8-8 (6oh) (40) J Bramhill 40/1: 060/00-7: Nvr btr than mid-div on reapp.   12   11
1285   **I GOT RHYTHM 6** [2]6-8-10 (45) K Darley 11/2: 4/16/60-08: Held up, nvr dngrs: qck reapp.   3   7
849   **COLONNADE 43** [1]5-9-0 (50) Darren Williams 12/1: 000-2039: Prom, wknd qckly 3f out: 6 wk abs.   1¾   9
1252   **AVEIRO 7** [3]8-9-2 (52) A Culhane 5/1 JT FAV: 3321200: 10th: Led till 7f out, wknd, t.o.: btr 937.   15   0
1285   **LAMPOS 6** [4]4-9-2 vis (54) D Allan(3) 5/1 JT FAV: 3125000: 11th: Held up, t.o. halfway.   22   0
1265   **MANNY 7** [7]4-8-8 (11oh)P (35) P Mathers(6) 40/1: 005/-00: 12th: Keen & prom till halfway, wknd   dist   0
qckly, t.o.: tried cheek pieces, stiff task.
12 Ran   Time 3m 27.47 ()   Owned: Mr Malcolm O'Hair   Trained: Middlesbrough

---

1397   8.20 Ramside Event Catering Classified Stakes 3yo+ 0-70 (E)
             £2426 £2426 £571   1m2f32y   Soft 93   -69 Slow   Far Side

1226   **RASID 9** [5] C A Dwyer 6-9-9 (75) K Darley 13/2: 53-10231: Prom, led 3f out, held on well fnl 1f,   78
joined by Jimmy Byrne on line: op 5/1: eff at 10/12f on fast, soft grnd & polytrack: handles a sharp or stiff/gall
trk, runs well fresh: in gd form, see 1226 & 434 (AW h'cap).
1254   **JIMMY BYRNE 7** [1] B Ellison 4-9-9 (68) R Winston 7/1: 2300-041: Prom, ev ch 2f out, kept on to   dht   73
join Rasid on the line: well clr rem: acts on firm & soft grnd, handles hvy: see 1254.
4992} **KONKER 175** [4] Mrs M Reveley 9-9-4 (67) T Eaves(5) 10/1: 114/00/6-3: ch g Selkirk - Helens   15   53
Dreamgirl (Caerleon) Held up, prog to chase ldrs 2f out, sn btn: won a h'cap hdle in Dec '03 (eff
at 2m on gd & hvy, rtd 127h): 6th on sole '03 Flat start (h'cap): dual h'cap wnr in '01: eff at 10/12f on gd & hvy
grnd: gd weight-carrier, capable of better. 2 Oct'01 Newc 10.1hvy 68-60 F: 2 Oct'01 Ayr 13g/s 62-56 F:
1214   **NEWCORP LAD 10** [6] Mrs G S Rees 4-9-5 (71) A Culhane 16/1: 51126-04: b g Komaite - Gleam of Gold   4   48
(Crested Lark) Chsd ldrs, left bhd 2f out: won 2 class stks in '03, has since been gelded: eff at 7f/1m on firm &
hvy grnd: likes Hamilton: capable of better. 2 Jul'03 Nott 8.2fm 74-(73) E: 1 Jul'03 Hami 8.3gd 74-(68) E:

1 Jun'03 Hami 8.3gd 67-(64) E: 2 Aug'02 Hayd 7.1hvy 72- D:
1109* **BENBYAS 16** [2]7-9-9 vis (75) D Tudhope(7) 4/7 FAV: 00/0/-6115: Led till 3f out, sn btn: hvly bckd 2 49
at odds-on: has been busy of late, much btr expected after 1109.
1000 **COME WHAT JULY 26** [3]3-8-1 bl (70) Dale Gibson 8/1: 23-12566: Keen & prom, wknd over 2f out. 12 29
6 Ran   Time 2m 22.71(16.21)   Owned: Mr Keith Middleton   Trained: Malton

Official Going Good (Good/Firm places)

1398   2.00 M J Church Maiden Stakes 3yo (D)
£3621 £1114 £557   1m2f46y   Good 45   -10 Slow   Inside

1022 **SOLOR 25** [19] D J Coakley 3-9-0   D Holland 25/1: 41: Handy, led over 2f out, hdd appr fnl 1f but 88
rallied gamely to get up again ins last, drvn out: much sharper for debut & apprec step up to 10f, 12f looks sure to
suit: acts on gd grnd: game eff, open to further improvement.
4732} **MAGNETIC POLE 196** [14] Sir Michael Stoute 3-9-0   J Murtagh 7/4 FAV: 3-2: b c Machiavellian - ½ 86
Clear Attraction (Lear Fan) Handy, hdwy to lead over 1f out, rdn & hdd ins last, not btn far: nicely bckd on reapp:
plcd sole '03 start (mdn): half-brother to a mid-dist wnr: stays 10f on gd & gd/firm: shown enough to win a mdn.
1130 **IKTITAF 15** [11] J H M Gosden 3-9-0   R Hills 33/1: 03: b c Alhaarth - Istibshar (Mr Prospector) 2½ 82+
In tch, rdn over 4f out, styd on well fnl 2f, nrst fin: much sharper for recent debut & stays 10f, looks sure to
apprec 12f: plenty to take about this, will rate higher & shld win soon.
1113 **GRAVARDLAX 17** [4] B J Meehan 3-9-0 (89) K Darley 6/1: 42-04: ch c Salse - Rubbiyati (Cadeaux ¾ 80
Genereux) In tch, eff 3f out, onepace: rnr-up on 2nd of 2 '03 starts (mdn): dam 1m wnr: eff at 7f, poss stays
10f: acts on gd grnd. 2 Oct'03 Newm 7fm 96- D:
4898} **MOONLIGHT TANGO 185** [13]3-8-9   L Dettori 6/1: 04-5: In tch, onepace 2f out: wants 12f h'caps. 1¼ 73
    MOTORWAY [1]3-9-0   D Sweeney 25/1: 6: b c Night Shift - Tadkiyra (Darshaan) Bhd, late gains, 3 75
nvr dngrs on debut: cost 270,000gns: half-brother to a smart 7f/10f scorer: v green here but shld apprec 10f &
looks sure to come on for this.
4942} **BELISCO 181** [10]3-9-0   Dane O'Neill 50/1: 50-7: In tch, wknd 2f out on reapp: longer trip. 2 72
    UIG [3]3-8-9   T E Durcan 200/1: 8: In tch, some late gains. hd 66
1086 **MASTER MAHOGANY 20** [18]3-9-0   V Slattery 80/1: 049: Nvr dngrs. 1¾ 68
496   **OPERA STAR 90** [8]3-8-9   Martin Dwyer 80/1: 0-50: 10th: In tch, wknd over 2f out: abs. 1 61
1258 **PRINCIPESSA 8** [9]3-8-9   S Drowne 12/1: 3-50: 11th: In tch, wknd over 2f out. ½ 60
2819} **AQUALUNG 291** [15]3-9-0   M Hills 4/1: 4-0: 12th: Led till over 2f out, wknd: longer trip. ½ 64
1108 Go Green 17 [6]3-8-9 R Price 200/1:0   1055 Grist Mist 22 [5]3-8-9 R Havlin 125/1:0
5018} House Of Blues 173 [12]3-9-0 S W Kelly 100/1:0   1136 Planters Punch 15 [20]3-9-0 R L Moore 50/1:0
1125 Justice Jones 15 [17]3-9-0 A Daly 150/1:0   Ballyliffin [7]3-9-0 J D Walsh(7) 125/1:0
1259 Regal Performer 8 [16]3-9-0 T Quinn 100/1:0   Forged [2]3-9-0 N Mackay(3) 40/1:0
20 Ran   Time 2m 11.54 (5.54)   Owned: Bolam Hurley Ross   Trained: West Ilsley

1399   2.30 Bet365 Call 08000 322365 Handicap Stakes Fillies 4yo+ 0-80 (D)   [80]
£3748 £3748 £882   1m3f144y   Good 45   -19 Slow   Inside

224* **WASTED TALENT 130** [9] J G Portman 4-9-4 p (70) R L Moore 6/1: 262531-1: Led, rdn & hdd over 1f 74
out, rallied to get up again ins last, ddhtd on line, drvn out: 4 days ago won a mares mdn hdle (2m2.5f, rtd 120h,
gd & gd/soft): eff at 1m, suited by 12f on firm, gd & fibresand: eff in cheek pieces: tough, learnt to win.
4620} **ETCHING 204** [2] J R Fanshawe 4-8-6 (58) E Ahern 7/2 FAV: 322210-1: b f Groom Dancer - Eternity dht 62
(Suave Dancer) Cl-up, hdwy to lead over 1f out till ins last, rallied for press to ddht on line: '03 h'cap wnr,
plcd several times: eff at 12f, shld relish a return to 2m: acts on firm & gd grnd, prob any trk: runs well fresh:
tough & genuine, shld be winning again over further shortly.
1 Sep'03 Nott 16.0g/f 59-53 F: 2 Sep'03 Warw 16.2fm 59-53 F: 2 Aug'03 Chep 16.2g/f 52-48 F:
2 Aug'03 Nott 16.0gd 49-45 F: 2 Jun'03 Thir 12g/f 45-42 E:
2417} **ALBAVILLA 307** [4] P W Harris 4-9-8 (74) T Quinn 12/1: 3/556-3: b f Spectrum - Lydia Maria nk 77
(Dancing Brave) In tch, eff & hung left over 1f out, kept on ins last, just held: op 9/1: unplcd all 3 '03 starts
(mdns, rtd 77): stays 12f on gd, poss handles firm & soft: shld win a race on this form.
936   **ANYHOW 32** [7] Miss K M George 7-8-9 (60) D Holland 4/1: 0021454: Held up, hdwy 2f out, keeping ½ 62
on when no room cl home: wld have gone close: clr rem: tough, eff: see 801.
498   **NUZZLE 90** [10]4-7-12 (50) F Norton 25/1: 631-0005: In tch, eff 2f out, no extra fnl 1f: 3 mth 5 45
abs: longer trip, prob best around 1m/10f as in 199, see 115.
1286 **MOST SAUCY 7** [1]8-9-0 (65) D Nolan(5) 7/1: 55500-66: Chsd ldrs, wknd 2f out: needs sharp trks. 3½ 55
1098 **SNINFIA 19** [12]4-8-8 (60) J Quinn 20/1: 40200-07: b f Hector Protector - Christmas Kiss (Taufan) 3 45
Slow away, bhd, nvr a factor: rnr-up on 1 of 6 '03 starts (h'cap, with L Cumani): stays 10f on fast grnd: now with
G Ham. 2 Aug'03 Ripo 10g/f 68-65 E:
876   **MAYSTOCK 39** [11]4-9-11 (77) L Dettori 9/2: 140-1038: Al bhd: nicely bckd, reportedly ran flat. 7 52
1056 **CLARADOTNET 22** [8]4-10-0 (80) T E Durcan 16/1: 210-09: Al bhd. 3 51
3999} **FULLY FLEDGED 239** [3]4-7-12 (1oh) (49) R Thomas(5) 40/1: 035-0: 10th: In tch, wknd over 3f out. 8 9
10 Ran   Time 2m 32.41 (7.41)   Owned: Dr Catherine Wills   Trained: Newmarket

---

1400   **3.00 Listed European Breeders Fund Lansdown Stakes Fillies 3yo+   (A)**
£17400 £6600 £3300   **5f11y rnd**   **Good 45**   **+23 Fast**   Far Side

1207 **RINGMOOR DOWN 11** [13] D W P Arbuthnot 5-9-0 (93) Dane O'Neill 11/2 CO FAV: 00243-61: Held up, gd   **105+**
hdwy over 1f out, styd on strongly to lead ins last, rdn clr, readily: fast time: caught the eye on reapp in 1207:
eff over this fast run/stiff 5f, prev suited by 6f: acts on firm & gd grnd, gall or sharp trk: useful eff, looks
imprvd & in fine heart, win again: see 1207.
1536* **LA CUCARACHA 347** [14] B W Hills 3-8-4   M Hills 6/1: 11-2: b f Piccolo - Peggy Spencer   ¾ **102+**
(Formidable) Held up, hdwy & bmpd over 2f out, styd on well to chall ins last, just held by wnr on reapp: won both
'03 starts (auct mdn & stks): eff over a stiff 5f, 6f looks sure to suit (dam multiple 6/7f wnr): acts on fast grnd
& runs well fresh: useful, improving with every run & only rcd 3 times, must be winning similar shortly.
1 May'03 Newb 5.2g/f 98- C: 1 Apr'03 Leic 5.0g/f 97- E:
883 **SPEED COP 38** [7] A M Balding 4-9-0 (100) Martin Dwyer 11/2 CO FAV: 64410-23: Led till over 1f   2½ **95**
out, rallied to lead again ins last, hdd & no extra fnl 100y: ran right up to best: tough & useful: see 883.
2844} **CURFEW 290** [6] J R Fanshawe 5-9-0 (95) J Murtagh 12.1: 104/505-4: b f Marju - Twilight Patrol   ¾ **93**
(Robellino) Slow away, in tch, kept on late: 5th on 2 of 3 '03 starts (h'cap, rtd 94): '02 hat-trick h'cap scorer:
eff at 5f, all 4 wins at trks: can carry big weights: useful, rate higher
over further. 1 Sep'02 Sali 6.9g/f 97-86 C: 1 Aug'02 Yarm 7fm 94-80 D: 1 Aug'02 Newm 7gd 84-75 D:
2 Aug'02 Yarm 7fm 82-75 D: 2 Jul'02 Redc 7g/f 76-73 C: 1 Jul'01 Yarm 7g/f 82- E:
1162 **SIMIANNA 13** [1]5-9-0 (88) F Norton 33/1: 36300-55: Chsd ldrs, prob just held when hmpd dist.   nk **91**
2644* **INCISE 298** [15]3-8-4 (93) J F Egan 12/1: 3201-6: ch f Dr Fong - Pretty Sharp (Interrex) Chsd   nk **91**
ldrs, hdwy over 2f out, led over 1f out, hdd & wknd ins last: joc received a 3-day careless riding ban: won last of
4 '03 starts (auct mdn), rnr-up in List: eff over a stiff or sharp 5f on firm & fast grnd.
1 Jul'03 Warw 5fm 87- E: 2 May'03 Sand 5.0g/f 90- A:
1159 **DRAGON FLYER 15** [4]5-9-0 (104) S Drowne 11/2 CO FAV: 0300-427: In tch, rdn but chall when badly   ¾ **89**
hmpd appr fnl 1f, not recover: forgive this: see 1159, 883.
1162* **PROUD BOAST 13** [5]6-9-0 (94) K Darley 8/1: 0360-018: In tch, short of room & wknd over 1f out.   1½ **85**
1162 **IKAN 13** [11]4-9-0 (89) T G McLaughlin 12/1: 2400-039: Bhd, late gains: needs h'caps, promise 1162.   ¾ **83**
4680} **VERMILLIANN 199** [10]3-8-4 (98) R L Moore 25/1: 116-0: 10th: Nvr a factor on reapp.   1¾ **78**
4347} **TENTATIVE 220** [16]3-8-4 (92) E Ahern 25/1: 121103-0: 11th: Keen, al bhd.   ¾ **76**
883 **DUSTY DAZZLER 38** [8]4-9-0 (87) L Dettori 14/1: 4202-160: 12th: In tch, wknd 2f out: btr 431 (aw).   ½ **74**
1216 **FLASHING BLADE 11** [9]4-9-0 (78) T Quinn 66/1: 005-000: 13th: In tch, wknd 2f out.   ¾ **72**
1175 **WITHORWITHOUTYOU 12** [3]3-8-4 (85) W Supple 40/1: 1054-650: 14th: Cl-up, wknd over 2f out.   5 **57**
14 Ran   Time 1m 01.38 (1.08)   Owned: Prof C D Green   Trained: Upper Lambourn

---

1401   **3.30 Exxon Mobil Maiden Auction Stakes 2yo   (F)**
£2975 £850 £425   **5f11y rnd**   **Good 45**   **-19 Slow**   Far Side

ELGIN MARBLES [11] R Hannon 2-8-9   Dane O'Neill 9/2: 1: b c Lujain - Bold Gem (Never So Bold)   **86+**
Slow away & bhd, hdwy 2f out, styd on strongly over 1f out to get up cl-home, rdn out on debut: April foal, cost
25,000gns: half-brother to a 7f juv wnr: dam 5f wnr: eff at 5f on gd grnd, runs well fresh: shld stay further &
showed a nice turn of foot here, can rate higher & win again.
1190 **THE CROOKED RING 12** [13] P D Evans 2-8-7   K Darley 11/2: 52: b g Magic Ring - My Bonus (Cyrano   shd **83**
de Bergerac) Chsd ldrs, hdwy to lead just ins last, collared cl-home: March foal, cost 9,000gns: half-brother to a
5f juv wnr: bred for speed & clearly has some: eff at 5f on gd grnd: can find similar.
ALSU [7] A M Balding 2-8-4   Martin Dwyer 14/1: 3: b f Fasliyev - Pourquoi Pas (Nordico) In   1½ **76**
tch, eff over 1f out, kept on ins last, not pace of front 2: debut: April foal, cost £35,000: dam 7/10f wnr: shld
apprec 6f & showed promise here, stable's 2yos tend to come on plenty for first run.
1123 **WITHERING LADY 15** [6] Mrs P N Dutfield 2-8-2   J F McDonald(3) 13/2: 34: Cl-up, led halfway, hdd   1 **71**
ins last, no extra: prob ran to form of 1123.
AL QUDRA [9]2-8-9 L Dettori 3/1 FAV: 5: b c Cape Cross - Alvilda (Caerleon) Chsd ldrs,   1¾ **74**
onepace over 1f out on debut: March foal, cost 16,000gns: bred to apprec 6/7f in time.
1325 **TURTLE MAGIC 4** [4]2-8-2 C Haddon(7) 11/1: 0236: Chsd ldrs, eff dist, no extra: qck reapp.   nk **66**
HAROLDINI [5]2-8-7 R Havlin 50/1: 7: Slow away, nvr a factor on debut.   1½ **67**
GRANARY GIRL [2]2-8-2 J F Egan 50/1: 8: Slow away & bhd, modest late gains on debut.   2 **56**
1097 **GOLDHILL PRINCE 19** [1]2-8-7 p A Daly 25/1: 049: In tch, wknd 2f out: see 1097.   2 **55**
1084 **SEASONS ESTATES 20** [10]2-8-4 S Drowne 9/1: 40: 10th: In tch, wknd 2f out.   1 **49**
Mystery Maid [8]2-8-2 J Quinn 66/1:0   **Grand Welcome** [14]2-8-7 E Ahern 16/1:0
1205 **Cree 11** [3]2-8-7 T Quinn 50/1:0   **Ahaz** [12]2-8-7 W Supple 50/1:0
14 Ran   Time 1m 03.5 (3.2)   Owned: Jumeirah Racing   Trained: Marlborough

---

1402   **4.00 Oval Of Bath Peugeot Selling Stakes 3yo+   (G)**
£2625 £750 £375   **1m2f46y**   **Good 45**   **-08 Slow**   Inside

972* **ABSOLUTE UTOPIA 29** [5] J L Spearing 11-10-0 (63) J Murtagh 11/4 FAV: 0223411: Held up, gd hdwy   **63**
to chall 2f out, led ent fnl 1f, just prevailed in a driving fin: nicely bckd, no bid: eff at 10/12f on firm,
gd/soft, loves polytrack/Lingfield: suited by plating class nowadays: see 972 (AW clmr).
1341* **OUR DESTINY 3** [8] A W Carroll 6-10-0 (47) S Hitchcott(3) 8/1: 0116312: Rear, hdwy to lead 2f out,   hd **62**
hdd ent fnl 1f, rallied & just btn in a tight fin: clr of rem: qck reapp & remains in fine form: see 1342 (1m AW).
1098 **SALFORD FLYER 19** [7] Jane Southcombe 8-9-10 bl (54) E Ahern 10/1: 405//-0603: Trkd ldrs, led 3f   7 **47**
out till over 2f out, left bhd by front 2 fnl 1f: see 1098 (C/D).
4702} **MOBO BACO 198** [1] R J Hodges 7-9-10 (60) S Drowne 3/1: 040030-4: ch g Bandmaster - Darakah   3 **43**
(Doulab) Keen & prom, led briefly 3f out, grad wknd: nicely bckd on reapp: won a seller & 2 class stks in '03:
h'cap wnr in '02: eff at 7/10f on firm, soft grnd & fibresand, any trk: can run well fresh, likes to run up
with/force the pace: 7yo, enjoys sell grade.
1 Jun'03 Bath 8.0fm 66-(64) E: 1 Apr'03 Pont 8.0g/f 66-(56) F: 1 Mar'03 Leic 7.0g/f 61-(53) G:
2 Jul'02 Warw 8.1gd 54-50 G: 1 Apr'02 Folk 9.6fm 52-47 E: 2 Apr'02 Warw 10.8g/f 50-45 F: 1 Sep'01 Bath 8fm 51-44 F:
1184 **CHAKRA 12** [3]10-9-10 (40) C Haddon(7) 66/1: 00000/-65: Keen & chsd ldrs 1m, wknd: see 1184.   2½ **39**

1160   **EVA PERON 13** [9]4-9-5 (49) A Daly 20/1: 6000-006: Slowly away, nvr nr ldrs: see 935. ½ 33
5029} **BREEZER 172** [6]4-9-10 (57) R Havlin 11/1: 0/5500-7: b g Forzando - Lady Lacey (Kampala) Nvr 1¾ 35
troubled ldrs: jumps fit, 4th in a juv hdle in Dec '03 (rtd 106h, eff at 2m on gd), subs tried a visor: lightly rcd
in '03, some mdn promise (rtd 68): prob eff at 1m on fast grnd: with G Balding.
924   **LUNAR LORD 33** [2]8-9-10 P (57) R Price 5/1: 3100/5-08: Chsd ldrs 7f, wknd: tried cheek pieces: 9 21
unplcd in a h'cap hdle since 924.
3477} **DEVOTE 982** [4]6-9-10 bl S Whitworth 25/1: 506//-9: b g Pennekamp - Radiant Bride (Blushing 3 17
Groom) Al bhd, t.o.: jumps fit, won a sell hdle at Taunton recently (rtd 102h, eff at 2m1f/2m4f on gd & hvy, wears
blnks): last rcd on the Flat in '01, modest form (with B Llewellyn, has been gelded): wears blnks.
1098   **JACK DURRANCE 19** [10]4-9-10 VIS (65) J Quinn 16/1: 50100-00: 10th: Keen & led till 3f out, wknd, 10 2
t.o.: much too free in first time visor.
10 Ran   Time 2m 11.28 (5.28)   Owned: Mr M T Lawrance   Trained: Kinnersley

---

1403   4.30 Nationwide Property Finance Handicap Stakes 3yo 0-75 (E)   [82]
£3777 £1162 £581   **1m2f46y**   **Good 45**   -05 Slow   Inside

1306* **ANOTHER CHOICE 5** [4] N P Littmoden 3-9-4 (6ex)t (72) K Darley 15/8 FAV: 6000-311: Chsd ldrs, styd 78
on strongly to lead cl-home, drvn out: well bckd, qck reapp: eff at 1m, suited by 10f: acts on firm & soft grnd,
likes a stiff fin: clearly in fine form, defied a poor draw in 1306.
1193   **JAKARMI 12** [1] B Palling 3-8-10 (64) T Quinn 9/1: 1613222: Chsd ldrs, hmpd & lost place 2f out, ½ 68
strong run fnl 1f & just failed: eff at 1m, styd this longer 10f trip well: v consistent & prob unlucky here.
1124   **DESERT IMAGE 15** [9] C Tinkler 3-9-0 (68) D Corby(3) 50/1: 0-126003: Chsd ldrs, ev ch 2f out, led hd 71
ins fnl 1f, collared cl-home: fine run from this rank outsider: earlier in gd form on the AW, clearly stays 10f
well: acts on gd grnd & on both AWs: see 337.
1099   **KESHYA 19** [8] D J Coakley 3-8-9 (63) Dane O'Neill 5/1: 0062-34: Chsd ldrs, led 2f out till ins nk 65
fnl 1f, no extra: sound run, btn under 1L: see 1099 (1m here).
1193* **GOBLIN 12** [14]3-8-8 (62) T E Durcan 15/2: 5000-415: Rear, sltly short of room & switched 2f out, 1¼ 62
styd on & nrst fin: stays 10f trip (see 1193 (1m, AW, class stks).
4530} **ALALOOF 210** [11]3-8-13 (67) R Hills 8/1: 605-6: b f Swain - Alattrah (Shadeed) Dwelt, hdwy wide nk 66+
2f out, fin well but too late: reapp/h'cap bow, bckd from 25/1: lightly rcd & promise in '03 (rtd 65): sure to
learn from this & will rate higher over 12f.
980   **ILLEANA 28** [12]3-8-10 (64) Martin Dwyer 33/1: 00-47: ch f Lomitas - Illyria (Nashwan) Chsd 3 59
ldrs, wknd fnl 1f: h'cap bow: unplcd on both juv starts: cost £130,000: with W Muir.
875   **SIMONOVSKI 39** [13]3-9-2 (70) S W Kelly 33/1: 55-08: b c Miswaki - Eartha (Rahy) Held up, nvr ½ 64
nr to chall: h'cap bow: 5th on both juv starts (AW mdn, rtd 72a): cost £50,000: with J Osborne.
4175} **RINNEEN 229** [10]3-8-3 (57) R Smith 40/1: 03000-9: Prom, lost pl after 3f, no ch after on reapp. 1½ 49
403   **DR CERULLO 104** [7]3-9-7 (75) S Drowne 20/1: 6301-330: 10th: Nvr troubled ldrs: top-weight, long 2 64
abs, has been gelded: see 403 & 238 (AW).
4808} **SMOOTHLY DOES IT 190** [2]3-8-13 (67) E Ahern 66/1: 530020-0: 11th: Al rear on reapp: gldd. 1 54
1124   **ANOTHER CON 15** [5]3-8-8 (62) R Havlin 25/1: 3-414500: 12th: Sn led, wknd 3f out. 1 48
4707} **NEAP TIDE 197** [3]3-9-7 (75) J Murtagh 6/1: 064-0: 13th: Early ldr, remained prom & regained lead 16 35
3f out till 2f out, wknd qckly, t.o. on reapp: jt top-weight, tchd 8/1, has been gelded: reportedly rcd too freely.
213   **SOLO SOLE 132** [6]3-9-4 (72) N Mackay(3) 28/1: 6003-0: 14th: Chsd ldrs 7f, wknd: reapp. 9 16
14 Ran   Time 2m 11.04 (5.04)   Owned: Mr A A Goodman   Trained: Newmarket

---

1404   5.00 Saffie Joseph & Sons Handicap Stakes 3yo 0-70 (E)   [76]
£3751 £1154 £577   **5f11y rnd**   **Good 45**   -12 Slow   Far Side

1102* **IVORY LACE 19** [15] S Woodman 3-9-3 (65) D Sweeney 9/2: 5201311: Chsd ldrs, chall strongly fnl 71
1f, just prevailed cl-home: op 6/1: eff at 5/6f on firm, gd/soft grnd & polytrack: prob handles any trk.
1228   **LACONIA 10** [10] J S Moore 3-9-7 (69) Martin Dwyer 10/1: 50-45262: Chsd ldrs, led after halfway, hd 74
overhauled cl-home: jt top-weight: fine eff & deserves similar, again just shaded by today's wnr in 1102 (C/D).
1031   **LAVISH TIMES 25** [8] A Berry 3-8-3 bl (51) F Norton 16/1: 0-053063: Front rank, ev ch till no 1½ 52
extra well ins fnl 1f: gd run back on turf: see 703 (AW seller).
5014} **BEST FORCE 173** [14] G A Butler 3-8-9 (57) T P Queally(3) 14/1: 500-4: b f Compton Place - ½ 56
Bestemor (Selkirk) Chsd ldrs, not qckn ins fnl 1f on reapp: h'cap bow: half-sister to a juv wnr: eff at 5f on gd
grnd, shld stay 6f: sharper next time.
1099   **BARABELLA 19** [9]3-9-1 (63) J F McDonald(3) 25/1: 4440-05: gr f Barathea - Thatchabella nk 61
(Thatching) Reared & slow away, short of rm halfway, styd on late wide, nrst fin: lost ch at the start on this big
drop in trip: 4th in 3 mdns in '03 (rtd 71): eff at 5f, stays 7f on gd & fast: return to 6f will suit.
76   **MAXIS PRINCESS 157** [5]3-8-8 (56) Dane O'Neill 16/1: 04000-6: b f Revoque - Harmer (Alzao) ½ 52
Slowly away, styd on late wide, nrst fin on reapp: bckd at long odds: AW mdn 4th in '03 (rtd 58a): eff at 6f on
fibresand, acts on turf: has tried a t-strap: sharper next time, esp over 6f.
3281} **GEMINI GIRL 271** [7]3-8-8 (56) T Quinn 12/1: 005366-7: Chsd ldrs, onepcd fnl 1f: tchd 20/1, reapp. 1 49
4887} **MALUTI 185** [1]3-8-5 (53) J Mackay 14/1: 0006-8: Nvr btr than mid-div on reapp: gelded. hd 45
1268   **A BID IN TIME 7** [4]3-8-2 (2ow) (48) W Supple 9/1: 000-0029: Held up, sltly short of room halfway, hd 41
no ch after: btr 1268.
1116   **AFTER THE SHOW 17** [6]3-9-7 (69) J Murtagh 100/30 FAV: 04051-00: 10th: Led till halfway, wknd: ¾ 58
well bckd, jt top-weight: btr expected after 1116.
703   **REHIA 64** [3]3-8-9 (57) R Hills 16/1: 0-065440: 11th: Chsd ldrs 4f, wknd: 9 wk abs. shd 45
1103   **IMPERIUM 19** [2]3-9-6 (68) S Drowne 12/1: 2: 46-40200: 12th: Hmpd start, no ch after: see 1023 (AW). ½ 54
1044   **Samara Sound 24** [11]3-8-7 (55) S Whitworth 12/1:0   1103 **Beau Jazz 19** [13]3-8-12 (60) S Righton 40/1:0
14 Ran   Time 1m 03.16(2.86)   Owned: Mr Christopher J Halpin   Trained: Chichester

Official Going Standard To Fast

1405
5.40 Littlewoods Bet Direct Apprentice Banded Stakes 3yo+ 0-45 (H)
£1435 £410 £205 **6f aw rnd** **Going 28** **+11 Fast** Inside

778 **LARKYS LOB 57** [2] J O'Reilly 5-9-7 (45) J D O'Reilly(5) 3/1 FAV: 5324631: Made all, pushed clr   **61a+**
ins fnl 1f, val 7L+: 8 wk abs, new stable: eff at 6/7f on fibresand/sharp trks, likes Southwell: goes well fresh:
apprec return to banded grade & can follow up: see 778 & 304 (P Johnson).
1201 **CLEVELAND WAY 11** [6] D Carroll 4-9-7 vis (45) D Tudhope(3) 7/2: 5645022: Prom, ev ch 2f out, no ch   5   **48a**
with easy wnr ins fnl 1f: see 1201 & again fin bhd today's wnr in 304 (7f).
1199 **VALAZAR 11** [4] D W Chapman 5-9-7 (45) P Makin 7/2: 00-00023: Handy & ev ch bef 1f out, sn wknd.   1¼   **44a**
1201 **INDIAN MUSIC 11** [3] A Berry 7-9-7 (45) P Mathers 6/1: 00-61544: Nvr nrr than mid-div: btr 982.   5   **29a**
1266 **MR UPPITY 8** [1]5-9-7 e (40) M Halford(5) 8/1: 00-00245: Chsd ldrs 3f, sn wknd: btr 982.   ¾   **27a**
1065 **COMPTON PRINCESS 21** [5]4-9-7 (40) S Donohoe 6/1: 00000-36: Handy 4f, sn fdd: btr 1065 (hvy).   6   **11a**
6 Ran Time 1m 14.32 (1.02) Owned: J O R Racing Trained: Barnsley

1406
6.10 Betdirect Co Uk Banded Stakes 3yo+ 0-35 (H)
£1442 £412 £206 **1m aw rnd** **Going 28** **-16 Slow** Inside

1262 **AMETHYST ROCK 8** [7] P L Gilligan 6-9-4 (35) F Lynch 4/1 FAV: 0060-031: Prom, led bef halfway,   **38a**
edgd left & hdd just ins fnl 1f, rallied to regain lead cl-home: enjoyed recent drop back to 1m/9.4f, acts on
fibresand: tough & game 6yo: see 1262.
791 **DALRIATH 55** [4] M C Chapman 5-9-4 (35) Andrew Webb(7) 11/2: 00-06642: Rear, gd prog to lead ins   shd   **37a**
fnl 1f, hdd under press cl-home: 7 wk jumps abs, unplcd (rtd 54h, mdn hdle): acts on fast & f/sand: mdn.
1286 **MATHMAGICIAN 7** [6] R F Marvin 5-9-4 bl (35) Dean McKeown 13/2: 4046603: Bhd, prog fnl 3f, sn   8   **23a**
no impress on clr front 2: qck reapp: btr 771.
894 **SARN 36** [8] M Mullineaux 5-9-4 (35) P Varley(7) 11/1: 40000-04: Handy 6f, sn no extra: see 894.   nk   **22a**
1335* **UN AUTRE ESPERE 4** [1]5-9-10 bl (30) B Swarbrick(7) 6/1: 6000515: Trkd ldrs 5f, sn no extra: qck   6   **17a**
reapp: disapp on return to 1m back on fibresand: btr 1335 (7f, soft).
1200 **CEZZARO 11** [2]6-9-4 (35) J Bramhill 6/1: 61040-56: Led till bef halfway, fdd: btr 1200.   shd   **10a**
909 **MISS OCEAN MONARCH 35** [3]4-9-4 (30) A Culhane 12/1: 30440-08: ch f Blue Ocean - Faraway Grey   2   **6a**
(Absalom) Handy 6f, fdd: plcd 5 times in '03 (h'caps, sellers & clmrs, rtd 44): sell wnr in '02 (M R Channon):
eff at 7.5f/1m, stays 10f: acts on fast & soft grnd: with D W Chapman.
2 Jun'03 Muss 8g/f 42-40 E: 1 Jul'02 Beve 7.4g/s 58- F:
827 **MORRIS DANCING 49** [10]5-9-4 p (30) Joanna Badger 14/1: 0000508: Chsd ldrs 5f, sn fdd: jumps fit.   ½   **5a**
1204 **MISTER RUSHBY 11** [5]4-9-4 (30) R Fitzpatrick 33/1: 0000-009: b g Hamas - Final Rush (Final   ½   **4a**
Straw) Chsd ldrs, fdd 2f out: unplcd in '03 (rtd 33a & 29, h'caps, D W Chapman): '02 dual sell wnr for current
stable & B Ellison: suited by sharp/turning 7f on gd grnd: likes to race with/force pace: with Miss V Haigh.
1 Aug'02 Catt 7gd 61- G: 1 Jul'02 Catt 7gd 58- G:
1244 **SPIDERS WEB 8** [9]4-9-4 bl (35) P Doe 11/1: 0B23000: 10th: Handy 4f, sn wknd: btr 906.   3½   **0a**
10 Ran Time 1m 42.92 (3.52) Owned: Mr John Peters Trained: Newmarket

1407
6.40 Special Offers @ Betdirect Co Uk Banded Stakes 4yo+ 0-45 (H)
£1442 £412 £206 **1m6f aw** **Going 28** **-29 Slow** Inside

1238 **SUNNYSIDE ROYALE 10** [4] R Bastiman 5-9-0 t (45) R Ffrench 7/1: 06/346-01: b g Ali Royal - Kuwah   **50a**
(Be My Guest) Prom, led after 7f, rdn out fnl 2f: earlier h'cap hdle wnr (rtd 91h at best, stays 2m1f on gd & soft
grnd, eff with t-strap): 3rd of 16 on first of 3 '03 Flat starts (rtd 47, h'cap, M W Easterby): h'cap rnr-up in
'02: eff around 12/14f on firm, gd & fibresand: eff with t-strap, tried blnks: apprec drop to banded grade.
2 Jun'02 Beve 12gd 50-47 F:
1263 **DOCTOR JOHN 8** [1] Andrew Turnell 7-9-0 (45) C Catlin 1/1 FAV: 0//-421622: Handy, chsd wnr ins   4   **45a**
fnl 2f, al held: well bckd: eff at 14f, will apprec return to 2m: see 1263 & 690.
918 **ILOVETURTLE 33** [2] M C Chapman 4-8-12 (40) G Duffield 14/1: 00000-03: b g Turtle Island - Gan   4   **41a**
Ainm (Mujadil) Handy, chsd wnr from 3f out, sn no extra: jumps fit, earlier rnr-up (juv nov hdle, rtd 100h, stays
2m1.5f on gd grnd): h'cap rnr-up twice in '03: auct mdn wnr in '02 (M Johnston): eff at 7.5f/1m, stays 12f: acts
on fibresand & gd/soft grnd: has tried blnks.
2 Jun'03 Pont 12.0g/s 61-57 F: 2 Feb'03 Sout 8af 61a-58 F: 1 Jul'02 Beve 7.4g/s 75- E:
1263 **BERKELEY HEIGHTS 8** [6] Mrs J Candlish 4-8-12 (45) N Chalmers 9/2: 5-406234: Handy, outpcd 4f   3   **38a**
out, modest late gains: btr 984.
1033 **BROUGHTONS FLUSH 25** [3]6-9-0 (45) F Lynch 13/2: 1150/-005: Rear, nvr a factor: btr 733.   2½   **36a**
1204 **KING PRIAM 11** [7]9-9-0 bl (30) R Fitzpatrick 20/1: 5654006: Led 7f, fdd: btr 353.   18   **21a**
1182 **EL PEDRO 12** [5]5-9-0 (45) M Savage(5) 9/1: 005-4347: Handy 12f, fdd: btr 575.   5   **16a**
7 Ran Time 3m 7.89 (8.09) Owned: S Durkin P Earnshaw & J Greenan Trained: Wetherby

1408
7.10 Bet In Running @ Betdirect Co Uk Banded Stakes 3yo+ 0-40 (H)
£1442 £412 £206 **5f aw str** **Going 28** **Inapplicable** Outside

1290+ **MAROMITO 6** [1] R Bastiman 7-9-12 (40) H Bastiman 8/11 FAV: 00-00311: Made just about all, drvn   **48a**
out to hold on: well bckd on qck reapp: eff at 5f on firm, gd & both AWs, handles soft grnd: gd weight carrier,
enjoys banded grade: see 1290 & 860.
844 **FINGER OF FATE 44** [2] M J Polglase 4-9-6 bl (40) R Fitzpatrick 10/1: 0000002: Prom, led briefly   shd   **42a**
halfway, ev ch fnl 1f, just held: 6 wk abs: stays 8.4f, back to form on drop to 5f: apprec drop to banded grade &
can find similar: see 844.
1309 **LEVELLED 5** [10] D W Chapman 10-9-6 (35) A Culhane 11/1: 0455023: Dwelt, prog after 3f, kept on   3½   **32a**
late: qck reapp: just btr 1309.
963 **MISS WIZZ 29** [3] W Storey 4-9-6 p (40) D Tudhope(7) 9/1: 60-04164: Chsd ldrs, onepcd fnl 1f.   1½   **28a**
1309* **TUSCAN DREAM 5** [7]9-9-12 (40) P Bradley(5) 8/1: 0022515: Handy till dist, no extra: qck reapp.   ½   **33a**
1309 **DANCING RIDGE 5** [9]7-9-6 vis (30) G Duffield 28/1: 6/00-0056: Handy 3f, sn no extra: qck reapp.   1¾   **22a**

SOUTHWELL   Fibresand   TUESDAY 27.04.04   Lefthand, Sharp, Oval Track

1199	**DANAKIM 11** [8]7-9-6 (40) D Fentiman(7) 16/1: 6100407: Chsd ldrs 3f, wknd: see 578.	1¼	18a
1201	**CARONTE 11** [6]4-9-6 h bl (40) J Bramhill 16/1: 0000108: Slow away, nvr a factor: btr 904.	2½	11a
963	**WILHEHECKASLIKE 29** [5]3-8-10 vis (40) D R McCabe 66/1: 0200-009: Prom, fdd 2f out: see 850.	1½	7a
907	**WUB CUB 35** [4]4-9-6 (35) A Beech(3) 66/1: 0400-600: 10th: Bhd, nvr a factor: btr 773.	shd	6a

10 Ran   Time 59.29 ()   Owned: Mrs P Bastiman   Trained: Wetherby

---

1409
7.40 Bet Direct On 0800 32 93 93 Banded Stakes 4yo+ 0-35 (H)
£1456 £416 £208   **1m3f aw**   **Going 28**   **-34 Slow**   Inside

1265	**RHETORIC 8** [1] D G Bridgwater 5-8-12 (35) D Nolan(4) 4/1: 0/005-041: Made all, drvn out fnl 1f: eff at 11/12f on fibresand: win again in this grade: see 1265.		36a
965	**MOYNE PLEASURE 29** [3] Paul Johnson 6-8-12 p (30) D Fentiman(7) 3/1 FAV: 0006002: Slow away, grad prog ins fnl half-mile, kept on fnl 1f but not quite get to wnr: waiting tactics prob overdone here: see 780.	2½	31a
1287*	**BUYING A DREAM 6** [2] Andrew Turnell 7-9-4 (35) C Catlin 7/2: 500/-5013: Chsd ldrs, chsd wnr from 2f out, kept on but just held for 2nd cl-home: qck reapp: see 1287.	hd	36a
1204	**ZELEA 11** [5] J Parkes 5-8-12 t (35) B Swarbrick(7) 9/2: 03500/-54: In tch 1m, sn outpcd, rallied late.	¾	28a
1286	**PARADISE GARDEN 7** [4]7-8-12 (35) A Culhane 5/1: 00050-05: Handy over 1m, sn no extra.	1¼	26a
1076	**ELLE ROYAL 21** [6]5-8-12 BL (35) G Duffield 16/1: 00/0-006: br f Ali Royal - Silvretta (Tirol) Cl-up 1m, sn fdd: first time blnks: unplcd sole '03 start (rtd 21, seller): modest form in '02 (rtd 66, mdn): plcd once in '01 (fills mdn, rtd 77): stays 1m on hvy grnd.	11	11a

6 Ran   Time 2m 28.14 (6.84)   Owned: Mr Alan A Wright   Trained: Winchcombe

---

1410
8.10 Bet Direct On Sky Active Tri-Banded Stakes 3yo 0-45 (H)
£1435 £410 £205   **7f aw rnd**   **Going 28**   **+04 Fast**   Inside

1147	**SAROS 15** [4] B Smart 3-9-0 (45) F Lynch 9/2: 00606-01: b c Desert Sun - Fight Right (Crystal Glitters) Prom, led halfway, pushed clr fnl 2f, val 12L+: unplcd in '03 (rtd 56, mdn): eff at 7f, tried further: acts on f/sand & a sharp trk: reportedly lost action last time, apprec this drop to banded grade.		56a+
1203*	**ROMAN THE PARK 11** [1] T D Easterby 3-9-0 (45) G Duffield 5/4 FAV: 600-312: Handy, styd on to chase wnr ins fnl 2f but al well held: well bckd: clr rem: eff at 7f, prob apprec return to 1m: ran to form of 1203.	9	39a
1311	**PLATINUM CHIEF 5** [2] A Berry 3-9-0 bl (45) A Culhane 11/2: 5-665053: Bhd, nvr nrr than mid-div.	5	29a
1108	**ROYAL NITE OWL 17** [3] J O'Reilly 3-9-0 (45) J D O'Reilly(7) 9/1: 00-004: Led 4f, fdd: see 839.	nk	28a
1314	**MYSTIC PROMISE 5** [6]3-8-4 t (35) Hayley Turner(5) 9/2: 0050345: Chsd ldrs 4f, fdd: qck reapp.	1½	15a
1312	**WEAVER SPELL 5** [5]3-8-9 (40) V Halliday 25/1: 0006-56: Handy 4f, wknd: qck reapp: see 1312.	shd	19a

6 Ran   Time 1m 28.32(17.2)   Owned: Pinnacle Desert Sun Partnership   Trained: Thirsk

---

LINGFIELD   Polytrack   TUESDAY 27.04.04   Lefthand, Very Sharp Track

Official Going STANDARD.

1411
5.25 Bet Direct No Q Demo 08000 837 888 Banded Stakes 4yo+ 0-40 (H)
£1274 £364 £182   **1m4f aw**   **Going 53**   **-21 Slow**   Inside

1204	**SERAPH 11** [5] John A Harris 4-8-9 p (40) D Holland 5/2 JT FAV: 3103321: Made most, drvn out to hold on: eff at 11/12f on fast & both AWs: eff with cheek pieces: see 1204 & 867.		41a
1287	**LEOPHIN DANCER 6** [3] P W Hiatt 6-8-10 (40) B Doyle 11/4: 00-60122: Keen mid-div, ev ch 2f out, kept on fnl 1f, just held: qck reapp: rider reported mount hung in closing stages: see 1287 & 1180.	shd	40a
1265*	**ERSAAL 8** [2] J Jay 4-9-1 t (40) N Callan 5/1: 00-03013: Held up, prog to lead briefly 2f out, kept on & just btn in 3-way photo: clr rem: tchd 13/2: acts on both AWs: just btr 1265.	nk	45a
2095}	**WAYWARD MELODY 320** [4] G L Moore 4-8-9 BL e (40) R L Moore 5/2 JT FAV: 60/0000-4: b f Merdon Melody - Dubitable (Formidable) Cl-up over 1m, sn fdd: jumps fit, earlier won a sell h'cap hdle on first start for present stable, prev juv nov hdle wnr for S Dow (stays 2m4f on fast & gd/soft): modest Flat form in '03 (rtd 38, h'cap): plcd in '02 (rtd 60, fills mdn): has tried visor, blnks & eye-sheild.	11	24a
1072	**SWEET REFLECTION 21** [1]4-8-9 (40) Lisa Jones(3) 14/1: 0000-005: Keen mid-div, prog & ev ch 4f out, hung badly & fdd ins fnl 3f: see 828.	16	2a

5 Ran   Time 2m 38.19 (8.99)   Owned: Mr M F Schofield   Trained: Melton Mowbray

---

1412
5.55 Bet Direct No Q On 08000 93 66 93 Banded Stakes 3yo+ 0-45 (H)
£1621 £463 £232   **1m2f aw**   **Going 53**   **-01 Slow**   Inside

1289*	**KINGS TOPIC 6** [5] P Burgoyne 4-9-13 (45) L Keniry(3) 3/1: 000/0-211: Prom, styd on under press to lead well ins fnl 1f, drvn out: qck reapp: eff arnd a sharp 10f, tried 12f, acts on polytrack in banded grade.		55a
1243+	**MONTOSARI 8** [2] P Mitchell 5-9-13 (45) D Holland 4/5 FAV: 00-16312: Dictated pace, hdd under press cl-home: well bckd: only just denied though ran a little below form of win here in 1243.	nk	54a
1182*	**HUSKY 12** [4] R M H Cowell 6-9-7 p (45) B Doyle 4/1: 0000-513: Keen cl-up, ev ch 2f out, kept on fnl 1f, not btn far in 3rd: op 5/2: just ahead of today's wnr in 1182.	2	45a
1013	**ROY MCAVOY 27** [1] Mrs G Harvey 6-9-7 (45) G Baker 11/1: 000-0004: Slow away, handy 7f, sn fdd.	13	25a
1072	**PLATINUM BOY 21** [3]4-9-7 p (35) V Slattery 33/1: 0003005: Handy 7f, fdd: btr 784.	5	17a

5 Ran   Time 2m 08.26 (5.46)   Owned: Topics Tarts   Trained: Marlborough

---

1413

6.25 Bet Direct No Q Banded Stakes 4yo+ 0-45 (H)
£1435 £410 £205 **7f aw rnd** **Going 53** **-06 Slow** Inside

1327+ **BAYTOWN FLYER 4** [2] P S McEntee 4-9-4 (40) T G McLaughlin 7/2: 0111211: Made all, drvn out to **53a**
hold on ins fnl 1f: qck reapp, tchd 2/1: eff at 6/7f, has tried 1m: acts on firm, gd/soft & both AWs: likes a
sharp trk: thriving in this grade, 5 wins in 12 days: see 1327, 1314 & 1288.

728 **CARGO 62** [7] B A Pearce 5-8-12 t P (45) R Miles(3) 4/1: 05-04202: Reared st, sn handy, styd on to hd **46a**
chase wnr ins fnl 1f, post came too sn: tchd 11/2, 8 wk abs, tried cheek pieces (often blnkd): only just denied on
first start for new yard, prev with D Flood: see 709.

1073 **SINGLE TRACK MIND 21** [1] J R Boyle 6-8-12 (45) D Holland 5/2 FAV: 2545023: Held up, prog bef 1f ½ **45a**
out, kept on & not btn far: ran to form of 2nd in 1073.

61 **A ONE 160** [6] B Palling 5-8-12 (45) M Fenton 10/1: 300000-4: b g Alzao - Anita's Contessa ½ **44a**
(Anita's Prince) Cl-up, rcd wide, no extra ins fnl 1f: tchd 14/1, long abs: plcd on reapp in '03 (rtd 55, h'cap):
claim & sell h'cap wnr in '02: eff at 6f/1m on fast, likes soft, hvy, handles fibresand: acts on any trk: only btn
arnd 1L here & spot on next time.
1 Oct'02 Leic 7sft 62-57 G: 2 Sep'02 Chep 8gd 54- F: 1 Jun'02 Chep 7hvy 68- F: 2 Jul'01 Wind 6g/f 79- D:

1201 **INDIAN WARRIOR 11** [8]8-8-12 (45) N Callan 8/1: 1004055: Chsd ldrs till no extra dist: btr 310. 1 **42a**
1248 **GENTLE RESPONSE 8** [4]4-8-12 bl (45) N Pollard 5/1: 0631056: Handy over 5f, wknd: btr 830. 3 **36a**
1997] **OSO NEET 686** [5]6-8-12 (30) L Keniry(3) 66/1: 06//0000/-7: b g Teenoso - Unveiled (Sayf El Arab) 2½ **31a**
Bhd, nvr a factor on reapp: missed '03: v mod in '02 (J C Fox): unplcd in '00 (rtd 71, mdn): has tried blnks.
969 **JANES VALENTINE 29** [3]4-8-12 (40) J Tate 25/1: 00-40408: Chsd ldrs over 4f, wknd: btr 708. 8 **15a**
8 Ran Time 1m 26.96 (4.16) Owned: Mr J Doxey Trained: Newmarket

---

1414

6.55 Avoid The Queues With Bet Direct No Q Banded Stakes 4yo+ 0-45 (H)
£1463 £418 £209 **2m aw** **Going 53** **-19 Slow** Inside

1373 **FLETCHER 2** [8] H Morrison 10-9-2 (45) R L Moore 6/1: 6204-051: Cl-up, led 2f out, sn clr, rdn **47a**
out to just hold on: op 4/1 on qck reapp: eff at 12/14f, stays 2m: acts on firm, soft grnd & polytrack: enjoyed
drop to banded grade: see 1373.

7 **PRINCE OF THE WOOD 169** [5] A Bailey 4-8-12 (45) M Fenton 9/1: 200064-2: ch g Woodborough - Ard shd **46a**
Dauphine (Forest Wind) Prom, chsd wnr ins fnl 1f, just held: op 12/1: earlier plcd once over hdles (rtd 102h at
best, juv nov, 2m): rnr-up once in '03 (h'cap): eff at 11.6f, now stays 2m: acts on gd/soft grnd & fibresand.
2 May'03 Wind 11.6g/s 53-51 E:

1329 **ANNIVERSARY GUEST 4** [2] Mrs Lucinda Featherstone 5-9-2 P (40) Derek Nolan(7) 12/1: 305-0343: Rear, 2½ **43a**
rcd keenly, hdwy fnl half-mile, onepcd fnl 1f: qck reapp & cheek pieces: acts on firm & fibresand, see 968 .
801 **WAVERLEY ROAD 54** [9] M Madgwick 7-9-2 (45) D Holland 8/1 FAV: 60510-04: Handy 13f, sn no extra: 7 **36a**
well bckd: recently jumps unplcd (rtd 104h): btr 137.
1076 **LITTLE RICHARD 21** [1]5-9-2 p (40) V Slattery 9/2: 3140235: Prom 13f, wknd: btr 1076. 3½ **32a**
1263 **MYSTERIUM 8** [6]10-9-2 vis (45) Steven Harrison(7) 11/1: 33-34156: Bhd, nvr able to chall: op 7/1. 1¾ **30a**
1064 **ANNAKITA 21** [3]4-8-12 (45) Lisa Jones(3) 10/1: 00060-07: Held up, nvr a factor: see 1064. nk **29a**
1204 **DASH FOR GLORY 11** [7]5-9-2 (30) N Callan 33/1: 0000-008: Led till 2f out, fdd: see 1204. 2 **27a**
1243 **CADWALLADER 8** [4]4-8-12 (45) R J Killoran(7) 33/1: 500-465U: Held up, prog & stumbled/u.r. 3f out. **0a**
9 Ran Time 3m 31.62 (11.62) Owned: Lady Margadale Trained: East Ilsley

---

1415

7.25 Bet In Running @ Betdirect Co Uk Banded Stakes 3yo+ 0-35 (H)
£1253 £358 £179 **6f aw rnd** **Going 53** **-00 Slow** Inside

1327 **GRAND VIEW 4** [4] J R Weymes 8-9-0 p (30) D Holland 1/1 FAV: 00-60421: Sn bhd, grad prog 2f out to **38a**
lead well ins fnl 1f, rdn out: qck reapp: well bckd: stays 7f, best at 5/6f on firm, soft & both AWs: see 1327.
1292 **TINY TIM 6** [3] A M Balding 6-9-0 (35) R J Killoran(7) 11/4: 4423522: Handy, led bef 1f out till ¾ **35a**
well ins fnl 1f, no extra: op 7/2 on qck reapp: eff at 6f, will apprec return to 7/8f: see 1292.
1290 **SECOND GENERATION 6** [6] R J Hodges 7-9-0 (30) R L Moore 7/1: 06/0//0-553: Rear & sn under press, 1¾ **30a**
prog 2f out, onepcd fnl 1f: qck reapp: see 1290.
1288 **MAHLSTICK 6** [1] D W P Arbuthnot 6-9-0 t (35) B Doyle 11/2: 406/-6344: Led early, styd cl-up, ev 4 **18a**
ch bef 1f out, sn fdd: op 7/1 on qck reapp: btr 1181.
637 **ALMARA 72** [3]4-9-0 t (30) S Carson 9/1: 000-0405: b f Wolfhound - Alacrity (Alzao) Bhd, nvr a shd **18a**
factor: 10 wk abs: modest form in '03 (rtd 26, tried cheek pieces): wears a t-strap.
1185 **TONG ICE 12** [2]5-9-0 bl (30) R Brisland 25/1: 0400/0-06: gr g Petong - Efficacious (Efisio) Sn 8 **0a**
led, hdd bef 1f out, fdd: unplcd sole '03 start (class stks): plcd twice in '02 (rtd 57$, seller): stays 7f on
fibresand: eff with visor, has tried blnks: with B A Pearce. 2 Feb'02 Sout 7af 57a- F:
6 Ran Time 1m 13.58 (3.18) Owned: Sporting Occasions Trained: Middleham

---

1416

7.55 Betdirect Co Uk Tri-Banded Stakes 3yo 0-45 (H)
£1610 £460 £230 **1m aw rnd** **Going 53** **+08 Fast** Outside

1246* **DIAL SQUARE 8** [2] P Howling 3-9-6 (6ex) (51) M Hills 4/7 FAV: 0132311: Held up, hdwy 3f out to **59a+**
lead ins fnl 1f, pushed out, val 4L+: fast time: well bckd: eff btwn 7f/1m, likes Lingfield/polytrack: easily
defied 6lb penalty & is thriving at present: see 1246.
761 **JOINT DESTINY 59** [4] E J O'Neill 3-9-0 (45) D Holland 7/2: 2340-502: Handy, styd on to lead 2½ **46a**
dist, sn hdd & no extra: 8 wk abs: eff at 6f/1m on firm, gd grnd & polytrack: can find similar, see 441.
1246 **STAGECOACH RUBY 8** [3] G L Moore 3-8-9 (40) R L Moore 8/1: 50-00543: Led till dist, wknd: op 5/1. 1½ **38a**
1134 **FRESH CONNECTION 15** [1] G G Margarson 3-8-4 (35) A McCarthy 16/1: 00054: Handy over 5f, wknd. 5 **23a**
238 **DAVIDS GIRL 127** [5]3-8-4 (35) S Carson 14/1: 406005-5: b f Royal Applause - Cheer (Efisio) 1 **21a**
Cl-up 6f, fdd: long abs: unplcd in 4 '03 starts (rtd 59, mdn): with D Morris.
5 Ran Time 1m 39.83(3.63) Owned: Mr Rory Murphy Trained: Newmarket

Official Going SOFT (GOOD/SOFT places).

1417

2.10 Sodexho Handicap Stakes 3yo 0-80 (D)
£6042 £1859 £930   **6f str**   **Soft 130**   -13 Slow   Stands Side   [87]

1154 **MOLCON 15** [11] N A Callaghan 3-9-4 (77) J Murtagh 15/2: 61150-51: Rear, plenty to do over 1f   86
out, strong run to lead cl-home, going away: eff over 5/6f on firm, enjoyed this soft grnd: likes a stiff trk &
apprec switch to waiting tactics: stable in tremendous early season form: see 1154.
1154 **ASK THE CLERK 15** [3] V Smith 3-8-12 (71) M Tebbutt 20/1: 0350102: Chsd ldrs, ev ch ent fnl 1f,   ½   78
led ins fnl 1f, not pace to repel wnr cl-home: rider gvn a 1 day whip ban: back to form, clrly relishes soft grnd.
1088 **MUY BIEN 21** [5] J R Jenkins 3-9-3 bl (76) D Holland 10/1: 2203123: Tried to make all, clr 1.5f   nk   82
out, collared ins fnl 1f & no extra: rider gvn a 2 day whip ban, clr of rem: tough & consistent, in fine form.
4605} **FLIPANDO 207** [9] T D Barron 3-9-3 (76) K Fallon 9/1: 310-4: b g Sri Pekan - Magic Touch (Fairy   3   75
King) Mid-div, styd on under press fnl 1f, nrst fin on reapp: clr of rem: won middle of 3 '03 starts (mdns),
highly tried on fnl outing: eff at 6f on fast & firm grnd, prob handles soft: handles a sharpish or stiff/gall trk:
promising reapp, spot on next time. 1 Sep'03 Newc 6g/f 88- D:
5014} **OUT AFTER DARK 174** [20]3-9-3 (76) R Smith 8/1: 042-5: b g Cadeaux Genereux - Midnight Shift   6   62
(Night Shift) Slowly away, hdwy from rear dist, nrst fin but nvr dngrs on reapp: rnr-up on fnl '03 start (mdn), has
since been gelded: eff at 6f on fast & gd/soft: sharper next time.
2 Nov'03 Nott 6.1g/s 78- D:
1116 **BOHOLA FLYER 18** [6]3-9-0 (73) Dane O'Neill 8/1: 002-146: Front rank, wknd dist: btr 1116 & 1044 (AW). hd   59
4971} **EPAMINONDAS 179** [12]3-9-2 (75) E Ahern 20/1: 053-7: ch c Miswaki - Nora Nova (Green Dancer)   5   49
Rear, late gains, nvr dngrs on reapp: plcd on fnl '03 start (Newmarket mdn, rtd 77): eff at 7f on gd grnd, sharper
next time & a rtn to further/faster grnd will suit: with R Hannon.
1119* **FINDERS KEEPERS 17** [4]3-9-7 (80) L Dettori 5/1 FAV: 320-2318: Rear, prog halfway, btn over 1f   2   49
out: bckd from 7/1, top-weight: not gvn a hard time once btn, much btr over 7f on fast grnd in 1119.
1116 **STORMY NATURE 18** [8]3-9-3 (76) T Quinn 8/1: 420-39: Chsd ldrs 4f: btr 1116.   1¾   41
1054 **NIGHT WORKER 23** [2]3-8-4 (63) R L Moore 20/1: 43040-60: 10th: Rear, nvr nr ldrs: see 1054.   1¼   25
1116 **MOTU 18** [19]3-9-2 (75) K Darley 20/1: 410-00: 11th: b g Desert Style - Pink Cashmere (Polar   hd   37
Falcon) Rdn in rear, nvr a factor: won middle of 3 '03 starts (mdn): eff at 6f on gd & fast grnd, 7f shld suit:
handles a sharpish or stiff/gall trk: can flash his tail, has been gelded since last year: with J Dunlop.
1 Aug'03 Ripo 6g/f 78- D:
4941} **RED SOVEREIGN 182** [7]3-9-3 (76) W Supple 33/1: 21366-0: 12th: Chsd ldrs till 2f out, wknd: reapp.   5   26
1116 **ALCHERA 18** [14]3-9-0 bl (73) S Carson 25/1: 50210-00: 13th: Front rank 4f, wknd.   ½   22
735   **SMOKIN JOE 62** [15]3-8-9 (68) I Mongan 25/1: 216-4050: 14th: Sn outpcd, nvr dngrs: 9 wk abs.   1¼   14
1154 **DELLAGIO 15** [13]3-9-2 (75) Helen Smith(7) 66/1: 010-000: 15th: Al outpcd.   1¼   18
1054 **TORQUEMADA 23** [16]3-8-6 (65) P Doe 40/1: 60-300: 16th: Cl up, wknd 3f out: 'struck into'.   23   0
1116 **HAYDN 18** [17]3-9-4 (77) J F Egan 16/1: 0000-500: 17th: Al bhd, t.o. in last.   2   0
17 Ran Time 1m 21.73 (8.63) Owned: Mr Mark Venus Trained: Newmarket

---

1418

2.40 Gr3 Bovis Homes Sagaro Stakes 4yo+ (A)
£29000 £11000 £5500   **2m45y**   **Soft 130**   -19 Slow   Inside

987   **RISK SEEKER 30** [13] E Lellouche 4-8-12 D Boeuf 11/2: 21120-21: b c Elmaamul - Robertet   119
(Roberto) Held up, smooth hdwy 3f out, led over 1f out, sn well clr, v impressive: French chall, won 3 times in
'03, incl 2 Gr 3s: eff around 2m & relishes soft grnd: runs well fresh: tough, v smart staying operation & will
prove hard to beat when the grnd rides soft.
2 Mar'04 Mais 15.5sft 107- : 2 Oct'03 Long 15sft 112- A: 1 Sep'03 Long 15sft 112- : 1 Jul'03 Deau 15g/s 109- A:
1005 **DUSKY WARBLER 28** [9] M L W Bell 5-8-13 (107) D Holland 16/1: 33325-22: Led early, remained prom   18   108
& regained lead 4f out, hdd over 1f out & sn left bhd by impressive wnr: bckd at long odds: not disgraced on this
step up in grade, revels in soft & hvy grnd: met a v smart rival here, see 1005.
4794} **MILLENARY 193** [5] J L Dunlop 7-9-4 (117) T Quinn 3/1 FAV: 221042-3: b c Rainbow Quest -   11   103
Ballerina (Dancing Brave) Held up, imprvd to chase ldrs halfway, wknd 2f out: not gvn a hard time, top-weight,
reapp: Gr 3 wnr in 1st time blnks in '03, also rnr-up sev times: eff at 12/14f, does stay 2m: acts on firm &
gd/soft, handles soft & any trk, loves Newmarket: runs well fresh: v smart, has fine rec in Jockey Club Stks.
2 Oct'03 Newm 16g/f 118-(118) A: 1 Jul'03 Newm 12g/f 119-(116) A: 2 May'03 Sain 12sft 119- A:
2 May'03 Newm 12gd 119-(116) A: 1 Jul'02 Newm 12g/s 119- A: 2 May'02 Newm 12g/f 119- A:
2 Sep'01 Curr 14g/f 120- A: 1 Jul'01 Newm 13.2fm 121- A: 1 May'01 Newm 12g 120- A:
1230 **LET ME TRY AGAIN 11** [4] T G Mills 4-8-9 (105) R Miles 20/1: 20540-04: b g Sadler's Wells -   11   88
Dathiyna (Kris) Chsd ldrs till wknd qckly 2f out: won twice in '03 (mdn & h'cap off 75), subs ran well in Gr
company, 7th in Gr 1 St Leger (rtd 108 at best, tried a visor): eff at 12f, shld stay further:acts on gd, fast grnd
& polytrack: do better on a sound surface.
2 May'03 Ling 11.8gd 105-(91) A: 1 Apr'03 Wind 11.6g/f 90-75 E: 1 Feb'03 Ling 12ap 72a- D: 2 Jan'03 Ling 10ap 79a-73 D:
2200*}**ROYAL REBEL 678** [3]8-8-13 J Murtagh 20/1: 043/001/-5: b g Robellino - Greenvera (Riverman) Rdn   17   73
in rear, nvr nr ldrs on comeback: last rcd when won Gr 1 Ascot Gold Cup in '02: only win in '01 again Gr 1 Ascot
Gold Cup: eff at 2m, best over a stiff 2m4f: acts on firm & gd/soft, any trk, loves Ascot: eff with/ without
blnks/visor: high-class but enigmatic stayer who is best when able to race prominently.
1 Jun'02 Asco 20g/f 119- A: 1 Jun'01 Asco 20g/f 119- A:
4934} **DARASIM 185** [8]6-9-4 vis (114) J Fanning 14/1: 131130-6: b g Kahyasi - Dararita (Halo) Chsd ldrs   dist 48
till after halfway, wknd & eased, t.o. on reapp: won a h'cap, a Gr 3 & a Gr 2 in '03, also plcd sev times: eff at
12f/2m, stays 2m2f: acts on firm & gd/soft grnd: loves to force the pace & eff with/without a visor: usually
consistent, capable of much btr.
1 Sep'03 Long 15.5g/s 115- : 1 Aug'03 Deau 15g/s 114- A: 1 Jul'03 Good 14gd 117-103 B:
2 Apr'03 Nott 14.1gd 108-(107) A: 1 Aug'02 Good 12fm 109-103 A: 2 Jul'02 Good 14fm 107-103 A:
1 Apr'02 Ripo 12.2g/f 108-100 : 1 Apr'02 Donc 14.6gd 103-100 B:
4794} **SAVANNAH BAY 193** [6]5-8-13 (111) L Dettori 12/1: 5/26355-7: Bhd, nvr dngrs, t.o. on reapp: has   dist 13
bee gelded since last term: controversially awdd this race last term, subs lost it on appeal: with B Meehan.
4840} **MAKTUB 136** [1]5-9-2 P Robinson 13/2: 111200-8: Trkd ldrs, wknd qckly 4f out, t.o. on reapp.   3   13
5009*}**MISTERNANDO 175** [12]4-8-9 (101) S Hitchcott 16/1: 122611-9: Rdn in rear, nvr trav & t.o. on reapp. dist 0
4494*}**SUPREMACY 213** [14]5-8-13 (104) K Fallon 11/1: 41/0021-0: 10th: Chsd ldrs till after halfway,   dist 0
wknd & t.o. on reapp: has been gelded since last term.
4794*}**PERSIAN PUNCH 193** [7]11-9-4 (118) Martin Dwyer 11/1: 114101-P: Sn led, hdd 4f out, rallying when   0

faltered & eased, tragically collapsed & died: v sad loss to connections & racing: high-class stayer who was as tough & genuine as we have seen.

1635} **MOROZOV 248** [10]5-8-13   I Mongan   20/1: 16/12U0-P: Chsd ldrs, wknd qckly 3f out, t.o./p.u. fnl 1f on reapp.   **0**

1230   **HILBRE ISLAND 11** [11]4-8-9 BL (110) S Drowne   33/1: 0310-30P: Keen & chsd ldrs till halfway, sn   **0**
wknd, t.o./p.u. fnl 1f: tried blnks & reportedly unsuited by this testing grnd.

13 Ran   Time 3m 49.97 (23.97)   Owned: Ecurie Wildenstein   Trained: France

---

1419   3.15 Listed Carey Group Swinley Stakes Fillies 3yo   (A)
£17400   £6600   £3300   **1m rnd**   **Soft 130**   -27 Slow   Inside

4501*}**SHADY REFLECTION 212** [3] J H M Gosden 3-8-11   (75) L Dettori   8/1: 501-1: b f Sultry Song -   **88**
Woodland Melody (Woodman)   Made most, held on gamely fnl 1f, all out on reapp: won fnl of 3 '03 starts (mdn auct):
eff at 1m, shld stay 10f: acts on gd, revels in soft grnd: handles a stiff/undul trk, runs well fresh: loves to
run up with/force the pace: useful filly, op to further improvement but must reportedly have rain-softened grnd.
1 Sep'03 Hami 8.3gd 78- E:

1039* **GLEN INNES 25** [6] D R Loder 3-8-11   J Murtagh   2/1 FAV: 12: Rear, short of room 2f out, switched   shd   **88+**
wide & styd on strongly fnl 1f, just btn in a thrilling fin: hvly bckd, clrly relishes soft & hvy grnd & imprvd in
defeat in this btr grade: unlucky, win a Listed sn, poss over further: see 1039 (fill mdn).

1171   **RED TOP 14** [7] R Hannon 3-8-11   Dane O'Neill   9/1: 3-23: Dwelt, chsd ldrs, styd on under press   1½   **85**
fnl 1f but not quite pace of front 2: stays 1m, acts on firm & soft grnd: must surely find a mdn, see 1171 (7f).

1131   **SOLAR POWER 16** [9] J R Fanshawe 3-8-11   (83) E Ahern   7/1: 1-24: Keen & chsd ldrs, sltly short of   1½   **82**
room 2f out, switched & styd on under press: op 11/2: did not really get the run of today's race & not disgraced in
the circumstances: acts on fast & soft grnd: will apprec further (dam stayed 12f): see 1131.

2727} **GLEBE GARDEN 295** [11]3-8-11   (89) I Mongan   25/1: 310-5: b f Soviet Star - Trounce (Barathea)   hd   **82**
Chsd ldrs, onepcd fnl 1f on reapp: won middle of 3 juv starts (fill mdn): eff at 6f, prob stays 1m: acts on gd &
fast, handles soft grnd: wants h'caps.   1 Jun'03 Wind 6gd 85- E:

1297   **DESERT CRISTAL 7** [5]3-8-11   Martin Dwyer   20/1: 25-26: Keen in rear, hdwy wide 2f out, wkng when   1   **80**
short of room ins fnl 1f: stiff task: mdn, see 1297.

4774} **NEPHETRITI WAY 194** [1]3-8-11   (87) S Drowne   20/1: 212-7: b f Docksider - Velvet Appeal (Petorius)   1   **78**
Chsd ldrs, ev ch 2f out, onepcd fnl 1f on reapp: won mid of 3 '03 starts (fill mdn auct), rnr-up on both other
outings: eff 6/7f on fast & firm, poss handles soft: sharper next time & on faster grnd in h'caps.
2 Oct'03 Newm 7g/f 85-(80) B: 1 Sep'03 Good 6fm 81- D: 2 Sep'03 Warw 6.1fm 79- F:

4952*}**CAVERAL 180** [4]3-8-11   R L Moore   11/1: 31-8: ch f Ashkalani - Melting Gold (Cadeaux Genereux)   3½   **72**
Rear, imprvd to chase ldrs 2f out, btn fnl 1f on reapp: won fnl of 2 juv starts (mdn): eff at 6f on gd & fast grnd,
shld stay 7f/1m this term: handles a stiff/gall trk: with R Hannon & worth another ch back on faster grnd.
1 Oct'03 Newm 6gd 94- D:

4851*}**FIRST CANDLELIGHT 189** [8]3-8-11   T Quinn   14/1: 21-9: Chsd ldrs 6f, wknd on reapp.   ¾   **70**

1171   **ATTUNE 14** [10]3-8-11   K Fallon   14/1: 4-40: 10th: Chsd ldrs, wknd 2f out: nicely bckd, see 1171.   19   **35**

1171   **HALABALOO 14** [2]3-8-11   D Holland   6/1: 3-50: 11th: Chsd ldrs till after halfway, wknd.   1   **33**

11 Ran   Time 1m 51.07 (12.57)   Owned: Maktoum Al Maktoum   Trained: Manton

---

1420   3.50 Listed Velcourt Group Paradise Stakes 4yo+   (A)
£17400   £6600   £3300   **1m rnd**   **Soft 130**   +11 Fast   Inside

4800} **PUTRA PEKAN 193** [6] M A Jarvis 6-9-0 bl (106) K Fallon   4/1: 610010-1: b c Grand Lodge - Mazarine   **113**
Blue (Bellypha)   Keen & prom, led dist, rdn clr fnl 1f: reapp, best time of day: won 2 h'caps & a cond stks in '03
(incl reapp), won first 2 '02 starts (h'cap & stks): eff at 1m/9f on firm & soft grnd, any trk, likes a RHd one &
racing round a bend: wears blnks & runs esp well fresh: smart, career best run today.
1 Sep'03 Newb 9fm 102-(106) B: 1 Jul'03 Sand 8.1g/f 106-100 B: 1 May'03 Kemp 8g/f 102-96 B:
1 May'02 Hayd 8.1gd 100- C: 1 May'02 Kemp 8g/f 104-95 B: 1 Jul'01 Newm 8gd 95-89 B:

3186+ **NEW SEEKER 277** [5] C G Cox 4-9-0   (103) J Murtagh   7/4 FAV: 321311-2: b c Green Desert - Ahbab   4   **106**
(Ajdal)   Led till dist, kept on for 2nd but no ch with wnr: well bckd, reapp: highly progressive in '03, won 3
h'caps, incl 2 val events here at Ascot: eff forcing the pace at 7f/1m on firm & soft grnd: tough & consistent.
1 Jul'03 Asco 7gd 104-95 B: 1 Jun'03 Asco 8g/f 97-87 B: 1 May'03 Newm 7gd 90-76 C: 2 Apr'03 Warw 8.1fm 90- D:

4624} **IKHTYAR 207** [3] J H M Gosden 4-9-3   (117) W Supple   3/1: 31210-3: b c Unfuwain - Sabria (Miswaki)   1¼   **107**
Chsd ldrs, onepcd fnl 1f on reapp: nicely bckd: won twice in '03 (stks & a List event by an impressive 6L): eff at
1m, stays 10f well & acts on gd & firm grnd, below best 2 starts on soft: v smart when conds in his favour, sharper
next time & a rtn to faster grnd/10f will suit.
1 Jul'03 Sand 10.0gd 121-(108) A: 2 May'03 Kemp 8fm 112- A: 1 Apr'03 Sand 8.1gd 108- C:

1225* **HERETIC 11** [2] J R Fanshawe 6-9-0   (105) O Urbina   3/1: 41000-14: Chsd ldrs, wknd qckly 2f out,   21   **74**
eased & fav.: puzzling run with conds in his favour & something surely amiss: see 1225.

4 Ran   Time 1m 48.03 (9.53)   Owned: HRH Sultan Ahmad Shah   Trained: Newmarket

---

1421   4.25 Listed Bovis Homes Pavilion Stakes 3yo   (A)
£17400   £6600   £3300   **6f str**   **Soft 130**   -12 Slow   Stands Side

4866} **MILLBAG 187** [3] M R Channon 3-8-11   (100) T E Durcan   3/1: 31313-1: b c Cape Cross - Play With   **107**
Fire (Priolo)   Trkd ldr, led halfway, styd on strongly fnl 1f despite drifting right, readily: nicely bckd, reapp:
'03 mdn & cond stks wnr, also 3rd in a Gr3 (rtd 101): suited by 6f, stays 7f: acts on firm & soft grnd, stiff/gall
trk: runs well fresh: smart colt, more to come & shld be winning in Group company.
1 Oct'03 Sali 6g/f 100-(95) C: 1 Sep'03 Hayd 5fm 85- D:

1167   **MOONLIGHT MAN 14** [6] R Hannon 3-8-11   (105) Dane O'Neill   2/1 FAV: 41113-22: Chsd ldrs, ev ch   3   **98**
halfway, drifted left fnl 1f & left bhd by wnr: nicely bckd: handles soft, poss over further: tough & useful.

1106   **CRAFTY FANCY 18** [7] D J S ffrench Davis 3-8-6   (88) T Quinn   4/1: 65655-23: Chsd ldrs, onepcd fnl 1f.   ¾   **90**

1018   **MAC LOVE 27** [8] J Akehurst 3-8-11   (105) J Quinn   10/1: 63232-54: b g Cape Cross - My Lass   2½   **89**
(Elmaamul)   Keen in rear, mdn impress fnl 1f: tchd 14/1: trained by M Channon in '03, mdn & dual h'cap wnr, also
plcd sev times, incl in List company: eff at 5/6f on gd & firm grnd: handles a gall or flat trk: tough last year.
2 Oct'03 Donc 6g/f 108-(100) A: 2 May'03 Kemp 5fm 93-87 D:
1 Aug'03 Hayd 5g/f 89-83 E: 1 Apr'03 Nott 5.1g/f 92- D: 2 Apr'03 Nott 5.1gd 79- D:

1206   **TREASURE HOUSE 12** [4]3-8-11   (91) D Holland   9/1: 2210-005: b c Grand Lodge - Royal Wolff (Prince   10   **64**
Tenderfoot)   Keen & chsd ldrs, hung right & btn dist: tchd 14/1: '03 mdn wnr, subs btn in Gr2 company: eff at 6f

on firm & gd/soft grnd: handles a gall or sharp/undul trk: capable of btr.
1 Aug'03 Brig 6.0fm 70-(88) D: 2 Aug'03 Sali 6g/f 95- D: 2 Aug'03 Ripo 6g/f 85- D:
1167 **RUSSIAN VALOUR 14** [2]3-9-4 (113) K Dalgleish 7/1: 31211-06: b c Fasliyev - Vert Val (Septieme Ciel) Led till halfway, wknd & eased: smart juv, won a mdn, List & Gr 3 Norfolk stks: suited by 5f on fast & gd/soft grnd: likes to force the pace: sprinting type, not handle mud? *23* **21**
1 Jun'03 Asco 5g/f 113- A: 1 May'03 Sand 5.0g/f 103- A: 2 May'03 Wind 5.0g/s 97- B: 1 Apr'03 Pont 5g/f 95- D:
6 Ran Time 1m 21.66 (8.56) Owned: Sheikh Ahmed Al Maktoum Trained: West Ilsley

1422

5.00 Bovis Homes Conditions Stakes 2yo (C)
£7192 £2728 £1364 **5f str** **Soft 130** **-40 Slow** Stands Side

1114* **PRINCE CHARMING 18** [1] J H M Gosden 2-9-1 L Dettori 15/8: 11: Chsd ldrs, qcknd to lead ins fnl 1f despite drifting right, cmftbly: bckd from 9/4: eff at 5f on gd/soft & soft, shld stay 6f: prob best juv seen out to date, Royal Ascot type if handling faster grnd: green here, shld be plenty more to come: see 1114. **102+**
1149* **CORNUS 15** [3] R Hannon 2-9-1 R L Moore 1/1 FAV: 112: Chsd ldrs, led briefly ent fnl 1f, not pace of wnr cl-home: well bckd & first defeat: acts on gd/soft & soft grnd: not disgraced, met a smart sort. *1¾* **96**
1190 **ALPAGA LE JOMAGE 13** [5] B J Meehan 2-8-11 J F McDonald(3) 14/1: 33: Led till ent fnl 1f, no extra: bckd at long odds: eff at 5f on fast & soft grnd: ran well for a long way, met a couple of above-average rivals & must find a mdn: see 1190. *1¾* **88**
1205 **DETONATE 12** [4] I A Wood 2-8-11 D Holland 40/1: 64: b c Mind Games - Bron Hilda (Namaqualand) Chsd ldrs, onepcd fnl 1.5f: Apr first foal: dam from a gd family, sire a high-class sprinter. *1¾* **84**
1001* **ALVARINHO LADY 28** [8]2-8-10 Paul Eddery 20/1: 15: Went right start, chsd ldrs 3f, sn btn: see 1001. *8* **63**
1237* **NORCROFT 11** [2]2-9-1 D Fox(5) 5/1: 216: Chsd ldr 3f, wknd: bckd from 8/1: btr 1237 (gd). *7* **53**
6 Ran Time 1m 07.53 (8.53) Owned: Sheikh Mohammed Trained: Manton

1423

5.30 Bovis Homes Stakes Handicap 3yo+ 0-80 (D) **[80]**
£5629 £1732 £866 **1m str** **Soft 130** **-24 Slow** Stands Side

26 **RETIREMENT 167** [7] M H Tompkins 5-9-9 (75) J Fanning 10/1: 024212-1: Trkd ldrs, smooth hdwy to lead ent fnl 1f, rdn clr: reapp: eff at 1m/10f on fast, soft grnd & both AWs: handles any trk & runs v well fresh: stable in fine form, impressed here & shld defy a pen: see 26. **83+**
4673} **LILLI MARLANE 200** [3] N A Callaghan 4-9-6 (72) L Dettori 4/1 FAV: 123350-2: b f Sri Pekan - Fiveofive (Fairy King) Held up, prog when short of room 2f out, switched dist, styd on well into 2nd but no ch with wnr: bckd from 6/1, reapp: '03 h'cap wnr for G Margarson, also plcd sev times: eff at 1m/10f on firm & soft grnd: likes a stiff/gall trk: did not get the best of runs & shld be winning similar soon. *5* **70**
2 Jul'03 Nott 10.0fm 76-70 E: 1 Jun'03 Nott 8.2gd 75-64 E: 2 May'03 Leic 8.0gd 67- F:
3111} **CRAIL 279** [6] C F Wall 4-9-6 (72) G Baker 40/1: 4/0010-3: b g Vettori - Tendency (Ballad Rock) Chsd ldrs, eff 2f out, just lost out on 2nd ins fnl 1f on reapp: gd run from this outsider on grnd considered softer than ideal: '03 mdn wnr: eff at 1m on firm & soft grnd, handles a gall trk: clrly runs well fresh. *½* **69**
1 Jul'03 Donc 8g/f 77-(63) D:
452 **J R STEVENSON 98** [9] M Wigham 8-9-11 (77) S W Kelly 6/1: 6351-204: Held up, hdwy when short of room 1.5f out, switched & styd on, nvr nrr: 3 month abs: closer with clr run: see 369 & 265 (AW). *1½* **71**
1138 **TERRAQUIN 16** [10]4-9-10 (76) K Dalgleish 50/1: 16-04005: Mid-div, hdwy to chall dist, sn no extra: more interesting at 7f: see 517. *2* **66**
1351 **OAKLEY RAMBO 4** [18]5-9-13 (79) Dane O'Neill 16/1: 0000-506: Chsd ldrs, led after 3f till ent fnl 1f, wknd. *2½* **65**
434 **BLUE TROJAN 102** [17]4-9-12 (78) J Daly(7) 25/1: 5644-227: Prom wide, wknd fnl 1f: long abs. *6* **54**
1219* **NIMELLO 11** [13]8-9-11 (77) S Whitworth 7/1: 121-0018: Rear, nvr nr to chall: btr 1219 (AW). *¾* **51**
1231 **HUXLEY 11** [19]5-10-0 T (80) P McCabe 50/1: 1010-009: b g Danehill Dancer - Biddy Mulligan (Ballad Rock) Hmpd start, nvr nr ldrs: top-weight, tried a t-strap: ex Irish, dual h'cap wnr in '03: winning form at 7f/1m on fast & soft grnd: now with M Quinlan. *1½* **51**
4818} **CRAIC SA CEILI 191** [15]4-9-9 (75) M Savage(5) 33/1: 0/50450-0: 10th: b f Danehill Dancer - Fay's Song (Fayruz) Chsd ldrs 6f, wknd on reapp: failed to win in '03, 4th in a val Goodwood h'cap (rtd 81): '02 nurs wnr for M Channon: eff at 7f/1m on fast & soft grnd: handles a sharp or stiff/gall trk. *hd* **46**
1 Oct'02 Ayr 8sft 79-72 D: 2 Sep'02 Muss 8g/f 74-68 D: 2 Sep'02 Hayd 7.1gd 64- E:
1057 **CLIMATE 23** [20]5-9-11 vis (77) R L Moore 16/1: 0S30-540: 11th: Chsd ldrs 6f, wknd: see 878. *2* **44**
4468} **BAND 215** [5]4-9-8 (74) G Gibbons 20/1: 630360-0: 12th: Chsd ldrs, wknd 2f out on reapp. *5* **31**
1057 **KRUGERRAND 23** [4]5-9-13 (79) Paul Eddery 11/1: 040-0000: 13th: Rear, wide, nvr dngrs. *5* **26**
1080 **PHOTOFIT 21** [8]4-9-6 (72) T Quinn 14/1: 62-60: 14th: Chsd ldrs, wknd 3f out on h'cap bow. *10* **4**
1057 **TOPTON 23** [1]10-10-0 bl (80) K Fallon 14/1: 01-43100: 15th: Al bhd, t.o.: nicely bckd, top-weight: much btr 714 (AW). *dist* **0**
4979} **OUT FOR A STROLL 179** [2]5-9-11 (77) Martin Dwyer 16/1: 0/00110-0: 16th: Led till bef halfway, wknd qckly, t.o. *nk* **0**
518 **JUST FLY 88** [12]4-10-0 (80) J Murtagh 10/1: 505-2220: 17th: Al bhd, t.o.: abs, btr 518 (AW). *dist* **0**
1020 **RED GALAXY 27** [11]4-9-9 t (75) E Ahern 50/1: 10/000-0P: Sn bhd, t.o./p.u. & dismounted fnl 1f. **0**
18 Ran Time 1m 51.07(12.37) Owned: Mr Ben Allen Trained: Newmarket

PONTEFRACT WEDNESDAY 28.04.04 Lefthand, Undulating Track, Stiff Uphill Finish

Official Going Heavy (Soft places)

1424

2.20 European Breeders Fund Thorne Maiden Stakes 2yo (D)
£5447 £1676 £838 **5f rnd** **Soft 123** **-13 Slow** Inside

1173 **KINGS GAIT 13** [6] T D Easterby 2-9-0 D Allan(3) 5/1: 61: b c Mujahid - Miller's Gait (Mill Reef) Led/dsptd lead, came stands side straight, kept on well for press, drvn out, gamely: April foal: half-brother to sev wnrs: dam styd 9f as 2yo: eff at 5f, 6f shld suit: much imprvd for debut & with forcing tactics on soft. **79**
1173 **LINCOLNEUROCRUISER 13** [2] J O'Reilly 2-9-0 D R McCabe 7/1: 52: Dwelt, sn chsd ldrs, eff appr fnl 1f, kept on, just held: imprvd for debut on this soft grnd: will apprec 6f & can win similar: see 1173. *nk* **78**
1173 **PRINCE NAMID 13** [9] Mrs A Duffield 2-9-0 G Duffield 9/4 FAV: 43: Cl-up, eff to chall appr fnl *½* **77**

1f, onepace ins last: clr rem, bckd: acts on soft grnd & shld be plcd to win similar: see 1173.
1161 **TARTATARTUFATA 14** [1] D Shaw 2-8-9 P Hanagan 20/1: 04: b f Tagula - It's So Easy (Shaadi) In   3   64
tch, eff over 1f out, no extra fnl 1f: May foal, cost 11,000gns: full sister to a 5/6f wnr: dam 7f scorer.
1274 **LANE MARSHAL 8** [5]2-9-0 T Eaves(5) 25/1: 65: gr c Danzig Connection - Evening Falls (Beveled)   10   51
Cl-up, led over 3f out till fnl out, wknd: Feb foal, cost 4,200gns: half-brother to a 7f/mid-dist wnr: dam sprint wnr.
        CAITLIN [8]2-8-9 F Lynch 6/1: 6: Dwelt, nvr a factor: ndd race.   ½   45
        ROBURY [3]2-9-0 T P Queally(3) 16/1: 7: Dwelt, al bhd on debut.   1¼   47
        BEACON STAR [4]2-9-0 R Ffrench 5/1: 8: Dwelt, in tch, wknd 2f out: op 3/1, scope, ndd race.   3½   40
        ELLENARE [7]2-8-9 B Swarbrick(7) 25/1: 9: Dwelt, al bhd: lkd fit.   ¾   33
9 Ran Time 1m 08.09 (6.79) Owned: Mrs E J Wills   Trained: Malton

1425   2.50 Ossett Selling Handicap Stakes 3yo+ 46-55 (F)   [57]
           £3513 £1081 £541   **1m4y rnd   Soft 123   -16 Slow   Inside**

1090 **ROCINANTE 21** [6] J J Quinn 4-9-3 (46) R Winston 4/1 FAV: 0-000301: Cl-up, led over 2f out, sn   51
clr, drvn out to hold on ins last, val bit further, no bid: op 6/1: best around 1m & acts on fast, gd/soft &
fibresand, any trk: enjoyed drop into the lowest grade: see 647.
1147 **PLAUSABELLE 16** [4] T D Easterby 3-8-6 (8oh)BL (49) D Allan(3) 11/1: 006-02: b f Royal Applause -   ¾   52
Sipsi Fach (Prince Sabo) Bhd, hdwy 2f out, kept on ins last, not btn far: unplcd all 3 '03 starts: stays a
stiff/undul 1m on soft grnd: imprvd for first time blnks & drop into sell company.
4321} **RYMERS RASCAL 223** [1] E J Alston 12-9-6 (49) G Duffield 6/1: 400302-3: b g Rymer - City Sound   2   49
(On Your Mark) Keen in tch, eff to chase wnr over 1f out, no extra ins last: lkd fit for reapp: plcd in 2 of 8 '03
starts (sell h'caps): won 2 sell h'caps in '02: eff over 7f/8.3f on firm, hvy & any trk, likes Redcar: stays 10yo.
2 Sep'03 Pont 8.0g/f 49-49 F: 2 Aug'02 Newc 8gd 55- E: 1 Aug'02 Hami 8.2hvy 56-54 G: 1 Aug'02 Thir 8gd 56-51 F:
1 Aug'01 Beve 7.4g/f 66-63 E: 2 Aug'01 Redc 8fm 63- E:
1278 **LORD CONYERS 8** [5] B Ellison 5-9-0 (3oh) (40) T Eaves(5) 10/1: 2504/-004: Bhd, eff over 1f out,   2½   39
kept on ins last: shld stay 1m: see 1047.
4854} **ASTRAL PRINCE 189** [2]6-9-5 bl (48) R Ffrench 12/1: 000/066-5: ch g Efisio - Val d'Erica (Ashmore)   1   42
In tch, outpcd over 2f out, some late gains: fit from nov chasing, rnr-up earlier (rtd 72c, 2m, gd): unplcd on the
Flat in '03 & '02 (rtd 50): stays 10f on fibresand & gd, handles fast & gd/soft: eff in blnks.
1 May'01 Wolv 7af 79a-69 E:
1314 **PEARTREE HOUSE 6** [3]10-9-5 (48) A Culhane 10/1: 00-00006: Held up, no impress fnl 2f: see 463.   2   39
1322 **FRANKS QUEST 5** [9]4-9-7 (50) L Keniry(3) 6/1: 2336047: Bhd, no dngr: boiled over in padd.   2   38
1160 **LORD OF METHLEY 14** [12]5-9-7 bl (50) V Halliday 11/2: 40036-08: Cl-up, wknd over 2f out.   ¾   37
1200 **DELAWARE TRAIL 12** [11]5-9-2 P (45) L Enstone(3) 33/1: 60006-09: Cl-up, wknd over 2f out: NH type.   19   2
1132 **WODHILL BE 16** [7]4-9-4 (47) T P Queally(3) 40/1: 0-56500: 10th: In tch, hung right after 2f, wknd.   18   0
1304 **LETS PARTY 6** [10]4-9-9 BL t (52) Dale Gibson 20/1: 00400-00: 11th: Led till 3f out, wknd: blnks.   7   0
11 Ran Time 1m 52.92 (11.12) Owned: Mrs Marie Taylor   Trained: Malton

1426   3.25 Ferrybridge Flyers Maiden Stakes 3yo+ (D)
           £5616 £1728 £864   **6f rnd   Soft 123   -45 Slow   Inside**

63   **GAME FLORA 161** [2] M E Sowersby 3-8-8 (50) T Eaves(4) 25/1: 445000-1: b f Mind Games - Breakfast   55
Creek (Hallgate) Cl-up, led over 3f out, kept on fnl 1f, rdn out: 4th at best in '03 (rtd 66): dam 5f wnr: much
imprvd on return at 6f & on first start on soft grnd: goes well fresh.
4534} **BORIS THE SPIDER 210** [1] M D Hammond 3-8-13 (62) A Culhane 9/1: 0000-2: b g Makbul - Try Vickers 3   54
(Fuzzbuster) Held up, hdwy well over 2f out, chsd wnr ins last, no impress: unplcd all 4 '03 starts (rtd 64):
imprvd on return at 6f on soft grnd.
1119 **CLOUDS OF GOLD 17** [5] J S Wainwright 3-8-8 J Tate 50/1: 03: b f Goldmark - Tongabezi   ¾   47
(Shernazar) Bhd, kept on late, nrst fin under hands & heels: eff at 6f, looks sure to stay further: handles soft
grnd: poss more to come.
1216 **BOLLIN ARCHIE 12** [8] T D Easterby 3-8-13 G Duffield 11/1: 504: Made most till over 3f out, no   nk   51
extra fnl 1f: scopey: stays 6f on soft grnd: see 953.
4264} **PALVIC MOON 225** [4]3-8-8 (60) R Fitzpatrick 14/1: 006006-5: ch f Cotation - Palvic Grey   hd   45
(Kampala) In tch, some late gains, nvr dngrs on reapp: unplcd '03 starts (rtd 62): prob stays 6f on fast & soft.
1585} **THE WARLEY WARRIOR 346** [3]3-8-13 bl P Mulrennan(5) 8/1: 5-6: Slow away, in tch, late gains.   1½   47
4952} **LIGNE DEAU 180** [10]3-8-13 R Havlin 10/1: 000-7: Nvr a factor: lkd burly on reapp.   nk   46
4740} **ARTISTIC STYLE 197** [9]4-9-10 (70) R Winston 1/1 FAV: 30223-8: Cl-up, wknd 2f out: bckd, shorter trip. ¾ 44
617   **LADY DOUBLE U 75** [7]4-9-5 D Allan(3) 33/1: 0/-009: In tch, wknd 2f out.   2   35
4871} **SOMEONES ANGEL 187** [6]3-8-8 W Ryan 11/1: 00-0: 10th: Keen, al bhd, t.o.   16   3
3401} **BOLSHEVIK 286** [11]3-8-13 P Hanagan 11/1: 06-0: 11th: In tch, wknd over 2f out, t.o.   16   0
11 Ran Time 1m 24.22 (10.12) Owned: The Southwold Set   Trained: York

1427   4.00 Pontefract Borough Handicap Stakes 3yo 0-85 (D)   [89]
           £9350 £3546 £1773   **1m2f6y   Soft 123   +03 Fast   No Stalls.**

1144 **WOODY VALENTINE 16** [1] M Johnston 3-8-13 (74) S Chin 11/2: 1400-421: Led till over 1f out,   85
rallied ins last to lead again, rdn out: eff at 10f, stays 12f: acts on firm & soft grnd, prob any trk: game win.
1105 **ODDSMAKER 18** [6] P D Evans 3-8-12 (73) Dean McKeown 5/1 JT FAV: 00015-32: In tch, hdwy to lead   1¼   82
over 1f out, rdn & hdd ins last, no extra: well clr of rem: stays 10f & can win a h'cap on this form: see 1105.
1108 **TYTHEKNOT 18** [4] Jedd O'Keeffe 3-9-0 (75) P Hanagan 8/1: 02-23: Prom, eff over 2f out, sn outpcd   18   66
by front 2: padd pick: not get home over this longer trip on testing grnd, worth another ch: see 1108 (1m).
1124 **MAMBINA 16** [10] M R Channon 3-8-5 (66) C Catlin 9/1: 50-044: Bhd, modest late gains, nvr dngrs: 1   56
small: much softer grnd: btr 1124 (gd).
1104 **WEET A HEAD 18** [3]3-9-7 (82) D Sweeney 8/1: 3263-535: In tch, outpcd fnl 2f: handled soft in 1104.   1   71
1019 **ABSOLUTELY SOAKED 27** [8]3-8-3 (64) Lisa Jones(3) 14/1: 30-56: b f Alhaarth - Vasilopoula   5   48
(Kenmare) In tch, wknd over 2f out: plcd on first of 2 '03 starts (mdn auct): stays 7f on gd grnd.
1019 **JUST A FLUKE 27** [7]3-9-2 T R Ffrench 14/1: 27-047: Handy, wknd 2f out: tried a t-strap, see 1019.   1¾   59
1163 **RIGONZA 14** [5]3-8-11 (72) D Allan(3) 25/1: 54346-08: ch g Vettori - Desert Nomad (Green Desert)   4   48
Nvr a factor: ndd race: plcd in an auct mdn in '03 (rtd 71): stays 7f on fast grnd, bred to stay at least 1m.
923   **MRS PANKHURST 34** [2]3-8-12 (73) M Hills 5/1 JT FAV: 010-59: In tch, wknd 2f out: see 923 (gd).   dist   0

4825*)**RED SKELTON 190** [9]3-9-2 (77) A Culhane 9/1: 01-0: 10th: ch c Croco Rouge - Newala (Royal   *dist* 0
Academy) Sn bhd, t.o./virtually p.u. 2 out: reapp: won a mdn auct on last of 2 '03 starts: ndd plenty of riding
when winning over 7f, shld stay 1m+: acts on fibresand & a sharp trk: something amiss here.
1 Oct'03 Sout 7af 78a- F:
10 Ran   Time 2m 20.1 (12)   Owned: Favourites Racing   Trained: Middleham

---

1428   4.35 Brian Hunter - A Lifetime In Racing Maiden Stakes 3yo (D)
£5590 £1720 £860   **1m2f6y**   **Soft 123**   -71 Slow   No Stalls

MASTER WELLS [6] J D Bethell 3-9-0   C Catlin 20/1: 5: b g Sadler's Wells - Eljazzi (Artaius)   84
Held up, hdwy well over 1f out, styd on to lead ins last, rdn out: eff at 10f, shld stay 12f: acts on soft grnd &
runs well fresh: v pleasing start, can rate higher.
BACKGAMMON [1] D R Loder 3-9-0   N Pollard 9/4: 2: b c Sadler's Wells - Game Plan (Darshaan)   1½   81
Prom, led 2f out till ins last, not pace of wnr: well clr of rem: half-brother to a smart mid-dist wnr: eff at
10f, 12f shld suit: acts on soft grnd: shld learn from this & win similar shortly.
4871} **BLAZE OF COLOUR 187** [5] Sir Michael Stoute 3-8-9   F Lynch 2/1 FAV: 0-3: ch f Rainbow Quest -   13   63
Hawait Al Barr (Green Desert) In tch, eff to chall over 2f out, no extra over 1f out: op 13/8, lkd fit: well btn
sole '03 start: dam 12f/2m winner: may do better.
1148 **MOONSHAFT 15** [7] E A L Dunlop 3-9-0   W Ryan 20/1: 004: Led till 2f out, no extra: scopey.   3   64
1213 **BOLLIN ANNABEL 12** [2]3-8-9   D Allan(3) 8/1: 0-25: Whipped round & lost 16L + start, al bhd.   5   53
1258 **EMPRESS EUGENIE 9** [4]3-8-9   J Tate 3/1: 46: Handy, wknd over 2f out: scope: btr 1258.   2½   49
6 Ran   Time 2m 28.5 (20.4)   Owned: Mr Jordan Ellison Lund   Trained: Middleham

---

1429   5.05 Susan & Brian Greenwood 40th Anniversary Handicap Stakes 3yo 0-80 (D)
£5330 £1640 £820   **1m4f8y**   **Soft 123**   -17 Slow   Inside   [83]

1193 **CONSIDINE 13** [4] J M P Eustace 3-8-4 (59) J Tate 12/1: 045-01: b c Romanov - Libeccio   69
(Danzatore) Led early, cl-up, led over 1f out, kept on, rdn clr: 4th at best from 3 '03 starts (AW mdns): much
imprvd for step up to 12f & first eff on soft grnd: acts on a stiff & an undul trk: prob more to come.
1051* **HABITUAL DANCER 23** [3] Jedd O'Keeffe 3-8-4 (59) P Hanagan 4/1: 000-612: Keen in tch, sltly   5   63
outpcd 3f out, rallied appr fnl 1f, nrst fin: stays 12f, shaped like further will suit: prob more to come: see 1051.
676 **CRACKLEANDO 70** [2] N P Littmoden 3-8-2 (57) J Bramhill 25/1: 000-303: Led after 4f till over 1f   ¾   60
out, no extra: 10 wk abs: back to form: prob stays 12f on polytrack & soft: see 291.
1124 **ZAFFEU 16** [5] N P Littmoden 3-9-1 (70) J P Guillambert(3) 11/2: 06624: Dwelt, in tch, eff over 2f   shd   73
out, hung right & no extra over 1f out: acts on polytrack & gd, poss soft: see 1124 (11f).
1192 **DAYTIME GIRL 13** [6]3-9-7 (76) M Hills 1/1 FAV: 51-35: In tch, wknd 3f out: not handle soft?   dist   0
1174 **HATHLEN 13** [1]3-9-7 (76) A Culhane 6/1: 3022-066: In tch, wknd 2f out, t.o.: not handle soft?   2½   0
6 Ran   Time 2m 50.95 (16.85)   Owned: Mr Elias Haloute   Trained: Newmarket

---

1430   5.35 Betfair Com Apprentice Series Round 2 Handicap Stakes 3yo+ 0-70 (E)
£4085 £1257 £629   **1m2f6y**   **Soft 123**   +10 Fast   No Stalls   [67]

1278 **JAKE BLACK 8** [2] J J Quinn 4-8-11 (50) D Tudhope 5/2 FAV: 0-011531: Cl-up, led over 3f out, sn   61
rdn clr: fast time: stays 10f well on soft & fibresand: thriving, shld defy a pen on similar grnd: see 1278, 893.
1254 **DICKIE DEADEYE 9** [3] G B Balding 7-9-3 (56) T Block(5) 11/4: 050-6522: Held up, hdwy over 2f out,   11   59
kept on same pace: well clr of rem & running well: see 1254, 924.
1112 **MIDSHIPMAN 18** [8] A W Carroll 6-9-12 BL (65) C Haddon 12/1: 0-000003: b c Executive Man - Midler   10   58
(Comedy Star) Bhd, modest late gains, no threat: well btn sole '03 start, dual h'cap & class stks wnr for P D'Arcy
in '02: suited by 9/12f on soft, hvy & loves fibresand/W'hampton: has tried visor & blnks.
2 Jan'02 Wolv 8.4af 98a- C: 1 Dec'01 Wolv 9.3af 99a-85 C: 1 Dec'01 Wolv 12af 88a- D: 1 Nov'01 Wolv 9.3af 84a-73 E:
2 Nov'01 Sout 8af 77a-69 D: 2 Oct'01 Yarm 7hvy 71-69 D:
964 **LIBRE 30** [5] R C Guest 4-10-0 bl (67) A Reilly(5) 7/2: 0140-054: Held up, eff 3f out, sn btn: nicely bckd.   1¼   59
4303] **LITTLE ENGLANDER 224** [4]4-9-9 (62) C Cavanagh(5) 14/1: 6240-5: b g Piccolo - Anna Karietta   5   49
(Precocious) Chsd ldrs, wknd over 2f out: rnr-up in '03 (mdn): poss stays 10f on soft grnd.
2 Aug'03 Wind 10.0g/f 69- D:
782 **MARENGO 58** [7]10-7-12 (7oh) K Ghunowa 16/1: 0-006006: b g Never So Bold - Born To Dance   11   13
(Dancing Brave) Slow away & al bhd: 2 mth abs: 4th at best in '03 (rtd 50): won 4 times at Southwell in '02: eff
at 5.5f/7f, stays 1m on firm & soft, loves fibresand/Southwell: gd weight-carrier.
2 Dec'02 Sout 8af 74a-70 C: 2 Sep'02 Sout 8af 73a-70 E: 1 Sep'02 Sout 8af 71a-64 F: 2 Mar'02 Sout 7af 69a-63 E:
1 Feb'02 Sout 6af 66a-56 E: 1 Feb'02 Sout 7af 56a- F: 2 Feb'02 Sout 6af 52a- F: 1 Jan'02 Sout 6af 53a- F:
2 Oct'01 Sout 5af 54a-51 F: 1 Aug'01 Warw 5.5gd 48- F: 2 Jul'01 Sout 7af 53a-52 F: 1 Feb'01 Sout 7af 56a- G:
1159} **FURNITURE FACTORS 372** [1]4-9-7 (60) J D O'Reilly(3) 50/1: 3400/00-7: In tch, wknd over 3f out.   24   14
1064 **TURFTANZER 22** [10]5-7-12 (2oh)t (35) Janice Webster 25/1: 0-504608: Handy, wknd over 3f out.   11   0
382 **BUSCADOR 107** [9]5-9-5 (58) Saleem Golam(3) 13/2: 11061-09: Led till 3f out, wknd: best 157 (aw).   17   0
9 Ran   Time 2m 19.4(11.3)   Owned: Mr G A Lucas   Trained: Malton

---

Official Going GOOD/SOFT.

1431   1.20 Group 3 Prix de Barbeville 4yo+   (A)
£25704 £10282 £7711   **1m7f110y**   **Good/Soft**

4934*)**WESTERNER 179** [6] E Lellouche 5-9-6   D Boeuf 1/1 FAV: 522211-1: b c Danehill - Walensee (Troy)   122+
Held up, gd prog to lead ins fnl 1f, pushed out, val 4L+: reapp: developed into high class stayer in '03, won 2 Gr
1's: eff at 2m/2m4f on gd/soft & v soft: acts on a stiff/gall trk & likes Longchamp: goes well fresh: heads for Gr
1 Ascot Gold Cup & big claims with give in grnd. 1 Sun'26 Long 15.5sft 118-: 1 Sun'05 Long 20sft 123- A:

LONGCHAMP   THURSDAY 22.04.04   Righthand, Stiff, Galloping Track

2 Sun'14 Long 15.5g/s 108- : 2 Sun'23 Deau 15g/s 110- A: 2 Sun'20 Mais 14g/s 110- A:
FORESTIER [4] E Danel 4-8-9   C-P Lemaire 17/4: 13151-12: ch c Nikos - Forest Hills (Sicyos)   **2**   **109**
Mid div, eff when hmpd dist, kept on ins fnl 1f, no ch with easy wnr: eff at 2m on soft grnd.
1202] **IDAHO QUEST 725** [5] H-A Pantall 7-8-11   O Peslier 16/1: /2321-3: b g Rainbow Quest - Javandra   **shd**   **107**
(Lyphard) Keen bhd, gd prog ins well ins fnl 1f, nrst fin: eff at 2m on soft: useful.
2 Sep'01 Long 12gd 119- :
3909} **SWING WING 243** [2]5-8-13 (109) I Mendizabal 11/1: /31533-5: b g In The Wings - Swift Spring   **hd**   **108**
(Bluebird) Cl up, ev ch 2f out, no extra well ins fnl 1f: reapp: List wnr in '03: List & stks wnr in '02: eff at
12/15.5f on fast, soft & fibresand: tough 5yo: sharper next time.
1 Tue'24 Long 15.5gd 110- A: 2 Sep'02 Long 15gd 107- : 1 Aug'02 Deau 15g/s 107- : 1 Apr'02 Epso 10g/f 105- B:
2 Oct'01 San 8g/s 105- : 1 Sep'01 Bath 8fm 91-84 C: 1 Aug'01 Hami 8.2sft 92- D: 2 Aug'01 Good 7g/f 87-79 C:
2 Jun'01 Sout 6af 80a- D: 2 May'01 Sout 6af 80a- D:
6 Ran   Time 3m 35.50 ()   Owned: Ecurie Wildenstein   Trained: France

LONGCHAMP   SUNDAY 25.04.04   Righthand, Stiff, Galloping Track

Official Going GOOD/SOFT.

1432
2.20 Group 3 Fillies Prix de la Grotte 3yo   (A)
£25704 £10282 £7711   **1m rnd**   **Good/Soft**

GREY LILAS [5] A Fabre 3-9-0   Gary Stevens 28/10: 62-11: gr f Danehill - Kenmist (Kenmare)   **113+**
Prom, hdwy to lead ins fnl 1f, pushed out, val 3L+: earlier won fillies event here at Longchamp: eff at 1m on
gd/soft, stiff/gall trk, likes Longchamp: lightly rcd, improving with every start: returns for French 1,000 Guineas.
1156 **PETIT CALVA 19** [2] R Gibson 3-9-0   T Jarnet 21/1: 64150-32: Led till hdd ins fnl 1f, sn outpcd   **1½**   **107**
by easy wnr: eff at 7f/1m on gd/soft: useful.
4631*)**DENEBOLA 203** [4] P Bary 3-9-0   C-P Lemaire 13/10 FAV: 4131-3: br f Storm Cat - Coup de Genie (Mr   **shd**   **106**
Prospector) In tch, prog dist, kept on & not btn far in 3rd: eff at 1m on gd/soft.
1 Sun'05 Long 8sft 114- A: 1 Sat'02 Deau 6g/s 105- A:
8 Ran   Time 1m 38.40 ()   Owned: Gestut Ammerland   Trained: France

1433
2.50 Group 3 Colts Prix de Fontainebleau 3yo   (A)
£25704 £10282 £7711   **1m rnd**   **Good/Soft**

1060* **AMERICAN POST 25** [2] Mme C Head-Maarek 3-9-2   C Soumillon 1/2 FAV: 2111-11: Made all, pushed out   **122+**
to assert fnl 1f, val 3L+: eff at 1m, mid dist bred & 10f+ will suit: acts on fast & soft grnd: high class
performer with gd turn of foot: now heads for French 2,000 Guineas where must have fine chance bef main target
of Epsom Derby in June: see 1060.
4797} **ANTONIUS PIUS 190** [4] A P O'Brien 3-9-2   J P Spencer 66/10: 110-2d: b c Danzig - Catchascatchcan   **1**   **114**
(Pursuit of Love) Bhd, prog to chase wnr when hung right ins fnl 1f, kept on for 2nd, disq & plcd last: reapp:
rider received 4 day careless riding ban: Irish raider, mdn & Gr 2 wnr in '03: eff at 6/7f, stays 1m: acts on gd &
gd/soft grnd: eff on a gall/undul trk & has gone well fresh: smart, met a high-class rival here.
1 Sun'29 Curr 6gd 102- A: 1 Wed'14 Gowr 7g/s 102- :
1060 **BLACKDOUN 25** [1] J-L Pelletan 3-9-2   F Spanu 101/10: 224-2132: Prom, no extra ins fnl 1f: plcd 2nd.   **2**   **110**
4 Ran   Time 1m 38.50 ()   Owned: K Abdulla   Trained: France

1434
3.20 Group 2 Prix Greffuhle 3yo   (A)
£42148 £16268 £7764   **1m2f110y**   **Good/Soft**

MILLEMIX [4] Mme C Head-Maarek 3-9-2   C-P Lemaire 6/4 JT FAV: 011-21: bl c Linamix - Milesime   **111**
(Riverman) Chsd ldrs, led bef 1f out, drvn out: won last 2 of 3 '03 starts (stks): eff at 1m, suited by 10.5f,
further will suit: acts on gd/soft & hvy grnd: improving 3yo who heads for French Derby in June.
ESPERANTO [6] A P O'Brien 3-9-2   J P Spencer 124/10: 5-12d: b c Sadlers Wells - River Missy   **2**   **106**
(Riverman) Mid div, hdwy wide 2f out, styg on when hmpd rival ins fnl 1f, fin 2nd, disq & plcd 5th: rider received
2 day careless riding ban: recent mdn wnr at The Curragh: eff at 10f, further will suit: acts on gd/soft grnd & a
gall trk: useful, shld win a List/Gr event.
9} **DAY OR NIGHT 169** [3] J E Pease 3-9-2   T Gillet 42/10: 143-12: gr c Daylami - Amaryllis (Sadlers   **snk**   **105**
Wells) Handy, styd on fnl 1f for 3rd, promoted to 2nd.
8 Ran   Time 2m 12.90()   Owned: Alec Head   Trained: France

NAVAN   SATURDAY 24.04.04   Lefthand, Galloping Track

Official Going Yielding (Yielding To Soft Places)

1435
4.00 Listed Irish EBF Fillies & Mares Salsabil Stakes 3yo+   (A)
£29737 £8690 £4140   **1m2f**   **Good/Soft**

ALL TOO BEAUTIFUL A P O'Brien 3-8-7   J P Spencer 4/7 FAV: 11: b f Sadlers Wells - Urban Sea   **112**
(Miswaki) In tch, gd prog to lead 2f out, pushed out, easily, val 5L+: rider received a 4 day ban for careless
riding: earlier won a mdn at Leopardstown: eff at 10f, 12f will suit: acts on gd/soft grnd & a gall trk: goes well
fresh: well regarded, win Gr races & looks an Oaks filly.
1630} **QUEEN ASTRID 344** D K Weld 4-9-13   P J Smullen 6/1: 4210-2: b f Revoque - Talina's Law (Law   **2½**   **106**
Society) Led till hdd 2f out, styd on byt no ch with easy wnr. 2 Fri'16 Cork 10.2g/s 99- A:
3340} **IMOYA 266** Enda Kelly 5-9-10 (97) P Cosgrove 16/1: 5050-3: b f Desert King - Urgent Liaison   **1**   **101**
(High Estate) Cl up, outpcd 3f out, rallied fnl 1f. 1 Apr'02 Wind 10g/f 87- D: 2 Oct'01 Donc 8hvy 84- D:

NAVAN   SATURDAY 24.04.04   Lefthand, Galloping Track

9 Ran   Time 2m 16.50()   Owned: Michael Tabor   Trained: Ballydoyle, Co Tipp

---

CURRAGH   SUNDAY 25.04.04   Righthand, Galloping Track

Official Going Soft

1436	**4.30 Group 3 Fillies EBF Athasi Stakes 3yo+ (A)**
	£38025 £11115 £5265 **7f rnd** **Soft**

LUCKY 10 [2] A P O'Brien 3-8-8   J A Hefferenan 11/8 FAV: 5-311: b f Sadlers Wells - Zummerudd   **107+**
(Habitat) Mase all, pushed out fnl 1f, val 3L : earlier mdn wnr at Tipperary: eff at 7f, 1m+ will suit: acts on
gd/soft & hvy grnd: goes well fresh: easily handled step up in grade & more Group prizes await.
952   **GOLDEN NUN 29** [1] T D Easterby 4-9-7 (99) K Darley 4/1: 02305-02: b f Bishop of Cashel - Amber   1½   **101**
Mill (Doulab) Handy, outpcd 3f out, rallied fnl 1f, not pace wnr: reported to have broken blood vessel: Gr 3 &
listed rnr up numerous times in '03: won 4 times in '02 (mdn, h'caps & stks): eff at 6f/7f on firm & soft grnd:
acts on any trk: eff with blnks or cheek pieces: tough & useful, fine return.
2 Wed'24 Ches 6.1g/s 100-98 A: 2 Fri'11 York 6.0fm 99-97 A: 2 Thu'17 Ripo 6g/f 96-100 A: 1 Oct'02 Donc 6sft 101- B:
1 Sep'02 Donc 6.5fm 96-82 B: 2 Aug'02 Newm 5gd 85-78 B: 1 Jul'02 Ches 5fm 78- E: 2 May'02 Hami 6gd 75- E:
2 Apr'02 Warw 5g/f 74- D:
MEGEC BLIS 28 [6] D K Weld 3-8-8   P J Smullen 4/1: 4-13: b f Soviet Star - Machaera   2½   **83**
(Machiavellian) Chsd ldrs, onepcd dist.
6 Ran   Time 1m 30.60()   Owned: Mrs John Magnier   Trained: Ballydoyle, Co Tipp

---

DIELSDORF   SUNDAY 25.04.04

Official Going Good

1437	**2.00 Super Grand Prix BMW 4yo+ ()**
	£10859 £4344 £3258 **1m3f110y**

3051] **MOONJAZ 999** K Klein 7-8-11 (92) E Wehrel 227/10: 3-3121: Just held on to repel 2nd.   **84**
1068* **AKASH 19** M Johnston 4-9-6 (90) J Fanning 23/10 CO FAV: 4/05220-12: Led, hdd under press cl   nk   **92**
home: only just denied on Swiss raid: see 1068.
SYNDACO M Weiss 5-8-9   R Havlin 28/1: 3: Onepace.   2½   **77**
13 Ran   Time 2m 28.9()   Owned: Stall Brunau   Trained: Germany

---

SHA TIN   SUNDAY 25.04.04   Righthand Track

Official Going Good/Firm

1438	**9.30 Group 1 Audemars Piquet QE II Cup 3yo+ (A)**
	£575540 £215827 £107914 **1m2f** **Good/Firm**

RIVER DANCER [8] J Size 5-9-0   G Schofield 57/1: -4434001: Led well ins fnl 1f, rdn out.   **122**
ELEGANT FASHION [2] D Hayes 6-8-10   G Mosse 39/10: 213-5212: Just held.   ¾   **116**
1139 **SCOTTS VIEW 13** [6] M Johnston 5-9-0 (115) S Chin 9/1: -4101313: Mid div, prog wide ins fnl 2f,   shd   **119**
nrst fin: fine eff on step up to Group 1 company, thriving: one to follow: see 1139.
14 Ran   Time 2m 1.40()   Owned: R J Arculli   Trained: Hong Kong

---

SOUTHWELL   Fibresand   THURSDAY 29.04.04   Lefthand, Sharp, Oval Track

Official Going Standard To Slow

1439	**2.30 Littlewoods Bet Direct Maiden Auction Stakes 2yo (F)**
	£2954 £844 £422 **5f aw str** **Going 61** **Inapplicable** Outside

1048 **UNLIMITED 4** [6] Mrs A Duffield 2-8-9   G Duffield 13/8 FAV: 21: Cl-up, led dist, rdn out: well   **75a**
bckd: eff at 5f, bred to get further: acts on fibresand/sharp trk: only lightly rcd & can improve.
1173 **URABANDE 14** [3] Julian Poulton 2-8-2 Lisa Jones(3) 50/1: 02: b f Tipsy Creek - La Belle Mystere   ½   **65a**
(Lycius) Led till dist, kept on fnl 1f but just held: clr rem: April foal, cost 2,600gns: dam unplcd: sire a
useful juv at sprint dists: eff at 5f, shaped as tho' 6f will suit: acts on fibresand: improved fr debut.
1091 **ETERNALLY 21** [6] R M H Cowell 2-8-9 P M Henry 20/1: 03: ch c Timeless Times - Nice Spice (Common   3   **63a**
Grounds) Handy, onepcd ins fnl 1f: AW bow: April foal, cost 4,500gns: dam unplcd: sire won numerous times at 2:
eff at 5f on fibresand: imprvd on debut eff with today's fitting of cheek pieces.
ZENDARO 0 [8] W M Brisbourne 2-8-9   B Swarbrick(7) 100/30: 4: b g Danzero - Countess Maud (Mtoto)   2½   **56a**
In tch till dist, sn wknd & hung left: tchd 9/2 on debut: April first foal, cost 6,500gns: dam unrcd.
MISSED TURN 0 [7]2-8-9   P Fessey 14/1: 5: Handy, no extra fnl 2f: debut.   3   **47a**
ALMOST PERFECT 0 [9]2-8-3 (1ow) E Ahern 6/1: 6: Nvr nrr than mid-div: debut.   1½   **37a**
DANEHILL ANGEL 0 [11]2-8-6   D Holland 14/1: 7: Rear, nvr nrr than mid-div on debut.   2½   **33a**
1048 **RONNIES LAD 24** [4]2-8-7   V Halliday 50/1: 58: Bhd, nvr able to chall: btr 1048.   nk   **33a**
1325 **LORD CHALFONT 6** [12]2-8-9 bl A Culhane 14/1: 09: Rear, nvr able to chall.   5   **20a**

KERESFORTH 0 [10]2-9-0 T E Durcan 12/1: 0: 10th: Slow away, nvr a factor.   **1**   **22a**
Metolica 0 [2]2-8-4 (2ow) R Fitzpatrick 40/1:0   1325 **Ryans Lil Ol Gal 6** [1]2-8-2 Dale Gibson 80/1:0
12 Ran Time 1m 1.74 () Owned: Mrs L J Tounsend Trained: Leyburn

---

1440   3.00 Betdirect Co Uk Claiming Stakes 3yo (F)
       £3213 £918 £459   **1m aw rnd**   **Going 61**   -35 Slow   Inside

1081* **DOCTORED 22** [5] B A Pearce 3-8-13 p (54) B Reilly(3) 11/2: 3-004611: Handy till led after 5f, rdn   **67a**
out fnl 1f to hold on: eff at 7f/1m on fast, gd/soft & fibresand: eff in blnks, t-strap or cheek pieces: see 1081.
983+***CASPIAN DUSK 30** [2] W G M Turner 3-9-1 (70) A Culhane 1/4 FAV: 406-2312: Led after 3f, hdd bef   ¾   **66a**
2f out, kept on ins fnl 1f, not pace of wnr: bckd at long odds-on: clr rem: below form of win here in 983 (mdn).
1292 **DIVINA 8** [1] S L Keightley 3-8-6 vis (30) F Norton 50/1: 000043: Handy 6f, sn no extra: see 1015.   6   **45a$**
1250 **BRETTON 10** [4] R Hollinshead 3-8-7 p (45) Dale Gibson 10/1: 44-26644: Rear, nvr a factor: btr 351.   4   **38a**
4816] **SHANGHAI SURPRISE 192** [3]3-8-9 (46) J Edmunds 25/1: 46000-5: b c Komaite - Shanghai Lil (Petong)   dist **15a**
Led, hdd 5f out, fdd 3f out: reapp: unplcd in '03 (rtd 39a & 63, mdns, I A Wood): tried blnks: with J Balding.
5 Ran Time 1m 47.09 (7.69) Owned: Mr T M J Keep Trained: Lingfield

---

1441   3.30 Special Offers @ Betdirect Co Uk Handicap Stakes Fillies 3yo 0-75 (E)   **[82]**
       £3741 £1151 £576   **6f aw rnd**   **Going 61**   -05 Slow   Inside

1239 **GENEROUS GESTURE 12** [3] M L W Bell 3-9-6 VIS (74) I Mongan 9/2: 604-1561: Bhd, grad prog from   **83a**
halfway, styd on to lead dist despite hanging left, rdn out: first time visor: eff at 6f, has tried 7f: acts on
fibresand, handles fast & gd grnd: imprvd eff here with application of visor: see 795.
1239 **MARINAITE 12** [4] S R Bowring 3-9-7 (75) J Bramhill 2/1 FAV: 21522: Cl-up, led trav well 2f out,   2   **77a**
hdd dist, not pace of wnr ins fnl 1f: clr rem: another gd eff: lightly rcd in h'cap grade & can find similar, see 1239.
1338 **OBE BOLD 5** [7] A Berry 3-8-11 (65) F Norton 25/1: 33000-43: Led till halfway, fdd fnl 2f: qck reapp.   7   **51a**
1146* **CHEEKY CHI 17** [5] P S McEntee 3-8-12 (66) N Callan 4/1: 44314: In tch, ev ch 2f out, sn wknd &   nk   **51a**
hung left from dist: btr 1146 (5f, soft).
177 **TURKISH DELIGHT 141** [6]3-8-3 (57) J Edmunds 16/1: 44430-5: b f Prince Sabo - Delicious   ½   **41a**
(Dominion) Handy frst outpcd after 2f, modest late gains: reapp: unplcd all 3 '03 starts (rtd 75, fills mdn, D
Morris): eff around 6f, handles fibresand, firm & fast grnd.
975 **VELVET TOUCH 30** [1]3-8-1 (55) J Quinn 14/1: 022-2606: Rear, nvr nrr than mid-div: btr 436.   ½   **38a**
1146 **QUEENS SQUARE 17** [8]3-7-12 (2oh) (50) Kim Tinkler 66/1: 44200-07: b f Forzando - Queens Check   8   **14a**
(Komaite) Handy, fdd 2f out: plcd 4 times in '03 (sellers & clmrs, rtd 54): eff at 6f on fast & gd grnd.
2 Jul'03 Hayd 6gd 54- F:
1338 **SAHARA SILK 5** [2]3-9-0 vis (68) D Holland 7/2: 6134128: Handy over 2f, sn fdd, eased fnl 1f: qck   dist **0a**
reapp: v disapp eff & surely something amiss: has won here 4 times: btr 1338 & 872.
8 Ran Time 1m 17.27 (3.97) Owned: Mr & Mrs J & P Ransley Trained: Newmarket

---

1442   4.00 Bet In Running @ Betdirect Co Uk Handicap Stakes 3yo+ 0-75 (E)   **[70]**
       £3760 £1157 £579   **5f aw str**   **Going61**   Inapplicable   Outside

1393 **FAR NOTE 3** [1] S R Bowring 6-10-0 bl (70) J Bramhill 8/1: 0046101: Slow away, prog & sn in tch,   **81a+**
led despite hanging right dist, pushed clr, val 4L+: qck reapp: suited by 5/6f, stays 1m: acts on firm, gd/soft &
likes fibresand/Southwell: eff with blnks: decisive wnr under top-weight & can follow up: see 1393 & 859.
1127* **DUNN DEAL 17** [4] W M Brisbourne 4-9-7 (63) T E Durcan 7/1: 660-3012: Held up, eff ins fnl 2f,   2   **66a**
nvr getting to wnr: ran to wng form of 1127 (gd).
749 **EMPRESS JOSEPHINE 62** [7] J R Jenkins 4-9-4 vis (60) D Corby(3) 11/1: 424-1253: Cl-up, led after   1½   **59a**
2f, hdd dist, sn no extra: 9 wk abs: rider received a 1 day whip ban: ran to form of 641 & 507.
1267 **ITALIAN MIST 9** [13] Julian Poulton 5-9-12 e (68) M Halford(7) 6/1 FAV: 2013104: Bhd, prog ins fnl   ½   **66a**
2f, nrst fin: back to form on return to fibresand & return to 6f will suit: see 1221.
960 **THE LEATHER WEDGE 31** [12]5-8-5 (47) F Norton 15/2: 6040525: Handy, ev ch dist, onepcd ins fnl 1f.   hd   **44a**
1408 **FINGER OF FATE 2** [5]4-7-12 bl (40) J F McDonald(3) 7/1: 0000026: Trkd ldrs, ev ch when short of   hd   **36a**
room dist, sn onepcd: qck reapp: just btr 1408.
1310 **SPEEDFIT FREE 7** [6]7-8-10 vis (52) Ann Stokell 40/1: 6240037: Nvr nrr than mid-div: new stable.   nk   **47a**
1336 **ATTORNEY 6** [3]6-9-0 (6ex)vis (56) D Holland 15/2: 3001128: Cl-up till hung left bef 2f out, no extra.   ½   **50a**
1011 **SEA THE WORLD 29** [11]4-9-7 vis (63) N Callan 7/1: 0-513269: Al bhd: btr 859.   ½   **56a**
643 **LADY PROTECTOR 73** [8]5-8-6 (48) J Edmunds 16/1: 0-410300: 10th: Led over 2f, styd cl-up & ev ch   ¾   **39a**
1f out, sn wknd: 10 wk abs: twice below 587.
1267* **AROGANT PRINCE 9** [9]7-9-2 bl (58) R Price 10/1: 0100010: 11th: Al in rear: btr 1267 (gd/soft).   7   **31a**
1012 **SOUNDS LUCKY 29** [10]8-8-12 bl (54) G Gibbons 33/1: 0126040: 12th: Rear, nvr a factor: btr 819 & 737.   1   **24a**
12 Ran Time 59.83 () Owned: Mrs Ann Potts Trained: Edwinstowe

---

1443   4.30 Bet Direct On 0800 32 93 93 Selling Stakes 3yo+ (G)
       £2534 £724 £362   **6f aw rnd**   **Going 61**   +04 Fast   Inside

1310 **ON THE TRAIL 7** [5] D W Chapman 7-9-11 (50) A Culhane 11/4: 0013121: Made all, rdn out ins fnl 1f   **58a**
to hold on: qk reapp: no bid: stays 7f, best up with/forcing the pace around 6f on both AWs: likes claim/sells.
1194 **BLAKESET 14** [3] T D Barron 9-9-11 (63) E Ahern 100/30: 1230532: Cl-up, styd on ins fnl 1f, just   ¾   **55a**
held by wnr: rider received a 2 day whip ban: back to form here, see 730 & 610.
1179 **NEVER WITHOUT ME 14** [7] P J McBride 4-9-11 (54) K Jackson(7) 9/4 FAV: 6452103: Handy, hung left   shd   **54a**
under press dist, kept on & not btn far in 3rd: well bckd: ran to form of win here in 1046 (h'cap, 5f).
1267 **BELLS BEACH 9** [2] P Howling 6-9-6 (54) T E Durcan 6/1: 0156104: Sn outpcd, sn struggling,   2   **43a**
rallied ins fnl 2f, nrst fin: btr 1012 (polytrack).
1032 **POLAR HAZE 27** [6]7-9-11 bl (55) R Price 9/1: 6150455: Handy, wknd fnl 2f: btr 533.   3½   **38a**
1327 **BOUND TO PLEASE 6** [1]9-9-6 vis (47) Ann Stokell 50/1: 50504/-06: b g Warrshan - Hong Kong Girl   17   **0a**
(Petong) Slow away, al in rear: qck reapp: unplcd sole start in late '02 (rtd 43a, seller, P J Makin): claim wnr
here in '02: h'cap wnr here in '01: eff at 5/6f, suited by 7f/1m on fast, gd/soft & polytrack: loves

SOUTHWELL Fibresand THURSDAY 29.04.04 Lefthand, Sharp, Oval Track

fibresand/Southwell: can go well fresh, eff with/without visor: with Miss A Stokell.
1 Feb'02 Sout 7af 62a- F: 2 Jan'02 Sout 7af 64a- F: 2 Mar'01 Sout 7af 69a-66 E: 1 Feb'01 Sout 8af 69a-62 E:
6 Ran Time 1m 16.74 (3.44) Owned: Mr J M Chapman Trained: York

1444 5.00 Bet Direct On Sky Active Handicap Stakes 3yo 46-55 (F) [64]
£2877 £822 £411 1m4f aw Going 61 -24 Slow Inside

1124 **PEPE** 17 [2] R Hollinshead 3-8-13 (49) Stephanie Hollinshead(7) 11/2: 06-66301: Made all, hung **56a**
right under press ins fnl 2f, rdn out: eff at 12f on fibresand: first win: see 1030.
1178 **PRINCESS KIOTTO** 14 [5] T D Easterby 3-9-3 (53) T E Durcan 9/2: 000-52: Handy till outpcd over 4 **53a**
1m, rallied ins fnl 1f, nvr getting to wnr: eff at 12f on fibresand: see 1178.
1280 **ATLANTIC BREEZE** 9 [3] Mrs N Macauley 3-8-11 (47) R Fitzpatrick 7/1: 0-000003: Handy till outpcd 3½ **42a**
over 1m, rallied fnl 1f: worth try over further: btr 159.
1250 **VALIANT AIR** 10 [8] J R Weymes 3-8-10 (1oh) (45) D Holland 11/4 FAV: 040-4524: Cl-up 10f, sn wknd: 1½ **38a**
below form on return to fibresand: btr 1250 (hvy).
1324* **ANGELOS PRIDE** 6 [7]3-9-11 (6ex) (61) G Duffield 4/1: 0233315: Mid-div, fdd fnl 2f: qck reapp: 10 **40a**
below par on step up to 12f: btr 1324 (9.4f).
1000 **NORTHERN SUMMIT** 29 [4]3-8-10 (6oh) (40) F Norton 50/1: 600-06: b g Danehill Dancer - Book Choice 10 **12a**
(North Summit) Slow away, cl-up over 1m, sn fdd: unplcd all 3 '03 starts (rtd 46, mdn).
1324 **REBEL ROUSER** 6 [6]3-8-11 (47) I Mongan 10/1: 000-557: Rear, nvr a factor: qck reapp. 3 **9a**
1240 **MISS HOOFBEATS** 12 [1]3-8-11 (47) B Reilly(3) 11/1: 030-08: b f Unfuwain - Oiselina (Linamix) Al 12 **0a**
in rear, nvr a factor: 3rd of 5 in 1 of 3 '03 starts (rtd 54 at best, mdn): with Miss J Feilden.
8 Ran Time 2m 44.60(10.3) Owned: Mr J D Graham Trained: Upper Longdon

AYR THURSDAY 29.04.04 Lefthand, Galloping Track

Official Going GOOD.

1445 5.50 Kidzplay Maiden Auction Stakes 2yo (H)
£1666 £476 £238 5f str Good/Soft 76 -14 Slow Far Side

HANDSOME LADY [4] I Semple 2-8-3 P Hanagan 5/1: 1: ch f Handsome Ridge - Il Doria (Mac's Imp) **80**
In tch, led trav well dist, clr fnl 1f, easily on debut: Feb foal, half-sister to several modest performers: dam a
sprinter, sire a high-class 1m/10f performer: eff at 5f on gd/soft grnd, runs well fresh: handles a gall trk:
decent debut eff, can hold her own in higher grade.
1173 **SMIDDY HILL** 14 [6] R Bastiman 2-8-3 R Ffrench 5/2: 32: Led till dist sn left bhd by easy wnr: 5 **66**
nicely bckd: acts on gd & gd/soft grnd, sharpish or gall trk: prob met an above average rival, see 1173.
1143 **SPEED DIAL HARRY** 17 [3] K R Burke 2-8-8 Darren Williams 7/4 FAV: 523: Prom, sltly outpcd 1¼ **67**
halfway, kept on again cl-home: consistent, see 1143.
BOND FINESSE [1] B Smart 2-8-7 (4ow) F Lynch 20/1: 4: b f Danehill Dancer - Funny Cut (Sure 1¼ **62**
Blade) Slowly away, modest late gains on debut: mkt drifter: £4,000 April foal: half-sister to sprint wnr Landing
Strip: dam a 1m wnr abroad; sire a smart sprinter: sure to learn from this.
1091 **BEVERLEY BEAU** 21 [5]2-8-8 R Winston 20/1: 55: b c Inchinor - Oriel Girl (Beveled) Speed 3.5f, 7 **43**
wknd: op 14/1: April foal, cost 3,000gns: dam a sprint winning juv, sire a high-class 7f performer.
1224 **MAUREENS LOUGH** 12 [2]2-8-3 J F Egan 13/2: 36: Chsd ldrs, btn halfway: bckd from 10/1. 2½ **32**
6 Ran Time 1m 01.14 (4.54) Owned: Mr David Platt Trained: Carluke

1446 6.20 Hats By Christine Selling Stakes 3yo+ (H)
£1264 £361 £181 1m rnd Good/Soft 76 -24 Slow Inside

1388 **FOREST AIR** 3 [6] Miss L A Perratt 4-8-12 (49) P Hanagan 5/1: 50300-01: br f Charnwood Forest - **49**
Auriga (Belmez) Prom, styd on well to lead cl-home, drvn out: qck reapp, no bid: plcd in a clmr in '03 (rtd 49):
eff at 1m/9f on fast & gd/soft grnd: handles a sharpish or gall trk: suited by sell grade.
1341 **DESERT HEAT** 5 [2] I Semple 6-9-8 bl (66) R Winston 3/1 FAV: 2120042: Dwelt, hdwy to lead when nk **58**
hung left dist, collared cl-home: qck reapp, bght for 4,000: see 467 (AW h'cap, first time visor).
1278 **SCURRA** 9 [3] A C Whillans 5-9-3 (51) P Mulrennan(5) 8/1: 0320-603: Held up, styd on fnl 1f, nrst fin. 1½ **50**
1160 **TINIAN** 15 [8] K R Burke 6-9-8 p (52) Darren Williams 4/1: 3030404: Keen & led early, ev ch till 2½ **50**
wknd dist: rcd too keenly with cheek pieces back on: see 586 & 239.
1160 **ROYAL WINDMILL** 15 [5]5-9-3 p (47) G Faulkner 6/1: 3206-005: b g Ali Royal - Salarya (Darshaan) 1 **43**
Led after 2f till dist, wknd: tchd 8/1: '03 sell wnr, also plcd several times: eff at 7f/1m on firm & soft grnd:
handles a gall or sharp trk, wears cheek pieces: btr than this.
2 Sep'03 Thir 8g/f 52-(43) E: 2 Jul'03 Catt 7fm 44-42 F: 1 Jul'03 Muss 8gd 40-(42) G: 2 Sep'01 Pont 5fm 72- E:
1292 **SENNEN COVE** 8 [7]5-9-3 (40) R Ffrench 16/1: 0-006366: Chsd ldrs, onepcd 2f out. 1¼ **40**
SMEORACH [1]3-7-12 A Nicholls 20/1: 7: ch f My Generation - Mohican (Great Nephew) Slowly 1½ **32**
away, nvr dngrs on debut: half-sister to mid-dist wnr Colonel Custer: with J Moffatt.
1279 **BETTYS VALENTINE** 9 [10]4-8-12 T (30) L Enstone(3) 66/1: 000/-408: Prom, wknd qckly dist: t-strap. 1¼ **29$**
WELCOME ARCHIE [4]4-9-3 T Eaves(5) 66/1: 9: Slowly away, al bhd on Flat debut. 5 **24**
772 **BLUE BIJOU** 60 [9]4-9-3 Dean McKeown 20/1: 0-050: 10th: Chsd ldrs wknd 5f, wknd: 9 wk abs. 11 **4**
10 Ran Time 1m 44.60 (8.00) Owned: Mrs Kathleen Anne Cullen Trained: Ayr

1447 6.50 T Lawrie And Partners Banded Stakes 3yo+ 0-45 (H)
£1628 £465 £233 6f str Good/Soft 76 +03 Fast Far Side

1277 **REDOUBTABLE** 9 [7] D W Chapman 13-9-6 (45) P Makin(7) 9/2: 6141001: Nvr far away, led after **52**
halfway, rdn clr fnl 1f: fair time: eff at 6/7f, stays a sharp 1m: acts on firm, soft grnd & on both AWs: 13yo
who has been in great form in banded company, see 783 & 541 (AW).
1147 **TIZ WIZ** 17 [2] W Storey 3-8-9 (45) K Dalgleish 20/1: 060-02: b f Wizard King - Dannistar 3 **43**

(Puissance) Chsd ldrs, styd on fnl 1f, no ch with wnr: cheaply bght March foal, lightly rcd & modest '03 form: drpd back in trip here, eff at 6f on gd/soft grnd, return to 7f in banded company shld suit.

4104} **JOSHUAS BOY 236** [3] K A Ryan 4-9-6 BL (45) R Winston 5/2 FAV: 600/0-3: ch c Bahhare - Broadway Rosie (Absalom): Prom, kept on under press fnl 1f: bckd from 4/1, tried blnks, reapp: unplcd sole '03 start: modest '02 form, incl in sell company: half-brother to several wnrs, incl smart sprinter Eastern Purple.   *shd*   **43**

1391   **PIRLIE HILL 3** [8] Miss L A Perratt 4-9-6 (45) R Ffrench 6/1: 46000-34: Led till after halfway, wknd fnl 1f: qck reapp since 1391.   *1*   **40**

4104}   **PETANA 236** [6]4-9-6 bl (45) F Lynch 14/1: 625020-5: Held up, some late hdwy, nvr dngrs on reapp.   *2½*   **33**

4497}   **ANDREYEV 214** [5]10-9-6 (45) J F Egan 10/1: 055000-6: Chsd ldrs 4f, sn left bhd: reapp.   *1¾*   **28**

1415*   **GRAND VIEW 2** [4]8-9-12 p (40) P Hanagan 3/1: 0-604217: Prom till halfway, wknd: top-weight: too sn?   *7*   **14**

2188}   **SQUARE DANCER 318** [1]8-9-6 t (40) D McGaffin 66/1: 200/000-8: Speed till halfway: reapp.   *5*   **0**

1146   **TAPLEON 17** [9]3-8-9 (40) T Eaves(5) 100/1: 000-69: Chsd ldrs, outpcd halfway.   *8*   **0**

9 Ran   Time 1m 13.69 (4.39)   Owned: Mr David W Chapman   Trained: York

---

1448   **7.20 Alan Macdonald Happy Birthday Banded Stakes 3yo+ 0-45 (H)**
£1624 £464 £232   **7f50y rnd**   **Good/Soft 76**   **-50 Slow**   Inside

1278   **STELLITE 9** [2] J S Goldie 4-9-7 (45) J F Egan 7/1: 0050-01: Handy, styd on to lead dist, drvn out: eff at 7f, has tried further: acts on gd/soft grnd: apprec drop to banded grade: see 1278.   **48**

3854}   **HEBENUS 248** [1] T A K Cuthbert 5-9-7 (45) F Lynch 8/1: 605250-2: b g Hamas - Stinging Nettle (Sharpen Up): Led, hdd dist, rallied ins fnl 1f, not btn far: reapp: rnr-up once in '03 (sell h'cap, R A Fahey): h'cap wnr in '02: eff at 6f/1m on fast & gd/soft grnd: has tried blnks & cheek pieces.   *1*   **45**
2 Aug'03 Yarm 8.0g/f 44-43 G: 2 Jul'02 Donc 6gd 50-53 D: 1 Jul'02 Hami 6gd 57-49 E:

4298}   **MOONLIGHT SONG 225** [4] John A Harris 7-9-7 (45) D Fentiman(7) 14/1: 000060-3: b f Mujadil - Model Show (Dominion): Cl-up, edged left under press ins fnl 2f, kept on & not btn far in 3rd: clr rem on reapp: unplcd in '03 (rtd 49, List): h'cap wnr in '02, also sand fnd in late '01 (rtd 50a, h'cap): suited by 7f, stays 1m: acts on fast, hvy & fibresand, likes Southwell & handles any trk: has tried cheek pieces.   *nk*   **44**
1 Jun'02 Ayr 7.2hvy 58-51 C: 2 Mar'01 Sout 7af 58a- E: 2 Jan'01 Sout 8af 66a-65 E: 1 Jan'01 Sout 7af 64a- F:

996   **TANCRED ARMS 29** [6] D W Barker 8-9-7 (45) L Enstone(3) 15/2: 01060-04: b f Clantime - Mischievous Miss (Niniski): Mid-div, outpcd after 4f, modest late gains: fills h'cap wnr in '03: won 2 appr h'caps, sell & clmr in '02: suited by 6/7.5f, stays 1m: acts on firm, hvy & fibresand: eff with/without visor: with D W Barker.   *5*   **34**
1 Jun'03 Ayr 7.2g/f 44-40 E: 1 Jul'02 Catt 7gd 55-49 F: 1 Jul'02 Ches 7.5fm 48-43 E: 1 May'02 Newc 7gd 46- F: 1 Mar'02 Catt 7g/s 49- G: 1 Apr'01 Sout 7af 43a-39 F:

4064}   **MERLINS PROFIT 238** [5]4-9-7 (45) R Winston 12/1: 40/0003-5: Mid-div till outpcd over 4f, modest late gains: reapp & new stable.   *nk*   **33**

97}   **GOODBYE MRS CHIPS 520** [3]5-9-7 t (45) T Eaves(5) 16/1: 043000/-6: Handy 5f, fdd: jumps abs.   *3½*   **26**

1164   **MEXICAN 15** [8]5-9-7 p (45) P Hanagan 7/1: 00500-07: Cl-up 5f, fdd: jumps abs.   *1¾*   **22**

776   **ROSTI 60** [7]4-9-7 (45) G Faulkner 11/4 FAV: 4-113068: Rear, nvr a factor: well bckd after 10 wk abs: v disapp on return to turf: btr 408 (polytrack).   *1¾*   **18**

8 Ran   Time 1m 32.64 (8.84)   Owned: Mr J S Goldie   Trained: Glasgow

---

1449   **7.50 Christine Sadler Designer Jewellery Banded Stakes 3yo+ 0-40 (H)**
£1449 £414 £207   **1m5f13y**   **Good/Soft 76**   **-16 Slow**   Inside

4414}   **RIGHTY HO 219** [9] W H Tinning 10-9-10 (40) R Winston 9/1: 60/3200-1: b g Reprimand - Challanging (Mill Reef): Prom, led 2f out, drvn out to hold on: reapp: plcd on first 2 of only 4 '03 starts (sellers, rtd 44): plcd 3 times in '02 (rtd 36, h'cap): h'cap & sell wnr in '01: eff at 10f/2m on firm & soft, any trk: eff with/without visor & goes well fresh: a gd weight-carrier who enjoyed drop to banded grade.   **42**
2 May'03 Catt 13.8fm 43-(43) G: 1 Aug'01 Redc 11g/f 43-38 E: 1 Apr'01 Ripo 10hvy 50- F:

1240   **TIMBUKTU 12** [2] C W Thornton 3-8-3 (40) P Hanagan 7/2 FAV: 006-0002: b g Efisio - Sirene Bleu Marine (Secreto): Mid-div, prog & ev chr 1f out, kept on but just held: op 5/1: clr rem: left prev modest form bhd on step up to13f, acts on gd/soft grnd: apprec drop to banded grade & can find similar.   *nk*   **41**

3679}   **HAYSTACKS 256** [4] James Moffatt 8-9-10 p (35) A Nicholls 9/2: 000060-3: b g Contract Law - Florissa (Persepolis): Slow away, prog ins fnl 2f, nvr rch ldrs: tchd 6/1: long jumps abs, earlier won 2 h'cap hdles (rtd 111h, stays 3m1.5f on firm & soft, eff with visor & cheek pieces): unplcd on Flat in '03 (rtd 48, class stks): h'cap wnr in '01: eff at 10/12f, stays 2m on firm & soft, eff with/without visor.   *5*   **35**
1 Sep'01 Newc 16fm 50-45 E:

1278   **BALALAIKA TUNE 9** [8] W Storey 5-9-10 (40) Darren Williams 16/1: 0-000604: Keen handy, edged left & no extra ins fnl 2f: see 852.   *1*   **34**

3007}   **NAUTICAL STAR 646** [6]9-9-10 (35) T Eaves(5) 16/1: 432050/-5: Led early, styd prom till fdd fnl 2f.   *1½*   **32**

353   **COPPLESTONE 112** [1]8-9-10 p (35) K Dalgleish 10/1: 26565-06: Handy, no room 3f out, sn no extra.   *½*   **31**

1329   **AMANPURI 6** [5]6-9-10 (35) Dean McKeown 5/1: 0-040627: Handy till no room 2f out, sn no extra.   *1*   **30**

1026   **IPLEDGEALLEGIANCE 27** [3]8-9-10 (35) P Makin(7) 7/1: 5000558: Rear, nvr a factor: btr 446.   *7*   **22**

1332   **JEZADIL 6** [7]6-9-10 p (35) Kristin Stubbs(7) 14/1: 430-0039: Led 10f out, hdd 2f out, fdd.   *10*   **12**

9 Ran   Time 2m 56.61 (12.01)   Owned: Mr W H Tinning   Trained: York

---

1450   **8.20 Racing Here On Saturday 22nd May Banded Stakes 3yo+ 0-40 (H)**
£1449 £414 £207   **1m2f**   **Good/Soft 76**   **+03 Fast**   Inside

1278   **KINGSDON 9** [4] T J Fitzgerald 7-9-7 vis t (40) J F Egan 1/1 FAV: 0-010441: Handy, led 2f out, pushed clr, val 11L+: well bckd: suited by 1m/10f on fast, soft & polytrack: eff in a t-strap, with/without a visor: hacked up on drop to banded grade & more prizes await: see 654.   **47+**

1287   **SMARTER CHARTER 8** [2] Mrs L Stubbs 11-9-7 (35) Kristin Stubbs(7) 10/1: 0000-502: Keen rear, styd on to chase wnr ins fnl 1f & al held: clr rem: see 1287.   *8*   **37**

1095   **OPTIMUM NIGHT 21** [7] P D Niven 5-9-7 (40) R Winston 5/1: 000-03: b g Superlative - Black Bess (Hasty Word): Handy & ev ch 3f out, sn no extra: unplcd all 3 '03 starts (rtd 52, mdn): mod jumps form prev.   *5*   **29**

1118   **HOWARDS DREAM 18** [6] D A Nolan 6-9-7 t (35) T Eaves(5) 25/1: 50060-04: b g King's Theatre - Keiko (Generous): Prom & ev ch 3f out, sn wknd: h'cap wnr in '03: missed '02: unplcd in '01 (rtd 53, l Semple, mdn): eff at 12f, has tried 2m: acts on fast grnd: eff with t-strap, has tried cheek pieces. 1 Jul'03 Hami 12.1g/f 45-40 F: *2½*   **26**

1213   **SIR BOND 13** [1]3-8-7 (3ow) (40) F Lynch 6/1: 0-045: Led over 7f, wknd: btr 1213.   *nk*   **28**

1118   **BRIDEWELL 18** [3]5-9-7 (30) P Hanagan 5/1: 0000-006: Rear, nvr a factor: btr 1118.   *7*   **15**

AYR   THURSDAY 29.04.04   Lefthand, Galloping Track

640   **ANACAPRI 74** [5]4-9-7   (35) L Enstone(3) 50/1: 0-0607: Cl-up 7f, fdd: 10 wk abs: btr 531.   1¾   **13**
7 Ran   Time 2m 11.72(7.32)   Owned: Mr Mike Browne   Trained: Malton

LINGFIELD   Polytrack   THURSDAY 29.04.04   Lefthand, Sharp, Undulating Track

Official Going Standard

1451   5.35 Littlewoods Bet Direct Amateur Riders' Banded Stakes 4yo+ 0-45 (H)
£1449 £414 £207   **1m**   **Going 46**   **-16 Slow**   Outside

747   **LITTLETON ZEPHIR 62** [11] Mrs P Townsley 5-11-0   (45) Mrs C Thompson(5) 14/1: 06-02001: In tch, eff   **46a**
to lead over 2f out, pushed out: 2 mth abs: eff at 1m/10f, tried 12f: acts on fast grnd & both AWs: eff
with/without cheek pieces & blnks, tried visor: runs well fresh: see 464.
828   **GRAN CLICQUOT 51** [4] G P Enright 9-11-0   (40) Mr J Pemberton(7) 16/1: 4500-002: Held up, hdwy 2f   1¾   **42a**
out, chsd wnr ins last, no impress: 7 wk abs: acts on firm & polytrack: see 770.
1090   **THEATRE LADY 22** [2] P D Evans 6-11-0   (40) Miss E Folkes(3) 11/4 FAV: 0363043: Led till over 3f   1½   **39a**
out, sn outpcd, some late gains: see 539.
1266   **ROBIN SHARP 10** [12] J Akehurst 6-11-0 p (45) Mr S Gascoyne(7) 12/1: 2605004: In tch wide, eff over   shd   **38a**
2f out, sn no extra: btr 457.
1413   **SINGLE TRACK MIND 2** [5]6-11-0 P (45) Mr M Pattinson(5) 3/1: 5450235: Dwelt, bhd, modest late gains.   2   **34a**
1379   **PRINCE MINATA 3** [10]9-11-0   (40) Miss A Hockley(7) 7/1: 0030406: Nvr a factor: qk reapp.   ¾   **32a**
1245   **LADY LIESEL 10** [3]4-11-0   (40) Miss Donna Handley(6) 12/1: 0030047: Led over 3f out till over 2f out.   3½   **25a**
1223   **MARAVEDI 12** [9]4-11-0 VIS (45) Miss A L Turner(5) 33/1: 0000-08: ch f Hector Protector - Manuetti   1   **23a**
(Sadler's Wells) Dwelt, al bhd: tried visor: unplcd in '03 (rtd 51).
1341   **MUTABARI 5** [7]10-11-0   (45) Mr John Evans(7) 25/1: 50000-09: In tch wide, wknd 2f out.   1¾   **19a**
1332   **MIDDLEMISS 6** [8]4-11-0   (40) Mr J J Best(5) 25/1: 0/5554-00: 10th: b f Midhish - Teresa Deevey   nk   **18a**
(Runnett) In tch, wknd over 2f out: poor form.
891   **SINGULARITY 38** [6]4-11-0   (40) Mr L Newnes(3) 10/1: 03055-00: 11th: Dwelt, in tch, wknd over 2f out.   5   **8a**
4460} **MR LOVERMAN 216** [1]4-11-0   (45) Miss V Haigh(4) 16/1: 000000-0: 12th: Reluctant to race & left 25L   10   **0a**
at start, al bhd.
12 Ran   Time 1m 41.14 (4.94)   Owned: Classic Security UK Ltd   Trained: Godalming

1452   6.05 Betdirect Co Uk Banded Stakes 4yo+ 0-40 (H)
£1439 £411 £206   **6f**   **Going 46**   **+00 Fast**   Inside

1261   **ALASTAIR SMELLIE 10** [2] S L Keightley 8-8-12 vis (35) P McCabe 8/1: 30-00221: Prom, hdwy to lead   **48a**
over 2f out, rdn clr: eff over 5/7f on fast, hvy & both AWs: see 1261, 847.
1413* **BAYTOWN FLYER 2** [4] P S McEntee 4-9-4   (40) L Dettori 4/11 FAV: 1112112: Led till over 2f out,   3½   **44a**
not pce of wnr: bckd at odds-on: btr expected after 1413.
1290   **ONEFORTHEBOYS 8** [5] D Flood 5-8-12   (40) S Whitworth 8/1: 4003063: Dwelt, bhd, modest late gains.   2   **32a**
1184   **SOTONIAN 14** [3] P S Felgate 11-8-12   (40) S Hitchcott(3) 12/1: 3305334: Chsd ldr till 3f out, no extra.   2   **26a**
1415   **TONG ICE 2** [1]5-8-12   (30) R Brisland 33/1: 400/0-065: Al bhd: see 1415.   ½   **24a**
5 Ran   Time 1m 13.15 (2.75)   Owned: Mrs C C Regalado-Gonzalez   Trained: Melton Mowbray

1453   6.35 Bet In Running @ Betdirect Co Uk Tri-Banded Stakes 3yo 0-45 (H)
£1607 £459 £230   **6f**   **Going 46**   **+01 Fast**   Inside

901   **YAMATO PINK 37** [7] Mrs H Sweeting 3-8-9   (40) G Baker 11/2: 04660-01: ch f Bijou d'Inde - Time Or   **48a**
Never (Dowsing) Slow away, held up, hdwy to lead over 1f out, rdn clr: unplcd in '03 (rtd 55, with K Burke):
imprvd for new stable back at 6f on fibresand.
1330   **FAYR FIRENZE 6** [2] M F Harris 3-9-0 vis (45) S Righton 4/1: 6-046252: In tch, lost place over 2f   2½   **46a**
out, rallied late: qck reapp: handles polytrack & fibresand: see 1312, 846.
1085   **PARALLEL LINES 22** [4] P D Evans 3-9-0   (45) K Fallon 9/4 FAV: 0004003: Held up, brief eff over 1f   ¾   **44a**
out, no impress: bckd: see 832, 767.
975   **JASMINE PEARL 30** [8] T M Jones 3-9-0   (45) S Whitworth 7/2: 55-36004: Cl-up, led 2f out till over   ½   **42a**
1f out, no extra: see 389 (fibresand).
703   **ANATOM 66** [1]3-8-4 T (35) L Dettori 15/2: 00660-05: Al bhd: 2 mth abs: now with D McEntee.   3   **23a**
735   **MUST BE SO 63** [3]3-9-0   (45) N Chalmers(5) 14/1: 31-50006: In tch, wknd well over 1f out: 2 mth abs.   hd   **32a**
1312   **INDRANI 7** [5]3-9-0 P (45) N Pollard 14/1: 0640047: Led till 2f out, wknd: cheek pieces: see 797.   3   **23a**
7 Ran   Time 1m 13.12 (2.72)   Owned: Mr P Sweeting   Trained: Marlborough

1454   7.05 Special Offers @ Betdirect Co Uk Tri-Banded Stakes 3yo 0-45 (H)
£1432 £409 £205   **1m2f**   **Going 46**   **-47 Slow**   Inside

1416+ **DIAL SQUARE 2** [3] P Howling 3-9-6 (6ex) (51) K Fallon 1/4 FAV: 1323111: Rcd keen in tch, hdwy   **52a**
over 1f out, led ins fnl 1f & rdn out: landed treble, qck reapp: eff btwn 7f/10f, likes Lingfield/polytrack: gd
run under top-weight, thriving at present: v tough: see 1246 & 535.
1324   **SCORCHIO 6** [1] M F Harris 3-9-0   (45) L Dettori 7/1: 60006-62: Led, rdn & hdd ins fnl 1f, just   ½   **44a**
held: stays 10f on polytrack: imprvd on drop into banded company: see 1324.
1240   **LENWADE 12** [2] G G Margarson 3-9-0   (45) J Mackay 7/1: 6000-003: gr f Environment Friend -   2½   **40a**
Branitska (Mummy's Pet) Trkd ldr, ch 2f out, onepcd over 1f out: fin unplcd all '03 starts (rtd 66).
971   **OUT OF MY WAY 31** [4] T M Jones 3-8-4   (30) S Whitworth 20/1: 400-0004: ch f Fraam - Ming Blue   5   **22a**
(Primo Dominie) Bhd, hdwy 3f out, wknd over 1f out: modest in '03 (unplcd in sellers & a mdn, rtd 26).
4 Ran   Time 2m 12.15 (9.35)   Owned: Mr Rory Murphy   Trained: Newmarket

LINGFIELD Polytrack THURSDAY 29.04.04 Lefthand, Sharp, Undulating Track

1455
7.35 Bet Direct On 0800 32 93 93 Claiming Stakes 3yo+ (H)
£1278 £365 £183 1m2f Going 46 -19 Slow Inside

1223 **MONDURU** 12 [2] G L Moore 7-9-10 bl e (50) R L Moore 4/5 FAV: 0122321: Trkd ldrs, led over 1f out, 52a
pushed out ins fnl 1f: eff around 7/10f on firm, soft & both AWs, acts on a sharp trk: made most of drop in grade.
1164 **SENOR TORAN** 15 [7] P Burgoyne 4-9-10 (47) L P Keniry(3) 2/1: 00-34302: Trkd ldr, onepcd over 1f out. 1¾ 48a
968 **FITZ THE BILL** 31 [6] N B King 4-9-2 BL (30) J Mackay 16/1: 6000-003: b f Mon Tresor - In The Sky 3 35a
(Imp Society) Led until over 1f out, sn no extra: fin unplcd all '03 starts (rtd 44): first time blnks.
450 **ISLAND STAR** 99 [4] G P Enright 4-9-7 (40) R Brisland 16/1: 060-0004: b g Turtle Island - 1¼ 38a
Orthorising (Aragon) Keen & trkd ldrs, outpcd 2f out: long abs, hdles unplcd since race 450 (nov clmr, rd 66h):
4th at best in '03 (h'cap, class stks, rtd 71a, with P Harris): well btn both '02 mdn starts (rtd 64a): stays 10f,
handles fast grnd: has tried a visor: new stable (prev with S Dow).
878 **SINK OR SWIM** 41 [5]6-9-5 N Chalmers(5) 16/1: 005: Rear, nvr nr ldrs: 6 wk abs. 3½ 31a
1291 **MISTER GRAHAM** 8 [3]9-9-10 p O Urbina 12/1: 046: Rear, chsd ldrs 5f out, wknd over 3f out, t.o. 13 16a
6 Ran Time 2m 09.33 (6.53) Owned: Pleasure Palace Racing Trained: Brighton

1456
8.05 Bet Direct On Sky Active Banded Stakes 3yo+ 0-40 (H)
£1477 £422 £211 1m5f Going 46 -19 Slow Inside

968 **ROYALE PEARL** 31 [9] R Ingram 4-9-9 (40) Dane O'Neill 14/1: 340-0041: gr f Cloudings - Ivy Edith 44a
(Blakeney) Keen in rear, hdwy 3f out, led well over 1f out, rdn out ins fnl 1f: 3rd 1 of 6 '03 starts (fills h'cap,
rtd 62 at best): first win here: eff at 13f on polytrack, acts on a sharp trk.
1265 **LADY LAKSHMI** 10 [8] R Guest 4-9-9 (40) J Mackay 9/1: 35030-32: Rear, outpcd 3f out, hdwy 3f out, 2 41a
chsd wnr ins fnl 1f & kept on for press: eff at 12/13f on fast & both AWs: see 1265.
1411 **LEOPHIN DANCER** 2 [4] P W Hiatt 6-9-10 (40) B Doyle 7/2: 0-601223: Trkd ldrs, onepace. 1 40a
967} **EAU PURE** 390 [5] G L Moore 7-9-10 (40) R L Moore 11/4 FAV: 000/0R//0-4: b f Epervier Bleu - Eau 2½ 36a$
de Nuit (Kings Lake) In tch, outpcd 4f out, mod late gains: reapp, hdles fit: won 2 h'cap hdles in 03/04 (eff at
2m1f/2m3.5f on gd & soft, rtd 107h at best): well beat sole '03 start (fills h'cap, rtd 3a, with B Pearce).
1244 **SYLVAN TWISTER** 10 [7]5-9-10 (35) N Pollard 50/1: 00-00-555: Rear, outpcd 5f out, onepcd fnl 2f. nk 36a
1289 **DAFA** 8 [2]8-9-10 bl (40) S W Kelly 14/1: ///0/-11606: Led till joined 6f out, hdd well over 1f out. 1¼ 34a
1414 **ANNIVERSARY GUEST** 2 [6]5-9-10 (40) C Catlin 6/1: 05-03437: Keen in rear, fdd 3f out. 1½ 32a
1244 **LADY XANTHIA** 10 [3]3-8-3 (35) P Doe 33/1: 0066-048: Keen & trkd ldr, ch 6f out, fdd 2f out. 3½ 27a
1411* **SERAPH** 2 [1]4-10-1 p (40) K Fallon 10/30: 1033219: Chsd ldrs, wknd over 5f out, t.o. dist 0a
9 Ran Time 2m 50.82(8.52) Owned: Mr Glen Antill Trained: Epsom

MUSSELBURGH FRIDAY 30.04.04 Righthand, Sharp Track

Official Going Good (Good/Firm places)

1457
2.20 East Lothian Handicap Stakes 3yo 0-75 (E) [76]
£4105 £1263 £632 5f str Good/Soft 73 -01 Slow Stands Side

1268* **HES A ROCKET** 10 [4] K R Burke 3-7-12 (6ex)(3oh)bl (46) Lisa Jones(3) 7/1: 003-6511: Bumped start, 61
in tch, hdwy to lead over 1f out, rdn clr: prev with Mrs C Dunnett: eff at 5f on gd/soft, prob fibresand: wears
blnks: fine start for new stable having been gelded, shld land qk-fire hat-trick: see 1268.
1102 **PRINCESS KAI** 22 [5] R Ingram 3-8-4 bl (55) G Duffield 7/2 FAV: 3-100342: Cl up, eff over 1f out, 3 58
not pace of wnr: acted another gd run: see 1102.
1374 **GARNOCK VENTURE** 4 [8] A Berry 3-8-4 bl (55) F Norton 12/1: 3-400103: Chsd ldrs, onepace over 1f shd 58
out: acts on gd/soft & fibresand: sell wnr in 871.
995* **LINDA GREEN** 30 [1] P A Blockley 3-8-9 (60) Dean McKeown 6/1: 42030-14: In tch, eff 2f out, no 2 57
impress: drifted from 7/2: btr 995 (gd, class stks).
1229 **PETERS CHOICE** 13 [7]3-9-7 P (72) N Callan 9/2: 2011-005: Led till over 1f out, wknd: cheekpieces. ½ 67
4887} **FEU DUTY** 188 [9]3-8-11 (62) R Havlin 12/1: 0010-6: b f Fayruz - Fire Reply (Royal Academy) In nk 56
tch, wknd 1f out: won 2nd of 4 juv starts (mdn auct fill): eff at 5f on fast grnd: likes dominating on a sharp trk.
1 Sep'03 Muss 5g/f 64- E:
1374 **BLADES DAUGHTER** 4 [2]3-7-13 (1ow)(4oh)P (45) P Fessey 14/1: 000-607: gr f Paris House - 4 32
Banningham Blade (Sure Blade) Al bhd: qck reapp, tried cheekpieces: poor form.
1116 **GLOBAL ACHIEVER** 20 [3]3-9-5 BL (70) R Ffrench 5/1: 322108: Swerved right start, al bhd: tried 5 37
blnks & now twice below 750 (fibresand).
4237} **OL LUCY BROON** 228 [6]3-8-5 (56) J F Egan 25/1: 62600-9: b f Royal Applause - Jay Gee Ell (Vaigly 8 0
Great) Al bhd on reapp: rnr-up in a mdn in '03: prob stays 6f on gd: sprint bred. 2 Aug'03 Ayr 6gd 56- D:
9 Ran Time 1m 01.25 (3.75) Owned: Mrs Lorraine Charge Trained: Leyburn

1458
2.50 Royal Bank Of Scotland Median Auction Maiden Stakes 2yo (E)
£4017 £1236 £618 5f str Good/Soft 73 -15 Slow Stands Side

1249 **MARY READ** 11 [2] B Smart 2-8-9 F Lynch 12/1: 31: Made virtually all, styd on well fnl 1f, rdn 81
out: eff at 5f on gd/soft & hvy: likes to force the pace: going the right way, see 1249.
1107 **CHISELLED** 20 [3] K R Burke 2-9-0 Darren Williams 3/1 FAV: 42: b c Rossini - Con Dancer (Shareef 1¼ 80
Dancer) In tch, hdwy to chall dist, not pace of wnr but clr of rem: Feb foal, cost 20,000gns: eff at 5f on gd/soft:
sharper for debut, shld win a race.
1117 **MONSIEUR MIRASOL** 19 [7] K A Ryan 2-9-0 N Callan 8/1: 33: Slow away, bhd, some late gains, no 2½ 75
threat: prob ran to form of 1117.
SECRET PACT [8] M Johnston 2-9-0 K Dalgleish 16/1: 4: br c Lend A Hand - Schust Madame (Second 3 67
Set) Cl up, wknd fnl 1f: Mar foal, cost 100,000 gns: half brother to a 6/7f juv wnr: dam 12f wnr.
CHILALI [1]2-8-9 F Norton 33/1: 5: b f Monashee Mountain - Pam Story (Sallust) Prom, wknd hd 61

411

appr fnl 1f: debut: Apr foal, cost E6,000: half sister to wnrs over 5/7f: dam plcd at 5f: bred to be speedy.

1091 **FORFEITER 22** [5]2-9-0 K Darley 7/2: 26: In tch, wknd over 1f out: btr 1091 (fast grnd, debut).   nk   65

  AZA WISH [4]2-8-9 S Righton 100/1: 7: b f Mujadil - Kilcsem Eile (Commanche Run) Slow away,   shd   59
al bhd: Mar foal, cost E8,000: half sister to smart hurdler Al Eile: bred to need 1m+.

1161 **TIFFIN DEANO 16** [9]2-9-0 G Faulkner 15/2: 58: Handy, wknd fnl 1f: see 1161.   ½   62

1149 **CAMPEON 17** [6]2-9-0 K Fallon 7/2: 059: In tch, wknd 2f out: bckd: btr 1149.   ½   60

9 Ran   Time 1m 01.91 (4.41)   Owned: S J F Racing   Trained: Thirsk

---

1459   3.20 Famous Grouse Handicap Stakes 3yo+ 0-85 (D)   [83]
£6747 £2076 £1038   **1m6f**   **Good/Soft 73**   **-45 Slow**   Inside

1252 **TONI ALCALA 11** [2] R F Fisher 5-8-9 (64) K Fallon 5/2 JT FAV: 3540231: Handy, hdwy trav well to   73
lead over 1f out, eased, val 5L+: apprec return to 1m, gd/soft & fibresand, any trk: tough.

4444} **HIGHLAND GAMES 218** [1] J G Given 4-10-0 (85) K Darley 6/1: 511060-2: b g Singspiel - Highland   3   87
Gift (Generous) Cl up, led over 3f out till over 1f out, onepace: clr rem, gelded: won 2 of 6 '03 starts (mdn &
3-rnr class stks, with Sir M Stoute): eff at 12f, stays 14f: acts on fast & gd/soft grnd, fair or sharp trks.
1 May'03 Wind 11.6g/f 88-(85) C: 1 May'03 Yarm 11.5gd 85- D:

424 **COMPTON ECLAIRE 105** [3] G A Butler 4-8-0 bl (57) P Hanagan 100/30: 01034-33: Hld up, eff over 3f   7   52
out, sn btn: bckd from 11/2: longer trip: btr 243, 24 (claimer, polytrack, visor).

2504} **AUTUMN FANTASY 307** [4] B Ellison 5-8-12 t (67) T Eaves(5) 7/1: 000000-4: In tch 11f, wknd: op   10   52
10/1: unplcd in '03 (rtd 58): plcd over hdls (rtd 78h): '02 wnr for J Gosden (h'cap): suited by a gall 2m on fast & gd.

3142*}**KAHYASI PRINCESS 280** [5]4-9-13 (84) R Ffrench 5/2 JT FAV: 101311-5: b f Kahyasi - Dungeon   3   65
Princess (Danehill) Led till over 3f out, wknd: won 4 of 11 '03 starts (claim & 3 h'caps): eff at 12f, suited by 2m:
handles soft, likes gd/soft & fm: best up with/forcing the pace on a stiff/gall trk: progressive, tough & genuine
last term.   1 Jul'03 Asco 16.2gd 85-72 D: 1 Jul'03 Hayd 16.2g/f 77-68 E: 1 Jul'03 Beve 16.2g/s 69-61 E:
1 Jun'03 Carl 11.9fm 62-(63) F: 2 Apr'03 Beve 12.1g/f 71- E:

5 Ran   Time 3m 13.02 (16.52)   Owned: Mr Alan Willoughby   Trained: Ulverston

---

1460   3.50 Royal Bank Of Scotland Handicap Stakes 3yo 0-95 (C)   [100]
£11505 £3540 £1770   **7f30y rnd**   **Good/Soft 73**   **+01 Fast**   Outside

955 **REDWOOD ROCKS 34** [1] B Smart 3-8-6 (78) F Lynch 12/1: 32100-01: b g Blush Rambler - Crisp and   83
Cool (Oggyian) Made all, kept on gamely for press ins last: '03 raced mdn wnr: eff over a stiff or sharp 7f on fast &
gd/soft: likes dominating but can be too keen (not here): back to form.
1 Oct'03 Newc 7gd 82-(80) F: 2 Sep'03 Donc 7gd 81-75 D:

1305 **MAN OF LETTERS 8** [3] M Johnston 3-8-1 (73) R Ffrench 5/2 FAV: 5-4322: In tch, strong run over 1f   ½   77
out, styd on ins last, just failed: another gd run: worth a try at 1m now: see 1305.

1094* **HATCH 22** [4] R M H Cowell 3-9-2 (88) P Hanagan 11/2: 0-221313: Slow away, hld up, hdwy over 1f   nk   91
out, kept on ins last, nrst fin: clr rem: acts on fm & gd/soft: another gd run having been raised 9lb for wng over
C/D in 1094: fast improving.

885 **RYDAL 41** [8] G A Butler 3-9-3 (89) T P Queally(3) 12/1: 42221-04: ch c Gilded Time - Tennis   5   84
Partner (Northern Dancer) In tch, eff over 1f out, sn wknd: won last of 5 '03 starts (mdn): stays 1m on fast, gd &
polytrack, any trk: won in first time blnks & for forcing tactics.
1 Nov'03 Muss 8g/f 89-(89) D: 2 Oct'03 Yarm 7.0gd 85-(83) D: 2 Oct'03 Ling 7ap 81a- D: 2 Sep'03 Newm 6g/f 82- E:

3635} **BESSEMER 259** [6]3-9-7 (93) K Dalgleish 16/1: 310-5: b g Carnegie - Chalna (Darshaan) Cl up,   2   84
wknd 2f out: gelded: won 2nd of 3 '03 starts (mdn): eff at 6f on fast & gd grnd, gall trk: shld stay 7f/1m (dam 12f
wnr).   1 Aug'03 Ayr 6gd 84- D:

1125* **RIVER TREAT 18** [2]3-8-13 (85) K Fallon 100/30: 524-16: In tch, wknd 2f out: bckd tho' op 2/1.   5   68

4605} **IMPERIAL ECHO 209** [5]3-8-13 (85) K Darley 7/1: 421433-7: b g Labeeb - Regal Baby (Northern Baby)   shd   68
In tch, wknd 2f out: op 12/1: acts on fm & gd/soft: won in '03, fine 3rd in Redcar 2yo Trophy:: eff at 6f/7f on fast & gd/soft,
gall trks.   1 Aug'03 Ayr 7.2g/f 82- E: 2 Aug'03 Redc 6g/f 88- F: 2 Apr'03 Newc 5g/f 85- D:

1206 **LOMMEL 14** [7]3-9-3 (89) D R McCabe 25/1: 15-08: b c Lomitas - Idrica (Rainbow Quest) Dwelt al   23   26
bhd: won first of 2 '03 starts (nov maid auct): eff at 6f (dam 1m/12f scorer) on fm, has disapp on polytrack: has run
well fresh.   1 Jun'03 Yarm 6.0fm 92- E:

8 Ran   Time 1m 30.13 (5.23)   Owned: Mr Dan Hall   Trained: Thirsk

---

1461   4.20 Edmonds Co Uk Classified Stakes 3yo+ 0-75 (D)
£5382 £1656 £828   **1m rnd**   **Good/Soft 73**   **+00 Fast**   Outside

964 **LOVE IN SEATTLE 32** [5] M Johnston 4-9-10 (78) K Dalgleish 14/1: 422-01: b c Seattle Slew -   80
Tamise (Time For A Change) Made all, styd on for press fnl 1f: rnr-up in 2 of 3 '03 starts (mdns): apprec return to
1m, stays 10f on fast & gd/soft, gall trks: goes well fresh: enjoys forcing the pace.
2 Apr'03 Newm 12gd 81- D: 2 Apr'03 Leic 10.0g/f 81- D:

1164 **TONY TIE 16** [3] J S Goldie 8-9-7 (75) J F Egan 11/2: 0060-622: Hld up, hdwy over 2f out, styd on   ½   75
well ins last, just held: clr rem: tough, see 1164, 964.

693 **HAIL THE CHIEF 69** [6] D Nicholls 7-9-8 (76) K Fallon 4/1 FAV: 650-1403: Chsd wnr, onepace fnl   4   68
2f: 10 wk abs: btr 360 (aw).

1095 **KHANJAR 22** [4] D R Loder 4-9-9 vis (77) D R McCabe 11/2: 24/22-24: Slow away, eff 2f out, onepace.   ¾   67

83 **ASTROCHARM 160** [8]5-9-4 bl (75) M Henry 6/1: 300400-5: b f Charnwood Forest - Charm The Stars   hd   61
(Roi Danzig) In tch, eff 2f out, onepace: op 7/2: rnr-up in a h'cap in '03: won 2 h'caps in '02: stays an easy 10f,
suited by 1m: acts on gd/soft & any trk: has tried blnks: slipped down the weights.
2 Aug'03 Newm 8fm 80-80 D: 1 Sep'02 Thir 8gd 88-81 C: 2 Jul'02 Yarm 7fm 83-78 D: 1 Jun'02 Pont 8fm 83-72 E:
1 Sep'01 Ling 7gd 76-68 E:

1131 **AIMEES DELIGHT 18** [7]4-9-7 (78) G Duffield 14/1: 0310-006: b f Robellino - Lloc (Absalom) In   ¾   62
tch, wknd 2f out: '03 dual h'cap wnr: stays 1m on fm, fast & fibresand, any trk: prob wants faster grnd.
1 Jun'03 Nott 8.2g/f 80-77 D: 1 May'03 Warw 7.1g/f 77-71 D: 1 Jul'02 Ripo 5g/f 77- F: 2 May'02 Wolv 5af 76a- E:

1214 **SARRAAF 14** [1]8-9-7 (72) N Callan 9/2: 2-423257: Al bhd: btr 1214.   3   56

928 **SAWWAAH 35** [2]7-9-12 (80) A Nicholls 14/1: 01030-08: In tch, wknd 2f out: tchd 20/1.   2   57

8 Ran   Time 1m 43.34 (5.84)   Owned: Mr M Doyle   Trained: Middleham

MUSSELBURGH FRIDAY 30.04.04 Righthand, Sharp Track

1462 **4.50 Royal Bank Of Scotland Maiden Stakes 3yo+ (D)**
£4716 £1451 £726 **1m1f** **Good/Soft 73** **-01 Slow** Outside

1130 **MACLEAN 18** [1] Sir Michael Stoute 3-8-9 K Fallon 4/9 FAV: 2-21: Handy, hdwy to lead over 1f out, rdn out: well bckd: stays 9f well on gd/soft grnd & prob any trk: open to further improvement in h'caps. **80**
1171 **SHARP NEEDLE 16** [5] J Noseda 3-8-4 K Darley 11/2: 02: b f Mark of Esteem - Blushing Sunrise (Cox's Ridge) Hld up, hdwy to chase wnr over 2f out, kept on: op 3/1: dropped in class & stays 9f on gd/soft grnd & a sharp trk: shld find a race. *1* **71**
1095 **KINGS ENVOY 22** [7] Mrs J C McGregor 5-9-10 (60) D McGaffin 33/1: 6/000/0-43: Hld up, eff 2f out, kept on same pace: acts on fast & gd/soft: clr rem: see 1095. *1* **74$**
1178 **QUEEN LUCIA 15** [4] J G Given 3-8-4 G Duffield 25/1: 44: Keen, led after 2f till dist, wknd. *5* **59**
4706} **SALAMBA 200** [8]3-8-9 M Henry 20/1: 53-5: ch c Indian Ridge - Towaahi (Caerleon) In tch, wknd 2f out: reapp: plcd in a mdn 2nd of 2 '03 starts (rtd 78): prob stays 7f on gd/soft. *5* **58**
4164} **BADR 233** [6]3-8-9 R Ffrench 8/1: 20-6: Cl up, wknd 2f out on reapp. *1½* **56**
COLUMBIAN EMERALD [2]3-8-9 R Havlin 150/1: 7: ch g Among Men - Sarabi (Alzao) Slow away, al bhd: dam 5f juv wnr: bred to apprec sprint trips. *12* **32**
7 Ran Time 1m 57.4 (6.7) Owned: The Queen Trained: Newmarket

1463 **5.20 Saffie Joseph & Sons Handicap Stakes 3yo+ 46-55 (F)** **[62]**
£2975 £850 £425 **7f30y rnd** **Good/Soft 73** **-19 Slow** Outside

188 **TAP 140** [11] Ian Emmerson 7-9-2 P (50) D Fentiman(7) 40/1: 142000-1: b g Emarati - Pubby (Doctor Wall) Prom, hdwy to lead over 1f out, rdn out: '03 dual sell h'cap wnr (with D Nicholls): suited by 7f, stays 1m on fast, soft & fibresand: acts on any trk: runs well fresh: back to form in first time cheekpieces. **58**
2 Jul'03 Ayr 7.2gd 57-(53) F: 1 Jul'03 Beve 7.5g/s 55-50 F: 1 Jun'03 Sout 7af 54a-51 G:
2 May'03 Ayr 7.2g/s 52-42 D: 2 May'03 Muss 7.1g/s 44-41 F: 2 Jan'03 Sout 8af 43a- G:
1319 **MOUNT ROYALE 7** [3] N Tinkler 6-9-3 vis t (51) Kim Tinkler 7/1: 1006222: Led till over 1f out, onepace: tchd 10/1: in gd form: 7f specialist: see 684. *¾* **57**
1132 **BALERNO 18** [14] R Ingram 5-9-3 (51) K Darley 9/2: 0450523: In tch, eff 2f out, onepace: clr rem: gd run: acts on fast, gd/soft & both aw's: see 1132, 408. *¾* **55**
1253 **SHIFTY 11** [7] D Nicholls 5-9-3 vis (51) Alex Greaves 7/1: 26-50004: In tch, eff over 1f out, no impress: tried a visor 1253, see 166, 86. *3* **50**
1391 **WALTZING WIZARD 4** [10]5-9-7 (55) F Lynch 6/1: 2-354555: Bhd, eff 2f out, no impress: longer trip. *1¼* **52**
1320 **EAST RIDING 7** [8]4-9-1 (49) Ann Stokell 66/1: 2005-566: In tch, wknd 2f out: see 1119 (7f). *1½* **43**
4767} **YORKSHIRE BLUE 197** [13]5-9-2 (50) J F Egan 10/1: 600000-7: b g Atraf - Something Blue (Petong) In tch, wknd 2f out: '03 sell wnr (with R Whitaker): '02 mdn wnr: eff at 6/7.5f on fast & fibresand, sharp or gall trk: has run well fresh: tried blnks. 1 May'03 Redc 7g/f 58-(52) F: 1 Jul'02 Wolv 6af 70a- D: *1* **42**
1391 **FRIAR TUCK 4** [5]9-9-4 (52) T Eaves(5) 20/1: 3200-008: Nvr a danger: qck reapp: see 1391. *2½* **40**
792 **MAGIC MAMMAS TOO 58** [12]4-9-4 VIS (52) T P Queally(3) 12/1: 26-25349: Al bhd: abs: tried a visor. *1* **38**
1119 **LUKE AFTER ME 19** [1]4-9-3 (51) K Fallon 8/1: 000-0230: 10th: Al bhd: btr 1119 (fast grnd). *1¾* **33**
1074 **PEREGIAN 24** [2]6-9-1 (49) G Duffield 10/1: 0005-530: 11th: In tch, wknd 2f out: changed stable. *1¼* **29**
4824} **Due Diligence 192** [6]5-9-2 (50) K Dalgleish 33/1:0 4856} **Xanadu 191** [4]8-9-2 (50) P Hanagan 33/1:0
13 Ran Time 1m 31.22(6.42) Owned: Trade Direct Bathrooms & Furniture Trained: Chester-Le-Street

NOTTINGHAM FRIDAY 30.04.04 Lefthand, Galloping Track

Official Going SOFT (HEAVY places).

1464 **2.10 Bestwood Park Maiden Stakes 3yo (D)**
£3747 £1153 £576 **6f15y str** **Soft 92** **-24 Slow** Stands Side

1108 **INCHLOSS 20** [9] B A McMahon 3-9-0 W Supple 11/2: 041: b g Imperial Ballet - Earth Charter (Slip Anchor) Held up, hdwy halfway, styd on well to lead cl-home, rdn out: op 9/2: apprec this drop back to 6f, prob stays 1m: acts on soft grnd & on a gall trk: improving with racing, see 1108. **76**
SNAP [12] M Johnston 3-9-0 J Fanning 6/1: 2: ch c Dr Fong - Reactress (Sharpen Up) Chsd ldrs, led halfway till ins fnl 1f, not pace of wnr on debut: half-brother to mid-dist wnr Shemozzle: eff at 6f, 7f/1m shld suit: acts on soft grnd & on a gall trk: decent first eff, sure to improve. *1¼* **71**
100 **SOVIET SCEPTRE 156** [7] G A Butler 3-9-0 K McEvoy 5/1 JT FAV: 56-3: ch c Soviet Star - Princess Sceptre (Cadeaux Genereux) Chsd ldrs, styd on under press fnl 1f, nrst fin on reapp/h'cap qual run: tchd 13/2: decent 5th in a Goodwood mdn on '03 debut, subs disapp on AW bow (rtd 82): 58,000gns Feb foal: eff at 6/7f, bred to stay 1m: acts on fast & soft grnd: interesting in h'caps over 7f+ now. *nk* **70+**
CALLED UP [5] H Candy 3-9-0 Dane O'Neill 9/1: 4: b g Easycall - Clued Up (Beveled) Dwelt, chsd ldrs, sltly outpcd 2f out, styd on under press on debut: dam a winning sprinter: eff at 6f on soft grnd, shld benefit from 7f: sharper next time. *1* **67**
1008 **INDIAN EDGE 30** [4]3-9-0 (65) D Sweeney 14/1: 666-05: Chsd ldrs, lost place halfway, rallying when short of room dist: tchd 20/1. *nk* **66**
1136 **DR SYNN 18** [11]3-9-0 P Doe 5/1 JT FAV: 6-06: Prom till wknd fnl 1f: op 8/1: now qual for h'caps & shld apprec further. *nk* **65**
1044 **ADORATA 27** [1]3-8-9 D Badel 66/1: 007: Chsd ldrs, onepcd fnl 2f. *¾* **57**
1177 **GHANTOOT 15** [8]3-9-0 N Mackay(3) 25/1: 08: Sn outpcd, nvr dangerous. *1¼* **58**
1210 **PRIVATE JESSICA 14** [2]3-8-9 J Murtagh 7/1: 09: Nvr nr ldrs. *nk* **52**
RENE BARBIER [6]3-9-0 P Robinson 25/1: 0: 10th: Dwelt, al bhd on debut. *10* **37**
5022} **SPARTAN SPEAR 175** [13]3-9-0 J Edmunds 16/1: 04-0: 11th: Held up, al bhd on reapp: new stable. *½* **36**
4527} **Baychevelle 213** [10]3-8-9 S Sanders 16/1:0 4536} **New Day Dawning 212** [3]3-8-9 (48) R Fitzpatrick 50/1:0
13 Ran Time 1m 17.76 (6.96) Owned: Mr R Thornhill Trained: Tamworth

---

1465   2.40 Nottinghamshire Chamber Of Commerce And Industry Handicap Stakes Fillies 3yo+ 0-70 (£70])
£3708 £1141 £570   6f15y str   Soft 92   -04 Slow   Stands Side

1221   **AMELIA** 13 [9] W M Brisbourne 6-8-8 (50) B Swarbrick(7) 8/1: 2555301: Mid-div, gd hdwy 2f out,   58
strong run to lead cl-home, won going away: deserved win, plcd several times on AW this winter: eff at 5/6f, stays
a sharp 7f: acts on firm & soft grnd, both AWs: wins her share of races, see 1024 & 246 (AW).

1239   **GOJO** 13 [8] B Palling 3-9-0 (67) S Sanders 6/1: 060-42: Chsd ldrs, drvn to lead ins fnl 1f, not   1   72
pace to repel wnr cl-home: fine run, knocking on the door & deserves similar: acts on gd & soft, prob firm: won
race on wrong side over C/D in 1239.

1179   **GRANDMA LILY** 15 [14] M C Chapman 6-9-4 (60) L Dettori 15/2: 3000003: Outpcd, styd on strongly   ¾   62
fnl 1f, not quite get there: acts on fast, gd grnd & fibresand: see 85 (AW h'cap).

1354   **PARK STAR** 6 [5] D Shaw 4-9-2 (58) J F McDonald(3) 11/1: 63200U4: Outpcd, styd on fnl 1f, not   3½   52
reach ldrs: qck reapp: see 740 & 587.

4997]   **BOWLING ALONG** 178 [16]3-8-7 (60) P Mulrennan(4) 40/1: 325300-5: b f The West - Bystrouska   shd   54
(Gorytus) Dwelt, recovered to chase ldrs, wknd fnl 1f on reapp: '03 sell wnr, subs plcd in h'cap company, also
tried a visor: eff at 5/7f on firm & gd/soft grnd: likes a sharp trk, esp Catterick: sharper next time.
2 Sep'03 Catt 7g/s 58-55 E: 1 May'03 Catt 6.0fm 58- G:

4616]   **GLENCOE SOLAS** 207 [6]4-9-12 (68) P Dobbs 8/1: 625600-6: ch f Night Shift - Boranwood   1   60
(Exhibitioner) Led till ins fnl 1f, wknd: reapp: '03 mdn (reapp) & fills h'cap wnr, also plcd sev times: eff at
6f on gd & fast: handles a sharp & gall trk, likes to run up with/force the pace: can run well fresh.
2 Aug'03 Ling 6g/f 72-73 D: 2 Jul'03 Sand 5.0g/f 74-70 D: 1 Jun'03 Wind 6g/f 71-64 E: 1 Mar'03 Kemp 6gd 68- D:

4416]   **TUSCARORA** 220 [10]5-9-1 (57) I Mongan 16/1: 646406-7: b f Revoque - Fresh Look (Alzao) Held up,   1¼   46
prog when short of room dist, nrst fin on reapp: won a clmr (reapp), h'cap & seller in '03: '02 AW claim wnr: eff
at 6f/1m on gd, firm grnd & polytrack: handles a sharp or gall trk, runs well fresh: suited by sell/claim grade.
1 Jun'03 Brig 8.0fm 47-(64) G: 2 May'03 Bath 8.0g/s 63-62 E: 2 May'03 Bath 8.0g/f 65-59 E: 1 Apr'03 Ling 7ap 61a-55 F:
1 Jan'03 Ling 6ap 51a- F: 2 Jul'02 Ayr 7.2gd 59-58 E: 1 Jan'02 Ling 6ap 62a- F:

1345   **SUGAR CUBE TREAT** 6 [13]8-7-12 (10oh)p (30) P Varley(5) 25/1: 00-00058: Dwelt, some prog halfway,   ¾   27
sn no impress: qck reapp.

1726]   **MEDUSA** 340 [12]4-10-0 (70) J Murtagh 20/1: 0/2300-9: Chsd ldrs, wknd 2f out: reapp, top-weight.   5   45

1015   **QUEEN OF BULGARIA** 29 [15]3-8-7 (60) R Price 40/1: 6202-000: 10th: Speed 4f, sn btn.   ½   34

874   **SILVER CHIME** 42 [2]4-9-13 (69) N Mackay(3) 9/1: 31050-00: 11th: Slow away, nvr dngrs: 6 wk abs.   2½   37

999   **LEOPARD CREEK** 30 [1]3-8-9 (62) A Culhane 20/1: 400-00: 12th: Al towards rear.   2½   24

2014]   **LADY JUSTICE** 328 [3]4-10-0 (70) D Tudhope(7) 16/1: 06/50-0: 13th: Slowly away, al bhd on reapp.   1¾   28

1337*   **BLAKESHALL QUEST** 6 [4]4-9-7 (6ex)vis (63) D Holland 11/2 FAV: 4451010: 14th: Speed till halfway,   nk   20
wknd: qck reapp: reportedly unsuited by this soft grnd, btr on the AW in 1337.

1726] Princess Erica 340 [11]4-9-2 (58) W Supple 20/1:0   1327 Sweet Talking Girl 7 [7]4-7-12 (40) J Quinn 25/1:0
16 Ran   Time 1m 16.60 (5.80)   Owned: Mr Raymond McNeill   Trained: Baschurch

---

1466   3.10 Damian Wakefield Stag Party Novice Median Auction Stakes 2yo   (F)
£3115 £890 £445   5f13y str   Soft 92   +11 Fast   Stands Side

1117*   **JOSEPH HENRY** 19 [7] M Johnston 2-9-6   J Fanning 4/11 FAV: 11: Chsd ldr, went on 2f out, pushed   98+
clr, easily: hvly back, v fast juv time under a big weight: eff at 5f on fast & soft grnd: impressive run in the
circumstances & deserves a step up in grade: prob none to follow, see 1117.

1353   **MAURO** 6 [4] P M Phelan 2-8-7   J Quinn 25/1: 42: Chsd ldrs, kept on fnl 1f for 2nd, no ch with   7   70
wnr: prob eff at 5f on soft grnd: caught a tartar, see 1353.

1325*   **ZIMBALI** 7 [6] J M Bradley 2-8-7   S Carson 4/1: 5413: Set fast pace till 2f out, wknd: op 10/3:   3   64
rtd higher in 1325 (gd/soft).

   OUR FUGITIVE [2] A W Carroll 2-8-12   D Holland 14/1: 4: gr c Titus Livius - Mystical Jumbo   ½   68
(Mystiko) Dwelt, outpcd till late gains on debut: 5,000gns Apr foal: half brother to 6/7f juv wnr Leitrim Lakes:
sire a high-class sprinter: modicum of promise on debut & shld learn from this.

1029   **SAHARA MIST** 28 [1]2-8-7   W Supple 25/1: 065: b f Desert Style - Tereed Elhawa (Cadeaux Genereux)   7   48
Al outpcd: 3,000gns Apr 1st foal: dam a 6f juv wnr, sire a smart 7f performer: with D Shaw.

1256   **WHISTLING ALONG** 11 [3]2-8-12   J Bramhill 25/1: 06: b c Atraf - Forest Song (Forzando) Hmpd   10   30
start & al bhnd: 3,500gns Apr foal: half brother to a 1m wnr: sire a high-class sprinter: with J Bradley.
6 Ran   Time 1m 02.57 (4.07)   Owned: John Brown & Megan Dennis   Trained: Middleham

---

1467   3.40 Dcm Apex Handicap Stakes Fillies 3yo+ 0-80   (D)   [80]
£5671 £1745 £873   1m1f213y   Soft 92   -48 Slow   Inside

1307   **OLIVIA ROSE** 8 [7] J Pearce 5-8-8 (60) J Quinn 13/2: 00452-01: b f Mujadil - Santana Lady   66
(Blakeney) Held up, gd hdwy to lead entr fnl 1f, styd on strongly, rdn out: failed to win in '03, tho' plcd sev
times, incl in first time visor: claim wnr for M Johnston in '02: eff btwn 1m & 12f, acts on fast, hvy & f/sand:
handles a sharp or gall trk, eff with/without a visor: well h'capped. 2 Nov'03 Nott 8.2sft 61-57 F:
2 Sep'03 Muss 9g/f 69-(60) E: 2 Aug'03 Yarm 10.1g/f 63-(62) F: 2 Jun'03 Muss 9g/f 58-(62) E: 1 Jun'02 Leic 8g/f 64- E:
2 Apr'02 Beve 7.4g/f 71-68 E: 1 Dec'01 Sout 7af 73a-66 E: 2 Nov'01 Catt 7g/s 72- E: 2 Oct'01 Newc 6hvy 72- D:

1164   **GREY CLOUDS** 16 [4] T D Easterby 4-9-1 (67) W Supple 5/2 FAV: 11430-42: Keen in rear, hdwy to   1   70
lead dist, collared entering fnl 1f, kept on but not pace of wnr: op 10/3: acts on fast & soft grnd: see 1164.

4848*]**POLAR JEM** 191 [3] G G Margarson 4-9-8 (74) A McCarthy 9/1: 6321-3: b f Polar Falcon - Top Jem   1¼   75
(Damister) Chsd ldrs, rdn & onepcd fnl 1f on reapp: pleased '03 with a mdn win here at Nottingham: eff at 10f on
firm & soft grnd, handles sharp or gall trks: has run well fresh: spot on next time.
1 Oct'03 Nott 10.0g/f 76- D: 2 Oct'03 Newc 10.1fm 76- D:

148*   **MAXILLA** 146 [6] L M Cumani 4-9-6 (72) D Holland 9/1: 004/241-4: b f Lahib - Lacinia (Groom   ½   72
Dancer) Chsd ldrs, led 2f out till dist, no extra: op 13/2, reapp: lightly rcd in '03, won fnl start (AW mdn):
eff at 1m/10f, has class on easy/gall trk: sharper next time.
1 Dec'03 Ling 10ap 66a-(63) D: 2 Apr'03 Yarm 8.0gd 73-67 D:

1307   **TRANSCENDANTALE** 8 [8]6-7-13 (1ow)(5oh) (45) C Catlin 13/2: 0000-235: Held up, late prog, nvr   1½   49
dngrs: clr of rem: see 1307 & 1135.

1348   **SIENNA SUNSET** 6 [10]5-8-8 (60) S Carson 11/1: 20200-06: Chsd ldr, led 3f out till 2f out, sn wknd.   7   48

4711} **PERUVIA 200** [5]4-9-10 (76) S Sanders 9/1: 30/4412-7: Chsd ldrs, wknd over 2f out: jumps fit. 5 57
1322+**SPARK UP 7** [9]4-9-1 (6ex) (67) S W Kelly 11/1: 0624418: Led till 3f out, sn wknd: disapp under a pen, reportedly hung right: see 1322 (AW). 2½ 45
4940} **SUMMER WINE 184** [2]5-9-9 (75) G Baker 16/1: 421/000-9: Slow away, nvr trbld ldrs on reapp. 9 40
9 Ran Time 2m 16.37 (14.07) Owned: Mr A Watford Trained: Newmarket

1468

4.10 Colwick Maiden Stakes Fillies 3yo (D)
£3739 £1150 £575 **1m54y rnd** **Soft 92** **-73 Slow** Inside

4056} **PONT ALLAIRE 239** [4] H Candy 3-8-11 Dane O'Neill 13/8 FAV: 4-1: b f Rahy - Leonila (Caerleon) 80
Trkd ldr, went on dist, styd on strongly, rdn out: nicely bckd, reapp, slow time: fill mdn 4th on sole '03 start (rtd 79): 150,000gns half sister to a wnr in France: eff at 1m on soft, handles fast grnd: handles a gall trk & runs well fresh: open to more improvement.
1210 **TREE TOPS 14** [2] J H M Gosden 3-8-11 L Dettori 5/2: 52: Set pace till collared dist, eased when held ins fnl 1f: prob stays a gall 1m on soft grnd: shld find a small race, see 1210. 3 73
1210 **PINCHING 14** [6] H R A Cecil 3-8-11 W Ryan 4/1: 43: Chsd ldrs, not qckn fnl 1f: op 10/3: in front to today's 2nd in 1210 & more at home on gd grnd? 2½ 68
LILLIANNA [7] H R A Cecil 3-8-11 Paul Eddery 25/1: 4: ch f Barathea - Machikane Akaiito (Persian Bold) Dwelt, hdwy 2f out, no impress fnl 1f on debut: stablemate of 3rd: cost 9,000gns: sire a high-class miler: bred to apprec 1m & may do better on faster grnd. 3½ 61
SOVIET SPIRIT [1]3-8-11 J Murtagh 11/1: 5: ch f Soviet Star - Kristina (Kris) Chsd ldrs till wknd dist on debut: dam a 1m wng juv: bred to apprec 1m: shld learn from this. nk 60
1177 **PURPLE RAIN 15** [3]3-8-11 I Mongan 40/1: 006: Keen & prom 6f, wknd on h'cap qual run. 1¾ 56
1177 **THARAA 15** [5]3-8-11 S Drowne 10/1: 0-27: Slowly away, keen in rear: btr 1177 (gd). 2½ 51
7 Ran Time 1m 52.63 (13.23) Owned: Britton House Stud Ltd Trained: Wantage

1469

4.40 Newark Handicap Stakes 4yo+ 0-70 (E) [70]
£3809 £1172 £586 **1m6f15y** **Soft 92** **-07 Slow** Inside

1286* **ISAAF 10** [15] P W Hiatt 5-8-13 (55) P Makin(7) 9/1: 602-1211: Nvr far away, led 2f out, styd on well fnl 1f, rdn out: continues in fine form & 3rd win from 4 starts this term: eff at 11/15.4f on firm, soft grnd & fibresand: handles a sharp or stiff/undul trk: in fine form & gets on well with P Makin: see 1286 & 891. 65
4938*}**CALAMINTHA 184** [9] M C Pipe 4-9-2 (60) N Mackay(3) 10/1: 503501-2: b f Mtoto - Calendula (Be My Guest) Chsd ldrs, styd on well fnl 1f but not pace of wnr: jumps fit, won 2 nov hdles this winter (eff at 2m/2m2f on gd & soft, rtd 131h, tried a visor): '03 sell wnr for R Beckett: eff at 12/14f on fast & soft: shld find similar. 1 Oct'03 Yarm 14.1sft 60-(60) G: 1¾ 67
1093 **MACARONI GOLD 22** [12] W Jarvis 4-9-2 (60) M Tebbutt 20/1: 2-044503: Ran in snatches, led 6f out & sn clr, hdd 2f out, no extra: clr of rem: see 813 & 67 (AW). 3½ 63
3480] **IMPISH JUDE 625** [17] J Mackie 6-8-7 (49) Dale Gibson 16/1: 0/00033/-4: b f Imp Society - Miss Nanna (Vayrann) Held up, late hdwy, nvr dngrs: jumps fit, h'cap hdle wnr in Dec '03 (eff around 2m on gd & soft, rtd 98h): missed '03 on the Flat, h'cap plcd prev term: eff at 12/14f on gd & soft grnd: modest, 2m shld suit. 7 43
1109 **NORTHERN NYMPH 20** [10]5-10-0 (70) Stephanie Hollinshead(7) 25/1: 5/4-23005: Rear, some late prog, nvr dngrs under top-weight: see 837 7 743 (AW). 1½ 62
666 **PIPSSALIO 73** [13]7-8-3 t (45) J F McDonald(3) 5/1 FAV: 0043-626: Rear, nvr nr ldrs: nicely bckd: won a mdn hdle (eff at 2m4f on gd/soft & soft, rtd 120h) since 666. hd 37
1320} **LUBINAS 363** [3]5-8-5 (1ow) (46) S W Kelly 20/1: 6622/20-7: b g Grand Lodge - Liebesgirl (Konigsstuhl) Rear, some hdwy when short of room 2f out, nvr dngrs: has been gelded: rnr-up in a h'cap hdle 9 days ago (eff at 2m4f on gd/soft, rtd 99h): lightly rcd on the Flat in '03, rnr-up in native Germany: stays 12f. 1¾ 37
1389 **GOLDEN BOOT 4** [5]5-9-11 p (67) T E Durcan 11/2: 02343-68: Rear, nvr nr ldrs: qck reapp. 1¾ 55
2103} **MIGRATION 322** [6]8-9-4 (60) L Vickers 40/1: 162////4-9: Slow away, nvr trbld ldrs on reapp. 6 40
1135 **MADHAHIR 18** [14]4-9-4 (62) D Holland 14/1: 20-00130: 10th: Chsd ldrs, wknd 2f out: reportedly ran in snatches: btr 979 (12f). 3 38
1030 **MASJOOR 28** [18]4-9-1 (59) L Dettori 12/1: 030-020: 11th: Chsd ldrs, wknd 3f out: btr 1030 (AW). 10 23
918 **BLACKTHORN 36** [2]5-9-3 (59) J Murtagh 11/2: 52002-40: 12th: Prom till wknd 3f out: see 918. ½ 22
1285 **LITTLE TOBIAS 10** [11]5-8-9 (51) C Catlin 16/1: 0/1010-60: 13th: Prom till halfway: see 1285. 9 2
1223 **DOWN TO THE WOODS 13** [4]6-8-3 (45) J Quinn 66/1: 60040-00: 14th: Held up, al bhd. 3½ 0
4931} **SAINTLY THOUGHTS 185** [8]9-8-8 p (50) S Drowne 50/1: 323200-0: 15th: Chsd ldrs till halfway. 3 0
1285 **STARRY MARY 10** [1]6-8-13 (55) S Sanders 9/1: 0006-220: 16th: Led till after halfway, wknd & eased. 4 0
3750} **St Jerome 254** [7]4-9-0 (58) T G McLaughlin 33/1:0 34 **Party Ploy 168** [16]6-9-7 (63) I Mongan 40/1:0
18 Ran Time 3m 12.17 (13.87) Owned: Miss Maria McKinney Trained: Banbury

1470

5.10 Carlton Hblb Handicap Stakes 3yo 0-70 (E) [77]
£3926 £1208 £604 **1m54y rnd** **Soft 92** **-53 Slow** Inside

1163 **RILEY BOYS 16** [4] J G Given 3-9-3 (66) S Sanders 13/2: 3000-121: Sn led, hdd ins fnl 1f, rallied gamely to regain lead on line in a thrilling fin: eff at 6f, stays 1m: acts on firm, soft grnd & fibresand: continues in fine form & a v game eff here: see 1163 & 892. 73
1253 **CHARMATIC 11** [12] J A Glover 3-8-11 (60) J Quinn 9/2 FAV: 00-522: Keen & prom, led ins fnl 1f, caught on line: op 11/2: fine run, certainly deserves similar: clearly relishes testing conds, see 1253. shd 66
1136 **EVALUATOR 18** [6] T G Mills 3-9-7 (70) L Dettori 6/1: 36-43: Slowly away, hdwy from rear 1.5f out, fin strongly & only just failed: fine h'cap bow, clearly stays 1m on soft grnd: shld win similar, see 1136. nk 75
1163 **AUROVILLE 16** [17] M L W Bell 3-9-3 (66) I Mongan 14/1: 050-04: Rear, prog 2f out, nrst fin: op 20/1: prob stays a gall 1m on soft grnd: see 1163. 1½ 68
1209 **WEE DINNS 14** [7]3-9-6 (69) P Dobbs 11/1: 000-05: b f Marju - Tir An Oir (Law Society) Slowly away, recovered to chase ldrs, onepcd fnl 1f: lightly rcd & some mdn promise in '03, caught the eye on fnl start (rtd 73): eff at 1m on soft grnd, has tried 10f & shld suit: with S Kirk. 1½ 68
1163 **CHARNOCK BATES ONE 16** [3]3-9-2 (65) T E Durcan 15/2: 53354-46: Early ldr, remained prom, onepcd fnl 1.5f: see 1163. ½ 63
4996} **SELEBELA 178** [10]3-8-11 (60) N Mackay(3) 20/1: 3605-7: ch f Grand Lodge - Risarshana (Darshaan) Mid-div, kept on under press but not pace to chall on reapp: plcd in Italy on '03 debut: cost 20,000gns: prob ¾ 56

NOTTINGHAM   FRIDAY 30.04.04   Lefthand, Galloping Track

handles gd & soft grnd, 10f may suit: likely to impr when stable hits form.

1283 **AMWELL BRAVE** 10 [8]3-9-2 (65) D Holland 10/1: 2335058: Rear, prog when short of room 2f out, nrst fin: see 601 (AW mdn).	1¼	58

4714} **MR INDEPENDENT** 200 [14]3-9-2 (65) E Ahern 20/1: 030-9: b g Cadeaux Genereux - Iris May (Brief   1½   55
Truce) Held up, nvr troubled ldrs on reapp: plcd on middle of 3 juv starts (mdn, rtd 70), has since been gelded:
prob eff at 1m on gd grnd: with E Dunlop.

1008 **AIRGUSTA** 30 [9]3-9-1 (64) P Robinson 10/1: 000-00: 10th: Prom, wknd over 1f out.   hd   54

1163 **MR MIDASMAN** 16 [18]3-9-6 (69) Dale Gibson 20/1: 041-600: 11th: Slowly away, nvr nr ldrs: see 923.   4   51

4344} **DOUBLE VODKA** 224 [5]3-9-4 (67) J Murtagh 20/1: 6035-0: 12th: Slowly away, keen in rear, nvr   1¾   47
dngrs on reapp: new stable, has been gelded.

1007 **MILITARY TWO STEP** 30 [11]3-9-2 (65) A Culhane 33/1: 35002-00: 13th: Keen & prom 6.5f, wknd.   hd   45

4942} **BEAUTIFUL NOISE** 184 [1]3-9-0 (63) W Supple 16/1: 0506-0: 14th: Held up, al bhd on reapp.   3½   37

4547} **Desert Battle** 212 [15]3-9-4 (67) D Sweeney 50/1:0   4737} **Washbrook** 199 [16]3-9-1 (64) C Catlin 40/1:0
4577} **Joey Perhaps** 210 [2]3-9-1 (64) S W Kelly 25/1:0   **Faith Healer** 174 [13]3-9-2 (65) M Tebbutt 18/1:0
18 Ran   Time 1m 51.17(11.77)   Owned: Mr Paul Riley   Trained: Gainsborough

---

THIRSK   SATURDAY 01.05.04   Lefthand, Flat, Oval Track

Official Going GOOD.

1471   2.05 European Breeders Fund Sutton Novice Stakes 2yo (D)
£5473 £1684 £842   **5f str**   Good/Soft 90   **-23 Slow**   Stands Side

1212 **WORLD AT MY FEET** 15 [5] N Bycroft 2-8-7   J Quinn 12/1: 21: Trkd ldrs, pushed along & hdwy to   87
lead ins last, sn asserted, hands & heels : imprvd from encouraging C/D debut: eff at 5f, sure to get 6f+: acts on
gd/soft grnd & a sharp/easy trk: progressing well, looks potentially useful: see 1212.

1091* **BOLD MARC** 23 [6] K R Burke 2-9-0   Darren Williams 5/6 FAV: 412: Handy, led 2f out till ins last   3½   84
& no ch with wnr: hvly bckd, clr rem, top-weight: acts on fast, gd/soft & handles soft: prob ran to form of 1091.

TWICE NIGHTLY [1] J D Bethell 2-8-12   P Hanagan 20/1: 3: b g Wolfhound - Dusty's Darling   2   76+
(Doyoun) Pushed along & bhd, hung left but styd on well from over 1f out: 10,000gns April foal, half-brother to a
useful sprint juv & a wnr abroad: eff at 5f, sure to apprec 6f+: handles gd/soft: ran green, expect improvement.

1107 **SPECIAL GOLD** 21 [4] T D Easterby 2-8-12   D Allan(3) 11/4: 54: b c Josr Algarhoud - Inya Lake   2   69
(Whittingham) Dsptd lead till 2f out, then dist: 26,000gns March foal, dam a smart sprinter: sire smart performer
at 7f/1m: poss do best when return to mdn company.

PIDDIES PRIDE [7]2-8-7   T P Queally(3) 40/1: 5: b f Indian Lodge - Fairybird (Pampabird) Dwelt   2   58
& sn pushed along, mod prog: April foal, cheaply bght: half-sister to wnrs abroad, dam a 5f juv wnr.

1071* **SMOKINCANON** 25 [3]2-8-12   R Miles(3) 7/1: 316: Dwelt & sn outpcd: btr 1071 (AW).   hd   63

MELANDRE [2]2-8-7   T Williams 50/1: 6: Dwelt, chsd ldrs till over 1f out, ddhtd for 6th.   dht   58
7 Ran   Time 1m 02.68 (5.68)   Owned: Cavalier Racing   Trained: Malton

1472   2.40 Rye Maiden Stakes 3yo+ (D)
£5525 £1700 £850   **1m4f**   Good/Soft 90   **-55 Slow**   Inside

1209 **KARAMEA** 15 [1] J L Dunlop 3-8-0 (82) J Quinn 1/2 FAV: 03-31: gr f Rainbow Quest - Karapucha   70+
(Kaldoun) Handy & led 7f out, pulled clr under hands & heels fnl 2f, val 4L+: well bckd at odds-on: eff at 10/12f,
could get further: acts on fast & gd/soft grnd: found this straightforward, likely type for fills mid-dist h'caps.

4989} **CALONNOG** 180 [6] H R A Cecil 4-9-5   Paul Eddery 10/3: 5-2: ch f Peintre Celebre - Meadow Spirit   2½   63
(Chief's Crown) Led 3f & remained handy, no impress on wnr from over 2f out: reapp, op 5/2: mdn unplcd sole '03
start (rtd 65): eff arnd 12f, could get further: acts on gd/soft grnd.

4973} **DAWN AIR** 182 [4] K A Ryan 3-8-0   P Fessey 25/1: 0-3: b f Diesis - Midnight Air (Green Dancer)   3   59
Pushed along towards rear, outpcd over 3f out, late gains, no threat to front pair: reapp: well btn sole '03 start
(mdn, rtd 44, D Daly): likely to apprec mid-dists this term.

1358 **LOGGER RHYTHM** 7 [2] R Dickin 4-9-10   M Fenton 50/1: 004: Rear, rdn 4f out, not able to chall: 1½   59
longer trip could well suit now in h'cap company.

4875} **HAVETOAVIT** 190 [3]3-8-5 (61) S Shaw(7) 14/1: 55400-5: Reared start, v slow away, sn keen & chsd   3   48
ldrs, btn 3f out: reapp.

1279 **PAULA** 11 [7]4-9-5 P T Hamilton(3) 100/1: 06: Prom, rdn & btn 3f out.   12   30

939 **ALBEE** 35 [5]4-9-10 p J Mongan 16/1: 6647: Led/dsptd lead till 7f out, sn btn: op 12/1.   6   26

4847} **ROCKY RAMBO** 192 [8]3-8-5   T Eaves(1) 100/1: 0-8: Held up & lost tch fnl 3f, reapp.   dist   0
8 Ran   Time 2m 47.21 (17.41)   Owned: Mrs S Egloff   Trained: Arundel

1473   3.15 B F C Brava Ltd Maiden Stakes 3yo (D)
£5785 £1780 £890   **7f rnd**   Good/Soft 90   **-09 Slow**   Inside

NIGHT AIR [13] D R Loder 3-9-0   T P Queally(3) 4/1: 1: b g Night Shift - Pippas Song (Reference   69
Point) Handy, rdn & led ins last, all out: op 7/2, debut: 110,000gns purchase: well bred newcomer: eff at 7f, 1m
cld suit: acts on gd/soft & an easy trk, goes well fresh: type to rate higher.

1196 **MY PARIS** 16 [5] K A Ryan 3-9-0   N Callan 12/1: 0-322: Handy & led 2f out till ins last, styd   shd   68
on gamely, just held: turf debut: eff at 7f/1m on fibresand & gd/soft grnd: see 1196, 381.

1129 **BURLEY FLAME** 19 [9] J G Given 3-9-0   M Fenton 25/1: 0-43: b g Marju - Tarsa (Ballad Rock)   ½   67
Handy, rdn & outpcd over 2f out, styd on well ins last & not btn far: clr of rem: unplcd sole '03 start (rtd 61,
mdn): eff arnd 7f, tried 1m, shld suit: handles gd & gd/soft grnd: type to apprec h'cap company & 1m.

4200} **SESSAY** 232 [7] D Nicholls 3-9-0 (69) A Nicholls 33/1: 320-4: b g Cyrano de Bergerac - Green   5   57
Supreme (Primo Dominie) Chsd ldrs, drvn & no extra over 1f out: reapp, has been gelded: mdn rnr-up '03: eff at
5f, not stay 7f? acts on fast & gd/soft, stiff/undul or easy trk: lightly rcd, apprec h'caps & 5/6f.
2 May'03 Hami 5.0g/s 76- D:

1228 **ICE PLANET** 14 [6]3-9-0   Alex Greaves 16/1: 035: Mid-div, drvn & no prog fnl 2f.   nk   56

1152 **MOORS MYTH** 18 [2]3-9-0 Dean McKeown 1/1 FAV: 0-36: Led till 2f out, sn hung left & btn: hvly 2 52
bckd: much btr 1152.
4651} **ADAIKALI** 206 [1]3-9-0 B Doyle 11/2: 0-7: Mid-div, drvn & btn 2f out: reapp. nk 42
1177 **TRYSTING GROVE** 16 [3]3-8-9 G Parkin 100/1: 08: Mid-div, ran wide on bend 3f out, sn no prog. 2 36
4240} **STORM CLOUDS** 229 [8]3-9-0 A Mullen(7) 100/1: 05-9: Mid-div, no prog fnl 3f, reapp/gelded. 5 37
1304 **ESTEPONA** 9 [12]3-9-0 D R McCabe 20/1: 40: 10th: Dwelt & sn bhd. ½ 36
1021 **ANTIGIOTTO** 29 [4]3-9-0 N Mackay(3) 33/1: 00: 11th: Dwelt & al towards rear. 1¾ 34
5022} **Ravel** 176 [10]3-9-0 I Mongan 33/1:0   1177 **Theatre Belle** 16 [15]3-8-9 D Allan(3) 66/1:0
192 **Mikes Mate** 140 [14]3-9-0 T Eaves(5) 100/1:0   **Warbreck** [11]3-9-0 P Hanagan 14/1:0
15 Ran   Time 1m 29.87 (6.97)   Owned: Sheikh Mohammed   Trained: Newmarket

---

1474

3.50 Totepool Handicap Stakes 3yo+ 0-90 (C)   **[89]**
£9783 £3010 £1505   **7f rnd**   **Good/Soft 90**   **-12 Slow**   Inside

998 **RAPHAEL** 31 [7] T D Easterby 5-9-0 (75) Dale Gibson 12/1: 65223-01: b f Perugino - Danny's 81
Miracle (Superlative) Held up, prog/short of room 2f out, styd on for press to lead cl-home: dual class stks scorer
'03, most consistent, 5 times h'cap rnr-up: h'cap scorer '02: eff at 7f/8.4f on firm, soft & handles hvy, any trk:
best without blnks: v tough & genuine.
2 Oct'03 Muss 7.1gd 78-73 C: 2 Sep'03 Muss 7.1gd 64-72 D: 2 Jul'03 Beve 7.5gd 75-72 D: 1 Jun'03 Beve 8.5g/f 73-(70) E:
2 Jun'03 Beve 7.5g/f 73-70 E: 1 May'03 Redc 7g/f 69-(70) E: 2 Mar'03 Catt 7g/f 72-71 D: 1 Oct'02 Donc 7sft 73-68 E:
1 Sep'01 Ripo 8g/f 78-73 D: 1 Aug'01 Thir 7gd 71- E: 2 Aug'01 Thir 7gd 74- E: 2 Jul'01 Redc 7fm 68-64 D:
887 **FIVEOCLOCK EXPRESS** 42 [11] Miss Gay Kelleway 4-9-3 p (78) I Mongan 8/1: 21300-42: Held up, hdwy nk 82
over 3f out & rdn/led well ins last, hdd cl-home: 6 wk abs: fine run, see 887.
17 **QUALITAIR WINGS** 171 [9] J Hetherton 5-8-11 (72) D McGaffin 20/1: 021026-3: b g Colonel Collins - ¾ 74+
Semperflorens (Don) Rear, hdwy/short of room 2f out, styd on well for press: reapp: h'cap scorer '03: dual h'cap
scorer '02: eff at 7f/8.4f on firm, gd/soft & polytrack, any trk, best without cheek pieces: fine return, shade
closer with a clr run/faster start.
2 Nov'03 Catt 7sft 73-68 D: 1 Sep'03 Hami 8.3gd 71-63 D: 2 Sep'03 Beve 7.5g/s 68-64 E: 2 May'03 Catt 7fm 74-69 D:
1 Oct'02 Catt 7g/s 71-65 E: 2 Sep'02 Beve 8.4g/f 65-62 E: 1 Sep'02 Yarm 8g/f 63-56 F:
1142 **YOUNG MR GRACE** 19 [12] T D Easterby 4-9-0 (75) D Allan(3) 12/1: 0460-034: Chsd ldrs, rdn & styd 1½ 74
on well fnl 2f: stablemate of wnr: see 1142.
998 **ATLANTIC QUEST** 31 [10]5-9-7 (82) P Mulrennan(5) 25/1: 00410-05: b g Woodman - Pleasant Pat hd 81+
(Pleasant Colony) Mid-div, short of room 2f out, styd on eyecatchingly under hands & heels: class stks & dual h'cap
wnr '03 (M Johnston): AW mdn & turf h'cap scorer '02: eff at 1m/10f on firm, gd & polytrack: eff with/without
visor or cheek pieces: spot on next time, prob at 1m.
1 Oct'03 Redc 8g/f 84-80 D: 2 Jul'03 Ayr 8g/f 86-(85) C: 1 Jun'03 Ayr 9.1g/f 86-80 D: 2 Jun'03 Hayd 8.1g/f 82-80 C:
1 May'03 Muss 8gd 82-(79) D: 1 May'02 Newm 8fm 84-79 C: 2 Mar'02 Ling 10ap 80a- D: 1 Jan'02 Ling 8ap 71a- D:
1035 **GO TECH** 28 [6]4-9-5 (80) A Mullen(7) 16/1: 0005-006: Bhd, swtchd wide & picked up strongly under hd 79+
inexperienced rider fnl 1f: s/mate of 1st & 4th: v well h'capped & looks to have come to hand: crying out for a
return to 1m & stronger handling will help: should not be missed next time.
928 **CARDINAL VENTURE** 36 [14]6-9-12 (87) N Callan 9/2 FAV: 0111-207: Handy & led over 3f out till ins hd 86
last: bckd: likes to dominate: see 141.
1214* **HARRY POTTER** 15 [5]5-8-10 vis (71) Darren Williams 13/2: 3-003018: Mid-div, onepace fnl 2f. hd 70
1231 **GOLDEN CHALICE** 14 [3]5-9-13 (88) N Chalmers(5) 13/2: 520-5609: Mid-div, no prog fnl 2f. 1¾ 84
1354 **TRUE NIGHT** 7 [13]7-9-2 (77) Alex Greaves 25/1: 4215-000: 10th: Mid-div, rdn & no impress dist. ¾ 71
4999*}**KING HARSON** 179 [4]5-9-7 vis (82) P Hanagan 8/1: 016331-0: 11th: Led 5f out till 3f out, wknd. dht 76
1214 **DISTANT COUNTRY** 15 [15]5-8-12 p (73) J Quinn 9/1: 1014-660: 12th: Mid-div, no prog fnl 2f: btr 998. 1¾ 64
1251 **Online Investor** 12 [8]5-8-6 (67) A Nicholls 14/1:0
4807} **Time To Remember** 196 [1]6-8-8 (69) D R McCabe 25/1:0
2399} **Wessex** 311 [16]4-10-0 (89) Dean McKeown 33/1:0   3829} **Coranglais** 252 [2]4-9-1 (76) S Carson 33/1:0
16 Ran   Time 1m 30.06 (7.16)   Owned: Mrs K Arton   Trained: Malton

---

1475

4.25 Hygicare Thirsk Hunt Cup Handicap 3yo+ 0-95 (C)   **[94]**
£12818 £3944 £1972   **1m rnd**   **Good/Soft 90**   **+05 Fast**   Inside

951 **BLUE SPINNAKER** 35 [18] M W Easterby 5-9-10 (90) P Mulrennan(5) 11/1: 14004-01: b g Bluebird - 102
Suedoise (Kris) Held up, hdwy 3f out, rdn & led over 1f out, sn asserted: best time of day: mdn & h'cap wnr '03:
ex-French prev: suited by 1m, tried 10f: acts on firm & gd/soft grnd, gall or easy trk: v useful gelding who
overcame awkward wide draw in fine style.
1 Aug'03 Hayd 8.1fm 90-81 C: 2 Jul'03 York 7.0fm 82-79 C: 1 Jun'03 Donc 5fm 83- D: 2 Apr'03 Pont 6g/f 81- D:
44 **VICIOUS WARRIOR** 166 [5] R M Whitaker 5-9-3 (83) Dean McKeown 20/1: 004020-2: b g Elmaamul - Ling2½ 88
Lane (Slip Anchor) Chsd ldrs & led 2f out, sn hdd, kept on but not pace of wnr: rest well held on reapp: 4 runner
class stks & subs h'cap rnr-up '03: dual h'cap wnr '02: eff at 1m/10f: handles firm grnd, enjoys give & gd/soft
prob ideal: handles any trk: well h'capped type, encouraging reapp, turn prob not far away.
2 Oct'03 Muss 8gd 86-82 D: 2 Jul'03 Ches 10.3fm 83-(85) D: 1 Sep'02 Donc 10.2fm 86-82 C:
1 Jun'02 Ripo 10g/s 83-76 D: 2 May'02 Nott 10gd 76-72 C: 2 May'02 Beve 9.9gd 78-72 D:
1104 **CATS WHISKERS** 21 [6] M W Easterby 5-9-1 (81) Dale Gibson 5/1 FAV: 20000-03: b g Catrail - Haut 2 81
Volee (Top Ville) Chsd ldrs & ev ch 2f out, rdn & no extra ins last: nicely bckd stablemate of wnr: dual h'cap
rnr-up '03: thrice h'cap wnr '02: eff at 7f/1m on fast & gd/soft grnd: handles a flat or stiff/gall trk: tough
type, looks to have come to hand.
2 May'03 Redc 10g/f 91-87 B: 2 May'03 Thir 8gd 89-84 C: 1 Aug'02 Thir 8gd 85-80 D: 1 Jul'02 Beve 8.4g/s 80-76 D:
1 Jun'02 Newc 8g/s 78-70 D: 2 May'02 Newc 8g/f 72-68 E: 1 Sep'01 Redc 7g/f 70-65 E:
1066 **CHERISHED NUMBER** 25 [1] I Semple 5-8-13 (79) I Mongan 14/1: 34004-04: Mid-div, prog & ch over 1f 1½ 77
out, no extra.
1151 **CHAPPEL CRESENT** 18 [10]4-9-7 (80) A Nicholls 9/1: 0-000525: Led till 2f out, wknd: see 1151 (7f). ½ 84
4666} **CRIPSEY BROOK** 204 [16]6-9-6 (86) Kim Tinkler 20/1: 511330-6: Rear, late gains for press, reapp. 1 81
1231 **UHOOMAGOO** 14 [7]6-9-2 bl (82) P Fessey 10/1: 3430-107: Dwelt, eff over 2f out, no prog dist. hd 77
1122 **SEA STORM** 20 [12]4-9-0 p (81) T P Quealy(3) 33/1: 0205-058: Prom, wknd fnl 2f: mid-div. 4 68
127 **MISTER ARJAY** 154 [17]4-8-12 (78) T Eaves 25/1: 535200-9: Mid-div, no prog fnl 3f, jumps fit. 1¾ 62
1126 **QUEENS RHAPSODY** 19 [8]4-9-5 (85) N Mackay(3) 10/1: 2024040: 10th: Mid-div, drvn & no prog fnl 3f. ¾ 67

928   **ATLANTIC ACE 36** [11]7-9-0 (80) F Lynch 16/1: 50105-00: 11th: Slow away & bhd, nvr able to chall.   nk   61
1151 **TEDSTALE 18** [2]6-9-4 (84) J Quinn 10/1: 22604-00: 12th: Mid-div, struggling fnl 2f.   hd   65
1231 **MYSTIC MAN 14** [3]6-9-5 (85) N Callan 9/1: 400-0000: 13th: Mid-div, short of rm halfway, sn btn.   1¾   62
945   **PENNY CROSS 35** [13]4-9-8 (88) M Fenton 20/1: 21333-00: 14th: Chsd ldrs till 2f out.   hd   65
1126 **TAKES TUTU 19** [4]5-9-0 vis (80) Darren Williams 11/1: 00065-00: 15th: Al towards rear: op 16/1.   1¾   53
1151 **TOUGH LOVE 18** [15]5-9-8 (88) D Allan(3) 8/1: 330-0000: 16th: Al towards rear.   hd   61
81   **GEM BIEN 161** [9]6-9-2 (82) P Hanagan 50/1: 0/01640-0: 17th: Mid-div, no ch fnl 2f, abs.   3   49
17 Ran   Time 1m 42.27 (6.87)   Owned: G Sparkes G Hart S Curtis & T Dewhirst   Trained: Sheriff Hutton

---

1476   5.00 Doug Moscrop Racing Journalist Of The Year Handicap Stakes 3yo+ 0-85 (D)   **[84]**
            £5707 £1756 £878   **5f str**   **Good/Soft 90**   **-05 Slow**   Stands Side

1293 **CHICO GUAPO 10** [10] J A Glover 4-9-3 (73) I Mongan 33/1: 15-05001: Made most in centre, drvn   79
out, gamely: suited by 5f on firm, gd/soft & both AWs, loves a sharp/easy trk, esp Chester & Thirsk: see 692.
1145 **ARTIE 19** [18] T D Easterby 5-9-3 (73) Dale Gibson 7/1: 0630-002: Al prom stands side & led that   ½   77
group dist, not pace of wnr: well bckd: back to form today, well h'capped: see 1145.
1276 **HIGHLAND WARRIOR 11** [11] J S Goldie 5-8-9 (65) N Mackay(3) 8/1: 133-3323: Slow away, in tch   ½   68
stands side, styd on for press: eff at 5f, 6f & poss Ayr ideal: see 967.
1393* **RAYMONDS PRIDE 5** [14] K A Ryan 4-9-12 (6ex)bl (82) T Eaves(5) 15/2: 0-005114: Dwelt, held up   nk   84
stands side, short of room dist, styd on well ins last: shade closer with a clr run: see 1393.
4353} **PALANZO 224** [4]6-8-12 (68) P M Quinn 50/1: 000000-5: b g Green Desert - Karpacka (Rousillon)   hd   70+
Held up far side, hdwy to lead that group ins last, kept on well: unplcd '03 (rtd 70, h'cap): cond stks rnr-up '02:
suited by 6f on firm or fast grnd, gall trk: best without blnks: 1st home on far side, well h'capped, keep in mind.
2 Apr'02 Thir 6fm 99- C: 2 Jul'01 Hayd 6fm 104- C: 2 Jun'01 Yarm 6g/f 107- C: 1 Jun'01 Newm 6fm 107-102 B:
2 May'01 Hayd 6g/f 104-99 A:
4541} **BRIGADORE 213** [8]5-8-12 (68) T Hamilton(3) 50/1: 030000-6: b g Magic Ring - Music Mistress   ¾   67
(Classic Music) Prom centre, kept on onepace, reapp: h'cap scorer '03: lightly rcd & unplcd '02 (rtd 84, h'cap):
eff at 5f on fast & gd/soft grnd, likes a stiff/gall trk & can force the pace. 1 Jul'03 Ayr 5g/f 75-71 C:
2 Jun'01 Beve 5gd 90- B: 1 May'01 Newc 5g/f 87- D: 1 May'01 Newc 5g/s 75- F: 2 Apr'01 Muss 5g/s 72- F:
1120 **CHAIRMAN BOBBY 20** [3]6-9-0 (70) D Allan(3) 10/1: 33062-57: Led far side till ins last: see 1120.   ¾   66
1217 **PAX 15** [7]7-9-10 (80) L Treadwell(7) 11/1: 1640-668: Chsd ldrs far side till dist: see 927.   nk   75
1179* **MYND 16** [1]4-8-11 (67) Dean McKeown 5/1: 1120219: Dwelt, prom far side till dist: nicely bckd.   shd   62
1120 **SIERRA VISTA 20** [16]4-9-8 p (78) P Hanagan 8/1: 3604-030: 10th: Led stand side till dist, wknd.   ½   72
1255 **SEVEN NO TRUMPS 12** [12]7-9-10 (80) S Carson 25/1: 000-2500: 11th: Chsd ldrs stands side till   hd   74
over 1f out: btr 944 (soft, reapp).
1120 **BEYOND THE CLOUDS 20** [13]8-9-9 (79) D R McCabe 33/1: 03000-00: 12th: Held up stands side &   nk   72+
keen, hung left but kept on under tender handling fnl 1f: jockey banned for 20 days, trainer fined & horse banned
for 40 days for failing to achieve best possible placing: v eyecatching.
3821} **ZUHAIR 252** [5]11-9-5 (75) Alex Greaves 40/1: 002200-0: 13th: Held up far side, nvr on terms.   nk   67
4874} **DISPOL KATIE 190** [15]3-9-6 (85) N Callan 10/1: 131022-0: 14th: Chsd ldrs stands side till dist.   nk   76
1145 **QUANTICA 19** [19]5-8-10 (66) Kim Tinkler 10/1: 00002-60: 15th: Dwelt stands side, al rear.   ½   56
1217 **JOHN OGROATS 15** [6]6-9-6 (76) F Lynch 50/1: 40000-00: 16th: Far side, nvr on terms.   nk   65
944   **Whistler 35** [9]7-9-8 p(78) M Fenton 33/1:0
4719} **Beyond Calculation 201** [20]10-8-11 (67) J Quinn 20/1:0
1293 **Izmail 10** [17]5-9-2 (72) A Nicholls 25/1:0   1217 **Tommy Smith 15** [2]6-9-5 bl(75) G Parkin 40/1:0
20 Ran   Time 1m 01.75 (4.75)   Owned: 2nd Carlton Partnership   Trained: Worksop

---

1477   5.35 Levy Board Classified Stakes 3yo 0-70 (E)
            £3604 £1109 £555   **6f str**   **Good/Soft 90**   **-21 Slow**   Stands Side

1392* **MR WOLF 5** [6] D W Barker 3-9-9 (70) T Eaves(5) 9/2: 500-2211: Led till over 1f out, styd on   82
gamely for press to lead again well ins last: qck reapp: likes to force the pace at 5/6f on gd/soft & soft grnd,
handles firm: see 1392.
4301* **MIS CHICAF 227** [4] J S Wainwright 3-9-1 (71) D Allan(3) 16/1: 053501-2: b f Prince Sabo -   1   70
Champagne Season (Vaguely Noble) Handy & led over 1f out, drvn & hdd cl-home: nicely bckd on reapp:
mdn scorer fnl '03 start: winning form at 5f, stays an easy 6f: acts on fast & gd/soft grnd.
1 Sep'03 Beve 5g/f 77-(63) D:
914   **TREASURE CAY 38** [2] P W D'Arcy 3-9-8 (75) Paul Eddery 9/2: 1-53: Held up, rdn & hdwy to chall   hs   77
over 1f out, no extra fnl 100y: well bckd: turf bow: eff at 5/6f, return to latter could suit: acts on polytrack
& gd/soft grnd: see 176 (5f, debut).
1023* **SHRINK 29** [1] M L W Bell 3-9-0 (70) I Mongan 6/1: 22-214: Trkd ldrs & ch over 1f out, rdn & no   shd   68
extra ins last: encouraging turf return, stays 6f but a return to 5f could suit: acts on fast, gd/soft & polytrack.
4923} **NEON BLUE 186** [3]3-9-3 (68) D Tudhope(7) 12/1: 204040-5: b g Atraf - Desert Lynx (Green Desert)   ¾   69
Dwelt & held up, hdwy to chall over 1f out, onepace: gelded, reapp: dual mdn rnr-up '03: eff at 5/6f on fast &
gd/soft grnd, gall/easy trks. 2 Aug'03 Thir 5g/s 69-(80) E: 2 Aug'03 Thir 5fm 72- D:
1228* **TIZZYS LAW 14** [5]3-9-0 (70) J Bramhill 13/2: 0-16: Trkd ldrs, rdn & ch over 1f out, no extra: 1   63
clr of rem: btr 1228 (5f).
1239 **ALICE BLACKTHORN 14** [8]3-9-0 (67) F Lynch 16/1: 44510-07: b f Forzando - Owdbetts (High Estate)   5   48
Dwelt & rear, nvr able to chall: auct mdn wnr '03: eff round 6f on firm & fast grnd, stiff/undul & gall trks.
1 Oct'03 Pont 6g/f 71-(70) F:
4534} **COMMANDER BOND 213** [7]3-9-7 (74) D McGaffin 20/1: 004-8: Dwelt, rear, nvr a factor: gelded.   1¾   50
1050 **MONTE MAJOR 26** [9]3-9-5 (72) N Callan 5/2 FAV: 6-342129: Prom, drvn & btn over 1f out, virtually   24   0
p.u.: well bckd, reportedly unsuited by crse: see 1050 & 875.
9 Ran   Time 1m 16.19(6.69)   Owned: Mr P Asquith   Trained: Richmond

Official Going GOOD.

1478   1.40 Countrywide Steel & Tubes Rated Stakes Handicap 4yo+ 0-100 (B)   [106]
£12360 £4688 £2344   1m2f   Good/Firm 20   -03 Slow   Stands Side

3332} **PROMOTION 273** [2] Sir Michael Stoute 4-8-7 (1oh) (85) M J Kinane 12/1: 132-1: b g Sadler's Wells **102+**
- Tempting Prospect (Shirley Heights) Dwelt, rear stands side, gd hdwy to lead dist, rdn clr: tchd 16/1, reapp:
'03 debut mdn wnr, subs rnr-up in class stks grade, has since been gelded: eff at 10/12f on fast & firm grnd:
likes a stiff/gall trk, runs well fresh: lightly rcd, type to prog further & more val h'caps to be won.
2 Aug'03 Thir 12fm 86-(85) D: 1 May'03 Sand 10.0g/f 85- D:
1111 **TIZZY MAY 21** [4] R Hannon 4-9-2 (95) P Dobbs 20/1: 23240-02: ch c Highest Honor - Forentia   2½   105
(Formidable) Chsd ldrs stands side, ev ch ent fnl 1f, kept on but not pace of wnr: failed to win in '03, tho' plcd
many times in h'cap company: mdn & stks wnr in '02: eff at 7/10f on firm & soft grnd: runs well fresh: fine run
in this competitive event, deserves similar.
2 Oct'03 Newm 10fm 99-95 B: 2 Sep'03 Hayd 10.5gd 97-96 B: 2 Aug'03 Good 9g/f 99-96 B:
2 Jul'03 Sand 7.1g/f 97-93 C: 1 May'02 Newm 5fm 96- D:
1111 **PUTRA KUANTAN 21** [16] M A Jarvis 4-8-13 (92) P Robinson 4/1 FAV: 01200-63: b c Grand Lodge -   ½   **101+**
Fade (Persepolis) Made all far side, kept on but no ch with front 2 on stands side: runs well fresh: '03 mdn
(debut) & class stks wnr: handles a sharp or stiff/gall trk: runs well fresh: handles gd/soft, prefers fast & firm
grnd: can set the pace & a fine run in the circumstances.
2 Aug'03 Yarm 10.1g/f 94-(95) C: 1 Aug'03 York 9.7g/f 96-(88) C: 1 May'03 Newm 10fm 91- D:
1296* **BLYTHE KNIGHT 10** [10] E A L Dunlop 4-9-10 (103) L Dettori 6/1: 0430-414: Slowly away stands   1½   109
side, hdwy 2f out, nrst fin under top-weight: nicely bckd: needs to come late, but nvr got into contention today.
1235 **ALRAFID 14** [3]5-8-7 (4oh) (82) R L Moore 40/1: 22426-05: Rear stands side, keeping on when short   hd   91
of room 1.5f out, nvr nrr: gd run from this outsider: see 134 (AW h'cap).
1296 **KINGS THOUGHT 10** [7]5-9-2 (95) J Murtagh 16/1: 310-6046: Led till over 1f out stands side, grad   1   98
wnkd: tough front runner: again bhnd today's 4th in 1296 (hvy).
1225 **MYSTERINCH 14** [8]4-9-1 (94) J F Egan 50/1: 4211/3-37: Chsd ldrs stands side, ev ch dist, sn   nk   96
onepcd: see 1225 (1m, soft).
1151 **ST PANCRAS 18** [12]4-8-11 (90) W Ryan 12/1: 2/5456-08: b c Danehill Dancer - Lauretta Blue   1½   90
(Bluebird) Slowly away stands side, styd on late, nvr dngrs: bckd from 20/1, swtg: lightly rcd & highly tried in
'03, often made the running: '02 nov wnr, also Gr 2 rnr-up: eff at 7f/1m on fast & firm grnd, shld stay 10f:
handles a stiff/gall trk & has run well fresh: gd run after getting warm & missing start, keep in mind.
2 Sep'02 Donc 7fm 107- A: 2 Aug'02 Sali 8g/f 93- C: 1 Jul'02 Newm 6g/f 87- D:
1235* **IONIAN SPRING 14** [14]9-8-11 (90) R Smith 14/1: 06530-19: Rear stands side, prog 3f out, btn fnl 1f.   1   88
1235 **BARRY ISLAND 14** [6]5-8-7 (8oh) (78) R Thomas(5) 40/1: 1524430: 10th: Mid-div stands side, btn dist.   1½   82
4041} **INTERCEPTOR 241** [19]4-8-9 (88) D Holland 16/1: 51/2030-0: 11th: Chsd ldrs 1m far side on reapp.   5   77
1437 **AKASH 6** [21]4-8-12 (91) J Fanning 10/1: 5220-120: 12th: Chsd ldr stands side, wknd 1.5f out: qck reapp.   1   78
928 **EVEREST 36** [15]7-8-7 (1oh) (85) J P Spencer 13/2: 23000-00: 13th: Rear stands side, nvr dngrs.   ¾   72
4894* }**PAGAN SKY 189** [13]5-8-7 (86) Lisa Jones(3) 12/1: 056161-0: 14th: Slow away stands side, al rear.   2   69
1115 **ALMAVIVA 21** [9]4-8-11 (90) E Ahern 50/1: 1/65-00: 15th: Prom, wknd 3f out stands side.   6   64
   Tresor Secret 266 [18]4-8-7 (1oh)(85) D Fox(5) 50/1:0   4599} **Famous Grouse 210** [17]4-9-7 (100) S Drowne 20/1:0
3809} **Barrissimo 252** [5]4-9-3 (96) K Fallon 33/1:0   1225 **Gala Sunday 14** [11]4-8-11 (90) P J Smullen 66/1:0
   19 Ran   Time 2m 04.35 (2.25)   Owned: The Queen   Trained: Newmarket

1479   2.15 Gr3 Victor Chandler Palace House Stakes 3yo+ (A)
£29000 £11000 £5500   5f str   Good/Firm 20   -01 Slow   Stands Side

1187 **FRIZZANTE 16** [1] J R Fanshawe 5-8-9 (105) J Murtagh 13/8 FAV: 14611-21: Rear, hdwy dist, strong   **116+**
run to lead nr line: hvly bckd from 2/1: eff at 5/6f on gd & firm grnd: likes Newmarket: needs to be held up as
late as poss & clearly a v smart & prog sprinter when everything goes right: just the type for the Golden Jubilee or
Kings Stand at R Ascot: see 1187.
4282} **AVONBRIDGE 231** [5] R Charlton 4-8-12 (113) S Drowne 7/1: 221343-2: b c Averti - Alessia   shd   **118+**
(Caerleon) Chsd ldrs, slightly short of room dist, led ins fnl 1f, caught cl home: clr of rem, reapp & reportedly
ndd this race: '03 List wnr, also Gr 1 plcd in France: v eff at 5/6f on firm & gd/soft: likes a stiff/gall trk: v
smart sprinter who hails from yard who handled brother Patavellian v well last season: exciting season to come.
1 Oct'02 York 6g/f 107- A: 2 May'03 Newb 6.0g/f 115-(108) A: 2 Apr'03 Asco 6gd 114-(108) A:
1 Oct'02 York 6g/f 107- A: 2 May'03 Newb 6.0g/f 115-(108) A: 2 Apr'03 Asco 6gd 114-(108) A:
4315* }**BOOGIE STREET 226** [9] R Hannon 3-8-3 t (107) R L Moore 11/1: 51341-3: b c Compton Place - Tart   4   106
And A Half (Distant Relative) Chsd ldrs, led dist till ins fnl 1f, no extra on reapp: '03 mdn auct & List wnr: eff
at 5/6f on fast grnd: likes a stiff/gall trk, wears a t-strap: fine reapp bhnd to v smart sprinters.
1 Sep'03 Ayr 5g/f 106-(94) A: 1 Aug'03 Sand 5.0g/f 91- E:
1207 **FROMSONG 15** [3] B R Millman 6-8-12 (95) L Dettori 25/1: 0000-244: Rear, short of room halfway,   hd   106$
fin well but too late: see 1207 & 1004.
1162 **MATTY TUN 17** [13]5-8-12 (87) K Fallon 33/1: 31100-05: b g Lugana Beach - B Grade (Lucky   ½   104$
Wednesday) Outpcd, late prog, nvr dngrs: fine run at today's weights, lost any realistic ch at the start: won 3
h'caps in '03 (incl reapp): '02 mdn auct & h'cap wnr: eff at 5f on firm, gd/soft & f/sand: loves a stiff trk, can
run well fresh: return to h'cap grade will suit.   1 May'03 Muss 5gd 89-83 C: 1 May'03 York 5.0fm 84-76 B:
1 Dec'02 Sout 5af 75a-72 D: 1 Aug'02 Sand 5g/s 71-64 D: 2 May'02 Carl 5g/s 63-62 E: 1 May'02 Newc 5g/f 65- F:
4775} **BALTIC KING 197** [14]4-8-12 t (105) D Holland 7/1: 043100-6: b c Danetime - Lindfield Belle (Fairy   ½   102
King) Rear, hdwy & ev ch dist, no extra on reapp: prog in '03, class stks reapp: eff at 5/6f on
gd & firm grnd, poss handles soft: wears a t-strap: sharper next time & prob up tp wng in List/Gr 3 class.
1 Sep'03 Asco 5g/f 108-98 B: 2 Jul'03 Newm 6g/f 98-94 B: 2 Jun'03 Asco 5g/f 94-90 B: 1 May'03 Leic 6.0g/f 95-(85) D:
1 Oct'02 Ling 5gd 87- D: 2 Aug'02 Wind 6g/f 86- E:
1137 **SMOKIN BEAU 19** [7]7-8-12 (98) T G McLaughlin 16/1: 5400-627: Chsd ldrs, onepcd fnl 1f: see 1137.   hd   101
4680} **FAST HEART 203** [2]3-8-3 t (99) J F McDonald 50/1: 131003-8: Nvr better than mid-div on reapp.   hd   100
1207 **PERUVIAN CHIEF 15** [12]7-8-12 vis (97) E Ahern 16/1: 0600029: Slow away, late prog when short of rm.   1½   95
1159 **COLONEL COTTON 19** [8]5-8-12 (109) W Ryan 9/1: 50130-60: 10th: Outpcd, short of room dist & again   nk   94
ins fnl 1f, nvr nrr: not much luck, may have fought out minor placings with a clr run: needs everything to fall right.
1207 **REPERTORY 15** [6]11-9-1 (108) J Fanning 25/1: 64010-00: 11th: Front rank, wknd fnl 1f.   2½   90

1207 **DUBAIAN GIFT 15** [4]5-8-12 (105) Martin Dwyer 20/1: 02216-00: 12th: Led till dist, wknd. ½ **86**
4362} **MORNIN RESERVES 224** [10]5-8-12 (108) R Winston 14/1: 113012-0: 13th: Front rank, wkng when hmpd fnl 1f: reapp, new stable. 5 **71**
13 Ran Time 59.24 (1.04) Owned: Mrs Jan Hopper & Mrs Elizabeth Grundy Trained: Newmarket

1480 **2.55 Gr1 Ultimatebet Com 2000 Guineas Stakes Colts & Fillies 3yo (A)**
£174000 £66000 £33000 **1m str** **Good/Firm 20** **+18 Fast** Centre

1188* **HAAFHD 16** [4] B W Hills 3-9-0 (120) R Hills 11/2: 1133-11: Trkd ldrs centre, went on over 2f out, styd on v strongly, rdn out for a famous win: well bckd, fast time: handles gd/soft, loves fast & firm grnd: much imprvd for 1m & forcing tactics this term: likes a stiff/gall trk, esp Newmarket: high-class & will prove v hard to beat arnd 1m this term: see 1188. **125+**
4797} **SNOW RIDGE 196** [14] Saeed bin Suroor 3-9-0 (113) L Dettori 8/1: 110-2: b c Indian Ridge - Snow Princess (Ela Mana Mou) Held up centre, hdwy & switched to far side 2f out, styd on well fnl 1f but cld nvr get to wnr: well bckd, reapp: trained by M Tregoning to win 2 of 3 '03 starts, stks (reapp) & notably Gr 2 Royal Lodge: eff at 1m, bred to relish 10f+: acts on fast & firm grnd, runs well fresh: real Derby type & one to follow. *1¾* **122+**
1 Sep'03 Asco 8fm 113- A: 1 Sep'03 Kemp 7g/f 108- C:
4742*}**AZAMOUR 202** [11] John M Oxx 3-9-0 M J Kinane 25/1: 11-3: b c Night Shift - Asmara (Lear Fan) Held up centre, hdwy 1.5f out, fin well into 3rd on reapp: Irish chall, unbtn in 2 '03 starts, both at The Curragh (incl Gr 2): eff at 1m, will relish 10f judged on this: acts on fast & gd/soft grnd: expected to take in the Irish 2000 Guineas on his way to the Derby & clearly v smart. 1 Oct'03 Curr 8g/s 110- : *1* **119**
1301* **GREY SWALLOW 13** [3] D K Weld 3-9-0 P J Smullen 10/1: 11-14: Slowly away, hdwy from rear centre over 1f out, nvr nrr: well bckd: prev unbtn Irish chall, acts on fast & soft: sure to run well in Irish 2000 Guineas. *1* **117**
1155* **WHIPPER 25** [8]3-9-0 C Soumillon 9/1: 41141-15: Trkd ldrs centre, ev ch 2f out, no extra fnl 1f: op 7/1: French chall, prob failed to stay this stiff 1m: handles firm, seems best on soft grnd: see 1155 (7f). *hd* **117**
1234+**SALFORD CITY 14** [6]3-9-0 (115) J Murtagh 11/2: 1-16: Outpcd, prog 2f out, flashed tail & onepcd fnl 1f: well bckd: again hmpd himself with a slow start & can not get away with that in top-class company: prob worth another chance if able to sort out breaking probs: see 1234. ½ **116**
4797} **BACHELOR DUKE 196** [9]3-9-0 (114) S Sanders 20/1: 334-7: b c Miswaki - Gossamer (Seattle Slew) Chsd ldrs centre, onepcd dist on reapp: lightly rcd & yet to win, tho' 4th in Gr 1 Dewhurt on fnl '03 start (rtd 114): eff at 7f on fast grnd, 1m+ shld suit this term: nailed on to find a mdn. *1½* **113**
1234 **MILK IT MICK 14** [1]3-9-0 (114) D Holland 12/1: 2511-258: Slowly away centre, keen in rear, nvr nr ldrs: bckd from 20/1, clr of rem: nvr really trav & reportedly failed to stay this 1m trip: will return to 6/7f now but has yet to recapture high-class juv form: see 1040 (AW). *3½* **106**
3904} **TUMBLEBRUTUS 230** [7]3-9-0 P Cosgrave 200/1: 62126-9: b c Storm Cat - Mariah's Storm (Rahy) Front rank centre, wknd fnl 1f on reapp: '03 mdn wnr, also rnr-up in a Gr 2: eff at 7f on fast & gd/soft grnd: smart, but prob pacemaker for fav One Cool Cat today. 2 Aug'03 Curr 7g/f 107- A: *8* **90**
1150 **GLARAMARA 18** [12]3-9-0 (96) T E Durcan 200/1: 013-020: 10th: Al outpcd centre: highly tried. *2½* **85**
1188 **THREE VALLEYS 16** [2]3-9-0 (117) K Fallon 20/1: 113D2-20: 11th: Mid-div centre, eff 2f out, sn btn: fin tired & most disapp: may do better back at sprint trips, but fine 5L 2nd to today's wnr on reapp in 1188. ½ **84**
1113 **BARBAJUAN 21** [10]3-9-0 (110) P Robinson 150/1: 45143-50: 12th: Rcd alone far side & chsd ldrs till 2f out: see 1113. *shd* **84**
4284*}**ONE COOL CAT 230** [13]3-9-0 J P Spencer 15/8 FAV: 41111-0: 13th: b c Storm Cat - Tacha (Mr Prospector) Held up centre, rdn & btn over 2f out, eased: Irish chall, reapp, hvly bckd from 9/4: top-class juv, dual Gr 1 wnr, Phoenix & National stks: eff at 7f on gd & fast grnd, shld stay 1m: has a fine turn of foot & held in high regard by powerful yard: reportedly suffered from an irregular heartbeat here & capable of much better. *dist* **44**
1 Sep'03 Curr 7g/f 122- : 1 Aug'03 Curr 6gd 119- A: 1 Jul'03 Curr 6.3gd 116- A: 1 Jun'03 York 6.0fm 111- D:
4661} **GOLDEN SAHARA 205** [5]3-9-0 VIS t (96) J Carroll 200/1: 122-0: 14th: Set pace 5f centre, wknd. *nk* **43**
14 Ran Time 1m 36.64 (0.14) Owned: Mr Hamdan Al Maktoum Trained: Lambourn

1481 **3.30 Ladbrokes Handicap Stakes 3yo+ 0-95 (C)** **[95]**
£29000 £11000 £5500 **6f str** **Good/Firm 20** **-01 Slow** Stands Side

1035 **MOAYED 28** [20] N P Littmoden 5-8-13 bl t (80) E Ahern 25/1: 0-126331: Chsd ldrs far side, imprvd to lead ent fnl 1f, styd on strongly, drvn out: trav smoothly in fast run races, stays 10f, clearly apprec this drop back to 6f: acts on fast, hvy & polytrack: eff in a visor & t-strap: Stewards Cup is his target & open to more improvement at this trip: see 1035 & 571 (AW sell). **89**
611 **ELLENS ACADEMY 79** [3] E J Alston 9-8-11 (78) J F Egan 33/1: 31-46342: Chsd ldrs stands side, prog to lead that group dist, styd on strongly, but not rch wnr far side: 11 wk abs: deserves similar, see 386 (AW). *1¾* **81**
1138 **POLAR KINGDOM 19** [23] T D Barron 6-8-7 (74) R Hills 20/1: 0-311003: Rear far side, fin strongly but too late: fit from AW, on a handy turf mark: see 611 (7f AW). *hd* **77**
1151 **GREENSLADES 18** [25] P J Makin 5-9-9 (90) S Sanders 10/1: 1/0105-44: Tried to make all far side, collared ent fnl 1f, no extra: sound run back over fav 6f trip: see 1151 (7f, reapp). *shd* **93**
4471} **TYCHY 217** [19]5-9-9 (90) B Reilly(3) 33/1: 052110-5: ch f Suave Dancer - Touch of White (Song) Chsd ldrs far side, ev ch dist, not qckn ins fnl 1f on reapp: won 3 h'caps & a class stks in '03: eff at 6/7f on firm & gd grnd, handles soft: runs well fresh, handles any trk: gd weight carrier, spot on next time. ½ **92**
1 Sep'03 Pont 6g/f 94-83 D: 1 Jul'03 Epso 7gd 85-(81) D: 2 Jul'03 Asco 6.5g/f 85-81 C: 1 May'03 Newb 6.0g/f 80-74 D:
1 May'03 Ling 5g/f 77-68 E: 1 Sep'02 Nott 6g/f 67-62 E: 1 Aug'02 Brig 6.9g/f 62- F: 2 Aug'02 Muss 7.1fm 63-57 E:
1138 **HIGH REACH 19** [6]4-9-8 (89) L Dettori 8/1: 43144-36: Chsd ldrs stands side, styd on under press fnl 1f: nicely bckd: see 1138. *shd* **91**
1293 **FRUIT OF GLORY 10** [7]5-9-9 (90) D Holland 12/1: 5-054437: Chsd ldrs stands side, onepcd fnl 1f. ¾ **89**
567 **BEAUVRAI 84** [29]4-8-8 (75) M Tebbutt 100/1: 0000-008: Chsd ldrs far side, ev ch dist, sn onepcd: 12 wk abs: prev trained by J J Quinn: both wins at 5f: see 567 (AW). *1¼* **70**
1104 **AVENTURA 21** [28]4-8-13 (80) C Soumillon 50/1: 0-004009: Outpcd halfway far side, styd on late. *nk* **74**
1354 **MR MALARKEY 7** [4]4-8-13 bl (80) T G McLaughlin 25/1: 04000-40: 10th: Front rank far side, wknd. *nk* **73**
5030} **NAJEEBON 175** [27]5-9-8 (89) S Hitchcott(3) 25/1: 001450-0: 11th: ch c Cadeaux Genereux - Jumairah Sun (Scenic) Chsd ldrs 5f far side, onepcd on reapp: won 3 h'caps in '03 (incl reapp): '02 mdn wnr: stays 7f, suited by 6f: acts on firm & fast grnd, any trk: eff with/without visor & t-strap: with M Channon. *shd* **82**
1 Oct'03 York 6.0g/f 92-85 B: 1 Sep'03 Good 6fm 88-80 C: 2 Aug'03 Hayd 6g/f 81-78 C: 2 May'03 Ling 7gd 82-80 B:
1 Apr'03 Pont 6g/f 82-74 C: 1 Sep'02 Yarm 6fm 76- D:
1276 **VIEWFORTH 11** [1]6-8-10 bl (77) S Drowne 25/1: 4600-440: 12th: Chsd ldrs 5f stands side. *nk* **69**
1138 **MARKER 19** [21]4-9-7 (88) R Havlin 40/1: 1600-600: 13th: Chsd ldrs far side, outpcd fnl 1f: see 945. *nk* **79**
1138 **PRINCE CYRANO 19** [30]5-9-2 (83) G Carter 50/1: 0200-000: 14th: b g Cyrano de Bergerac - Odilese *shd* **74**

(Mummy's Pet) Held up far side, nvr dngrs: rnr-up once in '03 (class stks): failed to win in '02, 7th in Wokingham (rtd 103): dual '01 wnr for S Williams: stays 7f, suited by 6f on fast/firm grnd, handles soft: best with blnks, handles any trk: on a winning mark. 2 Jun'03 Wind 6g/f 92-(90) C: 2 Sep'01 Chan 5.5sft 102- :
1 Sep'01 Kemp 6g/f 98- B: 1 Aug'01 Folk 6g/f 91- F: 2 Jul'01 Newm 7g/f 86- D:
618 **CELTIC MILL 78** [14]6-9-4 (85) L Enstone(3) 20/1: 0140-140: 15th: Led 4f stands side, wknd: 11 wk abs. ½ **75**
1120 **OBE ONE 20** [5]4-8-8 (75) F Norton 66/1: 10000-00: 16th: Chsd ldrs till halfway stands side. *nk* **64**
1138* **PERSARIO 19** [8]5-9-5 (86) J Murtagh 4/1 FAV: 62620-10: 17th: Chsd ldrs, wknd 1.5f out stands side: hvly bckd: more expected after 1138 (reapp). ½ **74**
2804} **MARSAD 295** [24]10-9-9 (90) P Doe 14/1: 505203-0: 18th: Chsd ldrs 4f far side on reapp: 5th in this race last year, won it in '01 & '02 (off rtd 90). *nk* **77**
1251 **CD FLYER 12** [11]7-9-4 (85) R Winston 14/1: 4110-520: 19th: Speed till halfway stands side: 3rd in this race off an 11lbs lower mark when trained by M Channon in '03: see 1251. *nk* **71**
1131 **CHEESE N BISCUITS 19** [18]4-8-12 (79) R L Moore 50/1: 33135-00: 20th: Nvr nr ldrs stands side. ¾ **62**
1138 **WINNING VENTURE 19** [22]7-9-5 (86) W Ryan 14/1: 46305-60: 21th: Prom 4f stands side: tchd 20/1. *shd* **69**
998 **WATCHING 31** [12]7-9-2 (83) P Dobbs 20/1: 00040-30: 22th: Chsd ldrs till halfway stands side. ¾ **63**
5030} **Bi Polar 175** [9]4-8-11 (78) M J Kinane 33/1:0
1151 **Master Robbie 18** [2]5-9-11 (92) T E Durcan 40/1:0
1138 **Steel Blue 19** [10]4-9-5 VIS(86) M Hills 25/1:0
1151 **Camberley 18** [13]7-9-11 (92) K Fallon 16/1:0
1383 **Devise 5** [16]5-8-11 (78) Martin Dwyer 40/1:0
921 **Plateau 37** [17]5-9-3 (84) J Carroll 25/1:0
1151 **Fantasy Believer 18** [15]6-9-11 (92) J Fanning 40/1:0
1251 **Arctic Burst 12** [26]4-9-4 VIS t(85) S Whitworth 100/1:0
30 Ran Time 1m 12.03 (1.23) Owned: Mr Nigel Shields Trained: Newmarket

1482

4.05 Listed Rolls-Royce Motor Cars London Newmarket Stakes Colts 3yo (A)
£17400 £6600 £3300 **1m2f** **Good/Firm 20** **-12 Slow** Stands Side

1318* **HAZYVIEW 8** [6] N A Callaghan 3-8-8 (84) D Holland 3/1: 031-2111: Made all, styd on strongly fnl 1f, rdn out: well bckd: completed hat-trick after 2 h'cap wins & clearly coped with this step into List company: eff at 10f, 12f shld suit: acts on fast & gd/soft grnd, any trk: fast improving, v useful colt who may have a crack at the Chester Vase while in this form: see 1318. **111**
1167 **TAHREEB 17** [4] M P Tregoning 3-8-8 (108) Martin Dwyer 4/1: 21344-42: Chsd ldrs, ev ch ent fnl 1f, kept on but not pace of wnr: nicely bckd: styd this longer 10f trip: rtd higher in 1167. *1½* **108**
1040 **CROCODILE DUNDEE 28** [3] Jamie Poulton 3-8-8 (93) J F Egan 20/1: 105-063: b c Croco Rouge - Miss Salsa Dancer (Salse) Keen in rear, hdwy & ev ch ent fnl 1f, no extra: '03 mdn wnr (reapp), in gd form in decent company on AW: eff at 7f/1m, prob stays 10f: acts on fast grnd & polytrack: runs well fresh: useful. *2½* **104**
1 Oct'03 Ling 7ap 85a- D:
1189 **ISIDORE BONHEUR 16** [5] B W Hills 3-8-8 bl (98) M Hills 9/1: 14-44: Trkd ldr, ev ch till wknd fnl 1f: not stay 10f? see 1189 (first time blnks). *2½* **100**
4557} **BAYEUX 212** [1]3-8-8 t (112) L Dettori 11/10 FAV: 102-5: b c Red Ransom - Elizabeth Bay (Mr Prospector) Chsd ldrs, wknd dist: hvly bckd, reapp: trained by D Loder & won 1st of 3 '03 starts (mdn), subs Gr 3 rnr-up to Milk It Mick: eff at 6/7f on fast grnd: eff with/without a t-strap & reportedly has wind probs: now with Saeed bin Suroor & a drop back in trip shld suit. 2 Oct'03 Newm 7g/f 111- A: 1 May'03 Good 6g/f 95- D: *1* **98**
5 Ran Time 2m 05.38 (3.28) Owned: Mr T Mohan Trained: Newmarket

1483

4.40 Ruinart Champagne Conditions Stakes 4yo+ (B)
£12267 £4653 £2327 **1m2f** **Good/Firm 20** **-02 Slow** Stands Side

1230 **BANDARI 14** [8] M Johnston 5-8-7 (114) J Fanning 9/2: 3/4442-01: b c Alhaarth - Miss Audimar (Mr Leader) Made all, styd on strongly fnl 2f, drvn out: failed to win in '03, Gr 2 rnr-up on fnl of 4 starts: '02 Gr 3 (2) & Gr 2 wnr, disapp in Derby: suited by 10/12f, just stays 14f: acts on firm, soft & on any trk: can run well fresh & best when able to dominate as he did today: v smart at best & can win more Gr races. **113**
2 Jul'03 Newm 12g/f 116-(117) A: 1 Aug'02 York 11.8gd 118- A: 1 Jul'02 Good 12fm 121- A: 1 May'02 Ling 11.4gd 115- A:
1 Oct'01 Pont 8sft 109- A: 1 Sep'01 Ayr 8g/f 102- D: 1 Aug'01 Beve 7.4gd 98- D:
884 **PRIVATE CHARTER 42** [10] B W Hills 4-8-7 (110) M Hills 10/1: 32645-02: b c Singspiel - By Charter (Shirley Heights) Chsd ldrs, chall over 1f out, kept on & not btn far: nicely bckd, 6 wk abs: '03 mdn wnr (reapp), also rnr-up in Gr 1 Italian Derby: eff at 10/12f on gd & fast: can run well fresh: smart, List/Gr races await. *1* **110**
2 May'03 Capa 12g/f 109- A: 1 Mar'03 Ling 10ap 79a- D: 2 Nov'02 Newm 7g/s 85- D:
1588*}**MUSANID 349** [3] Sir Michael Stoute 4-8-10 (100) R Hills 6/1: 33/1-3: ch c Swain - Siyadah (Mr Prospector) Rear, styd on fnl 2f, nrst fin on reapp: nicely bckd: won sole '03 start (mdn): eff at 9/10f, shld relish 12f: acts on firm & soft grnd: handles a stiff/gall or sharp trk, runs well fresh: smart & career best run, only lightly rcd & more improvement to come. 1 May'03 Ripo 9sft 89- D: ½ **105**
4955} **PERSIAN LIGHTNING 183** [7] J L Dunlop 5-8-7 (102) M J Kinane 13/2: 306200-4: b g Sri Pekan - Persian Fantasy (Persian Bold) Trkd wnr, ev ch ent fnl 1f, no extra: nicely bckd: '03 h'cap wnr, also stks plcd: won 2 h'caps & a class stks in '02: eff at 9/10f, stays 12/13f on gd & firm, likes a gall trk: tough, fine reapp. *1* **106**
2 Sep'03 Newb 9fm 101-(102) B: 2 Jun'03 Asco 10g/f 104-98 A: 1 May'03 Newm 10g/f 99-92 B:
1 Sep'02 Hayd 11.9gd 89-80 D: 1 Jun'02 Newc 10.1g/f 80- D: 2 Jun'02 Pont 10g/f 78-70 D: 1 Apr'02 Leic 8g/f 72-68 E:
4196} **SONGLARK 232** [2]4-8-7 VIS t (107) L Dettori 4/1 FAV: 5/20452-5: Held up, smooth prog 2f out, found less than expected under press in 1st time visor on reapp: bckd from 11/2. *2½* **101**
1523} **ORANGE TOUCH 352** [6]4-8-7 (101) K Fallon 20/1: 51/54-6: Keen & prom, slightly outpcd 1.5f out, rallied late on reapp. *2* **97**
4296} **QUIET STORM 227** [9]4-8-10 (94) D Holland 20/1: 021324-7: Held up, nvr nr ldrs on reapp. *shd* **100**
4805] **BEEKEEPER 420** [1]6-8-7 J P Spencer 9/2: 4/0163/0-8: Rear, nvr nr to chall: well bckd, new yard. *1¼* **95**
1364* **PUTRA SANDHURST 7** [4]6-9-1 (104) P Robinson 9/1: 22025-19: Chsd ldrs, wknd dist: btr 1364 (g/s). *2* **100**
1139 **ROCKET FORCE 19** [5]4-8-7 (102) E Ahern 66/1: 41/320-00: 10th: Slowly away, nvr dngrs. *5* **84**
10 Ran Time 2m 04.31 (2.21) Owned: Mr Hamdan Al Maktoum Trained: Middleham

---

1484   5.15 Curragh 'home Of The Irish Classics' Handicap Stakes 4yo+ 0-100 (C)   [98]
£8572 £3252 £1626   1m4f   Good/Firm 20   -13 Slow   Centre

1357 **DISSIDENT** 7 [5] D Flood 6-8-0 vis (70) J Mackay 20/1: 4U10221: Prom, went on over 2f out, rdn   78
clr: eff at 10/12f on fast, hvy & polytrack: tough & progressive: see 1357 & 1026 (AW sell).
1295 **PAGAN DANCE** 10 [16] Mrs A J Perrett 5-9-6 p (90) L Dettori 6/1: 1440-342: Held up, prog when   3   94
short of room 2f out & again dist, fin well but wnr had flown: nicely bckd: poss a shade unlucky tho' tricky ride
who thrives on trouble in running: see 1295.
1172 **PRINS WILLEM** 17 [1] J R Fanshawe 5-9-4 (88) J Murtagh 9/2: 52610-23: Rear, prog 2f out, nrst   hd   92
fin: bckd from 11/2, clr of rem: best held up, deserves a race: see 1172 (C/D).
1172 **BAGAN** 17 [7] H R A Cecil 5-9-2 (86) W Ryan 4/1 FAV: 20015-44: Keen & chsd ldrs, hung right &   5   82
onepcd fnl 1f: well bckd: again bhnd today's 3rd in 1172 (C/D).
1230 **PERFECT STORM** 14 [19]5-9-8 (92) F Norton 14/1: 0012-005: b c Vettori - Gorgeous Dancer (Nordico)   nk   87
Held up, short of room 2f out, nrst fin: '02 class stks wnr, also rnr-up in val November H'cap: '02 rtd h'cap wnr:
eff at 1m, stays 12f well: acts on firm & soft grnd: handles a stiff or easy trk: has tried blnks.
2 Nov'03 Donc 12gd 95-90 B: 1 Oct'03 Yarm 10.1sft 90-(86) C: 1 Oct'02 Sand 8g/f 94-87 C:
2 Sep'02 Newb 8fm 87-85 C: 1 Jul'02 Kemp 6fm 85- D:
1111 **TRUST RULE** 21 [13]4-10-0 (98) M Hills 11/1: 32102-06: b c Selkirk - Hagwah (Dancing Brave)   Keen   1¼   91
& chsd ldrs, hmpd dist & no ch after: won a mdn & h'cap in '03, also plcd sev times: eff at 10/12f on gd & firm
grnd: handles a sharp or gall trk: ran better than fin pos suggests today & shld be given another chance.
2 Oct'03 Newm 12g/f 100-96 B: 1 Sep'03 York 11.9g/f 99-86 B: 2 Aug'03 York 11.9fm 88-85 C:
1 Jun'03 Wind 10.0g/f 87-(84) D 2 Jun'03 Hayd 11.9g/f 87-(86) D: 2 Mar'03 Donc 10.3gd 89- D:
1295 **CHAMPION LION** 10 [9]5-8-1 (2ow) (69) S Hitchcott 9/1: 050-0057: Slow away, hdwy 2f out, nrst fin.   shd   64
1112 **ESTABLISHMENT** 21 [2]7-8-7 (77) S Whitworth 25/1: 02015-08: b g Muhtarram - Uncharted Waters   nk   69+
(Celestial Storm) Waited with, nrst fin: '03 h'cap wnr, also 2nd twice: suited by 2m/2m4f on gd & firm grnd,
handles soft: fairly h'capped & an encouraging reapp over this inadequate trip: keep in mind back over 2m+.
1 Oct'03 Newm 16gd 83-78 C: 2 Oct'03 Good 16fm 79-75 E: 2 Mar'03 Asco 16.2g/f 81-78 D:
2 Jul'02 Asco 16.2gd 81-77 B: 2 Jun'02 Asco 20g/f 78-73 C: 2 Sep'01 Asco 16.2g/s 66-65 C:
1 Jul'01 Asco 12gd 68-62 C: 2 Jul'01 Wind 10g/f 65- E: 2 Jun'01 Brig 11.8g/f 53- E:
4215} **MONTECRISTO** 231 [8]11-8-4 (74) Lisa Jones(3) 40/1: 6/35323-9: Waited with, styd on late, nvr nrr.   ¾   65
3914} **LARGO** 195 [12]4-9-7 (91) M J Kinane 33/1: 011005-0: 10th: Nvr nr ldrs on reapp.   3½   77
1172 **DOVEDON HERO** 17 [3]4-8-9 (79) S Sanders 50/1: 33016-00: 11th: Prog to chase ldrs 2f out, sn btn.   nk   64
979 **ENVIRONMENT AUDIT** 32 [10]5-7-12 (3oh)VIS (65) J Jeffrey(6) 100/1: 00/0-0000: 12th: Led till over   hd   53
2f out, wknd qckly: too keen in first time visor.
1397* **RASID** 5 [6]6-8-9 (4ex) (79) D Holland 20/1: 3-102310: 13th: Al in rear: too sn after 1397?   1   62
936 **SO VITAL** 36 [11]4-8-3 P (73) R Price 50/1: 62-1030: 14th: Chsd ldrs, wknd 2f out.   2½   52
1027 **BRILLIANT RED** 29 [20]11-8-1 (78) E Ahern 40/1: 0064050: 15th: Chsd ldrs 10f, wknd.   6   48
1172 **WAIT FOR THE WILL** 17 [15]8-9-5 bl (89) R L Moore 25/1: 02426-00: 16th: Held up, al bhnd.   ¾   58
3255} **FINANCIAL FUTURE** 276 [14]4-10-0 (98) J Fanning 14/1: 322110-0: 17th: Prom till halfway, wknd.   3½   62
731 **HIP HOP HARRY** 66 [18]4-9-2 (86) K Fallon 7/1: 31-02120: 18th: Chsd ldrs, wknd 2f out: 9 wk abs.   11   33
1068 **WAHCHI** 25 [17]5-9-1 (85) T Lucas 100/1: 1/23/40-00: 19th: Al rear, fin last.   1½   30
19 Ran   Time 2m 32.81(4.01)   Owned: Mrs Ruth M Serrell   Trained: Lingfield

---

Official Going GOOD.

1485   2.10 Freephone Stanleybet Flat V Jump Jockeys Handicap Stakes 4yo+ 0-70 (E)   [49]
£6988 £2150 £1075   1m30y rnd   Good/Firm 34   -04 Slow   Inside

1049 **STOIC LEADER** 26 [2] R F Fisher 4-11-3 (66) K Dalgleish 12/1: 4011401: Mid-div, hdwy to lead 2f   80
out, rdn clr despite flashing tail over 1f out, eased cl-home: eff at 6/7f, now suited by 7f/1m on firm & soft grnd,
both AWs: back to form, see 967 & 913.
945 **SANGIOVESE** 35 [5] H Morrison 5-11-3 (66) T J Murphy 5/1: 01-03352: Chsd ldrs, switched & styd on   4   70
for press fnl 2f, no threat to wnr: see 195.
1198 **REALISM** 16 [7] P W Hiatt 4-10-13 (62) K McEvoy 25/1: 4410503: Chsd ldrs, styd on onepace fnl 2f: 1   64
acts on fibresand & fast grnd: see 678 (AW mdn h'cap).
1059 **PHRED** 26 [11] R F Johnson Houghton 4-11-2 (65) G Lee 16/1: 60100-64: Prom & ch 2f out, no extra   1   65
ins last: see 1059.
4540} **OSCAR PEPPER** 213 [9]7-11-1 (64) N Fehily 12/1: 050404-5: b g Brunswick - Princess Baja   1¾   60
(Conquistador Cielo) Held up, eff over 2f out, sn onepace: reapp: class stks wnr '03, AW h'cap & cond stks rnr-up:
dual turf h'cap wnr '02: suited by 7/9f, stays 10f: acts on firm, gd/soft & f/sand, prob any trk: best without headgear.
1 Jun'03 Redc 7g/f 72-(67) E: 2 Apr'03 Newc 8.0g/f 65-65 D: 2 Feb'03 Wolv 8.5af 87a-87 C: 2 Jan'03 Sout 8af 88a- C:
2 Nov'02 Wolv 8.4af 88a-85 C: 2 Jul'02 Beve 8.4g/s 69-68 D: 1 Jun'02 Redc 9fm 70-65 E: 1 May'02 Redc 8fm 64-58 F:
2 May'01 Ayr 7g/f 68-64 D: 2 Mar'01 Sout 7af 95a-90 C: 1 Mar'01 Wolv 7af 95a- C: 2 Dec'00 Wolv 7af 84a-82 C:
1322 **ACTIVE ACCOUNT** 8 [3]7-11-3 (66) B Harding 12/1: 233-2256: Dwelt, kept on late, nvr a threat.   1¼   59
840 **YORKER** 49 [4]6-11-2 (65) A Culhane 16/1: 3422007: Mid-div, no impress fnl 3f: btr 752.   ½   57
1036 **REAP** 28 [12]6-11-4 (67) C Llewellyn 11/2: 1112-038: Led till 2f out, btn dist: see 1036.   ¾   57
1215 **ACOMB** 15 [1]4-10-13 (62) W Supple 9/2 FAV: 4150-069: b g Shaamit - Aurora Bay (Night Shift) V   ½   51
slow away & bhd, eff over 2f out, sn no impress: thrice h'cap wnr '03: unplcd '02 (rtd 59): eff at 7f/1m, tried
10f: acts on firm & gd/soft grnd, stiff/undul trks: lost ch at the start today.
1 Sep'03 Beve 8.5g/s 68-60 E: 1 Aug'03 Pont 8fm 63-50 F: 1 Jun'03 Redc 7fm 51-47 E:
1352 **SWIFT ALCHEMIST** 7 [8]4-11-4 (67) G Duffield 12/1: 52000-00: 10th: b f Fleetwood - Pure Gold   3   50
(Dilum) Chsd ldrs till over 2f out: '03 auct mdn wnr, subs dual h'cap rnr-up: h'cap rnr-up '02 (M D I Usher): eff
at 7f/1m on fast, soft & polytrack, prob any trk: can go well fresh. 2 Aug'03 Ling 7ap 75a-72 D:
2 May'03 Yarm 8.0gd 74-73 E: 1 Apr'03 Newc 8.0g/f 70-(73) F: 2 Sep'02 Ling 7sft 71-65 E: 2 Jul'02 Kemp 6g/s 70- D:
1298 **COOL TEMPER** 10 [10]8-11-6 P (69) Dane O'Neill 7/1: 0336-530: 11th: Sn rdn mid-div, no prog fnl   5   42
2f: cheek pieces: btr 1298.
1168*} **BUTHAINA** 375 [6]4-11-7 (70) A Dobbin 20/1: 5/31-0: 12th: Mid-div, strug fnl 2f: reapp, new yard.   19   13
12 Ran   Time 1m 43.61 (3.11)   Owned: Great Head House Estates Limited   Trained: Ulverston

1486   2.45 Listed Stanleybet Com Spring Trophy Stakes 3yo+   (A)
£17400 £6600 £3300   7f30y rnd   Good/Firm 34   -03 Slow   Inside

1356 **ROCKETS N ROLLERS 7** [2] R Hannon 4-9-3 (102) Dane O'Neill 9/1: 0-333231: Made all, held on all **109**
out cl-home: op 14/1: suited by 7f, stays 1m: acts on fast, soft & fibresand, prob any trk: tough, consistent & v
useful, deserved this: see 838.
1356 **POLAR BEN 7** [3] J R Fanshawe 5-9-10 (112) O Urbina 7/2 JT FAV: 53100-22: Held up, styd on for   *shd* **115**
press fnl 2f, just denied: nicely bckd, op 4/1: 2lb worse terms than when just ahd of today's wnr in 1356.
1349 **BABODANA 7** [8] M H Tompkins 4-9-7 (111) G Duffield 7/2 JT FAV: 4210-163: Mid-div, styd on   1¼ **109**
onepace for press fnl 2f: gd run, eff at 7f, return to 1m could suit: see 951 (1m h'cap).
1356 **MAKHLAB 7** [5] B W Hills 4-9-3 (108) W Supple 14/1: 1/001-554: Prom & ch over 1f out, no extra   *shd* **105**
when short of room nr fin: again bhnd today's 1st & 2nd in 1356, see 922.
1231* **EL COTO 14** [4]4-9-3 (101) G Gibbons 11/1: 0304-015: Chsd ldrs, keeping on for press when no room   ¾ **103**
ins last, not able to recover: closer with a clr run & prob ran to form of 1231 (val h'cap).
1126 **QUITO 19** [9]7-9-3 bl (103) A Culhane 16/1: 1062556: Rear, rdn & styd on fnl 2f, not able to   ½ **102**
chall: see 951, 618 & 64.
1356 **WILL HE WISH 7** [1]8-9-3 (95) K Dalgleish 50/1: 61-00567: Keen & held up, not able to chall: see 1043.   2½ **97**
3186} **MILLENNIUM FORCE 280** [6]6-9-3 (111) C Catlin 11/2: 344230-8: b g Bin Ajwaad - Jumairah Sun   ½ **96**
(Scenic) Trkd ldrs, btn 2f out: reapp scorer '03 in Gr 3 company, subs Gr 3 rnr-up: won 3 h'caps & a cond stks
'02: 7f specialist, stays 1m: acts on fast or hvy, any trk: can go v well fresh: tough & smart performer at best.
2 Jun'03 Long 7gd 114- A: 1 Apr'03 Curr 7gd 112- : 1 Oct'02 Donc 7sft 107- B: 2 Oct'02 Newm 7g/f 96-91 C:
1 Sep'02 Donc 7g/f 93-86 B: 1 Jul'02 Newc 7g/f 86-83 D: 1 May'02 Ling 7gd 83-80 B: 2 Sep'01 Hayd 7.1hvy 81- D:
1 Sep'01 Catt 7g/f 81- D: 2 Jul'01 Sali 8g/f 77-75 D:
2989+ **MESHAHEER 288** [7]5-9-3 t (106) K McEvoy 4/1: 16/0241-9: b c Nureyev - Race The Wild Wind (Sunny's   2 **92**
Halo) Keen & held up, no impress fnl 2f: reapp: lightly rcd '03, cond stks wnr, earlier Gr 3 rnr-up in France:
List scorer '02: suited by 7f on firm & gd/soft, handles soft: best in a t-strap: smart colt whose career has been
hmpd by injury problems. 1 Jul'03 Newb 7g/f 112-(111) B: 2 May'03 Long 7sft 112- A: 1 Sep'02 Newb 7fm 114- A:
1 Jul'01 Newm 6g/f 111- A: 1 May'01 Donc 6g/f 100- D:
9 Ran   Time 1m 29.70 (2.60)   Owned: Mr M Mulholland   Trained: Marlborough

1487   3.20 Freephone Stanleybet Conditions Stakes 3yo+   (C)
£8729 £3311 £1656   6f str   Good/Firm 34   +05 Fast   Centre

1062 **STEENBERG 27** [7] M H Tompkins 5-9-11 (110) G Duffield 2/1: 43401-21: In tch trav well, hdwy &   **119**
rdn/led over 1f out, decisively: nicely bckd, gd time: suited by 6/7f, tried 9f: acts on firm & soft grnd, loves a
stiff/gall trk: produced a v smart performance, keep on side when returned to Group company: see 1062.
1356 **BAHAMIAN PIRATE 7** [1] D Nicholls 9-9-7 (110) S W Kelly 11/2: 606-1442: Held up, hdwy & led over   3½ **106**
2f out, hdd over 1f out & sn no ch with wnr: see 1356, 1004.
1309} **MISTER LINKS 364** [4] Saeed bin Suroor 4-8-13 (109) K McEvoy 11/8 FAV: 1220/30-3: b c Flying Spur   1¾ **94**
- Lady Anna Livia (Ahonoora) Handy, rdn over 1f out, onepace: hvly bckd, reapp: lightly rcd '03 (plcd, rtd 111, Gr
3, R Hannon): mdn, stks & Gr 3 scorer '02: eff at 6/7f, has shaped as if 1m could suit: acts on firm & soft grnd:
handles an easy or gall trk, can go v well fresh: prev with R Hannon, an encouraging return.
2 Sep'02 Donc 6fm 113- B: 2 Aug'02 York 6g/f 107- A: 1 Jul'02 Newm 6g/s 106- A: 1 Jun'02 Newb 6sft 102- C:
1 Jun'02 Kemp 5sft 101- E:
1227 **CIRCUIT DANCER 14** [6] A Berry 4-8-13 (92) A Culhane 8/1: 22316-34: Trkd ldrs, onepace fnl 2f: *nk* **92**
bckd at long-odds, op 16/1: see 1227.
1293 **PRINCE OF BLUES 10** [2]6-8-13 p (58) P Varley(7) 100/1: 0004045: Led till halfway, btn over 1f out.   8 **67$**
1207 **TRINCULO 15** [3]7-8-13 p (86) J P Guillambert(3) 50/1: 0U25006: Led 3f out till 2f out, sn btn.   10 **37**
5037} **TOM TUN 175** [5]9-9-11 bl (97) K Dalgleish 20/1: 000010-7: b g Bold Arrangement - B Grade (Lucky   23 **0**
Wednesday) Dwelt & sn struggling: reapp: cond stks scorer in first time blnks '03 (J G Given), thrice h'cap & also
List wnr '02: suited by 5/6f, stays 7f: acts on firm, gd & fibresand, best when mud flying: eff with/without
blnks/t-strap, loves a stiff trk.
1 Sep'03 Hami 6.0gd 99-(88) B: 1 Nov'02 Donc 6hvy 101- A: 1 Jul'02 Hami 5.9sft 92-87 C: 2 Jun'02 Curr 6.2g/s 95-87 :
1 May'02 Ayr 6g/s 88-82 D: 1 Mar'02 Donc 6sft 84-76 C: 2 Jan'02 Sout 6af 80a-79 D: 1 Apr'01 Pont 6hvy 90-84 C:
2 Mar'01 Donc 6hvy 87-81 C: 1 Mar'01 Wolv 5af 85a-80 C: 2 Feb'01 Wolv 5af 81a-77 C: 1 Feb'01 Wolv 5af 81a-73 D:
7 Ran   Time 1m 13.04 (1.74)   Owned: Mr Kenneth MacPherson   Trained: Newmarket

1488   3.55 Freephone Stanleybet Handicap Stakes 3yo 0-85   (D)   **[89]**
£5792 £1782 £891   6f str   Good/Firm 34   -33 Slow   Centre

4680} **BENBAUN 203** [10] M J Wallace 3-9-6 (81) D Corby(3) 10/1: 016120-1: b c Stravinsky - Escape To   **91**
Victory (Salse) Handy & rdn/led 2f out, edged left & styd on strongly: reapp: dual nursery h'cap wnr '03: eff at
5/6f on firm & fast grnd, gall/undul trks: eff with/without visor & can go well fresh: progressive profile.
2 Oct'03 Epso 5gd 83-77 D: 1 Sep'03 Redc 5fm 78-62 E: 1 Aug'03 Chep 5.1g/f 62-56 D:
4078} **TIMES REVIEW 238** [9] T D Easterby 3-9-4 (79) W Supple 20/1: 132500-2: b c Crafty Prospector -   1½ **83**
Previewed (Ogygian) Chsd ldrs, styd on for press, nvr a threat to wnr: reapp: mdn scorer '03, subs h'cap rnr-up:
eff at 5f, stays 6f well & has tried 1m: acts on firm, gd/soft & fibresand, stiff/gall or sharp/turning trk:
encouraging return. 2 Jul'03 York 5.0fm 87-80 C: 1 Jun'03 Newc 5fm 81- D: 2 May'03 Wolv 6af 82a- D:
1383 **MORSE 5** [1] J A Osborne 3-9-7 (82) S W Kelly 3/1 FAV: 336-0223: Rear, styd on for press fnl 2f,   ½ **85**
not able to chall: nicely bckd tho' op 2/1: qck reapp: remains in gd heart after 1383 & 1116.
2262} **LUALUA 317** [5] T D Barron 3-9-1 (76) P Makin(7) 12/1: 105-4: ch g Presidium - Tawny (Grey Ghost)   1½ **75**
Led till 2f out, no extra ins last: reapp, has been gelded: lightly rcd '03, debut wnr (auct mdn, disapp 2 subs
starts): win came at 5f, return to that trip cld suit: acts on gd & fast, sharp or gall trk: spot on at 5f.
1 May'03 Muss 5gd 79- E:
1154 **PERUVIAN STYLE 18** [3]3-9-3 (78) K McEvoy 4/1: 401-1105: Sn pushed along & chsd ldrs, not able to   ½ **76**
chall: imprvd eff but much btr 914 (AW, Lingfield).
1360 **GEORGE THE BEST 3** [4]3-9-3 (78) A Culhane 16/1: 11000-06: Chsd ldrs till over 1f out.   1½ **72**
1239 **JUST ONE LOOK 14** [2]3-8-8 (69) D Sweeney 13/2: 6500-007: Mid-div, al outpcd.   3½ **53**
955 **WEST COUNTRY 35** [7]3-9-2 (77) K Dalgleish 7/1: 232-4308: Mid-div & sn outpcd, nvr a factor.   ¾ **58**
4997} **LUPINE HOWL 179** [8]3-8-1 (62) G Gibbons 20/1: 063060-9: Chsd ldrs till over 2f out, reapp.   *hd* **43**

1176 **ATTACCA 16** [6]3-9-2 p (77) G Duffield 10/1: 0021-60: 10th: Prom, btn 2f out: reportedly lame.   **6**   **40**
10 Ran   Time 1m 15.37 (4.07)   Owned: Mrs R G Hillen   P Ransley   A Skidmore   Trained: Newmarket

---

1489	**4.30 Stanleybet Com Maiden Stakes 3yo** **(D)**
	£5766 £1774 £887 **1m2f120y** **Good/Firm 34** **-21 Slow** Outside

4445} **DESTINATION DUBAI 219** [3] Saeed bin Suroor 3-9-0 VIS K McEvoy 4/9 FAV: 22-1: b c Kingmambo -   **84**
Mysterial (Alleged) Led/dsptd lead, went on over 2f out & rdn/in command dist: reapp, hvly bckd at odds-on: promise
when rnr-up both '02 starts (D Loder, mdns): half-brother to top-class miler Dubai Destination: eff at 1m, styd
longer 10/5f trip well: acts on fast & gd grnd, gall/undul trks: goes well fresh: found this straightforward.
2 Sep'03 Pont 8.0g/f 90- D: 2 Sep'03 Donc 8gd 94- D:
1275 **TWOFAN 11** [5] M Johnston 3-9-0   K Dalgleish 6/1: 22: Led/dsptd lead till over 2f out, sn outpcd   **2**   **80**
by wnr but well clr of rem: imprvd from intro, acts on fast grnd: clearly going the right way after 1275.
4872} **MUNGO JERRY 190** [1] J G Given 3-9-0   W Supple 12/1: 0-3: b c Tannenkonig - Mostly Sure (Sure   **6**   **71**
Blade) Held up, eff 3f out, no impress on front pair fnl 2f: reapp: unplcd sole '03 start (rtd 46, mdn): longer
10.5f trip could well suit this term.
     CORRAN ARD 202 [8] Mrs J Harrington 3-9-0   A Culhane 33/1: 000-4: Mid-div, no impress fnl 2f.   **1¼**   **69**
4138} **ROYAL APPROACH 235** [2]3-8-9   D Sweeney 33/1: 60-5: Trkd ldrs till over 1f out, reapp.   **2½**   **60**
     ACUZIO [4]3-9-0   G Duffield 40/1: 6: Dwelt, chsd ldrs, btn 2f out, debut.   **6**   **56**
1108 **GRANDE TERRE 21** [6]3-8-9   O Urbina 14/1: 000-P7: Rear, no impress fnl 3f.   **1¼**   **49**
     NOW LOOK AWAY [7]3-9-0   G Gibbons 16/1: 8: Dwelt, keen, lost tch fnl 3f: op 25/1, debut.   **14**   **34**
8 Ran   Time 2m 15.78(5.78)   Owned: Godolphin   Trained: Newmarket

---

Official Going GOOD.

1490	**1.30 Curtis Medical Rated Stakes Handicap 4yo+ 0-110 (B)**	**[114]**
	£12064 £4576 £2288 **6f str** **Firm 10** **-10 Slow** Stands Side	

1151 **ROYAL STORM 19** [2] Mrs A J Perrett 5-8-9 (95) M J Kinane 9/1: 32126-01: b c Royal Applause -   **102**
Wakayi (Persian Bold) Al cl-up & led 2f out, drvn & styd on strongly: nicely bckd: dual h'cap wnr '03: mdn & dual
h'cap scorer '02: stays 1m, suited by 6/7f on firm, gd & polytrack, any trk, likes Newmarket: suited by forcing
tactics: tough & v useful entire.
2 Oct'03 Newb 6.0g/f 97-92 B: 1 Oct'03 Newm 7g/f 95-88 C: 2 Oct'03 York 7.0g/f 93-88 B: 2 Aug'03 Good 7fm 88-80 B:
2 Aug'03 Kemp 7g/f 85-81 D: 2 Jun'03 Warw 7.1fm 83-(81) D: 1 May'03 Ling 7gd 82-79 B: 2 May'03 Warw 7.1g/f 85-(79) D:
1 Oct'02 Sand 7g/f 84-78 D: 1 Sep'02 Good 7fm 77-73 D: 2 Aug'02 Epso 8.5gd 73- D: 1 Jun'02 Warw 7.1g/f 79- D:
4350} **SEEL OF APPROVAL 225** [6] R Charlton 5-9-3   (103) D Holland 9/2: 416112-2: b g Magical Point -   hd   **109**
Petit Point (Petorius) Chsd ldrs, drvn to chall when edged right ins last, just held: bckd from 6/1, reapp: prog
in '03, won 2 h'caps & 2 class stks, also rnr-up in val Ayr Gold Cup: dual h'cap scorer '02: eff at 6/6.5f on firm
& gd grnd, loves a gall trk, prob handles any: developed into a v useful sprinter, keep on side.
2 Sep'03 Ayr 6fm 105-99 B: 1 Sep'03 Hayd 6fm 107-(92) C: 1 Sep'03 York 6.0g/f 103-92 B: 1 Aug'03 Hayd 6g/f 100-(87) C:
2 Jul'03 Newb 6.0g/f 86-83 C: 1 Apr'03 Kemp 6fm 85-77 C: 1 Sep'02 Kemp 6fm 79-71 C: 1 Sep'02 Ling 6fm 72-65 E:
1137 **MAZEPA 20** [7] N A Callaghan 4-8-9   (95) L Dettori 8/1: 00100-63: Mid-div, rdn to chall over 1f   ¾   **99**
out, no extra cl-home: see 1137.
1251* **ZILCH 13** [8] M L W Bell 6-8-7 (1oh) (92) I Mongan 9/2: 03-12214: Dwelt & held up, styd on for   **2**   **91**
press, not able to chall: ideally suited by an easier surface but not disgraced after 1251 (hvy).
952 **CHOOKIE HEITON 36** [3]6-9-4 (104) R Winston 4/1 FAV: 00010-45: Chsd ldrs, short of room over 1f   1½   **97**
out, sn onepace: nicely bckd: see 952.
2660} **BORDER SUBJECT 20** [5]7-9-7 (107) S Drowne 8/1: 0/64100-6: b g Selkirk - Topicality (Topsider)   **3**   **91**
Led till 2f out, wknd ins last: reapp: plcd in this race '03, subs rtd h'cap wnr: class stks & rtd h'cap wnr '02
(this race): stays 1m, best dominating at 6f on firm, gd/soft & any trk: spot on next time.
1 May'03 York 6.0fm 110-103 B: 2 Jun'02 Asco 6gd 107-100 B: 1 May'02 Newm 6fm 104-92 B:
1 Apr'02 Wind 6gd 108- C: 2 Apr'02 Beve 7.4g/f 92- C: 1 May'01 Ling 7g/f 96-92 B:
5037} **PRESTO VENTO 176** [9]4-8-7 (3oh) (90) K Darley 16/1: 050030-7: Dwelt & held up, nvr able to chall.   ½   **75**
1162 **BOND BOY 18** [1]7-8-7 (1oh) (92) F Lynch 7/1: 4004068: Held up, rdn & no impress dist: btr 1162.   ½   **73**
3940} **CRAFTY CALLING 248** [4]4-8-10 (96) K Fallon 16/1: 301054-9: Chsd ldrs till over 1f out on reapp.   **9**   **51**
9 Ran   Time 1m 12.00 (1.2)   Owned: The Cloran Family   Trained: Pulborough

---

1491	**2.00 Gr3 Letheby & Christopher Dahlia Stakes Fillies 4yo+ (A)**
	£29000 £11000 £5500 **1m1f str** **Firm 10** **-06 Slow** Stands Side

1115* **BENEVENTA 22** [6] J L Dunlop 4-8-9   (104) S Sanders 7/2: 11340-11: Trkd ldr, rdn & led over 1f   **110**
out, edged right but styd on strongly, in command ins last: hvly bckd: eff at 1m/9f, stays 10f well: tough &
progressive filly, more success likely: see 1115 (List).
1111* **SILENCE IS GOLDEN 22** [3] B J Meehan 5-8-9 (99) K Fallon 7/2: 22325-12: Dwelt, pushed along in   2½   **104**
tch halfway, styd on for press, no threat to wnr: op 5/2: up in grade, prob ran to form of 1111 (val h'cap).
     SPECIAL DELIVERY 21 [2] E Lellouche 4-8-9   D Bonilla 7/1: 010-143: b f Danehill - Seconde Bleue   nk1   **103**
(Glint of Gold) In tch, hung right & kept on onepace fnl 2f, no threat to wnr: well bckd, op 10/1: wnr at St-Cloud
earlier in '04: both career wins at 10.5f on gd & gd/soft grnd, clry handles firm well: useful filly.
4598+ **ECHOES IN ETERNITY 211** [5] Saeed bin Suroor 4-9-0 T (109) L Dettori 2/1 FAV: 1/03011-4: b f   ½   **105**
Spinning World - Magnificient Style (Silver Hawk) Led till over 1f out, no impress dist: hvly bckd, clr of rem:
reapp: List & Gr 2 scorer on fnl 2 '03 starts: wknd: slow start wnr '02 (fill mdn, J Gosden): wng form at 1m/10f on firm
& fast grnd, loves a stiff/gall trk: wore a t-strap today.
1 Oct'03 Newm 8fm 109-(93) A: 1 Sep'03 Yarm 10.1g/f 107-(93) A: 1 Sep'02 Newm 8g/f 97- D:
4983} **ZIETORY 182** [7]4-8-9 (102) S Drowne 33/1: 621242-5: b f Zieten - Fairy Story (Persian Bold)   **5**   **91**
Chsd ldrs, btn over 1f out: reapp: '03 h'cap & subs List wnr in France, also List AW rnr-up: eff at 7f/1m, prob
stays a gall 12f: acts on fast, gd/soft & polytrack, gall or sharp trk.
2 Nov'03 Ling 8ap 97a-(102) A: 2 Sep'03 Sain 8gd 92- : 1 Aug'03 Deau 8g/s 102- A: 2 Jul'03 Newm 7g/f 97-86 B:

1 May'03 Newb 7gd 92-79 D: 1 Oct'02 Leic 6sft 82- F:

1115 **NAJAABA 22** [1]4-8-9 (82) B Reilly 66/1: 1115156: Held up, rdn & no impress fnl 2f: see 861 (AW).   2½   83
5027} **FELICITY 159** [4]4-8-9 (97) M J Kinane 12/1: 313535-7: Trkd ldrs & keen, btn over 1f out, reapp.   3½   79
4226} **CHANTRESS 232** [8]4-8-9 (92) J Murtagh 16/1: 21413-8: Held up, strug fnl 3f: reapp, new yard.   7   67
8 Ran   Time 1m 50.65 (1.45)   Owned: Mr R N Khan   Trained: Arundel

---

1492   2.40 Gr1 Ultimatebet Com 1000 Guineas Stakes Fillies 3yo (A)
£187195 £71005 £35503   **1m str**   **Firm 10**   **+06 Fast**   Centre

2727*}**ATTRACTION 299** [8] M Johnston 3-9-0 (119) K Darley 11/2: 11111-1: b f Efisio - Flirtation   120
(Pursuit of Love) Made all, held on well for press fnl 1f: fast time, hvly bckd, reapp: unbtn juv, won 5 times,
incl a Gr 3 & & Gr 2 in an injury shortened season: eff at 5/6f, stays a stiff 1m well: acts on firm & gd/soft,
loves a stiff/ gall trk: best with forcing tactics: high class, a superb training feat & will prove hard to beat
1 Jul'03 Newm 6g/f 118- A: 1 Jun'03 Asco 5g/f 115- A: 1 Jun'03 Beve 5g/f 109- A: 1 May'03 Thir 5g/s 90- D:
1 Apr'03 Nott 5.1gd 92- F:
4470} **SUNDROP 218** [1] Saeed bin Suroor 3-9-0   K McEvoy 16/1: 12-2: b f Sunday Silence - Oenothera   ½   118
(Night Shift) Held up towards far side, styd on for press fnl 2f, not quite get there: reapp: lightly rcd '03, AW
mdn wnr, subs Gr 1 rnr-up (D Loder): eff at 7f/1m on firm grnd & polytrack, sharp, turning or stiff trk: goes well
fresh: has a mid-dist pedigree & holds leading Oaks claims following this.
2 Sep'03 Asco 8fm 109- A: 1 Sep'03 Ling 7ap 86a- D:
1110* **HATHRAH 22** [16] J L Dunlop 3-9-0 (111) R Hills 6/1: 4122-13: Trkd ldr far side, rdn & styd on   ½   117
fnl 2f, only btn 1L: well bckd: up in grade & imprvd in defeat: acts on firm & gd/soft: see 1110 (List, g/s).
4470* }**RED BLOOM 218** [7] Sir Michael Stoute 3-9-0 (113) K Fallon 4/1 FAV: 311-4: b f Selkirk - Red   1¼   114
Camellia (Polar Falcon) Keen & trkd ldrs far side, rdn & kept on fnl 2f on reapp: fill mdn & Gr 1 Fillies Mile wnr
in '03 (bt today's rnr-up): likes a stiff/gall trk: eff at 1m, further will suit: acts on gd & firm grnd: decent
reapp, will improve for 10f+ & each-way claims in the Oaks. 1 Sep'03 Asco 8fm 112- A: 1 Aug'03 Newm 7g/f 95- D:
4891*}**SECRET CHARM 190** [6]3-9-0   M Hills 14/1: 11-5: b f Green Desert - Viz (Kris S) Held up far   ½   113+
side, short of room & drpd rear over 2f out, styd on well ins last: reapp: unbtn both '03 starts, mdn & List: eff
at 7f, styd this stiff 1m well & breeding suggests mid-dists will suit: acts on firm & gd, stiff trks, goes well
fresh: smart reapp, imprve at 10f+ & prob one to follow. 1 Oct'03 Newb 7gd 105- A: 1 Oct'03 Newm 7fm 93- D:
4556*}**CARRY ON KATIE 213** [10]3-9-0 L Dettori 7/1: 111-6: br f Fasliyev - Dinka Raja (Woodman) Chsd   hd   112
ldrs far side, hung right & onepace over 1f out: tchd 11/1 & shorter priced stablemate of 2nd: unbtn in '03, fill
mdn, Gr 2 & Gr 1 Cheveley Park (J Noseda): all wins at 6f but styd stiff 1m today: acts on firm & gd grnd,
stiff/gall trks, goes well fresh: smart filly, only btn around 3L today.
1 Oct'03 Newm 6g/f 115- A: 1 Aug'03 York 6.0fm 111- A: 1 Jul'03 Asco 6gd 105- D:
1233 **NATALIYA 15** [14]3-9-0 (104) S Sanders 20/1: 13-37: In tch far side, rdn & no extra fnl 1f: see 1233.   1¼   109
1169* **SILCAS GIFT 18** [15]3-9-0   T E Durcan 16/1: 11000-18: Chsd ldrs far side, btn dist: ran well for   nk   108
a long way, prob not stay this longer 1m trip: btn 1169 (7f).
1233* **MAJESTIC DESERT 15** [3]3-9-0 (111) D Holland 7/1: 12312-19: Prom far side, btn dist: op 9/2.   hd   107
4799}**CAIRNS 197** [12]3-9-0   J Carroll 25/1: 11-0: 10th: Chsd ldrs far side till over 1f out, reapp.   2½   102
949   **KELUCIA 36** [4]3-9-0 (100) J F Egan 100/1: 21334-50: 11th: Held up far side, no impress fnl 2f.   2   98
4631}**NECKLACE 210** [13]3-9-0   J Murtagh 8/1: 2110-0: 12th: Chsd ldrs far side till over 1f out: well   ¾   97
bckd Irish chall: like stablemate show on Cool Cat in 2000 Guineas ran too bad to be true.
1169 **VALJARV 18** [5]3-9-0 (95) T G McLaughlin 200/1: 4031-000: 13th: Held up far side, no prog fnl 2f.   2½   92
1169 **INCHENI 18** [9]3-9-0 (103) S Drowne 25/1: 61-20: 14th: Held up far side, no impress fnl 2f: bckd.   3   86
4871*}**JATH 191** [11]3-9-0   N Callan 100/1: 1-0: 15th: Dwelt & held up, btn 2f out on reapp.   1½   83
1233 **SPOTLIGHT 15** [2]3-9-0 (101) E Ahern 33/1: 3121-40: 16th: Rcd alone centre, joined ldrs in far   shd   83
side group over 3f out, btn 2f out: see 1233.
16 Ran   Time 1m 36.78 (0.28)   Owned: Duke of Roxburghe   Trained: Middleham

---

1493   3.15 Gr2 Ultimatebet Com Jockey Club Stakes 4yo+ (A)
£58000 £22000 £11000   **1m4f rnd**   **Firm 10**   **+02 Fast**   Centre

1230 **GAMUT 15** [7] Sir Michael Stoute 5-8-9 t (117) K Fallon 7/4 FAV: 13123-21: Trkd ldrs, short of   120
room over 2f out, pushed along & hdwy to lead well ins last, styd on strongly: hvly bckd, gd time: eff at 11/14f on
fast or gd grnd, sharp or gall trk: v smart & tough: see 1230.
950   **SYSTEMATIC 36** [3] M Johnston 5-8-9 (109) K Darley 11/1: 11/255-32: Trkd ldr & ev ch fnl 3f, rdn   1¼   117
& led over 1f out till well ins last: op 14/1, left reapp well bhd: smart, see 950.
990   **WARRSAN 36** [6] C E Brittain 6-9-0 (117) D Holland 9/2: 26333-53: b c Caerleon - Lucayan Princess   1½   120
(High Line) Led, rdn & hdd over 1f out, no extra: well bckd: fine campaign '03, Gr 3, Gr 2 (this race) & Gr 1
scorer, so rnr-cap twice in similar company: rtd h'cap & cond stks wnr '02, subs Gr 3 rnr-up: suited by 12/14f on
firm & soft any trk: goes well fresh: high-class & genuine entire.
2 Jun'03 San 12fm 117- A: 1 Jun'03 Epso 12.0g/f 120-(116) A: 2 May'03 York 13.9fm 119-(115) A:
1 May'03 Newm 12gd 119-(115) A: 1 Apr'03 Newb 12.0fm 116-(115) A: 2 Oct'02 Newb 12sft 115- A:
2 Sep'02 Asco 12g/f 113- A: 2 Sep'02 Sali 14g/f 110- C: 1 Jul'02 Newm 12g/f 107- C:
1230* **DUBAI SUCCESS 15** [5] B W Hills 4-8-9 (110) M Hills 100/30: 105D3-14: In tch, rdn & styd on fnl   ¾   114
2f, not pace to chall: nicely bckd but below form of 1230 (Gr 3, bt today's wnr).
4489}**MARTALINE 36** [1]5-8-12 L Dettori 8/1: 32124-05: gr c Linamix - Coraline (Sadler's Wells) Held   1½   115
up, hung right & onepace from over 1f out: French raider, unplcd in Dubai earier in '04: prob best at 12/14f on gd & soft grnd, gall trks.
2 Sep'03 Long 12gs 115- : 1 Jul'03 Mais 14g/s 112- A: 2 Jun'03 Chan 12gd 112- A: 2 Aug'02 Deau 15g/s 106- :
1230 **JELANI 15** [2]5-8-9 M J Kinane 9/1: 22/541-/06: b c Darshaan - No Rehearsal (Baillamont) Chsd   4   106
ldrs till over 1f out: missed '03: lightly rcd '02, Gr 1 Epsom Derby 4th bef landing 3 rnr-up List event: suited by
12f on fast & gd/soft, stiff/gall or sharp/undul trk, likes Haydock: career hmpd by injuries.
1 Jul'02 Hayd 12g/f 108- A: 2 Oct'01 York 7g/s 102- B: 1 Sep'01 Ayr 7.2gd 95- C: 1 Sep'01 Hayd 7.1g/s 89- D:
4227}**MOMENTS OF JOY 232** [4]4-8-6 (105) S Sanders 8/1: 115-7: Held up, no impress fnl 2f on reapp.   6   94
7 Ran   Time 2m 29.77 (0.97)   Owned: Mrs G Smith   Trained: Newmarket

---

1494

3.50 Listed R L Davison Pretty Polly Stakes Fillies 3yo (A)
£17400 £6600 £3300   **1m2f str**   **Firm 10**   **+02 Fast**   Stands Side

4978} **OUIJA BOARD 183** [4] E A L Dunlop 3-8-8 (93) K Fallon 2/1 FAV: 313-1: b f Cape Cross - Selection   **115+**
Board (Welsh Pageant) Held up, hdwy to lead dist & sn rdn clr, decisively: hvly bckd, reapp: lightly rcd '03, nov
stks wnr, subs List plcd (rtd 98): eff at 7f/1m, relished step up to 10f & 12f will suit (half-sister to decent
stayer/hdler Spectrometer): acts on firm & gd, goes well fresh: smart display, good credentials for Epsom Oaks.
1 Oct'03 Yarm 7.0gd 92- D:
5018* **}SAHOOL 178** [6] M P Tregoning 3-8-8 (86) R Hills 13/2: 61-2: b f Unfuwain - Mathaayl (Shadeed)   6   **103**
Chsd ldr from over 2f out, kept on for press but sn well held: reapp: lightly rcd '03, won 2nd of just 2 starts
(mdn): wng form at 1m, mid-dists shld suit: handles firm & soft grnd: encouraging bhnd potentially v smart wnr.
1 Nov'03 Nott 8.2sft 84- D:
4895* **}RAVE REVIEWS 190** [8] J L Dunlop 3-8-8 (81) M J Kinane 16/1: 61-3: b f Sadler's Wells - Pieds de   ½   **102**
Plume (Seattle Slew) Held up, rdn & outpcd over 2f out, kept on ins last: reapp: lightly rcd '03 (won 2nd of just
2 starts, mdn): winning form at 1m, mid-dist pedigree: handles firm & gd grnd: appears useful & a likely improver
at 12f+. 1 Oct'03 Newb 8gd 78- D:
1101 **BRINDISI 24** [2] B W Hills 3-8-8 M Hills 12/1: 2-34: Led & clr over 2f out, hdd over 1f out,   1¼   **100$**
wknd: op 16/1, longer trip.
     KISSES FOR ME 200 [9]3-8-9 (1ow) J Murtagh 5/1: 1-5: Chsd ldrs, rdn & no impress over 1f out.   ½   **100**
4404} **OPERA COMIQUE 224** [7]3-8-8 T L Dettori 7/2: 13-6: Trkd ldr, btn 2f out: well bckd on reapp for   11   **85**
new yard, wore a t-strap.
2389} **LADY PEACHES 312** [5]3-8-8 J Fanning 100/1: 0-7: Dwelt, held up & no impress fnl 3f, reapp.   1¾   **83$**
19*   **RENDEZVOUS POINT 171** [1]3-8-8 K Darley 16/1: 1-8: Dwelt, chsd ldrs till over 2f out.   5   **76**
1236 **HE JAA 15** [3]3-8-8 D Holland 20/1: 0P: Held up, p.u. 3f out.   **0**
9 Ran   Time 2m 02.92 (0.82)   Owned: Lord Derby   Trained: Newmarket

---

1495

4.25 Hastings Maiden Stakes 3yo (D)
£7046 £2168 £1084   **1m str**   **Firm 10**   **-19 Slow**   Stands Side

1236 **REHEARSAL 15** [18] C G Cox 3-9-0 P Robinson 9/2: 21: Chsd ldrs & keen early, led dist, rdn out: **97**
well bckd tho' op 7/2: confirmed debut promise: eff at 1m, will relish 10f: acts on firm & gd grnd, stiff/gall trk:
lightly rcd & more to come over further: see 1236.
1119 **NEVER WILL 21** [24] M Johnston 3-9-0 J Fanning 14/1: 5-22: Led, rdn & hdd dist, not pace of wnr: 2½   **90**
styd longer 1m trip well: acts on firm & fast grnd, shld find a race: see 1119.
1100 **CREDIT 24** [3] R Hannon 3-9-0 K Fallon 10/1: 33: Chsd ldrs, chall over 2f out, onepace bef dist: shd   **90**
bckd, op 14/1: imprvd from intro on this firm grnd: find a race: see 1100.
4974} **SILENT HAWK 183** [20] Saeed bin Suroor 3-9-0 T L Dettori 11/2: 2-4: b c Halling - Nightbird   ½   **89**
(Night Shift) Chsd ldrs & ch over 2f out, onepace: reapp: rnr-up sole '03 start (mdn): eff at 7f/1m, 10f may
suit: acts on firm & gd grnd, stiff trk: ran well in t-strap today.
2 Nov'03 Newm 7g/f 91- D:
     MIKAO [16]3-9-0 Saleem Golam(7) 100/1: 5: b g Tagula - Oumaladia (Waajib) Held up, switched &   2½   **84+**
styd on fnl 2f, not able to chall: debut: eye-catching late hdwy under inexperienced rider: dam a 12f wnr:
expect improvement over mid-dists.
     NASSIRIA [19]3-8-9 T E Durcan 25/1: 6: b f Singspiel - Naskhi (Nashwan) Keen & prom, outpcd   2½   **74**
over 2f out, kept on ins last on debut: likely to apprec mid-dists on breeding, can improve.
116   **MASTER THEO 155** [9]3-9-0 (77) J Quinn 33/1: 335-7: Prom, no impress fnl 2f, reapp.   hd   **78**
1166 **DENOUNCE 18** [14]3-9-0 W Ryan 2/1 FAV: 28: Dwelt & held up, keen, hdwy to chall over 2f out, sn   ¾   **77**
rdn & no extra: hvly bckd, op 11/4: see 1166.
1279 **OH GOLLY GOSH 12** [23]3-9-0 P (76) K Darley 14/1: 30-229: Prom, no impress dist: cheek pieces.   1½   **74**
4868} **WANT 191** [22]3-9-0 M J Kinane 9/1: 6-0: 10th: Slow away, late gains, nrst fin: promising.   1¼   **71**
     HAWAAJES [15]3-9-0 R Hills 20/1: 0: 11th: Held up, eff to press ldrs 2f out, sn no extra.   nk   **70**
1171 **MISS INKHA 18** [12]3-8-9 S Drowne 100/1: 0: 12th: Held up & no impress on ldrs.   1   **63**
     DESERT HAWK [13]3-9-0 J Murtagh 33/1: 0: 13th: Pushed along rear, no impression.   1½   **65**
881   **SUSPICIOUS MINDS 43** [6]3-8-9 D Holland 50/1: 00: 14th: Held up, no impress on ldrs, abs.   nk   **59**
     MISS MERENDA [11]3-8-9 J Mackay 100/1: 0: 15th: Dwelt & al rear on debut.   2   **55**
     KILLMOREY [8]3-9-0 O Urbina 66/1: 0: 16th: Slow away & nvr on terms, debut.   nk   **59**
1166 **HINODE 18** [17]3-9-0 S Sanders 100/1: 00: 17th: Chsd ldrs till 3f out.   ¾   **58**
     MAGIC VERSE [10]3-8-9 C Lowther 100/1: 0: 18th: Dwelt & al rear on debut.   nk   **52**
     Unbridleds Dream [1]3-9-0 G Carter 66/1:0   **Crocolat** [4]3-8-9 A Mackay 50/1:0
     Glencalvie [5]3-9-0 E Ahern 33/1:0   **Eizawina Docklands** [2]3-9-0 T G McLaughlin 33/1:0
     Vicat Cole [21]3-9-0 N Callan 66/1:0   1258 **Mitzi Caspar 13** [7]3-8-9 J F Egan 100/1:0
24 Ran   Time 1m 38.8 (2.3)   Owned: Elite Racing Club   Trained: Hungerford

---

1496

5.00 Portland Lodge Handicap Stakes 3yo 0-100 (C)   **[101]**
£13962 £4296 £2148   **1m str**   **Firm 10**   **-03 Slow**   Stands Side

1095* **MASTER MARVEL 24** [16] M Johnston 3-8-9 (82) J Fanning 6/1: 211: Led till over 1f out, rallied   **90**
gamely to lead again well ins last: nicely bckd tho' op 9/2, h'cap bow: suited by 1m/9f on firm & gd grnd, could
get further: useful colt, likely to improve with racing, typical of the yard: see 1095 & 919.
4875* **}THYOLO 191** [19] C G Cox 3-9-3 (90) P Robinson 5/1 FAV: 411-2: ch c Bering - Topline (Acatenango)   ¾   **96**
Chsd ldrs, rdn & chall over 1f out, kept on well: reapp: mdn & h'cap wnr '03: eff at 1m, mid-dists could suit
this term, acts on firm & gd grnd, gall or sharp/undul trk: progressive type.
1 Oct'03 Donc 8g/f 90-82 C: 1 Sep'03 Good 8fm 84- D:
1206 **JEDBURGH 16** [15] J L Dunlop 3-9-6 (93) M J Kinane 25/1: 20111-03: Held up, hdwy & rdn/led over   nk   **98**
1f out, hdd well ins last: styd longer 1m trip well: see 1206.
1192 **SPIN KING 17** [11] M L W Bell 3-8-7 (80) J Mackay 20/1: 5613-04: b c Intikhab - Special Dissident   3½   **78**
(Dancing Dissident) Held up, rdn & styd on fnl 3f, not able to chall: op 33/1: lightly rcd '03, auct mdn scorer:

NEWMARKET   SUNDAY 02.05.04   Righthand, Stiff, Galloping Track

winning form at 7f, styd this stiff 1m: acts on firm & gd/soft grnd, stiff/undul trks. 1 Jul'03 Leic 7.0fm 81- E:

4763} **STATE DILEMMA 199** [8]3-9-2 (89) M Hills 20/1: 3314-5: b c Green Desert - Nuriva (Woodman) Trkd ldr, rdn & onepace fnl 2f: reapp: lightly rcd '03, mdn scorer: eff at 7f/1m on firm & fast grnd, stiff/gall trks, prob handles a sharp/turning one.	nk	86
1 Sep'03 Newb 7fm 90- D:		
1176* **GRANSTON 17** [3]3-8-6 (1ow) (78) S Drowne 12/1: 5401-316: Held up, kept on for press, not able to chall: op 10/1: see 1176.	½	75
4044*}**SECRETARY GENERAL 242** [17]3-9-1 (88) K Fallon 8/1: 241-7: Dwelt & held up, not able to chall.	hd	83
947 **ANUVASTEEL 36** [21]3-8-5 (78) A Mackay 25/1: 05132-68: Dwelt & held up, no impress on ldrs.	nk	72
1315 **OVERDRAWN 9** [18]3-9-7 (94) D Holland 33/1: 23415-09: Slow away, eff 2f out, no impress.	nk	87
1021+ **FANCY FOXTROT 30** [4]3-9-5 (92) L Dettori 12/1: 52326-10: 10th: Held up, no impress fnl 2f: see 1021.	2½	80
1105 **MOUNT VETTORE 22** [7]3-8-9 (82) J Murtagh 12/1: 5-1200: 11th: Held up, hung right for press 2f out, sn btn: twice below 955.	nk	69
1176 **ALFONSO 17** [6]3-8-3 (76) E Ahern 33/1: 04-100: 12th: Chsd ldrs, rdn & btn over 1f out: btr 617.	1	61
1236* **MUDAWIN 15** [1]3-9-3 (90) R Hills 11/2: 5-010: 13th: Held up, rdn & btn 2f out: btr 1236.	shd	75
1186 **MAHMOOM 17** [12]3-8-1 (90) T E Durcan 8/1: 211-00: 14th: In tch, btn & eased dist: bckd.	nk	74

1186 **Outer Hebrides 17** [2]3-8-8 vis(81) D R McCabe 50/1:0	1186 **Tranquil Sky 17** [5]3-8-13 (86) W Ryan 66/1:0
1176 **Magical Mimi 17** [13]3-8-3 (76) Leanne Kershaw(7) 50/1:04811}	**Tafaahum 195** [20]3-9-1 (88) W Supple 50/1:0
132 **Mountcharge 152** [9]3-8-7 (80) J Quinn 33/1:0	1186 **Mister Saif 17** [14]3-8-13 (86) K Darley 33/1:U

20 Ran   Time 1m 37.52(1.02)   Owned: Maktoum Al Maktoum   Trained: Middleham

---

SALISBURY   SUNDAY 02.05.04   Righthand, Galloping Track, Stiff Finish

Official Going Soft

1497   2.30 Butler & Co Equine Tax Planning Maiden Stakes 3yo+   (D)
£5844 £1798 £899   **6f str**   **Good/Soft 82**   -23 Slow   Centre, field rcd stands side

DAFORE 0 [17] R Hannon 3-8-12 R L Moore 12/1: 1: b c Dr Fong - Aquaglow (Caerleon) Mid-div, prog on rail ins fnl 2f, rdn out to get up on line: debut: cost 260,000gns: eff at 6f, 7f/1m shld suit: acts on gd/soft grnd & a stiff/gall trk: goes well fresh: improve with experience.		86
1044 **ALDERNEY RACE 29** [4] R Charlton 3-8-12 T Quinn 2/1 FAV: 4-52: ch c Seeking The Gold - Oyster Catcher (Bluebird) Handy till led ins fnl 1f, hdd under press cl-home: well bckd: close 4th of 19 on sole '03 start (mdn, rtd 85): eff at 6f, shld stay further: acts on fast & gd/soft grnd, has disapp on polytrack: only just denied & can find similar on this evidence.	nk	84
1191 **FAREWELL GIFT 17** [15] R Hannon 3-8-12 (87) P Dobbs 3/1: 200-43: Cl-up, short or room stands raid 1f out, switched & kept on, nrst fin: tchd 4/1: acts on gd & gd/soft grnd: gone close with with a clr run: see 1191.	1¼	80
1078 **MR HULLABALOU 25** [8] R Ingram 3-8-12 M Henry 66/1: 004: Handy, kept on fnl 1f, btn far in 4th: eff at 6f on gd/soft grnd: vastly imprvd eff here on 3rd start & now quals for h'caps: see 898.	1	77
1080 **ISAZ 25** [11]4-9-8 (74) Dane O'Neill 9/2: 025/4-55: Led, hdd ins fnl 1f, sn no extra: btr 1080.	2½	70
1136 **EL CHAPARRAL 20** [9]4-9-8 (74) M Tebbutt 16/1: 403/-06: b g Bigstone - Low Line (High Line) Cl-up over 4f, sn no extra: missed '03: plcd on last of 3 '02 starts (rtd 92 at best, auct stks, M A Jarvis): eff around 7f on fast & gd/soft grnd: all ages maiden: shld find a maiden: with D K Ivory.	2½	63
4761} **PLEASURE SEEKER 199** [3]3-8-7 A Daly 50/1: 00-7: Slow away, nvr nrr than mid-div on reapp.	½	57
49 **ROCKLEY BAY 166** [19]3-8-12 D Sweeney 25/1: 054-8: Handy over 4f, wknd: reapp.	½	61
1080 **GENEROUS SPIRIT 25** [14]3-8-12 Paul Eddery 16/1: 09: Handy till dist, wknd: btr 1080.	1¼	58
1210 **DULCIMER 16** [2]3-8-7 R Thomas(5) 50/1: 00: 10th: Rear, prog when short of room dist, sn onepcd.	1¼	50
BATCHWORTH BEAU 0 [1]3-8-12 S Carson 50/1: 0: 11th: Slow away, modest late gains.	2	49
536 **BOLD TRUMP 89** [5]3-8-12 S Hitchcott(3) 20/1: 0-40: 12th: Handy, short of room dist, wknd.	½	48
1136 **CEDRIC COVERWELL 20** [10]4-9-8 C Catlin 66/1: 400: 13th: Handy 4f, fdd: btr 973.	¾	46
4066} **MISS TILLY 240** [12]3-8-7 F Norton 66/1: 000-0: 14th: Mid-div 4f, sn wknd: reapp.	nk	40
TIPSY LADY 0 [16]3-8-7 N Pollard 10/1: 0: 15th: Slow away, al bhd on debut.	1	37
STRIDES OF FIRE 0 [6]3-8-12 R Havlin 9/1: 0: 16th: Slow away, nvr a factor on debut.	10	17
FAIR OPTIONS 0 [13]3-8-12 M Fenton 25/1: 0: 17th: Slow away, al in rear.	2½	10

17 Ran   Time 1m 18.40 (6.3)   Owned: Fieldspring Racing   Trained: Marlborough

1498   3.00 Sharp Minds Betfair Rated Stakes Handicap 3yo 0-100 (B)   [102]
£12238 £4642 £2321   **6f str**   **Good/Soft 82**   -12 Slow   Centre, field rcd stands side

4801*}**SPLIFF 197** [11] H Candy 3-8-13 (87) Dane O'Neill 4/1 CO FAV: 021-1: b c Royal Applause - Snipe Hall (Crofthall) Held up, prog bef 1f out, led well ins fnl 1f, pushed out, val 3L+: tchd 5/1 on reapp & h'cap bow: nov stks wnr on fnl '03 start: eff at 5f, imprvd here for step up to 6f: acts on firm & gd/soft: stiff/gall or sharp trk: goes well fresh: unexposed 3yo who qcknd up nicely here, more prizes await. 1 Oct'03 Catt 5g/f 88- D: 2 May'03 Sali 5fm 88- D:		98+
1152 **STAR PUPIL 19** [7] A M Balding 3-8-6 (80) Martin Dwyer 4/1 CO FAV: 02-42: Chsd ldrs, prog to lead just ins fnl 1f, hdd well ins fnl 1f, not pace wnr: stay 7f, ran to form on drop back to 6f: lost little in defeat on h'cap bow & can find simila or a mdn: see 1152 (mdn).	1¼	85
1370* **TARUSKIN 7** [10] N A Callaghan 3-8-13 (3ex) (87) D Fox(5) 4/1 CO FAV: 3231-313: Held up, prog halfway, ev ch dist, sn no extra: qck reapp: below par run on drop back to 6f, btr 1370 (1m).	3	83
4450} **ENFORD PRINCESS 219** [9] R Hannon 3-8-12 (90) R L Moore 20/1: 1100-4: b f Pivotal - Expectation (Night Shift) Rear, prog ins fnl 2f, nrst fin: reapp: mdn & stks wnr on first 2 of only 4 '03 starts: eff at 6f, shld stay further: acts on fast & gd/soft grnd: sharp or gall trk & has gone well fresh. 1 May'03 Wind 6g/f 89- C: 1 May'03 Newm 6g/f 87- D:	hd	85
4874*}**ENCHANTMENT 191** [8]3-8-7 (81) C Catlin 16/1: 01601-5: b f Compton Place - Tharwa (Last Tycoon) Cl-up, ev ch dist, sn wknd: reapp: auct mdn & sal sell stks wnr in '03 (at 5/6f on firm & fast grnd: acts on a stiff/gall trk: sharper for this: with J M Bradley. 1 Oct'03 Donc 6g/f 85- B: 1 Sep'03 Carl 5fm 80- F:	2½	69
1116 **BATHWICK BILL 22** [1]3-8-9 (83) A McCarthy 16/1: 11530-06: Prom, led halfway, hdd ins fnl 1f, wknd.	nk	70
4545} **KINGS CAPRICE 214** [4]3-9-0 (88) S Carson 13/2: 523-7: Cl-up till dist, fdd: op 5/1 on reapp.	1	72

1154	**COMPTONS ELEVEN** 19 [2]3-9-1 (89) S Hitchcott(3) 9/1: 10033-08: Sn handy, edged left & wknd dist.	nk 72
176	**ORO VERDE** 144 [6]3-9-3 (91) P Dobbs 20/1: 033402-9: Keen handy, wknd bef 1f out: reapp.	¾ 72
1154	**MAC THE KNIFE** 19 [5]3-8-9 (83) R Smith 25/1: 43420-00: 10th: Rear, nvr a factor.	13 34
1206	**FLIP FLOP AND FLY** 16 [3]3-8-11 BL (85) M Fenton 16/1: 01300-00: 11th: Led till halfway, wkng when	5 23
	short of room 2f out: first time blnks.	

11 Ran   Time 1m 17.78 (5.68)   Owned: Mr H R Mould   Trained: Wantage

---

1499   **3.35 Catisfield Hinton & Stud Conditions Stakes Fillies 2yo (C)**
£7308 £2772 £1386   **5f str**   **Good/Soft 82**   **+06 Fast**   Centre, rcd stands side

1212* **LADY FILLY** 16 [2] W G M Turner 2-9-1   A Quinn(5) 15/8 FAV: 111: Made all, pushed clr ins fnl 2f,   **93+**
v easily, val 8L+: well bckd tho' op 5/4: eff at 5f on gd/soft & soft grnd: likes forcing tactics: acts on a
stiff/gall trk: impressive win conceding weight all round & deserves step up to List/Gr grade: see 1212.

AZUREE 0 [3] R Hannon 2-8-6   R L Moore 9/2: 2: b f Almutawakel - Cappella (College Chapel)   4   73
Rear, prog to chase wnr despite edging right ins fnl 2f, al held: debut: Mar foal, cost E45,000: half-sister plcd
at 6f as a juv: dam won a couple of times over 5f at 2: sire high-class mid-dist performer: eff at 5f, 6f shld
suit: acts on gd/soft grnd: encouraging eff & can rate higher with more experience.

SPEED OF SOUND 0 [7] A M Balding 2-8-6   Martin Dwyer 3/1: 3: ch f Zafonic - Blue Siren   5   60
(Bluebird) Slow away, sn handy & chsd wnr bef 1f out, fdd fnl 1f: debut: Apr foal, half-sister to useful sprinter
Speed Top: dam top-class over sprint dists: sire high-class miler winning 2,000 Guineas: improve for this.

1084 **IAM FOREVERBLOWING** 25 [6] S C Burrough 2-8-9   L Keniry(3) 20/1: 54: ch f Dr Fong - Farhana   5   50
(Fayruz) Cl-up over 4f, fdd: Mar foal, cost 23,000gns: half-sister to 5f wnr as a juv: dam useful at sprint
dists: sire decent miler, later progressed into top-class performer at mid-dists.

FEMINIST 0 [4]2-8-6   C Catlin 9/2: 5: Handy 4f, fdd, debut.   1¾   42
SPREE 0 [5]2-8-6   Dane O'Neill 8/1: 6: Slow away, handy over 3f, sn fdd: debut.   13   13

6 Ran   Time 1m 3.60 (3.18)   Owned: Mrs M S Teversham   Trained: Sherborne

---

1500   **4.10 Goddards Fiat Handicap Stakes 3yo 0-100 (C)**
£9187 £3485 £1742   **1m1f198y**   **Good/Soft 82**   **+07 Fast**   Inside, rcd stands side bar wnr   **[100]**

759* **DANCING LYRA** 64 [5] J W Hills 3-8-6   (78) R L Moore 12/1: 0300-611: Chsd ldrs, rcd alone far   **94+**
rail, led 2f out, sn pushed clr, val 10L+: 9 wk abs: prev eff at 6f, now suited by 10f on fast, gd/soft &
polytrack: goes well fresh: prob had benefit of racing on best grnd but stil won easily: see 759.

1298* **TIGER TIGER** 11 [1] Jamie Poulton 3-8-12 (83) F Norton 100/30: 0-1312: Rcd stan side, held up,   8   89
prog 3f out, kept on & led stands side group ins fnl 1f, no ch with far rail wnr: eff over 1m, stays 10f: acts on
polytrack & gd/soft, revels in hvy grnd, in grand form.

1275* **KEELUNG** 12 [8] M A Jarvis 3-8-13 (85) M Henry 2/1 FAV: 0-42213: Led, rcd stands side, hdd under   1½   88
press ins fnl 1f, sn no extra: well bckd: not disgraced: just btr 1275 (mdn).

4480*\ARKHOLME 218 [4] W J Haggas 3-8-10 (82) M Fenton 7/1: 41-4: b g Robellino - Free Spirit   4   79
(Caerleon) Cl-up, rcd stands side, fdd fnl 1f: reapp & h'cap bow: mdn wnr on last of only 2 '03 starts: eff at
1m, appeared first to stay 10f here: acts on rain-softened grnd & a gall trk: 1 Sep'03 Hayd 8.1gd 85- D:

4205\ TORINMOOR 233 [3]3-9-7 (93) Dane O'Neill 9/1: 316-5: ch c Intikhab - Tochar Ban (Assert) Bhd,   2   87
rcd stands side, nvr nrr than mid-div: reapp: tchd 12/1: mdn wnr on 2nd of only 3 '03 starts: eff at 7f, bred to
be suited by mid-dists: acts on fast & firm grnd: eff on a gall trk: Mrs A J Perrett. 1 Aug'03 Newm 7fm 96- D:

727 **CHASING THE DREAM** 67 [10]3-8-2 (74) Martin Dwyer 7/1: 126: Rear, prog stands side 4f out, fdd   shd   67
fnl 1f: 10 wk abs & turf bow: btr 727 & 322 (polytrack).

1192 **MR TAMBOURINE MAN** 17 [6]3-8-11 (83) C Catlin 8/1: 261-67: Keen handy stands side 10f, sn fdd.   3½   71
1206 **SENESCHAL** 16 [2]3-8-9 (92) S Hitchcott(3) 14/1: 21-08: Handy stands side, fdd fnl 2f: see 1206.   6   72

8 Ran   Time 2m 12.08 (7.58)   Owned: Mr N N Browne   Trained: Lambourn

---

1501   **4.45 City Cabs Salisbury Maiden Stakes 3yo (D)**
£5668 £1744 £872   **1m4f**   **Good/Soft 82**   **-01 Slow**   Stands side, rcd far side

DAY FLIGHT 0 [8] J H M Gosden 3-9-0   P Dobbs 7/1: 1: b c Sadler's Wells - Bonash (Rainbow Quest)   **89+**
Held up, gd prog ins fnl 4f, led ins fnl 1f, pushed clr, val 9L+: tchd 12/1 on debut: dam won Group races at 1m &
12f in France: half-brother wnr at 7f: eff at 12f, shapes as tho' further will suit: acts on gd/soft grnd & a
stiff/gall trk: goes well fresh: impressive debut performance & can rate higher with more experience.

4981\ RIVER GYPSY 182 [7] D R C Elsworth 3-9-0   L Keniry(3) 8/1: 4-2: b c In The Wings - River Erne   6   78
(Irish River) Held up, prog 2f out, styd on fnl 1f, no ch with easy wnr: reapp: 4th of 12 on sole '03 start (mdn,
rtd 75a): eff at 1m, improve for step up to 12f: acts on polytrack & gd/soft grnd: win over mid dists.

1259 **IRISH BLADE** 13 [10] H Candy 3-9-0   Dane O'Neill 9/2: 0-43: Led, hdd 11f out, styd prom, ev ch 2f   nk   76
out, sn edged left & no extra: op 10/3: eff at 10f, poss stays 12f: now quals for h'caps: see 1259.

WATER TAXI 0 [3] R Charlton 3-9-0   D Sweeney 14/1: 4: ch c Zafonic - Trellis Bay (Sadler's   ½   76+
Wells) Rear, prog after 1m, staying on when short of room twice ins fnl 2f, no impress fnl 1f: debut: dam wnr at
12f, just sharper for today & improve on this.

LIGHT WIND 0 [5]3-8-9   Martin Dwyer 16/1: 5: Slow away, nvr nrr than mid-div: debut.   ½   70
1211 **STRIKE** 16 [11]3-9-0   R Havlin 6/4 FAV: 26: Led 11f out, hdd ins fnl 1f, wknd: well bckd: btr   nk   74
expected after promise shown in 1211 (debut, gd, 11f).

MASSIF CENTRALE 0 [1]3-9-0   N Pollard 6/1: 7: Slow away, prog inside fnl 4f, kept on under hands   1¾   72+
& heels: debut: ran green here & can improve with experience.

192 **VICTORY LAP** 141 [13]3-8-9   C Catlin 10/1: 3-8: Handy 10f, fdd: reapp.   2   64
1183 **SHALATI PRINCESS** 17 [12]3-8-9 (45) R Brisland 66/1: 006049: Al in rear.   10   51$
OPEN BOOK 0 [6]3-8-9   M Fenton 25/1: 0: 10th: Keen rear, nvr a factor on debut.   11   37
514 **Once Around** 92 [4]3-9-0   R Miles 40/1:0   1140 **Harry Came Home** 20 [2]3-9-0 R L Moore 66/1:0

12 Ran   Time 2m 42.42 (10.02)   Owned: Mr K Abdulla   Trained: Manton

428

1502   **5.20 102 Spire Fm Handicap Stakes 4yo+ 0-90 (C)**   [88]
£9628 £3652 £1826   **1m6f15y**   **Good/Soft 82**   **-38 Slow**   Flag Start

2605] **THE LAST CAST 666** [14] H Morrison 5-9-0 (74) M Fenton 7/1: 0/00226/-1: ch g Prince of Birds -   **82**
Atan's Gem (Sharpen Up) Made all, drvn out ins fnl 1f to hold on: 6 wk jumps abs, earlier h'cap hdle wnr (rtd 131h,
stays 2m5f on gd & hvy): eff at 10f, enjoyed step up to 14f: acts on gd & hvy grnd: goes well fresh: game 5yo who
is unexposed at this trip, win again. 2 Jun'02 Sand 10gd 74-70 D: 2 May'02 Wind 10sft 75-70 D: 2 Nov'01 Wind 8hvy 79- D:
1295 **BUCKS 11** [17] D K Ivory 7-8-9 (69) M Howard(7) 33/1: 125-0302: Held up, prog 3f out, styg on when   ¾   **75+**
no room 1f out, switched & kept on cl-home, nvr get to wnr: op 20/1: poss unlucky against a fav hcapped wnr.
1389 **SENTRY 6** [15] J H M Gosden 4-9-10 (85) Dane O'Neill 100/30 FAV: 4/231-143: Handy, ev ch bef 1f   shd   **90**
out, kept on, not btn far in 3rd: tchd 4/1: eff at 11/12f, stays 14f: fine run under top-weight: see 1389.
1056 **INVITATION 27** [10] A Charlton 6-8-10 (74) R Smith 25/1: 5500-064: Held up, prog when no room bef   2½   **73**
1f out, switched & kept on late: eff at 10f, now stays 14f: has slipped to a winning mark, see 1056.
1087 **SUN HILL 25** [16]4-8-11 (72) D Sweeney 25/1: 0-111005: Handy till dist, sn onepcd: btr 837.   ¾   **74**
1112 **MOSTARSIL 22** [2]6-8-10 p (70) R L Moore 25/1: 15206-06: ch g Kingmambo - Naazeq (Nashwan) Rear,   nk   **71+**
prog ins fnl 2f, nrst fin: won 4 h'caps in '03: suited by 10/12f, stays sharp 2m well: acts on firm, gd &
polytrack: eff with cheek pieces: tough 6yo: spot on next time.
2 Sep'03 Good 16fm 73-71 D: 1 Aug'03 Good 12g/f 71-65 D: 1 Jul'03 Epso 12.0gd 66-60 E: 2 Jun'03 Sali 12g/f 60-59 E:
1 May'03 Brig 11.9g/f 60-54 E: 2 Apr'03 Brig 11.9g/f 54-51 F: 1 Feb'03 Ling 12ap 49a-42 F: 2 Aug'02 Chep 10.1gd 50- F:
1 Jul'02 Bath 10.2g/f 53- F: 2 Aug'01 Newm 10gd 84-82 C: 1 Jun'01 Pont 12gd 81- D:
2894] **LAGGAN BAY 293** [9]4-9-2 (77) L Keniry(3) 16/1: 305212-7: Rear, nvr nrr than mid-div: long jumps abs.   1¼   **77**
5033] **STOOP TO CONQUER 176** [8]4-8-9 (70) T Quinn 15/2: 05356-8: Keen handy, fdd dist: reapp.   hd   **69**
1056 **CROWN AGENT 27** [19]4-8-9 (70) Martin Dwyer 33/1: 22U-0509: Nvr nrr than mid-div: btr 918.   3   **66**
1232 **SAN HERNANDO 15** [18]4-8-11 (72) N Pollard 4/1: 6060-640: 10th: Mid-div over 12f, sn wknd: btr 1232.   1¾   **66**
1357 **MAN THE GATE 8** [1]5-7-12 (58) Lisa Jones(3) 8/1: 5300-250: 11th: Mid-div over 13f, sn wknd: btr 979.   1   **51**
1109 **TURTLE VALLEY 22** [11]8-8-13 (73) Paul Eddery 9/1: 0-503100: 12th: Cl-up 13f, sn fdd: btr 1087.   1   **65**
1232 **MERSEY SOUND 15** [5]6-8-7 (67) P Dobbs 33/1: 03210-00: 13th: Al in rear.   1½   **58**
     Cloudy Sky 1675 [3]8-9-6 (80) G Baker 66/1:0   4957] **Theatre 184** [4]5-9-9 (83) F Norton 20/1:0
1295 **Stolen Hours 11** [7]4-8-12 (73) S Hitchcott(3) 50/1:0   936 **Grand Wizard 37** [13]4-8-10 (71) M Tebbutt 16/1:0
17 Ran   Time 3m 14.80(16.8)   Owned: Mr D P Barrie   Trained: East Ilsley

---

Official Going GOOD (GOOD/FIRM places).

1503   **1.45 Ian Stevenson E B F Maiden Stakes A Qualifier For Hamilton Park 2-Y-O Series Final 2yo (D)**
£4823 £1484 £742   **5f4y str**   **Good**   **-08 Slow**   Stands side

1237 **SEA HUNTER 15** [5] M R Channon 2-9-0 A Culhane 11/10 FAV: 01: b c Lend A Hand - Ocean Grove   **84**
(Fairy King) Prom, led ins fnl 1f, rdn out: well bckd: Feb foal, cost 110,000gns: half-brother to wnrs at 5/6f:
dam juv wnr at 6f: sire top-class at 6f/1m: eff at 5f, will apprec further: acts on gd grnd: impr with racing.
     DISTINCTLY GAME [6] K A Ryan 2-9-0 G Parkin 9/2: 2: b c Mind Games - Distinctly Blu   ½   **81**
(Distinctly North) Bhd, prog 2f out, styd on well fnl 1f, just denied: op 3/1 on debut: Jan first foal, cost
11,000gns: dam won a couple of times at 5f: sire top-class at sprint dists: eff at 5f, shld stay 6f: acts on gd
grnd: encouraging debut eff & can find similar.
     BECKERMET [2] R F Fisher 2-9-0 P Bradley(5) 33/1: 3: b g Second Empire - Razida (Last Tycoon)   2   **75**
Slow away, sn prom, led dist, hdd ins fnl 1f, sn no extra: debut: clr rem: May foal, cost E12,500: half-brother
to a wnr at 9f: dam smart at 7f/1m: sire top-class at 1m: eff at 5f, 6/7f will suit in time: acts on gd grnd:
showed promise here & can improve with racing.
1143 **KEEPASHARPLOOKOUT 20** [4] Mrs L Stubbs 2-9-0 P Hanagan 7/1: 44: Handy 3f, sn wknd: btr 1143.   7   **57**
962 **NO COMMISSION 34** [1]2-9-0 D Nolan(5) 25/1: 05: Led, hdd dist, sn fdd: see 962.   2½   **50**
1117 **NEE LEMON LET 21** [3]2-8-9 P Mathers(7) 100/30: 26: Keen prom, fdd bef 1f out, sn eased: 9   **21**
disappointing run, btr 1117 (debut).
6 Ran   Time 1m 0.78 (2.68)   Owned: Sheikh Mohammed   Trained: West Ilsley

1504   **2.15 Sunday Mail Annual Jump Jockeys Handicap NH Jockeys 4yo+ 0-70 (E)**   [39]
£4420 £1360 £680   **1m65y rnd**   **Good 45**   **-25 Slow**   Inside

1278 **DOUBLE RANSOM 12** [7] Mrs L Stubbs 5-11-3 bl (56) G Duffield 4/1 FAV: 2-231421: Bhd, grad prog to   **63**
lead dist, rdn out: tchd 5/1: eff at 1m/10f on polytrack, gd & soft: eff with blnks: in gd form, see 1278.
1122 **ANTHEMION 21** [13] Mrs J C McGregor 7-11-7 (60) W Dowling(3) 16/1: 00025-02: ch g Night Shift -   1   **64**
New Sensitive (Wattlefield) Mid-div, prog ins fnl 2f, kept on fnl 1f, not extra: nvr-nvr twice in '03 (h'cap &
class stks): modest form over hdles in 02/03 (rtd 82h, mdn hdle): Flat wnr back in '00 (2 h'caps, P Haslam): eff
at 7f/1m on firm, gd/soft & fibresand: encouraging run & is on a winning mark.
2 Sep'03 Carl 7.9fm 63-62 D: 2 Jul'03 Hami 8.3g/f 62-(59) E:
1319 **SPINDOR 9** [16] J A Osborne 5-11-8 bl (61) V Slattery 8/1: 3421033: Held up, prog ins fnl 2f, not   shd   **64**
btn far in 3rd: tchd 5/1: acts on fast, gd & both AWs: see 1010.
1314* **BEAUTEOUS 10** [3] M J Polglase 5-11-10 (63) L Vickers(3) 6/1: 4411114: Led, hdd dist, sn no extra: ½   **65**
rider received 2 day whip ban: not disgraced on bid for 5 timer back on turf: see 1314.
1198 **YENALED 17** [11]7-11-3 (56) J Crowley 8/1: 3050045: Slow away, prog 3f out, onepcd ins fnl 1f.   1¼   **56**
1388 **MILLENNIUM HALL 6** [15]5-11-4 (57) K Renwick 9/1: 10060-06: b g Saddlers' Hall - Millazure   2   **53**
(Dayjur) Rear, nvr nrr than mid-div: qck reapp: h'cap wnr here in '03: h'cap rnr-up here in '02 (L M Cumani):
eff btwn 1m/11.6f on fast & hvy grnd: with P Monteith. 1 Jul'03 Hami 9.2g/f 61-57 E: 2 May'02 Wind 11.6g/f 72-70 D:
4890] **FRANCIS FLUTE 190** [9]6-10-11 (50) A Dempsey 33/1: 046000-7: Prom over 6f, sn wknd: reapp.   1¼   **44**
1388 **LUCKY LARGO 6** [4]4-11-5 bl (58) B Gibson(3) 25/1: 020-0508: Handy 6f, sn wknd: qck reapp.   6   **40**
1366 **ONE LAST TIME 8** [14]4-11-10 (63) H Bastiman 18/1: 0660-009: Slow away, al in rear: btr 1049.   3½   **38**

128 **MEHMAAS 155** [12]8-11-2 (55) L Enstone 14/1: 535000-0: 10th: Handy 5f, sn wknd: long abs. 1½ 27
4711} **SKIDDAW JONES 202** [5]4-11-1 (54) L McGrath(3) 16/1: 254000-0: 11th: Handy 6f, fdd: reapp. 2½ 21
1295 **LUNAR LEADER 11** [10]4-11-7 t p (60) A Ross 25/1: 000-0000: 12th: Bhd, nvr a factor. nk 26
1366 **HULA BALLEW 8** [1]4-11-5 (58) R Garritty 12/1: 3366-050: 13th: Handy, fdd 3f out: btr 1366. nk 23
1442 **SPEEDFIT FREE 3** [8]7-10-13 (52) Ann Stokell(7) 14/1: 2400300: 14th: Chsd ldrs over 5f, sn fdd. 1½ 14
14 Ran Time 1m 49.65 (5.85) Owned: Tyme Partnership Trained: Malton

1505

2.50 52nd Lowland Regiment Claiming Stakes 3yo (E)
£3738 £1150 £575 **1m1f36y** **Good 45** **-29 Slow** Inside

934 **HAWKIT 37** [7] J A Osborne 3-9-3 (74) S W Kelly 1/1 FAV: 33-52101: Prom, led 2f out, pushed out, val 3L+: well bckd: clmd for 12,000: eff around 1m/9f on fast, gd grnd & fibresand: see 839. 67+
1144 **BARGAIN HUNT 20** [5] W Storey 3-8-3 (50) J Bramhill 12/1: 06403-02: b g Foxhound - Atisayin (Al Nasr) Prom, styd on ins fnl 1f, al held by wnr: plcd once in '03 (seller, rtd 57$ & 47): eff at 7f/9f on gd & gd/soft grnd: has tried visor & cheek pieces. 1¾ 48
1395 **TANCRED IMP 6** [8] D W Barker 3-7-12 (45) R Ffrench 7/1: 003-053: b f Atraf - Tancred Mischief (Northern State) Chsd ldrs, kept on ins fnl 1f, not btn far in 3rd: clr rem & qck reapp: 3rd of 7 at best on last of 3 '03 starts (rtd 52, seller): eff at 1m/9f, further shld suit: acts on gd grnd. nk 42
1387 **ONE N ONLY 6** [2] Miss L A Perratt 3-8-12 (55) P Hanagan 10/1: 5450-454: Handy 6f, sn no extra. 6 47
THE FOXS HEAD [4]3-8-12 J McAuley 50/1: 5: Chsd ldrs 6f, sn no extra: debut. 1¾ 45
1339 **CHASE THE RAINBOW 8** [1]3-8-7 (62) P Mathers(7) 4/1: 51002-66: Handy 7f, fdd: see 1339. 5 33
1275 **BEAVER DIVA 12** [6]3-7-12 B Swarbrick(7) 16/1: 0-47: Led, hdd 2f out, fdd: btr 1275. 1 22
1095 **LAPDANCING 24** [3]3-8-4 P Fessey 33/1: 00-08: Rear, nvr a factor. 14 10
8 Ran Time 2m 0.87 (6.77) Owned: Mr Paul J Dixon Trained: Upper Lambourn

1506

3.25 Totejackpot Handicap Stakes 4yo+ 0-85 (D) [84]
£7124 £2192 £1096 **1m5f9y** **Good 45** **+07 Fast** Stands side

3764] **COLORADO FALLS 615** [11] P Monteith 6-9-2 (72) L Enstone(3) 12/1: 215306/-1: b g Nashwan - Ballet Shoes (Ela Mana Mou) Handy, outpcd 2f out, rallied to lead ins fnl 1f, rdn out: tchd 25/1: 10 wk jumps abs, earlier plcd on 2 of 3 03/04 hdles starts (rtd 119h, h'cap, stays 2m1f on gd & hvy): missed '03: appr h'cap wnr in '02: eff over 12f, now stays 13f: acts on fast & gd/soft grnd, goes well fresh, made gd use of drop to fair mark. 80
1 Jul'02 Hayd 11.9g/s 82-81 E: 2 Jun'02 Ayr 15hvy 81-82 C: 1 May'01 Newm 12g/f 96- D:
1109 **NAKWA 22** [6] E J Alston 6-8-4 (60) D Allan(3) 8/1: 1225322: Led, hdd & hung right after 9f, rallied & ev ch ins fnl 1f, just held by wnr: remains in gd form: acts on gd, soft & fibresand: see 1109 & 1034. 1½ 65
1361* **GEORGE STUBBS 8** [3] M J Polglase 6-8-9 (65) J F McDonald(3) 11/2: 3640313: Keen mid-div, styd on to lead 3f out, hdd ins fnl 1f, no extra: tchd 13/2: just btr 1361 (2m). 3 65
1389 **SAHEM 6** [9] D Eddy 7-9-8 (78) P Hanagan 7/1: 1330-504: Rear, prog & ev ch dist, sn onepcd: btr 926. ½ 78
1118 **TBM CAN 21** [2]5-8-9 (65) B Swarbrick(7) 5/1 FAV: 31506-65: b g Rock City - Fire Sprite (Mummy's Game) Rear, prog & ev ch 3f out, no extra ins fnl 2f: prog in '03, won 4 h'caps & a class stks: unplcd in '02 (rtd 55a, no turf form): suited by 12/13f on firm & gd grnd: with W M Brisbourne. 3 61
1 Aug'03 Beve 12.1gd 67-(60) F: 1 Jul'03 Warw 12.6g/f 60-56 G: 1 Jun'03 Folk 12fm 50-47 F:
1 Jun'03 Hami 13.0gd 51-47 F: 1 Jun'03 Muss 12fm 48-41 E:
997 **TIYOUN 32** [5]6-9-5 (75) K Dalgleish 8/1: 42025-26: Chsd ldrs 12f, sn no extra: btr 997. 1 69
1118 **SPITTING IMAGE 21** [4]4-8-6 (62) S W Kelly 16/1: 0240-037: Prom, led 4f out, hdd 3f out, hung right & wknd fnl 2f: btr 1118. ½ 55
1092 **REPULSE BAY 24** [7]6-7-13 (55) Joanna Badger 25/1: 03500-68: Al bhd: btr 1092. 3 44
1469 **GOLDEN BOOT 2** [10]5-8-11 p (67) T Eaves(5) 7/1: 02343-609: Rear, nvr a factor: qck reapp: btr 1389. shd 55
1118* **TANDAVA 21** [1]6-9-3 (73) G Duffield 6/1: 20400-10: 10th: Handy over 12f, fdd: btr 1118. 1¾ 58
10 Ran Time 2m 50.44 (4.94) Owned: Mr J W D Campbell Trained: Rosewell

1507

4.00 Jacqui Dalgleish 40th Birthday Median Auction Maiden Stakes 3-5yo (E)
£3803 £1170 £585 **1m4f17y** **Good 45** **-09 Slow** Stands side

1174 **BUMPTIOUS 17** [3] M H Tompkins 3-8-7 (75) G Duffield 4/7 FAV: 346-331: Prom, styd on to lead 2f out, drvn out to hold on: well bckd: eff at 1m/10f, now suited by arnd 12f: acts on gd & gd/soft grnd: see 1017. 82
RECOGNISE [8] M Johnston 3-8-7 K Dalgleish 7/1: 2: ch g Groom Dancer - Broken Romance (Ela Mana Mou) Handy, outpcd 3f out, rallied dist, kept on ins fnl 1f, just held: debut: half-brother to a couple of wnrs around mid-dists/staying dists: eff at 12f, shld be suited by further: acts on gd grnd: showed signs of greeness here but can impr with experience & find similar. ½ 81
1279 **INTO THE SHADOWS 12** [9] Mrs M Reveley 4-9-7 A Culhane 11/2: 33: Chsd ldrs, ev ch 2f out, onepcd dist: eff at 1m/12f on gd & soft grnd: ran to form of 1279. 3 72
CAYMANS GIFT [1] A C Whillans 4-9-12 P Hanagan 66/1: 4: ch g Cayman Kai - Gymcrak Cyrano (Cyrano de Bergerac) Handy, wknd over 1f out: Flat debut: jumps fit, modest hdles form to date. 4 71
1260 **BLUE HILLS 13** [2]3-8-7 (73) R Ffrench 12/1: 052-05: Rear, nvr nrr than mid-div: rnr-up on last of 3 '03 starts (med auct mdn): eff around 1m on rain softened grnd: has been gelded since last term. 2½ 67
1390 **ARCHENKO 6** [6]4-9-12 P Bradley(5) 66/1: 006: Led after 2f till 2f out, fdd: qck reapp. 9 55$
1304 **ILLICIUM 10** [7]5-9-7 T Eaves(5) 33/1: 607: Rear, nvr a factor. 1¾ 48
LANGE BLEU 396 [5]5-9-12 e V Slattery 33/1: 2/50-8: Bhd, nvr a factor on debut. 23 23
1041} **DILIGENT LAD 386** [10]4-9-12 (57) L Enstone(3) 50/1: 600/0-9: Led early, styd prom, fdd fnl 3f. 30 0
9 Ran Time 2m 38.37 (6.57) Owned: Mrs Beryl Lockey Trained: Newmarket

1508

4.35 David Cooper Handicap Stakes 3yo+ 0-70 (E) [69]
£4469 £1375 £688 **6f5y str** **Good 45** **+04 Fast** Stands side

1463 **FRIAR TUCK 2** [15] Miss L A Perratt 9-8-9 (50) R Ffrench 12/1: 3200-0001: Rcd far side, bhd, prog centre ins fnl 2f, rdn out to lead cl-home: tchd 20/1: qck reapp: eff at 5f, suited by 6f: acts on firm & hvy grnd: v well h'capped on old form & this was first win since '02: see 1391. 56
1463 **XANADU 2** [14] Miss L A Perratt 8-8-9 p (50) P Mulrennan(5) 12/1: 120000-02: ch g Casteddu - ¾ 53

HAMILTON   SUNDAY 02.05.04   Righthand, Undulating Track, Stiff Uphill Finish

Bellatrix (Persian Bold) Rcd far side, handy, led dist, hdd cl-home: tchd 20/1 on qck reapp, stablemate of wnr: h'cap wnr in '03 (first time cheek pieces): appr h'cap wnr in '02: won 4 races back in '00: eff at 5/6f on firm & gd grnd: loves Hamilton & is eff with cheek pieces: well h'capped 8yo who could go one btr on this evidence.
2 Aug'03 Muss 5g/f 54-51 E: 1 Aug'03 Hami 6.0g/f 54-45 E: 2 Sep'02 Redc 6g/f 56-52 E: 1 May'02 Hami 5gd 55-49 F: 1 Jun'01 Hami 6g/f 68- E:

4716} **GOLDEN SPECTRUM 202** [5] D Nicholls 5-9-2 (57) Alex Greaves 25/1: 000000-3: ch g Spectrum - Plessaya (Nureyev) Handy stands side, styd on despite hanging right ins fnl 1f, no ch with far side: reapp: unplcd in '03 (rtd 62a & 63, h'caps & class stks, R Hannon): mdn wnr on turf in '02: eff at 6/7f on firm, gd & prob fibresand, tried cheek pieces, t-strap & blnks: gd eff on first start for D Nicholls & is well h'capped.			1	57+

2 Jul'02 Sand 7g/f 82-83 C: 1 May'02 Sali 6g/f 86- D: 2 Apr'02 Newm 7g/f 88- D: 2 Aug'01 Newb 7fm 90- D: 2 Aug'01 Good 7g/f 82- D:

1391 **TANCRED TIMES 6** [8] D W Barker 9-9-2 (57) L Enstone(3) 7/1: 1000-044: Cl-up far side, onepcd fnl 1f.	1	54
629 **FLYING EDGE 78** [2]4-9-6 (61) A Nicholls 12/1: 160-0205: Prom stands side, ev ch dist, sn onepcd.	nk	57
1218 **TELEPATHIC 15** [13]4-9-11 (66) P Bradley(5) 40/1: 000-0006: Rcd far side, handy till dist, onepcd.	nk	61
1391* **ULYSEES 6** [12]5-10-1 (6ex) (70) P Hanagan 7/2 FAV: 06600-17: Rear, prog ins fnl 2f, nrst fin: well bckd: disapp after easy win here in 1391.	½	63
1094 **PAGAN STORM 24** [6]4-9-12 bl (67) Kristin Stubbs(7) 25/1: 146-0008: Nvr nrr than mid-div stands side.	½	58
963 **ONLY ONE LEGEND 34** [9]6-9-3 p (58) A Culhane 9/1: 0000039: Rcd far side, handy till dist, wknd.	1½	45
4304} **BALLYBUNION 228** [16]5-9-13 (68) L Treadwell(7) 18/1: 326100-0: 10th: Led till dist far side.	½	53
1119 **ENVIRONMENTALIST 21** [10]5-8-9 t (50) D McGaffin 66/1: 20/006-00: 11th: Al bhd.	5	21
1074 **LEGAL SET 26** [4]8-9-0 (55) Ann Stokell 16/1: 0-405020: 12th: Led till dist stands side: btr 1074.	hd	25
4905} **ROSSELLI 188** [1]8-8-5 (46) P Mathers(4) 50/1: 360044-0: 13th: Rcd stands side, cl-up 4f, fdd.	nk	15
3802} **SMIRFYS PARTY 253** [3]6-9-1 (56) J Bramhill 33/1: 000100-0: 14th: Prom 4f stands side.	1¾	20
1179 **VIJAY 17** [7]5-9-4 bl (59) G Duffield 9/2: 60-03060: 15th: Rcd stands side, handy 4f, fdd: op 7/1.	3½	14

15 Ran   Time 1m 12.30 (2.5)   Owned: Cree Lodge Racing Club   Trained: Ayr

---

1509   5.10 Discover Scottish Racing Handicap Stakes 3yo 0-75 (E)   **[82]**
£3851 £1185 £593   **5f4y str**   **Good 45**   **-04 Slow**   Stands side

1338 **SCOTTISH EXILE 8** [1] K R Burke 3-8-11 vis (65) Darren Williams 9/2: 31-64431: Handy, styd on to lead dist, drvn out to hold on: eff at 5f, 6f shld suit: acts on both AWs, fast & gd/soft: eff with visor.		69
1229 **BARON RHODES 15** [8] J S Wainwright 3-9-2 (70) T Eaves(5) 7/1: 16042-22: Cl-up, styd on well ins fnl 1f, poss came too sn: op 5/2: ran to form of 2nd in 1229.	nk	73
1277 **LORD BASKERVILLE 12** [4] W Storey 3-8-3 (57) J Bramhill 7/1: 30-00603: br c Wolfhound - My Dear Watson (Chilibang) Trkd ldrs, styd on despite edging left ins fnl 1f, not btn far in 3rd: op 12/1: unplcd in '03 (rtd 69, auct mdn): eff at 5/6f on fast & gd grnd: encouraging eff here & can find similar.	¾	58
4382} **OPEN MIND 223** [2] E J Alston 3-8-0 (2ow) (52) A Nicholls 12/1: 24040-4: b f Mind Games - Primum Tempus (Primo Dominie) Cl-up, just no extra ins fnl 1f: reapp: rnr-up first time out in '03 (med auct mdn): eff at 5f on fast & gd grnd: has slipped down weights. 2 Apr'03 Pont 5g/f 68- E:	1¼	51
1119 **MUSIOTAL 21** [5]3-7-12 (4oh) (48) P Fessey 25/1: 50-05: Rear, kept on fnl 1f, nrst fin.	½	48
1404 **LAVISH TIMES 5** [7]3-7-12 (1oh)bl (51) P Hanagan 7/2 FAV: 0530636: Prom till dist, wknd: tchd 5/1.	hd	47
4247} **SIR ERNEST 230** [6]3-9-7 (75) J F McDonald(3) 5/1: 104000-7: Handy till dist, fdd: reapp.	nk	69
863 **SHAYMEES GIRL 46** [3]3-8-3 (57) Joanna Badger 10/1: 0-5338: Led, hdd dist, sn fdd: btr 863.	9	26

8 Ran   Time 1m 0.97(2.47)   Owned: Mrs Melba Bryce   Trained: Leyburn

---

KEMPTON   MONDAY 03.05.04   Righthand, Flat, Fair Track

Official Going HEAVY

1510   2.10 E B F Sharp Minds Betfair Maiden Stakes 2yo (D)
£5389 £1658 £829   **5f str**   **Heavy 167**   **+05 Fast**   Far side

1190 **TURNKEY 18** [4] M R Channon 2-9-0 T E Durcan 5/2: 21: Cl-up & led over 1f out, pulled clr under hands-and-heels, readily: nicely bckd, fast juv time: eff at 5f, 6f will suit: acts on fast, imprvd on hvy grnd today: handles a stiff/gall or easy trk: well regarded & looks useful: see 1190.		102+
1205 **PLANET TOMATO 17** [7] P F I Cole 2-9-0 K Fallon 6/4 FAV: 32: Led till over 1f out, sn no ch with wnr: hvly bckd, caught a tartar: handles gd, poss hvy grnd: see 1205.	11	80
WILKO [5] J Noseda 2-9-0 E Ahern 3/1: 3: ch c Awesome Again - Native Roots (Indian Ridge) Trkd ldrs & sn pushed along, no impress over 1f out: nicely bckd tho' op 2/1: Jan first foal, $35,000 purchase: dam a 3yo wnr, should suggests 1m/hdl could suit eventually.	½	78
STEDFAST MCSTAUNCH [1] B J Meehan 2-9-0 S Drowne 25/1: 4: gr g Desert Style - Aneydia (Kenmare) Dwelt, chsd ldrs till no impress fnl 2f: op 20/1: Feb foal, E32,000 purchase: half-brother to a plcd 12f/hdles performer: stay further in time.	3	69
FORTNUM [2]2-9-0 Dane O'Neill 16/1: 5: b c Forzando - Digamist Girl (Digamist) Dwelt, in tch till wknd dist: op 12/1: Apr foal, cost 35,000gns: half-brother to a 2 sprint wnrs: dam a prolific sprint wnr abroad.	3½	58
ATSOS [6]2-9-0 P Dobbs 20/1: 6: Dwelt, pushed along till wknd & lost tch from halfway.	1	55
FIRST RULE [8]2-9-0 J Quinn 33/1: 7: Dwelt, sn in tch till 2f out.	2	49
FLYING PASS [3]2-9-0 T Quinn 50/1: 8: Dwelt & sn outpcd, bhd halfway.	6	31

8 Ran   Time 1m 6.4 (8.1)   Owned: Sheikh Mohammed   Trained: West Ilsley

---

1511   2.40 Stpp Media Maiden Stakes Div 1 3yo (D)
£5616 £1728 £864   **1m rnd**   **Heavy 167**   **-19 Slow**   Outside

4651} **FIRST CENTURION 208** [11] J W Hills 3-9-0 E Ahern 11/1: 6-1: b c Peintre Celebre - Valley of Hope (Riverman) Mid-div, rdn & hdwy/switched 2f out, led ins last & sn rdn clr: reapp: unplcd sole '03 start (rtd 66+, AW mdn): relished step up to 1m on hvy grnd, handles polytrack & 10f+ will suit: goes well fresh.		88
1191 **PIZAZZ 18** [3] B J Meehan 3-9-0 D Holland 4/1: 0-52: ch c Pivotal - Clare Celeste (Coquelin) Led/dsptd lead, went on 3f out, sn strongly prsd & hdd ins last, no ch with wnr: rest well held, bckd: unplcd sole '03 starts (rtd 79, mdn): half-brother to wnrs at 6/10f: styd longer 1m trip well & handles fast & hvy grnd.	5	76

1101 **SAILMAKER 25** [4] R Charlton 3-9-0 S Drowne 7/2 FAV: 6-23: Prom & led over 2f out till over 1f 4 68
out, wknd: nicely bckd: ran well for a long way in these testing conds, but btr 1101 (gd/soft).
1236 **DANDYGREY RUSSETT 16** [10] G L Moore 3-8-9 R Brisland 33/1: 04: gr f Singspiel - Christian 3½ 56
Church (Linamix) Slow away & bhd, late gains, nvr threat to front trio: shapes as if mid-dists will suit.
    PASS THE PORT [9]3-9-0 J Murtagh 9/1: 5: Chsd ldrs 3f out, sn no impress: debut. 1 59
    LUCAYAN LEGEND [7]3-9-0 P Dobbs 9/1: 6: Rear, only mod gains fnl 2f on debut. 5 49
    HIGH VIEW [1]3-9-0 J Quinn 50/1: 7: Slow away & went left start, little hdwy on debut. 10 29
1297 **TSARBUCK 12** [12]3-9-0 P Doe 100/1: 0-008: Mid-div, no impress fnl 3f. 1½ 26
4265} **GREAT EXHIBITION 37** [5]3-9-0 T K McEvoy 4/1: 32-09: Led till 3f out, sn btn: nicely bckd, t-strap. 2 22
    HERIOT [6]3-9-0 Dane O'Neill 14/1: 0: 10th: Slow away & sn struggling rear on debut. 9 4
1100 **Captain Marryat 25** [8]3-9-0 Martin Dwyer 14/1:0   4943} **Rubaiyat 187** [2]3-9-0 T E Durcan 33/1:0
12 Ran   Time 1m 51.75 (14.95)   Owned: Mr D M Kerr and Mr N Brunskill   Trained: Lambourn

---

1512   **3.15 Jubilee Stakes Handicap 4yo+ 0-100 (C)**   [98]
        £9390 £3562 £1781   **1m rnd**   **Heavy 167**   +01 Fast   Outside

1231 **SHOT TO FAME 16** [5] P W Harris 5-9-5 (89) E Ahern 14/1: 6300-501: Made all, pulled clr 2f out, 111
cmftbly: fair time: eff at 1m on firm & hvy: enjoyed forcing tactics today: well h'capped, see 1066.
1231 **ST PETERSBURG 16** [1] M H Tompkins 4-9-9 (93) D Holland 11/2: 315-2102: Chsd wnr thr'out, kept on 11 100
fnl 2f but no impress on easy wnr: well clr of rem, nicely bckd: back to form, btr 1066.
1231 **DIGITAL 16** [2] M R Channon 7-9-6 (90) T E Durcan 12/1: 02-03403: Bhd, styd on fnl 2f, nvr 5 87
threaten front pair: op 16/1: see 945.
1296 **NORTON 12** [3] T G Mills 7-9-9 (93) W Ryan 8/1: 000-0504: Chsd ldrs, outpcd by ldrs fnl 3f: see 1231. 1 88
1231 **DESERT OPAL 16** [6]4-9-10 (94) S Drowne 7/2 FAV: 2110-005: Chsd ldrs, no impress fnl 2f: see 951. 1 87
1354 **HURRICANE COAST 9** [4]5-8-3 bl (73) J Mackay 14/1: 0410166: Keen, in tch, btn 2f out, reportedly 5 56
finished distressed: btr 1282 (7f, gd).
1151 **AUDIENCE 20** [17]4-9-11 (95) J Quinn 25/1: 0226-007: b g Zilzal - Only Yours (Aragon) Chsd ldrs, 2½ 73
btn 2f out: lightly rcd '03, dual stks rnr-up for W Haggas: won both starts '02, nov stks & val cond stks: both
wins at 7f, stays 1m well: acts on fast & gd grnd, stiff/gall trks: eff with/ without blnks: first home of those
who remained on ins of trk. 2 Sep'03 Donc 8gd 104-(103) C: 2 Aug'03 Chep 7.1g/f 103-(104) C:
1 Oct'02 Newm 7g/f 82- B: 1 Oct'02 Sal 7gd 82- D:
1151 **HURRICANE FLOYD 20** [7]6-9-4 (88) J Murtagh 16/1: 34003-08: ch g Pennekamp - Mood Swings (Shirley 12 42
Heights) Al rear, nvr factor: h'cap rnr-up '03 for M C Pipe: h'cap rnr '02 for D Nicholls: eff btwn 6f/1m on
firm, gd & any trk: eff with/without t-strap/visor: breathing prob reported in these testing conditions.
2 Jun'03 Asco 7g/f 88-81 B: 2 Jul'02 York 7g/f 90-86 C: 2 Aug'01 Yarm 6gd 96- C: 2 Jun'01 Newm 7fm 106- A:
836 **CORNELIUS 51** [16]7-10-0 (98) N Chalmers(5) 14/1: 00410-09: Led group on ins 5f, sn btn: 7 wk abs. 6 40
4689} **SRI DIAMOND 204** [12]4-8-10 (80) P Dobbs 33/1: 1/030-0: 10th: In tch no rail, btn 2f out: reapp, gldd. ½ 21
4939} **DEVANT 187** [9]4-9-1 (85) P Robinson 6/1: 010605-0: 11th: Rcd inner rail, in tch till 3f out, reapp. 9 8
1231 **JAY GEES CHOICE 16** [10]4-9-5 (89) B O'Neill(7) 20/1: 2600-600: 12th: Prom inner till 3f out: btr 951. 17 0
17   **Night Kiss 173** [8]4-7-12 (4oh)(64) Martin Dwyer 33/1:0   1231 **Yakimov 16** [14]5-9-5 (89) Dane O'Neill 25/1:0
14 Ran   Time 1m 50.15 (13.35)   Owned: The Conquistadors   Trained: Berkhamsted

---

1513   **3.45 Fulham F C Football And Community Scheme E B F Conditions Stakes Fillies 3yo (C)**
        £8384 £3180 £1590   **6f str**   **Heavy 167**   -06 Slow   Far side

4947*}**AUTUMN PEARL 186** [7] M A Jarvis 3-8-13 (87) P Robinson 9/2: 151-1: b f Orpen - Cyclone Flyer 95
(College Chapel) Made all, rdn clr over 1f out, held on well for press: op 11/2, reapp: lightly rcd '03, landed
auct mdn & AW cond stks: eff at 5f, now stays 6f well: acts on polytrack, gd & hvy grnd, sharp/stiff trk: likes to
force the pace & can go well fresh: useful filly. 1 Oct'03 Ling 5ap 88a- D: 1 Jun'03 Sand 5.0gd 88- E:
4978} **CUSCO 184** [1] R Hannon 3-8-13 (87) P Dobbs 11/2: 31305-2: ch f Titus Livius - John's Ballad 1 91
(Ballad Rock) Chsd wnr 2f out, kept on but al held: reapp: mdn scorer '03, subs cond stks plcd (rtd 86): eff at
6f, best last term at 7f/1m: acts on fast & hvy, stiff/gall or easy trks: encouraging rtn, can improve over
further. 1 Aug'03 Sand 8.1g/f 83- D:
4308} **HILITES 228** [4] J S Moore 3-8-9 (83) Martin Dwyer 16/1: 101004-3: ch f Desert King - Slayjay 1¼ 83
(Mujtahid) Held up in tch, kept on for press fnl 2f, al held: reapp: auct mdn, h'cap & nov auct wnr '03: suited
by 5.6f/6f, stays a sharp 7f: acts on firm & soft grnd, prob any trk: tough type, well clr of rem here.
1 Aug'03 Bath 5.7fm 87-(73) E: 1 Aug'03 Wind 6g/f 82-73 E: 1 Jul'03 Carl 5.9gd 69- E: 2 Jul'03 Warw 7.1g/f 71- E:
4921*}**LA CORUNA 188** [5] R Charlton 3-8-13 S Drowne 2/1 FAV: 11-4: Trkd wnr, struggling from 2f out: 9 60
well bckd on reapp but reportedly unsuited by hvy grnd.
1154 **DOLCE PICCATA 20** [6]3-8-9 (89) T Quinn 11/1: 30132-05: Chsd ldrs till over 2f out. 2 50
1997} **OUR GAMBLE 331** [3]3-8-13 (90) Dane O'Neill 11/1: 0410-6: Dwelt, nvr a factor: s/mate of 2nd. 10 24
4789*}**BREAD OF HEAVEN 199** [2]3-8-13 (81) D Holland 4/1: 3221-7: Sn rdn & struggling, no ch from dist 0
halfway, eased right down: op 3/1, reapp: reportedly never travelling.
7 Ran   Time 1m 21.5 (10.4)   Owned: Mr & Mrs Kevan Watts   Trained: Newmarket

---

1514   **4.20 Stpp Media Maiden Stakes Div 2 3yo (D)**
        £5616 £1728 £864   **1m rnd**   **Heavy 167**   -49 Slow   Outside

5031} **NIGHT FROLIC 177** [5] J W Hills 3-8-9 E Ahern 14/1: 00-1: b f Night Shift - Miss d'Ouilly 69
(Bikala) Chsd ldrs till lost pl 3f out, prog to lead ins fnl 1f, rdn out: reapp: unplcd both '03 starts (rtd
52, mdn): imprvd for today's step up to 1m, further shld suit: acts on hvy grnd & goes well fresh: has tried a
t-strap: only lightly rcd & can rate higher.
    CHARLESTON [3] J H M Gosden 3-9-0 J Murtagh 11/2: 2: ch c Pursuit of Love - Discomatic nk 74
(Roberto) Cl-up, ev ch 2f out, led bef 1f out till hdd cl-home: debut: well related, brother/half-brother to wnrs
at 7f/14f: eff at 1m, will apprec further: acts on hvy grnd: only just denied here & can find similar.
    ANATOLIAN QUEEN [2] J M P Eustace 3-8-9 J Tate 12/1: 3: b f Woodman - Imia (Riverman) Reared 1¾ 65
start, held up, prog & short of room just ins fnl 2f, switched & styd on ins fnl 1f, not pace front 2: debut: cost
$75,000: eff at 1m, shld be suited by further: acts on hvy grnd: encouraging eff & improve with experience.
37   **VERASI 170** [9] R Charlton 3-9-0 Dane O'Neill 33/1: 000-4: b g Kahyasi - Fair Verona (Alleged) shd 69$

432

Handy & ev ch after 6f, onepcd ins fnl 1f: reapp: unplcd in all 3 '03 starts (rtd 60, mdn): eff at 1m on hvy grnd.

MOTIVE [7]3-9-0 K Fallon 11/2: 5: Held up, prog ins fnl 2f, nvr nrr than mid-div: not		2	65

disgraced here on debut: with Sir Michael Stoute.

4686} **BAILAORA 204** [12]3-9-0 (79) T Quinn 9/2 FAV: 444302-6: Rear, hdwy when short of room dist, sn
onepcd: reapp: rider reported mount was unsuited by today's heavy grnd. — ½ — 64

MY PENSION [4]3-9-0 T E Durcan 20/1: 7: Bhd, nvr nrr than mid-div on debut. — 3 — 58

1377 **DEVIOUS AYERS 7** [6]3-9-0 W Ryan 14/1: 3-48: Led over 6f, sn fdd: qck reapp: just btr 1377. — 1 — 56

PETER PAUL RUBENS [1]3-9-0 D Holland 8/1: 9: Mid-div 6f, fdd: debut. — 6 — 44

4973} **MY HOPE 184** [11]3-8-9 S Drowne 5/1: 00-0: 10th: Mid-div, fdd fnl 3f: tchd 15/2 on reapp. — 8 — 23

BLACK SABBETH [10]3-9-0 J Quinn 20/1: 0: 11th: Chsd ldrs 5f, sn fdd: debut. — dist — 0

11 Ran Time 1m 54.15 (17.35) Owned: The Wandering Stars Trained: Lambourn

---

1515 4.50 Sharp Minds Betfair Handicap Stakes 3yo 0-85 (D) [89]
£5824 £1792 £896 1m1f rnd Heavy 167 -23 Slow Inside

1141 **ANOUSA 21** [8] P Howling 3-9-2 VIS (77) K Fallon 14/1: 2501-01: b c Intikhab - Annaletta (Belmez) — 84
Held up, gd prog ins fnl 2f, styd on to lead cl-home, drvn out: mdn wnr on fnl '03 start: eff at 1m/9f, further
shld suit: acts on firm & hvy grnd: goes well fresh & acts on a gall/stiff trk: left below par effort on
reapp bhd here with application of first time visor. 1 Oct'03 Newc 8gd 80-(78) D: 2 Jun'03 Newm 7fm 78- D:

1369 **GAVROCHE 8** [3] C A Dwyer 3-8-10 (71) J P Guillambert(3) 12/1: 0-123522: Rear, prog halfway, styd — 1¼ — 74
on well ins fnl 1f, just held by wnr: acts on fast, hvy grnd & fibresand: see 1369 & 441.

1206 **FREAK OCCURENCE 17** [2] Miss E C Lavelle 3-9-7 (82) S Drowne 20/1: 11420-03: Rear, prog to lead — nk — 84
just ins fnl 1f, hdd & no extra cl-home: acts on fast, hvy grnd & polytrack: btr 232.

1257 **HONEST INJUN 14** [6] B W Hills 3-9-3 (78) Martin Dwyer 7/1: 02-144: Led, hdd 6f out, styd cl-up — 2 — 76
till led again dist, hdd ins fnl 1f, no extra: eff at 7f/9f on gd/soft, hvy & fibresand: see 1257 & 381.

1108* **BAFFLE 23** [11]3-9-2 (77) T Quinn 6/1: 026-15: Led after 2f, hdd dist, sn wknd: op 9/2: btr 1108. — 2 — 71

4583} **PENZANCE 212** [4]3-9-3 (78) E Ahern 7/1: 13-6: ch c Pennekamp - Kalinka (Soviet Star) Handy when — 1¾ — 68+
hmpd bef 1f out, not recover: reapp: med auct mdn wnr on first of only 2 '03 starts: half-brother to top-class
filly Soviet Song: dam decent 1m/10f performer: eff at 1m, shld be suited by further: acts on firm grnd & goes
well fresh: lost any ch here with interference. 1 Sep'03 Hayd 8.1fm 80- E:

1007 **BALEARIC STAR 33** [12]3-8-7 (68) T E Durcan 10/1: 60000-07: Rear, nvr nrr than mid-div: btr 1007. — 2½ — 53

1141* **SHOW NO FEAR 21** [13]3-8-10 (71) W Ryan 3/1 FAV: 00552-18: Handy over 7f, wknd: well bckd: — 1½ — 53
disappointing on today's hvy grnd: btr 1141 (gd).

1206 **WATAMU 17** [9]3-9-5 (80) J Quinn 20/1: 01-09: b c Groom Dancer - Miss Golden Sands (Kris) Handy — 5 — 52
7f, fdd: auct mdn wnr on fnl of 2 '03 starts: eff at 7f, shld apprec further: acts on gd grnd & a sharp/ undul
trk. 1 Sep'03 Epso 7gd 80- E:

2690*)SALISBURY PLAIN 302 [1]3-9-7 (82) J Murtagh 12/1: 41-0: 10th: Mid-div, prog when hung badly bef — 1¾ — 50
1f out, sn onepcd: reapp.

4706} **SCHAPIRO 203** [14]3-9-2 (77) K McEvoy 20/1: 045-0: 11th: Bhd, nvr a factor: reapp. — 6 — 33

1318 **Laawaris 10** [5]3-9-7 (82) Dane O'Neill 33/1:0 4980} **Thirteen Tricks 183** [7]3-9-0 (75) D Holland 20/1:0

13 Ran Time 2m 7.2 (17.2) Owned: Arkland International (UK) Ltd Trained: Newmarket

---

1516 5.25 Keith William Elmslie Handicap Stakes 3yo+ 0-85 (D) [85]
£5746 £1768 £884 1m6f92y Heavy 167 -54 Slow Inside

1172 **JOROBADEN 19** [1] C F Wall 4-9-12 (83) J Quinn 7/2 J FAV: 4/-2161: Held up, prog 3f out & sn hung — 91
left, styd on to lead ins fnl 1f, rdn out: tchd 9/2: eff at 10/12f, imprvd here for step up to 14.4f: acts on
gd/soft, hvy & polytrack: gd weight carrier: apprec today's stamia test & more prizes await: see 1172 & 1019.

1271* **LINENS FLAME 13** [8] B G Powell 5-9-1 (71) K Fallon 7/2 J FAV: 6/000-112: Handy till led 3f out, — 3½ — 71
hdd ins fnl 1f, no extra: clr rem: acts on soft & hvy: another gd eff here, raised 7lb since recent win in 1271.

1172 **DANCE WORLD 19** [13] Miss J Feilden 4-9-7 (78) B Reilly(3) 20/1: 424-103: Mid-div, prog after 12f, — 8 — 66
fdd dist: btr 1030 (12f, fibresand).

1484* **DISSIDENT 2** [4] D Flood 6-9-6 (6ex)vis (76) J Mackay 6/1: U102214: Handy over 12f, sn fdd: qck — nk — 63
reapp: disapp on first try at 14f: btr 1484 (12f, fast).

4865} **STAR MEMBER 192** [9]5-9-7 (77) D Holland 16/1: 632050-5: b g Hernando - Constellation (Kaldoun) — 8 — 52
Handy 12f, fdd: reapp: rnr-up once in '03 (h'cap, rtd 81): mdn scorer on debut in '02: eff at 10f/14f, prob stays
2m: acts on fast, gd & polytrack: with A P Jarvis. 2 Sep'03 Hayd 14gd 81-76 C: 1 Jun'02 Ling 10ap 81a- F:

1232 **SONOMA 16** [14]4-8-13 (70) Hayley Turner(5) 16/1: 125-506: Led over 11f, sn wknd: btr 1003. — 6 — 36

1056 **KIROV KING 28** [5]4-9-4 (75) L Keniry(3) 50/1: 10460-07: b c Desert King - Nymphs Echo (Mujtahid) — 5 — 33
Nvr nrr than mid-div: ex Irish, mdn & stks wnr at Downpatrick in '03: eff at 12f on hvy grnd.

1056 **SKELLIGS ROCK 28** [11]4-9-6 (77) Dane O'Neill 25/1: 44/20-58: Mid-div, fdd 5f out: btr 1056. — 6 — 26

4687} **LAND N STARS 204** [7]4-9-4 (75) T Quinn 20/1: 0/422-9: b g Mtoto - Uncharted Waters (Celestial — 22 — 0
Storm) Bhd, nvr a factor: reapp: rnr-up on 2 of only 3 '03 starts (mdn, C A Cyzer): unplcd sole juv start: eff
around 14f on firm & fast gnrd: with Jamie Poulton.
2 Oct'03 Good 14fm 73-(70) D: 2 Jul'03 Catt 13.8g/f 73- F:

288 **TREASURE TRAIL 121** [10]5-9-3 (73) P Dobbs 16/1: 06000-50: 10th: Bhd, nvr a factor: long abs. — hd — 0

1016* **ARRESTING 32** [12]4-10-0 (85) J Murtagh 6/1: 3222-10: 11th: Mid-div, hdwy after 1m, fdd 3f out, — 6 — 0
eased fnl 1f: disapp under top-weight, reportedly unsuited by grnd: btr 1016 (11.8f, gd/soft).

672 **Rome 75** [2]5-8-13 (69) Martin Dwyer 25/1:0 877 **Dolzago 45** [3]4-8-12 bl(69) T E Durcan 12/1:0

13 Ran Time 3m 34.9(32.1) Owned: The Storm Again Syndicate Trained: Newmarket

DONCASTER MONDAY 03.05.04 Lefthand, Flat, Galloping Track

Official Going Good/Soft (Soft Places)

1517 **2.00 National Festival Circus Is Here Today Novice Auction Stakes 2yo (E)**
£3435 £1057 £529 **5f str** **Good/Soft 62** **-03 Slow** Stands Side

1107 **MYSTICAL LAND 23** [6] J H M Gosden 2-8-9 L Dettori 2/7 FAV: 21: Trkd ldrs, shaken up to lead dist, rdn out: fair juv time: hvly bckd at odd on, confirmed debut promise: eff at 5f, 6f will suit: acts on gd/soft & soft grnd, gall trks: type to improve with racing: see 1107. **91**
1143* **BIGALOS BANDIT 21** [1] J J Quinn 2-9-3 K Darley 9/1: 12: Led, rdn & hdd dist, kept on: acts on gd/soft & soft grnd: sound run conceding weight: see 1143. ¾ **96**
SPACE SHUTTLE [4] T D Easterby 2-8-7 D Allan(3) 25/1: 3: b c Makbul - Sky Music (Absalom) Slow away, rdn & kept on over 1f out, not able to chall: op 14/1: Mar foal, cheaply bght: half-brother to a 5/6f wnr, dam a 6/7f wnr: eff at 5f, will get further: handles gd/soft grnd: ran green, but not btn far & a likely improver. 1¾ **81**
1107* **APOLOGIES 23** [2] B A McMahon 2-8-12 G Gibbons 11/2: 014: Handy, rdn & no extra over 1f out. 1½ **81**
NORTHERN REVOQUE [3]2-8-2 Dale Gibson 100/1: 5: b f Revoque - Delia (Darshaan) Slow away & bhd from halfway, saddle slipped: cheaply bght Apr foal, half-sister to a juv wnr, dam plcd abroad. *dist* **0**
5 Ran Time 1m 01.47 (3.27) Owned: Sheikh Mohammed Trained: Manton

1518 **2.30 'unicyclist' Maiden Stakes 3yo+ (D)**
£6256 £1925 £963 **7f str** **Good/Soft 62** **-13 Slow** Stands Side

1236 **DR THONG 16** [14] P F I Cole 3-8-12 K Darley 6/4 FAV: 5-41: Made all, rdn & al holding rivals fnl 1f: well bckd: eff at 7f on fast & gd/soft grnd, likes a gall trk & suited by forcing tactics today: lightly rcd, type to progress & h'cap company could suit: see 1236. **81**
1130 **STAR MAGNITUDE 21** [19] J H M Gosden 3-8-12 L Dettori 7/1: 02: ch c Distant View - Stellaria (Roberto) Trkd ldrs, rdn & kept on fnl 2f, not able to chall wnr: left debut bhd: apprec drop to 7f, but shld stay 1m: acts on gd/soft grnd: clrly going the right way. 1½ **77**
1100 **PANSHIR 25** [20] C F Wall 3-8-12 (73) R L Moore 11/2: 0-503: Rear, switched & styd on fnl 2f, not pace of wnr: bckd: handles gd & gd/soft grnd: rtn to 1m could suit: ran to form of 919 (1m). 1¾ **74**
LITERATIM [5] L M Cumani 4-9-10 N Mackay(3) 20/1: 4: b c Polish Precedent - Annie Albright (Verbatim) Mid-div, shkn up & styd on onepace fnl 2f: clr of rem on debut: half-brother to a smart 5/6f 2yo wnr: eff at 7f, shapes as if 1m could suit: handles gd/soft grnd: pleasing start. 2½ **69**
1216 **AMANDAS LAD 17** [17]4-9-10 (65) L Vickers 33/1: 6466355: Chsd ldrs, no impress over 1f out. 5 **60**
IRUSAN [1]4-9-10 Leanne Kershaw(7) 66/1: 6: br g Catrail - Ostrusa (Rustan) Mid-div towards centre, no prog fnl 2f on debut: half-brother to a useful sprinter abroad. 2½ **55**
1220 **PURI 16** [6]5-9-10 M Fenton 40/1: 0-47: Trkd ldrs, no impress fnl 1f: see 1220. ¾ **54**
1152 **GUSTAVO 20** [16]3-8-12 R Hills 10/1: 08: Rear, switched & mod prog. 1½ **51**
1279 **NODS STAR 13** [15]3-8-7 Dale Gibson 50/1: 59: Bhd, mod late gains, nvr dngrs. *shd* **46**
1216 **GASPARINI 17** [18]3-8-12 D Sweeney 33/1: 2-00: 10th: Trkd ldrs till over 1f out, longer trip. *nk* **50**
1279 **ALCAIDESA 13** [9]3-8-12 D R McCabe 12/1: 40: 11th: Slow away & hmpd after 2f, nvr on terms. *nk* **49**
665 **LAURA LEA 76** [11]4-9-10 Dean McKeown 100/1: P0: 12th: Chsd ldrs till 2f out: abs, turf bow. 1 **47**
1279 **VIBE 13** [12]3-8-12 K Dalgleish 16/1: U00: 13th: Cl-up, hung left & btn over 1f out. 2½ **42**
1177 **WEDOWANNAGIVEUTHAT 18** [13]3-8-7 T Hamilton(3) 50/1: 00: 14th: Dwelt & al towards rear. ½ **36**
POINTED [7]3-8-7 D Allan(3) 33/1: 0: 15th: Dwelt, nvr threaten ldrs on debut. *shd* **36**
3686} **MACS ELAN 259** [3]4-9-10 J McAuley 66/1: 0-0: 16th: Mid-div, struggling from halfway, reapp. 1½ **38**
3684} **Mad Maurice 259** [8]3-8-12 S W Kelly 14/1:0
757 **Tata Naka 65** [10]4-9-5 (46) T G McLaughlin 50/1:0
1304 **Lucky Piscean 11** [2]3-8-12 G Gibbons 50/1:0
3764} **Ash Laddie 256** [4]4-9-10 (63) M Henry 50/1:0
20 Ran Time 1m 28.47 (5.27) Owned: Mr Frank Stella Trained: Whatcombe

1519 **3.05 William Hill 25 Year Service Handicap Stakes 3yo+ 0-90 (C)** **[90]**
£10270 £3160 £1580 **1m2f60y** **Good/Soft 62** **+02 Fast** Inside

1346 **TELEMACHUS 9** [6] J G Given 4-9-10 (86) M Fenton 13/2: 35530-61: b g Bishop of Cashel - Indian Imp (Indian Ridge) Mid-div, smooth hdwy 2f out & led dist, drvn out: best time of day: AW mdn & h'cap scorer '03, subs gelded: mdn rnr-up '02: eff at 1m, suited by 10.5f, tried 12f: acts on firm soft & fibresand, prob any trk: gd weight carrier. 1 Jul'03 Ches 10.3fm 89-84 D: 1 Apr'03 Wolv 8.5af 81a-(81) E: 2 Sep'02 Ling 6sft 87- F: **90**
1235 **BRIAREUS 16** [4] A M Balding 4-9-2 (78) K Darley 11/1: 324-0002: ch g Halling - Lower The Tone (Phone Trick) Al handy & led over 2f out till dist, kept on: mdn scorer '03, subs h'cap rnr-up: unplcd sole '02 starts (rtd 75, mdn): wng form at 10f, stays 12f & has tried 14f: acts on fast & gd/soft, stiff/gall or sharp trk. 2 Aug'03 Asco 12g/f 80-77 C: 1 Apr'03 Wind 10.0g/f 79- D: 1 **80**
928 **JABAAR 38** [18] D Nicholls 6-9-11 (87) Alex Greaves 33/1: 00420-03: gr g Silver Hawk - Sierra Madre (Baillamont) Mid-div, short of room over 2f out, kept on for press: h'cap rnr-up '03 (lady riders h'cap): '02 h'cap scorer (E Dunlop): eff at 10/11.7f on firm & gd/soft grnd, stiff/gall trks: can go well fresh: well h'capped, turn poss not far away. 2 Aug'03 Bath 11.7fm 89-87 C: 1 May'02 Newm 10g/f 98-84 D: 1 Oct'01 Pont 8g/s 89- D: 1 **88**
1092* **BRIEF GOODBYE 25** [11] John Berry 4-9-0 (76) K Dalgleish 11/1: 01663-14: Mid-div, rdn & styd on onepace fnl 2f: stays 10.3f: prog ran close to 1092 (1m). *nk* **76**
928 **COMPTON DRAGON 38** [3]5-9-1 (77) A Nicholls 16/1: 0000-005: ch g Woodman - Vilikaia (Nureyev) Slow away & rear, styd on for press, nvr threaten ldrs: unplcd '03 (tried blnks & chkpces, earlier with G Butler, rtd 85 at best, h'cap): '02 AW cond stks wnr, subs List rnr-up: best form around 1m, this longer 10f trip may yet suit: acts on firm, gd/soft & polytrack, stiff or sharp trk: likes Lingfield & can go well fresh. 2 Jun'02 Kemp 8fm 105- A: 1 Mar'02 Ling 8ap 105a- B: 1 Nov'01 Ling 8ap 95a- D: 2 Oct'01 Newm 7g/s 0- G: 6 **69**
4085} **GLIMMER OF LIGHT 240** [5]4-9-2 (78) R L Moore 20/1: 4150-6: Mid-div, switched & onepace fnl 2f. *hd* **69**
1474 **ATLANTIC QUEST 2** [2]5-9-6 (82) P Mulrennan(5) 7/1: 0410-057: Held up, eff over 2f out, no prog dist: qck reapp on grnd softer than ideal: caught the eye in 1474. ½ **72**
928 **DUNASKIN 38** [16]4-9-9 (85) F Norton 16/1: 05053-08: Led/dsptd lead till 2f out, best dominating. *nk* **74**
1346 **BROADWAY SCORE 9** [8]6-9-7 (83) T G McLaughlin 25/1: 0000-009: Held up, eff 2f out, sn btn. 4 **66**
4756} **MADAMOISELLE JONES 201** [17]4-8-4 (66) D Kinsella 33/1: 134100-0: 10th: Prom till over 1f out. ½ **48**

4374*}**BEST FLIGHT 226** [7]4-8-10 (72) R Hills 7/2 FAV: 0341-0: 11th: Chsd ldrs, btn dist: well bckd. *2* **51**
1066 **LES ARCS 27** [12]4-9-4 (80) J F McDonald(3) 28/1: 210-00: 12th: Al towards rear. *6* **51**
4664} **STALLONE 207** [10]7-8-11 (73) T Hamilton(3) 33/1: 552310-0: 13th: Nvr factor on reapp. *nk* **43**
1296 **PRAIRIE WOLF 12** [14]8-9-9 (85) N Pollard 33/1: 32320-00: 14th: Mid-div, struggling fnl 2f. *1½* **53**
1172 **HIGH ACTION 19** [20]4-10-0 (90) S W Kelly 40/1: 41106-00: 15th: Mid-div, no prog fnl 3f. *4* **52**
2334} **DERWENT 316** [15]5-9-8 (84) L Dettori 14/1: 0010/03-0: 16th: Al towards rear, reapp. *1* **45**
1172 **ISLAND LIGHT USA 19** [1]4-9-9 (85) D Allan(3) 25/1: 01350-00: 17th: Slow away & al bhd. *1¼* **44**
1231 **IBERUS 16** [13]6-9-4 BL (80) G Gibbons 33/1: 60505-00: 18th: Led till 3f out, wknd qckly: blnks. *4* **33**
1739*}**BISHOPRIC 343** [19]4-9-12 (88) D Sweeney 7/1: 41-0: 19th: Mid-div, struggling fnl 3f, reapp. *8* **30**
1346 **ARAWAN 9** [9]4-9-8 (84) Dale Gibson 50/1: 32/104-00: 20th: Chsd ldrs till halfway. *15* **6**
20 Ran Time 2m 12.58 (6.18) Owned: The Travellers Trained: Gainsborough

1520

3.35 Doncaster Racecourse Sponsorship Club Conditions Stakes 3yo (C)
£9151 £3247 £1624 **1m rnd** **Good/Soft 62** **-25 Slow** Outside

4797} **DUKE OF VENICE 198** [1] Saeed bin Suroor 3-9-1 T (106) L Dettori 4/6 FAV: 310-1: b c Theatrical - Rihan (Dayjur) Trkd ldr, led over 1f out, rdn out: hvly bckd, reapp: lightly rcd '03, impressive mdn wnr for M Johnston, subs well held in Gr 1: wng form at 1m, mid-dists shld suit: acts on fast & gd/soft grnd, stiff/gall trks: goes well fresh & suited by t-strap: smart & can win in better company. **109**
1 Sep'03 Sand 8.1g/f 104- D:
9} **HAPPY CRUSADER 177** [2] P F I Cole 3-8-12 (104) K Dalgleish 3/1: 331136-2: b c Cape Cross - Les Hurlants (Barathea) Led till over 1f out, kept on for press: op 9/4 on reapp: dual h'cap wnr '03, subs 3rd in a French Gr 3 (rtd 95): best at 7f/1m, mid-dists may suit this term: acts on firm & gd/soft, sharp/undul or stiff trk. 1 Aug'03 Newc 8.0g/f 93-87 B: 1 Aug'03 Good 7g/f 91-78 C: *1¾* **102**
1175 **BIRTHDAY SUIT 18** [3] T D Easterby 3-8-13 (102) K Darley 4/1: 113-33: Chsd ldrs, rdn & no impress over 1f out, eased: longer trip: btr 1175 (6f). *19* **69**
SES SELINE [4] John A Harris 3-8-4 Paul Eddery 66/1: 4: b f Salse - Absentee (Slip Anchor) Slow away & sn well bhd: half-sister to a smart stayer: highly tried. *15* **33**
4 Ran Time 1m 43.07 (6.97) Owned: Godolphin Trained: Newmarket

1521

4.10 Joe Sime Memorial Handicap Stakes 3yo 0-80 (D) **[87]**
£5395 £1660 £830 **1m6f132y** **Good/Soft 62** **-21 Slow** Inside

1355 **NESSEN DORMA 9** [4] J G Given 3-9-1 (74) M Fenton 7/2: 11-45521: Led/dsptd lead till went on over 3f out, styd on strongly for press: op 5/2: prev wins at 1m, now suited by 12f/14.7f, shld get 2m: acts on both AWs, gd & gd/soft grnd, stiff or sharp trks: progressive type: see 1355, 252. **82**
1260 **SIEGFRIEDS NIGHT 14** [1] M C Chapman 3-7-12 (2oh) (55) N Mackay(3) 5/1: 3233362: Held up, eff trav well over 3f out, rdn & no extra dist: op 8/1: prob stays gall 14.5f: see 1000, 923, 658 & 316. *2½* **60**
1272 **AL BEEDAA 13** [7] J L Dunlop 3-9-1 (74) R Hills 4/1: 03-43: Trkd ldrs, onepace fnl 2f: h'cap bow, longer 14.7f trip may yet suit: handles gd/soft & soft grnd: well clr of rem here: see 1272. *1¼* **75**
1260* **ITS BLUE CHIP 14** [2] P W D'Arcy 3-8-5 e (64) Paul Eddery 100/30 FAV: 0-3014: Held up, no impress from 3f out: bckd, op 4/1: btr 1260 (12f). *11* **51**
1165 **PRAIRIE SUN 19** [6]3-7-12 (57) Dale Gibson 6/1: 000-445: Led after 3f till 3f out, wknd: btr 1165. *2½* **40**
1211 **MUZIO SCEVOLA 17** [5]3-8-9 (68) S Hitchcott(3) 10/1: 2556: Slow away, mid-div till lost pl 4f out: h'cap bow: much btr 1211, 1016 & 873 (11/12f). *dist* **0**
3964} **OPERA BABE 248** [8]3-8-13 (72) L Dettori 12/1: 4005-7: b f Kahyasi - Fairybird (Pampabird) Slow away & sn bhd, t.o., reportedly gurgled on reapp: unplcd '03 (rtd 74, tried a t-strap, mdns). *dist* **0**
7 Ran Time 3m 15.22 (12.22) Owned: Hokey Cokey Partnership Trained: Gainsborough

1522

4.40 Cannons Health Club Claiming Stakes 4yo+ (E)
£3621 £1114 £557 **6f str** **Good/Soft 62** **-00 Slow** Stands Side

1215 **PAYS DAMOUR 17** [15] D Nicholls 7-9-0 (62) Alex Greaves 14/1: 4600-001: Trkd ldrs trav well, led over 1f out & sn rdn clr: op 12/1: suited by 6/7f, tried 1m: acts on firm, gd/soft & handles hvy, any trk, likes Epsom: see 853. **69**
1145 **TYPE ONE 21** [14] J J Quinn 6-9-10 P (75) K Darley 7/2 FAV: 0100002: Trkd ldrs, styd on for press fnl 2f, nvr threat to wnr: fair run in first time cheek pieces: see 492 (AW clmr). *3½* **67**
5000} **RED LEICESTER 181** [10] J A Glover 4-8-5 (50) G Gibbons 25/1: 46000-3: b f Magic Ring - Tonic Chord (La Grange Music) Handy & led 2f out, hdd over 1f out, not pace of wnr: reapp: unplcd '03 (rtd 60, mdn, subs tried blnks): eff at 6f on gd/soft grnd in claim grade. *nk* **47**
1319 **JUBILEE STREET 10** [3] Mrs A Duffield 5-8-10 (49) A Beech(3) 33/1: 60005-04: Towards rear, styd on for press, nrst fin: handles fast & gd/soft grnd, rtn to 7f in similar could suit: see 1319. *shd* **52$**
1049 **RAFTERS MUSIC 28** [13]9-8-10 (63) M Fenton 6/1: 26-30205: Chsd ldrs, onepace dist: see 153. *1½* **47**
1127 **RIVER LARK 21** [8]5-8-3 (45) D Allan(2) 8/1: 2-644606: Led till 2f out, wknd: best at 5f. *1* **37**
940 **RIPPLE EFFECT 37** [5]4-9-5 (75) N Mackay(3) 8/1: 2051567: In tch, outpcd dist: btr 799 (7f). *nk* **52**
1345 **GDANSK 9** [2]7-9-4 (70) F Norton 6/1: 2000-0U8: Dwelt, eff halfway, btn dist: see 1251. *2½* **44**
1310* **PEDRO JACK 11** [16]7-9-10 (72) J F McDonald(3) 10/1: 0300-019: Al towards rear: btr 1310. *3½* **40**
1405 **COMPTON PRINCESS 6** [1]4-7-13 (45) Dale Gibson 20/1: 0000-360: 10th: Outpcd halfway: see 1065. *1¼* **11**
751} **EFIMAC 425** [9]4-8-5 (45) N Pollard 50/1: 4/50500-0: 11th: b f Presidium - Efipetite (Efisio) Dwelt, chsd ldrs 4f, reapp: unplcd '03 (rtd 46a, clmr): late '02 AW clmr wnr, turf unplcd (rtd 60): winning form at 6f, acts on fibresand & a sharp trk: can go well fresh. 1 Nov'02 Sout 6af 50a- F: *1½* **12**
1465 **PRINCESS ERICA 3** [4]4-8-5 P (58) J Edmunds 16/1: 30305-00: 12th: Slow away, mid-div till 2f out: qck reapp in cheek pieces. *nk* **11**
1284 **METICULOUS 13** [6]6-8-4 (30) R L Moore 100/1: 0000000: 13th: Sn outpcd. *1¼* **6**
3624} **ZIETZIG 262** [12]7-8-10 (53) A Nicholls 14/1: 042306-0: 14th: Prom, rdn & btn over 1f out, eased, reportedly lost action on reapp. *1¼* **8**
14 Ran Time 1m 14.53 (3.73) Owned: The Inglenookers Trained: Thirsk

1523

5.15 'clowns' Handicap Stakes 3yo+ 0-85 (D)   [85]
£5931 £1825 £913   **6f str**   **Good/Soft 62**   +01 Fast   Stands Side

1354 **KINGSCROSS 9** [9] M Blanshard 6-9-2 (73) D Sweeney 9/2: 3000-421: Held up, short of room over 1f   **82**
out, strong run for press to lead well ins last, going away: eff at 5f/6f: handles fast, likes gd & soft grnd, any
trk: best delivered late: well h'capped: see 976.

1251 **LOYAL TYCOON 14** [16] D Nicholls 6-9-9 (80) T Hamilton(3) 16/1: 0000-002: Chsd ldrs, bmpd over 1f   1¼   **82**
out, not pace of wnr well ins last: back to form & on a decent mark: see 1251.

4560} **LOOK HERES CAROL 214** [18] B A McMahon 4-9-12 (83) G Gibbons 8/1: 010004-3: ch f Safawan -   shd   **85**
Where's Carol (Anfield) Chsd ldrs, switched & ch ins last, no extra: reapp: mdn scorer '03: lightly rcd '02, dual
mdn rnr-up: eff at 6f, winning form at 7f: acts on firm, likes gd/soft & soft grnd, prog any trk.
1 Jul'03 Thir 7sft 92-(92) D: 2 Jul'03 Hayd 7.1gd 90-(95) D: 2 May'03 Nott 6.1g/s 96-(95) A: 2 Apr'03 Leic 6.0g/f 91-(78)
2 Oct'02 Redc 7fm 80- D: 2 Sep'02 Pont 6fm 80- D:

1354 **PINCHBECK 9** [10] M A Jarvis 5-9-5 (76) M Henry 20/1: 41033-04: b g Petong - Veuve Hoornaert   shd   **77**
(Standaan) Handy & led over 1f out till well ins last: class stks wnr '03, subs dual h'cap plcd (rtd 77 at best):
landed 4 h'caps in '02: suited by 6f on firm & gd/soft grnd, held up or forcing the pace, prob any trk: best last
term in blnks/cheek pieces, neither worn today. 1 Jul'03 Leic 6.0gd 75-(68) E: 1 Jul'02 Donc 6gd 78-71 D:
1 May'02 Ripo 6g/s 71-62 E: 1 May'02 Hayd 6g/s 72-62 E: 1 May'02 Carl 5fm 64-57 E:

1474 **ONLINE INVESTOR 2** [15]5-8-10 (67) D R McCabe 14/1: 6000-005: b g Puissance - Anytime Baby   2½   **61 +**
(Bairn) Dwelt & keen rear, short of room 2f out, kept on late in eye-catching fashion, qck reapp: plcd '03 (rtd 77,
h'cap, C Cox): List rnr-up '02, subs disapp in blnks: eff at 5/6f on firm & gd/soft grnd, prog any trk: best held
up, looked a tricky ride at times: on a long losing run but well h'capped for shrewd yard.
2 Apr'02 Hayd 5g/f 97- A: 2 Jul'01 Newb 5.1fm 92- B: 1 May'01 Bath 5.7g/f 81- E:

1354 **BRANSTON TIGER 9** [14]5-9-2 (73) M Fenton 8/1: 04-50006: Mid-div, not able to chall: op 10/1.   ¾   **65**
1958} **RAGAMUFFIN 333** [17]6-9-6 (77) D Allan(3) 33/1: 000/200-7: Rear, mod gains, reapp.   hd   **68**
1138 **ARMAGNAC 21** [2]6-9-6 (77) K Dalgleish 16/1: 0460-008: Dwelt, eff halfway, no impress dist.   nk   **67**
4671} **MAGIC MUSIC 206** [6]5-9-2 (73) N Pollard 16/1: 011402-9: Led till over 1f out, wknd, reapp.   1½   **58**
4053} **MERLINS DANCER 242** [13]4-9-4 (75) Alex Greaves 33/1: 000400-0: 10th: Chsd ldrs till over 1f out.   shd   **60**
27   **MILLION PERCENT 171** [19]5-9-12 (83) Darren Williams 33/1: 215430-0: 11th: Nvr nr ldrs: reapp.   2   **62**
1383* **LINCOLN DANCER 7** [1]7-9-13 (7ex) (84) L Treadwell(7) 10/1: 0043410: 12th: Slow away, nvr on terms: 2½   **56**
qck reapp & lost all ch at the start: stablemate of 2nd: see 1383.

1217 **HICCUPS 17** [8]4-9-10 p (81) L Dettori 4/1 FAV: 10630-20: 13th: Unruly stalls & reared start, nvr   1   **50**
on terms with ldrs: joc reportedly gelding became upset in the stalls: well bckd & prob btr judged 1217 (5f).

921   **Musical Fair 39** [7]4-9-6 (77) R L Moore 25/1:0   4810} **Vigorous 196** [5]4-9-2 (73) C Cogan 33/1:0
1145   **Winthorpe 21** [4]4-9-4 (75) Dale Gibson 50/1:0   1215 **Sir Don 17** [11]5-8-7 vis(64) A Nicholls 33/1:0
17 Ran   Time 1m 14.45(3.65)   Owned: Mrs D Ellis   Trained: Upper Lambourn

Official Going Soft

1524

2.15 European Breeders Fund Primrose Maiden Stakes Fillies 2yo (D)
£4583 £1410 £705   **5f rnd**   **Soft 111**   -63 Slow   No stalls

1097 **LITTLE WIZZY 25** [7] P D Evans 2-8-11   Joanna Badger 33/1: 301: b f Wizard King - Little Unknown   **75**
(Known Fact) Cl-up, led 2f out, rdn out to hold on despite hanging left fnl 1f: Mar foal, dam unrcd: sire useful
around 1m: eff around 5f on gd & soft grnd: acts on a sharp/turning trk.

  ALEXANDER CAPETOWN [12] B W Hills 2-8-11   M Hills 7/2: 2: b f Fasliyev - Hawas (Mujtahid) Slow   shd   **74**
away, prog halfway, styd on well stands rail ins fnl 1f, post came too sn: debut: Feb foal, cost E180,000: half
sister to 7f Listed wnr: dam wnr at 1m: sire high-class sprinter as a juvenile: eff at 5f, shld apprec 6/7f: acts
on soft grnd: only just denied here & can rate higher with experience.

  UMNIYA [5] M R Channon 2-8-11   C Catlin 8/1: 3: b f Bluebird - Sparky's Song (Electric) Slow   nk   **73**
away, prog fnl 2f, styd on well, not btn far in 3rd: debut: Mar foal, cost 40,000 gns: half sister to useful 6f
wnr Lady Links: dam won at mid-dists: sire high-class at sprint dists: eff at 5f, shld stay 6f: acts on soft grnd.

  RUBYS DREAM [4] J M Bradley 2-8-11   S Carson 50/1: 4: Handy, edged right dist, styd on not btn   nk   **72**
far in 4th: debut: eff at 5f on soft grnd: encouraging effort.

  IVANA ILLYICH [8]2-8-11   J D Smith 12/1: 5: Bhd, prog halfway, no impress ins fnl 1f: debut.   2½   **65**
1170 **MISTY PRINCESS 19** [1]2-8-11   I Mongan 12/1: 056: Slow away, nvr nrr than mid-div: see 1170.   nk   **64**
1084 **ELVINA HILLS 26** [11]2-8-11   C Haddon(7) 33/1: 07: Nvr nrr than mid-div.   1   **61**
  KASHMAR FLIGHT [3]2-8-11   W Supple 16/1: 8: Cl-up when hung left after 3f, wknd: debut.   ½   **60**
  ROYAL ACCOLADE [13]2-8-11   S Sanders 6/1: 9: Prom over 3f, fdd: debut.   nk   **59**
1149 **GOGETTER GIRL 20** [6]2-8-11   N Callan 11/4 FAV: 6240: 10th: Led, hdd after 3f, sn wknd: well   2   **53**
bckd: disappointing effort: btr 1084.

1380   **Waterline Lover 7** [9]2-8-11 R Havlin 12/1:0   1325 **Mrs Willy Nilly 10** [2]2-8-11 J Bramhill 80/1:0
12 Ran   Time 1m 6.0 (8.7)   Owned: Mr E A R Morgans   Trained: Abergavenny

1525

2.45 Axminster Carpets Classified Stakes 3yo+ 0-80 (D)
£5798 £1784 £892   **7f26y rnd**   **Soft 111**   +18 Fast   Inside

1126 **JUST A GLIMMER 21** [11] L G Cottrell 4-9-2 (80) I Mongan 8/1: 0-301201: Cl-up, led 2f out, pushed   **83+**
clr despite edging left ins fnl 1f, val 4L+: fast time: eff arnd 7f on soft grnd & fibresand: likes a sharp trk &
racing up wndr/forcing the pace: acts on fast, soft grnd & polytrack: see 840.

1151 **DAWN PIPER 20** [4] D R Loder 4-9-7 vis (82) T P Queally(3) 8/1: 32-10202: Led 5f, kept on but no ch   2½   **82**
with wnr ins fnl 1f: acts on fast, soft grnd & polytrack: see 879 & 401.

1251 **CHATEAU NICOL 14** [6] B G Powell 5-9-5 vis (77) S Sanders 7/2 FAV: 3014133: Held up, kept on fnl   nk   **79**

1f, nrst fin: consistent performer: see 1251 & 1079.
1122 **H HARRISON 22** [12] I W McInnes 4-9-5 (80) P Mathers(7) 25/1: 1103-064: Cl-up over 5f, sn hung badly left & no extra: just btr 1122. *3½* **72**
4801} **HANDSOME CROSS 198** [8]3-8-12 (85) O Urbina 6/1: 321232-5: b c Cape Cross - Snap Crackle Pop (Statoblest) Mid-div, nvr nr ldrs: reapp, op 10/1: auct mdn wnr in '03 (also plcd 5 times, I A Wood): eff at 5f on firm & gd/soft grnd: with H Morrison. *4* **70**
2 Oct'03 Catt 5g/f 87-(86) D: 2 Sep'03 Redc 5fm 86-(83) E: 1 Aug'03 Folk 5g/f 84-(73) F: 2 Jul'03 Chep 6.1g/s 73- E:
1351 **CERTAIN JUSTICE 9** [9]6-9-5 (80) C Catlin 5/1: 06040-06: Cl-up 3f, sn no extra: op 4/1: btr 44. *½* **64**
1481 **AVENTURA 2** [2]4-9-5 (80) J Bramhill 9/1: 0040007: Slow away, nvr a factor: qck reapp: btr 800. *1¾* **60**
4919} **SAN ANTONIO 188** [10]4-9-7 (82) M Hills 8/1: 122000-8: b g Efisio - Winnebago (Kris) Rear, nvr a factor: reapp: mdn & h'cap wnr in '03: eff at 7f/1m on fast & gd/soft grnd: acts on a stiff/undul & gall trk. *5* **53**
2 Jul'03 Good 7gd 87-84 C: 2 Jul'03 Newm 8g/f 87-84 C: 1 May'03 Pont 8.0g/s 89-79 D: 1 May'03 Donc 7gd 88- D:
1036 **TAGULA BLUE 30** [5]4-9-5 VIS (80) W Supple 10/1: 21006-U9: b g Tagula - Palace Blue (Dara Monarch) Keen cl-up 5f, fdd: 1st time visor: won 2 h'caps in '03: unplcd in '02 (rtd 71, auct mdn): suited by around 1m on fast, best on gd & gd/soft grnd: eff with a t-strap: with J A Glover. *1¼* **49**
1 Jul'03 Nott 8.2gd 82-72 D: 2 Jun'03 Nott 8.2gd 76-70 E: 1 May'03 Thir 8g/s 71-63 D:
4666} **LIQUID FORM 206** [3]4-9-10 (85) A McCarthy 25/1: 614013-0: 10th: Bhd, nvr a factor on reapp. *8* **40**
10 Ran Time 1m 28.91 (6.51) Owned: Manor Farm Packers Ltd Trained: Cullompton

1526

3.20 Coventry Cup Handicap Stakes 3yo 0-80 (D) **[85]**
£8028 £2470 £1235 **7f26y rnd** **Soft 111** **-00 Slow** Inside

5034} **APEX 177** [2] E A L Dunlop 3-9-2 (73) W Supple 9/1: 333030-1: ch c Efisio - Royal Loft (Homing) Held up, prog halfway, led ins fnl 1f, rdn out to hold on: reapp: plcd 3 times in '03 (h'cap & mdns, rtd 78): eff at 6f, now stays 7f: acts on fast & soft grnd: goes well fresh: unexposed around this trip. **81**
973* **KAMANDA LAUGH 35** [6] B W Hills 3-9-2 (73) M Hills 5/1 JT FAV: 60-12: Cl-up, led 2f out till ins fnl 1f, kept on, just denied: h'cap bow: eff at 6f/7f on soft & polytrack: can find similar: see 973. *shd* **80**
4577} **MR JACK DANIELLS 213** [4] W R Muir 3-9-0 (71) R Miles(3) 33/1: 0100-3: b g Mujadil - Neat Shilling (Bob Back) Held up, prog 2f out, kept on well fnl 1f: reapp: auct mdn wnr in '03: eff at 7f, 1m shld suit: acts on fast & soft grnd: sharp/undul trk: encouraging run. 1 Aug'03 Folk 7g/f 74- F: *1¼* **76**
4773} **LEAPING BRAVE 199** [15] B R Millman 3-9-6 (77) A McCarthy 66/1: 530130-4: b g Indian Rocket - Island Heather (Salmon Leap) Cl-up 3f, sn outpcd, rallied ins fnl 1f: reapp: mdn wnr in '03: eff at 5f/7f, shapes as though further will suit : eff on soft grnd & polytrack, gall/undul trk. 1 Sep'03 Chep 6.1g/f 78-(78) D: *2½* **77**
1215* **COTOSOL 17** [12]3-9-6 (77) S Sanders 11/2: 3026-015: Handy over 5f, onepcd fnl 1f: btr 1215. *¾* **75**
135 **DANDOUCE 153** [14]3-8-13 (70) B Doyle 8/1: 423-6: Led early, onepcd fnl 2f on reapp. *½* **67**
1359 **PHLUKE 9** [11]3-9-2 (73) S Carson 5/1 JT FAV: 5305127: Cl-up & ev ch dist, wknd: btr 1359 & 1163. *¾* **68**
1360 **XPRES DIGITAL 9** [8]3-9-3 t (74) J Bramhill 20/1: 5610-048: Dwelt, nvr nrr than mid-div: btr 1360. *1¼* **67**
1116 **CARTRONAGEERAGHLAD 23** [13]3-9-7 bl (78) T P Queally(3) 16/1: 4160-009: Led after 2f till 2f out, fdd. *¾* **69**
1148 **DISTANT CONNECTION 20** [16]3-9-4 (75) E Stack 100/1: 04503-00: 10th: Cl-up & ev ch 3f out, fdd. *3* **60**
510 **DIAMOND GEORGE 94** [5]3-8-3 (60) D Fox(5) 33/1: 266-560: 11th: Rear, nvr a factor: long abs. *2* **41**
1054 **ARFINNIT 28** [10]3-8-13 (70) C Catlin 20/1: 3000-030: 12th: Mid-div till halfway, sn fdd. *nk* **50**
1007 **THADEA 33** [9]3-8-7 (1ow) (63) I Mongan 33/1: 30303-00: 13th: Mid-div when no room 3f out, wknd. *¾* **42**
1239 **URBAN ROSE 16** [7]3-8-8 (65) O Urbina 14/1: 01044-00: 14th: Rear, nvr nrr than mid-div. *3* **37**
337 **AMONG DREAMS 117** [3]3-8-9 (66) N Callan 16/1: 153-00: 15th: Bhd, nvr a factor: new stable. *3½* **31**
4639} **NINAH 209** [1]3-9-0 (71) G Duffield 40/1: 302240-0: 16th: Al in rear on reapp. *3½* **29**
1141 **HAZEWIND 21** [17]3-8-3 (60) Joanna Badger 9/1: 0-042100: 17th: Bhd, nvr able to chall: op 14/1. *7* **6**
17 Ran Time 1m 30.20 (7.8) Owned: Patrick Milmo and Stuart Tilling Trained: Newmarket

1527

3.50 Spring Membership Maiden Stakes Fillies 3yo+ (D)
£4128 £1270 £635 **1m22y rnd** **Soft 111** **-46 Slow** Inside

4721} **DREAMING OF YOU 203** [7] Sir Michael Stoute 3-8-8 B Doyle 14/1: 0-1: b f Spectrum - Gay Hellene (Ela Mana Mou) Cl-up, styd on to lead ins fnl 1f, rdn out: op 10/1 on reapp: unplcd sole '03 start (fills mdn, rtd 64): half sister to decent staying h'capper & Gr wnr over hdles Landing Light: eff at 1m, bred to apprec further: acts on soft grnd & a sharp/turning trk: goes well fresh: sure to rate higher. **76**
1129 **BEAUCHAMP STAR 21** [4] G A Butler 3-8-8 S Carson 7/1: 032: Keen mid-div, prog & ev ch just ins fnl 1f, kept on but just held by wnr: op 14/1: eff at 7f, imprvd for step up to 1m: acts on gd & soft grnd: imprvg with racing & can find similar: see 1129. *½* **75**
1186 **LYCA BALLERINA 18** [2] B W Hills 3-8-8 (73) M Hills 9/4 FAV: 64634-53: Mid-div, prog to lead dist, hdd ins fnl 1f, no extra: well bckd: acts on fast & soft grnd: see 1186. *½* **74**
1258 **NUKHBAH 14** [15] Lady Herries 3-8-8 (70) S Sanders 9/2: 43-34: Led till dist, no extra: btr 1258 (8.3f). *2½* **67**
1171 **CARA BELLA 19** [13]3-8-8 T P Queally(3) 100/30: 4-05: ch f Seeking The Gold - Cherokee Rose (Dancing Brave) Cl-up over 6f, sn wknd: 4th of 8 on sole '03 start (nov fills stks, rtd 80): eff at 6f, bred to apprec further: acts on firm grnd: with D R Loder. *3* **63**
MISS MONICA [10]3-8-8 W Supple 12/1: 6: ch f Grand Lodge - Bea's Ruby (Fairy King) Cl-up & ev ch bef 1f out, sn fdd: debut: dam wnr around 1m: sharper for today. *2* **59**
TREW CLASS [9]3-8-8 N Callan 20/1: 7: Held up, nvr nrr than mid-div on debut. *2* **55**
1340 **DARENEUR 9** [1]4-9-7 M Savage(5) 125/1: 08: Cl-up over 6f, fdd dist: see 1340. *1¼* **53**
DANETTIE [8]3-8-8 B Swarbrick(7) 100/1: 9: Nvr nrr than mid-div. *1¼* **51**
4772} **VIOLA DA BRACCIO 199** [3]3-8-8 C Catlin 66/1: 0-0: 10th: Rear, nvr a factor: reapp. *5* **42**
779 **My Little Sophia 63** [6]4-9-7 P Varley(7) 125/1:0 **Tetchy** [5]4-9-7 I Mongan 20/1:0
Kerristina [14]3-8-8 J D Smith 66/1:0 4657} **Light The Dawn 208** [11]4-9-7 G Baker 80/1:0
14 Ran Time 1m 49.39 (12.59) Owned: Mr M Tabor & Mrs John Magnier Trained: Newmarket

---

1528   **4.25 Edgecote Handicap Stakes 3yo 0-70 (E)**   [75]
£4583 £1410 £705   **1m4f134y**   Soft 111   -51 Slow   No Stalls

1124* **BILL BENNETT 21** [8] J Jay 3-9-6 (67) G Baker 11/2: 1-606511: Held up, prog to lead 2f out, sn   77+
pushed clr, val 10L+: slow time: eff at 9/11f, now stays 12.6f: acts on firm, gd/soft & firesand, reveled in soft
grnd today: likes Warwick: can complete hat-trick, see 1124 & 1000.
1240 **SAVANNAH RIVER 16** [9] C W Thornton 3-7-13 † (46) C Catlin 9/1: 000-032: Cl-up, ev ch 3f out, kept   7   **46**
on but al held by easy wnr ins fnl 2f: acts on gd & soft grnd: ran to form of 1240.
1240 **CALARA HILLS 16** [4] W M Brisbourne 3-8-3 (50) B Swarbrick(7) 40/1: 006-03: ch f Bluegrass Prince   ¾   **49**
- Atlantic Line (Capricorn Line) Rear, prog 3f out, sn onepcd: clr rem: unplcd in all 3 '03 starts (rtd 43 & 58a).
1306 **ATHOLLBROSE 11** [2] T D Easterby 3-8-9 (56) W Supple 5/1: 400-424: Cl-up over 10f, fdd: btr 1306 (10f). 5   **48**
1260 **JACKIE KIELY 14** [1]3-8-9 (56) R Miles(3) 10/1: 0-062055: Rear, prog after 1m, fdd fnl 1f: btr 676.   nk   **47**
1209 **CLOUDINGSWELL 17** [3]3-9-2 (63) D Corby(3) 20/1: 43006-06: b f Cloudings - L'Ancressaan (Dalsaan)   16   **33**
Rear, prog & ev ch 2f out, sn fdd: plcd once in '03 (mdn, rtd 70a, I A Wood): eff at 7f on fast grnd & polytrack.
1121 **STAGE TWO 22** [10]3-7-12 (45) R Ffrench 4/1 FAV: 0647: Nvr travelling & al bhd: btr 1121 (fast).   15   **0**
1339 **RUSSALKA 9** [7]3-8-10 (57) N Callan 33/1: 022-0058: Led halfway till 2f out, fdd: btr 1339.   11   **0**
1067 **CROCIERA 27** [11]3-9-7 (68) G Duffield 9/1: 00-49: Rear, nvr a factor: btr 1076.   2½   **1**
5022} **DUKES VIEW 178** [5]3-9-7 (68) I Mongan 9/2: 006-0: 10th: Mid-div 11f, fdd: reapp.   11   **0**
1283 **BONJOUR BOND 13** [6]3-9-1 (62) F Lynch 20/1: 400-400: 11th: Led till halfway, sn fdd: btr 983.   21   **0**
11 Ran   Time 2m 59.80 (20.5)   Owned: Mr & Mrs Jonathan Jay   Trained: Newmarket

---

1529   **4.55 Rowanna Handicap Stakes 3yo 46-55 (F)**   [65]
£3318 £948 £474   **1m22y rnd**   Soft 111   -63 Slow   Inside

1242 **THREE WELSHMEN 16** [4] B R Millman 3-9-1 bl (52) I Mongan 11/1: 050-0051: Led after 2f, made rest,   60
rdn out fnl 1f: prev eff at 5f, suited by arnd 1m now: acts on soft & polytrack: has mprvd recently with blnks.
656 **TURNBERRY 76** [12] J W Hills 3-9-4 VIS (55) M Hills 5/1: 004-4362: Rear, prog & ev ch ins fnl 1f,   2½   **58**
kept on but not pace wnr: tchd 7/1, 11 wk abs: eff at 7f/1m on soft & both AWs: gd eff in 1st visor, see 510.
1280 **SUMMERISE 13** [8] H J Collingridge 3-9-2 (53) Dean McKeown 9/2: 0610-063: Cl-up 6f, sn no extra.   2   **52**
1324 **LARAD 10** [7] J S Moore 3-8-10 bl (47) Derek Nolan(7) 11/2: 0551334: Led 2f, cl-up till no extra   1   **44**
dist: btr 1324 (fibresand).
1222 **FLYING SPUD 16** [3]3-8-10 (47) N Callan 14/1: 00-545: Cl-up over 6f, wknd: btr 863.   ½   **43**
213 **MR STROWGER 138** [1]3-8-13 (50) R Smith 33/1: 00000-6: b c Dancing Spree - Matoaka (Be My Chief)   1   **44**
Nvr nrr than mid-div: long abs: ex-Irish, mod form to date: with A Charlton.
1125 **ACCENDERE 21** [5]3-9-1 (50) W Supple 100/30 FAV: 0057: Held up, prog halfway, fdd fnl 1f: 3   **40**
disapp on step up to 1m for h'cap bow: see 1125 (mdn, 7.1f).
871 **BOOKIESINDEXDOTCOM 46** [11]3-8-13 vis (50) W Supple 16/1: 2-030668: Rear, nvr a factor: 7 wk abs.   4   **31**
4577} **MELINDAS GIRL 213** [15]3-9-1 (52) E Stack 25/1: 0650-9: b f Intikhab - Polish Honour (Danzig   ½   **32**
Connection) Cl-up over 5f, wknd: reapp: unplcd in '03 (rtd 65, auct mdn).
1222 **VENETIAN ROMANCE 16** [13]3-9-4 BL e (55) G Hannon 33/1: 00305-50: 10th: Rear, nvr a factor: blnks.   5   **26**
1242 **DELCIENNE 16** [2]3-8-10 (47) A McCarthy 20/1: 40020-00: 11th: Bhd, nvr a factor.   6   **7**
43 **ELITISTA 168** [14]3-9-1 (52) T P Queally(3) 25/1: 0555-0: 12th: Keen mid-div, fdd 3f out: reapp.   4   **5**
1099 **TROMPE LOEIL 25** [10]3-8-13 p (50) S Carson 6/1: 0-006000: 13th: Bhd, al adrift: btr 843.   dist   **0**
1085 **KNICKYKNACKIENOO 26** [6]3-9-2 (53) C Catlin 9/2: 0060-42W: Ran loose bef start & withdrawn.   **0**
14 Ran   Time 1m 50.72 (13.9)   Owned: Mouse Racing   Trained: Cullompton

---

1530   **5.25 Knowle Apprentice Handicap Stakes 3yo+ 0-85 (G)**   [84]
£3066 £876 £438   **1m22y rnd**   Soft 111   -19 Slow   Inside

4985} **HENESEYS LEG 183** [2] John Berry 4-8-4 (60) J D O'Reilly(5) 33/1: 122645-1: b f Sure Blade -   71
Away's Halo (Sunny's Halo) Rear, prog to lead dist despite edging right, rdn out to hold on: reapp: h'cap wnr in
'03 (also rnr-up twice): eff at 1m, wld apprec return to 10/12f: acts on firm & soft: goes well fresh.
2 Sep'03 Brig 11.9g/f 65-63 E: 2 Aug'03 Folk 9.7g/f 64-61 D: 1 Aug'03 Brig 9.9fm 65-55 F:
1385 **BEST BEFORE 7** [7] P D Evans 4-8-5 (61) Steven Harrison(5) 6/1: 65-00122: Keen cl-up, led halfway   nk   **70**
till styd, styd on ins fnl 1f, just held: qck reapp: acts on fast, soft & polytrack: remains in gd form: see 1385.
1385 **PARNASSIAN 7** [12] G B Balding 4-8-0 (56) R Thomas 12/1: 2500-003: Bhd, prog after 5f, onepcd dist.   5   **56**
1128 **PAY THE SILVER 21** [3] I A Wood 6-9-1 p(7) B Swarbrick(3) 25/1: 40230-04: gr g Petong -   ¾   **69**
Marjorie's Memory (Fairy King) Rear, prog 3f out, no impress fnl 1f: h'cap wnr in '03 (also plcd numerous times):
dual h'cap scorer in '02: h'cap wnr in '01 (A Jarvis): stays 12f, best arnd 7/10f: acts on fast, gd & polytrack:
poss fibresand: eff with cheek pieces: off a sharp/undul trk, esp Epsom.
2 Oct'03 Epso 12.0gd 77-71 E: 2 Jul'03 Epso 10.1g/f 73-73 E: 1 Jul'03 Epso 10.1g/f 74-69 E:
2 Jun'03 Chep 10.2g/f 68-66 E: 2 May'03 Brig 9.9g/s 65-63 F: 1 Sep'02 Brig 8.5gd 72-67 E:
2 Jul'02 Epso 10gd 70-64 E: 1 Jun'02 Good 9g/f 63-57 E:
1351 **NUIT SOMBRE 9** [10]4-9-11 (81) W Hogg(5) 6/1: 05600-05: b g Night Shift - Belair Princess (Mr   4   **72**
Prospector) Rear, eff halfway, fdd dist: won 2 h'caps in '03: aucn mdn & nurs h'cap wnr in '02: eff at 1m/10f on
firm & gd/soft grnd: has tried blnks: well h'capped on best of last years form: with M Johnston.
2 Jul'03 York 7.9fm 94-92 B: 1 Jul'03 Sand 10.0gd 92-89 B: 1 Jun'03 Ripo 8g/f 91-84 C: 2 Jun'03 York 10.4fm 89-84 B:
2 May'03 Beve 8.5gd 84-82 D: 1 Aug'03 Newc 7gd 86-79 E: 1 Jul'02 Ayr 6g/s 89- E:
1255 **FLEETWOOD BAY 14** [11]4-9-2 (72) D Fox 50/1: 0020-006: Led till halfway, fdd fnl 2f.   1½   **60**
1340+ **FIRST DYNASTY 9** [9]4-9-9 (79) A Quinn 8/1: 52/023-17: Cl-up over 6f, wknd: btr 1340 (fibresand).   1   **65**
1393 **HOV 7** [4]4-9-2 p (72) N Chalmers 7/2 FAV: 0-000268: Nvr nrr than mid-div: qck reapp: btr 1142.   nk   **57**
810 **EPHESUS 59** [5]4-9-9 vis (79) S Donohoe(3) 16/1: 30-30009: Cl-up over 6f, wknd fnl 2f: 8 wk abs.   1½   **61**
848 **MR DIP 50** [6]4-8-2 (58) C Haddon(3) 66/1: 050-060: 10th: Keen mid-div, wknd fnl 2f: 7 wk abs.   ¾   **38**
1381 **THE BONUS KING 7** [8]4-10-0 (84) A Elliott(7) 8/1: 0-452000: 11th: Cl-up over 5f, fdd: qck reapp.   ½   **63**
1235 **KENTUCKY KING 16** [1]4-9-13 (83) P Gallagher(3) 11/2: 601000: 12th: Slow away, al rear: btr 1057.   3   **56**
4452} **JOHANNIAN 220** [13]6-10-0 (84) C J Davies(5) 33/1: 054/005-0: 13th: Mid-div, wknd fnl 3f on reapp.   hd   **56**
4253} **Anna Walhaan 230** [17]5-9-5 (75) S Crawford(3) 33/1:0 4702} **Adobe 204** [16]9-8-13 (69) M Savage 16/1:0
15 Ran   Time 1m 47.24(10.4)   Owned: Mr Peter J Skinner   Trained: Newmarket

---

Official Going HEAVY. No Stalls & Hand Timed after race 2.

1531   2.00 European Breeders Fund Maiden Stakes 2yo   (D)
£5028 £1547 £774   **5f rnd**   **Heavy 149**   -37 Slow   Inside

1114 **EARL OF LINKS** 24 [4] R Hannon 2-9-0   P Dobbs   9/4: 31: Made all, hung right & held on for press   **80**
ins last: eff at 5f on gd/sot & hvy grnd, confirmed debut promise: see 1114.
   HARVEST WARRIOR [5] T D Easterby 2-9-0   D Allan(3)   12/1: 2: br c Mujahid - Lammastide   hd   **79**
(Martinmas) Cl-up. rdn & styd on well, just held: op 16/1, clr rem: Feb foal, cost 23,000gns: half-brother to a
multiple 7f wnr, also sev juv sprint wnrs: dam a 5f juv wnr: eff at 5f on hvy grnd.
   DRAMATICUS [6] D R Loder 2-9-0   J Murtagh   8/13 FAV: 3: b c Indian Ridge - Corinium (Turtle   3½   **72**
Island) Chsd ldrs, not pace of front pair over 1f out: well bckd at odds-on: Feb first foal, dam a 7f/1m wnr, sire
a high-class sprinter: prob handles hvy grnd.
1325 **NINAHS INTUITION** 11 [3] J M Bradley 2-9-0   A Nicholls   22/1: 44: Chsd ldrs till dist: see 1325.   ¾   **71**
   LIMONIA [2]2-8-9   I Mongan   33/1: 5: b f Perugino - Limoges (Konigsstuhl) Slow away, sn handy   6   **54**
till over 1f out: May foal, 8,000gns purchase: half-sister to smart 1m/10f German Flat performer & subs v smart
hdler Limerick Boy: dam a wnr in Germany: need further & more time.
   CLIPPER HOY [1]2-9-0   G Baker   33/1: 6: Prom till halfway, sn bhd on debut.   10   **39**
6 Ran   Time 1m 06.62 (9.32)   Owned: Coriolan Links Partnership VIII   Trained: Marlborough

---

1532   2.30 Warwick Racecourse Conference And Banqueting Centre Classified Stakes 3yo+ 0-60 (F)
£3262 £932 £466   **5f rnd**   **Heavy 149**   + 05 Fast   Inside

1345 **FULL PITCH** 10 [19] W Jenks 8-9-3   (55) M Hills   50/1: 1////-0061: ch g Cadeaux Genereux - Tricky   **67**
Note (Song) Dwelt & pushed along, hdwy halfway, led well ins last, going away: gd time: significant injury probs
prev to this yr, last rcd back in '99, won for W Haggas (sole start, mdn): both wins at 5f, enjoys soft & hvy.
1276 **KARMINSKEY PARK** 14 [10] T J Etherington 5-9-2   (62) J Fanning   9/2: 00440-62: Dwelt, chsd ldrs &   3   **64**
led 3f out till hdd well ins last, no extra: likes gd/soft & hvy grnd: on a fair mark for similar: see 1276.
1371 **PULSE** 9 [13] J M Bradley 6-9-3 p (60) S Carson   14/1: 256-0023: Chsd ldrs & led stands side group   2½   **60**
over 2f out, no extra dist: acts on both AWs, firm & hvy grnd: see 1221.
1145 **QUICKS THE WORD** 22 [12] C W Thornton 4-9-6 bl (63) J Murtagh   11/1: 1600-004: b g Sri Pekan - Fast   1   **61**
Tempo (Statoblest) Chsd ldrs, onepace over 1f out: class stks wnr '03 (first time blnks): dual h'cap rnr-up '02:
eff at 5/6f on fast & hvy: likes gd/soft trk: prob suited by blnks nowadays. 1 Aug'03 Nott 5.1g/f 75-(70) E:
2 May'03 Hayd 6sft 77-72 D: 2 Mar'03 Newc 5g/s 73-69 D: 2 Oct'02 Ayr 6sft 69-67 D: 2 Jul'02 Hayd 5gd 68-68 D:
1127 **BOANERGES** 22 [3]7-9-3   (59) C Catlin   28/1: 00005-05: Chsd ldrs, no extra dist.   2   **54**
1049 **BRIGADIER MONTY** 29 [7]6-9-3   (59) E Ahern   25/1: 060006-06: Chsd ldrs, btn dist.   hd   **53**
4856} **SHOLTO** 195 [2]6-9-5 bl (62) J D O'Reilly(7)   10/1: 066000-7: Led 2f & rem far side, wknd dist, reapp.   ½   **53**
1371 **GUNS BLAZING** 9 [16]5-9-4   (61) M Howard(7)   33/1: 01000-08: Hmpd start & towards rear, late gains.   1¼   **49**
1127 **BRANTWOOD** 22 [11]4-9-6 t (63) G Gibbons   20/1: 5000-009: Chsd ldrs till over 1f out.   ½   **50**
1127 **PLAYTIME BLUE** 22 [9]4-9-5   (62) G Baker   4/1 FAV: 6121430: 10th: Chsd ldrs till dist: new yard.   hd   **48**
1052 **PERCY DOUGLAS** 29 [8]4-9-3 vis (50) Ann Stokell   66/1: 063-0000: 11th: Slow away & outpcd, mod prog.   ½   **45**
1371 **TABOOR** 9 [17]6-9-3 h bl (57) K Fallon   11/1: 0050050: 12th: Chsd ldrs till over 1f out: btr 1371.   2   **41**
1293 **KINGS BALLET** 13 [1]6-9-3 p (54) J Quinn   11/1: 0204000: 13th: Dwelt, chsd ldrs, btn dist.   ½   **40**
1046 **Cark** 29 [5]6-9-3 p(47) R Pierrepont(7) 50/1:0   1371   **Panjandrum** 9 [18]6-9-3 (56) M Savage(5) 20/1:0
1320* **Lucius Verrus** 11 [6]4-9-3 (54) W Supple 16/1:0   1284   **Marabar** 14 [14]6-9-0 bl(60) A Culhane 14/1:0
17 Ran   Time 1m 04.49 (7.19)   Owned: Mr W Jenks   Trained: Bridgnorth

---

1533   3.00 Kingmaker Restaurant Handicap Stakes 3yo+ 0-70 (E)   [69]
£3916 £1205 £603   **6f21y rnd**   **Heavy 149**   -00 Slow   No Stalls

1255 **SAVILES DELIGHT** 15 [5] R Brotherton 5-9-9   (64) J Murtagh   9/2 JT FAV: 04-32431: Led/dsptd lead,   **72**
went on halfway, rdn & styd on strongly: stays 7f, best at 6f: acts on firm, hvy & both AWs, prob any trk: see 214.
1393 **CARLTON** 8 [3] C R Dore 10-9-4   (59) R Thomas(5)   7/1: 0245222: Chsd ldrs, styd on for press, not   1¾   **61**
pace of wnr: in gd heart & well h'capped for similar: see 1393, 1277 & 565.
1103 **WATERSIDE** 26 [4] J W Hills 5-9-13   (68) M Hills   9/2 JT FAV: 1404-003: Led 3f, onepace from dist: shd   **70**
op 7/1: acts on firm, hvy & polytrack: likes gd/soft trk: see 235.
1443 **NEVER WITHOUT ME** 5 [10] P J McBride 4-8-11   (52) J Quinn   9/1: 4521034: Chsd ldrs, hung left & no   3   **48**
extra dist: clr rem, qck reapp: stays 6f, poss just best at 5f: acts on fibresand & hvy grnd: see 1046, 168.
1354 **FULL SPATE** 10 [9]9-9-13   (68) J F Egan   13/2: 6061-605: Pushed along rear, no hdwy over 1f out.   6   **53**
1391 **OASES** 8 [8]5-9-5   (60) W Supple   11/2: 400-0206: Chsd ldrs till 2f out: btr 976.   6   **34**
1354 **RIDICULE** 10 [12]5-9-4 vis (59) A Culhane   10/1: 540-0007: Prom, wknd fnl 2f: see 1103.   hd   **32**
897 **JAGGED** 42 [13]4-9-2   (57) G Baker   10/1: 02630-08: b g Sesaro - Latin Mass (Music Boy) Held up,   5   **21**
nvr on terms with ldrs: new yard, abs: AW mdn & AW h'cap rnr-up '03, turf h'cap plcd (rtd 60, K R Burke): prob
best at 6f/sharp 7f on fast, gd/soft & polytrack, best efforts on a sharp trk.
2 Nov'03 Ling 7ap 61a-59 F: 2 Feb'03 Ling 5ap 61a- D:
4719} **HIGH RIDGE** 204 [6]5-9-3 p (58) S Carson   25/1: 035360-9: Sn struggling on reapp.   6   **11**
27 **COMPTON ARROW** 172 [1]8-9-8   (63) I Mongan   25/1: 440100-0: 10th: Slow away & al bhd: new yard.   23   **0**
10 Ran   Time 1m 19.7 (9.1)   Owned: Mr Roy Brotherton   Trained: Pershore

---

1534   3.30 Spring Membership Handicap Stakes 3yo 0-70 (E)   [75]
£4209 £1295 £648   **1m22y rnd**   **Heavy 149**   -46 Slow   No Stalls

1304 **PREMIER DREAM** 12 [10] M Johnston 3-9-6   (67) J Fanning   11/2: 6631: Made all, rdn & held on well   **72**
ins last: h'cap bow: eff arnd 1m: enjoys soft & hvy grnd, prob handles gd: handles a stiff or sharp/turning trk &
likes forcing tactics: type to prog with racing: see 1304.
1124 **SUCHWOT** 22 [4] F Jordan 3-8-9   (56) K Fallon   100/30 FAV: 600-062: b g Intikhab - Fairy Water   nk   **60**

(Warning) Handy & chsd wnr from 3f out, ev ch ins last, just held: bckd from 7/1: unplcd in '03 (rtd 61, debut): eff at 1m, has tried 11f: prob handles fast, likes hvy grnd.

1250 **GIVEN A CHANCE 15** [8] Mrs S Lamyman 3-7-12 (5oh) (40) R Thomas(5) 33/1: 00-45053: Chsd ldrs, styd 2½ 45
on onepace for press: stays a sharp 1m, has tried 12f: acts on hvy grnd: see 1250.

1339* **DARING AFFAIR 10** [11] K R Burke 3-9-5 (66) Lisa Jones(3) 9/2: 6-321514: Held up, eff 2f out, kept ¾ 65
on onepace: acts on fibresand, gd/soft & hvy grnd: see 1339 (AW h'cap).

1086 **PRINCE VALENTINE 27** [5]3-8-13 (60) M Tebbutt 14/1: 00-0035: Dwelt & held up, short of room ¾ 58
halfway, mod late gains: handles soft & hvy grnd: see 1086.

4996} **MISS ELOISE 182** [2]3-8-11 (58) D Allan(3) 74/1: 50052-6: b f Efisio - Zaima (Green Desert) Chsd nk 55
ldrs, btn dist: reapp: auct mdn rnr-up '03: eff at 7f, 1m may suit: prob handles firm & soft grnd.
2 Nov'03 Catt 7sft 60-(58) E:

804 **BIG BAD BURT 61** [15]3-9-5 (66) Dean Williams(7) 11/1: 00-42237: Dwelt & held up, no impress: 9 6 54
wk abs, new yard: btr 735 & 545 (AW).

88 **WAKE UP HENRY 162** [6]3-8-13 (60) D Sweeney 10/1: 006-8: Al towards rear, abs. 1¾ 46

1282 **MUNAAWESH 14** [1]3-9-5 (66) A Culhane 13/2: 05-03009: Held up, no impress halfway: btr 1050 (6f). ½ 51

1239 **CHORUS BEAUTY 17** [9]3-9-3 (64) J F Egan 14/1: 01-00: 10th: Held up, strug fnl 2f: btr 260 (AW, 6f). 10 36

1000 **THE STICK 34** [17]3-8-13 (60) T E Durcan 12/1: 656-000: 11th: Chsd ldrs till halfway. 22 2
11 Ran   Time 1m 52.6 (15.8)   Owned: Lucayan Stud   Trained: Middleham

---

1535   4.00 Zorn Handicap Stakes Div 1 4yo+ 0-70 (E)   [70]
£3738 £1150 £575   1m22y rnd   Heavy 149   -05 Slow   No Stalls

1128 **SUMMER BOUNTY 22** [1] F Jordan 8-9-6 (62) J Fanning 25/1: 22450-01: b g Lugana Beach - Tender 72
Moment (Caerleon) Held up, gd hdwy to lead over 1f out, styd on strongly: 03/04 jumps wnr (h'cap hdle, rtd 95h, 2m, firm & gd/soft): thrice h'cap rnr-up in '03: dual h'cap wnr '02: stays up to 12f, apprec this drop to 1m: acts on firm, hvy & both AWs, any trk: best without blnks/t-strap. 2 Apr'03 Warw 10.9fm 65-62 D:
2 Apr'03 Pont 10.0g/f 68-62 E: 2 Mar'03 Leic 11.8g/f 64-60 E: 2 Jun'02 Kemp 12g/s 62-61 D:
2 May'02 Wind 11.6sft 60-59 F: 1 May'02 Nott 10gd 59-53 F: 1 May'02 Pont 8gd 53-47 F:

1126 **DANCING KING 22** [6] P W Hiatt 8-8-4 (46) Lisa Jones(3) 8/1: 4006262: Trkd ldr & led after 2f till 2½ 50
over 1f out, not pace of wnr: clr of rem: acts on fast, gd/soft & f/sand, loves to race with/force the pace.

1334* **BOJANGLES 11** [15] R Brotherton 5-8-6 (48) E Ahern 9/2 FAV: 500-0013: led/dsptd lead till 2f out, 6 44
no extra dist: op 7/1: acts on gd/soft & soft, prob handles hvy: remains in gd heart after 1334.

1348* **COMMITMENT LECTURE 10** [10] M Dods 4-9-1 t (57) W Supple 5/1: 4200-514: Held up, eff 3f out, no 3 49
prog dist: see 1348 (gd/soft).

4542} **HILARIOUS 216** [5]4-8-9 (51) A McCarthy 33/1: 503440-5: b f Petorius - Heronwater (Ela Mana Mou) 4 37
Prom, chsd wnr till over 1f out: reapp: dual h'cap plcd in '03 (rtd 57): unplcd '02 (rtd 65, mdn): eff around 1m on fast grnd, handles a sharp/undul trk.

287 **ROUTE SIXTY SIX 123** [3]8-8-3 p (45) Leanne Kershaw(7) 16/1: 03500-06: Dwelt, nvr on terms, jumps fit. 5 24

1045 **KINDNESS 31** [14]4-8-10 (52) D Sweeney 33/1: 56003-67: Chsd ldrs till 3f out: btr 1045. 12 15

1322 **QUIET READING 11** [7]7-8-6 vis (48) Hayley Turner(5) 8/1: 3463228: Rdn rear, nvr a factor: btr 1322. 2 8

1388* **PHAROAHS GOLD 8** [2]6-8-13 (6ex)vis (55) T E Durcan 8/1: 0503019: Al towards rear: btr 1388 (gd). 2½ 11

1385 **DASH FOR COVER 8** [4]4-9-10 (66) P Dobbs 11/1: 001-2000: 10th: Mid-div, struggling halfway. 6 14

1254 **DAIMAJIN 15** [13]9-9-4 (60) C Catlin 50/1: 0540000: 11th: Keen & prom till over 3f out. 1 7

1282 **HORIZONTAL 14** [11]4-9-1 (57) M Tebbutt 11/1: 5-6600: 12th: Chsd ldrs, lost tch fnl 3f, longer trip. 1 3

1366 **PRIDE OF KINLOCH 10** [8]4-9-3 (59) K Fallon 8/1: 00-06040: 13th: In tch till over 2f out: op 10/1. 16 0

1298 **THE GAIKWAR 13** [12]5-9-12 bl (68) M Savage(5) 9/1: 425012U: Slow away, stumbled/u.r. 6f out. 0
14 Ran   Time 1m 49.3 (12.5)   Owned: Mr Tim Powell   Trained: Towcester

---

1536   4.30 Zorn Handicap Stakes Div 2 4yo+ 0-70 (E)   [70]
£3721 £1145 £573   1m22y rnd   Heavy 149   +01 Fast   No Stalls

1385 **SUPREME SALUTATION 8** [8] D K Ivory 8-9-12 (68) A Culhane 7/1: 60-01101: Held up, hdwy to lead 82
over 1f out & sn well clr, easily: fair time: earlier with D W Chapman: eff at 7f/9f, stays 11f well: acts on firm, hvy & both AWs, prob any trk: see 935 & 868.

1284* **FEN GYPSY 14** [4] P D Evans 6-9-4 (60) K Fallon 6/4 FAV: 4000212: Prom & led after 2f till over 10 63
1f out, sn no ch with wnr: bckd: acts on firm, gd/soft & prob hvy but btr 1284 (gd, 7f, seller).

1463 **EAST RIDING 4** [13] Miss A Stokell 4-8-3 (45) Ann Stokell 25/1: 005-5663: Held up, kept on late, 3½ 43
nvr a threat: qck reapp: see 1119.

5017} **EXPLODE 180** [15] Miss L C Siddall 7-8-10 (52) J Quinn 20/1: 000000-4: b g Zafonic - Didicoy 5 44
(Danzig) Prom till over 1f out on Flat reapp, jumps fit (no form): unplcd on the level '03 (rtd 71, cond stks, flattered): unplcd '02 (rtd 87, flattered).

1083 **TO WIT TO WOO 27** [3]4-8-11 p (53) M Hills 4/1: 014-2005: Chsd ldrs till 2f out: op 6/1: btr 513 (AW). 4 40

1098 **TALLY 26** [12]4-9-0 (56) J Murtagh 14/1: 46-00006: ch g Tagula - Sally Chase (Sallust) In tch 4 38
till 3f out: AW mdn, AW h'cap & turf h'cap wnr '03 for A Berry: suited by 6f on both AWs & fast grnd, stiff or sharp trk: more interesting when drpd in trip & on faster grnd.
1 Jun'03 Carl 5.9g/f 62-58 E: 2 Jun'03 Redc 6g/f 62-58 D: 1 Feb'03 Ling 6ap 74a-69 D: 1 Feb'03 Ling 6ap 70a- D:
2 Nov'02 Wolv 6af 57a- F: 2 Nov'02 Wolv 6af 62a- D:

1132 **PARISIAN PLAYBOY 22** [5]4-8-6 (48) J Fanning 20/1: 0003-007: Held up & nvr a factor. nk 29

1253 **PURE SPECULATION 15** [1]4-9-3 (59) I Mongan 7/1: 00-00648: In tch 5f: btr 978. 4 35

92 **BENEKING 161** [6]4-9-3 (59) W Supple 16/1: 604000-9: Held up, lost tch fnl 2f: new yard, abs. 6 27

1273 **DEXILEOS 14** [11]5-9-1 (57) D Sweeney 20/1: 4000-000: 10th: In tch 5f. dist 0

1059 **WOOD FERN 29** [10]4-9-9 (65) T E Durcan 20/1: 001-0000: 11th: Led 2f, strug halfway: btr 263 (AW). dist 0
11 Ran   Time 1m 48.8 (12)   Owned: Mr Dean Ivory   Trained: Radlett

---

1537   5.00 Herr Source Classified Stakes 3yo+ 0-65 (E)
£3933 £1210 £605   7f26y rnd   Heavy 149   -16 Slow   No Stalls

157 **AZREME 150** [12] D K Ivory 4-9-7 (68) I Mongan 22/1: 610006-1: ch c Unfuwain - Mariette (Blushing 72
Scribe) Chsd ldrs, led dist, in command when eased cl-home: 5 mth abs, prev with P W D'Arcy: lightly rcd in '03, h'cap wnr: 4-rnr nov stks rnr-up in '02, AW unplcd (rtd 74a, mdn): eff at 7f/1m on both AW's, gd/soft & hvy grnd: likes a sharp/undul or turning trk & goes well fresh: eff with/without a visor.

WARWICK   TUESDAY 04.05.04   Lefthand, Sharp, Turning Track

1 May'03 Ling 7sft 71-68 D: 2 Feb'03 Wolv 6af 69a- D: 2 Jul'02 Sand 7g/s 75- D:
1391 **BALAKIREF 8** [4] M Dods 5-9-4 (64) W Supple 15/8 FAV: 00-10222: Held up, rdn to chall when hung   2   66
left over 1f out, sn no extra: bckd: remains in gd form: acts on fast, hvy & f/sand: overdue another win, see 1391.
1485 **SWIFT ALCHEMIST 3** [15] Mrs H Sweeting 4-9-3 (67) G Baker 12/1: 2000-003: Held up, styd on for   3   61
press fnl 2f, not able to reach front pair: qck reapp: acts on fast, hvy & polytrack: on a fair mark: see 1485.
4606} **CASHNEEM 213** [1] W M Brisbourne 6-9-4 (61) D Allan(3) 25/1: 414100-4: b g Case Law - Haanem   2   59
(Mtoto) Chsd ldrs, no impress over 1f out: reapp: dual h'cap scorer '03: unplcd & mod form '02 (P W Harris): eff
btwn 6f/1m on firm & hvy grnd: encouraging return.
1 Sep'03 Chep 7.1gd 62-57 F: 1 Aug'03 Redc 8g/f 56-51 D: 1 Jul'01 Newb 6fm 83-77 C:
1010 **SIR FRANCIS 34** [14]6-9-4 (65) E Ahern 5/1: 60-00005: Held up, eff over 2f out, no prog dist: hd   58
prev best when dominating, well h'capped.
12* **DIDNT TELL MY WIFE 174** [16]5-9-4 (64) Lisa Jones(3) 5/1: 041021-6: Held up & nvr a threat: op 7/1.   6   49
115 **NICHOLAS NICKELBY 158** [17]4-9-4 (62) J Murtagh 14/1: 622-7: Led till over 1f out, abs, new yard.   9   37
4829* **IN THE PINK 196** [9]4-9-3 (67) T E Durcan 14/1: 504351-8: Held up & nvr a factor: reapp.   ½   35
1284 **JONNY EBENEEZER 14** [3]5-9-7 p (68) B Doyle 10/1: 02-00029: Cl-up, wknd over 1f out: btr 1284.   8   28
1393 **BUNDY 8** [5]8-9-4 (65) J Quinn 12/1: 1450-000: 10th: Held up & keen, btn 2f out.   ½   24
1371 **TAPPIT 9** [7]5-9-4 p (64) S Carson 40/1: 000-0000: 11th: Chsd ldrs, struggling fnl 3f.   nk   23
1385 **ONE WAY TICKET 8** [10]4-9-4 p (65) J F Egan 14/1: 41020-00: 12th: Chsd ldrs till over 1f out, fdd.   1   22
4979} **LOGISTICAL 185** [6]4-9-6 (67) D Sweeney 20/1: 054560-0: 13th: Al bhd & eased from dist, reapp.   dist   0
13 Ran   Time 1m 34.1(11.7)   Owned: Halcyon Partnership   Trained: Radlett

---

BATH   TUESDAY 04.05.04   Lefthand, Turning Track with Uphill Finish

Official Going SOFT (GOOD/SOFT places).

1538   2.20 European Breeders Fund Maiden Stakes 2yo   (D)
£4586 £1411 £706   **5f11y rnd**   **Soft 116**   -13 Slow   Far Side

JOHNNY JUMPUP [2] R M Beckett 2-9-0 S Sanders 12/1: 1: ch c Pivotal - Clarice Orsini (Common   90
Grounds) Handy, led over 2f out, asserted ins last: Feb foal, half-brother to a 6f/1m wnr: eff at 5f, get further:
acts on soft grnd & a turning trk: goes well fresh: decisive success, type to win more races.
ICEMAN [8] J H M Gosden 2-9-0 L Dettori 11/8 FAV: 2: b c Polar Falcon - Virtuous (Exit To   2½   84
Nowhere) Prom & chsd wnr 2f out, kept on but held ins last, no extra: March foal, half-brother to a
6f juv wnr & 10f 3yo wnr, dam a 1m juv wnr: eff at 5f, bred to stay further: acts on soft grnd: encouraging.
1367 **DUSTINI 9** [10] W G M Turner 2-9-0 BL A Daly 14/1: 353: Led till over 2f out, no impress over 1f   6   71
out: op 16/1: prob handles soft grnd: see 1077.
MS POLLY GARTER [4] J M Bradley 2-8-9 R L Moore 20/1: 4: b f Petong - Utopia (Primo Dominie)   1¼   63
Trkd ldr, no impress over 1f out: cheaply bght Feb first foal, dam related to a 7f juv wnr.
ABERDEEN PARK [9]2-8-9 Joanna Badger 40/1: 5: Towards rear, mod hdwy halfway, nvr a threat.   ¾   61
TROUBLESOME GERRI [12]2-8-9 V Slattery 66/1: 6: Sn rdn & mid-div at best.   3   54
MAKE IT HAPPEN NOW [3]2-8-9 D Corby(3) 50/1: 7: Chsd ldrs till halfway.   nk   53
ALRIGHT MY SON [7]2-9-0 Dane O'Neill 5/1: 8: V slow away, only mod prog, lost ch start.   2   53
AGILETE [6]2-9-0 S Drowne 13/2: 9: Prom, btn over 1f out: op 5/1.   2½   48
1325 **MUESTRA 11** [11]2-8-9 F Norton 50/1: 00: 10th: Slow away & al rear.   4   33
PIE CORNER [15]2-9-0 L Keniry(3) 40/1: 0: 11th: Mid-div, struggling from halfway.   2   33
1353 **LISTEN TO ME 10** [5]2-9-0 Paul Eddery 40/1: 50: 12th: Struggling halfway: see 1353.   5   30
Cleo Collins [13]2-8-9 Martin Dwyer 12/1:0   **Amalgam** [1]2-8-9 R Havlin 28/1:0
14 Ran   Time 1m 06.79 (6.49)   Owned: Mr & Mrs A Briars   Trained: Lambourn

1539   2.50 Saltwell Signs Claiming Stakes 3yo   (F)
£2912 £832 £416   **5f161y rnd**   **Soft 116**   -04 Slow   Far Side

543 **CORNWALLIS 90** [10] R Guest 3-8-5 (55) R L Moore 12/1: 06-01: b g Forzando - Up And Going (Never   68
So Bold) Rear, hdwy 2f out, led ins last, styd on strongly: clmd by J S King for 5,000, 3 mth abs, has been gelded:
first win on AW bow: eff at 5.5f on soft & a turning trk: goes well fresh & apprec drop to claim grade.
4874} **BORZOI MAESTRO 193** [4] J L Spearing 3-9-1 (77) A Daly 9/2: 430400-2: ch g Wolfhound - Ashkernazy   3½   69
(Salt Dome) Keen & trkd ldrs, led going well over 1f out, sn rdn & hdd ins last, no extra: reapp: AW seller, turf
& AW h'cap scorer '03: eff at 5/6f on fast, soft & fibresand, prob any trk, loves a sharp/turning one: loves to
force the pace: best last term in cheek pieces, not worn today: gd reapp.
1 Jul'03 Wolv 6af 79a-71 E: 1 Jul'03 Ling 5g/f 75-65 E: 1 Jul'03 Wolv 5af 69a- G: 2 Jun'03 Wolv 5af 64a- G:
1247 **ROCKET 15** [5] R Hannon 3-8-11 Dane O'Neill 11/1: 043: Cl-up & ch halfway, no extra over 1f out: 1¾   62
imprvd eff on drop to 5/8f on soft grnd.
4930} **JINKSONTHEHOUSE 189** [7] M D I Usher 3-8-4 (60) Martin Dwyer 12/1: 550000-4: Chsd ldrs, onepace.   shd   55
1404 **IMPERIUM 7** [9]3-9-3 (68) T Quinn 9/2: 6-402005: Narrow lead bef halfway, hdd over 1f out & wknd.   5   58
1321 **MARKSGOLD 11** [6]3-9-1 (60) L Dettori 11/2: 000-366: Sn strug & al outpcd: op 9/2: btr 1125 (7f).   5   46
1085 **JAOLINS 27** [8]3-8-6 (52) R Havlin 11/1: 1200507: Mid-div, outpcd halfway: btr 901 (AW, 7f).   ½   36
PRINCE RENESIS [3]3-8-11 Derek Nolan(7) 33/1: 8: Slow away & sn struggling: clmd for 8,000 by   1¾   38
I W McInnes: debut.
1015 **BARBILYRIFLE 33** [1]3-8-9 p (62) S Drowne 4/1 FAV: 000-0039: Rcd alone far side & bhd: btr 1015.   14   11
815 **RICKY MARTAN 57** [2]3-8-5 VIS (58) S Hitchcott(3) 12/1: 64-00000: 10th: Led/dsptd lead 2f: abs.   nk   6
10 Ran   Time 1m 15.99 (6.89)   Owned: The Bricklayers Partnership   Trained: Newmarket

1540   **3.20 Oswald Bailey Handicap Stakes Fillies 3yo+ 0-70 (E)**   [70]
£3692 £1136 £568   **5f161y rnd**   **Soft 116**   **-09 Slow**   Far Side

23   **GO GO GIRL 173** [10] L G Cottrell 4-9-7 (63) F Norton 16/1: 565330-1: ch f Pivotal - Addicted To   **71**
Love (Touching Wood) Mid-div, rdn & styd on to lead cl-home: 6 mth abs: mdn & h'cap plcd '03 (rtd 64): unplcd '02
(rtd 73): eff btwn 5/6f on firm & soft grnd, sharp/undul or turning trk: goes well fresh.
4184} **ANNIJAZ 236** [16] J M Bradley 7-8-12 (54) R L Moore 25/1: 010060-2: b f Alhijaz - Figment (Posse)   1   **60**
Held up, rdn & rapid prog to lead ins last, hdd cl-home: reapp: landed 3 fills h'caps in '03: dual h'cap plcd '02
(rtd 53): eff btwn 5.7f/1m & stays 10f: acts on firm, hvy & fibresand, any trk: fine return, could be set for
another productive season in similar grade.
1 Jun'03 Donc 7g/f 57-51 E: 1 Jun'03 Redc 8fm 52-48 E: 1 May'03 Yarm 6.0gd 46-44 F: 2 May'03 Bath 5.7g/f 48-44 E:
1 Dec'01 Wolv 7af 51a-48 F: 1 Jun'01 Folk 6.8g/f 62-55 E: 2 May'01 Ling 10ap 51a-48 E:
1465* **AMELIA 4** [2] W M Brisbourne 6-9-0 (66w) (56) B Swarbrick(7) 5/1: 5553013: Al handy & led over 1f   1¾   **58**
out, hdd ins last & kept on: nicely bckd under a 6lb pen, qck reapp: ran to form of 1465.
1024 **I WISH 32** [13] M Madgwick 6-9-2 (58) L Keniry(3) 10/1: 146-0504: Al handy, no extra ins last: 1¼   **57**
acts on fast, soft & polytrack: see 50.
151   **CALUSA LADY 150** [7]4-9-2 (58) R Havlin 20/1: 460005-5: Mid-div, not pace to chall, abs.   3   **50**
1348 **CLOUDLESS 10** [8]4-8-11 (53) Dane O'Neill 9/1: 2403366: Rear, kept on late, no dngr: op 12/1.   ½   **44**
1179 **BAHAMIAN BELLE 19** [14]4-9-0 t (56) L Dettori 7/1: 405-6047: Keen in mid-div, btn dist: bckd.   nk   **46**
1179 **YOMALO 19** [1]4-9-11 (67) S Sanders 14/1: 11220-08: Slow away, nvr on terms.   1   **55**
1465 **GOJO 4** [12]3-9-1 (67) T Quinn 7/2 FAV: 060-429: Led 1f, btn over 1f out: nicely bckd: btr 1465.   nk   **54**
1284 **RILEYS DREAM 14** [11]5-8-3 (45) D Kinsella 20/1: 0000-050: 10th: Dwelt, al mid-div: btr 1284.   nk   **31**
4022} **CHARLOTTEBUTTERFLY 245** [4]4-9-5 (61) J Mackay 33/1: 430353-0: 11th: Chsd ldrs till over 1f out.   nk   **46**
1371 **ELA FIGURA 9** [17]4-9-0 (56) S Hitchcott(3) 16/1: 20020-60: 12th: Al bhd: see 1371.   shd   **41**
767   **FIAMMA ROYALE 65** [3]6-8-8 (50) R Miles(3) 25/1: 000-40000: 13th: Dwelt, dsptd lead till dist: abs.   2½   **30**
1404 **BARABELLA 7** [18]3-8-11 (63) J F McDonald(3) 9/1: 4440-050: 14th: Al rear: op 12/1: btr 1404.   3   **36**
597   **Naughty Girl 84** [9]4-10-0 (70) K McEvoy 33/1:0   4388} **Royal Supremacy 225** [5]3-8-4 (56) J Bramhill 40/1:0
16 Ran   Time 1m 16.27 (7.17)   Owned: Mr H C Seymour   Trained: Cullompton

1541   **3.50 Oval Of Bath Peugeot Stakes 3yo+ 46-55 (F)**   [61]
£3581 £1023 £512   **1m2f46y**   **Soft 116**   **+13 Fast**   Inside

1379 **SAXE COBURG 8** [10] G A Ham 7-9-7 (54) J F McDonald(3) 28/1: 63540-51: Rear, hdwy halfway, led   **68**
over 1f out, sn asserted, pushed out: gd time: suited by 10/11.5f on both AWs, fast & soft grnd, likes a sharp or
turning trk: decisive success, win again on this evidence: see 1379.
827   **DIAMOND ORCHID 56** [6] P D Evans 4-9-0 (47) S Drowne 7/1: 62-32422: Chsd ldrs, rdn & kept on fnl   3½   **54**
2f, not pace of wnr: recent jumps runner (unplcd, rtd 72h, juv nov): see 827, 575 & 354.
1357* **ICANNSHIFT 10** [19] S Dow 4-9-8 (55) R L Moore 9/2: 0060213: Chsd ldr 3f out, led over 2f out   2½   **58**
till over 1f out, wknd: remains in gd heart: see 1357.
1402 **OUR DESTINY 7** [12] A W Carroll 6-9-2 (49) S Hitchcott(3) 7/1: 1163124: Chsd ldrs, drvn & onepace   1¼   **50**
over 1f out: consistent type: see 1341.
1430+ **JAKE BLACK 6** [1]4-9-3 (50) T Quinn 13/8 FAV: 0115315: Mid-div when hmpd after 3f, sn handy, rdn   ½   **50**
& btn over 1f out: qck reapp: btr 1430.
4855} **TIDAL 195** [7]5-9-8 (55) Derek Nolan(7) 25/1: 606000-6: br f Bin Ajwaad - So Saucy (Teenoso)   2   **52**
Dwelt & rear, some hdwy for press, nvr a threat: reapp: unplcd '03 (rtd 69 & 20a, tumbled down h'cap, tried blnks,
P Howling & B Meehan): h'cap scorer '02: suited by 10f, handles soft grnd, likes firm & a gall trk: well h'capped
& gave some encouragement today.   1 Jul'02 Newb 10fm 79-72 D:
3632} **DEEWAAR 263** [4]4-9-2 (49) R Smith 66/1: 532000-7: b g Ashkalani - Chandni (Ahonoora) Rear, eff   hd   **46**
3f out, nvr able to chall: Flat reapp, jumps fst (unplcd, rtd 90h, nov): sell grade rnr-up in '03 for J S Moore:
eff arnd 10/11f, handles firm, gd & polytrack, sharp/turning trks: best without visor & cheek pieces.
2 Apr'03 Ripo 10gd 53-(48) F: 2 Feb'03 Ling 10ap 68a- D:
1331 **QUARRY ISLAND 11** [18]3-7-12 (11oh) (35) Joanna Badger 40/1: 5200028: Led after 3f till 2f out.   nk   **42**
1128 **NAUTICAL 22** [11]6-9-8 (55) A Daly 100/1: 4310/0-09: Rear, kept on late, nvr a threat to ldrs.   ¾   **50**
1090 **ON GUARD 27** [5]6-9-5 vis (52) D Kinsella 25/1: 650-3600: 10th: Rear, hdwy halfway, nvr a threat.   15   **25**
4901} **DANEBANK 190** [16]4-9-5 (52) L Dettori 16/1: 064600-0: 11th: Mid-div, rdn & btn 2f out, 7 wk   5   **18**
jumps abs, new yard.
1140 **Nina Fontenail 22** [2]3-8-3 (1ow)(50) E Stack 40/1:0   542   **Esperance 90** [13]4-9-1 (48) S Sanders 25/1:0
1327 **Abbiejo 11** [3]7-8-13 (16oh)(30) R Miles(3) 80/1:0   1466} **Multicolour 358** [15]4-9-8 Dane O'Neill 66/1:0
1098 **In Tune 26** [8]4-9-3 BL(50) L Keniry(3) 100/1:0   1045 **Seejay 31** [9]4-9-2 (49) Martin Dwyer 33/1:0
17 Ran   Time 2m 18.67 (12.67)   Owned: Sally & Tom Dalley   Trained: Axbridge

1542   **4.20 Weatherbys Insurance Handicap Stakes 3yo+ 0-70 (E)**   [70]
£4456 £1371 £686   **1m5y rnd**   **Soft 116**   **-18 Slow**   Inside

726   **LOCKSTOCK 69** [16] M S Saunders 6-9-9 p (65) R Miles(3) 20/1: 0414-001: Trkd ldrs trav well & led   **75**
over 2f out, sn asserted & styd on strongly: 2 mth abs: eff at 7/9.3f on fast, hvy & fibresand, any trk: goes well
fresh & suited by blnks/cheek pieces: see 93.
1385 **AMNESTY 8** [4] G L Moore 5-9-6 bl e (62) R L Moore 7/4 FAV: 0061152: Keen & held up, prog/short of   3½   **64**
room over 2f out & sn switched, kept on, al held: bckd, op 5/2: remains in gd heart: see 1385, 1273.
1128 **EMBER DAYS 22** [15] J L Spearing 5-9-6 P (62) V Slattery 10/1: 5522-503: Keen & held up, kept on   2   **60**
fnl 2f, not pace of front pair: shown enough to find similar: see 178.
1402 **MOBO BACO 7** [15] R J Hodges 7-9-4 (60) S Drowne 10/1: 40030-44: Led till over 2f out, no extra   1¼   **56**
ins last: op 13/2: see 1402.
1059 **ENCHANTED PRINCESS 29** [13]4-10-0 VIS (70) L Dettori 10/1: 01-05: b f Royal Applause - Hawayah   ¾   **65**
(Shareef Dancer) Mid-div, eff 3f out, no extra ins last: nicely bckd tho' op 6/1: first time visor on h'cap bow:
lightly rcd in '03, landed a mdn for J Gosden: wng form over a sharp 1m on fast grnd, handles soft on this evidence:

can go well fresh.   1 Jul'03 Wind 8.3g/f 72- D:

1195 **CLANN A COUGAR 19** [5]4-9-7 BL (63) B Swarbrick(5) 14/1: 4404-006: Dwelt & keen, chsd ldrs till   ¾   57
over 1f out: tried blnks, op 12/1: yet to convince over 1m, of interest when returned to 6/7f: see 942.
1399 **SNINFIA 7** [11]4-9-4 (60) J F McDonald(3) 16/1: 0200-007: Dwelt, in tch till 2f out: see 1399.   2¼   51
344   **TUSCAN TREATY 118** [14]4-9-4 (60) J Mackay 66/1: 00000-08: b f Brief Truce - Fiorenz (Chromite)   1¼   49
Held up, no impress fnl 2f: dual '03 h'cap wnr: eff at 6/7f on firm & fast, likes a sharp/undul trk: impr on this
at 6/7f.   1 Jun'03 Brig 6.0fm 64-56 F: 2 Apr'03 Catt 7g/f 58-56 E: 1 Apr'03 Folk 7g/f 57-49 G: 2 Nov'02 Wolv 8.4af 54a- F:
1282 **B A HIGHFLYER 14** [1]4-9-9 (65) S Hitchcott(3) 7/1: 2216-059: Chsd ldrs till dist: btr 1282.   ½   53
1307 **KARATHAENA 12** [12]4-9-4 VIS (60) T Quinn 14/1: 03-00000: 10th: Trkd ldrs, strug fnl 2f in visor.   ½   47
4690} **PRINCESS MAGDALENA 205** [10]4-9-1 (57) R Havlin 25/1: 000010-0: 11th: Trkd ldrs till 2f out.   ¾   43
1319 Parker 11 [6]7-9-6 (62) S Sanders 14/1:0   2722} Night Driver 302 [3]5-9-10 (66) Dane O'Neill 14/1:0
13 Ran   Time 1m 49.04 (10.74)   Owned: Mr Chris Scott   Trained: Wells

---

1543   4.50 Www Saltwellsigns Co Uk Handicap Stakes 4yo+ 46-55 (F)   [69]
£3066 £876   £438   **1m3f144y**   **Soft 116**   **-20 Slow**   Inside

1238 **ONLY FOR SUE 17** [18] W S Kittow 5-8-12 bl (53) S Drowne 11/1: 061-0031: Led/dsptd lead, went on   61
3f out, held on well for press fnl 1f: eff at 12/14f on gd, fibresand & polytrack on soft grnd today: see 1238 & 244.
1373* **GREAT VIEW 9** [1] Mrs A L M King 5-9-6 (6ex)vis (61) D Corby(3) 9/2: 32-01212: Chsd ldrs, eff to   1½   66
chall over 1f out, no extra for press ins last: well clr of rem: remains in fine form: see 1373.
1402 **SALFORD FLYER 7** [7] Jane Southcombe 8-8-13 bl (54) A Quinn(5) 22/1: 05//-06033: Chsd ldrs, kept on   8   49
fnl 2f but not threat to front pair: see 1098.
1373 **SHORT CHANGE 9** [2] A W Carroll 5-8-13 (54) S Hitchcott(3) 10/1: 03222-04: Chsd ldrs, rdn & onepace.   1¼   47
1090 **PARADISE VALLEY 27** [15]4-8-6 t (47) S Sanders 25/1: 6050205: Mid-div, drvn & kept on, nvr a threat.   nk   39
1342* **RED FOREST 10** [10]5-8-12 t (53) L Dettori 3/1 FAV: 4560-316: Rear, eff from halfway, nvr able to   hd   45
threaten: op 7/2: btr 1342 (AW).
1128 **COOL BATHWICK 22** [12]5-9-0 BL (55) Martin Dwyer 14/1: 00-12607: Led after 1f till 3f out, blnks.   1½   45
873} **WESTERN RIDGE 404** [3]7-8-12 (53) R Havlin 25/1: 3214/00-8: b g Darshaan - Helvellyn (Gone West)   6   35
Mid-div, no prog fnl 2f: reapp, 6 mth jumps abs, 03/04 wnr of 3 h'cap hdles (2m, firm & gd, 102h): unplcd in early
'03 (rtd 48, h'cap): AW h'cap wnr late '02: suited by 12f/sharp 15f on firm, fast & fibresand, likes W'hampton,
prob handles any trk: eff in cheek pieces, not worn here.   1 Dec'02 Wolv 12af 58a-55 F:
2 Dec'02 Wolv 14.7af 59a- G: 2 May'02 Ches 12.3fm 57-55 D: 1 Apr'02 Wolv 14.7af 61a-54 F:
2 Mar'02 Wolv 12af 54a-50 F: 2 Mar'02 Wolv 12af 57a- D: 2 Feb'01 Wolv 9.3af 58a- D:
3152} **PURDEY 284** [17]4-8-9 (50) J F McDonald(3) 25/1: 6004-9: ch f Double Trigger - Euphorie (Feenpark)   5   26
Rear, mod gains for press, nvr a threat: reapp: unplcd '03 (rtd 62 & 39a): has tried up to 2m prev.
2184} **JAVA DAWN 323** [14]4-8-7 (48) A Daly 66/1: 020/000-0: 10th: Rear, nvr a factor, reapp/new yard.   ½   23
900   **COMPTON AVIATOR 42** [9]8-9-0 t (55) R L Moore 16/1: 30244-60: 11th: Al bhd, 6 wk abs.   ¾   29
1373 **FREE STYLE 9** [20]4-8-7 (48) Joanna Badger 12/1: 0145520: 12th: Keen, chsd ldrs till over 2f out.   18   0
972   **ITSONLYAGAME 36** [4]4-8-9 vis (50) Dane O'Neill 25/1: 1005020: 13th: In tch 7f, sn btn: btr 972.   2½   0
1406 **UN AUTRE ESPERE 7** [11]5-8-5 (1oh)bl (45) J Mackay 50/1: 0005150: 14th: Chsd ldrs till halfway.   7   0
4963} **CANATRICE 186** [5]4-9-0 p (55) J P Guillambert(3) 33/1: 420100-0: 15th: Dwelt & al bhd, jumps fit.   9   0
458   **KOMATI RIVER 103** [16]5-8-7 (48) T Quinn 8/1: 0/6256-00: 16th: Bhd, no ch from halfway: abs.   25   0
1082 **ANGELICA GARNETT 27** [6]4-8-6 (47) F Norton 33/1: 0600100: 17th: In tch till halfway: btr 827.   10   0
17 Ran   Time 2m 40.80(15.80)   Owned: Ms Susan Arnesen   Trained: Cullompton

---

Official Going GOOD

1544   2.10 Toteplacepot Banded Stakes 3yo+ 0-45 (H)
£1638 £468   £234   **5f59y rnd**   **Good**   **Slow**   Inside

1248 **HARBOUR HOUSE 15** [3] J J Bridger 5-9-7 (45) J Tate 9/1: 0-020631: Cl-up, led 3f out, rdn out: 47
eff around 6f/1m, imprvd here for drop back to 5f: acts on fast, gd/soft & polytrack: win again in banded grade.
1336 **AINTNECESSARILYSO 11** [2] N E Berry 6-9-7 (45) P Doe 2/1 FAV: 4363332: Chsd ldrs, rcd far rail in   ½   46
str, prog & ev ch dist, kept on but just held by wnr: op 7/2: another consistent run, see 1336 & 941.
889   **SO SOBER 43** [8] D Shaw 6-9-7 (45) N Callan 13/2: 1540043: Held up, prog halfway, kept on fnl 1f,   1¾   41
nrst fin: 6 wk abs: btr 312 (fibresand).
1336 **THREAT 11** [7] J M Bradley 8-9-7 (45) B Reilly(3) 13/2: 0400344: Cl-up over 4f, no extra fnl 1f.   1½   36
1290 **MANGUS 13** [4]10-9-7 bl (35) N Chalmers(5) 33/1: 0-306005: Bhd, nvr nrr than mid-div: see 749.   1   33
1368 **CRAFTY POLITICIAN 9** [6]7-9-7 bl (45) W Ryan 100/30: 00-41256: Nvr nrr than mid-div: btr 1288 & 1184.   hd   32
1270 **FRENCHMANS LODGE 14** [10]4-9-7 BL (45) K Ghunowa(7) 25/1: 0000-007: b g Piccolo - St Helena   2   26
(Monsanto) Keen rear, prog & cl-up halfway, no extra fnl 2f: first time blnks: 3rd of 7 at best in '03 (rtd 60a,
mdn, D J S Ffrench Davis): unplcd in '02 (rtd 71, mdn): eff at 5f on polytrack: with J M Bradley.
1368* **FLYING FAISAL 9** [5]6-9-13 bl (45) C J Davies(7) 11/1: 0304618: Rear, nvr able to chall: btr 1368 (6f).   3   23
1290 **AVIT 13** [9]4-9-7 (40) N Pollard 11/1: 00-00239: Handy over 3f, edged right & sn fdd: btr 832.   6   0
1327 **TOP PLACE 11** [1]3-8-12 p (40) J D Smith 14/1: 0-000550: 10th: Led 1f, kept far rail, fdd 2f out.   ¾   0
10 Ran   Time 1m 5.6 (5.6)   Owned: Mr Tommy Ware   Trained: Liphook

---

1545   2.40 Toteexacta Banded Stakes 4yo+ 0-35 (H)
£1288 £368   £184   **6f209y rnd**   **Good**   **Slow**   Inside

1415 **TINY TIM 7** [3] A M Balding 6-8-12 (35) T Block(7) 4/11 FAV: 4235221: Handy till led 2f out,   43+
pushed clr, val 6L+: qck reapp: well bckd at long odds-on: suited by 6/7f, stays a sharp 1m in banded grade:
acts on gd grnd & polytrack, handles firm: gd confidence boost: see 1415 & 1292.
1451 **MIDDLEMISS 5** [2] J W Mullins 4-8-12 p (35) S Righton 10/1: 5554-002: Handy till outpcd after 3f,   4   34
rallied ins fnl 2f, no ch with easy wnr: clr rem, qck reapp: eff at 7f on gd & with cheek pieces: see 1813.
1335 **MISS FAYE 11** [4] J M Bradley 4-8-12 p (35) B Reilly(3) 4/1: 00/466-03: b f Puissance - Bingo Bongo   12   10

BRIGHTON   TUESDAY 04.05.04   Lefthand, V Sharp, Undulating Track

(Petong) Cl-up, led after 4f, hdd 2f out, hung badly right & fdd: unplcd all 3 '03 starts (rtd 45, fills mdn):
unplcd both '02 starts: wears cheek pieces.
4423] **MAYFAIR MAUNDY 578** [1] W G M Turner 4-8-12 (35) C Haddon(7) 14/1: 00500/-4: ch f The West -   **5**   **0**
Mayfair Ballerina (King's Signet) Led, hdd 4f out, sn fdd: reapp: missed '03: modest form in '02 (rtd 47, sell).
4 Ran   Time 1m 27.6 (7.8)   Owned: Mr I A Balding   Trained: Kingsclere

1546   3.10 Totequadpot Banded Stakes 3yo+ 0-35 (H)
£1295 £370 £185   **7f214y rnd**   Good   Slow   Inside

782   **ADJIRAM 64** [4] A W Carroll 8-9-4 vis (30) W Ryan 15/8 FAV: 0/46/-3541: Led 6f, outpcd, rallied   **38**
ins fnl 1f to lead cl-home: 8 wk jumps abs, earlier unplcd (rtd 68h, nov h'cap hdle, stays 2m2f on firm): eff at
1m/12f on fast & gd grnd: eff with a visor & goes well fresh: see 782.
1292   **NEWCORR 13** [2] J J Bridger 5-9-4 (35) N Chalmers(5) 7/2: 0/0-00632: Handy, ev ch over 2f out, led   **1**   **35**
ins fnl 1f, hdd cl-home: tchd 11/2: eff at 1m/9f on gd, hvy grnd & polytrack: see 1292.
1261   **POINT MAN 15** [5] J W Payne 4-9-4 (30) N Callan 6/1: 00050-03: Cl-up & led 2f out, hdd ins fnl   **2**   **31**
1f, no extra: tchd 8/1: eff at 1m on gd grnd: see 1261.
1430   **MARENGO 6** [1] Paul Johnson 10-9-4 (30) K Ghunowa(7) 6/1: 0060064: Bhd, prog 2f out, onepcd fnl 1f.   **1½**   **28**
4024] **HAUNT THE ZOO 245** [3]9-9-4 (35) L Vickers 11/4: 332513-5: b f Komaite - Merryhill Maid (M Double   **30**   **0**
M) Reared leaving stalls & lost all ch: reapp: op 7/4: appr h'cap wnr in '03: won both starts in '02 (fills
h'caps): suited by 1m/9.4f on fast, loves fibresand/Southwell/W'hampton: gd weight-carrier who has gone well
fresh: eff with eye-shield: see John A Harris.
1 Aug'03 Wolv 9.4af 58a-55 F: 2 Jul'03 Wolv 8.5af 56a-(55) F: 1 May'02 Wolv 8.4af 70a-63 D:
1 May'02 Wolv 8.4af 64a-57 E: 1 Sep'01 Wolv 9.3af 61a-58 F: 1 Jul'01 Sout 8af 58a- F:
5 Ran   Time 1m 43.15 (11.15)   Owned: Mr K Marshall   Trained: Alcester

1547   3.40 Totewin Banded Stakes 3yo+ 0-40 (H)
£1491 £426 £213   **1m3f196y**   Good   Slow   Outside

1333   **BUZ KIRI 11** [6] A W Carroll 6-9-10 (35) P Doe 5/2 FAV: 2122621: Mid-div, grad prog to lead 2f   **42**
out, drvn out: tchd 7/2: suited by 10/12f, stays 14f/2m: acts on fast, soft & both AWs: enjoys banded grade.
1329   **DORA CORBINO 11** [8] R Hollinshead 4-9-10 (40) T G McLaughlin 16/1: 5320632: Led, hdd 2f out, no   **4**   **35**
extra dist: eff at 12f on gd grnd & fibresand: see 823.
1180   **DANCES WITH ANGELS 19** [4] Mrs A L M King 4-9-10 (40) N Callan 14/1: 4400-003: b f Mukaddamah -   **hd**   **34**
Lady of Leisure (Diesis) Chsd ldrs over 7f, outpcd 3f out, rallied despite edging left ins fnl 1f: plcd once in '03
(rtd 42, fills h'cap): unplcd in '02 (med auct mdn, rtd 59): eff at 10f, prob stays 12f: acts on gd & gd/soft grnd.
1456   **LEOPHIN DANCER 5** [3] P W Hiatt 6-9-10 (40) L Vickers 3/1: 6012234: Handy over 1m, sn no extra: **4**   **28**
qck reapp: disapp on return to turf: btr 1456 & 1411 (polytrack).
1250   **BUNINO VEN 15** [5]3-8-5 BL e (40) B Reilly(3) 10/1: 000-0405: Keen mid-div, outpcd halfway, mod   **3**   **23**
late gains: 1st time eye-sheild & blnks: btr 899.
1455   **ISLAND STAR 5** [1]4-9-10 (40) R Brisland 20/1: 60-00046: Rear, nvr a factor: qck reapp: btr 1455.   **11**   **7**
1409   **MOYNE PLEASURE 7** [7]6-9-10 p (40) K Ghunowa(7) 5/1: 0060027: Cl-up 1m, wknd: qck reapp: btr 1409.   **2**   **4**
1449   **TIMBUKTU 5** [2]3-8-5 (40) N Pollard 11/4: 06-00028: Cl-up, fdd 4f out, eased to walk ins fnl 1f.   **dist**   **0**
8 Ran   Time 2m 40.5 (12.3)   Owned: Mr Serafino Agodino   Trained: Alcester

1548   4.10 Toteplace Banded Stakes 3yo+ 0-40 (H)
£1442 £412 £206   **7f214y rnd**   Good   Slow   Inside

1328   **CHICKASAW TRAIL 11** [5] R Hollinshead 6-9-7 (40) Stephanie Hollinshead(7) 11/1: 0-000651: Held up,   **45**
gd prog to lead ins fnl 1f, rdn out: eff arnd 1m/10f on firm & gd, poss handles gd/soft & f/sand: see 862.
1328   **SEA JADE 11** [6] J W Payne 5-9-7 (40) N Callan 7/4 FAV: 26460-42: Keen handy, led 2f out till ins   **½**   **43**
fnl 1f, kept on but just held by wnr: clr rem: not btn far & can find similar: see 1328.
1402   **CHAKRA 7** [8] C J Gray 10-9-7 (40) C Haddon(7) 16/1: 0000/-653: Keen handy 6f, edged left & sn no   **6**   **31**
extra: qck reapp: btr 1402.
1288   **HARBOUR PRINCESS 13** [2] M F Harris 3-8-8 (35) S Righton 10/1: 066634: Chsd ldrs till outpcd   **3½**   **24**
halfway, modest late gains: btr 1288.
1335   **ZINGING 11** [7]5-9-7 (40) J Tate 3/1: 0640065: Led 6f, sn wknd: btr 328.   **2**   **20**
1073   **WILOM 28** [1]6-9-7 (40) N Pollard 7/1: 5450006: Keen cl-up, fdd 2f out: btr 343.   **11**   **0**
1335   **DEFINITELY SPECIAL 11** [3]6-9-7 p (35) P Doe 6/1: 0000647: Cl-up, fdd fnl 2f: see 500.   **2½**   **0**
1058   **KUMAKAWA 29** [4]6-9-7 bl (40) Liam Jones(7) 8/1: 0026008: Rear, nvr trav, rider lost whip 2f out.   **dist**   **0**
8 Ran   Time 1m 42.6 (10.6)   Owned: Mr Anthony White   Trained: Upper Longdon

1549   4.40 Totepool Tri-Banded Stakes 3yo 0-45 (H)
£1463 £418 £209   **6f209y rnd**   Good   Slow   Inside

1281   **PERERIN 14** [7] I A Wood 3-9-0 (45) N Callan 2/1 FAV: 000-01: b c Whittingham - Antithesis (Fairy   **50+**
King) Mid-div, outpcd after 4f, rallied to lead ins fnl 1f, pushed out, val 3L+: bckd from 7/1: modest form in '03
(rtd 45 & 22a, mdns): eff at 7f, shaped as tho' further will suit: acts on gd grnd: eff on a sharp/undul trk:
apprec drop to banded grade & can follow up.
1453   **FAYR FIRENZE 5** [3] M F Harris 3-9-0 vis (45) S Righton 5/1: 0462522: Handy till led dist, hdd ins   **1¼**   **46**
fnl 1f, no extra: qck reapp: eff at 6f/7f on gd grnd & both AWs: see 1453 & 1312.
1416   **STAGECOACH RUBY 7** [1] G L Moore 3-8-9 (40) W Ryan 11/4: 0-005433: Led & clr, till dist, no   **½**   **40**
extra: op 9/4: qck reapp: acts on firm & gd grnd: see 1073.
1085   **TARANAI 27** [2] B W Duke 3-9-0 (45) N Chalmers(5) 9/1: 6-400004: Cl-up & ev ch dist, no extra: op 6/1.   **1¾**   **42**
1330   **HEATHYARDS JOY 11** [4]3-8-4 (35) P Doe 5/1: 0-004425: Rear, nvr nrr than mid-div: btr 1330.   **1½**   **29**
1330   **BROTHER CADFAEL 11** [6]3-8-9 (40) N Pollard 9/2: 3032666: Bhd, no prog when rider lost whip halfway.   **nk**   **33**
1312   **SPARKLING CLEAR 12** [5]3-8-9 vis (40) J D Smith 20/1: 066-0067: Rear & seemed to lose action,   **dist**   **0**
eased fnl 2f: see 872.
7 Ran   Time 1m 27.85(8.05)   Owned: Tyrnest Ltd   Trained: Upper Lambourn

Official Going GOOD (GOOD/FIRM places).

1550   6.10 Brunton Hall Maiden Auction Stakes 2yo (E)
£3361 £1034 £517   **5f str**   **Good 60**   **-21 Slow**   Stands side

DANCE ANTHEM [5] M G Quinlan 2-8-8 P McCabe 7/2: 1: ch c Royal Academy - Statua (Statoblest)   **79+**
Handy, prog when hmpd dist, found room & led ins fnl 1f, pushed out, val 3L+: debut: Feb foal, cost 8,500gns:
dam smart performer abroad: eff at 5f, shld apprec 6f: acts on gd grnd & a sharp trk:
goes well fresh: showed a gd turn of foot here & can rate higher.
920 **WINDY PROSPECT 40** [9] P A Blockley 2-8-10 D Nolan(2) 11/4 FAV: 352: Dwelt, prog & ev ch dist,   1½   74
kept on ins fnl 1f, not pace of wnr: well bckd after 6 wk abs: can find similar: see 920.
LLAMADAS [1] M Dods 2-8-9 F Lynch 3/1: 3: b g Josr Algarhoud - Primulette (Mummy's Pet) Slow   nk   72
away, prog 2f out, nrst fin: debut: March foal, cost 16,000gns: half-brother to numerous wnrs at 2: dam wnr at
5f/1m: sire useful performer arnd 1m: eff at 5f, will apprec further: acts on gd grnd: sure to learn from this.
1237 **COLEORTON DANCER 17** [7] K A Ryan 2-8-7 G Parkin 11/2: 04: ch c Danehill Dancer - Tayovullin   ½   68
(Shalford) Led, hdd ins fnl 1f, no extra: April foal, cost 6,000gns: dam won numerous times at 7f: sire useful at
sprint dists: eff at 5f on gd grnd.
LADY HOPEFUL [3]2-8-3 T Hamilton 10/1: 5: Handy over 3f, sn onepcd: debut.   nk   63
1133 **MISS GOOD TIME 22** [4]2-8-2 P Hanagan 50/1: 06: Handy till dist, no extra.   1   59
NAMKING [2]2-8-8 Dean McKeown 50/1: 7: Slow away, nvr able to chall: debut.   1¼   61
1029 **VOICE OF AN ANGEL 32** [8]2-8-2 G Duffield 12/1: 58: Prom over 3f, wknd: btr 1029 (fibresand).   7   37
1212 **GYPSY FAIR 18** [6]2-8-5 K Darley 14/1: 09: Rear, nvr able to chall.   ¾   38
1173 **MORNING WORLD 19** [10]2-8-9 K Dalgleish 66/1: 00: 10th: Cl-up over 3f, fdd.   5   29
10 Ran   Time 1m 1.57 (4.07)   Owned: The Afternoon Syndicate   Trained: Newmarket

---

1551   6.40 Len Lothian Ltd Handicap Stakes 4yo+ 46-55 (F)   **[67]**
£2926 £836 £418   **2m**   **Good 60**   **-31 Slow**   Stands side

1118 **GARGOYLE GIRL 23** [4] J S Goldie 7-8-13 (52) K Darley 5/1: 0640-051: Held up, grad prog to lead   **59+**
dist, pushed clr, val 16L+: recent jumps unplcd: eff at 11/14f, now stays 2m: acts on firm & gd/soft grnd: loves
Musselburgh: back to winning form here with cheek pieces left off: win again on this evidence: see 1118.
1285 **ROMIL STAR 14** [3] K R Burke 7-8-11 BL (50) Darren Williams 6/1: 5560-002: b g Chief's Crown -   13   47
Romelia (Woodman) Handy till led after 11f, sn clr, hdd dist, sn edged left & no extra: earlier h'cap hdle wnr (rtd
109h, stays 2m5.5f on fast & gd/soft): h'cap wnr in '03 (R D Wylie): rnr-up 3 times in '02 (h'caps): eff at
12f/14f on gd, hvy & fibresand: goes well fresh, tried blnks here: has slipped back to winning mark.
1 Feb'03 Sout 14af 73a-66 D: 2 Dec'02 Wolv 12af 70a-64 D: 2 Jun'02 Muss 12gd 64-62 E: 2 Jun'02 Wolv 12af 63a-62 D:
1307 **DORMY TWO 12** [9] J S Wainwright 4-8-8 p (50) R Winston 20/1: 340-03: b f Eagle Eyed - Tartan Lady   ½   46
(Taufan) Keen rear, prog just ins fnl half-mile, onepcd fnl 2f: earlier plcd twice over hdles (rtd 92h, juv nov
hdles, stays 2m1.5f on gd, cheek pieces): eff at 1m on fast grnd.
1361 **CELTIC VISION 10** [10] M Appleby 8-8-11 t (50) P Hanagan 20/1: 66004: Rear, nvr nrr than mid div.   1½   45
1361 **MR FORTYWINKS 10** [8]10-9-2 (55) T Eaves(5) 5/1: 41406-05: ch g Fools Holme - Dream On (Absalom)   ½   49
Cl-up over 12f, no extra: tchd 7/1: amat rider h'cap wnr here in '03: dual h'cap wnr in '02: suited by 15f/2m on
firm & fibresand, likes gd & hvy: can go well fresh & handles any trk: likes to race up with/forcing the pace.
1 Jul'03 Muss 16gd 61-51 F: 2 Jul'02 Muss 16g/s 61-59 F: 1 Jul'02 Ayr 15g/s 60-53 F:
1 Jul'02 Donc 16.5gd 51-44 F: 2 Jul'01 Hami 13gd 61-60 E: 1 Apr'01 Ripo 16hvy 64-62 C:
2394] **WESTERN BLUEBIRD 676** [6]6-8-12 (51) P Mulrennan(5) 20/1: 426044/-6: Chsd ldrs 12f, fdd: jmps fit.   20   29
1449 **BALALAIKA TUNE 5** [7]5-8-7 (6oh) (40) D Fentiman(7) 20/1: 0006047: Keen rear, nvr a factor: btr 1449.   1¾   22
1238 **ASTROMANCER 17** [1]4-8-8 (50) Saleem Golam(6) 4/1 FAV: 244-0458: Led 11f, fdd: btr 137 (AW).   10   18
4812*]**ROUGE BLANC 197** [5]4-8-12 P (54) Dale Gibson 1/2: 424231-9: Handy, fdd 5f out: new stable.   28   0
1271 **MARINO MOU 14** [2]4-8-4 (1oh) (45) A Reilly(5) 12/1: 00630: 10th: Chsd ldrs 12f, fdd: btr 1271.   13   0
10 Ran   Time 3m 37.15 (14.65)   Owned: Mrs C Brown   Trained: Glasgow

---

1552   7.10 Hollies Claiming Stakes 4yo+ (F)
£2884 £824 £412   **1m4f**   **Good 60**   **-33 Slow**   Inside

866 **PLATINUM CHARMER 48** [1] K R Burke 4-8-7 p (58) Darren Williams 9/4: 04-21021: Handy, styd on to   56
lead ins fnl 1f, drvn out: 7 wk abs & new stable: suited by 12f, has tried further: acts on gd, soft & fibresand:
apprec refitting of cheek pieces here: win again in sell/claim grade: see 446 (K A Ryan).
4321] **ARMS ACROSSTHESEA 229** [8] A C Whillans 5-8-9 (40) J Carroll 16/1: 006000-2: b g Namaqualand -   3   53
Zolica (Beveled) Rear, grad prog to lead 2f out, hdd ins fnl 1f, no extra: clr rem, reapp: mod form in '03 (rtd 43,
amat h'cap, F P Murtagh): plcd over hdles in 02/03 (rtd 88h, nov claim hdle, stays 2m on firm & gd/soft): eff at
6f/1m, now stays 12f: acts on firm, gd/soft & fibresand: best without visor, tried blnks & cheek pieces.
1 May'02 Muss 8g/s 65-61 F: 2 May'02 Carl 7.9fm 66-57 E: 1 May'01 Newc 6g/f 69- F:
1047 **MIKASA 29** [6] R F Fisher 4-8-6 (3ow) (40) R Winston 25/1: 000-0003: b g Victory Note - Resiusa   6   41
(Niniski) Led 10f, sn wknd: unplcd sole 03/04 jump start (juv sell hdle): unplcd on Flat in '03 (rtd 59, mdn).
3872] **MINSTREL HALL 610** [5] P Monteith 5-9-4 L Enstone(3) 7/1: 460310/-4: b f Saddlers' Hall -   1½   50
Mindomica (Dominion) Rear, nvr nrr than mid-div: hdles fit, earlier sell hdle wnr (rtd 99h, stays 2m on fast grnd):
missed '03: claim wnr in '02 (C W Thornton): eff at 1m/12f on gd & hvy grnd: acts on an undul/stiff trk.
1 Jun'02 Hami 11hvy 54- E:
1064 **ETON 28** [2]8-9-9 (70) Alex Greaves 2/1 FAV: 3310-305: Prom, led 2f out till dist, fdd: btr 924.   nk   54
1425 **ASTRAL PRINCE 6** [3]6-8-5 bl (48) R Ffrench 11/1: 00/060-56: Handy 6f, wknd: qck reapp.   4   30
IRANOO 1326 [7]7-8-3 t P Hanagan 20/1: 004500///-7: Handy 1m, wknd: jumps fit.   ¾   26
1396 **WASHINGTON PINK 8** [4]5-8-5 (45) T Hamilton(2) 12/1: 40/0-0048: Rear, nvr a factor: btr 1396.   4   22
8 Ran   Time 2m 41.87 (11.27)   Owned: Platinum Racing Club Limited   Trained: Leyburn

MUSSELBURGH   TUESDAY 04.05.04   Righthand, Sharp Track

1553
7.40 Continental Airlines Big Apple Handicap Stakes 3yo+ 0-70 (E)   [67]
£4134 £1272 £636   **7f30y rnd**   **Good 60**   **-43 Slow**   Outside

1485* **STOIC LEADER** 3 [10] R F Fisher 4-10-5 (6ex) (72) D Nolan(5) 9/4 FAV: 0114011: Handy, led 2f out,   **80+**
pushed out ins fnl 1f, val 3L+: well bckd on qck reapp: eff at 6f, now suited by 7f/1m on firm & soft grnd, both
AWs: gd weight carrier: in fine form at present & easily defied 6lb pen: see 1485.
1393 **THE GAMBLER** 8 [1] Paul Johnson 4-8-11 p (50) D Fentiman(7) 33/1: 500-0002: Rear, prog 3f out, kept   1¾   51
on fnl 1f, no ch with easy wnr: encouraging eff here & has slipped to a fair mark: see 1393.
1214 **BAILIEBOROUGH** 18 [12] D Nicholls 5-10-0 (67) Alex Greaves 10/1: 000-0603: Handy, kept on from 2f   hd   67
out, just held for 2nd cl-home: see 1142.
1366 **EFIDIUM** 10 [4] N Bycroft 6-9-12 (65) Suzanne France(7) 12/1: 0046-204: Rear, prog after 4f, edged   1   63
right & onepcd distr: btr 1215 (reapp).
1393 **OLD BAILEY** 8 [6]4-8-8 bl (47) P Makin(5) 9/1: 2626-605: Keen cl-up over 5f, sn no extra: btr 1217.   1   43
1322 **HOHS BACK** 11 [13]5-9-10 p (63) Natalia Gemelova(7) 12/1: 0-000206: Cl-up over 5f, sn no extra.   nk   58
1092 **REGENTS SECRET** 26 [2]4-9-13 (66) K Darley 12/1: 00040-47: Rear, nvr nrr than mid-div: btr 1092.   shd   60
1463 **SHIFTY** 4 [5]5-8-12 (51) P M Quinn 10/1: 6-500048: Bhd, nvr a factor: qck reapp: btr 1463.   1¾   41
499 **SMITH N ALLAN OILS** 97 [8]5-9-7 p (60) R Winston 8/1: 0101-109: Mid-div over 5f, no extra: btr 266.   2   46
1253 **GENERAL SMITH** 15 [7]5-9-5 (58) K Dalgleish 33/1: 24655-00: 10th: b g Greensmith - Second Call   2   40
(Kind of Hush) Slow away, al in rear: h'cap wnr in '03 (J M Bradley): h'cap wnr in '02: eff at 5f/6f on fast,
gd/soft & fibresand: has tried cheek pieces: with G A Harker. 2 Aug'03 Warw 5.5fm 60-58 E:
1 Jun'03 Ling 5g/f 57-51 E: 2 Apr'03 Ripo 5g/f 59-58 E: 1 Jul'02 Catt 5g/f 56-54 E: 2 May'02 Catt 5.9gd 56-52 E:
1266 **LIONS DOMANE** 15 [11]7-9-2 (55) J Carroll 14/1: 0560P00: 11th: led 5f, sn fdd: btr 528.   5   27
858 **MON SECRET** 49 [9]6-9-4 (57) F Lynch 10/1: 1213-400: 12th: Cl-up 5f, fdd: 7 wk abs: btr 393.   3   23
1393 **AFRICAN SPUR** 8 [3]4-9-12 t (65) D Tudhope(7) 50/1: 2200000: 13th: Rear, nvr a factor: btr 775.   1¾   29
13 Ran   Time 1m 32.16 (7.26)   Owned: Great Head House Estates Limited   Trained: Ulverston

1554
8.10 Mill Lade Maiden Stakes 3yo (D)
£4056 £1248 £624   **7f30y rnd**   **Good 60**   **-42 Slow**   Outside

1460 **MAN OF LETTERS** 4 [4] M Johnston 3-9-0 (76) K Dalgleish 2/5 FAV: 5-43221: Cl-up, styd on to lead   75
1f out, rdn out: qck reapp: eff at 7f, will apprec return to 1m: acts on gd & soft: gd confidence boost: see 1460.
1070 **GRACEFUL AIR** 28 [5] R Weymes 3-8-9 (62) R Winston 33/1: 0303-452: Held up, outpcd 3f out,   2   64
rallied well ins fnl 1f, nvr get to wnr: eff at 6f/7f: see 1070.
815 **JOSHUAS GOLD** 57 [2] D Carroll 3-9-0 (58) D Tudhope(7) 20/1: 03555-23: Handy, led briefly dist, sn   ¾   67$
no extra: 8 wk abs: acts on gd/soft grnd & polytrack: see 815.
1070 **CRATHES** 28 [6] J G Given 3-8-9 M Fenton 12/1: 24: Handy over 5f, no extra: btr 1070 (6f, hvy).   3½   55
4948} **CANADIAN STORM** 187 [1]3-9-0 (70) G Duffield 16/1: 050-5: gr c With Approval - Sheer Gold   hd   59
(Cutlass) Led till dist, wknd: reapp: modest form in '03 (rtd 76 & 51a, mdns): half-brother to useful 5/6f wnrs.
4706} **SON OF THUNDER** 204 [8]3-9-0 L Enstone(3) 100/1: 00-6: ch g Dr Fong - Sakura Queen (Woodman)   ½   56
Rear, nvr nrr than mid-div: reapp: unplcd both '03 starts (rtd 50, mdn).
814 **TRENCH COAT** 57 [7]3-9-0 (72) K Darley 5/1: 253-27: Cl-up 5f, sn fdd: 8 wk abs: btr 814 (AW).   10   41
1281 **DAWN DUEL** 14 [3]3-8-9 F Lynch 66/1: 0-08: Slow away, al in rear.   dist   6
8 Ran   Time 1m 32.05 (7.15)   Owned: Jumeirah Racing   Trained: Middleham

1555
8.40 Goose Green Handicap Stakes 3yo+ 46-55 (F)   [65]
£3045 £870 £435   **5f str**   **Good 60**   **+05 Fast**   Stands side

1393 **CASH** 8 [13] Paul Johnson 6-9-4 p (55) K Dalgleish 20/1: 1350001: Rcd centre, prom till led dist,   61
drvn out: stays 6f, suited by 5f: acts on firm, hvy & loves f/sand: eff with cheek pieces, tried visor, see 749.
1179 **VALIANT ROMEO** 19 [2] R Bastiman 4-9-2 (53) R Ffrench 5/1 FAV: 00000-52: b c Primo Dominie -   1   55
Desert Lynx (Green Desert) Rcd stands side, prom & ev ch dist, styd on, just held by wnr: unplcd in '03 (rtd 70,
h'cap): mdn & dual nursery scorer for M R Channon in '02: eff at 6f, best over a stiff/gall 5f: acts on firm &
gd/soft, any trk: eff with/without visor: lost little in defeat here & is h'capped to win similar.
1 Oct'02 Newm 5fm 91-78 C: 1 Sep'02 Chep 5g/f 83-73 E: 2 Sep'02 Good 6fm 74-66 D: 1 Apr'02 Brig 5.2fm 76- D:
1132 **ROAN RAIDER** 22 [15] M J Polglase 4-8-9 (1oh)vis (45) T Hamilton(3) 50/1: 600-0003: gr g El Prado -   nk   47
Flirtacious Wonder (Wolf Power) Chsd ldrs centre, styd on ins fnl 1f, not btn far in 3rd: plcd at best in '03 (mdns
& sellers, rtd 50): eff at 6f/1m on fast & gd grnd: eff with visor & t-strap. 2 Sep'03 Wind 6g/f 50-(49) D:
1218 **BEST LEAD** 17 [4] Ian Emmerson 5-9-1 bl (52) D Fentiman(7) 10/1: 5-104434: Bhd, prog despite   nk   52
hanging right ins fnl 2f, nrst fin: just btr 1218 (fibresand).
1276 **MALAHIDE EXPRESS** 14 [8]4-9-4 (55) Dean McKeown 6/1: 4502055: Led, hdd dist, no extra: btr 793.   nk   54
1179 **COLLEGE MAID** 19 [7]7-8-13 bl (50) K Darley 8/1: 3006-406: Handy & ev ch dist, sn no extra: see 1096.   1   46
1442 **LADY PROTECTOR** 5 [5]5-8-11 (48) J Edmunds 11/1: 4103007: Nvr nrr than mid-div: qck reapp: btr 587.   1½   40
1179 **FAIRGAME MAN** 19 [16]6-8-12 (49) R Winston 16/1: 00000-08: Rcd centre, handy over 3f, no extra.   nk   40
1179 **TORRENT** 19 [17]9-8-10 bl (47) P Makin(7) 14/1: 3001009: Handy centre over 3f, no extra.   1½   34
1221 **LAUREL DAWN** 22 [1]6-9-1 (52) P Mathers(7) 12/1: 4103-000: 10th: Bhd, nvr able to chall: btr 1221.   ½   38
1276 **MYSTERY PIPS** 204 [6]4-9-1 vis (52) Kim Tinkler 16/1: 143415-0: 11th: Handy over 3f, sn wknd.   1¾   33
1276 **PROUD WESTERN** 14 [12]6-8-10 (47) T Eaves(5) 10/1: 00140-00: 12th: Rear, nvr a factor.   shd   27
1216 **STAVROS** 18 [9]4-8-9 (46) J Carroll 50/1: 60006-00: 13th: Rcd centre, al in rear.   3   17
5000} **ROBWILLCALL** 182 [3]4-9-1 (52) F Lynch 14/1: 640000-0: 14th: Handy 3f, fdd: reapp.   5   9
1391 **JOYCES CHOICE** 8 [11]5-9-3 p (54) A Reilly(7) 10/1: 0050-20R: Ref to race: cheek pieces; btr 1179.   0
15 Ran   Time 1m 0.89(2.79)   Owned: Insull White Pritchard & Johnson   Trained: Stanley

446

COLOGNE SUNDAY 02.05.04 Righthand, Fair Track

Official Going SOFT

1556 **4.10 Gr 2 Gerling Preis 4yo+** ()
£28169 £10563 £4225 **1m4f** **Soft**

OLASO [10] P Vovcenko 5-8-11 A Starke 16/10 FAV: 1: br h Law Society - Olaya (Acatenango) **119+**
Chsd ldrs, led over 2f out & soon asserted, readily: recent wnr of a Gr 3 event here in Germany: eff at 10.5/12f,
stays 15f: acts on gd & soft grnd: v smart & progressive entire.
4525} **WELL MADE** [3] H Blume 7-8-11 W Mongil 47/10: 416-1032: br h Mondrian - Well Known 3½ **113**
(Konigsstuhl) Held up in tch, hdwy to chse ldr over 1f out, kept on but no impress: eff at 12f on soft grnd:
smart. 1 Sep'02 Colo 12sft 118- : 1 May'02 Colo 12sft 114- :
4004} **SENEX** [5] H Blume 4-8-11 A de Vries 182/10: 23: Held up, styd on for press fnl 3f, no threat. 2½ **110**
987 **FOREIGN AFFAIRS 35** [2]6-8-11 (102) F Johansson 48/10: 46-40428135: Trkd ldr, wknd over 1f out: 8¾ **101**
Brit chall, disapp in this better grade: see 987 (List, 15f).
8 Ran Time 2m 30.89() Owned: Stall Silbersee Trained: Germany

LONGCHAMP SUNDAY 02.05.04 Righthand, Stiff, Galloping Track

Official Going Very Soft

1557 **2.20 Gr 3 Prix Vanteaux Fillies 3yo** ()
£25704 £10282 £7711 **1m1f55y** **Heavy**

4836*}**LATICE** [1] J M Beguigne 3-9-0 C Soumillon 7/10 FAV: 11-1: ch f Inchinor - Laramie (Gulch) **114**
Handy, led over 1f out, styd on strongly to make a wng reapp & remain unbtn from 3 career starts: Gr 3 wnr here at
Longchamp last term: eff at 9f, 10f+ lks sure to suit: acts on gd/sft & hvy grnd: goes well fresh: smart filly.
1 Oct'03 Long 9g/s 105- :
ASTI [3] E Lellouche 3-9-0 D Boeuf 44/10: 12: b f Sadler's Wells - Astorg (Lear Fan) Held up, 1 **112**
hdwy to chse ldr dist, kept on but always held: only 2nd start, eff at 9f on v soft grnd: v useful.
4631} **GREEN SWALLOW** [2] P Demercastel 3-9-0 T Gillet 152/10: 21314-63: b f Green Tune - Green Sails 1½ **110**
(Slip Anchor) Rear, kept on wide, nrst fin. 1 Aug'03 Deau 7gd 108- A:
6 Ran Time 2m 01.30 () Owned: E Ciampi Trained: France

1558 **3.05 Gr 1 Prix Ganay 4yo+** ()
£80479 £32197 £16099 **1m2f110y** **Heavy**

1061 **EXECUTE** [2] J E Hammond 7-9-2 T Gillet 219/10: 25326-21: ch h Suave Dancer - She's My Lovely **118**
(Sharpo) Mid-div, hdwy to led ins last, styd on strongly: rnr-up in this event last term: Gr 2 wnr '02 & also again
rnr-up in this event: suited by 10f on gd & hvy grnd: high class easy grnd performer.
2 Apr'04 Long 10gd 115- : 2 Apr'03 Long 10.5sft 115- : 2 Apr'02 Long 10.5gd 116- : 1 Mar'02 Long 10sft 116- :
4798} **VESPONE** [4] Saeed bin Suroor 4-9-2 C P Lemaire 42/10: 21110-22: ch c Llandaff - Vanishing 1½ **117**
Prairie (Alysheba) Tried to make all, not pace of wnr cl home: Gr 3 & dual Gr 1 wnr in '03 for N Clement, subs btn
in Gr 1 Champion Stks for current connections: loves to front run, eff at 1m, suited by 10f on gd & hvy: v smart,
further Gr success awaits. 1 Jun'03 Long 10gd 118- A: 1 Jun'03 Chan 9gd 118- A: 1 May'03 Sain 10sft 113- :
1255*}**FAIR MIX** [7] M Rolland 6-9-2 O Peslier 46/10: 1655-163: Chsd ldrs, styd on fnl 2f, not pace to ½ **116**
chall: won this race last term.
4837*}**VALLEE ENCHANTEE** [5] E Lellouche 4-8-13 D Boeuf 56/10: 371411-4: Held up, efft when short of ½ **112**
room ins last, kept on: reapp.
990* **POLISH SUMMER** [8]7-9-2 G Stevens 11/10 FAV: 2512-115: Held up, onepce fnl 2f: btr 990 (gd/fm). ½ **114**
1350* **CHANCELLOR 8** [6]6-9-2 (110) T Jarnet 50/1: /464-018: Trkd ldr, rdn & btn over 1f out: fin 4th in 4 **110**
this race last term: up in grade after 1350 (Gr 3).
8 Ran Time 2m 14.60() Owned: Ecurie Chalhoub Trained: France

CURRAGH MONDAY 03.05.04 Righthand, Galloping Track

Official Going GOOD.

1559 **3.00 Gr 3 EBF Tetrarch Stakes 3yo** ()
£39255 £11517 £5487 **7f str** **Good**

1040+**LEITRIM HOUSE 30** [2] B J Meehan 3-9-0 M J Kinane 5/2 JT FAV: 16-11: Made all, rdn & in command **114+**
over 1f out, eased nr line, readily: op 9/4: suited by 7f/1m on firm, gd & polytrk: v smart & progressive colt, shld
make presence felt in the Irish 2000 Guineas: see 1040 (AW).
4571} **GRAND REWARD 213** [3] A P O'Brien 3-9-0 P J Scallan 3/1: 1325-2: b c Storm Cat - Serena's Song 3½ **106**
(Rahy) Chsd ldr halfway, rdn & no impress dist: reapp: mdn wnr in '03, subs Gr 2 rnr up & cl 6th in Gr 1 Middle Park
(rtd 110): eff at 6f, prob stays 7f: acts on firm & gd: likes a gall trk & can go well fresh: met a smart rival here.
2 Sep'03 Newb 6.0g/f 108-0 A: 1 May'03 Newb 6.0gd 89-0 D:
1167 **MOKABRA 19** [4] M R Channon 3-9-3 (107) A Culhane 9/2: 31165-63: b c Cape Cross - Pacific Grove 2 **105**
(Persian Bold) Handy, outpcd over 2f out, kept on ins last: prog juv, auct mdn, stks & German Gr 2 wnr: eff at 6f,
prob stays 7f: handles fast & gd/sft grnd, sharpish or stiff/undul trk: v useful.
1 Sep'03 Bade 6gd 100- A: 1 Aug'03 Ripo 6g/f 101-100 C: 1 May'03 Newc 6g/f 85-0 E:
1063* **NEWTON 29** [5] A P O'Brien 3-9-0 P Cosgrave 5/2 JT FAV: 11053D2-14: Held up in tch, no impress ½ **101**
fnl 2f: shorter priced stablemate of rnr-up: btr 1167 (List, soft).
5 Ran Time 1m 22.30 () Owned: Gallagher Equine Ltd Trained: Upper Lambourn

CURRAGH MONDAY 03.05.04 Righthand, Galloping Track

1560 4.00 Gr 3 EBF Mooresbridge Stakes 4yo+ ()
£39195 £11457 £5427 1m2f Good/Soft

1350 **NYSAEAN 9** [6] R Hannon 5-9-4 (112) M J Kinane 6/4: 10-54521: Trkd ldrs, al trav well, led over **116**
1f out & readily asserted: op 7/4: stays 12f, suited by 10f: handles firm & gd, loves gd/soft & soft grnd: v smart
performer with cut in the ground, reportedly has the Arc as long term autumn target: see 1061.
4650} **LATINO MAGIC 8** [8] R J Osborne 4-9-0 R M Burke 12/1: 2126-502: ch c Lion Cavern - Tansy 2½ **105**
(Shareef Dancer) Held up, styd on fnl 2f, nvr threat to wnr: recent List 4th: dual wnr '03, incl List: stays 10f,
wng form at 1m/9f: acts on firm & gd/sft grnd: handles a sharp or stiff trk: v useful colt.
2 Oct'03 Tipp 7.5g/f 101- : 2 Aug'03 Leop 8g/f 101- A:
4599} **AKSHAR 36** [4] D K Weld 5-9-0 BL (103) P J Smullen 14/1: 13130-03: Chsd ldrs, rdn & kept on, nvr 1½ **103**
able to chall in first time blnks.
922 **MIDDLEMARCH 39** [5] J S Goldie 4-9-0 p (109) J F Egan 25/1: 25016-04: Led/dsptd lead till dist, sn btn. 2½ **99**
994* **BRIAN BORU 36** [7]4-9-7 t J A Heffernan 5/4 FAV: 304213-15: Dsptd lead halfway, wknd over 1f out: shd **106**
well bckd: '03 St Leger wnr & needs 12f+: btr 994.
7 Ran Time 2m 09.30() Owned: Fieldspring Racing Trained: East Everleigh

WOLVERHAMPTON Fibresand WEDNESDAY 05.05.04 Lefthand, Sharp Track

Official Going STANDARD.

1561 6.00 Wolverhampton-Racecourse Co Uk Amateur Riders' Banded Stakes 4yo+ 0-35 (H)
£1439 £411 £206 1m1f79y aw Going 53 -43 Slow Inside

1333 **LEYAALY 12** [1] B A Pearce 5-11-0 (30) Mr G Gallagher(7) 10/1: 0/00-6001: ch f Night Shift - Lower **36a**
The Tone (Phone Trick) Made all, held on gamely fnl 1f, drvn out: op 14/1, slow time: mod form '03 (lightly rcd):
no form '02: eff by forcing the pace at 9f on fibresand & a sharp trk in banded company.
1547 **MOYNE PLEASURE 1** [2] Paul Johnson 6-11-0 p (30) Miss Kelly Harrison(3) 5/2 FAV: 00600272: Trkd 1½ **33a**
ldrs, rdn & outpcd over 2f out, kept on cl-home for press, not able to chall: op 3/1, unplcd yesterday: see 1409.
1335 **DUNDONALD 12** [3] M Appleby 5-11-0 bl t (35) Mr L Newnes(3) 4/1: 0650333: Chsd wnr, rdn & no extra nk **32a**
over 1f out: see 1335.
2768} **CLASSICAL WALTZ 301** [4] J J Sheehan 6-11-0 (35) Mr J Pemberton(7) 16/1: 506/00/0-4: ch f In The 5 **25a**
Wings - Fascination Waltz (Shy Groom) In tch, eff 3f out, no impress: reapp: no form sole '03 start (rtd 12a).
4918} **ERUPT 190** [9]11-11-0 (35) Miss V Barr(7) 7/1: 000060-5: In tch till 3f out, reapp, new yard. 2½ **22a**
1332 **HELLBENT 12** [5]5-11-0 (35) Miss S Beddoes 11/4: 0056346: Dwelt & held up, hdwy wide 3f out, no 1¾ **20a**
prog fnl 2f: btr 784 (polytrack).
1406 **MORRIS DANCING 8** [8]5-11-0 (30) Mr E Dehdashti(3) 8/1: 0005007: Chsd ldrs, btn 5f out: btr 784. hd **20a**
1406 **MISS OCEAN MONARCH 8** [6]4-11-0 (30) Miss Rachel Clark(7) 9/1: 0440-008: Rear & no ch halfway. 8 **8a**
8 Ran Time 2m 07.17 (8.97) Owned: Mr Mervyn Merwood Trained: Lingfield

1562 6.30 Weddings And Receptions At Dunstall Park Banded Stakes 3yo+ 0-40 (H)
£1432 £409 £205 5f aw rnd Going 53 +01 Fast Inside

1199 **HAGLEY PARK 19** [5] M Quinn 5-9-6 (40) D Holland 7/4 FAV: 6543031: Made all, rdn & clr from dist: **50a**
suited by 5f on both AWs & loves W'hampton: see 286.
889 **WHITE O MORN 44** [4] J W Unett 5-9-6 p (40) R Winston 9/2: 0424102: Led/dsptd lead till over 1f 7 **39a**
out, sn btn: 6 wk abs: prev with B McMahon: see 781 (C/D).
1336 **TRAVELLERS JOY 12** [7] R J Hodges 4-9-6 (40) R L Moore 11/1: 5660-003: Bhd early, kept on late, shd **39a**
nvr a threat to wnr: handles fast & fibresand: see 1336.
1320 **MINIRINA 12** [2] C Smith 4-9-6 (40) R Fitzpatrick 14/1: 0540-044: Prom, rider lost whip over 1f ½ **38a**
out, sn no impress: see 1320.
1408 **TUSCAN DREAM 8** [1]9-9-6 (40) P Bradley(5) 7/1: 0225155: In tch, no impress dist: see 1309. ¾ **36a**
982 **EMARATIS IMAGE 36** [3]6-9-6 (40) A Culhane 9/4: 0-064646: In tch, btn over 1f out: new yard. 1¼ **33a**
1408 **DANCING RIDGE 8** [6]7-9-6 vis (30) Stephanie Hollinshead(7) 20/1: 00-00567: Struggling halfway. 1 **30a**
7 Ran Time 1m 02.84 (2.64) Owned: Mr Steven Astaire Trained: Wantage

1563 7.00 Come Evening Racing To Dunstall Park Banded Stakes 4yo+ 0-40 (H)
£1421 £406 £203 1m6f166y aw Going 53 -27 Slow Outside

3643} **MY LEGAL EAGLE 264** [3] E G Bevan 10-9-0 (40) B Swarbrick(5) 2/1 JT FAV: 22050//5-1: b g Law **41a**
Society - Majestic Nurse (On Your Mark) Held up, hdwy 6f out, rdn/led over 1f out, styd on strongly: reapp: unplcd
sole '03 start (h'cap, rtd 30a): 02/03 hdles wnr (h'cap, rtd 97h, 2m/2m1f, firm & gd/soft): eff at 10/12f, stays
2m: acts on fast, hvy & both AWs, with/without blnks & handles any trk. 2 Oct'01 Bath 17.1g/f 42-44 D:
2 Sep'01 Ches 15.8g/s 47-46 D: 2 Sep'01 Warw 16.1g/f 42-37 F: 2 Mar'01 Nott 14hvy 38-36 E:
1287 **THE LAST MOHICAN 14** [5] P Howling 5-9-0 p (30) R Winston 3/1: 2440032: Led, rdn & hdd over 1f 5 **34a**
out, sn no impress on wnr: see 537 & 395.
1329 **RIVER OF FIRE 12** [2] C N Kellett 6-9-0 (30) D Holland 13/2: 10360-03: ch g Dilum - Bracey Brook 5 **29a**
(Gay Fandango) In tch, rdn & no impress fnl 2f: h'cap scorer '03, AW h'cap plcd (rtd 44a): suited by 14f/2m on
firm, soft & fibresand, prob any trk: eff with/without visor & can force the pace. 1 Jul'03 Folk 16.4g/f 38-36 F:
2 Dec'02 Wolv 14.7af 43a-42 E: 2 Dec'02 Sout 14af 49a-50 D: 2 Oct'02 Yarm 14g/s 55- F: 2 Jul'02 Hami 12sft 48-49 E:
1414 **LITTLE RICHARD 8** [1] M Wellings 5-9-0 p (40) V Slattery 2/1 JT FAV: 1402354: In tch, btn 4f out. 10 **19a**
1180 **POLKA PRINCESS 20** [4]4-8-12 p (30) A Culhane 14/1: 0300005: Chsd ldr, struggling 4f out, t.o. dist **0a**
5 Ran Time 3m 21.40 (11.80) Owned: Mr E G Bevan Trained: Hereford

1564

7.30 June Summer Ball At Dunstall Park Banded Stakes 3yo+ 0-45 (H)
£1446 £413 £207   **1m1f79y aw**   **Going 53**   **+01 Fast**   Inside

1334 **IAMBACK 12** [5] Miss Gay Kelleway 4-9-7 (45) D Holland 7/1: 1604301: Made all, rdn & styd on well   **50a**
from over 1f out: eff around 1m/9.4f on fast grnd & fibresand: see 526 & 299.
1289 **GALEY RIVER 14** [10] J J Sheehan 5-9-7 (45) D Corby(3) 16/1: 0505162: Cl-up, rdn & no extra fnl   2½   **44a**
1f: acts on fast & both AWs: see 1072 & 770.
1332* **EUROLINK ARTEMIS 12** [3] Julian Poulton 7-9-7 p (45) N Callan 10/3: 0-040113: Held up, rdn & styd   2½   **40a**
on onepace fnl 2f, not able to threaten front pair: see 1332, 1262 & 970.
1289 **SIX PACK 14** [6] Andrew Turnell 6-9-7 (45) C Catlin 3/1 FAV: 0060-224: Rear, outpcd 3f out, late   2   **36a**
rally, no threat: op 9/2: see 1289 & 894.
3245} **SUPER DOMINION 280** [4]7-9-7 (40) Stephanie Hollinshead(7) 12/1: 000030-5: ch g Superpower -   1¾   **34a**
Smartie Lee (Dominion) Prom, btn dist: reapp: h'cap plcd '03 (rtd 49, AW unplcd, rtd 30a): h'cap plcd '02: eff
btwn 6/9f on fast, gd/soft & f/sand, likes W'hampton: suited by t-strap & eff in cheekpcs, neither worn tonight.
2 Jan'02 Wolv 8.4af 56a-57 E: 1 Dec'01 Wolv 7af 59a-55 F: 1 Nov'01 Nott 8.2g/s 66-60 F: 2 Oct'01 Leic 8g/s 66- F:
2 Aug'01 Beve 7.4g/f 59-59 E: 1 Aug'01 Beve 8.4gd 60- E: 1 Jul'01 Leic 6g/s 48-42 E: 1 Nov'00 Wolv 9.3af 71a- D:
2967} **TIME TO REGRET 292** [9]4-9-7 (45) R Winston 4/1: 024235-6: b g Presidium - Scoffera (Scottish   1¾   **32a**
Reel) Prom till over 1f out on reapp: clmr & sell rnr-up '03, AW unplcd (rtd 24a): unplcd '02 (rtd 68): eff btwn
7/9.3f on fast grnd, stiff or sharp/turning trk.   2 Jun'03 Carl 9.3g/f 54-(51) F: 2 Jun'03 Catt 7g/f 52-(51) F:
1313 **BEVIER 13** [8]10-9-7 (45) N Chalmers(5) 7/1: 5342047: In tch, btn 3f out: btr 821 (C/D).   2½   **28a**
1450 **OPTIMUM NIGHT 6** [2]5-9-7 (40) A Culhane 16/1: 000-038: Bhd, brief eff 3f out: qck reapp: see 1450.   1¾   **26a**
1342 **WESTERN COMMAND 11** [1]8-9-7 p (40) Joanna Badger 14/1: 0553359: Chsd ldrs till lost place hway.   5   **19a**
1451 **MUTABARI 6** [7]10-9-7 (40) Amy Myatt(7) 33/1: 0000-000: 10th: Held up, eff wide, btn 3f out.   5   **12a**
10 Ran   Time 2m 03.10 (4.90)   Owned: Twilight Racing   Trained: Newmarket

1565

8.00 Conferences With Racing At Dunstall Park Banded Stakes 3yo+ 0-40 (H)
£1432 £409 £205   **7f aw rnd**   **Going 53**   **-15 Slow**   Outside

1202 **NEUTRAL NIGHT 19** [2] R Brotherson 4-9-7 vis (40) D Holland 11/8 FAV: 5324331: Led 1f & remained   **47a**
handy, led ins last, styd on well for press: 1st win: eff at 6/7f, yet to convince at 1m: acts on fast, gd &
fibresand: suited by visor/blnks & banded company: see 1202, 297.
739 **MY GIRL PEARL 69** [8] M S Saunders 4-9-7 (40) M Savage(5) 10/1: 00400-02: b f Sri Pekan - Desert   3   **40a**
Bloom (Last Tycoon) Handy & led over 3f out till ins last, no extra: op 7/1, 10 wk abs: h'cap plcd '03 for J M
Bradley (rtd 50, AW h'cap unplcd, rtd 17a): plcd twice in '02 (auct mdn & nurs, rtd 67 & 51a): eff at 6/7f on firm,
gd & fibresand, sharp/undul or gall trk.
1368 **RATHMULLAN 10** [3] E A Wheeler 5-9-7 bl (40) Liam Jones(7) 7/1: 00-00343: Handy, short of room when   1½   **37a**
stumbled over 3f out, no impress over 1f btn: op 7/1, handy from 3f out: prob handles fibresand: see 905.
1129 **ROVING VIXEN 23** [1] J L Spearing 3-8-9 P (40) A Daly 10/1: 00-004: b f Foxhound - Rend Rover   nk   **36a**
(Monseigneur) Prom early, no impress fnl 2f: op 7/1, cheek pieces: unplcd prev up to 1m.
4622} **BEN KENOBI 212** [4]6-9-7 (30) R Ffrench 11/1: 004100-5: In tch till over 1f out, reapp.   2½   **31a**
1425 **PEARTREE HOUSE 7** [5]10-9-7 (30) A Culhane 6/1: 0-000066: Bhd halfway, nvr a factor: qck reapp.   1½   **28a**
1073 **WESTMEAD ETOILE 29** [7]4-9-7 vis (40) D Corby(3) 9/2: 300-0307: Led/dsptd lead till 3f out, sn btn.   8   **12a**
1328 **DUNMIDOE 12** [6]4-9-7 (35) G Carter 16/1: 00-00500-08: Sn bhd & no ch 3f out.   10   **0a**
8 Ran   Time 1m 31.00 (4.80)   Owned: Mr Raymond N R Auld   Trained: Pershore

1566

8.30 Stay At The Holiday Inn Dunstall Park Banded Stakes 3yo+ 0-35 (H)
£1435 £410 £205   **6f aw rnd**   **Going 53**   **-03 Slow**   Inside

1314 **WELSH WHISPER 13** [4] S A Brookshaw 5-9-6 (30) N Chalmers(5) 12/1: 4005661: b f Overbury - Grugiar   **42a**
(Red Sunset) Dwelt, in tch, rdn & led over 1f out, rdn clr: 1st win: eff at 6f, has tried up to 9.4f prev: acts
on fibresand & suited by banded company.
1314 **COUNTRYWIDE GIRL 13** [2] A Berry 5-9-6 (35) P Bradley(5) 3/1: 5364332: Led till over 1f out, edged   6   **27a**
left & no impress dist: op 4/1: acts on fast, hvy & fibresand: see 663.
1408 **LEVELLED 8** [5] D W Chapman 10-9-6 (35) A Culhane 5/2 FAV: 4550233: Chsd ldrs, wknd over 1f out.   ¾   **24a**
1415 **SECOND GENERATION 8** [7] R J Hodges 7-9-6 (30) R L Moore 4/1: 6/0//0-5534: Sn outpcd, kept on   hd   **24a**
late, nrst fnl: op 11/2: btr 1415 (polytrack).
1545* **TINY TIM 1** [1]6-9-6 BL (35) R J Killoran(7) 11/4: 42352215: Cl-up, carried left & no extra over 1f   nk   **23a**
out: 1st time blnks, scored on turf yesterday: see 1545.
2956} **MADAME ROUX 293** [6]6-9-6 (30) G Carter 14/1: 00/0000-6: Dwelt & sn bhd on reapp.   5   **8a**
1309 **VAUDEVIRE 13** [3]3-8-10 bl (30) T Hamilton(3) 14/1: 6-6037: Cl-up, ch 2f out, wknd: see 1309.   3   **0a**
7 Ran   Time 1m 16.19(3.39)   Owned: Mr S A Brookshaw   Trained: Shrewsbury

Official Going GOOD/SOFT.

1567

1.55 Joseph Heler Cheshire Cheese Lily Agnes Conditions Stakes 2yo (B)
£12325 £4675 £2338   **5f16y rnd**   **Good**   **Slow**   Inside

1161* **DANCE NIGHT 21** [1] B A McMahon 2-8-10 G Gibbons 15/8 FAV: 211: Trkd ldrs, switched right & rdn   **97**
to lead over 1f out, styd on strongly for press: hvly bckd, jockey gvn 1 day careless riding ban: eff at 5f on gd &
gd/soft grnd, sharp/turning or stiff trk: tough & useful colt: see 1161, 920.
1249 **SAPPHIRE DREAM 16** [2] A Bailey 2-8-5 T E Durcan 8/1: 22: Chsd ldrs, short of room over 1f out,   1½   **86**
kept on well for press ins last: acts on gd & hvy grnd, stiff/undul or sharp/turning trk: looks nailed on for a mdn.
1256* **BEAVER PATROL 16** [3] R F Johnson Houghton 2-8-13 S Carson 100/30: 13: Dwelt, keen, short of   hd   **93**
room on rail 2f out & again ins fnl 1f, fin well: acts on gd & gd/soft grnd: 6f sure to suit, wld have gone v

close with a clr run, keep in mind for more success: see 1256.

1041* **CANTON 32** [6] R Hannon 2-8-10   Dane O'Neill   7/1: 614: Slow away & bhd, rdn & styd on well wide   ½   88
fnl 1f, nrst fin: type to win again, poss at 6f: acts on polytrack & gd grnd, see 1041 (AW).

1386* **MONASHEE PRINCE 9** [5]2-8-10   N Pollard   14/1: 215: Led, rdn & hdd over 1f out, no extra: prob   nk   87
ran to form of 1386.

1149 **KING AFTER 22** [7]2-8-10   L Dettori   25/1: 166: Led/dsptd lead, rdn & no extra when bumped over 1f   ½   85
out: shwd gd speed from mod draw: prob handles gd grnd & polytrack: see 931.

1212 **IM AIMEE 19** [8]2-8-7 (2ow)   S Drowne   40/1: 2637: Chsd ldrs, btn dist: poor draw: see 1212, 882.   1¼   78

962* **TARA TARA 37** [9]2-8-8   R Winston   8/1: 18: Dwelt, nvr able to chall: bckd, poor draw.   hd   78

1037* **MITCHELLAND 32** [4]2-8-8   J Fanning   10/1: 419: Trkd ldrs, switched wide over 1f out, sn rdn/btn &   1¼   74
eased: much btr 1037 (hvy).

9 Ran   Time 1m 02.72 (2.92)   Owned: Mr J C Fretwell   Trained: Tamworth

---

1568   2.25 Listed Letheby & Christopher Cheshire Oaks Fillies 3yo   (A)
£29000 £11000 £5500   **1m3f79y**   **Good**   **Fast**   Inside

1258 **HIDDEN HOPE 16** [1] G Wragg 3-8-9   (75)   T E Durcan   14/1: 00-21: Chsd ldr trav well, rdn to lead   106
over 1f out, styd on strongly: 1st win: clearly liked this step up to 11.5f: acts on gd & gd/soft grnd: v
useful & prog filly, looks ready for the step into Gr 3 company: see 1258.

989 **MENHOUBAH 39** [2] C E Brittain 3-8-9 p   D Holland   7/1: 434-2302: Tried to make all, hdd dist & no   2½   101
extra: rest well held: fine front rng eff, stays 11.5f: acts on firm, gd & dirt: see 599.

4937* **CRYSTAL CURLING 189** [4] B W Hills 3-8-9   M Hills   7/2 FAV: 21-3: ch f Peintre Celebre - State   2   98
Crystal (High Estate): In tch, rdn & hdwy to chase front pair 3f out, no prog dist: well clr rem, hvly bckd, reapp:
won 2nd of just 2 '03 starts (mdn): half sister to a 12f scorer: wng form at 7f, stays 11.5f & cld get further:
acts on fast & soft grnd, gall or sharp/turning trks: encouraging return, entitled to progress.
1 Oct'03 Yarm 7.0sft 88- D: 2 Sep'03 Nott 6.1g/f 79- D:

4972* **SI SI AMIGA 186** [8] B W Hills 3-8-9   Martin Dwyer   12/1: 1-4: b f Desert Style - No Hard Feelings   6   89
(Alzao): Rear, pushed along halfway, only mod prog: reapp: sole start wnr '03 (mdn, impress): dam an 11/12f
performer: wng form at 7f, mid-dists shld suit: acts on gd grnd & a stiff/gall trk: can go well fresh: only 2nd
career start, type to progress at 12f+.   1 Nov'03 Newm 7g/f 85- D:

1169 **QASIRAH 21** [5]3-8-9 BL   (100)   P Robinson   12/1: 120-05: b f Machiavellian - Altaweelah (Fairy King)   5   82
Keen & held up, rdn & no impress 3f out: tried blnks & no improvement: '03 debut wnr (fills mdn), subs Listed
rnr-up: eff at 7f, mid-dist pedigree: acts on firm & fast grnd, stiff/gall trk & can go well fresh.
2 Aug'03 Newm 7fm 94- A: 1 Jul'03 Newb 7g/f 84- D:

1150 **ITHACA 22** [6]3-8-9   W Ryan   7/1: 120-36: Mid-div, rdn & no prog fnl 3f: btr 1150 (7f).   3   78
     ALEXANDER DUCHESS 17 [7]3-8-9   J Murtagh   11/1: 42161-67: Sn struggling in rear, Irish raider.   11   65

4526* **DERAASAAT 218** [9]3-8-9   (95)   R Hills   11/2: 01-8: Chsd ldrs, btn 3f out: op 9/2, reapp.   2   62

4408* **PROUD TRADITION 225** [3]3-8-9   L Dettori   5/1: 1-9: Chsd ldrs early, lost place halfway: reapp.   dist   0

9 Ran   Time 2m 27.3 (3.5)   Owned: Mrs Stephen Lussier   Trained: Newmarket

---

1569   2.55 Totesport Chester Cup Heritage Handicap 4yo+   (B)
£69600 £26400 £13200   **2m2f147y**   **Good**   **Slow**   Outside   [116]

1112* **ANAK PEKAN 25** [4] M A Jarvis 4-8-2   (90)   P Robinson   2/1 FAV: 21222-11: Keen, al well plcd trkg   103+
ldrs, led dist, rdn clr: hvly bckd: eff at 2m/2m2f & a thorough stayer: acts on fast & gd/soft, likes to race
with/force the pace: handles a gall or sharp/turning trk: useful & prog stayer on side: see 1112.

1418 **MISTERNANDO 7** [18] M R Channon 4-8-13   (101)   S Hitchcott(3)   33/1: 22611-02: b c Hernando -   5   107+
Mistinguett (Doyoun): Held up, hdwy wide halfway, rdn/chall 2f out, not pace of wnr fnl 1f: ultra-prog in '03, won
10 times, incl List fnl start: eff at 14f/2m2f on firm & gd, any trk: outstanding run from widest draw & had an
awkward passage: appeals as the type to progress into Gr company, should be followed.
1 Nov'03 Muss 16g/f 101-(94) A: 1 Oct'03 Newb 16g/f 98-90 C: 2 Sep'03 Asco 16.2fm 91-88 C:
2 Sep'03 Ayr 17.5g/f 89-85 D: 1 Sep'03 Good 16fm 83-80 D: 1 Aug'03 Ripo 16gd 82-73 E:
1 Aug'03 Ches 16.4g/f 80-75 F: 1 Aug'03 Sand 16.4g/f 74-70 D: 1 Aug'03 Nott 16.0gd 72-62 F:

4796* **BIG MOMENT 200** [11] Mrs A J Perrett 6-8-12   (96)   D Holland   7/1: 420440-3: ch g Be My Guest -   ¾   102+
Petralona (Alleged): Held up, rdn when short of room 3f out, styd on for press ins last, nrst fin: 7 wk jumps abs,
dual nov wnr (rtd 148h, eff at 2m/2m5f on firm & hvy): rnr-up in this race in '03: h'cap rnr-up in '02: suited by
14f/2m2f on firm & gd/soft, any trk: prob 2nd without trouble & deserves a change of luck in similar.
2 May'03 Ches 18.7fm 97-92 B: 2 Jul'02 Newm 16.1g/s 98-97 C: 1 Aug'02 Good 14g/f 92-89 B:
1 Jul'01 Donc 12g/f 92- D: 2 Jun'01 Good 11g/f 92- D: 2 May'01 Ches 10.3fm 92- D:

5033} **DISTANT PROSPECT 179** [5] A M Balding 7-8-6   (90)   Martin Dwyer   15/2: 4/00303-4: b g Namaqualand -   ½   95
Ukraine's Affair (The Minstrel): Held up, rdn & styd on fnl 3f, nvr pace to chall: 3 month jumps abs (nov wnr, rtd
126h, eff at 2m on gd & gd/soft): h'cap plcd '03: val h'cap plcd '02 (rtd 95): thorough stayer, best at 2m2f:
handles firm, likes gd/soft & hvy, any trk: useful performer on an easy surface.
2 Jun'02 Hayd 16.2sft 93-92 C: 1 Oct'01 Newm 18g/s 95-88 B:

1361 **MANA DARGENT 11** [10]7-8-5   (89)   J Fanning   28/1: 01433-05: Mid-div, hdwy halfway when short of   shd   94
room 3f out, sn onepace: thorough stayer, best at beloved Ascot.

1112 **PONDERON 25** [12]4-8-1   (89)   S Carson   13/2: 30131-06: Mid-div, hdwy to go handy halfway, led over   1½   92
4f out till over 1f out, wknd.

1232 **RANDOM QUEST 18** [3]6-8-4   (88)   F Norton   12/1: 23250-07: Towards rear, switched wide & short of   ¾   90
room over 3f out, kept on late for press: ran well for a long way & gave away plenty of grnd racing wide.

4796} **NUMITAS 200** [2]4-8-3   (91)   J Mackay   20/1: 302010-8: Mid-div, lost pl 7f out, kept on late for press.   nk   92

1361 **KRISTENSEN 11** [15]5-7-13 p   (83)   J Quinn   16/1: 56233-59: Mid-div when lost pl 4f out, no ch after.   2½   83

5009} **ALMIZAN 182** [8]4-8-0   (88)   C Catlin   33/1: 101564-0: 10th: Mid-div, rdn & btn 3f out, reapp.   9   79

5009} **COLLIER HILL 182** [9]6-8-12   (96)   E Ahern   25/1: 160303-0: 11th: Held up, hdwy halfway, btn 2f out.   ¾   87

695 **GRALMANO 74** [1]9-8-1   (85)   P Fessey   20/1: 03102-00: 12th: Prom, wknd 5f out, 7 wk jumps abs.   11   67

5008} **ARCHDUKE FERDINAND 182** [14]6-8-4   (88)   J F Egan   33/1: 052400-0: 13th: Mid-div, lost place when   9   62
short of room halfway, no threat after: reapp.

4280} **RAYSHAN 235** [6]4-9-2   (104)   R Winston   33/1: 521356-0: 14th: Mid-div, strug 6f out: jumps fit,   3   74
new yard & has been gelded.

743 **GRACILIS 69** [7]7-7-12 (2oh)   (80)   Lisa Jones(3)   25/1: 30000/-00: 15th: Sn bhd, jumps fit.   3   50

1431 **SWING KING 13** [16]5-9-10   (108)   K Fallon   16/1: 31533-50: 16th: Prom, wknd 5f out, eased: btr 1431.   6   71

926* **RAHWAAN 40** [13]5-8-3   (87)   P Hanagan   12/1: 55034-10: 17th: Led till 4f out, sn btn, lame: see 926.   22   33

17 Ran   Time 4m 10.9 (12)   Owned: HRH Sultan Ahmad Shah   Trained: Newmarket

---

1570   **3.30 Tess Graham Memorial Handicap Stakes 3yo 0-90 (C)**   **[97]**
£13065 £4020 £2010   **6f18y rnd**   **Good/Soft**   **Fast** Inside

1344 **LAKE GARDA 11** [1] B A McMahon 3-9-2 (85) G Gibbons 8/1: 2001-531: Led/dsptd lead, led over 3f   **93**
out, strongly prsd fnl 2f, drvn out, gamely: nicely bckd, fair time: eff at 5/6f on firm & gd/soft grnd, prob any
trk: tough & genuine, may most of v fav No 1 draw: see 1344.
1191* **FUN TO RIDE 20** [5] B W Hills 3-9-7 (90) M Hills 3/1 FAV: 22-12: Trkd ldrs, bumped dist but sn ev   *1*   **94**
ch, rdn & no extra nr fin: hvly bckd tho' op 9/4, h'cap bow: acts on fast & gd/soft grnd: see 1191 (mdn).
1473 **SESSAY 4** [6] D Nicholls 3-8-0 (69) A Nicholls 25/1: 320-43: Mid-div, hdwy trav well over 2f out,   *1*   **71**
no extra for press ins fnl 1f: h'cap bow, qck reapp: suited by 6f: win similar on this evidence: see 1473.
1186 **INSTANT RECALL 20** [2] B J Meehan 3-8-9 (78) D Holland 5/1: 3104: Rear, styd on for press, nrst   *1½*   **76**
fin: eff at 6f, return to 7f will suit: acts on polytack & gd/soft grnd: slow start gave away gd draw advantage.
4495*)**ACE CLUB 220** [12]3-8-6 (75) R Hills 16/1: 21-5: ch g Indian Rocket - Presently (Cadeaux   *1*   **71+**
Genereux) Held up, short of room 2f out, kept on ins last: reapp/h'cap bow: won 2nd of just 2 '03 starts (mdn):
wng form at 5f, 6f likely to suit: acts on polytack & gd grnd: gd run from poor high draw, keep in mind for
similar. 1 Sep'03 Muss 5gd 78- D: 2 Sep'03 Pont 5g/f 74- E:
898* **PRESTO SHINKO 43** [9]3-8-9 (78) K Fallon 7/1: 033-16: Trkd ldrs, hung left & btn ins last, saddle   *½*   **72**
slipped: tchd 12/1, 6 wk abs: ran well for a long way from poor draw, worth another look after 898 (AW mdn).
3368*)**BO MCGINTY 275** [15]3-8-10 (79) P Hanagan 25/1: 301-7: ch g Fayruz - Georges Park Lady (Tirol)   *3*   **67**
U.r. bef start, pushed along mid-div, nvr on terms: reapp/h'cap bow: won fnl start '03 (auct mdn, lightly rcd):
suited by stiff 5f, 6f shld suit this term: acts on fast grnd, stiff trks & can go well fresh: poor draw here.
1 Aug'03 Carl 5g/f 81- E:
1488* **BENBAUN 4** [3]3-9-4 (6ex) (87) D Corby(3) 5/1: 16120-18: Led, hdd bef halfway & bumped over 1f out, *3½*   **68**
sn btn: nicely bckd under a pen, quick reapp: btr 1488 (fast).
1344 **PICCOLO PRINCE 11** [10]3-7-13 (68) J Quinn 12/1: 1212129: Mid-div, no impress dist: poor draw.   *shd*   **49**
914 **LA VIE EST BELLE 42** [13]3-8-7 (76) A McCarthy 50/1: 16320-60: 10th: b f Makbul - La Belle Vie   *1½*   **54**
(Indian King) Mid-div, no impress fnl 2f: 6 wk abs: fills auct mdn scorer '03, subs h'cap plcd & nov auct rnr-up:
eff at 5.7f/6.5f on firm & gd grnd: can force the pace: poor draw here.
2 Oct'03 Nott 6.1fm 76-(78) F: 1 Aug'03 Bath 5.7fm 75-(77) E: 2 Jun'03 Warw 5g/f 68- E:
1186 **GO YELLOW 20** [4]3-8-4 (73) S Carson 16/1: 0626-00: 11th: Outpcd, hdwy when no room dist, eased.   *shd*   **51**
1216* **COMMANDO SCOTT 19** [11]3-8-9 (78) F Lynch 33/1: 4340-10: 12th: Al rear from poor draw.   *shd*   **55**
3185) **Catch The Wind 284** [16]3-8-13 (82) J Murtagh 40/1:0 919 **Ticero 41** [7]3-8-11 (80) T E Durcan 40/1:0
14 Ran   Time 1m 15.9 (2.8)   Owned: Mr J C Fretwell   Trained: Tamworth

---

1571   **4.05 Weatherbys Bank Maiden Stakes Div 1 2yo (D)**
£8288 £2550 £1275   **5f16y rnd**   **Good/Soft**   **Slow** Inside

1256 **CATWALK CLERIC 16** [3] M J Wallace 2-9-0 K Fallon 1/1 FAV: 41: b c Orpen - Ministerial Model   **83+**
(Shalford) Trkd ldrs, eff to chall over 1f out, briefly outpcd but styd on for press to lead well ins last, going
away: hvly bckd: confirmed debut promise: eff at 5f, looks sure to relish 6f+: acts on gd/soft grnd, sharp/turning
trks: still green but got the hang of things cl-home & looks set to improve with racing.
1123 **TOWN HOUSE 23** [5] B P J Baugh 2-8-9 J Fanning 33/1: 502: gr f Paris House - Avondale Girl (Case   *1*   **74**
Law) Led, rdn & hdd well ins last, no extra: Mar 1st foal, dam a 5/6f wnr, incl juv success & also a sister to a
7f/1m wnr: eff at 5f, acts on gd/soft grnd & a sharp trk: sharp type, shld sn be winning.
1401 **THE CROOKED RING 8** [7] P D Evans 2-9-0 K Darley 7/2: 523: Chsd ldrs, rdn & onepcd dist: nicely   *nk*   **78**
bckd: acts on gd & gd/soft grnd: see 1401, 1190.
VICTORIA PEEK [1] D Nicholls 2-8-9 A Nicholls 8/1: 4: b f Cape Cross - Night Spirit (Night   *2*   **69**
Shift) Pushed along, styd on from over 1f out, not rch ldrs: Feb foal, 20,000gns purchase: half sister to a 5f juv
wnr abroad, dam a 6f 3yo wnr: got the hang of things late on, handles gd/soft & looks a likely improver.
1458 **AZA WISH 5** [6]2-8-9 S Righton 33/1: 05: Dwelt, sn outpcd: qck reapp.   *5*   **59**
1123 **CHILLY CRACKER 23** [4]2-8-9 Dale Gibson 5/1: 26: Chsd ldrs, bumped dist, sn btn: btr 1123.   *3½*   **52**
THE TERMINATOR [2]2-9-0 F Norton 14/1: 7: Dwelt & sn outpcd on debut: op 11/1.   *15*   **27**
7 Ran   Time 1m 04.44 (4.64)   Owned: Favourites Racing   Trained: Newmarket

---

1572   **4.40 David M Robinson Diamond Design Handicap Stakes 3yo 0-100 (C)**   **[107]**
£13683 £4210 £2105   **5f16y rnd**   **Good/Soft**   **Slow** Inside

1154 **MOSS VALE 22** [7] B W Hills 3-9-7 (100) M Hills 5/1: 5163-41: Mid-div, styd on for press fnl 1f   **111+**
to lead nr fin: hvly bckd: eff at 5/6f on fast & gd/soft grnd, sharp or stiff trks: impressive effort under
top-weight, v useful sprinter & List/Gr 3 company will suit: see 1154.
914 **GREEN MANALISHI 42** [8] D W P Arbuthnot 3-7-13 (78) J Quinn 9/1: 2551-422: Handy, led over 1f   *½*   **86**
out, hung left & hdd cl-home: nicely bckd, 6 wk abs: acts on firm, gd/soft & polytack: met a smart rival, see 914.
4605) **WANCHAI LAD 214** [14] D Nicholls 3-8-9 (88) K Darley 50/1: 1160-3: b c Danzero - Frisson (Slip   *3*   **90+**
Anchor) Bhd, strong run wide from over 1f out, nrst fin: reapp: auct mdn & nov auct stks scorer '03 (A Jarvis):
both wins at 5f, tried 6f, shaped as if a return to that trip will suit: eye-catching late prog from poor high-draw, one to keep in mind. 1 Sep'03 Redc 5fm 91- E: 1 Aug'03 Ripo 5gd 82- E:
1 **EMBASSY LORD 177** [5] J O'Reilly 3-7-12 (1ow)(10oh)b(82) J D O'Reilly 50/1: 221500-4: b g Mind   *½*   **78$**
Games - Keen Melody (Sharpen Up) Mid-div, hdwy tho' hung left over 2f out, switched right & styd on for press ins
last: 6 month abs: clmg grade scorer '03 (B J Meehan): eff at 6f on fast, gd/soft & fibresand, sharp/turning for
fair trks: best blnkd & can force the pace: poor draw, one to note when dropped in grade.
1 Aug'03 Yarm 6.0g/f 67-(62) F: 2 Aug'03 Wolv 6af 68a-(64) F: 2 Jul'03 Yarm 6.0gd 59- G:
1344 **FOURSQUARE 11** [6]3-8-13 (99) N Callan 4/1: 5102-15: Led till dist, no extra: hvly bckd.   *nk*   **92**
1509 **SIR ERNEST 3** [3]3-8-0 (2ow)(2oh) (75) Martin Dwyer 12/1: 04000-06: b g Daggers Drawn - Kyra Crown   *½*   **78**
(Astronef) Pushed in rear, late gains, nvr a threat: quick reapp: dual nov stks scorer '03, incl C/D: both wins at
5f, acts on fast grnd & both AWs, loves a sharp trk: slow start lost gd draw advantage.
1 Jun'03 Ches 5.1g/f 85- D: 1 Jun'03 Catt 5g/f 83- D: 2 Mar'03 Sout 5af 63a- F:
1400 **INCISE 8** [11]3-9-0 (93) L Dettori 14/1: 3201-67: Hmpd early & bhd, some hdwy fnl 2f, nvr dngr.   *1½*   **89**
1150 **LOCAL POET 22** [15]3-9-2 (95) G Gibbons 33/1: 6224-158: Rear, mod prog from poor draw.   *½*   **90**

CHESTER   WEDNESDAY 05.05.04   Lefthand, Very Tight Track

1106 **HARRY UP 25** [1]3-8-11 (90) M Fenton 100/30 FAV: 1040-239: Cl-up till dist, wknd: hvly bckd.   2½   80
3739*}**TRIBUTE 259** [12]3-8-1 (80) T P Queally 25/1: 63261-0: 10th: Hmpd early & towards rear, nvr able   hd   69
to chall from poor high-draw on reapp: has been gelded.
1002* **JOHNNY PARKES 35** [9]3-8-4 (83) P Robinson 13/2: 22215-10: 11th: Mid-div, switched wide & btn   nk   71
over 1f out: modest draw: btr 1002.
4247*}**DIVINE SPIRIT 233** [10]3-8-4 (83) P Hanagan 50/1: 442161-0: 12th: Hmpd early & sn bhd: poor draw.   1½   68
1441 **CHEEKY CHI 6** [4]3-7-12 (11oh) (66) D Fox(5) 20/1: 443140: 13th: Cl-up, btn 2f out: qck reapp.   3   56
1229 **Jadan 18** [13]3-7-12 (5oh)(72) J Mackay 50/1:0
1031* **Demolition Molly 33** [2]3-7-12 (7oh)t p(70) Lisa Jones(3) 12/1:0
15 Ran   Time 1m 03.21 (3.41)   Owned: Mr John C Grant   Trained: Lambourn

1573   5.15 Weatherbys Bank Maiden Stakes Div 2 2yo (D)
£8255 £2540 £1270   **5f16y rnd   Good/Soft   Slow**   Inside

1117 **TIVISKI 24** [1] E J Alston 2-8-9 W Supple 12/1: 341: Chsd ldrs, pushed along halfway, rdn & styd   82
on to lead well ins last, going away: op 9/1: eff at 5f on a sharp/turning or gall trk: acts on fast & gd/soft
grnd: prog with racing: see 1117 & 954.
1422 **ALPAGA LE JOMAGE 7** [6] B J Meehan 2-9-0 L Dettori 4/6 FAV: 332: Sn cl-up, rdn to chall over 1f   1½   81
out, hung left & not pace of wnr well ins last: hvly bckd at odds-on: see 1422 & 1190.
1237 **ON THE WATERLINE 18** [9] P D Evans 2-8-9 S Drowne 6/1: 23: Trkd ldrs, rdn & styd on well ins   nk   75
last, not pace of wnr: fine eff from widest draw: acts on gd & gd/soft: find similar on this evidence: see 1237.
954 **THEATRE OF DREAMS 39** [3] D Nicholls 2-9-0 A Nicholls 7/1: 54: b c Averti - Loch Fyne   hd   79
(Ardkinglass) Keen & led, rdn & hdd well ins last, no extra: Mar foal, cost 8,000gns: brother to a plcd 5f juv, dam
related to useful sprinters: handles gd/soft grnd: imprvd with forcing tactics today.
       PIPER LILY [1]2-8-9 F Norton 12/1: 5: b f Piccolo - Polly Golightly (Weldnaas) Dwelt & sn   2½   69
pushed along, not able to chall: Feb 1st foal, dam a multiple sprint wnr: sire high-class sprinter.
1343 **MYTTONS DREAM 11** [7]2-8-9 S Hitchcott(3) 33/1: 66: br f Diktat - Courtisane (Persepolis) Outpcd   1¾   66
& nvr on terms: Mar foal, cost 15,000 gns: related to sprint wnrs & wnrs abroad, dam a 7f juv wnr.
1237 **SHARP N FROSTY 18** [8]2-9-0 T E Durcan 20/1: 47: Sn outpcd & bhd: btr 1237.   13   45
7 Ran   Time 1m 04.86(5.06)   Owned: The Selebians   Trained: Preston

FOLKESTONE   THURSDAY 06.05.04   Righthand, Sharpish, Undulating Track

Official Going SOFT (HEAVY places).

1574   2.05 Cross Channel Maiden Auction Stakes 2yo (E)
£3455 £1063 £532   **5f str   Soft 90   -37 Slow**   Stands Side

       STRIKING ENDEAVOUR [1] G C Bravery 2-8-10 S Sanders 11/2: 1: b c Makbul - Nineteenth of May   79
(Horning) Made all, hung right & jnd dist, rdn & styd on strongly to assert ins last: op 9/2: March foal, 16,000gns
purchase: half-brother to 4 wnrs incl useful 1m/10f AW wnr Zanay: dam a 1m 3yo wnr: eff at 5f, likely to need
further in time: acts on soft & a sharp/undul trk: goes well fresh: gd start, likely to progress.
1380 **AGENT KENSINGTON 10** [3] R Hannon 2-8-2 R L Moore 1/2 FAV: 22: Sn handy, rdn to chall over 1f   2½   65
out, no extra ins last: well bckd at odds-on: prob handles soft grnd but btr 1380 (gd, debut).
1084 **ARTADI 29** [2] P M Phelan 2-8-3 J Quinn 25/1: 03: b f Bien Bien - Gibaltarik (Jareer) Chsd   4   58
ldrs, outpcd from 2f out: some improvement from debut: cheaply bght April foal, half-sister to several sprint juv
wnrs, dam a 5f juv wnr: poss handles soft grnd.
       JOSEAR [5] S C Williams 2-8-9 N Callan 25/1: 4: Rear, only mod late prog on debut.   ¾   62
       DUSTY DANE [4]2-8-9 T A Daly 25/1: 5: Cl-up 2f, wknd from halfway, t-strap.   ½   61
       TAIPAN TOMMY [6]2-8-13 C Catlin 33/1: 6: Sn outpcd & struggling.   5   55
931 **JOE NINETY 41** [7]2-8-9 Derek Nolan(7) 12/1: 567: Prom 2f, sn struggling: op 10/1, abs.   3   45
7 Ran   Time 1m 04.79 (6.39)   Owned: Unicorn Free Spirit Partnership   Trained: Newmarket

1575   2.35 Trans-Manche Maiden Stakes 3yo (D)
£3741 £1151 £576   **5f str   Soft 90   -06 Slow**   Stands Side

       EISTEDDFOD [9] P F I Cole 3-9-0 S Sanders 3/1 FAV: 1: ch g Cadeaux Genereux - Ffestiniog   75
(Efisio) Led far side group & overall ldr ins last, styd on strongly: debut: half-brother to useful 1m wnr Boston
Lodge: eff at 5f, shld get further: acts on soft grnd & a sharp/undul trk: type to prog & win again.
1228 **URBAN CALM 19** [1] R M H Cowell 3-8-9 M Henry 5/1: 42: Led overall stands side till ins last, no   3   63
extra: op 7/2: prob ran to form of 1228.
4128} **GENERAL FEELING 241** [2] S Kirk 3-9-0 P Dobbs 7/2: 3-3: b g General Monash - Kamadara (Kahyasi)   nk   67
Chsd ldrs stands side, kept on for press: reapp, has been gelded: plcd sole '03 start (rtd 77, auct mdn): eff at
5/6f: handles firm & soft grnd, sharp/turning & undul trks.
146 **EX MILL LADY 152** [6] John Berry 3-8-9 N Callan 20/1: 5-4: Cl-up stands side, kept on for press   1¾   59
fnl 2f: 5 mth abs, turf bow: handles soft grnd, return to 6f+ could suit.
1441 **VELVET TOUCH 7** [12]3-8-9 (57) W Ryan 7/1: 22-26065: Chsd wnr halfway far side, no impress dist.   ½   58$
1270 **INDIAN LILY 16** [11]3-8-9 G Baker 33/1: 506: Bhd far side, late prog, nrst fin: needs 6f+ & h'caps.   2½   52
1497 **GENEROUS SPIRIT 4** [13]3-9-0 Paul Eddery 14/1: 007: Chsd ldrs far side till 2f out, qck reapp.   ½   56
3246} **CINNAMON RIDGE 281** [10]3-9-0 L Keniry(3) 16/1: 00-8: Chsd wnr far side till over 2f out, sn   1¾   53
wknd: reapp, op 20/1, gelded.
5013} **WILLHEGO 182** [8]3-9-0 N Pollard 16/1: 000-9: Stands side, nvr on terms: op 12/1, reapp.   1   50
1044 **RADLETT LADY 33** [4]3-8-9 M Howard(7) 25/1: 00: 10th: In tch stands side till halfway.   3   39
481 **NOBLE MOUNT 101** [5]3-9-0 J Mackay 25/1: 500: 11th: Towards centre, dwelt, nvr a factor.   3   38
1044 **Sapphire Sky 33** [3]3-8-9 B Doyle 50/1:0   1119 **Pass Go 25** [7]3-9-0 C Catlin 20/1:0
13 Ran   Time 1m 03.21 (4.81)   Owned: Elite Racing Club   Trained: Whatcombe

1576

3.05 Eurotunnel 10th Anniversary Handicap Stakes Fillies 3yo 0-75 (E) [80]
£3591 £1105 £553 **6f str** **Soft 90** -07 Slow Stands Side

1374* **MELAINA 10** [10] M S Saunders 3-8-10 (7ex)p (62) P Makin(5) 10/1: 61-20611: Made all, shaken up & 67
just held on ins last: eff at 6f on fibresand & soft: likes forcing tactics & a sharp trk: see 1374, 316 & 73.

4903} **PRINCESS GALADRIEL 192** [9] J R Best 3-7-12 (50) D Kinsella 25/1: 0040-2: b f Magic Ring - Prim hd 54
Lass (Reprimand) Rear, rdn & green over 1f out, switched & strong run cl-home, just failed: reapp: unplcd '03
(rtd 58 & 31a): eff at 6f, return to 7f in similar could suit: handles soft grnd & a sharp/undul trk.

268 **INTRIGUING GLIMPSE 128** [3] Miss B Sanders 3-9-5 (71) N Callan 11/1: 60113-3: Keen & handy, no 1½ 71
extra ins last: 4 mth abs: acts on polytrack & soft grnd: return to minimum trip shld suit: see 268 & 217 (5f).

1417 **BOHOLA FLYER 8** [8] R Hannon 3-9-7 (73) R Smith 3/1 JT FAV: 002-1464: Chsd ldr 2f out, no extra 1¼ 69
dist: acts on gd, soft & polytrack: see 1417, 1116 & 1044.

1338* **CREWES MISS ISLE 12** [2]3-9-3 (69) S Whitworth 10/1: 420-4615: Dwelt & rear, hmpd over 1f out, 1½ 61
kept on late: could impr on this in similar: handles firm, soft & fibresand: see 1338, 466.

1255 **RISE 17** [5]3-8-12 bl (64) B Swarbrick(5) 16/1: 0400-006: Sn pushed along: see 494. shd 56
1404 **BEST FORCE 9** [4]3-8-5 (57) C Catlin 9/1: 500-47: Chsd wnr, btn dist: btr 1404 (gd). ½ 48
1392 **LADY OF THE LINKS 10** [7]3-8-4 (56) J Quinn 11/1: 5400-48: Dwelt & sn struggling rear: see 1392. 7 32
1239 **WHISTFUL 19** [1]3-9-2 (68) S Sanders 3/1 JT FAV: 0542-39: Cl-up till 2f out, sn btn/eased: 3 38
reportedly unsuited by the soft grnd: btr 1239 (gd).

1239 **CHIQITITA 19** [6]3-8-3 bl (55) R L Moore 14/1: 600-0000: 10th: b f Saddlers' Hall - Funny Cut 6 13
(Sure Blade) Slowly away & sn rdn to race in tch, struggling halfway: unplcd '03 (rtd 67 & 24a, M Wigham).

10 Ran Time 1m 16.86 (5.86) Owned: Bali Royal Racing Trained: Wells

1577

3.40 Entente Cordiale Handicap Stakes 3yo 46-55 (F) [67]
£2968 £848 £424 **7f str** **Soft 90** -19 Slow Stands Side

1070 **PICKLE 30** [1] S C Williams 3-9-2 (55) S Sanders 13/2: 3041: b f Piccolo - Crackle (Anshan) In 63
tch, hdwy to lead over 1f out, rdn out: h'cap bow: op 11/1: unplcd prev at 6f, imprvd for step up to 7f: handles
soft grnd & polytrack, sharp/undul trks.

1529 **KNICKYKNACKIENOO 29** [4] A G Newcombe 3-9-0 (53) S Whitworth 4/1: 0060-422: Dwelt & rear, hdwy 2 56
to press wnr over 1f out, wknd cl-home: clr of rem: see 1085.

1529* **THREE WELSHMEN 3** [5] B R Millman 3-9-6 (7ex)bl (59) J Quinn 7/2 JT FAV: 50-00513: Keen & led till 6 52
over 1f out, wknd: op 4/1: qck reapp: btr 1529 (1m).

510 **VRISAKI 97** [8] Miss D Mountain 3-9-2 (55) G Carter 20/1: 00-204: Chsd ldrs, no impress over 1f 3½ 43
out: 3 mth abs: btr 284 (fibresand).

1359 **HEAD BOY 12** [7]3-9-2 (55) R L Moore 7/2 JT FAV: 0-400565: Chsd ldrs, lost pl halfway, no ch after. 1¾ 41
1529 **LARAD 3** [2]3-8-8 bl (47) Derek Nolan(6) 7/1: 5513346: Chsd ldr till over 2f out, fdd: qck reapp. 3½ 28
164 **BE MY ALIBI 150** [6]3-8-10 (49) B Swarbrick(5) 33/1: 405000-7: ch f Daggers Drawn - Join The Party 4 23
(Be My Guest) Rear, struggling fnl 3f: reapp: plcd '03 (rtd 69, auct mdn, AW unplcd, rtd 62a, J S Moore): eff at
5f, prob handles soft grnd & fibresand.

1330 **JESSE SAMUEL 13** [3]3-8-7 (1oh) (45) W Ryan 16/1: 0000-048: Al towards rear & t.o.. 27 0
1085 **LIVIA 29** [9]3-8-11 BL (50) R Havlin 11/1: 0604069: Prom, strug halfway: blnks: poor run. 6 0

9 Ran Time 1m 31.85 (7.65) Owned: Mr S P Tindall Trained: Newmarket

1578

4.15 Channel Tunnel Handicap Stakes 3yo+ 0-70 (E) [70]
£3523 £1084 £542 **6f str** **Soft 90** +14 Fast Stands Side

1221 **CAUSTIC WIT 19** [11] M S Saunders 6-9-0 P (56) P Makin(5) 12/1: 3030-101: Made all against far 68
rail, clr over 2f out, rdn to hold on well ins last: best time of day: all wins at 6f, eff at 5f: loves to race
with/force the pace on fast, soft or fibresand: suited by application of cheek pieces today: see 384.

1293 **ANOTHER GLIMPSE 15** [6] Miss B Sanders 6-9-11 t (67) N Callan 11/2: 50-41002: Mid-div & outpcd ½ 77
halfway, closed well ins last, no reach wnr: acts on fast, soft & polytrack: see 384.

1255 **TAYIF 17** [9] Andrew Reid 8-9-3 t (59) S Carson 5/1 CO FAV: 2602053: Prom till outpcd halfway, 1 66
kept on ins last, not reach wnr: clr of rem: likely type for similar: see 407, 340 & 328.

1465 **GLENCOE SOLAS 6** [4] S Kirk 4-9-10 (66) P Dobbs 5/1 CO FAV: 25600-64: Rear, late gains, nvr a 5 63
threat to leading trio: qck reapp: acts on fast & gd, prob handles soft: see 1465.

913 **LOCH LAIRD 43** [2]9-8-12 (54) G Baker 8/1: 00-00105: Rear, mod gains for press: abs: btr 846. 3½ 45
902 **FIREWORK 44** [3]6-9-7 p (63) C Catlin 14/1: 420-0006: Chsd wnr till over 1f out: abs: see 628. 3 48
1533 **OASES 2** [7]5-9-4 (60) S Whitworth 8/1 CO FAV: 00-02067: Dwelt & al bhd: qck reapp: btr 976. 3½ 39
1255 **ARABIAN KNIGHT 17** [5]4-9-2 (58) R L Moore 20/1: 06-00008: Struggling halfway: see 960. 1 35
1336 **FIRE CAT 13** [8]5-7-12 (40) D Kinsella 22/1: 000-0009: Chsd ldrs till 2f out: see 1201. 1 15
1440* **DOCTORED 7** [1]3-8-9 p (61) B Doyle 10/1: 0046110: 10th: Sn drvn & struggling halfway: btr 1440. 1¾ 33
1442 **SEA THE WORLD 7** [10]4-8-11 vis (53) J Quinn 12/1: 5132600: 11th: Chsd ldrs, hung left & btn 2f out. nk 24

11 Ran Time 1m 15.61 (4.61) Owned: Mrs Sandra Jones Trained: Wells

1579

4.50 Samphire Hoe Handicap Stakes 3yo+ 46-55 (F) [59]
£3066 £876 £438 **1m1f149y** **Soft 90** -65 Slow Outside

1307 **GOT TO BE CASH 14** [1] W M Brisbourne 5-9-0 (45) B Swarbrick(5) 3/1: 0260-421: Rear, smooth hdwy 57
to lead over 1f out, rdn clr despite hanging left: first win, slow time: eff btwn 1m/12.5f on firm & soft grnd,
prob any trk: see 893.

1342 **SHAPE UP 12** [6] T Keddy 4-9-5 bl (50) P Doe 8/1: 42640-32: Trkd ldr & briefly led over 1f out, sn 5 54
no impress on wnr: op 13/2: eff btwn 9.7 & 12f: see 1342.

1132 **LUCEFER 24** [4] G C H Chung 6-9-1 (46) Dean Williams(7) 12/1: 3412-003: Keen in rear, late gains, 1 48
nvr a threat to ldrs: prob stays a sharp 9.7f: could impr on this with more enterprising tactics: see 1132.

768 **SHAMAN 67** [5] G L Moore 7-9-0 (45) R L Moore 9/2: 6600-504: b g Fraam - Magic Maggie (Beveled) 2½ 44
Trkd ldrs, no impress fnl 2f: abs: 8 wk jumps abs (Jan '04 h'cap hdle wnr, rtd 107h, 2m, fast & soft): '03 AW
h'cap wnr, turf unplcd (rtd 47, h'cap): AW h'cap rnr-up '02, turf unplcd (rtd 61, clmr): eff at 1m/10f, stays a

FOLKESTONE THURSDAY 06.05.04 Righthand, Sharpish, Undulating Track

sharp 12f: acts on firm, soft & polytrack, any trk, likes Lingfield. 1 Jan'03 Ling 10ap 53a-51 F: 2 Aug'02 Ling 10ap 52a-50 F: 1 Dec'01 Ling 10ap 65a-58 F: 1 Oct'01 Sali 10gd 58-52 E: 2 Jun'01 Brig 10gd 56- F:

1379 **ENCORE ROYALE 10** [2]4-9-5 (50) N Callan 20/1: 25000-05: b f Royal Applause - Verbena (Don't Forget Me) Keen chasing ldrs, btn 2f out: appr h'cap rnr-up '03: unplcd '02 (rtd 61): eff over a stiff/undul 1m, handles firm & fast grnd. 2 Jun'03 Sali 8fm 57-56 E: *2* **46**

1273 **ROYAL RACER 16** [7]6-9-5 (50) N Pollard 5/2 FAV: 350/0-136: Led till dist, wknd qckly: bckd. *2* **43**

DALON 166 [8]5-9-8 (53) M Tebbutt 9/1: 241614-7: Prom, lost pl after 3f, no ch fnl 2f: ex-Polish. *¾* **45**

29 **VIVA ATLAS ESPANA 124** [3]4-9-0 (45) S Sanders 25/1: 0/0060-08: Al rear, eased fnl 2f: abs. *27* **0**

8 Ran Time 2m 12.92 (14.92) Owned: Mrs B Penton Trained: Nesscliffe

1580

5.25 Cote D'opale Median Auction Maiden Stakes Div 1 3-4yo (F)
£2954 £844 £422 **1m1f149y** **Soft 90** **-73 Slow** Outside

1321 **MAGIC AMIGO 13** [9] J R Jenkins 3-8-7 (73) W Ryan 11/2: 05420-21: Mid-div, hdwy to chall when hmpd over 1f out, switched & rdn to lead cl-home: op 4/1: eff at 6/7f, now stays a sharp 9.7f well: acts on fast, soft & fibresand: see 1321. **73**

1259 **EXTRA COVER 17** [2] R Charlton 3-8-7 (75) P Dobbs 2/5 FAV: 5-222: Led, hung left 4f out & veered sharply left over 1f out, hdd cl-home: well bckd at odds-on: acts on gd, soft & polytrack: has ability but lkd a tricky ride & threw this away today: see 1259 & 1021. *hd* **72**

PLAY THE MELODY [5] C Tinkler 3-8-7 J Quinn 14/1: 3: b g Revoque - Dumayla (Shernazar) Dwelt, rear, styd on for press fnl 2f, not reach front pair: encouraging intro: half-brother to wnrs at 12f/2m: stays a sharp 9f & looks sure to relish 10f+: one to note over further. *1¾* **70+**

53 **MAXIMINUS 170** [7] M Madgwick 4-9-8 L Keniry(3) 33/1: 0/00-4: b g The West - Candarela (Damister) Mid-div, eff 3f out, onepace: clr of rem on reapp, 8 wk jumps abs (plcd, rtd 108h, mdn hdle, 2m, fast grnd): unplcd & mod form prev on the level: stays a sharp 9f & handles soft grnd. *shd* **70$**

5018} **VICARIO 182** [3]3-8-7 J Mackay 33/1: 00-5: Chsd ldrs, struggling fnl 2f: abs, gelded. *6* **62**

KILINDINI [10]3-8-8 (1ow) S Sanders 16/1: 6: Trkd ldrs, chall 2f out, hmpd over 1f out & sn btn/eased: op 20/1, debut. *1½* **61**

BAYOU PRINCESS [4]3-8-2 C Catlin 40/1: 7: Mid-div, no ch fnl 2f, debut. *7* **45**

4948} **RAINSBOROUGH HILL 189** [6]3-8-7 V Slattery 33/1: 000-8: Slow away, al bhd, no ch 3f out: reapp. *7* **40**

1340 **SALFORD ROCKET 12** [1]4-9-8 T G McLaughlin 50/1: 0-09: Al bhd. *9* **28**

1130 **HEYWARD PLACE 24** [8]4-9-3 t P Doe 100/1: 000: 10th: Chsd ldr till halfway, wknd qckly & virt p.u. *dist* **0**

10 Ran Time 2m 13.69 (15.69) Owned: Mr Kevin Reddington Trained: Royston

1581

6.00 Cote D'opale Median Auction Maiden Stakes Div 2 3-4yo (F)
£2954 £844 £422 **1m1f149y** **Soft 90** **-74 Slow** Outside

1283 **AMANKILA 16** [6] M L W Bell 3-8-2 J Mackay 4/5 FAV: 031: Trkd ldr 4f out, ev ch going well when left clr over 2f out, easily: well bckd at odds-on: eff around 9.7f/10f on gd & soft grnd, sharp/undul trk: lkd the likely wnr when handed this race by rival's sad demise: see 1283. **62**

1398 **BALLYLIFFIN 9** [9] S Kirk 3-8-7 P Dobbs 33/1: 02: b g Daggers Drawn - Blues Quartet (Cure The Blues) Slow away & sn rdn rear, styd on for press fnl 2f to take remote 2nd: well bhd on debut prev. *11* **55**

1241 **MUSLIN 19** [7] J R Fanshawe 3-8-5 (3ow) O Urbina 7/1: 03: ch f Bien Bien - Moidart (Electric) Mid-div, eff to chase ldrs when hmpd over 2f out, sn no impress: well bhd debut earlier. *2½* **50**

1236 **LUCKY AGAIN 19** [2] J L Dunlop 3-8-7 G Carter 10/1: 04: Dwelt, rear, short of room over 3f out & hmpd over 2f out, sn no impress, longer trip. *5* **45**

1358 **BA CLUBMAN 12** [1]4-9-8 R L Moore 12/1: 05: Chsd ldr, struggling when hmpd over 2f out. *17* **25**

1308 **SERENGETI SKY 14** [4]3-8-7 A Beech(3) 9/1: 046: Mid-div, eff/badly hmpd over 2f out, no ch after. *18* **0**

1241 **MISS ST ALBANS 19** [5]3-8-2 Nicol Polli(7) 50/1: 07: Saddle slipped, chsd ldrs till halfway. *4* **0**

1259 **GOOD ARTICLE 17** [10]3-8-7 e S Whitworth 20/1: 00-0B: Hmpd & lost place after 1f, sn rear, mod hdwy when b.d. over 2f out. **0**

1220 **BANSHA BRU 19** [3]4-9-8 S Sanders 11/2: 3S: Led, hard rdn when collapsed 2f out, sadly died. **0**

9 Ran Time 2m 13.75(15.75) Owned: Mr Luke Lillingston Trained: Newmarket

CHESTER THURSDAY 06.05.04 Lefthand, Very Tight Track

Official Going GOOD/SOFT.

1582

1.55 Victor Chandler Handicap Stakes 3yo 0-95 (C) **[97]**
£10433 £3210 £1605 **1m4f66y** **Good 57** **-04 Slow** Inside

1174* **LOCHBUIE 21** [4] G Wragg 3-8-9 (78) J F Egan 7/2 FAV: 640-411: Held up in tch, pushed along halfway, led dist, rdn out: hvly bckd: suited by 12f, shld stay 14f+: acts on gd grnd, sharp/turning or gall trk: lightly rcd, progressing with racing, win again: see 1174. **90**

4927*} **ASIATIC 191** [1] M Johnston 3-8-11 (80) K Dalgleish 5/1: 241-2: ch c Lomitas - Potri Pe (Potrillazo) Led/dsptd lead early, went on 2f out, hdd dist, drvn & kept on: well clr of rem on reapp/h'cap bow: mdn win fnl '03 start: eff at 1m, styd longer 12f trip well: acts on gd & gd/soft grnd, sharp/turning or gall trk: fine reapp, likely type for similar. 1 Oct'03 Nott 8.2g/s 81- D: 2 Sep'03 Hayd 8.1gd 84- D: *½* **90**

1382 **DUMFRIES 10** [5] J H M Gosden 3-8-12 (81) L Dettori 5/1: 031-53: Handy & led after 3f till 2f out, no extra dist: nicely bckd: looks worth a try at 10f in similar: handles fast & gd grnd: see 1382. *7* **82**

4975} **AKRITAS 187** [10] P F I Cole 3-9-7 (90) T Quinn 12/1: 1P0-4: b c Polish Precedent - Dazzling Heights (Shirley Heights) Slow away & rear, kept on late, nvr a threat to ldrs: reapp: h'cap bow: debut scorer '03 (auct mdn), subs no form in stronger company: wng form at 1m, mid-dist pedigree: acts on fast grnd & a stiff/gall trk: can go well fresh. 1 Sep'03 Newm 8g/f 90- E: *¾* **90**

1427 **ODDSMAKER 8** [3]3-8-4 (73) Dean McKeown 6/1: 0015-325: Keen, trkd ldrs, no extra over 1f out: return to 10f in similar shld suit: see 1427 & 1105. *nk* **72**

1272* **MARINE CITY 16** [2]3-8-8 (77) P Robinson 11/2: 0-16: Chsd ldrs inner till lost place halfway, only mod hdwy after: h'cap bow: btr 1272 (mdn, soft). *1½* **74**

1382* **RAREFIED 10** [8]3-8-12 (6ex) (81) S Drowne 15/2: 62-017: Trkd ldrs, btn 2f out: bt this 3rd in 1382. *22* **48**

923 **INFIDELITY 42** [7]3-7-12 (2oh) (65) Lisa Jones(3) 50/1: 120-6008: Chsd ldrs till 3f out; 6 wk abs.   ½   33
1226 **RUTTERS REBEL 19** [6]3-8-3 (72) E Ahern 16/1: 00126-59: Led 2f, prom till wknd qckly 3f out.   21   8
9 Ran   Time 2m 43.9 (7.5)   Owned: Mollers Racing   Trained: Newmarket

---

1583   2.25 Freephone Stanleybet Stakes Handicap 3yo 0-100 (C)   [107]
£16457   £6243   £3121   **7f122y rnd**   **Good 57**   **+08 Fast**   Inside

1186* **OASIS STAR 21** [2] P W Harris 3-8-2 (81) Martin Dwyer 5/1: 1-11: Chsd ldrs inner, rdn to lead ins   88
last, all out: op 4/1, gd time: remains unbtn: eff at 7/7.6f, shld get 1m: acts on firm & gd grnd, stiff or
sharp/turning trks: genuine type who took full advantage of fav'ble low draw: see 1186.
1206 **ZONUS 20** [9] B W Hills 3-8-4 (83) R Hills 4/1 FAV: 2-142: Pushed along rear, hdwy 2f out, strong   hd   89
run ins last, just held: gd run from awkward draw, did not look at home on this tight trk: win again, prob at 1m+.
1480 **GLARAMARA 5** [4] A Bailey 3-9-3 (96) K Fallon 8/1: 013-0203: In tch, smooth hdwy to lead over 2f   ¾   101
out, rdn & hdd ins last, no extra: tchd 12/1, qck reapp: stays 7.6f, return to 6/7f could prove ideal: gd run.
4811} **SEWNSO CHARACTER 199** [5] M Blanshard 3-9-3 (96) F Norton 20/1: 326225-4: b c Imperial Ballet -   1¾   98
Hope And Glory (Well Decorated) Held up in tch, prog 2f, keeping on when hmpd cl home: reapp: '03 auct mdn
wnr, subs thrice rnr-up, incl h'cap: eff at 6f, prob suited by 7/7.6f & has tried 1m: acts on firm & gd/soft
grnd, stiff/gall or sharp trk: encouraging return. 2 Sep'03 Ches 7.6g/s 97-(99) C: 2 Aug'03 Ches 7.0gd 99-95 C:
2 Aug'03 Yarm 7.0g/f 90-(98) D: 1 Jul'03 Hayd 6gd 98- E: 2 Jun'03 Wind 6gd 84- E:
4163} **DESERT DREAMER 239** [16]3-9-0 (93) A Medeiros(5) 50/1: 415420-5: b g Green Desert - Follow That   1½   92+
Dream (Darshaan) Held up, kept on late for press, not able to chall: reapp, has been gelded: mdn wnr '03: eff at
6/7f, 1m may suit: acts on firm & fast grnd, sharp/turning or gall trk: can go well fresh: fine run from poor wide
draw, a likely improver & one to keep in mind. 2 Aug'03 Ches 6.1fm 92-(97) C: 1 Jul'03 Newb 7g/f 94- D:
1297* **CELLO 15** [1]3-8-3 (82) J F Egan 9/2: 6355-216: Trkd ldrs, awkward hld carriage, lost place over   7   69
2f out: hvly bckd, op 11/2: btr 1297 (hvy, mdn, 8.5f).
545* **ST SAVARIN 92** [12]3-7-12 (77) Dale Gibson 33/1: 51-25317: Chsd ldrs 5f: poor draw, abs.   2   60
1526 **DISTANT CONNECTION 3** [7]3-7-12 (2oh) (75) R Thomas(2) 50/1: 4503-008: b c Cadeaux Genereux -   ¾   59
Night Owl (Night Shift) Broke wl & led/dsptd lead 5f, wknd: qck reapp: h'cap plcd fnl '03 start (rtd 67):
eff at 7f, tried 1m: handles fast grnd & a gall trk.
1150 **MAKFOOL 23** [6]3-8-13 (92) T E Durcan 14/1: 243-0349: Chsd ldrs till 2f out: btr 949.   2½   69
1360 **BRIGHT SUN 12** [10]3-8-3 (82) Kim Tinkler 66/1: 52100-00: 10th: Nvr land a blow from mod draw.   1   57
3973*}**RINGSIDER 250** [8]3-8-3 (82) T P Queally(3) 16/1: 01-0: 11th: Hmpd start & al rear.   nk   56
1208 **WHITE HAWK 20** [18]3-9-7 (100) J Murtagh 50/1: 1214-40: 12th: Al bhd: poor draw: btr 1208.   3½   67
1186 **FREE TRIP 21** [17]3-8-7 (1ow) (85) L Dettori 12/1: 1120-160: 13th: Al towards rear from poor draw.   4   45
1315 **APPALACHIAN TRAIL 13** [15]3-8-7 (86) R Winston 9/1: 05-3120: 14th: In tch 6f, poor draw.   7   32
4160}**SKYHARBOR 239** [3]3-8-9 (88) D Holland 20/1: 413100-0: 15th: Led till halfway: reapp, gldd.   dist   0
15 Ran   Time 1m 36.13 (3.73)   Owned: Mr R J Creese   Trained: Berkhamsted

---

1584   2.55 Gr3 Mbna Europe Bank Chester Vase Colts & Geldings 3yo (A)
£37700   £14300   £7150   **1m4f66y**   **Good 57**   **-07 Slow**   Inside

1318 **RED LANCER 13** [5] R J Price 3-8-10 (88) R Miles 9/1: 1222221: In tch, smooth hdwy to lead 2f   109
out, rdn clr, eased cl-home: op 12/1: eff at 1m/10f, imprvd significantly for return to 12f today: acts on
fibresand, gd & soft grnd, prob any trk: has not fin out of the first 2 in last 8 starts: v prog & career best run
here: see 1318, 947 & 702.
1316 **PRIVY SEAL 13** [4] J H M Gosden 3-8-10 (110) L Dettori 5/2 JT FAV: 3155-122: Trkd ldrs, rdn to   5   102
chall over 2f out, sn no ch with wnr: hvly bckd: did not fully convince over this longer 12f trip.
1189 **TEMPLE PLACE 21** [1] M L W Bell 3-8-10 (100) J Murtagh 5/2 JT FAV: 513-33: Led/dsptd lead, went   1¾   100
on over 4f out till 2f out, sn no impress: hvly bckd: appeared not to see out this longer 12f trip: btr 1189.
1482 **ISIDORE BONHEUR 5** [6] B W Hills 3-8-10 bl (98) M Hills 25/1: 14-444: Led after 1f till over 4f   ½   99
out, mod rally for press fnl 2f, no threat: btr 1189 (9f).
1189 **ROEHAMPTON 21** [7]3-8-10 T (97) K Fallon 5/1: 01-65: Sn pushed along & strug halfway: nicely bckd   14   80
in first time t-strap, again disapp: see 1189.
1211* **GRAHAM ISLAND 20** [2]3-8-10 (84) D Holland 7/2: 05-16: Trkd ldrs, wknd qckly 3f out: btr 1211 (mdn).   10   66
6 Ran   Time 2m 44.33 (7.93)   Owned: Fox and Cub Partnership   Trained: Hereford

---

1585   3.30 Listed Breitling Watches & Waltons Of Chester Huxley Stakes For The Tradesman's Cup 4yo+ (A)
£20300   £7700   £3850   **1m2f75y**   **Good 57**   **-00 Slow**   Outside

1483* **BANDARI 5** [7] M Johnston 5-8-12 (114) R Hills 100/30: 4442-011: Mid-div, short of room over 4f   117
out, finished for press fnl 2f to lead well ins last: hvly bckd tho' op 5/2, qck reapp: suited by 10/12f, but
stays 14f: acts on firm, soft & any trk: prev best dominating but ran to best held up off a sound pace today: v
smart entire, seems rejuvenated this term: see 1483.
3032} **PARASOL 292** [1] D R Loder 5-8-12 vis (114) J Murtagh 2/1 FAV: 111262-2: br c Halling - Bunting   1¾   114
(Shaadi) Al handy & led after 3f till well ins last: well bckd on reapp: well plcd '03, 4 wins incl 3 List (incl
this race) & also a Gr 3 rnr-up: eff 10f specialist, tried 12f: acts on firm, gd/soft & polytrack, prob any trk: can
go well fresh & suited by visor: v smart entire, a fine return today.
2 Jul'03 Newb 10.0fm 116-(115) A: 2 May'03 Sand 10.0g/f 114-(114) A: 1 May'03 Ches 10.3fm 115-(114) A:
1 Apr'03 Kemp 10fm 117-(108) A: 1 Mar'03 Ling 10ap 111a-(105) A: 1 Feb'03 Ling 10ap 108a-(104) B:
2 Nov'02 Newm 10gd 108- A: 1 Aug'02 Epso 10g/f 108- C: 2 Jun'01 Asco 7g/f 105- A: 1 Jun'01 Hayd 6gd 94- D:
4219*}**LEPORELLO 236** [9] P W Harris 4-9-3 (114) T Quinn 5/1: 131111-3: b c Danehill - Why So Silent   1¼   117
(Mill Reef) Held up, smooth hdwy 4f out to press ldr over 1f out, no extra ins last: well bckd tho' op 7/2, reapp:
v prog '03, won 6 times, incl 2 val h'caps & 2 Gr 3 events: best arnd 10/10.5f: acts on soft grnd, relishes
firm/fast, prob any trk: can go well fresh: v encouraging return & spot on for Prince Of Wales' Stks.
1 Sep'03 Good 9.9fm 116-(110) A: 1 Aug'03 Wind 10.0g/f 115-(102) A: 1 Aug'03 Hayd 10.5fm 109-93 B:
1 Jul'03 Newb 12/g/f 100-(95) C: 1 Jun'03 Ling 10ap 91a-(80) D: 1 May'03 Ling 7sft 78- D:
1478 **KINGS THOUGHT 5** [11] S Gollings 5-8-12 (95) D Holland 33/1: 10-60464: Prom, hung right on bend   3½   107$
over 2f out, kept on at clr of rem, qck reapp: best when able to dominate, highly tried: see 1296.
1350 **BOURGAINVILLE 12** [5]6-8-12 (107) Martin Dwyer 12/1: 026-0455: Rear, not able to chall.   5   100
4493} **HAMBLEDEN 221** [3]7-8-12 (101) P Robinson 12/1: 325312-6: b g Vettori - Dalu (Dancing Brave) Led   2   97
3f, remained handy, no impress fnl 2f: bckd on reapp: h'cap & rtd h'cap wnr '03: 4 times rnr-up '02, incl rtd

h'cap: suited by 12/14f, stays 2m well: acts on firm, hvy & fibresand, prob any trk: best up with/forcing the
pace: most game & useful, tends to need reapp & will leave this bhd over further.
2 Sep'03 Asco 12g/f 102-99 B: 1 Sep'03 Kemp 12g/f 100-95 C: 2 Jul'03 York 11.9fm 98-95 B:
1 Jun'03 Thir 12g/f 98-92 C: 2 May'03 York 13.9fm 93-89 C: 2 Nov'02 Newm 16gd 91-90 B:
2 Jul'02 Newb 13.2fm 93-90 C: 2 Jun'02 Good 14g/f 87- C: 2 Jun'02 York 13.8g/f 92-90 C:

1168	**LAGO DORTA** 22 [10]4-9-1 (106) Dane O'Neill 12/1: 0121-647: Slowly away, little hdwy: btr 1168.			15	80
401	**MARGERY DAW** 113 [8]4-8-7 (64) Lisa Jones 150/1: 3/2252-58: Chsd ldrs till 5f out, abs/new yard.			5	65
884	**GRAND PASSION** 47 [12]4-8-12 (103) S Drowne 14/1: 032-2109: Chsd ldrs, lost place halfway: abs.			1¼	68
1139	**PIANO STAR** 24 [13]4-8-12 VIS K Fallon 14/1: 24103-00: 10th: Chsd ldrs, lost place after 2f			2	65

& sn struggling: tried visor, another poor display.
10 Ran   Time 2m 14.40 (5.9)   Owned: Mr Hamdan Al Maktoum   Trained: Middleham

1586   4.05 Walker Smith Way Solicitors Rated Stakes Handicap 4yo+ 0-95 (C)   [102]
£11933 £4526 £2263   **1m2f75y**   **Good 57**   **-00 Slow**   Outside

1235	**GUILDED FLYER** 19 [5] W S Kittow 5-8-6 (80) W Supple 14/1: 16500-01: b g Emarati - Mo Ceri				89

(Kampala) Made all, rdn & in command over 1f out, styd on strongly: dual h'cap wnr '03: thrice AW h'cap wnr '02:
best up with/forcing the pace at 9/12f on both AWs, firm, gd & gd/soft grnd, prob any trk: tough gelding with a
progressive overall profile, relished being able to dominate on this sharp trk.
1 Jul'03 Wind 10.0g/f 83-69 E: 2 Jul'03 Newb 9g/f 70-66 E: 1 May'03 Leic 10.0g/f 67-60 E: 2 Nov'02 Ling 10ap 85a-78 F:
1 Oct'02 Ling 10ap 78a-68 E: 1 Jul'02 Wolv 12af 76a-59 F: 1 Jun'02 Wolv 9.3af 60a-45 F:

4226}	**PETRULA** 236 [2] K A Ryan 5-8-4 (1oh)bl (77) P Fessey 7/1: 204034-2: ch g Tagula - Bouffant (High			2½	81

Top) Chsd wnr, rdn fnl 3f, kept on but al held: nicely bckd, 6 wk jumps abs (Dec '03 h'cap hdle wnr, rtd 123h at
best, 2m/2m4f, firm & gd/soft, cheek pieces & blnks): won this race in '03: dual h'cap rnr-up '02 (A Berry): gd
run in blnks, best without, has tried visor: acts on firm & soft, any trk, likes Chester. 2 Jun'03 Ripo 10g/f 81-79 D:
1 May'03 Ches 10.3fm 80-73 C: 2 Sep'02 Sand 8gd 81-77 C: 2 Jul'02 Carl 7.9g/s 79- D: 2 Jul'02 Ayr 8gd 79- D:
2 Jun'02 Leic 7gd 78-75 D: 2 Nov'01 Catt 6g/s 77-72 D: 1 Aug'01 Hayd 6sft 74- D: 2 Aug'01 Ches 7fm 76- D:

1296	**CROW WOOD** 15 [4] J G Given 5-9-4 (92) M Fenton 10/1: 01305-03: Chsd ldrs when hmpd after 2f,			1½	93

styd on for press fnl 2f, no threat: gd run: see 1296.

1295	**OFARABY** 15 [3] M A Jarvis 4-8-12 (86) P Robinson 5/2 FAV: 164-3164: Keen in mid-div, onepace for			3	83

press fnl 2f: hvly bckd: just btr 1295 & 964.

3893}	**SHAYADI** 254 [16]7-8-5 t P (79) F Norton 20/1: 046010-5: b g Kahyasi - Shayrdia (Storm Bird) Held			½	75

up in tch, late gains for press, no threat: jumps fit, dual Dec '03 wnr (seller & nov, rtd 119h, 2m, firm & soft,
t-strap): h'cap wnr on the level '03 (M Johnston): h'cap plcd '02 (rtd 88): winning form at 10f, stays up to 15f:
acts on firm & hvy, prob any trk: eff in blnks/cheek pieces & wore a t-strap today.
1 Jul'03 Ayr 10gd 79-75 E: 2 Jun'01 Ayr 15g/f 90-88 C: 1 Apr'01 Pont 10hvy 91- C:

4294}	**LOW CLOUD** 232 [14]4-8-4 (1oh) (77) A Nicholls 66/1: 016650-6: Held up, hmpd early, only mod prog:			nk	73

reapp for new yard, has been gelded.

4897}	**STRETTON** 194 [13]6-8-7 (81) T P Queally(3) 16/1: 403310-7: Rear, nvr mounted chall: reapp.			5	69
928	**LINNING WINE** 41 [15]8-8-9 (83) J Murtagh 14/1: 021-0248: Mid-div, btn 2f out, abs: btr 928 & 547.			2½	67
758*	**CONSONANT** 68 [7]7-9-2 (90) K Fallon 9/2: 0////-11119: Trkd ldrs, btn 2f out: nicely bckd, abs.			1¼	72
1296	**NORTHSIDE LODGE** 15 [10]6-8-6 (80) E Ahern 14/1: 4-220300: 10th: Chsd ldrs, lost place 3f out.			14	42
475	**BLUE PATRICK** 103 [8]4-8-12 (88) J Tate 66/1: 01600-00: 11th: Mid-div, lost place 3f out, abs.			4	42
1346	**FISIO THERAPY** 12 [1]4-8-7 (81) J Fanning 5/1: 4335-04P: Prom when broke down early, sadly died.				0

12 Ran   Time 2m 14.73 (6.23)   Owned: The Racing Guild   Trained: Cullompton

1587   4.40 Stratstone Aston Martin Maiden Stakes Fillies 3yo (D)
£8210 £2526 £1263   **7f2y rnd**   **Good 57**   **-28 Slow**   Inside

4973}	**SYDNEY STAR** 187 [7] B W Hills 3-8-11 M Hills 4/6 FAV: 2-1: b f Machiavellian - Sena Desert				80

(Green Desert) Trkd ldrs outer, led 2f out, rdn & al holding rival from dist: hvly bckd at odds-on on reapp: plenty
of promise sole '03 start (mdn rnr-up): eff at 7f, dam useful at up to 10f & 1m+ could suit: acts on fast & gd
grnd, stiff/gall or sharp/turning trk: goes well fresh: type to rate higher & win again.
2 Nov'03 Newm 7g/f 88- D:

5031}	**NOORA** 180 [2] M P Tregoning 3-8-11 R Hills 7/2: 0-2: ch f Bahhare - Esteraad (Cadeaux Genereux)			1¾	76

Trkd ldrs, rdn & chsd wnr over 1f out, al held: well clr of rem, nicely bckd tho' op 5/2: reapp: unplcd sole '03
start (mdn, rtd 58): dam 6f juv wnr, sire smart at 1m/10f: styd longer 7f trip, further could suit: acts on gd
grnd & a sharp trk: encouraging.

4887}	**ISLAND SPELL** 194 [3] C Grant 3-8-11 (76) J Murtagh 9/1: 003063-3: b f Singspiel - Shifty Mouse			6	64

(Night Shift) Led till 2f out, sn no impress on front pair: bckd at long odds, reapp: mdn & h'cap plcd '03 (rtd
77): eff at 5f, return to that trip could suit: handles firm & gd grnd, sharp or gall trk.

4462}	**KEEPERS LODGE** 223 [4] B A McMahon 3-8-11 (72) G Gibbons 10/1: 40504-4: Keen & handy till over 1f			shd	64

out: op 12/1, reapp.

	PRELUDE [8]3-8-11 T E Durcan 33/1: 5: Held up, lost tch fnl 2f on debut.			2½	59
3851}	**BALLYBORO** 256 [5]3-8-11 D Corby(3) 16/1: 5-6: Slow into stride & nvr on terms: op 25/1, reapp.			6	47

6 Ran   Time 1m 30.95(5.95)   Owned: Mr Mohamed Obaida   Trained: Lambourn

Official Going STANDARD

1588   2.15 Battle Of Wounded Knee Banded Stakes 3yo+ 0-45 (H)
£1449 £414 £207   **6f aw rnd**   **Going 50**   **+04 Fast**   Inside

1337	**BOISDALE** 12 [3] S L Keightley 6-9-6 (45) L Treadwell(7) 7/1: 60000-61: b g Common Grounds -				58a

Alstomeria (Petoski) Handy, led after 4f, rdn out: won class & claim stks here in '03 (D Nicholls): unplcd in '02
(rtd 53, h'cap, J R Toller): stays 7f, well suited by 6f on firm, soft & fibresand: loves Southwell, has tried a
t-strap: apprec drop to banded grade.
1 Jun'03 Sout 6af 62a-(54) F: 2 Apr'03 Sout 7g/f 58-(53) G: 1 Apr'03 Sout 6af 65a-(49) G:

1405+ **ŁARKYS LOB 9** [2] J O'Reilly 5-9-6 (45) J D O'Reilly(7) 4/7 FAV: 3246312: Slow away, prog & ev ch dist, kept on but just held by wnr: well bckd: only just denied on follow up bid, see 1405. — 1¼ 53a

1413 **CARGO 9** [7] B A Pearce 5-9-6 t p (45) B Reilly(3) 9/2: 5-042023: Played up at start, handy over 4f, sn onepcd: clr rem: op 10/1: see 1413 & 709. — 2 47a

1268 **PARDON MOI 16** [1] Mrs C A Dunnett 3-8-10 P (45) Hayley Turner(5) 25/1: 4-344004: Cl-up over 4f. — 5 32a

459 **LAKE EYRE 105** [4]5-9-6 (45) J Edmunds 11/1: 303-5005: Led, hdd 2f out, wknd: long abs: btr 91. — 1 29a

3660} **GLORY GIRL 264** [5]4-9-6 (45) D Tudhope(7) 33/1: 630-6: ch f Factual - Glory Gold (Hittite Glory) Handy, wknd ins fnl 2f: reapp: plcd on 1 of only 3 '03 starts (rtd 49, mdn): eff at 5f on gd/soft grnd. — ½ 27a

1363 **ZABADOU 12** [8]3-8-10 (40) T Eaves(5) 40/1: 00-067: Al in rear. — 1¼ 23a

1266 **ETERNAL BLOOM 17** [6]6-9-6 (45) T Williams 16/1: 2000338: Handy, fdd dist: btr 1266. — 2 17a

8 Ran   Time 1m 16.1 (2.8)   Owned: Ms Sue Gray   Trained: Melton Mowbray

---

1589   2.45 Hoorah For Hats & Horses Banded Stakes 3yo+ 0-45 (H)
£1460 £417 £209   1m3f aw   Going 50   +06 Fast   Inside

249] **LAGO DI COMO 866** [1] Mrs P Townsley 7-9-7 t (45) A Culhane 10/1: 511200//-1: b g Piccolo - Farmer's Pet (Sharrood) Made all, clr bef halfway, pushed clr, val 15L+: reapp & new stable: missed '03 & '02: seller & amat h'cap wnr in '01 (T J Naughton): auct mdn wnr in '00 (rtd 69): eff btwn 9f & 11.5f on firm, fast & both AWs: acts on a sharp/undul trk, tried blnks, eff with t-strap: goes well fresh: authoritative win. — 52a+
2 Sep'01 Wolv 9.3af 51a-49 F: 1 Aug'01 Brig 10fm 53-43 F: 1 Aug'01 Ling 10g/f 47-G:

48 **MELOGRANO 171** [6] Mark Campion 4-9-7 (45) D Nolan(5) 15/2: 060360-2: ch g Hector Protector - Just A Treat (Glenstal) Cl-up, hung left & no extra after 9f: op 9/1 on reapp, new stable: plcd once in '03 (rtd 58, clmr, R M Beckett): mdn plcd once in '02: eff at 1m, poss stays 11f: handles fast, hvy grnd & fibresand. — 11 38a
2 Oct'02 Nott 8.2hvy 75- D:

1407* **SUNNYSIDE ROYALE 9** [5] R Bastiman 5-9-13 t (45) H Bastiman 5/2: 6/346-013: Rear, prog after 5f, no impress fnl 2f: clr rem: below par eff on drop back to 11f: btr 1407 (14f). — 1¾ 41a

469* **MISTY MAN 104** [7] Miss J Feilden 6-9-7 bl (45) B Reilly(3) 4/1: 044-3514: Rear, nvr nrr than mid-div: reportedly hung right throughout: btr 469. — 10 20a

4638} **TIOGA GOLD 212** [4]5-9-7 P (40) V Halliday 16/1: 0/54400-5: Cl-up 6f, sn wknd: jumps fit. — 2½ 16a

906* **CUMWHITTON 44** [3]5-9-2 p (45) T Hamilton(3) 2/1 FAV: 6//60-5016: Dwelt, hdwy after 3f, fdd halfway: tchd 3/1, 6 wk abs: reportedly showed signs of coming into season: btr 906. — 4 10a

3090} **NOBLE PHILOSOPHER 288** [2]4-9-7 (45) Joanna Badger 20/1: 060-7: Cl-up over 5f, fdd: jumps abs. — dist 0a

7 Ran   Time 2m 26.15 (4.85)   Owned: Mr M J Caldwell   Trained: Godalming

---

1590   3.20 St Ava's Day Banded Stakes 3yo+ 0-45 (H)
£1460 £417 £209   7f aw rnd   Going 50   -02 Slow   Inside

776 **SANDORRA 67** [6] M Brittain 6-9-2 (45) T Williams 9/1: 0-316001: Made all, drvn out fnl 1f: op 7/1, 10 wk abs: eff at 7f on fibresand: likes forcing tactics & goes well fresh: likes banded grade: see 356. — 50a

1335 **TEE JAY KASSIDY 13** [3] Julian Poulton 4-9-2 (40) M Halford(7) 8/1: 004-1252: Rear, hdwy when short of room halfway, kept on ins fnl 2f, no pace of wnr: see 1264 & 909. — 3½ 41a

1405 **INDIAN MUSIC 9** [4] A Berry 7-9-2 (45) J Carroll 8/1: 0-615443: Rear, prog after 5f, onepcd fnl 2f. — 1¼ 38a

1200 **AIR OF ESTEEM 20** [7] Ian Emmerson 8-9-2 (45) D Fentiman(7) 2/1 FAV: 3-556024: Cl-up till dist, no extra: below form of 2nd in 1200 (1m). — nk 37a

1451* **LITTLETON ZEPHIR 7** [1]5-9-8 (45) A Culhane 4/1: 6-020015: Handy over 5f, wknd: qck reapp: disapp on drop back to 7f: btr 1451 (1m). — 2½ 38a

1405 **CLEVELAND WAY 9** [5]4-9-2 vis (45) D Tudhope(7) 7/2: 6450226: Dwelt, nvr nrr than mid-div: btr 1405. — 3 26a

4918] **NORTH LANDING 191** [2]4-9-2 (45) T Eaves(5) 14/1: 020000-7: b g Storm Bird - Tirol Hope (Tirol) Handy 4f, wknd: reapp: appr seller rnr-up in '03 (M Johnston, also with H A McWilliams): plcd once in '02 (auct mdn): eff at 7f/1m on fast & gd grnd: has tried cheek pieces: with R C Guest. — 6 14a
2 Jun'03 Ripo 8g/f 57-(61) E: 2 Aug'02 Thir 7gd 77- E:

7 Ran   Time 1m 30.25 (3.65)   Owned: Mr Mel Brittain   Trained: Warthill

---

1591   3.55 Sigmund Freud Birthday Tri-Banded Stakes 3yo+ 0-45 (H)
£1442 £412 £206   1m aw rnd   Going 50   -11 Slow   Inside

1410* **SAROS 9** [3] B Smart 3-9-6 (6ex) (51) M Stainton(7) 5/6 FAV: 0606-011: Led after 3f, pushed clr ins fnl 1f, val 4L+: well bckd: eff at 7f, now stays 1m: acts on fibresand & a sharp trk, loves Southwell: thriving in banded grade & hat-trick beckons: see 1410. — 55a+

1440 **DIVINA 7** [7] S L Keightley 3-8-4 vis (30) B Reilly(3) 12/1: 0000432: Cl-up, kept on ins fnl 2f, not pace of wnr: qck reapp: eff at 1m on fibresand: with visor: see 1440 & 873. — 2 34a

1410 **ROMAN THE PARK 9** [2] T D Easterby 3-9-0 (45) D Allan(3) 2/1: 600-3123: Slow away, handy till dist, wknd: also well btn by today's wnr in 1410. — 5 34a

1410 **PLATINUM CHIEF 9** [4] A Berry 3-8-9 bl (40) A Culhane 9/1: 6650534: Handy, fdd fnl 2f: btr 1410. — 10 9a

1196 **AIREDALE LAD 21** [6]3-8-4 (35) J Bramhill 18/1: 0-645: Nvr nrr than mid-div: btr 1196. — 7 0a

1147 **DELTA LADY 24** [5]3-9-0 (45) R Ffrench 20/1: 42600-06: b f River Falls - Compton Lady (Sovereign Dancer) Rear, nvr a factor: plcd twice in '03 (rtd 54, seller, C W Fairhurst): prob stays 7.5f, handles firm & gd/soft, tried blnks: with R Bastiman. 2 Jul'03 Beve 7.5g/s 50- F: — 2 0a

1280 **HYMNS AND ARIAS 16** [1]3-9-0 (45) S Righton 20/1: 10-04007: Led, hdd 5f out, sn fdd: btr 857. — 12 0a

7 Ran   Time 1m 44.35 (4.95)   Owned: Pinnacle Desert Sun Partnership   Trained: Thirsk

---

1592   4.30 Sack Of Rome Banded Stakes 3yo+ 0-35 (H)
£1439 £411 £206   1m4f aw   Going 50   -12 Slow   Inside

1563 **THE LAST MOHICAN 1** [5] P Howling 5-9-5 p (30) P McCabe 9/4 FAV: 24400321: Made all, rdn out ins fnl 2f: bckd: rnr-up yesterday in this grade at W'hampton: eff around 12f, stays 2m: acts on firm grnd & both AWs: eff with cheek pieces: first win: see 1563 & 1287. — 38a

1200 **MISS FLEURIE 20** [2] R Craggs 4-9-5 (35) D Allan(3) 14/1: 4/-0002: Keen cl-up, styd on ins fnl 2f, nvr getting to wnr: clr rem: imprvd eff on step up to 12f: acts on fibresand: can find similar. — 4 31a

SOUTHWELL Fibresand THURSDAY 06.05.04 Lefthand, Sharp, Oval Track

1561 **MOYNE PLEASURE 1** [3] Paul Johnson 6-9-5 p (30) L Enstone(3) 3/1: 06002023: Cl-up 10f, no extra: rnr-up yesterday at W'hampton in 1561, see 1409. *5* **24a**
1409 **ZELEA 9** [1] J Parkes 5-9-5 (35) A Culhane 6/1: 3500/-544: Rear, nvr nrr than mid-div: btr 1409. *7* **14a**
1326 **QUEEN EXCALIBUR 13** [6]5-9-5 (35) N Chalmers(5) 3/1: 0000635: Handy over 1m, sn wknd: btr 1326. *6* **5a**
1333 **DANCING DOLPHIN 13** [4]5-9-5 (30) M Halford(7) 8/1: 50646/-36: Slow away, al in rear: btr 1333. *3½* **0a**
6 Ran Time 2m 41.85 (7.55) Owned: Mr P Woodward Trained: Newmarket

1593
5.05 Rudolph Valentino Birthday Banded Stakes 4yo+ 0-35 (H)
£1439 £411 £206 **1m aw rnd** **Going 50** **-09 Slow** Inside

1406 **DALRIATH 9** [1] M C Chapman 5-8-12 (35) Andrew Webb(7) 5/2: 0-066421: Keen cl-up, led after 4f, pushed out ins fnl 1f, val 5L+: eff around 1m on fast grnd & fibresand: first win: see 1406. **42a+**
1307 **DESIRES DESTINY 14** [6] M Brittain 6-8-12 (35) T Williams 4/1: 0-606302: Led 4f, styd cl-up & ev ch 2f out, not pace of wnr ins fnl 1f: eff around 1m on fibresand: see 1200. *3* **35a**
1072 **SHAAMITS ALL OVER 30** [5] B A Pearce 5-8-12 BL (35) B Reilly(3) 12/1: 0600-003: br f Shaamit - First Time Over (Derrylin) Chsd ldrs over 5f, hung left & no extra: first time blnks: mod form to date. *3* **29a**
1409 **PARADISE GARDEN 9** [4] P L Clinton 7-8-12 vis (35) D Allan(3) 14/1: 0050-054: Nvr nrr than mid-div. *¾* **27a**
1406 **MATHMAGICIAN 9** [2]5-8-12 bl (35) Dean McKeown 8/1: 0466035: Cl-up over 4f, fdd: btr 1406. *3* **21a**
1406* **AMETHYST ROCK 9** [7]6-9-4 (35) A Culhane 7/4 FAV: 060-0316: Handy till 3f out, wknd: disapp eff & rider reported mount was nvr trav: btr 1406. *½* **26a**
1546 **MARENGO 2** [3]10-8-12 (30) Joanna Badger 14/1: 0600647: Slow away, al bhd, fin lame: qck reapp. *1¾* **17a**
7 Ran Time 1m 44.17(4.77) Owned: Mr Michael B Gielty Trained: Market Rasen

CHESTER FRIDAY 07.05.04 Lefthand, Very Tight Track

Official Going GOOD/SOFT.

1594
1.55 Bank Of Scotland Rated Stakes Handicap 4yo+ 0-100 (B) **[106]**
£15382 £5834 £2917 **5f16y rnd** **Good 48** **-00 Slow** Inside

1120 **PTARMIGAN RIDGE 26** [4] Miss L A Perratt 8-8-4 (1oh) (82) N Mackay(3) 14/1: 5001-001: b c Sea Raven - Panayr (Faraway Times) Chsd ldrs, sltly short of room dist, strong run to lead cl-home, rdn out: ended '03 with a h'cap win: rnr-up in '02 (h'cap) & dual '01 h'cap scorer: suited by 5f: acts on fast, loves gd & hvy, any trk: best up with the pace, tho' can come from bhd: wins his share of h'caps. **88**
1 Sep'03 Hayd 5gd 85-78 C: 2 Nov'02 Donc 5hvy 82-80 D: 1 Oct'01 Catt 5sft 87-76 D: 1 Aug'01 Hayd 5g/f 81-74 C:
1400 **SIMIANNA 10** [2] A Berry 5-8-9 p (88) F Norton 8/1: 6300-552: Chsd ldrs, strong run & ev ch ins fnl 1f, just btn in a thrilling fin: usually runs well here at Chester & this was a fine eff: see 1162. *hd* **92**
1217* **MAKTAVISH 21** [1] I Semple 5-8-6 p (85) P Hanagan 7/2 JT FAV: 00-11213: Fast away & tried to make all, collared cl-home: well bckd: fine front running eff, tho' was not helped by hanging right throughout. *¾* **86**
4471} **NATIVE TITLE 223** [9] D Nicholls 6-8-4 (2oh) (81) A Nicholls 50/1: 026/010-4: b g Pivotal - Bermuda Lily (Dunbeath) Held up, weaved through over 1f out, fin fast but too late: lightly rcd in '03, won mid of 3 starts, val Ayr Silver Cup: '02 h'cap wnr for M Blanshard: eff at 5f, btr suited by 6f/1m: acts on firm & soft: can force the pace: excellent reapp from a poor high draw, keep in mind back over further. *½* **83+**
1 Sep'03 Ayr 6g/f 83-77 B: 2 Sep'02 Bath 5.7fm 77-72 D: 1 Jun'02 Leic 6g/f 77-70 E: 1 Jun'01 Newb 7fm 86- D:
2 May'01 Newm 7g/f 86- D: 2 May'01 Kemp 8sft 85- D: 2 Apr'01 Newb 8sft 78- D:
4884} **CORRIDOR CREEPER 195** [5]7-8-11 p (90) D Holland 10/1: 122000-5: ch g Polish Precedent - Sonia Rose (Superbity) Chsd ldr till no extra ins fnl 1f: '03 h'cap wnr, also plcd sev times: won 2 h'caps in '02 & a val h'cap in '01 (with P Harris): eff at 6f, suited by 5f: acts on gd & firm, handles gd/soft & any trk: eff with/without a t-strap & cheek pieces, has tried blnks: encouraging reapp, likes Chester. *hd* **90**
2 Sep'03 Yarm 5.2g/f 95-90 C: 2 Sep'03 Donc 5.6gd 96-90 B: 1 Aug'03 Epso 5fm 92-85 B:
2 Jun'03 Sali 5fm 85-83 D: 2 Jun'03 Sali 5fm 85-83 D: 2 May'03 Muss 5gd 85-80 C:
2 May'03 Bath 5.0g/s 83-(79) D: 1 Sep'02 Ches 5fm 81-76 D: 2 Sep'02 Yarm 5.1fm 80-76 C:
1162 **JOHNSTONS DIAMOND 23** [3]6-8-10 (89) K Fallon 4/1: 1-001046: Chsd ldrs, onepcd fnl 1f: well bckd. *1* **86**
1293* **CAPE ROYAL 16** [6]4-8-9 (88) L Dettori 7/2 JT FAV: 220-0617: Held up, late hdwy, nrst fin: nicely bckd: hold-up tactics not conducive to this type of trk, rcd much more prominently in 1293. *1¾* **80**
4884} **TALBOT AVENUE 195** [7]6-8-4 (1oh) (82) W Supple 33/1: 000000-8: Keen in rear, nrst fin on reapp. *3* **66**
1162 **VITA SPERICOLATA 23** [12]7-8-7 (86) R Winston 25/1: 30000-09: Chsd ldrs 3.5f, eased when btn fnl 1f: speedy sort, poorly drawn. *1½* **65**
1479 **SMOKIN BEAU 6** [11]7-9-5 (98) T G McLaughlin 25/1: 400-6200: 10th: Nvr btr than mid-div: qck reapp: al struggling from poor high draw: much btr 1137. *shd* **77**
1138 **FURTHER OUTLOOK 25** [8]10-8-7 (86) A Culhane 25/1: 200-1300: 11th: Nvr btr than mid-div: mod draw. *1* **62**
1207 **WHITBARROW 21** [10]5-8-13 (92) K Darley 20/1: 00/056-50: 12th: Nvr nr ldrs: poor draw. *1¾* **64**
1293 **PALAWAN 16** [13]8-8-5 (84) M Hills 66/1: 02-00600: 13th: Al bhd from poor draw. *10* **26**
927 **POMFRET LAD 42** [14]6-9-7 (100) Alex Greaves 66/1: 51052-00: 14th: Al bhd: 6 wk abs, poor draw. *nk* **41**
14 Ran Time 1m 02.22 (2.42) Owned: The Hon Miss Heather Galbraith Trained: Ayr

1595
2.25 Gr3 Jardine Lloyd Thompson Dee Stakes Colts & Geldings 3yo (A)
£40600 £15400 £7700 **1m2f75y** **Good 48** **-61 Slow** Outside

1316* **AFRICAN DREAM 14** [2] P W Chapple Hyam 3-8-11 (113) J Quinn 2/5 FAV: 311111: Held up, qcknd to lead ent fnl 1f, styd on strongly, pushed out: slow time: completed 5-timer, has prog from wng a clmr to two Gr 3s: eff at 1m/10f on gd, soft grnd & polytrack, handles any trk: clearly thriving & a smart performer: see 1316. **110**
1317 **PUTRA SAS 14** [5] P F I Cole 3-8-8 (90) L Dettori 4/1: 21-22: Trkd ldr, went on over 2f out, not pace of wnr fnl 1f: lightly rcd, far from disgraced on this step up to Group company: eff at 1m/10f: see 1317. *¾* **103**
1316 **MUTAWASSEL 14** [4] B W Hills 3-8-8 (95) R Hills 6/1: 01-43: Led till over 2f out, sn onepcd: did not look at all at home on this tight trk: poss stays a sharp 10f: again bhd today's wnr in 1316. *1½* **100**
3 Ran Time 2m 19.74 (11.24) Owned: Franconson Partners Trained: Newmarket

1596   2.55 Gr3 Betdaq Ormonde Stakes 4yo+   (A)
£43500 £16500 £8250   **1m5f89y**   **Good 48**   **-00 Slow**   Inside

1493 **SYSTEMATIC 5** [7] M Johnston 5-8-11 (109) K Darley 5/2 FAV: 1/255-321: Chsd clr ldr, imprvd to   **117+**
lead over 3f out, rdn clr fnl 1f: hvly bckd tho' op 6/4, qck reapp: eff at 12/13f on firm & soft, gall or sharp
trk: loves to dominate & proved a class above today's rivals: smart & more decent prizes await, see 1493 & 950.

1230 **THE WHISTLING TEAL 20** [5] G Wragg 8-8-11 (107) D Holland 7/2: 1/4452-02: b g Rudimentary -   **1¾   112**
Lonely Shore (Blakeney) Mid-div, smooth prog to chall over 2f out, not pace of wnr ins fnl 1f: well bckd & clr rem:
failed to win in '03, List rnr-up on fnl start: won a stks & a Gr 3 in '02 & 3 h'caps in '01: eff at 10/13.5f: acts
on firm & f/sand, relishes gd or hvy: handles any trk, can run well fresh: decent eff, met a smart rival.
2 Nov'03 Donc 12gd 109-(109) A: 1 Oct'02 Newb 12sft 116- A: 2 Sep'02 Donc 12fm 114- A:
1 Aug'02 Newm 12gd 106- B: 2 Aug'02 Good 12fm 112-110 A: 1 Aug'01 York 10.3gd 109-95 B:
1 May'01 Redc 10g/f 96-87 B: 2 May'01 Ches 10.3fm 89-85 C: 1 Apr'01 Pont 8hvy 88-77 D:

990 **COMPTON BOLTER 41** [1] G A Butler 7-8-11 (108) L Dettori 15/2: 01-40503: Held up, hdwy to chase   **12   96**
front 2 2f out, sn no impress: 6 wk abs: acts on gd grnd, could nvr get competitive today: btr 82 (AW).

950+***ROYAL CAVALIER 41** [6] R Hollinshead 7-8-11 (98) W Supple 9/1: 0206-014: Chsd ldrs, outpcd 4f   **hd   96**
out, al struggling after: 6 wk abs: beat today's wnr in 950 (gall trk).

1230 **FOREST MAGIC 20** [8]4-8-11 (100) E Ahern 25/1: 5211/-405: Chsd ldrs, outpcd 4f out, no ch after: **1¾   94**
again bhd today's 1st & 4th in 950.

LIMERICK BOY 582 [10]6-8-11 T E Durcan 33/1: 005000/-6: b c Alwuhush - Limoges (Konigsstuhl)   **5   86**
Chsd ldrs, outpcd over 3f out on Flat comeback: jumps fit, won a Gr 2 nov hdle at Aintree 3 wks ago (rtd 133h, eff
at 2m on gd/soft & soft): former useful Flat performer in native Germany (Gr 3 scorer): eff at 1m/10f on soft & hvy
grnd: with Miss V Williams & shld be capable of btr.

990 **RAWYAAN 41** [2]5-8-11 bl (112) R Hills 14/1: 201-1607: b c Machiavellian - Raheefa (Riverman) Al   **¾   85**
rear: 6 wk abs: ended '03 with a stks win in first time blnks: won 3 times in '02, 2 h'caps & a List: eff at
1m/10f on firm & gd/soft, any trk: eff with/without visor, likes blnks: can run well fresh & this is not his form.
1 Sep'03 Donc 10.3gd 112-(108) B: 2 Jul'03 Epso 10.1g/f 107-(110) C: 2 May'03 Good 9.9g/f 107-(112) A:
1 Sep'02 Good 9.8fm 114- A: 1 Aug'02 Good 9g/f 107-100 B: 1 May'02 Nott 10gd 102-90 C:
1 Oct'01 Newm 8g/s 90- D:

4837} **NARRATIVE 201** [3]6-8-11 (108) T P Queally 12/1: 05/4300-8: Bolted & sn in clr lead, hdd 3f out,   **2   82**
wknd & eased: bckd from 20/1, reapp & new stable.

4633} **FIRST CHARTER 215** [4]5-8-11 (109) K Fallon 5/1: 0/31120-9: Nvr trav in rear, t.o. on reapp: **dist 37**
reportedly subs found to be coughing.
9 Ran   Time 2m 56.34 (6.54)   Owned: Maktoum Al Maktoum   Trained: Middleham

1597   3.30 Boodle & Dunthorne Maiden Stakes 3yo   (D)
£8288 £2550 £1275   **1m2f75y**   **Good 48**   **-36 Slow**   Outside

1398 **IKTITAF 10** [3] J H M Gosden 3-9-0   R Hills 3/1: 031: Trkd ldrs, short of room dist, strong run   **84**
to lead ins fnl 1f, drvn out: nicely bckd: eff at 10f, 12f looks sure to suit: acts on gd grnd, handles a tight
trk: lightly rcd & progressing well, see 1398.

LINE DRAWING [1] B W Hills 3-9-0 K Fallon 9/2: 2: b c Unfuwain - Fine Detail (Shirley Heights)   **½   82**
Rear, gd hdwy to lead dist, flashed tail & caught ins fnl 1f: debut & ran v green: mid-dist bred, eff over a sharp
10f, 12f shld suit: acts on gd grnd & runs well fresh: shld learn plenty from this debut & find similar.

1055 **LARKWING 32** [2] G Wragg 3-9-0   D Holland 5/4 FAV: 4-23: Held up, hdwy 2f out, staying on when   **1¼   79**
hmpd entering fnl 1f, switched & no extra cl-home: well bckd: carried head high, did not get the run of today's
race: sltly btr on reapp in 1055.

1177 **MOUFTARI 22** [8] B W Hills 3-9-0   M Hills 12/1: 0-54: b c Miswaki - Nature's Magic (Nijinsky)   **shd   79**
Led till dist, no extra: stablemate of rnr-up: unplcd sole '03 start, cost $200,000: half-brother to decent miler
Tough Speed: capable eff for a long way, may apprec a drop back to 1m.

4943} **PATRIXPRIAL 191** [4]3-9-0 N Callan 33/1: 0-5: gr c Linamix - Magnificent Star (Silver Hawk)   **1½   76**
Keen in rear, some late hdwy, nvr dngrs on reapp: well btn on sole '03 start: half-brother to hdles/chase wnrs:
dam a top-class mid-dist performer: stoutly bred, needs one more run to qual for h'caps.

1166 **BALIMAYA 23** [5]3-8-9 E Ahern 8/1: 06: Prom early, rallied & ev ch 2 out, sn btn.   **1½   68**

1398 **GO GREEN 10** [7]3-8-9 Joanna Badger 66/1: 0007: Slowly away, al bhd & hung right throughout.   **14   48**

5016} **PHOENIX EYE 183** [6]3-9-0 W Supple 100/1: 0-8: Keen & prom, hmpd halfway, no ch after on reapp.   **14   33**
8 Ran   Time 2m 17.20 (8.70)   Owned: Mr Hamdan Al Maktoum   Trained: Manton

1598   4.05 Warwick International Rated Stakes Handicap 4yo+ 0-90 (C)
£10379 £3937 £1968   **7f122y rnd**   **Good 48**   **-00 Slow**   Inside   **[97]**

1475 **CHAPPEL CRESENT 6** [1] D Nicholls 4-9-4 (87) A Nicholls 15/2: 0005251: Broke well & made all, clr   **98**
fnl 1f, readily: well bckd, qck reapp: suited by 7/7.5f on gd & gd/soft grnd, poss handles hvy: acts on a tight or
stiff/gall trk: made most of plum no. 1 draw & nvr saw another rival: see 1151 & 511.

1138 **NASHAAB 25** [4] P D Evans 7-9-4 (87) K Fallon 5/1: 05-00002: b g Zafonic - Tajannub (Dixieland   **3   90**
Band) Hmpd start, hdwy fnl 1.5f, fin well but no ch with wnr: well bckd: failed to win in '03, tho' plcd sev times
(h'caps): plcd sevl times in h'caps in '02: eff at 7f/1m on hvy & f/sand, likes fast & firm, any trk, likes
Chester: tries blnks/visor: on a decent mark but hold-up tactics are hard to pull off here.
2 Sep'03 Ayr 8fm 91-90 C: 2 Jun'03 Ches 7.0g/f 89-87 C: 2 Oct'02 York 8fm 93-91 B:
2 Jun'02 Newb 8sft 86-85 C: 2 Sep'01 Donc 7gd 86-82 C: 1 Aug'01 Ches 7.5fm 87-76 C:
1 May'01 Leic 8fm 74-67 D: 1 Jan'01 Sout 8af 80a-66 D: 1 Dec'00 Wolv 8.4af 65a- D:

1423* **RETIREMENT 9** [3] M H Tompkins 5-8-9 (3ex) (78) D Holland 2/1 FAV: 24212-13: Chsd ldrs, kept on   **½   80**
under press fnl 1f: will apprec a return to a stiff 1m, as in 1423 (soft grnd).

1094 **FLINT RIVER 29** [7] H Morrison 6-8-7 (2ow) (74) A Culhane 12/1: 2000124: Mid-div, kept on under   **1   76**
press fnl 1f: far from disgraced, continues in gd form: see 1094 & 940.

1525 **H HARRISON 4** [2]4-8-11 (80) E Ahern 14/1: 103-0645: Trkd ldrs, short of room entering straight,   **nk   79**
onepcd ins fnl 1f: qck reapp: see 1525 & 1122.

1512 **DIGITAL 9** [11]7-9-7 (90) S Hitchcott(3) 12/1: 2-034036: Rear, hdwy when short of room dist, nrst   **1½   86**
fin: qck reapp: jt top-weight: poor high-draw & did not get the run of today's race: see 1512.

952 **TIME N TIME AGAIN 41** [15]6-8-5 (74) J Quinn 33/1: 3331507: Prom 6f, wknd: 6 wk abs: poor high   **2½   65**

CHESTER FRIDAY 07.05.04 Lefthand, Very Tight Track

draw & not stay this longer 7.5f trip: loves Chester & 5f: see 807.
4178} **BANJO BAY 239** [9]6-9-3 (86) Alex Greaves 50/1: U10000-8: b g Common Grounds - Thirlmere (Cadeaux *hd* **77**
Genereux) Keen & prom, wknd fnl 1f on reapp: mod draw: '03 h'cap wnr for J Given: h'cap rnr-up for B McMahon in
'02: eff at 1m, suited by 6/7f on firm & soft, prob any trk: can run well fresh: tough & useful, now with D
Nicholls. 1 May'03 Good 6g/f 89-86 C: 2 Apr'02 Newm 7fm 92-88 B: 2 Aug'01 Ripo 6g/f 92-88 B:
2 Jul'01 Newm 8g/f 91-83 C: 1 Jun'01 Leic 7gd 85-76 D: 1 May'01 Pont 6sft 81- D:
1475 **QUEENS RHAPSODY 6** [6]4-9-2 (85) T E Durcan 12/1: 0240409: Rear, nvr nr ldrs: tchd 16/1, qck reapp. *¾* **74**
1255 **IDLE POWER 18** [8]6-8-4 (2oh)p (71) W Supple 20/1: 04000-00: 10th: Nvr btr than mid-div, hmpd dist. *nk* **61**
1474* **RAPHAEL 6** [12]5-8-9 (3ex) (78) Dale Gibson 16/1: 5223-010: 11th: Nvr btr than mid-div: qck *1¼* **63**
reapp, poor high draw: see 1474.
744 **RISKA KING 71** [16]4-8-5 (74) T Hamilton(2) 66/1: 0100-000: 12th: Rear, late gains: abs, poor draw. *½* **58**
1115 **DAME DE NOCHE 27** [10]4-9-7 (90) M Fenton 33/1: 10300-60: 13th: Trkd ldrs 6f, wknd: jt *1¾* **70**
top-weight: unable to dominate from poor high draw: see 1115.
1461 **HAIL THE CHIEF 7** [14]7-8-7 (76) M Hills 28/1: 50-14030: 14th: Al bhd from poor high draw. *3½* **49**
1474 **CARDINAL VENTURE 6** [18]6-9-4 (87) N Callan 25/1: 111-2000: 15th: Chsd ldrs, short of room 1.5f *nk* **59**
out, wknd: qck reapp: ran well for a long way from poor high draw: see 838.
1059 **SOLLER BAY 32** [17]7-8-6 (75) Darren Williams 25/1: 00466-20: 16th: Nvr nr ldrs, poorly drawn. *12* **22**
1227 **SMIRFYS SYSTEMS 20** [5]5-8-11 (80) R Hills 20/1: 50012-00: 17th: b g Safawan - Saint Systems *13* **2**
(Uncle Pokey) Al bhd, t.o.: '03 h'cap wnr: '02 mdn wnr: eff at 6/7f on fast & firm grnd: can run well fresh.
2 Aug'03 York 6.0fm 80-76 C: 1 Aug'03 Thir 6g/f 78-68 D: 1 Sep'02 Catt 7fm 73- D:
1195* **WARDEN WARREN 22** [13]6-8-4 (1oh)p (72) Hayley Turner(5) 33/1: 4610010: 18th: Al bhd: poor draw. *5* **0**
18 Ran Time 1m 36.03 (3.63) Owned: Mrs A D Coogan Trained: Thirsk

1599 **4.40 Cheshire Regiment Handicap Stakes Sponsored By The Elifar Foundation 3yo+ 0-80 (D) [80]**
£9165 £2820 £1410 **1m4f66y Good 48 -22 Slow** Inside

997* **COURT OF APPEAL 37** [4] B Ellison 7-9-12 t (78) T Eaves(5) 11/2: 02434-11: Prom, rdn to lead dist, **91**
styd on strongly, rdn out: op 9/2, top-weight: eff t 10/14f on fast, soft grnd & fibresand: runs well fresh, gd
weight-carrier: clearly likes Chester, won this race from an 8lb lower mark last term: in great form, see 997.
5033} **ALERON 181** [5] J J Quinn 6-9-2 (68) E Ahern 9/2 CO FAV: 033434-2: b c Sadler's Wells - High Hawk *2½* **76**
(Shirley Heights) Chsd ldrs, led over 2f out till dist, kept on but not pace of wnr on reapp: op 6/1: dual h'cap
wnr in '03, also plcd numerous times, incl 3rd in this race from an 8lb higher mark: eff at 12/14f, prob stays 2m:
acts on fast, soft grnd & fibresand: likes a sharp trk, handles any: fairly h'capped & spot on next time.
2 Apr'03 Catt 12.0g/f 79-72 D: 1 Apr'03 Muss 14g/f 74-64 E: 2 Mar'03 Catt 13.8g/f 64-62 D:
1 Feb'03 Sout 12af 61a-55 E: 1 Nov'02 Catt 13.7sft 63-56 E:
1295 **MEXICAN PETE 16** [9] P W Hiatt 4-9-8 (74) A Culhane 25/1: 21103-03: b g Atraf - Eskimo Nel (Shy *¾* **80**
Groom) Rear, styd on well fnl 1.5f, nrst fin: progressive in '03, won 3 h'caps: eff at 11/12f on gd & firm, any
trk: running into form. 1 Aug'03 Sali 12g/f 77-66 E: 1 Aug'03 Redc 11g/f 66-61 E: 2 Aug'03 Brig 9.9fm 68-61 F:
2 Jul'03 Warw 10.9g/f 63-61 D: 2 Jul'03 Hayd 11.9g/f 65-61 D: 1 Jul'03 Warw 10.9fm 61-55 F:
1128* **TRUE COMPANION 25** [7] N P Littmoden 5-9-5 (71) J P Guillambert(3) 12/1: 0130314: Rear, styd on *½* **76**
fnl 1f, nrst fin: see 1128.
1286 **TROUBLE MOUNTAIN 17** [6]7-9-3 bl (69) K Fallon 9/2 CO FAV: 023-3335: Mid-div, sltly short of room *1* **72**
2f out, styd on under press fnl 1f: see 1164.
1484 **CHAMPION LION 6** [2]5-9-3 (69) S Hitchcott(3) 9/2 CO FAV: 50-00506: Slowly away, kept on but not *½* **71**
pace to chall: qck reapp.
4114} **MOVIE KING 242** [8]5-9-5 (71) D Holland 16/1: 400450-7: ch g Catrail - Marilyn (Kings Lake) *13* **53**
Prom, led briefly halfway & again 4f out till 2f out, wknd on reapp: '03 AW h'cap wnr: won 2 h'caps & a mdn in '03:
suited by 1m/10f, best when able to dominate: acts on fast, fibresand & loves Lingfield/polytrack: fairly h'capped.
1 Feb'03 Ling 10ap 85a-79 C: 1 Apr'02 Wind 8.3g/f 82-75 D: 1 Feb'02 Ling 10ap 77a-67 E: 1 Feb'02 Ling 10ap 75a- D:
1361 **ALWAYS RAINBOWS 13** [12]6-9-4 p (70) M Fenton 50/1: 43000/-08: Nvr nr ldrs. *3½* **47**
4144} **MR LEAR 241** [3]5-9-6 (72) T Hamilton(3) 12/1: 121040-9: Led briefly halfway, wknd on reapp. *1¼* **47**
1295 **JEEPSTAR 16** [14]4-9-11 (77) W Supple 25/1: 21253-00: 10th: Led till halfway, again 5f out till 4f out. *2½* **48**
870 **SUDDEN FLIGHT 50** [10]7-9-2 (68) M Hills 10/1: 10-00030: 11th: Chsd ldrs 1m, grad wknd: abs. *16* **17**
1271 **BAKIRI 17** [1]6-9-1 (67) T E Durcan 16/1: 2/060/-040: 12th: Prom 1m, sn wknd: see 1271. *1¾* **14**
12 Ran Time 2m 44.96(8.56) Owned: Spring Cottage Syndicate No 2 Trained: Malton

HAMILTON FRIDAY 07.05.04 Righthand, Undulating Track, Stiff Uphill Finish

Official Going GOOD/SOFT

1600 **6.10 Mitie Amateur Classified Stakes Amateur Riders 4yo+ 0-65 (F)**
£3024 £864 £432 **6f5y str Good/Soft 81 +01 Fast** Far Side

1553* **STOIC LEADER 3** [7] R F Fisher 4-12-0 (66) Mr K Mercer(3) 9/4 FAV: 1140111: Held up, hdwy centre **79**
over 1f out, hmpd well ins last but sn led, styd on strongly: qck reapp, fair time: suited by 6f/1m on firm & soft
grnd, both AWs, any trk: most tough & genuine: see 1553 & 1485.
1215 **LORD OF THE EAST 21** [9] D Nicholls 5-11-7 (65) Mr J Gee(5) 10/1: 0502-032: Handy far side & led *nk* **70**
over 1f out, swerved badly left & hdd well ins last, just held: in good form, could win soon: see 1215.
1371 **WHIPPASNAPPER 12** [10] J R Best 4-11-7 (65) Mr E Dehdashti(3) 5/2: 1302103: Chsd ldrs, styd on fnl *1¼* **67**
2f: back to form, see 1354, 565 & 516.
1476 **HIGHLAND WARRIOR 6** [2] J S Goldie 5-11-7 (65) Mr G Goldie(7) 8/1: 33-33234: Switched far side & *1¾* **62**
held up, short of room & switched 2f out, kept on late: loves Ayr: see 1476 & 967.
960* **BLUEBERRY RHYME 39** [11]5-11-7 vis (62) Miss Faye Bramley(5) 20/1: 3-221015: Chsd ldrs, onepace *2* **56**
from dist: prev with P J Makin: see 960 & 742.
4698} **ALBASHOOSH 208** [1]6-11-9 (67) Miss Kelly Harrison(3) 20/1: 430006-6: b g Cadeaux Genereux - *1* **55**
Annona (Diesis) Led till over 1f out, sn no impress: reapp: class stks rnr-up '03 (J Goldie): h'cap wnr '02:
both wins at 7f, stays 1m: acts on firm & soft grnd, likes a gall trk: eff with/without a visor: well h'capped.
2 Jun'03 Ayr 8g/f 80-(78) D: 2 Aug'02 Newc 7gd 85-82 D: 1 Jul'02 York 7g/f 81-74 C: 2 Sep'01 Yarm 7g/s 83- D:
1 Aug'01 Chep 7sft 84- D:
1508 **TELEPATHIC 5** [3]4-11-8 BL (66) Ms C Williams 50/1: 00-00067: Held up, nvr able to chall: blnks. *2* **48**
1277 **QUIET TIMES 17** [5]5-11-7 bl (65) Mr M Seston(5) 13/2: 4041558: Chsd ldrs, btn dist: btr 834. *3½* **37**

4311} **TUSCAN FLYER 232** [8]6-11-7 (64) Miss R Bastiman(5) 25/1: 410142-9: b g Clantime - Excavator Lady 1½ 32
(Most Secret) Trkd ldrs, struggling fnl 2f: reapp: h'cap & class stks scorer '03: seller wnr for A Berry in '02,
subs landed a h'cap for current yard: acts at 5f, prob stays a sharp 6f: acts on firm, gd & polytrack: eff
with/without blnks: leave this bhd, prob at 5f/easier trk.
2 Sep'03 Yarm 6.0gd 65-60 F: 1 Sep'03 Brig 5.3g/f 55-(60) F: 1 Aug'03 Muss 5g/f 62-55 E: 2 Jul'03 Beve 5g/f 57-53 F:
1 Sep'02 Pont 5fm 58-52 E: 1 Jul'02 Muss 5gd 52- F: 1 May'01 Ayr 5g/f 65-60 D: 2 May'01 Muss 5gd 64-60 F:
4699} **ORANGINO 208** [6]6-11-7 (40) Miss R Davidson(5) 100/1: 020000-0: 10th: Chsd ldrs, outpcd halfway. nk 31
1447 **ANDREYEV 8** [12]10-11-7 p (45) Miss Dawn Rankin(5) 50/1: 55000-60: 11th: Sn bhd & nvr on terms. ½ 29
1447 **SQUARE DANCER 8** [4]8-11-7 t (40) Mr M Macdonald Wagstaffe(7) 150/1: 00/000-00: 12th: Sn strug. 9 2
12 Ran   Time 1m 14.6 (4.8)   Owned: Great Head House Estates Limited   Trained: Ulverston

---

1601 6.40 Mitie Maiden Auction Stakes A Qualifier For The Hamilton Park 2-Y-O Series Final 2yo (E)
£4160 £1280 £640   5f4y str   Good/Soft 81   -20 Slow   Far Side

MIDNIGHT TYCOON [2] B Smart 2-8-7 F Lynch 2/1 FAV: 1: b c Marju - Midnight Allure (Aragon) 81
Made all, rdn & al holding rival fnl 1f: cheaply bght Feb foal, dam a dual 1m 3yo wnr & sister to a smart 5f
sprinter: eff at 5f, 6f shld suit: acts on gd/soft & a stiff/undul trk, goes well fresh: sharp type, can win again.
EXTRA MARK [4] J R Best 2-8-7 N Pollard 9/2: 2: b c Mark of Esteem - No Comebacks (Last ¾ 78
Tycoon) Cl-up, rdn & outpcd halfway, rallied for press from over 1f out, al just held: April foal, half-brother to
prolific wnrs New Options & Steely Dan: dam plcd 6f juv & subs prolific 1m/12f wnr: eff at 5f, will get further in
time: acts on gd/soft grnd & a stiff trk: well clr of rem, a most encouraging start.
MISTER BELL [3] J G M O'Shea 2-8-11 D Sweeney 7/1: 3: gr c Lujain - Zaragossa (Paris House) 9 55
Dwelt, chsd ldrs till over 1f out: acts on gd/soft grnd, a stiff trk, dam a 5f juv wnr.
MRS KEPPLE [6] M Johnston 2-8-6 J Fanning 9/4: 4: Cl-up till outpcd from halfway. 2 44
962 **KRISTIKHAB 39** [1]2-8-9 F Norton 9/1: 05: Dwelt & sn outpcd, gelded. 3 38
5 Ran   Time 1m 3.15 (5.05)   Owned: Pinnacle Marju Partnership   Trained: Thirsk

---

1602 7.10 Mitie Mile Stakes Handicap Fillies 3yo+ 0-90 (C)
£9848 £3736 £1868   1m65y rnd   Good/Soft 81   +07 Fast   Inside   [98]

1141 **CELTIC HEROINE 25** [15] M A Jarvis 3-8-11 (81) K Darley 5/2 FAV: 51541-21: Trkd ldrs & led over 90
1f out, drvn out: best time of evening: eff at 1m/9f on fast, gd/soft & both AWs, stiff or sharp trk: lightly rcd
& progressive type: fine run against elders, keep on right side: see 1141 & 189.
1219 **LAURO 20** [14] Miss J A Camacho 4-9-2 (73) R Winston 14/1: 21214-32: Mid-div, drvn & styd on, not 1¼ 76
able to reach wnr: bckd at long odds: acts at fast, gd/soft & fibresand: see 1219.
1388 **DISPOL FOXTROT 11** [8] Miss V Scott 6-8-8 (65) R Ffrench 13/2: 12215/-23: Handy & led 3f out till 3 64
over 1f out, no extra: gd run, likes this trk, v testing grnd suits well: see 1388.
1024*}**SALAGAMA 392** [7] P F I Cole 4-10-0 (85) R Thomas(5) 11/2: 1-4: br f Alzao - Waffle On (Chief 3 78
Singer) Keen, led after 1f till 3f out, sn no extra: morning gamble, reapp/h'cap bow: sole start wnr '03 (debut,
fills mdn, impressive): eff forcing the pace at 7f, longer 8.5f trip shld suit: acts on fast, handles gd/soft grnd:
stiff/undul or gall trk. 1 Apr'03 Newb 7g/f 91- D:
1491 **NAJAABA 5** [1]4-9-11 (82) B Reilly(3) 25/1: 1151565: Held up, styd on onepace for press fnl 2f: nk 74
qck reapp: most progressive on last month, not disgraced tonight: see 861.
1423 **LILLI MARLANE 9** [2]4-9-1 (72) D Fox(5) 5/1: 23350-26: Towards rear, only mod prog towards centre. 2½ 59
1366 **MEGANS MAGIC 13** [5]4-8-12 (69) J Bramhill 10/1: 542-6127: Dwelt & bhd, late prog: btr 1307. shd 55
1279* **LYFORD LASS 17** [4]3-8-2 (72) P Hanagan 25/1: 218: Held up, no prog fnl 2f: hdwy bow: btr 1279 (mdn).1¾ 55
1131 **ODABELLA 25** [11]4-8-12 (69) J F Egan 20/1: 32340-39: Mid-div, no impress fnl 3f: btr 1131 (fast). 1¾ 49
1307 **UNO MENTE 15** [13]5-8-3 (60) Kim Tinkler 66/1: 01350-00: 10th: b f Mind Games - One Half Silver 1½ 37
(Plugged Nickle) Al bhd: '03 h'cap scorer for Mrs P M Dutfield, AW clmr plcd (rtd 54a): fills h'cap scorer '02:
eff at 1m/10f on firm, gd & polytrack: eff in cheek pieces, best without: can go well fresh.
1 Aug'03 Wind 8.3g/f 63-59 E: 1 Oct'02 Leic 8gd 64-57 E: 2 Sep'02 Bath 8fm 58-54 G:
5027} **MILLAGROS 182** [9]4-9-9 (80) D McGaffin 25/1: 106410-0: 11th: Chsd ldrs, btn 2f out, reapp. shd 56
1351 **RICHEMAUR 13** [12]4-9-6 BL (77) K Dalgleish 25/1: 0000-400: 12th: Keen, mid-div, hung right & btn ½ 52
2f out: blnks: twice below 1131 (fast).
1348 **ELLEN MOONEY 13** [10]5-8-4 BL (61) S Chin 33/1: 2-234000: 13th: Led 1f, cl-up till over 2f out: blnks. ½ 35
4289} Scotland The Brave 233 [6]4-8-12 (69) J Fanning 50/1:0 1039 **Shardda 34** [3]4-8-8 (65) B Swarbrick(5) 50/1:0
15 Ran   Time 1m 50.15 (6.35)   Owned: Mr P D Savill   Trained: Newmarket

---

1603 7.40 Mitie Scottish Handicap Stakes 3yo 0-70 (E)
£4339 £1335 £668   1m1f36y   Good/Soft 81   -14 Slow   Inside   [77]

1395* **ACE COMING 11** [3] D Eddy 3-8-12 (6ex)bl (61) P Hanagan 7/2: 000-0311: Keen handy, led 2f out, 71
drvn clr despite edging right ins fnl 1f: eff at 7f/1m, imprvd here for step up to 9f: acts on gd & soft grnd:
suited by blnks: progressing well & may not be at end of winning run: see 1395.
1306 **TIME TO RELAX 15** [10] J J Quinn 3-9-3 (66) K Darley 6/1: 00-24102: Rear, prog & ev ch dist, not 5 68
pace of wnr fnl 1f: clr rem: eff at 6f, stays 1m/9f: see 1099.
1311 **UPTHEDALE 15** [9] J R Weymes 3-7-12 (7oh) (40) D Fentiman(7) 33/1: 0500-043: b g General Monash - 7 35
Pimpinella (Reprimand) Keen, led till 2f out, wknd on front 2: unplcd in '03 (rtd 54 & 37a, mdns).
1198 **RARE COINCIDENCE 22** [2] R F Fisher 3-9-6 p (69) J F Egan 12/1: 0-113604: Led till 2f out, fdd. 1½ 54
1240 **PERFECT BALANCE 20** [4]3-8-11 (60) Kim Tinkler 12/1: 300-0165: Cl-up over 5f, fdd: btr 1147. 3 39
923 **ALWAYS FLYING 43** [5]3-9-7 (70) J Fanning 9/4 FAV: 355-1526: Prom 7f, fdd: 6 wk abs: btr 923. 1 47
1339 **MISKINA 13** [7]3-8-8 (57) B Swarbrick(5) 10/1: 024-037: Handy over 5f, wknd: btr 1339. ½ 33
4643} **MUSICAL LYRICS 213** [6]3-9-4 (67) R Ffrench 16/1: 4030-8: b f Quiet American - Foreign Courier 7 29
(Sir Ivor) Led till 1m out, fdd 3f out: reapp: plcd once in '03 (rtd 70, fills mdn): eff at 6f on firm grnd.
8 Ran   Time 2m 2.7 (8.6)   Owned: Mr I R Clements   Trained: Newcastle Upon Tyne

---

1604   **8.10 Mitie Median Auction Maiden Stakes 3yo (E)**
£3396 £1045 £523   **1m3f16y**   **Good/Soft 81**   **-14 Slow** Far Side

1241 **TUDOR BELL 20** [1] J G M O'Shea 3-9-0 (75) D Sweeney 11/4: 4-0231: Made all, pushed clr ins fnl   **77+**
2f, val 9L+: eff at 10f, apprec step up to 11f, further shld suit: acts on gd & hvy grnd: see 1241.
983   **GOLD CARD 38** [5] J R Weymes 3-9-0 (70) R Winston 10/1: 634-22: Handy, kept on ins fnl 2f but no   6   **65**
ch with wnr: eff at 1m, poss stays 11f: acts on gd & gd/soft grnd: see 983.
1095 **PAR INDIANA 29** [4] I Semple 3-8-9 (60) P Hanagan 11/2: 43-33: Cl-up over 1m, sn no extra: btr 1095. ¾ **60**
1507 **RECOGNISE 5** [2] M Johnston 3-9-0 K Dalgleish 5/6 FAV: 24: Prom 1m, wknd: qck reapp: btr 1507 (gd). 7 **55**
1275 **SILVER RHYTHM 17** [6]3-8-9 Darren Williams 33/1: 0-35: Mid-div, wknd fnl 2f: btr 1275.   1½ **48**
4943} **ROAMING VAGABOND 191** [3]3-9-0 D Fox(5) 25/1: 00-6: ch g Spectrum - Fiveofive (Fairy King) Rear, 15 **31**
nvr a factor: reapp: unplcd both '03 starts (rtd 66, mdn, G G Margarson).
6 Ran Time 2m 29.25 (10.45)   Owned: K W Bell & Son Ltd   Trained: Westbury On Severn

---

1605   **8.40 Mitie Handicap Stakes 3yo 46-55 (F)**   **[64]**
£2968 £848 £424   **5f4y str**   **Good/Soft 81**   **-09 Slow** Far Side

1374 **SHORT CHORUS 11** [7] J Balding 3-8-11 p (47) K Darley 8/1: 000-0401: Cl-up, styd on to lead dist,   **55**
rdn out: eff at 5f on firm & gd/soft grnd: acts with cheek pieces: see 1268.
1031 **DESERT LIGHT 5** [8] D Shaw 3-9-3 vis (52) P Hanagan 8/1: 0-130022: Cl-up, led after 3f, styd on   nk **60**
ins fnl 1f, just held: eff at 5/6f on gd/soft grnd & fibresand: see 1031.
1457* **HES A ROCKET 7** [10] K R Burke 3-9-12 (7ex)bl (62) B Swarbrick(5) 7/4 FAV: 03-65113: Handy, short nk **68+**
of room 2f out till ins fnl 1f, switched & styd on well, post came too sn: qck reapp: lkd unlucky here on bid for
hat-trick & surely would have won with a clr passage: see 1457 & 1268.
1374 **WENDYS GIRL 11** [1] R P Elliott 3-9-5 (55) S Chin 16/1: 0-0052P4: Cl-up till dist, no extra: see 1222. 2½ **54**
1509 **MUSIOTAL 5** [4]3-8-12 (48) J F Egan 6/1: 50-055: Rear, prog halfway, nrst fin: qck reapp: see 1509. shd **46**
1404 **A BID IN TIME 10** [2]3-8-13 (49) Darren Williams 10/1: 00-00206: Slow away, kept on fnl 1f, nrst fin. nk **46**
1457 **GARNOCK VENTURE 7** [3]3-9-5 bl (55) F Lynch 11/1: 4001037: Nvr nrr than mid-div: qck reapp. hd **51**
1509 **LAVISH TIMES 5** [9]3-9-1 bl (51) F Norton 9/1: 5306368: Led 3f, sn no extra: qck reapp: btr 1404. shd **46**
4996} **ICENASLICE 185** [5]3-9-5 (55) R Winston 12/1: 346-9: b f Fayruz - Come Dancing (Suave Dancer) Sn 1¾ **46**
handy, short of room 2f out, sn wknd: reapp: plcd once in '03 (rtd 65, auct mdn): with J J Quinn.
1031 **LOVEISDANGEROUS 35** [6]3-9-3 (53) Kim Tinkler 33/1: 35206-50: 10th: Handy over 3f, fdd: btr 1031. shd **43**
10 Ran Time 1m 2.6(4.5)   Owned: Watchman Racing   Trained: Doncaster

---

Official Going Soft, changed to Soft (Hvy Places) after 3.40

1606   **2.05 Come Racing Again Next Weekend Apprentice Handicap Stakes 3yo+ 46-55 (F)**   **[63]**
£3248 £928 £464   **6f15y str**   **Soft 123**   **-03 Slow** Stands side

1277 **KING NICHOLAS 17** [1] J Parkes 5-9-1 t p (50) Rory Moore(3) 4/1 FAV: 00-01041: Handy, led far side   **55**
group after 3f, drvn out: op 6/1: stay 7f/1m, apprec switch back to 6f this term: acts on firm, soft & both AWs:
eff with t-strap & cheek pieces: has slipped to a fair mark: see 1277 & 851.
1214 **SEMPER PARATUS 21** [7] V Smith 5-9-4 bl (53) Stephanie Hollinshead(3) 10/1: 140-4002: Rear far ½ **56**
side, prog ins fnl 2f, kept on & only just held: acts on firm, soft grnd & fibresand: back to form here & is
h'capped to find similar: see 459 & 74.
4741} **FENWICKS PRIDE 206** [9] R A Fahey 6-9-5 (54) D Swift(5) 20/1: 00000/0-3: b g Imperial Frontier - hd **56**
Stunt Girl (Thatching) Handy far side, ev ch dist, kept on & not btn far in 3rd: reapp: unplcd sole '03 start (rtd
35, h'cap): unplcd in '02 (rtd 57, h'cap, D F Rothwell): plcd in '01 (rtd 65, h'cap): eff at 5/6f on fast & hvy
grnd, prob any trk: eff with/without visor: lost little in defeat here on reapp & is well h'capped to find similar.
1426* **GAME FLORA 9** [6] M E Sowersby 3-8-12 (7ex) (57) P Mulrennan 11/1: 45000-14: Cl-up far side, ev ch 2½ **52**
dist, no extra fnl 1f: h'cap bow: btr 1426 (mdn).
1228 **DIAMOND SHANNON 20** [11]3-8-5 (50) Dawn Watson(5) 20/1: 2-005: b f Petorius - Balgren (Ballad nk **44**
Rock) Slow away far side, prog after 4f, nrst fin: rnr-up on sole '03 start (seller): eff at 6f, 7f shld suit:
acts on fast & soft grnd: only lightly rcd & can rate higher. 2 Sep'03 Ling 6g/f 47- G:
1588 **GLORY GIRL 1** [5]4-8-10 (45) D Tudhope 25/1: 630-66: Bhd far side, prog ins fnl 2f, nrst fin: ½ **38**
unplcd yesterday at Southwell in 1588.
1447* **REDOUBTABLE 8** [12]13-8-12 (7ex) (47) P Makin(3) 14/1: 1410017: Cl-up, led stands side group dist 1 **37+**
& kept on, no ch with far side group: won race on stands side: see 1447.
4311} **SPEED ON 232** [17]11-8-11 (46) C Cavanagh(4) 12/1: 000/606-8: b g Sharpo - Pretty Poppy (Song) ½ **35**
Rcd stands side, led that group till dist, no extra: reapp: unplcd in 3 '03 starts (rtd 42, h'caps): plcd once in
'02 (h'cap, rtd 58): h'cap rnr-up in '01: all wins at 5f, acts on firm & soft grnd, handles any trk: likes a
stiff/undul one: best without a visor & has gone well fresh. 2 Sep'01 Sand 5gd 62-60 E:
1267 **HALCYON MAGIC 17** [14]6-9-1 bl (50) Laura Pike(5) 8/1: 05060-29: Handy stands side 4f, no extra. nk **38**
1218 **STAR LAD 20** [16]4-8-13 bl (48) P Mathers(3) 16/1: 1001450: 10th: Trkd ldrs stands side, wknd dist. ½ **35**
1194 **ZAK FACTA 22** [8]4-9-1 (50) K Ghunowa(5) 33/1: 5524600: 11th: Cl-up far side, hung left & fdd dist. ½ **36**
1028 **ACE MA VAHRA 35** [13]6-8-12 BL (47) P Bradley 40/1: 6061600: 12th: Switched to far side, led 5f 1 **30**
out to 3f out, wknd fnl 2f: tried blnks.
1472* **WATERPARK 361** [15]6-8-13 (48) A Mullen(5) 8/1: 22/0131-0: 13th: Handy stands side, wknd fnl 2f. 1¾ **26**
1194 **ABOVE BOARD 22** [4]9-8-10 (10oh) (35) M Nem(7) 33/1: 0301060: 14th: Al bhd far side. 3 **14**
4185} **RUN ON 239** [2]6-9-5 (54) D Nolan 12/1: 653466-0: 15th: Cl-up far side 2f, fdd fnl 2f. 5 **10**
1336* **BALI STAR 14** [10]9-8-11 (46) C Haddon(5) 14/1: 2400410: 16th: Handy stands side 4f, hung left & fdd. nk **1**
1337 **ASTRAC 13** [3]13-9-1 (50) Derek Nolan(5) 10/1: 0115-500: 17th: Mid-div far side 4f, fdd. 25 **0**
17 Ran Time 1m 18.41 (7.61)   Owned: Mr M Wormald   Trained: Malton

---

1607

2.35 Become An Annual Member Median Auction Maiden Stakes 3yo (E)
£3751 £1154 £577   **6f15y str**   **Soft 123**   **+01 Fast**   Stands side

1152 **MISSION MAN 24** [7] R Hannon 3-9-0 (82) P Dobbs 8/11 FAV: 024-421: Cl-up, led after 3f, pushed   **84+**
clr ins fnl 1f, val 5L+: bckd at odds on: stay 7f/1m, imprvd here on drop back to 6f: acts on gd & soft grnd: gd
confidence boost: see 1152 & 925.
1464 **INDIAN EDGE 7** [11] B Palling 3-9-0 (65) D Kinsella 9/1: 666-052: ch g Indian Rocket - Beveled   3½   **74$**
Edge (Beveled) Slow away, prog despite hanging left after 4f, kept on ins fnl 1f, al held by wnr: op 12/1, qck
reapp: unplcd in '03 (rtd 74 & 55a, mdns): half-brother to a 6f List wnr: eff at 6f on soft grnd.
1270 **KENSINGTON 17** [10] R Guest 3-9-0 (72) J Carroll 9/1: 33064-63: Handy over 4f, wknd: see 1270.   2½   68
1464 **RENE BARBIER 7** [2] J A Glover 3-9-0 G Gibbons 66/1: 04: Cl-up over 4f, fdd: qck reapp.   4   57
1377 **CUNNING PURSUIT 11** [4]3-9-0 I Mongan 33/1: 065: Nvr nrr than mid-div: see 1377.   3   **49$**
      VICTORIANA [9]3-8-9 Dean McKeown 20/1: 6: b f Wolfhound - Silk St James (Pas de Seul) Trkd   1¼   41
ldrs, wknd bef 1f out: debut: half-sister to wnrs at 7f/10f: with H J Collingridge.
      WEIRS ANNIE [8]3-8-9 Dane O'Neill 5/1: 7: b f Puissance - Hyde Princess (Touch Paper) Handy   ½   40
over 4f, wknd: debut: op 10/3: sister/half-sister to numerous wnrs around 5f: dam won 3 times at 5f.
953   **ONYX 41** [1]3-9-0 S Righton 66/1: 68: Led 3f, sn wknd: 6 wk abs.   1   42
4766} **SAM THE SORCERER 204** [12]3-9-0 V Halliday 100/1: 000-9: Rear, nvr a factor: reapp.   nk   41
1497 **STRIDES OF FIRE 5** [6]3-9-0 BL R Havlin 25/1: 00: 10th: Slow away, al bhd: qck reapp & blnks.   5   28
      PETROLINA [3]3-8-9 J Mackay 14/1: 0: 11th: Slow away, al bhd: debut.   6   8
11 Ran   Time 1m 18.12 (7.32)   Owned: Lady Davis   Trained: Marlborough

---

1608

3.05 European Breeders Fund Novice Median Auction Stakes Fillies 2yo (F)
£3474 £1069 £535   **5f13y str**   **Soft 123**   **-00 Slow**   Stands side

1380 **CELTIC SPA 11** [4] Mrs P N Dutfield 2-8-8 R Havlin 11/2: 01: gr f Celtic Swing - Allegorica   84
(Alzao) Slow away, cl-up over 1f out, ev ch dist, led to lead cl-home: tchd 7/1: Feb foal, cost £10,000: dam
wnr at 5/7f: sire high-class performer around 12f: eff at 5f, bred to apprec further in time: acts on soft grnd &
a gall trk: can rate higher with more experience.
974* **BRIGHT MOLL 38** [3] M L W Bell 2-8-12 I Mongan 4/11 FAV: 12: Cl-up, led bef 2f out, hdd under   hd   86
press cl-home: bckd at odds on: clr of rem: ran to form of debut win in 974 here conceding 4lb to wnr.
      CASTELLETTO [1] B A McMahon 2-8-8 G Gibbons 9/2: 3: b f Komaite - Malcesine (Auction Ring)   5   70
Led over 2f, no extra dist: op 3/1 on debut: Apr foal, cost 15,500gns: sister to numerous wnrs at sprint dists:
dam 1m wnr: sire won at 7f: just btr for today.
      MONASHEE MISS [5] J A Pickering 2-8-8 Dean McKeown 33/1: 4: ch f Monashee Mountain - Most   10   45
Uppitty (Absalom) Handy over 2f, hung left & sn wknd: debut: Jan foal, cost 950gns: dam wnr at 5/6f.
4 Ran   Time 1m 4.67 (6.17)   Owned: Mr Steve Evans   Trained: Seaton

---

1609

3.40 Robin Hood Handicap Stakes 3yo+ 0-80 (D)   **[79]**
£6078 £1870 £935   **1m1f213y**   **Soft 123**   **-49 Slow**   Inside

1278* **PURE MISCHIEF 17** [1] W M Brisbourne 5-8-7 (58) D Allan(3) 2/1 FAV: 0030/-311: Cl-up, styd on to   65
lead dist, rdn out: eff at 10f on gd/soft, soft & both AWs: continues to run well & is on a fair mark: see 1278.
1083 **BLAZING THE TRAIL 30** [5] J W Hills 4-9-1 (66) S Whitworth 7/2: 4025132: Led till dist, kept on   1   70
but just held by wnr: acts on gd/soft, soft grnd & polytrack: see 1083 & 912.
1467* **OLIVIA ROSE 7** [6] J Pearce 5-9-0 (6ex) (65) J Mackay 11/4: 0452-013: Rear, prog after 7f, no   1   67
impress ins fnl 1f: op 9/4 on qck reapp: ran to form of win in 1467.
3167} **SMART JOHN 286** [2] W M Brisbourne 4-8-9 (60) Dane O'Neill 13/2: 6/03050-4: b g Bin Ajwaad - Katy   5   55
Q (Taufan) Cl-up over 1m, wknd: tchd 10/1 on reapp: plcd once in '03 (h'cap, rtd 62, B P J Baugh): unplcd in '02
(rtd 68, G J Given): eff at 10f on gd/soft grnd.
1352 **KARAOKE 13** [3]4-9-3 (68) J D Smith 6/1: 0010055: Keen cl-up over 1m, fdd: btr 803 (polytrack).   13   46
5 Ran   Time 2m 19.5 (17.2)   Owned: The Cartmel Syndicate   Trained: Nesscliffe

---

1610

4.15 Hblb Maiden Stakes Fillies 3yo (D)
£4979 £1532 £766   **1m54y md**   **Heavy 197**   **-27 Slow**   Inside

1365 **CITRINE SPIRIT 13** [4] J H M Gosden 3-8-11 R Havlin 13/8 FAV: 0-61: gr f Soviet Star - Casessa   **73+**
(Caro) Cl-up, led after 5f, pushed clr fnl 1f, val 8L+: well bckd: unplcd sole '03 starts (rtd 58, mdn): eff at
1m, has tried further: acts on hvy grnd & a gall trk: improve eff here on today's testing grnd.
5005} **DARK RAIDER 184** [7] A P Jones 3-8-11 S Whitworth 5/2: 00-2: br f Definite Article - Lady   6   64
Shikari (Kala Shikari) Cl-up, no extra ins fnl 1f: reapp: unplcd both '03 starts (rtd 74, List): eff at 1m, bred
to apprec mid-dists: acts on hvy grnd.
4138} **INMOM 241** [3] S R Bowring 3-8-11 G Baker 6/1: 50-3: b f Barathea - Zakuska (Zafonic) Rear,   1¼   59
prog after 6f, no impress fnl 1f: clr rem on reapp: unplcd both '03 starts (rtd 63, fill mdn).
983   **MARIA MARIA 38** [2] Mrs N Macauley 3-8-11 P McCabe 33/1: 0-004: Led till 3f out, fdd: see 438.   8   49
1520 **SES SELINE 4** [5]3-8-11 Dean McKeown 10/1: 45: Handy 4f, sn fdd: qck reapp: see 1520.   5   41
1125 **GOLNESSA 25** [1]3-8-11 R Fitzpatrick 25/1: 006: Cl-up 5f, fdd.   9   26
      CRIMSON STAR [6]3-8-11 Dane O'Neill 4/1: 7: b f Soviet Star - Crimson Shower (Dowsing) Cl-up   8   13
till 3f out, fdd on debut: dam wnr at 1m: sharper for today: with C Tinkler.
7 Ran   Time 1m 57.34 (17.94)   Owned: Mr Salem Suhail   Trained: Manton

---

1611	4.50 Nottingham Racecourse Conference Centre Handicap Stakes 3yo 46-55 (F)		[68]
	£3234 £924 £462 1m1f213y Heavy 197 +09 Fast Inside		

37   **ILWADOD** 174 [7] M R Channon 3-8-5 (1oh) (45) R Lappin 14/1: 006-1: b c Cadeaux Genereux - 56
Wedoudah (Sadler's Wells) Mid-div, gd prog to lead ins fnl 1f, rdn out: reapp: unplcd in '03 (rtd 57, mdn):
imprvd on step up to 10f, further shld suit: acts on hvy & a gall trk: goes well fresh: imprvd eff on h'cap bow.

1280   **PAY ATTENTION** 17 [11] T D Easterby 3-8-10 (51) D Allan(3) 7/1: 5300-402: Handy led after 1m, hdd   1½   57
ins fnl 1f, no extra: clr rem: eff at 7f/1m, now stays 10f: find similar on this evidence: see 1147.

999   **STRANGELY BROWN** 27 [12] S C Williams 3-9-0 (55) G Carter 4/1 FAV: 00-003: b g Second Empire -   6   52
Damerela (Alzao) Keen rear, prog halfway, kept on fnl 1f, no ch with front 2: well bckd: unplcd both '03 starts
(rtd 55, mdn): prob stays 10f on hvy grnd.

1534   **GIVEN A CHANCE** 3 [9] Mrs S Lamyman 3-8-5 (6oh) (40) Rory Moore(7) 11/2: 0-450534: Led till 2f out.   6   34
1363   **LET IT BE** 13 [10]3-8-5 (1oh) (45) J Mackay 15/2: 000-25: Handy, ev ch 3f out, sn wknd: btr 1363.   1¾   31
1339   **UNINTENTIONAL** 13 [16]3-9-0 (55) A Daly 16/1: 0652-606: Rear, nvr nrr than mid-div: btr 238.   hd   39
1373   **STEPPENWOLF** 12 [4]3-8-5 (1oh) (45) S Righton 50/1: 00-60007: Handy over 7f, wknd: see 696.   1   28
1529   **SUMMERISE** 4 [6]3-8-12 (53) Dean McKeown 15/2: 610-0638: Nvr nrr than mid-div: qck reapp.   1¼   33
1444   **ATLANTIC BREEZE** 8 [15]3-8-5 (1oh)P (45) R Fitzpatrick 10/1: 0000039: Handy over 7f, wknd: btr 1444.   shd   23
1365   **CTESIPHON** 13 [2]3-8-11 (52) I Mongan 16/1: 03-00: 10th: b f Arch - Beautiful Bedouin (His   1½   28
Majesty) Rear, nvr a factor: unplcd sole '03 starts (rtd 56, mdn): with J G Given.

4858}   **ROMEOS DAY** 197 [14]3-8-13 (54) L Harman(7) 33/1: 0000-0: 11th: Bhd, nvr a factor on reapp.   shd   29
1272   **ROVELLA** 17 [8]3-8-5 (6oh) (40) D Kinsella 40/1: 000-00: 12th: Rear, nvr a factor.   2   18
1150   **WELL KNIT** 24 [13]3-9-0 (55) L Keniry(3) 12/1: 20-00000: 13th: Bhd, nvr able to chall.   9   15
1280   **MYSTIC MOON** 17 [5]3-9-0 (55) S Whitworth 10/1: 0-006040: 14th: Slow away, nvr a factor.   12   0
1153   **INCHCONNEL** 24 [3]3-9-0 (55) V Slattery 20/1: 030-000: 15th: Cl-up, fdd 4f out.   17   0
1258   **CASHEMA** 18 [1]3-9-0 (55) R Havlin 10/1: 000-00: 16th: Slow away, al in rear.   1   0

16 Ran   Time 2m 21.12 (18.82)   Owned: Sheikh Ahmed Al Maktoum   Trained: West Ilsley

---

1612	5.20 Saffie Joseph & Sons Handicap Stakes 3yo 0-70 (E)		[74]
	£3653 £1124 £562 1m6f15y Heavy 197 -10 Slow Inside		

1429   **CRACKLEANDO** 9 [9] N P Littmoden 3-8-11 (57) Steven Harrison(7) 9/1: 000-3031: Cl-up, led after   63
6f, rcd far side in straight, edged left & right under press fnl 2f, all out to hold on: eff at 10 f/12f, stays 14f:
acts on polytrack, soft & hvy grnd: see 1429.

1528*   **BILL BENNETT** 4 [5] J Jay 3-9-13 (6ex) (73) G Baker 7/4 FAV: 6065112: Rear, prog after 1m, rcd   ½   78
stands side str, kept on despite hanging left, short of room ins fnl 1f, just held: qck reapp: eff at 9/12.6f,
stays 14f: acts on firm, hvy grnd & fibresand: not disgraced under top-weight with a 6lb pen, see 1528 & 1124.

658   **NOCATEE** 80 [10] P C Haslam 3-8-3 (49) Rory Moore(7) 8/1: 500-3343: Rear, prog 1m out, rcd stands   1   53
side straight, prog despite hanging left ins fnl 2f, not btn far in 3rd: clr of rem: eff at 9/11f, now stays 14f:
acts on hvy grnd & fibresand: see 608.

1213   **OVER THE YEARS** 21 [7] T P Tate 3-7-12 (4oh) (40) J Mackay 28/1: 00-54: Cl-up over 1m, sn outpcd,   10   36
mod late gains stands side fnl 2f: see 1213.

1308   **HOLLY WALK** 15 [1]3-8-2 bl (48) G Gibbons 10/1: 0004-025: Keen in tch 12f, wknd: btr 1308.   5   38
1240   **NORTHERN SPIRIT** 20 [2]3-8-7 (53) P Fessey 16/1: 0550-06: b g Kadeed - Elegant Spirit (Elegant   shd   42
Air) Rear, nvr nrr than mid-div: modest form in '03 (rtd 61, mdn): with K A Ryan.

1260   **CADEAUX ROUGE** 18 [8]3-9-3 (63) R Havlin 9/1: 5560-47: Mid-div, fdd 3f out: btr 1260.   13   41
1259   **LA CONCHA** 18 [6]3-8-9 (55) Dane O'Neill 7/1: 00008: Slow away, al in rear.   dist   0
1124   **SPECTESTED** 25 [3]3-9-1 (61) L Keniry(3) 11/1: 550-09: Rear, nvr a factor.   29   0
1444   **VALIANT AIR** 8 [4]3-7-13 (45) A McCarthy 4/1: 40-45240: 10th: Led, hdd 1m out, sn fdd: btr 1250.   dist   0

10 Ran   Time 3m 27.39(29.09)   Owned: The Headquarters Partnership Ltd   Trained: Newmarket

---

Official Going Standard

1613	2.15 Saturday Night Racing At Lingfield 29th May Handicap Stakes 3yo+ 0-75 (E)		[75]
	£3504 £1078 £539 1m aw rnd Inapplicable Fair Outside		

1352*   **LIFTED WAY** 13 [7] P R Chamings 5-9-13 (74) S Drowne 6/1: 5400-011: Al handy & led over 1f out,   80a
drvn out to hold on: eff at 7f/1m on firm, gd/soft & polytrack: in gd form: see 1352.

924*   **BRAVE DANE** 43 [8] A W Carroll 6-9-12 (73) W Ryan 11/2 JT FAV: 0-115612: Rear, hdwy wide 2f out,   hd   77a
strong run ins last, just failed: 6 wk abs: eff at 1m, 10f poss ideal: remains in gd heart: see 924.

932   **CONCER ETO** 42 [6] S C Williams 5-9-9 p (70) B Reilly(3) 6/1: 200-0023: Al handy & rdn/chall dist,   nk   73a
no extra cl-home in a tight fin: op 4/1: 6 wk abs: see 932 (C/D).

1536*   **SUPREME SALUTATION** 3 [4] D K Ivory 8-9-12 (7ex) (73) M Howard(7) 8/1: 0-011014: Mid-div, eff to   nk   75a
chase ldrs over 1f out, hung under press & onepace cl-home: op 9/2, qck reapp: remains in gd form: see 1536.

1027   **PARAGON OF VIRTUE** 35 [2]7-10-0 (75) R L Moore 11/2 JT FAV: 0-340365: Drpd rear & pushed along   2½   72a
early, mod late prog: btr 888.

1042   **COLLEGE DELINQUENT** 34 [5]5-9-5 t (66) Martin Dwyer 7/1: 3303-346: Trkd ldrs halfway, no impress   ½   62a
dist: op 9/1: btr 517.

1131   **ESTIMATION** 25 [9]4-9-5 (66) A Quinn(5) 25/1: 3635007: Keen in mid-div, onepcd fnl 1.5f.   ½   61a
4910}   **WILLHECONQUERTOO** 193 [3]4-9-6 t (67) S Carson 25/1: 056500-8: ch g Primo Dominie - Sure Care   2   58a
(Caerleon) Led till over 1f out, wknd, reapp: class stks scorer '03, subs h'cap rnr-up: auct mdn scorer '02, AW
h'cap rnr-up: eff at 5/6f, prob suited by sharp 7f, yet to convince at 1m: acts on fast, gd & polytrack, handles a
gall trk, loves a sharp/undul one: eff with/without t-strap, tried chkpcs.

2 Jul'03 Group 7gd 85-(80) D: 2 Jun'03 Ches 7.0g/f 82-76 C: 1 May'03 Brig 7.0g/f 77-(74) D: 2 Aug'02 Ling 5g/f 88- D:
2 Jul'02 Ling 6ap 86a-82 D: 1 Jun'02 Brig 5.2gd 79- F: 2 May'02 Muss 5gd 77- F: 2 May'02 Newc 5gd 74- F:

1042   **AGILIS** 34 [1]4-9-6 VIS (67) R Miles(3) 16/1: 46-06009: Rear, rdn & strug fnl 3f: visor, poor run.   shd   58a
714   **SUPERCHIEF** 73 [11]9-9-4 bl t (65) S Sanders 11/1: 4355250: 10th: Keen, in tch wide 6f: abs.   10   39a

674 **Learned Lad 79** [10]6-9-5 (66) C Catlin 20/1:0   1235 **Count Walewski 20** [12]4-9-9 (70) T Quinn 40/1:0
12 Ran   Time 1m 38.86 (2.66)   Owned: Mrs Alexandra J Chandris   Trained: Basingstoke

LINGFIELD Polytrack FRIDAY 07.05.04 Lefthand, Sharp, Undulating Track

Official Going Soft (Good/Soft Places)

1614	**2.45 European Breeders Fund Maiden Stakes 2yo (D)**

£4212 £1296 £648   **5f str**   **Good/Soft**   **Slow**   Stands Side

1205 **MOSCOW MUSIC 21** [4] M G Quinlan 2-9-0   S Drowne 4/7 FAV: 21: Made all & in command dist, pushed   75
out: hvly bckd at odds on, confirmed debut promise: acts on gd & gd/soft grnd, gall or sharp/undul trk: can force
the pace: type to rate higher: see 1205.
        BOGAZ [1] R M Beckett 2-9-0   S Sanders 8/1: 2: b c Rossini - Fastnet (Forzando) Chsd wrn, shkn   1½   69
up & kept on, al held by wnr: Feb foal, 17,000gns purchase: half-brother to a 5f plcd juv: eff at 5f, shld stay 6f:
handles gd/soft grnd: likely improver.
1510 **FORTNUM 4** [3] R Hannon 2-9-0   R L Moore 3/1: 53: Pushed along rear, kept on late, nvr a threat: ¾   67
op 9/2, qck reapp: see 1510.
1380 **HEART OF ETERNITY 11** [2] J R Boyle 2-8-9   Martin Dwyer 11/1: 04: b f Namid - Kurfuffle   1½   57
(Bluebird) Pushed along & green near, no impress fnl 2f: £31,000 Apr foal, half-sister to a dual juv wnr.
4 Ran   Time 1m 02.32 (5.52)   Owned: O'Connor Racing   Trained: Newmarket

1615	**3.20 Toteplacepot Handicap Stakes 3yo+ 0-85 (D)**	[85]

£7046 £2168 £1084   **5f str**   **Good/Soft**   **Fast**   Stands Side

1217 **FOREVER PHOENIX 21** [10] R M H Cowell 4-9-10 (81) A Quinn(5) 9/2 FAV: 6112131: Al trav well & trkd   96+
ldrs stands side, went on 2f out & sn asserted, readily: eff at 1m, imprvd significantly at 5/6f this term: acts on
fast, gd/soft & both AWs, likes sharp/undul trk: useful filly who travels well in her races, more to come.
1269 **ROXANNE MILL 17** [11] J M Bradley 6-9-3 (74) R L Moore 13/2: 40020-32: Handy & rdn to chall over   3½   77
1f out, sn outpcd by wnr: on a fair mark for similar, can win sn: see 1269.
1578 **ANOTHER GLIMPSE 1** [6] Miss B Sanders 6-8-10 t (67) S Sanders 5/1: 50-410023: Rdn rear early, styd   1¼   67
on late, not reach front pair: rnr-up yesterday: eff at 5f, 6/7f suits ideally: see 1578 & 880 (AW).
4218} **CERULEAN ROSE 237** [9] A W Carroll 5-8-11 (68) W Ryan 7/1: 111135-4: ch f Bluegrass Prince -   ¾   66
Elegant Rose (Noalto) Held up, hdwy halfway, nrst fin: reapp: most prog in '03, landed 3 h'caps: unplcd '02 (rtd
35, no sand form, tried t-strap & blnks): eff at 5/5.8f on firm & gd/soft, prob any trk: tough filly, encouraging rtn.
1 Aug'03 Newm 5fm 69-63 D: 1 Aug'03 Bath 5.0fm 64-56 E: 1 Jul'03 Good 5gd 61-51 D: 1 Jul'03 Chep 5.1g/s 52-37 E:
1 Jul'03 Donc 5gd 44-37 F:
1293 **MADRASEE 16** [3]6-9-6 (77) S Drowne 12/1: 2004505: Pushed along rear, eff to chase ldrs halfway,   2   70
no prog & position accepted ins last: likes Brighton: see 329.
1383 **OK PAL 11** [8]4-10-0 (85) R Miles(3) 9/1: 04-U3006: Led/dsptd lead till 2f out, fdd: btr 834 (AW).   4   68
4259} **ROSES OF SPRING 234** [7]6-10-0 p (85) B Doyle 25/1: 000100-7: gr f Shareef Dancer - Couleur de   ¾   66
Rose (Kalaglow) Mid-div, outpcd halfway on reapp: prog in '03, landed 3 AW h'caps, turf h'cap & dual turf class
stks scorer: '02 h'cap wnr: eff at 5/6f on firm, gd/soft & both AWs, any trk, likes Bath: best in cheek pieces,
with/without t-strap, has tried visor: likes to force the pace. 1 Aug'03 Bath 5.0fm 88-(83) D:
2 Jul'03 Bath 5.7fm 80-(85) C: 2 Jun'03 Bath 5.7fm 86-83 D: 1 May'03 Bath 5.0g/s 86-(84) D:
2 May'03 Ling 5gd 84-82 D: 1 May'03 Redc 5g/f 82-75 D: 1 Mar'03 Ling 5ap 83a-77 D: 1 Jan'03 Ling 5ap 81a-74 E:
1 Jan'03 Wolv 6af 76a-68 E: 1 Dec'02 Ling 5ap 71a-64 E: 1 Sep'02 Leic 5fm 71-65 D: 2 Sep'02 Good 6fm 66-63 C:
1293 **DANCING MYSTERY 16** [12]10-9-11 bl (82) Liam Jones(7) 11/1: 3-135008: Led till 3f out, sn btn.   1½   59
1371 **LADY PEKAN 12** [5]5-8-5 bl (62) Lisa Jones(3) 10/1: 6002209: Towards centre, prom till halfway.   ½   37
1269 **BYO 17** [1]6-8-13 (70) Martin Dwyer 14/1: 444-0620: 10th: Towards centre, sn strug: btr 1269.   nk   44
1476 **Seven No Trumps 6** [2]7-9-9 p(80) S Carson 12/1:0
740 **Blessed Place 71** [4]4-8-0 (2ow)(5oh)(50) C Catlin 40/1:0
12 Ran   Time 59.75 (2.95)   Owned: Mr J M Greetham   Trained: Newmarket

1616	**3.55 R R Richardson Classified Stakes 3yo+ 0-80 (D)**

£5639 £1735 £868   **7f140y str**   **Good/Soft**   **Slow**   Centre

1351 **SOYUZ 13** [3] M A Jarvis 4-9-9 (82) P Robinson 5/4 FAV: 3000-231: Trkd ldr, led 2f out & rdn clr,   90
decisively: slow time, hvly bckd thr' op 4/5: eff at 6f/1m on fast & soft grnd, prob any trk: see 1057.
1481 **CHEESE N BISCUITS 6** [2] G L Moore 4-9-4 (79) R L Moore 7/2: 3135-002: b f Spectrum - Bint   3½   77
Shihama (Cadeaux Genereux) Pushed rear, styd on to take 2nd cl-home, nvr a threat: bckd from 11/2, qck reapp:
AW mdn wnr '03 (C A Cyzer), subs AW h'cap scorer for current yard: suited by 7f, tried 9f: prob handles firm
& gd/soft grnd, likes polytrack, sharp/undul trk. 1 Oct'03 Ling 7ap 83a-75 D: 1 Feb'03 Ling 7ap 74a-70 D:
1351 **JOOLS 13** [4] D K Ivory 6-9-8 (81) R Miles(3) 7/2: 00-00153: Led, rdn & hdd 2f out, sn no impress.   ¾   80
1351 **IMPERSONATOR 13** [1] J L Dunlop 4-9-7 BL (78) T Quinn 5/1: 00040-04: b g Zafonic - Conspiracy   2   75
(Rudimentary) Trkd ldr, rdn & btn over 1f out: blnks: h'cap plcd '03 (rtd 83): nurs h'cap scorer '02: eff at
7f/1m on fast & hvy grnd, likes a stiff/gall trk. 1 Nov'02 Donc 7hvy 91-82 D: 2 Oct'02 Newm 8g/f 84-78 D:
4 Ran   Time 1m 37.77 (9.97)   Owned: Mr N R A Springer   Trained: Newmarket

1617	**4.30 Weatherbys Insurance Maiden Stakes 3yo+ (D)**

£4199 £1292 £646   **7f str**   **Good/Soft**   **Fast**   Stands Side

1210 **LUCKY SPIN 21** [17] R Hannon 3-8-7   R L Moore 11/4: 21: Handy stands side, led over 1f out & rdn   92
clr, readily: bckd, confirmed debut promise: eff at 7f, shld get 1m: acts on gd & gd/soft grnd, gall or
sharp/undul trk: looks potentially useful: see 1210.
3253} **CASTLETON 282** [8] H J Cyzer 3-8-12   Martin Dwyer 5/2 FAV: 34-2: b c Cape Cross - Craigmill (Slip   5   86

LINGFIELD **Polytrack** **FRIDAY 07.05.04** **Lefthand, Sharp, Undulating Track**

Anchor) Led till over 1f out, sn no ch with wnr but well clr of rem: reapp: promise both '03 starts (auct mdn plcd, rtd 85, subs Gr 2 4th, rtd 99): eff at 6/7f: handles firm & gd/soft grnd: likely type for similar.
4750} **WYOMING 205** [6] J A R Toller 3-8-7 W Ryan 100/1: 00-3: ch f Inchinor - Shoshone (Be My Chief) *7* **66$**
Mid-div, kept on late, nvr trbld front pair: reapp: mod form both '03 starts (rtd 56 & 26a, mdns): shapes as if 1m+ could suit, likely improver in h'cap company.
1514 **MY PENSION 4** [1] P Howling 3-8-12 S Drowne 25/1: 04: Dwelt, hdway halfway, no impress fnl 2f. *¾* **70$**
2611} **PRESUMPTIVE 309** [16]4-9-10 T Quinn 9/2: 0/3-5: Trkd ldrs, no impress fnl 2f: op 8/1, new yard. *3½* **63**
1136 **KEYAKI 25** [7]3-8-7 S Sanders 7/1: 66: Slow away, sn mid-div, btn over 1f out. *1½* **55**
1083 **MADAME MARIE 30** [11]4-9-5 (50) Lisa Jones(3) 66/1: 40003-07: Bhd halfway, late gains: cld improve. *nk* **54**
4575} **GREY BOY 217** [14]3-8-12 C Catlin 20/1: 0-8: Cl-up after 2f, wknd 2f out: reapp, gldd. *nk* **58**
734 **FORGE LANE 71** [12]3-8-12 R Brisland 66/1: 009: Mid-div & strugg fnl 2f: abs, new yard. *1½* **55**
829 **YOUNG DYNASTY 59** [15]4-9-10 BL (45) Liam Jones(7) 66/1: 0550: 10th: Went left start, handy till over 1f out, 2 month abs, blnks. *1½* **52$**
1010 **STAR FERN 37** [4]3-8-12 (57) N Chalmers(5) 50/1: 4-5500: 11th: Al bhd & no ch fnl 2f, turf rtn. *3* **46**
1518 **Mad Maurice 4** [9]3-8-12 P S W Kelly 33/1:0
1152 **Blake Hall Lad 24** [5]3-8-12 O Urbina 33/1:0
Wolf Cub [10]3-8-12 C Lowther 33/1:0
1130 **Spector 25** [3]4-9-10 D Corby(3) 50/1:0
798 **Night Storm 64** [13]3-8-7 (70) Paul Eddery 12/1:0
1220 **Zambezi River 20** [2]5-9-10 C J Davies(7) 100/1:0
17 Ran Time 1m 26.51 (6.11) Owned: Mr George C Scudder Trained: Marlborough

LINGFIELD **Polytrack** **FRIDAY 07.05.04** **Lefthand, V Sharp Track**

Official Going Standard

1618

5.05 Come To The Derby Trial Tomorrow Handicap Stakes Fillies 3yo+ 0-70 (E) **[70]**
£3474 £1069 £535 **1m2f aw** **Inapplicable** **Slow** Inside

1340 **STATE OF BALANCE 13** [9] K Bell 6-9-3 (59) C Catlin 12/1: 0040-041: ch f Mizoram - Equilibrium (Statoblest) Dwelt, keen in rear, switched wide & styd on for press to lead cl-home, all out: first win: unplcd '03 (rtd 53a, AW mdn): mod bmpr form back in 02/03: eff arnd a sharp 10f on polytrack. **61a**
1399 **ANYHOW 10** [6] Miss K M George 7-9-8 (64) D Nolan(5) 6/1: 0214542: Mid-div, drvn to chall ins last, not pace of wnr cl-home: op 9/2: loves this trk, could win again: see 801 (12f). *nk* **65a**
1045* **MY LILLI 34** [5] P Mitchell 4-8-12 (54) R L Moore 6/1: 3406413: Handy & led 3f out, rdn clr over 2f out, hdd well ins last: op 8/1: ran to form of 1045 (1m, made all). *hd* **54a**
1385 **MISS GRACE 11** [7] J J Sheehan 4-10-0 (70) D Corby(3) 25/1: 13360-04: ch f Atticus - Jetbeeah (Lomond) Handy, styd on for press fnl 2f, just held: clr of rem & btn less than 1L in a tight fin: C/D mdn wnr for B W Hills in '03, subs turf unplcd (rtd 63, h'cap): eff arnd 10f: acts on polytrack, handles fast & gd/soft, stiff or sharp trk. 1 Mar'03 Ling 10ap 70a-(72) D: 2 Mar'03 Ling 10ap 74a- D: *nk* **69a**
912 **FIGURA 44** [4]6-9-0 (56) S Sanders 4/1 FAV: 0356665: Trkd ldrs, short of room 2f out, no impress, abs. *6* **46a**
801 **ALISA 64** [2]4-9-1 t (57) S W Kelly 20/1: 03556: Chsd ldrs, no impress dist: 2 mnth abs: btr 801. *1* **46a**
1045 **WANNA SHOUT 34** [8]6-9-2 (58) Lisa Jones(3) 7/1: 4-212127: Trkd ldrs, wknd over 1f out: btr 1045. *shd* **47a**
1585 **MARGERY DAW 1** [1]4-9-8 (64) Derek Nolan(7) 16/1: 3/2252-588: U.r. & bolted on way to start, reluctant to enter stalls, mid-div, struggling fnl 2f: unplcd yesterday: see 269 & 148. *2* **50a**
53* **TETOU 171** [12]4-10-0 (70) J F McDonald(3) 12/1: 301-9: Trkd ldrs, btn 2f out: abs, h'cap bow. *1½* **54a**
1307 **ACOLA 15** [14]4-9-0 (56) B Doyle 14/1: 000-000: 10th: Mid-div wide, btn 3f out. *1* **39a**
1399 **NUZZLE 10** [10]4-8-8 (50) Martin Dwyer 14/1: 31-00050: 11th: Led after 2f till 3f out, sn btn. *2½* **29a**
4832} **HARIBINI 199** [13]4-8-6 (48) N Chalmers(5) 50/1: 043030-0: 12th: Slow away & al bhd: new yard. *1* **26a**
1098 **CASTAWAY QUEEN 29** [11]5-9-6 (62) S Drowne 11/1: 05620-20: 13th: Rear/wide, no ch fnl 2f. *1* **39a**
4870} **DREAMING WATERS 196** [3]3-8-6 (63) S Carson 20/1: 600-0: 14th: Reluctant to enter stalls, led 2f, lost pl from halfway: reapp: h'cap/AW bow. *1½* **38a**
14 Ran Time 2m 07.29(4.49) Owned: North Farm Stud Trained: Wantage

LINGFIELD **Polytrack** **SATURDAY 08.05.04** **Lefthand, Sharp, Undulating Track**

Official Going SOFT (GOOD/SOFT places).

1619

1.35 Listed Antonia Cridland Oaks Trial Fillies 3yo (A)
£29750 £11000 £5500 **1m3f106y** **Soft 116** **-43 Slow** Outside

BARAKA 238 [5] A P O'Brien 3-8-8 J P Spencer 9/4: 0-1: b f Danehill - Cocotte (Troy) Dwelt, sn trkd ldr & trav well, cruised through to lead over 1f out, any amount in hand: Irish raider, reapp: well btn sole '03 start (val stks, started at odds on): half sister to high class mid-dist performer Pilsudski: relished this step up to 11.5f & soft ground, shld get further: impeccably bred & one to follow. **113+**
1294 **BOWSTRING 17** [2] J H M Gosden 3-8-8 (95) L Dettori 10/11 FAV: 0-122: Led, rdn & jnd 2f out, hdd over 1f out & sn left bhnd: clr of rem, well bckd: caught a tartar: see 1294, 980. *6* **98**
3998} **RIO DE JUMEIRAH 250** [1] C E Brittain 3-8-8 (78) D Holland 16/1: 3035-3: b f Seeking The Gold - Tegwen (Nijinsky) Chsd ldrs, rdn & no impress fnl 3f: reapp: mdn plcd '03 (rtd 77): stays 7f, bred to appreciate mid-dists: handles fast & gd grnd, stiff or sharp/undul trk: appeared to struggle in these testing conditions. *10* **85$**
4631} **DONNA VITA 216** [4] G A Butler 3-8-8 (90) K Fallon 11/2: 10-4: b f Vettori - Soolaimon (Shareef Dancer) Held up, rdn & lost tch 3f out: reapp: AW mdn wnr on debut '03, subs well btn sole other start (Gr 1): eff at 7f, strong mid-dist pedigree: acts on polytrk: can go well fresh. 1 Sep'03 Ling 7ap 81a- D: *1* **83**
1382 **CHARA 12** [3]3-8-8 (66) E Ahern 25/1: 045-3105: Sn bhd & no ch fnl 3f: see 1165 (h'cap). *7* **73$**
5 Ran Time 2m 41.68 (18.28) Owned: Mrs David Nagle & Mrs John Magnier Trained: Ireland

---

1620 **2.05 Gr3 Totesport Chartwell Stakes Fillies 3yo+** **(A)**
£29000 £11000 £5500 **7f str** **Soft 116** **+11 Fast** Stands Side

1210* **ILLUSTRIOUS MISS 22** [11] D R Loder 3-8-5 T P Queally 4/1: 11: Rear when short of room over 1f   **114+**
out, swtchd & smooth/rapid prog to lead ins last, sn clr, wd 4L+ in a fast time: nicely bckd: confirmed debut
promise: eff at 7f, will get 1m: acts on gd & relished soft today: handles a gall or sharp/undul trk: unexposed
filly, poss a smart performance & one to follow in higher company.
4176} **GONFILIA 58** [1] Saeed bin Suroor 4-9-3 t L Dettori 3/1 FAV: 2251-012: b f Big Shuffle - Gonfalon   2½ 106
(Slip Anchor) Cl up & went on over 2f out, rdn & hdd ins last, no ch with wnr but rest well covered: bckd: val
stks wnr in Dubai earlier: List wnr in France in '03, earlier dual Listed rnr-up: dual German wnr '02: eff at 7f/1m
on firm, soft & dirt: can force the pace: tough & useful filly, win again in Listed company.
2 Aug'03 Deau 8g/s 101- A: 2 Aug'03 Good 7g/f 100- A: 2 Mar'03 Nad 8dirt 96a- :
1436 **GOLDEN NUN 13** [8] T D Easterby 4-9-3 p (96) T Quinn 7/1: 2305-023: Mid-div, styd on for press, no   4 99
threat to front pair: List/val h'cap company could be ideal: see 1436.
58 **BLAISE CASTLE 176** [9] G A Butler 4-9-3 (90) S Drowne 14/1: 003042-4: Keen early & trkd ldrs,   1¾ 97
styd on onepace for press: 6 mth abs: acts on gd, soft & polytrk: see 58.
4953* **DOWAGER 190** [3]3-8-5 (90) Martin Dwyer 12/1: 162461-5: b f Groom Dancer - Rose Noble (Vaguely   nk 96
Noble) Chsd ldrs, rdn & no extra over 1f out: reapp: mdn & List scorer '03: stays 7f well, poss a stiff 6f suits
best: acts on firm & gd, prob handles soft: handles a stiff or easy trk: useful filly, a fair return.
1 Oct'03 Newm 6gd 98-(98) A: 2 Sep'03 Sali 6fm 102-(91) A: 1 Jun'03 Kemp 7fm 86- D:
1151 **MISS IVANHOE 25** [2]4-9-3 (102) D Holland 9/2: 22612-06: Chsd ldrs, no impress fnl 2f: btr 1151.   shd 96
1356 **STARBECK 14** [12]6-9-3 (84) P McCabe 40/1: 05520-07: b f Spectrum - Tide of Fortune (Soviet Star)   nk 95$
Dwelt & rear, mod hdwy when short of room over 1f out, nvr a threat: List rnr-up '03 (P S McEntee): unplcd '02 (rtd
76, h'cap): eff at 6f/7f on firm & soft, has tried a t-strap: btr off in h'caps.
2 Oct'03 Asco 7gd 94-(62) A: 2 Jul'01 Newm 6gd 86-82 B:
1169 **MALVERN LIGHT 24** [10]3-8-5 (99) R Hills 7/1: 41-48: Chsd ldrs, no prog 2f out: see 1169.   2½ 91
1383 **MISS GEORGE 12** [3]6-9-3 (83) Dane O'Neill 33/1: 30-10039: Dwelt & bhd, nvr factor: see 879.   2½ 87$
1356 **RIVA ROYALE 14** [4]4-9-3 (84) J Fanning 50/1: 35001-00: 10th: Led till over 2f out, sn btn: see 1356.   2½ 83
1490 **PRESTO VENTO 6** [5]4-9-3 (90) P Dobbs 20/1: 50030-00: 11th: Dwelt, rear, keeping on when hmpd   3 79
over 1f out, position accepted: qck reapp: forgive this.
11 Ran Time 1m 27.77 (7.37) Owned: Sheikh Mohammed Trained: Newmarket

---

1621 **2.35 Totescoop6 Sprint Heritage Handicap 3yo 0-105 (B)**   [98]
£34800 £13200 £6600 **6f str** **Soft 116** **+04 Fast** Stands Side

1488 **MORSE 7** [4] J A Osborne 3-8-13 (83) L Dettori 9/2: 36-02231: Chsd ldrs, hdwy to lead over 1f   93
out, drvn out: bckd, gd time: eff at 6/7f on fast, soft & polytrk: has a progressive profile.
1360 **PETARDIAS MAGIC 14** [3] E J O'Neill 3-9-1 (85) K Fallon 6/1: 16-41302: Rear, hdwy halfway,   hd 94
drvn/styd on well ins last, just failed: acts on fast, soft & polytrk: back to best, see 1154 & 1116.
1570 **PRESTO SHINKO 3** [1] R Hannon 3-8-8 (78) D Holland 4/1: 033-163: Went left & dwelt start, sn trkd   3 80
ldrs, hung left & no impress from dist: op 6/1, qck reapp: acts on fast & polytrk, handles soft.
1018 **VIENNAS BOY 37** [5] R Hannon 3-9-5 (89) Dane O'Neill 12/1: 42020-44: Led, rdn & hdd over 1f out,   1 88
sn no impress: btr 1018 (stks).
1417* **MOLCON 10** [6]3-8-11 (81) D Fox(5) 3/1 FAV: 1150-515: Broke well & trkd ldrs, btn 2f out: well bckd.   ½ 79
1498 **ORO VERDE 8** [2]3-9-7 (91) P Dobbs 50/1: 33402-06: Went left start, rear, efft & no impress over   hd 88
1f out: qck reapp: see 176 (AW nov stks)
1498 **STAR PUPIL 6** [7]3-8-10 VIS (80) Martin Dwyer 100/30: 02-427: Dwelt, sn rdn/bhd & nvr trav: nicely   1¾ 73
bckd tho' op 11/4: never going well in 1st time vis: may want further but much btr 1498 (g/s).
7 Ran Time 1m 15.53 (6.73) Owned: Turf 2000 Limited Trained: Upper Lambourn

---

1622 **3.10 Gr3 Gallagher Group Ltd Derby Trial Stakes Colts & Geldings 3yo (A)**
£35700 £13200 £6600 **1m3f106y** **Soft 116** **-14 Slow** Outside

1153* **PERCUSSIONIST 25** [1] J H M Gosden 3-8-7 (88) L Dettori 11/4: 32-11: Trkd ldrs, smooth hdwy to   118
lead over 2f out, pulled well clr despite hanging badly right ins last: well bckd: confirmed reapp promise: suited by
11.5f/12f, shld stay further: acts on fast, likes good/soft & soft grnd, stiff or sharp/undul trk: clearly still
green but a useful colt who can continue to progress: see 1153.
1482* **HAZYVIEW 7** [5] N A Callaghan 3-8-7 (84) D Holland 11/10 FAV: 31-21112: Trkd ldr, led after 3f,   10 106
hdd over 2f out, sn no ch with wnr: hvly bckd: no match for this wnr over today's longer trip: btr 1482 (List).
4742} **FIVE DYNASTIES 209** [3] A P O'Brien 3-8-7 J P Spencer 9/4: 14-3: b c Danehill - Star Begonia   17 89
(Sadler's Wells) Held up in tch, rdn & lost tch with front pair over 3f out, eased: bckd from 3/1, reapp: Irish
raider, mdn wnr on debut '03, subs Gr 2 4th (rtd 100): eff at 1m, mid dist pedigree: acts on firm & gd/sft grnd:
connections reported colt did not handle the testing ground today.
1384 **MAIDSTONE MIDAS 12** [4] W S Kittow 3-8-7 S Drowne 100/1: 04: b c Nashwan - Be Mine (Wolfhound)   dist 0
Led 3f, sn lost tch: up in trip: highly tried & no form.
4 Ran Time 2m 38.30 (14.9) Owned: Exors of the late Mr R E Sangster Trained: Manton

---

1623 **3.40 Testers Of Edenbridge Maiden Stakes 3yo+ (D)**
£4407 £1356 £678 **1m2f** **Soft 116** **-59 Slow** Inside

4989} **FINE PALETTE 187** [7] H R A Cecil 4-9-12 W Ryan 7/2: 2-1: ch c Peintre Celebre - Filly Mignonne   84
(Nashwan) Keen, rear, hdwy over 2f out, rdn to lead well ins last: nicely bckd, reapp: mdn rnr up on sole start
'03: eff at 10f, 12f+ could suit: likes soft grnd, gall or sharp/undul trk: goes well fresh: lightly rcd colt.
2 Nov'03 Redc 10sft 74- D:
53 **SEVEN YEAR ITCH 172** [2] M P Tregoning 4-9-12 Martin Dwyer 13/2: 2-2: Keen & led till over 3f   1 82
out, rallied for press to lead again ins last, no extra when hdd & hung right well ins last: 6 mth abs: turf bow:
acts on soft & polytrk: handles a sharp/undul trk: should find a race: see 53.
4942} **PAGAN MAGIC 192** [6] J A R Toller 3-8-11 Lisa Jones(3) 7/1: 05-3: b c Diesis - Great Lady Slew   1½ 80

(Seattle Slew) Handy & led over 3f out, rdn & hdd ins last, no extra when carried right close home: op 10/1, reapp: unplcd but promise 2nd of just 2 '03 starts (rtd 77, mdn): styd longer 10f trip well, 12f may suit: acts on soft ground, sharp/undul & easy trks: now qual for h'caps.
759 **SWAINSON 70** [8] P Mitchell 3-8-11 D Holland 5/1: 34: Dwelt but sn trkd ldrs, onepace fnl 3f: *2½* **77**
bckd, turf bow: abs: handles soft ground & polytrk: see 759 (debut).
1166 **MAHARAAT 24** [3]3-8-11 t R Hills 9/4 FAV: 55: Chsd ldrs till dist: well bckd: btr 1166 (1m, gd). *1¾* **75$**
1259 **PERSIAN DAGGER 19** [4]3-8-11 G Carter 33/1: 0-006: Rear, only mod prog fnl 3f. *1¾* **73**
1384 **MASKED 12** [5]3-8-11 T Quinn 14/1: 07: Dwelt, al bhd: plenty of stamina in pedigree. *1* **71**
LUCKY ARTHUR [1]3-8-6 D Sweeney 66/1: 8: Al bhd on debut: cld need 12f+ in time. *2* **63**
873 **STARMIX 50** [9]3-8-11 K Fallon 20/1: 09: Chsd ldrs till halfway, lost tch: abs. *26* **42**
9 Ran Time 2m 21.72 (17.52) Owned: Mrs Angela Scott Trained: Newmarket

1624 **4.15 Lingfield-Racecourse Co Uk Handicap Stakes 4yo+ 0-105 (B)** **[100]**
£12319 £4673 £2336 **7f str** **Soft 116** **-04 Slow** Stands Side

1474 **GOLDEN CHALICE 7** [14] A M Balding 5-9-0 (86) K Fallon 8/1: 20-56001: Held up stands rail, short of room & swtchd over 3f out, hdwy to lead dist, in command ins last: op 10/1: returned to form with aid of favourable high draw: eff at 7f/1m on firm & soft, any trk, best without vis: useful gelding: see 431. **95**
1423 **OAKLEY RAMBO 10** [15] R Hannon 5-8-5 (77) R L Moore 12/1: 000-5062: Rear stands rail, swtchd *¾* **82**
towards centre & styd on well from over 2f out, al held by wnr: gd run from high draw tho' forced to race away from rail closing stages: acts on firm & soft: nicely h'capped, can win soon: see 1020.
4349*}**POLAR BEAR 231** [10] W J Haggas 4-9-2 (88) D Holland 5/2 FAV: 053/11-3: ch g Polar Falcon - Aim *½* **92**
For The Top (Irish River) In tch & short of room over 2f out, swtchd & styd on, not able to chall: hvly bckd on reapp: won both starts '03 (h'caps): plcd '02 (AW mdn, rtd 71a, turf unplcd, rtd 66): eff at 7f/1m on firm, soft & fibresand, gall or sharp trk: goes well fresh: lightly rcd & useful 4yo, continues to progress.
1 Sep'03 Ayr 8fm 90-80 C: 1 Aug'03 Newm 7gd 82-70 D:
1481 **MARKER 7** [2] G B Balding 4-8-13 (85) R Havlin 20/1: 600-6004: Chsd ldr, chall over 1f out, no *4* **82**
extra ins last: gd run from awkward low draw: acts on firm & soft: stiff 6f could be ideal: see 945.
1356 **KOOL 14** [8]5-9-9 (95) T Quinn 12/1: 1120/-305: Chsd ldrs, no impress fnl 2f: op 14/1: see 1126. *½* **91**
1481 **PRINCE CYRANO 7** [13]5-8-7 (79) G Carter 33/1: 200-0006: Reared start, bhd, late gains: see 1481. *1* **73**
1151 **MARSHMAN 25** [9]5-9-4 (90) P Robinson 7/2: 1534-037: Chsd ldrs till dist: bckd: btr 1151 (g/s). *1* **82**
1138 **TARANAKI 26** [11]6-8-11 (83) S Sanders 8/1: 01-04148: Handy, led 2f out till dist, wknd: bckd. *shd* **75**
262 **CAMP COMMANDER 131** [1]5-9-10 t (96) L Dettori 14/1: 000034-9: gr c Pennekamp - Khalatara *2* **85**
(Kalaglow) Dwelt, bhd, only mod prog: 4 mth abs: val h'cap wnr '03, AW h'cap plcd (rtd 99a): mdn wnr '02: suited by 7f/1m, stays 10f: acts on fast, gd & polytrk, any trk: suited by a t-strap: best held up off a strong pace: useful cot, should be spot on for repeat bid in Victoria Cup h'cap. 2 Jun'03 Asco 8g/f 99-92 B: 1 Apr'03 Asco 7gd 92-83 B:
1 Aug'02 Warw 7.1g/f 84- D: 2 Dec'01 Ling 7ap 81a- D: 2 Dec'01 Ling 8ap 81a-77 D:
1423 **OUT FOR A STROLL 10** [16]5-8-5 (77) J Mackay 66/1: 00110-00: 10th: b g Zamindar - The Jotter *nk* **65**
(Night Shift) Always rear: dual h'cap scorer '03 (lightly rcd, well bckd both wins): dual h'cap wnr '02: eff at 7f/1m on firm & gd grnd & a stiff/gall or undul trk: can go well fresh: merits attention when bckd.
1 Oct'03 Nott 8.2fm 78-71 E: 1 Sep'03 Leic 7.0g/f 75-68 E: 2 Sep'02 Hayd 8.1gd 76-70 E: 1 Aug'02 Pont 8g/f 72-66 C:
2 Aug'02 Bath 8g/f 70-65 D: 1 Jul'02 Newc 7g/f 71-62 F:
1138 **MATERIAL WITNESS 26** [6]7-9-0 (86) Martin Dwyer 33/1: 02100-00: 11th: Led/dsptd lead till 2f out. *1½* **72**
1356 **CRIMSON SILK 14** [12]4-9-12 P (98) Paul Eddery 25/1: 063-0000: 12th: Chsd ldrs till 3f out: chkpcs. *5* **76**
1474 **FIVEOCLOCK EXPRESS 7** [7]4-8-9 vis (81) S Drowne 11/1: 1300-420: 13th: Sn strugg: btr 1474. *8* **48**
1337 **VAL DE MAAL 14** [5]4-8-1 (73) A McCarthy 66/1: 15240-30: 14th: Led till 4f out, wknd: gldd. *5* **33**
14 Ran Time 1m 28.77 (8.37) Owned: Holistic Racing Ltd Trained: Kingsclere

1625 **4.45 Ocs Group Ladies Stakes Handicap Lady Amateur Riders 3yo+ 0-75 (E)** **[60]**
£2392 £2392 £563 **7f str** **Soft 116** **-38 Slow** Stands Side

1074* **SOMERSET WEST 32** [7] J R Best 4-10-3 (63) Miss J Ferguson(7) 20/1: 01-60011: Made most, held on gamely for press, joined on line: op 33/1: prev with Mrs L Stubbs: imprvd of late with forcing tactics at 7f: acts on fast, soft & polytrk: significant improv today on turf return for new yard: see 1074 (AW sell). **64**
1253 **HE WHO DARES 19** [12] A W Carroll 6-10-0 (60) Mrs S Bosley 5/2 FAV: 2-203431: Dwelt & bhd, strong *dht* **64**
run from over 1f out & forced a dead heat: nicely bckd: eff btwn 7/10f on fast, hvy & polytrk: tough, see 1253.
1530 **PARNASSIAN 5** [8] G B Balding 4-9-9 (55) Miss J Hannaford(7) 11/2: 500-0033: Rear, styd on fnl 2f, *¾* **58**
not pace to chall front pair: qck reapp: see 1253.
1010 **FEARBY CROSS 38** [3] W J Musson 8-10-7 (67) Miss J Pledge(7) 11/1: 4000-604: Chsd ldrs, kept on, *1¾* **67**
not pace of ldrs: bckd: see 698.
1339 **CARRIACOU 14** [13]3-10-1 (73) Miss R D'Arcy(5) 12/1: 2002-645: Chsd ldr over 2f out, sn no extra. *1½* **71**
1485 **PHRED 7** [5]4-10-4 (64) Miss E Johnson Houghton 14/1: 0100-646: Bhd, hdwy over 2f out, no impress *hd* **61**
from dist: see 1059.
1533 **CARLTON 4** [6]10-9-13 (59) Mrs Emma Littmoden(3) 13/2: 2452227: Bhd, styd on fnl 2f, nvr dngrs. *1* **54**
1298 **LYGETON LAD 17** [15]6-11-0 t (74) Miss E J Jones 13/2: 5565108: Chsd ldrs till 2f out: btr 1043. *3* **64**
1348 **OH SO ROSIE 14** [14]4-10-0 p (60) Mrs S Moore(3) 6/1: 020-4339: Dwelt & bhd, nvr a threat: btr 1348. *2½* **46**
33 **GIVERAND 176** [2]5-8-13 (45) Miss Sophie Doyle(7) 50/1: 0/0030-0: 10th: b f Royal Applause - *1* **29**
Petersford Girl (Taufan) Chsd ldrs 4f: mdn plcd '03 (rtd 45$): eff at 6f on fast grnd & a sharp trk.
1080 **GRUMPYINTMORNING 31** [9]5-9-7 (53) Mrs C Thompson(4) 33/1: 42054-00: 11th: Sn strugg: *5* **29**
685 **YELLOW RIVER 78** [11]4-9-0 (4ow)(2oh)p (40) Miss S Beddoes 66/1: 000-4000: 12th: Cl up 4f: jumps fit. *8* **10**
1195] **FREDERICK JAMES 1097** [1]10-8-10 (2oh) (40) Miss A Wallace(2) 66/1: 0/04000//-0: 13th: Al bhd. *14* **0**
765 **KARAOKE KING 69** [4]6-10-2 (62) Miss S Cassidy(7) 33/1: 00-6000P: Sn bhd, t.o./p.u. ins last. **0**
14 Ran Time 1m 31.15(10.75) Owned: Mr Roger Clarke Trained: Alcester

Official Going SOFT (HEAVY places).

1626   **1.50 Coachman Caravans Conditions Stakes 3yo+ (C)**
£12064 £4576 £2288   **5f str**   **Soft 121**   **+03 Fast**   Inside

1487 **BAHAMIAN PIRATE 7** [5] D Nicholls 9-9-2 (108) K Darley 9/4 FAV: 06-14421: Chsd ldrs, switched for   **107**
eff over 1f out & drvn to lead line, all out: bckd: gd time: eff at 5/6f: handles firm & fibresand, loves gd/soft
& hvy, any trk: can go well fresh: 9yo, but remains a v useful performer, esp of fav soft grnd: see 1004.

1207* **BISHOPS COURT 22** [8] Mrs J R Ramsden 10-9-9 (111) A Culhane 10/3: 64153-12: Trkd ldr & led dist,   hd   **112**
drvn & hdd line: op 5/2: clr of rem & ran to form of 1207 (rtd h'cap).

1594 **VITA SPERICOLATA 1** [3] J S Wainwright 9-9-7 (86) R Winston 22/1: 30000-093: Led till dist, no   5   **84**
extra: unplcd yesterday: see 1594.

1227 **HALMAHERA 21** [4] K A Ryan 9-8-12 bl (102) N Callan 5/2: 1044-024: Trkd ldrs, hung left & no impress.   1½   **86**

3351} **TEDBURROW 279** [2]12-8-12 (95) W Supple 20/1: 0/50605-5: b g Dowsing - Gwiffina (Welsh Saint)   6   **74**
Held up, rdn & btn over 1f out: reapp: lightly rcd & unplcd '03 (rtd 104, List): stks & Gr 3 wnr '02: suited by
6f, eff at 5f: acts on firm & soft, any trk, likes Chester: can go well fresh: v tough performer, 12yo.
1 Jun'02 Newc 6g/f 115- A: 1 May'02 Hayd 6g/s 114- C: 1 Jul'01 Hayd 6fm 114- C: 2 May'01 York 6g/f 114- A:

1479 **COLONEL COTTON 7** [6]5-9-9 (109) T E Durcan 6/1: 0130-606: Dwelt, nvr able to chall: see 1159.   2½   **77**

1508 **ROSSELLI 6** [1]8-8-12 (46) P Bradley(5) 200/1: 60044-07: b g Puissance - Miss Rossi (Artaius)   5   **46**
Chsd ldrs towards centre, struggling fnl 2f: qck reapp: h'cap plcd '03 (rtd 59, flattered in cond stks, tried cheek
pieces): stks rnr-up '02: stays 6f, suited by 5f: acts on firm, best on soft & hvy: can go well fresh: eff
with/without blnks, visor or t-strap. 2 Sep'02 Hami 6fm 64- B: 2 Jul'02 Bath 5.7g/f 87- C:

4884} **ABSENT FRIENDS 196** [7]7-9-5 (98) J Edmunds 20/1: 162500-8: b g Rock City - Green Supreme (Primo   dist   **23**
Dominie) Chsd ldr till lost pl halfway & sn bhd, virtually p.u.: reapp: rtd h'cap & stks scorer '03: rtd h'cap &
stks wnr '02: suited by 5f on gd & soft, loves firm & fast, any trk. 2 Sep'03 Beve 5g/s 100-(97) C:
1 Aug'03 Nott 5.1g/f 103-(89) C: 1 Jun'03 Donc 5fm 90-84 B: 1 Sep'02 Beve 5g/f 90- C: 1 Sep'02 Yarm 5.1fm 85-76 C:
2 Sep'02 Leic 5g/f 78- C: 2 Jul'02 Catt 5gd 75-69 D: 1 May'01 Redc 5g/f 72-65 C: 2 May'01 Beve 5fm 68-61 E:
8 Ran   Time 1m 07.21 (5.91)   Owned: Lucayan Stud   Trained: Thirsk

---

1627   **2.20 Leisure Furnishings Sprint A Rated Handicap Stakes 3yo+ 0-80 (D)**   **[84]**
£7712 £2925 £1463   **5f str**   **Soft 121**   **+07 Fast**   Inside

1476 **ARTIE 7** [18] T D Easterby 5-9-5 (75) Dale Gibson 7/2 FAV: 630-0021: Broke well & made all far   **86**
rail, styd on strongly for press: eff at 5/6f on firm & soft grnd, any trk: likes to dominate: make full use of
fav'able high draw, well h'capped: see 1145.

1393 **CATCH THE CAT 12** [13] J S Wainwright 5-8-12 bl (68) R Winston 7/1: 6050-302: Chsd wnr far side,   3½   **71**
over 2f out, kept on, al held: op 11/1: loves this trk, gd run: see 1179.

1532 **MARABAR 4** [16] D W Chapman 6-8-7 (3oh)bl (60) B Swarbrick(5) 50/1: 5001003: Bhd far side, styd on   1   **64**
for press in last, not reach ldrs: qck reapp, imprvd eff from fav'able high draw: acts on soft & hvy grnd: eff at
5f, suited by 6f: see 1065 (seller).

1393 **PADDYWACK 12** [20] D W Chapman 7-9-0 bl (70) A Culhane 10/1: 66100-04: Mid-div far side, kept on   2   **67**
from fav'able high draw: see 155 (AW).

1476 **RAYMONDS PRIDE 7** [15]4-9-12 bl (82) T Eaves(5) 9/2: 0051145: Mid-div far side, no impress dist.   2½   **74**

1532 **KARMINSKEY PARK 4** [9]5-8-7 (1oh) (62) O Urbina 12/1: 0440-626: Chsd ldrs towards centre, no   nk   **54**
impress over 1f out: qck reapp: not disgraced from moderate draw: see 1532 & 1276.

1025 **SHARP HAT 36** [10]10-8-8 (64) M Fenton 50/1: 0055007: Chsd ldr side till dist: see 70.   1¼   **53**

5013* **MISARO 184** [12]3-9-0 (79) D Nolan(3) 50/1: 351-8: b g Acambaro - Misniniski (Niniski) Mid-div,   2   **64**
nvr on terms: reapp/h'cap bow: mdn scorer fnl '03 start (lightly rcd): eff at 6f, has tried 10f (stoutly bred):
acts on gd/soft grnd & a gall trk: fair rtn from moderate draw. 1 Nov'03 Nott 6.1g/s 83- D:

1476 **MYND 7** [11]4-8-10 (66) Dean McKeown 12/1: 1202109: Mid-div far side, nvr able to chall: btr 1179.   nk   **50**

1921} **PRINCE PYRAMUS 339** [6]6-8-7 (18oh) (45) T E Durcan 100/1: 000000-0: 10th: b g Pyramus - Rekindled   ¾   **45**
Flame (Kings Lake) Bhd far side, mod prog: reapp from poor low draw: unplcd '03 (rtd 47, seller, tried cheek
pieces, t-strap & blnks): clmr rnr-up for E Alston '02: eff btwn 5/7f on firm, soft & any trk.
2 Oct'02 Leic 7sft 70- E:

1293 **AWAKE 17** [1]7-9-1 (71) A Nicholls 9/1: 500-0650: 11th: Led quartet stands side, postion accepted   1¼   **51**
from dist when no ch with ldrs far side: proved poorly drawn & this is probably best forgiven: see 1293 & 1251.

1145* **GREY COSSACK 26** [14]7-9-10 (80) G Parkin 7/1: 0000-010: 12th: Bhd far side, nvr factor.   1¼   **58**

2315} **CANDLERIGGS 322** [19]8-9-2 (72) Alex Greaves 16/1: 0/50650-0: 13th: on q Indian Ridge - Ridge   hd   **50**
Pool (Bluebird) Sn strug far side, no dngr on reapp: lightly rcd & unplcd '03 (rtd 75, h'cap): trained in Ireland
& mod form '02: last won back in '00 (h'cap, E Dunlop): eff at 5f, suited by 6f on fast & gd/soft: can go well
fresh. 2 May'01 York 6g/f 96-92 B:

5006} **SIR SANDROVITCH 185** [17]8-8-7 (3oh) (60) T Hamilton(3) 28/1: 066000-0: 14th: Sn strug far side.   5   **31**

1046 **SOAKED 33** [8]11-8-7 (3oh)bl (60) J Bramhill 50/1: 0402340: 15th: Chsd ldrs far side till halfway.   ¾   **29**

921   **Consensus 44** [7]5-9-10 (80) T Williams 25/1:0   1096* **Frascati 30** [3]4-9-1 (71) F Lynch 33/1:0
1194   **Queen Of Night 23** [2]4-9-0 (70) P Makin(5) 40/1:0   1120 **Piccled 27** [4]6-9-8 (78) D Allan(3) 28/1:0
19 Ran   Time 1m 07.00 (5.70)   Owned: Mr A Arton   Trained: Malton

---

1628   **2.55 Powerpart Handicap Stakes 3yo 0-75 (E)**   **[82]**
£4940 £1520 £760   **1m100y rnd**   **Soft 121**   **-10 Slow**   Inside

1470 **CHARMATIC 8** [17] J A Glover 3-8-8 (62) Dean McKeown 5/1: 00-5221: Led/dsptd lead, duelled with   **69**
rnr-up fnl 2f, narrowly led cl-home, all out: first win: eff at 1m on soft & hvy grnd, stiff/gall trks: loves to
race with/force the pace: made full use of far rail berth, on the upgrade: see 1470 & 1253.

1470* **RILEY BOYS 8** [14] J G Given 3-9-1 (69) M Fenton 7/2 FAV: 000-1212: Led/dsptd lead till narrowly   ½   **75**
went on over 2f out, hdd ins last, just held: tchd 5/1: just tchd off today's wnr in 1470 (1lb worse today).

1099 **MYSTICAL GIRL 30** [16] M Johnston 3-9-5 (73) K Dalgleish 11/2: 230-33: Trkd ldrs, drvn & styd on   shd   **79**
well fnl 1f, not reach wnr: fav'able draw: acts on fast & soft grnd, rest well covered: see 1099.

4996} **SILVERHAY 186** [6] T D Barron 3-9-0 (68) P Makin(5) 22/1: 523-4: b g Inchinor - Moon Spin (Night   3   **69+**

Shift) Mid-div, styd on under hand riding fnl 2f, not reach front trio: reapp/h'cap bow: auct mdn rnr-up '03: eff at 7f, styd longer 8.5f trip well: acts on gd & soft grnd, stiff/undul trk: fine eff under tender handling from awkward low draw, one to note in similar. 2 Oct'03 Newc 7gd 77- F:
1216 **TROJAN FLIGHT 22** [9]3-9-1 (69) A Culhane 7/1: 000-45: Trkd ldrs, no impress over 1f out: not quite see out this longer 8.5f trip, 7f could be ideal: see 1216 (mdn). *1½* **68**
4921} **FUTOO 193** [15]3-8-9 (63) N Pollard 33/1: 060106-6: b g Foxhound - Nicola Wynn (Nicholas Bill) *1½* **60**
Chsd ldrs 6f, sn no impress: reapp: seller (M Channon) & h'cap scorer '03 (current yard): suited by 6/7f, yet to convince at 1m: acts on fast & gd/soft, gall or sharp/turning trk: eff with/without visor.
1 Sep'03 Catt 7g/s 64-60 E: 1 Jul'03 Ripo 6g/f 68- E:
1163 **ORION EXPRESS 24** [10]3-8-11 (65) P Mulrennan(5) 12/1: 000-667: Switched right start, in tch 7f. *¾* **61**
4043} **JEROME 248** [7]3-9-7 (75) D Allan(3) 50/1: 204034-8: b c Nicolotte - Mim (Midyan) Mid-div, nvr able to chall: reapp: auct mdn rnr-up '03: eff btwn 6f/1m last term, handles firm & fast grnd, stiff or sharp trk: eff with/without blnks. 2 Jun'03 Thir 6g/f 72- E: *3½* **65**
1192 **GLENDALE 23** [12]3-8-8 (62) J D Smith 40/1: 000-1009: Bhd, only mod prog: btr 651 (AW). *9* **37**
1017 **CHARLIE TANGO 37** [4]3-9-2 (70) T E Durcan 20/1: 5030-300: 10th: Rear, wide & no dngr, poor draw. *1* **43**
1470 **EVALUATOR 8** [1]3-9-4 (72) K Darley 8/1: 36-430: 11th: Rear, eff wide, nvr factor, poor draw. *½* **44**
1198+**MISSION AFFIRMED 23** [8]3-9-0 (68) Dale Gibson 10/1: 55-01510: 12th: Mid-div, lost pl halfway. *5* **32**
1470 **Mr Midasman 8** [5]3-8-12 (66) W Supple 33/1:0
1176 **Dark Day Blues 23** [13]3-9-1 (69) P Hanagan 25/1:0
3968} **Gallas 252** [11]3-8-10 VIS(64) R Winston 50/1:0
1178 **Fossgate 23** [3]3-9-6 (74) C Catlin 28/1:0
16 Ran Time 1m 54.93 (11.13) Owned: Advanced Brickwork Ltd Trained: Worksop

1629

3.25 C G I Stayers Handicap Stakes 4yo+ 0-75 (E) **[78]**
£4654 £1432 £716 **2m35y** **Soft 121** **-39 Slow** Inside

1361 **DR SHARP 14** [12] T P Tate 4-9-6 (70) Dale Gibson 10/1: 0/0114-01: Trkd ldrs & led 2f out, drvn & styd on strongly: eff at 11/12f, now stays a stiff 2m well: acts on gd & soft grnd, can force the pace: see 1361. **81**
1252* **GREAT AS GOLD 19** [14] B Ellison 5-8-13 p (60) R Winston 9/4 FAV: 56203-12: Chsd ldrs & pushed along over 3f out, styd on for press, not pace of wnr: thorough stayer, clr of rem: see 1252 (2m5f). *3½* **66**
1361 **THE RING 14** [15] Mrs M Reveley 4-9-8 (72) K Darley 11/4: 4431-023: Held up, gd hdwy from 5f out, short of room over 2f out, sn no extra: see 1003. *7* **72**
1093 **OCEAN TIDE 30** [11] R Ford 7-10-0 vis (75) K Dalgleish 8/1: 00/0-3344: Led till 2f out, fdd: see 743. *6* **70**
4498} **IL CAVALIERE 223** [3]9-9-2 (63) J Carroll 20/1: 2/0000/4-5: b g Mtoto - Kalmia (Miller's Mate) *7* **52**
Bhd 4f out, only mod prog: 7 wk jumps abs (h'cap hdle rnr-up, rtd 128h, 2m/2m6f, gd & hvy): unplcd sole '03 Flat start (rtd 63, h'cap): unplcd '02 (rtd 65, h'cap): eff at 14f/2m on fast & soft, likes a gall trk.
2 Nov'01 Muss 16gd 74-69 C: 1 Oct'01 Redc 14gd 69-62 E: 2 Sep'01 Redc 14g/f 63-61 E: 2 Aug'01 Newc 14.4g/f 64-61 D:
1469 **NORTHERN NYMPH 8** [1]5-9-7 (68) Stephanie Hollinshead(5) 25/1: 4-230056: Rear, mod hdwy 4f out. *7* **51**
3252} **KAPAROLO 283** [2]5-9-7 (68) W Supple 10/1: 530650-7: ch g El Prado - Parliament House (General Assembly) Cl-up, btn over 1f out, eased: jump fit, nov hdle & h'cap hdle wnr 03/04 (rtd 122h, 2m/2m6.5f, fast & gd/soft): plcd on level '03 (rtd 76, h'cap, disapp in cheek pieces): '02 mdn scorer & h'cap rnr-up: eff at 12f, suited by 14/14.6f, yet to convince at 2m+: acts on fast & hvy, likes a stiff/gall trk. 2 Oct'02 Donc 14.6sft 81-78 D: *21* **33**
1 Jul'02 Sali 14gd 81- D: 2 Jun'02 Newb 12hvy 82-76 D: 2 Apr'02 Beve 12g/f 78- E: 2 Apr'02 Leic 10gd 77- D:
1469 **MADHAHIR 8** [4]4-8-12 (62) M Fenton 20/1: 0-001308: Chsd ldrs till over 2f out: btr 979 (12f, soft). *1½* **26**
1109 **RINGSIDE JACK 28** [9]8-8-3 (50) G Gibbons 8/1: 0344-309: Chsd ldrs till 3f out, eased: btr 1069. *6* **9**
1172 **THE PERSUADER 24** [10]4-9-10 (74) R Ffrench 10/1: 1210-000: 10th: Chsd ldrs, lost tch fnl 3f, eased. *4* **29**
1285* **GALANDORA 18** [13]4-7-13 (49) Lucy Russell(6) 16/1: 300-5610: 11th: Al rear, no ch fnl 3f: btr 1285. *9* **0**
11 Ran Time 3m 56.23 (25.93) Owned: The Ivy Syndicate Trained: Tadcaster

1630

4.00 Wanderer Selling Stakes 3yo (F)
£3077 £879 £440 **1m1f207y** **Soft 121** **-79 Slow** Inside

1250 **CIACOLE 19** [6] Ronald Thompson 3-8-7 (50) Dean McKeown 11/4: 40-04031: Led/dsptd lead, went on over 2f out, held on for press: no bid, v slow time: eff arnd 1m/10f, poss stays stiff 12f: handles fast, hvy & fibresand: best in sell grade: see 1250 & 596. **47**
1000 **ARGENT 38** [1] D Carroll 3-8-12 (58) D Tudhope(7) 4/1: 3550-P02: b g Barathea - Red Tiara (Mr Prospector) Led/dsptd lead, chsd wnr over 2f out, held ins last: op 7/2, has been gelded: clmd by Miss L Perrett for 6,000: plcd '03 (rtd 66, mdn, tried t-strap): styd stiff 10f in sell grade, tried 12f: handles soft grnd. *1½* **49**
1528 **BONJOUR BOND 5** [2] B Smart 3-8-12 BL (62) D McGaffin 7/1: 400-4003: ro g Portrait Gallery - Musical Essence (Song) Chsd ldrs, kept on for press but not quite rch wnr when no room nr fin: first time blnks: unplcd '03 (lightly rcd, rtd 66, mdn, debut): eff around 8.5f/10f, prob handles fast & soft grnd. *nk* **48**
1440 **BRETTON 9** [5] R Hollinshead 3-8-12 bl (45) Dale Gibson 7/1: 4-266444: Keen in rear, no prog fnl 2f. *5* **40**
116 **WARIF 161** [4]3-8-12 R Ffrench 2/1 FAV: 000-5: Held up, hung right & btn 2f out: op 6/4, reapp. *4* **34**
1241 **BAROQUE 21** [3]3-8-12 R Winston 25/1: 0006: Chsd ldrs till lost pl 4f out, t.o. *dist* **0**
6 Ran Time 2m 22.31 (20.01) Owned: Mr B Bruce Trained: Doncaster

1631

4.30 Coachman Amara Median Auction Maiden Stakes Div 1 2yo (E)
£4472 £1376 £688 **5f str** **Soft 121** **-89 Slow** Inside

MELALCHRIST [7] J J Quinn 2-9-0 P Hanagan 14/1: 1: b g Almaty - Lawless Bridget (Alnasr Alwasheek) Pushed along mid-div early, shkn up & strong run ins last to lead nr fin, going away: slow time: cheaply bght Jan 2nd foal, dam a mdn half-sister to a useful sprinter/1m performer: eff at 5f, 6f+ will suit on this evidence: acts on soft grnd & a stiff trk: goes well fresh: entitled to progress. **80**
TAGULA BAY [6] T D Easterby 2-8-9 D Allan(3) 14/1: 2: b f Tagula - Nezool Almatar (Last Tycoon) Trkd ldrs & led over 1f out, rdn & hdd/no extra nr fin: Feb foal, cost E8,500: half-sister to 2 wnr abroad at up to 1m, dam unplcd at 1m/9f as a 3yo: eff over a stiff 5f on soft grnd: likely to progress. *1½* **71**
1353 **LANGSTON BOY 14** [12] M L W Bell 2-9-0 I Mongan 6/4 FAV: 423: Led after 1f till over 1f out, no extra ins last: hvly bckd, op 9/4: handles gd/soft & soft grnd, just btr 1353. *3* **70**
1445 **BOND FINESSE 9** [8] B Smart 2-8-9 F Lynch 5/1: 44: Mid-div far rail, shkn up & kept on, not able to chall: handles soft grnd: see 1445. *shd* **65**
DIXIE QUEEN [10]2-8-9 L Enstone(3) 11/1: 5: b f King of Kings - Dixieline City (Dixieland Band) *2* **61**

BEVERLEY   SATURDAY 08.05.04   Righthand, Oval Track with Stiff Uphill Finish

Led 1f, no extra over 1f out: 13,000gns Feb first foal, dam unrcd half-sister to a useful sprinter: sire high-
class juv & subs 2,000 Guiness wnr: showed speed for a long way from fav high draw.

MING VASE [11]2-9-0   D Tudhope(7) 25/1: 6: Dwelt & v slow into stride, switched towards centre & *shd* **66** +
kept on under hands-and-heels half-way: nvr threat: green on intro, expect significant improvement.

DESERT BUZZ [4]2-9-0   M Tebbutt 50/1: 7: Dwelt, in tch till over 1f out.   3½   59

TIMMY [5]2-9-0   T Eaves(5) 33/1: 8: Chsd ldrs till halfway.   1½   56

1303 **STORY OF ONE 16** [9]2-9-0   K Darley 5/2: 29: Cl-up till lost pl halfway: new yard!: btr 1303.   6   44

1274 **VISION VICTORY 18** [2]2-9-0   Dale Gibson 16/1: 40: 10th: Sn outpcd & struggling: btr 1274.   ½   43

1091 **Favouring 30** [1]2-9-0 T Hamilton(3) 14/1:0   **Miller Hill** [3]2-9-0 T Lucas 33/1:0

12 Ran   Time 1m 11.82 (10.52)   Owned: Mr T G S Wood   Trained: Malton

---

1632   5.05 Coachman Amara Median Auction Maiden Stakes Div 2 2yo (E)
£4472 £1376 £688   **5f str**   **Soft 121**   **-64 Slow**   Inside

ROYAL ISLAND [10] M Johnston 2-9-0   K Dalgleish 4/1: 1: b c Trans Island - Royal House (Royal   **88** +
Academy) Led/dsptd lead, went on over 2f out & rdn clr, decisively: 14,000gns Apr foal, half-brother to a useful
7.5f juv wnr abroad, dam a 6f juv & subs 1m 3yo wnr: eff over a stiff 5f, stay further: acts on soft grnd & goes
well fresh: likely to progress with racing.

SKIPPIT JOHN [11] Ronald Thompson 2-9-0   Dean McKeown 14/1: 2: b g Abou Zouz - Lady Quinta   8   72
(Gallic League) Towards rear, kept on from halfway, nvr threat to wnr: op 11/1: cheaply bght Mar foal,
half-brother to a plcd juv, dam a 5f juv wnr: prob handles soft grnd.

OBE GOLD [5] M R Channon 2-9-0   T E Durcan 10/3: 3: b c Namaqualand - Gagajulu (Al Hareb)   ½   71 +
Dwelt & bhd, kept on late, nvr a threat: nicely bckd tho' op 5/2: Mar foal, half-brother to a 5f juv wnr, dam a
multiple 5f juv wnr: fair run from moderate draw, expect improvement.

LADY DAN [6] M W Easterby 2-8-9   T Lucas 25/1: 4: Mid-div, eff to chase wnr over 1f out, sn no   2   62
extra: some promise in these testing conditions.

1143 **PARIS BELL 26** [3]2-9-0   D Allan(3) 3/1 FAV: 35: Led after 1f till over 2f out, fdd: op 9/2: mod draw.   6   55

1237 **JOE JO STAR 21** [7]2-9-0   D Nolan(3) 9/2: 66: Chsd ldrs till over 1f out.   1½   52

NITEOWL LAD [2]2-9-0   J D O'Reilly(7) 25/1: 7: U.r. bef start, slow away, nvr on terms from mod draw.   5   42

11 **FANTASY DEFENDER 28** [4]2-9-0   P Hanagan 14/1: 08: Chsd ldrs till halfway.   3½   35

1303 **HUNIPOT 16** [8]2-8-9   G Parkin 50/1: 09: Chsd ldrs 2f, sn bhd.   ½   29

LA BELLA ROSA [1]2-8-9   L Enstone(3) 25/1: 0: 10th: Dwelt & al bhd, poor draw on debut.   29   0

10 Ran   Time 1m 10.53 (9.23)   Owned: Mr Markus Graff   Trained: Middleham

---

1633   5.35 Coachman Vip Lady Amateur Riders' Handicap Stakes 3yo+ 0-70 (E)   [55]
£3757 £1156 £578   **1m1f207y**   **Soft 121**   **-46 Slow**   Inside

1504 **YENALED 6** [11] K A Ryan 7-10-1 (56) Miss N Carberry(3) 7/1: 0500451: Held up, smooth hdwy to lead   64
dist & pulled clr, readily: eff at 7f/1m, now stays a stiff 10f well: acts on firm, soft & fibresand: see 457.

1254* **MELODIAN 19** [7] M Brittain 9-10-7 bl (62) Ms C Williams 11/8 FAV: 56-54512: Led till 5f out, no   3½   64
impress on wnr from dist: well bckd, op 7/4: just btr 1254.

4045] **SANTIBURI LAD 248** [8] N Wilson 7-9-13 (54) Mrs N Wilson(5) 16/1: 130460-3: b g Namaqualand -   1¼   54
Suggia (Alzao) Chsd ldrs, kept on ins last, no threat: reapp: clmr scorer '03: class stks rnr-up '02: eff at
1m/10f on firm, soft & handles fibresand, any trk: can go well fresh & enjoys claim grade.
1 Jun'03 Redc 10g/f 59-(58) F: 2 Jun'02 Carl 8fm 61- F: 1 Aug'01 Redc 8fm 70- E: 1 Jul'01 Hami 8.2gd 69- F:
2 Jun'01 Newc 8g/f 57- F: 1 Jun'01 Ripo 8g/f 56- E:

4476] **THE FAIRY FLAG 224** [12] A Bailey 6-10-4 p (59) Miss Kelly Harrison(3) 7/1: 103436-4: ch f Inchinor   2½   55
- Good Reference (Reference Point) Led/dsptd lead till dist, wknd: 7 wk jumps abs (lightly rcd, mod recent form,
h'cap hdles): ladies h'cap & amat riders h'cap wnr '03: eff at 10f, suited by 12f: acts on firm, likes gd & hvy,
any trk: can go well fresh & force the pace: suited by cheek pieces.   1 Aug'03 Ches 12.3gd 62-55 E:
2 Aug'03 Nott 10.0g/f 56-54 E: 2 Aug'03 Hayd 10.5g/f 58-54 D: 1 Jul'03 Hayd 11.9gd 56-49 D:
2 Jun'03 Ayr 10.9g/f 51-48 F: 1 Oct'01 Ayr 10.8hvy 53- E: 2 Sep'01 Redc 10g/f 45-43 E:
2 Sep'01 Hami 11gd 44-43 F: 1 May'01 Leic 8fm 52- F:

4739] **PENSION FUND 207** [3]10-9-8 (49) Miss J Coward(2) 9/1: 430000-5: Chsd ldrs, no impress dist.   1¼   43

4457] **INCHNADAMPH 225** [4]4-9-9 (50) Miss A Elsey 40/1: 500/000-6: Chsd ldrs, no impress fnl 2f, reapp.   ¾   43

4506] **WUXI VENTURE 222** [6]4-10-11 (66) Miss V Tunnicliffe(5) 15/2: 00///2160-7: Al bhd, 7 wk jumps abs.   1¼   57

1366 **SOFT MIST 14** [5]4-10-2 (57) Miss Dawn Rankin(5) 33/1: 200-6008: Mid-div, strug fnl 2f: btr 332.   10   34

791   **BLUE VENTURE 66** [1]4-10-0 (55) Miss A Armitage(5) 12/1: 43300-09: Held up, eff wide, no dngr.   ½   31

1289 **OUR GLENARD 17** [13]5-9-4 (45) Miss A L Turner(5) 7/2: 2205640: 10th: Slow away & strug fnl 2f.   15   1

5001] **LARKING ABOUT 186** [10]4-10-10 (65) Ms Amy Boeder(7) 25/1: 5420-0: 11th: Dwelt, al rear, t.o.   1¾   19

11 Ran   Time 2m 19.00(16.70)   Owned: The Fishermen   Trained: Hambleton

---

THIRSK   SATURDAY 08.05.04   Lefthand, Flat, Oval Track

Official Going GOOD. All Times Slow.

1634   6.05 Calverts Carpets Claiming Stakes 2yo (E)
£3624 £1115 £558   **5f str**   **Good**   **Slow**   Stands Side

1029* **NOVA TOR 36** [6] P C Haslam 2-8-8   Rory Moore(7) 9/2: 11: Made all, edged left, rdn & styd on   73
strongly ins last: jock given 3-day whip ban: clmd by N Shields for 15,000: eff at 5f, 6f shld suit: acts on
fibresand & gd grnd, likes a sharp/easy trk: see 1029.

1224* **LITTLE BISCUIT 21** [4] K R Burke 2-8-13   Darren Williams 2/1 FAV: 112: Slow away, chsd ldrs, eff   3   69
to chase wnr from dist, al held: handles gd, soft & fibresand: tough & consistent type: see 1224 & 938.

1303 **VON WESSEX 16** [3] W G M Turner 2-8-8   C Haddon(7) 8/1: 65163: Prom, styd on onepace for press: ½   63
rider given a 1-day ban for not riding to draw: btr to form, see 1303.

1439 **MISSED TURN 9** [8] K A Ryan 2-8-5   P Fessey 16/1: 54: b f Mind Games - Miss Beverley (Beveled)   1¾   55
Slow away, mid-div, kept on fnl 2f, no threat: 14,000gns Feb foal, sister to a 6f juv wnr, dam unrcd: eff at 5f,

---

6f+ will suit: handles gd grnd.
SNOOKERED AGAIN [11]2-9-0 P Mulrennan(5) 20/1: 5: b g Lujain - Highest Bid (Highest Honor) 1¼ 60
Slow away & bhd, kept on late, no threat: cheaply bght March foal: half-brother to 2 plcd 3yo performers: dam a 1m juv wnr & subs a wnr up to 10f: looks sure to apprec further, likely improver.
1303* **WHY HARRY 16** [1]2-8-8 R Winston 9/2: 3016: Mid-div, rdn & ch over 1f out, no extra when eased ins last: op 7/2: something poss amiss in the closing stages here: see 1303 (soft). 1¼ 50
1439 **KERESFORTH 9** [7]2-8-13 W Supple 25/1: 07: Handy, outpcd fnl 2f, gelded. ¾ 52
1394 **JOSHAR 12** [5]2-8-3 R Ffrench 33/1: 038: Mid-div, no impress fnl 2f: see 1394. nk 41
1224 **BORACAY BEAUTY 21** [9]2-7-12 D Fentiman(7) 66/1: 09: Mid-div, outpcd from halfway. 1 33
1224 **BOWLAND BRIDE 21** [2]2-8-2 F Norton 66/1: 50: 10th: Al towards rear. 2½ 30
1394* **KISSING A FOOL 12** [10]2-8-8 P Makin(5) 9/1: 510: 11th: Cl-up, strug fnl 2f: btr 1394 (soft). hd 36
11 Ran Time 1m 02.21 (5.21) Owned: Blue Lion Racing III Trained: Middleham

1635

6.35 Quadnetics Handicap Stakes 3yo+ 46-55 (F) **[62]**
£3101 £886 £443 **7f rnd** **Good** **Slow** Inside

1463* **TAP 8** [7] Ian Emmerson 7-9-6 p (54) D Fentiman(7) 8/1: 42000-11: Al handy & led over 2f out, drvn & held on gamely: suited by 7f, stays 1m: acts on fast, soft & fibresand, any trk: likes to race prom/force the pace: imprvd last twice in cheek pieces: see 1463. 60
1463 **LUKE AFTER ME 8** [9] G A Swinbank 4-9-3 (51) R Winston 11/1: 00-02302: Dwelt, mid-div & hdwy to chall over 1f out, just held cl-home: can find a race: see 1119, 996 & 577. ½ 55
1463 **MOUNT ROYALE 8** [4] N Tinkler 6-9-5 vis t (53) Kim Tinkler 11/2 JT FAV: 0062223: Handy & ev ch over 1f out, no extra cl-home: well h'capped on turf, poss best when able to dominate: see 1463 & 684 (AW). 1¼ 54
1132* **SCARROTTOO 26** [11] S C Williams 6-9-7 (55) B Reilly(3) 11/2 JT FAV: 5005514: Rear, styd on for press fnl 2f, not reach front trio: joc given 2-day whip ban: ran to form of 1132. ½ 55
760 **CLASSIC VISION 70** [12]4-9-7 (55) A Culhane 9/1: 53-10045: Held up, styd on, not pace to chall: abs: longer 7f trip looks likely to suit: acts on gd grnd & both AWs: not given a hard time from awkward draw, worth another look in similar: see 760 & 319. 1½ 52+
251 **SCRAMBLE 134** [3]6-9-4 t (52) T Eaves(5) 9/1: 413464-6: Dwelt, mid-div, onepace fnl 2f: abs: return to 1m+ will suit: see 84. ½ 48
1463 **WALTZING WIZARD 8** [15]5-9-7 (55) J Carroll 16/1: 3545557: Mid-div, eff fnl 3f, onepace: see 208. 1¼ 48
1522 **ZIETZIG 5** [10]7-9-5 (53) Alex Greaves 25/1: 42306-08: b g Zieten - Missing You (Ahonoora) nk 45
Mid-div, no prog over 1f out: qck reapp: '03 seller scorer for H McWilliams, h'cap rnr-up: '02 clmr rnr-up for T D Barron: eff at 6/7f on firm & fast, handles gd/soft: likes to race with/force the pace & enjoys a sharp/undul trk.
2 Jul'03 Catt 7g/f 55-50 D: 1 Mar'03 Catt 7g/f 53-(55) G: 2 Jun'02 Muss 7.1gd 56- F: 2 Sep'01 York 7g/f 67-68 E:
499 **MR BOUNTIFUL 101** [16]6-9-7 (55) S W Kelly 20/1: 12300-09: Towards rear, nvr a factor: see 22. 3 41
1393 **TRINITY 12** [5]8-9-3 (51) T Williams 14/1: 00040-00: 10th: Cl-up, struggling fnl 2f: see 1393. 1¾ 33
1606 **ZAK FACTA 1** [2]4-9-2 vis (50) Darren Williams 16/1: 55246000: 11th: Led till over 2f out, wknd: unplcd yesterday: see 444. hd 32
1282 **ZAMYATINA 18** [6]5-9-2 (50) D Allan(3) 25/1: 64000-00: 12th: Mid-div, btn 2f out: see 1282. 2½ 27
1020 **KELSEAS KOLBY 37** [8]4-9-7 vis (55) G Gibbons 12/1: 02120-00: 13th: b g Perugino - Notre Dame (Classic Music) Drpd rear early, nvr a factor: sell h'cap scorer '03, seller & h'cap rnr-up: mdn plcd '02 (debut, rtd 70): suited by 7f on fast & gd/soft: suited by visor, tried blnks & cheek pieces: likes a stiff/gall trk & sell grade. 2 Oct'03 Redc 7g/f 55-55 E: 1 Oct'03 Leic 7.0g/f 54-49 G: 2 Sep'03 Leic 7.0g/f 53-(41) G: 1 30
1366 **PEPPER ROAD 14** [1]5-9-2 (50) R Ffrench 12/1: 21060-00: 14th: Prom, btn 2f out. 3½ 18
1406 **SARN 11** [13]5-9-2 p (50) P Varley(7) 20/1: 0000-040: 15th: Sn struggling in rear: see 894. 6 6
15 Ran Time 1m 29.25 (6.35) Owned: Trade Direct Bathrooms & Furniture Trained: Chester-Le-Street

1636

7.05 Glisten Maiden Stakes 3yo+ (D)
£5798 £1784 £892 **1m rnd** **Good** **Slow** Inside

BLUE OASIS [2] R Guest 3-8-6 K Darley 10/1: 1: b f Sadler's Wells - Humble Eight (Seattle Battle) Dwelt & rear, hdwy halfway, styd on for press to lead cl-home: op 8/1, debut: related to a couple of useful performers abroad who were best on easy grnd: eff at 1m, shaped as if 10f+ will suit: acts on gd grnd & an easy trk, goes well fresh: most encouraging start, can rate higher. 75
4306} **CAPPED FOR VICTORY 233** [5] Sir Michael Stoute 3-8-11 (100) K Fallon 1/3 FAV: 232-2: b c Red Ransom - Nazoo (Nijinsky) Handy & led 5f out, drvn & hdd cl-home: hvly bckd, reapp: twice mdn rnr-up '03, in btwn fin 3rd of 7 in List company (rtd 102): eff at 7f/1m on firm & gd, stiff/gall or easy trk: shld find similar. ¾ 77
2 Sep'03 Yarm 8.0gd 89- D: 2 Jul'03 Sand 7.1gd 90- D:
5024} **ARRAN SCOUT 183** [9] Mrs L Stubbs 3-8-11 R Winston 33/1: 04-3: b g Piccolo - Evie Hone (Royal Academy) Trkd ldrs, ch 2f out, rdn & no extra well ins last: rest well covered: reapp: promise 2nd of just 2 '03 starts (mdn, rtd 81): eff at 1m on gd grnd, gall or easy trk: confirmed last yr's promise, interesting for h'caps. hd 77
1177 **LITTLE BOB 23** [11] J D Bethell 3-8-11 C Catlin 14/1: 0-44: Dwelt & bhd, drvn & kept on for press fnl 2f, not threaten front trio: now qual for h'caps, could impr: see 1177. 4 69
2873} **KELBROOK 300** [7]5-9-10 W Supple 25/1: 2-5: Dwelt, mid-div, no prog fnl 2f, reapp. ½ 66
1426 **ARTISTIC STYLE 10** [14]4-9-10 (68) T Eaves(5) 16/1: 30223-06: Led 1f, prom till 2f out, op 14/1. 1 66
4872} **COMMEMORATION DAY 197** [13]3-8-11 M Fenton 33/1: 60-6: Dwelt & bhd, drvn & late gains, gelded. 2 62
4676} **KOODOO 210** [6]3-8-11 L Enstone(3) 200/1: 000-8: Rear, late gains for press, nvr threat, reapp. ½ 61
170 **BLUE MARINER 151** [8]4-9-10 B Doyle 14/1: 2/0-9: Trkd ldrs, btn 2f out, reapp. 3 55
51 **LOCATOR 172** [12]3-8-11 J Tate 33/1: 5-0: 10th: Mid-div, struggling fnl 2f, 6 mth abs/turf bow. 2 51
Milly Golightly [4]3-8-6 S W Kelly 100/1:0
Grey Fortune [10]5-9-5 T Williams 100/1:0
4889} **Outward 196** [1]4-9-10 H Bastiman 66/1:0
5005} **Grey Orchid 185** [3]3-8-6 J Fanning 200/1:0
14 Ran Time 1m 43.34 (7.94) Owned: E Duggan & D Churchman Trained: Newmarket

THIRSK   SATURDAY 08.05.04   Lefthand, Flat, Oval Track

1637   7.35 Ripley Handicap Stakes 4yo+ 0-85 (D)   [81]
£5525 £1700 £850   2m   **Good**   Slow   Inside

1389 **LUCKY JUDGE 12** [9] G A Swinbank 7-8-2 (55) Dale Gibson 28/1: 535/4/-401: Held up, rapid hdwy for **64**
press over 3f out & led over 1f out, drvn out: eff at 13f/2m on fast & hvy grnd: nicely h'capped: see 1034.
1232 **MADIBA 21** [5] P Howling 5-8-2 (55) J Fanning 12/1: 6022202: Al handy & led over 3f out till over   1¾ **61**
1f out, kept on well: op 16/1, back to form, can find similar on turf: see 812, 690 & 306.
1361 **RIYADH 14** [6] M Johnston 6-9-3 vis (70) K Dalgleish 7/1: 60-00003: ch g Caerleon - Ausherra   1½ **74+**
(Diesis) Slow away & rear, styd on fnl 5f, not reach front papr: op 9/1: unplcd for J Fanshawe '03 (lightly rcd,
rtd 89, h'cap): '02 val h'cap wnr for M Pipe: eff at 12f, thorough stayer, last win came at 2m4f: acts on firm &
gd, handles gd/soft: best in blnks/visor, eff without: can go well fresh: one to note with a stiffer test.
1 Jun'02 Asco 20g/f 93-88 C: 1 Oct'01 Newm 14g/f 87-83 C: 1 Sep'01 Good 16g/f 84-79 D: 2 Jul'01 Ches 15.8fm 82-79 D:
2 Jun'01 Yarm 14g/f 82-75 E: 2 Jun'01 Sali 14gd 75-75 C: 1 May'01 Leic 11.8fm 76-69 E: 2 Mar'01 Ling 8ap 72a- D:
1109 **NOBRATINETTA 28** [4] Mrs M Reveley 5-9-9 (76) K Darley 25/1: 410-04: b f Celtic Swing -   2 **78**
Bustinetta (Bustino) Mid-div, styd on onepace for press fnl 2f: lightly rcd on the level '03, auct mdn scorer:
02/03 dual bmpr wnr (2m, gd & hvy): wng form at 12f, stays an easy 2m: acts on gd & gd/soft grnd, stiff/undul or
easy trk: lightly rcd, entitled to progress. 1 May'03 Hami 12.1g/s 76- E:
1093 **SONO 30** [12]7-9-6 p (73) P Hanagan 50/1: 20000-05: b g Robellino - Sweet Holland (Alydar) Rear,   2 **73**
drvn & kept on late, nrst fin: cheek pieces reapplied: recent jumps rnr (unplcd, rtd 94h, h'cap hdle): h'cap
rnr-up '03: ex-German Flat wnr: wng form at 1m/10f, stays 12f & shaped tonight as if 2m will suit: acts on fast &
hvy grnd, stiff/easy trks. 2 Jun'03 Pont 12.0g/f 81-78 D:
1459* **TONI ALCALA 8** [8]5-9-1 (68) K Fallon 11/2: 5402316: Mid-div, onepace for press fnl 3f: see 1459.   nk **67**
4685} **SKYES FOLLY 209** [1]4-9-10 (80) M Fenton 14/1: 501515-7: Led 1f, handy till fdd fnl 2f: new yard.   ½ **78**
605 **RED SCORPION 87** [2]5-9-5 (72) B Swarbrick(5) 11/1: 035-1658: Mid-div, no impress fnl 3f: abs.   4 **66**
1399* **ETCHING 11** [7]4-8-4 (60) E Ahern 11/4 FAV: 22210-19: Trkd ldrs, wknd qckly 3f out: btr 1399 (11.7f).   19 **34**
1361 **THEWHIRLINGDERVISH 14** [11]6-9-12 (79) A Mullen(7) 3/1: 2000-340: 10th: Led after 1f till 3f out.   nk **52**
681 **VANBRUGH 79** [10]4-8-8 t (64) Darren Williams 33/1: 226-1060: 11th: Trkd ldrs, wknd qckly 3f out.   ½ **36**
1459 **AUTUMN FANTASY 8** [3]5-8-11 t (64) T Eaves(5) 33/1: 00000-40: 12th: Rear & lost tch halfway.   dist **0**
12 Ran Time 3m 36.70 (13.90) Owned: Mrs I Gibson Trained: Richmond

1638   8.05 Dick Peacock Sprint Handicap Stakes 3yo+ 0-75 (E)   [75]
£5772 £1776 £888   6f str   **Good**   Slow   Stands Side

1393 **IF BY CHANCE 12** [8] R Craggs 6-9-7 bl (68) T Eaves(5) 12/1: 05-02441: Made all far side, held on   **75**
all out: suited by 6f on fast, soft & fibresand, any trk: see 967.
194 **HARTSHEAD 147** [13] G A Swinbank 5-9-2 (63) B Doyle 33/1: 304460-2: b g Machiavellian - Zalitzine   nk **69+**
(Zilzal) Dwelt, rdn & chsd ldrs stands side, led that group over 1f out, edged left & not rch wnr far side: pulled
well clr rem stands side, abs: unplcd '03 (rtd 68, mdn): eff at 6f/1m, has tried 12f: handles fast & gd grnd: fine
run, shld win similar on this evidence, poss at 7f.
1145 **PALACE THEATRE 26** [9] T D Barron 3-9-4 (75) P Makin(5) 14/1: 1-03: Rcd alone in centre, al prom &   1½ **77**
styd on for press: left reapp bhd: eff at 6f on fast & gd grnd: fine run, win again: see 1145.
1442* **FAR NOTE 9** [6] S R Bowring 6-9-5 bl (66) J Bramhill 8/1: 0461014: Al chsd ldrs far side, kept on   1¼ **64**
for press: eff at 6f, poss suited by 5f: see 1442 (AW, 5f).
1508 **PAGAN STORM 6** [2]4-9-6 (67) Kristin Stubbs(7) 50/1: 46-00005: Handy far side, onepce dist: qck reapp.   2½ **58**
4108} **MISTER SWEETS 244** [16]5-9-12 (73) D Tudhope(7) 16/1: 530000-8: ch g Nashwan - Keybeegia (Lyphard)'s   03
Mid-div stand side, kept on late, not able to chall on reapp: AW mdn & AW h'cap scorer for M C Chapman '03, turf
h'cap rnr-up, plcd several times (rtd 80, h'cap): AW mdn rnr-up late '02: eff btwn 6f/1m, both wins at 7f: acts on
firm, gd & both AWs, prob any trk: tough & genuine, an encouraging return for new yard.
1 Mar'03 Sout 7g/f 80-73 E: 2 Mar'03 Donc 6gd 78-73 C: 1 Feb'03 Ling 7ap 79a-(65) D: 2 Feb'03 Sout 7af 67a- D:
2 Jan'03 Sout 6af 65a- D: 2 Dec'02 Sout 8af 58a- D: 2 Nov'02 Sout 8af 56a- D:
1476 **PALANZO 7** [10]6-9-7 (68) A Nicholls 6/1 FAV: 00000-57: Mid-div stands side, drvn & onepace.   shd **58**
1391 **COUSTOU 12** [4]4-9-3 (64) P Fessey 100/1: 0005-608: Chsd wnr far side till dist: see 1094.   nk **53**
4468} **HILLTIME 225** [20]4-9-4 (65) R Winston 10/1: 44550/0-9: b g Danetime - Ceannanas (Magical Wonder)   ½ **53**
Dwelt, towards rear stands side, late gains: unplcd sole '03 start (rtd 57, mdn): dual nov wnr over hdles 02/03
(rtd 98h, stays 2m1f on fast grnd): has tried a visor.
1476 **ZUHAIR 7** [5]11-9-11 (72) Alex Greaves 25/1: 02200-00: 10th: Towards rear far side, mod prog.   ½ **59**
5025} **ROMAN MISTRESS 183** [14]3-9-1 (72) B Doyle 33/1: 020000-0: 11th: Prom stands side 4f, reapp.   ½ **54**
1277 **WILLIAMS WELL 18** [12]10-9-2 bl (63) Dale Gibson 25/1: 12020-00: 12th: Handy stands side 4f.   ½ **48**
4671} **MIMIC 211** [15]4-9-11 (72) R Mills(7) 16/1: 251140-0: 13th: Led/dsptd lead stand side till dist.   nk **56**
1474 **TIME TO REMEMBER 7** [14]6-9-6 (67) A Culhane 25/1: 0000R-00: 14th: Chsd ldrs stands side 4f.   ½ **50**
1476 **QUANTICA 7** [7]5-9-3 (64) Kim Tinkler 14/1: 0002-600: 15th: Dwelt, stands side, al towards rear.   1½ **43**
1553 **AFRICAN SPUR 4** [3]4-9-2 t (63) D Nolan(3) 66/1: 2000000: 16th: Sn bhd far side, qck reapp.   ¾ **39**
4712} **KINGS COLLEGE BOY 208** [19]4-9-2 (63) P Hanagan 20/1: 104260-0: 17th: Stands side, al rear.   shd **39**
1600 **QUIET TIMES 1** [11]5-9-4 bl (65) N Callan 8/1: 40415580: 18th: Sn struggling stands side.   1½ **37**
1476 **CHAIRMAN BOBBY 7** [17]6-9-8 (69) L Enstone(3) 7/1: 3062-500: 19th: Led stands side till halfway.   ¾ **38**
4698} **MIDNIGHT PARKES 209** [1]5-9-7 (68) W Supple 6/1: 304500-0: 20th: Cl-up far side 3f: reapp.   1¾ **33**
20 Ran Time 1m 13.80 (4.30) Owned: Mr Ray Craggs Trained: Sedgefield

1639   8.35 Catterick Garrison Maiden Guaranteed Sweepstakes 3yo+ (D)
£5200 £1600 £800   6f str   **Good**   Slow   Stands Side

1464 **SNAP 8** [7] M Johnston 3-8-11 J Fanning 9/4 FAV: 21: Handy & led over 1f out, drvn & styd on   **74**
well: nicely bckd, op 5/2, confirmed debut promise: eff at 6f, 7f+ could suit: acts on gd & soft grnd, gall or
easy trk: lightly rcd, type to prog: see 1464.
4495} **FLYING BANTAM 223** [8] R A Fahey 3-8-11 (71) T Hamilton(3) 20/1: 22503-2: b g Fayruz - Natural   ½ **72**
Pearl (Petong) Narrow lead till over 1f out, kept on for press: reapp: dual mdn rnr-up '03: eff at 5/6f on firm &
gd/soft grnd, stiff or easy trk: h'caps may suit best. 2 Jul'03 Beve 5g/s 73- D: 2 Jun'03 Carl 5fm 79- E:
869 **DARK CHAMPION 51** [9] R E Barr 4-9-7 (60) P Hanagan 5/1: 5-204653: Chsd ldrs, rdn & kept on: 7   nk **71$**
wk abs, prev with J O'Keeffe: offic rtd 60, treat rating with caution: see 313.
1191 **MIDNIGHT BALLARD 23** [13] R F Johnson Houghton 3-8-11 (82) S Carson 7/2: 536-64: b c Mister   nk **70**

473

THIRSK SATURDAY 08.05.04 Lefthand, Flat, Oval Track

Baileys - Shadow Music (Shadeed) Chsd ldrs, styd on for press: mdn plcd in '03 (rtd 90): eff at 6/7f on firm & gd grnd, gall or easy trk: gd run, 7f & h'caps could suit best.

2685}	**OEUF A LA NEIGE 308** [3]4-9-7 (70) R Ffrench 28/1: 0/50530-5: Mid-div, drvn & kept on, not able to chall: reapp, has been gelded, apprec 7f+.			2	64
	INTAVAC BOY [2]3-8-11 T Williams 100/1: 6: Slow away & bhd, styd on for press, nrst fin on debut.			½	63
47	**COMPTON PLUME 208** [16]4-9-7 (55) T Eaves(5) 14/1: 422026-7: Rcd alone stands side, chsd ldrs 4.5f.			2½	55
12	**MISTER REGENT 22** [10]3-8-11 N Callan 9/1: 38: Slow away, drvn & nvr pace to chall: btr 1216.			¾	52
1426	**BORIS THE SPIDER 10** [5]3-8-11 (61) A Culhane 25/1: 0000-29: Mid-div at best: btr 1426 (soft).			1¼	48
795	**RED MONARCH 66** [15]3-8-11 D Nolan(3) 50/1: 00: 10th: Prom stand side till over 1f out, abs.			hd	48
1426	**THE WARLEY WARRIOR 10** [11]3-8-11 bl P Mulrennan(5) 50/1: 5-60: 11th: Slow away, chsd ldrs 4f.			8	24
4482}	**SUJOISSE 224** [12]3-8-11 R Winston 100/1: 000-0: 12th: Sn struggling, reapp.			nk	23
1152	**SCIENTIST 25** [6]3-8-11 (80) K Fallon 7/2: 65-00: 13th: Dwelt, mid-div, strug halfway: op 11/4.			nk	22
4534}	**FROM THE NORTH 220** [14]3-8-6 C Catlin 100/1: P0-0: 14th: Sn bhd, t.o. on reapp.			29	0

14 Ran Time 1m 15.21(5.71) Owned: Lord Hartington Trained: Middleham

KEMPTON MONDAY 10.05.04 Righthand, Flat, Fair Track

Official Going HEAVY.

1640 2.10 Natwest Maiden Auction Stakes 2yo (H)
£1523 £435 £218 **5f str** **Heavy 145** **-02 Slow** Far Side

	GOLDEN ANTHEM [7] J Pearce 2-8-9 J Quinn 7/1: 1: ch f Lion Cavern - Bacinella (El Gran Senor)		79

Slow away & pushed along rear, short of room & switched over 2f out, rdn & strong run to lead ins last, going away: 4,500gns Mar foal, half-sister to a 1m US juv wnr: dam related to wnrs at 7f/12f: eff at 5f, shld stay 6f: acts on hvy grnd & an easy trk: goes well fresh.

1524	**RUBYS DREAM 7** [10] J M Bradley 2-8-9 R L Moore 4/1 FAV: 42: Handy & led over 1f out, hdd ins last, no pace of wnr: bckd tho' op 3/1: handles soft & hvy grnd: see 1524.	2½	71
1325	**WIZZSKILAD 17** [8] Mrs P N Dutfield 2-9-0 R Havlin 6/1: 0463: Led/dsptd lead till over 1f out, no extra: handles gd/soft & hvy grnd: see 1053.	5	66
1097	**GENERAL NUISANCE 32** [4] J S Moore 2-9-0 Derek Nolan(7) 8/1: 264: In tch, outpcd halfway, kept on ins last: handles gd & hvy grnd: prev with P G Murphy: see 929.	½	65
	TIPSY LILLIE [1]2-8-9 Lisa Jones(3) 20/1: 5: ch f Tipsy Creek - Belle de Nuit (Statoblest)	3½	53

Towards rear & outpcd halfway, mod late prog, nvr dngr: Apr foal, dam a 6/7f juv wnr & related to wnrs up to 12f.

	QUEENS GLORY [9]2-8-9 S Drowne 16/1: 6: b f Mujadil - Karenaragon (Aragon) Chsd ldrs, btn over 1f out: Mar foal, 5,000gns Mar 2yo: dam plcd at 5f as a juv.	2½	48
	RUSSIAN ROCKET [2]2-9-0 C Catlin 33/1: 7: Dwelt, nvr on terms.	1	51
1538	**MUESTRA 6** [5]2-8-9 T E Durcan 4/1: 008: Slow away & al bhd, qck reapp.	3	40
882	**BAMBOOZLED 51** [6]2-8-9 K Fallon 5/1: 69: Chsd ldrs till halfway, abs.	1¾	37
	SHERBOURNE [11]2-8-9 Paul Eddery 11/2: 0: 10th: Slow away, sn chsd ldrs till dist, eased.	5	27
1325	**ZACHY BOY 17** [3]2-9-0 Martin Dwyer 12/1: 6050: 11th: Led/dsptd lead till 2f out, sn hung & btn.	¾	31

11 Ran Time 1m 05.66 (7.36) Owned: Mr S Birdseye Trained: Newmarket

1641 2.40 Cbfm Tri-Banded Stakes 3yo 0-45 (H)
£1453 £415 £208 **6f str** **Heavy 145** **-27 Slow** Far Side

1588	**PARDON MOI 4** [9] Mrs C A Dunnett 3-9-0 (45) Hayley Turner(5) 6/1: 3440041: Led/dsptd lead, went on 2f out, rdn & styd on well: op 9/2, qck reapp: eff at 6/7f on fast, hvy & fibresand: best without chkpcs.		50
1453	**INDRANI 11** [7] John A Harris 3-9-0 (45) Paul Eddery 10/1: 6400402: Trkd ldrs, drvn & kept on fnl 2f, al held by wnr: handles fibresand, gd/soft & hvy grnd: see 797.	2½	43
1363	**LORD WISHINGWELL 16** [3] J S Wainwright 3-8-9 VIS (40) S Whitworth 20/1: 000-03: b g Lake Coniston - Spirito Libro (Lear Fan) Handy, rdn & onepace fnl 2f: first time visor, some improvement on drop in trip: unplcd '03 (rtd 50, mdn): eff over 6f in banded company in hvy grnd.	2½	33
1453	**ANATOM 11** [5] P S McEntee 3-8-5 (1ow)t (35) N Pollard 7/1: 0660-054: Led/dsptd lead 4f, wknd.	1¾	26
1549	**HEATHYARDS JOY 6** [1]3-8-4 (45) J Quinn 9/2: 0044255: Rdn rear, nvr pace to chall: qck reapp.	nk	24
1549	**TARANAI 6** [4]3-9-0 (45) N Chalmers(5) 7/2 FAV: 4000046: Sn rdn rear, only mod prog: qck reapp.	1	32
1258	**ST GEORGES GIRL 21** [6]3-8-4 (30) J Jeffrey(7) 33/1: 000-07: b f Muthahb - Nickelodeon (Nickel King) Reared apart & sn struggling rear: unplcd '03 (rtd 25 & 0a).	¾	21
1453	**MUST BE SO 11** [8]3-8-9 (40) J Tate 9/2: 1-500068: Chsd ldrs 4f.	1¾	23
1247	**SCENIC FLIGHT 21** [7]3-9-0 BL (45) C Catlin 10/1: 4000-009: Chsd ldrs till over 1f out, blnks.	½	27

9 Ran Time 1m 21.39 (10.29) Owned: Mr Andy Middleton Trained: Norwich

1642 3.15 Coutts & Co Banded Stakes 3yo+ 0-45 (H)
£1551 £443 £222 **7f rnd** **Heavy 145** **-36 Slow** Outside

1328*	**EXTEMPORISE 17** [10] T T Clement 4-9-5 (45) T G McLaughlin 10/1: 50-03511: Handy & led over 2f out, hung right but drvn/styd on strongly from over 1f out: op 7/1: eff btwn 6f/1m on fibresand, gd/soft & soft.		54
1328	**TOJONESKI 17** [12] I W McInnes 5-9-5 p (40) K Fallon 1/1 FAV: 0034222: Led/dsptd lead over 2f out, kept on, not pace of wnr: acts on fast, hvy & fibresand: see 1328, 1262 & 830.	4	47
1247	**HAPPY CAMPER 21** [16] M R Hoad 4-9-5 (45) D Sweeney 50/1: 45-00653: Rear, late gains, not able to reach front pair: handles fast & hvy grnd: eff 7f: see 902.	1¼	45
1245*	**DUE TO ME 21** [17] G L Moore 4-9-5 p (45) S Whitworth 14/1: 00-52514: Trkd ldrs, switched stands side 3f out & sn led that group, no ch with front trio inner: clr of rem: acts on gd, hvy & polytrack: see 1245.	nk	44
1334	**KANZ WOOD 17** [14]8-9-5 (45) S Hitchcott(3) 10/1: 00-05055: Dwelt, rear, drvn & only mod prog.	6	35
1075*	**SHIRLEY OAKS 34** [6]6-9-5 (45) N Chalmers(5) 9/1: 0500316: Trkd ldrs, no extra dist: btr 1075.	¾	34
1334	**CATCH THE FOX 17** [5]4-9-5 (45) J Tate 8/1: 0050-027: Handy till over 1f out: btr 1334.	8	23
1451	**SINGLE TRACK MIND 11** [7]6-9-5 (45) Martin Dwyer 14/1: 4502358: Rear, btn 2f out: btr 1413.	5	16
1267	**MUQTADI 20** [4]6-9-5 (45) L Dettori 13/2: 5004549: Rear, sn strug: failed to handle hvy grnd.	5	9
1565	**WESTMEAD ETOILE 5** [1]4-9-5 BL (45) C Lowther 50/1: 00-03000: 10th: Cl-up till over 2f out: blnks.	½	8

KEMPTON   MONDAY 10.05.04   Righthand, Flat, Fair Track

1075 **PACKIN EM IN 34** [2]6-9-5 (45) M Henry 16/1: 0-320100: 11th: Led/dsptd lead till over 2f out, 4 2
wknd qckly: reportedly failed to handle hvy grnd: btr 969 (AW).
1451 **ROBIN SHARP 11** [13]6-9-5 p (35) P Doe 25/1: 6050040: 12th: Led overall 4f, wknd qckly: btr 1451. 2½ 0
1590 **TEE JAY KASSIDY 4** [11]4-9-5 (40) Lisa Jones(3) 20/1: 04-12520: 13th: Held up, nvr land a blow. 3 0
890 **WATERLINE DANCER 49** [8]4-9-5 vis t (45) S Drowne 33/1: 0-000040: 14th: Prom 5f: abs: btr 890. 3½ 0
1413 **INDIAN WARRIOR 13** [15]8-9-5 (45) K McEvoy 16/1: 0040550: 15th: Dwelt, rear, nvr factor: btr 310. 9 0
1277 **FORMERIC 20** [3]8-9-5 vis (40) J Quinn 10/1: 000-0030: 16th: Al bhd: btr 1277. 1½ 0
1413 **JANES VALENTINE 13** [9]4-9-5 (35) N Pollard 50/1: 0-404000: 17th: Reared start, sn bhd, t.o. 15 0
17 Ran   Time 1m 36.75 (12.65)   Owned: Ms K Sadler   Trained: Newmarket

1643   3.50 One Account Banded Stakes 3yo+ 0-40 (H)
£1505 £430 £215   1m2f   Heavy 145   -32 Slow   Outside

1334 **UNSUITED 17** [9] J E Long 5-9-8 (40) Natalia Gemelova(7) 12/1: 0-032641: Rear, hdwy & led over 1f 55
out, sn rdn clr, easily: eff arnd 9/10f on fibresand, soft & hvy, sharp/easy trk: first win: see 668.
1332 **MR WHIZZ 17** [2] A P Jones 7-9-8 p (40) Derek Nolan 11/2: 0144322: Chsd ldr 3f out, ch 2f out, 17 38
sn no impress: prob handles soft, hvy & fibresand: see 442 (1m).
1273 **PRINCE ALBERT 20** [11] J R Jenkins 6-9-8 (35) W Ryan 16/1: 35/05-003: Mid-div, kept on fnl 3f. ¾ 37
1328 **ALL ON MY OWN 17** [4] I W McInnes 9-9-8 bl (35) L Vickers 16/1: 2400534: Dwelt, rear, mod prog. 2½ 35
1589 **MISTY MAN 4** [10]6-9-8 bl (40) B Reilly(3) 6/1: 44-35145: Keen & sn handy, led halfway & rdn clr nk 34
over 3f out, hdd over 1f out & wknd: op 8/1, qck reapp: btr 469 (AW, 12f).
1592 **DANCING DOLPHIN 4** [6]5-9-8 (30) Lisa Jones(3) 33/1: 0646/-366: Trkd ldrs till 2f out: qck reapp. 2 32
1450 **SMARTER CHARTER 11** [1]11-9-8 (35) Kristin Stubbs(7) 14/1: 000-5027: Dwelt, rear, little hdwy. 5 27
1333* **MARGARETS WISH 17** [8]4-9-8 (40) L Dettori 5/2 FAV: 0-040018: Chsd ldrs 3f out, sn btn: hvly bckd. hd 26
1413 **OSO NEET 13** [12]6-9-8 (30) L Keniry(3) 66/1: 6//0000/-09: Bhd halfway, t.o.: see 1413. 22 8
1244* **LADY AT LEISURE 21** [7]4-9-8 (40) S Whitworth 8/1: 0/5-60010: 10th: Led till halfway, sn bhd. ¾ 7
1548* **CHICKASAW TRAIL 6** [13]6-10-0 (40) Stephanie Hollinshead(5) 20/1: 0006510: 11th: Mid-div, ½ 12
struggling fnl 3f: qck reapp: btr 1548 (1m).
1409* **RHETORIC 13** [5]5-9-8 (40) D Nolan(3) 5/1: 005-0410: 12th: Prom, strug 4f out: btr 1409 (AW). 5 1
1565 **ROVING VIXEN 5** [3]3-8-7 p (40) A Daly 25/1: 00-0040: 13th: Dwelt & al bhd: see 1565. 3 0
13 Ran   Time 2m 20.02 (17.72)   Owned: Amaroni Racing   Trained: Woldingham

1644   4.20 Wealth Management Banded Stakes 3yo+ 0-45 (H)
£1495 £427 £214   5f str   Heavy 145   +03 Fast   Far Side

1269 **FOLEY MILLENNIUM 20** [10] M Quinn 6-9-3 (45) N Pollard 25/1: 00/0/6P-01: Made all towards centre, 51
clr dist, drvn out: fair time: eff at 5/6f on fast & hvy grnd: see 1269.
1336 **EJAY 17** [4] Julian Poulton 5-9-3 (40) Lisa Jones(3) 16/1: 6020002: Rear, styd on for press fnl 1½ 45
2f, not reach wnr: acts on fibresand & hvy grnd: see 720 & 582.
1544* **HARBOUR HOUSE 6** [1] J J Bridger 5-9-9 (45) J Tate 5/1: 0206313: Chsd wnr halfway, no impress 3 45
dist: qck reapp: acts on fast, hvy & polytrack: see 1544.
1248 **BADOU 21** [7] L Montague Hall 4-9-3 vis (45) K Fallon 2/1 FAV: 4100024: Mid-div, not pace to 1¾ 36
chall: 6/7f prob ideal: see 528 (7f).
1522 **RIVER LARK 7** [9]5-9-3 (45) K McEvoy 7/2: 6446065: Mid-div, no impress fnl 1f: see 253. ¾ 35
1544 **THREAT 6** [2]8-9-3 (45) Martin Dwyer 9/1: 4003446: Dwelt, outpcd, mod prog: qck reapp: see 541. ½ 34
1544 **FRENCHMANIC LODGE 6** [8]4-9-8 bl t (45) P Doe 80/1: 000 0007: Held up, nff halfway, no impress. 8 23
1012 **KILMEENA STAR 40** [5]6-9-3 bl (40) R L Moore 7/1: 0004128: Keen & chsd ldr 3f, sn btn: abs. 1 21
1269 **ABRAXAS 20** [3]1-6-9-3 p (40) C Catlin 20/1: 6-500009: Sn struggling: btr 183. 8 7
1545 **MAYFAIR MAUNDY 6** [6]4-9-3 (35) A Quinn(5) 33/1: 00500/-40: 10th: Sn bhd, t.o.: qck reapp. 8 0
10 Ran   Time 1m 05.38 (7.08)   Owned: Mrs S G Davies   Trained: Wantage

1645   4.50 Royalties Gold Banded Stakes 3yo+ 0-45 (H)
£1533 £438 £219   1m4f   Heavy 145   -55 Slow   Outside

546 **MAKE MY HAY 96** [3] J Gallagher 5-9-8 (40) T E Durcan 11/1: 4002-361: Rear, hdwy to lead over 2f 52
out, drvn/styd on well fnl 1f: earlier with J White: jumps fit (unplcd, rtd 99h, nov): eff arnd 10/12f on fast, hvy &
fibresand, with/without blnks: see 224.
1469 **PIPSSALIO 10** [5] Jamie Poulton 7-9-8 t (45) C Catlin 13/8 FAV: 043-6262: Held up, sn pushed 3 48
along, drvn to chall 2f out, no extra ins last: clr of rem & could find similar: see 206.
  SURE FUTURE 1342 [8] R M Stronge 8-9-8 (45) A Daly 7/1: /0050///-3: b g Kylian - Lady Ever So 13 37
Sure (Malicious) Rear, eff to chase ldrs over 3f out, no impress fnl 2f: v long Flat abs, recent jumps rnr (unplcd,
rtd 109h), h'cap hdle plcd 03/04 (rtd 119h, 2m6f/3m, gd & hvy): unplcd on the level back in '00.
1547 **DORA CORBINO 6** [11] R Hollinshead 4-9-8 (40) T G McLaughlin 16/1: 3206324: Led till over 2f out, 6 31
fdd: qck reapp: see 1547, 1329.
1287 **NEPTUNE 19** [1]8-9-8 (30) R L Moore 25/1: 0/-500245: Rear, only mod prog: btr 1180. nk 30
1358 **KALANISHA 6** [9]4-9-8 (45) Paul Eddery 11/2: 000-06: ch g Ashkalani - Camisha (Shernazar) Trkd 3 27
ldrs, lost pl 5f out: op 8/1: unplcd '03 (rtd 44, mdn).
3456] **SILVER MISTRESS 636** [7]5-9-8 (45) V Slattery 50/1: 0000/-7: gr f Syrtos - Galava (Graustark) 19 14
Keen in mid-div, chsd ldrs 4f out, btn 2f out: missed '03: unplcd '02 (rtd 64, debut).
1455 **SINK OR SWIM 11** [4]6-9-8 (30) J Tate 40/1: 0058: Chsd ldrs till 4f out, t.o. dist 0
1528 **STAGE TWO 7** [10]3-8-3 (45) J Fanning 7/1: 06409: Trkd ldr, wknd 4f out, virtually p.u.: op 5/1. 5 0
1411 **ERSAAL 13** [2]4-9-8 t P (45) K Fallon 5/1: 0-030130: 10th: Trkd ldrs, strugg halfway: btr 1411, 1265. 28 0
10 Ran   Time 2m 54.02(24.02)   Owned: Mrs Irene Clifford   Trained: Moreton-In-Marsh

Official Going SOFT (GOOD/SOFT places).

1646   5.45 Sandhurst Marquees Novice Stakes 2yo (D)
£4108 £1264 £632   5f10y str   Soft   Inapplicable   Inside.

1190* **BLUE DAKOTA 25** [4] J Noseda 2-9-5   L Dettori   1/8 FAV: 11: Made all, al in command, unchall fnl 102+
2f, any amount in hand: well bckd at long odds-on: eff at 5f on fast & soft grnd, stiff or sharp trk: remains
unbtn & potentially smart juv who heads for Norfolk stks next month: see 1190.
1538 **ALRIGHT MY SON 6** [5] R Hannon 2-8-12   Dane O'Neill 33/1: 02: b c Pennekamp - Pink Stone   6   78
(Bigstone) Sn rdn & chsd ldrs, took 2nd ins last, no ch with easy wnr: qck reapp: Mar 1st foal, cost E28,000: dam
plcd abroad around 1m/10f: looks sure to apprec further in time, likely imprvr.
1524* **LITTLE WIZZY 7** [2] P D Evans 2-9-0   J Murtagh 25/1: 3013: Went left start, sn chsd wnr, wknd fnl 1f.   2   75
   PERIANTH [3] B J Meehan 2-8-12 S Drowne 20/1: 4: ch c Bluebird - Meandering Rose (Irish River)   6   61
Chsd ldrs till outpcd halfway: Mar foal, cost 22,000gns: dam unrcd, related to high-class 1m/10f performer.
   COME GOOD [1]2-8-12 R Hughes 12/1: 5: ch c Piccolo - The Frog Lady (Al Hareb) Hmpd/carried   6   49
left start, sn in tch, btn over 1f out: op 10/1: Mar foal, brother to a useful multiple 6f juv wnr, also a 7f juv
wnr: dam plcd at 10f/2m & over hdles: stay further in time.
5 Ran   Time 1m 05.12 ()   Owned: Mr A F Nolan Mrs J M Ryan Mrs P Duffin   Trained: Newmarket

---

1647   6.15 Factortame Handicap Stakes 3yo 0-70 (E)   [76]
£3796 £1168 £584   1m67y rnd   Soft   Inapplicable   Inside.

940 **FOLEY PRINCE 44** [11] Mrs Stef Liddiard 3-9-3 (65) S Drowne 12/1: 146-0301: Made all, drvn & held   74
on gamely fnl 2f: op 16/1, 6 wk abs, prev with D Flood: eff around 7f/1m on firm, fast & both AWs, likes Windsor:
likes to force the pace & goes well fresh: see 804.
1403 **SMOOTHLY DOES IT 13** [4] Mrs A J Bowlby 3-9-2 (64) T E Durcan 25/1: 30020-02: b g Efisio - Exotic   hd   72+
Forest (Dominion) Hung left & strug early, styd on well from 2f out, just failed: h'cap rnr-up '03: eff arnd 1m on
fast & soft, has tried 10f, may yet suit: likely type for similar. 2 Oct'03 Wind 8.3g/f 67-68 E:
1403 **JAKARMI 13** [12] B Palling 3-9-3 (65) T Quinn 7/2 FAV: 6132223: Chsd wnr & ch over 1f out, no   1½   70
extra well ins last: nicely bckd, op 4/1: another gd run: acts on firm, soft & fibresand: see 1403, 1193 & 1007.
1359 **NANTUCKET SOUND 16** [15] M C Pipe 3-9-5 (67) Dane O'Neill 8/1: 634-04: b c Quiet American - Anna   ½   71
(Ela Mana Mou) Dwelt & bhd, styd on well for press fnl 2f, not able to reach wnr: clr of rem: plcd fnl '03 start
(lightly rcd, rtd 72, mdn): eff at 1m, 10f may suit: handles gd/soft, soft & polytrack, sharp or gall trk.
1318 **HABANERO 17** [9]3-9-6 (68) R L Moore 14/1: 0221-005: b c Cadeaux Genereux - Queen of Dance   12   54
(Sadler's Wells) Chsd ldrs, btn dist: '03 h'cap wnr fnl start: eff at 1m: acts on firm & fast, sharp/stiff trk.
1 Oct'03 Wind 8.3g/f 72-68 E: 2 Sep'03 Good 8fm 71-65 D: 2 Sep'03 Sali 8g/f 68-65 D:
1370 **ANDURIL 15** [2]3-9-7 (69) J Tate 14/1: 045-6036: Keen, bhd, mod late prog, no threat: btr 1370.   1   53
1220 **LANDUCCI 23** [1]3-9-6 (68) M Hills 8/1: 00-27: Chsd ldrs till 2f out: btr 1220 (AW).   1   50
1470 **AMWELL BRAVE 10** [16]3-9-0 vis (62) L Dettori 9/1: 3350508: Mid-div, eff 3f out, no impress: btr 1283.   shd   44
1417 **NIGHT WORKER 12** [18]3-8-12 (60) P Dobbs 25/1: 3040-609: Chsd ldrs till 3f out: up in trip.   4   36
1359 **SUSIEDIL 16** [7]3-9-1 (63) B Doyle 33/1: 00140-00: 10th: Chsd ldrs, btn over 2f out.   5   31
3136} **MOLINIA 290** [17]3-9-3 (65) S Sanders 33/1: 550-0: 11th: Dwelt, in tch till halfway then reapp.   4   27
226 **MUSIC MIX 143** [8]3-9-1 (63) J Murtagh 7/1: 466-0: 12th: Bhd, eff 3f out, sn btn: h'cap/turf bow.   1¾   23
1403 **SOLO SOLE 13** [10]3-9-7 (69) N Mackay(3) 33/1: 6003-00: 13th: Al bhd, dropped in trip.   ½   28
98 **INCHPAST 167** [14]3-9-3 (65) P Robinson 16/1: 050-0: 14th: Al rear: abs, h'cap bow.   ¾   23
1007 **The Job 40** [3]3-8-9 (57) J Quinn 12/1:0   1259 **Kitley 21** [13]3-9-3 (65) S Whitworth 25/1:0
365 **Lord Greystoke 121** [6]3-8-12 (60) R Havlin 66/1:0   1081 **Whiplash 33** [5]3-8-11 (59) R Smith 33/1:0
18 Ran   Time 1m 51.90 ()   Owned: Mrs Stef Liddiard   Trained: Hungerford

---

1648   6.45 Karina Lawford Memorial Handicap Stakes 3yo 0-70 (E)   [74]
£3738 £1150 £575   1m3f135y   Soft   Inapplicable   Inside.

1331* **FLEETFOOT MAC 17** [9] P D Evans 3-8-13 (59) N Callan 12/1: 0006-11: Made all, drvn & wandered   66
under press fnl 2f: styd on strongly, gamely: suited by 11.5f/12f, will get further: likes soft grnd, gall/undul
or sharp trk: well suited by forcing tactics: shows a willing attitude: see 1331.
1382 **LATE OPPOSITION 14** [14] E A L Dunlop 3-9-7 (67) L Dettori 4/1 FAV: 006-4222: Held up, smooth   3   68
hdwy & rdn/chsd wnr over 1f out, flashed tail under press & no extra nr fin: acts on gd & soft: see 1382, 1260.
1340 **GENERAL FLUMPA 16** [4] C F Wall 3-9-4 (64) G Baker 11/1: 0-633: Mid-div, smooth hdwy over 2f out,   ½   64
onepcd for press ins last: bckd at long morning odds on h'cap bow: styd longer 11.5f trip well: acts on soft grnd.
135 **PRENUP 160** [1] L M Cumani 3-8-12 (58) N Mackay(3) 12/1: 500-4: ch f Diesis - Mutual Consent   ½   57
(Reference Point) Chsd ldr 5f out, rdn & no impress dist: nicely bckd, h'cap bow, 5 month abs: mdn unplcd '03 (rtd
47): stays 11.5f, drop to 10f cld prove ideal: acts on soft: can be plcd to effect.
1427 **MAMBINA 12** [17]3-9-6 (66) T E Durcan 20/1: 50-0445: Chsd ldrs, onepcd for press fnl 2f: imprvd   3   61
eff, prob handles gd & soft grnd: see 1124.
1521 **ITS BLUE CHIP 7** [2]3-9-4 e (64) Paul Eddery 6/1: 0-30146: Rear, hdwy 3f out, not able to chall.   4   54
1470 **AIRGUSTA 10** [11]3-9-1 (61) P Robinson 14/1: 000-007: b c Danehill Dancer - Ministerial Model   ½   50
(Shalford) Chsd ldrs till 2f out: unplcd '03 (rtd 67a & 28): longer 11.5f trip today, mid-dists may yet suit.
1427 **ABSOLUTELY SOAKED 4** [18]3-9-2 (62) C Lowther 33/1: 30-568: Rear, eff 3f out, btn dist: see 1427.   3   47
1403 **RINNEEN 13** [6]3-8-8 (54) R L Moore 16/1: 03000-09: b f Bien Bien - Sparky's Song (Electric)   1¾   37
Rear, drvn 4f out, mod prog: op 33/1: unplcd '03 (rtd 71, prob flattered & 60a, h'cap): dam a mid-dist wnr.
51 **SCIENCE ACADEMY 174** [20]3-9-0 (60) K Fallon 6/1: 500-0: 10th: ch f Silver Hawk - Dance Design   shd   43
(Sadler's Wells) Mid-div, eff 3f out, sn no impress: bckd: 6 month abs, h'cap bow: unplcd '03 (rtd 70 & 57a):
mid-dist pedigree, may apprec a faster surface.
1124 **MISTER TRICKSTER 28** [13]3-9-1 (61) J Quinn 33/1: 6650-600: 11th: Rear, mod prog: longer trip.   6   36
1260 **BAKHTYAR 21** [16]3-9-1 (61) S Drowne 12/1: 005-00: 12th: Chsd ldr till 2f out.   3   32
1260 **LITTLESTAR 21** [10]3-8-10 BL (56) S Sanders 33/1: 000-000: 13th: Chsd ldrs, wknd fnl 2f: blnks.   3   23
1403 **ILLEANA 13** [15]3-9-1 (61) Martin Dwyer 33/1: 00-400: 14th: Chsd ldrs, strug fnl 4f: btr 908.   4   23
1165 **Varuni 26** [3]3-9-4 (64) P Dobbs 25/1:0

1165 Dolly Wotnot 26 [12]3-9-7 (67) T G McLaughlin 40/1:0

1398 **Grist Mist 13** [19]3-8-13 T(59) A McCarthy 100/1:0   120 **Polar Dancer 163** [8]3-9-5 (65) Dane O'Neill 20/1:0

1470 **Desert Battle 10** [5]3-9-4 (64) D Sweeney 66/1:0   1165 **Semelle De Vent 26** [7]3-8-12 (58) R Havlin 16/1:0

20 Ran Time 2m 42.68 () Owned: Mr M W Lawrence Trained: Abergavenny

---

1649   7.15 Listed Totesport Com Royal Windsor Stakes Colts & Geldings 3yo+   (A)
£19500 £6000 £3000   **1m67y rnd**   **Soft**   **Inapplicable**   Inside.

1420+ **PUTRA PEKAN 12** [4] M A Jarvis 6-9-7 bl (108) P Robinson 5/4 FAV: 10010-11: Pulled v hard early,   **113**
ran wide on bend but led after 2f, strongly chall over 1f out, styd on strongly for press to assert ins last: hvly
bckd, op 11/8: eff at 1m/9f on firm & soft grnd, any trk: needs strong handling but a smart entire, gvn an
intelligent ride tonight (made full use of fav rail position): see 1420.

     ANCIENT WORLD 214 [5] Saeed bin Suroor 4-9-2 T L Dettori 13/8: 4411-2: b c Spinning World -   2½   **102**
Headline (Machiavellian): Led, ran wide on bend & hdd after 2f, no extra ins last: ex-French, dual stks wnr at Longchamp in '03: eff at 1m/8.5f on gd/soft &
soft: can go well fresh: ran well in t-strap tonight, can be plcd to find similar.

922   **EXCELSIUS 46** [6] J L Dunlop 4-9-7 (106) T Quinn 14/1: 03301-03: Slow away, sn chsd ldrs, kept on   3½   **102**
to take 3rd, no threat to front pair fnl 2f: 7 wk abs: see 108 (Listed).

1486* **ROCKETS N ROLLERS 9** [3] R Hannon 4-9-7 (106) Dane O'Neill 6/1: 3332314: Trkd ldrs, wknd over 1f   hd   **102**
out: needs a return to 7f: btr 1486 (fast, made all).

4 Ran Time 1m 50.88 () Owned: HRH Sultan Ahmad Shah Trained: Newmarket

---

1650   7.45 Beechcroft Associates Classified Stakes 4yo+ 0-70 (E)
£4407 £1356 £678   **1m2f7y**   **Soft**   **Inapplicable**   Inside.

1296   **SCOTTISH RIVER 19** [15] M D I Usher 5-9-2 (72) Hayley Turner(5) 40/1: 5110561: Held up, hdwy 3f   **80**
out & drvn/led dist, hung badly left closing stages but held on well: eff at 1m/10f on firm, soft & both AWs, poss
handles hvy, any trk, likes a sharp one: holding form well, can win more races: see 1296, 747 & 699 (AW).

1502   **INVITATION 8** [8] A Charlton 6-9-0 (70) R Smith 12/1: 500-0642: Rear, drvn & styd on well fnl 2f,   ¾   **76**
not reach wnr: apprec drop to 10f, could find similar: see 1056.

1357   **STREET LIFE 16** [3] W J Musson 6-9-4 (74) K Fallon 9/4 FAV: 06-25233: Held up, hdwy 3f out, ch   1½   **78**
dist, sn no extra: well bckd, loves this trk & prevailing conditions, clr of rem: see 391.

1467   **POLAR JEM 10** [14] G G Margarson 4-9-1 (74) A McCarthy 10/1: 6321-34: Trkd ldrs, narrow lead over   5   **68**
1f out, sn hdd & no extra: see 1467.

1235   **SILVER PROPHET 23** [16]5-9-5 (75) G Baker 100/1: 43000-05: gr g Idris - Silver Heart (Yankee   1½   **70**
Gold) Chsd ldrs till over 1f out: appr h'cap plcd '03 (rtd 80): '02 mdn wnr: eff arnd 10/11f on fast & soft grnd,
prob any trk. 2 Jul'02 Sand 10g/s 85-81 D: 1 Jun'02 Good 11sft 86- D: 2 May'02 Wind 10sft 86- E:

4708* **PEQUENITA 210** [10]4-8-11 bl (69) R L Moore 14/1: 000421-6: b f Rudimentary - Sierra Madrona   shd   **62**
(Woodman) Chsd ldrs, ran wide on bend after 3f, remained handy, narrow lead 2f out, hdd dist & wknd: 4 month jumps
abs, 03/04 mdn hdle wnr (rtd 116h, 2m/2m1.5f, gd & gd/soft), eff in cheek pieces): '03 clmr wnr for J G Given: eff
arnd 11/12f on fibresand, gd/soft & soft grnd.

1 Oct'03 Ayr 10.9g/s 68-(50) F: 2 Aug'03 Wolv 12af 53a-50 G: 2 May'03 Ling 7sft 65- D:

1273   **MISS PEBBLES 20** [2]4-8-11 (68) N Pollard 12/1: 0056-147: Led 1f, remained handy till led again   2   **59**
over 2f out, hdd over 1f out & wknd: see 747.

1467   **MAXILLA 10** [12]4-8-13 (72) L Dettori 7/1: 04/241-48: Led after 1f till over 2f out, sn btn: btr 1467.   shd   **61**

4740} **SHREDDED 209** [19]4-9-5 (75) J Murtagh 14/1: 3/54-9: Chsd ldrs, btn 2f out.   shd   **67**

1357 SIR HAYDN 16 [0]4-9-0 (70) W Ryan 20/1: 6000 0001 10th: Dha, late gains for press, no danger.   ¾   01

1599   **SUDDEN FLIGHT 3** [17]7-9-0 (68) R Havlin 25/1: 0-000300: 11th: Mid-div, btn 3f out: quick reapp.   nk   **60**

1346   **WAR OWL 16** [13]7-9-2 (72) Lisa Jones(3) 8/1: 2011350: 12th: Chsd ldrs till 2f out: btr 1128 & 1098.   5   **55**

3890} **MY GALLIANO 259** [7]8-9-0 (68) L Keniry(3) 40/1: 660216-0: 13th: Mid-div, no prog fnl 2f: 2 mth jmps abs.   9   **41**

1352   **SKYLARKER 16** [18]6-9-2 (72) N Callan 12/1: 4-233000: 14th: Mid-div halfway, sn btn: btr 632.   1¾   **41**

1009   **MOON SHOT 40** [5]8-9-1 (71) V Slattery 40/1: 51/3-1240: 15th: Al bhd, 6 wk abs: btr 870 & 752.   12   **25**

     One Of Them 323 [11]5-9-0 BL(62) Derek Nolan(7) 100/1:056   **Chevrone 174** [20]4-9-0 BL(70) S Drowne 20/1:0

605 **Dusty Carpet 89** [1]6-9-0 (65) M Fenton 25/1:0   38 **Dens Joy 177** [6]8-8-11 (52) S Sanders 33/1:0

19 Ran Time 2m 17.33 () Owned: Mr M D I Usher Trained: Lambourn

---

1651   8.15 Bdl Group Median Auction Maiden Stakes 3yo (E)
£3669 £1129 £565   **1m2f7y**   **Soft**   **Inapplicable**   Inside.

4895} **INCURSION 198** [20] A King 3-9-0 (82) R Hughes 5/2 FAV: 063-1: b c Inchinor - Morgannwg (Simply   **84**
Great) Al handy & led going well against stands rail over 3f out, prsd over 2f out, rdn & asserted ins last: well
bckd, reapp: mdn plcd '03 (rtd 80, lightly rcd): eff at 1m, apprec step up to 10f, 12f+ could suit: acts on fast &
soft grnd, gall or sharp/easy trks: type to prog.

1259   **MIDSHIPMAN EASY 21** [14] P W Harris 3-9-0 N Callan 5/1: 0-32: Trkd ldrs & rdn to chall over 2f   3   **78**
out, not pace of wnr ins last: rest well covered: acts on gd/soft & soft, prob prog from latest: now qual for
h'caps, shld find a race: see 1259 (C/D).

1494   **LADY PEACHES 8** [7] D Mullarkey 3-8-9 L Dettori 12/1: 0-03: ch f Bien Bien - Upper Club (Taufan)   3½   **68**
Chsd ldrs, outpcd over 2f out, rallied to snatch 3rd, no danger: no form sole '03 start: now stays a sharp 10f,
may get further: handles soft grnd & a sharp trk: shown ability, h'caps likely to suit.

1258   **ELLINA 21** [1] J Pearce 3-8-9 R Price 25/1: 00-04: b f Robellino - Native Flair (Be My Native)   hd   **68**
Chsd ldrs & ch over 3f out, no extra bef dist: unplcd '03 (rtd 63, mdn): imprvd over longer 10f trip, handles soft
grnd: prog with racing, h'caps could suit.

     CULTURED [12]3-8-9 S Drowne 33/1: 5: Chsd ldrs, no impress fnl 2f on debut.   3   **63**

1140   **PELLA 28** [17]3-8-9 D Sweeney 100/1: 006: Chsd ldrs, btn over 1f out.   2½   **60**

     HONEYMOONING [8]3-8-9 W Ryan 10/1: 7: Rear & sn pushed along, late prog wide under hands &   hd   **60+**
heels: ran green: most encouraging debut, expect improvement.

4827} **YOUNG LOVE 202** [16]3-8-9 M Fenton 66/1: 00-8: Mid-div, struggling fnl 2f, reapp.   1¼   **58**

WINDSOR MONDAY 10.05.04 Sharp, Figure 8 Track

1495	**CROCOLAT 8** [11]3-8-9 A Mackay 66/1: 09: Bhd, mod late prog, no danger.			nk	57
1236	**LAABBIJ 23** [6]3-9-0 Martin Dwyer 7/2: 0-60: 10th: Rear, drvn & only mod prog: btr 1236 (1m).			½	61
1473	**ANTIGIOTTO 9** [13]3-9-0 N Mackay(3) 66/1: 000: 11th: Rear, late prog, no dngr: improve in h'caps.			hd	61
473	**WILD PITCH 107** [18]3-9-0 R L Moore 33/1: 6-00: 12th: Mid-div, no impress fnl 2f, abs.			1¼	59
1384	**SILENCIO 14** [9]3-9-0 V Slattery 25/1: 00: 13th: Mid-div, no impress fnl 3f.			2½	56
	HIGHLIGHT GIRL [4]3-8-9 S Hitchcott(3) 50/1: 0: 14th: Al towards rear on debut.			3	47
1258	**ST TROPEZ 21** [10]3-8-9 S Whitworth 100/1: 00-00: 15th: Keen, rear, eff 3f out, sn btn.			3½	43
1398	**JUSTICE JONES 13** [3]3-9-0 A Daly 66/1: 0000: 16th: Led 2f, prom till over 2f out.			¾	47
1527	**TREW CLASS 7** [2]3-8-9 P Robinson 20/1: 00: 17th: Al bhd, longer trip.			2½	39
	POUILLY FUME [15]3-8-9 A McCarthy 50/1: 0: 18th: Al bhd on debut.			14	21
1468	**SOVIET SPIRIT 10** [19]3-8-9 J Murtagh 7/1: 50: 19th: Keen & led after 2f, hdd 3f out, sn btn.			½	20
601	**SECOND USER 89** [5]3-9-0 J Jeffrey(7) 100/1: 000: 20th: Bhd halfway, 12 wk abs.			3½	20

20 Ran   Time 2m 21.04()   Owned: Mr Nigel Bunter   Trained: Barbury Castle

WOLVERHAMPTON Fibresand MONDAY 10.05.04 Lefthand, Sharp Track

Official Going STANDARD

1652 2.30 Mix Business With Pleasure At Dunstall Park Maiden Auction Stakes Fillies 2yo (E)
£3445 £1060 £530   **5f aw rnd**   **Going 51**   **+07 Fast**   Inside

1343 **RIGHTPRICE PREMIER 16** [7] K A Ryan 2-8-6 (1ow) N Callan 9/4 FAV: 321: Keen cl-up, led after 2f, **68a+**
pushed out ins fnl 1f, val 2L+: AW bow, fair time: eff at 5f, shld appr further: acts on gd/soft grnd & fibresand:
eff on a sharp or gall trk: improving with racing: see 1343 & 1091.
WISE WAGER [6] R A Fahey 2-8-3 T Hamilton 7/1: 2: b f Titus Livius - Londubh (Tumble Wind) ½ **62a**
Dwelt, prog to chase wnr dist, kept on despite edging left fnl 1f, just held: clr rem: debut: op 12/1, Mar foal ,
cost E3,500: half-sister plcd at 5f/1m: sire top-class at sprint dists: eff at 5f, shld stay further: acts on
fibresand: sure to improve with more experience.
1380 **BAILEYS APPLAUSE 14** [5] C A Dwyer 2-8-7 p S Sanders 3/1: 53: b f Royal Applause - Thicket 7 **45a**
(Wolfhound) Led, hdd 3f out, fdd dist: Feb foal, cost 12,000gns: dam 5f wnr as a juv: sire Gr 1 wnr at 6f.
1380 **LATERAL THINKER 14** [2] J A Osborne 2-8-4 J F McDonald(3) 3/1: 2234: Handy till halfway, sn ½ **40a**
outpcd, modest late gains: below par effort & reportedly lost action: btr 1380 & 1325.
DOCKLANDS GRACE [4]2-8-6 T P Queally(3) 12/1: 5: gr f Honour And Glory - Afarel (Runaway Groom) nk **41a**
Slow away, nvr nrr than mid-div: op 8/1 on debut: May foal, cost 9,000gns: half-sister to numerous wnrs abroad:
dam wnr in US: sire decent performrer around 6f/1m: with N P Littmoden.
1401 **TURTLE MAGIC 13** [1]2-8-3 C Haddon(7) 12/1: 02366: Rear, nvr a factor: btr 1325 & 1161. 4 **26a**
1458 **CHILALI 10** [3]2-8-4 F Norton 20/1: 57: Cl-up 3f, wknd: btr 1458 (debut). shd **26a**

7 Ran   Time 1m 2.4 (2.2)   Owned: Rightprice Racing   Trained: Hambleton

1653 3.00 Winning Post Special At Dunstall Park Claiming Stakes 2yo (F)
£2898 £828 £414   **5f aw rnd**   **Going 51**   **-08 Slow**   Inside

KEY SECRET [4] M D I Usher 2-8-3 J Mackay 12/1: 1: ch f Whittingham - Foxkey (Foxhound) Slow **68a**
away & bhd, prog to lead dist, rdn out to hold on: debut: Mar first foal, dam 5f wnr as a juv: sire speedily bred
performer: eff at 5f on fibresand: acts on a sharp trk & goes well fresh.
1401 **GOLDHILL PRINCE 13** [2] W G M Turner 2-8-6 p C Haddon(7) 9/2: 0402: Handy, styd on well despite shd **70a**
edging right ins fnl 1f, just held by wnr: eff at 5f on gd/soft grnd & fibresand: eff with cheek pieces: worth a
try at 6f in similar grade: see 1097.
1303 **STRAFFAN 18** [7] E J O'Neill 2-8-5 J Carroll 7/2: 633: Handy till dist, sn onepcd: AW bow: 1¼ **65a**
acts on soft grnd & fibresand: see 1303.
1212 **LADY ERICA 24** [8] K R Burke 2-8-9 Darren Williams 15/8 FAV: 254: Cl-up, ev ch dist, no extra. ½ **67a**
1550 **VOICE OF AN ANGEL 6** [3]2-8-5 F Norton 12/1: 505: b f Desert Style - Madame Curie (Polish nk **62a**
Precedent) Led, edging right & hdd dist, no extra: qck reapp: Mar foal, cost E4,000: sire top-class juv performer.
SHISH [1]2-8-3 J F McDonald(3) 8/1: 6: b f Rossini - Kebabs (Catrail) Rear, nvr a factor on 7 **39a**
debut: op 4/1: Mar first foal, cost E3,500: dam wnr at 6f: sire top-class at sprint dists as a juv.
1325 **ICE RUBY 17** [5]2-8-2 B Swarbrick(5) 20/1: 007: Slow away, handy over 3f, wknd. 2 **32a**
1343 **HOUDINI BAY 16** [6]2-8-7 T Hamilton(3) 25/1: 08: Cl-up over 3f, wknd. ¾ **35a**

8 Ran   Time 1m 3.15 (2.95)   Owned: Mr I Sheward   Trained: Lambourn

1654 3.35 Sponsor A Race At Dunstall Park Handicap Stakes 4yo+ 46-55 (F)
£2933 £838 £419   **1m6f166y aw**   **Going 51**   **-11 Slow**   Outside   **[68]**

1135 **TOLEDO SUN 28** [10] V Smith 4-8-11 (51) Joanna Badger 6/1: 0000-351: Cl-up, led 12f out, drvn out **57a**
ins fnl 1f to hold on: rider rec a 2 day whip ban: recently plcd over hdles (rtd 111h, juv nov, eff at 2m on firm
grnd): eff at 10/11f, improve for step up to around 15f: handles both AWs & a sharp trk: first win: see 595.
1459 **COMPTON ECLAIRE 10** [3] G A Butler 4-8-9 vis (49) T P Queally(3) 13/2: 1034-332: Slow away, prog 1 **53a**
halfway, kept on despite edging left fnl 1f, just held by wnr: op 5/1: suited by 12/14f, stays 15f: see 1459.
1313 **RED MOOR 18** [6] R Hollinshead 4-8-8 (48) A Culhane 5/1: 65-26123: Cl-up till dist, sn no extra: 1½ **50a**
eff at 11/12f, now stays 15f: see 1197.
1563* **MY LEGAL EAGLE 5** [4] R J Price 10-8-8 (6ex) (46) B Swarbrick(5) 5/1: 2050//5-14: Held up, prog shd **47a**
halfway, no impress dist: op 7/2, qck reapp: see 1563 (better)
1469 **LUBINAS 10** [1]5-8-8 (46) S W Kelly 8/1: 622/20-05: Cl-up over 12f, sn no extra: see 1469. 4 **43a**
1551 **CELTIC VISION 6** [8]8-8-12 t (50) S Righton 22/1: 660046: Nvr trav in mid-div, fdd after 12f. 30 **17a**
1460} **CALIBAN 364** [5]6-8-11 (49) M Fenton 12/1: 514550-7: ch g Rainbows For Life - Amour Toujours (Law 15 **1a**
Society) Led till hdd 12f out, fdd 1m out: op 8/1: reapp: AW h'cap wnr in '03: nov h'cap hdle wnr in 02/03 (rtd
110h, stays 2m on firm & soft): unplcd in '02 (rtd 37a, h'cap): eff at 9/11f, stays a sharp 2m well: acts on
fibresand & a sharp trk: eff with a visor.
1 Mar'03 Wolv 16.2af 53a-45 F: 1 Mar'01 Sout 11af 50a- G: 1 Feb'01 Sout 11af 51a-46 F: 2 Feb'01 Wolv 9.3af 43a- G:
1285 **THE BEDUTH NAVI 20** [2]4-8-8 (1ow) (47) S Sanders 7/2 FAV: 2212348: Cl-up 12f, sn fdd, rtn lame. 19 **0a**

478

WOLVERHAMPTON Fibresand MONDAY 10.05.04 Lefthand, Sharp Track

1332 **FORTUNA MEA 17** [9]4-8-5 (45) P Makin(3) 20/1: 60000-69: b f Mon Tresor - Veni Vici (Namaqualand) *dist* **0a**
Rear, nvr a factor: unplcd in '03 (rtd 44, h'caps): fill sell wnr in '02: eff at 1m on f/sand: handles a sharp trk.
1 Oct'02 Wolv 8.4af 58a- G:
9 Ran Time 3m 19.0 (9.4) Owned: Monkey a Month Racing Trained: Newmarket

---

1655 4.10 Come Racing Again Tomorrow At Dunstall Park Handicap Fillies 3yo 0-70 (E) [73]
£3396 £1045 £523 1m100y aw rnd Going 51 -11 Slow Inside

1534 **DARING AFFAIR 6** [1] K R Burke 3-9-7 (66) Darren Williams 9/4: 3215141: Mid-div, prog to lead bef **71a**
1f out, rdn out to hold on despite hanging right: qck reapp: eff btwn 6f & 8.5f on fibresand, gd/soft grnd & hvy:
likes Wolverhampton: see 1534 & 1339.
1403 **KESHYA 13** [3] D J Coakley 3-9-4 (63) T P Queally(3) 11/8 FAV: 0062-342: Cl-up, outpcd after 6f, *hd* **67a**
rallied ins fnl 1f, just held by wnr: well bckd: AW bow: eff at 1m/8.4f on gd/soft grnd & fibresand: see 1099.
798 **SOMEWHERE MY LOVE 67** [2] T G Mills 3-9-7 (66) R Miles(3) 7/1: 50-1003: Cl-up, kept on but just *1½* **67a**
held by front 2 ins fnl 1f: 10 wk abs: acts on both AWs: see 496.
4987} **STILETTO LADY 189** [5] J G Given 3-9-4 (63) M Fenton 13/2: 040-4: b f Daggers Drawn - Nordic *1¼* **61a**
Pride (Horage) Led till hdd bef 1f out, no extra: op 5/1 on reapp: unplcd in 3 '03 starts (rtd 67, auct mdn):
prob stays 8.4f on fibresand: just sharper for today.
1242 **LADY PREDOMINANT 23** [4]3-8-2 T (47) B Swarbrick(5) 10/1: 4060105: Cl-up 6f, fdd: tried t-strap. *20* **5a**
5 Ran Time 1m 51.55 (5.35) Owned: Mr Nigel Shields Trained: Leyburn

---

1656 4.40 Tattersalls Value Package At Dunstall Park Selling Stakes 3yo+ (G)
£2639 £754 £377 7f aw rnd Going 51 -11 Slow Outside

1341 **TURN AROUND 16** [8] B W Hills 4-9-8 (52) A Culhane 7/2: 000-0021: Cl-up, led halfway, drvn out **53a**
fnl 1f: op 5/2: bght in for 7,200gns: eff at 8.5f on gd/soft & fibresand, can win again in this grade.
1378 **CHANDELIER 14** [7] M S Saunders 4-9-8 p (48) R Miles(3) 6/1: 0-536032: Cl-up, outpcd halfway, *1¾* **49a**
rallied ins fnl 1f, no ch with wnr: tchd 8/1: eff at 7f/1m: cheek pieces refitted here: see 1378 & 571.
1378* **MIZHAR 14** [6] J J Quinn 8-9-13 p (52) Darren Williams 6/1: 5250013: Rear, prog after 5f, no *nk* **53a**
impress ins fnl 1f: top-weight: btr 1378 (C/D).
1627 **QUEEN OF NIGHT 2** [4] D W Chapman 4-9-3 (70) P Makin(5) 5/1: 515-0404: Led till halfway, no extra. *1* **41a**
1446 **TINIAN 11** [1]6-9-8 BL (45) S Bushby(7) 14/1: 0304045: Nvr nrr than mid-div: tried blnks, btr 1446. *8* **30a**
1080 **COMPTON EAGLE 33** [5]4-9-8 T P Queally(3) 8/1: 0-06: b g Zafonic - Gayane (Nureyev) Slow away, *7* **16a**
nvr a factor: unplcd sole '03 start (rtd 65, mdn): with G A Butler.
3887} **GOLDEN LEGEND 615** [2]7-9-8 (30) B Swarbrick(5) 66/1: 000000/-7: b g Last Tycoon - Adjalisa *6* **4a**
(Darshaan) Rear, nvr a factor: p.u. sole 03/04 hdle start: missed '03: mod form in '02 (rtd 40, h'cap): amat
h'cap wnr in '01 (A B Coogan): eff at 1m/9f on firm & fast: has tried t-strap: with R J Price.
2 Jul'01 Warw 8g/f 62-62 G: 1 Jul'01 Kemp 9fm 62-56 E: 2 May'01 Redc 6g/f 56-54 G:
869 **SHADOWFAX 53** [3]4-9-8 VIS (58) M Fenton 3/1 FAV: 2-400028: Cl-up 4f, sn fdd, eased ins fnl 1f: *dist* **0a**
disapp eff in first time visor & reportedly lost action: see 869.
8 Ran Time 1m 30.6 (4.4) Owned: Gryffindor (wwwracingtourscouk) Trained: Lambourn

---

1657 5.10 Teletext Racing 'hands And Heels' Apprentice Handicap Stakes 3yo+ 46-55 (F) [56]
£2947 £842 £421 1m1f79y aw Going 51 -01 Slow Inside

£00 **VANDENDERGIIE 140** [7] J A Osbome 5-9-0 (48) R Keogh(3) 4/1 C FAV: 0/00635-1: Rear, prog after 4f, **54a**
styd on to lead ins fnl 1f, rdn out: tchd 11/2: long abs: eff at 9f/12f on fibresand & fast grnd: goes well fresh
& has slipped to a fair mark: see 75.
1425 **FRANKS QUEST 12** [5] P Burgoyne 4-9-8 (50) R J Killoran(5) 11/2: 3360402: Cl-up, led 4f out, hdd *nk* **55a**
ins fnl 1f, kept on but just denied: clr rem: eff at 9/11f: can find similar: see 718.
1366 **ARJAY 16** [2] Andrew Turnell 6-9-9 (51) M Howard 12/1: 0000-003: b g Shaamit - Jenny's Call *6* **44a**
(Petong) Led over 5f, wknd fnl 2f: ran out once in '03 (class stks): class stks wnr in '02: eff at 6/7f, stays
slowly run 10f: acts on fast & gd, likes the mud: has tried blnks.
2 Jul'03 Beve 9.9gd 73-(70) E: 1 May'02 Thir 7g/s 83- D: 1 Sep'01 Ayr 7.2g/f 80-74 C:
1090 **CALL OF THE WILD 33** [6] R A Fahey 4-9-9 p (51) D Swift(3) 4/1 C FAV: 6-033364: Bhd, prog after 3f, *4* **36a**
fdd fnl 2f: cheek pieces refitted: btr 961 (fibresand).
1535 **DANCING KING 6** [4]8-9-4 (46) M Halford 4/1 C FAV: 0062625: Cl-up 6f, wknd: qck reapp: btr 1535. *hd* **30a**
956 **CHANTRY FALLS 42** [8]4-9-6 (48) Liam Jones 9/1: 50463-06: Rear, prog after 3f, fdd 2f out: 6 wk abs. *6* **20a**
1379 **CRUSOE 14** [1]7-9-9 bl (51) K May 5/1: 0400427: Cl-up 4f, sn fdd: btr 1379. *2½* **18a**
1535 **DAIMAJIN 6** [3]5-9-8 (50) T O'Brien(5) 20/1: 5400008: Slow away, nvr a factor: qck reapp: see 689. *3* **11a**
8 Ran Time 2m 3.15(4.95) Owned: Mr D Marks Trained: Upper Lambourn

---

REDCAR MONDAY 10.05.04 Lefthand, Flat, Galloping Track

Official Going Soft (Heavy Places)

1658 2.20 Crows Nest Restaurant Novice Median Auction Stakes 2yo (F)
£2934 £838 £419 5f str Soft 138 -33 Slow Stands side

1424 **PRINCE NAMID 12** [2] Mrs A Duffield 2-8-12 S Carson 1/4 FAV: 431: Made all, pushed out ins fnl **75+**
1f, val 7L+: eff at 5f, will apprec further: acts on soft grnd & a gall trk: can rate higher: see 1424.
MAS O MENOS 4 [4] Ms Deborah J Evans 2-8-12 I Mongan 20/1: 2: b g King's Theatre - Promising *5* **62**
Lady (Thunder Gulch) Prom, outpcd by easy wnr ins fnl 1f: debut: Mar first foal, cost 8,000gns: dam wnr at around
1m: sire high-class performer around 12f: improve with experience.
JANE JUBILEE 1 [1] M Johnston 2-8-7 R Ffrench 4/1: 3: b f Mister Baileys - Elsie Bamford (Tragic *1¾* **52**
Role) Prom over 3f, no extra: debut: Feb first foal, cost 5,500gns: dam staying wnr at 14/15f, sire top-class
performer at 1m: just sharper for today.

3 Ran Time 1m 5.05 (8.55) Owned: Mr S Adamson Trained: Leyburn

---

1659 **2.50 Classic Boxes Maiden Stakes Fillies 3yo+** **(D)**
£3624 £1115 £558 **6f str** **Soft 138** **-55 Slow** Stands side

1281 **EXTREMELY RARE 20** [7] T D Easterby 3-8-11 D Allan(3) 3/1: 201: Handy, led dist, all out to hold **65**
on: slow time eff at 6f, 7f shld suit: acts on gd & soft grnd: sharp & gall trk: see 999.
1 **GREEN RIDGE 182** [5] P W D'Arcy 3-8-11 (70) K Darley 11/4 FAV: 2506-2: b f Muhtarram - Top of The hd **63**
Morning (Keen) Led 4f out, hdd dist, kept on, just denied: op 9/4 on reapp: rnr-up first time out in '03 (auct
mdn): eff at 5/6f, shld stay further: acts on gd & soft grnd: only just denied on reapp & can find a race.
2 Apr'03 Yarm 5.2gd 73- F:
1426 **PALVIC MOON 12** [8] C Smith 3-8-11 (56) R Fitzpatrick 6/1: 06066-53: Handy, kept on ins fnl 1f, 1 **60$**
just held by front 2: op 9/2: stay 6f on fast & soft grnd: see 1426.
572 **AKIRAMENAI 93** [2] Mrs L Stubbs 4-9-7 R Winston 9/1: 04: Bhd, prog halfway, no impress ins fnl ¾ **58**
1f: op 16/1: long abs: eff at 6f on soft grnd.
25 **LA FONTEYNE 179** [6]3-8-11 T Eaves(5) 50/1: 00-5: b f Imperial Ballet - Baliana (Midyan) Handy shd **57**
over 4f, no extra dist: reapp: unplcd both '03 starts (rtd 46): with C B Booth.
3683} **PAY TIME 267** [1]5-9-7 (45) P Mulrennan(5) 33/1: 00/6000-6: ch f Timeless Times - Payvashooz 17 **22**
(Ballacashtal) Chsd ldrs 4f, sn fdd, eased fnl 1f: reapp & new stable: unplcd in '03 (rtd 53, mdn, M
Brittain); rnr-up in late '02 (mdn): eff at 5f on fibresand: with R E Barr. 2 Nov'01 Sout 5af 57a- F:
1774} **SAVANNAH SUE 348** [3]3-8-11 V Halliday 25/1: 0-7: Handy, wkng & hung badly left after 4f, sn btn. 5 **9**
4641} **CHAMPAGNE CRACKER 216** [4]3-8-11 (65) P Hanagan 3/1: 352622-8: Led 2f out, sn fdd, eased fnl 1f: 1½ **5**
disapp reapp tho' best form last year came on sound surface.
8 Ran Time 1m 20.49 (11.59) Owned: Mrs M H Easterby Trained: Malton

---

1660 **3.25 Toteexacta Stakes Handicap Fillies 3yo+ 0-80** **(D)** **[71]**
£7007 £2156 £1078 **7f str** **Soft 138** **-12 Slow** Stands side

1606 **WATERPARK 3** [8] R Craggs 6-8-5 (48) P Fessey 8/1: 2/0131-01: b f Namaqualand - Willisa (Polar **59+**
Falcon) Made all, pushed clr ins fnl 1f, val 6L+: qck reapp: won this race & an app fill h'cap on 2 of only 4 '03
starts: suited by 7f/1m on fast, soft grnd & fibresand: acts on a sharp or gall trk,
likes Redcar: still improving & can follow up on this evidence.
1 May'03 Redc 7g/f 49-42 D: 1 Mar'03 Sout 8af 45a-36 F: 2 Mar'02 Sout 8af 37a-36 F: 2 Feb'02 Sout 7af 42a- F:
1540 **ANNIJAZ 6** [15] J M Bradley 7-8-11 (54) S Carson 6/1 JT FAV: 10060-22: Held up, prog 3f out, styd 4 **56**
on to chase wnr ins fnl 1f, al held: qck reapp: see 1540 (reapp).
1277 **JUST ONE SMILE 20** [4] T D Easterby 4-9-5 (62) D Allan(3) 20/1: 32142-03: Chsd ldrs, ev ch bef 1f shd **63**
out, sn onepcd: acts on firm, soft grnd & polytrack, just btr 22.
1465 **PARK STAR 10** [11] D Shaw 4-8-13 (56) R Winston 14/1: 3200U44: Rear, prog halfway, no impress fnl 1f. nk **56**
1348 **CELTIC ROMANCE 16** [3]5-8-7 (50) P Hanagan 9/1: 000-0005: Rear, prog after 3f, onepcd: bckd. hd **49**
1590* **SANDORRA 4** [2]6-8-8 (6ex) (51) T Williams 12/1: 3160016: Cl-up 5f, no extra: qck reapp: btr 1590. 1¾ **46**
847 **JESSIE 57** [14]5-8-2 t (45) Kim Tinkler 6/1 JT FAV: 6522247: Nvr nrr than mid-div: 8 wk abs: btr 771. 2½ **35**
1239 **ANNIE HARVEY 23** [7]3-9-4 (73) F Lynch 14/1: 51D30-08: ch f Fleetwood - Resemblance (State ¾ **61**
Diplomacy) Nvr nrr than mid-div: auct mdn wnr in '03: eff at 6/7f, further shld suit: acts on fast & gd/soft.
1 Aug'03 Thir 7g/s 77- E:
1485 **BUTHAINA 9** [10]4-9-10 (67) T Eaves(3) 33/1: 5/31-09: b f Bahhare - Haddeyah (Dayjur) Nvr nrr 3 **49**
than mid-div: med auct mdn wnr on 1 of only 2 '03 starts (J L Dunlop): unplcd sole '02 start (rtd 47, fill mdn):
eff at 7f/1m, further shld suit: acts on fast grnd: with T H Caldwell. 1 Apr'03 Newc 8.0g/f 71- F:
1448 **MOONLIGHT SONG 11** [9]7-8-2 (45) D Fentiman(7) 11/1: 00060-30: 10th: Handy over 4f, wknd fnl 2f. 1¼ **25**
1388 **PHARAOH HATSHEPSUT 14** [5]6-7-12 (6oh)VIS (35) P M Quinn 50/1: 400/-0000: 11th: Handy 5f, wknd. ¾ **19**
1393 **HIGH CANE 14** [13]4-8-13 (56) K Dalgleish 20/1: 36-03000: 12th: Rear, nvr a factor: btr 966. 2 **30**
1282 **EAGER ANGEL 20** [6]6-8-11 p (54) Dean McKeown 14/1: 1510300: 13th: Mid-div 4f, wknd: btr 1195. ½ **27**
1344 **MRS SPENCE 16** [12]3-8-8 (63) Dale Gibson 40/1: 025-060: 14th: Bhd, nvr a factor: btr 1344. 3½ **29**
1348 **SABALARA 16** [1]4-9-1 (58) I Mongan 13/2: 5620-000: 15th: Prom over 3f, sn fdd, eased fnl 1f. dist **0**
15 Ran Time 1m 32.31 (10.51) Owned: Mr Ray Craggs Trained: Sedgefield

---

1661 **4.00 Classic Suite Handicap Stakes 3yo+ 46-55** **(F)** **[62]**
£3220 £920 £460 **1m str** **Soft 138** **-05 Slow** Stands side

1425* **ROCINANTE 12** [15] J J Quinn 4-9-3 (51) R Winston 11/1: 0003011: Chsd ldrs, styd on styd on to **56**
lead dist, rdn out: op 9/1: best around 1m, acts on fast & fibresand, likes a soft surface: thriving at present &
can win again in the mud: see 1425 (sell h'cap).
1164 **ARCHIRONDEL 26** [9] M D Hammond 6-8-12 (46) I Mongan 25/1: 0-60U002: b g Bin Ajwaad - Penang hd **48**
Rose (Kingdom Bay) Held up, prog after 6f, styd on well fnl 1f, post came too sn: unplcd sole 03/04 hdle start:
plcd twice in '03 (rtd 64, h'cap, J Berry): h'cap wnr in '02, also plcd twice: eff at 1m/10f on firm & soft
grnd: handles a sharp/ undul or gall trk: has gone well fresh: back to form here & is h'capped to win similar.
2 Aug'02 Brig 9.9g/f 69-66 D: 1 Jun'02 Brig 8.4gd 68-60 D: 2 Apr'02 Nott 8.2g/f 60-56 E: 1 Jul'01 Folk 9.6g/f 55-52 E:
1 Jul'01 Brig 10g/f 51-46 F: 1 Jun'01 Redc 10g/f 47-40 D:
1388 **ENCOUNTER 14** [3] J Hetherton 8-8-12 (1oh) (45) D Allan(3) 11/1: 6500-003: Rear, prog 3f out, styd shd **49**
on well fnl 1f, not btn far in 3rd: won this race 12 months ago (4lb higher mark): h'capped to win similar.
1366 **GOODBYE MR BOND 16** [12] E J Alston 4-9-4 (52) Dean McKeown 5/2 FAV: 4-563434: Handy, short of ½ **54+**
room halfway & lost pl, prog in fnl 2f, not btn far in 4th: well bckd: infrequent wnr, did not get run of today's
race: see 1366 & 387.
1553 **SHIFTY 6** [10]5-9-1 (49) P M Quinn 20/1: 5000405: Mid-div, prog & ev ch dist, sn onepcd: see 1463. ½ **50**
996* **ZHITOMIR 40** [18]6-9-3 (51) L Enstone(3) 14/1: 0-00000-16: Held up, prog halfway, no impress fnl 1f: 3 **46**
6 wk abs: btr 996 (7f, seller).
1448* **STELLITE 11** [14]8-8-13 (47) K Darley 9/1: 0050-017: Rear, prog after 4f, no impress fnl 1f: op 7/1. ¾ **40**
1446* **FOREST AIR 11** [14]4-9-1 (49) R Ffrench 25/1: 0300-018: Bhd, nvr nrr than mid-div: btr 1446. 2 **38**
1536 **EXPLODE 6** [11]7-9-4 (52) K Dalgleish 40/1: 00000-49: Led after 4f, hdd dist, fdd: btr 1536. 1½ **38**
4855} **NOBLE PENNY 201** [7]5-9-2 (50) S Chin 20/1: 360000-0: 10th: b f Pennekamp - Noble Form (Double ¾ **34**
Form} Prom till dist, fdd: reapp: plcd once in '03 (h'cap, rtd 57): unplcd in '02 (rtd 61 & 51a, J Hills, mdns):
eff around 7f/1m on gd grnd.

1348	**PRINTSMITH** 16 [13]7-8-12 (1oh) (45) J Bramhill 16/1: 4321050: 11th: Nvr able to chall: btr 908.		1	28

1278 **BUSINESS MATTERS 20** [17]4-8-12 (46) R Lappin 33/1: 3000-000: 12th: b f Desert Style - Hear Me ... 8 ... 14
(Simply Great) Rear, nvr a factor: plcd once in '03 (class stks, rtd 58, J C Fox): ex Irish, plcd on 2 of 4 starts
in '02 (mdns): eff at 6.5f/stiff 1m on firm & soft grnd: with H Alexander.

1379 **SMART MINISTER 14** [16]4-9-3 (51) Dale Gibson 20/1: 36420-00: 13th: Cl-up 5f, sn fdd. ... 7 ... 7
4321} **DARA MAC 235** [4]5-9-2 p (50) Suzanne France(7) 33/1: 4B2005-0: 14th: Handy 6f, fdd. ... nk ... 5
4646} **GEMINI LADY 216** [19]4-8-12 (1oh) (45) A Nicholls 20/1: 330420-0: 15th: Mid-div till halfway, fdd. ... 14 ... 0
1322 **THUNDERCLAP 17** [8]5-9-7 P (55) P Mulrennan(5) 12/1: 00-12000: 16th: Led 4f, sn fdd. ... 13 ... 0
1095 **ISLANDS FAREWELL 32** [2]4-9-2 (50) T Eaves(5) 50/1: 000-00: 17th: Mid-div 5f, fdd. ... nk ... 0
1504 **Mehmaas 8** [6]8-9-7 vis(55) P Hanagan 12/1:0   4697} **Hormuz 211** [5]8-9-0 (48) D Fentiman(7) 25/1:0
19 Ran   Time 1m 46.31 (11.51)   Owned: Mrs Marie Taylor   Trained: Malton

---

1662   4.30 Voltigeur Restaurant Claiming Stakes 3yo+   (F)
£3102 £886 £443   **6f str**   **Soft 138**   **+04 Fast**   Stands side

1145 **DIZZY IN THE HEAD 28** [2] J O'Reilly 5-9-5 e (67) J D O'Reilly(7) 5/1: 56000-01: b g Mind Games - ... 57
Giddy (Polar Falcon) Prom, led 4f out, rdn out: class stks wnr in '03: h'cap & sell wnr on first 2 starts in '02:
eff at 5/6f on firm & soft, apprec hvy: with blnks or visor, apprec today's fitting of first time eye-shield:
goes well fresh: enjoyed drop to claim grade.
1 May'03 Nott 6.1g/s 73-(70) E: 2 Jul'02 Ripo 6g/f 75-75 D: 1 Jun'02 Redc 6fm 74-70 D: 1 May'02 Leic 6gd 68- G:
2 May'01 Wind 5gd 88- B: 1 May'01 Wind 5g/s 84- D:

1277 **DOWNLAND 20** [10] N Tinkler 8-9-7 (50) Kim Tinkler 5/2 FAV: 06000-02: Rear, prog halfway, styd on ... ¾ ... 56
well ins fnl 1f, not pace wnr: well bckd on drop to clmg grade: see 1277.

1267 **SHADY DEAL 20** [3] J M Bradley 8-8-13 (49) K Dalgleish 12/1: 35-00003: Handy, chsd wnr bef 1f ... ½ ... 47
out, onepcd ins fnl 1f: clr rem: not disgraced here: see 775.

3706} **MALLIA 265** [1] T D Barron 11-9-1 (45) Laura Jayne Crawford(7) 12/1: 021406-4: b g Statoblest - ... 5 ... 48
Pronetta (Mr Prospector) Cl-up 4f, sn wknd: reapp: appr h'cap wnr in '03: dual claim wnr in '02: stay 7f, eff at
5f but suited by 6f on firm, hvy & fibresand: eff with/without cheek pieces.
1 Jul'03 Hami 6.0g/f 47-42 E: 2 Jul'03 Hami 6.0g/f 43-42 E: 2 Jun'03 Sout 7af 47a-45 G: 2 Jun'03 Sout 7af 43a-(45) F:
2 Apr'02 Sout 6af 53a- G: 2 Mar'02 Wolv 6af 55a- F: 2 Feb'02 Sout 6af 56a-54 E: 1 Feb'02 Wolv 6af 55a- F:
1 Jan'02 Sout 6af 52a- F: 1 Nov'01 Wolv 6af 62a-56 F: 2 Jun'01 Thir 6fm 55- F: 1 Mar'01 Wolv 6af 60a-56 D:

1194* **SERGEANT SLIPPER 25** [11]7-9-9 vis (46) R Fitzpatrick 10/1: 0312015: Nvr nrr than mid-div: btr 1194. ... hd ... 55$
1119 **FRIMLEYS MATTERRY 29** [7]4-8-13 (45) P Mulrennan(5) 12/1: 300-6066: Handy 4f, wknd. ... 3½ ... 36
1276 **PETONGSKI 20** [9]6-8-13 (47) T Eaves(5) 7/2: 5640-007: Chsd ldrs over 3f, wknd: btr 1276. ... 1 ... 33
1267 **SABANA 20** [4]6-9-5 (45) S Carson 16/1: 0130608: Led, hdd 4f out, fdd halfway: btr 844. ... 2 ... 33
1446 **WELCOME ARCHIE 11** [5]4-8-13 Dale Gibson 100/1: 09: Al in rear: see 1446. ... ½ ... 26
1600 **ANDREYEV 3** [6]10-8-13 vis (40) K Darley 14/1: 5000-600: 10th: Chsd ldrs till halfway, sn fdd. ... 3 ... 17
1606 **ABOVE BOARD 3** [8]9-8-13 t (35) Dean McKeown 25/1: 3010600: 11th: Rear, nvr a factor: qck reapp. ... 4 ... 6
11 Ran   Time 1m 16.99 (8.09)   Owned: Burntwood Sports Ltd   Trained: Barnsley

---

1663   5.00 Saffie Joseph & Sons Handicap Stakes 3yo 0-70   (E)   [77]
£3799 £1169 £585   **1m2f**   **Soft 138**   **+01 Fast**   Inside

1382 **MAGIC STING 14** [1] M L W Bell 3-9-0 (63) I Mongan 4/1 FAV: 5-5561: ch c Magic Ring - Ground Game ... 68
(Gildoran) Mid-div, prog ins fnl 2f, rdn out to lead cl-home: op 6/1: 5th of 13 on sole '03 start (rtd 74, mdn):
eff at 10f, has tried further: acts on soft grnd & a gall trk: still lightly rcd & up to more improvement.

1193 **IM DANCING 25** [5] T D Easterby 3-8-10 (59) D Allan(3) 16/1: 05360-02: Cl-up, led after 7f, hdd ... nk ... 63
under press cl-home: eff at 7f, imprvd for step up to 10f: acts on gd/soft & soft: can find similar: see 1193.

1174 **WING COLLAR 25** [3] T D Easterby 3-9-2 (65) P Hanagan 33/1: 4440-03: Held up, prog 3f out, kept ... 1¼ ... 67
on ins fnl 1f, not btn far in 3rd: stablemate of rnr-up: eff at 10f on soft grnd: see 1174.

1603 **PERFECT BALANCE 3** [4] N Tinkler 3-8-11 (60) Kim Tinkler 9/1: 001654: Chsd ldrs, ev ch bef 1f ... nk ... 60
out, sn onepcd: qck reapp: eff at 1m/10f: btr 1147 (1m).

1306 **PLATINUM PIRATE 18** [8]3-9-1 vis (64) P Mulrennan(5) 5/1: 2021365: Mid-div, prog & ev ch dist, wknd. ... 1¾ ... 62
1355 **ROCK LOBSTER 16** [7]3-9-2 (65) J Bramhill 14/1: 14-056: Rear, nvr nrr than mid-div: btr 1144. ... 3 ... 58
1306 **HERNANDOS BOY 18** [6]3-8-13 (62) T Eaves(5) 8/1: 000-507: Bhd, nvr nrr than mid-div: see 1067. ... 2½ ... 58
1144 **BOND MOONLIGHT 28** [9]3-8-11 P (60) F Lynch 9/1: 4-223208: Handy over 6f, sn fdd: cheek pieces. ... 22 ... 21
1144 **THIRD EMPIRE 28** [10]3-8-13 (62) R Winston 9/1: 4050-39: Rear, nvr a factor: well bckd: btr 1144. ... 10 ... 10
4443} **PEARL PRIDE 228** [11]3-9-7 (70) K Dalgleish 10/1: 6420-0: 10th: ch f Theatrical - Spotlight Dance ... 3 ... 13
(Miswaki) Led 7f, sn fdd: reapp: rnr-up once in '03 (fill mdn): eff at 7.5f, further shld suit: acts on fast
grnd: likes forcing tactics: with M Johnston. 2 Aug'03 Beve 7.5g/f 76- D:

1603 **UPTHEDALE 3** [2]3-7-12 (7oh) (40) D Fentiman(7) 14/1: 500-043U: Cl-up, hmpd & wkng when u.r. 3f out. ... 0
11 Ran   Time 2m 16.01(13.71)   Owned: Mrs P T Fenwick   Trained: Newmarket

---

YORK   TUESDAY 11.05.04   Lefthand, Flat, Galloping Track

Official Going GOOD/SOFT (GOOD places).

1664   1.30 Newton Investment Management Rated Stakes Handicap 3yo 0-100   (B)   [97]
£12841 £4871 £2435   **1m2f88y**   **Soft 109**   **-02 Slow**   Inside

1206 **FRANK SONATA 25** [5] M G Quinlan 3-9-5 (88) R L Moore 33/1: 01400-61: Chsd ldrs, short of room ... 99
over 2f out, switched & strong run for press to lead well ins last: eff at 7f, now stays gall 10.5f well, 12f+ cld
suit: acts on gd & soft grnd, stiff/gall trks: useful colt, type to prog over further: see 1206.

1241* **WOODCRACKER 24** [8] M L W Bell 3-9-4 (87) I Mongan 16/1: 0-12: Trkd ldrs, rdn & hdwy to lead ... 1 ... 97
dist, hdd ins last, no extra: bckd h'cap bow: eff at 10/10.5f on gd & soft grnd: lightly rcd & progressive type,
likely to find similar: see 1241 (mdn).

4652* **LORD MAYOR 216** [6] Sir Michael Stoute 3-9-5 (88) K Fallon 11/1: 631-3: b c Machiavellian - ... 1¾ ... 95
Misleading Lady (Warning) Trkd ldrs, styd on for press, not pace of front pair: reapp/h'cap bow: AW mdn scorer fnl

'03 start (lightly rcd, turf plcd, rtd 85, mdn): winning form at 7f, stays 10.5f, could get further: handles fast, soft & polytrack, stiff/undul or sharp trk: encouraging return. 1 Oct'03 Ling 7ap 88a- D:

1192 **GOLDEN GRACE 26** [7] E A L Dunlop 3-9-5 (88) L Dettori 20/1: 631-04: b c Green Desert - Chief Bee (Chief's Crown) Trkd ldr & chall over 3f out till no extra ins last: left reapp bhd: mdn wnr fnl '03 start (lightly rcd): wng form over a stiff 7f, clearly stays 10.4f: acts on fast & soft grnd, stiff/gall trk: encouraging, can be plcd to find similar. 1 Nov'03 Newm 7g/f 92- D: *hd* **92**

1358* **BAYHIRR 17** [3]3-9-4 (87) P Robinson 100/30: 0-315: Led till dist, wknd: hvly bckd, h'cap bow: acts on gd/soft & soft grnd: just btr 1358. *2* **91**

4911} **NIGHTSPOT 197** [1]3-8-13 (82) S Drowne 66/1: 5515-6: ch g Night Shift - Rash Gift (Cadeaux Genereux) Held up, rdn 3f out, not able to chall: gelded, reapp: '03 mdn scorer, AW unplcd (rtd 73a, nov): eff over a sharp 6f, shaped here as if 1m+ will suit: acts on fast grnd, prob handles soft: gave some encouragement, entitled to be sharper for this. 1 Oct'03 Wind 6g/f 89- D: *3½* **83**

1427 **WEET A HEAD 13** [2]3-8-11 (80) W Supple 33/1: 263-5356: Chsd ldrs, no impress over 2f out, ddhtd for 6th: btr 1104 (class stks). *dht* **81**

4763*} **TOP SPEC 208** [10]3-9-4 (87) Dane O'Neill 50/1: 322161-8: Slow away & bhd early, mod gains: gelded, reapp: lost ch start, should improve on this. *¾* **87**

1089* **CITY PALACE 34** [9]3-8-9 (78) R Hughes 10/1: 6-19: Trkd ldrs, btn 2f out: h'cap bow: btr 1089 (1m). *6* **72**

1496 **THYOLO 9** [11]3-9-7 (90) J Murtagh 3/1 FAV: 411-20: 10th: Chsd ldrs, eff wide over 2f out, sn btn: hvly bckd tho' op 5/2, top-weight: longer 10f trip, breeding suggests he wants it: rcd keenly today & btr 1496. *1¾* **82**

1192 **HELLO ITS ME 26** [13]3-9-2 (85) J Quinn 8/1: 331-20: 11th: Held up, eff 3f out, sn btn: nicely bckd. *1¾* **75**

3605*} **WHISPERED PROMISES 271** [4]3-8-13 (82) K Dalgleish 17/2: 4211-0: 12th: Rear, no ch 4f out: bckd. *shd* **72**

4172} **CARACARA 243** [12]3-9-2 (85) J Fanning 12/1: 210-0: 13th: Rdn in rear & no ch fnl 4f. *dist* **0**

13 Ran Time 2m 18.88 (11.58) Owned: Adams Flynn Arnold Trained: Newmarket

1665

2.00 Williamhillpoker Com Stakes Handicap 3yo 0-105 (B) **[111]**
£19500 £6000 £3000 **6f212y rnd** **Soft 109** **-30 Slow** Inside

1496 **STATE DILEMMA 9** [4] B W Hills 3-8-6 (89) M Hills 9/2: 3314-51: Held up, hdwy halfway, styd on for press to lead well ins last: hvly bckd: eff at 7f/1m on firm & soft grnd: lightly rcd, useful & progressive colt, prob more to come: see 1496. **96**

1369 **KEY PARTNERS 16** [13] P A Blockley 3-7-12 (11oh) (70) J Bramhill 66/1: 52-102: Rear, styd on wide for press fnl 3f, not pace of wnr: suited by 7f on fast & soft grnd: fine run at today's weights, see 1129 (mdn). *1¼* **85$**

946* **BYGONE DAYS 45** [2] W J Haggas 3-8-0 (83) P Hanagan 5/2 FAV: 02-13: Trkd ldr, led over 2f out till ins last, no extra nr fin: hvly bckd, 6 wk abs: styd longer 7f trip well: see 946 (sn led, mdn, 6f). *½* **86**

4717} **FINE SILVER 211** [10] P F I Cole 3-8-0 (83) J Quinn 25/1: 22146-4: gr c Intikhab - Petula (Petong) Trkd ldrs & ch over 1f out, onepace ins last: reapp: mdn scorer '03, 4th in a h'cap (rtd 84): winning form at 5.7f, stays stiff 7f well: acts on firm & soft grnd, stiff/gall trks: gd return. *1¼* **84**
1 Jun'03 Bath 5.7fm 85- D: 2 Apr'03 Leic 5.0g/f 85- E: 2 Apr'03 Newm 5gd 85- C:

1496 **MISTER SAIF 9** [11]3-8-3 (86) R L Moore 40/1: 0622-0U5: Rear when short of rm 3f out, kept on for press, not able to chall: acts on firm, soft & polytrack: fair run, worth another try at 1m: see 119 & 79. *½* **86**

3659} **DANESMEAD 269** [3]3-8-13 (96) K Darley 14/1: 212333-6: b c Danehill Dancer - Indian Honey (Indian King) Chsd ldrs, onepace fnl 2f: reapp: auct mdn wnr '03, subs val stks rnr-up in Ireland & Newbury Super Sprint plcd: eff at 5/6f, stays 7f: acts on firm & soft, sharpish or stiff/gall trk: proved tough & most consistent last term, plenty to like about this return. *shd* **96**
2 Jun'03 Curr 6.3g/s 93- : 1 Jun'03 Donc 6fm 78- E: 2 May'03 Ripo 5g/s 80- D: 2 Apr'03 Pont 5g/f 82- D:

1234 **BAHIANO 24** [6]3-9-3 (100) K Fallon 15/2: 2-212367: Held up in tch, short of room over 3f out, sn onepace & no impress: well bckd, op 9/1: btr 1234, 885. *nk* **99**

1154 **CONVINCE 28** [8]3-8-7 (90) S Drowne 25/1: 32104-08: ch g Mt Livermore - Conical (Zafonic) Rear, short of room over 2f out, only mod prog: '03 mdn scorer: winning form at 6f, 7f+ not certain to suit (sprinting pedigree): acts on fast grnd, sharp or stiff/gall trk. 1 Aug'03 Wind 6g/f 97- D: 2 Jul'03 Wind 6g/f 95- D: *2½* **85**

1360 **ISKANDER 17** [12]3-8-7 bl (90) N Callan 25/1: 36154-69: b g Danzero - Amber Mill (Doulab) Dwelt, bhd, only mod prog: auct mdn scorer '03, subs val stks 5th (rtd 92): eff at 6f, 7f/1m shld suit: acts on firm & soft, stiff/undul or easy trk: eff with/without blnks. 1 Aug'03 Hami 6.0g/f 81-(88) E: 2 Jun'03 Carl 5fm 79- E: *1¼* **83**

1583 **BRIGHT SUN 5** [5]3-7-13 (82) Kim Tinkler 50/1: 2100-000: 10th: Led till 2f out: qck reapp. *1¼* **73**

4596} **VARNAY 220** [1]3-8-6 vis (89) T P Queally(3) 8/1: 51263-0: 11th: Held up, eff 3f out, btn dist: bckd. *1¼* **78**

1167 **PARKVIEW LOVE 27** [7]3-9-7 (104) J Fanning 9/1: 2165-030: 12th: Chsd ldrs till dist, eased. *1¾* **90**

1460* **Redwood Rocks 11** [14]3-7-13 (82) C Catlin 12/1:0 1360 **Mrs Moh 17** [9]3-7-12 (81) Dale Gibson 33/1:0

14 Ran Time 1m 31.0 (9.7) Owned: Maktoum Al Maktoum Trained: Lambourn

1666

2.30 Gr3 Tattersalls Musidora Stakes Fillies 3yo (A)
£31900 £12100 £6050 **1m2f88y** **Soft 109** **-36 Slow** Inside

4470} **PUNCTILIOUS 227** [4] Saeed bin Suroor 3-8-8 T (110) L Dettori 8/11 FAV: 113-1: b f Danehill - Robertet (Roberto) Led, increased tempo halfway, al in command fnl 2f, styd on strongly: hvly bckd, padd pick, reapp & first time t-strap: v useful juv, fill mdn & nov stks wnr, also Gr 1 Fill Mile 3rd (rtd 109): stays 10.5f, 12f looks sure to suit acts on firm & soft, easy or stiff/gall trks: smart, genuine Oaks claims. **108+**
1 Sep'03 Sali 8fm 105- D: 1 Jul'03 Yarm 7.0gd 90- D:

1419 **GLEN INNES 13** [1] D R Loder 3-8-8 (91) K Fallon 9/4: 122: Keen & trkd wnr, kept on for press fnl 3f but lost grnd from dist: styd longer 10.5f trip, 12f+ may suit: lightly rcd, useful & progressive: return to List company shld suit: see 1419 & 1039. *6* **96**

1169 **BAY TREE 27** [2] D R Loder 3-8-8 (102) T P Queally 16/1: 1100-63: b f Daylami - My Branch (Distant Relative) Trkd ldrs, styd on for press fnl 3f, not able to chall: fills mdn & List scorer '03, subs well held in Gr 1/Gr 2 company: wins at 6/7f, prob styd longer 10.5f trip today: acts on firm & soft grnd, stiff/gall trks: can go well fresh: useful filly. 1 Aug'03 Newm 7fm 98- A: 1 Aug'03 Newb 6.0g/f 95- D: *1¾* **94**

1304 **CHANTELOUP 19** [3] J R Fanshawe 3-8-8 J Murtagh 25/1: 24: In tch, eff fnl 4f, not able to threaten: longer 10.5f trip likely to suit: highly tried after debut & shld win when sights lowered *2* **90**

4596} **ASIA WINDS 220** [5]3-8-8 (93) M Hills 20/1: 141155-5: ch f Machiavellian - Ascot Cyclone (Rahy) Held up, eff fnl 4f, no impress: progressive juv '03, mdn & dual h'cap scorer: eff at 7f last term, mid-dists may suit: acts on firm & gd grnd, stiff/gall or sharp/turning trk: needs a drop in trip/grade. *7* **82**
1 Aug'03 Ches 7.0gd 94-87 C: 1 Aug'03 Newb 7g/f 92-78 D: 1 Jul'03 Bath 5.0g/f 73- D:

1495 **NASSIRIA 9** [6]3-8-8 T E Durcan 33/1: 66: Reluctant to load, chsd ldrs till 3f out, sn bhd. *dist* **0**

6 Ran Time 2m 22.33 (15.03) Owned: Godolphin Trained: Newmarket

1667 **3.00 Gr2 Duke Of York Hearthstead Homes Stakes 3yo+ (A)**
£58000 £22000 £11000 **6f str** **Soft 109** **-08 Slow** Stands Side

1062* **MONSIEUR BOND 37** [5] B Smart 4-9-2 (114) F Lynch 4/1 FAV: 2125-511: Trkd ldr trav well, led over 1f out, drvn out, decisively: hvly bckd: stays 1m, best at 6/7f: acts on firm, loves gd/soft & soft, gall trks: progressed into a high-class sprinter when granted easy grnd, keep on side in similar conditions: see 1062. **119**
1487* **STEENBERG 10** [14] M H Tompkins 5-9-2 (110) P Robinson 10/1: 3401-212: Bmpd start, switched & rear, hdwy halfway, styd on well for press, al held: also bhd today's wnr on reapp: v smart performer, Group success awaits: see 1487 & 1062. *1½* **114**
1187* **ARAKAN 26** [9] Sir Michael Stoute 4-9-2 (111) K Fallon 11/2: 12263-13: Chsd ldrs, drvn & styd on, snatched 3rd line: nicely bckd, lkd superb: acts on firm & soft grnd: smart & consistent: see 1187. *1¾* **109**
1227+**WELSH EMPEROR 24** [10] T P Tate 5-9-2 bl (109) Dale Gibson 33/1: 42426-14: Led till over 1f out, lost 3rd on line: bold front running eff, loves easy grnd: spot on back in Gr 3/List company: see 1227. *hd* **108**
952* **GOLDEVA 45** [11]5-8-13 (100) A Culhane 66/1: 65620-15: Mid-div, switched & styd on for press, no threat: 6 wk abs, prob progressed again after 952 (List, ahd of today's wnr). *1¾* **102**
4629} **AIRWAVE 219** [8]4-8-13 (117) Dane O'Neill 6/1: 123360-6: b f Air Express - Kangra Valley (Indian Ridge) Rear/keen early, hdwy halfway, no prog fnl 1f: well bckd but ndd reapp: high-class '03 reapp, won a Gr 2, subs Gr 1 rnr-up & plcd twice further in Gr 1's: List & Gr 1 wnr '02: suited by 5/6f on firm & fast, handles soft: loves a stiff trk & can go well fresh: high-class sprinter at best, expected to leave this bhnd. *shd* **102**
2 Jun'03 Asco 6fm 119-(117) A: 1 May'03 Sand 5.0g/f 121-(117) A: 1 Oct'02 Newm 6fm 123- A: 1 Sep'02 Ayr 6gd 108- A: 1Jul'03 Hayd 6g/f 116-(110 1 Jul'02 Leic 6sft 84- E: 2 Jul'02 Kemp 6g/f 94- E:
4629} **SOMNUS 219** [6]4-9-9 (117) T E Durcan 12/1: 114210-7: b g Pivotal - Midnight's Reward (Night Shift) Chsd ldrs, no impress fnl 2f under hand riding: ndd this tho' clr of rem: cond stks, List & Gr 1 Haydock Sprint Cup wnr '03: won 4 times in '02, incl 2 val stks: acts on firm/fast, career best last term on rain softened gd grnd: loves a stiff/gall trk & can go well fresh: proven high-class, improve on this. *½* **111**
1 Sep'03 Hayd 6gd 123-(114) A: 2 Aug'03 Newm 6fm 114-(114) A: 1Jul'03 Newb 6.0fm 114-(114) A: 1Jul'03 Hayd 6g/f 116-(110) A: 1 Oct'02 Redc 6fm 116- B: 1 Sep'02 Donc 6fm 109- B: 1 Aug'02 Ripo 6g/f 97-83 D: 1 Jul'02 York 6g/f 88- E:
4775} **COUNTRY REEL 207** [7]4-9-2 VIS t (110) L Dettori 20/1: 114/205-8: b c Danzig - Country Belle (Seattle Slew) Chsd ldrs, btn over 1f out: reapp, tried visor: lightly rcd '03, Gr 3 rnr-up on reap: mdn & Gr 2 wnr for D Loder '02: eff over a stiff 6f: acts on firm & gd/soft grnd, can go well fresh: eff in a t-strap: smart sprinter. 2 Jun'03 Newc 6gd 109-(111) A: 1 Aug'02 York 6g/f 107- A: 1 Aug'02 Newm 6g/s 100- D: *3½* **96**
1227 **ORIENTOR 24** [12]6-9-2 (109) K Darley 28/1: 006-2459: Bhd, eff 2f out, no impress: btr 952. *1½* **93**
1626* **BAHAMIAN PIRATE 3** [13]9-9-2 (110) S W Kelly 25/1: 6-144210: 10th: Rear, no prog fnl 2f: qck reapp. *1* **91**
1187 **BONUS 26** [15]4-9-2 (108) M J Kinane 18/1: 12515-60: 11th: Went left start, chsd ldrs till 2f out. *5* **81**
1187 **ASHDOWN EXPRESS 26** [2]5-9-2 (111) S Sanders 12/1: 35410-30: 12th: Chsd ldrs till over 1f out. *2½* **76**
4775} **FAYR JAG 207** [4]5-9-2 (110) W Supple 33/1: 01510U-0: 13th: b g Fayruz - Lominda (Lomond) Chsd ldrs, btn/hmpd over 1f out: reapp: v prog '03, won 5 times, incl val Wokingham h'cap, List & Gr 3 contests: dual h'cap wnr '02: eff at 5f, suited by 6f on firm & gd/soft, loves a stiff/gall trk, prob handles any: v tough & progressive last term, shld prove much sharper for this. *1¾* **73**
1 Sep'03 Curr 6g/f 112- : 1 Aug'03 Newm 6fm 111-(110) A: 1 Jun'03 Asco 6fm 112-102 B: 1 Jun'03 York 6.0g/f 105-97 B: 1 Jun'03 Pont 6g/f 101-94 C: 2 Apr'03 Beve 5fm 93-(93) C: 2 Jul'02 Newm 6g/s 95-89 B: 1 Jun'02 Newm 6fm 93-84 C: 2 May'02 Newm 6fm 88-82 C: 1 Apr'02 Ripo 6g/f 87-74 C: 2 Sep'01 Ches 6gd 75- C: 1 Aug'01 Thir 5fm 76- D:
4795} **TRADE FAIR 206** [1]4-9-2 (120) R Hughes 12/1: 3/11615-0: 14th: b c Zafonic - Danefair (Danehill) Chsd ldrs trav well, lost place qckly dist, eased considerably: padd pick on reapp: dual List & Gr 3 wnr '03: mdn wnr '02: best over 7f on firm & fast grnd, trainer reports not suited by soft: can go well fresh: loves a stiff trk: reportedly broken blood vessels: expect major improv on a faster surface. 1 Sep'03 Newb 7g/f 123-(123) A: 1 Jun'03 Newm 7fm 125-(116) A: 1 May'03 Newm 7g/f 118-(116) A: 1 Sep'02 Newb 7fm 100- D: *2* **69**
4795*}**JUST JAMES 206** [3]5-9-6 (113) J Murtagh 11/1: 0/25201-0: 15th: Bhd, eff over 2f out, no impress. *½* **72**
15 Ran Time 1m 16.39 (6.99) Owned: Mr R C Bond Trained: Thirsk

1668 **3.35 Arriva Trains Stakes Handicap 4yo+ 0-95 (C)** **[94]**
£10738 £3304 £1652 **1m3f198y** **Soft 109** **+10 Fast** Inside

1235 **BALKAN KNIGHT 24** [4] D R Loder 4-9-0 vis (80) T P Queally(3) 5/1 JT FAV: 01/1-61: Mid-div, hdwy to lead over 1f out, held on gamely for press: fast time: well bckd: eff at 10f, imprvd for step up to 12f: acts on fast & soft grnd, stiff/undul or gall trks: lightly rcd, progressive colt: see 1235. **86**
1389 **CRUISE DIRECTOR 15** [8] W J Musson 4-9-3 (83) K Fallon 12/1: 0301002: Mid-div, rdn & hdwy to chall ins last, just held cl-home: nicely bckd & fine run despite boiling over in padd: acts on gd/soft, soft & polytrack: Windsor specialist: see 1056. *nk* **88**
1389 **GOLD RING 15** [1] G B Balding 4-9-7 (87) S Drowne 5/1 JT FAV: 2413-023: Chsd ldrs & ch over 1f out, no extra ins last: nicely bckd: acts on firm & soft grnd: consistent type, deserves a nice prize: see 1389. *1½* **90**
4879} **CRATHORNE 199** [16] J D Bethell 4-9-0 p (80) T Quinn 16/1: 045030-4: b g Alzao - Shirley Blue (Shirley Heights) Dwelt, towards rear, styd on for press fnl 3f, not able to chall: bckd at long odds: reapp, has been gelded: dual h'cap rnr-up '03, also plcd over C/D in a val h'cap: mdn scorer '02: winning form at 1m but suited by sharp or gall 12f, tried 14f: eff with/without cheek pieces: nicely h'capped, one to note in similar. *nk* **82+**
2 Jun'03 Ches 12.3g/f 83-83 D: 2 May'03 Ches 12.3fm 85-79 C: 1 Sep'02 Thir 8gd 84- D:
1346 **LA SYLPHIDE GB 17** [11]7-9-2 (82) S W Kelly 16/1: 11610-25: Led till over 1f out, no extra ins last: prob styd longer 12f trip but more convincing at 10.5f in 1346, see 1346 (reapp). *2½* **82**
388 **NOWELL HOUSE 119** [2]8-9-2 (82) P Mulrennan(5) 14/1: 41653-66: Keen & trkd ldrs trav well, ev ch 2f out, sn no extra: jumps fit, 03/04 dual h'cap hdle wnr (rtd 129h, 2m/2m4f, gd & hvy grnd, stiff/undul trks): clr of rem & gd run in fav conditions: see 277. *nk* **81**
1519 **DUNASKIN 8** [19]4-9-5 (85) J Murtagh 33/1: 5053-007: b g Bahhare - Mirwara (Darshaan) Dwelt & bhd, eff 4f out, no impress: thrice h'cap wnr '03 (made all each time): mdn & h'cap rnr-up '02: stays sharp 12f, best dominating at 1m/10f on fast & gd/soft grnd, prob any trk: not suited by hold-up tactics from awkward high draw, worth another look. 1 May'03 Ripo 8g/s 89-83 C: 1 Apr'03 Beve 9.9g/f 83-75 D: 2 Apr'03 Thir 12fm 71-(75) E: 1 Apr'03 Ripo 10g/f 78-66 E: 2 Sep'02 Donc 7fm 67-64 D: 2 Aug'02 Ripo 6gd 60- F: *12* **72**
5036} **SPORTING GESTURE 185** [3]7-8-9 (75) Dale Gibson 16/1: 612000-8: Mid-div, no prog fnl 2f, reapp. *3* **59**
918 **INDIAN SOLITAIRE 47** [7]5-8-7 vis (73) P Hanagan 7/1: 00200-39: Held up, hdwy 3f out, btn 2f out: nicely bckd, op 8/1: abs: btr 918. *1* **56**
1375* **MANIATIS 15** [13]7-8-10 vis (76) S Sanders 20/1: 465/-6110: 10th: Trkd ldrs, btn 2f out: new yard. *¾* **58**
1172 **RING OF DESTINY 27** [10]5-9-12 (92) Martin Dwyer 33/1: 03010-00: 11th: Rear & drvn halfway, no prog. *9* **65**

1346 **KENTUCKY BLUE 17** [18]4-9-5 (85) T E Durcan 25/1: 30550-30: 12th: Chsd ldrs, btn 2f out: btr 1346. **6** **52**
4879} **DOUBLE OBSESSION 199** [9]4-10-0 (94) K Dalgleish 20/1: 102000-0: 13th: Trkd ldrs, btn 2f out, eased. **6** **55**
4572} **KUSTER 221** [5]8-9-11 bl (91) N Mackay(3) 25/1: 310115-0: 14th: Rear, eff 4f out, sn lost pl, reapp. **3½** **49**
1389* **KING REVO 15** [12]4-9-5 (85) K Darley 6/1: 01604-10: 15th: Sn pushed & bhd, eased fnl 3f, t.o. **25** **23**
1484 **Wahchi 10** [17]5-8-12 (78) T Lucas 100/1:0 1226* **Captain Clipper 24** [20]4-8-13 (79) A Nicholls 25/1:0
4039} **Sovereign Dreamer 251** [15]4-9-2 (82) J Bramhill 40/1:0 **Harambee 219** [14]4-9-0 (80) R Winston 66/1:P
19 Ran Time 2m 38.72 (11.92) Owned: Sheikh Mohammed Trained: Newmarket

1669 4.10 Garbutt & Elliott Colin Foster E B F Novice Stakes Fillies 2yo (D)
£6871 £2114 £1057 **6f3y str** **Soft 109** **-62 Slow** Stands Side

1123* **JUSTAQUESTION 29** [2] I A Wood 2-8-12 T P Queally(3) 9/2: 011: Al handy & led over 1f out, held **93**
on all out: nicely bckd, op 11/2: eff at 5f, imprvd for step up to 6f, get further: acts on gd, relished soft
today: handles a gall or sharp/turning trk: leggy, scopey & clearly useful, win more races: see 1123.
1524 **UMNIYA 8** [3] M R Channon 2-8-8 T E Durcan 13/2: 32: Rdn & chsd ldrs, chall dist, just held: shd 88
imprvd for step up to 6f: sure to find a mdn on this evidence: see 1524.
1274* **ELSIE HART 21** [4] T D Easterby 2-9-1 W Supple 100/30: 13: Held up, switched for eff halfway, 1½ 92
onepace ins last: well bckd: leggy, attractive colt, styd longer 6f trip well: clear of rem & looks sure to win
more races: see 1274.
1380* **HIGH CHART 15** [5] G G Margarson 2-8-10 A McCarthy 9/2: 14: Keen & trkd ldrs, btn dist: longer 5 77
trip: poss handles soft: see 1380 (gd).
1380 **ASHES 15** [1]2-8-8 Darren Williams 28/1: 05: b f General Monash - Wakayi (Persian Bold) Unruly 6 63
& u.r. bef start, led till over 1f out, sn hung left & eased: cheaply bght Feb foal, half-sister to 7f performer
Royal Storm: dam a 5f juv wnr: highly tried, scopey type who could improve in time.
1499 **AZUREE 9** [6]2-8-9 (1ow) R Hughes 2/1 FAV: 26: Trkd ldrs, lost place qckly over 1f out, eased, dist 0
t.o.: hvly bckd but something prob amiss: eye-catching 1499 (5f, debut).
6 Ran Time 1m 19.64 (10.24) Owned: Mr Christopher Shankland Trained: Upper Lambourn

1670 4.45 Theripleycollection Com Racing Jewellery Maiden Stakes Colts & Geldings 2yo (D)
£4856 £1494 £747 **5f3y str** **Soft 109** **-73 Slow** Stands Side

BRECON BEACON [3] P F I Cole 2-8-11 K Fallon 100/30 FAV: 1: b c Spectrum - Ffestiniog (Efisio) **91**
Cl-up & led 2f out, rdn & styd on well ins last: well bckd tho' op 5/1: fit for debut: March foal, half-brother
to a useful 7f/1m wnr Boston Lodge, dam a multiple 6/7f juv wnr: eff at 5f, stay further: acts on soft grnd & a
gall trk: goes well fresh: looks useful, entitled to progress.
ASIAN TIGER [1] R Hannon 2-8-11 M J Kinane 11/2: 2: b c Rossini - Dry Lightning (Shareef ½ 88
Dancer) Chsd ldrs, chall dist, not pace of wnr cl-home: nicely bckd: 32,000gns April foal, half-brother to a pair
of 7f juv wnrs abroad: dam a 10f 3yo wnr: eff at 5f, looks sure to get further: acts on soft grnd, gall trk:
strong, scopey type, win races.
ADORATION [4] M Johnston 2-8-11 J Fanning 7/1: 3: b c Royal Applause - Unconditional Love 2 84+
(Polish Patriot) Chsd ldrs & rdn early, outpcd halfway but kept on strongly cl-home: April foal, half-brother to a
multiple 5f juv wnr, also a 9f 3yo wnr: dam a 5f juv scorer who styd 10f: scopey but ndd this intro, expect
significant improvement at 6f+.
BLUE KANDORA [2] M A Jarvis 2-8-11 P Robinson 11/2: 4: b c Cape Cross - Party Dress (Lahib) 1½ 81
Dwelt & held up, eff to chase ldrs 2f out, no extra ins last: nicely bckd, op 13/2: April first foal, cost
75,000gns: dam plcd abroad around 1m & related to a 12f List wnr: eff at 5f, likely to need much further in time:
lengthy, scopey type, gave encouragement & clr of rem here.
SKYWARDS [7]2-8-11 L Dettori 7/2: 5: Led till 3f out, sn no impress: nicely bckd but ndd this. 5 71
KOMAC [8]2-8-11 S Sanders 16/1: 6: Led/dsptd lead till 2f out, sn btn: op 25/1, ndd this. 1 69
MAC COIS NA TINE [6]2-8-11 K Darley 20/1: 7: Dwelt & sn rdn, nvr on terms. 1¼ 66
PROSPECT COURT [5]2-8-11 T Quinn 9/1: 8: In tch, rdn & btn 2f out: op 14/1, ndd this. 5 56
8 Ran Time 1m 05.88(9.08) Owned: Elite Racing Club Trained: Whatcombe

WOLVERHAMPTON Fibresand TUESDAY 11.05.04 Lefthand, Sharp Track

Official Going STANDARD.

1671 6.20 Evening Racing Is Fun At Dunstall Park Banded Stakes 3yo+ 0-40 (H)
£1446 £413 £207 **6f aw rnd** **Going 43** **+06 Fast** Inside

1565 **RATHMULLAN 6** [7] E A Wheeler 5-9-6 bl (40) Liam Jones(7) 6/1: 0-003431: Wide, in tch & prog to **42a**
lead dist, edged left under press ins last, held on all out: joc given 2-day careless riding ban: qck reapp: first
win: eff around 6f, tried 1m: acts on fibresand, eff in blnks, tried cheek pieces: suited by banded company.
1565* **NEUTRAL NIGHT 6** [5] R Brotherton 4-9-12 vis (40) I Mongan 5/2 JT FAV: 3243312: Trkd ldrs & chall nk 47a
when hmpd over 1f out & carried left ins last, just held: op 7/4, qck reapp: lkd an unlucky loser, see 1565.
1590 **INDIAN MUSIC 5** [6] A Berry 7-9-6 (40) J Carroll 5/1: 6154433: Wide & rear, late gains, nrst fin: 1½ 37a
op 3/1, qck reapp: see 982.
1442 **FINGER OF FATE 12** [1] M J Polglase 4-9-6 (40) R Fitzpatrick 5/2 JT FAV: 0000264: Led after 1f 1¼ 33a
till dist, fdd: btr 1408 (5f).
1248 **MANDYS COLLECTION 22** [3]5-9-6 (40) S Whitworth 5/1: 43/00-0U5: Led 1f, prom till dist: see 1248. 5 18a
1457 **BLADES DAUGHTER 11** [4]3-8-10 (40) N Callan 8/1: 000-6006: Mid-div, btn halfway: see 1457. ½ 17a
6 Ran Time 1m 15.04 (2.24) Owned: Mr E A Wheeler Trained: Pangbourne

---

1672   6.50 Stay In The Holiday Inn Dunstall Park Selling Stakes 3yo+   (H)
           £1463 £418 £209   **1m100y aw rnd**   **Going 43**   **-15 Slow**   Inside

1341   **FORTY FORTE 17** [5] Miss S J Wilton 8-9-8 t p (45) A Quinn(5) 6/1: 0003061: Sn handy & led after   **53a**
2f, hdd 2f out but rallied gamely for press to assert from dist: op 4/1: no bid: eff at 1m/10f on firm, hvy &
loves fibresand/W'hampton: eff in cheek pieces, now suited by t-strap & sell grade: see 128.
1656   **MIZHAR 1** [2] J J Quinn 8-9-13 p (52) M Fenton 10/3: 52500132: Chsd ldrs, hdwy to chall 2f out, no   2½   **53a**
extra for press ins last: op 9/4: plcd yesterday: stays 1m, prob best at 7f as in 1378.
1642   **KANZ WOOD 1** [6] A W Carroll 8-9-8 (50) I Mongan   9/4 FAV: 00-050553: Rear, smooth hdwy halfway,   1½   **45a**
rdn to lead 2f out, hdd dist & no extra: clr rem: unplcd yesterday: see 769.
1656   **TINIAN 1** [7] K R Burke 6-9-8 (45) N Callan   4/1: 03040454: Rear, eff 3f out, btn over 1f out: 5   **35a**
op 7/2, unplcd yesterday: see 417.
1223   **BETTER OFF 24** [4]6-9-8   (48) Joanna Badger 8/1: 00-50605: Lost tch halfway: see 558.   8   **19a**
1326   **YALLAMBIE 18** [3]5-9-3 t (50) D Nolan(3) 6/1 Revouque - Tahnee (Cadeaux Genereux)   13   **0a**
Led till 6f out, btn 3f out: missed '03: unplcd '02 (rtd 65, no sand form, R Wilman).
1443   **BOUND TO PLEASE 12** [1]9-9-8 vis (40) Ann Stokell 25/1: 0504/-067: Bhd from halfway: see 1443.   15   **0a**
7 Ran   Time 1m 51.15 (4.95)   Owned: John Pointon and Sons   Trained: Stoke-On-Trent

---

1673   7.20 Esp Experience Challenge Tri-Banded Stakes 3yo 0-45   (H)
           £1428 £408 £204   **1m4f aw**   **Going 43**   **-31 Slow**   Inside

1311   **TRUE TO YOURSELF 19** [6] J G Given 3-8-9 (40) M Fenton 5/2 FAV: 000-021: Held up, smooth hdwy to   **45a**
lead dist, rdn clr, decisively: first win: eff at 9f on f/sand, imprvd for step up to 12f in banded company.
486   **MIDDLEHAM ROSE 105** [5] P C Haslam 3-8-4 (35) Rory Moore(7) 3/1: 000-662: b f Dr Fong - Shallop   7   **30a**
(Salse)   Held up, hdwy to lead over 4f out, rdn & hdd dist, sn no ch with wnr: rest well covered: unplcd '03
(lightly rcd, rtd 42, mdn): poss stay longer 12f trip in banded company, handles fibresand.
1630   **BRETTON 3** [1] R Hollinshead 3-9-0 (45) N Callan 7/2: 2664443: Led, hdd 4f out, sn no impress: 5   **33a**
op 5/1, qck reapp: btr 351.
1547   **BUNINO VEN 7** [4] S C Williams 3-8-9   (40) R L Moore 4/1: 00-04054: Held up, no impress fnl 3f.   nk   **27a**
1454   **SCORCHIO 12** [3]3-9-0 (45) S Righton   4/1: 0006-625: Chsd ldrs, btn 3f out: btr 1454 (polytrk).   3   **28a**
1444   **NORTHERN SUMMIT 12** [2]3-8-4   (35) F Norton 20/1: 600-066: Trkd ldr, btn 4f out, t.o.: see 1444.   dist   **0a**
6 Ran   Time 2m 42.56 (8.96)   Owned: Mr Mike J Beadle   Trained: Gainsborough

---

1674   7.50 Corporate Hospitality Is A Winner At Dunstall Park Banded Stakes 3yo+ 0-45   (H)
           £1446 £413 £207   **1m1f79y aw**   **Going 43**   **+07 Fast**   Inside

1564*   **IAMBACK 6** [5] Miss Gay Kelleway 4-9-6   (45) Dean Williams(7) 11/4: 6043011: Handy & led over 5f   **50a**
out, pushed out to assert ins last: op 5/4: eff around 1m/9.4f on fast grnd & fibresand: see 1564, 526 & 299.
1363   **BALLYRUSH 17** [2] K R Burke 4-9-0 BL (45) R Keogh(7) 3/1: 0545652: Trkd ldr, eff to chase wnr over   2   **40a**
2f out trav neatly, no extra ins last: first time blnks: handles fibresand, stays 9.4f in banded company: see 700.
1564   **GALEY RIVER 6** [1] J J Sheehan 5-9-0   (45) D Corby(3) 2/1 FAV: 5051623:   2½   **37a**
1541   **ON GUARD 7** [3] P G Murphy 6-9-0   (40) D Kinsella   11/4: 50-36004: Held up, btn 2f out: op 7/2.   ¾   **36a**
1396   **MANNY 15** [4]4-9-0 p (35) P Mathers(7) 33/1: 005/-005: b g Emarati - Needwood Nymph (Bold Owl)   Led   dist   **6a**
till over 5f out, sn btn: missed '03: mod form '02 (rtd 39a & 27, A Berry).
5 Ran   Time 2m 01.64 (3.44)   Owned: Twilight Racing   Trained: Newmarket

---

1675   8.20 Sponsor A Race At Dunstall Park Tri-Banded Stakes 3yo 0-45   (H)
           £1425 £407 £204   **1m1f79y aw**   **Going 43**   **-17 Slow**   Inside

1185   **A BIT OF FUN 26** [3] J J Quinn 3-8-4 (35) P Hanagan 2/1 FAV: 000-5201: In tch, prog & led over 2f   **43a**
out, rdn clr ins last: first win: eff around 9.4f on fibresand in banded company: see 782.
1311   **ROYAL UPSTART 19** [1] W M Brisbourne 3-8-9 bl (40) B Swarbrick(5) 4/1: 5000-032: Chsd ldrs, outpcd   5   **41a**
halfway, kept on to take 2nd, no threat: prob stays 9.4f in banded company, handles fast & fibresand: see 1311.
1311*   **SECRET BLOOM 19** [5] J R Norton 3-9-0 vis (45) Darren Williams   9/4: 0542413: Led over 4f out till   ¾   **45a**
over 2f out, sn no extra: btr 1311.
1591   **PLATINUM CHIEF 5** [4] A Berry 3-8-9 P (40) P P Mathers(6) 14/1: 6505344: Pushed along rear, mod   1¾   **38a**
late gains: qck reapp, cheek pieces.
1246   **REGENCY MALAYA 22** [2]3-9-0 bl t (45) S Righton   11/2: 5200325: Led till over 4f out, btn 2f out.   5   **36a**
1410   **MYSTIC PROMISE 14** [6]3-8-4 t (35) Hayley Turner(5) 12/1: 0503456: Bhd, lost tch halfway: see   2½   **23a**
1203.
6 Ran   Time 2m 03.81 (5.61)   Owned: The Fun Seekers   Trained: Malton

---

1676   8.50 Tattersalls Value Package At Dunstall Park Banded Stakes 3yo+ 0-35   (H)
           £1456 £416 £208   **7f aw rnd**   **Going 43**   **-15 Slow**   Outside

1566   **COUNTRYWIDE GIRL 6** [6] A Berry 5-9-7 (35) F Norton 7/4 FAV: 3643321: Made all, hung left over 1f   **36a**
out, styd on strongly: prob best at 6/7f, tried 1m: acts on fast, likes soft, hvy & fbsnd: see 1566.
1565   **BEN KENOBI 6** [5] Mrs P Ford 6-9-7 (30) R Ffrench 17/2: 04100-52: ch g Accondy - Nour El Sahar   1   **33a**
(Sagace)   Pushed along towards rear, styd on wide, not reach wnr: qck reapp: '03 h'cap scorer, sand unplcd: unplcd
'02 (rtd 61): eff at 7f in banded company, winning form at 12f: acts on fast grnd, fibresand & a sharp/turning trk.
1 Jul'03 Warw 12.6g/f 47-44 F:
1566*   **WELSH WHISPER 6** [3] S A Brookshaw 5-9-13 (30) N Chalmers(5) 5/2: 0056613: Dwelt, hdwy to chase   1¾   **36a**
wnr over 2f out, no extra dist: qck reapp: just btr 1566.
1546   **POINT MAN 7** [8] J W Payne 4-9-7 (30) N Callan 13/2: 0050-034: Chsd ldrs, no prog fnl 2f: btr 1546.   6   **18a**
653   **ELLAMYTE 85** [4]4-9-7 (35) D Nolan(3) 11/2: 300-0005: b f Elmaamul - Deanta In Eirinn (Red Sunset)   2   **14a**
Trkd ldr, btn 2f out: 12 wk abs: t-strap omitted: h'cap plcd '03 (H Morrison, rtd 56, also clmr plcd): '02 nov

---

WOLVERHAMPTON Fibresand TUESDAY 11.05.04 Lefthand, Sharp Track

auct stks wnr, val auct stks plcd (rtd 80): eff at 5/6f on fast, gd/soft: eff with/without blnks, tried visor.
1 Jul'02 Wind 5g/f 77- E:
1297 **BOOZY DOUZ 20** [2]4-9-7 P (30) S Whitworth 20/1: 00/0-06: Sn struggling.		1¼	11a
1309 **MESMERISED 19** [7]4-9-7 p (30) Ann Stokell 16/1: 0-000067: Trkd ldrs till halfway.		1¼	8a
1548 **CHAKRA 7** [1]10-9-7 (30) C Haddon(7) 12/1: 000/-6538: Sn outpcd & no ch: btr 1548 (1m).		6	0a

8 Ran   Time 1m 30.26(4.06)   Owned: Galaxy Moss Side Racing Clubs Limited   Trained: Cockerham

NEWCASTLE WEDNESDAY 12.05.04 Lefthand, Stiff, Galloping Track

Official Going HEAVY (SOFT places).

1677   6.15 Dalton Park Top Brands Median Auction Maiden 2yo (E)
£3624 £1115 £558   **6f str   Soft 90   -18 Slow**   Centre

SELKIRK STORM [3] M W Easterby 2-9-0   P Mulrennan(5) 33/1: 1: b c Trans Island - Force Divine   79
(L'Emigrant) Slow away, switched to race far side halfway & led over 1f out, rdn & in command when eased cl-home:
Feb foal, 16,000 gns purchase: half brother to an unplcd juv, dam a juv wnr in France, subs 10f wnr: eff at 6f,
sure to get further: acts on hvy grnd & a stiff trk: goes well fresh.
1458 **SECRET PACT 12** [5] M Johnston 2-9-0   R Ffrench 11/4: 42: Led towards centre till hdd over 1f   1¼   74
out, kept on for press: op 4/1: handles gd/soft & hvy, styd longer 6f trip.
LORNA DUNE [8] Mrs J R Ramsden 2-8-9   A Culhane 14/1: 3: b f Desert Story - Autumn Affair   3½   62
(Lugana Beach) Held up, prog when switched far side 3f out, chall 2f out, no extra dist: op 12/1: 11,000 gns Feb
foal, half sister to a 10/11f 3yo wnr, dam a 6f juv wnr, subs useful at 7/10f: eff at 6f, will stay further: acts
on hvy grnd, stiff trk: encouraging start.
1343 **TANTIEN 18** [7] John A Harris 2-8-9   Dean McKeown 8/1: 54: b f Diktat - Tahilla (Moorestyle)   3   56
Chsd ldrs, outpcd/switched to far rail over 2f out, kept on ins last: Apr foal, half sister to sev wnrs, incl tough
multiple 7f/1m scorer Dandy Regent: dam a smart 6f/1m wnr: will need 6f+: handles hvy grnd.
1037 **MOUNT EPHRAM 39** [1]2-9-0   P Bradley(5) 25/1: 45: Cl-up centre till over 1f out: btr 1037 (5f).   1   59
1117 **PROCRASTINATE 31** [2]2-9-0   P Mathers(7) 10/1: 306: Cl-up, btn over 1f out: btr 1037.   hd   59
PROFITS REALITY [4]2-9-0   D Nolan(3) 8/1: 7: Chsd ldrs till outpcd halfway, debut.   1   57
1274 **ALMATY EXPRESS 22** [10]2-9-0   P Hanagan 5/2 FAV: 38: Held up, no impress fnl 2f: btr 1274.   1¼   54
RYEDANE [9]2-9-0   D Allan(3) 14/1: 9: Chsd ldrs till lost tch from halfway, eased.   15   24
1503 **KEEPASHARPLOOKOUT 10** [6]2-9-0   R Winston 10/1: 440: 10th: Chsd ldrs far side till halfway, eased.   ½   23
10 Ran   Time 1m 17.78 (6.48)   Owned: Morecool Racing   Trained: Sheriff Hutton

1678   6.45 Ing Real Estate Development Uk Handicap Stakes 3yo 0-70 (E)   [76]
£4349 £1338 £669   **7f str   Soft 90   -06 Slow**   Centre

1007 **INSUBORDINATE 42** [10] J S Goldie 3-8-8 (56) T Eaves(5) 12/1: 41006-01: ch c Subordination -   61
Manila Selection (Manila) Rear, hdwy/switched far side 2f out, led dist, rdn & styd on strongly: op 14/1, 6 wk abs:
sell scorer '03: eff at 6/7f, tried 1m: acts on fast & hvy, likes a stiff trk: eff with/without cheek pieces & can
go well fresh.   1 Aug'03 Redc 6g/f 67-(62) G:
1239 **IMPULSIVE BID 25** [6] Jedd O'Keeffe 3-9-0 (62) P Hanagan 16/1: 404-402: Chsd ldrs, hdwy to chall   2   62
dist, not pace of wnr: acts on gd & hvy grnd, styd longer 7f trip well: see 1050.
560 **TURF PRINCESS 96** [4] Ian Emmerson 3-8-9 (57) D Fentiman(7) 12/1: 26-12453: Led/dsptd lead till   1   55
went on halfway, hdd over 1f out & no extra: op 10/1, 3 month abs: acts on firm, hvy & fibresand: see 389 & 283.
1628 **TROJAN FLIGHT 4** [12] Mrs J R Ramsden 3-9-7 (69) K Fallon 6/4 FAV: 000-454: Held up, eff 3f out,   4   60
no impress dist: bckd, op 7/4, quick reapp: just btr 1628 & 1216.
1242 **REVERSIONARY 25** [9]3-8-5 BL (53) Dale Gibson 20/1: 0560-005: b c Poyle George - Harold's Girl   1¼   42
(Northfields) Chsd ldrs till outpcd fnl 2f: tried blnks: unplcd '03 (rtd 72, prob flattered, auct mdn): tried up
to 1m prev: poss handles hvy grnd.
1007 **KINGS ROCK 42** [1]3-8-13 (61) P Fessey 9/2: 30-26006: Chsd ldrs, hmpd over 2f out, sn btn, abs.   2½   46
1054 **PARTY PRINCESS 37** [8]3-8-12 (60) Dean McKeown 33/1: 0377: Chsd ldrs halfway, btn over 1f out.   3   40
1376 **COULD SHE BE MAGIC 16** [7]3-8-10 (58) D Allan(3) 9/1: 01-21028: Chsd ldrs, edged left & btn over   2   34
1f out: btr 1376 & 615 (AW, made mdn).
1470 **MILITARY TWO STEP 12** [13]3-9-0 p (62) Darren Williams 10/1: 5002-009: Sn strug rear, eased dist.   20   8
4047} **VICTORIAN DANCER 251** [11]3-8-11 (59) G Parkin 40/1: 04004-0: 10th: Dwelt & sn bhd, reapp.   6   0
1360 **FOX COVERT 18** [3]3-9-0 (64) L Enstone(3) 12/1: 3230-000: 11th: Led till over 3f out, sn edged   3   0
left & struggling, eased, longer trip.
11 Ran   Time 1m 30.84 (6.74)   Owned: Mr J S Goldie   Trained: Glasgow

1679   7.15 Dalton-Park Com Handicap Stakes 3yo 46-55 (F)   [68]
£3094 £884 £442   **1m3y str   Soft 90   -27 Slow**   Centre

1193 **DANCE TO MY TUNE 27** [4] M W Easterby 3-9-0 (54) P Mulrennan(5) 8/1: 40606-61: Swerved left start,   67
held up in tch, smooth prog 2f out, led dist, rdn to hold on: eff at 6f, now stays a stiff 1m well: acts on fast,
gd & appeared to relish hvy grnd tonight: best without visor: see 1193.
1611 + **NLWADOD 5** [6] M R Channon 3-8-11 (6ex) (51) R Lappin 11/10 FAV: 006-12: Trkd ldr & led over 2f   ¾   61
out till dist, kept on, not pace of wnr: nicely bckd under a 6lb pen, quick reapp: eff at 1m/10f, return to latter
will suit: well clr of rem, can win again: see 1611.
1178 **FOURSWAINBY 27** [5] B Ellison 3-8-8 (48) T Eaves(5) 14/1: 00-63: b g Foxhound - Arena (Sallust)   8   46
Dwelt & held up, eff over 2f out, no impress dist: lightly rcd & unplcd '03 (rtd 57, mdn).
1395 **SIR GALAHAD 16** [2] T D Easterby 3-8-12 (52) D Allan(3) 7/4: 6-00534: Dictated pace, qcknd tempo   9   36
halfway, hdd over 2f out & sn btn: op 2/1: btr 1395 (soft).
1576 **LADY OF THE LINKS 6** [1]3-9-1 VIS (55) Kim Tinkler 16/1: 5400-405: Trkd ldrs, rdn & lost place   1½   37
from 2f out, visor, op 12/1: quick reapp: much longer trip: btr 1392 (5f, soft).
986 **DANDY JIM 43** [3]3-8-6 (16oh) (30) A Culhane 25/1: 6-050056: Hmpd start & held up, strugg fnl 2f.   2½   25
6 Ran   Time 1m 46.43 (9.43)   Owned: R S Cockerill (Farms) Ltd   Trained: Sheriff Hutton

NEWCASTLE WEDNESDAY 12.05.04 Lefthand, Stiff, Galloping Track

1680 **7.45 Dalton Park 50% Off Best Brands Handicap Stakes 3yo+ 46-55 (F)** **[57]**
£3409 £974 £487 **1m4f93y** **Soft 90** **+22 Fast** Flag Start

2543} **ROYAL MELBOURNE 317** [8] Miss J A Camacho 4-9-8 (51) R Winston 25/1: 0000-1: ch g Among Men - Calachuchi (Martinmas) Keen & trkd ldr, led over 2f out, held on all out: reapp, gd time: unplcd '03 (rtd 45a & 51, mdns): eff at 12.5f, cld get further: relished hvy grnd tonight: handles a stiff trk & goes well fresh. **56**
156 **CANTEMERLE 158** [10] W M Brisbourne 4-9-8 bl (51) K Fallon 8/1: 000350-2: b f Bluebird - Legally Delicious (Law Society) Mid-div, rdn & styd on to chase wnr ins last, just held: 5 mnth abs: fills mdn rnr-up '03 (poss flattered): eff arnd 12f on a sharp or gall trk: likes soft & hvy & eff with/without blnks. *shd* **56**
2 May'03 Hayd 11.9sft 74- D:
1504 **MILLENNIUM HALL 10** [1] P Monteith 5-9-11 (54) K Renwick 8/1: 0060-063: Rear, hung left but styd on for press fnl 2f, not reach front pair. *3* **55**
1396* **NEXT FLIGHT 16** [6] R E Barr 5-9-9 (52) R Fitzpatrick 6/1: 6232314: Led, hdd 2f out & no extra. *1½* **51**
1388 **INCHINNAN 16** [7]7-9-11 (54) T Eaves(5) 16/1: 6500-505: Mid-div, not able to chall: longer trip. *shd* **53**
1278 **EAST CAPE 22** [5]7-9-3 (6oh) (40) Kim Tinkler 16/1: 3010006: Chsd front pair, no impress fnl 2f: some improvement: see 724 (banded). *1* **43**
1363* **FORTUNES FAVOURITE 18** [12]4-9-3 (1oh) (45) E Ahern 14/1: 5-034017: Rear, eff 2f out, sn no prog. *1½* **41**
2192} **MYTHICAL KING 331** [9]7-9-10 (53) B Swarbrick(5) 11/4 FAV: 406/350-8: Mid-div, eff 3f out, hung left & btn over 1f out: 6 wk abs. *¾* **47**
1425 **PLAUSABELLE 14** [4]3-8-4 bl (52) D Allan(3) 10/1: 006-029: Rear, drvn 5f out, btn 2f out: btr 1425. *2½* **43**
1551* **GARGOYLE GIRL 8** [3]7-10-1 (6ex) (58) K Darley 11/2: 640-0510: 10th: Keen, rear, no impress: btr 1551. *½* **48**
4418} **DUBONAI 232** [2]4-9-11 (54) C Catlin 25/1: 003230-0: 11th: Held up, eff 2f out, sn btn & eased. *1½* **42**
1388 **SUMMER SPECIAL 16** [13]4-9-7 (50) L Enstone(3) 12/1: 300-5530: 12th: Rear, eff wide over 2f out, sn btn & eased ins last: btr 1388 (gd, 9f). *2* **35**
12 Ran Time 2m 46.40 (8.50) Owned: Mr Jamie Spence Trained: Malton

1681 **8.15 Dalton Park Outlet Shopping Classified Stakes 3yo+ 0-65 (E)**
£3744 £1152 £576 **1m2f32y** **Soft 90** **-19 Slow** Far Side

1599 **ALERON 5** [1] J J Quinn 6-9-11 P (68) E Ahern 9/4 FAV: 33434-21: Led 1f & remained handy travelling well, led ins last, pushed out to assert: well bckd, qck reapp: eff at 12/14f & prob stays 2m, relished this drop to 10f in hvy grnd, also acts on fast & fibresand: handles any trk & well suited by cheek pieces tonight: travels well in a race, win again: see 1599. **72+**
TURTLE DANCER 917 [6] B Ellison 6-9-9 (66) T Eaves(5) 20/1: 222243//-2: b g Turtle Island - Love Me Please (Darshaan) Trkd ldrs & led over 2f out, hdd ins last & sn no impress on wnr: v long abs: last rcd 02/03 (nov hdle wnr, rtd 97h, 2m, fast grnd): last rcd on the Level in '01 in native Ireland (plcd, mdns): eff around 10f, poss stays 12.5f: likes gd/soft & soft grnd: encouraging after such a long break, find a race. *1½* **67**
1633 **MELODIAN 4** [2] M Brittain 9-9-8 bl (62) T Williams 9/2: 6-545123: Trkd ldrs & ch 2f out, onepace ins last: enjoying testing surfaces at present: see 1633 & 1254. *½* **65**
1389 **KIDZPLAY 16** [8] J S Goldie 8-9-8 (64) C Catlin 10/1: 3564-034: Sn led & dictated pace till hdd over 2f out, onepace: step up to 11/12f shld suit, likes Mussleburgh & Ayr: see 1389. *¾* **64**
1609* **PURE MISCHIEF 5** [4]5-10-0 (58) B Swarbrick(5) 7/2: 030/-3115: Held up in tch, eff over 2f out, no extra dist: quick reapp: just btr 1609. *7* **60**
1352 **MEDALLIST 18** [3]5-9-12 bl e (69) R Winston 14/1: 30330-66: b g Danehill - Obsessive (Seeking The Gold) Dwelt, sn chsd ldrs, rdn & btn over 1f out: stable-mate of rnr-up: class stks plcd '03 (rtd 78): '02 mdn scorer for Sir M Stoute, subs h'cap unplcd: wng form at 1m, stays a stiff 10f: acts on gd & gd/soft, likes a stiff/gall trk: eff with/without blnks, wore an eyeshield. 1 May'02 Hayd 8.1g/s 84- D: *¾* **57**
549 **COUNTYKAT 98** [5]4-9-13 (70) Donna Bashton(7) 33/1: 3630-607: Rear, lost tch fnl 3f: 3 mnth abs. *18* **34**
1226 **ZAN LO 25** [9]4-9-5 (60) P Hanagan 66/1: 52516-08: ch f Grand Lodge - Zanella (Nordico) Rear & lost tch fnl 3f: ex-French, '03 wnr in the provinces: wng form at 12f on fast grnd. *1¼* **24**
4707} **TRILEMMA 212** [7]3-8-5 (1ow)BL (63) S Sanders 4/1: 0006-9: Mid-div, rdn halfway & sn bhd, virtually p.u.: 1st time blnks on reapp. *dist* **0**
9 Ran Time 2m 17.47 (10.97) Owned: Mr Grahame Liles Trained: Malton

1682 **8.45 Pantheon Retail Asset Managers Dalton Park Median Auction Maiden 3-4yo (F)**
£3248 £928 £464 **5f str** **Soft 90** **-06 Slow** Centre

1267 **TATWEER 22** [6] D Shaw 4-9-9 vis (47) R Winston 7/2: 55000-51: b g Among Men - Sandystones (Selkirk) Chsd ldrs, led & hung left over 1f out, styd on well for press: nicely bckd, op 9/2: mod form '03 (lightly rcd, rtd 55a & 23): unplcd '02 (M P Tregoning 1st time visor, rtd 77, mdn): eff at 5f, tried up to 7f: acts on hvy & gd/soft grnd, stiff or sharp/undul trk. **59**
4917} **WESTBOROUGH 197** [8] N Tinkler 3-9-0 (56) Kim Tinkler 7/1: 040205-2: ch g Woodborough - Filey Brigg (Weldnaas) Chsd ldrs, edged left & kept on for press, no threat to wnr: reapp: h'cap rnr-up '03: eff at 5f on firm & hvy grnd, stiff/gall trks. 2 Sep'03 Redc 5fm 60-58 E: *2½* **53**
1392 **EL PALMAR 16** [9] T D Barron 3-9-0 (68) P Makin(5) 6/4 FAV: 62-33: Led/dsptd lead, no extra ins last: well bckd: btr 1392. *shd* **53**
4692} **TAKE GOOD TIME 213** [2] John Berry 4-9-9 S Chin 8/1: 6-4: Mid-div, outpcd halfway, kept on ins last: reapp: a apprec return to 6f+. *3½* **46**
1555 **STAVROS 8** [3]4-9-9 (46) P Hanagan 16/1: 0006-005: Led/dsptd lead till over 1f out, btn when hmpd ins last: has been gelded. *nk* **45**
GREY GURKHA [7]3-9-0 G Parkin 12/1: 6: Dwelt & bhd, kept on late on debut. *1¼* **42**
1242 **DR FOX 25** [5]3-9-0 (51) E Ahern 10/1: 0505-007: Mid-div, outpcd from halfway, kept on late. *1¼* **39**
1119 **CASEYS HOUSE 31** [4]4-9-4 T Eaves(5) 100/1: 08: Dwelt & bhd, only mod prog. *nk* **33**
865 **KNIGHT TO REMEMBER 56** [10]3-9-0 (48) Darren Williams 10/1: 600-3409: Switch left start & held up, nvr a factor: new stable, abs: btr 462. *5* **28**
1320 **MY WILD ROVER 19** [1]4-9-9 t P Mulrennan(5) 33/1: 0P-000: 10th: Mid-div till lost place over 2f out, sn struggling/eased. *24* **0**
10 Ran Time 1m 03.01(4.81) Owned: Swann Racing Ltd Trained: Newark

YORK   **WEDNESDAY 12.05.04**   Lefthand, Flat, Galloping Track

Official Going GOOD/SOFT (GOOD places).

1683
1.30 Totesport Com Handicap Stakes 3yo+ 0-110 (B) [108]
£14820 £4560 £2280   **5f str**   **Good/Soft 75**   **-24 Slow**   Stands Side

1120 **RIVER FALCON 31** [10] J S Goldie 4-7-12 (2oh) (78) N Mackay(3) 16/1: 0000-501: Sn trkd ldrs, rdn to   87
chall halfway, led over 1f out: duelled with rivals ins last, just prevailed: eff at 5/6f on firm or soft grnd,
loves gall trks: on a wng mark & cld follow up: see 927.
1481 **WATCHING 11** [12] D Nicholls 7-8-1 (83) A Nicholls 16/1: 0040-302: Chsd ldrs, rdn to chall dist,   ½   87
just held cl-home: well h'capped, relished this easy grnd, can win similar in these conditions: see 998.
1162 **HENRY HALL 28** [11] N Tinkler 8-8-11 (93) Kim Tinkler 25/1: 6513-303: Mid-div, rdn to chall dist,   nk   96
ev ch ins last, just held cl-home: well h'capped: has run well without success in this race prev: see 1004.
1594 **CORRIDOR CREEPER 5** [19] J M Bradley 7-8-8 p (90) C Catlin 12/1: 22000-54: Al prom & ev ch from   ¾   91
dist, no extra well ins last: op 10/1, qck reapp: see 1594.
1479 **MATTY TUN 11** [2]5-8-12 (94) K Fallon 8/1: 1100-055: Dwelt & outpcd, nrst fin: won this race   ½   93
from an 18lbs lower mark last term: prog h'capper, see 1479.
1594 **CAPE ROYAL 5** [9]4-8-6 (88) A Culhane 10/1: 20-06106: Trkd ldrs, onepcd from dist: quick reapp.   ½   85
1626 **BISHOPS COURT 4** [6]10-10-0 (110) L Dettori 9/1: 4153-127: Trkd ldrs, no extra fnl 1f: qck   nk   106
reapp: far from disgraced under top-weight: ran a similar race to this in this h'cap last year: see 1626.
1400 **DRAGON FLYER 15** [8]5-9-5 (101) J P Spencer 12/1: 300-4208: Handy/dsptd lead till over 1f out.   2½   90
1476 **SIERRA VISTA 11** [5]4-7-12 (2oh)p (78) P Hanagan 20/1: 604-0309: Chsd ldrs till dist: btr 1120.   1   67
1207 **FANNYS FANCY 26** [20]4-8-9 (91) S Sanders 11/2 FAV: 2/1143-00: 10th: b f Groom Dancer - Fanny's   1   76
Choice (Fairy King) Rear, nvr pace to chall: well bckd: lightly rcd '03, dual AW wnr (mdn & h'cap), turf plcd (rtd
93, List): juv rnr-up '02 (mdn): eff at 5f, both wins at 6f: acts on polytrack, fast & gd/soft, stiff/gall or
sharp/undul trk: can go well fresh: this trk doesn't favour hold up tactics, improve back at 6f next time.
1 Jul'03 Ling 6ap 93a-84 D: 1 Apr'03 Ling 6ap 86a- D: 2 Sep'02 Muss 5g/f 75- D:
4177} **NIGHT PROSPECTOR 234** [16]4-8-10 (92) N Callan 50/1: 125100-0: 11th: b c Night Shift - Pride of   1   75
My Heart (Lion Cavern) Chsd ldrs, no impress from halfway: reapp: mdn & h'cap scorer '03, dual rnr-up '02 (mdns):
eff at 5f on fast & gd, prob any trk: likes to dominate. 1 Aug'03 Wind 5.0gd 92-85 D: 2 May'03 Redc 5g/f 86-85 C:
1 May'03 Folk 5g/f 85-(85) D: 2 Apr'03 Newm 6gd 85- D: 2 Jul'02 Yarm 5.1g/f 85- D: 2 May'02 Ling 5gd 85- D:
1594 **WHITBARROW 5** [4]5-8-10 (92) S Drowne 18/1: 0/056-500: 12th: Chsd ldrs till 2f out: quick reapp.   nk   74
1487 **PRINCE OF BLUES 11** [1]6-7-12 (18oh)p (62) P Varley(7) 66/1: 0040450: 13th: Prom far side, btn 1f   1   60
out: v stiff task.
1479 **FAST HEART 11** [3]3-8-8 t (99) M Hills 25/1: 31003-00: 14th: b c Fasliyev - Heart of India (Try My   hd   78
Best) Dwelt & al outpcd: mdn & nurs h'cap scorer '03: suited by 5f on fast & gd grnd, prob any trk: best in
t-strap. 1 Aug'03 Ches 5.1g/f 97-90 D: 1 Aug'03 Hayd 5g/f 90- D:
1487 **TRINCULO 11** [7]7-8-3 p (85) J Bramhill 33/1: U250060: 15th: Led overall/dsptd lead till dist.   ¾   62
1400 **IKAN 15** [18]4-8-6 (88) E Ahern 33/1: 400-0300: 16th: In tch, no impress from halfway: btr 1162.   ¾   63
1476* **CHICO GUAPO 11** [15]4-7-12 (3oh) (77) J Quinn 18/1: 5-050010: 17th: Led/dsptd lead till halfway.   nk   54
1627* **ARTIE 4** [14]5-7-13 (6ex) (81) Dale Gibson 7/1: 30-00210: 18th: Restless stalls, dwelt & al bhd: 2   50
bckd, quick reapp: lost all ch at the start: prev in fine form, btr 1627 (well drawn, broke fast & made all).
4287} **Proud Native 238** [13]10-8-5 (87) K Darley 40/1:0   4884} **Salviati 200** [17]7-8-8 (90) S Carson 50/1:0
20 Ran   Time 1m 01.74 (4.94)   Owned: Mr S Bruce   Trained: Glasgow

1684
2.00 Gr3 Totepool Middleton Stakes Fillies 4yo+ (A)
£29000 £11000 £5500   **1m2f88y**   **Good/Soft 75**   **-06 Slow**   Inside

991 **CRIMSON PALACE 46** [4] Saeed bin Suroor 5-8-9 L Dettori 6/4 FAV: 101/4-141: b f Elliodor -   115+
Perfect Guest (Northern Guest) In tch, smooth prog over 3f out & led dist, rdn out: hvly bckd, 6 wk abs: earlier Gr
1 4th in Dubai & won a val stks: ex-SA, Gr 1 wnr back in '03: eff arnd 9f, stays 10.5f well: acts on fast & soft,
gall/fair trks, goes well fresh: smart mare with a fine turn of foot.
1491* **BENEVENTA 10** [3] J L Dunlop 4-8-12 (104) S Sanders 100/30: 1340-112: Handy & led over 3f out,   ¾   115
rdn & hdd 1f out, styd on well for press ins last: pulled well clr of rem: op 11/4: tough & prog filly, lost
nothing in defeat after 1491 & 1115.
4681} **SUMMITVILLE 214** [5] J G Given 4-8-9 (111) K Fallon 4/1: 035302-3: b f Grand Lodge - Tina Heights   11   101
(Shirley Heights) Chsd ldrs, outpcd by front pair from 3f out: bckd on reapp: Gr1 Epsom Oaks plcd '03 (rtd 114 at
best): fills mdn & Gr3 scorer '02: wng form at 7f/1m, best around 12f & has tried 14f+: handles a sharp/undul or
stiff/gall trk & can go well fresh: smart effort here in t-strap.
2 Oct'03 Asco 12gd 112-(110) A: 1 Sep'02 Donc 8fm 105- A: 2 Aug'02 Newm 7sft 101- A: 1 Jul'02 Newm 7g/f 90- D:
1139 **LANDINIUM 30** [2] C F Wall 5-8-9 (100) R Hughes 25/1: 05440-44: Chsd ldrs, rdn & no impress fnl 2f.   6   95
4162} **THINGMEBOB 245** [6]4-8-9 (104) P Robinson 12/1: 401320-5: b f Bob Back - Kip's Sister (Cawston's   9   86
Clown) Held up, lost tch from 4f out: reapp: landed a private stks & mdn '03, subs List rnr-up: best arnd 12f,
has tried 14f+: likes firm & gd grnd, stiff/gall trks: has gone well fresh.
2 Aug'03 York 11.9fm 105-(103) A: 1 Jul'03 York 11.9fm 97- D: 1 May'03 Newm 8gd 1- G: 2 Oct'02 Newm 7g/f 0- G:
2907} **SUN ON THE SEA 303** [1]4-8-9 (107) M J Kinane 9/1: 44146-6: Led, hdd over 3f out & sn btn, reapp.   2½   84
6 Ran   Time 2m 15.68 (8.38)   Owned: Godolphin   Trained: Newmarket

1685
2.30 Gr2 Totesport Dante Stakes 3yo (A)
£84100 £31900 £15950   **1m2f88y**   **Good/Soft 75**   **-06 Slow**   Inside

4429*}**NORTH LIGHT 231** [1] Sir Michael Stoute 3-8-11 K Fallon 6/1: 21-1: b c Danehill - Sought Out   117+
(Rainbow Quest) Keen, in tch, prog & led over 4f out, held on well under hands & heels: bckd: won fnl of 2 '03
starts (mdn, rdly): appr step up to 10.5f, breeding suggests 12f+ will suit: acts on fast & soft grnd, sharp/undul
or stiff trk: goes well fresh: smart colt, burst into Derby picture & solid each-way claims.
1 Sep'03 Good 8g/f 94- D: 2 Aug'03 Sand 7.1sft 92- D:
4469} **RULE OF LAW 228** [3] Saeed bin Suroor 3-8-11 T (110) L Dettori 8/1: 3113-2: b c Kingmambo -   ½   115
Crystal Crossing (Royal Academy) Mid-div, outpcd 3f out, styd on well for press fnl 1.5f, not btn far: reapp,
jockey given 4-day whip ban: mdn & List scorer '03, subs Gr 2 plcd (D Loder): stays 10.5f, 12f shld suit judged on
this: acts on firm & gd/soft grnd, stiff/gall trks: prev best in a visor, smart effort here in t-strap.

488

1 Aug'03 York 7.0fm 107- A: 1 Jul'03 York 7.0fm 97- D:
1208* **LET THE LION ROAR 26** [9] J L Dunlop 3-8-11 (108) M J Kinane 3/1 FAV: 12-13: Pushed along early in rear, styd on for press fnl 2f, nvr pace to chall: hvly bckd, padd pick: acts on fast & gd/soft grnd: progressed again & looks likely to relish 12f+: see 1208. *2½* **111**
1208 **TOP SEED 26** [6] M R Channon 3-8-11 (108) T E Durcan 8/1: 03624-24: Trkd ldrs, styd on onepace for press fnl 3f: just bhd today's 3rd in 1208. *1* **109**
1130* **ANDEAN 30** [7]3-8-11 T P Queally 4/1: 6-15: Keen, mid-div, smooth hdwy 3f out, rdn & no extra from 2f out: nicely bckd: handles fast & prob gd/soft grnd: this longer 10.5f trip may yet suit: imprving. *6* **104**
4839} **MOSCOW BALLET 206** [5]3-8-11 J P Spencer 5/1: 125-6: b c Sadler's Wells - Fire The Groom (Blushing Groom) Trkd ldrs, drvn & btn 2f out: hvly bckd on reapp, Irish raider: stks wnr on debut '03, subs Gr2 rnr-up & Gr1 5th (rtd 110 at best): eff at 1m, mid-dists shld suit this term: acts on firm & gd grnd, stiff/gall or sharpish trks: can go well fresh. 2 Sep'03 Asco 8fm 109- A: *3½* **100**
4866} **MUTAWAFFER 201** [8]3-8-11 (99) R Hills 33/1: 1510-7: b c Marju - Absaar (Alleged) Mid-div, rdn & btn 3f out: reapp: mdn & cond stks scorer '03, well held in a Gr3 subs: wng form at 6/7.6f, mid-dist pedigree: acts on gd/soft grnd, poss handles firm, stiff/gall or sharp trk: can go well fresh. *5* **95**
1 Sep'03 Ches 7.6g/s 102- C: 1 Jul'03 Asco 6g/s 95- D:
1480 **BARBAJUAN 11** [4]3-8-11 (110) P Robinson 33/1: 5143-508: Led 2f, rdn & btn 3f out: btr 1113 (1m). *5* **90**
1294 **SKIDMARK 21** [10]3-8-11 (102) R Hughes 25/1: 1-211349: Al bhd: much btr 1040 & 727 (AW). *5* **85**
3029*}**OMAN GULF 298** [2]3-8-11 M Hills 25/1: 1-0: 10th: Led after 2f till over 4f out, sn btn: reapp. *1½* **84**
10 Ran Time 2m 15.69 (8.39) Owned: Ballymacoll Stud Trained: Newmarket

1686 **3.00 Listed Bank Of Scotland Corporate Banking Hambleton Rated Hcap 4yo+ 0-110 (A)** **[115]**
£17400 £6600 £3300 **1m rnd** **Good/Soft 75** **+13 Fast** Inside

928* **AUTUMN GLORY 47** [12] G Wragg 4-8-7 (2oh) (94) S Drowne 9/2 FAV: 140-11: Trkd ldrs & rdn to lead ins last, styd on strongly in a fast time: bckd, abs: eff at 1m on a gall trk, shld get further: likes fast & gd/soft grnd: lightly rcd & v prog colt, one to follow: see 928. **103**
4976} **DUCK ROW 193** [5] J A R Toller 9-9-5 (108) S Sanders 25/1: 414440-2: ch g Diesis - Sunny Moment (Roberto) Trkd ldrs, rdn & led over 1f out, hdd ins last, kept on: reapp: '03 stks scorer: List & Gr 3 wnr in '02: stays 9f, ideally suited by 1m on firm & gd/soft grnd: tough, genuine & smart gldg, a fine reapp. *2* **112**
1 Aug'03 Newm 8gd 110-(110) B: 1 Sep'02 Donc 8fm 112- A: 2 Aug'02 Leop 8gd 112- : 1 Jun'02 Curr 8g/s 110- :
2 May'02 York 7.9fm 110-106 A: 1 Aug'01 Bath 8g/f 105- C: 2 Jul'01 Deau 8gd 109- :
1225 **MINE 25** [11] J D Bethell 6-8-10 vis (99) T Quinn 12/1: 03406-23: Held up, rdn & hdwy to chall dist, not pace of wnr: another solid run from this useful h'capper: see 1225. *hd* **102**
1475* **BLUE SPINNAKER 11** [17] M W Easterby 5-8-9 (98) J P Spencer 10/1: 4004-014: Held up, styd on wide for press fnl 3f, nrst fin: nicely bckd tho' op 8/1: ran close to form of 1475. *shd* **101**
1486 **EL COTO 11** [4]4-8-13 (102) W Supple 7/1: 304-0155: Mid-div, rdn to press ldrs over 1f out, no extra well ins last: nicely bckd: tough, useful & consistent: clr of rem here: see 1486 & 1231. *shd* **104**
951 **PENTECOST 46** [10]5-8-9 (98) K Fallon 14/1: 13240-06: ch g Tagula - Boughtbyphone (Warning) Rear, eff fnl 3f, no impress: 6 wk abs: rtd h'cap socrer '03, Listed rnr-up: R Ascot wnr '02 (Brittania h'cap): suited by 7f/1m, prob stays 9f: acts on firm, gd/soft & any trk, likes Ascot: best without a visor & likes to come late off a strong pace: tough & useful. 2 Sep'03 Hayd 8.1gd 104-(99) A: 1 Aug'03 Asco 8g/f 100-92 B: *5* **92**
1 Jun'02 Asco 8g/f 100-91 B: 2 May'02 Ayr 8g/s 92- C: 2 Apr'02 Sand 8g/s 97-90 C: 2 Aug'01 Newm 6g/f 87-84 B:
1 Aug'01 Epso 6fm 80- E: 2 Jul'01 Bath 5fm 84- D: 2 Jul'01 Beve 5fm 82- E: 2 Jun'01 Pont 5fm 85- F:
4176} **PLAY THAT TUNE 244** [9]4-8-7 (96) J Fanning 20/1: 4/12033-7: ch f Zilzal - Military Tune (Nashwan) Chsd ldr, ch 2f out, fdd under press: reapp: fills mdn wnr on reapp '03, subs dual Listed plcd (rtd 97 at best, H Cecil): fills mdn rnr-up '02: eff at 7f/1m on fast & gd/soft grnd, prob any trk: can go well fresh: showed up well for a long way for new yard, could improve. *3* **86**
2 Jun'03 Leic 7.0g/f 84-(85) C: 1 May'03 Newm 7gd 88- D: 2 Jul'02 Kemp 7g/s 88- D:
951 **CONVENT GIRL 46** [15]4-8-7 (1oh) (95) R Havlin 50/1: 23126-08: b f Bishop of Cashel - Right To The Top (Nashwan) Dwelt, bhd, kept on fnl 3f, no threat: 6 wk abs: prog '03, dual h'cap scorer, also landed a class stks, Listed rtd h'cap rnr-up: mdn scorer '02: eff at 9f, suited by 1m on firm & gd grnd, stiff/undul or easy trks. *2* **83**
2 Sep'03 Asco 8fm 98-95 A: 1 Sep'03 Sand 8.1g/f 95-87 C: 2 Aug'03 Kemp 8fm 87-84 C: 1 Jul'03 Kemp 8g/f 87-(83) D:
1 Jul'03 Sali 8g/f 86-78 D: 2 Oct'02 Leic 9.9gd 84- C: 2 Aug'02 Good 7g/f 82-77 C: 1 Jul'02 Leic 7g/f 77- E:
1349 **PABLO 18** [6]5-9-0 p (103) M Hills 12/1: 455-0109: Chsd ldrs 3f out, rdn & no impress fnl 2f: btr 1126. *½* **89**
1117*}**PRINCE TUM TUM 389** [18]4-9-2 (105) M J Kinane 16/1: 3311/1-0: 10th: b c Capote - La Grande Epoque (Lyphard) Rear, only mod late prog: landed sole start in '03 (Listed): mdn & stks wnr '02: eff at 1m on firm & fast grnd, any trk: can go well fresh: proved v smart prev but has had injury probs, a likely improver. *shd* **91**
1 Apr'03 Kemp 8fm 108-(96) A: 1 Oct'02 York 7fm 96- B: 1 Sep'02 Warw 7.1g/f 83- D:
1231 **KINGS COUNTY 25** [13]6-8-8 (1ow)(1oh) (95) R Hughes 7/1: 0/5512-30: 11th: Mid-div, btn 2f out. *1¾* **81**
4878} **ATAVUS 200** [2]7-8-8 (97) J Mackay 25/1: 030104-0: 12th: Led, hdd over 1f out, sn btn, reapp. *5* **73**
1151 **CALCUTTA 29** [7]8-8-10 (99) R Hills 25/1: 31314-00: 13th: Mid-div, struggling fnl 2f. *3* **71**
1115 **COTE QUEST 13** [3]4-8-7 (4oh) (92) Martin Dwyer 40/1: 3013-400: 14th: Bhd halfway. *5* **61**
1351 **JAZZ MESSENGER 18** [14]4-8-7 (1oh) (95) E Ahern 8/1: 11006-60: 15th: Mid-div, strugg fnl 2f, eased. *8* **49**
1486 **MILLENNIUM FORCE 11** [1]6-9-7 (110) C Catlin 50/1: 44230-00: 16th: Al bhd, 7f specialist. *6* **54**
2665} **EXCELLENTO 312** [19]4-8-13 (102) L Dettori 10/1: 2/1113-0: 17th: Rcd wide & prom, btn 3f out. *13* **28**
17 Ran Time 1m 40.75 (4.95) Owned: Mollers Racing Trained: Newmarket

1687 **3.35 European Breeders Fund Maiden Stakes 2yo (D)**
£4895 £1506 £753 **6f str** **Good/Soft 75** **-69 Slow** Stands Side

PIVOTAL FLAME [6] B A McMahon 2-9-0 S Sanders 14/1: 1: b c Pivotal - Reddening (Blushing Flame) Held up & hdwy halfway, led over 1f out, styd on strongly for press: 50,000 gns May 1st foal, dam a 2m 3yo wnr & sister to a useful 9/10f wnr abroad: sire a high-class sprinter: eff at 6f, get further: acts on gd/soft grnd & a gall trk: goes well fresh: scopey colt, clrly useful, type to prog in gd company. **101**
CRIMSON SUN [5] Saeed bin Suroor 2-9-0 L Dettori 7/2: 2: b c Danzig - Crimplene (Lion Cavern) Keen trkg ldrs, eff to chall dist, not pace of wnr: nicely bckd: Feb 1st foal, dam smart 6f juv & subs high-class 3yo at 1m/12f: eff at 6f, sure to get further: acts on gd/soft grnd & a gall trk: promising start, win races. *¾* **98**
CAPABLE GUEST [11] M R Channon 2-9-0 T E Durcan 14/1: 3: b c Cape Cross - Alexander Confranc (Magical Wonder) Pushed along towards rear, styd on well from over 1f out, nrst fin: 130,000 gns Mar foal, half brother to a useful 5/6f wnr, dam a 7f juv wnr: eff at 6f, get further on this evidence: green early but caught the eye late on, expect improvement & shld win sn. *½* **96+**
1237 **FIEFDOM 25** [2] M Johnston 2-9-0 J Fanning 4/1: 54: Led till over 1f out, kept on for press: *hd* **95**

nicely bckd: left debut bhd over this longer 6f trip: acts on gd/soft grnd: will stay further & shld find similar.
AMSTERDAM [8]2-9-0 J P Spencer 3/1 FAV: 5: b c Danehill - Dathiyna (Kris) Sn trkd ldrs 1½ **91+**
travelling well, shaken up & outpcd over 1f out: hvly bckd, op 7/2: Irish raider, Mar foal, half brother to 3yo wnrs at 10/12f, dam unrcd daughter of a high-class sprinter: eff at 6f, breeding suggests much further will suit in time: acts on gd/soft: sopey colt, improve, esp when tackling further.
COLEORTON DANE [3]2-9-0 N Callan 50/1: 6: Trkd ldrs & rdn to chall 2f out, no extra dist: ran well for a long way, land an ordinary mdn in the North. shd **91**
1510 **WILKO 9** [1]2-9-0 E Ahern 7/2: 37: Cl-up, btn over 1f out: hvly bckd after 1510 (hvy). 1½ **88**
AIRE DE MOUGINS [7]2-9-0 K Darley 25/1: 8: Towards rear, kept on late, nrst fin: well clr of rem: likely improver & interesting for minor trk mdns. hd **87**
SOWERBY [9]2-9-0 T Williams 66/1: 9: Sn struggling. 10 **62**
LOYALTY LODGE [10]2-9-0 T Quinn 50/1: 0: 10th: Sn outpcd. 6 **47**
LAUREN LOUISE [4]2-8-9 T R Winston 50/1: 0: 11th: Prom till halfway: t-strap. ¾ **40**
11 Ran Time 1m 18.03 (8.63) Owned: Mr R L Bedding Trained: Tamworth

1688 **4.10 Tadcaster Maiden Stakes 3yo (D)**
£4934 £1518 £759 **6f217y rnd** **Good/Soft 75** **-30 Slow** Inside

1191 **SOLDIERS TALE 27** [5] J Noseda 3-9-0 E Ahern 4/9 FAV: 21: Trkd ldrs, hdwy to lead dist, sn asserted under hands & heels, rdly: hvly bckd at odds-on to confirm debut promise: eff at 6f, stays 7f well & 1m shld suit: acts on fast & gd/soft, stiff/gall trks: looks useful & shld win more races: see 1191. **101**
1171 **CAPESTAR 28** [12] B G Powell 3-8-9 T Quinn 14/1: 62: b f Cape Cross - Sedulous (Tap On Wood) 5 **82**
Trkd ldrs 3f out, chsd wnr from over 1f out, sn well held but clr of rem: poss imprvd from encouraging debut: eff at 7f on gd & gd/soft grnd, 1m could suit: a likely type for similar.
NEW ORDER [8] B W Hills 3-8-9 R Hughes 7/2: 3: b f Singspiel - Eternal (Kris) Hmpd start, 9 **71**
mid-div, eff to chase ldrs 3f out, onepace: bckd tho' op 11/4, debut: bred to apprec 1m+: prob handles gd/soft grnd: some encouragement.
1514 **PETER PAUL RUBENS 9** [7] P F I Cole 3-9-0 K Darley 28/1: 04: ch c Belong To Me - Skybox (Spend A 1¾ **74**
Buck) Rcd keenly & sn led, clr halfway, rdn & hdd 2f out, fdd: left hvy grnd debut bhd & ran well for a long way here: half brother to wnrs in the US: could well apprec gd or faster grnd, shld find a race.
1152 **IMTALKINGGIBBERISH 29** [9]3-9-0 S W Kelly 25/1: 05: Mid-div, eff 3f out, edged right & no impress fnl 2f, has been gelded. 1¾ **72**
HUGGIN MAC [4]3-8-9 Suzanne France(7) 100/1: 6: Dwelt & bhd, mod late prog on debut. nk **66$**
258 **NOBLE DESERT 135** [6]3-8-9 Martin Dwyer 100/1: 0-7: Held up, eff from halfway, no impress, abs. 1½ **64**
4751} **OLIVANDER 210** [10]3-9-0 (80) L Dettori 14/1: 52U6-8: Chsd ldrs till 3f out, reapp. 2 **66**
1518 **GUSTAVO 9** [1]3-9-0 M Hills 50/1: 009: Dwelt, outpcd & al rear. 5 **59**
4997} **SHINKO FEMME 190** [11]3-8-9 (62) W Ryan 66/1: 624630-0: 10th: Mid-div, btn 2f out, reapp. 2½ **50**
4937} **ALBADI 196** [2]3-9-0 T E Durcan 66/1: 0-0: 11th: Al bhd, reapp. 6 **46**
DEE EN AY [3]3-9-0 S Sanders 66/1: 0: 12th: Prom, struggling fnl 3f on debut. 10 **31**
12 Ran Time 1m 28.63 (7.33) Owned: Mr Syd Belzberg Trained: Newmarket

1689 **4.45 Toteexacta Handicap Stakes 4yo+ 0-90 (C)** **[89]**
£11057 £3402 £1701 **1m5f197y** **Good/Soft 75** **-21 Slow** Inside

1516 **STAR MEMBER 9** [10] A P Jarvis 5-9-2 (77) K Fallon 14/1: 32050-51: Mid-div, pushed along & hdwy over 2f out, rdn to lead ins last, styd on strongly to assert: left hvy grnd reapp bhd: eff at 10f, suited by 14f & prob stays 2m: acts on fast, gd/soft & polytrack, sharp/undul or gall trk: decisive scorer. **88**
4373] **CAPTAIN MILLER 944** [18] N J Henderson 8-8-6 (67) T Quinn 9/1: /1206/0//-2: b g Batshoof - 3 **73**
Miller's Gait (Mill Reef) Handy & rdn to lead over 2f out, rdn & hdd ins last, not pace of wnr, rest well covered: remarkable performance after 3 year abs: unplcd sole '01 start (class stks): '00 h'cap wnr: eff around 14f/2m, has tried 2m4f: acts on fast & hvy grnd, prob any trk: excellent return, win races if able to repeat.
1112 **HIGH POINT 32** [7] G P Enright 6-9-5 (80) L Dettori 6/1: 1-000233: Held up, eff to chase ldrs 2f out, styd on onepace for press: nicely bckd: see 1112, 83. 3 **83**
1112 **MOON EMPEROR 32** [9] J R Jenkins 7-9-5 vis (80) M J Kinane 25/1: 500-0604: Rear, rdn & kept on. 3½ **79**
1506 **GEORGE STUBBS 10** [17]6-8-4 (65) G Gibbons 20/1: 6403135: Chsd ldrs, drvn & no extra over 1f out. ½ **64**
1232 **NAWOW 25** [6]4-9-0 (76) K Dalgleish 12/1: 326-0356: Rear, kept on late for press, nrst fin. 1½ **73**
1506 **SAHEM 10** [13]7-9-1 (76) R Hughes 14/1: 330-5047: Held up, eff wide 3f out, no impress fnl 2f. ¾ **72**
1516* **JOROBADEN 9** [19]4-9-11 (4ex) (87) J Quinn 11/2 FAV: 4/-21618: Rear, hdwy 5f out, no prog when hung left 2f out: hvly bckd under a pen: btr 1516 (hvy). 8 **75**
1232 **PROMOTER 25** [5]4-9-12 (88) E Ahern 9/1: 21404-09: ch g Selkirk - Poplina (Roberto) Led till 1¾ **74**
over 2f out, sn btn: mdn scorer '03, subs h'cap plcd (rtd 92): wng form at 10f, best eff over a gall 2m: acts on firm & fast grnd, stiff/gall trks. 1 Jun'03 Newm 10fm 87- D: 2 Jun'03 Sand 10.0gd 81- D:
1389 **GRAN DANA 16** [3]4-9-4 (80) J Fanning 20/1: 2100: 10th: Prom, btn 2f out: btr 1121 (fast, 12f). 1¾ **64**
1569 **MANA DARGENT 7** [14]7-10-0 (89) W Hogg(7) 16/1: 1433-050: 11th: Mid-div,btn 3f out: btr 1569. 5 **68**
1361 **FREEDOM NOW 18** [1]6-9-0 (75) S Drowne 33/1: 4/3660-00: 12th: b g Sadler's Wells - Free At Last 10 **44**
(Shirley Heights) Chsd ldrs, btn 3f out: unplcd 03/04 (rtd 108h, nov): h'cap plcd '03 (rtd 80, h'cap): '01 mdn wnr for L Cumani: eff at 10/12f on fast & gd grnd, stiff or sharp trk.
1 Jul'01 Wind 10g/f 86- D: 2 Jun'01 Ripo 12g/f 79- D:
1459 **HIGHLAND GAMES 12** [11]4-9-9 (85) K Darley 16/1: 11060-20: 13th: Mid-div, eff wide 4f out, sn btn. 5 **49**
1232 **BID FOR FAME 25** [8]7-9-5 P (80) W Ryan 33/1: 0621-000: 14th: Al rear: cheek pieces, poor run. 3 **41**
1112 **SNOWS RIDE 32** [4]4-9-3 (79) Martin Dwyer 50/1: 5011-000: 15th: Sn bhd: btr 140 (AW). 4 **36**
1361 **GREENWICH MEANTIME 18** [2]4-9-4 (80) J P Spencer 6/1: 3221-030: 16th: Rear, eff 3f out, sn btn. ¾ **36**
856 **TEMPSFORD 57** [12]4-9-12 (88) S Sanders 16/1: 31511-50: 17th: Cl-up till 4f out: abs: see 856. 6 **38**
22] **WEET FOR ME 909** [20]8-9-10 (85) W Supple 100/1: 311033//-0: 18th: Chsd ldrs, struggling halfway. dist **0**
18 Ran Time 3m 06.09(13.39) Owned: Jarvis Associates Trained: Twyford

Official Going Good/Firm (Firm Places)

1690 2.10 Hardings Bar And Catering Services Maiden Stakes 3yo+ (D)
£3465 £1066 £533 **5f213y rnd** Firm 18 +10 Fast Inside

1228 **BUY ON THE RED 25** [5] W R Muir 3-8-12 (72) R Miles(3) 5/2: 424-221: Cl-up, led after 4f, drvn out **88**
fnl 1f to hold on despite edging right: bckd: eff at 5/6f, acts on polytrack & soft grnd, imprvd today on firm
grnd: acts on a v sharp/undul trk: op to more improvement: see 1228 & 973.
1281 **GET TO THE POINT 22** [1] P W D'Arcy 3-8-12 (72) R L Moore 4/1: 0050-022: Handy, chsd wnr bef 1f *2* **80$**
out, kept on but al held: acts on firm & gd grnd: another gd eff & can find similar: see 1281.
4302} **ALL QUIET 238** [8] R Hannon 3-8-7 P Dobbs 14/1: 000-3: b f Piccolo - War Shanty (Warrshan) *3½* **65**
Mid-div, prog 2f out, kept on fnl 1f, no impress on front 2: reapp: unplcd all 3 '03 starts (rtd 73, mdn).
2151} **FAIR COMPTON 333** [4] R Hannon 3-8-8 (1ow) Dane O'Neill 8/1: 04-4: b f Compton Place - Fair *½* **65**
Eleanor (Saritamer) Handy over 4f, no extra: tchd 14/1 on reapp: unplcd both '03 starts (rtd 64, auct mdn): eff
at 6f on fast grnd: now quals for h'caps.
3899} **WYCHBURY 260** [2]3-8-12 (79) D Corby(3) 2/1 FAV: 532-5: ch c Swain - Garden Rose (Caerleon) Cl-up *1¾* **64**
when short of room & lost footing after 2f, styd in tch, wknd 1f out: well bckd on reapp: plcd on 2 of only 3 '03
starts (rtd 80, mdn): eff at 5f/6f, 7f shld suit: acts on fast grnd: did not get run of race & can rate higher.
2 Aug'03 Yarm 5.2g/f 80- D:
1575 **GENEROUS SPIRIT 6** [6]3-8-12 Paul Eddery 20/1: 0006: Mid-div, nvr able to chall: quick reapp. *1* **61**
1497 **FAIR OPTIONS 10** [12]3-8-12 G Carter 66/1: 07: Nvr nrr than mid-div: see 1497. *2½* **54**
1101 **BOLD RIDGE 34** [7]4-9-8 D Sweeney 50/1: 00-08: Bhd, mod late gains. *½* **53**
1575 **CINNAMON RIDGE 6** [14]3-8-12 BL L Keniry(3) 25/1: 00-09: Led despite hanging left 4f, wknd. *2½* **46**
1339 **COMPASSION 18** [9]3-8-7 P (62) A McCarthy 33/1: 54450-00: 10th: Mid-div over 3f, wknd. *½* **40**
1222 Son Of Rembrandt 25 [13]3-8-12 (60) M Howard(7) 33/1♦730} Quarrymount 211 [10]3-8-12 S Archer(7) 16/1:0
Flying With Eagles [15]3-8-12 Lisa Jones(3) 50/1:0 946 Our Sion 46 [3]4-9-8 A Daly 100/1:0
14 Ran Time 1m 8.33 (0.53) Owned: Mr R Haim Trained: Lambourn

1691 2.40 Racecourse Video Services Handicap Stakes 3yo+ 0-75 (E) [72]
£3822 £1176 £588 **7f214y rnd** Firm 18 -05 Slow Inside

1298 **KATIYPOUR 21** [6] Miss B Sanders 7-10-0 (72) Lisa Jones(3) 8/1: 6-031201: Mid-div, prog to lead **77+**
ins fnl 1f, pushed out, val 2L+: tchd 12/1: eff btwn 1m/11f on firm, gd/soft & both AWs: see 1042 & 932.
122 **ANALYZE 165** [5] B G Powell 6-10-0 (72) R L Moore 16/1: 331506-2: b g Anabaa - Bramosia *1* **74**
(Forzando) Mid-div, prog to chase wnr ins fnl 1f, just held cl-home: plcd twice over hdles in chd 03/04 (rtd 103h, mdn
hdle, eff at 2m1f on firm & fast): won 2 h'caps in '03 (M R Channon), h'cap & clmg wnr in '02: eff at 1m, suited
by 10f on firm, soft or polytrack, any trk: only just denied under top weight.
1 Aug'03 Ayr 10g/f 74-70 E: 2 May'03 Nott 10.0gf f 77-(75) D: 2 Apr'03 Leic 10.0gd 76-73 E:
1 Apr'03 Newc 10.1g/f 76-68 E: 2 Apr'03 Nott 10.0gd 71-(69) E: 2 Dec'02 Ling 10ap 70a-70 F:
1 Dec'02 Ling 10ap 70a- D: 2 Oct'02 Nott 10g/f 70-67 E: 1 Apr'02 Leic 10g/f 70-65 E:
1219 **SAMUEL CHARLES 25** [11] W M Brisbourne 6-9-5 (63) N Pollard 8/1: 4000-123: Cl-up, ev ch & hung *shd* **64**
badly left after 6f, led briefly dist, kept on but just held by front 2: in gd form tho' not look str-forward.
1613 **CONCER ETO 5** [2] S C Williams 5-9-12 p (70) B Reilly(3) 7/2 FAV: 00-00234: Handy & short of room *4* **63**
after 6f, prog when short of room dist, no impress fnl 1f: quick reapp: shade closer with clr passage: btr 1613.
1535 **DASH FOR COVER 8** [9]4-9-6 (64) P Gallagher(7) 20/1: 01-20005: Led till dist, no extra: btr 978. *¾* **55**
1504 **SPINDOR 10** [15]5-9-3 bl (61) V Slattery 11/1: 4210336: Mid-div, nvr able to chall: btr 1504. *1* **50**
1214 **CAPTAIN DARLING 26** [12]4-9-7 p (65) A Quinn(5) 9/1: 43-60207: Chsd ldrs 6f, sn no extra: btr 1049. *½* **53**
1036 **NIGHT WOLF 39** [14]4-9-11 (69) S Hitchcott(3) 14/1: 4415-608: Handy wide 6f, no extra: btr 932. *1¼* **55**
520 **TREETOPS HOTEL 102** [3]5-9-2 (60) N Chalmers(5) 14/1: 00000-29: Held up, nvr nrr than mid-div. *¾* **44**
1298 **DEEPER IN DEBT 21** [10]6-9-11 (69) G Carter 9/1: 2-243350: 10th: Bhd, nvr a factor: rider *1* **51**
reported mount was nvr travelling: btr 1042 & 932.
1530 **PAY THE SILVER 9** [13]6-9-13 p (71) I Mongan 10/1: 0230-040: 11th: Rear, nvr able to chall: btr 1530. *2* **49**
1613 **AGILIS 5** [4]4-9-4 bl (62) R Miles(3) 33/1: 6-060000: 12th: Mid-div 6f, wknd: qck reapp. *nk* **39**
132 **CHUBBES 162** [8]3-9-3 vis (74) Dane O'Neill 13/2: 614230-0: 13th: Rear, nvr a factor: long abs. *2½* **46**
4877} Ziet Dalsace 201 [7]4-8-11 (55) S Righton 33/1:0 902 Salon Prive 50 [1]4-9-5 BL(63) S Whitworth 25/1:0
15 Ran Time 1m 33.85 (1.85) Owned: Mr Peter Crate Trained: Epsom

1692 3.10 Alexander Catering Selling Stakes 3yo+ (G)
£2548 £728 £364 **1m3f196y** Firm 18 -15 Slow Outside

1373 **BANNINGHAM BLAZE 17** [3] C R Dore 4-9-3 vis (50) R Thomas(5) 3/1: 000-0041: Held up, prog 2f out, **50**
styd on to lead fnl 1f, drvn out: recent hdles unplcd (rtd 32h): eff around 12f on firm, fast & polytrack: eff
with a visor: apprec drop to sell grade: see 1373.
896 **CHOCOLATE BOY 50** [5] G L Moore 5-10-0 bl (57) R L Moore 7/4 FAV: 5244102: Mid-div, prog to lead *½* **59**
2f out, hdd ins fnl 1f, kept on & only just held: well bckd after 7 wk abs: on firm grnd & polytrack: see 842.
1541 **OUR DESTINY 8** [1] A W Carroll 6-10-0 (62) S Hitchcott(3) 7/2: 1631243: Cl-up, led 6f out, hdd *8* **48**
after 12f, wknd: best form has come at shorter trips: btr 1402 & 1341.
1543 **PARADISE VALLEY 8** [2] Mrs Stef Liddiard 4-10-0 t (47) R Miles(3) 8/1: 0502054: Bhd, late gains. *1½* **45**
1455 **SENOR TORAN 13** [6]4-9-8 P (53) L Keniry(3) 9/1: 0-343025: Cl-up 12f, fdd: btr 1455 (polytrack). *6* **30**
1373 **BIRTH OF THE BLUES 17** [4]8-9-8 (45) P Gallagher(7) 10/1: 0631466: Led 6f, fdd 3f out: btr 1076. *11* **16**
6 Ran Time 2m 32.25 (4.05) Owned: Crown Select Trained: Spalding

BRIGHTON   WEDNESDAY 12.05.04   Lefthand, V Sharp, Undulating Track

---

1693   3.45 Celebpoker Com Handicap Stakes 3yo+ 0-70 (E)   **[70]**
£3803 £1170 £585   **1m3f196y**   **Firm 18**   **+06 Fast**   Outside

3445} **FLYING SPIRIT 279** [15] G L Moore 5-9-2 (58) R L Moore 4/1: 123102-1: b g Flying Spur - All   **71+**
Laughter (Vision) Led 10f out, pushed clr ins fnl 2f, val 6L+: earlier won 2 nov hdles (rtd 122h at best, stays 2m2f
on firm grnd): clmr, sell & appr h'cap wnr in '03: suited by around 12f on firm & gd/soft grnd: loves a sharp/undul
trk, esp Brighton: goes well fresh, eff with/without cheek pieces: easy wnr & more races await.
2 Aug'03 Brig 11.9fm 59-56 D: 1 Jul'03 Epso 12.0g/f 59-54 E: 2 Jun'03 Brig 11.9g/f 56-(55) E:
1 May'03 Brig 11.9fm 58-(55) E: 1 May'03 Brig 11.9g/f 57-(66) G: 2 May'03 Sout 12g/f 46-(66) G: 1
1 Jun'02 Nott 10g/s 72- F: 2 Jun'02 Ches 10.3gd 73- D: 2 May'02 Thir 6fm 74- E:
1295 **DANAKIL 21** [8] S Dow 9-10-0 (70) P Dobbs 14/1: 30-00002: Keen rear, prog after 1m, styd on well   4   **75**
ins fnl 1f, no ch with easy wnr: acts on firm & soft: not disgraced here & is on a wng mark: see 1295.
936 **PRIVATE BENJAMIN 47** [6] Jamie Poulton 4-8-7 (49) F Norton 14/1: 64-01063: Keen mid-div, prog to   shd   **53**
chase wnr bef 1f out, no extra ins fnl 1f: btr 672 (mdn).
3996} **MERRYMAKER 254** [7] W M Brisbourne 4-9-3 (59) N Pollard 10/1: 003433-4: b g Machiavellian - Wild   3½   **58**
Pavane (Dancing Brave) Handy over 10f, hung left & no extra: op 20/1 on reapp: plcd 3 times in '03 (h'caps &
class stks, rtd 65 at best, Sir M Stoute): eff at 12/14f on fast grnd: eff with a visor, has tried blnks.
1399 **MOST SAUCY 15** [9]8-9-6 (62) L Keniry(3) 14/1: 5500-665: Rear, prog fnl 2f, nrst fin: see 1286.   1¼   **59**
1385 **EASTBOROUGH 16** [1]5-9-4 (60) D Sweeney 7/1: 0343466: Dwelt, nvr nrr than mid-div: op 10/1.   ¾   **55**
711 **CANTRIP 78** [17]4-8-11 (53) A Daly 20/1: 2660-007: b f Celtic Swing - Circe (Main Reef) Led, hdd   1½   **45**
12f out, wknd ins fnl half mile: 11 wk abs: h'cap wnr in '03: showed promise on sole '02 start (rtd fills mdn, rtd
73): eff at 12/14f on firm & fast grnd: likes to force the pace.
2 Jul'03 Pont 12.0g/f 65-62 E: 2 Jun'03 Yarm 14.1fm 64-61 E: 1 May'03 Ling 11.8g/f 63-57 F:
1083 **FOREST TUNE 35** [16]6-9-3 (59) Dane O'Neill 25/1: 6106-008: Keen bhd, nvr nrr than mid-div.   1¼   **49**
1135* **WELLINGTON HALL 30** [4]6-9-7 (63) A McCarthy 7/4 FAV: 00500-19: Chsd ldrs, short of room halfway,   nk   **52**
no extra fnl 2f: well bckd: trainer reported that 6yo was unsuited by trk: rtd higher in 1135 (reapp).
1118 **MAJLIS 31** [11]7-9-9 bl (65) A Quinn(5) 33/1: 01-00500: 10th: Rear, prog halfway, fdd 2f out, no ch   nk   **53**
when no room ins fnl 1f: btr 877.
1618 **Margery Daw 5** [14]4-9-8 (64) Lisa Jones(3) 66/1:0   1375 **Mandoob 16** [3]7-9-13 p(69) J P Guillambert(3) 16/1:0
3582} **North Point 273** [5]6-8-13 P(55) R Miles(3) 25/1:0   218 **Gabor 147** [18]5-9-2 (58) R Brisland 16/1:0
686} **Summer Cherry 442** [12]7-8-3 t(45) P Doe 33/1:0   1148 **Young Patriarch 29** [13]3-8-2 (63) D Kinsella 20/1:0
16 Ran   Time 2m 29.71 (1.5)   Owned: Richard Green (Fine Paintings)   Trained: Brighton

---

1694   4.20 Toteplacepot Handicap Stakes 3yo 0-70 (E)   **[77]**
£3666 £1128 £564   **5f59y rnd**   **Firm 18**   **-13 Slow**   Inside

1539 **IMPERIUM 8** [6] Mrs Stef Liddiard 3-9-2 (65) F Norton 11/1: 4020051: Handy, grad styd on to lead   **72**
cl-home, rdn out: eff at 5/6f on firm, gd/soft & polytrack: 1st win: see 1023.
1457 **PRINCESS KAI 12** [5] R Ingram 3-8-6 bl (55) S Hitchcott(2) 6/1: 1003422: Cl-up, ev ch bef 1f out,   ¾   **58**
kept on but just held cl-home: continues to run well: see 1457.
1404 **REHIA 15** [1] J W Hills 3-8-4 (53) S Whitworth 15/2: 0654403: Led, hdd under press cl-home: nk   **55**
handles firm, gd & both AWs: see 703.
1404* **IVORY LACE 15** [10] S Woodman 3-9-7 (70) D Sweeney 6/1: 2013114: Sn bhd, prog despite hanging   nk   **71**
left ins fnl 2f, nrst fin: op 9/2: far from disgraced on hat-trick bid: just btr 1404.
914 **CUT AND DRIED 49** [4]3-9-5 (68) L Keniry(3) 11/2 JT FAV: 00-11605: Handy till dist, no extra: ½   **67**
bckd from 10/1, 7 wk abs: btr 712 (polytrack).
735 **ALIZAR 76** [8]3-8-10 (59) Dane O'Neill 12/1: 2314236: Bhd, prog ins fnl 2f, nrst fin: 11 wk abs.   1   **55**
1572 **CHEEKY CHI 7** [2]3-9-3 (66) Lisa Jones 12/1: 4431407: Nvr nrr than mid-div: quick reapp.   ½   **60**
1374 **SAVERNAKE BRAVE 16** [3]3-7-13 bl (48) Joanna Badger 9/1: 6500-528: Keen rear & sn hung right, nvr   1   **39**
a factor: op 12/1: btr 1374 (fibresand).
1404 **MAXIS PRINCESS 15** [9]3-8-5 (54) R L Moore 6/1: 04000-69: Mid-div over 4f, wknd: btr 1404.   1¼   **41**
944 **EASILY AVERTED 46** [7]3-9-2 P (65) I Mongan 16/1: 6-550000: 10th: Mid-div till halfway, wknd.   2   **46**
10 Ran   Time 1m 1.67 (1.67)   Owned: The Cross Keys Racing Club   Trained: Hungerford

---

1695   4.55 Teletext Racing 'hands And Heels' Apprentice Handicap Stakes 3yo+ 0-55 (G)   **[55]**
£2674 £764 £382   **1m1f209y**   **Firm 18**   **-27 Slow**   Outside

1219 **BANK ON HIM 25** [7] G L Moore 9-9-4 (45) Jemma Marshall(8) 7/1: 1222251: Keen handy, styd on to   **51**
lead ins fnl 1f, pushed out: suited by 1m/10f on firm, gd/soft & fibresand, loves polytrack: see 1027 & 498.
1267 **HOLLY ROSE 22** [5] D E Cantillon 5-9-11 p (52) M Howard 15/2: 34100-02: Led, hdd ins fnl 1f, no   2½   **53**
extra: tchd 10/1: another gd eff here at Brighton: see 1267 (reapp).
1132 **FANTASY CRUSADER 30** [2] J A Gilbert 5-9-6 (47) M Halford 12/1: 10000-03: ch g Beveled -   4   **42**
Cranfield Charger (Northern State) Chsd ldrs over 1m, sn onepcd: h'cap wnr in '03: unplcd in '02 (rtd 29, J
Cullinan): eff at 7f/10f on firm & fast grnd: eff with cheek pieces: has tried a t-strap.
1 Aug'03 Ling 10g/f 52-47 F: 2 Jul'03 Ling 10.3g/f 47-45 F: 2 Jun'03 Brig 8.0fm 45-(34) G: 1 Jun'01 Ling 7fm 72- E:
1579 **LUCEFER 6** [8] G C H Chung 6-9-5 (46) Dean Williams(3) 11/2: 412-0034: Bhd, prog 2f out, onepcd fnl 1f.   1   **39**
1657* **VANDENBERGHE 2** [10]5-9-7 (48) R Keogh(3) 11/2: 00635-15: Nvr nrr than mid-div: qck reapp, btr 1657.   shd   **40**
498 **FIFE AND DRUM 105** [3]7-9-8 p (49) Laura Pike 20/1: 2U00-006: b g Rahy - Fife (Lomond) Cl-up over   hd   **40**
1m, wknd: long abs: sell wnr in '03 (J Akehurst): eff at 1m, suited by 10/12f on firm & gd grnd: eff with cheek
pieces, has tried blnks: with Miss J Feilden. 2 Oct'03 Ling 8ap 59a-(54) G: 2 Sep'03 Good 8g/f 55-54 F:
2 Sep'01 Ling 10ap 55a-52 G: 1 Jul'03 Yarm 10.1fm 51-(56) G: 2 Aug'02 Sali 9.9g/f 63-59 E:
2 Sep'01 Chep 10.1fm 62-61 F: 1 Aug'01 Nott 10gd 61-58 E: 1 Dec'00 Ling 10ap 66a-60 E:
1412* **KINGS TOPIC 15** [1]4-10-0 (55) R J Killoran(3) 11/1: 00/0-2117: Handy till short of room after 6f,   ¾   **44**
wknd fnl 2f: btr 1412 & 1289 (polytrack).
1402 **EVA PERON 15** [9]4-9-4 (45) B O'Neill 33/1: 000-0068: Handy 7f, sn hung left & wknd: jumps fit.   1   **32**
1128 **BURGUNDY 30** [6]7-10-0 vis (55) Steven Harrison 9/2 FAV: 0-634209: Nvr trav in rear, btn fnl 2f.   ¾   **40**
1579* **GOT TO BE CASH 6** [4]5-9-10 (6ex) (51) Samantha Davies(8) 7/1: 260-4210: 10th: Mid-div over 7f, fdd.   nk   **35**

492

BRIGHTON
WEDNESDAY 12.05.04   Lefthand, V Sharp, Undulating Track

1373   **Sammys Shuffle 17** [11]9-9-7 bl(48) K Jackson 16/1:0   842   **Sholay 59** [12]5-9-9 (50) Crystal Caetano(8) 33/1:0
12 Ran   Time 2m 2.37(4.57)   Owned: Vetlab Supplies Ltd   Trained: Brighton

SAINT CLOUD
WEDNESDAY 05.05.04   Lefthand, Galloping Track

Official Going GOOD/SOFT.

1696	**1.35 Gr 3 Prix la Force 3yo** ()
	£25704 £10282 £7711 **1m2f** **Good/Soft**

     DELFOS [1] C Laffon Parias 3-9-2   O Peslier 2/1: -2111: ch c Green Tune - Akhla (Nashwan) Trkd   **114+**
ldr, led over 1f out & sn asserted under hand riding: recent wnr in French provs: eff at 10f, expected by trainer to
relish 12f: acts on good/soft & soft grnd, gall trks: lightly rcd & progressive colt: smart & cld be supplemented
for the French Derby: type to win more Group races & rate higher.
     YOUNG TIGER [4] F Rohaut 3-9-2   J B Eyquem 34/10: 5-1142: Rear, hdwy to chse ldr dist, rdn &   2½   **109**
styd on, always held: eff at 10f on gd/soft: v useful.
     KURM [3] J C Rouget 3-9-2   I Mendizabal 18/10 FAV: 34211-13: Led after 1f till dis, no extra.   2½   **105**
4 Ran   Time 2m 08.40()   Owned: L Marinopoulos   Trained: France

JAGERSRO
THURSDAY 06.05.04

Official Going FAST.

1697	**7.40 Listed Pramms Memorial 4yo+** ()
	£46583 £15528 £7764 **1m120y rnd** **Fast**

1231   **VORTEX 19** [7] Miss Gay Kelleway 5-9-6 t (97) N Cordrey 147/10: 11111001: Mid-hdwy to lead dist,   **104**
held on all out: suited by 1m/8.5f on firm, gd & both AWs: loves a sharp/turning trk: best held up: smart & prog AW
performer: well plcd to land this v val prize, see 836, 700.
     MANDRAKE EL MAGO [3] F Castro 5-9-6   M Santos 4/5 FAV: 2: Just denied by a most game wnr: well   hd   **103**
clr of rem: eff at 8.5f on AW: useful.
3550*)**ORGANIZER 270** [10] W Neuroth 4-9-6   F Johansson 57/10: 13: No impress on front pair ins fnl 1f.   8½   **91**
1057   **TE QUIERO GB 31** [1]6-9-6 t (82) F Lynch 153/10: 0-0002277: Dwelt, sn mid-div, btn 2f out: s/mate   7   **81**
of wnr: poss best when up with/forcing the pace: see 846 & 141.
12 Ran   Time 1m 49.00()   Owned: Coriolis Partnership   Trained: Newmarket

LONGCHAMP
THURSDAY 06.05.04   Righthand, Stiff, Galloping Track

Official Going HOLDING.

1698	**2.50 Gr 3 Prix d'Hedouville** ()
	£25704 £10282 £7711 **1m4f** **Soft**

1061   **SHORT PAUSE 32** [6] A Fabre 5-8-12   G Stevens 6/4 JT FAV: 34142-31: b c Sadler's Wells - Interval   **114**
(Habitat) Trkd ldrs, rdn to chall dist, led ins last, drvn out: Listed wnr & Gr 2 rnr-up in '03: dual wnr '02: eff
at 10/12f on fast, likes soft grnd: smart entire.   2 Oct'03 Long 10sft 111- A: 2 Oct'02 Long 9.7g/f 107- :
4838} **KINDJHAL 200** [2] E Lellouche 4-8-9   D Boeuf 34/10: 222-2312: Held up, rdn/chall dist, no extra cl home. ¾   **109**
     MAREDSOUS [4] D Sepulchre 4-8-6   I Mendizabal 21/1: 40112-53: Held up, styd on fnl 2f, nvr nrr.   ½   **105**
8 Ran   Time 2m 39.10()   Owned: K Abdulla   Trained: France

CHANTILLY
FRIDAY 07.05.04   Righthand, Galloping Track

Official Going SOFT.

1699	**2.00 Gr 3 Prix Allez France (Fillies & Mares) 4yo+** ()
	£25704 £10282 £7711 **1m2f** **Soft**

5027} **PRIDE 182** [5] A de Royer Dupre 4-8-7 (80) D Bonilla 155/10: 3/210-41: b f Peintre Celebre -   **115**
Specificity (Alleged) Trkd ldrs, edged right & bmpd 2f out, drvn to lead dist, drvn out: '03 mdn wnr for G Butler,
subs List unplcd (rtd 92): suited by 10f on gd & soft grnd, prob handles polytrk: useful & much imprvd filly.
1 Oct'03 Newb 10.0gd 82-0 D: 2 Oct'03 Ling 8ap 67-0 D:
     RUSSIAN HILL [9] A Fabre 4-8-7   Gary Stevens 53/10: 3214-222: Led till dist, kept on.   1½   **112**
833   **SAMANDO 62** [6] F Doumen 4-8-9   C P Lemaire 56/10: 0131-363: Held up, kept on for press, nrst fin.   shd   **114**
11 Ran   Time 2m 06.90()   Owned: Np Bloodstock Ltd   Trained: France

LEOPARDSTOWN   SUNDAY 09.05.04   Lefthand, Galloping Track

Official Going GOOD/YIELDING

1700   4.00 Gr 2 Derrinstown Stud Derby Trial 3yo   ()
£57620   £16549   £7839   **1m2f   Good/Soft**

1302* **YEATS 21** [5] A P O'Brien 3-9-0   J P Spencer   1/5 FAV: 1-11: Made all, shkn up & in command fnl   **117+**
2f, val 4L+: eff at 1m/10f, expected to relish 12f: acts on fast & soft grnd: only doing just enough here &
connections predict plenty more to come at Epsom, remains the one to beat in the Derby: see 1302 (Gr 3, impressive).
4742} **RELAXED GESTURE 197** [2] D K Weld 3-9-0   P J Smullen   11/2: 3120-2: ch c Indian Ridge - Token   1½   **110**
Gesture (Alzao) Rear, effort to chase ldr over 1f out, kept on but always well held: reapp: '03 mdn wnr, subs Gr 2
rnr-up & unplcd in an US Gr 1: eff at 7f/1m, stays 10f: acts on fast & gd/sft grnd: useful & well regarded,
reportedly has many options, including Belmont Stakes in US. 2 Oct'03 Curr 8g/s 108- :
MEDICINAL 21 [3] D K Weld 3-9-0   P Shanahan 20/1: 1-43: gr c Linamix - Pharmacist   1   **109**
(Machiavellian) Chsd ldrs, outpcd over 2f out, kept on for press, nvr dngrs: mdn scorer '03: wng form at 7f,
mid-dists shld suit: acts on fast & soft.
4 Ran   Time 2m 10.30 ()   Owned: Mrs John Magnier   Trained: Ballydoyle

1701   4.30 Gr 3 Derrinstown Stud 1000 Guineas Trial (Fillies) 3yo   ()
£37074   £10877   £5182   **7f rnd   Good/Soft**

895* **ALEXANDER GOLDRUN 49** [1] J S Bolger 3-8-11   K J Manning   4/1: 01221-11: Dwelt & hmpd early, rear,   **110**
hdwy 2f out & styd on for press to lead well ins last: eff at 7f/1m on fast & hvy grnd, expected to stay further but
Irish Guineas is next target: see 895 (List, 1m).
1300 **MISTY HEIGHTS 21** [5] D K Weld 3-8-11   P J Smullen   5/1: 3142-32: b f Fasliyev - Mountains Of Mist   shd   109
(Shirley Heights) Trckd ldrs, rdn & led dist, drvn & just hdd close home: op 4/1: '03 Tipperary mdn scorer, subs
Gr 1 4th & Gr 3 rnr-up: 7f specialist on fast & soft grnd, stiff/gall trk: smart. 2 Sep'03 Curr 7g/f 102- A:
4172} **MISS CHILDREY 35** [8] F Ennis 3-8-11   J A Heffernan   14/1: 15004-53: Led till hdd dist, kept on   nk   108
well for press, just held & clr of rem.
9 Ran   Time 1m 31.40()   Owned: Mrs N O'Callaghan   Trained: Coolcullen

DUSSELDORF   SUNDAY 09.05.04

Official Going SOFT

1702   3.35 Gr 2 German 1000 Guineas (Fillies) 3yo   ()
£80989   £30986   £16197   **1m rnd   Soft**

SHAPIRA [13] A Lowe 3-9-2   J Palik   514/10: 1: ch f Kornado - Semplice (Common Grounds) Rear,   107
strong run wide 2f out & led over 1f out, styd on strongly: well suited by 1m on soft grnd: smart German filly.
5011} **LA INA 187** [5] A Trybuhl 3-9-2   A de Vries   53/10: 32332: Held up, styd on wide, not pace to chall wnr.   1¾   103
1110 **COQUETERIA 29** [1] G Wragg 3-9-2   (80) S Drowne   124/10: 0441-23: Trckd ldrs, narrow lead briefly   ¾   101
dist, kept on: acts on fast, prog last twice on soft & gd/sft grnd: useful filly, see 1110 (List).
15 Ran   Time 1m 42.21()   Owned: Stall Granum   Trained: Germany

YORK   THURSDAY 13.05.04   Lefthand, Flat, Galloping Track

Official Going GOOD/SOFT (GOOD places).

1703   1.30 Langleys Solicitors Rated Stakes Handicap 4yo+ 0-105 (B)   [110]
£12818   £4862   £2431   **6f str   Good/Soft 69   -03 Slow   Stands Side**

1486 **QUITO 12** [12] D W Chapman 7-9-7 bl (103) A Culhane   12/1: 0625561: Held up, hdwy halfway, styd on   110
strongly to lead ins last, rdn clr: stays 1m, eff at 5f but best at 6/7f: acts on firm, loves gd/soft, soft &
fibresand, any trk: v smart, most tough & genuine & this was a tremendous run in a h'cap: see 618, 64.
1487 **TOM TUN 12** [10] J Balding 9-8-11 bl (93) Dean McKeown   25/1: 00010-02: Led/dsptd lead till went on   3   95
halfway, hdd ins last, no extra: left reapp bhd on fav'd easy grnd: see 1487.
1481 **MARSAD 12** [4] J Akehurst 10-8-7 (1oh) (88) P Doe   14/1: 05203-03: ch g Fayruz - Broad Haven (Be My   1¾   86
Guest) Dwelt, switched & hdwy halfway, styd on onepace ins last: imprvd from reapp: C/D rtd h'cap rnr-up '03: val
h'cap wnr '02: 6f specialist on firm, hvy & any trk, can go well fresh: genuine 10yo, slipping to a handy mark.
2 Jun'03 York 6.0g/f 91-88 B: 1 May'02 Newm 6fm 96-90 C: 2 Jul'01 Newb 6g/f 95-93 B: 2 May'01 Good 6fm 93-90 C:
1 May'01 Newm 6g/f 91-85 C: 2 Apr'01 Kemp 7hvy 89-83 C:
1137 **INDIAN SPARK 31** [5] J S Goldie 10-8-13 (95) K Fallon   8/1: 0500-404: ch g Indian Ridge - Annes   ¾   90
Gift (Ballymoss) Short of room & drpd rear early, styd on for press from halfway, nvr able to chall: h'cap scorer
'03: cond stks wnr '02: eff at 5/6f on any grnd/trk, loves York & Doncaster: now slipping to a handy mark.
1 May'03 Hayd 5sft 105-100 B: 2 Apr'03 Thir 6fm 104-(102) C: 2 Mar'03 Donc 5g/s 102-101 B: 1 Apr'02 Thir 6fm 106- C:
2 Sep'01 Leop 5gd 110- : 1 Jun'01 Newc 5g/f 108-99 B:
1598* **CHAPPEL CRESENT 6** [9]4-8-8 (3ex) (90) A Nicholls   4/1 FAV: 0052515: Dsptd lead till outpcd 2f out: 2½   77
nicely bckd: eff at 6f, forcing tactics at 7f poss ideal: btr 1598 (7.5f, made all).
1626 **HALMAHERA 5** [6]9-9-6 bl (102) R Winston   12/1: 044-0246: Trckd ldrs, no impress fnl 1f: qck reapp.   ½   87
1481 **CD FLYER 12** [8]7-8-7 (4oh) (85) T Eaves(4)   12/1: 110-5207: Mid-div, not pace to chall ldrs: see 1251.   hd   73
1490 **MAZEPA 11** [14]4-8-13 (95) L Dettori   7/1: 0100-638: Trckd ldrs, rdn & btn dist: btr 1490 (firm).   2   73
1400 **PROUD BOAST 16** [3]6-8-11 (93) K Darley   16/1: 360-0109: Pushed along rear, nvr pace to threaten.   4   60
4956} **PIVOTAL POINT 195** [7]4-8-9 (91) S Sanders   11/2: 21352-0: 10th: b g Pivotal - True Precision   3½   48
(Presidium) Keen & trckd ldr, wknd qckly halfway: reapp: nicely bckd, op 6/1: '03 mdn scorer, subs h'cap plcd &

494

stks rnr-up: eff at 5f, suited by 6f on firm & gd, sharp or stiff trk: useful sprinter, sharper next time.
2 Oct'03 Newm 6gd 94-(88) C: 1 Jun'03 Wind 6g/f 91- D: 2 May'03 Sali 6g/f 82- D:
4674} MUTAWAQED 201 [15]6-8-7 (3oh)t (86) E Ahern 14/1: 103630-0: 11th: Mid-div trav well, shaken up &   1¼   43
no impress when hmpd over 1f out, no ch after: trav well for a long way on reapp, likely to be sharper for this.
1594 POMFRET LAD 6 [1]6-9-4 (100) Alex Greaves 50/1: 1052-000: 12th: Cl-up, btn 2f out, qck reapp.   2½   47
1227 Dazzling Bay 26 [13]4-9-7 (103) J F Egan 25/1:0   1487 Circuit Dancer 12 [11]4-8-10 (92) J Carroll 25/1:0
14 Ran   Time 1m 13.71 (4.31)   Owned: Mr Michael Hill   Trained: York

---

1704   2.00 Sharp Minds Betfair Rated Stakes Handicap 4yo+ 0-105 (B)   [112]
£13247 £5025 £2512   1m2f88y   Good/Soft 69   +05 Fast   Inside

884   VINTAGE PREMIUM 54 [7] R A Fahey 7-9-0 (98) P Hanagan 16/1: 320-0601: b g Forzando - Julia Domna   104
(Dominion) Made all, rdn & strongly pressed over 2f out, held on gamely ins last, all out: gd time, 8 wk abs: nov
hdle rnr-up 03/04 (rtd 116h): List & stks rnr-up '03: won 3 h'caps '02: best arnd 10f, stays 11f: acts on firm &
f/sand, enjoys gd or soft, any trk: goes well fresh: genuine & v useful entire, loves to dominate.
2 Jun'03 Donc 10.3fm 108-(107) C: 2 May'03 Ches 10.3fm 109-(109) A: 2 Sep'02 Ayr 10.8gd 110- A:
2 Sep'02 Donc 10.2fm 106-100 B: 1 Jul'02 York 10.3g/f 111-101 B: 1 Jun'02 Epso 10gd 107-97 B:
1 May'02 Wind 10sft 100-92 B:
1296   SHAHZAN HOUSE 22 [5] M A Jarvis 5-8-10 (94) P Robinson 6/1: 60410-32: Trkd ldrs trav well, chall   nk   99
fnl 2f, drvn & just btn in a tight fin: nicely bckd: useful & consistent, remains on the upgrade: see 1296.
1111   DUMARAN 33 [10] W J Musson 6-8-8 (92) K Fallon 4/1 FAV: 403-0023: Held up, rdn & hdwy to press   1   95
ldrs fnl 1f, just held cl-home: hvly bckd: confirmed improvement of 1111 & can find a nice prize.
1484   BAGAN 12 [12] H R A Cecil 5-8-4 (2oh) (86) W Ryan 15/2: 0015-444: Rear, styd on for press, not   nk   90
able to reach front trio: see 1172 (12f).
1519   JABAAR 10 [3]6-8-4 (1oh) (87) A Nicholls 12/1: 0420-035: Mid-div, hdwy to press ldrs 2f out, no extra.   ¾   90
1475   CRIPSEY BROOK 12 [2]6-8-4 (2oh) (86) Kim Tinkler 25/1: 11330-66: ch g Lycius - Duwon (Polish   1¾   88
Precedent) Trkd ldr, rdn & no extra over 1f out: most progressive '03, landed 4 h'caps & 2 class stks: h'cap scorer
'02: suited by 10/10.5f on firm & gd grnd, any trk: can go well fresh.
1 Aug'03 Ripo 10gd 86-80 C: 1Aug'03 Hayd 10.5g/f 85-79 D: 1Jul'03 Hayd 10.5g/f 79-75 C:
1Jun'03 Newc 10.1g/f 77-(73) D: 1 Jun'03 Nott 10.0g/f 76-67 D: 2 Jun'03 Newc 10.1fm 68-64 E:
1 May'03 Newc 10.1g/f 66-(57) E: 2 Oct'03 York 10.3fm 59- D: 1 Sep'02 Redc 10g/f 58-54 G:
1351   ALWAYS ESTEEMED 19 [4]4-8-13 (97) Martin Dwyer 6/1: 40000-27: Trkd ldrs, btn 2f out: btr 1315 (1m).   6   89
1478   ST PANCRAS 12 [14]4-8-4 (88) E Ahern 14/1: 5456-008: Rear, eff 3f out, no impress: see 1478.   5   74
1111   PRINCE NUREYEV 33 [11]4-8-11 (95) J P Spencer 16/1: 02440-09: b g Desert King - Annaletta   2½   77
(Belmez) Rear, eff 3f out, nvr a threat: h'cap scorer '03, subs 6 rnr class stks rnr-up: mdn scorer '02: eff at
11/12f on firm & gd/soft grnd, loves a stiff/gall trk.
2 Jul'03 Asco 12g/f 101-(99) B: 1 May'03 Newb 11.0gd 97-93 C: 1 Jul'02 Sand 7g/s 92- D:
1519* TELEMACHUS 10 [8]4-8-5 (3ex) (89) M Fenton 13/2: 5530-610: 10th: Chsd ldrs, btn 2f out: btr 1519.   1½   69
1478   BARRISSIMO 12 [1]4-8-8 (92) M J Kinane 33/1: 01/35-00: 11th: b g Night Shift - Belle de Cadix   3   68
(Law Society) Chsd ldrs, rdn & btn 3f out: unplcd '03 (lightly rcd, rtd 101, 4 rnr stks): mdn scorer for P Harris
in '02 (made all): winning form at 7f, stays 10f: acts on fast & soft grnd, prob firm. 1 Oct'02 Donc 7sft 93- D:
1478   GALA SUNDAY 12 [13]4-8-4 (1oh) (87) Dale Gibson 66/1: 5100-000: 12th: Al bhd.   hd   63
1560   MIDDLEMARCH 10 [9]4-9-7 (105) J F Egan 25/1: 5016-040: 13th: In tch, btn 3f out: btr 1560.   6   72
1350   SIR GEORGE TURNER 19 [6]5-9-6 (104) K Dalgleish 25/1: 04632/-00: 14th: Led/dsptd lead, btn 3f out.   hd   70
14 Ran   Time 2m 13.99 (6.69)   Owned: Mr J C Parsons   Trained: Malton

---

1705   2.30 Gr2 Emirates Airline Yorkshire Cup 4yo+ (A)
£81200 £30800 £15400   1m5f197y   Good/Soft 69   +10 Fast   Inside

1418   MILLENARY 15 [1] J L Dunlop 7-8-13 bl (117) T Quinn 9/2: 21042-31: Held up, smooth hdwy to lead   120+
dist, rdn clr, impressive: nicely bckd, fast time: eff at 12/14f, does stay 2m: acts on firm & gd/soft, handles
soft/any trk: suited by blnks nowadays: produced a high-class staying performance today, hard to beat in Gr 1
comp if repeating this: see 1418.
1005* ALCAZAR 43 [2] H Morrison 9-8-10 (118) M Fenton 7/1: 11024-12: Trkd ldrs, hdwy trav well 4f out   3   114
& led over 1f out, hdd dist & sn no ch with wnr: rest well covered, 6 wk abs: up in grade & progressed again.
1493   JELANI 11 [7] Andrew Turnell 5-8-10 (106) M J Kinane 11/1: 2/541/-063: Led/dsptd lead, went on   4   108
over 2f out, rdn & hdd over 1f out, kept on for press: stays gall 14f: imprvd efft, smart entire whose career has
been blighted by injuries, with Gr 3/List on this evidence: see 1493.
4628} MR DINOS 221 [5] P F I Cole 5-9-1 (122) K Fallon 4/1 JT FAV: 151/116-4: b c Desert King - Spear   2   110+
Dance (Gay Fandango) Rear, rdn & styd on fnl 2f, nrst fin on reapp: lightly rcd '03, Gr 2 reapp wnr & notably Gr 1
Ascot Gold Cup: 4 times wnr '02, inc Gr 3/Gr 1: thorough stayer, needs 2m+, career best at 2m4f: acts on fast &
hvy, stiff trks: top-class, highly encouraging return over this inadequate 14f, one to be on back at 2m+.
1 Jun'03 Asco 20g/f 124-(115) A: 1 May'03 Sand 16.4g/f 123-(115) A: 1 Oct'02 Long 15.5hvy 119- :
1 Jul'02 Vich 15gd 111- : 2 Jun'02 Newc 16g/f 111-103 B: 2 Jun'02 Asco 16.2g/f 106- A:
1 May'02 York 13.8g/f 102- B: 1 Apr'02 Newm 12g/f 97- D: 2 Jul'01 Asco 7g/f 98- D:
1230   DUTCH GOLD 26 [4]4-8-9 BL (111) D Holland 50/1: 06-02005: ch c Lahib - Crimson Conquest (Diesis)   7   96
Handy & led halfway till over 2f out, sn btn: first time blnks & longer trip: AW mdn & Gr 3 scorer '03, subs Epsom
Derby 6th: mdn rnr-up '02: eff at 10/12f on firm/fast & polytrack, loves a sharp/easy trk, prob handles a stiff
one: has tried t-strap prev: v useful but needs trip & sights lowering. 1 May'03 Ches 12.3fm 110-(100) A:
2 Apr'03 Kemp 8fm 104-(89) A: 1 Mar'03 Ling 10ap 86a-(89) D: 2 Aug'02 Ches 7.5fm 90- C:
1418   MAKTUB 15 [10]5-8-10 P Robinson 16/1: 11200-06: b c Love The Groom - Carmen The Best (Waajib)   3½   91
Held up, gd hdwy over 3f out, rdn & no prog over 2f out: lightly rcd '03, Gr 3 scorer, subs Gr 1 rnr-up (Italian
trained): multiple wnr '02: appears best btwn 11/14f on fast & hvy grnd.
2 Oct'03 San 12gd 116- : 1 Oct'03 San 11gd 104- :
2327} HIGHEST 327 [3]5-8-10 L Dettori 4/1 JT FAV: 2/10325-7: b c Selkirk - Pearl Kite (Silver Hawk)   6   83
Held up in tch, eff 4f out, btn 3f out: reapp: lightly rcd '03, Gr 1 Coronation Cup rnr-up: '02 mdn & class stks
wnr for Sir M Stoute, subs Gr 2 & Gr 1 St Leger rnr-up: suited by 12/14f on gd/soft, likes firm & fast grnd, any
trk, loves a gall one: tough & v smart when on song, cld leave this bhd on a faster surface.
2 Jun'03 Epso 12.0g/f 119-(115) A: 2 Sep'02 Donc 14.6fm 118- A: 2 Aug'02 York 11.8gd 117- A:1 Jul'02 Asco 12gd 104- B:
2 Jun'02 Asco 12g/f 104-94 B: 1 May'02 Leic 11.8g/s 88- D: 2 May'02 Ches 10.3fm 97- D: 2 Oct'01 Newm 8g/s 92- D:
1230   SALSALINO 26 [9]4-8-9 (107) R Hughes 7/1: 43243-68: Wide & dsptd lead 2f, rdn & btn 4f out.   12   68
2293*}SHANTY STAR 328 [8]4-8-9 (105) K Darley 8/1: 01/131-9: Trkd ldrs, lost tch qckly 4f out, reapp.   dist   0

1418 **MOROZOV 15** [6]5-8-10 I Mongan 50/1: 6/12U0-PP: In tch, wkng when hung left 2f out, sn p.u..   0
10 Ran   Time 3m 01.61 (8.21)   Owned: Mr L Neil Jones   Trained: Arundel

---

1706   3.00 Listed Michael Seely Memorial Glasgow Stakes Colts & Geldings 3yo   (A)
£18600   £6600   £3300   **1m2f88y**   **Good/Soft 69**   **-09 Slow**   Inside

1501* **DAY FLIGHT 11** [1] J H M Gosden 3-8-11   R Hughes   5/2: 11: Handy & led 4f out, readily pulled well   119+
clr fnl 2f under hand riding, v easily: nicely bckd: remains unbeaten after impressive mdn success: eff at 10/12f,
further cld suit: 2 clear cut victories to date & this v smart colt's future lies in Group company.
1208 **MAC REGAL 27** [4] M G Quinlan 3-8-11   L Dettori   20/1: 1-32: Sn handy, readily outpcd by wnr from   20   86
over 3f out: caught a tartar: see 1208.
      GO FOR GOLD 326 [2] A P O'Brien 3-8-11   J P Spencer   11/2: 1-3: b c Machiavellian - Kithanga   4   81
(Darshaan) Led, rdn & hdd 4f out, left bhnd fnl 2f: reapp, Irish raider: sole start mdn wnr '03: half-brother to
a top-class 12/14f performer Milan: expected to need mid-dists this term: wng form at 7f on gd.
1234 **FORT DIGNITY 26** [3] Sir Michael Stoute 3-8-11   (108) K Fallon   4/6 FAV: 1-44: In tch, rdn & btn   6   73
over 2f out: longer trip, much more expected after 1234 (Gr 3, 7f,gd) & something prob amiss.
4 Ran   Time 2m 15.39 (8.09)   Owned: Mr K Abdulla   Trained: Manton

---

1707   3.35 Sharp Minds Betfair Stakes Handicap 3yo 0-95 (C)   [89]
£10966   £3374   £1687   **1m rnd**   **Good/Soft 69**   **-01 Slow**   Inside

1582 **ODDSMAKER 7** [8] P D Evans 3-9-2   (77) Dean McKeown   9/1: 015-3251: Al handy & rdn/led dist, styd   88
on strongly for press: bckd: suited by 1m/10f, tried 12f: acts on fast, prog this term on gd/soft & soft grnd,
loves a stiff/gall trk: tough, the type his trainer does esp well with, keep on side: see 1427 & 1105.
1464* **INCHLOSS 13** [3] B A McMahon 3-8-12   (73) G Gibbons   10/1: 0412: Trkd ldrs, rdn & styd on for   1   83
press, not pace of wnr: h'cap bow, fine eff over longer 1m trip: likes gd/soft & soft grnd: see 1464 (6f mdn).
1315* **BARATHEA DREAMS 20** [1] J S Moore 3-9-4   (79) Martin Dwyer   5/2 FAV: 11413: Led, drvn & hdd dist,   ½   87
kept on: remains in gd form: see 1315.
1515 **FREAK OCCURENCE 10** [6] Miss E C Lavelle 3-9-7   (82) D Holland   6/1: 1420-034: Mid-div, lost place   2½   85
& drpd towards rear over 4f out, kept on for press fnl 2f, no dngr: bckd: see 1515 & 232.
1360 **POPPYS FOOTPRINT 19** [4]3-9-0   (75) P Fessey   33/1: 620-0005: ch f Titus Livius - Mica Male (Law   3   72
Society) Held up, eff to chase ldrs 2f out, sn no impress: '03 auct mdn & nov stks scorer, subs h'cap rnr-up:
winning form at 6f, stays gall 1m well: acts on fast & gd grnd, stiff/gall trks, likes Hamilton.
2 Sep'03 Ayr   8g/f 84-83 C: 1 Aug'03 Hami   6.0gd 84-(73) D: 1 Jul'03 Hami   6.0g/f 78- E:
3894} **CHARLOTTE VALE 261** [9]3-8-7   (68) A Culhane   50/1: 4246-6: ch f Pivotal - Drying Grass Moon (Be My   hd   64
Chief) Rear, styd on for press fnl 2f, nrst fin: reapp: auct fills mdn rnr-up '03: best eff over a stiff 6f, 1m
not sure to suit (sprinting influence in pedigree): handles fast & gd grnd, stiff/undul trks.
2 Jun'03 Hami   6.0gd 78- E:
13   **APERITIF 183** [11]3-9-0   (75) R Hills   14/1: 663-7: ch g Pivotal - Art Deco Lady (Master Willie)   nk   70
Unruly stalls, slow away, kept on late for press, nvr a dngr: 6 mth abs, h'cap bow: turf unplcd '03 (rtd 75, AW mdn
plcd, rtd 80a): eff at 5f, 7f+ may yet suit: handles polytrack & poss firm grnd, sharp/turning trk.
1526 **COTOSOL 10** [15]3-9-2   (77) I Mongan   20/1: 026-0158: Chsd ldrs 3f out, btn dist: btr 1215 (7f).   1¾   69
1257 **RONDELET 24** [10]3-9-2   (77) S Sanders   10/1: 064-29: Mid-div, eff to chase ldrs over 2f out, sn   2   65
hung left & wknd: btr 1257.
1192 **BREATHING SUN 28** [7]3-9-3 t   (78) K Fallon   7/1: 03011-00: 10th: Dwelt & al towards rear: bckd.   5   57
1257* **PLAY MASTER 24** [5]3-8-13   (74) W Ryan   12/1: 212010: 11th: Chsd ldrs, btn 2f out: btr 1257.   11   33
1315 **CERTIFIABLE 20** [13]3-8-12   (73) A Nicholls   25/1: 41150: 12th: Mid-div wide, btn 2f out: btr 934 (AW).   2½   27
3763} **SWIFT SAILING 266** [14]3-9-5   (80) M Hills   20/1: 015-0: 13th: Al bhd on reapp.   4   27
1105 **GJOVIC 33** [12]3-9-3 BL   (78) K Darley   25/1: 342-250: 14th: Chsd ldrs, wknd qckly 3f out: blnks.   5   16
14 Ran   Time 1m 41.40 (5.6)   Owned: Mr D Maloney   Trained: Abergavenny

---

1708   4.10 Swisscom Eurospot Stakes Handicap 3yo 0-85 (D)   [92]
£6611   £2034   £1017   **1m3f198y**   **Good/Soft 69**   **-04 Slow**   Inside

1318 **CUTTING CREW 20** [8] P W Harris 3-9-3   (81) Martin Dwyer   9/1: 402-31: Made all, rdn & styd on   99
strongly fnl 2f: first win: eff at 10f, imprvd for step up to 12f, got further: acts on fast, gd/soft & polytrack,
prob any trk: enjoyed forcing tactics today: lightly rcd, type to prog: see 1318.
1174 **ABSOLUTELYTHEBEST 28** [3] E A L Dunlop 3-9-0   (78) E Ahern   8/1: 004-122: Mid-div, hdwy to press   4   88
ldr 2f out, sn outpcd but kept on: another gd run: acts on gd, gd/soft & polytrack: see 1174 & 367.
1521* **NESSEN DORMA 10** [7] J G Given 3-9-1 (5ex)   (79) M Fenton   20/1: 1-455213: Handy, lost place after   1¾   87
2f, drpd rear, switched wide & styd on for press fnl 3f: eff at 12f, will relish a return to 14f+: see 1521.
1347* **DALLOOL 19** [1] M A Jarvis 3-9-1   (79) P Robinson   100/30: 514: Trkd ldrs trav well, rdn & no   nk   86
impress from dist: hvly bckd, op 9/2, h'cap bow: clr of rem but just btr 1347 (4 runner mdn).
1515 **GAVROCHE 10** [9]3-8-9   (73) J P Guillambert(3) 33/1: 1235225: Mid-div, eff over 2f out, no prog   5   74
from dist: prob best returned to 9/10f: see 1515, 1369 & 441.
1382 **JOMACOMI 17** [11]3-9-3   (81) J Fanning   14/1: 136: Trkd ldrs, no impress fnl 2f: btr 1382 & 701 (12f).   3   78
1305 **ROYAL DISTANT 21** [2]3-8-12   (76) Dale Gibson   50/1: 3124-607: Eff to chase ldrs 3f out, sn wknd.   1¾   71
1428* **MASTER WELLS 15** [4]3-9-7   (85) L Dettori   16/1: 18: Dwelt, rear, only mod hdwy: h'cap bow.   9   69
4344} **SAIDA LENASERA 237** [5]3-8-12   (76) A Culhane   100/1: 43140-9: b f Fasliyev - Lanasara (Generous)   nk   59
Held up, nvr a factor: reapp: mdn scorer '03 (M Channon), subs h'cap unplcd: eff at 7f, stays 1m: acts on
firm & fast grnd, gall or sharp/turning trks.   1 Aug'03 Catt 7fm 78- D:
1140 **SCARRABUS 31** [10]3-8-11   (75) T Quinn   100/1: 560-40: 10th: Restrained start & al towards rear.   4   52
1515* **ANOUSA 10** [6]3-9-4 (5ex)vis   (82) K Fallon   12/1: 2501-010: 11th: Sn bhd: btr 1515 (hvy).   26   24
1124 **GLIDE 31** [14]3-8-7   (71) K Darley   9/1: 045-30: 12th: Mid-div, hdwy wide halfway, btn 3f out: btr 1124.   20   0
1582 **ASIATIC 7** [13]3-9-2   (80) K Dalgleish   11/4 FAV: 241-20: 13th: Prom, sn pushed along, rdn & btn 3f   6   0
out: qck reapp, hvly bckd tho' op 2/1: much btr 1582 (dsptd lead).
1153 **BORDER SAINT 30** [12]3-9-1   (79) I Mongan   25/1: 3040: 14th: Chsd ldrs, rdn & btn over 3f out: op   dist   0
33/1 on h'cap bow: btr 1153 & 873.
14 Ran   Time 2m 35.57 (8.77)   Owned: Mrs P W Harris   Trained: Berkhamsted

YORK THURSDAY 13.05.04 Lefthand, Flat, Galloping Track

1709 **4.45 Constant Security Maiden Stakes Fillies 2yo (D)**
£4875 £1500 £750 **5f str** **Good/Soft 69** **-22 Slow** Stands Side

1170 **DANCE AWAY 29** [4] M L W Bell 2-8-11 J Mackay 9/2: 21: Handy & led over 1f out, readily asserted from dist: nicely bckd, confirmed debut promise: eff at 5f on gd/soft & gd grnd, stiff/gall trks: useful filly, could make her mark in a higher grade: see 1170. **97+**

MIZZ TEE [8] T D Easterby 2-8-11 D Allan(3) 16/1: 2: b f Orpen - D D's Jakette (Deputy Minister) Chsd ldrs, switched & rdn/kept on fnl 1f, no threat to wnr: op 25/1: 15,000gns Mar foal, half-sister to a 7f 3yo wnr, dam a multiple US wnr: eff at 5f, get further: acts on gd/soft & a gall trk, promising start. *4* **86**

NUFOOS [1] M Johnston 2-8-11 R Hills 11/2: 3: b f Zafonic - Desert Lynx (Green Desert) Handy & ch 2f out, sn outpcd by wnr: bckd tho' op 4/1: Feb foal, cost 100,000gns: half-sister to a multiple 5f juv wnr: dam a 6f wnr: handles gd/soft grnd, showed ability on debut. *nk* **85**

1445 **SMIDDY HILL 14** [6] R Bastiman 2-8-11 R Ffrench 25/1: 324: Led, rdn & no extra over 1f out: handles gd & gd/soft grnd: see 1445 & 1173. *2* **79**

1524 **ALEXANDER CAPETOWN 10** [3]2-8-11 M Hills 4/1: 25: Pushed along towards rear, kept on from halfway, nvr able to chall: nicely bckd: handles gd/soft & soft grnd: see 1524. *3½* **69**

TESARY [7]2-8-11 E Ahern 12/1: 6: b f Danehill - Baldemara (Sanglamore) Mid-div, rdn & btn 2f out: op 10/1: April foal, half-sister to a 7f/1m wnr: dam unrcd. *1* **66**

BURTON ASH [10]2-8-11 M Fenton 25/1: 7: Struggling from halfway. *2½* **59**

DEPUTY OF WOOD [5]2-8-11 K Fallon 9/4 FAV: 8: Trkd ldrs, btn dist: nicely bckd, op 11/4. *1* **56**

1471 **MELANDRE 12** [9]2-8-11 T Williams 50/1: 69: Chsd ldrs, fdd halfway. *1½* **53**

1117 **NEXT TIME 32** [2]2-8-11 L Dettori 16/1: 450: 10th: Swerved badly left start & sn bhd: see 1117. *11* **25**

10 Ran Time 1m 01.34(4.54) Owned: Cheveley Park Stud Trained: Newmarket

LINGFIELD Polytrack THURSDAY 13.05.04 Lefthand, Very Sharp Track

Official Going STANDARD.

1710 **6.00 Radio Mercury Roadshow Apprentice Banded Stakes 3yo+ 0-40 (H)**
£1435 £410 £205 **7f aw rnd** **Going 47** **-31 Slow** Inside

1199 **BALLYGRIFFIN KID 27** [1] T P McGovern 4-9-7 (40) R Lucey Butler(3) 5/2: 563-0341: Rear, in tch, hdwy over 1f out & led ins last, styd on well under hand riding: bckd, op 3/1: eff at 6/7f, tried 1m: likes a sharp/undul trk: acts on firm & polytrack: see 783. **44a**

1548 **SEA JADE 9** [2] J W Payne 5-9-7 (40) D Tudhope 6/4 FAV: 6460-422: Dictated pace, rdn & flashed tail over 1f out, hdd ins last, no extra: bckd: acts on fast, gd/soft & polytrack: see 1548 & 1328. *1¼* **40a**

1671* **RATHMULLAN 2** [4] E A Wheeler 5-9-13 bl (40) Liam Jones(5) 4/1: 0034313: Handy wide, outpcd by front pair from over 1f out: qck reapp: acts on both AWs, stays 7f: see 1671. *1½* **42a**

1546 **NEWCORR 9** [3] J J Bridger 5-9-7 (35) M Halford(5) 9/2: 0-006324: Cl-up, ch halfway, wknd dist. *nk* **35a**

4 Ran Time 1m 28.30 (5.50) Owned: Mr Tommy Breen Trained: Lewes

1711 **6.30 Book A Box At Lingfield Banded Stakes 3yo+ 0-40 (H)**
£1435 £410 £205 **1m aw rnd** **Going 47** **-17 Slow** Outside

412 **TARKWA 119** [2] R M H Cowell 5-9-7 (40) B Doyle 10/1: 3260-601: gr f Doyoun - Shining Fire (Kalaglow) Chsd ldrs, drvn & styd on to lead cl-home, all out: '03 fills h'cap rnr-up on turf: '02 fills h'cap scorer: eff at 1m/12f on firm, gd & polytrack: can go well fresh. **43a**
2 Aug'03 Ling 10g/f 44-43 F: 2 Aug'02 Epso 12gd 49-50 E: 1 Jul'02 Bath 10.2g/f 48-43 E:

1642 **ROBIN SHARP 3** [3] J Akehurst 6-9-7 p (40) J Quinn 5/2: 0500402: Sn pushed along, outpcd over 3f out, rdn & hdwy to lead 2f out till well ins last, just held: clr rem, nicely bckd, qck reapp: see 846 & 457. *shd* **42a**

1182 **MYTHICAL CHARM 28** [1] J J Bridger 5-9-7 (40) J Tate 9/4 FAV: 6000633: Led till over 2f out, no extra dist: bckd: btr 1182. *5* **32a**

1073 **BRANDYWINE BAY 37** [4] A P Jones 4-9-7 p (40) G Baker 5/1: 53504-04: Slow away, nvr able to chall. *¾* **30a**

1245 **BENJAMIN 24** [5]6-9-7 bl t (40) V Slattery 7/2: 3426-225: Trkd ldrs, btn 2f out: btr 1245 & 1185. *7* **16a**

5 Ran Time 1m 41.36 (5.16) Owned: Mr J B Robinson Trained: Newmarket

1712 **7.00 Saturday Night Racing Here Starts Soon Banded Stakes 3yo+ 0-45 (H)**
£1663 £475 £238 **1m2f aw** **Going 47** **+04 Fast** Inside

1450* **KINGSDON 14** [7] T J Fitzgerald 7-9-7 vis t (45) J F Egan 4/1 FAV: 0104411: Trkd ldr trav well, rdn & hdwy to lead dist, sn asserted: best time of day: suited by 1m/10f on fast, soft & polytrack, sharp or gall trk: relishing banded company: see 1450 & 654. **55a**

1289 **RYANS BLISS 22** [12] T D McCarthy 4-9-7 (45) R Miles(3) 12/1: 0-002532: Held up, eff wide from halfway & led over 2f out, hdd dist, no ch with wnr: see 970. *4* **49a**

FAIRLAND 257 [14] S Dow 5-9-7 (45) L Smith(7) 50/1: 400/040-3: b g Blues Traveller - Massive Powder (Caerleon) Slow away, rear/wide, styd on for press, snatched 3rd line: Flat reapp, jumps fit (p.u., c.j. h'cap): ex-Irish, modest form: worth a try at 12f+ in similar, prob handles polytrack. *3* **44a**

893 **MRS CUBE 52** [10] P Howling 5-9-7 (45) P McCabe 11/1: 60-11334: Tkrd ldrs wide halfway, led 3f out till over 2f out, sn no impress: 7 wk abs: btr 826 (fibresand, 8.5f). *½* **43a**

1674 **GALEY RIVER 2** [11]5-9-7 p (45) D Corby(3) 10/1: 0516235: Mid-div, onepace fnl 3f: qck reapp. *3* **38a**

1642 **DUE TO ME 3** [3]4-9-7 p (45) S Whitworth 7/1: 0-525146: Trkd ldrs till lost place halfway, no impress after: qck reapp: btr 1642 & 1245 (1m). *hd* **38a**

1633 **OUR GLENARD 5** [2]5-9-7 (45) L Treadwell(7) 10/1: 2056407: Rear, eff 3f out, no dngr: op 16/1. *1* **36a**

1469 **DOWN TO THE WOODS 13** [8]6-9-7 P (45) T Eaves(5) 20/1: 0040-008: Rdn early, mid-div, btn 3f out: cheek pieces: see 1223. *nk* **35a**

1674* **IAMBACK 2** [6]4-9-13 (45) D Holland 11/2: 0430119: Trkd ldrs, btn 2f out: op 7/2, qck reapp. *½* **40a**

LINGFIELD Polytrack THURSDAY 13.05.04 Lefthand, Very Sharp Track

1564 **SIX PACK 8** [13]6-9-7 (45) C Catlin 11/1: 060-2240: 10th: Rear, no ch fnl 2f: btr 1289 & 894. ... 1 32a
829 **MR FLEMING** 65 [5]5-9-7 bl (45) C Lowther 33/1: 00044-30: 11th: Led/dsptd lead till 3f out: abs. ... 3 27a
1136 **MANDAHAR 31** [1]5-9-7 (45) J Quinn 25/1: 00000: 12th: Rdn & rear early, sn bhd: longer trip. ... 5 19a
1412 **HUSKY 16** [4]6-9-7 p (45) B Doyle 8/1: 000-5130: 13th: Led after 2f till 4f out, sn btn & eased. ... nk 18a
4802} **LOST SPIRIT 208** [9]8-9-7 (45) Natalia Gemelova(7) 20/1: 414250-0: 14th: b g Strolling Along - ... 23 0a
Shoag (Affirmed) Reluctant to go to start, chsd ldrs till halfway, reapp: amat riders h'cap scorer '03: h'cap &
appr h'cap wnr '02, AW h'cap plcd (rtd 45a): suited by 10/13f on firm, gd/soft & both AWs: best dominating.
2 Sep'03 Hami 12.1g/f 42-40 E: 1 Aug'03 Catt 12.0g/f 39-32 F: 2 Mar'03 Folk 12gd 46-45 E: 2 Jul'03 Hami 11g/s 50-47 E:
1 Jul'02 Hami 11gd 54-47 E: 2 Jun'02 Thir 12g/f 46-45 D: 1 Jun'02 Catt 12g/f 43-36 E: 2 Apr'02 Ripo 12.2gd 38-39 F:
2 Jul'01 Sout 12fm 55-54 E: 1 Feb'01 Ling 12ap 65a-60 C: 1 Feb'01 Ling 12ap 61a-55 C: 1 Feb'01 Ling 12ap 58a-51 D:
14 Ran   Time 2m 07.11 (4.31)   Owned: Mr Mike Browne   Trained: Malton

---

1713 7.30 New Site @ Lingfield-Racecourse Co Uk Tri-Banded Stakes 3yo 0-45 (H)
£1439 £411 £206   **1m2f aw**   **Going 47**   **-22 Slow**   Inside

1416 **JOINT DESTINY 16** [4] E J O'Neill 3-9-0 (45) D Holland 7/2: 340-5021: Keen, rear, smooth hdwy to ... 49a
lead over 1f out & sn rdn clr, al holding rivals ins last: eff at 6f/1m, now stays a sharp 12f: acts on firm, gd &
polytrack: see 1416 & 441.
1591 **DIVINA 7** [2] S L Keightley 3-8-4 vis (35) B Reilly(2) 11/2: 0004322: Keen in mid-div, lost place ... 1 37a
halfway, styd on for press fnl 2f, no threat to wnr: op 7/2: acts on both AWs: styd longer 10f trip: see 1591.
1501 **SHALATI PRINCESS 11** [7] J C Fox 3-9-0 (45) P McCabe 12/1: 0060403: Chsd ldrs, outpcd fnl 2f. ... 3 42a
1331 **OKTIS MORILIOUS 20** [1] A W Carroll 3-9-0 (45) J Quinn 2/1 FAV: 0041234: Mid-div, outpcd over 2f ... ½ 41a
out, kept on late: bckd, op 3/1: see 1331, 1183 & 970.
796 **SIR FRANK GIBSON 71** [3]3-9-0 (45) C Catlin 9/1: 0-042305: Trkd ldr, lost place 4f out, kept on ... 2 38a
late, no dngr: op 7/1: prev with M Johnston: needs a return to 11f+: see 614 & 486.
1675 **REGENCY MALAYA 2** [6]3-9-0 bl t (45) S Righton 7/1: 2003256: Dwelt, keen & hdwy to lead after 4f, ... shd 38a
hdd over 1f out & fdd: op 10/1: btr 1246 & 1183.
1454 **LENWADE 14** [8]3-8-9 BL (40) N Pollard 10/1: 000-0037: Led 4f, chsd ldrs till btn 2f out: blnks. ... 12 15a
1548 **HARBOUR PRINCESS 9** [5]3-8-4 VIS (35) R Miles(3) 25/1: 0666348: Keen, mid-div, btn 3f out: visor. ... 1 8a
8 Ran   Time 2m 09.77 (6.97)   Owned: Mr T F Brennan   Trained: Newmarket

---

1714 8.00 Come Evening Racing 29th May Banded Stakes 4yo+ 0-35 (H)
£1281 £366 £183   **1m4f aw**   **Going 47**   **-06 Slow**   Inside

1409 **BUYING A DREAM 16** [7] Andrew Turnell 7-9-0 (35) C Catlin 11/4 FAV: 00/-50131: Rear, pushed along ... 36a
& hdwy from 4f out, styd on for press to lead well ins last: eff at 7f, suited by 12f on fast, gd/soft & fibresand,
likes polytrack/Lingfield & banded company: see 1409, 1287 & 780.
1546* **ADJIRAM 9** [6] A W Carroll 8-9-6 vis (30) J Quinn 7/1: 46/-35412: Keen, sn trkd ldr & led over 4f ... ¾ 40a
out, hdd over 3f out, rallied for press & led again over 1f out till well ins last: acts on fast, gd & polytrack.
1456 **SYLVAN TWISTER 14** [10] P Mitchell 5-9-0 (30) J F Egan 16/1: 0/00-5553: br g First Trump - Storm ... ½ 33a
Party (Bluebird) Dwelt, kept on for press, nrst fin: unplcd '03 (rtd 31a, AW h'cap): no form '02.
539 **ITALIAN COUNSEL 100** [8] L A Dace 7-9-0 (30) D Holland 11/2: 0000/0/-04: b g Leading Counsel - ... ½ 32a
Mullaghroe (Tarboosh) Chsd ldrs, onepcd for press fnl 3f: 6 wk jumps abs, landed 4 h'cap hdles in 03/04 (rtd 123h,
2m/2m3.5f on firm & hvy): only mod form on the level, 2m could suit in similar.
1561 **HELLBENT 8** [2]5-9-0 (30) V Slattery 7/1: 0563465: Keen in mid-div, onepace fnl 2f. ... 2 29a
414 **RIPCORD 119** [5]6-9-0 (30) N Pollard 14/1: 0000/-56: Keen, led/dsptd lead & went on trav well ... 1¼ 27a
over 3f out, hdd & wknd over 1f out: prev with Lady Herries, 4 mth abs: needs a drop in trip on this evidence.
1656 **GOLDEN LEGEND 3** [4]7-9-0 (30) R Miles(3) 20/1: 00000/-07: Dwelt, mid-div, no impress fnl 3f. ... 10 12a
1450 **BRIDEWELL 14** [1]5-9-0 P (30) T Eaves(5) 14/1: 000-0068: Sn rdn rear, no ch 3f out. ... ¾ 11a
1333 **SUPERCLEAN 20** [3]4-9-0 vis (30) B Swarbrick(5) 33/1: 055-0069: Struggling from halfway, t.o.. ... 14 0a
1592* **THE LAST MOHICAN 7** [9]5-9-6 p (30) P McCabe 7/2: 4003210: 10th: Led after 1f till over 4f out, ... shd 0a
wknd qckly: reportedly ran too free today: see 1592.
10 Ran   Time 2m 35.57 (6.37)   Owned: Robinson Webster (Holdings) Ltd   Trained: Malton

---

1715 8.30 Lingfield Leisure Club Banded Stakes 3yo+ 0-35 (H)
£1439 £411 £206   **6f aw rnd**   **Going 47**   **+02 Fast**   Inside

3632} **BRONX BOMBER 272** [4] Dr J D Scargill 6-9-0 BL (35) C Lowther 13/2: 00/0/600-1: ch g Prince Sabo - ... 40a
Super Yankee (Superlative) Trkd ldr & rdn to lead over 1f out, held on well for press: reapp in first time blnks:
lightly rcd & unplcd '03: eff over a sharp 6f on polytrack: appreciate drop to banded grade.
1566 **TINY TIM 8** [1] A M Balding 6-9-6 (35) T Block(7) 11/10 FAV: 3522152: Trkd ldrs trav well, eff to ... 1¾ 40a
chase wnr dist, kept on but al held: clr of rem: btr 1545 (7f, gd).
1548} **CRUSTY LILY 363** [5] R M H Cowell 8-9-0 P (30) B Doyle 7/1: 000000-3: gr f Whittingham - Miss ... 5 19a
Crusty (Belfort) Cl-up, led over 2f out till over 1f out, wknd: reapp in first time cheek pieces: unplcd '03 (rtd
35, P D Evans): fills h'cap plcd '02 (rtd 42): eff at 5.5f/6f on fast & gd grnd, likes a sharp/turning trk.
53 **MRS BOZ 177** [2] A W Carroll 4-9-0 (35) J Quinn 8/1: 060-4: Rear, hdwy halfway, no prog fnl 2f. ... 2 13a
1566 **MADAME ROUX 8** [7]6-9-0 (30) G Carter 14/1: 0/0000-65: Dwelt & al towards rear/outpcd. ... 3½ 4a
1642 **JANES VALENTINE 3** [3]4-9-0 VIS (35) N Chalmers(5) 5/1: 4040006: Led till 2f out, wknd: visor. ... ¾ 1a
1181 **KAFIL 28** [6]10-9-0 bl (30) J Tate 16/1: 0/500-007: In tch wide till halfway. ... 3½ 0a
7 Ran   Time 1m 13.10(2.70)   Owned: Mr R A Dalton   Trained: Newmarket

Official Going GOOD (GGOD/FIRM places).

1716   1.40 'Jamaica Inn At Salisbury Playhouse' Maiden Stakes Div 1 2yo   (D)
£4664 £1435 £718   **5f str**   **Good/Firm 36**   -22 Slow   Far side

1632 **OBE GOLD 5** [5] M R Channon 2-9-0 T E Durcan 11/2: 31: Handy, ev ch halfway, rdn out to lead   **91**
cl-home: op 9/2 on qck reapp: eff at 5f on fast: acts on a stiff/gall trk: imprvd today, see 1632.

1237 **GRAND OPTION 26** [4] B W Duke 2-9-0 T P Queally(3) 8/1: 03232: Led, hdd under press cl-home, no   ¾ **88**
extra: acts on fast & soft grnd: continues to run well & deserves to find similar: see 1237 & 1114.

ANGEL SPRINTS [9] L G Cottrell 2-8-9 A Daly 50/1: 3: b f Piccolo - Runs In The Family (Distant   2   **77**
Relative) Chsd ldrs, kept on fnl 1f, not pace of front 2: debut: Feb foal, cost 16,000gns: half-sister won
numerous times at 5f: dam won numerous times at 5/6f, sire Gr 1 wng sprinter: eff at 5f, shld stay 6f: acts on
fast grnd: encouraging eff & can find a mdn.

GALEOTA [2] R Hannon 2-9-0 P Dobbs 4/6 FAV: 4: b c Mujadil - Refined (Statoblest) Handy, sn   shd **81**
hung right, outpcd halfway, rallied ins fnl 1f, no threat to front 3: well bckd on debut: April foal, cost
150,000gns: eff at 5f on fast grnd: lkd in need of today's experience & can rate higher.

EMPIRES GHODHA [10]2-9-0 L Keniry(3) 20/1: 5: b c Mujadil - La Caprice (Housebuster) Cl-up, ev   ¾ **79**
ch after 3f, no extra fnl 1f: debut: Feb first foal, cost 25,000gns: dam wnr at 5f, sire speedily bred.

WOOD SPIRIT [1]2-8-9 R Havlin 50/1: 6: Bhd, nvr nrr than mid-div: debut.   ½   **73**

DARTANIAN [3]2-9-0 N Callan 66/1: 7: Nvr nrr than mid-div: debut.   1¾   **73**

HEIDIS DASH [6]2-8-9 S Drowne 7/1: 8: Rear, nvr a factor: op 5/1 on debut.   ¾   **66**

BLACK DRAFT [11]2-9-0 M O'Hara 66/1: 9: Slow away, al bhd.   1¾   **66**

DONT TELL TRIGGER [8]2-8-9 J D Smith 33/1: 0: 10th: Rear, nvr a factor.   nk   **60**

10 Ran   Time 1m 2.74 (2.94)   Owned: Mr M Channon   Trained: West Ilsley

---

1717   2.10 'Jamaica Inn At Salisbury Playhouse' Maiden Stakes Div 2 2yo   (D)
£4648 £1430 £715   **5f str**   **Good/Firm 36**   -07 Slow   Far side

BLACK VELVET [9] M P Tregoning 2-9-0 W Supple 5/1: 1: br c Inchinor - Three Owls (Warning)   **96+**
Made all, drvn out fnl 1f: debut, gd juv time: Feb first foal, cost 165,000gns: dam 1m wnr, sire Gr performer arnd
7f: eff at 5f, bred to apprec further: acts on fast grnd & a stiff/gall trk: goes well fresh: won here with
authority & reportedly heads for Gr 3 Coventry Stks at Royal Ascot.

BRAG [1] R Charlton 2-9-0 S Drowne 8/1: 2: b f Mujadil - Boast (Most Welcome) Handy, chsd wnr   2   **82**
dist, kept on but al held fnl 1f: op 6/1 on debut: March first foal, dam smart at sprint dists: sire speedily bred:
eff at 5f, 6f shld suit: acts on fast grnd: encouraging eff & can impr on today.

AGE OF KINGS [4] J H M Gosden 2-9-0 J Murtagh 6/5 FAV: 3: b c Kingmambo - Everhope (Danzig)   ½   **86**
Slow away, prog halfway, styd on well ins fnl 1f, nrst fin: well bckd on debut: Jan foal, cost $280,000: dam List
wnr abroad: sire Gr 1 wnr at 1m: eff at 5f, will apprec further: acts on fast grnd: promising eff after showing
signs of greenness, impr for today & find a mdn.

VERITABLE [7] S Kirk 2-8-9 P Dobbs 25/1: 4: Sn handy, onepcd bef 1f out: debut.   1½   **77**

1256 **CALY DANCER 24** [6]2-9-0 N Pollard 16/1: 05: Handy 3f, no extra dist: see 1256.   1   **79**

1510 **ATSOS 10** [3]2-9-0 Dane O'Neill 8/1: 66: Rear, prog after 2f, wknd 1f out.   3½   **69**

NANTON [8]2-9-0 R L Moore 8/1: 7: Handy till 2f out, sn wknd.   1   **66**

INCHCAPE ROCK [5]2-9-0 R Havlin 16/1: 8: Slow away, nvr a factor.   1½   **62**

KENWYN [11]2-9-0 F Norton 33/1: 9: Rear, nvr a factor.   hd   **61**

1538 **PIE CORNER 9** [2]2-9-0 L Keniry(3) 100/1: 00: 10th: Cl-up till halfway, fdd.   1¾   **56**

10 Ran   Time 1m 1.97 (2.17)   Owned: Lady Tennant   Trained: Lambourn

---

1718   2.40 Wise Catering Maiden Stakes Div 1 Fillies 3yo+   (D)
£5551 £1708 £854   **1m1f198y**   **Good/Firm 36**   +01 Fast   Inside

3789} **QUIFF 265** [1] Sir Michael Stoute 3-8-7 B Doyle 7/2: 5-1: b f Sadler's Wells - Wince (Selkirk)   **90+**
Handy al trav well, styd on to lead ins fnl 1f, pushed out, val 3L+: reapp: 5th of 8 on sole '03 start (fills mdn,
rtd 71): dam top-class miler, sire top-class mid-dist performer: eff at 10f, 12f shld suit: acts on fast grnd & a
stiff/gall trk: goes well fresh: showed a gd turn of foot here on only 2nd start, can rate higher.

4871} **DAWN SURPRISE 202** [9] Saeed bin Suroor 3-8-7 K McEvoy 11/8 FAV: 3-2: b f Theatrical - Lignify   1   **84**
(Confidential Talk) Cl-up, led after 1m, hdd ins fnl 1f, not pace easy wnr: clr rem, well bckd on reapp: 3rd of 22
on sole '03 start (mdn): dam top-class performer in Argentina: sire Breeders Cup turf wnr: eff at 1m/10f, further
shld suit: acts on fast grnd & a gall trk: lost little in defeat here on only 2nd start, can find similar.

FEAAT [2] J H M Gosden 3-8-7 W Supple 8/1: 3: b f Unfuwain - Trois Heures Apres (Soviet Star)   5   **79$**
Slow away, sn mid-div, kept on fnl 1f, no ch with front 2: debut: cost 190,000gns: not disgraced, improve.

4871} **SANTA CATERINA 202** [3] J L Dunlop 3-8-7 Dane O'Neill 50/1: 000-4: Held up, prog after halfway,   1   **77**
no impress fnl 1f: reapp: not disgraced on step up in trip & h'caps will suit.

1398 **MOONLIGHT TANGO 16** [4]3-8-7 (76) R Havlin 10/1: 04-55: Cl-up over 1m, wknd: see 1398.   nk   **76**

1019 **CRYSTAL CHOIR 42** [6]4-9-8 J Murtagh 50/1: 0-06: Led 1m, fdd: 6 wk abs.   5   **69**

1365 **BUBBLING FUN 19** [5]3-8-7 R L Moore 40/1: 02-47: Rear, nvr nrr than mid-div: btr 1365.   ¾   **66$**

1398 **UIG 16** [7]3-8-7 T E Durcan 100/1: 08: Keen mid-div, prog halfway, short of room 2f out, sn wknd.   5   **60**

1209 **APRON 27** [10]3-8-7 S Drowne 40/1: 09: Rear, prog halfway, fdd fnl 2f.   1½   **58**

2417} **FORCE OF NATURE 323** [8]4-9-8 Paul Eddery 4/1: 2-0: 10th: Keen handy 7f, wknd: reapp.   2   **55**

10 Ran   Time 2m 8.06 (3.56)   Owned: Mr K Abdulla   Trained: Newmarket

---

1719   3.10 Wise Catering Maiden Stakes Div 2 Fillies 3yo+   (D)
£5551 £1708 £854   **1m1f198y**   **Good/Firm 36**   -24 Slow   Inside

4070} **WELL KNOWN 251** [5] R Charlton 3-8-7 S Drowne 11/8 FAV: 2-1: b f Sadler's Wells - Danefair   **85**
(Danehill) Dictated pace, eased when clr ins fnl 1f, drvn out cl-home to hold on: well bckd on reapp: rnr-up on
sole '03 start (fills stks): half-sister to smart 7f/1m performer Trade Fair, dam high-class 10/12f performer in
France: eff at 7f, enjoyed step up to 10f: acts on fast grnd & a stiff/gall & easy trk: goes well fresh.

2 Sep'03 Kemp 7g/f 87- C:
1236 **ANNA PALLIDA 26** [9] P W Harris 3-8-7 T P Queally(3) 7/2: 02: b f Sadler's Wells - Masskana (Darshaan) Al cl-up, lkd held ins fnl 1f till styd on after wnr eased, just btn: tchd 13/2: mid-dist bred: eff at 10f, 12f shld suit: acts on fast grnd: prob shade flattered here tho' this was encouraging. *hd* **81**
GOSLAR [8] H Candy 3-8-7 Dane O'Neill 16/1: 3: ch f In The Wings - Anna of Brunswick (Rainbow Quest) Slow away, prog after 7f, kept ins fnl 1f, not btn far in 3rd: debut: well bred, eff at 10f, shld apprec further: acts on fast grnd: encouraging eff & can find similar. *nk* **80**
3648} **WOU OODD 271** [3] M R Channon 3-8-7 T E Durcan 33/1: 0-4: ch f Barathea - Abyaan (Ela Mana Mou) Slow away, styd on fnl 1f, not btn far: clr rem, reapp: unplcd sole '03 start (rtd 42, fill mdn): eff at 10f on fast. *¾* **78**
4871} **GARRYURRA 202** [7]3-8-7 B Doyle 7/2: 26-5: Chsd ldrs over 1m, sn no extra: op 5/2 on reapp. *4* **72**
881 **LEBENSTANZ 54** [4]4-9-8 N Mackay(3) 10/1: 66: Handy over 7f, no extra: op 20/1, 8 wk abs. *1¾* **69**
1384 **TWELVE BAR BLUES 17** [6]3-8-7 R Havlin 25/1: 07: Handy 1m, no extra. *nk* **68**
808 **SPOT IN TIME 69** [2]4-9-8 R Price 100/1: 08: Cl-up over 7f, wknd: 10 wk abs. *nk* **67**
759 **HIGHFLUTING 75** [1]3-8-7 D Kinsella 100/1: 09: Rear, nvr a factor: 11 wk abs. *28* **27**
9 Ran Time 2m 10.53 (6.03) Owned: Mr K Abdulla Trained: Beckhampton

1720

3.45 'racing Welfare Ken Carey Lifetime In Racing' Claiming Stakes 3yo (E)
£3536 £1088 £544 **6f212y str** **Good/Firm 36** **-13 Slow** Far side

1647 **WHIPLASH 3** [15] R Hannon 3-8-5 (59) R L Moore 16/1: 000-0401: Handy, styd on to lead ins fnl 1f, rdn out: qck reapp, clmd for 5,000: eff at 5/7f on fast: handles a sharp/undul & stiff/gall trk: first win. **58**
975 **JOY AND PAIN 44** [13] G L Moore 3-9-5 (58) T P Queally(3) 16/1: 0060162: Mid-div, prog & short of room after 4f, switched wide & kept on well ins fnl 1f, post came too sn: 6 wk abs: acts on fast & polytrack. *½* **70$**
1339 **LADY MO 19** [10] K A Ryan 3-9-0 (65) N Callan 4/1 FAV: 5110123: Handy, styd on to lead dist, hdd ins fnl 1f, no extra: clmd for 12,000: see 1339 & 1222. *1½* **62**
1081 **CITY GENERAL 36** [11] J S Moore 3-8-11 p (56) Derek Nolan(7) 12/1: 2550-334: Led till dist, no extra: op 20/1, clr rem: see 1081 & 996. *1¾* **55**
623 **THE FOOTBALLRESULT 89** [14]3-8-2 (58) Joanna Badger 50/1: 060-005: b f The West - Bunny Gee (Last Tycoon) Rear, nvr nrr than mid-div: unplcd in '03 (rtd 69, mdn). *6* **34**
1526 **ARFINNIT 10** [8]3-9-1 (70) T E Durcan 6/1: 000-0306: Chsd ldrs over 5f, wknd: btr 1054. *nk* **46**
824} **CLOUD CATCHER 418** [12]3-8-2 S Righton 33/1: 0-7: br f Charnwood Forest - Notley Park (Wolfhound) Slow away, nvr nrr than mid-div: reapp: unplcd sole '03 start (auct mdn). *2* **29**
1239 **DEIGN TO DANCE 26** [3]3-8-12 P (70) W Supple 8/1: 2620-508: Handy over 4f, wknd: cheek pieces. *1* **37**
1008 **FARNBOROUGH 43** [4]3-9-5 N Pollard 20/1: 0-509: Bhd, nvr a factor: btr 841. *½* **43**
1539 **MARKSGOLD 9** [7]3-8-7 (60) S Drowne 12/1: 000-3660: 10th: Handy till halfway, fdd. *nk* **30**
1539 **ROCKET 9** [9]3-8-11 Dane O'Neill 6/1: 0430: 11th: Handy 5f, fdd: btr 1539. *4* **26**
1577 **LIVIA 7** [1]3-8-6 P (50) R Miles(3) 50/1: 6040600: 12th: Trkd ldrs till halfway, wknd; pieces. *1* **19**
1054 **Spring Dancer 38** [5]3-9-0 (58) J Murtagh 20/1:0 671 **City Affair 85** [2]3-8-11 (60) V Slattery 14/1:0
14 Ran Time 1m 28.96 (3.46) Owned: Dr Thomas & Mrs Thelma Wade Trained: Marlborough

1721

4.20 Portway Rated Stakes Handicapfillies 4yo+ 0-95 (C) **[97]**
£8474 £3214 £1607 **1m4f** **Good/Firm 36** **+12 Fast** Stands side

1381 **DESERT ROYALTY 17** [2] E A L Dunlop 4-8-13 (82) W Supple 5/2 FAV: 13123-21: Held up, prog 3f out, styd on to lead ins fnl 1f, rdn out: gd time: wng form over 1m/12f: acts on firm & gd/soft, see 1381. **95**
1381* **TAWNY WAY 17** [7] W Jarvis 4-9-0 (83) S Drowne 9/2: 1220-512: Mid-div, prog after 1m, led bef 1f out, hdd ins fnl 1f, no extra: eff at 9/10f, imprvd here on step up to 12f: can find similar: see 1381. *1¾* **90**
3757} **PONGEE 266** [9] L M Cumani 4-9-4 (87) N Mackay(3) 15/2: 4/11110-3: b f Barathea - Puce (Darshaan) Held up, prog 3f out, onepcd fnl 1f: reapp: won first 4 of only 5 '03 starts (h'caps & class stks): 4th at best in '02 (nursery, rtd 67): eff at 10f, suited by around 12f: acts on firm, gd/soft & polytrack: acts on a stiff or easy trk: has gone well fresh: not disgraced here. *3* **92**
1 Jun'03 Sali 12fm 82-75 D: 1 Jun'03 Nott 10.0g/f 81-(75) F: 1 May'03 Ling 10ap 78a-70 E:
1 Apr'03 Yarm 10.1gd 76-(67) E:
1381 **DESERT ISLAND DISC 17** [10] J J Bridger 7-8-7 (76) R L Moore 13/2: 6030-044: Handy, led 3f out, hdd bef 1f out, wknd: just btr 1381. *2½* **77**
1484 **LARGO 12** [8]4-9-7 (90) K McEvoy 12/1: 11005-05: ch f Selkirk - Lady of The Lake (Caerleon) Handy 10f, wknd: reapp: fills mdn & class stks wnr in '03: dual mdn rnr-up in '02: proved eff at 7f/1m, stays 12f on fast & gd/soft grnd: sharper for today. 1 Jul'03 Wind 11.6g/f 93-(92) C:
1 Jun'03 Chep 12.1g/f 94-(83) D: 2 Oct'02 Wind 8.3g/s 85- D: 2 Oct'02 Leic 7gd 85- D: *1¼* **89**
1056 **RIBBONS AND BOWS 38** [4]4-8-6 (75) S Whitworth 25/1: 05600-06: gr f Dr Devious - Nichodoula (Doulab) Rear, nvr nrr than mid-div: unplcd in '03 (rtd 86, List): fills mdn wnr in '02: eff at 6/7f on fast & gd/soft grnd: acts on a stiff trk: with C A Cyzer. 2 Jul'02 Sand 7g/f 93- A: 1 Jun'02 Sali 6g/s 86- E: *½* **73$**
1027* **TIGHT SQUEEZE 41** [1]7-8-11 (80) C Catlin 8/1: 3001017: Handy 11f, wknd. *1¼* **76**
1399 **CLARADOTNET 16** [5]4-8-6 (75) T E Durcan 33/1: 210-008: Al in rear. *¾* **69**
1009 **DORIS SOUTER 43** [6]4-8-4 (3oh) (70) R Smith 12/1: 153-2059: Led till 3f out, fdd dist: 6 wk abs. *1½* **64**
1399 **MAYSTOCK 16** [3]4-8-8 vis (77) T P Queally(3) 14/1: 40-10300: 10th: Cl-up, ev ch after 1m, fdd fnl 2f. *3½* **63**
10 Ran Time 2m 35.29 (2.89) Owned: Mrs Janice Quy Trained: Newmarket

1722

4.55 Dutton Gregory Handicap Stakes 3yo 0-75 (E) **[82]**
£3757 £1156 £578 **6f str** **Good/Firm 36** **-06 Slow** Far side

615 **BRIDGEWATER BOYS 90** [9] K A Ryan 3-8-8 bl (62) N Callan 9/1: 215-4131: Handy, styd on to lead dist, drvn out: long abs: eff at 5/6f on firm, gd & loves fibresand: eff with blnks & goes well fresh: see 510. **72**
1539* **CORNWALLIS 9** [4] J S King 3-8-7 (6ex) (61) Hayley Turner(5) 14/1: 06-012: Mid-div, prog halfway, styd on well fnl 1f, just held: op 8/1, new stable: eff at 5.5f/6f on fast & soft grnd: only just denied from poor low draw & can find similar: see 1539 (R Guest). *½* **68**
1464 **DR SYNN 13** [5] J Akehurst 3-8-11 (65) S Hitchcott(3) 20/1: 6-063: Held up, prog wide after 4f, kept on fnl 1f, not btn far in 3rd: eff at 6f on fast grnd: not disgraced here on h'cap bow from low draw. *1½* **68**
1070 **ESTIHLAL 37** [14] E A L Dunlop 3-8-6 (60) W Supple 14/1: 60-04: b f Green Desert - Ta Rib (Mr Prospector) Held up, prog halfway, kept on fnl 1f, nrst fin: unplcd both '03 starts (rtd 61, mdn): eff at 6f, *shd* **63**

looks in need of 7f+: acts on fast grnd: encouraging run & can rate higher.
1102 **KRYSSA 35** [17]3-8-6 (60) R L Moore 7/2: 41335: Held up, prog halfway, onepcd ins fnl 1f: tchd 9/2. ½ **62**
119 **MOSCOW TIMES 166** [13]3-9-3 (71) J Murtagh 5/2 FAV: 600-6: b g Soviet Star - Bargouzine (Hotfoot) 2½ **66**
Chsd ldrs over 4f, no extra: well bckd on reapp: unplcd all 3 '03 starts (rtd 83, mdn): with D R C Elsworth.
1023 **SIMPSONS MOUNT 41** [12]3-9-1 (69) D Sweeney 25/1: 6537: Rear, nvr nrr than mid-div: 6 wk abs. *hd* **63**
4892} **SIGNOR PANETTIERE 201** [18]3-8-13 (67) P Dobbs 12/1: 400005-8: b c Night Shift - Christmas Kiss *shd* **60**
(Taufan) Handy over 4f, wknd dist: reapp: mdn wnr first time out in '03, subs shade disapp: eff at 5f on gd grnd: acts on an easy trk & goes well fresh: has had a wind operation. 1 Mar'03 Kemp 5gd 91- D:
1576* **MELAINA 7** [1]3-8-7 (6ex)p (61) P Makin(5) 12/1: 1-206119: Cl-up, led halfway, hdd dist, wknd. *nk* **53**
1054 **INSTINCT 38** [11]3-8-8 (62) Dane O'Neill 14/1: 0-50300: 10th: Slow away, al bhd. ½ **53**
4761} **ONE UPMANSHIP 210** [8]3-9-1 p (69) K McEvoy 33/1: 502430-0: 11th: Handy 4f, wknd. 3½ **51**
933 **DISCO DIVA 48** [7]3-9-0 (68) F Norton 25/1: 60152-00: 12th: Bhd, nvr a factor. 1½ **46**
4613} **BAHAMA BELLE 220** [16]3-8-8 (62) T E Durcan 50/1: 0000-0: 13th: Rear, nvr a factor. ½ **39**
5034} **BERTOCELLI 187** [15]3-9-7 (75) N Pollard 20/1: 550610-0: 14th: Handy 4f, fdd. *shd* **51**
1417 **RED SOVEREIGN 15** [3]3-9-4 (72) T P Queally(3) 25/1: 21366-00: 15th: Led 4f out, hdd halfway, fdd. 2½ **41**
1539 **JINKSONTHEHOUSE 9** [2]3-8-6 (60) A Daly 40/1: 50000-40: 16th: Al bhd: btr 1539. *1* **26**
1116 **KURINGAI 33** [10]3-9-3 (71) O Urbina 14/1: 20-04300: 17th: Led till 4f out, fdd: btr 1002. *3* **28**
17 Ran Time 1m 14.63 (2.53) Owned: Bishopthorpe Racing Trained: Hambleton

1723

5.25 Tryon Handicap Stakes 3yo+ 0-80 (D) **[80]**
£5980 £1840 £920 **6f212y str** **Good/Firm 36** **-04 Slow** Far side

1025 **GOODENOUGH MOVER 41** [19] J S King 8-9-1 (67) Hayley Turner(5) 5/1 JT FAV: 30000-21: Made all far **74**
rail, rdn out to hold on fnl 1f: 6 wk abs: eff at 6f, suited by 7f & stays 1m: acts on firm, soft & polytrack, likes Chepstow & Salisbury: goes well for today's pilot: see 1025 (reapp).
1024 **AND TOTO TOO 41** [5] P D Evans 4-9-0 bl (66) N Callan 12/1: 5-062442: Handy, kept on well ins fnl ½ **71**
1f, just held by wnr: 6 wk abs: not btn far here & can find similar: see 1024 & 760.
1525 **CHATEAU NICOL 10** [14] B G Powell 5-9-11 vis (77) J Murtagh 5/1 JT FAV: 0141333: Handy, styd on to *hd* **81**
chase wnr 1f out, not btn far in 3rd: proving consistent: see 1525 & 1251.
136 **RESONATE 163** [12] A G Newcombe 6-9-5 (71) Dane O'Neill 14/1: 152006-4: b c Erins Isle - *shd* **74**
Petronelli (Sir Ivor) Held up, prog wide after 5f, kept on fnl 1f, nrst fin: reapp: lady rider h'cap wnr in '03: ex-Irish, mdn wnr in '00 (J Bolger, rtd 104, rnr-up in List): eff btwn 5f & 7f, does stay 9f: acts on both firm & soft grnd, encouraging eff & can find similar.
2 Sep'03 Sali 7.0g/f 71-71 D: 1 Jul'03 Asco 7gd 71-65 C: 1 Oct'02 Donc 7sft 71- E:
1138 **LITTLE VENICE 31** [8]4-9-10 (76) Lisa Jones(3) 16/1: 63240-05: b f Fumo di Londra - Petrine *hd* **78**
(Petorius) Mid-div, hdwy when short of room after 5f, switched & styd on well fnl 1f, not btn far: h'cap & class stks wnr in '03: plcd on 4 of 6 '02 starts (mdns, rtd 72): suited by 7f & likes firm & gd, handles soft grnd, prob any trk: likes to force the pace.
2 Aug'03 Newm 7fm 79-75 C: 1 Jul'03 Newm 7fm 77-73 D: 1 Jun'03 Warw 7.1g/f 72-(73) D:
1530 **EPHESUS 10** [17]4-9-13 vis (79) W Supple 16/1: 0-300006: Rear, prog 3f out, hdwy when short of 1½ **79+**
room ins fnl 1f, not recover: poss plcd without interference: see 511.
1322 **DANIELLES LAD 20** [13]8-9-5 bl (71) T P Queally(3) 16/1: 0413037: Handy over 5f, no extra: btr 1322. *nk* **70**
1079 **MICHELLE MA BELLE 36** [1]4-9-9 (75) R L Moore 9/1: 655-0228: Mid-div, prog when hung badly right 3½ **67**
bef 1f out, no impress & sn eased: btr 1079 & 1024.
1512 **NIGHT KISS 10** [7]4-8-12 (64) R Smith 16/1: 00220-09: Rear, nvr nrr than mid-div: see 1512. 1¾ **52**
1354 **KEW THE MUSIC 19** [11]4-8-10 (62) T E Durcan 16/1: 0000-000: 10th: Bhd, nvr nrr than mid-div. *hd* **49**
1020 **MISTRAL SKY 42** [15]5-9-2 vis (68) S Drowne 13/2: 10-20020: 11th: Handy over 5f, sn wknd. 1¾ **51**
4438] **THREEZEDZZ 586** [3]6-8-13 (65) R Havlin 40/1: 0/00000/-0: 12th: Slow away, al in rear. ½ **47**
1474 **CORANGLAIS 12** [4]4-9-7 (73) S Carson 50/1: 62050-00: 13th: Handy 4f, wknd. ¾ **53**
1059 **Oh Boy 38** [10]4-8-13 (65) P Dobbs 33/1:0
1533 **Compton Arrow 9** [9]8-8-11 (63) S Hitchcott(3) 50/1:0
1344 **Point Calimere 19** [20]3-9-0 (78) K McEvoy 25/1:0 1423 **Craic Sa Ceili 15** [18]4-9-6 P(72) P Makin(5) 12/1:0
1151 **Secret Formula 30** [16]4-9-13 (79) L Keniry(3) 33/1:0 1481 **Bi Polar 12** [6]4-9-10 (76) N Pollard 14/1:0
19 Ran Time 1m 28.35(2.85) Owned: D Goodenough Removals & Transport Trained: Swindon

YARMOUTH FRIDAY 14.05.04 Lefthand, Flat, Fair Track

Official Going GOOD/FIRM.

1724

2.10 Betfred Com Now Online Selling Stakes 3-4yo (G)
£2569 £734 £367 **1m2f21y** **Good/Firm 39** **-14 Slow** Inside

489 **ESTIMATE 108** [10] John A Harris 4-9-2 vis (62) Paul Eddery 10/1: 264-0001: Dwelt, sn trkd ldrs, **53**
led over 3f out, in command when eased cl-home: op 8/1: eff at 8.5f/10f on fast: apprec drop to sell: see 489.
1611 **ROMEOS DAY 7** [1] M R Channon 3-8-6 (54) S Hitchcott(1) 6/1: 0000-02: ch g Pursuit of Love - *1* **54**
Daarat Alayaam (Reference Point) Chsd ldrs, rdn & kept on, not pace of wnr: lightly rcd & unplcd '03 (rtd 60, auct mdn): stays an easy 10f in sell grade on fast grnd.
1455 **FITZ THE BILL 15** [4] N B King 4-9-2 bl (30) J Mackay 20/1: 000-0033: Held up, eff to chase wnr *2* **46$**
over 2f out, no impress ins last: clr of rem: stays an easy 10f in sell grade on fast grnd: see 1455.
934 **STYLISH SUNRISE 49** [9] M L W Bell 3-8-6 (70) D Holland 7/2 JT FAV: 036-04: Prom, btn 2f out. *10* **37**
1193 **REGULATED 29** [7]3-8-12 (69) S Sanders 7/2 JT FAV: 50-20155: Dwelt, chsd ldrs till over 2f out. 2½ **39**
774 **SHATIN SPECIAL 75** [11]4-9-8 p (51) Dean Williams(7) 12/1: 2F41666: Led 1f, prom till 2f out: abs. *2* **31**
1630 **WARIF 6** [8]3-8-6 B Doyle 20/1: 000-57: ch c Diesis - Alshoowg (Riverman) Dwelt, led after 1f ¾ **29**
till over 3f out, fdd: qck reapp: lightly rcd & unplcd '03 (rtd 67 & 63a, J Dunlop).
DOVEDON LASS [5]3-8-1 J Quinn 40/1: 8: Slow away & al bhd on debut. *5* **17**
1160 **GOOD LOSER 30** [3]4-9-7 t (60) M Tebbutt 4/1: 20244-09: Slow away, sn struggling. *23* **0**
1130 **BYRD ISLAND 32** [6]3-8-1 J F Egan 25/1: 000: 10th: Held up, rdn & btn 3f out. *6* **0**
10 Ran Time 2m 09.51 (5.31) Owned: Mrs A E Harris Trained: Melton Mowbray

---

1725   **2.40 Lord Nelson - Royal Navy Maiden Stakes 3yo** (D)
£3533 £1087 £544   1m3f101y   Good/Firm 39   +08 Fast   Inside

1209 **MODESTA 28** [6] H R A Cecil 3-8-9   W Ryan 7/2: 41: Held up, eff to chase ldr over 2f out, rdn &   85
styd on to lead well ins last: eff at 10f, fast time: eff at 3/1, imprvd for step up to 11.5f: acts on fast & gd grnd,
gall/easy trks: lightly rcd filly, potentially useful: see 1209.
4736} **NEW MORNING 213** [8] M A Jarvis 3-8-9   P Robinson 8/11 FAV: 4-2: b f Sadler's Wells - Hellenic   1   82
(Darshaan) Trkd ldrs & keen, led over 2f out till well ins last: rest well covered: hvly bckd on reapp: promise
sole '03 start (rtd 73, mdn): strong mid-dist pedigree, styd longer 11.5f trip, shld get further: acts on fast &
gd/soft grnd, gall/easy trks: likely to be plcd to find similar.
1358 **TALWANDI 20** [5] Sir Michael Stoute 3-9-0   B Doyle 16/1: 63: b c Alhaarth - Talwara (Diesis)   5   80
Chsd ldrs, rdn/hung left & no impress dist: prob stays 11.5f & handles fast grnd, mid-dist pedigree.
        SHONGWENI [1] P J McBride 3-9-0   S Sanders 100/1: 4: gr g Desert King - Spend A Rubble (Spend A   2½   76
Buck) Dwelt & held up, kept on late, nrst fin on debut: shaped as if 12f+ will suit, mid-dist pedigree.
4971} **FORT CHURCHILL 195** [10]3-9-0   N Callan 100/1: 00-5: Held up, hung left & no impress fnl 2f: shd 76
reapp: has been gelded.
1358 **SUNSET MIRAGE 20** [7]3-8-9   W Supple 13/2: 0-26: Cl-up, wknd fnl 2f: btr 1358.   6   62
1495 **MISS MERENDA 12** [3]3-8-9   J Mackay 66/1: 07: Held up, struggling fnl 2f.   4   56
1370 **VAMOSE 19** [4]3-9-0 (69) D Holland 16/1: 0230-48: Led 1m, btn over 1f out, longer trip.   1   60
1140 **CLEAVER 32** [2]3-9-0   M Tebbutt 25/1: 0-59: Keen & prom, btn 2f out.   3½   55
        GLANWORTH [9]3-9-0   A Mackay 80/1: 0: 10th: Dwelt, pushed rear, strug halfway on debut.   dist 0
10 Ran   Time 2m 26.32 (3.52)   Owned: Mr K Abdulla   Trained: Newmarket

---

1726   **3.10 Betfred Sprint Series Qualifier A Handicap Stakes 3yo+ 0-85** (D)   **[85]**
£5434 £1672 £836   6f str   Good/Firm 39   -13 Slow   Stands Side

1523 **PINCHBECK 11** [11] M A Jarvis 5-9-5 p (76) P Robinson 9/3 JT FAV: 1033-041: Rdn & chsd ldrs, styd   82
on for press to lead well ins last: eff at 6f on firm & gd/soft grnd, apprec reapp of cheek pieces today: see 1523.
1255 **PRINCE HECTOR 25** [13] W J Haggas 5-9-7 (78) S Drowne 9/1: 30010-02: Held up, styd on well ins   ½   82
last, just failed: imprvd from reapp: eff at 6f, winning form at 1m: see 1255.
1523 **ARMAGNAC 11** [2] M A Buckley 6-9-6 (77) J Quinn 11/2: 460-0003: Held up, hdwy to chall ins last,   shd 80
just held cl-home: gd run, looks to have come to hand, likes Haydock: see 1138.
1481 **MR MALARKEY 13** [7] Mrs C A Dunnett 4-9-8 bl (79) T G McLaughlin 9/2 JT FAV: 4000-404: Led, hung   1¾   78
badly left over 1f out & hdd well in last: lost winning ch with steering problems late on: see 1354.
1400 **DUSTY DAZZLER 17** [12]4-10-0 (85) A Quinn(5) 9/1: 202-1605: Chsd ldrs, no extra fnl 1f: see 431 (AW). 1   81
1217 **WILLHEWIZ 28** [10]4-10-0 (85) J F Egan 15/2: 5101:056: Cl-up & ch dist, no extra: see 1217.   1¾   76
4925} **COMPLICATION 199** [5]4-8-10 bl (67) Lisa Jones(3) 33/1: 312000-7: b f Compton Place - Hard Task   hd   57
(Formidable) Chsd ldrs, btn dist: reapp: mdn scorer '03, subs h'cap rnr-up: eff at 6f on firm & fast grnd, easy
or stiff trk: eff in blnks. 2 Sep'03 Thir 6fm 43-67 E: 1 Sep'03 Thir 6g/f 68-(67) D:
1523 **MUSICAL FAIR 11** [8]4-9-6 (77) D Holland 10/1: 1340-008: b f Piccolo - Guarded Expression   ½   65
(Siberian Express) Held up, no impress dist: progressive '03, landed 4 h'caps: stays 6f, best at 5f: acts on firm
& fast grnd, prob any trk. 1 Aug'03 Wind 5.0g/f 77-71 E: 2 Jul'03 Donc 6g/f 71-69 D: 1 Jul'03 Catt 5fm 69-60 E:
2 Jul'03 Catt 6.0g/f 65-64 D: 1 Jul'03 Redc 5gd 57-54 E: 1 Jun'03 Warw 6.1fm 56-46 E:
1522 **PEDRO JACK 11** [3]7-9-1 (72) S Hitchcott(3) 22/1: 300-0109: Dwelt & held up, no impress fnl 2f.   3½   49
1267 **GONENDUNNETT 24** [4]5-7-13 (1ow)(5oh) (50) R Miles 25/1: 3-000000: 10th: Prom 4f, fdd.   hd   32
4818} **MANDARIN SPIRIT 207** [9]4-9-6 (77) S Sanders 25/1: 411000-0: 11th: Dwelt & al rear, reapp.   shd 53
1598 **Warden Warren 7** [6]6-9-1 p(72) B Reilly(3) 16/1:0   1255 **A Teen 25** [1]6-8-5 (62) Paul Eddery 14/1:0
13 Ran   Time 1m 13.49 (3.09)   Owned: Mr T G Warner   Trained: Newmarket

---

1727   **3.45 Saltwell Signs Maiden Auction Stakes Div 1 2yo** (F)
£2926 £836 £418   6f str   Good/Firm 39   -46 Slow   Stands Side

        HIGHLAND CASCADE [4] J M P Eustace 2-8-2   J Tate 16/1: 1: ch f Tipsy Creek - Highland Hannah   77
(Persian Heights) Chsd ldrs, led dist, styd on strongly: cheaply retained Feb foal: sire smart juv/sprinter: eff
at 6f, acts on fast grnd & an easy trk: goes well fresh: entitled to progress
        ACTIVE ASSET [12] M R Channon 2-9-0   S Hitchcott(3) 7/4 FAV: 2: ch c Sinndar - Sacristy   ½   86
(Godswalk), half-brother to several wnrs from 5f/1m, dam plcd at 5f: eff at 6f on fast grnd & an easy trk: gd
run conceding plenty of weight * shld find similar.
        KANAD [11] B Hanbury 2-8-11 T W Supple 10/1: 3: b c Bold Edge - Multi Sofft (Northern State)   ½   81
In tch racing keenly, chall over 1f out, kept on: 13,000gns April foal, half-brother to a 1m juv wnr, dam plcd at
13f: eff at 6f, could well apprec 1m+ in time: handles fast grnd & an easy trk: promising start.
1401 **HAROLDINI 17** [10] Mrs P N Dutfield 2-8-7   D Holland 7/2: 04: Led 3f, no extra ins last: op   1½   72
11/2, rest well covered: styd longer 6f trip.
1133 **SILVER VISAGE 32** [8]2-8-9   B Reilly(3) 12/1: 55: Chsd ldrs halfway, no extra dist.   3½   63
1380 **BE BOP ALOHA 18** [9]2-8-2 Lisa Jones(3) 25/1: 06: Dwelt, prom till hmpd & no extra 2f out.   2   50
1048 **DANES ROCK 39** [6]2-8-9   N Pollard 10/1: 47: Chsd ldrs, hung left & no impress over 1f out.   shd 57
        LADY SUESANNE [7]2-8-4   J F Egan 14/1: 8: Slow away & al outpcd: op 12/1.   ¾   50
        CRY OF THE WOLF [3]2-8-9 Steven Harrison(7) 33/1: 9: Dwelt & sn outpcd.   1   52
1538 **DUSTINI 10** [5]2-9-0 P A Quinn(5) 8/1: 3530: 10th: Chsd ldrs till over 1f out: op 6/1, cheek pieces. nk   56
        DAVALA [2]2-8-7   W Ryan 40/1: 0: 11th: Dwelt, sn outpcd on debut.   3½   38
11 Ran   Time 1m 16.09 (5.69)   Owned: Mr J M Ratcliffe   Trained: Newmarket

1728

4.20 Saltwell Signs Maiden Auction Stakes Div 2 2yo (F)
£2926 £836 £418 **6f str** **Good/Firm 39** **-37 Slow** Stands Side

1249 **ALTA PETENS 25** [6] M L W Bell 2-8-2 J Mackay 9/4 FAV: 41: Led/dsptd lead, went on 4f out, rdn clr dist, decisively: nicely bckd, confirmed debut promise: eff at 5f, relished this step up to 6f & shld get further: acts on fast & hvy, stiff or easy trk: progressive filly, looks potentially useful: see 1249. **82+**

1249 **MEGELL 25** [5] M G Quinlan 2-8-2 Lisa Jones(3) 3/1: 62: ch f Entrepreneur - Shalwell (Shalford) Handy, rdn & outpcd by wnr fnl 1f: well bckd, left hvy grnd debut bhd: clr of rem: E7,500 April foal, dam related to an Irish/French 2,000 Guineas wnr: imprvd for step up to 6f & fast grnd. *5* **66**

1190 **GRYSKIRK 29** [11] P W D'Arcy 2-8-9 Paul Eddery 14/1: 463: b c Selkirk - Gryada (Shirley Heights) Chsd ldrs, no impress dist: 9,000gns Feb foal: brother to a mid-dist wnr: dam a useful 7f/1m juv. *5* **58**

FONG SHUI [7] P J Makin 2-8-9 S Sanders 14/1: 4: ch c Dr Fong - Manila Selection (Manila) Dwelt, in tch, no impress fnl 2f: 8,000gns March foal, half-brother to a 6f juv wnr, dam unrcd. *2½* **50**

1380 **CLINET 18** [10]2-8-2 J Quinn 13/2: 05: Led 2f, btn over 1f out. *¾* **41**
1325 **FAITHISFLYING 21** [8]2-8-7 N Callan 66/1: 06: Prom till halfway. *1¼* **42**
LORD NORMACOTE [9]2-8-11 S Drowne 50/1: 7: Dwelt & sn outpcd. *nk* **45**
1256 **FAIR ALONG 25** [4]2-8-9 M Tebbutt 16/1: 08: Chsd ldrs till halfway. *½* **41**
UGLY SISTER [2]2-8-4 J F Egan 33/1: 9: Chsd ldrs, struggling halfway. *2* **30**
PACIFIC STAR [1]2-9-0 W Supple 4/1: 0: 10th: Held up & no impress from halfway: bckd. *hd* **39**
KERRYS BLADE [3]2-8-9 N Pollard 33/1: 0: 11th: Dwelt & sn outpcd. *12* **2**
11 Ran Time 1m 14.94 (4.54) Owned: Joy and Valentine Feerick Trained: Newmarket

1729

4.50 Hkb Wiltshires Legal Services Classified Stakes 3yo 0-65 (E)
£3630 £1117 £559 **7f str** **Good/Firm 39** **-32 Slow** Stands Side

4596} **SFORZANDO 223** [10] J A R Toller 3-8-11 (65) Lisa Jones(3) 25/1: 6500-1: Held up & hdwy over 1f out, led ins last, rdn out: first win, reapp: lightly rcd & unplcd '03 (rtd 67, mdn): eff at 7f, related to a 10f wnr & 1m+ could suit: acts on fast grnd & an easy trk, goes well fresh. **70**

1171 **SPEEDBIRD 30** [5] G Wragg 3-9-2 (70) J F Egan 15/2: 20-02: ch f Sky Classic - Egoli (Seeking The Gold) In tch, hdwy to lead over 1f out till ins last, kept on: mdn rnr-up '02: eff at 6/7f, 1m+ may suit: acts on fast grnd, sharp/easy trk. 2 Oct'03 Wind 6g/f 78- D: *1* **74**

1526 **DANDOUCE 11** [13] P W Chapple Hyam 3-9-2 (70) B Doyle 5/1: 423-63: Chsd ldrs, chall over 1f out, not pace of front pair: bckd: stays 7f: acts on polytrack & fast grnd: see 13. *1½* **71**

4577} **BEST DESERT 224** [2] J R Best 3-9-0 (65) N Pollard 20/1: 35602-4: Chsd ldrs & ch over 1f out, no extra: reapp: nursery h'cap rnr-up '03: eff over a sharp 7f, acts on fast grnd, sharp or stiff trk. *3* **63**

1359 **AESCULUS 20** [4]3-9-2 (70) N Mackay(3) 25/1: 051-05: Chsd ldrs, onepace fnl 2f. *2½* **60**
1129 **RIVER OF BABYLON 32** [16]3-8-11 (64) J Mackay 9/2 FAV: 50-26: Led 5f, btn dist: bckd: btr 1129. *hd* **54**
1554 **CANADIAN STORM 10** [12]3-9-5 (70) P Robinson 33/1: 050-57: Dwelt & held up, nvr on terms. *4* **54**
697 **GREEN FALCON 83** [14]3-9-1 (66) D Holland 11/2: 0338: Dwelt, handy till dist: op 13/2, abs. *shd* **50**
1359 **KING OF KNIGHT 20** [1]3-9-4 (69) O Urbina 20/1: 000-459: Chsd ldrs 5f: see 1130 (1m). *hd* **52**
1086* **HASAYIS 37** [11]3-9-2 (70) W Supple 11/2: 00-10: 10th: In tch, btn dist: op 3/1: btr 1086. *1* **48**
4462} **CARLA MOON 231** [6]3-8-11 (65) W Ryan 33/1: 600-0: 11th: Al rear: reapp, has been gelded. *1¾* **40**
631 **ORCHESTRATION 90** [7]3-9-4 (69) S Hitchcott(3) 33/1: 26-440: 12th: Prom, btn 2f out, abs. *6* **37**
111 **NEW YORK 168** [9]3-9-2 (70) S Drowne 20/1: 324-0: 13th: Chsd ldrs till 2f out, 5 mth abs. *hd* **34**
1007 **Fools Entire 44** [3]3-9-1 (66) J Quinn 14/1:0 1457 **Global Achiever 14** [17]3-9-0 (65) T G McLaughlin 66/1:0
1417 **Dellagio 16** [8]3-9-3 (68) S Sanders 40/1:0 455 **Fubos 114** [15]3-9-1 vis(66) N Callan 66/1:0
17 Ran Time 1m 27.54 (4.94) Owned: Mr P C J Dalby Trained: Newmarket

1730

5.20 Howards Holdings Handicap Stakes Fillies 3yo+ 46-55 (F) **[74]**
£3017 £862 £431 **6f str** **Good/Firm 39** **-30 Slow** Stands Side

1576 **PRINCESS GALADRIEL 8** [15] J R Best 3-8-4 (50) N Pollard 10/1: 0040-21: Pushed along towards rear, strong run for press from over 1f out & led well ins last, going away: eff at 6f, 7f will suit: acts on fast & soft grnd, sharp/undul or easy trk: type to prog: see 1576. **63**

2810} **COME AWAY WITH ME 308** [12] M A Buckley 4-9-2 (52) J Quinn 6/1 JT FAv: 012-2: b f Machiavellian - Vert Val (Septieme Ciel) Led/dsptd lead, went on over 1f out, edged right & hdd well ins last, no extra: op 7/1, reapp: mdn scorer '03, subs AW h'cap rnr-up: eff at 6/7f, has tried 1m: acts on fast grnd & fibresand, sharp/turning or easy trk: gd return. 2 Jul'03 Wolv 6af 52a-50 E: 1 Jun'03 Thir 7g/f 53- D: *1½* **59**

436 **VENDORS MISTAKE 116** [17] Andrew Reid 3-8-2 (48) J F Egan 40/1: 600-063: b f Danehill - Sunspangled (Caerleon) Led/dsptd lead, onepace for press ins last: 4 mth abs: lightly rcd & unplcd '03 (rd 63a, AW mdn): eff at 6f, has tried 1m: acts on fast grnd & an easy trk: promising turf debut. *1¼* **51**

4311} **MANNORA 239** [14] P Howling 4-9-3 (53) S Drowne 8/1: 100430-4: b f Prince Sabo - Miss Bussell (Sabrehill) In tch far side, kept on for press: reapp: '03 fills mdn scorer, subs h'cap plcd (rtd 53): eff at 6f on fast grnd, stiff or sharp/undul trk. 1 Jun'03 Newc 6g/f 58-(49) D: *shd* **56**

4824} **EMMERVALE 206** [11]5-9-0 vis (50) B Doyle 50/1: 036100-5: Chsd ldrs, kept on, reapp. *shd* **52**
1132 **RANNY 32** [4]4-8-13 (49) N Chalmers(5) 12/1: 00-42206: In tch, not pace to chall: btr 913 & 799. *1½* **46**
1577* **PICKLE 8** [6]3-9-1 (6ex) (61) D Holland 6/1 JT FAV: 30417: Chsd ldrs, onepace: btr 1577 (soft). *¾* **56**
1085 **DOCKLANDS BLUE 37** [20]3-8-6 BL (52) Steven Harrison(7) 25/1: 0364308: Dwelt & bmpd start, late gains, nrst fin, blnks. *2* **41**
4877} **CAERPHILLY GAL 203** [3]4-9-5 (55) R Miles(3) 20/1: 513040-9: Chsd ldrs till dist, reapp. *nk* **43**
4618} **ESSEX STAR 221** [10]3-8-7 (53) B Reilly(3) 50/1: 0000-0: 10th: Held up, no impress, reapp. *1¾* **36**
1220 **PRINCESS BANKES 27** [19]3-8-9 (55) Dean Williams(7) 33/1: 0605-060: 11th: Sn outpd . *½* **36**
1522 **RED LEICESTER 11** [9]4-9-0 (50) W Ryan 14/1: 46000-30: 12th: Chsd ldrs 5f: btr 1522. *shd* **31**
1641* **PARDON MOI 4** [1]3-8-5 (6ex) (51) Lisa Jones(3) 14/1: 4400410: 13th: Prom, kept on. *½* **30**
958 **INCHING 46** [18]4-8-12 t (48) A Quinn(5) 10/1: 26-44000: 14th: Chsd ldrs till halfway, 6 wk abs. *1¼* **23**
911 **JOANS JEWEL 51** [16]3-8-8 (54) J Tate 7/1: 5560: 15th: Prom 3f, abs, h'cap bow. *6* **11**
1374 **ANISETTE 18** [13]3-8-7 (1ow)VIS (52) N Callan 50/1: 2-3060: 16th: Prom till halfway: tried a visor. *2* **4**
5015} **Scarlett Breeze 190** [2]3-8-7 (53) P Robinson 10/1:0

YARMOUTH   FRIDAY 14.05.04   Lefthand, Flat, Fair Track

4728} Cut Ridge 214 [8]3-8-11 (47) W Supple 20/1:0
1540 **Cloudless 10** [5]4-9-3 (53) S Hitchcott(3) 12/1:0   129 **Gunnhildr 167** [7]4-9-4 (54) S Sanders 40/1:0
20 Ran   Time 1m 14.52 (4.12)   Owned: Mrs Pam Akhurst   Trained: Maidstone

---

1731   5.50 Custom Kitchens Classified Stakes 4yo+ 0-60 (F)
£2905 £830 £415   **7f str**   **Good/Firm 39**   **-22 Slow**   Stands Side

685 **WARLINGHAM 84** [4] P Howling 6-9-0 (57) S Sanders 5/2: 0011501: Held up, hdwy & led dist, rdn   **60**
out: bckd, 12 wk abs: eff at 6f, suited by 7f on firm, gd & both AWs, loves a sharp/easy trk & can go well fresh.
1366 **CRYFIELD 20** [1] N Tinkler 7-9-0 (58) Kim Tinkler 15/8 FAV: 605-0062: Trkd ldrs, rdn to chall ins   nk **59**
last, just held: nicely bckd: see 1214.
1319 **AGUILA LOCO 21** [2] Mrs Stef Liddiard 5-9-0 p (56) S Drowne 4/1: 0620303: Led 5f, kept on ins last.   ½ **57**
1542 **TUSCAN TREATY 10** [5] T T Clement 4-8-11 (57) J Mackay 11/2: 0000-004: Chsd ldrs, lost tch fnl 2f.   11 **24**
1518 **TATA NAKA 11** [3]4-8-11 (45) Lisa Jones 16/1: 0650-005: Chsd ldr, btn 2f out: see 757.   2 **18**
5 Ran   Time 1m 26.90(4.3)   Owned: Mr David Andrew Brown   Trained: Newmarket

---

NEWBURY   FRIDAY 14.05.04   Lefthand, Flat, Galloping Track

Official Going GOOD (GOOD/SOFT places).

1732   1.30 Listed Cantor Sport Carnarvon Stakes 3yo (A)
£17400 £6600 £3300   **6f8y str**   **Good 42**   **+ 07 Fast**   Stands Side

1234 **SO WILL I 27** [8] M P Tregoning 3-8-11 (109) R Hills 15/8 FAV: 41-31: Waited with, prog wide over   **107**
1f out, srtong run to lead ins fnl 1f, drvn out: well bckd, best time of day: stays 7f, apprec this return to 6f:
acts on gd & fast grnd: v useful, got the run of today's race: see 1234 (7f Greenham).
1421 **MAC LOVE 16** [5] J Akehurst 3-8-11 (102) G Carter 40/1: 3232-542: Mid-div, short of room fnl 1f,   1 **104**
styd on strongly & not btn far: fine run from this outsider, found trouble: see 1421.
1106 **NIGHTS CROSS 34** [4] M R Channon 3-9-1 (104) A Culhane 20/1: 03212-43: Held up, short of room sev   hd **108**
times fnl 1.5f, fin strongly but too late: stays a gall 6f well: another to find trouble, consistent & ran to v best.
4833*}**RUM SHOT 206** [2] H Candy 3-8-11 (97) Dane O'Neill 8/1: 611-4: b c Efisio - Glass (Bering) Nvr   ½ **102**
far away, led ent fnl 1f, no extra cl home: sound reapp: won 2 of 3 '03 starts (mdn & stks): eff at 6f on gd & fast
grnd: handles a flat or sharp trk: spot on next time.   1 Oct'03 Yarm 6.0gd 100- C: 1 Oct'03 Wind 6g/f 99- D:
3874}**BOTANICAL 263** [7]3-8-11 (104) T L Dettori 14/1: 1204-5: b c Seeking The Gold - Satin Flower (Shadeed)   1 **99**
Nvr far away, led after halfway till ent fnl 1f, no extra: reapp, tried a t-strap: '03 debut wnr (mdn), subs 8L 2nd
to Three Valleys in Gr 3 Coventry then disapp twice, incl in a visor (D Loder): eff at 6f on fast & firm grnd: can
run well fresh: now with Saeed bin Suroor.   2 Jun'03 Asco 6g/f 102- A: 1 May'03 York 6.0fm 100- D:
1400 **LA CUCARACHA 17** [9]3-8-6 (99) M Hills 3/1: 11-26: Rear, no room fnl 2f, eased ins fnl 1f: op   hd **94+**
9/4: no run at any stage, rider given a 4-day careless riding ban: must be given another chance, see 1400.
1387 +**SEVILLANO 18** [3]3-8-11 (106) T E Durcan 6/1: 2132-117: Front rank, wknd fnl 1f: see 1387 (5f).   2 **93**
1421 **CRAFTY FANCY 16** [11]3-8-6 (93) T Quinn 40/1: 5655-238: Sn outpcd & nvr dngrs: see 1421 (soft).   7 **68**
1106 +**IF PARADISE 34** [10]3-9-1 (105) R Hughes 14/1: 16205-19: Led till after halfway, wkng when hmpd   2½ **70**
dist: bt today's 3rd in 1106 (5f soft).
4947}**INNCLASSIC 197** [6]3-8-6 (104) E Ahern 100/1: 03-0: 10th: b f Stravinsky - Kyka (Blushing John) Chsd   25 **0**
ldrs till halfway, wknd & eased, t.o.: plcd on 2nd of 2 '03 starts (stks, rtd 77a): eff at 5f on polytrk, 6f shld suit.
1167 **VENABLES 30** [1]3-9-1 t (104) J Murtagh 33/1: 1140-500: 11th: Sn well bhnd, t.o. & eased.   10 **0**
11 Ran   Time 1m 13.73 (2.13)   Owned: Mr Hamdan Al Maktoum   Trained: Lambourn

---

1733   2.00 Listed Swettenham Stud Trial Stakes Fillies 3yo (A)
£17400 £6600 £3300   **1m2f6y**   **Good 42**   **-21 Slow**   Centre

1494 **RAVE REVIEWS 12** [2] J L Dunlop 3-8-9 (81) K Darley 7/1: 61-31: Chsd ldrs, rdn to chall dist,   **105**
styd on strongly to get up cl home, drvn out: eff at 10f on gd & firm, 12f shld suit: lightly rcd & improving.
1494 **SAHOOL 12** [4] M P Tregoning 3-8-9 (86) R Hills 4/1: 61-22: Prom, went on over 3f out till worn   ¾ **103**
down cl home: well bckd: eff at 10f on firm & soft grnd: deserves similar, bt today's wnr in 1494.
1568 **CRYSTAL CURLING 9** [7] B W Hills M Hills 9/2: 21-33: Held up, styd on fnl 1f, not trouble   2½ **98**
front 2: return to 12f will suit judged on this: see 1568 (11.5f, reapp).
1209* **WINDS OF MARCH 28** [5] J H M Gosden 3-8-9 (95) L Dettori 5/4 FAV: 14: Chsd ldrs, eff & bmpd 2f   2 **95**
out, sn onepcd: hvly bckd: progressive in season & this shld be forgiven: see 1209 (debut).
1568 **ITHACA 9** [1]3-8-9 (102) R Hughes 16/1: 120-365: Waited with, nvr nr ldrs: again bhnd today's   3 **90**
3rd in 1568, see 1150 (7f, reapp).
1101 **FIRE FINCH 36** [8]3-8-9 T E Durcan 100/1: 66: ch f Halling - Fly For Fame (Shaadi) Held up, nvr   6 **81**
a factor: highly tried: with M Channon.
1468* **PONT ALLAIRE 14** [6]3-8-9 (79) Dane O'Neill 12/1: 4-17: Led till 3f out, wknd: up in grade after   8 **69**
1468 (fill mdn, 1m soft, slow time).
7 Ran   Time 2m 09.16 (6.36)   Owned: Prince A A Faisal   Trained: Arundel

---

1734   2.30 Scottish Equitable/Jockeys Association Of Great Britain Stakes Handicap 3yo 0-85 (D)   [92]
£6188 £1904 £952   **6f8y str**   **Good 42**   **+03 Fast**   Stands Side

1154 **WYATT EARP 31** [9] J A R Toller 3-8-10 (74) J Murtagh 12/1: 046-01: b g Piccolo - Tribal Lady   **78**
(Absalom) Waited with, hdwy 2f out, led ins fnl 1f, drvn out: fair time, tchd 6/1: lightly rcd juv, 4th in a
Newmarket mdn (rtd 81): half-brother to wnrs around 1m: eff at 6f, shld stay 7f: acts on gd & fast grnd, handles
a stiff/gall trk: does not look harshly treated & could follow up.
1239 **MISSUS LINKS 27** [6] R Hannon 3-8-6 (70) R Hills 6/1: 1-52: Tried to make all, battled on well &   nk **74**
only just btn: acts on gd, soft grnd & polytrack: lightly rcd, loves to front run: see 1239 & 135.

1281* **PRIMO WAY** 24 [8] B W Hills 3-9-2 (80) M Hills 7/2: 435-13: Mid-div, short of room dist, switched **shd 84**
& fin well but too late: nicely bckd: fine eff in the circumstances, worth a try over 7f now: see 1281.

    DELPHIE QUEEN 215 [10] S Kirk 3-9-3 (81) R Hughes 20/1: 454410-4: ch f Desert Sun - Serious **hd 85+**
Delight (Lomond) Mid-div, short of room dist & again ins fnl 1f, fin strongly: reapp: ex-Irish, mdn wnr at
Listowel in '03: winning form at 6f on gd grnd: lkd a shade unlucky here & one to keep in mind.

1570 **INSTANT RECALL** 9 [4]3-9-0 (78) L Dettori 10/3 FAV: 31045: Held up, hdwy wide fnl 1f, nrst fin. **hd 81**

1404 **AFTER THE SHOW** 17 [2]3-8-5 (1ow) (68) T E Durcan 25/1: 4051-606: Keen & prom, onepcd fnl 1f. **1 68**

4773} **JIMMY RYAN** 210 [3]3-9-6 (84) J P Guillambert(3) 16/1: 314-7: b c Orpen - Kaysama (Kenmare) Keen **1½ 80**
& front rank, wknd fnl 1f on reapp: won middle of 3 juv starts (mdn), subs nursery h'cap 4th: eff at 6f on fast
grnd, handles a sharp or gall trk: sharper next time. 1 Sep'03 Nott 6.1g/f 85- D:

4729} **I WONT DANCE** 213 [5]3-9-4 (82) R Smith 25/1: 012-8: b c Marju - Carnelly (Priolo) Dwelt, keen **¾ 75**
in rear, keeping on when hmpd cl-home: reapp: lightly rcd in '03, mdn auct wnr, subs stks rnr-up: eff at 6f, prob
stays a gall 7f: acts on fast grnd & a stiff/gall trk: can run well fresh: with R Hannon & longer priced
stablemate of rnr-up. 2 Oct'03 Leic 7.0g/f 82-(81) C: 1 Sep'03 Newm 6g/f 83- E:

494* **KABREET** 107 [7]3-9-7 (85) Dane O'Neill 7/1: 3101-319: Held up, prog wide 2f out, btn dist: **3½ 68**
top-weight: long abs since 494 (AW).

1488 **PERUVIAN STYLE** 13 [1]3-8-12 (76) K Darley 10/1: 01-11050: 10th: Chsd ldrs, wknd over 1f out. **½ 58**

1513 **HILITES 11** [11]3-9-5 (83) D Nolan(7) 12/1: 01004-30: 11th: Slowly away, al rear: see 1513. **5 50**

11 Ran   Time 1m 13.96 (2.36)   Owned by Byculla Thoroughbreds   Trained: Newmarket

---

1735

3.00 Sanctuary Group Conditions Stakes Fillies 2yo (C)
£7517 £2851 £1426   **5f34y str**   **Good 42**   **-12 Slow**   Stands Side

1170* **SIENA GOLD** 30 [2] B J Meehan 2-8-11 L Dettori 3/10 FAV: 11: Trkd ldr, went on over 1f out, styd **98+**
on strongly, readily under hands & heels riding: hvly bckd, fair juv time: highly regarded, v speedy filly, eff at
5f on gd grnd: likes to run up with or force the pace & looks an ideal Queen Mary type, see 1170.

    INDIANNIE STAR [4] M R Channon 2-8-5 T E Durcan 25/1: 2: b f Fraam - Ajig Dancer (Niniski) **1 86**
Chsd ldrs, kept on well fnl 1f but not pace of wnr: Jan first foal: dam a 7f wnr, sire a smart miler: eff at 5f on
gd, 6f shld suit: plenty to like about this encouraging debut, met an above average rival: shld find similar.

1362* **POLLY ALEXANDER** 20 [5] M J Wallace 2-8-11 K Darley 10/1: 5113: Led till over 1f out, no extra: **1 89**
far from disgraced under jt top-weight, acts on gd & soft grnd: see 1362.

    SPIRIT OF CHESTER [1] Mrs P N Dutfield 2-8-5 R Havlin 25/1: 4: b f Lend A Hand - It Takes Two **nk 82**
(Alzao) Slowly away, styd on late, nvr dngrs on debut: £30,000 April foal: half-sister to sprint wnr Final Exam:
sire a high-class sprinter/miler: 6f will suit judged on this & sure to benefit from this experience.

    BENTLEYS BUSH [3]2-8-5 R Smith 33/1: 5: ch f Baratheа - Veiled Threat (Be My Guest) Slowly **2½ 75**
away, nvr a factor tho' some late hdwy on debut: 45,000gns April foal: sister to a wnr in France: sir a top-class
miler: bred to apprec 6/7f+ given time: lost all chance at the start today, sure to improve.

    UNREAL [6]2-8-5 M Hills 6/1: 6: b f Dansili - Illusory (Kings Lake) Chsd ldrs, wknd & eased **1 72**
fnl 1f on debut: Feb foal, half-sister to numerous wnrs: dam a sprint wnr, sire a top-class miler: with B Hills.

6 Ran   Time 1m 03.03 (2.73)   Owned: Mr N Attenborough & Mrs L Mann   Trained: Upper Lambourn

---

1736

3.35 Tkp Surfacing Handicap Stakes 3yo+ 0-80 (D)   **[80]**
£6370 £1960 £980   **1m2f6y**   **Good 42**   **-27 Slow**   Centre

4614} **HAWRIDGE PRINCE** 221 [12] L G Cottrell 4-9-10 (76) S Carson 12/1: 0312-1: b g Polar Falcon - **85**
Zahwa (Cadeaux Genereux) Trkd ldrs, imprvd to lead 2f out, styd on strongly fnl 1f, rdn out: tchd 16/1, reapp: '03
mdn wnr, subs h'cap rnr-up: eff at 1m/10f on gd & fast grnd: handles a sharp or stiff/gall trk, clearly runs v well
fresh: gd weight-carrier, only lightly rcd & open to more improvement.
2 Oct'03 Wind 10.0g/f 76-73 D: 1 Aug'03 Wind 8.3gd 76- D:

1650 **SHREDDED** 4 [5] J H M Gosden 4-9-9 (75) R Havlin 25/1: 3/54-02: b c Diesis - Shiitake (Green **1¼ 81**
Dancer) Chsd ldrs, styd on strongly to snatch 2nd cl-home, not reach wnr: qck reapp: twice rcd in '03, mdn 4th
(rtd 72): eff at 10f on gd & gd/soft grnd, handles a stiff/gall trk: shld find similar if repeating this.

1430 **DICKIE DEADEYE** 16 [16] G B Balding 7-8-4 (56) R Thomas(5) 14/1: 50-65223: Prom, led 4f out till **hd 62**
2f out, caught for 2nd cl-home: another consistent run: see 1430 & 1254.

1352 **TODLEA** 20 [2] J A Osborne 4-9-7 (73) J Murtagh 14/1: 0000-644: Chsd ldrs, kept on under press **1¾ 76**
fnl 1f, nrst fin: acts on gd & firm grnd, eff at 1m/10f: not much luck here: see 1352.

1346 **DREAM MAGIC** 20 [15]6-9-11 (77) S Whitworth 12/1: 0044-405: Chsd ldrs, onepcd fnl 1f: see 1235 (C/D). **½ 79**

1423 **J R STEVENSON** 16 [8]8-9-10 (76) L Dettori 7/1: 351-2046: Mid-div, styd on late, nvr dngrs: see 1423. **1¾ 75**

1519 **BRIAREUS** 11 [7]4-9-12 (78) K Darley 7/1: 24-00027: Led early, remained prom, left bhd fnl 1f. **nk 76**

1650 **INVITATION** 4 [13]6-9-4 (70) R Smith 8/1: 00-06428: Rear, hdwy wide fnl 2f, not rch ldrs: qck reapp. **nk 67**

1478 **BARRY ISLAND** 13 [3]5-9-12 (78) K Fallon 11/2 FAV: 5244309: Held up, short of room over 2f out, **hd 75**
nvr nr to chall: bckd from, 7/1: btr 1235.

1296 **CLASSIC ROLE** 23 [9]5-9-11 vis (77) R Hughes 11/1: 3412200: 10th: Chsd ldrs, rdn & btn dist. **3 69**

1056 **LADY MCNAIR** 39 [11]4-9-10 (76) T E Durcan 14/1: 04446-40: 11th: Rdn in rear, nvr nr ldrs: see 1056. **nk 67**

1098 **TRAVELLERS TALE** 36 [4]5-9-2 (68) D Kinsella 16/1: 034-0060: 12th: Chsd ldrs, wknd after 1m. **3½ 54**

3695} **FACTUAL LAD** 270 [17]6-9-2 (68) T Quinn 50/1: 245110-0: 13th: b g So Factual - Surprise Surprise **1¾ 54**
(Robellino) Led after 2f, hdd 4f out, sn wknd on reapp: won 3 h'caps in '03: likes to race with/force the pace
around 10f on firm, fast & prob hvy grnd, handles both AWs: likes a sharp/undul trk: has tried cheek pieces, btr
without: with B Millman. 1 Aug'03 Brig 9.9fm 69-67 E: 1 Jul'03 Folk 9.7g/f 68-61 F: 2 Feb'03 Ling 10ap 58a-56 F:

2108} **MAJOR BLADE** 336 [18]6-8-9 (61) R Hills 50/1: 203/006-0: 14th: Nvr nr ldrs on reapp. **nk 44**

1519 **BEST FLIGHT 11** [1]4-9-6 (72) M Hills 16/1: 0341-00: 15th: Nvr btr than mid-div. **nk 54**

1650 Dens Joy **4** [6]8-8-0 (52) D Fox(5) 33/1:0   3108} Aragons Boy 295 [10]4-9-5 (71) Dane O'Neill 33/1:0

1423 Huxley 16 [19]5-9-11 (77) P McCabe 50/1:0   1056 Royal Trigger 39 [14]4-9-4 T(70) E Ahern 50/1:0

19 Ran   Time 2m 09.77 (6.97)   Owned: Mr Eric Gadsden   Trained: Cullompton

1737   4.10 Dickie Gaskell Maiden Stakes 3yo (D)
£6240 £1920 £960   1m2f6y   **Good 42**   -19 Slow   Centre

REMAADD [15] M P Tregoning 3-9-0 K Darley 5/1: 1: gr c Daylami - Bint Albaadiya (Woodman)   102
Chsd ldrs, imprvd to lead 2f out, styd on strongly, drvn out: tchd 13/2, debut: sire a high-class mid-dist
performer: eff over a gall 10f on gd, runs well fresh: reportedly held in some regard & open to improvement.
1501 **MASSIF CENTRALE 12** [5] D R C Elsworth 3-9-0 J Murtagh 10/3 FAV: 02: ch c Selkirk - Madame   1¾   98
Dubois (Legend of France) Rear, switched wide & hdwy 2f out, kept on but not quite get there: bckd from 11/2, clr
of rem: half-brother to several wnrs: dam a high-class mid-dist performer, sire a v smart miler: eff at 10f on gd
grnd: looks sure to find similar.
HAADEF [17] J H M Gosden 3-9-0 R Hills 8/1: 3: b c Sadler's Wells - Taqreem (Nashwan) Pushed   4   92
in rear, switched wide & styd on well fnl 1f, nrst fin on debut: ran green: mid-dist bred, holds several big race
entries: 12f shld now suit & sure to improve.
DOUBLE ASPECT [13] Sir Michael Stoute 3-9-0 S Whitworth 33/1: 4: b c Dr Fong - Spring   shd   92+
(Sadler's Wells) Slowly away, staid on nicely closing stages, nrst fin on debut: crying out for 12f judged on this:
plenty to like about this most encouraging first effort.
4559} **PRESENT ORIENTED 225** [10]3-9-0 P Doe 14/1: 56-5: Prom, led 3f out till 2f out, wknd fnl 1f on   3½   87
reapp: now qual for h'caps.
1166 **KASKA 30** [16]3-8-9 M Hills 12/1: 06: Chsd ldrs, btn 2f out.   1¼   80
DUNE RAIDER [4]3-9-0 R Havlin 10/1: 7: Mid-div, onepcd when short of room fnl 1f: shorter   3   80
priced stablemate of 4th, bckd from 25/1.
4906} **FU FIGHTER 200** [8]3-9-0 E Ahern 33/1: 54-8: Led till 3f out, wkng when hmpd 2f out on reapp.   6   71
GOLDEN KEY [3]3-9-0 K Fallon 8/1: 9: Chsd ldrs, btn 2f out on debut: s/mate of 4th.   ¾   70
SINISTRA [11]3-8-9 T Quinn 14/1: 0: 10th: Chsd ldrs, rdn & btn 2f out on debut: op 10/1.   6   56
GIFT VOUCHER [2]3-9-0 S Carson 25/1: 0: 11th: Nvr nr ldrs on debut.   ½   60
5024} **PURR 189** [9]3-9-0 T E Durcan 50/1: 0-0: 12th: Al towards rear on reapp: has been gelded.   6   51
1166 **TUMBAGA 30** [6]3-9-0 R Hughes 6/1: 00: 13th: Prom, wknd 3f out: op 9/2.   nk   50
4652} **Plovers Lane 219** [1]3-9-0 Dane O'Neill 100/1:0   873 **Ocean Rock 56** [14]3-9-0 P McCabe 100/1:0
1511 **High View 11** [18]3-9-0 R Smith 100/1:0   4445} **True Patriot 232** [19]3-9-0 D Kinsella 100/1:0
17 Ran   Time 2m 08.95(6.15)   Owned: Sheikh Ahmed Al Maktoum   Trained: Lambourn

Official Going GOOD/SOFT.

1738   2.20 European Breeders Fund Novice Stakes 2yo (D)
£4823 £1484 £742   6f15y str   **Soft 103**   -13 Slow   Inside

1353* **GOODRICKE 20** [4] D R Loder 2-9-2 T P Queally(3) 4/9 FAV: 211: Held up, prog halfway, styd on to   99+
lead dist, pushed out, val 4L+: well bckd at odds-on: eff at 5f, improvd for step up to 6f: acts well on gd/soft &
soft grnd: imprvg juv who showed a gd turn of foot here, deserves step up to Listed grade: see 1353.
1510 **STEDFAST MCSTAUNCH 11** [1] B J Meehan 2-8-12 L Keniry(3) 22/1: 42: Handy, outpcd halfway, rallied 3   84
ins fnl 1f, no ch with easy wnr: eff at 6f, will apprec further: acts on soft grnd: encouraging eff, see 1510.
1424 **LINCOLNEUROCRUISER 16** [7] J O'Reilly 2-8-12 J D O'Reilly(7) 12/1: 523: Carried right after   1¼   80
start, handy 4f, sn outpcd, rallied ins fnl 1f: see 1424.
1424* **KINGS GAIT 16** [3] T D Easterby 2-9-5 D Allan(3) 25/1: 614: Cl-up & ev ch after 4f, wknd dist.   shd   86
1173 **DANTES DIAMOND 29** [6]2-8-12 S W Kelly 5/1: 225: Led till dist, wknd: below form on today's   3½   70
soft grnd: btr 1173 (gd) & 1001 (firm).
1367* **IM SPARTACUS 19** [5]2-9-5 D Nolan(3) 25/1: 0216: Handy 4f, wknd & sn eased: btr 1367 (fast).   5   64
1422 **NORCROFT 16** [2]2-9-5 P Dobbs 12/1: 2167: Slow away, al in rear: twice below win of 1237 (gd).   5   51
7 Ran   Time 1m 17.78 (6.98)   Owned: Sheikh Mohammed   Trained: Newmarket

1739   2.50 West Bromwich Albion Football Club Median Auction Maiden Stakes 2yo (E)
£3715 £1143 £572   6f15y str   **Soft 103**   -32 Slow   Inside

ROYAL ALCHEMIST [6] M D I Usher 2-8-9 A Daly 25/1: 1: b f Kingsinger - Pure Gold (Dilum) Slow   89+
away, prog after 4f, styd on to lead well ins fnl 1f, pushed out, val 4L+: debut: Feb foal, half sister wnr at 1m:
sire useful performer at around 1m: eff at 6f, bred to apprec 7f+ in time: acts on soft grnd & a gall trk: goes
well fresh: won here with authority & looks sure to rate higher.
1571 **THE CROOKED RING 9** [10] P D Evans 2-9-0 S W Kelly 2/1 FAV: 5232: Rear, prog halfway, styd on to   3   82
lead ins fnl 1f, hdd cl-home & no extra: well bckd: acts on gd & soft: continues to run well: see 1571 & 1401.
ENGLISH FELLOW [2] B A McMahon 2-9-0 J Carroll 9/2: 3: b c Robellino - Q Factor (Tragic Role)   1   79
Handy when short of room after 4f, kept on but no ch with front 2: op 6/1 on debut: Jan foal, cost 9,000 gns: half
brother wnr at 10f, dam won numerous times at 6f/1m: sire top class performer as a juv: eff at 6f, bred to apprec
further: acts on soft grnd.
DOCTOR HILARY [9] M L W Bell 2-9-0 I Mongan 5/1: 4: b c Mujahid - Agony Aunt (Formidable)   ¾   77
Slow away, grad prog from halfway to lead dist, hdd ins fnl 1f, wknd: debut: Apr foal, cost 21,000 gns: half
brother to wnrs at 5/8f: dam 10f wnr: sire Gr1 wnr as a juv: sharper for today.
1123 **LADY MISHA 32** [7]2-8-9 D Allan(3) 9/1: 55: Handy, led after 4f, hdd dist, fdd: see 1123.   1¾   67
MALINSA BLUE [1]2-8-9 Dean McKeown 20/1: 6: Handy when short of room after 4f, sn no extra.   1¾   63
1401 **GRAND WELCOME 17** [5]2-9-0 P Dobbs 33/1: 07: Chsd ldrs till halfway, wknd.   1   65
TRUCKLE [4]2-9-0 K Dalgleish 15/2: 8: Led 4f, fdd: op 11/2 on debut.   shd   64
1550 **MISS GOOD TIME 10** [11]2-8-9 J Bramhill 20/1: 069: Rear, nvr able to chall.   1¼   55
1190 **COUNTRYWIDE SUN 29** [3]2-9-0 V Slattery 22/1: 00: 10th: Cl-up over 4f, fdd.   1¾   55
TYSON RETURNS [8]2-9-0 D Nolan(3) 14/1: 0: 11th: Slow away, handy over 4f, fdd.   1¾   50
11 Ran   Time 1m 18.90 (8.1)   Owned: The Ridgeway Partnership   Trained: Lambourn

---

1740   **3.25 Clumber Park Selling Handicap Stakes 3yo 46-55 (F)**   **[64]**
£2898 £828 £414   **1m54y rnd   Soft 103   -24 Slow**   Outside

1529 **FLYING SPUD** 11 [6] J L Spearing 3-8-11 (47) A Daly 9/2: 00-5451: Handy, styd on to lead dist,   **54**
rdn out: eff at 1m on soft grnd: acts on a gall trk: imprvd here for drop to sell grade: see 863.
1395 **BISCAR TWO** 18 [1] R M Whitaker 3-8-13 VIS (49) V Halliday 5/2 FAV: 00-46222: Handy 6f, sn outpcd,   1¼   **53**
rallied ins fnl 1f, no ch with wnr: well bckd: ran to form in 1st time visor: shaped as tho' 10f will suit: see 1395.
1376 **FARAWAY ECHO** 18 [4] M L W Bell 3-9-2 VIS (52) Hayley Turner(5) 4/1: 500-063: gr f Second Empire -   1¾   **51**
Salalah (Lion Cavern) Handy, led after 6f, hdd dist, no extra: 1st time visor: unplcd in '03 (rtd 67, fills mdn):
eff at 1m on soft grnd.
1410 **WEAVER SPELL** 17 [7] J R Norton 3-8-7 (8oh) (35) A Mullen(7) 25/1: 0006-564: Nvr nrr than mid-div.   4   **35**
1240 **PRINCESS ISMENE** 27 [3]3-9-0 bl (50) D Nolan(3) 4/1: 2433405: Nvr nrr than mid-div: btr 1134.   3½   **35**
1416 **DAVIDS GIRL** 17 [2]3-8-9 (45) D McGaffin 10/1: 06005-56: Handy over 5f, wknd: see 1416.   nk   **29**
1549 **BROTHER CADFAEL** 10 [8]3-8-7 (3oh) (40) Dean McKeown 10/1: 0326667: Rear, nvr a factor: btr 1242.   3½   **21**
1440 **SHANGHAI SURPRISE** 15 [5]3-9-2 bl (52) P Dobbs 20/1: 46000-58: Led till 2f out, fdd.   17   **2**
8 Ran   Time 1m 49.60 (10.2)   Owned: Mr M Bishop   Trained: Kinnersley

---

1741   **4.00 Browne Jacobson Classified Stakes 3yo 0-85 (C)**
£10192 £3136 £1568   **1m54y rnd   Soft 103   +03 Fast**   Outside

1192 **CIMYLA** 29 [6] C F Wall 3-9-2 (83) G Baker 5/1: 41-301: Held up, prog halfway, rdn out to lead   **89**
cl-home: op 7/1: eff at 1m/9f on polytrack, soft grnd, prob fast: back to form after losing action last time out:
only lightly rcd & can rate higher: see 947.
1496 **SECRETARY GENERAL** 12 [3] P F I Cole 3-9-5 (88) C Catlin 15/8 FAV: 241-02: b c Fasliyev - Katie   ½   **90**
McLain (Java Gold) Led 7f out, edged right under press bef 1f out, hdd cl-home: well bckd, clr rem: mdn wnr on fnl
'03 start: eff at 7f/1m on fast & soft grnd: acts on a stiff/gall trk: lost little in defeat here.
1 Sep'03 York 7.0g/f 89- D: 2 Jul'03 Newm 7g/f 93- D:
4288] **FORT** 240 [2] M Johnston 3-9-7 (90) K Dalgleish 12/1: 13-3: ch g Dr Fong - Chief's Quest (Chief's   6   **80**
Crown) Handy, ev ch halfway, fdd ins fnl 2f: reapp: med auct mdn wnr on 1st of only 2 '03 starts: eff at 7f,
around 1m shld suit: acts on fast grnd & goes well fresh, acts on a sharp/undul trk: just sharper for today.
1 Aug'03 Epso 7g/f 87- E:
1315 **BAILEYS DANCER** 21 [7] M Johnston 3-8-13 (85) S Chin 16/1: 51140-04: Led till 7f out, outpcd   ½   **71**
halfway, mod late gains: see 1315.
1419 **GLEBE GARDEN** 16 [5]3-9-3 (89) I Mongan 7/2: 310-55: Handy 6f, wknd: btr 1419.   3   **69**
1513 **CUSCO** 11 [4]3-9-1 (87) P Dobbs 7/2: 31305-26: Handy over 5f, wknd: btr 1513 (6f, hvy).   2   **63**
1110 **ZERLINA** 34 [1]3-9-0 (86) P Gallagher(7) 18/1: 201-07: b f Singspiel - Tass (Soviet Star) Slow   4   **54**
away, nvr a factor: fills mdn wnr on fnl '03 start: eff at 7f on fast grnd & polytrack, stiff or sharp trk.
1 Oct'03 Ling 7ap 88a- D: 2 Sep'03 Leic 7.0g/f 83- D:
7 Ran   Time 1m 47.43 (8.03)   Owned: Mr Peter Botham   Trained: Newmarket

---

1742   **4.35 Colwick Park Maiden Stakes 3yo+   (D)**
£4193 £1290 £645   **1m6f15y   Soft 103   -17 Slow**   Inside

1489 **TWOFAN** 13 [1] M Johnston 3-8-6 S Chin 8/13 FAV: 221: Made all, pushed out fnl 1f, val 4L+:   **74+**
well bckd: eff around 10f, imprvd here for step up to 14f: acts on fast & soft grnd: op to more improvement at
staying dists: see 1489 & 1275.
1390 **SADLERS PRIDE** 18 [8] Andrew Turnell 4-9-12 (72) J Carroll 5/1: 30-22: Keen mid-div, prog   2   **70**
halfway, styd on ins fnl 1f, not pace wnr: eff at 11/14f on gd & soft grnd: see 1390.
 WATCHFUL WITNESS 336 [10] Dr J R J Naylor 4-9-12 D Sweeney 50/1: 0-3: ch c In The Wings -   1¼   **69$**
Eternal (Kris) Handy over 12f, sn onepcd: earlier juv hdle wnr at Plumpton (rtd 107h, stays 2m on soft, tried
blnks, G L Moore): unplcd on sole Flat start in native France: eff at 14f on soft grnd.
 WODHILL HOPE 9 [9] D Morris 4-9-7 D McGaffin 66/1: 4: Rear, nvr nrr than mid-div on debut.   5   **59**
1384 **BROUGH SUPREME** 18 [5] H Morrison 3-8-6 P Dobbs 4/1: 0-54: Mid-div, hdwy 4f out, wknd fnl 1f.   dht   **64**
1291 **INDIAN CHASE** 23 [11]7-9-13 vis Lucy Russell(7) 20/1: 26: Keen handy 13f, fdd.   1¾   **62**
 GREAT GIDDING [4]3-8-6 C Catlin 28/1: 7: Nvr nrr than mid-div on debut.   5   **57**
43 **PATTERN MAN** 179 [2]3-8-6 J Bramhill 100/1: 000-8: Handy 11f, wknd.   ½   **56**
1358 **COURT EMPEROR** 20 [3]4-9-12 G Baker 100/1: 009: Rear, nvr able to chall.   ½   **55**
 MEADOW HAWK 384 [7]4-9-12 M Henry 20/1: 0/00-0: 10th: Handy 3f, wknd.   25   **34**
10 Ran   Time 3m 15.15 (16.85)   Owned: Mr A Al-Rostamani   Trained: Middleham

---

1743   **5.05 Wollaton Park Classified Stakes 3yo+ 0-70 (E)**
£3702 £1139 £570   **6f15y str   Soft 103   +09 Fast**   Inside

1251 **ANTONIO CANOVA** 25 [6] Bob Jones 8-9-4 (70) T Williams 33/1: 000/0-001: ch g Komaite - Joan's   **80**
Venture (Beldale Flutter) Rear far side, prog halfway, styd on to lead well ins fnl 1f, rdn out: unplcd sole '03
start (rtd 58, h'cap): mod form in '02: prog in '01, won 3 h'caps incl val Great St Wilfrid: eff at 5f, suited by
6f on firm, soft & any trk: likes Newmarket & goes well fresh: has slipped to a decent mark.
1 Aug'01 Ripo 6g/f 92-85 B: 1 Aug'01 Newm 6g/s 88-82 C: 1 May'01 Kemp 6fim 82-78 C:
1239 **UNDER MY SPELL** 27 [2] P D Evans 3-8-5 (70) S Chin 14/1: 3555-002: b f Wizard King - Gagajulu (Al   2½   **70**
Hareb) Handy far side, kept on fnl 1f, no ch with wnr: sell wnr 1st time out in '03 (also plcd twice): eff at 5/6f
on firm & soft: acts on a gall trk & goes well fresh: win similar off this mark. 1 Apr'03 Nott 5.1g/f 78- G:
1269* **MADDIES A JEM** 24 [15] J R Jenkins 4-9-6 (75) S W Kelly 4/1 FAV: 3460-113: Handy stands side   nk   **74+**
group, led that group halfway, kept on fnl 1f, no ch with far side: not disgraced here on bid for hat-trick & prob
disadvantaged by racing on stands side: btr 1269 & 976.
1533 **FULL SPATE** 10 [13] J M Bradley 9-9-4 (68) K Dalgleish 14/1: 061-6054: Rear stands side, prog   hd   **71**
halfway, kept on fnl 1f: see 1354.
1523 **MERLINS DANCER** 11 [5]4-9-9 (75) A Nicholls 25/1: 00400-05: Rcd far side, led till ins fnl 1f, wknd.   1   **73**
1598 **TIME N TIME AGAIN** 7 [10]6-9-8 p (74) Dean McKeown 14/1: 3315006: Handy far side 4f, no extra.   2   **66**

507

NOTTINGHAM   FRIDAY 14.05.04   Lefthand, Galloping Track

1354	**DORCHESTER 20** [9]7-9-8 (74) G Carter 13/2: 3053-657: Nrr than mid-div far side: btr 1354.	3	57
1417	**ASK THE CLERK 16** [16]3-8-11 (73) Joanna Badger 8/1: 3501028: Handy stands side 4f, wknd: btr 1417.	3	47
1079	**AMONG FRIENDS 37** [12]4-9-4 (70) I Mongan 40/1: 00/036-69: Rcd stands side, led that gr 4f, wknd.	nk	43
4818}	**CAPE ST VINCENT 207** [11]4-9-6 (72) P Dobbs 9/1: 212024-0: 10th: Handy stands side 4f, wknd.	¾	43
1533	**WATERSIDE 10** [14]5-9-4 (68) J Carroll 10/1: 404-0030: 11th: Handy stands side 4f, wknd.	1	38
1354	**CASHEL MEAD 20** [8]4-9-3 (72) A Daly 12/1: 3-500600: 12th: Nvr nrr than mid-div far side.	shd	36
1345	**FREE WHEELIN 20** [4]4-9-6 (72) C Catlin 14/1: 0000-030: 13th: Rear far side, nvr able to chall.	3½	30
71	**MONTE MAYOR LAD 175** [7]4-9-4 (70) D Allan(3) 50/1: 330334-0: 14th: Rear, nvr a factor far side.	½	27
1345	**SEWMUCH CHARACTER 20** [3]5-9-4 (70) D Sweeney 9/1: 50304-40: 15th: Al bhd far side.	½	26
1103	**HARD TO CATCH 36** [1]6-9-4 (69) M Howard(7) 20/1: 4104550: 16th: Handy far side till 2f out, wknd.	hd	25

16 Ran   Time 1m 16.49(5.69)   Owned: The Antonio Canova Partnership   Trained: Newmarket

HAMILTON   FRIDAY 14.05.04   Righthand, Undulating Track, Stiff Uphill Finish

Official Going GOOD/SOFT

1744

6.20 Sky Bet Watch & Bet Press Red Maiden Auction Stakes 2yo 2yo (E)
£3868 £1190 £595   6f str   Good 55   -49 Slow   Stands side

1401	**ALSU 17** [2] A M Balding 2-8-4 Martin Dwyer 7/4: 31: Cl-up & led halfway, rdn & clr over 1f out,		70
	edged left but al in command ins last: confirmed debut promise: eff at 5f, apprec step up to 6f & shld get further: acts on gd grnd & a stiff/undul trk: appeals as the type to prog: see 1401.		
	TRICKSHOT [5] T D Easterby 2-8-2 Dale Gibson 25/1: 2: ch f Mister Baileys - Zizi (Imp Society)	1¾	62+
	Slowly away & well bhd, styd on strongly from over 1f out, nvr threatened wnr: cheaply bought Mar foal, dam a 5f juv wnr: sire a 2,000 Guineas wnr: eff over a stiff 6f, further could suit: acts on fast grnd & a stiff trk: caught the eye after slow start, likely imprvr in similar company.		
1386	**EXIT SMILING 18** [7] M Johnston 2-8-9 R Ffrench 4/6 FAV: 23: Cl-up, rdn & outpcd by wnr from	nk	68
	over 1f out: prob stays 6f: see 1386.		
	MELVINO [6] T D Barron 2-8-8 P Makin(5) 25/1: 4: b c Josr Algarhoud - Safe Secret (Seclude)	shd	66
	Led till halfway, no impress fnl 1f: Apr foal, half brother to a 7f juv wnr, dam plcd at 12f & subs hdles wnr: stay further in time, shld improve.		
1161	**DRAMATIC REVIEW 30** [3]2-8-8 L Enstone(3) 33/1: 05: b c Indian Lodge - Dramatic Shift (Night	nk	65
	Shift) Outpcd, kept on late, nrst fin: 10,000gns Feb 1st foal, dam related to a 10f 3yo wnr: need further in time.		
1401	**AHAZ 17** [4]2-8-7 B Swarbrick(5) 50/1: 06: Chsd ldrs till outpcd from halfway.	6	46
	FRANSISCAN [1]2-8-7 Rory Moore(7) 33/1: 7: Sn outpcd & struggling.	5	31

7 Ran   Time 1m 16.05 (6.25)   Owned: Columbus Costa Del Sol   Trained: Kingsclere

1745

6.50 Mcgrattan Piling Handicap Stakes 3yo 0-95 (C)
£9326 £3538 £1769   6f str   Good 55   -05 Slow   Stands side   [94]

1570	**BO MCGINTY 9** [5] R A Fahey 3-8-13 (79) T Hamilton(3) 11/4 FAV: 301-01: Chsd ldrs, rdn & led over		87
	1f out, held on all out: eff at 5/6f on fast & gd grnd, likes a stiff trk: see 1570.		
1360	**LETS GET IT ON 20** [2] J J Quinn 3-8-9 (75) R Winston 11/1: 502-0052: Held up, styd on well ins	shd	82
	last, just held: clr of rem, can win similar: see 1360.		
1229	**LOUISIADE 27** [3] T D Easterby 3-8-2 (68) Dale Gibson 20/1: 20000-03: b g Tagula - Titchwell Lass	4	63
	(Lead On Time) Held up, styd on for press, not pace to chall: '03 mdn scorer, subs h'cap rnr-up: eff at 5f, stays a stiff 6f: acts on fast & gd grnd, stiff/undul trks. 2 Aug'03 Newm 5g/f 79-73 C: 1 Jun'03 Hayd 5g/f 75- D:		
1488	**GEORGE THE BEST 13** [11] M D Hammond 3-8-9 (75) A Culhane 11/2: 1000-064: b g Imperial Ballet -	¾	68
	En Retard (Petardia) Mid-div, kept on onepace, no threat: eff at 5/6f acts on fast, likes gd & soft grnd, stiff/undul trks, prob handles any.		
	1 Jul'03 Hami 6.0gd 87-78 D: 1 Jun'03 Pont 5g/s 79- E: 2 May'03 Hami 5.0sft 77- E:		
4643}	**FIORE DI BOSCO 220** [8]3-9-2 (82) P Makin(5) 20/1: 013002-5: Held up, short of room over 1f out,	1¼	71
	sn no impress, reapp.		
112	**SWEET CANDO 168** [1]3-7-12 (64) R Ffrench 40/1: 610334-6: In tch till over 1f out, reapp.	½	51
1387	**A LITTLE BIT YARIE 18** [9]3-9-0 VIS (80) Darren Williams 8/1: 123-3047: Led till over 1f out,	2½	59
	wknd: visor: btr 1387 & 1229 (5f).		
1154	**GRANATO 31** [4]3-9-7 (87) Martin Dwyer 7/2: 221-08: Mid-div, no impress dist.	4	54
	MADRA RUA 202 [10]3-7-12 (nh) (63) P Fessey 33/1: 040050-9: Chsd ldrs till 2f out, reapp.	6	13
1305	**VADEMECUM 22** [7]3-9-0 (80) F Lynch 11/2: 0413-60: 10th: Held up, strug halfway: btr 1305.	5	14
1488	**ATTACCA 13** [6]3-8-9 BL (75) J Fanning 33/1: 0021-600: 11th: Sn bhd, nvr factor: blnks: btr 1176 (1m).	5	0

11 Ran   Time 1m 13.4 (3.6)   Owned: Paddy McGinty & Bo Turnbull   Trained: Malton

1746

7.25 Listed Saffie Joseph & Sons Braveheart Rated Stakes Handicap 4yo+ 0-110 (A)
£20300 £7700 £3850   1m4f17y   Good 55   +10 Fast   Stands side   [116]

1569	**COLLIER HILL 9** [4] G A Swinbank 6-8-8 (96) R Winston 9/1: 60303-01: ch g Dr Devious - Polar		104
	Queen (Polish Precedent) Held up, prog when short of room 3f out, styd on to lead ins fnl 1f, rdn out: won 2 h'caps in early '03: won 2 class stks & a h'cap in '02, also rnr-up 5 times: eff at 12/13f, stays 2m: handles firm, likes fast & gd/soft grnd: likes Hamilton: talented performer when on song.		
	1 Jul'03 Hayd 11.9g/f 94-89 B: 1 May'03 Hami 13.0gd 92-81 D: 2 Oct'02 York 13sft 85-81 C: 1 Sep'02 Ayr 13gd 83-77 C: 2 Aug'02 York 11.8gd 76-74 C: 2 Aug'02 Pont 12sft 76-73 D: 2 Jun'02 Carl 12fm 75-67 D: 1 Jun'02 Newc 12.4g/s 66- F: 1 May'02 Ayr 13g/s 64- F: 2 May'02 Hami 11sft 58- D:		
1704	**VINTAGE PREMIUM 1** [6] R A Fahey 7-8-13 (3ex) (101) T Hamilton 8/1: 320-06012: Led, hdd 2f out,	nk	108
	rallied & ev ch fnl 1f, just held by wnr: best arnd 10f, now stays 12f: fine run in defeat after a gallant win yesterday at York in 1704: others h'caps await on this evidence.		
1068	**BOURGEOIS 38** [10] T D Easterby 7-8-7 (95) F Lynch 9/2 J FAV: 30350-23: Mid-div, prog ins fnl 3f,	2½	98
	kept on but no pace front 2 fnl 1f: just btr 1068.		
1484	**PERFECT STORM 13** [12] M Blanshard 5-8-7 (4oh) (91) F Norton 10/1: 012-0054: Rear, gd prog to lead	1	96$
	2f out, edged right & hdd ins fnl 1f, no extra: clr rem: see 1484.		

4796} **SUN BIRD 209** [3]6-9-1 (103) A Culhane 16/1: 012502-5: ch g Prince of Birds - Summer Fashion **10** **89**
(Moorestyle) Rear, nvr nrr than mid-div: reapp: prog in '03, won 3 h'caps, also rnr-up in val Ebor & Cesarewitch
h'caps: rnr-up on sole 02/03 hdles start (rtd 105h, stay 2m on hvy): won 2 h'caps in '02: eff at 10/12f, imprvd
last term for step up to 2m/2m2f: acts on firm & soft: sharper next time over further.
2 Oct'03 Newm 18g/f 103-98 B: 2 Aug'03 York 13.9fm 99-92 B: 1 Aug'03 Ches 18.7fm 93-85 B:
1 Jun'03 Ayr 15g/f 87-84 C: 1 May'03 Muss 16gd 86-79 D: 1 Jul'02 Hayd 11.9gd 85-77 B:
1 Jun'02 Muss 12gd 74-71 E: 1 Aug'01 Ches 10.3g/s 75-70 C: 1 Aug'01 Redc 11g/f 70-66 C:
1364 **GRAMPIAN 20** [11]5-9-0 (102) M Fenton 10/1: 11525/-26: Handy 9f, wknd: btr 1364. **1¼** **86**
4716* }**DESERT QUEST 214** [7]4-8-7 (60h)vis (89) Martin Dwyer 25/1: 3/1461-7: b g Rainbow Quest - Jumilla **1¼** **77**
(El Gran Senor) Nvr nrr than mid-div: reapp: mdn & h'cap wnr on 2 of only 4 '03 starts (Sir M Stoute): showed
promise on sole '02 start (plcd, mdn, rtd 71): eff around 10f, has tried 12f: acts on fast & soft grnd: goes well
fresh & eff with/without visor: has been gelded since last term: with A M Balding.
1 Oct'03 Wind 10.0g/f 90-84 C: 1 Apr'03 Wind 10.0g/s 83- D:
2248} **FIGHT YOUR CORNER 330** [9]5-9-7 (109) K McEvoy 6/1: 015/520-8: Handy over 9f, wknd. **½** **90**
1296 **BONECRUSHER 23** [2]5-9-5 (107) T P Queally 9/2 J FAV: 0-640529: Rear, prog when hmpd & jockey **6** **79**
lost iron 2f out, not recover: 1st try at 12f: only just denied in 1296 (10f).
1364 **LEGAL APPROACH 20** [8]5-9-7 (109) R Ffrench 25/1: 11/131/-40: 10th: Chsd ldrs over 1m, fdd. **2** **78**
1273 **EASTER OGIL 24** [1]9-8-7 (55) P Makin 200/1: 0002650: 11th: Rear, nvr able to chall. **11** **48**
2817* }**MORSON BOY 308** [5]4-8-11 (99) J Fanning 7/1: 54/1151-0: 12th: Cl-up, outpcd when short of room **16** **28**
3f out, sn eased: reapp: gelded over winter.
12 Ran Time 2m 37.23 (5.43) Owned: Mr R H Hall & Mr Ashley Young Trained: Richmond

1747 7.55 Luddon Construction Maiden Stakes 3yo+ (D)
£6240 £1920 £960 **1m1f36y** **Good 55** **-26 Slow** Inside

1495 **NEVER WILL 12** [4] M Johnston 3-8-9 J Fanning 8/11 FAV: 5-221: Made all, rdn out ins fnl 1f: **87**
eff at 7f/9f on firm & gd grnd: gd confidence boost: see 1495.
5007} **RESERVOIR 191** [1] W J Haggas 3-8-9 (77) Martin Dwyer 11/2: 043-2: b g Green Desert - Spout **1** **84**
(Salse) Handy, outpcd after 7f, rallied ins fnl 1f, just held by wnr on reapp: plcd in '03 (rtd 81, mdn): eff at
7f/9f, further shld suit: acts on fast & soft grnd: has been gelded since last term, can find similar.
1428 **BACKGAMMON 16** [5] D R Loder 3-8-9 T P Queally(3) 11/4: 23: Cl-up & ev ch after 7f, no extra fnl **¾** **82**
1f: eff at 9/10f on gd & soft grnd: ran to form of 1428.
1507 **INTO THE SHADOWS 12** [3] Mrs M Reveley 4-9-4 T Eaves(5) 20/1: 334: Rear, nvr nrr than mid-div. **3** **71**
1507 **CAYMANS GIFT 12** [6]4-9-9 P Mulrennan(5) 50/1: 45: Chsd ldrs 6f, fdd: btr 1507. **8** **60**
4340} **KINTORE 238** [7]3-8-9 M Fenton 100/1: 000-6: ch c Inchinor - Souadah (General Holme) Handy 7f, **15** **30**
fdd: reapp: plcd all 3 '03 starts (rtd 53, mdn): with J S Goldie.
HOWARDS ROCKET 0 [2]3-8-9 R Winston 33/1: 7: Slow away, al in rear on debut. **9** **12**
7 Ran Time 2m 1.45 (7.35) Owned: Maktoum Al Maktoum Trained: Middleham

1748 8.30 Sky Vegas On Channel 295 Handicap A Qualifier For Tote Handicap Final 3yo+ 0-75 (E) [74]
£4371 £1345 £673 **1m65y rnd** **Good 55** **-29 Slow** Inside

1388 **JORDANS ELECT 18** [11] Semple 4-9-5 (65) T Eaves(5) 7/1: 10500-51: Cl-up, styd on to lead dist, **73**
drvn out: eff at 1m/9.3f on firm & gd/soft grnd: see 1388.
1385 **MEELUP 18** [13] Jane Southcombe 4-8-11 p (57) L Enstone(3) 16/1: 2210002: Led, hdd dist, kept on **¾** **63**
fnl 1f, not btn far from the front: see 820.
1164 **MOUNT PEKAN 30** [4] J S Goldie 4-8-0 (46) F Norton 20/1: 05000-03: b c Sri Pekan - The Highlands **nk** **50**
(High Line) Keen rear, prog ins fnl 2f, not btn far in 3rd: unplcd in '03 (rtd 65, h'cap): 4th at best in '02 (rtd
75, mdn): eff around 1m on gd grnd: this was encouraging & has slipped to a decent mark.
1553 **BAILIEBOROUGH 10** [7] D Nicholls 5-9-7 (67) Alex Greaves 14/1: 00-06034: Mid-div, prog when short **2** **68+**
of room ins fnl 2f, switched & kept on fnl 1f, ch had gone: closer here with clr passage: just btr 1553.
1461 **SARRAAF 14** [12]8-9-11 (71) A Culhane 9/1: 4232505: Cl-up over 6f, sn no extra: just btr 1122. **½** **71**
1633 **WUXI VENTURE 6** [6]9-9-6 (66) T Hamilton(3) 8/1: 0///2160-06: b g Wolfhound - Push A Button (Bold **shd** **65**
Lady) Chsd ldrs over 6f, sn no extra: quick reapp: earlier beginner chase wnr (rtd 117c, styd 2m4f on fast & hvy
grnd): h'cap wnr on 1 of only 4 '03 Flat starts: h'cap hdle wnr in 02/03 (rtd 113h, h'cap): eff at 1m/10.4f on fast
& hvy grnd: eff without blnks or visor. 1 Aug'03 Hami 9.2g/f 66-64 C: 2 Jul'03 Hami 9.2g/f 64-62 E:
1535 **PHAROAHS GOLD 10** [5]6-8-8 vis (54) Darren Williams 20/1: 5030107: Rear, nvr nrr than mid-div. **hd** **52**
1542 **CLANN A COUGAR 10** [14]4-9-3 bl (63) B Swarbrick(5) 14/1: 404-0068: Handy over 6f, wknd: see 1542. **1½** **58**
1366 **LATE ARRIVAL 20** [10]7-8-7 (47) Dale Gibson 66/1: 1606/5-09: Handy, fdd fnl 2f: see 1366. **1** **40**
1164 **GIFTED FLAME 30** [9]5-9-5 (65) P Makin(5) 8/1: 04006-00: 10th: Rear, nvr able to chall. **1** **56**
1504 **ANTHEMION 12** [8]7-9-0 (60) R Ffrench 9/1: 0025-020: 11th: Cl-up, fdd ins fnl 2f: btr 1504. **1½** **48**
1366 **BASINET 20** [3]6-8-10 (56) R Winston 66/1: 46506-00: 12th: Rear, nvr able to chall. **shd** **43**
1603* **ACE COMING 7** [1]3-8-8 (6ex)bl (67) P Mulrennan(5) 7/2 FAV: 00-03110: 13th: Rear, nvr a factor: v **nk** **53**
disapp on hat-trick bid: btr 1603 (gd/soft) & 1395 (soft).
1214 **CRESKELD 28** [2]5-9-12 (72) F Lynch 25/1: 100-3000: 14th: Handy 6f, fdd: btr 836. **3½** **51**
14 Ran Time 1m 50.95 (7.15) Owned: Mr Ian Crawford Trained: Carluke

1749 9.05 Cmpe Glasgow Classified Stakes 3yo+ 0-70 (E)
£3803 £1170 £585 **5f4y str** **Good 55** **-06 Slow** Stands side

1269 **THE FISIO 24** [6] A M Balding 4-9-8 vis (70) Martin Dwyer 4/1: 3002041: Cl-up, led bef 2f out, rdn **77**
out to hold on: eff at 5f/sharp 6f on fast, gd/soft & both AWs: eff with/without visor: see 1103 & 415.
1627 **FRASCATI 6** [3] A Berry 4-9-6 (71) F Lynch 12/1: 0004102: Handy, prog & kept on ins fnl 1f, just **½** **73**
held by wnr: quick reapp: ran to form of win in 1096.
1638 **CHAIRMAN BOBBY 6** [8] D W Barker 6-9-8 (69) Rory Moore(7) 4/1: 062-5003: Led till bef 2f out, **nk** **74**
rallied ins fnl 1f, not btn far: quick reapp: see 1120.
4805} **TWICE UPON A TIME 209** [7] B Smart 5-9-8 (73) A Culhane 9/2: 000210-4: ch f Primo Dominie - **nk** **73**
Opuntia (Rousillon) Mid-div, prog ins fnl 2f, kept on cl-home: reapp: won 2 h'caps in '03: class stks wnr in '02:
eff at 5f/5.7f on firm & gd/soft grnd: prob acts on any trk, likes Bath & goes well fresh: not disgraced here.
1 Oct'03 York 5.0g/f 75-70 D: 2 Oct'03 Redc 5gf 70-(70) E: 1 Jul'03 Nott 5.1fm 73-63 D: 1 Jun'02 Bath 5.7g/f 72- E:
2 Oct'01 Catt 5g/s 68- D: 2 Aug'01 Hayd 6g/f 60 D:

HAMILTON FRIDAY 14.05.04 Righthand, Undulating Track, Stiff Uphill Finish

1523 **VIGOROUS 11** [4]4-9-8 (73) Alex Greaves 10/1: 00440-05: b f Danetime - Merrily (Sharrood) Handy   hd   71
till dist, kept on same pace: auct mdn & stks wnr in early '03 (M R Channon): 4th of 13 on sole '02 start (mdn, rtd
75): eff at 5/6f on fast & gd/soft grnd: acts on a sharp/undul trk & has gone well fresh: encouraging eff here &
can be plcd to gd eff by D Nicholls. 1 Apr'03 Hami 5.0g/s 82-(82) C: 1 Apr'03 Folk 6g/f 80- F:
1615 **ROXANNE MILL 7** [2]6-9-9 (74) B Swarbrick(5) 3/1 FAV: 0020-326: Chsd ldrs over 3f, edged left & no   2½   65
extra: quick reapp: btr 1615 & 1269.
4919} **MARSHALLSPARK 199** [1]5-9-8 (70) T Hamilton(3) 20/1: 131600-7: b g Fayruz - Lindas Delight   nk   63
(Batshoof) Mid-div, no extra fnl 2f: reapp: 2 class stks in '03: h'cap wnr in '02: eff at 6/7f on firm, gd/soft
& fibresand, sharp or stiff trk: with R A Fahey. 1 Sep'03 Redc 7fm 72-(69) E: 1 Aug'03 Brig 7.0fm 60-(68) E:
2 May'03 Carl 5.9fm 70-68 E: 2 Jun'02 Ches 7fm 70- C: 1 May'02 Ches 6fm 73-66 C: 2 Oct'01 Newc 6g/s 73- D:
944   **REGAL SONG 48** [5]8-9-8 bl (68) R Winston 10/1: 005-0008: Rear, nvr a factor: 7 wk abs.   6   45
8 Ran   Time 1m 1.15(3.05)   Owned: Mr D H Caslon   Trained: Kingsclere

SOUTHWELL Fibresand SATURDAY 15.05.04 Lefthand, Sharp, Oval Track

Official Going Standard

1750	6.00 Saffie Joseph Handicap Stakes 3yo+ 46-55 (F)				**[64]**
	£2982 £852 £426	**6f aw rnd**	**Going 55**	**+11 Fast** Inside	

819   **ROMAN EMPIRE 68** [5] K A Ryan 4-9-0 bl (50) N Callan 13/2: 0000-041: Handy, prog despite edging   61a+
right dist, pushed out to lead cl-home, val 3L+: 10 wk abs & new stable: eff at 6f/7f on both AWs, has tried 1m:
apprec refitting of blnks: goes well fresh: follow-up on this evidence: see 819 (T J Etherington).
1588 **LARKYS LOB 9** [13] J O'Reilly 5-9-1 (51) J D O'Reilly(7) 9/2 FAV: 2463122: Prom, led after 3f, hdd   2   55a
well ins fnl 1f, no extra: op 6/1: gd eff in defeat: see 1588 & 1405 (banded).
1267 **LARGS 25** [14] J Balding 4-8-12 (48) J Edmunds 9/1: 5-033263: Handy, chsd ldr dist, sn no extra.   1½   48a
1504 **SPEEDFIT FREE 13** [8] Miss A Stokell 7-9-0 vis (50) R Winston 12/1: 4003004: Mid-div, prog   1   47a
halfway, kept on fnl 1f: visor refitted: just btr 1310.
1532 **LUCIUS VERRUS 11** [2]4-9-4 VIS (54) Darren Williams 12/1: 34-30105: Mid-div, hdwy after 4f, kept   nk   50a
on fnl 1f: first time visor: btr 1320 (mdn clmr).
1337 **SCARY NIGHT 21** [3]4-9-4 p (54) T Hamilton(3) 10/1: 0016006: Handy 4f, no extra: btr 793 (clmr).   ¾   48a
956* **BULAWAYO 47** [4]7-8-13 bl (49) G Gibbons 12/1: 3030617: Rear, nvr nrr than mid-div: abs, btr 956.   hd   42a
1553 **THE GAMBLER 11** [15]4-8-12 p (48) D Fentiman(7) 11/1: 00-00028: Held up, prog after 4f, onepcd fnl 1f.   ¾   39a
1221 **KENNINGTON 28** [12]4-9-5 vis (55) J Mackay 7/1: 1040349: Led 3f, sn wknd: btr 1052.   ¾   44a
1379 **DESERT FURY 19** [11]7-8-12 (48) R Ffrench 14/1: 05000-00: b g Warning - Number One Spot   4   25a
(Reference Point) Slow away, al in rear: plcd twice in '03 (h'caps, rtd 66 & 69a): plcd 4 times in '02 (h'caps &
clmr, earlier with B Hanbury): class stks wnr in '01: eff at 7f/1m, prob stays a gall 10f: acts on firm, soft &
fibresand, sharp or gall trk: has gone well fresh, tried cheek pieces: well h'capped 7yo.
2 Jan'03 Sout 7af 69a-68 E: 2 Dec'02 Wolv 8.4af 70a- F: 2 Jun'02 Warw 7.1gd 79- E: 2 Sep'01 Ayr 7.2g/f 78-79 C:
1 Jul'01 Ayr 7sft 81- D: 2 May'01 Hayd 8.1g/f 76-72 C: 2 May'01 Newm 8g/f 80-72 C:
1522 **PRINCESS ERICA 12** [10]4-8-12 p (48) J Bramhill 25/1: 0305-000: 11th: b f Perpendicular -   3½   15a
Birichino (Dilum) Bhd, nvr a factor: plcd twice in '03 (h'caps, rtd 64 & 62a, T D Easterby): rnr-up in '02 (nov
stks): eff at 5/6f on gd grnd & fibresand: with J Balding. 2 Oct'02 Sout 5af 65a- D:
1371 **LOUIS GEORGIO 20** [16]5-9-0 (50) J F Egan 33/1: 05400-00: 12th: Mid-div when no room after 3f, fdd.   2½   10a
1541 **IN TUNE 11** [7]4-9-0 bl (50) D Corby(3) 33/1: 00/55-000: 13th: Mid-div 4f, fdd.   1¼   6a
1452 **BAYTOWN FLYER 16** [9]4-9-2 (52) T G McLaughlin 33/1: 1121120: 14th: Handy over halfway, wknd.   3½   0a
1452* **ALASTAIR SMELLIE 16** [1]8-8-12 vis (48) P McCabe 10/1: 0-002210: 15th: Handy, no room after 3f, fdd.   6   0a
15 Ran   Time 1m 15.95 (2.65)   Owned: Yorkshire Racing Syndicates IV   Trained: Hambleton

1751	6.30 Discovery Of Cape Cod Selling Stakes 2yo (G)			
	£2513 £718 £359	**6f aw rnd**	**Going 55**	**-33 Slow** Inside

1445 **SPEED DIAL HARRY 16** [6] K R Burke 2-8-12 VIS Darren Williams 6/4 FAV: 5231: Prom, led 3f out,   75a+
pushed clr, val 9L+: well bckd, bght in for 15,500gns: eff at 5f, improved for step up to 6f: acts on soft grnd &
fibresand: apprec fitting of 1st time visor & drop to sell grade: see 1445 & 1143.
1631 **MILLER HILL 7** [5] M W Easterby 2-8-12 P Mulrennan(5) 20/1: 02: b g Prince Sabo - Atlantic   6   57a
Heiress (Thowra) Handy, kept on ins fnl 2f, no ch with easy wnr: Apr foal, cost 2,200gns: half-brother plcd as a
juv abroad: sire top-class performer as a juv: eff at 5f on fibresand.
1634 **JOSHAR 7** [7] M W Easterby 2-8-7 Dale Gibson 10/1: 0303: Dwelt, prog after 4f, no impress fnl 1f.   1¼   48a
1634 **MISSED TURN 7** [2] K A Ryan 2-8-7 P Fessey 7/2: 544: Prom 4f, fdd: qck reapp: btr 1634 (5f).   hd   47a
1634 **KISSING A FOOL 7** [4]2-9-3 L Treadwell(7) 10/1: 5105: Handy till halfway, wknd: btr 1394 (soft).   6   41a
1653 **SHISH 5** [3]2-8-7 N Callan 9/1: 66: Prom 4f, fdd: qck reapp: see 1653.   2   25a
1380 **NUTTY TIMES 19** [1]2-8-7 A Daly 7/2: 23307: Led 3f, sn fdd: op 5/2: v disapp: btr 1097 & 1029 (5f).   5   0a
7 Ran   Time 1m 18.62 (5.32)   Owned: Mr J C S Wilson   Trained: Leyburn

1752	7.00 Maguire & Batty Median Auction Maiden Stakes 2yo (F)			
	£3393 £1044 £522	**5f aw str**	**Going 55**	**Inapplicable** Outside

   ROSEIN 0 [11] Mrs G S Rees 2-8-12 J Fanning 7/1: 1: b f Komaite - Red Rosein (Red Sunset)   76a
Dwelt, prom & led after 3f, rdn out to hold on despite hanging left dist: op 5/1 on debut: Apr foal, cost 20,000
gns: sister to sprint wnr Proud Boast: dam val h'cap winner at 6f: sire won at 6f: eff at 5f, shld apprec further:
acts on fibresand & a sharp trk: goes well fresh: improve with experience.
1601 **EXTRA MARK 8** [1] J R Best 2-9-3 N Pollard 2/1 FAV: 02: Handy, styd on ins fnl 1f, not pace wnr: ¾   78a
acts on gd/soft grnd & fibresand, again lost little in defeat & can find similar: see 1601.
   FORZEEN 0 [5] J A Osborne 2-9-3 S Sanders 3/1: 3: ch c Forzando - Mazurkanova (Song) Trkd   2½   71a
ldrs, prog & ev ch dist, no extra fnl 1f: tchd 6/1 on debut: Mar foal, cost 19,000gns: brother/ half-brother
to juv wnrs at 5/6f: dam 6f wnr as a juv: eff at 5f on fibresand: learn from this.
1550 **COLEORTON DANCER 11** [3] K A Ryan 2-9-3 N Callan 5/1: 044: Led 3f, wknd dist: tchd 7/1: btr 1550.   2½   64a
1439 **ETERNALLY 16** [9]2-9-3 p M Henry 25/1: 035: Rear, nvr nrr than mid-div: btr 1439.   3   55a

PEE JAYS DREAM 0 [2]2-9-3 Dale Gibson 25/1: 6: Chsd ldrs over 3f, no extra: debut.	½	**54a**
ROKO 0 [8]2-9-3 P Mulrennan(5) 25/1: 7: Dwelt, nvr nrr than mid-div: debut.	hd	**53a**

1274 **UREDALE 25** [10]2-9-3 R Ffrench 33/1: 58: Slow away, al bhd. — ¾ **51a**
KERNY 0 [4]2-9-3 R Winston 12/1: 9: Chsd ldrs 3f, fdd. — 10 **26a**
1439 **URABANDE 16** [7]2-8-12 Lisa Jones(3) 7/1: 020: 10th: Chsd ldrs till halfway, fdd: btr 1439. — hd **20a**
KENTUCKY BANKES 0 [6]2-9-3 A Daly 20/1: 0: 11th: Handy 3f, wknd on debut. — ¾ **23a**
11 Ran Time 1m 0.02 () Owned: Mr Tom Murray Trained: Preston

1753   7.30 Mansfield 103 2 Handicap Stakes 4yo+ 0-70 (E)   [68]
£3790 £1166 £583   **2m aw**   **Going 55**   **-32 Slow**   Inside

4422} **HERNE BAY 234** [8] A Bailey 4-9-2 (56) R Winston 10/1: 500140-1: b g Hernando - Charita (Lycius) — **64a**
Handy, prog to lead 2f out, drvn out: reapp: mdn & sell h'cap wnr in '03 (M Johnston): 3rd of 2nd on 1 of only 2
'02 starts (mdns, rtd 74a & 57): eff at 8.4f/11f, now suited by around 2m: acts on fast grnd & fibresand: likes a
sharp trk, esp Southwell: has tried cheek pieces: goes well fresh: can win again.
1 Aug'03 Beve 16.2g/f 57-53 F: 1 Jan'03 Sout 11af 60a- D:

1637 **MADIBA 7** [4] P Howling 5-9-9 (60) J Fanning 11/4 FAV: 0222022: Prom, led after 11f, hdd 2f out, — 2 **65a**
kept on ins fnl 1f, not pace wnr: clr rem: op 9/2: continues to run well: see 1637 & 812.
1469 **MACARONI GOLD 15** [5] W Jarvis 4-9-10 (64) M Tebbutt 9/2: 0445033: Rear, prog after 12f, no — 16 **55a**
impress fnl 2f: op 10/3: btr 1469 & 107.
690 **SPORTSMAN 85** [7] M W Easterby 5-8-3 bl (40) Dale Gibson 16/1: 0500/3-44: Handy 13f, wknd: — 2½ **29a**
recently u.r. over hdles: btr 690 (reapp).
1252 **JAMAICAN FLIGHT 26** [11]11-8-8 (45) J Quinn 7/1: 0-344445: Led 11f, sn badly outpcd, mod gains. — shd **33a**
1238 **JUNGLE LION 28** [12]6-9-1 t (52) Dean McKeown 12/1: 0101606: Chsd ldrs over 12f, wknd: op 8/1. — 2½ **38a**
1323 **MYRTUS 22** [6]5-8-8 (45) D Fentiman(7) 40/1: 0/0-37: Nvr nrr than mid-div: see 1323. — 6 **26a**
1589 **SUNNYSIDE ROYALE 9** [9]5-8-12 t (49) R Ffrench 12/1: 346-0138: Held up, prog after 10f, fdd 3f — 17 **15a**
out.
1563 **RIVER OF FIRE 10** [3]6-7-12 (5oh)vis (30) Natalia Gemelova(7) 16/1: 0360-039: Prom 10f, sn fdd. — 10 **0a**
1469 **MIGRATION 15** [2]8-9-4 (55) L Vickers 12/1: 162////4-00: 10th: b g Rainbow Quest - Armeria — 13 **2a**
(Northern Dancer) Bhd, nvr a factor: op 8/1: 4th of 13 on sole '03 start (seller, rtd 43a): missed '02, '01 &
'00: mdn wnr on 1 of 3 '99 starts (R Charlton, also listed rnr up, rtd 106): eff at 10f/12f on gd & soft.
1238* **BEST PORT 28** [1]8-9-2 (53) N Callan 6/1: 3054-010: 11th: Handy over 12f, fdd: btr 1238. — 1¾ **0a**
TINTA 210 [14]4-9-1 (55) M Fenton 15/1: 250000-0: 12th: b f Robellino - Albahaca (Green Dancer) — dist **0a**
Rear, nvr a factor: reapp: rider reported mount was nvr travelling: Brit bow, ex French, rnr up on 1 of 8 starts
to date in native country: with P A Blockley.
12 Ran Time 3m 40.00 (14.0) Owned: Mr T R Pearson Trained: Tarporley

---

1754   8.00 Margaret Simpson's 50th Birthday Claiming Stakes 3yo+ (F)
£2898 £828 £414   **1m3f aw**   **Going 55**   **-16 Slow**   Inside

1440 **CASPIAN DUSK 16** [7] W G M Turner 3-8-9 (70) C Haddon(7) 3/1: 06-23121: Handy, styd on to lead 3f — **64a**
out, drvn out: eff at 1m/10f, stays sharp 11f on both AWs: see 1440 & 983.
1326 **HEATHERS GIRL 22** [2] D Haydn Jones 5-9-4 (54) Paul Eddery 7/1: 0/-016242: Chsd ldrs, prog to — 1¾ **53a**
chase wnr 1f out, al held ins fnl 1f: 10/1: eff at 8.5f/11f: see 862 & 633.
1324 **FOX HOLLOW 22** [4] M J Haynes 3-8-5 (51) R Miles(3) 10/1: 0032623: Prom, led after 7f, hdd 3f out, — 2½ **53a**
sn no extra: eff at 7f/9.4f, prob stays 11f: just btr 1324 (9.4f).
1552* **PLATINUM CHARMER 11** [5] K R Burke 4-10-0 p (55) Darren Williams 2/1 FAV: 4-210214: Mid-div, prog — 1¼ **57a**
4f out, onepcd dist: top weight: see 1552 (gd).
1286 **GAME GURU 25** [6]5-9-12 p (70) Dean McKeown 11/4: 1461055: Mid-div, nvr able to chall: btr 857. — 1 **53a**
JAZIL 1834 [3]9-9-11 t R Winston 11/1: 313/0////-6: b g Nashwan - Gracious Beauty (Nijinsky) — 15 **27a**
Led 7f, sn fdd: op 6/1: last seen on racecourse in 01/02 over hdles (rtd 107h, h'cap rnr-up, stays 2m4f on firm &
gd/soft, wears t-strap): unplcd sole '99 Flat start (J H Gosden, h'cap, rtd 90): h'cap mdn wnr back in '98: prev
eff at 10/12f on firm & gd grnd, eff with/without visor.
6 Ran Time 2m 29.17 (7.87) Owned: Mr P Nabavi Trained: Sherborne

---

1755   8.30 Flight Of The 1st British Turbojet Handicap Stakes 3yo+ 46-55 (F)   [62]
£2982 £852 £426   **1m aw rnd**   **Going 55**   **+03 Fast**   Inside

1633* **YENALED 7** [12] K A Ryan 7-9-12 (60) N Callan 6/1: 5004511: Rear, prog & ev ct dist, led ins fn — **70a**
1f, rdn out: eff at 7f/1m, stays a stiff 10f well: acts on fm, soft & fibresand: land hat-trick: see 1633.
1282 **SPY GUN 25** [6] T Wall 4-9-4 (52) S Sanders 9/2 FAV: 0504062: Handy, prog to lead bef 1f out, hdd — 3 **54a**
ins fnl 1f, no extra: wel bckd from 12/1: best eff for a while & is h'capped to find similar: see 864 & 165.
1334 **KENNY THE TRUTH 22** [9] Mrs J Candlish 5-9-2 t (50) K Fallon 6/1: 3451433: Bhd, prog after 6f, — 3½ **45a**
kept on but no ch with front 2: see 1334 & btr 850 (banded).
1657 **CALL OF THE WILD 5** [14] R A Fahey 4-9-3 BL (51) T Hamilton(3) 12/1: 0333644: Dwelt, prog after 5f, — 1½ **43a**
nrst fin: qck reappp in first time blnks: btr 961.
1223 **SORBIESHARRY 28** [7]5-9-2 p (50) R Fitzpatrick 12/1: 1501405: Mid-div, prog halfway, no impress fnl 2f. — ¾ **40a**
1591* **SAROS 9** [11]3-8-9 (1ow)(4oh) (55) F Lynch 11/2: 606-0116: Prom, led after 5f, hdd bef 1f out, — shd **45a**
wknd: disapp on hat-trick bid: btr 1591 & 1410 (banded).
1341 **XALOC BAY 21** [13]6-9-6 (54) Darren Williams 14/1: 1236037: Prom over 5f, sn wknd: btr 1341. — shd **42a**
1223 **WILSON BLUEBOTTLE 28** [8]5-9-1 bl (49) Dale Gibson 20/1: 6102208: Chsd ldrs 6f, sn no extra. — nk **36a**
1661 **PRINTSMITH 5** [4]7-9-0 (48) J Bramhill 20/1: 3210509: Nvr nrr than mid-div: qck reapp: btr 908. — 4 **27a**
1553 **HOHS BACK 11** [5]5-9-3 p (51) Lisa Jones(3) 10-1: 0002060: 10th: Handy over halfway, sn wknd. — ¾ **28a**
4970} **NIGHT MARKET 196** [10]6-8-12 (1oh) (45) R Winston 10/1: 000600-0: 11th: ch g Inchinor - Night — 13 **0a**
Transaction (Tina's Pet) Led 5f, fdd on reapp: appr h'cap & sell wnr in '03: plcd 4 times in '02 (rtd 59 & 47a,
h'caps): eff at 7f/10f on firm, fast grnd & fibresand: handles stiff or sharp trk: has tried blnks.
1 Apr'03 Pont 10.0g/f 59-54 E: 1 Apr'03 Beve 8.5fm 58-(54) G: 2 Jul'02 Wind 8.3g/f 59-58 E: 2 Nov'01 Sout 8af 62a- D:
2 Jul'01 Ripo 9g/f 70- E: 2 Jun'01 Beve 8.4fm 71- E:
1100 **BENNANABAA 37** [1]5-9-7 t (55) D Corby(3) 50/1: 05000: 12th: Al in rear. — 4 **0a**
1660* **WATERPARK 5** [3]6-9-6 (6ex) (54) P Fessey 6/1: 0131-010: 13th: Mid-div, prog halfway, fdd 2f out: — 2 **0a**
op 9/2: v disappointing back at 1m & surely something amiss: btr 1660 (7f, soft).

SOUTHWELL Fibresand SATURDAY 15.05.04 Lefthand, Sharp, Oval Track

1374 **Kedross** 19 [15]3-8-4 (8oh)(51) J Quinn 33/1:0
1047 **Mystery Solved** 40 [2]4-8-12 (1oh)(45) D Nolan(3) 25/1:0
15 Ran   Time 1m 43.61(4.21)   Owned: The Fishermen   Trained: Hambleton

NEWBURY SATURDAY 15.05.04 Lefthand, Flat, Galloping Track

Official Going Good (Good/Soft Places)

1756 **1.35 London Paddy Power Gold Cup Handicap Stakes 3yo 0-95 (C)** **[99]**
£11536 £4376 £2188   **1m3f5y**   **Good/Firm 27**   **-11 Slow**   Inside

120* **PUKKA** 168 [8] L M Cumani 3-8-7 (1ow) (78) L Dettori 11/1: 0431-1: Mid-div, hdwy to lead over 1f   **99+**
out, rdn out: 4 month abs: eff at 10/11f, 12f will suit: acts on soft & polytrack, gall or sharp trk: lightly
rcd & v progressive, one to keep on your side: see 120.
4811} **MARAAHEL** 208 [1] Sir Michael Stoute 3-9-7 (93) R Hills 16/1: 414-2: b c Alzao - Nasanice   1¼   **111+**
(Nashwan) Dwelt, chsd ldrs, looking for gap & switched when hmpd over 3f out, styd on for press, not able to reach
wnr: reapp & h'cap bow: mdn scorer '03: stays 11f well, further will suit: acts on fast & soft, stiff trks: wld
have gone v close with clr run, useful & one to keep in mind. 1 Sep'03 Pont 8.0g/f 93- D:
1664* **FRANK SONATA** 4 [3] M G Quinlan 3-9-6 (4ex) (92) J Murtagh 11/2: 1400-613: Trkd ldrs & led over 2f   2   **106**
out, sn hdd, not pace of front pair: nicely bckd under a pen, qck reapp: stays 11f, acts on fast & soft.
1140* **BUKIT FRASER** 33 [6] P F I Cole 3-9-0 (86) K Fallon 10/1: 34-14: Pushed along rear, in tch   3   **96**
halfway, kept on for press, no threat: apprec further in similar: see 1140.
1192 **MOCCA** 30 [5]3-8-4 (76) Martin Dwyer 10/1: 34152-45: Led/dsptd lead till till over 2f out, wknd.   1¼   **84**
1365* **MAGANDA** 21 [10]3-8-12 (84) P Robinson 11/1: 20-16: Rear, eff 3f out, no prog over 1f out: h'cap   4   **86**
bow: jockey reported filly was hanging left: btr 1365 (g/s).
1259* **VINANDO** 26 [11]3-8-12 (84) S Drowne 8/1: 5-17: In tch wide, btn 2f out: h'cap bow: btr 1259 (10f, g/s).   13   **68**
1398 **GRAVARDLAX** 18 [2]3-8-13 BL (85) M Hills 40/1: 42-048: Led/dsptd lead till 4f out, sn btn: blnks.   4   **63**
947 **LE TISS** 49 [4]3-8-9 (81) T E Durcan 25/1: 10162-49: Rear & no ch fnl 2f: abs: see 947 (9f).   11   **46**
1403* **ANOTHER CHOICE** 18 [7]3-8-7 (1ow)t (78) D Holland 12/1: 000-3110: 10th: Rear, eff wide 3f out, sn   ½   **42**
btn: reportedly hanging right thr'out: much btr 1403 (gd, 10f).
1355* **SWAGGER STICK** 21 [9]3-9-4 (90) K Darley 13/8 FAV: 0014-11W: Withdrawn on vets advice (lost a shoe).   **0**
11 Ran   Time 2m 20.0 (4.2)   Owned: Fittocks Stud   Trained: Newmarket

---

1757 **2.05 Listed Paddy Power Stakes Registered As The Aston Park Stakes 4yo+ (A)**
£17400 £6600 £3300   **1m5f61y**   **Good/Firm 27**   **-02 Slow**   Inside

1596 **THE WHISTLING TEAL** 8 [2] G Wragg 8-8-12 (107) D Holland 5/4 FAV: 4452-021: Held up, smooth hdwy   **114**
from 4f out & led over 2f out, sn asserted, readily: hvly bckd: eff at 10f, suited by 12/13.5f on firm, hvy &
fibresand: v tough, genuine & smart in Listed/Gr 3 class: see 1596.
990 **DELSARTE** 49 [6] Saeed bin Suroor 4-8-12 T L Dettori 9/4: 12034-02: b c Theatrical - Delauncy   4   **108**
(Machiavellian) Held up in tch, hdwy to lead over 3f out, hdd over 2f out & sn no impress on wnr: well bckd: op
3/1: t-strap, 7 wk abs: mdn & List scorer '03, subs Gr 2 rnr-up (M Johnston): v eff at 10f, stays 13.4f: acts on
fast & gd grnd, loves a stiff/gall trk & can go well fresh: smart colt.
2 Jun'03 Asco 12g/f 111- A: 1 May'03 Newm 10gd 113- A: 1 Apr'03 Leic 10.0g/f 91- D:
1112 **GULF 35** [4] D R C Elsworth 5-8-12 (97) J Murtagh 33/1: 60606-03: ch g Persian Bold - Broken   ½   **107**
Romance (Ela Mana Mou) Rear, eff 3f out, drvn & kept on, nvr threatened wnr: cond stks scorer '03, subs val h'cap
plcd & Gr 2 unplcd (rtd 106 at best): '02 mdn scorer: eff at 14f/2m on firm & fast grnd, handles gd, stiff or
sharp/undul trk: can go well fresh: back to useful best on a sound surface.
1 Jun'03 Good 14fm 104-(100) C: 2 May'02 York 13.8g/f 99- B: 1 May'02 Sali 12g/f 97- D:
1418 **SAVANNAH BAY** 17 [5] B J Meehan 5-8-12 bl (111) R Hughes 10/1: 26355-04: ch g In The Wings - High   3   **103**
Savannah (Rousillon) Chsd ldrs, no impress fnl 2f: op 12/1: '03 Gr 3 wnr (fin rnr, awdd race, subs Gr 2 plcd): Gr
3 scorer '02: suited by 2m on firm or gd/soft grnd, stiff/gall or sharp/undul trk: eff with/without t-strap & can go
well fresh: best without blnks: smart stayer when on song, apprec a return to 2m.
1 Apr'03 Asco 16.2gd 112-(103) A: 1 Sep'02 Long 15gd 106- 2 Jul'02 Newm 14.7g/s 107- A: 1 Aug'01 Newm 7fm 94- D:
2 Jul'01 Sand 7g/f 85- D:
1230 **DISTINCTION** 28 [8]5-8-12 (107) K Fallon 6/1: 34015-05: b g Danehill - Ivy Leaf (Nureyev) Trkd   8   **91**
ldrs & led after 5f, hdd over 3f out, sn btn: '03 cond stks scorer: mdn wnr '02, subs dual val h'cap plcd (rtd 97):
eff btwn 12f/2m on firm & gd/soft grnd, stiff or sharp/undul trk.
1 Sep'03 Sali 14.1fm 107-(101) C: 1 Jun'02 Newm 10g/f 86- D: 2 May'02 Ripo 10g/s 90- D:
4554} **GOLD MEDALLIST** 226 [7]4-9-1 (102) Dane O'Neill 14/1: 151603-6: Rear, eff 3f out, no impress: gelded.   5   **87**
1596 **FOREST MAGIC** 8 [3]4-8-12 (100) Paul Eddery 33/1: 211/-4057: Led 5f, btn 3f out: btr 1596 & 1230.   2½   **80**
1350 **YAWMI** 21 [1]4-9-1 (109) R Hills 25/1: 110-08: Chsd ldrs, wknd qckly 4f out, t.o, reportedly distressed.   dist   **0**
8 Ran   Time 2m 48.97 (3.87)   Owned: Mrs F A Veasey   Trained: Newmarket

---

1758 **2.40 Gr1 Juddmonte Lockinge Stakes 4yo+ (A)**
£116000 £44000 £22000   **1m str**   **Good/Firm 27**   **+24 Fast**   Centre

4798} **RUSSIAN RHYTHM** 210 [3] Sir Michael Stoute 4-8-11 (117) K Fallon 3/1 FAV: 2/11125-1: ch f   **120**
Kingmambo - Balistroika (Nijinsky) Mid-div, hdwy to chall over 1f out, drvn to prevail well ins last, gamely: hvly
bckd: v fast time: reapp: thrice Gr 1 wnr '03 (incl 1,000 Guineas): mdn, Gr 3 & Gr 2 wnr '02: eff at 1m/sharp
10f: acts on firm & gd, stiff or sharp trk: goes v well fresh: tough & genuine, high-class filly
2 Sep'03 Asco 8fm 118-(120) A: 1 Aug'03 Good 9.9g/f 120-(120) A: 1 Jun'03 Asco 8g/f 120-(120) A:
1 May'03 Newm 8g/f 122- A: 1 Oct'02 Newm 8fm 117- A: 1 Aug'02 York 6g/f 116- A:
1 Jul'02 Asco 6g/f 117- A: 1 Jun'02 Newm 6fm 103- D:
1349 **SALSELON** 21 [8] L M Cumani 5-9-0 BL (113) J Murtagh 66/1: 32310-02: Rear, rapid prog to chall   ½   **121**
over 1f out, drvn & just held cl-home: unruly once again in preliminaries but left reapp well bld: acts on fast &
hvy grnd: galvanized by first time blnks: sure to win Gr prizes for talented handler: see 1349.
1349 **NORSE DANCER** 21 [14] D R C Elsworth 4-9-0 (117) T Quinn 10/1: 40360-43: Rear, rapid prog for   nk   **120**
press & led ins last, sn hdd & no extra cl-home: op 14/1: lkd the likely wnr at the dist but is not

512

straightforward: high-class at best: see 1439.

988* **FIREBREAK** 49 [10] Saeed bin Suroor 5-9-0 T K McEvoy 16/1: 21005-14: Trkd ldrs & led over 2f out,   *1*   **118**
hdd ins last, kept on: 7 wk abs: fine rtn to turf, drop to Gr 2/Gr 3 level will suit: see 988 (dirt, Gr 2).

1349+**HURRICANE ALAN** 21 [15]4-9-0 (116) P Dobbs 14/1: 5205-315: Mid-div, eff fnl 2f, not pace to   *1*   **116**
chall: remains in gd heart after 1349 (Gr 2, g/s).

1420 **IKHTYAR** 17 [12]4-9-0 (117) R Hills 11/2: 31210-36: Mid-div, eff over 1f out, onepace ins last: ¾   **115**
up in grade, imprvd eff on this faster surface: Gr 2/Gr 3 company ideal: see 1420.

1349 **CHECKIT** 21 [6]4-9-0 (112) T E Durcan 25/1: 0-433607: br c Mukaddamah - Collected (Taufan) Rear,   ½   **114**
switched & kept on fnl 2f, not pace to chall: cond stks wnr '03, val h'cap & Gr 3 plcd, also List rnr-up: won thrice
'02, incl Gr 2: best btwn 7f/9f on firm & soft, any trk & can go well fresh: smart.
2 Nov'03 Newm 8g/f 109-(113) A: 1 Sep'03 Donc 8gd 110-(105) C: 2 Oct'02 San 8sft 102- :   1 Aug'02 Bade 6sft 106- :
2 Jul'02 Newb 6fm 102- A: 1 May'02 Pont 6g/f 95- C: 1 May'02 Nott 6g/s 95- E: 2 May'02 Newm 5fm 93- D:

991 **REFUSE TO BEND** 49 [9]4-9-0 T L Dettori 5/1: 10100-08: b c Sadler's Wells - Market Slide (Gulch)   1½   **111**
Chsd ldrs, no impress over 1f out: 7 wk abs & t-strap fitted: List, Gr 1 2,000 Guineas & Gr 3 wnr '03 for D Weld:
Gr 1 wnr in '02: best at 1m, tried 12f: acts on fast & gd grnd, stiff/gall trks: goes well fres: proved v smart
miler last term, has gone off the boil.
1 Aug'03 Leop 8g/f 118- A: 1 May'03 Newm 8g/f 119- A: 1 Apr'03 Leop 8g/f 117- :   1 Sep'02 Curr 7g/f 111- :

1349 **INDIAN HAVEN** 21 [1]4-9-0 (114) D Holland 20/1: 10100-59: Cl-up, rdn & no extra dist: likes   ¾   **110**
softer grnd: see 1349 (g/s).

1703* **QUITO 2** [4]7-9-0 bl (103) A Culhane 25/1: 6255610: 10th: Dwelt & bhd, little prog: qck reapp: see 1703.   ¾   **109**
1349 **GATEMAN** 21 [7]7-9-0 (115) K Dalgleish 16/1: 2602120: 11th: Led 2f, remained prom till over 1f out.   *shd*   **109**
1487} **KRATAIOS** 14 [11]4-9-0 O Peslier 25/1: 2/123-140: 12th: b c Sabrehill - Loxandra (Last Tycoon)   ½   **108**
Rear, eff 3f out, no impress: French raider, earlier this term landed a cond stks in native land: wnr '03, subs
List rnr-up & Gr 1 plcd: eff at 7f/1m on gd & soft grnd.

4436*]**WITH REASON** 233 [13]6-9-0 T R Hughes 25/1: 216121-0: 13th: Cl-up, btn 2f out: reapp in t-strap: *5*   **98**
progressive '03, AW mdn, List & dual Gr 3 scorer for D Loder: stays 1m, best at 7f: acts on firm, gd/soft &
fibresand, any trk: best up with/forcing the pace: needs sights lowering & drop to 7f.

2201} **DESERT DEER** 333 [2]6-9-0 (114) K Darley 16/1: 211/210-0: 14th: Led/dsptd lead till over 2f out,   *15*   **70**
sn wknd, sadly broke leg & unlikely to run again.

1356* **TOUT SEUL** 21 [5]4-9-0 (113) S Carson 12/1: 30605-10: 15th: Chsd ldrs, rdn & btn 2f out, well bhd   *6*   **58**
when badly hmpd cl-home: see 1356 (7f, g/s).

15 Ran   Time 1m 37.00 (0.2)   Owned: Cheveley Park Stud   Trained: Newmarket

---

1759   3.10 Paddypower Com Stakes Handicap 3yo+ 0-100 (C)   **[98]**
£17400 £6600 £3300   **1m4f5y**   Good/Firm 27   **-01 Slow**   Inside

1068 **SWIFT TANGO** 39 [17] E A L Dunlop 4-9-6 (90) L Dettori 16/1: 3-102341: Rear, short of room when   **102**
hdwy over 2f out, switched & squeezed thr' gap to lead well ins last, all out: eff at 1m/10f, progressed again on
step up to 12f today: acts on firm, soft & polytrack: best without visor: well suited by waiting tactics & given a
superb ride today, progressive profile, keep on side.

1295* **COLD TURKEY** 24 [10] G L Moore 4-9-1 (85) S Whitworth 9/2 FAV: 1132412: Rear, forced to switch 2f   *shd*   **96+**
out, strong run ins last, just denied: hvly bckd, remains on an upward curve & shld be kept on side.

1346* **RED FORT** 21 [7] M A Jarvis 4-9-10 (94) P Robinson 8/1: 0140-13: Trkd ldrs & rdn to lead over 2f   *1*   **104**
out, hdd well ins last, no extra: op 7/1: fine run: see 1346.

1111 **TURBO 35** [5] G B Balding 5-9-9 (93) S Drowne 16/1: 0021-004: b g Piccolo - By Arrangement (Bold   2½   **96**
Arrangement) Rear, styd on for press fnl 2f, not pace to chall: val November h'cap wnr fnl '03 start: h'cap wnr
fnl '02 start: eff at 10/12f on firm, likes gd & gd/soft, loves a gall trk, esp Doncaster: eff with/without cheek
pieces: seasonal best on step up to 12f.
1 Nov'03 Donc 12gd 95-89 B: 2 Oct'03 Newb 10.0gd 89-86 B: 1 Jul'02 Donc 10.2gd 88-83 C:
2 Apr'02 Hayd 10.5g/f 82-80 C: 1 Jul'01 Warw 7.1g/s 81- E: 2 Jun'01 Wind 8gd 87- E:

1172 **MEPHISTO** 31 [6]5-9-2 (86) D Holland 11/2: 3216-05: b g Machiavellian - Cunning (Bustino) Trkd   1½   **90**
ldrs trav well & led over 3f out till over 2f out, no extra dist: lightly rcd '03, mdn scorer: eff at 10/12f on
fast grnd & a stiff/undul trk: lightly rcd type, more to come.
1 Jul'03 Pont 12.0g/f 86- D: 2 Jun'03 Donc 10.3g/f 88- D:

1502 **LAGGAN BAY** 13 [14]4-8-5 (75) L Keniry(1) 25/1: 05212-06: b g Alzao - Green Lucia (Green Dancer)   *2*   **76**
Rear, kept on for press, not able to chall: unplcd over hdles 03/04 (rtd 85h, juv nov): mdn h'cap wnr in first
time visor '03 (R Hannon): dual mdn rnr-up '02: prob best around 10/12f, may get further: acts on firm, gd/soft &
polytrack, prob any trk: off in visor, not worn as yet this term: gd run.
2 Jul'03 Wind 11.6g/f 76-75 D: 1 Jul'03 Bath 11.7g/f 76-70 E: 2 Jul'03 Sali 12g/f 73-70 D: 2 Jan'03 Ling 8ap 77a-77 D:
2 Sep'02 Bath 8fm 80- D: 2 Jul'02 Sand 7g/s 84- D:

1172 **FLOTTA** 31 [18]5-9-2 (86) A Culhane 7/1: 1210-457: Rear, kept on for press fnl 2f, not able to chall.   *hd*   **86**
1381 **LION HUNTER** 19 [19]5-9-3 (87) R Hughes 16/1: 51/-06038: Mid-div, smooth hdwy to press ldrs over   ¾   **86**
2f out, sn rdn & no extra dist: appeared not to get home over this longer 12f trip: one to note in similar at 10f.
1172 **WUNDERWOOD** 31 [15]5-9-6 (90) T Quinn 6/1: 22014-09: Chsd ldrs, btn dist: bckd: 'nvr trav'.   ½   **88**
770*] **MANORSON** 731 [16]5-9-11 (95) Martin Dwyer 33/1: 52/115-/0: 10th: Trkd ldr, ch 4f out, btn 2f out.   *6*   **84**
3650] **DEFINING** 273 [2]5-9-11 (95) J Murtagh 16/1: 11/0203-0: 11th: Rear, eff 3f out, sn no prog, reapp.   *1*   **83**
1389 **GENERAL GB** 19 [8]7-8-2 (72) S Carson 33/1: 1205200: 12th: Rear, eff 3f out, btn 2f out: btr 1295.   *6*   **51**
2161*]**THUNDERING SURF** 697 [13]7-9-9 (93) P Dobbs 33/1: 60/0631-/0: 13th: Mid-div, btn 2f out: long abs.   *5*   **65**
1296 **HARCOURT** 24 [3]4-9-2 (86) K Fallon 12/1: 52/310-00: 14th: Chsd ldrs till over 2f out.   3½   **53**
1484 **FINANCIAL FUTURE** 14 [9]4-9-12 (96) J Fanning 33/1: 22110-00: 15th: Chsd ldrs till 3f out.   *4*   **57**
3150*]**VALIANT EFFORT** 656 [11]5-8-5 (75) K McEvoy 100/1: 0521-/0: 16th: Led till over 3f out, sn btn.   ¾   **35**
1381 **WIGGY SMITH** 19 [1]5-8-10 (80) Dane O'Neill 6/1: 615/41-50: 17th: Mid-div, btn 4f out: btr 1381.   *2*   **37**

17 Ran   Time 2m 32.63 (3.33)   Owned: Mr Khalifa Sultan   Trained: Newmarket

---

1760   3.45 David Wilson Homes Maiden Stakes 2yo (D)
£5164 £1589 £795   **6f8y str**   Good/Firm 27   **-11 Slow**   Centre

1538 **ICEMAN** 11 [7] J H M Gosden 2-9-0 L Dettori 5/2: 21: Trkd ldrs & led over 1f out, rdn & asserted   **97+**
from dist, decisively: hvly bckd & confirmed debut promise: eff at 5f, relished step up to 6f & will get further:
acts on soft, clry enjoyed fast grnd, gall trk: looks useful & a Royal Ascot type.

SCREWDRIVER 0 [6] R Hannon 2-9-0 Dane O'Neill 66/1: 2: b c Entrepreneur Luot (Pursuit of   *2*   **88**
Love) Trkd ldrs, pushed along & kept on from over 1f out, no threat to wnr: 30,000gns May foal, half-brother to a
7/14f wnr: eff at 6f, sure to get further: acts on fast grnd & a gall trk: likely to progress & win similar soon.

MUSHAJER 0 [4] M P Tregoning 2-9-0   R Hills 8/1: 3: gr c Linamix - Luxurious (Lyphard) Chsd   nk   87
ldrs & ch 2f out, not pace of wnr from dist: op 10/1: Apr foal, 78,000gns purchase: half-brother to numerous wnrs,
incl a smart 10f+ US wnr: dam well related to a top-class 10f performer abroad: eff at 6f, will need further in
time: acts on fast grnd: promising start, should be winning soon.

WITCHRY 0 [10] M A Jarvis 2-9-0   P Robinson 5/1: 4: b c Green Desert - Indian Skimmer (Storm   2½   79
Bird) Mid-div, eff to press ldrs over 1f out, no extra ins last: bckd, op 6/1: Jan foal, dam a multiple Gr 1
mid-dist wnr, sire a smart juv & top-class sprint/1m performer: well bred, shld win races.

AL GARHOUD BRIDGE 0 [8]2-9-0   A Culhane 20/1: 5: b c Josr Algarhoud - Pluck (Never So Bold)   1   76
Rear, some late gains: E40,000 Feb foal, half-brother to 6/7f wnr Balakiref, dam a 6f wnr.

SHAHEER 0 [9]2-9-0   L Keniry(3) 66/1: 6: Rear, kept on from halfway, not able to chall.   2   70
PERFECT CHOICE 0 [13]2-9-0   D Holland 11/1: 7: Dwelt & bhd, late gains, no threat, shld improve.   ¾   68
LEAGUE OF NATIONS 0 [2]2-9-0   K Fallon 10/1: 8: Chsd ldrs till over 1f out: op 20/1.   1   65
BAKKE 0 [12]2-9-0   S Drowne 50/1: 9: Rear, eff 2f out, no impression.   ½   63
1538 ABERDEEN PARK 11 [1]2-8-9   Joanna Badger 66/1: 50: 10th: Chsd ldrs, hung badly left & btn 1f out.   3½   47
RUSKY DUSKY 0 [5]2-9-0   R Hughes 20/1: 0: 11th: Mid-div, no impress fnl 2f, op 25/1.   2½   44
1114 ART LEGEND 35 [2]2-9-0   J Murtagh 20/1: 40: 12th: Keen & led till over 1f out, wknd qckly, op 20/1.   4   32
BLA SHAK 0 [11]2-9-0   Martin Dwyer 9/4 FAV: P: Pushed along rear, p.u./dismounted halfway, lame.   0
13 Ran   Time 1m 13.9 (2.3)   Owned: Cheveley Park Stud   Trained: Manton

---

1761   4.20 Catridge Farm Stud & Manor Farm Packers Handicap Stakes Fillies 3yo 0-80 (D)   [85]
£6318 £1944 £972   7f str   Good/Firm 27   -00 Slow   Centre

4592*}RED SAHARA 224 [7] W J Haggas 3-8-13 (70) K Fallon 13/2: 01-1: ch f Desert Sun - Red Reema (Red   81+
Sunset) Held up, hdwy when short of room over 2f out & again over 1f out, sn led & asserted ins last, cosily:
nicely bckd: reapp/h'cap bow: auct mdn wnr '03 (lightly rcd, turf unpled, rtd 61): eff at 6f, apprec step up to 7f
& shld get 1m: acts on fibresand & fast, sharp/turning or gall trk: goes well fresh: looks one to follow.
1 Oct'03 Wolv 6af 74a- F:

4558} GO BETWEEN 226 [6] E A L Dunlop 3-9-7 (78) S Drowne 33/1: 543210-2: b f Daggers Drawn -   2   83
Pizzicato (Statoblest) Mid-div, eff to press ldrs over 1f out, not pace of wnr ins last: reapp: fill mdn wnr '03:
eff at 6/7f on fast & gd grnd, gall or sharp/undul trks: fine rtn, can find a race.
1 Sep'03 Yarm 6.0g/f 80-(81) D: 2 Aug'03 Epso 7g/f 79-(82) E:

1321* ANDALUZA 22 [10] P D Cundell 3-8-13 (70) S Carson 25/1: 413: Mid-div, styd on well for press ins   ½   74
last, not pace of wnr: h'cap/turf bow: acts on fibresand & fast grnd, lightly rcd & clrly on the up-grade after 1321.
1527 LYCA BALLERINA 12 [19] B W Hills 3-9-2 (73) K May(7) 7/1: 4634-534: Chsd ldrs & ch over 1f out,   2½   72
onepace ins last: see 1527 & 1186.
5013} HERE TO ME 191 [11]3-9-1 (72) R Hughes 25/1: 203502-5: ch f Muhtarram - Away To Me (Exit To   hd   70
Nowhere) Chsd ldrs, btn dist: reapp: thrice mdn rnr-up '03: best at 5/6f last term but prog stays a stiff 1m:
acts on fast & gd/soft grnd, prob any trk: shown enough to find a race.
2 Nov'03 Nott 6.1g/s 75-(66) D: 2 Jul'03 Sand 5.0g/f 67- E: 2 Jul'03 Epso 6g/f 75- E:
1099 HANA DEE 37 [8]3-8-10 (67) T O'Brien(7) 50/1: 030-006: b f Cadeaux Genereux - Jumairah Sun   1½   62
(Scenic) Rear, eff when short of room over 1f out, kept on ins last: shade closer with a clr run: lightly rcd '03,
mdn plcd (rtd 72): stays a gall 7f, tried 1m, shld suit on this evidence: handles fast grnd.
1305 WAVERTREE GIRL 23 [5]3-9-4 (75) J Fanning 25/1: 404-3057: Prom, ch over 1f out, no extra.   ½   69
1281 ELA PAPAROUNA 25 [12]3-9-2 (73) Dane O'Neill 13/2: 543-38: Rear, short of room 2f out, switched   ½   66
& kept on late: see 1281.
4869} FILLIEMOU 204 [9]3-8-8 (65) R Hills 50/1: 440400-9: Rear, eff when short of room over 1f out, late prog.   nk   57
4709} NINE RED 215 [17]3-8-7 (64) M Hills 20/1: 5550-0: 10th: Rear, late gains, no threat on reapp.   1   54
1258 TRUE 26 [2]3-9-2 (73) Martin Dwyer 10/1: 43-00: 11th: Led/dsptd lead till over 1f out, op 12/1.   hd   62
1376* FARRIERS CHARM 19 [15]3-8-8 (65) L Keniry(3) 25/1: 644-10: 12th: Chsd ldrs, btn over 1f out: btr 1376.   1¼   51
1186 FADEELA 30 [1]3-8-13 (70) Paul Eddery 20/1: 5210-500: 13th: Mid-div, no impress fnl 2f: btr 1186.   1   54
2151*}BLUE DAZE 336 [4]3-9-3 (74) P Dobbs 25/1: 01-0: 14th: Prom, wknd over 1f out: reapp, h'cap bow.   1¾   55
54 ABINGTON ANGEL 179 [16]3-9-7 (78) L Dettori 13/2: 32660-0: 15th: Nvr on terms with ldrs: well bckd.   shd   59
4946} CYFRWYS 198 [3]3-9-7 (78) K Darley 33/1: 42524-0: 16th: Chsd ldrs till over 1f out, reapp.   shd   58
1441* GENEROUS GESTURE 16 [20]3-9-4 vis (75) D Holland 10/1: 04-15610: 17th: Led/dsptd lead 5f, sn btn.   3   49
4450} COCONUT COOKIE 232 [14]3-9-7 (78) J Murtagh 33/1: 200-0: 18th: Chsd ldrs till over 2f out, reapp.   4   38
4105} WAAEDAH 251 [13]3-9-7 (78) A Culhane 33/1: 01620-0: 19th: Al bhd on reapp.   ½   43
1239* BEEJAY 28 [18]3-9-4 (75) T Quinn 5/1 FAV: 31-10: 20th: Mid-div, struggling 2f out: rider   1¼   37
reported filly ran flat: much btr 1239 (6f).
20 Ran   Time 1m 26.17 (1.87)   Owned: Shortgrove Manor Stud   Trained: Newmarket

---

1762   4.55 Paddy Power Dial-A-Bet Maiden Stakes Div 1 3yo (D)
£5902 £1816 £908   1m str   Good/Firm 27   -09 Slow   Centre

MADID 0 [15] J H M Gosden 3-9-0   R Hills 7/1: 1: br c Cape Cross - Waffle On (Chief Singer)   97+
Dwelt & rear, smooth hdwy to lead over 1f out, sn asserted, hands-and-heels: op 6/1, debut: 150,00gns purchase,
brother to a 7f List wnr & half-brother to wnrs abroad: dam a 6f wnr: eff over a gall 1m on fast grnd: goes well
fresh: most promising start: looks useful & can win more races.
1166 GRAND BUT ONE 31 [9] B W Hills 3-9-0   M Hills 9/1: 62: Led till over 1f out, not pace of wnr but   1   89
kept on ins last: op 15/2: progressed from eye-catching debut: acts on fast & gd: win sn.
4972} SECRET FLAME 196 [1] W J Haggas 3-8-9   L Dettori 9/2: 5-3: b f Machiavellian - Secret Obsession   2   80
(Secretariat) Mid-div, eff to press ldrs over 1f out, kept on onepace: well bckd: reapp: mdn promise '03 (sole
start, rtd 77): stays a gall 1m, bred to apprec 10/12f: handles fast grnd: promising, shld win races.
1236 PRINCIPAL WITNESS 28 [4] W R Muir 3-9-0   Martin Dwyer 66/1: 04: b c Definite Article - Double   nk   82
Eight (Common Grounds) Chsd ldrs & drvn/chall over 1f out, kept on onepace: rest well covered, left debut bhd: eff
at 1m, half-brother to a 12f wnr & dam a dual 12f wnr: acts on fast grnd, type to progress at 10f+: shld win a mdn.
1236 WHITSBURY CROSS 28 [11]3-9-0   J Murtagh 4/1 FAV: 0-55: Mid-div, eff to chase ldrs over 3f out,   3   78
no impress over 1f out: well bckd, op 9/2: see 1236.
1384 SOUND OF FLEET 19 [12]3-9-0   K Fallon 5/1: 2-46: Cl-up, ev ch & no extra bef dist: see 1384 (10f).   ½   77
1495 EIZAWINA DOCKLANDS 13 [5]3-9-0   T K Darley 66/1: 07: b g Zilzal - Sandrella (Darshaan) Rear,   3   71$
kept on late, nvr a threat: first time t-strap & imprvd from intro: cheaply bght foal, half-brother to a 12f 3yo
wnr: dam unrcd & half-sister to high-class mid-dist performer Storming Home.
1514 BAILAORA 12 [16]3-9-0 bl (79) T Quinn 16/1: 44302-68: Chsd ldrs till over 1f out.   nk   70
CHICA ROCA 205 [3]3-8-9 (80) L Keniry(3) 50/1: 350-9: Chsd ldrs, btn over 1f out, ex French.   ½   64

NEWBURY SATURDAY 15.05.04 Lefthand, Flat, Galloping Track

1495	**WANT 13** [6]3-9-0 R Hughes 12/1: 6-00: 10th: Mid-div, no prog fnl 2f.	½	68
1236	**FUEL CELL 28** [13]3-9-0 Dane O'Neill 9/1: 00: 11th: Dwelt, rdn mid-div, nvr factor.	1¾	65
	ALJAAREH 0 [7]3-9-0 S Drowne 8/1: 0: 12th: Mid-div, struggling fnl 2f, eased ins last, op 10/1, debut.	½	64
	SHAABAN 0 [2]3-9-0 A Culhane 16/1: 0: 13th: Dwelt & al bhd on debut.	2½	59
	SOLIPSIST 0 [17]3-9-0 P Dobbs 33/1: 0: 14th: Rear, nvr a factor on debut.	nk	58
	WODHILL GOLD 0 [10]3-9-0 O Urbina 66/1: 0: 15th: Mid-div at best on debut.	6	47
1497	**BATCHWORTH BEAU 13** [8]3-9-0 S Carson 100/1: 00: 16th: Prom 4f, longer trip.	3½	40
1636	**LOCATOR 7** [14]3-9-0 J Tate 66/1: 5-00: 17th: Chsd ldrs till over 2f out.	hd	39

17 Ran Time 1m 39.7 (2.8) Owned: Mr Hamdan Al Maktoum Trained: Manton

1763 5.25 Paddy Power Dial-A-Bet Maiden Stakes Div 2 3yo (D)
£5876 £1808 £904 **1m str** **Good/Firm 27** -07 Slow Centre

1495	**CREDIT 13** [9] R Hannon 3-9-0 K Fallon 6/4 FAV: 331: Trkd ldrs halfway, rdn & led ins last, held on for press: hvly bckd, op 7/4: eff at 1m on firm & gd/soft grnd, stiff/gall or turning trks: useful.		86
	LONG ROAD 0 [10] J Noseda 3-9-0 P Robinson 12/1: 2: b c Diesis - Tuviah (Eastern Echo) Dwelt, towards rear, hdwy from over 2f out & chall well ins last, just held cl-home on debut: brother to a 10/11f 3yo wnr: eff at 1m, shld get further: acts on fast grnd & a gall trk: promising start, can find a race.	hd	85
	SILVERSTEIN 0 [6] J H M Gosden 3-9-0 L Dettori 5/1: 3: b c Seeking The Gold - Salchow (Nijinsky) Dwelt, sn mid-div, drvn & led over 1f out till well ins last, no extra: nicely bckd: debut: $40,000 purchase: brother to a French 1m juv Gr 1 wnr, dam unrcd half-sister to sev Gr 1 wnrs: eff at 1m on fast grnd: well bred & this was an encouraging start.	½	84
	DIFFERENT PLANET 0 [4] J W Hills 3-9-0 T Quinn 20/1: 4: b c Inchinor - Take Heart (Electric) Mid-div, keeping on when short of room dist & again ins last, closer with a clr run on debut: op 16/1: 60,000gns purchase, half-brother to a 6/7f wnr, also a dual 10f wnr: dam a multiple wnr at 7f/10f: eff at 1m, stay further: acts on fast grnd & a gall trk: plenty to like here.	1¼	80+
1511	**PIZAZZ 12** [12]3-9-0 (79) M Hills 6/1: 0-525: Chsd ldrs, chall dist, no extra ins last.	¾	80
	LOST SOLDIER THREE 0 [5]3-9-0 D Holland 12/1: 6: Mid-div, outpcd halfway, kept on late: op 10/1: mid-dist pedigree, 10f+ will suit in similar.	1¼	77
4251}	**ZUMA 242** [15]3-9-0 P Dobbs 33/1: 00-7: Trkd ldr & ch over 2f out, bmpd dist, onepace, reapp.	nk	76
1514	**MY HOPE 12** [2]3-8-9 S Drowne 33/1: 00-08: Rear, switched & kept on late, nvr threat to ldrs.	nk	70$
	GENTLE RAINDROP 0 [7]3-8-9 Martin Dwyer 50/1: 9: Chsd ldrs till over 1f out, debut.	½	69
4872}	**THREE SHIPS 204** [11]3-9-0 R Hughes 14/1: 0-0: 10th: Led till over 1f out, bmpd & sn btn.	1	72
1495	**DESERT HAWK 13** [3]3-9-0 Dane O'Neill 20/1: 00: 11th: Rear, eff over 2f out, sn no impress.	hd	71
1617	**FORGE LANE 8** [1]3-9-0 R Brisland 50/1: 0000: 12th: Sn struggling, gelded.	5	62$
	COUNT BORIS 0 [14]3-9-0 S Carson 50/1: 0: 13th: Chsd ldrs 6f on debut.	¾	61
	KINGS MINSTREL 0 [8]3-9-0 A Culhane 14/1: 0: 14th: Dwelt & al bhd on debut.	18	28
	GOVERNMENT 0 [13]3-9-0 K Darley 12/1: 0: 15th: Slow away & sn bhd on debut.	1½	25

15 Ran Time 1m 40.31(3.51) Owned: Highclere Thoroughbred Racing XV Trained: Marlborough

THIRSK SATURDAY 15.05.04 Lefthand, Flat, Oval Track

Official Going Good/Firm

1764 2.15 European Breeders Fund Carlton Miniott Novice Stakes Fillies 2yo (D)
£5577 £1716 £858 **5f str** **Good/Firm 27** -30 Slow Stands Side

	MISS MEGGY 0 [8] T D Easterby 2-8-10 D Allan(3) 20/1: 1: Dwelt, sn mid-div, rdn & led ins last, styd on strongly: £25,000 April first foal, dam a 5/6f wnr & sire high-class sprinter: eff at 5f on fast grnd & an easy trk: goes well fresh: sharp type, potentially useful.		90
1608	**BRIGHT MOLL 8** [1] M L W Bell 2-8-12 I Mongan 15/8 FAV: 122: Trkd ldrs & ch 2f out, rdn & no extra ins last: nicely bckd, op 3/1: acts on fast & soft grnd, proving consistent , see 1608 & 974.	1¼	87
1471*	**WORLD AT MY FEET 14** [9] N Bycroft 2-9-3 J Quinn 3/1: 213: Led/dsptd lead & narrow lead over 1f out, hdd ins last & no extra: bckd, op 9/2: acts on fast & gd/soft grnd: just btr 1471.	1½	87
	COLONIAL GIRL 0 [3] T D Easterby 2-8-10 W Supple 25/1: 4: b f Desert Style - Telemania (Mujtahid) Dwelt, towards rear, drvn & kept on late, not able to chall: op 33/1: £21,000 April foal, dam a 6f juv wnr & 7f plcd: sire proved best at 7f: eff at 5f, looks sure to apprec 6f+ in similar: handles fast grnd.	2½	72
1380	**ELISHA 19** [5]2-8-10 S W Kelly 16/1: 45: Cl-up till no extra ins last.	nk	71
1445*	**HANDSOME LADY 16** [4]2-8-10 N Callan 3/1: 16: Trkd ldrs, no extra dist: nicely bckd tho' op 6/4: disappointing effort on today's fast grnd: btr 1445 (gd/soft).	1	68
	AFRICAN BREEZE 0 [10]2-8-10 Dean McKeown 25/1: 7: b f Atraf - Luanshya (First Trump) Dwelt, rear, nvr pace to chall: Feb first foal, dam 5f juv plcd & subs 6f 3yo wnr, a half-sister to useful sprint h'capper Magic Rainbow, sire a high-class sprinter: with R M Whitaker.	1	65
1173	**SERENE PEARL 30** [2]2-8-10 N Pollard 100/1: 08: Al towards rear.	1	62
1343*	**FLOSSYTOO 21** [6]2-9-3 J D O'Reilly(7) 9/1: 019: Dwelt, led till hung left & hdd over 1f out, fdd.	¾	67
	AMANDERICA 0 [7]2-8-10 Andrew Webb(7) 100/1: 0: 10th: Slow away & sn bhd on debut.	dist	0

10 Ran Time 59.84 (2.84) Owned: Mr David W Armstrong Trained: Malton

1765 2.50 Sally Walpole 30th Birthday Handicap Stakes 3yo+ 0-80 (D)
£5746 £1768 £884 **5f str** **Good/Firm 27** -02 Slow Stands Side [79]

1371	**POLISH EMPEROR 20** [17] P W Harris 4-9-5 e (70) N Callan 9/1: 4225031: Made most stands side, drvn & styd on strongly ins last: bckd, op 11/1: stays 6f, best at 5f: acts on firm, gd/soft & both AWs: suited by blnks/eye-shield & forcing tactics, loves a sharp/easy trk: see 1371 & 109.		81
1523	**ONLINE INVESTOR 12** [18] D Nicholls 5-9-0 (65) Alex Greaves 9/2 FAV: 000-0052: Trkd ldrs stands side, chall dist, no extra cl-home: nicely bckd: gd effort but on long losing run: see 1523.	1	73
1476	**BRIGADORE 14** [19] J R Weymes 5-9-2 (67) T Hamilton(3) 8/1: 30000-63: Al prom stands side, not pace of front pair ins last: back on a winning mark: see 1476 (reapp).	3½	64
4286*	**RACCOON 241** [6] T D Barron 4-9-9 (74) T P Queally(3) 13/2: 02011-4: b g Raphane - Kunucu	1¼	67+

515

(Bluebird) Chsd ldrs far side, led that group ins last, no threat to ldrs stands side: bckd tho' op 5/1, reapp: progressive '03, landed mdn h'cap & h'cap: both wins at 5f on fast grnd, stiff or easy trk: gd return on 'wrong side', keep in mind. 1 Sep'03 Sand 5.0g/f 75-68 D: 1 Sep'03 Thir 5g/f 69-60 F: 2 Jul'03 Hami 6.0g/f 54- D:
1683 **CHICO GUAPO 3** [4]4-9-12 (77) I Mongan 13/2: 0500105: Led far side, no extra ins last. qk reapp. *½* **68**
1371+**ERRACHT 20** [13]6-9-0 (65) G Baker 10/1: 030-0516: Chsd ldrs stands side, no prog dist: btr 1371. *½* **54**
927 **KANGARILLA ROAD 50** [1]5-9-5 (70) Dean McKeown 18/1: 56/600-07: b g Magic Ring - Kangra Valley *shd* **59**
(Indian Ridge) Mid-div far side, kept on late, no dngr: 7 wk abs: lightly rcd & unplcd '03 (h'cap, rtd 73): suited by 5f on fast & gd/soft grnd, any trk: with Mrs J R Ramsden.
1 Aug'02 York 5g/f 77-74 C: 1 May'02 Thir 5gd 73-69 C: 1 Apr'02 Catt 5g/f 73-58 E: 2 Apr'02 Nott 5g/s 60-55 E:
1476 **TOMMY SMITH 14** [3]6-9-7 bl (72) D McGaffin 14/1: 2630-008: ch g Timeless Times - Superstream *nk* **60**
(Superpower) Prom far side till over 1f out: dual h'cap rnr-up '03: class stks & dual h'cap wnr '02: best at 5/6f, loves firm & fast grnd, with/without visor, tried blnks: loves to dominate: well h'capped.
2 Jul'03 Pont 5g/f 79-77 D: 2 May'03 Beve 5gd 80-76 D: 1 Jul'02 York 5g/f 85-78 C: 1 Jun'02 Ripo 5fm 79-71 D:
1 Jun'02 Pont 5g/f 74- E: 1 Aug'01 Beve 5g/f 69-63 E: 1 Jul'01 Redc 5fm 63-58 F: 2 Jun'01 Muss 5g/f 57-56 E:
2 Jun'01 Leic 6g/f 58- G:
1476 **WHISTLER 14** [5]7-9-10 p (75) Darren Williams 25/1: 4500-009: Handy far side till over 1f out. *hd* **62**
1518 **AMANDAS LAD 12** [8]4-9-0 (65) N Pollard 66/1: 4663550: 10th: Chsd ldrs far side, no prog dist. *1¾* **47**
1476 **JOHN OGROATS 14** [20]6-9-7 (72) S W Kelly 40/1: 0000-000: 11th: Dwelt, rear stands side, late prog. *½* **52**
4670} **CHARLIE PARKES 218** [10]6-9-12 (77) W Supple 14/1: 500000-0: 12th: Prom far side till over 1f out. *shd* **57**
1627 **CANDLERIGGS 7** [7]8-9-3 (68) L Treadwell(7) 33/1: 50650-00: 13th: Rear far side, nvr a factor. *shd* **47**
1627 **SIR SANDROVITCH 7** [15]8-8-7 p (58) G Parkin 20/1: 66000-00: 14th: Al rear stands side. *2* **31**
1508 **BALLYBUNION 13** [9]5-9-0 (65) A Nicholls 28/1: 26100-00: 15th: Dwelt & al bhd far side. *nk* **37**
1638 **TIME TO REMEMBER 7** [2]6-8-13 (64) J Carroll 50/1: 000R-000: 16th: Rear far side throughout. *½* **34**
187 **STRENSALL 155** [14]7-9-12 (77) R Fitzpatrick 33/1: 001420-0: 17th: Dwelt & al bhd stands side: abs. *1* **44**
1555* **CASH 11** [12]6-8-8 p (59) L Enstone(3) 18/1: 3500010: 18th: Chsd ldrs stands side, btn over 1f out. *2½* **18**
1638 **African Spur 7** [16]4-8-7 t(58) D Tudhope(3) 66/1:0 4313} **Elvington Boy 240** [11]7-9-9 (74) T Lucas 25/1:U
20 Ran Time 58.43 (1.43) Owned: Edrich Graves Harris Trained: Berkhamsted

1766

3.20 Rectangle Group Handicap Stakes 3yo 0-100 (C) **[105]**
£9822 £3022 £1511 **5f str** **Good/Firm 27** **-00 Slow** Stands Side

1570 **BENBAUN 10** [2] M J Wallace 3-8-10 vis (87) D Corby(3) 14/1: 6120-101: Made all, rdn & styd on **99**
strongly fnl 2f, op 12/1: eff at 5/6f on firm & fast grnd, gall/undul trks: best dominating & showed fine speed to overcome tricky low draw, progressive & useful: see 1488.
1488 **LUALUA 14** [10] T D Barron 3-7-12 (75) P Fessey 22/1: 105-42: Dwelt & held up, styd on for press, *1½* **81**
not pace of wnr: imprvd eff on drop back to 5f: again fin bhd today's wnr in 1488.
1572 **JOHNNY PARKES 10** [13] Mrs J R Ramsden 3-8-6 (83) I Mongan 15/2: 2215-103: Trkd ldrs, styd on *¾* **88**
onepace for press: 8lb higher than win in 1002 (reapp).
1150 **TWO STEP KID 32** [9] J Noseda 3-8-11 (88) E Ahern 9/4 FAV: 1-64: Trkd ldrs & ch over 1f out, no *nk* **92**
extra ins last: hvly bckd on h'cap debut: handles fast & polytrack: prob apprec return to sprinting: eff at 5/6f.
4881} **TRAYTONIC 203** [4]3-9-7 (98) F Lynch 14/1: 240410-5: b c Botanic - Lady Parker (Nordico) Rear & *1½* **97**
rdn, nrst fin on reapp: mdn seller, cond stks & h'cap scorer '03 (progressive): eff at 5/6f, tried 7f: acts on firm & gd grnd, prob handles gd/soft: prob handles any trk, likes a gall one: prob sharper for this at 6f next time.
1 Oct'03 York 6.0g/f 102-94 C: 2 Aug'03 Ling 5g/f 93-(90) D: 1 Jul'03 Yarm 5.2gd 95- C: 1 Mar'03 Donc 5gd 85- F:
1477* **MR WOLF 14** [1]3-8-2 (79) A Nicholls 10/1: 00-22116: Handy & ch over 1f out, no extra: btr 1477. *½* **76**
1572 **TRIBUTE 10** [11]3-8-2 (79) T P Queally 6/1: 63261-07: b g Green Desert - Zooming (Indian Ridge) *shd* **76**
Slow away & held up, not pace to chall: op 5/1: mdn scorer '03: eff at 5/6f on fast & gd grnd, sharp/undul trk.
1 Aug'03 Ling 5g/f 80-(85) D: 2 Jul'03 Ling 6gd 86- D:
1154 **WHOS WINNING 32** [14]3-7-12 (2oh) (73) J F McDonald(3) 25/1: 40436-08: Mid-div, not pace to chall. *1½* **67**
1387 **CELTIC THUNDER 19** [7]3-8-7 (84) D Allan(3) 11/2: 31246-29: Chsd ldrs, btn when hmpd ins last. *½* **74**
4548*}**PARADISE ISLE 227** [3]3-8-13 (90) G Baker 14/1: 22211-0: 10th: Slow away & rear, nvr a factor. *nk* **79**
3524} **Self Belief 278** [12]3-7-12 (8oh)(67) D Fox(5) 100/1:0 1572 **Divine Spirit 10** [5]3-8-6 (83) W Supple 25/1:0
4247} **Fyodor 243** [8]3-8-8 (85) S W Kelly 12/1:0 3895} **Molly Moon 263** [6]3-8-12 (89) F Norton 40/1:0
14 Ran Time 58.33 (1.33) Owned: Ransley Skidmore Birks Trained: Newmarket

1767

3.55 Toteexacta Handicap Stakes 4yo+ 0-95 (C) **[95]**
£9997 £3076 £1538 **6f str** **Good/Firm 27** **+01 Fast** Stands Side

1481 **CELTIC MILL 14** [2] D W Barker 6-9-3 (84) L Enstone(3) 10/1: 140-1401: Made all far side, strongly **97**
pressed dist, held on gamely for press: gd time: best dominating at 6/7f, stays 1m: acts on firm, gd & fibresand, any trk: v tough & useful performer: see 482 (reapp).
1391 **MINE BEHIND 19** [1] J R Best 4-8-11 (78) N Pollard 16/1: 2263-162: Trkd ldrs trav well far side, *¾* **86**
chall ins last, no extra fnl 100y: lost little in defeat & can find similar: see 1255.
1523 **HICCUPS 12** [19] Mrs J R Ramsden 4-9-0 p (81) I Mongan 7/1: 0630-203: Dwelt, trkd ldrs stands *3* **82+**
side, rdn & led that group ins last, not pace of front pair far side: gd run, likely type for similar: see 1217.
1481 **ELLENS ACADEMY 14** [14] E J Alston 9-8-13 (80) W Supple 4/1 FAV: 1-463424: Trkd ldrs stands side *½* **79**
& led that group over 1f out till ins last, kept on: nicely bckd: on a fair mark & threatening to win similar.
1251 **INTER VISION 26** [4]4-9-5 (86) A Beech(3) 33/1: 2054-005: b c Cryptoclearance - Fateful (Topsider) *½* **83**
Chsd ldrs far side, kept on: '03 h'cap wnr: thrice wnr '02, incl cond stks: eff at 5f, suited by 6f on firm & gd/soft, prob any trk, likes Ripon/Chester: with A Dickman.
2 Aug'03 Ches 6.1g/f 90-87 C: 1 Aug'03 Ripo 6g/f 90-80 D: 1 Jul'02 Ches 5fm 98- B: 1 Jun'02 Ripo 5g/f 96- E:
1 Jun'02 Ches 5gd 86- D: 2 May'02 Carl 5g/s 84- E: 2 May'02 Redc 5fm 83- F:
1523 **MILLION PERCENT 12** [12]5-9-1 (82) Darren Williams 16/1: 15430-06: b g Ashkalani - Royal Jade *shd* **79**
(Last Tycoon) Mid-div stands side, eff to chall over 1f out, no extra ins last: class stks, rtd h'cap & h'cap wnr '03 (progressive, rtd 84 at best, h'cap): class stks rnr-up '02: 6f specialist, stays 7f: acts on fm & fast, handles soft & polytrack: prob handles any trk & best without cheek pieces.
1 Aug'03 Newm 6gd 82-75 D: 2 Jul'03 Leic 6.0gd 75-(70) E: 1 Jul'03 Ayr 6gd 76-70 D: 1 Jun'03 Warw 6.1fm 75-(68) E:
2 Jun'02 Kemp 6g/f 80- D: 2 Aug'01 Ripo 6g/f 98- A: 1 Aug'01 Ripo 6gd 91- D: 1 May'01 Yarm 6g/f 90- D:
4471} **LAFI 231** [16]5-9-11 (92) L Treadwell(7) 16/1: 1/14310-7: Rear stands side, short of room 2f out, *hd* **88+**
kept on late: eye-catching late prog for new yard on reapp, has been gelded, prob impr at 7f.

4990*}**CD EUROPE 194** [7]6-9-11 (92) N Callan 11/1: 202021-8: Rear far side, late gains on reapp. *hd* **87**
1481 **VIEWFORTH 14** [3]6-8-8 bl (75) J Carroll 14/1: 600-4409: Chsd wnr far side till over 1f out: btr 1276. *nk* **69**
1120 **SEAFIELD TOWERS 34** [10]4-8-11 p (78) N Mackay(3) 33/1: 13160-00: 10th: Led stands side till dist. *2½* **64**
1481 **OBE ONE 14** [13]4-8-5 (72) F Norton 33/1: 0000-000: 11th: Dwelt, stands side, nvr pace to chall. *1½* **54**
1474 **TRUE NIGHT 14** [18]7-8-9 (76) P M Quinn 25/1: 215-0000: 12th: Rcd stands side, al bhd. *½* **56**
1523 **RAGAMUFFIN 12** [20]6-8-6 (73) D Allan(3) 14/1: 00/200-00: 13th: Mid-div stands side, drvn & no prog. *nk* **52**
1598 **BANJO BAY 8** [8]6-9-3 (84) Alex Greaves 16/1: 10000-00: 14th: Prom stands side till over 1f out. *½* **61**
1481 **NAJEEBON 14** [11]5-9-6 (87) S Hitchcott(3) 7/1: 01450-00: 15th: Rdn towards rear stands side, nvr a factor: well bckd, op 9/1, prefers stiffer trk. *¾* **62**
1627 **Paddywack 7** [6]7-8-0 bl(67) J Quinn 11/1:0
874 **Awarding 57** [5]4-8-11 (78) Lucy Russell(7) 50/1:0
2511} **Prince Dayjur 322** [15]5-8-12 (79) E Ahern 14/1:0
1120 **No Time 34** [17]4-9-11 (92) T G McLaughlin 20/1:0
19 Ran Time 1m 11.03 (1.53) Owned: Mr P Asquith Trained: Richmond

1768

4.30 Grapes Great Habton Maiden Stakes 3yo+ (D)
£5681 £1748 £874 **1m4f** **Good/Firm 27** **-14 Slow** Inside

1272 **PORTRAIT OF A LADY 25** [8] H R A Cecil 3-8-0 (74) J Quinn 11/2: 540-31: Trkd ldrs & rdn/led over 1f out, held on gamely for press cl-home: now suited by 12f: acts on fast & soft grnd, sharp/undul or easy trk. **74**
1140 **SUNNY LADY 33** [2] E A L Dunlop 3-8-0 (73) N Mackay(3) 11/2: 60-22: Mid-div, drvn & styd on well ins last, just denied: styd longer 12f trip well: acts on fast & gd grnd: see 1140. *shd* **73**
SUNDAY CITY 0 [7] D R Loder 3-8-5 T P Queally(3) 11/4 FAV: 3: ch c Sunday Silence - Diamond City (Mr Prospector) Mid-div, onepace for press fnl 3f but kept on: debut: half-brother to a useful dirt performer: styd an easy 12f, could get further: acts on fast grnd. *¾* **77**
1347 **CUMBRIA 21** [9] M Johnston 3-8-0 S Chin 100/30: 34: Led/dsptd lead, rdn & hdd over 1f out & no extra: nicely bckd tho' op 9/4: handles fast & gd/soft grnd: see 1347. *1½* **70**
1429 **HATHLEN 17** [4]3-8-5 (76) R Lappin 11/2: 022-0665: Led till 2f out, btn dist: clr rem, prob stays 12f. *1* **74**
1501 **VICTORY LAP 13** [11]3-8-2 (2ow) S Hitchcott 14/1: 3-06: Held up, eff 4f out, no prog fnl 3f. *5* **64**
3277] **AWWAL MARRA 650** [10]4-9-5 Dean McKeown 25/1: 2/-7: ch f King of Kings - Secretariat Lass (Secretariat) Held up, rdn & btn 3f out: long abs: missed '03: rnr-up sole prev start in '02 (M Johnston, mdn): eff over a sharp/turning 7f, 1m+ may yet suit: acts on fast grnd. *9* **50**
2 Aug'02 Ches 7g/f 73- D:
JIDIYA 201 [12]5-9-10 I Mongan 33/1: 52-8: Slow away, chsd ldr till 3f out, jumps fit. *2½* **51**
307 **ASHTAROUTE 132** [1]4-9-5 (49) Andrew Webb(7) 50/1: 30050-69: Al bhd. *1* **45**
1472 **DAWN AIR 14** [13]3-8-0 P Fessey 20/1: 0-30: 10th: Sn struggling. *2½* **41**
IM A DARK HORSE 0 [5]3-8-5 G Parkin 50/1: 0: 11th: Slow away & al bhd on debut. *1½* **44**
5024} **ZAMEEL 190** [6]3-8-5 D Allan(3) 100/1: 00-0: 12th: Mid-div, btn 5f out, gelded, reapp. *2½* **40**
3173} **LAGOSTA 294** [3]4-9-10 (46) N Pollard 50/1: 00005-0: 13th: Chsd ldrs till 5f out, t.o., new yard. *dist* **0**
13 Ran Time 2m 34.72 (4.92) Owned: Mr J Shack Trained: Newmarket

1769

5.00 Sun Inn Normanby Handicap Stakes 3yo 0-80 (D) **[87]**
£5785 £1780 £890 **1m rnd** **Good/Firm 27** **-17 Slow** Inside

1628 **MYSTICAL GIRL 7** [8] M Johnston 3-9-2 (75) S Chin 5/1 FAV: 230-331: Handy & led over 2f out, readily asserted, val 4L+: bckd: eff at 7f/1m on fast & soft: progressive, win again: see 1628. **90+**
1130 **LA PERSIANA 33** [11] W Jarvis 3-8-13 (72) J Quinn 11/1: 40-52: gr f Daylami - La Papagena (Habitat) Mid-div, kept on for press ins last, no threat to wnr: h'cap bow: unplcd '03 (rtd 74, mdn): stays 1m, shaped as if 10f could suit: handles fast grnd: can find a race. *2* **79**
1473 **BURLEY FLAME 14** [3] J G Given 3-8-13 (72) M Fenton 10/1: 0-433: Led till over 2f out, kept on for press: h'cap bow & apprec return to 1m: acts on fast & gd/soft grnd: see 1473. *3* **73**
1495 **OH GOLLY GOSH 13** [4] N P Littmoden 3-9-3 p (76) J P Guillambert(3) 25/1: 30-2204: Chsd ldrs over 2f out, no extra bef dist: handles fast & soft grnd: see 1089. *1* **75**
1186 **HEZAAM 30** [7]3-9-4 (77) W Supple 8/1: 01-05: b c Red Ransom - Ashraakat (Danzig) Held up, kept on late for press, not able to chall: h'cap bow: lightly rcd '03, mdn scorer: winning form over a stiff 7f, 1m likely to suit: acts on fast & gd grnd: with J L Dunlop. *shd* **76**
1 Nov'03 Newm 7g/f 79- D:
1470 **DOUBLE VODKA 15** [1]3-8-5 (64) D Allan(3) 25/1: 6035-06: b g Russian Revival - Silius (Junius) Slow away & held up, eff 3f out, only mod prog: mdn plcd in '03 for M Dods (rtd 68): dam a 1m/10f wnr: eff over a stiff 7f, 1m+ shld suit: handles fast grnd. *1½* **60**
1470 **AUROVILLE 15** [14]3-8-7 (66) I Mongan 16/1: 050-047: Chsd ldrs over 2f out, sn no extra: op 12/1. *nk* **61**
1105 **THE VIOLIN PLAYER 35** [18]3-9-7 (80) M Tebbutt 50/1: 0313-08: Bhd, late gains, no threat. *1½* **72**
1176 **CATHERINE HOWARD 30** [12]3-9-1 (74) S Hitchcott(3) 9/1: 1-49: Chsd ldrs till 2f out: btr 1176. *2* **62**
1370 **ON THE WATERFRONT 20** [15]3-8-8 (67) J Carroll 14/1: 55420: 10th: Bhd, mod prog: btr 1370. *1½* **52**
1515 **SHOW NO FEAR 12** [6]3-8-12 (71) W Ryan 7/1: 0552-100: 11th: Held up, nvr a factor: btr 1141. *¾* **55**
1515 **HONEST INJUN 12** [17]3-9-4 (77) E Ahern 14/1: 02-1440: 12th: Mid-div, hmpd early, keeping on when hmpd ins last: luckless run, can do better: see 1515, 1257 & 381. *1* **59+**
1176 **DISPOL VELETA 30** [10]3-8-9 (68) N Mackay(3) 7/1: 3014130: 13th: Prom till 2f out: much btr 1176. *3* **44**
4686} **STEVEDORE 216** [5]3-9-6 (79) J F McDonald(3) 20/1: 0214-0: 14th: Mid-div, btn 3f out, reapp. *2* **51**
798 **NORWEGIAN 72** [13]3-8-6 vis (65) T P Queally(3) 10/1: 51430: 15th: Mid-div, struggling fnl 2f, abs. *2½* **32**
1306 **NAMED AT DINNER 23** [9]3-9-0 (73) A Beech(3) 66/1: 04224-00: 16th: Prom till 4f out. *nk* **39**
1146 **Lady Sunset 33** [16]3-8-1 (60) F Norton 66/1:0
4988} **Hearthstead Dream 194** [2]3-8-13 (72) A Nicholls 40/1:0
18 Ran Time 1m 38.9 (3.5) Owned: T T Bloodstocks Trained: Middleham

THIRSK   SATURDAY 15.05.04   Lefthand, Flat, Oval Track

1770   5.30 Boltby Classified Stakes 3yo 0-80 (D)
£5577 £1716 £858   1m rnd   Good/Firm 27   -47 Slow   Inside

1419 **ATTUNE 17** [6] B J Meehan 3-8-9 (80) J F McDonald(3) 9/1: 4-401: Handy & led ins last, held on all   81
out: slow time: eff at 7f, now stays a slowly run 1m: acts on fast & gd grnd: see 1171.
5028} **ALEKHINE 190** [4] P W Harris 3-9-1 (83) E Ahern 11/2: 16-2: b g Soviet Star - Alriyaah (Shareef   *hd*   **87**
Dancer) Dwelt, sn in tch, styd on well for press cl-home, just held: bckd on reapp, has been gelded: debut wnr '03
(mdn, subs unplcd, cond stks): winning form at 7f, stays a slowly run 1m: acts on fast grnd, gall/easy trk & goes
well fresh: only lightly rcd & more improvement is likely. 1 Oct'03 Donc 7g/f 82- D:
4845} **ALSHAWAMEQ 206** [8] J L Dunlop 3-8-13 (81) W Supple 13/2: 615-3: b g Green Desert - Azdihaar (Mr   *shd*   **85**
Prospector) Trkd ldrs & led over 1f out till ins last, just held: reapp, has been gelded: lightly rcd '03, mdn
scorer in first time blnks: winning form over a stiff 1m, related to wnrs btwn 5f/12f: acts on fast grnd.
1 Oct'03 Sali 8g/f 85- D:
4420} **MAJOR EFFORT 234** [5] Sir Michael Stoute 3-8-12 (80) F Lynch 3/1: 052-4: b c Rahy - Tethkar   *1¼*   **81**
(Machiavellian) In tch, kept on for press fnl 2f, not pace to chall: well bckd, op 5/1, reapp: mdn rnr-up fnl '03
start: eff at 7f, styd slowly run 1m & a stronger gall at this trip will suit: handles fast & gd/soft grnd,
sharp/turning or easy trks: with Sir Michael Stoute.
2 Sep'03 Ches 7.0g/s 81- D:
1186 **SWEET REPLY 30** [3]3-8-9 (78) L Enstone(3) 22/1: 45104-05: Led till 2f out, no extra.   2   **74**
1152* **DAVORIN 32** [7]3-9-1 (83) T P Queally(3) 7/4 FAV: 16: Dwelt, sn handy & narrow lead 2f out till   *nk*   **79**
over 1f out, wknd: well bckd tho' op 5/4: btr 1152 (debut, 7f, g/s).
947   **HEVERSHAM 49** [1]3-8-12 (80) S W Kelly 9/1: 41207: Trkd ldrs, onepace fnl 2f: 7 wk abs: btr 694.   *nk*   **75**
7 Ran   Time 1m 41.28(5.88)   Owned: Wyck Hall Stud   Trained: Upper Lambourn

NOTTINGHAM   SATURDAY 15.05.04   Lefthand, Galloping Track

Official Going Good (Good/Soft places)

1771   1.50 Totepool Classified Stakes 3yo 0-90 (C)
£13813 £4250 £2125   6f15y   Good/Soft 72   -07 Slow   Inside

1570* **LAKE GARDA 10** [4] B A McMahon 3-8-13 (91) G Gibbons 11/4 FAV: 001-5311: Keen cl-up, duelled with   95
ldr ins fnl 1f, drvn out to lead cl-home: bckd tho' op 9/4: eff at 5/6f on firm & gd/soft grnd, prob any trk:
genuine, improving & useful: see 1570 & 1344.
1621* **MORSE 7** [2] J A Osborne 3-8-12 (88) S Sanders 3/1: 6-022312: Led, under press ins fnl 1f, just   *shd*   **93**
hdd cl-home, saddle slipped slightly: rider received 2 day whip ban: well bckd on qck reapp: imprvd on win in 1621
(h'cap), just denied here & can return to winning ways.
1572 **HARRY UP 10** [3] J G Given 3-8-12 (90) M Fenton 10/1: 040-2303: Handy, kept on ins fnl 1f, not   2   **87**
pace frm disgraced: far frm disgraced: just btr 1106, see 1018.
4557} **MANDOBI 226** [6] A C Stewart 3-9-1 (93) P McCabe 6/1: 32120-4: ch c Mark of Esteem - Miss Queen   *3½*   **80**
(Miswaki) Rear, prog halfway, no impress fnl 1f: reapp: med auct mdn wnr in '03 (also plcd on 3 of other 4
starts): eff at 6f, will apprec return to 7f: acts on gd & fast grnd: acts on a stiff/gall trk: not disgraced.
2 Sep'03 York 7.0g/f 95-89 C: 1 Aug'03 Newm 7gd 87- E: 2 Jul'03 Newm 6g/f 92- E:
2503* **)PROMENADE 322** [7]3-8-9 (89) J Mackay 15/2: 1161-5: b f Primo Dominie - Hamsah (Green Desert)   1   **71**
Held up, al in rear: reapp: won 3 of only 4 '03 starts (auct mdn, auct nov stks & stks, unplcd in Gr 3): eff at
5f, 6f shld suit: acts on fast grnd & a gall trk: has gone well fresh: with M L W Bell.
1 Jun'03 Donc 5g/f 92- D: 1 May'03 Redc 5g/f 89- F: 1 Apr'03 Leic 5.0g/f 83- F:
1496 **MAHMOOM 13** [1]3-8-12 (87) C Catlin 11/2: 211-006: ch c Dr Fong - Rohita (Waajib) Handy till   *¾*   **72**
halfway, sn wknd: med auct mdn & stks wnr on 2 of only 3 '03 starts: eff at 6/7f (bred for speed): acts on fast
grnd: can force the pace: just sharper for today.
1 Oct'03 Newm 7g/f 88- B: 1 Sep'03 Newm 6g/f 88- E: 2 Sep'03 Good 6g/f 74- D:
4224} **SILVER PRELUDE 245** [5]3-8-12 (90) D Sweeney 25/1: 215250-7: Handy 4f, fdd: reapp.   9   **54**
7 Ran   Time 1m 15.55 (4.75)   Owned: Mr J C Fretwell   Trained: Tamworth

1772   2.20 Totesport Com Handicap Stakes 3yo+ 0-80 (D)
£8600 £2646 £1323   1m6f15y   Good/Soft 72   +10 Fast   Inside   **[80]**

1502 **BUCKS 13** [15] D K Ivory 7-9-4 (70) M Howard(7) 7/1: 25-03021: Handy, short of room over 2f out,   79
styd on well fnl 1f, rdn out to lead cl-home: eff at 12f/2m on firm, gd/soft & polytrack: see 1502 & 1056.
5008} **CLARINCH CLAYMORE 192** [3] J M Jefferson 8-9-3 (69) T Eaves(5) 16/1: 100046-2: b g Sabrehill -   *shd*   **77**
Salu (Ardross) Dwelt, prog after 6f, styd on to lead dist, hdd on line: reapp: h'cap wnr in '03: won 4 h'caps in
'02, also plcd 7 times: eff btwn 12f/2m on fast & fibresand, likes soft grnd: acts on any trk, loves Southwell: gd
weight- carrier who goes well fresh: only just denied here on reapp, is on a winning mark & can find similar.
1 Jul'03 Beve 16.2g/f 73-70 C: 2 Nov'02 Muss 16sft 79-75 C: 1 Oct'02 Ayr 13sft 76-65 C:
1 Aug'02 Beve 16.1 g/s 66-58 D: 2 Jun'02 Ayr 10.8g/s 59-57 F: 1 Jun'02 Hayd 10.5sft 59-53 G:
2 May'02 Pont 12g/f 52-51 E: 2 May'02 Hami 13sft 52-51 D: 2 Feb'01 Sout 12af 65a-65 D:
918   **GLORY QUEST 51** [18] Miss Gay Kelleway 7-8-13 (65) M Fenton 14/1: 3522103: Rear, prog over 10f,   1   **71**
kept on fnl 1f, not btn far in 3rd: 7 wk abs: back to form: just btr 870.
936   **CROSSWAYS 50** [5] P D Evans 6-9-2 (68) R Havlin 25/1: 034-4104: Handy, ev ch 3f out, no extra ins   *1¾*   **72**
fnl 1f: 7 wk abs: eff t 10/13f, now stays 14f: acts on firm, gd/soft grnd & polytrack: see 762.
1599 **BAKIRI 8** [17]6-8-8 (60) G Gibbons 66/1: 060/-0405: Led 3f out, hdd bef 1f out, wknd: lngr trip.   2   **61**
1252 **MOONSHINE BEACH 26** [10]6-8-8 P (60) P Makin(5) 16/1: 6105-406: Handy over 12f, no extra: pieces.   *1¼*   **59**
1469 **PARTY PLOY 15** [4]6-8-8 (60) V Halliday 25/1: 42606-07: b g Deploy - Party Treat (Millfontaine)   *1¾*   **57**
Led, hdd after 1f, styd in tch, no extra bef 1f out: claim & h'cap wnr in '03: rnr-up 4 times in '02: h'cap wnr in
'01: suited by 12f/14f on firm, soft & both AWs: eff with/without visor: tried cheek pieces: prob handles any trk.
2 Oct'03 Redc 14.1g/f 69-66 E: 1 Jul'03 Hami 12.1gd 60-54 E: 1 Jul'03 Catt 12.0fm 67-(49) F: 2 Jul'02 Ayr 13gd 60- E:
2 Jul'02 Hami 12g/s 59-55 F: 2 Jun'02 Hami 13sft 57-55 E: 2 Nov'01 Ling 12ap 66a-62 G: 2 Oct'01 Sout 12af 63a-59 E:
1 May'01 Wind 11.6gd 66-62 E:

1599 **MEXICAN PETE 8** [16]4-9-8 (75) R Miles(3) 9/1: 1103-038: Held up, nvr nrr than mid-div: btr 1599.   1¼ 70
1516 **SONOMA 12** [7]4-9-1 (68) J Mackay 14/1: 225-5069: Cl-up, led after 10f, hdd 3f out, wknd: btr 1003.   3½ 58
1295 **FOOTBALL CRAZY 24** [9]5-10-0 (80) B Swarbrick(5) 10/1: 33200-00: 10th: b g Mujadil - Schonbein   shd 70
(Persian Heights) Handy, ev ch after 10f, fdd 2f out: hdles fit, earlier rnr-up twice (rtd 114h at best, stays
2m3.5f on firm grnd, eff with cheek pieces, tried blnks): h'cap & claim wnr on Flat in '03 (N Callaghan, also plcd
for S Gollings): likes to force the pace around 10f, prob stays 12f: acts on fast grnd, likes gd/soft.
2 Sep'03 Ayr 9.1g/f 80-(88) B: 1 Aug'03 Yarm 10.1g/f 78-(93) F: 1 May'03 Ayr 10g/s 89-88 C:
2 Jul'02 Newm 10g/f 94-92 B: 1 Jul'02 Sand 10g/s 93-83 D: 1 Jun'02 Wind 10g/f 82-77 D:
1 Jun'02 Sand 9g/s 85-71 C: 1 Jun'02 Leic 8g/f 71- E: 1 Oct'01 York 8g/s 79-70 C:
1516 **TREASURE TRAIL 12** [13]5-9-4 (70) J D Smith 25/1: 6000-500: 11th: Rear, nvr nrr than mid-div.   ½ 59
1502 **SUN HILL 13** [11]4-9-3 (70) D Sweeney 14/1: 1110050: 12th: Bhd, nvr able to chall: btr 926.   ¾ 58
1637 **VANBRUGH 7** [8]4-8-7 vis t (60) Dale Gibson 50/1: 26-10600: 13th: Handy over 12f, wknd.   6 40
1056 **SAHAAT 40** [12]6-9-8 (74) V Slattery 50/1: 000-0000: 14th: Held up, nvr a factor.   1½ 52
1637 **NOBRATINETTA 7** [2]5-9-9 P (75) R Winston 12/1: 410-040: 15th: Handy 7f, wknd.   ½ 52
1295 **INDIVIDUAL TALENTS 24** [14]4-9-1 (68) C Catlin 6/1 FAV: 22513-00: 16th: Bhd, nvr able to chall.   3½ 40
4685} **HEAD TO KERRY 216** [1]4-9-0 (67) J F Egan 14/1: 213513-0: 17th: Mid-div, fdd 3f out.   20 19
3405* **ASTYANAX 283** [6]4-9-7 (74) S Sanders 15/2: 0/13241-0: 18th: Led 13f out, hdd 4f out, sn wknd,
eased fnl 2f: disapp effort on reapp & surely somethng amiss.   dist 0
18 Ran Time 3m 07.04 (8.74) Owned: Mr M Murphy Trained: Radlett

1773 2.55 Listed Totesport Stakes Registered As The Kilvington Stakesfillies 3yo+ (A)
     £23200 £8800 £4400 **6f15y** **Good/Soft 72** -43 Slow Inside

1620 **GOLDEN NUN 7** [8] T D Easterby 4-9-3 bl (100) R Winston 7/1: 305-0231: Dwelt, prog when short of   97
room halfway, again short of room dist, styd on well fnl 1f to lead cl-home: qck reapp: fin cl 4th in this race 12
months ago: best at 6f, stays 7f on fm & soft: has been in gd form & apprec return to listed.
1615* **FOREVER PHOENIX 8** [2] R M H Cowell 4-9-3 (81) B Doyle 13/2: 1121312: Handy trav well, short of   shd 96
room after 4f, styd on to lead ins fnl 1f, hdd on line: useful, gd run: see 1615 (h'cap).
1523 **LOOK HERES CAROL 12** [9] B A McMahon 4-9-3 (83) G Gibbons 12/1: 10004-33: Cl-up, styd on to lead   1½ 91
dist, hdd ins fnl 1f, not pace front 2: fin 2nd in this race 12 mths ago: see 1523.
4745} **MILLYBAA 10** [4] R Guest 4-9-3 (100) S Sanders 7/2: 13020-24: b f Anabaa - Millyant (Primo   2½ 84
Dominie) Handy till dist, no extra: recently rnr-up on reapp in Irish List event at Naas: mdn wnr first time out
in '03 (also close 3rd in this race & List rnr-up): unplcd sole '02 start (rtd 75): eff at 6f on gd & gd/soft grnd:
has gone well fresh & likes Nottingham: shade better expected here.
2 Oct'03 Curr 6g/s 103- : 1 Apr'03 Nott 6.1gd 89- D:
1492 **SILCAS GIFT 13** [5]3-8-13 (109) C Catlin 25/1: 6000-011: Cl-up, led halfway, hdd dist, wknd: ¾ 88
well bckd: disapp on drop back to 6f on first run against older horses: btr 1169 (3yo Gr 3, 7f).
4148} **INDIAN STEPPES 249** [7]5-9-3 (70) Lisa Jones 100/1: 522003-6: b f Indian Ridge - Ukraine Venture   3 73$
(Slip Anchor) Rear, prog halfway, wknd fnl 1f: reapp: fills h'cap wnr in early '03 (also plcd 3 times): mdn wnr
in late '02: stays 10f, suited by 6f on fast, soft & both AWs, likes fibresand: eff with/without cheek pieces.
2 Jul'03 Yarm 6.0g/f 72-69 E: 2 Jan'03 Sout 7af 71a-67 E: 1 Jan'03 Wolv 6af 77a-67 E:
1 Dec'02 Sout 7af 63a- D: 2 Dec'02 Wolv 7af 67a- D: 2 Nov'02 Sout 6af 59a- D: 2 Nov'02 Wolv 7af 62a- D:
2 Oct'02 Ling 7ap 63a- E: 2 Oct'02 Yarm 7sf 64- D:
1175 **NEEDLES AND PINS 30** [3]3-8-11 (102) J Mackay 22/1: 26125-47: Cl-up, outpcd when short of room   1½ 73
halfway, modest late gains: btr 1175 (reapp).
1175 **PETITE ROSE 30** [1]3-8-7 (95) R Havlin 12/1: 127: Led till halfway, fdd: up in grade: btr 1175.   2½ 62
1400 **VERMILLIANN 18** [6]3-8-7 (93) R Smith 40/1: 116-09: b f Majadil - Refined (Statoblest) Cl-up 3f,   6 44
wknd: worst first 2 of only 3 '03 starts (fills mdn & stks): eff over a stiff gall 5f on fast & gd grnd: has gone
well fresh: with R Hannon. 1 May'03 Sali 5g/f 93- C: 1 Apr'03 Newm 5gd 94- D:
9 Ran Time 1m 15.7 (6.9) Owned: Mr T G & Mrs M E Holdcroft Trained: Malton

1774 3.25 Go Racing In The Midlands Handicap Stakes 3yo+ 0-75 (E)   [70]
     £3741 £1151 £576 **5f13y** **Good/Soft 72** +02 Fast Inside. 2 Groups.

1532 **GUNS BLAZING 11** [9] D K Ivory 5-9-2 bl (58) M Howard(7) 25/1: 1000-001: Rcd far side, made all,   66
rdn out fnl 1f to hold on: suited by around 5f on firm & soft grnd, eff with blnks: h'capped to win sn: see 1371.
1533* **SAVILES DELIGHT 11** [17] R Brotherton 5-9-12 (68) J F Egan 8/1: 4-324312: Cl-up stands side, led   ½ 74
stands side group ins fnl 1f, kept on, just held by wnr far side: eff at 6/7f, fine run back at 5f: in fine form.
1127 **PRIME RECREATION 33** [6] P S Felgate 7-9-5 (61) Dale Gibson 20/1: 6060003: Cl-up far side, kept   ½ 65
on despite edging right bef 1f out, not btn far: lost little in defeat here & is h'capped to win sn: see 660.
1532 **BRANTWOOD 11** [3] B A McMahon 4-9-2 t P (58) G Gibbons 8/1: 000-0004: b g Lake Coniston - Angelic   ½ 61
Sounds (The Noble Player) Handy far side, kept on fnl 1f, not btn far: cheek pieces: plcd once in '03 (List h'cap,
rtd 87 at best): auct mdn wnr in '02: eff at 5f, stays a sharp 7.5f, acts on firm & v soft grnd: sharp/turning or
gall trk: has gone well fresh: best eff for a while today in cheek pieces & is v well h'capped.
2 Oct'02 Catt 5g/s 92- D: 1 May'02 Hayd 5g/s 87- E:
1522 **RAFTERS MUSIC 12** [2]9-9-4 (60) G Carter 18/1: 6-302055: Bhd stands side, prog halfway, nrst fin.   hd 62
1532 **PULSE 11** [12]6-9-7 p (63) S Sanders 4/1: 56-00236: Handy stands side, onepcd ins fnl 1f: btr 1532.   hd 64
1442 **DUNN DEAL 16** [10]4-9-9 (65) B Swarbrick(5) 15/2: 60-30127: Mid-div, prog 2f out, styd on fnl 1f.   hd 65
1627 **CATCH THE CAT 7** [16]5-9-13 bl (69) R Winston 11/2 FAV: 050-3028: Rcd stands side, led that group   ¾ 67
until ins fnl 1f, no extra, saddle slipped: btr 1627.
4616} **PARKSIDE PURSUIT 222** [15]6-9-12 (68) Hayley Turner(5) 33/1: 060200-9: b g Pursuit of Love - Ivory   2½ 59
Bride (Domynsky) Handy stands side till dist, no extra: reapp: h'cap wnr in '03: landed a hat-trick of h'caps in
'02, incl rtd h'cap: eff at 5/6f on gd & firm grnd: likes Salisbury.
2 Aug'03 Sand 5.0sft 69-67 E: 2 Jul'03 Newm 6g/f 66-67 C: 1 Jul'03 Sali 6g/f 69-62 E: 2 Aug'02 Newm 6g/s 77-74 C:
1 Jul'02 Ayr 6gd 77-67 D: 1 Jul'02 Sali 6gd 70-61 E: 1 Jun'02 Nott 6gd 61-58 F: 1 Jul'01 Bath 5fm 70- F:
1 Jun'01 Bath 5.7fm 72- E: 1 Jun'01 Bath 5.7g/f 66- F:
1497 **EL CHAPARRAL 13** [11]4-10-0 (70) D Sweeney 25/1: 403/-060: 10th: Bhd, nvr a factor.   1¼ 57
967 **WAINWRIGHT 47** [8]4-9-6 (62) D Nolan(3) 14/1: 331-1000: 11th: Al in rear: 7 wk abs.   hd 48
1023 Multahab 43 [4]5-9-7 (63) C Lowther 14/1:0   1532* Full Pitch 11 [13]8-10-0 (70) V Slattery 11/1:0
1441 Marinaite 16 [14]3-9-9 (74) J Bramhill 11/1:0
1540 Bahamian Belle 11 [7]4-8-13 (55) Lisa Jones(3) 16/1:0
1476 Beyond Calculation 14 [1]10-9-8 (64) C Catlin 25/1:0

3274] **Smirlys Night 651** [5]5-9-7 (63) T Eaves(5) 33/1:0
17 Ran   Time 1m 02.0 (3.5)   Owned: Mr R D Hartshorn   Trained: Radlett

1775   4.00 Konica East Classified Stakes 3yo+ 0-70 (E)
£3751 £1154 £577   **1m54y**   **Good/Soft 72**   **+02 Fast**   Outside

1131 **BRAZILIAN TERRACE** 33 [8] M L W Bell 4-9-3 (73) Hayley Turner(5) 8/1: 150-3401: ch f Zilzal -   77
Elaine's Honor (Chief's Crown) Held up, prog 3f out, styd on for press to lead well ins last: op 7/1: 1m specialist
on fast, gd/sft grnd & polytrack, prob any trk: see 800 (reapp). 1 Sep'03 Thir 8g/f 77-74 C:
2 Jun'03 Newm 8g/f 71-(82) E: 2 Jun'03 Nott 8.2g/f 79-80 D: 1 May'03 Yarm 8.0gd 80-72 E:
1 Sep'02 Yarm 8g/f 74-64 E:
1352 **MR VELOCITY** 21 [10] A C Stewart 4-9-3 (70) S Sanders 5/2 FAV: 33330-32: Held up, rdn when short   1¼   73
of room & switched 2f out, chall ins last, not pace of wnr: nicely bckd tho' op 2/1: see 1352.
1219 **SKIBEREEN** 28 [7] I W McInnes 4-9-3 (70) P Mathers(7) 28/1: 2-564503: Dwelt & held up, hdwy wide   nk   73
to lead over 1f out, hdd ins last & no extra: return to turf, gd run: see 1006 & 476.
1519 **MADAMOISELLE JONES** 12 [5] H S Howe 4-9-0 (64) D Kinsella 12/1: 34100-04: b f Emperor Jones -   3½   63
Tiriana (Common Grounds) Trkd ldrs, short of room over 1f out, kept on, not pace to chall: dual h'cap scorer '03,
AW unplcd (rtd 48a, h'cap): mdn plcd '02 (rtd 59a, turf unplcd, rtd 66): suited by 1m, tried 10f: acts on fast,
handles polytrack: handles a sharp or gall/undul trk.
1 Aug'03 Wind 8.3g/f 69-64 E: 1 Jun'03 Chep 8.1g/f 66-60 E:
1537* **AZREME** 11 [9]4-9-3 (70) D Sweeney 4/1: 10006-15: Trkd ldrs & keen, ev ch trav well over 2f out,   2   62
wknd dist: needs a return to 7f on this evidence: btr 1537 (7f, hvy).
1359 **LADY GEORGINA** 21 [3]3-8-2 (71) J Mackay 11/4: 34300-36: Led & keen, hdd 2f out, sn btn: btr 1359.   4   52
1366 **PRINCE OF GOLD** 21 [6]4-9-3 (67) Dale Gibson 8/1: 000-0507: Cl-up & led 2f out, sn hdd/btn: see 1006.   5   44
1176 **BETHANYS BOY** 30 [1]3-8-6 (72) R Winston 14/1: 0251-008: Chsd ldrs, btn 2f out, eased: btr 192 (AW).   10   26
8 Ran   Time 1m 45.16 (5.76)   Owned: Mrs GRowland-Clark/MLWBell Racing   Trained: Newmarket

1776   4.35 Midlands Racing-9 Great Venues-Handicap Stakes Div 1 3yo+ 0-70 (E)   [70]
£3673 £1130 £565   **1m1f213y**   **Good/Soft 72**   **-15 Slow**   Inside

1613 **SUPREME SALUTATION** 8 [3] D K Ivory 8-10-8 (78) M Howard(7) 16/1: 0110141: Trkd ldrs & keen, led   85
2f out, held on well for press: acts on firm, hvy & both AWs, any trk: eff at 7/10f, stays 11f well: tough 8yo,
enjoying some of the best form of his career: see 1536, 935 & 868.
1164 **GRAFT** 31 [2] M W Easterby 5-9-4 BL (60) Dale Gibson 13/2: 4000-062: Held up, smooth hdwy to chall   1   65
2f out, not pace of wnr from dist: op 9/2: gd run in first time blnks: well h'capped, likely type for similar.
1599 **CHAMPION LION** 8 [6] M R Channon 5-9-10 (66) C Catlin 100/30 FAV: 0-005063: Dwelt, styd on for   ¾   69
press fnl 3f, not able to chall: eff at 10f, return to 12f+ could suit: see 1295.
1223 **CHAMPAIN SANDS** 28 [5] W M Brisbourne 5-9-1 (57) P Makin(7) 14/1: 00062-34: Mid-div, styd on   ¾   58
onepace fnl 3f: stays 10f: see 1223.
1253 **APACHE POINT** 26 [8]7-9-2 (58) Kim Tinkler 28/1: 0024-005: ch g Indian Ridge - Ausherra (Diesis)   1½   56
Trkd ldrs & keen, led 3f out till 2f out, no extra ins last: h'cap & class stks scorer '03: dual h'cap wnr '02:
acts on fast & hvy grnd, suited by 7m/9f, poss stays 10f: handles any trk, likes a stiff/gall one: tough & genuine,
looks to be coming to hand: with N Tinkler.
2 Oct'03 Redc 9g/f 61-59 F: 1 Jul'03 Hami 8.3g/f 64-(65) E: 2 Jul'03 Hayd 8.1gd 66-62 E: 1 May'03 Redc 9g/f 62-58 E:
1 Aug'02 Newc 9g/s 59-53 E: 2 Aug'02 Hayd 8.1hvy 53-51 E: 1 Aug'02 Ayr 9sft 53-46 E: 2 Oct'01 Newc 8g/s 52-51 E:
1 May'01 Redc 7hvy 61- F:
1504* **DOUBLE RANSOM** 13 [13]5-9-3 bl (59) R Winston 13/2: 2314216: Rear, hdwy after 4f, onepcd fnl 2f.   1   55
1286 **SIR NINJA** 25 [10]7-9-5 (61) A Daly 9/1: 000/4-247: Mid-div wide, drvn & hung left 3f out, sn onepcd.   nk   57
1273 **MCQUEEN** 25 [4]4-8-13 (55) G Gibbons 16/1: 3310-068: Chsd ldrs till over 1f out: btr 99.   1   49
1541+ **SAXE COBURG** 11 [1]7-9-8 (64) S Sanders 9/1: 3540-519: Chsd ldrs, btn/short of room over 2f out.   ½   57
1430 **MIDSHIPMAN** 17 [7]6-9-6 (62) C Haddon(7) 28/1: 0000030: 10th: Rear, eff over 2f out, no impress.   1¾   52
1388 **LENNEL** 19 [11]6-9-10 (66) V Slattery 11/1: 114-5040: 11th: Slow away & al bhd: btr 1388 & 1128.   3   51
932 **ZEIS** 50 [12]4-9-12 T (68) J F Egan 8/1: 1/00-000: 12th: ch g Bahhare - Zoom Lens (Caerleon) Chsd   6   44
ldrd, btn 2f out: t-strap, 7 wk abs: lightly rcd & unplcd '03 (earlier with H Cecil, rtd 71, class stks): sole
start mdn wnr '02: eff at 1m, bred for mid-dists: acts on soft grnd & a gall trk: has gone well fresh.
1 Oct'02 Newb 8sft 85- D:
1430 **BUSCADOR** 17 [14]5-8-13 (55) B Swarbrick(5) 16/1: 1061-000: 13th: Led till 3f out, sn lost place & bhd.   12   15
1393 **NEW OPTIONS** 19 [9]7-8-10 (52) G Carter 66/1: 5030300: 14th: Al bhd: longer trip: btr 1247 (AW).   shd   12
14 Ran   Time 2m 10.99 (8.69)   Owned: Mrs Karen Graham   Trained: Radlett

1777   5.05 Midlands Racing-9 Great Venues-Handicap Stakes Div 2 3yo+ 0-70 (E)   [70]
£3663 £1127 £564   **1m1f213y**   **Good/Soft 72**   **-06 Slow**   Inside

1535* **SUMMER BOUNTY** 11 [12] F Jordan 8-9-12 (68) R Miles(5) 12/1: 2450-011: Held up, hdwy to lead 2f   79
out, styd on strongly ins last: op 10/1: confidence boosted by latest: eff at 1m/10f, stays up to 12f: acts on
firm, hvy & both AWs, any trk: see 1535.
4461* **PERFECT PUNCH** 232 [8] C F Wall 5-9-6 (62) S Sanders 12/1: 102540-2: b g Reprimand - Aliuska   1¼   70
(Fijar Tango) Rear, short of room 4f out, switched & drvn/styd on fnl 2f, not able to chall: reapp: AW h'cap wnr
'03, subs turf h'cap rnr-up: mdn unplcd '02 (rtd 61a): eff at 10f, prob suited by 12f: acts on polytrack, gd &
gd/soft grnd, stiff/gall or sharp trk: gd return, shd go on at 12f in similar.
2 May'03 Newc 12.4gd 64-61 E: 1 Mar'03 Ling 12ap 64a-58 F:
1064 **JAIR OHMSFORD** 39 [1] W J Musson 5-9-10 (66) G Carter 4/1 FAV: 0-141143: Mid-div, kept on onepace   4   67
fnl 3f: well h'capped on turf: handles soft, gd/soft & enjoys fibresand: see 683.
281 **ESCALADE** 134 [2] W M Brisbourne 7-9-1 p (57) B Swarbrick(5) 14/1: 40450-04: b g Green Desert -   hd   57
Sans Escale (Diesis) Dwelt, kept on wide fnl 3f, not pace to threaten: 4 mth abs: cheek pieces reapplied: class
stks rnr-up '03, class stks wnr '02, dual AW h'cap rnr-up: eff btwn 1m/11f on firm, soft & both AWs, any trk: eff
with/without cheek pieces: on a long losing run but well h'capped.
2 Sep'03 Leic 10.0g/f 59-58 E: 2 May'03 Newc 10.1g/f 62-(62) E: 2 Dec'02 Ling 10ap 55a-53 F:
2 Dec'02 Wolv 9.3af 55a-52 F: 2 Oct'02 Redc 9sft 60-63 E (earlier with J Osborne): 2 Oct'02 Ayr 10sft 61-60 D:
1 Apr'02 Epso 8.5g/f 73- E: 1 Sep'01 Hayd 8.1sft 67-62 D: 1 Sept'01 Leic 8sft 72- F:
1389 **CALATAGAN** 19 [6]5-9-7 (63) T Eaves(5) 5/1: 230/-3155: Mid-div, outpcd over 2f out, styd on well   nk   62

NOTTINGHAM SATURDAY 15.05.04 Lefthand, Galloping Track

cl-home: needs a return to 12f on this evidence: see 1389 & 1164.
1680 **MYTHICAL KING 3** [7]7-8-11 (53) D Sweeney 15/2: 06/350-06: b g Fairy King - Whatcombe (Alleged) ½ 51
Chsd ldrs, hung left & onepace fnl 2f: qck reapp: h'cap plcd '03 (lightly rcd, rtd 53): 03/04 jumps wnr (h'cap
hdle, rtd 124h, 2m/2m4f, soft & hvy): '02 Flat h'cap plcd (rtd 59, h'cap): eff at 10f, stays 12f: acts on firm &
gd/soft, any trk, likes a sharp one & forcing tactics.
2 Oct'01 Redc 10gd 74-72 D: 2 Jul'01 Leic 11.8gd 83-79 C: 1 Jun'01 Ches 10.3fm 81-78 D:
1543 **COOL BATHWICK 11** [11]5-8-7 bl (49) R Havlin 20/1: 0-126007: Chsd ldrs, no impress over 1f out. 2 44
1128 **BURLEY FIREBRAND 33** [14]4-9-1 VIS (57) Dale Gibson 33/1: 12020-08: b g Bahamian Bounty - ¾ 51
Vallauris (Faustus) Chsd ldrs, drvn & no impress fnl 2f: first time visor: '03 h'cap wnr, AW h'cap rnr-up:
lightly rcd & unplcd '02 (rtd 70): eff at 9f, prob stays sharp 12f: acts on gd grnd, prob fibresand & any trk.
2 Sep'03 Wolv 12af 60a-60 F: 2 Jul'03 Carl 9.3g/f 62-60 E: 1 Jul'03 Muss 9gd 63-54 E:
912 **WELSH WIND 52** [13]8-9-3 t p (59) B Doyle 9/1: 2031049: Rear, eff 3f out, no impress: 7 wk abs. 1 51
903 **ADALAR 53** [9]4-9-11 (67) S Donohoe(7) 16/1: 0-000060: 10th: Mid-div, eff wide, btn 2f out: abs. hd 58
1633 **THE FAIRY FLAG 7** [10]6-9-3 p (59) V Slattery 20/1: 03436-40: 11th: Cl-up & chall over 4f out, btn ½ 49
2f out: 6 wk abs: btr 912, 768.
1056 **FORTUNE POINT 40** [5]6-9-4 (60) A Daly 16/1: 0213200: 12th: Led till 2f out, sn btn: btr 912 & 768. nk 49
1064 **ARCHIE BABE 39** [4]8-9-10 (66) R Winston 13/2: 000-0150: 13th: Chsd ldrs, short of room over 2f hd 54
out till ins last, no ch after: no luck in running, prob best forgiven, btr 1034.
4488} **NO CHANCE TO DANCE 231** [3]4-8-13 (55) C Catlin 50/1: 0050-0: 14th: Rear, nvr a factor on reapp. 19 13
14 Ran Time 2m 10.12 (7.83) Owned: Mr Tim Powell Trained: Towcester

1778 5.35 Children Come Racing Free Apprentice Maiden Handicap Stakes 3yo+ 0-70 (G) [70]
£2856 £816 £408 1m54y Good/Soft 72 -10 Slow Outside

1625 **PARNASSIAN 7** [7] G B Balding 4-9-0 (56) R Thomas(3) 100/30 FAV: 00-00331: Held up, no room 2f 62
out, switched right & strong run to lead well ins last: op 3/1: eff btwn 7f/1m on gd & soft, handles firm & fast.
1617 **MADAME MARIE 8** [13] S Dow 4-8-8 (50) Lisa Jones 20/1: 0003-002: Rear, styd on wide for press fnl 1¼ 53
2f, not reach wnr: eff around 1m on gd/soft grnd: see 1083.
1534 **BIG BAD BURT 11** [10] Miss Gay Kelleway 3-8-9 P (64) Dean Williams(5) 7/1: 0-422303: Trkd ldrs, 1½ 64
ch/hung left 2f out & sn onepace: chkpcs: stays 1m, prob best at 7f: acts on polytrack & gd/soft.
1073 **COODEN BEACH 39** [3] M L W Bell 4-8-6 (48) Hayley Turner(3) 10/1: 032-0444: Trkd ldr trav well & 1 46
led over 2f out, hdd well ins last: op 12/1: acts on firm & gd/soft grnd: see 828.
1258 **LORIEN HILL 26** [9]3-9-0 (69) A Medeiros(3) 8/1: 034-65: b f Danehill - Lothlorien (Woodman) Chsd hd 66
ldrs, no extra over 1f out: lightly rcd '03, mdn plcd (rtd 74, AW unplcd, rtd 68a): eff around 7f on polytrack &
gd/soft grnd, sharp/turning trk: with B W Hills.
1661 **NOBLE PENNY 5** [4]5-8-8 (50) W Hogg(5) 16/1: 60000-06: Chsd ldrs, no extra over 1f out, qck reapp. ½ 46
969 **SHAMWARI FIRE 47** [14]4-8-6 (48) Natalia Gemelova(5) 16/1: 400-4607: Held up, eff 3f out, no extra nk 43
when short of room ins last, abs.
1636 **ARTISTIC STYLE 7** [2]4-9-11 (67) T Eaves(3) 10/1: 0223-068: Led till over 2f out, sn btn: btr 1636. 3½ 55
1083 **ZALKANI 38** [11]4-8-11 (53) R Miles 12/1: 00-33009: Rear, eff wide over 3f out, no impress: btr 476. ½ 40
1098 **SPRINGALONG 37** [18]4-9-7 (63) S Donohoe(5) 16/1: 04-04500: 10th: Rear, mod hdwy wide: op 20/1. 2 46
1304 **TOP ACHIEVER 23** [12]3-8-7 (62) Kristin Stubbs(7) 14/1: 5-000: 11th: Unruly start, bhd, mod late prog. shd 44
1536 **DEXILEOS 11** [6]5-8-0 T (52) N Chalmers(3) 25/1: 000-0000: 12th: Chsd ldrs till over 1f out. 1¼ 32
427 **SUERTE 120** [15]4-9-1 (57) P Makin(5) 25/1: 00/040-00: 13th: b f Halling - Play With Me (Alzao) 1 35
Al bhd, 4 mth abs: unplcd '03 (rtd 62, sole start, J Given): unplcd both '02 start (rtd 51, mdn).
1266 **LIEUDAY 26** [1]5-8-6 p (48) B Swarbrick(5) 15/2: D5053-50: 14th: Chsd ldrs till lost place over 3f out. ½ 25
1214 Rocky Reppin 29 [5]4-8-12 bl(54) K Pierrepont(3) 33/1:0 4252} Lady Redera 242 [17]3-8-5 (60) B Reilly 14/1:0
2338} Guardian Spirit 328 [16]5-8-11 (53) Dawn Watson(7) 50/1:0
1241 Stop The Nonsense 28 [8]3-8-5 T(60) K Jackson(7) 33/1:0
18 Ran Time 1m 46.17(6.77) Owned: Miss B Swire Trained: Andover

RIPON SUNDAY 16.05.04 Righthand, Sharpish Track

Official Going Good (Good/Firm Places)

1779 2.00 Skybet Com Wooden Spoon Charity Selling Guaranteed Sweepstakes 2yo (F)
£3900 £1200 £600 6f str Good/Firm 20 -64 Slow Stands side

1653 **GOLDHILL PRINCE 6** [9] W G M Turner 2-9-0 p C Haddon(7) 9/4: 04021: Cl-up, led after 4f, rdn out 69
despite edging left: op 3/1 on qck reapp: bght in for 3,600gns: eff at 5f, apprec step up to 6f: acts on fast,
gd/soft grnd & fibresand: eff with cheek pieces: see 1653.
1343 **STANS GIRL 22** [3] M R Channon 2-8-9 S Hitchcott(3) 5/4 FAV: 032: Led, hung right & hdd after 4f, 2½ 56
kept on but not pace of wnr: well bckd: clmd for 6,000: eff around 6f on gd/soft grnd: see 1343.
  COIS NA TINE EILE 0 [6] K A Ryan 2-8-9 N Callan 12/1: 3: br f Cois Na Tine - Water Pixie (Dance 3½ 46
of Life) Slow away, prog 3f out, no impress & eased well ins fnl 1f: op 9/1 on debut: April foal, cost 1,200gns:
half-sister to a couple of 1m wnrs abroad: dam unrcd: sire useful at sprint dists: played up in padd bef race.
1634 **BOWLAND BRIDE 8** [4] A Berry 2-8-9 P P Mathers(7) 40/1: 504: b f Raise A Grand - Red Riding Hood ½ 45
(Mummy's Pet) Handy over 4f, sn onepcd: April foal, cost £1,200: half-sister to juv wnrs abroad: dam unplcd:
sire top-class performer around 7f: with A Berry.
1386 **STEAL THE THUNDER 20** [5]2-9-0 F Lynch 9/1: 055: Cl-up 4f, edged left & wknd: see 1386. 2 44
  RIVERWELD 0 [2]2-9-0 Nicola Topper 50/1: 6: ch g Weldnaas - Riverain (Bustino) Handy till ¾ 42
halfway, sn no extra: debut: April foal, cost 1,500gns: dam 7f wnr, also won over hdles: sire useful around 7f.
  SABO PRINCE 0 [11]2-9-0 S Carson 33/1: 7: Slow away, al in rear: looked burly on debut. 4 30
1632 **LA BELLA ROSA 8** [12]2-8-9 VIS A Reilly(7) 80/1: 08: Handy till halfway, fdd. 9 1
  LADY INDIANA 0 [7]2-8-9 R Winston 14/1: 9: Slow away, al bhd: burly on debut. 2½ 0
  SINGHALONGTASVEER 0 [10]2-9-0 J Bramhill 66/1: 0: 10th: Rear, nvr a factor. 1 0
1439 **RYANS LIL OL GAL 17** [8]2-8-9 J McAuley 80/1: 000: 11th: Chsd ldrs 4f, fdd. hd 0
11 Ran Time 1m 15.04 (5.04) Owned: Gold Hill Racing Trained: Sherborne

1780

2.30 Giving For Sight Maiden Guaranteed Sweepstakes 2yo (D)
£5200 £1600 £800   **6f str**   Good/Firm 20   **-32 Slow**   Stands side

	HEARTHSTEAD WINGS 0 [4] M Johnston 2-9-0 J Fanning 8/1: 1: b c In The Wings - Inishdalla (Green			96+

Desert) Handy, styd on to lead dist, pushed clr despite edging left, val 6L+: debut: March foal, cost 27,000gns: half-brother to wnrs abroad: dam useful 6/7f wnr: sire top-class performer around mid-dists: eff at 6f, further will suit in time: acts on fast grnd & goes well fresh: acts on a sharp trk: impressive, win better races.

1503	**DISTINCTLY GAME** 14 [8] K A Ryan 2-9-0 N Callan 1/1 FAV: 22: Led till dist, kept on but no ch	4	81

with easy wnr: well bckd: eff at 5/6f on fast & gd grnd: another gd eff & deserves to find similar: see 1503.

1471	**TWICE NIGHTLY** 15 [1] J D Bethell 2-9-0 T Quinn 9/2: 33: Tracked wnr over 4f, sn onepcd: see 1471.	2½	74
	DAHTEER 0 [11] M R Channon 2-9-0 C Catlin 11/1: 4: b c Bachir - Reematna (Sabrehill) Trkd ldrs	hd	73

over 4f, sn onepcd: debut: Feb first foal, dam plcd at 7f: sharper for this.

	KILMOVEE 0 [6]2-8-9 K Darley 12/1: 5: gr f Inchinor - Christmas Rose (Absalom) Slow away, nvr	3	59

nrr than mid-div: debut: March foal, cost 7,000gns: half-sister plcd at 5/6f: dam unpcld.

	WOLDS DANCER 0 [9]2-8-9 D Allan(3) 16/1: 6: Slow away, prog halfway, nrst fin: debut.	1½	55
	ELLIS CAVE 0 [12]2-9-0 R Winston 16/1: 7: Rcd far side, led that group 4f out, kept on fnl 1f,	3	51+

no ch with stands side: not disgraced from unfavoured far side.

	ESKDALE 0 [10]2-9-0 D Nolan(3) 50/1: 8: Handy 4f, wknd.	1¼	47
	DANCING DEANO 0 [13]2-9-0 V Halliday 66/1: 9: Slow away, nvr nrr than mid-div.	¾	45
1466	**WHISTLING ALONG** 16 [5]2-9-0 S Carson 100/1: 060: 10th: Bhd, nvr able to chall.	1¼	41
1439	Metolica 17 [18]2-8-9 R Fitzpatrick 80/1:0	1631 **Timmy** 8 [3]2-9-0 G Parkin 50/1:0		
1517	Northern Revoque 13 [14]2-8-9 P Mathers(7) 100/1:0	**Frogs Gift** 0 [16]2-8-9 Nicola Topper 66/1:0		
1424	Lane Marshal 18 [15]2-9-0 T Eaves(5) 50/1:0	1571 **Aza Wish** 11 [17]2-8-9 S Righton 33/1:0		

16 Ran   Time 1m 13.14 (3.14)   Owned: Hearthstead Homes Ltd   Trained: Middleham

1781

3.00 Middleham Trainers Association Handicap Stakes 3yo+ 0-85 (D)   **[84]**
£6388 £1966 £983   **1m2f**   Good/Firm 20   **+11 Fast**   Inside

1346	**INTRICATE WEB** 22 [7] E J Alston 8-9-4 (74) D Allan(3) 20/1: 1124601: Rear, prog when short of		81

room 3f out, styd on to lead ins fnl 1f, rdn out: suited by 9.4f/10f on firm, soft & fibresand: tough performer.

4954*)	**SHAMARA** 179 [17] C F Wall 4-9-11 (81) S Sanders 7/1: 431310-2: b f Spectrum - Hamara (Akarad)	½	86

Handy, styd on to lead dist, hdd ins fnl 1f, not btn far: reapp: mdn & h'cap wnr in '03: eff at 10f/12f on firm & gd grnd, acts on any trk: still unexposed in h'cap grade & can find similar.
1 Oct'03 Newm 12gd 83-77 C: 1 Sep'03 Good 9.9g/f 77- D:

1519	**STALLONE** 13 [8] N Wilson 7-9-2 (72) T Hamilton(3) 50/1: 52310-03: ch g Brief Truce - Bering	½	76

Honneur (Bering) Held up, prog 3f out, kept on fnl 1f, not btn far: progressive in '03 winning 3 h'caps: nov hdle plcd in 02/03 (rtd 90h, t-strap): unplcd on Flat in '02 (rtd 50a & 30, h'caps, earlier with D Nicholls): eff at 1m/12f on firm & gd grnd: encouraging run, win again.
1 Sep'03 Thir 12fm 75-70 E: 2 Aug'03 Beve 12.1g/f 69-64 E: 1 Jun'03 Newc 10.1fm 62-56 E:
1 May'03 Newc 10.1g/f 57-52 G: 2 Apr'03 Beve 8.5fm 53-(53) G:

3982)	**NEVADA DESERT** 260 [19] R M Whitaker 4-9-1 (71) M Hills 16/1: 133425-4: b g Desert King - Kayanga	nk	74

(Green Desert) Led 6f, led again when hung badly left 2f out, hdd dist, sn onepcd: reapp: h'cap wnr in '03 (also plcd 5 times): plcd on 1 of 6 '02 starts (mdns): eff at 1m/11f on firm & gd/soft grnd: handles a stiff trk.
2 Aug'03 Pont 8.0g/f 71-70 C: 1 Jun'03 Beve 8.5g/f 69-66 D: 2 May'03 Carl 7.9fm 65-63 E:

1104	**LEIGHTON** 36 [9]4-9-10 P (80) T Quinn 25/1: 43403-05: Chsd ldrs, short of room 2f out, onepace fnl 1f.	3½	78
1586	**PETRULA** 10 [18]5-9-11 bl (81) N Callan 9/2 JT FAV: 04034-26: Handy, no room after 1m, sn onepcd.	1	77
1475	**TAKES TUTU** 15 [12]5-9-6 (76) Darren Williams 28/1: 0065-007: Nvr nrr than mid-div: sweated bef race.	¾	70
1467	**GREY CLOUDS** 16 [14]4-8-13 (69) K Darley 13/2: 1430-428: Handy, ev ch after 6f, wknd dist: btr 1467.	hd	62
1057	**ANGLO SAXON** 41 [15]4-10-0 (84) T P Queally(3) 12/1: 101-09: Chsd ldrs, prog 4f out, no extra fnl 2f.	1	75
1478	**EVEREST** 15 [20]7-9-13 (83) R Winston 10/1: 3000-000: 10th: Rear, nvr nrr than mid-div.	3	70
1586	**LOW CLOUD** 10 [6]4-9-6 (76) Alex Greaves 33/1: 16650-60: 11th: Bhd, nvr able to chall: btr 1586.	3	59
1519	**COMPTON DRAGON** 13 [10]5-9-5 (75) J Fanning 16/1: 000-0050: 12th: Al in rear.	½	57
1519	**BROADWAY SCORE** 13 [2]6-9-10 (80) P Mulrennan(5) 25/1: 000-0000: 13th: Bhd, nvr able to chall.	1½	59
1296	**SILVALINE** 25 [13]5-9-4 (74) K Fallon 9/2 JT FAV: 3-604550: 14th: Chsd ldrs, wknd 3f out.	1½	50
1599	**MOVIE KING** 9 [1]5-8-12 (68) J Quinn 25/1: 00450-00: 15th: Prom 7f, wknd.	¾	42
1519	**ISLAND LIGHT USA** 13 [11]4-9-10 (80) T Eaves(5) 50/1: 1350-000: 16th: Slow away, nvr nrr than mid div.	4	48
998	**RIFLEMAN** 46 [4]4-9-8 (78) G Duffield 33/1: 35340-00: 17th: Bhd, nvr a factor.	¾	44
3852)	**BOND MAY DAY** 266 [12]4-9-2 (72) F Lynch 25/1: 400160-0: 18th: Prom, led after 6f, hdd 2f out, wknd.	1¼	36
1519	**ARAWAN** 13 [5]4-9-7 (77) Dale Gibson 80/1: 2/104-000: 19th: Bhd, nvr a factor.	dist	16

19 Ran   Time 2m 4.24 (0.94)   Owned: Morris Oliver Pierce   Trained: Preston

1782

3.30 Toteplacepot Rated Stakes Handicap Fillies 3yo+ 0-95 (C)   **[94]**
£11014 £4178 £2089   **6f str**   Good/Firm 20   **-04 Slow**   Stands side

4905)	**ENCHANTED** 202 [3] N A Callaghan 5-9-8 (88) W Ryan 8/1: 060463-1: b f Magic Ring - Snugfit Annie		99+

(Midyan) Handy stands side, prog to lead dist, pushed out, val 4L+: tchd 11/1 on reapp: plcd first time out in '03 (List fills stks, rtd 93 at best, G G Margarson): h'cap scorer in '02: dual h'cap wnr in '01 (present trainer): eff at 6/7f on firm & gd grnd, has tried a t-strap: goes v well fresh: impressive display.
1 Aug'02 Newm 7fm 85-82 C: 1 Jul'01 Sali 7g/f 83-77 E: 1 Jun'01 Warw 5g/f 79- D:

1498	**ENCHANTMENT** 14 [5] J M Bradley 3-8-4 (3oh) (79) C Catlin 8/1: 01601-52: Prom stands side, led	2½	81

after 4f, hdd dist, kept on, not pace of wnr: not disgraced in defeat & can find similar: see 1498.

4982)	**BANDIT QUEEN** 196 [12] W Jarvis 4-9-5 (85) P Robinson 22/1: 016500-3: b f Desert Prince -	hd	86+

Wildwood Flower (Distant Relative) Prom far side, led far side group dist, kept on fnl 1f, just held by ldrs stands side: reapp: class stks wnr in ' 03 (M A Jarvis): mdn & h'cap wnr in '02 (J Gosden): suited by 6f on fast & soft grnd: has tried a gall trk & has gone well fresh: has tried blnks: first home on far side & can win again.
1 Jul'03 Kemp 6g/f 87-(82) D: 1 Oct'02 Ayr 6sft 87-79 D: 1 Oct'02 Nott 6g/f 80- D:

1749	**TWICE UPON A TIME** 2 [8] B Smart 5-8-7 (73) F Lynch 10/1: 000210-44: Dwelt, sn switched to stands	1	71

side, prog halfway, nrst fin: fin 4th just 2 days ago in 1749.
1683 **SIERRA VISTA 4** [16]4-8-12 p (78) L Enstone(3) 8/1: 04-03005: Rcd far side, led that group till *nk* **75**
dist, no extra: qck reapp: just btr 1120.
887 **GAELIC PRINCESS 57** [14]4-9-7 (87) R Winston 16/1: 4030-006: Handy far side over 4f, sn onepcd. *1* **81**
1476 **DISPOL KATIE 15** [2]3-8-8 (83) K Darley 6/1 JT FAV: 31022-06: ch f Komaite - Twilight Time *dht* **77**
(Aragon) Handy stands side over 4f, sn onepcd: auct mdn & nursery h'cap wnr in '03: eff at 5/6f on firm & fast grnd: acts on prob any trk, loves a stiff finish: with T D Barron. 2 Oct'03 Donc 6g/f 84-(77) B: 2 Sep'03 Ripo 5g/f 88-83 D: 1 Aug'03 Beve 5g/f 84-77 B: 1 Jul'03 Carl 5g/f 74- E: 2 Jul'03 Ripo 5g/f 70- F:
1594 **SIMIANNA 9** [11]5-9-10 (90) G Duffield 6/1 JT FAV: 300-5528: Rcd centre, chsd ldrs over 4f, sn no extra. *1* **81**
720 **SAFRANINE 82** [6]7-8-7 (3oh) (70) Ann Stokell 33/1: 000-0009: Bhd, nvr nrr than mid-div. *5* **50**
4269} **LINDENS LADY 243** [15]4-8-7 (1oh) (72) D Fentiman(7) 33/1: 464405-0: 10th: Prom far side 4f, wknd. *½* **49**
5025} **COLLEGE QUEEN 191** [1]6-8-7 (6oh) (67) J Quinn 33/1: 055400-0: 11th: Rcd stands side, led 4f, fdd. *nk* **48**
1400 **FLASHING BLADE 19** [10]4-8-12 T (78) S Sanders 14/1: 005-0000: 12th: Handy stands side, wknd 3f out. *2* **47**
1627 **CONSENSUS 8** [13]5-8-13 (79) T Williams 8/1: 0600-400: 13th: Sn handy stands side, fdd after 4f. *3½* **38**
1620 **RIVA ROYALE 8** [9]4-9-4 (84) T P Queally(3) 20/1: 5001-000: 14th: Handy stands side 4f, fdd. *1¾* **38**
1251 **BOLLIN JANET 27** [7]4-8-8 BL (74) K Fallon 10/1: 41500-00: 15th: Chsd ldrs 4f, fdd: 1st time blnks. *8* **8**
15 Ran Time 1m 11.44 (1.44) Owned: Norcroft Park Stud Trained: Newmarket

1783 **4.05 True Temper Maiden Stakes Div 1 3yo (D)**
£4805 £1478 £739 **1m1f** **Good/Firm 20** **+07 Fast** Inside

1398 **AQUALUNG 19** [13] B W Hills 3-9-0 M Hills 9/1: 4-01: b c Desert King - Aquarelle (Kenmare) Led, **89+**
rcd keenly, pushed out fnl 2f, val 6L+: op 12/1: 4th of 12 on sole '03 start (mdn, rtd 80): eff at 9f, further shld suit: acts on fast grnd: won in pleasing style & can progress in h'caps.
1166 **MARBUSH 32** [2] M A Jarvis 3-9-0 P Robinson 7/4: 32: Keen cl-up, kept on despite hanging right *4* **85**
ins fnl 2f, al held by wnr: well bckd: padd pick: eff at 1m/9f on fast & gd grnd: see 1166.
1398 **MAGNETIC POLE 19** [6] Sir Michael Stoute 3-9-0 K Fallon 4/5 FAV: 3-23: Handy, onepcd ins fnl 2f: *1¾* **83**
bckd at odds-on: clr of rem but more expected on slight drop back in trip: btr 1398.
PROTECTIVE 0 [10] J G Given 3-9-0 M Fenton 66/1: 4: ch c Hector Protector - You Make Me Real *11* **68**
(Give Me Strength) Chsd ldr 6f, sn outpcd, modest late gains: debut: cost 13,000gns: half-brother to numerous wnrs at 5/10f: imprv for today.
1304 **SNOWED UNDER 24** [8]3-9-0 C Catlin 66/1: 0-55: Nvr nrr than mid-div. *1* **64**
KALAMANSI 0 [4]3-8-9 S W Kelly 50/1: 6: Rear, nvr nrr than mid-div. *3* **57**
4482} **QUAY WALLOPER 232** [9]3-9-0 Darren Williams 100/1: U000-7: Handy 6f, fdd. *5* **55$**
1275 **BLUE NUN 26** [5]3-8-9 G Duffield 125/1: 58: Sn in tch, wknd 2f out. *nk* **49**
BELSHAZZAR 0 [1]3-9-0 Dale Gibson 100/1: 9: Slow away, al bhd: sweated bef race. *1½* **51**
DALMARNOCK 0 [3]3-9-0 F Lynch 100/1: 0: 10th: Mid-div 6f, fdd. *¾* **50**
TORNADO BAY 0 [7]3-8-9 T P Queally(3) 100/1: 0: 11th: Slow away, nvr a factor. *3½* **40**
98 **CELTIC SOLITUDE 173** [12]3-8-9 K Darley 100/1: 60-0: 12th: Rear, nvr able to chall. *dist* **10**
12 Ran Time 1m 51.54 (1.54) Owned: Mr K Abdulla Trained: Lambourn

1784 **4.35 True Temper Maiden Stakes Div 2 3yo (D)**
£4796 £1476 £738 **1m1f** **Good/Firm 20** **-24 Slow** Inside

1211 **YAAHOMM 30** [11] D R Loder 3-9-0 T P Queally(3) 11/10 FAV: 31: Prom, styd on for press to lead **74**
cl-home: well bckd: eff at 9f, stays 11f: acts on fast & gd grnd: only lightly rcd & can rate higher: see 1211.
1473 **MY PARIS 15** [1] K A Ryan 3-9-0 (73) N Callan 7/2: 0-3222: Led, under press ins fnl 2f, sn edged *nk* **73**
right, hdd cl-home: clr rem: eff at 7f/9f on fast & gd/soft grnd: proving consistent: see 1473 & 1196.
ALWAYS WAINING 0 [2] M Johnston 3-9-0 J Fanning 7/1: 3: b c Unfuwain - Glenarff (Irish River) *7* **63**
Chsd ldrs 7f, sn onepcd: debut: cost 9,000gns: half-brother to numerous wnrs: just sharper for today.
1152 **UNPRECEDENTED 33** [8] T T Clement 3-9-0 VIS (50) J Quinn 50/1: 600-004: Handy 6f, sn no extra. *5* **56**
1365 **JALOUSIE DREAM 22** [6]3-8-9 S W Kelly 100/1: 05: Trkd ldrs 5f, sn no extra. *5* **44**
5018} **REDMARLEY 192** [10]3-9-0 M Fenton 20/1: 00-6: Bhd, nvr nrr than mid-div. *4* **43**
EAGLE FEATHERS 0 [9]3-8-9 D Allan(3) 16/1: 7: Al in rear. *½* **37**
MANHATTAN JACK 0 [3]3-9-0 R Winston 25/1: 8: Bhd, nvr able to chall. *nk* **41**
1236 **SAHARAN SONG 29** [4]3-8-9 M Hills 7/1: 4-09: Handy 6f, fdd. *1¾* **33**
DONT TELL SIMON 0 [12]3-9-0 T Eaves(5) 66/1: 0: 10th: Slow away, al in rear. *15* **17**
1426 **CLOUDS OF GOLD 18** [5]3-8-9 P M Quinn 25/1: 030: 11th: Keen handy, wide turning for home & fdd. *7* **2**
1473 **MIKES MATE 15** [7]3-9-0 D Nolan(3) 150/1: 0-00: 12th: Slow away, rcd v wide on home straight, fdd. *23* **0**
12 Ran Time 1m 54.39 (4.39) Owned: Sheikh Ahmed Al Maktoum Trained: Newmarket

1785 **5.05 Garden Racecourse Handicap Stakes 3yo 0-75 (E)** **[82]**
£6271 £1930 £965 **1m4f60y** **Good/Firm 20** **-07 Slow** Inside

1521 **SIEGFRIEDS NIGHT 13** [12] M C Chapman 3-8-4 (58) D Fox(5) 11/2: 2333621: Handy, prog to lead 1f **68**
out, rdn out: suited by around 10/12f, prob stays 14.5f: acts on fast, gd/soft & fibresand.
1369* **MEADAAF 21** [4] A C Stewart 3-9-7 (75) K Fallon 7/2: 045-12: Handy, led 3f out, hung right under *2* **80**
press & hdd 1f out, not pace of wnr: bckd: eff at 10f, ran to form on step up to 12f: see 1369.
1472 **HAVETOAVIT 15** [9] J D Bethell 3-8-6 (60) T Quinn 12/1: 55400-53: Led 11f, no extra ins fnl 2f. *2½* **61**
1724 **ROMEOS DAY 2** [5] M R Channon 3-7-13 (1ow) (52) C Catlin 14/1: 0000-024: Chsd ldrs, outpcd & hung *1¾* **51**
right after 9f, rallied late: qck reapp: just btr 1724.
1604 **GOLD CARD 9** [3]3-8-12 (66) R Winston 14/1: 634-225: Slow away, prog & ev ch 3f out, sn no extra. *1* **62**
1403 **ALALOOF 19** [1]3-8-13 (67) R Hills 100/30 FAV: 605-66: Rear, nvr nrr than mid-div: well bckd: *shd* **62**
disappointing effort on step up to 12f: btr 1403 (10f, reapp).
1505 **BARGAIN HUNT 14** [13]3-7-12 (2oh) (50) J Bramhill 33/1: 6403-027: Handy over 1m, no extra: btr 1505. *2½* **43**
1306 **THE KING OF ROCK 24** [10]3-8-2 (56) J Quinn 7/1: 000-0548: Held up, nvr nrr than mid-div. *2½* **43**
1612 **NORTHERN SPIRIT 9** [6]3-7-12 (2oh) (50) P Fessey 50/1: 0550-069: Bhd, nvr nrr than mid-div: btr 1612. *4* **33**
1000 **CLASSIC EVENT 46** [15]3-8-9 (63) K Darley 10/1: 0350-00: 10th: Slow away, al bhd: btr 1000. *1* **42**
1306 **OUR KID 24** [2]3-8-8 BL (62) D Allan(3) 40/1: 6640-00: 11th: Slow away, al in rear. *1¾* **39**
1505 **Tancred Imp 14** [8]3-7-12 (7oh)(45) R Ffrench 66/1:0 1099 **Desert Daisy 38** [14]3-8-8 (62) T P Queally(3) 50/1:0

RIPON   SUNDAY 16.05.04   Righthand, Sharpish Track

1209 **Calomeria 30** [7]3-8-12 (66) S Sanders 50/1:0   1369 **Canni Thinkaar 21** [11]3-8-13 (67) N Callan 16/1:0
15 Ran   Time 2m 37.35(3.85)   Owned: Mr K D Blanch   Trained: Market Rasen

BATH   MONDAY 17.05.04   Lefthand, Turning Track with Uphill Finish

Official Going Good/Firm (Good Places)

1786	**2.10 Bath Ales Hop Pole E B F Novice Stakes 2yo (D)**

£4105 £1263 £632   **5f11y rnd**   **Good/Firm 29**   **-75 Slow**   Far Side

RUSSIAN GENERAL 0 [5] P F I Cole 2-8-12   K Fallon 4/11 FAV: 1: b c Soviet Star - Azra (Danehill)   **75**
Cl-up & went on after 2f, hung left over 1f out, asserted under hands-and-heels ins last: bckd at odd on: slow
time: Feb foal, £55,000 purchase: half-brother to a dual 1m 3yo wnr, dam a smart 5/7f juv wnr: eff at 5f, will get
further: acts on fast grnd & a stiff trk: goes well fresh: can rate higher.
DREAMERS LASS 0 [8] J M Bradley 2-8-7   S Carson 14/1: 2: b f Pyramus - Qualitair Dream (Dreams   1½   **62**
To Reality) Pushed along chasing ldrs, took 2nd cl-home, nvr threat to wnr: Mar foal, half-sister to a multiple
5/7f wnr, dam a dual 6f juv wnr: eff at 5f, shld get further on this evidence: handles fast: will improve.
1538 **TROUBLESOME GERRI 13** [2] S C Burrough 2-8-7   L Keniry(3) 25/1: 63: b f Thowra - Sid's Pretence   nk   **61**
(Southern Music) Dsptd lead 2f, ch over 1f out, sn no extra: May first foal, dam plcd over hdles.
1538 **MAKE IT HAPPEN NOW 13** [6] S C Burrough 2-8-7   D Corby(3) 20/1: 04: Chsd ldrs, hung left & btn dist.   2   **55**
DORN HILL 0 [3]2-8-7   V Slattery 10/1: 5: V slow away & well bhd, mod late prog, op 8/1.   2   **49**
DOMINER 0 [7]2-8-12 C Catlin 11/1: 6: Mid-div, hung right & btn over 2f out: op 9/1.   6   **38**
6 Ran   Time 1m 05.47 (5.17)   Owned: The Blandford Partnership   Trained: Whatcombe

1787	**2.40 Bath Ales Spa Median Auction Maiden Stakes 3-4yo (F)**

£2975 £850 £425   **5f11y rnd**   **Good/Firm 29**   **-04 Slow**   Far Side

1320 **NANNA 24** [6] R Hollinshead 3-8-8 (48) J Mackay 22/1: 5203021: Made all, drvn & held on well ins   **68**
last: eff at 5/6f: handles fibresand, improved on first start on turf & likes fast grnd: see 1320 & 466.
1337 **BOAVISTA 23** [1] P D Evans 4-9-2 (54) S Donohoe(4) 10/1: 4534422: Chsd wnr, kept on, al just held.   1   **64**
1575 **GENERAL FEELING 11** [12] S Kirk 3-8-13   P Dobbs 11/2: 3-33: Mid-div, switched & kept on fnl 2f,   nk   **68**
not pace to chall: well worth another try at 6f: see 1575.
4513} **SPEARIOUS 231** [9] B R Millman 3-8-13 T (70) S Drowne 9/2 FAV: 06022-4: b g Tagula - Gloria Crown   ¾   **66**
(Waajib) Chsd ldrs, kept on onepace: gelded, bckd on reapp in first time t-strap: dual h'cap rnr-up '03: eff at
5f on fast grnd & fibresand, sharp trks. 2 Sep'03 Wind 5.0g/f 73-70 D: 2 Sep'03 Sout 5af 49-36 E:
1722 **SIMPSONS MOUNT 4** [13]3-8-13 (69) D Sweeney 14/1: 65305: Rear, hung left but kept on ins last, no   1¼   **62**
threat: qck reapp: prob handles fast grnd & polytrack: rtn to low-grade h'caps shld suit: see 1722 & 1023.
1404 **LACONIA 20** [15]3-8-12 (73) Martin Dwyer 5/1: 0-452626: Chsd ldrs, no impress dist: btr 1404, 1102.   nk   **56**
1639 **RED MONARCH 9** [14]3-8-13 D Nolan(3) 66/1: 007: ch g Woodborough - Sans Ceriph (Thatching) Bhd,   1½   **56**
late gains for press, no dngr: now quals for h'caps, will apprec a rtn to 6f +, could improve.
ARIANS LAD 0 [5]3-8-13 S Sanders 50/1: 8: Chsd ldrs halfway, btn dist, eased on debut.   nk   **55**
DANCE TO THE BLUES 0 [2]3-8-8 C Catlin 7/1: 9: br f Danehill Dancer - Blue Sioux (Indian Ridge)   nk   **49**
Rear, short of room bef halfway, late gains, op 16/1: likely improver over further.
1290 **PHILLY DEE 26** [7]3-8-8 (49) Lisa Jones(3) 66/1: 3-300000: 10th: Fly-jumped start, bhd, nvr hdwy.   2   **43**
3911} **HUMILITY 264** [4]3-8-8   K Fallon 9/1: 0-0: 11th: Chsd ldrs till over 1f out, hung left, no reappt, op 7/1.   ½   **41**
2548} **EVEN HOTTER 322** [8]3-8-8 T Quinn 33/1: 0-0: 12th: Chsd ldrs 3f, sn btn, reapp.   2½   **33**
832   **SOMETHINGABOUTHER 69** [17]4-9-2 (48) B Doyle 66/1: 4503050: 13th: Al outpcd, 10 wk abs: btr 653.   shd   **33**
1404 **BEAU JAZZ 20** [11]3-8-13 (55) S Righton 66/1: 5306000: 14th: Prom early, sn struggling.   ½   **26**
197   **LYRICAL LADY 154** [10]3-8-8 (57) E Ahern 50/1: 0546-0: 15th: Dwelt & sn bhd, 5 mth abs.   1½   **26**
1607 **WEIRS ANNIE 10** [3]3-8-8 Dane O'Neill 5/1: 00: 16th: Chsd ldrs till halfway, op 4/1.   3   **17**
LORD ZINC 0 [16]3-8-13 S Hitchcott(3) 66/1: 0: 17th: Slowly away & sn bhd on debut.   5   **8**
17 Ran   Time 1m 01.94 (1.64)   Owned: Mrs G A Weetman   Trained: Upper Longdon

1788	**3.10 Bath Ales Rare Hare Handicap Stakes 3yo+ 46-55 (F)**	[65]

£3444 £984 £492   **5f16y rnd**   **Good/Firm 29**   **-03 Slow**   Far Side

1533 **HIGH RIDGE 13** [11] J M Bradley 5-9-4 p (55) Dane O'Neill 33/1: 35360-01: ch g Indian Ridge -   **64**
Change For A Buck (Time For A Change) Bhd, rapid prog wide from halfway, edged left & led nr fin: dual h'cap plcd
'03, earlier mdn plcd (rtd 68): unplcd '02 (H Cecil, rtd 69, mdn): suited by 5.8f/7f, tried up to 10f: acts on fast
grnd: eff in cheek pieces: jock rec 2 day careless riding ban: first win today.
1025 **ILLUSIVE 45** [13] M Wigham 7-9-4 bl (55) T Quinn 12/1: 5002262: Rear, hdwy to chall ins last, carr   hd   **61**
left & just held cl-home: 6 wk abs: on a long losing run but well h'capped & turn poss not far away: see 628.
1442 **ATTORNEY 18** [6] D Shaw 6-8-13 vis (50) K Fallon 8/1: 0011203: Mid-div, hdwy to chall ins last, no   2   **52**
extra when short of room cl-home: likes banded: see 1336 & 1248 (banded).
1267 **DAVIDS MARK 27** [8] J R Jenkins 4-9-3 (54) S Sanders 6/1 JT FAV: 5030-034: Led, hdd well ins   1½   **51**
last, no extra: see 1267 & 897.
1127 **DOUBLE M 35** [1]7-8-10 vis (47) R Hughes 6/1 JT FAV: 2421065: In tch, short of room when hmpd   nk   **43**
dist, kept on late, nrst fin: gone closer with a clr run: see 902 (AW).
1267 **LONG WEEKEND 27** [3]6-8-9 vis (46) Dawn Watson(7) 16/1: 2114606: Rdn & rear, nrst fin: see 832.   nk   **41**
4728} **PASCALI 217** [5]4-9-4 (55) S Drowne 13/2: 014-7: b f Compton Place - Pass The Rose (Thatching)   ½   **48+**
Held up, prog when hmpd ins last, not able to recover: reapp: lightly rcd '03, mdn scorer, subs h'cap plcd (rtd 54):
eff at 6f on fast, stiff or sharp trk: much closer with clr run, encouraging. 1 Sep'03 Wind 6g/f 49- D:
1533 **JAGGED 13** [10]4-9-3 (54) G Baker 16/1: 2630-008: Chsd ldr, btn dist: see 1533.   ¾   **45**
1606 **BALI STAR 10** [15]9-8-9 (46) P Dobbs 33/1: 4004109: Rear/wide, only mod prog: see 1336 (banded).   nk   **36**
1025 **MAYZIN 45** [18]4-9-4 p (55) D Sweeney 15/2: 1233140: 10th: Cl-up, btn dist: abs: btr 1025 & 897.   shd   **45**
1533 **RIDICULE 13** [12]5-9-4 vis T (55) E Ahern 14/1: 40-00000: 11th: Chsd ldrs, btn/ bmpd dist: t-strap.   1½   **40**
1606 **RUN ON 10** [7]6-9-2 (53) D Nolan(3) 40/1: 53466-00: 12th: b c Runnett - Polar Storm (Law Society)   shd   **38**
Chsd ldrs till over 1f out: h'cap rnr-up '03, class stks plcd (rtd 55): h'cap wnr '02, AW unplcd (rtd 12a, h'cap):

524

BATH MONDAY 17.05.04 Lefthand, Turning Track with Uphill Finish

eff at 5/6f on firm, gd & fibresand, loves a sharp/undul or easy trk: best without a t-strap.
2 May'03 Brig 5.3fm 49-47 E: 1 Jul'02 Yarm 6g/f 45-45 E: 1 Nov'01 Wolv 6af 52a- D:
1578 **Arabian Knight 11** [14]4-9-4 (55) Martin Dwyer 16/1:0   1662 **Shady Deal 7** [9]8-8-12 (49) C Catlin 14/1:0
1080 **Pompey Chimes 40** [17]4-9-4 (55) S Carson 33/1:0
1102 **Danifah 39** [16]3-8-5 (4oh)(51) Joanna Badger 16/1:0
319 **Brave Chief 133** [2]3-8-7 (2oh)(53) B Doyle 50/1:0
1540 **Royal Supremacy 13** [4]3-8-6 (3oh)(52) S Hitchcott(3) 50/1:0
18 Ran   Time 1m 10.94 (1.84)   Owned: James Leisure Ltd   Trained: Chepstow

1789 3.40 Bath Ales Barnstormer Handicap Stakes Fillies 3yo+ 0-75 (E)   [73]
£3809 £1172 £586   **1m5f22y   Good/Firm 29   -36 Slow**   Inside

1618 **ANYHOW 10** [6] Miss K M George 7-9-2 (61) D Nolan(3) 5/1: 2145421: Rear, hdwy fnl 3f & drvn to   **68**
lead line: op 4/1: eff at 9/10f, now suited by 12/13f on firm, soft & both AWs, prob any trk, loves Lingfield:
best with extreme waiting tactics, tough & genuine: see 1618 & 801.
813 **FLEETING MOON 70** [10] A M Balding 4-9-4 (63) Martin Dwyer 12/1: 0-22132: Mid-div, eff to press   shd **69**
ldrs 2f out, drvn & narrow lead nr fin, hdd line: 10 wk abs: acts on both AWs & fast grnd: see 813 & 772.
1285 **SASHAY 27** [1] R Hollinshead 6-8-0 (45) J Mackay 9/1: 434-5203: b f Bishop of Cashel - St James's   ½ **49**
Antigua (Law Society) Led till over 2f out, rallied & narrow lead again ins last till cl-home: AW h'cap & class stks
scorer '03: suited by 13f/2m on fast & polytrack, likes fibresand/W'hampton: h'capped to win.
2 Mar'04 Ling 16ap 58a-56 E:1 Sep'03 Wolv 14.8af 61a-(54) F:1 Jan'03 Wolv 16.2af 61a-58 D:2 Dec'02 Wolv 14.7af 56a-60 E
1 Apr'02 Nott 16g/f 54-50 D: 1 Mar'02 Wolv 16.2af 64a-58 D:1 Feb'02 Wolv 16.2af 59a-51 F: 2 Feb'02 Wolv 12af 59a-50 F:
1 Aug'01 Wolv 12af 50a-46 G: 2 Jun'01 Newm 10g/f 50- E:
1654 **COMPTON ECLAIRE 7** [5] G A Butler 4-8-10 vis (55) E Ahern 8/1: 034-3324: In tch, briefly outpcd   shd **60**
over 2f out, switched & styd on well cl-home, btn less than 1L in a v tight fin: see 1654, 243 & 24.
1342 **CLASSIC MILLENNIUM 23** [7]6-8-13 (58) Lisa Jones(3) 9/2: 155-0225: Chsd ldrs, outpcd over 2f out,   ½ **62**
rallied late on, not able to chall: won this in '03 off a 13lb lower mark: see 1342 & 896.
1469 **CALAMINTHA 17** [2]4-9-5 (64) K Fallon 3/1 FAV: 03501-26: Chsd ldr, onepace for press fnl 3f: see 1469. 1½ **66**
342 **BEECHY BANK 131** [3]6-9-10 (69) V Slattery 16/1: 01/431-07: Chsd ldrs 6f out & led over 2f out,   nk **70**
hdd ins last & wknd: 4 month abs: see 342.
1082 **AONINCH 40** [1]4-9-0 (59) R Havlin 15/2: 113-6058: Rear, eff wide 3f out, not able to chall: abs: see 801.1   **59**
1456 **ANNIVERSARY GUEST 18** [4]5-7-12 (3oh) (40) J F McDonald(3) 25/1: 5-034309: Keen, rear, no impress. 2½ **39**
1238 **MISS KOEN 30** [8]5-8-6 t (51) C Catlin 25/1: 3103000: 10th: Rear, eff 3f out, sn btn: btr 979 (soft). 9 **35**
10 Ran   Time 2m 53.97 (8.47)   Owned: Stableline   Trained: Crediton

1790 4.10 Bathales Com Median Auction Maiden Stakes 3yo (E)
£3556 £1094 £547   **1m2f46y   Good/Firm 29   -01 Slow**   Inside

4676} **CAUSE CELEBRE 219** [2] B W Hills 3-8-9 (78) R Hills 2/1 FAV: 0324-1: Made all & in command from   **75+**
dist, pushed out: nicely bckd tho' op 13/8: mdn rnr-up '03 (lightly rcd): eff at 1m, styd longer 10f trip well,
should get further: acts on fast grnd, stiff/gall or turning trks: goes well fresh & suited by forcing tactics today.
1514 **CHARLESTON 14** [7] J H M Gosden 3-9-0 R Hughes 5/2: 22: Chsd ldr over 2f out, kept on for press   1¾ **75**
but al redd: rest well covered: bckd: styd longer 10f trip, acts on fast grnd: shld find a race.
4138} **VELVET WATERS 251** [13] R F Johnson Houghton 3-8-9 (59) S Carson 33/1: 600-3: b f Unfuwain -   3½ **64$**
Gleaming Water (Kalaglow) Chsd wnr, no impress from over 2f out: reapp: unplcd at up to 1m in '03 (lightly rcd,
rtd 66, mdn): breeding suggests mid-dists will suit this term: prob stays 10f & handles fast grnd.
4875} **MAN AT ARMS 206** [6] R Hannon 3-9-0 (69) P Dobbs 5/1: 0003-4: b c Daggers Drawn - Punta Gorda   nk **68**
(Roi Danzig) Bhd, drvn & kept on fnl 2f, nrst fin: reapp: h'capp plcd '03 (rtd 69): eff at 1m/10f, shaped here as
if 12f will suit: acts on fast grnd, gall or turning trk.
1623 **LUCKY ARTHUR 9** [5]3-8-9 D Sweeney 50/1: 05: ch f Grand Lodge - Soltura (Sadler's Wells) Dwelt   3 **59**
& bhd, kept on late, no threat: some improvement from debut, shapes as if 12f+ will suit.
4717} **AVESOMEOFTHAT 217** [17]3-9-0 (74) R Havlin 20/1: 4520-6: Chsd ldrs, btn 3f out, reapp.   3 **60**
1321 **NOUNOU 24** [16]3-9-0 C Catlin 33/1: 057: Chsd ldr 2f, btn 2f out, longer trip.   shd **60**
1163 **LOOKS THE BUSINESS 33** [11]3-9-0 (65) C Haddon(7) 11/1: 5-245008: Chsd ldrs, no impress fnl 3f.   1 **59**
4751} **AUTUMN FLYER 215** [9]3-9-0 R Smith 25/1: 000-9: Mid-div, no impress over 2f out, reapp, gelded.   1¼ **57**
1240 **RUMOUR MILL 30** [12]3-9-0 (50) M Savage(4) 100/1: 00000-500: 10th: Mid-div, struggling fnl 3f.   7 **48**
1501 **OPEN BOOK 15** [4]3-8-9 S Drowne 28/1: 0: 00: 11th: Al bhd.   4 **37**
1611 **STEPPENWOLF 10** [3]3-9-0 (40) S Righton 100/1: 0-600000: 12th: Al rear.   ¾ **41$**
     SILKEN JOHN 0 [10]3-9-0 E Ahern 25/1: 0: 13th: Sn struggling rear on debut.   2 **38**
1166 **DORSET 33** [8]3-8-9 Martin Dwyer 20/1: 00: 14th: Mid-div, btn 3f out, longer trip.   6 **24**
     SOVEREIGN GIRL 0 [1]3-8-9 S Sanders 100/1: 0: 15th: Dwelt, sn mid-div, btn 4f out, debut.   2 **21**
1719 **HIGHFLUTING 4** [15]3-8-9 D Kinsella 100/1: 000: 16th: Al bhd, qck reapp.   26 **0**
16 Ran   Time 2m 08.98 (2.98)   Owned: The Hon Mrs J M Corbett & Mr C Wright   Trained: Lambourn

1791 4.40 Bath Ales Salamander Classified Stakes 3yo 0-70 (E)
£3426 £1054 £527   **1m2f46y   Good/Firm 29   -01 Slow**   Inside

1176 **ETMAAM 32** [14] M Johnston 3-9-3 (75) R Hills 9/2: 4-151: Rear, hdwy wide from over 2f out & styd   **87**
on strongly for press to lead cl-home: bckd: prev eff at 7f, now stays 10f well & shld get further on this
evidence: acts on fast & soft grnd: lightly rcd & progressive type: see 966.
1236 **ALBINUS 30** [7] A M Balding 3-8-13 BL (71) Martin Dwyer 8/1: 03-02: Trkd ldrs, ran wide on bend 5f   shd **80**
out, hdwy for press to lead well ins last, hdd line: op 9/1: left reapp bhd in first time blnks: eff at 1m, stays
longer 10f trip well & could get further: acts on polytrack & fast grnd: see 175.
1403 **DESERT IMAGE 20** [11] C Tinkler 3-8-12 (69) D Corby(3) 7/1: 1260033: Rear, styd on for press fnl   1½ **77**
2f, not pace of front pair ins last: acts on fast, gd & both AWs: see 1403 & 337.
4808} **KYTHIA 210** [13] H Morrison 3-8-11 (72) M Fenton 18/1: 315-4: b f Kahyasi - Another Rainbow   hd **75**
(Rainbows For Life) Rear, styd on to chase ldrs fnl 2f, not able to chall: reapp: auct mdn scorer '03: winning
form at 7.5f, stays 10f & could get further: acts on firm, fast, sharp/turning or stiffish trk.
1 Sep'03 Beve 7.5g/f 67- E:
1369 **KRISTALS DREAM 22** [4]3-8-13 (74) T Quinn 4/1 FAV: 56031-35: Led after 2f till ins last, no exra.   1¼ **75**

BATH MONDAY 17.05.04 Lefthand, Turning Track with Uphill Finish

1369 **SLAVONIC 22** [2]3-9-0 bl (72) R Hughes 10/1: 554-5446: Mid-div, short of room when trav well 2f out & again dist, not able to recover: looked sure to go close with a clr passage: another gd run in visor, stays 10f & can improve on this: see 1369, 1101 & 947. *1* **73+**
1511 **SAILMAKER 14** [3]3-9-3 (75) S Drowne 9/2: 6-237: Chsd ldrs, short of room when rdn 2f out, no extra. *shd* **78**
1398 **MASTER MAHOGANY 20** [6]3-8-12 (69) V Slattery 25/1: 0408: Dwelt, mid-div, not pace to chall. *1¾* **71**
1398 **PRINCIPESSA 20** [5]3-8-9 (69) K Fallon 16/1: 3-509: Chsd ldrs till lost pl 4f out, no threat after. *2* **65**
1359 **MORAG 23** [12]3-8-9 (70) S Carson 20/1: 10050-40: 10th: Chsd ldrs till 2f out: btr 1359 (1m). *¾* **64**
1628 **CHARLIE TANGO 9** [1]3-8-12 (67) S Hitchcott(3) 16/1: 030-3000: 11th: Mid-div, btn over 1f out: btr 817. *½* **66**
1283 **MARIA BONITA 27** [7]3-8-9 (70) S Sanders 50/1: 03-40: 12th: b f Octagonal - Nightitude (Night Shift) Led 2f & remained prom till wknd qckly 2f out: mdn plcd '03 (lightly rcd, rtd 79): half-sister to a 1m wnr: eff over a stiff 1m on fast grnd. *3* **59**
1258 **REIGN OF FIRE 28** [8]3-8-9 (64) L Keniry(3) 100/1: 46-00: 13th: Mid-div, btn 2f out: longer trip. *6* **50**
13 Ran Time 2m 09.03 (3.03) Owned: Mr Hamdan Al Maktoum Trained: Middleham

1792 **5.10 Bath Ales Gem Bitter Handicap Stakes 3yo+ 0-70 (E)** **[69]**
£4004 £1232 £616 **1m rnd** **Good/Firm 29** **+10 Fast** Inside

1298 **VOICE MAIL 26** [11] A M Balding 5-9-13 (68) L Keniry(3) 17/2: 4550-001: Rear, short of room over 2f out, switched wide & strong run for press to lead cl-home: best time of day: suited by 7f/1m on firm, gd & polytrack: prob handles any trk, loves Bath: see 978. **72**
1010 **ZAFARSHAH 47** [9] P D Evans 5-9-7 (62) K Fallon 7/2 FAV: 0-141462: Trkd ldrs, drvn & chall ins last, narrow lead cl-home, hdd line: 7 wk abs: fine run: tough, see 565. *nk* **65**
1485 **SANGIOVESE 16** [8] H Morrison 5-9-11 (66) S Drowne 4/1: 1-033523: Led, hdd well ins last: gd front running eff on a trk which tends to suit those delivered late: see 1485 & 195 (made all). *shd* **69**
1352 **BISHOPSTONE MAN 23** [10] H Candy 7-9-13 (68) C Cavanagh(7) 11/1: 2240-004: b g Piccolo - Auntie Gladys (Great Nephew) Keen trkg ldrs, short of room over 1f out & again ins last, not recover: h'cap scorer '03, subs dual h'cap rnr-up: h'cap wnr '02: best around 7f/8.5f on firm, soft & both AWs, prob any trk: goes well for an appr rider: poss unlucky & can win again. *1¼* **68**
2 Sep'03 York 7.9g/f 76-71 D: 2 Aug'03 Nott 8.2g/f 72-69 D: 1 Jun'03 Beve 7.5fm 69-65 E: 1 May'02 Brig 6.9g/f 66-60 E:
2 Sep'01 Chep 7g/f 63-60 F: 2 May'01 Ling 7g/f 65-65 E: 2 Apr'01 Sout 7af 55a- F: 2 Mar'01 Wolv 7af 60a-58 E:
1625 **PHRED 9** [13]4-9-8 (63) S Carson 11/1: 100-6465: Chsd ldr & chall 3f out till dist, no extra: see 1625. *½* **61**
1485 **REALISM 16** [12]4-9-6 (61) B Doyle 14/1: 4105036: Chsd ldrs, no impress ins last: see 1485, 678. *½* **59**
1657 **DAIMAJIN 7** [6]5-9-0 (55) D Nolan(3) 66/1: 4000007: Rear, eff over 2f out, no impress: btr 362 (AW sell). *1* **51**
1010 **QUANTUM LEAP 47** [15]7-9-10 (65) Lisa Jones(3) 12/1: 3-063038: Rear, only mod late prog: 7 wk abs. *hd* **60**
1542 **MOBO BACO 13** [3]7-9-2 (57) Martin Dwyer 7/1: 0030-449: Rear, mod late prog, no dngr: see 1402. *shd* **52**
1542 **EMBER DAYS 13** [4]5-9-6 p (61) V Slattery 25/1: 522-5030: 10th: Well bhd halfway, mod prog: see 178. *nk* **55**
1535 **The Gaikwar 13** [1]5-9-13 bl(68) M Savage(5) 11/1:0 1691 **Spindor 5** [2]5-9-7 bl(62) R Hughes 12/1:0
12 Ran Time 1m 40.8(1.5) Owned: Mr Roger Parry Trained: Kingsclere

MUSSELBURGH MONDAY 17.05.04 Righthand, Sharp Track

Official Going Good/Firm (Firm Places)

1793 **6.20 Budweiser Apprentice Handicap Stakes 4yo+ 46-55 (F)** **[65]**
£2912 £832 £416 **2m** **Good 60** **-20 Slow** Stands side

1629 **GALANDORA 9** [7] Dr J R J Naylor 4-8-10 (47) Lucy Russell(7) 6/1: 00-56101: Held up, prog after 12f, styd on to lead ins fnl 1f, rdn out: eff at 13f, stays 2m well: acts on fast & gd, tried soft grnd: likes a sharp trk: back to form today here on a sound surface; see 1285. **54**
1373 **JOELY GREEN 22** [3] N P Littmoden 7-8-10 bl (45) Steven Harrison(7) 9/2: 5066602: Rear, gd prog to lead 2f out, hdd ins fnl 1f, kept on, not pace wnr: clr rem: back to form on rtn to 2m: see 813 & 358. *1* **50**
1506 **REPULSE BAY 15** [6] J S Goldie 6-9-2 (51) J Currie(7) 13/2: 3500-603: b g Barathea - Bourbon Topsy (Ile de Bourbon) Handy 14f, sn no extra: op 5/1: won 2 h'caps in '03: lightly rcd in '02 (rtd 69, mdn): eff at 1m/12f, poss stays 2m: acts on firm & hvy grnd: acts on a stiff/gall trk, enjoys being held up, has tried a visor. *5* **51**
1 Jun'03 Newc 10.1g/f 63-58 F: 2 Jun'03 Muss 12g/f 60-58 F: 1 Jun'03 Donc 12fm 58-47 D: 2 Jul'01 Hami 8.2fm 67- E:
1551 **WESTERN BLUEBIRD 13** [4] Miss Kate Milligan 6-8-10 BL (45) P Mulrennan(3) 16/1: 26044/-64: b g Bluebird - Arrastra (Bustino) Led 14f, wknd: first time blnks: recent jumps unplcd (rtd 41h, sell h'cap): sell h'cap hdle wnr in 03/04 (rtd 78h, stays 2m4.5f on fast grnd, eff with cheek pieces): rnr-up once in '02 (h'cap, H Morrison): stays 2m, suited by 10/12f on firm, soft & fibresand, stiff or sharp trk: best without visor. *1* **44**
2 Apr'02 Folk 15.4fm 54-53 E: 1 Dec'01 Wolv 12af 59a-53 G: 2 Jun'01 Beve 12gd 57-54 F: 1 May'01 Newb 10gd 57- E:
1197 **SEA COVE 32** [8]4-8-8 (45) A Mullen(7) 5/1: 6500-45: Prom, hung badly left & wknd after 13f: see 1197. *hd* **43**
1551 **DORMY TWO 13** [1]4-8-11 p (48) T Eaves(3) 7/1: 340-036: Held up, nvr a factor: tchd 9/1: btr 1551. *1¾* **44**
1449 **HAYSTACKS 18** [2]8-8-7 (2oh)p (40) L Enstone 4/1 FAV: 06060-37: In tch, btn/hmpd 2f out. *hd* **37**
1414 **CADWALLADER 20** [5]4-8-5 (4oh) (40) T Hamilton 14/1: 00-465U8: Handy till hmpd after 14f, wknd. *2* **35**
8 Ran Time 3m 35.40 (12.9) Owned: Mr Michael Olpin Trained: Shrewton

1794 **6.50 John Smith's Extra Smooth Handicap Stakes 3yo+ 0-70 (E)** **[68]**
£4261 £1311 £656 **7f30y rnd** **Good 60** **-19 Slow** Outside

1214 **BORDER ARTIST 31** [5] D Nicholls 5-9-5 (59) A Nicholls 4/1 FAV: 0000-001: ch g Selkirk - Aunt Tate (Tate Gallery) Mid-div, prog to lead bef 1f out, rdn out to hold on: well bckd: won 4 h'caps in '03 incl this race: plcd once in '02 (slipped down h'cap, rtd 63, M Blanshard): mdn wnr in '01: eff btwn 6f/1m on fast, gd & fibresand, acts on any trk, likes Musselburgh: on a handy mark. **66**
1 Jul'03 Beve 7.5gd 67-63 D: 1 Jul'03 Epso 6g/f 64-60 D: 1 May'03 Muss 7.1g/f 61-55 D: 1 May'03 Muss 7.1g/s 59-52 F:
2 Apr'03 Ripo 8gd 56-52 E: 1 Jul'01 Wind 6g/f 76- D:
1122* **KIRKBYS TREASURE 36** [2] A Berry 6-9-4 (58) F Norton 9/1: 26005-12: Rear, gd prog to chase wnr dist, kept on fnl 1f, just held: only just denied on follow-up bid after recent C/D win in 1122. *nk* **63**
4883} **KILLALA 205** [9] I Semple 4-9-11 (65) T Eaves(5) 16/1: 040436-3: b g Among Men - Hat And Gloves *2* **66**

(Wolver Hollow) Handy, kept on fnl 1f, not btn far: reapp & new stable: med auct mdn wnr in '03 (M H Tompkins): mdn rnr up on 1 of only 2 '02 starts: eff at 6/7f on firm & gd, any trk: gd return.
1 Jul'03 Catt 7fm 67-(66) F: 2 Jun'02 Carl 6g/f 75- D:
1638 **COUSTOU 9** [8] A R Dicken 4-9-5 (59) P Fessey 33/1: 005-6004: Handy, prog 2f out, onepcd fnl 1f. *shd* **59**
1049 **SEA MARK 42** [4]8-9-7 (61) R Winston 11/2: 0/0000/-35: Held up, prog after 4f, onepace fnl 1f. *1¼* **59**
1553 **MON SECRET 13** [11]6-9-1 (55) F Lynch 10/1: 213-4006: Bhd, prog halfway, nrst fin: btr 193. *¾* **51**
1553 **SMITH N ALLAN OILS 13** [7]5-9-5 p (59) L Enstone(3) 16/1: 101-1007: Nvr nrr than mid-div: btr 323. *shd* **54**
1366 **BARZAK 23** [1]4-9-3 t (57) J Bramhill 14/1: 5-053008: Rear, nvr nrr than mid-div: btr 551. *½* **51**
1319 **DISPOL PETO 24** [12]4-9-3 p (57) Dean McKeown 25/1: 0-052059: Led 4f, sn wknd: btr 629. *¾* **49**
2171} **JEDEYDD 337** [3]7-9-7 t (61) Dale Gibson 33/1: 000000-0: 10th: Bhd, nvr a factor: reapp. *½* **52**
1536 **TALLY 13** [6]4-9-0 (54) K Dalgleish 14/1: 6-000060: 11th: Handy, led 3f out, hdd bef 1f out, fdd. *1½* **42**
152 **ROMAN MAZE 163** [14]4-9-13 (67) N Pollard 8/1: 05514-0: 12th: Dwelt, sn handy, fdd 2f out: op 12/1. *1½* **52**
1508 **Xanadu 15** [13]8-8-13 p(53) P Mulrennan(5) 12/1:0 1378 **Bella Beguine 21** [10]5-9-1 vis(55) G Duffield 16/1:0
14 Ran Time 1m 30.48 (5.58) Owned: F F Racing Services Partnership V Trained: Thirsk

1795

7.20 Gordons Gin Maiden Auction Stakes 2yo (F)
£3380 £1040 £520 **5f str** **Good 60** **-29 Slow** Stands side

POLLY PERKINS 0 [6] N P Littmoden 2-8-9 K Darley 4/1 FAV: 1: b f Pivotal - Prospering (Prince Sabo) Handy, grad prog to lead dist, rdn out to assert despite edging left: bckd on debut: Feb foal, cost 25,000gns: half-sister plcd at 7f: dam 7f wnr: sire top-class performer at sprint dists: eff at 5f, 6f shld suit: acts on gd grnd & a sharp trk: goes well fresh: can rate higher. **76**
SWEET ROYALE 0 [1] Miss L A Perratt 2-8-7 R Winston 9/1: 2: b f Royal Applause - Sorara (Aragon) Led 4f out, hdd under press dist, sn sltly short of room, switched & kept on, not pace wnr: op 7/1 on debut: Jan foal, cost 15,000gns: sire Gr 1 wnr at 6f: eff at 5f, 6f will suit: acts on gd grnd: pleasing eff. *1½* **68**
KATIE BOO 0 [2] A Berry 2-8-5 F Norton 7/1: 3: br f Namid - Misty Peak (Sri Pekan) Handy, prog when short of room dist, switched & kept on ins fnl 1f, not btn far: op 9/1 on debut: Mar first foal, cost E11,000: dam plcd at 6/7f: sire top-class sprinter: eff at 5f, shapes as tho' 6f will suit: acts on gd grnd: can improve. *nk* **65**
1550 **LADY HOPEFUL 13** [5] R P Elliott 2-8-5 T Hamilton(3) 5/1: 54: Handy 4f, onepcd ins fnl 1f: op 3/1: eff at 5f on gd grnd: see 1550. *nk* **64**
ALCHARINGA 0 [7]2-8-10 T Eaves(5) 25/1: 5: Led till 4f out, no extra dist: debut. *½* **68**
1632 **SKIPPIT JOHN 9** [8]2-8-8 Dean McKeown 9/2: 26: Prom 3f, sn no extra: btr 1632 (soft). *½* **65**
1161 **LORD JOHN 33** [3]2-8-8 Dale Gibson 9/2: 047: Bhd, nvr able to chall: see 1161. *2* **59**
1550 **NAMKING 13** [4]2-8-10 P Mulrennan(5) 12/1: 08: Early speed, sn badly outpcd, modest gains: see 1550. *½* **60**
8 Ran Time 1m 1.96 (4.46) Owned: Miss Vanessa Church Trained: Newmarket

1796

7.50 Courvoisier V S O P Handicap Stakes 3yo+ 0-75 (E) **[72]**
£5460 £1680 £840 **1m4f** **Good 60** **-30 Slow** Inside

1069 **RAJAM 41** [10] D Nicholls 6-9-11 VIS (69) Alex Greaves 22/1: 000-0601: Cl-up, styd on to lead 3f out, hdd ins fnl 1f, rallied to lead cl-home, rdn out: 6 wk abs: suited by 12/14f, has tried 2m+: acts on firm, hvy & prob any trk: goes well fresh: game effort in first time visor: see 997. **76**
1034 **EASIBET DOT NET 44** [3] I Semple 4-9-0 p (58) R Winston 10/1: 3215-402: Handy, styd on to lead ins fnl 1f, sn carr head high under press, hdd cl-home: 6 wk abs: has ability but does not look straightforward. *nk* **63**
1064 **CALL ME SUNSHINE 41** [9] P C Haslam 4-9-2 (60) G Faulkner 25/1: 02-10503: Held up, prog after 7f, no impress fnl 1f: 6 wk abs: eff at 1m/10f, now stays 12f: see 561. *3* **61**
1006 **OLDENWAY 47** [7] R A Fahey 5-10-0 (72) T Hamilton(3) 4/1: 00-00224: Mid-div, prog after 1m, onepcd dist: 7 wk abs: just below 1006 & 924 (10f). *hd* **72**
1462 **KINGS ENVOY 17** [5]5-9-7 (65) D McGaffin 14/1: 000/0-435: Chsd ldrs 10f, sn no extra: btr 1462 (9f). *2½* **61**
1506 **TBM CAN 15** [8]5-9-4 (62) N Pollard 7/2 JT FAV: 1506-656: Nvr nrr than mid-div: btr 1506. *½* **57**
1307 **UNTIDY DAUGHTER 25** [1]5-8-8 bl (52) T Eaves(4) 7/1: 050/00-57: Held up, nvr able to chall: btr 1307. *5* **40**
1278 **BORDER TERRIER 27** [2]6-8-9 (53) K Darley 14/1: 05010-08: b g Balnibarbi - Ring Side (Alzao) Rear, nvr a factor: h'cap wnr in '03: rnr-up once back in '00 (rtd 64, clmr): eff at 1m/10f on fast & soft grnd. *2* **38**
1 Oct'03 Newc 10.1gd 57-51 F: 2 Apr'03 Newc 10.1g/f 49-45 E:
1064 **PISTE BLEU 41** [6]4-8-9 (53) D Fentiman(7) 25/1: 3165-009: b f Pistolet Bleu - Thamissia (Riverman) Held up, nvr a factor: earlier jumps unplcd (rtd 84h, juv mdn hdle): h'cap wnr in '03: unplcd in '02 (rtd 70, mdn): eff at 10/12f on fast & gd grnd, eff with/without t-strap. *5* **31**
1 Aug'03 Catt 12.0g/f 59-51 F:
1093 **PLUTOCRAT GB 39** [4]8-9-13 VIS (71) K Dalgleish 7/2 JT FAV: 31/10///-20: 10th: Led 11f, wknd: recent hdles unplcd (rtd 117h, h'cap): disappointing here with 1st time visor: btr 1093. *17* **26**
10 Ran Time 2m 41.46 (10.86) Owned: A A Bloodstock Ltd Trained: Thirsk

1797

8.20 Arthur Mckay Building Services Selling Stakes 3yo+ (G)
£2933 £838 £419 **5f str** **Good 60** **+07 Fast** Stands side

1065 **AMERICAN COUSIN 41** [3] D Nicholls 9-9-9 (58) A Nicholls 7/2: 4140-101: Bhd, prog 2f out, styd on to lead ins fnl 1f, pushed clr, val 5L+: bght in for 7,500gns: 6 wk abs: suited by 5f, stays 6f: acts on firm, soft & fibresand, v disapp last time on hvy: goes well fresh: more prizes await in sell/claim grade: see 963. **63+**
1508 **VIJAY 15** [8] I Semple 5-9-4 VIS (57) R Winston 3/1 JT FAV: 0-030602: Prom, led 2f out, hdd ins fnl 1f, no extra: blnks left off & first time visor fitted: acts on firm, gd grnd & fibresand: just btr 748. *3* **50**
1555 **BEST LEAD 13** [1] Ian Emmerson 5-9-9 bl (52) D Fentiman(7) 3/1 JT FAV: 1044343: Dwelt, prog halfway, onepcd fnl 1f: just btr 1218 (fibresand). *2* **49**
1555 **ROAN RAIDER 13** [5] M J Polglase 4-9-4 vis (47) T Hamilton(3) 6/1: 00-00034: Chsd ldrs 3f, no extra. *4* **32**
1555 **ROBWILLCALL 13** [4]4-8-13 (49) F Norton 15/2: 40000-05: b f Timeless Times - Lavernock Lady (Don't Forget Me) Prom 3f, wknd: class stks wnr in '03: auct mdn & nov auct stks wnr in '02, h'cap plcd subs: eff at 5/6f on fast & gd/soft grnd: acts on any trk, likes a stiff/undul one: can force the pace: has tried cheek pieces & blnks: with A Berry. 1 Jun'03 Muss 5fm 70-(56) E: 1 Jun'02 Carl 5g/s 78- E: 1 May'02 Hami 5g/s 73- E: *2* **21**
781 **ATTILA THE HUN 77** [9]5-9-4 vis (40) T Eaves(5) 50/1: 00000-46: Dwelt, sn led, hdd 2f out, wknd. *1* **23**
1408 **CARONTE 20** [2]4-9-9 bl (40) J Bramhill 25/1: 0001007: Prom 3f, wknd: btr 904. *nk* **27**
4112} **RHINEFIELD BOY 252** [6]3-8-10 K Darley 20/1: 000-8: ch g Wolfhound - Rhinefield Beauty *5* **9**

(Shalford) Handy till halfway, fdd: reapp: unplcd all 3 '03 starts (rtd 55, auct mdn): with J S Goldie.
1074 **OUT OF TUNE** 41 [7]4-9-4 (40) G Faulkner 66/1: 00/500-09: Dwelt, albhd, 6 wk abs & new stable.   5   0
9 Ran   Time 1m 0.19 (2.69)   Owned: Middleham Park Racing XIV   Trained: Thirsk

---

1798   8.50 Edinburgh Evening News Handicap Stakes 3yo 46-55 (F)   [64]
£2947 £842 £421   1m rnd   Good 60   -08 Slow   Outside

1554 **SON OF THUNDER** 13 [5] M Dods 3-9-0 (50) L Enstone(3) 10/1: 00-61: Held up, short of room after   56
4f, grad prog to lead ins fnl 1f, rdn out: imprvd for step up to 1m on h'cap bow: acts on gd grnd & a sharp trk: gd
performance on only 4th start & can rate higher: see 1554.
1357 **SONDERBORG** 23 [4] Miss A M Newton Smith 3-9-5 e (55) Dale Gibson 13/2: 3222002: Chsd ldrs, styd   ½   59
on & ev ch ins fnl 1f, just held by wnr: acts on fast, gd grnd & both AWs: see 846 & 804.
1242 **WELSH EMPRESS** 30 [7] P L Gilligan 3-9-0 (50) F Lynch 6/1: 06603-03: b f Bahamian Bounty - Azola   ½   53
(Alzao) Rear, gd prog & ev ch dist, just held ins fnl 1f: plcd once in '03 (seller, rtd 51): eff around 1m on gd &
gd/ soft grnd: can find similar.
1242 **BREEZIT** 30 [1] S R Bowring 3-9-3 (53) J Bramhill 7/2 JT FAV: 60300-44: Rear, prog to lead after   2½   51
6f, hdd ins fnl 1f, no extra: see 1242.
656   **ABROGATE** 90 [8]3-8-13 (49) G Faulkner 4/1: 003-0245: Handy, prog & ev ch bef 1f out, wknd: long abs. 4   39
1196 **MR MOON** 32 [9]3-8-10 (11oh) (35) K Dalgleish 25/1: 000-66: b g Pursuit of Love - Sound of Sleat   2   32
(Primo Dominie) Led 6f, wknd: modest form in '03 (rtd 30, med auct mdn).
1630 **ARGENT** 9 [2]3-9-3 (53) R Winston 9/1: 550-P027: Handy, wn ch 2f out, wknd dist: new stable: 2½   34
btr 1630 (10f, soft, D Caroll).
1086 **DANTES DEVINE** 40 [6]3-9-4 (54) G Duffield 7/2 JT FAV: 055-0658: Prom 6f, fdd: btr 1086 (soft).   shd   34
8 Ran   Time 1m 42.94(5.44)   Owned: Mr Russ Mould   Trained: Darlington

---

Official Going Standard

1799   2.30 Enabled Day At Dunstall Park Banded Stakes 3yo+ 0-40 (H)
£1442 £412 £206   5f rnd   Going 46   +03 Fast   Inside

1566 **LEVELLED** 12 [9] D W Chapman 10-9-3 (35) A Culhane 10/1: 5502331: Mid-div, strong run for press   44a
to lead cl-home: eff at 6f, suited by 5f on fm, gd/soft & both AWs, any trk: eff with/without blnks.
1590 **CLEVELAND WAY** 11 [7] D Carroll 4-9-3 vis (40) D Tudhope(7) 4/1 JT FAV: 4502262: Handy & led   nk   43a
halfway, rdn & hdd cl-home: clr rem: see 1405, 304 & 296 (6f).
982   **BELLS BOYS** 48 [8] K A Ryan 5-9-3 p (40) N Callan 11/1: 3350403: Chsd ldr halfway, no impress   5   30a
dist: 7 wk abs: mdn: see 667 & 447.
1336 **BRIGHT MIST** 24 [2] B Palling 5-9-3 (40) P Doe 33/1: 30000/-04: b f Anita's Prince - Out On Her   1¼   26a
Own (Superlative) Dwelt, rear, kept on wide, nrst fin: missed '03: AW plcd '02 (rtd 56a, no turf form in a visor):
eff around 6/7f on fibresand.
1452 **SOTONIAN** 18 [12]11-9-3 (40) Stephanie Hollinshead(5) 8/1: 3053345: Mid-div, not pace to chall.   1¼   22a
1544 **AVIT** 13 [10]4-9-3 (40) J F Egan 8/1: 0-002306: Chsd ldrs till over 1f out: btr 1290, 832 (polytrack). shd 22a
1562 **MINIRINA** 12 [5]4-9-3 (35) R Fitzpatrick 33/1: 540-0447: Led till halfway, sn struggling: btr 1562. 1   19a
1562 **TRAVELLERS JOY** 12 [3]4-9-3 (40) T P Queally(3) 9/1: 660-0038: Hmpd early, nvr pace to threaten.   1   16a
1671 **MANDYS COLLECTION** 6 [11]5-9-3 P (40) S Whitworth 12/1: 3/00-0U59: Al outpcd, op 10/1, chkpcs.   ½   14a
501   **BACK IN SPIRIT** 109 [6]4-9-3 t (40) G Gibbons 6/1: 40/00-000: 10th: ch g Primo Dominie - Pusey   ¾   12a
Street Girl (Gildoran) Dwelt sn outpcd: op 12/1, 4 month abs: unplcd '03 (lightly rcd, rtd 33a): AW mdn wnr
'02, mod turf form (rtd 62, flattered): winning form at 6f on fibresand. 1 May'02 Wolv 6af 84a- D:
1562 **TUSCAN DREAM** 12 [1]9-9-3 (40) P Bradley(5) 16/1: 2251550: 11th: Prom when badly hmpd early, no ch. 3½   2a
1562 **WHITE O MORN** 12 [4]5-9-3 p (40) D Holland 4/1 JT FAV: 4241020: 12th: Rein broke early, went badly   14   0a
left, position sn accepted: btr judged 781.
12 Ran   Time 1m 02.37 (2.17)   Owned: Mr David W Chapman   Trained: York

---

1800   3.00 Winning Post Special At Dunstall Park Banded Stakes 3yo+ 0-35 (H)
£1442 £412 £206   1m1f79y   Going 46   -00 Slow   Inside

1592 **MOYNE PLEASURE** 11 [1] Paul Johnson 6-9-7 p (35) D Holland 6/4 FAV: 0020231: Made all & rdn/in   43a
command fnl 2f: bckd: eff btwn 1m/12f on firm, soft & fibresand, any trk, likes W'hampton: see 780.
1676 **BEN KENOBI** 6 [5] Mrs P Ford 6-9-7 (30) R Ffrench 9/4: 4100-522: Chsd wnr, rdn & no prog fnl 2f: 9   29a
qck reapp: longer trip: see 1676 (7f).
1561 **CLASSICAL WALTZ** 12 [6] J J Sheehan 6-9-7 (30) D Tudhope(7) 14/1: 06/00/0-43: Bhd, mod hdwy, nvr   2½   25a
threaten to chall: op 10/1, clr of rem: see 1561.
      ROYAL EXPOSURE 183 [3] M Wigham 7-9-7 (30) Paul Eddery 7/1: 060005-4: b g Emperor Jones - Blue   7   15a
Garter (Targowice) Dwelt, sn struggling: long abs: seller rnr-up back in '00: stays a stiff 10f on hvy grnd.
1566 **SECOND GENERATION** 12 [2]7-9-7 (30) T P Queally(3) 7/2: 0//0-55345: Chsd ldrs, btn 2f out: btr 1415. 1   13a
821   **DIAGON ALLEY** 70 [4]4-9-7 (30) P Bradley(5) 25/1: 0/0000-06: Slow away & sn bhd, 10 wk abs.   21   0a
6 Ran   Time 2m 02.49 (4.29)   Owned: P and Mrs D M Johnson   Trained: Stanley

---

1801   3.30 Norway's Independence Day Banded Stakes 3yo+ 0-40 (H)
£1446 £413 £207   1m100y rnd   Going 46   -20 Slow   Inside

1564 **SUPER DOMINION** 12 [10] R Hollinshead 7-9-2 p (40) Stephanie Hollinshead(5) 3/1 CO FAV: 00030-51:   46a
Handy & led 4f out, rdn clr bef dist: eff btwn 6/9f on fast, gd/soft & fibresand, likes W'hampton & cheekpieces.
1593 **AMETHYST ROCK** 11 [4] P L Gilligan 6-9-2 (40) J F Egan 3/1 CO FAV: 60-03162: Led till 5f out,   4   40a
kept on for press, no ch with wnr from dist: see 1406.
1643 **ROVING VIXEN** 7 [6] J L Spearing 3-8-4 BL (40) A Daly 10/1: 00-00403: Reared start & well bhd,   ¾   38a

late gains, nrst fin in first time blnks: stays 1m: handles fibresand: see 1565.
1456 **DAFA 18** [3] B J Curley 8-9-2 P (40) T P Queally(3) 3/1 CO FAV: 0/-116064: Bhd, late gains, nrst fin. *nk* **37a**
1710 **RATHMULLAN 4** [2]5-9-8 bl (40) Liam Jones(7) 10/1: 0343135: Trkd ldr, no impress fnl 2f: qck reapp. *1½* **40a**
2284} **TOMSK 332** [9]4-9-2 (40) P Mathers(7) 20/1: 0/04-6: b g Definite Article - Merry Twinkle (Martinmas) Mid-div, no impress fnl 2f: 6 month jumps abs (no form): lightly rcd & mod form '03 on the level (rtd 37): no form '02: AW bow tonight. *hd* **33a**
1611 **ROVELLA 10** [7]3-8-4 (40) G Gibbons 16/1: 000-007: b f Robellino - Spring Flyer (Waajib) Prom 5f: op 10/1: unplcd '03 (rtd 46, mdn). *8* **19a**
1660 **MOONLIGHT SONG 7** [8]7-9-2 (40) Paul Eddery 7/1: 0060-308: Trkd ldrs & led 5f out till 4f out, btn over 1f out: op 5/1: btr 1448. *nk* **18a**
1561 **MISS OCEAN MONARCH 12** [1]4-9-2 (30) A Culhane 12/1: 440-0009: Sn struggling rear. *1½* **15a**
826 **FOREST QUEEN 70** [5]7-9-2 (30) P Bradley(5) 50/1: 00/0/00-00: 10th: b f Risk Me - Grey Cree (Creetown) Al bhd, 10 wk abs: unplcd '03 (rtd 12, no sand form): no form '02. *3½* **8a**
10 Ran Time 1m 51.79 (5.59) Owned: Mrs Norman Hill Trained: Upper Longdon

1802

4.00 Mix Business With Pleasure At Dunstall Park Banded Stakes 4yo+ 0-45 (H)
£1446 £413 £207 **2m46y** **Going 46** **-12 Slow** Inside

1414 **PRINCE OF THE WOOD 20** [3] A Bailey 4-8-12 (45) D Holland 3/1: 00064-21: Held up, prog to lead 5f out, rdn & in command from dist: op 4/1: eff at 11.6f, now suited by 2m on gd/soft & fibresand in banded company. **48a**
1654 **MY LEGAL EAGLE 7** [6] R J Price 10-9-0 (45) R Miles(3) 4/1: 050//5-142: Trkd wnr 4f out, styd on for press, not impress ins last but clr of rem: op 9/4: see 1563 (14f). *1¾* **45a**
575 **FAIRY WIND 99** [4] B J Curley 7-9-0 (45) T P Queally(3) 9/4 FAV: 0020-003: b c Dashing Blade - Fairy Bluebird (Be My Guest) Trkd ldr & led halfway till 5f out, btn 2f out: bckd, op 6/1: 3 month abs: AW h'cap rnr-up '03, disapp in blnks & visor, turf unplcd (rtd 61, h'cap): multiple wnr abroad '02 (h'caps): eff at 11/12f on fibresand, soft & hvy grnd, yet to convince at 14f+. 2 Oct'03 Sout 12af 49a-48 F: *11* **34a**
1329 **MERCURIOUS 24** [5] J Mackie 4-8-12 (45) A Culhane 5/2: 334-4154: Trkd ldr halfway, btn 4f out: bckd. *24* **10a**
1263 **UNLEADED 28** [1]4-8-12 (35) P Doe 14/1: 2125045: Trkd ldrs till 4f out: op 10/1: see 576 & 395. *4* **6a**
650 **OULTON BROAD 91** [2]8-9-0 p (30) S W Kelly 14/1: 016/-0566: Struggling from halfway: jumps fit. *dist* **0a**
824 **TON CHEE 70** [7]5-9-0 (30) P Bradley(5) 33/1: 0/0043-67: Dwelt, sn led till halfway, sn bhd: op 16/1, abs. *dist* **0a**
7 Ran Time 3m 38.63 (9.43) Owned: The Four Of Us Trained: Tarporley

1803

4.30 Racing For All At Dunstall Park Tri-Banded Stakes 3yo 0-45 (H)
£1439 £411 £206 **6f rnd** **Going 46** **-14 Slow** Inside

1607 **SAM THE SORCERER 10** [1] J R Norton 3-9-0 (45) Darren Williams 12/1: 000-01: b g Wizard King - Awham (Lear Fan) Chsd ldr halfway, styd on for press to lead well ins last: first win: unplcd '03 (rtd 41a & 35): eff at 6f on fibresand & a sharp/turning trk. **48a**
1312 **DRESS PEARL 25** [6] R P Elliott 3-8-4 BL (35) G Gibbons 7/1: 0000-032: Mid-div, outpcd over 2f out, styd on well ins last, not reach wnr: op 6/1, imprvd eff in first time blnks: handles soft grnd & fibresand. *1* **34a**
1495 **MITZI CASPAR 15** [7] P L Gilligan 3-8-5 (1ow) (30) R Price 10/1: 00003: Held up, kept on wide, nrst fin: unplcd prev at 1m: eff at 6f in banded company, 7f shld suit in similar. *nk* **34a**
1203 **NITEOWL EXPRESS 31** [4] J O'Reilly 3-8-9 BL (40) D Allan(3) 4/1 FAV: 0-0654: Led after 1f till well ins last, no extra: first time blnks: see 1203. *hd* **37a**
1577 **BE MY ALIBI 11** [2]3-8-9 (40) S W Kelly 6/1: 05000-05: Chsd ldrs, no extra dist: see 1577. *1* **34a**
1641 **HEATHYARDS JOY 7** [5]3-8-4 (35) Stephanie Hollinshead(5) 6/1: 0442556: Mid-div, btn dist: btr 1330. *¾* **27a**
1679 **DANDY JIM 5** [9]3-8-4 BL (30) R Miles(3) 7/1: 0500567: Slow away & al rear: op 11/1, qck reapp, blnks. *10* **0a**
1641 **INDRANI 7** [8]3-8-9 (40) Paul Eddery 5/1: 4004028: Wide, outpcd, nvr factor: op 4/1: btr 1641. *1* **0a**
1641 **ANATOM 7** [3]3-8-4 VIS t (35) T P Queally(2) 8/1: 660-0549: Led till after 1f, sn struggling: op 7/1, visor. *9* **0a**
9 Ran Time 1m 16.39 (3.59) Owned: Mr Tim Simcox & Exors of Mrs P Farrow Trained: Barnsley

1804

5.00 Sponsor A Race At Dunstall Park Banded Stakes 3yo+ 0-45 (H)
£1435 £410 £205 **7f rnd** **Going 46** **-04 Slow** Outside

1627 **MARABAR 9** [2] D W Chapman 6-9-5 bl (45) A Culhane 2/1: 0010031: Handy & led 3f out, drvn & styd on to assert ins last: op 3/1: eff at 6/7f on firm, hvy & fibresand: see 1065 & 555. **57a**
1671 **NEUTRAL NIGHT 6** [5] R Brotherton 4-9-5 vis (45) D Holland 6/5 FAV: 2433122: Chsd ldrs, outpcd 3f out, styd on wide for press, no threat: well bckd: see 1671 & 1565. *2½* **51a**
1642 **SHIRLEY OAKS 7** [6] Miss Z C Davison 6-9-5 (45) N Chalmers(5) 4/1: 5023163: In tch, outpcd over 2f out, kept on ins last: acts on firm, gd/soft & both AWs: see 1075. *1* **49a**
1565 **MY GIRL PEARL 12** [1] M S Saunders 4-9-5 (40) P Makin(5) 8/1: 0400-024: Led till 3f out, no extra fnl 1f. *½* **48a**
1617 **YOUNG DYNASTY 10** [3]4-9-5 bl (45) Liam Jones(7) 28/1: 05505: Keen & al bhd: flattered 1617. *6* **32a**
1160 **GWAZI 33** [4]4-9-5 t (40) Darren Williams 20/1: 000-0306: Slow away & sn bhd, virt p.u,' lost action'. *dist* **0a**
6 Ran Time 1m 29.72(3.52) Owned: Miss N F Thesiger Trained: York

WINDSOR MONDAY 17.05.04 Sharp, Figure 8 Track

Official Going GOOD/FIRM

1805

6.05 Copthorne Hotel Slough/Windsor E B F Maiden Fillies Stakes Fillies 2yo (D)
£5330 £1640 £820 **5f10y** **Good/Firm** **Inapp** Inside

SALSA BRAVA 0 [12] N P Littmoden 2-8-11 J P Guillambert(3) 16/1: 1: b f Almutawakel - Ridotto (Salse) Prom, styd on to lead dist, rdn out: bckd from 50/1 on debut: Feb first foal, cost E16,000: dam plcd at best: sire high-class mid-dist performer: eff at 5f, further shld suit: acts on fast grnd & a sharp trk: goes well fresh: can improve for today's experience & rate higher. **84+**
GODSEND 0 [8] R Hannon 2-8-11 Dane O'Neill 7/1: 2: b f Royal Applause - Gracious Gift (Cadeaux *1¼* **79**

Genereux) Bhd, hdwy halfway, styd on to chase wnr ins fnl 1f, al held: op 5/1 on debut: Mar foal, dam wnr at 6/7f:
sire Gr 1 wnr at 6f: eff at 5f, shld apprec 6/7f in time: acts on fast grnd: can improve on today & find similar.
1640   **RUBYS DREAM 7** [17] J M Bradley 2-8-11 R L Moore 11/2: 423: Handy stands rail, kept on ins fnl   shd   78
1f, not btn far in 3rd: qck reapp: acts on fast & hvy grnd: continues to run well: see 1640 & 1524.
1466   **MAURO 17** [10] P M Phelan 2-8-11   J Quinn 20/1: 424: Led, rcd keenly, hdd dist, sn wknd: acts on   2½   70$
fast & soft grnd: just btr 1466 (soft).
        TOUCH OF SILK 0 [2]2-8-11 M Hills 16/1: 5: ch f Night Shift - Blew Her Top (Blushing John)   nk   69
Handy over 3f, sn onepcd: debut: Apr foal, cost £110,000: half-sister to a wnr at 6/10f: sire speedily bred.
1531   **LIMONIA 13** [3]2-8-11 M Howard(7) 33/1: 56: Dwelt, sn prom, no extra ins fnl 1f: see 1531.   ½   67
1380   **ASPEN RIDGE 21** [18]2-8-11 J F Egan 6/1: 07: Prom till dist, sn no extra.   shd   66
        STEPHANIES MIND 0 [4]2-8-11 I Mongan 12/1: 8: Bhd, hdwy halfway, nrst fin under hands & heels: 1½   61 +
debut: ran green here & sure to improve with experience.
1524   **IVANA ILLYICH 14** [9]2-8-11 J D Smith 25/1: 59: Keen mid-div, nvr able to chall: btr 1524.   hd   60
        ROMANTIC GIFT 0 [14]2-8-11 J Tate 5/1 FAV: 0: 10th: Slow away, nvr nrr than mid-div: op 7/1.   ¾   58
        ENCANTO 0 [19]2-8-11 Derek Nolan(7) 33/1: 0: 11th: Slow away, nvr nrr than mid-div.   1¼   54
1538   **MS POLLY GARTER 13** [5]2-8-11 S Whitworth 66/1: 40: 12th: Cl-up over 3f, wknd: btr 1538.   nk   53
        DIKTATIT 0 [7]2-8-11 T E Durcan 12/1: 0: 13th: Rear, nvr a factor.   nk   52
1524   **MISTY PRINCESS 14** [13]2-8-11 J F McDonald(3) 40/1: 0560: 14th: Al bhd.   shd   51
        ISLAND SWING 0 [15]2-8-11 Hayley Turner(5) 50/1: 0: 15th: Rear, nvr a factor.   ½   49
1524   **ROYAL ACCOLADE 14** [11]2-8-11 T J Mackay 10/1: 00: 16th: Handy till sn wknd: op 7/1.   1   46
        BLUE LINE 0 [1]2-8-11 G Baker 100/1: 0: 17th: Al in rear.   1   43
    Orpen Annie 0 [16]2-8-11 B Reilly(3) 40/1:0   **Divani 0** [6]2-8-11 L Dettori 12/1:0
19 Ran   Time 1m 1.05 ()   Owned: Miss Vanessa Church   Trained: Newmarket

---

1806   6.35 Smith & Milton Claiming Stakes 3yo+   (F)
£3073 £878 £439   **6f**   **Good/Firm**   **Inapp**   Inside

1540   **I WISH 13** [11] M Madgwick 6-8-13 (56) G Baker 10/1: 46-05041: Sn handy, styd on well to lead   60
cl-home, rdn out: eff btwn 5f/8.5f, has tried 10f: acts on fast, soft & polytrack: apprec drop to claim grade.
1221   **EFFECTIVE 30** [2] A P Jarvis 4-9-8 (62) K Fallon 9/1: 3050152: Held up, hdwy halfway, styd on to   shd   68
lead dist, hdd cl-home: acts on fast, gd grnd & both AWs: only just denied here with visor left off: see 1025.
648   **IVY MOON 91** [13] B J Llewellyn 4-8-7 (50) R Thomas(5) 40/1: 030-3603: Slow away, hdwy when short   2   47 +
of room ins 2f, switched & kept on, nrst fin: long abs: would have gone close with a clr passage & is worth
keeping in mind for similar: see 398.
1443   **BELLS BEACH 13** [9] P Howling 6-8-9 (45) M Hills 14/1: 1561044: Mid-div, hdwy & ch dist, sn no extra.   ½   47
1096   **TENDER 39** [12]4-8-9 (57) C Catlin 7/1: 40060-35: Led 3f, sn outpcd, rallied fnl 1f: claimed 6,000.   ½   45
1731   **AGUILA LOCO 3** [17]5-9-8 p (56) S Drowne 7/1: 6203036: Handy over 4f, hung under press & no extra   1   55
dist: qck reapp: just btr 1731.
1644   **THREAT 7** [3]8-8-12 (45) B Reilly(3) 25/1: 0034467: Clk-up, led 3f out, hdd dist, wknd: qck reapp.   shd   44
1255   **PORT ST CHARLES 28** [15]7-9-2 (66) J Quinn 6/1 FAV: 0004408: Held up, short of room halfway till   1¾   43 +
dist, sn no impress: did not get run of race & is worth another ch: claimed for 7,000: btr 1103.
1540   **RILEYS DREAM 13** [7]5-8-7 (45) R Havlin 50/1: 000-0509: Handy, hung left after halfway, sn no extra.   nk   33
1544   **FLYING FAISAL 13** [16]6-8-12 bl (47) R L Moore 16/1: 3046100: 10th: Bhd, nvr nrr than mid-div.   shd   37
1662   **SABANA 7** [4]6-9-2 bl (45) S Whitworth 50/1: 1306000: 11th: Slow away, al in rear: qck reapp.   1   38
976   **PHECKLESS 48** [8]5-9-8 (58) Dane O'Neill 12/1: 3400030: 12th: Rear, nvr a factor: btr 976.   ¾   42
1269   **TICKLE 27** [6]6-8-7 t (54) D Sweeney 25/1: 0-403660: 13th: Cl-up, ev ch dist sn wknd: btr 652.   ½   25
3477}   **LAKE VERDI 283** [18]5-9-8 t (60) S Sanders 40/1: 0/00006-0: 14th: ch g Lake Coniston - Shore Lark   nk   39
(Storm Bird) Cl-up over 3f, wknd: op 12/1 on reapp: unplcd in '03 (rtd 64, h'cap): unplcd in '02 (rtd 78,
h'caps): mdn & stks wnr in '01: winning form at 5/6f, has tried 7f: best without blnks & t-strap.
1 Jun'01 Newb 6fm 93- C: 1 May'01 Newm 5g/f 97- D:
1540   **NAUGHTY GIRL 13** [5]4-8-9 vis (65) Joanna Badger 12/1: 60-00000: 15th: Chsd ldrs over 4f, fdd.   ½   24
1532   **KINGS BALLET 13** [1]6-8-12 VIS (52) J F McDonald(3) 33/1: 2040000: 16th: Mid-div 4f, sn wknd.   ½   25
4771}   **MACS TALISMAN 214** [14]4-9-10 (67) M Tebbutt 10/1: 432003-0: 17th: ch c Hector Protector -   4   25
Inherent Magic (Magical Wonder) Rear, appeared to lose action halfway, nvr a factor: reapp: med auct mdn wnr in
'03 (W A O Gorman): eff at 6/7f on fast, gd grnd & fibresand: tried blnks & t-strap.
2 Aug'03 Newm 6gd 69-67 D: 2 Mar'03 Sout 7af 72a-70 E: 1 Jan'03 Sout 7af 67a- F:
        HERES HARRY 0 [10]4-9-2 J D Smith 100/1: 0: 18th: b c Most Welcome - Nahla (Wassl) Al in rear.   7   0
18 Ran   Time 1m 12.7 ()   Owned: Mrs Gail Gaisford   Trained: Denmead

---

1807   7.05 Addleshaw Goddard Handicap Stakes 3yo 0-85 (D)   [90]
£5639 £1735 £868   **1m3f135y**   **Good/Firm**   **Inapp**   Inside

1604*   **TUDOR BELL 10** [10] J G M O'Shea 3-8-13 (75) D Sweeney 4/1 FAV: 4-02311: Led after 1f, drvn out   82
ins fnl 1f to hold on: eff at 10/11.5f, further shld suit: acts on fast & hvy grnd: continues in fine form: see 1604.
1174   **COVENTINA 32** [4] J L Dunlop 3-9-4 (80) T Quinn 6/1: 5310-002: Handy, prog & ev ch bef 1f out,   nk   86
styd, just held by wnr: eff at 1m, imprvd here for step up to 11.5f: op to more improvement at this trip: see 923.
1515   **SCHAPIRO 14** [8] J H M Gosden 3-8-13 (75) L Dettori 7/1: 045-03: b g Nureyev - Konvincha   hd   80
(Cormorant) Sn cl-up, ev ch bef 1f out, hung left under press ins fnl 1f, not btn far in 3rd: unplcd in 3 '03
starts (rtd 85, mdn): eff at 11.5f on fast grnd: op to more improvement in h'cap grade, though does not look too
keen under pressure & is worth a try in headgear.
1206   **HORNER 31** [5] P F I Cole 3-9-4 (80) S Sanders 8/1: 446-04: b c Rahy - Dynashore (Dynaformer)   1¾   82
Held up, prog after 1m, kept on ins fnl 1f, not pace front 3: unplcd all 3 '03 starts (rtd 86, mdn): prev eff at
6f, now stays 11.6f: acts on firm & fast grnd: not disgraced.
1355   **VANTAGE 23** [3]3-9-4 (80) J P Guillambert(3) 4/1 J FAV: 0-223145: Mid-div, prog & ev ch 2f out, no   shd   81
extra fnl 1f: clr rem: just btr 1355 & see 1038.
1017   **NICK THE SILVER 46** [6]3-8-3 (65) S Carson 14/1: 030-06: gr c Nicolotte - Brillante (Green   6   57
Dancer) Held up, nvr able to chall: 7 wk abs: plcd on 1 of 3 '03 starts (mdn, rtd 76): ett at 1m, shld apprec
mid-dists: acts on fast grnd: with G B Balding.
1241   **MUSTANG ALI 30** [1]3-8-11 (73) P Dobbs 20/1: 22003-67: Mid-div over 1m, sn wknd: btr 1241.   hd   64
1260   **WILFRED 28** [9]3-8-8 (70) E Ahern 10/1: 0630-08: Led 1f, sn lost plg, fdd 3f out: btr 1260.   15   39
1177   **HOH NELSON 32** [7]3-8-8 (70) R L Moore 7/1: 000-39: Handy 1m, sn fdd: step up in trip: btr 1177 (1m).   1   37
9 Ran   Time 2m 30.15 ()   Owned: K W Bell & Son Ltd   Trained: Westbury On Severn

WINDSOR MONDAY 17.05.04 Sharp, Figure 8 Track

1808 7.35 Court House Clinics Conditions Stakes 2yo (B)
£12151 £4609 £2305 **5f10y** **Good/Firm** **Inapp** Inside

1646* **BLUE DAKOTA 7** [6] J Noseda 2-9-3 E Ahern 2/9 FAV: 111: Made all, pushed out ins fnl 1f, val 5L+: qck reapp: well bckd at odds on: eff at 5f on fast & soft, stiff or sharp trk, likes Windsor: unbtn, useful & improving, just the type for Gr 3 Norfolk Stks at Royal Ascot: see 1646 & 1190. **110+**
1567 **BEAVER PATROL 12** [2] R F Johnson Houghton 2-9-0 S Carson 7/1: 132: Cl-up, kept on ins fnl 1f, al held by easy wnr: clr rem: not disgraced bhd a smart looking rival: 6f shld suit: see 1567. *2½* **97**
1499 **SPEED OF SOUND 15** [4] A M Balding 2-8-6 Martin Dwyer 14/1: 33: Handy over 3f, sn no extra. *5* **74**
1503* **SEA HUNTER 15** [3] M R Channon 2-9-0 T E Durcan 20/1: 014: Nvr nrr than mid-div: disapp, btr 1503. *6* **64**
COURAGEOUSLY 0 [1]2-8-8 K Fallon 20/1: 5: b c Aljabr - Eishin Eleuthera (Sadler's Wells) Sn in rear, nvr a factor: debut: Jan foal, cost 14,000gns: half-brother juv wnr abroad: dam wnr at 9f: sire top-class performer around 1m: sharper for today: with P F I Cole. *1* **55**
1646 **LITTLE WIZZY 7** [5]2-8-9 Joanna Badger 66/1: 30136: Sn in rear, nvr a factor: btr 1524 (soft). *6* **38**
6 Ran Time 1m 0.4 (1.6) Owned: Mr A F Nolan Mrs J M Ryan Mrs P Duffin Trained: Newmarket

1809 8.05 Ufj International Plc Handicap Stakes 3yo 0-85 (D) **[92]**
£5623 £1730 £865 **5f10y** **Good/Firm** **Inapp** Inside

1572 **GREEN MANALISHI 12** [7] D W P Arbuthnot 3-9-3 (81) T Quinn 4/1: 551-4221: Keen mid-div, prog to lead dist, rdn out to assert despite hanging left ins fnl 1f: eff around 5f on firm, gd/soft & polytrack: in fine form. **92**
1576 **INTRIGUING GLIMPSE 11** [1] Miss B Sanders 3-8-7 (71) S Sanders 20/1: 60113-32: Slow away, hdwy halfway, styd on to chase wnr ins fnl 1f, al held: acts on fast, soft grnd & polytrack: apprec drop back to min trip. *1¼* **77**
1539 **BORZOI MAESTRO 13** [2] J L Spearing 3-8-9 (73) A Daly 20/1: 30400-23: Keen bhd, prog after 3f, no impress fnl 1f: gd run but needs to settle better: see 1539 (clmr). *1¾* **74**
1513 **DOLCE PICCATA 14** [9] B J Meehan 3-9-7 (85) J F McDonald(3) 14/1: 0132-054: ch f Piccolo - Highland Rhapsody (Kris) Handy, outpcd halfway, rallied dist: med auct fill mdn wnr in '03 (also plcd 7 times): eff at 5f on firm, gd & fibresand: eff with/without blnks: can find similar this term. *nk* **85**
2 Aug'03 Ches 6.1g/f 91-(93) B: 1 Jul'03 Muss 5gd 82-(77) E: 2 Jun'03 Sout 5af 77a- F: 2 May'03 Nott 5.1g/f 73- F: 2 Apr'03 Ripo 5gd 73- E: 2 Apr'03 Warw 5fm 70- D:
1154 **TAG TEAM 34** [13]3-8-8 (72) Martin Dwyer 3/1 FAV: 0-11305: Led over 2f, no extra dist: btr 735. *nk* **71**
1417 **ALCHERA 19** [4]3-8-6 bl (70) S Carson 14/1: 0210-006: b c Mind Games - Kind of Shy (Kind of Hush) Keen cl-up, led bef 2f out, hdd dist, sn wknd: nurs h'cap wnr in late '03: eff at 5/6f, has tried 7f: acts on fast & gd grnd, sharp/undul trk: eff with blnks. *½* **67**
1 Sep'03 Epso 6gd 76-76 D: 2 Jul'03 Wind 5.0g/f 80- D:
1383 **MIRASOL PRINCESS 21** [6]3-9-0 (78) I Mongan 9/1: 41100-07: Rear, nvr nrr than mid-div: see 1383. *hd* **74**
1576 **CREWES MISS ISLE 11** [12]3-8-3 (67) S Whitworth 10/1: 20-46158: Held up, nvr able to chall: btr 1338. *hd* **62**
1229 **FIDDLE ME BLUE 30** [5]3-8-13 (77) S Drowne 9/2: 31-59: Keen rear, nvr a factor: btr 1229. *1¼* **68**
1509* **SCOTTISH EXILE 15** [11]3-8-4 vis (68) Lisa Jones(3) 10/1: 1-644310: 10th: Cl-up over 3f, wknd: btr 1509. *1¼* **55**
1694 **Cheeky Chi 5** [8]3-8-2 (66) J Quinn 33/1:0
1383 **Bahamian Breeze 21** [10]3-8-12 VIS(76) E Ahern 14/1:0
12 Ran Time 1m 0.55 () Owned: Mr Derrick C Broomfield Trained: Upper Lambourn

1810 8.35 E-Trinsic Performance Challenge Maiden Stakes Fillies 3yo+ (D)
£4433 £1364 £682 **1m67y** **Good/Firm** **Inapp** Inside

1166 **DIAMOND LODGE 33** [17] J Noseda 3-8-9 S W Kelly 11/4 FAV: 41: Handy, styd on to lead dist, pushed out, val bit more: eff around 1m, further shld suit: acts on fast grnd & a sharp trk: open to more improvement , see 1166 (debut). **80+**
1468 **PINCHING 17** [3] H R A Cecil 3-8-9 VIS W Ryan 8/1: 432: Mid-div, prog & ev ch dist, rider sn lost whip, kept on but no ch with wnr: eff at 7f/1m on fast & gd grnd: eff with a visor: can find a mdn: see 1210. *1¼* **76**
980 **KALI 48** [2] R Charlton 3-8-9 D Sweeney 12/1: 2-33: Prom, styd on to lead after 6f, hdd dist, no extra: 7 wk abs: acts on fast grnd & polytrack: encouraging eff & can be seen to btr eff over further: see 980. *1¼* **73**
4993} **TENNYS GOLD 196** [9] B W Hills 3-8-9 M Hills 8/1: 02-4: b f Marju - Itatinga (Riverman) Led, hdd 6f out, styd cl-up, no extra dist: reapp: mdn rnr up once in '03 (rtd 72): eff at 7f/1m, 10f will suit: acts on fast grnd & ploytrack: now qual for h'caps. 2 Nov'03 Redc 7sft 72- D: *1* **71**
1462 **SHARP NEEDLE 17** [16]3-8-9 E Ahern 11/1: 025: Cl-up, no extra ins fnl 2f: just btr 1462 (9f, gd/soft). *1* **69**
1171 **SEA OF GOLD 33** [12]3-8-9 R L Moore 100/1: 06: Handy, ev ch 2f out, sn onepcd: see 1171. *¾* **67**
4611} **BONSAI 224** [15]3-8-9 M Tebbutt 100/1: 0-7: b f Woodman - Karakia (Sadler's Wells) Dwelt, prog halfway, kept on fnl 1f: reapp: unplcd sole '03 start (rtd 34): did best work here at fin & mid-dists shld suit. *shd* **66**
4721} **ADAPTABLE 217** [13]3-8-9 Dane O'Neill 9/1: 03-8: b f Groom Dancer - Adeptation (Exceller) Led 6f out, hdd 2f out, sn wknd: reapp: plcd on last of only 2 '03 starts (fill mdn, rtd 84): eff at 7f, bred to apprec further: handles fast grnd: with H Candy. *5* **56**
PALABELLE 0 [18]3-8-9 Martin Dwyer 16/1: 9: Rear, nvr nrr than mid-div: debut. *3* **50**
1468 **LILLIANNA 17** [1]3-8-9 Paul Eddery 33/1: 40: 10th: Nvr nrr than mid-div. *nk* **49**
2083} **TORCHLIGHT 340** [8]4-9-7 L Dettori 4/1: 5-0: 11th: Handy 6f, sn wknd: reapp. *1* **47**
119 **GOLDEN DRIFT 170** [6]3-8-9 D Holland 16/1: 0-0: 12th: Rear, nvr a factor. *shd* **46**
Land Army 0 [10]3-8-9 B Reilly(3) 100/1:0
Lady Taverner 0 [7]3-8-9 G Carter 66/1:0
Favourable 0 [14]3-8-9 L Keniry(3) 66/1:0
4895} **Eva Jean 205** [11]3-8-9 S Drowne 14/1:0
Agouti 0 [5]3-8-9 T Quinn 50/1:0
Tytherley 0 [4]3-8-9 J F McDonald(3) 100/1:P
18 Ran Time 1m 45.85(3.55) Owned: Mrs J Harris Trained: Newmarket

Official Going Good

1811   2.10 Marriott Goodwood Park Hotel Conditions Stakes 3yo+   (C)
£8445 £3203 £1602   **7f rnd**   **Good/Firm 30**   **+06 Fast**   Inside

4675*}**NAAHY 220** [2] M R Channon 4-9-1 (103) S Hitchcott(3) 5/1: 050001-1: ch c Bahamian Bounty - 　　　　**104**
Daffodil Fields (Try My Best) Allowed to dominate, made all, rdn/in command from dist, pushed out cl home: op 7/2:
fast time: 3-time h'cap wnr in '03: auct mdn & dual h'cap wnr '02: best dominating & all 7 wins at 7f: acts on frm &
gd/soft, any trk, loves Goodwood: can go well fresh: v useful and genuine, made full use of easy lead.
1 Oct'03 York 7.0g/f 105-100 B:2 Jun'03 Epso 7g/f 106-(104) A:1 May'03 Good 7g/f 105-98 B:1 Apr'03 Newm 7gd 101-93 C:
2 Sep'02 Good 7fm 93- C: 1 Aug'02 Sand 7g/f 92-86 D: 1 Aug'02 Good 7g/f 92-80 C: 2 Jul'02 Ayr 7.2gd 83-80 E:
2 Jul'02 Sali 6.9g/s 84-78 E: 1 Jun'02 Thir 7g/f 80- E: 2 Apr'02 Newm 5fm 74- D:
1187 **SUGGESTIVE 33** [5] W J Haggas 6-9-10 bl (107) M Hills 6/1: 4415-452: Rear, hung right & styd on 　　1¾　**109**
well for press ins last, nvr threatened wnr: smart effort giving 9lbs to wnr: see 922.
3341* **COURT MASTERPIECE 290** [4] E A L Dunlop 4-9-12 (106) J Murtagh 8/1: 1/42301-3: b c Polish 　　¾　**109**
Precedent - Easy Option (Prince Sabo) Keen & in tch, hdwy over 2f out, rdn & no prog bef dist: op 7/1, reapp: val
h'cap rnr-up & subs List scorer '03: lightly rcd '02, mdn scorer: eff at 7f/1m on fast grnd & any trk: smart colt,
gd return under topweight. 1 Aug'03 Good 8g/f 107-(105) A: 2 Jun'03 Epso 7g/f 105-96 C: 1 Aug'02 York 6g/f 93- D:
　　　STATE CITY 52 [6] Saeed bin Suroor 5-9-1 T (110) L Dettori 6/1: 15355-04: ch c Carson City - 　　hd　**97**
Wajna (Nureyev) Trkd ldrs, rdn & no impress over 1f out: t-strap, 7 wk abs: '03 List & Gr 1 wnr in Dubai:
multiple wnr '02: winning form btwn 5f/1m on dirt surfaces, handles fast grnd: clearly a v smart sand performer,
drop to 5/6f on turf could suit.
1098} **MAGHANIM 397** [7]4-9-1 (102) T Quinn 12/1: 210/0-5: b c Nashwan - Azdihaar (Mr Prospector) 　　shd　**97**
tch, eff over 2f out, hung right & no impress bef dist: reapp: unplcd sole '03 start (Gr 3, rtd 95): juv stks nwr
'02: eff at 7f, tried 1m, shld suit: acts on firm grnd & a gall trk: useful.
1 Sep'02 Donc 7fm 100- C: 2 Aug'02 Newm 7fm 102- D:
1768*}**MUSTAJED 356** [3]3-8-6 R Hills 6/4 FAV: 1-6: Held up in tch wide, no impress over 1f out: hvly 　　5　**89**
bckd on reapp: sole start wnr '03 (impressive, mdn, subs slight a pastern): winning form at 5f, 6f+ shld suit: goes
well fresh on fast grnd & a gall trk: well regarded & better clearly expected today.
1419 **CAVERAL 20** [1]3-8-1 (88) Martin Dwyer 20/1: 31-07: Keen & chsd wnr, btn over 2f out. 　　9　**66**
7 Ran   Time 1m 26.24 (1.7)   Owned: Kuwait Racing Syndicate   Trained: West Ilsley

---

1812   2.40 Mitsubishi Diamond Vision Stakes Handicap 4yo+ 0-100 (C)   **[98]**
£10010 £3080 £1540   **1m rnd**   **Good/Firm 30**   **+01 Fast**   Inside

4894} **HIGHLAND REEL 206** [6] D R C Elsworth 7-9-1 (85) T Quinn 40/1: 610000-1: ch g Selkirk - Taj 　　**91**
Victory (Final Straw) Rear, hdwy wide 2f out & drvn to lead well ins last: reapp: 5 mth jumps abs (unplcd, rtd
103h, nov): rtd h'cap scorer '03 on the level: h'cap plcd '02 (rtd 88): stays 10f, suited by 1m on fast or hvy
grnd, prob any trk & can go well fresh: best held up off a strong pace: showed turn of foot here.
1 Jun'03 Sali 8fm 91-84 C: 2 Mar'01 Donc 8hvy 97-92 B:
1351 **AMANDUS 24** [17] D R Loder 4-9-10 (94) K Fallon 7/1 JT FAV: 0214-002: b g Danehill - Affection 　　½　**100**
Affirmed (Affirmed) Trkd ldrs, drvn to lead ins last, hdd well ins last: bckd, op 9/1: lightly rcd '03, AW mdn
scorer, turf unplcd (rtd 96), h'cap): mdn rnr-up '02 (first time visor): eff at 1m/10f on firm, gd & both AWs,
prob any trk: eff with/without visor & can go well fresh: gd run from fav'ble high draw, could win soon.
1 Aug'03 Wolv 9.4af 96a-(85) D: 2 May'03 Ling 10ap 83a-(98) D: 2 Jul'02 Asco 7g/f 98- D:
1598 **NASHAAB 11** [15] P D Evans 7-9-4 (88) R Havlin 8/1: 5-000023: Rear, short of room 2f out, styd on 　　shd　**94**
strongly cl-home, nrst fin: threatening to win similar after 1598.
4599} **ABLE BAKER CHARLIE 227** [9] J R Fanshawe 5-9-7 (91) J Murtagh 8/1: 025110-4: b g Sri Pekan - 　　shd　**96**
Lavezzola (Salmon Leap) Trkd ldrs, kept on fnl 2f: reapp: progressive '03, h'cap & class stks scorer: auct mdn
wnr '02, subs dual h'cap rnr-up: eff at 1m/10f on firm, gd/soft & polytrack, loves a gall trk, prob handles any:
fine run, remains on an upward course & could prove sharper for this.
1 Aug'03 Asco 8g/f 90-(85) D: 1 Aug'03 Newb 9fm 88-78 D: 2 Jun'03 Newm 10g/f 79-77 C: 2 Aug'02 Newm 8gd 79-75 D:
2 Aug'02 Leic 9.9g/s 79-75 D: 1 Jul'02 Leic 10gd 77- F:
1231 **FINISHED ARTICLE 31** [8]7-9-6 (90) Dane O'Neill 10/1: 52204-05: b g Indian Ridge - Summer Fashion 　　nk　**94**
(Moorestyle) Rear, strong run wide for press fnl 1f, nrst fin: stablemate of wnr: h'cap scorer '03 (C/D, also
thrice h'cap rnr-up): C/D h'cap wnr '02: eff at 10f, suited by strongly run 1m on firm & gd/soft grnd, any trk,
Goodwood specialist: best delivered late, usually requires luck in running, promise here.
2 Sep'03 Asco 8g/f 90-85 B: 2 Sep'03 Good 9g/f 88-85 C: 1 Jul'03 Good 8g/s 87-82 D: 2 Jun'03 Good 8fm 82-80 C:
2 Oct'02 Newm 8fm 89- C: 2 Jul'02 Sand 8g/s 91-89 B: 2 Jun'02 Sali 8fm 92-89 C: 1 Jun'02 Good 8gd 88-83 D:
2 May'02 Good 8g/s 85- C: 2 Sep'01 Good 9g/f 82-79 C: 1 Aug'01 Good 9.8g/s 79-71 E: 2 Jun'01 Bath 8fm 73-72 D:
1478 **ALRAFID 17** [12]5-9-1 (85) R L Moore 16/1: 2426-056: Rear/wide, switched & styd on well ins last, 　　¾　**87**
not able to chall: gd run from poor low draw, likes this trk: worth noting in similar: see 134.
1231 **IMPELLER 31** [14]5-9-3 (87) S Drowne 8/1: 10022-07: ch g Polish Precedent - Almaaseh (Dancing 　　nk　**88+**
Brave) Mid-div, short of room over 2f out & again dist, not pace to chall: shade closer with a clr rur: class stks
& h'cap scorer '03, thrice h'cap rnr-up: h'cap & dual class stks rnr'up '02 (disapp in blnks): suited by 1m/9f on
firm & gd grnd, any trk, tough. 2 Oct'03 Nott 8.2g/s 89-86 C: 2 Oct'03 Newm 8g/f 87-84 C:
1 Sep'03 Good 9g/f 88-83 C: 1 Aug'03 Sand 9g/f 83-(79) D: 2 Jul'03 Brig 8.0g/f 80-77 D: 2 Oct'02 Brig 8gd 84- D:
2 Sep'02 Yarm 7fm 85- D: 2 Apr'02 Newb 8g/f 84-83 B: 1 Aug'02 Sali 7g/f 81- E:
1512 **SRI DIAMOND 15** [19]4-8-8 (78) J F Egan 20/1: 1/030-08: b g Sri Pekan - Hana Marie (Formidable) 　　1¼　**76**
Cl-up & drvn/led over 1f out till ins last, no extra: lightly rcd '03, AW h'cap plcd (rtd 83a, turf unplcd, rtd 76,
C/D h'cap): sole start wnr '02 (mdn): winning form at 7f, has tried 10f: acts on fast grnd & polytrack,
sharp/undul or turning trks: can go well fresh: spot on back at 7f. 1 Sep'02 Warw 7.1g/f 85- D:
1057 **WELCOME STRANGER 43** [7]4-8-8 (78) J Tate 20/1: 11034-09: V slow away & rear, styd on fnl 2f, 　　2　**72+**
not able to chall: lost cl start, 6 wk abs, can improve.
1042 **OMAHA CITY 45** [12]10-8-2 (72) J Quinn 20/1: 05600-00: 10th: Mid-div, eff wide, no prog fnl 2f: abs. 　nk　**65**
1475 **PENNY CROSS 17** [5]4-9-2 (86) R Hills 40/1: 1333-000: 11th: Led 6f, poor draw for forcing tactics. 　nk　**78**
1512 **DESERT OPAL 15** [10]4-9-8 VIS (92) R Hughes 7/1 JT FAV: 110-0050: 12th: Trkd ldrs, wknd 2f out: vis. 　1¼　**81**
1231 **SPANISH DON 31** [11]6-9-2 (86) T E Durcan 20/1: 06141-00: 13th: Chsd ldrs, no impress fnl 2f. 　hd　**74**
3673} **CAPTAIN SAIF 275** [18]4-9-8 (92) P Dobbs 33/1: /56635-0: 14th: Dwelt, rear, only mod prog, reapp. 　½　**79**
1126 **Hits Only Money 36** [3]4-9-13 (97) D Nolan(3) 33/1:0   1483 **Quiet Storm 17** [7]4-10-0 (98) D Holland 16/1:0
951 **Our Teddy 52** [4]4-9-6 (90) Martin Dwyer 33/1:0

4890} **Cal Mac 206** [1]5-8-7 (77) S Hitchcott(2) 66/1.0
18 Ran   Time 1m 39.75 (2.34)   Owned: Sir Gordon Brunton   Trained: Whitsbury

1813   3.15 Totesport Stakes Heritage Handicap 3yo 0-105 (B)   [104]
£43500 £16500   £8250   **1m1f rnd**   **Good/Firm 30**   **-21 Slow**   Inside

1206 **GATWICK 32** [11] M R Channon 3-8-11 (87) T Quinn 9/4 FAV: 3-131: Pushed along towards   **99+**
rear early, hdwy wide to lead over 1f out, rdn out: hvly bckd, op 11/4: eff at 1m/9f, 10f will suit: acts
on fast & gd, any trk: lightly rcd & v progressive, more to come over further & remains one to keep on side.

1500* **DANCING LYRA 16** [4] J W Hills 3-8-11 (87) K Fallon 10/1: 300-6112: Mid-div, rdn & styd on well   1½   **94**
from 2f out, not pace of wnr ins last: op 12/1: eff at 9/10f, progressive, fine run from poor low draw.

1294 **MUTAFANEN 27** [2] E A L Dunlop 3-9-7 (97) R Hills 12/1: 4331-133: Rear, hdwy wide to press ldrs   ½   **103**
ins last, not pace of wnr but kept on well: prob apprec return to sounder surface: fine run under top-weight from
poor low draw: useful colt, win more races: see 923.

756 **ROYAL WARRANT 80** [15] A M Balding 3-8-7 (83) Martin Dwyer 14/1: 10-36134: Trkd ldrs, drvn & styd   hd   **88**
on fnl 2f, not pace of wnr: 12 wk abs & turf return: styd longer 9f trip, shaped as if 10f+ could suit: see 694.

1496 **TRANQUIL SKY 16** [12]3-8-7 (83) D Fox(5) 33/1: 1310-005: b f Intikhab - Tranquillity (Night Shift)   hd   **87+**
Slow away & rear, short of room over 2f out & again over 1f out, styd on strongly, nrst fin: prob plcd with a clr
passage: bckd at long odds: '03 nov auct stks scorer & subs h'cap wnr: eff at 6/7f, styd this sharp 9f well:
likes fast grnd, sharp/undul trks: handles a stiff one: caught the eye here.
1 Jul'03 Brig 7.0g/f 88-82 E: 1 Jun'03 Good 6g/f 86- E:

1427* **WOODY VALENTINE 20** [16]3-8-4 (80) S Chin 15/2: 400-4216: Trkd ldrs, sltly outpcd when short of   ¾   **83**
room 2f out, kept on ins last: return to 10f+ will suit, ran to form of 1427.

1500 **TIGER TIGER 16** [6]3-8-9 (85) J F Egan 25/1: 0-13127: Rear, kept on wide for press, not able to   shd   **88**
chall: acts on fast, hvy & polytrack: see 1500.

1583 **DESERT DREAMER 12** [3]3-9-3 (93) M Hills 10/1: 15420-58: Rear, eff wide over 2f out, no impress   2   **90**
ins last: not see out this longer 9f trip from mod draw, return to 7f/1m could prove ideal: caught the eye 1583.

1315 **MOMTIC 25** [10]3-8-4 (80) J Quinn 12/1: 0321-339: Trkd ldrs, trav well when no run 2f out till   1   **77+**
ins last, not recover: much closer with any sort of run: see 1315.

1583 **SEWNSO CHARACTER 12** [19]3-9-6 (96) F Norton 16/1: 26225-40: 10th: Trkd ldrs, no room over 2f out   ½   **92+**
till ins last, not able to recover: much closer with a clr run: see 1583.

1623 **PAGAN MAGIC 10** [13]3-7-13 (75) Lisa Jones(3) 16/1: 05-30: 11th: Rear, only mod prog fnl 3f: h'cap bow.   nk   **70**

1747* **NEVER WILL 4** [1]3-9-4 (6ex) (94) J Fanning 16/1: 5-2210: 12th: Dsptd lead till over 1f out from   5   **80**
poor low draw: qck reapp: see 923.

1460 **HATCH 18** [14]3-9-0 (90) D Holland 16/1: 2213130: 13th: Trkd ldrs, btn over 1f out: btr 1460 & 1094 (7f).   nk   **75**

1496 **FANCY FOXTROT 16** [18]3-9-0 (90) R Hughes 16/1: 2326-100: 14th: Led/dsptd lead till over 1f out.   1¼   **72**

794 **Blue Empire 76** [8]3-7-13 (75) J Bramhill 66/1:0   1022* **Instructor 46** [5]3-8-3 (79) R L Moore 25/1:0
4891} Zweibrucken 206 [17]3-8-7 (83) P Dobbs 50/1:0   1515 Salisbury Plain 15 [9]3-8-4 (80) T E Durcan 33/1:0
18 Ran   Time 1m 55.10 (4.6)   Owned: Mr W H Ponsonby   Trained: Mel Ilsley

1814   3.45 Listed Letheby & Christopher Predominate Stakes Colts & Geldings 3yo (A)
£17400 £6600   £3300   **1m3f**   **Good/Firm 30**   **-62 Slow**   Outside

1208 **MANYANA 32** [3] M P Tregoning 3-8-8 T (100) Martin Dwyer 10/1: 1-51: b c Alzao - Sometime (Royal   **108**
Academy) Held up, rdn & hdwy over 2f out, hung right but drvn to lead ins last: slow time: bckd: left reapp bhd in
first time t-strap (breathing problems reported latest): styd slowly run 11f: acts on fast & gd grnd, stiff or
sharp/undul trk: can go well fresh: lightly rcd & v useful colt, open to improvement. 1 Jul'03 Sand 7.1gd 91- D:

1482 **CROCODILE DUNDEE 17** [5] Jamie Poulton 3-8-8 (96) J F Egan 25/1: 105-0632: Held up in tch, drvn &   hd   **107**
hdwy to lead 3f out, hdd ins last, styd on gamely, just denied: stays 11f, shaped as if further may suit: up in
grade & a career best: see 1482, 1040.

1584* **RED LANCER 12** [6] R J Price 3-9-0 (110) R Miles 100/30: 2222213: Hld up, kept on fnl 2f, not   2½   **109**
pace of front pair: well bckd: acts on fast, soft & fibresand: ran to smart best conceding 6lb all round.

1520 **HAPPY CRUSADER 15** [1] P F I Cole 3-8-8 (104) K Fallon 3/1: 31136-24: Led & dictated pace, qcknd   ½   **102**
over 4f out, hdd 3f out & no extra frm dist: op 7/2, longer trip, poss stays 11f: see 1520.

1113 **MUTAHAYYA 38** [7]3-8-8 (105) R Hills 2/1 FAV: 14212-25: Rear, eff 3f out, no prog over 1f out: 5   **95**
hvly bckd: bred to apprec this longer 11f trip: btr 1113 (1m, gd/soft).

1584 **GRAHAM ISLAND 12** [5]3-8-8 (84) D Holland 7/1: 05-166: Trkd ldrs, wandered under press 3f out &   5   **85**
btn/hmpd 2f out: well bckd: acts on fast grnd: btr 1584 & 1211.

4336} **ZOUAVE 242** [2]3-8-8 (92) M Hills 33/1: 103-7: b c Spectrum - Lady Windley (Baillamont) Chsd   1¾   **86**
ldr, btn 3f out: reapp: debut wnr '03 (mdn, subs List unplcd): winning form at 1m, mid-dist pedigree: acts on firm
& fast grnd, gall or easy trk: can go well fresh. 1 Aug'03 Kemp 8fm 87- D:
7 Ran   Time 2m 28.01 (10.11)   Owned: Sheikh Mohammed   Trained: Lambourn

1815   4.20 Casco Maiden Stakes 3yo (D)
£5577   £1716   £858   **1m rnd**   **Good/Firm 30**   **-01 Slow**   Inside

4514} **DUBOIS 232** [7] Saeed bin Suroor 3-9-0 VIS T R Hills 9/4 FAV: 25-1: b c Sadler's Wells - Dazzle   **88**
(Gone West) Dwelt, sn led, rdn & al holding rivals from dist: well bckd on reapp, visor & t-strap fitted: mdn
rnr-up '03 (lightly rcd, D Loder): eff at 7f/1m, 10f shld suit: acts on fast grnd, sharp/undul or easy trk: goes
well fresh & suited by forcing tactics: lightly rcd, sharpened up by visor. 2 Sep'03 Yarm 7.0g/f 80- D:

1152 **GOLD MASK 35** [10] J H M Gosden 3-9-0 D Holland 5/2: 0-62: b c Seeking The Gold - Leo's Gypsy   1¼   **84**
Dancer (Leo Castelli) Chsd wnr, eff to press wnr dist, no extra ins last: op 7/4: unplcd sole '03 start (rtd 74):
styd longer 1m trip, handles fast & gd/soft grnd, stiff or sharp/undul trk: shld find a race.

1511 **LUCAYAN LEGEND 15** [9] P F I Cole 3-9-0 K Fallon 13/2: 63: b c Docksider - Capo di Monte (Final   1¾   **81**
Straw) Sn pushed along mid-div, kept on, not pace of front pair: left hvy grnd debut bhd: eff at 1m, 10f could
suit on this evidence: handles fast grnd & a sharp/undul trk: clearly has ability, entitled to progress.

1623 **STARMIX 10** [4] P F I Cole 3-9-0 T Quinn 40/1: 004: Rear, eff 3f out, no prog on ldrs dist: 3   **73**
drpd in trip & career best: stays 1m, tried 12f: handles fast grnd: may do better in mid-dist h'caps.

GOODWOOD   **TUESDAY 18.05.04   Righthand, Sharpish, Undulating Track**

RIDGE BOY 0 [6]3-9-0 P Dobbs 33/1: 5: Mid-div, outpcd 3f out, no threat after on debut. *½* **74**
1166 **HIGH FREQUENCY 34** [3]3-9-0 Martin Dwyer 25/1: 06: Trkd ldr, wknd over 2f out. *3* **68**
ZILMY 0 [8]3-9-0 J Murtagh 4/1: 7: Dwelt & held up, eff 3f out, no prog over 1f out, eased: op 6/1. *½* **67**
INNOCENT REBEL 0 [2]3-9-0 T E Durcan 12/1: 8: Rear, nvr a factor on debut. *½* **66**
911 **BAHAMA REEF 55** [1]3-9-0 (63) Dane O'Neill 50/1: 06400-09: Mid-div, btn 3f out, abs. *2* **62**
2640} **BLAISE WOOD 319** [5]3-9-0 R L Moore 40/1: 6-0: 10th: Al rear: reapp, new yard & gelded. *hd* **61**
10 Ran Time 1m 39.9 (2.5) Owned: Godolphin Trained: Newmarket

1816

4.55 Avtrade Maiden Auction Stakes 2yo (D)
£4797 £1476 £738 **5f str** **Good/Firm 30** **-47 Slow** Stands Side

GORTUMBLO 0 [8] D J S ffrench Davis 2-8-7 T Quinn 25/1: 1: b c Sri Pekan - Evergreen (Lammtarra) Sn prom towards centre, led over 1f out, rdn out: bckd at long odds, op 33/1: Feb first foal, cost 8,000gns: dam a 3yo 1m wnr & half-sister to a List 1m scorer: eff at 5f, will get further: acts on fast grnd & a sharp/undu trk: goes well fresh: most promising start, could prove useful. **90**
1670 **ASIAN TIGER 7** [7] R Hannon 2-8-10 R Hughes 1/1 FAV: 22: Led, rdn & hdd over 1f out, not pace of wnr: hvly bckd: acts on fast & soft grnd: see 1670 (debut). *1½* **88**
1716 **EMPIRES GHODHA 5** [3] B J Meehan 2-8-9 K Fallon 9/2: 53: Cl-up & ch over 1f out, not pace of wnr: nicely bckd, op 13/2: qck reapp: imprvd from debut: acts on fast grnd, stiff/undul or sharp trk. *nk* **86**
RAGGED GLORY 0 [6] R Hannon 2-8-9 P Dobbs 33/1: 4: br c Foxhound - Resurgence (Polar Falcon) Dwelt, held up in tch, kept on late, nvr pace to threaten: Feb first foal, 25,000gns purchase: dam unrcd sister to top-class sprint peformer Pivotal & also half-sister to a useful 1m wnr: handles fast grnd, likely improver at 6f+. *2* **80+**
SHUJUNE AL HAWAA 0 [5]2-8-5 T E Durcan 14/1: 5: ch f Grand Lodge - Bank On Her (Rahy) Pushed along chasing ldrs, not pace to chall fnl 2f: Feb foal, 35,000gns purchase: dam a 7f 3yo wnr, sire top-class at 1m/10f: looks sure to apprec 6f+ & shld improve. *shd* **76**
1401 **WITHERING LADY 21** [1]2-8-2 J Quinn 10/1: 346: Held up in tch, outpcd fnl 2f: see 1123. *hd* **72**
1422 **DETONATE 20** [2]2-8-7 D Holland 100/30: 647: Keen in rear, hmpd halfway & no prog dist: bckd. *1½* **73**
IN DREAMS 0 [4]2-8-10 Martin Dwyer 50/1: 8: Cl-up 2f, sn outpcd on debut. *2½* **68**
8 Ran Time 1m 00.55 (3.85) Owned: Mr K Corrigan Trained: Lambourn

1817

5.30 Singleton Stakes Handicap 4yo+ 0-90 (C) **[90]**
£9965 £3066 £1533 **7f rnd** **Good/Firm 30** **-04 Slow** Inside

1624 **TARANAKI 10** [13] P D Cundell 6-9-6 (82) Lisa Jones(3) 9/1: 1-041401: Mid-div, switched & styd on well for press to lead ins last, sn asserted, decisively: nicely bckd, op 12/1: suited by 6/7f, stays 1m: acts on firm, gd/soft & both AWs: v tough & genuine, go close in Victoria Cup H'cap at Ascot on Sat (unlucky 3rd last year). **91**
1624 **MATERIAL WITNESS 10** [11] W R Muir 7-9-7 (83) Martin Dwyer 16/1: 2100-002: b g Barathea - Dial Dream (Gay Mecene) Led, hdd ins last, not pace of wnr but back to form: class stks scorer '03: dual turf h'cap & AW h'cap wnr '02: stays 1m, best at 6/7f: acts on fast, soft & polytrack, prob any trk, likes a sharp one: loves to dominate. 1 Jul'03 Chep 6.1g/f 89-(84) C: 2 Jul'03 Epso 6gd 90-84 C: 2 Apr'03 Wind 6g/s 87-(84) D: 1 Nov'02 Ling 7ap 79a-70 E: 1 Sep'02 Sand 7gd 84-77 D: 2 Jul'02 Epso 7gd 80- D: 2 Jun'02 Good 7g/s 76- D: 1 Jun'02 Good 7sft 76-72 C: 2 Jan'02 Ling 8ap 64a-67 D: 2 Dec'01 Ling 8ap 67a-66 E: 2 Sep'01 Hami 8.2gd 80-78 C: *2* **88**
1423 **JUST FLY 20** [16] S Kirk 4-9-2 (78) P Dobbs 12/1: 05-22203: Rear, hdwy & switched dist, strong run ins last, nrst fin: op 7/1: best delivered late, looks nicely weighted on turf, likely to find similar: see 518. *¾* **81**
1481 **FRUIT OF GLORY 17** [12] J R Jenkins 5-10-0 (90) D Holland 11/2 JT FAV: 0544304: Trkd ldrs, ch 2f out, onepace ins last: nicely bckd: eff at 7f, poss a stiff 6f just ideal, loves Newmarket: see 1137. *nk* **92**
4178} **LAST APPOINTMENT 250** [8]4-9-4 (80) J Tate 14/1: 4210-5: b c Elusive Quality - Motion In Limine (Temperence Hill) Chsd ldr, onepace ins last: reapp: lightly rcd '03, mdn scorer (C/D): eff at 7f on firm & fast grnd, handles polytrack, gall or sharp/undul trk: encouraging return from moderate draw. 1 Jun'03 Good 7fm 81- D: 2 Jun'03 Newb 7g/f 81- D: *nk* **81**
1042 **GREENWOOD 45** [7]6-9-1 (77) J F Egan 33/1: 0-030066: Rear, eff when short of room over 1f out, kept on, nrst fin: 6 wk abs: encouraging turf return, well h'capped: keep in mind: see 518. *½* **77**
1282 **PERFECT PORTRAIT 28** [1]4-8-11 VIS (73) K Fallon 14/1: 1-307: Settled rear, hdwy 2f out, not pace to chall from poor low draw: h'cap bow, wore vis: improve on this in similar when better drawn. *shd* **73**
1598 **DIGITAL 11** [4]7-9-12 (88) S Hitchcott(3) 6/1: 0340368: Settled rear, kept on late, nvr able to land blow: poor draw & prob requires stiffer track at this trip: see 945. *hd* **87**
1600* **STOIC LEADER 11** [15]4-9-4 (80) J Fanning 11/2 JT FAV: 1401119: Cl-up, btn when hmpd ins last. *1½* **76**
1598 **FLINT RIVER 11** [3]6-8-12 (74) R Hughes 14/1: 0001240: 10th: Mid-div, eff over 2f out, no impress. *3* **64**
3651} **GIFT HORSE 276** [9]4-9-6 (82) J Murtagh 14/1: 216-0: 11th: ch g Cadeaux Genereux - Careful Dancer (Gorytus) Chsd ldrs till over 1f out on reapp: lightly rcd '03, mdn scorer: eff at 1m, stiff or sharp/turning trk: acts on firm & fast grnd. 1 Jul'03 Sand 8.1g/f 84- D: 2 Jul'03 Warw 8.1fm 75- D: *1½* **69**
4925} **POLAR IMPACT 121** [10]5-8-10 (72) T E Durcan 10/1: 01011-10: 12th: Keen in rear, eff 2f out, no impress. *1½* **56**
1525+ **JUST A GLIMMER 15** [6]4-9-8 (84) F Norton 14/1: 3012010: 13th: Chsd ldrs till over 1f out: btr 1525. *2½* **63**
1624 **OAKLEY RAMBO 10** [2]5-9-4 (80) R L Moore 10/1: 00-50620: 14th: Al bhd: btr 1624 (soft). *¾* **58**
4897} **Yeoman Lad 206** [14]4-9-0 (76) S Whitworth 20/1:0 688 **Ile Michel 88** [5]7-9-9 (85) R Miles(3) 33/1:0
16 Ran Time 1m 26.91(2.41) Owned: Mr Eric Evers Trained: Compton

REDCAR   **TUESDAY 18.05.04   Lefthand, Flat, Galloping Track**

Official Going Firm (Good/Firm Places)

1818

2.00 European Breeders Fund Median Auction Maiden Stakes Fillies 2yo (F)
£3644 £1041 £521 **6f str** **Good/Firm 26** **-22 Slow** Centre

1669 **UMNIYA 7** [9] M R Channon 2-8-11 A Culhane 4/5 FAV: 321: Prom, styd on to lead dist, rdn out: well bckd on qck reapp: eff at 5f, imprvd for recent step up to 6f: acts on fast & soft grnd: gd confidence boost. **81**
TARAS TREASURE 0 [2] J J Quinn 2-8-11 R Winston 14/1: 2: b f Desert King - Oklahoma (Shareef Dancer) Handy, styd on to chase wnr ins fnl 1f, al held: debut: Feb foal, cost E48,000: half-sister won numerous *2½* **72**

times at sprint dists: dam unrcd: eff at 6f on fast: win a race.

1631 **TAGULA BAY 10** [12] T D Easterby 2-8-11 D Allan(3) 9/2: 23: Prom, led halfway, hdd dist, no *3½* **62**
extra: not disgraced on step up to 6f tho' drop back to 5f shld suit: ran to form of 2nd in 1631 (5f, soft).

KNOCK BRIDGE 0 [10] M J Wallace 2-8-11 S Sanders 6/1: 4: b f Rossini - Touraneena (Robellino) *nk* **61**
In tch, ev ch dist, sn no extra: debut: March foal, cost 5,500gns: half-sister to a 9f wnr: sire top-class performer over sprint dists at 2: just sharper for today.

MISSPERON 0 [7]2-8-11 N Callan 20/1: 5: b f Orpen - Secret Hideaway (Key To The Mint) Handy *hd* **60**
4f, sn no extra: debut: Feb foal, cost 18,000gns: half-sister to wnrs at 6f/1m: dam unrcd: sire Gr 1 wnr at 6f: not given a hard time here & can rate higher with experience.

UNDERTHEMISTLETOE 0 [11]2-8-11 F Lynch 33/1: 6: Slow away, sn handy, fdd dist: debut: unruly *2* **54**
in padd bef race & just ndd today's experience.

1524 **KASHMAR FLIGHT 15** [3]2-8-11 A Mullen(7) 33/1: 07: Slow away, nvr nrr than mid-div: debut. *1¼* **50**
FALCON GOER 0 [13]2-8-11 Kim Tinkler 66/1: 8: Bhd, nvr a factor. *½* **49**
DORN DANCER 0 [4]2-8-11 L Enstone(3) 33/1: 9: Slow away, nvr able to chall. *¾* **47**
THREE PENNIES 0 [5]2-8-11 S W Kelly 50/1: 0: 10th: Slow away, al bhd. *1¾* **42**
CANARY DANCER 0 [8]2-8-11 G Faulkner 66/1: 0: 11th: Mid-div till halfway, wknd. *1½* **38**
1123 **FANTASTIC STAR 36** [1]2-8-11 M Fenton 66/1: 00: 12th: Led till halfway, wknd. *2½* **31**
LIVE IN HOPE 0 [6]2-8-11 N Pollard 100/1: 0: 13th: Bhd, nvr a factor. *2* **25**
13 Ran Time 1m 11.82 (2.92) Owned: Kuwait Racing Syndicate Trained: West Ilsley

1819

2.30 Wilton Claiming Stakes 3yo+ (F)
£2919 £834 £417 **1m3f** **Good/Firm 26** **-22 Slow** Inside

1552 **ARMS ACROSSTHESEA 14** [1] A C Whillans 5-9-8 (50) A Mullen(7) 13/2: 06000-21: Held up, grad prog **54**
to led dist, drvn out: eff at 6f/1m, now stays 11/12f: acts on firm, gd/soft & fibresand.

1754 **PLATINUM CHARMER 3** [5] K R Burke 4-9-12 p (55) Darren Williams 5/2 FAV: 2102142: Handy, ev ch *1½* **55**
trav well bef 1f out, kept on but al held ins fnl 1f: qck reapp: top-weight: eff at 11/12f on fast, soft & fibresand.

1449* **RIGHTY HO 19** [2] W H Tinning 10-9-6 (45) R Winston 7/2: 0/3200-13: Led till dist, no extra: see 1449. *3½* **44**

1448 **MERLINS PROFIT 19** [4] M Dods 4-9-6 (40) L Enstone(3) 12/1: 0/0003-54: b g Wizard King - Quick *¾* **42**
Profit (Formidable) Rear, prog after 7f, ev ch bef 1f out, sn no extra: clr rem: 3rd of 7 best in '03 (rtd 42, M Todhunter): unplcd in '02 (rtd 70, flattered, last of 5, nov stks): prob stays 11f on fast grnd.

PERCY VERANCE 1359 [6]6-9-10 M Fenton 16/1: 000///-5: ch g Dolphin Street - Sinology (Rainbow *8* **35**
Quest) Held up, nvr nrr than mid-div: earlier unplcd sole 03/04 hdles start (rtd 100h, nov): unplcd both 01/02 starts (juv nov hdle, rtd 89h): modest Flat form back in '00 (rtd 54, auct mdn).

3490} **DOUBLE BLADE 283** [3]9-9-10 (45) A Culhane 9/1: 406404-6: b g Kris - Sesame (Derrylin) Handy *shd* **34**
over 1m, sn wknd: won 2 claim hdles in 03/04 (rtd 115h, stays a sharp 2m on firm & gd, handles soft): plcd once in '03 (h'cap, rtd 47, Mrs M Reveley): h'cap rnr-up in '02 (h'cap, also sand unplcd, rtd 56a): eff at 10f, suited by 11/14f on fast, gd/soft & polytrack: best without blnks: with N Wilson.
2 Apr'02 Ripo 12.2gd 59-58 E: 2 Jul'01 Redc 9fm 63- E: 2 Jun'01 Redc 10g/f 69-68 C:

1561 **ERUPT 13** [10]11-9-5 (45) T Eaves(5) 25/1: 00060-57: Rear, nvr able to chall: see 1561. *1¾* **26**
1552 **MIKASA 14** [8]4-9-8 (40) S Sanders 14/1: 00-00038: Cl-up 9f, wkng when lost balance dist, eased. *6* **21**
1430 **TURFTANZER 20** [9]5-9-5 t (35) Kim Tinkler 50/1: 5046009: Chsd ldrs 6f, wknd. *2½* **14**
1680 **FORTUNES FAVOURITE 6** [7]4-9-3 (45) S W Kelly 11/2: 0340100: 10th: Slow away, prog halfway, fdd *dist* **0**
after 1m, eased fnl 1f: qck reapp: btr 1363 (gd/soft).
10 Ran Time 2m 20.82 (5.32) Owned: Play Fair Partnership Trained: Hawick

1820

3.05 Marske Handicap Stakes 3yo+ 0-80 (D) **[80]**
£6533 £2010 £1005 **7f str** **Good/Firm 26** **+04 Fast** Centre

1461 **SAWWAAH 18** [13] D Nicholls 7-9-12 (78) Alex Greaves 20/1: 1030-001: b g Marju - Just A Mirage **84**
(Green Desert) Mid-div, prog to lead dist, rdn out to hold on despite hanging left: h'cap & claim wnr in '03: claim wnr on fnl '02 start: missed '01: eff at 1m/10.3f, enjoyed drop back to 7f today: acts on firm or hvy grnd: sharp/undul or gall trk: has gone well fresh: quirky & inconsistent but has ability.
1 Jun'03 Good 8fm 81-77 C: 2 May'03 Pont 8.0g/s 71-(82) E: 1 Apr'03 Hami 9.2g/s 84-(80) E: 1 Sep'02 Ayr 9gd 78- E:

1600 **WHIPPASNAPPER 11** [12] J R Best 4-8-13 (65) N Pollard 8/1: 3021032: Mid-div, prog halfway, kept *¾* **68**
on ins fnl 1f, just held by wnr: padd pick: remains in gd form: see 1600 & 1354.

1535 **PRIDE OF KINLOCH 14** [9] J Hetherton 4-8-5 (57) J McAuley 66/1: 0-060403: Handy, styd on to lead *nk* **59**
after 5f, hdd dist, not btn far in 3rd: see 385.

1660 **ANNIJAZ 8** [20] J M Bradley 7-8-5 (57) B Reilly(3) 10/1: 0060-224: Bhd, prog after 4f, no impress fnl 1f. *1¼* **57**
1523 **BRANSTON TIGER 15** [1]5-9-4 (70) M Fenton 20/1: 4-500065: Chsd ldrs till dist, no extra: btr 1354. *2* **66**
1537 **CASHNEEM 14** [16]6-8-8 (60) S W Kelly 14/1: 14100-46: Mid-div, prog 2f out, onepcd fnl 1f: btr 1537. *shd* **55**
1519 **IBERUS 15** [14]6-9-8 p (74) T Eaves(5) 33/1: 0505-007: b g Monsun - Iberica (Green Dancer) Bhd, *shd* **68+**
kept on well late, nrst fin: unplcd & p.u. in 2 03/04 hdles start (rtd 82h, nov h'cap): unplcd in '03 (rtd 102$ & 88, M C Pipe): dual German List wnr in '02: both wins at 1m on gd & hvy: slipped down weights, keep in mind at 1m.

1474 **GO TECH 17** [2]4-9-13 (79) D Allan(3) 5/1 FAV: 005-0068: Hld up, hard rdn but staying on when hmpd *hd* **72+**
over 1f out, not recover: op 7/1: ignore this: well h'acpped: btr 1474.

1393 **TRE COLLINE 22** [18]5-8-13 (65) Kim Tinkler 20/1: 320-0009: b g Efisio - Triple Joy (Most *¾* **56**
Welcome) Nvr nrr than mid-div: h'cap wnr in '03 (C F Wall): won fnl of just 2 '02 starts (h'cap): eff at 6/7f on firm, fast grnd & fibresand: with M Tinkler.
2 Jul'03 Donc 6g/f 75-(74) D: 1 Jun'03 Donc 7fm 74-68 D: 1 May'02 Wolv 7af 70a-65 E:

1345 **UP TEMPO 24** [11]6-9-11 bl (77) N Callan 7/1: 3111420: 10th: Handy, short of room after 5f till *½* **67+**
ins fnl 1f, ch had gone: much closer with clr passage & is worth another ch: btr 1345 & 1142.

1092 **QUEEN CHARLOTTE 40** [7]5-9-2 (68) R Winston 14/1: 106/10-20: 11th: Prom over 5f, wknd: 6 wk abs. *¾* **56**
1519 **ATLANTIC QUEST 15** [19]5-10-0 (80) J Carroll 12/1: 410-0500: 12th: Rear, nvr able to chall: btr 1474. *shd* **67**
1537 **ONE WAY TICKET 14** [8]4-8-8 p (60) L Enstone(3) 25/1: 1020-000: 13th: Led, hdd 2f out, wknd: btr 1385. *¾* **45**
1508 **FLYING EDGE 16** [6]4-8-8 (60) A Nicholls 10/1: 60-02050: 14th: Cl-up 4f, wknd. *½* **44**
1319* **MY BAYARD 25** [5]5-8-7 (59) P Fessey 20/1: 0-625010: 15th: Prom, led after 3f, hdd 2f out, wknd. *¾* **41**
1160 **Weet Watchers 34** [10]4-8-8 (60) A Culhane 16/1:0 1251 **Bond Playboy 29** [15]4-9-1 (67) S Sanders 25/1:0
1578 **Oases 12** [17]5-8-6 (58) Darren Williams 40/1:0 1598 **Riska King 11** [3]4-9-7 (73) T Hamilton(3) 20/1:0
19 Ran Time 1m 23.40 (1.60) Owned: Fayzad Thoroughbred Limited Trained: Thirsk

REDCAR   TUESDAY 18.05.04   Lefthand, Flat, Galloping Track

1821
3.35 Whitby Handicap Stakes 3yo+ 0-75 (E)   [75]
£3689 £1135 £568   **1m2f**   **Good/Firm 26**   -10 Slow   Inside

1609 **OLIVIA ROSE 11** [6] J Pearce 5-9-4 (65) S Sanders 6/1: 452-0131: Mid-div, prog to lead dist, drvn   73
out: eff btwn 1m/12f, acts on fast, hvy & fibresand: continues in fine form: see 1609 & 1467.
1599 **TROUBLE MOUNTAIN 11** [14] M W Easterby 7-9-6 bl (67) Dale Gibson 11/2 FAV: 23-33352: Rear, prog   ½   73
after 7f, chsd wnr fnl 1f, just held: continues to run well & on a fair mark: see 1164 & 196.
443 **MICHAELS DREAM 119** [10] J Hetherton 5-7-12 (5oh)vis (40) J McAuley 20/1: 00300-63: Cl-up, ev ch   3½   46
bef 1f out, sn no extra: hdles fit, earlier plcd (rtd 101h, mdn hdle): eff at 10f, return to 12/14f will suit: see 443.
4855} **SIR NIGHT 209** [15] Jedd O'Keeffe 4-8-6 (53) N Pollard 10/1: 434000-4: b g Night Shift - Highly   nk   53
Respected (High Estate) Bhd, eff 2f out, nrst fin: hdles fit, juv nov hdle wnr on fnl 03/04 start (rtd 105h, stays
2m1f on gd grnd, sharp/undul trks): won 2 sellers in '03 (J D Bethell): plcd at best in '02 (rtd 64, h'cap): eff
at 7f, stays 10f well: acts on fast, gd & fibresand: tried visor, cheek pieces & blnks: sharper for today.
2 Jun'03 Nott 10.0gd 60-60 D: 2 Jun'03 Pont 10.0g/f 62-57 D: 1 May'03 Beve 9.9gd 57-(52) F: 2 Apr'03 Nott 8.2g/f 52-51 F:
1 Mar'03 Sout 7af 54a-(48) G: 2 Feb'03 Sout 7af 51a- G:
4607} **STEPASTRAY 227** [17]7-8-1 (48) C Cogan 33/1: 310000-5: gr g Alhijaz - Wandering Stranger (Petong)   ¾   45
Held up, prog after 7f, no impress fnl 1f: hdles unplcd on sole 03/04 start (rtd 38h, nov hdle): mdn h'cap wnr in
'03: plcd several times in '02 (rtd 42, h'cap): eff at 10/12f, has tried 2m: acts on firm, soft & fibresand, any
trk: has tried blnks & cheek pieces: with R E Barr.
1 Aug'03 Redc 10g/f 50-45 E: 2 Jan'03 Sout 11af 45a- F: 2 Aug'02 Newc 10.1g/f 42-40 E: 2 Jul'01 Beve 10fm 44-44 E:
4920} **MARKET AVENUE 203** [2]5-9-1 (62) T Hamilton(3) 8/1: 600006-6: b f Factual - The Lady Vanishes   1¾   57+
(Robin des Pins) Held up, prog when short of room 2f out, again short of room dist, kept on late: reapp: won 3
h'caps & a class stks in '03: h'cap wnr in '02: h'cap rnr-up in '01: eff at 9/11f on firm & gd, handles gd/soft
grnd: acts on any trk: much closer with clr run & is on a handy mark now.
1 Jul'03 Beve 9.9gd 73-(69) E: 2 Jul'03 Ripo 10g/f 72-69 D: 1 Jul'03 Ches 10.3fm 70-64 D: 1 Jun'03 Muss 9fm 64-61 E:
1 May'03 Sout 10g/f 62-57 E: 2 Jul'02 Redc 11g/f 62-60 D: 1 Jun'03 Redc 10fm 64-54 F: 2 Aug'01 Ches 7g/s 65-65 C:
1397* **JIMMY BYRNE 22** [11]4-9-11 (72) T Eaves(5) 10/1: 300-0417: Nvr nrr than mid-div: btr 1397 (soft).   nk   66
1602 **UNO MENTE 11** [13]5-8-11 (58) Kim Tinkler 40/1: 1350-008: Bhd, nvr nrr than mid-div.   1¼   50
143* **TRANCE 167** [9]4-10-0 (75) P Fessey 22/1: 0/02001-9: Nvr nrr than mid-div: abs, btr 143 (1m, a/w).   1¼   65
1536 **EAST RIDING 14** [4]4-8-0 (2ow) (45) Ann Stokell 33/1: 05-56630: 10th: Mid-div, nvr able to chall.   ¾   35
1883} **LARA BAY 351** [8]4-9-3 (64) A Culhane 14/1: 50/05-0: 11th: Cl-up 1m, wknd.   1½   49
1777 **ESCALADE 3** [5]7-8-10 p (57) S W Kelly 10/1: 0450-040: 12th: Mid-div, short of room bef 1f out, sn btn.   2½   38
1278 **THE LOOSE SCREW 28** [16]6-7-12 (45) D Fentiman(7) 50/1: 6200-000: 13th: Led 7f out, hdd dist, fdd.   shd   25
1164 **EVERY NOTE COUNTS 34** [12]4-9-6 (67) R Winston 12/1: 4520-000: 14th: Cl-up, wknd 2f out.   1¼   45
1541 **JAKE BLACK 14** [3]4-8-12 (59) D Tudhope(7) 8/1: 1153150: 15th: Handy when short of room after 5f,   nk   36
short of room again 2f out, not recover: ignore this: btr 1430.
4534] **NIFTY ROY 582** [1]4-8-0 (2ow) (45) P Mathers 100/1: 26560/-0: 16th: Led, hdd 7f out, prom when   dist   0
short of room after 5f, sn fdd on reapp.
16 Ran   Time 2m 5.95 (3.65)   Owned: Mr A Watford   Trained: Newmarket

1822
4.10 Captain Cook Rating Related Maiden Stakes 3yo+ 0-70 (E)
£3455 £1063 £532   **7f str**   **Good/Firm 26**   -01 Slow   Centre

4799} **PERLE DOR 213** [4] W J Haggas 3-8-8 (70) A Culhane 11/4: 450-1: b f Entrepreneur - Rose Society   74
(Caerleon) Held up, hdwy over 1f out, lead cl-home, drvn out: well bckd on reapp: unplcd on all 3 '03 starts (rtd
75, md auct mdn): eff at 7f, bred to apprec mid-dists: acts on fast grnd & a gall trk: goes well fresh.
1022 **BALLINGER EXPRESS 46** [3] A M Balding 4-9-5 BL (64) N Chalmers(5) 22/1: 0532: Dwelt, sn in tch, led   nk   69
2f out, hdd dist, ev ch ins fnl 1f, just held by wnr: 7 wk abs & first time blnks: acts on fast grnd & polytrack.
1393 **PAWAN 22** [5] Miss A Stokell 4-9-8 (61) Ann Stokell 10/1: 5220353: Led 5f, styd on to lead again   nk   71
dist, hdd cl-home: padd pick: see 1276 & 1145.
1002 **FLASH RAM 48** [9] T D Easterby 3-8-11 (70) D Allan(3) 33/1: 333-64: Bhd, some late gains.   1½   68
1570 **SESSAY 13** [11]3-8-11 (69) A Nicholls 2/1 FAV: 320-435: Cl-up, ev ch dist, sn no extra: bckd tho'   nk   67
op 13/8: unplcd reapp to 6f: btr 1570 (6f).
1537 **NICHOLAS NICKELBY 14** [2]4-9-8 (60) T Hamilton(3) 50/1: 622-06: Prom, ev ch dist, sn no extra.   nk   65
1088 **TYZACK 41** [10]3-8-11 (69) M Fenton 15/2: 25240-57: Cl-up 5f, wknd: btr 1088.   2½   61
1639 **OEUF A LA NEIGE 10** [1]4-9-8 (67) S Sanders 10/1: 50530-58: Chsd ldrs till halfway, sn no extra.   nk   60
670 **LITTLE EYE 90** [7]3-8-11 (66) N Pollard 8/1: 234-4039: Rear, nvr a factor: long abs: btr 670 (polytrack).   2   56
1321 **ALIBA 25** [8]3-8-11 (66) R Winston 25/1: 354-40: 10th: Rear, prog halfway, wknd bef 1f out.   ¾   54
1464 **SPARTAN SPEAR 18** [6]3-8-11 (68) J Edmunds 50/1: 04-00: 11th: Mid-div 4f, fdd.   25   14
11 Ran   Time 1m 23.74 (1.94)   Owned: The Perle d'Or Partnership   Trained: Newmarket

1823
4.45 Saltburn Classified Stakes 3yo+ 0-65 (E)
£3562 £1096 £548   **1m str**   **Good/Firm 26**   -00 Slow   Centre

1691 **SAMUEL CHARLES 6** [2] W M Brisbourne 6-9-2 (63) S W Kelly 15/2: 000-1231: Led, hdd ins fnl 1f,   70
rallied to lead on line, drvn out: qck reapp: eff at 8/8.5f on firm, fast grnd & both AWs: see 1691 & 1219.
1553 **EFIDIUM 14** [8] N Bycroft 6-9-2 (64) Suzanne France(7) 7/1: 046-2042: Rear, prog to lead in fnl   shd   68
1f, hdd cl-home: tchd 9/1: back on a fair mark: just btr 1215.
1142 **EASTERN HOPE 36** [10] Mrs L Stubbs 5-9-2 bl (63) M Fenton 14/1: 5060-003: b g Danehill Dancer -   ¾   65
Hope And Glory (Well Decorated) Rear, prog after 5f, kept on fnl 1f, not btn far in 3rd: unplcd in '03
(h'caps, rtd 70): h'cap wnr in '02: eff at 7f/stiff 1m on fast & gd/soft grnd: eff with blnks.
1 Jun'02 Sand 7g/f 78-72 D:
1352 **STEELY DAN 24** [1] J R Best 5-9-4 (67) N Pollard 8/1: 1211604: Held up, prog & ev ch 1f out, no   shd   67
extra cl-home: last 5 wins have all come on polytrack: see 1042 & 1009.
1241 **BLAEBERRY 31** [3]3-8-1 (57) A Nicholls 25/1: 00-005: b f Kirkwall - Top Berry (High Top) Handy   1   60
over 6f, sn onepcd: unplcd both '03 starts (auct mdn, rtd 68): prob stays 1m on fast.
1485 **REAP 17** [9]6-9-4 (67) S Sanders 11/2: 112-0306: Prom, ev ch dist, sn wknd: btr 1036 (hvy).   1¼   63
1778 **ARTISTIC STYLE 3** [3]4-9-4 (67) T Eaves(5) 50/1: 223-0607: b c Anabaa - Fine Detail (Shirley   hd   62
Heights) Rear, nvr nrr than mid-div: qck reapp: plcd on both '03 starts (rtd 69, mdns): ex-French, plcd prev in
native country: eff at 5.5f/1m on fast & soft grnd: with B Ellison. 2 Sep'03 Muss 8g/f 68- D:

1748 **BAILIEBOROUGH 4** [6]5-9-5 (68) Alex Greaves 9/2 FAV: 0-060348: Handy over 6f, sn wknd: op 6/1.   *1*   **61**
1397 **NEWCORP LAD 22** [7]4-9-6 (69) A Culhane 10/1: 1126-049: Chsd ldrs over 6f, wknd: just btr 1397.   *3½*   **55**
1530 **HOV 15** [5]4-9-7 (70) R Winston 15/2: 0002600: 10th: Chsd ldrs 5f, fdd.   *5*   **47**
1385 **DUELLING BANJOS 22** [12]5-9-2 (65) G Carter 8/1: 0001-040: 11th: Cl-up 5f, wknd: op 6/1: btr 1385.   *½*   **41**
1194 **GIVE HIM CREDIT 33** [11]4-9-2 bl (65) J Carroll 66/1: 00400-50: 12th: Keen mid-div, short of room   *19*   **6**
7f out, wknd ins fnl 3f, eased cl-home: btr 1194.
12 Ran   Time 1m 36.90 (2.1)   Owned: Mr J F Thomas   Trained: Nesscliffe

---

1824   5.15 Horserace Betting Levy Board Handicap Stakes 3yo+ 0-75 (E)   [74]
£3660 £1126 £563   **6f str**   **Good/Firm 26**   **+03 Fast**   Centre

4856} **PLAYFUL DANE 209** [18] W S Cunningham 7-8-9 (55) D Fentiman(7) 20/1: 043100-1: b g Dolphin Street   **61**
- Omicida (Danehill) Prom, led after 3f, all out cl-home to hold on: reapp: won 2 h'caps in '03: unplcd in 4 '02
starts (rtd 41, mdns): stays 7f, suited by forcing tactics around 6f: acts on fast & gd grnd: likes a gall trk &
goes well fresh: fine start to campaign & can win again. 1 Aug'03 Newc 6g/f 57-50 F: 1 May'03 Redc 6g/f 51-42 G:
1504 **ONE LAST TIME 16** [14] R Bastiman 4-8-13 (59) P Fessey 33/1: 660-0002: b g Primo Dominie - Leap   *hd*   **63**
of Faith (Northiam) Mid-div, prog after 4f, styd on well ins fnl 1f, just held: unplcd in '03 (rtd 78, h'cap, R
Hannon): mdn wnr in '02: eff at 5/6f, has tried further: acts on fast grnd & a stiff/gall trk: back to form on
drop back to sprint dists, well h'capped on best form. 2 Jun'02 Asco 5g/f 97- B: 1 May'02 Sali 5g/f 89- D:
1639 **COMPTON PLUME 10** [12] W H Tinning 4-8-9 (55) V Halliday 20/1: 22026-03: ch g Compton Place -   *¾*   **57**
Brockton Flame (Emarati) Cl-up, ev ch dist, kept on & not btn far: plcd numerous times in '03 (rtd 58, h'caps &
auct mdn): modest form in '02: eff at 5/6f on firm & gd grnd: eff with/without blnks or a visor: generally
consistent but remains a mdn.
2 Oct'03 Catt 6.0g/f 58-(52) F: 2 Sep'03 Thir 5g/f 50-50 F: 2 Aug'03 Thir 6fm 50-48 F:
1465 **SILVER CHIME 18** [1] D M Simcock 4-9-7 (67) M Fenton 25/1: 1050-004: Led 3f, ev ch dist, no extra.   *nk*   **68**
1145 **CERTA CITO 36** [2]4-8-10 (56) D Allan(3) 12/1: 1300-005: Rear, prog 2f out, nrst fin: btr 1145.   *hd*   **56**
1743 **FULL SPATE 4** [16]9-9-7 (67) L Enstone(3) 11/2: 61-60546: Bhd, prog halfway, no impress fnl 1f.   *1¾*   **62**
1638 **ZUHAIR 10** [9]11-9-10 (70) L Treadwell(7) 14/1: 2200-007: Bhd, nvr nrr than mid-div: btr 1638.   *1*   **62**
1606 **FENWICKS PRIDE 11** [17]6-8-9 vis (55) T Hamilton(3) 7/1: 0000/0-38: Cl-up 4f, sn wknd: btr 1606.   *nk*   **46**
1639 **DARK CHAMPION 10** [4]4-9-4 (64) J Carroll 20/1: 2046539: Handy over 4f, wknd: btr 1639.   *1¼*   **51**
1638 **PAGAN STORM 10** [8]4-9-5 (65) Kristin Stubbs(7) 16/1: 6-000050: 10th: Nvr nrr than mid-div.   *nk*   **51**
1277 **RONNIE FROM DONNY 28** [15]4-9-7 (67) R Winston 12/1: 00U5500: 11th: Al in rear.   *shd*   **52**
1522* **PAYS DAMOUR 15** [10]7-9-8 (68) Alex Greaves 5/1 FAV: 600-0010: 12th: Mid-div till halfway, wknd.   *nk*   **52**
1600 **TUSCAN FLYER 11** [5]6-9-4 (64) Dale Gibson 16/1: 10142-00: 13th: Handy over 4f, fdd.   *1¾*   **43**
1522 **TYPE ONE 15** [7]6-9-12 (72) D Tudhope(7) 9/1: 1000020: 14th: Chsd ldrs 4f, sn wknd.   *3½*   **41**
1393 **DRURY LANE 22** [11]4-9-0 bl (60) A Culhane 8/1: 00-00000: 15th: Al in rear.   *2*   **23**
4416} **ZAP ATTACK 238** [20]4-8-8 (68) N Pollard 25/1: 310200-0: 16th: Rcd alone stands side, cl-up 4f, fdd.   *5*   **18**
16 Ran   Time 1m 10.30(1.40)   Owned: Ann and David Bell   Trained: Yarm

---

Official Going GOOD/FIRM

1825   6.15 Fenwick Of Leicester Handicap Stakes 3yo 0-80 (D)   [87]
£5850 £1800 £900   **7f9y**   **Good/Firm 31**   **-08 Slow**   Stands side

1078 **WARDEN COMPLEX 41** [6] J R Fanshawe 3-9-2 (75) O Urbina 11/2: 3-321: Held up, gd prog to lead ins   **87+**
fnl 1f, pushed out, v readily, val 3L+: 6 wk abs & h'cap bow: eff at 6/7f, 1m will suit: acts on fast, gd/soft grnd
& polytrack, any trk stiff/gall trk: goes well fresh: impressive, stable do well with these types, keep on your side.
1639 **MIDNIGHT BALLARD 10** [16] R F Johnson Houghton 3-9-4 (77) S Carson 16/1: 536-642: Handy, led 3f   *1¾*   **80**
out, hdd ins fnl 1f, not pace of wnr: encouraging eff on h'cap bow & can find similar: see 1639 & 1191.
955 **GO SOLO 52** [5] B W Hills 3-9-4 (77) K May(7) 7/1: 21516-03: b c Primo Dominie - Taza (Persian   *1½*   **77**
Bold) Trckd ldrs, onepcd from dist: bckd from 14/1: 7 wk abs: mdn & h'cap wnr in '03: suited by a sharp 7f, stays
1m on firm & gd/soft grnd: likes Chester.
1 Sep'03 Ches 7.0g/s 80-70 C: 1 Aug'03 Ches 7.0fm 71- D: 2 Jul'03 Hayd 6g/f 72- D:
4763} **BOULE DOR 215** [13] R Ingram 3-9-2 (75) N Day 5/1: 1300-4: b c Croco Rouge - Saffron Crocus   *½*   **74**
(Shareef Dancer) Handy, ev ch bef 1f out, sn no extra: reapp: mdn wnr first time out in '03: eff around 7f,
further dista suit: acts on gd grnd & a stiff/gall trk: has gone well fresh. 1 Aug'03 Leic 7.0gd 80- D:
1473* **NIGHT AIR 17** [15]3-9-1 (74) T P Queally(3) 6/1: 15: Sn handy, no extra fnl 1f: btr 1473 (gd/soft).   *½*   **72**
1470 **BEAUTIFUL NOISE 18** [7]3-8-1 (60) J F McDonald(3) 16/1: 0506-06: Cl-up 6f, wknd: see 1470.   *2*   **54**
1526 **HAZEWIND 15** [4]3-8-0 (1ow)t (58) C Catlin 25/1: 0421007: Handy over 5f, wknd: btr 765.   *½*   **52**
1665 **KEY PARTNERS 7** [2]3-8-11 (70) D Nolan(3) 5/1: 52-1028: Nvr nrr than mid-div: op 7/2: btr 1665 (soft).   *nk*   **62**
1007 **MR BELVEDERE 48** [1]3-8-9 (68) A Daly 33/1: 05030-09: Rear, nvr able to chall: 7 wk abs.   *shd*   **59**
1554 **TRENCH COAT 14** [9]3-8-11 (70) W Ryan 20/1: 253-200: 10th: Led, hdd 3f out, sn wknd: btr 814.   *nk*   **60**
1496 **SPIN KING 16** [8]3-9-7 (80) I Mongan 7/2 FAV: 5613-040: 11th: Handy over 5f, hung right & sn   *3*   **64**
wknd: bckd from 13/2: below form on drop back in trip: btr 1496 (1m).
1488 **LUPINE HOWL 17** [12]3-7-13 (58) J Mackay 50/1: 63060-00: 12th: Handy when short of room 2f, wknd.   *nk*   **41**
1359 **Danish Monarch 24** [11]3-8-12 (71) D Sweeney 40/1:0
904 **Burkees Graw 56** [3]3-7-12 (10oh)(47) R Thomas(1) 66/1:0
1054 **Perfect Hindsight 43** [14]3-8-1 (60) R Smith 20/1:0   1526 **Thadea 15** [10]3-8-1 (60) M Henry 25/1:P
16 Ran   Time 1m 24.75 (2.75)   Owned: Park Farm Racing   Trained: Newmarket

---

1826

6.45 Bbc Radio Leicester Maiden Stakes 2yo (D)
£5499 £1692 £846   **5f2y**   **Good/Firm 31**   **-01 Slow**   Stands side

1256 **CHATEAU ISTANA 29** [4] N P Littmoden 2-9-0   T P Queally(3) 11/2: 61: Cl-up, led despite hanging   **95+**
right dist, pushed clr, val 6L+: op 7/1: eff at 5f, apprec 6f: acts on fast grnd & a stiff/gall trk: won with
authority & more races await: see 1256.

1458 **CHISELLED 18** [11] K R Burke 2-9-0   Darren Williams 100/30 FAV: 422: Led, hdd under press dist,   4   82
not pace easy wnr: acts on fast & gd/soft grnd: can find similar: see 1458.

1205 **MARCHING SONG 32** [3] R Hannon 2-9-0   R Smith 7/2: 53: b c Royal Applause - Marl (Lycius) Slow   nk   81
away, prog after 3f, no impress fnl 1f: Feb foal, half-brother to wnrs at 6/8f: dam 5f wnr: eff at 5f on fast.

1524 **GOGETTER GIRL 15** [6] J Gallagher 2-8-9   N Callan 20/1: 62404: Handy over 3f, no extra: btr 1149.   1¼   72

INSIGNIA 0 [8]2-9-0   R Havlin 4/1: 5: b c Royal Applause - Amathea (Exit To Nowhere) Dwelt, nvr   3½   66
nrr than mid-div: op 3/1 on debut: Jan first foal, cost 250,000gns: dam 1m wnr: sire Gr 1 wnr at 6f.

DOVE COTTAGE 0 [10]2-9-0   I Mongan 25/1: 6: b c Great Commotion - Pooka (Dominion) Cl-up over   2½   58
2f, sn hung left & grad wknd: debut: April foal, cost 20,000gns: half-brother to a couple of wnrs over sprint
dists: dam plcd at 5f: sire top-class performer at 6f/1m: sharper for today.

DHEFAAF 0 [2]2-9-0   W Supple 16/1: 7: Al in rear.   1¼   54

1601 **MRS KEPPLE 11** [5]2-8-9   K Dalgleish 16/1: 48: Handy over 3f, fdd: see 1601.   1   46

1573 **ON THE WATERLINE 13** [7]2-8-9   S Drowne 15/2: 239: Handy over 3f, sn wknd: btr 1573 & 1237.   ½   44

TIP TOES 0 [9]2-8-9   C Catlin 33/1: 0: 10th: Slow away, nvr in rear.   5   29

10 Ran   Time 59.95s (1.6)   Owned: Mr Ivan Allan   Trained: Newmarket

---

1827

7.15 E A S Windows Anniversary Selling Stakes 3yo+ (G)
£3010 £860 £430   **7f9y**   **Good/Firm 31**   **-24 Slow**   Stands side

1635 **KELSEAS KOLBY 10** [4] J A Glover 4-9-7 vis (53) I Mongan 6/1: 2120-001: Mid-div, prog to lead dist   57
despite veering under press, rdn out: op 4/1: sold for 3,000gns: suited by 7f on fast & gd/soft grnd: eff with
visor: enjoyed drop back to sell grade: see 1635.

1537 **JONNY EBENEEZER 14** [10] R M H Cowell 5-9-7 (63) B Doyle 9/2: 2-000202: Handy, ev ch dist, kept   2   52
on but not pace of wnr: cheek pieces left off: see 1537.

1425 **WODHILL BE 20** [13] D Morris 4-9-2 (45) M Tebbutt 25/1: 0-565003: Held up, prog despite hanging   ½   46
right ins fnl 2f, onepcd fnl 1f: eff at 7f on fast grnd: see 910.

664 **LOVES DESIGN 91** [3] Miss S J Wilton 7-9-7 (45) A Quinn(5) 12/1: 0600554: Slow away, prog halfway,   1   49
onepcd fnl 1f: earlier jumps unplcd (rtd 64h, nov sell hdle): btr 465.

4833} **WATERLINE BLUE 210** [3] M N Callan 7/2 FAV: 262466-5: b g Mujadil - Blues Queen (Lahib)   nk   48
Cl-up over 5f, no extra: clr rem: reapp: med auct wnr in '03: eff at 5.7f/7f on firm & gd/soft grnd: tried
visor. 2 Aug'03 Bath 5.7fm 77-(91) E: 2 Jul'03 Asco 7g/s 91- C: 1 Jun'03 Leic 6.0g/f 85- E:

1284 **MY COUNTRY CLUB 28** [11]7-9-7 (53) Dane O'Neill 11/1: 22442-66: Slow away, nvr nrr than mid-div.   6   36

1635 **ZAK FACTA 10** [5]4-9-7 vis (47) C Cogan 14/1: 2460007: Handy over 4f, sn hung right & wknd: btr 1194.   3½   29

1642 **HAPPY CAMPER 8** [6]4-9-7 (45) D Sweeney 10/1: 5-006538: Cl-up, ev ch after 5f, sn wknd: btr 1642.   1¾   25

39 **KALLISTAS PRIDE 185** [15]4-9-2   Joanna Badger 33/1: 00-9: Keen handy 5f, sn wknd.   1½   17

1412 **ROY MCAVOY 21** [2]6-9-7 (40) G Baker 16/1: 00-00040: 10th: Al in rear.   3   16

1378 **FINE FRENZY 22** [7]4-9-2 p (45) M Howard(7) 7/1: 3640-040: 11th: Handy, led 2f out, hdd dist, fdd.   1¼   8

530 **LAGGAN MINSTREL 105** [14]6-9-7 p (52) R Havlin 25/1: 00000-00: 12th: Led 4f, fdd.   1¼   10

890 **TODDEANO 57** [1]8-9-7 t   V Slattery 50/1: 00-00: 13th: Al bhd: jumps fit.   12   0

13 Ran   Time 1m 25.9 (3.9)   Owned: Mr J A Glover   Trained: Worksop

---

1828

7.45 Rectangle Group Handicap Stakes 4yo+ 0-85 (D)   **[85]**
£5668 £1744 £872   **1m1f218y**   **Good/Firm 31**   **+02 Fast**   Inside

1623* **FINE PALETTE 10** [3] H R A Cecil 4-9-8 (79) W Ryan 7/1: 2-11: Held up, prog to lead 1f out, rdn   89
out: eff at 10f, 12f+ shld suit: acts on fast & soft grnd: improving with ev start & is unexposed in h'cap grade.

5019} **FRONTIER 194** [8] B J Llewellyn 7-8-9 (66) R Havlin 15/2: D60000-2: b g Indian Ridge - Adatiya   2½   70
(Shardari) Led, hdd 9f out, styd cl-up, led 2f out, hdd 1f out, kept on but held by wnr when short of room cl-home:
recent hdles rnr-up (nov, rtd 112h, stays 2m1f on fast & gd/soft): h'cap wnr on Flat in '03: eff at 10f, poss stays
11.5f: acts on firm & soft grnd: tried t-strap: h'capped to find similar.
2 Jul'03 Ches 10.3fm 76-73 D: 1 Jun'03 Wind 10.0g/f 75-68 D: 2 May'03 Leic 10.0g/f 73-68 E:

1586 **NORTHSIDE LODGE 12** [7] P W Harris 6-9-6 (77) D Holland 11/4 FAV: 2203003: Rear, prog 3f out,   1½   79
kept on fnl 1f: tchd 9/2: btr 758 (polytrack).

1098 **SAY WHAT YOU SEE 40** [14] J W Hills 4-9-0 (71) E Ahern 11/2: 0-042154: Slow away, led 9f out, hdd   nk   72
2f out, sn no extra: op 15/2: btr 900 (polytrack).

877 **COUP DE CHANCE 60** [1]4-9-13 bl (84) D Nolan(3) 18/1: 10411-05: ch f Ashkalani - Tout A Coup (Ela   nk   84
Mana Mou) Rear, eff when short of room after 7f, kept on ins fnl 1f: 9 wk abs: won last 2 of only 4 '03 starts
(h'caps): ex-Irish, won a mdn & 2 clmrs earlier in '03: eff at 11/2f on firm & gd, likes Brighton: suited by blnks.
1 Oct'03 Brig 11.9fm 86-81 F: 1 Oct'03 Brig 11.9fm 82-75 E:

4655} **PIRI PIRI 223** [5]4-8-9 (66) S Sanders 20/1: 513660-6: Rear, prog 3f out, onepcd ins fnl 1f.   1¼   64

1777 **ADALAR 3** [12]4-8-10 (65) S Drowne 25/1: 0000607: Handy 1m, sn wknd: qck reapp: btr 903.   2   62

1721 **TIGHT SQUEEZE 5** [10]7-9-9 (80) B Doyle 9/1: 0010108: Nvr nrr than mid-div: qck reapp: bt 1027.   1¼   73

1519 **PRAIRIE WOLF 15** [4]8-9-9 (80) I Mongan 14/1: 2320-009: Al in rear: btr 1296.   shd   72

HORS LA LOI 1735 [6]8-9-3 (74) C Catlin 50/1: 1/064////-0: 10th: Al bhd: jumps fit.   2   63

1618 **TETOU 11** [13]4-8-12 (69) J F McDonald(3) 33/1: 301-00: 11th: Handy till 3f out, wknd.   1   56

4515} **URSA MAJOR 585** [11]10-7-12 (3oh) (52) M Henry 66/1: 030000/-0: 12th: Handy over 7f, wknd.   1¾   39

1461 **KHANJAR 18** [9]4-9-4 vis (75) T P Queally(3) 14/1: 24/22-240: 13th: Al in rear.   3   54

1484 **HIP HOP HARRY 17** [2]4-9-11 vis (82) K Fallon 7/1: 1-021200: 14th: Bhd, nvr able to chall: btr 716.   10   46

14 Ran   Time 2m 5.45 (2.95)   Owned: Mrs Angela Scott   Trained: Newmarket

---

1829

8.15 First Aid Maiden Stakes 3yo (D)
£5642 £1736 £868   **5f218y**   **Good/Firm 31**   **+01 Fast**   Stands side

1497 **ALDERNEY RACE 16** [1] R Charlton 3-9-0 (84) S Drowne 9/4 J FAV: 4-521: Handy, styd on to lead   **100+**
dist, pushed clr, val 7L+: eff at 6f, further will suit: acts on fast & gd/soft grnd, has disapp on polytrack: won
with authority, gd confidence boost & more prizes await: see 1497.
1191 **MAJORCA 33** [9] J H M Gosden 3-9-0 K Fallon 9/4 J FAV: 0-32: Slow away, prog halfway, styd on to   5   **83**
lead dist sn hdd & no extra: eff at 6f, further shld suit: acts on fast grnd: can find a race: see 1191.
1464 **ADORATA 18** [18] J Jay 3-8-9   O Urbina 66/1: 0003: Cl-up over 4f, no impress, kind ride.   4   **66**
     LASKA 0 [10] M J Wallace 3-8-9   D Corby(3) 50/1: 4: br f Fasliyev - Dacian (Diesis) Handy 3f, sn   shd   **65**
outpcd, modest late gains: debut: looks in need of further.
1690 **GET TO THE POINT 6** [19]3-9-0 (72) D Holland 8/1: 050-0225: Trkd ldrs, ev ch bef 1f out, sn fdd.   ½   **68**
1281 **HALF A HANDFUL 28** [12]3-9-0   R Havlin 66/1: 0006: Slow away, nvr nrr than mid-div: see 1281.   1   **65**
1464 **CALLED UP 18** [16]3-9-0   D Sweeney 25/1: 47: Rear, nvr nrr than mid-div: showed more in 1464 (soft).   ¾   **63**
     ZAMEYLA 0 [17]3-8-9   P Robinson 8/1: 8: b f Cape Cross - Angelic Sounds (The Noble Player) Slow   ¾   **56**
away, nvr able to chall: debut: with M A Jarvis.
2677} **WILLOFCOURSE 318** [2]3-9-0 Dane O'Neill 7/1: 62-9: Led, hdd dist, fdd.   ¾   **59**
     CHATSHOW 292 [3]3-9-0   P Doe 25/1: 6-0: 10th: Cl-up 4f, fdd: debut.   ¾   **57**
925   **PINK SUPREME 53** [5]3-8-9 T T P Queally(3) 25/1: 2-00: 11th: Mid-div 4f, sn wknd.   1¼   **48**
     Petrion 0 [14]3-8-9 C Lowther 50/1:0   1473 **Ravel 17** [20]3-9-0 I Mongan 50/1:0
1690 **Flying With Eagles 6** [8]3-9-0 G Baker 100/1:0   2382} **Shifty Night 329** [11]3-8-9 C Catlin 100/1:0
15 Ran   Time 1m 11.65 (1.85)   Owned: Britton House Stud Ltd   Trained: Beckhampton

---

1830

8.45 Caribbean Evening Handicap Stakes 4yo+ 0-70 (E)   **[70]**
£3669 £1129 £565   **1m3f183y**   **Good/Firm 31**   **+06 Fast**   Inside

1238 **FIELD SPARK 16** [6] J A Glover 4-8-12 p (54) D Holland 6/1: 46616-61: Rear, prog 3f out, styd on   **60**
to lead dist, rdn out to hold on: eff around 12f on gd & fast grnd: eff with cheek pieces: see 1238 (reapp).
529   **REMINISCENT 105** [11] R F Johnson Houghton 5-8-13 vis (55) S Carson 16/1: 53522-42: Slow away,   nk   **60**
prog after 1m, styd on well fnl 1f, only just held: earlier hdles rnr-up (rtd 111h, mdn, stays 2m1f on gd grnd):
well h'capped on earlier polytrack form & can find similar: see 259 & 201.
1502 **MAN THE GATE 16** [9] P D Cundell 5-9-0 (56) S Sanders 9/2 J FAV: 300-2503: Rear, prog & ev ch   2   **58**
dist, kept on same pace: another gd run here at Leicester: see 979.
1543 **GREAT VIEW 14** [15] Mrs A L M King 5-9-9 vis (65) D Corby(3) 9/2 J FAV: 2-012124: Cl-up, led 2f   2½   **63**
out, hdd dist, sn wknd: btr 1543 & 1373.
2343} **TRUSTED MOLE 331** [5]6-8-10 (52) K Fallon 7/1: 155353-5: b g Eagle Eyed - Orient Air (Prince   1   **48**
Sabo) Slow away, prog 3f out, onepcd fnl 1f: h'cap wnr back in '03: dual rnr-up in '02 (clmrs, S
Keithley): eff at 10/12f, prob stays slowly run 14f: acts on firm, soft & polytrack, any trk: eff with/without
blnks, has gone well fresh. 1 Apr'03 Ripo 12.3g/f 57-50 E: 2 Mar'02 Ling 12ap 52a- F: 2 Feb'02 Ling 13ap 51a- F:
2 Nov'01 Ling 12ap 52a- F: 1 Jul'01 Leic 10gd 66- F: 1 Jun'01 Newm 10g/f 62- E: 2 May'01 Ling 10g/f 62-61 F:
1 May'01 Beve 10fm 59- F:
1693 **FOREST TUNE 6** [17]6-9-3 (59) W Supple 25/1: 106-0006: Handy 10f, sn wknd: qck reapp.   ¾   **54**
1693 **MOST SAUCY 6** [12]8-9-6 (62) E Ahern 9/1: 500-6657: Rear, nvr nrr than mid-div: qck reapp: btr 1693.   6   **48**
711   **LAZZAZ 84** [1]6-8-7 (49) M Henry 14/1: 5333028: Handy 10f, sn wknd: 12 wk abs: btr 711 (polytrack).   shd   **34**
1430 **LITTLE ENGLANDER 20** [16]4-9-3 (59) Dane O'Neill 33/1: 6240-59: Cl-up 10f, sn fdd: btr 1430.   2   **41**
1629 **MADHAHIR 10** [19]4-9-4 (60) T P Queally(3) 25/1: 0013000: 10th: Cl-up, short of room after 1m, sn wknd.   ½   **41**
937   **FIGHT THE FEELING 52** [13]6-8-9 (51) A Daly 33/1: 4220050: 11th: Rer, nvr a factor.   shd   **31**
4806} **RED RIVER REBEL 213** [8]6-9-2 (58) Darren Williams 33/1: 126340-0: 12th: b g Inchinor - Bidweaya   4   **32**
(Lear Fan) Led 10f, fdd: reapp: h'cap wnr in '03: h'cap scorer in '02: stays 14f, suited by 12f on firm & gd,
likes Newcastle & Beverley: likes to dominate: capable of better.
2 Aug'03 Beve 12.1gd 58-(60) F: 1 Jul'03 Beve 12.1g/f 61-55 E: 1 Aug'02 Beve 12g/f 69-64 E:
2 Jul'02 Beve 12gd 65-61 E: 2 Jul'02 Ripo 12.2gd 64-60 D: 1 Sep'01 Beve 12gd 66-59 E:
1 Aug'01 Newc 12.4g/f 58-58 E: 1 Aug'01 Newc 12.4gd 59-50 E:
1472 **Logger Rhythm 17** [14]4-9-4 (60) M Fenton 22/1:0   948   **Go Classic 52** [8]4-9-6 (62) C Catlin 50/1:0
1469 **St Jerome 18** [7]4-9-1 (57) N Callan 33/1:0   1357 **Ipsa Loquitur 24** [3]4-9-2 (58) S Drowne 7/1:P
16 Ran   Time 2m 31.4(3.1)   Owned: G Taylor & J P Burton   Trained: Worksop

---

Official Going Good/Firm

1831

2.20 New Fixture Next Monday Selling Stakes 2yo (F)
£3396 £1045 £523   **5f**   **Good/Firm 27**   **-90 Slow**   Inside

1573 **MYTTONS DREAM 13** [6] A Bailey 2-8-6   T P Queally(3) 5/1: 661: Hmpd start & rear, switched & styd   **63**
on wide for press to lead well ins last: op 4/1, bght in for 10,000gns: eff at 5f, 6f likely to suit on this
evidence: acts on fast grnd & a stiff trk: apprec drop to sell grade: see 1573 & 1343.
1634 **KERESFORTH 10** [4] T D Easterby 2-8-11 BL W Supple 18/1: 002: b g Mind Games - Bullion   1½   **63**
(Sabrehill) Chsd ldrs, rdn & led ins last: first time blnks: Feb foal, 13,000gns purchase:
half-brother to a 6f juv & 1m 3yo/hdles wnr Maunby Rocker: dam a 1m juv wnr: eff at 5f, get further: handles fast
grnd & a stiff trk: imprvd for drop to sell grade: clmd by I Wood for 6,000: see 1634.
929   **CONCERT TIME 53** [1] P T Midgley 2-8-6   R Fitzpatrick 50/1: 03: ch f Timeless Times - Thalya   3½   **48**
(Crofthall) Bhd, kept on late, not pace to chall: 8 wk abs: imprvd from intro & clmd for 6,000 by C Dore: cheaply
bght March foal, half-sister to a juv sprint wnr, dam unrcd: 6f in similar could suit, handles fast grnd.

1394 **EMMAS VENTURE 22** [9] M W Easterby 2-8-6   G Duffield 6/1: 5264: Went left start, held up in tch,   ¾   46
kept on late: op 9/1: btr 1224 (soft).
1303 **OUR LOUIS 26** [10]2-8-6   E Ahern 16/1: 605: b f Abou Zouz - Ninfa of Cisterna (Polish Patriot)   1   43
Led till ins last, fdd: op 20/1: cheaply bght Feb foal, half-sister to a 7f plcd 3yo, dam a multiple wnr abroad.
1634 **WHY HARRY 10** [11]2-9-2 K Darley 11/8 FAV: 30166: Chsd ldrs, keeping on onepace when hmpd ins   2   47
last: closer with a clr run, would not have troubled wnr: bckd, op 2/1: btr 1303 (soft).
         HOLLINGWOOD SOUL 0 [5]2-8-6 Dean McKeown 20/1: 7: Hmpd start, bhd, only mod prog.   ¾   35
1751 **MILLER HILL 3** [3]2-8-11 P Mulrennan(5) 9/1: 028: Dwelt & sn struggling: btr 1751 (AW).   8   24
1394 **ALICE KING 22** [2]2-8-6   C Haddon(7) 14/1: 449: Chsd ldrs till 2f out: btr 1394 & 1224 (soft).   5   9
1161 **RUBY REBEL 34** [7]2-8-6 G Parkin 50/1: 00: 10th: Swerved left start & sn bhd.   1¾   4
1303 **FOLD WALK 26** [8]2-8-6 G Gibbons 12/1: 04U: Swerved right & bmpr start, u.r.: see 1303.   0
11 Ran   Time 1m 07.16 (5.86)   Owned: Mr Gordon Mytton   Trained: Tarporley

---

1832   2.55 Jockeys Loft For Great Food Maiden Stakes 3yo   (D)
£4251 £1308 £654   7f100y   Good/Firm 27   -20 Slow   Inside

4761} **ALI DEO 215** [12] W J Haggas 3-9-0 P Robinson 7/2: 00-1: ch c Ali Royal - Lady In Colour   78
(Cadeaux Genereux) Unruly bef start, led/dsptd lead, styd on for press to lead well ins last: op 3/1, reapp:
unplcd both '03 starts (rtd 74, val auct stks, earlier rtd 87, mdn, flattered): dam a well related mdn: eff at
7.5f, 1m looks sure to suit: acts on fast grnd & a stiff trk, goes well fresh: lightly rcd, open to improvement.
1518 **STAR MAGNITUDE 15** [3] J H M Gosden 3-9-0 K Darley 4/1 FAV: 022: Trkd ldrs, drvn & styd on for   ¾   75
press, not able to reach wnr: hvly bckd: acts on fast & gd/soft grnd, return to 1m+ will suit: see 1518.
1495 **HAWAAJES 16** [13] B Hanbury 3-9-0 W Supple 11/2: 03: b g Royal Applause - Aegean Blue (Warning)   shd   75
Rdn early & sn led, hdd well ins last, no extra: op 4/1: 90,000gns purchase, dam uncrd sister to a prolific 5/7f
wnr: stays 7.5f, return to 6/7f might suit: handles fast grnd.
1518 **VIBE 15** [8] M Johnston 3-9-0 R Ffrench 25/1: U004: gr g Danzero - Courting (Pursuit of Love)   ½   73
Chsd ldrs till rdn & outpcd 2f out, kept on well ins last: significant improvement today on this fast grnd, shld
apprec return to 1m+ on this evidence.
1617 **GREY BOY 11** [1]3-9-0 G Duffield 40/1: 0-05: Chsd ldrs wide, no impress over 1f out.   2   70
         REMONSTRATE 0 [4]3-9-0 G Gibbons 25/1: 6: Switched & rear from start, late prog on debut.   2   66
1464 **GHANTOOT 18** [6]3-9-0 N Mackay(3) 16/1: 007: Held up in tch, no impress fnl 2f.   shd   66
         CHISEL 0 [11]3-9-0 K Dalgleish 8/1: 8: Chsd ldrs till over 1f out on debut, op 10/1.   5   56
2013} **KNOT IN DOUBT 346** [5]3-9-0 I Mongan 66/1: 00-9: Al bhd on reapp, longer trip.   4   48
4535} **BALLIN ROUGE 230** [7]3-8-9 E Ahern 50/1: 00-0: 10th: Sn struggling on reapp.   1½   40
10 Ran   Time 1m 34.31 (3.51)   Owned: Mrs J Dye   Trained: Newmarket

---

1833   3.25 Peter Holmes Lifetime In Racing Rated Stakes Handicap 3yo+ 0-95   (C)   [98]
£8498 £3223 £1612   1m100y   Good/Firm 27   +11 Fast   Inside

1066 **FLIGHTY FELLOW 42** [8] T D Easterby 4-9-6 (90) W Supple 10/1: 4322-061: Chsd ldrs, hdwy & no room   94
2f out, styd on to lead ins last, rdn out: past time: abs: suited by 1m/8.5f on fast & soft, any trk, with/without
blnks: likes Beverley: see 1066.
1351 **ACE OF HEARTS 24** [10] C F Wall 5-8-10 (1oh) (79) G Duffield 5/1: 362-0502: Chsd ldrs wide, kept   1¾   83
on for press well ins last, would not threaten wnr: back to form: see 1057.
4760} **ICE PALACE 215** [6] J R Fanshawe 4-9-10 (94) E Ahern 4/1 FAV: 2/31140-3: ch f Polar Falcon -   nk   96
White Palace (Shirley Heights) Hld up, switched wide & styd on fnl 2f, not pace to threaten: bckd, op 5/1, reapp:
auct mdn & subs h'cap wnr '03 (lightly rcd): rnr-up sole '02 start (mdn): eff at 1m/8.5f on firm & gd grnd, prob
any trk: gd return, likely type for a fills h'cap.
1 Sep'03 Kemp 8g/f 95-90 C: 1 Aug'03 Nott 8.2gd 89- F: 2 Aug'02 Ling 6g/f 83- E:
1351 **IRONY 24** [2] A M Balding 5-9-3 (87) K Darley 8/1: 0163-004: Led till ins last, onepace: see 945.   ½   88
1231 **STAR SENSATION 31** [9]4-9-2 (86) I Mongan 11/2: 25400-65: Held up, eff when hung left over 1f   hd   86
out, not pace to threaten: op 4/1: see 1231.
1586 **STRETTON 12** [1]6-8-10 (80) P Robinson 20/1: 03310-06: br g Doyoun - Awayil (Woodman) Bhd, kept   ¾   78
on late: only btn around 3L: h'cap scorer '03: h'cap wnr '02: eff at 1m, suited by 10f: acts on firm, gd &
handles soft: likes Chester & York: best delivered late off a strong pace, has a useful turn of foot.
1 Oct'03 York 10.4g/f 81-78 C: 1 May'02 Ches 10.3fm 88-80 C: 1 Jul'01 Ches 10g/f 84-78 D: 1 May'01 Good 9g/f 78-73 D:
1 May'01 York 8g/f 76-70 C:
1530 **THE BONUS KING 15** [7]4-8-10 (80) K Dalgleish 14/1: 4520007: Chsd ldrs & ch 3f out, wknd from dist.   ½   77
1475 **VICIOUS WARRIOR 17** [4]5-9-2 (86) Dean McKeown 17/2: 04020-28: Trkd ldrs, onepace when hmpd over 2   79
1f out: see 1475 (g/s).
1525 **DAWN PIPER 15** [3]4-8-13 vis (83) T P Queally(3) 10/1: 2-102029: Trkd ldrs & keen, ev ch over 2f   7   62
out, sn wandered under press & btn, eased: much btr 1525 & 879.
4364} **SPURADICH 241** [5]4-9-9 (93) N Mackay(3) 7/1: 510110-0: 10th: b c Barathea - Svanzega (Sharpen Up)   5   62
Rear, eff wide over 3f out, sn hung right & no impress: op 11/2, reapp: progressive '03, dual h'cap wnr, incl val
h'cap at this venue: best at 9/10f on fast & gd grnd: shld do better.
1 Aug'03 Beve 9.9g/f 94-84 B: 1 Aug'03 Ayr 9.1gd 82-70 E:
10 Ran   Time 1m 45.15 (1.35)   Owned: Mr David W Armstrong   Trained: Malton

---

1834   4.00 Rapid Lad Handicap Stakes 3yo 0-75   (E)   [82]
£4729 £1455 £728   1m1f207y   Good/Firm 27   -03 Slow   Inside

1403 **GOBLIN 21** [10] D E Cantillon 3-8-8 (62) G Duffield 7/2 JT FAV: 000-4151: Held up, hdwy when   72
short of room 6f out & again 2f out, led ins last & sn asserted, rdn out: op 9/2: eff at 1m, imprvd again here at
10f: acts on fast, gd & handles fibresand: lightly rcd, type to prog in similar company: see 1404 & 1193.
1259 **FITTING GUEST 29** [1] G G Margarson 3-8-11 (65) P Robinson 14/1: 40-62: ch c Grand Lodge - Sarah   1½   72
Clare (Reach) Led till ins last, kept on: rest well covered on h'cap bow: lightly rcd & unplcd '03 (4th, mdn,
debut): eff at 10f, 12f could suit: imprvd here on fast grnd, poss handles gd/soft: enjoyed forcing tactics.
5016} **MA YAHAB 194** [8] L M Cumani 3-9-3 (71) N Mackay(3) 8/1: 020-3: ch c Dr Fong - Bay Shade (Sharpen   3   73
Up) Mid-div when short of room over 2f out, switched & kept on, no threat: op 6/1, reapp/h'cap bow: mdn rnr-up
'03: styd this longer 10f trip, mid-dist pedigree & 12f+ could suit: acts on fast & gd/soft grnd: likely improver
in similar, prob over further. 2 Oct'03 Nott 8.2g/s 73- D:

BEVERLEY   TUESDAY 18.05.04   Righthand, Oval Track with Stiff, Uphill Finish

955   **RED BIRR 52** [9] A M Balding 3-9-7 (75) K Darley 8/1: 043-04: b g Bahhare - Cappella (College   ½   76
Chapel) Trkd ldrs, styd on onepace fnl 3f: 7 wk abs: mdn plcd '03 (rtd 76): eff at 6f, this longer 10f trip may
yet suit: handles fast & gd grnd, stiff trks: some encouragement.
1528   **ATHOLLBROSE 15** [5]3-8-2 (56) G Gibbons 10/1: 400-4245: Trkd ldrs, rdn & no extra dist: btr 1306.   ¾   56
1582   **INFIDELITY 12** [7]3-8-8 (62) D Kinsella 33/1: 20-60006: Rear, eff 2f out, no prog dist: see 568.   1   60
1462   **BADR 18** [3]3-9-1 (69) R Ffrench 11/1: 20-67: Trkd ldrs till over 1f out: h'cap bow & longer trip.   2½   63
1148   **SHARAAB 35** [4]3-9-7 t (75) W Supple 7/1: 30-68: Cl-up & ch over 2f out, sn wknd, h'cap bow.   3½   64
4885} **GAIETY GIRL 206** [6]3-8-11 (65) P Doe 20/1: 4430-9: Dwelt, eff wide, no impress, reapp.   2½   50
1628   **ORION EXPRESS 10** [2]3-8-9 (63) P Mulrennan(5) 14/1: 000-6600: 10th: Trkd ldrs till over 2f out.   2½   44
1648   **LATE OPPOSITION 8** [11]3-8-13 (67) E Ahern 7/2 JT FAV: 06-42220: 11th: Dwelt, eff wide & no   6   39
impress 2f out, eased: btr 1648 & 1382 (gd & soft).
11 Ran   Time 2m 05.34 (3.04)   Owned: Mrs E M Clarke   Trained: Newmarket

---

1835   4.35 Colin Stamford Is Our Painter Maiden Stakes Fillies 3yo+ (D)
£4225 £1300 £650   **1m1f207y**   **Good/Firm 27**   -08 Slow   Inside

1258   **PORTMANTEAU 29** [6] Sir Michael Stoute 3-8-10 F Lynch 8/1: 0-01: b f Barathea - Dayanata   88+
(Shirley Heights) Handy & led over 2f out, in command dist, hands & heels, readily: mdn unplcd sole start '03 (rtd
73): imprvd for step up to 10f & return to fast grnd: lightly rcd & the type to prog into a useful filly.
4012} **TARANDOT 259** [4] G G Margarson 3-8-10 A McCarthy 16/1: 0-2: b f Singspiel - Rifada (Ela Mana   2½   85+
Mou) Held up, hdwy to chase wnr dist, kept on, al held: pulled well clr of rem on reapp: well held sole '03 start
(mdn, flashed tail, rtd 53): apprec step up to 10f, 12f+ looks likely to suit (dam a 12f wnr): acts on fast grnd:
plenty to like about this, expect further progress at 12f+.
1468   **TREE TOPS 18** [1] J H M Gosden 3-8-10 K Darley 15/8 FAV: 523: Trkd ldrs, eff to chase wnr over   6   75
1f out, sn no impress: hvly bckd: thought likely to apprec this longer 10f trip but btr 1468 & 1210 (gd & soft).
1272   **HIGH SCHOOL 28** [12] P H Morris 3-8-10 A Beech(3) 4/1: 264: Rear, prog when bmpd over 3f out, nvr   2½   71+
pace to threaten: sister to a high-class mid-dist performer, well bred filly, one to note in 12f+ h'caps: see 980.
1527   **DARENEUR 15** [9]4-9-10 P Makin(5) 66/1: 005: Chsd ldrs, eff wide 2f out: longer trip.   4   64
1472   **PAULA 17** [5]4-9-10 G Gibbons 100/1: 066: Rear, eff wide 4f out, sn no impress, low grade h'caps.   2½   60$
4937} **RAINBOW COLOURS 202** [11]3-8-10 G Duffield 9/1: 6-7: gr f Linamix - Mill Rainbow (Rainbow Quest)   shd   60
Led till over 2f out, sn struggling: reapp: some promise sole '03 start (mdn, rtd 55+): mid-dist pedigree.
1178   **SWEET REPOSE 33** [10]3-8-10 E Ahern 20/1: 5-08: Mid-div, btn 2f out, longer trip.   1¾   57
1472   **CALONNOG 17** [8]4-9-10 Paul Eddery 7/2: 5-29: Rear & sn pushed along, nvr a factor: bckd, op 5/1.   2½   53
1518   **POINTED 15** [2]3-8-10 R Ffrench 33/1: 00: 10th: Mid-div till over 3f out, sn struggling.   6   43
1304   **ADEES DANCER 26** [3]3-8-10 D McGaffin 20/1: 4-00: 11th: Rear, hung badly left on bend over 3f   1¾   40
out & sn bhd, longer trip.
11 Ran   Time 2m 05.78 (3.48)   Owned: Maktoum Al Maktoum   Trained: Newmarket

---

1836   5.05 Come Racing At Beverley Handicap Stakes 3yo 46-55 (F)
£3504 £1078 £539   **1m4f16y**   **Good/Firm 27**   -61 Slow   Inside   [69]

1521   **PRAIRIE SUN 15** [12] Mrs A Duffield 3-9-0 (55) G Duffield 8/1: 000-4451: Led/dsptd lead till went   59
on 4f out & rdn clr over 1f out, held on for press cl-home: first win: eff at 12f, tried 14f latest: acts on
gd/soft, imprvd today on fast grnd & enjoys forcing tactics: see 1165.
1240   **DANEFONIQUE 31** [8] D Carroll 3-8-13 (54) R Fitzpatrick 8/1: 050-0322: Towards rear, hdwy to   ¾   57
chase ldr over 1f out, kept on well, not able to chall: styd longer 12f trip well, acts on fast & gd/soft grnd: on
an upward curve, could find similar: see 1240 & 1051.
1250* **CEASAR 29** [5] P A Blockley 3-9-0 (55) G Faulkner 8/1: 04-21013: Held up, eff when short of room   shd   58
over 2f out, styd on well ins last, nrst fin: op 13/2: acts on fast, hvy & fibresand: see 1250.
1241   **WINSLOW BOY 31** [14] C F Wall 3-9-0 (55) K Darley 14/1: 000-04: b g Expelled - Acusteal (Acaroid)   2   55
Dwelt & bhd, late gains, no dngr: unplcd '03 (rtd 67, subs gelded): styd this longer 12f trip & handles fast grnd.
1612   **HOLLY WALK 11** [3]3-8-5 bl (46) G Gibbons 14/1: 004-0255: Keen & dsptd lead, ran wide on bend   1½   43
early & hdd after 4f, onepace fnl 2f: impr on this when learning to settle: see 1308 (mdn).
4532} **XPRESSIONS 231** [1]3-8-9 (50) G Parkin 16/1: 4015-6: b g Turtle Island - Make Ready (Beveled)   nk   46
Drvn & bhd, eff when short of room over 1f out, kept on late, no dngr on reapp: seller scorer '03 (lightly rcd):
eff at 7f/1m, mid-dists may suit this term: handles fast grnd & a gall trk: enjoys sell grade.
1 Sep'03 Ayr 8g/f 56- E:
1280   **AVERTAINE 28** [6]3-8-12 (53) P Doe 10/1: 00527: Chsd ldrs & chsd wnr 2f out, hung right & fdd dist.   nk   49
1306   **NAFFERTON HEIGHTS 26** [4]3-8-8 (49) P Mulrennan(5) 3/1 FAV: 000-058: Keen & trk ldrs, short of   hd   45
room over 2f out & sn no impress: longer trip & mkt mover, op 7/1: see 1306.
1144   **SPRING BREEZE 36** [2]3-8-12 P (53) F Lynch 16/1: 04030-69: Bhd, eff over 2f out, no impress: chkpcs.   hd   49
1428   **BOLLIN ANNABEL 20** [13]3-9-0 (55) N Mackay(3) 13/2: 0-250: 10th: Mid-div, btn 2f out: h'cap bow.   1¾   48
1630   **BONJOUR BOND 10** [9]3-8-13 bl (54) D McGaffin 16/1: 00-40030: 11th: Chsd ldrs 9f: btr 1630 (sell).   ½   46
1528   **Calara Hills 15** [11]3-8-8 (49) P Makin(5) 12/1:0   **1630*** **Ciacole 10** [10]3-8-9 (50) Dean McKeown 12/1:0
13 Ran   Time 2m 41.83(10.53)   Owned: Miss Helen Wynne   Trained: Leyburn

---

SOUTHWELL   Fibresand   WEDNESDAY 19.05.04   Lefthand, Sharp, Oval Track

Official Going Standard

1837   2.20 Royal Bank Of Scotland Banded Stakes 4yo+ 0-45 (H)
£1449 £414 £207   **6f rnd aw**   **Going 57**   -01 Slow   Inside

1799   **CLEVELAND WAY 2** [10] D Carroll 4-8-12 vis (40) D Tudhope(7) 9/2: 5022621: Sn prom & led over 2f   49a
out, rdn out: quick reapp: suited by 6f, tried 1m: acts on firm, soft, likes fibresand: see 296.
1804* **MARABAR 2** [8] D W Chapman 6-9-4 bl (45) A Culhane 11/4 FAV: 0100312: Trkd ldrs, drvn & not pace   1¼   51a
of wnr fnl 2f: op 9/4: return to 7f could suit: see 1804.
1405   **MR UPPITY 22** [7] Julian Poulton 5-8-12 e (40) M Halford(7) 28/1: 0-002453: Dwelt, sn dsptd lead   1   42a

till outpcd halfway, kept on fnl 1f: see 982.

1277	**PILGRIM PRINCESS** 29 [2] E J Alston 6-8-12 P (45) D Allan(3) 6/1: 5460004: Dsptd lead to 2f out.	2	36a
1588	**LAKE EYRE** 13 [6]5-8-12 (45) J Edmunds 12/1: 03-50055: Chsd ldrs, btn over 1f out: see 91.	2	30a
1671	**FINGER OF FATE** 8 [1]4-8-12 bl (40) R Fitzpatrick 8/1: 0002646: Dwelt, outpcd, nvr able to chall.	shd	29a
1644	**EJAY** 9 [3]5-8-12 (45) Lisa Jones(3) 7/1: 0200027: Outpcd, nvr on terms: btr 1644 (5f, hvy).	3	20a
1799	**AVIT** 2 [4]4-8-12 (40) G Faulkner 25/1: 0023068: Cl-up, btn over 1f out: btr 1290 (polytrack).	3½	10a
1447	**PIRLIE HILL** 20 [5]4-8-12 (45) R Winston 7/1: 6000-349: Dwelt, chsd ldrs till over 1f out: see 1391.	1	7a
4360}	**MISS CEYLON** 242 [9]4-8-12 (45) Dale Gibson 50/1: 000000-0: 10th: b f Brief Truce - Five Islands (Bairn) Dwelt & sn outpcd on reappr: unplcd & mod form '03 (Miss A Stokell, rtd 58 & 10a, tried cheek pieces & visor): fills auct mdn wnr '02 for G M Moore, sand unplcd, rtd 49a): wng form at 5f, stays 6f on fast & gd.	7	0a

2 Aug'02 Hayd 5g/s 76-75 E: 1 Jul'02 Beve 5gd 74- F: 2 Jul'02 Redc 6g/f 71-67 D:
10 Ran Time 1m 16.8 (3.5) Owned: The Boot & Shoe Ackworth Partnership Trained: Warthilll

---

1838	2.50 Spanish Premier Properties Amateur Riders' Selling Stakes 4yo+ (H)
	£1442 £412 £206 **1m3f aw** **Going 57** **-28 Slow** Inside

1551	**ROMIL STAR** 15 [4] K R Burke 7-11-0 vis (65) Mr S Dobson(3) 4/6 FAV: 560-0021: Trkd ldrs & cruised into lead over 4f out, sn clr, any amount in hand: bought in for 6,600 gns: bckd at odds-on: eff at 12/14f on gd, hvy & fibresand: apprec drop to sell grade.		58a+
1407	**EL PEDRO** 22 [2] N E Berry 5-11-0 (40) Mr Joshua Harris(7) 9/1: 05-43402: Dwelt, sn handy & chsd wnr from 3f out, nvr any impress: rest well covered: see 347.	13	39a
1561	**MORRIS DANCING** 14 [9] B P J Baugh 5-11-0 VIS (30) Mr E Dehdashti(3) 33/1: 0050003: Led 6f, no ch from 3f out: tried a visor: see 784.	5	32a
1363	**LITTLETON VALAR** 25 [8] J R Weymes 4-11-0 bl e (30) Mr K Mercer 12/1: 0060-044: Dwelt, no impress.	5	25a
1643	**MISTY MAN** 9 [3]6-11-5 bl (45) Miss Fiona Brown(7) 6/1: 4-351455: Pushed along chsg ldrs, btn 4f out.	nk	29a
	MISS DANBYS 0 [6]9-10-9 Mr Nicky Tinkler 14/1: 6: b f Charmer - Dohty Baby (Hittite Glory) Dwelt, in tch, btn/eased 2f out, saddle slipped: jumps fit (mod form).	13	1a
1291	**REGAL REPOSE** 28 [5]4-10-9 (50) Mr G Tumelty(7) 40/1: 00200-07: b f Classic Cliche - Ideal Candidate (Celestial Storm) Unruly stalls, prom till halfway: '03 clmr scorer, turf clmr rnr-up (C Cyzer): wng form at 12f, stays 2m in clmg grade: acts on fibresand & gd/soft grnd, gall/undul or sharp trks.	nk	0a

2 Jul'03 Chep 16.2g/s 42-(45) F: 1 May'03 Wolv 12af 51a- F:

1244	**TE ANAU** 30 [7]7-10-9 (30) Ms Amy Boeder(7) 50/1: 0/00/-0668: Prom till halfway, sn bhd.	½	0a
1561	**DUNDONALD** 14 [1]5-11-0 bl t (35) Mr L Newnes(3) 14/1: 6503339: Cl-up 4f, struggling halfway: btr 1264.	9	0a

9 Ran Time 2m 30.63 (9.33) Owned: Mr M R Johnson Trained: Leyburn

---

1839	3.25 Fasthandle Limited Building Land Purchase Banded Stakes 3yo+ 0-35 (H)
	£1453 £415 £208 **7f rnd aw** **Going 57** **-12 Slow** Inside

1715*	**BRONX BOMBER** 6 [5] Dr J D Scargill 6-9-10 bl (35) C Lowther 7/2 JT FAV: 0/0/600-11: Trkd ldrs & led 3f out, sn hdd but rallied for press to lead again ins last, drvn out: eff at 6/7f on both AWs.		50a
1715	**TINY TIM** 6 [8] A M Balding 6-9-4 (35) T Block(7) 7/2 JT FAV: 5221522: Trkd ldrs & led over 2f out, hdd ins last & no extra: op 9/4, clr of rem: acts on gd & both AWs: see 1545.	4	36a
1642	**WESTMEAD ETOILE** 9 [4] J R Jenkins 4-9-4 vis T (35) S W Kelly 11/2: 0-030003: Chsd ldrs, no impress over 1f out: tried a t-strap, visor reapplied: mdn, see 597.	5	26a
1564	**OPTIMUM NIGHT** 14 [3] P D Niven 5-9-4 P (35) R Winston 9/1: 000-0304: Dwelt, prom till 3f out.	3½	19a
1676*	**COUNTRYWIDE GIRL** 8 [6]5-9-10 (35) F Norton 9/2: 6433215: Dsptd lead till over 2f out: btr 1676.	hd	24a
1522	**METICULOUS** 16 [2]6-9-4 (30) L Vickers 25/1: 0000006: gr g Eagle Eyed - Careful (Distinctly North) Sn outpcd & nvr factor: unplcd '03 (rtd 43a & 12, tried blnks): no form '02.	2½	13a
996	**MAGIC EAGLE** 49 [10]7-9-4 (35) G Parkin 11/1: 0/-500007: Led/dsptd lead 4f, sn btn: jumps fit, op 14/1.	11	0a
906	**SAMBA BEAT** 57 [7]5-9-4 (35) Dean McKeown 20/1: 050-0008: Slow away & sn outpcd, 8 wk abs.	6	0a
3946}	**SEA TERN** 285 [9]4-9-4 (35) S Righton 16/1: 00/00-9: b f Emarati - Great Tern (Simply Great) Slow away & sn outpcd: reapp, new yard, mod form.	2½	0a
3168}	**LILLS STAR LAD** 298 [1]6-9-4 (30) A Nicholls 66/1: 0P/0000-0: 10th: Sn struggling on reapp.	11	0a

10 Ran Time 1m 31.43 (4.83) Owned: Mr R A Dalton Trained: Newmarket

---

1840	4.00 Nspcc Full Stop Banded Stakes 4yo+ 0-40 (H)
	£1442 £412 £206 **1m6f aw** **Going 57** **-25 Slow** Inside

1407	**BERKELEY HEIGHTS** 22 [1] Mrs J Candlish 4-8-12 (40) N Callan 3/1 FAV: 4062341: Dwelt & sn pushed along rear, hdwy from halfway & led over 2f out, drvn out: eff at 14f/2m on fibresand: has worn blnks/visor.		44a
1645	**DORA CORBINO** 9 [7] R Hollinshead 4-8-12 (40) A Culhane 9/2: 2063242: Led 3f & led again 5f out till over 2f out, kept on for press: see 1547 & 823.	1	42a
1456	**SERAPH** 20 [6] John A Harris 4-8-12 p (40) Dean McKeown 100/30: 0332103: Chsd ldrs, ch over 2f out, no extra from dist: bckd, op 4/1: clr rem: see 1411.	1	41a
1197	**STAFF NURSE** 34 [2] Don Enrico Incisa 4-8-12 (40) Kim Tinkler 9/1: 2353-004: b f Night Shift - Akebia (Trempolino) Trkd ldrs & keen, rear after 4f & no impress on ldrs after: sell grade rnr-up '03 for N Tinkler: h'cap scorer in '02 for R Charlton: wng form at 7f, stays 14f on fm & soft: tried vis.	5	34a

2 Sep'03 Catt 13.8g/s 46-(50) G: 1 Oct'02 Leic 7sft 65-59 E:

1564	**WESTERN COMMAND** 14 [8]8-8-12 (35) Joanna Badger 10/1: 5533505: In tch till 4f out: btr 1313.	5	27a
1643	**RHETORIC** 9 [3]5-8-12 (40) B Swarbrick(5) 11/2: 05-04106: Keen & prom, btn 3f out: btr 1409.	6	19a
2683}	**SORRENTO KING** 679 [4]7-8-12 t (30) R Havlin 20/1: 6/0606/0/-7: ch g First Trump - Star Face (African Sky) Keen sn bhd, jumps fit (mod form), long Flat abs.	11	5a
1451	**MARAVEDI** 20 [5]4-8-12 vis (40) F Norton 14/1: 0000-008: Led over 10f out till 5f out, sn btn: Ingr trip.	8	0a

8 Ran Time 3m 11.32 (11.52) Owned: Mr A J Cartlich Trained: Leek

---

1841

4.35 Southwell Sponsorship Banded Stakes 3yo+ 0-45 (H)
£1449   £414   £207   **1m rnd aw**   **Going 57**   **-09 Slow**   Inside

1674   **BALLYRUSH 8** [7] K R Burke 4-9-7 bl (45) R Keogh(7) 4/1: 5456521: Handy & led 3f out, rdn clr & in   **48a**
command when hung left over 1f out, eased cl-home: eff around 1m/9.4f tried 11f: acts on fibresand in blnks.
1593*   **DALRIATH 13** [5] M C Chapman 5-9-7 (40) Andrew Webb(7) 3/1 FAV: 0664212: Chsd wnr 3f out, no   3   **42a**
impress bef dist: op 4/1: ran to form of 1593.
1448   **MEXICAN 20** [3] M D Hammond 5-9-7 vis (40) Darren Williams 14/1: 0500-003: b c Pine Bluff - Cuando   6   **30a**
Quiere (Affirmed) Dwelt, chsd ldrs till 2f out: unplcd '03 (rtd 50, tried cheek pieces, h'cap): dual mdn rnr-up C
Brittain in '02: best effs around 11f/11.5f on firm grnd, handles gd: eff with/without blnks or visor, handles a
sharp or stiff trk: has tried a t-strap. 2 Aug'02 Bath 11.6fm 84- D: 2 May'02 Thir 12fm 82- D:
1642   **TEE JAY KASSIDY 9** [2] Julian Poulton 4-9-7 (40) M Halford(7) 8/1: 4-125204: Held up, btn 2f out.   4   **22a**
4530}   **FABULOSO 232** [8]3-8-9 (45) M Tebbutt 6/1: 500000-5: Chsd ldrs & led over 3f out, sn hdd & btn 2f out.   nk   **21a**
1245   **CUMBRIAN PRINCESS 30** [1]7-9-7 (45) D Sweeney 11/2: 4001136: Outpcd, no impress fnl 2f: btr 1185.   15   **0a**
1673   **BRETTON 8** [6]3-8-9 bl (45) Stephanie Hollinshead(5) 9/1: 6644437: Led till over 3f out, sn hmpd & btn.   3½   **0a**
1185   **SUNSET BLUES 34** [4]4-9-7 bl e (40) A Culhane 7/1: 50038: Chsd ldrs, struggling fnl 3f: btr 1185.   11   **0a**
8 Ran   Time 1m 44.65 (5.25)   Owned: Mrs B Keogh   Trained: Leyburn

---

1842

5.10 Entertain With Racing At Southwell Tri-Banded Stakes 3yo 0-45 (H)
£1446   £413   £207   **7f rnd aw**   **Going 57**   **+01 Fast**   Inside

1511   **TSARBUCK 16** [9] R M H Cowell 3-9-0 (45) G Faulkner 9/2: 0-0001: b c Perugino - Form At Last   **56a**
(Formidable) Chsd ldrs & led over 2f out, sn rdn clr, decisively: 1st win & sign of any form on this AW debut:
unplcd in mdns earlier: eff at 7f, tried up to 8.5f prev may yet suit: acts on fibresand & apprec drop in class.
1803   **MITZI CASPAR 2** [5] P L Gilligan 3-8-4 (30) R Price 15/2: 000032: Led 4f, no impress fnl 2f: op   5   **35a**
6/1: quick reappp: prob stays 7f: see 1803.
1330   **MONKEY OR ME 26** [6] P T Midgley 3-8-4 (35) R Fitzpatrick 7/2 FAV: 0-004233: Held up, some late gains. 2   **31a**
1320   **CAMPBELLS LAD 26** [7] A Berry 3-9-0 (45) F Norton 12/1: 0540-54: Prom, outpcd fnl 2f: see 1320.   nk   **40a**
1529   **BOOKIESINDEXDOTCOM 16** [3]3-9-0 vis (45) S W Kelly 6/1: 0306605: Prom, btn over 1f out: needs 6f.   5   **30a**
1395   **NUMPTY 23** [8]3-8-9 t (40) Kim Tinkler 10/1: 0-550006: Dwelt, chsd ldrs till halfway: see 316.   3½   **18a**
1505   **BEAVER DIVA 17** [10]3-8-4 (30) B Swarbrick(5) 16/1: 0-407: Held up & keen, btn 2f out: dropped in trip.   5   **0a**
1803   **DANDY JIM 2** [4]3-8-4 bl (30) J Bramhill 25/1: 5005608: Slow away & sn outpcd, nvr factor, quick reappp.   7   **0a**
1803*   **SAM THE SORCERER 2** [2]3-9-6 (6ex) (51) Darren Williams 5/1: 000-019: Chsd ldrs till 2f out: btr 1803.   2   **0a**
1447   **TAPLEON 20** [1]3-8-9 (40) T Eaves(5) 66/1: 000-600: 10th: Prom till 4f out, sn bhd, AW bow.   2   **0a**
10 Ran   Time 1m 30.53(3.93)   Owned: Mr S P Shore   Trained: Newmarket

---

Official Going Good/Firm

1843

2.10 M-Real Conditions Stakes 4yo+ (C)
£9883   £3749   £1874   **1m4f**   **Good/Firm 26**   **+05 Fast**   Outside

1915}   **PAPINEAU 353** [12] Saeed bin Suroor 4-8-9 T (103) K McEvoy 8/1: 2115-1: ch c Singspiel - Early   **114+**
Rising (Grey Dawn II) Held up, switched when short of room twice 2f out, strong run for press to lead ins last,
readily: reappp, gd time: ex-French, with A Fabre in '03, 2 wins incl Listed: eff at 12f, get futher: acts on fast &
soft: suited by t-strap here & goes well fresh: smart, impressed here, one to be with in GR class.
1483   **SONGLARK 18** [14] Saeed bin Suroor 4-8-9 vis t (107) T E Durcan 25/1: 20452-52: br c Singspiel -   2½   **107**
Negligent (Ahonoora) Trkd ldrs, led over 1f out, hdd ins last, not pace of wnr: completed stable one-two: Gr2 UAE
Derby rnr-up '03, subs cond stks rnr-up in UK: Gr3 wnr for A Fabre in '02: eff at 10/12f on firm, gd & dirt
surfaces: eff in visor/t-strap, likes a stiff/gall or sharp/undul trk: gd run, v useful colt.
2 Sep'03 Donc 10.3gd 108-(109) B: 2 Mar'03 Nad 10dirt 109a- A: 1 Oct'02 Sain 8gd 110- :
1350   **PERSIAN MAJESTY 25** [13] P W Harris 4-9-5 (108) J Murtagh 10/1: 1/1-63: Prom, rdn & styd on   ¾   **116**
onepace fnl 2f: op 9/1: stays a sharp 12f & an improved/smart run conceding weight: see 1350.
1483   **PERSIAN LIGHTNING 18** [6] J L Dunlop 5-8-9 (102) M J Kinane 7/1: 06200-44: Mid-div, eff when   ½   **105**
short of room from over 3f out & again 2f out, onepcd for press ins last: poss a shade closer with a clear run.
1478   **TIZZY MAY 18** [4]4-8-9 (98) Dane O'Neill 33/1: 3240-025: Rear, rdn/styd on, nvr ffl: try 12f?   3   **101**
1296   **CORRIOLANUS 28** [5]4-8-9 (100) D Holland 100/1: 63-30006: Cl-up, btn dist: blnks omitted: see 693.   1¼   **99**
1139   **TUNING FORK 37** [7]4-8-9 (98) T Quinn 66/1: 26650-07: b c Alzao - Tuning (Rainbow Quest) Led   1¾   **97**
till over 1f out, fdd: mdn scorer '03 (H Cecil), subs Gr2 rnr-up: eff at 10f/10.5f on firm & soft grnd, stiff/gall
trks: best without visor.
2 May'03 York 10.4fm 108- A: 1 May'03 Hayd 10.5sft 95- D:
1230   **PUGIN 32** [2]6-8-9 (105) K Fallon 11/2 JT FAV: 0060-558: Dwelt, eff & no impress fnl 3f: see 1230.   1¾   **95**
1585   **HAMBLEDEN 13** [10]7-8-9 (101) P Robinson 7/2: 25312-69: Trkd ldrs, btn over 1f out: see 1585.   1½   **93**
1483   **PRIVATE CHARTER 18** [3]4-8-9 (110) M Hills 11/2 JT FAV: 2645-020: 10th: Mid-div, btn over 1f out.   ½   **92**
433   **ULUNDI 123** [8]9-8-9 (107) R Hughes 20/1: 40/000-00: 11th: b g Rainbow Quest - Flit (Lyphard)   3   **88**
Held up & al bhd: 4 month abs: unplcd over hdles last winter (rtd 104h, Gr 1 hdle): lightly rcd & unplcd on the
Level '03 (rtd 103, Gr3): Listed h'cap wnr '02, subs close 4th in a US Gr1 (rtd 118): eff at 10/12f: handles soft &
fibresand, loves firm/fast grnd, prob any trk: can go well fresh: 9yo.
1 Jun'02 Asco 10g/f 115-109 A: 1 Jul'01 Sand 10fm 109-105 B: 1 May'01 Good 12fm 109- B:
1705   **SALSALINO 6** [11]4-8-9 (107) K Darley 7/1: 3243-600: 12th: Rear & sn rdn, nvr factor, quick reappp.   5   **81**
1596   **RAWYAAN 12** [9]5-9-5 bl (112) R Hills 14/1: 01-16000: 13th: Slow away & sn bhd: btr 990.   ¾   **90**
1585   **BOURGAINVILLE 13** [1]6-8-9 (105) Martin Dwyer 14/1: 26-04550: 14th: Prom, btn 3f out: btr 1350 & 884. 5   **73**
14 Ran   Time 2m 34.33 (2.53)   Owned: Godolphin   Trained: Newmarket

1844

2.40 Listed Normandie Stud Lupe Stakes Fillies 3yo (A)
£17400 £6600 £3300   1m1f192y rnd   Good/Firm 26   -03 Slow   Inside

1110 **HALICARDIA 39** [6] P W Harris 3-8-8 (97) D Holland 7/2 FAV: 311-31: Held up, hdwy & green/wandered fnlk 2f but reeled in ldr cl-home, drvn out: nicely bckd: improved stepped up to 10f, shld get further: acts on fm & gd/soft, any trk: v useful & unexposed at mid-dists, reportedly needs a gap between races.   **106**

1492 **SPOTLIGHT 17** [4] J L Dunlop 3-8-11 (101) M J Kinane 9/2: 3121-402: Chsd ldrs & prog to lead 3f out, rdn & hdd nr line: well clr rem: styd longer 10f trip well: handles a stiff or sharp/undul trk: v useful.   nk   **108**

4845*)**CARINI 210** [3] H Candy 3-8-8 Dane O'Neill 11/2: 11-3: b f Vettori - Secret Waters (Pharly) Led after 1f till over 7f out, not pace of front pair from over 2f out: reapp: unbtn in 2 '03 starts, mdn & nov stks: eff at 7f/1m, dam wnr over mid-dists & 10f+ shld suit: acts on fast grnd, stiff/undul or gall trk: can go well fresh. 1 Oct'03 Nott 8.2g/f 95- D: 1 Aug'03 Sali 7.0g/f 75- E: 6   **96**

4597)**MADAEH 228** [1] J L Dunlop 3-8-8 (94) R Hills 11/2: 3115-4: b f Swain - Tamgeed (Woodman) Chsd ldrs & prog to lead 7f out till 3f out, fdd: bckd, op 7/1, reapp: lightly rcd '03, auct mdn & h'cap scorer, subs Listed unplcd (rtd 99): both wins at 7f, breeding suggests mid-dists shld suit: acts on firm & gd grnd, likes a sharp/undul trk. 1 Aug'03 Good 7g/f 92-83 C: 1 Jul'03 Ling 7g/f 84- E: 2½   **92**

1419* **SHADY REFLECTION 21** [7]3-8-11 (91) K Fallon 11/2: 501-15: Chsd ldrs, btn 2f out: bckd: see 1419.   3   **91**

1568 **DERAASAAT 14** [5]3-8-8 (93) W Supple 12/1: 01-06: ch f Nashwan - Nafhaat (Roberto) Led 1f, chsd ldrs till 3f out: fills mdn scorer '03 (lightly rcd): wng form at 1m, bred for mid-dists: acts on fast grnd & a gall trk. 1 Sep'03 Nott 8.2g/f 80- D: 2½   **84**

3998*)**AL SIFAAT 261** [2]3-8-8 T (90) K McEvoy 6/1: 21-7: ch f Unfuwain - Almurooj (Zafonic) Keen, rear, hung wide on bend over 3f out & sn struggling, t.o.: wore a t-strap on reapp: lightly rcd '03, fills mdn scorer: eff at 6f, bred to apprec 7f/1m: acts on fast grnd, stiff/gall trks: something clrly amiss today. 1 Sep'03 Leic 6.0gd 88- D: 2 Aug'03 Newb 6.0g/f 88- D: 26   **47**

7 Ran Time 2m 07.13 (2.93)   Owned: Persistent Partners   Trained: Berkhamsted

1845

3.15 Vodafone 'dash' Trial Stakes Handicap 3yo+ 0-110 (B)   [107]
£12093 £4587 £2294   5f str   Good/Firm 26   -08 Slow   Stands Side

1683 **WHITBARROW 7** [11] J M Bradley 5-8-11 (90) R L Moore 9/1: 056-5001: Broke well & sn settled to trk ldrs, led ins last, drvn out: nicely bckd, op 10/1: eff at 5/6f on fm & gd, any trk: new trainer has reportedly cured his foot probs: extremely well h'capped on best of form & v interesting in Epsom Dash under a pen (crse wnr).   **97+**

235 **TEXAS GOLD 151** [7] W R Muir 6-8-8 (87) S Drowne 8/1: 360113-2: Chsd ldrs travelling well, eff to chall dist, not pace of wnr: 5 month abs, excellent return, spot on next time.   ¾   **91**

1615 **ROSES OF SPRING 12** [10] R M H Cowell 6-8-4 p (83) E Ahern 14/1: 00100-03: Al handy & led 2f out, rdn & hdd ins last, no extra: left turf reapp bhd, prolific wnr '03 & shld win more races: see 1615.   1½   **82**

1683 **CORRIDOR CREEPER 7** [2] J M Bradley 7-8-11 p (90) C Catlin 9/2 FAV: 2000-544: Prom towards stands side, not pace of ldrs towards centre from dist: hvly bckd tho' op 7/2: stable-mate of wnr: see 1594.   1   **86**

1207 **LITTLE EDWARD 33** [1]6-9-4 (97) J Murtagh 7/1: 0225-505: gr g King's Signet - Cedar Lady (Telsmoss) Dsptd lead stands side till 2f out, no extra: dual cond stks scorer '03, subs val h'cap rnr-up at the Curragh: dual h'cap wnr '02: best at 5/5.8f on firm & gd/soft grnd, prob any trk, loves a stiff one. 2 Sep'03 Curr 5g/f 101-97: 2 Aug'03 Sand 5.0g/s 98-95 B: 1 Jul'03 Bath 5.7fm 99-(97) C: 1 Jun'03 Sand 5.0fm 99-(97) C: 2 Aug'02 Newb 5.1fm 95-92 C: 1 Jul'02 Warw 5.5g/f 93-83 C: 1 Jul'02 Warw 5g/f 82-76 D: 1 Aug'01 Sand 5gd 80- D: 2 Jul'01 Sali 6g/f 78- D: shd   **93**

5006*)**MALAPROPISM 196** [4]4-8-9 (88) B O'Neill(7) 16/1: 003001-6: ch g Compton Place - Mrs Malaprop (Night Shift) Slow away, eff when short of room over 1f out, sn outpcd: reapp: landed 3 h'caps '03, auct mdn wnr '02: best btwn 5/5.7f & stays 6f: acts on firm or soft grnd, any trk: likely to prove sharper for this. 1 Nov'03 Muss 5g/f 92-83 D: 1 Aug'03 Good 5g/f 84-78 D: 2 Jul'03 Bath 5.0g/f 78-75 E: 1 May'03 Bath 5.7g/f 77-69 E: 2 Oct'02 Sand 5g/f 77-77 D: 2 Aug'02 Sand 5sft 84-82 D: 1 Jul'02 Redc 5g/f 84- E: 2 Jul'02 Yarm 5.1g/f 82- D: 2 May'02 Wind 5sft 80- D: 1   **81**

1479 **DUBAIAN GIFT 18** [9]5-9-10 (103) Martin Dwyer 7/1: 2216-007: b g Bahamian Bounty - Hot Lavender (Shadeed) Sn prom till over 1f out: most prog '03, dual h'cap scorer bef landing a Listed contest: dual AW h'cap wnr '02, subs landed 2 turf h'caps: suited by 5f & loves to force the pace: acts on firm, gd/soft & both AWs, any trk: useful, best when able to dominate. 1 Sep'03 Donc 5gd 107-(95) A: 2 Aug'03 Nott 5.1g/f 96-(95) C: 2 Aug'03 Hayd 5fm 95-92 C: 1 May'03 Ling 5gd 89-79 D: 1 May'03 Hayd 5g/f 82-76 C: 1 Aug'02 Good 5fm 75-72 C: 2 Jul'02 Kemp 5g/s 70-72 E: 1 Feb'02 Ling 5ap 74a-68 E: 1 Jan'02 Sout 5af 72a-65 E: nk   **95**

1011 **TURIBIUS 49** [6]5-8-1 (1ow) (79) J F Egan 7/1: 021-6138: Chsd ldrs, no impress fnl 2f, abs: btr 755 (AW).   ½   **70**

1479 **PERUVIAN CHIEF 18** [8]7-9-3 vis (96) D Holland 11/2: 6000209: Outpcd early, nvr able to chall: on 9/2.   ½   **84**

1479 **REPERTORY 18** [5]11-9-12 (105) R Miles(3) 16/1: 4010-000: 10th: Led/dsptd lead till halfway, sn btn.   1¾   **88**

1594 **FURTHER OUTLOOK 12** [3]10-8-5 (84) T P Queally(3) 25/1: 00-13000: 11th: Prom early, outpcd halfway.   nk   **66**

11 Ran Time 58.39 (1.69)   Owned: Seasons Holidays   Trained: Chepstow

1846

3.45 Chichester Festival Theatre Maiden Stakes Fillies 3yo (D)
£5512 £1696 £848   7f rnd   Good/Firm 26   +02 Fast   Inside

2415)**ANOTHER FAUX PAS 329** [1] R Hannon R L Moore 100/1: 0-1: b f Slip Anchor - Pirie (Green Dancer) Towards rear, rdn & styd on strongly fnl 2f to lead cl-home: shock win: unplcd & only mod form sole '03 start (rtd 55, fills mdn): eff at 7f, 1m+ looks sure to suit (mid-dist pedigree): acts on gd/firm grnd & a sharp/undul trk: goes well fresh: clrly learned from last year, potentially useful.   **76**

1690 **ALL QUIET 7** [10] R Hannon 3-8-11 R Hughes 25/1: 000-32: Dwelt, sn mid-div, hdwy & rdn/led ins last, hdd cl-home: shorter priced stable-mate of wnr: left reapp bhd at 7f: shld win a race.   nk   **75**

1419 **HALABALOO 21** [9] G Wragg 3-8-11 (78) D Holland 4/1: 3-503: Prom, styd on onepace from dist: handles fast, gd & polytrack, sharp/undul or stiff trk, eff at 7f, worth another try at 1m: see 1171 & 49.   1   **73**

4556)**INDIANA BLUES 230** [11] A M Balding 3-8-11 (93) Martin Dwyer 100/30: 040-4: ch f Indian Ridge - Blue Raven (Bluebird) Led, hdd ins last & wknd nr fin: nicely bckd, op 5/2, reapp: unplcd '03 (mdn 4th, rtd 83, subs Gr1 unplcd, rtd 97, prob flattered): eff at 6f, stays a sharp 7f, tho' return to former could suit: acts on fast, gall or sharp/undul trk: ran well for a long way, spot on back at 6f.   1   **71**

CUT SHORT 0 [6]3-8-11 J P Murtagh 12/1: 5: b f Diesis - Sun And Shade (Ajdal) Rear, kept on ins last, not pace to chall: encouraging debut: sister to a high-class 6/7f juv wnr, dam a 6f juv wnr & related to a high-class mid-dist performer: stays 7f, shaped as if 1m+ could suit: handles fast grnd, encouraging.   1   **69**

4972} **GIRL WARRIOR 200** [4]3-8-11 K Darley 8/1: 3-6: ch f Elusive Quality - Qhazeenah (Marju) Held   *1*   **66**
up, kept on late for press, nvr threat on reapp: promise sole '03 start (mdn plcd, rtd 82+): eff at 7f, related to
mid-dist wnrs & 1m+ will suit: handles gd grnd, prob fast: likely improve on this at 1m+.
1497 **TIPSY LADY 17** [5]3-8-11 T Quinn 25/1: 07: Slow away, nvr on terms with ldrs.   ½   **60**
      SAN LORENZO 0 [3]3-8-11 T E Durcan 10/1: 8: Mid-div, no impress over 1f out on debut.   *3*   **59**
946 **SCRUNCH 53** [7]3-8-11 K Fallon 25/1: 69: Trkd ldrs, hung badly left & btn over 1f out, abs.   ½   **57**
1587 **NOORA 13** [8]3-8-11 R Hills 9/4 FAV: 0-20: 10th: Keen, mid-div, struggling fnl 3f, reportedly lost action.   *1*   **56**
    Bonnetts 0 [12]3-8-11 Dane O'Neill 33/1:0   1497 **Dulcimer 17** [2]3-8-11 S Drowne 100/1:0
12 Ran   Time 1m 26.19 (1.69)   Owned: Jubert Family   Trained: Marlborough

---

1847   4.20 Baker Tilly Trophy Stakes Handicap 3yo 0-100 (C)   [104]
£10400 £3200 £1600   **7f rnd**   **Good/Firm 26**   **-26 Slow**   Inside

1186 **SECRET PLACE 34** [13] E A L Dunlop 3-8-6 (82) E Ahern 6/1: 02-11301: Chsd ldrs & led over 1f out,   **93**
sn rdn clr, decisively, gd time: op 5/1 stays 1m, all 3 wins at 7f: acts on both AWs & fast grnd, likes a
sharp/undul trk: made full use of fav high-draw, win again on this evidence: see 694 & 432.
1518* **DR THONG 16** [6] P F I Cole 3-8-2 (78) R L Moore 5/1: 5-412: Keen in mid-div, hdwy to lead over   *3*   **81**
2f out, edged right & hdd over 1f out, sn no impress on wnr: nicely bckd: fine run: see 1518.
1496 **JEDBURGH 17** [4] J L Dunlop 3-9-7 (97) M J Kinane 9/4 FAV: 0111-033: Held up, eff when short of   nk   **99**
room 3f out, kept on for press, not pace to chall: well bckd: return to a stiffer 7f could prove ideal: see 1496.
4160} **LORD LINKS 252** [5] R Hannon 3-8-10 (86) R Hughes 33/1: 13040-4: ch g Daggers Drawn - Lady From *2*   **84**
Limerick (Rainbows For Life) Slow away, bhd, kept on late, kind ride: reapp, has been gldd: debut scorer '03 (mdn,
subs rtd 93 at best, 3rd of 7, cond stks): wng form at 5f, stays a sharp 7f: handles firm & fast grnd, stiff/gall
or sharp/undul trks: can go well fresh: spot on for this encouraging return. 1 May'03 Newm 5g/f 88- D:
1040 **BRAVO MAESTRO 46** [7]3-9-5 (95) T Quinn 7/1: 011-605: Keen & trkd ldr, chall over 2f out, sn bmpd   nk   **92**
& no extra dist: op 8/1, 6 wk abs: btr 885 & 15 (AW).
1583 **DISTANT CONNECTION 13** [11]3-7-12 (2oh) (72) J Quinn 16/1: 503-0006: Keen, held up, no impress   2½   **66**
over 2f out: see 1583.
1498 **COMPTONS ELEVEN 17** [1]3-8-11 (87) T E Durcan 33/1: 0033-007: gr g Compton Place - Princess Tara *1*   **77**
(Prince Sabo) Mid-div, no impress fnl 2f: mdn & h'cap scorer '03, subs cond stks plcd: eff at 5/6f, 7f shld suit
this term: acts on fast & gd grnd, sharp/undul or easy trks. 1 Sep'03 Good 6g/f 93-83 D: 1 Aug'03 Yarm 5.2g/f 90- D:
1421 **TREASURE HOUSE 21** [3]3-8-12 (88) D Holland 25/1: 210-0058: Mid-div, btn 3f out, reportedly hung right.½   **77**
1496 **ANUVASTEEL 17** [8]3-8-10 (76) D Fox/5 4/1: 5132-609: Mid-div, no impress fnl 2f: well bckd: btr 229.   shd   **65**
4683} **HOH BLEU DEE 221** [10]3-8-12 (88) Martin Dwyer 33/1: 11666-0: 10th: b g Desert Style - Ermine   *4*   **69**
(Cadeaux Genereux) Rear, nvr factor: gldd, reapp: won 1st 2 '03 starts (auct mdn & nov stks, subs Listed unplcd,
rtd 92 at best): wng form at 5.7f/6f, dam a 1m wnr: acts on fast grnd, sharpish or turning trk: can go well fresh.
1 Aug'03 Ripo 6g/f 88- D: 1 Jul'03 Bath 5.7g/f 83- F:
1513 **Our Gamble 16** [12]3-8-10 (86) Dane O'Neill 33/1:0   3513} **King Carnival 283** [2]3-9-5 (95) P Dobbs 25/1:0
12 Ran   Time 1m 28.15 (3.65)   Owned: Mr Khalifa Sultan   Trained: Newmarket

---

1848   4.55 Delta International E B F Maiden Stakes 2yo (D)
£4771 £1468 £734   **6f str**   **Good/Firm 26**   **-33 Slow**   Stands Side

    HENRIK 0 [5] M R Channon 2-9-0 T E Durcan 5/1: 1: b c Primo Dominie - Clincher Club (Polish   **98**
Patriot) Sn trkd ldr travelling well & led over 1f out, rdn & just held on: nicely bckd: Mar foal, 100,000 gns
purchase: half brother to wnrs at 6f/1m, dam a 5f juv & subs 7f 3yo wnr: eff over a sharp 6f, return to 5f might
suit at present: acts on fast grnd & goes well fresh: showed plenty of speed, looks potentially useful.
    QADAR 0 [1] M P Tregoning 2-9-0 T R Hills 6/4 FAV: 2: b c Xaar - Iktidar (Green Desert) Trkd   shd **97+**
ldrs, short of room & switched over 1f out, rdn to chall ins last, just denied: hvly bckd: 250,000 gns Mar foal,
half brother to 3 useful 5/6f juv wnrs, dam plcd at 7f as a 3yo: eff at 6f on a sharp/undul trk & goes well fresh:
suited by t-strap here: looks useful & must be way sn.
1256 **CHALISON 30** [4] R Hannon 2-9-0 R Hughes 5/2: 23: Led, rdn & hdd over 1f out, not pace of front   1¼   **93**
pair: rest well covered: nicely bckd: acts on fast & gd/soft grnd, styd longer 6f trip: find a race: see 1256.
    SILVER WRAITH 0 [2] N A Callaghan 2-9-0 J Murtagh 14/1: 4: b c Danehill Dancer - Alpine Lady   *4*   **81**
(Tirol) Chsd ldrs, outpcd fnl 2f: £180,000 Mar foal: half brother to a 5f juv & subs 7f 3yo wnr, dam lightly rcd &
unplcd at 1m/10f: shaped here as if 7f+ will suit in time.
    SAFENDONSEABISCUIT 0 [3]2-9-0 P Dobbs 14/1: 5: b c Danzig Connection - The Fugative (Nicholas)   3½   **70**
Slow away, sn chsd ldrs, btn over 1f out: 13,000 gns Mar 1st foal, dam a multiple 5/6f wnr, none as a 2yo: sire
hig-class US mid-dist dirt performer: expected to need further in time & can improve.
    PART TIME LOVE 0 [6]2-9-0 C Catlin 16/1: 6: b c Royal Applause - Keen Melody (Sharpen Up) Sn   1¾   **65**
outpcd, longer priced stable-mate of wnr: Jan foal, half brother to a prolific 5/6f 3yo wnr, dam plcd at 7f as a 3yo.
    WISE DENNIS 0 [7]2-9-0 D Holland 16/1: 7: Slow away, sn in tch, outpcd fnl 2f.   hd   **64**
7 Ran   Time 1m 13.54 (3.54)   Owned: Mr John Breslin   Trained: West Ilsley

---

1849   5.30 Cucumber Stakes Handicap 3yo+ 0-80 (D)   [80]
£5811 £1788 £894   **1m rnd**   **Good/Firm 26**   **-03 Slow**   Inside

1723 **EPHESUS 6** [17] Miss Gay Kelleway 4-9-10 vis (76) W Supple 4/1 FAV: 3000061: Chsd ldrs against far   **83**
rail, drvn & narrow lead over 1f out, just prevailed, all out: bckd, op 5/1, quick reapp: confirmed return to form
in eye-catching eff latest: eff at 1m/10f & likes both AWs, fast & gd grnd, prob any trk: best in a visor.
12 **PANGO 189** [11] H Morrison 5-9-5 (71) P Dobbs 10/1: 210500-2: ch g Bluegrass Prince - Riverine   shd **77+**
(Risk Me) Mid-div, short of room 2f out, switched & styd on strongly ins last, just denied: 6 month abs, op 14/1:
h'cap scorer '03: class stks wnr '02, AW h'cap rnr-up: eff at 1m/11f on fast, gd/soft & both AWs, prob any trk:
fine return, lkd unlucky & likely to find similar. 1 Sep'03 Epso 8.5g 75-68 D: 2 Aug'03 Good 9.9g/f 71-68 E:
2 Jun'03 Kemp 9fm 70-69 E: 2 Nov'02 Sout 11af 71a-69 E: 2 Oct'02 Ling 10ap 70a-69 E: 1 Jun'02 Chep 8g/s 76- D:
2 May'02 Brgh 8g/f 76-72 E:
1792 **QUANTUM LEAP 2** [7] S Dow 7-8-13 vis (65) D Holland 11/1: 0630303: Keen & held up, hdwy to chall   hd   **70**
over 1f out, just held cl-home: nicely bckd, op 12/1: on a fair mark & has a decent record at this venue: see 101.
697 **PRIORS DALE 88** [9] K Bell 4-9-0 (66) Dane O'Neill 25/1: 020-2664: Rear, styd on for press fnl   ½   **70**

GOODWOOD   WEDNESDAY 19.05.04   Righthand, Sharpish, Undulating Track

2f, nrst fin: 12 wk abs: acts on fast, gd & polytrack, gd turf return, shown enough to find a race: see 430 & 17.

1296 **MAD CAREW 28** [18]5-9-10 (76) S Whitworth 12/1: 2-510405: Held up, eff/short of room over 2f out	1¾	77+

till over 1f out, kept on ins last: would have gone close with a clr run: see 674 & 122.

1385 **SPIRITS AWAKENING 23** [8]5-8-6 (58) J Quinn 20/1: 60422-06: b g Danzig Connection - Mo Stopher ... 3 ... 53
(Sharpo) Trkd ldrs & ch 2f out, sn no extra: dual h'cap rnr-up '03: h'cap wnr '02: suited by 1m on firm or hvy
grnd, prob any trk. 2 Oct'03 Newb 9g/f 60-58 F: 2 Sep'03 Wind 8.3g/f 60-56 E: 1 Oct'02 Bath 8gd 55-51 F:

1650 **MISS PEBBLES 9** [20]4-9-2 (68) N Pollard 14/1: 056-1407: Prom, no extra over 1f out: btr 978 (soft). ... ¾ ... 62

1542* **LOCKSTOCK 15** [19]6-9-6 p (72) R Miles(3) 10/1: 414-0018: Led after 2f till over 2f out, fdd: op 8/1. ... nk ... 65

1381 **CAROUBIER 23** [15]4-9-10 (76) T E Durcan 16/1: 2120109: Dwelt, rear, only mod prog: btr 1059 (g/s). ... nk ... 68

1691 **AGILIS 7** [4]4-8-7 bl (50) I Mongan 40/1: 0600000: 10th: Held up, some hdwy, nvr factor: see 547.- ... hd ... 50

1024 **POPPYLINE 47** [10]4-8-3 (55) Martin Dwyer 33/1: 54440-00: 11th: b f Averti - Shalverton ... hd ... 45
(Shalford) Mid-div when short of room 3f out, no impress fnl 2f: 7 wk abs: dual h'cap rnr-up '03: auct mdn rnr-up
'02: best eff around 7f/8.5f on firm & gd/soft grnd, prob any trk: remains a mdn.
2 Jul'03 Brig 8.0g/f 70-(64) D: 2 Jun'03 Wind 8.3g/f 65-64 E: 2 Apr'03 Leic 8.0g/f 65-64 E: 2 Sep'02 Bath 5.7fm 67- E:

1352 **REBATE 25** [6]4-8-12 (64) R Hughes 25/1: 00-05000: 12th: Rear, short of room over 2f out, little hdwy. ... ¾ ... 53

1542 **AMNESTY 15** [16]5-8-10 bl e (62) R L Moore 8/1: 0611520: 13th: Rear, eff 3f out, sn no impress. ... ¾ ... 50

1542 **NIGHT DRIVER 15** [14]5-8-7 (59) R Brisland 33/1: 0105/0-00: 14th: Rear, eff 2f out, no impress. ... hd ... 46

1423 **BLUE TROJAN 21** [12]4-9-12 (78) E Ahern 12/1: 644-2200: 15th: Mid-div, btn 2f out: btr 434 & 294. ... nk ... 64

1530 **BEST BEFORE 16** [3]4-8-13 (65) S Drowne 25/1: 5-001220: 16th: Trkd ldrs, wknd qckly over 2f out. ... 8 ... 37

1723 **Danielles Lad 6** [13]8-9-5 bl(71) T Quinn 14/1:0   1817 **Stoic Leader 1** [1]4-10-0 (80) D Nolan(3) 16/1:0

18 Ran   Time 1m 39.75(2.35)   Owned: Ionian Partnership   Trained: Newmarket

SAINT CLOUD   TUESDAY 11.05.04   Lefthand, Galloping Track

Official Going Soft

1850   1.50 Gr 3 Prix Cleopatre 3yo Fillies   ()
£25704 £10282 £7711   1m2f110y   Soft

STEEL PRINCESS R Gibson 3-8-9 T Jarnet 17/2: 1-11: b f Danehill - Champaka (Caerleon) Chsd ... 112
ldrs, styd on for press to lead well ins last: reapp: unbeaten filly who earlier landed a Fillies event at Longchamp:
eff at 10/11f on soft ground: progressive filly who reportedly could head for the French Oaks next.

LOVE AND BUBBLES R Collet 3-8-9 S Maillot 74/1: 052121-2: Led over 1f out till cl home. ... ¾ ... 110

BARANCELLA F Head 3-8-9 O Peslier 4/1: 13: Handy, led 3f out, sn rdn & hdd over 1f out, kept on. ... snk ... 109

10 Ran   Time 2m 16.30()   Owned: R F Barnes   Trained: France

LONGCHAMP   THURSDAY 13.05.04   Righthand, Stiff, Galloping Track

Official Going V Soft

1851   1.20 Gr 3 Prix de Guiche 3yo Colts   ()
£25704 £10282 £7711   1m1f55y rnd   Soft

MISTER SACHA J C Rouget 3-9-2 I Mendizabal 11/10 FAV: 111: b c Tiger Hill - Miss Sacha (Last ... 112
Tycoon) Held up, swtchd & hdwy over 1f out, drvn to lead ins last, styd on strongly, decisively: remains unbeaten:
eff at 1m/9.4f on soft, shld stay further: lightly raced, smart & progressive.

RED TUNE Mme C Head Maarek 3-9-2 O Peslier 42/10: 122: Handy, chance ins last, not pace of wnr. ... 1½ ... 108

CHARMO P Demercastel 3-9-2 S Pasquier 39/1: 236-4203: Mid-div, styd on wide for press, not pace wnr.1 ... 106

7 Ran   Time ()   Owned: Lagardere Family   Trained: France

1852   2.20 Gr 2 Prix Hocquart 3yo Colts & Fillies   ()
£42148 £16268 £7765   1m4f   Soft

LORD DU SUD J C Rouget 3-9-2 E Legrix 56/10: 1-111: gr c Linamix - Marseillaise (Esprit Du ... 118+
Nord) Trkd ldrs, led 2f out, drvn out: suited by 12f on gd & soft: lightly raced, unbtn, smart & progressive, heads
for the French Derby.

4836} **PROSPECT PARK** C Laffon Parias 3-9-2 O Peslier 6/4 FAV: 33-112: Rear, styd on wide for press. ... ¾ ... 116

1158 **CHERRY MIX 32** A Fabre 3-9-2 Gary Stevens 37/10: 12-323: Mid-div, onepace fnl 2f. ... 3 ... 112

6 Ran   Time ()   Owned: Mme B Hermelin   Trained: France

LONGCHAMP   SUNDAY 16.05.04   Righthand, Stiff, Galloping Track

Official Going Good/Soft

1853   2.15 Gr 1 Prix Lupin 3yo Colts & Fillies   ()
£80479 £32197 £16099   1m2f110y   Good/Soft

1158* **VOIX DU NORD 35** D Smaga 3-9-2 D Boeuf 14/10 FAV: 12421-11: Rear, drvn to chall dist, all out ... 120
to lead line: suited by 10.5f/11f, 12f shld suit: acts on gd/sft & soft ground: v smart & improving, connections
bullish on French Derby prospects.

1434* **MILLEMIX 21** Mme C Head Maarek 3-9-2 C P Lemaire 23/10: 011-212: Chsd ldrs, led over 1f out ... nse ... 119
till joined ins last, just denied in a thrilling fin: smart & progressive: see 1434.

LONGCHAMP   SUNDAY 16.05.04   Righthand, Stiff, Galloping Track

4400} **VALIXIR** A Fabre 3-9-2 Gary Stevens 16/10: 112-13: b c Tremolino - Vadlamixa (Linamix) Trkd **2   116**
ldr & led 2f out till over 1f out, no extra ins last: 9f wnr on reapp: Gr 3 rnr up last term: stays 10.5f, handles gd
& soft ground: smart colt. 2 Sep'03 Long 8gd 99- A:

1434 **ESPERANTO 21** A P O'Brien 3-9-2 J P Spencer 79/10: 5-12D4: Led 2f, bumped when chall over 2f **6   108**
out, no impress over 1f out & eased ins last when held: also behind today's rnr up in 1434.
5 Ran   Time ()   Owned: Baron T de Zuylen de Nyevelt   Trained: France

---

1854 **2.50 Gr 1 French 1000 Guines 3yo Fillies** ()
£140838 £56345 £28173   **1m rnd**   **Good/Soft**

TORRESTRELLA F Rohaut 3-9-0 O Peslier 97/10: 22-111: b f Orpen - Sea Ring (Bering) Trkd ldr **117+**
& led over 2f out, drvn & styd on strongly, decisively: unbeaten this term & supplemented for this event after
scoring in a Listed event here at Longchamp last month: well suited by 1m/9f, will get further: acts on gd/sft & soft
ground: lightly raced, v smart & progressive, v strong French Oaks claims.

1432* **GREY LILAS 21** A Fabre 3-9-0 Gary Stevens 6/5 FAV: 62-112: Trkd ldrs, pressed wnr over 1f out, **1½   114**
not pace to chall ins last: smart filly, win more Gr races: see 1432 (Gr 3, C/D).

MISS MAMBO E Libaud 3-9-0 C Soumillon 38/10: 13-113: b f Kingmambo - Troika (Strawberry Road) **2   110**
Held up in tch, styd on wide for press, not pace to chall: recent Chantilly stks wnr: well suited by 1m on gd & hvy
grnd: smart filly, win a Gr 3 sn.

1233 **NYRAMBA 29** 3-9-0 (109) I Mendizabal 6/5 FAV: 12110-25: Mid-div, kept on for press, not pace to **½   109**
chall: wants Gr 3 class in 1233.

1492 **CAIRNS 14** 3-9-0 T Gillet 7/2: 11-06: b f Cadeaux Genereux - Tanami (Green Desert) Rear, styd **shd 109**
on well from over 1f out, nvr threatened wnr: well held in Newmarket 1000 Guineas earlier this month: won both
starts '03 (mdn & Gr 2, M Channon): winning form at 6/7f, 1m shld suit this term: acts on fast & gd/sft ground:
likes a stiff/undul trk & can go well fresh: useful. 1 Oct'03 Newm 7g/f 108-0 A: 1 Sep'03 Sali 6g/f 84-0 D:

1492 **CARRY ON KATIE 14** 3-9-0 L Dettori 7/2: 111-69: Led till over 2f out, btn dist: btr 1492 (held up, firm). **2¾   104**
13 Ran   Time ()   Owned: B Bargues   Trained: France

1855 **3.30 Gr 1 French 2000 Guineas 3yo Colts** ()
£140838 £56345 £28173   **1m rnd**   **Good/Soft**

1433* **AMERICAN POST 21** Mme C Head-Maarek 3-9-2 R Hughes 4/10 FAV: 2111-111: Trkd ldrs, drvn to chall dist, **121**
not pace of wnr but keeping on when left in lead well ins last, drvn out: fortunate wnr following Antonius Pius
strange swerve: eff at 1m, mid-dist pedigree & may improve for 10f+: acts on fast & soft, connections blamed drying
ground for unimpressive performance today, high-class.

4272} **DIAMOND GREEN FR** A Fabre 3-9-2 G Stevens 34/10: 111-32: Held up, hdwy to chall dist, slightly **½   119**
hampered ins last, not pace of wnr fnl 100yds: unbeaten juv, 3 wins incl Gr 3 Longchamp success: eff at 7f/1m on
gd/soft & soft ground: smart colt, win in Gr 2/3.

4335*}**BYRON 240** Saeed bin Suroor 3-9-2 (100) L Dettori 82/10: 133D1-3: b c Green Desert - Gay **nk   118**
Gallanta (Woodman) Sn cl up, led over 1f out till ins last, kept on: mdn & Gr 2 wnr '03 for D Loder: both wins at
6f, styd this lngr 1m trip: acts on gd/gall trks: goes well fresh: fine reapp, win more Gr races just
below top-class. 1 Sep'03 Newb 6.0g/f 111-100 A: 1 Jun'03 Newm 6fm 95-0 D:

1433 **ANTONIUS PIUS 21** J P Spencer 15/1: 110-2D5: Held up, hdwy to chall dist out, qcknd to lead **¾   118+**
ins last & asserting for press when veered sharply right & hit rail well ins last, sn hdd & no time to recover:
looked an unlucky loser although displayed similar steering problems bhd this wnr in 1433: clearly top-class & Gr 1
races to be won if 'kink' is ironed out.

1559 **NEWTON 13** 3-9-2 bl P J Scallan 15/1: 053D2-146: Led till over 1f out, no extra: see 1063. **1½   115**
7 Ran   Time ()   Owned: K Abdulla   Trained: France

1856 **4.00 Gr 3 Prix de Saint-Georges 3yo+** ()
£25704 £10282 £7711   **5f str**   **Good/Soft**

4629} **THE TRADER 224** M Blanshard 6-9-2 bl (109) J P Spencer 56/10: 661426-1: ch g Selkirk - Snowing **115**
(Tate Gallery) Twds rear, hdwy halfway & drvn to lead ins last, styd on strongly: reapp: dual cond stks wnr '03, Gr
1 C/D rnr up final start (career best): '02 Listed wnr (Gr 2 4th): stays 6f, 5f specialist on any ground, loves a
stiff/gall trk & best from off the pace in blnks: goes well fresh: loves Longchamp, win more val prizes.
2 Oct'03 Long 5sft 116- A: 1 Sep'03 Leic 5.0g/f 108-109 C: 1 Jul'03 Newm 5g/f 113-110 C: 2D Jun'03 Chan 5gd 112- A:
1 Jun'02 Kemp 5fm 114- A: 1 Sep'01 Newb 5.1fm 114- A: 1 Sep'01 Leic 5g/f 107- C: 1 Aug'01 Newb 5.1fm 100-88 C:
2 Apr'01 Nott 5hvy 98- C:

4775} **THE TATLING 212** J M Bradley 7-9-7 (113) L Dettori 82/10: 12655342: b g Perugino - Aunty Eileen **2   113**
(Ahonoora) Trkd ldrs, led over 1f out till ins last, kept on, not pace of wnr: Listed & Gr 3 wnr '03, Gr 1 rnr up &
Gr 1 plcd over C/D (just bhd this wnr): thrice wnr '02, incl val h'cap: eff at 6f, prob best at 5f: acts on firm or
soft, any trk: best without t-strap: fine return, developed into a smart sprinter & shld win in Gr comp this term.
2 Aug'03 York 5.0fm 115-109 A: 1 Jul'03 Good 5gd 115-109 A: 1 Jul'03 Sand 5.0g/f 110-104 A:
2 May'03 York 6.0fm 106-100 B: 2 May'03 Newm 6g/f 106-100 B: 2 Apr'03 Kemp 6fm 98-101 C:
1 Oct'02 York 6g/f 103-95 B: 2 Sep'02 Ayr 6gd 97-90 B: 1 Aug'02 Sand 5g/f 88-85 B:

4629*}**PATAVELLIAN 224** R Charlton 6-9-11 bl (95) S Drowne 23/10 CO FAV: 111-151113: b g Machiavellian - **1½   112**
Alessia (Caerleon) Led/dsptd lead till over 1f out, kept on for press on reapp: v prog '03, winning 4 of 5 starts,
incl Stewards Cup h'cap & Gr 1 Prix l'Abbaye over C/D: thrice wnr '02 (2 h'caps & class stks): eff at 7f, best has
come at 5/6f in blnks (eff without): goes well fresh on fm, soft & any trk: high-class, spot on for this.
1 Oct'03 Long 5sft 121- A: 1 Aug'03 Good 6g/f 117-95 B: 1 Jul'03 Newm 7fm 98-90 B: 1 Apr'03 Wind 6g/s 94-82 D:
1 Oct'02 Newm 6fm 86-74 D: 1 Sep'02 Chep 7g/f 80- E: 1 Sep'02 Chep 7gd 69-64 F: 2 Aug'01 Sand 9gd 71- D:
12 Ran   Time ()   Owned: Mrs C J Ward   Trained: Upper Lambourn

CORK   FRIDAY 14.05.04   Righthand, Galloping Track, Long Run In

Official Going Good/Firm (Firm Places)

1857   7.20 Gr 3 EBF Blue Wind Stakes Fillies & Mares 3yo+   ()
£39195 £11457 £5427   1m2f50y   Good/Firm

HAZARISTA 12 J M Oxx 3-8-9   F M Berry 7/1: 0-411: b f Barathea - Hazaradjat (Darshaan)   110
Mid-div, rdn to lead ins last, sn asserted, readily: recent Gowran Park mdn wnr: eff at 1m/10f on fast & good/soft
ground: likes a galloping trk: lightly rcd, v useful & progressive filly.
4599} **CACHE CREEK** 33 P Hughes 6-9-10 (89) J A Heffernan 10/1: U350-042: Mid-div, kept on for press   2   104
fnl 2f, no threat to wnr.
1491 **FELICITY** 12 J H M Gosden 4-9-10 (97) P Shanahan 5/1: 13535-03: b f Selkirk - Las Flores   1½   102
(Sadler's Wells) Led till hdd ins last & no extra: op 4/1: belatedly a mdn scorer '03 (placed many times prev), subs
Listed plcd (rtd 101): eff at 10f, 12f could suit: acts on gd & fast ground, prob any trk: useful filly.
1 Aug'03 Wind 10.0g/f 82-90 D: 2 Jun'03 Newb 10.0g/f 84-97 D:
9 Ran   Time 2m 09.80()   Owned: H H Aga Khan   Trained: Currabeg

CAPANELLE   SUNDAY 16.05.04   Righthand, Flat, Galloping Track

Official Going Good/Soft

1858   4.55 Gr 1 Premio Presidente della Repubblica 4yo+   ()
£213380 £105458 £60915   1m2f   Good/Soft

59   **ALTIERI** 182 V Caruso 6-9-2 M Esposito : 1302-111: ch c Selkirk - Minya (Blushing Groom) Held   119
up, efft/hmpd over 1f out, led ins last & sn clr, decisively: Gr 1 3rd last term (rtd 116): Gr 3 wnr '02: eff at 1m,
suited by 10/12f on gd & soft ground, galloping trk: decisive wnr who posted a high class performance here.
2 Nov'03 Capa 10g/s 114- : 1 Jul'02 Deau 8sft 115- : 2 Jun'02 Chan 8gd 113- :
1558 **VESPONE** 14 Saeed bin Suroor 4-9-2 K McEvoy : 1110-222: Led after 1f till wandered under press   3   115
& hdd ins last, no chance with wnr after: ran cl to best: see 1558 (Gr 1).
NONNO CARLO M Grassi 4-9-2 M Belli : 100201-3: Trkd ldr, chall 2f out, sn hung left & no impress.   2   112
7 Ran   Time 1m 58.70()   Owned: Scuderia Incolinx   Trained: Italy

KRANJI   SUNDAY 16.05.04

Official Going Good

1859   1.30 Gr 1 Singapore Airlines International Cup 3yo+   ()
£523026 £197368 £98684   1m2f   Good

3395} **EPALO** 287 A Schutz 5-9-0 A Starke 64/10: 11222-11: b c Lando - Evening Kiss (Kris) Sn led &   120
rdn clr over 1f out, readily: List & Gr 2 wnr '03, subs Gr 1 rnr up: eff at 9/11f on gd grnd & an AW surface: goes
well fresh: loves to dominate & enjoyed an easy lead today: high class entire who could head for the King Geoge.
2 Aug'03 Muni 10gd 112- A:
SURVEYOR M F de Kock 4-9-0 bl B Vorster 126/10: 20-32102: Trkd ldr, rdn & kept on fnl 2f.   5   112
BOWMANS CROSSING D Oughton 5-9-0 M J Kinane 54/10: 02-33543: Mid-div wide, late gains.   ¾   111
1230 **IMPERIAL DANCER** 29 6-9-0 (117) T E Durcan 23/1: 164110-36: Sn twds rear & pshd along, forced   2½   107
wide 3f out, late gains: jockey reported that 12f is his minimum requirement now.
16 Ran   Time 2m 02.60()   Owned: Gary A Tanaka   Trained: Germany

COLOGNE   SUNDAY 16.05.04   Righthand, Fair Track

Official Going Good

1860   4.10 Gr 2 German 2000 Guineas 3yo Colts & Fillies   ()
£70423 £26761 £12676   1m   Good

1167* **BRUNEL** 32 W J Haggas 3-9-2 (105) D Holland 1/1 FAV: 2215-11: Made all, & always holding rivals   117+
under hand riding ins last, shade cosily: earlier decisive wnr of European Free h'cap at Newmarktet: eff at 7f, now
stays 1m well: acts on fast & gd, handles gd/sft grnd: loves to dominate & this v smart colt looks set to make his
presence felt in the St James Palace.
LAZIO A Trybuhl 3-9-2 A de Vries 92/10: 2: Prom, styd on for press fnl 2f, not pace of wnr: ½   113
ASSIUN A Suborics 3-9-2 P Schiergen 26/10: 3: Trkd ldrs, drvn & chall dist, no extra ins last.   hd   112
15**MOKABRA** 13 3-9-2 (107) A Culhane 105/10: 31165-638: Held up, rdn & no impress over 1f out: btr 1559. 5   102
9 Ran   Time 1m 36.30()   Owned: Highclere Thoroughbred Racing X   Trained: Newmarket

Official Going Good/Firm

1861 2.10 Sunseeker Stakes Rated Stakes Handicap 4yo+ 0-100 (B) [107]
£12853 £4875 £2438 1m6f Good/Firm 26 -13 Slow Inside

1230 **BAROLO** 33 [12] P W Harris 5-9-5 (98) Martin Dwyer 7/1: 13114-01: b g Danehill - Lydia Maria 109+
(Dancing Brave) Trkd ldr, rem handy & led over 2f out, rdn clr, readily: bckd, op 10/1: most prog '03, landed 3
h'caps: mdn rnr-up '02: eff at 10f, suited by 12/14f on firm & gd gnrd, stiff/undul or sharp trks: smart effort &
clearly done well this winter, looks up to Listed/Gr 3 class. 1 Jun'03 York 13.9g/f 99-92 C:
1 May'03 Newm 12fm 95-83 C: 1 May'03 Newm 10gd 87-75 D: 2 Oct'02 Wind 8.3g/s 78- D:
1569 **ARCHDUKE FERDINAND** 15 [10] P F I Cole 6-8-7 (86) S Sanders 20/1: 52400-02: ch g Dernier Empereur 5 89
- Lady Norcliffe (Norcliffe) Keen early, chsd ldrs, styd on for press, no threat to wnr: lightly rcd '03, rtd h'cap
rnr-up, disapp in cheek pieces: dual cond stks rnr-up '02: eff at 14f, suited by 2m/2m6f on firm, gd & any trk:
can go well fresh: slipping to an attractive mark, spot on in similar at 2m. 2 Sep'03 York 13.9g/f 92-88 C:
2 Sep'02 Pont 17.9fm 96- C: 2 Jun'02 Asco 22.1gd 103- B: 1 Jun'01 Newc 16fm 109-100 B:
4796} **ROMANY PRINCE** 215 [13] D R C Elsworth 5-9-7 (100) Dane O'Neill 14/1: 002330-3: b g Robellino - nk 103
Vicki Romara (Old Vic) Towards rear, styd on for press fnl 2f, nrst fin: reapp, op 20/1: C/D h'cap rnr-up '03:
mdn scorer '02, h'cap rnr-up: sole win at 12f, prob suited by 14f/2m on firm & soft gnrd, gall or sharp/undul trks:
gd return, stronger pace &/or 2m will suit.
2 Jul'03 Good 14gd 100-91 B: 2 Sep'02 Kemp 12fm 91-86 C: 1 Aug'02 Newm 12sft 85- D:
1759 **COLD TURKEY** 5 [2] G L Moore 4-8-6 (85) S Whitworth 11/4 FAV: 1324124: Rear, stumbled over 4f ½ 87+
out, hdwy when short of room over 1f out, styd on: quick reapp: stays a sharp 14f, poss best at 12f: much closer but
for mishaps, has a turn of foot: see 1759.
1112 **REVEILLEZ** 40 [3]5-8-13 (92) J Murtagh 7/1: 43613-65: Led till over 2f out, onepace: 6 wk abs. ½ 93
1668 **GOLD RING** 9 [4]4-8-8 (87) S Drowne 13/2: 413-0236: Trkd ldrs, rdn & no extra 1f out: btr 1668 & 1389. hd 87
1109 **CARA FANTASY** 40 [8]4-8-4 (3oh) (80) W Supple 20/1: 3/1661-47: Slow away, held up, rapid hdwy to 5 76
go handy over 3f out, no extra fnl 2f: 6 wk abs: made gnrd up too qckly here after tardy start.
5008*}**ESCAYOLA** 197 [1]4-8-9 vis (88) T Quinn 10/1: 111211-8: b g Revoque - First Fling (Last Tycoon) 2 78
Held up, eff 3f out, no impress: op 8/1, reapp: v prog '03, landed 5 h'caps: lightly rcd & unplcd '02 (rtd 62 &
42a): suited by 14f/2m1.5f on firm & gd gnrd, prob any trk: suited by blnks/visor & a gd weight carrier.
1 Nov'03 Muss 16g/f 90-82 C: 1 Oct'03 Newc 16.2g/f 92-76 C: 2 Oct'03 Newc 16.1gd 72-67 E:
1 Sep'03 Ayr 17.5g/f 69-62 D: 1 Sep'03 Yarm 14.1g/f 62-55 E: 1 Aug'03 Chep 16.2g/f 56-49 F:
1569 **ALMIZAN** 15 [7]4-8-7 (86) T E Durcan 8/1: 01564-09: Keen & held up, no impress fnl 3f: op 10/1. nk 75
1484 **WAIT FOR THE WILL** 19 [6]8-8-7 (86) R L Moore 9/1: 2426-000: 10th: Mid-div, no impress over 2f out. 10 61
1232 **KING FLYER** 33 [5]8-8-4 (3oh) (80) D Holland 20/1: 036-0230: 11th: Rear, btn 3f out: btr 1232. nk 57
1502 **THEATRE** 18 [9]5-8-4 (3oh) (80) P Doe 20/1: 40004-0S: Held up, wide when slipped up on bend after 2f. 0
12 Ran Time 3m 04.27 (5.47) Owned: Mrs P W Harris Trained: Berkhamsted

---

1862 2.40 Listed Peters Fairline Festival Stakes 4yo+ (A)
£17400 £6600 £3300 1m1f192y Good/Firm 26 +05 Fast Inside

1231 **ALKAADHEM** 33 [8] M P Tregoning 4-8-12 (102) R Hills 100/30: 121-541: Mid-div, smooth hdwy 3f 107
out, led dist, drvn out: well bckd: gd time: eff at 1m, improved for step up to sharp 10f, could get further
acts on fm & gd, any trk: smart & improving, prob only just does enough, type to progress again & win a Gr race.
1596 **COMPTON BOLTER** 13 [9] G A Butler 7-9-1 (108) R Hughes 16/1: 1-405032: Trkd ldrs travelling well, nk 109
led over 1f out, drvn & joined dist, just held cl-home: fine run: see 82 (AW, Listed).
4402} **BIG BAD BOB** 242 [5] J L Dunlop 4-9-4 (112) J Murtagh 7/1: 201110-3: br c Bob Back - Fantasy Girl ½ 111
(Marju) Trkd ldrs, stumbled on bend 5f out, chall over 2f out, onepace: op 11/2, reapp: prog '03, cond stks wnr
bef Listed & Gr3 success abroad: won 4 times '02, incl Listed fnl start: well suited by 10f, yet to convince at
12f: acts on firm & gd/soft gnrd & loves to force the pace: prob handles any trk: genuine & smart colt.
1 Aug'03 Bade 10gd 115- A:1 Aug'03 Deau 10g/s A:1 Jul'03 Hayd 10.5g/f 115-(106) C:
2 May'03 Ches 10.3g/f 115-(106) A: 1 Oct'02 Asco 8g/f 106- A: 1 Sep'02 Ches 7.5fm 104- C:
1 Aug'02 Ches 7.5fm 99- D: 1 Aug'02 Newc 7g/f 93- E: 2 Oct'03 Folk 7g/f 84- E:
1349 **SUBLIMITY** 26 [7] Sir Michael Stoute 4-9-1 t (110) K Fallon 9/2: 1144-104: Rear, hdwy 2f out, styd ¾ 107
on, nrst fin: bckd: stays 10f: set plenty to do, encouraging: see 922.
1350 **ISLAND HOUSE** 26 [3]8-8-12 (111) D Holland 15/2: 4432-305: Rear when outpcd 3f out, kept on late, 1¾ 102
nvr able to land blow: won a weaker renewal of this in '03: set plenty to do here, gd run.
1230 **ANANI** 33 [10]4-9-1 (106) E Ahern 12/1: 2-034206: Led 2f & rem handy, led again over 2f out till 3½ 100
over 1f out, no extra: see 884 (AW).
3290} **FOODBROKER FOUNDER** 293 [6]4-8-12 (103) T Quinn 33/1: 150200-7: ch g Groom Dancer - Nemea 3 93
(The Minstrel) Mid-div, no impress fnl 3f, reapp: h'cap scorer '03, stks wnr & mdn wnr '02: eff at 9/10f,
tried 12f: acts on firm & gd/soft gnrd, easy or stiff trk: can go well fresh & a gd weight carrier.
2 Jun'03 Asco 10g/f 108-(88) A: 1 Apr'03 Kemp 9fm 89-84 D: 1 Oct'02 Sali 8gd 85- D: 2 Sep'02 Kemp 8fm 83- D:
1585 **LAGO DORTA** 14 [4]4-9-1 (104) Dane O'Neill 33/1: 121-6408: Slow away & rear, no prog fnl 3f: btr 1168. 6 87
1585 **PARASOL** 14 [1]5-8-12 vis (114) T P Queally 5/2 FAV: 11262-29: Took keen hold & led after 2f, 5 77
slipped badly bend 5f out, hdd over 2f out & sn btn: hvly bckd: this run best forgiven: a tricky ride for an
apprentice, L Dettori undefeated from 4 starts on this colt: see 1585.
1168 **WAKE** 36 [2]4-8-12 (90) S Drowne 66/1: 2/-160: 10th: Rear, btn 3f out: highly tried: see 881 (AW mdn). 3½ 72
10 Ran Time 2m 06.13 (1.93) Owned: Mr Hamdan Al Maktoum Trained: Lambourn

---

1863 3.15 Listed Excel Schroders London Boat Show Ebf Conqueror Stakes Fillies 3yo+ (A)
£17400 £6600 £3300 1m rnd Good/Firm 26 +05 Fast Inside

1620 **GONFILIA** 12 [4] Saeed bin Suroor 4-9-6 t (100) K McEvoy 9/4: 251-0121: Led/dsptd lead till went 107
on over 2f out, rdn & in command dist, styd on strongly: eff at 7f/1m on firm, soft & dirt: likes to race
with/force the pace: smart: see 1620.
1258* **CLASSICAL DANCER** 31 [2] H Candy 3-8-5 (84) T Quinn 9/1: 3-12: Held up, hung right & styd on for ¾ 102
press from over 1f out, nvr threatened wnr: up in grade & improved: open to further improvement, see 1258 (mdn).
1492 **INCHENI** 18 [3] G Wragg 3-8-5 (103) S Drowne 8/1: 61-203: Held up, styd on for press fnl 2f, not 1 100
able to chall: left stains bhd: acts on fast, gd & polytrack: see 1169.

1686 **COTE QUEST 8** [8] S C Williams 4-9-3 (92) Martin Dwyer 33/1: 013-4004: Chsd ldrs & chsd wnr 2f   nk   99$
out, no extra ins last: handles fast & soft grnd: see 1115.
1620 **STARBECK 12** [7]6-9-3 (88) P McCabe 40/1: 5520-005: Slow away, keen rear, hung left & btn 2f out.   4   91
4682*)**CHIC 222** [5]4-9-6 (97) K Fallon 6/4 FAV: 113621-6: ch f Machiavellian - Exclusive (Polar Falcon)   2½   89
Trkd ldrs, ch over 2f out, sn rdn & wknd: hvly bckd, op 7/4: reapp: prog '03, fills mdn, h'cap & Listed scorer:
eff at 7f, easy 1m on firm & gd grnd, prob any trk: can go well fresh.
1 Oct'03 Asco 7gd 101-(97) A: 2 Sep'03 Donc 7gd 98-(97) A: 1 Jun'03 Kemp 8fm 98-87 C: 1 May'03 Ches 7.0fm 89- D:
  IANINA 19 [6]4-9-3 J Murtagh 25/1: 3430-607: b f Eagle Eyed - Ice Dream (Mondrian) Led after   3½   79
2f till over 2f out, sn btn: German raider, recent Gr3 unplcd: '03 stks wnr in Italy: wng form at 6f/1m on gd & soft.
1491 **ZIETORY 18** [1]4-9-6 (102) D Holland 8/1: 21242-58: Rear, haning & no impress from 3f out: btr 1491.   10   62
8 Ran   Time 1m 39.06 (1.66)   Owned: Godolphin   Trained: Newmarket

---

1864   3.45 De Novo Raymarine Maiden Stakes Fillies 3yo (D)
£5499 £1692 £846   **1m1f rnd**   **Good/Firm 26**   **-34 Slow**   Inside

1153 **SPRINGTIME ROMANCE 37** [9] E A L Dunlop 3-8-11 K Fallon 100/30: 361: Chsd ldrs, led over 2f out,   79
drvn out to hold on: hvly bckd: eff at 9/10f, tried 12f (bred to stay): imprvd on this fast grnd today, handles a
sharp/undul trk: relished a positive ride under K Fallon: see 1153 & 1055.
4126} **AL SHUUA 255** [11] C E Brittain 3-8-11 D Holland 14/1: 36-2: b f Lomitas - Sephala (Mr   hd   79
Prospector) Al handy & ev ch fnl 2f, rdn & just held: reapp: mdn plcd '03 (rtd 73, debut): eff at 7f, now stays
sharp 9f, may get further: acts on fast grnd, sharp/undul trk: shld find a mdn.
4972} **GOLDEN ISLAND 201** [5] J W Hills 3-8-11 R Hills 8/1: 0-3: ch f Selkirk - Daftiyna (Darshaan)   2½   74
Rear, hdwy/no room over 3f out, switched & kept on well ins last, nrst fin: op 10/1, reapp: unplcd sole '03 start:
dam plcd at 9f as a 3yo: styd this longer 9f trip & 10f+ may suit: handles fast grnd: luckless run, caught the eye
late on, likely improver.
1527 **MISS MONICA 17** [14] H R A Cecil 3-8-11 W Ryan 10/1: 64: Mid-div, eff fnl 2f, onepace: stays 9f   1½   71
& imprvd on this fast grnd: see 1527.
4736} **APPETINA 219** [10]3-8-11 (77) M Fenton 11/2: 2303-5: b f Perugino - Tina Heights (Shirley   2   67
Heights) Led till over 2f out, hmpd sn after when fading: op 9/2, reapp: fills mdn rnr-up on debut '03, subs dual
mdn plcd (rtd 78 at best): half sister to a smart mid-dist performer, dam a 10f wnr: stays 1m, handles fast &
gd/soft grnd, gall trks. 2 May'03 Redc 6g/f 76- E:
1651 **CULTURED 10** [3]3-8-11 E Ahern 12/1: 56: Mid-div, no impress fnl 3f, dropped in trip.   6   55
1272 **OLYMPIAS 30** [8]3-8-11 S Drowne 33/1: 507: Towards rear, little hdwy, dropped in trip.   ½   54
1055 **COOL CLEAR WATER 45** [6]3-8-11 W Supple 50/1: 008: Chsd ldr after 1f till over 2f out, fdd, 6 wk abs.   nk   53
  TOPPLE 0 [2]3-8-11 Dane O'Neill 25/1: 9: Dwelt & sn pushed along, nvr factor on debut.   9   37
  RUGGTAH 0 [13]3-8-11 T E Durcan 11/1: 0: 10th: Al bhd on debut.   7   25
  PRAIRIE OYSTER 0 [12]3-8-11 J Murtagh 16/1: 0: 11th: Sn struggling rear, debut.   4   17
1258 **COLLADA 31** [7]3-8-11 R Hughes 14/1: 00: 12th: Prom, struggling halfway.   5   7
12 Ran   Time 1m 55.90 (5.4)   Owned: Maktoum Al Maktoum   Trained: Newmarket

---

1865   4.20 Motor Boat & Yachting Centenary Stakes Handicap 3yo 0-85 (D)   [92]
£5551 £1708 £854   **1m3f**   **Good/Firm 26**   **-46 Slow**   Outside

1515 **WATAMU 17** [12] P J Makin 3-9-0 (78) S Sanders 12/1: 01-001: Trkd ldr, rdn & led over 1f out, rdn   90
out: well bckd at long odds, op 25/1: slow time: apprec step up to 11f, shld stay further: acts on gd, enjoyed
fast grnd & likes a sharp/undul trk: see 1515.
1769* **MYSTICAL GIRL 5** [9] M Johnston 3-9-2 (5ex) (80) S Chin 11/4: 230-3312: Led, rdn clr over 4f out,   1¼   89
hdd over 1f out, kept on for press: hvly bckd, op 10/3, quick reapp under pen: styd longer 11f trip well.
1318 **CAMROSE 27** [11] J L Dunlop 3-9-5 (83) T Quinn 7/2: 4321-43: Mid-div, hdwy to chall 2f out, not   2½   88
pace of front pair: rest well covered, nicely bckd: stays a sharp 11f, see 1318.
1213* **OBAY 34** [2] E A L Dunlop 3-9-7 (85) K Fallon 7/1: 0-414: Chsd ldrs, rdn & onepace/held fnl 2f: see 1213. 3   86
4871} **MOMMKIN 209** [6]3-8-13 (77) T E Durcan 20/1: 425-5: b f Royal Academy - Walimu (Top Ville)   1¼   76
Mid-div, not pace to chall on reapp: h'cap bow: mdn rnr-up '03: eff at 1m, dam a 1m/12f wnr: handles fast &
gd/soft grnd: looks likely to apprec 12f+ in similar. 2 Oct'03 Ayr 8g/s 77- D:
1708* **CUTTING CREW 7** [10]3-9-8 (5ex) (86) Martin Dwyer 5/2 FAV: 402-316: Rear, eff from 3f out, only   1   84
mod late prog: hvly bckd on reapp under pen: btr 1708 (made all, gd/soft).
886 **LORD OF THE SEA 61** [1]3-8-6 (70) P Doe 20/1: 55-33407: Mid-div, btn 3f out: abs: btr 798 & 568 (AW).   12   52
1055 **GROUND PATROL 48** [8]3-8-5 (1ow) (68) S Drowne 16/1: 0-34368: Dwelt & al rear: abs: btr 676 (AW).   hd   50
1515 **LAAWARIS 17** [5]3-9-2 (80) S W Kelly 33/1: 1-009: Slow away & al bhd: see 1318.   shd   61
4125} **CARLBURG 255** [4]3-8-7 (71) E Ahern 33/1: 00200-0: 10th: b g Barathea - Ichnusa (Bay Express)   13   35
Trkd ldrs, btn when no room over 2f out: reapp: mdn rnr-up '03: eff over a stiff 7f, dam a 7f wnr & sire a top
class miler: acts on gd grnd. 2 Jul'03 Sand 7.1gd 77- D:
10 Ran   Time 2m 25.80 (7.9)   Owned: Mr R A Henley   Trained: Marlborough

---

1866   4.55 Finning Power Ebf Maiden Stakes Fillies 2yo (D)
£4797 £1476 £738   **6f str**   **Good/Firm 26**   **-30 Slow**   Stands Side

  BALTIC DIP 0 [1] R Hannon 2-8-11 R Hughes 3/1: 1: b f Benny The Dip - Drei (Lyphard) Made all   93
against stands rail, strongly prsd fnl 2f, rdn & just prevailed in a thrilling fin: bckd: Feb foal, cost 38,000
gns: related to sev wnrs, incl a 5f juv wnr & also a 10f/hdles scorer: dam unplcd sole start, eff at 6f, get
further: acts on fast & a sharp/undul trk: goes well fresh: potentially useful.
  PARK ROMANCE 0 [2] B J Meehan 2-8-11 K Fallon 5/2 FAV: 2: b f Dr Fong - Park Charger (Tirol)   shd   92
Trkd ldrs & chall from 2f out, just denied: hvly bckd, rest well covered: Feb foal, 200,000 gns purchase: half
sister to a useful 6f juv & subs 7f 3yo wnr Rum Charger: dam plcd 7f juv, subs useful 1m/10f 3yo wnr: eff at 6f,
will get further: acts on fast grnd, sharp/undul trk: fine start, shld be wng sn.
  SHIVAREE 0 [5] M R Stoute 2-8-11 T E Durcan 4/1: 3: ch f Rahy - Shmoose (Caerleon) Trkd ldrs   2½   84
& ch over 2f out, not pace of front pair: clr of rem, op 5/2: Apr foal, dam a 6f juv wnr & half sister to a smart
1m performer: eff at 6f, get further: handles fast grnd: likely improver.
  MARIANIS 0 [6] J G Portman 2-8-11 R L Moore 7/1: 4: b f Lujain - Without Warning (Warning)   6   68
Dwelt, sn outpcd & no impress on front trio: bckd at long odds, op 14/1: Apr foal, cost 13,000 gns: half sister to
7f wnr: dam related to a useful 10/12f performer: stay further & could improve in time.

GOODWOOD THURSDAY 20.05.04 Righthand, Sharpish, Undulating Track

SOME NIGHT 0 [3]2-8-11 J Murtagh 9/2: 5: Sn outpcd & no impress halfway. ½ 66
1401 **MYSTERY MAID** 23 [4]2-8-11 S Drowne 25/1: 06: Cl-up till over 2f out, wknd qckly, longer trip. 8 45
6 Ran Time 1m 13.34 (3.34) Owned: Thurloe Thoroughbreds VIII Trained: Marlborough

---

1867	5.30 Avon Inflatables Apprentice Stakes Handicap 3yo+ 0-70 (E)				[70]
	£3916 £1205 £603 **5f str** **Good/Firm 26** **-19 Slow** Stands Side				

1774 **PARKSIDE PURSUIT** 5 [1] J M Bradley 6-9-12 (68) C J Davies(5) 50/1: 60200-01: Held up stands side, 72
smooth hdwy halfway & led dist, drvn out: quick reapp: left reap bhd: eff at 5/6f on firm & gd: see 1774.
1544 **AINTNECESSARILYSO** 16 [14] N E Berry 6-8-3 (45) M Halford(5) 10/1: 3633322: Rear towards centre, nk 49
hdwy to chall ins last, just held: most consistent, deserved to win again: see 1544, 1336 & 501.
1774* **GUNS BLAZING** 5 [18] D K Ivory 5-9-9 (7ex)bl (65) M Howard(5) 5/1 CO FAV: 000-0013: Led/dsptd lead nk 68
till went on halfway, hdd dist & just held cl-home: nicely bckd: quick reapp: prob prog again after 1774.
4964} **REDWOOD STAR** 202 [13] P L Gilligan 4-9-1 e (57) D Fox 12/1: 021030-4: b f Piccolo - Thewaari ¾ 58
(Eskimo) Al prom, ch ins last, just held cl-home: reapp, op 10/1, C/D h'cap scorer '03, sand unplcd (rtd 37, tried
t-strap): suited by a sharp 5f, tried 7f: acts on fast grnd & polytrack, eff in eye-shield, has tried blnks.
1 Sep'03 Good 5g/f 59-51 E: 2 Sep'03 Good 5fm 51-44 E: 2 Nov'02 Ling 5ap 62a- E:
1788 **DOUBLE M** 3 [10]7-8-5 vis (47) R Thomas 8/1: 4210655: Held up, keeping on when hmpd ins last, not nk 47+
able to recover: closer with a clr run: quick reapp: well h'capped on turf, likely type for similar: see 902 (AW).
1774 **PULSE** 5 [11]6-9-7 p (63) A Quinn 6/1: 6-002366: Al prom towards centre, onepace ins last: nk 62
stable-mate of wnr, bckd: quick reapp: see 1532 & 1371.
1336 **HENRY TUN** 27 [5]6-7-12 p (40) D Fentiman(5) 33/1: 2130207: Prom stands side, carried right & no nk 38
extra from dist: btr 1046.
1532 **PANJANDRUM** 16 [12]6-8-13 (55) M Savage 20/1: 0600408: Held up centre, not pace to chall: see 1371. nk 52
1615 **CERULEAN ROSE** 13 [4]5-9-12 (68) Liam Jones(5) 5/1 CO FAV: 11135-49: Dwelt, in tch stands side, shd 65
switched halfway, only mod prog: see 1615.
1408* **MAROMITO** 23 [17]7-8-13 (55) D Tudhope(5) 5/1 CO FAV: 0-003110: 10th: Cl-up centre, wkng when 1 49
hmpd well ins last: wtr 1408 (a/w).
1578 **FIRE CAT** 14 [6]5-7-12 (5oh) (35) Hayley Turner 50/1: 00-00000: 13th: Led/dsptd lead till over 1f out. 3 25
4384} **LOCH INCH** 14 [3]7-9-1 bl (57) N Chalmers 40/1: 101000-0: 14th: ch g Inchinor - Carrie Kool shd 42
(Prince Sabo) Chsd ldrs, no prog fnl 2f, reapp: landed 3 h'caps in '03: eff at 5/5.7f on firm & soft grnd, prob
any trk: suited by blnks, tried cheek pieces, no head gear worn today: sharper for this with headgear reapplied.
1 Sep'03 Leic 5.0gd 59-51 E: 1 Aug'03 Yarm 5.2g/f 54-48 D: 1 Aug'03 Bath 5.7fm 49-41 E:
1544 **CRAFTY POLITICIAN** 16 [8]7-8-3 bl (45) Steven Harrison(5) 50/1: 0-412560: 15th: Cl-up stands side 3f. ¾ 28
1765 **ERRACHT** 5 [2]6-9-9 (65) B Swarbrick(3) 20/1: 30-05160: 16th: Stands side, prom till halfway: qck reapp. shd 48
4432} **Indian Bazaar** 239 [16]8-8-8 (50) P Makin(3) 14/1:0
1354 **Goodwood Prince** 26 [9]4-9-6 VIS(62) J Coffill Brown(7) 33/1:0
1442 **Arogant Prince** 21 [7]7-9-4 bl(60) Saleem Golam(5) 25/1:0
1774 **Bahamian Belle** 5 [15]4-8-13 bl(55) Dean Williams(5) 33/1:0
18 Ran Time 58.94(2.24) Owned: Mr J M Bradley Trained: Chepstow

---

NEWCASTLE THURSDAY 20.05.04 Lefthand, Galloping, Stiff Track

Official Going Good/Firm (Good places)

1868	2.20 Saltwell Signs Novice Stakes 2yo (D)				
	£3536 £1088 £544 **5f str** **Good 46** **-02 Slow** Centre				

1632* **ROYAL ISLAND** 12 [3] M Johnston 2-9-2 K Dalgleish 1/6 FAV: 11: Made all, rdn over 1f out & in 88+
command ins last, eased nr fin: well bckd at long odds-on: eff at 5f on a stiff trk, will get further: acts on gd
& soft grnd: useful, rate higher & win more races: see 1632.
1439* **UNLIMITED** 21 [5] Mrs A Duffield 2-9-0 G Duffield 8/1: 212: Chsd wnr, drvn & no impress from 2 75
dist: turf bow: acts on fibresand & gd grnd: prob ran to form of 1439 (mdn auct).
REGAL LUSTRE 0 [4] J R Weymes 2-8-7 R Winston 25/1: 3: b f Averti - Noble Lustre (Lyphard's 5 53
Wish) Dwelt, sn chsd front pair, no impress fnl 2f: Feb foal, cost 11,500 gns: sister to a 7f 3yo wnr, also
prolific 6f wnr Doctor Dennis: dam a 6f wnr: get further, could improve.
GRACIES GIFT 0 [1] P C Haslam 2-8-12 G Faulkner 10/1: 4: b c Imperial Ballet - Settle Petal hd 58
(Roi Danzig) Bhd & drvn, al outpcd: op 12/1: Feb foal, 8,000 gns 2yo: half brother stayed 1m.
4 Ran Time 1m 0.6 (2.4) Owned: Mr Markus Graff Trained: Middleham

---

1869	2.50 Culture 10 Claiming Stakes 2yo (F)				
	£3087 £882 £441 **6f str** **Good 46** **-26 Slow** Centre				

1439 **RONNIES LAD** 21 [5] J R Norton 2-8-7 Darren Williams 33/1: 501: b g Lake Coniston - Lycius Touch 63
(Lycius) Sn rdn chsg ldrs, switched & styd on strongly ins last to lead cl-home: claimed by G L Moore for 7,000:
cheaply bought Mar foal, brother to a 6f juv wnr, dam a 5f juv wnr: apprec step up to a stiff 6f, get further
on this evidence: acts on gd grnd: imprvd here on turf bow & drop to clmg grade.
1653 **STRAFFAN** 10 [4] E J O'Neill 2-8-8 J Carroll 6/1: 6332: Led, rdn & hdd nr fin: op 4/1: styd nk 63
stiff 6f well: acts on gd, soft & fibresand: could land similar: see 1653 & 1303.
1751 **JOSHAR** 5 [12] M W Easterby 2-8-4 Dale Gibson 11/1: 03033: Chsd ldrs & ch over 1f out, no extra 2½ 52
ins last: handles gd & soft grnd, poss fibresand: stays a stiff 6f in clmg grade: see 1751 & 1394.
1652 **TURTLE MAGIC** 10 [11] W G M Turner 2-8-8 C Haddon(7) 2/1 FAV: 023664: Trkd ldrs & ch over 1f out, shd 55
no extra ins last: styd longer 6f trip on this drop to clmg grade: handles gd & soft grnd: see 1161.
1677 **PROCRASTINATE** 8 [10]2-8-13 P Mathers(7) 7/1: 3065: Slow away, sn handy & ch over 1f out, no extra. 1¾ 55
1677 **MOUNT EPHRAM** 8 [1]2-8-13 P Bradley(5) 9/1: 456: Held up, short of room halfway, prog when hmpd ½ 53
2f out, kept on late, closer with a clr run: op 16/1: see 1037.
LOJO 0 [3]2-8-8 T Hamilton(3) 16/1: 7: ch f Pivotal - Myhat (Factual) Slow away & rear, kept on 3½ 38
late, nvr threat: cheaply bought Apr 1st foal, dam a 6f juv wnr, sire high-class sprinter.
1744 **FRANSISCAN** 6 [8]2-9-1 G Faulkner 20/1: 08: ch g Fraam - Ordained (Mtoto) Mid-div, no prog fnl 2 39

2f: left debut bhd: Feb 1st foal, 6,000 gns purchase: dam a multiple 10/12f wnr & half sister to a 9/12f wnr.
SAMALAN 0 [2]2-8-9 G Duffield 33/1: 9: Drvn & al rear. 5 **18**
1303 **FRISBY RIDGE 28** [9]2-8-8 BL K Dalgleish 10/1: 050: 10th: Dwelt, handy till over 2f out, blnks, op 7/1. 1½ **13**
1831 **Fold Walk 2** [6]2-8-8 P Mulrennan(5) 12/1:0 1653 **Voice Of An Angel 10** [7]2-8-8 F Norton 12/1:0
12 Ran Time 1m 15.52 (4.32) Owned: The Matthewman Partnership Trained: Barnsley

1870

3.25 Putter & Flutter Handicap Stakes 4yo+ 0-70 (E) **[70]**
£4105 £1263 £632 **2m19y** **Good 46** **-08 Slow** Centre

2839} **RED SUN 313** [6] J Mackie 7-8-6 t (48) R Winston 100/30 FAV: 00/3/244-1: b g Foxhound - Superetta (Superlative) Made all & rdn clr from 5f out, in command fnl 2f, rdly: nicely bckd on Flat reapp, jumps fit (prog 03/04, landed 3 h'caps, 2m/2m3f, fast & hvy, rtd 129h): lightly rcd '03, h'cap rnr-up: AW h'cap plcd '02 (rtd 46a, A Streeter): eff at 14f/2m1f on firm, fast & fibresand, prob any trk: suited by forcing tactics & a t-strap. **59**
2 Jun'03 Pont 17.1g/f 43-41 E: 1 May'01 Sout 14af 50a-43 F: 2 Apr'01 Sout 11af 43a-42 G:
107 **ACADEMY 176** [8] Andrew Turnell 9-9-0 (56) C Catlin 5/1: 220240-2: ch g Archway - Dream Academy (Town And Country) Held up, rdn & styd on fnl 2f, no impress on wnr: bckd: reapp: multiple h'cap rnr-up '03, prog '02, landed 5 h'caps: suited by 14f/2m3f on firm, gd, handles fibresand, any trk, likes Catterick: can go well fresh: most consistent & tough, a gd return, could find similar. 2 Oct'03 Pont 17.1g/f 60-58 E: 5 **59**
2 Sep'03 Newc 16.1g/f 59-57 E:2 Aug'03 Pont 17.1g/f 59-56 F:2 Jul'03 Redc 16.0gd 55-53 E:
1 Oct'02 Catt 15.8fm 58-55 F:1 Aug'02 Pont 17.1g/f 53-51 F:1 Aug'02 Catt 13.7g/f 51-46 E:
1396 **BERRYWHITE 24** [4] C Grant 6-7-12 (40) J Mackay 8/1: 200-0033: Chsd ldrs, rdn & chsd wnr over 3f out, no impress bef dist: bckd, op 9/1, prob stays 2m: handles gd & soft grnd: see 867. 1½ **42**
1252 **GREEN N GOLD 31** [5] M D Hammond 4-8-13 (57) K Darley 11/2: 0400-104: Held up, drvn & kept on fnl 2f, short of room cl-home but nvr a threat: ran to form of 1069 (hvy). hd **59**
965 **ALMNADIA 52** [2]5-8-8 P (50) I Mongan 4/1: 15005/-05: b f Alhaarth - Mnaafa (Darshaan) Chsd ldrs, drvn & btn 2f out: bckd tho' op 5/1: tried cheek pieces, jumps fit (unplcd, rtd 109h, h'cap): missed '03 on the Level: AW sell & turf sell h'cap wnr '02: eff at 12f yet to convince beyond (get 3m over timber): acts on polytrack & fast, sharp or stiff trk: wore cheek pieces today, wng form without. 4 **48**
1 Jul'02 Pont 12g/f 54-51 F: 1 Jun'02 Ling 12ap 51a- G:
4931} **ROYAL CASTLE 205** [1]10-8-4 (46) R Ffrench 7/1: 140030-6: Mid-div, outpcd fnl 4f: reapp. 2½ **41**
1637 **AUTUMN FANTASY 12** [3]5-9-4 (60) T Eaves(5) 16/1: 0000-407: Prom till over 2f out: btr 1459. 4 **51**
478 **DANCE LIGHT 117** [7]5-9-6 (62) T G McLaughlin 8/1: 6/0600-08: Held up, chsd wnr 2f out, wknd qckly. 5 **48**
1551 **MARINO MOU 16** [10]4-8-1 (45) A McCarthy 20/1: 006309: Held up, eff 4f out, sn btn. 9 **22**
9 Ran Time 3m 34.26 (8.76) Owned: Bulls Head Racing Club Trained: Church Broughton

1871

4.00 Northumberland Plate Three Day Festival Median Auction Maiden Stakes 3yo (E)
£3526 £1085 £543 **1m2f32y** **Good 46** **-01 Slow** Far Side

WHATS UP DOC 202 [5] M Johnston 3-9-0 (82) K Dalgleish 4/5 FAV: 533-1: b c Dr Massini - Surprise Treat (Shalford) Made all, hung left fnl 2f but al in command, rdly: hvly bckd, op 13/8: reapp: Brit bow, ex-Irish: dual mdn plcd '03 (lightly rcd): eff at 1m, apprec step up to 10f with forcing tactics, further shld suit: acts on gd & soft, sharp or stiff trk: goes well fresh: type to progress with racing. **83+**
4786} **ATLANTIC CITY 216** [2] W J Haggas 3-9-0 (71) K Darley 11/4: 622-2: ch g First Trump - Pleasuring (Good Times) Handy & chsd wnr from 4f out, rdn & no impress fnl 2f: op 2/1, well clr of rem on reapp: dual auct mdn rnr-up '03 (small fields, rtd 77 at best, mdn, debut): eff at 1m, this longer 10f trip could suit: acts on fast & gd grnd, stiff/undul or sharp trk. 2 Oct'03 Redc 8g/f 74- E: 2 Sep'03 Muss 8g/f 73- E: 5 **73**
1241 **DANCING BEAR 33** [4] Julian Poulton 3-9-0 (62) N Pollard 11/1: 0-403: Chsd ldrs, no impress on front pair fnl 2f: likely to apprec low grade mid-dist h'caps: see 930. 12 **53**
ASTON LAD 0 [3] M D Hammond 3-9-0 Darren Williams 25/1: 4: b c Bijou d'Inde - Fishki (Niniski) Held up, rdn 3f out, no impress on debut: half brother to a 6f sell wnr, also a wnr over fences & a 2m2f wnr on the Level: dam a multiple wnr on the Level & hdles/fences: stoutly bred. 2 **50**
1428 **EMPRESS EUGENIE 22** [6]3-8-9 J Carroll 7/1: 465: Cl-up, rdn & btn 3f out: btr 1258 (debut, 1m). 6 **35**
1636 **MILLY GOLIGHTLY 12** [1]3-8-9 L Enstone(3) 50/1: 06: Held up, drvn & no prog 4f out: longer trip. hd **35**
MATRIMONY 0 [7]3-9-0 T I Mongan 14/1: P: Dwelt, sn rdn rear, no ch fnl 2f, p.u. & dismounted: op 8/1, wore a t-strap on debut. **0**
7 Ran Time 2m 11.17 (4.67) Owned: Mr James Monaghan Trained: Middleham

1872

4.30 Bbc Radio Newcastle Handicap Stakes 3yo 0-70 (E) **[77]**
£4053 £1247 £624 **1m3y rnd** **Good 46** **-12 Slow** Centre

1395 **EGO TRIP 24** [6] M W Easterby 3-8-1 (50) Dale Gibson 20/1: 60000-01: Pushed along towards rear, styd on for press from over 2f out & switched/led cl-home: first win: eff at 6f, now stays a stiff 1m well, could get further: acts on firm & gd grnd, sharp or stiff trk: see 1395. **57**
1124 **CHARLIE BEAR 38** [12] E A L Dunlop 3-9-4 (67) J Carroll 9/1: 500-02: ch c Bahamian Bounty - Abi (Chief's Crown) Led till rdn & hdd cl-home: op 7/1: left reapp bhd: lightly rcd & unplcd '03 (rtd 70): dam a 10f wnr: eff over stiff 1m, tried 11f, may yet suit: acts on gd grnd: enjoyed forcing tactics today. 1 **71**
1603 **TIME TO RELAX 13** [3] J J Quinn 3-9-3 (66) K Dalgleish 6/1: 0-241023: Mid-div, eff from over 2f out, no extra when bmpd cl-home: op 11/2: remains in gd heart: see 1603 & 1099. ¾ **68**
1603 **RARE COINCIDENCE 13** [14] R F Fisher 3-9-4 p (67) J F Egan 12/1: 1136044: Handy & ch 2f out, no extra/bmpd well ins last, also bhd today's 3rd latest: acts on fibresand & gd grnd: see 564 (AW). hd **67**
1628 **FUTOO 12** [7]3-8-12 (61) N Pollard 12/1: 60106-65: Chsd ldrs over 2f out, no extra ins last: wants 7f. 1¾ **58**
1554 **JOSHUAS GOLD 16** [4]3-8-9 (58) R Fitzpatrick 13/2: 3555-236: Held up, eff 2f out, not pace to chall. 2 **51**
1679* **DANCE TO MY TUNE 8** [13]3-8-11 (6ex) (60) P Mulrennan(5) 13/2: 0606-617: Dwelt & held up, not pace to chall: btr 1679 (soft). 3 **47**
4997} **COBALT BLUE 198** [10]3-8-6 (55) K Darley 4/1 FAV: 0000-8: b g Bluebird - Amy Hunter (Jade Hunter) Mid-div, no prog fnl 2f: nicely bckd on reapp: unplcd '03 (rtd 61, mdn): bred to apprec this 1m trip. 1½ **40**
1577 **VRISAKI 14** [8]3-8-4 P (53) T Williams 33/1: 00-2049: Cl-up when hmpd after 2f, btn 3f out: cheekpieces. 5 **28**
190 **RESTART 159** [11]3-9-0 (63) L Enstone(3) 25/1: 6030-0: 10th: b g Revoque - Stargard (Polish Precedent) Held up, nvr a factor on reapp: lightly rcd '03, AW mdn plcd (rtd 68a, turf unplcd, rtd 50, debut): stays 7f on fibresand. nk **37**

NEWCASTLE THURSDAY 20.05.04 Lefthand, Galloping, Stiff Track

1628 **DARK DAY BLUES 12** [9]3-9-3 (66) Darren Williams 25/1: 6230-000: 11th: In tch, btn 2f out: btr 1176.   1¼   37
1147 **REEDSMAN 38** [5]3-8-1 (50) F Norton 25/1: 0000-200: 12th: Al bhd: btr 495 (6f, AW).   3½   14
1171 **SHEBAAN 36** [2]3-8-6 (55) A McCarthy 50/1: 2U050-00: 13th: Dwelt & al bhd: btr 1171.   7   5
1534* **PREMIER DREAM 16** [1]3-9-7 (70) J Fanning 5/1: 66310: 14th: Cl-up till 3f out, sn bhd: ran as if   12   0
something amiss after 1534 (hvy, made all).
14 Ran   Time 1m 41.68 (4.68)   Owned: Mr K Hodgson & Mrs J Hodgson   Trained: Sheriff Hutton

1873   5.05 Shields Gazette Handicap Stakes Fillies 3yo+ 0-75 (E)   [74]
       £3799 £1169 £585   **5f str**   **Good 46**   +10 Fast   Centre. 2 Groups.

1555 **LADY PROTECTOR 16** [12] J Balding 5-7-13 (45) Dale Gibson 14/1: 1030001: Held up stands side, led   54
ins last, rdn out: op 12/1, best time of day: eff at 5/6f on fast, gd/soft & fibresand: see 374.
1726 **MUSICAL FAIR 6** [14] J A Glover 4-10-0 (74) S Carson 10/1: 340-0002: Trkd ldrs stands side & led   1½   77
ins last, sn hdd, kept on: imprvd eff for this drop to 5f: quick reapp: acts on firm & gd grnd: see 1726.
1615 **LADY PEKAN 13** [10] P S McEntee 5-9-1 bl (61) T G McLaughlin 14/1: 0022003: Led stands side till   ½   62
ins last, onepace: see 1293, 1096 & 234.
1638 **ROMAN MISTRESS 12** [7] T D Easterby 4-9-6 (66) K Dalgleish 8/1: 20000-04: ch f Titus Livius -   shd   67+
Repique (Sharpen Up) Held up far side, styd on for press to lead that group ins last, not reach ldrs stands side:
h'cap wnr '03: mdn wnr '02: eff at 5/6f, stays a sharp 7f: acts on fast & gd/soft grnd, prob any trk: first home
on unfavoured side, h'capped to win & one to keep in mind. 2 Aug'03 Thir 5g/s 77-76 D: 1 Jun'03 Hayd 5g/f 78-75 D:
2 Aug'02 Catt 6gd 80-76 D: 2 Jun'02 Ripo 5g/f 81- E: 1 Jun'02 Newc 5g/s 79- D:
1627 **KARMINSKEY PARK 12** [4]5-9-2 (62) R Winston 3/1 FAV: 440-6265: Slow away & bhd far side, hdwy to   shd   63
dspte lead in that group ins last, not pace of ldrs stands side: gd run: see 1532.
1782 **COLLEGE QUEEN 4** [3]6-9-7 P (67) I Mongan 11/1: 55400-07: b f Lugana Beach - Eccentric Dancer   ½   66
(Rambo Dancer) Prom far side & led that group over 1f out till ins last: quick reapp: improvement here in 1st time
cheek pieces: dual fills h'cap wnr '03 (apprec blnks): dual fills h'cap wnr '02: loves to force the pace at 6f on
firm & gd grnd, prob any trk: best blnkd, has tried t-strap. 1 Aug'03 Nott 6.1g/f 71-62 D:
1 Aug'03 Folk 6g/f 67-56 F: 2 Aug'02 Newm 6fm 62-60 E: 1 Aug'02 Folk 6fm 60-54 F: 1 Jul'02 Thir 6g/f 52-49 D:
1555 **COLLEGE MAID 16** [6]7-8-2 bl (48) J F Egan 8/1: 006-4067: Mid-div, far side, not pace to chall: see 1096.   ½   46
1508 **TANCRED TIMES 18** [2]9-8-10 (56) L Enstone(3) 7/1: 000-0448: Led far side till over 1f out, wknd.   ½   52
3747} **BETTYS PRIDE 274** [1]5-9-2 (62) Darren Williams 20/1: 0/00600-9: Trkd ldrs, short of room over 1f out.   1   55
1555 **MYSTERY PIPS 16** [11]4-8-5 vis (51) Kim Tinkler 20/1: 43415-00: 10th: Mid-div stands side, hung   1¾   39
left & btn over 1f out.
1441 **OBE BOLD 21** [13]3-8-6 (60) F Norton 14/1: 3000-430: 11th: Prom stands side till over 1f out: btr 1441.   ½   46
1096 **TAMARELLA 42** [5]4-8-10 (56) A McCarthy 16/1: 00-00050: 12th: Prom far side till 2f out, abs: see 767.   4   30
4528} **BLUES PRINCESS 233** [9]4-8-10 (56) T Hamilton 20/1: 7/1: 04/0000-0: 13th: Strugg halfway, op 12/1.   2½   23
13 Ran   Time 59.98(1.78)   Owned: Simon Mapletoft Racing II   Trained: Doncaster

DONCASTER THURSDAY 20.05.04 Lefthand, Flat, Galloping Track

Official Going Good/Firm (Firm Places)

1874   6.20 Sky Bet Press Red To Bet Now Maiden Auction Stakes 2yo (E)
       £3591 £1105 £553   **6f str**   **Good/Firm 20**   -27 Slow   Stands side

962 **INDIBRAUN 52** [13] P C Haslam 2-8-7   G Faulkner 7/2 FAV: 51: b g Indian Rocket - The Aspecto Girl   84
(Alzao) Made all, edged left ins fnl 2f, rdn out: well bckd after 7 wk abs: Apr foal, cost 10,500 gns: half
brother to wnrs at 6/8f: dam mdn: sire high-class performer at sprint dists: eff at 6f, 7f shld suit: acts on
fast grnd & a gall trk: goes well fresh: imprvd eff here after being gldd since debut: can rate higher.
1249 **ROCKBURST 31** [8] K R Burke 2-8-2   A Nicholls 8/1: 52: b f Xaar - Topwinder (Topsider) Keen   1½   72
handy, chsd ldr ins fnl 1f, al held: op 13/2: Mar foal, cost 7,500 gns: half sister to wnrs at 5/10f: dam unplcd:
sire high-class performer as a juv: eff at 6f, 7f shld suit: acts on fast grnd: encouraging run & can improve.
     MR KALANDI 0 [14] P W D'Arcy 2-8-9   Paul Eddery 12/1: 3: gr c Grand Lodge - Singhana (Mouktar)   2   73
Handy, onepcd from dist: debut: Mar foal, cost 22,000 gns: dam 14f wnr: sire high-class performer at 1m/10f: eff
at 6f, further will suit in time: acts on fast grnd: gd start.
1212 **MIMI MOUSE 34** [7] T D Easterby 2-8-4   D Allan(3) 8/1: 64: Handy over 4f, sn onepcd: see 1212.   1½   64
     SATIN ROSE 0 [12]2-8-2   J Mackay 33/1: 5: Rear, prog halfway, nrst fin: debut.   1¾   57
1471 **PIDDIES PRIDE 19** [1]2-8-2   G Duffield 16/1: 56: Handy over 4f, wknd: see 1471.   1½   53
     SHINGLE STREET 0 [11]2-8-9   P Robinson 15/2: 7: Rear, prog halfway, sn ran green & hung left,   2½   53
wknd: op 10/1 on debut: with M H Tompkins.
     BOND CITY 0 [2]2-8-9   F Lynch 9/1: 8: Cl-up over 4f, wknd: op 15/2 on debut.   1   50
     SAINT CLEMENTS 0 [5]2-8-11   R Ffrench 6/1: 9: Handy 4f, edged left & sn wknd: debut.   nk   51
1161 **MIRAGE PRINCE 36** [4]2-8-7   C Catlin 25/1: 60: 10th: Handy, wknd fnl 2f.   ½   46
     Zarova 0 [3]2-9-0 A Culhane 16/1:0   **Hamburg Springer 0** [9]2-8-7 J F McDonald(3) 33/1:0
     Belton 0 [10]2-8-7 Dean McKeown 33/1:0   **Dishdasha 0** [6]2-8-9 G Gibbons 16/1:0
14 Ran   Time 1m 13.63 (2.83)   Owned: Mr D Browne   Trained: Middleham

1875   6.50 South Yorkshire Times Stakes Handicap 3yo+ 0-75 (E)   [74]
       £3552 £1093 £547   **1m4f**   **Good/Firm 20**   -23 Slow   Inside

1357 **MARITIME BLUES 26** [9] J G Given 4-8-12 (58) A Culhane 11/2: 560-0001: Handy, prog to lead 2f   66+
out, pushed clr, val 7L+: eff at 1m/10f, apprec step up to 12f: acts on firm, gd & fibresand: well h'capped 4yo
who now here in fine style, unexposed at this trip & can follow up: see 1164.
5010} **SWYNFORD PLEASURE 197** [3] J Hetherton 8-8-7 (53) D Allan(3) 14/1: 100050-2: b f Reprimand -   5   55
Pleasuring (Good Times) Held up, prog after 7f, short of room 2f out, styd on to chase wnr ins fnl 1f, al held:
reapp: won 3 h'caps in '03: h'cap wnr in '02 (also plcd 5 times): suited by 10/12f on firm or gd grnd, handles
gd/soft: enjoys a strong pace: likes Beverley: sharper for this gd return & is on winning mark.

1 Aug'03 Ripo 12.3g/f 62-58 D: 1 Aug'03 Beve 12.1g/f 58-52 E: 1 Jun'03 Pont 12.0g/f 53-49 D:
2 May'03 Yarm 10.1g/f 53-50 F: 2 Aug'02 Beve 9.9g/f 61-60 D: 1 Jun'02 Beve 9.9g/f 62-59 D:
2 Jun'02 Redc 10fm 61-59 C: 2 Jun'02 Beve 8.4gd 60-59 D: 2 Oct'01 Leic 8g/s 64-63 E:

1821 **MICHAELS DREAM** 2 [8] J Hetherton 5-7-12 (4oh) (40) J McAuley 15/2: 0300-633: Handy 10f, sn onepcd: quick reapp: op 13/2: just btr 1821.	2½	42
918 **PERESTROIKA** 56 [4] B Ellison 6-9-0 (60) T Eaves(5) 28/1: 5050/-004: ch g Ashkalani - Licentious (Reprimand) Held up, prog 3f out, nrst fin: 8 wk abs: missed '03: rnr-up 1st time out in '02 (h'cap, subs disapp, E A L Dunlop): won 2 h'caps in '01: eff at 14f on soft, likes fast & firm grnd: likes Yarmouth: has gone well fresh: not disgraced here & is well h'capped for new yard.	¾	56

2 May'02 Kemp 14.4g/f 77-76 D: 1 Jul'01 Yarm 14fm 76-73 E: 1 Jun'01 Yarm 14g/f 77-67 E:

1009 **DISTANT COUSIN** 50 [7]7-9-4 vis (64) D Holland 7/1: 22256-05: Handy, no extra 2f out: 7 wk abs.	shd	59
1693 **MERRYMAKER** 8 [10]4-8-13 bl (59) G Baker 7/1: 03433-46: Slow away, prog after 5f, no impress fnl 2f.	shd	53
1516 **KIROV KING** 17 [2]4-9-10 (70) P Robinson 11/2: 0460-007: Keen handy, wknd fnl 2f: bckd from 10/1.	5	57
1254 **LIBERTY SEEKER** 31 [5]5-9-0 P (60) S Hitchcott(3) 14/1: 3/0000-08: ch g Machiavellian - Samara (Polish Patriot) Rear, nvr a factor: won 2 nov hdles in 03/04 (rtd 122h, G A Swinbank): unplcd in '03 (rtd 75): plcd in 2 of only 3 '02 starts (rtd 52a & 83, M R Channon): eff at 1m, prob stays 12f: acts on fibresand & soft.	1¼	45
4664} **NIGHT SIGHT** 224 [11]7-9-7 (67) C Catlin 8/1: 650004-9: Keen handy, led 3f out, hdd 2f out, fdd.	nk	51
1361 **JADEERON** 26 [6]5-9-4 p (64) Lisa Jones(3) 5/1 FAV: 2234400: 10th: Mid-div, wknd 2f out: btr 1118.	3½	43
1610 **INMOM** 13 [1]3-7-12 (61) J Bramhill 33/1: 50-30: 11th: Led till 3f out, sn fdd: btr 1610 (1m, hvy).	dist	15

11 Ran   Time 2m 35.02 (5.22)   Owned: Downlands Racing   Trained: Gainsborough

---

1876   7.20 Lakeside Village Median Auction Maiden Stakes 3-4yo (E)
£3582 £1102 £551   6f str   Good/Firm 20   -29 Slow   Stands side, rcd two groups

1477 **NEON BLUE** 12 [12] R M Whitaker 3-8-9 (68) M Hills 9/2: 04040-51: Handy stands side, led dist, rdn out: op 6/1: eff at 5/6f on fast & gd/soft grnd: gd confidence boost: see 1477.		72
1607 **KENSINGTON** 13 [10] R Guest 3-8-9 (67) J Carroll 15/2: 3064-632: Handy stands side, prog & ev ch ins fnl 1f, just held by wnr: eff at 6f on fast & gd: see 1607 & 1270.	1	68
1690 **FAIR OPTIONS** 8 [7] H J Cyzer 3-8-9 G Carter 14/1: 003: gr c Marju - Silver Singing (Topsider) Rcd far side, slow away, prog 2f out, kept on fnl 1f, just held by stands side: eff at 6f, further shld suit: acts on fast grnd: gd eff fin 1st home on unfav far side, can rate higher & now quals for h'caps.	nk	66+
1765 **AMANDAS LAD** 5 [9] M C Chapman 4-9-4 (65) L Vickers 33/1: 6635504: Led stands side group till dist, kept on & not btn far in 4th: away reapp: see 999.	shd	66
1497 **ISAZ** 18 [13]4-9-4 (73) D Sweeney 4/1 JT FAV: 025/4-555: Handy stands side, kept on ins fnl 1f.	½	65
1228 **TRUE MAGIC** 33 [1]3-8-4 (65) P Robinson 16/1: 3306-56: b f Magic Ring - True Precision (Presidium) Led far side group, hdd ins fnl 1f: plcd once in '03 (rtd 71, auct mdn): eff at 5/6f on fast & gd.	¾	58
4308} **TRUMAN** 245 [16]3-8-9 S Sanders 7/1: 5-7: b c Entrepreneur - Sabria (Miswaki) Mid-div stands side, prog dist, nrst fin: reapp: 5th of 6 on side '03 start (cond stks, rtd 65): eff at 6f, bred to apprec further.	nk	62
1518 **IRUSAN** 17 [2]4-9-4 Leanne Kershaw(7) 66/1: 68: Cl-up far side, onepcd fnl 1f: see 1518.	shd	61
3147} **ALFELMA** 300 [19]4-8-13 (47) A Nicholls 100/1: 0/3000-9: Handy stands side over 4f, wknd.	8	34
1464 **SOVIET SCEPTRE** 20 [3]3-8-9 (73) K Darley 4/1 JT FAV: 56-30: 10th: Handy far side, wknd dist: better expected after recent 3rd in 1464 (soft).	1½	35
RAETIHI 0 [15]3-8-6 (2ow) N Callan 66/1/:0: 11th: Mid-div stands side, wknd fnl 2f.	1	29

973 Quintillion 52 [20]3-8-9 T Eaves(5) 50/1:0		Parliament Act 0 [4]3-8-9 T G Gibbons 25/1:0	
1575 Radlett Lady 14 [6]3-8-4 C Catlin 50/1:0		Judda 0 [17]3-8-9 Dean McKeown 33/1:0	
1345} Feed The Meter 382 [14]4-8-13 J Mackay 66/1:0		Lord Of The Fens 0 [11]4-9-4 G Baker 100/1:0	
1230 Tikitano 388 [5]3-8-4 R Ffrench 25/1:0		Barholm Charlie 0 [18]3-8-9 J Bramhill 33/1:0	

19 Ran   Time 1m 13.74 (2.94)   Owned: Country Lane Partnership   Trained: Scarcroft

---

1877   7.50 Stoneacre Group Classified Stakes 3yo+ 0-80 (D)
£5688 £1750 £875   1m str   Good/Firm 20   +04 Fast   Stands side

1475 **MYSTIC MAN** 19 [7] K A Ryan 6-9-4 (82) N Callan 16/1: 00-00001: Handy, styd on to lead dist, pushed clr, readily: suited by 7f/1m, has tried 10f: acts on firm, soft & fibresand: back to best.		90+
4619} **LANGFORD** 227 [12] M H Tompkins 4-9-2 (79) G Duffield 16/1: 223136-2: ch g Compton Place - Sharpening (Sharpo) Chsd ldrs, styd on to lead 2f out, hdd dist, not recover: reapp: mdn wnr in '03 (also plcd 7 times): rnr-up fnl '02 start (h'cap): eff at 1m, will apprec return to 9.7f/10f: acts on firm & gd grnd: decent start to campaign & can find similar bef long. 4 May'03 Folk 9.7g/f 78-(75) D:	2½	81

2 Jul'03 Leic 10.0g/f 76-(75) F: 2 Jul'03 Sand 10.0g/f 76-73 D: 2 Apr'03 Pont 10.0g/f 73-70 D:
2 Apr'03 Yarm 10.1gd 76-(70) E: 2 Oct'02 Wind 8.3g/f 71-68 E: 2 Sep'02 Yarm 8g/f 69-65 E:

1664 **WEET A HEAD** 9 [2] R Hollinshead 3-8-4 (80) W Supple 16/1: 63-53563: In tch, prog 2f out, onepcd fnl 1f.	nk	80
1512 **DEVANT** 17 [6] M A Jarvis 4-9-2 (83) P Robinson 7/1: 10605-04: b f Zabeel - Frenetic (Truly Vain) Held up, prog 2f out, onepcd ins fnl 1f: won 2 h'caps in '03: mdn wnr on last of only 2 '02 starts: suited by 7f/1m, has tried 10f: acts on fast & gd/soft grnd, likes to race with/force the pace: gd effort.	hd	79
1475 **TEDSTALE** 19 [5]6-9-4 bl (82) D Allan(3) 20/1: 2604-005: ch g Irish River - Carefree Kate (Lyphard) Bhd, prog halfway, onepcd fnl 2f: h'cap wnr 1st time out in '03: h'cap wnr in '01, also plcd sev times: stays 11f, suited by 1m/10f on firm or gd grnd, eff with/without blnks: has gone well fresh.	3	75

2 Jun'03 York 8.9fm 88-84 B: 2 Jun'03 Newc 8fm 86-83 D: 1 Apr'03 Newc 8.0g/f 81-78 D: 2 Aug'02 Thir 8g/s 85-84 C:
2 May'02 Ripo 8g/s 85-84 C: 1 May'02 Thir 8fm 87-80 C: 1 Oct'01 Pont 8g/s 80-73 D: 1 Jul'01 Beve 8.4fm 76-72 D:

1586 **LINNING WINE** 14 [8]8-9-4 (82) K Darley 9/2: 21-002406: Rear, no run fnl 2f, not recover, late gains: forgive this: see 928.	nk	74
1475 **ATLANTIC ACE** 19 [3]7-9-2 (78) F Lynch 33/1: 0105-007: Dwelt, nvr nrr than mid-div.	2	68
2895} **MORNING AFTER** 311 [16]4-8-13 (78) O Urbina 14/1: 3122/43-8: Handy 6f, sn wknd: reapp.	½	64
1423 **TOPTON** 22 [15]10-9-2 bl (78) R Winston 14/1: 1-431009: Slow away, al in rear: btr 714.	¾	65
4478} **OBRIGADO** 236 [4]4-9-2 (80) D Holland 7/2 FAV: 4216-0: 10th: Keen cl-up, wknd ins fnl 2f, sn eased: better expected here on reapp.	6	53
1530 **KENTUCKY KING** 17 [9]4-9-3 (81) A Culhane 20/1: 0103000: 11th: Bhd, nvr a factor: btr 1057.	1¼	52
1461* **LOVE IN SEATTLE** 20 [10]4-9-2 (80) K Dalgleish 5/1: 422-010: 12th: Led till 6f out, wknd fnl 3f:	¾	49

v disappointing here back on a fast surface: btr 1461 (good/soft).
1530 **JOHANNIAN** 17 [13]6-9-2 (79) S Carson 33/1: 54/005-00: 13th: Led 6f out, hdd 2f out, fdd.   ¾   47
1586 **BLUE PATRICK** 14 [1]4-9-2 (80) T G McLaughlin 66/1: 1600-000: 14th: Handy 6f, fdd.   9   31
14 Ran   Time 1m 37.79 (1.29)   Owned: R J H Limited   Trained: Hambleton

---

1878   8.20 Hatfields Chrysler Crossfire Handicap Fillies 3yo+ 0-80 (D)   [88]
£5736 £1765 £883   **6f str**   **Good/Firm 20**   **+00 Fast**   Stands side

1477 **MIS CHICAF** 19 [10] J S Wainwright 3-8-10 (70) R Winston 9/2 CO FAV: 53501-21: Made all, al trav   80+
well, rdn out fnl 1f: eff at 5f/6f on fast & gd/soft grnd: fine win here against older rivals: unexposed in h'cap
grade & more prizes await: enjoyed dominating: see 1477.
4979} **FAVOUR** 201 [8] Mrs J R Ramsden 4-9-6 (71) I Mongan 13/2: 610223-2: b f Gothenberg - Prejudice   1½   73
(Young Generation) Keen mid-div, prog halfway, kept on ins fnl 1f, al held by easy wnr: reapp: h'cap wnr in '03
(also plcd 3 times): won sole '02 start (fills mdn): eff at 6f/7f on firm & soft grnd: acts on Flat & stiff/gall
trk: far from disgraced here & can find similar.
2 Oct'03 Newc 6gd 69-67 E: 2 Oct'03 Leic 6.0g/f 71-67 E: 1 Sep'03 Thir 6fm 42-62 E: 1 Oct'02 Redc 6sft 70- D:
1782 **CONSENSUS** 4 [9] M Brittain 5-10-0 (79) T Williams 9/2 CO FAV: 600-4003: Handy, hung left & no   1¾   76
extra from dist: quick reapp: not disgraced under top weight: btr 921.
1750 **PRINCESS ERICA** 5 [5] J Balding 4-8-0 (2ow)(1oh)p (48) F Norton 33/1: 305-0004: Trkd ldrs till   1½   44
dist, no extra: quick reapp: see 1750.
1337 **BINT ROYAL** 26 [6]6-8-9 p (60) D Holland 8/1: 20010-55: Handy, outpcd halfway, rallied fnl 1f.   ¾   51
1660 **JUST ONE SMILE** 10 [2]4-8-11 (62) D Allan(3) 9/2 CO FAV: 2142-036: Slow away, prog when short of   nk   52+
room 2f out, mod late gains: btr 1660.
1046 **PLAYFUL SPIRIT** 45 [4]5-7-12 (2oh)vis (47) J Bramhill 12/1: 6330037: Handy 4f, sn wknd: 6 wk abs.   2   33
1465 **BOWLING ALONG** 20 [7]3-7-12 (58) R Ffrench 25/1: 25300-58: Bhd when no room after 2f, nvr a factor.   3½   32
1269 **TAPAU** 30 [3]6-9-6 (71) S Carson 11/1: 32130-59: Handy, wknd fnl 2f: btr 1269.   ¾   43
5006} **OFFICERS PINK** 197 [1]4-9-5 t (70) K Darley 6/1: 624135-0: 10th: ch f Grand Lodge - Arethusa   23   2
(Primo Dominie) Handy till halfway, sn hung left & wknd, eased fnl 1f: reapp: mdn wnr in '03: fills mdn rnr-up in
'02: eff at 5/6f on firm & gd grnd: prob any trk: eff with a t-strap: with P F I Cole.
1 Aug'03 Ripo 5g/f 65-(69) D: 2 Aug'03 Thir 6g/f 69-65 E: 2 Aug'02 Beve 5gd 70- D:
10 Ran   Time 1m 12.04 (1.24)   Owned: Mr Anthony D Copley   Trained: Malton

---

1879   8.50 Sky Vegas Live On Channel 295 Stakes Handicap 3yo 0-85 (D)   [89]
£5899 £1815 £908   **7f str**   **Good/Firm 20**   **-05 Slow**   Stands side

1526 **KAMANDA LAUGH** 17 [2] B W Hills 3-9-2 (77) M Hills 7/4 FAV: 60-121: In tch, prog to lead bef 1f   86
out, rdn out to hold on: eff at 6f/7f on fast grnd, soft & polytrack: only lightly rcd & improving: see 1526.
1360 **REIDIES CHOICE** 26 [3] J G Given 3-8-11 (72) A Culhane 14/1: 20000-02: b g Royal Applause - Fairy   nk   79
Ring (Fairy King) Slow away, prog when short of room 2f out, swtchd & kept on fnl 1f, just held: med auct mdn wnr
1st time out in '03: eff at 5f, apprec step up to 7f: acts on firm & fast grnd, has disapp on soft: tried cheek
pieces: long way to find similar. 2 Jun'03 Beve 5g/f 89- D: 1 Jun'03 Kemp 5fm 86- E:
1707 **POPPYS FOOTPRINT** 7 [6] K A Ryan 3-9-0 (75) N Callan 9/1: 20-00053: Slow away, prog when short of   nk   81
room 2f out, kept on fnl 1f, not btn far in 3rd: quick reapp: apprec return to fast surface & is well h'capped.
1496 **OUTER HEBRIDES** 18 [4] D R Loder 3-9-2 (77) T P Queally(3) 7/1: 221-004: b g Efisio - Reuval   1   81
(Sharpen Up) Handy, edged right & onepcd from dist: med auct mdn wnr on fnl '03 start (also rnr-up twice): eff at
6/7f on fast grnd &fibresand, sharp/turning or undul trks: eff with/without visor: has been gldd since last term.
1 Aug'03 Wolv 6af 75a- F: 2 Jul'03 Folk 7g/f 84- E: 2 Jul'03 Catt 7g/f 76- E:
1488 **TIMES REVIEW** 19 [12]3-9-6 (81) K Darley 11/2: 32500-25: Led, hdd dist, wknd: btr 1488 (6f).   3½   78
1105 **WESTERN ROOTS** 40 [9]3-9-2 (77) S Sanders 12/1: 40-24006: Chsd ldrs, outpcd halfway, mod late gains.1½   71
4709} **SKY GALAXY** 220 [10]3-9-7 (82) D Holland 12/1: 215000-7: ch f Sky Classic - Fly To The Moon   1   74
(Blushing Groom) Handy 5f, sn wknd: reapp: med auct mdn wnr in '03: eff at 6f on firm grnd: acts on a stiff/gall
trk: with E A L Dunlop. 1 Jun'03 Redc 6fm 85- E: 2 May'03 Newm 6fm 86- D:
1348 **CAPETOWN GIRL** 26 [11]3-8-12 (73) G Faulkner 14/1: 2025-108: Handy, wknd fnl 2f.   2   61
1305 **KINGSMAITE** 28 [7]3-8-9 (70) J Bramhill 18/1: 4212-049: Keen handy, short of room after 2f, wknd fnl 3f.   7   44
1628 **MR MIDASMAN** 12 [5]3-8-2 (63) J Mackay 25/1: 41-60000: 10th: Slow away, prog halfway, wknd fnl 2f.   1¾   33
4293} **Nesnaas** 246 [8]3-8-11 (72) W Supple 20/1:0   1477 **Commander Bond** 19 [1]3-8-11 (72) F Lynch 33/1:0
12 Ran   Time 1m 24.99(1.79)   Owned: Mr John Sillett   Trained: Lambourn

---

HAYDOCK   FRIDAY 21.05.04   Lefthand, Flat, Galloping Track

Official Going Good/Firm

1880   2.00 Stella Molony Maiden Auction Stakes 2yo (E)
£3692 £1136 £568   **5f**   **Good/Firm 20**   **-18 Slow**   Centre

1503 **BECKERMET** 19 [5] R F Fisher 2-8-7 P Bradley(5) 8/1: 31: Dwelt, sn trkd ldrs, narrow lead ins   81
last, just prevailed, rdn out: confirmed debut promise: eff at 5f, get further: acts on fast & gd grnd, stiff/gall trks.
1517 **SPACE SHUTTLE** 18 [2] T D Easterby 2-8-7 D Allan(3) 6/4 FAV: 32: Al prom, rdn & outpcd 2f out,   shd   80
styd on well for press cl-home, just denied: handles fast & gd/soft grnd, crying out for 6f+: shld win sn.
1386 **GIFTED GAMBLE** 25 [10] K A Ryan 2-8-7 BL N Callan 12/1: 033: Dwelt, carried left start, sn handy   hd   79
& led 3f out till well ins last, just held: gd run in 1st time blnks: acts on fast & gd grnd: see 1386.
1567 **IM AIMEE** 16 [11] P D Evans 2-8-2 G Duffield 11/4: 26304: Went left start, led, hdd 3f out,   1½   69
short of room when onepace ins last: acts on polytrack, gd/soft & fast grnd: see 1212 & 882.
          AMPHITHEATRE 0 [1]2-8-7 S Carson 20/1: 5: b g Titus Livius - Crimson Ring (Persian Bold)   1   71
Mid-div, not able to chall: cheaply bought Apr foal, half brother to 2 juv wnrs abroad, dam unplcd: eff at 5f,
shaped as if 6f will suit: well clr of rem, gave encouragement.
1550 **MORNING WORLD** 17 [6]2-8-9 K Dalgleish 66/1: 006: b c Bahamian Bounty - Snap Cracker (Inchinor)   10   46
Trkd ldrs, no impress fnl 2f: well btn 2 starts prev: Jan 1st foal, 16,000 gns purchase: dam a multiple juv 5f wnr.

555

BOLD MINSTREL 0 [4]2-8-7   F Norton 8/1: 7: br c Bold Fact - Ponda Rosa (Case Law)   Sn outpcd: hd   43
bckd: Apr 1st foal, E7,000 purchase: dam 6f plcd juv & subs 6f 3yo wnr.
DANS HEIR 0 [9]2-8-7   G Faulkner 33/1: 8: Slow away & hmpd start, sn struggling.   2   37
COURTINTIME 0 [3]2-8-2   J Quinn 33/1: 9: Dwelt, mid-div, sn outpcd.   1½   27
OLDSTEAD FLYER 0 [7]2-8-7   R Fitzpatrick 50/1: 0: 10th: Slow away & al towards rear.   2   26
COUNTRYWIDE DREAM 0 [8]2-8-7   D Holland 20/1: 0: 11th: Dwelt, went right start, sn outpcd.   3   17
11 Ran   Time 1m 0.72 (1.92)   Owned: Great Head House Estates Limited   Trained: Ulverston

---

1881	2.35 Performance Car Hire Handicap Stakes 3yo 0-85 (D)	[88]
	£6078 £1870 £935 6f Good/Firm 20 -06 Slow Centre	

1722* **BRIDGEWATER BOYS 8** [3] K A Ryan 3-8-7 (5ex)[67] N Callan 10/1: 15-41311: Mid-div, rdn & hdwy   79
to lead ins last, drvn out: eff at 5/6f on firm, gd & fibresand, stiff or sharp trks: prog type: see 1722 & 510.
1417 **FLIPANDO 23** [2] T D Barron 3-9-1 (75) D Holland 7/1: 310-42: Mid-div & sn pushed along, ch dist,   shd   86
styd on for press: fine run, lightly raced: see 1417.
1734 **DELPHIE QUEEN 7** [11] S Kirk 3-9-7 (81) R Hughes 11/2: 54410-43: Held up, switched & styd on well   hd   91
ins last, nrst fin: op 4/1: acts on fast & gd grnd: caught the eye when unlucky latest: see 1734.
1360 **RED ROMEO 27** [9] G A Swinbank 3-9-1 (75) Dale Gibson 7/1: 2016-24: Led, edged left & hdd ins   hd   84
last, just held nr line: in gd form: see 1360.
1477 **TREASURE CAY 20** [5]3-9-1 BL T (75) Paul Eddery 14/1: 1-535: Slow away, rear, eff from over 2f   nk   83
out, no extra ins last: handles fast, gd/soft & polytrack: stays 6f: fair run in blnks/t-strap.
1605 **HES A ROCKET 14** [10]3-8-3 bl (63) J Quinn 12/1: 3-651136: Cl-up, no extra from dist: btr 1605 & 1457.   3½   60
1745 **LETS GET IT ON 7** [12]3-9-1 (75) K Dalgleish 13/2: 02-00527: Chsd ldrs, carried right dist, no extra.   ½   70
1570 **COMMANDO SCOTT 16** [4]3-9-2 (76) P Bradley(5) 33/1: 4340-108: Led/dsptd lead, no extra over 1f out.   ¾   69
1570 **ACE CLUB 16** [7]3-8-13 (73) M Hills 9/2 FAV: 21-59: Keen, mid-div, no impress over 1f out: see 1570.   2   60
1417 **STORMY NATURE 23** [1]3-9-1 (75) E Ahern 16/1: 420-300: 10th: Prom, btn dist: btr 1116.   nk   61
4503} **MIND ALERT 235** [6]3-8-12 (72) D Allan(3) 50/1: 521006-0: 11th: b g Mind Games - Bombay Sapphire   nk   57
(Be My Chief) Prom, btn over 1f out: reapp: nurs h'cap wnr '03: eff at 6f on fast & gd grnd, gall or sharpish
trk: likes to force the pace. 1 Aug'03 Ripo 6gd 78-69 D: 2 Jul'03 Redc 6g/f 73-67 D:
63   **Shamrock Tea 184** [8]3-8-0 (60) Natalia Gemelova(7) 25/13890}   **Orpenberry 277** [13]3-8-12 (72) J Edmunds 40/1:0
13 Ran   Time 1m 12.87 (1.57)   Owned: Bishopthorpe Racing   Trained: Hambleton

---

1882	3.05 Haydock Park Annual Badgeholders Maiden Stakes 3yo (D)	
	£6019 £1852 £926 1m30y Good/Firm 20 -01 Slow Inside	

1494 **BRINDISI 19** [5] B W Hills 3-8-9 (89) M Hills 2/5 FAV: 2-341: Trkd ldrs & went on 2f out, pushed   85
out, cmftbly: well bckd at long odds-on: eff at 1m, shld stay further: acts on fm & gd/soft: more to come, will
rate higher: see 1494 & 1101.
1473 **ADAIKALI 20** [3] Sir Michael Stoute 3-9-0   B Doyle 14/1: 0-02: b c Green Desert - Adaiyka   1½   86
(Doyoun) Chsd ldrs, rdn & chsd wnr over 1f out, hung left & kept on, nvr able to chall: unplcd sole '03 start (AW
mdn, rtd 71a): half brother to a high-class 10f 3yo performer, dam a high-class 9f performer: styd this longer 1m
trip, 10f will suit: acts on fast grnd & prob polytrack: type to prog in h'caps, prob over further.
NORDWIND 0 [1] P W Harris 3-9-0   D Holland 10/1: 3: b c Acatenango - Narola (Nebos)   Slow away &   2   77+
bhd, styd on fnl 2f despite rng green, kind ride: 110,000 gns purchase, half brother to a smart 11f wnr: eff at 1m,
will relish 10f+: acts on fast: caught the eye, v interesting over further.
1108 **FOOLISH GROOM 41** [10] R Hollinshead 3-9-0   Dale Gibson 16/1: 34: Held up, outpcd 3f out, kept on   1¾   79
ins last: shaped as if 10f+ may suit: handles fast & soft grnd: see 1108 (C/D).
FIRST COUNSEL 0 [7]3-9-0   P Robinson 12/1: 5: b c Wolfhound - Supreme Kingdom (Take A Reef)   shd   79
Held up, onepace & no impress fnl 2f: half brother to wnrs at 6/10f, juv wnr.
1489 **ACUZIO 20** [8]3-9-0   B Swarbrick(5) 100/1: 66: Mid-div, eff over 2f out, sn no impress, dropped in trip.   2   75$
1297 **MOSCOW BLUE 30** [9]3-9-0   R Hughes 12/1: 0-67: Prom, ch 2f out, wknd.   1   73
DESERT LEADER 0 [2]3-9-0   G Gibbons 40/1: 8: Slow away & bhd, btn 2f out on debut.   4   65
159 **CALCULAITE 165** [6]3-9-0   N Mackay(3) 100/1: 000-9: Led till 2f out, sn btn, reapp.   ½   64
9 Ran   Time 1m 42.17 (1.67)   Owned: Mr M H Dixon   Trained: Lambourn

---

1883	3.40 Golborne Rated Stakes Handicap 4yo+ 0-90 (C)	[93]
	£10151 £3123 £1562 1m30y Good/Firm 20 +11 Fast Inside	

1849 **BLUE TROJAN 2** [1] S Kirk 4-8-13 (78) F Norton 14/1: 44-22001: Led 1f & rem handy till led dist,   89
rdn clr & eased nr fin, val 3/4L: op 16/1, fast time: stays a sharp 10f, suited by 1m: acts on firm, gd/soft &
fibresand, stiff or sharp trks: see 294.
1474 **YOUNG MR GRACE 20** [2] T D Easterby 4-8-9 (74) D Allan(3) 14/1: 460-0342: Trkd ldr & led 2f out   1¼   78
till dist, not pace of wnr but kept on: stays 1m: see 1142.
1781+ **INTRICATE WEB 5** [8] E J Alston 8-8-12 (3ex) (77) J Quinn 10/1: 1246013: Held up, short of room   ¾   80
over 2f out, styd on well fnl 1f, nrst fin: remains in gd heart after 1781 (10f).
1131* **FLOWERDRUM 39** [12] W J Haggas 4-9-4 (83) R Hughes 5/1: 1101-014: Mid-div, styd on late.   nk   85
4492} **ETTRICK WATER 236** [10]5-9-7 vis (86) D Holland 9/2 FAV: 142113-5: ch g Selkirk - Sadly Sober (Roi   hd   87
Danzig) Led after 1f till 2f out, no extra: reapp, op 15/2: prog '03, mdn & dual h'cap scorer: plcd sev times
'02, dual h'cap rnr-up: suited by dominating at 7f/1m on firm, sof, & any trk: best in visor, tried blnks: tough,
sharper for this. 1 Sep'03 Wolv 9.4af 74a-72 E: 1 Sep'03 Warw 8.1fm 74-(73) F: 2 Aug'03 Thir 8g/s 74-71 D: 2 Jul'03 Donc 8g/f 74-70 D:
2 Jul'03 Warw 8.1g/f 71-70 E: 2 Jun'03 Newb 8fm 72-(70) D: 2 May'03 Warw 7.1g/f 72-69 D: 2 Oct'02 Ling 7gd 67-63 E:
1 Jun'03 Ayr 7.2g/f 80-(78) D: 2 Sep'02 Hami 9.1fm 81- D: 2 Sep'02 Yarm 8g/f 81-80 D: 2 Nov'01 Muss 8gd 81- D:
1474 **HARRY POTTER 20** [9]5-8-6 vis (71) D Sweeney 16/1: 0030106: Chsd ldrs, hung left & onepace dist: hd   71
prob handles fast, soft & polytrack: see 1214.
1475 **UHOOMAGOO 20** [3]6-9-2 bl (81) N Callan 9/1: 430-1007: Held up, eff over 2f out, mod late prog   1½   78
when short of room ins last, position accepted: see 744.
4820} **SHERIFFS DEPUTY 214** [11]4-8-7 (72) S W Kelly 25/1: 221042-8: b g Atraf - Forest Fantasy (Rambo   ¾   68
Dancer) Held up, not able to chall: reapp: auct mdn wnr '03, AW h'cap rnr-up: h'cap rnr-up '02: eff at 1m, tried
10f, may yet suit: acts on firm, gd & fibresand, prob any trk.
2 Oct'03 Wolv 9.4af 74a-72 E: 1 Sep'03 Warw 8.1fm 74-(73) F: 2 Aug'03 Thir 8g/s 74-71 D: 2 Jul'03 Donc 8g/f 74-70 D:
2 Jul'03 Warw 8.1g/f 71-70 E: 2 Jun'03 Newb 8fm 72-(70) D: 2 May'03 Warw 7.1g/f 72-69 D: 2 Oct'02 Ling 7gd 67-63 E:

HAYDOCK   FRIDAY 21.05.04   Lefthand, Flat, Galloping Track

1475 **CHERISHED NUMBER 20** [4]5-9-0 (79) K Dalgleish 10/1: 4004-049: Held up, eff 3f out, no impress.   nk   74
1035 **NAMROUD 48** [6]5-9-7 (86) E Ahern 11/2: 1210-060: 10th: Chsd ldrs, btn when short of room ins last.   nk   60
1474 **QUALITAIR WINGS 20** [7]5-8-8 (73) G Duffield 12/1: 21026-30: 11th: Slow away, al bhd, btr 1474.   3½   60
1423 **BAND 23** [5]4-8-7 (72) G Gibbons 33/1: 30360-00: 12th: b g Band On The Run - Little Tich (Great
Nephew) Mid-div, eff 3f out, sn btn: mdn rnr-up '03, h'cap plcd (C/D, rtd 83): eff at 7f/1m: acts on fast,
relished soft grnd last term: remains a mdn but shown ability. 2 Apr'03 Hayd 7.1g/f 74- D:
12 Ran   Time 1m 41.24 (0.74)   Owned: The Ex Katy Boys   Trained: Upper Lambourn

---

1884   4.10 George Formby Centenary Stakes Handicap 4yo+ 0-75 (E)   [75]
£3770 £1160 £580   1m2f120y   Good/Firm 20   -28 Slow   Inside

1609 **SMART JOHN 14** [2] W M Brisbourne 4-8-13 (60) S W Kelly 10/1: 03050-41: Mid-div, rdn & hdwy to
lead over 1f out, styd on strongly for press: eff at 10f on fast & gd/soft grnd: likes a gall trk: 1st win today.   64
1618 **NUZZLE 14** [10] M Quinn 4-8-0 (47) F Norton 14/1: 1-000502: Prom & led over 2f out, hdd over 1f out.   1   53
1388 **ROTUMA 25** [7] M Dods 5-9-1 bl (62) E Ahern 11/2: 104-0503: Chsd ldrs, ch over 2f out, kept on.   nk   67
1226 **LAWOOD 34** [4] K A Ryan 4-10-0 (75) N Callan 9/2 JT FAV: 30-40124: Held up, styd on for press fnl 2f.   shd   79
1781 **COMPTON DRAGON 5** [11]5-10-0 (75) A Nicholls 9/1: 00-00505: Held up, eff 2f out, styd on onepace: ½   79
now stays 10f, best prev around 1m: clr of rem today: see 1519.
3017} **GLEN VALE WALK 307** [3]7-8-0 bl (47) N Mackay(3) 16/1: 504034-6: ch g Balla Cove - Winter Harvest   5   44
(Grundy) Slow away & held up, nvr able to chall, eased ins last: reapp: dual h'cap plcd '03 (rtd 48, C/D): h'cap
rnr-up twice '02: eff at 1m, prob suited by 10/12f on firm & gd/soft grnd, gall or sharp/turning trk: eff
with/without blnks. 2 Oct'02 York 11.8fm 51-48 E: 2 Jul'02 Catt 12g/s 42-40 E: 1 Jul'01 Warw 10.8g/f 52-41 F:
1821 **SIR NIGHT 3** [8]4-8-6 (53) D Holland 9/2 JT FAV: 34000-47: Mid-div, btn 2f out: btr 1821.   3½   45
924 **MI ODDS 57** [6]8-9-6 (67) P Robinson 8/1: 12-15008: Mid-div, lost place from halfway: 8 wk abs.   1¾   57
3875} **IFTIKHAR 270** [5]5-9-2 (63) K Dalgleish 20/1: 0224-9: b g Storm Cat - Muhbubh (Blushing Groom)   ½   52
Slow away & held up, rdn 4f out, no impress: reapp, longer priced stable-mate of wnr: lightly rcd '03, dual mdn
rnr-up: unplcd '02: eff at 1m/sharp 12f on fast grnd, easy or sharp/turning trk.
2 Aug'03 Catt 12.0g/f 65- D: 2 Aug'03 Thir 8g/f 68- D:
1430 **LIBRE 23** [9]4-9-3 p (64) Dean McKeown 8/1: 140-0540: 10th: Prom, btn 2f out: btr 1430 & 964.   nk   52
4666} **LUXOR 224** [1]7-7-12 (5oh)p (40) B Swarbrick(5) 20/1: 060000-0: 11th: Led till over 2f out, sn btn: 6   25
reapp: unplcd '03 (rtd 44): dual h'cap wnr '02: best at 10f without cheek pieces, blnks, visor or t-strap: acts
on firm & gd/soft grnd, prob any trk: best dominating.
11 Ran   Time 2m 15.04 (5.04)   Owned: Mr & Mrs D J Smart   Trained: Nesscliffe

---

1885   4.45 Crankwood Maiden Stakes 3yo+ (D)
£5668 £1744 £872   1m3f200y   Good/Firm 20   -25 Slow   Inside

1501 **STRIKE 19** [5] J H M Gosden 3-8-9 R Hughes 2/1 FAV: 261: Dwelt & held up, hdwy 4f out & led over   81
1f out, rdn out: nicely bckd: eff 11/12f on fast & gd grnd, below par latest on gd/soft: likes a gall trk:
lightly rcd & the type to prog: see 1501, 1211.
1347 **WOOLLY BACK 27** [9] R Hollinshead 3-8-9 Dale Gibson 11/2: 22: Keen & chsd ldrs, not pace of wnr   ¾   79
over 2f out, kept on: bckd: eff at 12f on fast & gd/soft grnd, shaped as if 14f+ could suit: see 1347.
1365 **STOCKING ISLAND 27** [3] B Hanbury 3-8-9 A Duffield 3/1: 023: Keen & prom, led 4f out till over   nk   73
1f out, no extra: nicely bckd: styd longer 12f trip: acts on fast & gd/soft grnd: see 1365.
POPES HILL 215 [1] L M Cumani 3-8-9 D Holland 7/2: 0-4: b c Sadler's Wells - Ghost Tree   1½   75
(Caerleon) Mid-div, lost place 4f out, rider dropped whip dist but kept on well ins last, nrst fin: nicely bckd on
reapp: clr rem: Brit bow, well btn sole start in Italy last term: styd lngr 12f trip, shaped as if 14f+ will suit:
acts on fast ground: encouraging.
2333} **DOUBLE TURN 334** [2]4-9-12 K Dalgleish 50/1: 5-5: ch g Double Trigger - Its My Turn (Palm Track)   5   66
Led till 4f out, sn btn, reapp: unplcd sole '03 start (rtd 40, mdn, J H M Gosden): has been gelded.
4757} **TURNER 219** [7]3-8-9 (73) S W Kelly 20/1: 360-6: gr g El Prado - Gaily Royal (Royal Academy)   ¾   65
Held up, eff 3f out, no impress: reapp, longer trip, unplcd '03 (rtd 74 & 69a, J H M Gosden): eff at 1m, mid-dists
shld suit: handles fast ground: has been gelded.
4896} **HEART SPRINGS 209** [8]4-9-7 D Sweeney 100/1: 00-7: Prom, wknd over 3f out, reapp.   11   40
1636 **KELBROOK 13** [4]5-9-12 V Slattery 16/1: 2-58: Slow away & al bhd, longer trip.   12   23
1581 **BA CLUBMAN 15** [6]4-9-12 P B Doyle 50/1: 059: Chsd ldrs till 5f out, cheek pieces, longer trip.   28   0
9 Ran   Time 2m 33.22 (5.42)   Owned: Duke of Devonshire   Trained: Manton

---

1886   5.15 Monks Heath Apprentice Handicap Stakes 3yo+ 0-75 (E)   [75]
£3939 £1212 £606   5f   Good/Firm 20   -01 Slow   Centre

1615 **BYO 14** [8] M Quinn 6-9-8 (69) K May(5) 9/1: 44-06201: Al handy, narrow lead dist, just prevailed,   74
all out: eff at 5/5.7f & likes fast grnd, acts on hvy & polytrack: see 1269.
1555 **VALIANT ROMEO 17** [9] R Bastiman 4-8-7 vis (54) Saleem Golam(5) 9/2 FAV: 0000-522: Led, just hdd   hd   57
dist, styd on well, just held: nicely bckd, op 6/1: see 1555.
1765 **WHISTLER 6** [3] J M Bradley 7-10-0 p (75) C J Davies(5) 13/2: 500-0003: Held up, rdn & hdwy to   ½   77
chall ins last, no extra cl-home: quick reapp: on a fair mark, looks to have come to hand: see 944.
1555 **MALAHIDE EXPRESS 17** [2] E J Alston 4-8-8 (55) J D O'Reilly(3) 8/1: 5020554: Chsd ldrs & ch ins   hd   56
last, no extra: acts on firm, fast & fibresand: see 793 & 198.
1774 **DUNN DEAL 6** [4]4-9-4 (65) B Swarbrick 6/1: 0-301205: Pushed along towards rear, kept on late,   ½   64
not able to chall: quick reapp: see 1127.
1532 **BOANERGES 17** [6]7-8-10 (57) P Makin 15/2: 0005-056: br g Caerleon - Sea Siren (Slip Anchor)   1¾   51
Held up, onepace fnl 2f: unplcd '03 (rtd 70, h'cap): '02 dual h'cap scorer for R Guest: stays 7f, best at 5f on
fast/firm, handles soft: handles any trk: tried a visor, best without: can go well fresh: well h'capped.
2 May'02 York 5fm 90-88 B: 1 Apr'02 Thir 5fm 88-82 C: 1 Apr'02 Kemp 5fm 85-78 D: 2 Jul'01 Newm 5gd 83-78 C:
1 Jun'01 Muss 5g/f 79-74 C:
1774 **BEYOND CALCULATION 6** [5]10-9-3 (64) L Treadwell 20/1: 6000-007: ch g Geiger Counter - Placer   1   55
Queen (Habitat) Mid-div, nvr pace to chall, quick reapp: h'cap rnr-up '03: dual h'cap & a class stks scorer in
'02: stays 7f, suited by 6f/stiff 5f on firm & gd/soft, handles fibresand & any trk.
2 Jun'03 Ripo 5g/f 77-75 D: 1 Sep'02 Sali 5g/f 78-72 E: 1 Jul'02 Warw 6g/f 78- E: 1 Jun'02 Newc 5g/f 72-66 E:
2 Jun'02 Bath 5.7g/f 71- E: 1 Sep'01 Redc 6g/f 79-73 D: 2 Aug'01 Brig 5.2g/f 74-72 E: 2 Jul'01 Bath 5fm 74-71 D:

557

HAYDOCK   FRIDAY 21.05.04   Lefthand, Flat, Galloping Track

1 Jun'01 Ches 5fm 72-67 D:
4741} **LOUGHLORIEN 220** [7]5-8-7 (54) Natalia Gemelova 9/1: 450006-8: b g Lake Coniston - Fey Lady   nk   **44**
(Fairy King) Mid-div, nvr pace to chall: reapp: h'cap scorer '03 (K Ryan): class stks & h'cap wnr '02: eff at
5/6f on firm & gd/soft grnd, prob any trk: best without cheek pieces & blnks.
1 Jun'03 Beve 5g/f 60-53 E: 2 Jun'02 Carl 5fm 67-64 E: 2 Jun'02 Muss 5g/s 67-64 E: 1 May'02 Catt 5.9gd 65-60 E:
1 Mar'02 Catt 5g/s 61- F: 2 Jun'01 Redc 5g/f 73- D:
1532 **QUICKS THE WORD 17** [10]4-9-2 bl (63) D Fentiman(3) 11/1: 600-0049: Mid-div, nvr pace to chall.   3   **44**
1600 **TELEPATHIC 14** [1]4-9-3 (64) P Mathers 25/1: 0-000600: 10th: Held up, nvr on terms, dropped in trip.   1   **42**
1765 **TOMMY SMITH 6** [11]6-9-11 bl (72) S Donohoe 8/1: 630-0000: 11th: Chsd ldrs, btn over 1f out.   ½   **48**
11 Ran   Time 59.86(1.06)   Owned: Mr J G Dooley   Trained: Wantage

NEWMARKET   FRIDAY 21.05.04   Righthand, Stiff, Galloping Track

Official Going Good/Firm

1887	2.10 Postts Vodafone Top-Up Voucher Maiden Stakes Fillies 2yo (D)

£4745 £1460 £730   **6f**   **Good 53**   **-32 Slow**   Inside

HERES THE PLAN 0 [9] M G Quinlan 2-8-11 P McCabe 25/1: 1: b f Revoque - Fanciful (Mujtahid) In   **80**
tch, hdwy & edged left ins fnl 1f, styd on well to lead nr line, rdn out: Feb foal, cost 4,500gns: half-sister to 2
7f juv scorer: eff over a stiff 6f, 7f shld suit: goes well fresh on gd grnd: fine start, shld win more races.
BEAUTIFUL MOVER 0 [7] J W Hills 2-8-11 R Hills 5/1: 2: ch f Spinning World - Dancer's Glamour   shd   **77**
(Danzig Connection) Held up, hdwy to lead over 1f out, edged right & hdd nr line on debut: Mar foal, cost $32,000:
half-sister to wnrs on dirt in US: dam sprint wnr in US: eff over a stiff 6f on gd: fine start, bckd from 10/1, win sn.
CATCH A STAR 0 [10] N A Callaghan 2-8-11 J Murtagh 7/2: 3: ch f Giant's Causeway - Amy Hunter   1½   **74**
(Jade Hunter) With ldrs, led 2f out till over 1f out, onepcd in last: bckd tho' op 11/4 on debut: Apr foal, cost
180,000gns: eff at 6f, bred to stay further: gd speed on debut, likely to be placed to win a race.
THUNDER CALLING 0 [4] P F I Cole 2-8-11 K Fallon 3/1 FAV: 4: b f Thunder Gulch - Glorious   ½   **72**
Calling (Nijinsky) In tch, eff to chall over 1f out, sn onepace: nicely bckd on debut: May foal: half-sister to
wnrs over 6/11f: dam wn at up to 9f: bred to need 7f in time & type to improve for this.
ABERDOVEY 0 [6]2-8-11 I Mongan 10/1: 5: In tch, eff & short of room over 1f out, kept on ins last.   nk   **71**
1652 **BAILEYS APPLAUSE 11** [1]2-8-11 S Drowne 14/1: 536: Held up, short of room over 1f out, no impress.   2   **65**
MOON MISCHIEF 0 [11]2-8-11 T G McLaughlin 7/1: 7: Led after 1f till 2f out, wknd: op 9/2.   2½   **58**
LADRUCA 0 [2]2-8-11 R L Moore 10/1: 8: Al bhd.   5   **43**
JAY 0 [5]2-8-11 W Ryan 25/1: 9: Slow away & al bhd.   nk   **42**
TIME FOR YOU 0 [8]2-8-11 S Sanders 33/1: 0: 10th: Handy, wknd over 2f out.   3½   **32**
10 Ran   Time 1m 15.93 (5.13)   Owned: Mr Liam Mulryan   Trained: Newmarket

1888	2.45 Robinsons Mercedes-Benz A-Class Conditions Stakes 3yo (C)

£8398 £3186 £1593   **1m**   **Good 53**   **+12 Fast**   Inside

4469} **ALMURAAD 237** [6] Sir Michael Stoute 3-8-12 R Hills 11/10 FAV: 16-1: b c Machiavellian -   **108**
Wellspring (Caerleon) Cl-up, hdwy to lead over 1f out, styd on well, rdn out: hvly bckd: won first of 2 juv starts
(mdn): stays a stiff 1m well on gd, poss firm grnd, gall trks: runs well fresh: useful, did this in a gd time.
1 Sep'03 Leic 7.0gd 90- D:
1234 **MUKAFEH 34** [3] J L Dunlop 3-8-12 (100) W Supple 7/1: 13-02: Set pace till over 1f out, kept on,   ½   **106**
just held: well clr of rem & career best stepped up to 1m: acts on firm & gd grnd: useful, see 1234.
1482 **BAYEUX 20** [5] Saeed bin Suroor 3-8-12 t (112) K McEvoy 7/2: 1542-03: Chsd ldr over 5f, no extra   4   **98**
over 1f out: see 1482.
1189 **PSYCHIATRIST 36** [4] R Hannon 3-8-12 (102) R L Moore 7/1: 1412-324: Handy, no impress over 1f out.   shd   **102**
4850*)**COY 212** [2]3-8-7 K Fallon 01: 01-5: b f Danehill - Demure (Machiavellian) Slow away & went   nk   **92**
left, prom, outpcd over 2f out, modest late gains on reapp: op 7/1: lesser fancied stablemate of wnr: won
last of 2 juv starts (mdn): eff at 6f, shld stay 1m: acts on gd grnd & a stiff trk: prob capable to btr.
1 Oct'03 Newc 6gd 97- D:
1189 **NAADDEY 36** [1]3-8-12 vis (92) T E Durcan 33/1: 54353-06: b c Seeking The Gold - Bahr (Generous)   11   **75**
Slow away & hmpd start, sn rdn & nvr a factor: '03 nov stks wnr: eff at 1m on fm & gd/soft, gall trks: tried vis.
2 Jul'03 Newb 7fm 98- C: 1 Jul'03 Beve 7.5g/s 89- D: 2 Jun'03 Sali 7.0fm 87- D:
6 Ran   Time 1m 39.75 (3.25)   Owned: Mr Hamdan Al Maktoum   Trained: Newmarket

1889	3.15 Robinsons Mercedes-Benz Slk Handicap Stakes 3yo+ 0-90 (C)	[87]

£9412 £2896 £1448   **1m4f**   **Good 53**   **-20 Slow**   Outside

1461 **ASTROCHARM 21** [1] M H Tompkins 5-9-0 (73) R Hills 11/1: 00400-51: Hld up, trav well, hdwy to   **81**
lead over 1f out, styd on well, rdn out: prev best at 1m, stays a gall 12f well: likes firm & fast grnd, handles
gd/soft & any trk: has slipped to a v handy mark: see 1461.
1484 **DOVEDON HERO 20** [7] P J McBride 4-9-4 bl (77) S Sanders 7/1: 3016-002: ch g Millkom - Hot Topic   1¼   **82**
(Desse Zenny) Slow away, held up, hdwy 2f out, kept on ins last: '03 mdn & h'cap wnr: winning form over
10/12f & acts on fast & gd grnd, polytrk: eff with/without blnks: gd run, on last winning mark here.
1 Oct'03 Leic 11.8g/f 81-76 C: 1 Jul'03 Bath 10.2g/f 76- D: 2 Jun'03 Nott 8.2gd 60- D:
4602} **VALANCE 230** [6] C R Egerton 4-9-3 (76) S Drowne 6/1: 3/04103-3: br g Bahhare - Glowlamp (Glow)   nk   **80**
Held up, hdwy to chall over 1f out, sn onepace on reapp: op 8/1: juv mdn hdle wnr last winter (rtd 123?, 2m,
gd & fast): '03 mdn wnr: eff over 12/14f on firm & polytrack, gall or sharp trk. 1 Sep'03 Ling 12ap 80a-(80) D:
4783*)**STEALING BEAUTY 217** [8] L M Cumani 4-9-3 (76) J Murtagh 8/1: 5/01-4: b f Sadler's Wells -   2   **77**
Imitation (Darshaan) In tch, hdwy & no room 2f out till 1f out, kept on late: reapp: won last of 2 '03 starts
(mdn): stays 12f on any trk: acts well on fresh & firm grnd: lightly rcd, do better.
1 Oct'03 Brig 11.9fm 79- D:
1232 **RAVENGLASS 34** [3]5-9-8 (81) R Havlin 6/1: 6100-065: Chsd ldr, led over 2f out till over 1f out, no extra.   2   **79**
1650 **SIR HAYDN 11** [4]4-8-11 (70) W Ryan 10/1: 033-3606: Hld up, eff to chall over 1f out, sn no extra.   nk   **67**
1172 **PRAIRIE FALCON 37** [5]10-9-11 (84) A Medeiros(5) 4/1 JT FAV: 00010-37: Led over 9f, no extra: btr 1172. 6   **72**

1772 **INDIVIDUAL TALENTS 6** [2]4-8-9 (68) K Fallon 4/1 JT FAV: 2513-008: In tch, chall over 2f out,   *dist* 0
wknd & eased over 1f out: nicely bckd: another poor run & surely something amiss: see 1295.
8 Ran   Time 2m 37.53 (8.73)   Owned: Mystic Meg Limited   Trained: Newmarket

---

1890   3.50 Essex And Suffolk Chamber Of Commerce Classified Stakes 3yo+ 0-80 (D)
£5408 £1664 £832   **1m2f**   **Good 53**   **-16 Slow**   Inside

4109} **TRUENO 257** [1] L M Cumani 5-9-3 (80) T P Queally(3) 15/2: 51/2524-1: b g Desert King - Stitching   85
(High Estate) Handy, hdwy to lead over 1f out, styd on well, drvn out: rnr-up on 2 of 4 '03 starts (h'caps):
French province wnr in '02: eff at 10f, likes fm, soft grnd & likes gall trks: runs well fresh: lightly
rcd & improving. 2 Aug'03 Newm 14.8fm 80-75 C: 2 Jul'03 Sali 12g/f 76-75 E:
4572} **SOLO FLIGHT 231** [8] H Morrison 7-9-8 (85) S Drowne 7/1: 060206-2: gr g Mtoto - Silver Singer   1   88+
(Pharly) Held up, hdwy & short room 2f out, styd on well, nrst fin: mr-up in a class stks on 1 of 11 '03 starts for
B Hills: dual stk h'cap wnr in '02: wng form over 10/12f: handles soft, likes fm & fast, any trk: best coming late
off a strong pace: h'capped to win more for smart new trainer, keep in mind.
2 Sep'03 Donc 10.3gd 86-(85) C: 1 Sep'03 Newb 10fm 96-89 B: 2 Sep'02 Donc 12fm 92-89 B: 2 Jun'02 Epso 12gd 92-92 B:
1 Apr'02 Newm 12fm 93-88 C: 1 Jun'01 Donc 12g/f 91-81 D: 2 May'01 Ches 12.3fm 81-79 D:
1381 **KENS DREAM 25** [7] Ms A E Embiricos 5-9-3 (77) P McCabe 33/1: 11015/-03: b g Bin Ajwaad - Shoag   ¾   82
(Affirmed) Held up, keen, hdwy over 1f out, kept on ins last: unplcd sole '03 start: mr-up in a hdle in 02/03
(rtd 116h, 2m, soft): '02 mdn & dual h'cap wnr: suited by 10/11f on fast & gd, easy or gall trks, likes Nottingham:
back to best here. 1 Sep'02 Warw 10.8g/f 83-75 E: 1 Jul'02 Nott 9.9g/f 73-69 E: 1 Jun'02 Nott 9.9gd 71-62 E:
1381 **BARKING MAD 25** [5] M L W Bell 6-9-6 (83) K Fallon 7/2: 10350-64: b g Dayjur - Avian Assembly   hd   84
(General Assembly) Led, rdn & hdd over 1f out, no extra: nicely bckd: '03 dual h'cap wnr: suited by 10f on firm &
gd grnd, handles soft & any trk: tough. 1 Jul'03 Newm 10g/f 85-82 C: 1 Jun'03 Wind 10.0g/f 83-77 D:
2 Jun'03 Wind 10.0g/f 83-77 D: 2 Oct'02 Newm 7fm 85-83 B: 2 Aug'02 Newm 7sft 88-83 B: 2 Jul'02 Ling 8ap 80a- D:
1478 **TRESOR SECRET 20** [9]4-9-3 (80) R L Moore 12/1: 01010-05: Held up, flashed tail & no impress 2f out.   5   73
4873} **JAMES CAIRD 210** [2]4-9-5 (82) R Hills 3/1 FAV: 551162-6: Chsd ldr, wknd appr fnl 1f: bckd.   1¼   73
1697 **TE QUIERO GB 15** [4]6-9-3 t (80) M Fenton 12/1: 0022007: In tch, wknd 2f out: btr 846, 141.   2   68
1616 **JOOLS 14** [3]6-9-3 (80) T Quinn 8/1: 0-001538: Prom, wknd well over 1f out: best 1057.   8   56
1714*}**ULTIMATA 361** [6]4-9-2 (82) J Murtagh 10/1: 1-9: Al bhd on reapp: longer trip.   7   45
9 Ran   Time 2m 09.05 (6.95)   Owned: Mrs Liz Jones   Trained: Newmarket

---

1891   4.20 Robinsons Mercedes-Benz M-Class Handicap Stakes 3yo+ 0-80 (D)
£5746 £1768 £884   **1m**   **Good 53**   **-12 Slow**   Inside   [80]

1059 **TIBER TIGER 46** [7] N P Littmoden 4-9-8 bl (74) T G McLaughlin 8/1: 60500-41: Slow away, held up,   84
hdwy over 1f out, styd on to lead ins last, rdn out: wk abs: eff over 7f/1m on firm & gd/soft, gall trks: tough,
took advantage of winning mark: see 1059.
888* **HARRISON POINT 62** [9] P W Chapple Hyam 4-9-12 (78) K Fallon 3/1 JT FAV: 0230-112: Prom, hdwy to   1½   84
lead over 1f out till ins last, no extra: hvly bckd after 2 month abs: continuing in fine heart: see 888, 698.
1778* **PARNASSIAN 6** [5] G B Balding 4-8-4 (56) R Thomas(5) 3/1 JT FAV: 0-003313: Held up, sltly outpcd   2½   57
over 2f out, styd on fnl 1f, nrst fin: nicely bckd: op'd reapp: apprec easier grnd: see 1778.
1130 **HABSHAN 39** [1] N A Graham 4-9-4 (70) J Murtagh 25/1: 52-04: ch g Swain - Cambara (Dancing Brave)   shd   70
Led till over 1f out, no extra: mr-up on 2nd of 2 '03 starts (mdn): stays 1m on fast & gd/soft, gall trks.
2 Sep'03 Hayd 8.1g/s 77- D:
4907*}**LEOBALLERO 207** [4]4-9-12 (78) M Tebbutt 12/1: 352231-5: ch g Lion Cavern - Ball Gown (Jalmood)   ½   77
Handy, eff well over 1f out, no extra ins last: won last of 6 '03 starts for H Collingridge (mdn, rtd 81 when plcd
on turf): eff over 7/8.2f on fast, gd & polytrack, sharp or gall trks: suited by a t-strap (not worn here): sharper
for this, poss more to come. 1 Oct'03 Ling 7ap 71a-(78) D: 2 Aug'03 Nott 8.2gd 80-(83) F: 2 May'03 Leic 8.0gd 80- F:
1691 **DASH FOR COVER 9** [6]4-8-12 (64) R L Moore 16/1: 1-200056: In tch, eff over 1f out, no extra.   ¾   61
1625 **LYGETON LAD 13** [3]6-9-6 t (72) M Fenton 5/1: 5651007: nicely bckd, eff over 1f out, no impress.   2½   64
1351 **ISLAND RAPTURE 27** [2]4-9-11 (77) Lisa Jones(3) 8/1: 23055-08: b f Royal Applause - Gersey   ½   68
(Generous) Chsd ldr, wknd over 1f out: won first of 8 '03 starts (mdn, with Mrs A Perrett, plcd in h'caps): suited
by 10f & acts on firm, soft & polytrack, stiff or sharp trks: tried cheek pieces. 2 Jul'03 Asco 10g/f 81-80 C:
2 Jun'03 Sali 9.9fm 81-(80) D: 1 Feb'03 Ling 10ap 83a-(83) D: 2 Sep'02 Ling 7sft 85- D: 2 Aug'02 Sali 6.9g/f 85- D:
912 **MUST BE MAGIC 58** [8]7-8-9 vis (61) S Sanders 16/1: 120-4509: Held up, no extra 2f out: 2 month abs.   ¾   50
9 Ran   Time 1m 41.67 (5.17)   Owned: Mr Mark Harniman   Trained: Newmarket

---

1892   4.55 Robinsons Mercedes-Benz S-Class Maiden Stakes 3yo (D)
£5512 £1696 £848   **1m2f**   **Good 53**   **-14 Slow**   Inside

1495 **SILENT HAWK 19** [5] Saeed bin Suroor 3-9-0 t K McEvoy 10/11 FAV: 2-41: Led till over 7f out, led   91
again over 1f out, wandered appr fnl 1f but styd on, rdn out: hvly bckd: stays 10f on firm & gd grnd, gall trks:
useful, still green & is open to improvement: see 1495.
1719 **ANNA PALLIDA 8** [6] P W Harris 3-8-9 T Quinn 7/2: 022: With ldr, led over 7f out till over 1f   2   82
out, not pace of wnr: op 7/4, clr mr: prob ran to form of 1719 & shld find similar.
DAZE 0 [2] Sir Michael Stoute 3-8-9 K Fallon 7/1: 3: b f Daylami - Proud Titania (Fairy King)   4   76
In tch, no impress fnl 2f on debut: half-sister to a 12f wnr: bred to apprec mid-dists & will learn from this.
4676} **ON EVERY STREET 223** [4] H R A Cecil 3-9-0 VIS W Ryan 9/1: 5-4: b g Singspiel - Nekhbet (Artaius)   3½   76
In tch, wknd 2f out: op 7/1: rtd 70 when 5th sole '03 start for C Cyzer: been gelded & tried a visor here.
1358 **RACE THE ACE 27** [1]3-9-0 J Murtagh 10/1: 45: Dwelt, nvr a factor: see 1358.   8   64
4044} **WAVERTREE SPIRIT 261** [3]3-9-0 T G McLaughlin 20/1: 6-6: ch g Hector Protector - Miss Clarinet   6   55
(Pharly) Held up, nvr a factor on reapp: 6th sole '03 (mdn, rtd 67).
6 Ran   Time 2m 08.83 (6.73)   Owned: Godolphin   Trained: Newmarket

Official Going Good/Firm

1893
2.20 Dm Hall Median Auction Maiden Stakes 2yo (E)
£3666 £1128 £564 **6f str Good/Firm 25 -44 Slow** Stands side

1739 **DOCTOR HILARY 7** [7] M L W Bell 2-9-0 J Mackay 4/7 FAV: 41: Made all, pushed clr fnl 1f despite **83+**
edging left, val 4L+: well bckd on quick reapp: eff at 6f, 7f shld suit: acts on fast grnd & a gall trk: win again
in this form: see 1739 (debut).
1670 **MAC COIS NA TINE 10** [3] K A Ryan 2-9-0 G Parkin 13/2: 02: b c Cois Na Tine - Berenice **2½ 74**
(Marouble) Chsd ldrs, styd on fnl 1f, at held by easy wnr: Feb foal, cost 17,000 gns: brother/half brother to wnrs
at 5/6f: sire useful sprinter as a juv: eff at 6f, shld stay further: acts on fast grnd: can improve with racing.
1084 **AUNTY EURO 44** [4] E J O'Neill 2-8-9 J Carroll 12/1: 433: Handy till dist, sn onepcd: op 6/1 **shd 68**
after 6 wk abs: eff at 6f on fast grnd: see 1084.
1503 **NO COMMISSION 19** [6] R F Fisher 2-9-0 J F Egan 100/1: 054: b g General Monash - Price of **1½ 69**
Passion (Dolphin Street) Keen handy till dist, no extra: Feb 1st foal, cost 18,000 gns: dam wnr at 5f.
  SOUND AND VISION 0 [2]2-9-0 F Lynch 14/1: 5: Rear, nvr nrr than mid-div: debut. **1½ 65**
  BALLYCROY GIRL 0 [1]2-8-9 R Winston 20/1: 6: Al in rear: debut. **2 54**
  TOSS THE CABER 0 [5]2-9-0 K Darley 5/1: 7: ch c Dr Devious - Celtic Fling (Lion Cavern) Prom **2 53**
4f, sn hung left & wknd, eased fnl 1f: op 11/4: debut: Apr foal, half brother to wnrs at 7/8f: dam 1m wnr.
7 Ran Time 1m 13.49 (4.19) Owned: HESheikh Rashid Bin Mohammed Trained: Newmarket

---

1894
2.55 Kidzplay Maiden Stakes 3yo+ (D)
£5512 £1696 £848 **1m2f Good/Firm 25 -13 Slow** Inside

1140 **TANNOOR 39** [1] M A Jarvis 3-8-11 (77) K Darley 2/5 FAV: 033-31: Made all, pushed out fnl 1f, val **79+**
5L+: bckd at odds-on: till 4/10/11f on firm & soft grnd: still only lightly rcd & can rate higher: see 1140.
1039 **MISS ADELAIDE 48** [2] B W Hills 3-8-6 (77) A Culhane 9/4: 43-442: Handy, styd on to chase wnr bef **2½ 69**
1f out, al held fnl 1f: well bckd, clr rem: 7 wk abs: apprec step-up here to 10f: see 881.
  AFRICAN SUNSET 681 [4] J Howard Johnson 4-9-11 R Winston 40/1: 0/-3: b g Danehill Dancer - **10 60**
Nizamiya (Darshaan) Cl-up till 3f out, sn wknd: p.u. sole 03/04 hdle start (J W F Ainsley).
1462 **COLUMBIAN EMERALD 21** [6] T J Etherington 3-8-11 T Eaves(5) 100/1: 04: Cl-up 7f, sn wknd: see 1462. **1½ 58**
  SHARABAD 0 [5]6-9-11 J F Egan 100/1: 5: b g Ela Mana Mou - Sharbada (Kahyasi) Chsd ldrs, wknd **1¾ 55**
ins fnl 3f: flat debut, earlier nov hdle plcd (rtd 79h, 2m4f).
391} **LORD LAHAR 492** [3]5-9-11 T O'Brien(7) 50/1: 0/00-6: b g Fraam - Brigadiers Bird (Mujadil) Al in **6 46$**
rear: unplcd both '03 starts (rtd 43a, mdn): M R Channon.
6 Ran Time 2m 8.29 (3.89) Owned: Sheikh Ahmed Al Maktoum Trained: Newmarket

---

1895
3.25 Dawn Construction Stakes Handicap 3yo+ 0-95 (C) **[95]**
£8607 £3265 £1632 **1m2f Good/Firm 25 +13 Fast** Inside

4226} **ARCALIS 251** [8] J Howard Johnson 4-9-7 (88) R Winston 4/1 JT FAV: 132412-1: gr g Lear Fan - **97+**
Aristocratique (Cadeaux Genereux) Mid-div, prog to lead 2f out, pushed out, cmftbly: reapp: prog in '03 wng 3
h'caps (Miss J R Ramsden): nurs h'cap wnr at end of '02: eff at 10/12f on firm & gd/soft grnd, likes a strong pace &
goes well fresh: showed a gd turn of foot here on first start for current trainer, more h'caps await.
2 Sep'03 Donc 10.3g/f 89-84 C: 1 Aug'03 Newm 10fm 86-79 C: 2 Jul'03 Donc 10.3g/f 80-76 C:
1 Jun'03 Pont 10.0g/f 80-71 D: 1 Jun'03 Leic 10.0g/f 72-66 D: 1 Oct'02 Pont 8g/s 71-65 E:
1796 **OLDENWAY 4** [6] R A Fahey 5-8-5 (72) T Hamilton(3) 6/1: 0-002242: Prom, ev ch bef 1f out, kept on **2 76**
but al held: tchd 8/1, quick reapp: continues in gd form: see 1006 & 924.
951 **BLUE SKY THINKING 55** [4] K R Burke 5-10-0 (95) Darren Williams 9/2: 34-15603: Mid-div, prog when **1½ 96**
short of room 2f out, sn switched, onepace when hung left dist: 8 wk abs & top weight: btr 519 (polytrack).
1602 **MILLAGROS 14** [5] I Semple 4-8-11 (78) J Carroll 20/1: 06410-04: b f Pennekamp - Grey Galava **1½ 76**
(Generous) Rear, late gains: won 2 h'caps & a fills mdn in '03: eff at 1m/10f: acts on firm & gd/soft grnd, sharp
or stiff trk: lives a RH'd trk: do better. 1 Oct'03 Muss 8gd 80-74 D: 1 Aug'03 Carl 7.9fm 76-70 E:
1 Jun'03 Hami 9.2g/f 73-(65) D: 2 May'03 Hami 9.2g/s 65- D: 2 Apr'03 Muss 9g/f 76- D:
1461 **TONY TIE 21** [3]8-8-9 (76) J F Egan 7/1: 060-6225: Handy 1m, sn no extra: btr 1461 & 1164. **½ 75**
1704 **JABAAR 8** [1]6-9-6 VIS (87) Alex Greaves 9/2: 420-0356: Keen handy 1m, sn wknd: well bckd tho' op **1 84**
7/2, disapp here in 1st time visor: btr 1519.
4788* }**KIRKHAM ABBEY 217** [2]4-7-12 vis (65) M Henry 4/1 JT FAV: 531011-7: b g Selkirk - Totham **8 51**
(Shernazar) Led, hdd 2f out, fdd: prog in '03 wng no less than 5 h'caps: unplcd '02 (rtd
39a): eff btwn 8.5f/12f, shaped as tho' further will suit: acts on firm, fast grnd & firesand: acts on a
sharp/undul & gall trk: eff with visor, tried blnks & cheek pieces. 1 Oct'03 Redc 9g/f 65-59 F:
1 Oct'03 Brig 9.9g/f 64-50 F: 1 Sep'03 Redc 10fm 54-46 E: 1 Jun'03 Wolv 9.4af 53a-48 F:
1 Apr'03 Sout 12af 48a-41 F:
4889* }**DEVINE LIGHT 209** [7]4-7-12 (65) P Fessey 100/1: 000501-8: Cl-up 6f, fdd: reapp. **16 31**
8 Ran Time 2m 5.68 (1.28) Owned: Andrea & Graham Wylie Trained: Crook

---

1896
4.00 Biggart Baillie Classified Stakes 3yo 0-60 (F)
£3346 £956 £478 **1m rnd Good/Firm 25 -33 Slow** Inside

1376 **SHOWTIME ANNIE 25** [8] A Bailey 3-8-9 (58) J Fanning 8/1: 00-61041: Handy, styd on to lead 2f **65**
out, pushed out: eff at 6f, stays a gall trk: well: acts on fast, gd or fibresand: see 863.
1554 **GRACEFUL AIR 17** [5] J R Weymes 3-8-11 (62) R Winston 6/1: 303-4522: Prom, ev ch bef 1f out, kept **1 64**
on but just held by wnr cl-home: eff at 6/7f, now stays 1m: see 1554.
1505 **ONE N ONLY 19** [4] Miss L A Perratt 3-8-9 (55) R Ffrench 25/1: 450-4543: Mid-div, prog 2f out, **shd 61**
staying on when short of room cl-home: eff at 6/7f, now stays 1m: shade closer with clr run: see 1119.
1119 **COLLOSEUM 40** [2] T J Etherington 3-8-12 (59) T Eaves(5) 16/1: 56-04: b g Piccolo - Trig Point **1¾ 60**
(Rudimentary) Keen cl-up till dist, no extra: 6 wk abs: plcd both '03 starts (rtd 60, med auct mdn): prob stays
1m on fast grnd: only lightly rcd.

1304 **KALISHKA 29** [6]3-9-1 (63) K Darley 9/2 FAV: 000-65: Held up, prog 2f out, no impress fnl 1f. ½ **62**
1163 **MENAI STRAIGHTS 37** [1]3-9-1 (63) J F Egan 9/1: 0553-606: Cl-up over 6f, wknd: btr 939. ¾ **60**
1534 **THE STICK 17** [3]3-8-9 (57) R Lappin 14/1: 656-0007: Slow away, prog after 2f, wknd fnl 2f: see 901. *nk* **53**
1279 **INDI ANO STAR 31** [7]3-9-0 (62) D Tudhope(7) 14/1: 6668: Rear, nvr nrr than mid-div: btr 1108. *1½* **55**
1387 **BALWEARIE 25** [10]3-9-1 p (63) J Carroll 20/1: 44254-69: Bhd, nvr able to chall: see 1387. *1½* **54**
3801} **VIOLET AVENUE 272** [13]3-8-11 (62) S Chin 20/1: 204-0: 10th: ch f Muhtarram - Ivoronica *3* **44**
(Targowice) Prom 6f, fdd: reapp: rnr-up 1st of only 3 '03 starts (med auct mdn): eff at 6f on gd grnd: acts on a gall trk: with J G Given. 2 Jul'03 Ayr 6gd 70- E:
1397 **COME WHAT JULY 25** [9]3-9-3 bl (65) L Enstone(3) 13/2: 3-125660: 11th: Chsd ldrs 5f, sn wknd. *hd* **49**
1505 **CHASE THE RAINBOW 19** [12]3-8-9 (59) F Lynch 50/1: 1002-660: 12th: Led, hdd 2f out, sn fdd: btr 1339. *3½* **34**
1534 **MUNAAWESH 17** [11]3-9-2 (64) A Culhane 7/1: 5-030000: 13th: Mid-div, 5f, sn wknd: btr 1193. *shd* **40**
1489 **GRANDE TERRE 20** [14]3-9-0 (65) J Mackay 20/1: 000-P00: 14th: b f Grand Lodge - Savage (Polish *2* **34**
Patriot) Al in rear: unplcd all 3 '03 starts (rtd 74, fills stks).
14 Ran Time 1m 41.25 (4.65) Owned: Showtime Ice Cream Concessionaire Trained: Tarporley

1897

4.30 'strip The Willow' Handicap Stakes 3yo+ 46-55 (F) **[64]**
£3626 £1036 £518 **7f50y rnd** **Good/Firm 25** **-05 Slow** Inside

1662 **DOWNLAND 11** [6] N Tinkler 8-9-0 (50) K Darley 6/1 JT FAV: 6000-021: Handy, styd on to lead dist, **58**
drvn out: eff at 6/7f, stays 1m: acts on firm, likes hvy grnd: well h'capped: see 1662.
1504 **FRANCIS FLUTE 19** [13] B Mactaggart 6-8-11 (47) P Mulrennan(5) 14/1: 46000-02: b g Polar Falcon - *nk* **53**
Darshay (Darshaan) Chsd ldrs, prog & ev ch despite edging left dist, kept on, just denied: unplcd in '03 (rtd 54, class stks): mdn wnr in '02: unplcd for E Alston in '01 (rtd 65): eff at 7f/9f on fast & gd/soft grnd: likes a stiff trk: has slipped to a fair mark & can find similar on this evidence. 1 Aug'02 Newc 7g/s 57- D:
1522 **JUBILEE STREET 18** [14] Mrs A Duffield 5-9-2 (52) A Beech(3) 12/1: 0005-043: Held up, prog after *1½* **53**
5f, kept on ins fnl 1f, not btn far: bckd from 20/1: see 1522.
1635 **MR BOUNTIFUL 13** [8] M Dods 6-9-4 p (54) F Lynch 14/1: 2300-004: Held up, prog bef 1f out, nrst *1½* **54**
fin: back on a wng mark: see 22.
1635 **WALTZING WIZARD 13** [16]5-9-3 (53) J Fanning 14/1: 5455505: Rear, prog 3f out, no impress fnl 1f. ½ **52**
1661 **ZHITOMIR 11** [3]6-9-1 (51) L Enstone(3) 7/1: 0000-166: Cl-up, outpcd after 4f, rallied ins fnl 1f. *1* **48**
1463 **YORKSHIRE BLUE 21** [18]5-8-12 (48) J F Egan 12/1: 00000-07: Rear, nvr nrr than mid-div: see 1463. *3* **39**
1447 **JOSHUAS BOY 22** [4]4-8-10 (1oh)P (45) G Parkin 33/1: 600/0-38: Handy, wknd dist: cheekpieces. *1* **35**
1553 **OLD BAILEY 17** [2]4-8-10 (1oh)bl (45) P Fessey 8/1: 626-6059: Keen cl-up 6f, fdd: btr 1393. *2* **31**
1284 **SILVER MASCOT 31** [7]5-9-5 (55) T Eaves(5) 10/1: 2514230: 10th: Led 5f out, hdd dist, fdd. ½ **39**
1606 **REDOUBTABLE 14** [17]13-9-0 (50) A Culhane 25/1: 4100100: 11th: Al in rear: btr 1447. ½ **33**
1635 **LUKE AFTER ME 13** [12]4-9-4 (54) R Winston 6/1 JT FAV: 0-023020: 12th: Mid-div, prog & trav well *nk* **36+**
when short of room & badly hmpd 2f out, not recover: lost all chance here after being hmpd & this is best forgotten.
1508 **ENVIRONMENTALIST 19** [9]5-8-10 (1oh)t (45) D McGaffin 100/1: 0/006-000: 13th: Al in rear: stiff task. *7* **15**
1662 **ANDREYEV 11** [15]10-8-10 (6oh) (40) J Currie(7) 50/1: 000-6000: 14th: Al in rear. *nk* **14**
1508 **LEGAL SET 19** [11]8-9-2 (52) Ann Stokell 25/1: 4050200: 15th: Chsd ldrs till 5f, wknd: btr 1074. ½ **19**
1600 **SQUARE DANCER 14** [5]8-8-10 (11oh)t (35) J McAuley 100/1: 0/000-000: 16th: Led, hdd 5f out, wkng *1* **11**
when short of room 2f out: faced stiff task.
890} **PROCREATE 420** [1]4-8-10 (46) W J O'Connor 8/1: 500-0: 17th: b g Among Men - Woodbury Princess *5* **2**
(Never So Bold) Keen handy, fdd 2f out: reapp: Irish raider, unplcd in 3 '03 starts (rtd 44a, J A Osborne): lost all chance here by bolting to start: with Miss A M Winters.
1450 **HOWARDS DREAM 22** [10]6-8-10 (16oh)t (30) J Mackay 66/1: 0060-040: 18th: Al well adrift. *20* **0**
18 Ran Time 1m 28.98 (2.18) Owned: Mr A Graham Trained: Malton

1898

5.05 Duke Of Perth Handicap Stakes 3yo+ 0-85 (D) **[85]**
£5629 £1732 £866 **6f str** **Good/Firm 25** **+02 Fast** Stands side

1600 **HIGHLAND WARRIOR 14** [8] J S Goldie 5-8-9 (66) J F Egan 6/1: 3-332341: Mid-div, prog to lead **76**
dist, drvn out: best at 6f, does stay 9f: acts on fm & soft: loves Ayr.
1767 **MINE BEHIND 6** [6] J R Best 4-9-7 (78) N Pollard 4/1 FAV: 263-1622: Prom, led travelling well ¾ **84**
dist, sn hdd, kept on fnl 1f, just held: well bckd on quick reapp: remains in gd form: see 1767 & 1255.
1132 **SNOW BUNTING 39** [10] Jedd O'Keeffe 6-7-12 (5oh) (50) Leanne Kershaw(7) 20/1: 6560-003: Held up, *2* **55$**
prog 2f out, nrst fin: encouraging eff here & is back on a wng mark: see 1000.
1508* **FRIAR TUCK 19** [12] Miss L A Perratt 9-7-12 (55) R Ffrench 12/1: 00-00014: Cl-up till dist, no *shd* **54**
extra: raised 5lbs since recent win in 1508.
1145 **UNDETERRED 39** [9]8-9-6 (77) K Darley 10/1: 24000-05: ch g Zafonic - Mint Crisp (Green Desert) *2* **70**
Rear, prog 2f out, nrst fin: h'cap wnr in '03: also plcd numerous times: plcd form in '02 (rtd 80 at best, incl 3rd in Steward's Cup, D Nicholls): best at 6f, stays 7f: acts on firm & gd grnd, handles soft & any trk, likes Goodwood: eff with/without visor: worth keeping in mind back at Goodwood.
2 Aug'03 Ripo 6g/f 82-78 B: 1 Aug'03 Good 6g/f 82-73 B: 2 Jul'03 Hami 6.0g/f 78-73 B: 2 Jul'03 York 6.0fm 77-73 C:
2 Jul'02 Donc 6gd 76- D: 1 Jun'01 Newc 6fm 94-85 C: 2 Jun'01 Epso 6fm 88-80 C:
1726 **ARMAGNAC 7** [4]6-9-3 (74) A Culhane 5/1: 60-00036: Dwelt, sn mid-div, onepcd dist: quick reapp. *1¾* **62**
3488} **MACHINIST 286** [13]4-9-11 (82) Alex Greaves 50/1: 31/040-7: br g Machiavellian - Athene *3* **61**
(Rousillon) Cl-up, short of room after 2f outill dist, no impress: reapp: ladies h'cap plcd on 1 of only 3 '03 starts (rtd 81, Sir M Stoute): mdn wnr in '02: eff at 7f, further shld suit: acts on gd & polytrack: not disgraced here on first start for D Nicholls, not get best of runs & can rate higher over further. 1 Oct'02 Ling 7ap 86a- D:
1638 **KINGS COLLEGE BOY 13** [14]4-8-4 (61) T Hamilton(2) 25/1: 04260-08: Led, hung left & hdd dist, fdd. *shd* **39**
1794 **XANADU 4** [11]8-7-12 (2oh)p (53) P Fessey 20/1: 000-0209: Handy over halfway, sn no extra: qk reapp. *1¾* **28**
1345* **ZOOM ZOOM 27** [3]4-9-6 (77) R Winston 9/1: 31/-10: 10th: Prom till dist, fdd: btr 1345 (gd/soft). *2½* **43**
1822 **PAWAN 3** [2]4-8-4 (61) Ann Stokell 14/1: 2203530: 11th: Cl-up 4f, fdd. ½ **26**
1627 **GREY COSSACK 13** [5]7-9-9 (80) G Parkin 20/1: 000-0100: 12th: Chsd ldrs 4f, fdd. *1¼* **41**
967 **NEMO FUGAT 53** [1]5-8-9 (66) J Carroll 33/1: 00400-00: 13th: Mid-div 3f, wknd. *1½* **23**
1765 **JOHN OGROATS 6** [7]6-9-1 P (72) F Lynch 14/1: 000-0000: 14th: Cl-up 4f, fdd. *7* **10**
14 Ran Time 1m 10.72(1.42) Owned: Frank & Annette Brady Trained: Glasgow

Official Going FIRM

1899   6.05 Bathwick Tyres Lady Riders' Handicap Stakes 4yo+ 0-70 (F)   [54]
£3395 £970 £485   **1m2f46y**   **Firm 19**   **-32 Slow**   Inside

1792+ **VOICE MAIL 4** [4] A M Balding 5-11-5 (5ex) (73) Miss M Sowerby(5) 9/2: 550-0011: Dwelt, bhd, hdwy   81
from over 2f out & led ins last, sn in command, decisively: qck reapp under a pen: eff at 7f/1m, now stays 10f
well: acts on firm, gd & polytrack: loves Bath: see 1792 & 978.
1625* **HE WHO DARES 13** [11] A W Carroll 6-10-9 (63) Mrs S Bosley 9/2: 2034312: Dwelt, bhd, hdwy to   1¾   67
chase ldr ins last, not pace to chall: in gd form: see 1625.
1776 **SAXE COBURG 6** [5] G A Ham 7-10-10 (64) Miss S Brotherton 10/1: 540-5103: Rear, eff to chase ldrs   2   65
over 1f out, onepace ins last: qck reapp: see 1541.
1695 **HOLLY ROSE 9** [6] D E Cantillon 5-9-12 p (52) Ms C Williams 3/1 FAV: 4100-024: Chsd ldr 3f out, onepace hd   52
1379 **RAINSTORM 25** [7]9-9-5 (45) Mrs S Owen(3) 11/1: 11400-65: Handy & led 5f out, hdd ins last, wknd.   ½   44
961 **LANDESCENT 53** [2]4-9-10 (50) Mrs S Moore(3) 12/1: 0451156: Led till 5f out, btn 2f out: jumps fit.   5   41
1286 **TOP OF THE CLASS 31** [3]7-10-2 vis (56) Miss E Folkes(3) 14/1: 0350407: Chsd ldrs, btn 2f out: btr 1128.   3½   42
3683} **SENIOR MINISTER 278** [9]6-10-9 (63) Mrs Marie King(5) 40/1: 003000-8: b g Lion Cavern - Crime   shd   48
Ofthecentury (Pharly) Chsd ldrs & keen, hung right & btn over 2f out: reapp: h'cap plcd '03 (rtd 66): unplcd '02
(rtd 85, List, tried blnks): winning form at 5f, stays a stiff 6f: handles firm & fast grnd, prob any trk.
1633 **LARKING ABOUT 13** [1]4-10-8 (62) Ms Amy Boeder(7) 50/1: 5420-09: ch f Silver Hawk - Milly Ha Ha   5   39
(Dancing Brave) Dwelt & al bhd: lightly rcd '03, AW mdn rnr-up for H Cecil, turf unplcd (rtd 64): stays a sharp
13f, handles polytrack. 2 Oct'03 Ling 13ap 69a- D:
1676 **CHAKRA 10** [8]10-9-0 (40) Miss Faye Bramley(5) 50/1: 00/-65300: 10th: Chsd ldrs till halfway, up in trip.   shd   16
1402* **ABSOLUTE UTOPIA 24** [12]11-10-9 (63) Miss E J Jones 11/2: 223411P: P.u. & dismounted early on.   0
11 Ran   Time 2m 11.17 (5.17)   Owned: Mr Roger Parry   Trained: Kingsclere

---

1900   6.35 E B F / Chloe Two Years On Maiden Stakes 2yo (D)
£4401 £1354 £677   **5f161y**   **Firm 19**   **-09 Slow**   Far side

HOH HOH HOH 0 [1] A M Balding 2-9-0 Martin Dwyer 5/2 FAV: 1: ch c Piccolo - Nesting (Thatching)   95+
Keen & trkd ldrs, short of room 2f out, switched to lead over 1f out & sn asserted, readily: cost
21,000gns purchase: dam unplcd 4yo, sister to a 7f 2yo wnr: sire a high-class sprinter: eff at 5.8f, get further:
acts on firm grnd & a turning/stiffish trk: well regarded, win better races.
1646 **COME GOOD 11** [7] R Hannon 2-9-0 Dane O'Neill 11/4: 52: Chsd ldrs, chall/bmpd over 1f out, sn no   7   76
ch with easy wkt: left debut bhd: prob handles firm grnd: see 146.
1538 **AGILETE 17** [5] L G Cottrell 2-9-0 S Drowne 7/2: 03: b c Piccolo - Ingerence (Akarad) Trkd ldr   5   61
& led over 2f out till over 1f out, no extra: 22,000gns Mar foal, brother to useful 5/6f wnr Pan Jammer, also
half-brother to a 10f/hdles wnr: get further in time & can improve.
MASTER JOSEPH 0 [8] M R Channon 2-9-0 C Catlin 5/1: 4: b c Komaite - Petit Peu (Kings Lake)   4   49
Outpcd & bhd, late gains: Apr foal, 18,000gns purchase: half-brother to a 10f 3yo wnr, also a 6f juv
wnr abroad: dam unplcd sole start.
1499 **IAM FOREVERBLOWING 19** [3]2-8-9 L Keniry(3) 9/1: 545: Led till over 2f out, sn btn.   2½   36
1786 **DOMINER 4** [6]2-9-0 S Carson 33/1: 66: Chsd ldrs, wknd qckly from halfway, qck reapp.   2   35
SARAH BROWN 0 [2]2-8-9 T P Queally(3) 14/1: 7: Sn bhd & outpcd.   ¾   28
7 Ran   Time 1m 10.68 (1.58)   Owned: Mr D F Allport   Trained: Kingsclere

---

1901   7.05 Toteexacta Classified Stakes 3yo 0-80 (D)
£6643 £2044 £1022   **5f11y**   **Firm 19**   **+19 Fast**   Far side

1782 **ENCHANTMENT 5** [4] J M Bradley 3-8-13 (79) C Catlin 9/4 FAV: 1601-521: Made all, rdn clr from   92
dist, styd on strongly: qck reapp, fast time: eff at 5/6f, likes firm & fast grnd, stiff/ gall or sharpish trk:
likes to force the pace: decisive scorer, can win again: see 1782 & 1498.
1498 **BATHWICK BILL 19** [3] B R Millman 3-9-2 (80) G Baker 5/1: 1530-062: ch g Stravinsky - Special   2½   85
Park (Trempolino) Chsd ldrs, eff to chase wnr over 1f out, al held: was 5/6f h'cap scorer '03, subs disapp in
blnks: eff at 5/6f on firm & gd grnd, sharp/undul or stiff/turning trk: clr rem, gd run.
1 Jul'03 Ling 6gd 86-79 E: 1 Jun'03 Bath 5.0fm 88- D:
1154 **SHIELALIGH 38** [6] Miss Gay Kelleway 3-8-13 t (80) D Holland 5/1: 1243-003: ch f Aragon - Sheesha   5   68
(Shadeed) Chsd ldrs & outpcd halfway, kept on late, nvr a threat: debut wnr '03 for H Candy (auct mdn, subs h'cap
plcd, rtd 85, lightly rcd): has been gelded: suited by 6f on firm & gd grnd, sharp or sharp/turning trks: can go
well fresh: worn s-trap last twice. 2 Jul'03 Sali 6g/f 83- F: 1 Jun'03 Wind 6gd 80- E:
1809 **MIRASOL PRINCESS 4** [2] D K Ivory 3-8-13 (78) Dane O'Neill 12/1: 1100-004: Pushed along & outpcd,   ½   66
kept on late, no dngr: see 1383.
1570 **CATCH THE WIND 16** [7]3-8-13 (79) T P Queally(3) 16/1: 3140-05: b f Bahamian Bounty - Tinkerbird   shd   65
(Music Boy) Chsd wnr, btn dist: lightly rcd juv '03, auct mdn scorer: eff over a stiff/undul 5f, acts on fast &
soft grnd. 1 Jun'03 Pont 5g/f 80- F:
1255 **TRICK CYCLIST 32** [9]3-9-2 (78) Martin Dwyer 3/1: 200-2406: Outpcd, late gains: btr 818 (AW).   ½   66
4926*} **CORPS DE BALLET 206** [5]3-9-2 (83) S Sanders 11/2: 5431-7: b f Fasliyev - Dwell (Habitat) Chsd   5   51
ldrs till halfway: reapp: lightly rcd '03, mdn scorer on fnl start: eff at 6f, sole win at 5f: acts on firm &
gd/soft grnd, sharp/undul or gall trk. 1 Oct'03 Nott 5.1g/s 79-(77) D:
SOLVED 229 [1]3-8-13 (79) D Nolan(3) 25/1: 63230-8: Prom early, no impress from halfway, Brit bow.   1   45
8 Ran   Time 1m 0.26 (u0.04)   Owned: Ms A M Williams   Trained: Chepstow

BATH   FRIDAY 21.05.04   Lefthand, Turning Track with Uphill Finish

1902   **7.35 Charles Saunders Foodservice Claiming Stakes 3yo** (F)
£3164 £904 £452   **5f11y**   **Firm 19**   **-12 Slow**   Far side

1722 **JINKSONTHEHOUSE 8** [7] M D I Usher 3-8-2 (57) Hayley Turner(5) 10/1: 0000-401: b f Whittingham - **59**
Aldwick Colonnade (Kind of Hush) Chsd ldrs, styd on to lead over 1f out, drvn out to hold on: plcd first time out
in '03 (rned auct stks, rtd 72): eff around 5f on firm & gd grnd: first win.
1268 **ONLY IF I LAUGH 31** [5] B J Meehan 3-8-5 bl (70) J F McDonald(3) 7/4 FAV: 504-3402: Rear, prog & ev   1¼ **57**
ch dist, kept on but not pace wnr fnl 1f: acts on firm grnd, fast grnd & both AWs: claimed for 5,000.
256 **BLUE MOON HITMAN 146** [3] R Brotherton 3-8-11 (55) D Holland 10/1: 454636-3: Handy, led 2f out,   shd **62**
hdd 1f out, sn no extra: long abs & new stable, see 256 (A Berry).
1694 **CUT AND DRIED 9** [6] D M Simcock 3-9-5 (68) Martin Dwyer 11/4: 0-116054: Rear, prog 2f out, no   3 **61**
impress fnl 1f: btr 712 (polytrack).
1694 **REHIA 9** [2]3-8-4 (53) S Whitworth 7/2: 6544035: Cl-up, led 3f out, hdd 2f out, sn wknd: btr 1694.   2½ **38**
1453 **PARALLEL LINES 22** [4]3-8-5 bl (46) E Ahern 14/1: 0040036: Handy till halfway, wknd: btr 1453.   ½ **37**
1690 **CINNAMON RIDGE 9** [1]3-8-5 bl L Keniry(1) 16/1: 00-007: b g Indian Ridge - Savoury (Salse) Led   9 **10**
2f, sn fdd: modest form to date.
7 Ran   Time 1m 1.88 (1.58)   Owned: Midweek Racing   Trained: Lambourn

1903   **8.05 Cauda Equina Handicap Stakes 3yo 0-75** (E)   **[79]**
£4300 £1323 £662   **5f161y**   **Firm 19**   **-19 Slow**   Far side

1809 **TAG TEAM 4** [7] A M Balding 3-9-7 (72) Martin Dwyer 7/4 FAV: 0-113051: Made all, drvn out to hold   **78**
on fnl 1f: qck reapp: eff at 5f, best around 6f: acts on firm grnd & polytrack, disapp on gd/soft: still only
lightly rcd & is open to more improvement: see 818 & 735.
1722 **SIGNOR PANETTIERE 8** [1] R Hannon 3-9-2 (67) P Dobbs 9/2: 00005-02: Mid-div, prog & ev ch 1f out,   hd **72**
kept on, just denied: eff at 5/6f on firm & gd grnd: left reapp eff bhd here, can find similar: see 1722.
1054 **MELODY KING 46** [9] P D Evans 3-9-2 bl (67) S Drowne 14/1: 03140-03: b g Merdon Melody -   3 **63**
Retaliator (Rudimentary) Cl-up till dist, sn no extra: 7 wk abs: h'cap wnr in '03: eff at 5/6f on firm & fast
grnd: eff with visor & blnks: best when able to dominate. 1 Aug'03 Chep 6.1g/f 68-63 E: 2 Jun'03 Donc 5.6fm 70- D:
1540 **BARABELLA 17** [3] R J Hodges 3-8-9 (60) J F McDonald(3) 7/1: 440-0504: Slow away, onepcd.   ¾ **54**
1720 **ARFINNIT 8** [8]3-9-2 vis (67) T Dean(7) 13/2: 00-03065: Slow away, sn handy, wknd dist: btr 1054 (gd/soft).½ **59**
1044 **NEBRASKA CITY 48** [6]3-8-13 (64) Dane O'Neill 16/1: 55050-06: b g Piccolo - Scarlet Veil   3½ **46**
(Tyrnavos) Al in rear: 7 wk abs: unplcd in '03 (rtd 70, mdns): has tried visor & cheek pieces.
1054 **OFF BEAT 46** [5]3-9-7 bl (72) S Carson 11/2: 610-6307: Handy till halfway, wknd: btr 729 (7f).   4 **42**
4899} **JAILBIRD 207** [4]3-8-7 (58) S Sanders 14/1: 505-8: Handy 3f, wknd: reapp: unplcd all 3 '03   1 **25**
starts (rtd 61, med auct mdn): with R M Beckett.
8 Ran   Time 1m 11.22 (2.12)   Owned: Magic Moments   Trained: Kingsclere

1904   **8.35 Weatherbys Bank Median Auction Maiden Stakes 3yo** (F)
£3437 £982 £491   **1m5y**   **Firm 19**   **-36 Slow**   Inside

1241 **OUR JAFFA 34** [1] D J Daly 3-8-9   J Murtagh 100/30: 41: Slow away, sn mid-div, styd on to lead   **84+**
ins fnl 1f, pushed out, val 3L+: eff at 1m, prob stays 10f: acts on firm & gd grnd: decisive wnr here, only
lightly rcd & can rate higher: see 1241.
1210 **VAMP 35** [11] R M Beckett 3-8-9   S Sanders 5/1: 02: Held up, prog 3f out, styd on to chase wnr   1¼ **79**
fnl 1f, al held: eff at 1m, further shld suit: acts on firm grnd: encouraging run.
MAGIC MERLIN 0 [9] P W Harris 3-9-0   D Holland 3/1 FAV: 3: b c Magic Ring - St James's Antigua   1 **83**
(Law Society) Handy, styd on to lead dist, hdd ins fnl 1f, no extra: debut: eff at 1m, further shld suit: acts on
firm grnd: not disgraced & sharper for this.
1377 **DELIGHTFULLY 25** [6] B W Hills 3-8-9 (69) Martin Dwyer 5/1: 0-024: Cl-up, led 2f out, hdd dist,   1¾ **75$**
no extra: see 1377 (fibresand).
1610 **DARK RAIDER 14** [3]3-8-9 (63) D Corby(3) 10/1: 00-25: Handy, outpcd 3f out, rallied fnl 1f: see 1610.   nk **74**
1321 **CARRY ON DOC 28** [7]3-9-0 (73) S Whitworth 7/1: 5355-36: Led 6f, sn wknd: btr 1321 (7f).   ¾ **77**
98 **IPHIGENIA 178** [5]3-8-9 (50) R Miles(3) 66/1: 023000-7: b f Orpen - Silver Explosive (Rock Hopper)   1 **70$**
Handy 6f, wknd: reapp: plcd on 2 of 4 '03 starts (rtd 67 & 66a, mdns): eff at 5/6f on fast grnd & fibresand.
2 Jun'03 Chep 6.1g/f 67- E:
1054 **MY MICHELLE 46** [8]3-8-9 (72) E Ahern 11/1: 553-08: b f Ali Royal - April Magic (Magic Ring) Al   2 **66**
in rear: 7 wk abs: plcd on 1 of 3 '03 starts (mdn, rtd 80): eff at 6f on fast & gd grnd: with B Palling.
1497 **PLEASURE SEEKER 19** [4]3-8-9   A Daly 20/1: 00-09: Slow away, al bhd.   ½ **65**
1384 **SEAGOLD 25** [10]3-8-9   S Drowne 40/1: 0-00: 10th: Chsd ldrs 5f, sn fdd.   3½ **58**
1501 **HARRY CAME HOME 19** [2]3-9-0 L Keniry(1) 66/1: 0000: 11th: Rear, nvr a factor.   5 **53**
11 Ran   Time 1m 42.76(4.46)   Owned: Miss A H Marshall   Trained: Newmarket

AYR   SATURDAY 22.05.04   Lefthand, Galloping Track

Official Going Firm (Good/Firm Places)

1905   **1.00 Dobbie Electrical Handicap Stakes 4yo+ 0-70** (E)   **[70]**
£2324 £2324 £547   **1m5f13y**   **Firm**   **Slow**   Inside

1637 **TONI ALCALA 14** [7] R F Fisher 5-9-10 (66) P Mulrennan(5) 7/2 FAV: 4023161: Rear, stdy hdwy over   **68**
3f out & chall ins last, drvn & ddhtd line: bckd: eff at 12f, suited by 13/14f, stays 2m1f: acts on firm, gd/soft &
fibresand, any trk: tough & genuine: see 1459, 752.
5010} **COSMIC CASE 199** [4] J S Goldie 9-8-3 (45) A Nicholls 11/2: 155300-1: b f Casteddu - La   dht **47**
Fontainova (Lafontaine) Held up, rdn & hdwy 2f out, dsptd lead ins last, ddhtd line: op 9/2: jmps fit (no form):
flat reapp, '03 h'cap wnr: h'cap wnr '02: eff at 12f/2m on firm & gd, handles gd/sft, any trk: eff with/without a

563

vis: best held up: tough 9yo, back on a fair mark. 1 Jun'03 Muss 14fm 50-47 F: 1 Sep'02 Hami 12g/f 51-48 F:
2 Apr'02 Muss 14g/f 51-49 E: 2 Jul'01 Hayd 14fm 60-56 D: 2 Jun'01 Newc 12.4g/f 61-58 C:
1 Jun'01 Hami 12g/f 58-54 E: 1 Jun'01 Muss 12g/f 56-48 E: 1 May'01 Pont 12fm 48-40 E: 2 May'01 Hami 13gd 52-42 E:

1796* **RAJAM 5** [2] D Nicholls 6-10-5 (6ex)vis (75) Alex Greaves 5/1: 00-06013: Trkd ldr & led over 2f out till ins last, just held when short of room cl home: nicely bckd:, qck reapp under a pen, gd run.		1	75
581 **MAGIC CHARM 103** [8] Jedd O'Keeffe 6-7-12 (40) Leanne Kershaw(7) 20/1: 105-0004: Trkd ldrs, led over 3f out till over 2f out, no extra dist: 4 mth abs, new stable: see 581 (AW).		1½	38
1396 **EXALTED 26** [3]11-8-12 (54) Dale Gibson 8/1: 42200-55: Chsd ldrs, outpcd fnl 2f: likes easy grnd.		shd	52
762 **FOREVER MY LORD 84** [1]6-8-7 (49) J P Guillambert(3) 4/1: 430-0006: Led till over 3f out, sn no impress.	7		38
1551 **ASTROMANCER 18** [5]4-8-7 BL (49) M Henry 7/1: 44-04507: Twds rear & no impress fnl 3f: see 137 & 11.		nk	37
4735} **ALAFDAL 221** [6]4-9-12 (68) K Renwick 25/1: 62000-8: b c Gone West - Aqaarid (Nashwan) Always rear: reapp: mdn rnr up '03 (J Dunlop): eff over a stiff 10f on fast ground. 2 Apr'03 Newc 10.1g/f 70- D:	24		24

8 Ran   Time 2m 50.23 (5.63)   Owned: The Cosmic Cases   Trained: Glasgow

AYR   SATURDAY 22.05.04   Lefthand, Galloping Track

3151} **WOOD DALLING 302** [3]6-8-4 (56) P Mathers(7) 50/1: 404305-7: Dwelt & bhd, mod prgo, new yard.   ½   53
4792} **POP UP AGAIN 218** [12]4-9-9 (75) F Lynch 8/1: 320513-8: Held up, rdn & nvr pace to threaten: reapp.   2   68
1750 **SPEEDFIT FREE 7** [1]7-7-12 (2oh)vis (48) Ann Stokell 33/1: 0030049: Dsptd lead till halfway, sn btn.   2½   38
1824 **PAGAN STORM 4** [7]4-8-13 (65) Kristin Stubbs(7) 20/1: 0000500: 10th: Always bhd: qck reapp: btr 1638.   2½   48
1765 **ONLINE INVESTOR 7** [11]5-9-3 (69) A Nicholls 6/1: 00-00520: 11th: Hld up & keen, btn 2f out: 6   41
nicely bckd: up in trip & not settle early: best at 5/6f, but hard to win with: see 1765.
1225 **CARIBE 35** [5]5-8-13 (65) J Carroll 50/1: 01046-60: 12th: Trkd ldrs, btn 2f out.   16   8
12 Ran   Time 1m 28.52 (1.72)   Owned: The Mathieson Partnership   Trained: Carluke

---

1910   3.45 Laburnam Classified Stakes 3yo+ 0-60 (F)
£3206 £916 £458   **7f50y rnd**   **Firm**   **Fair**   Inside

1242 **SHES OUR LASS 35** [6] D Carroll 3-8-3 (60) R Fitzpatrick 4/1: 42-00131: Mid-div, hdwy 3f out &   64
rdn/led over 1f out, styd on strongly: nicely bckd: stays 1m, suited by 7f on firm, soft & fibresand, sharp or gal
trk: tough & bang in form filly: see 1242 & 1085.
1820 **WHIPPASNAPPER 4** [9] J R Best 4-9-8 (65) J P Guillambert(3) 11/4 FAV: 0210322: Held up, styd on   1¾   68
for press, not pace to chall wnr: nicely bckd, tho' op 9/4: acts on firm, gd/soft & polytrk: see 1354 (6f).
1794 **COUSTOU 5** [1] A R Dicken 4-9-3 (59) T Eaves(5) 10/1: 05-60043: Pushed along chasing ldrs, kept on   1½   60
for press: acts on firm & gd grnd: see 1094.
1897 **LUKE AFTER ME 1** [3] G A Swinbank 4-9-3 (54) F Lynch 5/1: 0-0230204: Rear, prog/short of room 2f   hd   59
out, onepace: nicely bckd: handles firm & gd/sft grnd; see 1635, 996 & 577.
1508 **GOLDEN SPECTRUM 20** [2]5-9-3 (58) Alex Greaves 6/1: 00000-35: Trkd ldrs, no impress bef dist.   1   57
1765 **TIME TO REMEMBER 7** [5]6-9-3 (60) A Nicholls 12/1: 00R-0006: b g Pennekamp - Bequeath (Lyphard)   hd   56
Led till over 1f out, wknd, op 16/1: h'cap wnr '03: thrice h'cap plcd '02 (rtd 80): eff at 6/7f on firm & gd grnd,
gall trks, likes York. 1 Jun'03 York 6.0fm 74-69 D: 1 Aug'01 Redc 7fm 79-75 D:
1553 **REGENTS SECRET 18** [7]4-9-8 (65) P Mulrennan(5) 10/1: 0040-407: Held up, efft over 1f out, btn dist.   shd   61
1602 **ELLEN MOONEY 15** [8]5-9-0 bl (57) T Hamilton(3) 20/1: 2340008: Al twds rear: see 163.   5   44
1508 **LEGAL SET 20** [4]8-9-3 (52) Ann Stokell 40/1: 4050209: Trkd ldr, btn 2f out: see 728.   2½   42
9 Ran   Time 1m 28.68(1.88)   Owned: We-Know Partnership   Trained: Warthilll

---

KEMPTON   SATURDAY 22.05.04   Righthand, Flat, Fair Track

Official Going Good/Firm

1911   6.05 New Fixture Maiden Auction Stakes 2yo (E)
£3562 £1096 £548   **6f str**   **Good/Firm 30**   **-17 Slow**   Stands Side

AASTRAL MAGIC 0 [16] R Hannon 2-8-2   R L Moore 20/1: 1: b f Magic Ring - Robanna (Robellino)   70
Rear, hdwy over 1f out & rdn/led well ins last: cheaply retained Apr first foal, dam plcd at 13/14f: eff at 6f, shld
get further: acts on fast grnd & goes well fresh: can rate higher.
1760 **SHAHEER 7** [1] B J Meehan 2-8-9   L Keniry(3) 4/1: 62: b c Shahrastani - Atmospheric Blues (Double   nk   76
Schwartz) In tch, rdn & styd on well fnl 1f, just held: imprvd from debut: Feb foal, 14,000gns purchase:
half-brother to wnrs at 6/7f, dam a stayer: eff at 6f, get further: acts on fast: win sn.
1510 **FLYING PASS 19** [6] D J S ffrench Davis 2-8-9   T Quinn 20/1: 03: b g Alzao - Complimentary Pass   ¾   74
(Danehill) Prom & led over 2f out, hdd well ins last: left hvy grnd debut bhd: Apr foal, 17,000gns purchase: dam
a 1m plcd 3yo & related to a multiple 5/7f sprint h'cap wnr: eff at 6f on fast grnd: promise today.
RIDDER 0 [14] D J Coakley 2-8-10   D Holland 20/1: 4: b c Dr Fong - Frond (Alzao) Prom, ch dist,   ½   73
rdn & no extra nr fin: Jan foal, 20,000gns purchase: half-brother to plcd juvs, dam 7f juv wnr & related to wnrs
mainly at 1m+: eff at 6f, get further: acts on fast grnd: rider reported colt was hanging left.
CLOANN 0 [12]2-8-2 R Smith 33/1: 5: Slow away, kept on late, nrst fin: stablemate of wnr.   2   59
1439 **ZENDARO 23** [8]2-8-8 W Supple 12/1: 46: Cl-up, wknd ins last, turf bow.   3½   54
WHATATODO 0 [17]2-8-2 Hayley Turner(5) 25/1: 7: Bhd, mod late prog.   hd   47
MISSED A BEAT 0 [19]2-8-3 F Norton 10/1: 8: Slow away & rdn nr on terms: op 7/1.   1¾   43
KING OF FIRE 0 [7]2-8-7 S Carson 66/1: 9: Mid-div, sn outpcd.   hd   46
MISTER AZIZ 0 [11]2-8-8 J Tate 16/1: 0: 10th: Chsd ldrs, btn over 1f out.   ¾   45
FLY TO DUBAI 0 [4]2-8-8 J Quinn 7/2 FAV: 0: 11th: Mid-div, btn 2f out.   hd   44
SPACED 0 [5]2-8-10 R Hughes 9/1: 0: 12th: Rear, only mod late prog.   ½   44
YOUNG THOMAS 0 [3]2-8-8 M Fenton 14/1: 0: 13th: Outpcd thru'out.   2   36
MILL BY THE STREAM 0 [18]2-8-9 N Callan 20/1: 0: 14th: Mid-div, in tch 4f.   1¼   33
DON PELE 0 [21]2-8-9 J F Egan 10/1: 0: 15th: Prom till over 1f out, 'lost action'.   nk   32
1538 **AMALGAM 18** [10]2-8-2 D Kinsella 66/1: 00: 16th: Al rear & outpcd.   nk   24
1053 **BIG BAMBO 47** [2]2-8-7 R Havlin 100/1: 00: 17th: Led till over 2f out, sn btn, 7 wk abs.   3   20
PIPS PEARL 0 [20]2-8-3 R Miles(3) 33/1: 0: 18th: Sn bhd & struggling.   4   4
SMART DAWN 0 [9]2-8-4 S Chin 33/1: 0: 19th: Rear & hmpd halfway, nvr factor.   10   0
19 Ran   Time 1m 13.89 (2.79)   Owned: Green Pastures Partnership   Trained: Marlborough

---

1912   6.35 Fuller's London Pride Maiden Stakes 3yo (D)
£5642 £1736 £868   **7f rnd**   **Good/Firm 30**   **+01 Fast**   Inside

1171 **KIND 38** [9] R Charlton 3-8-9 (80) R Hughes 4/5 FAV: 34-31: Keen, led & sn clr, v easily: hvly   88+
bckd tho' op 8/13: gd time: well suited by forcing tactics at 7f, 1m+ should suit: acts on firm & gd grnd: lightly
rcd, impressed, win again.
1497 **FAREWELL GIFT 20** [4] R Hannon 3-9-0 (84) R L Moore 2/1: 200-432: Trkd ldrs, eff to chase wnr   6   77
over 1f out, kept on but al well held: nicely bckd, op 7/2: handles fast & gd/soft: prob stays 7f.
4850} **TROPICAL STORM 213** [5] J Noseda 3-9-0 E Ahern 14/1: 24-3: ch g Alhaarth - Rainstone (Rainbow   ¾   75+
Quest) Chsd ldrs, short of room 2f out, onepace, kind ride: lightly rcd, mdn rnr-up on debut: eff at 6f, bred
to apprec 7f/1m+: handles fast & gd/soft: plenty of improvement likely in 7f+ h'caps. 2 Sep'03 Hayd 6g/s 74- D:
1125 **SNOW JOKE 40** [8] Mrs P N Dutfield 3-8-9 (57) R Havlin 100/1: 000-04: b f Desert Sun - Snowcap   ½   69$
(Snow Chief) Slow away, in tch, outpcd fnl 2f: 6 wk abs: unplcd '03 (rtd 67): this trip shld suit.

KEMPTON   SATURDAY 22.05.04   Righthand, Flat, Fair Track

1497 **MR HULLABALOU 20** [7]3-9-0 (79) N Day 10/1: 0045: Chsd wnr, no impress over 1f out: longer trip.   **2**   **70**
    PURE IMAGINATION 0 [2]3-9-0 S Carson 66/1: 6: ch g Royal Academy - Ivory Bride (Domynsky) Al   **7**   **56**
rear: 10,000gns 2yo purchase: half-brother to a 5/7f wnr: dam 6f scorer.
    ILTRAVITORE 0 [6]3-9-0 N Pollard 40/1: 7: Slow away & al bhd.   **¾**   **55**
    SYLVATICUS 0 [3]3-9-0 R Smith 66/1: 8: Sn bhd & t.o. 3f out: reportedly hung right thr'out on debut.   **29**   **0**
  8 Ran Time 1m 26.25 (1.95)   Owned: Mr K Abdulla   Trained: Beckhampton

1913   7.05 Sharp Minds Betfair Handicap Stakes 3yo+ 0-70 (E)   **[69]**
    £3650 £1123 £562   **1m2f**   **Good/Firm 30**   **-14 Slow**   Inside

1027 **GIUNCHIGLIO 50** [9] W M Brisbourne 5-9-7 (62) K Fallon 7/1: 65600-31: Mid-div, prog to lead over   **68**
1f out, drvn out: 7 wk abs: eff at 10f on fast & gd grnd, handles polytrack: goes well fresh: confidence boost.
4306] **SWELLMOVA 603** [6] J R Boyle 5-9-3 (58) A Quinn(5) 14/1: 1204/-2: b g Sadler's Wells - Supamova   **¾**   **62**
(Seattle Slew) Trkd ldrs & led over 1f out, sn hdd, kept on for press: gelded, abs, fine run: missed '03: '02
debut wnr (3 rnr mdn, P Cole, subs h'capped plcd, rtd 64): eff at 1m/10f, tried 12f, may yet suit: acts on fast &
gd/soft grnd, stiff or sharpish trk: goes well fresh: excellent rtn, win similar if repeating.
2 Aug'02 Redc 6g/s 61- F: 1 Aug'02 Ripo 10g/s 55- D:
1609 **BLAZING THE TRAIL 15** [2] J W Hills 4-9-12 (67) S Whitworth 9/1: 0251323: Held up, styd on for   **¾**   **70**
press fnl 2f, not pace to chall: continues in gd form: acts on fast, soft & polytrack: see 1609, 1083 & 912.
1609 **KARAOKE 15** [4] S Kirk 4-9-10 (65) J F Egan 10/1: 0100554: Held up, styd on for press fnl 2f, not   **hd**   **67**
able to chall: slipped to a handy mark on turf.
4889] **QABAS 210** [1]4-10-0 (69) R Hughes 16/1: 462222-5: b g Swain - Classical Dance (Regal Classic)   **shd**   **71**
Rear, rdn/styd on well fnl 2f, nrst fin, saddle slipped: bckd at long odds, gelded, Flat reapp, 6 wk jumps abs
(unplcd, rtd 70h, nov): 5 times rnr-up '03 for A C Stewart (mdns): promise sole '02 start (rtd 73, mdn): eff btwn
9/11f on firm & gd grnd, prob any trk: clr rem here & shown enough to find a race.
2 Oct'03 Muss 9gd 71-(69) D: 2 Oct'03 Nott 10.0fm 62-(74) D: 2 Sep'03 Pont 10.0g/f 71-(77) D:
2 Aug'03 Bath 11.7fm 73-(78): 2 Apr'03 Yarm 8.0gd 81- D:
498 **CASTAIGNE 115** [14]5-9-2 (57) R Havlin 25/1: 0020-006: Rear, late gains, nvr threat: see 101.   **5**   **52**
900 **LYRICAL WAY 60** [17]5-9-7 bl (62) F Norton 16/1: 221-4057: Rear, eff 3f out, onepace: abs: see 236.   **nk**   **56**
1618 **CASTAWAY QUEEN 15** [5]5-9-7 BL (62) E Ahern 16/1: 5620-208: Mid-div, btn over 1f out, blnks btr 1098.   **2**   **53**
4704] **BILLY BATHWICK 223** [10]7-9-3 (58) D Holland 10/1: 446553-9: ch g Fayruz - Cut It Fine (Big   **1**   **48**
Spruce) Trkd ldrs, btn over 1f out: reapp: dual h'cap scorer '03 (l Wood, earlier with Dr Naylor): dual h'cap
plcd '02 (rtd 53): eff at 1m, prob best at 10/12f: acts on soft, likes firm & fast grnd, any trk: best without
cheek pieces. 1 Jun'03 Muss 12g/f 63-59 E: 1 Jun'03 Beve 9.9fm 59-51 D: 2 May'03 Muss 12gd 50-49 E:
1 Jun'01 Wind 10g/f 63-60 D: 2 May'01 Bath 8g/f 63-58 D:
1642 **CATCH THE FOX 12** [19]4-8-4 (45) J Tate 33/1: 050-0200: 10th: Rear, rdn & btn 2f out: btr 1334 (1m).   **½**   **34**
1098 **BLUEGRASS BOY 44** [11]4-9-8 (53) S Carson 10/1: 25300-30: 11th: Slow away, eff 3f out, no prog   **hd**   **51**
fnl 2f: bckd: abs: btr 1098.
1541 **ICANNSHIFT 18** [8]4-9-0 (55) R L Moore 6/1 FAV: 0602130: 12th: Led till over 1f out, sn btn: btr 1541.   **5**   **36**
1382 **BOSCO 26** [3]3-8-7 BL (62) P Dobbs 25/1: 605-000: 13th: br c Petardia - Classic Goddess (Classic   **8**   **32**
Secret) Prom till 3f out, sn btn: blnks: highly rcd & unplcd '03 (rtd 72, mdn): half-brother to a 6f juv wnr.
1273 **Havantadoubt 32** [13]4-9-5 (60) G Baker 25/1:0   1736 **Major Blade 8** [12]6-9-3 (58) D Sweeney 33/1:0
1618 **Haribini 15** [15]4-8-4 (44) N Chalmers(3) 10/1:0   1385 **Seal Of Office 26** [18]5-9-8 (63) C Catlin 25/1:P
17 Ran Time 2m 06.7 (4.4)   Owned: Mr Nev Jones   Trained: Nesscliffe

1914   7.35 Happy Birthday Don Chadwick Handicap Stakes 3yo+ 0-80 (D)   **[79]**
    £5512 £1696 £848   **5f str**   **Good/Firm 30**   **+06 Fast**   Stands Side

1481 **DEVISE 21** [1] M S Saunders 5-9-11 (76) R Miles(3) 10/1: 600-1601: Mid-div, short of room when   **80**
switched 2f out, hdwy to lead over 1f out, rdn out: best time of night: eff at 5/5.7f on firm & gd/soft grnd.
1293 **BLUE KNIGHT 31** [11] A P Jarvis 5-9-7 (72) K Fallon 7/1: 00-24062: Held up, styd on for press ins   **¾**   **73**
last, not pace of wnr: gd run, wng form has come at 6/7f: see 655.
1615 **SEVEN NO TRUMPS 15** [13] J M Bradley 7-9-11 (76) R L Moore 12/1: 0-250003: Mid-div, kept on for   **nk**   **76**
press fnl 2f, no extra cl-home: best run since reapp: see 944 (C/D).
1354 **HOLLOW JO 28** [4] J R Jenkins 4-9-4 (69) R Hughes 8/1: 1120-004: Held up, no room fnl 2f, nrst   **1¾**   **64+**
fin:- gone close with any sort of run, keep in mind: eff at 5f, spot on at 6/7f.
3947] **YORKIES BOY 268** [6]9-8-5 (56) C Catlin 25/1: 600400-5: gr g Clantime - Slipperose (Persepolis)   **¾**   **49**
Prom, onepace from dist: reapp: class stks plcd '03: h'cap plcd '02 (rtd 88, J G Given): best up with/forcing the
pace at 5/6f, stays 7f well: acts on firm & gd/soft, any trk: gd rtn from this genuine 9yo.
1 May'01 York 6g/f 105-100 B:
1532 **PLAYTIME BLUE 18** [12]4-8-11 (62) G Baker 12/1: 1214306: Prom & ch dist, no extra: btr 1127.   **½**   **53**
4850] **SNOW WOLF 213** [7]3-9-6 (79) Dane O'Neill 16/1: 023-7: ch g Wolfhound - Christmas Rose (Absalom)   **1**   **67**
Rear, mod late gains on reapp: h'cap rcd '03, mdn rnr-up: eff at 5/6f on firm & gd grnd, stiff/ gall
trks: prev with M Tregoning. 2 Oct'03 Nott 5.1fm 80- D:
1638* **IF BY CHANCE 14** [5]6-9-9 bl (74) D Holland 9/2 FAV: 5-024418: Held up, eff/hmpd over 1f out, sn   **hd**   **61**
no impress: op 11/2: closer with a clr run & worth another look after 1638.
1774 **PRIME RECREATION 7** [2]7-8-11 (62) L Keniry(3) 10/1: 0600039: Led 3f out till over 1f out, 'hanging'.   **nk**   **48**
1743 **HARD TO CATCH 8** [14]6-9-1 bl (66) M Howard(7) 12/1: 1045500: 10th: Prom, no extra dist: see 628.   **1**   **49**
1481 **BEAUVRAI 21** [10]4-9-8 (73) M Tebbutt 8/1: 000-0000: 11th: Slow away, eff when hmpd over 1f out,   **shd**   **56+**
no ch after: closer without interference: well h'capped & lkd to be coming to hand latest: see 1481 & 567.
1867 **GOODWOOD PRINCE 2** [3]4-8-11 (62) T Quinn 14/1: 06-50000: 12th: Held up, nvr a factor, qck reapp.   **nk**   **44**
4053] **FORMALISE 261** [9]4-9-3 (68) S Carson 20/1: 405060-0: 13th: b g Forzando - Esilam (Frimley Park)   **2**   **44**
Prom till over 1f out, reapp: h'cap unplcd '03 (rtd 78, disapp in cheek pieces): lightly rcd '02 (landed a mdn):
eff at 5/6f on firm & fast grnd, stiff/undul or sharp trk. 1 Oct'02 Wind 6g/f 87- D:
4053] **TOMTHEVIC 261** [8]6-8-9 (60) M Fenton 20/1: 550220-0: 14th: Led till sn btn 3f out, sn btn, new yard.   **1½**   **31**
14 Ran Time 59.51 (1.21)   Owned: Mr D Naylor   Trained: Wells

566

1915   8.05 Rectangle Group Classified Stakes 3yo+ 0-70 (E)
£3591 £1105 £553   1m rnd   Good/Firm 30   -16 Slow   Inside

1385* **SALINOR** 26 [1] A C Stewart 4-9-8 (75) K Fallon 1/1 FAV: 41323-11: Held up, hdwy when hmpd over   81
1f out, led ins last, rdn out: hvly bckd, op 11/8: eff around 1m on firm & gd grnd.
1423 **CLIMATE** 24 [13] J R Boyle 5-9-7 vis (74) D Sweeney 14/1: S30-5402: Held up, eff/short of room &   nk   78
switched over 2f out, styd on well cl-home: apprec rtn to faster grnd: well h'capped, win again: see 878.
1691 **ANALYZE** 10 [5] B G Powell 6-9-6 (73) R L Moore 15/2: 31506-23: Prom, ch dist, no extra well ins last.   1½   74
1650* **SCOTTISH RIVER** 12 [2] M D I Usher 5-9-10 (77) Hayley Turner(5) 12/1: 1105614: Slow away, mid-div,   1   76
hung left & onepace fnl 2f: jockey reported gelding was hanging left in the closing stages: see 1650.
1322 **SUMMER SHADES** 29 [9]6-9-0 (70) T Quinn 16/1: 21620-65: Led till ins last, no extra: see 1322.   hd   65
54 **WIZARD LOOKING** 186 [12]3-8-6 t (71) P Dobbs 33/1: 60526-6: b g Wizard King - High Stepping   1   67
(Taufan) Trkd ldrs, no extra over 1f out: gelded, abs: lightly rcd '03 (auct mdn rnr-up): eff at 6f, shld get 1m:
acts on fast grnd, stiff/undul trks. 2 Oct'03 Pont 6g/f 73-(75) F:
1530 **ANNA WALHAAN** 19 [7]5-9-6 (73) C Catlin 20/1: 64205-07: b g Green Desert - Queen's Music   hd   68
(Dixieland Band) Rear, eff 2f out, onepace: h'cap rnr-up '03, earlier h'cap plcd for M Channon (rtd 83): class
stks wnr '02: eff around 1m on firm & gd/soft grnd, with/without visor, handles any trk, likes a gall one.
2 Aug'03 Brig 8.0fm 78-76 D: 1 May'02 Ayr 8g/s 96- C: 2 May'02 Thir 8gd 94- B: 1 Jun'01 Nott 6g/f 90- D:
1461 **AIMEES DELIGHT** 22 [11]4-9-4 (74) M Fenton 12/1: 310-0068: Held up, eff 2f out, not pace to chall.   1   64
1526 **CARTRONAGEERAGHLAD** 19 [6]3-8-10 bl (75) Dane O'Neill 25/1: 160-0009: b g Mujadil - Night Scent   ½   67
(Scenic) Rear, only mod prog when hmpd over 1f out: AW auct mdn scorer '03 (subs landed a h'cap in first time
blnks): eff at 6/7f, stays gall 1m: acts on gd, soft & fibresand, sharp or gall trk.
1 Nov'03 Donc 7gd 80-68 D: 1 Jun'03 Sout 6af 67a- F:
1823 **STEELY DAN** 4 [3]5-9-3 (67) N Pollard 11/1: 2116040: 10th: Al bhd, qck reapp: btr 1823.   nk   61
517 **BOUNDLESS PROSPECT** 112 [8]5-9-5 (72) E Ahern 20/1: 5500-000: 11th: Rear, eff over 2f out, sn   shd   63
short of room & position accepted: 4 mth abs: set plenty to do & not given a hard time, do better.
406* **MUYASSIR** 129 [4]9-9-3 (63) J Quinn 16/1: 0100-010: 12th: Trkd ldr, btn/hmpd over 1f out, eased,   5   52
4 month abs: btr 406 (AW).
12 Ran   Time 1m 40.68 (3.68)   Owned: M J C Hawkes & A Goddard   Trained: Newmarket

1916   8.35 Sharp Minds Betfair Stakes Handicap 3yo+ 0-80 (D)   [80]
£7020 £2160 £1080   1m4f   Good/Firm 30   -06 Slow   Inside

3420*}**OCEAN AVENUE** 290 [6] C A Horgan 5-9-10 (76) D Holland 9/2: 10/2431-1: b g Dolphin Street -   86
Trinity Hall (Hallgate) Made all, keen early, rdn & in command over 1f out, styd on strongly: nicely bckd, op 7/1,
reapp: lightly rcd '03, plcd 3 of 4 starts, incl h'cap success: landed 2 h'caps '02: likes to dominate at 12/14.5f
on firm or gd, any trk, likes Kempton: goes well fresh & a gd weight carrier: most tough & genuine.
1 Aug'03 Kemp 14.4g/f 78-75 D: 2 Jun'03 Sand 14gd 76-71 D: 1 Aug'02 Sali 12g/f 72-68 E: 1 Aug'02 Folk 12fm 69-58 F:
1689 **CAPTAIN MILLER** 10 [9] N J Henderson 8-9-4 (70) T Quinn 7/2 FAV: 1206/0//-22: Trkd wnr, eff from   3½   74
2f out, al held: bckd: may have caught a tartar & still likely type for similar after 1689.
1736 **BARRY ISLAND** 8 [3] D R C Elsworth 5-9-11 (77) Dane O'Neill 7/1: 2443003: Dwelt & held up, kept   1¼   78
on fnl 2f, nvr a threat: often set plenty to do but shown enough to find similar: see 429.
1693 **DANAKIL** 10 [2] S Dow 9-9-4 (70) R L Moore 9/2: 0-000024: Held up, switched & kept on fnl 2f, no dngr.   nk   71
1650 **SILVER PROPHET** 12 [4]5-9-7 (73) G Baker 20/1: 3000-055: Rear, eff halfway, no prog fnl 2f: see 1650.   2½   70
4263} **HONOR ROUGE** 249 [13]5-9-8 (74) D Nolan(3) 25/1: 016000-6: ch f Highest Honor - Ayers Rock (In The   5   64
Wings) Mid-div, no prog 3f out: reapp: fill rtd h'cap wnr '03 for P W Harris: progress '02, laned 3 h'caps: eff
at 10/12f: likes firm/fast grnd, handles any trk: fillies/mares events will suit.
1 May'03 Sali 12fm 85-81 C: 2 Aug'02 Pont 12g/f 91-87 C: 1 Jul'02 Hayd 11.9g/f 89-80 C: 1 Jun'02 Kemp 12g/f 80-76 D:
1 Jun'02 Pont 10g/f 82-72 D: 1 Sep'01 Muss 8g/f 78- F:
1295 **EZZ ELKHEIL** 31 [14]5-9-6 (72) R Hughes 7/1: 0-243007: Keen & trkd ldrs, btn 2f out: btr 731 (AW).   1   61
1502 **STOLEN HOURS** 20 [8]4-9-4 (70) G Carter 50/1: 6434-008: Rear, little hdwy, drpd in trip.   nk   58
1295 **PERSIAN KING** 31 [10]7-9-12 (78) V Slattery 33/1: 2/050-009: Al bhd.   1   65
3957} **DEFERLANT** 983 [11]7-9-4 vis (70) E Ahern 25/1: 52311/5//-0: 10th: Bhd, nvr a factor, 7 wk jumps abs.   4   51
1484 **SO VITAL** 21 [12]4-9-4 p (70) J Quinn 25/1: 62-10300: 11th: Al bhd: btr 936 (AW).   7   41
1543 **KOMATI RIVER** 18 [5]5-8-0 (2ow) (5oh) (45) C Catlin 50/1: 6256-000: 12th: Keen & chsd ldrs, btn 2f out.   5   16
557 **SQUIRTLE TURTLE** 106 [7]4-9-2 bl T (68) K Fallon 11/1: 3503-100: 13th: Dwelt, sn handy till over   11   17
2f out, eased: abs, t-strap: jockey reported gelding was unable to dominate: btr 331 (AW).
13 Ran   Time 2m 34.27(4.27)   Owned: Mr A Kinghorn   Trained: Ogbourne Maizey

Official Going Good/Firm

1917   1.30 Option Hygiene Handicap Stakes 3yo+ 0-105 (B)   [96]
£14092 £4336 £2168   5f   Good/Firm 25   -12 Slow   Centre

1765 **RACCOON** 7 [8] T D Barron 4-8-6 VIS (74) K Darley 5/1: 02011-41: Handy far side, styd on to lead   88+
dist despite edging left, rdn clr: qck reapp & first time visor: stays 6f, all wins come at 5f: acts on fast grnd,
stiff/gall or easy trk: apprec today's fitting of a visor, unexposed in h'cap grade & more prizes await: see 1765.
4764} **CONNECT** 219 [7] M H Tompkins 7-9-4 bl (86) G Duffield 12/1: 306006-2: b g Petong - Natchez Trace   3   89
(Commanche Run) Rear far side, prog 2f out, kept on fnl 1f, not pace of wnr: reapp: class stks & h'cap wnr in '03:
h'cap wnr in '02 (also plcd 4 times): won 2 h'caps in '01: loves to come late over a stiff 5f, stays a sharp 6f
well: acts on firm, gd grnd & polytrack: eff with/without blnks: likes Yarmouth: pleasing eff.
2 Jul'03 Asco 5g/f 88-86 C: 2 Jun'03 Ches 5.1g/f 85-83 C: 1 Jun'03 York 5.0g/f 85-76 C: 1 Feb'03 Ling 6ap 75a- E:
2 Sep'02 Sand 5g/f 84- D: 1 Aug'02 Ches 5fm 82-75 D: 1 Aug'01 Yarm 5.1gd 83-80 C: 2 Aug'01 Asco 5gd 84-79 D:
1 Jun'01 Yarm 5.1g/f 77-72 D:
1767 **SEAFIELD TOWERS** 7 [1] Miss L A Perratt 4-8-9 p (77) N Mackay(3) 20/1: 3160-003: ch g Compton Place   ¾   78
- Midnight Spell (Night Shift) Cl-up far side, onepace dist: qck reapp: rider received a 2-day whip ban: won 2

h'caps in '03: auct mdn rnr-up in '02, also h'cap plcd (rtd 74): eff at 6f, prob best around 5f: acts on firm &
fast grnd, eff in cheek pieces, prob handles any trk: likes to race with/force the pace: is back on a winning mark.
1 Aug'03 York 5.0fm 78-73 C: 1 Jul'03 Ripo 6g/f 73-67 D: 2 Jul'03 Hayd 6g/f 71-67 C: 2 Jun'03 Carl 5fm 67-66 E:
2 Jun'03 Carl 5fm 69-65 E: 2 Aug'02 Carl 5fm 75- F:

1703 **INDIAN SPARK 9** [13] J S Goldie 10-9-11 (93) T E Durcan 12/1: 500-4044: Rear stands side, prog		nk	93+

halfway, kept on fnl 1f: won race on stands side, another promising eff & is h'capped to find similar: see 1703.
1594 **TALBOT AVENUE 15** [12]6-8-12 (80) S Righton 28/1: 00000-05: b g Puissance - Dancing Daughter   nk   79
(Dance In Time) Rear stands side, prog halfway, nrst fin: h'cap wnr in '03: dual h'cap scorer in '02: eff at 5/6f
on firm & gd grnd: acts on any trk, likes a stiff/gall one, & York: now now very fav h'capped, win soon.
1 Jul'03 York 5.0fm 92-85 C: 1 Oct'02 York 6g/f 86-78 B: 2 Oct'02 York 5fm 82-78 D: 1 Aug'02 Newb 5.1fm 79-73 C:
2 Jul'02 Good 5gd 79-72 D: 2 Sep'01 Good 5g/f 78-74 E: 1 Jul'01 Sand 5g/f 76-71 D:
1626 **ABSENT FRIENDS 14** [11]7-9-13 (95) J Edmunds 33/1: 62500-06: Cl-up stands side, led stands side   ½   92+
group 2f out, no extra fnl 1f: bold effort.
1683 **MATTY TUN 10** [15]5-9-11 (93) R Hughes 11/2: 100-0557: Slow away stands side, nvr nrr than   ½   88+
mid-div: little ch here with tardy start: btr 1683.
1683 **PRINCE OF BLUES 10** [2]6-7-12 (2oh)p (64) P Varley(7) 40/1: 0404508: Rcd far side, led till dist, wknd.   2½   54
1765 **CHICO GUAPO 7** [5]4-8-8 (76) T P Queally(3) 12/1: 5001059: Cl-up far side till dist, fdd: qck reapp.   nk   63
1572 **FOURSQUARE 17** [14]3-9-2 (92) Dean McKeown 9/1: 5102-150: 10th: Led stands side group 3f, sn wknd.   shd   78
1765 **CHARLIE PARKES 7** [4]6-8-5 (73) D Allan(3) 16/1: 00000-00: 11th: Handy far side till dist, sn wknd.   1¼   55
1683 **SALVIATI 10** [10]7-9-7 (89) K Dalgleish 16/1: 04205-00: 12th: Al in rear far side.   3½   61
4161} **ATLANTIC VIKING 255** [6]9-10-0 (96) S W Kelly 50/1: 105060-0: 13th: Nvr nrr than mid-div far side.   2   62
1594 **MAKTAVISH 15** [9]5-9-3 p (85) R Winston 4/1 FAV: 0-112130: 14th: Cl-up stands side till 1f out, sn   shd   50
wknd & eased: well bckd: btr expected after fine 3rd in 1594 (gd): forgive this.
1594 **PALAWAN 15** [3]8-9-0 (82) Martin Dwyer 25/1: 2-006000: 15th: Handy far side 3f, sn wknd.   ½   45
15 Ran   Time 1m 0.67 (1.87)   Owned: Mr P D Savill   Trained: Thirsk

---

1918   2.00 Listed Dave Jones For Mortgages Stakes Registered As The Sandy Lane Stakes 3yo (A)
£17400 £6600 £3300   **6f**   Good/Firm 25   +12 Fast   Centre

1572* **MOSS VALE 17** [9] B W Hills 3-8-11 (106) K Darley 5/2: 5163-411: Keen cl-up, led trav well 2f   117
out, rdn clr fnl 1f: well bckd: eff at 5/6f on fast & gd/soft grnd: acts on a sharp or stiff/gall trk:
progressive 3yo who showed a gd turn of foot here, well up to winning in Group company: see 1572.
1479 **BOOGIE STREET 21** [4] R Hannon 3-9-0 t (107) R Hughes 11/2: 51341-32: Handy, kept on ins fnl 1f,   3   111
no ch with wnr: op 4/1: not disgraced on return to own age group conceding 3lbs to progressive wnr: see 1479.
1360* **HIGH VOLTAGE 28** [3] K R Burke 3-8-11 t (99) Darren Williams 16/1: 22020-13: Set gd pace 3f, styd   3   99
handy, wknd bef 1f out: not disgraced on return in age group: just btr 1360 (h'cap, gd/soft).
1683 **FAST HEART 10** [1] B J Meehan 3-8-11 t (99) J F McDonald 40/1: 1003-004: Handy over 4f, no extra.   shd   98
1572 **LOCAL POET 17** [2]3-8-11 (92) G Gibbons 28/1: 224-1505: Handy till dist, wknd: btr 1150.   2½   91
1234 **NEROS RETURN 35** [8]3-9-0 (105) K Dalgleish 16/1: 11-606: Mid-div, hung left halfway, nvr able to chall.   3½   84
1421* **MILLBAG 24** [6]3-9-0 (107) T E Durcan 7/4 FAV: 31313-17: Handy 4f, sn wknd: well bckd: disapp   2   78
here on return to a fast surface: btr 1421 (reapp, soft).
1572 **EMBASSY LORD 17** [5]3-8-11 bl (80) J D O'Reilly 140/1: 21500-48: Al in rear: see 1572.   1¼   71
1732 **RUM SHOT 8** [7]3-8-11 (97) D Sweeney 7/1: 611-49: Handy 4f, sn fdd: btr 1732.   2½   64
9 Ran   Time 1m 12.11 (0.81)   Owned: Mr John C Grant   Trained: Lambourn

---

1919   2.30 Totesport Silver Bowl Heritage Handicap 3yo 0-110 (B)
£52200 £19800 £9900   **1m30y**   Good/Firm 25   +10 Fast   Inside   **[110]**

1813* **GATWICK 4** [17] M R Channon 3-8-13 (8ex) (95) S Hitchcott(3) 11/2: 3-1311: Dwelt, prog halfway,   107+
short of room ins fnl 2f, styd on with strong run to lead ins fnl 1f, rdn out: op 4/1 on qck reapp: eff at 1m/9f,
10f will suit: acts on fast & gd grnd: v progressive 3yo who showed a gd turn of foot after not getting the best of
runs, improve again over further & win in listed/Gr company: see 1813.
1583 **MAKFOOL 16** [10] M R Channon 3-8-8 (90) T E Durcan 40/1: 43-03402: Handy, styd on to lead dist,   1¾   96
hdd ins fnl 1f, no extra: stablemate of wnr: apprec today's return to 1m: can find similar, see 1150.
1583 **ZONUS 16** [12] B W Hills 3-8-5 (87) K Darley 5/2 FAV: 2-1423: Dwelt, prog 3f out, short of room   shd   93
ins fnl 2f & sn switched wide, styd on well fnl despite hanging badly left & carrying hd high: nrst fin: v well
bckd: would have fin closer with clr run but shapes as though further will suit: not straightforward but has
plenty of ability: see 1583 & 1206.
1583 **APPALACHIAN TRAIL 16** [2] I Semple 3-8-4 (86) G Duffield 12/1: 05-31204: Handy, edged left just   shd   92
ins fnl 2f, kept on & not btn far in 4th: back to form after disapp at Chester (poor draw): can find similar.
1583+ **OASIS STAR 16** [11]3-8-4 (86) Martin Dwyer 6/1: 1-115: Handy till dist, sn onepcd: gd effort   2   88
here on hat-trick bid: prob stays 1m, return to sltly shorter will suit: raised 5lb since recent win in 1583.
1707 **FREAK OCCURENCE 9** [4]3-8-0 (82) J F McDonald(3) 25/1: 420-0346: Handy 6f, no extra bef 1f out.   nk   83
1636 **CAPPED FOR VICTORY 14** [3]3-8-6 (88) B Swarbrick(5) 12/1: 232-27: Led 7f out, hdd dist, no extra.   ½   88
1741 **SECRETARY GENERAL 8** [5]3-8-10 (92) R Thomas(5) 12/1: 241-028: Held up, eff when no room 3f out,   ½   90
prog bef 1f out, nrst fin: not get run of race here & is better than this: see 1741.
1666 **ASIA WINDS 11** [15]3-8-11 (93) W Ryan 25/1: 41155-59: Slow away, prog when short of room 2f out   1   90+
till dist, kept on fnl 1f, ch had gone: lot closer here with clr passage & is worth another ch: btr 1666.
1496 **OVERDRAWN 20** [8]3-8-10 (92) S W Kelly 12/1: 3415-000: 10th: Nvr nrr than mid-div: see 1315.   hd   88
1186 **BENNY THE BALL 37** [1]3-8-1 (83) J Bramhill 50/1: 4261-00: 11th: Handy, ev ch 2f out, sn fdd.   3½   72
1665 **PARKVIEW LOVE 11** [18]3-9-7 (103) K Dalgleish 66/1: 165-0300: 12th: Handy till halfway, sn wknd.   nk   91
1665 **CONVINCE 11** [7]3-8-5 (87) Dean McKeown 50/1: 2104-000: 13th: Al in rear: btr 1665.   shd   75
1621 **STAR PUPIL 14** [13]3-8-1 (83) F P Ferris(3) 40/1: 02-4200: 14th: Bhd & nvr a factor, saddle   ½   70
slipped: first try at 1m: btr 1498 (6f).
1315 **COLOUR WHEEL 29** [6]3-8-8 T (90) R Hughes 20/1: 0122-60: 15th: Led till 7f out, styd handy till   1¾   73
wknd fnl 2f: first time t-strap: btr 1315 (reapp).
1583 **WHITE HAWK 16** [14]3-8-13 (95) T P Queally(3) 50/1: 1214-400: 16th: Al in rear: see 1208.   shd   77
1665 **Bahiano 11** [16]3-9-2 (98) Dean Williams(7) 33/1:0   1167 **Spanish Ace 38** [9]3-9-2 (98) D Sweeney 66/1:0
18 Ran   Time 1m 41.73 (1.23)   Owned: Mr W H Ponsonby   Trained: West Ilsley

1920   3.05 E B F Bollin Maiden Stakes Fillies 2yo (D)
£5369 £1652 £826   6f   Good/Firm 25   -34 Slow   Centre

1567 **SAPPHIRE DREAM 17** [6] A Bailey 2-8-11 R Winston 10/11 FAV: 221: Made all, rdn out ins fnl 1f: **86**
well bckd: eff around 5f, imprvd here for step up to 6f: acts on fast & hvy grnd, stiff/undul, gall or
sharp/turning trk: gd confidence boost: see 1567.

   MYTTONS BELL 0 [4] A Bailey 2-8-11   J Bramhill 33/1: 2: b f Bold Edge - Ionian Secret (Mystiko)   1¾   **79**
Handy, kept on ins fnl 2f, al held by wnr: debut: March foal, cost 7,000gns: dam plcd at 10f: sire high-class
performer at sprint dists: eff at 6f, shaped as tho' further will suit: acts on fast grnd: encouraging eff.

   EASY FEELING 0 [7] R Hannon 2-8-11 R Hughes 6/1: 3: b f Night Shift - Talena (Zafonic) Handy,   hd   **78**
kept on despite edging left ins fnl 1f, just held for 2nd: debut: Feb first foal, cost £30,000: dam plcd abroad:
sire speedily bred: eff at 6f on fast grnd: not disgraced here & can rate higher with experience.

   WASALAT 0 [5] M R Channon 2-8-11   T E Durcan 5/1: 4: b f Bahri - Saabga (Woodman) Slow away, sn   1¼   **74**
handy, outpcd halfway, rallied fnl 1f: debut: clr rem: Jan foal, sister to a 7f/1m wnr: dam plcd at 7f: sire
high-class performer at 1m: impr on today's experience when tried over further.

   SWEET MARGUERITE 0 [8] 2-8-11   D Allan(3) 14/1: 5: Handy 3f, sn edged left & no extra fnl 2f.   4   **62**
1716 **DONT TELL TRIGGER 9** [2] 2-8-11   J D Smith 25/1: 06: Handy 4f, sn wknd.   shd   **62**
1343 **MAKE US FLUSH 28** [3] 2-8-11 P Bradley(5) 20/1: 47: In tch 4f, wknd.   3½   **52**
   SUKUMA 0 [1] 2-8-11 Martin Dwyer 10/1: 8: Al in rear.   hd   **51**
1343 **GLORIA NIMBUS 28** [9] 2-8-11 S Righton 66/1: 09: Keen handy, wknd halfway.   20   **0**
9 Ran   Time 1m 14.84 (3.54)   Owned: Mr P T Tellwright   Trained: Tarporley

1921   3.35 Listed E B F Joan Westbrook Pinnacle Stakes Fillies 4yo+ (A)
£23200 £8800 £4400   1m3f200y   Good/Firm 25   -11 Slow   Outside

1721 **PONGEE 9** [1] L M Cumani 4-8-11   (87) T E Durcan 3/1: 11110-31: Cl-up, styd on to lead dist, drvn   **103**
out: suited by around 12f: acts on firm, gd/soft grnd & polytrack: tough & progressive 4yo, see 1721.
1721+ **DESERT ROYALTY 9** [2] E A L Dunlop 4-8-11   (82) R Hughes 5/2 FAV: 3123-212: In tch, prog when   2½   **97**
short of room 2f out, styd on onepcd ins fnl 1f: well bckd: fin ahead of today's wnr off 5lbs better terms in 1721.
1491 **CHANTRESS 20** [6] Mrs J R Ramsden 4-8-11 P (92) Martin Dwyer 15/2: 21413-03: b f Peintre Celebre -   2   **95**
Up Anchor (Slip Anchor) Handy, ev ch 3f out, no extra bef 1f out: cheek pieces: mdn & h'cap wnr in '03 (also plcd
twice, M Johnston): eff aroun 10.4f, prob stays 12f: acts on firm & gd grnd, prob any trk: has gone well fresh:
not disgraced here on step up in grade with fitting of cheek pieces.
   1 Aug'03 Ches 10.3gd 89-82 C: 1 Jun'03 Carl 9.3fm 83- D: 2 May'03 Muss 8gd 82- D:
1857 **FELICITY 8** [3] J H M Gosden 4-8-11   (97) R Havlin 9/2: 3535-034: Led, hdd dist, no extra: below   shd   **95**
par run on step up to 12f: btr 1857 (Gr 3, 10f).
1684 **THINGMEBOB 10** [5] 4-8-11   (104) G Duffield 100/30: 01320-55: Keen handy over 1m, sn no extra: clr   shd   **94**
rem: yet to reach heights of last term in both effs this term: see 1684.
1467 **TRANSCENDANTALE 22** [4] 6-8-11   (47) T P Queally 100/1: 000-2356: Chsd ldrs over 1m, sn fdd.   17   **64**
1527 **MY LITTLE SOPHIA 19** [7] 4-8-11 S W Kelly 200/1: 507: Al well adrift: v stiff task.   dist   **0**
7 Ran   Time 2m 32.16 (4.36)   Owned: Fittocks Stud   Trained: Newmarket

1922   4.10 Mtb Group Maiden Stakes 3yo (D)
£5707 £1756 £878   1m2f120y   Good/Firm 25   -24 Slow   Outside

1358 **NUNKI 28** [5] H R A Cecil 3-9-0   W Ryan 11/4: 31: Handy, styd on to lead ins fnl 1f, rdn out to   **89**
hold on: well bckd, eff at 10/10.5f, 12f shld suit: acts on fast & gd/soft grnd: eff on a stiff/gall trk: lightly
rcd & there shld be more to come: see 1358.
1384 **IDEALISTIC 26** [6] L M Cumani 3-8-9   Martin Dwyer 16/1: 02: b f Unfuwain - L'Ideale (Alysheba)   hd   **84**
Chsd ldrs, on grad to lead dist, hdd ins fnl 1f, kept on, just held: clr rem: rider received a 1-day whip ban:
eff at 10.5f, 12f shld suit: acts on fast grnd: only just denied & can find similar when stepped up to 12f.
1784 **ALWAYS WAINING 6** [8] M Johnston 3-9-0   K Dalgleish 7/1: 33: Led 2f, cl-up when hung right on   4   **82**
bend 5f out, styd on to lead 2f out despite hanging right, hdd dist, onepcd when eased ins fnl 1f: op 5/1: qck
reapp: eff at 9/10.5f: shown enough to win similar: see 1784.
1707 **GJOVIC 9** [4] B J Meehan 3-9-0   (75) J F McDonald(3) 4/1: 342-2504: Held up, nvr nrr than mid-div.   3   **78**
1597 **MOUFTARI 15** [9] 3-9-0   (84) K Darley 5/2 FAV: 0-545: Handy, led 3f out, hdd 2f out, sn wknd: well   1¾   **75**
bckd: drop back to a mile shld suit: btr 1597.
1489 **MUNGO JERRY 21** [10] 3-9-0   G Duffield 10/1: 0-36: Keen handy 1m, sn wknd: see 1489.   2   **72**
1783 **PROTECTIVE 6** [7] 3-9-0   T E Durcan 20/1: 47: Slow away, al in rear: qck reapp.   7   **62**
1597 **PHOENIX EYE 15** [3] 3-9-0 S W Kelly 100/1: 0-08: Led after 2f till 3f out, sn fdd: see 1597.   8   **50**
   TWILIGHT YEARS 0 [1] 3-9-0   D Allan(3) 40/1: 9: Slow away, al in rear.   ½   **49**
1617 **MAD MAURICE 15** [2] 3-9-0 p   T P Queally(3) 40/1: 0-000: 10th: Held up, prog 5f out, fdd 2f out.   5   **42**
10 Ran   Time 2m 15.49 (5.19)   Owned: Niarchos Family   Trained: Newmarket

1923   4.40 Mary Page Birthday Handicap Stakes 4yo+ 0-75 (E)   [75]
£3640 £1120 £560   1m6f   Good/Firm 25   -08 Slow   Inside

1506 **NAKWA 20** [9] E J Alston 6-9-2   (63) D Allan(3) 7/2 FAV: 2253221: Led, hdd after 5f, styd cl-up &   **73+**
led again 4f out, rdn clr ins fnl 2f, eased cl-home, val 7L+: well bckd: eff at 12/14f on fast, soft grnd &
fibresand: has been running well & this was a deserved success: see 1506 & 1109.
1629 **NORTHERN NYMPH 14** [4] R Hollinshead 5-9-5   (66) Stephanie Hollinshead(5) 6/1: 2300562: Held up,   5   **68**
grad prog to chase wnr ins fnl 1f, kept on but al held: encouraging eff here & is back on a winning mark. see 743.
2069) **ONCE 346** [2] J A Osborne 4-10-0   (75) S W Kelly 11/1: 23/2300-3: gr g Hector Protector - Moon   1¼   **75**
Magic (Polish Precedent) Handy, onepcd bef 1f out: reapp & new stable: rnr-up once in '03 (h'cap, M L W Bell):
plcd on 2 of 3 juv starts (mdn, rtd 78): prev eff at 7f/10f, poss stays 14f: acts on fast & gd grnd.
   2 Apr'03 Newm 10gd 80-76 C: 2 Sep'02 Warw 7.1g f 78- D:
4664} **FANTASTICO 226** [6] Mrs K Walton 4-9-3   (64) K Dalgleish 20/1: 561430-4: b f Bahhare - Minatina   1¼   **62**
(Ela Mana Mou) Chsd ldrs, no extra ins fnl 2f: recent hdles unplcd (rtd 63h, h'cap): plcd twice in 03/04 (rtd 93h,

juv nov, stays 2m on gd & gd/soft): h'cap wnr in '03: plcd 4 times in '02 (mdns, rtd 74 & 71a): eff at 10/12f, has tried 2m: acts on firm, soft grnd & both AWs.
1 Aug'03 Folk 12g/f 64-60 F: 2 Sep'02 Bath 10.2fm 74- D: 2 Sep'02 Sout 8af 71a- F:
1034 **BRAMANTINO 49** [7]4-8-11 bl (58) G Parkin 7/1: 0-531025: Handy over 12f, sn no extra: 7 wk abs. ¾ **56**
1721 **CLARADOTNET 9** [5]4-9-9 (70) T E Durcan 8/1: 210-0006: Held up, nvr nrr than mid-div. 2½ **64**
1793 **REPULSE BAY 5** [10]6-8-4 (51) N Mackay(3) 11/2: 500-6037: Handy 12f, sn wknd: qck reapp: btr 1793. 3 **41**
1361 **VICARS DESTINY 28** [3]6-9-8 p (69) G Duffield 6/1: 626-2208: Held up, nvr a factor: recent wnr over hdles (h'cap, rtd 130h): btr 1069 (2m2f, hvy). 2 **56**
3208} **CIRCUS MAXIMUS 299** [1]7-8-11 bl (58) K Darley 12/1: 0/5/5020-9: b g Pleasant Colony - Crockadore (Nijinsky) Al in rear: recent hdles unplcd (rtd 86h, claim hdle): nov chase & claim hdle wnr in first 2 of 4 03/04 starts (rtd 103c & 120h, eff with/without blnks): rnr-up on Flat on 1 of 4 '03 starts (h'cap): eff around 14f on fast grnd: eff with blnks, has tried cheek pieces. 4 **39**
2 Apr'03 Nott 14.1g/f 56-54 F:
1772 **VANBRUGH 7** [8]4-8-8 vis t (55) Darren Williams 16/1: 6-106000: 10th: Keen cl-up, led after 5f, hdd 4f out, sn hung left & fdd: qck reapp. 7 **27**
10 Ran Time 3m 02.63(4.63) Owned: Mr Alan Dick Trained: Preston

ASCOT SATURDAY 22.05.04 Righthand, Stiff, Galloping Track

Official Going Good/Firm

1924 — 1.45 First National Stakes Handicap 3yo 0-90 (C) [97]
£9851 £3031 £1516 **1m2f** **Good/Firm 20** **-30 Slow** Inside

1496 **MUDAWIN 20** [4] M P Tregoning 3-9-7 (90) S Whitworth 11/1: 5-0101: Slow away, held up, gd hdwy over 3f out to lead 1f out, rdn clr, going away: op 8/1: relished step up to 10f, 12f sure to suit: acts on fast & gd grnd, gall trk: v useful & progressive, just the type for King George V at Royal Ascot: see 1236. **100+**
1213 **GANYMEDE 36** [10] M L W Bell 3-8-11 (80) M Fenton 16/1: 63-232: Cl-up, eff over 1f out, kept on but not pace of wnr: gd run, must win a mdn: see 1019. 3½ **83**
4811} **SPRING GODDESS 215** [2] A P Jarvis 3-8-13 (82) N Callan 50/1: 03160-3: b f Daggers Drawn - Easter Girl (Efisio) Held up, hdwy 2f out, kept on ins last, not pace of wnr on reapp: '03 fills mdn wnr: eff at 7.5f, stays 10f on fast grnd & a stiff or fair trk: gd return. 1 Sep'03 Beve 7.5g/f 82- D: ½ **84**
1664 **GOLDEN GRACE 11** [6] E A L Dunlop 3-9-5 (88) J F Egan 5/1 JT FAV: 631-044: Slow away, keen & sn chsd ldrs, hdwy to lead over 1f out till dist, no extra: prob ran to form of 1664. *nk* **89**
4978} **SHALAYA 203** [3]3-9-4 (87) B Doyle 10/1: 16-5: b f Marju - Shalama (Kahyasi) Keen, cl-up, led over 2f out till over 1f out, no extra: won first of 2 '03 starts (fills mdn): eff at 1m, prob stays 10f: acts on fast grnd: lightly rcd. 1 Sep'03 Leic 8.0g/f 79- D: *hd* **87**
1619 **RIO DE JUMEIRAH 14** [11]3-8-9 (78) D Holland 16/1: 3035-36: Held up, eff & short of room over 2f out, late gains: could rate higher: see 1619. ¾ **77**
1597* **IKTITAF 15** [8]3-9-4 (87) W Supple 13/2: 0317: Chsd ldrs, wknd over 1f out: btr 1597 (mdn, gd). *nk* **85**
1511* **FIRST CENTURION 19** [5]3-9-4 (87) T Quinn 5/1 JT FAV: 6-18: Held up, stumbled bend over 2f out, no impress: see 1511 (1m, hvy). 2½ **81**
1741 **BAILEYS DANCER 8** [12]3-8-12 (81) S Chin 8/1: 1140-049: In tch, btn over 2f out: see 1315. ¾ **73**
1651* **INCURSION 12** [13]3-9-1 (84) V Slattery 17/2: 063-10: 10th: Held up, wknd over 2f out: btr 1651 (soft). *nk* **75**
1664 **TOP SPEC 11** [1]3-9-2 (85) R L Moore 16/1: 22161-00: 11th: b g Spectrum - Pearl Marine (Bluebird) In tch, wknd 2f out: '03 dual h'cap wnr: stays 1m well on firm & gd grnd: likes a gall trk, does handle any, likes Newmarket: needs 1m? 3½ **71**
1 Oct'03 Newm 8g/f 87-82 D: 1 Aug'03 Newm 8fm 85-80 C: 2 Aug'03 Newb 7g/f 85-75 D: 2 Jul'03 Newm 7g/f 76-72 D:
4830} **STANLEY CRANE 214** [7]3-8-9 t (78) O Urbina 50/1: 435-0: 12th: Keen, sn clr ldr, hdd & wknd over 2f out. 4 **57**
1580* **MAGIC AMIGO 16** [14]3-8-5 (74) F Norton 33/1: 5420-210: 13th: Al bhd: btr 1580 (soft, mdn auct). *shd* **52**
1141 **GRETNA 40** [9]3-8-13 (82) G Carter 25/1: 6-100: 14th: In tch, wknd qckly over 4f out, t.o.: twice below 977 (mdn fills, soft). *21* **30**
14 Ran Time 2m 09.01 (5.01) Owned: Mr Hamdan Al Maktoum Trained: Lambourn

1925 — 2.15 Ritz Club London Conditions Stakes Fillies 4yo+ (B)
£11948 £4532 £2266 **7f str** **Good/Firm 20** **+04 Fast** Stands Side

1782* **ENCHANTED 6** [4] N A Callaghan 5-8-5 (88) F Norton 10/11 FAV: 60463-11: Keen held up, hdwy to lead appr fnl 1f, rdn clr, going away: 2nd win in under a week: suited by 6/7f on firm & gd, any trk: thriving, career best run & can win a List fills event shortly: see 1782. **97**
1620 **BLAISE CASTLE 14** [2] G A Butler 4-8-5 (90) R L Moore 4/1: 03042-42: Handy, eff to chall over 1f out, not pace of wnr: acts on fast, soft & polytrack: useful, ran to best: see 1620, 58. 2 **91**
1598 **DAME DE NOCHE 15** [3] J G Given 4-8-9 (88) M Fenton 7/1: 0300-603: Set pace, hdd appr fnl 1f, wknd: far from disgraced at these weights & will do btr with an uncontested lead back in h'cap company. 2½ **90**
1863 **STARBECK 2** [5] P Howling 6-8-6 (1ow) (88) N Callan 9/1: 520-0054: Slow away, keen, held up, eff 2f out, onepace: qck reapp: see 1863. 1 **85**
1775 **MADAMOISELLE JONES 7** [7]4-8-5 (64) W Supple 33/1: 4100-045: Handy, wknd over 1f out: flattered. ½ **83$**
1094 **HIGH FINANCE 44** [6]4-8-9 (79) T Quinn 12/1: 10455-56: Keen held up, brief eff 2f out, no extra: abs. 2½ **82$**
1806 **TENDER 5** [1]4-8-5 (57) J F Egan 66/1: 0060-357: Keen cl-up, wknd over 1f out: flattered: see 1096 (5f). ¾ **76$**
7 Ran Time 1m 27.13 (1.13) Owned: Norcroft Park Stud Trained: Newmarket

1926 — 2.45 Totesport Victoria Cup Heritage Handicap 4yo+ 0-110 (B) [106]
£34800 £13200 £6600 **7f str** **Good/Firm 20** **+10 Fast** Stands Side. 2 Groups.

1686 **MINE 10** [16] J D Bethell 6-9-7 vis (99) T Quinn 5/1 FAV: 3406-231: Held up far side, strong run over 1f out to lead ins last, rdn out: stays 1m, best at 7f now & enjoys a gall trk: thrives off a strong pace/big field: career best, has a fine turn of foot, smart enough for List/Gr 3 now: see 1225. **110**
1481 **GREENSLADES 21** [20] P J Makin 5-8-13 (91) S Carson 10/1: 0105-442: Chsd ldrs far side, gd hdwy ¾ **99**

over 1f out, kept on ins last, al held by wnr: excellent eff with more restrained tactics & can land a val h'cap.
1697* **VORTEX 16** [6] Miss Gay Kelleway 5-9-5 e t (97) N Cordrey 16/1: 1110013: Handy stands side, led that group 2f out, styd on well, al held by far side: most progressive & a fine run on poss unfav'd side: thriving, shld not be underestimated in Royal Hunt Cup: see 1697, 836. *1¼* **103+**
1624 **CAMP COMMANDER 14** [12] C E Brittain 5-9-2 t (94) B Doyle 16/1: 00034-04: Dwelt, held up stands side, gd hdwy 2f out, styd on well ins last in centre: won this race last term off an 11lb lower mark & a fine eff again on poss unfav'd side: tough & useful with a turn of foot: see 1624. *hd* **100**
1624 **KOOL 14** [13]5-9-0 (92) S Chin 16/1: 120/-3055: With ldrs far side, onepcd over 1f out: gd run, see 1126. *2* **93**
1686 **ATAVUS 10** [18]7-9-3 (95) A McCarthy 25/1: 30104-06: b c Distant Relative - Elysian (Northfields) Led far side group & overall ldr over 1f out, hdd & no extra ins last: sole '03 win in a stks, List rnr-up: '02 List & Gr 3 wnr: best at 7f, stays 1m on firm & gd, poss soft: acts on any trk, loves Newmarket: has run well fresh: tough & genuine, best when dominating. *shd* **96**
1 Sep'03 Yarm 6.0g/f 100-(102) C: 2 May'03 Wind 8.3g/s 110-(107) A: 1 Sep'02 Epso 7g/f 109- A:
1 Jun'02 Newm 7fm 109- A: 1 Aug'01 Newb 7.2fm 113- A: 1 Jul'01 Asco 7fm 100-93 B: 1 Jul'01 Newm 7g/f 97-86 B:
2 May'01 Good 7fm 90-82 C: 1 May'01 Newm 8g/f 87-78 C:
1512 **AUDIENCE 19** [14]4-9-0 P (92) M Fenton 20/1: 226-0007: Held up far side, eff well over 1f out, no impress. *1* **91**
1481 **MASTER ROBBIE 21** [15]5-8-12 (90) R Lappin 12/1: 160-0008: b g Piccolo - Victoria's Secret (Law Society) Held up far side, no impress over 1f out: '03 seven time wnr (5 h'caps & 2 class stks): eff over 6.5/7f & loves firm or gd grnd, any trk, likes Ascot: most tough, progressive & useful last term. *1* **87**
1 Oct'03 York 7.0g/f 96-90 B: 2 Oct'03 Newm 7fm 91-87 B: 1 Sep'03 Asco 7fm 91-85 B: 1 Aug'03 Ayr 7.2g/f 85-(85) D:
2 Aug'03 Sand 7.1g/f 85-84 C: 2 Aug'03 Newm 7fm 86-84 B: 1 Jul'03 Asco 6.5g/f 87-81 C: 1 Jun'03 Warw 7.1fm 84-(79) D:
1 May'03 Newb 7g/f 81-74 E: 2 May'03 Good 7g/f 73-69 C: 1 May'03 Sali 7.0fm 71-64 D: 2 Apr'03 Folk 7g/f 66-(65) E:
1686 **EL COTO 10** [8]4-9-10 (102) B Reilly(3) 11/1: 04-01559: Handy stands side, no extra over 1f out. *1¼* **97**
1686 **CALCUTTA 10** [3]8-9-6 (98) K May(7) 33/1: 1314-000: 10th: b c Indian Ridge - Echoing (Formidable) Held up stands side, no impress over 1f out: '03 stks & h'cap wnr: '02 stks & 3 time h'cap scorer: eff at 7f, last 10 wins have come at 1m: likes firm & fast, handles gd/soft: best without blnks & likes a gall trk: gd weight-carrier who has run well fresh: best held up, has a turn of foot: useful & tough. *hd* **92**
1 Oct'03 York 7.9g/f 101-97 B: 1 Sep'03 Bath 8.0fm 99-(95) C: 1 Sep'02 Bath 8fm 107- C: 2 Sep'02 Donc 8fm 105-100 B:
1 Jul'02 Newb 8fm 102-96 B: 1 Jul'02 York 8g/f 95-94 B: 1 Jun'02 Sali 8fm 95-92 C: 1 Sep'01 Donc 8g/f 98-91 B:
1 May'01 Sand 8gd 96-91 B: 2 May'01 Good 8fm 95-91 C:
1043 **HIDDEN DRAGON 49** [4]5-9-8 (100) D Nolan(3) 20/1: 4000-220: 11th: With ldrs stands side, wknd over 1f out: 7 wk abs, btr 1043, 887. *½* **93**
4950} **VINDICATION GB 205** [19]4-9-1 t (93) O Urbina 25/1: 065110-0: 12th: In tch far side, no extra fnl 2f. *nk* **85**
1225 **SELECTIVE 35** [11]5-9-8 (100) D Holland 8/1: 22230-40: 13th: In tch stands side, short of room 2f out but sn no extra: rnr-up in this race off a 1lb lower mark last term. *1* **90**
1481 **FANTASY BELIEVER 21** [10]6-8-12 (90) F Norton 50/1: 041-0000: 14th: Handy stands side, wknd 2f out. *4* **72**
MAKSAD 35 [7]4-9-3 (95) W Supple 6/1: 5121-20: 15th: Bo dngr stands side: bckd, French raider. *shd* **77**
1812 **CAPTAIN SAIF 4** [2]4-9-0 bl (92) R L Moore 25/1: 56635-00: 16th: Dwelt, in tch, short of room over 2f out, no extra. *½* **73**
1490 **CRAFTY CALLING 20** [17]4-9-2 t (94) L Keniry(3) 33/1: 01054-00: 17th: Handy, wknd qckly far side 2f out. *1¼* **73**
1486 **WILL HE WISH 21** [5]8-9-3 (95) N Callan 33/1: 1-005600: 18th: Led stands side till 2f out, wknd: see 1043. *2½* **69**
1624* **GOLDEN CHALICE 14** [1]5-8-13 (91) J F Egan 16/1: 0-560010: 19th: Dwelt, in tch stands side, wknd qckly 2f out: btr on soft grnd in 1624. *10* **45**
3974} **INTO THE BREEZE 266** [9]4-9-3 (95) S Whitworth 33/1: 265125-0: 20th: Held up stands side, wknd 2f out. *¾* **47**
20 Ran Time 1m 26.7 (0.7) Owned: Mr M J Dawson Trained: Middleham

1927

3.20 Brunswick Group Handicap Stakes Fillies 3yo+ 0-80 (D) **[80]**
£7118 £2190 £1095 **1m str** **Good/Firm 20** **-06 Slow** Stands Side. 2 Groups.

1542 **ENCHANTED PRINCESS 18** [15] W J Haggas 4-9-1 BL (67) D Holland 12/1: 01-051: Held up far side, hdwy over 1f out, led ins last, rdn out: imprvd over this stiff/straight 1m & best on fast grnd, handles soft: clearly enjoyed blnks, tried a visor last time: reportedly in foal: see 1542. **77**
1116 **PINK SAPPHIRE 42** [13] D R C Elsworth 3-8-5 (69) O Urbina 33/1: 510-02: ch f Bluebird - Highbrook (Alphabatim) Made most far side, overall ldr 2f out, hdd & not pace of wnr ins last: 6 wk abs: won 1 of 3 '03 starts (fills mdn): eff at 6f, clearly stays 1m: acts on fast grnd & a sharp or stiff trk: lightly rcd, v encouraging. 1 Aug'03 Wind 6g/f 72- D: *1½* **75**
1610* **CITRINE SPIRIT 15** [6] J H M Gosden 3-8-10 (74) F Norton 9/1: 0-613: Led stands side group throughout, styd on well ins last, not reach far side pair: v encouraging on prob unfav'd side of crse: acts on fast & hvy grnd: lightly rcd, one to keep on your side next time: see 1610. *2½* **74**
4344*}**FLORIDA HEART 246** [11] A M Balding 3-8-12 (76) L Keniry(3) 12/1: 054221-4: ch f First Trump - Miami Dancer (Seattle Dancer) Held up far side, hdwy & short of room over 2f out, eff over 1f out, onepace: won last of 7 '03 starts (nursery h'cap): eff at 7f/1m on fast & gd grnd, likes gall trks: consistent, gd return. *2* **73**
1 Sep'03 Ayr 8g/f 75-71 C: 2 Sep'03 York 7.9g/f 74-(72) E: 2 Aug'03 Yarm 8.0g/f 75-(73) E:
1849 **MISS PEBBLES 3** [5]4-9-1 VIS (67) N Pollard 12/1: 56-14005: In tch stands side, kept on over 1f out, no dngr: qck reapp & a gd run in a visor. *nk* **63**
1467 **SPARK UP 22** [19]4-8-13 bl (65) T Quinn 25/1: 6244106: Handy far side, eff over 1f out, sn no extra. *hd* **60**
1711 **MYTHICAL CHARM 9** [1]5-8-3 t (55) J Tate 20/1: 0006337: With ldrs stands side, outpcd over 2f out, some late gains: see 427. *3* **44**
1616 **CHEESE N BISCUITS 15** [18]4-9-10 (76) R L Moore 7/1 JT FAV: 135-0028: Held up far side, late gains. *hd* **64**
1465 **TUSCARORA 22** [16]5-8-3 (1ow) (54) P Doe 14/1: 46406-09: Held up far side, no extra over 1f out. *1¾* **39**
1723 **NIGHT KISS 9** [3]4-8-10 (62) R Smith 10/1: 0220-000: 10th: ch f Night Shift - Roxy (Rock City) In tch stands side, no extra over 1f out: '03 fills h'cap wnr: eff at 7f/1m on firm, gd & polytrack, acts on any trk, likes Ascot. 2 Oct'03 Ling 7ap 59a-(56) E: 2 Sep'03 Asco 8g/f 65-63 D: 1 Mar'03 Asco 7g/f 66-60 D: *hd* **45**
1 Oct'02 Newm 7g/f 64- E: 2 Sep'02 Ling 6fm 59- G:
1618 **MISS GRACE 15** [8]4-8-5 (57) D Corby(3) 14/1: 3360-040: 11th: In tch stands side, wknd over 1f out. *2* **36**
3915} **STRATEGY 269** [4]4-10-0 (80) S Whitworth 25/1: 416123-0: 12th: Held up stands side, wknd over 1f out. *hd* **58**
4255} **MUSIC MAID 249** [20]6-8-10 (62) N Callan 16/1: 145115-0: 13th: With ldrs far side, wknd 2f out on reapp. *shd* **40**
1723 **MICHELLE MA BELLE 9** [2]4-9-9 (75) A Daly 14/1: 55-02200: 14th: Cl-up stands side, hung badly right over 2f out, wknd: btr 1079, 1024. *4* **45**
1527* **DREAMING OF YOU 19** [14]3-8-11 (75) B Doyle 7/1 JT FAV: 0-10: 15th: Held up far side, wknd over 3f out, eased: not enjoy faster grnd? btr 1527 (fills mdn, soft). *¾* **43**
1587 **KEEPERS LODGE 16** [17]3-8-8 (72) W Supple 40/1: 40504-40: 16th: Al bhd. *1¼* **37**
1537 **IN THE PINK 18** [10]4-8-13 (65) R Lappin 20/1: 04351-00: 17th: Al bhd. *1¼* **27**
1470 **FAITH HEALER 22** [12]3-7-12 (2oh)P (60) A McCarthy 50/1: 30460-00: 18th: Al bhd far side. *½* **23**

5027} **HELDERBERG 197** [7]4-9-4 (70) M Fenton 40/1: 002210-0: 19th: Al bhd far side: now with B Rothwell.   nk   **30**
1255   **MARGALITA 33** [9]4-9-6 BL t (72) J F Egan 25/1: 1300-600: 20th: With ldr far side till over 2f   9   **14**
out, wknd, reportedly lost action: tried blnks.
20 Ran   Time 1m 40.83 (2.13)   Owned: Mrs Susan J Jensen   Trained: Newmarket

1928	3.55 Bonusprint Com Handicap Stakes 4yo+ 0-85 (D)			[87]
	£8323 £2561 £1281 2m45y Good/Firm 20 -12 Slow Inside			

1516   **LAND N STARS 19** [14] Jamie Poulton 4-8-13 (72) P Doe 66/1: 0/422-01: In tch, gd hdwy over 2f   **83**
out, led over 1f out, rdn clr: enjoyed step up to 2m: acts on firm & fast grnd: handles any trk, clearly enjoyed
this gall one: only 4yo, unexposed at this trip, win more staying h'caps: see 1516.
1700} **GOT ONE TOO 364** [9] N J Henderson 7-9-1 (72) D Holland 7/2 FAV: 101///113-2: ch g Green Tune -   5   **77**
Gloria Mundi (Saint Cyrien) Led after 1f & sn clr, given breather over 4f out, rdn again 3f out, hdd over 1f out,
not pace of wnr: nicely bckd: fit from chasing, useful, earlier won at Cheltenham (rtd 151c, 2m/2m3f, fast & hvy),
multiple wnr prev: won 2 h'caps on the Flat in '03: suited by 14f/2m on fast or soft grnd, any trk: gd run.
1 May'03 Kemp 14.4g/f 72-66 D: 1 Apr'03 Nott 14.1g/f 64-56 F:
1502   **MOSTARSIL 20** [5] G L Moore 6-8-11 p (68) R L Moore 7/1: 5206-063: In tch, hdwy over 2f out, late   ¾   **72**
gains, no threat: encouraging, acts on any trk, likes sharp/undul ones: see 1502.
1689* **STAR MEMBER 10** [10] A P Jarvis 5-10-1 (86) N Callan 8/1: 2050-514: Held up, trav well over 3f   1¾   **88+**
out but only asked for eff 2f out when plenty to do, onepace: big weight: prob stays 2m & looks the type to do btr.
1087   **DON FERNANDO 45** [6]5-9-7 (78) J F Egan 20/1: 0/0000-05: b c Zilzal - Teulada (Riverman) Held   2½   **77**
up, hdwy over 2f out, onepace: earlier won a nov chase (rtd 128c, 2m4f, firm & soft): unplcd on the Flat in '03
(rtd 82): '01 mdn wnr: prob stays 2m4f on gd & firm, acts on soft over hdles.
2 May'02 York 10.3g/f 92-89 B: 1 Sep'01 Sand 7gd 89- D:
1569   **KRISTENSEN 17** [12]5-9-10 p (81) B Doyle 10/1: 6233-506: In tch, eff over 2f out, no impress: see 1361.   1¾   **78**
1502   **SAN HERNANDO 20** [3]4-8-12 (71) T Quinn 8/1: 060-6407: Held up, some late gains, nvr dngrs.   hd   **68**
1484   **ESTABLISHMENT 21** [7]7-9-6 (77) S Whitworth 8/1: 2015-008: Held up, no impress fnl 2f: likes Ascot.   1   **73**
1753   **MADIBA 7** [2]5-8-3 (60) S Carson 16/1: 2220229: In tch, wknd well over 1f out: btr 1753 (fibresand).   shd   **56**
1502   **STOOP TO CONQUER 20** [11]4-8-9 (68) G Carter 14/1: 05356-00: 10th: b g Polar Falcon - Princess   1¼   **63**
Genista (Ile de Bourbon) Al bhd: plcd in a mdn in '03: poss stays 2m on fast grnd.
      SIMPLY HONEST 15 [8]9-8-1 (58) F Norton 7/1: 00100-40: 11th: In tch, eff & short of room over 2f   2½   **50**
out, sn no extra: Irish raider.
2911} **DOMENICO 312** [1]6-9-3 (74) W Supple 66/1: 50/6002-0: 12th: In tch, wknd over 2f out.   3½   **63**
3193} **GRAND FROMAGE 661** [4]6-8-13 (70) V Slattery 33/1: 30521P/-0: 13th: Al bhd: changed stable.   26   **33**
1637   **SKYES FOLLY 14** [13]4-9-5 (78) M Fenton 16/1: 01515-00: 14th: Chsd ldr till over 3f out, wknd.   8   **33**
14 Ran   Time 3m 31.23 (5.23)   Owned: Mr Kenneth Wilkinson   Trained: Lewes

1929	4.30 Wyndham Maiden Stakes 3yo (D)			
	£6825 £2100 £1050 7f str Good/Firm 20 -00 Slow Stands Side			

1688   **PETER PAUL RUBENS 10** [7] P F I Cole 3-9-0 D Holland 14/1: 041: Keen, made all, rdn clr over 1f   **100**
out, cmftbly: stays 7f & relished this fast grnd: looks useful & open to plenty of improvement: see 1688.
1419   **RED TOP 24** [6] R Hannon 3-9-0 (87) R L Moore 10/11 FAV: 3-232: Trkd wnr, eff over 2f out, easily   5   **84**
outpcd by wnr: hvly bckd: another plcd run: see 1419.
2887} **AWESOME LOVE 313** [8] M Johnston 3-9-0 S Chin 3/1: 2-3: br c Awesome Again - Circus Toons (Wild   1   **87**
Again) In tch, rdn & sltly outpcd 2f out, sn onepace: rnr-up sole juv start: eff at 6f, prob stays 7f
(half-brother to a smart 1m wnr): acts on fast grnd: can find a mdn in the north. 2 Jul'03 Ayr 6g/f 87- D:
1236   **LATIF 35** [4] J H M Gosden 3-9-0 T W Supple 10/1: 4-04: b c Red Ransom - Awaamir (Green Desert)   2   **83**
Keen in tch, onepcd fnl 2f: op 6/1: 4th in a nov stks sole juv start: bred to apprec 7f/1m (dam 1m scorer).
1763   **GENTLE RAINDROP 7** [2]3-8-9 J F Egan 10/1: 05: Sn rdn bhd, no dngr: bred to apprec 7f/1m.   1¾   **74**
      PINE BAY 0 [3]3-8-9 M Fenton 66/1: 6: Dwelt, al bhd.   3   **68**
4393} **FIRST DAWN 243** [9]3-8-9 R Lappin 25/1: 06-7: In tch, btn over 2f out.   1½   **65**
      NIKIFOROS 0 [1]3-9-0 T Quinn 25/1: 8: Al bhd.   11   **48**
1688   **ALBADI 10** [5]3-9-0 B Doyle 50/1: 0-09: Handy, wknd qckly 2f out.   5   **38**
9 Ran   Time 1m 27.37(1.37)   Owned: Richard Green (Fine Paintings)   Trained: Whatcombe

Official Going Good/Firm

1930	1.50 Newmarket Countryside Raceday Handicap Stakes 3yo 0-90 (C)			[92]
	£9763 £3004 £1502 1m Good/Firm 23 -08 Slow Far Side			

1206   **RED SPELL 36** [3] R Hannon 3-8-13 (77) Paul Eddery 10/1: 1-051: Sn prom, led over 1f out, rdn &   **85**
kept on gamely to hold on cl-home: eff over 1m on fast & polytrack, sharp or stiff/gall trk: career best here in a
messy race: see 1206 (race working out well).
1318   **LETS ROLL 29** [8] C W Thornton 3-8-6 (70) T Williams 12/1: 2251-262: Chsd ldrs, short of room &   shd   **77+**
lost place over 6f out, hdwy & not clr run over 1f out, hmpd & kept on ins fnl 1f: unlucky, win sn.
1462* **MACLEAN 22** [1] Sir Michael Stoute 3-8-12 (76) K Fallon 9/2 FAV: 2-213: Handy, kept on for press   hd   **82**
ins fnl 1f: handles fast & gd/soft: ran to winning form of 1462, see 1130.
1419   **SOLAR POWER 24** [4] J R Fanshawe 3-9-6 (84) E Ahern 9/1: 1-244: Chsd ldrs, ev ch fnl 1f, kept on.   nk   **89**
1526* **APEX 19** [10]3-9-0 (78) Dane O'Neill 10/1: 33030-15: Bhd, hdwy over 2f out, kept on: stays 1m.   nk   **82**
1526   **MR JACK DANIELLS 19** [12]3-8-9 (73) R Miles(3) 8/1: 0100-36: Bhd, little room fnl 2f, kept on   nk   **76+**
under a kind ride: stays 1m: rate higher: see 1526.
3804} **SWEET INDULGENCE 273** [14]3-9-6 (84) K McEvoy 25/1: 13-7: ch c Inchinor - Silent Indulgence   nk   **86+**
(Woodman) In tch, staying on when hmpd over 1f out, no room ins fnl 1f, kept on: reapp: won 1 of 2 '03 starts
(mdn, with B Hanbury): eff btwn 7f/1m on fast, acts on a stiff/gall trk: goes well fresh: now with J Scargill,
would have gone v close with a clr run, keep in mind for similar. 1 Aug'03 Newm 7g/f 86- D:
1417   **MOTU 24** [13]3-8-8 (72) P Robinson 20/1: 410-008: Midfield, not clr run ins fnl 1f, kept on: stays 1m.   nk   **71**

1192 **MUHAYMIN** 37 [7]3-9-7 (85) R Hills 16/1: 031-09: ch c A P Indy - Shadayid (Shadeed) Led over 6f,   ¾   84
no extra ins fnl 1f: top-weight: won fnl '03 start (mdn): eff at 1m, shld stay further: acts on fast & gd,
stiff/gall trk: not btn far under top-weight, imprvd for a drop back to 1m. 1 Oct'03 Leic 8.0g/f 82- D:
1665 **FINE SILVER** 11 [6]3-9-5 (83) J Quinn 10/1: 22146-40: 10th: Mid-div, hmpd over 2f out, late   hd   81
gains: winning form at 5.7f, stays 1m: see 1665.
1518 **PANSHIR** 19 [9]3-8-9 (73) M Hills 12/1: 0-5030: 11th: Rear, hdwy over 1f out, sn onepcd: see 1518.   1¼   68
1315 **JUST TIM** 29 [11]3-8-12 (76) P Dobbs 12/1: 602-4140: 12th: Handy, onepcd over 1f out: see 1101.   1   69
1761 **HANA DEE** 7 [5]3-8-1 (65) C Catlin 25/1: 030-0060: 13th: Al bhd: see 1761.   20   18
4834} **SANBONAH** 214 [2]3-8-4 (72) Lisa Jones(3) 25/1: 000125-0: 14th: b f King of Kings - Oh Nellie   2   21
(Tilt The Stars) Handy over 5f, wknd: reapp: won a fills nursery in '03: eff btwn 7f/1m on fast grnd.
2 Oct'03 Newm 8g/f 73-69 D: 1 Sep'03 Yarm 7.0g/f 71-63 D:
14 Ran   Time 1m 38.97 (2.47)   Owned: Mrs John Lee   Trained: Marlborough

---

1931   2.20 Listed Haven And British Holidays Fairway Stakes 3yo   (A)
£17400   £6600   £3300   **1m2f**   **Good/Firm 23**   **+00 Fast**   Far Side

1622 **HAZYVIEW** 14 [4] N A Callaghan 3-9-3 (103) E Ahern 11/2: 1-211121: Chsd ldrs, hdwy to lead 1f   114
out, rdn out: gd handy conceding weight: eff at 10f, tried 11.5f: acts on fast & gd/soft, any trk: gd
weight-carrying performance & back to winning form on drop in grade: v useful: see 1482 & 1017.
1520* **DUKE OF VENICE** 19 [1] Saeed bin Suroor 3-8-12 t (109) K McEvoy 10/11 FAV: 310-12: Chsd ldr, led   1¾   105
over 2f out, hdd 1f out, no extra ins fnl 1f: nicely bckd, clr of rem: winning form at 1m, stays 10f: shade btr
expected after 1520 (cond stks, 1m).
1617 **CASTLETON** 15 [2] H J Cyzer 3-8-12 (100) K Fallon 10/1: 34-23: Handy, ev ch 2f out, onepcd fnl   2½   101
1f: prob stays 10f & must win a mdn: see 1617 (mdn).
1568 **SI SI AMIGA** 17 [3] B W Hills 3-8-7 (92) M Hills 18/1: 1-44: Led over 7f, no extra fnl 1f: see 1568.   ¾   94
1495* **REHEARSAL** 20 [6]3-8-12 (94) P Robinson 7/2: 215: Rear, hdwy over 2f out, sn wknd: up in trip.   ¾   97
1492 **JATH** 20 [5]3-8-7 (85) R Hills 40/1: 1-06: b f Bishop of Cashel - Night Trader (Melyno) Rear,   17   62
nvr a factor: won sole '03 start (fills mdn): eff at 1m, 10f could suit: acts on fast grnd: has run well fresh.
1 Oct'03 Donc 8g/f 88- D:
6 Ran   Time 2m 04.42 (2.32)   Owned: Mr T Mohan   Trained: Newmarket

---

1932   2.50 Listed Cheveley Park Stud King Charles Ii Stakes 3yo   (A)
£17400   £6600   £3300   **7f str**   **Good/Firm 23**   **+04 Fast**   Far Side

1234 **FOKINE** 35 [4] B W Hills 3-8-12 (114) M Hills 4/1: 1620-221: Rcd in 2nd, led over 1f out, rdn   111
out: eff btwn 6/7f on firm, fast & polytrack, gall or sharp/turning trk: useful, made most of drop in grade.
1188 **PEAK TO CREEK** 37 [8] J Noseda 3-9-5 (111) E Ahern 7/1: 31111-32: Rear, hdwy & ev ch over 1f out,   nk   117
kept on ins fnl 1f: enjoyed return to 7f & a fine/smart run conceding plenty of weight: poised tro run well in R
Ascot engagement: see 1188.
4680} **CARTOGRAPHY** 224 [2] Saeed bin Suroor 3-8-12 (104) K McEvoy 14/1: 1310-3: b c Zafonic - Sans   ¾   108
Escale (Diesis) Led over 5f, kept on: reapp: won 2 of 4 '03 starts (nov stks, mdn, with M Jarvis): eff btwn 5f/7f
on firm & gd/soft, stiff/gall trks: runs well fresh: useful, well clr rem.
1 Sep'03 Beve 5g/s 104- D: 1 Jun'03 Donc 5.6fm 90- D:
4571} **AUDITORIUM** 232 [6] Sir Michael Stoute 3-9-2 (113) K Fallon 7/2: 01123-4: b c Royal Applause -   4   104
Degree (Warning) Rear, outpcd after 3f, kept on ins fnl 1f: reapp: won 2 of 5 '03 starts (List, mdn, 1.5L 4th in
Gr 1 Middle Park, rtd 112): eff at 6/7f on firm & gd, sharp or stiff/undul trks: useful, better than this.
2 Sep'03 Donc 7gd 112- A: 1 Aug'03 Ripo 6g/f 112- A: 1 Aug'03 Pont 6fm 97- D:
670* **SAINT ETIENNE** 94 [3]3-8-7 P Robinson 14/1: 15: Handy, keen, no impress over 1f out: long abs.   2   91
1150* **IQTE SAAB** 39 [1]3-8-12 (104) R Hills 11/8 FAV: 12-16: Trkd ldrs & keen, no impress over 1f out: nk   95
hvly bckd: much btr on gd/soft in 1150.
1421 **MOONLIGHT MAN** 24 [7]3-8-12 (105) Dane O'Neill 20/1: 1113-227: Handy over 5f, sn btn: see 1421.   2   91
9} **SGT PEPPER** 196 [5]3-9-2 (100) P Dobbs 50/1: 31140-8: b c Fasliyev - Amandine (Darshaan) Al bhd: 2½   90
reapp: won 2 of 4 '03 starts (mdn, List): eff at 7f/1m, acts on firm & fast, likes Salisbury.
1 Aug'03 Sali 8g/f 100- A: 1 Jul'03 Sali 7.0g/f 96- D:
8 Ran   Time 1m 24.58 (1.38)   Owned: Sangster Family   Trained: Lambourn

---

1933   3.25 Coral Sprint Handicap 3yo 0-100   (C)
£26000   £8000   £4000   **6f str**   **Good/Firm 23**   **+08 Fast**   Far Side   [104]

1690+ **BUY ON THE RED** 10 [2] W R Muir 3-8-1 (77) R Miles(3) 10/1: 424-2211: Chsd ldrs centre, led group   88
over 1f out, hung right 1f out, kept on for press ins fnl 1f: op 16/1: eff btwn 5/6f on polytrack, firm & soft, prob
any trk: imprvg & bang in-form for the Balmoral h'cap at R Ascot.
15 **BIG BRADFORD** 192 [6] P G Murphy 3-8-9 VIS (85) D Kinsella 66/1: 432420-2: b g Tamure - Heather   ¾   91
Honey (Insan) Keen & led centre over 4f, hmpd 1f out, kept on ins fnl 1f: long abs: won a mdn in '03 (with E
James): eff at 5/6f on firm, gd/soft & polytrack, acts on a stiff trk: has tried blnks, imprvd here in a 1st time
visor: gd agent for new stable. 2 Oct'03 Uing 6ap 88a-(85) D: 2 Aug'03 Newm 6fm 89-86 B: 1 Jun'03 Carl 5fm 82- E:
2 May'03 Nott 6.1g/s 82- E: 2 Apr'03 Nott 5.1g/f 80- D:
1621 **MOLCON** 14 [3] N A Callaghan 3-8-5 (81) P Robinson 20/1: 150-5153: In tch centre, kept on for   1   86
press over 1f out: see 1417 & 1154.
1665 **BYGONE DAYS** 11 [16] W J Haggas 3-8-9 (85) K Fallon 9/2 JT FAV: 02-134: Chsd ldrs far side, led   2   84+
group ins fnl 1f, kept on no ch with centre group: first home from high no's: see 1665 & 946.
4503* }**PARTNERS IN JAZZ** 236 [14]3-8-12 (88) E Ahern 9/1: 2221-5: gr c Jambalaya Jazz - Just About   nk   86
Enough (Danzig) Made most far side, no extra ins fnl 1f: reapp: won fnl '03 start (nurs): eff at 5f/6f on fast &
rain softened grnd, acts on a stiff & undul trk: gd run.
1 Sep'03 Hami 6.0gd 88-73 B: 2 Sep'03 Beve 5g/f 73- D. 2 Jun'03 Ayr 5g/f 77- E: 2 Jun'03 Hami 6.0g/f 87- D:
1621 **VIENNAS BOY** 14 [18]3-8-10 (88) P Dobbs 20/1: 2020-446: Chsd ldrs far side, onepcd over 1f out.   1¼   80
1498* **SPLIFF** 20 [19]3-9-5 (95) Dane O'Neill 5/1: 021-17: Held up far side, hdwy 2f out, onepcd fnl 1f.   ½   87
1771 **MORSE** 7 [7]3-9-1 (91) C Catlin 20/1: 0223128: Chsd ldrs centre, outpcd over 1f out: see 1621.   hd   82
1460 **IMPERIAL ECHO** 22 [9]3-8-7 (83) P Fessey 33/1: 21433-09: Held up far side, no pace to chall.   shd   73
1492 **VALJARV** 20 [17]3-9-5 (95) T G McLaughlin 33/1: 031-0000: 10th: b f Bluebird - Iktidar (Green   1   82
Desert) Held up far side, late prog but not dangerous: won fnl '03 start (mdn fills): eff over 6/6.5f on firm & gd

NEWMARKET   SATURDAY 22.05.04   Righthand, Stiff, Galloping Track

grnd: gd run. 1 Oct'03 Newm 6fm 95-(96) D: 2 Jun'03 Leic 6.0g/f 81- E: 2 Jun'03 Nott 5.1g/f 77- D:

1665	**DANESMEAD 11** [1]3-9-5 (95) K McEvoy 16/1: 12333-60: 11th: Held up centre, nvr a factor.	shd	82
1191	**SWINBROOK 37** [10]3-8-7 (83) Lisa Jones(3) 50/1: 52-00: 12th: Chsd ldrs far side, wknd ins fnl 1f.	hd	69
1360	**DISTANT TIMES 28** [11]3-8-3 (79) R Ffrench 16/1: 223-5130: 13th: Held up far side, hdwy over 1f out, sn wknd: btr 1088.	¾	63
1766	**TRAYTONIC 7** [5]3-9-7 (97) N Chalmers(5) 12/1: 40410-50: 14th: Held up far side, not clr run over 1f out, nvr a factor.	½	79
1734	**KABREET 8** [4]3-8-6 (82) R Hills 20/1: 101-3100: 15th: With ldr centre over 4f, sn no extra.	1	61
1154	**DANZIG RIVER 39** [15]3-9-6 (96) M Hills 9/2 JT FAV: 46115-20: 16th: Chsd ldrs far side, wknd 1f out.	1¾	70
1766	**DIVINE SPIRIT 7** [13]3-8-6 (82) I Mongan 66/1: 2161-000: 17th: Chsd ldrs far side, wknd over 1f out.	¾	54
1154*	**SARISTAR 39** [8]3-8-8 (84) J Quinn 10/1: 51010-10: 18th: With ldrs far side, wknd over 1f out.	5	41

18 Ran   Time 1m 11.68 (0.88)   Owned: Mr R Haim   Trained: Lambourn

---

1934   4.00 Persimmon Homes E B F Maiden Stakes 2yo (D)
£4716 £1451 £726   6f str   Good/Firm 23   -37 Slow   Far Side

1190	**DESTINATE 37** [1] R Hannon 2-9-0 P Dobbs 16/1: 01: b c Desert Style - Double Eight (Common Grounds) Led over 3f, led again ins fnl 1f, rdn out: eff at 6f on fast, acts on a stiff/gall trk: much imprvd from debut run & apprec step up to 6f: win again.		99
	JUANTORENA 0 [4] M L W Bell 2-9-0 I Mongan 8/1: 2: ch c Miswaki - Millyant (Primo Dominie) With ldrs, led over 2f out, hung left 1f out & hdd ins fnl 1f, no extra: op 12/1 on debut: bred for speed: -	¾	96
1687	**CAPABLE GUEST 10** [7] M R Channon 2-9-0 C Catlin 4/5 FAV: 33: With ldrs, kept on for press ins fnl 1f: hvly bckd: acts on fast & gd/soft: win a mdn: see 1687.	hd	95
	DARKO KARIM 0 [5] D R Loder 2-9-0 K Fallon 4/1: 4: b c Groom Dancer - Russian Rose (Soviet Lad) With ldrs, onepcd when short of room ins fnl 1f: clr of rem on debut: half brother to a 2yo 1m wnr (Hanami): eff at 6f on fast: good gd start, win a mdn sn.	1	90
	ARC OF LIGHT 0 [6]2-9-0 M Hills 12/1: 5: Keen in rear, wknd 2f out on debut.	5	77
	DESERT LOVER 0 [3]2-9-0 E Ahern 8/1: 6: Keen, sn handy, wknd 2f out on debut.	2½	70
1386	**OUR CHOICE 26** [4]2-9-0 T G McLaughlin 20/1: 047: Al bhd.	¾	68$
1727	**CRY OF THE WOLF 8** [2]2-9-0 Dane O'Neill 20/1: 08: Chsd ldrs, wknd after halfway.	¾	66

8 Ran   Time 1m 14.42 (3.62)   Owned: Mr Michael Pescod & Mr Justin Dowley   Trained: Marlborough

---

1935   4.35 Countryside Alliance Maiden Stakes 3yo (D)
£5629 £1732 £866   1m str   Good/Firm 23   -02 Slow   Far Side

	MOON DAZZLE 0 [8] W J Haggas 3-8-9 R Hills 12/1: 1: b f Kingmambo - June Moon (Sadler's Wells) Mid-div, hdwy to lead 1f out, going away, v readily: op 20/1: half sister to 2 German 2,000 Guineas wnr (Dupont & Pacimo): eff at 1m on fast grnd, shld stay further: runs v well fresh: v useful start, win in better company.		96+
1763	**LONG ROAD 7** [10] J Noseda 3-9-0 E Ahern 5/4 FAV: 22: Trkd ldrs, led over 1f out, sn hdd & onepcd under hands & heels: nicely bckd, clr of rem: can win similar: see 1763.	3	90
4568}	**ARRGATT 232** [12] M A Jarvis 3-9-0 K McEvoy 22/1: 0-3: gr c Intikhab - Nuit Chaud (Woodman) Led over 6f, no extra ins fnl 1f: reapp: unplcd sole '03 start (mdn, rtd 64): better run.	4	82
4851}	**TELEFONICA 213** [13] Sir Michael Stoute 3-8-9 K Fallon 7/2: 42-4: b f Distant View - Call Account (Private Account) With ldr, ev ch over 1f out, sn no impress: reapp: rnr-up fnl '03 start (mdn): handles fast & gd grnd: sharper for this next time. 2 Oct'03 Newc 7gd 80- D:	5	67
1527	**VIOLA DA BRACCIO 19** [6]3-8-9 Dane O'Neill 66/1: 0-05: Handy, wknd 2f out.	¾	65
	LADY LEXIE 0 [2]3-8-9 I Mongan 33/1: 6: Slowly away in rear, nvr a factor on debut.	8	49
1763	**KINGS MINSTREL 7** [7]3-9-0 C Catlin 40/1: 07: Al bhd.	1	52
1171	**ANTIGUA BAY 38** [5]3-8-9 Lisa Jones(3) 4/1: 08: Rear, nvr a factor.	1¾	43
	CAYMAN CALYPSO 0 [11]3-9-0 P Robinson 10/1: 9: Handy, wknd over 2f out on debut.	nk	47
	BOLD PHOENIX 0 [4]3-9-0 J McAuley 33/1: 0: 10th: Handy, wknd over 2f out on debut.	¾	45
1495	**SUSPICIOUS MINDS 20** [1]3-8-9 M Hills 50/1: 000: 11th: Al bhd.	5	30
1762	**EIZAWINA DOCKLANDS 7** [3]3-9-0 t T G McLaughlin 50/1: 000: 12th: Al bhd.	1	33
	KARASHINKO 0 [9]3-9-0 C Lowther 33/1: 0: 13th: Nvr a factor on debut.	28	0

13 Ran   Time 1m 38.51 (2.01)   Owned: Wentworth Racing (Pty) Ltd   Trained: Newmarket

---

1936   5.10 Ngk Spark Plugs/Fmi Maiden Stakes 3yo (D)
£5421 £1668 £834   1m4f   Good/Firm 23   -28 Slow   Centre

1597	**LARKWING 15** [1] G Wragg 3-9-0 (85) K Fallon 8/13 FAV: 4-231: Mid-div, hdwy to lead over 1f out, pushed out: eff at 10f/12f on fast & gd/soft, stiff/gall trk: see 1055. going the right way: see 1763.		82
1211	**TURNSTILE 36** [3] R Hannon 3-9-0 P Dobbs 10/1: 4-42: Rcd in 2nd, ev ch over 1f out, sn onepcd: stays 12f on fast: shld win a race: see 1211.	1¾	78
1501	**WATER TAXI 20** [5] R Charlton 3-9-0 Dane O'Neill 100/30: 43: Chsd ldrs, not clr run over 1f out, onepcd ins fnl 1f: stays 12f on fast: see 1501.	½	77
1651	**HONEYMOONING 12** [6] H R A Cecil 3-8-9 Paul Eddery 12/1: 04: Rear, hdwy 2f out, no impress ins fnl 1f: stays 12f on fast: imprvd from debut: see 1651.	hd	71
5032}	**IVY LEAGUE STAR 196** [4]3-8-9 M Hills 20/1: 06-5: b f Sadler's Wells - Ivy (Sir Ivor) Led till over 1f out, no extra ins fnl 1f: reapp: unplcd both '03 starts (mdns, rtd 64): mid-dist bred.	2½	65
1725	**GLANWORTH 8** [2]3-9-0 A Mackay 66/1: 06: ch c Woodman - Leo Girl (Seattle Slew) Chsd ldrs, wknd over 3f out: well btn on earlier debut: N Callaghan.	dist	0
	FLAMINGO PALACE 0 [7]3-9-0 T G McLaughlin 40/1: 7: ch g Croco Rouge - Chantilly (Sanglamore) Rear, wknd 5f out on debut: with P McBride.	dist	0

7 Ran   Time 2m 34.98 (6.18)   Owned: Mollers Racing   Trained: Newmarket

574

Official Going Good/Firm (ALL TIMES SLOW)

1937   2.20 E B F /Hardings Bar And Catering Services Novice Median Auction Stakes 2yo   (E)
£3712   £1142   £571   **6f rnd**   **Good/Firm**   **V Slow**   Inside

1670* **BRECON BEACON** 12 [5] P F I Cole 2-9-6   S Drowne 4/9 FAV: 11: Trkd ldr & led 2f out, sn strongly   **86**
pressed, held on gamely, all out: hvly bckd: eff at 5f, apprec step up to 6f: acts on soft & fast grnd, any trk:
fine run conceding weight. see 1670.
1640   **QUEENS GLORY** 13 [1] W R Muir 2-8-7   J Quinn 25/1: 62: Trkd ldrs, switched to chall over 1f out,   *shd*   **72**
just held: left hvy grnd debut bhd: eff at 6f, imprvd on fast grnd & a sharp/undul trk: see 1640.
943   **BRIDGE PLACE** 57 [4] B J Meehan 2-8-12   Dane O'Neill 7/2: 03: b c Polar Falcon - Dark Eyed Lady   *1¼*   **73**
(Exhibitioner) Chsd ldrs, wandered under press over 1f out, not able to chall: 8 wk abs: imprvd from intro:
27,000gns Feb foal, related to 3 2yo sprint wnrs: dam a multiple sprint wnr: imprvd on this fast grnd & stays 6f.
1466   **ZIMBALI** 23 [2] J M Bradley 2-8-7   S Carson 8/1: 54134: Led till 2f out, sn no impress: btr 1325 (g/s).   *5*   **54**
1779   **SABO PRINCE** 7 [3]2-8-12   C Catlin 50/1: 05: ch g Atraf - Moving Princess (Prince Sabo) Keen,   *7*   **39**
btn 2f out: cheaply bght May foal, dam plcd btwn 6/10f: been gelded.
5 Ran   Time 1m 11.51 (3.71)   Owned: Elite Racing Club   Trained: Whatcombe

---

1938   2.50 Burgess Hill Selling Stakes 3yo+   (G)
£2590   £740   £370   **7f rnd**   **Good/Firm**   **Slow**   Inside

1827   **JONNY EBENEEZER** 5 [2] R M H Cowell 5-9-6   (63) B Doyle 5/2 FAV: 0002021: U.r. bef start, reared   **60**
start, sn mid-div, drvn to lead well ins last: bght in for 5,000gns: bckd tho' op 7/4: qck reapp: often bhd 5/7f,
stays stiff 1m: acts on firm, soft & fibresand, any trk: eff with/without cheek pieces: suited by sell grade.
1691   **ZIET DALSACE** 11 [8] A W Carroll 4-9-1   (52) I Mongan 9/2: 10054-02: b f Zieten - Providenc Mill   *nk*   **54**
(French Stress)   Handy & led 2f out, drvn & hdd well ins last, just held: clr rem: dual seller wnr for G C Bravery
in '03: eff at 6f/1m, both wins at 7f on firm, fast & polytrack, prob handles any trk, likes Yarmouth & sell grade.
1 Sep'03 Yarm 7.0g/f 58-(51) G: 2 Jul'03 Wind 8.3g/f 56-55 E: 1 Jul'03 Yarm 7.0g/f 57-(48) G:
1720   **CITY GENERAL** 10 [9] J S Moore 3-8-9 p (55) Derek Nolan(7) 3/1: 550-3343: Rear/wide, onepace.   *5*   **49**
1385   **ESPADA** 27 [10] J A Osborne 8-9-6   (58) S W Kelly 5/1: 02-00004: Led 2f, outpcd from over 1f out: op 7/2.   *2½*   **44**
1806   **THREAT** 6 [3]8-9-6   (45) C Catlin 16/1: 0344605: Led/dsptd lead 5f, wknd, qck reapp, longer trip.   *nk*   **43**
1694   **EASILY AVERTED** 11 [7]3-8-9 p (59) A Daly 20/1: 5500006: Dwelt & bhd, nvr able to chall, needs 5/6f.   *2*   **39**
4901] **CAFE AMERICANO** 209 [6]4-9-6   (49) T Quinn 16/1: 605000-7: b g Labeeb - Coffee Ice (Primo Dominie)   *5*   **29**
Held up, rdn & btn over 1f out, reapp: unplcd '03 (rtd 45 & 54, disapp in a visor): mdn rnr-up '02: eff at 7f on
gd grnd & a gall/undul trk, tried up to 10f previously. 2 Sep'02 Chep 7gd 72- D:
1443   **POLAR HAZE** 24 [1]7-9-12 vis (40) J Quinn 16/1: 1504558: Prom 2f, sn lost pl: btr 941 (AW).   *1¼*   **32**
1806   **FLYING FAISAL** 6 [4]6-9-12 bl (47) S Carson 16/1: 0461009: Led/dsptd lead till 2f out: btr 1368 (6f).   *½*   **31**
651   **COSTA DEL SOL** 97 [5]3-8-9   (45) J Tate 25/1: 05-00040: 10th: Sn bhd & outpcd: 3 month abs.   *dist*   **0**
10 Ran   Time 1m 23.41 (3.61)   Owned: Mrs J M Penney   Trained: Newmarket

---

1939   3.20 Donatellos Family Raceday Sunday 6th June Maiden Stakes 3yo+   (D)
£3790   £1166   £583   **12f**   **Good/Firm**   **Slow**   Outside

1725   **TALWANDI** 9 [6] Sir Michael Stoute 3-8-10   B Doyle 6/4 FAV: 631: Handy & led dist, flashed tail   **83**
under press, rdn out to hold on: hvly bckd, op 5/2: eff at 11.5f/12f on fast grnd, may get further: improving.
1768   **SUNNY LADY** 8 [1] E A L Dunlop 3-8-5   (73) E Ahern 2/1: 60-222: Trkd ldrs & ev ch dist, just held: *hd*   **77**
nicely bckd tho' op 7/4: consistent: see 1768 & 1140.
1521   **AL BEEDAA** 20 [7] J L Dunlop 3-8-5   (73) T Quinn 3/1: 03-433: Led, flashed tail & hdd dist, no   *2*   **74**
extra but well clr of rem: op 5/2: handles fast & soft grnd: see 1521 (h'cap).
1384   **OH SO HARDY** 27 [5] M A Allen 3-8-5   C Catlin 66/1: 04: Rear, no impress fnl 4f.   *14*   **57**
1719   **TWELVE BAR BLUES** 10 [9]3-8-5   F Norton 10/1: 005: ch f Nashwan - Throw Away Line (Assert)   *2*   **54**
Dwelt, chsd ldrs till over 2f out: mid-dist bred.
1580   **SALFORD ROCKET** 17 [4]4-9-13   S Sanders 33/1: 0-006: b g Slip Anchor - Mysterious Maid   *21*   **29**
(L'Emigrant)   Chsd ldrs, lost tch fnl 3f, longer trip, modest.
1790   **HIGHFLUTING** 6 [2]3-8-5   D Kinsella 100/1: 0007: Sn bhd & t.o., qck reapp.   *dist*   **0**
7 Ran   Time 2m 33.61 (5.41)   Owned: HH Aga Khan   Trained: Newmarket

---

1940   3.50 Southern Fm Challenge Cup Handicap Stakes 3yo+ 46-55 (F)   **[62]**
£3101   £886   £443   **10f**   **Good/Firm**   **V Slow**   Outside

1692   **OUR DESTINY** 11 [4] A W Carroll 6-9-3   (51) I Mongan 10/1: 6312431: Held up & hmpd early,   **58**
hdwy/forced to switch over 1f out, styd on for press to lead well ins last: eff btwn 1m/11f on fast, soft &
fibresand, any trk: tough, 8 wins from 59 starts: see 1341, 957 & 905.
1357   **KERNEL DOWERY** 29 [12] P W Harris 4-9-6 e (54) T Quinn 5/1 JT FAV: 0043-002: Led, drvn & hdd well   *½*   **59**
ins last: gd run in first time eye-shield, cheek pieces omitted: acts on firm, fast & polytrack: see 1357.
1695   **FANTASY CRUSADER** 11 [18] J A Gilbert 5-8-13 p (47) J Quinn 10/1: 0000-033: Al prom, drvn & ch   *½*   **51**
dist, not pace of wnr cl-home: likes Lingfield (turf): see 1695.
1712   **FAIRLAND** 10 [11] S Dow 5-8-12 (1oh) (45) L Smith(5) 25/1: 00/040-34: Bhd & wide, kept on late,   *shd*   **50+**
nrst fin: again caught the eye under inexperienced rider: eff at 10f: handles fast & polytrack.
1451   **THEATRE LADY** 24 [15]6-8-12 (46) S Drowne 12/1: 3630435: Keen, mid-div, styd on onepace for press.   *nk*   **49**
1099   **EVEN EASIER** 45 [10]3-8-7 (5oh) (55) S Whitworth 10/1: 26-00506: Chsd ldrs 2f out, no extra ins   *shd*   **58**
last, abs: stays a sharp 10f: see 603.
1451   **GRAN CLICQUOT** 24 [13]9-8-12 (1oh) (45) C Catlin 14/1: 500-0027: Chsd ldrs, no extra fnl 1f: see 1451.   *2*   **46**
1695   **BURGUNDY** 11 [7]7-9-7 bl (55) E Ahern 11/1: 6342008: Mid-div, short of room 2f out, no onepace.   *nk*   **54**
1693   **PRIVATE BENJAMIN** 11 [2]4-9-1   (49) F Norton 5/1 JT FAV: 4-010639: Led/dsptd lead, ch over 1f out,   *1*   **47**
no extra when short of room & eased ins last: btr 1693.
1712   **MRS CUBE** 10 [1]5-8-12 (1oh) (45) S Sanders 16/1: 0-113340: 10th: Chsd ldrs till dist, eased cl-home.   *1¼*   **42**
1289   **PRIVATE SEAL** 32 [19]9-8-12 (1oh)t (45) M Halford(7) 33/1: 2202050: 11th: Late prog, nvr a dngr: see 916.   *¾*   **41**

BRIGHTON   SUNDAY 23.05.04   Lefthand, V Sharp, Undulating Track

1125 **DON ARGENTO 41** [14]3-7-12 (15oh) (45) F P Ferris(3) 25/1: 000-00: 12th: gr g Sri Pekan - Grey   ¾   40
Galava (Generous) Keen & held up, eff 2f out, no impress: abs: plcd '03 (rtd 60, mdn): h'cap bow today.
1241 **PEARL OF YORK 36** [3]3-8-7 (5oh) (55) T P Queally(3) 33/1: 000-00: 13th: b f Richard of York -   ¾   48
Laser Show (Wassl) Mid-div, no prog 2f out: plcd '03 (rtd 61 & 56a, mdns).
766 **PIQUET 84** [9]6-8-12 (1oh) (45) J Tate 20/1: 3166000: 14th: Prom, btn over 1f out, 12 wk abs.   hd   38
3738} **LYSANDERS QUEST 277** [6]6-8-12 (6oh) (40) N Day 33/1: 050000-0: 15th: Al bhd, new yard.   1½   36
1618 **FIGURA 16** [8]6-9-1 (49) Dane O'Neill 7/1: 3566650: 16th: Rear, nvr a factor, long losing run.   2½   35
1695 **FIFE AND DRUM 11** [5]7-9-0 p (48) B Reilly(3) 14/1: U00-0060: 17th: Mid-div, btn/eased over 1f out.   shd   34
1529 **Venetian Romance 20** [16]3-8-2 (10oh)P(50) G Hannon 33/1:0
937 **Coolfore Jade 57** [17]4-9-1 (49) M Savage(5) 25/1:0
19 Ran   Time 2m 03.81 (6.01)   Owned: Mr Dennis Deacon   Trained: Alcester

1941   4.20 Ebony Room Brighton Marina 1st Anniversary Handicap Stakes 3yo+ 0-70 (E)   [64]
£4163 £1281 £641   **7f rnd**   Good/Firm   V Slow   Inside

1024 **A WOMAN IN LOVE 51** [8] Miss B Sanders 5-9-8 (58) S Drowne 4/1 FAV: 25640-61: Keen mid-div, hdwy   67
to lead ins last, rdn out: 7 wk abs: suited by 7f, stays 1m: acts on firm, gd & polytrack, loves a sharp trk:
goes well fresh: see 1024.
1013 **LONDONER 53** [1] S Dow 6-9-3 (53) T Quinn 8/1: 6-000032: Led till ins last, no extra: 8 wk abs: gd run.   1¾   58
761* **ALAZAR 85** [6] P D Evans 6-9-9 bl t (59) E Ahern 5/1: 0-401313: Chsd ldr & ch dist, no extra: 12   1   62
wk abs, gd rtn to turf: see 761.
698 **TEMPER TANTRUM 92** [4] Andrew Reid 6-9-10 p (60) J P Guillambert(3) 5/1: 23-55204: Mid-div, short   hd   62
of room 2f out, kept on ins last: 3 month abs, loves this trk, another gd run: see 151.
1548 **ZINGING 19** [10]5-8-0 (1ow) (35) F Norton 16/1: 6400655: Chsd ldrs, drvn & no extra dist: see 216.   1   36
1267 **GUN SALUTE 33** [2]4-8-11 (47) S Whitworth 9/1: 0-104606: Rear, short of room over 1f out, kept on.   1¼   44
1849 **AGILIS 4** [9]4-9-5 bl (55) R Miles(3) 10/1: 6000007: Mid-div, short of room 2f out till over 1f   shd   52
out, not able to recover: qck reapp: well h'capped, no luck in running today: see 234.
844 **DOCTOR DENNIS 70** [5]7-8-13 vis (49) N Pollard 14/1: 446-5168: Keen towards rear, nvr a factor: abs.   ¾   44
798 **ELSINORA 80** [3]3-8-10 (57) P Dobbs 33/1: 0300-09: Prom till over 1f out, sn btn: 12 wk abs: turf rtn.   1   50
1731* **WARLINGHAM 9** [7]6-9-8 (58) S Sanders 9/2: 0115010: 10th: Keen in rear, struggling over 1f out.   hd   50
10 Ran   Time 1m 23.84 (4.04)   Owned: High & Dry Racing   Trained: Epsom

1942   4.50 Bet365 Call 0800 322365 Handicap Stakes 3yo 0-75 (E)   [78]
£4410 £1357 £679   **5f59y rnd**   Good/Firm   V Slow   Inside

1694* **IMPERIUM 11** [9] Mrs Stef Liddiard 3-9-5 (69) F Norton 4/1: 0200511: Dwelt, sn mid-div & led over   76
1f out, went badly left under press, held on gamely: eff at 5/6f on firm, gd/soft & polytrack, likes Brighton.
1809 **INTRIGUING GLIMPSE 6** [3] Miss B Sanders 3-9-7 (71) S Sanders 1/1 FAV: 0113-322: In tch, drvn to   hd   77
chall dist, just held: hvly bckd, qck reapp: clr of rem: see 1809 & 1576.
1376 **MISS MADAME 27** [7] R Guest 3-8-11 (61) T P Queally(3) 9/1: 060-33: Led till over 1f out, no   3½   56
extra: acts on fast & fibresand: eff at 5.5f, rtn to 6f+ shld suit: see 1376 (7f).
1729 **DELLAGIO 9** [6] C A Dwyer 3-8-10 (60) S Drowne 8/1: 10-00004: b c Fasliyev - Lady Ounavarra   1   52
(Simply Great) Rear, kept on late for press, no threat: op 12/1: lightly rcd '03, mdn wnr (D Nicholls, subs
injured): winning form at 5f on fast grnd & a gall trk. 1 Jun'03 York 5.0g/f 86- D:
4578} **MOUSEMAN 233** [8]3-8-10 (60) I Mongan 20/1: 630310-5: b g Young Ern - Scottish Royal (Night   2   46+
Shift) Cl-up, ch when badly hmpd dist, not able to recover: ran well for a long way & much closer but for
interference on reapp: seller scorer '03, AW unplcd (rtd 44a): eff at 6f, stays 7f: acts on firm & polytrack,
sharp/undul trks: suited by forcing tactics & blnks in sell grade: has been gelded.
1 Sep'03 Ling 6g/f 61-(58) G:
1044 **SUSSEX STYLE 50** [2]3-8-3 (53) D Kinsella 33/1: 0-00606: Bhd, nvr pace to threaten, abs: btr 1044.   1¼   35
1694 **ALIZAR 11** [5]3-8-8 (58) T Quinn 13/2: 3142367: Trkd ldrs, ch when hmpd dist & not able to   nk   39
recover, position accepted: luckless run: prob btr judged 1694 & 735.
1809 **CHEEKY CHI 6** [1]3-9-0 (64) S W Kelly 16/1: 3140008: Dwelt, chsd ldrs till 2f out: btr 1146 (soft).   2½   37
8 Ran   Time 1m 03.35(3.35)   Owned: The Cross Keys Racing Club   Trained: Hungerford

BEVERLEY   MONDAY 24.05.04   Righthand, Oval Track With Stiff, Uphill Finish

Official Going Good/Firm (Firm Places)

1943   2.30 Windmill Banded Stakes 3yo+ 0-40 (H)
£1470 £420 £210   **1m100y rnd**   Good/Firm 36   -04 Slow   Inside

1446 **SENNEN COVE 25** [8] R Bastiman 5-9-2 t (40) R Ffrench 15/2: 0063661: Chsd ldrs, hdwy to lead over   46
1f out, rdn out: op 13/2: eff btwn 1m/9f on fast grnd & fibresand, stiff or sharp trk: eff in t-strap: first win.
1801 **MISS OCEAN MONARCH 7** [9] D W Chapman 4-9-2 (40) A Nicholls 4/1 JT FAV: 40-00002: Held up, styd   1½   42
on wide for press, not able to chall wnr: apprec rtn to turf: see 1406.
2191} **LITTLE TASK 343** [7] J S Wainwright 6-9-2 (30) R Winston 8/1: 0000/0/5-3: b g Environment Friend   1¾   39
- Lucky Thing (Green Desert) Slow away & bhd, took 3rd cl-home, nvr threat: Flat reapp, jumps fit (03/04 nov chase
wnr, rtd 101c, 2m, gd & fast grnd): unplcd sole '03 Flat start (17, appr h'cap): stays a stiff 1m on fast grnd.
1800* **MOYNE PLEASURE 7** [4] Paul Johnson 6-9-8 p (40) I Mongan 4/1 JT FAV: 0202314: Led till over 1f   1¾   42
out, sn outpcd, op 9/4: just btr 1800 (9f, AW).
1839 **OPTIMUM NIGHT 5** [6]5-9-2 p (35) G Parkin 16/1: 00-03045: Chsd ldrs, no impress fnl 2f: qck reapp.   3   30
4995} **MISS LEHMAN 202** [5]6-9-2 (40) T Eaves(5) 25/1: 060-6: ch f Beveled - Lehmans Lot (Oats) Keen,   1   28
trkd ldrs, no extra fnl 2f: reapp: unplcd '03 (rtd 46, tried up to 12f prev).
1200 **SEA YA MAITE 38** [10]10-9-2 t (40) J Bramhill 7/1: 5450247: Keen in rear, eff wide, no impress: btr 905.   ¾   27
1713 **DIVINA 11** [3]3-8-4 vis (40) D Fentiman(7) 5/1: 0043228: Dwelt, trkd ldrs till 2f out: btr 1713 & 1591 (a/w).   2½   22
1643 **ALL ON MY OWN 14** [2]9-9-4 (2ow)bl (35) L Vickers 12/1: 4005349: Dwelt & al bhd: op 10/1: btr 1328.   nk   23
3602} **DALYAN 284** [1]7-9-2 (30) P Fessey 33/1: 0/040//00-0: 10th: Chsd ldrs till over 2f out: reapp.   4   14
10 Ran   Time 1m 47.22 (3.42)   Owned: Border Rail & Plant Limited   Trained: Wetherby

1944   3.00 Beverley Conservative Club Maiden Claiming Stakes 3yo+   (H)
£1509 £431 £216   7f100y rnd   Good/Firm 36   + 07 Fast   Inside

1778 **SHAMWARI FIRE 9** [13] I W McInnes 4-9-5 (46) R Ffrench 11/2: 00-46001: Mid-div, switched & styd **54**
on for press to lead late: fair time: off around 7f/1m on fm & gd/soft: first win on 21st start.
1564 **TIME TO REGRET 19** [14] J J Quinn 4-9-5 (53) R Winston 11/4 FAV: 24235-62: Trkd ldrs, smooth prog *shd* **53**
to lead over 2f out, drvn & hdd cl-home: bckd, op 7/2: see 1564.
1774} **SEYED 723** [11] V Smith 4-9-5 M Tebbutt 7/1: 5/-3: b g Desert Prince - Royal Bounty (Generous) *2* **49**
Rear, styd on wide for press, not able to chall: gelded, long abs: missed '03: unplcd sole '02 start (cond stks, D
Loder, rtd 60, sole start): dam a 7f juv wnr, sire a top-class miler: stays a stiff 7.5f on fast grnd in banded stks.
1716} **NITEOWL DREAM 364** [10] J O'Reilly 4-9-0 (58) J D O'Reilly(7) 25/1: 0205/00-4: ch f Colonel *2½* **39**
Collins - Nite Owl Dancer (Robellino) Staying on when short of room 2f out, nrst fin: reapp: lightly rcd '03
(unplcd, rtd 30 & 24a): mdn rnr-up 2002, disapp in blnks: eff at 5/6f, tried 7f: handles firm, soft & fibresand,
stiff/gall or sharp trks: best without blnks. 2 May'02 Wolv 6af 66a- D:
1682 **KNIGHT TO REMEMBER 12** [5]3-8-8 (45) G Faulkner 20/1: 00-34005: Led to 2f out, fdd: btr 613 (AW). ½ **43**
3270} **DELIGHTFUL GIFT 298** [9]4-9-0 (48) T Williams 25/1: 00640-6: Chsd ldrs till over 2f out, reapp. *hd* **37**
1661 **SMART MINISTER 14** [7]4-9-5 (49) P Fessey 6/1: 6420-007: Mid-div, eff wide, no impress. ½ **41**
1803 **HEATHYARDS JOY 7** [6]3-8-3 (35) Dale Gibson 20/1: 4425568: Mid-div, eff over 2f out, sn no impress. *1½* **33**
490 **SOLEIL DHIVER 118** [8]3-8-2 (40) Rory Moore(7) 20/1: 0400-059: Mid-div wide, hmpd 2f out, no impress. *1½* **29**
1662 **WELCOME ARCHIE 14** [15]4-9-2 A Nicholls 40/1: 000: 10th: Dwelt, nvr on terms with ldrs. *hd* **31**
   COTTAM KARMINSKI 0 [12]3-8-3 P M Quinn 25/1: 0: 11th: Dwelt, nvr a factor on debut. *nk* **28**
1446 **BETTYS VALENTINE 25** [3]4-9-0 (30) T Eaves(5) 50/1: 000/-4000: 12th: Chsd ldrs 5f: btr 1446. *7* **16**
580 **GOOD TIMING 105** [4]6-9-5 (45) L Vickers 25/1: 00/0-2000: 13th: Mid-div, struggling fnl 2f: abs. *2* **17**
1522 **COMPTON PRINCESS 21** [2]4-8-13 BL (40) J Mackay 16/1: 000-3600: 14th: Keen & wide, in tch till 2f *14* **0**
out: blnks: btr 1065 (hvy, 6f).
1042 **SPINNING DOVE 51** [1]4-9-0 (65) I Mongan 6/1: 23-32R5R: Ref to race & took no part: see 697 & 514. **0**
15 Ran   Time 1m 32.98 (2.18)   Owned: Ivy House Racing   Trained: Catwick

1945   3.30 Beaver Banded Stakes 3yo+ 0-45 (H)
£1491 £426 £213   1m4f16y   Good/Firm 36   -12 Slow   Inside

1307 **LIFE IS BEAUTIFUL 32** [9] W H Tinning 5-9-8 (45) R Winston 6/4 FAV: 62010-61: Mid-div, prog/short **50**
of room over 3f out & over 2f out, switched to lead ins last, styd on strongly: bckd, op 2/1: eff at 12f on fast &
gd/soft grnd: likes Beverley & apprec drop to banded company: see 1307.
1645 **STAGE TWO 14** [13] M Johnston 3-8-5 (40) R Ffrench 15/2: 064002: Rear, hdwy to lead over 2f out, *1¾* **47**
hdd ins last & no extra: clr rem: eff around 12f in banded company, acts on fast grnd: see 1121.
1840 **DORA CORBINO 5** [12] R Hollinshead 4-9-8 (40) Stephanie Hollinshead(5) 9/1: 0632423: Chsd ldrs, *4* **41**
not able to chall ins last: mdn: see 1840.
1838 **EL PEDRO 5** [2] N E Berry 5-9-8 (40) M Savage(5) 7/1: 5-434024: Chsd ldrs trav well, onepace. *2½* **37**
1663 **UPTHEDALE 14** [11]3-8-5 (40) D Fentiman(7) 33/1: 00-043U5: Bhd, mod late gains for press: see 1311. *nk* **36**
1307 **DASH OF MAGIC 32** [7]6-9-8 (45) M Tebbutt 6/1: 1625106: Slow away, eff wide, not able to chall. *1½* **34**
1611 **LET IT BE 17** [1]3-8-5 (45) A Nicholls 14/1: 000-257: Rear, eff 3f out, btn 2f out: btr 1363. *3* **30**
1801 **ROVELLA 7** [10]3-8-5 (40) Dale Gibson 5/1: 000-0008: Mid-div, hung right & btn 2f out: see 1801. *2* **27**
1547 **DANCES WITH ANGELS 20** [4]4-9-8 (40) I Mongan 16/1: 400-0039: Rear, eff wide halfway, btn 2f out. *3* **23**
984 **QUINN 55** [5]4-9-8 (40) G Faulkner 50/1: 05050-00: 10th: ch g First Trump - Celestine (Skyliner) *2½* **19**
Rear, eff 3f out, no prog: abs: unplcd '03 (rtd 46, auct mdn).
1406 **CEZZARO 27** [3]6-9-8 (45) J Bramhill 16/1: 1040-560: 11th: Btn 4f out. *1¾* **17**
3323] **HIBERNATE 657** [8]10-9-8 (45) T Eaves(5) 22/1: 000265/-0: 12th: Led till over 2f out, sn bhd: abs. *5* **10**
4355] **SEA OF HAPPINESS 247** [6]4-9-8 (45) P Fessey 40/1: 0-0404-0: 13th: Chsd ldrs till 4f out, sn bhd, gelded. *29* **0**
13 Ran   Time 2m 38.26 (6.96)   Owned: W H & Mrs J A Tinning   Trained: York

1946   4.00 Dog And Duck Walkington Banded Stakes 3yo+ 0-45 (H)
£1502 £429 £215   1m2f   Good/Firm 36   -04 Slow   Inside

1577 **LARAD 18** [9] J S Moore 3-8-8 bl (45) Derek Nolan(7) 5/1: 5133461: Trkd ldrs & led over 1f out, **49**
styd on well for press: op 7/1: eff at 1m/10f on both AWs, fast & soft grnd: first win: see 1529, 1324.
1819 **MERLINS PROFIT 6** [5] M Dods 4-9-8 (40) T Eaves(5) 8/1: 0003-542: Bhd, eff to chase ldrs 2f out, *1½* **46**
not pace of wnr but kept on: mdn: see 1819.
1819 **RIGHTY HO 6** [7] W H Tinning 10-9-8 (45) R Winston 5/2 FAV: 3200-133: Mid-div, styd on wide for *nk* **45**
press, not pace of wnr: qck reapp: see 1819 & 1449 (13f).
1712 **OUR GLENARD 11** [11] S L Keightley 5-9-8 (45) D Fentiman(7) 7/1: 0564004: Slow away, rear, styd on *1¾* **43**
late, no threat: op 11/2: see 330 & 84.
1507 **ARCHENKO 22** [1]4-9-8 (45) P Bradley(5) 33/1: 0065: Led till over 1f out, wknd: drpd in trip. *6* **34**
1028 **SUNRIDGE FAIRY 52** [2]5-9-8 (35) P Fessey 33/1: 3060/0-06: b f Definite Article - Foxy Fairy *3½* **29**
(Fairy King) Rear & pushed along, nvr factor: jumps fit (mod): no form on the level '03: dual seller wnr for P C
Haslam in '02 (incl h'cap, turf unplcd, rtd 31): both wins at 1m on fibresand.
1 Feb'02 Sout 8af 57a- F: 1 Jan'02 Sout 8af 61a-49 F:
1711* **TARKWA 11** [10]5-9-8 (45) G Faulkner 3/1: 260-6017: Chsd ldrs till over 1f out: btr 1711 (polytrack, 1m). *5* **22**
1593 **DESIRES DESTINY 18** [3]6-9-8 (45) T Williams 10/1: 6063028: Keen, handy, eff wide & btn 2f out. *2* **19**
1591 **DELTA LADY 18** [8]3-8-8 (45) R Ffrench 16/1: 2600-069: Trkd ldrs & keen, btn 2f out. *1¾* **17**
782 **RILEYS ROCKET 84** [6]5-9-8 (40) J Mackay 25/1: 60005-00: 10th: Bolted bef start, trkd ldrs, hung *dist* **0**
on bend over 4f out & sn bhd, abs, new yard.
10 Ran   Time 2m 06.29 (3.99)   Owned: Mr A P Crook   Trained: Hungerford

BEVERLEY MONDAY 24.05.04 Righthand, Oval Track With Stiff, Uphill Finish

1947 **4.30 Eager Beaver Tri-Banded Stakes 3yo 0-45 (H)**
£1484 £424 £212 **1m100y rnd** **Good/Firm 36** **-17 Slow** Inside

1591 **ROMAN THE PARK 18** [11] T D Easterby 3-8-9 (40) P M Quinn 5/1: 00-31231: Trkd ldrs & led 2f out, pushed out: eff around 7f/1m on fibresand on fast grnd in banded company, stiff/turning or sharpish trk: see 1410. **46**
1611 **GIVEN A CHANCE 17** [3] Mrs S Lamyman 3-9-0 (45) R Winston 17/2: 4505342: Rear, styd on for press, not threat wnr: eff around 1m on fast & hvy grnd: see 1534 & 1250. *1½* **46**
1529 **DELCIENNE 21** [5] G G Margarson 3-9-0 (45) A Beech(3) 16/1: 0020-003: Rear, styd on fnl 3f, not able to chall: handles fast grnd & polytrack: see 77. *nk* **45**
1842 **MONKEY OR ME 5** [13] P T Midgley 3-8-4 (35) R Fitzpatrick 9/2: 0042334: Rear, eff 3f out, styd on onepace: qck reapp: handles fibresand & fast grnd: see 1203. *nk* **34**
1842* **TSARBUCK 5** [12]3-9-6 (6ex) (51) G Faulkner 100/30 FAV: 0-00015: Led 6f, fdd: qk reapp: btr 1842 (aw). *2* **46**
1607 **CUNNING PURSUIT 17** [1]3-9-0 (45) I Mongan 10/1: 0656: Swerved left start, held up wide, nvr on terms. *1½* **37**
1441 **QUEENS SQUARE 25** [9]3-9-0 (45) T Eaves(5) 20/1: 4200-007: Mid-div, no impress fnl 2f: see 1441. *¾* **36**
1675* **A BIT OF FUN 13** [6]3-9-0 (45) R Ffrench 7/1: 00-52018: Prom till over 1f out: btr 1675 (AW). *1¾* **33**
1395 **JOHNNY ALLJAYS 28** [2]3-9-0 (45) Derek Nolan(7) 25/1: 0000-09: b g Victory Note - It's Academic (Royal Academy) Held up, eff/no room over 1f out, no impress: little form '03 (rtd 56, prob flattered). *hd* **32**
1675 **PLATINUM CHIEF 13** [7]3-9-0 (45) P Bradley(5) 14/1: 5053440: 10th: Chsd ldrs 6f, saddle slipped. *9* **16**
662 **PEACE TREATY 97** [4]3-8-4 (35) J Bramhill 66/1: 00-00000: 11th: Chsd ldrs, btn 2f out, 3 month abs. *2* **2**
662 **Major Project 97** [10]3-8-4 (30) Rory Moore(7) 50/1:0 1842 **Dandy Jim 5** [8]3-8-4 bl(30) A Nicholls 25/1:0
13 Ran Time 1m 48.31 (4.51) Owned: Middleham Park Racing II Trained: Malton

1948 **5.00 Rose And Crown Banded Stakes 3yo+ 0-45 (H)**
£1502 £429 £215 **5f str** **Good/Firm 36** **-12 Slow** Inside

4311} **MOLOTOV 249** [18] I W McInnes 4-9-3 (45) R Ffrench 16/1: 300000-1: b g Efisio - Mindomica (Dominion) Cl-up & led over 1f out, held on for press: op 28/1, reapp: AW clmr plcd '03 (rtd 46a, C Thornton, tried blnks earlier): unplcd sole turf start '02 (rtd 63, subs landed an AW clmr): eff at 5/6f, tried 7f: acts on fast grnd & fibresand, stiff or sharp/turning trk: can go well fresh. 1 Dec'02 Wolv 6af 70a- F: **47**
1555 **FAIRGAME MAN 20** [8] J S Wainwright 6-9-3 p (45) G Parkin 14/1: 0000-002: ch g Clantime - Thalya (Crofthall) Chsd ldrs, kept on for press: cheek pieces reapplied: imprvd effort: h'cap rnr-up '03, AW unplcd (rtd 16a, h'cap): clmr rnr-up '02: eff at 5/6f on firm, gd & any trk: gd run with headgear reapplied, prev with A Berry. 2 Jun'03 Hami 6.0g/f 60-62 E: 2 Sep'02 Sand 5g/f 71- E: 2 Jul'01 Ches 5g/f 89-87 C: *¾* **44**
1290 **LAW MAKER 33** [19] M A Buckley 4-9-3 vis (40) J Bramhill 8/1: 0060423: Led till over 1f out, kept on: acts on polytrack & fast grnd: see 1290 & 1075 & 897. *shd* **44**
1799 **WHITE O MORN 7** [10] J W Unett 5-9-3 p (40) B Reilly(3) 33/1: 2410204: Mid-div, styd on for press: acts on fibresand & fast grnd: see 781. *hd* **43**
1248 **LYDIAS LOOK 35** [13]7-9-3 (45) Kristin Stubbs(7) 10/1: 00-05545: Mid-div, short of room 2f out, kept on. *½* **41**
1867 **HENRY TUN 4** [11]6-9-3 p (40) M Savage(5) 10/1: 1302006: Chsd ldrs, onepace for press: qck reapp. *½* **39**
1374 **SMART DANNY 28** [16]3-8-9 (45) R Winston 5/1 JT FAV: 40-0557: Went left start, chsd ldrs 4f. *½* **37**
1544 **SO SOBER 20** [5]6-9-3 (45) I Mongan 25/1: 5400438: Went left start, rear, late gains: just btr 1544. *1* **34**
1730 **CUT RIDGE 10** [9]5-9-3 (45) P Bradley(5) 33/1: 15020-09: Mid-div, short of room halfway, no dngr. *hd* **33**
1606 **ACE MA VAHRA 17** [4]6-9-3 bl (45) A Beech(3) 50/1: 0616000: 10th: Hmpd start & bhd, nrst fin. *nk* **32**
1797 **ATTILA THE HUN 7** [2]5-9-3 P (40) M Tebbutt 66/1: 0000-460: 11th: Rear, eff twds centre, nvr factor. *1½* **28**
1447 **PETANA 25** [12]4-9-3 bl (45) Joanna Badger 20/1: 25020-50: 12th: Mid-div, no impress from halfway. *hd* **27**
1837 **FINGER OF FATE 5** [20]4-9-3 bl (45) J F McDonald(3) 5/1 JT FAV: 0026460: 13th: Chsd ldrs till 2f out. *shd* **27**
1336 **DIAMOND RING 31** [15]5-9-3 (45) A Daly 11/1: 05360-50: 14th: Hmpd start & bhd, only mod prog. *shd* **26**
1426 **LADY DOUBLE U 26** [6]4-9-3 (45) P M Quinn 50/1: 0/-0000: 15th: Swerved left start, nvr a factor. *2½* **18**
1555 **PROUD WESTERN 20** [7]6-9-3 t (45) T Eaves(5) 14/1: 0140-000: 16th: Dwelt & al outpcd. *nk* **17**
1730 **INCHING 10** [17]4-9-3 t (45) G Faulkner 7/1: 6-440000: 17th: Cl-up till halfway, sn bhd. *1* **14**
1627 **PRINCE PYRAMUS 16** [3]6-9-3 (45) J Mackay 40/1: 00000-00: 18th: Al bhd. *3* **5**
1682 **Stavros 12** [14]4-9-3 (45) D McGaffin 33/1:0 1659 **Pay Time 14** [1]5-9-3 (40) Rory Moore(7) 66/1:0
20 Ran Time 1m 03.69(2.39) Owned: Ivy House Racing Trained: Catwick

CARLISLE MONDAY 24.05.04 Righthand, Stiff & Undulating Track

Official Going Firm

1949 **2.20 Viacom Outdoor Rating Related Maiden Stakes 3yo 0-60 (F)**
£3262 £932 £466 **5f193y** **Firm 15** **-20 Slow** Inside

1722 **ESTIHLAL 11** [13] E A L Dunlop 3-8-11 (60) W Supple 6/4 FAV: 60-041: Held up, prog to lead over 1f out, sn asserted, hands-and-heels: hvly bckd tho' op 5/4: eff at 6f, 7f shld suit: acts on firm grnd, likes a stiff trk: decisive scorer, type to improve again: see 1722. **69+**
1678 **FOX COVERT 12** [8] D W Barker 3-9-0 VIS (59) F Lynch 14/1: 230-0002: b g Foxhound - Serious Contender (Tenby) Led till over 1f out, kept on, no ch with wnr: rest well covered: h'cap & auct mdn rnr-up '03, plcd sev times: suited by 6/7f on firm & gd, prob not gd/soft & hvy: handles any trk: apprec visor. 2 Sep'03 Catt 6.0g/f 73-(73) F: 2 Aug'03 Ripo 6gd 76-69 D: *2½* **61**
1509 **OPEN MIND 22** [12] E J Alston 3-8-11 (52) F Norton 12/1: 24040-43: Rdn chasing ldrs, kept on, nvr threat: longer trip: btr 1509 (5f). *4* **47**
1395 **BEAMSLEY BEACON 28** [9] G M Moore 3-9-0 bl (49) K Darley 40/1: 6200-004: ch g Wolfhound - Petindia (Petong) Chsd ldr, hung right & no extra fnl 2f: AW auct mdn rnr-up '03 (turf unplcd, rtd 58, debut): eff around 6f, tried 10f: prob handles firm & fibresand: prob eff in blnks. 2 Jun'03 Sout 6af 61a- F: *1½* **46**
995 **WILLJOJO 54** [3]3-8-11 vis (57) T Hamilton(3) 7/1: 23503-35: In tch, outpcd fnl 2f: 8 wk abs: see 995. *½* **41**
995 **KILLERBY NICKO 54** [2]3-9-0 (57) D Allan(3) 25/1: 00-606: Outpcd, only mod prog: 8 wk abs. *shd* **44**
1509 **LORD BASKERVILLE 22** [11]3-9-0 (57) Darren Williams 8/1: 0-006037: Mid-div, nvr pace to threaten. *1½* **40**

1639 **BORIS THE SPIDER 16** [4]3-9-0 (58) A Culhane 14/1: 0000-208: Well bhd, only mod late prog: btr 1426. *1½* **36**
1825 **LUPINE HOWL 6** [7]3-9-0 P (58) G Gibbons 25/1: 3060-009: Mid-div, struggling from halfway: chkpcs. *¾* **34**
327 **RED ROCKY 139** [6]3-8-11 (55) J Carroll 66/1: 5655-00: 10th: Outpcd, nvr a factor: new yard, abs. *7* **17**
1769 **LADY SUNSET 9** [5]3-8-11 P (55) Donna Caldwell(7) 33/1: 200-0000: 11th: Chsd ldrs 4f, chkpcs. *3½* **7**
1470 **JOEY PERHAPS 24** [14]3-9-0 (60) J Fanning 12/1: 0450-00: 12th: Chsd ldrs till over 2f out, drpd in trip. *5* **0**
1688 **SHINKO FEMME 12** [10]3-8-11 (60) Kim Tinkler 9/1: 24630-00: 13th: V slow away & al t.o. *11* **0**
13 Ran Time 1m 12.8 (2.1) Owned: Mr Hamdan Al Maktoum Trained: Newmarket

1950

2.50 Viacom Outdoor Median Auction Maiden Stakes 2yo (E)
£3835 £1180 £590 **5f** **Firm 15** **-20 Slow** Inside

CARTE ROYALE 0 [14] M Johnston 2-9-0 S Chin 5/1: 1: ch c Loup Sauvage - Noble One (Primo Dominie) Chsd ldrs & led over 1f out, styd on strongly ins last: Feb foal, 22,000gns purchase: dam a 5f juv scorer: eff over a stiff 5f on firm, will get further: goes well fresh: useful, type to progress. **93+**

TAGULA SUNRISE 0 [12] R A Fahey 2-8-9 T Hamilton(3) 9/1: 2: ch f Tagula - Lady From Limerick (Rainbows For Life) Led till over 1f out, styd on, no ch with wnr: Feb foal, 35,000gns purchase: sister to a multiple 7f/1m juv wnr: dam plcd at 5/6f as a juv: eff over a stiff 5f on fm: win sn. *2* **81**

JERRYS GIRL 0 [10] Miss L A Perratt 2-8-9 R Miles(3) 25/1: 3: ch f Danehill Dancer - Lurgoe Lady (Spectrum) Outpcd, styd on well fnl 2f, nrst fin: Jan first foal, dam unrcd: eff at 5f, looks sure to apprec 6f+: acts on firm grnd & a stiff trk: encouraging start. *1½* **77**

1739 **ENGLISH FELLOW 10** [2] B A McMahon 2-9-0 G Gibbons 5/1: 34: Chsd ldrs & sn rdn, onepace. *2* **76**
1458 **MONSIEUR MIRASOL 24** [7]2-9-0 W Supple 4/1 FAV: 335: Mid-div, not pace to chall: longer 6f trip. *1¾* **71**
1256 **GLASSON LODGE 35** [5]2-8-9 Darren Williams 6/1: 456: Mid-div wide, not able to chall: op 9/2. *½* **64**
1677 **ALMATY EXPRESS 12** [4]2-9-0 R Thomas(5) 16/1: 307: Chsd ldrs till over 1f out: btr 1274 (5f, soft). *1* **66**
1632 **PARIS BELL 16** [9]2-9-0 D Allan(3) 7/1: 358: Keen, mid-div, no impress fnl 1f: btr 1143 (5f, soft). *hd* **65**
HYMN OF VICTORY 0 [3]2-9-0 J Fanning 28/1: 9: Cl-up till over 1f out on debut. *1¾* **60**
TILLINGBORN DANCER 0 [8]2-9-0 A Culhane 20/1: 0: 10th: Outpcd, nvr a factor. *nk* **59**
MOSSMANN GORGE 0 [11]2-9-0 K Darley 12/1: 0: 11th: Slow away & nvr a factor. *3* **50**
BLACK COMBE LADY 0 [6]2-8-9 F Norton 25/1: 0: 12th: Outpcd, nvr on terms. *9* **27**
ANTLEY COURT 0 [1]2-9-0 J Carroll 33/1: 0: 13th: V slow away & al t.o. *dist* **0**
13 Ran Time 1m 01.24 (1.74) Owned: Mr & Mrs Heywood & Mr & Mrs Bovingdon Trained: Middleham

1951

3.20 Mark Petersen Racegoers Club Handicap Stakes 3yo 0-70 (E) **[70]**
£3770 £1160 £580 **5f** **Firm 15** **-15 Slow** Inside

1457 **FEU DUTY 24** [7] T J Etherington 3-9-4 (60) J Fanning 6/1: 0010-61: Made all, edged left under press but rdn clr from dist, decisively: op 4/1: eff at 5f on firm & fast, stiff or sharp trk: best dominating: see 1457. **72**

1465 **LEOPARD CREEK 24** [1] Mrs J R Ramsden 3-8-13 P (55) D Allan(3) 8/1: 400-002: ch f Weldnaas - Indigo (Primo Dominie) Rear & rdn, kept on late, no threat: unplcd '03 (rtd 65, debut, lightly rcd): related to smart sprinters Astonished & Bishops Court: eff over a stiff 5f on fm: improved for cheekpieces. *4* **57**

1268 **BLUE POWER 34** [5] K R Burke 3-9-0 (56) Darren Williams 7/2: 13-00353: Keen & chsd ldrs, styd on onepace: nicely bckd, op 4/1: handles firm grnd & fibresand: see 169. *shd* **58**

4923} **THORNABY GREEN 209** [4] T D Barron 3-9-7 (63) K Darley 100/30 FAV: 415600-4: Chsd ldrs till over 1f out: bckd, reapp: '03 seller wnr, subs h'cap unplcd: eff at 5f, handles fast & gd, stiff or sharp trk: gelded. *1* **62**

1682 **WESTBOROUGH 12** [2]3-8-13 (55) Kim Tinkler 7/2: 40205-25: Held up, nvr pace to threaten: see 1682. *hd* **54**
1605 **LAVISH TIMES 17** [6]3-8-8 bl (50) F Norton 7/1: 3063606: Chsd ldrs till over 1f out: btr 1404 (gd). *1¾* **44**
1745 **MADRA RUA 10** [3]3-9-4 P (60) W Supple 10/1: 40050-07: Chsd ldrs to 2f out: cheek pieces: ex-Irish. *3* **45**
7 Ran Time 1m 0.99 (1.49) Owned: Miss M Greenwood A Watson K Hart Trained: Malton

1952

3.50 Azure Claiming Stakes 3yo+ (F)
£2982 £852 £426 **1m3f206y** **Firm 15** **+02 Fast** Outside

1541 **QUARRY ISLAND 20** [1] P D Evans 3-7-12 (40) B Swarbrick(5) 14/1: 2000201: Made all, rdn out: op 12/1, clmd by P G Airey for 5,000: first win: says a stiff 12f in claim grade: handles both AWs, fm & soft, prob any trk: eff with/without vis, tried blnks: enjoyed forcing tactics. **52**

1769 **HEARTHSTEAD DREAM 9** [3] M Johnston 3-8-3 (69) S Chin 3/1: 0320-02D: Chsd ldrs, short of room over 2f out, squeezed thr' gap & styd on ins last, fin 2nd & plcd 3rd: bckd, op 4/1: clmd by J O'Shea for 5,000: 4-rnr nov auct stks rnr-up in '03: stays 12f in mod claiming grade, handles firm & gd grnd. *1½* **54**

1506 **SPITTING IMAGE 22** [2] Mrs M Reveley 4-9-8 (61) A Culhane 11/8 FAV: 240-0303: Handy & ch over 2f out, hmpd ins last when no impress on wnr: fin 3rd, plcd 2nd: bckd: see 1118. *shd* **56**

1819 **PLATINUM CHARMER 6** [4] K R Burke 4-9-13 p (55) Darren Williams 7/4: 1021424: Keen & trkd ldrs, ch over 1f out, no extra: op 11/8, see 1819. *1½* **58**

4 Ran Time 2m 32.36 (1.56) Owned: Mr G E Amey Trained: Abergavenny

1953

4.20 Altham Builders Merchant Handicap Stakes Fillies 3yo 0-70 (E) **[75]**
£3738 £1150 £575 **1m1f61y** **Firm 15** **-02 Slow** Inside

1725 **SUNSET MIRAGE 10** [5] E A L Dunlop 3-9-7 (68) W Supple 7/2 JT FAV: 0-261: Trkd ldrs, led over 1f out, rdn out: bckd: 1st win on h'cap bow: eff around 9/10f on fm & gd/soft: see 1725 & 1358. **74**

497* **IVORY COAST 117** [3] W R Muir 3-8-12 (59) R Miles(3) 5/1: 004-412: Chsd ldrs, kept on for press, just held: op 11/2, 4 month abs: turf debut, gd run: acts on polytrack & firm grnd, stiff or sharp trk: eff at 1m/10f. *nk* **64**

1514* **NIGHT FROLIC 21** [6] J W Hills 3-9-5 (66) K Darley 5/1: 00-13: Trkd ldrs, hung left over 2f out, kept on for press, not able to chall: h'cap bow: styd longer 9f trip: handles firm & hvy grnd: see 1514. *1½* **68**

1099 **RABITATIT 46** [4] J G M O'Shea 3-9-2 (63) B Swarbrick(5) 9/2: 21150-24: Chsd ldrs, onepace & held over 1f out: 6 wk abs: handles firm & gd/soft grnd: see 1099. *nk* **64**

3424} **FAIRLIE 292** [7]3-9-6 (67) A Culhane 7/1: 41046-5: b f Halling - Fairy Flax (Dancing Brave) Chsd ldrs, onepace fnl 2f: reapp: fill mdn wnr '03, subs h'cap unplcd: winning form at 6f, shld apprec 1m/10f this term: handles fast grnd & a stiff/undul trk. 1 Jun'03 Pont 6g/f 79- D: *1* **66**

1216 **DAME NOVA 38** [1]3-8-0 (47) C Cogan 16/1: 000-06: b f Definite Article - Red Note (Rusticaro) *shd* **46**

Held up, outpcd 3f out, kept on late, no threat: unplcd '03 (rtd 58, auct mdn): half-sister to a multiple front
running h'cap wnr Sir Francis: shld get 1m/10f this term.
1611   **PAY ATTENTION 17** [2]3-8-10 (57) D Allan(3) 7/2 JT FAV: 300-4027: Chsd ldrs till 2f out, eased: btr 1611. 13   30
7 Ran   Time 1m 56.98 (1.98)   Owned: Maktoum Al Maktoum   Trained: Newmarket

---

1954	4.50 Viacom Outdoor Apprentice Handicap Stakes 3yo+ 46-55 (F)				[62]
	£3108 £888 £444 7f200y Firm 15 +00 Fast Inside				

520   **ZAWRAK 114** [16] I W McInnes 5-9-7 (55) Natalia Gemelova(3) 8/1: 003-6301: Unruly start & held up,   60
prog & led over 1f out, styd on strongly: 1½ wk jumps abs (mod form): eff at 1m/10f on firm, gd & polytrack, stiff
or sharp/undul trk: goes well fresh: see 236.
1661   **SHIFTY 14** [7] D Nicholls 5-9-0 (48) L Treadwell(3) 11/2: 0004052: Dwelt & held up, prog to chall   2   50
dist, not pace of wnr: acts on firm, gd & fibresand: on a handy mark: see 86.
4419} **WELL MEET AGAIN 244** [14] M W Easterby 4-9-5 (53) P Mulrennan 12/1: 031065-3: ch g Bin Ajwaad –   ¾   53
Tantalizing Song (The Minstrel) Held up, styd on fnl 2f, not able to chall: reapp: h'cap wnr '03 (no sand form):
auct mdn rnr-up '02: eff at 7f/1m on firm & fast grnd, stiff or easy trk.
1 Jun'03 Thir 7g/f 58-54 E: 2 Jun'02 Thir 7g/f 72- E:
1090   **HEATHYARDS PRIDE 47** [5] R Hollinshead 4-9-2 (50) H Fellows(7) 20/1: 4-104: Mid-div, styd on   1½   47
onepace: 7 wk abs: eff at 1m/9f on fibresand & firm grnd: stiff or sharp trk: see 299 (AW mdn).
1661   **ENCOUNTER 14** [17]6-8-13 (47) T Hamilton 4/1 FAV: 500-0035: Chsd ldrs trav well, onepace.   ½   43
1940   **THEATRE LADY 1** [18]6-8-12 (46) M Howard(5) 9/2: 36304356: Cl-up, no impress dist: unplcd yesterday.   3   36
1748   **LATE ARRIVAL 10** [2]7-8-12 (1oh) (45) D Tudhope(5) 16/1: 606/5-007: b g Emperor Jones – Try Vickers   3   30
(Fuzzbuster) Bhd, short of room over 2f out, keeping on when hmpd ins last, no threat: closer with a clr run:
unplcd '03 (rtd 38a, AW h'cap): sell h'cap & h'cap scorer '02: suited by 7f, stays 10f: acts on firm, gd/soft &
fibresand: prob handles any trk: likes Beverley: eff in a visor or blnks.
1 Sep'02 Beve 7.4g/f 53-47 E: 2 Jul'02 Carl 6.8gd 49-47 E: 1 Jul'02 Beve 7.4g/s 49-40 F: 2 Aug'01 Muss 9g/f 49-44 F:
1575   **WILLHEGO 18** [9]3-8-6 (6oh) (52) J P Guillambert 14/1: 000-08: Dwelt, nvr on terms with ldrs: longer trip.   ½   35
1633   **BLUE VENTURE 16** [3]4-9-5 (53) D Wakenshaw(7) 16/1: 3000-00: Prom till 2f out.   ¾   34
1426   **BOLSHEVIK 26** [10]3-8-4 (8oh) (50) D Allan 16/1: 06-00: 10th: Led till over 1f out, fdd on h'cap bow.   nk   30
4820} **ENCORE 217** [1]5-4-9-0 (48) B Swarbrick(3) 8/1: 306065-0: 11th: Mid-div, btn 2f out, reapp.   5   18
1798   **MR MOON 7** [12]3-8-0 (23oh) (35) Leanne Kershaw(3) 25/1: 000-660: 12th: Al bhd: btr 1798 & 1196.   nk   15
1821   **NIFTY ROY 6** [11]4-8-12 (1oh) (45) K Ghunowa(5) 66/1: 26560/-00: 13th: Chsd ldrs till 3f out, qck reapp.   18   0
1849   **POPPYLINE 5** [1]4-9-7 (55) R Miles 9/1: 4440-00U: Reins broke, u.r. start: qck reapp.   0
14 Ran   Time 1m 38.88(1.18)   Owned: New Century Windows Ltd   Trained: Catwick

---

Official Going GOOD/FIRM

1955	6.15 Allen & Overy Llp E B F Novice Stakes 2yo (D)			
	£5122 £1576 £788 5f10y Good/Firm Inapplicable Inside			

       PIKE BISHOP 0 [3] R Charlton 2-8-12   S Drowne 8/1: 1: b c Namid – Pink Cashmere (Polar Falcon)   91 +
Keen handy, carr left after 2f, styd on to lead dist, rdn out: tchd 14/1 on debut: Mar foal, cost 62,000gns:
half-brother to a couple of juv wnrs at 6f: dam unrcd: sire top-class performer at sprint trips: eff at 5f, shld
apprec 6f: acts on fast grnd & a sharp trk: goes well fresh: fine start, win more races.
1816   **EMPIRES GHODHA 6** [4] B J Meehan 2-8-12   K Fallon 11/2: 532: Handy, hung left after 2f, kept on   1¾   84
to chase wnr from dist, al held: qck reapp: continues to run well & deserves to find similar: see 1816.
1567   **MONASHEE PRINCE 19** [1] J R Best 2-9-2   N Pollard 7/2 J FAV: 2153: Led, hdd dist, no extra: tchd   hd   87
9/2: acts on fast & gd grnd: ran to form under top-weight: see 1386.
1669   **HIGH CHART 13** [2] G G Margarson 2-8-9   A McCarthy 11/2: 144: Handy & carr left after 2f, onepcd.   ½   78
1816   **ASIAN TIGER 6** [8]2-8-12   D Holland 7/2 J FAV: 225: Cl-up, outpcd bef 1f out, rallied well ins   shd   80
fnl 1f: well bckd tho' op 11/4: below par eff here: btr 1816 & 1670.
       RUBYANNE 0 [1]2-8-7   T E Durcan 5/1: 6: b f Fasliyev - Phyliel (Lyphard) Dwelt & reared leaving   2½   67
stalls, lost around 8L, sn in tch & ev ch dist, wknd ins fnl 1f & eased: tchd 13/2: debut: May foal, cost
26,000gns: half-sister sprint plcd as a juv: dam 6f wnr: sire top-class at sprint dist: lost any ch here at start.
       ARCHIE GLENN 0 [5]2-8-12   P McCabe 50/1: 7: b c Lake Coniston – La Ballerine (Lafontaine) Keen   3   63
handy 3f, sn wknd: debut: May foal, cost 12,500gns: half-brother 6f wnr as a juv: dam wnr at 9/15f: sire Gr 1 at
sprint dists: with Miss P N Dutfield.
       LORD ELROND 0 [6]2-8-12   J Quinn 16/1: 8: Chsd ldrs till halfway, wknd on debut.   hd   62
8 Ran   Time 1m 1.37 ()   Owned: Mr Michael Pescod   Trained: Beckhampton

---

1956	6.45 Finspreads Handicap Stakes 3yo 0-70 (E)				[77]
	£3660 £1126 £563 1m67y Good/Firm Inapplicable Inside				

1515   **BALEARIC STAR 21** [7] B R Millman 3-9-3 (66) K Fallon 5/1: 0000-601: Hld up, prog halfway, styd   72
on to lead dist, drvn out: op 7/1: eff around 1m on fm & fast, disapp last time on hvy.
1647* **FOLEY PRINCE 14** [12] Mrs Stef Liddiard 3-9-6 (69) S Drowne 4/1: 46-03012: Handy, short of room   ½   75
after 6f till dist, kept on & ev ch well ins fnl 1f, just denied: acts on fm, soft & both AWs: loves Windsor.
1647   **HABANERO 14** [8] R Hannon 3-9-3 (66) R L Moore 6/1: 221-0053: Prom, led 2f out, hdd dist, kept on   nk   71
& not btn far in 3rd: back to form on return to fast grnd: see 1647.
1729   **DANDOUCE 10** [3] P W Chapple Hyam 3-9-5 (68) B Doyle 7/2 FAV: 423-634: Prom, ev ch dist, kept on   nk   72
& not btn far: prev eff at 5/6f, now suited by 7f/1m: only lightly rcd & can be plcd to gd effect.
4596} **DAMI 233** [11]3-9-5 (68) D Holland 10/1: 4400-5: b f Dynaformer - Trampoli (Trempolino) Keen   ½   71
handy, not handle bend after 2f & sn bhd, prog ins fnl 2f, nrst fin: reapp: unplcd in '03 (rtd 75, fill mdn): eff
at 7f/1m on fast & gd grnd: fair return, lightly raced.
1647   **LANDUCCI 14** [6]3-9-3 (66) M Hills 10/1: 00-206: Mid-div, prog & ev ch bef 1f out, wknd fnl 1f.   5   59
1193   **RAJAYOGA 39** [10]3-8-13 (62) Saleem Golam(7) 50/1: 440-07: ch c Kris - Optimistic (Reprimand)   nk   54
Rear when not handle bend after 2f & lost pl, prog 2f out, nvr nrr than mid-div: unplcd in 3 '03 starts (rtd 67, mdn).

580

1791   **MORAG 7** [5]3-9-7   (70) L Enstone(3) 16/1: 0050-408: Mid-div, wknd ins fnl 2f: qck reapp: btr 1359.   *1¼*   **59**
1099   **GABANA 46** [4]3-9-4   (67) S Sanders 8/1: 003-069: Bhd when hmpd after 2f, nvr nrr than mid-div.   *½*   **55**
1339   **SWORN TO SECRECY 30** [13]3-9-1   (64) P Dobbs 33/1: 435-0000: 10th: Handy, eff/no room 2f out, wknd. *1*   **50**
1470   **WASHBROOK 24** [9]3-8-12   (61) C Catlin 20/1: 00640-00: 11th: b g Royal Applause - Alacrity (Alzao)   *1¼*   **44**
Keen mid-div, not handle bend after 2f & sn bhd & no impress: unplcd '03 (rtd 67, mdn): with A Turnell.
1618   **DREAMING WATERS 17** [14]3-8-11   (60) S Carson 50/1: 600-00: 12th: Led 6f, sn fdd.   *4*   **35**
1526   **Among Dreams 21** [1]3-9-0 (63) Dane O'Neill 33/1:0   1655   **Stiletto Lady 14** [2]3-8-12 (61) M Fenton 16/1:0
14 Ran   Time 1m 45.58 ()   Owned: Mr G W Dormer   Trained: Cullompton

---

1957
7.15 French Horn Classified Stakes 3yo+ 0-90 (C)
£9432   £2902   £1451   **6f**   **Good/Firm**   **Inapplicable**   Inside

1811   **CAVERAL 6** [1] R Hannon 3-8-5   (88) R L Moore 15/2: 31-001: Held up, prog after 3f, styd on to   **100+**
lead dist, pushed clr, shade cmftbly: bckd on qck reapp: relished return to 6f, tried further: acts on fast & gd,
stiff or sharp trks: op to further improvement at this trip.
1817   **FRUIT OF GLORY 6** [5] J R Jenkins 5-9-0   (90) D Holland 5/4 FAV: 5443042: Led, edged left & hdd   *3*   **92**
dist, sn outpcd by easy wnr: well bckd on qck reapp: continues to run with credit: see 1817 & 1137.
1498   **KINGS CAPRICE 22** [2] G B Balding 3-8-8   (87) S Carson 14/1: 523-03: ch c Pursuit of Love - Palace   *2½*   **87**
Street (Secreto) Slow away, prog after 3f, onepace: rnr-up on 1 of only 3 '03 starts (mdn): eff at 6f, shld apprec
step up to 7f: acts on fast grnd & a gall trk. 2 Sep'03 Newb 6.0g/f 91- D:
1479   **FROMSONG 23** [3] B R Millman 6-9-8   (95) S Drowne 100/30: 000-2444: Rear, hdwy trav well 3f out,   *1*   **89**
fdd under press dist: op 2/1: won this contest 12 months ago: something amiss? btr 1004.
1703   **MAZEPA 11** [4]4-9-8   (95) K Fallon 7/2: 100-6305: Sn cl-up, fdd 2f out, eased ins fnl 1f: again   *dist*   **0**
disappointing & surely something amiss: twice below 1490.
5 Ran   Time 1m 11.65 ()   Owned: Mr A L Stalder   Trained: Marlborough

---

1958
7.45 Listed Telectronics Systems Leisure Stakes 3yo+ (A)
£17400   £6600   £3300   **6f**   **Good/Firm**   **Inapplicable**   Inside

1767*   **CELTIC MILL 9** [1] D W Barker 6-9-1   (91) L Enstone 16/1: 40-14011: Made all, rdn out fnl 1f: **109**
best dominating at 6/7f, stays 1m: acts on firm, gd & fibresand, any trk: tough & useful 6yo who produced career
best eff to land this: v useful & thriving at present: see 1767 (h'cap).
1667   **ASHDOWN EXPRESS 13** [3] C F Wall 5-9-8   (111) S Sanders 7/2: 5410-302: Held up, hdwy 2f out, styd   *1¼*   **112**
on to chase wnr ins fnl 1f: al held: well bckd: back to smart best on faster grnd: win a nice prize.
1732   **LA CUCARACHA 10** [5] B W Hills 3-8-1   (99) Martin Dwyer 9/2: 11-263: Cl-up, ev ch bef 1f out, no   *2*   **94**
extra fnl 1f: op 3/1: eff at 5/6f: not disgraced on first run outside of own age group: see 1732 & 1400.
1667   **COUNTRY REEL 13** [8] Saeed bin Suroor 4-9-1 vis t (107) K McEvoy 7/1: 14/205-04: Cl-up 4f, sn no extra. *1¾*   **94**
4795}   **TWILIGHT BLUES 219** [7]5-9-1   (114) D Holland 2/1 FAV: 410000-5: ch c Bluebird - Pretty Sharp   *hd*   **93**
(Interrex) Handy over 4f, sn no extra: reapp: Gr 2 wnr at best in '03: List h'cap wnr in '02 (also 5th in 2,000
Guineas, rtd 113): best at 6f, stays 7f/1m on firm & gd/soft grnd: acts on stiff/gall or easy trk: has gone well
fresh: inconsistent but smart performer at best: with B J Meehan. 1 May'03 York 6.0fm 116-(110) A:
1 Apr'02 Newm 7fm 110-106 A: 2 Sep'01 Kemp 6g/f 102- A: 1 Jun'01 Newb 5.1g/f 94- D:
1620   **MISS GEORGE 16** [6]6-8-10   (82) Dane O'Neill 25/1: 0-100306: Held up, nvr nrr than mid-div: see 1383.   *½*   **83**
4775}   **STORMONT 74** [9]4-9-11   J Quinn 50/1: 6310-407: gr c Marju - Legal Steps (Law Society) Bhd, hdwy   *7*   **80**
halfway, fdd dist: 10 wk abs: earlier unplcd in both starts at Nad Al Sheba (h'caps): Gr 2 wnr in Germany in '03:
juv mdn stks wnr in '02: all winning form at 6f: acts on fm & gd/soft: with H J Collingridge.
1 Sep'03 Bade 6gd 104- A: 2 Jun'03 York 6.0fm 93-89 B: 2 Nov'02 Newm 6g/s 84- C: 1 Oct'02 Ling 6ap 101a- D:
1 Oct'02 Ling 6gd 95- D: 2 Aug'02 Ling 5g/f 83- D: 2 Jul'02 Newm 6g/f 91- E:
1479   **BALTIC KING 23** [2]4-9-1 t (104) S Drowne 10/1: 43100-68: Handy 4f, sn wknd: btr 1479.   *1¾*   **65**
1667   **BONUS 13** [4]4-9-8   (105) R Hughes 8/1: 2515-609: Handy 4f, sn fdd: btr 1187 (reapp).   *5*   **57**
9 Ran   Time 1m 11.00 ()   Owned: Mr P Asquith   Trained: Richmond

---

1959
8.15 Ruinart Champagne Maiden Stakes 3yo (D)
£4498   £1384   £692   **1m2f7y**   **Good/Firm**   **Inapplicable**   Inside

1514   **MOTIVE 21** [19] Sir Michael Stoute 3-9-0   K Fallon 3/1: 51: ch c Machiavellian - Mistle Song   **86**
(Nashwan) Cl-up, styd on to lead 1f out, drvn out to hold on despite hanging: cost 250,000gns: eff at 10f, 12f
shld suit: acts on fast grnd & a sharp trk: only lightly rcd & there shld be more improvement to come.
1148   **COMING AGAIN 41** [11] B W Hills 3-9-0   M Hills 7/4 FAV: 2-52: b c Rainbow Quest - Hagwah (Dancing   *shd*   **85**
Brave) Led, hdd 1m out, styd cl-up, ev ch bef 1f out, sn edged left under press, just held: 6 wk abs: rnr-up on
sole '03 start (mdn): half-brother to mid-dist 9-furlong wnr Trust Rule: sire top-class over mid-dists: prev eff at
6f, enjoyed step up here to 10f, 12f shld suit: acts on fast grnd: shown enough to find similar.
2 Oct'03 Newb 6.0g/f 86- D:
1718   **UIG 11** [18] H S Howe 3-8-9   D Kinsella 100/1: 003: ch f Bien Bien - Madam Zando (Forzando) Led   *1½*   **78**
1m out, hdd 1f out, sn edged left & no extra: imprvd eff here on 3rd start, eff at 10f on fast grnd: qual for h'caps.
   PLUMMET 0 [14] J H M Gosden 3-8-9   R Hughes 10/1: 4: b f Silver Hawk - Fairy Heights (Fairy   *2½*   **74**
King) Mid-div, prog & ev ch dist, sn wknd: debut: dam Gr 1 wnr at 1m: eff at 10f on fast grnd: improve.
1384   **NIETZSCHE 28** [10]3-9-0   S W Kelly 7/2: 025: Handy, hung left 2f out, sn no extra: btr 1384 (gd).   *3*   **74**
   DOUBLE DAGGER LADY 0 [16]3-8-9   D Holland 8/1: 6: Dwelt, nvr nrr than mid-div: debut.   *3½*   **64**
   SHASTYE 0 [3]3-8-9   R Havlin 25/1: 7: Held up, nvr nrr than mid-div: debut.   *1*   **62**
1790   **LUCKY ARTHUR 7** [17]3-8-9   D Sweeney 40/1: 000: Mid-div 1m, sn no extra: qck reapp: btr 1790.   *shd*   **61**
1737   **HIGH VIEW 10** [13]3-9-0   G Baker 66/1: 009: Cl-up 7f, sn wknd: see 1737.   *1¾*   **63**
1790   **OPEN BOOK 7** [12]3-8-9   S Drowne 100/1: 000: 10th: Nvr nrr than mid-div.   *2½*   **54**
   Stylish Dancer 0 [20]3-8-9 J Quinn 50/1:0   **Charnwood Pride 0** [2]3-9-0 T M Fenton 25/1:0
   Pearnickity 0 [8]3-8-9 P Doe 100/1:0   1651   **Silencio 14** [9]3-9-0 V Slattery 50/1:0
1495   **Magic Verse 22** [4]3-8-9 C Lowther 66/1:0   1783   **Kalamansi 8** [7]3-8-9 W Ryan 40/1:0
   Imtouchingwood 0 [6]3-8-9 Dane O'Neill 66/1:0

1651 **Second User 14** [5]3-9-0 S Sanders 100/1:0

18 Ran   Time 2m 10.57 ()   Owned: Highclere Thoroughbred Racing X   Trained: Newmarket

---

1960	8.45 Saffie Joseph Handicap Stakes 3yo+ 46-55 (F)						[59]
	£3129 £894 £447	1m3f135y	Good/Firm	Inapplicable	Inside		

1541 **DIAMOND ORCHID 20** [18] P D Evans 4-9-4 vis (49) K Fallon 4/1 FAV: 2-324221: Mid-div, styd on to lead dist, rdn out, edged left: suited by 9/12f on fast, soft grnd & both AWs: eff with cheek pieces, apprec refitting of visor: has been in gd form & this was deserved: see 1541 & 827. — **56**

1645* **MAKE MY HAY 14** [14] J Gallagher 5-9-1 (46) T E Durcan 8/1: 002-3612: Held up, hdwy & ev ch dist, kept on ins fnl 1f, just held: continues in gd form: see 1645 (banded). — ½ **51**

546 **VANILLA MOON 110** [12] J R Jenkins 4-9-3 vis (48) W Ryan 25/1: 405-5243: Led over 1m out, hdd 6f out, led again 4f out, hdd dist, no extra: long abs: acts on fast grnd & polytrack: see 409. — 3 **48**

1579 **SHAPE UP 18** [20] T Keddy 4-9-5 bl (50) P Doe 10/1: 2640-324: Handy, ev ch 2f out, no extra dist. — 2½ **46**

1680 **SUMMER SPECIAL 12** [7]4-9-3 (48) L Enstone(3) 14/1: 00-55305: Held up, prog 4f out, no impress fnl 2f. — 1¼ **42**

1373 **LISSAHANELODGE 29** [10]5-9-1 (46) S Whitworth 10/1: 060-1206: Rear, prog after 6f, onepace fnl 2f. — hd **39**

1777 **COOL BATHWICK 9** [1]5-9-2 P (47) S Drowne 14/1: 1260007: Led 1f, styd cl-up, fdd fnl 3f: cheekpieces. — 5 **32**

1680 **DUBONAI 12** [9]4-9-6 t (51) C Catlin 12/1: 03230-08: ch c Peintre Celebre - Web of Intrigue (Machiavellian) Held up, prog 4f out, fdd ins fnl 2f: ran without declared t-strap here: plcd twice in '03 (h'caps, rtd 57): eff at 10/12f on fast grnd: has tried a t-strap.
2 Aug'03 Newc 12.4g/f 57-55 E: — ¾ **35**

1724 **SHATIN SPECIAL 10** [8]4-9-2 p (47) J Quinn 33/1: F416669: Bhd, nvr nrr than mid-div: btr 746. — 1½ **29**

1736 **DENS JOY 10** [11]8-9-5 (50) Martin Dwyer 14/1: 0056-000: 10th: b f Archway - Bonvin (Taufan) Led, nvr nrr than mid-div: class stks wnr in '03 (Miss D A McHale): won 2 h'caps in late '02: won 4 h'caps in '01 incl 3 here at Windsor: eff at 1m/10f on firm, gd/soft & fibresand, best without visor: likes a sharp/easy trk, esp Windsor & W'hampton: has tried cheek pieces: with V Smith. 1 May'03 Wind 10.0g/s 68-(68) E:
1 Nov'02 Wolv 9.3af 77a-70 E: 1 Nov'02 Wolv 9.3af 66a-58 F: 1 Sept'01 Thir 8g/f 78-76 C:
1 Aug'01 Wind 8.3g/f 79-70 D: 1 Aug'01 Wind 8.3gd 72-63 D: 1 Aug'01 Wind 8.3gd 62-57 E: — 6 **23**

1618 **ALISA 17** [17]4-9-10 t (55) Lisa Jones(3) 25/1: 035560: 11th: Handy 1m, sn wknd. — 1¼ **26**

1776 **MCQUEEN 9** [6]4-9-7 (52) J F Egan 14/1: 310-0600: 12th: Cl-up 7f, sn wknd. — 2 **20**

1412 **MONTOSARI 27** [16]5-9-9 (54) D Holland 11/2: 0-163120: 13th: Keen cl-up 1m, sn wknd. — 1½ **20**

2886} **GREGORIAN 315** [5]7-9-6 (51) D Sweeney 20/1: 510/415-0: 14th: Led after 1f, hdd over 1m out, sn wknd. — ½ **16**

1674 **ON GUARD 13** [19]6-9-3 (48) D Kinsella 14/1: 0-360040: 15th: Held up, nvr a factor. — nk **12**

1543 **SALFORD FLYER 20** [2]8-9-4 bl (49) A Quinn(5) 20/1: 5//-060330: 16th: Led 6f out, hdd 4f out, fdd. — ¾ **12**

1693 **Cantrip 12** [13]4-9-4 (49) S Sanders 10/1:0

1604 **Roaming Vagabond 17** [15]3-8-7 (8oh)(55) N Pollard 14/1:0

18 Ran   Time 2m 30.08()   Owned: Diamond Racing Ltd   Trained: Abergavenny

---

Official Going GOOD/FIRM

1961	2.10 Hunt Staff Benefit Society Maiden Stakes 3yo (D)						
	£5551 £1708 £854	1m3f183y	Good/Firm 25	-17 Slow	Inside		

1725 **NEW MORNING 10** [6] M A Jarvis 3-8-9 P Robinson 1/16 FAV: 4-21: Made most, clr 3f out, v easily, val 15L+: eff around 12f on fast & gd/soft, gall or easy trk: useful, shld win in higher grade: see 1725. — **73+**

4019} **DEVITO 265** [7] A King 3-9-0 V Slattery 66/1: 0-2: ch g Trempolino - Snowy (Wollow) Handy, outpcd 4f out, took poor 2nd ins fnl 1f: reapp & new stable: unplcd sole '03 start (M Harris). — 11 **58$**

1742 **GREAT GIDDING 10** [8] H Morrison 3-9-0 S Drowne 10/1: 03: b g Classic Cliche - Arcady (Slip Anchor) Cl up, no extra from 3f out. — 1¾ **55**

4409} **GREEK STAR 244** [4] K A Morgan 3-9-0 P Makin(5) 25/1: 0-4: b g Soviet Star - Graecia Magna (Private Account) Bhd, mod late gains: reapp & new stable: unplcd sole '03 start (mdn, rtd 44, Sir M Stoute). — 1 **53**

1755 **KEDROSS 9** [1]3-8-9 (58) O Urbina 14/1: 000-0005: Bhd, nvr a factor. — 14 **27**

1790 **SOVEREIGN GIRL 7** [5]3-8-9 S Sanders 150/1: 06: Rear, nvr a factor: qck reapp. — 1¼ **25**

5016} **TOUT LES SOUS 200** [2]3-9-0 S W Kelly 150/1: 0-7: Rear, hdwy after 2f, wknd 3f out on reapp. — 7 **19**

1610 **SES SELINE 17** [3]3-8-9 Paul Eddery 66/1: 458: Cl up 6f, sn wknd. — shd **13**

8 Ran   Time 2m 33.34 (5.04)   Owned: Mr N R A Springer   Trained: Newmarket

---

1962	2.40 Quorn Hunt Conditions Stakes 3yo+ (D)						
	£6553 £2325 £1163	7f9y	Good/Firm 25	+05 Fast	Stands side		

1487 **MISTER LINKS 23** [1] Saeed bin Suroor 4-9-4 (104) K McEvoy 4/6 FAV: 220/30-31: Made all, rdn out fnl 1f: eff btwn 6/7f, tried 1m but shld suit: acts on firm & soft grnd, easy or a gall trk: a gall trk: app return to 7f, gd confidence boost & deserves return to higher grade: useful: see 1487. — **92**

4528} **ST ANDREWS 590** [2] M A Jarvis 4-9-4 P Robinson 12/1: 314/-2: b c Celtic Swing - Viola Royale (Royal Academy) Cl up, not pace of wnr fnl 1f: reapp: missed '03: won 1 of 3 '02 starts (auct mdn): eff at 7f/1m, further shld suit: acts on fast & gd grnd, stiff/gall trk: lightly rcd, entitled to need this & can rate higher next time. 1 Sep'02 Newm 8g/f 93- E: — 6 **78**

2231} **COLISAY 341** [4] A C Stewart 5-9-4 (103) D Holland 13/8: 20/4210-3: b g Entrepreneur - La Sorrela (Cadeaux Genereux) Handy fdd fnl 1f: reapp: won 1 of 4 '03 starts (h'cap): won a mdn & a h'cap in '02: suited by around 1m on firm or gd/soft grnd, prob any trk: can carry big weights: just sharper for this.
1 May'03 Sand 8.1g/f 105-98 B: 2 Apr'03 Sand 8.1gd 103-93 C: 2 Aug'02 Wind 8.3g/f 94-89 C:
1 Jul'02 Sand 8.1gf 105-98 B: 2 Jul'02 Newm 8g/s 92-82 C: 1 Jun'02 Kemp 8fm 83- D: — 5 **68**

1723 **MISTRAL SKY 11** [3] Mrs Stef Liddiard 5-9-4 vis (67) S Drowne 50/1: 0-200204: Handy , fdd 2f out. — 12 **44**

4 Ran   Time 1m 23.43 (1.43)   Owned: Godolphin   Trained: Newmarket

LEICESTER   MONDAY 24.05.04   Righthand, Stiff, Galloping Track

1963
3.10 Fernie Hunt Selling Stakes 3-5yo (G)
£2982 £852 £426 **5f218y** Good/Firm 25 -40 Slow Stands side

1806 **RILEYS DREAM 7** [2] B J Llewellyn 5-8-7 (45) R Havlin 7/1: 00-05001: Rear, prog halfway, led ins **45**
fnl 1f, rdn out: bght in for 4,400 gns: eff btwn 5/7f on fast & gd/soft, stiff trks: apprec drop in grade.
1644 **FRENCHMANS LODGE 14** [4] J M Bradley 4-9-2 bl (35) P Doe 50/1: 00-00002: Bhd, hdwy 4f out, ev ch ½ **52$**
ins fnl 1f, just held: eff btwn 5/6f on fast & polytrack: imprvd eff here out of banded grade: see 1544.
1537 **TAPPIT 20** [1] J M Bradley 5-9-10 p (57) D Holland 13/2: 00-00003: b g Mujadil - Green Life (Green 1½ **56**
Desert) Prom, led dist, hdd ins fnl 1f, no extra: won a h'cap in '03: rnr-up twice in '02 (h'caps): eff btwn
5.8f/7f, acts on firm, soft & fibresand, sharp, undul or turning trks, likes Brighton: wears cheek pieces.
1 Jul'03 Bath 5.7fm 71-65 E: 2 Jun'03 Good 6g/f 66-63 E: 2 May'03 Brig 7.0g/s 63-62 E: 2 Jun'02 Chep 5sft 68-67 D:
2 May'02 Hami 6g69-62 E: 1 Jun'01 Brig 6g/f 81- E:
197 **CHARLIEISMYDARLING 161** [5] J A Osborne 3-8-3 (55) Martin Dwyer 10/1: 40560-4: b g Mind Games - 1 **41**
Blessed Lass (Good Times) Bhd, prog 2f out, not pace to chall: long abs: 4th at best in '03 (mdn, rtd 60a): eff
at 6f on fast: not disgraced on turf debut.
1730 **RED LEICESTER 10** [14]4-8-11 ViS (48) Dean McKeown 7/1: 6000-305: Led, hdd dist, sn no extra. 1½ **35**
1617 **ZAMBEZI RIVER 17** [13]5-9-10 C J Davies(6) 40/1: 00:0006: ch g Zamindar - Double River (Irish River) hd **47**
Bhd, nvr nrr than mid div: modest form prev: with J Bradley.
1682 **DR FOX 12** [3]3-8-7 P P Makin(5) 20/1: 505-0007: Rear & outpcd, modest late gains: cheekpieces. ½ **37**
4136} **MICKLEDOR 258** [11]4-9-5 vis (47) L Enstone(3) 14/1: 060034-8: Bhd, nvr nrr than mid div. shd **39**
1676 **WELSH WHISPER 13** [12]5-8-12 (45) N Chalmers(5) 15/2: 0566139: Bhd, hdwy over 2f out, wknd fnl 1f. ½ **30**
1797 **ROAN RAIDER 7** [8]4-9-10 vis (47) K Fallon 10/1: 0-000340: 10th: Chsd ldrs, wknd ins fnl 1f: 2 **36**
rider reported mount was unsuited by fast grnd: see 1555.
1239 **BACK AT DE FRONT 37** [10]3-9-1 (67) C Catlin 8/1: 5456000: 11th: Cl up, wknd 2f out. 2 **30**
1312 **SIMPLY RED 32** [7]3-8-11 (40) V Slattery 33/1: 00-0000: 12th: Handy, wknd over 2f out. 9 **0**
1465 **QUEEN OF BULGARIA 24** [6]3-8-10 (56) J Quinn 6/1 FAV: 202-0000: 13th: Handy, wknd 2f out. 2 **0**
661 **JACKS DELIGHT 97** [15]4-8-12 S Sanders 50/1: 00-00: 14th: In tch, lost pl halfway, fdd: long 16 **0**
abs: rider reported mount had lost action.
14 Ran   Time 1m 13.72 (3.92)   Owned: Mr Greg Robinson and Mr A N Jay   Trained: Bargoed

1964
3.40 Pytchley Hunt Maiden Stakes 2yo (D)
£5616 £1728 £864 **5f218y** Good/Firm 25 -17 Slow Stands side

1709 **NUFOOS 11** [3] M Johnston 2-8-9 R Hills 5/6 FAV: 31: Made all, pushed out fnl 1f, val 3L: op **89+**
1/2: eff at 6f on fast & gd/soft grnd, acts on a stiff/gall trk: only lightly rcd & can imprve: see 1709.
SATCHEM 0 [4] D R Loder 2-9-0 K Fallon 11/10: 2: br c Inchinor - Mohican Princess (Shirley 2 **86**
Heights) Cl up, kept on but not pace easy wnr fnl 1f: nicely bckd from 2/1, debut, clr of rem: cost 100,000 gns:
Feb first foal, sire high class at 7f, eff at 6f, shld stay further: acts on fast grnd: pleasing eff & can find similar.
HAWRIDGE KING 0 [2] W S Kittow 2-9-0 M Fenton 66/1: 3: b g Erhaab - Sadaka (Kingmambo) Cl up, 5 **71**
hung left & wknd ins fnl 2f: Feb first foal, dam wnr at 1m: sire went on to win Epsom Derby at 12f: can improve.
YOURS SINCERELY 0 [7] P A Blockley 2-9-0 D Nolan(3) 40/1: 4: ch c Mark of Esteem - Evrobi (Grand 7 **50**
Lodge) Handy, fdd fnl 2f: debut: dam plcd over 1m as a juvenile, 7f wnr at 3.
GAVIOLI 0 [1]2-9-0 C Catlin 50/1: 5: Al in rear: debut: J M Bradley. 1½ **45**
1574 **TAIPAN TOMMY 18** [6]2-9-0 J F Egan 40/1: 66: Keen cl up, fdd fnl 2f. 2½ **37**
FLYING TARA 0 [5]2-8-9 Paul Eddery 100/1: 7: Al bhd on debut. 11 **0**
7 Ran   Time 1m 12.36 (2.56)   Owned: Mr Hamdan Al Maktoum   Trained: Middleham

1965
4.10 Belvoir Hunt Handicap Stakes 3yo 0-80 (D)
£5785 £1780 £890 **1m1f218y** Good/Firm 25 -05 Slow Inside   **[84]**

1762 **SOUND OF FLEET 9** [2] P F I Cole 3-9-7 (77) K Fallon 11/2: 2-461: Cl up, styd on to lead dist, **83+**
pushed out fnl 1f, val 3L+: eff at 7f, app return to 10f acts on firm & fast grnd: eff on a stiff/gall, trk: fine
win under top weight: open to more improvement at this trip: see 1384.
1554* **MAN OF LETTERS 20** [8] M Johnston 3-9-6 (76) K Dalgleish 6/4 FAV: 5-432212: Handy, led 3f out, 1¾ **78**
hdd bef 1f out, sn no extra: eff at 7f, app step up 10f, acts on fast grnd: clr of rem: cost little in debut: see 1554.
1534 **WAKE UP HENRY 20** [11] R Charlton 3-8-2 (58) N Mackay(3) 25/1: 006-03: ch g Nashwan - River Saint 2½ **56**
(Irish River) Handy, onepcd fnl 1f: bhd at best in '03 (nov, rtd 52a): not disgraced on step up in trip.
1647 **ANDURIL 14** [12] J M P Eustace 3-8-12 (68) J Tate 14/1: 45-60364: Bhd, hdwy 2f out, nrst fin. ½ **65**
1651 **LAABBIJ 14** [9]3-9-6 (76) Martin Dwyer 9/2: 0-605: ch c Shuailaan - United Kingdom (Danzig) Bhd, 1¼ **71**
outpcd 2f out, some late gains: 7th sole '03 start (mdn, rtd 74): poss needs further.
1769 **SHOW NO FEAR 9** [4]3-9-0 W Ryan 12/1: 552-1006: Bhd, hdwy 3f out, onepcd fnl 1f: see 1141. nk **64**
5023} **DHEHDAAH 199** [10]3-8-9 (65) R Hills 40/1: 600-7: b c Alhaarth - Carina Clare (Slip Anchor) nk **58**
Mid-div, onepcd 2f out: reapp: unplcd all '03 starts (mdns, rtd 68): with N Graham.
1470 **MR INDEPENDENT 24** [5]3-8-7 (63) P Robinson 12/1: 030-08: Bhd, nvr a factor: reportedly hung right. 3 **51**
4847} **PENNY STALL 215** [6]3-8-6 (62) S Sanders 8/1: 044-9: Bhd, nvr a factor: op 5/1 on reapp: was 5 **42**
reportedly unsuited by this fast grnd.
1691 **CHUBBES 12** [7]3-9-1 vis (71) T Quinn 16/1: 14230-00: 10th: Led, hdd 3f out, fdd dist. 11 **34**
10 Ran   Time 2m 5.58 (3.08)   Owned: Meyrick Smith Landis & Cole   Trained: Whatcombe

1966
4.40 Susie And Jim Celebration Claiming Stakes 3yo+ (F)
£3504 £1078 £539 **1m9y** Good/Firm 25 Inapplicable Inside

1164 **BEN HUR 40** [6] W M Brisbourne 5-9-10 (56) S W Kelly 7/2: 10050-01: b g Zafonic - Gayane **63**
(Nureyev) Cl up, led after 3f, rdn out fnl 1f: 6 wk abs: won a mdn h'cap in '03 (1st time cheek pieces): 3rd 2 of
7 '02 starts (h'cap, mdn, rtd 76): eff btwn 1m/10f on firm, soft & fibresand, acts on any trk: runs well fresh,
with/without cheek pieces: imprvd for drop to clmg grade.
1 Sep'03 Wolv 8.5af 66a-60 F: 2 Sep'03 Hami 8.3g/f 62-60 C: 2 Aug'03 Carl 7.9g/f 60-60 E: 2 May'03 Carl 9.3fm 63-58 E:
1822 **NICHOLAS NICKELBY 6** [8] M J Polglase 4-9-10 (60) T Quinn 11/2: 622-062: Keen & led 3f, ev ch 1 **61**

dist, not pace wnr: qck reapp: acts on fast & fibresand: see 115 & 71.
1672 **TINIAN 13** [9] K R Burke 6-9-2 (50) K Dalgleish 8/1: 0404543: Rear, hdwy over 1f out, kept on: handles fast, soft & fibresand: see 417. *1¼* **50**
1827* **KELSEAS KOLBY 6** [5] P A Blockley 4-9-2 vis (53) D Nolan(3) 2/1 FAV: 120-0014: Rear, hdwy over 2f out, hung left & right over 1f out, no impress: quick reapp, clr of rem: suited by 7f, stays 1m: new stable (prev with J Glover): see 1827 & 1635. *½* **49**
1720 **CITY GENERAL 11** [1]3-8-8 p (55) J D Smith 8/1: 550-3345: Bhd, some late gains: see 996. *6* **41**
1348 **THUMAMAH 30** [4]5-9-3 t (49) J F Egan 20/1: 600-0006: Bhd, prog halfway, wknd 1f out: see 820. *3½* **31**
1385 **BIJOU DANCER 28** [3]4-9-6 (56) G Baker 11/1: 00560-07: ch g Bijou d'Inde - Dancing Diana (Raga Navarro) Handy 6f, sn wknd: unplcd all '03 starts (class stks, clmrs, mdns, rtd 63, with R Hannon): unplcd sole '02 start (mdn): eff at 5f on fast grnd. *½* **33**
IRISH CHAPEL 0 [7]8-9-10 N Chalmers(5) 100/1: 8: b g College Chapel - Heart of Flame (Top Ville) Bhd, prog after 2f, wknd 3f out: Flat debut, long bmpr abs: unplcd sole 02/03 bmpr start. *5* **27**
221 **RELATIVE HERO 157** [2]4-9-10 (62) A Quinn(5) 14/1: 011650-9: Bhd, prog halfway, fdd 2f out: long abs. *10* **7**
9 Ran Time 1m 42.4 () Owned: D C Rutter & H Clewlow Trained: Nesscliffe

1967 **5.10 Sandicliffe Motor Group Handicap Stakes Fillies 3yo+ 0-70 (E)** **[82]**
£4085 £1257 £629 **1m3f183y** **Good/Firm 25** **-02 Slow** Inside

1470 **SELEBELA 24** [5] L M Cumani 3-8-4 (58) N Mackay(3) 6/1: 3605-01: In tch, led 3f out, rdn clr fnl 1f: op 7/2: imprvd for step up to 12f on fast, prob soft grnd: acts on stiff/ gall trk: won with authority, see 1470. **74**
1692* **BANNINGHAM BLAZE 12** [6] A W Carroll 4-8-13 (50) S Hitchcott(3) 9/4 FAV: 00-00412: Rear, prog 3f out, hung right & no impress 1f out: op 4/1, new stable (prev with C Dore): see 1692 & 1373. *8* **52**
1830 **MOST SAUCY 6** [1] I A Wood 8-9-10 (61) D Nolan(3) 11/2: 00-66503: Bhd, hdwy 3f out, fdd dist. *1½* **61**
1543 **FREE STYLE 20** [4] Mrs H Sweeting 4-8-13 (50) G Baker 7/1: 1455204: Handy, fdd 2f out: op 9/1. *4* **44**
1648 **SCIENCE ACADEMY 14** [7]3-8-4 (58) T Quinn 4/1: 500-05: In tch, wknd over 3f out: see 1648. *8* **40**
1693 **MARGERY DAW 12** [3]4-9-9 (60) T G McLaughlin 33/1: 52-50006: Led, hdd 3f out, sn fdd. *13* **22**
1680 **CANTEMERLE 12** [2]4-9-4 (55) S W Kelly 5/1: 00350-27: Mid-div, fdd after 1m: btr 1680. *26* **0**
7 Ran Time 2m 31.55(3.25) Owned: Scuderia Rencati Srl Trained: Newmarket

THIRSK **MONDAY 24.05.04 Lefthand, Flat, Oval Track**

Official Going Firm

1968 **6.30 Milly's Selling Stakes Fillies 2yo (E)**
£3575 £1100 £550 **6f str** **Good/Firm 22** **-66 Slow** Stands side

1906 **BOWLAND BRIDE 2** [10] A Berry 2-8-9 P Mathers(7) 14/1: 50441: Handy, al trav well, led dist, drvn out: no bid: quick reapp: eff at 6f, shld stay 7f: acts on fast grnd: 1st win: see 1779. **55**
MERMAIDS CRY 0 [6] J A Glover 2-8-9 T P Queally(3) 8/1: 2: b f Danzero - Little Tramp (Trempolino) Dwelt, sn mid-div, prog when short of room bef 1f out, swtchd & kept on fnl 1f, nrst fin: claimed for 6,000: Feb foal, half sister wnr at 5f: eff at 6f on fast: lkd unlucky, gd debut. *1* **51+**
SHUCHBAA 0 [13] K A Ryan 2-8-9 P Fessey 7/1: 3: b f Zaha - Little Miss Rocker (Rock Hopper) Slow away, prog after 3f, kept on fnl 1f: debut: Mar foal, cost 8,000 gns: dam wnr at 12f, also wnr over hdles: sire Gr1 wnr abroad at 9f: eff at 6f, wants 7f already: acts on fast grnd. *2½* **44**
1869 **JOSHAR 4** [8] M W Easterby 2-8-9 Dale Gibson 6/1: 030334: Prom, ev ch 2f out, no extra fnl 1f. *nk* **43**
1869 **FRISBY RIDGE 4** [5]2-8-9 G Gibbons 10/1: 0505: Prom, no extra dist: quick reapp: see 1303. *shd* **42**
1831 **CONCERT TIME 6** [7]2-8-9 R Thomas(5) 5/1: 036: Chsd ldrs 4f, sn no extra: quick reapp: btr 1831 (5f). *1¼* **38**
DICTION 0 [4]2-8-9 Darren Williams 6/1: 7: br f Diktat - Waft (Topsider) Dwelt, prog halfway, onepcd ins fnl 2f: debut: Apr foal, cost 3,000 gns: half sister plcd at 10f: dam plcd at 1m. *¾* **36**
1831 **EMMAS VENTURE 6** [11]2-8-9 K Darley 7/2 FAV: 52648: Led till dist, fdd: well bckd, btr 1224 (5f). *2* **30**
1831 **HOLLINGWOOD SOUL 6** [1]2-8-9 Dean McKeown 14/1: 09: Bhd, nvr a factor: quick reapp. *1¾* **25**
1831 **RUBY REBEL 6** [9]2-8-9 BL R Fitzpatrick 50/1: 000: 10th: Bhd, hung badly left & fdd ins fnl 2f. *9* **1**
1634 **BORACAY BEAUTY 16** [3]2-8-9 D Fentiman(7) 25/1: 000: 11th: Handy 4f, fdd. *2* **0**
11 Ran Time 1m 14.82 (5.32) Owned: Mr A B Parr Trained: Cockerham

1969 **7.00 Herriot Happening Handicap Stakes 3yo+ 0-100 (C)** **[99]**
£9490 £2920 £1460 **1m4f** **Good/Firm 22** **+00 Fast** Inside

1746 **BOURGEOIS 10** [3] T D Easterby 7-9-10 (95) R Winston 4/1 FAV: 0350-231: Handy, prog & ev ch dist, rdn out to lead cl-home: tchd 5/1: eff at 10/12f, stays 14f: acts on firm & hvy, eff with/without blnks/visor. **102**
1689 **HIGHLAND GAMES 12** [7] J G Given 4-9-0 (85) K Darley 7/1: 1060-202: Held up, prog to lead 2f out, hdd under press cl-home: back to form on a fast surface: shld find similar: see 1459. *nk* **92**
1599* **COURT OF APPEAL 17** [1] B Ellison 7-9-0 t (85) T Eaves(5) 9/2: 2434-113: Mid-div, prog after 1m, kept on well ins fnl 1f, not btn far: only just denied here on hat-trick bid: in fine form: see 1599. *½* **91**
1772 **GLORY QUEST 9** [8] Miss Gay Kelleway 7-7-12 (2oh) (67) Dean Williams(6) 10/1: 5221034: Trkd ldrs, ev ch 2f out, onepcd well ins fnl 1f: not btn far: gd run: see 1772. *nk* **74**
1668 **SPORTING GESTURE 13** [4]7-8-3 (74) Dale Gibson 11/2: 12000-05: ch g Safawan - Polly Packer (Reform) Chsd ldrs, onepcd ins fnl 1f: landed 3 h'caps in '03 (also plcd 6 times): plcd fnl 2 starts (h'cap, rtd 59): landed hat-trick in h'caps in '01: eff at 10/12f on firm & gd grnd, not soft or hvy: handles any trk: much more encouraging, tough & can win again. 2 Sep'03 Thir 12g/f 78-75 C: 1 Sep'03 York 11.9g/f 80-72 D: 2 Jun'03 Carl 11.9fm 76-71 D: 1 Jun'03 York 11.9fm 73-69 C: 2 May'03 York 11.9fm 71-65 C: 2 May'03 Ches 12.3g/f 69-65 D: 1 Apr'03 Pont 10.0g/f 68-60 E: 1 Aug'01 Pont 12gd 75-62 C: 1 Jul'01 Nott 10g/f 62-53 E: *hd* **78**
1668 **SOVEREIGN DREAMER 13** [9]4-8-9 t (80) J Bramhill 18/1: 06110-06: b c Kingmambo - Spend A Dream (Spend A Buck) Led, hdd 2f out, sn wknd: won 3 h'caps in '03: rnr up fnl start in '02 (h'cap): eff at 12f on gd/soft grnd: imprvd last term for fitting of t-strap, has tried blnks: best when able to dominate. 1 Aug'03 Newc 12.4g/f 84-75 E: 1 Aug'03 Ripo 12.3g/f 78-71 C: 1 Apr'03 Ripo 12.3g/f 80-72 D: *6* **75**

2 Oct'02 Wind 8.3g/s 74-70 D:
1668 **DOUBLE OBSESSION 13** [2]4-9-7 (92) S Chin 9/1: 02000-07: Handy over 1m, sn no extra. 2 84
1172 **ANNAMBO 40** [5]4-8-12 vis (83) T P Queally(3) 9/2: 20100-08: ch c In The Wings - Anna Matrushka 3 70
(Mill Reef) Handy 1m, sn fdd: mdn & class stks wnr in '03: eff around 11.5f/12f, has tried 2m: acts on firm & soft
grnd, eff in a visor: has gone well fresh: with D R Loder.
1 Jul'03 Bath 11.7fm 87-(85) C: 2 May'03 Ripo 12.3sft 87-82 D: 1 Apr'03 Thir 12fm 87- D:
1519 **DERWENT 21** [6]5-8-9 (80) W Supple 25/1: 010/03-09: Handy, wknd ins fnl 3f: see 1519. hd 66
9 Ran   Time 2m 32.47 (2.67)   Owned: Mr C H Stevens   Trained: Malton

---

1970   7.30 Skybet Press Red - Bet Now Classified Stakes 3yo+ 0-80 (D)
£5499 £1692 £846   **7f rnd**   **Good/Firm 22**   **-02 Slow**   Inside

1820 **ATLANTIC QUEST 6** [9] G A Harker 5-9-3 p (80) P Mulrennan(5) 9/2: 10-05001: Handy, prog to lead ins 83
fnl 1f, rdn out: well bckd on quick reapp: suited by 7f/1m, stays 10f on fm, gd & polytrack: eff with/without
visor, apprec refitting of cheek pieces here: tough, back on wng mark here: see 1519 & 1474.
1474 **KING HARSON 23** [8] J D Bethell 5-9-5 vis (82) J Fanning 7/1: 16331-02: b g Greensmith - Safari nk 83
Park (Absalom) Led, hdd under press ins fnl 1f, just held: prog back end of '03 wng 3 h'caps: thrice h'cap rnr-up
in '02: eff at 6f, 7f specialist on firm & hvy grnd, any trk: gd weight carrier who is suited by a visor: likes to
force the pace: genuine, fine return & shld continue to run well.
1 Nov'03 Catt 7sft 83-77 D: 1 Sep'03 York 7.0g/f 76-73 E: 1 Aug'03 Newc 7g/f 74-66 D: 2 Sep'02 Hayd 7.1fm 80-79 C:
2 Jul'02 Pont 6g/f 83-80 C: 2 Jul'02 Beve 7.4g/f 83-80 D: 1 Oct'01 Donc 6hvy 90- B: 1 Jun'01 Pont 5fm 75- F:
1820* **SAWWAAH 6** [7] D Nicholls 7-9-9 (78) Alex Greaves 8/1: 030-0013: Chsd ldrs, ev ch when edged left 1 85
dist, styd on fnl 1f, not btn far: quick reapp: clr rem, gd run: see 1820.
1598 **H HARRISON 17** [3] I W McInnes 4-9-3 (78) P Mathers(7) 3/1 FAV: 03-06454: Handy & ev ch bef 2f 3 73
out, no extra dist: op 9/2: slightly better expected: btr 1598.
1383 **ENDLESS SUMMER 28** [4]6-9-3 T (80) F Lynch 13/2: 4004-355: In tch, no extra when no room bef 1f ½ 72
out: first time t-strap: btr 921 (6f, reapp).
1474 **WESSEX 23** [1]4-9-6 (83) Dean McKeown 33/1: 010-06: ch c Gone West - Satin Velvet (El Gran Senor) shd 74+
Dwelt, prog when short of room 2f out, switched & kept on well fnl 1f: mdn wnr on 1 of only 3 '03 starts (M
Johnston): eff at 1m on firm grnd: much closer with a clr passage: with James Moffatt.
1 Jun'03 York 7.9fm 88- D:
1624 **FIVEOCLOCK EXPRESS 16** [5]4-9-4 vis (81) T P Queally(3) 7/1: 300-4207: Handy 5f, sn no extra: btr 1474. ¾ 70
1094 **WHAT A DANCER 46** [6]7-9-3 (77) R Winston 11/2: 01-43148: Held up, prog when short of room 2f out ½ 68+
& again dist, onepace fnl 1f: 6 wk abs: did not get best of runs: btr 887.
1782 **SAFRANINE 8** [2]7-9-0 (70) Ann Stokell 50/1: 00-00009: Cl-up 5f, sn wknd. 3 59
1035 **SILVER SEEKER 51** [10]4-9-7 p (84) T Eaves(5) 20/1: 310/0-500: 10th: Slow away, al bhd. 7 53
10 Ran   Time 1m 24.46 (1.70)   Owned: Mr A Polignone   Trained: Middleham

---

1971   8.00 Carleton Furniture Group Maiden Stakes 3yo+ (D)
£5512 £1696 £848   **7f rnd**   **Good/Firm 22**   **-11 Slow**   Inside

4829} **MUTAMARED 216** [6] M P Tregoning 4-9-11 W Supple 3/1: 226-1: ch c Nureyev - Alydariel (Alydar) 86+
Keen handy, styd on to lead dist, pushed clr, val 7L+: reapp & new stable: rnr-up on 1 of only 2 '03 starts (mdn,
Saeed Bin Suroor): prev rnr-up on sole start in Dubai (1m stks, dirt): eff at 7f on fast & dirt, shld apprec 1m:
eff with/without t-strap: goes well fresh: lightly rcd, can go on to better things. 2 Aug'03 Ling 7g/f 66- D:
1690 **WYCHBURY 12** [3] M J Wallace 3-9-0 (77) K Darley 6/5 FAV: 532-52: Led till hdd dist, kept on but 5 75
no ch with easy wnr: stays 7f: caught a useful sort: see 1690.
1636 **BLUE MARINER 16** [12] P W Harris 4-9-11 J Fanning 11/1: 2/0-03: Cl-up, ev ch bef 1f out, sn wknd. 1 73
SWAINSWORLD 0 [7] T D Easterby 3-9-0 D Allan(3) 40/1: 4: b g Swain - Highest Dream (Highest ¾ 71
Honor) Mid-div, prog halfway, onepcd fnl 1f: debut.
1587 **ISLAND SPELL 18** [8]3-8-9 (75) P Fessey 8/1: 03063-35: Handy 5f, sn no extra: btr 1587. 7 52
1636 **KOODOO 16** [1]3-9-0 (62) V Halliday 66/1: 000-06: Nvr nrr than mid-div. 2½ 52
KENTUCKY EXPRESS 0 [9]3-9-0 R Winston 25/1: 7: Slow away, nvr nrr than mid-div: debut. 1¼ 50
PURE VINTAGE 0 [5]3-9-0 T Hamilton(3) 16/1: 8: b g Fasliyev - Tootling (Pennine Walk) Slow 1¼ 47
away, stumbled 5f out, prog ins fnl 2f, nrst fin: debut: not disgraced here & can improve with more experience.
4642} **MISSIE 230** [2]4-9-6 (50) F Lynch 50/1: 00/5045-9: Handy till halfway, wknd. shd 41
1659 **AKIRAMENAI 14** [4]4-9-6 T P Queally(3) 20/1: 040: 10th: Chsd ldrs till halfway, fdd. shd 40
1587 **Ballyboro 18** [11]3-8-9 D Corby(3) 50/1:0   1639 **Mister Regent 16** [10]3-9-0 N Callan 11/1:0
12 Ran   Time 1m 25.21 (2.31)   Owned: Mr Hamdan Al Maktoum   Trained: Lambourn

---

1972   8.30 Calverts Carpets Handicap Stakes 3yo+ 0-70 (E)   [70]
£3741 £1151 £576   **1m rnd**   **Good/Firm 22**   **-06 Slow**   Inside

1485 **ACOMB 23** [5] M W Easterby 4-9-6 (62) K Darley 5/1 FAV: 150-0601: Made all, rdn out to assert ins 70
fnl 2f: eff at 7f/1m, has tried 10f: acts on firm & gd/soft: enjoyed switch to forcing tactics: see 1485.
1425 **RYMERS RASCAL 26** [3] E J Alston 12-8-7 (49) W Supple 16/1: 00302-32: Mid-div, prog halfway, styd 2 52
on to chase wnr ins fnl 1f, al held: remains in gd form despite age: see 1425 (reapp).
1823 **EFIDIUM 6** [10] N Bycroft 6-9-8 (64) G Faulkner 6/1: 46-20423: Mid-div, prog halfway, onepace fnl 1f. 1¼ 65
1731 **CRYFIELD 10** [1] N Tinkler 7-9-1 (57) Kim Tinkler 15/2: 05-00624: Chsd ldrs, onepcd from dist. hd 57
1775 **SKIBEREEN 9** [13]4-9-13 (69) P Mathers(7) 7/1: 5645035: Slow away, hdwy halfway, nrst fin: btr 1775. shd 68
4741} **ALCHEMIST MASTER 223** [6]5-8-13 (55) Dean McKeown 20/1: 140000-6: b g Machiavellian - Gussy ¾ 52
Marlowe (Final Straw) Handy over 6f, no extra: reapp: h'cap wnr in early '03: h'cap wnr in '02 (subs disq & plcd
last): eff over a sharp 1m, acts on both AWs: has slipped back to a decent mark.
1 Feb'03 Sout 8af 80a-68 E: 2 Nov'02 Ling 8ap 69a-64 E:
1794* **BORDER ARTIST 7** [4]5-9-9 (6ex) (65) A Nicholls 13/2: 000-0017: Handy, wknd bef 1f out: quick ½ 61
reapp: btr expected after recent win in Ire.
1794 **SMITH N ALLAN OILS 7** [15]5-9-3 p (59) F Lynch 20/1: 01-10008: Nvr nrr than mid-div: quick reapp. 1 53
4322} **ARIES 249** [2]4-10-0 (70) D Corby(3) 14/1: 0/32000-9: ch f Big Shuffle - Auenlust (Surumu) 5 54
Mid-div, wknd ins fnl 2f: reapp: plccd twice in '03 (h'caps, rtd 73): medn auct mdn wnr in '02 (M Channon): eff at
6/7f, prob stays 1m: acts on firm & gd/soft grnd: M J Wallace. 2 Aug'03 Nott 6.1g/f 72-73 D:

THIRSK MONDAY 24.05.04 Lefthand, Flat, Oval Track

2 Oct'02 Newm 7fm 80-75 B: 2 Sep'02 Redc 7fm 77-73 E: 1 Jul'02 Folk 7g/s 70- F: 2 Jul'02 Hami 6sft 70- E:
1485 **OSCAR PEPPER 23** [17]7-9-7 (63) P Makin(5) 11/1: 50404-50: 10th: Chsd ldrs, outpcd halfway, mod gains *2* **43**
1633 **SOFT MIST 16** [16]4-8-12 (54) R Winston 66/1: 00-60000: 11th: Rear, mod late gains. *nk* **33**
1748* **JORDANS ELECT 10** [12]4-9-13 (69) T Eaves(5) 9/1: 0500-510: 12th: Prom 6f, sn fdd. *¾* **46**
4967} **Northern Games 205** [7]5-9-3 (59) C Williams(7) 50/1:0 1635 **Scramble 16** [11]6-8-10 t(52) T Hamilton(3) 16/1:0
1660 **Buthaina 14** [8]4-9-7 (63) J Fanning 40/1:0
1553 **General Smith 20** [14]5-8-13 (55) P Mulrennan(5) 80/1:0
1636 **Outward 16** [9]4-9-6 (62) R Ffrench 100/1:0 1661 **Mehmaas 14** [18]8-8-9 vis(51) C Cogan 66/1:0
18 Ran Time 1m 37.69 (2.29) Owned: Mr Giles W Pritchard-Gordon Trained: Sheriff Hutton

1973

9.00 Buck Inn Thornton Watlass Handicap Stakes Fillies 3yo+ 0-80 (D) **[76]**
£5525 £1700 £850 **5f str** **Good/Firm 22** **+07 Fast** Stands side

1873 **MUSICAL FAIR 4** [9] J A Glover 4-9-11 (73) R Winston 13/8 FAV: 40-00021: Handy, prog when short of room dist, styd on to lead ins fnl 1f, rdn out to hold on despite edging left: quick reapp: stays 6f, suited by 5f: acts on firm & fast grnd: in gd form: see 1873. **81**
1509 **BARON RHODES 22** [11] J S Wainwright 3-9-2 (72) T Eaves(5) 7/1: 6042-222: Prom, ev ch bef 1f out, kept on just held by wnr cl-home: acts on fast & soft grnd: another gd run: see 1509 & 1229. *1¼* **77**
1749 **FRASCATI 10** [8] A Berry 4-9-8 (70) F Lynch 10/1: 0041023: Led, edged left & hdd ins fnl 1f, no extra. *hd* **74**
1873 **BETTYS PRIDE 4** [5] M Dods 5-9-0 (62) Darren Williams 14/1: 00600-04: b f Lion Cavern - Final Verdict (Law Society) Slow away, prog halfway, kept on fnl 1f: quick reapp: unplcd in '03 (rtd 62, fills h'cap): mdn & h'cap wnr in '02: suited by 5/6f on firm & gd grnd, acts on gall or sharp trk: tried a t-strap: encouraging eff here & is v well h'capped now. 2 Sep'02 Hayd 5g/f 85-80 C: 1 Aug'02 Thir 5gd 79-74 D: 2 Jul'02 Ches 5fm 73-68 C: 1 Jun'02 Muss 5g/f 68- D: 2 Jun'02 Redc 6fm 68- D: 2 Jun'02 Muss 5g/f 65- D: 2 Aug'01 Ripo 5fm 68- F: *3* **57**
91 **SHAROURA 182** [10]8-9-0 (62) T Hamilton(3) 14/1: 233505-5: ch f Inchinor - Kinkajoo (Precocious) Rear, prog halfway, styd on fnl 1f: reapp: won 2 h'caps in '03: dual h'cap wnr in '02 (J M Bradley): dual h'cap wnr in '01: eff at 5/7f on firm, soft & fibresand: acts on any trk: with R A Fahey. *nk* **56**
2 Jul'03 Newc 6g/s 64-60 D: 1 Jul'03 Thir 6g/s 58-52 D: 1 Jul'03 Hami 6.0g/f 54-48 E: 2 Jun'03 Muss 7.1g/f 52-48 D: 2 Aug'02 Sali 6g/f 54-52 E: 2 Jul'02 Wind 6g/f 55-54 D: 2 Nov'01 Wolv 6af 62a-57 F: 1 Sep'01 Pont 6fm 59-53 D:
1873 **ROMAN MISTRESS 4** [1]4-9-4 (66) K Dalgleish 6/1: 0000-046: Prom till halfway, no extra dist. *1* **57**
1873 **MYSTERY PIPS 4** [6]4-8-3 vis (51) Kim Tinkler 33/1: 3415-007: Handy 3f, wknd. *3* **33**
1749 **VIGOROUS 10** [7]4-9-8 (70) Alex Greaves 5/1: 0440-058: Handy 3f, sn wknd: btr 1749. *1* **49**
4487} **REWAYAAT 240** [2]3-9-10 (80) W Supple 14/1: 52100-9: Chsd ldrs till 4f, wknd: reapp. *1¼* **55**
1676 **MESMERISED 13** [3]4-7-13 (1ow)(11oh) (35) Ann Stokell 100/1: 0000600: 10th: Bhd, nvr a factor. *13* **0**
10 Ran Time 57.79(57.0) Owned: P and S Partnership Trained: Worksop

RIPON TUESDAY 25.05.04 Righthand, Sharpish Track

Official Going Good/Firm

1974

2.10 E B F Spa Welter Maiden Stakes 2yo (D)
£5590 £1720 £860 **5f str** **Good/Firm 37** **-42 Slow** Stands Side

1709 **MIZZ TEE 12** [10] T D Easterby 2-8-9 D Allan(3) 5/4 FAV: 21: Sn handy, rdn & asserted ins last, styd on strongly: hvly bckd, op 11/8: confirmed debut promise: eff at 5f on gd/soft & fast grnd, sharpish or gall trk: will get further & can rate higher: see 1709. **81**
HANSEATIC LEAGUE 0 [6] M Johnston 2-9-0 J Fanning 11/4: 2: b c Red Ransom - Rhine Valley (Danzig) Sn led, hdd ins last, not pace of wnr: nicely bckd: Feb foal, dam 5/6f wnr: eff at 5f on fast grnd & a sharpish trk, encouraging start. *¾* **83**
STRATHTAY 0 [4] P C Haslam 2-8-9 G Faulkner 16/1: 3: ch f Pivotal - Cressida (Polish Precedent) Chsd ldrs, kept on ins last, nrst fin: 20,000gns March first foal, dam unrcd: eff at 5f, looks sure to apprec 6f+: acts on fast: type to rate higher over further. *1½* **73**
1669 **ASHES 14** [8] K R Burke 2-8-9 K Dalgleish 25/1: 054: Went left start, sn handy & ch over 1f out, no extra: handles fast grnd: see 1669. *1¼* **69**
HIGH PETERGATE 0 [3]2-8-9 Dale Gibson 33/1: 5: Mid-div, rdn & kept on, nrst fin: E40,000 March foal, half-sister to a wnr abroad, dam unplcd: 6f+ shld suit. *½* **67**
RICH ALBI 0 [9]2-9-0 W Supple 16/1: 6: Chsd ldrs, outpcd fnl 2f. *hd* **71**
HIGH MINDED 0 [5]2-9-0 Darren Williams 16/1: 7: Slow away & bhd, kept on late & shld imprve: scope. *1½* **66+**
SAFFA GARDEN 0 [7]2-8-9 D Holland 8/1: 8: Bmpd start, chsd ldrs, sn outpcd. *½* **59**
MILL END CHATEAU 0 [12]2-9-0 P Mulrennan(5) 50/1: 9: Chsd ldrs till 2f out. *3½* **53**
MIST OPPORTUNITY 0 [2]2-9-0 K Darley 20/1: 0: 10th: Sn outpcd in rear. *16* **8**
MICKEY BOGGITT 0 [1]2-9-0 J Carroll 25/1: 0: 11th: Dwelt & sn struggling. *3* **0**
HIGHBURY LASS 0 [11]2-8-9 A Culhane 66/1: 0: 12th: Dwelt & al bhd. *19* **0**
12 Ran Time 1m 01.72 (3.92) Owned: Salifix Trained: Malton

1975

2.40 Markington Claiming Stakes 3yo (F)
£3255 £930 £465 **6f str** **Good/Firm 37** **-26 Slow** Stands Side

1903 **ARFINNIT 4** [2] M R Channon 3-8-11 vis (64) A Culhane 3/1 JT FAV: 0-030651: Handy & led over 2f out, rdn & styd on well ins last: qck reapp: eff at 5/6f on fast & soft grnd, gall or sharpish trk: eff with/without visor: apprec drop to claim grade: see 1054. **67**
1873 **OBE BOLD 5** [4] A Berry 3-8-4 (60) J Carroll 9/2: 000-4302: Trkd ldrs, styd on for press, not pace of wnr: qck reapp: stays 6f: see 1338. *1½* **54**
1257 **WARES HOME 36** [1] K R Burke 3-9-3 VIS (67) Darren Williams 5/1: 006-0603: b c Indian Rocket - Pepilin (Coquelin) Led, hdd over 2f out, sn onepace: op 7/1: first time visor, drpd in trip: '03 nov auct stks scorer: eff at 5/6f, tried 1m: acts on fast & gd grnd, stiff/undul trks: can force the pace. *shd* **66**
1 Jul'03 Hami 6.0gd 85- E: 2 Jun'03 Hami 6.0gd 81- D: 2 May'03 Hami 5.0gd 74- D:

337 **MAUNBY RAVER 139** [5] P C Haslam 3-9-7 (65) G Faulkner 4/1: 41215-04: Chsd ldrs till dist.	3	62
1678 **COULD SHE BE MAGIC 13** [6]3-8-2 bl (55) Dale Gibson 3/1 JT FAV: 1-210205: Chsd ldrs 5f, bckd.	7	23
1408 **WILHEHECKASLIKE 28** [3]3-8-3 vis T (35) J Bramhill 33/1: 200-0006: Sn bhd: tried a t-strap: see 850.	14	0

6 Ran   Time 1m 13.75 (3.75)   Owned: Mr Tim Corby   Trained: West Ilsley

---

1976   3.10 Black Sheep Brewery Handicap Stakes 3yo 0-70 (E)   **[77]**
         £4310 £1326 £663   **1m2f**   **Good/Firm 37**   **-03 Slow**   Inside

1242 **DAGGERS CANYON 38** [6] Julian Poulton 3-8-9 (58) Lisa Jones(2) 33/1: 0540-201: Led 3f & remained handy till led again over 2f out, rdn out: first win: eff at 10f, shld stay 12f: acts on fast, gd/sft & polytrk: see 1051.		67
1834 **FITTING GUEST 7** [5] G G Margarson 3-9-2 (65) P Robinson 3/1 FAV: 40-622: Trkd ldrs, drvn & chsd wnr over 1f out, no extra nr fin: paddock pick: ran to form of 1834 (led).	½	72
1663 **WING COLLAR 15** [9] T D Easterby 3-9-2 (65) W Supple 14/1: 4440-033: Held up, styd on for press, nrst fin: acts on fast & soft grnd, worth another try at 12f in similar: see 1663 & 1174.	1½	70
1042 **REDI 52** [12] L M Cumani 3-9-4 (67) D Holland 7/2: 4054-04: Chsd ldrs, kept on onepace fnl 2f: 8 wk abs: stays 10f: see 1042.	nk	71
1160 **HEARTBEAT 41** [14]3-7-12 (47) Dale Gibson 22/1: 6-400445: Mid-div, kept on late, nrst fin: shld stay 10f: handles fast & gd/soft grnd: see 1160, 1051 & 645.	3	47
1603 **ALWAYS FLYING 18** [8]3-9-7 (70) K Dalgleish 9/1: 55-15266: Dsptd lead & led after 3f till 3f out, wknd.	nk	69
1398 **PLANTERS PUNCH 28** [1]3-8-13 (62) Martin Dwyer 20/1: 00-007: b c Cape Cross - Jamaican Punch (Shareef Dancer) Rear, late gains, no threat: unplcd '03 (rtd 67, mdn).	½	60
1740 **BISCAR TWO 11** [11]3-8-0 (49) J Bramhill 8/1: 0-462228: Rear, mod gains for press: see 1740, 1395.	1¼	45
1611 **STRANGELY BROWN 18** [10]3-8-6 (55) B Reilly(3) 7/1: 00-0039: Keen & trkd ldrs, stumbled badly on home turn over 4f out, btn 2f out: see 1611.	1	50
1769 **DISPOL VELETA 10** [13]3-9-4 (67) K Darley 8/1: 0141300: 10th: Held up, eff & no impress over 2f out.	2	59
4526} **EUIPPE 238** [2]3-9-1 (64) M Fenton 33/1: 456-0: 11th: b f Air Express - Myth (Troy) Al bhd on reapp/h'cap bow: unplcd '03 (rtd 68, lightly rcd, mdns): half-sister to a smart 1m/14f wnr, dam mid-dist wnr.	2½	52

1663 Pearl Pride 15 [7]3-9-7 (70) J Fanning 25/1:0   1473 Storm Clouds 24 [4]3-8-3 (52) D Allan(2) 40/1:0
4787} Acca Larentia 221 [15]3-8-8 (57) V Halliday 50/1:0   1306 Raheed 33 [3]3-9-2 (65) A Culhane 25/1:0
15 Ran   Time 2m 07.28 (3.98)   Owned: Mr S M Kemp   Trained: Newmarket

---

1977   3.40 Nick Wilmot-Smith Memorial Handicap Stakes 3yo+ 0-95 (C)   **[88]**
         £9100 £3452 £1726   **6f str**   **Good/Firm 37**   **+02 Fast**   Stands Side

1481 **STEEL BLUE 24** [10] R M Whitaker 4-9-11 (85) A Culhane 10/1: 200-1001: Sn led far side & overall ldr, drvn out, decisively: visor omitted after latest: eff at 5/6f on fast, soft & dirt surfaces: prob handles any trk: seems best when able to dominate: see 921.		93
1594 **JOHNSTONS DIAMOND 18** [9] E J Alston 6-10-0 (88) W Supple 8/1: 0010462: Sn handy far side, not pace of wnr ins last: see 687.	1½	90
1743 **TIME N TIME AGAIN 11** [12] E J Alston 6-8-10 p (70) D Allan(3) 12/1: 3150063: Chsd ldrs far side, kept on onepace ins last: see 807 & 551.	1½	67
1354 **ROMANY NIGHTS 31** [4] J W Unett 4-9-2 vis (76) D Holland 7/2 FAV: 00-50434: Trkd ldrs stands side, led that group ins last, no ch with front trio far side: fair run, remains in sound form: see 1354 & 807.	¾	71 +
4888} **BLYTHE SPIRIT 213** [1]5-9-1 (75) T Hamilton(3) 7/1: 005045-5: b g Bahamian Bounty - Lithe Spirit (Dancing Dissident) Led stands side till dist, not pace of ldrs far side: reapp: op 11/1: h'cap wnr '03: dual h'cap wnr '02: eff at 6f, suited by 7f/1m on firm & gd/soft grnd, loves a stiff/gall trk, prob handles any: eff with/without blnks or eye-shield, tried cheek pieces: no headgear worn today.	¾	68

1 Jun'03 Newc 8fm 82-76 D: 2 Aug'02 Ripo 6gd 82-78 D: 1 Jun'02 Redc 7fm 81-72 D: 2 Jun'02 Newc 8g/s 74-71 D: 1 May'02 Carl 7.9fm 69-67 E: 2 Jun'01 Thir 6fm 81- D:

1767 **OBE ONE 10** [8]4-8-9 (69) J Carroll 16/1: 000-0006: b g Puissance - Plum Bold (Be My Guest) Chsd ldrs far side, no extra dist: h'cap scorer '03: auct mdn wnr '02: suited by 5f on firm or gd/soft grnd, prob any trk: slipped down the weights, sharper at 5f.	1½	57

1 Aug'03 Good 5g/f 83-76 C: 2 Aug'02 Newc 5g/s 81- D: 2 Jun'02 Catt 5g/f 80- D: 1 May'02 Muss 5gd 76- F:

1898 **UNDETERRED 4** [2]8-9-3 (77) K Darley 4/1: 4000-057: Trkd ldrs, short of room over 1f out, switched & no impress last: qck reapp: see 1898.	¾	63
1898 **ARMAGNAC 4** [11]6-9-5 (79) Martin Dwyer 7/1: 0-000368: Bhd stands side, nvr a factor: btr 1726.	1	62
967 **EXTINGUISHER 57** [5]5-8-6 (66) A Nicholls 16/1: 00000-09: ch g Zamindar - Xaymara (Sanglamore) Chsd ldrs till 2f out stands side: 8 wk abs: unplcd '03 (rtd 73, h'cap): ex-French, '01 St Cloud wnr (stks): best at 5f on gd/soft grnd.	2	43
1745 **FIORE DI BOSCO 11** [7]3-8-11 (80) P Makin(5) 20/1: 13002-50: 10th: Chsd ldrs stands side till 1f out.	2	51
1774 **WAINWRIGHT 10** [6]4-8-0 (60) J Bramhill 33/1: 31-10000: 11th: Chsd ldrs, stands side, btn 2f out.	nk	30

11 Ran   Time 1m 12.11 (2.11)   Owned: Country Lane Partnership   Trained: Scarcroft

---

1978   4.10 Grantley Maiden Stakes 3yo (D)
         £4882 £1502 £751   **1m rnd**   **Good/Firm 37**   **-01 Slow**   Inside

1815 **LUCAYAN LEGEND 7** [4] R Hannon 3-9-0 Martin Dwyer 10/1: 631: Chsd ldrs, led over 1f out, rdn out: op 8/1: eff around 1m, 10f could suit: handles fast grnd, sharp & undul trks: see 1815.		91
1762 **GRAND BUT ONE 10** [12] B W Hills 3-9-0 A Culhane 4/7 FAV: 622: Handy & led over 2f out, hdd over 1f out, kept on: clr of rem: hvly bckd at odds-on: see 1762 & 1166.	1¼	87
MURBAAT 0 [11] A C Stewart 3-9-0 P McCabe 40/1: 3: b c Deploy - Ozette (Dancing Brave) Rear, switched wide & kept on for press, nrst fin: eye-catching late hdwy on debut: half-brother to a 7f/1m juv wnr, dam a useful stayer in Ireland: sure to apprec 10f+, handles fast grnd, scopey colt, expect improvement.	5	78 +
2856} **BLUETORIA 318** [3] J A Glover 3-8-9 J Fanning 100/1: 0-4: b f Vettori - Blue Birds Fly (Rainbow Quest) Rear, kept on late, nrst fin on reapp: clr of rem: dam a 10f 3yo wnr: stays 1m, 10f+ looks likely to suit: handles fast grnd: better effort.	nk	72
SOVIET TREAT 254 [10]3-8-9 (95) K Dalgleish 7/2: 62502-5: b f Ashkalani - Mystery Treat (Plugged Nickle) Led till 3f out, fdd: reapp: op 4/1: ex-Irish: '03 auct mdn rnr-up: eff around 7f/1m on fast & gd grnd.	7	60
1787 **RED MONARCH 8** [14]3-9-0 Dean McKeown 66/1: 0006: Mid-div, drvn & btn 3f out.	5	56

1784 **UNPRECEDENTED 9** [1]3-9-0 vis (50) T G McLaughlin 100/1: 600-0047: Chsd ldrs 6f: btr 1784. *nk* **55**

4617} **FANLING LADY 232** [5]3-8-9 (74) A Nicholls 20/1: 303032-8: In tch 5f on reapp, new yard. *5* **41**

1518 **NODS STAR 22** [2]3-8-9 Dale Gibson 66/1: 509: Al bhd. *6* **31**

1783 **BLUE NUN 9** [8]3-8-9 J Carroll 100/1: 500: 10th: Sn struggling rear. *1¾* **28**

1832 **GHANTOOT 7** [6]3-9-0 K Darley 25/1: 0000: 11th: Mid-div, btn 3f out. *1½* **30**

1473 **ESTEPONA 24** [7]3-9-0 G Parkin 66/1: 400: 12th: Sn bhd: btr 1304 (debut, soft). *1¾* **27**

12 Ran Time 1m 40.56 (3.06) Owned: Lucayan Stud Trained: Marlborough

1979

4.40 Galphay Classified Stakes 3yo+ 0-70 (E)
£4105 £1263 £632 **1m2f** **Good/Firm 37** **+01 Fast** Inside

1650 **POLAR JEM 15** [6] G G Margarson 4-9-3 (73) A McCarthy 6/1: 6321-341: Dictated pace, styd on strongly for press fnl 2f: op 5/1: eff at 10f on firm & soft grnd, sharp or gall trks: enjoyed forcing the pace. **79**

1681* **ALERON 13** [3] J J Quinn 6-9-5 (72) K Darley 11/4 FAV: 3434-212: Chsd ldrs, outpcd over 2f out, kept on ins last, no threat: gelded: eff at 10f tho' ideally suited by testing grnd at this trip, gets 12f+ well. *4* **74**

625 **STATEROOM 101** [7] J A R Toller 6-9-5 bl (72) Lisa Jones(3) 7/1: 00154-53: Trkd ldrs, styd on for press, not able to chall: see 625. *nk* **73**

1781 **STALLONE 9** [4] N Wilson 7-9-5 (72) R Winston 100/30: 2310-034: Held up, eff to chase wnr over 1f out, no impress ins last: see 1781 (C/D). *½* **72**

1821 **JIMMY BYRNE 7** [2]4-9-5 (72) T Eaves(5) 25/1: 00-04105: Handy, drvn & no extra over 1f out: btr 1397. *5* **65**

4922*}**OPENING CEREMONY 210** [1]5-9-0 (68) T Hamilton(3) 8/1: 130531-6: br f Quest For Fame - Gleam of Light (Danehill) Cl-up, fdd under press fnl 2f: reapp: h'cap & class stks scorer '03: unplcd '02 (rtd 69, Mrs A J Perrett): suited by 10f, tried 12f: acts on fast & gd/soft grnd, likes a stiff/gall trk: has gone well fresh. *2½* **56**
1 Oct'03 Redc 10g/f 72-(65) E: 1 Aug'03 Newc 10.1g/f 64-60 E: 1 Oct'01 Leic 7g/s 89- D:

1602 **MEGANS MAGIC 18** [5]4-9-0 (69) J Bramhill 4/1: 42-61207: Dwelt, held up in tch, eff wide, btn 2f out. *1½* **54**

7 Ran Time 2m 06.87 (3.57) Owned: Norcroft Park Stud Trained: Newmarket

1980

5.10 Studley Royal Handicap Stakes 3yo+ 0-75 (E) **[88]**
£4095 £1260 £630 **1m4f60y** **Good/Firm 37** **-34 Slow** Inside

1791 **ALBINUS 8** [1] A M Balding 3-8-11 bl (71) Martin Dwyer 9/4 FAV: 03-021: Made all & dictated pace, ran wide on bend over 5f out, rdn & in command fnl 2f: nicely bckd, first win: eff at 1m/10f, now stays a slowly run 12f with forcing tactics: enjoyed being able to dictate on a trk which favours front runners: see 1791. **90**

1633 **SANTIBURI LAD 17** [4] N Wilson 7-8-11 (54) T Hamilton(3) 12/1: 30460-32: Keen & trkd ldrs, eff to chase wnr over 1f out, no impress: op 14/1: prefer claim grade & 10f: see 1633. *6* **62**

1875 **DISTANT COUSIN 5** [3] M A Buckley 7-9-7 vis (64) J Fanning 10/1: 2256-053: Trkd ldrs, styd on onepace fnl 3f, nvr a threat: see 1009. *hd* **71**

1821 **TROUBLE MOUNTAIN 7** [5] M W Easterby 7-9-10 bl (67) K Darley 7/2: 3-333524: In tch, eff over 2f out, sn no impress: btr 1821, 1164 & 196. *2½* **70**

1830* **FIELD SPARK 7** [7]4-9-3 (6ex)p (60) D Holland 5/2: 6616-615: Rear, drvn 3f out, no impress over 1f out. *hd* **62**

1680+**ROYAL MELBOURNE 13** [6]4-8-12 (55) R Winston 7/1: 0000-16: Chsd wnr halfway, btn over 2f out. *10* **44**

6 Ran Time 2m 42.24(8.74) Owned: Miss K Rausing Trained: Kingsclere

LINGFIELD Polytrack TUESDAY 25.05.04 Lefthand, Sharp, Undulating Track

Official Going Good/Firm

1981

2.20 Lingfield Leisure Club Median Auction Maiden Stakes 2yo (F)
£3031 £866 £433 **5f str** **Good/Firm** **Slow** Stands Side

1735 **INDIANNIE STAR 11** [7] M R Channon 2-8-9 T E Durcan 2/5 FAV: 21: Handy & led 2f out, drvn & styd on well: nicely bckd at odds-on, confirmed debut promise: eff at 5f on fast & gd grnd, gall or sharp/undul trk. **81**

KWAME 0 [6] Miss E C Lavelle 2-8-9 S W Kelly 66/1: 2: b f Kingsinger - Admire (Last Tycoon) Held up rear, hdwy to chase wnr dist, kept on but al held: March foal, dam a 1m juv wnr: eff at 5f, 6f will suit: acts on fast grnd, sharp/undul trk: pleasing intro, entitled to prog & find similar. *1½* **76**

1256 **EDGE FUND 36** [1] B R Millman 2-9-0 S Sanders 7/1: 333: Towards centre & prom, hung left & styd on for press fnl 2f, not pace of wnr: op 11/2: type to apprec h'cap company in time: see 1256 & 1001. *nk* **80**

TURKS WOOD 0 [3] M H Tompkins 2-9-0 F P Ferris(3) 33/1: 4: b c Charnwood Forest - Nairasha (Niniski) Slow away & rear, styd on for press from over 1f out, nrst fin: E15,000 March foal, half-brother to wnrs abroad: looks sure to apprec 6f+ & caught the eye late on, improve. *hd* **79+**

1640 **RUSSIAN ROCKET 15** [2]2-9-0 Hayley Turner(5) 66/1: 05: b g Indian Rocket - Soviet Girl (Soviet Star) Dwelt, sn chsd ldrs, outpcd over 1f out: left hvy grnd debut bhd: cheaply bght April foal: gd start. *½* **77**

RIDE SAFARI 0 [9]2-9-0 P Doe 40/1: 6: V slow away & well bhd rear, gd late hdwy: will improve. *1¾* **72+**

1880 **IM AIMEE 4** [4]2-8-9 S Carson 12/1: 263047: Prom till over 1f out, qck reapp. *½* **65**

1716 **BLACK DRAFT 12** [11]2-9-0 T P Queally(3) 50/1: 08: Cl-up, wknd dist. *nk* **69**

1646 **PERIANTH 15** [5]2-9-0 S Drowne 12/1: 49: Chsd ldrs till 2f out: see 1646. *½* **67**

KEMPSEY 0 [12]2-9-0 J Tate 50/1: 0: 10th: Sn outpcd & struggling. *2½* **60**

HALLUCINATE 0 [10]2-9-0 R L Moore 20/1: 0: 11th: Dwelt, sn outpcd, op 16/1. *shd* **59**

1367 **MAJESTICAL 30** [8]2-9-0 R Miles(3) 20/1: 340: 12th: Led till 2f out, wknd qckly: 'lost shoe'. *1* **56**

12 Ran Time 59.9 (3.1) Owned: Timberhill Racing Partnership Trained: West Ilsley

LINGFIELD Polytrack TUESDAY 25.05.04 Lefthand, Sharp, Undulating Track

1982

2.50 First Title Classified Stakes 3yo 0-65 (E)
£3689 £1135 £568 **7f str** **Good/Firm** **Fair** Stands Side

1775 **LADY GEORGINA 10** [16] J R Fanshawe 3-8-13 (70) O Urbina 8/1: 4300-361: Al trav well & handy, led over 1f out, rdn clr: op 13/2: first win: eff at 7f/1m on firm & gd/soft grnd: see 1359. **78**

1729 **BEST DESERT 11** [12] J R Best 3-8-11 (65) N Pollard 6/1 JT FAV: 35602-42: Mid-div, styd on for press fnl 2f, nvr any threat to wnr: confirmed promise of reapp: see 1729. *3½* **67**

1761 **HERE TO ME 10** [13] R Hannon 3-8-13 (70) P Dobbs 6/1 JT FAV: 03502-53: Mid-div, eff 2f out, onepace. *½* **69**

1778 **BIG BAD BURT 10** [3] Miss Gay Kelleway 3-8-11 T p (63) S Sanders 8/1: 4223034: Prom, rdn & onepace dist: prob ran to form of latest in first time t-strap: acts on fast, gd/soft & polytrack: see 1778, 545. *1¼* **64**

1720 **DEIGN TO DANCE 12** [5]3-8-8 (64) T E Durcan 25/1: 620-5005: b f Danetime - Lady Montekin (Montekin) Towards rear, kept on late, nrst fin: imprvd eff with cheek pieces omitted: dual auct mdn rnr-up in '03: eff at 5.7f/6f, prob stays a sharp 7f: handles firm & fast grnd, sharp/undul trks. *hd* **60**
2 Sep'03 Good 6fm 77-(75) D: 2 Aug'03 Bath 5.7fm 76- E:

1647 **KITLEY 15** [2]3-8-11 (63) S Whitworth 14/1: 0643-006: b c Muhtarram - Salsita (Salse) Rear, kept on late, no dngr: op 25/1: h'cap plcd fnl '03 start (rtd 65, nursery, AW h'cap unplcd, rtd 61a): eff at 7f/1m on fast & gd grnd, easy/sharp trks. *½* **62**

1534 **CHORUS BEAUTY 21** [9]3-8-8 (61) S Drowne 20/1: 01-007: Prom till dist, see 260 (6f, AW mdn). *nk* **58**

111 **PICCLEYES 179** [4]3-8-11 (65) R L Moore 20/1: 260353-8: Led/dsptd lead till over 1f out: 6 mth abs. *¾* **59**

1825 **HAZEWIND 7** [14]3-8-11 VIS t (58) S Carson 12/1: 4210009: Rear, little hdwy in first time visor: see 765. *hd* **58**

1729 **NEW YORK 11** [8]3-8-11 T (68) S W Kelly 20/1: 324-00: 10th: Led till 3f out, btn dist. *¾* **56**

1607 **INDIAN EDGE 18** [15]3-8-11 (65) D Kinsella 8/1: 666-0520: 11th: Dwelt & rear, eff 2f out, no prog. *shd* **55**

1281 **VELOCITAS 35** [11]3-8-11 (58) T P Queally(3) 9/1: 0-400: 12th: Rear, no room over 2f out, sn no prog. *nk* **54**

3471} **Yashin 291** [17]3-8-11 (65) F P Ferris(3) 20/1:0 229 **Red Contact 157** [6]3-9-0 (68) R Smith 33/1:0

1617 **Star Fern 18** [10]3-8-11 (55) T Quinn 50/1:0 713 **Dream Of Dubai 91** [7]3-8-8 (62) G Gibbons 20/1:0

16 Ran Time 1m 23.36 (2.96) Owned: Byerley Turf Trained: Newmarket

1983

3.20 Lingfield Park Handicap Stakes 3yo 0-85 (D) **[91]**
£5769 £1775 £888 **7f str** **Good/Firm** **Fair** Stands Side

1498 **FLIP FLOP AND FLY 23** [10] S Kirk 3-9-2 (79) R L Moore 25/1: 1300-001: b g Woodborough - Angelus Chimes (Northfields) Rear, hdwy 2f out & styd on well to lead well ins last, going away, v readily: blnks omitted: mdn scorer '03 (List 3rd of 7, rtd 91): eff at 6/7f on fast & gd: follow-up in this form. 1 Jun'03 Newc 6gd 87- D: **88+**

1583 **FREE TRIP 19** [2] J H M Gosden 3-9-6 (83) R Havlin 8/1: 120-1602: Led pair on far side & sn clrr, kept on well ins last, not pace of wnr stands side: op 7/1: imprvd eff, enjoyed forcing tactics: see 955. *1½* **88**

1720 **JOY AND PAIN 12** [12] G L Moore 3-8-2 (65) T P Queally 15/2: 0601623: Trkd ldrs, ch dist, onepace. *1½* **67**

1607* **MISSION MAN 18** [8] R Hannon 3-9-5 (82) P Dobbs 7/1: 024-4214: Prom, styd on onepace for press: acts on fast & soft grnd: see 1607. *¾* **82**

1525 **HANDSOME CROSS 22** [9]3-9-7 (84) S Drowne 8/1: 21232-55: Led, hdd ins last, no extra: see 1525. *hd* **83**

1762 **BAILAORA 10** [11]3-8-12 bl (75) S Sanders 20/1: 4302-606: b c Shinko Forest - Tart (Warning) Mid-div, not pace to chall: h'cap rnr-up fnl '03 start (first time blnks, earlier mdn 4th, rtd 82): eff at 7f, breeding suggests mid-dists may suit: handles firm & fast grnd, handles a sharp/undul or gall trk. *1* **72**
2 Oct'03 Good 7fm 81-77 D:

1576 **RISE 19** [5]3-7-12 (1oh)bl (60) D Kinsella 25/1: 400-0067: Towards centre, not pace to threaten: see 494. *2* **54**

1417 **FINDERS KEEPERS 27** [3]3-9-0 (77) T Quinn 7/1: 20-23108: Trkd ldrs trav well, found little over 1f out. *1¼* **67**

855 **JOMUS 70** [13]3-8-2 (65) C Cogan 10/1: 05-52129: Slow away & sn bhd, late gains: 10 wk abs: progressive earlier on AW, needs 1m & strong handling: see 855 & 798. *1¾* **51**

1722 **DISCO DIVA 12** [15]3-8-3 (66) R Thomas(5) 25/1: 0152-000: 10th: Al rear, sn struggling: see 933. *nk* **51**

1707 **SWIFT SAILING 12** [4]3-9-0 BL (77) T E Durcan 25/1: 015-00: 11th: b c Storm Cat - Saytarra (Seeking The Gold) Chsd ldrs till 3f out: tried blnks: lightly rcd '03, mdn scorer: eff over a stiff 6f on gd/soft grnd. 1 Jul'03 Sali 6g/s 82- D: *nk* **61**

351 **ONE ALONE 138** [6]3-7-12 (16oh) (45) M Henry 66/1: 0000-00: 12th: Al rear, 5 mth abs, new yard. *1¼* **42**

1583 **ST SAVARIN 19** [1]3-8-11 (74) N Pollard 14/1: 1-253100: 13th: Chsd sole rival far side, no ch fnl 3f. *1¼* **52**

1722 **BERTOCELLI 12** [14]3-8-10 (73) J Mackay 12/1: 50610-00: 14th: Chsd ldrs till 2f out. *1½* **48**

1825 **MIDNIGHT BALLARD 7** [7]3-9-0 (77) S Carson 4/1 FAV: 536-6420: 15th: Prom, btn over 1f out: rider reported colt unsuited by gd/firm grnd but much btr 1825 (g/f). *3* **46**

15 Ran Time 1m 23.16 (2.76) Owned: Mr Mike Browne Trained: Upper Lambourn

1984

3.50 Saturday Night At Lingfield On 29th May Claiming Stakes 3yo+ (E)
£3465 £1066 £533 **7f str** **Good/Firm** **Slow** Stands Side

935 **LADY PISTE 60** [7] P D Evans 3-8-0 vis t (61) F P Ferris(3) 9/2: 4253101: Al handy & led over 1f out, sn in command, hands & heels: clmd by G Margarson for 6,000: 2 mth abs: eff at 5/6f, now suited by sharp/undul 7f: acts on firm, gd/soft & polytrack: loves claim grade: see 804 & 233. **55**

1588 **CARGO 19** [1] B A Pearce 5-9-0 t p (48) R Miles(3) 7/1: 0420232: Al handy trav well, led over 2f out, found little & hdd over 1f out, held on for 2nd: see 1413, 709 & 544. *3* **50**

1413 **A ONE 28** [8] B Palling 5-9-4 (51) D Sweeney 20/1: 00000-43: Led 5f, sn outpcd but kept on cl-home: more gall trk in similar company will suit: likes Chepstow: see 1413. *nk* **53**

1549 **FAYR FIRENZE 21** [3] M F Harris 3-8-3 (45) S Righton 16/1: 4625224: Pushed along rear, styd on late, no threat: handles fast, gd & both AWs: see 1549 & 1453. *½* **48**

1806 **IVY MOON 8** [9]4-8-9 (50) R Thomas(5) 11/4 FAV: 30-36035: Pushed along rear, eff over 2f out, no impress dist: bckd: see 1806 & 398. *1¾* **39**

1750 **BULAWAYO 10** [2]7-9-0 bl (49) G Gibbons 7/1: 0306106: Chsd ldrs 5f: btr 956 (AW). *1* **42**

1720 **FARNBOROUGH 12** [6]3-8-13 (59) T Quinn 12/1: 0-5007: b c Lear Fan - Gretel (Hansel) Sn struggling rear, little hdwy: only mod form in mdns & clmrs prev. *1* **50**

1498 **MAC THE KNIFE 23** [4]3-8-13 (79) P Dobbs 7/1: 3420-008: b c Daggers Drawn - Icefern (Moorestyle) Slow away & well bhd from halfway: op 4/1: debut wnr '03 in auct mdn company, subs cond stks rnr-up: eff at 5/6f, handles fast & gd/soft: has gone well fresh: reportedly has a breathing prob. *16* **18**

LINGFIELD Polytrack TUESDAY 25.05.04 Lefthand, Sharp, Undulating Track

2 Jun'03 Pont 6g/s 84- C: 2 Apr'03 Newb 5.2g/f 84- D: 1 Mar'03 Donc 5gd 85- E:
323 **PHRENOLOGIST 140** [5]4-9-10 (65) S Sanders 8/1: 5613-09: Prom till halfway, sn struggling &   *14*   **0**
eased: 5 mth abs, reportedly unsuited by this fast grnd on return to turf: prev with J Fanshawe: see 23 (aw).
9 Ran   Time 1m 23.67 (3.27)   Owned: Mrs S J Lawrence   Trained: Abergavenny

---

1985	4.20 Furlongs And Fairways At Lingfield Park Handicap Stakes 3yo 46-55 (F)					**[69]**
	£3038 £868 £434	**6f str**	**Good/Firm**	**Slow**	Stands Side	

1324 **CHEROKEE NATION 32** [17] P W D'Arcy 3-8-12 (53) T Quinn 5/1 JT FAV: 006-441: Trkd ldrs, hdwy to   **59**
lead over 1f out & asserted under hands & heels: eye-shield omitted after latest: apprec drop to 6f, tried at up to
10f prev this term: acts on fast grnd, poss handles fibresand, likes a sharp/undul trk: see 1240.
1453* **YAMATO PINK 26** [15] Mrs H Sweeting 3-8-9 (50) G Baker 11/1: 4660-012: Mid-div, eff to chase wnr   *¾*   **54**
from dist, hung but kept on, al held: op 7/1: up in grade on turf return, gd run: acts on polytrack & fast grnd.
973 **MISS JUDGEMENT 57** [4] W R Muir 3-8-11 (52) R Miles(3) 16/1: 0006-53: b f Revoque - Mugello   *nk*   **55**
(Emarati) Towards centre mid-div, styd on for press, nrst fin: 8 wk abs, gd run on h'cap bow from awkward low draw:
unplcd '03 (rtd 49 & 16a): stays 6f, 7f could suit: acts on fast grnd & a sharp/undul trk.
1730 **PARDON MOI 11** [8] Mrs C A Dunnett 3-8-7 (48) Hayley Turner(5) 20/1: 4004104: Towards centre &   *nk*   **50**
trkd ldrs, onepace from dist: back to form after disapp latest: see 1641 (banded).
472 **DUBAIAN MIST 122** [2]3-8-12 (53) N Chalmers(5) 25/1: 05-05: b f Docksider - Robellino Miss   *¾*   **53**
(Robellino) Sn chsd ldrs, no extra when short of room cl-home: h'capper ran well for a long way on drop in trip:
unplcd sole '03 turf start (rtd 64, AW unplcd, rtd 55a, mdns): eff at 6f, tried up to 1m: handles fast grnd.
1404 **MALUTI 28** [14]3-8-9 (50) J Mackay 5/1 JT FAV: 0006-06: ch g Piccolo - Persian Blue (Persian   *1¼*   **46**
Bold) Prom & ch over 1f out, no extra when hmpd ins last: op 7/1: unplcd '03 (rtd 64, mdn, subs gelded): prob
stays a sharp 6f on fast grnd.
1730 **JOANS JEWEL 11** [3]3-8-10 (51) J Tate 25/1: 55607: Pushed along rear, mod late prog.   *2½*   **40**
1268 **BLACK OVAL 35** [10]3-9-0 (55) R L Moore 13/2: 6-445038: Chsd ldrs till outpcd fnl 2f: btr 1268 (5f).   *shd*   **44**
1902 **PARALLEL LINES 4** [11]3-8-5 bl (46) S Drowne 20/1: 0400369: Led & clr over 2f out, hdd & wknd 2f out.   *nk*   **34**
975 **MISTER COMPLETELY 56** [6]3-8-8 (49) N Pollard 10/1: 40-26600: 10th: Chsd ldrs 5f, little prog.   *nk*   **36**
1085 **I WISH I KNEW 48** [5]3-8-9 (50) T P Queally(3) 16/1: 000-600: 11th: Rear, sn rdn, little hdwy: 7 wk abs.   *¾*   **35**
1539 **JAOLINS 21** [12]3-8-7 (48) R Havlin 14/1: 2005000: 12th: Chsd ldrs 5f: btr 901 (AW).   *hd*   **32**
1730 **SCARLETT BREEZE 11** [7]3-8-10 (51) S Whitworth 3/1: 40065-00: 13th: Bhd, no impress.   *¾*   **33**
1374 **BOLD WOLF 29** [13]3-8-11 (52) A Daly 13/2: 020-4440: 14th: Cl-up till over 2f out: btr 1374 & 898.   *1½*   **30**
1942 **Sussex Style 2** [9]3-8-12 (53) D Sweeney 14/1:0   1453 **Jasmine Pearl 26** [16]3-8-8 (49) D Corby(3) 14/1:0
16 Ran   Time 1m 11.83 (3.03)   Owned: Mr Walt Sylvester   Trained: Newmarket

---

1986	4.50 Ladbrokes Com Amateur Riders' Handicap Stakes 4yo+ 0-75 (E)				**[50]**
	£3552 £1093 £547	**1m4f**	**Good/Firm**	**Inapp** Inside	

1916 **DANAKIL 3** [10] S Dow 9-10-13 (63) Mr D Hutchison(7) 9/2: 0000241: Rear, hdwy to lead over 2f out,   **73a**
pulled clr under hand riding: qck reapp: eff at 12f on firm, soft & both AWs, any trk: best held up: see 1295.
1691 **PAY THE SILVER 13** [8] A Wood 6-10-4 p (56) Mr G Bartley(7) 12/1: 230-0402: Held up, hdwy when   *5*   **57a+**
short of room over 3f out & lost place, staying on when no room again 2f out, wnr had flown: luckless run.
1695* **BANK ON HIM 13** [13] G L Moore 9-10-12 (62) Mr J Jones(5) 11/2: 2222513: Rear, hdwy to chase wnr   *1½*   **62a**
over 2f out, no extra ins last: stays 12f, suited by 1m/10f: see 1695, 1027 & 498.
1830 **REMINISCENT 7** [5] R F Johnson Houghton 5-11-1 vis (65) Miss E J Jones 4/1 FAV: 3522-424: Held up,   *hd*   **65a**
switched wide & styd on fnl 2f, not pace of wnr: see 1830, 259 & 201.
1543 **COMPTON AVIATOR 21** [3]8-10-3 t (53) Mrs S Bosley 9/1: 0244-605: ch g First Trump - Rifada (Ela   *1½*   **50a**
Mana Mou) Dwelt, rear, kept on onepace fnl 3f: AW unplcd '03: class stks rnr-up '02: suited by
10/12f, tried 2m: acts on firm, gd & polytrack, eff in a t-strap, prob handles any trk, likes a sharp/easy one.
2 Sep'03 Good 12g/f 56-53 E: 2 Feb'03 Ling 12app 57a-55 D: 2 Apr'02 Folk 7gd 69- E: 2 Jul'01 Donc 10.2gd 74- E:
2 Nov'00 Ling 10ap 76a-70 G:
4263} **OPTIMAITE 252** [9]7-11-7 t (71) Miss M Sowerby(5) 20/1: 000050-6: b g Komaite - Leprechaun Lady   *5*   **61a**
(Royal Blend) Slow away & rear, under hand riding: no prog 2f out: Flat reapp, 4 mth jumps abs: 03/04 nov hdle wnr (2m, rtd
120h at best, fast & gd, stiff/gall trks): Flat unplcd '03 (rtd 75, h'caps): dual h'cap wnr '02: eff btwn 10/14f,
tried 2m: acts on firm & gd/soft, any trk: can go well fresh: tried visor, suited by t-strap: best held up.
1 Aug'02 Newb 11g/f 90-86 B: 1 Jun'02 Donc 10.2g/f 86-83 B: 2 Sep'01 Kemp 12g/f 76- C: 2 Jul'01 Sand 10g/f 90-90 C:
1 Jun'01 Folk 9.6g/f 92- C:
1899 **TOP OF THE CLASS 4** [1]7-9-4 vis (60) Miss E Folkes(3) 16/1: 3504007: Lost pl early, no impress.   *½*   **29a**
1721 **RIBBONS AND BOWS 12** [4]4-11-6 BL (70) Mr S Walker 14/1: 5600-068: Chsd ldrs 4f out, wknd, blnks.   *5*   **52a**
1589* **LAGO DI COMO 19** [2]7-10-10 t (60) Mrs C Thompson(5) 12/1: 11200//-19: Led & sn clr, hdd 2f out,   *1*   **41a**
wknd.
1197 **LIGHT BRIGADE 40** [11]5-9-11 (2ow) (45) Miss Joanna Rees 6/1: 06/03-600: 10th: Chsd ldrs 9f, abs.   *1½*   **26a**
1650 **ONE OF THEM 15** [6]5-10-7 bl (57) Mrs S Moore(3) 50/1: 05600-00: 11th: Chsd clr ldr till 3f out, sn   *4*   **30a**
btn.
1821 **Lara Bay 7** [12]4-11-0 (64) Mr S Goswell(7) 33/1:0   747 **Paso Doble 88** [7]6-10-11 (61) Mr J Millman(7) 20/1:0
13 Ran   Time 2m 36.35(1.95)   Owned: The Danakilists   Trained: Epsom

---

NOTTINGHAM   TUESDAY 25.05.04   Lefthand, Galloping Track

Official Going Good/Firm

NOTTINGHAM TUESDAY 25.05.04 Lefthand, Galloping Track

1987 **2.30 Quicksilver-Slotz Median Auction Maiden Stakes 2yo (H)**
£1656 £473 £237 **5f13y str** **Good 48** **-01 Slow** Stands side

1571 **TOWN HOUSE 20** [5] B P J Baugh 2-8-9 J F Egan 20/1: 5021: Made all stands rail, drvn out fnl 1f: eff at 5f on gd & gd/soft grnd: acts on a gall or sharp trk: likes to force the pace: see 1571. **74**
1727 **KANAD 11** [14] B Hanbury 2-9-0 t R Hills 8/1: 32: Mid-div, prog 2f out, short of room & switched ins fnl 1f, nrst fin: op 6/1: eff at 5f, will apprec return to 6f: acts on fast & gd grnd, prob wnr here with clr run & can find similar: see 1727. ¾ **77+**
1014 **LACONICOS 54** [13] D R Loder 2-9-0 K Fallon 4/9 FAV: 23: Cl-up, onepcd ins fnl 1f: well bckd at odds-on: 8 wk abs: acts on gd & gd/soft grnd: reportedly lost action here: btr 1014 (debut). *hd* **76**
1805 **RUBYS DREAM 8** [11] J M Bradley 2-8-9 Dane O'Neill 6/1: 4234: Slow away, sn cl-up, no extra dist. *1½* **67**
ZOLASH 0 [8]2-9-0 Derek Nolan(7) 66/1: 5: b c General Monash - Zolba (Classic Secret) Slow away, prog ins fnl 2f, nrst fin: debut: April foal, cost 8,000gns: sire Gr winning sprinter as a juv. *1* **69**
1631 **DESERT BUZZ 17** [2]2-9-0 J Quinn 66/1: 06: b c Desert Story - Sugar (Hernando) Mid-div, no impress ins fnl 1f: Jan first foal, cost E3,000: dam unrcd: sire useful performer around 1m/10f: with J Hetherton. *hd* **68**
1728 **FAIR ALONG 11** [6]2-9-0 M Tebbutt 80/1: 007: Mid-div, prog when no room ins fnl 1f, sn onepcd. *1¼* **65**
1640 **WIZZSKILAD 15** [9]2-9-0 Amy Baker(7) 50/1: 04638: Nvr nrr than mid-div: btr 1640. *1* **62**
1786 **DREAMERS LASS 8** [10]2-8-9 C Catlin 33/1: 29: Handy till halfway, wknd: btr 1786. *1½* **53**
1640 **SHERBOURNE 15** [3]2-8-9 Paul Eddery 14/1: 00: 10th: Handy 3f, wknd. *1¾* **48**
1728 **FAITHISFLYING 11** [4]2-9-0 N Callan 66/1: 060: 11th: Al in rear. *hd* **52**
Debs Broughton 0 [12]2-8-9 G Carter 50/1:0 1394 **Belle Largesse 29** [7]2-8-9 J McAuley 100/1:0
13 Ran Time 1m 0.95 (2.45) Owned: Mr J H Chrimes Trained: Stoke On Trent

1988 **3.00 Quicksilver Gaming Centres Selling Stakes 3yo+ (H)**
£1519 £434 £217 **6f15y str** **Good 48** **+07 Fast** Stands side

1408 **DANAKIM 28** [7] J R Weymes 7-9-10 (35) D Fentiman(7) 33/1: 1004001: Made all, rdn out to assert fnl 2f despite edging left: bought in for 4,200 gns: eff at 5/6f on firm, hvy & fibresaand: see 578. **51**
1405 **VALAZAR 28** [17] D W Chapman 5-9-5 (45) K Fallon 9/2: 0-000232: Cl-up, ev ch dist, kept on but not pace of wnr: op 11/2: continues in form & can find similar: see 1405 & 1199. *2½* **42**
1508 **ONLY ONE LEGEND 23** [10] K A Ryan 6-9-5 bl (55) N Callan 7/2 FAV: 0000303: Bhd, prog 2f out, kept on fnl 1f: op 9/2: blinks refitted & cheekpieces left off: btr 963. *nk* **41**
1938 **THREAT 2** [16] J M Bradley 8-9-5 bl (45) L Keniry(3) 8/1: 3446054: Handy till dist, sn onepcd: qck reapp. ¾ **39**
1963 **ROAN RAIDER 1** [8]4-9-5 vis (47) K Ghunowa(7) 20/1: 0-0003405: Mid-div, eff 3f out, onepcd fnl 1f. ¾ **37**
1837 **MR UPPITY 6** [15]5-9-5 e (40) M Halford(7) 16/1: 0024536: Handy over 4f, no extra: qck reapp: see 1837. ½ **36**
1788 **SHADY DEAL 8** [12]8-9-5 (47) C Catlin 20/1: 0000307: Nvr nrr than mid-div: btr 1662. *hd* **35**
OSLA 0 [1]3-8-8 (3ow) Dane O'Neill 14/1: 8: ch f Komaite - Orlaith (Final Straw) Bhd far side, modest late gains: debut: claimed for 4,000: with H Candy. *2* **27**
1368 **JALOUHAR 30** [11]4-9-5 p (49) M Tebbutt 12/1: 6505029: Mid-div 4f, sn wknd. *1¼* **25**
1878 **PRINCESS ERICA 5** [2]4-9-0 p (45) J Edmunds 8/1: 05-00040: 10th: Cl-up 4f far side, sn wknd. *shd* **19**
317 **TRAVELLING TIMES 141** [3]5-9-5 bl (49) L Enstone(3) 12/1: 3200-560: 11th: Led far side 3f, sn wknd. ½ **23**
1750 **LOUIS GEORGIO 10** [6]5-9-5 (45) J F Egan 33/1: 5400-000: 12th: Al in rear. ½ **22**
1938 **FLYING FAISAL 2** [5]6-9-10 bl (47) C J Davies(7) 22/1: 4610000: 13th: Al bhd far side. *1¼* **23**
1368 **LONE PIPER 30** [14]9-9-5 (40) Hazel Boyd(7) 20/1: 4366060: 14th: Nvr a factor. *1½* **14**
1876 **ALFELMA 5** [9]4-9-0 (47) D Tudhope(7) 66/1: 0/3000-00: 15th: Mid-div till halfway, wknd. *5* **0**
1672 **MIZHAR 14** [13]8-9-10 p (52) S Hitchcott(3) 8/1: 500132P: Sn bhd, p.u: broke blood vessel. **0**
16 Ran Time 1m 13.31 (2.51) Owned: Miss K Buckle Trained: Middleham

1989 **3.30 Quicksilver-Slotz Leaders Banded Stakes 3yo+ 0-40 (H)**
£1509 £431 £216 **6f15y str** **Good 48** **-15 Slow** Stands side

1799 **SOTONIAN 8** [9] P S Felgate 11-9-5 (40) Stephanie Hollinshead(5) 14/1: 0533451: Cl-up, rdn out to lead cl-home: eff at 5f/6f on fast, gd/soft grnd & fibresand, poss polytrack: best without blnks: see 667. **43**
1266 **MASTER RATTLE 22** [15] Jane Southcombe 5-9-5 (40) L Enstone(3) 9/1: 5200012: Cl-up, ev ch ins fnl 1f, just held: recent wnr in Jersey (5.5f, h'cap): eff at 5.5f/7f on gd, gd/soft grnd & polytrack: see 709. *nk* **41**
1799 **BELLS BOYS 8** [11] K A Ryan 5-9-5 p (40) N Callan 17/2: 3504033: Led, hdd under press cl-home. *shd* **40**
1938 **POLAR HAZE 2** [8] J Pearce 7-9-5 bl (40) J Quinn 6/1: 5045504: Handy, ev ch dist, kept on, not btn far: op 13/2: qck reapp: all wins have come on fibresand: btr 533. ½ **38**
1327 **MOONGLADE 32** [13]4-9-5 BL (30) J McAuley 50/1: 000-0005: Sn cl-up, no extra well ins fnl 1f: eff at 6f on gd grnd: imprvd eff here in first time blnks: see 1327. *nk* **37**
1799 **TRAVELLERS JOY 8** [12]4-9-5 (40) M Savage(5) 8/1: 60-00305: Rear, prog halfway, no impress fnl 1f. *shd* **36**
1447 **GRAND VIEW 26** [5]8-9-5 p (40) K Fallon 3/1 FAV: 6042107: Rear, prog ins fnl 2f, nrst fin: btr 1415. *1½* **32**
1065 **GRUFF 49** [10]5-9-5 (30) R Fitzpatrick 66/1: 00-00008: ch g Presidium - Kagram Queen (Prince Ragusa) Slow away, nvr nrr than mid-div: 7 wk abs: modest form in '03 (rtd 29, stks): AW h'cap wnr in early '02 (D W Barker): eff at 5/6f on firm, gd & fibresand, handles soft grnd: acts on a sharp trk. *hd* **31**
1 Feb'02 Sout 6af 61a-55 F: 2 Aug'01 Muss 5g/f 69- F:
1588 **ETERNAL BLOOM 19** [7]6-9-5 (40) D Tudhope(7) 14/1: 0003309: Handy till dist, wknd: btr 1266. *nk* **30**
1545 **MISS FAYE 21** [16]4-9-5 p (30) Dane O'Neill 25/1: 0/466-030: 10th: Slow away, al bhd: btr 1545. *1¾* **25**
1625 **FREDERICK JAMES 17** [14]10-9-5 (35) B Swarbrick(5) 33/1: 04000//-00: 11th: Bhd, nvr a factor. *nk* **24**
769 **VLASTA WEINER 86** [4]4-9-5 bl (40) C Catlin 10/1: 5046460: 12th: Mid-div 4f, wknd. *nk* **23**
1715 **Crusty Lily 12** [6]8-9-5 p(35) L P Keniry(3) 12/1:0 1625 **Yellow River 17** [2]4-9-5 BL(40) S Hitchcott(3) 11/1:0
1690 **Our Sion 13** [1]4-9-5 (35) V Slattery 66/1:0 1682 **My Wild Rover 13** [3]4-9-5 VIS t(30) J F Egan 33/1:0
16 Ran Time 1m 14.63 (3.83) Owned: Mr F Dean Trained: Melton Mowbray

NOTTINGHAM   TUESDAY 25.05.04   Lefthand, Galloping Track

1990
4.00 Brydons Nose Baggers Banded Stakes 4yo+ 0-45 (H)
£1663 £475 £238   1m6f15y   Good 48   -02 Slow   Inside rail

1329* **COURT ONE 32** [6] R J Price 6-9-0 (45) J F McDonald(3) 9/1: 000-0011: Slow away, prog halfway, rdn
out to lead cl-home: op 6/1: eff at 14f/2m on fast & gd/soft grnd: enjoys banded grade: see 1329.   **47**
1654* **TOLEDO SUN 15** [15] V Smith 4-9-0 (45) Joanna Badger 7/2 FAV: 000-3512: Led 3f out, hdd cl-home.   nk **46**
1692 **PARADISE VALLEY 13** [8] Mrs Stef Liddiard 4-9-0 t (45) J Quinn 9/1: 5020543: Rear, prog 3f out,   1 **45**
kept on from dist, not btn far: op 6/1: see 1026 & 347.
1456* **ROYALE PEARL 26** [4] R Ingram 4-9-0 (45) Dane O'Neill 12/1: 40-00414: Mid-div, prog ins fnl 4f, nrst fin. 2 **43**
1789 **ANNIVERSARY GUEST 8** [12]5-9-0 (40) D Nolan(3) 14/1: 0343005: Cl-up, no extra bef 1f out: see 1414. 1 **42**
705 **PROMOTE 92** [5]8-9-0 (40) S Hitchcott(3) 40/1: 000/00-06: gr g Linamix - Rive (Riverman) Rear,   hd **41**
nvr nrr than mid-div: long abs: unplcd sole '03 start (h'cap, rtd 22): unplcd in '02 (rtd 54a, h'cap): prev wnr in
native France: eff at 1m on soft grnd: with Ms A E Embiricos.
1414* **FLETCHER 28** [11]10-9-0 (45) K Fallon 5/1: 204-0517: Nvr nrr than mid-div: btr 1414.   1¼ **40**
1407 **DOCTOR JOHN 28** [13]7-9-0 p (45) C Catlin 9/2: 4216228: Cl-up over 12f, grad wknd: btr 1407 & 1263. nk **39**
     WATERSHIP DOWN 1471 [3]7-9-0 (45) V Slattery 33/1: 000/0///-9: b g Dolphin Street - Persian Myth   ¾ **38**
(Persian Bold): Rear, nvr a factor: rnr-up twice over fences in 02/03 (h'caps, rtd 93c, stays 3m on firm & gd/soft
grnd): nov chase wnr in 01/02 (rtd 104c): modest Flat form prev on 4 Irish starts.
1414 **ANNAKITA 28** [9]4-9-0 (45) G Carter 20/1: 0060-000: 10th: Al in rear.   1¼ **37**
1243 **QUEST ON AIR 36** [2]5-9-0 (45) W Ryan 11/1: 42103-20: 11th: Handy, led after 12f, sn hdd, fdd fnl 1f. shd **36**
1945 **DANCES WITH ANGELS 1** [14]4-9-0 (40) N Callan 12/1: 400-00300: 12th: Mid-div, prog when short of 8 **28**
room 3f out, fdd: unplcd yesterday in 1945, btr 1547.
1793 **CADWALLADER 8** [1]4-9-0 (40) L Keniry(3) 28/1: 0-465U00: 13th: Led 12f, fdd: 'breathing prob'.   13 **16**
13 Ran   Time 3m 5.30 (7.0)   Owned: Derek & Cheryl Holder   Trained: Hereford

1991
4.30 Lawrences London Marauders Apprentice Banded Stakes 3yo+ 0-35 (H)
£1477 £422 £211   1m1f213y   Good 48   -29 Slow   Inside rail

1943 **LITTLE TASK 1** [6] J S Wainwright 6-9-7 (30) A Reilly(5) 4/1: 0000/0/5-31: Slow away, prog 4f out,   **38**
rdn out to lead cl-home: 3rd yesterday at Beverley: eff at 1m, now stays 10f: acts on fast & gd grnd: 1st win.
8   **EDDIES JEWEL 197** [13] H Alexander 4-9-7 (35) R Keogh(5) 16/1: 000300-2: b g Presidium -   hd **36**
Superstream (Superpower): Handy, styd on to lead 2f out, hdd cl-home: reapp: plcd once in 03 (mdn, J S
Wainwright): apprec step up here to 10f: acts on gd grnd: has tried cheek pieces.
1593 **PARADISE GARDEN 19** [3] P L Clinton 7-9-7 (30) R Kennemore(7) 8/1: 050-0543: Held up, prog after 2 **33**
6f, kept on ins fnl 1f: see 1286.
1753 **RIVER OF FIRE 10** [2] C N Kellett 6-9-7 vis (30) W Hogg 9/1: 360-0304: Mid-div, prog halfway, led   ¾ **31**
2f out, sn hdd, no extra bef 1f out: see 1563.
1449 **IPLEDGEALLEGIANCE 26** [1]8-9-7 (35) C Haddon 3/1 FAV: 0005505: Held up, prog after 5f, onepcd dist. ½ **30**
909 **GALAXY FALLON 63** [9]6-9-7 (30) A Mullen(3) 20/1: 00/00/-606: b f Dancing Spree - No Comebacks   3 **26**
(Last Tycoon): Rear, nvr nrr than mid-div: 9 wk abs: p.u. sole 03/04 hdles start: modest form prev.
1838 **LITTLETON VALAR 6** [14]4-9-7 (30) D Fentiman 5/1: 060-0447: Nvr nrr than mid-div: qck reapp.   ½ **25**
1676 **BOOZY DOUZ 14** [10]4-9-7 (30) B O'Neill(5) 40/1: 00-0068: Mid-div 6f, sn no extra: see 1676.   2½ **21**
1800 **CLASSICAL WALTZ 8** [7]6-9-7 (30) K May(3) 16/1: 6/00/0-439: Rear, prog 4f out, wknd bef 1f out.   1 **19**
640 **DIVA DANCER 100** [8]4-9-7 BL (35) M Howard 20/1: 0/00-000: 10th: Handy 1m, wknd: 1st time blnks. 3½ **14**
1412 **PLATINUM BOY 28** [11]4-9-7 p (35) Dean Williams 20/1: 0030050: 11th: Led 1f, styd cl-up, led 3f   ¾ **12**
out, hdd 2f out, wknd: btr 1412.
1643 **DANCING DOLPHIN 15** [4]5-9-7 (30) M Halford(5) 12/1: 646/-3660: 12th: Cl-up 1m, fdd: op 8/1: btr 1333.12 **0**
1839 **LILLS STAR LAD 6** [15]6-9-7 (30) Steven Harrison(5) 80/1: P/0000-00: 13th: Bhd, nvr a factor.   nk **0**
1839 **SEA TERN 6** [5]4-9-7 (35) Derek Nolan 25/1: 00/00-00: 14th: Cl-up, hung right & rcd wide round   6 **0**
bend 5f out, wknd: qck reapp: mod form to date.
1283 **LAWGIVER 35** [12]3-8-7 P (35) D Tudhope 33/1: 000-00: 15th: Led after 1f, hdd 3f out, fdd.   13 **0**
15 Ran   Time 2m 10.07 (7.77)   Owned: Mr Keith Jackson   Trained: Malton

1992
5.00 Waldrons Waifs & Strays Banded Stakes 4yo+ 0-45 (H)
£1509 £431 £216   1m54y rnd   Good 48   -05 Slow   Inside rail

903 **MY MAITE 63** [11] R Ingram 5-9-0 bl t (45) N Day 13/2: 36-24001: Held up, prog halfway, rdn out to   **48**
lead cl-home: rider received a 1 day careless riding ban: 9 wk abs: eff at 1m, stays 12f on fast & gd, likes
polytrack: suited by t-strap & blnks, goes well fresh: app drop to banded company: see 498.
1661 **GEMINI LADY 15** [8] Mrs G S Rees 4-9-0 (45) J F Egan 14/1: 30420-02: b f Emperor Fountain -   shd **47**
Raunchy Rita (Brigadier Gerard): Keen bhd, gd prog to lead 1f out, hdd cl-home: plcd 3 times in 03 (h'caps, rtd
48): lightly rcd in 02 (mdns, rtd 58): eff at 1m/10f on firm & fast: apprec drop in grade & can find similar.
2 Sep'03 Redc 10fm 47-47 E:
1642 **TOJONESKI 15** [15] I W McInnes 5-9-0 p (45) R Ffrench 4/1: 0342223: Cl-up, led halfway, hdd 1f   nk **46**
out, kept on & not btn far: bckd from 7/1: see 1642 & 1548.
1695 **LUCEFER 13** [7] G C H Chung 6-9-0 (45) K Fallon 7/2 FAV: 12-00344: Mid-div, prog when short of   ½ **45**
room 2f out, switched & ev ch ins fnl 1f, just held: just btr 1579 (10f).
1643 **CHICKASAW TRAIL 15** [10]6-9-0 (45) Stephanie Hollinshead(5) 16/1: 0065105: Held up, prog 4f out,   1¼ **43**
no impress ins fnl 1f: btr 1548.
1565 **PEARTREE HOUSE 20** [18]10-9-0 (45) S Hitchcott(3) 10/1: 0000666: Rear, prog halfway, onepcd fnl 1f. 2½ **38**
1536 **PARISIAN PLAYBOY 21** [2]4-9-0 (45) J Quinn 14/1: 003-0007: Led till halfway, wknd dist: see 956.   ½ **37**
1541 **SEEJAY 21** [1]4-9-0 (45) C Catlin 25/1: 600-308: Nvr nrr than mid-div: btr 1045.   nk **36**
1755 **KENNY THE TRUTH 10** [9]5-9-0 t (45) P M Quinn 7/1: 4514339: Rear, nvr a factor: btr 1755 & 1334. 1¾ **32**
1710* **BALLYGRIFFIN KID 12** [13]4-9-0 (45) Dane O'Neill 16/1: 63-03410: 10th: Keen bhd, nvr a factor.   1 **30**
1711 **MEGADIM 12** [16]6-9-0 t (45) L Enstone(3) 25/1: 426-2250: 11th: Keen cl-up 6f, wknd: btr 1245.   1¾ **26**
1841* **BALLYRUSH 6** [4]4-9-6 bl (45) R Keogh(7) 7/1: 4565210: 12th: Rear, prog halfway, fdd fnl 2f: qck reapp. shd **31**
1334 Over To You Bert 32 [14]5-9-0 (45) V Slattery 25/1:0
1642 Indian Warrior 15 [5]8-9-0 bl(45) B Swarbrick(5) 25/1:0
1676 Ellamyte 14 [3]4-9-0 (45) D Nolan(3) 50/1:0
356   Landofheartsdesire 138 [17]5-9-0 vis(45) D McGaffin 33/1:0

NOTTINGHAM TUESDAY 25.05.04 Lefthand, Galloping Track

1128 **Ace in The Hole 43** [12]4-9-0 p(45) J F McDonald(3) 66/1:0
1045 **Taiyo 52** [6]4-9-0 (45) N Callan 16/1:P
18 Ran Time 1m 43.65(4.25) Owned: The Stargazers 2nd XI Trained: Epsom

BADEN BADEN SATURDAY 22.05.04 Lefthand, Sharpish, Turning Track

Official Going Good

1993
3.25 Gr 3 Betty Barclay-Rennen 4yo+ ()
£26761 £12676 £5634 **2m Good**

1418 **DARASIM 24** [3] M Johnston 6-9-2 vis (114) J Fanning 18/10: 131130-61: Made all, rdn & styd on **113**
strongly fnl 2f: eff at 12f/2m, stays 2m2f: acts on firm & gd/sft ground: loves to be able to dominate: tough & smart
when on song, left reapp well bhd today: see 1418.
    BAILAMOS [7] P Schiergen 4-8-12 A Suborics 102/10: 2: Chsd ldrs, styd on late. 1½ **106**
    KING OF BOXMEER [5] W Baltromei 5-8-12 bl I Ferguson : 3: Rear, kept on late, nvr a threat. 2½ **104**
1418 **DUSKY WARBLER 24** [5]5-8-12 (107) J Mackay 16/10 FAV: 33325-228: Cl up, btn over 2f out, eased 13 **84**
fnl 1f: well ahead of this wnr in 1418 (soft), something amiss?
8 Ran Time 3m 21.59() Owned: Markus Graff Trained: Middleham Moor

CURRAGH SATURDAY 22.05.04 Righthand, Galloping Track

Official Going Good/Firm (Good Places)

1994
2.45 Listed Marble Hill Stakes 2yo ()
£25298 £5478 £5478 **5f Good/Firm**

RUSSIAN BLUE 19 [2] A P O'Brien 2-9-0 J P Spencer 1/5 FAV: 111: b c Danehill - Soviet Artic **110+**
(Bering) Made all, shaken up & always holding rivals fnl 1f, readily: remains unbeaten, earlier won twice over C/D:
eff at 5f, 6f will suit: acts on fast & hvy grnd, all 3 wins at The Curragh: can go well fresh: v useful juvenile who
should prove a leading player in the Coventry Stakes at Royal Ascot.
    LALTRO MONDO 48 [3] M Halford 2-9-0 T P O'Shea 12/1: 412: Trkd ldrs, rdn & chall over 1f out, 1 **102**
always held by wnr, ddheated for 2nd: 7 wk abs: behind this wnr on debut earlier this season.
    KAY TWO 37 [4] Miss F M Crowley 2-9-0 P J Smullen 20/1: 22: Held up, kept on fnl 2f, no dngr. dht **102**
    JOYCE 37 [1] A P O'Brien 2-9-0 J A Hefferman 5/1: 14: Cl up, wknd halway & eased ins last.. 4 **90**
4 Ran Time Notime taken () Owned: Exors Of The Late R E Sangster Trained: Ballydoyle

1995
3.20 Gr 1 Irish 2000 Guineas 3yo Colts & Fillies ()
£156244 £51724 £24924 **1m Good/Firm**

1480 **BACHELOR DUKE 21** [8] J A R Toller 3-9-0 (114) S Sanders 12/1: 334-71: Held up, swtchd wide & **121**
drvn/strong run to lead well ins last: op 10/1: 1st career win: earlier 7th in Newmarket 1000 Guineas (this 2nd & 3rd
in front): eff over a stiff/gall 1m on fast: improved/high-class performance today, lightly rcd & shld continue to
run well in the top mile races: see 1480.
1480 **AZAMOUR 21** [5] John M Oxx 3-9-0 M J Kinane 6/4 FAV: 11-32: Trkd ldrs, rdn & led just ins last, 1 **118**
hdd well ins last: ahead of today's wnr in 2000 Guineas but prob ran to that smart form: see 1480.
1480 **GREY SWALLOW 21** [3] D K Weld 3-9-0 P J Smullen 2/1: 11-143: Trkd ldrs, rdn & ch dist, not pace ½ **117**
of wnr cl home: op 7/4: smart, earlier 3rd in English 2000 Guineas: shld stay further: see 1480.
1559* **LEITRIM HOUSE 19** [2] B J Meehan 3-9-0 S Drowne 5/1: 16-114: Handy & rdn to lead from 2f out, sn 1½ **114**
hdd & no extra ins last: fine run & will relish a return to 7f: v interesting for Gr 3 Jersey at R Ascot: see 1559.
1559 **GRAND REWARD 19** [6]3-9-0 J P Spencer 14/1: 1325-25: Led till ins last, wknd: see 1559. 3 **108**
1855 **NEWTON 6** [4]3-9-0 bl P J Scallan 50/1: 053D2-1466: Chsd ldrs 6f: see 1063 (7f, soft). 1½ **105**
8 Ran Time 1m 40.00 () Owned: Exors Of The Late Duke Of Devonshire Trained: Newmarket

1996
3.55 Gr 3 Weatherbys Greenland Stakes 3yo+ ()
£34840 £10184 £4824 **6f Good/Firm**

1187 **THE KIDDYKID 37** [9] P D Evans 4-9-6 (104) J P Spencer 12/1: 15365-371: Trkd ldrs, chsd ldr over **112**
1f out, led dist, all out: op 10/1: eff at 6f on firm or soft ground: likes to dominate/race prom: tough, improved
run & v smart now: see 952.
1667 **ARAKAN 11** [3] Sir M Stoute 4-9-6 (111) Gary Stevens 4/5 FAV: 12263-132: Held up, efft over 2f hd **111**
out, styd on well for press, just failed: smart, prob needs return to 7f now: see 1667.
1400+**RINGMOOR DOWN 25** [4] D W P Arbuthnot 5-9-3 (93) J P Murtagh 10/1: 00243-613: Held up, styd on 1½ **103**
late, no threat to wnr: not disgraced: see 1400 (Listed).
4745*}**HANABAD 223** [4] J M Oxx 4-9-6 M J Kinane 7/2: 224512214: ch c Cadeaux Genereux - Handaza (Be My 1½ **101**
Guest) Chsd ldrs, rdn to chall over 1f out, no extra fnl 100yds: op 3/1: reapp: Listed wnr '03: eff at 5/6f, stays
1m: acts on fast & gd/sft ground: smart sprinter last term, entitled to be sharper for this.
1 Oct'03 Curr 6g/s 108- : 2 Sep'03 Curr 6g/f 111- : 2 Jun'03 Curr 8gd 111- A:
1667 **ORIENTOR 11** [6]6-9-9 (109) S Sanders 16/1: 006-24595: Rear, efft fnl 2f, not pace to chall: nk **103**
ideally suited by more give: see 952 (Listed).
10 Ran Time 1m 11.80 () Owned: Mrs Claire Massey Trained: Pandy

1997   **4.55 Gr 2 Ridgewood Pearl Stakes 4yo+**   ()
£54873 £16549 £7839   **1m str**   **Good/Firm**

1349 **SOVIET SONG 28** [4] J R Fanshawe 4-8-11   (114) J P Murtagh 11/1: 1/4245-231: Trkd ldrs, smooth   **120+**
prog to lead over 1f out, sn asserted, readily: eff at 7f/1m on fast & soft ground, any trk: v smart filly who was
back to best today: heads to Royal Ascot in fine form: see 1349 & 1115.
1492} **LIVADIYA 8** [5] H Rogers 8-8-11   (87) M J Kinane 14/1: 313-0042: b m Shernazar - Lilissa (Doyoun)   6   **108**
Rear, styd on to take 2nd ins last, nvr threat to wnr: op 10/1: most progressive last term, landing 3 val h'caps & 2
Listed contests: eff at 1m, poss ideally suited by 9/10f: acts on fast & soft ground, prob any trk: v useful 8yo.
4598} **HANAMI 231** [2] J A R Toller 4-9-0   (110) S Sanders 8/1: /56100-3: b f Hernando - Russian Rose   3   **105**
(Soviet Lad)   Trkd ldrs, rdn & no impress fnl 2f: op 7/1, reapp: Gr 2 wnr here at The Curragh in '03, English & Irish
Oaks unplaced: Listed juv wnr '02: eff at 1m/10f, sort of h'cap contests at 12f: acts on good & gd/sft ground: likes a
stiff/galloping trk: proved v useful last term, sharper for this over 10f+.
1 Jun'03 Curr 10gd 109- A: 1 Nov'02 Newm 8g/s 104- A:
1491 **ECHOES IN ETERNITY 20** [3] Saeed bin Suroor 4-9-0 t (109) J P Spencer 7/4 FAV: 1/03011-44: Led   2½   **100**
till over 1f out, fdd: btr 1491.
2570} **HYMN OF LOVE 251** [1] 4-8-11 bl P J Smullen 12/1: 315321-5: Cl up, wknd qckly fnl 2f, eased: op 10/1.   25   **52**
5 Ran   Time 1m 39.50()   Owned: Elite Racing Club   Trained: Newmarket

Official Going Good

1998   **2.20 Listed Coppa d'Oro 3yo+**   ()
£24648 £10845 £5915   **1m7f**   **Good**

1569 **SWING WING 18** P F I Cole 5-9-7   (108) D Holland 34/100: 31533-501: Held up, hdwy to lead 2f out,   **110**
rdn & styd on strongly: eff at 12f, best around 15f on fast, soft & firesand: tough & v useful gelding: see 1431.
   AROUND ALONE M Gasparini 7-9-7   M Esposito   : 2: Styd on but not able to overhaul wnr.   ½   **108**
   IL BIMBO DE ORO M Ciciarelli 5-9-7   L Panici   : 3: No impress on front pair closing stages.   8   **100**
7 Ran   Time 3m 11.70 ()   Owned: Sir Martyn Arbib   Trained: Whatcombe

1999   **3.50 Gr 1 Italian Oaks 3yo Fillies**   ()
£251127 £133768 £79789   **1m3f**   **Good**

1568 **MENHOUBAH 18** [1] C E Brittain 3-8-12 p (100) D Holland 207/100: 434-23021: Trkd ldrs, led over 1f   **105**
out, styd on strongly: now suited by 11/11.4f on firm, gd & dirt: best in chkpcs: v useful, confidence boost.
   STEP DANZER [4] A Botti 3-8-12   E Botti 20/1: 131-3322: Chall over 1f out, no extra.   1¼   **102**
   LORIANA [3] R Brogi 3-8-12   G Temperini 132/10: 13-31513: Rear, late gains, nrst fin.   1¾   **100**
417 **TAMARILLO 255** [6] 3-8-12   (90) M Fenton 13/10 FAV: 22155: gr f Daylami - Up And About (Barathea)   1¼   **98**
Trkd ldr & led 2f out, hdd over 1f out & no extra: earlier this year landed the UAE Oaks at Nad Al Sheba (well ahead
of todays wnr): mdn wnr '03, subs Gr 2 unpled (rtd 92): winning form at 1m/9f, prob styd this 11f trip (mid dist
pedigree): acts on firm, gd & dirt: likes a galloping trk & can force the pace.
1 Aug'03 Nott 8.2g/f 86-0 D: 2 Jul'03 Kemp 7g/f 90-0 D: 2 Jun'03 Kemp 7fm 85-0 D:
11 Ran   Time 2m 15.10()   Owned: C E Brittain   Trained: Newmarket

Official Going Good

2000   **2.20 Gr 2 Prix Vicomtesse Vigier 4yo+**   ()
£42148 £16268 £7764   **1m7.5f**   **Good**

1431 **FORESTIER 31** [5] E Danel 4-8-12   C P Lemaire 8/1: 3151-121: ch c Nikos - Forest Hills (Sicyos)   **118**
Trkd ldrs, drvn & led over 1f out, held on gamely for press: earlier this term scored at Saint Cloud: dual wnr '03,
incl a Listed success at Maisons Laffitte: prev eff at 12f, now seems best around 2m: likes good & good/soft ground:
has developed into a smart 4yo stayer. 2 Apr'04 Long 15.5g/s 109- A:
1431* **WESTERNER 31** [2] E Lellouche 5-9-2   D Boeuf 30/100 FAV: 22211-12: Chsd ldrs, chall over 1f out,   nk   **121**
no extra ins last: high class & consistent stayer, wld enjoy soft grnd in the Ascot Gold Cup: see 1431.
4627} **CLEAR THINKING** [1] A Fabre 4-8-12   Gary Stevens 64/10: 233-1533: Chsd ldrs, styd on for press.   ¾   **116**
6 Ran   Time 3m 29.90 ()   Owned: Mme R J Wattinne   Trained: France

2001   **2.55 Gr 1 Prix Saint Alary 3yo Fillies**   ()
£80479 £32197 £16099   **1m2f**   **Good**

1157* **ASK FOR THE MOON 44** [2] J C Rouget 3-9-0   I Mendizabal 3/5 JT FAV: 221-1111: Prom, hdwy & chall   **116**
over 1f out, led ins last, drvn out: remains unbeaten this term: eff at 10f/10.5f, 12f shld suit: acts on good &
gd/sft ground: smart filly with a winning habit, sound claims for the French Oaks next month: see 1157 (Gr 3).
1557 **ASTI 21** [5] E Lellouche 3-9-0   D Boeuf 34/10: -122: b f Sadler's Wells - Astorg (Lear Fan)   Trkd   nk   **115**
ldr & keen early, efft over 1f out, styd on well ins last, just held: debut winner earlier this term at Saint Cloud:
eff at 9/10.5f on good & v soft ground: likes a gall trk: lightly raced filly, open to further improvement, big
runner in French Oaks. 2 May'04 Long 9.3hvy 109- :

LONGCHAMP SUNDAY 23.05.04 Righthand, Stiff,. Galloping Track

4932} **AGATA** [7] Y de Nicolay 3-9-0 D Bonilla 21/1: 323-233: Held up, styd on late to take 3rd.		½	114
1157 **SUPER LINA 44** [4] Y de Nicolay 3-9-0 C Soumillon 3/5 JT FAV: 21-224: Led till ins last, onepace.		1½	112
OMETSZ [1]3-9-0 Gary Stevens 86/10: -125: Held up, efft over 1f out, btn ins last.		nk	111
AUSTRALIE [3]3-9-0 T Jarnet 58/10: 1-16: Trkd ldrs, no extra fnl 1f.		¾	110
1557 **GREEN SWALLOW 21** [6]3-9-0 T Gillet| 12/1: 1314-637: Rear & keen early, not able to chall.		½	109

7 Ran Time 2m 05.10 () Owned: J P Dubois Trained: France

2002 3.30 Gr 1 Prx d'Ispahan 4yo+ ()
£42148 £16268 £7764 **1m1f** **Good**

3709} **PRINCE KIRK** [3] E Borromeo 4-9-2 BL M Monteriso 25/1: 3302-131: b c Selkirk - Princess Manila **122**
(Manila) Hld up rear, rdn & hdwy to lead ins last, jinked right nr the line, styd on strongly: Italian raider, Gr1
rnr up in '03: well suited by 9/10f on gd & gd/sft: likes a gall trks: improved for first time blnks & this was a
high-class effort. 2 Jun'03 Chan 9gd 110- A: 2 Apr'03 Capa 8gd 109- :
4914*)**SIX PERFECTIONS 211** [2] P Bary 4-8-13 T Thulliez 8/11 FAV: 122211-2: bl f Celtic Swing - Yogya ½ **117**
(Riverman) Held up, hdwy to lead dist, hdd ins last & no extra: rest well covered on reapp: '03 English & Irish 1000
Guineas rnr-up bef Gr 1 success in France and US Breeders Cup Mile: eff at 9f, 1m suits ideally on fm & v soft, prob
any trk: tough & top class miler, spot on next time.
1 Oct'03 Sant 8fm 124- A: 1 Aug'03 Deau 8g/s 124- A: 2 Aug'03 Deau 8g/s 118- A: 2 May'03 Curr 8sft 119- A:
2 May'03 Newm 8g/f 119-0 A: 1 Apr'03 Mais 7gd 119- : 1 Oct'02 Long 8gd 118- : 1 Aug'02 Deau 7gd 110- :
1758 **CHECKIT 8** [1] M R Channon 4-9-2 (112) S Hitchcott 20/1: -4336003: Led till rdn & hdd dist, kept 2½ **115**
on for press: drop to Gr2/Gr 3 shld bring success: see 1758.
1350 **SUNSTRACH 29** [4] L M Cumani 6-9-2 L M Cumani 10/1: 43103-34: Trkd ldrs, rdn & onepace over 1f 1½ **112**
out: eff at 9f, return to 10f will suit in Gr2/Gr3 company: see 1350.
3712} **NEBRASKA TORNADO 280** [5]4-8-13 Gary Stevens 13/8: 11161-5: Trkd ldr, btn over 1f out on reapp. 4 **101**

5 Ran Time 1m 52.00() Owned: Scuderia Pieffegi Trained: Italy

---

CURRAGH SUNDAY 23.05.04 Righthand, Galloping Track

Official Going Good/Firm

2003 2.05 Boylesports EBF Maiden 2yo ()
£8723 £2559 £1219 **6f str** **Good/Firm**

ORATORIO [2] A P O'Brien 2-9-2 J P Spencer 4/5 FAV: 1: b c Danehill - Mahrah (Vaguely Noble) **100+**
Made all, pressed from halfway, rdn & asserted over 1f out, readily: op 4/6 on debut: well bred newcomer, eff over a
gall 6f on fast ground: goes well fresh: well regarded & looks smart, a likely contender for Royal Ascot next month.
SHAMOAN [5] G M Lyons 2-8-13 P Cosgrave(3) 7/1: 222: Cl up/dsptd lead, outpcd by wnr bef dist. 2½ **85**
BACK TO PARIS [7] J S Bolger 2-9-2 K J Manning 7/2: 3: Trkd ldrs, outpcd halfway, kept on late. 1 **85**
7 Ran Time 1m 14.00 () Owned: Mrs John Magnier Trained: Ballydoyle

---

2004 3.05 Gr 1 Tattersalls Gold Cup 4yo+ ()
£108004 £33098 £15678 **1m2f110y** **Good/Firm**

4280} **POWERSCOURT 253** [3] A P O'Brien 4-9-0 J P Spencer 100/30: 2/6113-1: b c Sadler's Wells - **121+**
Rainbow Lake (Rainbow Quest) Made all, rdn & qcknd clr 2f out, styd on strongly, impressive: op 5/2 on reapp: cond
stks & Gr 2 wnr '03: mdn wnr '02, Gr 1 rnr up: suited by 10/12f on firm & soft ground, loves a stiff/gall trk: goes
well fresh: high class entire, come s right into the Prince Of Wales Stks frame.
1 Aug'03 York 11.9fm 120-0 A: 2 Oct'02 Donc 8sft 111- A: 2 Oct'02 Newm 8fm 106- D:
1997 **LIVADIYA 1** [2] H Rogers 8-8-11 (87) J A Heffernan 16/1: 313-00422: Rear, rdn & kept on well for 6 **111**
press fnl 2f, no threat to easy wnr: Gr 2 rnr up over 1m here yesterday: smart mare.
1560* **NYSAEAN 20** [1] R Hannon 5-9-0 (112) M J Kinane 9/10 FAV: 10-545213: Trkd ldrs, rdn & kept on fnl ½ **113**
2f, no impress on easy wnr: ideally suited by 10/12f here: see 1560 (Gr 3).
994 **NAPPER TANDY 28** [5] J S Bolger 4-9-0 bl K J Manning 8/1: 5414-254: Keen, trkd ldrs, rdn & kept ½ **112**
on, nvr pace to threaten: see 994.
4800} **NAHEEF 78** [7]5-9-0 TBL (113) K McEvoy 6/1: 23125-35: b c Marju - Golden Digger (Mr Prospector) 1½ **110**
Trkd ldr, rdn & impress over 1f out, eased when btn ins last: 10 wk abs: '03 Gr 3 wnr, subs Gr 2 rnr up in Germany:
Gr 3 wnr in '02: eff at 9/10f, tried 12f: acts on firm, gd/sft & any trk: well suited by t-strap & visor, wore blnks
today: smart performer.
2 Sep'03 Fran 10sft 112- A: 1 Sep'03 York 8.9g/f 112-113 A: 2 Jun'03 Long 10g/s 113- A: 1 Aug'02 Wind 10g/f 110- A:
2 Sep'01 Curr 7g/f 113- : 1 Aug'01 Good 7fm 111- A: 1 Jul'01 Epso 7g/s 86- E:
1843 **PRIVATE CHARTER 4** [4]4-9-0 (110) M Hills 16/1: 645-0206: In tch, btn 2f out: qck reapp. 4½ **104**

6 Ran Time 2m 11.00 () Owned: Mrs John Magnier Trained: Ballydoyle

---

2005 3.40 Gr 1 Irish 1000 Guineas (Fillies) ()
£150884 £51724 £24924 **1m** **Good/Firm**

1492* **ATTRACTION 21** [5] M Johnston 3-9-0 (119) K Darley 2/1 FAV: 11111-11: Made all, always rivals ins **120**
last, v game: op 5/2: well suited by a stiff/galloping 1m & loves to force the pace: 1st filly to complete
English/Irish 1000 Guineas double: unbtn, v hard not to see her landing the Coronation Stakes at Royal Ascot.
1701* **ALEXANDER GOLDRUN 14** [12] J S Bolger 3-9-0 K J Manning 8/1: 01221-112: Prom in chasing group, 1 **116**
rdn & chsd wnr fnl 3f, kept on, always held: return to 1m & an excellent run: has progressed into a v smart filly &
more Group success awaits this term: see 1701 (Gr 3).
1620+ **ILLUSTRIOUS MISS 15** [6] D R Loder 3-9-0 K Fallon 9/2: 113: Held up, kept on well from over 1f 2 **112**
out, not able to chall: styd longer 1m trip well: acts on fast & soft: lightly raced, win another Gr 2/3.
4172*)**KINNAIRD 255** [9] P C Haslam 3-9-0 (99) M J Kinane 16/1: 115111-4: ch f Dr Devious - Ribot's 1 **110**
Guest (Be My Guest) Trkd ldrs, onepace for press over 1f out: reapp: most progressive juv, 5 wins, culminating in Gr

CURRAGH **SUNDAY 23.05.04 Righthand, Galloping Track**

2 May Hill stks: acts on fast & soft, prob any trk, loves a stiff one: goes well fresh: eff over a gall 1m: v tough & smart filly, a fine return, will enjoy a drop into Gr3/Gr 2 company. 1 Sep'03 Donc 8gd 107-99 A:
1 Aug'03 Asco 7g/f 101-86 B: 1 Jul'03 Thir 7sft 98-0 C: 1 Jun'03 Hami 6.0g/f 86-0 E: 1 Jun'03 Hami 6.0gd 88-0 E:
1492 **SECRET CHARM 21** [15]3-9-0 M Hills 4/1: 11-55: Trkd ldrs, prog over 2f out, soon no extra. ½ **109**
1492 **NECKLACE 21** [8]3-9-0 J A Heffernan 16/1: 2110-06: b f Darshaan - Spinning The Yarn (Barathea) *1½* **106**
Trkd ldrs, no extra over 1f out: Gr 3 & Gr 1 wins here at the Curragh during '03: both wins at 7f, 1m+ shld suit this term: likes fast ground & a gall trk. 1 Aug'03 Curr 7g/f 110- A: 1 Aug'03 Curr 7g/f 105- A:
1492 **MAJESTIC DESERT 21** [7]3-9-0 (111) T E Durcan 12/1: 12312-197: Chsd ldrs, onepace & no impress. **106**
1701 **MISTY HEIGHTS 14** [13]3-9-0 P J Smullen 20/1: 3142-328: Held up, rdn & nvr able to land blow: see 1701. **106**
15Ran Time 1m 37.60 () Owned: Duke Of Roxburghe Trained: Middleham Moor

2006

5.15 Gr 3 Gallinule Stakes 3yo ()
£34893 £10237 £4877 **1m2f** **Good/Firm**

1301 **MEATH 35** [3] A P O'Brien 3-9-0 J P Spencer 11/8: 31-221: Made all, rdn & styd on strongly fnl 2f: imprvd for this step up to 10f & shld stay 12f: acts on firm & soft ground: likes a galloping trk: lightly raced & progressive, an Irish Derby possible. **112**
CAIRDEAS [5] D K Weld 3-9-0 P J Smullen 4/5 FAV: 212: b c Darshaan - Sabaah (Nureyev) Chsd ldrs, styd on press, no threat: up in grade following a recent Naas mdn success: eff at 1m/10f, shld stay 12f: acts on fast & soft ground, stiff/gall trks: lightly raced & useful. *1½* **108**
BARATI [6] J M Oxx 3-9-0 M J Kinane 9/1: 143: b c Sadlers Wells - Oriane (Nashwan) Chsd ldrs, chsd wnr briefly dist, no extra: earlier this term landed a Curragh mdn on debut: winning form at 1m, stays 10f & 12f+ could suit: acts on fast & soft ground, gall trks: has run well fresh: v useful & the type to progress at 12f+. *nk* **107**
5 Ran Time 2m 10.90() Owned: Mrs John Magnier Trained: Balldoyle

RIPON **WEDNESDAY 26.05.04 Righthand, Sharpish Track**

Official Going Good/Firm

2007

6.25 Lishman Sidwell Campbell & Price Classified Stakes 4yo+ 0-70 (E)
£4056 £1248 £624 **6f str** **Good/Firm 23** **-02 Slow** Stands Side

1743 **MERLINS DANCER 12** [6] D Nicholls 4-9-0 (72) Alex Greaves 5/1: 0400-051: b g Magic Ring - La Piaf (Fabulous Dancer) Handy stands side & led after 1f, in command dist, styd on strongly: op 9/1: mdn & h'cap wnr for W R Muir '03, disapp in blnks: auct mdn rnr-up '02: eff at 5f, prob stays 7f, all wins at 6f: acts on firm & gd/soft grnd: eff held up or forcing the pace: returned with cut off-fore. **81**
1 Jun'03 Newm 6fm 82-77 C: 1 Jun'03 Ling 6g/f 78-(77) D: 2 Jun'03 Nott 6.1g/f 77-75 D: 2 Jul'02 Wind 5g/f 82- E:
1749 **CHAIRMAN BOBBY 12** [9] D W Barker 6-8-12 (70) L Enstone(3) 15/2: 62-50032: Rcd alone far side & sn cl up, kept on, not pace of wnr from dist: op 6/1: not disgraced: see 1120. *3½* **71**
874* **PRINCE AARON 68** [7] C N Allen 4-9-0 (72) G Carter 4/1 JT FAV: 2-116213: Trkd ldrs stands side, kept on, al held from dist: op 9/4: 10 wk abs: well treated on turf: acts on fast & polytrack, loves Lingfield. *hd* **72**
1624 **VAL DE MAAL 18** [8] G C H Chung 4-8-13 (71) R Ffrench 14/1: 5240-304: Prom, no extra fnl 2f: see 1337. *3* **62**
1767 **RAGAMUFFIN 11** [1]6-8-12 (70) K Darley 10/1: 0/200-005: ch g Prince Sabo - Valldemosa (Music Boy) Chsd ldrs stands side, not pace to chall: '03 rnr-up (lightly rcd, h'cap): h'cap wnr in 1st time blnks '02: eff at 6f on fast or soft grnd, any trk, likes Newcastle: suited by waiting tactics, eff with/without blnks: can go well fresh. 2 Apr'03 Newc 5g/f 78-75 D: 2 Jul'02 Pont 6g/s 81-78 D: 1 Jun'02 Newc 6g/f 80-73 C: *nk* **60**
2 May'02 Hami 6gd 74-72 E: 2 May'01 Redc 5g/f 89-86 C:
1782 **LINDENS LADY 10** [5]4-8-11 (72) R Winston 11/1: 64405-06: Prom stands side till halfway. *1½* **55**
1977 **TIME N TIME AGAIN 1** [2]6-8-12 p (70) J Quinn 5/1: 31500637: Led stands side 1f, cl-up 4f. *nk* **55**
1638 **HARTSHEAD 18** [3]5-8-12 (68) B Doyle 4/1 JT FAV: 04460-28: Dwelt & al outpcd stands side: btr 1638. *7* **41**
92 **BLESSINGINDISGUISE 183** [4]11-8-12 bl (49) P Mulrennan(5) 33/1: 022240-9: Dwelt, al bhd, abs. *15* **7**
9 Ran Time 1m 11.52 (1.52) Owned: Chalfont Foodhalls Ltd Trained: Thirsk

2008

6.55 Ripon Spring Festival Selling Handicap Stakes 4-5yo 46-55 (F) **[69]**
£3276 £936 £468 **1m4f60y** **Good/Firm 23** **-24 Slow** Inside

1796 **PISTE BLEU 9** [9] R Ford 4-8-12 (53) P Hanagan 7/1: 165-0001: Held up, hdwy & switched to lead over 1f out, drvn out: no bid: eff at 10/12.5f on fast & gd grnd, apprec drop to sell grade: see 1796. **55**
4321} **FAIRY MONARCH 251** [6] P T Midgley 5-8-5 p (46) R Fitzpatrick 16/1: 050000-2: b g Ali Royal - Cookawara (Fairy King) Held up, rdn & chall over 1f out, drvn & no extra well ins last: reapp: unplcd '03 (tried t-strap, rtd 56 & 37a, h'caps, earlier with I W McInnes & J S Wainwright): unplcd '02 (rtd 80, J Cullinan, blnks): stays 12f in sell grade nowadays on fast grnd: gd run in cheek pieces tonight. *1* **46**
1 Jul'01 Newm 7g/f 89-82 D: 1 Jul'01 Epso 6g/f 79- E: 2 Jul'01 Epso 7fm 78- E:
443 **MARGOLD 127** [10] R Hollinshead 4-8-9 (50) A Culhane 11/1: 3306-003: Trkd ldr & led 4f out till over 1f out, kept on onepace: clr rem: abs: eff at 12/14f on firm & fast grnd. *1½* **49**
1954 **BLUE VENTURE 2** [1] P C Haslam 4-8-12 (53) G Faulkner 8/1: 300-0004: ch g Alhaarth - September Tide (Thatching) Bhd, short of room 3f out, switched & kept on, nrst fin, nvr threat: quick reapp: plcd '03 (rtd 58a, clmr, turf unplcd, rtd 60, turf unplcd, rtd 60, turf h'cap): plcd '02 (rtd 74 & 74a, mdns): eff at 6/7f on firm grnd & fibresand: eff in cheek pieces. 2 Oct'02 Sout 6af 74a- D: *5* **45**
4724} **KARYON 226** [13]4-8-6 (1ow)(6oh) (40) R Winston 20/1: 5/60003-5: Handy, no extra 2f out, jumps fit. *hd* **38**
1334 **GRADY 33** [5]5-8-5 (6oh) (40) B Swarbrick(5) 9/1: 00600-66: Bhd, late gains for press, nvr threat. *½* **36**
1425 **LORD OF METHLEY 28** [12]5-8-7 (48) V Halliday 6/1: 0036-007: Trkd ldrs, btn 2f out, needs 1m. *1½* **36**
1960 **SHATIN SPECIAL 2** [2]4-8-6 p (47) R Ffrench 17/2: 4166608: Rear, eff wide 4f out, no impress 2f out. *shd* **35**
1840 **SERAPH 7** [7]4-8-5 (6oh)p (40) T Eaves(1) 9/2 FAV: 3321039: Chsd ldrs till 2f out: op 11/2: btr 1411. *1¾* **31**
1551 **BALALAIKA TUNE 22** [3]5-8-5 (11oh) (35) J Bramhill 16/1: 0060400: 10th: Chsd ldrs & ch 3f out, sn fdd. *2* **28**
1753 **SPORTSMAN 11** [11]5-8-5 (11oh)bl (35) Dale Gibson 10/1: 500/3-440: 11th: Dwelt & al bhd: btr 690. *2* **25**
1819 **TURFTANZER 8** [4]5-8-5 (11oh)t (35) Kim Tinkler 33/1: 0460000: 12th: Chsd ldrs, btn/hmpd 3f out. *7* **15**
1507 **DILIGENT LAD 24** [8]4-9-0 (55) L Enstone(3) 33/1: 600/0-00: 13th: Keen & sn led till 4f out, sn fdd. *24* **0**
13 Ran Time 2m 39.35 (5.85) Owned: Mr M Dunlevy & Mr N Morgan Trained: Tarporley

---

2009   7.25 Ripon Farm Services Handicap Stakes 4yo+ 0-80 (D)   [80]
£5421 £1668 £834   2m   Good/Firm 23   +04 Fast   Stands Side

1506 **TIYOUN** 24 [8] Jedd O'Keeffe 6-9-8 (74) A Culhane 11/2: 2025-261: In tch, eff to chase wnr 3f   86
out, led ins last, rdn out: op 8/1: best time of night: eff btwn 11f/2m on firm, soft & any trk: well h'capped.
1870* **RED SUN** 6 [2] J Mackie 7-8-2 (6ex)t (54) P Hanagan 15/8 FAV: 0/3/244-12: Led & qcknd tempo from   *1*   64
5f out, drvn & hdd ins last, no extra: nicely bckd under 6lb pen, quick reapp: well clr of rem & ran to form of 1870.
1772 **MOONSHINE BEACH** 11 [6] P W Hiatt 6-8-6 p (58) P Makin(5) 13/2: 105-4063: Handy, no extra fnl 3f.   12   58
1637 **SONO** 18 [7] P D Niven 7-9-4 p (70) D Allan(3) 20/1: 0000-054: Held up, mod late gains for press.   ¾   69
1689 **GEORGE STUBBS** 14 [5]6-8-11 (63) K Darley 100/30: 4031355: In tch, btn 2f out: btr 1361 (gd/sft, C/D). 4   58
1689 **FREEDOM NOW** 14 [4]6-9-6 (72) K Dalgleish 14/1: 3660-006: Bhd, eff wide 4f out, no impress: see 1689. 10   59
1551 **ROUGE BLANC** 22 [9]4-8-0 T (54) J Quinn 12/1: 24231-07: b f King of Kings - Style n' Elegance   *dist*   0
(Alysheba) Chsd ldrs, struggling fnl 3f: t-strap, poor run: h'cap wnr fnl '03 start for P J McBride, AW unplcd,
(rtd 37a, D Bridgwater, disapp in a visor): eff at 14f/2m2f on fast & gd grnd, stiff/undul or easy trks.
1 Oct'03 Pont 18.0g/f 57-51 E: 2 Sep'03 Nott 16.0g/f 48-45 F: 2 Aug'03 Yarm 14.1g/f 48-46 E:
1870 **AUTUMN FANTASY** 6 [3]5-8-8 (60) J Carroll 33/1: 000-4008: Al bhd: quick reapp: see 1459.   5   0
1689 **WEET FOR ME** 14 [1]8-10-0 (80) R Winston 25/1: 11033//-09: b g Warning - Naswara (Al Nasr) Chsd   2½   0
ldr, fdd 3f out: missed '03: missed '02, plcd late '01 (cond stks, rtd 90a): former mulitple h'cap wnr: eff btwn
12f/2m on hvy, loves firm, fast & both AWs, any trk: gd weight carrier who likes to dominate.
1 Jul'01 Redc 16fm 90-85 D: 1 Jul'01 Hayd 14fm 89-82 D: 1 Jan'01 Sout 11af 98a-88 C: 1 Dec'00 Sout 12af 90a-83 C:
2 Dec'00 Wolv 14.7af 93a-81 D: 1 Nov'00 Wolv 16.2af 82a-76 D:
9 Ran   Time 3m 27.81 (3.01)   Owned: Miss Sharon Long   Trained: Leyburn

---

2010   8.00 Cocked Hat Farm Foods Handicap Stakes 3yo+ 0-90 (C)   [82]
£9031 £3425 £1713   1m rnd   Good/Firm 23   -01 Slow   Inside

1877 **LANGFORD** 6 [7] M H Tompkins 4-9-11 (79) P Robinson 9/2 FAV: 23136-21: Made all & grabbed fav ins   87
rail, rdn & al in command fnl 1f under a well judged tactical ride: suited by 1m/10f on firm & gd, eff with forcing
tactics: open to more improvement: see 1877 (reapp).
1474 **DISTANT COUNTRY** 25 [9] Mrs J R Ramsden 5-9-3 p (71) J Quinn 13/2: 014-6602: Rear, hdwy when short *2* 74
of room over 1f out & again ins last, styd on well cl-home, no threat to wnr: stays 1m: caught the eye in 998.
1877* **MYSTIC MAN** 6 [3] K A Ryan 6-10-6 (6ex) (88) P Mahorman(5) 13/2: 0-000013: Held up, smooth prog   *shd*   91
towards centre 3f out, ch over 1f out, sn no extra: beat today's wnr in 1877.
4846} **BLONDE STREAK** 217 [12] T D Barron 4-9-9 (77) P Makin(5) 9/1: 013204-4: ch f Dumaani - Katiba   *shd*   79
(Gulch) Chsd ldrs, styd on for press fnl 2f, no threat to wnr: reapp: mdn & h'cap scorer '03: mdn rnr-up '02:
eff at 7f, both wins at 1m: acts on firm & gd/soft grnd, prob any trk: gd return.
2 Sep'03 Pont 8.0g/f 79-(80) D: 1 Aug'03 Thir 8g/s 82-74 D: 1 Jun'03 Nott 8.2gd 79-(75) D: 2 Aug'02 Newc 7g/f 77- E:
1781 **NEVADA DESERT** 10 [5]4-9-3 (71) Dean McKeown 7/1: 33425-45: Trkd ldrs, ev ch 2f out, sn no extra. hd   72
1883 **CHERISHED NUMBER** 5 [14]5-9-11 VIS (79) R Winston 13/2: 004-0406: Held up, not pace to chall fnl 2f. 1¼   77
1530 **ADOBE** 23 [4]9-9-1 (69) B Swarbrick(5) 16/1: 20002-07: b g Green Desert - Shamshir (Kris) Held   2½   62
up, eff halfway, no impress over 1f out: dual h'cap scorer '03: plcd 5 times in '02 (rtd 65a & 77, h'caps): best
around 1m on any trk, loves firm, gd/soft & fibresand, handles soft.
2 Oct'03 Bath 8.0fm 72-68 E: 2 Sep'03 Thir 8fm 72-70 D: 1 Jul'03 Bath 8.0fm 74-69 E: 1 May'03 Bath 8.0g/s 70-67 E:
2 Mar'02 Wolv 8.4af 65a-62 E: 1 Aug'01 Ripo 8g/f 83-77 C: 1 Aug'01 Thir 8fm 80-75 C: 2 Jun'01 Newc 8g/f 78-77 C:
2 May'01 Leic 8fm 79-76 D:
4297} **JUSTE POUR LAMOUR** 252 [6]4-9-8 (76) B Doyle 33/1: 424500-8: Chsd ldrs, btn over 2f out, reapp. 2   65
1820 **QUEEN CHARLOTTE** 8 [2]5-9-0 (68) J Fanning 22/1: 06/10-209: Handy & chall 4f out, sn fdd.   2   53
1915 **AIMEES DELIGHT** 4 [13]4-9-6 (74) M Fenton 12/1: 10-00600: 10th: Chsd ldrs, btn over 2f out: btr 1461. 1½   56
1794 **SEA MARK** 9 [11]8-8-7 (61) T Eaves(3) 10/1: 0000/-350: 11th: Mid-div, no prog fnl 3f: btr 1049. hd   42
1066 **Unicorn Reward** 50 [1]4-9-10 (78) A Culhane 25/1:0   1525 **Tagula Blue** 23 [8]4-9-10 t(78) K Darley 16/1:P
13 Ran   Time 1m 39.43 (1.93)   Owned: Marlborough Electronics   Trained: Newmarket

---

2011   8.30 Black Sheep Brewery Handicap Stakes 3yo 0-70 (E)   [76]
£4280 £1317 £659   6f str   Good/Firm 23   -31 Slow   Stands Side

1678 **PARTY PRINCESS** 14 [8] J A Glover 3-8-9 (57) Dean McKeown 5/1: 253-001: b f Orpen - Summer Queen   66
(Robellino) Far side & led overall from halfway, rdn clr from over 1f out, decisively: auct mdn rnr-up '03, AW
unplcd (rtd 48a): eff at 5f, now stays 6f well, tried 7f: acts on fast grnd, stiff or sharpish trk: likes to race
with/force the pace: 1st win tonight, more success to come, poss in fills h'caps. 2 Jul'03 Beve 5g/f 70- E:
1570 **PICCOLO PRINCE** 21 [4] E J Alston 3-9-6 (68) J Quinn 9/2: 2121202: Trkd ldrs stands side & led   2½   71
that group ins last, no ch with wnr far side: back to form: can find similar: see 1344 & 1050.
1730* **PRINCESS GALADRIEL** 12 [10] J R Best 3-8-9 (57) N Pollard 7/2 FAV: 0040-213: Held up far side,   hd   59
drvn & kept on from halfway, not pace to chall wnr: type to prog but may need a stiffer trk: see 1730 & 1576.
1477 **TIZZYS LAW** 25 [2] M A Buckley 3-9-7 (69) J Bramhill 12/1: 0-164: Led stands side till hdd ins   3   62
last, no extra: handles fast & sharpish grnd, stays 6f, could prove spot on back at 5f: see 1228.
4668} **CARIBBEAN BLUE** 229 [6]3-8-4 (52) R Ffrench 14/1: 600-5: b f First Trump - Something Blue   hd   44
(Petong) Bhd stands side, styd on for press, nrst fin: reapp/h'cap bow: unplcd at 6f '03 (rtd 63, debut): shaped
here as if 7f+ may suit: prob handles fast grnd: with R M Whitaker.
4618} **DELUSION** 233 [11]3-9-3 (65) D Allan(3) 25/1: 204040-6: b f Hennessy - Another Fantasy (Danehill)   1¾   52
Led far side 2f, btn over 2f out: reapp: mdn rnr-up '03: eff at 6f, handles firm & fast grnd, stiff/gall trks.
2 Jul'03 Nott 6.1fm 70- D:
252 **WEET AN HAUL** 151 [9]3-8-7 (55) P Hanagan 14/1: 000120-7: Chsd ldrs far side till halfway, sn wknd. shd   42
1605 **LOVEISDANGEROUS** 19 [7]3-8-2 (50) Kim Tinkler 16/1: 5206-508: Prom far side, no impress halfway. ¾   35
1606 **GAME FLORA** 19 [1]3-8-10 (58) T Eaves(3) 14/1: 5000-149: Cl-up stands side till over 2f out: btr 1426. 1¾   38
1678 **REVERSIONARY** 14 [12]3-8-2 bl (50) Dale Gibson 8/1: 560-0050: 10th: Dwelt & al bhd far side: bckd. nk   29
1039 **SARATOGA SPLENDOUR** 53 [13]3-8-1 (49) Leanne Kershaw(7) 50/1: 00-60: 10th: Mid-div far side,   3   19
struggling from halfway: h'cap bow & 8 wk abs.
1216 **Compton Micky** 40 [5]3-8-12 (60) J Edmunds 22/1:0
1639 **The Warley Warrior** 18 [3]3-8-4 (1ow)bl(51) P Mulrennan 20/1:0

RIPON   WEDNESDAY 26.05.04   Righthand, Sharpish Track

13 Ran   Time 1m 13.23 (3.23)   Owned: Mr Derrick Bloy   Trained: Worksop

2012
9.00 Accountant Online Maiden Stakes 3yo+   (D)
£4862 £1496 £748   **1m2f**   **Good/Firm 23**   -14 Slow   Inside

MUTASALLIL 454 [3] Saeed bin Suroor 4-9-10 T J Carroll 5/1: 3-1: b c Gone West - Min Alhawa | | 90
(Riverman) Trkd ldrs & rdn/led over 1f out, rdn out: lkd fit & well after long abs: Brit bow: 3rd of 7 sole start
prev in Dubai (cond stks): eff at 10f, may get further: acts on fast grnd & a sharpish trk: goes well fresh &
suited by t-strap tonight: could prove useful.
1623 **SEVEN YEAR ITCH** 18 [4] M P Tregoning 4-9-10 BL K Darley 6/4 FAV: 2-22: Led/dsptd lead till went | ½ | 89
on 4f out, drvn & hdd over 1f out, kept on: 1st time blnks: handles fast, soft & polytrack: strong colt, padd pick
& has shown enough to find similar, fin well clr of rem tonight: see 1623 & 53.
1719 **WOU OODD** 13 [2] M R Channon 3-8-5 A Culhane 7/2: 0-43: Chsd ldrs, no impress on front pair from | 8 | 72
2f out: lengthy, scopey filly, qual for h'caps & 12f+ may yet suit: see 1719.
1783 **BELSHAZZAR** 10 [7] T P Tate 3-8-10 J Edmunds 100/1: 04: b c King of Kings - Bayou Bidder | 2 | 74
(Premiership) Prom, no impress fnl 3f: longer trip, still ndd this: bhd on debut prev: half brother to a 3yo wnr
in US, dam a multiple US wnr.
1784 **MANHATTAN JACK** 10 [6]3-8-10 R Winston 66/1: 05: Mid-div, no impress fnl 3f. | nk | 74
ROMAN FORUM 0 [8]3-8-10 W Ryan 5/2: 6: b c Selkirk - Flit (Lyphard) In tch, pushed along & no | shd | 74
impress fnl 3f, debut: strong, impressive looking newcomer: brother to 1000 Guineas winner Wince & half brother
to a smart 10f performer/hdler Ulundi: dam a 10f wnr: well bred newcomer who can do better in time.
CUTTHROAT 0 [5]4-9-10 Dale Gibson 66/1: 7: Missed break & sn bhd, t.o. 2f out, jumps fit. | 21 | 44
2932} **BLUE VIKING** 315 [1]3-8-10 D Fentiman(7) 80/1: 4-8: Keen & led after 1f till 4f out, sn bhd. | 8 | 32
8 Ran   Time 2m 06.97(3.67)   Owned: Godolphin   Trained: Newmarket

LINGFIELD   Polytrack   WEDNESDAY 26.05.04   Lefthand, Sharp, Undulating Track

Official Going Firm (Good/Firm Places)

2013
2.25 Come Racing At Lingfield Maiden Stakes 3yo   (D)
£3838 £1181 £591   **1m1f**   **Good/Firm**   Slow   Inside

HASAIYDA 0 [8] Sir Michael Stoute 3-8-9 K Fallon 3/1: 1: b f Hector Protector - Hasainiya (Top | | 78
Ville) Dwelt, in tch, hdwy to lead dist, styd on strongly to assert under hands & heels: op 2/1: debut: half
sister to a 11/13f 3yo wnr & subs hdles scorer: acts at 9f, acts on fast grnd: looks sure to get 10f+: improve.
1297 **RESPLENDENT KING** 35 [3] T G Mills 3-9-0 (65) R Miles(3) 11/2: 0-335532: Led, rdn & hdd dist, no | 2½ | 77
extra: rest well covered: eff around 1m/9f on fast, hvy & polytrack: improved run.
1762 **FUEL CELL** 11 [7] R Hannon 3-9-0 Dane O'Neill 6/1: 003: b c Desert Style - Tappen Zee (Sandhurst | 4 | 69
Prince) Prom, styd on onepace for press, no threat to front pair: stay 9f, handles fast grnd: dam 7f scorer.
3189} **MICHABO** 305 [2] D R C Elsworth 3-9-0 T Quinn 14/1: 0-4: b g Robellino - Mole Creek (Unfuwain) | nk | 68
Keen & trkd ldrs, onepace fnl 2f: reapp, gelded: unplcd sole '03 start (rtd 45, mdn): dam an 11f 3yo scorer & half
sister to top mid-dist performer Terimon: stay further.
SHUHEB 0 [5]3-8-9 D Holland 11/1: 5: Keen, in tch, outpcd over 2f out on debut. | ½ | 62
1651 **YOUNG LOVE** 16 [4]3-8-9 S Drowne 20/1: 00-06: Held up, no impress fnl 3f. | 2 | 58
4715} **TELL THE TREES** 226 [6]3-8-9 T P Queally(3) 66/1: 000-7: Trkd ldr, btn 2f out, reapp. | nk | 57
SAFA PARK 0 [1]3-9-0 K McEvoy 9/4 FAV: 8: Slow away & rear, hung left & btn 2f out: bckd on | 6 | 50
debut, connections reported afterwards that the colt may have been unsuited by the ground.
8 Ran   Time 1m 56.13 (5.63)   Owned: HH Aga Khan   Trained: Newmarket

2014
3.00 Family Celebrations At Lingfield Park Handicap Stakes 3yo 46-55   (F)
£2996 £856 £428   **1m3f106y**   **Good/Firm**   Slow   Outside   [64]

1580 **VICARIO** 20 [3] M L W Bell 3-9-0 (50) I Mongan 10/1: 00-51: gr g Vettori - Arantxa (Sharpo) | | 63
Rear, stumbled bend over 3f out, squeezed thro' gap & led dist, rdn out: op 12/1: h'cap bow: unplcd '03 (rtd 31):
apprec step up to 11.5f, will get further: enjoyed fast grnd & sharp/undul trk: lightly rcd, rate higher.
1398 **REGAL PERFORMER** 29 [7] S Kirk 3-9-4 (54) P Dobbs 16/1: 00-002: b g Ali Royal - Khatiynza | 4 | 59
(Nishapour) Held up, switched & hdwy over 3f out, styd on to chase wnr, not able to chall: rest well covered:
h'cap bow: unplcd '03 (rtd 67, mdns, subs gelded): stays 11.5f on fast grnd: likely type for similar.
1785 **ROMEOS DAY** 10 [4] M R Channon 3-9-2 (52) T E Durcan 7/2 FAV: 000-0243: Held up, hdwy from | 3½ | 52
halfway, styd on onepace fnl 3f: bckd, op 6/1: stays 11.5f: see 1724 (sell).
1528 **JACKIE KIELY** 23 [14] T G Mills 3-9-2 (52) R Miles(3) 7/1: 0620554: Trkd ldrs & led 2f out till | 1¼ | 50
dist, fdd under press: prob handles fast grnd & polytrack: return to 10f could suit: see 676 (AW).
1648 **RINNEEN** 16 [10]3-9-1 VIS (51) Dane O'Neill 12/1: 3000-005: Slow away & rear, mod late gains in visor. | ¾ | 48
1836 **WINSLOW BOY** 8 [8]3-9-5 (55) G Baker 6/1: 000-046: Chsd ldrs, no extra when bmpd over 1f out. | ½ | 51
1872 **VRISAKI** 6 [13]3-9-3 (53) A McCarthy 20/1: 00-20407: Sn trkd ldr & led 4f out till 2f out, wknd: | hd | 48
quick reapp: cheek pieces omitted: btr 284 (7f, AW).
497 **EL MAGNIFICO** 119 [11]3-8-12 (48) K Fallon 8/1: 006-608: Mid-div, btn when hmpd dist: see 497. | nk | 42
1089 **SAUCY** 49 [6]3-9-0 BL (50) J F McDonald(3) 20/1: 0-669: b f Muhtarram - So Saucy (Teenoso) Keen & | 9 | 32
trkd ldr 2f, btn 2f out: h'cap bow, blnks: unplcd '03 (sole start, rtd 63, mdn): mid-dist breeding.
886 **CLARE GALWAY** 67 [12]3-9-0 (50) J P Guillambert(3) 25/1: 0500: 10th: Chsd ldrs, btn 2f out, 2 | 1¾ | 30
month abs, h'cap bow, longer trip.
1258 **DONASTRELA** 37 [5]3-9-3 (53) Martin Dwyer 16/1: 0-600: 11th: Sn rdn & al rear, h'cap bow, longer trip. | 2½ | 29
1648 **LITTLESTAR** 16 [9]3-9-2 bl (52) T Quinn 16/1: 0-000000: 12th: Led till 4f out, sn btn. | 1½ | 26
1611 **WELL KNIT** 19 [1]3-9-0 (50) J F Egan 12/1: 0-000000: 13th: Mid-div, struggling fnl 2f: op 20/1. | 2 | 21
1611 **UNINTENTIONAL** 19 [2]3-9-2 (52) D Holland 10/1: 652-6060: 14th: Mid-div, struggling from halfway | dist | 0
& eased 2f out: jockey reported filly slipped on the 1st bend: btr 238.
14 Ran   Time 2m 32.04 (8.64)   Owned: Mr T Redman Mr P Philips & Mr P Coe   Trained: Newmarket

2015 3.35 Dormansland Handicap Stakes Fillies 3yo+ 0-85 (D) [78]
£5460 £1680 £840 **1m2f** **Good/Firm** **Slow** Inside

1530* **HENESEYS LEG** 23 [6] John Berry 4-9-1 (65) Lisa Jones(3) 6/1: 22645-11: Trkd ldrs, led 2f out, 75
styd on strongly under hands riding ins last: eff at 1m/12f on firm & soft: progressive: see 1530.
1736 **LADY MCNAIR** 12 [4] P D Cundell 4-9-10 (74) K Fallon 5/1: 4446-402: Rear, styd on for press, not 1¾ 79
able to chall wnr: op 6/1: nicely h'capped, 10f poss best trip: see 1056.
1721 **DORIS SOUTER** 13 [3] R Hannon 4-9-6 (70) R L Moore 6/1: 53-20503: Trkd ldr, no extra over 1f out: 1 73
likes to dominate, unable to do so today: see 736.
912 **LARA FALANA** 63 [7] Miss B Sanders 6-9-2 (66) T Quinn 9/2: 500-0254: Rear, in tch, short of room 1 69+
over 2f out & no impress ins last: shade closer with a clr run: see 799.
1283* **FLING** 36 [1]3-9-2 (80) Dane O'Neill 2/1 FAV: 15: Held up, eff 3f out, no impress: hvly bckd on ½ 82
h'cap bow tho' op 7/4: btr 1283 (auct mdn, gd).
1828 **TIGHT SQUEEZE** 8 [2]7-10-0 (78) K McEvoy 12/1: 0101006: Mid-div, eff wide, btn 2f out: btr 1027 (AW). 1½ 78
1131 **JUBILEE TREAT** 44 [5]4-9-12 (76) D Holland 10/1: 55120-07: b f Seeking The Gold - Dance Treat ½ 75
(Nureyev) Led till 2f out, sn btn: 6 wk abs: made all to land fillies h'cap '03: suited by 10f on fast grnd,
stiff or sharpish trk: can go well fresh.
2 Sep'03 Sand 10.0g/f 80-74 D: 1 Aug'03 Ripo 10g/f 76-70 D:
7 Ran Time 2m 11.65 (7.45) Owned: Mr Peter J Skinner Trained: Newmarket

Official Going Standard

2016 4.10 Marsh Green Claiming Stakes 3yo+ (F)
£2975 £850 £425 **6f aw rnd** **Going** **Inapplicable** Inside

1806 **BELLS BEACH** 9 [1] P Howling 6-8-9 (53) K Fallon 5/1: 5610441: Trkd ldrs, switched & hdwy to lead 56a
dist, rdn out: suited by 5/6f on fast, gd/soft & fibresand, loves Lingfield/polytrack & sell/clmg grade: see 1012.
1867 **AINTNECESSARILYSO** 6 [8] N E Berry 6-9-8 (58) M Savage(5) 9/1: 6333222: Dwelt, sn chsd, ldrs, styd 1¼ 64a
on for press, al held: quick reapp: frequently plcd, win record less impress but could find similar: see 1867.
1743 **WATERSIDE** 12 [9] J W Hills 5-9-12 (82) S Whitworth 3/1 FAV: 04-00303: Held up, short of room shd 68a
over 1f out, styd on onepace ins last: shade closer with a clr run: clmd by N Shields for 12,000.
1806 **LAKE VERDI** 9 [5] B Hanbury 5-9-4 t (60) D Holland 16/1: 00006-04: Led till dist, kept on: acts 1 57a
on firm, gd & polytrack: see 1806.
1815 **BAHAMA REEF** 8 [7]3-8-10 (1ow) (63) Dane O'Neill 33/1: 6400-005: b g Sri Pekan - Caribbean Dancer 1 55a
(Shareef Dancer) Chsd ldrs, no extra ins last: dual auct mdn rnr-up '03, subs disapp in a visor: eff at 5/6f:
handles firm, fast & polytrack, has tried up to 1m prev: handles a sharp/undul or turning trk.
2 May'03 Brig 6.0fm 80- E: 2 Apr'03 Bath 5.0g/f 76- E:
1588* **BOISDALE** 20 [4]6-9-6 (53) L Treadwell(7) 16/1: 0000-616: Chsd ldrs, outpcd fnl 1f: see 1588 (fbsnd). 1 53a
1644 **KILMEENA STAR** 16 [3]6-8-12 bl (54) R L Moore 12/1: 0041207: Chsd ldrs till over 1f out: see 844. hd 44a
1806 **AGUILA LOCO** 9 [11]5-9-6 p (56) S Drowne 12/1: 2030368: Chsd ldrs, no impress over 1f out: see 739. ½ 50a
1788 **ILLUSIVE** 9 [2]7-9-12 bl (60) T Quinn 9/2: 0022629: Chsd ldrs, no impress fnl 2f: op 11/2: btr 1788. ¾ 54a
1806 **MACS TALISMAN** 9 [6]4-9-10 (67) M Tebbutt 33/1: 32003-00: 10th: Al bhd under minimal press: eff 1¾ 47a
in blnks & t-strap, of more interest when headgear reapplied: see 1806.
1827 **WATERLINE BLUE** 8 [12]3-8-5 t (76) R Havlin 10/1: 62466-50: 11th: Sn outpcd: op 8/1: see 1827. 2 31a
1481 **ARCTIC BURST** 25 [10]4-9-12 vis (78) Darren Williams 20/1: 4/10-0000: 12th: b g Royal Academy - 3½ 32a
Polar Bird (Thatching) Switched ins, al bhd & no impress: op 14/l: lightly rcd '03, mdn scorer for B Hills:
rnr-up in a mdn '02: eff at 5/6f on fast & gd/soft grnd, stiff/undul trk: can go well fresh & eff in a t-strap,
omitted today: no form in visor to date. 1 May'03 Pont 6g/s 87-(94) D: 2 Aug'02 York 6g/f 92- D:
12 Ran Time 1m 13.67 (3.27) Owned: Mr Richard Berenson Trained: Newmarket

2017 4.45 Play A Round At Lingfield Golf Club Selling Stakes 2yo (G)
£2534 £724 £362 **5f aw rnd** **Going** **Inapplicable** Outside

1631 **STORY OF ONE** 18 [3] N P Littmoden 2-8-11 D Holland 7/2: 201: Trkd ldrs & led ins last, drvn 69a
out: bckd, op 4/1: bought in for 6,000 gns, 1st win: eff at 5f, will get 6f: acts on polytrack & soft grnd.
1831 **ALICE KING** 8 [4] W G M Turner 2-8-6 C Haddon(7) 33/1: 4402: Dwelt, sn mid-div, styd on for 1¼ 59a
press, not able to reach wnr: AW bow: eff at 5f, 6f in similar will suit: prob handles soft & polytrack: see 1224.
1653 **LADY ERICA** 16 [9] K R Burke 2-8-6 Darren Williams 100/30: 2543: Led till ins last: handles both AWs. ¾ 57a
1751 **SHISH** 11 [5] J A Osborne 2-8-6 S W Kelly 25/1: 664: Rdn rear, late gains, nrst fin: needs a nk 56a
return to 6f in similar: prob handles polytrack: see 1653.
1471 **SMOKINCANON** 25 [7]2-9-2 R Miles(3) 13/8 FAV: 3165: Prom wide, no extra dist: bckd: btr 1071. hd 65a
  JONNY FOXS 0 [1]2-8-11 D Sweeney 16/1: 6: ch c Foxhound - Lala Salama (College Chapel) Outpcd shd 60a
early, rapid prog wide halfway, btn dist: Mar 1st foal, dam only mod, half sister to sev juv wnrs.
1640 **BAMBOOZLED** 16 [6]2-8-6 VIS S Drowne 8/1: 607: Cl-up, lost place bef dist: tried visor. ¾ 53a
929 **DIATONIC** 61 [8]2-8-11 Lisa Jones(3) 25/1: 08: b g Deploy - Vic Melody (Old Vic) Dwelt & sn hd 57a
outpcd: Mar foal, half brother to wnrs in Eastern Europe, dam unrcd: sire a high-class 12f performer.
1071 **FAITHFULL GIRL** 50 [10]2-8-6 N Chalmers(4) 40/1: 09: Sn outpcd, 7 wk abs. hd 51a
1133 **SHES MY DREAM** 44 [2]2-8-6 Derek Nolan(7) 50/1: 000: 10th: Al outpcd & bhd. 1¼ 47a
10 Ran Time 1m 03.12 (5.32) Owned: Richard Green (Fine Paintings) Trained: Newmarket

LINGFIELD Polytrack WEDNESDAY 26.05.04 Lefthand, V Sharp Track

2018 5.20 Dunsdale Handicap Stakes 3yo+ 0-70 **(E)** [70]
£3513 £1081 £541 **1m aw rnd** **Going** **Inapplicable** Outside

1915 **CLIMATE** 4 [7] J R Boyle 5-9-12 vis (68) D Sweeney 7/2 JT FAV: 30-54021: Mid-div & al travelling 79a
well, smooth prog to lead ins last, rdn out: op 9/2: quick reapp: eff at 7.5f/9f on firm, soft & polytrack: in gd
form, well h'capped, can follow-up: see 878.
1812 **OMAHA CITY** 8 [6] B Gubby 10-10-0 (70) M Tebbutt 20/1: 5600-002: Prom & led over 2f out, hdd ins 2 75a
last & outpcd by wnr: acts on firm, gd/soft & polytrack: capable 10yo, well h'capped for similar: see 1042.
1849 **REBATE** 7 [5] R Hannon 4-9-13 (69) P Dobbs 12/1: 0-050003: Dictated pace, hdd over 2f out, kept 1½ 71a
on: had the run of the race in front, imprvd eff: see 903 & 716.
2775} **ROYAL ADVOCATE** 321 [4] J W Hills 4-9-7 (63) S Whitworth 16/1: 00654-4: b g Royal Applause - Kept nk 64a
Waiting (Tanfirion) Keen in mid-div, onepcd fnl 2f: reapp: unplcd '03 (rtd 67, mdn): eff around 1m, prob handles
fast grnd & polytrack, sharp/undul or gall trk: has been gelded, made an encouraging return.
1247* **FREE OPTION** 37 [2]9-9-9 (65) Laura Pike(7) 10/1: 0-503315: Rear, short of room when prog ins ½ 65a
last, nvr a threat: weak ride: see 1247.
1537 **DIDNT TELL MY WIFE** 22 [3]5-9-8 (64) Lisa Jones(3) 4/1: 41021-66: Keen, mid-div, no impress dist. 1¾ 61a
1613 **COLLEGE DELINQUENT** 19 [9]5-9-9 t (65) Dane O'Neill 13/2: 303-3467: Slow away & rear, nvr on terms shd 62a
with ldrs: lost ch start, op 10/1: see 517.
1792 **ZAFARSHAH** 9 [11]5-9-6 (62) S Drowne 7/2 JT FAV: 1414628: In tch, btn over 1f out: btr 565 (7f). hd 58a
1792 **SPINDOR** 9 [8]5-9-5 bl (61) S W Kelly 14/1: 1033609: Al rear: btr 1504 & 1010 (7f). ¾ 56a
1613 **ESTIMATION** 19 [12]4-9-8 (64) I Mongan 20/1: 6350000: 10th: Chsd ldrs, btn 2f out: btr 255 (fbsd). 3½ 52a
1535 **QUIET READING** 22 [10]7-9-11 vis (67) Hayley Turner(5) 14/1: 4632200: 11th: Trkd ldr, lost place ½ 54a
from over 2f out: btr 1322 & 1198 (fibresand).
11 Ran Time 1m 40.57(4.37) Owned: Inside Track Racing Club Trained: Epsom

GOODWOOD WEDNESDAY 26.05.04 Righthand, Sharpish, Undulating Track

Official Going Str course - Good, Rnd Course - Good/Firm

2019 6.10 Solent Sky - Home Of The Spitfire Selling Stakes Handicap 3yo 46-55 **(F)** [74]
£3387 £1042 £521 **1m3f** **Good/Firm** 31 **-64 Slow** Outside

1372 **GARSTON STAR** 31 [7] J S Moore 3-8-6 (52) Martin Dwyer 6/1: 50006-31: Made all, pushed out ins 60+
fnl 2f, val 4L+: eff at 10f, apprec step up here to 11f: acts on fast grnd & a sharp/undul trk: 1st win: see 1372.
1713 **OKTIS MORILIOUS** 13 [6] A W Carroll 3-8-0 (1oh) (45) J F McDonald(3) 7/2 JT FAV: 0412342: Handy, 2 50
prog to chase wnr ins fnl 1f, al held: op 9/2: clr rem: eff at 10/11f on fast grnd & polytrack: see 1183 & 970.
1529 **MR STROWGER** 23 [2] A Charlton 3-8-1 (47) R L Moore 7/2 JT FAV: 00000-63: Cl-up, no extra ins fnl 2f. 5 44
1740 **PRINCESS ISMENE** 12 [4] P A Blockley 3-8-1 bl (47) F P Ferris(3) 8/1: 4334054: Handy 1m, sn no extra. nk 43
1720 **SPRING DANCER** 13 [8]3-8-7 (52) T Quinn 13/2: 600-0005: b f Imperial Ballet - Roxy Music (Song) 4 43
Missed break, sn in mid-div, wknd 3f out: op 8/1: fills auct mdn wnr in '03 (A P Jarvis, also rnr-up twice): eff at
6f, bred to apprec further: acts on fast & gd grnd: tried visor & cheek pieces, with B G Powell.
2 Jul'03 Asco 6g/f 79-76 D: 1 Jun'03 Pont 6g/f 79- E: 2 May'03 Yarm 6.0gd 72- F:
1648 **GRIST MIST** 16 [3]3-8-9 t (55) R Havlin 14/1: 00-0006: Chsd ldrs 1m, sn wknd: see 1398. 3½ 40
1740* **FLYING SPUD** 12 [5]3-8-4 (50) A Daly 5/1: 00-54517: Sn bhd, nvr a factor: btr 1740 (1m, soft). 3½ 30
1737 **TRUE PATRIOT** 12 [9]3-8-7 BL (53) J F Egan 20/1: 000-08: b g Rainbow Quest - High Standard (Kris) 17 9
Al in rear: 1st time blnks: mod form in 3 '03 starts (rtd 55, E A L Dunlop): tried visor: with P Mitchell.
894 **ALTARES** 65 [1]3-8-0 (1oh) (35) C Catlin 33/1: 000-0009: Rear, al adrift: 9 wk abs. 3½ 0
9 Ran Time 2m 28.35 (10.45) Owned: East Garston Racing Trained: Hungerford

2020 6.40 Goodwood Flying School Maiden Auction Stakes 2yo **(E)**
£4076 £1254 £627 **5f str** **Good** 41 **-12 Slow** Stands side

1764 **ELISHA** 11 [6] D M Simcock 2-8-4 C Catlin 8/1: 451: Made all, drvn out ins fnl 1f: eff at 5f on 71
gd grnd: acts on a sharp/undul trk: enjoyed front-running: see 1380.
1728 **CLINET** 12 [7] P M Phelan 2-8-2 J F Egan 16/1: 052: b f Docksider - Oiche Mhaith (Night Shift) 1½ 64
Slow away, prog halfway, chsd wnr ins fnl 1f, al held: Apr foal, cost £8,000: half sister to a couple of sprint
wnrs abroad: dam 6f wnr: sire high-class performer at 1m: eff at 5f, shld be suited by further: acts on gd grnd.
ELSIE WAGG 0 [8] M J Wallace 2-8-9 K Fallon 10/3: 3: b f Mt Livermore - Hoedown Honey (Country 1¾ 66
Light) Handy, prog to chase wnr halfway, no extra ins fnl 1f: tchd 4/1 on debut: Feb foal, sire decent sprinter at
sprint/mid-dists: sire decent sprinter abroad: eff at 5f, shld apprec further: acts on gd: encouraging.
BLUE MARBLE 0 [11] C E Brittain 2-8-13 D Holland 12/1: 4: b c Fraam - Fizzy Fiona (Efisio) 2½ 61
Handy 3f, no extra bef 1f out: debut: Mar foal, cost 14,000 gns: half brother to a couple of 5f wnr: dam unrcd:
sire useful performer around 1m: sharper for today.
1716 **GRAND OPTION** 13 [4]2-8-9 T P Queally(3) 3/1 JT FAV: 032325: Cl-up, fdd dist: bckd, btr 1716. 1½ 55
1816 **RAGGED GLORY** 8 [3]2-8-13 P Dobbs 3/1 JT FAV: 46: In tch when short of room after 2f, sn outpcd, ½ 58
mod late gains: well bckd: failed to build on promise shown in 1816 (debut).
TIGHT CIRCLE 0 [9]2-8-2 J Mackay 50/1: 7: Handy 3f, sn wknd. 3 38
CHEK OI 0 [2]2-8-13 Martin Dwyer 16/1: 8: Al in rear. hd 48
SECRET DIVA 0 [1]2-8-2 J F McDonald(3) 40/1: 9: Bhd, nvr a factor. nk 36
LILY LENAT 0 [10]2-8-5 (1ow) T Quinn 50/1: 0: 10th: Slow away, al rear. ¾ 37
LAKESDALE 0 [5]2-8-4 T E Durcan 16/1: 0: 11th: Slow away, al bhd. nk 35
11 Ran Time 59.39 (2.69) Owned: Good Connection II Trained: Newmarket

2021 7.10 Woodward At Goodwood 60th Birthday Stakes Handicap 3yo 0-95 (C) [98]
£9487 £2919 £1460 1m4f Good/Firm 31 -14 Slow Stands side

1236 **ADMIRAL 39** [2] Sir Michael Stoute 3-8-6 (76) K Fallon 9/2: 64-01: b c Alhaarth - Coast Is Clear 85+
(Rainbow Quest) Rear, prog halfway, styd on to lead 2f out, drvn out to hold rival ins fnl 1f: 4th of 14 in 1 of
only 2 '03 starts (rtd 88+, mdns): dam dual mid-dist wnr: apprec today's step up to 12f: acts on fast grnd & a
sharp/undul trk: lightly rcd, genuine & open to improvement.
1865* **WATAMU 6** [5] P J Makin 3-8-13 (5ex) (83) D Holland 6/4 FAV: 01-0012: Handy, prog when edged left nk 90
dist, ev ch ins fnl 1f, just held by wnr: well bckd on quick reapp: suited by 11/12f: lost little in defeat: useful.
1489* **DESTINATION DUBAI 25** [4] Saeed bin Suroor 3-9-7 vis (91) K McEvoy 6/1: 22-13: Led, hdd 9f out, 1½ 95
styd cl-up till led halfway, hdd 2f out, no extra well ins fnl 1f: op 9/2: first try at 12f, prob stays: see 1489 (mdn).
1582 **AKRITAS 20** [1] P F I Cole 3-9-4 (88) T Quinn 15/2: 1P0-44: Rear, prog when no room bef 2f sn no 1¾ 89
impress: op 13/2: just btr 1582 (reapp).
1612 **BILL BENNETT 19** [6]3-8-7 (77) O Urbina 20/1: 0651125: Rear, nvr a factor: btr 1612 (hvy) & 1528. 15 57
1708 **ABSOLUTELYTHEBEST 13** [3]3-8-12 (82) W Supple 4/1: 004-1226: Cl-up, led 9f out, hdd halfway, fdd 16 41
just ins fnl half mile: tchd 7/1: v disapp, not handle sharper grnd? btr 1708.
6 Ran Time 2m 37.20 (5.4) Owned: Highclere Thoroughbred Racing XI Trained: Newmarket

2022 7.45 Listed On The House Stakes 3yo+ (A)
£17850 £6600 £3300 1m rnd Good/Firm 31 +13 Fast Inside

1168 **KALAMAN 42** [5] Sir Michael Stoute 4-9-5 (116) K Fallon 2/5 FAV: 11202-21: Handy, styd on for 112
press to lead ins last, rdn out: hvly bckd, 6 wk abs: eff at 1m, stays a stiff 9f & has tried 10f: acts on fm or
gd: gd confidence boosting win, v smart at best: see 1168 (reapp).
4431+ **IMTIYAZ 245** [2] Saeed bin Suroor 5-9-8 t (109) W Supple 7/2: 2/10631-2: ro c Woodman - Shadayid ¾ 110
(Shadeed) Led, hdd under press well ins fnl 1f, not pace wnr: reapp: Listed wnr on fnl of 4 '03 Brit starts
(earlier wnr in Dubai): Listed wnr on '02 reapp (visored), subs Gr1 2nd: eff at 1m, will apprec return to 10f:
acts on firm & soft: goes esp well fresh: eff with/without visor, eff in t-strap: likes G'wood.
1 Sep'03 Good 9.9g/f 110-(110) A: 2 Sep'02 Good 9.8fm 112- A: 2 Jun'02 Chan 9gd 114- :
1 May'02 York 10.3fm 114- A: 1 Jun'01 Sand 7sft 94- D:
1043 **VANDERLIN 53** [4] A M Balding 5-9-8 (105) Martin Dwyer 20/1: 22040-33: Prom, ev ch dist, kept on nk 109
but not pace front 2 well ins fnl 1f: clr rem: 7 wk abs: eff at 6f, prob best at 7f, now stays 1m: useful.
1585 **GRAND PASSION 20** [3] G Wragg 4-9-5 (103) S Drowne 16/1: 32-21004: Hld up, prog halfway, wknd dist. 5 96
1234 **KINGS POINT 39** [1]3-8-12 (104) Dane O'Neill 20/1: 4116-505: Keen handy 6f, wknd: btr 1040 (reapp). 7 87
5 Ran Time 1m 38.51 (1.51) Owned: HH Aga Khan Trained: Newmarket

2023 8.15 Goodwood Aerodrome Stakes Handicap 3yo+ 0-80 (D) [80]
£5616 £1728 £864 6f str Good 41 +11 Fast Stands side

1598 **IDLE POWER 19** [14] J R Boyle 6-9-4 p (70) Martin Dwyer 13/2: 4000-001: Handy, styd on to lead 78
well ins fnl 1f, rdn out: eff at 6/7f on firm, gd/soft & polytrack, any trk: eff with cheekpieces: gd confidence
restorer after long losing run, h'capped to follow-up: see 1598 (reapp).
2949+ **DEVON FLAME 314** [11] R J Hodges 5-9-0 (66) J F McDonald(3) 8/1: 00/4111-2: b g Whittingham - Uae nk 72
Flame (Polish Precedent) Keen cl-up, led 2f out, hdd under press cl-home: reapp: prog in early '03 wng last 3 of
only 4 starts (h'caps): well btn on all 3 '02 mdn starts: stays 1m, suited by around 6f on fast & gd/soft grnd:
prob acts on any trk: excellent return, improving & spot-on for this.
1 Jul'03 Leic 6.0g/f 69-60 E: 1 Jul'03 Wind 6g/f 62-53 E: 1 Jun'03 Chep 6.1g/f 55-43 E:
1867 **DOUBLE M 6** [16] Mrs L Richards 7-7-12 (3oh)vis (47) R Thomas(5) 7/1: 2106553: Chsd ldrs, prog & ¾ 54
styd on ins fnl 1f, not btn far: quick reapp: another encouraging eff & is on a wng mark: see 1867 & 902.
1824 **FULL SPATE 8** [2] J M Bradley 9-9-3 (69) R L Moore 10/1: 1-605464: Slow away, prog halfway, nrst fin. 1 70
1578 **FIREWORK 20** [10]6-8-9 p (61) T Quinn 16/1: 20-00065: Led 4f, no extra dist: see 628. shd 61
1788 **ATTORNEY 9** [9]6-7-12 vis (50) Hayley Turner(5) 16/1: 0112036: Mid-div, late gains. nk 49
1255 **NIVERNAIS 37** [7]5-10-0 (80) Dane O'Neill 9/1: 0/1336-07: b g Forzando - Funny Wave (Lugana 1¼ 75
Beach) Held up, nvr nrr than mid-div: h'cap wnr 1st time out from only 4 '03 starts (also plcd twice): plcd thrice
in '02 (h'caps, rtd 74, well btn in visor): eff at 5/6f, stays 7f: acts on firm & gd/soft grnd: likes to force the
pace & eff with a t-strap: has run well fresh.
1 Jun'03 Sali 6g/f 79-73 C: 2 Sep'01 Chep 5fm 79-74 E: 1 Aug'01 Folk 5g/f 74- F:
1723 **CORANGLAIS 13** [8]4-9-3 (69) C Catlin 25/1: 2050-008: ch g Piccolo - Antonia's Folly (Music Boy) 2½ 57
Chsd ldrs 4f, sn no extra: mdn wnr in '03 (T D Easterby): plcd on 2 of 3 '02 starts (mdns, rtd 82): eff at 5/7f on
fast & gd/soft grnd: has a sharpish or stiff/undul trk: has tried blnks: with J M Bradley.
2 Jun'03 Redc 7g/f 82-79 D: 1 Apr'03 Pont 6g/f 82-(80) D:
1788 **LONG WEEKEND 9** [12]6-7-12 (4oh)vis (46) J Mackay 25/1: 1146069: Slow away, nvr nrr than mid-div. ½ 37
1787 **SIMPSONS MOUNT 9** [5]3-8-5 (66) S Dweney 33/1: 653050: 10th: Slow away, nvr nrr than mid-div. 1¼ 49
1914 **BLUE KNIGHT 4** [4]5-9-6 (72) K Fallon 50/30 FAV: 0-240620: 11th: Rear, nvr able to chall: v ¾ 53
disapp here on follow up bid, returned home lame: fin close 2nd in this race 12 months ago off 2lb higher mark.
1542 **B A HIGHFLYER 22** [6]4-8-11 (63) T E Durcan 20/1: 216-0500: 12th: Al rear stands side: btr 1282. ¾ 42
976 **Ben Lomand 57** [13]4-9-8 c(74) P Dobbs 33/1:0 698 **Currency 95** [17]7-9-12 (78) D Holland 16/1:0
1255 **Stokesies Wish 37** [15]4-8-12 (64) S Hitchcott(3) 20/1:0 1726 **A Teen 12** [3]6-8-8 (60) Lisa Jones(3) 25/1:0
16 Ran Time 1m 11.81 (1.81) Owned: The Idle B'S Trained: Epsom

---

2024   **8.45 Aviation Industries Stakes Handicap 3yo 0-80 (D)**   [86]
£5681 £1748 £874   **1m1f**   **Good/Firm 31**   **-33 Slow**   Inside

1825 **BOULE DOR 8** [9] R Ingram 3-9-3 (75) N Day 5/1 JT FAV: 1300-41: Held up, prog when hmpd after 3f   84+
out, prog when again short of room dist, swtchd & qcknd to lead cl-home, going away: eff at 7f, imprvd here for step
up to 9f: acts on fast & gd, any trk: showed a gd turn of foot to land this & more h'caps await.
1915 **CARTRONAGEERAGHLAD 4** [10] J A Osborne 3-9-3 (75) T P Queally(3) 12/1: 60-00002: Held up, prog 3 1   77
out, ev ch ins fnl 1f, not pace wnr: quick reapp: improved at 9f: acts on fast, soft grnd & fibresand: lost little
in defeat & deserves to find similar: see 1915.
1651 **WILD PITCH 16** [12] P Mitchell 3-8-2 (60) R L Moore 20/1: 6-003: ch g Piccolo - Western Horizon   nk   61
(Gone West) Rear, prog halfway, styd on to lead dist, hdd well ins fnl 1f, no extra: clr rem: unplcd sole '03
start (stks, rtd 58): eff at 9f, has tried further: acts on fast grnd: gd h'cap bow.
1526 **PHLUKE 23** [5] R F Johnson Houghton 3-9-1 (73) S Carson 11/1: 3051204: Cl-up, led 3f out, hdd   4   66
dist, wknd: did not get home on 1st try at 9f: btr 1359 (1m, gd/soft).
1257 **THE WAY WE WERE 37** [1]3-9-3 (75) K Fallon(3) 10/1: 31-65: Led 6f, sn wknd: see 1257 (reapp).   3½ 62
1791 **MASTER MAHOGANY 9** [6]3-8-11 (69) V Slattery 25/1: 04006: Chsd ldrs, no extra ins fnl 3f: see 1086.   hd   55
189 **UNCLE JOHN 165** [7]3-8-9 (67) J F Egan 33/1: 00105-7: b g Atraf - Bit O' May (Mummy's Pet) Nvr   ¾   51
nrr than mid-div: reapp: auct mdn wnr in '03: eff at 8.4f on fibresand: has gone well fresh.
1 Nov'03 Wolv 8.5af 70a- E:
1527 **BEAUCHAMP STAR 23** [2]3-9-2 (74) D Holland 6/1: 0328: Slow away, sn mid-div, hung right & wknd   1   56
fnl 2f: btr expected here on h'cap bow: btr 1527 (1m, soft).
1647 **SMOOTHLY DOES IT 16** [13]3-8-9 (67) T E Durcan 5/1 JT FAV: 0020-029: Slow away, hdwy when short   ½   48
of room ins fnl half mile, sn no impress: disappointing: btr 1647 (1m, soft).
1500 **CHASING THE DREAM 24** [14]3-9-0 (72) Martin Dwyer 15/2: 1260: 10th: Handy over 6f, wknd.   1   51
1257 **DUMNONI 37** [4]3-9-7 (79) N Callan 9/1: 631-0630: 11th: Handy till halfway, sn hung left & wknd.   15   37
1577 **KNICKYKNACKIENOO 20** [3]3-7-12 (56) C Catlin 10/1: 060-4220: 12th: Keen mid-div, wknd 3f out.   4   7
1965 **MR INDEPENDENT 2** [8]3-8-5 VIS (63) W Supple 16/1: 030-000: 13th: Handy 5f, sn lost action & wknd.   24   0
13 Ran   Time 1m 56.26(5.76)   Owned: Friends and Family   Trained: Epsom

---

Official Going Good/Firm (Firm places)

2025   **2.30 Arran Rating Related Maiden Stakes 3yo 0-70 (E)**
£3595 £1106 £553   **1m1f20y**   **Good/Firm 22**   **Inapp**   Inside

955 **ANOTHER BOTTLE 61** [2] T P Tate 3-9-0 (70) Dale Gibson 11/8 FAV: 033-01: b g Cape Cross - Aster   86+
Aweke (Alzao) Keen early, trkd ldrs, smooth hdwy to lead over 1f out, rdn clr & eased cl-home, readily: well bckd:
2 mth abs: plcd fnl '03 start (rtd 74, auct mdn): eff at 7f, imprvd for step up to 9f on fast grnd.
1636 **LITTLE BOB 19** [1] J D Bethell 3-9-0 (70) T Quinn 8/1: 0-442: In tch, rdn & outpcd 2f out, styd   5   75
on to take 2nd cl-home, nvr threat to wnr: stays 9f: handles fast & gd: may want further:see 1177.
1791 **CHARLIE TANGO 10** [3] M R Channon 3-9-0 (67) T E Durcan 9/1: 30-30003: Trkd ldr, outpcd over 1f   nk   74
out & lost 2nd nr fin: handles polytrack & fast grnd: see 817.
901 **LA PETITE CHINOISE 65** [4] R Guest 3-8-11 (66) R Winston 16/1: 3406-604: ch f Dr Fong - Susi Wong   shd   71
(Selkirk) Chsd ldrs till outpcd 2f out, kept on late: unplcd '3 (rtd 72, 4th, auct mdn): eff at 5f, prob stays
gall 9f: handles firm & gd/soft grnd: blnks omitted today after latest.
1527 **NUKHBAH 24** [5]3-8-11 (70) F Lynch 13/8: 43-345: Led till over 1f out, sn btn: well bckd: btr 1258.   shd   71
5 Ran   Time 1m 54.75 ()   Owned: Mr J Hanson   Trained: Tadcaster

---

2026   **3.00 European Breeders Fund Crosshill Classified Stakes 3yo 0-85 (C)**
£8922 £3166 £1583   **1m rnd**   **Good/Firm 22**   **-01 Slow**   Inside

1930 **FINE SILVER 5** [2] P F I Cole 3-8-11 (83) T Quinn 2/1: 2146-401: Chsd ldrs, outpcd 3f out,   95
rallied for press ins last to lead nr line: well bckd, op 3/1: qck reapp: eff at 7f/1m on firm & soft grnd: see 1665.
1602* **CELTIC HEROINE 20** [1] M A Jarvis 3-8-12 (89) P Robinson 11/8 FAV: 1541-212: Trkd ldrs & smooth   hd   95
prog to lead over 1f out, rdn & hdd cl-home: bckd: clr rem, ran to form: see 1602 & 1141.
4336} **MBOSI 251** [3] M Johnston 3-8-12 (86) J Fanning 10/1: 15-3: b g Kingmambo - April Starlight   4   86
(Storm Bird) Led till over 2f out, no impress in last: op 8/1, gelded, eapp: lightly rcd '03, mdn wnr on debut,
subs last of 5 in a conds event: winning form at 1m on fast grnd & an easy trk: has gone well fresh.
1 Sep'03 Thir 8g/f 74- D:
1685 **OMAN GULF 15** [4] B W Hills 3-8-13 (87) A Culhane 3/1: 1-04: b c Diesis - Dabaweyaa (Shareef   3   82
Dancer) Keen & handy, led over 2f out till over 1f out, sn btn: nicely bckd tho' op 9/4: drpd in grade but a
disapp run: mdn wnr sole start '03: brother to 1m h'capper Faithful Warrior, dam a smart 1m wnr: winning form at
6f, this trip shld suit: acts on firm grnd & a stiff trk: has gone well fresh: needs to learn restraint.
1 Jul'03 Newm 6fm 87- D:
4 Ran   Time 1m 38.44 (1.84)   Owned: SIV Corporation   Trained: Whatcombe

---

2027   **3.30 Macdonalds Solicitors Handicap Stakes 3yo+ 0-80 (D)**   [78]
£5525 £1700 £850   **7f50y rnd**   **Good/Firm 22**   **Inapp**   Inside

1897 **YORKSHIRE BLUE 6** [4] J S Goldie 5-7-12 (2oh) (48) N Mackay(3) 9/2: 0000-001: Keen chasing ldrs,   56
smooth hdwy to lead 2f out, rdn out to hold on: op 7/2: eff at 6f, suited by 7/7.5f on fast grnd & fibresand: see 1463.
1833 **THE BONUS KING 9** [2] M Johnston 4-10-0 (80) A Elliott(7) 8/1: 5200002: Led/dsptd lead, styd on   ½   83
for press, not pace of wnr: op 6/1: turn prob not far away: see 1066 & 688.
1602 **SCOTLAND THE BRAVE 20** [5] J D Bethell 4-9-1 (67) T Quinn 12/1: 14050-03: ch f Zilzal - Hunters   ½   68
of Brora (Sharpo) Led/dsptd lead till over 2f out, kept on for press: imprvd from reapp: impressive mdn wnr on

---

debut '03, subs unplcd & lightly rcd: winning form at 7f, tried 1m, shld suit: acts on fast grnd & a gall trk: goes well fresh: looks well h'capped on best of last yr's form, this was encouraging.
1 May'03 Redc 7g/f 77- E:
1897 **WALTZING WIZARD 6** [8] A Berry 5-8-1 (53) J Fanning 6/1: 4555054: Held up, styd on onepace fnl 2f. ½ 55
1794 **ROMAN MAZE 10** [3]4-9-1 (67) S W Kelly 8/1: 05514-05: Dwelt, eff 2f out, no extra dist: handles both AWs & fast grnd: see 71. nk 66
1898 **FRIAR TUCK 6** [1]9-8-3 (55) R Ffrench 12/1: 0-000146: Keen & prom, no extra dist: see 1508 (6f). ¾ 54
1909 **SEA STORM 5** [9]6-9-13 (79) P Mulrennan(5) 3/1 FAV: 05-05037: Held up wide, no impress over 1f out: qck reapp: bckd: btr expected after 1909 (C/D). hd 77
1898 **JOHN OGROATS 6** [6]6-9-1 (67) F Lynch 33/1: 00-00008: b g Distinctly North - Bannons Dream (Thatching) Struggling rear halfway, nvr a factor: qck reapp: cheek pieces omitted: unplcd '03 (rtd 81, cond stks, slipped down h'cap): class stks & dual h'cap scorer '02, incl val Ayr Silver Cup: eff at 5f, suited by 6f on firm, gd/soft & hvy, loves a stiff/gall trk: has gone well fresh: yet to find form this term. 7 51
1 Sep'02 Ayr 6gd 91-83 B: 1 Sep'02 Sand 5g/f 86- D: 2 Aug'02 Beve 5g/s 77-76 D: 1 Aug'02 Pont 5g/s 75-69 E:
2 Jun'01 Newc 6g/f 83-80 D: 1 May'01 Hayd 6sft 81-75 D: 1 Apr'01 Nott 5hvy 84- F:
1909 **SPEEDFIT FREE 5** [10]7-8-1 (3ow)(2oh)vis (48) Ann Stokell 50/1: 0300409: Keen & led after 2f till over 2f out, sn btn, qck reapp: btr 1750 (AW). ½ 36
1878 **JUST ONE SMILE 7** [7]4-8-10 (62) D Allan(3) 5/1: 142-0360: 10th: Prom, btn over 1f out: btr 1660. 1¾ 41
10 Ran Time 1m 28.85 () Owned: Mr John Mc C Hodge Trained: Glasgow

2028

4.00 European Breeders Fund Ayr Maiden Stakes 2yo (D)
£5473 £1684 £842 **6f str** **Good/Firm 22** **-07 Slow** Stands Side

LEOS LUCKY STAR 0 [3] M Johnston 2-9-0 J Fanning 1/2 FAV: 1: b c Forestry - Leo's Lucky Lady (Seattle Slew) Cl-up & led halfway, in command when hung left over 1f out, al in command, readily: well bckd at long odds-on: $200,000 Feb foal, half-brother to a smart juv/10f wnr Leos Luckyman: eff at 6f, further will suit: acts on fast: potentially useful, win more races. 92+
SUNSET STRIP 0 [1] M R Channon 2-9-0 T E Durcan 9/4: 2: b c Josr Algarhoud - Shady Street (Shadeed) Chsd ldrs, kept on to chase wnr over 1f out, nvr any impress: bckd: 52,000gns April foal, half-brother to a sprint wnr abroad: eff at 6f, 7f shld suit: handles fast grnd: gd start. 3 80
GENERAL MAX 0 [6] A Crook 2-9-0 V Halliday 33/1: 3: b c General Monash - Sawaki (Song) Pushed along chasing ldrs, kept on ins last, nvr a threat: 23,000gns 2yo purchase, April foal: half-brother to wnrs at 5f/1m, dam a 7f 3/4yo wnr: shaped as if 7f+ will suit: handles fast grnd, encouraging start. ¾ 78
1601 **KRISTIKHAB 20** [2] A Berry 2-9-0 F Lynch 25/1: 054: Led till halfway, sn outpcd. 1¾ 73
WEB RACER 0 [5]2-8-9 R Winston 33/1: 5: Outpcd, nvr a factor. 5 53
ROYAL FLYNN 0 [4]2-9-0 L Enstone(3) 40/1: 6: Sn bhd. 11 25
6 Ran Time 1m 11.06 (1.76) Owned: Mrs S J Brookhouse Trained: Middleham

2029

4.30 17th June Is Ladies Night Handicap Stakes 3yo+ 0-70 (E) [70]
£3653 £1124 £562 **5f str** **Good/Firm 22** **+01 Fast** Stands Side

1867* **PARKSIDE PURSUIT 7** [14] J M Bradley 6-9-9 (65) C J Davies(7) 4/1: 0200-011: Mid-div stands side, prog & led that group dist, rdn out: nicely bckd: eff at 5/6f on fir, & gd grnd, prob any trk: in great heart. 73
1765 **KANGARILLA ROAD 12** [5] Mrs J R Ramsden 5-9-10 (66) T Quinn 3/1 FAV: 6/600-002: Al prom far side & rdn/led that group ins last, not pace of wnr stands side: nicely bckd: come to hand, h'capped to win. 1 70+
1794 **TALLY 10** [15] M J Polglase 4-8-12 (54) J Fanning 25/1: 0000603: Led stands side till dist, kept on well: drpd in trip, an imprvd eff: eff at 5/6f: nicely h'capped, could find similar: see 1536. ½ 56
1627 **SOAKED 19** [2] D W Chapman 11-9-3 bl (59) A Culhane 20/1: 4023404: Led far side, hdd dist & no extra cl-home: see 335. nk 60
1908 **PIRLIE HILL 5** [16]4-8-3 (45) R Ffrench 16/1: 00-34025: Prom, short of room over 1f out, kept on: mdn. shd 46
1765 **BRIGADORE 12** [6]5-9-10 (66) T Hamilton(3) 7/1: 0000-636: Chsd ldrs far side, not pace to chall. ½ 65
1873 **COLLEGE MAID 7** [10]7-8-6 VIS (48) J Currie(7) 12/1: 06-40607: Prom stands side, onepace ins last: vis. hd 46
1600 **BLUEBERRY RHYME 20** [9]5-9-4 vis (60) D Nolan(3) 25/1: 2210158: Prom stands side, no extra dist. ¾ 56
1797 **VIJAY 10** [12]5-9-1 (57) A Mullen(7) 16/1: 0306029: Prom stands side 4f: btr 1797. 2 47
1898 **XANADU 6** [13]8-8-11 p (53) R Winston 16/1: 00-02000: 10th: Prom stands side till dist: btr 1508. ¾ 41
1392 **SEA FERN 31** [7]3-8-3 (53) P Hanagan 33/1: 000-50: 11th: b g Petong - Duxyana (Cyrano de Bergerac) Outpcd far side, nvr a factor: lightly rcd & unplcd '03 (rtd 59, mdn). nk 40
1457 **PETERS CHOICE 27** [4]3-9-5 (69) T Eaves(3) 25/1: 011-0050: 12th: Chsd ldrs far side 4f: btr 1457 (g/s). ¾ 54
1532 **PERCY DOUGLAS 23** [11]4-8-8 vis (50) Ann Stokell 66/1: 63-00000: 13th: Dwelt, prom stands side 3f. 1 32
1886 **DUNN DEAL 6** [8]4-9-9 (65) T E Durcan 10/1: 3012050: 14th: Outpcd far side: btr 1442 (fibresand). ½ 45
1898 **SNOW BUNTING 6** [3]6-8-8 (50) Leanne Kershaw(7) 7/1: 560-0030: 15th: Outpcd, nvr a factor far side. 2½ 23
4502} **NORTHERN SVENGALI 241** [1]8-7-12 t (40) J McAuley 66/1: 054000-0: 16th: Reared start & sn bhd. 3½ 3
16 Ran Time 57.67 (1.07) Owned: Mr J M Bradley Trained: Chepstow

2030

5.00 Hansel Foundation Handicap Stakes 3yo+ 0-80 (D) [80]
£5473 £1684 £842 **1m2f** **Good/Firm 22** **-50 Slow** Inside

800 **HIAWATHA 84** [2] P A Blockley 5-9-5 (71) D Nolan(3) 9/1: 1-413001: Made all, dictated pace, pressed 2f out, carried right but held on well for press ins last: slow time: abs: eff at 9/12f on fast & fibresand: can go well fresh: tough & genuine, enjoyed forcing tactics today under a well judged ride: see 423. 74
1776 **CHAMPAIN SANDS 12** [1] W M Brisbourne 5-8-5 (57) B Swarbrick(5) 4/1 CO FAV: 0062-342: Trkd ldrs, pressed wnr from 2f out, hung right ins last, just held: bckd: acts on fast, gd/soft & fibresand. ½ 59
1796 **EASIBET DOT NET 10** [3] I Semple 4-8-6 BL (58) R Winston 5/1: 215-4023: Cl-up, onepace when carried right ins last: op 9/2, fair run in first time blnks: see 1796 & 75. shd 60
1781 **LEIGHTON 11** [7] J D Bethell 4-10-0 (80) T Quinn 4/1 CO FAV: 3403-054: b g Desert Story - Lady Fern (Old Vic) Rear, styd on onepace, not able to chall: nicely bckd tho' op 3/1: lightly rcd '03, plcd fnl start (rtd 84, h'cap): auct mdn scorer '02: winning form at 7.4f, stays gall 10.3f well: acts on firm & gd grnd, stiff/gall or sharpish trk. 1 Sep'02 Beve 7.4gd 87- E: 2 Aug'02 Ripo 6fm 88- E: 2½ 78
1504 **SKIDDAW JONES 25** [5]4-8-0 (52) R Ffrench 12/1: 54000-05: b g Emperor Jones - Woodrising (Nomination) Chsd ldrs, no extra dist: reapp wnr '03 (h'cap, rtd 61 at best, h'cap): unplcd '02 (rtd 51, mdn): winning form at 9f, stays a slowly run 10.5f: acts on fast & gd grnd, gall trks: has gone well fresh. ½ 49

AYR   THURSDAY 27.05.04   Lefthand, Galloping Track

2 Aug'03 Ayr 9.1gd 56-54 E: 1 Jun'03 Ayr 9.1g/f 55-46 E:
1388 **STING LIKE A BEE 31** [6]5-7-12 (1oh) (49) N Mackay(3) 4/1 CO FAV: 1024466: In tch, onepace fnl 2f: ½   46
prob would have preferred stronger gall: see 924 & 464.
1776 **LENNEL 12** [4]6-9-0 bl (66) T E Durcan 6/1: 14-50407: Held up in tch, btn dist: see 1388 & 1128.   1¼   60
7 Ran   Time 2m 11.64(7.24)   Owned: Mr Nigel Shields   Trained: Southwell

BATH   THURSDAY 27.05.04   Lefthand, Turning Track With Uphill Finish

Official Going Firm

2031   2.20 European Breeders Fund Maiden Stakes Fillies 3yo (D)
£6929 £2132 £1066   1m5y   Firm 10   -31 Slow   Inside

4973} **PEERESS 208** [3] Sir Michael Stoute 3-8-11 K Fallon 10/11 FAV: 3-1: ch f Pivotal - Noble One   79+
(Primo Dominie) Dwelt, sn keen trkg ldrs & led over 1f out, edged out to assert, readily: hvly bckd on reapp:
fills mdn plcd sole '03 start (rtd 81): stays 1m well on fm & gd, further shld suit: goes well fresh: progress in h'caps.
3789} **GRAND APOLLO 279** [5] J H M Gosden 3-8-11 F Norton 20/1: 6-2: ch f Grand Lodge - Narva (Nashwan) 1¼   71
Slow away, rear, keeping on when short of room ins last, nrst fin, nvr threat: unplcd sole '03 start (fills mdn,
rtd 73): half-sister to a 1m wnr: eff at 1m on fm, 10f will suit: gd run, win a race.
1846 **ALL QUIET 8** [9] R Hannon 3-8-11 (67) R Hughes 3/1: 000-323: Led, strongly pressed over 3f out &   1¼   68
hdd over 1f out, no extra when hmpd ins last & lost 2nd: bckd, op 7/2: styd longer 1m trip: handles firm & fast.
1846 **GIRL WARRIOR 8** [10] P F I Cole 3-8-11 S Drowne 12/1: 3-64: Chsd ldrs, kept on onepace, no   1   66
threat: stays 1m & handles firm & gd grnd: see 1846.
1904 **IPHIGENIA 6** [11]3-8-11 (50) R Miles(3) 66/1: 23000-05: Chsd ldrs halfway, no impress fnl 2f: see 1904.   1¼   63$
4610} **LA PROFESSORESSA 234** [4]3-8-11 (66) R Havlin 50/1: 03005-6: b f Cadeaux Genereux - Fellwah   ¾   62
(Sadler's Wells) Mid-div, not pace to chall: reapp: unplcd '03 (rtd 68, mdn): dam related to a high-class miler:
prob stays a sharp 1m, handles fast & gd grnd.
1810 **PALABELLE 10** [6]3-8-11 Martin Dwyer 10/1: 07: Chsd ldrs 6f.   ½   61
1733 **FIRE FINCH 13** [1]3-8-11 S Hitchcott(3) 20/1: 668: Dwelt, bhd, no impress.   1¼   58
1280 **HSI WANG MU 37** [7]3-8-11 (47) J F Egan 100/1: 00-25059: Mid-div, btn 2f out, drpd in trip.   ½   57$
4870} **FATAYAAT 216** [8]3-8-11 W Supple 41/1: 0-0: 10th: Trkd ldr, ch 4f out, wknd over 1f out, reapp.   1¼   54
1527 **KERRISTINA 24** [2]3-8-11 C Catlin 100/1: 00: 11th: Al bhd, no ch fnl 2f.   14   29
11 Ran   Time 1m 41.59 (3.29)   Owned: Cheveley Park Stud   Trained: Newmarket

2032   2.50 Betfred Com In-Running Classified Claiming Stakes 3yo+ 0-60 (F)
£3101 £886 £443   1m5y   Firm 10   -13 Slow   Inside

1578 **DOCTORED 21** [12] B A Pearce 3-8-13 p (60) B Reilly(3) 16/1: 0461101: Prom, narrow lead ins last,   61
all out: clmd by P D Evans for 10,000: eff at 7f/1m on firm, gd/soft & fibresand: likes claim grade: see 1440.
1045 **MARNIE 54** [2] J Akehurst 7-9-4 (51) C Catlin 7/1: 00-01302: Chsd ldrs & rdn to chall over 1f   hd   53
out, narrow lead bef dist till ins last, just held: 8 wk abs: gd run: see 845.
792 **LORD CHAMBERLAIN 85** [8] J M Bradley 11-9-11 bl (53) R L Moore 11/1: 4402203: Mid-div, kept on for   nk   59$
press, just held cl-home: 12 wk abs, gd turf return: see 379.
1938 **ESPADA 4** [7] J A Osborne 8-9-1 BL (58) Martin Dwyer 10/1: 2-000044: Led & sn clr, hdd bef dist &   1¾   46
no extra: first time blnks, qck reapp, rcd freely: see 216.
1597 **GO GREEN 20** [3]3-8-2 (59) F P Ferris(3) 12/1: 00005: ch f Environment Friend - Sandra Mac (Marju)   shd   45
Rear, kept on late, not able to chall: return to 10f & poss h'cap company may suit: handles fm: unplcd prev.
i1642 **MUQTADI 17** [9]6-9-1 (45) K May(7) 8/1: 0045406: Bhd, late gains, nrst fin: see 717.   nk   45
1695 **EVA PERON 15** [5]4-8-12 P (45) C Haddon(7) 20/1: 00-00607: Mid-div, not pace to threaten: chkpces.   1½   39
1128 **LEITRIM ROCK 45** [16]4-9-1 (52) S Whitworth 28/1: 03000-08: b g Barathea - Kilshanny (Groom   3½   35
Dancer) V slow away & bhd, late gains: jumps fit (no form): dual AW h'cap rnr-up '03 for D Arbuthnot, turf h'cap
plcd (rtd 38): juv nov stks wnr '02: eff around 1m, winning form at 5f: acts on fast, soft & fibresand, gall or
sharp trk: best without cheek pieces/blnks: lost ch start today, could do better in similar.
2 Mar'03 Ling 8ap 55a-53 E: 2 Feb'03 Ling 7ap 55a-53 E: 2 Jan'03 Sout 8af 55a-53 G: 1 May'02 Wind 5sft 82- D:
1792 **MOBO BACO 10** [15]7-9-7 (57) S Drowne 7/2 FAV: 030-4409: Mid-div, wide 3f out, no impress: see 452.   1½   38
913 **DARK SHAH 64** [1]4-9-1 p (55) L Keniry(3) 10/1: 4000-500: 10th: Mid-div, hdwy 3f out, no prog dist: abs.   ½   31
2085} **LEGION OF HONOUR 350** [13]5-9-11 (60) A Quinn(5) 50/1: 260/000-0: 11th: Al bhd, reapp.   ½   40
1938 **LIGHT DALSACE 4** [4]4-9-4 (52) I Mongan 6/1: 0054-020: 12th: Chsd ldrs 6f: qck reapp: btr 1938 (7f).   ¾   32
851 **EMPEROR CAT 74** [6]3-8-5 bl (54) Dean McKeown 33/1: 05-23000: 13th: Al bhd, abs: btr 661 (7f, AW).   8   15
469 **TOBEROE COMMOTION 125** [11]6-9-1 BL (45) R Havlin 66/1: 40006-00: 14th: Al bhd: blnks: jumps abs.   7   1
1656 **CHANDELIER 17** [10]4-9-5 p (45) M Savage(5) 20/1: 5360320: 15th: Dwelt & al rear: btr 1656 & 1378.   4   0
189 **BUCHANAN STREET 166** [14]3-8-7 bl (56) K Fallon 66/1: 0: 0206-0: 16th: Al bhd, 6 mth abs.   15   0
16 Ran   Time 1m 40.14 (1.84)   Owned: Mr T M J Keep   Trained: Lingfield

2033   3.20 Betfred Com Now Online Median Auction Maiden Stakes Fillies 2yo (F)
£2989 £854 £427   5f11y   Firm 10   +01 Fast   Far Side

DONT TELL MUM 0 [7] R Hannon 2-8-11 R Hughes 1/1: 1: b f Dansili - Zinnia (Zilzal) Prom & led   87
over 2f out, just hdd ins last but rallied gamely for press to prevail nr line: op 12/1, gd juv time: 20.000gns Feb
first foal, dam an unplcd juv & a half-sister to a 5f juv wnr: eff at 5f, will get further: acts on firm grnd & a
stiff/turning trk: goes well fresh: likeable attitude, potentially useful.
ROODEYE 0 [1] R F Johnson Houghton 2-8-11 K Fallon 4/1: 2: b f Inchinor - Roo (Rudimentary)   hd   86
Led/dsptd lead throughout, narrow lead ins last till close home: op 3/1: Feb first foal, dam a useful sprinter:
eff at 5f, shld get further: acts on fm grnd & a stiff/turning trk: fine start, win sn.
1716 **ANGEL SPRINTS 14** [2] L G Cottrell 2-8-11 A Daly 9/2: 33: Cl-up, not pace to chall from dist: 1½   81
op 13/2, clr rem: prob imprvd from debut: handles fm & fast: type to find a race sn: see 1716.
1717 **BRAG 14** [8] R Charlton 2-8-11 S Drowne 8/11 FAV: 24: Cl-up, switched & btn bef dist: bckd, see 1717.   4   69
MADAM CAVERSFIELD 0 [4]2-8-11 P Dobbs 33/1: 5: b f Pursuit of Love - Madam Alison (Puissance)   3   60
Slow away & bhd, late gains, nvr a threat: longer priced stablemate of wnr: March first foal, dam a 6f juv wnr &

subs useful 1m h'cap performer: crying out for 6f+, likely improver.
1805　**MS POLLY GARTER 10** [3]2-8-11　R L Moore　25/1: 406: Chsd ldrs, no impress from halfway.　　　　6　44
1640　**MUESTRA 17** [5]2-8-11　R Havlin　100/1: 0007: Sn rdn & outpcd, nvr a factor.　　　　1¼　40
　　　　INDIAN PEARL 0 [6]2-8-11　M Savage(4) 66/1: 8: Went right start & sn outpcd.　　　　2　34
8 Ran　Time 1m 0.83 (0.53)　Owned: Mrs Teresa M Moriarty　Trained: Marlborough

---

2034　　3.50 Betfred Sprint Series Qualifier A Handicap Stakes Fillies 3yo+ 0-75 (E)　　　**[69]**
　　　　£4479 £1378 £689　　**5f161y**　　Firm 10　　+04 Fast　Far Side

1787　**BOAVISTA 10** [9] P D Evans 4-8-13 (54) R Havlin　11/2: 5344221: Made all, drvn out: best time of　63
day: first career success at 23rd attempt, plcd numerous times prev: eff at 5/6f, stays 7f: acts on firm, gd/soft
& both AWs: eff with/without t-strap: enjoyed forcing tactics today: well deserved success: see 593.
1578　**GLENCOE SOLAS 21** [5] S Kirk 4-9-10 BL (65) P Dobbs　11/2: 5600-642: Chsd ldr from over 1f out,　　　1¾　70
kept on but al held: first time blnks, gd run: acts on firm & gd, prob handles soft: both wins at 6f.
1729　**AESCULUS 13** [3] L M Cumani 3-9-3 (67) K Fallon　6/1: 051-053: Pushed along & bhd, kept on wide　　　1　69
late, no threat: handles firm & polytrack: return to 6f+ will suit: see 1729 & 49 (6f).
913　**LILY OF THE GUILD 64** [7] W S Kittow 5-8-13 (54) I Mongan　6/1: 60-00244: Missed break, sn in tch　　　¾　54
racing keenly, outpcd over 1f out: 2 mth abs, op 15/2: handles firm, gd/soft & polytrack: see 270.
1540　**YOMALO 23** [1]4-9-10 (65) R Miles(3) 4/1 FAV: 1220-005: ch f Woodborough - Alkariyh (Alydar) Bhd　　nk　64
& sn pushed along, keeping on when hmpd ins last, nrst fin: op 13/2, closer with a clr passage: mdn & h'cap wnr
'03, AW mdn rnr-up: eff at 5/6f, stays 7f: acts on fibresand & fast, any trk. 2 Oct'03 Wind 6g/f 69-66 E:
2 Sep'03 Pont 6g/f 67-66 D: 1 Sep'03 Ling 6g/f 67-62 E: 1 Aug'03 Beve 5g/f 63-(57) D: 2 Jun'03 Sout 7af 55a- F:
1787*　**NANNA 10** [6]3-8-4 (6ex) (54) J Mackay　5/1: 2030216: Dwelt, sn chsd wnr, no impress fnl 2f: beat　¾　51
today's wnr in 1787 (clmr, 5f, made all).
1820　**ANNIJAZ 9** [2]7-9-2 (57) R L Moore　6/1: 060-2247: Rear, nvr able to chall: btr 1540 (soft).　　　1½　49
1710　**SEA JADE 14** [4]5-8-4 (45) J F Egan　11/1: 460-4228: Chsd wnr, wknd qckly 2f out: btr 1710 & 1548.　3½　26
8 Ran　Time 1m 09.42 (0.31)　Owned Mr D Healy　Trained: Abergavenny

---

2035　　4.20 Betfred In Shops On Phone & Online Handicap Stakes 4yo+ 0-70 (E)　　　**[70]**
　　　　£3643 £1121 £561　　**2m1f34y**　　Firm 10　　-31 Slow　　Inside

1772　**TREASURE TRAIL 12** [6] S Kirk 5-9-9 (65) J F Egan　6/1: 000-5001: b g Millkom - Forever Shineing　69
(Glint of Gold) Held up, switched wide & hdwy to lead dist, rdn & styd on strongly: 03/04 mdn hdle wnr (rtd 96h,
2m, fast & gd/soft): h'cap rnr-up on the level '03: dual h'cap wnr '02: eff at 11/14f, now stays 2m1f well: acts
on firm & gd/soft grnd, prob any trk: unexposed at this trip. 2 Jul'03 Asco 12g/s 83-80 C:
2 Jul'02 Sand 14g/f 82-80 D: 1 Jul'02 Folk 12g/s 80-71 E: 1 Jul'02 Bath 11.6g/s 68-65 E:
2 Jun'02 Brig 11.8g/s 68-61 E:
1373　**DELTA FORCE 32** [4] P A Blockley 5-8-7 (49) Dean McKeown　5/1: 2144532: Chsd ldrs & ch 3f out, led　1½　50
over 2f out till dist, not pace of wnr: op 4/1: acts on firm, gd & likes fibresand: see 456.
　　　　DONALD 340 [7] M Pitman 4-8-12 (56) R Hughes　8/1: 146/124-3: b g Enjoy Plan - Dahira (Dakota)　1　56
Rear, kept on for press fnl 2f, not able to chall front pair: Brit bow, 1 yr abs: ex-Polish, '03 wnr in native
land: a wnr at up to 1m prev, stays 2m1f on this evidence: handles firm & soft grnd: encouraging start.
477　**NOBLE CALLING 124** [5] R J Hodges 7-8-10 (52) S Drowne　6/1: 60006-03: b c Caller I D -　　　dht　52
Specificity (Alleged) Rear, prog when hmpd 2f out, kept on, not able to threaten front pair: ddhtd for 3rd: jumps
fit (nov hdle wnr, rtd 118h, 2m/2m6.5f, fast & gd/soft): dual amat h'cap wnr on the level '03: thrice h'cap rnr-up
'02: eff btwn 9f/2m1f, well suited by strongly run 10f last term: acts on firm & gd grnd, prob any trk.
1 Jun'03 Newb 10.0g/f 57-52 E: 1 May'03 Bath 10.2g/f 56-48 F: 2 Aug'02 Chep 8gd 52-49 E: 2 Jul'02 Bath 10.2g/f 50- F:
2 Jun'02 Good 9g/f 57-47 E: 1 Jul'01 Good 8gd 60-56 F:
1291*　**SARIBA 36** [2]5-7-12 (40) Hayley Turner(5) 9/2: 410-0615: Chsd ldr, short of room over 1f out &　　1½　38
lost place, kept on late: closer with a clr run: fair turf return after 1291 (AW seller).
1789　**SASHAY 10** [3]6-8-3 (45) J Mackay　100/30 FAV: 34-52036: Chsd ldrs, onepace for press fnl 2f: op 5/1.　2　41
1271　**HENRY ISLAND 37** [8]11-9-12 (68) Martin Dwyer　15/2: 14443-57: Keen & chsd ldrs, btn over 1f out.　1　63
1693　**NORTH POINT 15** [1]6-8-9 BL (51) R Miles(3) 16/1: 0/0666-08: Led till over 2f out: op 12/1, blnks.　½　26
8 Ran　Time 3m 47.88 (6.98)　Owned: Mr T Neill & Mrs John Lee　Trained: Upper Lambourn

---

2036　　4.50 Betfred Com Early Prices From 9 A M Handicap Stakes 3yo+ 0-70 (E)　　　**[84]**
　　　　£3634 £1118 £559　　**1m2f46y**　　Firm 10　　-02 Slow　　Inside

1647　**NANTUCKET SOUND 17** [8] M C Pipe 3-8-11 (67) K Fallon　5/2 JT FAV: 634-041: Pushed along in tch,　71
hdwy to lead dist, rdn out: first win: eff at 1m, imprvd for step up to 10f: acts on firm, soft & polytrack.
1913　**KARAOKE 5** [2] S Kirk 4-9-9 (65) J F Egan　9/2: 1005542: Rear, prog/short of room 2f out, switched　　nk　69
& chall ins last, just held: qck reapp: acts on firm, gd & both AWs: see 803.
1899*　**VOICE MAIL 6** [4] A M Balding 5-10-3 (5ex) (73) L Keniry(3) 5/2 JT FAV: 50-00113: Rear, keeping on　1　76+
well when short of room dist, switched & styd on well nr line, shade unlucky: would have gone v close with a clr
passage: qck reapp under a 5lb pen: loves this trk, in fine form: see 1899 & 1792.
1650　**SKYLARKER 17** [5] W S Kittow 6-10-0 (70) I Mongan　9/1: 2330004: Chsd ldrs & led 6f out till dist,　½　72
no extra nr fin but clr of rem: imprvd eff with forcing tactics: see 273.
1618　**WANNA SHOUT 20** [11]6-9-2 (58) Lisa Jones(3) 20/1: 2121205: Rear, eff wide, no impress on ldrs.　7　51
1884　**NUZZLE 6** [3]4-8-5 (49) F Norton　10/1: 0005026: Chsd ldrs, btn dist: op 8/1: btr 1884.　4　34
1913　**CASTAIGNE 5** [7]5-9-1 (57) R Havlin　20/1: 020-0067: Chsd ldrs till over 1f out: qck reapp: see 101.　4　38
1913　**BILLY BATHWICK 5** [9]7-9-2 (58) R L Moore　14/1: 46553-08: Chsd ldrs till 2f out, qck reapp: see 1913.　¾　38
2152‡　**WOOD STREET 348** [6]5-9-2 (58) V Slattery　66/1: 400/000-9: b g Eagle Eyed - San Catrinia　　1¼　36
(Knesset) Al bhd: Flat reapp, jumps fit (unplcd, rtd 61h, h'cap): unplcd '03 on the level (lightly rcd, rtd 51a &
44, h'caps): mdn h'cap scorer '02 for Mrs A J Bowlby: eff at 1m/10f on firm, gd & polytrack, prob any trk.
1 Jul'02 Epso 65-(60): 2 Jun'02 Nott 8.2gd 60-58 E:
1736　**FACTUAL LAD 13** [10]6-9-12 (68) G Baker　20/1: 45110-00: 10th: Led till 6f out, btn 2f out: see 1736.　3　42
1643　**Mr Whizz 17** [12]7-7-13 (1ow)p(40) C Catlin　22/1:0　　1056　**Bowing 52** [1]4-9-4 (60) D Kinsella　40/1:0
12 Ran　Time 2m 07.22(1.22)　Owned: Mr T M Hely-Hutchinson　Trained: Wellington

Official Going GOOD/FIRM

2037   6.35 Buttercross Claiming Stakes 4yo+   (E)
£3731 £1148 £574   **1m4y**   **Good/Firm 38**   **-05 Slow**   Inside

1823 **BAILIEBOROUGH 10** [2] D Nicholls 5-9-2 vis (68) Alex Greaves 11/10 FAV: 0603401: Mid-div, prog   73+
halfway, styd on to lead dist, pushed clr fnl 1f, val 7L+: eff at 7f/8.5f on firm & gd/soft grnd: eff with a visor.
1681 **COUNTYKAT 16** [3] K R Burke 4-9-2 (68) Donna Bashton(7) 7/2: 630-6002: Handy, short of room bef 2f   5   61
out, switched & led over 1f out, hdd dist, no extra: btr 467.
      GOOD TIME BOBBY 0 [5] J O'Reilly 7-8-11 D Allan(3) 16/1: 3: b g Primitive Rising - Goodreda   3   50
(Good Times) Slow away, prog 3f out, no impress fnl 1f: Flat bow, unplcd sole 02/03 hdles start (rtd 65h, nov):
plcd fnl 01/02 hdles start (nov hdle, well btn, rtd 76h, G A Swinbank).
1425 **LORD CONYERS 30** [4] B Ellison 5-8-1 P (40) P Hanagan 15/2: 504/-0044: Handy over 5f, sn wknd.   6   28
1657 **DANCING KING 18** [1]8-8-6 (48) P Makin(4) 4/1: 0626255: Led, hdd dist, fdd: btr 1535 (hvy).   hd   32
      HOLDERNESS GIRL 2176 [6]11-8-1 (30) R Ffrench 50/1: 0000/////-6: b f Lapierre - Isobel's Choice dist 0
(Green God) Cl-up, wkng when short of room 2f out, sn btn: modest form over hdles & on Flat to date.
6 Ran   Time 1m 45.29 (3.49)   Owned: Middleham Park Racing XVIII   Trained: Thirsk

2038   7.05 Msk Handicap Stakes Fillies 3yo+ 0-70 (E)   [70]
£5603 £1724 £862   **1m2f6y**   **Good/Firm 38**   **-25 Slow**   Inside

1781 **GREY CLOUDS 12** [3] T D Easterby 4-9-13 (69) W Supple 11/2: 430-4201: Mid-div, prog halfway, styd   78
on to lead dist, rdn out: stays 13f, suited by 10f on fast & gd/soft grnd: likes a stiff trk.
1821* **OLIVIA ROSE 10** [6] J Pearce 5-10-0 (5ex) (70) J Quinn 5/1: 52-01312: Mid-div, prog halfway, led 1¾   75
well over 1f out, hdd dist, kept on, not pace of wnr: top-weight: in gd form, see 1821.
1796 **UNTIDY DAUGHTER 11** [2] B Ellison 5-8-10 p (52) T Eaves(3) 14/1: 50/00-503: Rear, prog 3f out, styd 2   54
on ins fnl 1f, nrst fin: acts on fast & soft grnd: see 1307.
2047} **DREAMS FORGOTTEN 353** [4] G G Margarson 4-9-1 (57) A McCarthy 40/1: 00/3200-4: b f Victory Note - shd 58
Sevens Are Wild (Petorius) Led, hdd over 1f out, no extra: reapp: plcd on first 2 of only 4 '03 starts (h'caps,
rtd 60, S Kirk): eff at 7f/1m, poss stays 10f: acts on fast & gd/soft grnd: encouraging eff here for new stable &
shld find a mod race. 2 May'03 Wind 8.3g/s 60-56 E:
1695 **GOT TO BE CASH 16** [5]5-8-10 (52) D Allan(3) 11/1: 60-42105: Rear, prog 3f out, kept on ins fnl 1f.   ¾   52
1681 **ZAN LO 16** [7]4-9-2 (58) P Hanagan 40/1: 2516-006: Rear, prog 3f out, styd on fnl 1f: btr 1681.   ¾   56
1082 **DANCE PARTY 51** [9]4-9-7 P (63) K Fallon 11/2: 0-330047: Handy, under press & wkng when short of   1   60
room bef 1f out: 7 wk abs & cheek pieces: btr 1082.
1602 **ODABELLA 21** [12]4-9-12 (68) Lisa Jones(3) 9/1: 2340-308: Held up, nvr nrr than mid-div: btr 1131 (reapp)nk 64
1921 **TRANSCENDANTALE 6** [11]6-8-5 (47) J Fanning 14/1: 00-23569: Chsd ldrs 7f, sn wknd: qck reapp.   3   38
1834 **INFIDELITY 10** [10]3-8-6 (62) C Catlin 14/1: 0-600060: 10th: Handy 1m, sn wknd: btr 1834.   shd 52
1821 **EAST RIDING 10** [8]4-8-3 (45) Ann Stokell 50/1: 5-566300: 11th: Cl-up 7f, sn wknd: btr 1536.   2   32
1724* **ESTIMATE 14** [13]4-9-6 vis (62) Paul Eddery 14/1: 64-00010: 12th: Chsd ldrs 7f, wknd: btr 1724.   5   41
1899 **HOLLY ROSE 7** [1]5-8-12 p (54) Hayley Turner(5) 9/2 FAV: 100-0240: 13th: Held up, prog halfway, fdd   7   22
3f out.
13 Ran   Time 2m 14.4 (6.3)   Owned: Vintage Partners   Trained: Malton

2039   7.35 Youngsters Conditions Stakes 2yo   (C)
£9210 £3494 £1747   **6f**   **Good/Firm 38**   **-25 Slow**   Inside

      TONY JAMES 0 [5] C E Brittain 2-8-8 D Holland 6/1: 1: b c Xaar - Sunset Ridge (Green Tune)   102+
Prom, led just ins fnl 2f, pushed out, val 2L+: debut: Feb first foal, cost E22,000: sire Gr 1 wnr as a juv: eff
at 6f, further will suit: acts on fast grnd & goes well fresh: win more races.
1149 **DARIO GEE GEE 45** [6] K A Ryan 2-8-13 N Callan 6/4: 122: Keen handy, prog & ev ch dist, sn   1   100
edged left & not pace of wnr: clr rem: 6 wk abs: eff at 5/6f on fast & gd/soft grnd: fine run in defeat conceding
weight to wnr & can sn return to winning ways: see 1149.
1249* **SOCIETY MUSIC 39** [4] M Dods 2-8-8 L Enstone(3) 100/30: 13: Handy 4f, sn no extra: btr 1249 (5f, hvy). 6   77
1874* **INDIBRAUN 8** [3] P C Haslam 2-8-13 G Faulkner 3/1: 514: Led, hdd just ins fnl 2f, no extra: btr 1874. shd 81
      FOREST VIKING 0 [2]2-8-8 T Eaves(3) 50/1: 5: b g Orpen - Berhala (Doyoun) Slow away, al in   11   43
rear: debut: 8.000gns: half-brother to a couple of wnrs abroad: sire Gr 1 sprint wnr as a juv.
      MIDNIGHT IN MOSCOW 0 [1]2-8-8 Rory Moore(7) 25/1: 6: b c Soviet Star - Solar Display (Diesis)   7   22
Handy over halfway, jinked & hit rail 2f out, not recover on debut: March foal, cost E25,000: dam plcd abroad.
6 Ran   Time 1m 17.92 (3.82)   Owned: Mr A J Richards   Trained: Newmarket

2040   8.05 Sky Bet Press Red To Bet Handicap Stakes 3yo 0-85 (D)   [92]
£10712 £3296 £1648   **1m4y**   **Good/Firm 38**   **+09 Fast**   Inside

4730*}**PENRITH 227** [3] M Johnston 3-9-7 (85) J Fanning 11/2: 1-1: b c Singspiel - Queen Mat (Fairy   91
King) Held up, hdwy inner from over 2f out & rdn/chall ins last, just prevailed in a driving fin, all out: reapp &
h'cap bow: sole start mdn wnr '03: dam a 1m French wnr, sire top-class at mid-dists: eff at 7f/1m, will get
further: acts on fast grnd, stiff/undul & gall trks: goes v well fresh & can force the pace: type to progress.
1 Oct'03 Leic 7.0g/f 82- D:
1813 **TRANQUIL SKY 10** [5] N A Callaghan 3-9-5 (83) K Fallon 5/2 FAV: 310-0052: Chsd ldrs halfway,   shd 88
pushed along & hdwy over 2f out, rdn & hung badly left from over 1f out, narrow lead ins last, just hdd line in a
thrilling fin: deserves to find similar sn: see 1813.
1770 **ALEKHINE 13** [4] P W Harris 3-9-7 (85) P Hanagan 10/1: 16-23: Dwelt, rear, switched wide & styd   1   88
on well for press fnl 2f, not pace to chall front pair: set plenty to do but styd this longer 10f trip well: fine
h'cap bow, lightly raced & shld be wng sn: see 1770.
1877 **WEET A HEAD 8** [6] R Hollinshead 3-8-13 (77) W Supple 16/1: 3-535634: Trkd ldrs, rdn & chall over 2½   75
2f out, not pace of front pair when badly squeezed out ins last, no extra: shade closer with clr run.
1784 **MY PARIS 12** [11]3-8-9 (73) N Callan 16/1: 0-32225: Trkd ldrs, rdn & no extra when short of room   1¼   68

606

PONTEFRACT   FRIDAY 28.05.04   Lefthand, Undulating Track, Stiff Uphill Finish

ins last: worth another try over this longer 10f trip: h'cap bow tonight: see 1784, 1473 & 1196.

1496 **GRANSTON** 26 [1]3-9-0 (78) P Robinson 4/1: 401-3166: Sn handy, no extra when hmpd ins last.   ½   72
1879 **REIDIES CHOICE** 8 [7]3-8-8 (72) M Fenton 10/1: 0000-027: Held up, hdwy wide to press ldrs 2f out,   1   64
sn rdn & no extra: appeared not to see out this longer 10f trip: of more interest at 1m in similar: see 1879.
1496 **MOUNT VETTORE** 26 [2]3-9-2 (80) D Holland 8/1: 5-12008: Bhd, little hdwy, no threat: btr 955 (7f).   shd   71
1770 **HEVERSHAM** 13 [10]3-9-0 (78) A Culhane 33/1: 412009: Sn led, rdn & edged right over 1f out, hdd   3½   62
dist & fdd: prob much another try over longer 10f trip, had to work hard from outside stall to dominate: see 694.
1707 **INCHLOSS** 15 [9]3-8-13 (77) J Quinn 12/1: 04120: 10th: Mid-div, eff wide 2f out, sn btn: btr 1707.   5   51
1163 **WINGS OF MORNING** 44 [8]3-8-3 (67) J Bramhill 50/1: 02-15630: 11th: Chsd ldrs, fdd fnl 3f: 6 wk abs.   5   31
11 Ran   Time 1m 44.14 (2.34)   Owned: Sheikh Mohammed   Trained: Middleham

---

2041   8.35 St John Ambulance Handicap Stakes 3yo+ 0-70 (E)   [68]
£5018 £1544 £772   1m4f8y   Good/Firm 38   -06 Slow   Inside

1543 **RED FOREST** 24 [4] J Mackie 5-8-8 t (48) Dale Gibson 9/1: 560-3161: Chsd ldrs, rdn & hdwy to chall   60
over 1f out, duelled with rnr-up & asserted for press fnl 100y: eff at 1m, now suited by 12f on fast, gd &
fibresand, below best on soft latest: handles a stiff or sharp trk: see 1342 & 1197.
1875 **NIGHT SIGHT** 8 [6] Mrs S Lamyman 7-9-13 (67) K Fallon 10/1: 50004-02: b g Eagle Eyed - El Hamo   2   73
(Search For Gold) Rear, smooth hdwy to lead over 1f out, sn duelled with wnr & no extra well ins last: clr of rem:
h'cap rnr-up in '03, AW h'cap unplcd (rtd 70a): landed 5 h'caps in '02 for M C Chapman: suited by 10/12f on firm,
gd/soft & fibresand, any trk: loves Doncaster: best without blnks: well h'capped, spot on back at Town Moor.
2 Jun'03 Donc 12fm 70-69 D: 1 Jun'02 Donc 12g/f 86-76 D: 1 Jun'02 Donc 12fm 75-65 D: 1 May'02 Donc 10.2fm 66-58 C:
1 Apr'02 Catt 12g/f 63-53 D: 2 Apr'02 Sout 11gd 55-52 G: 1 Feb'02 Sout 11af 87a-78 D: 2 Jan'02 Sout 12af 81a-77 D:
1 Mar'01 Sout 12af 88a-81 C: 1 Feb'01 Sout 11af 89a-73 D: 1 Dec'00 Sout 7af 61a- D:
1469 **BLACKTHORN** 28 [7] Mrs J R Ramsden 5-9-4 (58) D Holland 6/1: 2002-403: Bhd, hdwy when hmpd over   5   57
1f out, switched & kept on, no threat: see 918.
1830 **RED RIVER REBEL** 11 [11] J R Norton 6-9-4 (58) Darren Williams 25/1: 26340-04: Chsd ldr & led   3   52
over 2f out till over 1f out, no extra bef dist: loves Beverley: see 1830.
1875 **SWYNFORD PLEASURE** 8 [2]8-8-13 (53) D Allan(3) 11/2: 00050-25: Held up, eff fnl 3f, held dist.   1¼   45
1636 **COMMEMORATION DAY** 20 [1]3-8-7 (64) R Winston 8/1: 60-06: b g Daylami - Bequeath (Lyphard)   nk   55
Mid-div, not able to chall fnl 3f on h'cap bow: unplcd '03 (lightly rcd, rtd 79, debut): half-brother to wnrs at
7f/1m, sire might prove ideal.
1923 **BRAMANTINO** 6 [5]4-9-4 bl (58) P Hanagan 10/1: 5310257: Keen early, trkd ldrs, outpcd fnl 3f: btr 1034.   shd   48
4704} **TASNEEF** 229 [10]5-9-9 (63) J P Guillambert(3) 40/1: 026140-8: b g Gulch - Min Alhawa (Riverman)   6   44
Keen & sn led till over 2f out, fdd: 5 mth jumps abs (plcd, rtd 82h, mdn hdle): h'cap scorer '03 on the level,
disapp in blnks: mdn wnr for M P Tregoning in '02: loves to race with/force the pace at 12f on firm or gd/soft.
1 Aug'03 Folk 12g/f 67-59 E: 2 Jun'03 Folk 12fm 59-60 F: 2 Jul'02 Asco 12g/f 81-81 D: 1 Jun'02 Ripo 12.2g/f 81- D:
1875* **MARITIME BLUES** 8 [8]4-9-9 (5ex) (63) M Fenton 3/1 J FAV: 60-00019: Mid-div, rdn & btn 3f out.   ¾   43
1469* **ISAAF** 28 [9]5-9-10 (64) P Makin(5) 9/2 J FAV: 02-12110: 10th: Mid-div, no prog fnl 2f: btr 1469 (14f, soft).   2½   40
1875 **MICHAELS DREAM** 8 [3]5-8-0 bl (40) J McAuley 16/1: 300-6330: 11th: Held up wide, eff 3f out, sn btn.   10   0
11 Ran   Time 2m 39.45 (5.35)   Owned: Mr P Riley   Trained: Church Broughton

---

2042   9.05 Barbican Maiden Stakes 3yo (D)
£5616 £1728 £864   6f   Good/Firm 38   +02 Fast   Inside

1178 **EMTILAAK** 43 [5] B Hanbury 3-9-0 (78) W Supple 13/8 FAV: 023-231: Trkd ldr & led halfway, clr   79
over 1f out, readily: 6 wk abs: poss stays 1m, well suited tonight by forcing tactics at 6f: acts on fast, gd &
polytrack, stiff/undul or sharp trk: could make mark in h'cap company.
3423} **WRENLANE** 296 [4] R A Fahey 3-9-0   P Hanagan 16/1: 30-2: ch g Fraam - Hi Hoh (Fayruz) Held up,   5   65
styd on to take 2nd ins last, nvr a threat to wnr: reapp: lightly rcd '03, mdn unplcd (rtd 73, auct mdn): brother
to a 5/7f wnr Zinging: eff over a stiff 6f, handles fast grnd: qual for h'caps.
1281 **FOUR KINGS** 38 [3] J M P Eustace 3-9-0 T J Tate 9/1: 503: Rear, styd on fnl 2f, nrst fin, nvr a   nk   64
threat: qual for h'caps, 7f could suit.
1829 **LASKA** 10 [6] M J Wallace 3-8-9 K Fallon 100/30: 44: br f Fasliyev - Dacian (Diesis) Held up,   hd   58
eff to chase wnr over 1f out, hung badly left & no impress from dist: dam unplcd at 6f/1m.
1525} **FIREBIRD RISING** 379 [7]3-8-9 D Holland 5/2: 3-5: b f Stravinsky - Capable (Capote) Chsd ldrs,   6   40
btn/eased over 1f out: reapp: 3rd of 6 sole start '03 (mdn, rtd 81): half-sister to a 7f juv wnr.
1636 **GREY ORCHID** 20 [1]3-8-9 T Eaves(3) 50/1: 00-06: Led till hdd halfway, sn btn.   6   22
ESTOILLE 0 [2]3-8-9 J Quinn 50/1: 7: Chsd ldrs, outpcd from halfway on debut.   2   16
7 Ran   Time 1m 16.27(2.17)   Owned: Mr Hamdan Al Maktoum   Trained: Newmarket

---

BRIGHTON   FRIDAY 28.05.04   Lefthand, V Sharp, Undulating Track

Official Going Firm

2043   2.10 E B F /Yell Ltd Median Auction Maiden Stakes 2yo (E)
£3406 £1048 £524   5f213y rnd   Good/Firm 26   -15 Slow   Inside

1780 **DAHTEER** 12 [1] M R Channon 2-9-0 T E Durcan 11/4: 41: Led after 1f, rdn clr despite edging   92
right ins last, pushed ou: stays a sharp/undul 6f, 7f sure to suit: acts on fast: more to come, see 1780.
1848 **SILVER WRAITH** 9 [5] N A Callaghan 2-9-0 J Murtagh 13/8 FAV: 42: Cl-up, hung left over 1f out,   1¾   85
sltly hmpd but onepace ins last: nicely bckd: prob ran to form of 1848 & shld find a small race.
1738 **STEDFAST MCSTAUNCH** 14 [4] B J Meehan 2-9-0 L Keniry(3) 9/2: 423: In tch, eff over 1f out,   ½   83
onepace: acts on fast & soft grnd: see 1738.
1646 **ALRIGHT MY SON** 18 [3] R Hannon 2-9-0 R L Moore 11/2: 024: In tch, no extra over 1f out: showed   3½   73
more on soft grnd over 5f in 1646.
RANSACKER 0 [2]2-9-0 S Sanders 25/1: 5: b c Bahamian Bounty - Hazy Heights (Shirley Heights)   6   55
Slow away & al bhd: March first foal, cost 25,000gns: dam 1m wnr.
1237 **COLONEL BILKO** 41 [7]2-9-0 BL S Drowne 14/1: 206: Hung right throughout, chsd wnr till 2f out,   5   40

607

BRIGHTON   FRIDAY 28.05.04   Lefthand, V Sharp, Undulating Track

wknd: abs, blnks: twice below 974 (5f, soft).
1640 **TIPSY LILLIE 18** [6]2-8-9   N Pollard 33/1: 57: Chsd ldrs, hmpd over 4f out, sn wknd: 'struck into'. 2 29
2017 **FAITHFULL GIRL 2** [2]2-8-9   F P Ferris(3) 100/1: 008: b f Second Empire - Cairde Nua (Mukaddamah) 8 7
Handy, hmpd after 2f, sn bhd: March first foal, cost E5,000.
8 Ran   Time 1m 10.26 (2.46)   Owned: Sheikh Ahmed Al Maktoum   Trained: West Ilsley

---

2044	2.40 Betfred Sprint Series Qualifier A Handicap Stakes 3yo+ 0-80 (D)	**[78]**
	£5421 £1668 £834 **5f59y rnd** **Good/Firm 26** **-01 Slow** Inside	

1914 **HARD TO CATCH 6** [8] D K Ivory 6-9-2 bl (66) M Savage(5) 5/1: 0455001: Squeezed out early, bhd, gd 74
hdwy 2f out, short of room 1f out but styd on strongly to lead ins last, rdn clr: also landed this race last
term off a 1lb lower mark: stays 7f, suited by 5/6f on firm & fast, both AWs, handles soft: loves a sharp & undul
trk, has a fine record here at Brighton: tough, see 628, 516.
1371 **YORKIE 33** [3] P A Blockley 5-8-3 (53) J F Egan 7/1: 00-10002: Handy, hdwy to lead 1f out, hdd 1½ 57
ins last, not pace of wnr: eff at 5f, both wins at 6f, stays 1m: on a handy mark, see 819 (seller).
482   **JAYANJAY 123** [5] Miss B Sanders 5-10-0 (78) S Sanders 5/1: 6602-043: Handy, eff over 1f out, 1¼ 78
kept on same pace: encouraging eff after 4 mth abs, loves sharp/undul trks: see 482, 149.
1806 **PORT ST CHARLES 11** [4] C R Dore 7-9-2 (66) R Thomas(5) 20/1: 0044004: Sn bhd, hdwy over 1f out, ¾ 64
hung left ins last, kept on: showed some promise again for new stable: slipped down the weights: see 1806, 1103.
1873 **LADY PEKAN 8** [1]5-8-11 bl (61) F P Ferris(3) 7/1: 0220035: Set pace till 1f out, no extra: see 1293, 1096. nk 58
1867 **GUNS BLAZING 8** [10]5-8-12 bl (62) M Howard(7) 11/2: 00-00136: Sn chsd ldr, chall over 1f out, no ½ 57
extra: shade btr expected off a 3lb lower mark than 1867, see 1774.
1886* **BYO 7** [9]6-9-5 (69) J Murtagh 6/1: 4-062017: In tch, btn 2f out: btr expected after 1886 ¾ 62
(unpenalized here) but 1 plcd run from 5 starts here now: see 1269.
1925 **TENDER 6** [7]4-8-7 (57) S Drowne 12/1: 060-3508: Al bhd: qck reapp: see 1096. 2 44
1867 **LOCH INCH 8** [6]7-8-7 bl (57) R L Moore 20/1: 01000-09: In tch, wknd 2f out: see 1867. ½ 42
1886 **BEYOND CALCULATION 7** [2]10-8-10 P (60) T E Durcan 10/1: 000-0000: 10th: Hmpd after 1f, no impress. 6 27
10 Ran   Time 1m 01.46 (1.46)   Owned: Mrs Karen Graham   Trained: Radlett

---

2045	3.10 Weatherbys Bank Rated Stakes Handicap 4yo+ 0-85 (D)	**[89]**
	£4737 £1797 £898 **6f209y rnd** **Good/Firm 26** **+08 Fast** Inside	

2023* **IDLE POWER 2** [6] J R Boyle 6-8-12 (3ex)p (73) J Murtagh 6/4 FAV: 000-0011: Handy trav well, led 82
over 1f out, drvn to hold on ins last: hvly bckd: qck reapp: eff at 6/7f on firm & gd/soft, polytrack & any trk:
eff in cheek pieces: confidence fully restored now & in grand heart: see 2023, 1255.
1817 **GREENWOOD 10** [7] P G Murphy 9-9-2 (77) S Drowne 4/1: 0300662: In tch, hdwy to chase wnr over 1f hd 85
out, chall ins last, just held for press: well clr of rem & confirmed promise of 1817: win sn, see 1817.
4171} **CONCUBINE 260** [2] J R Boyle 5-8-4 (5oh) (60) R L Moore 9/1: 240300-3: b f Danehill - Bye Bold 7 59
Aileen (Warning) Held up, modest late gains: rnr-up twice in '03 (h'caps): '02 h'cap wnr: suited by 7f on fast or
gd grnd, likes sharp/undul trks.
2 Jun'03 Good 7g/f 67-66 D: 2 Jun'03 Brig 7.0g/f 69-66 E: 2 Sep'02 Epso 7gd 69-66 D: 1 Jul'02 Epso 7gd 68-60 E:
1833 **DAWN PIPER 10** [5] D R Loder 4-9-7 vis (82) T P Queally(3) 9/2: 1020204: Chsd ldr till over 2f out, wknd. 1¾ 72
1726 **MANDARIN SPIRIT 14** [3]4-9-0 bl (75) S Sanders 15/2: 110000-5: b g Primo Dominie - Lithe Spirit 2½ 59
(Dancing Dissident) Led till over 1f out, wknd: '03 4-time h'cap scorer (once for Sir M Prescott): eff over
7f/8.5f on fast, gd & fibresand, likes sharp/undul trks: tough & progressive last term, wears blnks.
1 Sep'03 Epso 7gd 79-71 D: 1 Sep'03 Folk 7g/f 72-64 E: 1 Jul'03 Wolv 8.5af 66a-58 E: 1 Jul'03 Catt 7g/f 60-54 E:
2 Jun'03 Muss 7.1g/f 57-54 F:
1941 **AGILIS 5** [4]4-8-4 (10oh)bl (45) J F Egan 16/1: 0000000: Handy, wknd 2f out: 'hung left'. 7 35
1642 **SINGLE TRACK MIND 18** [1]6-8-4 (20oh) (45) M Henry 50/1: 5023507: Slow away, bhd: 'not handle trk'. nk 34
7 Ran   Time 1m 21.09 (1.29)   Owned: The Idle B'S   Trained: Epsom

---

2046	3.40 Brighton Square Handicap Stakes Fillies 3yo 0-75 (E)	**[75]**
	£3780 £1163 £582 **1m1f209y** **Good/Firm 26** **-12 Slow** Outside	

1648 **PRENUP 18** [7] L M Cumani 3-8-11 (58) J Murtagh 5/2 FAV: 500-41: Cl-up, led halfway, styd on 69
gamely for press when pressed ins last, drvn out: well bckd: relished drop back to 10f, poss just stays 11.5f:
handles soft, enjoyed this fast grnd & sharp/undul trk: confidence boosting first win: see 1648.
1470 **WEE DINNS 28** [1] S Kirk 3-9-6 (67) J F Egan 13/2: 000-052: In tch, chsd wnr 2f out, chall ins nk 77
last, just held: op 9/2: well clr of rem & an encouraging eff stepped up to 10f on fast grnd, handles soft.
3066*}**MUNAAWASHAT 311** [2] M Johnston 3-9-7 (68) R Hills 9/2: 261-3: b f Marju - Simaat (Mr Prospector) 4 71
Slow away, held up, hdwy wide over 2f out, kept on ins last, no threat: reapp: won last of 3 '03 starts (auct
mdn): eff over a gall 7f, bred to stay 1m+ (dam 1m wnr): acts on fast & gd grnd: shld do btr.
1 Jul'03 Ayr 6gd 71- E: 2 Jun'03 Ripo 6g/f 71- D:
1718 **BUBBLING FUN 15** [3] E A L Dunlop 3-9-4 (65) S Drowne 20/1: 02-404: b f Marju - Blushing Barada nk 67
(Blushing Groom) Keen in tch, lost place over 2f out, modest late gains: poss stays 10f on fast grnd: modest juv
form. 2 Oct'03 Newm 7g/f 0- G:
1648 **DOLLY WOTNOT 18** [6]3-9-3 (64) T P Queally(3) 12/1: 0445-505: Held up, eff 2f out, sn btn: see 1165. 1 64
1790 **VELVET WATERS 11** [4]3-8-12 (59) S Sanders 5/1: 600-36: Led to halfway, wknd over 2f out: btr 1790. 2 56
4443} **TARDIS 246** [8]3-9-3 (64) I Mongan 9/1: 661524-7: ch f Vettori - Time Lapse (The Noble Player) 13 39
In tch, chall over 2f out, sn hmpd/wknd: '03 mdn auct wnr: eff over 7f/1m on gd & fast grnd, fair/sharp trks.
2 Sep'03 Yarm 8.0gd 64-61 E: 1 Jul'03 Muss 7.1gd 61-(65) E:
1648 **MAMBINA 18** [5]3-9-4 (65) T E Durcan 6/1: 50-04458: Keen in tch, wknd 2f out: see 1648 (gd), 1427. 3 36
8 Ran   Time 2m 01.59 (3.79)   Owned: Fittocks Stud   Trained: Newmarket

2047

4.10 Pleasure Palace Racing Lady Riders Series Claiming Stakes 4yo+ (F)
£2884 £824 £412 1m3f196y Good/Firm 26 -18 Slow Outside

1506 **GOLDEN BOOT 26** [6] A Bailey 5-10-10 vis (63) Miss V Cottrill(7) 5/2 FAV: 343-6001: Slow away, held 68
up, plenty to do over 3f out, strong hdwy well over 1f out to lead ins last, rdn clr: eff over 1m/12f, stays 2m:
acts on firm & gd/soft, prob any trk: relished drop into claim grade & for considerate handling: see 1389.
1967 **BANNINGHAM BLAZE 4** [5] A W Carroll 4-10-3 vis (50) Mrs S Bosley 3/1: 0-004122: Held up, hdwy well 4 53
over 1f out, styd on to take 2nd ins last: qck reapp: ran to form of 1967 (h'cap), 1692.
1967 **MARGERY DAW 4** [1] P S McEntee 4-10-1 (60) Miss J C Duncan(5) 20/1: 2-500063: Sn clr ldr, tired & shd 51
hdd ins last, no extra: qck reapp: apprec a return to 10f: see 269, 148.
1838* **ROMIL STAR 9** [3] K R Burke 7-10-6 bl (50) Ms C Williams 9/2: 60-00214: Bhd, modest late gains: 3 52
btr 1838 (seller, fibresand).
1692 **CHOCOLATE BOY 16** [2]5-10-6 bl (60) Miss H Grissell(5) 9/4: 2441025: Chsd clr ldr, wknd over 2f out. 2 49
1940 **PIQUET 5** [4]6-10-9 (45) Miss Donna Handley(7) 50/1: 1660006: Keen bhd, no impress. 8 40
6 Ran Time 2m 33.53 (5.21) Owned: Mr Peter G Freeman Trained: Tarporley

2048

4.40 Rendezvous Casino Classified Stakes 3yo 0-70 (E)
£3361 £1034 £517 5f213y rnd Good/Firm 26 -06 Slow Inside

1809 **BORZOI MAESTRO 11** [6] J L Spearing 3-9-0 p (73) S Sanders 4/1: 0400-231: Keen, handy, hdwy to 75
lead over 1f out, styd on well ins last, drvn out: winning form over 5/6f: acts on fast, soft & fibresand, prob any
trk, likes a sharp one: tough, imprvd run here this season, see check pieces: see 1539.
4892} **SWEET PICKLE 216** [3] D J Coakley 3-8-8 (70) T P Queally(3) 25/1: 3010-2: Keen, led till over 1f nk 69
out, kept on for press, just held on reapp: '03 auct mdn wnr: stays a sharp/undul 6f, shld get further: acts on
fast grnd: encouraging return.
1743 **ASK THE CLERK 14** [9] V Smith 3-9-0 (73) M Tebbutt 9/1: 5010203: In tch, eff over 1f out, onepace. 1¼ 71
1477 **SHRINK 27** [1] M L W Bell 3-8-8 (69) I Mongan 7/2 FAV: 22-2144: In tch, eff over 1f out, onepace. ½ 63
999* **PLACE COWBOY 58** [7]3-9-2 (75) S W Kelly 5/1: 2-15: Bhd, some late gains, carried hd high: abs. shd 71
1690 **FAIR COMPTON 16** [8]3-8-8 (65) P Dobbs 12/1: 04-46: Cl-up, onepace over 1f: see 1690. 1¼ 59
5015} **AVERRLLINE 204** [5]3-8-11 (73) D Kinsella 14/1: 332210-7: Held up, some late gains on reapp: '03 1¼ 58
mdn wnr, plcd several times: eff at 6f, poss stays 7f: acts on firm & gd/soft, likes sharp/undul trks.
1722 **ONE UPMANSHIP 15** [2]3-8-11 e (68) R L Moore 16/1: 0240-08: Bhd, modest late gains. nk 57
1829 **GET TO THE POINT 10** [10]3-8-13 (72) J Murtagh 9/2: 50-02259: Slow away & nvr a factor. 1 56
1722 **KURINGAI 15** [4]3-8-11 (69) A Quinn(5) 12/1: 0-043000: 10th: Handy, wknd over 2f out. 3½ 44
10 Ran Time 1m 09.75(1.95) Owned: The Square Milers Trained: Kinnersley

Official Going Standard

2049

2.30 Peter Gent - Nightfreight Handicap Stakes Fillies 3yo+ 46-55 (F) [76]
£2947 £842 £421 7f aw rnd Going 40 -31 Slow Outside

1603 **MISKINA 21** [7] W M Brisbourne 3-8-7 (2oh) (55) B Swarbrick(5) 11/2: 024-0301: Mid-div, drvn & styd 61a
on to lead cl-home: first win: eff btwn 7/8.5f on fast grnd & fibresand, sharp trks: see 1339.
1750 **LARGS 13** [11] J Balding 4-8-10 (47) J Edmunds 5/1: 0332632: Held up, hdwy to lead over 2f out, nk 52a
sn rdn clr, drvn & hdd nr line: see 858, 659 & 562.
1266 **DASAR 39** [10] M Brittain 4-8-11 vis (48) D Tudhope(7) 7/1: 06-64023: Cl-up, ch over 2f out, onepace. 1 51a
1535 **HILARIOUS 24** [9] B R Millman 4-8-12 (49) G Baker 13/2: 03440-54: Prom, lost pl after 3f, late 2½ 47a
rally, no threat: handles fast grnd & fibresand, rtn to 1m shld suit: see 1535 (1m).
1948 **ACE MA VAHRA 4** [8]6-8-10 (47) J Bramhill 20/1: 6160005: Led till over 2f out, fdd: blnks omitted. 3½ 38a
1379* **MAGGIES PET 32** [3]7-8-13 t (50) S Whitworth 7/2 FAV: 5224516: Chsd ldrs, no impress fnl 2f: btr 1379. ½ 40a
1961 **KEDROSS 4** [12]3-7-12 (11oh) (46) C Haddon(3) 25/1: 00-00057: Slow away & nvr on terms with ldrs. 2 32a
   RED MELODICA 26 [6]4-9-4 (55) R Winston 25/1: 000-08: b f Red Ransom - Melodica (Machiavellian) 2 37a
Bhd, brief eff wide 3f out, no dngr: ex Irish, lightly rcd mdn in '03, has tried up to 10f prev: AW bow today.
1730 **CLOUDLESS 14** [5]4-9-3 (54) G Gibbons 7/1: 0336609: Prom, wknd fnl 2f: btr 958 & 864. 1¾ 33a
1730 **PRINCESS BANKES 14** [1]3-8-2 (7oh) (50) Dean Williams(7) 12/1: 605-0600: 10th: b f Vettori - Lady 1¼ 26a
Bankes (Alzao) AI outpcd: mod form in Britain to date at up to 8.5f, ex French mdn.
158 **DUNCANBIL 172** [4]3-8-5 (4oh) (53) Derek Nolan(6) 12/1: 050066-0: 11th: Chsd ldrs till 3f out, sn btn, abs. 5 20a
1395 **SATSU 32** [2]3-8-4 (5oh) (52) M Fenton 10/1: 05-0060: 12th: Sn struggling rear. nk 18a
12 Ran Time 1m 31.14 (4.94) Owned: The Blacktoffee Partnership Trained: Nesscliffe

2050

3.00 D A Constable Ltd Liability Underwriters Claiming Stakes 3yo (F)
£2905 £830 £415 1m4f aw Going 40 -33 Slow Inside

1359 **BOLD BLADE 34** [1] M J Polglase 3-9-1 bl (70) G Gibbons 8/1: 13-25001: Made all, rdn & in command 73a
over 2f out, eased cl-home: prev with B Smart: eff at 1m, apprec step up to 12f in claim grade, could get further:
likes fibresand & a sharp trk: best blnkd: see 190.
1612 **SPECTESTED 21** [5] B J Meehan 3-8-5 P (56) J F McDonald(3) 10/1: 550-002: ch g Spectrum - Nisibis 9 52a
(In The Wings) Dwelt & held up, drvn & kept on fnl 3f, nvr threat to wnr: clmd by A W Carroll for 5000: wore cheek
pieces: lightly rcd & unplcd in '03 (rtd 65a & 70, tried blnks): tried up to 14f prev, mid-dists shld suit.
1754* **CASPIAN DUSK 13** [3] W G M Turner 3-9-5 (70) C Haddon(7) 6/5 FAV: 6-231213: Held up, eff to chase 3½ 61a
wnr 3f out, sn no impress: op 11/8: btr 1754 (11f).
1444* **PEPE 29** [7] R Hollinshead 3-9-0 (57) Stephanie Hollinshead(5) 2/1: 6-663014: Cl-up, btn 2f out: btr 1444. 10 42a
1713 **SIR FRANK GIBSON 15** [6]3-8-9 (45) S Whitworth 16/1: 0423055: Held up in rear, left bhd fnl 4f: btr 658. 16 17a
1785 **OUR KID 12** [4]3-8-11 bl (62) R Winston 7/1: 6640-006: ch g Pursuit of Love - Flower Princess dist 0a

(Slip Anchor) In tch till 5f out, t.o. on AW bow: unplcd '03 (lightly rcd, rtd 69, mdn).
1783 **TORNADO BAY 12** [2]3-8-4 B Swarbrick(5) 50/1: 07: Held up in tch, bhd from halfway, longer trip. *dist* **0a**
7 Ran Time 2m 42.3 (8.7) Owned: Mr Paul J Dixon Trained: Newark

2051 3.30 European Breeders Fund Maiden Stakes 2yo (D)
£4046 £1245 £623 **6f aw rnd** **Going 40** **-14 Slow** Inside

1550 **WINDY PROSPECT 24** [7] P A Blockley 2-9-0 D Nolan(3) 9/4: 3521: Led after 1f, prsd fnl 2f, held on well for press: op 3/1: eff at 5f, styd longer 6f trip well: acts on gd grnd & both AWs: improving. **85a**
1780 **DISTINCTLY GAME 12** [10] K A Ryan 2-9-0 J Carroll 7/4 FAV: 222: Al handy, ev ch over 1f out, no extra cl-home: clr of rem: nicely bckd on AW bow: acts on fast, gd & fibresand: consistent: see 1780. *1½* **79a**
1920 **MYTTONS BELL 6** [6] A Bailey 2-8-9 J Bramhill 4/1: 23: Prom, not pace of front pair over 1f out: clr of rem on AW bow: prob handles fibresand but btr 1920 (debut, fast). *5* **61a**
ZANTERO 0 [3] R P Elliott 2-9-0 T Hamilton(3) 33/1: 4: b c Danzero - Cruinn A Bhord (Inchinor) Slow away, hdwy wide halfway, no prog dist, op 6/1: 9,000gns Feb foal, dam a multiple 7f wnr. *10* **40a**
1760 **LEAGUE OF NATIONS 13** [11]2-9-0 A Culhane 4/1: 05: b c Indian Danehill - Athens Belle (Groom Dancer) Rdn & outpcd early, nvr on terms: AW bow: Jan foal, E42,000 purhcase: half-brother to a 7f/1m 3yo wnr, dam a useful 7f juv & subs 10f 3yo wnr. *1½* **36a**
KALIKA 0 [8]2-8-9 G Gibbons 25/1: 6: Chsd lrs till 2f out. *1* **28a**
1744 **DRAMATIC REVIEW 14** [5]2-9-0 G Faulkner 16/1: 057: Chsd ldrs, btn 2f out, AW bow. *1¾* **28a**
ZANDO 0 [1]2-9-0 Rory Moore(7) 25/1: 8: Sn outpcd & nvr factor. *1½* **24a**
1424 **ELLENARE 30** [4]2-8-9 B Swarbrick(5) 50/1: 09: Al outpcd on AW bow. *3* **10a**
1900 **IAM FOREVERBLOWING 7** [9]2-8-9 D Corby(3) 33/1: 5450: 10th: Led 1f, strugg halfway, AW bow. *2* **4a**
1658 **MAS O MENOS 18** [2]2-9-0 Dean McKeown 20/1: 20: 11th: Sn bhd, AW bow: btr 1658 (soft). *1½* **4a**
11 Ran Time 1m 16.04 (3.24) Owned: bellhouseracingcom Trained: Southwell

2052 4.00 Wolverhampton & Dudley Breweries Selling Stakes 3yo+ (G)
£2611 £746 £373 **1m100y aw rnd** **Going 40** **-22 Slow** Inside

1657 **FRANKS QUEST 18** [6] P Burgoyne 4-9-7 (53) S Hitchcott(3) 5/1: 3604021: In tch, rdn to lead over 1f out, duelled with rnr-up, prevailed all out: bght in for 7,500gns: eff btwn 8.5f & 11f on fibresand, fast & gd/soft. **58a**
400} **CELTIC THATCHER 498** [9] N P Littmoden 6-9-7 vis G Gibbons 11/4 FAV: 60060/0-2: b g Celtic Swing - Native Thatch (Thatching) Stumbled start & sn pushed along, hdwy to chall dist, just held: long abs: nicely bckd, op 9/2: clr of rem: no form sole '03 start: C/D cond stks rnr-up in '02: former useful AW performer: eff at 8.5f/9.3f, loves fibresand & W'hampton: can force the pace & best in a visor: could win similar if staying sound. *hd* **57a**
2 Feb'02 Wolv 8.4af 94a- C: 1 Dec'01 Wolv 8.4af 96a-80 C: 1 Dec'01 Wolv 8.4af 93a- D: 1 Oct'01 Wolv 8.4af 75a-66 E: 1 Jul'01 Wolv 9.3af 71a- F:
1801 **ROVING VIXEN 11** [3] J L Spearing 3-8-4 bl (35) R Miles(3) 7/1: 0-004033: Led/dsptd lead, went on over 3f out till over 1f out, hung right & no extra: op 14/1: see 801 & 1565. *3½* **45a**
1672 **KANZ WOOD 17** [5] A W Carroll 8-9-7 (45) A Daly 10/1: 0505534: Slow away & well bhd, kept on late. *¾* **49a**
36 **FREDS FIRST 195** [4]3-8-9 M Fenton 33/1: 0-5: b g Nomination - Perecapa (Archway) Well bhd, mod late gains: 6 month abs: no form sole prev start. *8* **35a**
1755 **XALOC BAY 13** [13]6-9-12 (53) Darren Williams 11/2: 2360306: Led/dsptd lead 5f, fdd: btr 1341. *2½* **35a**
1827 **MY COUNTRY CLUB 10** [11]7-9-7 (53) N Chalmers(5) 25/1: 2442-667: Chsd ldrs till 2f out: AW bow. *hd* **29a**
1451 **MR LOVERMAN 29** [7]4-9-7 (40) R Fitzpatrick 50/1: 00000-08: ch g Spectrum - Soviet Artic (Bering) Rider slow to remove blindfold & v slow away, nvr a factor: unplcd in '03 (rtd 63, mdn, flattered, tried blnks). *4* **22a**
1672* **FORTY FORTE 17** [10]8-9-12 t p (52) B Swarbrick(5) 10/1: 0030619: Mid-div, sn rdn, nvr factor: btr 1672. *nk* **26a**
1819 **MIKASA 10** [12]4-9-7 P (40) D Nolan(3) 25/1: 0-000300: 10th: Cl-up till over 2f out, saddle slipped. *10* **4a**
1812 **CAL MAC 10** [8]5-9-7 (77) R Winston 4/1: 60034-00: 11th: b g Botanic - Shifting Mist (Night Shift) Prom, btn/eased over 2f out: appr h'cap wnr '03, subs disapp in a visor: AW mdn scorer '02, turf h'cap rnr-up: eff around 1m on firm, fast & fibresand, sharp or stiff trk: has gone v well fresh. *½* **3a**
1 May'03 Warw 8.1g/f 86-80 G: 2 May'02 Newm 8fm 86-83 C: 1 Apr'02 Wolv 8.4af 87a- E:
1720 **Cloud Catcher 15** [1]3-8-4 J F McDonald(3) 16/1:0 1195 **Banners Flying 43** [2]4-9-7 (70) A Culhane 12/1:0
13 Ran Time 1m 51.43 (5.23) Owned: Fun & Fantasy & Andrew Haynes Racing Ltd Trained: Marlborough

2053 4.30 Ladbrokes Com Handicap Stakes 3yo+ 0-75 (E) **[73]**
£3760 £1157 £579 **6f aw rnd** **Going 40** **+14 Fast** Inside

1743 **CAPE ST VINCENT 14** [12] H Morrison 4-9-11 VIS (70) A Culhane 5/1: 12024-01: gr c Paris House - Cape Merino (Clantime) Chsd ldrs, rdn to chall over 1f out & styd on for press well ins last: fast time: AW auct mdn wnr '03 (C/D, subs dual h'cap rnr-up): stays 7f, best at 6f on both AWs & fast grnd, stiff/gall or sharp trk, likes W'hampton: galvanized by vis today. **79a**
2 Oct'03 Ling 6ap 74a-72 E: 2 Aug'03 Newm 6g/f 72-70 D: 1 Jul'03 Wolv 6af 70a- F: 2 Jul'03 Wolv 6af 65a- D:
1615 **ANOTHER GLIMPSE 21** [4] Miss B Sanders 6-10-0 t (73) R Miles(3) 9/2: 4100232: Held up, rdn & hdwy to lead over 1f out, hdd well ins last: clr rem: consistent type, remains in gd heart: acts on both AWs, fast & gd. *nk* **81a**
1526 **XPRES DIGITAL 25** [9] S R Bowring 3-9-5 t (73) J Bramhill 14/1: 610-0403: Prom, kept on onepace. *5* **68a**
1218* **GILDED COVE 41** [3] R Hollinshead 4-9-5 (64) Stephanie Hollinshead(5) 6/1: 0335114: Slow away, kept on wide, not able to land blow: 6 wk abs, lost ch here with slow start, worth another look after 1218 & 941. *1½* **55a**
1542 **PARKER 24** [7]7-9-0 bl (59) S Hitchcott(3) 12/1: 4360605: Prom, outpcd over 1f out: best dominating. *½* **48a**
1726 **GONENDUNNETT 14** [1]5-9-5 p (64) Darren Williams 14/1: 0000006: Led 1f, prom, no extra dist. *½* **51a**
1729 **GLOBAL ACHIEVER 14** [10]3-9-1 (69) Dean Williams(7) 14/1: 2210007: Led after 1f till over 1f out. *hd* **55a**
1465 **BLAKESHALL QUEST 28** [5]4-9-12 vis (71) R Winston 8/1: 4510108: Prom, btn 2f out: btr 1337. *2½* **49a**
1127 **ST IVIAN 46** [8]4-9-8 p (67) R Fitzpatrick 12/1: 2002009: Sn bhd & nvr factor: abs: btr 864. *½* **43a**
1442 **ITALIAN MIST 29** [11]5-9-9 e (68) B Doyle 4/1 FAV: 0131040: 10th: Al towards rear: op 6/1: btr 1442. *1* **41a**
1195 **TEEHEE 43** [6]6-9-5 bl (64) M Fenton 20/1: 0150-460: 11th: Bhd, nvr on terms: abs: prefer 7f: see 280. *7* **18a**
1774 **FULL PITCH 13** [13]8-9-9 (68) Kirby Harris(7) 20/1: ////-006100: 12th: Al outpcd: btr 1532 (hvy, 5f). *½* **20a**
1337 **NOBLE LOCKS 34** [2]6-9-6 (65) Joanna Badger 8/1: 1-000040: 13th: Sn bhd: op 11/1: btr 1337 (C/D). *½* **15a**
13 Ran Time 1m 14.34 (1.54) Owned: Barbara Jamet and Templeton Stud Trained: East Ilsley

WOLVERHAMPTON   Fibresand   FRIDAY 28.05.04   Lefthand, Sharp, Oval Track

2054   5.00 Winning Post Special At Dunstall Park Handicap Stakes 3yo+ 46-55 (F)   [61]
£2996 £856 £428   1m1f79y aw rnd   Going 40   -19 Slow   Inside

1819* **ARMS ACROSSTHESEA 10** [11] J Balding 5-9-9 (6ex) (56) J Edmunds 9/1: 6000-211: Held up, rdn & hdwy   **64a**
to lead over 1f out, rdn out: op 7/1: 6lb pen for latest: eff btwn 9/12f on firm, gd/soft & fibresand: prev with
A C Whillans, remains in great heart for new stable: see 1819.
1755 **CALL OF THE WILD 13** [8] R A Fahey 4-9-3 p (50) T Hamilton(3) 9/2: 3336442: Held up, eff to chase   2   **52a**
ldrs over 3f out, not pace of wnr from dist: mdn: see 961, 747 & 421.
1695 **VANDENBERGHE 16** [5] J A Osborne 5-9-5 (52) V Slattery 7/2 FAV: 0635-153: Bhd, kept on fnl 2f.   3   **49a**
1801* **SUPER DOMINION 11** [12] R Hollinshead 7-8-13 (6ex)p (46) Stephanie Hollinshead(5) 9/2: 0030-514:   ¾   **42a**
Held up, prog to lead over 4f out, sn rdn clr, hdd over 1f out & no extra: op 6/1: rtn to 1m shld suit: clr of rem.
1657 **ARJAY 18** [6]6-9-1 (48) J Carroll 10/1: 000-0035: Mid-div, lost pl 4f out, mod late prog: btr 1657.   7   **33a**
1579 **ENCORE ROYALE 22** [9]4-9-0 (47) O Urbina 16/1: 5000-056: V slow away, hdwy wide halfway, btn 2f out. 1¾   **29a**
839 **ROYALTEA 76** [7]3-8-5 (8oh) (51) Joanna Badger 33/1: 66407: Prom, no ch from 3f out: 11 wk abs.   5   **24a**
1661* **ROCINANTE 18** [13]4-9-6 (53) R Winston 4/1: 0030118: Chsd ldrs, btn 2f out: much btr 1661 & 1425.   3   **20a**
1712 **IAMBACK 15** [1]4-9-8 (55) Dean Williams(7) 7/1: 4301109: Cl-up, btn 3f out: btr 1674 & 1564.   8   **9a**
1430 **FURNITURE FACTORS 30** [3]4-9-3 P (50) Dean McKeown 40/1: 400/00-00: 10th: b g Magic Ring - Make   9   **0a**
Hay (Nomination) Led till 6f out, struggling from halfway: tried cheek pieces: unplcd '03 (lightly rcd, no form,
tried a t-strap): thrice mdn plcd in '02: eff at 6/7f on fast & gd/soft grnd, stiff or sharp/turning trk.
1827 **Zak Facta 10** [4]4-9-0 vis(47) S Hitchcott(3) 16/1:0   1778 **Suerte 13** [2]4-9-2 P(49) B Doyle 12/1:0
12 Ran   Time 2m 03.74(5.54)   Owned: Mr J Carter   Trained: Doncaster

YORK   FRIDAY 28.05.04   Lefthand, Flat, Galloping Track

Official Going Good/Firm

2055   2.20 Sportingoptions Co Uk 08702 070707 Handicap Stakes 3yo 0-70 (E)   [77]
£3907 £1202 £601   6f3y str   Good/Firm 39   +06 Fast   Centre

1878* **MIS CHICAF 8** [16] J S Wainwright 3-9-13 (6ex) (76) K Fallon 11/4 FAV: 3501-211: Cl-up, led   **93+**
halfway, pushed out fnl 1f, easily: well bckd: top-weight: eff at 5/6f on fast & gd/soft: easily destroyed rivals
on rtn to own age: interesting for William Hill Trophy here shortly: see 1878.
1881* **BRIDGEWATER BOYS 7** [6] K A Ryan 3-9-10 (6ex)bl (73) N Callan 5/1: 5-413112: Held up, prog   7   **76**
halfway, kept on ins fnl 1f, no ch with easy wnr: tchd 13/2 on qck reapp: continues in fine form: see 1881 & 1722.
1949 **FOX COVERT 4** [10] D W Barker 3-8-10 vis (59) L Enstone(3) 7/1: 30-00023: Led till halfway, edged   1   **59**
left over 1f out, kept on: qk reapp: shld find a h'cap: just btr 1949.
1216 **VOLATICUS 42** [7] D Nicholls 3-8-11 (60) A Nicholls 14/1: 0-204: Handy, carr left dist, onepace.   ½   **59**
1570 **GO YELLOW 23** [1]3-9-7 (70) S Donohoe(7) 16/1: 0626-005: b g Overbury - Great Lyth Lass (Waajib)   shd   **68**
Chsd ldrs far side over 4f, sn carr left & onepcd: rnr-up once in '03 (mdn): eff over a sharp 6f on fast grnd:
enjoys forcing tactics: with P D Evans. 2 Oct'03 Wind 6g/f 83- D:
1441 **TURKISH DELIGHT 29** [8]3-9-2 (65) W Supple 25/1: 44430-56: Held up, prog halfway, no impress fnl 1f.   1   **60**
1605 **GARNOCK VENTURE 31** [15]3-8-6 bl (55) F Norton 33/1: 0010307: Handy 4f, sn no extra: btr 1457.   ½   **49**
1878 **BOWLING ALONG 8** [5]3-8-9 (58) T Eaves(3) 50/1: 5300-508: Nvr nrr than mid-div: btr 1465.   2   **46**
1949 **KILLERBY NICKO 4** [11]3-8-8 (57) D Allan(3) 33/1: 00-6069: ch g Pivotal - Bit of A Tart (Distant   3   **36**
Relative) Never handy, sn wknd: qck reapp: unplcd in '03 (rtd 67, mdn): with T D Easterby.
1605 **MUSIOTAL 21** [12]3-7-13 (48) N Mackay(3) 9/1: 50-0550: 10th: Slow away, modest late gains: btr 1509.   ¾   **25**
999 **UHURU PEAK 58** [14]3-8-13 (62) P Mulrennan(5) 20/1: 3050: 11th: Al in rear: 8 wk abs.   1¼   **35**
1518 **Gasparini 25** [4]3-9-1 (64) D Holland 25/1:0   1949 **Shinko Femme 4** [2]3-8-11 (60) W Ryan 20/1:0
4923} **Fitzwarren 213** [3]3-9-6 vis(69) C Catlin 25/1:0   2011 **Reversionary 2** [13]3-8-1 (50) Dale Gibson 25/1:0
1679 **Lady Of The Links 16** [18]3-8-0 vis(49) Kim Tinkler 33/1:0
1682 **El Palmar 16** [19]3-9-5 (68) P Makin(5) 16/1:0
1729 **Fools Entire 14** [17]3-9-0 (63) J Quinn 33/1:0   1769 **Named At Dinner 13** [20]3-9-5 (68) J Fanning 66/1:0
19 Ran   Time 1m 11.43 (2.03)   Owned: Mr Anthony D Copley   Trained: Malton

2056   2.50 Sportingoptions Co Uk Commission Cutters Maiden Auction Stakes Fillies 2yo (F)
£3136 £896 £448   5f3y str   Good/Firm 39   -10 Slow   Centre

1709 **SMIDDY HILL 15** [7] R Bastiman 2-8-4   R Ffrench 5/2 FAV: 3241: Made all, clr ins fnl 2f, rdn out: **85**
well bckd: eff at 5f on gd/soft, improved on fast here: nursery type.
1795 **KATIE BOO 11** [15] A Berry 2-8-4   F Norton 9/2: 32: Handy stands side, kept on ins fnl 1f, not   5   **70**
pace wnr: acts on fast & gd grnd: will appreciate 6f: see 1795 (reapp).
1632 **LADY DAN 20** [11] M W Easterby 2-8-4   T Lucas 25/1: 43: b f Danzero - Dubai Lady (Kris) Handy,   nk   **69**
kept on ins fnl 1f: Feb foal, cost 7,500gns: dam plcd over mid-dists: sire decent juv performer abroad: eff at
5f, shapes as tho' further will suit: acts on fast grnd.
1709 **MELANDRE 15** [10] M Brittain 2-8-4   T Williams 50/1: 604: b f Lujain - Talighta (Barathea)   ¾   **67**
Handy, onepcd: Jan foal, cost 6,200gns: sharper for this.
1818 **TAGULA BAY 10** [2]2-8-4   W Supple 7/2: 235: In tch over 3f, sn no extra: btr 1818 (6f).   ½   **66**
1826 **GOGETTER GIRL 10** [4]2-8-4   J Quinn 15/2: 624046: Handy 4f, no extra: btr 1826.   1   **63**
OCHIL HILLS DANCER 0 [9]2-8-7   L Enstone(2) 20/1: 7: b f Bluebird - Classic Dilemma (Sandhurst   1¼   **62**
Prince) In tch till halfway, sn outpcd, trailed fnl 1f: debut: Apr foal, cost 5,000gns: half-sister to a couple
of wnrs: dam 2yo wnr abroad: sire high-class performer at sprint dists: with A Crook.
974 **JUSTENJOY YOURSELF 59** [1]2-8-4   Hayley Turner(5) 33/1: 68: Chsd ldrs till halfway, sn no extra.   5   **45**
MISS JELLYBEAN 0 [14]2-8-4   Kim Tinkler 25/1: 9: Handy stands side till dist, fdd.   nk   **47**
TOMOBEL 0 [12]2-8-4   P Robinson 12/1: 0: 10th: Slow away, al in rear.   ½   **43**

611

MARIANS GIFT 0 [5]2-8-4 Dale Gibson 33/1: 0: 11th: Slow away, al bhd. *5* **29**
First Rhapsody 0 [13]2-8-4 T Eaves(2) 33/1:0 1029 **Kilkenny Kitten 56** [3]2-8-4 t A Nicholls 50/1:0
Lanas Turn 0 [8]2-8-4 D Allan(3) 20/1:0 1394 **Danehill Fairy 32** [6]2-8-4 bl J Fanning 33/1:0
15 Ran Time 59.25 (2.45) Owned: Mr I B Barker Trained: Wetherby

2057

3.20 Sportingoptions Co Uk 2nd Anniversary Handicap Stakes 3yo+ 0-80 (D) **[78]**
£5883 £1810 £905 **6f217y rnd** **Good/Firm 39** **-02 Slow** Inside

1972 **EFIDIUM 4** [10] N Bycroft 6-9-0 (64) C Catlin 9/1: 6-204231: Rear, prog 3f out, styd on to lead well ins fnl 1f, rdn out: qck reapp: eff at 7f/1m on firm, gd/soft & fibresand: tough, deserved win. **72**
5021} **MAGIC AMOUR 204** [9] Ian Williams 6-8-10 (60) P Robinson 16/1: 112020-2: ch g Sanglamore - Rakli (Warning) Led 5f, rallied to lead dist, hdd well ins fnl 1f, no extra: won 2 h'caps in '03: mdn plcd in '02 (rtd 69): loves to force the pace at 7f/1m on firm & fast grnd: encouraging eff here on reapp & can find similar. *2½* **61**
2 Oct'03 Nott 8.2fm 61-59 E: 2 Sep'03 Leic 7.0g/f 60-58 E: 1 Aug'03 Nott 8.2g/f 60-55 D: 1 Jul'03 Folk 7g/f 56-49 D: 2 Jul'03 Donc 7g/f 50-49 E:
1748 **SARRAAF 14** [13] J S Goldie 8-9-6 (70) K Fallon 10/1: 2325053: Handy wide, styd on ins fnl 1f: tough. *shd* **70**
1255 **KAREEB 39** [3] W J Musson 7-9-12 (76) G Carter 8/1: 000-6004: Handy, ev ch dist, sn no extra: op 6/1. *½* **75**
1824 **RONNIE FROM DONNY 10** [11]4-9-3 (67) T Eaves(3) 33/1: 0U55005: Held up, prog when short of room 3f out, switched & kept on fnl 1f, nrst fin: on a fair mark: btr 241. *nk* **65**
1775 **PRINCE OF GOLD 13** [12]4-9-0 (64) W Supple 16/1: 00-05006: In tch wide 4f, sn short of room, onepcd. *hd* **61**
1820 **PRIDE OF KINLOCH 10** [4]4-8-7 (57) K McEvoy 12/1: 0604037: Cl-up, led 2f out, hdd dist, wknd. *1¼* **52**
1794 **JEDEYDD 11** [8]7-8-11 t (61) L Enstone(3) 33/1: 00000-08: b g Shareef Dancer - Bilad (Riverman) Nvr nrr than mid-div: unplcd in '03 (rtd 63, h'cap): h'cap wnr in '02 (B Hanbury): eff at 1m, suited by 7f: acts on firm & gd grnd, loves a straight 7f: has gone well fresh: long losing run but well h'capped. *1½* **53**
1 Jul'02 Leic 7gd 80-76 D: 2 Jul'01 Newb 6fm 91-88 C: 2 Jul'01 Hayd 7.1fm 86-86 C: 1 May'01 Yarm 7g/f 86- D: 2 May'01 Thir 8g/f 80- D:
1878 **FAVOUR 8** [14]4-9-7 (71) D Holland 7/2 FAV: 10223-29: Handy over 5f, sn no extra: well bckd: btr expected on rtn to 7f: btr 1878 (reapp, 6f). *shd* **62**
1379 **PAS DE SURPRISE 32** [15]6-8-5 (55) S Chin 33/1: 3055400: 10th: Bhd, modest late gains: btr 910. *hd* **45**
1820 **UP TEMPO 10** [16]6-9-13 bl (77) N Callan 14/1: 1114200: 11th: Bhd, prog when short of room halfway, modest late gains: btr 1345. *½* **66**
1094 **NO GROUSE 50** [7]4-9-9 (73) P Hanagan 10/1: 0-050030: 12th: Mid-div 5f, sn wknd: btr 1094. *2* **58**
1755 **SPY GUN 13** [2]4-8-0 (50) R Ffrench 11/1: 5040620: 13th: Chsd ldrs over 4f: 'broke blood vessel'. *2½* **30**
1941 **ALAFZAR 5** [6]6-8-9 vis t (59) R Havlin 8/1: 4013130: 14th: Handy over 5f, wknd. *3½* **32**
1820 **Tre Colline 10** [5]5-9-1 VIS(65) Kim Tinkler 25/1:0 1972 **Mehmaas 4** [1]8-8-1 vis(51) C Cogan 33/1:0
16 Ran Time 1m 24.18 (2.88) Owned: Hambleton Racing Partnership Trained: Malton

2058

3.50 Val Greaves - A Lifetime In Racing Maiden Stakes 3yo+ (D)
£3595 £1106 £553 **1m3f198y** **Good/Firm 39** **-31 Slow** Inside

1835 **TARANDOT 10** [2] G G Margarson 3-8-3 A McCarthy 6/4 FAV: 0-21: Handy, prog to lead ins fnl 1f, rdn out: well bckd: eff at 10f, apprec step up to 12f: acts on fast grnd & a stiff/gall trk: see 1835. **87**
1718 **FORCE OF NATURE 15** [5] H R A Cecil 4-9-6 W Ryan 7/2: 2-02: b f Sadler's Wells - Yashmak (Danzig) Led, eff under press 2f out, hdd ins fnl 1f, no extra: rnr-up on sole '03 start (fill mdn): eff at 10/12f on firm & fast grnd: left debut eff bhd with a solid display & can find similar. 2 Jun'03 Kemp 10fm 82- D: *¾* **85**
1272 **LIGHT OF MORN 38** [3] R Guest 3-8-5 (2ow) D Holland 2/1: 23: Cl-up, no extra from 1f out: op 5/4: acts on fast & soft grnd: riders 2lb overweight proved costly: see 1272. *1½* **84**
1742 **WATCHFUL WITNESS 14** [4] Dr J R J Naylor 4-9-11 Lucy Russell(7) 12/1: 0-34: Keen handy 1m, sn wknd. *20* **57**
DARING GAMES 0 [6]3-8-3 P Hanagan 33/1: 5: b f Mind Games - Daira (Daring March) Slow away, al in rear: debut: with B Ellison. *1* **50**
GREY SAMURAI 0 [1]4-9-11 L Enstone(3) 100/1: 6: gr g Gothenberg - Royal Rebeka (Grey Desire) Handy 1m, sn fdd: Flat debut, recent hdles unplcd: with P T Midgley. *20* **29**
6 Ran Time 2m 35.20 (8.4) Owned: Norcroft Park Stud Trained: Newmarket

2059

4.20 Sarah Lunn Memorial Stakes Handicap 3yo+ 0-85 (D) **[85]**
£6435 £1980 £990 **6f3y str** **Good/Firm 39** **+05 Fast** Centre

1476 **PAX 27** [11] D Nicholls 7-9-7 (78) L Treadwell(7) 7/1 FAV: 640-6601: Handy, prog to lead ins fnl 1f, rdn out: bckd: eff over a stiff 5f & 6f on firm, gd/soft grnd & any trk: enjoys a strong pace: see 1217 & 927. **87**
1977 **ROMANY NIGHTS 3** [1] J W Unett 4-9-5 vis (76) D Holland 8/1: 0-504342: Trkd ldrs, styd on to chase wnr ins fnl 1f, not btn far: qck reapp: continues to run well & winning turn shld not be far away: see 1977. *1* **81**
1767 **PADDYWACK 13** [14] D W Chapman 7-8-7 bl (64) J Quinn 25/1: 100-0403: Cl-up, led 2f out, hdd ins fnl 1f, sn no extra: gd run, h'capped to win: see 1627 & 155. *1* **66**
1523 **WINTHORPE 25** [8] J J Quinn 4-9-1 (72) K Dalgleish 50/1: 0-000004: Handy, styd on ins fnl 1f: first signs of encouragement this term & has slipped back to a winning mark: see 482. *1¼* **71**
1917 **TALBOT AVENUE 6** [15]6-9-9 (80) S Righton 8/1: 0000-055: Keen in tch, short of room & hung right after halfway, kept on onepace: qck reapp: not disgraced & another on a handy mark: see 1917. *½* **77**
4925} **BOLLIN EDWARD 213** [6]5-8-6 (63) D Allan(3) 20/1: 400000-6: b g Timeless Times - Bollin Harriet (Lochnager) Bhd, styd on late, nrst fin: plcd 3 times in '03 (h'caps, rtd 74): mdn wnr in '02: eff at 6f on fast & gd grnd, prob any trk: eff with/without visor: has tried blnks: encouraging reapp, slipped to a handy mark, sharper next time. 2 May'03 Donc 6gd 74-71 D: 1 Jun'02 Ripo 6g/f 72- D: 2 May'02 Pont 6gd 78- D: *shd* **59+**
1767 **VIEWFORTH 13** [16]6-9-2 (73) K Fallon 9/1: 00-44007: Trkd ldrs, not extra dist: btr 1276. *shd* **68**
1594 **NATIVE TITLE 21** [4]6-9-12 (83) A Nicholls 9/1: 26/010-48: Rear, prog halfway, no extra ins fnl 1f. *shd* **77**
1977 **EXTINGUISHER 3** [9]5-8-9 (66) W Supple 25/1: 0000-009: Led 4f, sn wknd: qck reapp: see 1977. *1¼* **56**
1970 **ENDLESS SUMMER 4** [7]6-9-9 (80) P Robinson 8/1: 004-3550: 10th: Rear, nvr nrr than mid-div: op 14/1. *¾* **68**
1824 **ZUHAIR 10** [3]11-8-13 (70) F Norton 33/1: 200-0000: 11th: ch g Mujtahid - Ghzaalh (Northern Dancer) Rear, modest late gains: plcd 4 times in '03 (h'caps): h'cap wnr in '02, won that race at Goodwood 4 times in a row: suited by waiting tactics over 5/6f: handles gd/soft & fibresand, loves firm & gd grnd: tried blnks: *nk* **57**

tough 10yo, comes good at Goodwood.
2 Aug'03 Beve 5gd 78-76 D: 2 Aug'03 Good 6g/f 78-72 B: 2 Aug'02 Good 6fm 71-70 B: 1 Jul'02 Good 5gd 78-70 D:
1 Aug'01 Good 5fmn 84-79 D: 2 Jul'01 Kemp 6fm 78- D:

1726 **PEDRO JACK** 14 [5]7-8-10 (67) J Fanning 66/1: 00-01000: 12th: Nvr nrr than mid-div: btr 1310.	1¼	50
1383 **BLACKHEATH** 32 [20]8-9-9 (80) Alex Greaves 16/1: 023-0440: 13th: Bhd, nvr able to chall: btr 1383.	3	54
1600 **LORD OF THE EAST** 21 [18]5-8-10 (67) Lisa Jones(3) 10/1: 502-0320: 14th: Handy 4f, edged left & fdd.	2½	34
1749 **Marshallspark** 14 [10]5-8-10 (67) P Hanagan 20/1:0		
1797* **American Cousin** 11 [2]9-8-7 (6ex)(64) P M Quinn 25/1:0		
1683 **Proud Native** 16 [12]10-10-0 (85) N Callan 33/1:0 1215 **Colemanstown** 42 [19]4-8-13 (70) T Eaves(3) 33/1:0		
2007 **Chairman Bobby** 2 [17]6-8-13 (70) L Enstone(3) 11/1:0 1878 **Consensus** 8 [13]5-9-8 (79) T Williams 16/1:0		

20 Ran   Time 1m 11.85 (2.05)   Owned: Mr D Nicholls   Trained: Thirsk

---

2060   4.50 Sportingoptions Co Uk Max 3% Apprentice Handicap Stakes 4yo+ 46-55 (F)   [63]
£3094 £884 £442   1m5f197y   Good/Firm 39   -26 Slow   Inside

1802 **MY LEGAL EAGLE** 11 [9] R J Price 10-8-10 (45) Hayley Turner 5/1 JT FAV: 50//5-1421: Held up, prog 4f out, rdn out to lead cl-home: eff at 10/12f, suited by 14f/2m: acts on fast, hvy grnd & both AWs: see 1802.		49
1793* **GALANDORA** 11 [5] Dr J R J Naylor 4-9-4 (6ex) (53) Lucy Russell(5) 7/1: 0-561012: Rear, prog 3f out, kept on well ins fnl 1f, just held: just denied on follow up bid after recent win in 1793.	½	55
1905 **ASTROMANCER** 6 [12] M H Tompkins 4-9-0 (49) Saleem Golam(5) 7/1: 4-045003: Handy, prog & ev ch dist, kept on & not btn far: qck reapp: mdn: see 1238 & 733.	hd	50
1802* **PRINCE OF THE WOOD** 11 [1] A Bailey 4-9-2 (6exr)P (51) P Makin(3) 5/1 JT FAV: 0064-214: Led, hdd well ins fnl 1f, no extra: acts on fast, gd/soft grnd & fibresand: see 1802 (banded, a/w).	nk	51
4154] **KRISTINEAU** 976 [6]6-8-13 t (48) P Mathers(3) 14/1: 520000//-5: ch f Cadeaux Genereux - Kantikoy (Alzao) Handy, ev ch 2f out, no extra ins fnl 1f: recent hdles plcd (mdn hdle, rtd 96h, stays 2m1.5f on gd & gd/soft grnd, eff with t-strap): rnr-up once back in '01 (rtd 62, h'cap): prev eff at 1m, now stays 14f: acts on fast & hvy grnd: with Mrs Dianne Sayer. 2 Apr'01 Nott 8.2hvy 61-58 F:	1½	47
1643 **SMARTER CHARTER** 18 [3]11-8-10 (15oh) (30) Kristin Stubbs(3) 25/1: 00-50206: Nvr nrr than mid-div.	4	40
1635 **SARN** 20 [8]5-8-10 (45) P Varley(7) 25/1: 000-0407: Bhd, nvr able to chall: btr 1406.	1¼	39
1551 **MR FORTYWINKS** 24 [4]10-9-1 (50) Suzanne France(5) 8/1: 1406-058: Chsd ldrs 12f, no extra: btr 1551.	hd	43
1396 **BULGARIA MOON** 32 [11]4-8-10 (5oh) (40) P Bradley 50/1: 060/00-09: ch g Groom Dancer - Gai Bulga (Kris) Handy 9f, wknd: unplcd both '03 starts (rtd 34, h'cap): with C Grant.	8	30
1552 **WASHINGTON PINK** 24 [7]5-8-10 (5oh) (40) M Halford(5) 16/1: 0/0-00400: 10th: Al bhd: btr 1396.	14	18
1793 Western Bluebird 11 [10]6-8-10 bl(45) Leanne Kershaw(3) 16/1:0		
1821 The Loose Screw 10 [2]6-8-10 (45) D Fentiman(5) 16/1:0		
2009 Rouge Blanc 2 [13]4-9-5 BL t(54) P Mulrennan 14/1:0 1507 **Illicium** 26 [14]5-8-10 (5oh) (40) D Fox 20/1:P		

14 Ran   Time 3m 2.54(9.14)   Owned: Mr E G Bevan   Trained: Hereford

---

Official Going Good/Firm

2061   6.05 European Breeders Fund Maiden Stakes Fillies 2yo (D)
£5801 £1785 £893   6f str   Good/Firm   Inapplicable   Stands Side

MASA 0 [5] Saeed bin Suroor 2-8-11 L Dettori 4/1 FAV: 1: b f Dixie Union - My Yellow Diamond (Housebuster) Made all, readily asserted from over 1f out, val 7L+: op 5/1: $95,000 Feb foal, dam a 3yo wnr & half-sister to several smart performers: sire top-class US dirt performer at up to 9f: eff at 6f, get further: acts on fast grnd & a sharp/undul trk: goes well fresh: impressive debut, useful, win more races.		92+
1709 **TESARY** 16 [11] E A L Dunlop 2-8-11 T E Durcan 7/1: 62: Prom, eff to chase wnr over 1f out, kept on but al well held: imprvd from debut: apprec fast grnd & step up to 6f, get further: see 1709.	5	76
1805 **STEPHANIES MIND** 12 [9] C N Allen 2-8-11 I Mongan 8/1: 03: b f Mind Games - Adorable Cherub (Halo) Chsd ldrs, rdn halfway, kept on for press, no threat to wnr: imprvd from debut: 15,000gns Feb foal, sister to a useful 3yo sprinter Dazzling Bay, also a prolific 6/7f wnr abroad: imprvd for step up to 6f & fast grnd.	nk	75
1805 **IVANA ILLYICH** 12 [13] S Kirk 2-8-11 J F Egan 20/1: 504: ch f Tipsy Creek - Tolstoya (Northfields) Prom, rdn & onepace fnl 2f: bckd at long odds: £25,000 April foal, half-sister to numerous wnrs, incl sprinters: dam a 5f juv wnr: this longer 6f trip shld suit: prob handles fast & soft grnd, sharp/undul trks.	nk	74
KISSING LIGHTS 0 [4]2-8-11 J Mackay 10/1: 5: Chsd wnr till dist: op 9/1.	1½	69
EXTREME BEAUTY 0 [10]2-8-11 D Holland 16/1: 6: Mid-div, outpcd over 2f out, kept on late.	1	66
GONE FISHING 0 [8]2-8-11 P Robinson 9/2: 7: Dwelt, chsd ldrs till outpcd from halfway.	¾	64
1805 **ROMANTIC GIFT** 12 [6]2-8-11 J Tate 12/1: 08: Chsd ldrs, no impress fnl 2f, longer trip.	nk	63
ROCK CHICK 0 [3]2-8-11 J Murtagh 9/1: 9: Outpcd twds rear, late gains, awkward head carriage.	1¼	59
COUNTY CLARE 0 [12]2-8-11 Martin Dwyer 7/1: 0: Dwelt, outpcd, mod late prog, op 9/2.	¾	57
IMPERIAL MISS 0 [7]2-8-11 S Carson 66/1: 0: 11th: Slow away & well bhd, nvr a factor.	1	54
ROSIELLA 0 [2]2-8-11 J Quinn 100/1: 0: 12th: U.r. bef start, dwelt, sn bhd.	11	24
JUST BEWARE 0 [1]2-8-11 N Chalmers(3) 100/1: 0: 13th: Slow away & sn outpcd, t.o..	10	0

13 Ran   Time 1m 10.61 (1.81)   Owned: Godolphin   Trained: Newmarket

---

2062   6.40 Mid Sussex Timber 75th Anniversary Handicap Stakes Fillies 3yo+ 0-70 (E)   [68]
£3494 £1075 £538   5f str   Good/Firm   Inapplicable   Stands Side

1873+ **LADY PROTECTOR** 9 [6] J Balding 5-8-12 (52) D Holland 8/1: 0300011: Chsd ldrs towards centre, styd on for press to lead cl-home, all out: eff at 6f, suited by 5f: acts on fast, gd/soft & fibresand, stiff or sharp trk.		59
1948 **INCHING** 5 [4] R M H Cowell 4-8-5 (45) Martin Dwyer 33/1: 4400002: Al prom towards centre, drvn & led well ins last, hdd cl-home: qck reapp: see 740 & 242.	nk	51
2044 **LADY PEKAN** 1 [2] P S McEntee 5-9-7 bl (61) T G McLaughlin 10/1: 02200353: Led/dsptd lead in	hd	66

centre, hdd well ins last, just held cl-home: op 12/1: unplcd yesterday: see 274.
1102 **COMERAINCOMESHINE 51** [11] T G Mills 3-8-12 (60) R Miles(3) 16/1: 030-364: Prom stands side, kept on, not pace of ldrs towards centre: 8 wk abs: eff at 5f, spot on in similar at 6f: handles fast grnd & polytrack. ½ **63**
1806* **I WISH 12** [14]6-9-2 (56) L Dettori 4/1 FAV: 6-050415: Rear, kept on late, not able to chall: see 1806. ¾ **57**
1694 **PRINCESS KAI 17** [1]3-8-9 bl (57) S Hitchcott(3) 16/1: 0034226: Dwelt & towards rear centre, late gains. *shd* **58**
1873 **TAMARELLA 9** [3]4-8-12 VIS (52) A McCarthy 25/1: 0-000507: Prom centre, no extra dist: visor. *shd* **52**
1878 **PLAYFUL SPIRIT 9** [7]5-8-7 (1ow)vis (46) J Edmunds 16/1: 3300308: Twds rear, late gains, no threat. *nk* **46**
3529} **MINIMUM BID 292** [13]3-8-8 (56) J Quinn 25/1: 063-9: b f First Trump - La Noisette (Rock Hopper) Bhd centre halfway, late gains, nrst fin: h'cap bow on reapp: unplcd '03 (rtd 60, auct mdn): half-sister to wnrs at 7f/1m: likely improver on return to 6f+. *nk* **54**
2034* **BOAVISTA 2** [9]4-9-12 (7ex) (66) S Donohoe(7) 6/1: 3442210: 10th: Prom stands side, no extra dist. 1¼ **60**
1867 **ERRACHT 9** [5]6-9-10 (64) N Chalmers(5) 20/1: 0-051600: 11th: Prom stands side till dist: btr 1371. ½ **56**
1867 **REDWOOD STAR 9** [15]4-9-3 e (57) J F Egan 9/2: 21030-40: 12th: Prom stands side, btn over 1f out. 1 **46**
1867 **BAHAMIAN BELLE 9** [10]4-9-0 t (54) S W Kelly 50/1: 6040000: 13th: Dwelt, keen & rear, nvr a factor. ¾ **41**
1442 **Empress Josephine 30** [12]4-9-2 vis(56) T E Durcan 25/11023 **Ryans Quest 57** [8]5-8-5 (45) P Doe 25/1:0
15 Ran Time 57.63 (0.83) Owned: Simon Mapletoft Racing II Trained: Doncaster

2063

7.10 Derek Burridge Racing & Golf Trophies Handicap Stakes 3yo+ 0-75 (E) **[74]**
£4014 £1235 £618 **7f str** **Good/Firm** **Inapplicable** Stands Side

1849 **QUANTUM LEAP 10** [12] S Dow 7-9-6 vis (66) R L Moore 8/1: 6303031: Led/dsptd lead & rdn clr from over 1f out: op 9/1: eff btwn 6f/10f, 7f suits now: acts on firm, gd/soft & polytrack, loves a sharp/undul trk, esp Lingfield: eff with/without visor: tough & genuine 7yo: see 1849 & 101. **75**
1723* **GOODENOUGH MOVER 16** [14] J S King 8-9-9 (69) Hayley Turner(5) 5/1 JT FAV: 0000-212: Al prom, kept on for press, not pace of wnr from dist: ran to form of 1723 (made all). 2½ **72**
1962 **MISTRAL SKY 5** [11] Mrs Stef Liddiard 5-9-7 P (67) J F Egan 16/1: 2002043: Chsd ldrs, switched & styd on for press ins last, not able to chall: back to form in first time cheek pieces: see 1020 & 121. ½ **69**
1723 **AND TOTO TOO 16** [17] P D Evans 4-9-7 bl (67) S Donohoe(7) 5/1 JT FAV: 0624424: Mid-div, styd on late. ¾ **67**
1691 **CAPTAIN DARLING 17** [4]4-9-3 VIS (63) E Ahern 14/1: 3-602005: Trkd ldrs, onepace fnl 1f: visor. *shd* **63**
765 **ADANTINO 90** [9]5-8-8 bl (54) S Drowne 14/1: 6341336: Chsd ldrs, no extra dist, abs: see 536 (banded). 1 **52**
1775 **AZREME 14** [16]4-9-10 (70) M Howard(7) 14/1: 0006-157: Trkd ldrs trav well, found little dist: btr 1537. ½ **67**
1788 **MAYZIN 12** [15]4-8-7 p (53) T E Durcan 12/1: 2331408: Dwelt, sn keen & prom, btn dist: btr 1025 & 897. *nk* **49**
1915 **STEELY DAN 7** [3]5-9-5 (65) L Dettori 13/2: 1160409: Rear, late prog, no threat: op 8/1: btr 1823. 1½ **58**
1537 **LOGISTICAL 25** [2]4-9-5 (65) S Whitworth 20/1: 54560-00: 10th: b c Grand Lodge - Magic Milly (Simply Great) Bhd, only mod late prog: class stks wnr '03: mdn wnr '02: prob suited by 7f: handles gd & soft grnd, poss firm grnd, stiff or sharp/undul trk. ¾ **56**
1 Jul'03 Leic 7.0gd 76-(68) E: 1 May'02 Bath 5gd 76- D: 2 Apr'02 Folk 5gd 79- D:
1691 **Treetops Hotel 17** [1]5-8-11 (57) N Chalmers(5) 33/1:0 1774 **El Chaparral 14** [8]4-9-6 P(66) R Miles(3) 33/1:0
607 **Power Bird 108** [7]4-9-2 (62) J Murtagh 20/1:0 1723 **Compton Arrow 16** [5]8-8-13 (59) I Mongan 33/1:0
4692} **Old Harry 230** [6]4-8-6 (52) L Keniry(1) 33/1:0 4564} **Franksalot 240** [13]4-9-5 (65) J Quinn 16/1:0
16 Ran Time 1m 22.06 (1.66) Owned: Mrs M E O'Shea Trained: Epsom

LINGFIELD Polytrack SATURDAY 29.05.04 Lefthand, V Sharp Track

Official Going Standard

2064

7.45 Rapporteur Handicap Stakes 3yo 46-55 (F) **[69]**
£3024 £864 £432 **1m2f aw** **Going** **Inapplicable** Inside

1372* **INCISOR 34** [7] S Kirk 3-8-11 (52) P Dobbs 7/2 FAV: 056-511: Trkd ldrs trav well, shaken up to lead ins last, readily, val 3L+: nicely bckd: well suited by 10f on fast grnd & polytrack, progressive. **62a+**
1954 **WILLHEGO 5** [10] J R Best 3-8-11 (52) Martin Dwyer 20/1: 000-002: ch g Pivotal - Woodrising (Nomination) Led, rdn & hdd ins last, no ch with wnr: qck reapp: plcd '03 (rtd 53, mdn): styd this longer 10f trip with forcing tactics: enjoyed polytrack tonight & handles a sharp/undul trk: best eff to date. 2½ **57a**
1395 **ASK THE DRIVER 33** [11] D J S ffrench Davis 3-8-13 (54) S Whitworth 6/1: 050-243: Short of room & drpd rear from start, hdwy for press fnl 2f, not able to chall: stays a sharp 10f: handles gd grnd & polytrack, poss soft: see 1395 & 1242. 1½ **57a**
2014 **CLARE GALWAY 3** [6] T D McCarthy 3-8-9 (50) R Miles(3) 12/1: 05004: b f Compton Place - Oublier L'Ennui (Bellman) Trkd ldrs, rdn & styd on onepace: qck reapp, bckd, op 14/1: stays a sharp 10f on polytrack. ½ **52a**
2014 **SAUCY 3** [13]3-8-9 bl (50) J F McDonald(3) 25/1: 0-6605: Chsd ldr, no extra dist: qck reapp: see 2014. 2 **49a**
1836 **AVERTAINE 11** [12]3-8-11 (52) R L Moore 8/1: 005206: Rear, mod prog for press: op 14/1: btr 1280. 1½ **49a**
863 **LADY STRIPES 73** [1]3-8-11 (52) T E Durcan 12/1: 060-0607: Rdn in tch, hmpd 2f out, no impress. *shd* **49a**
1324 **NAFFERTON GIRL 36** [8]3-8-9 (50) S W Kelly 20/1: 03-408: Chsd ldrs, drvn & btn over 1f out: btr 1078. 2½ **43a**
1985 **MISTER COMPLETELY 4** [5]3-8-8 (49) I Mongan 10/1: 0-265009: Rear, struggling fnl 4f: qck reapp. *shd* **42a**
1376 **SHARPLAW DESTINY 33** [2]3-8-12 (53) S Drowne 10/1: 004-50: 10th: Al towards rear & no ch fnl 3f. *hd* **45a**
1611 **MYSTIC MOON 22** [4]3-8-13 (54) D Holland 20/1: 0060400: 11th: Chsd ldrs, btn 2f out: btr 1280. ½ **45a**
1129 **DAYDREAM DANCER 47** [14]3-8-12 (53) P Robinson 9/1: 000-50: 12th: Al bhd, no ch fnl 3f: 7 wk abs. ¾ **43a**
1340 **ADEEBA 35** [9]3-9-0 (55) W Supple 25/1: 000-60: 13th: b f Alhaarth - Nedaarah (Reference Point) Al bhd: up in trip: unplcd '03 (rtd 65, mdn): mid-dists shld suit this term. 1¾ **43a**
1136 **SUNSET DREAMER 47** [3]3-8-11 (52) E Ahern 10/1: 6000: 14th: Al towards rear & no ch fnl 3f: abs. 4 **34a**
14 Ran Time 2m 07.99 (5.19) Owned: Mr R Gander Trained: Upper Lambourn

LINGFIELD **Polytrack SATURDAY 29.05.04 Lefthand, V Sharp Track**

2065

8.20 Mott Macdonald Selling Stakes 3yo (G)
£2562 £732 £366 **1m4f aw Going Inapplicable** Inside

1390 **PERUVIAN BREEZE 33** [2] N P Littmoden 3-8-12 (59) E Ahern 4/1: 066-561: Trkd ldr, chall from 2f out & narrowly asserted for press well ins last: bght in for 6,400gns: first win: lightly rcd & unplcd '03 (rtd 68, mdn): now stays a sharp 12f in sell grade: acts on polytrack: see 1141. **63a**

1403 **ANOTHER CON 32** [3] Mrs P N Dutfield 3-8-13 P (66) R Havlin 100/30: 4145002: Led, rdn & pressed fnl 2f, hdd well ins last & no extra: clr of rem: op 4/1: stays a sharp 12f in sell grade: fair run in cheek pieces. *½* **62a**

1896 **COME WHAT JULY 8** [5] R Guest 3-9-4 VIS (73) D Holland 9/4 FAV: 1256603: Trkd ldrs, outpcd over 2f out, sn no impress: bckd in first time visor: btr 702 & 601 (10f). *5* **60a**

1250 **FRAMBO 40** [9] J G Portman 3-8-7 T p (45) R L Moore 20/1: 5-005064: Mid-div, not pace to chall: t-strap. *7* **40a**
1720 **MARKSGOLD 16** [8]3-8-12 (57) S Drowne 12/1: 00-36605: Held up, drvn & nvr a factor: longer trip. *6* **37a**
1250 **SIGNORA PANETTIERA 40** [6]3-8-7 (58) S Hitchcott(3) 6/1: 640-606: Trkd ldrs, btn over 2f out: 6 wk abs. *4* **26a**
1501 **ONCE AROUND 27** [4]3-8-12 (51) R Miles(3) 14/1: 0-0007: Rear, no ch fnl 3f: mod form at up to 12f prev. *1¾* **29a**
1724 **WARIF 15** [1]3-8-12 BL (53) B Doyle 16/1: 000-508: Keen & prom early, struggling from halfway: blnks. *2½* **25a**
8 Ran Time 2m 35.53 (6.33) Owned: M C S D Racing Ltd Trained: Newmarket

2066

8.50 Music After Racing Maiden Stakes 3yo (D)
£3994 £1229 £615 **1m2f aw Going Inapplicable** Inside

1623 **SWAINSON 21** [6] P Mitchell 3-9-0 D Holland 9/4: 341: Made all, qcknd over 1f out, rdn & al holding rival ins last: op 4/1: eff at 10f, 12f may suit: handles soft grnd & polytrack, sharp/undul trks: enjoyed forcing tactics tonight under a well judged ride: see 1623 & 759. **83a**

1169 **ST FRANCIS WOOD 45** [10] J Noseda 3-8-9 E Ahern 13/8 FAV: 2-02: ch f Irish River - Francisco Road (Strawberry Road) Keen & cl-up trav well, shaken up ins last & found less than lkd likely, not pace of wnr cl-home: bckd tho' op evens: 6 wk abs: highly tried 2 prev starts, List rnr-up sole '03 start: eff at 1m/10f, a drop in trip could suit: acts on fast grnd & polytrack, stiff or sharp trk: better expected. *½* **76a**
2 Nov'03 Newm 8g/f 97- A:

SUPAMACH 0 [3] P F I Cole 3-8-9 S Drowne 10/1: 3: b f Machiavellian - Supamova (Seattle Slew) Cl-up, ch dist, kept on onepace on debut: half-sister to a 10f 3yo wnr, dam a 1m 3yo wnr: eff over a sharp 10f, could get further: acts on polytrack: pleasing debut, shld improve. *2½* **72a**

1815 **INNOCENT REBEL 11** [8] E A L Dunlop 3-9-0 T E Durcan 12/1: 04: ch c Swain - Cadeaux d'Amie (Lyphard) Keen & prom, not pace of front pair fnl 2f: op 14/1, AW bow: half-brother to a top-class 1m/10f performer Hatoof: dam well related: well bred colt, mid-dists shld suit: prob handles polytrack. *3* **73a**

1622 **MAIDSTONE MIDAS 21** [9]3-9-0 B Doyle 50/1: 045: Cl-up till over 2f out, no extra. *3* **69a**
1008 **PINS N NEEDLES 59** [4]3-8-9 J F Egan 20/1: 06: Keen & cl-up, outpcd fnl 2f: 2 mth abs, longer trip. *¾* **63a**
JOHNNY ROOK 0 [12]3-9-0 I Mongan 14/1: 7: Pushed along rear, kept on late, nvr threat on debut. *1¾* **66a**
3511} **BEE DEES LEGACY 293** [2]3-9-0 R Brisland 50/1: 0-8: Pushed along towards rear, nvr factor: new stable. *1½* **64a**
SAILORMAN 0 [7]3-9-0 Martin Dwyer 10/1: 9: U.r. bef start, pushed along mid-div, nvr a factor: op 8/1. *hd* **63a**
BREAKING THE RULE 0 [5]3-8-9 R L Moore 33/1: 0: 10th: Mid-div, chsd ldr till over 2f out, debut. *1¼* **56a**
16**CRIMSON STAR 22** [1]3-8-9 R Miles(3) 20/1: 00: 11th: Prom, short of room after 2f, wknd fnl 2f. *7* **47a**
Surface To Air 0 [11]3-9-0 R Havlin 66/1:0 **Amazonic 0** [14]3-8-9 R Price 100/1:0
13 Ran Time 2m 08.65(4.45) Owned: Mr Richard J Cohen Trained: Epsom

KEMPTON **SATURDAY 29.05.04 Righthand, Flat, Fair Track**

Official Going Good/Firm

2067

1.35 Totesport Handicap Stakes 3yo+ 0-90 (C) **[90]**
£9760 £3003 £1502 **1m2f Firm 04 -30 Slow** Inside

1979* **POLAR JEM 4** [1] G G Margarson 4-9-3 (6ex) (79) A McCarthy 12/1: 321-3411: Made all, rdn clr 2f out, cmftbly, val 3/4L: op 8/1, qck reapp: v eff at 10f on firm or fast grnd, easy or gall trks: relished forcing tactics last twice & thriving at present, can land quick-fire hat-trick: see 1979. **88**

2036 **KARAOKE 2** [6] S Kirk 4-8-3 (65) R L Moore 13/2: 0055422: Held up, hdwy 2f out, styd on over 1f out, no impress on wnr: bckd, qk reapp, another gd run: win again, see 2036, 803. *1½* **69**

1736 **TODLEA 15** [4] J A Osborne 4-8-10 (72) R Hughes 10/1: 000-6443: In tch, hdwy 2f out, kept on, no threat to cmftble wnr: gd run: see 1736, 1352. *nk* **76**

1650 **STREET LIFE 19** [16] W J Musson 6-8-12 (74) G Carter 16/1: 6-252334: Held up, kept on late, nrst fin: tough, handles firm grnd, likes soft, hvy & Windsor: see 1650, 391. *2* **75**

1828 **NORTHSIDE LODGE 11** [2]6-9-1 (77) Martin Dwyer 8/1: 2030035: Prom, chsd wnr over 3f out, onepace. *1¾* **75**
1781 **SILVALINE 13** [8]5-8-12 (74) P Doe 25/1: 6045506: Held up, late gains, nvr dngrs: may do btr. *½* **71**
1296 **ARRY DASH 38** [3]4-9-10 (86) T E Durcan 14/1: 15-40207: Chsd ldrs, sltly outpcd 2f out, late gains. *nk* **82**
1721 **DESERT ISLAND DISC 16** [10]7-8-13 (75) J F McDonald(3) 16/1: 030-0448: In tch, eff 2f out, no impress. *nk* **70**
1602 **LILLI MARLANE 22** [7]4-8-10 BL (72) P Dobbs 7/1: 3350-269: Bhd, modest late gains: tried blnks. *1* **65**
1828 **PRAIRIE WOLF 11** [13]8-9-2 (78) I Mongan 14/1: 320-0000: 10th: With ldrs, wknd 2f out: see 1296. *½* **70**
1777* **SUMMER BOUNTY 14** [11]8-9-0 (76) R Miles(3) 16/1: 450-0110: 11th: Slow away, al bhd: nvr trav. *¾* **67**
179* **WINDY BRITAIN 171** [5]5-9-12 (88) D Holland 11/2 FAV: 313131-0: 12th: In tch, wknd 2f out: long abs: prev v consistent & much btr than this: see 179, 82. *1¼* **77**
1484 **RASID 28** [15]6-8-13 (75) S Drowne 50/1: 1023100: 13th: Chsd ldrs, wknd over 2f out: btr 1397 (soft). *¾* **62**
1849 **CAROUBIER 10** [12]4-9-0 (76) J Quinn 16/1: 1201000: 14th: Al bhd: btr 1059 (gd/soft, 1m). *1¼* **61**
1895 **TONY TIE 8** [9]8-8-13 (75) J F Egan 20/1: 60-62250: 15th: Keen in tch, wknd 2f out: too free. *2* **57**
15 Ran Time 2m 05.57 (3.37) Owned: Norcroft Park Stud Trained: Newmarket

---

2068 2.05 Listed Favourites Racing Achilles Stakes 3yo+ (A)
£17400 £6600 £3300 **5f str** **Firm 04** **-09 Slow** Centre

1918 **BOOGIE STREET** 7 [10] R Hannon 3-8-13 t (107) R Hughes 4/1: 1341-321: Handy, led over 1f out, styd **113**
on strongly, rdn out: caught a high-class sort last time: v eff over 5/6f on firm & fast grnd, fair or stiff trks:
wears a t-strap: progressive & smart now, win a Group race in this form: see 1479.
4629} **LOCHRIDGE** 237 [5] A M Balding 5-9-2 (106) Martin Dwyer 9/2: 161130-2: ch f Indian Ridge - **1** **104+**
Lochsong (Song) Handy, rdn 2f out, styd on fnl 1f, not pace of wnr: '03 dual h'cap & List wnr: '02 mdn & h'cap
wnr: suited by 6f, stays 7f, likes firm & fast grnd, stiff trks: can dominate: progressive & v useful, fine rtn,
will be winning gd race shortly with a rtn to 6f. 1 Aug'03 Pont 6g/f 103-(89) A: 1 Aug'03 Asco 6g/f 99-89 B:
1 Jul'03 Newb 6.0fm 92-84 C: 1 Oct'02 Newm 6fm 88-81 B: 1 Jun'02 Sali 7fm 77- D: 2 Sep'01 Kemp 7g/f 82- D:
1856 **THE TATLING** 13 [8] J M Bradley 7-9-10 (112) D Holland 2/1 FAV: 55340-23: In tch, hdwy & sltly **½** **110**
short or room 2f out, kept on late, not threat to wnr: hvly bckd: ran close to smart best conceding weight.
1957 **FROMSONG** 5 [6] B R Millman 6-9-3 (95) T E Durcan 25/1: 00-24444: In tch, onepace fnl 1f: qk reapp. **1¼** **99**
1626 **COLONEL COTTON** 21 [3]5-9-7 (103) P Robinson 12/1: 130-6065: Held up, late gains, nrst fin: much **shd** **102**
more encouraging on this faster grnd: see 1159.
4764} **BALI ROYAL** 226 [9]6-9-2 (104) R Miles 10/1: 422124-6: b f King's Signet - Baligay (Balidar) **¾** **95**
With ldrs, led over 3f out till over 1f out, no extra: reapp: '03 List fill wnr: won 2 val h'caps in '02: suited
by 5f, stays 6f: loves fm & fast, handles hvy & fibresand, any trk: genuines & useful, much sharper for this.
2 Oct'03 Newm 5g/f 100-(105) A: 1 Sep'03 Hami 5.0g/f 103-(102) A: 2 Jul'03 Newm 5g/f 100-(102) C:
2 Jul'03 Sand 5.0g/f 103-(98) A: 2 Jun'03 York 5.0g/f 99-95 C: 1 Jun'02 Muss 5g/f 99-95: 1 May'02 Hayd 5gd 98-90 B:
2 Apr'02 Thir 5fm 89-88 C: 1 Aug'01 Good 5g/f 88-85 C: 2 Jul'01 Bath 5fm 87-83 C: 1 Jul'01 Ches 5g/f 85-77 C:
1845 **PERUVIAN CHIEF** 10 [7]7-9-3 vis (96) G Carter 20/1: 0002007: Bhd, late hdwy, nrst fin: won this in '03. **shd** **95**
1845 **LITTLE EDWARD** 10 [2]6-9-3 (97) J Murtagh 20/1: 225-5058: With ldrs, wknd dist: needs h'caps. **1¼** **91**
1490 **BORDER SUBJECT** 27 [4]7-9-3 BL (105) S Drowne 12/1: 64100-69: Led till over 3f out, wknd appr fnl **1** **88**
1f: below best in blnks: see 1490.
4585} **BOLEYN CASTLE** 238 [1]7-9-3 (96) S W Kelly 33/1: 000000-0: 10th: ch g River Special - Dance Skirt **6** **70**
(Caucasus) Slow away, in tch, wknd over 2f out: plcd in a List on '03 reapp (rtd 104), subs below best incl in a
visor: '02 stks & val h'cap wnr: eff at 5f on firm & gd/soft, any trk: has run well fresh & can force the pace:
prev with T Mills, now with P McEntee.
1 Jul'02 Asco 5g/f 116-108 B: 1 Jul'02 Sand 5g/s 109- A: 1 Jun'02 Sand 5g/s 109- C: 1 Aug'01 Epso 5g/f 96-88 B:
10 Ran Time 58.96 (0.66) Owned: Hippodrome Racing Trained: Marlborough

---

2069 2.40 Listed Byrne Group Heron Stakes 3yo (A)
£17400 £6600 £3300 **1m rnd** **Firm 04** **-08 Slow** Inside

1482 **TAHREEB** 28 [5] M P Tregoning 3-8-12 (108) Martin Dwyer 3/1: 1344-421: Led over 2f out, styd on **112**
gamely for press when prsd ins last: bckd: eff over 1m/10f on fm & gd/soft, any trk: genuine & improving.
4469} **LEICESTER SQUARE** 245 [4] Saeed bin Suroor 3-8-12 T (107) L Dettori 9/4 FAV: 1204-2: ch c Gone **nk** **111**
West - Stage Manner (In The Wings) In tch, hdwy over 2f out, styd on to chall when carr head high & not go past ins
last: nicely bckd on reapp: '03 mdn wnr for M Johnston, plcd in Group company: stays 1m on firm & gd grnd, stiff or
fair trks: wears a t-strap: v useful, win races if taking to headgear.
2 Jul'03 Curr 6.3gd 103- A: 1 Jun'03 Leic 6.0g/f 88- D:
4672} **ORCADIAN** 231 [6] J M P Eustace 3-8-12 (103) J Tate 16/1: 31220-3: b g Kirkwall - Rosy Outlook **3** **104**
(Trempolino) Set pace till over 2f out, onepace on reapp: won 1 of 5 '03 starts (mdn): eff at 6f, prob stays 1m on
firm & gd grnd, gall or easy trks: useful.
2 Sep'03 Yarm 6.0gd 102-(100) C: 2 Aug'03 Newb 7fm 104- A: 1 Jul'03 Wind 6g/f 96- D:
1167 **AZAROLE** 45 [3] J R Fanshawe 3-8-12 (108) J Murtagh 11/4: 21144-54: b c Alzao - Cashew (Sharrood) **nk** **103**
In tch, onepace fnl 2f: well bckd tho' op 7/4: '03 nov auct wnr, 4th in Gr 2: eff at 6/7f, prob stays 1m on firm
& fast grnd, sharp or gall trk: shade btr expected here.
1 Aug'03 Wind 6g/f 106-(90) E: 1 Jul'03 Newm 6g/f 97- E: 2 Jul'03 Yarm 6.0g/f 94- D:
1492 **KELUCIA** 27 [1]3-8-7 (100) J F Egan 14/1: 1334-505: Held up, swished tail fnl 2f, onepace. **1** **96**
4067*}**RESPLENDENT ONE** 267 [7]3-8-12 R Miles 20/1: 01-6: b c Marju - Licentious (Reprimand) Held up, **hd** **100**
rdn 3f out, some late gains, no dngr: '03 mdn wnr: half-brother to a dual 14f scorer: stays 1m, further will suit:
acts on fast grnd: poss more to come in lesser grade. 1 Sep'03 Kemp 8g/f 87- D:
1685 **BARBAJUAN** 17 [8]3-9-3 (102) P Robinson 20/1: 143-5007: In tch, wknd 2f out: see 1113. **2½** **100**
1811 **MUSTAJED** 11 [2]3-8-12 VIS W Supple 14/1: 1-68: In tch, wknd qckly 2f out: visor, see 1811. **¾** **93**
8 Ran Time 1m 37.76 (0.96) Owned: Sheikh Ahmed Al Maktoum Trained: Lambourn

---

2070 3.15 Totetrifecta Wokingham Trial Handicap Stakes 3yo+ 0-90 (C)
£12760 £4840 £2420 **6f str** **Firm 04** **+17 Fast** Centre. 2 Groups.

2007 **PRINCE AARON** 3 [17] C N Allen 4-8-11 (72) G Carter 7/1: 1162131: Handy far side, overall ldr **90**
over 1f out, pushed clr, readily: fast time: suited by 6f: acts on fm & poly track: easy trks, loves Lingfield: gd
weight carrier: took advantage of v handy turf mark & thriving at present: see 874.
1909 **TRUE NIGHT** 7 [20] D Nicholls 7-8-13 (74) T E Durcan 14/1: 5-000042: Chsd ldrs far side, kept on **2½** **84**
over 1f out, no threat to wnr: encouraging, h'capped to win, prob over 7f/1m: see 1909.
1820 **ONE WAY TICKET** 11 [16] J M Bradley 4-7-12 (2oh)p (57) Hayley Turner(5) 25/1: 020-0003: ch c **2½** **62**
Pursuit of Love - Prima Cominna (Unfuwain) Handy far side, led that group over 3f out till over 1f out, onepace:
'03 mdn wnr: eff over 6/7f on firm, gd/soft & prob any trk: eff in cheek pieces: gd rtn.
2 Sep'03 Chep 7.1g/f 66-(70) E: 1 Aug'03 Warw 7.1fm 71-(70) D: 2 Jul'03 Ripo 6g/f 73-70 E:
2 May'03 Redc 7g/f 71-(70) E: 2 May'03 Sali 7.0fm 69-(70) E:
1703 **MUTAWAQED** 16 [6] M A Magnusson 6-9-10 t (85) J Murtagh 10/1: 03630-04: ch g Zafonic - Waqood **¾** **86+**
(Riverman) Bhd stands side, styd on nicely late, no ch with far side group: '03 dual h'cap wnr: '02 h'cap scorer:
v eff at 6f, has won at 1m: acts on fast & rain-softened grnd, both AWs, any trk: wears a t-strap: keep in mind.
1 Jun'03 Newc 6gd 86-78 C: 2 May'03 Kemp 6fm 79-76 C: 1 Jan'03 Ling 6ap 84a-79 D: 2 Dec'02 Ling 7ap 81a-77 C:
1 Jan'02 Ling 7ap 76a-69 E: 1 Dec'01 Sout 8af 64a-56 F: 2 Nov'01 Wolv 6af 59a-52 F:
1 Nov'01 Sout 7af 57a-45 F:
1523 **LOYAL TYCOON** 26 [14]6-9-6 (81) L Dettori 5/1 FAV: 000-0025: Chsd ldrs far side, onepace over 1f **shd** **82**
out: s/mate of 2nd, poised for a big run at Epsom (won in '03, 3lb lower now): see 1523.

KEMPTON   SATURDAY 29.05.04   Righthand, Flat, Fair Track

1914 **SEVEN NO TRUMPS 7** [8]7-9-2 p (77) R L Moore 20/1: 2500036: Led stands side group over 2f out till ins last, no extra: s/mate of 3rd, another gd run: see 944. nk 77

1774 **SAVILES DELIGHT 14** [4]5-8-9 (70) J F Egan 14/1: 3243127: Led stands side group till over 2f out, onepace: in gd form: see 1774, 1533. ½ 68

1703 **MARSAD 16** [10]10-9-13 (88) P Doe 12/1: 5203-038: In tch stands side, some late gains: see 1703. hd 85

1624 **MARKER 21** [9]4-9-8 (83) R Havlin 20/1: 00-60049: Bhd stands side, some late gains, nvr dngr. nk 79

361 **CANTERLOUPE 141** [5]6-9-3 T (78) D Holland 25/1: 30516-00: 10th: In tch stands side, no impress fnl 1f: tried a t-strap, long abs: see 41 (fibresand). ½ 72

4394* **THURLESTONE ROCK 250** [19]4-9-3 (78) J F McDonald(3) 20/1: 021001-0: 11th: ch g Sheikh Albadou - Don't Smile (Sizzling Melody) Handy, wknd fnl 1f on reapp: '03 dual h'cap wnr: eff over 5f, suited by 6f on firm & fast grnd, both AWs: likes sharp trks & eff with/without blnks. ¾ 70
1 Sep'03 Kemp 6g/f 80-75 C: 1 Aug'03 Ling 6g/f 73-69 D: 2 Jul'03 Epso 6g/f 71-69 D: 2 Oct'02 Ling 5ap 78a- D: 1 Oct'02 Wolv 6af 79a-67 D: 2 Sep'02 Chep 5g/f 70-61 E:

1103 **ZARZU 51** [7]5-8-13 (74) J Bramhill 20/1: 3543430: 12th: In tch stands side, wknd dist: 7 wk abs. nk 65

4544} **DANEHILL STROLLER 241** [13]4-9-13 (88) Lisa Jones(3) 25/1: 101243-0: 13th: b g Danetime - Tuft Hill (Grundy) Slow away, in tch, wknd 2f out on reapp: '03 h'cap & class stks wnr: eff over 5/6f on firm, gd/soft & polytrack: handles any trk & eff in cheek pieces: has run well fresh: shld do btr with headgear on. ½ 77
2 Aug'03 Asco 6g/f 87-85 D: 1 Aug'03 Newc 6g/f 88-(84) D: 1 Jul'03 Donc 6g/f 84-81 D: 2 Jul'03 Hayd 6g/f 82-81 D: 2 Jul'03 Ripo 6g/f 80-78 D: 2 Jul'02 Beve 5g/s 85- D: 1 Jun'02 Ling 5ap 80a- E:

4286} **HEY PRESTO 255** [15]4-8-13 (74) P Robinson 20/1: 060040-0: 14th: b g Piccolo - Upping The Tempo (Dunbeath) Led far side after 1f till over 3f out, wknd: '03 h'cap wnr: eff over 5/6f on firm & gd grnd, prob any trk: tried blnks. 2 May'03 Newm 6g/f 82-79 C: 1 May'03 Sali 6fm 82-73 E: 2 Sep'02 Folk 5gd 74- D: nk 62

1523* **KINGSCROSS 26** [2]6-9-4 (79) J Quinn 10/1: 000-4210: 15th: Slow away stands side, nvr a factor. 2½ 60

1767 **NAJEEBON 14** [12]5-9-10 (85) S Hitchcott(3) 12/1: 1450-000: 16th: Al bhd far side: see 1481. shd 65

4544} **DOMIRATI 241** [11]4-9-4 (79) S Drowne 12/1: 302234-0: 17th: In tch, wknd 2f out. 1¼ 55

1845 **TURIBIUS 10** [1]5-9-4 (79) R Hughes 16/1: 21-61300: 18th: Al bhd stands side: reportedly nvr trav. 4 43

1782 **GAELIC PRINCESS 13** [3]4-9-10 (85) S Whitworth 33/1: 030-0060: 19th: Nvr a factor stands side. 2½ 42

19 Ran   Time 1m 10.28 (u0.82)   Owned: Black Star Racing   Trained: Newmarket

---

2071   **3.50 Platinum Security Conditions Stakes 2yo   (C)**
£7291 £2765 £1383   **6f str**   **Firm 04**   **-29 Slow**   Centre

1808 **BEAVER PATROL 12** [6] R F Johnson Houghton 2-9-0 S Carson 1/1 FAV: 1321: Handy, hdwy over 1f out, styd on well for press to get up cl-home: hvly bckd: clrly stays 6f & acts on firm & gd/soft, easy trks: useful, genuine, going the right way: see 1567, 1256. 104

1893* **DOCTOR HILARY 8** [5] M L W Bell 2-8-10 J Mackay 7/1: 412: Led, rdn but kept on over 1f out, collared cl-home: acts on fm & fast: imprvd stepped up in class & shld be wng again shortly: see 1893. hd 99

1818* **UMNIYA 11** [2] M R Channon 2-8-5 T E Durcan 7/2: 3213: Chsd ldrs, eff over 1f out, kept on ins last, not btn far: clr of rem & prob ran to best: see 1818. ¾ 92

BANKNOTE [1] A M Balding 2-8-7 Martin Dwyer 7/1: 4: b c Zafonic - Brand (Shareef Dancer) Slow away, in tch, eff 2f out, sn no extra on debut: Apr foal: half-brother to wnrs over 6f/hdles: learn from this. 7 73

1738 **IM SPARTACUS 15** [3]2-9-0 I Mongan 25/1: 02165: In tch, wknd 2f out: twice below 1367. 2 74

BIBI HELEN [7]2-8-2 D Fox(5) 50/1: 6: b f Robellino - Tarry (Salse) Slow away & al bhd on debut: Apr foal, cheaply bght: half-brother to a 9f wnr: dam 7f/14f scorer: bred to need 7f+. nk 61

DOCTORS CAVE [4]2-8-7 D Holland 14/1: 7: Al bhd on debut. 1¼ 62

7 Ran   Time 1m 13.06 (1.96)   Owned: Mr G C Stevens   Trained: Didcot

---

2072   **4.25 Bjorn Again Here Wednesday June 2nd Maiden Stakes 3yo   (D)**
£5720 £1760 £880   **1m rnd**   **Firm 04**   **-41 Slow**   Inside

1688 **CAPESTAR 17** [9] B G Powell 3-8-10 (1ow) J Murtagh 9/4 FAV: 621: Cl-up, hdwy to lead over 1f out, styd on, rdn out: well bckd: apprec step up to 1m: acts on firm & gd/soft, gall or fair trks: confidence boost. 77

SERRE CHEVALIER [8] P W Harris 3-9-0 Martin Dwyer 20/1: 2: b g Marju - Ski Lodge (Persian Bold) Held up, hdwy well over 1f out, kept on ins last on debut: dam 7f juv scorer: stays 1m, further shld suit: acts on firm grnd & a fair trk: v encouraging first run, learn plenty from this & shld be winning soon. ½ 79+

1763 **ZUMA 14** [13] R Hannon 3-9-0 D Holland 5/1: 00-003: b c Grand Lodge - Paradise Waters (Celestial Storm) Slow away, sn in tch, outpcd over 2f out, kept on late: unplcd both juv starts: eff at 1m on firm. 1 77

4149} **ZWADI 263** [12] H Candy 3-8-9 (75) S Whitworth 20/1: 34324-4: b f Docksider - Local Custom (Be My Native) Sn led, hdd appr fnl 1f, no extra: plcd in a mdn for B Hills in '03: eff at 6f, stays 1m on firm, prob fibresand & on any trk. 2 Aug'03 Folk 7g/f 76- D: nk 71

1737 **TUMBAGA 15** [1]3-9-0 T R Hughes 7/1: 005: Handy, outpcd 2f out, late gains: btr run in t-strap. 2½ 71

4971} **PRE EMINANCE 210** [5]3-9-0 S Drowne 6/1: 4-6: In tch, wknd over 1f out: op 9/1. ½ 70

1762 **SHAABAN 14** [6]3-9-0 T E Durcan(3) 25/1: 07: Slow away, bhd, modest late gains. ½ 69

4774} **HUNTERS VALLEY 225** [10]3-8-9 (80) P Dobbs 12/1: 0523-8: Nvr a factor on reapp. ¾ 62

4713} **CHIGORIN 229** [2]3-9-0 J Tate 25/1: 03-9: In tch, no impress fnl 2f. nk 66

1495 **KILLMOREY 27** [4]3-9-0 J Quinn 66/1: 00: 10th: Slow away, al bhd. 1 64

1327} **POWERFUL PARRISH 230** [3]3-8-9 L Dettori 9/2: 25-0: 11th: Chsd ldrs, wknd over 2f out: op 3/1. 4 51

1965} **KARMA CHAMELIAN 359** [7]3-8-9 Lisa Jones(3) 50/1: 0-0: 12th: In tch, wknd over 2f out. 7 37

4547} **COURT CHANCELLOR 241** [11]3-9-0 R L Moore 100/1: 000-0: 13th: Al bhd. 18 6

13 Ran   Time 1m 40.39 (3.59)   Owned: D & J Newell   Trained: Winchester

---

2073   **4.55 Wednesday Evening Series Handicap Stakes 3yo+ 0-85   (D)**
£5486 £1688 £844   **2m**   **Firm 04**   **-35 Slow**   Inside   [80]

921} **QUEDEX 424** [6] R J Price 8-8-8 (60) R Miles(3) 8/1: 0/065/06-1: b g Deploy - Alwal (Pharly) Held up, hdwy over 2f out, styd on strongly to lead over 1f out, rdn out: recent sell & h'cap hdle wnr (2m1f, gd & soft), styd 2m3.5f, rtd 114h): lightly rcd & modest Flat form since '01 (rtd 80): former h'cap wnr: suited by 2m on firm or soft & any trk, tough, v well h'capped now, can win again. 68

1861 **THEATRE 9** [7] Jamie Poulton 5-10-0 (80) P Doe 8/1: 0004-0S2: b g Theatrical - Fasta (Seattle Song) Chsd ldrs, lost pl over 4f out, styd on to lead over 2f out till 1f out, not pace of wnr: '03 h'cap wnr: '02 mdn scorer: stays 2m on firm, gd & polytrack, any trk: right back to best. 2 May'03 Good 14g/f 86-81 B: 1½ 86

KEMPTON SATURDAY 29.05.04 Righthand, Flat, Fair Track

1 Apr'03 Newb 16fm 82-76 C: 1 Dec'02 Ling 12ap 79a- D: 2 Oct'02 Ling 13ap 80a- D: 2 Jun'02 Yarm 14fm 75- D:

1689 **HIGH POINT 17** [9] G P Enright 6-10-0 (80) S Hitchcott(3) 4/1 JT FAV: 0002333: Chsd ldrs, rdn over 2f out, some late gains, no threat: another gd run: acts on fm, gd/soft & polytrack: see 1112.	1	84
1650 **SUDDEN FLIGHT 19** [10] P D Evans 7-8-13 (65) R Havlin 25/1: 0003004: In tch, eff when hmpd over 2f out, rallied ins last, no dngr: prob stays 2m on fm, likes gd, soft & both a/w's: see 870.	nk	70
1232* **MALARKEY 42** [2]7-9-10 (76) S Drowne 4/1 JT FAV: 06/-51215: Held up, hdwy well over 2f out, no extra over 1f out: 6 wk abs: prob better expected after impressive win in 1232 (gd grnd).	5	76
2035* **TREASURE TRAIL 2** [3]5-9-4 (5ex) (70) J F Egan 9/2: 00-50016: Held up, eff over 2f out, sn wknd.	3	67
4755} **PEAK PARK 227** [8]4-7-12 (4oh) (48) Lisa Jones(3) 25/1: 000360-7: br g Dynaformer - Play Po (Play On) Keen, al bhd on reapp: plcd in an appr h'cap in '03: stays 2m on fast grnd & on a sharp/undul trk.	3	46
1772 **HEAD TO KERRY 14** [4]4-8-11 (65) R Hughes 8/1: 13513-08: Keen in tch, wknd over 2f out.	½	58
1689 **SNOWS RIDE 17** [1]4-9-7 BL (75) D Holland 25/1: 011-0009: Led after 1f till 2f out, wknd: blnks.	13	55
1516 **LINENS FLAME 26** [5]5-9-9 (75) J Murtagh 8/1: 000-1120: 10th: Chsd ldr till wknd qckly 3f out: not handle firm grnd?: much btr 1516, 1271 (soft).	25	31

10 Ran   Time 3m 30.53(6.33)   Owned: Fox and Cub Partnership   Trained: Hereford

DONCASTER SATURDAY 29.05.04 Lefthand, Flat, Galloping Track

Official Going Good/Firm (Firm places in Str)

2074 1.50 Skybet Com Classified Stakes 3yo+ 0-80 (D)
£5509 £1695 £848   **6f str**   **Good/Firm 31**   **-09 Slow**   Stands Side

1767 **HICCUPS 14** [5] Mrs J R Ramsden 4-9-2 p (80) R Winston 4/1: 630-2031: Dwelt, keen, hdwy when short of room dist, led ins fnl 1f, drvn out: deserved win, now race on wrong side last time: eff at 5/6f on firm & gd/soft grnd, likes a gall trk: wears cheek pieces: see 1767 & 1217.		82
1767 **MILLION PERCENT 14** [7] K R Burke 5-9-2 (80) K Fallon 3/1 FAV: 5430-062: Chsd ldrs, no room over 1f out till entering fnl 1f, kept on, no impress fnl 50y: bckd: shade closer to wnr with clr run, encouraging: see 1767.	½	82
1767 **BANJO BAY 14** [6] D Nicholls 6-9-4 (82) L Treadwell(7) 16/1: 0000-003: Chsd ldrs, led entering fnl 1f, hdd & no extra cl-home: on a decent mark & return to form here: see 1568.	1½	79
1767 **ELLENS ACADEMY 14** [2] E J Alston 9-9-2 (80) R Hills 4/1: 4634244: Slowly away, styd on fnl 1f.	hd	77
1598 **SMIRFYS SYSTEMS 22** [3]5-9-2 (78) B Swarbrick(5) 14/1: 0012-005: Dwelt, chsd ldrs, onepcd fnl 1f.	1¼	73
1726 **MR MALARKEY 15** [8]4-9-2 bl (78) M Hills 7/1: 000-4046: Led till entering fnl 1f, wkng when short of room cl-home: see 1726.	3½	63
1726 **WILLHEWIZ 15** [4]4-9-4 BL (82) J P Guillambert(3) 16/1: 101-0567: Prom, wknd dist: tried blnks.	1¾	60
1817 **MATERIAL WITNESS 11** [1]7-9-6 (84) M Fenton 11/2: 100-0028: Prom till halfway, sn bhd: btr 1817.	hd	61

8 Ran   Time 1m 13.22 (2.42)   Owned: J M & Mrs E E Ranson   Trained: Thirsk

2075 2.25 Lakeside Median Auction Maiden Stakes 3yo (E)
£3465 £1066 £533   **5f str**   **Good/Firm 31**   **-32 Slow**   Stands Side

1216 **CATHERINE WHEEL 43** [2] J R Fanshawe 3-8-9 K Fallon 1/3 FAV: 21: Held up, strong run to lead cl-home, drvn out: well bckd at odds-on, 6 wk abs: eff at 5/6f on fast & gd/soft grnd: runs well fresh.		68
1575 **EX MILL LADY 23** [9] John Berry 3-8-9 N Callan 16/1: 5-42: Tried to make all, worn down cl-home: bckd at long odds: eff at 5f on fast, handles soft grnd: return to 6f may suit, see 1575.	nk	67
1146 **FISHLAKE FLYER 47** [1] J G Given 3-8-9 (66) M Fenton 8/1: 20432-43: Chsd ldrs, ev ch fnl 1f, just btn in a close fin: 7 wk abs: eff 5/6f on gd grnd: lightly raced & should run well: see 1146.	nk	66
HARRINGTON BATES 0 [6] R M Whitaker 3-9-0 Dean McKeown 8/1: 4: ch g Wolfhound - Fiddling (Music Boy) Slowly away, recovered to chase ldrs, short of room ins fnl 1f & only btn around 1L on debut: op 4/1: cost 26,000gns: sprint bred, eff at 5f on fast grnd & h'capped now & one to keep in mind.	½	69+
1639 **FROM THE NORTH 21** [4]3-8-9 VIS A Beech(3) 100/1: P0-05: ch f Foxhound - Best Swinger (Ela Mana Mou) Held up, switched & styd on late, nrst fin: imprvd form in first time visor: eff at 6f on fast grnd.	1	61$
1464 **NEW DAY DAWNING 29** [7]3-8-9 (48) J Fanning 100/1: 04600-06: Held up, prog when hmpd dist, no ch after: offic rtd 48, treat this rating with caution.	1¾	56$
1949 **OPEN MIND 5** [3]3-8-9 (52) R Hills 22/1: 4040-437: Prom, lost pl halfway: qck reapp: see 1949.	¾	54$
1740 **SHANGHAI SURPRISE 15** [5]3-9-0 bl (45) E Ahern 100/1: 6000-508: Front rank till halfway.	2½	52$

8 Ran   Time 1m 01.34 (3.14)   Owned: Cheveley Park Stud   Trained: Newmarket

2076 2.55 Sky Vegas Live On Channel 295 Handicap Stakes 3yo+ 0-100 (C)   [100]
£9958 £3064 £1532   **7f str**   **Good/Firm 31**   **+08 Fast**   Stands Side

1883 **UHOOMAGOO 8** [1] K A Ryan 6-8-8 bl (80) N Callan 7/1: 30-10001: Held up, hdwy 2f out, led entering fnl 1f, rdn clr, going away: gd time: eff at 6f, suited by 7f, stays 1m well: acts on firm, soft grnd & fibresand, any trk: suited by blnks & runs well fresh: impressed here, could go well Royal Hunt Cup, see 744.		90
1351 **FLYING EXPRESS 35** [9] B W Hills 4-8-12 (84) M Hills 7/2: 0644-602: Chsd ldrs, led briefly dist, kept on but no ch with wnr: bckd from 6/1: sound run, a bold eff clearly expected & deserves similar: see 1151.	3	87
1512 **JAY GEES CHOICE 26** [6] M R Channon 4-9-0 (86) C Catlin 10/1: 600-6003: b g Barathea - Llia (Shirley Heights) Hmpd start, recovered to chase ldrs, onepcd fnl 1f: failed to win in '03, class stks rnr-up: juv mdn & stks wnr in '02: stays 1m, prob best at 7f: acts on firm & soft grnd, likes a gall trk: hinted at a return to form, extremely well h'capped now & one to keep in mind.	1	87+
2 Jul'03 Sali 8g/f 98-(99) B: 1 Oct'02 Leic 7sft 94- C: 1 Sep'02 Hayd 7.1g/f 96- D: 2 Jul'02 Asco 6g/f 82- D:		
1970 **WHAT A DANCER 5** [11] G A Swinbank 7-8-5 (77) R Winston 10/1: 1-431404: Held up, short of room halfway & again 2f out, kept on fnl 1f: qck reapp & did not get the run of today's race: see 1970.	½	77
1151 **MANAAR 46** [8]4-8-13 (85) E Ahern 9/1: 12220-05: Chsd ldrs, outpcd after halfway, rallied fnl 1f: abs.	½	84
1726 **PRINCE HECTOR 15** [2]5-8-8 (80) K Fallon 11/4 FAV: 600-0005: Rdn in rear, some late hdwy, nvr nr to chall: well bckd & much btr expected after encouraging rnr-up in 1726 (6f).	1¾	75
1812 **PENNY CROSS 11** [10]4-8-12 (84) M Fenton 22/1: 333-0007: b f Efisio - Addaya (Persian Bold) Chsd ldrs, stumbled halfway, no ch after: v consistent for M Johnston in '03, won a mdn, a h'cap & a class stks, also plcd numerous times: eff at 7/8.5f on gd & firm grnd: loves to dominate, handles an easy or gall trk, likes	3½	72

618

Beverley: now with J Given. 1 Aug'03 Beve 8.5g/f 87-(83) D: 2 Aug'03 Redc 8g/f 85-82 D: 2 Jun'03 Newc 8g/f 83-80 D:
1 Jun'03 Carl 6.9fm 87-74 E: 1 Jun'03 Beve 7.5g/f 80-(72) D: 2 May'03 Thir 7gd 71- D:
3974} **PIETER BRUEGHEL 273** [4]5-9-0 (86) R Hills 50/1: 300000-8: b g Citidancer - Smart Tally (Smarten) 3½ **67**
Led till 2f out, wknd on reapp: mainly out of form in '03, tho' plcd once in a val Newcastle h'cap (rtd 93): '02 h'cap wnr for P Cole: eff at 6/7f on gd & firm grnd, acts on any trk, likes Chester: has worn a t-strap, not today: with D Nicholls & slowly slipping down the h'cap.
1 Jun'02 Ches 7fm 99- C: 1 Sep'01 Ches 6gd 100- C: 1 May'01 Newb 5.1gd 93- D:
1812 **HITS ONLY MONEY 11** [7]4-9-9 (95) Dean McKeown 16/1: 1130-009: Nvr btr than mid-div: see 1126. nk **75**
1926 **HIDDEN DRAGON 7** [3]5-9-12 (98) K McEvoy 14/1: 000-2200: 10th: Chsd ldrs 5f, sn wknd. ½ **77**
1970 **KING HARSON 5** [5]5-8-10 vis (82) J Fanning 8/1: 6331-020: 11th: Chsd ldr 5.5f, wknd into last: too sn? 5 **51**
11 Ran Time 1m 24.86 (1.66) Owned: Mr J Duddy & Mr T Fawcett Trained: Hambleton

2077

3.30 European Breeders Fund Zetland Maiden Stakes 2yo (D)
£4791 £1474 £737 **6f str** **Good/Firm 31** **-39 Slow** Stands Side

1687 **CRIMSON SUN 17** [3] Saeed bin Suroor 2-9-0 K McEvoy 8/11 FAV: 21: Broke well & made all, styd on strongly fnl 1f, rdn out: hvly bckd: eff at 6f, 7f looks sure to suit: acts on fast & gd/soft grnd, gall trk: confirmed debut promise, useful juv who can win in better grade: see 1687. **88**
1670 **ADORATION 18** [4] M Johnston 2-9-0 J Fanning 9/2: 32: Chsd ldrs, kept on fnl 1f despite drifting left, not pace of wnr: decent run bhd a potentially smart rival, eff at 6f on fast grnd: win similar: see 1670. 1½ **83**
1848 **SAFENDONSEABISCUIT 10** [5] S Kirk 2-9-0 E Ahern 11/1: 53: Chsd ldrs, onepcd fnl 1f: op 14/1: eff at 6f on fast grnd: far from disgraced bhd 2 prob above average rivals: shld find similar, see 1848. hd **82**
MISS ROSIE 0 [8] T D Easterby 2-8-9 R Winston 25/1: 4: b f Xaar - Disallowed (Distinctly North) ¾ **75+**
Slowly away, v green in rear, styd on nicely fnl 1f, nrst fin on debut: 24,000gns April foal: dam a 9f & hdles wnr: sire a top-class juv: eff at 6f on fast, 7f looks sure to suit: plenty to like about this, will improve.
1677 **PROFITS REALITY 17** [1]2-9-0 Dean McKeown 66/1: 05: br c Key of Luck - Teacher Preacher (Taufan) hd **79**
Prom, onepcd fnl 1f: 25,000gns March foal: brother to 7f wnr Key Partners: dam a 7f wnr.
TOM FOREST 0 [9]2-9-0 V Halliday 28/1: 6: b c Forest Wildcat - Silk Masque (Woodman) Prom ½ **77**
early, lost place halfway, rallied late on debut: March foal, cost 60,000gns: half-brother to several wnrs in the US: dam a 6f 2yo scorer, sire a high-class sprinter: with A Crook.
MIGHTY EMPIRE 0 [10]2-9-0 R Hills 50/1: 7: b c Second Empire - Barnabas (Slip Anchor) Chsd 1½ **73**
ldrs, wknd fnl 1f on racecourse bow: Feb foal, cost E15,000: dam unrcd, sire a v smart 1m juv performer.
1874 **BELTON 9** [6]2-9-0 N Callan 100/1: 08: Prom early, sn bhd. 19 **33**
1424 **ROBURY 31** [2]2-9-0 J D O'Reilly(7) 100/1: 09: Chsd ldrs till halfway. 1 **30**
COUNTRY RAMBLER 0 [7]2-9-0 M Hills 9/2: 0: 10th: Slowly away, al bhd & fin last on debut. ¾ **28**
10 Ran Time 1m 15.02 (4.22) Owned: Godolphin Trained: Newmarket

2078

4.05 Meadowhall Handicap Stakes 3yo+ 0-85 (D) **[83]**
£5606 £1725 £863 **1m4f** **Good/Firm 31** **+00 Fast** Inside

1357 **LUCKY LEO 35** [8] Ian Williams 4-8-9 (64) C Catlin 25/1: 00/300-01: Held up, prog 3f out, led entering fnl 1f, styd on strongly, drvn out: first win: lightly rcd in recent seasons, apprec this step up to 12f: acts on fast grnd & on a gall trk: open to further improvement, see 1357. **71**
1772 **MEXICAN PETE 14** [2] P W Hiatt 4-9-5 (74) E Ahern 7/1: 103-0302: Chsd ldrs, imprvd to lead dist, sn hdd, kept on & just btn in a close fin: back to form & deserves similar: see 1599. nk **80**
1668 **CRATHORNE 18** [4] J D Bethell 4-9-11 p (80) K McEvoy 9/2: 45030-43: Held up, prog 2f out & ev ch fnl 1f, not qckn cl-home: drifted from 3/1 & well clr rem: ran to form of 1668. 1¾ **83**
816 **CARROWDORE 82** [7] C N Allen 4-8-13 p (68) Dean McKeown 10/1: 45220-24: Chsd ldrs, btn over 1f out: 12 wk abs & new stable (prev with R Hannon): see 816 (AW clmr). 10 **56**
1516 **DISSIDENT 26** [9]6-9-8 vis (77) L Treadwell(7) 5/1: 1022145: Chsd ldrs, led 2f out till dist, sn wknd. 2½ **61**
1599 **JEEPSTAR 22** [3]4-9-6 (75) G Gibbons 13/2: 1253-006: b g Muhtarram - Jungle Rose (Shirley 3 **55**
Heights) Led till 3f out, grad wknd: dual h'cap wnr in '02: winning form at 10/12f, acts on gd & firm grnd: likes to race up with/force the pace on a sharpish trk, handles any: capable of better.
2 Sep'03 Ripo 10g/f 79-75 C: 1 Sep'03 Muss 12g/f 77-71 C: 2 Sep'03 York 11.9g/f 72-70 D: 1 Aug'03 Ripo 10g/f 72-65 E:
1889* **ASTROCHARM 8** [6]5-9-7 (76) R Hills 7/2 FAV: 0400-517: Held up, nvr nr ldrs: bckd from 5/1, 5 **49**
top-weight: much btr expected after 1889 (gd grnd, slow time).
1599 **MR LEAR 22** [5]5-9-1 (70) T Hamilton(3) 16/1: 21040-08: b g Lear Fan - Majestic Mae (Crow) Front shd **43**
rank, wknd qckly 3f out: nov & h'cap hdle wnr in 03/04 (eff around 2m on soft & hvy grnd, rtd 119h): won 3 h'caps for T Barron in '03: suited by 10/12f & front running tactics: acts on gd, fast grnd & fibresand, hvy over hdles: likes a sharpish trk, esp Ripon: with R Fahey. 1 Aug'03 Ripo 12.3g/f 73-70 E: 2 Jul'03 Beve 12.1g/f 74-70 E:
1 Jul'03 Ripo 10g/f 70-65 D: 2 Jul'03 Hami 13.0g/f 66-65 E: 1 May'03 Muss 12gd 65-59 E: 1 Feb'02 Sout 8af 66a-49 F:
3181] **TRIPHENIA 669** [1]6-9-6 (75) K Fallon 8/1: 40/6100/-9: b g Ashkalani - Atsuko (Mtoto) Held up, 6 **38**
al bhd & fin last on comeback: missed '03, prev term won a Goodwood class stks (rtd 83): '02 mdn wnr: ef at 14f on firm, soft grnd & fibresand, likes a sharp trk: clearly has had plenty of injury problems.
1 Jun'02 Good 14g/f 83- C: 1 Apr'01 Sout 11af 87a- D:
9 Ran Time 2m 33.55 (3.75) Owned: B and S Vaughan Trained: Alvechurch

2079

4.40 Merlin Land Rover Handicap Stakes 3yo 0-85 (D) **[90]**
£5850 £1800 £900 **1m2f60y** **Good/Firm 31** **-07 Slow** Inside

1708 **GAVROCHE 16** [8] C A Dwyer 3-8-11 (73) J P Guillambert(3) 11/1: 2352251: Dwelt, hdwy from rear dist, drvn to lead fnl strides: deserved win & apprec this return to 10f: eff at 9/10f on fast, hvy grnd & fibresand: has worn a visor, best without: handles a sharp or gall trk: see 1515 & 441 (with M Wallace). **84**
1791* **ETMAAM 12** [4] M Johnston 3-9-4 (80) R Hills 6/4: 4-1512: Held up, gd hdwy to lead briefly dist, rallied to regain lead ins fnl 1f, just btn in a thrilling fin: well bckd: fine run under top-weight & conceding 7lb to today's wnr: imprvd in defeat, see 1791. hd **90**
1220* **SUNISA 42** [3] B W Hills 3-9-0 (76) M Hills 8/1: 624-213: Held up, gd hdwy to lead dist, hdd ins fnl 1f & no extra cl-home: op 12/1, 6 wk abs & clr of rem: stays a gall 10f & runs well fresh: see 1220. 1 **83**
1340 **STRIDER 35** [2] Sir Michael Stoute 3-9-2 (78) K Fallon 7/2: 00-24: Chsd ldrs, ev ch dist, wknd fnl 1f on h'cap bow: may benefit from a return to 1m: see 1340 (AW). 5 **78**
1429 **ZAFFEU 31** [6]3-8-8 (70) J Fanning 11/1: 066245: Slowly away, hdwy when short of room & lost 1¾ **67+**

place 2f out, not recover/hands & heels: op 14/1: improve: see 1124.
1708 **SAIDA LENASERA 16** [9]3-8-10 (72) T Hamilton(3) 33/1: 43140-06: Prom, led 2f out till dist, wknd. ½ **67**
1729 **GREEN FALCON 15** [1]3-8-1 (63) C Catlin 10/1: 03307: Prom, short of rm 2f out, wknd: see 697. 1½ **56**
1494 **RENDEZVOUS POINT 27** [7]3-9-1 (77) K McEvoy 10/1: 1-08: Chsd ldrs, ev ch 2f out, sn wknd: see 19. 1 **68**
1708 **ROYAL DISTANT 16** [11]3-8-12 (74) Dale Gibson 16/1: 124-6009: Led till 2f out, wknd. 13 **43**
9 Ran Time 2m 10.39 (3.99) Owned: Mr J L Guillambert Trained: Newmarket

2080

5.15 Cantley Apprentice Handicap Stakes 4yo+ 0-70 (E) **[70]**
£3591 £1105 £553 **7f str** **Good/Firm 31** **-13 Slow** Stands Side

1897 **JUBILEE STREET 8** [11] Mrs A Duffield 5-8-10 (52) Saleem Golam 9/2 JT FAV: 005-0431: Held up, strong run to lead dist, drifted right but styd on well fnl 1f, rdn out: suited by 7f, poss stays 9f: acts on fast & gd/soft grnd: handles a gall trk, see 1897 & 1319. **61**
1778 **NOBLE PENNY 14** [17] Mrs K Walton 5-8-6 (48) A Elliott(5) 15/2: 0000-062: Slowly away, gd hdwy from rear when short of room dist, fin well but wnr had flown: set plenty to do & a gd run in the circumstances. 2½ **51**
1536 **BENEKING 25** [16] R Hollinshead 4-8-13 (55) H Fellows(5) 12/1: 04000-03: b g Wizard King - Gagajulu (Al Hareb) Held up, styd on fnl 1f, nrst fin: trained by J Gallagher & plcd several times in '03 (h'caps), also tried blnks & cheek pieces: eff at 6/7f on fast, gd/soft grnd & a polytrack. ½ **57**
2 Jul'03 Ling 7g/f 72-(69) E: 2 Jun'03 Ling 7g/f 71-68 D: 2 Aug'02 Chep 6gd 75-71 D: 2 Jun'02 Leic 6gd 72- E:
1726 **WARDEN WARREN 15** [14] Mrs C A Dunnett 6-9-13 p (69) Steven Harrison 10/1: 1001004: Mid-div, imprvd to chase ldrs 2f out, onepace fnl 1f: op 7/1: see 1195 (AW). 1½ **68**
1366 **OPEN HANDED 35** [6]4-9-1 t (57) A Mullen 25/1: 0-600105: Slowly away, gd hdwy 2f out, btn fnl 1f. 2½ **51**
1773 **INDIAN STEPPES 14** [7]5-10-0 (70) M Halford 10/1: 22003-66: Prom, short of room dist, sn btn. shd **64**
1750 **KENNINGTON 14** [13]4-8-12 vis (54) Laura Pike 20/1: 0403407: Chsd ldrs, led 3f out till dist, wknd. hd **47**
5029} **TEDSDALE MAC 204** [15]5-8-10 p (52) Suzanne France 11/1: 643304-8: ch g Presidium - Stilvella (Camden Town) Prom, btn when short of room dist: reapp, clr of rem: failed to win in '03, plcd sev times (h'caps): '02 mdn auct wnr: eff at 5f, stays 1m: acts on firm & gd/soft: wears cheek pieces, has tried blnks: with N Bycroft. 2 May'03 Carl 5fm 59-(58) F: 1 Apr'02 Nott 5g/s 70- F: hd **44**
1801 **RATHMULLAN 12** [10]5-7-12 bl (40) Liam Jones 20/1: 3431359: Chsd ldrs, wknd over 2f out. 5 **22**
1564 **MUTABARI 24** [1]10-7-12 (5oh) (35) Amy Myatt(5) 50/1: 000-0000: 10th: Dwelt, nvr nr ldrs: stiff task. 1 **20**
4339] **STONE CREST 964** [8]6-7-12 (10oh) (30) S Yourston 100/1: 660//-0: 11th: b f Bigstone - Hillcrest (Thatching) Led till 3f out, wknd: comeback, stiff task: missed prev 2 seasons: lightly rcd & some mdn promise '01. ¾ **18**
1878 **BINT ROYAL 9** [18]6-9-2 p (58) Dawn Watson 9/2 JT FAV: 0010-550: 12th: Prom 5f, wknd. 1 **34**
1010 **SUPER CANYON 59** [12]6-9-0 (56) Kirsty Milczarek(5) 16/1: 532-4200: 13th: Nvr btr than mid-div: abs. nk **31**
4106} **ALPINE HIDEAWAY 265** [5]11-8-7 (49) A Reilly 33/1: 0/06140-0: 14th: Front rank till halfway: reapp. 1¾ **20**
4381*} **Boing Boing 250** [9]4-9-0 (56) B O'Neill 14/1:0 1927 **Spark Up 7** [2]4-9-7 bl(63) K Ghunowa 16/1:0
1778 **Rocky Reppin 14** [3]4-8-9 (51) K Pierrepont(5) 66/1:0 788 **Indian Shores 88** [4]5-8-11 (53) P Varley(5) 33/1:0
18 Ran Time 1m 26.3(3.1) Owned: Mr D W Holdsworth & Mr J A McMahon Trained: Leyburn

MUSSELBURGH SATURDAY 29.05.04 Righthand, Sharp Track

Official Going Good/Firm (Firm places)

2081

1.45 One Maiden Stakes 3yo+ (D)
£4745 £1460 £730 **1m rnd** **Firm 12** **-21 Slow** Outside

1783 **MARBUSH 13** [6] M A Jarvis 3-8-12 S Sanders 1/1 JT FAV: 321: Trkd ldr, rdn to chall 2f out, led over 1f out, drvn out: hvly bckd: eff at 1m/9f on firm & gd grnd, sharp or gall trk: lightly rcd & improving. **85**
1929 **AWESOME LOVE 7** [4] M Johnston 3-8-12 K Dalgleish 1/1 JT FAV: 2-32: Led, hdd over 1f out, styd on well for press, not pace of wnr: well bckd & well clr of rem: stays 1m on fm & fast: win a mdn. ¾ **83**
1896 **MENAI STRAIGHTS 8** [2] R F Fisher 3-8-12 (62) F Norton 33/1: 553-6063: ch g Alhaarth - Kind of Light (Primo Dominie) Prom, no impress on front pair fnl 2f: plcd fnl '03 start (mdn, rtd 71): eff around 1m, handles gd & gd/soft grnd: apprec rtn to h'caps. 11 **61$**
1504 **LUCKY LARGO 27** [7] Miss L A Perratt 4-9-10 bl (53) D McGaffin 66/1: 20-05004: Chsd ldrs, no impress. nk **60$**
966 **YOUNG WARRIOR 61** [5]3-8-12 A Nicholls 100/1: 06: Bhd halfway, abs, longer trip. ½ **59**
1747 **CAYMANS GIFT 15** [1]4-9-10 T Eaves(3) 50/1: 457: Al bhd: btr 1507 (12f, debut). 5 **49**
3561} **TAILI 290** [3]3-8-7 J McAuley 100/1: 000-8: b f Taipan - Doubtfire (Jalmood) Sn bhd & t.o. 3f out, reapp: unplcd '03 (rtd 27). dist **0**
7 Ran Time 1m 40.15 (2.65) Owned: Sheikh Ahmed Al Maktoum Trained: Newmarket

2082

2.20 Victor Chandler Scottish Sprint Cup Heritage Handicap 3yo+ 0-105 (B) **[100]**
£29000 £11000 £5500 **5f str** **Firm 12** **+18 Fast** Stands Side

1917* **RACCOON 7** [1] T D Barron 4-8-12 vis (84) S Sanders 11/4 FAV: 2011-411: Led/dsptd lead & went on 2f out, drvn & styd on strongly: hvly bckd, op 7/2: v fast time: stay 6f, all wins at 5f: acts on fm & fast, stiff or sharp trk: wears vis: most speedy, useful & progressive, prob even more to come. **91**
1845 **CORRIDOR CREEPER 10** [4] J M Bradley 7-9-3 p (89) R Ffrench 10/1: 000-5442: Trkd ldr trav well & chall over 1f out, not pace of wnr ins last: consistent type & deserves a val prize: see 1594. ¾ **93**
1120* **MAGIC GLADE 48** [10] C R Dore 5-9-1 (87) R Thomas(5) 6/1: 00-01213: Sn handy, styd on well for press, not pace of wnr: acts on firm, fast & fibresand: v speedy & firmly on the up-grade: see 1120 & 660. 1¼ **87**
1917 **CONNECT 7** [13] M H Tompkins 7-9-1 bl (87) F P Ferris(3) 16/1: 06006-24: Mid-div, short of room & switched over 1f out, kept on late: in gd heart & a sltly stiffer trk may suit: gd run from an awkward draw. nk **86**
1626 **VITA SPERICOLATA 21** [8]7-8-13 vis (85) P Hanagan 20/1: 000-0035: b f Prince Sabo - Ahonita (Ahonoora) Handy & ch over 1f out, no extra ins last: op 25/1: List rnr-up '03: List wnr '02, rtd h'cap & List rnr-up: eff at 5/6f on firm & hvy grnd, any trk, loves Chester: eff with/without visor: well h'capped. nk **83**
2 Aug'03 Ches 6.1fm 95-(91) A: 2 Aug'02 Pont 6g/f 98- A: 2 Aug'02 Asco 6g/s 98-95 B: 1 Aug'02 Ches 6g/f 98- A:
1 Aug'01 Ches 6fm 106- A: 1 Jul'01 Newm 5g/f 99- C: 2 May'01 Beve 5fm 100- C:

1782 **SIMIANNA** 13 [7]5-9-4 p (90) F Norton 33/1: 00-55206: Rear, short of room & nrst fin: on a fair mark. ½ 86
1845* **WHITBARROW** 10 [3]5-9-10 (96) K Dalgleish 12/1: 56-50017: Trkd ldrs stands side, not pace to chall. nk 91
1898 **MINE BEHIND** 8 [12]4-8-10 P (82) N Pollard 10/1: 63-16228: Chsd ldrs, not able to chall: ckpcs, wants 6f. ½ 75
1809* **GREEN MANALISHI** 12 [2]3-8-8 (88) J Carroll 8/1: 51-42219: Slow away & rear, short of room & 1¼ 77+
late gains, best forgiven after fluffing start: ready winner latest & remains one to keep on side: see 1809.
1481* **MOAYED** 28 [6]5-9-1 bl t (87) T P Queally(3) 14/1: 1263310: 10th: Dwelt, rear, late prog: needs 6f. ½ 74
1683* **RIVER FALCON** 17 [14]4-8-12 (84) N Mackay(3) 16/1: 000-5010: 11th: Chsd ldrs, outpcd over 1f out. shd 71
1594* **PTARMIGAN RIDGE** 22 [5]8-9-0 (86) T Eaves(3) 33/1: 001-0010: 12th: Chsd ldrs to 2f out: btr 1594. shd 72
1917 **ABSENT FRIENDS** 7 [9]7-9-8 (94) P Mathers(7) 28/1: 2500-060: 13th: Mid-div, outpcd from halfway. nk 79
1917 **SEAFIELD TOWERS** 7 [11]4-8-5 p (77) D Allan(3) 33/1: 160-0030: 14th: Sn outpcd & nvr factor: btr 1917. shd 61
1845 **MALAPROPISM** 10 [15]4-9-1 (87) A Culhane 20/1: 03001-60: 15th: In tch till over 1f out: moderate draw. nk 70
1917 **SALVIATI** 7 [16]7-9-1 (87) Darren Williams 66/1: 4205-000: 16th: b g Lahib - Mother Courage 1¾ 65
(Busted) Dwelt & nvr on terms from poor draw: dual h'cap wnr '03: h'cap wnr '02: eff at 5f, stays 6f: acts on
firm & gd/soft, any trk, likes Ascot: tough 7yo.
2 Sep'03 Asco 5g/f 91-90 B: 1 Jul'03 Asco 5g/s 91-88 B: 1 Jul'03 Catt 5fm 91-83 D: 2 May'03 Muss 5gd 84-81 C:
2 Jun'02 Newc 5g/f 92-90 B: 1 Jun'02 Redc 5fm 94-85 C: 1 Aug'01 Bath 5.7g/f 89-83 C: 1 Aug'01 Asco 5gd 90-77 D:
2 Jul'01 York 6g/f 78-77 C: 2 Jun'01 Redc 6g/f 78-73 C:
1845 **ROSES OF SPRING** 10 [17]6-8-11 p (83) A Quinn(3) 40/1: 0100-030: 17th: Sn struggling from poor draw. ¾ 59
17 Ran Time 57.81 (u0.31) Owned: Mr P D Savill Trained: Thirsk

---

2083 **2.50 Santini Selling Stakes 2yo (E)**
£6734 £2072 £1036 **5f str** **Firm 12** **-32 Slow** Stands Side

1573 **THEATRE OF DREAMS** 24 [9] D Nicholls 2-8-11 A Nicholls 13/8 FAV: 541: Sn cl-up & led 2f out, rdn 79+
clr, readily: bght in for 22,000gns: well bckd, first win: eff at 5f, handles gd & gd/soft grnd, imprvd for firm
today & drop to sell grade: cut above this grade, win again: see 1573 & 954.
1818 **KNOCK BRIDGE** 11 [1] M J Wallace 2-8-6 D Corby(3) 5/2: 42: Chsd ldrs, switched & kept on fnl 1f, 3½ 63
no impress on easy wnr: bckd, op 3/1: handles firm & fast grnd: rtn to 6f in similar shld suit: see 1818.
1652 **CHILALI** 19 [3] A Berry 2-8-6 F Norton 25/1: 503: Led till 2f out, not pace of wnr. 1¾ 58
1868 **GRACIES GIFT** 9 [2] P C Haslam 2-8-11 L Enstone(3) 12/1: 44: Prom, outpcd from halfway: see 1868. 2 57
1634 **LITTLE BISCUIT** 21 [2]2-8-11 Darren Williams 4/1: 1125: Towards rear, only mod pog: op 3/1. nk 56
1727 **DANES ROCK** 15 [5]2-8-11 VIS G Faulkner 25/1: 406: Chsd ldrs till halfway: visor, op 33/1: see 1048. nk 55
1362 **CHICAGO NIGHTS** 35 [8]2-8-6 Rory Moore(7) 25/1: 47: Cl-up till over 1f out: see 1362. ¾ 48
1779 **STEAL THE THUNDER** 13 [6]2-8-11 F Lynch 50/1: 0558: Al bhd. 1 50
  SHATIN LEADER 0 [7]2-8-6 N Mackay(3) 28/1: P: b f Atraf - Star Dancer (Groom Dancer) Hmpd start 0
& slow away, hung badly right when bhd halfway, t.o. & dismounted dist: cheaply bght Jan foal.
9 Ran Time 59.73 (2.23) Owned: Mr D Nicholls Trained: Thirsk

2084 **3.25 Victor Chandler Sprint Trophy Handicap Stakes 3yo+ (C)**
£10082 £3102 £1551 **5f str** **Firm 12** **-16 Slow** Stands Side [80]

1774 **CATCH THE CAT** 14 [12] J S Wainwright 5-9-3 bl (69) G Parkin 16/1: 50-30201: Sn handy & led dist, 77
drvn & held on all out: stays 5f, suited by sharp or stiff 5f on firm, soft & any trk, tough Beverley: best up
with/forcing the pace: tough & genuine, an impressive display from a potentially awkward draw: see 1774.
1765 **STRENSALL** 14 [4] R E Barr 7-9-10 (76) R Fitzpatrick 25/1: 01420-02: Rdn chasing ldrs, drvn & shd 83
strong chall ins last, just denied: right back to form from fav'able low draw: loves Catterick: see 124.
1749 **ROXANNE MILL** 15 [8] J M Bradley 6-9-9 (75) P Hanagan 20/1: 020-3263: Broke fast & sn led till nk 81
dist, kept on for press: on a handy mark: see 1269.
1977 **OBE ONE** 4 [1] A Berry 4-9-3 (69) F Norton 8/1: 00-00064: Chsd ldrs, drvn & keeping on when short nk 74
of room ins last: gd run from fav'able low draw: h'capped to win: see 1977.
1909 **ONLINE INVESTOR** 7 [11]5-9-3 (69) Alex Greaves 13/2: 0-005205: Chsd ldrs, rdn to press ldrs dist, shd 73
no extra & eased/lost 4th cl-home: on long losing run: see 1765 & 1523.
1898* **HIGHLAND WARRIOR** 8 [10]5-9-7 (73) N Mackay(3) 10/1: 3323416: Dwelt, bhd, switched & short of room nk 75
over 1f out, nrst fin: crying out for rtn to 6f, keep on side at Ayr: see 967.
1886 **WHISTLER** 8 [2]7-9-9 p (75) S Sanders 6/1 CO FAV: 00-00037: Chsd ldrs, short of room dist, kept on. ½ 75
1973 **FRASCATI** 5 [3]4-9-4 (70) A Culhane 20/1: 0410238: Mid-div, ch over 1f out, no extra: see 1749. shd 70
2029* **PARKSIDE PURSUIT** 2 [3]6-9-5 (71) C J Davies(7) 6/1 CO FAV: 200-0119: Reared start, bhd, nvr on terms. 1¼ 67
1476 **IZMAIL** 28 [15]9-9-3 (69) K Dalgleish 33/1: 0015-000: 10th: Chsd ldrs, wknd dist: see 1293. ¾ 63
1765 **BALLYBUNION** 14 [14]5-8-10 (62) A Nicholls 33/1: 6100-000: 11th: ch g Entrepreneur - Clarentia 1 53
(Ballad Rock) Dwelt & al rear: dual h'cap & also a class stks scorer '03: class stks plcd '02 (rtd 62, no sand
form): eff at 5f/sharp 6f on firm & fast grnd, prob any trk, likes Catterick.
1 Aug'03 Catt 6.0g/f 69-(65) E: 2 Aug'03 Bath 5.7fm 72-65 E: 1 Jul'03 Folk 5g/f 65-62 F: 2 Jul'03 Catt 5g/f 62-58 E:
1 Jun'03 Catt 6.0g/f 60-53 E: 1 Oct'01 Newm 6g/f 86-78 C: 1 Sep'01 Catt 6g/f 81- D:
2029 **BRIGADORE** 2 [17]5-9-0 (66) D Fentiman(7) 25/1: 000-6360: 12th: In tch, btn 2f out, awkward draw. 1½ 53
2029 **KANGARILLA ROAD** 2 [16]5-9-0 (66) T P Queally(3) 6/1 CO FAV: 600-0020: 13th: Keen, in tch till nk 52
over 1f out: moderate draw, qck reapp: see
1782 **Twice Upon A Time** 13 [6]5-9-6 (72) F Lynch 12/1:0 1914 **If By Chance** 7 [5]6-9-8 bl(74) T Eaves(3) 16/1:0
15 Ran Time 58.93 (1.43) Owned: Mr T W Heseltine Trained: Malton

---

2085 **4.00 Sheraton Grand Cup A Handicap Stakes 3yo+ 0-85 (D)**
£13572 £4176 £2088 **1m6f** **Firm 12** **-26 Slow** Inside [85]

4498} **JACK DAWSON** 266 [6] John Berry 7-9-0 (71) F Norton 7/2 JT FAV: 243540-1: b g Persian Bold - 80
Dream of Jenny (Caerleon) Held up, switched & hdwy over 2f out, led over 1f out, drvn out: bckd: jumps fit (plcd,
rtd 126h, List h'cap hdle, 2m1f, fast & gd): class stks rnr-up '03, h'cap plcd (rtd 74 at best): eff at 10f, suited
by 14f/2m on firm & gd/soft, any trk, loves Musselburgh: tough & genuine: tough & genuine. 2 Jul'03 Epso 10.1gd 72-(75) D:
2 Sep'02 Muss 16g/f 76-76 C:2 Aug'02 Warw 16.1g/f 78-76 D:1 Jun'02 Muss 16g/f 81-74 D: 1 May'02 Hami 13gd 75-71 D:
2 May'02 Thir 16g/f 70-70 C: 1 Sep'01 Muss 16g/f 70-66 C: 1 Jul'01 Ches 15.8fm 71-66 D:
1 Jun'01 Ayr 15g/f 68-64 C:
1928 **KRISTENSEN** 7 [11] D Eddy 5-9-8 p (79) P Hanagan 8/1: 233-5062: Chsd ldrs, ch dist, not pace of wnr. 2 85

MUSSELBURGH   SATURDAY 29.05.04   Righthand, Sharp Track

1905* **TONI ALCALA** 7 [12] R F Fisher 5-8-11 (68) D Nolan(2) 14/1: 0231613: Trkd ldrs, short of room 2f   3   70
out, drvn & kept on, not pace to chall: op 16/1: remains in gd heart: see 1905.
1759 **FLOTTA** 14 [2] M R Channon 5-10-0 (85) A Culhane 7/2 JT FAV: 210-4504: Trkd ldrs, outpcd over 2f   ½   86
out, kept on onepace: see 877.
1506 **TANDAVA** 27 [1]6-9-1 P (72) T P Queally(3) 16/1: 0400-105: Led, hdd 2f out, no extra: cheekpieces.   ½   72
1680 **GARGOYLE GIRL** 17 [4]7-8-3 (60) N Mackay(3) 20/1: 40-05106: Bhd, switched/kept on, not able to chall.   ½   59
1905 **RAJAM** 7 [5]6-9-4 vis (75) Alex Greaves 20/1: 0-060137: Handy & led 2f out till over 1f out, wknd.   ½   73
1875 **PERESTROIKA** 9 [3]6-8-3 (60) R Ffrench 12/1: 050/-0048: Held up, eff fnl 3f, no impress: op 14/1.   4   54
1637 **RIYADH** 21 [9]6-8-13 bl (70) K Dalgleish 13/2: 0-000039: Dwelt & bhd, outpcd over 3f out: needs   hd   63
2m+: well h'capped & more interesting if getting into 2m4f Ascot Stakes h'cap at Royal Ascot next month.
1272 **SEA PLUME** 39 [7]5-9-3 (74) S Sanders 33/1: 02000-50: 10th: b f Slip Anchor - Fine Quill   1½   65
(Unfuwain) Chsd ldr, rdn/btn when hmpd over 1f out: lightly rcd '03 (h'cap rnr-up): unplcd '02 (rtd 70, mdn): eff
at 10f, imprvd last term for step up to 2m: handles fast & gd/soft grnd, likes a gall trk. 2 Oct'03 Newm 16gd 73-73 C:
1296 **Recount** 38 [8]4-9-6 (77) N Pollard 16/1:0
1772 **Clarinch Claymore** 14 [10]8-9-2 (77) T Eaves(3) 14/1:0
12 Ran   Time 3m 01.87 (5.37)   Owned: The Premier Cru   Trained: Newmarket

2086   4.30 Vcpoker Com Handicap Stakes 3yo+ 0-85 (D)   [76]
£6734 £2072 £1036   **7f30y rnd**   **Firm 12**   **-32 Slow**   Outside

1794 **KIRKBYS TREASURE** 12 [1] A Berry 6-9-0 (62) F Lynch 7/1: 6005-121: Rear, switched & hdwy for   68
press to lead dist, drvn out: eff btwn 6f/1m, 7f seems ideal: acts on firm, hvy & any trk, likes Musselburgh: best
delivered late: in gd form: see 1122.
1898 **PAWAN** 8 [6] Miss A Stokell 4-8-13 (61) Ann Stokell 20/1: 2035302: Trkd ldrs, rdn & chall over 1f   ½   65
out, rider not as strong as winning joc, no extra: win similar: a stronger rider: acts on firm, soft & fibresand.
1691 **NIGHT WOLF** 17 [2] M R Channon 4-9-4 (66) A Culhane 8/1: 415-6003: Held up in tch, rdn & hdwy to   1¼   67
lead over 1f out, sn hung right & hdd dist, onepace: see 932.
1909 **BALLYHURRY** 7 [4] J S Goldie 7-9-10 (72) N Mackay(3) 5/1: 0154-064: b g Rubiano - Balakhna   1½   70
(Tyrant) Rear, short of room over 1f out, kept on, nvr able to chall: shade closer with a clr run: most
progressive '03, landed 5 h'caps: h'cap wnr '02: eff at 1m/10f, best at 7f last term: acts on firm & hvy, any trk,
likes Musselburgh & Ayr: can go well fresh.
1 Sep'03 Ayr 7.2gd 75-70 C: 1 Jul'03 Muss 7.1gd 71-66 D: 1 Jun'03 Muss 7.1g/f 68-62 D: 2 Jun'03 Ayr 7.2g/f 63-61 C:
1 May'03 Ayr 7.2g/s 65-55 D: 2 May'03 Muss 7.1g/f 59-55 D: 1 Apr'03 Muss 8g/f 56-52 E: 1 Jul'03 Ayr 10g/s 53-49 E:
2 Jul'02 Hami 9.1gd 50-47 E: 2 Jun'02 Muss 9gd 47-45 E:
1794 **KILLALA** 12 [3]4-9-3 (60) T Eaves(3) 8/1: 40436-35: Trkd ldrs & ch over 2f out, carr right & no   2½   58
extra from over 1f out: op 6/1: see 1794.
1909 **ALBASHOOSH** 7 [7]6-9-2 (64) Alex Greaves 7/2: 0006-656: Trkd ldr & smooth prog to lead over 2f   ½   56
out, rdn & hdd over 1f out, wknd: found less than lkd likely today: see 1600.
1910 **WHIPPASNAPPER** 7 [9]4-9-5 (67) N Pollard 3/1 FAV: 2103227: Chsd ldrs, short of room when no extra   hd   58
over 1f out: see 1910 & 1354.
1820 **RISKA KING** 11 [5]4-9-8 (70) P Hanagan 16/1: 00-00008: Rear, drvn 3f out, no prog: see 318.   4   53
1253 **LOCOMBE HILL** 40 [8]8-9-0 (62) A Nicholls 14/1: 100-0209: Led, rdn & hdd 3f out, sn btn: abs: see 417.   17   11
9 Ran   Time 1m 27.97 (3.07)   Owned: Kirkby Lonsdale Racing   Trained: Cockerham

2087   5.05 Akd 15 Years At The Top Of It Classified Stakes 3yo+ 0-75 (D)
£5421 £1668 £834   **1m rnd**   **Firm 12**   **-04 Slow**   Outside

2027 **SEA STORM** 2 [6] D R MacLeod 6-9-7 p (79) T P Queally(3) 10/1: 5-050301: Handy & led 3f out, sn   84
strongly prsd, drvn & styd on gamely: qck reappr: suited by 7f/sharp 1m on firm, gd & polytrack, any trk, loves a
sharp one: back to form with cheekpieces reapplied & on a handy mark.
1781 **TAKES TUTU** 13 [4] K R Burke 5-9-3 bl (73) Darren Williams 7/1: 065-0002: b g Afternoon Deelites -   1   78
Lady Affirmed (Affirmed) Trkd ldrs, rdn to chall over 1f out, no extra well ins last: blnks reapp: h'cap plcd for M
Johnston '03 (rtd 89): progressive '02, won 5 times, incl 3 val turf h'caps: suited by 7f/1m, stays slow run 10.5f:
acts on firm, gd/soft & both AWs, any trk, with/without blnks or vis: well h'capped, should be winning soon.
1 Sep'02 Hayd 10.5g/f 92-87 B: 2 Aug'02 Good 9g/f 90-86 B: 1 Aug'02 Good 7g/f 85-82 C: 1 May'02 Newm 7g/f 84-80 C:
1 Feb'02 Ling 7ap 86a- D: 1 Feb'02 Sout 7af 78a- D: 2 Jan'02 Sout 7af 83a- D: 2 Nov'01 Ling 7ap 84a-77 B:
1877 **JOHANNIAN** 9 [7] J M Bradley 6-9-3 (74) R Ffrench 33/1: 4/005-003: b g Hernando - Photo Call   1¼   75
(Chief Singer) Held up, rdn to chase ldrs over 1f out, onepace: lightly rcd '03 (unplcd, rtd 79, class stks, l
Wood, tried a t-strap): rtd h'cap wnr '02 for M Jarvis: eff at 1m, suited by 10.5f on firm & soft, gall trks:
formerly useful, now v well h'capped & looks to have come to hand, shld find a race.
2 Jun'02 Donc 10.2g/f 101- C: 2 Jun'02 Donc 10.2g/f 102- C:1 May'02 York 10.3fm 104-98 B:1 May'01 Hayd 10.5g/f 88- D:
1895 **MILLAGROS** 8 [2] I Semple 4-9-1 (76) J Carroll 11/2: 6410-044: Bhd, switched & kept on for press,   ¾   71
not able to chall: stiffer 1m prob ideal: see 1895.
1883 **YOUNG MR GRACE** 8 [1]4-9-3 (74) D Allan(3) 7/2 FAV: 60-03425: Chsd ldrs, no extra for press bef   ¾   71
dist: well bckd, op 9/2: btr 1883.
1877 **ATLANTIC ACE** 9 [9]7-9-4 (76) F Lynch 9/1: 105-0006: b g First Trump - Risalah (Marju) Dwelt,   3½   65
bhd, little hdwy: class stks wnr '03, disapp in cheek pieces: class stks & h'cap scorer '02: eff btwn 7/9f on
firm, soft & fibresand, any trk: likes Goodwood: likes to come late off a strong pace.
1 Sep'03 Pont 8.0g/f 84-(80) D: 1 Sep'02 Good 9fm 98-89 C: 2 Aug'02 Good 8fm 92-86 B: 1 Apr'02 Beve 7.4g/f 92- C:
1 Oct'01 Redc 7sft 85-76 D: 1 Jun'01 Good 7g/f 77-73 C:
1877 **LOVE IN SEATTLE** 9 [8]4-9-7 (79) K Dalgleish 7/1: 422-0107: Led till 3f out, sn btn: well bckd: btr 1461.   5   58
1519 **BRIEF GOODBYE** 26 [5]4-9-4 (76) F Norton 9/2: 1663-148: Mid-div, rdn & btn 2f out: op 11/2: btr 1519.   3   49
517 **RUDOOD** 119 [3]4-9-6 (78) S Sanders 6/1: 42/410-59: In tch, rdn & btn 2f out: bckd: abs.   6   39
9 Ran   Time 1m 38.8(1.3)   Owned: Mr Maurice W Chapman   Trained: Lauder

Official Going Good/Firm

2088   2.05 Win #1 000's At Breckland Bingo Ladies Handicap For Lady Riders 3yo+ 0-70 (E)   [56]
£3630 £1117 £559   1m4f   Firm 12   -21 Slow   Centre

1960 **SHAPE UP 6** [13] T Keddy 4-9-8 bl (50) Miss Lynsey Hanna 14/1: 640-3241: Cl-up, al trav well, led   61 +
dist, pushed clr ins fnl 1f, val 5L+: qck reapp: eff btwn 9.7f & 12f on firm, soft grnd & polytrack: eff with
blnks: has slipped to a decent mark: 1st win: see 1579 & 1342.
1287 **ROYAL AXMINSTER 39** [15] Mrs P N Dutfield 9-8-12 (40) Miss A Wallace(5) 16/1: 1605-052: Led, hdd   3   45
dist, kept on but al held: gd eff from the front on return to turf, shld find similar: see 1287.
1834* **GOBLIN 12** [20] D E Cantillon 3-9-12 (71) Miss E J Jones 5/1: 00-41513: Bhd, prog after halfway,   1¼   74
ev ch dist, no extra when short of room cl-home: bckd: poss stays 12f, return to 10f will suit: see 1834.
2041 **MICHAELS DREAM 2** [9] J Hetherton 5-9-3 bl (45) Mrs S Bosley 14/1: 300-63304: Handy, onepcd.   hd   47
3934] **GREYFIELD 992** [8]8-9-13 (55) Miss Dawn Rankin(5) 33/1: 12/0400//-5: b g Persian Bold - Noble Dust   ¾   55
(Dust Commander) Slow away, prog after 1m, no impress fnl 1f: 3rd of 6 on 1 of 2 02/03 chase starts (rtd 109c, nov
chase, stays 2m3f on firm & soft grnd): plcd on 1 of 4 '01 Flat starts (rtd 63, h'cap): h'cap wnr in '00 (M R
Channon): eff at 10/12f, poss stays 14f on firm & soft grnd, acts on any trk.
1830 **MAN THE GATE 12** [4]5-10-0 (56) Miss C Nosworthy(7) 5/1: 00-25036: Rear, prog after 7f, fdd dist.   5   49
549 **REVIEWER 116** [7]6-11-0 (70) Miss V Sturgis(5) 20/1: 60/116/-07: b g Sadler's Wells - Clandestina   nk   62
(Secretariat) Rear, nvr nrr than mid-div: 9 wk hdles abs, earlier plcd (h'cap, rtd 124h, eff at 2m1f, prob stays
2m6f, acts on gd/soft & hvy): won first 2 of only 3 '02 starts (h'caps, H Morrison): mdn h'cap wnr in '01: stays
12f, has tried further: acts on fast & soft grnd, any trk: eff with/without blnks, has gone well fresh.
1 Jul'02 Asco 12gd 75-70 C: 1 Jul'02 Warw 12.6gd 75-65 E: 1 Jul'01 Bath 11.6gd 70-65 E:
4684] **KING HALLING 585** [17]5-10-9 (65) Miss Caroline Hurley(7) 40/1: 516400/-8: b c Halling - Flower   ½   56
Fairy (Fairy King) Handy, wknd 2f out: reapp: missed '03: mdn wnr in '02 (B Hanbury): eff at 10f, tried further:
acts on polytrack & a sharp trk: with R Ford. 1 Jul'02 Ling 10ap 75a- D:
1055} **WIZARD OF THE WEST 412** [2]4-10-0 (56) Ms D Goad(5) 50/1: 3/03600-9: In tch 10f, wknd: jumps abs.   1½   44
1830 **GREAT VIEW 12** [14]5-10-8 vis (46) Ms C Williams 7/2 FAV: 0121240: 10th: Rear, prog 5f out, wknd fnl 2f.   nk   51
4318] **SHALBEBLUE 255** [11]7-9-8 bl (50) Miss L Ellison(3) 20/1: 250325-0: 11th: Mid-div 9f, sn wknd.   1   35
1990 **FLETCHER 5** [1]10-9-3 (45) Miss L J Harwood(3) 14/1: 04-05100: 12th: Al in rear: qck reapp: btr 1414.   3   26
1899 **LARKING ABOUT 9** [12]4-10-1 (57) Ms Amy Boeder(7) 33/1: 5420-000: 13th: Bhd, nvr a factor: btr 1633.   1¾   35
1776 **GRAFT 15** [5]5-10-6 (62) Miss S Brotherton 8/1: 000-0620: 14th: Bhd, prog after 1f, fdd 2f out.   shd 39
1905 **Magic Charm 8** [16]6-8-12 (40) Miss J Waring(7) 16/1:0
2047 **Margery Daw 2** [6]4-10-4 (60) Miss J C Duncan(5) 25/1:0
1243 **Little Sky 41** [10]7-9-3 (45) Miss J Ellis(5) 33/1:0
1059 **Trusted Instinct 55** [18]4-10-11 t(67) Mrs Emma Littmoden(3) 40/1:0
18 Ran   Time 2m 32.18 (3.98)   Owned: Mr Andrew Duffield   Trained: Newmarket

---

2089   2.35 Play At Breckland Bingo Brandon Maiden Stakes 2yo   (D)
£4774 £1469 £735   5f str   Firm 12   -10 Slow   Stands side

1670 **SKYWARDS 19** [7] Saeed bin Suroor 2-9-0 L Dettori 4/1: 51: b c Machiavellian - Nawaiet (Zilzal)   91 +
Made all, pushed clr, going away: well bckd: Jan foal, brother to high-class miler Excuse Needed & a 10f wnr:
dam won at 6f: eff at 5f, further will suit: acts on fm grnd, poss not soft: acts on a stiff trk: goes
well fresh: impressive, real R Ascot type.
1670 **KOMAC 19** [10] B A McMahon 2-9-0 S Sanders 16/1: 62: b c Komaite - Star of Flanders (Puissance)   5   73
Cl-up, not pace easy wnr ins fnl 1f: March foal, cost 5,500gns: half-brother to a 6f wnr, also half-brother plcd at
7/9f: dam unrcd: sire won at 7f: eff at 5f, shld apprec further: acts on fm: caught a useful sort.
1760 **WITCHRY 15** [6] M A Jarvis 2-9-0 P Robinson 4/6 FAV: 43: Handy, no extra 1f out: bckd: btr 1760.   1½   69
 DIAMOND HOMBRE 0 [9] J W Hills 2-9-0 M Hills 14/1: 4: gr c Two Punch - Flowing (El Gran Senor)   2½   62
Cl-up till dist, fdd: op 10/1 on debut: Feb foal, cost $105,000: half-brother to wnrs at 5/10f: dam decent sprint
performer: sire useful around 6f: just sharper for today.
 TOWN END TOM 0 [1]2-9-0 M Fenton 50/1: 5: Slow away, sn handy, wknd ins fnl 2f: debut.   hd   61
 HEDINGHAM KNIGHT 0 [3]2-9-0 Dane O'Neill 25/1: 6: Slow away & bhd, modest late gains: debut.   shd 60
 COOL PANIC 0 [5]2-9-0 D Holland 15/2: 7: Cl-up over 3f, wknd: debut.   2   54
 LOWESTOFT PLAYBOY 0 [8]2-9-0 T P Queally(3) 33/1: 8: Al in rear: debut.   4   42
 LIGHTHORNE LAD 0 [4]2-9-0 S Kelly 80/1: 9: Bhd, nvr a factor.   1¾   37
 WHATSHEWORTH 0 [2]2-9-0 P McCabe 66/1: 0: 10th: Al in rear.   11   7
10 Ran   Time 59.30 (1.10)   Owned: Godolphin   Trained: Newmarket

---

2090   3.10 Brecklandbingo Co Uk Handicap Stakes 3yo+ 0-105 (B)   [99]
£13780 £4240 £2120   7f str   Firm 12   -03 Slow   Stands side

1926 **MASTER ROBBIE 8** [10] M R Channon 5-9-3 (88) S Hitchcott(3) 8/1: 60-00001: Handy, styd on to lead   95
1f out, rdn out: op 6/1: eff at 6.5f/7f & loves fm or gd, any trk: most tough & game.
1877 **OBRIGADO 10** [13] W J Haggas 4-8-9 (80) R Hills 20/1: 4216-02: b g Bahri - Glorious Diamond (His   ½   84
Majesty) Rcd alone middle of trk, led after 2f, hdd 1f out, kept on, not btn far: mdn wnr in '03: eff at 7f/1m,
10f shld suit: acts on firm & soft grnd: left reapp eff bhd with a solid display, unexposed in h'cap grade.
1 Aug'03 Pont 8.0g/f 81- D: 2 Jul'03 Donc 8g/f 74- D:
1686 **KINGS COUNTY 18** [2] L M Cumani 6-9-10 (95) D Holland 5/2 FAV: 5512-303: Cl-up, outpcd after   nk   98+
halfway, styling when short of room dist, styd on well: bckd: gd run, relish return to 1m: see 1231.
2010 **JUSTE POUR LAMOUR 4** [8] P L Gilligan 4-8-5 (76) J F Egan 33/1: 24500-04: ch g Pharly - Fontaine   1   76
Lady (Millfontaine) Handy, kept on onepace: qck reapp: rnr-up once in '03 (h'cap, J R Fanshawe): nursery h'cap wnr
in '02 (M Ryan): eff at 7f, has tried further: likes fm & fast, gall trks: better run.
2 May'03 Sand 7.1g/f 84-80 D: 1 Sep'02 Donc 7fm 84-76 D:
1817* **TARANAKI 12** [1]6-9-3 (88) S Sanders 8/1: 0414015: Handy, eff when short of room bef 1f out, sn onepcd.½   88
1926 **VINDICATION GB 8** [6]4-9-7 t (92) L Dettori 9/1: 65110-06: ch g Compton Place - Prince's Feather   hd   91
(Cadeaux Genereux) Nvr nrr than mid-div: won 3 h'caps in '03: AW h'cap rnr-up in '02, unplcd on turf (rtd 82, auct
mdn): suited by 7f, shld get 1m: acts on firm, soft grnd & polytrack: acts on any trk, suited by t-strap, tried
visor. 1 Oct'03 Newm 7fm 92-84 B: 1 Sep'03 Good 7fm 93-81 D: 2 Jun'03 Leic 7.0g/f 86-80 D:

1 Jun'03 Ling 7g/f 83-75 D: 2 Oct'02 Ling 6ap 79a-78 D:
1925* **ENCHANTED 8** [5]5-9-10 (95) K Fallon 4/1: 0463-117: Rear, prog after 5f, no impress ins fnl 1f: *1*   **92**
tchd 11/4: disapp under jt top-weight for hat-trick bid: btr 1925 & 178 (fills).
1624 **MARSHMAN 22** [3]5-9-5 (90) Saleem Golam(7) 16/1: 534-0308: Slow away, nvr a factor: btr 1151.   *1*   **85**
1068 **WING COMMANDER 54** [9]5-9-8 (93) P Hanagan 10/1: 0233-439: Al in rear: 8 wk abs: see 1068.   *3½*   **81**
1512 **HURRICANE FLOYD 27** [12]6-9-1 (86) T P Queally(3) 11/1: 4003-000: 10th: Slow away, al bhd: see 1512. *1¼*   **71**
1624 **PRINCE CYRANO 22** [11]5-8-5 (76) G Carter 20/1: 00-00060: 11th: Bhd, nvr a factor: see 1481.   *8*   **46**
11 Ran   Time 1m 24.31 (1.11)   Owned: Mr Alec Tuckerman   Trained: West Ilsley

2091   3.45 Play At Breckland Bingo Thetford Classified Stakes 3yo+ 0-80 (D)
     £6747 £2076 £1038   **1m str**   **Firm 12**   **+14 Fast**   Stands side

1833 **ACE OF HEARTS 12** [7] C F Wall 5-9-3 (80) S Sanders 9/2: 62-05021: Cl-up, led dist, rdn out to   **88**
hold on despite edging left: eff at 7f/1m, stays 10f well: acts on firm, soft grnd & both AWs: see 1833 & 1057.
1704 **ST PANCRAS 17** [2] N A Callaghan 4-9-7 (84) E Ahern 100/30: 456-0002: Led, hdd dist, kept on, not   *1½*   **88**
pace of wnr: well bckd: gd run back at 1m: see 1478.
2598*}**UNSCRUPULOUS 333** [6] J R Fanshawe 5-9-3 (80) L Dettori 2/1 FAV: 54/0321-3: ch g Machiavellian -   *1¾*   **80**
Footlight Fantasy (Nureyev): Keen rear, short room 3f out till over 1f out, kept on: well bckd on reapp: h'cap wnr on
fnl '03 start: promise both '02 starts (rtd 78): eff at 7f/1m on fm & gd: suited by waiting tactics: lightly rcd,
will rate higher. 1 Jul'03 Yarm 8.0g/f 83-75 D: 2 Jun'03 Good 7g/f 78-(72) D:
1877 **TOPTON 10** [3] P Howling 10-9-3 bl (76) K Fallon 16/1: 4310004: Held up, prog after 6f, no impress fnl 1f. *2*   **76**
1970 **FIVEOCLOCK EXPRESS 6** [5]4-9-4 (81) D Holland 20/1: 00-42005: Handy over 6f, wknd: qck reapp.   *2½*   **72**
4289} **HONORINE 256** [8]4-9-0 (80) P Robinson 10/1: 121243-6: b f Mark of Esteem - Blue Water (Bering)   *nk*   **67**
Al in rear: op 6/1 on reapp: won 2 h'caps in '03 (also plcd 4 times): plcd twice in '02 (mdns, rtd 72): suited by
1m on fast grnd, acts on an easy or gall trk: consistent performer last term, sharper for this.
2 Aug'03 Newm 8g/f 82-80 D: 1 Aug'03 Donc 8g/f 80-77 D: 2 Jul'03 Sali 8g/f 79-77 D: 1 May'03 Yarm 8.0g/f 81-73 E:
2 Apr'03 Brig 8.0g/f 70-71 D:
1891* **TIBER TIGER 9** [1]4-9-3 bl (80) T G McLaughlin 5/1: 0500-417: Handy 6f, sn wknd: btr 1891 (C/D, gd). *1½*   **67**
7 Ran   Time 1m 36.32 (u 0.17)   Owned: Lady Stuttaford & Mr W G Bovill   Trained: Newmarket

2092   4.20 Play Bingo At Bury St Edmunds Maiden Stakes 3yo (D)
     £5577 £1716 £858   **7f str**   **Firm 12**   **-02 Slow**   Stands side

1171 **ARICIA 46** [13] J H M Gosden 3-8-9 K Fallon 11/8 FAV: 01: b f Nashwan - Rahaam (Secreto) Slow   **90+**
away, sn in tch, led after 4f, clr ins fnl 1f, impressive: well bckd after 7 wk abs: dam 7f wnr: eff at 7f, 1m will
suit: acts on fm grnd & a stiff/gall trk: goes well fresh: taking perfomance, win in much better grade.
1829 **ZAMEYLA 12** [14] M A Jarvis 3-8-9 P Robinson 11/1: 02: b f Cape Cross - Angelic Sounds (The   *5*   **74**
Noble Player) Handy, kept on from dist, not pace easy wnr: op 7/1: cost 150,000: dam 5f wnr: eff at 7f, shld be
suited by further: acts on firm grnd: shown enough to find similar.
1511 **GREAT EXHIBITION 27** [18] Saeed bin Suroor 3-9-0 t (85) L Dettori 5/2: 32-003: b c Gone West -   *¾*   **77**
Touch of Greatness (Hero's Honor) Led, hdd, no extra dist: well bckd: earlier unplcd in Nad Al Sheba (Gr 2): plcd
on both '03 starts (rtd 90, mdn, D L Loder): eff at 6/7f, further shld suit: acts on firm grnd: wears a t-strap.
2 Sep'03 Thir 7fm 90- D:
5023} **BARONS SPY 205** [3] A W Carroll 3-9-0 M Hills 50/1: 00-4: b c Danzero - Princess Accord   *6*   **65**
(D'Accord) Rear, prog 3f out, hung right & wknd ins fnl 2f: unplcd both '03 starts (rtd 68): tried t-strap.
1834 **SHARAAB 12** [16]3-9-0 t (74) R Hills 11/2: 30-605: Handy over halfway, sn no extra: btr 1148.   *hd*   **64**
     POLAR SUN 0 [9]3-9-0 E Ahern 16/1: 6: Nvr nrr than mid-div: debut: well bred: with J R Fanshawe.   *3½*   **57**
46}**MOON LEGEND 239** [19]3-8-9 D Holland 20/1: 06-7: Cl-up, fdd 2f out: reapp.   *nk*   **51**
     EIJAAZ 0 [12]3-9-0 W Supple 20/1: 8: Rear, prog after 3f, wknd 2f out: debut.   *1¼*   **54**
1829 **PETRION 12** [6]3-8-9 S Sanders 100/1: 09: Al in rear.   *2½*   **44**
1270 **RAWALPINDI 40** [1]3-9-0 Lisa Jones(3) 66/1: 0-00: 10th: Al bhd.   *nk*   **48**
1876   **Judda 10** [2]3-9-0 T G McLaughlin 100/1:0   1959 **Kalamansi 6** [11]3-8-9 D Fox(5) 66/1:0
     Mary Carleton 0 [8]3-8-9 B Doyle 66/1:0   1876 **Tikitano 10** [17]3-8-9 C Catlin 40/1:0
1581 **Miss St Albans 24** [15]3-8-9 R Price 100/1:0   **Electras Dream 0** [10]3-8-9 Hayley Turner(5) 66/1:0
16 Ran   Time 1m 24.18 (0.98)   Owned: Mr George Strawbridge   Trained: Manton

2093   4.50 Winnersbingo Co Uk Handicap Stakes Fillies 3yo+ 0-85 (D)
     £6838 £2104 £1052   **6f str**   **Firm 12**   **-23 Slow**   Stands side   **[85]**

1824 **SILVER CHIME 12** [8] D M Simcock 4-8-10 (67) M Fenton 7/1: 050-0041: Made all, drvn out ins fnl   **72**
1f to hold on: tchd 9/1: suited by 6f, has tried 7f: acts on firm & gd grnd, prob handles polytrack: see 874.
2034 **GLENCOE SOLAS 3** [6] S Kirk 4-8-8 bl (65) P Dobbs 4/1 FAV: 600-6422: Handy, ev ch dist, kept on   *hd*   **69**
ins fnl 1f, just held: well bckd on qck reapp: acts on firm & gd, prob handles soft: can find similar: see 2034.
2080 **BINT ROYAL 1** [4] Miss V Haigh 6-8-1 p (58) R Miles(2) 9/1: 0010-5503: Held up, prog despite   *shd*   **61**
hanging left from 1f out, just denied in 3-way photo: bckd from 12/1: fin unplcd yesterday at Doncaster: prob wnr
in another couple of strides, rider's 1lb overweight proved costly: see 1337.
1782 **BANDIT QUEEN 14** [5] W Jarvis 4-10-1 (86) P Robinson 11/2: 16500-34: Cl-up, hung right & no extra dist. *2*   **83**
1743 **MADDIES A JEM 14** [7] D M Simcock 4-9-5 (75) S W Kelly 5/1: 460-1135: Mid-div, prog & ev ch bef 1f out, sn no extra. *shd*   **71**
1726 **COMPLICATION 16** [10]4-8-6 bl (63) Lisa Jones(3) 7/1: 12000-06: Handy, outpcd after 4f, rallied fnl 1f. *shd*   **58**
1761 **FADEELA 15** [11]3-8-1 (67) C Catlin 10/1: 210-5007: Cl-up till dist, no extra: btr 1110.   *1¼*   **58**
1772*}**SPARKLING JEWEL 368** [1]4-9-6 (77) R L Moore 7/1: 2/31-8: b f Bijou d'Inde - Jobiska (Dunbeath)   *nk*   **67**
Rear, eff when hung left dist, sn onepcd: reapp: mdn wnr on 1 of only 2 '03 starts: rnr-up sole '02 start (AW auct
mdn): eff at 5/6f on fast grnd & polytrack: has gone well fresh: with R Hannon.
1 May'03 Newb 5.2g/f 72- D: 2 May'02 Ling 5ap 82a- F:
1782 **FLASHING BLADE 14** [3]4-9-3 t P (74) S Sanders 25/1: 05-00009: Handy over 4f, sn no extra.   *½*   **63**
1970 **SAFRANINE 6** [7]7-8-10 (67) Ann Stokell 33/1: 0-000000: 10th: Slow away, al in rear.   *nk*   **55**
1731 **TATA NAKA 16** [9]4-7-12 (15oh)VIS (40) Hayley Turner(5) 66/1: 650-0050: 11th: Handy 3f, sn wknd.   *5*   **28**
11 Ran   Time 1m 12.95(2.15)   Owned: Tick Tock Partnership   Trained: Newmarket

Official Going Good/Firm (Firm places on sprint crse)

2094   **1.45 Listed Bonusprint Com National Stakes 2yo   (A)**
£14500 £5500 £2750   **5f6y str**   **Good/Firm 37**   -04 Slow   Far Side

1795* **POLLY PERKINS 14** [2] N P Littmoden 2-8-7 K Darley 25/1: 11: Slow away, held up, gd hdwy over 1f   **98+**
out, qcknd to lead ins last, going away, rdly: v eff over a stiff or sharp 5f, 6f shld suit: acts on fast & gd
grnd: useful, tidy turn of foot here, win more races & merits respect in Queen Mary at R Ascot: see 1795.
1614* **MOSCOW MUSIC 24** [1] M G Quinlan 2-9-1 S Drowne 9/1: 212: Handy, hdwy over 1f out, chall ins   1½   **98**
last, not pace of wnr: imprvd stepped up in class & on this fast grnd, acts on gd/soft: win more races: see 1614.
882* **BUNDITTEN 42** [5] Andrew Reid 2-8-12 J F Egan 33/1: 13: Made most, rdn & hdd ins last, no extra: nk   **94**
10 wk abs: gd run up in class: acts on fast grnd & polytrack: win another stks race: see 882.
1573 **ALPAGA LE JOMAGE 26** [3] B J Meehan 2-8-12 K Fallon 20/1: 3324: With ldr, eff over 1f out,   1   **91**
onepcd: win a minor trk mdn: see 1422, 1190.
1149 **NEXT TIME AROUND 48** [6]2-9-3 M Fenton 20/1: 135: Hung right thr'out, bhd, some late gains: 7   nk   **95**
wk abs, not disgraced under joint top weight & handles fast & gd/soft: see 1149, 920.
1981* **INDIANNIE STAR 6** [7]2-8-7 T E Durcan 8/1: 216: Handy travelling well, wknd appr fn l 1f: just   shd   **84**
too sn after 1981 (auct mdn)?
1608* **CELTIC SPA 24** [4]2-8-7 R Havlin 33/1: 017: Slow away, hung right thr'out, eff well over 1f out,   ½   **82**
no extra: btr 1608 (nov auct, soft grnd).
1422* **PRINCE CHARMING 33** [8]2-9-3 L Dettori 4/11 FAV: 118: In tch, wknd well over 1f out: hvly bckd,   3   **83**
jnt top-weight: 1st start on fast grnd & prob not enjoy it: looked useful on soft earlier in 1422.
8 Ran   Time 1m 01.65 (2.05)   Owned: Miss Vanessa Church   Trained: Newmarket

2095   **2.20 Gr2 Bonusprint Com Henry Ii Stakes 4yo+   (A)**
£63220 £23980 £11990   **2m78y**   **Good/Firm 37**   +10 Fast   Inside

1843* **PAPINEAU 12** [2] Saeed bin Suroor 4-8-12 t (111) L Dettori 9/4: 2115-11: Handy, trav well over 2f   **118**
out, styd on to lead dist, kept on despite edging right, drvn out: fast time, hvly bckd: styd this stiff 2m well &
shld get further: acts on fast & soft: thriving, fast imprvg & smart: will be 5lb worse off with Mr Dinos in Gold
Cup (2m4f) but shld give him a race if staying that extended trip: see 1843.
1705 **MR DINOS 18** [7] P F I Cole 5-9-5 (122) K Fallon 2/1 FAV: 51/116-42: Prom, rdn 3f out, kept on   1½   **122+**
for press fnl 2f, 1L bhd when hmpd by wnr ins last, not recover: bckd: back to form (won this in '03) on a fast
surface: excellent run conceding weight & closer to this wnr but for interference: will take all the beating again in
Gold Cup (6L wnr last term) where he doesn't have a pen: see 1705.
5026*)**NEW SOUTH WALES 206** [5] Saeed bin Suroor 4-8-12 t (105) K McEvoy 20/1: 11/6401-3: b c In The   1½   **114**
Wings - Temora (Ela Mana Mou): Led 1f, led again over 2f out till over 1f out, kept on same pace: s/mate of wnr:
won last of 4 '03 starts (stks): '02 mdn & Gr 3 wnr: eff at 14.5f, stays 2m on fast & gd/soft: runs well fresh in
a t-strap: smart, fine return & shld find a staying Gr 3 contest this term.
1 Nov'03 Donc 14.6gd 109- C: 1 Oct'02 Leop 7g/s 102- :
1418* **RISK SEEKER 33** [9] E Lellouche 4-8-12 t D Boeuf 4/1: 1120-214: In tch, eff over 2f out, onepace: ¾   **113**
handles fast grnd, produced career best/impress performance on v soft last time in 1418 & would be interesting in the
Gold Cup on fav soft grnd: see 1418.
1418 **HILBRE ISLAND 33** [4]4-8-12 (110) M Hills 66/1: 310-30P5: Held up, eff over 2f out, sn no extra.   2   **111**
1569 **MISTERNANDO 26** [3]4-8-12 (105) S Hitchcott 8/1: 2611-026: In tch, wide, rdn & no impress over 2f   1¼   **110**
out: highly tried & more interesting back in 1under l/rtd h'caps: see 1569 (auct mdn).
1418 **ROYAL REBEL 33** [8]8-9-0 (112) J Murtagh 20/1: 43/001-/-57: In tch, outpcd 3f out, mod late gains: shd   **110**
lightly rcd in recent seasons, former dual Ascot Gold Cup wnr: see 1418.
1757 **SAVANNAH BAY 16** [1]5-9-0 bl (111) T E Durcan 33/1: 6355-048: Led after 1f till over 2f out, wknd.   2½   **107**
1705 **SHANTY STAR 18** [10]4-8-12 (105) K Darley 16/1: 01/131-0P: gr c Hector Protector - Shawanni   **0**
(Shareef Dancer) Slow away & al bhd, t.o./p.u. bef line: won 2 of 3 '03 starts (stks & Gr 3 Queens Vase): stays
a stiff 2m well on firm & fast grnd: has run well fresh: lkd v useful last term, something surely amiss.
1 Jun'03 Asco 16.2g/f 108-(101) A: 1 Apr'03 Catt 12.0g/f 99-(87) C: 1 Oct'02 Pont 10fm 91- D:
9 Ran   Time 3m 34.17 (4.37)   Owned: Godolphin   Trained: Newmarket

2096   **2.55 Doubleprint Handicap Stakes 3yo+ 0-105   (B)**   [105]
£15413 £5847 £2923   **1m14y rnd**   **Good/Firm 37**   +00 Fast   Inside

1478 **PUTRA KUANTAN 30** [13] M A Jarvis 4-9-3 (94) P Robinson 5/2 FAV: 1200-631: Led early, cl-up, led   **103**
again dist & sn rdn clr, styd on strongly, rdn out: hvly bckd: caught the eye last time: stays 10f, suited by a
stiff 1m now: likes firm & fast, handles gd/soft: can front run & handles any trk: thriving, v useful & must come
right into the Royal Hunt Cup frame under only a 7lb penalty: see 1478.
1812 **IMPELLER 13** [6] W R Muir 5-8-10 (87) S Drowne 13/2: 0022-002: Keen held up, hdwy to chase wnr   2   **90**
over 1f out, not wnr's pace: likes Sandown & another gd run: see 1812.
1812 **FINISHED ARTICLE 13** [9] D R C Elsworth 7-8-13 (90) K Darley 15/2: 2204-053: Held up, kept on   nk   **92**
late, nrst fin: v tough: requires luck in rng & will relish a return to fav course Goodwood: see 1812.
1883+ **BLUE TROJAN 10** [2] S Kirk 4-8-7 (84) J F Egan 9/1: 4-220014: In tch, eff well over 1f out, kept   ½   **85**
on, not pace of wnr: another fine run: see 1883.
1812 **OUR TEDDY 13** [3]4-8-10 BL (87) Martin Dwyer 33/1: 000-4005: Dwelt, bhd, kept on late, nrst fin: nk   **87**
btr run in 1st time blnks, tried visor earlier: shaped like further will suit & has slipped down the weights: see 547.
1586 **CONSONANT 25** [8]7-8-13 (90) K Fallon 16/1: ////-111106: Prom, onepcd over 1f out: btr 758 (aw).   hd   **89**
1847 **KING CARNIVAL 12** [4]3-8-3 (92) R Smith 66/1: 05112-07: ch c King of Kings - Miss Waki Club   1   **89**
(Miswaki) Keen held up, hdwy & hung right over 1f out, onepace: '03 mdn & nurs h'cap wnr: eff at 6f, shld stay
further: acts on fast grnd & a gall trk: useful last term.
2 Aug'03 Wind 6g/f 92-(93) C: 1 Jul'03 Asco 6g/f 95-89 D: 1 Jun'03 Hayd 6g/f 94- D:
1926 **CALCUTTA 9** [1]8-9-5 (96) M Hills 12/1: 314-0008: Held up, mod late gains: see 1926.   hd   **92**
1686 **EXCELLENTO 19** [7]4-9-11 (102) L Dettori 10/1: 2/1113-09: ch c Rahy - Golden Opinion (Slew O'   1¼   **95**
Gold) Led after 1f till over 1f out, no extra: won first 3 in '03 (mdn & 2 h'caps): suited by 1m on firm or
gd/soft, sharp or stiff trk: useful & genuine last term, can front run.
1 May'03 Thir 8g/s 103-(99) B: 1 May'03 Newm 7g/f 102-(95) B: 1 Apr'03 Ripo 8g/f 95- D: 2 Sep'02 Pont 8fm 80- D:

SANDOWN   MONDAY 31.05.04   Righthand, Galloping Track, Stiff Finish

1231 **CHINKARA** 44 [11]4-9-1 (92) L Keniry(3) 16/1: 14110-00: 10th: Held up, hung right fnl 2f, no impress.	hd	84
1812* **HIGHLAND REEL** 13 [10]7-8-10 (87) J Murtagh 14/1: 10000-10: 11th: Held up, btn 2f out: btr 1812.	nk	78
1686 **CONVENT GIRL** 19 [5]4-9-3 (94) R Havlin 12/1: 3126-060: 12th: Dwelt, sn handy, wknd over 2f out.	2	81
4338} **BINANTI** 255 [12]4-9-0 (91) M Fenton 33/1: 420140-0: 13th: In tch, wknd well over 1f out.	shd	78
1613* **LIFTED WAY** 24 [14]5-8-3 (80) K McEvoy 11/1: 400-0110: 14th: Prom, wknd over 2f out: too keen.	3	61

14 Ran   Time 1m 41.99 (2.99)   Owned: HRH Sultan Ahmad Shah   Trained: Newmarket

---

2097   3.30 Bonusprint European Breeders Fund Maiden Stakes Fillies 2yo (D)
£4875 £1500 £750   **5f6y str**   **Good/Firm 37**   **-18 Slow**   Far Side

JEWEL IN THE SAND [3] R Hannon 2-8-11   P Dobbs 9/1: 1: b f Bluebird - Dancing Drop (Green   **76+**
Desert) Front rank, went on dist, styd on strongly despite drifting right, rdn out: tchd 9/1: debut: Mar foal,
cost £65,000: half sister to a 6f wnr abroad: dam a useful 7f/1m performer, sire a top class sprinter: eff at 5f
on fast grnd, clrly runs well fresh: overcame greeness today, 6f shld suit & can go on & win again.
1805 **TOUCH OF SILK** 14 [5] B W Hills 2-8-11   M Hills 7/2: 52: Trkd ldrs, ev ch fnl 1f, just btn   ¾   73
cl-home: bckd from 5/1: eff at 5f on fast grnd: still showed signs of greeness today, shld find similar: see 1805.
LIWAS LAKE [4] Saeed bin Suroor 2-8-11   L Dettori 5/4 FAV: 3: ch f Greenwood Lake - Champagne   2   67
Sweep (End Sweep) Tried to make all, collared dist, held when short of room cl-home on debut: hvly bckd tho'
drifted from 8/11: Feb 1st foal, cost $300,000: sire a top class juv in the US on the dirt: eff at 5f on fast grnd:
showed plenty of speed & sure to learn from this for powerful yard.
1716 **HEIDIS DASH** 18 [2] R Charlton 2-8-11   S Drowne 5/1: 04: b f Green Desert - Child Prodigy (Ballad   2½   60
Rock) Chsd ldrs, btn fnl 1f: 140,000 gns Mar foal: half sister to 1m juv wnr Menuhin: dam a 1m wnr in the USA,
sire a top class sprinter/miler: some improvement on debut here.
XEERAN [7]2-8-11   P Robinson 11/2: 5: b f Xaar - Cyclone Flyer (College Chapel) Slow away,   ½   58
keen in rear, btn fnl 1f on debut: bckd from 9/1: Mar foal, cost 60,000gns: half sister to dual 5f juv wnr Autumn
Pearl: dam a sprint wnr, sire a top class juv: clrly showing something at home, lost all ch at the start today.
1380 **CHUTNEY MARY** 35 [6]2-8-11   K Darley 25/1: 06: Dwelt, hung badly left halfway, al bhd.   7   37

6 Ran   Time 1m 02.26 (2.76)   Owned: Sand Associates   Trained: Marlborough

---

2098   4.05 Tripleprint Handicap Stakes 3yo 0-80 (D)   [86]
£5759 £1772 £886   **7f16y rnd**   **Good/Firm 37**   **-14 Slow**   Inside

1847 **DISTANT CONNECTION** 12 [8] A P Jarvis 3-8-12 (70) K McEvoy 6/1: 03-00061: Front rank, led dist,   79
held on drvn out: nicely bckd: tried 1m, seems best at 7f: acts on fast grnd & on a gall trk: 1st success, see 1583.
1763 **PIZAZZ** 16 [2] B J Meehan 3-9-7 (79) M Hills 10/1: 0-5252: Held up, hdwy 1.5f out, fin strongly &   shd   87+
just failed in a thrilling fin: jnt top weight: eff at 7f/1m on fast & gd/soft: shld find similar, prob at 1m.
4686} **LOVE TRIANGLE** 232 [4] D R C Elsworth 3-9-7 (79) L Keniry(3) 14/1: 214600-3: ch g Titus Livius -   1¼   83
Kirsova (Absalom) Prom, ev ch 2f out, no extra cl-home: op 10/1, has been gldd: '03 Galway mdn wnr, also plcd sev
times, incl in a nurs h'cap: eff arnd 7f on fast & gd/soft, handles a sharp or gall trk: sound reapp under jnt top
weight. 1 Aug'03 Galw 7g/s 86- : 2 Jul'03 Sali 7.0g/f 86-79 E: 2 May'03 Good 5g/f 84- D:
1927 **PINK SAPPHIRE** 9 [6] D R C Elsworth 3-9-1 (73) J Murtagh 9/2: 510-024: Chsd ldrs, kept on under   nk   77
press fnl 1f: well bckd stable-mate of 3rd: prob ran to form of 1927 (1m) & a return to that trip will suit.
1734 **MISSUS LINKS** 17 [12]3-8-13 (71) K Darley 5/1: 1-525: Led till dist, no extra: see 1734 (6f).   hd   74
4066} **KINBRACE** 269 [1]3-8-3 (61) Martin Dwyer 10/1: 050-6: b f Kirkwall - Cache (Bustino) Dwelt, hdwy   ¾   62
wide fnl 2f, nrst fin on reapp/h'cap bow: lightly rcd & some mdn promise in '03 (rtd 66 at best): 9,000gns half
sister to sev wnrs, incl mid-dist h'cappers Swan Hunter & Lunar Lord: nothing much went right today, improve.
1163 **WHITGIFT ROCK** 47 [13]3-9-3 (75) J F Egan 11/1: 631-1207: Chsd ldrs, onepcd fnl 1f: 7 wk abs.   hd   75
1761 **ANDALUZA** 16 [10]3-9-0 (72) K Fallon 100/30 FAV: 4138: Mid-div, nov pace to chall: well bckd, btr 1761.   nk   71
1761 **NINE RED** 16 [5]3-8-3 (61) K May(7) 16/1: 5550-09: b f Royal Applause - Sarcita (Primo Dominie)   1¾   56
Held up, nvr nr to chall: some mdn promise in '03 (rtd 67): 40,000gns half sister to a couple of useful sprinters.
1915 **WIZARD LOOKING** 9 [9]3-8-11 t (69) P Dobbs 20/1: 60526-60: 10th: Rear, short of rm halfway, nvr dngrs.   shd   64
1956 **SWORN TO SECRECY** 7 [7]3-8-6 BL (64) S Drowne 33/1: 35-00000: 11th: Al rear in 1st time blnks.   hd   58
2031 **LA PROFESSORESSA** 4 [3]3-8-8 (66) R Havlin 33/1: 03005-60: 12th: Mid-div, btn 2f out: qck reapp.   2½   55

12 Ran   Time 1m 29.98 (3.58)   Owned: Mrs Ann Jarvis   Trained: Twyford

---

2099   4.40 Bonusprint Handicap Stakes 4yo+ 0-80 (D)   [80]
£5733 £1764 £882   **1m2f7y**   **Good/Firm 37**   **-05 Slow**   Inside

3848*}**FAAYEJ** 281 [14] Sir Michael Stoute 4-9-12 (78) R Hills 6/1: 521-1: b g Sadler's Wells - Russian   84+
Ballet (Nijinsky) Mid-div, smooth prog to lead ent fnl 1f, styd on strongly, rdn out: op 9/2 on reapp: won fnl of
3 juv starts (mdn), has since been gldd: eff at 10/12f on fast & gd/soft grnd, clrly runs well fresh: can force the
pace: been gelded: poss the type to only just do enough & more to come.
1 Aug'03 Beve 9.9g/f 75- D: 2 Jul'03 Newc 12.4g/s 77- D:
1599 **TRUE COMPANION** 24 [7] N P Littmoden 5-9-5 (71) J P Guillambert(3) 12/1: 1303142: Rear, hdwy 1.5f   ½   76
out, fin strongly & only just btn: op 16/1: remains in fine form, see 1128.
1913 **ICANNSHIFT** 9 [5] S Dow 4-8-2 (54) R Miles(3) 25/1: 6021303: Led till ent fnl 1f, kept on well: see 1357.   nk   58
2015 **LADY McNAIR** 5 [12] P D Cundell 4-9-8 (74) K Fallon 9/2 FAV: 446-4024: Trkd ldrs, sltly short of   nk   77
room dist, kept on under press & only btn around 1L: nicely bckd, qck reapp: see 2015.
3773} **TENDER FALCON** 284 [4]4-9-1 (67) J Murtagh 20/1: 333214-5: br g Polar Falcon - Tendresse (Tender   nk   69
King) Front rank, sltly outpcd ent fnl 1f, kept on under press cl-home on reapp: won 2 h'caps in '03, also plcd sev
times: eff at 10f, stays 12f: acts on firm & gd/soft, poss any trk: tough & consistent, can set the pace.
1 Aug'03 Sand 10.0g/f 69-62 D: 2 Jul'03 Asco 10gd 66-62 D: 1 May'03 Nott 10.0g/f 63-59 F:
1789 **AONINCH** 14 [3]4-8-5 (1ow) (56) R Havlin 20/1: 13-60506: Stdd start, styd on fnl 1f, nrst fin.   nk   58
1235 **BEST BE GOING** 44 [6]4-9-10 (76) T E Durcan 9/1: 3451-07: b g Danehill - Bye Bold Aileen   nk   76
(Warning) Chsd ldrs, onepcd fnl 1f: 6 wk abs: ended '03 with a Goodwood h'cap win (fast time): eff at 1m, prob
stays 10f: acts on firm grnd & on a sharp/undul trk: slowly coming to hand. 1 Oct'03 Good 8fm 79-71 D:
1916 **BARRY ISLAND** 9 [11]5-9-11 (77) K Darley 7/1: 4430038: Held up, nvr nr to chall.   2   73
1812 **WELCOME STRANGER** 13 [8]4-9-11 (77) J Tate 12/1: 1034-009: Chsd ldrs, btn over 1f out: btr 1812.   3½   68
1913 **BLAZING TRAIL** 9 [2]4-9-1 (67) M Fenton 7/1: 2513230: 10th: Al towards rear: btr 1913.   3   53
1541 **DEEWAAR** 27 [13]4-7-12 (3oh) (47) D Fox(5) 100/1: 32000-00: 11th: Held up, nvr a factor.   1¼   34
1613 **LEARNED LAD** 24 [9]6-8-4 (56) J F Egan 16/1: 50-25000: 12th: Held up, nvr a factor.   nk   39

SANDOWN   MONDAY 31.05.04   Righthand, Galloping Track, Stiff Finish

1736 **DREAM MAGIC 17** [1]6-9-11 (77) Martin Dwyer 7/1: 044-4050: 13th: Front rank 1m, wknd: bckd from   1½   57
9/1: much btr expected after 1736, see 1235.
1890 **JOOLS 10** [10]6-10-0 (80) M Howard(7) 16/1: 0015300: 14th: Al towards rear under top weight.   nk   59
1875 **KIROV KING 11** [15]4-9-4 (70) L Keniry(3) 25/1: 460-0000: 15th: Mid-div, btn 2f out.   2   46
15 Ran   Time 2m 08.34(4.24)   Owned: Mr Hamdan Al Maktoum   Trained: Newmarket

---

REDCAR   MONDAY 31.05.04   Lefthand, Flat, Galloping Track

Official Going GOOD/FIRM (FIRM places).

2100   2.00 Enter Today's Racecard Competition Novice Auction Stakes 2yo (E)
     £3504 £1078 £539   5f str   Good/Firm 33   -27 Slow   Centre

1471 **BOLD MARC 30** [2] K R Burke 2-8-13   Darren Williams 13/8 FAV: 4121: Trkd ldrs trav well, qcknd to   92+
lead dist, sn asserted under hands-and-heels: nicely bckd: eff at 5f on fast & gd/soft grnd, handles soft: handles
a sharp or gall trk: speedy with a useful turn of foot, win again: see 1471.
1631* **MELALCHRIST 23** [5] J J Quinn 2-8-13   R Winston 9/2: 12: Al prom, briefly led over 1f out, kept   1¾   82
on for press, not pace of wnr: op 7/2: acts on fast & soft grnd, likely type to apprec 6f: see 1631.
1677 **RYEDANE 19** [1] T D Easterby 2-8-9   D Allan(3) 28/1: 03: b c Danetime - Miss Valediction   2½   71
(Petardia) Prom, rdn & outpcd over 1f out: op 33/1: 9,000gns Apr foal, dam uncrd half-sister to 2 juv wnrs, sire
high-class sprinter: eff at 5f on fast grnd, 6f shld suit: one to note in ordinary mdn company.
1955 **MONASHEE PRINCE 7** [3] J R Best 2-9-1   N Pollard 7/4: 21534: Led till over 1f out, sn btn: ¾   74
nicely bckd, top-weight: reportedly needs a short rest, btr 1955 & 1386.
     JUN FAN [4]2-8-9   T Eaves(3) 16/1: 5: br c Artax - Ringside Lady (Clay Hero)   Dwelt, outpcd   nk   67
early, kept on late, nvr threat: Mar foal, 13,000gns purchase: half-brother to a List wnr in Australia: dam a List
Australian wnr: sire top-class dirt sprinter in US.
1752 **UREDALE 16** [6]2-8-9   J Carroll 50/1: 506: b c Bahhare - Baileys First (Alzao)   Chsd ldrs, outpcd   1½   63
halfway: £18,000 Mar foal, half-brother to wnrs abroad, incl a 10f German wnr: dam related to a Gr 3 mid-dist wnr:
likely to need further & more time.
     KIMBERLEY HALL [7]2-8-4 (2ow) Dean McKeown 16/1: 7: Chsd ldrs till halfway on debut.   4   46
7 Ran   Time 59.52 (3.02)   Owned: Market Avenue Racing Club 1   Trained: Leyburn

---

2101   2.35 Totesport Zetland Gold Cup Heritage Handicap 3yo+ 0-105 (B)   [105]
     £32500 £10000 £5000   1m2f   Good/Firm 33   +15 Fast   Inside

1686 **BLUE SPINNAKER 19** [1] M W Easterby 5-9-7 (98) P Mulrennan(5) 5/1: 004-0141: Held up, hdwy & short   104
of room 2f out, switched & drvn to lead cl-home: nicely bckd, fast time: eff at 1m/10f on firm & gd/soft, gall or
easy trk: useful & progressive with a fine turn of foot: prob val for more than may margin, see 1475.
1890 **JAMES CAIRD 10** [4] M H Tompkins 4-8-5 (82) F P Ferris(3) 10/1: 51162-62: ch g Catrail - Polish   nk   87
Saga (Polish Patriot) Held up, rdn & hdwy wide to lead over 1f out, edged left under press & hdd cl-home: h'cap &
class stks scorer '03: suited by 10f, tried 12f: acts on fast, polytrack & a stiff/undul or sharp trk, likes
Pontefract: progressive profile.
2 Oct'03 Donc 10.3g/f 80-80 D: 1 Sep'03 Pont 10.0g/f 80-(67) E: 1 Sep'03 Pont 10.0g/f 80-67 E: 2 Apr'03 Ling 8ap 75a- F:
1586 **CROW WOOD 25** [7] J G Given 5-9-1 (92) N Pollard 11/1: 1305-033: Trkd ldrs, switched & rdn to   shd   97
chall ins last, just held: fine run in a v comp h'cap: see 1296.
1104* **ZERO TOLERANCE 51** [2] T D Barron 4-8-13 (90) D Holland 4/1 FAV: 01304-14: Mid-div, rdn & staying   nk   94
on well when short of room dist, not pace of wnr cl-home: hvly bckd & not btn far in a v tight fin: 7 wk abs &
remains on the up-grade: see 1104.
1833 **VICIOUS WARRIOR 13** [14]5-8-8 (85) Dean McKeown 20/1: 4020-205: Trkd ldr, led over 2f out, hdd   shd   89
dist, no extra cl-home: only btn arnd 1L, ideally suited by more give but well h'capped: see 1475.
4599 **MILLAFONIC 240** [9]4-9-4 (95) A Culhane 11/1: 31150-6: b c Zafonic - Milligram (Mill Reef)   1¼   97+
Mid-div, eff when short of room over 1f out, keeping on when hmpd ins last, nrst line: reapp: mdn & class stks
scorer '03: both wins at 1m, now stays a gall 10f well: acts on fast & gd/soft grnd: little luck today & likely to
win more races.   1 May'03 Ayr 8g/s 98-(89) C: 1 May'03 Kemp 8g/f 95- D:
1704 **CRIPSEY BROOK 18** [12]6-8-9 (86) Kim Tinkler 11/1: 1330-667: Trkd ldrs, onepace fnl 3f.   ½   87
1704 **SIR GEORGE TURNER 18** [3]5-9-9 (100) J Fanning 11/1: 4632/-008: ch g Nashwan - Ingozi (Warning)   1½   99
Trkd ldrs, short of room when no extra dist: missed '03: List & Gr 3 rnr-up in '02, disapp in blnks: former v
useful juv, val class wnr: both wins at 7f, stays 10f well: acts on firm & gd grnd, sharp or gall trk, prob
prefers latter: slipping to a fair mark & ran well for a long way.   2 Sep'02 Good 10fm 104- A:
2 May'02 Ches 10.3fm 103- A: 1 Oct'01 Newm 7gd 108- B: 2 Aug'01 Asco 7gd 91- B: 1 Jul'01 Leic 7gd 89- E:
1833 **STRETTON 13** [5]6-8-2 (79) J Mackay 8/1: 3310-069: Held up, eff when no room over 2f out, not   shd   78
pace to chall: shade closer with a clr run: see 1833.
1704 **TELEMACHUS 18** [10]4-8-13 (90) F Lynch 25/1: 530-6100: 10th: Chsd ldrs, hmpd early, nvr factor after.   2   86
4666] **CASTLESHANE 234** [11]7-8-12 (89) R Winston 25/1: 100000-0: 11th: Led till 2.5f out, wkng when   2   82
hmpd: jumps fit.
1843 **Ulundi 12** [8]9-9-11 (102) P Hanagan 28/1:0
1843 **Bourgainville 12** [15]6-9-11 (102) N Chalmers(5) 16/1:0
1704 **Always Esteemed 18** [17]4-9-6 (97) J Carroll 16/1:0   1478 **Pagan Sky 30** [13]5-8-9 (86) Lisa Jones(3) 16/1:0
15 Ran   Time 2m 04.13 (1.83)   Owned: G Sparkes G Hart S Curtis & T Dewhirst   Trained: Sheriff Hutton

---

2102   3.10 Go Racing In Yorkshire On Bank Holiday Selling Stakes 3-5yo (F)
     £2989 £854 £427   7f str   Good/Firm 33   -05 Slow   Centre

     SEDGE [3] P T Midgley 4-9-7   R Fitzpatrick 66/1: 1: b g Lure - First Flyer (Riverman) Rdn in   60
rear, styd on well for press fnl 1f to lead line: no bid, Flat debut: jumps fit (mod form in bmprs): eff over a
gall 7f, 1m+ will suit on this evidence: acts on fast grnd & goes well fresh in sell grade.
1970 **SILVER SEEKER 7** [11] I Semple 4-9-7 (84) D Holland 5/1 JT FAV: 10/0-5002: Al prom, rdn & led ins   hd   59
last, hdd line: drpd in grade: could find similar: see 838.

864   **TANTRIC 75** [1] J O'Reilly 5-9-7 (60) J D O'Reilly(7) 10/1: 1000-003: Prom, rdn & led 2f out till   1¼   56
dist, no extra: 11 wk abs: see 864.
1944   **TIME TO REGRET 7** [6] J J Quinn 4-9-7 (53) R Winston 6/1: 4235-624: Chsd ldrs, kept on onepace.   ½   54
1820   **WEET WATCHERS 13** [8]4-9-12 (56) Alex Greaves 9/1: 0-164305: Led till 2f out, no extra dist: 2   55
prob handles fast grnd: see 1160 & 555.
1977   **WAINWRIGHT 6** [14]4-9-12 p (60) G Parkin 10/1: 1-100006: Chsd ldrs till dist: 6f prob ideal.   1¼   52
1884   **LIBRE 10** [13]4-9-7 p (61) Dean McKeown 6/1: 40-05407: Mid-div, nvr pace to chall: recent jmps rnr.   hd   47
708*   **CAYMAN BREEZE 98** [5]4-9-12 (60) A Culhane 5/1 JT FAV: 00-05418: Held up, short of room 2f out,   ½   51
sn onepace & held: op 10/1, new yard, abs.
1944   **COMPTON PRINCESS 7** [12]4-9-2 (39) J Mackay 33/1: 00-36009: Hmpd start, keen, nvr dngrs.   2½   36
1522   **EFIMAC 28** [15]4-9-2 (43) Suzanne France(7) 28/1: 50500-00: 10th: Mid-div, btn 3f out: see 1522.   ½   35
1949   **BEAMSLEY BEACON 7** [7]3-8-10 P (49) N Pollard 14/1: 200-0040: 11th: Bhd halfway: cheek pieces.   8   24
1142   **LOOKING DOWN 49** [10]4-9-2 (67) G Faulkner 15/2: 04030-00: 12th: Slow away, chsd ldrs 5f.   4   11
170   **Matriarchal 174** [2]4-9-2 (34) Kim Tinkler 100/1:0   1463   **Due Diligence 31** [9]5-9-7 (45) J Fanning 25/1:0
14 Ran   Time 1m 24.48 (2.68)   Owned: Mr Peter Mee   Trained: Westow

---

2103   3.45 Carlsberg Lager Handicap Stakes 3yo 0-80 (D)   [84]
£5996 £1845 £923   **1m3f**   **Good/Firm 33**   **-01 Slow**   Inside

1382   **ZEITGEIST 35** [2] L M Cumani 3-9-7 (77) D Holland 6/4 FAV: 01-41: Handy, prog to lead bef 1f out,   82
rdn out: well bckd: eff at 7f, now suited by 11/11.5f: acts on fast & soft grnd: unexposed at this trip in h'cap
grade & more prizes await: see 1382.
1628   **SILVERHAY 23** [5] T D Barron 3-8-12 (68) P Hanagan 13/8: 523-42: Prom, led 3f out till dist, not   2   68
pace wnr: well bckd: eff at 7/8.5f, apprec step up to 11f: acts on fast & soft: eyecatching in 1628.
4736}   **SAND AND STARS 230** [1] M H Tompkins 3-8-13 (69) F P Ferris(3) 20/1: 540-3: ch f Dr Devious -   ¾   67
Charm The Stars (Roi Danzig) In tch, hdwy 2f out, onepace fnl 1f: reapp: unplcd in 3 '03 starts (rtd 70, mdn):
eff at 1m, now stays 11f: acts on fast grnd: eff in blnks: sharper from this.
1582   **RUTTERS REBEL 25** [3] A G Swinbank 3-9-2 (72) R Winston 14/1: 0126-504: Rear, prog 4f out, onepcd   hd   70
fnl 1f: eff at 1m, now stays 11f: see 1226.
1834   **BADR 13** [4]3-8-9 (65) J Fanning 9/1: 20-605: b c Theatrical - Bejat (Mr Prospector) Led 1m,   5   55
wknd fnl 2f: op 11/1: rnr-up on first of only 2 '03 starts (mdn): eff at 1m, bred to be suited by further: acts
on gd grnd & a stiff trk: with Mark Johnston.   2 Aug'03 Hami 8.3gd 78- D:
1582   **MARINE CITY 25** [3]3-9-5 (75) A Culhane 15/2: 0-166: Handy over 1m, sn fdd: btr 1272 (soft).   3   60
6 Ran   Time 2m 19.26 (3.76)   Owned: Mr L Marinopoulos   Trained: Newmarket

---

2104   4.20 Stokesley Median Auction Maiden Stakes 3yo (E)
£3474 £1069 £535   **6f str**   **Good/Firm 33**   **-08 Slow**   Centre

1914   **SNOW WOLF 9** [1] J M Bradley 3-9-0 (76) D Holland 10/11 FAV: 023-01: Made all, pushed out ins fnl   81+
1f, val bit more: well bckd: eff at 5/6f on firm & gd grnd: gd confidence boost: see 1914.
1639   **FLYING BANTAM 23** [5] R A Fahey 3-9-0 (71) P Hanagan 6/4: 22503-22: Prom, kept on ins fnl 1f, not   2½   72
pace wnr: well bckd: ran to form of 2nd in 1639.
   OTAGO [6] J R Best 3-9-0 N Pollard 14/1: 3: b c Desert Sun - Martino (Marju) Handy, no extra   2½   65
dist: debut: cost 14,000gns: just sharper for this.
   KEY FACTOR [4] M W Easterby 3-8-9 P Mulrennan(5) 20/1: 4: b f Defacto - Onemoretime (Timeless   shd   60
Times) Dwelt, prog halfway, nrst fin: debut: improve for today's experience.
5031}   **BORODINSKY 205** [3]3-9-0 T Eaves(3) 50/1: 000-5: b g Magic Ring - Valldemosa (Music Boy) Handy   7   45
over 3f, sn fdd: reapp & new stable: modest form in 3 '03 starts (A Berry, rtd 29): has been gelded over winter.
1896   **BALWEARIE 10** [2]3-9-0 p (40) J Carroll 16/1: 4254-606: Handy 3f, sn fdd: btr 1387.   8   21
6 Ran   Time 1m 11.41 (2.51)   Owned: Mr E A Hayward   Trained: Chepstow

---

2105   4.55 Redcar Handicap Stakes 3yo+ 0-70 (E)   [65]
£3474 £1069 £535   **1m6f19y**   **Good/Firm 33**   **-04 Slow**   Inside

1753   **BEST PORT 16** [2] J Parkes 8-9-7 (58) M Lawson(5) 9/2: 054-0101: Held up, prog to lead trav well   68+
dist, pushed clr, ran 7L+: eff at 12f, suited by 14f/2m on firm & soft, v disapp last time out on fibresand: won in
gd style & can follow up on this evidence: see 1238.
1772   **PARTY PLOY 16** [4] K R Burke 6-9-6 (57) Darren Williams 7/2 FAV: 2606-002: Mid-div, prog to lead   5   59
over 2f out, hdd dist, no extra: on a winning mark: see 1772 (reapp).
1680   **NEXT FLIGHT 19** [1] R E Barr 5-9-1 (52) D Holland 9/2: 2323143: Led 7f, styd prom & led again 3f   ½   53
out, hdd over 2f out, sn no extra: btr 1396 (soft).
1952   **SPITTING IMAGE 7** [3] Mrs M Reveley 4-9-10 (61) A Culhane 5/1: 40-03024: Ev ch 2f out, sn no extra.   ½   61
1033   **MORVERN 59** [7]4-8-11 (48) J Fanning 12/1: 0004-405: ch g Titus Livius - Scotia Rose (Tap On   5   40
Wood) Cl-up, ev ch 3f out, sn fdd: 8 wk abs: plcd once in '03 (h'cap, rtd 62): plcd in '02, rnr-up in a match
(rtd 66, nov stks): eff at 10f, has tried further: acts on firm & fast: eff with a visor, tried cheek pieces.
2 Sep'02 Leic 7frm 66- D:
1870   **ALMNADIA 11** [6]5-8-7 p (48) R Winston 9/1: 5005/-056: In tch, led after 7f, hdd 3f out, sn fdd.   4   34
1796   **CALL ME SUNSHINE 14** [8]4-9-8 (59) G Faulkner 4/1: 2-105037: Al in rear: btr 1796 (12f).   4   39
1870   **GREEN N GOLD 11** [5]4-9-6 (57) P Hanagan 9/1: 400-1048: Handy, fdd 4f out: btr 1870.   15   15
1589   **TIOGA GOLD 25** [9]5-7-12 (35) J Mackay 33/1: 54400-59: b g Goldmark - Coffee Bean (Doulab) Rear,   11   0
nvr a factor: earlier hdles plcd (rtd 94h, nov): plcd in '03 (rtd 47a, h'cap): sell wnr in late '01 (B J Meehan):
eff at 1m/10f on fast grnd & fibresand: has tried blnks.   1 Dec'01 Sout 8af 62a- G:
9 Ran   Time 3m 03.03(5.23)   Owned: Mr M Wormald   Trained: Malton

628

Official Going Good/Firm (Firm Places)

2106   1.55 Mrs B A Spencer Median Auction Maiden Stakes 3yo (F)
£3611 £1111 £556   **1m rnd**   **Firm 18**   **Inapplicable**   Inside

925   **TABLEAU 66** [3] B W Hills 3-9-0 R Hughes 9/4 FAV: 5-31: Made all, shkn up & in command from   **84**
dist, shade cosy: 2 month abs: eff at 7f, imprvd for step up to 1m & further shld suit: acts on firm & gd grnd,
stiff/gall trks: goes well fresh: lightly rcd, open to improvement in h'caps: see 925.
1762   **PRINCIPAL WITNESS 16** [9] W R Muir 3-9-0 S Sanders 3/1: 042: Prom, short of room over 1f out,   ½   80
kept on, not able to reach wnr: closer to cosy wnr with clr run: op 7/2: eff at 1m, 10f looks sure to suit:
promise last twice, can find a race: see 1762.
1495   **MASTER THEO 29** [7] H J Collingridge 3-9-0   (77) J Quinn 12/1: 335-03: b c Southern Halo - Lilian   1¾   77
Bayliss (Sadler's Wells) Chsd wnr, onepace for press dist: dual mdn plcd '03 (rtd 80a & 78): eff around 7f/1m on
firm, gd & polytrack, sharp/undul or stiff trk: shown enough to find a race.
1763   **DIFFERENT PLANET 16** [4] J W Hills 3-9-0 E Ahern 5/2: 44: Chsd ldrs, kept on onepace: btr 1763.   3½   70
   DAN DI CANIO 0 [12]3-9-0 P Doe 33/1: 5: b g Bahri - Khudud (Green Desert) Dwelt & held up,   nk   69
kept on late, not able to chall: shaped here as if 10f+ would suit: handles firm grnd, encouraging intro.
4981   **KENTMERE 211** [2]3-9-0 T (71) S Carson 20/1: 22500-6: b c Efisio - Addaya (Persian Bold) Chsd   ¾   68
ldrs, outpcd fnl 2f: t-strap on reapp: dual mdn rnr-up '03, sand unplcd (rtd 61a): half-brother to smart 1m wnr
Priors Lodge: eff around 7/7.2f, 1m shld suit this term: handles fast grnd.
2 Sep'03 Muss 7.1g/f 76- D: 2 Aug'03 Ayr 7.2g/f 80- E:
4407   **FIFTH COLUMN 251** [10]3-9-0 O Urbina 14/1: 0-7: Prom, no impress fnl 2f: op 20/1, reapp.   shd   68
   AFTER LENT 0 [15]3-9-0 J Bramhill 100/1: 8: Held up, eff over 2f out, no impress on debut.   ½   67
4694   **SUPER KING 232** [6]3-9-0 W Supple 14/1: 02-9: Prom 5f, reapp.   3   61
1832   **CHISEL 13** [14]3-9-0 R Ffrench 33/1: 00: 10th: In tch till 2f out, longer trip.   1½   58
1340   **KNIGHT OF HEARTS 37** [13]3-9-0 P McCabe 150/1: 550: 11th: Al bhd.   6   47
   ZALEBE 0 [5]3-8-9 R Price 50/1: 0: 12th: Sn struggling rear on debut.   dist   0
12 Ran Time 1m 40.53 () Owned: Mr K Abdulla Trained: Lambourn

2107   2.25 Geraldine Hauke Selling Stakes 3-5yo (G)
£2954 £844 £422   **1m2f**   **Firm 18**   **-28 Slow**   Inside

1724   **REGULATED 17** [9] D B Feek 3-8-12 (65) Dane O'Neill 5/1: 0-201551: Held up, hdwy & hung right   64
over 1f out, styd on for press to lead well ins last: op 4/1, bght in for 7,000gns: prev with J Osborne: suited by
10f, could get further: acts on firm & both AWs, likes sell grade: see 899.
2944   **LABELLED WITH LOVE 319** [10] W G M Turner 4-9-7 L Treadwell(7) 40/1: 0-2: ch g Zilzal - Dream   1¼   56
Baby (Master Willie) Dwelt & keen, sn handy, led 3f out & rdn clr, hdd well ins last: reapp: mod form sole '03
start (rtd 23, C/D mdn): eff at 10f, rtn to 1m might suit: handles firm grnd: encouraging run dropped to sell grade.
1724   **STYLISH SUNRISE 17** [5] M L W Bell 3-8-7 T (65) E Ahern 5/1: 036-043: Held up, outpcd over 2f out,   2½   52
kept on ins last: op 4/1, first time t-strap: stays a stiff 10f in sell grade: handles firm & fast grnd.
   UNCLE BATTY 0 [4] G A Harker 4-9-7 R Ffrench 10/1: 4: b g Bob Back - Aunt Sadie (Pursuit of   ½   51
Love) Dwelt & held up, kept on late, nvr a threat: bckd: clmd for 6,000: Flat debut, 8 wk jumps abs (unplcd,
bmprs): stays 10f on the level, shapes as if 12f+ in similar will suit: handles firm grnd.
   ALI BRUCE 0 [11]4-9-7 T G McLaughlin 7/2 FAV: 5: b g Cadeaux Genereux - Actualite (Polish   ¾   50
Precedent) Trkd ldrs & keen, onepace for press fnl 2f: gamble from 12/1: Flat debut, jumps fit (mod form, bmprs).
1284   **ENNA 41** [8]5-9-2 (51) B Swarbrick(5) 15/2: 01013-46: Chsd ldr, hdwy over 1f out: clmd for 6,000.   1½   43
1724   **FITZ THE BILL 17** [1]4-9-2 bl (42) S Sanders 11/2: 00-00337: Held up, btn 2f out: flattered 1724.   6   34
1966   **RELATIVE HERO 7** [7]4-9-7 p (62) A Quinn(5) 8/1: 11650-08: Prom till over 1f out: longer trip.   1½   37
1270   **BUCKENHAM STONE 41** [2]5-9-2 J Quinn 33/1: 00-09: Bhd halfway: 6 wk abs, longer trip.   11   17
353   **FIRST CLASS GIRL 144** [3]5-9-2 G Carter 50/1: 0/-40: 10th: Struggling halfway, 5 month abs.   1¾   15
2120} **WAFANI 353** [12]5-9-7 bl B Reilly(3) 40/1: 00U/0-0: 11th: Led till 3f out, sn btn, reapp.   2½   16
1973   **Mesmerised 7** [6]4-9-2 p(35) Ann Stokell 25/1:0   1058   **Jems Law 56** [13]5-9-2 vis J Jeffrey(7) 66/1:0
13 Ran Time 2m 07.11 (4.61) Owned: Mr D R Hunnisett Trained: Brightling

2108   3.00 New Street Chambers Handicap Stakes Fillies 3yo+ 0-85 (D)   [84]
£6832 £2102 £1051   **1m rnd**   **Firm 18**   **Inapplicable**   Inside

1925   **MADAMOISELLE JONES 9** [6] H S Howe 4-8-8 (64) D Kinsella 20/1: 100-0451: Made all, rdn & held on   70
well ins last: op 16/1: suited by 1m, tried 10f: acts on firm, fast & polytrack: likes to force the pace: see 1775.
1915   **SUMMER SHADES 9** [8] W M Brisbourne 6-8-13 (69) B Swarbrick(5) 9/1: 1620-652: Chsd ldrs, hung   nk   74
right & chall from dist, just held: op 10/1: tough, loves fast grnd: see 1322.
1625   **OH SO ROSIE 23** [7] J S Moore 4-8-2 (58) S Carson 20/1: 20-43303: In tch, outpcd 2f out, styd on   1¾   60
for press ins last, not reach front pair: acts on firm & gd/soft: see 1020.
2010   **BLONDE STREAK 5** [5] T D Barron 4-9-7 (77) R Hughes 5/1: 13204-44: In tch, styd on onepce: qck reapp.½   78
5021} **SHARP SECRET 207** [4]6-7-13 (55) J Quinn 14/1: 134265-5: b f College Chapel - State Treasure   ½   55
(Secretariat) Chsd ldrs, no extra from dist: reapp: fill h'cap scorer '03, plcd sev times: sell h'cap, appr h'cap
& h'cap scorer '02 for M Johnston: acts on gd/soft, loves firm/fast grnd, prob any trk.
2 Sep'03 Thir 8g/f 57-55 C: 1 Jul'03 Yarm 8.0fm 58-53 E: 2 Jun'03 Newm 8fm 54-51 E: 2 Sep'02 Good 8fm 53-53 E:
2 Jul'02 Carl 7g/s 57-53 E: 1 Jul'02 Yarm 7fm 55-47 E: 1 Jul'02 Thir 8g/f 54-47 E: 1 Jul'02 Muss 8g/f 48-43 F:
2 Jul'02 Beve 7.4g/s 45-43 F:
1761* **RED SAHARA 16** [9]3-8-10 (78) S Sanders 11/8 FAV: 01-16: Trkd ldr & keen, no extra from dist: 1   76
hvly bckd, op 7/4: more expected against older rivals today: btr 1761 (7f, 3yo h'cap).
1877   **DEVANT 16** [2]4-9-10 (80) M Henry 9/2: 0605-047: Pushed along rear, nvr able to chall: op 7/2.   1½   75
2063   **AND TOTO TOO 2** [3]4-8-11 bl (67) Dane O'Neill 8/1: 06244248: Held up, rdn & btn 2f out: 'lost action'.   ½   61
1723   **CRAIC SA CEILI 18** [1]4-8-12 (68) T G McLaughlin 33/1: 0450-009: Held up & struggling from 3f out.   12   42
9 Ran Time 1m 40.24 () Owned: Horses Away Racing Club Trained: Tiverton

LEICESTER MONDAY 31.05.04 Righthand, Stiff, Galloping Track

2109 3.35 Foxy's Lucky Peg & Concrete Shuffle Median Auction Maiden Stakes 2yo (E)
£4154 £1278 £639 5f str Firm 18 +04 Fast Stands Side

SAFARI SUNSET 0 [5] P Winkworth 2-9-0 P Doe 20/1: 1: b c Fayruz - Umlani (Great Commotion) 92
Chsd ldrs & led over 1f out, edged right but rdn & styd on strongly to win in a fast juv time: Mar first foal, cost E25,000: eff over a stiff 5f, 6f shld suit: acts on fm grnd & goes well fresh: potentially useful & worth following.
DRUM DANCE 0 [17] R F Johnson Houghton 2-9-0 S Carson 7/1: 2: b c Namid - Socialite (Alzao) *1* 88
Chsd ldrs, eff to chall over 1f out, not pace of wnr nr fin: op 5/1: E35,000 Apr foal, half-brother to a 9/10f wnr.
1955 **EMPIRES GHODHA 7** [12] B J Meehan 2-9-0 BL J F McDonald(3) 6/1: 5323: Prom & led halfway till over *1½* 84
1f out, onepace: op 4/1: prob ran to form of latest in first time blnks: acts on firm & fast: see 1955 & 1816.
LOADERFUN 0 [15] H Candy 2-9-0 Dane O'Neill 14/1: 4: br c Danehill Dancer - Sideloader Special *2* 78
(Song) Outpcd, kept on from over 1f out, not able to chall: Feb foal, half-brother to 5/6f juv wnrs, dam a 6f 3yo scorer: eff at 5f, crying out for 6f: acts on firm grnd & a stiff trk: v enouraging start, must win sn.
1738 **DANTES DIAMOND 17** [10]2-9-0 G Baker 13/2: 2255: Led till halfway, hung right & no extra from dist. *hd* 77
BELLY DANCER 0 [2]2-8-9 J Quinn 4/1 FAV: 6: gr f Danehill Dancer - Persian Mistress (Persian *½* 70
Bold) Chsd ldrs, not pace to chall: bckd, op 6/1: 20,000gns Apr foal, half-sister to a 6f 3yo wnr, dam unrcd.
1744 **MELVINO 17** [16]2-9-0 P Makin(5) 16/1: 47: Prom, no impress fnl 2f: see 1744. *3* 66
1614 **BOGAZ 24** [6]2-9-0 S Sanders 8/1: 28: Prom till over 2f out: btr 1614 (g/s). *1½* 62
1795 **ALCHARINGA 14** [7]2-9-0 D Kinsella 33/1: 59: Prom 3f: btr 1795. *½* 60
THREE STRIKES 0 [9]2-8-9 O Urbina 10/1: 0: 10th: Mid-div, nvr pace to threaten. *2½* 47
1911 **CLOANN 9** [11]2-8-9 R Hughes 10/1: 50: 11th: Chsd ldrs till halfway,'slipped just after start'. *½* 45
MONASH LAD 0 [13]2-9-0 Saleem Golam(7) 50/1: 0: 12th: Slow away & al outpcd. *1½* 46
1786 **Dorn Hill 14** [1]2-8-9 B Swarbrick(5) 50/1:0
Balthasar 0 [18]2-9-0 J Bramhill 66/1:0
Sastre 0 [3]2-8-9 E Ahern 66/1:0
Tit For Tat 0 [8]2-8-9 R Ffrench 10/1:0
Indian Smoke 0 [14]2-9-0 L Enstone(3) 100/1:0
Hidden Jewel 0 [4]2-9-0 W Supple 33/1:0
18 Ran Time 58.99 (0.69) Owned: Mr P Winkworth Trained: Godalming

2110 4.10 June Hall Claiming Stakes 2yo (F)
£3377 £1039 £520 5f str Firm 18 -24 Slow Stands Side

1653* **KEY SECRET 21** [5] M D I Usher 2-9-2 J F McDonald(3) 9/2: 11: Chsd ldr & led over 1f out, rdn 76
out: clmd for 14,000: remains unbtn: eff at 5f on fibresand & fm: improving.
1727 **HAROLDINI 17** [6] Mrs P N Dutfield 2-9-3 B Swarbrick(5) 9/4 FAV: 042: Held up, outpcd bef *1½* 72
halfway, switched & kept on ins last, no threat: bckd, op 11/4: rtn to 6f in similar shld suit, handles fm & fast.
1634 **VON WESSEX 23** [1] W G M Turner 2-8-13 C Haddon(7) 100/30: 651633: Led & hung right, hdd over 1f *½* 66
out, no extra: op 5/2: acts on firm & gd grnd: see 1133.
1445 **BEVERLEY BEAU 32** [7] Mrs L Stubbs 2-8-13 Dane O'Neill 10/1: 554: Keen & prom till outpcd *¾* 64
halfway, mod late rally: prob handles firm grnd & eff at 5f in claim grade, 6f could suit: see 1445.
1640 **GENERAL NUISANCE 21** [2]2-8-13 Derek Nolan(7) 100/30: 2645: Dwelt, chsd ldrs till over 1f out. *4* 52
1987 **FAITHISFLYING 6** [4]2-8-9 S Sanders 16/1: 0606: ch c Wolfhound - Niggle (Night Shift) Sn bhd & *3½* 37
outpcd, 'hung': qck reapp: cheaply retained Mar foal, half-brother to a 5f juv wnr, dam modest.
6 Ran Time 1m 0.40 (2.1) Owned: Mr I Sheward Trained: Lambourn

2111 4.45 Jeanette Brassil Handicap Stakes 3yo+ 0-75 (E) [75]
£5629 £1732 £866 6f str Firm 18 -04 Slow Stands Side

1578+ **CAUSTIC WIT 25** [10] M S Saunders 6-8-13 p (60) P Makin(5) 8/1: 030-1011: Prom & led halfway till 72
over 1f out, rallied for press to lead again ins last, all out: eff at 5f, all wins at 6f: acts on firm, soft or fibresand: suited by cheek pieces last twice: thriving, see 1578 & 384.
1820 **ONE WAY TICKET 2** [15] J M Bradley 4-8-10 p (57) R Ffrench 100/30 FAV: 20-00032: Al prom & rdn/led *nk* 68
over 1f out till ins last, just held: bckd, op 5/1, qck reapp: in fine form & well clr of rem: see 1820.
1774 **BRANTWOOD 16** [8] B A McMahon 4-8-11 t (58) W Supple 9/1: 00-00043: Chsd ldrs, kept on late. *3½* 59
1540 **CHARLOTTEBUTTERFLY 27** [1] T T Clement 4-8-11 (58) J F McDonald(3) 20/1: 30353-04: b f Millkom - *nk* 58
Tee Gee Jay (Northern Tempest) Pushed along rear, kept on, not able to chall: plcd sev times '03 (rtd 70, mdn, also rtd 57a, class stks): unplcd sole '02 start (rtd 46a, h'cap, R Ingram): eff around 6f, tried 7f: prob handles firm, fast & fibresand, sharp or stiff trk: mdn.
1988* **DANAKIM 6** [3]7-7-12 (7ex)(3oh) (42) D Fentiman(7) 5/1: 0040015: Led till halfway, hung right & no *shd* 45
extra bef dist: bckd, op 8/1: qck reapp: btr 1988 (seller, banded).
2027 **SPEEDFIT FREE 4** [12]7-8-2 (2ow)p (47) Ann Stokell 25/1: 3004006: Outpcd, mod gains, qck reapp. *1½* 44
1743 **MONTE MAYOR LAD 17** [11]4-9-3 bl (64) D Kinsella 20/1: 30334-07: b g Sesaro - Alcalali (Septieme *1½* 55
Ciel) Dwelt, in tch, sn rdn, not pace to chall: blnks reapp: lightly rcd '03 (AW plcd, rtd 64a, mdn): mdn rnr-up '02 (rtd 81): eff at 6/7f: handles both AWs, fast & gd/soft grnd, sharp or stiff trk.
2 Aug'02 Hayd 6g/s 76- E:
328 **TOPPLING 146** [2]6-8-11 (58) B Swarbrick(5) 18/1: 00000-08: Prom to halfway, sn no extra: 5 mth abs. *1* 46
1914 **HOLLOW JO 9** [14]4-9-7 (68) G Gibbons 7/2: 120-0049: Chsd ldr, btn over 1f out: btr 1914. *3½* 45
1214 **SUPER SONG 45** [6]4-9-9 t (70) S Donohoe(7) 33/1: 201-0000: 10th: Dwelt & al outpcd: abs, drpd in trip. *shd* 47
168 **BABY BARRY 174** [9]7-8-10 vis (57) J Quinn 16/1: 042300-0: 11th: Dwelt, chsd ldrs till halfway: op 9/1, abs *1½* 29
1374 **WONKY DONKEY 35** [13]3-7-12 T (54) M Henry 8/1: 0-3430: 12th: In tch when hmpd after 2f: 'lost action'. *6* 9
12 Ran Time 1m 11.11 (1.3) Owned: Mrs Sandra Jones Trained: Wells

LEICESTER   MONDAY 31.05.04   Righthand, Stiff, Galloping Track

2112   5.15 Steven Abraham Apprentice Handicap Stakes 4yo+ 46-55 (F)   [68]
£3494 £1075 £538   1m3f183y   Firm 18   -41 Slow   Inside

1830 **TRUSTED MOLE** 13 [7] W M Brisbourne 6-8-12 (52) B Swarbrick 11/4 FAV: 55353-51: Trkd ldrs & led
over 4f out, styd on strongly, rdn out: well bckd, op 3/1: slow time: eff at 10/12f, prob stays slowly run 14f,
acts on firm, soft & polytrack: see 1830.   **58**

3988] **CRACOW** 631 [4] A M Hales 7-8-5 (45) P Makin 16/1: 0/05300/-2: b g Polish Precedent - Height of   ¾   **49**
Secrecy (Shirley Heights) In tch, eff to chall over 1f out, not pace of wnr ins last: v long abs: missed '03:
unplcd '02 (rtd 70, lightly rcd, N Hawke): val h'cap rnr-up back in '01 for J Hills: eff around 10/12f on firm,
gd/soft & any trk: can force the pace: formerly useful, potentially v well h'capped. 2 Jun'01 Epso 12fm 93-91 B:

1884 **GLEN VALE WALK** 10 [2] Mrs G S Rees 7-8-5 bl (45) C Haddon(3) 8/1: 04034-63: Keen & prom, onepace.   nk   **48**
1238 **TOM BELL** 44 [1] J G M O'Shea 4-8-7 (47) P Mathers 15/2: 0005-204: Held up, rdn & kept on fnl 2f,   nk   **49**
not able to chall: 6 wk abs: prob handles firm & hvy grnd: mdn, see 1064.

2060 **SMARTER CHARTER** 3 [6]11-8-5 (15oh) (30) Kristin Stubbs 10/1: 0-502065: Held up, eff fnl 3f, not   1¾   **45$**
able to land blow: qck reapp: see 1287.

2008* **PISTE BLEU** 5 [11]4-8-11 (6ex) (51) A Mullen(5) 100/30: 65-00016: Trkd ldr, ch over 1f out, no   nk   **50**
extra: bckd, op 4/1: qck reapp: just btr 2008 (sell h'cap).

1396 **AVEIRO** 35 [13]8-8-7 (47) Dean Williams(3) 9/1: 3212007: Held up, eff & onepace fnl 4f: btr 937 (AW).   4   **40**
1894 **LORD LAHAR** 10 [12]5-8-5 (45) T O'Brien(7) 33/1: 0/00-68: Keen & prom till over 2f out: see 1894.   6   **29**
     PERTINO 2074 [9]8-8-13 p (53) C Williams(7) 16/1: 050/////-9: b g Terimon - Persian Fountain   2½   **33**
(Persian Heights) Held up & keen, struggling fnl 3f: recent jumps rnr (unplcd, h'cap chase).

4587] **SHERZABAD** 240 [3]7-8-5 (1oh) (44) Saleem Golam(4) 20/1: 461000-0: 10th: Dwelt & al bhd, abs.   11   **9**
1712 **LOST SPIRIT** 18 [5]8-8-5 (5oh) (40) Steven Harrison(5) 16/1: 14250-00: 11th: Led till over 4f out, virt p.u.   dist   **0**
11 Ran   Time 2m 35.35(7.05)   Owned: Mr PG Evans & David Manning Associates   Trained: Nesscliffe

---

CHEPSTOW   MONDAY 31.05.04   Lefthand, Undulating, Galloping Track

Official Going Good/Firm (Good Places)

2113   2.15 Pete Smith Carsales@Wyvern-Carsales Co Uk Maiden Stakes 3yo (D)
£3614 £1112 £556   1m4f23y   Good 56   -07 Slow   Inside

1922 **ALWAYS WAINING** 9 [3] M Johnston 3-9-0 K Dalgleish 11/4: 331: Sn led, styd on well fnl 1f, rdn   **88**
out: v 10.9.5f, imprvd for today's step up to 12f: acts on fast & gd, undul /gall trk: prog again in h'caps.

1807 **HORNER** 14 [6] P F I Cole 3-9-0 (80) R L Moore 5/2 FAV: 446-042: Mid-div, prog 4f out, kept on   1   **85**
fnl 1f, not pace wnr: now suited by 11.6f/12f: acts on fast & gd grnd: shld find a mdn: see 1807.

1398 **FORGED** 34 [8] L M Cumani 3-9-0 N Mackay(3) 33/1: 03: b c Peintre Celebre - Imitation (Darshaan)   ½   **84**
Slow away, prog after 1m, kept on ins fnl 1f, nrst fin: mid-dist bred: at 12f, shapes as tho' further will
suit: acts on gd grnd: lft debut eff well bhd today: open to more improvement.

1428 **BLAZE OF COLOUR** 33 [7] Sir Michael Stoute 3-8-9 B Doyle 3/1: 0-34: Cl-up, no extra bef 1f out: 2½   **75**
op 2/1: longer trip, may do better in h'caps: see 1428.

947   **SONG OF VALA** 65 [1]3-9-0 (80) S Whitworth 9/1: 042-05: ch g Peintre Celebre - Yanka (Blushing   nk   **79**
John) Led, sn hdd, styd cl-up & ev ch bef 1f out, wknd ins fnl 1f: clr rem, 9 wk abs: rnr-up on last of only 3 '03
starts (mdn): eff over a gd/gall 1m, hld stay further: acts on gd & soft grnd. 2 Nov'03 Nott 8.2sft 80- D:

977   **ON CLOUD NINE** 62 [2]3-8-9 Hayley Turner(5) 7/1: 26: Keen mid-div over 7f, grad wknd: btr 977 (10f).   10   **60**
1580 **BAYOU PRINCESS** 25 [4]3-8-9 A McCarthy 100/1: 07: Al bhd: see 1580.   2   **57**
1737 **PLOVERS LANE** 17 [5]3-9-0 P A Daly 33/1: 00-08: Bhd, nvr a factor: cheek pieces.   5   **55**
8 Ran   Time 2m 38.72 (7.62)   Owned: The Always Trying Partnership   Trained: Middleham

2114   2.50 European Breeders Fund Handicap Stakes Fillies 3yo+ 0-80 (D)   [76]
£6760 £2080 £1040   1m4f23y   Good 56   +14 Fast   Inside

1541 **TIDAL** 27 [9] A W Carroll 5-8-7 (55) R Thomas(5) 16/1: 06000-61: Cl-up, led 2f out, rdn out: gd   **67**
time: eff at 10f, now stays 12f: handles soft grnd, likes firm & gd: well h'capped mare: see 1541.

1399* **WASTED TALENT** 34 [1] J G Portman 4-9-10 VIS (72) R L Moore 5/1: 62531-12: Led 10f, styd cl-up &   1   **81**
ev ch fnl 1f, just held by wnr: ran to form with 1st time visor fitted: see 1399 (cheekpieces).

1768* **PORTRAIT OF A LADY** 16 [3] H R A Cecil 3-8-9 (74) Paul Eddery 4/1: 540-313: Rear, prog after   shd   **82**
halfway, kept on ins fnl 1f, not btn far: did little wrong on h'cap bow: see 1768 (mdn).

1718 **MOONLIGHT TANGO** 18 [7] J H M Gosden 3-8-7 (72) K Dalgleish 6/1: 04-554: br f Benny The Dip -   2   **77**
Summer Dance (Sadler's Wells) Rear, prog after 7f, no impress from dist: clr rem: 4th at best in '03 (mdn, rtd
74): eff at 12f on gd grnd.

1789* **ANYHOW** 14 [8]7-9-0 (62) K Dalgleish(3) 6/1: 1454215: Held up, nvr nrr than mid-div: 10th: Dwelt.   10   **53**
1789 **COMPTON ECLAIRE** 14 [3]4-8-7 vis (55) S W Kelly 8/1: 34-33246: Slow away, al in rear: btr 1654.   3½   **41**
1889 **STEALING BEAUTY** 10 [10]4-10-0 (76) N Mackay(3) 4/1 FAV: 5/01-47: Cl-up 9f, sn wknd: btr 1889.   1¾   **60**
1986 **TOP OF THE CLASS** 6 [4]7-8-6 vis (54) Joanna Badger 18/1: 5040008: Rear, prog halfway, fdd 3f out.   5   **31**
1285 **CASTANET** 41 [2]5-7-12 (2oh) (44) A McCarthy 16/1: 65043/-59: Cl-up till halfway, grad wknd: 6 wk abs.   hd   **22**
1719 **GARRYURRA** 18 [6]3-8-9 (74) B Doyle 14/1: 26-50: 10th: Rear, btn when eased dist, saddle slipped.   25   **16**
10 Ran   Time 2m 36.14 (5.04)   Owned: Mrs B Quinn   Trained: Alcester

2115   3.25 British Racing School Selling Stakes 2yo (G)
£2527 £722 £361   6f16y str   Good 56   -38 Slow   Stands side

1920 **DONT TELL TRIGGER** 9 [7] J S Moore 2-8-6 J D Smith 11/4: 061: b f Mujadil - Ordinate (Nashwan)   **62**
Made all, edged left ins fnl 2f, rdn out: bckd: bt in for 5,200gns: Feb foal, cost £3,000: sister plcd at 6f/1m: dam
9f wnr: eff at 6f, further shld suit: acts on gd & an undul/gall trk: enjoyed drop to sell grade.

2020 **LAKESDALE** 5 [6] M R Channon 2-8-6 R L Moore 13/2: 02: b f Desert Style - Option (Red Ransom)   2   **63**

631

Bhd, prog halfway, styd on to chase wnr ins fnl 1f, al held: qck reapp: clmd for 6,000: Feb first foal, sire
top-class performer as a juv: eff at 6f, shapes as tho' 7f will suit: acts on gd grnd: encouraging eff.

1950 **GLASSON LODGE 7** [2] P D Evans 2-8-7 (1ow) S W Kelly 5/4 FAV: 4563: Cl-up over 4f, sn no extra:	2	58

well bckd on qck reapp: btr expected on step up to 6f on drop to sell grade: btr 1256.

1325 **PRINCELY VALE 38** [4] W G M Turner 2-8-11 B O'Neill(7) 10/1: 04: b c Princely Heir - Lomalou	2½	55

(Lightning Dealer)   Handy over 4f, sn wknd: Apr foal, cost 30,000gns: dam unrcd.

ROYAL COZYFIRE 0 [1]2-8-11 K Dalgleish 8/1: 5: Sn handy, ev ch 2f out, edged left & fdd dist: op 4/1.	3	46
17 **KENTUCKY BANKES 16** [5]2-8-11 A Daly 25/1: 06: Cl-up, hung left halfway, sn wknd: op 8/1.	5	33
2017 **SHES MY DREAM 5** [3]2-8-6 S Whitworth 33/1: 0007: Al in rear: qck reapp.	6	12

7 Ran   Time 1m 14.46 (5.66)   Owned: Bigwigs Bloodstock Racing Club V   Trained: Hungerford

---

2116   4.00 Western Daily Press Race Club Classified Stakes 3yo+ 0-75 (D)
£5473   £1684   £842   **1m14y str**   **Good 56**   **-05 Slow**   Stands side

1930 **JUST TIM 9** [3] R Hannon 3-8-5 (74) R L Moore 9/2: 02-41401: Mid-div, prog to lead dist, rdn out:		79

stays 10f, suited by around 1m on fast, gd/soft grnd & polytrack: settled better today.

1526 **LEAPING BRAVE 28** [1] B R Millman 3-8-6 (76) A McCarthy 13/2: 30130-42: Led, hdd 7f out, styd	2½	73

cl-up, led again 2f out, hdd dist, no extra: apprec step up to 1m: acts on gd, soft & polytrack.

1832* **ALI DEO 13** [6] W J Haggas 3-8-7 (77) S W Kelly 11/2: 00-13: Cl-up, led after 2f, hdd 2f out,	½	74

edged left & no extra dist: op 4/1: eff at 7.5f/1m on fast & gd grnd: remains in gd fettle: see 1832.

2027 **THE BONUS KING 4** [7] M Johnston 4-9-5 (77) A Elliott(7) 5/2 FAV: 2000024: Cl-up over 5f, sn	1	72

outpcd, rallied ins fnl 1f: qck reapp: see 2027 & 1066.

1525 **CERTAIN JUSTICE 28** [5]6-9-5 (77) N De Souza(5) 9/1: 6040-065: Rear, prog halfway, no impress dist.	½	71
1817 **OAKLEY RAMBO 13** [4]5-9-8 (80) P Gallagher(7) 4/1: 0-506206: Rear, prog halfway, fdd bef 1f out.	4	66
1890 **TRESOR SECRET 10** [2]4-9-3 BL (75) K Dalgleish 14/1: 1010-057: b g Green Desert - Tresor (Pleasant	14	35

Tap) Bhd, nvr a factor: disapp in first time blnks: ex French, won 2 h'caps in '03: eff at 9/10f on gd & gd/soft.
7 Ran   Time 1m 36.79 (4.89)   Owned: Mr D J Walker   Trained: Marlborough

---

2117   4.35 Britishhorseracing Com Information Stand Maiden Stakes 3yo+ (D)
£3799   £1169   £585   **1m14y str**   **Good 56**   **-05 Slow**   Stands side

1904 **MAGIC MERLIN 10** [15] P W Harris 3-8-12 B Doyle 15/8 FAV: 31: Keen cl-up, led after 5f, pushed		83+

clr fnl 1f, val 2L+: well bckd: eff at 1m, shld apprec further: acts on firm & gd grnd, undul/gall trk: lightly
rcd & improving 3yo, type to progress again in h'caps: see 1904.

1707 **RONDELET 18** [3] R M Beckett 3-8-12 (76) M Tebbutt 9/2: 064-202: Rear, prog 3f out, styd on to	¾	79

chase wnr ins fnl 1f, al held: acts on gd & gd/soft grnd: lost little in defeat & shld find similar: see 1257.

MINORITY REPORT 0 [4] L M Cumani 4-9-10 N Mackay(3) 10/1: 3: b g Rainbow Quest - Queen Sceptre	2	75+

(Fairy King)   Slow away, prog 3f out, nrst fin: debut: eff at 1m, 10f looks sure to suit: learn plenty from this.

1623 **MASKED 23** [6] J W Hills 3-8-12 N Day 25/1: 004: Slow away, prog 2f out, nrst fin: eff at 1m,	2	71

rtn to further in h'caps will suit.

71 **BLAINA 192** [7]4-9-5 (75) R Thomas(5) 7/1: 032260-5: ch f Compton Place - Miss Silca Key (Welsh	nk	65

Saint)   Keen mid-div, prog halfway, no impress from dist: reapp: plcd 3 times in '03 (rtd 81, fill mdn): eff at
7f/1m on fast & gd/soft grnd: showed ability last term but did not al impress with attitude: with D R C Elsworth.
2 Aug'03 Sali 7.0g/f 65-(80) D: 2 Jul'03 Asco 8g/s 81- D:

1815 **RIDGE BOY 13** [11]3-8-12 R L Moore 9/2: 56: Cl-up 6f, sn no extra: see 1815.	¾	68
1815 **HIGH FREQUENCY 13** [17]3-8-12 K Dalgleish 8/1: 067: Cl-up 6f, sn wknd.	1	66
1101 **CHAMBRAY 53** [5]3-8-7 T Block(7) 50/1: 5-08: Nvr nrr than mid-div.	nk	59
1210 **COTTON EASTER 45** [1]3-8-7 Paul Eddery 66/1: 09: Rear, modest late gains.	1¾	59
INK IN GOLD 0 [16]3-8-12 D Nolan(3) 25/1: 0: 10th: Nvr nrr than mid-div.	nk	60
4563} **TOTAL FORCE 242** [2]3-8-12 P Gallagher(7) 33/1: 05-0: 11th: Rear, nvr able to chall on reapp.	shd	59
1257 **ROOD BOY 42** [14]3-8-12 (55) Hayley Turner(5) 16/1: 043-4550: 12th: Led 5f, sn wknd: 6 wk abs.	2½	54
4389} **SWEET AZ 252** [10]4-9-5 (39) S Whitworth 100/1: 000500-0: 13th: Cl-up over 5f, sn wknd.	2	45$

1541 Nina Fontenail 27 [9]3-8-7 (45) A Beech 100/1:0		1829 Chatshow 13 [12]3-8-12 A McCarthy 100/1:0			
1617 Spector 24 [8]4-9-10 D Corby(3) 66/1:0		1876 Lord Of The Fens 11 [13]4-9-10 S W Kelly 100/1:0			

17 Ran   Time 1m 14.46 (5.66)   Owned: The Magic Circle   Trained: Berkhamsted

---

2118   5.10 Bet365 08000 322 365 Stakes Handicap Fillies 3yo 0-75 (E)   [82]
£4222   £1299   £650   **6f16y str**   **Good 56**   **-17 Slow**   Stands side

1125 **VERKHOTINA 49** [11] R Charlton 3-9-4 (72) B Doyle 5/1: 550-61: b f Baratnea - Alusha (Soviet		85+

Star)   Rear, prog halfway, styd on to lead bef 1f out, pushed clr, val 5L+: 7 wk abs: unplcd in '03 (rtd 81, mdn):
has tried 7f, enjoyed rtn to 6f: acts on fast & gd grnd: eff on an undual/gall trk & goes well fresh: showed a gd
turn of foot to oblige on h'cap bow, more progress await.

1743 **UNDER MY SPELL 17** [2] P D Evans 3-9-2 (70) S W Kelly 9/2 FAV: 555-0022: Handy, styd on ins fnl	3½	71

1f, no ch with easy wnr: caught a decent sort: see 1743.

1526 **URBAN ROSE 28** [12] J W Unett 3-8-10 (64) D Corby(3) 8/1: 1044-003: b f Piccolo - Blue Lamp	shd	64

(Shadeed)   Cl-up, no extra fnl 1f: auct mdn wnr in '03: eff at 6f on firm & gd grnd. 1 Sep'03 Warw 6.1fm 72- F:

1570 **LA VIE EST BELLE 26** [4] B R Millman 3-9-5 (73) A McCarthy 8/1: 6320-604: Cl-up, wknd appr fnl 1f.	1¾	68
1722 **MELAINA 18** [8]3-8-12 p (66) A Beech(3) 12/1: 2061105: Led 4f, sn wknd: btr 1576 & 1374.	1¾	56
1942 **ALIZAR 8** [6]3-8-4 (58) R L Moore 14/1: 1423606: Rear, prog halfway, eased when no impress ins fnl 1f.	shd	47
1902* **JINKSONTHEHOUSE 10** [7]3-8-6 (60) Hayley Turner(5) 10/1: 000-4017: Cl-up, ev ch after 4f, sn wknd.	¾	47
1788 **DANIFAH 14** [1]3-7-12 (5oh) (47) Joanna Badger 22/1: 000-0008: b f Perugino - Afifah (Nashwan)	1¾	34

Handy 4f, sn wknd: auct mdn & h'cap wnr in '03: eff at 5f, has tried further: acts on firm & gd.
1 Aug'03 Chep 5.1gd 72-67 D: 1 Jun'03 Warw 5g/f 70- E: 2 Jun'03 Bath 5.0fm 68- E: 2 Jun'03 Ling 5g/f 69- F:

1809 **CREWES MISS ISLE 14** [3]3-8-10 (64) S Whitworth 7/1: 0-461509: Rear, nvr a factor: op 10/1: btr 1338.	4	34
1787 **LYRICAL LADY 14** [9]3-7-13 BL (53) R Thomas(2) 50/1: 0546-00: 10th: Al bhd: first time blnks:	3½	13

unplcd both '03 starts (rtd 56): with Mrs A J Bowlby.

1526 **NINAH 28** [10]3-9-0 (68) K Dalgleish 10/1: 02240-00: 11th: Cl-up, sn fdd: see 1526.	1¼	24
1761 **BEEJAY 16** [5]3-9-7 (75) N De Souza(5) 8/1: 31-100: 12th: Slow away, al in rear: twice below 1239 (reapp).	2	25

CHEPSTOW   MONDAY 31.05.04   Lefthand, Undulating, Galloping Track

12 Ran   Time 1m 13.20(4.4)   Owned: Mr A E Oppenheimer   Trained: Beckhampton

REDCAR   TUESDAY 01.06.04   Lefthand, Flat, Galloping Track

Official Going Firm (Good/Firm places)

2119   2.15 European Breeders Fund Median Auction Maiden Stakes Fillies 2yo   (E)
£3988 £1227 £614   **6f str**   **Good/Firm 32**   **-31 Slow**   Centre

1887 **ABERDOVEY 11** [2] M L W Bell 2-8-11 J Mackay 5/2 FAV: 51: b f Mister Baileys - Annapurna (Brief   **79**
Truce) Handy, hdwy to lead over 1f out, styd on, drvn out: Feb first foal, cost 50,000gns: dam useful over 7/10f:
stays a gall 6f well, 7f sure to suit: acts on fast grnd: going the right way.
 ARABIAN DANCER 0 [5] M R Channon 2-8-11 T E Durcan 7/2: 2: b f Dansili - Hymne (Saumarez)   *shd* **78+**
Dwelt, held up, hdwy over 1f out, styd on ins last, just held on debut: Feb first foal, cost 3,000gns: dam mid-dist
wnr: eff over a gall 6f, 7f+ sure to suit: acts on fast: plenty to like about this, ran green, learn plenty & win sn.
1818 **MISSPERON 14** [6] K A Ryan 2-8-11 N Callan 12/1: 53: Led till appr fnl 1f, kept on for press,   *hd*   **77**
just held: op 20/1: eff over a gall 6f on fast: imprvd from debut & can win similar with a repeat of this.
1709 **BURTON ASH 19** [4] J G Given 2-8-11 M Fenton 14/1: 04: b f Diktat - Incendio (Siberian Express)   *1¼*   **73**
Cl-up, onepace appr fnl 1f: April foal: half-sister to smart sprinter Baron's Pit: dam mutliple wnr: speedily
bred & imprvd for debut here over 6f on fast.
1658 **JANE JUBILEE 22** [10]2-8-11 R Ffrench 20/1: 35: In tch, eff over 1f out, onepace: btr run, see 1658.   *hd*   **72**
1818 **TARAS TREASURE 14** [1]2-8-11 R Winston 11/4: 26: Keen held up, some late gains, nvr dngrs: see 1818.*shd* **71**
1780 **WOLDS DANCER 16** [9]2-8-11 D Allan(3) 20/1: 67: Held up, no impress over 2f out.   *2*   **65**
1780 **AZA WISH 16** [8]2-8-11 S Righton 66/1: 0508: Bhd, modest late gains: see 1458.   *1¼*   **61**
1780 **KILMOVEE 16** [7]2-8-11 A Culhane 12/1: 59: Cl-up, wknd 2f out: see 1780.   *hd*   **60**
1739 **LADY MISHA 18** [11]2-8-11 P Hanagan 25/1: 550: 10th: Handy, wknd well over 1f out.   *½*   **58**
 ELLIEBOW 0 [12]2-8-11 F Lynch 50/1: 0: 11th: Slow away & al bhd: debut.   *nk*   **57**
 SPECTRUM OF LIGHT 0 [3]2-8-11 Dean McKeown 100/1: 0: 12th: Handy, wknd 2f out.   *1¼*   **53**
12 Ran   Time 1m 12.69 (3.79)   Owned: Usk Valley Stud   Trained: Newmarket

2120   2.45 Levy Board Handicap Stakes 3yo+ 0-70 (E)   [69]
£3572 £1099 £550   **1m1f**   **Good/Firm 32**   **-00 Slow**   Inside

1661 **ARCHIRONDEL 22** [5] M D Hammond 6-8-6 (1ow) (47) A Culhane 4/1 FAV: 60U0021: Held up, hdwy to lead   **57**
over 1f out, styd on well, drvn out: well bckd: eff over 1m/10f & likes fm & fast, handles soft & any trk: in gd
heart for new connections & well h'capped: well bckd: see 1661.
1055 **SCRIPTORIUM 57** [11] L M Cumani 3-8-4 (58) N Mackay(3) 13/2: 0-602: b c Singspiel - Annie Albright   *2*   **63**
(Verbatim) In tch, eff over 2f out, kept on ins last, no pace of wnr: 2 mth abs: imprvd for h'cap bow & stays 9f
on fast grnd, further shld suit: shld win a small race.
2054 **ARJAY 4** [4] Andrew Turnell 6-8-6 (48) J Carroll 16/1: 00-00353: Held up, hdwy well over 1f out,   *2½*   **48**
kept on ins last, not pace of wnr 2: qck reapp: see 1657.
1776 **APACHE POINT 17** [13] N Tinkler 7-9-1 (57) Kim Tinkler 5/1: 024-0054: Handy, onepace over 1f out.   *¾*   **55**
1927 **HELDERBERG 10** [9]4-9-11 (67) M Fenton 33/1: 02210-05: b f Diesis - Banissa (Lear Fan) In tch,   *nk*   **64**
eff 2f out, sn no impress: '03 h'cap wnr (with C Brittain): stays 11f, last win at 7f: acts on firm & gd, likes gall
trks: with C Brittain last term, now with B Rothwell.
 1 Oct'03 Redc 7g/f 70-65 E: 2 Oct'03 Pont 8.0g/f 67-(66) D: 2 Sep'03 Hami 9.2gd 69-(66) D:
1972 **OSCAR PEPPER 8** [1]7-9-7 (63) G Faulkner 5/1: 0404-506: Handy, wknd over 1f out: see 1972.   *1½*   **57**
1049 **MERDIFF 57** [14]5-9-4 (60) S W Kelly 8/1: 03201-07: Handy, wknd well over 1f out: 2 mth abs: see 39.   *2*   **50**
1748 **BASINET 18** [15]6-8-12 p (54) R Winston 12/1: 6506-008: b g Alzao - Valiancy (Grundy) Slow away &   *½*   **43**
bhd, some late gains: '03 h'cap wnr: '02 class stks & h'cap scorer: suited by 7/9f on firm & gd grnd, handles soft
& fibresand, any trk: has run well fresh & comes late: win on cheek pieces last term: well h'capped now if
returning to form. 1 Jun'03 Wind 8.3g/f 61-60 E: 2 Sep'02 Hami 8.2fm 64-63 E: 1 Sep'02 Muss 9g/f 62-60 F:
 1 Aug'02 Carl 6.8g/f 61- F: 1 Oct'01 Wolv 8.4af 70a-56 F: 2 Jul'01 Newc 8g/f 60-57 E: 1 Jun'01 Newc 8g/f 58-52 E:
1776 **BUSCADOR 17** [8]5-8-11 (53) B Swarbrick(5) 16/1: 061-0009: Keen cl-up, led 3f out till over 1f out, wknd. *1*   **40**
678   **CRYPTOGAM 103** [6]4-8-5 (47) T Eaves(1) 100/1: 440-0000: 10th: Bhd, nvr a factor: long abs: see 678.   *2*   **30**
1518 **ASH LADDIE 29** [7]4-9-2 (58) D Allan(3) 100/1: 0/050-00: 11th: Bhd, nvr a factor.   *1¼*   **38**
1755 **WILSON BLUEBOTTLE 17** [12]5-8-3 bl (45) Dale Gibson 7/1: 1022000: 12th: Led till 3f out, wknd.   *1½*   **22**
1821 **STEPASTRAY 14** [2]7-8-4 (46) C Cogan 16/1: 10000-50: 13th: Keen, chsd ldrs, wknd over 2f out: btr 1821. *1*   **21**
1781 **ARAWAN 16** [3]4-10-0 (70) T Lucas 50/1: 104-0000: 14th: Al bhd.   *21*   **5**
1835 **PAULA 14** [10]4-8-11 VIS (53) L Enstone(3) 66/1: 0660: 15th: Al bhd: visor.   *10*   **0**
15 Ran   Time 1m 51.7 (2.9)   Owned: The Archi Partnership   Trained: Middleham

2121   3.15 Constant Security Sprint Stakes Handicap 3yo 0-90 (C)   [96]
£10452 £3216 £1608   **5f str**   **Good/Firm 32**   **+08 Fast**   Centre

1901+ **ENCHANTMENT 11** [1] J M Bradley 3-9-3 (85) R Ffrench 5/2 FAV: 601-5211: Trkd ldr, led over 1f   **99**
out, rdn clr, hvly bckd: eff over 5/6f & loves firm & fast grnd, gall trks, prob handles any: best up with/forcing
the pace: useful & fast improving, shld land hat-trick: see 1901.
1876 **TRUE MAGIC 12** [3] J D Bethell 3-7-12 (4oh) (62) N Mackay(3) 25/1: 3306-562: Bhd, hdwy over 1f out,   *2½*   **71**
kept on ins last: gd run: see 1876.
1933 **DIVINE SPIRIT 10** [8] M Dods 3-8-12 (80) F Lynch 66/1: 161-0003: b g Foxhound - Vocation (Royal   *shd* **85+**
Academy) Held up, hdwy well over 1f out, nrst fin: won 2 h'caps in late '03: stays 6f, both wins at 5f on firm &
fast grnd, prob handles any trk, likes an easy time: may need one now: clearly come to head, back on a winning mark & one to be with
back in fav'd cheek pieces next time. 1 Sep'03 Muss 5g/f 84-81 C: 1 Aug'03 Catt 5g/f 82-(70) F:
2 Aug'03 Muss 5g/f 74-71 D:
1771 **HARRY UP 10** [10] J G Given 3-9-7 (89) M Fenton 7/1: 40-23034: Held up, late gains, nrst fin: gd   *hd*   **93**
run back at 5f: on a fair mark: see 1771, 1106.
1766 **CELTIC THUNDER 17** [5]3-9-2 (84) R Winston 10/1: 1246-205: In tch, eff over 2f out, onepace.   *nk*   **87**
1229 **TYNE 45** [11]3-9-1 (83) P Hanagan 9/1: 216-06: b c Komaite - High Typha (Dowsing) Handy, no   *2½*   **79**

633

impress over 1f out: 6 wk abs: won 1 of 3 '03 starts (mdn): eff at 5f on fast grnd & on a gall trk.
1 Jun'03 Redc 5g/f 84- D: 2 May'03 Redc 5g/f 85- F:
1766 **JOHNNY PARKES 17** [9]3-9-1 (83) A Culhane 6/1: 215-1037: In tch, wknd over 1f out: btr 1766, 1002. *nk* **78**
1771 **SILVER PRELUDE 17** [2]3-9-5 (87) N Callan 25/1: 15250-08: gr c Prince Sabo - Silver Blessings *1* **79**
(Statoblest) Led till over 1f out, wknd: won 1 of 8 '03 starts (auct mdn): loves to dominate over 5f & acts on firm & fast grnd, prob any trk.
2 Aug'03 Thir 5fm 87-86 C: 1 Jul'03 Wind 5.0g/f 90- E: 2 Jun'03 Ling 5g/f 83- D: 2 Jun'03 Nott 5.1g/f 70- F:
2048* **BORZOI MAESTRO 4** [6]3-8-10 (6ex)p (78) A Daly 17/2: 400-2319: Held up, btn 2f out: btr 2048 (6f). *shd* **70**
1771 **PROMENADE 17** [4]3-9-4 (86) J Mackay 11/2: 1161-50: 10th: In tch, wknd 2f out: see 1771. *3* **69**
1572 **SIR ERNEST 27** [7]3-8-7 (75) G Gibbons 20/1: 4000-060: 11th: In tch, wknd over 2f out: see 1572. *1½* **54**
11 Ran Time 57.69 (1.19) Owned: Ms A M Williams Trained: Chepstow

2122

3.45 Great Value Yorkshire Season Ticket Classified Stakes 3yo+ 0-70 (E)
£3377 £1039 £520 **7f str** **Good/Firm 32** **-10 Slow** Centre

2080 **WARDEN WARREN 3** [1] Mrs C A Dunnett 6-9-0 p (69) B Reilly(3) 100/30: 0010041: Handy, hdwy over 1f **76**
out, led ins last, rdn out: joc received a 1-day whip ban: qck reapp: likes to race up with/force the pace over 6/7f on firm, gd & fibresand, gall or sharp trk: reportedly best without being crowded: tough: see 3574, 3124.
1909 **SAMUEL CHARLES 10** [3] W M Brisbourne 6-9-2 (72) S W Kelly 5/2 FAV: 0-123122: Led 1f, led over 2f *3* **74**
out till ins last, no extra: consistent: see 1909, 1823.
4353} **BANDOS 255** [2] I Semple 4-9-5 t (75) P Hanagan 11/4: 110220-3: ch g Cayman Kai - Lekuti (Le Coq *6* **65**
d'Or) Missed break, keen, led after 1f till over 2f out, wknd: nicely bckd on reapp: '03 class stks & h'cap wnr: suited by 7f, stays 1m: acts on fast grnd & likes Ayr: wears a t-strap & has run well fresh.
2 Aug'03 Ayr 8g/f 76-74 D: 2 Aug'03 Newc 7g/f 75-73 D: 1 Jul'03 Ayr 7.2g/f 75-69 E: 1 Jun'03 Ayr 7.2g/f 67-(53) F:
1817 **PERFECT PORTRAIT 14** [4] D R Loder 4-9-2 vis (72) D R McCabe 11/4: 1-3004: Keen, chsd ldrs, wknd *1* **60**
qckly 2f out: see 1817, 1079.
4 Ran Time 1m 24.75 (2.95) Owned: Annwell Inn Syndicate Trained: Norwich

2123

4.15 Redcarracing Co Uk Maiden Handicap Stakes 3yo 35-55 (F) **[60]**
£2975 £850 £425 **1m6f19y** **Good/Firm 32** **-33 Slow** Centre

1612 **NOCATEE 25** [1] P C Haslam 3-9-6 p (52) G Faulkner 7/1: 00-33431: Trkd ldrs trav well, rdn & led **59**
over 1f out, sn hard drvn & held on all out: op 9/2: prev eff around 9/11f, now seems suited by 14f & shld get 2m: acts on fast, hvy & fibresand, sharp or gall trks: eff with/without visor or cheek pieces: see 1612 & 608.
1836 **SPRING BREEZE 14** [16] M Dods 3-9-5 p (51) L Enstone(3) 16/1: 4030-602: Keen, trkd ldrs, switched & *hd* **57**
drvn/styd on well ins last, just denied: styd this longer 14f trip well: now eff in cheek pieces.
1785 **NORTHERN SPIRIT 16** [7] K A Ryan 3-9-0 P (46) N Callan 20/1: 550-0603: Handy & led over 3f out *½* **51**
till over 1f out, kept on for press: first time cheek pieces: stays a gall 14f on fast grnd: see 1612.
1836 **BOLLIN ANNABEL 14** [4] T D Easterby 3-9-7 (53) D Allan(3) 16/1: 0-2504: Mid-div, styd on for press *2* **55**
fnl 3f, not pace to chall: stays 14f, 2m shld suit: acts on fast, prob handles gd/soft: clr of rem, see 1213.
1528 **SAVANNAH RIVER 29** [15]3-8-13 t (45) P Hanagan 10/1: 000-0325: Rear, hdwy 3f out, sn no extra. *7* **37**
1675 **ROYAL UPSTART 21** [2]3-8-8 bl (40) B Swarbrick(5) 25/1: 000-0326: Mid-div, not able to chall: btr 1675. *1¾* **29**
1612 **VALIANT AIR 25** [5]3-8-10 (42) R Winston 10/1: 0-452407: Prom, btn 2f out: btr 1444 & 1250 (12f). *nk* **31**
1945 **STAGE TWO 8** [9]3-8-8 VIS (40) R Ffrench 11/2: 0640028: Chsd ldrs wide, btn 3f out: tried visor. *1½* **27**
1836 **NAFFERTON HEIGHTS 14** [3]3-9-1 (47) Dale Gibson 6/1: 000-0509: Keen & led till over 3f out, sn btn. *7* **24**
1945 **UPTHEDALE 8** [6]3-8-7 (39) D Fentiman(7) 25/1: 0-043U50: 10th: Al bhd & no impress: see 1945 & 1603. *3* **12**
2014 **ROMEOS DAY 6** [11]3-9-6 (52) T E Durcan 5/1 FAV: 00-02430: 11th: Mid-div halfway, btn 3f out: bckd. *hd* **25**
1783 **QUAY WALLOPER 16** [12]3-9-4 (50) Darren Williams 25/1: U000-00: 12th: b g In Command - Myrrh *3½* **18**
(Salse) Chsd ldrs, btn 3f out: longer trip: unplcd at up to 8.5f in '03 (lightly rcd, rtd 50).
1783 **Celtic Solitude 16** [14]3-9-0 (46) A Culhane 33/1:0 1630 **Baroque 24** [10]3-8-2 (14oh)(20) J Bramhill 100/1:0
14 Ran Time 3m 06.86 (9.06) Owned: Middleham Park Racing & Middleham Turf Trained: Middleham

2124

4.45 Kirkleatham Maiden Stakes 3yo+ (D)
£3552 £1093 £547 **1m2f** **Good/Firm 32** **-16 Slow** Centre

1718 **FEAAT 19** [5] J H M Gosden 3-8-6 J Carroll 4/6 FAV: 31: Trkd ldr, pushed along/outpcd 3f out, **81**
chall 2f out & led ins last, outstayed rival: hvly bckd at odds-on: eff at 10f on fast grnd, gall/undul trks: see 1718.
1935 **ARRGATT 10** [1] M A Jarvis 3-8-11 N Callan 5/2: 0-32: Led, joined & rdn from over 2f out, no *¾* **84**
extra when hdd ins last: well clr of rem: styd longer 10f trip: handles fast grnd, gall trks: see 1935.
1835 **POINTED 14** [4] T D Easterby 3-8-6 R Winston 100/1: 003: br f Selkirk - Tragic Point (Tragic *19* **49**
Role) Trkd ldrs, no impress on front pair from over 3f out: unplcd & mod form prev, now qual for h'caps.
4482} **RIVER LINE 248** [9] C W Fairhurst 3-8-11 Dean McKeown 33/1: 000-4: b g Keos - Portio (Riva *¾* **52**
Ridge) Held up, lost tch with front pair from over 3f out: reapp: unplcd at up to 1m in '03 (rtd 56, mdns).
SWAHILI DANCER 0 [7]3-8-11 N Mackay(3) 7/1: 5: b c Swain - Bella Ballerina (Sadler's Wells) *3½* **47**
Held up, rdn & lost tch from 4f out: debut, mid-dist breeding.
4482} **BAY SOLITAIRE 248** [2]3-8-11 D Allan(3) 50/1: 000-6: Reared start, sn in tch till 4f out. *shd* **47**
1784 **DONT TELL SIMON 16** [6]3-8-11 T Eaves(3) 100/1: 07: Bhd & no ch from halfway. *17* **23**
INDIBAR 0 [8]3-8-11 A Nicholls 16/1: 8: Prom till over 4f out on debut. *shd* **23**
8 Ran Time 2m 07.15 (4.85) Owned: Mr Hamdan Al Maktoum Trained: Manton

2125

5.15 Redcar Amateur Riders' Maiden Handicap Stakes 3yo+ 35-55 (G) **[41]**
£2688 £768 £384 **6f str** **Good/Firm 32** **-43 Slow** Centre

1122 **DESERT ARC 51** [6] W M Brisbourne 6-11-0 (55) Mr C Davies(7) 14/1: 46600-01: b g Spectrum - Bint **64**
Albadou (Green Desert) Rear, styd on strongly from over 1f out, nrst fin: fin 2nd, plcd 1st: 7 wk abs: unplcd '03 (rtd 71, mdn, prob flattered, A M Balding): eff at 6f, 7f shld suit, has tried 8.5f: acts on fast grnd & a gall trk.
1600 **ORANGINO 25** [10] J S Haldane 6-9-12 (39) Miss R Davidson(5) 33/1: 20000-02: b g Primo Dominie - *nk* **47**
Sweet Jaffa (Never So Bold) Al prom & ch ins last, not pace of wnr nr line: fin 3rd & plcd 2nd: amat riders mdn

h'cap rnr-up '03: amat class stks rnr-up '02: eff btwn 6f/1m on firm & gd/soft grnd: best without blnks.
2 Jun'03 Redc 8g/f 43-43 G: 2 Jul'02 Redc 7g/f 67- G:
1641 **LORD WISHINGWELL 22** [12] J S Wainwright 3-9-3 (5oh)vis (38) Miss Kelly Harrison(3) 33/1: 000-033: Al prom, rdn & kept on onepace fnl 2f: handles fast & hvy grnd: see 1641. *2* **40**
1410 **ROYAL NITE OWL 35** [8] J O'Reilly 3-9-5 (3oh) (40) Mr S Dobson(3) 50/1: 00-0044: Led till halfway, no extra ins last: eff around a gall 6f on fast grnd: see 839. *1* **39**
1963 **FRENCHMANS LODGE 8** [18]4-9-8 bl (35) Miss E J Jones 6/1: 0-000025: Pulled hard early, led from halfway till dist, edged left & no extra ins last: bckd: btr 1963. *1* **31**
1662 **FRIMLEYS MATTERRY 22** [7]4-10-4 (45) Miss V Barr(7) 25/1: 00-60666: b g Bluegrass Prince - Lonely Street (Frimley Park) Prom, edged left & no extra dist: AW seller plcd in '03 for A Jarvis (rtd 54a, first time visor): eff at 6/7f on fast & both AWs. *¾* **39**
1948 **LADY DOUBLE U 8** [5]4-10-4 (45) Miss A Elsey 50/1: 0/-00007: Bhd, late prog, nrst fin. *¾* **37**
1065 **VALUABLE GIFT 56** [2]7-9-8 (5oh)p (30) Mr G Bartley(7) 33/1: 00-00008: Prom, no extra dist: 8 wk abs. *nk* **26**
1988 **PRINCESS ERICA 7** [13]4-10-4 p (45) Miss Lynsey Hanna 10/1: 5-000409: Chsd ldrs till over 1f out. *nk* **35**
1951 **LEOPARD CREEK 8** [1]3-10-6 p (55) Miss S Brotherton 10/1: 400-0020: 10th: Prom, no impress bef dist. *2* **39**
1657 **CHANTRY FALLS 22** [19]4-10-7 (48) Ms C Williams 16/1: 0463-060: 11th: Nvr on terms with ldrs. *1* **29**
4330} **FIZZY LIZZY 256** [9]4-9-12 (39) Miss J Waring(7) 50/1: 050000-0: 12th: Chsd ldrs till over 2f out: reapp. *nk* **19**
1963 **MICKLEDOR 8** [4]4-10-6 bl (47) Miss L Ellison(3) 33/1: 60034-00: 13th: Dwelt, sn prom, btn 2f out. *shd* **27**
1989 **BELLS BOYS 7** [3]5-9-10 p (37) Miss N Carberry(3) 3/1 FAV: 5040330: 14th: Cl-up, wknd 2f out: hvly bckd. *3½* **8**
1872 **REEDSMAN 12** [14]3-9-11 VIS (46) Mrs S Bosley 25/1: 000-2000: 15th: Mid-div, nvr on terms, visor. *hd* **16**
110} **CHARLATAN 550** [16]6-9-8 (5oh) (30) Miss J C Duncan(5) 33/1: 000000/-0: 16th: In tch, lost place from 2f out, 7 wk jumps abs. *1½* **0**
1947 **QUEENS SQUARE 8** [11]3-9-10 (45) Miss A Rothery(7) 50/1: 200-0000: 17th: Prom till halfway. *2* **0**
1784 **CLOUDS OF GOLD 16** [17]3-10-1 (50) Mr P Callaghan(5) 25/1: 0300: 18th: Sn bhd, h'cap bow. *1¾* **0**
1824 **COMPTON PLUME 14** [15]4-11-0 (55) Mr Nicky Tinkler 4/1: 2026-031D: 19th: Prom, rdn & led ins last, lost weight cloth cl home, fin 1st, wng margin 0.5L, disqual & plcd last: most unfortunate, weight differential reportedly v small: see 1824. **0**
19 Ran Time 1m 13.42(4.52) Owned: Mr Steve Roberts Trained: Nesscliffe

SANDOWN TUESDAY 01.06.04 Righthand, Galloping Track, Stiff Finish

Official Going GOOD/SOFT (GOOD places).

2126 6.15 Sharp Minds Betfair: Best Odds Classified Stakes 3yo 0-80 (D)
£5603 £1724 £862 **1m14y rnd** **Good/Soft 80** **-17 Slow** Inside

1865 **MYSTICAL GIRL 12** [8] M Johnston 3-9-2 (85) S Chin 2/1 FAV: 30-33121: Made all, clr 1.5f out, styd on well, drvn out: hvly bckd: stays 11f well, best form poss at 7f/1m: acts on fast & soft grnd: likes to run up with/force the pace & handed an uncontested lead today: remains in great form, see 1865 & 1769. **94**
1810* **DIAMOND LODGE 15** [10] J Noseda 3-8-11 (79) E Ahern 9/2: 412: Dwelt, sn rdn along, hdwy to chase wnr fnl 1f, nvr going to get there: gd run, 10f shld suit: acts on fast & gd/soft: more to come. *1½* **84**
1919 **FREAK OCCURENCE 10** [9] Miss E C Lavelle 3-9-1 (81) S Drowne 6/1: 20-03463: Mid-div, styd on under press fnl 1f: tchd 8/1: another consistent run: see 1515 & 232 (AW). *1½* **84**
1318 **SAFFRON FOX 39** [1] J G Portman 3-9-0 (83) L Dettori 14/1: 0120-404: Chsd ldrs wide, sltly outpcd 2f out, rallied fnl 2f: has tried 10f, again suggested that trip may suit: see 1105. *¾* **82**
1141 **WINNERS DELIGHT 50** [13]3-9-0 (80) R Miles(3) 25/1: 6165-005: ch g First Trump - Real Popcorn (Jareer) Dwelt, hdwy wide 2f out, nvr nr ldrs: 7 wk abs: '03 mdn auct wnr, subs held in nursery h'caps: eff at 7f, prob stays 1m: acts on fast & gd/soft: banned under non-triers rule in 1141 & prob has a race in him. *shd* **81**
1 Jun'03 Ling 7g/f 81- E:
1847 **HOH BLEU DEE 13** [3]3-9-4 (84) J F Egan 33/1: 11666-06: Rear, nvr nr to chall: see 1847. *3½* **79**
1769 **STEVEDORE 17** [4]3-9-0 (77) L Keniry(3) 66/1: 0214-07: ch c Docksider - La Belle Katherine (Lyphard) Held up, nvr a factor: '03 mdn auct wnr, subs 4th in a nursery h'cap (rtd 81): eff at 6/7f on fast & firm grnd, handles a sharp or undul trk: with B Meehan. *2* **71**
1 Sep'03 Folk 7g/f 79- F: 2 Aug'03 Kemp 6g/f 79- D:
1847 **COMPTONS ELEVEN 13** [5]3-9-3 (83) S Hitchcott(3) 33/1: 033-0008: Hld up, short of rm 2f out, nvr dngrs. *nk* **73**
1665 **MISTER SAIF 21** [7]3-9-5 (85) R Hughes 14/1: 622-0U59: Prom 6.5f, wknd. *½* **74**
1931 **JATH 10** [11]3-9-2 (85) N Pollard 20/1: 1-060: 10th: Prom till dist, wknd: see 1931. *nk* **70**
1846* **ANOTHER FAUX PAS 13** [2]3-8-11 (79) R L Moore 14/1: 0-10: 11th: Al rear: btr 1846 (gd/fm). *2* **61**
1770 **MAJOR EFFORT 17** [12]3-9-0 (80) K Fallon 13/2: 052-40: 12th: Prom till halfway, sn btn: see 1770. *1½* **61**
1770* **ATTUNE 17** [6]3-8-11 (80) D Holland 20/1: 4-4010: 13th: Prom till halfway, wknd: btr 1770 (gd/fm). *½* **57**
13 Ran Time 1m 46.76 (7.76) Owned: T T Bloodstocks Trained: Middleham

2127 6.45 Sharp Minds Call 0870 90 80 121 Handicap Stakes 3yo 0-90 (C) [92]
£10010 £3080 £1540 **1m2f7y** **Good/Soft 80** **-15 Slow** Inside

4980} **ODIHAM 212** [10] H Morrison 3-9-0 (78) S Drowne 14/1: 002-1: b g Deploy - Hug Me (Shareef Dancer) Mid-div, hdwy & drvn to lead ent fnl 1f, styd on strongly, going away: reapp: rnr-up on fnl of 3 juv starts (AW mdn): eff at 1m, apprec this step up to 10f & 12f will suit: acts on gd/soft & polytrack: handles a sharp or stiff/gall trk: runs well fresh: lightly rcd, impressed here, win again, esp at 12f. 2 Nov'03 Ling 8ap 77a- D: **88+**
1500 **KEELUNG 30** [7] M A Jarvis 3-9-7 (85) P Robinson 7/1: 0-422132: Held up, switched stands side ent str, led dist till ins fnl 1f, no extra: bckd from 10/1, jt top-weight: another consistent run: see 1500 & 1275. *2* **90**
1174 **SETTLEMENT CRAIC 47** [6] T G Mills 3-9-7 (85) R Miles(3) 12/1: 2-143: Held up, styd on fnl 1.5f, nrst fin: 7 wk abs: prob handles fast, gd/soft & polytrack: return to 12f will suit: see 1174 & 873 (12f, AW). *1* **89**
1813 **MOMTIC 14** [11] W Jarvis 3-9-2 (80) J Murtagh 9/2: 321-3304: Prom, ev ch dist, fdd cl-home: nicely bckd, clr of rem: showed more in 1813. *2½* **80**
1965 **MAN OF LETTERS 8** [9]3-8-12 (76) K Dalgleish 5/1: 4322125: Prom, wkng when short of room dist, no ch after: see 1965. *4* **70**
1930 **MACLEAN 10** [2]3-8-13 (77) K Fallon 9/4 FAV: 2-2136: Trkd ldrs, wknd fnl 1f: hvly bckd from 3/1: prob not stay this longer 10f trip on easy grnd: btr 1930 & 1462 (9f). *2* **68**
1500 **MR TAMBOURINE MAN 30** [5]3-9-2 (80) S Sanders 25/1: 261-607: Nvr btr than mid-div: see 1192. *6* **62**
1708 **ANOUSA 19** [1]3-9-5 vis (83) J Fanning 25/1: 501-0108: Held up, al rear: btr 1515 (hvy). *1* **63**

2025 **CHARLIE TANGO 5** [8]3-8-1 (65) T Dean(7) 25/1: 0-300039: Dwelt, al rear: qck reapp.   nk   44
1815* **DUBOIS 14** [3]3-9-4 vis t (82) L Dettori 11/2: 25-10: 10th: Led & trav strongly, hdd dist & wknd v   6   52
qckly: well bckd: form prev on fast grnd, something surely amiss here: much btr 1815 (mdn).
1924 **RIO DE JUMEIRAH 10** [4]3-9-0 (78) D Holland 25/1: 3035-360: 11th: Prom, wknd over 2f out.   2½   44
11 Ran   Time 2m 13.61 (9.51)   Owned: Odiham Partnership   Trained: East Ilsley

---

2128   **7.15 Gr3 Betfair Com Brigadier Gerard Stakes 4yo+   (A)**
          £29000 £11000 £5500   **1m2f7y**   **Good/Soft 80**   **+15 Fast**   Inside

1585* **BANDARI 26** [3] M Johnston 5-8-10 (114) W Supple 7/2: 442-0111: Trkd ldr, went on halfway, chall   119
fnl 2f, forged ahead cl-home, drvn out in a fine duel: well bckd, fast time: suited by 10f now, just stays 14f: acts
on firm, soft & any trk: v smart & thriving term, major claims in the Prince of Wales's Stks at R Ascot.
1758 **IKHTYAR 17** [5] J H M Gosden 4-8-10 (113) R Hills 7/2: 1210-362: Mid-div, hdwy to chall 2f out,   nk   118
ev ch fnl 1f & just btn in a tight fin: well bckd, apprec this drop back to Gr 3 company, acts on firm & gd/soft
grnd: well clr rem, fine run, win a Gr race sn: see 1420.
2002 **SUNSTRACH 9** [4] M Cumani 6-8-10 (112) J Murtagh 10/1: 3103-343: Mid-div, kept on to chase   7   108
front pair fnl 1f, no impress: not disgraced bhd 2 v smart rivals, tho' poss a shade below best: see 1350 (C/D).
2004 **NYSAEAN 9** [2] R Hannon 5-8-13 (114) R Hughes 12/1: 5452134: Prom, ev ch 3f out till fdd over 1f   2½   107
out: tchd 16/1: likes easy grnd: see 2004 & 1560.
3421} **COMFY 300** [1]5-8-10 (113) K Fallon 12/1: 315//103-5: b c Lear Fan - Souplesse (Majestic Light)   3½   98
Keen in rear, some late prog tho' nvr dngrs on comeback: lightly rcd in early '03, stks wnr on reapp: missed '02
with leg problems: List wnr in '01: stays 10f, acts on fast & gd/soft grnd: likes a gall trk & has run well fresh.
1 May'03 Leic 7.0g/f 105- C: 1 Aug'01 York 7gd 107- A:
4798} **KAIETEUR 227** [8]5-8-10 (117) D Holland 7/1: 063230-6: b c Marlin - Strong Embrace (Regal   1   96
Embrace) Held up, nvr nr ldrs on reapp: failed to win in '03, tho' plcd in decent company, notably when ddhtd for
2nd in Gr 1 Arlington Million & 3rd in Coral Eclipse (rtd 120): stks & German Gr 1 wnr in '02: eff at 1m/10f, has
tried 12f: acts on fast & firm, likes gd & soft grnd, any trk: tough & v smart at best.
2 Aug'03 Arli 10gd 118- A: 1 Aug'02 Mais 10sft 117- : 2 Jul'02 Mais 10sft 117- : 2 Apr'02 Sand 10g/s 107- A:
1 Mar'02 Kemp 10gd 102- C: 1 Oct'01 Bath 8g/s 94- E: 2 Sep'01 Newb 7frm 91- D:
3238* }**LATEEN SAILS 310** [7]4-8-13 T (114) L Dettori 3/1 FAV: 1/0141-7: ch c Elmaamul - Felucca (Green   6   90
Desert) Keen & trkd ldrs, btn 2f out on reapp: best when able to dominate, rcd too keenly in first time t-strap
today: capable of much better. 1 Jul'03 Mais 9sft 113- A: 1 May'03 York 10.4fm 113- A: 1 Oct'02 Newm 8fm 111- D:
1746 **EASTER OGIL 18** [9]9-8-10 (55) N Pollard 200/1: 0026508: Dwelt, al bhd, t.o.: highly tried.   21   57
1558 **CHANCELLOR 30** [4]6-8-13 (112) S Sanders 20/1: 464-0109: Led till halfway, wknd & eased, t.o.   5   52
9 Ran   Time 2m 10.65 (6.55)   Owned: Mr Hamdan Al Maktoum   Trained: Middleham

---

2129   **7.50 Sharp Minds Betfair Handicap Stakes 3yo+ 0-80 (D)**   [80]
          £5603 £1724 £862   **1m14y rnd**   **Good/Soft 80**   **-01 Slow**   Inside

1972* **ACOMB 8** [9] M W Easterby 4-9-1 (5ex) (67) K Fallon 3/1 FAV: 50-06011: Cl-up, led 3f out, clr ins   82+
fnl 2f, eased cl-home, val 7L+: well bckd under 5lb pen: eff at 7f/1m, has tried 10f: acts on firm & gd/soft grnd:
in fine form & hat-trick awaits: see 1972 & 1485.
1915 **ANNA WALHAAN 10** [2] Ian Williams 5-9-4 (70) T Quinn 10/1: 4205-002: Slow away, hdwy halfway,   5   71
kept on ins fnl 1f, no ch with easy wnr: gd run in defeat: see 1915.
1849 **SPIRITS AWAKENING 13** [3] J Akehurst 5-8-4 (56) J Quinn 8/1: 0422-063: Mid-div, hdwy 3f out, kept   nk   56
on ins fnl 1f, just held for 2nd: gd run: see 1849.
1536 **FEN GYPSY 28** [11] P D Evans 6-8-8 (60) R Havlin 7/1: 0002124: Handy, wknd ins fnl 1f.   ½   59
1723 **OH BOY 19** [12]4-8-8 (60) R L Moore 20/1: 0/040-005: b c Tagula - Pretty Sally (Polish Patriot)   3½   52
Nvr nrr than mid-div: 4th oin 1 of 3 '03 starts (rtd 72, auct mdn): with R Hannon.
1812 **SRI DIAMOND 14** [6]4-9-10 (76) J F Egan 7/1: 1/030-006: Handy over 6f, sn no extra: btr 1812.   ½   67
1423 **CRAIL 34** [1]4-9-6 (72) G Baker 7/1: 4/0010-37: Rear, hdwy ins fnl 2f, nrst fin: btr 1423 (sft).   hd   63
1813 **INSTRUCTOR 14** [10]3-9-0 (77) R Hughes 12/1: 042-2108: Cl-up 5f, sn wknd: btr 1022 (polytrack).   hd   68
632   **INVADER 108** [4]8-10-0 bl t (80) S Drowne 25/1: 43-00609: In tch bfd, sn wknd: top-weight, abs, gelded. 6 59
1748 **MEELUP 18** [13]4-8-7 p (59) N Pollard 20/1: 1000220: 10th: Led 5f, sn fdd: btr 1748 & 1385.   ½   37
1823 **EASTERN HOPE 14** [7]5-8-11 bl (63) D Holland 5/1: 060-0030: 11th: Al bhd: well bckd: btr 1823.   5   31
1849 **NIGHT DRIVER 13** [5]5-8-3 (55) R Brisland 50/1: 105/0-000: 12th: b g Night Shift - Highshaan   14   0
(Pistolet Bleu) Slow away, plcd twice over hdles in 03/04 (rtd 103h, h'caps, stays 2m1f on gd/soft
grnd, P J Hobbs): unplcd sole '03 Flat start (h'cap): mdn & class stks wnr in '02 (B Hills): suited by 10f on
firm, fast grnd & polytrack, handles a stiff or sharp trk: with G L Moore.
1 Sep'02 Pont 10fm 71- E: 1 Jul'02 Ling 10ap 78a- D: 2 Jul'01 Newm 6g/f 75- E:
12 Ran   Time 1m 45.54 (6.54)   Owned: Mr Giles W Pritchard-Gordon   Trained: Sheriff Hutton

---

2130   **8.20 Bet 'in Running' At Betfair Handicap Stakes 3yo 0-80 (D)**   [87]
          £5486 £1688 £844   **1m6f**   **Good/Soft 80**   **-40 Slow**   Outside

1174 **GOLDEN QUEST 47** [10] M Johnston 3-9-5 (78) J Fanning 13/2: 0-1101: Handy, styd on to lead bef 2f   86
out, drvn out to hold on: 7 wk odds, nicely bckd: eff at 12f, apprec step up to 14f: acts on gd/soft grnd & both
AWs, goes well fresh: lightly rcd performer who is unexposed at staying dists: see 1174.
1429* **CONSIDINE 34** [6] J M P Eustace 3-8-8 (67) J Tate 12/1: 045-012: Led 4f, styd in tch, ev ch ins   ¾   73
fnl 1f, just held by wnr: eff at 12f, imprvd for step up to 14f: acts on gd/soft & soft grnd: lost little in
defeat & is open to more improvement: see 1429.
1708 **NESSEN DORMA 19** [5] J G Given 3-9-7 (80) M Fenton 5/1: 4552133: Cl-up, led after 6f, hdd 5f out,   ½   85
styd cl-up & ev ch dist, onepcd ins fnl 1f: nicely bckd: remains in gd form: see 1521.
1507* **BUMPTIOUS 30** [2] M H Tompkins 3-9-2 (75) P Robinson 5/1: 346-3314: Held up, prog after 12f, kept   ½   79
on ins fnl 1f: op 7/1: eff arnd 12f, now stays 14f: just btr 1507.
1737 **FU FIGHTER 18** [13]3-8-13 (72) E Ahern 25/1: 54-05: b g Unfuwain - Runelia (Runnett) Cl-up, led   hd   76
after 11f, hdd bef 2f out, no extra fnl 1f: unplcd both '03 starts (rtd 76a, auct mdn): stayed this much longer 14f
trip: acts on gd/soft grnd & polytrack: encouraging eff on h'cap bow.
1768 **HATHLEN 17** [14]3-9-0 (73) S Hitchcott(3) 20/1: 22-00656: Mid-div, prog 3f out, onepcd dist.   1½   75
2021 **BILL BENNETT 6** [9]3-9-4 (77) G Baker 14/1: 6511257: Held up, nvr nrr than mid-div: qck reapp.   ¾   78

1648* **FLEETFOOT MAC 22** [12]3-8-6　(65) K Fallon　4/1 FAV: 0006-118: In tch, led after 4f, hdd 1m out,　**15**　**46**
wknd ins fnl half-mile: well bckd: v disapp on step up in trip: btr 1648 (12f, soft).
1936　**TURNSTILE 10** [11]3-9-1　(74) P Dobbs　5/1: 4-429: Handy over 12f, sn wknd: btr 1936 (12f, fast).　**1¾**　**53**
1174　**LIQUIDATE 47** [7]3-8-7　(66) S Drowne　10/1: 006-100: 10th: Al in rear: 7 wk abs: btr 1000 (12f, gd).　**1¼**　**43**
1507　**BLUE HILLS 30** [3]3-8-11　(70) K Dalgleish　33/1: 052-050: 11th: Bhd, nvr a factor: btr 1507.　**3½**　**43**
11 Ran　Time 3m 11.88 (16.88)　Owned: Syndicate 2002　Trained: Middleham

---

2131
8.50 Sharp Minds Betfair Maiden Stakes 3yo+　(D)
£5772　£1776　£888　　**1m2f7y**　　**Good/Soft 80**　　**-27 Slow**　　Inside

1737　**HAADEF 18** [9] J H M Gosden 3-8-11　R Hills　1/1 FAV: 31: Mid-div, hdwy to lead dist, pushed out,　**94+**
val 2L+: bckd from 6/4: eff at 10f, 12f+ shld suit: acts on gd/soft grnd & a stiff/gall trk: plenty to like about
this performance & can rate higher when tried over further: see 1737.
　　ELMUSTANSER [3] Saeed bin Suroor 3-8-11 T L Dettori　5/1: 2: b c Machiavellian - Elfaslah (Green　**1¼**　**88**
Desert) Cl-up, ev ch dist, kept on fnl 1f, al held by wnr: debut, op 3/1: half-sister to high-class mid-dist
performer White Muzzle: eff at 10f, further will suit: acts on gd/soft, eff with a t-strap: can find a race.
　　SHAMBAR 768 [2] P R Chamings 5-9-10　J Murtagh　20/1: 4/-3: gr g Linamix - Shamawna (Darshaan)　**3**　**83**
Keen cl-up, led 3f out, hdd dist, no extra: reapp: Brit bow, ex-French: missed '03: 4th of 12 on sole '02 start
(10f mdn): eff at 10f, further shld suit: acts on gd/soft grnd: encouraging run after such a long lay-off.
4972} **MAID TO TREASURE 213** [14] J L Dunlop 3-8-6　T Quinn　5/1: 2-4: b f Rainbow Quest - Maid For The　**shd**　**78**
Hills (Indian Ridge) Mid-div, outpcd after 6f, rallied ins fnl 1f: clr rem: reapp: rnr-up sole '03 start (fills
mdn): prev eff at 7f, enjoyed step up to 10f, shaped as tho' further will suit: acts on gd & gd/soft grnd.
2 Nov'03 Newm 7g/f 82- D:
4126} **SHOOTING LODGE 267** [1]3-8-6　K Fallon　12/1: 0-5: Handy over 1m, sn no extra: reapp.　**4**　**72**
976}　**SECRET JEWEL 421** [15]4-9-5　S Sanders　66/1: 0/0-6: Bhd, prog ins fnl 2f, nrst fin: reapp.　**2**　**69**
　　ENHANCER [10]6-9-10　J F Egan　66/1: 7: Keen in tch 1m, sn no extra: 9 wk jumps abs.　**¾**　**72**
4147} **SONG OF THE SEA 266** [12]3-8-6　S Whitworth　66/1: 0-8: Nvr nrr than mid-div: reapp.　**½**　**66**
1810　**BONSAI 15** [8]3-8-6　E Ahern　33/1: 0-09: Cl-up 1m, sn fdd.　**½**　**65**
3275} **MY SUNSHINE 306** [7]3-8-6　P Robinson　20/1: 00-0: 10th: Handy 1m, sn wknd.　**1**　**63**
1651　**MIDSHIPMAN EASY 22** [13]3-8-11　(77) D Holland　15/2: 0-320: 11th: Led 3f, wknd: btr 1651.　**3**　**62**
1742　**INDIAN CHASE 18** [11]7-9-10 vis　Lucy Russell(7) 100/1: 260: 12th: Al in rear.　**3**　**52**
1737　**Ocean Rock 18** [6]3-8-11 P McCabe 100/1:0　　980　**Alianna 63** [5]3-8-6 R L Moore 100/1:0
　　Delfinia [16]3-8-6 S Drowne 100/1:0　　1581　**Good Article 26** [4]3-8-11 e D Corby(3) 100/1:0
16 Ran　Time 2m 14.82(10.72)　Owned: Mr Hamdan Al Maktoum　Trained: Manton

---

Official Going Good

2132
2.30 E B F Wolvey Maiden Stakes Fillies 2yo　(D)
£5590　£1720　£860　　**5f str**　　**Good 52**　　**-03 Slow**　　Stands Side

　　SHARPLAW STAR 0 [7] W J Haggas 2-8-11　M Hills　7/4 FAV: 1: b f Xaar - Hamsah (Green Desert)　**92+**
Trkd ldrs & led over 1f out, hands & heels, readily: hvly bckd, op 2/1: 92,000gns April foal, half-brother to
multiple 5f juv wnr Promenade, dam a dual 5f juv wnr: eff over a stiff 5f, 6f may suit: acts on gd grnd & goes well
fresh: clearly speedy, posted a fair juv time, useful & can win more races.
　　MOLLY MARIE 0 [1] T D Easterby 2-8-11　T Quinn　9/1: 2: b f Fasliyev - Snoozeandyoulose (Scenic)　**2½**　**81**
Prom, switched & kept on, not pace of wnr: op 6/1: 34,000gns April foal, half-sister to a 1m juv wnr, dam 7f wnr:
eff at 5f, get further: handles gd grnd: pleasing start, rate higher.
1920　**EASY FEELING 10** [3] R Hannon 2-8-11　R L Moore　3/1: 33: Trkd ldr halfway & led over 1f out, sn　**nk**　**80**
hdd & not pace of wnr: bckd: eff at 5f, return to 6f shld suit: acts on fast & gd grnd: see 1920.
2020　**ELSIE WAGG 6** [6] M J Wallace 2-8-11　K Fallon　5/2: 34: Led till over 1f out, fdd: op 3/1: see 2020.　**2**　**74**
　　MISS COTSWOLD LADY 0 [2]2-8-11　P Doe　66/1: 5: b f Averti - Celtic Bay (Green Dancer) Al　**12**　**42**
outpcd, not land blow: March first foal, cheaply bght: dam an uncrd juv.
　　DANCING MOONLIGHT 0 [4]2-8-11　R Fitzpatrick　80/1: 6: Slowly away & sn outpcd.　**5**　**29**
1968　**MERMAIDS CRY 8** [5]2-8-11　J F Egan　33/1: 27: Chsd ldrs till halfway, wknd qckly: new stable: btr 1968.　**1½**　**24**
7 Ran　Time 1m 01.07 (2.77)　Owned: Miss Tina Miller　Trained: Newmarket

---

2133
3.00 Hathern Claiming Stakes 3yo　(F)
£3367　£1036　£518　　**1m rnd**　　**Good 52**　　**Inapplicable**　　Inside

1879　**WESTERN ROOTS 12** [8] P F I Cole 3-9-10　(74) T Quinn　5/2 FAV: 0-240061: In tch, prog to lead over　**78**
1f out, edged left & held on well for press ins last: clmd by K Morgan for 15,000: eff at 7f/1m, tried 10f: likes
polytrack & gd grnd: apprec drop to claim grade: see 432.
1952　**HEARTHSTEAD DREAM 8** [4] J G M O'Shea 3-8-8　(69) D Sweeney　12/1: 0320-032: Held up, hdwy to　**nk**　**61**
chall ins last, styd on well, just held: clr of rem: claimed for 7,000: eff at 1m/12f in claim company: see 1952.
1678　**KINGS ROCK 20** [5] K A Ryan 3-9-4　(58) P Fessey　5/1: 0-260063: Held up, eff & hung right over 1f　**7**　**58**
out, nvr threatened front pair: mdn: see 553.
4443} **PAPEETE 250** [1] W J Haggas 3-9-5　(73) K Fallon　7/2: 33100-4: b f Alzao - Prairie Vela (Persian　**2½**　**54**
Bold) Dwelt, pushed along rear, nvr able to chall ldrs: reapp: op 3/1: auct mdn scorer '03: eff at 7f,
sharp/undul or stiff trk: acts on fast grnd.　1 Aug'03 Newc 7g/f 75- E:
1949　**RED ROCKY 8** [6]3-8-5　(55) Martin Dwyer　66/1: 5655-005: b f Danzero - Post Mistress (Cyrano de　**1¼**　**37**
Bergerac) Led/dsptd lead, went on 2f out, sn hdd & no extra dist: unplcd '03 (rtd 57, fills mdn, J Gallagher).
1359　**ERTE 38** [10]3-9-0　(62) K Darley　14/1: 03406-06: ch g Vettori - Cragreen (Green Desert) Led　**1½**　**43**
after 2f till 2f out, wknd: auct mdn plcd '03 (rtd 73, M Channon): eff around a stiff/gall 7f on fast & gd grnd.
1690　**COMPASSION 20** [3]3-8-1 p　(58) A McCarthy　40/1: 4450-007: Held up, btn over 1f out.　**¾**　**29**
1611　**CASHEMA 25** [9]3-8-9 P　(52) R Havlin　33/1: 000-008: Chsd ldrs till over 1f out, cheek pieces.　**nk**　**36**

1785 **DESERT DAISY 16** [7]3-7-13 (59) J Quinn 6/1: 2260-009: Chsd ldr, btn over 1f out: bckd: btr 1099.   3½   19
1825 **MR BELVEDERE 14** [2]3-9-0 bl (65) Dane O'Neill 7/1: 5030-000: 10th: Prom, struggling fnl 2f: op 6/1.   3½   27
10 Ran   Time 1m 42.89 (No Std Time)   Owned: Mr David Murrell   Trained: Whatcombe

---

2134	3.30 Sheff Wilson Lifetime In Racing Handicap Stakes 3yo 0-70 (E)	[74]
	£4300 £1323 £662 1m3f183y Good 52 +12 Fast Inside	

1967* **SELEBELA 8** [15] L M Cumani 3-9-3 (5ex) (63) J Murtagh 10/11 FAV: 3605-011: Trkd ldrs & led over   83+
2f out, readily drew clr, val 10L+: hvly bckd, fast time: eff around 12f on fast, gd & prob soft grnd: likes
Leicester: most progressive, keen on side for the hat-trick: see 1967 (C/D).
1679 **ILWADOD 20** [1] M R Channon 3-8-10 (56) K Darley 11/2: 006-122: Held up, outpcd over 4f out, styd   7   61
on late: stays 12f: has been gelded: acts on gd & hvy: see 1679.
1785* **SIEGFRIEDS NIGHT 16** [12] M C Chapman 3-9-6 (66) D Fox(5) 9/1: 3336213: Held up, kept on fnl 2f,   2   68
nvr a threat to wnr: consistent type: see 1785.
1729 **CANADIAN STORM 18** [4] M H Tompkins 3-9-0 (60) D Holland 25/1: 050-504: Held up & keen, prog to   ½   61
lead after 4f till over 2f out, sn no extra: 1m could prove ideal: see 1554 (7f).
1836 **DANEFONIQUE 14** [7]3-8-11 (57) R Fitzpatrick 25/1: 50-03225: Dwelt & held up, late prog, no threat.   hd   57
1124 **DARN GOOD 50** [13]3-9-6 BL (66) R L Moore 33/1: 00-00306: Chsd ldrs, btn 3f out: tried blnks, abs.   1¾   64
4532} **CHANFRON 245** [8]3-9-5 (65) A McCarthy 80/1: 0360-7: ch g Double Trigger - Mhargaidh Nua (Thowra)   1   62
Prom, btn 3f out: lightly rcd '03, mdn plcd (rtd 70): eff around a sharp 1m, mid-dists shld suit: handles fast.
1673* **TRUE TO YOURSELF 21** [5]3-8-1 (47) J Quinn 20/1: 000-0218: Held up, eff 4f out, no impress: btr 1673.   hd   43
1976 **HEARTBEAT 7** [2]3-8-1 (47) F P Ferris(3) 20/1: 4004459: Dwelt, al towards rear: btr 1976 & 1051 (10f).   2½   39
1514 **VERASI 29** [3]3-9-7 (67) S Drowne 8/1: 000-40: 10th: Chsd ldrs till 3f out: op 11/2: flattered 1514 (1m).   1   58
2014 **EL MAGNIFICO 6** [6]3-8-2 VIS (48) Lisa Jones(3) 50/1: 006-6000: 11th: Led 4f, btn 2f out: vis, qck reapp.   ½   38
473 Waltzing Beau 129 [17]3-8-13 (59) T Quinn 66/1:0
1577 Three Welshmen 26 [10]3-8-11 (57) S Sanders 25/1:0
1927 Faith Healer 10 [11]3-8-9 p(55) Joanna Badger 80/1:0   1612 Cadeaux Rouge 25 [14]3-9-0 (60) R Havlin 50/1:0
15 Ran   Time 2m 33.04 (4.74)   Owned: Scuderia Rencati Srl   Trained: Newmarket

---

2135	4.00 Forest Handicap Stakes 3yo+ 0-70 (E)	[82]
	£4280 £1317 £659 1m2f Good 52 -00 Slow Inside	

1976 **PLANTERS PUNCH 7** [5] R Hannon 3-8-8 (62) K Fallon 9/2: 00-0001: Mid-div, pushed along & hdwy to   70+
lead over 1f out, styd strongly, going away: bckd: first win: eff at 10f, 12f looks sure to suit: acts on gd &
a stiff trk: gd confidence boost, win again over 10f+: see 1976.
1781 **MOVIE KING 16** [11] S Gollings 5-9-10 P (65) D Holland 13/2: 0450-002: Led & sn clr, hdd over 1f   3   67
out, kept on: bckd at morning odds, first time cheek pieces: enjoys an uncontested lead, well h'capped: see 1599.
1895 **KIRKHAM ABBEY 11** [12] M A Jarvis 4-9-10 vis (65) K Darley 7/2: 31011-03: Prom, styd on   ½   67
onepace for press fnl 2f: well bckd: left reapp bhd: return to 12f in similar could suit: see 1895.
2054* **ARMS ACROSSTHESEA 4** [7] J Balding 5-9-4 (5ex) (59) J Edmunds 11/2: 000-2114: Held up, eff from 3f   1¼   59
out, styd on onepace: qck reapp under a pen: see 2054.
1541 **DANEBANK 28** [10]4-8-7 (48) G Carter 14/1: 64600-05: b g Danehill - Snow Bank (Law Society) Held   3½   43
up, kept on late, no threat: h'cap plcd '03 (rtd 55, disapp in a visor, J Hills): unplcd '02 (rtd 64a & 71, mdns):
stays a sharp 12f, may get further: handles fast & firm grnd, sharp/undul trks.
1913 **LYRICAL WAY 10** [8]5-9-5 bl (60) S Drowne 7/1: 21-40506: Chsd ldrs, btn over 1f out: btr 900 (AW).   shd   55
4372} **LUCKY ARCHER 255** [2]11-8-13 (54) R L Moore 33/1: 0200-07: b g North Briton - Preobrajenska   3   45
(Double Form) Held up, nvr land a blow: reapp: amat h'cap rnr-up '03: dual h'cap rnr-up '02: suited by 1m/9f on
firm & gd grnd, prob any trk: best without blnks: 11yo.
2 Jun'03 Good 9fm 64-60 E: 2 Jun'02 Bath 8g/f 67-65 E: 2 May'02 Bath 8g/f 66-60 E: 1 Jul'01 Sand 8g/f 64- E:
1 Jun'01 Leic 8g/f 59- F:
1830 **LITTLE ENGLANDER 14** [1]4-9-0 (55) Dane O'Neill 10/1: 6240-508: Held up, struggling fnl 2f: btr 1430.   1¼   44
  SACHSENWALZER 205 [9]6-8-12 (53) Martin Dwyer 20/1: 501445-9: Chsd ldr, btn 2f out: jumps fit.   1¾   40
498 **KYLE OF LOCHALSH 125** [3]4-9-2 (57) A McCarthy 16/1: 3000-300: 10th: Al rear: abs: btr 406 (AW).   hd   43
1946 **RILEYS ROCKET 8** [6]5-8-2 (3ow) (40) Paul Eddery 66/1: 0005-000: 11th: Dwelt & held up, keen, al bhd.   5   22
11 Ran   Time 2m 07.73 (5.23)   Owned: Lucayan Stud   Trained: Marlborough

---

2136	4.30 Leicester Racecourse Conference Centre Conditions Stakes Fillies 3yo (C)	
	£8538 £3238 £1619 7f str Good 52 -07 Slow Stands Side	

1617* **LUCKY SPIN 25** [6] R Hannon 3-8-9 (90) R L Moore 1/1 FAV: 211: Made all, rdn & styd on strongly   101+
ins last, pushed out: op 6/4: eff at 7f, shld get 1m: acts on gd/soft: v progressive & useful, win again.
1888 **COY 11** [7] Sir Michael Stoute 3-8-9 (92) K Fallon 3/1: 01-52: Dwelt, sn chsd ldrs, outpcd over   1¼   95
2f out, rallied fnl 1f: eff at 6/7f, well worth another try at 1m: see 1888.
4799} **SURF THE NET 227** [4] R Hannon 3-8-9 Dane O'Neill 10/1: 16-3: b f Cape Cross - On The Tide (Slip   ¾   94
Anchor) Chsd ldrs, onepace & held bef dist: reapp: lightly rcd '03, fills mdn wnr on debut, subs Gr 2 unplcd (rtd
94): eff at 6/7f, half-sister to a useful 10f wnr: acts on fast & gd grnd, stiff/gall trks: can go well fresh:
useful. 1 Jun'03 Newm 6g/f 92- D:
1169 **TOTALLY YOURS 48** [8] W R Muir 3-8-7 (90) Martin Dwyer 11/2: 02210-04: b f Desert Sun - Total   nk   91
Aloof (Groom Dancer) Chsd wnr, rdn & no extra from dist: 7 wk abs: auct mdn scorer '03, earlier val stks rnr-up in
Ireland: winning form at 6f, stays gall 7f well: acts on fast & gd grnd, sharp/undul or gall trk: clr of rem here.
1 Sep'03 Epso 6gd 87- E: 2 Aug'03 Curr 6g/f 72- D: 4 Aug'03 Wind 6g/f 72- D:
1419 **NEPHETRITI WAY 34** [1]3-8-9 (87) S Drowne 8/1: 212-05: Prom till over 1f out: see 1419.   7   78
1896 **CHASE THE RAINBOW 11** [2]3-8-7 (55) P Bradley(4) 150/1: 002-6606: Held up, struggling fnl 2f.   3   73$
6 Ran   Time 1m 26.10 (4.1)   Owned: Mr George C Scudder   Trained: Marlborough

---

2137   **5.00 Coronation Classified Stakes 3yo 0-80 (D)**
£5610 £1726 £863   **6f str**   **Good 52**   **-19 Slow**   Stands Side

1879 **TIMES REVIEW 12** [4] T D Easterby 3-8-12 (81) K Darley 4/1: 2500-251: Chsd ldrs, styd on for   **86**
press to lead line, all out: op 7/2: eff at 5/6f, tried 1m: acts on firm, gd/soft & fibresand: see 1488.
4953} **CHANCE FOR ROMANCE 214** [5] W R Muir 3-8-11 (83) Martin Dwyer 12/1: 106050-2: ch f Entrepreneur - *shd* **84**
My First Romance (Danehill) Prom & led over 2f out till hdd line: reapp: auct fills mdn scorer '03, subs Gr 2
unplcd (rtd 91, flattered, disapp in cheek pieces): eff at 5.7f/6f on firm & gd grnd, gall/turning trks: gd return.
1 Jul'03 Bath 5.7fm 73- F: 2 Jun'03 Sali 5fm 80- D:
1734 **HILITES 18** [9] J S Moore 3-8-10 (82) S Whitworth 20/1: 1004-303: Held up, styd on fnl 2f, not   ½ **81**
pace of wnr: back to form after latest: consistent juv, shld find a race this term: see 1513.
1933 **VIENNAS BOY 10** [3] R Hannon 3-9-1 (84) Dane O'Neill 5/2 FAV: 020-4464: Keen & prom, went on over 1¾ **81**
2f out, sn hdd, onepace dist: hvly bckd, op 4/1: see 1018.
1809 **DOLCE PICCATA 15** [8]3-8-12 (84) T Quinn 8/1: 132-0545: In tch, bmpd when outpcd halfway, keeping ¾ **76**
on when short of room over 1f out, not able to chall: shade closer with a clr run: 6f looks set to suit this term.
1766 **FYODOR 17** [7]3-9-1 (84) M Hills 11/2: 2312-06: b c Fasliyev - Royale Figurine (Dominion Royale) ¾ **77**
Held up, eff fnl 2f, no impress in last: lightly rcd '03, mdn scorer, spells well '03 & '04: best
at 5f, stiff/undul or sharp trks. 2 Sep'03 Muss 5g/f 86-84 C: 1 Aug'03 Pont 5g/f 87- D: 2 Jun'03 Newc 6gd 80- D:
1387 **BAYLAW STAR 36** [6]3-8-11 (75) J Edmunds 20/1: 3003-637: Chsd ldrs, no impress over 1f out: op 16/1.2 **67**
1975 **OBE BOLD 7** [10]3-8-8 (57) P Bradley(5) 100/1: 00-43028: Chsd ldrs till over 1f out: see 1975 & 1338. 1½ **59**
1919 **BENNY THE BALL 10** [2]3-8-11 (80) J P Guillambert(3) 6/1: 4261-009: Dwelt, nvr able to chall: 3½ **51**
bckd, op 11/1: drpd in trip: see 98 (7f, AW).
5015+ **LITTLE RIDGE 208** [1]3-9-0 (83) L Fletcher 8/1: 36011-0: 10th: b g Charnwood Forest - Princess 10 **27**
Natalie (Rudimentary) Led till halfway, sn btn: op 6/1, reapp: won 2 '03 starts (h'caps): both wins at 5f, stays
a gall 6f: handles fast & gd/soft grnd, gall or sharp trk: can force the pace.
1 Nov'03 Nott 5.1g/s 85-73 E: 1 Oct'03 Muss 5gd 77-65 E:
10 Ran Time 1m 14.04(4.24) Owned: Times of Wigan Trained: Malton

---

Official Going GOOD/FIRM (GOOD places).

2138   **8.00 Listed Saval Beg Stakes 3yo+ ()**
£21809 £6399 £3048   **1m6f**   **Good/Firm**

1911} **WINDERMERE 360** T M Walsh 5-9-9 (105) J P Murtagh 14/1: 12/152-1: b c Lear Fan - Madame **116**
L'Enjoleur (L'Enjoleur) Made all & sn clr, in command fnl 4f & eased cl home: 10 wk jumps hdler 03/04):
with J Gosden in '03, cond stks wnr & List rnr-up: won thrice in '02, Gr 2 plcd: eff at 12/15f, 2m+ shld suit: acts
on fast & gd/sft gnd: loves to force the pace & given a well judged ride today: smart staying entire.
2 Jun'03 Chan 15gd 110- A: 1 Apr'03 Ripo 12.3gd 109-105 B: 2 Oct'02 Long 15g/s 108- : 1 Sep'02 Newb 13.2fm 98-92 C:
1 Aug'02 Newb 13.2g/f 94-85 C: 1 May'02 Bath 10.2g/s 86- E: 2 May'02 Hayd 10.5g/s 86- D:
4934} **VINNIE ROE 213** D K Weld 6-10-2 P J Smullen 1/2 FAV: 4/1154-2: b h Definite Article - Kayu (Tap 4½ **115**
On Wood) Held up, well adrift of wnr halfway, kept on well fnl 2f, nvr a threat: reapp: lightly rcd in '03, List &
Gr 1 Irish St Leger wnr: won the same 2 races in '02: suited by 14f+, stays stiff 2m4f: acts on fast & hvy,
stiff/gall trks: set plenty to do tonight, improve on this & shld run well in Ascot Gold Cup (rnr-up in '02).
1 Sep'03 Curr 14g/f 121- : 1 Aug'03 Leop 12g/f 113- A: 1 Sep'02 Curr 14g/f 121- : 1 Aug'02 Leop 12gd 118- :
2 Jun'02 Asco 20g/f 118- A: 1 Oct'01 Long 15.5hvy 122- : 1 Sep'01 Curr 14g/f 123- : 1 Aug'01 Curr 14gd 115- :
1 Jul'01 Leop 14gd 113- : 1 Nov'00 Leop 9sft 108- :
4449+ **MY RENEE 243** M J Grassick 4-9-9 N G McCullagh 7/1: 3151-3: Well adrift halfway, kept on late. 3 **104**
6 Ran Time 3m 02.20() Owned: W Hennessy Trained: Kill

Official Going GOOD/SOFT.

2139   **2.20 Gr 3 Prix du Palais Royal 3yo+ ()**
£25704 £10282 £7711   **7f**   **Good/Soft**

  PUPPETEER A de Royer-Dupre 4-9-4 C Soumillon 8/5 FAV: 1121-621: b c Singspiel - Pidona **111**
(Baillamont) Held up, hdwy wide over 2f out, led ins last, drvn out: '03 List wnr: eff btwn 7/11f on gd & soft:
likes a gall trk: smart.
4749} **SARATAN** M Delzangles 7-9-4 bl E Legrix 15/2: 24433-02: b g Tirol - Sarafiya (Dalsaan) Held nk **110**
up, rdn & hdwy to chall ins last, not pace of wnr close home: eff at 7f on gd/soft: smart.
2 Aug'03 Colo 8gd 113- A: 1 May'03 Long 7sft 114- A:
4472} **CRYSTAL CASTLE** J E Hammond 6-9-4 (94) T Gillet 89/10: 40300-33: b g Gilded Time - Wayage (Mr nk **109**
Prospector) Mid-div, styd on fnl 2f & just btn in a tight fin.
1 Sep'02 Asco 6g/f 115- A: 1 Aug'02 Deau 6sft 114- : 1 Jul'02 Asco 7g/f 102-94 B:
1649 **ROCKETS N ROLLERS 17** 4-9-4 (106) Dane O'Neill 14/1: 33323145: Mid-div, chsd ldrs 2f out, no 1½ **106**
extra ins last: English chall, see 1486.
1758 **INDIAN HAVEN 12** 4-9-4 (114) D Holland 59/10: 10100-596: Held up, nvr nr to chall: reportedly ½ **105**
found the grnd a shade too fast: capable of much better & a return to 1m shld suit: see 1349 (Gr 2).
10 Ran Time 1m 19.80() Owned: 6C Racing Ltd Trained: France

BADEN BADEN   FRIDAY 28.05.04   Lefthand, Sharpish Track

Official Going GOOD.

2140   **3.24 Gr 3 Benazet Rennen 3yo+**   ()
£26751 £10563 £5634   **6f rnd**   **Good**

4188} **LUCKY STRIKE** A Trybuhl 6-9-6 A de Vries 7/10 FAV: 40-2111531: br g Petong - Urania (Most   **114**
Welcome) Led, hung & wide into str, styd on strongly, drvn out: List German wnr earlier this term: French Gr 3 wnr
in '03: eff at 6/7f on gd & gd/sft grnd: smart performer. 1 Jun'03 Long 7gd 112- A:
4168} **TOPKAMP** 260 M L W Bell 4-9-2 (104) A Suborics 56/10: 01134232: b f Pennekamp - Victoria Regia   2   **104**
(Lomond) Sn chsd wnr, rdn & kept on, but not pace to chall: clr of rem, reapp: stks & List wnr in '03: auct mdn &
nov fill scorer '02: suited by 6f, stays a sharp 7f: acts on firm & gd grnd: tough & useful sprinter, an excellent
return. 2 Aug'03 Hopp 6.5gd 100- A: 1 Jun'03 Hayd 6g/f 104-100 A: 1 May'03 Kemp 6g/f 102-94 C:
1 Jul'02 Donc 5g/f 96- D: 1 Jun'02 Nott 5gd 84- F: 2 Jun'02 Redc 6fm 81- E:
     SACHO W Kujath 6-9-6 A Helfenbein 24/1: 3: Prom, kept on fnl 2f, not pace of front pair.   4½   **94**
952   **CAPRICHO** 62 J Akehurst 7-9-6 (110) P Doe 43/10: 014140-04: gr g Lake Coniston - Star Spectacle   nk   **93**
(Spectacular Bid) Chsd ldrs, onepcd fnl 1f: 2 mth abs: rtd h'cap & Gr 3 wnr in '03: won 2 val h'caps in '02,
notably Wokingham: eff at 6/7f on firm & soft grnd: likes a stiff trk & loves to come late off a strong pace:
capable of better. 1 Jul'03 Hamb 6sft 109- A: 1 May'03 Newm 6g/f 107-101 B: 1 Aug'02 Good 7fm 104-98 B:
1 Jun'02 Asco 6gd 100-87 B: 2 Jul'01 Chep 6g/f 90- C:
10 Ran   Time 1m 07.94 ()   Owned: Stall Lucky Stables International   Trained: Germany

BADEN BADEN   SUNDAY 31.05.04   Lefthand, Sharpish Track

Official Going GOOD.

2141   **3.25 Gr 2 Grosser Preis 4yo+**   ()
£26761 £10563 £5634   **1m3f**   **Good**

4401} **TOUCH OF LAND** 253 H A Pantall 4-8-12 C P Lemaire 54/10: 031124031: b c Lando - Touch Of Class   **117**
(Be My Guest) Trkd ldrs, swtchd & hdwy for press to lead ins last, drvn out: eff at 10/12f on gd & soft grnd, this
11f trip reportedly ideal: smart colt. 2 May'03 Long 12sft 108- :
     ROTTECK H Steguweit 4-8-12 J Palik 125/10: 2: Mid-div, styd on for press fnl 2f, not btn far.   ¾   **116**
1438   **SCOTTS VIEW** 35 M Johnston 5-8-12 (115) S Chin 7/10 FAV: -41013133: Prom, led over 1f out, hdd &   hd   **115**
not pace of wnr ins last: reportedly unsuited by steady pace: tough & most prog earlier, worth another chance.
1843   **TUNING FORK** 11 4-8-12 (98) J Quinn 28/1: 26650-070: 10th: Led till over 1f out, sn btn: fin   8½   **94**
10th & reportedly not stay this 11f trip: highly tried, off rtd 95: see 1843.
10 Ran   Time 1m 07.94 ()   Owned: Gary A Tanaka   Trained: France

CAPANNELLE   SUNDAY 30.05.04   Righthand, Flat, Galloping Track

Official Going GOOD.

2142   **4.20 Gr 1 Derby Italiano 3yo**   ()
£425662 £221007 £130437   **1m4f**   **Good**

     GROOM TESSE L Camici 3-9-2 bl D Vargiu 10/1: 3101-121: ch c Groom Dancer - Vicomtesse Mag   **116**
(Highest Honour) Mid-div, hdwy wide & led dist, styd on strongly: Gr 3 wnr earlier this term: eff at 9f, suited by
step up to 12f, prob get further: acts on gd & v soft grnd: apprec reapp of blnks today: v smart & prog 3yo.
     DAYANO A Wohler 3-9-2 E Pedroza 39/10: 2-112: b c Lomitas - Dawn Side (Bold Forbes) Keen   2½   **112**
early & al handy, led over 2f out till dist, not pace of wnr: German raider, 1st defeat this term.
1584   **PRIVY SEAL** 24 J H M Gosden 3-9-2 vis (110) J P Murtagh 33/10: 155-1223: Chsd ldrs, slightly hmpd   3   **108**
over 1f out, kept on, not pace to chall: stays 12f well & prob back to best: see 1584 & 1113.
1595   **PUTRA SAS** 23 3-9-2 (90) S Drowne 62/10: 21-226: Trkd ldrs, no extra fnl 2f: fin 6th: this   3¼   **103**
longer 12f trip shld suit: see 1595 (Gr 3).
1706   **MAC REGAL** 17 3-9-2 A Polli 28/1: 1-320: 14th: Mid-div, btn 3f out: see 1706 & 1208.   11½   **86**
15 Ran   Time 2m 27.68 ()   Owned: Scuderia L3C   Trained: Italy

SAINT-CLOUD   MONDAY 31.05.04   Lefthand, Galloping Track

Official Going GOOD/SOFT.

2143   **2.50 Gr 2 Prix Corrida (Fillies) 4yo+**   ()
£42148 £16268 £7764   **1m2f110y**   **Good/Soft**

4936} **ACTRICE** E Lellouche 4-8-9 O Peslier 54/10: 3141-161: b f Danehill - Ange Bleu (Alleged)   **112**
Rear, hdwy 2f out, led over 1f out, rdn out: List wnr earlier this term: List wnr in '03, subs Gr 3 plcd (rtd
109): eff btwn 9/13f on gd & hvy grnd: smart filly.
4936* **VISORAMA** A Fabre 4-8-11 C Soumillon 18/10 FAV: 43211-52: gr f Linamix - Visor (Mr Prospector)   1½   **111**
Held up, hdwy to chall over 1f out, not pace of wnr: eff at 10.5f on gd/soft. 1 Oct'03 Sain 10.5sft 113- :
1699* **PRIDE** 24 A de Royer Dupre 4-8-11 (80) D Bonilla 54/10: /210-413: Held up, prog to chall dist, no extra.   ½   **110**
1115   **MONTURANI** 51 5-8-9 (104) T Jarnet 24/1: 23422-36: Chsd ldrs, ch dist, sn no extra & fin 6th: 7   5   **101**
wk abs: English chall, capable of better: see 57.

SAINT-CLOUD MONDAY 31.05.04 Lefthand, Galloping Track

1491 **SILENCE IS GOLDEN 29** 5-8-9 (99) M J Kinane 13/1: 2325-129: Trkd ldr, led over 3f out till over   5   94
2f out, wknd & fin 9th: btr 1491& 1111 (h'cap).
10 Ran   Time 2m 13.50()   Owned: Trained:

YARMOUTH WEDNESDAY 02.06.04 Lefthand, Flat, Fair Track

Official Going FIRM.

2144   2.20 European Breeders Fund/Vauxhall Holiday Park Novice Stakes 2yo (D)
           £4784 £1472 £736   6f str   Firm 12   -13 Slow   Stands Side

1687 **WILKO 21** [5] J Noseda 2-8-12   E Ahern   7/2: 301: Keen early, trkd ldrs, qckd to lead ins last,   90
styd on strongly: eff at 5f, now suited by 6f & will get further: poss handles hvy, apprec switch to firm today:
likes an easy trk: showed a decent turn to foot, potentially useful.
1550* **DANCE ANTHEM 29** [3] M G Quinlan 2-9-2   P McCabe   11/4: 12: Held up, hdwy to chall when hung right 1   89
ins last, not pace of wnr: acts on firm & gd grnd: sound run giving wnr 4lbs: see 1550.
1751* **SPEED DIAL HARRY 18** [2] K R Burke 2-8-12 BL G Faulkner 20/1: 52313: Led after 1f, edged left &   2½   78
hdd ins last, no extra: first time blnks: acts on firm, soft & fibresand: up in grade, see 1751 (seller).
1014 **EMERALD PENANG 62** [7] P W Chapple Hyam 2-8-12   S Whitworth   80/1: 54: b g Alzao - Run To Jane nk   77
(Doyoun) Led 1f, remained cl-up, no extra when hmpd ins last: prev with B Millman, has been gelded, 2 month abs:
38,000gns Feb first foal: sire useful at 1m/12f: prob handles firm grnd, type to apprec 7f+.
1205 **SIMPLIFY 47** [6]2-8-12   D Holland   2/1 FAV: 45: Pushed along & handy, short of room & ouptcd when ¾   75
hmpd over 1f out, no impress ins last: nicely bckd, 7 wk abs: see 1205.
1574* **STRIKING ENDEAVOUR 21** [4]2-9-2   S Drowne   9/2: 16: Chsd ldrs, short of room when no impress dist.   2   73
PARSLEYS RETURN [1]2-8-12   W Ryan   33/1: 7: b c Danzero - The Frog Queen (Bin Ajwaad) Dwelt &   16   27
sn outpcd: 9,000gns Feb first foal: dam a 7f juv wnr, sire top-class Australian juv.
7 Ran   Time 1m 11.87 (1.47)   Owned: Mrs Susan Roy   Trained: Newmarket

2145   2.50 Express Cafes Selling Stakes 2yo (G)
           £2541 £726 £363   6f str   Firm 12   -51 Slow   Stands Side

1848 **PART TIME LOVE 14** [1] M R Channon 2-8-11   S Hitchcott(3) 11/10 FAV: 61: Outpcd, hdwy halfway,   63
rdn/led over 1f out, sn hung right but in command, rdn out: nicely bckd, bght in for 20,000gns, slow time: eff at
6f on fast grnd: apprec drop to sell grade: see 1848.
1937 **ZIMBALI 10** [4] J M Bradley 2-8-12   R Ffrench   9/2: 541342: Trkd ldrs, kept on for press, no   2½   55
threat: stays an easy 6f in sell grade: handles firm & gd/soft grnd: see 1325.
2017* **STORY OF ONE 7** [2] N P Littmoden 2-9-3   D Holland   2/1: 2013: Led 4f, no extra dist: op 5/2:   shd   60
prob handles firm grnd but btr 2017 (5f, polytrack).
938   **PETITE ELLE 67** [6] P J McBride 2-8-6 VIS   J Quinn   22/1: 34: Prom, hung left & no impress over 1f ¾   47
out: 2 month abs, first time visor on turf now: bckd: see 938.
2017 **ALICE KING 7** [3]2-8-6   C Haddon(7) 10/1: 44025: Chsd ldrs, wknd dist: btr 2017 (5f, polytrack).   3½   36
5 Ran   Time 1m 14.15 (3.75)   Owned: Mr Graeme Love   Trained: West Ilsley

2146   3.20 Rca/Bhb Sponsorship Day Handicap Stakes 4yo+ 35-55 (F)   [63]
           £3507 £1002 £501   1m2f21y   Firm 12   -23 Slow   Inside

1940 **KERNEL DOWERY 10** [3] P W Harris 4-9-5 e (54) D Holland   11/4 FAV: 043-0021: Handy, led 3f out, rdn   61
out to hold on: stays 10f on firm, fast & polytrack: apprec recent fitting of eye-shield: first win: see 1490.
1966 **TINIAN 9** [13] K R Burke 6-9-1 (50) G Faulkner 25/1: 4045432: Rear, prog halfway, ev ch bef 1f   ½   55
out, just held by wnr: eff at 7f/1m, now stays 10f: acts on firm, soft grnd & fibresand: has drpd down
the weights & can find similar: see 1966 & 417.
1940 **BURGUNDY 10** [14] P Mitchell 7-9-6 bl (55) O Urbina 14/1: 3420003: Rear, prog 2f out, kept on well   shd   60
despite hanging left ins fnl 1f, not btn far: gd eff here & is back on a winning mark: see 903.
1695 **SAMMYS SHUFFLE 21** [11] Jamie Poulton 9-8-12 bl (47) P Doe 50/1: 5-040004: Mid-div, prog 2f out,   3½   47
onepcd from dist: btr 718.
1778 **ZALKANI 18** [8]4-9-2 (51) V Slattery 20/1: 0-330005: Slow away, prog after 1m, nrst fin: btr 476.   1¼   49
4859*)**ROJABAA 223** [5]9-9-4 (53) L Treadwell(7) 8/1: 453411-6: b g Anabaa - Slava (Diesis) Rear, prog   nk   50
3f out, onepcd fnl 1f: op 12/1: unplcd over hdles in 03/04 (rtd 71h, sell, tried blnks & t-strap): won 2 sell
h'caps at backend of '03: eff at 10/11.5f on firm & gd, enjoys sell grade: tried cheek pieces.
1 Oct'03 Brig 9.9fm 52-43 G: 1 Oct'03 Yarm 11.5gd 50-37 G: 2 Apr'03 Bath 10.2g/f 40-(39) G:
1828 **URSA MAJOR 15** [1]10-9-1 (50) S Drowne   14/1: 30000/-07: b g Warning - Double Entendre (Dominion) ¾   46
Cl-up, no extra bef 1f out: missed '03: AW h'cap wnr in early '02 (C N Allen): won 4 h'caps in '00: suited by
10/12f on firm, soft & both AWs, loves Lingfield: enjoys a strong pace, best without blnks.
1 Jan'02 Ling 12ap 84a-75 C: 2 Dec'01 Ling 10ap 74a-72 G: 1 Dec'00 Ling 12ap 81a-75 C:
1940 **FIGURA 10** [4]6-9-0 (49) P Robinson   8/1: 5666508: Nvr nrr than mid-div: see 520.   1   44
1940* **OUR DESTINY 10** [10]6-9-8 (6ex) (57) S Hitchcott(3) 6/1: 3124319: Handy over 7f, sn wknd: btr   ¾   51
expected after finishing in front of today's wnr in 1940.
1940 **FANTASY CRUSADER 10** [6]5-8-12 p (47) J Quinn 5/1: 000-0330: 10th: Cl-up when short of room after   1¾   39
7f, sn wknd: rider reported mount slipped on bend: btr 1940 & 1695.
1960 **Dens Joy 9** [16]8-9-1 (50) L Keniry(3) 18/1:0
1940 **Fife And Drum 10** [15]7-8-13 p(48) B Reilly(3) 28/1:0
1618 **Acola 26** [12]4-9-5 P(54) W Ryan 50/1:0   1940 **Mrs Cube 10** [9]5-8-10 (45) S Whitworth 28/1:0
1342 **French Risk 39** [7]4-8-10 (45) S W Kelly 25/1:0
3365} **Stars At Midnight 303** [2]4-9-0 (49) R Ffrench 50/1:0
16 Ran   Time 2m 07.65 (3.45)   Owned: The Treasure Hunters   Trained: Berkhamsted

---

2147 3.50 Pkf Accountancy Services Handicap Stakes 3yo+ 0-70 (E) [67]
£3790 £1166 £583 1m3f101y Firm 12 -29 Slow Inside

997 **DUCS DREAM 63** [3] D Morris 6-9-0 (53) J Mackay 4/1: 3000-001: b g Bay Tern - Kala's Image (Kala 59
Shikari) Cl-up, styd on well to lead cl-home, rdn out: 9 wk abs: h'cap wnr in '03 (also plcd 7 times): won 3
times in '02 (2 h'caps & clmr): eff at 10/14f on firm & soft grnd, loves Southwell & fibresand: has tried visor:
goes well fresh & likes Yarmouth: made full use of drop back to winning mark. 1 Sep'03 Yarm 11.5g/f 61-55 D:
2 Jul'03 Epso 12.0gd 55-54 E: 2 Jul'03 Epso 12.0gd 55-52 E: 2 Jun'03 Sout 12af 60a-60 E:
1 Dec'02 Sout 11af 68a- F: 1 Mar'02 Sout 11af 74a-67 E: 2 Feb'02 Sout 12af 65a- E: 1 Feb'02 Sout 11af 69a-63 E:
1828 **PIRI PIRI 15** [9] P J McBride 4-9-12 (65) S Whitworth 7/1: 13660-62: b f Priolo - Hot Curry hd 70
(Sharpen Up) Keen rear, prog 4f out, styd on to lead dist, hdd under press cl-home: h'cap wnr in '03: eff at 9/10f,
now stays 11.5f: acts on firm & fast grnd: only just denied under top-weight & can find similar.
1 Aug'03 Folk 9.7g/f 71-67 D:
1725 **FORT CHURCHILL 19** [8] M H Tompkins 3-9-2 (69) P Robinson 7/1: 00-53: b g Barathea - Brisighella 1¼ 72
(Al Hareb) Led 1f, led again 1m out, hdd dist, no extra ins fnl 1f: op 9/2: unplcd both '03 starts (rtd 57, mdn):
eff at 11.5f on firm grnd: has been gelded since last term: decent eff on h'cap bow against older horses.
1875 **MERRYMAKER 13** [6] W M Brisbourne 4-9-2 (55) S W Kelly 6/1: 3433-464: Rear, styd on fnl 1f. 1¼ 56
1956 **DAMI 9** [5]3-9-1 (68) D Holland 100/30 FAV: 4400-55: Mid-div, outpcd after 1m, rallied fnl 1f: 1½ 67
rider reported mount ran in snatches: btr 1956 (1m).
1990 **QUEST ON AIR 8** [10]5-8-5 (44) D Corby(2) 10/1: 2103-206: Handy 9f, sn wknd: btr 1243. 5 36
1713* **JOINT DESTINY 20** [1]3-7-13 (52) J Quinn 12/1: 40-50217: Nvr nrr than mid-div: btr 1713 (10f). 3 40
1991 **RIVER OF FIRE 8** [2]6-7-12 (7oh)vis (30) C Haddon(7) 25/1: 60-03048: Led briefly after 2f, fdd 3f out. 1½ 23
1776 **MIDSHIPMAN 18** [7]6-9-7 vis T (60) W Ryan 28/1: 0000309: Led early, in tch, ev ch dist, sn fdd: hd 45
1st time t-strap: btr 1430 (soft).
1502 **GRAND WIZARD 31** [4]4-10-0 T (67) M Tebbutt 9/1: 001-400: 10th: Mid-div, wknd fnl 2f: t-strap. 2½ 48
10 Ran Time 2m 27.55 (4.75) Owned: Mrs S I Parry Trained: Newmarket

---

2148 4.20 Racing Ahead Magazine Maiden Stakes 3yo+ (D)
£3413 £1050 £525 7f str Firm 12 +11 Fast Stands Side

1080 **ROYAL PRINCE 56** [9] J R Fanshawe 3-8-11 (77) D Holland 8/11 FAV: 34-41: Handy, styd on to lead 83+
dist, pushed clr, val 4L+: 8 wk abs, fast time: eff at 7f, 1m shld suit: acts on firm grnd, handles gd/soft &
polytrack: goes well fresh: improving performer & can make presence felt in h'cap grade: see 1080.
MR MISTRAL [2] G Wragg 5-9-7 S Drowne 20/1: 2: b g Zilzal - Miss Sancerre (Last Tycoon) Rear, 2½ 76
prog 2f out, kept on well under hands-&-heels, nrst fin: debut: eff at 7f on firm grnd, 1m+ is sure to suit:
encouraging debut & shld find similar.
4882} **RIVER NUREY 221** [10] B W Hills 3-8-11 (72) P Robinson 9/2: 60052-3: gr c Fasliyev - Dundel shd 76$
(Machiavellian) Cl-up, onepcd dist: tchd 6/1 on reapp: rnr-up on fnl '03 start (h'cap): eff at 6/7f on firm &
fast grnd: will apprec rtn to h'cap grade. 2 Oct'03 Donc 7g/f 73-66 C:
KABEER [4] P S McEntee 6-9-7 D R McCabe 66/1: 4: ch g Unfuwain - Ta Rib (Mr Prospector) Led, hd 75
hdd dist, sn no extra: clr rem: 7 wk jmps abs, rnr-up sole 02/03 bmpr start (stays 2m on fast, J Poulton): eff at
7f, shld stay further: acts on firm grnd.
1924 **STANLEY CRANE 11** [11]3-8-11 (75) S W Kelly 10/1: 435-05: Handy 5f, sn no extra: see 1924. 6 63
CRONKYVODDY [1]3-8-11 T J Quinn 66/1: 6: Slow away, prog ins fnl 2f, nrst fin: debut. hd 62
4147} **ICE DRAGON 267** [3]3-8-6 M Henry 14/1: 62-7: In tch fdd 2f out, wknd: reapp. 2½ 52
3 **KING OF MUSIC 205** [14]3-8-11 (72) O Urbina 28/1: 350-8: Nvr nrr than mid-div on reapp. ¾ 55
23 **ARRAN 202** [6]4-9-7 G Carter 100/1: U000-9: Slow away, al bhd on reapp. hd 54
215 **BOOGIE MAGIC 168** [7]4-9-2 (68) B Reilly(3) 66/1: 00400-0: 10th: Handy over halfway, wknd. ½ 48
WHITE SAIL [13]3-8-6 W Ryan 8/1: 0: 11th: Al bhd on debut. 3 42
2104 **OTAGO 2** [5]3-8-11 N Pollard 25/1: 30: 12th: Mid-div 4f, sn fdd. 1½ 44
1829 **FLYING WITH EAGLES 15** [8]3-8-11 C Haddon(7) 100/1: 000: 13th: Al bhd. 5 34
3166} **ABSOLUTELY FAB 312** [12]3-8-6 (35) Hayley Turner(5) 100/1: 00000-0: 14th: Mid-div 4f, sn fdd. shd 29
14 Ran Time 1m 22.65 (0.05) Owned: Mr Abdulla BuHaleeba Trained: Newmarket

---

2149 4.50 Grays Dry Lining Handicap Stakes 3yo+ 35-55 (F) [55]
£3542 £1012 £506 1m str Firm 12 +01 Fast Stands Side

1013 **PRIME OFFER 63** [11] J Jay 8-9-12 (53) O Urbina 16/1: 530-0241: Made all, pushed out fnl 1f, val 65+
4L+: 9 wk abs: suited by 7f/1m on firm, fast grnd & both AWs: made gd use of drop back to fav'able turf mark.
982 **BRILLIANTRIO 64** [12] M C Chapman 6-9-10 (51) L Vickers 40/1: 406U362: Rear, prog 4f out, kept on 3 56
but no with wnr fnl 1f: 9 wk abs: on fair mark: see 847 & 303.
1954 **POPPYLINE 9** [16] W R Muir 4-9-12 (53) S Drowne 20/1: 440-00U3: Rear, prog 3f out, kept on fnl 2f. 1¼ 55
2032 **LORD CHAMBERLAIN 6** [14] J M Bradley 11-9-12 bl (53) C J Davies(7) 9/1: 4022034: Slow away, prog 1¼ 52
after 5f, kept on fnl 1f: qck reapp: 11yo, just btr 2032.
1132 **MISS PEACHES 51** [7]6-9-5 (46) P Robinson 14/1: 0135465: Cl-up 2f, sn outpcd, rallied ins fnl 1f. nk 44
1750 **DESERT FURY 18** [2]7-9-3 (44) R Ffrench 10/1: 5000-006: Mid-div, prog after 5f, onepcd fnl 1f. ½ 41
1463 **BALERNO 33** [6]5-9-10 (51) G Carter 13/2 FAV: 4505237: Mid-div, prog halfway, no impress dist. ½ 47
1618 **MY LILLI 26** [10]4-9-8 (49) J Mackay 7/1: 4064138: Handy 6f, sn no extra: btr 1045 (polytrack). shd 45
1535 **KINDNESS 29** [17]4-9-9 (50) S Whitworth 50/1: 6003-609: Nvr nrr than mid-div: btr 1045. 1 44
1777 **NO CHANCE TO DANCE 18** [8]4-9-9 T (50) N Pollard 66/1: 050-00: 10th: b g Revoque - Song of The nk 43
Glens (Horage) Slow away, modest late gains: unplcd all '03 starts (rtd 63, mdn): with H J Collingridge.
1635 **CLASSIC VISION 25** [20]4-9-12 P (53) D Holland 9/1: 3-100450: 11th: Handy 6f, sn wknd: pieces. ¾ 45
2032 **ZIET DALSACE 6** [3]4-9-11 (52) W Ryan 14/1: 054-0200: 12th: Handy 6f: qck reapp: btr 1938. 1¼ 41
1660 **SABALARA 23** [15]4-10-0 e (55) S Carson 25/1: 620-0000: 13th: Cl-up, fdd fnl 2f: eye-shield. 3 38
1282 **BALLARE 43** [19]5-9-6 (47) T Williams 8/1: 3461040: 14th: Al in rear: 6 wk abs: btr 1282. 3 24
1606 **HALCYON MAGIC 26** [5]6-9-9 bl (50) Laura Pike(7) 16/1: 5060-200: 15th: Mid-div 5f: btr 1267. 1¼ 24
1045 **TITIAN LASS 60** [1]5-9-7 bl (48) L Keniry(3) 16/1: 0-415250: 16th: Al rear: btr 1012 (polytrk). 1 20
1511 **RUBAIYAT 30** [4]3-9-3 (55) J Quinn 40/1: 06-00: 17th: Cl-up, wknd ins fnl 2f. ¾ 26
1992 **TAIYO 8** [9]4-9-4 (45) S W Kelly 50/1: 54400P0: 18th: Prom 6f, sn wknd: btr 561. 4 8
1992 **PEARTREE HOUSE 8** [13]10-9-4 (45) G Faulkner 25/1: 0006660: 19th: Handy 6f, fdd. ½ 7

YARMOUTH WEDNESDAY 02.06.04 Lefthand, Flat, Fair Track

1778 **COODEN BEACH 18** [18]4-9-5 (46) Hayley Turner(5) 9/1: 32-04440: 20th: Al rear: btr 1778 & 1073. **6** **0**
20 Ran Time 1m 35.95 (0.85) Owned: Miss K A Bartlett Trained: Newmarket

---

2150 5.20 Racing Welfare 'arthur Taylor' Lifetime Amateur Riders' Handicap Stakes 3yo+ 0-70 (F) **[45]**
£3332 £952 £476 7f str Firm 12 -24 Slow Stands Side

1820 **CASHNEEM 15** [5] W M Brisbourne 6-10-13 (58) Mr C Davies(7) 3/1 CO FAV: 4100-461: Sn in tch, styd **64**
on to lead dist, rdn out: eff at 6f/1m on firm & hvy grnd: see 1537.
1941 **LONDONER 10** [9] S Dow 6-10-8 (53) Mr D Hutchison(5) 3/1 CO FAV: 0000322: Handy, styd on ins fnl ¾ **57**
2f, not btn far: remains in gd form: see 1013.
1824 **TUSCAN FLYER 15** [8] R Bastiman 6-11-3 (62) Miss R Bastiman(5) 16/1: 0142-003: Trkd ldrs, ev ch ½ **65**
dist, onepcd ins fnl 1f: stays 7f, all wins have come around 5f: see 1600.
2093 **BINT ROYAL 3** [3] Miss V Haigh 6-10-13 p (58) Miss V Haigh(5) 3/1 CO FAV: 10-55034: Mid-div, prog shd **61**
after halfway, ev ch dist, sn onepcd: well bckd on qck reapp: see 2093.
1535 **HORIZONTAL 29** [6]4-10-10 T (55) Mr R H Fowler 10/1: 56-56005: Cl-up 3f, sn outpcd, mod late gains. 1¼ **55**
1267 **FEAST OF ROMANCE 43** [7]7-10-2 bl (47) Miss A Pacault 16/1: 2150306: Led till dist: 6 wk abs. ½ **46**
1778 **DEXILEOS 18** [4]5-10-2 t (47) Mrs S Bosley 33/1: 00-00007: Al bhd: see 1273. 4 **38**
1072 **PRINCE DU SOLEIL 57** [10]8-9-4 (35) Mr N Soares(7) 33/1: 000-6608: Rear, nvr a factor: see 1072. 2 **22**
1625* **SOMERSET WEST 25** [1]4-11-7 (66) Miss J Ferguson(5) 5/1: 1-600119: Cl-up, ev ch 2f out, sn fdd: 1 **51**
below form on hat-trick bid & 1074 (polytrack).
9 Ran Time 1m 25.11(2.51) Owned: Law Abiding Citizens Trained: Nesscliffe

---

NOTTINGHAM WEDNESDAY 02.06.04 Lefthand, Galloping Track

Official Going Good/Firm

2151 2.10 European Breeders Fund Maiden Stakes Fillies 2yo (D)
£5005 £1540 £770 5f str Good/Firm Fair Stands Side

GLOVED HAND 0 [11] J G Given 2-8-11 K Fallon 20/1: 1: b f Royal Applause - Fudge (Polar Falcon) **90+**
Sn prom, rdn & edged left over 1f out, led ins last, just prevailed cl-home: fair juv time: op 16/1: Mar foal,
half-sister to a plcd 10f 3yo, dam unrcd: acts at 5f, will stay further: goes well
fresh: useful debut, can rate higher & win better races.
1608 **CASTELLETTO 26** [2] B A McMahon 2-8-11 G Gibbons 16/1: 32: Handy & led 2f out, rdn & hdd ins hd **89**
last, kept on well, just held: left soft grnd debut bhd: eff at 5f on fast: well clr of rem, useful, win sn.
1764 **COLONIAL GIRL 18** [8] T D Easterby 2-8-11 W Supple 9/1: 43: Pushed along chasing ldrs, outpcd by 7 **71**
front pair over 1f out: op 8/1: looks in need of 1st run.
1808 **SPEED OF SOUND 16** [4] A M Balding 2-8-11 M Hills 9/4 FAV: 334: Led till 2f out, no extra from dist. ¾ **69**
DUBAI ESCAPADE 0 [1]2-8-11 L Dettori 11/4: 5: b f Awesome Again - Sassy Pants (Saratoga Six) 1½ **64**
Sn prom, no extra over 1f out: bckd tho' op 9/4: May foal, half-sister to a smart US Gr 1 wnr, dam a US stks wnr.*
NELLA FANTASIA 0 [10]2-8-11 S Sanders 12/1: 6: ch f Giant's Causeway - Paper Moon (Lake ½ **62**
Coniston) Chsd ldrs, outpcd fnl 2f: £55,000 Mar fillies foal, dam a 1m 3yo wnr: will need further & can improve.
1805 **LIMONIA 16** [5]2-8-11 M Howard(7) 16/1: 567: Keen chasing ldrs, outpcd from halfway, op 10/1. 1¼ **58**
ENCOURAGEMENT 0 [6]2-8-11 R Hughes 13/2: 8: Dwelt, al outpcd towards rear, op 11/2, 'lost action'. 5 **43**
GREAT OPINIONS 0 [9]2-8-11 J Murtagh 12/1: 9: Slow away, nvr a factor in rear, op 10/1. 1¼ **39**
FRANTIC 0 [7]2-8-11 T Quinn 40/1: 0: 10th: Slow away & al bhd. 1½ **34**
BEECHES THEATRE 0 [3]2-8-11 J F Egan 100/1: 0: 11th: Dwelt & sn struggling. 7 **13**
11 Ran Time 1m 0.51 (2.01) Owned: Mrs M V Chaworth-Musters Trained: Gainsborough

---

2152 2.40 Hblb Median Auction Maiden Stakes 3-5yo (E)
£3604 £1109 £555 5f str Good/Firm Slow Stands Side

1963 **RED LEICESTER 9** [1] J A Glover 4-9-2 vis (48) Dean McKeown 9/1: 000-3051: Made all racing alone **59**
far side, drvn out: eff at 5/6f on fast & gd/soft: improved for an intelligent ride: see 1522.
1787 **LACONIA 16** [3] J S Moore 3-8-9 (72) Derek Nolan(7) 11/4 FAV: 4526262: Al prom, led stands side 2f 1¼ **54**
out, edged left ins last, not pace of wnr far side: nicely bckd: handles fast, gd/soft & polytrack: see 802.
1787 **DANCE TO THE BLUES 16** [7] B De Haan 3-8-9 P Dobbs 8/1: 03: Prom, onepace fnl 2f, not pace of 1 **51**
front pair: imprvd from debut: eff at 5f, 6f shld suit: acts on fast grnd: also bhd rnr-up in 1787.
1465 **LADY JUSTICE 33** [4] W Jarvis 4-9-2 (65) K Fallon 13/2: 06/50-04: b f Compton Place - Zinzi nk **50**
(Song) In tch, kept on fnl 2f, no threat: lightly rcd & unplcd '03 (rtd 66): unplcd '02 (lightly rcd, rtd 69):
eff at 5f, rtn to 6f could suit: acts on fast grnd & a gall trk.
481 **DANE RHAPSODY 128** [9]3-8-9 S Sanders 40/1: 05: b f Danetime - Hil Rhapsody (Anshan) Held up, 1¾ **45**
kept on late, not able to chall: 4 month abs: turf bow: no form prev: eff at 5f, shapes as 6f will suit: handles fast.
1639 **INTAVAC BOY 25** [13]3-9-0 J Murtagh 9/2: 66: Dwelt & outpcd, nrst fin: bckd, op 6/1: needs 6f+. 1 **47**
1948 **LAW MAKER 9** [8]4-9-7 vis (40) J Bramhill 8/1: 0604237: Led stands 3f, sn no extra. 1 **44**
1876 **PARLIAMENT ACT 13** [11]3-9-0 t G Gibbons 33/1: 08: Prom till over 1f out, gelded. nk **43**
4547} **THEMESOFGREEN 245** [12]3-9-0 I Harman(7) 20/1: 0-9: Dwelt, nvr on terms, saddle slipped, reapp. ½ **41**
665 **RADMORE SPIRIT 106** [14]4-9-2 J F Egan 100/1: 00: 10th: Outpcd & nvr on terms, new yard, abs. ½ **34**
1497 **CEDRIC COVERWELL 31** [15]4-9-7 (51) M Howard(7) 20/1: 4000: 11th: Hung left, in tchl till over 1f out. ½ **37**
1787 **Arians Lad 16** [10]3-9-0 D Sweeney 14/1:0 1787 **Weirs Annie 16** [6]3-8-9 Dane O'Neill 14/1:0
1876 **Barholm Charlie 13** [2]3-9-0 J Fanning 100/1:0 1575 **Sapphire Sky 27** [5]3-8-9 R Miles(3) 50/1:0
15 Ran Time 1m 02.07 (3.57) Owned: Mr Philip A Jarvis Trained: Worksop

2153   3.10 Cliff Smith 70th Birthday Celebration Handicap Stakes Fillies 3yo 0-80 (D)   [86]
£5980 £1840 £920   1m54y rnd   Good/Firm   Slow   Inside

1904* **OUR JAFFA 12** [3] D J Daly 3-9-5 (77) J Murtagh 4/1: 411: Mid-div, smooth hdwy 3f out & rdn/led   85
2f out, drvn & asserted ins last, nicely bckd on h'cap bow: stays 10f, suited by 1m last twice: acts on firm & gd:
lightly rcd & progressive: see 1904.

1651 **PELLA 23** [7] M Blanshard 3-8-0 (58) F Norton 50/1: 0062: ch f Hector Protector - Norpella   1   64
(Northfields) Dwelt, bhd, strong run wide for press from over 1f out, nrst fin: unplcd in mdns at up to 11f prev
this term: op 12/1, rtn to further will suit: handles fast: encouraging, shld find a race.

1774 **MARINAITE 18** [8] S R Bowring 3-9-1 (73) J Bramhill 25/1: 2152203: Led, rdn & hdd 2f out, no   1¼   76
extra ins last: enjoyed forcing tactics over this longer 1m trip: eff btwn 6f/1m on fibresand, fast & gd/soft grnd.

1769 **CATHERINE HOWARD 18** [11] M R Channon 3-8-13 (71) K Fallon 9/1: 1-404: Mid-div, styd on onepace   nk   73
for press: op 12/1: stays 1m: see 1176.

1628* **CHARMATIC 25** [5]3-8-7 (65) Dean McKeown 5/1: 00-52215: Trkd ldrs, short of room over 2f out,   nk   66
onepace for press dist: handles fast grnd but just btr 1628 (well drawn, soft).

1647 **SUSIEDIL 23** [6]3-8-2 (60) R Miles(3) 20/1: 0140-006: b f Mujadil - Don't Take Me (Don't Forget   5   51
Me) Bhd, hdwy when hung left over 1f out, sn no prog: '03 auct mdn scorer (h'cap unplcd, rtd 68): eff over a
sharp/undul 7f, 1m shld suit: acts on fast grnd. 1 Sep'03 Brig 7.0g/f 66- E:

1729 **SPEEDBIRD 19** [12]3-9-0 (72) J F Egan 11/2: 20-027: In tch, btn over 1f out: reportedly did not stride out.   3   57

1496 **MAGICAL MIMI 31** [4]3-9-0 (72) Leanne Kershaw(7) 66/1: 5130-008: b f Magic Ring - Naval Dispatch   2   53
(Slip Anchor) Mid-div at best: '03 fill mdn scorer for N Littmoden, subs val auct event plcd: suited by 6f & 1m +
may yet suit: acts on fast grnd, stiff/gall trk. 1 Sep'03 Nott 6.1g/f 80- D:

1927 **CITRINE SPIRIT 11** [14]3-9-2 (74) L Dettori 3/1 FAV: 0-6139: Cl-up from wide stall, fdd fnl 2f: ½   54
bckd tho' op 9/4: forcing tactics not suited to this wide stall but joc reported fill unsuited by the grnd.

1879 **SKY GALAXY 13** [15]3-9-7 (79) W Supple 50/1: 15000-00: 10th: Held up, eff 3f out, no impression.   ¾   58

1761 **COCONUT COOKIE 18** [13]3-8-11 (69) P Dobbs 50/1: 200-00: 11th: Al bhd, longer trip.   1   46

1924 **BAILEYS DANCER 11** [1]3-9-6 (78) J Fanning 8/1: 140-0400: 12th: Trkd ldrs till 2f out: btr 1741.   shd   55

1761 Abington Angel 18 [9]3-9-3 (75) M Hills 50/1:0   1647 Molinia 23 [10]3-8-4 (62) J F McDonald(3) 66/1:P
14 Ran   Time 1m 45.34 (5.94)   Owned: Miss A H Marshall   Trained: Newmarket

2154   3.40 Illuma - The Dawn Of A New Era Conditions Stakes 3yo+   (C)
£12296 £4664 £2332   1m54y rnd   Good/Firm   Slow   Inside

1512* **SHOT TO FAME 30** [5] P W Harris 5-9-1 (101) J Murtagh 15/8: 300-5011: Made all, drvn out: nicely   108
bckd: eff at 1m on fm & hvy: improved last twice for forcing tactics & well rdn here: useful.

1649 **ANCIENT WORLD 23** [1] Saeed bin Suroor 4-9-7 (100) L Dettori 4/6 FAV: 4411-22: Chsd wnr, rdn &   1½   110
styd on fnl 2f, al just held: well bckd at odds on: acts on fast & soft: useful & improving.

1811 **MAGHANIM 15** [2] J L Dunlop 4-9-1 (98) R Hills 8/1: 210/0-53: Keen & prom, onepace for press fnl   nk   103
2f: stays 1m, poss just best at 7f: see 1811.

1596 **NARRATIVE 24** [4] D R Loder 6-9-1 (106) K Fallon 20/1: 5/4300-04: b c Sadler's Wells - Barger   hd   102
(Riverman) Keen, in tch, rdn 3f out, late gains: Gr 1 plcd in '03 (rtd 111): Gr 2 wnr '02: rnr-up: best efforts at
14f, acts on fast, soft & dirt: been without a t-strap: v headstrong & a hard puller prev but settled well for drop
in trip & strong handling today, could improve on this over further.
2 Jun'02 San 12fm 116- : 1 May'02 Capa 14g/f 116- :

178 **SOPHRANO 175** [6]4-9-1 (63) S Yourston(7) 150/1: 600620-5: Al bhd, t.o. from halfway: new yard: see 96.   21   60

1988 **JALOUHAR 8** [3]4-9-4 (47) N Callan 250/1: 5050206: Sn bhd, t.o.: outclassed: see 1368 (6f).   20   23

6 Ran   Time 1m 44.10 (4.7)   Owned: The Conquistadors   Trained: Berkhamsted

2155   4.10 Byron Handicap Stakes 3yo 0-85 (D)   [90]
£5801 £1785 £893   6f str   Good/Firm   Slow   Stands Side

1901 **CORPS DE BALLET 12** [11] J L Dunlop 3-9-7 (83) S Sanders 33/1: 5431-01: Made all stands side,   90
drvn out: eff at 5f: suited by 6f: acts on fm & gd/soft: enjoyed switch to forcing tactics: see 1901.

1621 **PRESTO SHINKO 25** [4] R Hannon 3-9-1 (77) R Hughes 6/1: 033-1632: Sn clr on far side, rdn & styd   ¾   82+
on fnl 2f, not pace of wnr stands side cl-home: fine front-running eff & beat rem far side decisively, can win soon.

1766 **LUALUA 18** [10] T D Barron 3-9-1 (77) K Fallon 4/1: 105-423: Trkd wnr stands side, drvn & ch over   ¾   79
1f out, no extra nr fin: stays a gall 6f: see 1766 & 1488.

1665 **BRIGHT SUN 22** [1] N Tinkler 3-9-2 (78) Kim Tinkler 11/1: 100-0004: b c Desert Sun - Kealbra Lady   2   75
(Petong) Chsd ldr far side, al held: C/D auct mdn scorer for W Jarvis in '03: eff at 6f on firm & gd/soft.
1 Aug'03 Nott 6.1g/f 89- E: 2 Aug'03 Newm 6g/s 89- D:

1879 **KINGSMAITE 13** [5]3-8-4 (66) J Bramhill 40/1: 212-0405: Chsd ldr far side, no impress bef dist: ½   61
imprvd eff drpd in trip: see 226 & 184 (fibresand).

1734 **PRIMO WAY 19** [2]3-9-5 (81) M Hills 13/8 FAV: 435-136: Chsd ldrs far side till halfway, sn lost   2½   68
pl but mod late rally: hvly bckd, op 2/1: btr 1734 & 1281.

1734 **JIMMY RYAN 19** [3]3-9-7 (83) J P Guillambert(3) 13/2: 314-07: Held up far side, nvr on terms: see 1734.   5   55

1745 **LOUISIADE 19** [7]3-8-5 (67) W Supple 9/1: 0000-038: Far side, btn over 1f out: btr 1745.   1¾   34

2048 **GET TO THE POINT 5** [8]3-8-10 (72) J Murtagh 14/1: 0-022509: Sn outpcd far side: btr 1690.   ¾   37

1901 **SHIELALIGH 12** [6]3-9-1 t (77) L Dettori 12/1: 243-0030: 10th: Hld up far side, no impress fnl 2f: btr 1901.   2½   34

1881 **ORPENBERRY 12** [9]3-8-6 (68) J Edmunds 66/1: 3100-00: 11th: b f Orpen - Forest Berries   7   4
(Thatching) Sn outpcd stands side: lightly rcd '03 (auct mdn scorer for K Burke): winning form over a sharp 5f:
acts on firm & gd grnd. 1 Jul'03 Muss 5gd 73- E:

11 Ran   Time 1m 13.97 (3.17)   Owned: Mrs P G M Jamison   Trained: Arundel

2156	4.40 Watson Fothergill Handicap Stakes 3yo+ 0-70 (E)				[69]

£3751 £1154 £577   **1m6f15y**   Good/Firm   Slow   Inside

2060* **MY LEGAL EAGLE** 5 [12] R J Price 10-8-4 (45) R Miles(3) 3/1 FAV: 0//5-14211: Held up, styd on for   **54**
press to lead dist, sn asserted: nicely bckd: qck reapp: eff at 14f/2m on fast, hvy & both AWs: tough 10yo.
1772 **CROSSWAYS** 18 [11] P D Evans 6-10-0 (69) R Havlin 9/1: 34-41042: In tch, hdwy to lead 3f out till   1¾ **75**
dist, no extra: well clr of rem: gd run under top-weight: see 1772 & 762.
1899 **SAXE COBURG** 12 [13] G A Ham 7-9-7 (62) S Sanders 16/1: 40-51033: Held up, styd on onepace fnl   7 **59**
2f: no threat to front pair: longer trip: acts on firm, soft & both AWs: see 1899 & 1541.
1542 **SNINFIA** 29 [14] G A Ham 4-9-0 (55) A Daly 40/1: 200-0004: Bhd, rdn & kept on onepace fnl 3f, no threat. nk **51**
1543 **PURDEY** 29 [4]4-8-4 (45) D Kinsella 20/1: 6004-05: Bhd, kept on late, nrst fin, reportedly lost a shoe.   1½ **39**
1830 **FIGHT THE FEELING** 15 [16]6-8-6 (47) G Gibbons 25/1: 2200506: In tch, no impress fnl 2f: btr 937 (AW).   1½ **39**
1402 **LUNAR LORD** 36 [15]8-8-12 (53) R Price 25/1: 100/5-007: Held up, eff 3f out, only mod prog: see 924.   ½ **44**
1543* **ONLY FOR SUE** 29 [7]5-9-5 bl (60) N Callan 10/1: 61-00318: Keen & prom till 2f out: btr 1543 (11f, soft). 1½ **49**
1960 **COOL BATHWICK** 9 [3]5-8-6 bl (47) F Norton 33/1: 2600009: Mid-div, no impress fnl 2f: see 380 & 359.   nk **35**
1654 **CALIBAN** 23 [17]6-8-5 (46) R Fitzpatrick 20/1: 14550-00: 10th: Mid-div, brief eff 3f out, sn btn: 'lost action'. ½ **33**
1928 **MADIBA** 11 [2]5-9-5 (60) K Fallon 5/1: 2202200: 11th: Held up, short of room over 1f out when no impress.5 **40**
1772 **SONOMA** 18 [8]4-9-11 (66) M Hills 12/1: 25-50600: 12th: Led till 3f out, sn btn: btr 1232.   3 **42**
1923 **VANBRUGH** 11 [5]4-8-10 vis t (51) P Dobbs 40/1: 1060000: 13th: In tch, btn 4f out: prefers fibresand.   ¾ **26**
1753* **HERNE BAY** 18 [1]4-9-7 (62) Derek Nolan(7) 12/1: 00140-10: 14th: Held up, hmpd after 3f, sn bhd.   3½ **32**
1980 **DISTANT COUSIN** 8 [18]7-9-6 vis (61) J Bramhill 12/1: 256-0530: 15th: Keen, led 7f out till 3f out, wknd.   4 **25**
1637 **ETCHING** 25 [10]4-9-5 (60) J Murtagh 9/2: 2210-100: 16th: Led early, remained prom till wknd 2f out.   ½ **23**
1830 **ST JEROME** 15 [9]4-9-0 (55) J P Guillambert(3) 33/1: 0105-000: 17th: ch g Danzig Connection -   dist **0**
Indigo Dawn (Rainbow Quest) Bhd, on ch halfway, lost action: lightly rcd '03, auct mdn scorer: unplcd '02 (td 60,
mdn): eff over a sharp 14f, tried 2m: acts on firm grnd. 1 Jul'03 Catt 13.8fm 60-(51) E:
17 Ran   Time 3m 06.61 (8.31)   Owned: Mr E G Bevan   Trained: Hereford

2157	5.10 Teletext Racing 'hands And Heels' Apprentice Handicap Stakes 3yo+ 0-75 (F)				[75]

£3087 £882 £441   **1m2f**   Good/Firm   V Slow   Inside

1792 **REALISM** 16 [8] P W Hiatt 4-8-13 (60) Steven Harrison 14/1: 1050361: Mid-div, hdwy under hand   **67**
riding to lead ins last, narrowly asserted cl-home: eff at 1m/10f on fibresand & fast grnd: goes well for an appr.
1828 **SAY WHAT YOU SEE** 15 [7] J W Hills 4-9-10 (71) H Gemberlu(3) 11/4: 0421542: Trkd ldr, led over 1f   nk **77**
out till ins last: kept on: bckd: poss best when able to dominate: see 900 (made all).
679 **FIRST MAITE** 104 [6] S R Bowring 11-8-3 (50) M Nem(5) 16/1: 02-66643: Held up, styd on onepace.   4 **50**
2024 **CARTRONAGEERAGHLAD** 7 [1] J A Osborne 3-8-12 (72) K May 3/1: 0-000024: Rear, late prog.   ¾ **71**
1215} **ASWAN** 403 [5]6-9-3 (64) A Reilly 25/1: 503440-5: ch g Ashkalani - Ghariba (Final Straw) Led   ¾ **62**
till over 1f out: wknd: long abs: h'cap plcd '03 (rtd 66, disapp in a t-strap, AW unplcd, rtd 67a, h'cap, T J
Etherington): dual AW h'cap rnr up '03: eff btwn 7/10f on firm, fast & polytrack, prob any trk: best without blnks.
2 Dec'02 Ling 8ap 67a-67 E: 2 Nov'02 Ling 7ap 65a-65 E: 1 Sep'01 Kemp 8g/f 85-79 D: 1 Aug'01 Newc 8g/f 83- D:
1235 **KYLKENNY** 46 [9]4-9-10-0 t (75) R J Killoran(5) 8/1: 004-3006: Prom till lost pl 2f out: op 6/1, abs.   nk **72**
1777 **PERFECT PUNCH** 18 [2]5-9-6 (67) S O'Hara(3) 7/4 FAV: 02540-27: Prom, outpcd fnl 3f: op 5/2: btr 1777. 4 **58**
1940 **PRIVATE SEAL** 10 [3]9-7-12 (4oh)t (41) M Halford(3) 33/1: 2020508: Al bhd: see 539.   5 **29**
8 Ran   Time 2m 10.84(8.54)   Owned: Miss Maria McKinney   Trained: Banbury

Official Going Good

2158	2.30 St James Security Maiden Stakes 2yo (D)				

£3624 £1115 £558   **5f str**   Good/Firm 36   -03 Slow   Stands Side

COUNCIL MEMBER 0 [8] Saeed bin Suroor 2-9-0 K McEvoy 7/2: 1: b c Seattle Slew - Zoe Montana   **95**
(Seeking The Gold) Made virtually all, kept on well ins last, drvn out: bckd: Apr foal, cost $800,000: eff over a
stiff 5f, 6f+ sure to suit: acts on gd/firm & goes well fresh: useful, likely plenty more to come.
1934 **JUANTORENA** 11 [6] M L W Bell 2-9-0 K Darley 1/2 FAV: 22: ch c Miswaki - Millyant (Primo   ½ **92**
Dominie) Dsptd lead, kept on ins last for press, a just held by wnr: hvly bckd: May foal, cost 66,000 gns half
brother to a useful 6f wnr: confirmed useful impress of debut: eff at 5/6f on fast: well clr of
rem here, mdn shld prove a formality: 2 May'04 Newm 6g/f 91- D:
1670 **PROSPECT COURT** 22 [10] J D Bethell 2-9-0 S Chin 33/1: 03: ch c Pivotal - Scierpan (Sharpen Up)   6 **72**
Prom, not pace of front 2 over 1f out: Apr foal, cost 42,000 gns: half brother to sev wnr over 5f/1m: bred to
apprec 6/7f in time & improved from debut here.
SENTIERO ROSSO 0 [7] B Ellison 2-9-0 T Eaves(3) 9/1: 4: b c Intidab - Kheyrah (Dayjur) Sn bhd,   ½ **70**
brief eff 2f out, no impress on debut: op 5/1: Jan foal, cost £30,000: dam 6f juv wnr: learn from this.
1950 **HYMN OF VICTORY** 9 [9]2-9-0 M Fenton 100/1: 05: In tch, no impress over 1f out.   shd **70**
MOZAFIN 0 [5]2-9-0 T E Durcan 16/1: 6: Sn rdn & nvr a factor on debut: green.   1½ **66**
DAVY CROCKETT 0 [2]2-9-0 P Fessey 100/1: 7: Sn bhd, nvr a factor on debut.   1¾ **61**
1143 **MISTY MILLER** 51 [1]2-9-0 R Winston 33/1: 58: Went left start, bhd, brief eff when no run over 2f out. 3 **52**
FORPETESAKE 0 [3]2-9-0 VIS A Culhane 66/1: 9: Al bhd.   9 **28**
1143 **HIATS** 51 [4]2-9-0 J D O'Reilly(7) 200/1: 060: 10th: In tch, wknd 2f out, abs.   2 **22**
10 Ran   Time 1m 0.14 (1.94)   Owned: Godolphin   Trained: Newmarket

2159   3.00 Gosforth Decorating & Building Services Handicap 3yo+ 0-75 (E)   [73]
£4193 £1290 £645   1m rnd   Good/Firm 36   -18 Slow   Inside

1661 **GOODBYE MR BOND** 23 [4] E J Alston 4-8-7 (52) K Darley 9/4 JT FAV: 5634341: Chsd ldrs, chall over   60
1f out, styd on to lead ins last, drvn out: hvly bckd: eff around 1m/9f on fast, soft & fibresand, any trk:
deserved win after some promising efforts: game: see 387.
1214 **TOP DIRHAM** 47 [10] M W Easterby 6-9-12 (71) Dale Gibson 9/4 JT FAV: 0000-232: Held up, hdwy to   1¼   76
lead over 1f out, hdd ins last, not pace of wnr: well bckd: 7 wk abs & on a wng mark: see 1036.
4752* **MALLARD** 231 [2] J G Given 6-9-5 (64) M Fenton 8/1: 011101-3: b g Tagula - Frill (Henbit) In   ¾   67
tch, hdwy to lead over 2f out till over 1f out, onepace: '03 5 time h'cap scorer: '02 h'cap wnr for D Cantillon:
suited by 7f/8.5f on both a/w's, fast & gd, loves W'hampton & sharp trks: has run well fresh: tough & prog.
1 Oct'03 Ling 8ap 75a-71 E: 1 Sep'03 Epso 7gd 62-56 E: 1 Aug'03 Wolv 7af 72a-65 E: 1 Jul'03 Wolv 7af 67a-62 E:
1 Apr'03 Wolv 8.5af 63a-53 G: 2 Feb'03 Wolv 8.4af 53a-52 F: 2 Jan'03 Wolv 7af 53a- G-: 1 Apr'02 Wolv 8.4af 63a-56 G:
1897 **FRANCIS FLUTE** 12 [6] B Mactaggart 6-8-6 (51) P Mulrennan(3) 6/1: 6000-024: Keen held up, hdwy   1   52
over 1f out, onepace: shade btr expected after promising reapp in 1897.
1898 **NEMO FUGAT** 12 [5]5-9-3 (62) A Nicholls 25/1: 0400-005: b g Danehill Dancer - Do The Right Thing   nk   62
(Busted) Slow away, held up, hdwy & short of room 2f out, some late gains: 4th at best in '03 (rtd 79): stks & rtd
h'cap scorer for R Hannon in '02: eff at 5/6f on firm & gd, any trk: has run well fresh: tried blnks: more
encouraging & is v well h'capped if returning to form.
1 Jul'02 Newb 6fm 92-86 C: 1 Apr'02 Newm 7fm 89- C: 1 Sep'01 Ling 6gd 91- F: 2 Jul'01 Asco 6fm 91- D:
1954 **ENCOUNTER** 9 [1]8-8-2 (47) D Allan(1) 9/1: 00-00356: Held up, eff 2f out, sn no extra: see 1661, 1388.   1½   44
1755 **HOHS BACK** 18 [7]5-9-4 p (63) L Enstone(3) 20/1: 0020607: Slt lead till over 2f out, wknd: see 1214.   10   40
1215 **WAHOO SAM** 47 [3]4-9-6 (65) P Makin(5) 40/1: U0000-08: ch g Sandpit - Good Reputation (Gran Zar)   shd   42
Dsptd lead till over 2f out, wknd: 7 wk abs: well abs all '03 starts (rtd 66): '02 auct mdn & stks wnr: eff at
6/7f on fast & fibresand, easy trks. 1 Jul'02 Thir 7g/f 84- C: 1 Jul'02 Sout 6af 81a- F:
1504 **HULA BALLEW** 31 [9]4-8-11 (56) R Winston 20/1: 366-0509: Handy, wknd over 2f out.   10   13
1748 **ANTHEMION** 19 [8]7-9-1 (60) D McGaffin 25/1: 025-0200: 10th: In tch, wknd over 2f out: see 1504.   11   0
10 Ran Time 1m 43.36 (4.36)   Owned: Mr Peter J Davies   Trained: Preston

2160   3.30 Betfred Sprint Series Qualifier A Handicap Stakes 3yo+ 0-85 (D)   [77]
£5421 £1668 £834   6f str   Good/Firm 36   +05 Fast   Stands Side

2029 **TALLY** 6 [6] M J Polglase 4-8-1 (50) R Thomas(5) 5/1: 0006031: Handy, hdwy over 1f out to lead ins   60
last, drvn out: suited by 6f on fast & both AWs, any trk: confirmed encouraging run of 2029 & on a handy mark.
2029 **SNOW BUNTING** 6 [5] Jedd O'Keeffe 6-8-6 (55) M Fenton 14/1: 60-00302: Bhd, hdwy & short of room   shd   64
over 2f out, kept on ins last, just held: quick reapp: shade unlucky & another that is back on a wng mark.
1508 **ULYSEES** 31 [12] I Semple 5-9-7 (70) R Winston 7/1: 6600-103: Handy, eff well over 1f out, kept   1½   75
on same pace: btr run: -acts on fast & soft: see 1391.
2027 **FRIAR TUCK** 6 [9] Miss L A Perratt 9-8-6 (55) D McGaffin 25/1: 0001464: Handy, hdwy to lead over   shd   59
1f out till ins last, no extra: gd run: see 1508.
2010 **DISTANT COUNTRY** 7 [2]5-9-8 p (71) A Culhane 4/1: 14-66025: Held up, short of room when hdwy 2f   nk   74+
out, kept on ins last, nrst fin: onepace over 7f/1m+: see 2010 (1m), 998.
2023 **FULL SPATE** 7 [8]9-9-5 (68) Darren Williams 8/1: 6054646: Missed break, held up, some late gains.   ½   69
2084 **HIGHLAND WARRIOR** 4 [10]5-9-10 (73) T E Durcan 11/4 FAV: 3234167: Held up, hdwy & no room over   nk   73+
2f out till ins last, styd on, not recover: wld have gone close, in gd form: see 2084, 967.
2029 **PIRLIE HILL** 6 [1]4-8-1 (50) P Fessey 33/1: 0-340258: In tch, wknd over 1f out: see 2029, 1391.   1¾   45
1638 **WILLIAMS WELL** 25 [4]10-8-12 bl (61) Dale Gibson 25/1: 2020-009: ch g Superpower - Catherines Well   1¼   52
(Junius) In tch, wknd well over 1f out: '03 dual h'cap wnr: multiple wnr back in '00: eff at 5/6f, stays 7f &
handles soft, likes gd & firm grnd: suited by blnks & likes Newcastle: tough 10yo.
2 Oct'03 Ayr 6g/s 64-62 E: 2 Aug'03 Redc 6g/f 62-(63) F: 1 Aug'03 Newc 6g/f 64-59 E: 1 Apr'03 Newc 7g/f 63-59 E:
1910 **LEGAL SET** 11 [11]8-8-0 t (49) Ann Stokell 50/1: 5020000: 10th: Led till over 1f out, no extra: see 728.   1   37
2007 **RAGAMUFFIN** 7 [3]6-9-7 (70) K Darley 10/1: 200-0050: 11th: Held up, btn over 2f out: see 2007.   2½   51
2059 **COLEMANSTOWN** 5 [7]4-9-7 (70) T Eaves(3) 7/1: 056-0000: 12th: Handy, wknd 2f out.   ¾   49
12 Ran Time 1m 13.14 (1.84)   Owned: General Sir Geoffrey Howlett   Trained: Newark

2161   4.00 Rectangle Claiming Stakes 3yo+ (F)
£3101 £886 £443   5f str   Good/Firm 36   -01 Slow   Stands Side

2029 **SOAKED** 6 [9] D W Chapman 11-8-10 bl (59) A Culhane 3/1 FAV: 0234041: Made all, styd on fnl 1f,   61
rdn out: stays 6f, suited by 5f: acts on firm, soft & both AWs: eff in blnks: most tough 11yo (18th win from 149).
2059 **AMERICAN COUSIN** 5 [4] D Nicholls 9-9-2 (64) A Nicholls 9/2: 40-10102: Held up, hdwy well over 1f   2   60
out, kept on ins last, no threat to wnr: quick reapp: see 1797 (sell).
1797 **BEST LEAD** 16 [7] Ian Emmerson 5-9-2 bl (52) D Fentiman(7) 14/1: 0443433: Handy, onepace over 1f out.   1   57
1408 **MISS WIZZ** 36 [10] W Storey 4-8-5 p (37) Rory Moore(7) 50/1: 0-041644: In tch, wknd over 1f out: btn see 637.   1   43
1555 **JOYCES CHOICE** 29 [6]5-8-12 (53) G Parkin 25/1: 050-20R5: Handy, wknd over 1f out: see 1179.   shd   50
1662* **DIZZY IN THE HEAD** 23 [3]5-9-6 e (65) J D O'Reilly(5) 5/1: 6000-016: Handy, wknd well over 1f out: ½   56
claimed for 10,000: btn 1662 (soft).
963 **FLYING TACKLE** 65 [5]6-9-2 (49) L Enstone(3) 33/1: 5003-007: ch g First Trump - Frighten The Life   ¾   50
(Kings Lake) In tch, wknd over 1f out: 2 month abs: ddhtd in a h'cap in '03: plcd in '02: eff at 5/6f on fast &
hvy grnd: eff in blnks/visor or cheek pieces: likes gall trks. 1 Aug'03 Newc 6g/f 54-49 E:
2 Jul'03 Pont 5g/f 57-58 E: 1 Oct'01 Redc 6gd 64- D: 2 Oct'01 Ayr 5hvy 50-47 E: 2 Sep'01 Hami 5gd 44-42 F:
2059 **PROUD NATIVE** 5 [1]10-9-12 (85) K Darley 7/2: 1105-008: b g Imp Society - Karamana (Habitat)   hd   59
Bhd, nvr a factor: '03 dual clmr & dual h'cap scorer: multiple wnr prev season: eff at 5/6f on firm & hvy, any
trk, loves a stiff one: has tried blnks: gets on well with D Holland. 1 Aug'03 Newb 5.2fm 90-84 D:
1 Aug'03 Bath 5.7fm 84-(84) E: 1 Jul'03 Newm 5g/f 85-80 D: 1 Jun'03 Sand 5.0g/f 78-(85) E:
2 Oct'02 Sand 5g/f 88- E: 1 Sep'02 Sand 5g/f 84- E: 1 Aug'02 Bath 5.7g/f 93- D: 1 Jun'01 Sand 5sft 103- C:
1963 **TAPPIT** 9 [2]5-9-0 BL (50) Darren Williams 8/1: 0-000039: In tch, wknd well over 1f out: btr 1963.   shd   46
NEEDWOOD BUCOLIC 775 [8]6-8-12 D Tudhope(7) 100/1: 210/013/-0: 10th: In tch, wknd over 2f out.   ½   42
10 Ran Time 1m 0.05 (1.85)   Owned: Mr David W Chapman   Trained: York

NEWCASTLE   WEDNESDAY 02.06.04   Lefthand, Galloping, Stiff Track

2162

4.30 Nitex Co Uk Handicap Stakes 3yo+ 0-75 (E)   **[75]**
£3926   £1208   £604   **1m2f32y**   **Good/Firm 36**   **-48 Slow**   Far Side

1884   **ROTUMA 12** [7] M Dods 5-9-1 bl (62) L Enstone(3) 4/1: 04-05031: Handy, hdwy to lead over 2f out,   **69**
rdn out: suited by 10f, stays 11f on firm & hvy grnd, prob any trk: suited by blnks, tried visor: in gd form.
1884   **COMPTON DRAGON 12** [6] D Nicholls 5-9-12 VIS (73) A Nicholls 10/1: 0-005052: Held up, hdwy over 1f   ¾   **78**
out, kept on ins last, no threat to wnr: gd run in 1st time visor: see 1884, 1519.
1834   **MA YAHAB 15** [8] L M Cumani 3-8-12 (72) K Darley 2/1 FAV: 020-33: Chsd ldr, eff to chall over 2f   nk   **76**
out, sn no extra: hvly bckd tho' op 11/8: in gd form: see 1834.
1821   **TRANCE 15** [11] T D Barron 4-10-0 (75) P Makin(5) 25/1: 02001-04: Handy, onepcd over 1f out: prob   1   **77**
stays 10f on fast, gd/soft & fibresand: see 143 (mdn, fibresand).
937   **DISABUSE 67** [3]4-8-3 (50) Dale Gibson 3/1: 6-213445: In tch, outpcd over 2f out, some late   nk   **51**
gains, bckd from 5/1: 2 month abs, needs 12f+: see 937, 867.
1943   **MOYNE PLEASURE 9** [10]6-7-12 (3oh)p (42) D Fentiman(7) 20/1: 2023146: Held up, mod late gains.   1½   **43**
964   **SILVERTOWN 65** [4]9-9-7 (68) P Mulrennan(5) 10/1: 303/11-07: b g Danehill - Docklands (Theatrical)   ¾   **65**
Keen bhd, no danger: op 7/1: p.u. in 2 hdles last winter, 3 time h'cap wnr in 02/03 (2m4f, fast grnd, rtd 129h): won
both Flat '03 starts (h'caps): suited by 12f on firm, gd/soft & fibresand, any trk: loves to dominate.
1 Jun'03 Carl 11.9fm 72-65 D: 1 May'03 Muss 12g/f 69-60 D:
2030   **SKIDDAW JONES 6** [1]4-8-5 (52) G Parkin 25/1: 4000-058: Handy, wknd 2f out: see 2030.   5   **41**
1796   **KINGS ENVOY 16** [9]5-9-3 (64) D McGaffin 20/1: 00/0-4359: Nvr a factor: see 1462 (9f), 1095.   1¼   **51**
1668   **WAHCHI 22** [2]5-9-11 (72) T Lucas 50/1: 3/40-0000: 10th: ch g Nashwan - Nafhaat (Roberto) Led   ¾   **58**
till over 2f out, wknd: fin last both '03 starts: Listed rnr-up in '02: eff at 1m/11.5f on firm & gd, gall trks:
has run well fresh: with E Dunlop in '03, now with G Kelly.
2 Apr'02 Newm 9fm 105- A: 1 Sep'01 Donc 8g/f 91- D:
10 Ran   Time 2m 14.99 (8.49)   Owned: Denton Hall Racing Ltd   Trained: Darlington

2163

5.00 Jumbrella Apprentice Classified Stakes 3yo+ 0-60 (G)
£2548   £728   £364   **1m4f93y**   **Good/Firm 36**   **-26 Slow**   Far Side

1648   **ILLEANA 23** [8] W R Muir 3-8-3 (58) P Makin 8/1: 00-4001: ch f Lomitas - Illyria (Nashwan) Hld   **58**
up, hdwy 2f out, styd on to lead ins last, rdn out: 1st win: well btn '03 starts: imprvd on this fast grnd & stays 12.4f.
1772   **BAKIRI 18** [5] Andrew Reid 6-9-7 (59) Rory Moore 13/2: 60/-04052: Handy, hdwy to lead appr fnl   nk   **60**
1f, kept on till collared cl-home, just btn: stays 12.4f: see 1271.
2041   **BLACKTHORN 5** [7] Mrs J R Ramsden 5-9-7 (58) A Mullen(5) 3/1 FAV: 002-4033: Held up, hdwy well   ¾   **58**
over 1f out, kept on ins last, not btn far: quick reapp: gd run: see 918.
1821   **JAKE BLACK 15** [3] J J Quinn 4-9-7 (59) D Tudhope(3) 11/2: 1531504: Keen, led till appr fnl 1f, no extra.   2½   **54**
1785   **GOLD CARD 17** [1]3-8-9 (63) D Fentiman(3) 15/2: 634-2255: In tch, outpcd over 2f out, some late gains.   1¼   **55**
1830   **MADHAHIR 15** [6]4-9-7 (57) Stephanie Hollinshead 11/1: 0130006: With ldr, wknd over 1f out: see 979.   3   **48**
1836* **PRAIRIE SUN 15** [2]3-8-3 (59) Dean Williams(3) 9/2: 00-44517: Handy, wknd 2f out: btr 1836 (dsptd lead).   1¾   **42**
1952   **PLATINUM CHARMER 9** [4]4-9-7 p (56) S Bushby(7) 9/1: 0214248: In tch, wknd 3f out: btr 1819 (clmr).   8   **33**
8 Ran   Time 2m 45.52(7.62)   Owned: Foursome Thoroughbreds   Trained: Lambourn

BEVERLEY   WEDNESDAY 02.06.04   Righthand, Oval Track with Stiff, Uphill Finish

Official Going GOOD/FIRM (FIRM back straight).

2164

6.35 Big Screen Is Here Tonight Stakes A Handicap 3yo 0-70 (E)   **[76]**
£3952   £1216   £608   **1m4f16y**   **Good/Firm 30**   **-09 Slow**   Inside

4858} **ZALDA 223** [4] R Charlton 3-8-11 (59) R Winston 14/1: 006-1: ch f Zilzal - Gold Luck (Slew O'   **68**
Gold) Trkd ldr, styd on under press to lead cl-home, rdn out: reapp: unplcd on all 3 juv mdn starts, some promise
on fnl outing (mdn, rtd 60): clrly benefited for step up to 12f & h'cap company, runs well fresh: acts on fast grnd
& on a stiff trk: unexposed over mid-dists & can improve further.
1785   **HAVETOAVIT 17** [2] J D Bethell 3-8-12 (60) T Quinn 9/2: 5400-532: b g Theatrical - Summer Crush   1¼   **66**
(Summer Squall) Tried to make all, caught cl-home: tchd 6/1: 4th of 10 at best in '03 (AW mdn, rtd 65a, wore an
eye-shield): likes to front run & stays a stiff 12f well: acts on fast grnd, handles gd/soft & fibresand: bold
front running eff, prob caught a fairly h'capped rival: deserves similar.
2014* **VICARIO 7** [1] M L W Bell 3-8-8 (6ex) (56) D Allan(3) 13/8 FAV: 00-513: Rdn in rear, styd on late,   ¾   **61**
nrst fin: nicely bckd, clr of rem: nvr really lkd happy today, see 2014.
1306   **DUNLEA DANCER 41** [6] M Johnston 3-8-8 (56) J Fanning 9/2: 50500-34: Chsd ldrs, rdn & btn over 1f   6   **52**
out, tchd 7/2, 6 wk abs: see 1306 (10f here, soft grnd).
1768   **VICTORY LAP 18** [3]3-9-5 (67) T E Durcan 11/1: 3-065: Nvr trbld ldrs: best 192 (1m AW mdn).   1   **61**
1836   **XPRESSIONS 15** [8]3-8-2 (50) P Hanagan 11/2: 4015-66: Chsd ldrs, btn 2f out: see 1836 (C/D).   nk   **43**
1784   **REDMARLEY 17** [7]3-8-11 (59) M Fenton 25/1: 00-67: b g Croco Rouge - Dazzling Fire (Bluebird)   28   **12**
Rdn in rear, al bhd, t.o. on h'cap bow: unplcd on both juv mdn starts: half-brother to a sprint wnr.
1428   **MOONSHAFT 35** [5]3-9-7 (69) E Ahern 12/1: 0048: br c Capote - Moonshine Girl (Shadeed) Rear &   6   **13**
rcd wide, chsd ldrs halfway, wknd qckly 2f out, t.o. on h'cap bow: lightly rcd & well btn to date: top-weight.
8 Ran   Time 2m 36.00 (4.70)   Owned: Mr D J Deer   Trained: Beckhampton

2165

7.05 Listed Hilary Needler Trophy Fillies 2yo (A)
£14500   £5500   £2750   **5f str**   **Good/Firm 30**   **-17 Slow**   Inside

1764* **MISS MEGGY 18** [1] T D Easterby 2-8-11 D Allan 16/1: 11: Dwelt, hdwy wide over 1f out, strong   **92+**
run to lead cl-home: unbtn filly, eff at 5f on fast grnd: handles an easy or stiff trk, goes well fresh: gd turn
of foot from poor draw: hds for the Queen Mary at R Ascot & a lively outsider: see 1764.
1950   **TAGULA SUNRISE 9** [10] R A Fahey 2-8-8 P Hanagan 10/1: 22: Trkd ldrs, led ins fnl 1f, not pace   nk   **86**

to repel wnr cl-home: acts on fast & firm grnd: useful run from gd draw & must win sn.

1458* **MARY READ** 33 [5] B Smart 2-8-8 F Lynch 25/1: 313: Tried to make all, collared ins fnl 1f, just
btn in a close fin: fine front running eff from a modest draw, acts on fast & hvy grnd: speedy filly, see 1458. nk 85

1764 **AFRICAN BREEZE** 18 [14] R M Whitaker 2-8-8 Dean McKeown 28/1: 04: Hmpd start, mid-div, styd on
under press fnl 1f & nrst fin: lost all draw advantage whn hmpd early on & this was a fine effort in the
circumstances: eff at 5f on fast grnd: nailed on for a mdn, see 1764. ½ 83+

1974* **MIZZ TEE** 8 [15]2-8-11 W Supple 2/1 FAV: 215: Stumbled leaving stalls, sn well bhd, 'flew home'
fnl 1.5f: shorter priced stablemate of wnr: acts on fast & gd/soft: reportedly held in some regard, prob unlucky
today & an eyecatching run, keep on your side: see 1974. hd 86+

1920* **SAPPHIRE DREAM** 11 [11]2-8-11 T E Durcan 5/2: 2216: Chsd ldrs, kept on under press despite
drifting right fnl 1f: sound run, consistent & btn only just over 1L: see 1920 (6f). ½ 84

1752* **ROSEIN** 18 [9]2-8-8 J Fanning 8/1: 17: Chsd ldrs, sltly short of room dist, kept on: did not
get the run of this race: prob handles fast grnd: see 1752 (AW, debut). 1½ 76

1573* **TIVISKI** 28 [13]2-8-11 E Ahern 9/1: 3418: Hmpd start, recovered to chase ldrs, onepcd fnl 1f. ½ 77

1677 **TANTIEN** 21 [7]2-8-8 N Callan 10/1: 549: Nvr nr ldrs: highly tried: see 1677 (soft grnd). 2 68

1764 **HANDSOME LADY** 18 [8]2-8-8 T Quinn 10/1: 160: 10th: Chsd ldrs, fdd fnl 1f: best 1445 (gd/soft). hd 68

1634* **NOVA TOR** 25 [12]2-8-8 J Carroll 16/1: 110: 11th: Front rank, btn fnl 1f: up in grade for new
stable, won a clmr for P Haslam in 1634. ¾ 65

1764 **FLOSSYTOO** 18 [6]2-8-11 J D O'Reilly 33/1: 0100: 12th: Dwelt, prog wide when saddle slipped sn
after halfway, eased considerably & virtually p.u.: forgive this: see 1343 (mdn, gd/soft). dist 28

12 Ran Time 1m 03.66 (2.36) Owned: Mr David W Armstrong Trained: Malton

---

2166 7.35 Sky Bet Press Red To Bet Now Stakes A Handicap 3yo 0-80 (D) [87]
£6906 £2125 £1063 **7f100y rnd** **Good/Firm 30** **+10 Fast** Inside

1769 **BURLEY FLAME** 18 [7] J G Given 3-8-13 (72) M Fenton 8/1: 0-4331: Trkd ldr, styd on strongly to
lead well ins fnl 1f, drvn out: fast time: first success: eff at 7f/1m on fast & gd/soft grnd: game. 80

1270* **DOCTORATE** 43 [6] E A L Dunlop 3-9-7 (80) E Ahern 11/2: 4-012: Trkd ldr, went on dist, not pace
to repel wnr cl-home: top-weight, 6 wk abs, drifted from 3/1: eff at 6/7.5f, has tried 1m: improving. nk 87

1639* **SNAP** 25 [3] M Johnston 3-9-0 (73) J Fanning 7/4 FAV: 213: Trkd ldrs, drifted right & onepcd fnl
1f: well bckd from 5/2 on h'cap bow: stays a stiff 7.5f, acts on fast & soft grnd: see 1639 (6f mdn). 2 76

1879 **POPPYS FOOTPRINT** 13 [5] K A Ryan 3-9-4 (77) N Callan 7/2: 0-000534: Trkd ldrs, onepcd when short
of room ent fnl 1f: clr of rem: see 1879. nk 79

1627 **MISARO** 25 [1]3-9-3 (76) D Nolan(3) 25/1: 351-05: Led till dist, no extra: see 1627 (5f). 4 70

1678 **TROJAN FLIGHT** 21 [4]3-8-7 P (66) A Culhane 8/1: 000-4546: Keen in rear, hdwy 2f out, onepcd when
short of room fnl 1f: op 11/1, tried cheek pieces: see 1628 (8.5f here). ½ 59

1876* **NEON BLUE** 13 [8]3-8-9 (68) M Hills 7/1: 4040-517: Al towards rear: btr expected over this longer trip. hd 61

4988] **EBORACUM** 212 [2]3-8-6 (65) D Allan(3) 25/1: 4520-8: b f Alzao - Fire of London (Shirley Heights)
Held up, nvr nr ldrs & fin last on reapp: rnr-up on 4 of 4 '03 starts (mdn auct): stays a sharp 1m, acts on fast
grnd. 2 Sep'03 Ripo 8g/f 69- E: 7 43

8 Ran Time 1m 32.31 (1.51) Owned: Burley Appliances Ltd Trained: Gainsborough

---

2167 8.10 Brian Yeardley Continental Two Year Old Trophy Conditions Stakes Colts & Geldings 2yo (B)
£11670 £4426 £2213 **5f str** **Good/Firm 30** **-12 Slow** Inside

 BOLTON HALL [6] R A Fahey 2-8-6 P Hanagan 10/1: 1: b g Imperial Ballet - Muneera (Green
Dancer) Chsd ldrs, hard rdn to lead cl-home, just prevailed on debut: Feb foal, cost 22,000gns: sire a useful
miler: eff over a stiff 5f on fast grnd, fdd early fast: runs well fresh: scopey gelding, op to improvement. 90

1205* **TOURNEDOS** 47 [4] M R Channon 2-8-13 T E Durcan 6/4 FAV: 12: Prom, led ent fnl 1f, just shaded
cl-home: 7 wk abs, fdd fast: acts on gd & fast: runs well fresh: just found weight concession to wnr too much. nk 95

1601* **MIDNIGHT TYCOON** 26 [8] B Smart 2-8-11 F Lynch 2/1: 13: Led till ent fnl 1f, just btn in a close
fin: acts on fast & gd/soft grnd: going the right way: see 1601. nk 92

1517 **BIGALOS BANDIT** 30 [3] J J Quinn 2-8-13 R Winston 7/2: 124: Trkd ldrs, rdn but ev ch when short
of room ent fnl 1f, no ch after: well clr rem, jt top-weight: acts on fast & soft: wld have gone close. 1¾ 89+

 WAGGLEDANCE [2]2-8-6 J Carroll 25/1: 5: b g Mujadil - Assertive Lass (Assert) Slowly away,
nvr nr ldrs on debut: £16,000 Apr foal: half-brother to numerous juv wnr abroad: dam a 7f wnr, sire a decent juv. 9 57

 DEN PERRY [1]2-8-6 P Bradley 40/1: 6: ch c Tipsy Creek - Beverley Monkey (Fayruz) Dwelt & al
bhd on debut: Apr foal, cost 2,800gns: first foal, dam a sprint winning juv: sire a smart sprinter. 2½ 51

1780 **LANE MARSHAL** 17 [5]2-8-9 T Eaves 100/1: 6507: Al outpcd & hung right thr'out: highly tried. 8 30

7 Ran Time 1m 03.43 (2.13) Owned: Mr J J Staunton Trained: Malton

---

2168 8.40 Weatherbys Insurance Handicap Stakes 3yo 0-75 (E) [79]
£4729 £1455 £728 **1m100y rnd** **Good/Firm 30** **-03 Slow** Inside

1628 **RILEY BOYS** 25 [5] J G Given 3-9-6 (71) M Fenton 7/4 FAV: 00-12121: Set pace, qcknd 2f out, held
on well drvn out: well bckd from 9/4: eff at 6f, stays 8.5f well: acts on firm, soft grnd & fibresand: continues
in terrific form & gvn a fine enterprising front running ride: see 1628 & 1470. 77

1769 **DOUBLE VODKA** 18 [9] Mrs J R Ramsden 3-8-11 (62) A Culhane 6/1: 6035-062: Held up, short of room
after halfway, gd hdwy over 1f out, kept on & not btn far: gd eff in a race almost certainly not run to suit: stays
a stiff 8.5f: deserves similar, see 1769. ½ 66

1628 **FOSSGATE** 3 [3] J D Bethell 3-9-6 (71) T Quinn 8/1: 05-203: Front rank, not qckn ins fnl 1f:
sound run, only btn 1L: acts on fast & soft grnd: see 1178 (reapp, mdn). ½ 74

1834 **ATHOLLBROSE** 15 [7] T D Easterby 3-8-4 (55) W Supple 8/1: 00-42454: Chsd ldrs, onepcd fnl 1f. 1¾ 54

1769 **AUROVILLE** 18 [4]3-9-0 (65) T E Durcan 6/1: 050-0405: Held up, short of room 2f out, kept on &
nrst fin: unsuited by waiting tactics in a tactically run race: prob handles fast grnd: see 1470. ½ 62

1947 **GIVEN A CHANCE** 9 [8]3-7-12 (6oh) (43) R Thomas(2) 14/1: 5053426: Trkd ldrs, short of room 2f out,
onepcd fnl 1f: see 1947. ¾ 45

1628 **GLENDALE** 25 [2]3-8-8 P (59) N Callan 16/1: 00-10007: Keen & prom, btn fnl 1f: cheek pieces. 1½ 52

1813 **BLUE EMPIRE** 15 [6]3-9-7 (72) D Nolan(3) 20/1: 5142608: Stdd start, hdwy from rear 2f out, sn btn. 4 57

1953 **RABITATIT** 9 [1]3-8-12 (63) R Miles(3) 11/2: 1150-249: Rear, nvr nr to chall: op 13/2: btr 1099 (gd/sft). 3½ 41

9 Ran Time 1m 46.66 (2.86) Owned: Mr Paul Riley Trained: Gainsborough

2169 9.10 Next Meeting Is Wednesday 9 June Maiden Stakes Fillies 3yo+ (D)
£4160 £1280 £640 7f100y rnd Good/Firm 30 -16 Slow Inside

1778 **LORIEN HILL** 18 [2] B W Hills 3-8-9 (67) M Hills 15/8 FAV: 034-651: Trkd ldrs, imprvd to lead ins 73
fnl 1f, won going away: nicely bckd: deserved first win: eff around 7/7.5f on fast, gd/soft grnd & polytrack:
handles a sharp/turning or stiff trk: see 1778.
1131 **VAS Y CARLA** 51 [1] D R Loder 3-8-9 (80) T E Durcan 4/1: 626-02: ch f Gone West - Lady Carla 2 67
(Caerleon) Held up, hdwy wide halfway, took 2nd cl-home, no ch with wnr: 7 wk abs, drifted from 7/4: trained by J
Dunlop in '03, shthd 2nd on middle of 3 starts (fill mdn): eff at 7f on fast grnd, handles a stiff/gall trk: 1m
will suit judged on this. 2 Oct'03 Leic 7.0g/f 86- D:
1171 **KHAFAYIF** 49 [6] B Hanbury 3-8-9 W Supple 9/2: 03: b f Swain - Copper Play (Fast Play) Trkd ¾ 65
ldrs, led dist till ins fnl 1f, no extra: op 7/1, 7 wk abs: mid-dist bred, eff at 7.5f on fast grnd.
1896 **GRACEFUL AIR** 12 [5] J R Weymes 3-8-9 (62) R Winston 11/4: 03-45224: Led after 2f till dist, no 3 59
extra: bckd from 4/1: ran to form of 1896 & 1554.
4440} **NEQAAWI** 251 [4]3-8-9 T Charlotte Kerton(7) 33/1: 00-5: br f Alhaarth - Jinsiyah (Housebuster) 2 55
Keen & led 2f, left bhd 1f out: reapp/h'cap qual run, tried a t-strap: well btn in 2 juv mdn starts: half-sister
to a sprint wnr: with B Hanbury.
1518 **WEDOWANNAGIVEUTHAT** 30 [3]3-8-9 D Allan(3) 25/1: 006: Held up, nvr trbld ldrs. 2½ 50
1688 **HUGGIN MAC** 21 [7]3-8-9 Suzanne France(7) 20/1: 67: Dwelt, some hdwy halfway, sn btn. 1½ 47
1944 **COTTAM KARMINSKI** 9 [8]3-8-9 P M Quinn 50/1: 08: Slowly away, nvr troubled ldrs & fin last. 4 39
8 Ran Time 1m 34.26(3.46) Owned: Mr D M James Trained: Lambourn

Official Going Good (Good/Firm Places)

2170 6.20 Wednesday Night Is Race Night Apprentice Handicap Stakes 3yo+ 0-70 (E) [69]
£3611 £1111 £556 1m1f Good 45 -10 Slow Inside

1643* **UNSUITED** 23 [12] J E Long 5-8-9 (50) Natalia Gemelova 12/1: 0326411: Held up, gd prog to lead 66+
dist, pushed clr fnl 1f, val 7L+: eff at 9/10f on gd, hvy grnd & fibresand: likes Kempton: thriving, land hat-trick.
1792 **EMBER DAYS** 16 [6] J L Spearing 5-9-4 p (59) R Lucey Butler(3) 20/1: 22-50302: Rear, prog after 6f, 5 64
kept on fnl 1f & grabbed 2nd, no ch with easy wnr: continues to run with credit: see 1542 & 178.
1927 **MISS GRACE** 11 [11] J J Sheehan 4-8-13 (54) B O'Neill(5) 20/1: 360-0403: Rear, kept on late. hd 58
1913 **CATCH THE FOX** 11 [4] J J Bridger 4-8-2 (43) Lucy Russell(5) 33/1: 50-02004: Handy, no extra dist. 1 44
2057 **PAS DE SURPRISE** 5 [2]6-9-0 (55) S Donohoe 14/1: 0554005: Mid-div, prog 3f out, onepcd fnl 1f. 1 55
2099 **ICANNSHIFT** 2 [14]4-8-13 (54) L Smith(7) 9/2: 0213036: Cl-up, led after 5f, hdd dist, sn wknd. ½ 53
1712 **GALEY RIVER** 20 [15]5-8-0 (41) Liam Jones(5) 16/1: 5162357: Nvr nrr than mid-div: just btr 1913. 1¾ 37
1992 **LUCEFER** 8 [13]6-8-4 (45) Saleem Golam(3) 10/1: 2-003448: Nvr nrr than mid-div: btr 1579. ¾ 39
1891 **DASH FOR COVER** 12 [8]4-9-6 (61) P Gallagher 16/1: 2000569: Rear, modest late gains: btr 978. 1¼ 53
3864} **EXPECTED RESPONSE** 282 [10]5-9-0 bl (55) K Ghunowa(5) 7/2 FAV: 000000-0: 10th: b g Kris S - Nidd hd 46
(Known Fact) Led 5f, styd cl-up, fdd dist: weld bckd on reapp: modest form in '03 (rtd 43 & 62a, h'caps): unplcd
in '02 (rtd 88, h'caps, B W Hills): eff at 7f on gd, prob gd/soft grnd: has tried blnks: with S C Williams.
1 Sep'01 Kemp 7gd 93- C: 2 Aug'01 York 6gd 92- D:
1927 **MYTHICAL CHARM** 11 [9]5-8-12 t (53) M Howard(3) 12/1: 0063300: 11th: Handy over 6f, sn wknd. nk 43
1913* **GIUNCHIGLIO** 11 [1]5-9-9 (64) B Swarbrick 7/1: 5600-310: 12th: Al in rear: btr expected after 1913. 7 44
1718 **CRYSTAL CHOIR** 20 [7]4-9-10 (65) W Hogg(3) 16/1: 0-060: 13th: Handy 6f, hung left & sn fdd: btr 1718. 3½ 40
1891 **MUST BE MAGIC** 12 [5]7-9-4 vis (59) Nicol Polli 10/1: 20-45000: 14th: Handy 7f, fdd: btr 674. 2 31
1073 **SILVER LOUIE** 57 [3]4-8-4 (45) T Block(5) 66/1: 000R-00R: Ref to race: 8 wk abs. 0
15 Ran Time 1m 54.96 (4.96) Owned: Amaroni Racing Trained: Woldingham

2171 6.50 Hh Associates E B F Median Auction Maiden Stakes 2yo (E)
£3455 £1063 £532 5f str Good 45 -06 Slow Stands side

SOAR 0 [8] J R Fanshawe 2-8-9 J Murtagh 9/2: 1: b f Danzero - Splice (Sharpo) Cl-up, led bef 94+
1f out, pushed clr, impressive: op 7/4 on debut: Feb foal, half-sister to a couple of wnrs at 5f: dam smart
sprinter: eff at 5f on gd: goes well fresh: showed a decent turn of foot & will be winning better races.
SAFSOOF 0 [7] Saeed bin Suroor 2-9-0 L Dettori 8/11 FAV: 2: b c Gilded Time - Halcyon Bird 3 85
(Storm Bird) Led, hdd bef 1f out, kept on but al held by impressive wnr: well bckd on debut: Feb foal: dam unrcd:
sire high-class juv performer in USA: eff at 5f, 6f shld suit: acts on gd grnd: win similar.
1499 **FEMINIST** 31 [4] M R Channon 2-8-9 K Fallon 13/2: 53: b f Alhaarth - Miss Willow Bend (Willow 1½ 76
Hour) Handy over 3f, no extra dist: Apr foal, close 3rd on debut: sister/half-sister to numerous wnrs: dam dual wnr
abroad: sire decent performer around 1m: eff at 5f, will apprec further: acts on gd grnd: fair start.
2020 **LILY LENAT** 7 [1] J R Boyle 2-8-9 D Sweeney 20/1: 04: Slow away, prog after 3f, kept on fnl 1f. 1 73
TRANSVESTITE 0 [3]2-9-0 R L Moore 20/1: 5: Bhd, nvr nrr than mid-div on debut. ¾ 76
ANFIELD DREAM 0 [5]2-9-0 C Lowther 33/1: 6: Handy over 3f, edged right & fdd dist: debut. 3½ 66
1325 **HIGGYS PRINCE** 40 [6]2-9-0 Dane O'Neill 50/1: 07: Al in rear: 6 wk abs. 5 53
1574 **JOSEAR** 27 [2]2-9-0 A McCarthy 14/1: 48: Chsd ldrs till halfway, fdd: btr 1574. shd 52
8 Ran Time 1m 0.87 (2.57) Owned: Cheveley Park Stud Trained: Newmarket

---

2172   7.20 Pemberton Greenish Redfern Handicap Stakes 4yo+ 0-90 (C)   [90]
£9601 £2954 £1477   7f rnd   Good 45   +00 Fast   Inside

1883 **ETTRICK WATER 12** [4] L M Cumani 5-9-10 vis (86) D Holland 11/2: 42113-51: Made all, styd on   99
strongly fnl 1f, rdn out: suited by dominating at 7f/1m on firm, soft & any trk: tough & improving.
1817 **GIFT HORSE 15** [10] J R Fanshawe 4-9-4 (80) J Murtagh 20/1: 216-02: Chsd ldrs, styd on to chase   1   89
wnr dist, kept on fnl 1f, al held: acts on fm & gd: shown enough to find similar: see 1817.
1926 **KOOL 11** [11] P F I Cole 5-10-0 (90) S Sanders 5/1 FAV: 20/-30553: Rear, prog halfway, onepcd ins   1¾   95
fnl 1f: bckd from 8/1: gd run under top-weight: see 1926 & 1126.
1723 **CHATEAU NICOL 20** [2] B G Powell 5-9-2 vis (78) L Dettori 9/1: 1413334: Rear, kept on late.   ¾   81
1616* **SOYUZ 26** [13]4-9-11 (87) P Robinson 6/1: 000-2315: Chsd ldrs over 5f, wknd dist: btr 1616 (1m, gd/soft).2½   85
2063³ **QUANTUM LEAP 4** [3]7-8-10 (6ex)vis (72) R L Moore 11/1: 3030316: Cl-up till dist, wknd: qck reapp.   nk   69
1231 **CRAIOVA 46** [8]5-9-11 (87) R Hills 10/1: 1250-007: b c Turtle Island - Velvet Appeal (Petorius)   1   62
Handy 5f, sn wknd: mdn, class stks & h'cap wnr in '03: eff at 7f/1m on
fast, soft grnd & polytrack: has gone well fresh: with B W Hills. 2 Jul'03 Asco 8g/s 92-86 C:
1 Jul'03 Hayd 7.1gd 89-82 C: 1 May'03 Warw 7.1g/f 87-(80) D: 1 Mar'03 Newc 7g/s 86-(80) D:
2 Jul'02 Asco 8gd 82- D: 2 Jul'02 Hayd 7.1g/f 79- D: 2 Jun'02 Newb 7sft 88- D:
1817 **DIGITAL 15** [7]7-9-11 (87) S Hitchcott(3) 9/1: 3403608: Rear, eff when short of room 2f out &   nk   81
again dist, sn no impress: btr 1512 & 945.
1817 **FLINT RIVER 15** [9]6-8-11 (73) R Hughes 12/1: 0012409: Handy, chsd ldr bef 1f out, sn wknd: btr 1598.   nk   66
1512 **YAKIMOV 30** [1]5-9-10 (86) Dane O'Neill 50/1: 023-0000: 10th: ch g Affirmed - Ballet Troupe   ½   78
(Nureyev) Bhd, nvr a factor: recent jumps unplcd (rtd 60h): won 3 h'caps on Flat in '03 (P F I Cole): dual h'cap
& claim wnr in '02: suited by 1m/9.4f on fast, soft grnd & fibresand: acts on any trk: with D J Wintle.
2 Aug'03 Ripo 8gd 88-(92) D: 1 Aug'03 Leic 8.0gd 92-84 D: 1 Jul'03 Beve 8.5g/s 83-78 D: 2 May'03 Hayd 8.1sft 78-77 C:
1 Apr'03 Wolv 8.5af 88a-74 E: 2 Sep'02 Hami 9.1g/f 80- D: 1 Aug'02 Folk 9.6gd 78-73 D: 1 Aug'02 Newb 8g/f 78- D:
1 Aug'02 Pont 8sft 67-62 F: 2 Jul'02 Beve 7.4g/f 63- E:
1927 **CHEESE N BISCUITS 11** [12]4-8-13 P (75) K Fallon 8/1: 35-00200: 11th: Al in rear: cheekpieces.   7   53
1817 **JUST FLY 15** [6]4-9-2 (78) J F Egan 9/1: 5-222030: 12th: Handy over 5f, sn wknd: btr 1817 (fast).   5   46
1423 **TERRAQUIN 35** [5]4-8-12 (74) J Tate 33/1: 6-040050: 13th: Cl-up till halfway, fdd.   1¾   38
13 Ran   Time 1m 27.28 (3.18)   Owned: Mrs E H Vestey   Trained: Newmarket

---

2173   7.55 Williamhpoker Com Classified Stakes 3yo 0-80 (D)
£5525 £1700 £850   6f str   Good 45   +13 Fast   Stands side

1912* **KIND 11** [9] R Charlton 3-8-10 (82) R Hughes 10/11 FAV: 34-311: Veered badly right start, sn cl   86
up, led halfway, rdn out fnl 1f to hold on: suited by forcing tactics at 6f/7f, 1m will suit if learning to settle:
acts on firm & gd grnd: likes Kempton: lightly raced: see 1912.
1933 **SWINBROOK 11** [4] J A R Toller 3-8-11 (80) S Sanders 11/1: 52-002: ch g Stravinsky - Dance Diane   hd   85
(Affirmed) Rear, prog halfway, kept on well ins fnl 1f, just held by wnr: rnr-up on 1 of only 2 '03 starts (stks):
eff at 6f on gd grnd: lightly rcd performer who lost little in defeat, can find similar.
2 Oct'03 Yarm 6.0gd 85- C:
1912 **FAREWELL GIFT 11** [1] R Hannon 3-8-11 (80) K Fallon 7/1: 200-4323: Handy when short of room 5f   hd   84
out, outpcd after 3f, ralllied well fnl 1f, post came too sn: remains in gd form: apprec rtn to 7f: see 1912.
1734 **INSTANT RECALL 19** [3] B J Meehan 3-8-11 (78) D Holland 5/1: 310454: Rear, prog 2f out, styd on   ¾   82
ins fnl 1f, not btn far: clr of rest: acts on gd, gd/soft grnd & polytrack: see 1703.
914 **TROTTERS BOTTOM 70** [6]3-8-11 (79) J F Egan 25/1: 06326-05: b g Mind Games - Fleeting Affair   5   67
(Hotfoot) Handy when short of room 5f out, wknd: 10 wk abs: auct mdn wnr in '03 (also plcd 4 times): eff at
5/6f on fast, gd & polytrack. 2 Oct'03 Ling 5ap 84a-(76) D: 2 Sep'03 Good 6g/f 78-76 D: 1 Jul'03 Ling 6gd 76- E:
1983 **HANDSOME CROSS 8** [8]3-9-1 (84) S Drowne 5/1: 1232-556: Sn rcd stands rail, led 3f, wknd ins fnl 2f.   ¾   69
1912 **MR HULLABALOU 11** [2]3-8-11 (77) N Day 66/1: 00457: Al bhd: btr 1497.   ½   64
15 **BINNION BAY 203** [5]3-9-1 (84) R Smith 50/1: 3100-8: b g Fasliyev - Literary (Woodman) Bhd, nvr   5   53
a factor on reapp: auct mdn wnr on 3 '03 starts: eff at 5f on fast & gd grnd: acts on a sharp trk: has been
gelded since last term: with R Hannon. 1 May'03 Good 5g/f 85- D:
1847 **OUR GAMBLE 14** [7]3-8-10 (82) Dane O'Neill 20/1: 0410-609: Cl-up 3f, sn fdd: btr 1513.   1¾   43
9 Ran   Time 1m 13.07 (1.97)   Owned: Mr K Abdulla   Trained: Beckhampton

---

2174   8.25 Williamhillcasino Com Handicap Stakes Fillies 3yo 0-75 (E)   [82]
£3611 £1111 £556   7f rnd   Good 45   -08 Slow   Inside

1722 **KRYSSA 20** [12] G L Moore 3-8-5 (59) P Robinson 11/2: 413351: Handy, prog 2f out, drvn out to   67
lead cl-home: eff at 5f, suited by 6/7f: acts on gd, gd/soft grnd & polytrack: lightly rcd performer who is
unexposed in h'caps: apprec well judged P Robinson ride: see 1102.
1810 **KALI 16** [2] R Charlton 3-9-4 (72) D Sweeney 8/1: 2-332: Rear, gd prog to lead 1f out, hdd   nk   78
cl-home: eff at 7f, rtn to 1m will suit: acts on fast, gd grnd & polytrack: can find similar: see 1810 & 980.
1730 **PICKLE 19** [11] S C Williams 3-8-8 (62) S Sanders 11/1: 304103: Held up, prog after 5f, kept on   2   64
ins fnl 1f: acts on gd, soft grnd & polytrack: enjoyed return to 7f: see 1577.
1982 **HERE TO ME 8** [8] R Hannon 3-9-0 (70) R Hughes 14/1: 3502-534: Handy over 5f, sn onepcd: see 1982.   shd   71
1468 **THARAA 33** [1]3-9-1 (69) S Drowne 20/1: 0-205: Held up, prog & short of room 2f out, again short   1¼   68+
of room dist, switched & kept on fnl 1f: much closer with clr passage, apprec rtn to 1m: see 1177.
1761 **ELA PAPAROUNA 18** [3]3-9-3 (71) Dane O'Neill 9/1: 543-306: Rear, prog 3f out, nrst fin: shd   69
encouraging effort & looks sure to apprec further: see 1281.
126 **UNITED SPIRIT 186** [5]3-8-6 (60) K Fallon 12/1: 504-7: b f Fasliyev - Atlantic Desire (Ela Mana   1   56
Mou) Handy till halfway, sn outpcd, rallied bef 1f out: reapp: unplcd in '03 (rtd 66, mdn).
1912 **SNOW JOKE 11** [10]3-8-6 (60) R Havlin 50/1: 000-048: Handy 5f, sn no extra: btr 1912.   ¾   54
1956 **DANDOUCE 9** [17]3-9-0 BL (68) R L Moore 4/1 FAV: 423-6349: Led, hdd 1f out, fdd: disapp in blnks.   ¾   60
1024 **SAHARA STORM 61** [13]3-9-4 (72) D Holland 14/1: 3340-00: 10th: b f Desert Prince - Deluge   1   62
(Rainbow Quest) Cl-up over 5f, sn wknd: 9 wk abs: plcd in 2 of 4 '03 starts (fill mdn, rtd 76): eff at 6/7f on fm.
1929 **FIRST DAWN 11** [6]3-9-2 (70) S Hitchcott(3) 25/1: 06-00: 11th: Rear, nvr nrr than mid-div.   1   58
1985 **BLACK OVAL 8** [14]3-8-1 (55) Lisa Jones(3) 25/1: 4450300: 12th: Handy 5f, sn wknd.   nk   42
1720 **LADY MO 20** [15]3-8-9 (63) A McCarthy 11/1: 1101230: 13th: Al in rear: btr 1720 & 1339.   2½   45

KEMPTON   WEDNESDAY 02.06.04   Righthand, Flat, Fair Track

1239 **Man Crazy 46** [7]3-8-11 (65) M Tebbutt 50/1:0
1762 **Chica Roca 18** [9]3-9-7 (75) L Dettori 16/1:0
17 Ran   Time 1m 27.84 (3.74)   Owned: Mr D J Deer   Trained: Brighton

1488 **Just One Look 32** [4]3-9-0 (68) J Murtagh 33/1:0
1099 **Archerfield 55** [16]3-8-12 (66) R Hills 14/1:0

2175	8.55 Be A Wednesday Winner Handicap Stakes 3yo 0-85 (D)				[91]
	£5642 £1736 £868	1m4f	Good 45	-16 Slow Inside	

1813 **PAGAN MAGIC 15** [8] J A R Toller 3-8-11 (74) Lisa Jones(3) 6/1: 05-301: Chsd ldrs, styd on to lead   79
bef 1f out, all out: eff at 10f, now stays a slowly run 12f: acts on gd & soft grnd: open to more improvement.
1756 **LE TISS 18** [5] M R Channon 3-9-1 (78) S Hitchcott(3) 20/1: 0162-402: Held up, prog 3f out, styd   ¾   82
on to chase wnr ins fnl 1f, al held: eff at 1m, stays slowly run 12f: see 947.
1807 **MUSTANG ALI 16** [1] S Kirk 3-8-5 (68) J F Egan 25/1: 2003-603: ch g Ali Royal - Classic Queen   ½   70
(Classic Secret) Rear, prog when carr badly left over 1f out, kept on ins fnl 1f, not btn far: rnr-up twice in '03
(auct mdns): eff at 7f, now stays slowly run 12f: acts on firm, gd grnd & polytrack.
2 Sep'03 Brig 7.0g/f 68- E: 2 Aug'03 Folk 7g/f 70- F:
1807 **SCHAPIRO 16** [4] J H M Gosden 3-9-0 BL (77) L Dettori 10/1: 045-034: Held up, prog 3f out, onepcd   nk   79
ins fnl 1f: first time blnks: just btr 1807.
1377 **PEAK OF PERFECTION 37** [9]3-8-10 (73) P Robinson 9/1: 00-535: Led, hdd bef 1f out, sn no extra.   1¼   73
1871* **WHATS UP DOC 13** [3]3-9-5 (82) K Dalgleish 7/2: 533-16: Cl-up 10f, sn edged left & no extra: btr 1871.   1¾   79
1756 **BUKIT FRASER 18** [6]3-9-7 (84) D Holland 15/8 FAV: 34-147: Handy, edged left & wknd bef 1f out.   1¾   78
4732} **LAWAAHEB 232** [2]3-8-7 (70) R Hills 7/1: 056-8: b c Alhaarth - Ajayib (Riverman) Keen rear, nvr   2½   60
able to chall: reapp: unplcd all 3 '03 starts (rtd 75, mdns): with J L Dunlop.
1790 **AVESOMEOFTHAT 16** [7]3-8-9 (72) R Havlin 33/1: 4520-69: Handy over 1m, fdd: btr 1790.   13   45
9 Ran   Time 2m 37.32(7.32)   Owned: The Gap Partnership   Trained: Newmarket

HAMILTON   THURSDAY 03.06.04   Righthand, Undulating, Stiff Uphill Finish

Official Going Good/Firm (Good Places)

2176	2.10 Lord Advocate Handicap Stakes 4yo+ 0-75 (E)				[74]
	£3884 £1195 £598	1m5f9y	Good 48	-16 Slow Stands side	

2105 **PARTY PLOY 3** [1] K R Burke 6-8-11 (57) Darren Williams 7/2 JTFAV: 606-0021: Keen cl-up, led 3f   67
out, drvn out to hold on: qck reapp: suited by 12f/14f on firm, soft & both AWs: likes Hamilton.
2041 **ISAAF 6** [6] P W Hiatt 5-9-3 (63) P Mathers(7) 10/1: 2-121102: Keen in tch, ev ch ins fnl 1f,   hd   71
edged left under press & just held: qck reapp: lost little in defeat & shld sn return to winning ways: see 1469.
1680 **MILLENNIUM HALL 22** [4] P Monteith 5-8-8 (54) L Enstone(3) 12/1: 060-0633: Keen cl-up, kept on   1½   59
from dist, not pace front 2: eff btwn 1m/11.6f, now stays 13f: see 1504.
2085 **TANDAVA 5** [2] J Semple 6-9-12 p (72) G Duffield 11/1: 400-1054: Led 12f, no extra dist: see 1118.   1½   73
2085 **TONI ALCALA 5** [10]5-9-0 (58) D Nolan(3) 6/1: 2316135: Cl-up, outpcd 3f out, rallied dist: qck reapp.   ¾   68
2112* **TRUSTED MOLE 3** [9]6-8-6 (52) B Swarbrick(5) 7/2 JT FAV: 5353-516: Mid-div, nvr able to chall: 1   50
qck reapp: btr 2112 (appr h'cap).
1905* **COSMIC CASE 12** [5]9-8-1 (47) A Nicholls 6/1: 55300-17: Rear, nvr a dngr: btr 1905.   nk   44
1905 **EXALTED 12** [8]11-8-8 (54) Dale Gibson 20/1: 2200-558: Rear, nvr able to chall: btr 1396.   7   41
1923 **FANTASTICO 12** [7]4-9-2 (62) R Winston 10/1: 61430-49: Handy 9f, sn wknd: btr 1923.   3   45
9 Ran   Time 2m 43.87 (8.37)   Owned: Mr Ian A McInnes   Trained: Leyburn

2177	2.40 Claiming Stakes A Qualifier For The Hamilton Park 2-Y-O Series Final 2yo (E)				
	£3884 £1195 £598	5f4y str	Good 48	-17 Slow Stands side	

1906* **GOLDHILL PRINCE 12** [3] W G M Turner 2-8-9 p C Haddon(7) 7/4 FAV: 0402111: Led/dsptd lead, hung   69
right throughout, went on from halfway, drvn & held on all out: no bid: wckd bckd, op 9/4: eff at 5/6f on firm,
gd/soft & fibresand: likes sell/claim grade: see 1906 & 1779.
2028 **KRISTIKHAB 7** [4] A Berry 2-9-3 F Lynch 7/1: 0542: ch g Intikhab - Alajyal (Kris) Rdn chasing   shd   75
ldrs, drvn & styd on well in last, just failed: £20,000 Feb foal, half-brother to a 10f wnr & a juv wnr abroad:
eff over a stiff 5f, return to 6f in similar shld suit: handles fast & gd: gd run at the weights.
1869 **PROCRASTINATE 14** [7] R F Fisher 2-8-7 P Mathers(7) 11/1: 30653: Bhd, eff over 2f out, no impress.   3½   55
1818 **CANARY DANCER 16** [2] P C Haslam 2-8-12 G Faulkner 14/1: 04: b f Groom Dancer - Bird of Time   ½   59
(Persian Bold) Chsd ldrs, no impress dist: some improvement from debut: 12,000gns April foal, half-sister to a US
multiple sprint scorer, dam a 7f/1m 3yo wnr: prob stay further.
1869 **STRAFFAN 14** [8]2-8-6 J Carroll 7/2: 63325: Cl-up, btn over 1f out: op 2/1: btr 1869 (6f).   5   39
2056 **DANEHILL FAIRY 6** [5]2-8-2 G Duffield 33/1: 0206: Dsptd lead till halfway, sn btn: btr 1394.   ½   34
1107 **DROOPYS JOEL 54** [6]2-8-13 T Hamilton(3) 33/1: 007: b g Primo Dominie - Zaima (Green Desert)   5   31
Chsd ldrs, outpcd halfway: abs, mod form.
1117 **CITY TORQUE 53** [1]2-8-9 P Makin(5) 7/2: 68: ch f Marquetry - Citiscape (Citidancer) Sn bhd, op   15   0
5/1: abs: cheaply bght Feb first foal: bred to need 7f+.
8 Ran   Time 1m 1.38 (3.28)   Owned: Gold Hill Racing   Trained: Sherborne

2178	3.10 Ben Raceday Maiden Auction Stakes A Qualifier For The Hamilton Park 2-Y-O Series 2yo (E)				
	£3998 £1230 £615	6f5y str	Good 48	-19 Slow Stands side	

1874 **ROCKBURST 14** [9] K R Burke 2-8-3 A Nicholls 9/2: 521: Gd speed to bag fair rail position & make   77
all, held on well for press: op 7/1: eff at 6f, shld get 7f: acts on fast & gd: likes to force the pace: see 1874.
1362 **EVANESCE 40** [4] M R Channon 2-8-4 (1ow) S Hitchcott 7/2: 22422: Keen & sn handy, chall over 1f   1¼   73
out, onepace: bckd: 6 wk abs: styd stiff 6f well: acts on fast, gd/soft & polytrack: shld find a race.

1439 **ALMOST PERFECT 35** [6] T D Barron 2-8-2 P Fessey 50/1: 63: ch f Priolo - Talbiya (Mujtahid) Sn ½ 70
cl-up & ev ch over 1f out, just held cl-home: turf bow, left debut bhd: cheaply bght Feb first foal, dam unplcd on
sole start, related to smart 10/11f wnrs: sire a top-class miler: eff over a stiff 6f & shld get further.
1920 **MAKE US FLUSH 12** [7] A Berry 2-8-2 P Mathers(3) 100/1: 404: Mid-div, rdn & styd on fnl 2f, not nk 69
able to chall: acts on gd: imprvd eff, interesting for h'caps or sellers/clmrs: see 1343.
2056 **OCHIL HILLS DANCER 6** [8]2-8-6 V Halliday 25/1: 05: Prom, rdn & no extra fnl 1f: stays 6f. ½ 72
  HILL FAIRY 0 [3]2-8-9 Dale Gibson 16/1: 6: ch f Monsun - Homing Instinct (Arctic Tern) Bhd, ½ 74
prog when short of room over 1f out, styd on well cl-home, nrst fin: op 14/1: £46,000 Jan foal, dam a mutliple
mid/staying dist wnr: improve plenty for this.
1631 **DIXIE QUEEN 26** [11]2-8-6 (1ow) R Winston 14/1: 57: Hmpd early & bhd, late prog, nvr a threat: shd 70
this longer 6f trip looks set to suit: see 1631.
1974 **STRATHTAY 9** [12]2-8-6 G Faulkner 10/11 FAV: 38: Trkd ldrs far rail when short of room over 2f nk 69
out, sn rdn & no impress: hvly bckd & more expected after 1974 (5f, debut).
  SPINNAKERS GIRL 0 [2]2-8-2 P Hanagan 40/1: 9: Sn rdn & bhd, only mod prog: bckd at long odds. ¾ 63
2083 **CHICAGO NIGHTS 5** [5]2-8-4 Rory Moore(7) 40/1: 400: 10th: Dwelt, mid-div, no impress from halfway. 5 50
1149 **Comintrue 51** [1]2-8-5 (2ow) J Carroll 50/1:0 **Eminence Gift 0** [10]2-8-4 T Hamilton(1) 50/1:0
12 Ran Time 1m 13.83 (4.03) Owned: Mrs Sally L Jones Trained: Leyburn

---

<table>
<tr><td rowspan="2">2179</td><td>3.40 Hamilton Park Series Handicap Stakes 3yo+ 0-75 (E)</td><td></td><td>[75]</td></tr>
<tr><td>£4290 £1320 £660   1m1f36y   Good 48   +09 Fast Inside</td><td></td><td></td></tr>
</table>

1972 **JORDANS ELECT 10** [7] I Semple 4-9-8 (69) T Eaves(3) 8/1: 500-5101: Al handy & led over 2f out, 77
drvn & styd on strongly in last: best time of day: back to form after racing prom from poor wide draw latest: eff
at 1m/9f on firm & gd/soft grnd, loves Hamilton: see 1748 & 1388.
2087 **TAKES TUTU 5** [3] K R Burke 5-9-12 bl (73) Darren Williams 7/4 FAV: 65-00022: Held up, smooth hdwy 2 76
trav well 2f out, rdn & no extra from dist: hvly bckd, op 9/4: qck reapp: prob best at 7f/1m: on a handy mark.
2120 **OSCAR PEPPER 2** [9] T D Barron 7-9-2 vis (63) R Winston 11/2: 404-5063: In tch, switched & styd on shd 65
for press fnl 2f, not able to chall: nicely bckd, qck reapp: clr of rem, looks to have come to hand: see 1485.
1872 **RARE COINCIDENCE 14** [2] R F Fisher 3-8-9 (1ow) (67) D Nolan 10/1: 1360444: Led till 3f out, fdd dist. 6 59
2030 **CHAMPAIN SANDS 7** [1]5-8-10 (57) B Swarbrick(5) 7/1: 062-3425: Trkd ldrs & ch 2f out, no extra bef dist. ½ 47
2030 **SKIDDAW JONES 7** [5]4-8-5 (52) J Carroll 16/1: 4000-056: Held up, no impress fnl 3f: see 2030. 3 36
1748 **MOUNT PEKAN 20** [6]4-8-0 (47) P Hanagan 5/1: 5000-037: Keen & trkd ldrs, wknd fnl 2f: btr 1748 (1m). 1½ 28
1781 **RIFLEMAN 18** [8]4-10-0 P (75) G Duffield 12/1: 5340-008: ch g Starborough - En Garde (Irish River) 5 47
Prom, rdn & btn 2f out: cheek pieces, no improvement: h'cap scorer '03, subs disapp in a visor: dual AW wnr late
'02: eff at 7f, prob best around 1m & has tried 10f: acts on both AWs, firm & fast grnd, prob any trk: well h'capped.
1 Apr'03 Ripo 8g/f 87-82 C: 1 Dec'02 Ling 7ap 79a- D: 1 Dec'02 Wolv 8.4af 81a- F:
8 Ran Time 1m 57.65 (3.55) Owned: Mr Ian Crawford Trained: Carluke

---

<table>
<tr><td rowspan="2">2180</td><td>4.10 Howard Mcdowall Memorial Classified Stakes 3yo+ 0-65 (E)</td><td></td><td>[65]</td></tr>
<tr><td>£3819 £1175 £588   1m3f16y   Good 48   -13 slow Stands side</td><td></td><td></td></tr>
</table>

1663* **MAGIC STING 24** [5] M L W Bell 3-8-9 (66) J Mackay 5/1: 5-55611: Keen trkg ldrs & smooth prog to 73
lead over 1f out, rdn out to assert: step up to 11f & 12f+ shld suit: acts on soft, enjoyed
gd today, likes a stiff/undul or gall trk: lightly rcd & progressive 3yo, likely more to come: see 1663.
1681 **KIDZPLAY 22** [6] J S Goldie 8-9-8 (64) T Eaves(3) 9/4: 564-0342: Led, rdn & hdd over 1f out, 1¾ 68
switched & kept on for press, not pace of wnr: well bckd: see 1681 & 1389.
1923 **CLARADOTNET 12** [4] M R Channon 4-9-7 (67) S Hitchcott(3) 7/2: 10-00063: b f Sri Pekan - 3 62
Lypharitissima (Lightning) Chsd ldrs, rdn 2f out, onepace: bckd: '03 fills mdn scorer (lightly rcd, H Cecil):
winning form at 11.7f, tried 14f: acts on fast grnd & a stiff/turning trk.
1 Sep'03 Bath 11.7g/f 82- D: 2 Aug'03 Nott 10.0g/f 76- F:
1390 **TEMPLET 38** [1] I Semple 4-9-13 (70) P Hanagan 2/1 FAV: 4-234: Sn pushed along, rdn & btn 2f out: 14 48
hvly bckd, op 5/2: much btr expected after 1390 & 1038.
1226 **SASPYS LAD 47** [3]7-9-8 (65) B Swarbrick(5) 12/1: 55506/-65: Held up in tch, rdn & btn 3f out: abs. nk 42
1897 **HOWARDS DREAM 13** [2]6-9-8 t (30) J McAuley 100/1: 060-0406: Cl-up, btn over 2f out: see 1450. 30 0
6 Ran Time 2m 25.54 (6.74) Owned: Mrs P T Fenwick Trained: Newmarket

---

<table>
<tr><td rowspan="2">2181</td><td>4.40 Rectangle Group Maiden Handicap Stakes 3yo+ 35-55 (F)</td><td></td><td>[53]</td></tr>
<tr><td>£3094 £884 £442   5f4y str   Good 48   +04 Fast Stands side</td><td></td><td></td></tr>
</table>

2160 **PIRLIE HILL 1** [2] Miss L A Perratt 4-9-11 (50) J Carroll 5/1: 0-3402501: Sn cl-up stands side 55
trav well, led overall over 1f out, drifted badly right to far rail but sn in command: nicely bckd, unplcd
yesterday: eff at 5/6f on firm & gd grnd, poss handles gd/soft: handles a stiff/undul or gall trk: see 1391.
1787 **SOMETHINGABOUTHER 17** [4] P W Hiatt 4-9-6 (45) Darren Williams 20/1: 5030502: Prom stands side, 1¾ 44
drvn & kept on, not pace of wnr: clr rem: see 653.
1575 **NOBLE MOUNT 28** [10] R Guest 3-9-9 (55) J Mackay 9/1: 5003: b g Muhtarram - Our Poppet (Warning) 3 45
Held up far side, styd on for press, not pace of wnr: first home from far side group: h'cap bow: unplcd prev at
5/6f: eff over a stiff 5f on gd grnd in mdn h'cap company.
1948 **PETANA 10** [7] M Dods 4-9-3 bl (42) Natalia Gemelova(7) 10/1: 5020-504: gr f Petong - Duxyana ½ 31
(Cyrano de Bergerac) Switched far side & bhd, styd on from halfway, nvr able to chall: bckd: mdn rnr-up in '03:
unplcd '02 (Mrs Rees): eff around 5/6f on fast grnd, stiff or easy trk: seems best in blnks.
2 Aug'03 Thir 5g/f 43-42 E: 2 Jul'03 Hami 5.0g/f 45-(43) D:
1948 **ATTILA THE HUN 10** [14]5-8-10 (35) P Hanagan 4/1 FAV: 000-4605: Chsd ldrs far side, no impress dist. 1 21
1908 **AMBER FOX 12** [6]3-9-8 (54) F Lynch 10/1: 56004-56: Led stands side till over 1f out, sn no impress. 1½ 36
1605 **WENDYS GIRL 27** [12]3-9-7 (53) T Hamilton(3) 9/2: 0052P47: Cl-up far side & led that group over 2f ¾ 33
out till over 1f out, sn btn.
1799 **MINIRINA 17** [1]4-8-10 (35) P Makin(5) 25/1: 40-04408: Prom stands side till 2f out: btr 1562 (AW). 1¾ 10
1948 **PAY TIME 10** [9]5-9-1 (40) L Enstone(3) 33/1: 6000-609: Led far side 3f, sn btn. nk 14
1803 **BE MY ALIBI 17** [11]3-8-10 (35) B Swarbrick(5) 7/1: 5000-050: 10th: Chsd ldrs far side 3f out: btr 1803 (AW). 2½ 7
1797 **RHINEFIELD BOY 17** [3]3-9-2 (48) T Eaves(3) 33/1: 000-00: 11th: Chsd ldrs stands side 3f. 1¾ 11
1971 **Missie 10** [8]4-9-11 (50) R Winston 16/1:0

HAMILTON THURSDAY 03.06.04 Righthand, Undulating, Stiff Uphill Finish

1801 **Forest Queen 17** [13]7-8-5 (10oh) (20) P Mathers(5) 50/1:0
13 Ran   Time 1m 0.30(2.2)   Owned: The Hon Miss Heather Galbraith   Trained: Ayr

HAYDOCK THURSDAY 03.06.04 Lefthand, Flat, Galloping Track

Official Going Good/Firm - Good/Soft after Race 2184

2182

2.20 Littlewoods Bet Direct Maiden Stakes 3yo+   (D)
£5883 £1810 £905   **6f str   Good/Firm   Inapp**   Centre

1832 **HAWAAJES 16** [11] B Hanbury 3-8-13   W Supple 7/1: 031: Prom, hdwy to lead ins fnl 1f, edged left   77
but styd on, rdn out: imprvd back at 6f, stays 7.5f: acts on fast grnd & on a stiff trk: open to improvement.
1971 **KENTUCKY EXPRESS 10** [9] T D Easterby 3-8-13   D Allan(3) 66/1: 02: b c Air Express - Hotel   1¼   73
California (Last Tycoon) Dwelt, in tch, eff dist, kept on: half-brother to wnrs over 6f/hdles: dam 7f scorer:
much imprvd from debut back at 6f, 7f looks sure to suit: acts on fast grnd & a gall trk: type to win a race.
1846 **SAN LORENZO 15** [8] M R Channon 3-8-8   A Culhane 12/1: 03: ch f Machiavellian - Sanchez   ½   66
(Wolfhound) Led, rdn & hdd ins last, no extra: imprvd from debut & eff at 6f on fast, shld stay further.
1829 **MAJORCA 16** [7] J H M Gosden 3-8-13 (78) L Dettori 1/1 FAV: 0-324: In tch, rdn & onepace fnl 2f: hd   70
bckd from 7/4: btr expected but prob ran close to form of 1829, 1191.
4973} **TROIS ETOILES 215** [13]3-8-8 M Hills 66/1: 00-5: ch f Grand Lodge - Stardance (Rahy) Bhd, late   2   59+
gains, kind ride: well btn both juv starts: caught the eye here, sure to relish a step up to 7f+ & interesting in a
h'cap next time, keep in mind.
      GRAND RAPIDE [6]3-8-8   K McEvoy 20/1: 6: Held up, nvr a factor on debut.   7   41
1527 **LIGHT THE DAWN 31** [14]4-9-2   S W Kelly 66/1: 0-07: Chsd ldrs, wknd 2f out.   shd   40
      BUNKHOUSE [12]4-9-7   J Murtagh 33/1: 8: Dwelt, nvr a factor on debut.   ½   43
1682 **GREY GURKHA 22** [17]3-8-13   R Fitzpatrick 66/1: 69: Held up, hung left over 1f out, btn.   2   37
5014} **ALPHA ZETA 210** [16]3-8-13   Dean McKeown 100/1: 0-0: 10th: In tch, wknd 2f out: gelded.   1   34
1846 **INDIANA BLUES 15** [1]3-8-8 (89) K Darley 3/1: 040-40: 11th: Keen in tch, wknd 2f out: btr 1846.   nk   28
1070 **DESIGNER CITY 58** [10]3-8-8 (52) P Bradley(5) 66/1: 44660-00: 12th: In tch, wknd 2f out.   hd   27
1876 **IRUSAN 14** [5]4-9-7   Leanne Kershaw(7) 20/1: 600: 13th: Handy, wknd 2f out.   1   29
      RED HOT RUBY [15]3-8-8   G Parkin 33/1: 0: 14th: Dwelt, al bhd.   ½   22
4694} **LUKE SHARP 235** [4]3-8-13   N Callan 66/1: 000-0: 15th: Handy, wknd over 2f out on reapp.   4   15
      BRAIN WASHED [3]3-8-8   S Sanders 50/1: 0: 16th: Slow away & al bhd.   1   7
16 Ran   Time 1m 13.45 (2.15)   Owned: Mr Hamdan Al Maktoum   Trained: Newmarket

2183

2.50 Skybet Com Selling Stakes 2yo   (F)
£3108 £888 £444   **6f str   Good/Firm   Inapp**   Centre

1805 **ISLAND SWING 17** [3] J L Spearing 2-8-6   S Carson 4/1 CO FAV: 01: ch f Trans Island - Farmers   71
Swing (River Falls) Made all, rdn clr over 1f out: March first foal, cost 7,500gns: dam 1m wnr: imprvd from debut &
eff at 6f with forcing tactics on fast: relished drop to sell grade: bt in for 13,500gns, win another seller.
2083 **DANES ROCK 5** [8] P C Haslam 2-8-11 BL K Darley 4/1 CO FAV: 4062: Prom, eff to chase wnr 2f out,   5   60
onepace: not disgraced in blnks & eff at 6f on fast grnd: see 2083 (visor), 1048.
1869 **LOJO 14** [4] R P Elliott 2-8-6   W Supple 11/2: 03: In tch, no impress over 1f out: see 1869.   1½   51
1906 **TONIGHT 12** [1] W M Brisbourne 2-8-13   S W Kelly 12/1: 34: In tch, lost pl halfway, no impress.   nk   55
1968 **DICTION 10** [2]2-8-6   K McEvoy 4/1 CO FAV: 05: Handy, wknd 2f out: see 1968.   2½   43
      CASH TIME [7]2-8-6   R Fitzpatrick 20/1: 6: ch f Timeless Times - Cashmirie (Domynsky) Slow   6   25
away, nvr a factor on debut: May foal, dam 10f wnr: bred to need 6f+.
1968* **BOWLAND BRIDE 10** [5]2-8-11   P Bradley(5) 6/1: 504417: In tch, wknd 2f out: btr expected after 1968.   2   24
      ETERNAL SUNSHINE [6]2-8-6   S Chin 10/1: 8: Handy, wknd qckly over 2f out.   25   0
8 Ran   Time 1m 17.1 (5.8)   Owned: Mr J Spearing   Trained: Kinnersley

2184

3.20 Listed Bank Of Scotland Corporate Stakes Registered As The John Of Gaunt Stakes 4yo+   (A)
£17400 £6600 £3300   **7f30y rnd   Good   Inapp**   Inside

1811 **SUGGESTIVE 16** [5] W J Haggas 6-8-12 bl (107) M Hills 9/2: 415-4521: In tch, hdwy 2f out, styd on   110
well to lead cl-home, drvn out: stays 1m, best at 6/7f: acts on firm & soft, any trk: eff in blnks/visor: smart.
1486 **MAKHLAB 33** [2] B W Hills 4-8-12 (105) W Supple 16/1: 001-5542: Chsd ldr, eff to chall appr fnl   ½   109
1f, kept on for press, just held: ran to best but prob prefers even easier grnd: see 922.
4604} **THREE GRACES 84** [8] Saeed bin Suroor 4-8-12 vis T (109) L Dettori 9/2: 1512-103: ch g Peintre   shd   109
Celebre - Trefoil (Kris) Set pace, rdn over 1f out but kept on till collared cl-home, not btn far: smart run after
3 mth abs in first time t-strap, Dubai val h'cap wnr earlier: '03 mdn, h'cap & dual class wnr (with M Tregoning):
suited by 7f/1m, stays 9f & loves fm/fast, any trk: tried vis, t-strap here, gelded: useful, remains on upgrade.
2 Oct'03 Redc 7g/f 102-(99) A: 1 Sep'03 Newm 7g/f 101-(97) B: 1 Aug'03 Sali 8g/f 99-(93) C: 2 Aug'03 Newb 9fm 95-87 D:
1 Aug'03 Hayd 8.1g/f 89-81 C: 2 Jul'03 Nott 8.2gd 83-81 D: 1 Jun'03 Good 8g/f 82- D:
1686 **MILLENNIUM FORCE 22** [10] M R Channon 6-8-12 (107) K Darley 20/1: 4230-004: Slow away, sn rdn   ¾   107+
bhd, plenty to do over 2f out, "flew home", nrst fin: back to form & a 7f specialist: caught the eye here, keep in
mind, esp on soft grnd: see 1486.
1811 **COURT MASTERPIECE 16** [12]4-8-12 (106) J Murtagh 5/1: 42301-35: Held up, hdwy over 1f out, hung   2   103
left, onepace fnl 1f: closer to this wnr in 1811.
1758 **QUITO 19** [1]7-8-12 bl (111) A Culhane 6/1: 2556106: Keen, in tch, short of room when onepace fnl 1f.   ¾   101
3762} **DESERT DESTINY 287** [6]4-8-12 vis (107) K McEvoy 16/1: 0/15054-7: b g Desert Prince - High   4   93
Savannah (Rousillon) Held up, rdn & no impress over 1f out on reapp: gelded: '03 stks wnr, 5th in French 2,000
Guineas (with D Loder): '02 mdn wnr: eff at 7f, stays 1m on firm & gd/soft: eff with/without a visor: useful.
1 Apr'03 Newm 7gd 109-(92) C: 1 Jul'03 Newm 7g/f 92- D:
1926 **EL COTO 12** [7]4-8-12 (102) S Sanders 11/1: 4-015508: In tch, wknd 2f out: see 1686.   5   83
1624 **CRIMSON SILK 26** [3]4-8-12 p (94) P Robinson 40/1: 63-00009: ch g Forzando - Sylhall (Sharpo) In   nk   82
tch, wknd well over 1f out: 3rd in a List in '03: '02 mdn & auct stks scorer: suited by 6f on firm or gd grnd,
sharp or gall trk: too highly tried. 1 Aug'02 Wind 6g/f 97- E: 1 Jul'02 Wind 6g/f 93- D:

2086 **PAWAN 5** [9]4-8-12 (61) Ann Stokell 150/1: 0353020: 10th: In tch, wknd 2f out: needs h'caps, see 2086.   1   **80$**
1758 **TOUT SEUL 19** [4]4-9-3 (110) S Carson 4/1 FAV: 0605-100: 11th: Held up, rdn & wknd over 2f out: 8   **69**
now twice well below smart effort of 1356.
11 Ran   Time 1m 29.57 (2.47)   Owned: Mrs Barbara Bassett   Trained: Newmarket

---

2185 3.50 Betfred The Bonus King Handicap Stakes 3yo+ 0-95 (C)   **[93]**
£9978 £3070 £1535   **1m2f120y**   **Good/Soft**   **Inapp**   Outside

1478 **IONIAN SPRING 33** [7] C G Cox 9-9-11 (90) R Smith 8/1: 6530-101: Held up, hdwy to lead 2f out,   **97**
styd on gamely for press: eff over 10/12f on firm & soft grnd, fibresand & any trk, loves Newbury: best coming
late: tough, useful & game: see 1235.
1586 **OFARABY 28** [6] M A Jarvis 4-9-7 (86) P Robinson 5/2 FAV: 64-31642: In tch, hdwy to chase wnr   shd   **92**
over 1f out, kept on for press, just held in a fine duel: well bckd: apprec return to easy surface: see 964.
1736 **BRIAREUS 20** [9] A M Balding 4-9-0 (79) K Darley 13/2: 4-000203: In tch, eff over 1f out, onepace.   3½   **80**
1235 **FREELOADER 47** [4] J W Hills 4-8-9 (74) M Hills 11/2: 11260-04: Held up, eff dist, onepace.   ½   **74**
4720*}**BALTIC BLAZER 234** [2]4-8-11 (76) J Murtagh 8/1: 21-5: b g Polish Precedent - Pine Needle (Kris)   2½   **72**
In tch, eff over 2f out, no impress: '03 mdn wnr: eff at 8.3f on fast & gd/soft, shld stay further: acts on a gall
or easy trk: lightly rcd.   1 Oct'03 Wind 8.3g/f 70- D: 2 Sep'03 Hayd 8.1g/s 80- D:
1668 **LA SYLPHIDE 23** [3]7-9-3 (82) S W Kelly 11/4: 1610-256: Set pace till 2f out, no extra: bckd   nk   **77**
from 11/2: clearly btr expected after 1668, see 1346.
1525 **LIQUID FORM 31** [5]4-9-6 (85) W Supple 14/1: 14013-07: br g Bahhare - Brogan's Well (Caerleon)   1   **79**
Held up, btn 2f out: '03 dual h'cap wnr: '02 mdn auct scorer: eff over 1m/11f & likes firm & fast grnd, handles
gd/soft & any trk.   1 Sep'03 Good 11g/f 85-79 D: 1 Aug'03 Kemp 10g/f 80-72 E: 1 Aug'02 Good 8fm 81- E:
1226 **VICIOUS PRINCE 47** [8]5-8-9 (74) Dean McKeown 14/1: 00000-48: Handy, wknd well over 1f out: abs.   hd   **68**
1781 **ISLAND LIGHT USA 18** [1]4-8-11 (76) A Culhane 25/1: 350-0009: ch g Woodman - Isla Del Rey   30   **20**
(Nureyev) Held up, al bhd: '03 class stks wnr for E Dunlop: '02 mdn wnr: eff at 1m/10f on firm & gd/soft, gall or
fair trks: has tried a visor & cheek pieces: now with Mrs M Reveley.
1 Jun'03 Chep 10.2g/f 94-(88) C: 1 Sep'02 Kemp 8fm 90- D:
9 Ran   Time 2m 18.5 (8.5)   Owned: Elite Racing Club   Trained: Hungerford

---

2186 4.20 E B F Princess Royal Trust For Carers Unisys Classified Stakes 3yo+ 0-90 (C)
£8851 £3357 £1679   **6f str**   **Good/Soft**   **Inapp**   Centre

1933 **TRAYTONIC 12** [5] J R Fanshawe 3-8-12 (95) J Murtagh 9/2: 0410-501: Held up, hdwy over 1f out,   **104+**
led ins last, pushed clr, v readily: eff at 5/6f on firm, relished this gd/soft: handles any trk, likes a gall one:
impressed here for smart new trainer (prev with H Cyzer), keep on your side.
1977* **STEEL BLUE 9** [6] R M Whitaker 4-9-7 (85) A Culhane 11/2: 00-10012: Led, rdn & hdd ins last, no   2½   **95**
extra: well clr of rem & another fine run under top-weight: useful & improving: see 1977.
1626 **TEDBURROW 26** [2] E J Alston 12-9-1 (90) W Supple 14/1: 50605-53: Chsd ldrs, onepace over 1f out.   5   **79**
1708} **DANECARE 20** [11] J G Burns 4-9-6 (95) K Darley 7/1: 100-00024: b c Danetime - Nordic Flavour   2   **80**
(Nordico) Bhd, eff well over 1f out, no impress: recently rnr-up in an Irish h'cap: '03 dual h'cap wnr: suited by
6f on fast or hvy grnd.
951 **ONLYTIME WILL TELL 68** [10]6-9-4 (93) S W Kelly 9/2: 2500-005: Dwelt, held up, eff over 1f out,   2½   **73**
no impress: nicely bckd after a 10 wk abs: see 888.
1917 **INDIAN SPARK 2** [8]10-9-3 (82) K Dalgleish 100/30 FAV: 00-40446: Held up, no extra over 1f out.   1¼   **70**
2154 **JALOUHAR 1** [7]4-9-1 (47) M Tebbutt 200/1: 5050207: In tch, wknd over 2f out: unplcd yesterday.   ¾   **66$**
1703 **TOM TUN 21** [3]9-9-5 bl (94) Dean McKeown 3/1: 0010-028: Handy, wknd over 1f out: btr 1703, 1487.   1¾   **66**
1886 **TELEPATHIC 13** [9]4-9-1 (62) P Bradley(5) 200/1: 0006009: In tch, wknd over 2f out: see 1600, 1218.   2½   **57**
2111 **SPEEDFIT FREE 3** [9]7-9-1 vis (47) Ann Stokell 200/1: 0040060: 10th: Al bhd: see 1750, 1310.   7   **43**
1626 **ROSSELLI 26** [4]8-9-1 (46) C Ely(7) 150/1: 0044-000: 11th: Handy, wknd over 2f out: see 1626.   14   **15**
2052 **XALOC BAY 6** [1]6-9-1 (49) N Callan 100/1: 3603060: 12th: Handy 4f: see 675 (polytrack, slr).   1   **13**
12 Ran   Time 1m 14.36 (3.06)   Owned: Colin Davey Racing   Trained: Newmarket

---

2187 4.50 Betfred In-Shops Or On-Phone Handicap Stakes 3yo+ 0-85 (D)   **[85]**
£5707 £1756 £878   **6f str**   **Good/Soft**   **Inapp**   Centre

1598 **CARDINAL VENTURE 27** [2] K A Ryan 6-10-0 (85) N Callan 3/1: 11-20001: Made all, rdn clr appr fnl   **98**
1f: prev suited by 7f/8.5f, relished this drop back to 6f: acts on firm, gd/soft & loves fibresand, any trk: loves
to dominate: fine run under a big weight, follow up in this form: see 141, 2.
2059 **ROMANY NIGHTS 6** [7] J W Unett 4-9-5 BL (76) S W Kelly 3/1: 5043422: Handy, hdwy to go 2nd 3f out,   5   **78**
hung right & not pace of wnr ins last: another gd run in first time blnks: see 1354, 807.
1917 **PRINCE OF BLUES 12** [4] M Mullineaux 6-8-5 p (62) W Supple 16/1: 4045003: Chsd ldrs, onepcd 1f out.   1¾   **60**
1703 **CD FLYER 21** [3] B Ellison 7-10-0 (85) P Mulrennan(5) 11/4 FAV: 10-52004: Held up, eff well over   1½   **80**
1f out, onepace: btr 1251, 921.
1898 **GREY COSSACK 13** [1]7-9-8 (79) R Fitzpatrick 6/1: 00-01005: Held up, brief eff 2f out, no impress.   shd   **74**
2023 **ATTORNEY 8** [8]6-7-12 (50h)vis (50) Joanna Badger 11/1: 1120366: Nvr a factor: see 1788, 1336.   4   **42**
1824 **TYPE ONE 16** [6]6-8-13 vis (70) K Dalgleish 16/1: 0000207: Handy, wknd 2f out: btr 1522, 492.   10   **37**
7 Ran   Time 1m 14.76(3.46)   Owned: Mr Tony Fawcett   Trained: Hambleton

Official Going GOOD (GOOD/FIRM places Rnd Crse).

2188   6.20 Helical Bar Maiden Auction Stakes 2yo (E)
£4085 £1257 £629   **5f6y str**   **Good**   Slow   Far Side

KINGS QUAY [3] R Hannon 2-8-11 Dane O'Neill 9/2: 1: b c Montjeu - Glen Rosie (Mujtahid)			**100+**

Dwelt, sn trkd ldrs, short of rm dist, switched & strong run to lead cl-home, going away: debut: Feb 1st foal, cost 32,000gns: dam a decent miler, sire a top-class mid-dist performer: eff at 5f, will stay 6f: acts on gd & on a gall trk, runs well fresh: nice turn of foot here, will improve & win more races.

1274   **SPIRIT OF FRANCE 44** [8] M Johnston 2-8-11   J Fanning 7/2: 22: Front rank, led briefly dist, kept   1¼   90
on but not pace of wnr cl-home: op 11/4, 6 wk abs: acts on gd & soft grnd: shld apprec 6f now: win a mdn.
1717   **CALY DANCER 21** [1] D R C Elsworth 2-8-9   T Quinn 33/1: 053: ch g Entrepreneur - Mountain Dancer   1¾   83
(Rainbow Quest) Rear, rdn halfway, styd on late, nrst fin: Feb first foal, cost 18,000gns: dam a 12f wnr, sire a high-class miler: crying out for 6f+ & one to keep in mind in nursery h'caps: see 1717.
1752   **EXTRA MARK 19** [4] J R Best 2-8-7   N Pollard 6/1: 224: Trkd ldrs, ev ch till fdd ins fnl 1f: see 1752.   nk   80$
2094   **ALPAGA LE JOMAGE 3** [5]2-8-9 BL   L Dettori 3/1 FAV: 33245: Led till dist, wknd: qck reapp & tried   2   76
blnks, nicely bckd tho' op 2/1: much btr 2094 (C/D, List, without blnks).
   GEISHA LADY [7]2-8-2   Martin Dwyer 33/1: 6: b f Raise A Grand - Mitsubishi Style (Try My Best)   1½   65
Dwelt, nvr nr ldrs on debut: E11,500 April foal: half-sister to sev juv wnrs: dam styd 1m, sire a high-class juv.
   PITCH UP [2]2-9-0   K Fallon 7/2: 7: b c Cape Cross - Uhud (Mujtahid)   Dwelt, veered left sn   1   74
after start & sn well bhd, no ch: bckd from 9/2, debut: 40,000gns Feb foal: half-brother to a juv wnr abroad: dam unrcd, sire a high-class miler: with T Mills & btr clearly expected, threw this away at the start.
   OUR NIGEL [9]2-8-7   S Drowne 50/1: 8: Front rank 3.5f, wknd on debut.   7   47
8 Ran   Time 1m 03.25 (3.65)   Owned: Mr J R May   Trained: Marlborough

2189   6.50 Numis Securities Handicap Stakes 3yo+ 0-85 (D)
£5551 £1708 £854   **5f6y str**   **Good**   **Fair**   Far Side   **[85]**

2084   **WHISTLER 5** [1] J M Bradley 7-9-4 p (75)   R Hills 5/1: 0-000301: Mid-div, strong run to lead ent   83
fnl 1f, styd on well, rdn out: op 7/2, qck reapp: eff at 5/6f on firm, soft & any trk: on fair mark.
1532   **TABOOR 30** [9] J W Payne 6-7-12 (2oh)h bl T (53)   Lisa Jones(3) 14/1: 0500502: Trkd ldrs, ev ch   1½   57
entering fnl 1f, not pace of wnr cl-home: back to form in first time t-strap: see 748.
2044   **PORT ST CHARLES 6** [4] C R Dore 7-8-6 (63)   R Thomas(5) 15/2: 0440043: Hmpd start & bhd, styd on   1   62
strongly into 3rd, nrst fin: on a v handy mark & all wng form has come over 6f: turn shld not be far away.
1845   **FURTHER OUTLOOK 15** [6] D K Ivory 10-9-11 (82)   T Quinn 16/1: 0-130004: Led till ent fnl 1f, no extra.   nk   80
1898   **ZOOM ZOOM 13** [5]4-9-5 (76)   M Fenton 12/1: 31/-105: Nvr btr than mid-div: btr 1345 (6f, gd/sft).   ½   73
1927   **MARGALITA 12** [8]4-8-12 t (69)   J F Egan 33/1: 300-6006: Rdn in rear, staying on when short of room   ¾   63
fnl 1f: relish a return to 6f+: see 1927 (blnks).
2063   **MAYZIN 5** [10]4-7-12 (2oh)p (53)   J F McDonald(3) 13/2: 3314007: Front rank, wknd fnl 1f: tchd 8/1,   shd   49
qck reapp: rtd higher 897 (AW).
1749*   **THE FISIO 20** [7]4-9-2 vis (73)   Martin Dwyer 5/1: 0020418: Prom, rdn & hmpd over 1f out, not   1½   63
recover: no luck, btr 1749 (class stks).
2023   **NIVERNAIS 8** [3]5-9-9 (80)   Dane O'Neill 4/1 FAV: 1336-009: Swerved start, al rear: see 2023.   ½   69
5025}   **WICKED UNCLE 209** [2]5-9-5 bl (76)   D Holland 10/1: 002320-0: 10th: b g Distant Relative - The   1½   61
Kings Daughter (Indian King) Front rank 3.5f, wknd on reapp: failed to score in '03, plcd in several h'caps: '02
h'cap wnr for J Toller: eff at 5/6f on gd & firm grnd, sharp or stiff/gall trk: eff with/without blnks/visor, likes
to dominate: on a handy mark if returning to form. 2 Nov'03 Muss 5g/f 80-73 D: 2 Oct'03 Newc 5gd 75-70 D:
2 Aug'02 Bath 5fm 80- D: 1 May'02 Wind 5g/f 83-78 D: 2 Aug'01 Kemp 6fm 80-76 D: 1 Jul'01 Donc 5g/f 78-70 D:
10 Ran   Time 1m 02.12 (2.52)   Owned: Mr Raymond Tooth   Trained: Chepstow

2190   7.20 Listed Ig Index 30th Anniversary Surrey Stakes 3yo (A)
£17400 £6600 £3300   **7f16y rnd**   **Good/Firm 36**   +03 Fast   Inside

1762*   **MADID 19** [6] J H M Gosden 3-8-11   R Hills 11/2: 11: Held up, imprvd 2f out, strong run to lead   **114+**
cl-home, going away: handled drop back to 7f, return to 1m will suit: acts on fast & on a gall trk: smart & impressed
here, type to progress further & one to be with in Gr company next time, prob in Gr 3 Jersey: see 1762.
4086* }**PASTORAL PURSUITS 271** [4] H Morrison 3-9-3 (110)   S Drowne 9/1: 2111-2: b c Bahamian Bounty -   ½   116
Star (Most Welcome) Waited with, hdwy to lead dist, tired up & caught close home on reapp: op 6/1: highly
progressive juv, won 3 of 4 starts, notably Gr 3 Sirenia stks: eff at 6/7f on firm & gd/soft grnd: handles a sharp
or gall trk: has a decent turn of foot: excellent reapp coming after wnr weight, win more Gr races.
1 Sep'03 Kemp 6fm 115-(100) A: 1 Aug'03 Wind 6g/f 110- C: 1 Jul'03 Chep 6.1g/s 99- E: 2 Jun'03 Wind 6g/f 84- F:
1932   **PEAK TO CREEK 12** [5] J Noseda 3-9-3 (115)   E Ahern 5/6 FAV: 1111-323: Chsd ldrs, led briefly   2½   111
dist, not qckn ins fnl 1f: well bckd, clr of rem: fair run, stiff fin just against him: see 1932.
989   **JACK SULLIVAN 68** [7] G A Butler 3-8-11   M J Kinane 20/1: 2615-244: Front rank, led 2f out till   6   93
dist, wknd: 10 wk abs: see 989 & 598 (AW).
599*   **CATSTAR 117** [1]3-8-6 T (107)   K McEvoy 11/2: 12-15: Set decent pace, hdd 2f out, wknd: long abs,   8   72
tried a t-strap: btr 599 (1m).
1040   **ROSENCRANS 61** [2]3-9-1 vis t (100)   L Dettori 7/1: 1-31146: Keen & prom, btn 2f out, eased: 9 wk   13   56
abs: seems btr on the AW: see 1040 & 885.
6 Ran   Time 1m 28.73 (2.33)   Owned: Mr Hamdan Al Maktoum   Trained: Manton

2191   7.55 Numis Securities Rated Stakes Handicapfillies 4yo+ 0-95 (C)
£9256 £2848 £1424   **1m1f**   **Good/Firm 36**   -02 Slow   Inside   **[100]**

2067*   **POLAR JEM 5** [3] G G Margarson 4-8-4 (3ex)(2oh) (76)   A McCarthy 11/8 FAV: 21-34111: Made all, styd   87
on, hands & heels, cosily: well bckd tho' drifted from 10/11: completed qck hat-trick, eff at 9/10f on fast or firm
grnd: handles an easy or gall trk: thriving front runner, see 2067 & 1979.
1781   **SHAMARA 18** [2] C F Wall 4-8-9 (83)   S Sanders 9/4: 31310-22: Chsd ldrs, went after wnr 2f out,   nk   89

styd on all the way to the line, just failed: wng form over 10/12f & a return to further will suit: met an in-form rival.
1602 **SALAGAMA** 27 [1] P F I Cole 4-8-11 (85) K Fallon 9/2: 1-43: Chsd wnr 7f, onepcd fnl 1f: see 1602. — 3 — 86
1891 **ISLAND RAPTURE** 13 [5] J A R Toller 4-8-4 (4oh) (74) Lisa Jones(3) 14/1: 3055-004: Held up, nvr nr ldrs. — 1¾ — 75
1686 **PLAY THAT TUNE** 22 [4]4-9-7 (95) J Fanning 8/1: 12033-05: Keen & prom, wknd dist: top-weight. — 3 — 88
5 Ran   Time 1m 54.68 (3.48)   Owned: Norcroft Park Stud   Trained: Newmarket

---

2192	8.25 Binarybet Com Handicap Stakes 3yo+ 0-85 (D)						[79]
	£5460 £1680 £840	**1m6f**	**Good/Firm 36**	**-57 Slow**	Outside		

1736 **SHREDDED** 20 [7] J H M Gosden 4-9-11 (76) L Dettori 5/2 FAV: 3/54-021: Keen & prom, trav well & — — 82+
led dist, rdn out: tchd 7/2: much apprec this step up to 14f, shld stay 2m+: acts on fast & gd/soft grnd:
unexposed young stayer who is lightly rcd & open to plenty more improvement: see 1736.
1736 **INVITATION** 20 [3] A Charlton 6-9-7 (72) R Hughes 10/1: 0-064202: Slowly away, hdwy from rear 2f — ¾ — 75
out, fin well but not quite get to wnr: eff at 10f, stays a stiff 14f well: acts on fast grnd, likes gd or softer.
1516 **ROME** 31 [6] G P Enright 5-9-0 (65) Dane O'Neill 33/1: 4530-303: Prom, kept on under press fnl — shd — 68
1f, caught for 2nd cl-home: solid run, btn around 1L: clearly stays a gall 14f, acts on fast grnd & polytrack.
1928 **MOSTARSIL** 12 [2] G L Moore 6-9-3 p (68) R L Moore 7/2: 206-0634: Mid-div, eff when short of room — 1 — 69
1.5f out, kept on: tchd 9/2: return to 2m will suit judged on this, does not look the most straightforward ride.
5001*`TILLA 212 [5]4-9-2 (67) L Fletcher(3) 7/1: 062131-5: b f Bin Ajwaad - Tosca (Be My Guest) Trav — ¾ — 67
well in rear, prog 2f out, onepcd when short of room ins fnl 1f on reapp: op 11/2: dual h'cap wnr in '03: eff btwn
12f & 2m on fast & soft grnd: handles a sharp or gall trk: fair reapp, sharper for this.
1 Nov'03 Catt 13.8sft 70-65 E: 1 Oct'03 Pont 12.0g/f 66-60 F: 2 Sep'03 Folk 12g/f 60-(60) F:
1689 **MOON EMPEROR** 22 [9]7-9-11 (76) M J Kinane 6/1: 00-06046: Held up, late hdwy, nrst fin: op 9/2. — ¾ — 75
1916 **PERSIAN KING** 12 [8]7-9-5 (70) V Slattery 33/1: 050-0007: ch g Persian Bold - Queen's Share (Main — 5 — 61
Reef) Held up, nvr nr ldrs: beginners chase wnr in Sept '03 (eff around 2m on gd & firm, rtd 120c): lightly rcd on
the Flat in '03: dual nov hdle wnr in 02/03: '02 class stks wnr: eff around 10f on gd & fast, likes a sharp/undul
trk, esp Epsom. 2 Sep'02 Epso 10gd 86- C: 1 Aug'02 Epso 10g/f 87- D:
2073 **LINENS FLAME** 5 [11]5-9-10 (75) D Sweeney 20/1: 00-11208: Led till 1.5f out, wknd: btr 1516 & 1271. — 2½ — 63
1689 **GREENWICH MEANTIME** 22 [10]4-9-12 (77) K Fallon 5/1: 221-0309: Nvr btr than mid-div, btn/eased — 9 — 53
fnl 1f: top-weight: twice below encouraging eff of 1361 (2m, gd/soft).
4853} **THE VARLET** 225 [1]4-9-7 (72) S Sanders 50/1: 262605-0: 10th: b g Groom Dancer - Valagalore — 11 — 33
(Generous) Chsd ldrs 12f, wknd on reapp: rnr-up on a couple of '03 h'cap starts (incl in first time visor, M
Tregoning): mod mdn form in '02: eff at 12/14f on fast grnd: eff in a visor, has worn a t-strap: now with B Case.
2 Aug'03 Hayd 11.9g/f 72-73 D: 2 Jun'03 Good 14g/f 70-70 E:
10 Ran   Time 3m 08.11 (13.11)   Owned: Mr George Strawbridge   Trained: Manton

---

2193	8.55 June Maiden Stakes 3yo (D)						
	£5759 £1772 £886	**1m2f7y**	**Good/Firm 36**	**-45 Slow**	Inside		

1148 **BUCKEYE WONDER** 51 [2] M A Jarvis 3-9-0 (92) P Robinson 8/11 FAV: 24-21: Made all, held on gamely — — 84
fnl 1f, drvn out: hvly bckd from 1/1, slow time, 7 wk abs: eff at 10f on fast & gd/soft grnd, 12f will suit: put
prev experience to gd use here & deserved win: runs well fresh: see 1148.
1864 **GOLDEN ISLAND** 14 [3] J W Hills 3-8-9   K Fallon 11/4: 0-32: Nvr far away, chall fnl 1f, just btn: — hd — 78
clr of rem: eff at 9/10f on fast grnd: prob caught an above average rival & shld find a minor mdn: see 1864.
759 **ZANGEAL** 96 [5] C F Wall 3-9-0   J Quinn 16/1: 43: Keen in rear, hdwy to chall 2f out, not qckn — 3½ — 78
fnl 1f: 3 mth abs: rcd too keenly today & not disgraced in the circumstances: half-brother to High Accolade & shld
be capable of btr, encouraging in 759 (AW, debut).
WARNINGCAMP [9] Lady Herries 3-9-0   S Sanders 50/1: 4: b g Lando - Wilette (Top Ville) Dwelt, — 1¾ — 76
hdwy from rear to chall 2f out, btn fnl 1f on debut: clr of rem: mid-dist bred: prob eff at 10f on fast grnd.
QUDRAAT [11]3-9-0 R Hills 10/1: 5: b c In The Wings - Urgent Liaison (High Estate) Held up, — 4 — 70
styd on steadily, nrst fin on racecourse bow: 230,000gns purchase & bred to apprec mid-dists: encouraging.
1815 **BLAISE WOOD** 16 [7]3-9-0 P R L Moore 100/1: 6-06: b g Woodman - Castellina (Danzig Connection) — 3½ — 63
Keen & prom early, rdn & btn 2f out: tried cheek pieces: 6th of 7 on sole juv start (R Hannon).
1210 **SHAZANA** 48 [6]3-8-9   Martin Dwyer 20/1: 67: Keen & prom, wknd 2f out: 7 wk abs. — 2 — 57
4912} **MASTERMAN READY** 220 [8]3-9-0   E Ahern 66/1: 6-8: Nvr btr than mid-div on reapp: gelded. — ½ — 61
ENCOMPASS [12]3-8-9 R Hughes 14/1: 9: Prom, wknd 2f out on debut: op 8/1. — ½ — 55
LAUGH N CRY [5]3-8-9 Dane O'Neill 100/1: 0: 10th: Keen in rear, nvr dngrs on racecourse bow. — 6 — 46
1959 **CHARNWOOD PRIDE** 10 [10]3-9-0 t M Fenton 100/1: 0: 11th: Chsd ldrs 1m, sn btn. — 3½ — 46
PAINT THE LILY [4]3-8-9 Lisa Jones(3) 66/1: 0: 12th: Slowly away, al bhd & fin last on debut. — nk — 40
12 Ran   Time 2m 12.27(8.17)   Owned: Mr John W Phillips   Trained: Newmarket

---

Official Going Good (Good/Firm Places)

2194	2.30 Wendy Fair Markets Maiden Auction Stakes 2yo (E)						
	£3591 £1105 £553	**6f16y str**	**Good 60**	**-05 Slow**	Stands Side		

CAESAR BEWARE 0 [14] H Candy 2-8-11   Dane O'Neill 7/2 FAV: 1: b g Daggers Drawn - Red Shareef — — 106+
(Marju) Trkd ldrs & readily qcknd to lead ins last, v easily: bckd: Feb first foal, dam a multiple 1m/11f wnr
abroad, incl as a juv: eff at 6f, will enjoy 7f: acts on gd grnd & a gall/undul trk: goes well fresh: showed a
fine turn of foot, useful & can win more races.
1911 **DON PELE** 12 [16] S Kirk 2-8-11   J F Egan 12/1: 02: b c Monashee Mountain - Big Fandango — 3 — 94
(Bigstone) Chsd ldrs, rdn & led over 1f out, hdd ins last, no ch with wnr but clr rem: op 25/1, left debut bhd:
18,000gns March foal, half-brother to a 9f scorer: eff at 6f on gd: win a race.
HOLBECK GHYLL 0 [18] A M Balding 2-8-10 L Keniry(3) 5/1: 3: ch c Titus Livius - Crimada — 4 — 83
(Mukaddamah) Keen & led till over 1f out, no extra: op 7/2: April foal, 13,000gns purchase: half-brother to a 5f
wnr: dam unrcd: learn from this.
MUSICO 0 [12] B R Millman 2-8-13   S Drowne 25/1: 4: ch c Bold Fact - Scherzo Impromptu (Music — 3½ — 75

Boy) Mid-div, kept on late: 28,000gns Feb foal, half-brother to a juv wnr abroad, also 2 winning jumpers: dam unplcd half sister to a smart sprinter: improve over further.
1325 **LADY CHEF 41** [6]2-8-2 A McCarthy 66/1: 05: Chsd ldrs till hung badly left from halfway, no impress bef dist: 6 wk abs, can impr on this when correcting steering. *3* **55**
1805 **ENCANTO 17** [7]2-8-3 Martin Dwyer 20/1: 06: Chsd ldrs till over 1f out. *1* **53**
1760 **AL GARHOUD BRIDGE 19** [2]2-8-13 T E Durcan 5/1: 57: In tch, nvr able to chall: btr 1760 (fast). *1* **60**
1401 **GRANARY GIRL 37** [4]2-8-2 R Miles(1) 40/1: 08: Dwelt, nvr on terms. *½* **47**
HES A STAR 0 [5]2-8-9 R L Moore 20/1: 9: Dwelt & bhd, only mod prog. *½* **52**
1574 **JOE NINETY 28** [17]2-8-9 Derek Nolan(7) 66/1: 5600: 10th: Chsd ldrs till halfway. *¾* **50**
ALZARMA 0 [13]2-8-7 B Reilly(3) 50/1: 0: 11th: In tch 3f. *nk* **47**
1911 **SHAHEER 12** [3]2-8-10 D Holland 5/1: 620: 12th: Mid-div, no prog bef 2f out: btr 1911 (fast). *½* **48**
954 **CHAMPAGNE BRANDY 68** [11]2-8-3 F P Ferris(3) 66/1: 00: 13th: Sn struggling, 10 wk abs. *1½* **36**
BARNBROOK EMPIRE 0 [8]2-8-3 R Thomas(5) 66/1: 0: 14th: Dwelt & al outpcd. *1* **33**
1107 **VENEER 54** [15]2-8-10 R Hughes 25/1: 400: 15th: Sn outpcd, abs: see 974. *hd* **39**
1880 **AMPHITHEATRE 13** [10]2-8-7 J Quinn 9/1: 50: 16th: In tch till halfway, reportedly hung right. *1½* **31**
1640 **ZACHY BOY 24** [9]2-8-7 E Ahern 66/1: 60500: 17th: Chsd ldrs till halfway. *1½* **26**
1964 **GAVIOLI 10** [1]2-8-10 S Whitworth 50/1: 50: 18th: Prom to halfway: 'breathing prob'. *6* **0**
18 Ran Time 1m 12.67 (3.87) Owned: Mill House Partnership Trained: Wantage

2195

3.00 Fifehead Group Handicap Stakes 3yo 0-75 (E) **[77]**
£3585 £1103 £552 **5f16y str** **Good 60** **-20 Slow** Stands Side

1694 **IVORY LACE 22** [7] S Woodman 3-9-7 (70) D Sweeney 6/1: 0131141: Held up in tch, hdwy to lead ins last, pushed out cl-home: eff at 5/6f on firm, gd/soft & polytrack: thriving: see 1404 & 1102. **79**
1903 **MELODY KING 13** [6] P D Evans 3-9-3 bl (66) F P Ferris(3) 10/1: 3140-032: Led till hdd ins last, kept on for press: acts on firm & gd grnd: see 1903. *1½* **69**
1942* **IMPERIUM 11** [8] Mrs Stef Liddiard 3-9-12 (6ex) (75) S Drowne 9/2: 2005113: Trkd ldrs, rdn to chall over 1f out, no extra ins last: op 7/2: btr 1942 (fast, Brighton). *3* **70**
1809 **ALCHERA 17** [4] R F Johnson Houghton 3-9-5 bl (68) K Fallon 11/4 FAV: 210-0064: Trkd ldrs, hung left & no impress bef dist: bckd, op 10/3: see 1809. *¾* **61**
2048 **FAIR COMPTON 6** [3]3-9-2 (65) Dane O'Neill 12/1: 04-465: Chsd ldrs till dist: qck reapp: btr 2048. *2½* **50**
1942 **MISS MADAME 11** [2]3-8-12 (61) D Holland 11/2: 060-336: Bhd, hung left & no impress over 1f out. *1¾* **41**
1575 **PASS GO 28** [9]3-8-11 T (60) Martin Dwyer 20/1: 3-007: Dwelt, outpcd: t-strap, h'cap bow: btr 176 (AW). *2½* **32**
1809 **SCOTTISH EXILE 17** [5]3-9-5 vis (68) E Ahern 8/1: 6443108: V slow away & al bhd: filly reportedly put head down as the stalls opened, this prob best forgiven: see 1509. *nk* **39**
4584} **ARDKEEL LASS 243** [1]3-9-3 (66) M Howard(7) 10/1: 12306-9: ch f Fumo di Londra - Wot A Noise (Petorius) Prom 3f, btn over 1f out: reapp, op 15/2: debut wnr '03 (C/D auct mdn, B Palling): eff over a gall/undul 5f on fast grnd: can go well fresh. *5* **23**
2 Jul'03 Chep 5.1g/f 77- D: 1 Jun'03 Chep 5.1g/f 77- G:
9 Ran Time 1m 0.78 (3.98) Owned: Mr Christopher J Halpin Trained: Chichester

2196

3.30 Blackhorse Motor Finance Maiden Stakes 3yo+ (D)
£3572 £1099 £550 **1m2f36y** **Good 60** **-10 Slow** Inside

1763 **LOST SOLDIER THREE 19** [10] L M Cumani 3-8-11 D Holland 5/1: 61: Dwelt, sn keen & chsd ldrs, smooth hdwy to lead over 2f out, v easily: op 7/2: relished step up to 10f, 12f+ shld suit: acts on gd & prob fast grnd: looks useful, type to win h'caps. **89**
1790 **CHARLESTON 17** [7] J H M Gosden 3-8-11 R Hughes 15/8 FAV: 222: Led/dsptd lead till over 2f out, flashed tail & no ch with wnr bef dist: bckd, op 15/2: consistent: see 1790 & 1514. *7* **75+**
1016 **HASHID 63** [5] P C Ritchens 4-9-10 bl (77) Martin Dwyer 33/1: 53-63: b g Darshaan - Alkaffeyeh (Sadler's Wells) Led/dsptd lead till over 3f out, no impress on front pair when veered left ins last: 2 mth abs: unplcd '03 (lightly rcd, rtd 82, M Tregoning): best effs over a gall 12f on fast grnd: h'cap company may suit. *3½* **70**
ROSSALL POINT 0 [2] J L Dunlop 3-8-11 S Drowne 33/1: 4: b g Fleetwood - Loch Clair (Lomond) Rear, kept on late, nvr a threat to front pair on debut: cheaply bght gelding, half-brother to a couple of mid-dist wnrs: looks set to apprec 12f+ & could improve. *nk* **69**
4336} **GELLER 258** [4]3-8-11 (83) R L Moore 8/1: 2204-5: b g Mind Games - Time To Tango (Timeless Times) Keen & held up, eff from 3f out, no impress when hmpd ins last: op 9/1, reapp: dual mdn rnr-up in '03 (lightly rcd): eff at 6f/1m, not bred for mid-dists: acts on fast grnd, handles a gall or sharp trk. *½* **68**
2 Aug'03 Nott 6.1g/f 83- E: 2 Aug'03 Wind 8.3g/f 78- F:
1864 **COOL CLEAR WATER 14** [3]3-8-6 T E Durcan 25/1: 0006: Chsd ldrs till over 2f out. *1½* **61**
1959 **SILENCIO 10** [1]3-8-11 V Slattery 50/1: 0007: Bhd, pushed along & mod late prog. *1* **65$**
1737 **PRESENT ORIENTED 20** [6]3-8-11 (82) W Ryan 5/1: 56-58: Sn bhd, op 4/1. *12* **48**
1810 **ADAPTABLE 17** [9]3-8-6 (75) Dane O'Neill 20/1: 03-09: In tch till 3f out, longer trip. *9* **31**
1737 **GOLDEN KEY 20** [8]3-8-11 K Fallon 5/1: 00: 10th: Keen, chsd ldrs 3f out, wknd qckly over 2f out & eased: joc reported colt lost his action. *3* **32**
PRIDEWOOD DOVE 0 [11]5-9-5 R Miles(3) 100/1: 0: 11th: Dwelt, sn chsd ldrs till 5f out, t.o: jumps fit. *dist* **0**
11 Ran Time 2m 11.21 (7.11) Owned: Sheikh Mohammed Obaid Al Maktoum Trained: Newmarket

2197

4.00 Listen To Real Radio 105-106fm Classified Stakes 3yo+ 0-80 (D)
£5447 £1676 £838 **1m2f36y** **Good 60** **-11 Slow** Inside

2710+ **SKI JUMP 332** [2] R Charlton 4-9-5 bl (82) R Hughes 9/2: 03/1601-1: gr g El Prado - Skiable (Niniski) Rdn to lead early, styd on strongly from over 1f out, rdn out: op 7/2, reapp, gelded: won 2 of 4 '03 starts (h'caps): plcd fnl '02 start (rtd 75, auct mdn): eff at 10f, yet to convince beyond: acts on fast & gd/soft grnd, stiff/gall trks: goes esp well fresh & loves to force the pace in blnks: improving. **87**
1 Jul'03 Bath 10.2g/f 83-79 D: 1 Apr'03 Leic 10.0g/f 81-72 D:
1890* **TRUENO 13** [1] L M Cumani 5-9-6 (83) D Holland 10/11 FAV: 1/2524-12: Trkd ldrs, eff to press wnr from over 2f out, kept on but al held: nicely bckd: prob ran to form of 1890. *1½* **85**
1781 **ANGLO SAXON 18** [3] D R Loder 4-9-5 (82) K Fallon 13/2: 101-003: b c Seeking The Gold - Anna Palariva (Caerleon) In tch, eff over 1f out, no extra ins last: lightly rcd '03, mdn & h'cap scorer: wng form at 7.5f/1m, now stays gall 10f well: acts on fm & gd, enjoys a stiff fin & can go well fresh: has had breathing probs. *1¾* **82**

CHEPSTOW THURSDAY 03.06.04 Lefthand, Undulating, Galloping Track

1 Aug'03 Bath 8.0fm 84-80 D: 1 May'03 Beve 7.5gd 82- D:

1817 **ILE MICHEL 16** [6] J G M O'Shea 7-9-5 (82) D Sweeney 50/1: 3210-004: Rear, eff 2f out, no dngr.	2	79
1924 **TOP SPEC 12** [4]3-8-7 (83) Dane O'Neill 10/1: 2161-005: Rdn early, chsd ldrs till 3f out: see 1924.	4	74
1915 **SCOTTISH RIVER 12** [7]5-9-3 (77) Hayley Turner(5) 14/1: 1056146: Slow away & rear, eff wide from 5f out, btn 2f out: btr 1915 & 1650.	5	64
1516 **DANCE WORLD 31** [5]4-9-3 (76) B Reilly(3) 12/1: 424-1037: Chsd ldrs, btn 3f out: btr 1516 & 1030.	hd	63
1767 **AWARDING 19** [8]4-9-3 t (74) Lucy Russell(7) 100/1: 06-50008: Keen & chsd wnr till 3f out, sn btn.	nk	62

8 Ran   Time 2m 11.37 (7.27)   Owned: Mr K Abdulla   Trained: Beckhampton

---

2198   4.30 Weatherbys Insurance Handicap Stakes 3yo+ 0-85 (D)   [82]
£5772 £1776 £888   2m2f   Good 60   -02 Slow   Inside

1789 **CALAMINTHA 17** [13] M C Pipe 4-8-9 (63) D Holland 8/1: 3501-261: Led, rdn clr 4f out, drvn out to hold on: op 7/1: stayed this gall 2m2f well: acts on fast & soft: enjoyed front-rng & a fine ride.		69
1861 **KING FLYER 14** [3] Miss J Feilden 8-10-0 (80) S Whitworth 16/1: 36-02302: Rear, styd on well from over 1f out, not able to reach wnr: thorough stayer, likes Newmarket: see 813.	½	85
2073 **MALARKEY 5** [4] Mrs Stef Liddiard 7-9-10 (76) S Drowne 9/1: 6/-512153: Rear, kept on fnl 3f, no threat to wnr: better run back on gd grnd: see 1232.	hd	80
1861 **ALMIZAN 14** [9] M R Channon 4-10-0 (82) T E Durcan 16/1: 1564-004: b c Darshaan - Bint Albaadiya (Woodman) Handy from halfway, chsd wnr 3f out, no impress ins last: mdn & h'cap scorer '03: winning form at 12/15f, clearly stays 2m2f: acts on fast & gd grnd: looks nicely h'capped.	½	84
1 Sep'03 Ayr 15g/f 91-88 C: 2 Jul'03 Good 14gd 92-84 C: 1 May'03 Thir 12gd 85- D:		
2073* **QUEDEX 5** [14]8-8-13 (5ex) (65) R Miles(3) 11/4 FAV: 065/06-15: Rear, kept on wide for press fnl 3f, not able to chall: qck reapp under a pen, nicely bckd: stays 2m2f & ran to form of 2073 (2m).	½	67
2009 **MOONSHINE BEACH 8** [10]6-8-6 p (58) E Ahern 15/2: 05-40636: Mid-div, eff 3f out, no extra dist.	1½	58
2060 **PRINCE OF THE WOOD 6** [2]4-7-12 (6oh)p (46) D Kinsella 10/1: 064-2147: Chsd ldrs, btn over 1f out.	5	44
1629 **OCEAN TIDE 26** [8]7-9-7 vis (73) K Fallon 9/2: 0/0-33448: Chsd ldrs till 3f out: op 15/2: btr 1093 & 926.	8	55
1928 **GRAND FROMAGE 12** [1]6-9-1 (67) V Slattery 100/1: 0521P/-09: ch g Grand Lodge - My First Paige (Runnett) Mid-div, no impress fnl 3f: missed '03: '02 h'cap scorer for P Webber: eff at 14f/2m on gd, likes firm & fast grnd: eff in a visor & handles any trk.	shd	49
1 Jul'02 Ches 15.8fm 70-64 D: 2 Jun'02 Warw 16.1fm 67-59 D: 1 Sep'01 Kemp 16g/f 69-64 E: 2 Jul'01 Sali 14g/f 66-63 E:		
1928 **ESTABLISHMENT 12** [11]7-9-9 (75) Dane O'Neill 14/1: 015-0000: 10th: Bhd, some hdwy from halfway, btn 3f out: op 12/1: see 1484.	13	39
1090 **IMTIHAN 57** [12]5-7-12 (1oh)T (49) F P Ferris(3) 16/1: 00000-00: 11th: Chsd ldrs till 5f out: t-strap, jumps fit.	3	10
2429} **Laffah 343** [5]9-8-6 bl(58) R L Moore 33/1:0 1889 **Ravenglass 13** [6]5-9-13 (79) R Havlin 20/1:P		

13 Ran   Time 4m 02.25 (10.45)   Owned: Mr David Jenks   Trained: Wellington

---

2199   5.00 Saffie Joseph & Son Handicap Stakes 3yo+ 0-70 (E)   [79]
£3721 £1145 £573   7f16y str   Good 60   -04 Slow   Stands Side

1648 **MISTER TRICKSTER 24** [14] R Dickin 3-8-7 (58) S Righton 20/1: 650-6001: b c Woodborough - Tinos Island (Alzao) Chsd ldrs, styd on for press to lead wel ins last: first win: unplcd '03 (rtd 69, mdn): eff at 7f, tried up to 12f prev this term: acts on gd grnd & a gall/undul trk.		66
2063 **GOODENOUGH MOVER 5** [5] J S King 8-10-0 (69) Hayley Turner(5) 9/2: 000-2122: Trkd ldrs & narrow lead 3f out till well ins last: op 7/2: remains in here form: likes Salisbury: see 2063 & 1723.	¾	75
1020 **MIDDLETON GREY 63** [6] A G Newcombe 6-9-7 bl (62) L Keniry(3) 12/1: 64-03203: Dwelt, bhd, styd on well from over 4f out, nvr able to chall wnr: 2 mth abs: well h'capped on turf: see 840, 807 & 255.	nk	67
1792 **PHRED 17** [13] R F Johnson Houghton 4-9-7 (62) J Quinn 7/2 FAV: 00-64654: Chsd ldrs, onepace.	1¾	64
1788* **HIGH RIDGE 17** [9]5-9-5 p (60) F P Ferris(3) 12/1: 5360-015: Chsd ldrs, no impress bef dist: see 1788.	shd	62
1379 **BOUGHT DIRECT 38** [10]5-9-2 (57) A Beech(3) 17/2: 0-006546: Rear, kept on late, not able to chall.	shd	57
1723 **THREEZEDZZ 21** [1]6-9-7 (62) S Donohoe(7) 25/1: 00000/-07: ch g Emarati - Exotic Forest (Dominion) Prom racing alone far side, no extra dist: missed '03: unplcd '02 (lightly rcd, rtd 64, h'cap, Mrs P N Dutfield): h'cap rnr-up '01 for J G Portman, disapp in blnkrs: eff at 5/6f on firm & gd grnd, any trk: can go well fresh.	½	60
2 Apr'01 Newm 6g/s 96-92 C:		
1790 **NOUNOU 17** [13]5-9-0 (65) S Whitworth 16/1: 0508: b c Starborough - Watheeqah (Topsider) Bhd, only mod prog on h'cap bow: unplcd prev at up to 10f.	1¼	62
820 **BLUE QUIVER 87** [7]4-9-1 (56) Paul Eddery 4/1: 06-629: Cl-up, wknd under press dist: op 7/1, abs.	1¼	50
2053 **PARKER 6** [4]7-9-4 bl (59) D Sweeney 25/1: 3606050: 10th: Sn bhd: breathing problems reported.	8	39
4869} **FIVE GOLD 223** [12]3-9-2 (67) G Baker 20/1: 062410-0: 11th: b g Desert Prince - Ceide Dancer (Alzao) Chsd ldrs till 3f out, reapp/gelded: AW auct mdn scorer '03, turf h'cap 4th (rtd 73): eff at 1m on firm & fibresand, sharp/undul trks.	2	43
1 Oct'03 Sout 8af 73a-(74) F: 2 Sep'03 Sout 8af 75a- D:		
1722 **INSTINCT 21** [2]3-8-10 (61) P Gallagher(6) 20/1: 0-503000: 12th: Outpcd, nvr a factor: btr 975 (6f, soft).	2½	32
1730 **CAERPHILLY GAL 20** [3]4-8-13 (54) R Miles(3) 14/1: 13040-00: 13th: Led til 3f out, btn sn after.	½	24
1940 **DON ARGENTO 11** [8]3-7-12 (4oh) (45) D Kinsella 33/1: 000-000: 14th: Sn struggling in rear.	10	3

14 Ran   Time 1m 24.30(4.5)   Owned: The Tricksters   Trained: Stratford-On-Avon

---

WOLVERHAMPTON Fibresand   FRIDAY 04.06.04   Lefthand, Sharp Track

Official Going Standard

2200   1.55 Rooftop Housing Claiming Stakes 4yo+ (F)
£2926 £836 £418   1m6f166y   Going 41   -50 Slow   Inside

2047 **ROMIL STAR 7** [2] K R Burke 7-8-11 vis (65) K Dalgleish 5/6 FAV: 0-002141: Hld up, hdwy 4f out, led over 1f out, pushed clr, easily: eff at 12/14.7f on gd, hvy & f/sand: in gd form in sell/clmrs: see 1838.		67a
4690} **DESERT QUILL 236** [8] W M Brisbourne 4-8-6 (50) B Swarbrick(5) 16/1: 000030-2: ch f In The Wings - Aljood (Kris) Handy, lost plc 6f out, rallied to go 2nd 1f out, outpcd by wnr: mod form prev for D Elsworth.	10	48a

658

4182} **GORDYS JOY 267** [4] G A Ham 4-8-6 (35) C Catlin 66/1: 064-3: b f Cloudings - Beatle Song (Song) *7* **39a**
Hld up, hdwy to lead over 2f out till over 1f out, wknd: p.u. in a hdle recently (mod form): mod Flat form.
AMUSEMENT 0 [6] D G Bridgwater 8-9-5 D Nolan(3) 33/1: 4: ch g Mystiko - Jolies Eaux (Shirley Heights) Led over 4f out till over 2f out, wknd: long jumps abs, mod form back in 02/03. *½* **51a**
2112 **AVEIRO 4** [3]8-9-5 (62) I Mongan 11/8: 2120005: Led till 4f out, wknd: qk reapp: btr 866 (h'cap). *5* **44a**
1838 **REGAL REPOSE 16** [5]4-8-0 (50) A Mackay 80/1: 0200-006: In tch, wknd 4f out: see 1838. *24* **0a**
2037 **GOOD TIME BOBBY 7** [1]7-9-1 J D O'Reilly(7) 16/1: 37: Slow away, al bhd: btr 2037 (turf). *10* **0a**
7 Ran Time 3m 22.99 (13.39) Owned: Mrs Elaine M Burke Trained: Leyburn

2201 **2.30 Touchstone Housing Association Handicap Stakes 3yo+ 35-55 (F)** **[56]**
£3003 £858 £429 **5f rnd** **Going 41** **+09 Fast** Inside

1750 **LARKYS LOB 20** [13] J O'Reilly 5-9-11 (53) J D O'Reilly(7) 5/1: 4631221: Cl up, led over 3f out, sn clr, rdn out: gd time: eff at 5/7f on fibresand/sharp trks, likes Southwell: see 1405. **66a**
1750 **LUCIUS VERRUS 20** [3] D Shaw 4-9-10 vis (52) S Whitworth 8/1: 4-301052: In tch, eff 2f out, no ch with wnr: gd run: see 1750, 1320. *5* **52a**
1606 **STAR LAD 28** [11] R Brotherton 4-9-5 bl (47) I Mongan 14/1: 0014503: In tch, hdwy over 2f out, onepace: fair run: see 773 (6f). *1¼* **43a**
1788 **DAVIDS MARK 18** [8] J R Jenkins 4-9-11 (53) D Corby(3) 8/1: 030-0344: Cl up, chsd wnr over 1f out, sn no extra: see 1267, 897. *hd* **48a**
2016 **BOISDALE 9** [10]6-9-11 (53) L Treadwell(7) 14/1: 000-6165: Bhd, late gains: see 1588 (bndd, 6f). *2* **42a**
2152* **RED LEICESTER 2** [7]4-9-12 (6ex)vis (54) Dean McKeown 5/1: 00-30516: With ldrs, wknd fnl 1f: qck reapp, AW bow & reportedly struck into. *½* **41a**
1606 **SPEED ON 28** [9]11-9-10 (52) D Sweeney 14/1: 00/606-07: Nvr a factor: see 1606. *1¾* **34a**
1615 **BLESSED PLACE 28** [6]4-9-8 (50) C Catlin 33/1: 50-00008: ch g Compton Place - Cathedra (So Blessed) Cl up, wknd fnl 1f: won 2 h'caps in '03 (with J R Auvray): eff at 5/6f on fast & both a/w's: eff with/without cheekpieces. 2 Apr'03 Bath 5.0g/f 65-61 E: 2 Mar'03 Bath 5.0g/f 62-61 E:
1 Mar'03 Ling 5ap 62a-56 D: 2 Mar'03 Ling 5ap 57a-(56) D: 2 Jan'03 Wolv 6af 52a-51 F: *1¼* **28a**
1867 **MAROMITO 15** [4]7-9-5 (47) K Dalgleish 4/1 FAV: 0031109: In tch, wkng when hmpd ins last: btr 1408. *½* **23a**
1948* **MOLOTOV 11** [1]4-9-9 (6ex) (51) L Vickers 16/1: 00000-10: 10th: Handy, wknd 2f out: btr 1948 (bndd). *3½* **17a**
1562* **HAGLEY PARK 30** [5]5-9-7 (49) P Mulrennan(5) 10/1: 5430310: 11th: Cl up, wknd 2f out: btr 1562. *nk* **14a**
171} **DISPOL VERITY 542** [12]4-9-7 (49) B Swarbrick(5) 33/1: 234000/-0: 12th: Al bhd. *6* **0a**
1750 **SCARY NIGHT 20** [2]4-9-9 p (51) J Edmunds 7/1: 0160060: 13th: Al bhd, t.o.: see 793. *22* **0a**
13 Ran Time 1m 01.79 (1.59) Owned: J O R Racing Trained: Barnsley

2202 **3.05 St Helens Housing Association Selling Stakes 3yo+ (G)**
£2625 £750 £375 **6f rnd** **Going 41** **-07 Slow** Inside

1662 **MALLIA 25** [8] T D Barron 11-9-7 (46) Laura Jayne Crawford(7) 9/1: 21406-41: Handy, styd on to lead ins last, drvn out: eff at 5/7f, suited by 7f: acts on fm, hvy, loves fibresand, Southwell/ Wolverhampton. **48a**
1671 **INDIAN MUSIC 24** [7] A Berry 7-9-12 (38) J Bramhill 16/1: 1544332: Hld up, hdwy over 2f out, styd on well ins last, just failed: improved eff if not flattered: see 982 (banded). *hd* **52a$**
1443* **ON THE TRAIL 36** [5] D W Chapman 7-9-12 (56) A Nicholls 3/1: 0131213: Led, rdn & hdd ins last. *3* **43a**
1774 **RAFTERS MUSIC 20** [9] Julian Poulton 9-9-7 (66) G Carter 6/5 FAV: 3020554: In tch, eff 2f out, kept on ins last: bckd: reportedly nvr trav: see 153. *1* **35a**
1788 **BRAVE CHIEF 18** [4]3-8-13 (51) B Doyle 20/1: 002-005: Slow away, hld up, eff 3f out, onepace: btr 256. *½* **33a**
1337 **PIPS SONG 41** [11]9-9-12 (47) R Miles(3) 14/1: 0030506: In tch, wknd 2f out. *shd* **37a**
983 **PLATTOCRAT 66** [6]4-9-7 T Hamilton(3) 50/1: 57: b g Dancing Spree - No Comebacks (Last Tycoon) Handy, wknd 2f out: 10 wk abs: mod form. *2½* **25a**
1963 **BACK AT DE FRONT 11** [1]3-8-13 (58) C Catlin 12/1: 4560008: Al bhd: btr 422. *1* **22a**
1963 **WELSH WHISPER 11** [3]5-9-7 (44) N Chalmers(5) 16/1: 5661309: Slow away, al bhd: btr 1566 (banded). *nk* **21a**
1963 **JACKS DELIGHT 11** [10]4-9-7 VIS L Vickers 66/1: 00-000: 10th: Chsd ldr, wknd 2f out: visor: see 1963. *3½* **11a**
2054 **ZAK FACTA 7** [2]4-9-7 vis (45) I Mongan 10/1: 6000000: 11th: Al bhd. *6* **0a**
11 Ran Time 1m 15.7 (2.9) Owned: Harrowgate Bloodstock Ltd Trained: Thirsk

2203 **3.40 Extracare Charitable Trust Handicap Stakes 3yo 0-70 (E)** **[77]**
£3770 £1160 £580 **1m4f** **Going 41** **-06 Slow** Inside

1372 **QUEENS FANTASY 40** [4] D Haydn Jones 3-8-7 vis (56) S Whitworth 14/1: 00-04021: Slow away, sn handy, led after 4f till over 2f out, rallied to lead again ins last, rdn clr: 6 wk abs: eff at 10f, improved stepped up to 12f & further shld suit: acts on fast & fibresand: eff in vis: on the upgrade, see 1372. **65a**
1647 **JAKARMI 25** [8] B Palling 3-9-7 (70) R Miles(3) 7/2: 1322232: Cl up, led over 2f out, rdn & hdd ins last, no extra: stayed this longer 12f trip: see 1647, 1403. *3* **74a**
1663 **ROCK LOBSTER 25** [9] J G Given 3-9-5 (68) B Doyle 11/1: 14-0563: Handy, chall when ran wide over 1f out, onepace: improved stepped up to 12f: see 1144. *1¼* **70a**
1648 **ITS BLUE CHIP 25** [10] P W D'Arcy 3-8-13 e (62) Paul Eddery 6/1: 0-301464: Slow away, hld up, hdwy 4f out, onepace: see 1260. *1¾* **61a**
1648 **GENERAL FLUMPA 25** [11]3-9-2 (65) G Baker 2/1 FAV: 0-6335: In tch, eff 3f out, no impress: see 1648. *½* **63a**
1581* **AMANKILA 29** [1]3-9-5 (68) I Mongan 8/1: 0316: Hld up, btn 2f out: btr 1581 (10f, soft). *16* **46a**
1647 **AMWELL BRAVE 25** [6]3-9-2 (65) D Corby(3) 16/1: 3505007: Al bhd: btr 601 (10f), 325. *10* **28a**
4906} **EQUUS 221** [12]3-9-2 (65) L Treadwell(7) 40/1: 500-8: b g Desert Style - Iolanta (Danehill) Al bhd: well btn all 3 '03 starts (with R Hannon, rtd 69$): been gelded. now with L Dace. *1¾* **25a**
1398 **HOUSE OF BLUES 38** [5]3-8-11 (60) G Gibbons 25/1: 000-09: b g Grand Lodge - Sartigila (Efisio) In tch, wknd 4f out: unplcd all 3 '03 starts. *1½* **18a**
1936 **IVY LEAGUE STAR 13** [7]3-9-2 (65) K Dalgleish 12/1: 06-50: 10th: Led 4f, wknd 3f out: see 1936. *5* **16a**
1663 **PERFECT BALANCE 25** [2]3-8-11 (60) Kim Tinkler 14/1: 0-016540: 11th: Al bhd, t.o: btr 1663 (10f, sft). *19* **0a**
1124 **OUR LITTLE ROSIE 53** [3]3-8-11 (60) D Sweeney 12/1: 00510P: Al bhd, t.o./p.u. & dismounted 1f out: clearly something amiss: 7 wk abs: rcd similarly 1124, see 959. **0a**
12 Ran Time 2m 39.3 (5.7) Owned: Mr Mick White Trained: Pontypridd

2204 4.25 Arena Housing Association Handicap Stakes 3yo+ 35-55 (F) [54]
£3038 £868 £434 **7f rnd** **Going 41** -15 Slow Outside

1897 **OLD BAILEY** 14 [7] T D Barron 4-10-0 VIS (54) P Mulrennan(5) 9/2 JT FAV: 26-60501: Hld up, hdwy **61a**
over 3f out, styd on for press to lead cl home: eff at 5/7f on fast & fibresand, handles soft: acts on any trk, eff
in blnks, enjoyed a visor today: on a fair mark, see 1277.
1837 **MARABAR** 16 [12] D W Chapman 6-9-10 bl (50) A Nicholls 7/1: 1003122: Handy, hdwy to lead 1f out, nk **56a**
edged left & hdd cl home: in gd form: see 1837, 296.
2052 **KANZ WOOD** 7 [5] A W Carroll 8-9-5 VIS (45) D Nolan(3) 8/1: 5055343: Slow away, hld up, kept on 2½ **46a**
late, nrst fin: gd run in a visor: see 769.
1984 **BULAWAYO** 10 [4] Andrew Reid 7-9-9 bl (49) D Corby(3) 12/1: 3061064: Handy, outpcd 4f out, rallied nk **49a**
over 1f out, kept on: see 956.
1656* **TURN AROUND** 25 [6]4-9-12 (52) I Mongan 4/1: 00-00215: Led till 1f out, wknd: btr 1656 (seller). 3 **46a**
1266* **GILLYS GENERAL** 46 [11]4-9-9 (50) A J Gibbons 16/1: 050-4016: Cl up, wknd over 1f out: 8 wk abs. 1¾ **39a**
1776 **NEW OPTIONS** 20 [10]7-9-10 bl (50) G Carter 16/1: 0303007: Hld up, eff 3f out, no impress: see 1247. 2½ **35a**
1625 **CARLTON** 27 [2]10-9-12 (52) R Thomas(5) 9/2 JT FAV: 4522208: In tch, wknd 3f out: btr 1533 (hvy). 2 **33a**
2054 **SUPER DOMINION** 7 [3]7-9-5 p (49) Stephanie Hollinshead(5) 10/1: 030-5149: In tch, wknd 3f out. 4 **18a**
1518 **PURI** 32 [1]5-9-13 (53) B Doyle 12/1: 0-400: 10th: Al bhd. ¾ **24a**
4728} **TOKEWANNA** 235 [4]5-9-4 (54) B Swarbrick(5) 16/1: 464040-0: 11th: b f Danehill - High Atlas 9 **7a**
(Shirley Heights) In tch, wknd 3f out: reapp: 4th at best in '03 (rtd 57, with C Brittain): plcd in '02: eff at
5/7f on fm & gd/soft: tried a visor & cheekpieces: now with W Brisbourne.
2 Jul'02 Sand 5g/f 71- E:
2054 **ENCORE ROYALE** 7 [9]4-9-7 BL (47) O Urbina 16/1: 000-0560: 12th: Reluctant to leave stalls, al bhd. 11 **0a**
12 Ran Time 1m 30.14 (3.94) Owned: Mr J Baggott Trained: Thirsk

2205 5.00 Homezone Housing Association Handicap Stakes 3yo 35-55 (F) [63]
£3024 £864 £432 **1m100y rnd** **Going 41** -02 Slow Inside

2064* **INCISOR** 6 [12] S Kirk 3-9-9 (6ex) (58) J D Smith 2/1: 056-5111: In tch, hdwy to lead over 2f out, **71a**
drvn out: eff at 8.5f/10f on fast & both AW's: lightly rcd & fast improving, front 2 well clr here, win again.
1216 **RAYSOOT** 49 [13] A C Stewart 3-9-4 (53) P McCabe 6/4 FAV: 000-02: b c Cape Cross - Mashkorah 2½ **60a**
(Miswaki) Slow away, in tch, led 5f out till over 2f out, onepace: 7 wk abs, bckd: unplcd all 3 '03 starts:
improved stepped up to 8.5f on fibresand: well clr of rem, shld find similar.
2019 **SPRING DANCER** 9 [10] B G Powell 3-9-4 (53) R Miles(3) 20/1: 00-00053: Slow away, in tch, eff over 13 **40a**
3f out, sn no extra: see 2019 (gd/fm).
1798 **DANTES DEVINE** 18 [1] A Bailey 3-9-3 (52) O Urbina 10/1: 55-06504: b g Ashkalani - Basilea (Frere 1½ **36a**
Basile) Led till 5f out, wknd: rtd 67 when 5th in '03 (1m, fast).
1468 **PURPLE RAIN** 35 [3]3-9-4 (53) I Mongan 33/1: 0065: b f Celtic Swing - Calypso Grant (Danehill) nk **36a**
Sn rdn bhd, no dngr: unplcd to date.
1730 **ANISETTE** 21 [8]3-9-0 (49) G Carter 10/1: 2-30606: Handy, wknd 4f out: see 1730, 126. hd **31a**
2019 **FLYING SPUD** 9 [6]3-9-1 (50) A Daly 12/1: 0-545107: In tch, wknd 3f out: btr 1740 (sell h'cap). 5 **22a**
2011 **WEET AN HAUL** 9 [4]3-9-6 (55) D Nolan(3) 14/1: 00120-08: With ldrs, wknd 3f out: see 203, 158 (7f). 1 **25a**
1283 **KELTIC RAINBOW** 45 [9]3-9-6 VIS (55) Paul Eddery 14/1: 0033-469: Al bhd: 6 wk abs: visor. ¾ **23a**
1611 **CTESIPHON** 28 [7]3-9-1 BL (50) B Doyle 33/1: 03-000: 10th: Al bhd: blnks. 6 **6a**
1790 **Rumour Mill** 18 [11]3-9-1 (50) M Savage(5) 33/1:0 1690 **Son Of Rembrandt** 23 [2]3-9-3 (52) M Howard(7) 33/1:0
12 Ran Time 1m 49.88(3.68) Owned: Mr R Gander Trained: Upper Lambourn

Official Going GOOD.

2206 1.45 Gr2 Vodafone Temple Stakes 3yo+ (A)
£63800 £24200 £12100 **5f str** **Good/Firm 21** -15 Slow Flip Start - Hand Timed.

1683 **NIGHT PROSPECTOR** 23 [9] J W Payne 4-9-4 (89) J Murtagh 33/1: 25100-01: Dsptd lead, led over 1f **107**
out, styd on strongly, drvn out: eff at 5f on gd & fast grnd: handles any trk: vastly imprvd form, rider took full
advantage of unsatisfactory start: see 1683.
1513* **AUTUMN PEARL** 32 [11] M A Jarvis 3-8-8 (93) P Robinson 10/1: 151-12: Broke well & sn led on rail, 1¼ **100**
hdd dist, no extra cl-home: imprvd in defeat, acts on fast, hvy grnd & polytrack: loves to run up with/force the
pace, does stay 6f: see 1513.
1683 **BISHOPS COURT** 23 [10] Mrs J R Ramsden 10-9-4 (110) L Dettori 3/1 FAV: 153-1203: Trkd ldrs on ½ **102**
rail, no room entering fnl 1f, kept on: well bckd: class performer in this race, usually runs v well here at Epsom,
but come from bhd tactics leave him liable to meet trouble: see 1207.
790 **BOSTON LODGE** 85 [7] G A Butler 4-9-4 BL (97) M J Kinane 25/1: 41-32324: Chsd ldrs, onepncd fnl 1 **99**
1f: tried blnks: 12 wk abs & has been gelded since 790 (6f).
2068 **COLONEL COTTON** 6 [12]5-9-4 bl (100) D Holland 9/1: 30-60655: Prom, lost place bef halfway, fin ¾ **96**
well but too late: qck reapp: has plenty of ability, but is not an easy ride: see 1479 & 1159.
1732 **IF PARADISE** 21 [3]3-8-11 (105) R Hughes 12/1: 6205-106: Mid-div, wknd & eased fnl 1f: btr 1106. 2 **90**
1845 **REPERTORY** 16 [4]11-9-4 (105) T G McLaughlin 14/1: 010-0007: b g Anshan - Susie's Baby (Balidar) 1¼ **86**
Dsptd lead till wknd over 1f out: 11yo now, '03 List wnr in Ireland: rtd h'cap & dual stks wnr in '02: Gr 3 & List
wnr in '01: loves dominating around 5f: acts on firm & fast, likes gd/soft & hvy grnd: handles any trk, loves
Epsom: can run well fresh: poorly drawn today.
2 May'03 Sand 5.0g/f 109-(111) A: 1 Apr'03 Cork 5g/f 110- : 2 Apr'03 Newb 5.2g/f 112-110 B:
2 Apr'03 Nott 5.1gd 113-(110) B: 1 Oct'02 Newm 5g/f 112-104 B: 1 Sep'02 Leic 5g/f 100- C:
1 Jul'02 Newm 5g/f 111- C: 1 Oct'01 Long 5hvy 115- : 1 Jul'01 Curr 5g/s 116- :
1845 **DUBAIAN GIFT** 16 [6]5-9-4 (103) Martin Dwyer 14/1: 216-0008: Dwelt, rushed to dspt lead, wknd fnl 1 **83**
1f: loves to dominate, lost ch at start: see 1845.

1400 **SPEED COP 38** [5]4-9-1 (99) K Darley 8/1: 4410-239: Slowly away, nvr nr ldrs: lost all ch start.   *1*   77
1572 **INCISE 30** [1]3-8-8 (90) K Fallon 33/1: 3201-600: 10th: Slowly away, prog to dspt lead halfway,   *4*   65
hung left & wknd fnl 1.5f: another inconvenienced by the unsatisfactory start: see 1400.
1683 **DRAGON FLYER 23** [2]5-9-1 (98) S Drowne 16/1: 00-42000: 11th: V slowly away & al detached: *5*   50
caught out at the start & this shld be ignored: see 1151.
1773 **FOREVER PHOENIX 20** [8]4-9-1 (92) E Ahern 9/2: 121312R: Whipped round start & ref to race: well   0
bckd: lost all ch at the start: much btr 1773 & 1615.
12 Ran   Time 56.1 (1.8)   Owned: Mr C Cotran   Trained: Newmarket

---

2207   **2.15 Vodafone Mile Handicap 3yo+ 0-105 (B)**   **[98]**
        £23200 £8800 £4400   **1m114y rnd**   **Good/Firm 21**   **-08 Slow**   Inside

2076+ **8HOOMAGOO 6** [8] K A Ryan 6-9-1 (5ex)bl (85) N Callan 7/1: 0-100011: Held up, prog wide 2f out,   98
led wll ins fnl 1f, shot clr: well bckd: eff at 6f, suited by 7/8.5f: acts on firm, soft grnd & fibresand, any
trk: suited by blnks: clearly in tremendous form & escapes with a pen in the Royal Hunt Cup: see 2076 & 744.
1812 **ALRAFID 17** [11] G L Moore 5-9-1 (85) R L Moore 7/1: 426-0562: Held up, prog wide 2f out, ev ch   *3*   88
entering fnl 1f, not quite good enuff nr cl-home: continues to run well in defeat: see 1812 & 134.
4492} **DEFINITE GUEST 250** [7] R A Fahey 6-8-12 (82) P Hanagan 20/1: 113565-3: gr g Definite Article -   *1½*   83
Nicea (Dominion) Trkd ldrs, sltly short of room after halfway, styd on fnl 1f on reapp: dual h'cap wnr in '03: eff
at 7f/1m on firm & gd/soft, handles polytrack: handles any trk, has tried blnks, best without: encouraging reapp.
1 Jul'03 Newb 8fm 83-77 B: 1 Jul'03 York 7.9fm 80-71 D: 2 Jun'03 Carl 7.9g/f 74-70 D:
1 Sep'01 Folk 7gd 76-69 E: 1 Jul'01 Ling 7g/f 70-64 F:
1970 **SAWWAAH 11** [3] D Nicholls 7-8-12 (82) J Fanning 12/1: 30-00134: Nvr far away, led dist, drifted   *¾*   81
left & hdd ins fnl 1f, no extra: see 1820 (7f).
1704 **DUMARAN 22** [9]6-9-8 vis (92) K Fallon 5/1 FAV: 03-00235: Lost 5L+ start, rdn & prog over 1f out,   *nk*   90
fin well but too late: well bckd: won this race from a 5lb lower mark 2 yrs ago: lost all ch at the start today.
2096 **IMPELLER 4** [5]5-9-3 (87) S Drowne 13/2: 022-0026: Mid-div wide, onepcd dist: op 5/1, qck reapp.   *nk*   84
2096 **CONVENT GIRL 4** [6]4-9-0 (94) R Havlin 33/1: 126-0007: Slowly away, sltly short of room entering   *nk*   90
straight, nvr dngrs: qck reapp & top-weight: see 1686 (1m).
1478 **MYSTERINCH 34** [10]4-9-8 (92) J F Egan 25/1: 211/3-308: Prom, led over 2f out till dist, wkng   *hd*   88
when short of room: see 1225 (reapp).
2076 **JAY GEES CHOICE 6** [2]4-9-2 (86) S Hitchcott(3) 7/1: 00-60039: Led till after halfway, wknd 2f   *½*   81
out: showed much more 2076 (7f).
      OCEAN OF STORMS 50 [1]9-8-10 T (80) Martin Dwyer 25/1: 643R-210: 10th: b c Arazi - Moon Cactus   *1*   73
(Kris) Nvr btr than mid-div: 7 wk abs: UAE challenger, won a h'cap at Nad Al Sheba 7 wks ago: winning form btwn
1m & 15f & on fast & soft grnd: versatile performer, wears a t-strap.
2036 **VOICE MAIL 8** [13]5-8-8 (78) L Keniry(3) 16/1: 0-001130: 11th: Dwelt, nvr nr ldrs: btr 1899.   *1*   69
2096 **BLUE TROJAN 4** [4]4-9-0 (84) F Norton 5/1: 2200140: 12th: Prom, wknd 3f out: qck reapp.   *shd*   75
1833 **IRONY 17** [12]5-9-2 (86) K Darley 10/1: 163-0040: 13th: Front rank, led halfway till 2f out, wkng   *shd*   77
when short of room 1.5f out, eased: btr 1833.
13 Ran   Time 1m 44.30 (2.50)   Owned: Mr J Duddy & Mr T Fawcett   Trained: Hambleton

---

2208   **2.50 Vodafone Rose Bowl Handicap 4yo+ (B)**   **[114]**
        £23200 £8800 £4400   **1m2f18y**   **Good/Firm 21**   **-04 Slow**   Inside

1843 **PERSIAN LIGHTNING 16** [1] J L Dunlop 5-9-2 (102) M J Kinane 11/2: 6200-441: Mid-div, prog to lead   109
1.5f out, rdn clr, eased cl-home & v nrly caught: eff at 9/10f, stays 12/13f: acts on gd & firm, handles a gall or
sharp/undul trk: v smart h'capper, has shown enough to win in List company, rnr-up at Royal Ascot last year.
1746 **DESERT QUEST 21** [3] A M Balding 4-8-3 BL (89) Martin Dwyer 20/1: 3/1461-02: Rdn in rear, prog   *hd*   94
1.5f out, hung left, fin fast & only just failed: tried blnks: may well have won this race on a more conventional trk,
hmpd himself by hanging left fnl 2f: deserves similar, see 1746.
1704 **SHAHZAN HOUSE 22** [7] M A Jarvis 5-8-10 P (96) P Robinson 9/2 FAV: 0410-323: Chsd ldrs, imprvd to   *2*   98
lead over 2f out till 1.5f out, onepace fnl 1f: nicely bckd in first time cheek pieces: another consistent run, prob
ideally suited by sltly softer grnd: see 1704 & 1296.
1111 **COUNSELS OPINION 55** [8] C F Wall 7-9-4 (104) S Sanders 11/2: 00110-34: Dwelt, hdwy from rear 2f   *1¾*   104
out, onepcd ins fnl 1f: 8 wk abs: see 1111.
1862 **COMPTON BOLTER 15** [11]7-9-10 (110) R Hughes 8/1: 4050325: Mid-div, hmpd entering fnl 1f, onepace   *1½*   108
after: nicely bckd under top-weight: see 1862 (List).
1478 **BLYTHE KNIGHT 34** [6]4-9-3 (103) L Dettori 5/1: 430-4146: Mid-div going well, hmpd 3f out & again   *½*   100
dist, no ch after: tchd 13/2: whilst not up to the run of today's race: btr 1486.
928 **DANELOR 70** [5]6-8-0 (86) P Hanagan 5/1: 4220-457: Front rank, led over 3f out till 2f out, wknd: *1¼*   81
bckd from 13/2, 10 wk abs: rnr-up in this race from a 2lb lower mark last term: see 836.
2091 **ST PANCRAS 5** [9]4-7-12 BL (84) D Fox(5) 14/1: 56-00028: Sn rdn in rear, prog when veered left 3f   *5*   71
out, no ch after: qck reapp & first time blnks: rider reportedly given a 9-day careless riding ban: btr 2091 (1m).
1586* **GUILDED FLYER 29** [10]5-8-11 (87) J F Egan 16/1: 6500-019: Set qck pace till over 3f out, wknd: *nk*   73
went off to fast, see 1586.
2101 **SIR GEORGE TURNER 4** [4]5-9-0 (100) J Fanning 33/1: 632/-0000: 10th: Al rear, t.o.: qck reapp.   *28*   41
1483 **ROCKET FORCE 34** [2]4-8-11 VIS (97) K Fallon 50/1: 1/320-000: 11th: on c Spinning World - Pat Us   *1½*   36
(Caucasus) Dsptd lead, wknd 3f out, eased & t.o.: much too keen in first time visor: lightly rcd in '03, List
rnr-up on middle start: '02 mdn scorer: eff at 10f on gd & fast grnd, handles a gall trk: with E Dunlop.
2 May'03 Newm 10g/f 104-(104) A: 1 Oct'02 Newc 8g/f 82- D:
11 Ran   Time 2m 06.36 (2.56)   Owned: Windflower Overseas Holdings Inc   Trained: Arundel

---

2209   **3.30 Gr1 Vodafone Coronation Cup 4yo+ (A)**
        £145000 £55000 £27500   **1m4f10y**   **Good/Firm 21**   **+12 Fast**   Outside

1493 **WARRSAN 33** [5] C E Brittain 6-9-0 (117) D Holland 7/1: 6333-531: Held up, prog 2f out, led ent   122
fnl 1f, rdn clr: fast time, op 11/2: right back to v best, won this race last yr: suited by 12/14f on firm & soft,
any trk: genuine, high-class & most tough performer who looks sure to give a gd account in the King George.
4633} **DOYEN 243** [1] Saeed bin Suroor 4-9-0 (121) L Dettori 9/2: 5/11124-2: b c Sadler's Wells - Moon   *1¾*   118
Cactus (Kris) Mid-div going well, prog when short of room 1.5f out, kept on but no ch with wnr: well bckd, reapp:

'03 Gr 3 wnr, also 4th in Gr 1 Arc (A Fabre): eff at 12f on fast & soft, gall or sharp trk: runs well fresh: met trouble at a crucial time today but unlikely to have caught impressive wnr anyway: high-class.
2 Sep'03 Long 12g/s 124- : 1 Jun'03 Long 12gd 120- A:

1558	**VALLEE ENCHANTEE 33** [3] E Lellouche 4-8-11 D Boeuf 6/1: 01411-43: b f Peintre Celebre - Verveine (Lear Fan) Held up, prog when no room 1.5f out, fin well under hands & heels riding: won a couple of Gr 2s in '03: eff at 1m, suited by 12/13.5f: acts on fast & hvy, handles a gall or sharp/undul trk: v smart filly, owner reportedly so dissatisfied with this ride that joc will not ride this horse again: more Gr 2's surely await.				shd	115+

1 Oct'03 Long 12g/s 115- : 1 Aug'03 Deau 13.5g/s 114- A:

4893}	**HIGH ACCOLADE 223** [11] M P Tregoning 4-9-0 (116) Martin Dwyer 4/1 FAV: 626212-4: b c Mark of Esteem - Generous Lady (Generous) Prom, led over 2f out till dist, no extra on reapp: hvly bckd from 13/2: highly progressive in '03, won a class stks, List & Gr 3 & 2, also rnr-up in Gr 1 St Leger: eff at 12/14.6f, acts on gd & firm grnd: has tried blnks/visor, prob btr without: can force the pace: high-class, spot on next time.				shd	118

2 Oct'03 Newb 12.0gd 118-(116) A: 1 Sep'03 Asco 12g/f 118-(115) A: 2 Sep'03 Donc 14.6g/f 118-(115) A:
2 Jul'03 Good 12gd 117-(115) A: 1 Jun'03 Asco 12g/f 115- A: 1 May'03 Good 11g/f 113-(98) A:
1 May'03 Bath 10.2g/f 102-(93) B: 1 Jul'02 Newb 7fm 93- D:

1560	**BRIAN BORU 32** [10]4-9-0 t J P Spencer 9/1: 4213-155: Held up last, prog wide 2f out, nrst fin: sweating: set plenty to do for a confirmed stayer, last season's St Leger wnr: v smart & will win more races when more enterprisingly rdn, over further: see 1560 & 994.				1½	116+
3721}	**MAGISTRETTI 290** [12]4-9-0 (121) J Murtagh 7/1: 5/11022-6: dc Diesis - Ms Strike Zone (Deputy Minister) Trkd ldrs, onepcd fnl 1.5f on reapp: List & Gr 2 Dante wnr: subs rnr-up in Gr 1 Juddmonte at York: eff at 9/10f on firm & gd/soft grnd: likes a gall trk, esp York: high-class at best, sharper next time & keep in mind back at fav'd York.				1	114

2 Aug'03 York 10.4fm 122-(115) A: 2 Jun'03 Long 10gd 115- A: 1 May'03 York 10.4fm 110-(109) A:
1 Apr'03 Newm 9gd 111-(102) A: 2 Sep'02 Donc 7fm 95- C: 2 Jul'02 Newm 7g/s 97- A: 1 Jun'02 Sand 7g/s 91- D:

2141	**SCOTTS VIEW 5** [4]5-9-0 (115) K Fallon 10/1: 0131337: Prom, led 3f out till over 2f out, wknd ins fnl 1f: nicely bckd & qck reapp: has been busy, see 1438 & 1139.				shd	114
1493	**DUBAI SUCCESS 33** [8]4-9-0 (113) M Hills 25/1: 05D3-148: Trkd ldrs, rdn & btn 2f out: hung left.				½	113
1859	**IMPERIAL DANCER 19** [6]6-9-0 (117) T E Durcan 11/1: 4110-369: Held up, nvr nr ldrs: btr 1230.				3	108
1596*	**SYSTEMATIC 28** [9]5-9-0 (113) K Darley 10/1: 255-3210: 10th: Set decent pace till hdd 2f out, wknd: much btr 1596 (13.4f, gd grnd).				1¼	106
82	**SUNNY GLENN 195** [2]6-9-0 (78) R Havlin 100/1: 0/25000-0: 11th: Dwelt, al bhd, fin last on reapp.				6	97$

11 Ran   Time 2m 35.96 (1.16)   Owned: Mr Saeed Manana   Trained: Newmarket

---

2210	4.10 Gr1 Vodafone Oaks Fillies 3yo (A)
	£203000 £77000 £38500 **1m4f10y** Good/Firm 21 +16 Fast Outside

1494*	**OUIJA BOARD 33** [3] E A L Dunlop 3-9-0 (110) K Fallon 7/2: 313-11: b f Cape Cross - Selection Board (Welsh Pageant) Held up, gd prog to lead 2f out, powered clr fnl 1f for a highly impressive victory: well bckd, fast time: clearly relished this step up to 12f, acts on gd & firm grnd: handles a gall or sharp/undul trk & runs well fresh: high-class filly who will be hard to beat over mid-dists this term judged on this: see 1494.					123+

1 May'04 Newm 10fm 116-(93) A: 1 Oct'03 Yarm 7.0gd 95- D:

1435*	**ALL TOO BEAUTIFUL 41** [6] A P O'Brien 3-9-0 J P Spencer 11/4 FAV: 112: Mid-div, hdwy to lead 2.5f out, sn hdd, kept on but no ch with impressive wnr: well bckd from 4/1, 6 wk abs: decent eff from this lightly rcd filly in this much higher grade: prob stays 12f & acts on fast & gd/soft grnd: met a top-class rival, still learning & Group success looks assured: see 1435.				7	114
1666*	**PUNCTILIOUS 24** [2] Saeed bin Suroor 3-9-0 t (110) L Dettori 10/3: 113-13: Chsd ldrs, led halfway till 2.5f out, wknd: well bckd tho' op 5/2: reportedly hated this switch-back trk: must be given another ch on a more conventional trk, see 1666 (soft grnd).				3½	109
2005	**NECKLACE 12** [5] A P O'Brien 3-9-0 J Murtagh 10/1: 2110-064: Held up, hdwy & ch 3f out, sn left bhd: well clr rem: longer priced s/mate of 2nd: longer 12f trip, stays 1m/10f shld suit: see 2005.				1½	107
1384*	**CRYSTAL 39** [7]3-9-0 (93) M Hills 25/1: 0-215: Chsd ldrs, wknd over 3f out, t.o.: highly tried & lkd out of her depth: mdn wnr in 1384 (10f, gd grnd).				18	80
1492	**SUNDROP 33** [4]3-9-0 (117) K McEvoy 3/1: 12-26: V keen & prom, wknd qckly over 3f out, eased & t.o.: hvly bckd: reportedly ran away with joc & this is not her form: much longer 12f trip, 1,000 Guineas rnr-up.				4	74
1494	**KISSES FOR ME 12** [1]3-9-0 Paul Scallan 66/1: 1-507: Set pace till halfway, wknd & t.o.				dist	34

7 Ran   Time 2m 35.41 (0.61)   Owned: Lord Derby   Trained: Newmarket

---

2211	4.50 Gr3 Princess Elizabeth Stakes Sponsored By Vodafonefillies 3yo+ (A)
	£29000 £11000 £5500 **1m114y rnd** Good/Firm 21 -24 Slow Inside

1863*	**GONFILIA 15** [10] Saeed bin Suroor 4-9-6 t (102) L Dettori 11/10 FAV: 51-01211: Made all, clr 2f out, styd on strongly, readily: hvly bckd from 13/8 under top-weight: eff at 7f/1m on firm, soft grnd & dirt: handles a gall/undul or gall trk, loves to race with/force the pace: tough & smart filly who wears a t-strap.					105
4953}	**KUNDA 18** [1] R Hannon 3-8-8 (96) R Hughes 20/1: 23152-62: b f Intikhab - Ustka (Lomond) Trkd ldrs, went after wnr 2f out, sn no impress: recently 6th in a List race in France: '03 fills mdn wnr, also List rnr-up: eff at 6f, styd this longer 1m trip well: acts on gd & firm grnd, handles a sharp or sharp/undul trk: reportedly hung left & will apprec a return to a more conventional trk.				2½	98

2 Oct'03 Newm 6gd 93-(86) A: 1 Aug'03 Newb 6.0fm 86- D: 2 Jul'03 Newb 6.0g/f 91- D:

1568	**QASIRAH 30** [5] M A Jarvis 3-8-8 bl (98) P Robinson 20/1: 120-053: Chsd ldrs, onepcd fnl 1f: reportedly failed to handle this trk: see 1568.				1	96
1169	**TOP ROMANCE 51** [7] Sir Michael Stoute 3-8-8 (102) K Fallon 13/2: 11-04: ch f Entrepreneur - Heart's Harmony (Blushing Groom) Rear, late hdwy despite hanging left, nrst fin: 7 wk abs: won both '03 starts, mdn & List: eff at 7f on fast & firm, shld stay 1m+: can run well fresh & has a stiff/gall trk: capable of better.				¾	94

1 Oct'03 Newm 7fm 104- A: 1 Sep'03 Yarm 7.0g/f 83- D:

1636*	**BLUE OASIS 27** [6]3-8-8 (77) K Darley 20/1: 15: Dwelt, nvr trbld ldrs: up in grade after 1636.				3	88
	TIZDUBAI 300 [8]3-8-8 T K McEvoy 8/1: 11-6: b f Cee's Tizzy - Cee's Song (Seattle Song) Trkd wnr, wknd over 1f out, eased on reapp: op 5/1, longer priced stablemate of wnr, wore a t-strap: won both starts in the US last yr: eff at 6/6.5f on fast grnd.				shd	88
1666	**GLEN INNES 24** [2]3-8-8 (101) D Holland 11/2: 1227: Held up in last, nvr nr ldrs: op 4/1, reportedly hung left: much btr on soft grnd in 1666 & 1419.				2	84
1305+	**IMPERIALISTIC 43** [4]3-8-8 p (94) Darren Williams 7/1: 423-4118: Mid-div, btn 2f out: 6 wk abs: hung left: prev progressive on soft grnd: see 1305.				6	72

8 Ran   Time 1m 45.61 (3.81)   Owned: Godolphin   Trained: Newmarket

EPSOM
FRIDAY 04.06.04   Lefthand, Very Sharp, Undulating Track

2212   **5.25 Vodafone Group Services Handicap Stakes 3yo 0-100 (C)**   [107]
£23200 £8800 £4400   **7f rnd**   **Good/Firm 21**   -26 Slow   Inside

1919   **MAKFOOL 13** [8] M R Channon 3-9-0   (93) T E Durcan   9/1: 3-034021: Prom, went on 2f out, held on   101
well fnl 1f, drvn out: bckd from 12/1: eff at 7f/1m on fast & gd/soft grnd: handles any trk: likes to run up with
the pace, see 1919 & 949.
1771   **MANDOBI 20** [14] A C Stewart 3-8-13   (92) K Fallon   14/1: 32120-42: Dwelt, hdwy wide halfway, styd   ¾   98
on fnl 1f & only just btn: turn shld not be far away, see 1771.
1813   **FANCY FOXTROT 17** [11] B J Meehan 3-8-8   (87) M J Kinane   40/1: 326-1003: Dwelt, keen in rear, styd   nk   91
on wide fnl 1.5f, nrst fin: change of tactics, usually best forcing the pace, as in 1021.
2126   **MISTER SAIF 3** [4] R Hannon 3-8-6   (85) P Dobbs   20/1: 22-0U504: Mid-div, short of room briefly   hd   90
halfway, kept on under press fnl 1f: qck reapp: see 1665.
1983   **FREE TRIP 10** [13]3-8-4   (83) R Havlin   14/1: 20-16025: Prom, ev ch till wknd fnl 1f: see 1983.   2½   83
1813   **DESERT DREAMER 17** [15]3-8-13   (92) M Hills   8/1: 5420-506: Rear, prog wide 2f out, btn fnl 1f: op 13/2.   ¾   90
1983*   **FLIP FLOP AND FLY 10** [10]3-8-5 (5ex)   (84) J F Egan   8/1: 300-0017: Mid-div, nvr nr to chall.   hd   82
1919   **PARKVIEW LOVE 13** [12]3-9-7   (100) J Fanning   25/1: 65-03008: Chsd ldrs, no impress fnl 2f: top-weight.   1   96
1583   **CELLO 29** [5]3-8-3   (82) R L Moore   12/1: 355-2169: Dwelt, hdwy when short of room 2f out, no ch   1   76
after: btr 1297 (hvy grnd).
1919   **SPANISH ACE 13** [6]3-8-13 VIS   (92) Martin Dwyer   16/1: 260-0000: 10th: b g First Trump - Spanish   ¾   84
Heart (King of Spain) Keen & led 5f, wknd qckly: much too keen in first time visor: '03 Ascot stks wnr, also Gr 2
rnr-up: eff at 5/6f on gd & firm grnd: with A Balding.
2 Jun'03 Curr 6gd 97- A: 1 Apr'03 Asco 5gd 90- B: 2 Apr'03 Kemp 5fm 88- D:
1498   **TARUSKIN 33** [9]3-8-7   (86) F Norton   10/1: 231-3130: 11th: Dwelt, nvr nr ldrs: btr 1370.   nk   77
1186   **BETTALATETHANNEVER 50** [16]3-8-13   (92) Dane O'Neill   16/1: 061-1400: 12th: Rdn in rear, nvr dngrs.   shd   83
1919   **OVERDRAWN 13** [2]3-8-11   (90) S W Kelly   20/1: 415-0000: 13th: Nvr btr than mid-div.   1½   78
1665   **ISKANDER 24** [7]3-8-8   (87) N Callan   40/1: 6154-600: 14th: Chsd ldrs, wkng when short of room 2f out.   nk   74
1732   **BOTANICAL 21** [17]3-9-5 t   (98) L Dettori   16/1: 1204-50: 15th: Prom trav well, wknd qckly 1.5f out,   6   73
eased: ran as tho' something was amiss: see 1732.
1847*   **SECRET PLACE 16** [3]3-8-11   (90) E Ahern   5/2 FAV: 2-113010: 16th: Trkd ldrs 5f, wknd & eased: 2   61
hvly bckd: something amiss? much btr 1847.
1419   **FIRST CANDLELIGHT 37** [1]3-8-6   (85) M Fenton   25/1: 21-00: 17th: Prom till halfway, wknd & eased.   ½   55
17 Ran   Time 1m 23.39(3.29)   Owned: Sheikh Ahmed Al Maktoum   Trained: West Ilsley

---

THIRSK   **FRIDAY 04.06.04**   Lefthand, Flat, Oval Track

Official Going GOOD/FIRM (GOOD places). All Times Slow.

2213   **2.05 European Breeders Fund Novice Stakes 2yo (D)**
£4290 £1320 £660   **5f str**   **Good/Firm**   **Slow**   Stands Side

1880*   **BECKERMET 14** [5] R F Fisher 2-9-2   P Bradley(5)   14/1: 311: Dwelt, sn trkd ldrs, rdn to lead ins   82
last, drvn out: eff at 5f, shld get 6f: acts on fast & gd grnd, stiff/gall or easy trks: see 1880.
1677*   **SELKIRK STORM 23** [4] M W Easterby 2-9-2   Dale Gibson   8/1: 12: Prom, rdn to chall dist, not pace   ¾   79
of wnr ins last: acts on fast & hvy grnd: eff at 5/6f, shld win again after 1677.
1037   **BIBURY FLYER 62** [2] M R Channon 2-8-7   A Culhane   7/2: 223: Slow away, styd on for press fnl 2f,   hd   69
not able to chall: 9 wk abs: handles fast & hvy grnd: see 1037 & 943.
2056*   **SMIDDY HILL 7** [7] R Bastiman 2-8-9   R Ffrench   4/5 FAV: 32414: Led till hdd ins last & no extra.   ¾   69
1868   **UNLIMITED 15** [6]2-9-0   G Duffield   9/1: 2125: Cl-up, hung left & btn over 1f out: handles fast,   2   68
fibresand & gd grnd: see 1868 & 1439.
1567   **MITCHELLAND 30** [3]2-9-0   T Eaves(3)   16/1: 4106: In tch, btn over 1f out: btr 1037 (hvy).   3   59
     OUTRAGEOUS FLIRT 0 [8]2-8-7   A Beech   50/'1: 7: b f Indian Lodge - Sofia Aurora (Chief Honcho)   7   31
Slow away & sn outpcd in rear: £14,000 April foal, half-sister to a 6f juv wnr, dam a juv wnr abroad.
     OUR KES 0 [1]2-8-7   P Mathers(7)   100/1: 8: b f Revoque - Gracious Gretclo (Common Grounds) Slow   ¾   29
away, sn btn: April foal, 40,000gns: half-sister to a 6f juv wnr & also a 7f juv/1m 3yo scorer Granston.
8 Ran   Time 59.75 (2.75)   Owned: Great Head House Estates Limited   Trained: Ulverston

---

2214   **2.40 Leslie Petch Handicap Stakes 3yo+ 0-70 (E)**   [69]
£3819 £1175 £588   **6f str**   **Good/Firm**   **Fair**   Flip Start

1578   **TAYIF 29** [11] Andrew Reid 8-9-4 t (59) S Carson   9/1: 6020531: Broke well from flip start & made   73
all stands side, rdn clr ins last: op 12/1: eff at 6/7f on fast, hvy & polytrack, handles fibresand: likes a
sharp/easy trk: see 407.
2160*   **TALLY 2** [5] M J Polglase 4-9-1 (6ex) (56) K Ghunowa(7)   7/1: 0060312: Held up far side, styd on for   3   59
press to lead that group ins last, no ch with wnr stands side: qck reapp under a pen: op 5/1: remains in gd heart.
2125   **COMPTON PLUME 3** [6] W H Tinning 4-9-0 (55) Dale Gibson   11/2 JT FAV: 026-03D3: Al prom far side &   ½   57
led that group 2f out, no extra ins last: qck reapp: see 2125 & 1824.
1824   **DRURY LANE 17** [13] D W Chapman 4-9-3 bl (58) A Culhane   25/1: 0-000004: Handy stands side, outpcd   1½   55
by wnr bef dist: well h'capped & encouragement here: see 585.
1824*   **PLAYFUL DANE 17** [17]7-9-3 (58) D Fentiman(7)   11/2 JT FAV: 43100-15: Chsd ldrs stands side, not   2½   47
pace to chall from dist.
1822   **OEUF A LA NEIGE 17** [18]4-9-8   (63) R Ffrench   20/1: 0530-506: b g Danehill - Reine de Neige (Kris)   nk   51
Drvn towards rear stands side, late gains: h'cap plcd '03 (rtd 72): lightly rcd '02 (mdn plcd, rtd 79, AW unplcd,
rtd 74a, E Dunlop): eff btwn 6f/1m, 7f may prove ideal: handles fast & gd grnd, gall or easy trks: looks well
h'capped & this was more encouraging.
1532   **BRIGADIER MONTY 31** [4]6-9-2   (57) G Duffield   33/1: 6000-067: b g College Chapel - Miss St Cyr   2   39
(Brigadier Gerard) Prom far side & chall over 1f out, sn no extra: ex-Irish, '03 h'cap scorer at Navan: winning
form at 6f on soft grnd, poss handles fast.
2111   **TOPPLING 4** [20]6-9-3   (58) B Reilly(3)   11/1: 0000-008: b g Cadeaux Genereux - Topicality   1¼   36

(Topsider) Dwelt sltly from flip start, nvr on terms stands side, qck reapp: dual h'cap scorer '03, no AW form:
h'cap plcd (rtd 58, no sand form): suited by 6f, eff at 1m: likes firm & gd grnd, prob handles any trk.
2 Jul'03 Wind 6g/f 63-62 E: 1 Jun'03 Nott 6.1gd 63-55 F: 1 Jun'03 Yarm 6.0fm 58-50 E: 2 Jun'03 Chep 7.1g/f 52-50 E:
1 Jun'01 Wind 8.3g/f 86- D:

1277*	**MISTER MAL 45** [10]8-8-13 bl e (54) V Halliday 16/1: 053-0619: Led far side till 2f out, fdd: abs.				shd	32
1878	**TAPAU 15** [9]6-10-0 (69) C J Davies(7) 28/1: 2130-500: 10th: Trkd ldrs stands side till dist.				nk	46
1897	**SILVER MASCOT 14** [7]5-8-12 (53) T Eaves(3) 10/1: 5142300: 11th: Mid-div far side, btn dist: btr 1194.				½	28
5000}	**RUM DESTINY 213** [1]5-8-12 vis (53) G Parkin 66/1: 000000-0: 12th: Chsd ldrs far side till dist.				2	22
1638	**HILLTIME 27** [12]4-9-7 (62) R Winston 40/1: 4550/0-00: 13th: Rdn rear stands side, nvr a factor.				1¼	27
1909	**PAGAN STORM 13** [16]4-9-5 (60) Kristin Stubbs(7) 33/1: 0005000: 14th: Chsd ldrs stands side till dist.				1½	20
124	**INTELLIBET ONE 188** [8]4-9-5 (60) S Donohoe(7) 33/1: 000000-0: 15th: Far side, mid-div at best.				1¾	15
1973	**BETTYS PRIDE 11** [3]5-9-4 (59) W Supple 9/1: 0600-040: 16th: Al rear far side: btr 1973.				¾	12
1910	**TIME TO REMEMBER 13** [2]6-9-3 (58) Alex Greaves 10/1: 0R-00060: 17th: Far side & sn bhd.				2	5
1972	**GENERAL SMITH 11** [14]5-9-0 (55) J Carroll 16/1: 655-0000: 18th: Stands side & sn bhd, t.o..				24	0

18 Ran　Time 1m 12.00 (2.5)　Owned: Mr A S Reid　Trained: Mill Hill London

---

2215	3.15 Blue Bell At Kirby Hill Claiming Stakes 3yo (F)				
	£3129 £894 £447　**7f rnd**　**Good/Firm**　**Slow**　Inside				

2055	**EL PALMAR 7** [3] T D Barron 3-9-1 (68) P Makin(5) 16/1: 62-3301: Trkd ldrs & smooth prog to lead 2f out, rdn out: op 12/1: clmd by P Blockley for 10,000: eff at 5f, now stays easy 7f well in claim grade: acts on fast & soft grnd: see 1392.		73
1761	**TRUE 20** [11] M P Tregoning 3-8-10 (70) W Supple 2/1 FAV: 43-002: ch f Barathea - Bibliotheque (Woodman) Mid-div, hdwy but hung left under press from over 1f out, not able to chall wnr: nicely bckd, op 5/2: promise '03 (lightly rcd mdn, rtd 74, Sir Michael Stoute, unplcd): eff around 6/7f on fast grnd, stiff/gall or easy trk: has ability but lkd an awkward ride today.	2	63
2011	**DELUSION 9** [4] T D Easterby 3-8-4 (65) D Allan(3) 8/1: 04040-63: Prom, ch 2f out, not pace of front pair: poss stays an easy 6f in claim grade: see 2011 (6f).	4	49
1975	**WARES HOME 10** [5] K R Burke 3-9-1 vis (67) L Enstone(3) 8/1: 06-06034: Dwelt, sn mid-div, not pace to chall over 1f out: see 1975 (6f).	1¼	57
1946	**DELTA LADY 11** [7]3-8-0 (43) R Ffrench 50/1: 600-0605: Rear, only mod prog: see 1591.	hd	41
1975*	**ARFINNIT 10** [1]3-9-1 vis (64) A Culhane 11/4: 0306516: Led till 2f out, fdd: bckd: btr 1975 (6f).	¾	54
1678	**TURF PRINCESS 23** [10]3-8-10 (56) D Fentiman(7) 6/1: 6-124537: Sn handy, wknd dist: btr 1678.	hd	48
1147	**SALUT SAINT CLOUD 53** [8]3-8-5 (48) A McCarthy 66/1: 00045-68: b g Primo Dominie - Tiriana (Common Grounds) Keen rear early, hdwy halfway, btn over 1f out, abs: unplcd in '03 (rtd 69 & 42a, prob flattered, tried cheek pieces, blnks & visor, earlier with G C Bravery).	1	41
1944	**KNIGHT TO REMEMBER 11** [13]3-8-5 (45) R Fitzpatrick 33/1: 0-340059: Al towards rear: new yard..	2	37
1591	**HYMNS AND ARIAS 29** [12]3-8-0 P (43) P Fessey 50/1: 0-040000: 10th: Dwelt & al bhd, chkpcs.	9	16
1954	**BOLSHEVIK 11** [6]3-8-5 (50) R Winston 50/1: 06-000: 11th: Sn cl-up till 2f out, btn/eased dist.	6	11
1832	**KNOT IN DOUBT 17** [2]3-8-5　G Duffield 28/1: 00-00: 12th: Sn bhd.	10	0

12 Ran　Time 1m 28.76 (5.86)　Owned: Mr J G Brown　Trained: Thirsk

---

2216	3.50 Ellery Hill Rating Related Maiden Stakes Div 1 3yo+ 0-60 (F)				
	£3059 £874 £437　**7f rnd**　**Good/Firm**　**Slow**　Inside				

1099	**CARTE NOIRE 57** [9] J G Portman 3-8-5 (60) A Culhane 11/8 FAV: 6030-51: b f Revoque - Coffee Cream (Common Grounds) Handy & led over 1f out, drvn out: hvly bckd, op 7/4: 8 wk abs: mdn plcd in '03 (rtd 68, auct mdn): eff around 7f/1m on firm & fast grnd, sharp/undul or easy trks.		61
1876	**AMANDAS LAD 15** [7] M C Chapman 4-9-4 (60) W Supple 3/1: 6355042: Held up & keen, hdwy to press wnr bef dist, no extra ins last: op 7/2: stays an easy 7f well: see 487.	½	62
1778	**LIEUDAY 20** [3] W M Brisbourne 5-9-4 p (46) G Duffield 9/1: 5053-503: Dwelt, rear, kept on late for press, no threat to front pair: off rtd 46, treat rating with caution: see 1266.	2½	57$
1253	**ESTEBAN 46** [5] J J Quinn 4-9-4 (54) R Winston 12/1: 00450-04: b g Groom Dancer - Ellie Ardensky (Slip Anchor) Cl-up, led 2f out, sn hdd & outpcd: abs, drop in trip: h'cap plcd '03 (rtd 58, sand unplcd, rtd 58a): no form sole start '02: stays a gall 10f on firm grnd, has tried 12f.	1¾	53
1896	**INDI ANO STAR 14** [2]3-8-8 (60) R Fitzpatrick 7/1: 66605: Chsd ldrs, drvn & outpcd fnl 2f, op 9/2.	1¼	50
3878}	**REGAL FLIGHT 284** [8]3-8-8 (57) R Ffrench 12/1: 505-6: Mid-div, drvn & no prog fnl 2f, new yard.	½	49
4739}	**CANLIS 234** [1]5-9-4 (45) P Bradley(5) 66/1: 05/0000-7: Mid-div, drvn & btn 3f out, gelded.	½	48$
1778	**STOP THE NONSENSE 20** [6]3-8-8 BL t (53) J Carroll 20/1: 000-5008: Rear when bmpd halfway, nvr a factor, tried blnks: flattered 1003.	2½	43
4463}	**POLAR GALAXY 252** [4]3-8-5 (54) P Fessey 12/1: 505400-9: Led till 2f out, sn btn, reapp.	5	30

9 Ran　Time 1m 29.29 (6.39)　Owned: Mr A H Robinson　Trained: Compton

---

2217	4.35 Weatherbys Insurance Services Handicap Stakes 3yo+ 0-70 (E)			[65]
	£3595 £1106 £553　**1m4f**　**Good/Firm**　**Slow**　Inside			

2041*	**RED FOREST 7** [5] J Mackie 5-9-3 (6ex)t (54) Dale Gibson 9/4 FAV: 60-31611: Held up in tch, smooth hdwy to lead over 2f out & rdn clr bef dist, eased cl-home, val 8L: nicely bckd, op 11/4: qck reapp under a pen: eff at 1m, relishing 12f now on fast, gd & fibresand, disapp on soft this term: v progressive at present, winning run could continue: see 2041, 1342 & 1197.		67+
1980	**FIELD SPARK 10** [10] J A Glover 4-9-7 p (58) G Duffield 9/2: 616-6152: Mid-div, keen early, styd on for press fnl 2f, nvr a threat to wnr: in gd heart: see 1830.	6	63
2163	**BAKIRI 2** [7] Andrew Reid 6-9-8 (59) Rory Moore(7) 5/1: 0/-040523: Cl-up & led 5f out till over 2f out, kept on for press: clr of rem: qck reapp: could pinch similar if continuing in this form: see 2163 & 1271.	nk	63
2041	**SWYNFORD PLEASURE 7** [6] J Hetherton 8-9-4 (55) D Allan(3) 8/1: 0050-254: Held up, eff 3f out, no impress on front trio: see 1875.	5	52
1821	**ESCALADE 17** [2]7-9-6 VIS (57) A Culhane 14/1: 450-0405: Held up, short of room 3f out, mod prog.	nk	53
2088	**MAGIC CHARM 5** [11]6-8-11 (38) Leanne Kershaw(7) 20/1: 5-000406: Led after 1f till 5f out, sn no impress.	nk	33
1990	**ANNIVERSARY GUEST 10** [4]5-8-0 (37) R Ffrench 16/1: 3430057: Led 1f, prom till 4f out: see 1414.	nk	31
2038	**EAST RIDING 7** [3]4-8-3 (40) Ann Stokell 50/1: 5663008: Keen in mid-div, btn 3f out: btr 1536 (1m, hvy).	1½	32
2030	**EASIBET DOT NET 8** [8]4-9-10 bl (61) R Winston 11/2: 15-40239: Cl-up 4f out, wknd over 2f out.	1¼	51

THIRSK   FRIDAY 04.06.04   Lefthand, Flat, Oval Track

2038 **ZAN LO 7** [1]4-9-7 (58) W Supple 14/1: 516-0060: 10th: Held up, btn 3f out: op 12/1: see 1681. | | 5 | 42
4610] **NORMA SPEAKMAN 595** [9]4-8-11 (48) P Fessey 100/1: 0220/-0: 11th: ch f Among Men - Bride Bank | | 15 | 14

(Statoblest) Rear, no ch fnl 3f: v long abs: missed '03: dual juv seller rnr-up in '02 for A Berry: eff at 6/7f
on firm & fast grnd, easy to gall trk. 2 Jun'02 Redc 7fm 48- G: 2 Jun'02 Thir 6g/f 50- E:
11 Ran   Time 2m 39.22 (9.42)   Owned: Mr P Riley   Trained: Church Broughton

---

2218   5.10 Ellery Hill Rating Related Maiden Stakes Div 2 3yo+ 0-60 (F)
£3052 £872 £436   **7f rnd**   **Good/Firm**   **Slow**   Inside

4823} **MISS PORCIA 227** [7] P W Chapple Hyam 3-8-5 (59) A McCarthy 9/2: 0060-1: ch f Inchinor - Krista **60**
(Kris) Handy, rdn & led over 1f out, held on well for press: well bckd tho' op 9/4: reapp: unplcd in '03 for M
Wighan & M G Quinlan (rtd 66 & 31a, lightly rcd, disapp in a t-strap): eff at 7f, has tried 1m, may yet suit:
acts on fast grnd & an easy trk: goes well fresh.
1661 **DARA MAC 25** [6] N Bycroft 5-9-4 (47) J Quinn 40/1: B2005-02: b g Presidium - Nishara (Nishapour) **1¼** **59$**
Rear, styd on for press fnl 2f, al held by wnr: cheek pieces omitted: sell h'cap rnr-up in '03, also seller plcd
(rtd 51 at best): appr h'cap & mdn h'cap rnr-up '02: eff around 7f/1m, tried 10f: handles fast & gd/soft grnd,
prob any trk: best without blnks & cheek pieces.
2 Aug'03 Thir 8g/s 53-50 F: 2 Sep'02 Yarm 8g/f 56-53 F: 2 Jul'02 Beve 8.4g/f 53-50 F:
1910 **LUKE AFTER ME 13** [8] G A Swinbank 4-9-4 (55) R Winston 11/4 FAV: 2302043: Held up, eff to chase **1¼** **56**
ldrs over 1f out, sn rdn & no extra: nicely bckd, op 9/2: just btr 1910.
1359 **ABLAJ 41** [4] E A L Dunlop 3-8-8 VIS (57) W Supple 3/1: 400-04: ch g Horse Chestnut - Passe Passe **½** **55**
(Lear Fan) Led till over 1f out, no extra: bckd: tried visor, 6 wk abs: lightly rcd & unplcd '03 (rtd 64, mdn):
dam mid-dist plcd: may impr over further in h'cap company: handles fast grnd.
2011 **COMPTON MICKY 9** [2]3-8-8 P (60) D Allan(3) 50/1: 0-0605: Keen & trkd ldrs, short of room after 2f, **¾** **54**
rdn & no extra dist: clr of rem, cheek pieces.
1798 **SONDERBORG 18** [1]3-8-5 bl e (58) Dale Gibson 5/1: 2220026: Dwelt & rear, drvn & btn 2f out. **8** **37**
677 **MIDDLEHAM PARK 106** [3]4-9-4 (60) G Faulkner 8/1: 20060-07: Keen & trkd ldrs, btn 2f out: abs. **nk** **39**
2011 **CARIBBEAN BLUE 9** [5]3-8-5 (52) R Ffrench 14/1: 600-58: Mid-div, btn 2f out: btr 2011 (6f). **nk** **35**
1678 **MILITARY TWO STEP 23** [9]3-8-8 p (58) L Enstone(3) 20/1: 002-0009: Al towards rear. **1½** **35**
9 Ran   Time 1m 29.13 (6.23)   Owned: Mr Charles Alan McKechnie   Trained: Newmarket

---

2219   5.40 Racing Post Apprentice Handicap Stakes 3yo 35-55 (G)   [61]
£2583 £738 £369   **5f str**   **Good/Firm**   **Slow**   Stands Side

1605 **ICENASLICE 28** [2] J J Quinn 3-9-4 (51) D Tudhope(3) 9/2: 346-01: Broke well & made all, crossed **69+**
to stands rail halfway & sn rdn clr, readily: first win: eff at 5f, stays a stiff 7f: handles fast & gd grnd,
stiff or easy trk: enjoyed forcing tactics today: one to note if reappearing quickly.
1825 **BURKEES GRAW 17** [9] Mrs S Lamyman 3-9-0 (47) D Fentiman(3) 7/1: 00-00002: Dwelt & held up, styd **6** **49**
on for press fnl 2f, nvr ch with easy wnr: see 619.
1730 **VENDORS MISTAKE 21** [1] Andrew Reid 3-9-1 (48) Rory Moore 4/1 JT FAV: 600-0633: Prom, edged right **½** **48**
& onepace/held over 1f out: bckd tho' op 7/2: eff at 5f, return to 6f could suit: just btr 1730.
853 **CELLINO 80** [5] Andrew Turnell 3-9-0 (47) P Makin 14/1: 0050-04: b f Robellino - Celandine **nk** **46**
(Warning) Chsd ldrs, onepace for press: abs: lightly rcd & unplcd '03 (rtd 65, debut): eff around 6/7f wnr.
1881 **SHAMROCK TEA 14** [6]3-9-4 (55) Natalia Gemelova 11/2: 55000-05: b g Imperial Ballet - Yellow **shd** **54**
Ribbon (Hamas) Mid-div, no impress halfway: gelded, sell grade wnr '03 for D Cosgrove: wng form at 6f &
relishes soft grnd. 1 May'03 Ripo 6sft 78- F:
1947 **PEACE TREATY 11** [10]3-8-2 (35) C Haddon(3) 33/1: 0-000006: Rear, only mod late prog, nvr a dngr. **1** **31**
2075 **SHANGHAI SURPRISE 6** [4]3-8-12 P (45) K Pierrepont(7) 20/1: 000-5007: Chsd ldrs till halfway, chkpcs. **¾** **39**
1985 **PARALLEL LINES 10** [8]3-8-13 bl (46) S Donohoe 4/1 JT FAV: 4003608: Prom till 2f out, fdd: btr 1453. **1** **37**
1404 **GEMINI GIRL 38** [7]3-9-7 (54) M Lawson 7/1: 05366-09: Chsd ldrs till halfway. **nk** **44**
9 Ran   Time 59.93(2.93)   Owned: Miss D A Johnson   Trained: Malton

---

GOODWOOD   FRIDAY 04.06.04   Righthand, Sharpish, Undulating Track

Official Going GOOD/FIRM.

2220   6.20 Elm Farm Research Centre Stakes Handicap For Amateur Riders 3yo+ 0-70 (F)   [48]
£3838 £1181 £591   **1m1f rnd**   **Good 42**   **-54 Slow**   Inside

1940 **GRAN CLICQUOT 12** [9] G P Enright 9-9-11 (45) Mr J Pemberton(7) 14/1: 00-00201: In tch, kept on **52**
from 2f out, rdn out to lead cl-home: suited by 1m/10f on firm, gd grnd & polytrack: see 1451.
1849 **BEST BEFORE 16** [4] P D Evans 4-11-3 (65) Miss E Fokes(3) 10/1: 0012202: Led, under press ins fnl **hd** **71**
1f, hdd cl-home: now suited by 1m/9f: find similar on this evidence: see 1530 & 1385.
1298 **LIBERTY ROYAL 44** [14] P J Makin 5-11-2 P (64) Mr S Walker 7/1: 000-6063: Mid-div, prog halfway, **1½** **67**
ev ch clsg, sn onepcd: 6 wk abs: acts on gd grnd & polytrack, handles firm: gd eff with cheek pieces: see 1298.
1986 **BANK ON HIM 10** [12] G L Moore 9-10-2 (50) Mr J Jones(3) 5/2 FAV: 2225134: Mid-div, prog 3f out, **1¾** **50**
no impress ins fnl 1f: best recent form has come on polytrack: btr 1986.
1986 **PASO DOBLE 10** [15]6-10-9 (57) Mr J Millman(3) 20/1: 5026205: Rear, prog after 6f, onepcd fnl 1f. **1¼** **55**
1899 **RAINSTORM 14** [13]9-9-10 (44) Mrs S Owen(3) 7/1: 1400-656: Mid-div 7f, sn no extra: btr 1899. **shd** **41**
1946 **TARKWA 11** [2]5-9-10 (44) Mr G Arizkorreta 16/1: 60-60107: Nvr nrr than mid-div: btr 1711 (polytrk). **2½** **37**
1891 **PARNASSIAN 14** [6]4-10-11 (59) Miss J Hannaford(7) 6/1: 0033138: Bhd, nvr nrr than mid-div: btr 1891. **1½** **49**
718 **TINTAWN GOLD 101** [10]4-10-2 (50) Miss R Woodman(7) 25/1: 02500-09: b f Rudimentary - Clear Ahead **½** **39**
(Primo Dominie) Cl-up 7f, sn wknd: long abs: plcd 4 times in '03 (h'caps & clmr, Mrs P N Dutfield): plcd on one
of 4 '02 starts (fills nov auct): eff around 9.7f/10f on fast & gd grnd: with S Woodman.
2 Sep'03 Folk 9.7g/f 58-56 F: 2 Jul'03 Sand 10.0gd 58-(56) E: 2 May'02 Nott 6gd 71- F:
1986 **PAY THE SILVER 10** [16]6-11-7 p (69) Mr G Bartley(7) 4/1: 30-04020: 10th: Rear, nvr a factor: btr 1986. **1¼** **56**
4515} **SOMAYDA 249** [7]9-9-13 (47) Mr J Doyle(7) 33/1: 425000-0: 11th: Bhd, nvr a factor: reapp. **3½** **29**
2099 **LEARNED LAD 4** [5]6-10-8 BL (56) Mr S Dobson(3) 20/1: 0-250000: 12th: Mid-div, prog 6f out, fdd fnl 3f. **5** **29**
1411 **SWEET REFLECTION 38** [11]4-9-6 t (40) Miss J Pledge(7) 33/1: 000-0050: 13th: Rear, nvr a factor. **nk** **12**

464   **MUTARED 133** [3]6-10-4 (52) Mrs Emma Littmoden(3) 20/1: 00000-00: 14th: Bhd, nvr a factor.   1½   21
2019 **Grist Mist 9** [1]3-9-9 t(55) Miss A Wallace(5) 33/1:0   1804 **Young Dynasty 18** [8]4-9-11 bl(45) Mr J J Best(5) 50/1:0
16 Ran   Time 1m 59.20 (8.7)   Owned: Mrs M Enright   Trained: Lewes

---

2221   6.50 Green & Black's Organic Chocolate E B F Maiden Stakes 2yo   (D)
£4833 £1487   £744   **6f str**   **Good 42**   **-16 Slow**   Stands side

   DUBAWI 0 [3] Saeed bin Suroor 2-9-0   L Dettori   11/4: 1: b c Dubai Millennium - Zomaradah   102
(Deploy) Slow away, prog & ev ch after halfway, styd on to lead dist, rdn out: debut: Feb 1st foal, dam won
numerous Gr races around mid-dists: sire high-class performer at 1m/10f: eff at 6f, will apprec further in time:
acts on gd & a sharp/undul trk: goes well fresh: gd eff to defy greenness, can rate higher.
   FOX 0 [4] C E Brittain 2-9-0   D Holland   11/2: 2: b c Diktat - Badawi (Diesis) Cl-up, ev ch   1½   96
dist, kept on not pace wnr: debut: May foal, half brother to wnrs around 6/7f: dam useful performer around 1m:
sire high-class at sprint dists: eff at 6f, shaped as if 7f will suit: acts on gd grnd: encouraging run.
1848 **QADAR 16** [1] M P Tregoning 2-9-0 t   R Hills   1/2 FAV: 23: Led 5f out, hdd dist, sn no extra: clr   nk   95
rem: acts on fast & gd grnd: btr expected & failed to prog from debut in 1848.
1524 **WATERLINE LOVER 32** [2] P D Evans 2-8-9   S Drowne   50/1: 6004: ch f Efisio - Food of Love (Music   12   60
Boy) Led 1f, fdd ins fnl 2f: Apr foal, cost 18,000 gns: half sister to wnrs at 6/8f: dam wnr at sprint dists:
sire useful performer around 6/8f.
   BUZZ MAITE 0 [5]2-9-0   P Doe   50/1: 5: Al well adrift: debut.   dist   30
5 Ran   Time 1m 13.51 (3.51)   Owned: Godolphin   Trained: Newmarket

---

2222   7.20 Amberley Working Museum Maiden Stakes 3yo   (D)
£5538 £1704   £852   **1m3f**   **Good 42**   **-42 Slow**   Outside

1747 **RESERVOIR 21** [2] W J Haggas 3-9-0   (80) Martin Dwyer   2/1: 043-21: Sn handy & led over 3f out,   84
duelled with rnr-up sn after, drvn & styd on to assert ins last: eff 7/9f, styd this sharp 11f well & shld get 12f:
acts on fast & soft grnd, stiff or sharp/undul trk: showed admirable resolution, the type to prog: see 1747.
1924 **GANYMEDE 13** [7] M L W Bell 3-9-0   (81) D Holland   5/4 FAV: 63-2322: Trkd ldr, drvn to chall 3f   ½   82
out, no extra well ins last but clr of rem: prob met a prog type & shld win similar: stays 11f, return to 10f cld suit.
1892 **ON EVERY STREET 14** [5] H R A Cecil 3-9-0 vis   R Hughes   6/1: 5-43: Led till over 3f out, no   13   64
impress on front pair fnl 2f: likely to apprec mid-dist h'caps: see 1892.
   PORT N STARBOARD 0 [3] C A Cyzer 3-9-0   Lisa Jones(3) 20/1: 4: ch g Polar Falcon - Sally Slade   2½   60
(Dowsing) Rear, took mod 4th late on, nvr a threat: debut: 4,000 gns purchase, half brother to wnrs at 6/9f.
1959 **STYLISH DANCER 11** [6]3-8-9   R Havlin   33/1: 05: b f Muhtarram - Iltimas (Dayjur) Chsd ldrs, btn   1¾   52
2f out: well bhd debut earlier: 8,000 gns purchase, half sister to 2 5f juv wnrs incl a confirmed soft grnd lover:
dam a juv & 3yo sprint scorer.
1737 **PURR 21** [4]3-9-0   P Doe   22/1: 0-06: b g Pursuit of Love - Catawba (Mill Reef) Prom, btn 3f out: 3   51
well btn sole '03 start (rtd 56, mdn): half brother to sev mid-dist wnrs, dam a useful 10f 3yo scorer: shown
little today but a likely imprvr in mid-dist h'caps.
   SHARADI 280 [8]3-9-0   (77) M Tebbutt   14/1: 0456-7: Rear & al bhd, Brit bow, abs.   ¾   51
1959 **OPEN BOOK 11** [1]3-8-9   S Drowne   66/1: 0008: Wide & rear, nvr a factor.   6   38
8 Ran   Time 2m 27.21 (9.31)   Owned: Highclere Thoroughbred Racing XVI   Trained: Newmarket

---

2223   7.55 Hildon Stakes Handicap 3yo+ 0-85   (D)   [85]
£6825 £2100   £1050   **7f rnd**   **Good 42**   **+04 Fast**   Inside

2074 **MATERIAL WITNESS 6** [8] W R Muir 7-9-13   (84) Martin Dwyer   9/2: 00-00201: Made all, drvn & styd on   92
well from dist: fair time: stays 1m, best at 6/7f on fast, soft & polytrack: loves to dominate on a sharp/undul
trk, loves Goodwood: see 1817.
1891 **HARRISON POINT 14** [4] P W Chapple Hyam 4-9-10   (81) R Hughes   11/4 FAV: 230-1122: Keen, rear,   1   86
smooth hdwy 3f out & eff to chase wnr over 1f out, awkward head-carriage & no extra well ins last: not the most
convincing in a fin but plenty of ability & can win again: see 1891 & 888.
2018 **ZAFARSHAH 9** [5] P D Evans 5-8-7 (1ow)   (63) S W Kelly   10/1: 4146203: Rear, outpcd over 2f out,   2½   64
kept on late, no threat to front pair: see 565.
1849* **EPHESUS 16** [3] Miss Gay Kelleway 4-9-7 vis   (78) K Fallon   4/1: 0000614: Trkd ldrs, hmpd when   1¼   76
outpce 2f out, no impress after: return to 1m in similar will suit: see 1849.
1625 **FEARBY CROSS 27** [2]8-8-9   (66) Lisa Jones(3) 7/1: 000-6045: Rear, nvr able to chall: bckd from 12/1.   shd   63
5030] **GIOCOSO 209** [9]4-10-0   (85) E Ahern   25/1: 212060-6: b c Bahri - Wing My Chimes (Flying Paster)   1   80
Chsd ldrs, btn when short of room over 1f out: promise sole '02 start (rtd
78, unplcd, mdn): eff at 1m/9f on firm & gd/soft grnd, stiff/undul or easy trk.
2 Jun'03 Sand 9fm 90-88 C: 1 May'03 Chep 8.1g/s 85- D: 2 May'03 Kemp 8g/f 92- D:
1817 **LAST APPOINTMENT 17** [7]4-9-8   (79) D Holland   5/1: 4210-57: Trkd wnr, btn over 1f out: btr 1817.   2   70
7 Ran   Time 1m 27.22 (2.72)   Owned: Mr M J Caddy   Trained: Lambourn

---

2224   8.30 Jomati Anniversary Maiden Stakes Fillies 3yo   (D)
£5577 £1716   £858   **1m rnd**   **Good 42**   **+11 Fast**   Inside

1846 **CUT SHORT 16** [9] J H M Gosden 3-8-11   J Murtagh   5/2 FAV: 51: Chsd ldr & led over 2f out, rdn &   83
styd on strongly ins last: eff at 7f, imprvd for step up to 1m & 9f+ may suit: handles fast grnd, sharp/undul trk:
likely rcd & going the right way: see 1846.
   NOUVEAU RICHE 0 [8] H Morrison 3-8-11   D Holland   10/1: 2: ch f Entrepreneur - Dime Bag (High   1½   81
Line) Mid-div, eff to chase wnr ins last, kept on, al held: 47,000 gns purchase, half sister to v smart performers
bwtn 7/10f, dam a multiple 12f/2m wnr: eff at 1m, will get further: acts on fast grnd & a sharp/undul trk: nicely
bred, a most promising start & likely to win races.
   POSTERITAS 0 [6] H R A Cecil 3-8-11   R Hughes   9/1: 3: b f Lear Fan - Imroz (Nureyev) Mid-div,   nk   80
rdn & outpcd 2f out, kept on well ins last: debut: half sister to a dual wng juv, dam a useful 6/7f performer:
stays 1m, shaped as if further may suit: handles fast grnd & a sharp/undul trk: promising start.

GOODWOOD FRIDAY 04.06.04 Righthand, Sharpish, Undulating Track

MERWAHA 0 [10] M P Tregoning 3-8-11 R Hills 100/30: 4: b f Green Desert - Samheh (Private Account) Held up, kept on fnl 2f, not pace to chall on debut: half sister to a useful 7f juv wnr: dam plcd as a juv & related to a top class US performer: stays 1m on fast grnd & a sharp trk. *1¼* **78$**
4302} **GWEN JOHN 261** [1]3-8-11 S Drowne 9/2: 5-5: Mid-div, not pace to chall fnl 2f, reapp. *1¾* **74**
4943} **HEARTS DESIRE 219** [2]3-8-11 M Hills 9/2: 52-6: Trkd ldrs, no impress bef dist, reapp. *½* **73**
1929 **PINE BAY 13** [11]3-8-11 M Fenton 25/1: 67: Mid-div, btn over 1f out. *2½* **68**
1587 **PRELUDE 29** [7]3-8-11 S W Kelly 33/1: 58: Keen & al bhd. *nk* **67**
5022} **KINISKA 210** [5]3-8-11 E Ahern 50/1: 40-9: Led till over 2f out, sn wknd, reapp. *5* **57**
SATANS SISTER 0 [4]3-8-11 R Thomas(5) 50/1: 0: 10th: Dwelt, al bhd & t.o. *20* **22**
10 Ran Time 1m 39.92 (2.52) Owned: Cliveden Stud Trained: Manton

2225

9.00 Soil Association Stakes Handicap 3yo 0-80 (D) **[82]**
£5655 £1740 £870 **1m1f192y** **Good 42** **-20 Slow** Inside

21 **WAZIRI 204** [9] H Morrison 3-9-6 (74) S Drowne 12/1: 464-1: b g Mtoto - Euphorie (Feenpark) Slow away, hdwy to chase ldr over 2f out, led dist, drvn out: h'cap/turf bow, 7 month abs, has been gelded: promise in mdns late '03 (rtd 79a, AW mdn): eff at 1m, relished step up to 10f & shld get further: handles polytrack & enjoyed fast grnd tonight: likes a sharp/undul trk & goes well fresh: the type to progress. **79**
1982 **HAZEWIND 10** [8] P D Evans 3-8-2 vis t (56) F P Ferris(3) 14/1: 2100002: Led & sn clr, hdd dist, styd on well for press: styd this longer 10f trip well with frocing tactics: acts on fast grnd & polytrack: eff in a t-strap & visor: appears tough & genuine, shld win again after 765 (7f). *nk* **59**
1922 **GJOVIC 13** [10] B J Meehan 3-9-7 (75) K Fallon 3/1: 42-25043: Keen & trkd ldrs, styd on for press, not pace of wnr: comfirmed recent return to form: eff around 10f on firm, fast & polytrack: see 1105. *½* **77**
1791 **SLAVONIC 18** [7] J H M Gosden 3-9-5 bl (73) R Hughes 4/1: 54-54464: Held up, switched & kept on onepace fnl 2f: see 1791. *¾* **73**
1427 **MRS PANKHURST 37** [3]3-9-5 (73) M Hills 20/1: 010-505: Rear, kept on wide, not pace to chall: this longer 10f trip shld suit: see 923. *shd* **72**
1708 **SCARRABUS 22** [4]3-9-2 (70) J Murtagh 16/1: 560-406: Rear, short of room 2f out, sn no extra. *1½* **66**
1260 **PANGLOSS 46** [6]3-9-2 (70) R L Moore 6/1: 0300-37: Al rear, abs: btr 1260. *½* **65**
1769 **HEZAAM 20** [5]3-9-7 (75) R Hills 11/4 FAv: 01-058: Mid-div, outpcd fnl 2f: btr 1769 (1m). *½* **69**
1865 **LORD OF THE SEA 15** [1]3-8-13 (67) P Doe 16/1: 5-334009: Mid-div, btn over 1f out: btr 798 (AW). *1* **59**
1761 **FILLIEMOU 20** [2]3-8-8 (62) R Thomas(5) 14/1: 40400-00: 10th: gr f Goldmark - St Louis Lady (Absalom) Keen & trkd ldr, wknd qckly 2f out: unplcd '03 (rtd 73, mdn): dam a 6f/1m scorer. *12* **38**
10 Ran Time 2m 10.63(6.23) Owned: Ashley House Racing Trained: East Ilsley

HAYDOCK FRIDAY 04.06.04 Lefthand, Flat, Galloping Track

Official Going GOOD/SOFT.

2226

6.35 Patricia Thompson Surprise Birthday Handicap For Lady Amateur Riders 3yo+ 0-70 (G) **[52]**
£2744 £784 £392 **1m2f120y** **Good/Soft 65** **-31 Slow** Outside

1980 **SANTIBURI LAD 10** [6] N Wilson 7-10-2 (54) Mrs N Wilson(5) 4/1 FAV: 0460-321: Made all, styd on ins fnl 1f, just held on: poss stays 12f, apprec drop back to around 10f: acts on firm, soft & handles fibresand. **69**
1633 **INCHNADAMPH 27** [3] T J Fitzgerald 4-9-9 T (47) Miss A Elsey 11/1: 00/000-62: b g Inchinor - Pelf (Al Nasr) Keen cl-up, styd on ins fnl 1f, just held: clr rem: unplcd all 3 '03 starts (rtd 47, h'cap): 5th at best in '02 (rtd 71, prob flattered): eff at 10.5f on gd/soft grnd: imprvd eff here with fitting of t-strap. *nk* **60**
1945 **DASH OF MAGIC 11** [4] J Hetherton 6-9-3 (41) Miss S Brotherton 7/1: 6251063: Rear, prog 4f out, no impress dist: btr 852 (banded). *5* **47**
2060 **SARN 7** [9] M Mullineaux 5-9-7 (45) Miss M Mullineaux(7) 9/1: 00-04004: Rear, eff 3f out, nrst fin. *1* **49**
1633 **PENSION FUND 27** [8]10-9-11 (49) Miss J Coward(1) 8/1: 30000-55: b g Emperor Fountain - Navarino Bay (Averof) Rear, nvr nrr than mid-div: plcd twice in '03 (h'cap & sell, rtd 57): unplcd in '02 (rtd 67, h'cap): won 2 h'caps in '01: eff at 1m/10.3f, stays 12f: acts on firm, soft & any trk: tried blnks: can go well fresh. *1½* **50**
2 Aug'01 Ripo 10fm 79-76 C: 1 Jun'01 York 9g/s 76-73 B: 1 May'01 Ches 10.3fm 76-68 C: 2 Feb'01 Wolv 9.3af 71a-70 E:
2411} **DOUBLE SPEY 345** [11]5-9-3 (41) Miss A Armitage 12/1: 0/00600-6: Keen rear, prog when no room dist. *3* **38**
1946* **LARAD 11** [2]3-8-12 (5ex)bl (50) Mrs S Moore(3) 5/1: 1334617: Cl-up 1m, sn fdd: btr 1946. *2½* **43**
1991 **PARADISE GARDEN 10** [1]7-8-10 (7oh) (27) Miss Kelly Harrison(3) 10/1: 50-05438: Handy over 7f, wknd. *1* **25**
1796 **BORDER TERRIER 18** [5]6-9-12 (50) Ms C Williams 7/1: 5010-009: Al in rear. *hd* **40**
1643 **MARGARETS WISH 25** [7]4-9-5 (43) Miss V Cottrill(5) 8/1: 0400100: 10th: Chsd ldrs, saddle sn slipped, fdd 4f out: btr 1333. *dist* **0**
1657 **CRUSOE 25** [12]7-9-13 bl (51) Miss E J Jones 10/1: 4004200: 11th: Cl-up 6f, sn fdd. *15* **0**
11 Ran Time 2m 20.21 (10.21) Owned: Mrs Karan Ridley Trained: York

2227

7.05 Dean Moor Handicap Stakes 3yo 0-75 (E) **[82]**
£3770 £1160 £580 **5f str** **Good/Soft 65** **-31 Slow** Flip Start

1908 **CHAMPAGNE CRACKER 13** [8] Miss L A Perratt 3-8-6 (60) R Ffrench 16/1: 2622-031: Handy, styd on to lead dist, rdn out: eff at 5f, stays 6f, acts on firm & gd, improved here on gd/soft grnd: see 1908. **69**
2121 **SIR ERNEST 3** [11] M J Polglase 3-9-7 (75) A Culhane 9/1: 000-0602: Broke fast from flag start, led till dist, sn no extra: quick reapp: acts on fast & gd/soft grnd: see 1572. *2* **78**
1973 **BARON RHODES 11** [9] J S Wainwright 3-9-4 (72) T Eaves(3) 4/1 FAV: 042-2223: Veered left start, sn in tch, kept on ins fnl 1f: lost wng ch due flip start, can find similar: see 1973 & 1509. *1½* **71**
2137 **BAYLAW STAR 3** [10] J Balding 3-9-7 (75) P Mulrennan(5) 8/1: 003-6304: Cl-up over 3f, sn no extra. *¾* **72**
2011 **TIZZYS LAW 9** [4]3-9-1 (69) J Bramhill 5/1: 0-1645: Hmpd start, sn in tch, wknd fnl 1f. *¾* **64**
4301} **ABELARD 261** [3]3-8-13 (67) T Hamilton(3) 12/1: 333-6: b g Fasliyev - Half Hitch (Diesis) Rear, nvr nrr than mid-div: reapp: plcd on all 3 '03 starts (rtd 71, mdn): eff at 5f, 6f shld suit: acts on fast grnd. *1* **59**
1881 **HES A ROCKET 14** [7]3-8-9 bl (63) K Dalgleish 5/1: 6511367: Handy 3f, sn wknd: btr 1605 & 1457. *1¾* **50**
2137 **OBE BOLD 3** [5]3-8-8 (5ow) (57) J Carroll 12/1: 0-430208: Rear, nvr a factor: qck reapp: btr 1975. *2½* **42**
1951* **FEU DUTY 11** [6]3-8-12 (6ex) (66) R Winston 6/1: 0010-619: Slow away, prog halfway, hung left & *8* **25**

fdd dist: disappointing under a penalty: btr 1951 (firm).
4495} **SIR LOIN** 250 [1]3-8-6 (60) Kim Tinkler 33/1: 20600-0: 10th: ch g Compton Place - Charnwood Queen   1½   **15**
(Cadeaux Genereux) Whipped round start, al bhd: lost all ch on reapp: rnr-up 1st time out in '03 (med auct): eff
at 5f on gd grnd: acts on a stiff trk: with N Tinkler.   2 May'03 Newc 5gd 86- F:
10 Ran   Time 1m 3.60 (4.8)   Owned: Mr Jim McLaren   Trained: Ayr

---

2228   7.35 David Reilly's Getting Hitched E B F Maiden Stakes 2yo   (D)
£5857 £1802 £901   **6f str**   **Good/Soft 65**   **-35 Slow**   Centre

WHERE WITH ALL 0 [6] Saeed bin Suroor 2-9-0   K McEvoy   100/30: 1: b c Montjeu - Zelding (Warning)   **93**
Dsptd lead, led over all dist, rdn out: debut: Jan foal, dam List wnr at 5f: sire high-class mid-dist performer:
eff at 6f, further will suit: acts on gd/soft grnd & goes well fresh: sure to rate higher with experience.
1920 **WASALAT** 13 [2] M R Channon 2-8-9   A Culhane   5/2 FAV: 42: Dsptd lead, no extra ins fnl 1f: acts   2½   **78**
on fast & gd/soft grnd: looks in need of further: see 1920.
AFRICAN GIFT 0 [10] J G Given 2-8-9   T Quinn   9/1: 3: b f Cadeaux Genereux - African Light   2½   **71**
(Kalaglow) Handy, hung left & no extra dist: debut: Mar foal, half sister to numerous wnr abroad: dam plcd around
9f: sire high-class at sprint dists: sharper for today.
WEDLOCK 0 [8] T D Easterby 2-9-0   W Supple   33/1: 4: b c Pursuit of Love - Promise Fulfilled (Bet   2½   **69**
Twice) Sn handy, edged left & fdd dist: debut: Mar foal, dam won a couple of times at 6f: sire decent performer
around 6f/1m: improve for today.
GROUP CAPTAIN 0 [11]2-9-0   Dean McKeown   20/1: 5: V slow away, sn keen in tch, no impress ins fnl   1¾   **64**
2f under minimal press: debut: expect significant improvement next time.
PEVENSEY 0 [4]2-9-0   J Carroll   10/1: 6: Dwelt, nvr nrr than mid-div on debut.   ½   **63**
1893 **NO COMMISSION** 14 [3]2-9-0   D Nolan(3)   33/1: 0547: Keen handy 4f, sn wknd.   1¾   **58**
NOODLES 0 [5]2-9-0   R Winston   12/1: 8: Slow away, al bhd.   shd   **57**
ISITLOVEYOURAFTER 0 [7]2-8-9   T Hamilton(3)   66/1: 9: Sn prom, fdd halfway   19   **12**
1571 **THE TERMINATOR** 30 [1]2-9-0   P Bradley(5)   16/1: 00: 10th: Al well adrift.   dist   **0**
10 Ran   Time 1m 17.35 (6.05)   Owned: Godolphin   Trained: Newmarket

---

2229   8.10 Rectangle Group Handicap Stakes 3yo+ 0-85   (D)
£5590 £1720 £860   **1m6f**   **Good/Soft 65**   **+02 Fast**   Inside   **[82]**

1969 **GLORY QUEST** 11 [7] Miss Gay Kelleway 7-8-13 (67) I Mongan   2/1: 2210341: Cl-up, swtchd centre &   **77**
rcd alone in str, led 3f out, rdn clr fnl 1f: eff at 10f/2m on fast, hvy & loves fibresand: tough & consistent.
1923* **NAKWA** 13 [5] E J Alston 6-9-6 (74) D Allan(3)   7/4 FAV: 2532212: Led, styd far rail in str, hdd 3f   8   **75**
out, no extra ins fnl 2f, eased cl-home: continues in form: see 1923 (fast).
1923 **NORTHERN NYMPH** 13 [2] R Hollinshead 5-9-0 (68) Stephanie Hollinshead(5)   4/1: 3005623: Handy 13f.   3½   **68**
1742 **SADLERS PRIDE** 21 [6] Andrew Turnell 4-9-4 (72) J Carroll   11/2: 30-224: Al rear: btr 1742 & 1390.   12   **62**
4 Ran   Time 3m 6.89 (8.89)   Owned: WRB Racing 40 (wrbracingcom)   Trained: Newmarket

---

2230   8.45 Central Recycling Group Maiden Stakes 3yo+   (D)
£6097 £1876 £938   **1m3f200y**   **Good/Soft 65**   **-09 Slow**   Outside

1922 **PROTECTIVE** 13 [7] J G Given 3-8-7   W Supple   50/1: 401: Mid-div, prog 3f out, led dist, pushed   **81 +**
clr, val 7L+: imprvd for step up to 12f, shld stay further: acts on gd/ soft grnd & a gall trk: op to more
improvement & can make presence felt in h'cap grade: see 1783.
HISTORIC PLACE 0 [1] G B Balding 4-9-8   J Carroll   10/1: 2: b g Dynaformer - Captive Island   5   **74**
(Northfields) Slow away, prog 4f out, kept on ins fnl 1f, no ch with easy wnr: Flat bow, 9 wk hdles abs, earlier
bmpr wnr (2m, hvy): eff at 12f, will improve, poss at 14f+: acts on gd/soft grnd: encouraging run.
1892 **ANNA PALLIDA** 14 [12] P W Harris 3-8-4 (2ow) (81) T Quinn   9/4: 0223: Led, hdd dist, sn wknd: poss   ½   **70**
stays 12f, enjoy return to 10f: just btr 1892.
FARNE ISLE 0 [5] G A Harker 5-9-3   P Mulrennan(5)   66/1: 4: ch f Midnight Legend - Biloela   1½   **65**
(Nicholas Bill) Slow away, prog 3f out, no impress dist: Flat bow, hdles fit: unplcd in 03/04 (rtd 100h, eff
around 2m on gd & hvy, eff with cheek pieces, tried t-strap): improve on today.
4930} **IMPERIAL ROYALE** 220 [2]3-8-7 (60) J Bramhill   50/1: 630052-5: ch g Ali Royal - God Speed Her (Pas   5   **63**
de Seul) Nvr nrr than mid-div: reapp: rnr-up once in '03 (sell, M R Channon): eff around 1m on gd & gd/soft grnd.
2 Oct'03 Nott 8.2g/s 59-(69) G:
1885 **WOOLLY BACK** 14 [14]3-8-7   Dale Gibson   5/1: 226: Cl-up, ev ch 2f out, wknd: btr 1885 (fast).   ¾   **61**
MOLEHILL 0 [3]3-8-2   J Mackay   25/1: 7: Slow away, nvr a factor: debut.   2½   **52**
1153 **CHAPLIN** 52 [11]3-8-7   A Culhane   11/10 FAV: 0-28: Unruly in preliminaries, handy 9f, sn wknd on   shd   **56**
debut: prob lost ch before start: btr 1153 (reapp).
BRAVELY DOES IT 0 [6]4-9-8   R Winston   50/1: 9: Mid-div 1m, sn wknd.   4   **50**
1885 **DOUBLE TURN** 14 [8]4-9-8   B Swarbrick(5)   50/1: 5-50: 10th: Cl-up over 1f, sn wknd.   2   **47**
170 **TROFANA FALCON** 178 [13]4-9-8   Dean McKeown   100/1: 00-0: 11th: Rear, nvr a factor.   6   **39**
2058 Grey Samurai 7 [9]4-9-8 R Fitzpatrick 150/1:0   1784 Mikes Mate 19 [4]3-8-7 P Bradley(4) 100/1:0
13 Ran   Time 2m 36.68 (8.88)   Owned: Mr Peter Onslow   Trained: Gainsborough

---

2231   9.15 Mtb Group Maiden Stakes 3yo+   (D)
£6078 £1870 £935   **1m30y rnd**   **Good/Soft 65**   **+06 Fast**   Inside

4514} **INVASIAN** 249 [1] H R A Cecil 3-8-7   W Ryan   10/1: 0-1: ch c Desert Prince - Jarrayan   **88 +**
(Machiavellian) Made all, pushed out hands & heels ins fnl 1f, rdly: reapp: unplcd sole '03 start (mdn, rtd 69):
eff at 1m on gd/soft grnd: acts on a gall trk & goes well fresh: won in nice style & can progress.
CANTARNA 239 [16] J Mackie 3-8-2 (78) R Ffrench   12/1: 555-2: ch f Ashkalani - Lancea (Generous)   2½   **78**
Chsd ldrs, outpcd halfway, rallied ins fnl 2f, no ch with wnr: reapp: unplcd all 3 '03 Irish starts: eff at 1m,
shaped as tho' further will suit: acts on gd/soft grnd: encouraging start to Brit career.
1882 **FIRST COUNSEL** 14 [14] M A Jarvis 3-8-7   P Robinson   7/2: 53: Chsd ldrs, eff halfway, onepcd dist.   2   **79**
1882 **NORDWIND** 14 [5] P W Harris 3-8-7   T Quinn   3/1: 34: Handy 6f, sn no extra: btr 1882 (fast).   1¾   **75**

HAYDOCK FRIDAY 04.06.04 Lefthand, Flat, Galloping Track

1882 **FOOLISH GROOM 14** [7]3-8-7 Dale Gibson 12/1: 345: Cl-up 6f, sn hung left & wknd: quals for h'caps. *1* **73**
1971 **PURE VINTAGE 11** [9]3-8-7 T Hamilton(3) 33/1: 06: Nvr nrr than mid-div. *6* **61**
1882 **DESERT LEADER 14** [13]3-8-7 G Gibbons 50/1: 07: Rear, nvr nrr than mid-div. *½* **60**
1882 **ACUZIO 14** [8]3-8-7 B Swarbrick(5) 50/1: 668: Al bhd. *5* **50**
1832 **REMONSTRATE 17** [12]3-8-7 W Supple 25/1: 69: Rear, nvr a factor. *½* **49**
NARCISO 0 [4]4-9-4 P Mulrennan(5) 66/1: 0: 10th: Dwelt, al in rear. *1* **47**
4760] **SUCCESSOR 583** [3]4-9-4 A Culhane 5/2 FAV: 2/-0: 11th: ch c Entrepreneur - Petralona (Alleged) *5* **37**
Sn handy, fdd 2f out: reapp: mised '03: rnr-up sole '02 start (mdn): eff at 7f, bred to apprec mid-dists: acts on gd/soft grnd: with B W Hills. 2 Oct'02 Yarm 7g/s 82- D:
RICH CHIC 0 [2]3-8-2 J Mackay 50/1: 0: 12th: Al in rear. *1¾* **28**
1959 **High View 11** [6]3-8-7 Dean McKeown 66/1:0 1527 **Tetchy 32** [10]4-8-13 J Bramhill 20/1:0
14 Ran Time 1m 45.29(4.79) Owned: Dr K Sanderson Trained: Newmarket

DONCASTER SATURDAY 05.06.04 Lefthand, Flat, Galloping Track

Official Going GOOD (GOOD/FIRM Straight Crse).

2232

1.50 Tattenham Corner Handicap Stakes Fillies 4yo+ 0-80 (D) **[78]**
£5509 £1695 £848 **6f str** **Good 44** **-59 Slow** Flip Start - Hand Timed

2093 **GLENCOE SOLAS 6** [3] S Kirk 4-9-2 (66) M Fenton 11/2 JT FAV: 00-64221: Nvr far away, went on dist, held on drvn out: qck reapp, slow time: deserved win with blnks left off: eff at 5f, all wins at 6f: acts on gd & firm, prob handles soft grnd: eff with/without blnks: in gd form, see 2093 & 1465. **74**
2029 **COLLEGE MAID 9** [5] J S Goldie 7-8-0 (2ow)(1oh)bl (47) C Catlin 33/1: 6-406002: Bhd, hdwy 2f out, styd on strongly fnl 1f, nrst fin: back to form with blnks back on, tried cheekpieces & vis: change of tactics, usually best up with/forcing the pace: v well h'capped, see 1873. *¾* **55**
1973 **ROMAN MISTRESS 12** [13] T D Easterby 4-9-1 (65) D Allan(3) 7/1: 000-0463: Sn prom, onepace. *2* **64**
2080 **INDIAN STEPPES 7** [8] Julian Poulton 5-9-4 (68) Lisa Jones(3) 7/1: 2003-664: Well in rear, late gains. *¾* **64**
1873 **COLLEGE QUEEN 16** [4]6-9-2 bl (66) P Mulrennan(5) 20/1: 5400-065: Set pace till dist, no extra. *½* **61**
2093 **MADDIES A JEM 6** [12]4-9-11 (75) S W Kelly 8/1: 60-11356: Chsd ldrs 5f: btr 1743. *¾* **67**
2150 **BINT ROYAL 3** [11]6-8-6 p (56) J Quinn 6/1: 0-550347: Chsd ldrs, onepcd dist: qck reapp: btr 2150. *5* **33**
1878 **OFFICERS PINK 16** [7]4-9-6 (70) N De Souza(5) 25/1: 24135-08: Rdn in rear, nvr dngrs: see 1878. *¾* **44**
1822 **BALLINGER EXPRESS 18** [6]4-9-0 bl (64) N Chalmers(5) 12/1: 05329: V slowly away, no ch after. *½* **37**
1523 **MAGIC MUSIC 33** [10]5-9-7 (71) B Swarbrick(5) 11/2 JT FAV: 11402-00: 10th: b f Magic Ring - *nk* **43**
Chiming Melody (Cure The Blues) Trkd ldrs, wknd 1.5f out: new stable, prev with Mrs H Dalton: dual h'cap wnr in '03: eff at 6/7f on fast & hvy grnd: prob handles any trk: now with W Brisbourne & back on a wng mark.
2 Oct'03 York 6.0g/f 74-(74) D: 1 Jun'03 Donc 6g/f 77-71 D: 1 Jun'03 Leic 6.0g/f 76-67 E: 2 Apr'03 Nott 6.1gd 65-66 E:
1 Sep'02 Nott 6g/f 65-57 E: 2 Aug'02 Brig 6.9g/f 56- F:
2062 **PLAYFUL SPIRIT 7** [2]5-7-12 (3oh)vis (45) J Bramhill 40/1: 3003000: 11th: Al rear. *2½* **13**
2059 **CONSENSUS 8** [1]5-9-13 (77) T Williams 20/1: 0-400300: 12th: Mid-div 3f, sn wknd & eased, t.o. *18* **2**
1824 **CERTA CITO 18** [9]4-8-6 (56) J Carroll 11/1: 300-0050: 13th: Slow away & al bhnd, t.o. *1* **0**
13 Ran Time 1m 13.0 (6.2) Owned: Mr Eddie Tynan Trained: Upper Lambourn

2233

2.20 Doncaster Rovers 'champions' Handicap Stakes 4yo+ 0-85 (D) **[85]**
£7105 £2186 £1093 **1m4f** **Good 44** **-02 Slow** Inside

2162 **TRANCE 3** [4] T D Barron 4-9-4 (75) P Makin(5) 11/1: 2001-041: Mid-div, prog to lead ent fnl 1f, just prevailed in a tight fin: qck reapp: eff at 1m, apprec this step up to 12f: acts on fast, gd/soft & fibresand: handles a sharp or gall trk: game run, unexposed at this trip: see 143 (AW mdn). **86**
4782} **LOVES TRAVELLING 232** [6] L M Cumani 4-9-3 (74) N Mackay(3) 13/2: 401123-2: b g Blues Traveller - *nk* **82**
Fast Love (Second Set) Prom, led trav well 3f out till ent fnl 1f, rallied well & only just btn: clr of rem, reapp: won a claim (J Hills) & h'cap in '03, also plcd sev times: suited by 12f on fast, firm & polytrack, may stay further: handles any trk: decent reapp, shld sn go one better.
2 Oct'03 York 11.9g/f 73-71 E: 1 Sep'03 Beve 12.1g/f 74-62 E: 1 Aug'03 Brig 11.9fm 66-(62) F:
2041 **NIGHT SIGHT 8** [8] Mrs S Lamyman 7-8-11 (68) J Quinn 3/1 FAV: 0004-023: Rear, prog when no room 2f out till dist, styd on well but too late: well bckd: won this race in '02: well h'capped & loves Doncaster. *3* **71**
1602 **RICHEMAUR 29** [11] M H Tompkins 4-9-4 (75) F P Ferris(3) 33/1: 000-4004: Led till 3f out, no extra fnl 1.5f: too keen over this longer 12f trip: tried blnks in 1602, see 1131. *3* **73**
1923 **REPULSE BAY 14** [7]6-8-0 (2ow)(5oh) (50) C Catlin 20/1: 00-60305: Rear, styd on late, nvr dngrs: won this race last term off a 1lb higher mark: see 1793 (2m). *shd* **55$**
1890 **SOLO FLIGHT 15** [3]7-10-0 (85) M Fenton 11/2: 60206-26: Keen in mid-div, chsd ldrs 2f out, sn btn: op 4/1, top-weight: better expected from this well h'cappped gelding after encouraging reapp in 1890 (10f). *1½* **81**
2078 **MEXICAN PETE 7** [5]4-9-6 (77) Lisa Jones(3) 11/2: 03-03027: Nvr better than mid-div: btr 2078. *1* **71**
1889 **DOVEDON HERO 15** [2]4-9-7 bl (78) J Mackay 8/1: 016-0028: Al mid-div: btr 1889. *½* **71**
4374] **COALITION 613** [1]5-9-6 (77) S Whitworth 12/1: 111162/-9: b g Polish Precedent - Selection Board *1½* **68**
(Welsh Pageant) Rear, nvr a factor on comeback: op 20/1: missed '03, prev term trained by Sir M Prescott & completed a 4-timer (3 h'caps & a class stks), has since been gelded: eff at 12/14f on fast, gd/soft & polytrack.
2 Oct'02 Nott 16g/f 82-80 D: 1 Aug'02 Sand 14g/f 81-76 D: 1 Aug'02 Newc 12.4g/f 78-65 E:
1 Aug'02 Beve 12g/s 67- F: 1 Aug'02 Ling 12ap 70a-59 E:
4777*}**BARMAN 232** [9]5-9-10 (81) N De Souza(5) 20/1: 342251-0: 10th: ch g Atticus - Blue Tip (Tip Moss) *5* **64**
Al bhnd on reapp: dual claim wnr in '03 (incl in 1st time t-strap): eff at 12f on firm, gd/soft & polytrack: handles any trk: eff in a t-strap, has tried blnks & cheek pieces: with P Cole & suited by claim grade.
1 Oct'03 Newm 12g/f 86-(76) D: 2 Sep'03 Muss 12g/f 78-75 C: 2 Sep'03 Hayd 11.9fm 76-74 C:
1 Jul'03 Sali 12g/s 75-(80) D: 1 Apr'02 Warw 8.1g/f 85- D: 2 Nov'01 Nott 8.2g/s 89- D:
1969 **SOVEREIGN DREAMER 12** [10]4-9-7 t (78) J Bramhill 16/1: 6110-060: 11th: Prom, wknd 3f out, t.o. *11* **46**
11 Ran Time 2m 35.30 (5.50) Owned: Mr Nigel Shields Trained: Thirsk

2234

2.50 Carling Extra Cold Conditions Stakes 3yo+ (C)
£8720 £3308 £1654 **1m2f60y Good 44 +10 Fast** Inside

1350 **MUQBIL 42** [4] J L Dunlop 4-9-2 (113) R Hills 1/1 FAV: 10234-01: ch c Swain - Istiqlal (Diesis) **116+**
Hld up, smooth hdwy to lead 2f out, v readily: well bckd, best time of day, 6 wk abs: won Gr 3 Greenham on reapp in
'03, subs plcd twice more in Gr 3 company: eff at 7f, stays 10.3f well: acts on gd & fm, any trk: runs well fresh:
smart, dropped in grade for a confidence boosting win, win another Gr race.
2 Sep'03 Good 9.9fm 115-(116) A: 1 Apr'03 Newb 7fm 116- A: 2 Oct'02 Newm 7fm 110- A: 1 Aug'02 Newb 7g/f 106- A:
1740 **GRAMPIAN 22** [2] J G Given 5-9-2 (100) M Fenton 7/1: 1525/-262: Dwelt, hdwy to chase wnr 1.5f **5 106**
out, sn no impress: back to form, met a smart rival: see 1364.
1364 **SILVER GILT 42** [7] J H M Gosden 4-9-2 (102) J Quinn 14/1: 212/34-33: Chsd ldrs, onepcd fnl 2f: abs. **1 104**
1585 **KINGS THOUGHT 30** [3] S Gollings 5-9-2 (98) C Catlin 12/1: 0-604644: Set fast pace till 2f out, **3½ 99**
no extra: loves to dominate & ran as well as could be expected at today's weights: see 1585.
4547*}**KINGSWORD 248** [6]3-8-6 B Doyle 5/1: 41-5: bl c Dynaformer - Western Curtsey (Gone West) Rdn in **4 96**
rear, nvr dngrs on reapp: won fnl of 2 juv starts (nov): eff at 7f on fast grnd, 10f shld suit: handles a
stiff/gall trk: only lightly rcd & prob capable of better. 1 Oct'03 Sali 7.0g/f 93- D:
4225}**SHAMROCK CITY 266** [1]7-9-2 (93) J Mackay 40/1: 0/02400-6: b g Rock City - Actualite (Polish **5 85**
Precedent) Chsd ldrs 1m, wknd on reapp: '03 stks rnr-up: lightly rcd in recent seasons, '00 List wnr: eff at
1m/10f on gd & firm grnd: likes a stiff/gall trk & can force the pace. 2 Aug'03 Newm 8gd 98-(102) B:
1888 **BAYEUX 15** [8]3-8-4 (1owt) (105) J Carroll 11/2: 102-537: Front rank 1m, wknd: btr 1888. **5 78**
1476} **DHABYAN 389** [5]4-9-2 (98) S W Kelly 33/1: 0133/56-8: Al bhnd, t.o. & eased on reapp. **dist 42**
8 Ran Time 1m 09.86 (3.46) Owned: Mr Hamdan Al Maktoum Trained: Arundel

2235

3.25 Alfea San Rossore Handicap Stakes 3yo+ 0-80 (D)
£5671 £1745 £873 **7f rnd Good 44 -09 Slow** Inside **[79]**

2027* **YORKSHIRE BLUE 9** [13] J S Goldie 5-8-1 (52) N Mackay(3) 11/2: 000-0011: Prom, went on dist, styd **58**
on strongly, rdn out: eff at 6f, suited by 7/7.5f: acts on gd, fast grnd & fibresand: in fine form.
4367} **BORREGO 259** [4] C E Brittain 4-9-9 (74) R Hills 13/2: 402112-2: br c Green Desert - Pripet **1 78**
(Alleged) Trkd ldrs, chall ent fnl 1f, no extra cl home: op 8/1, reapp: dual h'cap wnr in '03: eff at 7/10f on
firm & gd grnd: likes a stiff/gall trk & runs well fresh: progressive.
2 Sep'03 Newb 7fm 76-70 C: 1 Aug'03 Hayd 8.1g/f 68-54 E: 2 Aug'03 Pont 8.0fm 57-57 F:
1781 **LOW CLOUD 20** [10] D Nicholls 4-9-10 VIS (75) J Carroll 16/1: 6650-603: b g Danehill - Raincloud **1¾ 75**
(Rainbow Quest) Trkd ldrs, slightly short of room dist, kept on in 1st time visor: '03 mdn wnr for A Stewart, has
since been gelded: eff at 7f, return to 1m will suit, has tried 10f: acts on gd & fast grnd: sharper next time.
1 Jun'03 Hayd 8.1g/f 84- F:
2150* **CASHNEEM 3** [5] W M Brisbourne 6-8-13 (6ex) (64) D Allan(3) 9/1: 100-4614: Chsd ldrs, onepcd fnl 1f. **hd 64**
2057* **EFIDIUM 8** [7]6-9-5 (70) C Catlin 11/2: 2042315: Trkd ldrs, onepcd fnl 1f: bckd, btr 2057. **2 66**
1743 **SEWMUCH CHARACTER 22** [6]5-9-2 (67) J Quinn 22/1: 0304-406: Led till dist, no extra: see 1345. **hd 63**
1525 **AVENTURA 33** [8]4-9-10 (75) L Fletcher(3) 18/1: 0400007: Chsd ldrs, switched dist, sn no impress. **nk 70**
2160 **SNOW BUNTING 3** [3]6-8-4 (1ow) (54) M Fenton 9/2 FAV: 0-003028: Hmpd early on, styd on late, nvr **1 48**
nrr: qck reapp: struggled to get into pace after early incident: see 2160.
2122*}**WARDEN WARREN 4** [2]6-9-9 (6ex)p (74) B Reilly(3) 10/1: 0100419: Rcd far side & sn prom, wknd & **3½ 60**
eased fnl 1f: qck reapp: see 2122.
2080 **NOBLE PENNY 7** [1]5-7-12 (49) Lisa Jones(3) 11/1: 000-0620: 10th: Sn hmpd, no ch after: btr 2080. **½ 34**
2063 **COMPTON ARROW 7** [12]8-8-4 (55) S Righton 50/1: 100-0000: 11th: Al bhnd. **¾ 38**
1537 **BALAKIREF 32** [11]5-8-13 (64) L Enstone(3) 15/2: 0-10222U: Dwelt, hmpd & u.r. after 1f. **0**
12 Ran Time 1m 26.91 (3.71) Owned: Mr John Mc C Hodge Trained: Glasgow

2236

4.00 Errol Taylor Meningitis Research Foundation Challenge Maiden Auction Stakes 2yo (E)
£3601 £1108 £554 **6f str Good 44 -20 Slow** Stands Side

1880 **SPACE SHUTTLE 15** [12] T D Easterby 2-8-7 BL D Allan(3) 11/8 FAV: 321: Made all stands side, held **81**
on well drvn out: well bckd from 2/1 in 1st time blnks: apprec step up to 6f & sharpened up by blnks: acts on fast
& gd/soft grnd: handles a gall trk: see 1880 & 1517.
1739 **MALINSA BLUE 22** [2] J A Glover 2-8-2 J Quinn 14/1: 62: b f Desert Style - Talina's Law (Law **1 71**
Society) Trkd ldrs, kept on fnl 1f but not pace of wnr: clr of rem: £20,000 Mar foal: half sister to a useful 14f
wnr: dam wng hdler: eff at 6f on gd, relish 7f+: improve & win.
2043 **RANSACKER 8** [5] C E Brittain 2-8-10 R Hills 14/1: 53: V slowly away, styd on well wide fnl 1f, **6 64**
no ch with front 2: lost all ch at the start: prob eff at 6f on gd: see 2043.
1687 **AIRE DE MOUGINS 24** [6] P C Haslam 2-8-10 G Faulkner 5/1: 04: b c Pennekamp - Colouring **nk 63**
(Catrail) Chsd ldrs, onepcd fnl 1.5f: 6,500 Mar foal: sire a top-class miler.
SACRED NUTS [8]2-8-10 J Mackay 14/1: 5: b c Sri Pekan - Sagrada (Primo Dominie) Dwelt, chsd **nk 62**
ldrs 4f, sn onepcd on debut: Mar foal, cost 28,000gns: half brother to a 2yo wnr abroad: dam a German wnr.
1893 **SOUND AND VISION 15** [14]2-8-10 L Enstone(3) 25/1: 56: Chsd ldrs, outpcd halfway, rallied late. **1 59**
1874 **MR KALANDI 16** [11]2-8-10 J Carroll 11/2: 37: Trkd ldrs, wknd 1.5f out: see 1874. **5 44**
1632 **FANTASY DEFENDER 28** [3]2-8-7 S W Kelly 66/1: 008: Chsd ldrs till after halfway. **hd 41**
1874 **SHINGLE STREET 16** [9]2-8-7 F P Ferris(3) 20/1: 09: Chsd ldrs 4f. **¾ 38**
1874 **SAINT CLEMENTS 16** [7]2-8-10 Dean McKeown 12/1: 00: 10th: Chsd ldrs, wknd 1.5f out. **hd 41**
2043 **TIPSY LILLIE 8** [10]2-8-2 Lisa Jones(3) 50/1: 500: 11th: Mid-div 4f: see 1640. **1½ 29**
1780 **ELLIS CAVE 20** [13]2-8-10 M Fenton 16/1: 00: 12th: Slowly away, al bhnd. **2½ 30**
SLATE GREY [1]2-8-7 V Halliday 50/1: 0: 13th: V slowly away, al t.o. on debut. **12 2**
13 Ran Time 1m 14.63 (3.83) Owned: Jennifer Pallister & Jonathan Gill Trained: Malton

DONCASTER SATURDAY 05.06.04 Lefthand, Flat, Galloping Track

2237 | 4.40 Doncaster-Racecourse Com Maiden Stakes 3yo+ (D)
£5574 £1715 £858   **5f str   Good 44   -28 Slow**   Stands Side

1607 **RENE BARBIER 29** [12] J A Glover 3-9-0 Dean McKeown 8/1: 041: b g Desert Style - Sweet Decision **69**
(Common Grounds) Chsd ldrs, prog to lead dist, held on well despite drifting right, drvn out: apprec drop back to
5f, acts on gd grnd: handles a gall trk: only lightly raced.
1575 **URBAN CALM 30** [5] R M H Cowell 3-8-9 M Henry 4/1: 422: Chsd ldrs, chall fnl 1f, just btn in a v **hd 63**
tight fin: eff at 5f on gd & soft grnd: see 1575 & 1228 (debut).
1988 **ROAN RAIDER 11** [9] M J Polglase 4-9-7 vis (45) K Ghunowa(7) 33/1: 0034053: Chsd ldrs, not qckn **1½ 64$**
fnl 1f: offic rtd just 45, treat rating with caution: eff at 5f/1m: see 1555.
2152 **LAW MAKER 3** [1] M A Buckley 4-9-7 vis (43) P Mulrennan(5) 16/1: 6042304: Chsd ldrs, onepcd fnl 1f. **1 61$**
4723} **SHIBUMI 236** [7]3-8-9 S W Kelly 16/1: 0-5: ch f Cigar - Hurricane Rose (Windjammer) Mid-div, **shd 56**
styd on late on reapp: unplcd sole juv start: dam from a mid-dist family: with H Morrison.
MILLINSKY [2]3-8-9 M Fenton 11/1: 7: ch f Stravinsky - Millyant (Primo Dominie) Mid-div, styd **shd 56**
on late wide, nvr nrr on debut: clr of rem: half sister to useful 6f performer Millybaa: modicum of promise here.
2152 **LACONIA 3** [11]3-8-9 (72) Derek Nolan(7) 5/2 FAV: 5262628: Chsd ldrs, wknd dist: tchd 7/2, qck reapp. **4 44**
2042 **FIREBIRD RISING 8** [13]3-8-9 P Makin(5) 3/1: 3-59: Chsd ldrs, wknd dist. **1¾ 39**
1829 **SHIFTY NIGHT 18** [4]3-8-9 Hayley Turner(5) 80/1: 00-00: 10th: Chsd ldrs 3f. **1 36**
1774 **MULTAHAB 21** [8]5-9-7 BL (58) C Lowther 15/2: 5-242400: 11th: Led till dist, wknd: keen in blnks. **nk 40**
4937} **Trinaree 220** [6]3-9-0 C Catlin 50/1:0   2042 **Estoille 8** [10]3-8-9 J Quinn 66/1:0
621 **Cobalt Runner 112** [14]3-9-0 B Doyle 50/1:0   1935 **Karashinko 14** [3]3-9-0 J Carroll 40/1:0
14 Ran Time 1m 01.81(3.61)   Owned: Mrs Janis MacPherson   Trained: Worksop

HAYDOCK SATURDAY 05.06.04 Lefthand, Flat, Galloping Track

Official Going Good (Good/Soft Places)

2238 | 1.35 Sharp Minds Betfair Rated Stakes Handicap 3yo 0-100 (B)   [104]
£12388 £4699 £2349   **1m3f200y   Good 53   +13 Fast**   Flip Start

1756 **FRANK SONATA 21** [4] M G Quinlan 3-9-3 (93) R L Moore 11/2: 400-6131: Held up, hdwy & rdn/led **108+**
over 2f out, rdn out to assert: nicely bckd: stays 12f well, shld get further: acts on fast & soft: proving tough,
useful & v progressive: see 1756, 1664.
1725+**MODESTA 22** [5] H R A Cecil 3-8-7 (83) W Ryan 9/2: 412: Trkd ldrs wide, smooth hdwy to press wnr **1¾ 92**
from 2f out, rdn & no extra ins last: bckd, tho op 7/2: excellent h'cap bow despite awkward wide route, stays 12f:
the type to progress & win again, keep on side: see 1725.
2021* **ADMIRAL 10** [6] Sir Michael Stoute 3-8-4 (80) F Lynch 5/1: 64-013: Keen early & led after 2f, hdd **3 87**
over 4f out, trav best till rdn & onepace fnl 2f: op 4/1: acts on fast & gd: gd run: see 2021.
1708 **DALLOOL 23** [11] M A Jarvis 3-8-4 (80) P Robinson 5/1: 5144: In tch, onepace fnl 2f: apprec 14f. **2½ 83**
2021 **AKRITAS 10** [1]3-8-12 (88) A Culhane 14/1: 1P0-445: Led/dsptd lead till over 2f out, btn dist: see 2021. **2½ 87**
1582 **DUMFRIES 30** [3]3-8-4 (80) R Havlin 16/1: 031-536: Mid-div trav well, rdn & no impress fnl 2f: **1¼ 77**
again shaped as if drop in trip would suit: see 1582.
1708 **JOMACOMI 23** [8]3-8-4 (80) R Ffrench 33/1: 1367: Trkd ldrs, no impress over 2f out: btr 1382 & 701. **¾ 76**
1708 **MASTER WELLS 23** [2]3-8-6 (82) T P Queally(3) 40/1: 108: Held up, rdn & hdwy over 3f out, no impress. **1½ 76**
4736}**MEKURIA 235** [9]3-8-7 (83) J Fanning 20/1: 241-9: b f Carnegie - Noble Air (Lycius) Chsd ldrs **8 65**
till over 2f out: reapp, h'cap bow: mdn scorer '03 (lightly rcd): winning form at 1m, dam a 1m wnr but shld get at
least 10f: acts on good, relished gd/sft last term: likes a gall trk.
1 Oct'03 Ayr 8g/s 84- D: 2 Sep'03 Nott 8.2g/f 66- D:
1790* **CAUSE CELEBRE 19** [7]3-8-22 (78) F Norton 14/1: 0324-10: 10th: Chsd ldrs, btn 2f out: h'cap bow. **nk 59**
1924 **FIRST CENTURION 14** [13]3-8-9 (85) G Duffield 16/1: 6-100: 11th: Mid-div till lost place 5f out, **5 59**
sn strugg: btr 1511 (1m, hvy).
1814 **Zouave 18** [10]3-9-2 (92) S Drowne 66/1:0   1500 **Arkholme 34** [12]3-8-4 (80) W Supple 16/1:0
13 Ran Time 2m 32.6 (4.8)   Owned: Adams Flynn Arnold   Trained: Newmarket

2239 | 2.05 Shank Lane Stakes Handicap 4yo+ 0-100 (C)   [98]
£13878 £4270 £2135   **2m45y   Good 53   -10 Slow**   Inside

2693*]**DANCING BAY 696** [3] N J Henderson 7-9-6 (90) W Ryan 13/2: 6010/31/-1: b g Suave Dancer - Kabayil **101**
(Dancing Brave) Rear, smooth hdwy over 2f out, rdn clr: well bckd, op 9/1: long Flat abs, jmps fit (rnr
up, val h'cap hdle, rtd 137h, dual h'cap wnr 03/04 (2m/2m5f, firm & hvy): '02 Flat h'cap wnr: suited by gall 2m on
fast & hvy, prefers cut: goes well fresh: useful stayer.
1 Jul'02 Newm 16.1g/s 91-86 C: 1 Oct'01 Ayr 13hvy 86-80 C:
1569 **DISTANT PROSPECT 31** [6] A M Balding 7-9-6 (90) D Sweeney 7/1: 00303-42: Held up, rdn & hdwy to **3½ 96**
chall 2f out, rdn but pulled clr of rem: op 9/1: thorough stayer, likes easy grnd & 2m+.
1502 **SENTRY 34** [4] J H M Gosden 4-9-1 (86) P Robinson 7/1: 231-1433: Keen early in mid div, still **5 87**
trav well when no room 2f out, swtchd & kept on for press in last: shade closer without trouble in running but would
not have troubled wnr: this longer 2m trip is likely to suit: a v consistent & prog styr: see 1502 & 1172 (12/14f).
1484 **PRINS WILLEM 35** [12] J R Fanshawe 5-9-6 (90) G Duffield 12/1: 2610-234: Chsd ldrs trav well, rdn **¾ 90**
& no extra bef dist: op 10/1: remains unconvincing at this trip: see 1172 (12f).
2085 **CLARINCH CLAYMORE 7** [2]8-8-2 (72) R Ffrench 20/1: 0046-205: Mid-div, chall 2f out, no extra. **1 71**
1689 **JOROBADEN 24** [14]4-9-5 (90) G Baker 16/1: 4/-216106: Prom & ch over 2f out, sn no extra. **2½ 87**
1969 **DOUBLE OBSESSION 12** [9]4-9-5 (90) T P Queally(3) 20/1: 2000-007: b c Sadler's Wells - Obsessive **shd 87**
(Seeking The Gold) Mid-div, lost plce 6f out, nvr threat: dual h'cap wnr '03: mdn wnr '02: suited by 12f: acts on
fast & gd/sft, handles firm, any trk, loves a stiff one, esp Ascot: both wins last term in blnks, eff without, has
tried vis: keep in mind at Ascot with hdgr reapp.

671

2 Aug'03 Pont 12.0g/f 98-95 C: 1 Jul'03 Asco 12g/s 96-91 C: 1 Jul'03 Asco 12g/f 94-86 C: 1 Jul'02 Ayr 7.2gd 89- D:
1569 **RANDOM QUEST 31** [5]6-9-2 (86) R Havlin 12/1: 3250-008: Held up, prog 4f out, rdn & btn over 1f out.   hd   **82**
1889 **PRAIRIE FALCON 15** [1]10-9-0 (84) A Medeiros(5) 33/1: 0010-309: Keen early, trk ldrs, rdn & led 3f   ½   **79**
out, hdd 2f out, wknd: see 1172.
4117*)**DOROTHYS FRIEND 271** [10]4-8-8 (79) S Drowne 6/1: 60/5111-0: 10th: b g Grand Lodge - Isle of   3½   **71**
Flame (Shirley Heights) Held up, prog 6f out, rdn & btn 3f out: bckd, reapp: prog autumn '03, landing 3 h'caps in
qck succession: unplcd '02 (mdns, rtd 67): eff btwn 12f/2m on fast grnd, any trk.
1 Sep'03 Newc 16.1g/f 77-67 E: 1 Sep'03 Kemp 14.4g/f 84-68 D: 1 Sep'03 Brig 11.9g/f 74-62 E:
1569 **PONDERON 31** [8]4-9-3 (88) S Carson 13/2: 0131-060: 11th: Prom, btn over 2f out: op 5/1: btr 1569.   13   **69**
1746 **MORSON BOY 22** [11]4-10-0 (99) J Fanning 14/1: 4/1151-00: 12th: Led till 3f out, wknd: op 12/1.   ¾   **79**
1928 **SKYES FOLLY 14** [7]4-8-4 (75) W Supple 33/1: 1515-000: 13th: Trkd ldrs wide, wknd 3f out.   nk   **54**
1861 **ARCHDUKE FERDINAND 16** [13]6-9-2 (86) A Culhane 12/1: 2400-020: 14th: Held up, btn 3f out.   dist   **0**
14 Ran   Time 3m 37.2 (10.2)   Owned: Elite Racing Club   Trained: Lambourn

---

2240   **2.35 Listed Joseph Heler Cheese Cecil Frail Stakes Fillies 3yo+   (A)**
£17400 £6600 £3300   **6f str**   **Good 53**   **+12 Fast**   Centre

4795} **TANTE ROSE 231** [9] R Charlton 4-9-0 (107) S Drowne 7/4: 603040-1: b f Barathea - My Branch   **104**
(Distant Relative) Held up, smooth prog halfway, chall dist & drvn to lead cl home, all out: nicely bckd on reapp:
prev with B Hills, Gr 3 scorer '03, subs Gr 2 plcd (rtd 109): mdn wnr '02: suited by 6/7f, gall or sharp/undul trk:
likes firm & good ground: goes v well fresh: v useful filly.   1 Apr'03 Newb 7fm 105- A: 1 Nov'02 Newm 6gd 88- D:
1233 **RUBY ROCKET 49** [10] H Morrison 3-8-10 (105) G Duffield 5/1: 11314-52: Held up, smooth hdwy &   nk   **107**
rdn/led over 1f out, hdd close home: 7 wk abs, op 7/1: acts on firm & gd grnd: smart effort back at 6f: see 1233.
1773* **GOLDEN NUN 21** [11] T D Easterby 4-9-4 bl (100) P Robinson 9/2: 05-02313: Rear, styd on fnl 2f: tough. 1½   **102**
5037] **DANI RIDGE 210** [8] E J Alston 6-9-0 (81) R Havlin 80/1: 000030-4: b f Indian Ridge - Daniella   5   **84**
Drive (Shelter Half) Chsd ldrs & chance over 1f out, wknd in last: reapp: h'cap wnr '03, AW h'cap plcd (rtd 83):
mdn & class stks wnr '02: suited by 6f, stays 7f: acts on firm, soft & polytrk: prob handles any trk, loves a
sharp/turning one: gd return & should make presence felt back in h'caps.
1 May'03 Ripo 6sft 85-76 D: 1 Sep'02 Ches 6fm 83- D: 1 Mar'02 Catt 6g/s 75- D:
1773 **NEEDLES AND PINS 21** [7]3-8-6 (97) F Lynch 25/1: 6125-405: Handy & led halfway till over 1f out,   nk   **83**
wknd in last: op 33/1: fair run but yet to fully convince at 6f: see 1175.
1773 **LOOK HERES CAROL 21** [5]4-9-0 (87) G Gibbons 20/1: 0004-336: Mid-div, rdn & no extra dist: see 1523. 1   **80**
2082 **SIMIANNA 7** [3]5-9-0 p (90) F Norton 16/1: 0-552067: Mid-div, btn over 1f out: btr 2082, 1594.   6   **63**
1620 **MALVERN LIGHT 28** [4]3-8-6 (97) A Culhane 14/1: 41-408: Mid-div, btn over 1f out: btr 1169.   1½   **58**
1233 **UNSHOODA 49** [1]3-8-6 (95) W Supple 14/1: 2126-09: ch f Machiavellian - Rawaabe (Nureyev) Chsd   3   **49**
ldrs & ch over 2f out, sn edged left & btn: 7 wk abs: fills mdn wnr '03, subs Listd rnr up (lightly rcd): winning
form at 6f, shld get further: likes firm ground, easy or gall trk.
2 Sep'03 Ayr 6fm 94- A: 1 Sep'03 Kemp 6fm 92- D: 2 Aug'03 York 6.0fm 88- D:
1957* **CAVERAL 12** [2]3-8-6 (85) R L Moore 7/1: 31-0010: 10th: Held up, btn over 1f out: btr 1957.   3   **40**
1925 **BLAISE CASTLE 14** [6]4-9-0 BL (90) T P Queally 33/1: 3042-420: 11th: Led till halfway, sn btn: blnks.   1½   **35**
11 Ran   Time 1m 13.75 (2.45)   Owned: Mr B E Nielsen   Trained: Beckhampton

---

2241   **3.10 Brian Dunn's Birthday E B F Maiden Stakes 2yo   (D)**
£5184 £1595 £798   **5f str**   **Good 53**   **-22 Slow**   Centre

1573 **PIPER LILY 31** [4] M Blanshard 2-8-9 F Norton 9/1: 51: Chsd ldrs, styd on for press to lead cl   **82**
home: imprvd from debut, eff at 5f on good grnd, handles gd/sft: likes a gall trk: 6f shld suit.
1974 **HANSEATIC LEAGUE 11** [9] M Johnston 2-9-0 J Fanning 1/1 FAV: 22: Led, rdn & hdd close home: well   hd   **86**
bckd: acts on fast & gd grnd: rest well covered & still a likely type for similar: see 1974.
TURNAROUND 0 [3] Mrs J R Ramsden 2-9-0 A Culhane 25/1: 0: gr c Highest Honor - Tamacana   2   **80+**
(Windwurf) Held up, shkn up & styd on well from over 1f out, not rch front pair: op 33/1: Jan foal, 48,000 euros
purchase: related to useful winners abroad, sire high class at 7/10f: eff at 5f, 6f+ sure to suit on this evidence:
acts on gd grnd, gall trk: promising start & likely to progress in similar.
2132 **EASY FEELING 4** [2] R Hannon 2-8-9 R L Moore 11/4: 334: Chsd ldrs & ch dist, no extra ins last: 2½   **67**
well bckd: qck reapp: poss too soon after 2132.
1173 **WONDERFUL MIND 51** [5]2-9-0 P Robinson 15/2: 05: b c Mind Games - Signs And Wonders (Danehill)   ½   **70**
Sn prom & rcd keenly, no extra from dist: bckd, op 9/1: abs: Feb 1st foal, cost 25,000gns: dam 10f wnr.
NE OUBLIE 0 [8]2-9-0 Dale Gibson 20/1: 6: ch c Makbul - Parkside Prospect (Piccolo) Dwelt, sn   8   **49**
handy, rdn & wknd over 1f out: Apr 1st foal, cost 14,000gns: dam a 5/6f juv wnr.
TOLDO 0 [1]2-9-0 P Bradley(5) 33/1: 7: In tch, edged left & btn over 1f out.   3   **43**
FELLBECK FRED 0 [7]2-9-0 T Eaves(7) 66/1: 8: Dwelt, sn outpcd.   5   **29**
8 Ran   Time 1m 02.53 (3.73)   Owned: Mr David Sykes   Trained: Upper Lambourn

---

2242   **3.40 Security Guard Company 0870 0347333 Handicap Stakes 3yo+ 0-95 (C)**   **[92]**
£10010 £3080 £1540   **1m30y rnd**   **Good 53**   **-03 Slow**   Inside

1519 **BISHOPRIC 33** [1] H Candy 4-9-10 (88) D Sweeney 12/1: 41-01: b g Bishop of Cashel - Nisha   **97**
(Nishapour) Al prom, remained far side in straight & led over 1f out, rdn out: op 10/1: lightly rcd '03, landed a
mdn: eff over a gall & undul 1m on fast, likes good & good/soft ground: lightly raced & improving.
1 May'03 Chep 8.1g/s 90- D:
1231 **PRIZEMAN 49** [3] G B Balding 6-10-0 (92) R Havlin 33/1: 05000//-02: b g Prized - Shuttle   1½   **97**
(Conquistador Cielo) Held up, styd on well for press far rail fnl 2f, al held: 7 wk abs: left reapp from a long abs
well bhd: last rcd '01, unplcd (rtd 106, Listed): dual juv wnr (inc Listed): eff at 7f/1m, tried up to 2m prev: acts
on firm & gd/sft grnd, likes a stiff/gall trk & can go well fresh: encouraging for similar.
1883 **INTRICATE WEB 15** [8] E J Alston 8-9-0 (78) F Norton 9/2: 2460133: Rear, hdwy in centre 3f   3½   **76+**
out & styd on for press to take 3rd, nvr a threat: best of those in centre.
1530 **NUIT SOMBRE 33** [2] M Johnston 4-9-1 (79) J Fanning 5/1: 5600-054: Led, rem far rail in straight,   2½   **72**
hdd over 1f out & no extra: acts on an easy surface but poss best on firm/fast ground: now well h'capped: see 1530.
1066 **MEZUZAH 60** [10]4-9-5 (83) S Drowne 10/1: 30406-05: b g Barathea - Mezzogiorno (Unfuwain) Held   1   **74**
up, rdn & some prog centre, nvr land blow: abs: val h'cap plcd '03 (rtd 89): mdn scorer '02: winning form at 7f,
stays 10f well, tried 12f: acts on firm & hvy grnd, sharp/undul or gall trk: can go well fresh.

HAYDOCK SATURDAY 05.06.04 Lefthand, Flat, Galloping Track

1 Nov'02 Donc 7hvy 93- D:
1820 **GO TECH 18** [7]4-9-0 (78) P Robinson 5/1: 05-00606: Prom, wknd centre fnl 2f: bckd, btr 1820. *nk* **68**
2057 **PRINCE OF GOLD 8** [9]4-7-13 (63) Dale Gibson 8/1: 0-050067: Held up, efft centre 3f out, sn btn. *½* **52**
2067 **SILVALINE 7** [4]5-8-9 (73) P Doe 7/1: 0455068: Mid-div, rcd centre, rdn & btn dist, eased: drop in trip. *½* **61**
1883 **HARRY POTTER 15** [5]5-8-7 BL (71) Darren Williams 13/2: 0301069: Mid-div, btn over 1f out: blnks. *2½* **54**
1972 **BUTHAINA 12** [6]4-7-12 (3oh) (59) S Yourston(7) 100/1: 5/31-0000: 10th: Prom till over 2f out. *9* **29**
10 Ran Time 1m 45.06 (4.56) Owned: Girsonfield Ltd Trained: Wantage

2243 4.10 Hilary Lindsay 40th Birthday Handicap Stakes 3yo 0-70 (E) [77]
£3952 £1216 £608 **1m30y rnd** **Good 53** **-10 Slow** Inside

1872 **FUTOO 16** [5] G M Moore 3-8-10 (59) F Lynch 10/1: 0106-651: Prom & led over 2f out, drvn & held on all out, most gamely: eff at 6/7f, now stays a gall 1m well: tough performer on this evidence, could win again. **63**
1534 **MISS ELOISE 32** [10] T D Easterby 3-8-7 (56) A Mullen(7) 8/1: 50052-62: Mid-div, styd on well for press ins last, nrst fin: op 11/1: now stays gall 1m well & could get further: encouraging for similar events. *½* **60**
1359 **ERMINE GREY 42** [2] D Haydn Jones 3-9-7 vis (70) Paul Eddery 14/1: 1016-003: Trkd ldrs, rdn & chall dist, kept on for press, al just held by wnr, 6 wk abs: vis reapp: acts on fast, good & fibresand: see 29. *shd* **74**
1769 **ON THE WATERFRONT 21** [3] J W Hills 3-9-3 (66) G Duffield 9/1: 554204: Dwelt, mid-div, swtchd & chall dist, drvn/no extra nr fin: acts on fast, gd & polytrk: better run from a fav low draw, mod draw latest. *nk* **68**
1707 **CHARLOTTE VALE 23** [8]3-9-3 (66) A Culhane 6/1 FAV: 4246-65: Mid-div, hung left & onepace. *1* **67**
1872 **COBALT BLUE 16** [11]3-8-3 BL (52) G Gibbons 9/1: 0000-06: Mid-div, rdn & kept on onepace fnl 2f: blnks. *2* **49**
1242* **DAGOLA 49** [13]3-8-13 (62) R Smith 13/2: 0000-17: Rear, only mod gains: op 5/1: abs: btr 1242. *6* **48**
1842 **CAMPBELLS LAD 17** [4]3-7-12 (5oh) (42) P M Quinn 66/1: 0540-548: Dwlet & held up, eff 3f out, sn btn. *1* **31**
1982 **VELOCITAS 11** [7]3-8-8 (57) J Fanning 25/1: 0-4009: Prom, wknd dist: see 953. *2* **37**
1017 **ASHSTANZA 65** [1]3-8-9 (58) P Robinson 13/2: 04-43400: 10th: Led till over 2f out, sn btn: abs: btr 796. *1¾* **35**
1907 **MY PENSION 14** [17]3-9-5 (68) S Drowne 12/1: 0430: 11th: Held up, efft 3f out, no impress: h'cap bow. *1½* **42**
1956 **STILETTO LADY 12** [15]3-8-10 (59) Dale Gibson 20/1: 040-400: 12th: Mid-div, btn 3f out: btr 1655 (AW). *1¼* **30**
1693 **YOUNG PATRIARCH 24** [18]3-9-0 (63) D Sweeney 50/1: 44-000: 13th: b c Silver Patriarch - Mortify (Prince Sabo) Held up, rdn & btn 2f out: unplcd but promise '03 (rtd 73+, mdn, lightly rcd): stays 7f on fast. *1¼* **31**
3980} **Schinken Otto 280** [14]3-8-4 (53) R Ffrench 66/1:0
871 **Maybe Someday 79** [12]3-8-11 p(60) J Edmunds 16/1:0
1648 **Desert Battle 26** [6]3-8-11 BL(60) F Norton 25/1:0 1659 **La Fonteyne 26** [16]3-8-9 (58) T Eaves(3) 50/1:0
17 Ran Time 1m 45.63(5.13) Owned: Mr M K Roddis Trained: Middleham

NEWMARKET SATURDAY 05.06.04 Righthand, Stiff, Galloping Track

Official Going Good/Firm

2244 6.30 Handicap Stakes For Gentleman Amateur Riders 4yo+ 0-75 (E) [46]
£3348 £1030 £515 **1m4f** **Good/Firm 18** **-36 Slow** Centre

1772+**BUCKS 21** [3] D K Ivory 7-12-0 (74) Mr Michael Murphy(7) 5/1: 5-030211: Cl-up, hdwy & edged right but styd on to lead ins last, rdn out: op 7/2: eff over 12f/2m on firm, gd/soft & polytrack, sharp or gall trks. **84**
1986* **DANAKIL 11** [6] S Dow 9-11-12 (72) Mr D Hutchison(5) 2/1 FAV: 0002412: Held up, hdwy to lead over 2f out, rdn & hdd ins last, not pace of wnr but clr of rem: well bckd: another gd run in an amat h'cap: v tough. *1¾* **78**
1928 **DOMENICO 14** [7] J R Jenkins 6-11-11 (71) Mr N Soares(7) 18/1: 0/6002-03: b g Sadler's Wells - Russian Ballet (Nijinsky) Handy, led over 3f out till 2f out, no extra: 03/04 dual h'cap hdle wnr (rtd 123h, 2m, firm & hvy): rnr-up in a h'cap on the Flat in '03: stays 2m on fast & soft grnd. 2 Jul'03 Beve 16.2g/f 75-74 C: *7* **67**
1916 **SQUIRTLE TURTLE 14** [10] P F I Cole 4-11-7 bl (67) Mr O Cole(5) 20/1: 503-1004: In tch, hmpd & lost place over 3f out, rallied over 1f out, no impress: see 1916, poss best when dominating as in 331 (fibresand). *1* **62**
1407 **ILOVETURTLE 39** [9]4-10-8 (54) Mr J Morgan(5) 14/1: 0000-035: In tch, onepace fnl 2f: see 1407. *nk* **49**
3764} **CYBER SANTA 649** [11]6-10-2 (48) Mr L Newnes(3) 12/1: 432430/-6: b g Celtic Swing - Qualitair Ridge (Indian Ridge) Held up, brief eff 3f out, no impress: gelded since last seen in '02, plcd in h'caps: '01 dual h'cap wnr: suited by 12/13f & acts on fast, gd/soft, polytrack & gall or sharp trk. *3½* **38**
2 Jul'02 Newm 10g/f 57-56 E: 2 Jun'02 Newm 12g/f 62-54 E: 2 May'02 Newc 12.4gd 54-51 E:
2 Apr'02 Pont 12fm 52-47 E: 1 Nov'01 Ling 13ap 50a-45 E: 1 Jul'01 Newc 12.4gd 45-44 E:
4268} **El El 263** [1]9-10-0 (46) Mr E Dehdashti(3) 13/2: 40500///0-7: b g North Briton - Branitska (Mummy's Pet) Keen, led after 1f till over 3f out, wknd: fit from chasing, 03/04 h'cap hdle & 2-time h'cap chase wnr (loves to dominate at 2m, stays 2m5.5f on firm, soft & any trk, likes sharp ones): modest Flat form since winning an appr mdn back in '98: tough over fences. *7* **26**
1802 **FAIRY WIND 19** [8]7-10-4 (50) Mr D Queally(7) 8/1: 020-0038: In tch, wknd over 2f out: see 1802. *2½* **26**
1801 **AMETHYST ROCK 19** [5]6-9-10 (2oh) (40) Mr M A Hammond(2) 20/1: 0-031629: In tch, wknd 3f out. *5* **10**
886} **BHUTAN 435** [2]9-10-4 (50) Mr J J Best(4) 14/1: 415130-0: 10th: Al bhd: changed stable. *¾* **17**
1754 **JAZIL 21** [4]9-11-0 t (60) Mr N Pearce(5) 50/1: 13/0////-60: 11th: Keen, handy, wknd 3f out: see 1754. *3½* **22**
11 Ran Time 2m 35.3 (6.5) Owned: Mr M Murphy Trained: Radlett

2245 7.00 E B F Frank Butters Maiden Stakes Fillies 2yo (D)
£4735 £1457 £729 **6f str** **Good/Firm 18** **-22 Slow** Stands Side

1866 **PARK ROMANCE 16** [4] B J Meehan 2-8-11 K Fallon 2/1 JT FAV: 21: With ldr, led & kept on despite hanging fnl 2f, rdn out: bckd: eff over a gall or sharp/undul 6f on fast, shld get further: useful, improving. **92**
1735 **BENTLEYS BUSH 22** [9] R Hannon 2-8-11 R Hughes 11/2: 52: Led till 2f out, not pace of wnr: sharper for debut & eff over a stiff 6f on fast grnd: win similar on a minor trk with a repeat of this: see 1735. *1¼* **86**
ALMENDRADOS 0 [1] J Noseda 2-8-11 E Ahern 8/1: 3: b f Desert Prince - Sevi's Choice (Sir Ivor) In tch, eff well over 1f out, kept on same pacet: op 9/2: Feb foal, cost 260,000gns: half-sister to a 5f juv scorer: eff at 6f, 7f shld suit: acts on fast grnd: plenty to like about this despite being a big drifter, win sn. *¾* **84**
ALL FOR LAURA 0 [5] D R Loder 2-8-11 T P Queally(3) 12/1: 4: ch f Cadeaux Genereux - Lighthouse (Warning) In tch, eff 2f out, onepace: March foal: dam 1m wnr: eff at 6f, 7f sure to suit: acts on fast grnd: *¾* **82**

sharper for this & shld win a race.
1887 **CATCH A STAR** 15 [2]2-8-11 L Dettori 2/1 JT FAV: 35: Slow away, held up, late gains, nvr dngrs:　　　nk　81
well bckd: clearly btr expected but prob ran to form of 1887 & shaped like further will suit.
　　　IMPROVISE 0 [6]2-8-11 D Holland 8/1: 6: b f Lend A Hand - Mellow Jazz (Lycius) In tch, wknd　　5　66
well over 1f out: Feb first foal: dam 6/8f scorer.
2033 **MADAM CAVERSFIELD** 9 [3]2-8-11 R L Moore 33/1: 57: Slow away, sn rdn & al bhd.　　　1¼　62
　　　TOP FORM 0 [8]2-8-11 W Supple 33/1: 8: Keen, handy, wknd & hung right over 1f out.　　1¼　58
1887 **JAY** 15 [7]2-8-11 W Ryan 100/1: 09: Slow away & al bhd.　　　6　40
9 Ran   Time 1m 13.19 (2.39)   Owned: Mr F C T Wilson   Trained: Upper Lambourn

---

2246   7.30 Fifty Years Of Twinning Classified Stakes 3yo+ 0-90 (C)
　　　　£9204 £2832 £1416   1m4f   Good/Firm 18   -26 Slow   Flip Start

1759 **WUNDERWOOD** 21 [5] Lady Herries 5-9-4 (89) S Sanders 11/2: 2014-001: b g Faltaat - Jasoorah　　98
(Sadler's Wells) Made all, styd on well over 1f out, drvn out: '03 mdn, class stks & h'cap scorer: eff over 10/12f &
likes firm, gd & polytrack, stiff or sharp trks: runs well fresh: tough, useful & still improving, genuine.
1 Oct'03 Donc 12g/f 91-83 C: 2 Sep'03 Kemp 12g/f 84-82 C: 2 Aug'03 Ayr 10gd 83-(80) D:
2 May'03 Newm 10fm 81-(79) D: 1 May'03 Nott 10.0g/f 79-(75) D: 1 Jan'03 Ling 10ap 74a- D:
4725} **ALKAASED** 236 [3] L M Cumani 4-9-7 (93) D Holland 7/2: 44/2122-2: b c Kingmambo - Chesa Plana　hd　100+
(Niniski) Trkd wnr, eff over 1f out, styd on to chall ins last, just held under a kind ride: won a mdn in '03,
rnr-up other 3 starts (Sir M Stoute): eff at 12f, stays 14f on firm & gd grnd, sharpish or stiff trks: shade over
confident ride today: returned in fine heart, useful & prob more to come, esp over further.
2 Oct'03 Leic 11.8g/f 93-90 C: 2 Oct'03 Newm 14fm 92-87 C: 1 Aug'03 Ripo 12.3g/f 81-(87) D:
2 Jul'03 Yarm 11.5gd 88- D:
1759 **DEFINING** 21 [6] J R Fanshawe 5-9-9 (95) O Urbina 25/1: 1/0203-03: b g Definite Article -　　2　99
Gooseberry Pie (Green Desert) Held up, hdwy well over 1f out, kept on but not pace of front 2: plcd on 2 of 4 '03
starts (class stks): '02 class stks & 4-time h'cap wnr: well suited by 12f & acts on firm, gd & both AWs, any trk,
likes Lingfield & Newmarket: has run well fresh: useful, encouraging return.
2 Jul'03 Wind 11.6g/f 97-(94) C: 1 Oct'02 Newm 12g/f 95-86 B: 1 Sep'02 Thir 12gd 88-79 C:
1 Aug'02 Newm 12gd 81-76 C: 1 Jul'02 Ling 12ap 81a-69 D: 1 Jun'02 Ripo 10fm 75- E: 1 Jun'02 Ling 10ap 71a-68 E:
1969 **HIGHLAND GAMES** 12 [7] J G Given 4-9-4 (87) K Fallon 4/1: 060-2024: Cl-up, eff over 1f out, sn　　2　91
hung left & no extra: well bckd: prob ran to form of 1969 & 1459.
1828* **FINE PALETTE** 18 [4]4-9-4 (87) W Ryan 9/4 FAV: 2-115: Held up, eff well over 1f out, sn no extra:　　½　89
hvly bckd: not disgraced but even btr expected stepped up to 12f after 1828 & 1623.
1516 **ARRESTING** 33 [2]4-9-4 (85) E Ahern 20/1: 3222-106: Handy, wknd dist: btr run on fast grnd.　nk　89
5026} **MAMCAZMA** 211 [9]6-9-9 (95) M Tebbutt 11/1: 200002-7: In tch, wknd over 2f out: reapp.　　4　88
1538* }**UROWELLS** 386 [1]4-9-6 (92) T E Durcan 25/1: 6/41-8: In tch, wknd over 1f out: reapp, gelded.　1¼　83
1759 **THUNDERING SURF** 21 [8]7-9-4 (90) R Hughes 33/1: 0/0631/-09: Keen, held up, wknd over 2f out.　10　66
9 Ran   Time 2m 34.07 (5.27)   Owned: Mr Tony Perkins   Trained: Littlehampton

---

2247   8.00 Newmarket Carnival Night Handicap Stakes 3yo 0-95 (C)　　　　　　　　　　[97]
　　　　£9646 £2968 £1484   1m str   Good/Firm 18   +02 Fast   Stands Side

1770 **ALSHAWAMEQ** 21 [9] J L Dunlop 3-9-0 (83) R Hills 20/1: 615-31: Dwelt, held up, hdwy 2f out, styd　　90
on well ins last to get up cl-home, rdn out: later stages: stays a stiff 1m well, shld get further: acts on fast grnd:
useful, lightly rcd & prob more to come: see 1770.
1930* **RED SPELL** 14 [2] R Hannon 3-8-10 (79) R Hughes 7/1: 1-0512: Handy, rcd stands side from halfway,　hd　85
led 3f out, kept on for press till collared cl-home: ran right up to form of 1930.
1930 **MR JACK DANIELLS** 14 [8] W R Muir 3-8-4 (73) R Miles(3) 7/2 FAV: 0100-363: In tch, rdn & outpcd　hd　78
over 1f out, rallied well ins last, styd on, just held: caught the eye 1930 & well worth a try over further now.
1745 **GRANATO** 22 [5] A C Stewart 3-9-2 (85) L Dettori 20/1: 221-004: b c Cadeaux Genereux - Genevra　　1　88
(Danehill) Led till 3f out, kept on same pace: won last of 3 '03 starts (mdn), rnr-up other 2: eff at 6f, clearly
stays 1m on firm & fast grnd, stiff & undul trks: useful, back to form on a sound surface.
1 Sep'03 Pont 6g/f 89- D: 2 Aug'03 Newm 6fm 89- D: 2 Aug'03 Pont 6fm 87- D:
1919 **SECRETARY GENERAL** 14 [13]3-9-7 (90) K Fallon 5/1: 241-0205: In tch, eff to chall 2f out, no extra.　2　89
4212* }**KIBRYAA** 266 [7]3-8-9 (78) M Henry 40/1: 021-6: ch c Silver Hawk - Fleur de Nuit (Woodman) In　2　73
tch, wknd well over 1f out: '03 mdn wnr: eff at 7f on firm & fast grnd, sharp trks: sharper for this.
1 Sep'03 Muss 7.1g/f 77- D: 2 Sep'03 Chep 7.0fm 80- D:
2040 **TRANQUIL SKY** 8 [3]3-9-4 (87) D Holland 6/1: 10-00527: Held up, hdwy over 2f out, hung left & no　nk　81
extra ins 1f: stays 9f, later stages after 2040 & 1813.
1769 **THE VIOLIN PLAYER** 21 [4]3-8-9 (78) W Ryan 66/1: 0313-008: b g King of Kings - Silk Masque　2½　67
(Woodman) Slow away, held up, hung right over 2f out but styd on over 1f out, nvr dngrs: '03 mdn wnr: stays 7f
well on firm & gd grnd, gall trks. 1 Sep'03 Chep 7.1gd 79- D:
1587* **SYDNEY STAR** 30 [10]3-9-3 (86) M Hills 7/1: 2-19: In tch, wknd dist: see 1587 (7f, mdn fills).　¾　73
1741* **CIMYLA** 22 [11]3-9-5 (88) S Sanders 9/1: 41-3010: 10th: In tch, eff well over 1f out, sn wknd &　6　63
eased: btr expected after 1741 (soft grnd).
1359* **TOPARUDI** 42 [12]3-8-4 (73) F P Ferris(3) 40/1: 3330-010: 11th: Slow away, in tch, wknd 2f out: abs.　½　47
1930 **APEX** 14 [1]3-8-9 (78) W Supple 12/1: 3030-150: 12th: Dwelt, al bhd: btr 1930, 1526.　¾　50
1756 **MAGANDA** 21 [6]3-9-0 (83) P Robinson 20/1: 20-160: 13th: Slow away, nvr a factor: see 1756, 1365.　1¾　51
13 Ran   Time 1m 37.8 (1.3)   Owned: Mr Hamdan Al Maktoum   Trained: Arundel

---

2248   8.30 Ngk Spark Plugs Maiden Stakes 3yo (D)
　　　　£5642 £1736 £868   1m str   Good/Firm 18   +01 Fast   Stands Side

1931 **CASTLETON** 14 [1] H J Cyzer 3-9-0 (100) K Fallon 1/2 FAV: 34-231: Made all, rdn clr over 1f out,　　94
easily: sweating, hvly bckd: prob stays 10f, apprec this stiff 1m: acts on firm & gd/soft: enjoyed forcing
tactics here: v useful, gd confidence boost: see 1931, 1617.
　　　MUSICANNA 0 [8] J R Fanshawe 3-8-9 O Urbina 10/1: 2: b f Cape Cross - Upend (Main Reef) Held　5　76
up, eff to go 2nd over 1f out, not pace of wnr: debut: half-sister to a 10f wnr: dam 12f scorer: eff at 1m, sure
to relish a step up to 10f: acts on fast grnd, encouraging start, will rate higher over further.
　　　RED SAIL 0 [9] J R Fanshawe 3-8-9 J D Smith 25/1: 3: ch f Dr Fong - Manhattan Sunset (El Gran　¾　74

Senor) Slow away, held up, hdwy over 1f out, no threat to wnr on debut: cost 22,000gns: half-sister to wnrs over 5/11f: dam styd 12f: acts at 1m, 10f looks sure to suit: acts on fast grnd: encouraging start, rate higher.

4678▶ **FLAMJICA** 238 [3] J A R Toller 3-8-9 Lisa Jones(3) 9/1: 35-4: ch f Real Quiet - Fiamma (Irish River) In tch, wknd 2f out on reapp: plcd on first of 2 '03 starts (auct mdn): poss stays 1m on fast grnd.	1¾	70
1810 **GOLDEN DRIFT** 19 [6]3-8-9 T E Durcan 40/1: 0-05: In tch, wknd 2f out.	3½	58
ZURI 0 [7]3-8-9 D Holland 13/2: 6: In tch, btn 2f out on debut.	6	51
1929 **ALBADI** 14 [2]3-9-0 BL J P Guillambert(3) 50/1: 0-007: With wnr, wknd well over 1f out: blnks.	3	50
919 **HOOPS AND BLADES** 72 [4]3-9-0 T E Ahern 66/1: 08: In tch, wknd over 2f out: abs, t-strap.	2½	45
MESAYAN 0 [5]3-9-0 T Laura Wells(7) 40/1: 9: Slow away, al bhd.	½	44
PHONE TAPPING 0 [11]3-9-0 P Robinson 33/1: 0: 10th: Slow away & al bhd.	1¾	40
1936 **GLANWORTH** 14 [10]3-9-0 F Norton 66/1: 060: 11th: Al bhd.	28	0

11 Ran   Time 1m 37.87 (1.37)   Owned: Mrs Charles Cyzer   Trained: Newmarket

---

2249   9.00 E B F Cecil Boyd Rochfort Handicap Stakes Fillies 3yo 0-85 (D)   **[91]**
£9055 £2786 £1393   **7f str**   **Good/Firm 18**   **-04 Slow**   Stands Side

1881 **DELPHIE QUEEN** 15 [10] S Kirk 3-9-6 (83) J F Egan 9/2: 4410-431: In tch, hdwy to lead over 1f out, rdn out: deserved win: apprec step up to 7f & acts on fast & gd grnd, likes gall trks: useful & improving.		93
1982* **LADY GEORGINA** 11 [7] J R Fanshawe 3-8-12 (75) O Urbina 5/1: 300-3612: Prom, eff & short of room over 2f out, kept on to chase wnr ins last, not her pace: another fine run & handles any trk: going the right way.	1½	81
1527 **CARA BELLA** 33 [13] D R Loder 3-8-12 (75) T P Queally(3) 9/1: 4-053: Held up, eff to chall over 1f out, no extra ins last: poss just stays 7f: see 1527.	3	75
2024 **DUMNONI** 10 [5] Julian Poulton 3-9-1 (78) N Callan 33/1: 31-06304: Keen cl-up, no extra appr fnl 1f: btr run: see 1257, 1020.	shd	77
1729▶ **SFORZANDO** 22 [6]3-8-6 (69) Lisa Jones(3) 10/1: 6500-15: Slow away, in tch, late gains, nvr dngrs.	nk	67
2108 **RED SAHARA** 5 [2]3-9-1 (78) M Hills 11/2: 01-166: Slow away, nvr a factor: qck reapp: btr 2108.	4	68
1761 **GO BETWEEN** 21 [3]3-9-4 (81) L Dettori 7/1: 43210-27: Keen, led 5f out till dist, wknd: btr 1761.	1	69
4450▶ **BEE MINOR** 253 [12]3-8-10 (73) R L Moore 66/1: 653500-8: b f Baratheca - Bee Off (Wolfhound) Al bhd on reapp: rnr-up in a fills mdn in '03: eff at 6f on fast grnd & on a sharp trk. 2 May'03 Ling 6g/f 75- D:	1½	58
4643▶ **DRY WIT** 242 [8]3-8-2 (65) F Norton 50/1: 24260-9: b f Desert Prince - Nawasib (Warning) Led early, handy till wknd over 2f out on reapp: rnr-up in 2 of 6 '03 starts (mdn aucts): stays an easy 7f on fast grnd. 2 Aug'03 Thir 7g/f 68- E: 2 Jul'03 Warw 7.1g/f 68- E:	nk	50
1281 **SCARLETT ROSE** 46 [9]3-8-5 (68) J Quinn 33/1: 360-60: 10th: In tch, wknd over 2f out: 6 wk abs.	¾	50
1935 **TELEFONICA** 14 [11]3-9-0 (77) K Fallon 3/1 FAV: 42-40: 11th: In tch, eff over 2f out, sn wknd: hvly bckd: clearly btr expected than 1935.	3½	52
1761 **BLUE DAZE** 21 [1]3-8-9 (72) R Hughes 25/1: 01-00: 12th: Handy, wknd over 2f out.	4	39

12 Ran   Time 1m 24.77(1.57)   Owned: Mr N Hartery   Trained: Upper Lambourn

---

Official Going GOOD (GOOD/FIRM places).

2250   2.00 Vodafone Live! Stakes Handicap 3yo 0-100 (C)   **[97]**
£43500 £16500 £8250   **1m2f18y**   **Firm 05**   **-28 Slow**   Inside

1664 **LORD MAYOR** 25 [1] Sir Michael Stoute 3-9-5 (88) K Fallon 11/2: 631-31: Held up, 'flew home' from over 1f out despite drifting left fnl 1f to lead cl-home, going away: well bckd: fine run, came from an almost impossible position: eff at 7/10f, 12f shld suit: acts on fm, soft, polytrk & any trk: lightly rcd & v progressive, excellent turn of foot here, v strong King George V H'cap claims.		102+
1813 **ROYAL WARRANT** 18 [14] A M Balding 3-9-1 (84) Martin Dwyer 16/1: 0-361342: Nvr far away, chsd ldr dist, kept on well but not pace of wnr cl-home: stays a sharp 10f: tough & consistent h'capper, see 1813 & 694.	1¾	91
2126* **MYSTICAL GIRL** 4 [16] M Johnston 3-9-7 (5ex) (90) D Holland 10/1: 0-331213: Sn led, clr 2f out & lkd to have a winning advantage, tired & caught cl-home: qck reapp: fine front running eff under jt top-weight: stays 11f, prob best at 1m: loves to force the pace: proving tough & useful.	hd	96
1813 **DANCING LYRA** 18 [2] J W Hills 3-9-7 (90) T Quinn 6/1: 00-61124: Slowly away, styd on fnl 1f, nrst fin: well bckd, jt top-weight: struck by rival's whip & caught the eye, 12f suit: see 1813.	3	91+
1192 **PRIME POWERED** 51 [8]3-9-6 (89) R Hughes 20/1: 021-55: Chsd ldrs, onepace fnl 1.5f: 7 wk abs: longer 10f trip: see 1192.	¾	89
1141 **MALIBU** 54 [5]3-8-7 (76) S Sanders 33/1: 51500-46: Held up, hdwy wide 2f out, no impress fnl 1f.	nk	75
1813 **TIGER TIGER** 18 [11]3-9-2 (85) J F Egan 20/1: 0-131207: Nvr btr than mid-div, short of room 3f out, some late hdwy: had a rough time in mid-div & shld be given another chance: see 1500 (gd/soft).	½	83
1496* **MASTER MARVEL** 34 [6]3-9-6 (89) K Darley 7/2 FAV: 2118: Trkd ldrs, lost place 3f out, no ch after: hvly bckd s/mate of 3rd: not at home on this easier surface, back-to-back trk & capable of btr, see 1496 (1m).	¾	86
1924 **SPRING GODDESS** 14 [4]3-8-13 (82) K McEvoy 33/1: 03160-39: Held up, nvr nr ldrs: see 1924.	nk	78
886* **OVER THE RAINBOW** 77 [18]3-9-4 (87) M Hills 33/1: 230-10: 10th: Held up, modest late gains, nvr dngrs: 11 wk abs: see 886 (AW).	hd	83
1741 **FORT** 22 [13]3-9-4 (87) K Dalgleish 33/1: 13-30: 11th: Slowly away, hdwy when short of room dist & sn stumbled, no ch after: wld have fin a gd deal closer & must be given another chance.	shd	83
1892* **SILENT HAWK** 15 [10]3-9-7 VIS t (90) L Dettori 11/1: 2-410: 12th: Prom, wknd fnl 1f: tried a vis.	¾	85
1807 **VANTAGE** 19 [17]3-8-10 BL (79) E Ahern 40/1: 2231450: 13th: Slowly away, sn chsd ldrs, wknd 2f out: tried blnks: see 1308 (12f, soft grnd).	1	72
2126 **FREAK OCCURENCE** 4 [7]3-8-12 (81) J F McDonald(3) 16/1: 0-034630: 14th: Nvr btr than mid-div.	5	66
923 **IN DEEP** 72 [9]3-8-6 (75) D Kinsella 66/1: 5562-00: 15th: b f Deploy - Bobbie Dee (Blakeney) Chsd ldrs wide, wkng when hmpd dist: 10 wk abs: mdn rnr-up on fnl of 4 '03 starts: eff at 7f/1m on fast grnd, shld stay further: with Mrs P Dutfield. 2 Oct'03 Sali 8g/f 73-(90) D:	1½	58
2040 **ALEKHINE** 8 [12]3-9-4 (87) I Mongan 7/1: 16-230: 16th: Wide in rear, imprvd to chase ldrs 2f out, sn btn: well bckd: longer 10f trip: btr 2040 & 1770 (1m).	½	69
1583 **RINGSIDER** 30 [15]3-8-11 (80) J P Spencer 40/1: 01-00: 17th: ch g Docksider - Red Comes Up (Blushing Groom) Mid-div, wknd 2f out, eased & t.o.: won fnl of 2 juv starts (mdns): £65,000 half-brother to sev wnrs over 1m/12f: eff at 7f on firm grnd, handles a v tight trk: with G Butler. 1 Aug'03 Ches 7.0fm 82- D:	16	37
1907 **OH GOLLY GOSH** 14 [3]3-8-5 p (74) T E Durcan 66/1: 0-220420: 18th: Led early, sn bhd, t.o.	1½	29

EPSOM   SATURDAY 05.06.04   Lefthand, Very Sharp, Undulating Track

18 Ran   Time 2m 07.08 (3.28)   Owned: Mr J M Greetham   Trained: Newmarket

2251
2.30 Listed Vodafone Woodcote Stakes 2yo (A)
£20300 £7700 £3850   **6f rnd**   **Firm 05**   **-32 Slow**   Outside

1760 **SCREWDRIVER** 21 [1] R Hannon 2-8-11 R Hughes 7/2: 21: Nvr far away, went on 2f out till collared **100**
dist, rallied gamely to regain lead ins fnl 1f, drvn strongly, drvn out: well bckd: eff at 6f, 7f+ will suit:
acts on fm, fast & any trk: reportedly held in some regard & clearly useful, win more races: see 1760.
1868* **ROYAL ISLAND** 16 [7] M Johnston 2-9-0 K Dalgleish 6/5 FAV: 112: Nvr far away, led dist till ins nk **101**
fnl 1f, just btn in a tight fin: hvly bckd, clr of rem: fine run conceding wnr 3lb, eff at 5/6f on firm & soft
grnd: handles a stiff or v sharp trk: clearly v useful, shld find a Listed: see 1868, 1632.
1816* **GORTUMBLO** 18 [5] D J S ffrench Davis 2-9-0 T Quinn 12/1: 13: Outpcd, styd on to chase leading 2 4 **89**
fnl 1f, nvr going to get there: eff at 5/6f on fast & firm grnd, will apprec 7f: rate higher: see 1816.+
1716* **OBE GOLD** 23 [3] M R Channon 2-9-0 T E Durcan 9/1: 314: Outpcd, styd on late, nvr dngrs: did 3½ **79**
not look at all at home on this unique trk, apprec a more gal one like 1716.
2077 **ADORATION** 7 [4]2-8-11 K Darley 8/1: 325: Slowly away, well bhd till styd on late: longer nk **75**
priced stablemate of rnr-up: best chance at the start: much btr 2077.
2020 **BLUE MARBLE** 10 [8]2-8-11 D Holland 20/1: 46: Chsd ldrs, lost place tattenham corner, no ch 3½ **65**
after: failed to handle this unique trk & not given a hard time: see 2020.
1709 **NEXT TIME** 23 [2]2-8-6 Martin Dwyer 66/1: 4507: Chsd ldrs, wknd 1.5f out: highly tried: see 954. 1¼ **56**
1571 **VICTORIA PEEK** 31 [6]2-8-6 M J Kinane 12/1: 48: Led till 2f out, wknd qckly, eased: see 1571. 3 **47**
8 Ran   Time 1m 10.03 (2.23)   Owned: Mr Raymond Tooth   Trained: Marlborough

2252
3.00 Gr3 Vodafone Diomed Stakes 3yo+ (A)
£43500 £16500 £8250   **1m11⁄4y rnd**   **Firm 05**   **-02 Slow**   Inside

4747} **PASSING GLANCE** 174 [3] A M Balding 5-9-9 (115) Martin Dwyer 20/1: 212160-1: br c Polar Falcon - **118**
Spurned (Robellino) Broke sharply & made all, clr 2f out, held on well fnl 1f, rdn out on reapp: highly prog in '03,
won a h'cap here at Epsom, a List contest & a Gr 2 in Germany: v eff with forcing tactics arnd 1m, stays 10f: acts on
fm & gd/soft, any trk, loves a sharp/undul one: runs well fresh: v smart, gd ride here & in top form.
1 Sep'03 Bade 8gd 115- A: 2 Aug'03 Good 8fm 116-(103) A: 1 Aug'03 Sali 8g/f 116-(103) A:
2 Jun'03 Good 8g/f 106-(97) A: 1 Jun'03 Epso 8.5g/f 99-89 B: 1 Oct'02 Newm 8fm 94- C:
2 Aug'02 Sali 8g/f 89- C: 1 May'02 Good 9g/f 91-87 B: 1 Jun'01 Sali 7g/f 90- D:
1705 **DUTCH GOLD** 23 [1] C E Brittain 4-9-4 bl (110) D Holland 33/1: 6-020052: Chsd ldrs till lost place 1¼ **110+**
halfway, prog when short of room 2f out, fin well but not quite reach wnr: big drop in trip & fine run in the
circumstances: prev best arnd 10/12f (5th in '03 Derby) & a return to further looks sure to suit: see 1705.
1758 **GATEMAN** 21 [10] M Johnston 7-9-7 (113) K Dalgleish 8/1: 6021203: Chsd wnr, kept on well fnl 1f hd **113**
but just caught for 2nd: usually front runs, unable to do so today: won this race last yr: tough & smart.
2002 **CHECKIT** 13 [8] M R Channon 4-9-4 (112) T E Durcan 9/1: 3360034: Chsd ldrs, onepace. 1 **108**
2022 **VANDERLIN** 10 [4]5-9-4 (105) K Darley 25/1: 2040-335: Keen & prom, no extra fnl 1f: s/mate wnr. nk **107**
3714} **BEAUCHAMP PILOT** 294 [11]6-9-4 M J Kinane 33/1: 31/3020-6: ch g Inchinor - Beauchamp Image 1 **105+**
(Midyan) Hld up last, styd on strongly late, nrst fin: lightly rcd in '03, List AW wnr, subs Gr 3 rnr-up: won 3
h'caps in '02, incl val Cambridgeshire: eff at 7f, suited by 1m/10f on firm, soft & polytrack, any trk: stable have
been out of form but this was eyecatching, keep in mind.
2 Jul'03 Asco 8g/f 111- A: 1 Nov'02 Ling 10ap 111a- A: 1 Oct'02 Newm 9fm 111-99 B: 1 Jul'02 Asco 10g/f 105- B:
1 May'02 Hayd 8.1g/s 96-84 C: 1 Nov'01 Newm 7gd 86-78 D: 1 Oct'01 Redc 8sft 81-72 E: 1 Sep'01 Asco 8gd 70-64 D:
1585 **LEPORELLO** 30 [7]4-9-7 (114) T Quinn 3/1 FAV: 31111-37: Rear & wide, nvr troubled ldrs: hvly 1½ **105**
bckd: inconvenienced by this drop back to 1m on this v tight trk: shld prove a different prospect back over 10f+
next time: see 1585.
1858 **VESPONE** 20 [9]4-9-4 VIS T (118) L Dettori 7/2: 110-2228: Stumbled start, some late hdwy tho' nvr nk **101**
dngrs: hvly bckd in first time visor/t-strap: lost all chance at the start today: see 1858 & 1558.
1686 **DUCK ROW** 24 [5]9-9-4 (108) S Sanders 15/2: 14440-29: Nvr btr than mid-div: much btr 1686. 2 **97**
1862 **PARASOL** 16 [2]5-9-4 vis (110) J P Spencer 12/1: 1262-200: 10th: Prom, rdn & hung left & found 3½ **90**
little 2f out: much btr over 10f, see 1585.
1862 **SUBLIMITY** 16 [6]4-9-4 t (110) K Fallon 7/1: 144-1040: 11th: Slowly away, al bhd, fin last: 1¾ **87**
boiled over in the preliminaries: btr judged on 1862, see 922.
11 Ran   Time 1m 42.40 (0.60)   Owned: Kingsclere Stud and Mr M E Wates   Trained: Kingsclere

2253
3.30 Vodafone 'dash' Stakes Heritage Handicap 3yo+ 0-105 (B)
£43500 £16500 £8250   **5f str**   **Firm 05**   **-06 Slow**   Stands Side   **[101]**

1162 **CARIBBEAN CORAL** 52 [8] J J Quinn 5-9-5 (92) R Winston 20/1: 0012-021: Mid-div, fin v strongly **99**
fnl 1f to force hd in front nr line: bckd at long odds: eff at 5/6f on firm & gd/soft grnd: handles any trk: best
held up for a late run & has a turn of foot, useful & in fine form: see 1162 & 927.
1481 **PLATEAU** 35 [10] D Nicholls 5-8-9 (82) M Hills 25/1: 0000-602: Stumbled start, just about last shd **88+**
halfway, fin v strongly & just failed in a thrilling fin: v well h'capped & this was a tremendous eff in the
circumstances: must be bckd to gain comp in the nr future & cld reward ante-post support for the Wokingham.
1481 **TYCHY** 35 [2] S C Williams 5-9-3 (90) J P Spencer 20/1: 52110-53: Prom far side, led halfway, nk **95**
collared dying strides: eff at 5/7f: fine run & deserves similar: see 1481.
1845 **TEXAS GOLD** 17 [3] W R Muir 6-9-0 (87) Martin Dwyer 50/1: 60113-24: Front rank far side, ev ch hd **91**
fnl 1f, just btn in a bunched fin: another consistent run: see 1845 & 106.
1683 **WATCHING** 24 [13]7-8-10 (83) A Nicholls 16/1: 040-3025: Front rank stands side, kept on well & shd **86**
just btn in a fin of hds: knocking on the door, acts on firm & hvy grnd: see 1683 & 998.
2082 **CORRIDOR CREEPER** 7 [17]7-9-3 p (90) D Holland 4/1: 00-54426: Front rank, ev ch fnl 1f, btn under hd **92**
1L in a v tight fin: bckd from 11/2: useful & in-form: see 2082.
2082 **WHITBARROW** 7 [1]5-9-10 (7ex) (97) Dane O'Neill 25/1: 6-500107: Front rank far side, ev ch fnl 1f, nk **98**
btn under 1L in a v close fin: see 1845.
2059 **TALBOT AVENUE** 8 [11]6-8-7 (80) P Dobbs 33/1: 000-0558: Chsd ldrs, kept on under press, only btn nk **80**
around 1L: sound run from this well h'capped sort: see 2059.
1683 **HENRY HALL** 24 [20]8-9-6 (93) Kim Tinkler 12/1: 513-3039: Chsd ldrs, sltly short of room dist, kept on. ½ **91**
1917 **ATLANTIC VIKING** 14 [12]9-9-9 (96) S Sanders 20/1: 05060-00: 10th: b g Danehill - Hi Bettina 1¼ **90**

676

(Henbit) Dwelt & outpcd, fin strongly, nvr nrr: won this h'cap from a 2lb lower mark last term: h'cap wnr in '02 & '01: suited by 5/6f, stays 7f: acts on firm & gd/soft, any trk, likes Epsom: gd weight-carrier, eff with/without blnks: best up with/forcing the pace, lost chance at the start today: stablemate of 2nd.
1 Jun'03 Epso 5fm 101-94 A: 2 Apr'03 Epso 5g/f 96-91 C: 1 Aug'02 Epso 5g/f 91-86 B: 2 Jul'02 Asco 5g/f 88-84 B: 2 May'02 Donc 6fm 84-83 D: 1 Jun'01 Ripo 5g/f 87-80 D:
1683 **CAPE ROYAL 24** [4]4-9-0 (87) L Dettori 20/1: 0-061060: 11th: Front rank centre, no extra ins fnl 1f. *nk* **80**
2082 **SEAFIELD TOWERS 7** [6]4-8-5 p (78) T E Durcan 66/1: 60-00300: 12th: Outpcd centre, late hdwy. *½* **70**
2206 **BOSTON LODGE 1** [19]4-9-10 bl (97) M J Kinane 16/1: 41-323240: 13th: Dwelt, nvr nr ldrs: bckd at long odds: 4th over 6f here at Epsom yesterday in 2206. *hd* **89**
1917 **MAKTAVISH 14** [5]5-8-12 p (85) P Hanagan 33/1: 1121300: 14th: Front rank centre, wknd fnl 1f. *hd* **77**
2082 **MAGIC GLADE 7** [7]5-9-0 (87) R Thomas(5) 16/1: 0-012130: 15th: Outpcd centre, nvr dngrs: reportedly broke a blood vessel & did not handle this trk: see 2082 & 1120. *¾* **76**
2082+**RACCOON 7** [9]4-8-8 (7ex)vis (81) K Darley 3/1 FAV: 011-4110: 16th: Prom centre, wknd dist: hvly bckd tho' op 5/2: much btr clearly expected under 7lb pen for 2082. *nk* **69**
64 **KATHOLOGY 199** [14]7-8-11 (84) T Quinn 20/1: 600530-0: 17th: b g College Chapel - Wicken Wonder (Distant Relative) Front rank till halfway, wknd on reapp: '03 h'cap wnr here at Epsom: won 2 h'caps in early '02: stays 7f, suited by 5/6f: acts on firm, hvy & fibresand, any trk: gd weight-carrier, best up with/forcing the pace: btr than this. 1 Apr'03 Epso 5g/f 92-84 C: 2 Aug'02 Sand 5g/f 88-86 B: 1 Jun'02 Sali 6g/s 87-82 C: 1 May'02 Brig 5.2g/f 85-77 D: 2 Jun'01 Hayd 7.1gd 86- C: *¾* **69**
4585} **BRAVE BURT 245** [18]7-8-10 (83) E Ahern 20/1: 400013-0: 18th: ch g Pips Pride - Friendly Song (Song) Led till halfway stands side, wknd on reapp: '03 h'cap wnr: won 2 h'caps in '02: loves to force the pace over 5f, acts on fast/firm, likes gd & gd/soft grnd: handles any trk, likes a stiff one: runs well fresh. *hd* **68**
1 Sep'03 Ayr 5g/f 84-80 D: 1 Jul'02 Asco 5gd 86-81 C: 1 Jul'02 Newm 5g/s 83-76 D: 2 Jul'01 Asco 5gd 89-84 C: 1 Jul'01 Newm 5gd 87-79 D:
2082 **PTARMIGAN RIDGE 7** [16]8-8-13 (86) J Murtagh 14/1: 01-00100: 19th: Front rank till halfway. *2* **65**
1917 **PALAWAN 14** [15]8-8-9 BL (82) L Keniry(3) 50/1: 0060000: 20th: Speed till halfway: tried blnks. *10* **31**
20 Ran Time 54.86 (0.56) Owned: Dawson Green Quinn Roberts Trained: Malton

2254 **4.20 Gr1 Vodafone Derby Stakes Colts & Fillies 3yo (A)**
£804118 £305010 £152505 **1m4f10y** **Firm 05** **+14 Fast** Centre

1685* **NORTH LIGHT 24** [6] Sir Michael Stoute 3-9-0 (115) K Fallon 7/2 JT FAV: 21-11: b c Danehill - Sought Out (Rainbow Quest) Trkd ldr, went on 3f out & kicked for home, styd on strongly, drvn out: fast time, fine positive ride: eff at 10f, relished this step up to 12f: acts on fm & soft, any trk: runs well fresh: lightly rcd, progressive, genuine & top-class: unexposed at this trip, can win more Gr 1's & prove hard to beat in Irish Derby. **123+**
1 May'04 York 10.4g/s 118- A: 1 Sep'03 Good 8g/f 96- D: 2 Aug'03 Sand 7.1sft 97- D:
1685 **RULE OF LAW 24** [11] Saeed bin Suroor 3-9-0 t (114) K McEvoy 20/1: 3113-22: Held up & still last halfway, prog 3f out, styd on strongly to take 2nd cl-home despite handing left: did not look completely at home on this switch-back trk & came from way back: stays 12f well, 14f will suit: v smart, Gr 1 success surely awaits on a more galloping track: again bhd today's wnr 1685. *1½* **119+**
1685 **LET THE LION ROAR 24** [3] J L Dunlop 3-9-0 VIS (110) M J Kinane 14/1: 12-133: Dwelt, sn mid-div, lost place ent str, switched & styd on strongly fnl 1f, nrst fin: fine run in 1st time visor: stays 12f well, will relish 14f: v smart, will improve on a gall trk & shld give North Light more to think about in the Irish Derby: v smart, ideal St Leger type, see 1685 (bhd this wnr & 2nd again). *hd* **119+**
1622* **PERCUSSIONIST 28** [5] J H M Gosden 3-9-0 (113) K Darley 7/1: 32-114: Sn pushed along prom, sltly lost place entering straight, went after wnr again entering fnl 1f, caught for 2nd cl-home: nicely bckd: fine run, shapes like a strong stayer who will relish a return to easier grnd: win more staying Gr races: see 1622 (soft). *hd* **119**
1480 **SALFORD CITY 35** [8]3-9-0 (115) J Murtagh 8/1: 1-165: Held up, hdwy wide 2f out, wknd fnl 1f: well bckd: made grnd v qckly & poss just failed to stay this longer 12f trip: 10f may prove ideal: see 1480. *3* **114**
1855* **AMERICAN POST 20** [13]3-9-0 R Hughes 13/2: 111-1116: Keen & prom, ev ch 3f out, wknd fnl 1f: bckd from 9/1: trav strongly but stamina lkd to give out: 10f in the Juddmonte at York could prove ideal. *1½* **112**
1480 **SNOW RIDGE 35** [7]3-9-0 (120) L Dettori 7/2 JT FAV: 110-27: Held up, prog to chase ldrs 2f out, wknd fnl 1f: hvly bckd: another with suspect stamina & failed to get this longer 12f trip: will reportedly return to 1m now & the Sussex stks looks a sensible target: 2,000 Guineas rnr-up in 1480. *1¾* **110**
1931* **HAZYVIEW 14** [12]3-9-0 (110) E Ahern 40/1: 2111218: Prom till wknd over 1f out: prev most progressive but this lkd a class too high: a credit to connections, see 1931 (List). *hd* **110**
1756* **PUKKA 21** [2]3-9-0 (86) D Holland 10/1: 0431-19: Trkd ldrs, wknd over 1f out: bckd from 16/1, also supported ante-post: imprvd in defeat here, won a h'cap off 78 in 1756 & this was a massive step up in class. *1½* **108**
1919+**GATWICK 14** [9]3-9-0 (104) T Quinn 16/1: 3-13110: 10th: Chsd ldrs, wknd 2f out: supplemented for a cost of 75,000 & failed to stay this 12f trip: prev most progressive, won a h'cap of 95 in 1919. *2½* **104**
1737 **MASSIF CENTRALE 22** [10]3-9-0 Dane O'Neill 100/1: 020: 11th: Dwelt & wide, al towards rear: highly tried mdn: see 1737 (mdn). *nk* **103**
1959 **COMING AGAIN 12** [14]3-9-0 M Hills 80/1: 2-520: 12th: Dwelt, mid-div, wknd 3f out & t.o. *19* **73**
4678} **ELSHADI 238** [4]3-9-0 VIS (96) Martin Dwyer 25/1: 114-0: 13th: b c Cape Cross - Rispoto (Mtoto) Dwelt, keen in rear, t.o. fnl 2f: tried a visor, reapp: won first 2 of 3 juv starts, mdn & stks, subs 4th in Gr 3 company: eff at 1m on fast grnd, handles a gall or undul trk: prev blnkd, tried a visor today: with M Tregoning. *1¼* **71**
1 Sep'03 Newb 8g/f 97- B: 1 Aug'03 Beve 8.5g/f 81- E:
2006* **MEATH 13** [1]3-9-0 J P Spencer 16/1: 31-2210: 14th: Led till 3f out, wknd & eased, t.o.: see 2006. *7* **61**
14 Ran Time 2m 33.72 (u1.08) Owned: Ballymacoll Stud Trained: Newmarket

2255 **5.05 Vodafone Rated Stakes Handicap 4yo+ 0-105 (B)** **[111]**
£23200 £8800 £4400 **1m4f10y** **Firm 05** **+01 Fast** Centre

4361*}**STARRY LODGE 259** [10] L M Cumani 4-8-9 (92) K Fallon 9/2: 164121-1: b c Grand Lodge - Stara (Star Appeal) Held up, prog to chase ldrs 2f out, went on dist, held on gamely, all out: op 7/2, decent time, reapp: won 5 h'caps in '03 & progressed from a mark of 60 to 88: wng form at 10/13.3f & acts on firm & gd/soft: handles a stiff/gall or sharp/undul trk, runs well fresh: tough, v genuine & most progressive. **99**
1 Sep'03 Newb 13.3fm 92-88 C: 2 Sep'03 York 11.9g/f 91-83 B: 1 Aug'03 Carl 11.9g/f 85-77 D: 1 May'03 Ayr 10.9g/s 80-73 D: 1 May'03 Redc 11g/f 73-66 E: 1 Apr'03 Warw 10.9fm 70-60 E:
1759* **SWIFT TANGO 21** [12] E A L Dunlop 4-8-13 (96) L Dettori 7/2 FAV: 1023412: Held up, gd prog to chase wnr 1.5f out, ev ch ins fnl 1f & just btn in a thrilling fin: hvly bckd from 9/2: v useful & in-form. *hd* **102**
4796} **ZIBELINE 231** [3] B Ellison 7-8-6 bl (89) K McEvoy 12/1: 230020-3: b g Cadeaux Genereux - Zia (Shareef Dancer) Held up, wide & prog 2f out, styd on late into 3rd: won a nov & a val Aintree h'cap this winter *1½* **92**

EPSOM   SATURDAY 05.06.04   Lefthand, Very Sharp, Undulating Track

(eff at 2m4f on gd & fast, rtd 138h): rnr-up twice in '03, incl in this h'cap (1lb lower): '01 h'cap wnr (1st time blnks): eff at 10/14f, stays 2m well: acts on gd & firm, any trk: eff with/without blnks, tried cheek pieces.
2 Sep'03 Ayr 13.1fm 92-89 C: 2 Jun'03 Epso 12.0fm 90-88 B: 1 Aug'01 Newb 13.2g/f 85-79 C:
2 Jul'01 Kemp 12fm 79-78 D: 2 Jun'01 Donc 12g/f 82-81 D:

877 **ANTICIPATING 78** [8] A M Balding 4-8-4 (3oh) (84) Martin Dwyer 14/1: 21460-04: Mid-div, prog 2f out, onepcd fnl 1f: 11 wk abs: sound run after break, spot on next time: see 877.		1	87

1484 **TRUST RULE 35** [9]4-9-0 (97) M Hills 15/2: 2102-065: Trkd ldrs, sltly short of room 2f out, onepcd fnl 1f: op 11/2: reportedly hung left: often runs well at York, see 1484.   nk   97

2078 **DISSIDENT 7** [1]6-8-4 (11oh)vis T (76) D Fentiman(7) 33/1: 0221456: Prom, sltly short of room 2f out, on onepcd: tried a t-strap: gd run from out of the h'cap, treat rating with caution: see 1484.   nk   86$

1483 **PUTRA SANDHURST 35** [11]6-9-7 (104) D Holland 8/1: 2025-107: Led early, regained lead 3f out till 3 dist, wknd: bckd from 16/1: btr 1364 (reapp, gd/soft grnd).   3   08

1668 **RING OF DESTINY 25** [13]5-8-6 (89) T Quinn 14/1: 3010-008: b g Magic Ring - Canna (Caerleon)   1¼   81
Held up, nvr nr ldrs: '03 h'cap wnr, won 3 h'caps in '02: suited by 10/12f on fast & gd grnd, poss gd/soft: handles any trk, likes Ripon: with P Harris & badgered to drop down the h'cap.
1 Sep'03 Thir 12g/f 94-88 C: 2 Sep'02 Pont 10fm 90-89 C: 1 Aug'02 Ripo 12.2g/f 88-82 D: 2 Jul'02 Ripo 10gd 83-79 D:
1 Jun'02 Sali 9.9g/f 80-73 D: 2 Apr'02 Sout 7g/f 76- D: 2 Jul'01 Folk 6.8g/f 73- F:

1111 **GALLERY GOD 56** [6]8-9-1 (98) J Murtagh 11/1: 10030-09: ch g In The Wings - El Fabulous (Fabulous   14   70
Dancer) Led after 2f till 3f out, wknd: 8 wk abs: won twice in '03, in France & this h'cap here at Epsom (4lb higher mark): with G Wragg in '02, '01 reapp h'cap wnr: eff at 12/14f, has tried 2m: acts on firm & gd/soft, handles hvy & any trk: gd weight-carrier, runs well fresh: capable of better.
1 Jun'03 Epso 12.0fm 106-102 B: 1 Jun'01 Thir 12fm 96-93 C:

1843 **TIZZY MAY 17** [7]4-9-1 (98) Dane O'Neill 8/1: 240-0250: 10th: Mid-div, btn 2f out: well bckd.   ¾   69
1759 **MANORSON 21** [2]5-8-7 T (90) E Ahern 25/1: 52/115/-00: 11th: Front rank till wknd 2f out: t-strap.   5   53
1759 **FINANCIAL FUTURE 21** [5]4-8-7 (90) M J Kinane 12/1: 2110-000: 12th: Trkd ldrs, wknd 3f out, t.o.   17   28
1037J **HERODOTUS 420** [4]6-8-4 (87) A Nicholls 66/1: 600050-0: 13th: Dwelt, al bhd, t.o.: reapp, new yard.   dist   0
13 Ran   Time 2m 35.25 (0.45)   Owned: Mr R C Thompson   Trained: Newmarket

---

2256   5.40 Vodafone Stakes Handicap 3yo+ 0-100 (C)   [94]
£23200 £8800 £4400   6f rnd   Firm 05   -16 Slow   Outside

2059 **NATIVE TITLE 8** [1] D Nicholls 6-9-2 (82) P Hanagan 11/1: 6/010-401: Trkd ldrs, imprvd to lead   93
dist, styd on strongly fnl 1f, drvn out: confirmed reapp promise: eff at 5f, suited by 6f/1m: acts on firm & soft grnd: likes to run up with/force the pace & handles a stiff/gall or v sharp trk: see 1594.

2070 **MUTAWAQED 7** [13] M A Magnusson 6-9-4 t (84) J Murtagh 8/1: 3630-042: Dwelt, outpcd, fin v   1½   89+
strongly: fin 3rd from a 6lb lower mark in this race last yr: fine run from a high draw, keep in mind.

1767 **LAFI 21** [9] D Nicholls 5-9-11 (91) Alex Greaves 14/1: 14310-03: ch g Indian Ridge - Petal Girl   nk   95+
(Caerleon) Mid-div, short of room 2f out, switched wide & chall ent fnl 1f, caught for 2nd cl-home: stablemate of wnr: dual Sandown h'cap wnr for A Stewart in '03: eff at 6f, stays 7f/1m well: acts on firm & gd/soft grnd: suited by hold-up tactics & likes Sandown: keep in mind back at 7f.
1 Aug'03 Sand 7.1g/f 94-85 C: 1 Jun'03 Sand 7.1fm 86-79 C: 1 Aug'02 Pont 8g/s 81- D:

2044 **JAYANJAY 8** [11] Miss B Sanders 5-8-11 (77) K McEvoy 16/1: 602-0434: Rear, styd on well fnl 1f,   ¾   78
nrst fin: gd run from modest draw: likes Epsom: see 2044.

2070+ **PRINCE AARON 7** [17]4-9-1 (81) G Carter 6/1 JT FAV: 1621315: Held up wide, styd on under press   ½   81
fnl 1f, nrst fin: well bckd & gd run from poor high draw: see 2070 & 874.

2059 **BLACKHEATH 8** [12]8-8-12 (78) P Dobbs 25/1: 23-04406: Bhd, short of room 1.5f out, nrst fin: ½   77
stablemate of 1st & 3rd: did not get the run of today's race from modest draw: see 1383 & 1217.

2082 **MINE BEHIND 7** [5]4-9-2 (82) N Pollard 11/1: 3-162207: Trkd ldrs, wknd ins fnl 1f: nicely bckd,   nk   80
has been gelded: see 1898 & 1767.

2059* **PAX 7** [15]7-9-3 (83) L Treadwell(7) 20/1: 40-66018: Keen in rear, some late gains: poor draw,   ½   80
stablemate of 1st & 3rd: btr 2059.

1926 **FANTASY BELIEVER 14** [4]6-9-6 (86) K Dalgleish 16/1: 41-00009: Trkd ldrs, fdd ins fnl 1f.   ½   82
1977 **UNDETERRED 11** [3]8-8-9 vis (75) K Darley 12/1: 000-0500: 10th: Slowly away, keeping on when hmpd   1¼   67
fnl 1f: slow start forfeited benefit of gd draw: likes Goodwood, see 1898.

2074 **BANJO BAY 7** [2]6-9-0 (80) Dane O'Neill 14/1: 000-0030: 11th: Led till 2f out, wknd: s/mate 1st & 3rd.   ¾   69
2082 **MALAPROPISM 7** [8]4-9-6 (86) S Hitchcott(3) 25/1: 3001-600: 12th: Chsd ldrs, btn dist: see 1845.   hd   75
1765* **POLISH EMPEROR 21** [6]4-8-12 e (78) N Callan 10/1: 2250310: 13th: Front rank, led 2f out till dist.   ¾   64
2045+ **IDLE POWER 8** [10]6-8-11 p (77) Martin Dwyer 10/1: 00-00110: 14th: At rear: mod draw: btr 2045 (7f).   shd   63
2070 **LOYAL TYCOON 7** [7]6-9-1 (81) A Nicholls 6/1 JT FAV: 00-00250: 15th: Trkd ldrs, wkng when badly   6   49
hmpd 2f out & again dist, eased: nicely bckd: s/mate of 1st & 3rd, won this race from a 3lb higher mark last year.

2068 **LITTLE EDWARD 7** [16]6-10-0 (94) T Quinn 33/1: 25-50500: 16th: Front rank 3f, wkng when hmpd   2½   55
dist, eased: top-weight, poor high draw.

2082 **VITA SPERICOLATA 7** [14]7-9-4 vis (84) R Winston 16/1: 00-00350: 17th: Dwelt, prog wide to chall   1   42
after 1f, wkng when hmpd dist, eased & fin last: poor high draw: btr 1626.
17 Ran   Time 1m 09.04 (1.24)   Owned: Mr C McKenna   Trained: Thirsk

---

BRIGHTON   SUNDAY 06.06.04   Lefthand, V Sharp, Undulating Track

Official Going FIRM. All Times Slow

2257   2.20 European Breeders Fund/Pietro Addis & Sons Median Auction Maiden Stakes 2yo (F)
£2905 £830 £415   5f59y rnd   Firm   Slow   Inside

2043 **SILVER WRAITH 9** [7] N A Callaghan 2-9-0   K Fallon 8/13 FAV: 421: In tch, hdwy wide to lead ins   91
last, rdn out: well bckd at odds-on: eff at 5.3f/6f on firm & fast grnd, sharp/undul trk: see 2043 & 1848.

1981 **RUSSIAN ROCKET 12** [5] Mrs C A Dunnett 2-9-0   Hayley Turner(5) 12/1: 052: Handy & briefly led   2½   82
dist, sn outpcd by wnr: handles firm & fast grnd: see 1981.

1987 **RUBYS DREAM 12** [3] J M Bradley 2-8-9   R L Moore 5/1: 42343: Chsd ldrs, chall over 1f out, kept   1¼   73
on onepace: acts on firm & hvy grnd: see 1805, 1640 & 1524.

TALCEN GWYN [1] M F Harris 2-9-0   J F Egan 40/1: 4: b c Fayruz - Cheerful Knight (Mac's Imp)   1½   73
Chsd ldrs, no extra dist: 8,000 gns 2yo, May foal: brother to a mod 3/4yo sprint wnr.

1805 **BLUE LINE 20** [8]2-8-9 G Baker 80/1: 05: gr f Bluegrass Prince - Out Line (Beveled) Rdn & bhd, mod late prog: Apr 1st foal, dam a multiple 6/7f wnr. *½* **66**
1937 **QUEENS GLORY 14** [4]2-8-9 J Quinn 9/2: 626: Led till dist, wknd qckly: btr 1937. *shd* **66**
ANGELAS GIRL [2]2-8-9 S Whitworth 50/1: 7: Sn outpcd. *9* **41**
IVORY WOLF [9]2-9-0 S Sanders 16/1: 8: Wide & al outpcd. *1¼* **42**
1937 **SABO PRINCE 14** [6]2-9-0 C Catlin 66/1: 059: Slow away & sn bhd. *1¾* **37**
9 Ran Time 1m 03.18 (3.18) Owned: Mr M Tabor Trained: Newmarket

2258

2.50 Donatello Ristorante Handicap Stakes 3yo+ 0-70 (E) **[66]**
£3504 £1078 £539 **7f rnd** **Firm** **Slow** Inside

1941* **A WOMAN IN LOVE 14** [2] Miss B Sanders 5-9-11 (63) S Sanders 5/1 FAV: 5640-611: Mid-div, hdwy & led ins last, rdn out: stays 1m, suited by 7f: acts on firm, gd & polytrack, likes Brighton: see 1941 & 1024. **71**
1841 **TEE JAY KASSIDY 18** [13] Julian Poulton 4-7-12 (1oh) (35) M Halford(7) 66/1: 1252042: Wide, rcd alone stands rail in str, kept on to take 2nd, not pace of wnr: reportedly lost a shoe: acts on firm grnd & fibresand: gd run, could find similar: see 909. *¾* **41**
1712 **DUE TO ME 24** [12] G L Moore 4-8-7 p (45) S Whitworth 40/1: 5251463: Al prom, styd on onepace for press: eff at 7f/1m on firm, hvy & polytrack: see 1642 & 1245 (banded). *2½* **45**
2057 **ALAFZAR 9** [6] P D Evans 6-9-7 bl t (59) S Donohoe(7) 7/1: 0131304: Keen, chsd ldrs, styd on onepace. *nk* **58**
1941 **WARLINGHAM 14** [1]6-9-6 (58) K Fallon 10/1: 1150105: Keen & trkd ldr, led 2f out till ins last. *shd* **57**
1941 **ZINGING 14** [9]5-7-13 (1ow)(1oh) (35) J Quinn 25/1: 4006556: Keen, rear, late gains, nrst fin. *shd* **35**
2045 **CONCUBINE 9** [15]5-9-8 (60) D Sweeney 10/1: 40300-37: Held up, hung left over 1f out, no dngr. *½* **57**
2016 **AGUILA LOCO 11** [10]5-9-3 p (55) F Norton 33/1: 0303608: Led till over 2f out, btn dist: btr 1731. *½* **51**
1938* **JONNY EBENEEZER 14** [16]5-9-6 (58) B Doyle 10/1: 0020219: Held up, eff over 2f out, no impress. *nk* **53**
1578 **LOCH LAIRD 31** [3]9-9-0 (52) G Baker 20/1: 0-001050: 10th: Mid-div, short of rm halfway, nvr dngrs. *¾* **45**
1956 **MORAG 13** [4]3-9-5 (67) T P Queally(3) 25/1: 050-4000: 11th: Mid-div, no impress: see 1359. *¾* **58**
1635 **SCARROTTOO 29** [11]6-9-3 (55) R L Moore 6/1: 0055140: 12th: Dwelt & al bhd: see 1132. *nk* **45**
2023 **B A HIGHFLYER 11** [7]4-9-9 (61) C Catlin 12/1: 16-05000: 13th: Chsd ldrs till halfway, sn bhd. *1½* **48**
2080 **MUTABARI 8** [5]10-7-12 (1oh) (35) J F McDonald(3) 66/1: 00-00000: 14th: Al bhd: see 1341. *nk* **22**
1613 **WILLHECONQUERTOO 30** [8]4-9-12 t (64) J F Egan 8/1: 56500-00: 15th: Reared, chsd ldrs till 3f out. *6* **38**
1876 **FAIR OPTIONS 17** [14]3-9-3 (65) G Carter 7/1: 0030: 16th: Chsd ldrs till 2f out: h'cap bow: btr 1876. *1½* **36**
16 Ran Time 1m 23.07 (3.27) Owned: High & Dry Racing Trained: Epsom

2259

3.20 Fat Leo Pizzeria Classified Stakes 3yo 0-75 (D)
£5395 £1660 £830 **7f rnd** **Firm** **Slow** Inside

1770 **SWEET REPLY 22** [3] I A Wood 3-8-8 (75) T P Queally(3) 12/1: 5104-051: ch f Opening Verse - Sweet Revival (Claude Monet) Handy & led 2f out, held on gamely ins last, all out: auct mdn scorer '03: eff at 6/7f, tried 1m: acts on firm & fast grnd, gall or sharp/undul trk. 1 Aug'03 Redc 6g/f 84-(83) F: **75**
1971 **WYCHBURY 13** [4] M J Wallace 3-8-11 (74) K Fallon 11/4: 532-522: Chsd ldrs & chall from over 1f out, drvn & just held: acts on firm & fast grnd: see 1971 & 1690. *hd* **77**
1688 **OLIVANDER 25** [5] G A Butler 3-8-11 BL (75) S Sanders 12/1: 52U6-03: b c Danzero - Mystic Goddess (Storm Bird) Rear, late gains, nrst fin: op 10/1, 1st time blnks, imprvd run: auct mdn rnr-up '03, AW unplcd (rtd 74a, mdn): eff at 6/7f on firm grnd, prob handles polytrack, sharp/undul or gall trk. 2 Jul'03 York 6.0fm 86- E: *½* **76**
2040 **HEVERSHAM 9** [6] W J Haggas 3-8-11 (74) R L Moore 9/1: 4120004: Led 3f, onepace fnl 2f: see 2040. *1* **74**
934 **CATALINI 72** [1]3-8-11 (75) S Hitchcott(3) 15/2: 5363-255: Held up, nvr chall: gldd, abs. *½* **73**
1761 **GENEROUS GESTURE 22** [8]3-8-8 vis (75) J Mackay 12/1: 4-156106: Keen & led 4f out till 2f out. *hd* **69**
1734 **I WONT DANCE 23** [7]3-9-2 (80) P Dobbs 5/2 FAV: 012-07: Al bhd: see 1734. *1¼* **74**
1983 **FINDERS KEEPERS 12** [2]3-8-11 (74) E Ahern 11/2: 0-231008: Keen, in tch till over 1f out, eased. *13* **47**
8 Ran Time 1m 23.16 (3.27) Owned: Mr C S Tateson Trained: Upper Lambourn

2260

3.50 Toteplacepot Handicap Stakes 3yo+ 0-70 (E) **[69]**
£4420 £1360 £680 **1m2f** **Firm** **Slow** Outside

2036 **FACTUAL LAD 10** [4] B R Millman 6-9-12 (67) G Baker 12/1: 5110-001: Mid-div, hdwy to lead over 1f out, rdn out: op 10/1: eff around 10f on firm, fast & prob hvy grnd, handles both AWs: gd wght carrier: see 1736. **74**
2015 **LARA FALANA 11** [5] Miss B Sanders 6-9-11 (66) S Sanders 9/2: 00-02542: Rear, styd on wide for press fnl 2f, not able to chall wnr: see 799. *1¼* **70**
2146 **FANTASY CRUSADER 4** [12] J A Gilbert 5-8-7 p (48) J Quinn 11/1: 00-03303: Keen & prom, ch dist, not pace of wnr: quick reapp: back to form & plcd all 3 starts at Brighton this term: see 1940 & 1695. *1½* **50**
1534 **PRINCE VALENTINE 33** [11] D B Feek 3-8-4 BL (58) F Norton 20/1: 00-00354: Led till over 1f out, kept on: fair run in 1st time blnks: prob stays a sharp 10f, return to 1m might suit: acts on firm & soft grnd. *1¼* **57**
1543 **SHORT CHANGE 33** [7]5-8-6 (47) T P Queally(2) 6/1: 3222-045: Mid-div, no extra dist: see 1543. *hd* **46**
1992* **MY MAITE 12** [9]5-8-6 bl t (47) E Ahern 6/1: 6-240016: Keen, rear, nvr chall: btr 1992 (1m). *shd* **46**
1778 **SPRINGALONG 22** [8]4-9-5 (60) S Donohoe(7) 25/1: 4-045007: Held up, eff over 2f out, no impress. *1* **58**
1913 **QABAS 15** [2]4-10-0 (69) R L Moore 9/2: 62222-58: Al bhd under top-weight: btr 1913. *hd* **66**
1830 **FOREST TUNE 19** [6]6-8-11 (52) K Fallon 4/1 FAV: 06-00069: Keen & al bhd, op 7/2: see 1083. *¾* **48**
1651 **JUSTICE JONES 27** [1]3-7-12 (2oh) (50) J F McDonald(3) 50/1: 00000: 10th: b g Emperor Jones - Rally For Justice (Dominion) Prom early, struggling halfway: mod form & unplcd prev. *17* **24**
1690 **BOLD RIDGE 25** [10]4-8-12 bl (53) J F Egan 12/1: 00-000: 11th: b g Indian Ridge - Cutting Ground (Common Grounds) Held up & hmpd after 3f, no ch fnl 3f, eased: h'cap bow, unplcd prev. *19* **0**
11 Ran Time 2m 03.30 (5.5) Owned: Tarka Racing Trained: Cullompton

2261
4.20 Pinocchio Ristorante Median Auction Maiden Stakes 3-4yo (E)
£3465 £1066 £533   **1m rnd**   Firm   **Slow**   Inside

2066 **ST FRANCIS WOOD 8** [7] J Noseda 3-8-6 (90) E Ahern 1/1 FAV: 2-021: Led till dist, rallied gamely **81**
to lead again ins last: nicely bckd: eff at 1m/10f on firm, fast & polytrack, stiff or sharp trk.
3790} **SOUTHERN BAZAAR 289** [2] B W Hills 3-8-11 K Fallon 5/4: 5-2: ch c Southern Halo - Sunday Bazaar ¾ **84**
(Nureyev) Chsd wnr, led over 1f out, awkward head-carriage & hdd ins last, no extra: well bckd, op 7/4: reapp:
promise sole '03 start (mdn, rtd 84): half brother to smart mid-dist performer Perfect Sunday: eff at 1m, 10f+ may
suit: acts on firm grnd, sharp/undul or stiff trk.
3275} **FRANGIPANI 294** [5] P F I Cole 3-8-6 N De Souza(5) 10/1: 334-3: b f Sri Pekan - Sharkashka 1£ **50**
(Shardari) Trkd ldrs, rdn & no impress fnl 2f: reapp: plcd 2nd of just 2 '03 starts (mdn, rtd 74): dam a
12f/hdles wnr: eff at 7f, breeding suggests 1m+ shld suit: handles gd grnd.
337 **PREGNANT PAUSE 151** [1] S Kirk 3-8-11 (64) J D Walsh(7) 16/1: 2402-404: Keen & al rear, no ch fnl 3 **58**
3f: abs, has been gelded: btr 268 & 15 (AW, 6/7f).
4 Ran   Time 1m 35.04 (3.04)   Owned: Mr Sanford R Robertson   Trained: Newmarket

2262
4.50 Great Grandma Betty Handicap Stakes 3yo+ 35-55 (F)   [57]
£2989 £854 £427   **6f rnd**   Firm   **Slow**   Inside

1941 **DOCTOR DENNIS 14** [2] J Pearce 7-9-4 vis (47) S Sanders 10/1: 46-51601: Rear, hdwy when short of **54**
room 2f out, drvn to lead cl-home: stays 7f, best at 6f on firm, soft & both AWs, likes a sharp/undul trk: see 767.
1886 **BOANERGES 16** [11] J M Bradley 7-9-12 (55) R L Moore 9/1: 005-0562: Mid-div, styd on wide to lead ¾ **59**
dist, rdn & hdd cl-home: fine run conceding wnr 8lbs: see 1886.
1052 **JAZZY MILLENNIUM 62** [13] B R Millman 7-9-10 bl (53) N Callan 8/1: 01500-03: ch g Lion Cavern - 1¼ **53**
Woodcrest (Niniski) Sn cl-up & led over 2f out till dist, kept on: sell & h'cap scorer '03: sell h'cap wnr '02:
suited by 6/7f on firm, soft & polytrack: loves Brighton: best when able to dominate, sped on similar when
granted a lower draw. 1 Jun'03 Brig 7.0g/f 57-54 E: 1 Apr'03 Brig 7.0g/f 56-(52) G: 1 Aug'02 Brig 6gd 55-50 F:
1 Sep'01 Brig 6sft 57-48 E: 1 Aug'01 Ling 6g/f 48-45 F: 2 Aug'01 Leic 7gd 48- G: 1 Jul'01 Brig 7g/f 51- G:
2016 **AINTNECESSARILYSO 11** [16] N E Berry 6-9-4 (47) M Savage(5) 10/1: 3332223: Rear, styd on for press dht **47**
fnl 2f, nrst fin & ddhtd for 3rd: most consistent: see 2016, 1867.
2044 **TENDER 9** [10]4-9-12 (55) F Norton 20/1: 60-35005: Mid-div, switched & keeping on ins last when 1¾ **50+**
hmpd, not able to recover: plcd with a clr run: nicely h'capped & could be wng sn: see 1096.
2053 **GONENDUNNETT 9** [12]5-9-7 vis (50) Hayley Turner(5) 20/1: 0000066: Prom, no extra from dist. hd **44**
1731 **TUSCAN TREATY 23** [3]4-9-10 VIS (53) B Doyle 14/1: 000-0047: Held up, short of room around 3 **38**
halfway, late prog in 1st time visor.
1540 **ELA FIGURA 33** [6]4-9-7 (50) J F McDonald 25/1: 0020-608: Mid-div, no extra dist: see 1371. ½ **33**
1730 **EMMERVALE 33** [8]5-9-7 vis (50) E Ahern 12/1: 36100-59: b f Emarati - Raintree Venture (Good ½ **31**
Times) Held up, rdn & no prog fnl 2f: C/D h'cap & fills h'cap scorer '03: sell rnr-up '02 for J G Portman: eff
btwn 5/7f on firm & gd/soft grnd, loves a sharp/undul trk, often goes well at Brighton: eff in a visor.
1 Sep'03 Catt 7g/s 51-44 F: 1 Jul'03 Brig 6.0g/f 44-43 F: 2 Sep'02 Brig 6.9fm 51- F: 2 Jul'01 Ling 6g/f 68- E:
1914 **GOODWOOD PRINCE 15** [15]4-9-12 (55) J F Egan 16/1: 6-500000: 10th: b g Emperor Jones - Scarlet 1 **33**
Lake (Reprimand) Wide & nvr on terms with ldrs: thrice h'cap rnr-up '03 (J Dunlop): C/D mdn scorer in '02: eff at
6/7f on fast & soft grnd, likes a sharp/undul trk: eff in cheek pieces, not worn this term.
2 Jul'03 Epso 7gd 80-77 D: 2 Jul'03 Epso 6g/f 80-77 D: 2 Jun'03 Epso 6g/f 78-73 D: 1 Aug'02 Brig 5.9g/f 85- D:
2 Aug'02 Epso 6g/f 81- E:
1941 **GUN SALUTE 14** [4]4-9-3 p (46) S Whitworth 7/2 FAV: 1046060: 11th: Stove away, switched rail, nvr dngr. ¾ **22**
1730 **MANNORA 23** [5]4-9-10 (53) K Fallon 5/1: 00430-40: 12th: Mid-div, btn 2f out: btr 1730. ½ **27**
1788 **RUN ON 20** [7]6-9-7 (50) S Righton 25/1: 3466-000: 13th: Al bhd: see 1788. nk **23**
1662 **SERGEANT SLIPPER 27** [14]7-9-3 vis (46) R Fitzpatrick 28/1: 3120150: 14th: Al rear: btr 1194 (AW). 3 **10**
1644 **HARBOUR HOUSE 27** [1]5-9-3 (46) J Quinn 9/2: 2063130: 15th: Mid-div, hmpd over 1f out, sn btn: ¾ **8**
bckd, op 14/1: see 1544 (banded).
1199 **PLEASURE TIME 51** [9]11-9-5 vis (48) P Dobbs 25/1: 5-500160: 16th: Led till over 2f out: abs. 1 **7**
16 Ran   Time 1m 10.50(2.7)   Owned: Mrs Lydia Pearce   Trained: Newmarket

Official Going Good/Firm

2263
6.30 Littlewoods Bet Direct E B F Median Auction Maiden Stakes 2yo (F)
£3572 £1099 £550   **6f rnd**   Good/Firm 25   **-30 Slow**   Inside

HAPPY EVENT [5] B R Millman 2-9-0 S Drowne 20/1: 1: b c Makbul - La Belle Vie (Indian King) **87+**
Held up, hdwy well over 1f out, styd on to lead ins last, rdn out: debut: Feb foal, cost 15,000gns: full brother
to useful sprinter Maktavish: dam 6/7f scorer: eff over a sharp 6f, 7f shld suit: acts on fast grnd & runs well
fresh: v pleasing start, potentially useful, will rate more highly & win more races.
1937 **BRIDGE PLACE 15** [7] B J Meehan 2-9-0 BL L Dettori 7/1: 032: Slt lead till over 3f out, rallied ¾ **85**
to chall ins last, kept on but not pace of wnr: gd run in first time blnks: shld find a race: see 1937.
MY PRINCESS [8] N A Callaghan 2-8-9 R L Moore 14/1: 3: b f Danehill Dancer - Shanoora (Don't 1¼ **76+**
Forget Me) Slow away, bhd, hdwy over 1f out, kept on ins last, nrst fin on debut: May foal, cost 24,000gns:
half-sister to a 7f wnr: dam 5f scorer: eff at 6f, 7f shld suit: acts on fast grnd, encouraging start, will learn
from this, rate more highly & shld find a race.
SPACE MAKER [2] M L W Bell 2-9-0 D Holland 12/1: 4: b c Almutawakel - Into Orbit (Safawan) hd **80**
Keen, handy, led over 3f out till ins last, no extra on debut: Feb foal, cost 23,000gns: eff at 6f on fast grnd:
showed some pace here & shld learn from this.
DRY ICE [12]2-9-0 Dane O'Neill 11/2: 5: b c Desert Sun - Snowspin (Carwhite) Slow away, bhd, nk **79**
hdwy 2f out, kept on ins last, nrst fin on debut: Mar foal, cost 18,000gns: dam 12f wnr: sire smart over 6f/1m:
learn plenty from this, 7f shld suit & will rate higher.
1900 **COME GOOD 17** [15]2-9-0 R Hughes 3/1 FAV: 526: Cl-up, hung left appr fnl 1f, no extra: hvly bckd. 3½ **69**

DREEMON [3]2-9-0 R Smith(5) 50/1: 7: Slow away, hung left & bhd, some late gains: debut. *shd* **68**
1911 **FLYING PASS 16** [6]2-9-0 Paul Eddery 9/1: 038: In tch, onepace when hmpd just ins last, not recover. *nk* **67**
1614 **FORTNUM 31** [16]2-9-0 P Dobbs 8/1: 539: In tch, onepace over 1f out: btr 1614, see 1510. *2½* **60**
1981 **PERIANTH 13** [9]2-9-0 N Callan 25/1: 400: 10th: Nvr a factor. *1¼* **56**
MAKEPEACE [11]2-9-0 S Hitchcott(3) 12/1: 0: 11th: In tch, wknd 2f out on debut. *nk* **55**
2194 **CHAMPAGNE BRANDY 4** [13]2-8-9 R Winston 66/1: 000: 12th: In tch, wknd 2f out. *2* **44**
MERRYMADCAP [10]2-9-0 D Sweeney 20/1: 0: 13th: In tch, wknd over 2f out on debut. *½* **47**
ROWAN LODGE [17]2-9-0 F P Ferris(3) 50/1: 0: 14th: Al bhd on debut. *2* **41**
1955 **ARCHIE GLENN 14** [18]2-9-0 R Havlin 10/1: 00: 15th: With ldrs, wknd 2f out. *¾* **39**
15 Ran Time 1m 13.61 (3.31) Owned: Mr Robin Lawson Trained: Cullompton

2264

7.00 Tote Supports Tonight's Charities Classified Stakes 3yo+ 0-70 (E)
£3591 £1105 £553 **1m67y rnd** **Good/Firm 25** **-06 Slow** Inside

1079 **BAKER OF OZ 61** [1] R Hannon 3-8-6 (70) R L Moore 14/1: 460-2641: Led early, cl-up, eff over 2f out, styd on well ins last to lead cl-home, rdn out: 2 month abs: eff over 7f/8.3f on firm, fast & polytrack, disapp on fibresand: acts on any trk: runs well fresh: game effort: see 734. **74**
1849 **PANGO 19** [6] H Morrison 5-9-5 (72) P Dobbs 10/11 FAV: 10500-22: Handy, hdwy to lead well over 1f out, hdd & no extra well ins last: hvly bckd: another fine run, deserves similar: see 1849. *¾* **75**
2024 **CHASING THE DREAM 12** [3] A M Balding 3-8-3 (69) J Quinn 12/1: 12603: Led after 1f till over 1f out, onepcd: acts on fast grnd & polytrack: see 322. *1¼* **67**
1691* **KATIYPOUR 26** [8] Miss B Sanders 7-9-8 (75) Lisa Jones(3) 2/1: 0312014: Held up, hdwy & hung right over 1f out, kept on ins last, no threat: nicely bckd: shade btr expected after 1691. *1¼* **72**
2087 **JOHANNIAN 9** [2]6-9-7 (74) D Holland 8/1: 005-0035: Held up, brief eff over 2f out, wknd dist. *1¾* **67**
1528 **CLOUDINGSWELL 35** [5]3-8-3 (60) N De Souza(5) 50/1: 3006-066: Keen in tch, wknd 2f out: see 1528. *8* **44**
3447] **LADY JEANNIE 665** [7]7-9-0 (48) R Miles(3) 66/1: 600400/-7: b f Emarati - Cottonwood (Teenoso) Slow away & al bhd on rtn: 02/03 nov hdle wnr (rtd 85h, 2m, hvy): last seen on the Flat in '02, unplcd (rtd 53): stay 10f on fast & gd grnd. 2 Sep'01 Ling 7.6gd 60- E: 1 Jul'01 Wind 8.3g/f 53-49 D: 2 Nov'00 Ling 8ap 39a-40 E: *6* **32**
7 Ran Time 1m 45.6 (2.6) Owned: The Mystery Partnership Trained: Marlborough

2265

7.30 Newsmith Capital Partners Handicap Stakes 3yo+ 0-85 (D) **[82]**
£5655 £1740 £870 **1m2f7y** **Good/Firm 25** **+00 Fast** Inside

1650 **WAR OWL 28** [15] Ian Williams 7-9-2 (70) Lisa Jones(3) 8/1: 0113501: In tch, hdwy 2f out, styd on strongly ins last to lead cl-home, rdn out: suited by 10f & acts on fast, gd/soft & both AWs: right back to best. **75**
82 **CZARINA WALTZ 198** [13] C F Wall 5-10-0 (82) G Baker 14/1: 351040-2: b f Emperor Jones - Ballerina Bay (Myjinski) Handy, hdwy to lead well over 1f out, kept on till collared cl-home: '03 dual h'cap wnr: '02 fill h'cap wnr: suited by 10f on fm, soft or polytrack, loves a sharp trk, esp Lingfield: tough, fine return. 1 Jul'03 Ling 10ap 86a-82 D: 1 May'03 Ling 10.3g/f 82-77 D: 2 May'03 Newm 10gd 81-72 D: 1 Jul'02 Ling 10ap 77a-71 D: 2 Jun'02 Ling 10ap 72a- D: *½* **85**
1890 **BARKING MAD 17** [14] M L W Bell 6-10-0 (82) D Holland 5/1: 0350-643: Led after 1f till over 1f out, rallied & not btn far: well bckd: fine run under a big weight: see 1890. *½* **84**
1890 **KENS DREAM 17** [2] Ms A E Embiricos 5-9-11 (79) S Hitchcott(3) 12/1: 1015/-034: Lost pl after 3f, hdwy over 2f out, chall ins last, no extra cl-home: gd run: see 1890. *nk* **80**
4207} **SECLUDED 269** [4]4-9-1 (69) S Sanders 8/1: 4355-5: b g Compton Place - Secret Dance (Sadler's Wells) Slow away & bhd, late gains, nvr dngrs: plcd in a mdn in '03 (rtd 74a at best): imprvd today at 10f on fast grnd & has been gelded since last term. *1¾* **67**
2067 **TODLEA 9** [10]4-9-4 (72) L Dettori 3/1 FAV: 00-64436: In tch, hdwy 2f out, onepace: nicely bckd. *hd* **69**
2030* **HIAWATHA 11** [5]5-9-7 (75) D Nolan(3) 12/1: 4130017: Chsd ldrs, wknd appr fnl 1f: btr 2030, 423. *½* **71**
1736 **CLASSIC ROLE 24** [7]5-9-9 vis (77) N Callan 12/1: 4122008: Slow away, in tch, no extra dist. *3½* **68**
1916 **STOLEN HOURS 16** [1]4-8-6 (60) J Quinn 25/1: 434-0009: b c Silver Deputy - Fasta (Seattle Song) Bhd, eff to 2f out, no threat: unplcd in hdles last winter: plcd in a mdn in '03 (rtd 79): stays 14f on firm & fast grnd, sharp trks: tried a visor. *hd* **50**
2015 **DORIS SOUTER 12** [3]4-9-2 (70) R Hughes 12/1: 3-205030: 10th: Led early, held up, btn dist. *1* **58**
1817 **YEOMAN LAD 20** [9]4-9-4 VIS (72) S Whitworth 20/1: 30000-00: 11th: In tch, wknd & hmpd 2f out. *8* **48**
2135 **KYLE OF LOCHALSH 6** [12]4-8-3 (57) A McCarthy 33/1: 000-3000: 12th: In tch, wknd 3f out. *1½* **30**
1519 **GLIMMER OF LIGHT 35** [6]4-9-8 (76) R L Moore 9/1: 4150-60: 13th: In tch, wknd over 2f out: bckd. *hd* **48**
4711} **VICTORY VENTURE 238** [8]4-9-9 (77) S W Kelly 33/1: 210030-0: 14th: In tch 1m, wknd: new yard. *14* **21**
14 Ran Time 2m 08.56 (2.56) Owned: Mrs Glennie Braune Trained: Alvechurch

2266

8.00 Sunley Handicap Stakes 3yo+ 0-85 (D) **[83]**
£6988 £2150 £1075 **5f10y rnd** **Good/Firm 25** **+09 Fast** Inside

2023 **DEVON FLAME 12** [5] R J Hodges 5-8-13 (68) J F McDonald(3) 6/1: 0/4111-21: Mid-div, prog when no room 2f out, hdwy & led ins last, styd on strongly: stays 1m, best at 5/6f on fast & gd/soft grnd: handles any trk, likes Windsor: v progressive profile, won this in a fast time, keep on side. **79**
2189 **FURTHER OUTLOOK 4** [4] D K Ivory 10-9-13 (82) Dane O'Neill 33/1: 1300042: Al prom & led over 1f out till ins last, not pace of wnr: see 944 (soft). *1½* **87**
4022] **SUNLEY SENSE 635** [6] M R Channon 8-9-10 (79) B O'Neill(7) 50/1: 111000/-3: b g Komaite - Brown Velvet (Mansingh) Mid-div, eff to chall bef dist, kept on onepace: long abs: missed '03: dual h'cap wnr '02, also landed a class stks: eff at 5/6f on firm & soft grnd, prob handles any trk: best without visor & a gd weight carrier: fine rtn after such a long break. 1 Aug'02 Bath 5fm 89- D: 1 Aug'02 Kemp 5fm 87-77 D: 1 Aug'02 Sali 6g/f 86-77 E: 2 Apr'02 Kemp 5fm 83-79 D: 1 Aug'01 Sand 5sft 86-76 D: 2 May'01 Bath 5g/f 82-77 D: *1* **81**
1914 **YORKIES BOY 16** [2] J M Bradley 9-7-13 (54) J Quinn 33/1: 00400-54: Dwelt & bhd, kept on fnl 2f, not able to chall: confirmed promise of recent rtn, can find a race sn: see 1914. *nk* **55**
1973* **MUSICAL FAIR 14** [12]4-9-9 (78) R Winston 7/2 JT FAV: 0-000215: Chsd ldrs, onepcd dist: see 1973. *shd* **79**
2137 **VIENNAS BOY 6** [3]3-9-8 (84) R L Moore 8/1: 20-44646: Mid-div, not pace to chall: see 2137 & 1018. *nk* **84**
2189 **PORT ST CHARLES 4** [7]7-8-8 (63) S Sanders 10/1: 4400437: Bhd, kept on late, not pace to threaten: see 2189 & 113. *1¾* **58**
2256 **POLISH EMPEROR 2** [8]4-9-9 e (78) N Callan 7/2 JT FAV: 2503108: Chsd ldrs till dist: btr 1765. *nk* **72**
2062 **LADY PEKAN 9** [1]5-8-7 bl (62) F P Ferris(3) 25/1: 2003539: Cl-up & led dist, sn hdd & no extra. *hd* **55**

2070 **SEVEN NO TRUMPS 9** [10]7-9-8 (77) D Holland 7/1: 5000360: 10th: Bhd, not pace to chall: btr 1914. *1* **67**
1255 **MR SPLIFFY 49** [13]5-8-0 (55) Hayley Turner(5) 25/1: 5100500: 11th: Chsd ldrs, short of room over 1f out when onepace: 7 wk abs. *½* **43**
765 **ITS ECCO BOY 99** [9]6-8-9 (64) Lisa Jones(3) 33/1: 4410000: 12th: Al outpcd: abs, needs 6/7f. *½* **50**
4608} **DELEGATE 247** [14]11-8-12 (67) W Ryan(5) 20/1: 152330-0: 13th: ch g Polish Precedent - Dangora (Sovereign Dancer) Outpcd & nvr a factor on reapp: h'cap scorer '03: h'cap & clmr scorer '02: suited by 5/6f, poss stays 7f: acts on firm or hvy, any trk. *3* **44**
2 Aug'03 Nott 5.1g/f 64-(67) E: 1 Aug'03 Brig 5.3fm 70-65 E: 1 Jul'02 Bath 5g/f 69- F: 1 Jul'02 Newm 5g/f 78-71 C: 1 Nov'01 Redc 5g/f 79- D: 2 Sep'01 Donc 5gd 77-74 D: 1 Aug'01 Newm 5g/f 75-69 D:
1615 **DANCING MYSTERY 31** [15]10-9-11 bl (80) S Carson 16/1: 1350000: 14th: Led till dist, sn btn. *2* **51**
14 Ran Time 59.83 (0.83) Owned: Mrs Angela Tincknell Trained: Somerton

2267

8.30 Deloitte Claiming Stakes 3yo+ (F)
£2996 £856 £428 1m3f135y Good/Firm 25 -02 Slow Inside

1990 **PARADISE VALLEY 13** [7] Mrs Stef Liddiard 4-9-5 t (45) S Drowne 8/1: 0205431: Rear, hdwy 3f out & strong run for press ins last to lead cl-home: eff btwn 10/15f on firm, gd & both AWs, poss handles soft: suited by t-strap & claim grade: see 347. **56**
4513] **COSI FAN TUTTE 606** [2] M C Pipe 6-9-4 vis T D Holland 5/2 FAV: 225410/-2: b g Inchinor - Bumpkin (Free State) Chsd ldr 4f out, drvn & ch 2f out, hdd ins last but hdd cl-home: v long abs, missed '03: '02 h'cap scorer (first time visor): eff btwn 1m/12f on fast & soft grnd, stiff/gall or sharp trk: gd weight carrier: eff in blnks/visor & gd run in t-strap tonight. 1 Oct'02 Nott 10g/f 77-70 E: 2 Jul'02 Newc 12.4g/f 74- D: 2 Jul'02 Newm 12sft 74-70 C: 2 May'02 Leic 8g/s 64- F: 2 May'02 Hami 9.1sft 52- E: *nk* **54**
1056 **RAINBOW WORLD 63** [9] Andrew Reid 4-10-0 P (65) J F Egan 12/1: 60-03003: Prom & led over 4f out till ins last, no extra: 2 month abs, fair run in cheek pieces: acts on fast, polytrack & soft grnd: see 816. *¾* **62**
1402 **JACK DURRANCE 41** [14] G A Ham 4-9-6 (55) J F McDonald(3) 50/1: 0100-004: b g Polish Precedent - Atlantic Desire (Ela Mana Mou) Bhd, kept on late for press, not able to chall: jumps fit (unplcd, mod): class stks wnr for M Johnston in '03: eff at 10f on gd/soft grnd & a stiff/turning trk: imprvd eff with visor omitted tonight. 1 May'03 Bath 10.2g/s 76-(70) E: *6* **45**
1047 **BLUE SAVANNA 63** [5]4-9-4 bl (45) R L Moore 10/1: 3-642105: Chsd ldrs, no extra dist: jmps fit. *1¾* **40**
2107* **REGULATED 7** [12]3-8-8 (65) Dane O'Neill 4/1: 2015516: Rear, mod prog for press: see 217 (10f). *1¾* **42**
1542 **PRINCESS MAGDALENA 34** [4]4-9-3 (55) I Mongan 8/1: 00010-07: Chsd ldrs till 2f out. *1½* **34**
2065 **ANOTHER CON 9** [1]3-8-3 (58) Lisa Jones(3) 7/1: 1450028: Led till 4f out, btn 2f out: new stable. *½* **34**
1754 **FOX HOLLOW 23** [11]3-8-4 (38) R Miles(3) 20/1: 0326239: Chsd ldrs, hung left & btn 3f out: btr 1754. *6* **26**
4592] **REAL ESTATE 600** [16]10-10-0 (52) S Whitworth 33/1: 2000//00/-0: 10th: Al bhd, long abs. *7* **24**
4828} **RARE PRESENCE 230** [6]5-9-5 vis t (50) S Carson 50/1: 340/000-0: 11th: Al bhd, jumps fit. *5* **8**
Hickerthriftcastle [13]5-9-7 M Tebbutt 40/1:0 845 **Introduction 85** [15]3-8-4 (45) Paul Eddery 20/1:0
782 **Red Acer 98** [10]3-8-4 (25) F P Ferris(3) 66/1:0 1247 **Last Rebel 49** [8]5-9-4 (70) R Hughes 16/1:0
15 Ran Time 2m 30.46 (3.16) Owned: Valley Fencing Trained: Hungerford

2268

9.00 E B F Retraining Of Racehorses Handicap Stakes Fillies 3yo 0-75 (E) **[82]**
£4407 £1356 £678 6f rnd Good/Firm 25 -19 Slow Inside

1576 **BOHOLA FLYER 32** [6] R Hannon 3-9-3 (71) R Hughes 20/1: 02-14641: Mid-div, eff to chall dist, narrow lead ins last, all out: suited by 6f on fast, gd & polytrack, handles soft, sharp/undul or gall trks. **77**
2062 **COMERAINCOMESHINE 9** [5] T G Mills 3-8-6 (60) R Miles(3) 14/1: 030-3642: Led/dsptd lead & went on halfway, edged sharply right over 1f out & hdd ins last, just denied: see 2062 & 51. *shd* **65**
1576 **WHISTFUL 32** [2] C F Wall 3-9-0 (68) S Sanders 33/1: 0542-303: Chsd ldrs, drvn & chall dist, no extra well ins last: see 1239. *1* **70**
2011* **PARTY PRINCESS 12** [4] J A Glover 3-8-10 (64) R Winston 12/1: 253-0014: Bhd, hdwy & chall dist, onepace ins last: see 2011. *1¼* **62**
2118 **UNDER MY SPELL 7** [8]3-9-2 (70) S W Kelly 9/1: 55-00225: Mid-div, switched & kept on, not able to chall. *¾* **66**
2098 **SWORN TO SECRECY 7** [7]3-8-7 bl (61) J F Egan 25/1: 5-000006: Bhd, prog halfway, hung badly left & no impress over 1f out: see 1339. *shd* **56**
1983 **RISE 13** [1]3-8-3 bl (57) S Carson 33/1: 00-00607: Chsd ldrs, no extra dist: see 494. *1½* **48**
2118 **URBAN ROSE 7** [18]3-8-10 (64) Dane O'Neill 14/1: 044-0038: Led 3f, no extra dist: see 2118. *¾* **53**
2118* **VERKHOTINA 7** [3]3-9-10 (6ex) (78) S Drowne 11/4 FAV: 550-619: Dwelt & bhd, only mod prog. *shd* **66**
1829 **PINK SUPREME 20** [11]3-9-2 t (70) T P Queally(3) 33/1: 2-000: 10th: ch f Night Shift - Bright Spells (Salse) Bhd, nvr pace to chall: h'cap bow: promise on sole '03 start (rnr-up, fill mdn, subs training probs): eff at 5f on gd grnd, sprint pedigree. 2 May'03 Wind 5.0gd 78- D: *½* **56**
268 **SWEETEST REVENGE 160** [9]3-9-7 (75) Hayley Turner(5) 16/1: 104254-0: 11th: Chsd ldrs till 2f out: 5 month abs: btr 135. *¾* **59**
2055 **TURKISH DELIGHT 10** [12]3-8-8 (62) N Callan 25/1: 4430-560: 12th: Outpcd, nvr a factor: see 1441. *hd* **45**
2062 **PRINCESS KAI 9** [16]3-8-3 bl (57) S Whitworth 25/1: 0342260: 13th: Chsd ldrs 4.5f: btr 1694. *¾* **38**
1809 **FIDDLE ME BLUE 21** [14]3-9-7 (75) R L Moore 8/1: 31-500: 14th: ch f Bluebird - Fiddle Dee Dee (Mujtahid) Chsd ldrs, btn when hmpd over 1f out: lightly rcd '03, C/D mdn scorer: eff at 5/6f on fast & gd/soft grnd, sharp or gall trk. 1 Oct'03 Wind 6g/f 78- D: *nk* **55**
1540 **GOJO 34** [15]3-9-2 (70) L Dettori 9/2: 060-4200: 15th: Prom early, sn bhd: btr 1465 (soft). *1¼* **46**
2048 **SHRINK 10** [17]3-8-13 BL (67) D Holland 11/2: 22-21440: 16th: Sn strug: blnks: btr 1023 (5f, AW). *½* **41**
1732 **Innclassic 24** [13]3-9-7 (75) J F McDonald(3) 33/1:0 2118 **Alizar 7** [10]3-8-3 (57) J Quinn 50/1:0
18 Ran Time 1m 13.08(2.78) Owned: Mr William Durkan Trained: Marlborough

FOLKESTONE   MONDAY 07.06.04   Righthand, Sharpish, Undulating Track

Official Going Good/Firm (Firm Places)

2269 2.20 Sandgate Handicap Stakes 3yo+ 0-75 (E) **[75]**
£3484 £1072 £536   **5f str**   **Good/Firm 20**   +02 Fast   Stands Side. 2 Groups.

2044* **HARD TO CATCH** 10 [12] D K Ivory 6-9-11 bl (72) M Savage(5) 8/1: 4550011: Dwelt, rear far side, **80**
hdwy halfway & led ins last, pushed out: op 7/1: eff at 5/6f on firm & fast, both AWs & handles soft: loves a
sharp/undul trk: tough & in fine form at present: see 2044, 628 & 516.
2023 **DOUBLE M** 12 [8] Mrs L Richards 7-8-6 vis (53) N Callan 6/1: 1065532: Mid-div far side, short of   ½ **59+**
room over 1f out, kept on ins last, wnr had first run: poss unlucky: see 2023.,
2237 **LAW MAKER** 2 [10] M A Buckley 4-7-12 (2oh)vis (43) J Quinn 12/1: 0423043: Dsptd lead far side &   1 **47**
went on halfway, hdd ins last, not pace of wnr: acts on fast, gd & polytrack: mdn: see 2237.
1867 **PULSE** 18 [5] J M Bradley 6-9-1 p (62) R L Moore 9/2 FAV: 0023664: Chsd ldrs stands side & led   1½ **60+**
that group over 1f out, no impress on ldrs far side: first home from unfav'd stands side group: see 1532 & 1221.
1914 **BEAUVRAI** 16 [3]4-9-8 (47) Martin Dwyer 8/1: 00-00005: U.r. bef start, dwelt & held up stands side,   ¾ **65**
kept on late, nvr a threat: op 7/2: see 1914, 1481 & 567.
2062 **INCHING** 9 [7] M Fenton (2oh) (47) Martin Dwyer 8/1: 4000026: Led far side till halfway, sn btn: btr 2062. 1¾ **38**
1914 **PLAYTIME BLUE** 16 [6]4-9-0 (61) G Baker 13/2: 2143067: Led stands side till over 1f out, wknd: btr 1127. hd **51**
1743 **AMONG FRIENDS** 24 [4]4-9-6 BL (67) T Quinn 16/1: 0/036-608: Trkd ldrs stands side till over 1f out. ½ **55**
1806 **NAUGHTY GIRL** 21 [1]4-8-13 BL (60) F P Ferris(3) 50/1: 0-000009: Rear stands side, no impress: blnks. ½ **46**
1867 **INDIAN BAZAAR** 18 [13]8-8-3 (50) R Miles(3) 20/1: 03145-00: 10th: ch g Indian Ridge - Bazaar   1¼ **32**
Promise (Native Bazaar) Mid-div far side, no impress when hmpd over 1f out: h'cap scorer '03 for J M Bradley:
unplcd '03 (rtd 53, h'cap, disapp in blnks): suited by 5f, stay 6f: acts on firm & soft grnd, prob any trk, likes
Chepstow. 1 Sep'03 Chep 5.1gd 51-45 E: 2 May'03 Good 5g/f 47-45 E: 1 Sep'01 Chep 5g/f 61-54 E:
1 Jun'01 Ling 5fm 52-48 E: 1 May'01 Yarm 5.1gd 46-41 F: 1 May'01 Good 5fm 50-43 E:
1914 **Tomthevic** 16 [11]6-8-12 (59) M Fenton 20/1:0   2044 **Loch Inch** 10 [7]7-8-6 bl(53) S Carson 20/1:0
12 Ran   Time 59.31 (0.91)   Owned: Mrs Karen Graham   Trained: Radlett

2270 2.50 Pilgrims Hospice Raceday On 25th June Selling Stakes 2yo (G)
£2506 £716 £358   **5f str**   **Good/Firm 20**   -39 Slow   Stands Side

1831 **KERESFORTH** 20 [4] I A Wood 2-9-0 bl N Callan 11/10 FAV: 0021: Made all stands side & sn clr of   **66**
rivals, styd on strongly: prev with T D Easterby, bght in for 7,200gns: well bckd: eff at 5f on fast grnd, stiff or
sharp/undul trk: likes to force the pace, suited by sell grade & blnks: see 1831.
SONGGARIA 0 [3] B Palling 2-8-9 T Quinn 5/2: 2: b f Kingsinger - Paula's Joy (Danehill) Sn   3½ **49**
pushed along chasing wnr stands side, kept on late, nvr threat: bckd, op 7/2: cheaply bght Feb foal, dam a 5f juv
wnr: sire smart juv/1m performer: claimed for 6,000.
2017 **SHISH** 12 [5] J A Osborne 2-8-9 S W Kelly 6/1: 6643: Led far side & sn clr of other pair, no   1½ **44**
impress on wnr from dist: op 4/1: btr 2017 (AW).
SAPPHIRE PRINCESS 0 [6] I A Wood 2-8-9 J F McDonald(3) 10/1: 4: b f Namaqualand - Breakfast   3 **35**
Creek (Hallgate) Outpcd far side, nvr a factor: stablemate of wnr: cheeply bght Apr foal, half-sister to a 5f juv
wnr & also a 6f 3yo wnr: dam a 5f juv wnr.
2017 **BAMBOOZLED** 12 [1]2-8-9 BL Joanna Badger 12/1: 6005: Dwelt, stands side, al outpcd: blnks, op 8/1. 6 **19**
2089 **WHATSHEWORTH** 8 [2]2-9-0 B Reilly(3) 25/1: 06: Dwelt, went right start, nvr on terms far side. 8 **2**
6 Ran   Time 1m 01.37 (2.97)   Owned: Neardown Stables   Trained: Upper Lambourn

2271 3.20 Toteexacta Handicap Stakes 3yo 0-80 (D) **[86]**
£8327 £2562 £1281   **6f str**   **Good/Firm 20**   +06 Fast   Stands Side. 2 Groups.

2023 **SIMPSONS MOUNT** 12 [2] R M Flower 3-8-4 (62) R L Moore 20/1: 6530501: Trkd ldrs stands side & led   **68**
over 1f out, rdn out: fair time: first win: eff at 5/6f on fast grnd & polytrack, sharp/undul trk.
2104* **SNOW WOLF** 7 [6] J M Bradley 3-9-10 (6ex) (82) Dane O'Neill 11/1: 023-012: Led far side, hung   1¾ **84**
badly left to stands side fnl 2f, no impress on wnr cl-home: see 2104 (auct mdn).
1903* **TAG TEAM** 17 [1] A M Balding 3-9-4 (76) Martin Dwyer 11/2: 1130513: Led stands side till over 1f   ½ **76**
out, edged right & no extra ins last: fair run: see 1903.
2048 **ASK THE CLERK** 10 [7] V Smith 3-9-1 (73) M Tebbutt 9/1: 0102034: Rear far side, nvr on terms: op   2½ **65**
7/1: handles fast grnd, loves soft: see 975 (C/D).
1766 **TRIBUTE** 23 [8]3-9-7 (79) T P Queally(3) 9/2: 3261-005: Trkd ldrs far side, no impress dist: see 1766. shd **71**
1766 **WHOS WINNING** 23 [4]3-8-12 (70) J F McDonald(3) 16/1: 0436-006: ch g Docksider - Quintellina   hd **61**
(Robellino) Chsd ldrs stands side till over 1f out: hcap scorer '03 in mdn company, subs h'cap plcd (rtd 74):
winning form at 5f, stays 6f well: acts on firm & fast grnd, sharp/undul or stiff trks: best without cheek pieces &
has gone well fresh. 1 Apr'03 Folk 5g/f 84- D:
1985* **CHEROKEE NATION** 13 [9]3-7-13 (57) J Quinn 6/1: 006-4417: Chsd ldrs far side till over 1f out: btr 1985. 3 **39**
1985 **SUSSEX STYLE** 13 [3]3-7-12 (6oh)T (50) D Kinsella 66/1: 0060608: Stands side & al rear: 'breathing prob'. ½ **36**
2042* **EMTILAAN** 10 [5]3-9-6 (78) R Hills 15/8 FAV: 023-2319: Dwelt, far side, trkd ldrs till over 2f   5 **44**
out, sn btn: hvly bckd: much btr 2042 (mdn, gall trk).
9 Ran   Time 1m 11.83 (0.83)   Owned: CSimpson ZMount TJLowe RMFlower   Trained: Jevington

2272 3.50 Rose & Crown Stelling Minnis Classified Stakes 3yo+ 0-70 (E)
£3494 £1075 £538   **7f str**   **Good/Firm 20**   -08 Slow   Stands Side

2016 **WATERSIDE** 12 [6] G L Moore 5-9-3 (68) R L Moore 100/30 FAV: 4-003031: Made all against far rail,   **76**
rdn & holding rivals ins last: prev with J Hills: suited by 6/7f on firm, soft & polytrack, prob any trk, likes a
sharp one: well suited by forcing tactics today: see 235.
1723 **BI POLAR** 25 [1] D R C Elsworth 4-9-6 (73) Dane O'Neill 5/1: 6020-002: b g Polar Falcon - Doctor   ¾ **77**
Bid (Spectacular Bid) Cl-up, rdn & ch dist, no extra ins last: mdn scorer '03, subs a h'cap rnr-up: unplcd '02
(rtd 83, mdn): best at 7f, tried 1m: acts on firm & fast grnd, stiff/gall or sharp/undul trk.

683

FOLKESTONE   MONDAY 07.06.04   Righthand, Sharpish, Undulating Track

2 Nov'03 Newm 7g/f 80-75 D: 1 Apr'03 Kemp 7fm 81-(78) D:
1983 **BERTOCELLI** 13 [7] G G Margarson 3-8-7 (70) A McCarthy 7/1: 0610-003: ch c Vettori - Dame Jude   1¾   70
(Dilum) Rdn & bhd early, kept on late, nvr factor: h'cap scorer '03: winning form at 7f, worth another try at 1m
on this evidence: acts on firm & fast grnd, stiff or sharp/undul trk: has run well fresh.
1 Oct'03 Leic 7.0fm 75-69 E:
4874} **SPRING JIM** 227 [3] J R Fanshawe 3-8-9 (72) O Urbina 4/1: 450-4: b g First Trump - Spring   hd   72
Sixpence (Dowsing) Slow away, sn in tch, onepace & held on over 1f out: op 3/1, reapp: lightly rcd & unplcd '03
(rtd 70, mdn): full brother to a useful sprinter Torosay Spring, dam 7f/12f wnr: styd longer 7f trip & shld get
further: acts on fast grnd, stiff or sharp/undul trk.
2045 **MANDARIN SPIRIT** 10 [4]4-9-5 bl (72) S Sanders 4/1: 1000-055. Tikd ldrs, btn over 1f out: boldt: see 2015.6   61
2085 **RECOUNT** 9 [2]4-9-8 (75) N Pollard 9/1: 1450-006: Chsd ldrs, struggling from halfway: dropped in trip.   4   57
613* **FIZZY LADY** 116 [5]3-8-4 t (67) R Miles(3) 12/1: 54-4417: Sn outpcd & bhd: abs: new yard: btr 613 (sell).   hd   48
27 Ran   Time 1m 26.18 (1.98)   Owned: Mr Nigel Shields   Trained: Brighton

2273   4.20 Ted Stannard Wedding Present Handicap Stakes 4yo+ 35-55 (F)   [60]
£3052 £872 £436   1m4f   Good/Firm 20   -42 Slow   Stands Side

1960 **CANTRIP** 14 [2] Miss B Sanders 4-8-13 (45) S Sanders 13/2: 60-00001: Led, ran wide on bend after   52
3f, sn chsd clr ldr & drvn to lead dist, styd on well for press: eff at 12/14f on firm & fast grnd, sharp/undul
trks: likes to race with/force the pace: see 1693.
1693 **SUMMER CHERRY** 26 [6] Jamie Poulton 7-8-9 t (41) P Doe 14/1: 40/503-02: b g Summer Squall -   1¼   46
Cherryrob (Roberto) Keen & prom & led after 4f, sn clr, hdd dist, no extra: left reapp bhd under a positive ride:
h'cap plcd '03 (rtd 49a): AW & turf amat h'cap wnr '02: suited to 10/12f on fast, gd & polytrack, handles gd/soft &
any trk, likes Lingfield: best in a t-strap & a gd weight carrier: has gone well fresh.
1 Sep'02 Hayd 10.5gd 53-47 E: 2 Aug'02 Ches 12.3g/f 48-48 E: 1 May'02 Ling 12ap 53a-50 E:
2 May'02 Brig 10g/s 50-45 F: 2 Feb'02 Ling 12ap 52a-51 F: 1 Nov'01 Ling 10ap 53a-49 F:
2 Apr'01 Ling 10ap 50a-44 E: 1 Feb'01 Ling 10ap 47a-43 E: 2 Jan'01 Ling 8ap 42a- D:
1342 **AMBERSONG** 44 [11] A W Carroll 6-8-9 (41) I Mongan 4/1 FAV: 0-330643: Pushed along rear, kept on   2½   42
late to take 3rd, nvr threat to front pair: 6 wk abs: see 342 & 75.
2054 **VANDENBERGHE** 10 [9] J A Osborne 5-9-2 (48) V Slattery 9/2: 635-1534: Mid-div, late gains, nvr   shd   49
threat to front pair: see 1657 (fibresand).
1967 **FREE STYLE** 14 [10]4-9-2 (48) N Chalmers(5) 5/1: 4552045: Mid-div, eff to chase ldrs 3f out, no impress.   shd   48
1940 **COOLFORE JADE** 15 [8]4-8-13 (45) R Miles(3) 14/1: 50500006: Chsd ldrs 4f out, btn over 1f out.   2½   41
1991 **CLASSICAL WALTZ** 13 [1]6-8-2 (4oh) N Mackay 25/1: 00/0-4307: Rear, only mod prog: see 1800. ¾   29
4859} **ABSINTHER** 228 [4]7-9-0 (46) G Baker 12/1: 144000-8: b g Presidium - Heavenly Queen (Scottish   nk   40
Reel) Rear & well bhd halfway, little hdwy: op 7/1, reapp: h'cap wnr '03, AW h'cap unplcd (rtd 40a): C/D h'cap
scorer '02: eff at 11/12f on fast, soft & fibresand: acts on any trk.
1 Jul'03 Wind 11.6g/f 50-48 E: 1 Aug'02 Folk 12g/f 51-46 E: 2 Aug'02 Brig 10g/f 57- E: 1 Aug'01 Folk 12gd 59-54 E:
2 Aug'01 Hayd 10.5sft 54-52 E: 2 Jul'01 Ling 11.4g/f 53-51 F: 2 Jan'01 Wolv 9.3af 58a- F: 2 Dec'00 Wolv 9.4af 57a-55 F:
1693 **GABOR** 26 [3]5-9-8 bl (54) R L Moore 7/1: 04500-09: Chsd ldrs, lost pl from 4f out, t.o.: op 4/1.   24   16
972} **ESTILO** 427 [7]4-8-2 (4oh) D Kinsella 66/1: 00/0000-0: 10th: Held up, wide on bend after 3f &   23   0
sn lost pl, t.o. 4f out: long abs.
757 **SILISTRA** 100 [5]5-9-4 (50) S W Kelly 50/1: 0000-000: 11th: Dsptd lead 4f, btn 3f out, t.o: jumps abs.   11   0
11 Ran   Time 2m 38.92 (7.42)   Owned: Mr A C Verdie   Trained: Epsom

2274   4.50 Come To Ladies Night On 5th August Median Auction Maiden Stakes 3-4yo (E)
£3601 £1108 £554   1m1f149y rnd   Good/Firm 20   -40 Slow   Stands Side

1762 **WHITSBURY CROSS** 23 [3] D R C Elsworth 3-8-8 (77) T Quinn 2/1 FAV: 0-551: Mid-div, rdn & outpcd   84
2f out, styd on for press to lead line, all out: eff at 1m/9.7f, 10f will suit: acts on fast & gd, any trk: see 1236.
1623 **MAHARAAT** 30 [1] Sir Michael Stoute 3-8-8 VIS t R Hills 4/1: 552: Sn cl-up & drvn/led 2f out, hdd   shd   83
line: op 5/2: gd run in first time visor: eff around 1m/9.7f on fast & gd grnd, prob handles soft: see 1623, 1166.
1904 **VAMP** 17 [4] R M Beckett 3-8-3 J Quinn 3/1: 023: Mid-div, styd on for press fnl 2f, not pace of   1   76
wnr cl-home: bckd, op 5/1: stays 9.7f, acts on firm & fast grnd: now qual for h'caps: see 1904.
1651 **ANTIGIOTTO** 28 [7] L M Cumani 3-8-8 N Mackay(3) 20/1: 0004: ch g Desert Story - Rofool (Fools   1½   78
Holme) Rear, outpcd 3f out, some late hdwy, nrst fin: imprvd eff on this fast grnd, stays a sharp 9.7f, rtn to 10f
will suit: clr of rem & interesting for h'caps.
1864 **APPETINA** 18 [13]3-8-4 (1ow) (75) M Fenton 4/1: 2303-55: Led/dsptd lead 7f, wknd: see 1864.   5   65
1021 **LAURENS GIRL** 66 [11]3-8-3 D R McCabe 66/1: 06: Keen in mid-div, no impress fnl 2f, 2 month abs.   1½   61
1581 **LUCKY AGAIN** 32 [5]3-8-8 G Carter 25/1: 047: Dwelt, rear, only mod late prog, nvr threat.   6   55
1961 **GREAT GIDDING** 14 [9]3-8-8 J F Egan 50/1: 038: Prom, btn 3f out: btr 1961 (12f).   1   53
1725 **MISS MERENDA** 24 [10]3-8-4 (1ow) P Doe 100/1: 009: Al bhd & no ch 4f out.   3   43
2092 **MISS ST ALBANS** 8 [12]3-8-5 (2ow) B Reilly 100/1: 0000: 10th: Prom, btn 3f out, modest form.   8   30
1580 **KILINDINI** 32 [6]3-8-8 S W Kelly 33/1: 6U: Reared start & u.r.   0
11 Ran   Time 2m 03.78(5.78)   Owned: McDowell Racing   Trained: Whitsbury

PONTEFRACT   MONDAY 07.06.04   Lefthand, Undulating Track, Stiff Uphill Finish

Official Going GOOD/FIRM (GOOD places).

2275   6.45 Enjoy The Craic Maiden Auction Stakes Fillies 2yo (E)
£4290 £1320 £660   6f rnd   Good/Firm 20   -36 Slow   Inside

2061 **EXTREME BEAUTY** 9 [5] C E Brittain 2-8-3 (1ow) E Ahern 4/1 FAV: 61: ch f Rahy - Mediation   75
(Caerleon) Nvr far away, led dist, rdn clr: bckd from 6/1: $15,000 Apr foal: dam a smart miler, sire a smart
miler on dirt: eff over 6f on fast grnd: much imprvd for debut.
2177 **CANARY DANCER** 4 [7] P C Haslam 2-8-4-6 G Faulkner 33/1: 042: Led till dist, kept on but not pace   3   65
of wnr: qck reapp: imprvd form on this rtn to 6f & fast grnd: see 2177.
1911 **WHATATODO** 16 [17] M L W Bell 2-8-2 J Mackay 18/1: 03: b f Compton Place - Emerald Dream   shd   63

(Vision) Prom, ev ch dist, not qckn ins fnl 1f: cheaply bght Apr foal: half-sister to a 7f wnr: sire a top-class sprinter: eff at 6f on fast grnd: far from disgraced from the widest draw.
1920 **SWEET MARGUERITE 16** [8] T D Easterby 2-8-4 D Allan(2) 9/1: 54: b f Diktat - Margaret's Gift *shd* **65**
(Beveled) Nvr far way, ev ch ent fnl 1f, no extra cl-home: Feb foal, cost 10,000gns: half-sister to a 5f winning juv: dam a sprint wnr, sire a top-class sprinter: eff at 6f on fast grnd: could find a small race.
FLAMAND [3]2-8-8 K Fallon 9/2: 5: ch f Miswaki - Sister Sorrow (Holy Bull) Dwelt, styd on *nk* **68**
under press fnl 1f, nrst fin on debut: E45,000 Mar foal: half-sister to a hdle wnr: dam unrcd, sire a top-class juv: with L Cumani & sure to learn plenty from this.
1677 **LORNA DUNE 26** [11]2-8-4 P Hanagan 5/1: 36: Rdn in mid-div, nvr nr ldrs: see 1677 (soft grnd). *1* **61**
TEQUILA SHEILA [1]2-8-2 C Catlin 14/1: 7: Rear, keeping on when hmpd ins fnl 1f on debut. *1* **56**
PATXARAN [14]2-8-2 Rory Moore(7) 33/1: 8: Nvr btr than mid-div on racecourse bow. *5* **41**
LARAS GIRL [15]2-8-2 G Duffield 25/1: 9: Dwelt, rdn in rear, nvr nr ldrs on debut. *1¼* **37**
1818 **LIVE IN HOPE 20** [10]2-8-2 J Fanning 100/1: 00: 10th: Prom 4f, wknd. *2* **31**
2056 **FIRST RHAPSODY 10** [6]2-8-4 (2ow) T Eaves 100/1: 00: 11th: Nvr nrr than mid-div. *1* **30**
2051 **KALIKA 10** [12]2-8-2 G Gibbons 66/1: 60: 12th: Slowly away, nvr a factor. *½* **27**
HARBOUR LEGEND [7]2-8-2 J Bramhill 18/1: 0: 13th: Slowly away, al bhd on debut. *nk* **26**
SCORPIO SALLY [9]2-8-2 P M Quinn 50/1: 0: 14th: Chsd ldrs 4f, wknd on debut. *shd* **26**
FRENCH KISSES [2]2-8-4 Dean McKeown 40/1: 0: 15th: Slowly away, al bhd on racecourse bow. *½* **27**
1744 **TRICKSHOT 24** [13]2-8-2 Dale Gibson 5/1: 20: 16th: Sn bhd, fin last: something clrly amiss? btr 1744. *½* **24**
16 Ran Time 1m 17.47 (3.37) Owned: Dr Ali Ridha Trained: Newmarket

2276

7.15 Tony Bethell Memorial Handicap Stakes 4yo+ 0-70 (E) **[71]**
£6971 £2145 £1073 **2m1f22y** **Good/Firm 20** **+07 Fast** Inside

1928 **STOOP TO CONQUER 16** [6] J L Dunlop 4-9-9 (66) K Fallon 15/2: 5356-001: Chsd ldrs, went on over **77**
2f out, rdn clr: op 5/1, best time of eve: first win, eff at 2m1f, acts on fast grnd: thorough stayer who in poss well h'capped & can follow up, see 1928.
2176 **TONI ALCALA 4** [2] R F Fisher 5-9-12 (68) L Fletcher(3) 12/1: 3161352: Mid-div, styd on under *5* **72**
press to take 2nd ins fnl 1f, no ch with wnr: qck reapp, jt top-weight: tough & genuine stayer, see 1905.
2085 **RIYADH 9** [5] M Johnston 6-9-12 vis (68) K Dalgleish 8/1: 0000303: Mid-div, hmpd after halfway, *1½* **70**
styd on under press fnl 2f, nrst fin: jt top-weight: thorough stayer, v well h'capped: see 1637.
2098] **HERNANDITA 723** [8] Miss E C Lavelle 6-9-8 (64) A Culhane 16/1: 1002/00/-4: b f Hernando - Dara *¾* **65**
Dee (Dara Monarch) Chsd ldrs, outpcd 4f out, rallied fnl 1f: 4th in a h'cap hdle 11 wk ago (rtd 103h, eff around 2m on gd & soft, has tried a visor): missed '03 on the Flat, lightly rcd & unplcd for M Pipe prev term: '01 class stks wnr (with J Dunlop, rtd 75): eff at 10/12f on gd/soft & hvy grnd, prob stays 2m1f on fast: sharper next time.
2 Oct'01 Bath 11.6g/s 75-72 D: 1 Apr'01 Nott 10hvy 75- D:
2198 **PRINCE OF THE WOOD 4** [9]4-8-8 p (51) P Makin(5) 12/1: 64-21405: Prom, outpcd 2f out: qck reapp. *½* **51**
2009 **RED SUN 12** [12]7-9-4 t (60) P Hanagan 3/1 FAV: 3/244-126: Keen & sn led, hdd 2f out, wknd: well bckd. *¾* **59**
2060 **KRISTINEAU 10** [11]6-8-5 t (47) P Mathers(4) 25/1: 20000//-57: Bhd, modest late gains: see 2060. *11* **36**
1629 **IL CAVALIERE 30** [1]9-9-6 (62) K Darley 16/1: 0000/4-58: Rear, nvr troubled ldrs: rnr-up in an *1¾* **49**
inter chase since 1629.
2156 **VANBRUGH 5** [7]4-8-8 t (51) Darren Williams 50/1: 0600009: Led early, rem prom, btn over 2f out. *1* **37**
1923 **VICARS DESTINY 16** [13]6-9-12 (68) L Vickers 14/1: 26-22000: 10th: Chsd ldrs, wknd 3f out. *¾* **53**
1870 **ACADEMY 18** [10]9-9-1 (57) C Catlin 7/2: 20240-20: 11th: Chsd ldrs, lost tch halfway, t.o.: well *25* **17**
bckd from 9/2 & something clrly amiss: much btr 1870.
1793 **Joely Green 21** [4]7-8-6 bl(48) E Ahern 12/1:0 1916 **So Vital 16** [3]4-9-6 (63) R Price 50/1:0
13 Ran Time 3m 42.55 (2.25) Owned: I H Stewart-Brown & M J Meacock Trained: Arundel

2277

7.45 Toteplacepot Handicap Stakes 3yo 0-80 (D) **[87]**
£6955 £2140 £1070 **1m2f6y** **Good/Firm 20** **-01 Slow** Inside

1882 **ADAIKALI 17** [2] Sir Michael Stoute 3-9-6 (79) K Fallon 9/4 FAV: 0-021: Chsd ldrs, prog to lead **88**
ent fnl 1f, styd on strongly, drvn out: well bckd, first success: apprec this step up to 10f, acts on fast grnd & prob polytrack: lightly rcd & progressive colt, see 1182.
1040 **ILE FACILE 65** [9] N P Littmoden 3-8-8 T (67) E Ahern 50/1: 2424102: Mid-div, styd on well under *1¼* **73**
press fnl 1f, not quite reach wnr: tried a t-strap, 9 wk abs & has been gelded: acts on fast grnd: stayed this longer 10f trip, see 706 (AW mdn auct).
1785 **MEADAAF 22** [10] A C Stewart 3-9-6 (79) K Darley 4/1: 045-123: Chsd ldrs, styd on under press fnl *nk* **84**
1.5f, not btn far: bckd from 11/2: another consistent run, see 1785 & 1369.
2153 **CHARMATIC 5** [5] J A Glover 3-8-6 (65) Dean McKeown 12/1: 0-522154: Prom, led 2f out till ent fnl *½* **69**
1f, no extra: nicely bck tho' op 8/1, clr rem, qck reapp: longer 10f trip, prev btr on soft & hvy as in 1628.
1894* **TANNOOR 17** [12]3-9-7 (80) P Robinson 6/1: 033-315: Keen & led till 2f out, wknd: top-weight. *6* **75**
1834 **GAIETY GIRL 20** [11]3-8-5 (64) D Allan(3) 50/1: 4430-06: b f Swain - Knoosh (Storm Bird) Slow *1¼* **57**
away, late gains, nvr dngrs: plcd on 1 of 4 '03 starts (mdn auct, rtd 70): eff at 7f on firm grnd: with T Easterby.
1359 **HATCH A PLAN 44** [1]3-8-7 (66) G Duffield 40/1: 000-0U7: b g Vettori - Fast Chick (Henbit) Nvr *¾* **58**
btr than mid-div: 6 wk abs: unplcd on all 3 juv starts: longer 10f trip today.
2079 **ROYAL DISTANT 9** [13]3-8-13 (72) Dale Gibson 50/1: 24-60008: Rear in rear, nvr a factor. *1* **62**
2040 **MOUNT VETTORE 10** [7]3-9-5 (78) K McEvoy 10/1: 5-120009: Held up, nvr dngrs. *shd* **68**
955 **ALPINE SPECIAL 72** [6]3-8-12 (71) G Faulkner 20/1: 03210-60: 10th: gr g Orpen - Halomix (Linamix) *1½* **59**
Al rear after 10 wk abs: '03 mdn auct wnr, also plcd sev times: eff at 1m on fast & firm, handles any trk.
1 Sep'03 Muss 8g/f 74-(71) E: 2 Aug'03 Newm 8fm 74-70 C: 2 Jun'03 Donc 6fm 70- E:
1832 **VIBE 20** [4]3-9-1 (74) J Fanning 10/1: U0040: 11th: Prom, wknd qckly 3f out, t.o. *12* **47**
1864 **AL SHUUA 18** [8]3-9-6 (79) B Doyle 7/1: 36-20: 12th: Chsd ldrs 1m, wknd qckly: much btr 1864. *6* **43**
12 Ran Time 2m 10.27 (2.17) Owned: HH Aga Khan Trained: Newmarket

2278

8.15 Listed Weatherbys Bank Pipalong Stakes Fillies 4yo+ (A)
£20300 £7700 £3850   **1m4y rnd**   **Good/Firm 20**   **+05 Fast**   Inside

4681} **CHORIST 240** [7] W J Haggas 5-9-2 (111) K Fallon 4/7 FAV: 211013-1: ch f Pivotal - Choir Mistress   **115**
(Chief Singer) Made just about all, clr fnl 1f, readily, val 3L+: gd time, hvly bckd, reapp under top-weight: won
a List & 2 Gr 3's in '03: eff at 1m, suited to 10f, has tried 12f: acts on firm & gd/soft, handles soft: likes a
stiff/gall trk, runs well fresh: smart, tough & genuine, as good as ever.
1 Sep'03 Curr 10g/f 111-: 1 Jul'03 Chep 10.2g/s 108-(104) A: 1 Jun'03 Newc 10.1gd 106-(104) A:
2 May'03 York 10.4fm 106-(104) A. 2 Sep'02 Curr 10g/f 100-. 1 Aug'02 Bali 0.0g/f 107 A:
1 Jul'02 Newm 10g/f 98-89 B: 2 Jun'02 Asco 8gd 95-84 A: 1 Jun'02 Newb 8sft 87- D:

1833 **ICE PALACE 20** [1] J R Fanshawe 4-8-11 (94) E Ahern 5/2: 31140-32: Trkd ldrs, went after wnr fnl   1¼   **101**
1f, sn no impress: clr rem: far from disgraced at today's weight, met a smart rival: see 1833.

1812 **QUIET STORM 20** [5] G Wragg 4-8-11 (96) K Darley 18/1: 1324-003: b f Desert Prince - Hertford   5   **91**
Castle (Reference Point) Trkd ldrs, ev 2f out, wknd fnl 1f: '03 h'cap & class stks wnr, also rnr-up sev times:
eff at 1m/10f, prob stays a stiff 12f: acts on fast, gd/soft & polytrk: handles a stiff/gall or sharp trk: better
off in h'caps. 2 Aug'03 Sali 9.9g/f 100-(85) A: 1 Jun'03 Sali 9.9g/f 85-(84) C: 2 May'03 Nott 8.2g/s 86-(85) C:
1 Apr'03 Ling 7ap 79a-74 E: 2 Nov'02 Ling 6ap 74a- D:

1863 **COTE QUEST 18** [8] S C Williams 4-8-11 (92) P Robinson 18/1: 13-40044: Rear, nvr nr to chall.   ½   **90**
2027 **SCOTLAND THE BRAVE 11** [4]4-8-11 (67) K McEvoy 66/1: 4050-035: Led early, remained prom 6f, wknd. 5   **80$**
1927* **ENCHANTED PRINCESS 16** [3]4-8-11 bl (74) A Culhane 16/1: 01-0516: Held up, nvr troubled ldrs: ¾   **78**
highly tried: btr 1927 (h'cap, offic rtd 67, first time blnks).
2038 **TRANSCENDANTALE 10** [6]6-8-11 (47) C Catlin 20/1: 0-235607: Al rear, fin last: stiff task.   1¼   **75$**
7 Ran   Time 1m 43.03 (1.23)   Owned: Cheveley Park Stud   Trained: Newmarket

2279

8.45 Emerald Isle Classified Stakes 3yo+ 0-65 (E)
£4134 £1272 £636   **5f rnd**   **Good/Firm 20**   **-11 Slow**   Inside

1886 **TOMMY SMITH 17** [2] J S Wainwright 6-9-5 bl (67) Darren Williams 7/1: 30-00001: Made all, rdn over   **75**
1f out & kept on well, eased nr line: op 9/2: best at 5/6f, loves firm & fast grnd: won this race 2 years ago:
able to dominate today & back to form: see 1765.

1532 **SHOLTO 34** [1] J O'Reilly 6-9-3 bl (59) J D O'Reilly(7) 6/1: 66000-02: b g Tragic Role - Rose Mill   1½   **66**
(Puissance) Rcd in 2nd, asked for eff over 1f out, no impress on wnr: won a h'cap & a class stks in '03:
eff at 5/6f on firm & soft, acts on any trk: goes well fresh: eff blnkd, has tried a t-strap.
1 Jun'03 Pont 5g/f 68-(64) E: 1 Apr'03 Warw 5fm 65-56 E: 1 Aug'02 Catt 5g/f 54-52 F: 2 Aug'01 Redc 6g/f 55- F:
1 Aug'01 Nott 6sft 54-45 F:

1873 **KARMINSKEY PARK 18** [11] T J Etherington 5-9-0 (62) J Fanning 5/1: 40-62653: In tch, hdwy 2f out,   ¾   **60**
styd on ins fnl 1f but no pace to reach 1st 2: see 1532 & 1276.
1638 **FAR NOTE 30** [5] S R Bowring 6-9-3 bl (65) J Bramhill 5/1: 4610144: In tch, hdwy 2f out, no   nk   **62**
impress ins fnl 1f: see 1638 & 1442.
2084 **ONLINE INVESTOR 9** [8]5-9-7 (69) Alex Greaves 4/1 FAV: 0052055: Bhd, hdwy over 2f out, no impress   ¾   **63**
ins fnl 1f: top weight: see 1523.
1627 **MYND 30** [9]4-9-3 (65) Dean McKeown 7/1: 2021006: Handy, no impress fnl 1f: op 10/1: see 1179.   2   **53**
1555 **LAUREL DAWN 34** [13]6-9-3 (49) Natalia Gemelova(7) 40/1: 103-0007: Nvr btr than mid-div: btr 187.   2½   **46**
719 **BLUE MAEVE 104** [12]4-9-3 (27) G Duffield 100/1: 06-40408: Handy, fdd over 1f out: long abs.   hd   **46$**
1465 **SUGAR CUBE TREAT 38** [10]8-9-0 (31) S Righton 100/1: 0-000509: b f Lugana Beach - Fair Eleanor   shd   **43$**
(Saritamer) Bhd, nvr a factor: lightly rcd & mod form recent seasons: eff at 6/7f on fast, likes gd/soft & soft,
sharp or stiff trk: has tried cheek pieces.
2027 **JOHN OGROATS 11** [4]6-9-3 (62) F Lynch 20/1: 0-000000: 10th: Al bhd: see 2027.   1½   **42**
1774 **SMIRFYS NIGHT 23** [6]5-9-3 (58) K Dalgleish 50/1: 21005/-00: 11th: b g Tina's Pet - Nightmare   shd   **42**
Lady (Celestial Storm) Chsd ldrs, wknd over 1f out: missed '03: mdn scorer in '02 (with B McMahon): eff at 5/6f
on firm, gd/soft & a gall trk: lightly rcd 5yo. 1 Jun'02 Donc 5g/f 76- D: 2 May'02 Hayd 6g/s 63-60 E:
1682* **TATWEER 26** [7]4-9-3 vis (60) K Fallon 9/1: 5000-510: 12th: Bhd, btn when eased ins fnl 1f.   5   **27**
1824 **DARK CHAMPION 20** [3]4-9-3 (62) P Hanagan 33/1: 0465300: 13th: Saddle slipped & al bhnd, t.o.   dist   **0**
13 Ran   Time 1m 02.89 (1.59)   Owned: Mr T W Heseltine   Trained: Malton

2280

9.15 Shamrock And Leprechaun Handicap Stakes 3yo+ 0-75 (E)
£4290 £1320 £660   **6f rnd**   **Good/Firm 20**   **-07 Slow**   Inside   **[75]**

2086 **ALBASHOOSH 9** [3] D Nicholls 6-9-2 (63) Alex Greaves 7/1: 006-6561: Handy, hdwy to lead over 1f   **75**
out, kept on well ins fnl 1f, eased nr line: wng form at 6/7f, stays 1m: acts on firm & soft, likes a gall trk,
handles a stiff/undul one: apprec return to 6f & back to a wng mark.
1877 **BLUE PATRICK 18** [2] J M P Eustace 4-10-0 P (75) J Tate 20/1: 600-0002: gr g Wizard King - Great   2½   **76**
Intent (Aragon) In tch, hdwy over 1f out, styd on well ins fnl 1f to go 2nd fnr line: not btn far under top weight:
won a clmg stks in '03: won 1st '02 start (mdn): eff at 6f, stays a stiff 1m: acts on fast, handles firm: prob
handles any trk: has run well ungeared: occ fitted of cheek pieces.
1 Jul'03 Asco 8g/f 89-(88) D: 1 Aug'02 Yarm 8g/f 89- D:
2161 **FLYING TACKLE 5** [6] M Dods 6-8-2 p (49) C Catlin 33/1: 003-0003: Chsd ldrs, ev ch 1f out, no   1   **47**
impress ins fnl 1f: qck reapp: see 2161.
1638 **MIDNIGHT PARKES 30** [5] E J Alston 5-9-5 (66) K Darley 10/1: 04500-04: br g Polar Falcon -   1   **61**
Summerhill Spruce (Windjammer) Handy, led 2f out, sn hdd, sn no impress: plcd once in '03 (h'cap, rtd 73, with M
Jarvis): h'cap & mdn scorer in '02: best at 6f, acts on firm & fast, prob not easy grnd, stiff/undul or sharp trks:
has tried blnks & cheek pieces. 1 Jun'02 Ripo 6g/f 81-73 C: 1 May'02 Pont 6g/f 82- D:
2059 **BOLLIN EDWARD 10** [11]5-9-0 (61) D Allan(3) 3/1 FAV: 00000-65: Mid-div, hdwy over 2f out, no   hd   **56**
iimpress ins fnl 1f: see 2059.
1897* **DOWNLAND 17** [10]8-8-9 (56) Kim Tinkler 7/1: 000-0216: In tch, some late gains but not dangerous: nk   **50**
fin clr of rem: just btr 1897.
2063 **CAPTAIN DARLING 9** [12]4-9-1 vis (62) E Ahern 9/1: 6020057: In tch, not pace to chall: op 14/1.   3   **47**
1886 **LOUGHLORIEN 17** [9]5-8-6 (53) P Hanagan 16/1: 50006-08: Mid-div, wknd fnl 1f: see 1886.   hd   **38**
2059 **MARSHALLSPARK 10** [4]5-9-3 (64) G Parkin 16/1: 1600-009: Al bhd: see 1749.   hd   **49**
1638 **PALANZO 30** [15]6-9-6 (67) L Treadwell(7) 9/1: 0000-500: 10th: Nvr a factor: tchd 14/1: see 1476.   2   **46**

PONTEFRACT MONDAY 07.06.04 Lefthand, Undulating Track, Stiff Uphill Finish

2007 **LINDENS LADY 12** [8]4-9-6 (67) J Fanning 25/1: 4405-060: 11th: b f Compton Place - Jubilee Place **2 40**
(Prince Sabo) Led to 2f out, sn no extra: rnr-up 2 of 13 '03 starts (both class stks): won a nurs & an auct mdn in
'02: eff at 5/6f, tried 7f: acts on firm & gd/soft, stiff, undul or easy trks: has tried a visor.
2 Jul'03 Wind 6g/f 78-(79) D: 2 Jun'03 Kemp 6fm 81-(78) D: 1 Oct'02 Pont 6fm 80-70 E: 1 Aug'02 Newc 6gd 70- F:
2 Jul'02 Yarm 6fm 62- G:
2023 **LONG WEEKEND 12** [7]6-7-12 vis (45) B Swarbrick(5) 18/1: 1460600: 12th: Al bhd. **2 12**
1508 **SMIRFYS PARTY 36** [13]6-8-7 (54) J Bramhill 33/1: 00106-00: 13th: Al bhd. **2½ 14**
1837* **Cleveland Way 19** [17]4-8-1 vis(48) D Fentiman(7) 33/1:**2**057 **No Grouse 10** [14]4-9-11 (72) T Hamilton(3) 12/1:0
15 Ran Time 1m 15.75(1.65) Owned: Mr M J Pipe Trained: Thirsk

CHESTER TUESDAY 08.06.04 Lefthand, Very Tight Track

Official Going GOOD/FIRM.

2281 6.20 Kemira Grow How E B F Maiden Stakes 2yo (D)
£5343 £1644 £822 5f16y rnd Good 60 -25 Slow Inside

1818 **DORN DANCER 21** [1] D W Barker 2-8-9 L Enstone(3) 16/1: 01: b f Danehill Dancer - Appledorn **85**
(Doulab) Cl-up, led over 2f out, styd on well, shade cosily, val 2L: March foal, cost E12,000: half-sister to wnrs
over 7f/1m: dam 6/7f scorer: eff over a sharp 5f on gd: imprvd from debut & took advantage of plum draw.
1531 **HARVEST WARRIOR 35** [4] T D Easterby 2-9-0 D Allan(3) 8/13 FAV: 22: Led till over 2f out, short **½ 84**
of room & outpcd over 1f out, rallied for press ins last, just held: hvly bckd: acts on gd & hvy grnd: going the
right way & can certainly find similar: see 1531.
1880 **GIFTED GAMBLE 18** [8] K A Ryan 2-9-0 bl N Callan 3/1: 0333: With ldr, chall over 1f out, no extra **2½ 77**
ins last: plcd again, gd effort from mod draw: see 1880, 1586.
CUTLASS GAUDY [2] R Hollinshead 2-9-0 Stephanie Hollinshead(5) 25/1: 4: br c Nomination - **2½ 70**
Cutlass Princess (Cutlass) Slow away & bhd, some late gains, no dngr on debut: May foal, half-brother to sprint
wnrs: speedily bred & shld learn plenty from this.
MENNA [9]2-8-9 E Ahern 25/1: 5: b f Mark of Esteem - Pounelta (Tachypous) In tch, lost place **2½ 63$**
over 2f out, modest late gains: March foal, cost E36,000: half-sister to a 7f wnr: dam 7f juv scorer.
1920 **GLORIA NIMBUS 17** [3]2-8-9 S Righton 100/1: 006: Keen in tch, wknd over 1f out. **½ 61**
OCEANICO DOT COM [6]2-8-9 F Norton 20/1: 7: In tch, wknd well over 1f out on debut. **½ 59**
MADAME TOPFLIGHT [5]2-8-9 G Duffield 10/1: 8: In tch, wknd over 1f out on debut. **1 56**
DOUGHTY [7]2-9-0 V Slattery 66/1: 9: Slow away & al bhd on debut. **15 31**
9 Ran Time 1m 04.04 (4.24) Owned: The Ebor Partnership Trained: Richmond

2282 6.50 Park Travel Rated Stakes Handicap 3yo+ 0-95 (C) **[96]**
£8720 £3308 £1654 7f2y rnd Good 60 +11 Fast Inside

1970 **H HARRISON 15** [1] I W McInnes 4-8-8 (76) R Ffrench 15/2: 3-064541: Led early, cl-up, led again **86**
over 2f out, styd on well fnl 1f, rdn out: suited by a sharp 7f on firm & gd, acts on gd/soft: tough, see 1122.
2093 **BANDIT QUEEN 9** [8] W Jarvis 4-9-4 (86) P Robinson 16/1: 6500-342: Held up, eff & short of room **2½ 90**
over 2f out, kept on over 1f out, nrst fin: stays a sharp 7f well: gd run from mod draw: see 2093.
2070 **TRUE NIGHT 10** [4] D Nicholls 7-8-9 (77) E Ahern 7/4 FAV: 0000423: Chsd ldrs, rdn 2f out, kept on **hd 80**
late, no threat to wnr: hvly bckd: likes this trk & h'capped to win, tho' tends to go off at v short prices.
2186 **ONLYTIME WILL TELL 5** [2] D Nicholls 6-9-11 (93) R Winston 16/1: 500-0054: In tch, eff to chase **1 94**
wnr over 1f out till ins last, no extra: see 888.
2057 **UP TEMPO 11** [7]6-8-8 bl (76) N Callan 22/1: 1142005: Bhd, hdwy & short of room over 2f out, late **hd 76**
hdwy: short of room sev times & this must be forgiven.
2090* **MASTER ROBBIE 9** [3]5-9-9 (3ex) (91) S Hitchcott(3) 4/1: 0-000016: Held up, hdwy & short of room **2½ 86**
over 2f out, wknd ins last: v tough, prefers racing prominently on gall trks: see 2090, 1926.
2007 **VAL DE MAAL 13** [5]4-8-8 (7oh) (69) Dean Williams(7) 50/1: 240-3047: Led till over 2f out, wknd. **1 69**
2076 **FLYING EXPRESS 10** [9]4-9-3 (85) M Hills 4/1: 644-6028: In tch, wknd 2f out: poor draw. **5 68**
1925 **DAME DE NOCHE 17** [6]4-9-6 (88) G Duffield 9/1: 300-6039: Cl-up, wknd 2f out: needs to lead. **2 67**
9 Ran Time 1m 28.47 (3.47) Owned: Ivy House Racing Trained: Catwick

2283 7.20 Ernst & Young Classified Stakes 3yo 0-75 (D)
£5421 £1668 £824 1m2f75y Good 60 -11 Slow Outside

1429 **DAYTIME GIRL 41** [4] B W Hills 3-8-12 (76) M Hills 5/1: 51-351: Made virtually all, kept on well **79**
fnl 1f, rdn out: 6 wk abs: right back to form with forcing tactics on this sounder surface: eff at 1m, stays 10.3f
well on gd & fast grnd, gall or sharp trks: lightly rcd & improving: see 1192.
1924 **MAGIC AMIGO 17** [3] J R Jenkins 3-9-0 (71) E Ahern 20/1: 420-2102: In tch, eff to chase wnr 3f **2 77**
out, onepace fnl 1f: stays 10.4f: imprvd run, see 1580, 1321.
1885 **TURNER 18** [2] W M Brisbourne 3-9-0 (73) G Duffield 40/1: 360-63: Held up, short of room 3f out **2½ 73**
till over 2f out, kept on ins last, nvr dngrs: shade closer with a clr run & stays 10.4f on fast & gd: see 1885.
1515 **PENZANCE 36** [5] J R Fanshawe 3-9-3 (78) J Murtagh 7/2 JT FAV: 13-64: Chsd ldrs, onepace over 1f **½ 75**
out: not disgraced, may do btr: see 1515.
1865 **MOMMKIN 19** [6]3-8-12 (76) S Hitchcott(3) 17/2: 425-55: Held up, btn 2f out: see 1865. **½ 69**
2040 **WEET A HEAD 11** [8]3-9-4 (79) N Callan 11/2: 5356346: In tch, wknd well over 2f out: see 2040 (1m), 1104. **8 63**
1791 **KRISTALS DREAM 22** [4]3-8-11 (74) K Darley 7/2 JT FAV: 6031-357: Handy, wknd 2f out: btr 1369. **5 49**
1784* **YAAHOMM 23** [7]3-9-4 (79) T P Queally(3) 9/2: 318: Al bhd: much btr 1784 (mdn). **½ 55**
8 Ran Time 2m 15.94 (7.44) Owned: Bonnycastle Concord Racing Morton Trained: Lambourn

---

2284　　7.50 Bank Of Scotland Handicap Stakes 3yo+ 0-80　(D)　　　　　　　　　　　[80]
　　　　　　£5538　£1704　£852　　**1m2f75y**　　**Good 60**　　**-12 Slow**　Inside

1828　**FRONTIER 21** [5] B J Llewellyn 7-9-3 t (69) D Sweeney　9/2 JT FAV: 60000-21: Trkd ldrs till lost　　76
place 4f out, hdwy & switched to lead over 1f out, all out to hold on: eff at 10f, poss stays 11.5f on fm & soft.
2162　**COMPTON DRAGON 6** [3] D Nicholls 5-9-7 vis (73) A Nicholls　11/2: 0050522: Mid-div, drvn & styd on　shd　79
well ins last, just failed: gd run: see 2162, 1884 & 1519.
2067　**SUMMER BOUNTY 10** [8] F Jordan 8-9-10 (76) J Murtagh 20/1: 50-01103: Dwelt & held up, hdwy when　1　80
hmpd dist, switched & kept on onepace: back to form: tough, clr rem: see 1777 & 1505.
1980　**TROUBLE MOUNTAIN 14** [2] M W Easterby 7-9-4 bl (70) K Darley 6/1: 3335243: Held up, no room dist,　3　69+
switched & kept on: much closer with a clr run: see 1821, 1164 & 196.
731　**GALLANT BOY 104** [9]5-9-8 vis t (74) F P Ferris(3) 16/1: 0-004005: Held up, no room over 2f out,　1½　70
kept on onepace ins last: imprvd eff after 3 mth abs, visor reapplied: on a fair mark: see 549.
2162*　**ROTUMA 6** [12]5-9-2 (6ex)bl (68) L Enstone(3) 12/1: 4-050316: Mid-div, carried left dist, no extra.　½　64
1916　**EZZ ELKHEIL 17** [13]5-9-4 (70) T P Queally(3) 25/1: 2430007: Led till 4f out, btn/no room dist.　1　64
1823　**NEWCORP LAD 21** [4]4-9-0 (66) G Duffield 50/1: 126-0408: Prom when stumbled 4f out, btn when　5　53
short of room over 1f out: see 1397.
1781　**EVEREST 23** [1]7-10-0 (80) F Norton 10/1: 000-0009: Held up, nvr a factor: see 928.　nk　66
1972　**SKIBEREEN 15** [10]4-9-3 (69) R Ffrench 16/1: 6450350: 10th: Held up, rdn & btn 2f out: btr 1972.　3　51
4476}　**RANI TWO 255** [7]5-9-8 (74) N Chalmers(5) 14/1: 060410-0: 11th: b f Wolfhound - Donya (Mill Reef)　3　52
Mid-div, rdn & btn 2f out: reapp: progressive '03, landed 3 h'caps & a class stks: fills mdn scorer '02, h'cap
plcd (rtd 58): suited by 9/10f on firm & gd grnd, prob handles gd/soft, any trk.
1 Sep'03 Ayr 10g/f 74-69 C: 1 Jun'03 Wind 10.0gd 71-(65) E: 1 Jun'03 Hami 9.2gd 65-60 E:
2 Jun'03 Nott 10.0g/f 68-60 D: 1 Jun'03 Ches 10.3g/f 62-55 D: 1 Jul'02 Ches 7.5fm 56- D:
1884　**LAWOOD 18** [11]4-9-9 (75) N Callan 14/1: 0-401240: 12th: Trkd ldrs, wknd dist: much btr 1226.　½　52
2135　**MOVIE KING 7** [6]5-8-13 p (65) D Holland　9/2 JT FAV: 450-0020: 13th: Rcd keenly, dsptd lead till　¾　41
went on 4f out, hdd over 1f out & sn btn/hmpd, eased: unable to gain uncontested lead as in 2135.
13 Ran　Time 2m 16.04 (7.54)　Owned: Mr F Jeffers　Trained: Bargoed

---

2285　　8.20 Edwards Homes & Bryn Thomas Handicap Stakes　Lady Amateur Riders 3yo+ 0-75　(E)　　　[60]
　　　　　　£3523　£1084　£542　　**1m4f66y**　　**Good 60**　　**-35 Slow**　Inside

2088*　**SHAPE UP 9** [7] T Keddy 4-9-7 (3ex)bl (53) Miss Lynsey Hanna　5/2 FAV: 40-32411: Sn trkd front pair　　64
& smooth hdwy to lead over 1f out, sn strongly pressed & hdd ins last, rdn & rallied to lead on line: eff at 10f,
well suited by 12f on firm, stiff & polytrack, sharp or stiff/gall trk: in fine form, see 2088.
1755*　**YENALED 24** [6] K A Ryan 7-10-3 (63) Miss N Carberry 5/1: 0045112: Rdn & hdwy 2f out & led ins　shd　73
last, just held line: clr rem: in fine form, given a strong ride & this rider looks worth following in these races.
467　**DICK THE TAXI 137** [11] R J Smith 10-10-7 (67) Miss E J Jones 8/1: 52132-33: Led till over 1f　5　70
out, not pace of front pair: recently p.u. in a h'cap chase: see 467.
2030　**LENNEL 12** [9] A Bailey 6-10-4 p (64) Miss J Ellis(5) 14/1: 4-504004: Slow away & bhd, kept on　shd　67
late, nrst fin: cheek pieces reapplied: see 1388 & 1128.
4664}　**SUALDA 243** [14]5-9-13 (59) Miss V Tunnicliffe(5) 14/1: 150500-5: b g Idris - Winning Heart　1　60
(Horage)　Trkd ldrs till lost place over 2f out, late rally, no dngr on reapp: h'cap scorer '03, subs disapp in
blnks: landed 3 h'caps in '02 for C Cox: eff at 1m, prob suited by 10/12f on firm & gd grnd, sharp/turning or gall
trk: slipped to a handy mark. 1 Jul'03 Donc 12gd 68-64 D: 1 Jun'02 Redc 11fm 74-70 D:
1 May'02 Redc 10fm 72-66 E: 1 May'02 Warw 8.1fm 67-60 F: 2 Sep'01 Nott 8.2gd 78- E:
2085　**RAJAM 10** [10]6-11-0 vis (74) Miss Kelly Harrison(3) 12/1: 0601306: Mid-div, eff 3f out, no extra dist.　hd　75
2220　**RAINSTORM 4** [5]9-8-12 (44) Miss S Owen(3) 16/1: 400-6567: Dwelt & bhd, kept on late, no dngr.　4　39
2226　**SARN 4** [1]5-8-10 (1oh) (41) Miss M Mullineaux(6) 16/1: 0-040048: Held up, mod prog, nvr a threat.　hd　36
2088　**SHALBEBLUE 9** [4]7-9-4 bl (50) Miss L Ellison(3) 20/1: 50325-09: b g Shalford - Alberjas (Sure　1¾　41
Blade)　Mid-div, eff 3f out, sn no impress: amat rider's h'cap scorer '03, plcd numerous times, AW unplcd (rtd 44a,
h'cap): unplcd '02 (rtd 51a, no turf form, h'caps): eff btwn 9/12f on firm, fast & fibresand, stiff or sharp trk:
suited by blnks. 2 Sep'03 Carl 11.9fm 51-47 F: 2 Jul'03 Pont 10.0g/f 46-42 F:
1 Jun'03 Muss 12g/f 43-37 F: 2 Jun'03 Ripo 12.3g/f 40-37 F: 1 Jan'01 Sout 11af 55a- F:
1828　**ADALAR 21** [13]4-10-3 (63) Miss E Folkes(3) 50/1: 0006000: 10th: Prom, btn over 1f out.　5　47
1960　**SUMMER SPECIAL 15** [2]4-9-1 (47) Miss C Williams 9/1: 0-553050: 11th: Mid-div, eff 3f out, btn dist.　4　25
2008　**GRADY 13** [8]5-8-10 (4oh) (38) Miss A Elsey 33/1: 0600-660: 12th: Mid-div, strug fnl 2f: btr 2008.　hd　19
4702}　**Honeystreet 240** [3]4-9-9 (55) Miss S Brotherton 16/1:0
2130　**Fleetfoot Mac 7** [12]3-9-4 (65) Miss M Sowerby(5) 12/1:0
14 Ran　Time 2m 48.22 (11.82)　Owned: Mr Andrew Duffield　Trained: Newmarket

---

2286　　8.50 Saffie Joseph & Sons Rated Stakes Handicap 3yo+ 0-85　(D)　　　　　　　　　[84]
　　　　　　£4904　£1860　£930　　**5f16y rnd**　　**Good 60**　　**-14 Slow**　Inside

1627　**AWAKE 31** [3] D Nicholls 7-9-0 (70) E Ahern　4/1 JT FAV: 00-06501: Sn trkd ldrs trav well, led　　82
over 1f out, rdn clr: eff at 5/6f on firm & hvy, any trk: well h'capped, win again: see 1251.
2187　**ROMANY NIGHTS 5** [10] J W Unett 4-9-8 bl (78) S Hitchcott(3) 11/1: 0434222: Held up, rdn & styd on　2½　81
well from over 1f out, nvr threatened wnr: gd run from awkward wide draw: eff at 5/6f, deserves similar.
2187　**PRINCE OF BLUES 5** [9] M Mullineaux 6-8-6 p (62) P Varley(7) 25/1: 0450033: Mid-div, rdn & styd on　nk　64
fnl 2f, not able to chall: gd run from awkward draw, on a long losing run but well h'capped: see 453.
2070　**DOMIRATI 10** [4] R Charlton 4-9-8 (78) R Winston 5/1: 02234-04: b g Emarati - Julia Domna　nk　79+
(Dominion)　Trkd ldrs, no room & lost place over 1f out, switched left & kept on cl-home: prob plcd with a clr run:
AW h'cap scorer '03, subs thrice rnr-up in turf h'caps: AW mdn scorer on debut late '02: eff at 5/6f on firm, fast
& both AWs, stiff or sharp/turning trk: proved v consistent last term, keep in mind. 2 Sep'03 Sand 5.0g/f 80-76 D:
2 Aug'03 Sand 5.0g/f 76-76 D: 2 May'03 Ches 6.1fm 77-75 C: 1 Apr'03 Ling 5ap 78a-70 D: 1 Nov'02 Wolv 6af 66a- F:
2195　**MELODY KING 5** [1]3-8-3 (2oh)bl (66) F P Ferris(3) 11/2: 140-0325: Led/dsptd lead till over 1f out,　nk　66
no extra: qck reapp: best draw, see 2195.
3971}　**PERFECT SETTING 283** [5]4-8-10 (66) D Sweeney 28/1: 2/4000-6: b g Polish Precedent - Diamond Park　1　63
(Alzao)　Held up, eff 2f out, no impress on reapp: lightly rcd & unplcd '03 (rtd 74, mdn, disapp in blnks, h'cap):
rnr-up on sole '02 start (mdn): eff at 5f on fast grnd, 6f may suit: can force the pace & handles a stiff trk.

CHESTER   TUESDAY 08.06.04   Lefthand, Very Tight Track

2 Sep'02 Sand 5g/f 83- D:
2189* **WHISTLER 5** [6]7-9-8 (3ex)p (78) R Ffrench 4/1 JT FAV: 0003017: Held up, nvr land a blow: btr 2189.   ¾   73
2084 **OBE ONE 10** [11]4-8-13 (69) F Norton 16/1: 0-000648: Dwelt, short of rm ins last, nvr threat: poor draw.   ½   62
2189 **WICKED UNCLE 5** [2]5-9-6 P (76) K Darley 7/1: 02320-09: Cl-up/dsptd lead till over 1f out, sn btn.   2½   62
1627 **PICCLED 31** [7]6-9-7 (77) D Allan(3) 20/1: 00-03000: 10th: Slow away & al bhd, lost ch start: btr 927.   nk   62
1917 **CHICO GUAPO 17** [8]4-9-5 (75) I Mongan 12/1: 0010500: 11th: Cl-up wide till over 1f out: loves   8   36
to front run but poorly drawn for such tactics tonight, forgive this: see 1476 & 692.
11 Ran   Time 1m 03.51(3.71)   Owned: Lucayan Stud & D Nicholls   Trained: Thirsk

SALISBURY   TUESDAY 08.06.04   Righthand, Galloping Track, Stiff Finish

Official Going GOOD/FIRM (FIRM places).

2287   2.15 Eddie Reavey Maiden Auction Stakes 2yo (E)
£3731 £1148 £574   6f str   Firm 18   -18 Slow   Centre

2178 **EVANESCE 5** [8] M R Channon 2-8-2 C Catlin 5/1: 224221: Made just about all, kept on gamely,   79
all-out: qck reapp & most deserved win after numerous rnr-up placings: eff at 5/6f on firm, gd/soft & polytrack:
handles a stiff/gall or sharp trk, likes to force the pace: most consistent, see 2178 & 931.
   POLAR DAWN [9] B R Millman 2-8-2 A McCarthy 33/1: 2: b f Polar Falcon - Leave At Dawn (Slip   shd   78+
Anchor) Mid-div, prog 2f out, fin strongly under hands & heels riding & just failed in a thrilling fin: debut:
2,500gns April foal: half-sister to 1m scorer Nassau Night: eff over a stiff/gall 6f on fm, 7f sure to suit: plenty
to like about this kind debut, improve & win sn.
2188 **CALY DANCER 5** [10] D R C Elsworth 2-8-10 T Quinn 3/1 FAV: 0533: Chsd ldrs, went after wnr 2f   2   80
out, no impress ins fnl 1f: nicely bckd, qck reapp: not disgraced conceding 8lb to front 2, stays a stiff/gall 6f.
1911 **MISSED A BEAT 17** [14] M Blanshard 2-8-2 J Mackay 9/2: 04: b f Mister Baileys - Lonely Heart   2½   65
(Midyan) Chsd ldrs, onepcd fnl 1f: March foal, cost 9,000gns: half-sister to 7f wnr Leitrim House & miler Ace Of
Hearts: dam a 10f wnr, sire a top-class miler: shld apprec 7f given time, handles firm grnd.
   HES A DIAMOND [8]2-9-0 R Miles(3) 4/1: 5: ch c Vettori - Azira (Arazi) Slowly away, styd on   3½   67
late, nvr dngrs on debut: Feb first foal, cost 25,000gns as a 2yo: sire a v smart miler: attracted mkt support &
some encouragement here, sure to learn from this.
920 **PENNESTAMP 75** [7]2-8-7 R Havlin 20/1: 06: b c Pennekamp - Sopran Marida (Darshaan) Chsd ldrs,   2½   53
rdn & onepcd fnl 2f: 11 wk abs: E12,000 Jan foal: half-brother to a 6f juv wnr: dam a wnr abroad.
   KINGSGATE BAY [11]2-9-0 N Pollard 33/1: 7: Slow away, nvr dngrs on racecourse bow.   1   57
   MABELLA [2]2-8-5 S Carson 20/1: 8: Keen in rear, ran v green, nvr a factor: s/mate 2nd.   nk   47
1987 **ZOLASH 14** [5]2-8-7 J D Smith 9/1: 59: Slowly away, al bhd.   2½   42
   BEE STINGER [1]2-8-7 S W Kelly 25/1: 0: 10th: Prom wide, wknd over 1f out on debut.   1¼   38
1727 **DAVALA 25** [13]2-8-7 A Daly 100/1: 00: 11th: Al bhd.   1   35
2020 **SECRET DIVA 13** [4]2-8-2 J F McDonald(3) 80/1: 00: 12th: Al rear.   1   27
1717 **ATSOS 26** [3]2-9-0 R Hughes 7/1: 660: 13th: Front rank till halfway, wknd & eased: fin last,   nk   38
tchd 12/1: much btr expected, with R Hannon.
13 Ran   Time 1m 14.26 (2.16)   Owned: Dave and Gill Hedley   Trained: West Ilsley

2288   2.45 Numerica Claiming Stakes For Amateur Riders 3yo+ (F)
£3627 £1116 £558   6f212y str   Firm 18   -33 Slow   Centre

1804 **SHIRLEY OAKS 22** [4] Miss Z C Davison 6-10-9 (43) Miss G D Gracey Davison(7) 14/1: 0231631: Trkd   54
ldrs, rdn to lead ins fnl 1f, going away: eff at 6f/1m on firm, gd/soft grnd & polytrack: handles a stiff/gall or
sharp trk: runs well for an amat: career best run today, see 1075 (AW banded).
1804 **MY GIRL PEARL 22** [2] M S Saunders 4-10-6 (50) Mr L Tibbatts(3) 14/1: 400-0242: Trkd ldrs, went on   1¼   47
over 2f out, collared ins fnl 1f & no extra cl-home: op 20/1: mdn after 24: see 1565 (AW banded).
2133 **MR BELVEDERE 7** [10] R Hannon 3-10-2 P (65) Mr J J Best(5) 15/2: 030-0003: b g Royal Applause -   nk   52
Alarming Motown (Warning) Early ldr, remained prom, kept on fnl 1f: plcd in a nov auct & a h'cap in '03, has since
been gelded: eff at 6/7f on firm & gd/soft grnd: has tried blnks/visor, tried in cheek pieces today & does not look
a straightforward ride. 2 Jun'03 Wknd 6g/f 72- E:
2220 **PASO DOBLE 4** [7] B R Millman 6-11-7 (57) Mr J Millman(7) 6/1: 0262054: Rear, late hdwy, nrst fin.   1½   58
1536 **WOOD FERN 35** [5]4-11-2 (62) Mr M Walford(5) 11/2 FAV: 01-00005: Chsd ldrs, onepcd fnl 1f: op   1   51
7/1: has been gelded since 1536, see 263 (AW mdn).
1748 **CLANN A COUGAR 25** [12]4-10-13 (60) Mr G Bartley(7) 6/1: 04-00606: Rdn in rear, hdwy, nvr dngrs.   hd   48
1966 **CITY GENERAL 15** [8]3-10-2 p (53) Mrs S Moore(3) 7/1: 0-334357: Led till 2f out, wknd: see 1938.   7   32
1984 **MAC THE KNIFE 14** [3]3-10-2 (70) Mr L Newnes(3) 8/1: 420-0008: Rdn in rear, nvr dngrs: see 1984.   2   28
2258 **MUTABARI 2** [6]10-10-11 (35) Mr John Evans(7) 25/1: 0-000009: Slowly away, al bhd: qck reapp.   shd   27
1650 **CHEVRONNE 29** [1]4-11-0 P (68) Mr L Jefford 13/2: 30350-00: 10th: b g Compton Place - Maria   1½   27
Isabella (Young Generation) Slowly away, sn prom, btn 2f out: tried cheek pieces, has prev worn blnks: '03 mdn
plcd (rtd 76 & 66a): eff at 1m on gd, fast grnd & polytrack: with L Cottrell.
1720 **THE FOOTBALLRESULT 26** [11]3-9-13 (54) Miss E J Jones 20/1: 060-0050: 11th: Chsd ldrs to halfway.   ½   21
1989 **FREDERICK JAMES 14** [9]10-11-0 (31) Mr James White(3) 66/1: 4000//-000: 12th: Al bhd, fin last.   1¼   23
12 Ran   Time 1m 20.09 (3.59)   Owned: The Secret Circle   Trained: East Grinstead

2289   3.15 South West Racing Experience Stakes Handicap 3yo+ 0-90 (C)   [89]
£8793 £3335 £1668   6f str   Firm 18   +06 Fast   Centre

2111* **CAUSTIC WIT 8** [4] M S Saunders 6-8-5 (6ex)p (66) R Miles(3) 8/1: 30-10111: Qckly away & made just   82
about all, clr fnl 1f, readily: gd time: eff at 5f, all wins at 6f: acts on firm, soft & f/sand: suited by cheek
pieces: has now won 4 of last 5 starts, clearly thriving & wng run may not yet be at an end: see 2111 & 384.
2093 **COMPLICATION 9** [6] J A R Toller 4-8-2 bl (63) Lisa Jones(3) 12/1: 2000-062: Prom, went after wnr   2   70
fnl 1f, no impress cl-home: op 16/1: caught an in-form rival, see 1726.
2070 **NAJEEBON 10** [2] M R Channon 5-9-8 (83) T E Durcan 8/1: 450-0003: Waited with, styd on fnl 1f,   2½   83
nrst fin: fairly h'capped & this was a btr run than of late: see 1489.

2084 **PARKSIDE PURSUIT 10** [9] J M Bradley 6-8-10 (71) R L Moore 4/1 FAV: 00-01104: Rear, hdwy 2f out, onepcd fnl 1f: nicely bckd: see 2029 (5f). *nk* **70**
2070 **THURLESTONE ROCK 10** [10]4-9-2 (77) J F McDonald(3) 13/2: 21001-05: Front rank, btn fnl 1f. *nk* **75**
2093 **SPARKLING JEWEL 9** [12]4-9-2 (77) Dane O'Neill 8/1: 2/31-06: Front rank 4.5f, wknd: see 2093. *¾* **72**
1914 **FORMALISE 17** [3]4-8-4 (65) S Carson 25/1: 05060-07: Rdn in rear, modest late prog: see 1914. *hd* **60**
2023 **CORANGLAIS 13** [11]4-8-4 (65) C Catlin 14/1: 050-0008: Rear, some late gains. *hd* **60**
2070 **GAELIC PRINCESS 10** [8]4-9-7 (82) S Whitworth 20/1: 30-00609: Chsd ldrs 4.5f, wknd. *¾* **74**
2070 **HEY PRESTO 10** [7]4-8-11 (72) R Smith 15/2: 60040-00: 10th: Keen & chsd ldrs, btn dist: see 2070. *hd* **64**
5030*}**TAHIRAH 207** [1]4-10-0 (89) S Sanders 11/1: 040110-0: 11th: b f Green Desert - Kismah (Machiavellian) Rear, short of room 2f out, nvr dngrs on reapp: top-weight: fills mdn & dual h'cap wnr in '03: eff at 7f/1m on gd, fast grnd & any trk, likes Doncaster: sharper next time & a return to 7f will suit. *2½* **74**
1 Nov'03 Donc 7gd 91-82 E: 1 Oct'03 Donc 7g/f 88-75 E: 1 Jun'03 Brig 8.0g/f 77- D: 2 Jun'03 Hayd 7.1g/f 77- D:
1042 **THE BEST YET 66** [5]6-8-9 (70) D Corby(3) 8/1: 3022-400: 12th: Dwelt, keen rear, al bhd: 10 wk abs. *5* **40**
12 Ran Time 1m 12.86 (0.76) Owned: Mrs Sandra Jones Trained: Wells

2290

3.45 E B F Margadale Classified Stakes 3yo 0-85 (C)
£10645 £3777 £1889 **1m1f198y** **Firm 18** **+03 Fast** Inside

4978} **MANGO MISCHIEF 220** [4] J L Dunlop 3-8-11 (85) R Hughes 9/1: 10-1: ch f Desert King - Eurolink Mischief (Be My Chief) Held up, smooth hdwy over 1f out, led well ins fnl 1f, rdn to assert: op 6/1, fair time, reapp: won first of 2 juv starts (fills mdn): half-sister to useful wnrs over 1m/10f: apprec this step up to 10f, acts on fast & fm: likes a stiff/undul trk, esp Salisbury & runs v well fresh: lightly rcd, open to improvement. **91**
1 Aug'03 Sali 7.0g/f 86- D:
1865 **CAMROSE 19** [2] J L Dunlop 3-9-0 (85) T Quinn 9/4: 4321-432: Tried to make all, kept on well fnl 1f, just btn by longer priced stablemate: well clr rem: consistent: see 1865. *nk* **92**
2040+**PENRITH 11** [3] M Johnston 3-9-5 (90) J Fanning 4/7 FAV: 1-13: Trkd ldr, ev ch halfway till 3f out, sn wknd: hvly bckd: longer 10f trip, reportedly returned lame: see 2040. *13* **77**
2196 **GELLER 5** [1] R Hannon 3-9-0 (83) R L Moore 25/1: 2204-54: Chsd ldrs 7f, sn wknd: qck reapp. *2½* **69**
4 Ran Time 2m 06.08 (1.58) Owned: Antoniades Family Trained: Arundel

2291

4.15 Champagne Duval-Leroy Maiden Stakes 3yo (D)
£6078 £1870 £935 **6f212y str** **Firm 18** **+06 Fast** Centre

CAMBERWELL [10] T G Mills 3-9-0 R Miles(3) 12/1: 1: b g Royal Applause - Into Orbit (Safawan) Rcd in 2nd, led appr fnl 3f, clr over 1f out, cmftbly on debut: op 9/1, gd time: cost E30,000: stays 7f, shld get further: acts on firm & a stiff/gall trk: runs v well fresh: fine start, win more races. **86**
2072 **HUNTERS VALLEY 10** [11] R Hannon 3-8-9 (78) P Dobbs 15/8 FAV: 0523-02: b f Nicolotte - Down The Valley (Kampala) Led till over 3f out, no ch with wnr ins fnl 1f: tchd 9/4: plcd on 2 of 4 '03 starts (mdns): eff at 7f on fast & firm grnd: capable of better. 2 Sep'03 Kemp 7g/f 82- D: *8* **67**
1912 **PURE IMAGINATION 17** [7] J M Bradley 3-9-0 R L Moore 40/1: 63: Mid-div, hdwy to dspt 2nd 2f out, wknd ins fnl 1f: see 1912. *2½* **66**
1722 **BAHAMA BELLE 26** [1] H S Howe 3-8-9 (57) D Kinsella 16/1: 0000-04: b f Bahamian Bounty - Barque Bleue (Steinlen) Chsd ldrs, keen, onepcd over 2f out: mdn unplcd in '03 (rtd 71). *¾* **57**
TROMP [6]3-9-0 S Sanders 9/1: 5: Rear, modest late gains on debut: tchd 12/1. *2* **60**
1864 **COLLADA 19** [13]3-8-9 R Havlin 25/1: 006: Chsd ldrs, wknd 2f out. *nk* **54**
BENNY BATHWICK [3]3-9-0 S Drowne 25/1: 7: Handy, wknd 2f out on debut. *½* **58**
1912 **ILTRAVITORE 17** [4]3-9-0 T Quinn 14/1: 08: Rear, modest late gains: has been gelded. *1¾* **54**
1829 **CALLED UP 21** [9]3-9-0 Dane O'Neill 11/4: 409: In tch, nvr nr ldrs. *2½* **49**
1762 **SOLIPSIST 24** [5]3-9-0 R Hughes 6/1: 00: 10th: Chsd ldrs, fdd 2f out: op 8/1. *2½* **44**
1846 **Dulcimer 20** [8]3-8-9 R Thomas(5) 50/1:0
2066 **Crimson Star 10** [14]3-8-9 C Catlin 50/1:0
3217} **Tartiruga 316** [12]3-9-0 S Carson 100/1:0
1089 **Summer Joy 62** [2]3-8-9 M Howard(4) 66/1:0
14 Ran Time 1m 26.38 (0.88) Owned: Welcocks Skips Ltd Waste Management Trained: Epsom

2292

4.45 Knights & Co Handicap Stakes 3yo 35-55 (F) **[59]**
£3744 £1152 £576 **6f212y str** **Firm 18** **-21 Slow** Centre

1529 **ACCENDERE 36** [3] R M Beckett 3-9-7 (52) S Sanders 12/1: 00501: b g Machiavellian - Littlewick (Green Desert) Rear, hdwy 3f out, styd on strongly ins fnl 1f to lead nr line: op 9/1, 1st win: unplcd all earlier mdn & sole h'cap start: eff at 7f on firm, acts on stiff/gall trk: lightly rcd, imprvd here for a drop back to 7f. **59**
1529 **TURNBERRY 36** [13] J W Hills 3-9-10 vis (55) T Quinn 7/2 FAV: 04-43622: Trkd ldrs, hdwy to lead ins fnl 3f, styd on ins fnl 1f but hdd nr line: op 13/2: handles firm, soft & both AWs: running well, see 1529. *nk* **61**
2024 **KNICKYKNACKIENOO 13** [9] A G Newcombe 3-9-10 (55) S Whitworth 9/1: 60-42203: Bhd, hdwy 3f out, onepcd ins fnl 1f: handles firm & soft: see 1085 & 871. *1¼* **58**
1940 **EVEN EASIER 16** [2] G L Moore 3-9-10 BL (55) R L Moore 8/1: 6-005064: Rear, hdwy over 1f out, styd on ins fnl 1f but no ch with ldrs: handles firm & fast: tried blnks: see 603. *1¼* **55**
1985 **YAMATO PINK 14** [10]3-9-7 (52) G Baker 8/1: 660-0125: Sn handy, wknd fnl 1f: see 1985 & 1453. *2½* **47**
1740 **DAVIDS GIRL 25** [15]3-8-9 (40) J Mackay 33/1: 6005-566: Rear, hdwy 2f out, not pace to chall. *¾* **33**
1985 **I WISH I KNEW 14** [5]3-9-0 VIS (45) Dane O'Neill 33/1: 000-6007: br g Petong - Hoh Dancer (Indian Ridge) Led till ins fnl 3f, sn no extra: tried a visor: mod in '03 (rtd 68a, mdns, nov stks, with P Makin). *hd* **38**
1963 **CHARLIEISMYDARLING 15** [16]3-9-6 (51) R Hughes 8/1: 40560-48: Bhd, hdwy 2f out, sn switched left, kept on but not pace of ldrs: poss not stay this 7f: see 1963. *½* **43**
1549* **PERERIN 35** [19]3-9-3 (48) S W Kelly 12/1: 000-019: Chsd ldrs, not much room 3f out, wknd over 1f out: just btr 1549 (banded). *shd* **40**
1947 **JOHNNY ALLJAYS 15** [11]3-8-11 BL (42) J D Smith 50/1: 0000-000: 10th: Rear, switched left over 2f out, nvr dngrs: first time blnks: see 1947. *nk* **33**
2136 **CHASE THE RAINBOW 7** [14]3-9-10 (55) J Fanning 25/1: 02-66060: 11th: Handy, not much room & no impress over 1f out: now with Miss K George: see 87. *½* **45**
2064 **SHARPLAW DESTINY 10** [8]3-9-5 BL (50) J F McDonald(3) 20/1: 004-500: 12th: Nvr a factor: blnks. *1¼* **37**
1147 **DALIDA 57** [12]3-9-5 (50) N Pollard 9/2: 00-U550: 13th: ch f Pursuit of Love - Debutante Days *½* **36**

SALISBURY TUESDAY 08.06.04 Righthand, Galloping Track, Stiff Finish

(Dominion) Handy, wknd 2f out: op 11/2, 8 wk abs: unplcd both '03 starts (mdns, rtd 61): with P Haslam.
1985 **JAOLINS 14** [7]3-8-13 (44) S Drowne 25/1: 0050000: 14th: Handy, wknd over 2f out. *hd* **30**
2049 **Kedross 11** [17]3-9-10 BL(55) C Catlin 33/1:0
1904 **Harry Came Home 18** [1]3-8-4 (35) A McCarthy 80/1:0
1497 **Miss Tilly 37** [18]3-9-1 (46) R Thomas(5) 66/1:0
2205 **Son Of Rembrandt 4** [4]3-9-10 (55) M Howard(7) 20/1:0
18 Ran Time 1m 28.27 (2.77) Owned: AWA Partnership Trained: Lambourn

2293

5.15 Alan Blencowe Motor Racing Handicap Stakes 4yo+ 0-70 (E) **[70]**
£3523 £1084 £542 **1m4f** **Firm 18** **-29 Slow** Stands Side

1940 **PRIVATE BENJAMIN 16** [2] Jamie Poulton 4-8-7 (49) P Doe 7/1: 0106301: In tch, hdwy over 2f out, **54**
led well ins fnl 1f, drvn out: eff at 10/12f on firm, fast & polytrack, prob any trk: back to form, see 672.
1180 **GIKO 36** [10] Jane Southcombe 10-7-12 (2oh) (38) Lisa Jones(3) 33/1: 0306062: Handy, led well over *½* **43**
1f out, hdd well ins fnl 1f & no extra: gd eff from 2lb out of the h'cap & up from banded grade: see 707.
2114 **ANYHOW 8** [9] Miss K M George 7-9-6 (62) J Fanning 9/2 JT FAV: 4542153: Midfield, hdwy 2f out, *nk* **64**
not clr run appr fnl 1f, kept on well ins fnl 1f & btn under 1L: ran to winning form of 1789.
1967 **MOST SAUCY 15** [11] I A Wood 8-9-3 (59) S W Kelly 5/1: 0-665034: Rear, hdwy 2f out, styd on ins *¾* **59**
fnl 1f, nrst fin: op 7/1: see 1286.
1986 **REMINISCENT 14** [8]5-9-2 vis (58) S Carson 5/1: 522-4245: Rear, hdwy 3f out, kept on: see 56. *1¼* **56**
1219} **AFRICAN DAWN 407** [4]6-8-11 t (53) L Keniry(3) 14/1: U2//4022-6: b g Spectrum - Lamu Lady (Lomond) *½* **50**
Chsd ldrs, wknd fnl 1f: reapp: rnr-up fnl 2 '03 starts (clmr & sell, with N Littmoden & P Webber): mdn scorer in
'02 (J Gosden): suited by 12/14f on both AWs & firm, likes a sharp trk: tried a t-strap: now with L Cottrell.
2 Apr'03 Wolv 12af 60a-(60) F: 2 Apr'03 Ling 13ap 52a-(65) G: 2 Dec'01 Sout 14af 66a-64 F: 1 Nov'01 Ling 12ap 66a- D:
1736 **TRAVELLERS TALE 25** [6]5-9-10 (66) D Kinsella 16/1: 34-00607: Led till dist, no extra: see 249. *½* **62**
2099 **AONINCH 8** [5]4-9-0 (56) S Whitworth 9/2 JT FAV: 3-605068: Rear, hdwy 3f out, wknd fnl 1f: see 801. *½* **51**
72 **TOP TREES 200** [3]6-8-4 (46) J Mackay 33/1: 2/50010-9: b g Charnwood Forest - Low Line (High *2* **38**
Line) Rcd in 2nd, chall 5f out, lost place 3f out, drpd reins 2f out & wknd: reapp: won a mdn h'cap in '03:
rnr-up in a h'cap in '02: eff at 9/13f on fast & fibresand: likes a sharp trk: with W Kittow.
1 Sep'03 Bath 13.1g/f 47-43 E: 2 Dec'02 Wolv 12af 58a-57 F:
2156 **SAXE COBURG 6** [1]7-9-6 (62) J F McDonald(3) 8/1: 0-510330: 10th: Bhd, hdwy 5f out, onepcd when *hd* **54**
not much room 2f out, btn & eased fnl 1f: qck reapp: see 2156.
1019 **ENCHANTED OCEAN 68** [7]5-9-4 (60) R Havlin 16/1: 40//-00: 11th: b f Royal Academy - Ocean Jewel *1¼* **50**
(Alleged) In tch, wknd 3f out: 10 wk abs: missed '03 & '02: 4th on '01 reapp (mdn, rtd 73, M Johnston).
11 Ran Time 2m 38.09(5.69) Owned: Mrs J Wotherspoon Trained: Lewes

REDCAR TUESDAY 08.06.04 Lefthand, Flat, Galloping Track

Official Going Firm (Good/Firm Places) ALL TIME SLOW

2294

2.30 Magnum Selling Stakes 2yo (G)
£2947 £842 £421 **7f str** **Firm** **V Slow** Centre

1445 **MAUREENS LOUGH 40** [4] T D Barron 2-8-6 P Fessey 3/1: 361: Made all, drvn & al holding rivals **59**
fnl 2f: bght in for 5,800gns, first win: 6 wk abs, v slow time: apprec step up to 7f, acts on firm grnd, handles
soft: apprec drop to sell grade: btr 1224.
1880 **DANS HEIR 18** [2] P C Haslam 2-8-11 P G Faulkner 9/4 FAV: 02: b g Dansili - Million Heiress *1½* **60**
(Auction Ring) Trkd wnr, drvn & kept on, al held by wnr: nicely bckd, op 11/4: clr of rem: imprvd eff in first
time cheek pieces: cheaply bght Jan foal, half-brother to prolific 7f+ wnr Colway Ritz: stays 7f on fm.
2194 **JOE NINETY 5** [5] J S Moore 2-8-11 Derek Nolan(7) 7/2: 56003: ch g Daggers Drawn - Sea Idol *5* **51**
(Astronef) Trkd ldrs, no impress on front pair over 1f out: qck reapp: op 11/4: 12,000gns March foal.
1779 **RIVERWELD 23** [6] G M Moore 2-8-11 F Lynch 4/1: 64: Prom, no impress fnl 2f: op 11/2. *hd* **50**
1779 **SINGHALONGTASVEER 23** [1]2-8-11 J Bramhill 33/1: 05: Prom, btn over 1f out, longer trip. *¾* **49**
1974 **HIGHBURY LASS 14** [7]2-8-6 Rory Moore(7) 20/1: 06: Dwelt & al rear, no ch fnl 2f. *9* **28**
1974 **MICKEY BOGGITT 14** [3]2-8-11 F Norton 14/1: 07: Rdn & sn bhd, no ch fnl 2f. *7* **21**
7 Ran Time 1m 26.72 (4.92) Owned: Oghill House Stud Trained: Thirsk

2295

3.00 East Cleveland Advertiser Handicap Stakes 3yo 0-70 (E) **[75]**
£3936 £1211 £606 **7f str** **Firm** **Slow** Centre

1872 **DARK DAY BLUES 19** [2] M D Hammond 3-9-2 (63) Darren Williams 20/1: 230-0001: ch c Night Shift - **68**
Tavildara (Kahyasi) Mid-div, rdn & hdwy to lead 2f out, drvn out: first win: h'cap rnr-up in '03 for R Hannon:
eff at 6/7f on firm & gd/soft grnd, gall or sharp/undul trk. 2 Sep'03 Hayd 6g/s 74-70 D: 2 Aug'03 Hayd 6g/f 72- E:
1829 **ADORATA 21** [6] J Jay 3-9-2 (63) O Urbina 7/1: 00032: Trkd ldrs, rdn & kept on fnl 2f, not pace *1¼* **65**
of wnr: h'cap bow, imprvd eff: eff at 6/7f, 1m may suit: acts on firm & fast grnd, stiff/gall trks.
1956 **WASHBROOK 15** [4] Andrew Turnell 3-8-11 (58) J Carroll 22/1: 0640-003: Rear, keen early, hdwy to *nk* **59**
press front pair when hmpd dist, kept on ins last: wld have gone close with a clr run : eff over a gall 7f, return
to 1m may suit: handles firm grnd: see 1956.
1834 **ORION EXPRESS 21** [12] M W Easterby 3-9-1 (62) P Mulrennan(5) 6/1 JT FAV: 00-66004: Dwelt & held *hd* **62**
up, eff to press ldrs over 1f out, sn onepace: handles firm & gd/soft grnd: see 1163.
2081 **MENAI STRAIGHTS 10** [3]3-8-13 P (60) F Norton 8/1: 53-60635: Prom, rdn & no extra over 1f out: *½* **59**
bckd: first time cheek pieces: handles firm & gd/soft grnd but just btr 2081 (mdn).
2218 **COMPTON MICKY 4** [15]3-8-11 p (58) J Edmunds 20/1: 0-06056: ch c Compton Place - Nunthorpe *½* **56**
(Mystiko) Keen & trkd ldrs, onepace fnl 2f: qck reapp: unplcd sole '03 start (rtd 36, mdn): prob eff around a
gall 7f on firm grnd: only btn around 3L today.
2055 **UHURU PEAK 11** [7]3-8-10 (57) Dale Gibson 16/1: 30507: Cl-up till over 1f out. *1* **53**
1142 **TOP LINE DANCER 57** [8]3-9-7 (68) K Dalgleish 6/1 JT FAV: 54-408: Mid-div, not able to chall: op 10/1. *shd* **64**
1745 **SWEET CANDO 25** [9]3-9-1 (62) P Hanagan 7/1: 10334-69: Prom, fdd under press fnl 2f. *1½* **55**
1395 **KILLOCH PLACE 43** [14]3-7-12 (3oh)vis (42) B Swarbrick(5) 20/1: 500-0000: 10th: Led/dsptd lead 5f: abs. *½* **37**

1930 **HANA DEE 17** [13]3-9-1 (62) A Culhane 9/1: 30-00600: 11th: Dwelt, sn rdn & towards rear, nvr a factor. 4 46
1896 **COLLOSEUM 18** [11]3-8-12 (59) K McEvoy 9/1: 56-040: 12th: Led/dsptd lead till halfway, sn btn. 3½ 36
1949 **Lupine Howl 15** [1]3-8-1 (48) S Righton 25/1:0   4230} **Speed Racer 267** [5]3-9-1 (62) Kim Tinkler 33/1:0
14 Ran   Time 1m 25.20 (3.4)   Owned: Mr Mike Newbould   Trained: Middleham

---

2296   3.30 Anderson Barrowcliff Handicap Stakes Fillies 3yo+ 0-70 (E)   [70]
£4277 £1316 £658   1m str   Firm   Slow   Centre

2149 **BRILLIANTRIO 6** [6] M C Chapman 6-8-9 (51) P Makin(5) 7/1: 06U3621: Dwelt, held up, smooth hdwy to 59
lead 2f out, rdn & sn in command, decisively. eff at 7f/1m, stays 10fl aets on firm, gd/soft & fibresand
2108 **OH SO ROSIE 8** [3] J S Moore 4-9-2 (58) Derek Nolan(7) 6/1: 0-433032: Rear, eff to chase wnr dist, 2½ 60
kept on but al held: op 5/1: gd run: see 2108 & 1020.
4360} **WESTCOURT DREAM 262** [11] M W Easterby 4-8-4 (46) Dale Gibson 5/1: 0333-3: ch f Bal Harbour - 1¾ 44
Katie's Kitty (Noble Patriarch) Chsd ldrs, outpcd 3f out, styd on late for press to snatch 3rd line: bckd, op 13/2,
reapp: h'cap & auct mdn plcd in '03 (rtd 47 at best): eff at 7f, stays a gall 1m well & further shld suit: handles
firm & gd/soft grnd, sharp/turning or gall trks: encouraging return.
2108 **SUMMER SHADES 8** [9] W M Brisbourne 6-9-13 (69) B Swarbrick(5) 5/2 FAV: 620-6524: Trkd ldrs trav shd 67
well & led over 2f out, hdd over 1f out & sn no extra: nicely bckd tho' op 2/1: see 2108 & 1322.
1841 **DALRIATH 20** [12]5-7-12 (1oh) (39) C Haddon(7) 9/1: 6642125: Keen & trkd ldrs trav well, shaken up 2 34
& onepace fnl 2f: turf return: see 1593 (AW banded).
1821 **UNO MENTE 21** [2]5-8-13 (55) Kim Tinkler 14/1: 350-0006: Trkd ldrs, outpcd fnl 3f: see 1602. 1½ 46
2010 **AIMEES DELIGHT 13** [8]4-10-0 (70) M Fenton 10/1: 0-006007: Dwelt & towards rear, little hdwy: op 8/1. 1¼ 58
1660 **CELTIC ROMANCE 29** [4]5-8-7 (49) J Carroll 12/1: 00-00058: Dwelt & held up, eff 3f out, btn dist. hd 36
1943 **MISS OCEAN MONARCH 15** [1]4-7-12 (40) D Fentiman(7) 14/1: 0-000029: Led till over 2f out, sn btn. 1½ 24
1976 **ACCA LARENTIA 14** [5]3-7-13 (52) Hayley Turner(5) 33/1: 0062-00: 10th: gr f Titus Livius - Daisy nk 35
Grey (Nordance) Prom till 3f out: clmr rnr-up in '03, lightly rcd: eff over a gall 7f, 1m may suit: handles fast
grnd. 2 Oct'03 Redc 7g/f 54-(53) F:
2120 **CRYPTOGAM 7** [10]4-8-5 (47) T Eaves(2) 66/1: 40-00000: 11th: Prom, btn 3f out: see 678. 6 20
11 Ran   Time 1m 37.27 (2.47)   Owned: Mr Jack Wilson   Trained: Market Rasen

---

2297   4.00 Methuselah Median Auction Maiden Stakes 2yo (E)
£3660 £1126 £563   6f str   Firm   Slow   Centre

1738 **LINCOLNEUROCRUISER 25** [4] J O'Reilly 2-9-0   J D O'Reilly(7) 12/1: 5231: Made all, rdn & stumbled 85
over 1f out, held on gamely ins last: eff at 5/6f: handles soft grnd, clearly relished firm conditions today:
likes a stiff & uphill trk: enjoyed front running & genuine: see 1738 & 1424.
     GOLDEN LEGACY 0 [8] R A Fahey 2-8-9   P Hanagan 14/1: 2: b f Rossini - Dissidentia (Dancing nk 79+
Dissident) Dwelt, sn pushed along trkg ldrs when no room 2f out till over 1f out, strong run ins last, just failed:
op 25/1: April foal, half-sister to a sprint wnr abroad, dam a multiple 5f wnr abroad: eff at 6f, 7f shld suit:
acts on firm grnd & a gall trk: rcd green, but a wnr here with a clr run, one to note in similar.
1887 **BEAUTIFUL MOVER 18** [13] J W Hills 2-8-9   D Holland 4/6 FAV: 23: Keen & trkd ldrs, ch dist, no 1¼ 75
extra: well bckd at odds-on: better on gd grnd in 1887 (debut, gd).
1950 **ENGLISH FELLOW 15** [14] B A McMahon 2-9-0   G Gibbons 14/1: 344: Handy, rdn & no extra from dist: ¾ 78
stays 6f: see 1950 & 1739.
     KAGGAMAGIC 0 [7]2-9-0   Darren Williams 100/1: 5: ch g Abou Zouz - Meadmore Magic (Mansingh) 2½ 70
Mid-div, rdn & onepace fnl 2f: cheaply bght April foal, half-brother to a dual 1m juv wnr, dam a dual 5f.
2100 **JUN FAN 8** [11]2-9-0   K McEvoy 14/1: 56: Trkd ldrs trav well, no extra from dist: see 2100 (5f). nk 69
     ROYAL PARDON 0 [6]2-8-9   I Mongan 20/1: 7: b f Royal Applause - Miss Mercy (Law Society) Chsd 3 55
ldrs till outpcd halfway, no impress after: op 16/1: Feb foal, half-sister to 5/6f juv wnrs, dam a 6f juv wnr.
1987 **DESERT BUZZ 14** [3]2-9-0   T Hamilton(3) 50/1: 068: Prom, btn over 1f out: btr 1987 (gd). 1 57
     TAKHMIN 0 [5]2-9-0   R Hills 5/1: 9: Sn prom, rdn & outpcd from halfway: bckd. 1½ 52
1631 **VISION VICTORY 31** [12]2-9-0   Dale Gibson 10/1: 400: 10th: Al bhd & outpcd: btr 1274 (soft). hd 51
     MISTER BUZZ 0 [2]2-9-0   A Culhane 100/1: 0: 11th: Bhd, nvr a factor. ¾ 49
     SPEAGLE 0 [1]2-9-0   J Carroll 100/1: 0: 12th: Dwelt & sn outpcd. ½ 47
     JESSICAS STYLE 0 [9]2-8-9   M Fenton 25/1: 0: 13th: Prom 4f, sn lost place. 1¼ 38
1880 **COUNTRYWIDE DREAM 18** [10]2-9-0   F Lynch 100/1: 00: 14th: Slow away & al bhd. 9 18
14 Ran   Time 1m 11.65 (2.75)   Owned: Peter Smith P C Coaches Limited   Trained: Barnsley

---

2298   4.30 Half Bottle Claiming Stakes 4yo+ (F)
£3262 £932 £466   2m4y   Firm   Slow   Inside

2105 **SPITTING IMAGE 8** [5] Mrs M Reveley 4-8-12 (60) A Culhane 11/4: 0-030241: Led till over 6f out, 63
led again 4f out, drifted right under press, drvn out: nicely bckd, first win: eff at 12/14f, stays a slowly run 2m
in claim grade: acts on firm & gd grnd, prob any trk: see 1118.
1637 **RED SCORPION 31** [3] W M Brisbourne 5-9-0 (69) B Swarbrick(5) 11/10 FAV: 35-16502: Held up, hdwy 1 62
3f out & drvn/chsd wnr fnl 2f, al just held: nicely bckd, op 11/8: see 238.
3856} **LORD LAMB 288** [2] Mrs M Reveley 12-8-7 (3ow) (70) D Holland 11/2: /2/5//014-3: gr g Dunbeath - ¾ 54
Caroline Lamb (Hotfoot) Held up, switched wide & hdwy to lead over 6f out, hdd 4f out, kept on for press: op 4/1,
reapp, longer priced stablemate of wnr: lightly rcd '03, clmr scorer: eff at 12f/2m on firm & soft grnd: suited by
claim grade. 1 Aug'03 Redc 14.1g/f 72-(80) F:
2008 **BALALAIKA TUNE 13** [6] W Storey 5-7-13 (35) J Bramhill 20/1: 0604004: Held up, eff to press ldrs 3½ 43
2f out, sn no extra: see 852.
1870 **BERRYWHITE 19** [1]6-9-0 (40) T Hamilton(3) 12/1: 00-00335: Trkd ldrs, btn over 1f out: offic rtd 40. shd 58
1870 **ROYAL CASTLE 19** [7]10-8-4 (44) T Eaves 10/1: 40030-66: b g Caerleon - Sun Princess (English hd 47
Prince) Prom till outpcd 3f out: h'cap scorer '03, AW h'cap unplcd (rtd 51a): dual claim wnr '02, AW h'cap rnr-up:
eff btwn 12f/2m on firm & fibresand, handles soft & any trk: can go well fresh.
1 Apr'03 Nott 16.0gd 56-47 D: 2 Aug'02 Wolv 16.2af 57a-56 F: 1 Jul'02 Muss 16g/f 49- E: 1 Jun'02 Redc 16fm 63- F:
2060 **BULGARIA MOON 11** [8]4-8-3 (35) P Bradley(1) 100/1: 60/00-007: Prom, btn 2f out: see 2060. 1¼ 46
1991 **DIVA DANCER 14** [9]4-7-12 bl (30) D Fentiman(7) 66/1: 0/00-0008: ch f Dr Devious - Catina (Nureyev) 1¼ 40
Rear, no prog fnl 3f: unplcd '03 (rtd 42, lightly rcd): no form '02 (rtd 40, R Beckett).

REDCAR TUESDAY 08.06.04 Lefthand, Flat, Galloping Track

1945 **SEA OF HAPPINESS** 15 [4]4-8-3 (41) P Hanagan 100/1: 0404-09: Lost tch from 4f out, eased. 29 22
9 Ran   Time 3m 31.08 (6.28)   Owned: The Mary Reveley Racing Club   Trained: Saltburn

2299	**5.00 Salmanazar Handicap Stakes** 3yo 35-55 (F)					[63]
	£3591 £1 ¦05 £553	**1m2f**	**Firm**	**Slow**	Inside	

4110} **RICHTEE** 275 [15] R A Fahey 3-9-6 (55) P Hanagan 12/1: 060-1: ch f Desert Sun - Santarene 64
(Scenic) Hld up, hdwy wide from 3f out & styd on for press to lead well ins last, going away: first win on
reapp/h'cap bow: unplcd at up to 6f in '03 (rtd 55): apprec step up to 10f on fm: runs well fresh.
1940 **PEARL OF YORK** 16 [4] R Guest 3-9-3 (52) M Fenton 25/1: 000-002: Mid-div, hdwy & rdn/led over 1f 1 59
out, hdd well ins last & no extra: now stays a gall 10f on firm grnd: see 1940.
1872* **EGO TRIP** 19 [6] M W Easterby 3-9-4 (53) Dale Gibson 11/4 FAV: 0000-013: Pushed along towards 1¾ 58
rear, hdwy to chase ldrs 4f out, onepace & held ins last: well bckd, op 4/1: styd longer 10f trip: see 1872 (1m).
1836 **HOLLY WALK** 21 [9] M Dods 3-8-11 VIS (46) Darren Williams 9/1: 04-02554: Led till over 1f out, nk 50
kept on for press: drpd in trip, gd run with forcing tactics in first time visor, settled much better today: stays
10f, return to 12f+ may suit: handles firm & soft grnd: see 1836 & 1308.
1945 **LET IT BE** 15 [1]3-8-5 (40) T Eaves(1) 14/1: 000-2505: Mid-div, outpcd 3f out, kept on late: see 1363. 1 43
2226 **LARAD** 4 [12]3-8-13 bl (48) Derek Nolan(7) 13/2: 3346106: Mid-div, eff to press ldrs 2f out, no extra dist. ½ 50
1785 **BARGAIN HUNT** 23 [5]3-8-12 (47) J Bramhill 12/1: 403-0207: Trkd ldr, fdd fnl 2f: btr 1505. ½ 48
1971 **KOODOO** 15 [3]3-9-6 (55) V Halliday 9/1: 000-068: gr c Fasliyev - Karsiyate (Kahyasi) Mid-div, 1 55
no impress fnl 2f: unplcd '03 (rtd 50, debut, mdn).
1947 **DELCIENNE** 15 [10]3-8-9 (44) A Beech(3) 12/1: 020-0039: Mid-div, no prog fnl 3f: see 1947 (banded). ¾ 43
1954 **MR MOON** 15 [11]3-8-0 (35) P M Quinn 100/1: 000-6600: 10th: Dwelt & held up, keen, btn 3f out. ¾ 33
1829 **RAVEL** 21 [8]3-8-12 (47) I Mongan 11/2: 00-000: 11th: b c Fasliyev - Lili Cup (Fabulous Dancer) 1¼ 43
Chsd ldrs, btn 3f out: longer trip: unplcd at up to 7f prev, incl in '03 (rtd 59, mdn).
1896 **THE STICK** 18 [7]3-9-6 (55) A Culhane 14/1: 56-00000: 12th: Mid-div, no impress from halfway. 7 42
4639} **Snow Chance** 245 [14]3-8-2 (37) B Swarbrick(5) 50/1:0
1673 **Middleham Rose** 28 [13]3-8-0 (2oh)(33) Rory Moore(5) 20/1:0
14 Ran   Time 2m 06.37(4.07)   Owned: Terence Elsey and Richard Mustill   Trained: Malton

LEOPARDSTOWN WEDNESDAY 02.06.04 Lefthand, Galloping Track

Official Going GOOD.

2300	**5.30 EBF Irish Stallion Farms Maiden** 2yo ()			
	£8723 £2559 £1219	**6f rnd**	**Good**	

1687 **AMSTERDAM** 21 [3] A P O'Brien 2-9-2 J P Spencer 2/7 FAV: 51: Made all, rdn & strongly pressed 95
fnl 1f, held on well for press, gamely: op 1/2: eff at 6f, likely to stay futher in time: acts on gd & gd/sft
grnd: not impressive tonight but the type to progress in stronger company, could be R Ascot bound: see 1687.
KING OF TORY [2] D K Weld 2-9-2 P J Smullen 5/1: 3: br f Diktat - Wars (Green Desert) 1½ 82
(General Holme) Trkd ldrs, rdn & prsd wnr fnl 1f, just held: op 7/2: most encouraging debut: eff over a gall 6f on ½ 92
gd grnd, will get futher: a likely type for similar.
REDRIGHTRETURNING [1] J S Bolger 2-8-11 K J Manning 5/1: 3: br f Diktat - Wars (Green Desert) 1½ 82
Dsptd lead, rdn & no extra ins last: clr of rem on debut: eff at 6f on gd grnd.
6 Ran   Time 1m 15.40()   Owned: Michael Tabor   Trained: Ballydoyle

SAN SIRO WEDNESDAY 02.06.04 Righthand, Stiff, Galloping Track

Official Going GOOD/FIRM.

2301	**2.20 Premio Stradella** 3yo+ ()		
	£8803 £3873 £2113	**1m4f**	**Good/Firm**

1684 **LANDINIUM** 21 C F Wall 5-9-0 (100) C Colombi 58/100 FAV: 05440-441: Led over 1f out & easily 94+
drew clr: eff at 10/12f on fast & hvy grnd: outclassed these rivals: see 1139 (List).
ENTUSIASMO J Heloury 3-8-7 G Bietolini : 2: ch f Masad - Emy Delight (Aloma's Ruler) No 6 77
match for this easy wnr in the closing stages.
MUSICAL SCORE M Gonnelli 5-9-11 M Esposito : 3: Finished 3rd but well adrift of front pair. 7 85
5 Ran   Time 2m 29.60()   Owned: Ettore Landi   Trained: Newmarket

CAPANNELLE FRIDAY 04.06.04 Righthand, Flat, Galloping Track

Official Going GOOD.

2302	**3.05 Listed Premio Alessandro Perrone** 2yo Fillies ()		
	£24648 £10845 £5915	**5f110y**	**Good**

TENDERLIT [4] R Menichetti 2-8-11 D Vargiu : 1: b f Lit de Justice - Tender Moment (Copy 98
Chief) Decisive scorer here & looks a useful Italian trained juv filly: eff at 5.5f on gd grnd.
1735 **POLLY ALEXANDER** 21 [6] M J Wallace 2-8-11 F Lynch 24/10: 51132: Cl up & ev ch dist, not pace of 2½ 89
wnr ins last but kept on: eff at 5/5.5f: see 1735 & 1362.
SHALIMAR [5] L Brogi 2-8-11 M Pasquale : 3: Just denied 2nd place. nse 88

CAPANNELLE   FRIDAY 04.06.04   Righthand, Flat, Galloping Track

7 Ran   Time 1m 05.60 ()   Owned: Scuderia Razza Dell'olmo   Trained: Italy

2303	4.05 Listed Premio Alberto Giubilo 2yo Colts & Geldings ()
	£24648 £10845 £5915 5f110y Good

GOLDEN STRAVINSKY [4] G Fratini 2-8-11 D Vargiu : 1 : b c Stravinsky - Shagadellic (Devil's Bag) Clear-cut wnr over this sprint trip: eff at 5.5f on gd grnd: Italian trained colt who cld prove useful. **95**

1571* **CATWALK CLERIC** 30 [8] M J Wallace 2-8-11 F Lynch 39/10: 412: Chsd ldrs, styd on well ins last, not pace of wnr: eff at 5/5.5f, 6f will suit: acts on gd & gd/sft grnd: see 1571, 1256. **2** **88**

PATAPAN [6] R Brogi 2-8-11 G Temperini : 3: Italian trained juvenile colt, fair 3rd today. **¾** **86**
8 Ran   Time 1m 05.60()   Owned: Scuderia Golden Horse   Trained: Italy

CHANTILLY   SATURDAY 05.06.04   Righthand, Galloping Track

Official Going GOOD/SOFT.

2304	2.50 Gr 3 Prix de Royaumont 3yo Fillies ()
	£25704 £10282 £7711 1m4f Good/Soft

SILVERSKAYA [7] J C Rouget 3-9-0 I Mendizabal 6/10 FAV: 1111: b f Silver Hawk - Boubskaia (Niniski) Rear, styd on strongly for press to lead well ins last: unbtn, incl in a List event at Toulouse: suited by 12f on gd & gd/sft, likes a gall trk: lightly rcd & improving filly who has developed into a smart performer. **111**

KALATUNA [2] J Van Handenhove 3-9-0 T Thulliez 24/1: 143-3512: ch f Green Tune - Kalasinger (Cheif Singer) Trkd ldr, led over 1f out, hdd ins last & not pace of wnr: eff at 12f on gd/soft: smart. **1** **108**

REVERIE SOLITAIRE [5] C Laffon Parias 3-9-0 O Peslier 14/1: 413: Held up, styd on late. **1½** **106**
7 Ran   Time 2m 36.20 ()   Owned: Earl Champ Gignoux   Trained: France

CHANTILLY   SUNDAY 06.06.04   Righthand, Galloping Track

Official Going GOOD/SOFT.

2305	2.10 Gr 2 Prix du Gros Chene 3yo+ ()
	£42148 £16268 £7764 5f str Good/Soft

1479 **AVONBRIDGE** 36 [9] R Charlton 4-9-2 (113) S Drowne 74/10: 221343-21: Made all, styd on strongly, drvn out: eff at 6f, has looked a potentially top-class sprinter at 5f on both starts this term: acts on firm & gd/sft grnd: progressive sprinter who shld be noted for his chosen engagement at R Ascot: see 1479. **117**

4629} **PORLEZZA** [7] Y de Nicolay 5-9-5 C Soumillon 24/10: 01D15-12: ch f Sicyos - Pupsi (Matahawk) Trkd wnr, rdn & kept on fnl 1f, not btn far: wnr of a C/D List event back in April: won this race prev 2 seasons, also Gr 1 wnr last term: eff btwn 5/6.5f on gd & hvy grnd, likes a gall trk & can go well fresh: v smart sprinter whose targets this summer reportedly include the July Cup at Newmarket. 1 Aug'03 Deau 6.5g/s 115- A: 1 Jun'03 Chan 5gd 115- A: 1 Jun'02 Chan 5gd 108- : 2 May'02 Long 5sft 111- : 2 Sep'01 Chan 5.5sft 99- : **½** **117**

1856* **THE TRADER** 21 [1] M Blanshard 6-9-2 bl (109) J P Spencer 6/5 FAV: 661426-13: Rear, swtchd & styd on strongly ins last, nrst fin: btn under 1L: rnr-up in this in '03: just btr 1856. **nk** **113**

2068 **THE TATLING** 8 [4] J M Bradley 7-9-2 (112) D Holland 61/10: 55340-234: Held up, kept on fnl 2f, not able to chall: also bhd todays 3rd in 1856. **1½** **108**

1773 **MILLYBAA** 22 [2]4-8-9 (100) L Dettori 20/1: 13020-247: Sn pshd along & chsd ldrs, no impress dist: fin 7th: needs a drop to List company: see 1773. **2** **95**
8 Ran   Time 58.10 ()   Owned: D J Deer   Trained: Beckhampton

2306	2.45 Gr 2 Prix de Sandringham 3yo Fillies ()
	£42148 £16268 £7764 1m rnd Good/Soft

BAQAH [7] F Head 3-8-11 D Bonilla 8/1: 42-31211: ch f Bahhare - Filfilah (Cadeaux Genereux) Held up, rdn & hdwy to chall over 1f out, styd on for press to lead nr fin: recent List wnr here at Chantilly, earlier stks wnr: eff btwn 5.5f/1m on gd & v soft grnd: likes a gall trk: smart & prog filly. **114**

1854 **MISS MAMBO** [8] E Libaud 3-8-11 C Soumillon 4/5 FAV: 13-1132: Keen & prom, rdn & briefly led dist, not pace of wnr close home: recent 3rd in French 1000 Guineas: see 1854. **½** **112**

1156 **DOLMA** [9] N Clement 3-8-11 C P Lemaire 24/1: 10-22123: Led, strongly pressed from 2f out & briefly hdd dist, kept on gamely but hdd & no extra cl home: also just bhd today's wnr last time. **snk** **111**

1854 **NYRAMBA** 21 [1]3-8-11 (109) L Dettori 22/1: 12110-255: Mid-div, rdn & no extra fnl 1f: see 1854. **1** **109**
9 Ran   Time 1m 35.80 ()   Owned: Hamdan Al Maktoum   Trained: France

2307	3.55 Gr 1 Prix Jean Prat 3yo Colts & Fillies ()
	£80479 £32197 £16099 1m1f rnd Good/Soft

5003*}**BAGO** 218 [5] J E Pease 3-9-2 T Gillet 6/4 FAV: 1111-1: b/br c Nashwan - Moonlight's Box (Nureyev) Mid-div, smooth prog to lead dist, readily asserted: reapp: unbtn in '03, wins included a Gr 3 & a Gr 1: suited by 1m/9f, shld stay 10f+: acts on gd & v soft grnd: likes a gall trk: reportedly been suffering from a virus, but this was a high-class display & clearly one to follow at the highest level. 1 Nov'03 Sain 8hvy 119- : 1 Sep'03 Long 8gd 104- A: **123+**

CACIQUE [3] A Fabre 3-9-2 Gary Stevens 39/10: -112: b c Danehill - Hasili (Kahyasi) Rear, late prog to take 2nd, no ch with easy wnr: prev unbtn in 2 starts: eff at 7/9f: acts on gd & gd/soft grnd: **3** **114**

CHANTILLY   SUNDAY 06.06.04   Righthand, Galloping Track

lightly raced & smart colt, Group success awaits.

4272} **ERSHAAD** [7] J E Hammond 3-9-2 C Soumillon 68/10: 1364-143: Held up, kept on late to take 3rd.		2	110
1685 **MOSCOW BALLET 25** [6]3-9-2 J P Spencer 21/1: 125-66: Mid-div, btn over 1f out: see 1685.		3½	103
4839* }**PEARL OF LOVE 231** [8]3-9-2 D Holland 77/10: 2111317: b c Peintre Celebre - Aunt Pearl (Seattle		½	102

Slew) Handy & led after 3f, hdd over 1f out, wknd on reapp: won 4 of 6 juv starts, incl List, Gr 2 & Gr 1: suited by 7f/1m, shld stay further: likes firm & gd grnd, stiff/gall trks: v smart juv who is likely to be sharper next time & will prob apprec a return to faster grnd.   1 Oct'03 San 8gd 117- : 1 Aug'03 Curr 7g/f 117- A: 1 Jun'03 Asco 7g/f 110-0 A: 1 May'03 Donc 6gd 107-0 D: 2 May'03 York 6.0fm 95-0 D:
8 Ran   Time 1m 46.60 ()   Owned: Niarchos Family   Trained: France

---

2308   **4.40 Gr 1 French Derby 3yo   ()**
£442634 £177085 £88542   **1m4f**   **Good/Soft**

BLUE CANARI [10] P Bary 3-9-2   T Thulliez 332/10: 31-3431: ch c Acatenango - Delicieuse Lady   **119**
(Trempolino) Rear, hdwy wide for press fnl 2f, styd on to lead on line, all out: fin bhd some of today's rivals in 3 starts this term: stks wnr in '03: stays 12f well, may get further: acts on gd & soft grnd: posted a high class performance & reportedly may now be supplemented for the Irish Derby.

1852 **PROSPECT PARK 24** [8] C Laffon Parias 3-9-2   O Peslier 28/10 JT FAV: 33-1122: b c Sadler's Wells   hd   **119**
- Brooklyn's Dance (Shirley Heights) Mid-div, hdwy & rdn to chall over 1f out, narrow lead ins last, hdd close home: stks & List wnr earlier this term, also Gr 2 rnr-up: suited by 10/12f on gd/soft & soft grnd: v smart colt who shld find Gr success this term.   2 May'04 Long 12sft 113- :

1853 **VALIXIR 21** [1] A Fabre 3-9-2   E Legrix 89/10: 112-133: Mid-div, styd on well for press from over   ½   **118**
1f out, nrst fin: styd longer 12f trip well: see 1853.

1706* **DAY FLIGHT 24** [2] J H M Gosden 3-9-2   R Hughes 28/10 JT FAV: 114: Cl up, led over 3f out tll hdd   ¾   **117**
well ins last: only btn just over 1L & has progressed into a smart performer who should bag Gr prizes this season: reportedly needs gd or softer grnd: see 1706 & 1501.

ANGE GARDIEN [3]3-9-2   C Soumillon 81/10: 25-125: Held up, styd on well for press fnl 2f.   2½   **113**
1852* **LORD DU SUD 24** [12]3-9-2   I Mendizabal 9/2: 1-1116: Mid-div, kept on fnl 2f, not able to chall.   shd   **113**
REEFSCAPE [7]3-9-2   Gary Stevens 28/10 JT FAV: 225-3117: Rear, kept on late, not able to chall.   shd   **112**
1622 **FIVE DYNASTIES 29** [9]3-9-2   J P Spencer 75/1: 14-38: Held up, drvn & nvr a threat: see 1622.   ¾   **111**
1814* **MANYANA 19** [16]3-9-2   (100) Martin Dwyer 64/1: 1-510: 11th: Held up, little hdwy: see 1814 (List).   3   **107**
1685 **TOP SEED 25** [5]3-9-2   (108) T E Durcan 42/1: 3624-240: 13th: Prom, lost pl 4f out, sn btn: see 1685.   9½   **93**
15 Ran   Time 2m 25.20()   Owned: Ecurie Jean Louis Bouchard   Trained: France

---

NEWBURY   WEDNESDAY 09.06.04   Lefthand, Flat, Galloping Track

Official Going Good/Firm

2309   **6.35 Green Energy Environmental Maiden Stakes 3yo   (D)**
£6500 £2000 £1000   **6f8y str**   **Good/Firm 24**   **-09 Slow**   Centre

4601} **KSCHESSINKA 249** [2] W J Haggas 3-8-9   M Hills 11/4: 0-1: br f Nureyev - Gran Dama (Rahy) Held   **83+**
up, switched right to stands side over 2f out, qcknd to lead over 1f out, held on for hands & heels: well bckd on reapp: eff over a gall 6f on fast grnd, runs well fresh: clrly done well over the winter, win more races.

2173 **FAREWELL GIFT 7** [10] R Hannon 3-9-0   (80) K Fallon 13/8 FAV: 00-43232: Handy, led over 2f out   1½   82
till over 1f out, kept on but not pace of wnr: another gd run, shld find a minor trk mdn.

1876 **TRUMAN 20** [3] J A R Toller 3-9-0   S Sanders 12/1: 5-03: b c Entrepreneur - Sabria (Miswaki)   3½   72
Handy, eff to chall over 1f out, no extra ins last: eff at 6f on fast grnd: imprvd run: see 1876.

1957 **KINGS CAPRICE 16** [6] G B Balding 3-9-0   (87) S Carson 11/4: 523-034: Keen in tch, eff to chall   ½   70
well over 1f out, wknd ins last: well bckd: shade more expected after 1957 (sharp).

1787 **EVEN HOTTER 23** [1]3-8-9   T Quinn 66/1: 0-05: b f Desert Style - Level Pegging (Common Grounds)   5   50
Sn bhd, late gains, nvr dangerous: well btn sole juv start: shapes like further will suit in h'caps.

2174 **CHICA ROCA 7** [9]3-8-9   (75) L Keniry(3) 25/1: 350-006: In tch, wknd over 1f out: plcd in native   shd   50
France last term: stays 6f on soft grnd.

2152 **THEMESOFGREEN 7** [5]3-9-0   T O'Brien(7) 100/1: 0-07: Keen, led over 3f out till over 2f out, wknd.   ¾   53
LOVEYOULONGTIME [7]3-8-9   S Drowne 18/1: 8: In tch, wknd 2f out on debut.   3   39
1762 **BATCHWORTH BEAU 25** [4]3-9-0   A Daly 100/1: 009: Led till over 3f out, wknd.   1   41
ROYAL LOGIC [8]3-8-9   T E Durcan 20/1: 0: 10th: Al bhd on debut.   6   18
10 Ran   Time 1m 13.56 (1.96)   Owned: Lael Stable   Trained: Newmarket

---

2310   **7.05 Wedgewood Estates Maiden Auction Stakes Fillies 2yo   (E)**
£4761 £1465 £733   **6f8y str**   **Good/Firm 24**   **-21 Slow**   Centre

WHAZZAT [6] B W Hills 2-8-9   R Hughes 7/1: 1: b f Daylami - Wosaita (Generous) Slow away, held   **91+**
up, hdwy to lead appr fnl 1f, sn hdd but rallied gamely for press to get up again cl-home: gambled from 16/1: Feb foal, cost 30,000 gns: half sister to a 1m juv wnr: dam stays 12f: eff over a gall 6f, 7f sure to suit: acts on fast grnd & runs well fresh: genuine, plenty more to come over further.

MAIDS CAUSEWAY [4] B W Hills 2-8-9   M Hills 16/1: 2: ch f Giant's Causeway - Vallee des Reves   nk   90
(Kingmambo) Slow away, held up, hdwy over 2f out, styd on well to lead just ins last, collared cl-home, just btn by well bckd stable-mate: Mar foal: dam unrcd: sire top class over 7f/10f: eff at 6f, 7f sure to suit: acts on fast grnd: pleasing start, learn from this & will be wng sn.

COURS DE LA REINE [10] P W Chapple Hyam 2-8-9   J Quinn 9/4 FAV: 3: b f Fasliyev - Society Queen   nk   89
(Law Society) In tch, hdwy to lead well over 1f out, sn hdd but kept on ins last, not btn far: hvly bckd on debut: Mar foal, cost 30,000 gns: dam 1m/10f scorer: eff at 6f, 7f sure to suit: acts on fast grnd: clrly held in some regard & will be wng similar shortly.

2061 **STEPHANIES MIND 11** [2] C N Allen 2-8-4   K McEvoy 5/1: 034: In tch, eff over 2f out, ev ch till   ¾   82
no extra ins last: confirmed of 2061, minor trks will suit.

1574 **AGENT KENSINGTON 34** [9]2-8-2   R L Moore 9/2: 225: In tch, wknd dist: see 1574, 1380 (5f).   3½   70
LADY LE QUESNE [8]2-8-5 (1ow)   S Drowne 25/1: 6: ch f Alhaarth - Lady Moranbon (Trempolino)   1½   69

Made most till over 1f out, no extra: Mar foal, cost 16,000 gns: half brother to a 10f wnr: dam won in France.

MISS MALONE [13]2-8-6 P Dobbs 33/1: 7: In tch, some late gains, nvr dangerous on debut.	1¾	65
YOU FOUND ME [17]2-8-9 E Ahern 25/1: 8: Bhd, some late gains, nvr dangerous on debut.	½	66
GUINEA A MINUTE [15]2-8-6 T Quinn 11/1: 9: In tch, wknd over 1f out on debut.	nk	62

1866 **MARIANIS 20** [12]2-8-4 J Mackay 11/1: 40: 10th: With ldrs, wknd over 1f out: see 1866.   hd 59
SHOSOLOSA [18]2-8-4 J F McDonald(3) 33/1: 0: 11th: Slow away & bhd, mod late gains on debut.   ½ 57

1866 **Mystery Maid 20** [7]2-8-2 D Kinsella 100/1:0   **Dara Girl** [16]2-8-4 R Havlin 66/1:0
Flying Ridge [11]2-8-6 L Keniry(3) 40/1:0   1987 **Debs Broughton 15** [3]2-8-2 Lisa Jones(3) 66/1:0
Bazelle [14]2-8-6 Paul Eddery 50/1:0   **Sirce** [5]2-8-2 F P Ferris(3) 25/1:0
Kapaje [1]2-8-2 G Catlin 20/1:0   **Spinning Coin** [19]2-8-2 R Miles(3) 50/1:0
19 Ran   Time 1m 14.33 (2.73)   Owned: Mr W J Gredley   Trained: Lambourn

---

2311   7.35 Sunley Handicap Stakes 3yo+ 0-75 (E)   **[72]**
£4713 £1450 £725   **1m5f61y**   **Good/Firm 24**   **-19 Slow**   Outside

2156* **MY LEGAL EAGLE 7** [6] R J Price 10-8-8 (6ex) (52) R Miles(3) 5/1 JT FAV: 5-142111: Held up, hdwy to   60
lead 3f out, styd on well ins last, pushed out: eff over 14f/2m on fast, hvy & both AWs, gall or sharp trks: v
tough 10yo & thriving at present despite advancing years: see 2156, 1563.
2156 **CROSSWAYS 7** [4] P D Evans 6-9-11 (69) R Havlin 13/2: 4-410422: Prom, eff 2f out, kept on to go   1½ 74
2nd ins last, no threat to wnr: in gd form but again bhd this wnr in 2156.
2078 **CARROWDORE 11** [1] C N Allen 4-9-7 p (65) I Mongan 16/1: 5220-243: In tch, bmpd over 2f out but sn   hd 70
hdwy, no extra well ins last: just stays 13.3f: encouraging but only 1 win from 24 starts: see 2078, 816.
1928 **SAN HERNANDO 18** [3] D R C Elsworth 4-9-11 (69) T Quinn 13/2: 60-64004: Held up, hdwy over 2f   ½ 73
out, no extra ins last, not btn far: see 1232, 948.
1916 **SILVER PROPHET 18** [7]5-9-12 (70) G Baker 40/1: 000-0555: Slow away, bhd, hdwy well over 2f out,   2½ 69
onepace fnl 1f: poss stays 14f, prob btr over shorter: see 1650.
1960 **LISSAHANELODGE 16** [9]5-7-13 (43) C Catlin 11/1: 60/-12066: Slow away, eff 2f out, no dngr.   ½ 42
1789 **CLASSIC MILLENNIUM 23** [11]6-9-0 (58) Lisa Jones(3) 8/1: 55-02257: Slow away, held up, eff 2f out,   nk 57
sn no impress: see 1197, 896.
2147* **DUCS DREAM 7** [12]6-9-1 (6ex) (59) J Mackay 20/1: 000-0018: Handy, eff 2f out, sn wknd: too sn.   9 44
340} **CHIVITE 518** [15]5-9-9 (67) K Fallon 5/1 JT FAV: 34555/0-9: b g Alhaarth - Laura Margaret   8 40
(Persian Bold) Chsd ldrs, eff to chase wnr over 2f out, wknd well over 1f out, eased: recent h'cap hdle wnr for P
Hobbs (tch 129h, 2m4f, firm & gd/soft), former multiple hdle scorer: unplcd sole Flat start in '03, rtd 80 for Mrs A
Perrett prev term: eff at 10f on gd/soft, tried a visor: has been gelded.
1807 **NICK THE SILVER 23** [2]3-8-2 (1ow) (60) S Carson 50/1: 030-060: 10th: Bhd, eff over 2f out, wknd.   nk 36
948 **POLANSKI MILL 74** [8]5-9-4 (62) Paul Eddery 66/1: 0/0000-P0: 11th: b g Polish Precedent - Mill On   ¾ 34
The Floss (Mill Reef) Nvr a factor: unplcd in '03 (rtd 67): poss stays 13.3f on firm.
2088 **REVIEWER 10** [14]6-9-12 (70) S Drowne 20/1: 0/116/-000: 12th: In tch, wknd qckly 2f out: see 2088.   hd 41
1629 **THE PERSUADER 32** [5]4-9-13 (71) K Dalgleish 8/1: 210-0000: 13th: b g Sadler's Wells - Sister Dot   ½ 41
(Secretariat) In tch, wknd qckly over 2f out: '03 4 time h'cap scorer: eff at 12/14f on firm & gd grnd, likes gall
trks: game & prog last term, slipped down the weights after some mod effs this term: op 14/1.
1 Sep'03 Hayd 14gd 81-75 C: 2 Aug'03 Leic 11.8gd 74-(75) D: 1 May'03 Beve 12.1gd 76-69 E:
1 May'03 York 11.9fm 74-60 D: 1 May'03 Nott 14.1g/f 65-55 E:
2035 **DONALD 13** [13]4-8-12 (56) R Hughes 10/1: 46/124-30: 14th: Chsd ldr, wknd 3f out: btr 2035 (2m).   14 4
1916 **DEFERLANT 18** [10]7-9-2 vis (60) E Ahern 50/1: 2311/5//-00: 15th: Led till 3f out, wknd.   ¾ 7
15 Ran   Time 2m 50.88 (5.78)   Owned: Mr E G Bevan   Trained: Hereford

---

2312   8.05 City Index Handicap Stakes Fillies 3yo+ 0-85 (D)   **[82]**
£6279 £1932 £966   **7f str**   **Good/Firm 24**   **-03 Slow**   Centre

1927 **MUSIC MAID 18** [4] H S Howe 6-8-8 (62) D Kinsella 9/1: 45115-01: b f Inzar - Richardstown Lass   68
(Muscatite) Held up, gd hdwy 2f out to lead dist, flashed tail under press but held on well: '03 4 time h'cap wnr:
below best in '02: eff at 7f/1m & likes firm & fast grnd, handles gd/soft & any trk, likes a gall one, esp
Salisbury: flashes tail but genuine, tough & in fine heart.   1 Sep'03 Sali 7.0fm 64-57 C:
1 Aug'03 Sali 8g/f 58-54 D: 1 Jul'03 Sali 8g/f 56-53 E: 2 Jun'03 Newb 7fm 55-53 D: 1 May'03 Ling 7g/f 52-47 E:
2108 **AND TOTO TOO 9** [1] P D Evans 4-8-13 bl (67) K Fallon 5/1: 2442402: Held up, hdwy to chall over 1f   ½ 72
out, kept on ins last, just held by wnr: back to form: tough & genuine, see 270.
1723 **LITTLE VENICE 27** [3] C F Wall 4-9-8 (76) S Sanders 100/30 FAV: 3240-053: In tch, hdwy well over   nk 80
1f out, kept on ins last, no extra cl-home but not btn far: gd run, decent trk at 7f: see 1723.
1782 **RIVA ROYALE 24** [2] I A Wood 4-10-0 (82) T P Queally(3) 14/1: 001-0004: Set pace, rdn & hdd dist,   1 84
onepace: top-weight: btr run with uncontested lead: likes Yarmouth, see 1356.
4601} **HOT LIPS PAGE 249** [5]3-8-6 (70) R Smith 33/1: 005-5: b f Hamas - Salt Peanuts (Salt Dome) In   hd 71
tch, rdn & sltly outpcd over 2f out, kept on ins last on reapp: 5th on last of 3 mdn '03 starts (rtd 77): some
promise here over 7f, shld stay further: acts on fast grnd.
1169 **DANCLARE 56** [6]3-9-6 (84) K McEvoy 4/1: 4210-06: ch f Stravinsky - Beyond Temptation (Sunny's   nk 84
Halo) In tch, eff & short of room 2f out, kept on ins last: shade closer with clr run: 8 wk abs: won 1 of 4 '03
starts (fills mdn): stays 7f, shld get further: acts on firm & fast, easy or gall trks: expect more next time.
1 Sep'03 Kemp 7g/f 86- D: 2 Sep'03 Kemp 6fm 83- D:
2169* **LORIEN HILL 7** [8]3-8-9 (6ex) (73) M Hills 11/2: 034-6517: In tch, wknd dist: btr 2169 (mdn).   1 71
2117 **BLAINA 9** [10]4-9-7 (75) T Quinn 16/1: 32260-58: With ldr, wknd well over 1f out: mdn, see 2117.   shd 72
1540 **CALUSA LADY 36** [7]4-8-1 (55) R Thomas(5) 10/1: 60005-59: Nvr a factor.   2 48
1465 **MEDUSA 40** [9]4-8-12 (66) M Tebbutt 66/1: 0/2300-00: 10th: Al bhd: 6 wk abs.   6 47
10 Ran   Time 1m 26.21 (1.91)   Owned: Mr R J Parish   Trained: Tiverton

NEWBURY WEDNESDAY 09.06.04 Lefthand, Flat, Galloping Track

2313 **8.35 Rundle & Co Classified Stakes 3yo+ 0-80 (D)**
£5590 £1720 £860 **1m rnd** **Good/Firm 24** **-16 Slow** Outside

2087 **BRIEF GOODBYE 11** [8] John Berry 4-9-3 (76) M Fenton 20/1: 663-1401: Made all, hdwy over 1f out, flashed tail but kept on well for press ins last: suited by 1m, stays 10.3f on firm & fast grnd, handles gd/soft: career best eff with switch to forcing tactics: see 1092. **81**
2076 **PRINCE HECTOR 11** [2] W J Haggas 5-9-3 (80) K Fallon 7/2 FAV: 010-0262: Held up, hdwy 2f out, strong run ins last, just failed: looks poised to strike & apprec return to 1m: see 1255. *hd* **80**
2067 **ARRY DASH 11** [4] M R Channon 4-9-7 (84) T E Durcan 8/1: 5-402003: Held up, hdwy over 1f out, styd on ins last, not pace of front 2: gd run: see 1104, 758. *1* **82**
1877 **LINNING WINE 20** [9] B G Powell 8-9-5 (82) J Murtagh 4/1: 1-024064: In tch, hung left 2f out, carried head high & no extra ins last: does not look straightforward now: see 1877, 928. *shd* **80**
1812 **SPANISH DON 22** [5]6-9-7 (84) L Keniry(3) 7/1: 6141-005: b g Zafonic - Spanish Wells (Sadler's Wells) In tch, outpcd 2f out, rallied ins last: '03 dual h'cap wnr: unplcd in '02: eff over 1m/9f on fast & soft grnd, sharp or gall trks: has run well fresh: can carry big weights: gd run. *nk* **81**
1 Oct'03 Newb 9gd 87-82 D: 1 Sep'03 Wind 8.3g/f 85-75 E:
1833 **STAR SENSATION 22** [6]4-9-5 e (85) R L Moore 9/2: 5400-656: Slow away, in tch, wknd over 1f out. *12* **55**
1497* **DAFORE 38** [7]3-8-11 (85) R Hughes 4/1: 17: Slow away & al bhd: reportedly lost action: btr 1497. *7* **44**
1475 **GEM BIEN 39** [3]6-9-3 (80) C Catlin 33/1: 01640-08: b g Bien Bien - Eastern Gem (Jade Hunter) Chsd wnr to 3f out, wknd: '03 h'cap scorer: class stks & h'cap wnr in '02: stays 10f, best around 1m on fast, soft & any trk, likes Beverley: goes well fresh & a gd weight carrier: can front run. 1 Jul'03 Ayr 8gd 84-79 D: *¾* **37**
1 Jul'02 Beve 8.4g/s 82- D: 1 May'02 Beve 8.4gd 80-74 D: 1 Jul'01 Nott 8.2g/f 78-72 D: 2 Apr'01 Wind 8.3g/s 75-73 D:
8 Ran Time 1m 38.96 (3.16) Owned: Mr J McCarthy Trained: Newmarket

2314 **9.05 Sodexho Prestige Handicap Stakes 3yo 0-75 (E)** **[82]**
£4537 £1396 £698 **7f str** **Good/Firm 24** **+12 Fast** Centre

1930 **PANSHIR 18** [9] C F Wall 3-9-4 (72) S Sanders 12/1: 0-50301: Held up, gd hdwy over 2f out, styd on well to lead ins last, pushed out, cmftbly: 1st win, gd time: imprvd run & clrly enjoys a gall 7f on fast grnd, acts on gd/soft: gd confidence boost: see 919. **84**
2098* **DISTANT CONNECTION 9** [1] A P Jarvis 3-9-8 (6ex) (76) K McEvoy 8/1: 3-000612: Led till 3f out, led again over 1f out till well ins last, not pace of wnr, not btn far: well clr of rem & proving prog: see 2098, 1583. *¾* **84**
1639 **SCIENTIST 32** [7] J H M Gosden 3-9-7 (75) J Fortune 20/1: 65-003: ch c Dr Fong - Green Bonnet (Green Desert) Chsd ldrs, hdwy 2f out, onepace fnl 1f: rtd 83 when 5th on 2nd of 2 juv starts: eff at 7f on fast. *4* **75**
2153 **MOLINIA 7** [4] R M Beckett 3-8-8 (62) J Quinn 66/1: 550-0P4: b f Nicolotte - Themeda (Sure Blade) Slow away, sn in tch, onepcd over 1f out: 5th at best in '03 (auct mdn, rtd 65): shld stay 7f. *3* **56**
1825 **BEAUTIFUL NOISE 22** [6]3-8-3 (57) J F McDonald(3) 20/1: 0506-065: b f Piccolo - Mrs Moonlight (Ajdal) Handy, led 3f out till over 1f out, wknd: unplcd in '03 (rtd 70): half sister to a 7f/1m wnr. *1½* **49**
1628 **EVALUATOR 32** [13]3-9-4 (72) R Miles(3) 10/1: 36-4306: In tch, wknd dist: btr 1470 (1m, soft). *¾* **62**
1930 **MOTU 18** [19]3-9-3 (71) J Murtagh 4/1: 410-0007: In tch, wknd over 2f out: see 1930, 1417. *1* **59**
1417 **TORQUEMADA 42** [17]3-8-6 (60) P Doe 33/1: 60-3008: Slow away & bhd, nvr a factor: see 1417, 898. *1½* **45**
175 **BLUE JAVA 182** [20]3-8-12 (66) S Drowne 20/1: 040-9: In tch, wknd over 2f out: been gldd. *1½* **48**
1983 **SWIFT SAILING 15** [10]3-9-5 (73) M Hills 40/1: 015-000: 10th: In tch, wknd 2f out: see 1983. *shd* **54**
2048 **ONE UPMANSHIP 12** [2]3-8-12 (66) E Ahern 33/1: 2430-000: 11th: In tch, wknd qckly 2f out. *1½* **44**
1982 **PICCLEYES 15** [5]3-8-9 (63) R L Moore 33/1: 60353-00: 12th: In tch, wknd over 2f out. *nk* **40**
1647 **NIGHT WORKER 30** [18]3-8-3 (57) R Smith 20/1: 040-6000: 13th: In tch, nvr a factor: see 1054. *shd* **34**
4941} **AMERICAN DUKE 224** [14]3-9-2 (70) Paul Eddery 66/1: 4400-0: 14th: Slow away & al bhd: been gldd. *1½* **44**
1497 **ROCKLEY BAY 38** [8]3-8-11 (65) D Sweeney 33/1: 054-00: 15th: In tch, wknd 2f out. *½* **38**
2098 **WIZARD LOOKING 9** [3]3-9-1 t (69) P Dobbs 28/1: 0526-600: 16th: In tch, wknd over 2f out. *1½* **39**
1417 **EPAMINONDAS 42** [11]3-9-5 (73) P Gallagher(7) 25/1: 053-00: 17th: In tch, wknd 2f out: abs. *nk* **42**
1903 **OFF BEAT 19** [12]3-9-0 bl (68) S Carson 25/1: 10-63000: 18th: In tch, wknd over 2f out. *½* **36**
1403 **NEAP TIDE 43** [16]3-9-7 (75) R Hughes 9/1: 064-00: 19th: Keen, in tch till wknd over 2f out. *7* **29**
2034 **AESCULUS 13** [15]3-8-13 (67) K Fallon 3/1 FAV: 051-0530: 20th: In tch, wknd over 2f out: well bckd: much better expected & something amiss: see 2034 (5.7f). *1½* **18**
20 Ran Time 1m 25.15(0.85) Owned: Mr Ettore Landi Trained: Newmarket

HAMILTON WEDNESDAY 09.06.04 Righthand, Undulating Track, Stiff Uphill Finish

Official Going GOOD/FIRM.

2315 **6.50 Western Saab Amateur Riders' Handicap Stakes 3yo+ 0-70 (E)** **[48]**
£3754 £1155 £578 **6f5y str** **Good/Firm 24** **-19 Slow** Stands Side

2125* **DESERT ARC 8** [4] W M Brisbourne 6-11-0 (7ex) (62) Mr C Davies(5) 6/1: 6600-011: Rear, gd hdwy over 1f out, fin fast to lead on line: op 8/1: gd win under a pen for recent mdn h'cap victory: eff at 6f, shld stay 7f: acts on fast grnd & on a gall trk: runs well for an amat & in fine form: see 2125. **67**
1537 **BUNDY 36** [7] M Dods 8-10-13 (61) Mr S Dobson(3) 14/1: 450-0002: b g Ezzoud - Sanctuary Cove (Habitat) Pushed in rear, gd hdwy to chall ent fnl 1f, just btn in a thrill fin: dual h'cap wnr in '03 (incl here at Hamilton): stays 7f, all wins at 6f: acts on fast & hvy, suited by a stiff/gall trk: on a wng mark. *shd* **64**
1 Sep'03 Newc 6g/f 68-61 F: 1 May'03 Hami 6.0g/s 67-62 E: 1 Sep'02 Newc 6g/s 64-58 F: 2 Jul'02 Hami 5.9g/s 63-59 E:
1 Jun'02 Carl 6g/s 57-53 E: 2 May'02 Hami 6g/s 54- F: 2 Jul'01 Leic 6g/s 61-58 E:
2161 **DIZZY IN THE HEAD 7** [14] Paul Johnson 5-11-3 bl (65) Mr P Evans(5) 12/1: 000-0163: Mid-div, hdwy to lead ins fnl 1f, caught cl-home: just btn in a bunched fin on first start for new stable, prev with J O'Reilly. *hd* **67**
2232 **COLLEGE MAID 4** [6] J S Goldie 7-9-13 bl (47) Ms C Williams 5/1: 4060024: Chsd ldrs, ev ch fnl 1f, just btn in a fin of heads: qck reapp & reportedly in season: see 2232. *shd* **49**
2086 **LOCOMBE HILL 11** [13]8-10-12 (60) Miss Kelly Harrison(3) 16/1: 00-02005: Trkd ldrs, styd on under press, btn under 1L: eff at 6f, btr at 7f/1m & rtn to further will suit: see 417 (1m AW clmr). *½* **60**
2029 **XANADU 13** [11]8-10-3 p (51) Miss P Robson 13/2: 0-020006: Led till ent fnl 1f, no extra: see 1508. *1* **48**

1448 **HEBENUS 41** [8]5-9-11 (45) Miss H Cuthbert(5) 11/1: 05250-27: Mid-div, kept on under press, nvr nrr: abs. **shd** 42
2160 **COLEMANSTOWN 7** [9]4-11-4 (66) Miss L Ellison(3) 14/1: 56-00008: Rear, nvr nr to challenge. 1 60
2111 **ONE WAY TICKET 9** [1]4-10-9 p (57) Miss E J Jones 10/3 FAV: 0-000329: Dsptd lead 4.5f, wknd: well bckd.3 42
1909 **CARIBE 18** [12]5-10-12 (60) Miss S Brotherton 25/1: 1046-600: 10th: Nvr btr thn mid-div. 1½ 41
4473] **SAIF SAREEA 610** [10]4-11-0 (14ow) (48) Mr G Gibson 200/1: 256000/2-0: 11th: b g Atraf - Slipperose 1½ 39
(Persepolis) Al bhd on comeback: missed '03, prev term nov auct rnr-up for A Berry, had since been gelded: eff at
5f on hvy grnd: has tried blnks: now with K Hogg. 2 Jun'02 Ayr 5hvy 60- E:
4829] **ABLE MIND 232** [3]4-11-7 (69) Mr S Irving(7) 25/1: 223233-0: 12th: Al bhd on reapp: new stable. 2½ 39
4739] **UNSHAKEN 239** [2]10-10-9 (57) Mr M Macdonald Wagstaffe(7) 66/1: 433430-0: 13th: Al bhd: new yard. 24 0
12 Ran   Time 1m 12.42 (2.62)   Owned: Mr Steve Roberts   Trained: Nesscliffe

---

2316 7.20 Redrow Homes Champagne Maiden Qualifier For Hamilton 2-Y-O Series Final 2yo (D)
£5532 £1702 £851   **6f5y str**   Good/Firm 24   -08 Slow   Stands Side

ABRAXAS ANTELOPE [6] J Howard Johnson 2-9-0   R Winston 4/1: 1: b c Imperial Ballet - Lypharden 90+
(Lyphard's Special) Made all, well clr fnl 1f, easily on debut: nicely bckd tho' op 10/3: Mar foal, cost 5,000gns
as a 2yo: half-brother to sev wnrs abroad, sire a decent mile h'capper: eff over a stiff/undul 6f, acts on fast
grnd: runs well fresh: easy wnr, worth a try in btr company.
ARTHUR WARDLE [5] M L W Bell 2-9-0   A Nicholls 7/2: 2: b c Stravinsky - Avanti Sassa 6 75
(Sassafras) Outpcd, styd on fnl 1f, no ch with wnr on debut: 3,000gns May foal: half-brother to sev decent wnrs in
the US: dam a wnr in the US, sire a top-class sprinter: prob met an above-average rival here.
MCELDOWNEY [2] M Johnston 2-9-0   S Chin 10/1: 3: b c Zafonic - Ayodhya (Astronef) Outpcd, some hd 75
late hdwy, nvr dngrs on debut: op 14/1: 2,000gns Apr foal: half-brother to sev wnrs, incl fair sprinter Ambitious:
dam a juv wnr in France, sire a top-class miler: shld learn from this.
LOVE BEAUTY [4] M Johnston 2-9-0   J Fanning 5/2 FAV: 4: b c Seeking The Gold - Heavenly Rhythm 2½ 68
(Septieme Ciel) Chsd ldrs, outpcd halfway, no ch after on debut: shorter priced stablemate of 3rd: 9,000gns Apr
foal: half-brother to 7f juv wnr Rebel Storm: dam unrcd, sire a top-class dirt performer in this US.
GOLBAND [3]2-8-9   J Carroll 3/1: 5: Tckd ldr 4.5f, wknd: nicely bckd, debut. 3 54
ALEXIA ROSE [1]2-8-9   F Norton 25/1: 6: Chsd ldrs, hung right & btn 1.5f out on debut. 5 39
6 Ran   Time 1m 11.75 (1.95)   Owned: Andrea & Graham Wylie   Trained: Crook

---

2317 7.50 Walter Scott Saints & Sinners Challenge Cup Handicap Stakes 3yo+ 0-85 (D) [83]
£6396 £1968 £984   **1m65y rnd**   Good/Firm 24   +05 Fast   Inside

2159* **GOODBYE MR BOND 7** [2] E J Alston 4-8-3 (6ex) (58) F Norton 8/1: 6343411: Prom, lost pl after 66
halfway, rallied to lead dist, rdn clr: best time of eve: eff around 1m/9f on fast, soft grnd & fibresand, handles
any trk: now has the winning habit, see 2159 & 387.
2067 **TONY TIE 11** [9] J S Goldie 8-9-4 (73) D Holland 8/1: 0-622502: Trkd ldrs, sltly outpcd after 1½ 76
halfway, styd on over 1f out: tchd 11/1: settled btr & back to form: on a wng mark, see 1164 &n 964.
2010 **CHERISHED NUMBER 14** [3] I Semple 5-9-8 vis (77) R Winston 15/2: 04-04063: b g King's Signet - ½ 79
Pretty Average (Skyliner) Trkd ldrs, ev ch fnl 1f, not qckn cl-home: h'cap & class stks wnr in '03: mdn & dual
h'cap wnr in '02: stays 10f, best form arnd 7f/1m: acts on fm & hvy, likes Ayr: eff with/without a vis: gd run.
1 Jun'03 Ayr 8g/f 83-(81) D: 1 May'03 Hami 8.3g/s 81-75 E: 2 Oct'02 Ayr 8sft 84- C: 1 Jul'02 Ayr 8g/s 75-71 D:
1 Jul'02 Ayr 7.2gd 72-65 E: 2 Jun'02 Hami 8.2sft 66- E: 1 May'02 Catt 7g/f 64- F: 2 Apr'02 Thir 7fm 62- E:
2179+§**JORDANS ELECT 6** [11] I Semple 4-9-6 (6ex) (75) L Enstone(3) 11/2: 00-51014: Trkd ldrs, onepcd fnl 1f. nk 76
2179 **TAKES TUTU 6** [8]5-9-8 P (77) Darren Williams 15/2: 5-000225: Held up, prog 2f out, no impress fnl ½ 77
1f: quick reapp & tried cheek pieces: see 2179 & 2087.
2159 **NEMO FUGAT 7** [10]5-8-7 (62) J Carroll 20/1: 400-0056: Held up, short of room sev times fnl 2f, nk 60
kept on: again showed promise, well h'capped: see 2159.
2129* **ACOMB 8** [5]4-9-6 (6ex) (75) K Darley 7/4 FAV: 0-060117: Keen & led till dist, no extra: well 2½ 69
bckd: much btr 2129 (gd/soft).
1970 **WESSEX 16** [6]4-9-11 (80) S Chin 25/1: 010-068: Slow away, nvr nr ldrs: top weight, has been gldd. 1 72
1972 **BORDER ARTIST 16** [4]5-8-9 (64) A Nicholls 20/1: 00-00109: Held up, nvr a factor: btr 1794. 1¾ 52
2087 **LOVE IN SEATTLE 11** [1]4-9-9 (78) J Fanning 25/1: 22-01000: 10th: Front rank 6.5f, wknd. 1 64
4614] **BIG SMOKE 247** [7]4-9-5 (74) P Hanagan 14/1: 320300-0: 11th: gr g Perugino - Lightning Bug 5 50
(Prince Bee) Rdn in rear, nvr a factor: jumps fit, mod nov hdle form: plcd in 3 h'caps for B Meehan in '03: '02
mdn wnr: eff around 1m on fast & gd/soft grnd: handles a gall trk, has tried blnks: now with J H Johnson.
2 Jun'03 Sand 8.1g/f 78-75 D: 1 Jul'02 Sali 6g/s 86- D:
11 Ran   Time 1m 45.40 (1.60)   Owned: Mr Peter J Davies   Trained: Preston

---

2318 8.20 Sky Bet Press Red To Bet Now Handicap Stakes 3yo+ 0-90 (C) [82]
£9065 £3439 £1719   **1m4f17y**   Good/Firm 24   -01 Slow   Stands Side

2176 **MILLENNIUM HALL 6** [2] P Monteith 5-7-13 (53) P Fessey 20/1: 60-06331: Chsd ldrs, imprvd to lead 64
dist, rdn clr, eased cl home: val 2L, qk reapp: eff btwn 1m & 13f: acts on fast & hvy grnd: likes a stiff/undul
trk, esp Hamilton: see 2176 & 1504.
2103* **ZEITGEIST 9** [4] L M Cumani 3-9-0 (6ex) (83) D Holland 8/11 FAV: 01-412: Nvr far away, ev ch fnl ¾ 90
2f, not btn far: hvly bckd & not disgraced under 6lb pen for recent win 2103: progressive.
2147 **PIRI PIRI 7** [1] P J McBride 4-8-11 (65) K Darley 8/1: 3660-623: Held up, styd on under press fnl 1½ 70
1.5f, nvr nrr: op 6/1: see 2147.
2176 **ISAAF 6** [8] P W Hiatt 5-8-8 (62) B Swarbrick(5) 7/1: 1211024: Trkd ldrs, sltly short of room 3f ½ 66
out, onepcd fnl 1f: quick reapp: in front of today's wnr in 2176.
1506* **COLORADO FALLS 38** [5]6-9-10 (78) L Enstone(3) 11/1: 15306/-15: Chsd ldrs, onepcd fnl 1f: top weight. ½ 81
1807* **TUDOR BELL 23** [3]3-8-9 (78) R Winston 10/1: 4-023116: Prom, led 2f out till dist, wknd on hd 81
hat-trick bid: unable to dominate today as in 2 wins in 1807 & 1604.
2103 **RUTTERS REBEL 9** [6]3-8-3 (72) Dale Gibson 14/1: 126-5047: Held up, nvr nr ldrs. 5 67
1689 **GRAN DANA 28** [7]4-9-9 (77) J Fanning 22/1: 21008: Led till 2f out, wknd: btr 1121. 5 64
8 Ran   Time 2m 34.86 (3.06)   Owned: Mrs Elizabeth Ferguson   Trained: Rosewell

HAMILTON WEDNESDAY 09.06.04 Righthand, Undulating Track, Stiff Uphill Finish

2319 **8.50 Tennent Caledonian Breweries Claiming Stakes 3yo (E)**
£4079 £1255 £628 **1m3f16y** **Good/Firm 24** **-24 Slow** Stands Side

2133 **HEARTHSTEAD DREAM 8** [2] J G M O'Shea 3-8-9 BL (65) B Swarbrick(5) 6/1: 320-0321: Prom, went on 2f out, kept on well despite wandering fnl 1f, rdn out: tried blnks, rider reportedly gvn a 2 day careless riding ban: eff at 1m/12f in clmg company: acts on gd & firm: looks a hard ride, apprec blnks today: see 2133 & 1952. **66**
2012 **MANHATTAN JACK 14** [6] G A Swinbank 3-9-3 R Winston 14/1: 052: ch g Forzando - Manhattan Diamond (Primo Dominie) Held up, gd hdwy to chall fnl 1f, not btn far: only 3rd start, eff at 11f on fast grnd: handles a stiff/undul trk: could find a clmr/sell. ¾ **72**
2046 **DOLLY WOTNOT 12** [1] N P Littmoden 3-8-9 (62) K Darley 3/1: 445-5053: Prom, onepcd fnl 1f: see 1165. 1½ **62**
1663 **PLATINUM PIRATE 30** [3] K R Burke 3-9-0 vis (63) Darren Williams 6/1: 0213654: Led till 2f out, wknd. 3 **62**
2107 **STYLISH SUNRISE 9** [5]3-8-6 (1ow)t (65) D Holland 9/2: 036-0435: Prom, ev ch when hmpd dist, no ch after: op 7/1, clr of rem: unlikely to have won but may well have fin in the frame: claimed for 6,000: see 2107. 1¼ **52**
1604 **PAR INDIANA 33** [4]3-8-9 (60) P Hanagan 5/2 FAV: 43-336: Chsd ldrs 1m, wknd: well bckd: btr 1604. 11 **38**
1505 **THE FOXS HEAD 38** [7]3-8-9 J McAuley 33/1: 57: b f Imperial Ballet - Lovely Leitrim (Erin's Hope) Chsd ldrs 1m, sn btn & t.o.: no form yet. 12 **20**
1446 **SMEORACH 41** [8]3-7-13 P Fessey 66/1: 08: ch f My Generation - Mohican (Great Nephew) Al bhd, t.o. in last: 6 wk abs: no form. 3½ **5**
8 Ran Time 2m 24.13 (5.33) Owned: Mr Gary Roberts Trained: Westbury On Severn

2320 **9.20 Thistle Mining Handicap Stakes 3yo+ 0-80 (D)** **[76]**
£5707 £1756 £878 **5f4y str** **Good/Firm 24** **+02 Fast** Stands Side

1886 **MALAHIDE EXPRESS 19** [4] E J Alston 4-8-7 (55) J D O'Reilly(7) 11/1: 0205541: Broke well & made all, held on well cl-home: fair time: suited by 5/6f, has tried further: likes fast grnd & fibresand, handles a sharp/turning or stiff/undul trk: likes to force the pace, see 198 (AW). **60**
2059 **CHAIRMAN BOBBY 12** [1] D W Barker 6-9-8 (70) L Enstone(3) 10/1: 5003202: Chsd ldrs stands side, styd on well fnl 1f, just tchd off in a tight fin: back to form & turn shld not be far away: see 2007. hd **74**
1898 **KINGS COLLEGE BOY 19** [5] R A Fahey 4-8-10 bl (58) P Hanagan 17/2: 4260-003: b g College Chapel - The Kings Daughter (Indian King) Outpcd stands side, fin strongly & not btn far in a tight fin: bckd from 14/1: '03 class stks wnr: eff at 5/6f on firm & soft grnd: back to form with reapplication of blnks tonight. nk **61**
2 Sep'03 Ches 5.1g/s 64-61 D: 1 Aug'03 Nott 5.1gd 63-(63) E: 2 Jul'03 Hami 6.0g/f 61-60 E:
2 Jun'03 Hami 5.0gd 62-60 F: 2 May'03 Hami 5.0sft 61-59 F:
2023 **CURRENCY 14** [6] J M Bradley 7-9-13 (75) D Holland 10/1: 3240004: Held up stands side, styd on strongly fnl 1f, just btn in a bunched fin: top weight: see 453. shd **78**
1276 **AAHGOWANGOWAN 50** [12]5-8-10 t (58) F Lynch 7/1: 0230-005: Made all far side, not quite rch ldrs stands side: abs: loves to dominate: on wrong side. 1¼ **57+**
2181* **PIRLIE HILL 6** [3]4-8-5 (6ex) (53) J Carroll 11/2: 4025016: Prom stands side, onepcd fnl 1f: see 2181. shd **52**
2029 **VIJAY 13** [13]5-8-7 (1ow)vis (54) R Winston 11/1: 3060207: Chsd ldrs far side, onepcd fnl 1f: op 14/1. hd **54**
2160 **HIGHLAND WARRIOR 7** [9]5-9-11 (73) K Darley 3/1 FAV: 2341608: Dwelt, some late hdwy far side, nvr dangerous: tchd 9/2: on the wrong side & lost ch start today: see 1898. 1¾ **67**
2160 **LEGAL SET 7** [7]8-8-1 t (49) Ann Stokell 66/1: 0200009: Al bhd far side. 1¾ **38**
1276 **ROSIES RESULT 50** [10]4-8-2 (50) Dale Gibson 33/1: 00000-00: 10th: ch g Case Law - Precious Girl (Precious Metal) Chsd ldrs 3.5f far side: 7 wk abs: failed to win in '03, h'cap rnr-up once: '02 mdn wnr: eff at 5f on fast & firm grnd: has tried a visor, seems btr without. ¾ **36**
2 Apr'03 Thir 5fm 65-64 C: 2 May'02 Thir 5fm 87- D: 1 Apr'02 Ripo 5g/f 78- D:
1344 **ELLIOTS CHOICE 46** [8]3-9-1 (70) D Tudhope(7) 12/1: 3020-440: 11th: Chsd ldrs 3.5f: abs, gelded. ¾ **53**
2227 **FEU DUTY 5** [2]3-8-13 (68) J Fanning 10/1: 010-6100: 12th: Prom 3.5f stands side: qck reapp. 1 **48**
2029 **NORTHERN SVENGALI 13** [11]8-7-12 (10oh)t P (36) J McAuley 100/1: 54000-00: 13th: Speed till halfway far side: tried cheek pieces, stiff task. 7 **6**
13 Ran Time 59.22(1.12) Owned: The Steady Eddie Partnership Trained: Preston

BEVERLEY WEDNESDAY 09.06.04 Righthand, Oval Track with Stiff, Uphill Finish

Official Going Good (Good/Soft Places)

2321 **2.20 Sportingoptions Co Uk Claiming Stakes 2yo (F)**
£3400 £1046 £523 **5f str** **Good/Soft 64** **-96 Slow** Inside

2110 **VON WESSEX 9** [14] W G M Turner 2-9-1 C Haddon(7) 15/8 FAV: 6516331: Made all, drvn out to hold on: op 5/2: slow time: eff at 5f on firm & gd/soft grnd, stiff or easy trk: likes to force the pace. **65**
2178 **COMINTRUE 6** [10] E J O'Neill 2-8-10 K Darley 12/1: 0002: Outpcd, styd on for press from halfway, not reach wnr: eff over a stiff 5f on gd/soft grnd, shaped as if a return to 6f & similar company will suit. ¾ **57**
2177 **DANEHILL FAIRY 6** [11] Mrs A Duffield 2-8-6 VIS G Duffield 12/1: 02063: Swerved right start, chsd ldrs, styd on to take 3rd, no threat: 1st time visor: handles gd/soft & soft grnd: see 1394. 1¾ **48**
1677 **KEEPASHARPLOOKOUT 28** [2] Mrs L Stubbs 2-8-13 D Holland 16/1: 4404: Mid-div, kept on for press, nvr a threat from mod low draw: handles gd/soft grnd: see 1143. shd **55**
1968 **FRISBY RIDGE 16** [9]2-8-6 D Allan(3) 12/1: 05055: Chsd ldrs till no extra over 1f out: see 1303. 2 **43**
1752 **URABANDE 25** [13]2-8-4 (1ow) N Pollard 13/2: 0206: Chsd ldrs, btn over 1f out: btr 1439 (AW). 2½ **33**
2177 **PROCRASTINATE 6** [5]2-8-13 P P Mathers(7) 7/1: 306537: Swerved left start & bhd, only mod prog. 1 **40**
2017 **JONNY FOXS 14** [15]2-8-11 N Callan 7/1: 68: Prom, btn when hmpd over 1f out: turf bow, new yard. hd **37**
1968 **HOLLINGWOOD SOUL 16** [7]2-8-0 J Quinn 40/1: 009: ch f Timeless Times - Crystal Chandelier (Pivotal) Mid-div, hung right & btn over 1f out: cheaply bought Mar 1st foal, dam unplcd. 3 **18**
1780 **TIMMY 24** [12]2-8-5 T Eaves(1) 20/1: 000: 10th: b c Timeless Times - Ohnonotagain (Kind of Hush) Swerved left start, mid-div, btn over 1f out: only mod form prev: cheaply bought Mar foal, dam plcd at 5/6f. 2½ **16**
1632 **HUNIPOT 32** [8]2-8-2 R Ffrench 33/1: 000: 11th: Chsd ldrs till 2f out. 2 **8**
2083 **Steal The Thunder 11** [6]2-8-10 BL F Lynch 20/1:0 **Taks Girl 0** [4]2-8-10 R Fitzpatrick 40/1:0

13 Ran   Time 1m 09.31 (8.01)   Owned: Mr Darren Coombes   Trained: Sherborne

---

2322   2.50 Sportingoptions Co Uk 08702 070707 Handicap Stakes 3yo 0-75 (E)   **[75]**
£4209 £1295 £648   1m4f16y   Good/Soft 64   -28 Slow   Inside

2046* **PRENUP** 12 [6] L M Cumani 3-9-1 (62) D Holland 10/11 FAV: 500-411: Made all & allowed to dictate   **78+**
pace, rdn clr fnl 2f, eased well ins last, val 8L+: well bckd, op 5/4: eff at 10f, stays 12f: acts on fast &
gd/soft, handles gd, prov or stiff/undul trk: enjoyed an easy lead today but a prog filly who is one to follow.
1976 **WING COLLAR** 15 [1] T D Easterby 3-9-5 (66) K Darley 5/2: 440-0332: Rear, styd on for press fnl   6   70
2f lo take 2nd, nvr threat to wnr: prob stays 12f: see 1976 & 1663.
1965 **DHEHDAAH** 16 [5] N A Graham 3-9-2 (63) R Hills 10/1: 600-03: Trkd wnr, rdn & no impress fnl 2f.   3½   62
2123 **SAVANNAH RIVER** 8 [2] C W Thornton 3-7-12 t (45) P Hanagan 9/1: 00-03254: Chsd ldrs, hung right &   4   38
btn over 1f out: btr 1528 & 1240.
1783 **SNOWED UNDER** 24 [3]3-9-4 (65) G Duffield 25/1: 0-555: gr g Most Welcome - Snowy Mantle (Siberian   1¼   56
Express) Dwelt, chsd ldrs till 2f out: h'cap bow & longer trip: unplcd sole '03 start (rtd 41, mdn).
4988] **BEACON BLUE** 219 [4]3-9-7 (68) R Ffrench 16/1: 5055-6: ch f Peintre Celebre - Catch The Blues   25   21
(Bluebird) Chsd ldrs, lost place from 3f out, t.o.: op 9/1, reapp: unplcd in '03 (lightly rcd, rtd 69, h'cap):
half sister to a 7f wnr, dam class at sprint dists.
6 Ran   Time 2m 42.36 (11.06)   Owned: Fittocks Stud   Trained: Newmarket

---

2323   3.20 Sportingoptions Max 3% Rated Stakes Handicap 4yo+ 0-80 (D)   **[87]**
£6116 £2320 £1160   1m2f rnd   Good/Soft 64   +08 Fast   Inside

1895 **OLDENWAY** 19 [4] R A Fahey 5-8-13 (72) P Hanagan 7/2 FAV: 0022421: Chsd ldrs, led over 1f out,   80
duelled with rnr-up, just prevailed on line: op 4/1, suited by 9/10f on firm & gd/soft, any trk: tough & game.
2038* **GREY CLOUDS** 12 [5] T D Easterby 4-9-2 (75) D Allan(3) 5/1: 30-42012: Trkd wnr & led over 1f out,   shd   82
sn hdd but duelled with wnr ins last, just hdd line: remains in gd heart: see 2038.
2038 **OLIVIA ROSE** 12 [3] J Pearce 5-9-0 (73) J Quinn 7/1: 2-013123: Rear, eff 2f out, onepace.   2½   76
1602 **LAURO** 33 [10] Miss J A Camacho 4-9-4 (77) P Mulrennan(5) 4/1: 1214-324: Trkd ldrs, led briefly 2f   1¾   78
out, not pace of front pair: clr of rem: shows 10f, more convincing at 1m/9f: see 1602 & 1219.
1650 **MAXILLA** 30 [2]4-8-12 (71) D Holland 11/2: 4/241-405: Chsd ldrs, hung right & lost place from 3f out.   10   59
1475 **MISTER ARJAY** 39 [7]4-9-3 (76) T Eaves(3) 16/1: 35200-06: b c Mister Baileys - Crystal Stepper   3½   59
(Fred Astaire) Handy, btn 2f out: recent jumps rnr (plcd, nov, rtd 113h): turf h'cap wnr '03 for G Butler, debut
wnr late '02 (AW nov stks): eff around 1m/10f on firm, fast & polytrack, any trk: eff in blnks, best without.
2 Oct'03 Nott 10.0g/f 79-76 C: 1 May'03 York 7.9fm 81-76 C: 2 May'03 Brig 7.0g/f 77-(72) D: 1 Dec'02 Ling 6ap 74a- D:
1704 **GALA SUNDAY** 27 [8]4-9-7 (80) Dale Gibson 12/1: 100-0007: b g Lear Fan - Sunday Bazaar (Nureyev)   ½   62
Led, hung left & hdd 2f out, fdd: op 16/1: auct mdn & cond stks wnr '03 for B Hills: eff at 9/10f on firm & fast
grnd, any trk: has shown v useful form, now well h'capped: one to note when the subject of a significant mkt move.
1 Jul'03 Hami 9.2g/f 100-(102) C: 2 Apr'03 Epso 10.1g/f 103-(95) B: 1 Apr'03 Pont 10.0g/f 90- E:
2 Sep'02 Hami 7fm 96- C: 2 Aug'02 Good 7fm 96- D:
1969 **DERWENT** 16 [1]5-9-2 bl (75) G Duffield 25/1: 10/03-008: Held up, eff wide 3f out, sn btn.   5   51
1781 **BROADWAY SCORE** 24 [6]6-9-7 (80) T Lucas 10/1: 00-00009: Chsd ldrs wide, lost place from over 2f out.   10   43
1668 **HARAMBEE** 29 [9]4-9-7 (80) T Hamilton(3) 8/1: 20116-PU: Stumbled & u.r leaving stalls.   0
10 Ran   Time 2m 07.87 (5.57)   Owned: Mr J J Staunton   Trained: Malton

---

2324   3.50 Sportingoptions Commission Cutters Stakes A Handicap 3yo+ 0-70 (E)   **[70]**
£4290 £1320 £660   7f100y rnd   Good/Soft 64   -08 Slow   Inside

2242 **PRINCE OF GOLD** 4 [8] R Hollinshead 4-9-7 P (63) N Callan 11/1: 0500601: Chsd ldrs, styd on for   70
press to lead nr line: op 12/1: quick reapp: eff around 7.5f/1m on firm, gd/soft & fibresand: see 1006.
1972 **ALCHEMIST MASTER** 16 [10] R M Whitaker 5-8-12 (54) Dean McKeown 12/1 JT FAV: 40000-62: Trkd ldrs   nk   60
& led over 1f out, hung left under press & hdd cl-home: op 10/1: nicely h'capped on turf, poss needs holding
up till as late as poss: acts on both AWs & gd/soft grnd: see 1972.
2037* **BAILIEBOROUGH** 12 [15] D Nicholls 5-9-11 vis (67) Alex Greaves 7/1 JT FAV: 6034013: Mid-div, styd   1½   70
on onepace for press: ran to form of 2037 (clmr).
2057 **JEDEYDD** 12 [1] M Dods 7-9-1 t (57) P Hanagan 40/1: 0000-004: Dwelt, styd on onepace fnl 3f, not   1¼   57+
able to chall: acts on firm & gd/soft grnd: gd run from poor low draw, well h'capped, keep in mind for similar.
2057 **RONNIE FROM DONNY** 12 [2]4-9-10 (66) T Eaves(3) 4/1: U550055: Keen trkg ldrs, onepace for press.   shd   66
1944* **SHAMWARI FIRE** 16 [13]4-8-9 (51) R Ffrench 12/1: 0-460016: Trkd ldrs, hmpd early, no extra bef dist.   nk   50
1972 **CRYFIELD** 16 [3]7-9-1 (57) Kim Tinkler 4/1: 5-006247: Mid-div, eff wide, not able to chall: mod draw.   2   52
2059 **EXTINGUISHER** 12 [7]5-9-6 (62) D R McCabe 28/1: 000-0008: Chsd ldrs till over 1f out: see 1977.   shd   57
2129 **EASTERN HOPE** 8 [11]5-9-7 bl (63) D Holland 8/1: 60-00309: Rear, eff wide, no prog bef dist: see 1823.   hd   57
1972 **SMITH N ALLAN OILS** 16 [5]5-9-1 p (57) Dale Gibson 16/1: 1-100000: 10th: Mid-div, hmpd 2f out, sn btn.   shd   51
1736 **ARAGONS BOY** 26 [12]4-10-0 (70) D Sweeney 10/1: 054-00: 11th: ch g Aragon - Fancier Bit (Lion   nk   63
Cavern) Sn led till over 1f out, wknd: lightly rcd & unplcd '03 (rtd 74, mdn): stays a stiff 1m, tried 10f: acts
on fast grnd: jock rec a 5-day careless riding ban.
1954 **WELL MEET AGAIN** 16 [9]4-8-11 (53) P Mulrennan(5) 8/1: 31065-30: 12th: Held up, no room & lost   5   37
place halfway, no impress: see 1954.
1966* **BEN HUR** 16 [14]5-9-6 (62) S W Kelly 9/1: 0050-010: 13th: Missed break, brushed up to go handy   12   25
when badly hmpd bef 1f, sn dropped rear & position accepted: op 7/1, this best forgiven after 1966 (clmr).
1794 **MON SECRET** 23 [6]6-8-11 (53) F Lynch 20/1: 13-40060: 14th: Chsd ldrs till over 2f out, eased: btr 1794.   ¾   15
1794 **BARZAK** 23 [4]4-8-13 t (55) K Darley 25/1: 0530000: 15th: Prom till lost plc 2f out, sn bhd & eased.   24   0
15 Ran   Time 1m 36.17 (5.37)   Owned: Horne Hollinshead Johnson   Trained: Upper Longdon

2325
4.20 Sportingoptions Supporting Racing Maiden Stakes 3yo+ (D)
£5525 £1700 £850 **7f100y rnd** Good/Soft 64 -17 Slow Inside

1761 **LYCA BALLERINA 25** [3] B W Hills 3-8-6 (71) R Hills 11/4: 634-5341: Chsd ldrs, smooth hdwy & led **73**
over 1f out, rdn out: eff at 7.5f/1m on fast & soft grnd: gd confidence boost: see 1527, 1186.
2081 **AWESOME LOVE 11** [4] M Johnston 3-8-11 (83) D Holland 10/11 FAV: 2-322: Chsd ldrs, eff to chall 2½ **74**
over 1f out, not pace of wnr: hvly bckd: acts on gd/soft, rated higher on fast grnd prev.
2106 **MASTER THEO 9** [11] H J Collingridge 3-8-11 (77) J Quinn 5/1: 335-033: Trkd ldrs, no room 2f out, 1 **72**
kept on ins last, not pace to chall: poss shade closer with a clr run: acts on firm & gd/soft & polytrack: see 2106.
PREMIER ROUGE 0 [12] A C Stewart 3-8-11 K Darley 12/1: 4: b g Croco Rouge - Petit Point 1½ **69**
(Petorius) Bhd, late gains wide, nvr threaten front trio: debut, op 14/1, 90,000 gns yearling purchase: styd 7.5f,
shaped as if 1m+ may suit: handles gd/soft grnd: encouraging start.
1651 **SOVIET SPIRIT 30** [7]3-8-6 O Urbina 16/1: 505: Trkd ldrs when no room over 2f out till over 1f 2 **60**
out, styd on onepace: op 14/1: now qual for h'caps, type to improve: see 1468.
2106 **CHISEL 9** [8]3-8-11 R Ffrench 40/1: 006: chs stablemate of rnr-up, longer priced stablemate of rnr-up: low grade h'caps will suit, unplcd prev. 1¾ **62**
Precedent) Chsd ldrs till over 1f out: longer priced stablemate of rnr-up: low grade h'caps will suit, unplcd prev.
SCOTT 0 [6]3-8-11 C Haddon(7) 66/1: 7: gr g Polar Falcon - Circled (Cozzene) Dwelt, eff when 1¾ **59**
short of room over 1f out, sn no impress on debut: dam a 7f juv wnr, plcd at 12f.
2231 **NARCISO 5** [9]4-9-7 T Lucas 100/1: 08: Dwelt, chsd ldrs till 4f out, quick reapp. 1 **57**
1922 **PHOENIX EYE 18** [5]3-8-11 S Righton 100/1: 0-009: Cl-up till over 1f out. 1 **55**
2104 **KEY FACTOR 9** [10]3-8-6 P Mulrennan(2) 50/1: 40: 10th: Led till over 1f out, sn btn/eased: see 2104. ¾ **49**
SONEARSOFAR 0 [1]4-9-7 M Lawson(5) 100/1: 0: 11th: Went left start, in tch till over 1f out, debut. 11 **34**
11 Ran Time 1m 36.89 (6.09) Owned: Letitia Lucas & Mr R J McCreery Trained: Lambourn

2326
4.50 Sportingoptions Co Uk Sponsoring On Friday Handicap Stakes Fillies 3yo+ 35-55 (F) [55]
£4030 £1240 £620 **5f str** Good/Soft 64 -55 Slow Inside

1948 **LYDIAS LOOK 16** [17] T J Etherington 7-9-4 (45) T Eaves(3) 9/2 FAV: 0-055451: Trkd ldr travelling **52**
well, led 2f out, drvn out: currently in foal: suited by 5/6f on fast, soft & both AWs, any trk: see 653.
2125 **LEOPARD CREEK 8** [6] Mrs J R Ramsden 3-9-6 p (54) D Allan(3) 25/1: 00-00202: Switched right from ¾ **59**
start & held up, styd on well for press against far rail in last, not reach wnr: acts on firm & gd/soft grnd: see 1951.
2125 **MICKLEDOR 8** [13] M Dods 4-9-4 P (45) S W Kelly 20/1: 0034-003: ch f Lake Coniston - Shamasiya 1¾ **45**
(Vayrann) Mid-div, hmpd halfway, styd on wide for press, nrst fin: mdn plcd in '03 (rtd 54): eff at 5/6f, stiff or
sharp trk: handles fast & gd/soft: eff in blnks, has tried visor, improved here in cheekpieces.
1281 **BOND SHAKIRA 50** [18] B Smart 3-9-7 (55) F Lynch 7/1: 5-304: Led, hdd 2f out & drifted left under nk **54**
press, kept on: op 9/1: 7 wk abs, h'cap bow: handles gd/soft & soft grnd: eff at 5f: see 1146.
2161 **MISS WIZZ 7** [10]4-8-10 p (37) Rory Moore(7) 14/1: 0416445: Chsd ldrs, switched & kept on ins last, nk **35**
not able to chall: acts on fast, gd/soft & fibresand: return to 6f will suit: see 637 (AW banded).
1605 **A BID IN TIME 33** [3]3-8-13 (47) N Callan 25/1: 0-002066: Swtchd right & bhd, kept on late but no dngr. shd **45**
2102 **EFIMAC 9** [15]4-9-8 (43) Suzanne France(7) 20/1: 0500-007: Bmpd start & bhd, hdwy halfway, nvr nk **40**
threat: blnks: acts on gd/soft & fibresand: see 1522.
2181 **PETANA 6** [19]4-8-13 bd (40) Joanna Badger 11/2: 020-5048: Chsd ldrs halfway, nvr pace to chall. shd **37**
2049 **ACE MA VAHRA 12** [14]6-9-2 bd (43) J Bramhill 10/1: 1600059: Went right start, hmpd early, mod 1¾ **35**
late prog: blnks reapplied: see 677 (1m, AW).
1948 **WHITE O MORN 16** [5]5-9-2 p (43) G Gibbons 20/1: 4102040: 10th: Mid-div, nvr on terms: btr 1948. ½ **33**
1973 **MYSTERY PIPS 16** [4]4-9-8 vis (49) Kim Tinkler 40/1: 415-0000: 11th: b f Bin Ajwaad - Le Shuttle 2½ **32**
(Presidium) Chsd ldrs till over 1f out: sell & h'cap wnr '03, AW unplcd (rtd 33a): suited by 5f on firm & fast
grnd, blnks/visor. 1 Sep'03 Good 5fm 52-46 E: 1 Jun'03 Muss 5g/f 44-(38) F:
253 **COLLEGE HIPPIE 165** [12]5-9-7 (48) P Makin(5) 15/2: 004060-0: 12th: Chsd ldrs, btn over 1f out, reapp. 3 **23**
1644 **RIVER LARK 30** [7]5-9-2 p (43) R Ffrench 12/1: 4460650: 13th: Chsd ldrs 3f: btr 1522. hd **17**
1873 **BLUES PRINCESS 20** [9]4-9-11 (52) T Hamilton(3) 16/1: 4/0000-00: 14th: Mid-div, sn struggling. 2½ **19**
2042 **GREY ORCHID 12** [8]3-9-1 (49) G Duffield 66/1: 00-060: 15th: Al outpcd & bhd. 2 **11**
2075 **New Day Dawning 11** [11]3-9-0 (48) R Fitzpatrick 33/1:01948 **Cut Ridge 16** [2]5-9-2 (43) P Bradley(5) 25/1:0
1988 **Alfelma 15** [1]4-9-0 (41) Natalia Gemelova(7) 100/1:0 1682} **Comic Times 382** [16]4-8-13 (40) S Righton 33/1:0
19 Ran Time 1m 07.26(5.96) Owned: Callers And Clerks Trained: Malton

Official Going GOOD/FIRM.

2327
4.00 Listed Naas Sprint Stakes 3yo+ ()
£21809 £6399 £3048 **5f** Good/Firm

2574} **OSTERHASE 16** [7] J E Mulhern 5-9-5 bl (94) F M Berry 3/1 FAV: 3261-061: b g Flying Spur - Ostrusa **114**
(Rustan) Led/dsptd lead, prevailed close home, rdn out: op 4/1: val h'cap scorer '03, also dual List rnr-up & plcd
in this event: suited by 5/6f on fast & soft grnd: likes a stiff/gall trk: v useful sprinter.
2 Jun'03 Curr 5gd 110- A: 2 Apr'03 Cork 5g/f 113- : 2 Jul'02 Curr 5sft 100-94 :
1766* **BENBAUN 23** [1] M J Wallace 3-8-12 BL (87) D Corby 6/1: 6120-1012: Led/dsptd lead, went on shd **106**
halfway, rdn & just hdd cl home: fine run against elders in 1st time blnks: see 1766 (h'cap).
GLOCCA MORRA 239 [8] W T Farrell 6-9-5 J P Murtagh 7/1: 041U41-3: b g Catrail - Delphinus 2½ **105**
(Soviet Star) Dwelt, kept on for press from halfway, not pace to chall front pair: reapp, all wins at 6/7f.
13 Ran Time 58.40 () Owned: Michael Rosenfeld Trained: Curragh

---

2328   4.30 Listed Swordlestown Stud Sprint Stakes 2yo Fillies   ()
£34893 £10238 £4878   **6f**   **Good/Firm**

DAMSON 56 [4] D Wachman 2-8-11   J P Spencer   15/8: 11: b f Entrepreneur - Tadkiyra (Darshaan)   112+
Trkd ldrs, smooth prog to lead over 1f out & sn rdn clr, eased close home: earlier clr-cut debut mdn wnr: dam
a 10f wnr & related to smart performers at 1m/12f+: appeared to apprec step up to 6f & will get further: acts
on fast & gd/sft ground: useful juv, Gr comp beckons.
PICTAVIA 12 [1] J S Bolger 2-8-11   K J Manning   11/8 FAV: 012: Led/dsptd lead till over 1f out,   2   102
kept on but no ch with wnr: earlier landed a 7f mdn at Leopardstown: eff at 6f on fast.
2071 **UMNIYA** 9 [6] M R Channon 2-8-11   T E Durcan   7/2: 32133: Chsd ldrs, rdn & onepace/held from over   1½   97
1f out: consistent up in grade: see 2071, 1818.
6 Ran   Time 1m 10.80()   Owned: Mrs John Magnier   Trained: Carrrick On Shore

---

Official Going FIRM. All Times Slow

2329   6.30 Pleasure Palace Racing Lady Riders' Series Classified Stakes 4yo+ 0-65   (E)
£3348 £1030 £515   **1m3f196y**   **Firm**   **Slow**   Outside

1693* **FLYING SPIRIT** 29 [2] G L Moore 5-10-8 (66) Miss Hayley Moore(7) 4/9 FAV: 23102-11: Nvr far away,   80
led halfway, clr fnl 2f, easily: well bckd: won a h'cap hdle at Stratford 19 days ago (rtd 130h, eff at 2m/2m4f on
firm & fast): suited by 12f on firm & gd/soft: loves a sharp/undul trk, esp Brighton: in fine form, see 1693.
3750} **NEEDWOOD MYSTIC** 295 [4] Mrs A J Perrett 9-10-6   (67) Miss L J Harwood(3) 8/1: 5/31102-2: b f Rolfe   5   67
- Enchanting Kate (Enchantment)   Rear, styd on late into 2nd, no ch with wnr: op 9/2 on reapp: dual h'cap wnr in
'03: '02 class stks & amat h'cap wnr: eff at 12f, prob btr suited by 14f/2m now: acts on firm, soft & polytrack:
best up with/forcing the pace, loves Brighton: can run well fresh: sharper next time over further.
2 Aug'03 Carl 14.1fm 67-66 E: 1 Jul'03 Donc 16.5g/f 68-60 E: 1 Jun'03 Hami 13.0g/f 62-54 E:
1 Aug'02 Carl 14.1fm 57-54 E: 1 Jun'02 Brig 11.8g/s 59- E: 1 Aug'01 Brig 12frm 62-55 E:
1 May'01 Brig 11.8g/s 56-50 E: 2 May'01 Brig 11.8g/s 53-49 F: 1 Apr'01 Brig 12sft 53-42 F:
2220 **PAY THE SILVER** 6 [3] I A Wood 6-10-11 p (69) Ms C Williams 5/1: 0-040203: Waited with, imprvd to   ½   71
chase wnr 1.5f out, sn no impress & caught for 2nd cl-home: qck reapp: see 1986 (AW).
2135 **LYRICAL WAY** 9 [5] P R Chamings 5-10-7 bl (60) Mrs S Bosley 20/1: 1-405064: Nvr far away, wknd 2f   4   61
out: return to 10f will suit: see 236.
2244 **SQUIRTLE TURTLE** 5 [1]4-10-9 bl (67) Mrs H Clubb(5) 20/1: 03-10045: Sn led, rcd v wide & hdd after   12   45
halfway, btn qckly: qck reapp: inexperienced rider steered an erratic crse: see 331 (AW).
5 Ran   Time 2m 34.10 (5.90)   Owned: Richard Green (Fine Paintings)   Trained: Brighton

---

2330   7.00 Karma Brighton Marina Claiming Stakes 2yo   (F)
£3017 £862 £431   **5f213y rnd**   **Firm**   **V Slow**   Inside

2177* **GOLDHILL PRINCE** 7 [1] W G M Turner 2-9-1 p   C Haddon(7) 11/4 JT FAV: 4021111: Made most, idled fnl   69
1f & just held on: op 2/1, v slow time: completed 4-timer, eff at 5/6f on firm, gd/soft & fibresand: suited by
sell/claim grade & cheek pieces: val for further than winning margin, see 2177 & 1779.
1869* **RONNIES LAD** 21 [2] G L Moore 2-8-11 P   R L Moore   11/4 JT FAV: 5012: Mid-div, went after wnr dist,   ½   62
fin well but too late: clr of rem, first time cheek pieces: prev trained by J Norton, clmd by A Reid for 8,000 here.
1752 **ETERNALLY** 26 [3] R M H Cowell 2-8-13 p   E Ahern   7/1: 0353: Front rank, rdn & found little dist.   5   49
2177 **STRAFFAN** 7 [6] E J O'Neill 2-8-8   S Sanders   7/2: 633254: Chsd ldrs wide, wknd & drifted left dist.   2½   37
2145 **STORY OF ONE** 8 [5]2-9-1   Dane O'Neill 5/1: 20135: Keen & prom, wknd after halfway: btr 2017 (AW).   2½   37
882 **ITSA MONKEY** 82 [4]2-8-11   J P Guillambert(3) 16/1: 06: b g Merdon Melody - Gracious Imp (Imp   3   24
Society) Al bhd, fin last: 12 wk abs: 6,000gns Apr foal: brother to a couple of juv wnrs: sire a smart sprinter.
6 Ran   Time 1m 13.40 (5.60)   Owned: Gold Hill Racing   Trained: Sherborne

---

2331   7.30 Bet365 Call 08000 322 365 Handicap Stakes Fillies 3yo+ 35-55   (F)   [53]
£2884 £824 £412   **5f59y rnd**   **Firm**   **Slow**   Inside

1837 **AVIT** 22 [6] P L Gilligan 4-8-10   (35) J F Egan   16/1: 0230601: Trkd ldrs, imprvd to lead dist,   40
held on well, drvn out: first win: eff at 5f, has tried further: acts on fast grnd & polytrack: handles a sharp
trk: has tried blnks, seems btr without: see 832.
4964} **LUCKY VALENTINE** 223 [9] G L Moore 4-9-5 p (44) R L Moore 10/1: 300100-2: b f My Best Valentine -   nk   48
Vera's First (Exodal) Mid-div, went after wnr dist, fin well & only just btn: reapp: '03 Windsor mdn wnr: eff at
5/6f on fast, firm grnd & polytrack: eff with/without cheek pieces, has tried blnks & an eye hood: runs well fresh.
1 Sep'03 Wind 6g/f 46-(48) D:
2262 **ELA FIGURA** 4 [10] A W Carroll 4-9-11 P (50) V Slattery 10/1: 020-6003: Held up, hdwy to chall   1½   50
entering fnl 1f, no extra cl-home: qck reapp & first time cheek pieces: acts on fast & firm grnd: mdn.
1641 **MUST BE SO** 31 [8] J J Bridger 3-8-5 T (37) A Daly 25/1: 5000604: Outpcd, fin well but too late: 1¾   32
tried a t-strap: return to 6f will suit judged on this & also to sell grade, as in 233 (6f seller, AW).
2174 **BLACK OVAL** 8 [4]3-9-6 (52) Dane O'Neill 9/2: 4530005: Dwelt, late hdwy, nvr dngrs: tchd 6/1.   ½   46
2219 **VENDORS MISTAKE** 6 [5]3-9-2 (48) S Sanders 5/1: 00-06336: Prom, sltly short of room/wknd fnl 1f.   nk   41
2269 **INCHING** 3 [2]4-9-8 (47) E Ahern 7/2 FAV: 0000267: Prom, wknd fnl 1f: qck reapp: btr 2062.   1¼   36
2062 **BAHAMIAN BELLE** 12 [3]4-9-11 (50) Laura Pike(7) 16/1: 0400008: Dwelt, recovered to trk ldrs   ½   38
halfway, sn short of room & not recover: did not get the run of today's race: see 1179 (first time t-strap).
2181 **SOMETHINGABOUTHER** 7 [7]4-9-6 (45) C Catlin 9/1: 0305029: Nvr btr than mid-div: btr 2181.   2½   26
1902 **REHIA** 20 [1]3-9-7 (53) S Whitworth 7/1: 5440350: 10th: Led till dist, wknd qckly.   ¾   31
10 Ran   Time 1m 04.03 (4.03)   Owned: Treasure Seekers 2000   Trained: Newmarket

2332
8.00 G&S Mechanical Services Selling Stakes 3-5yo (G)
£2562　£732　£366　　**1m1f209y**　　**Firm**　　**V Slow**　Outside

1913　**BOSCO 19** [6] R Hannon 3-8-5　(59) R L Moore　11/2: 605-0001: Held up, hard rdn to impr dist, styd　　　　　**57**
on to lead cl-home: op 7/1, v slow time, bght by P McEntee for 5,200gns: first win, eff at 10f on firm grnd:
handles a sharp/undul trk: apprec this drop to sell grade, see 1913.
2014　**JACKIE KIELY 15** [4] T G Mills 3-8-5　(50) E Ahern　11/4 FAV: 6205542: Trkd ldrs, badly hmpd dist,　　nk　**55**
rallied fnl 1f & only just btn: nicely bckd, clmd by P McEntee for 6,000: most unlucky here, see 2014.
633　**BONTADINI 117** [7] D Morris 5-9-4　(34) S Sanders　16/1: 000-5003: b g Emarati - Kintail (Kris)　　1¼　**53$**
Front rank, led entering fnl 1f till caught cl-home: clr of rem, long abs: '03 h'cap rnr-up, subs tried a visor:
'02 mdn wnr: eff at 9/10f on firm grnd & both AWs: likes a sharp trk.
2 Feb'03 Ling 10ap 59a-61 F:　1 Aug'02 Wolv 9.3af 65a- D:
2032　**LEITRIM ROCK 14** [5] A G Newcombe 4-9-4　(49) S Whitworth　6/1: 3000-004: Dwelt, sn chsd ldrs, ev　　5　**45**
ch 2f out, sn onepcd: see 2032.
2107　**LABELLED WITH LOVE 10** [2]4-9-4　L Treadwell(7) 4/1: 0-25: Keen & prom, led 3f out & sn wandered,　　¾　**43**
hdd entering fnl 1f & wknd qckly: clmd by J Boyle for 6,000: see 2107.
2133　**ERTE 9** [3]3-8-5　(62) C Catlin　11/2: 3406-066: Rdn in rear, nvr dngrs: big drifter from 11/4.　　　　½　**42**
2088　**MARGERY DAW 11** [1]4-8-13　(55) Laura Pike(7) 13/2: 0006307: Led till 3f out, wknd qckly.　　　　14　**17**
7 Ran　Time 2m 06.22 (8.42)　Owned: Mr Louis Stalder　Trained: Marlborough

2333
8.30 Laurent Perrier Handicap Stakes 3yo 0-70 (E)　　　　　　　　　　　　　　**[77]**
£3387　£1042　£521　　**1m3f196y**　　**Firm**　　**Slow**　Outside

1790　**MAN AT ARMS 24** [4] R Hannon 3-9-6　(69) R L Moore　7/2 CO FAV: 0003-41: Waited with, stdy prog to　　　**80**
lead 2f out, rdn well clr: this step up to 12f, acts on fast & firm grnd: handles a gall or sharp/undul trk:
interesting under a pen, see 1790.
2019*　**GARSTON 15** [5] J S Moore 3-8-8　(57) Derek Nolan(6) 12/1: 0006-312: Led till 2f out, sn left　　8　**60**
bhd by wnr: op 9/1: acts on fast & firm grnd: likes sell h'caps, see 2019.
2013　**RESPLENDENT KING 15** [2] T G Mills 3-9-7　(70) S Sanders　7/2 CO FAV: 3355323: Chsd ldr 1m, sn　　1¾　**70**
outpcd: bckd from 11/2: top-weight & fairly consistent: see 2013.
1965　**WAKE UP HENRY 17** [6] R Charlton 3-8-9　(58) S Drowne　7/2 FAV: 006-034: Trkd ldrs, btn 2f out.　　5　**50**
1623　**PERSIAN DAGGER 33** [3]3-9-2　(65) G Carter　5/1: 0-0065: b c Daylami - Persian Fantasy (Persian　　nk　**56**
Bold) Rdn in rear, nvr dngrs: with J Dunlop & mod form to date: related to sev wnrs & staying may be his game.
2019　**OKTIS MORILIOUS 15** [7]3-7-12 (1oh) (46) J F McDonald(3) 10/1: 4123426: Chsd ldrs 1m, wknd qckly.　　2½　**34**
2065*　**PERUVIAN BREEZE 12** [1]3-8-11　(60) E Ahern　8/1: 066-5617: Prom, wknd 2f out: btr 2065 (AW).　　nk　**46**
7 Ran　Time 2m 32.58 (4.38)　Owned: The Waney Racing Group Inc　Trained: Marlborough

2334
9.00 Racing's Big Day Out August 3rd Handicap Stakes 3yo+ 35-55 (F)　　　　　　**[55]**
£3003　£858　£429　　**6f209y rnd**　　**Firm**　　**Slow**　Inside

2150　**LONDONER 8** [3] S Dow 6-10-0　(55) R L Moore　7/2 FAV: 0003221: Made all, in command fnl 1f, rdn　　　**63**
out: v well h'capped nowadays & long overdue win: eff at 7/10f on firm, gd grnd & polytrack: handles a stiff or
sharp/undul trk: has worn a t-strap, eff without: gd confidence boost: see 2150 & 1013.
2149*　**PRIME OFFER 8** [10] J Jay 8-10-4 (6ex) (59) O Urbina　6/1: 30-02412: Nvr far away, kept on fnl 1f　　1¼　**62**
but not pace of wnr: op 4/1: not disgraced under big weight, see 2149 (1m).
761　**MISTER CLINTON 103** [4] D K Ivory 7-9-12　(53) Dane O'Neill　12/1: 0-000063: Mid-div, styd on under　　1　**54**
press fnl 1f, nvr nrr: long abs: usually runs well here at Brighton, see 761.
2258　**DUE TO ME 4** [5] G L Moore 4-9-4 p (45) S Whitworth　10/1: 2514634: Rear, styd on late, nvr nrr.　　½　**45**
2258　**TEE JAY KASSIDY 4** [11]4-8-8　(35) M Halford(7)　11/2: 2520425: Dwelt, eff 2f out, onepcd.　　½　**34**
935　**KINSMAN 76** [7]7-9-12 bl (53) J P Guillambert(3) 12/1: 00-21546: Slowly away, some late hdwy, nvr dngrs.　1½　**49**
2031　**IPHIGENIA 14** [1]3-9-1　(52) R Miles(3) 20/1: 3000-057: Trkd ldrs, btn fnl 1f: prob flattered last twice.　¾　**46**
2292　**PERERIN 2** [2]3-8-11 BL (48) S Sanders　12/1: 000-0108: Dwelt, al towards rear: qck reapp & blnks.　　1¾　**38**
1644　**BADOU 31** [9]4-9-2　(43) E Ahern　13/2: 1000249: Chsd ldrs 5f, wknd.　　　　　　　　　　　　2　**29**
2258　**AGUILA LOCO 4** [8]5-10-0 p (55) S Drowne　17/2: 3036000: 10th: Front rank 5.5f, wknd & eased.　　6　**29**
515　**SEKWANA 131** [12]5-9-4 bl t (45) V Slattery　80/1: 2360-/000-: 11th: Mid-div, btn 2f out: jumps fit.　　1　**17**
11 Ran　Time 1m 24.34(4.54)　Owned: Mr P McCarthy　Trained: Epsom

Official Going Standard

2335
2.30 Festival Of The Forgotten Herb Handicap Stakes Fillies 3yo+ 35-55 (F)　　　　**[65]**
£3168　£905　£453　　**7f aw rnd**　　**Going 63**　　**-03 Slow**　Inside

1606　**DIAMOND SHANNON 34** [13] D Carroll 3-8-12　(49) D Tudhope(7) 6/1: 2-0051: Chsd ldrs & led over 1f　　**61a+**
out, rdn clr, decisively: first win: AW bow: eff at 6/7f on fast, soft & enjoyed fibresand today: can win again.
1561*　**LEYAALY 36** [11] B A Pearce 5-8-11 p (38) P Makin(5) 20/1: 00-60012: Led till over 1f out, not pace　　5　**40a**
of wnr: eff at 7/9f: in gd form: see 1561 (bdband).
1730　**ESSEX STAR 27** [14] Miss J Feilden 3-8-13　(50) G Duffield　14/1: 0000-03: b f Revoque - Touch of　　1¾　**49a**
White (Song) Chsd ldrs wide, kept on onepace, no threat: AW bow: unplcd '03 (rtd 69, fills mdn): half-sister to a
5/7f wnr, dam a multiple 5f wnr: eff around 7f, handles fibresand.
1160　**SHOTLEY DANCER 57** [16] N Bycroft 5-8-10　(37) Suzanne France(7) 40/1: 060-4004: Bhd, late gains,　　½　**35a**
nrst fin: 8 wk abs: eff at 7f, needs a return to 1m: see 677.
1660　**JESSIE 31** [10]5-8-13 VIS (40) Kim Tinkler　8/1: 5222405: Dwelt & bhd, nrst fin: tried visor, t-strap omitted.　nk　**37a**
2204　**MARABAR 6** [1]6-9-9 bl (50) A Culhane　7/2 FAV: 0031226: Chsd ldrs, no impress dist: well bckd.　　¾　**46a**
1799　**BRIGHT MIST 24** [8]5-8-11　(38) D Sweeney　40/1: 0000/-047: Chsd ldrs till over 1f out: see 1799 (5f).　1¼　**31a**

1804 **NEUTRAL NIGHT 24** [6]4-9-4 vis (45) F P Ferris(3) 8/1: 4331228: Cl-up, drvn & btn over 1f out: btr 1565. 2½ **33a**
2107 **ENNA 10** [15]5-9-10 (51) F Norton 16/1: 1013-469: Mid-div, sn rdn, nvr a factor: new stable: AW bow. 5 **31a**
597 **JESSINCA 121** [5]8-8-8 (35) D Kinsella 14/1: 460-0060: 10th: Outpcd, nvr a factor: abs: see 597. 5 **7a**
1966 **THUMAMAH 17** [9]5-8-10 (1ow)VIS (36) M Tebbutt 40/1: 00-00060: 11th: Chsd ldrs 5f, vis: 'stiff' after race. 2 **5a**
1660 **SANDORRA 31** [2]6-9-6 (47) M Lawson(5) 13/2: 1600160: 12th: Chsd ldrs 5f, sn btn: btr 1590 (banded). 6 **5a**
1944 **Niteowl Dream 17** [12]4-10-0 (55) J D O'Reilly(7) 16/1:0
1270 **Pats Nemisis 51** [3]3-7-12 (10oh)(35) D Fentiman(7) 50/1:0
1801 **Moonlight Song 24** [4]7-8-8 (1oh)(34) R Ffrench 16/1:0 2049 **Red Melodica 13** [7]4-9-9 (50) R Winston 14/1:0
16 Ran Time 1m 31.24 (4.64) Owned: Diamond Racing Ltd Trained: Warthilll

2336

3.05 St Olive Of Palermo Maiden Stakes 2yo (D)
£3601 £1108 £554 **6f aw rnd** **Going 63** **-40 Slow** Inside

1634 **SNOOKERED AGAIN 33** [3] M W Easterby 2-9-0 P Mulrennan(5) 3/1 FAV: 51: Dwelt, sn rdn chasing ldrs, hdwy to lead ins last, rdn out: AW bow: apprec step up to 6f, handles fibresand & gd grnd, sharp trks. **75a**
1424 **CAITLIN 43** [4] B Smart 2-8-9 F Lynch 6/1: 62: ch f Intikhab - Esteraad (Cadeaux Genereux) Chsd ldrs, kept on for press, not pace of wnr: 6 wk abs, AW bow: E28,000 March foal, dam a 6f juv wnr, subs plcd at 10f & related to smart 1m/10f performers: apprec step up to 6f, will get further: acts on fibresand: clr of rem. 1½ **64a**
LOVELORN 0 [10] M W Easterby 2-9-0 T Lucas 20/1: 3: b g Mind Games - Love Letters (Pursuit of Love) Trkd ldrs wide & led over 2f out till ins last, no extra: longer priced stablemate of wnr: cheaply bght Feb first foal, dam a 7f juv wnr & plcd at 5/6f: eff at 6f on fibresand: showed up well for a long way. 4 **59a**
DESERT FERN 0 [11] Ms Deborah J Evans 2-8-9 N Callan 16/1: 4: Chsd ldrs, onepace fnl 2f. 2 **49a**
1161 **BRACE OF DOVES 57** [2]2-9-0 P Makin(5) 4/1: 05: Led till over 2f out, btn dist, abs, gelded. 1½ **51a**
2109 **HIDDEN JEWEL 10** [6]2-9-0 G Gibbons 33/1: 06: Chsd ldrs, drvn & no impress from halfway, AW bow. 1½ **48a**
GARDASEE 0 [9]2-9-0 Dale Gibson 10/1: 7: Hmpd start & bhd, mod late prog. 3 **40a**
2236 **TIPSY LILLIE 5** [5]2-8-9 G Duffield 10/1: 5008: Chsd ldrs till over 2f out, AW bow. ½ **33a**
1739 **TYSON RETURNS 27** [1]2-9-0 D Nolan(3) 9/1: 09: Chsd ldrs, btn 2f out, AW bow. ¾ **36a**
1048 **MINDFUL 66** [8]2-9-0 T G McLaughlin 12/1: 060: 10th: Went right start, chsd ldrs till halfway, eased. 5 **24a**
2132 **MERMAIDS CRY 9** [7]2-8-9 F P Ferris(3) 8/1: 200: 11th: Swerved right start, sn strugg, AW bow. 5 **7a**
11 Ran Time 1m 19.48 (6.18) Owned: Mr R Edmonds & Mr J Wade Trained: Sheriff Hutton

2337

3.35 Red Rose Festival Classified Claiming Stakes 3yo+ 0-60 (F)
£3003 £858 £429 **7f aw rnd** **Going 63** **+01 Fast** Inside

1988 **ONLY ONE LEGEND 16** [5] K A Ryan 6-9-3 bl (60) N Callan 6/1: 0003031: Rdn & in tch early, hdwy to lead over 1f out, rdn out: eff at 5/6f, stays 7f on fast, gd/soft & fibresand, likes polytrack/Lingfield. **62a**
1794 **DISPOL PETO 24** [10] Ian Emmerson 4-9-3 p (57) D Tudhope(7) 5/1 JT FAV: 0520502: Chsd ldrs, kept on for press, not pace of wnr: see 556. 2½ **56a**
1824 **PAYS DAMOUR 23** [8] D Nicholls 7-9-11 (57) Alex Greaves 5/1 JT FAV: 00-00103: Chsd ldrs, onepace bef dist: clr rem: acts on firm, gd/soft & handles hvy/fibresand: see 1522. 1½ **61a**
2202 **ON THE TRAIL 6** [3] D W Chapman 7-8-11 (56) A Culhane 11/2: 1312134: Led/dsptd lead till over 1f out. 4 **39a**
1590 **AIR OF ESTEEM 35** [7]8-8-11 (43) D Fentiman(7) 14/1: 5560245: Sn rdn towards rear, mod late gains. 1 **37a**
1966 **BIJOU DANCER 17** [11]4-8-11 P (51) G Baker 20/1: 0560-006: Chsd ldrs wide till halfway, mod late rally. 2½ **32a**
4699} **SKYLARK 242** [12]7-8-8 (58) Kim Tinkler 10/1: 036204-7: ch f Polar Falcon - Boozy (Absalom) Rdn/bhd & wide, only mod prog: reapp: turf h'cap rnr-up '03: fills h'cap for J Spearing '02: eff at 5/6f, suited by 7f: handles any trk, likes gd & firm grnd, eff with/without an eye-shield. ¾ **28a**
2 Sep'03 Nott 6.1g/f 60-57 E: 1 Jul'02 Yarm 7fm 69-64 D: 2 Sep'01 Chep 5g/f 66-62 E: 2 Sep'01 Bath 5.7fm 63-62 D: 2 Aug'01 Nott 5gd 65- E: 2 Jul'01 Folk 5g/f 62-60 E:
2063 **POWER BIRD 12** [6]4-9-2 VIS (56) L Keniry(3) 8/1: 00-20008: Chsd ldrs till over 2f out: visor: btr 450. 6 **26a**
2243 **MAYBE SOMEDAY 5** [1]3-9-1 bl (60) I Mongan 7/1: 6330209: Sn bhd & t.o. fnl 2f: 'never trav'. dist **0a**
1253 **EASTERN DAGGER 52** [4]4-8-11 (56) R Winston 25/1: 04060-00: 10th: b g Kris - Shehana (The Minstrel) Dwelt, hung badly right on bend 4f out & sn well bhd: jumps fit (no form): AW mdn & subs turf clmr scorer for M Johnston in '03, subs disapp for Mrs N Macauley & R Wilman, incl in visor: eff at 7f/1m on fast grnd & both AWs, stiff/gall or sharp trk. 1 May'03 Leic 8.0g/f 73-(71) F: 1 Feb'03 Wolv 7af 78a- D: 1½ **0a**
4116} **MISS NOTERIETY 276** [2]4-8-8 (25) T Eaves(3) 100/1: 000/0-0: 11th: Led till over 3f out, sn bhd, t.o., reapp, breathing problems reported. 5 **0a**
2052 **MR LOVERMAN 13** [9]4-9-7 (40) G Gibbons 66/1: 0000-000: 12th: Virtually ref to race, t.o.. dist **0a**
12 Ran Time 1m 30.92 (4.32) Owned: Sunpak Potatoes Trained: Hambleton

2338

4.10 Doreen Paterson 1st Time Racing Handicap Stakes 3yo+ 0-70 (E) **[67]**
£3591 £1105 £553 **1m aw rnd** **Going 63** **+01 Fast** Inside

2057 **TRE COLLINE 13** [14] N Tinkler 5-9-7 (60) G Baker 11/1: 0-000001: b g Efisio - Triple Joy (Most Welcome) Held up, v smooth hdwy to lead over 1f out, sn asserted, any amount in hand: eff at 6/7f, now stays 1m: acts on firm, fast & relished this return to fibresand: well h'capped, win again if able to repeat: see 1820. **75a+**
2 Jul'03 Donc 6g/f 75-(74) D: 1 Jun'03 Donc 7fm 74-68 D: 1 May'02 Wolv 7af 70a-65 E:
2226 **CRUSOE 6** [2] A Sadik 7-8-12 bl (51) I Mongan 14/1: 0042002: Sn prom & led 2f out, sn hdd, drvn & kept on, no ch with easy wnr: return to form, well h'capped: see 699. 7 **53a**
1485 **YORKER 40** [1] Ms Deborah J Evans 6-9-12 (65) N Callan 9/1: 4220003: Led till 2f out, drvn & kept on, no ch with wnr: 6 wk abs: see 752 & 241. 1½ **64a**
1875 **INMOM 21** [10] S R Bowring 3-8-10 (60) J Bramhill 12/1: 50-304: Mid-div, kept on wide, not able to chall: AW bow: handles fibresand: see 1610. 3 **53a**
2159 **HOHS BACK 8** [9]5-8-9 p (48) N Chalmers(5) 13/2: 0206005: Dwelt & bhd, mod late prog: btr 1553. 1½ **38a**
1007 **BOOK MATCHED 71** [8]3-9-6 (70) F Lynch 11/1: 03-31406: Chsd ldrs till over 1f out: abs: btr 751. 3 **54a**
2053 **TEEHEE 13** [5]6-9-8 bl (61) D Sweeney 12/1: 150-4607: Chsd ldrs, no impress dist: best at 6/7f. nk **44a**
1546 **HAUNT THE ZOO 37** [6]9-9-6 (59) L Fletcher(3) 16/1: 32513-58: Chsd ldrs 6f: see 1546. shd **42a**
1896 **MUNAAWESH 20** [15]3-8-6 (56) G Duffield 40/1: 0300009: Dwelt, wide, nvr on terms: see 1050. hd **38a**
2111 **MONTE MAYOR LAD 10** [13]4-9-11 P (64) F Norton 12/1: 0334-000: 10th: Wide & held up, nvr a factor. nk **45a**
2179 **RARE COINCIDENCE 7** [12]3-9-5 p (69) D Nolan(3) 9/2 FAV: 3604440: 11th: Chsd ldrs, btn 2f out. 5 **41a**
1606 **SEMPER PARATUS 34** [11]5-9-3 (56) M Tebbutt 12/1: 40-40020: 12th: Al bhd: btr 1606 (6f, soft). 2½ **23a**

744 **ZARIN 105** [7]6-9-13 (66) A Culhane 7/1: 6023-030: 13th: Dwelt, sn struggling: abs: btr 744 & 195. *11* **15a**
1944 **DELIGHTFUL GIFT 17** [4]4-8-6 (45) T Williams 50/1: 00640-60: 14th: b f Cadeaux Genereux - *12* **0a**
Delightful Chime (Alzao) Led early, sn struggling & bhd: unplcd '03 (rtd 74, flattered, cond stks).
1660 **HIGH CANE 31** [3]4-8-13 (52) Darren Williams 28/1: 6-030000: 15th: Dwelt & al bhd, eased fnl 2f: 'sore'. *15* **0a**
15 Ran Time 1m 44.34 (4.94) Owned: Peter Alderson Mike Gosse Adrian Mornin Trained: Malton

2339 4.40 National Black Cow Day Median Auction Maiden Stakes 3yo (F)
£3038 £868 £434 **7f aw rnd** Going 63 -26 Slow Inside

1842 **MITZI CASPAR 22** [11] P L Gilligan 3-8-9 (37) R Price 8/1: 0000321: Chsd ldr halfway, hung left **54a**
but led over 1f out, rdn out: eff at 6/7f on fibresand, has tried 1m: see 1842 & 1803.
4395} **GO FREE 262** [9] A M Hales 3-9-0 A Nicholls 22/1: 00-2: gr g Easycall - Miss Traxdata (Absalom) *1½* **56a**
Chsd ldrs, kept on onepace into last: reapp: unplcd both '03 starts (rtd 60a & 37, mdns, J Cullinan): stays 7f,
return to 1m may suit: handles fibresand.
2092 **PETRION 11** [5] R Guest 3-8-9 C Lowther 25/1: 003: Chsd ldrs till outpcd over 2f out, kept on *3* **45a**
late: AW bow: eff at 7f, 1m shld suit on this evidence: handles fibresand: see 1078 (6f).
1078 **WUNDERBRA 64** [12] M L W Bell 3-8-9 I Mongan 2/1 FAV: 34: Trkd ldrs & led over 4f out till over *½* **44a**
1f out, wknd: 2 mth abs, AW bow: see 1078 (6f).
TOO KEEN 0 [10]3-8-9 P Hanagan 25/1: 5: Dwelt, bhd, mod late prog on debut. *8* **30a**
2148 **FLYING WITH EAGLES 8** [7]3-9-0 G Baker 28/1: 0006: Bhd & rdn, little hdwy: 'not handle kick-back'. *1¼* **32a**
2152 **ARIANS LAD 8** [3]3-9-0 D Sweeney 10/1: 007: Prom till over 2f out, AW bow, longer trip. *hd* **31a**
1951 **WESTBOROUGH 17** [6]3-9-0 (53) Kim Tinkler 4/1: 0205-258: Led till over 4f out, sn bhd: btr 1682 (5f). *2½* **26a**
1659 **SAVANNAH SUE 31** [4]3-8-9 P Mulrennan(5) 8/1: 0-09: Sn outpcd & struggling, AW bow. *5* **12a**
1988 **OSLA 16** [1]3-8-9 F P Ferris(3) 16/1: 00: 10th: Dwelt, wide, nvr a factor, AW bow, new yard. *2½* **7a**
1822 **ALIBA 23** [8]3-9-0 (62) F Lynch 3/1: 354-400: 11th: Cl-up till over 3f out, sn bhd/eased: 'lost action'. *5* **3a**
2092 **JUDDA 11** [2]3-9-0 Dean McKeown 66/1: 000: 12th: Drvn & sn struggling. *nk* **2a**
12 Ran Time 1m 32.82 (6.22) Owned: Dr Susan Barnes Trained: Newmarket

2340 5.15 Howlin' Wolf Birthday Handicap Stakes 4yo+ 35-55 (F) [56]
£2996 £856 £428 **1m4f aw** Going 63 -19 Slow Inside

2226 **DASH OF MAGIC 6** [3] J Hetherton 6-8-12 (40) M Tebbutt 11/1: 2510631: Bhd, hdwy wide from 4f out **48a**
& led dist, rdn out: qck reapp: eff at 12f, suited by 11/12f on firm, gd/soft & likes fibresand/Southwell.
1754 **HEATHERS GIRL 26** [7] D Haydn Jones 5-9-8 (50) F Norton 7/1: 0162422: Chsd ldrs, kept on for *2* **54a**
press, not pace of wnr: stays 12f: see 1754, 862 & 633.
2008 **SHATIN SPECIAL 15** [10] G C H Chung 4-8-12 p (40) R Ffrench 25/1: 1666003: Chsd ldrs halfway, hung *1½* **42a**
left but led over 1f out, sn hdd & no extra ins last: apprec return to fibresand: see 666 (banded).
590 **ELA RE 122** [5] C R Dore 5-9-1 (43) R Thomas(5) 8/1: 606/0-404: Chsd ldrs, outpcd over 2f out, *nk* **44a**
kept on late: 6 wk jumps abs (mod, h'cap hdle): see 421.
1793 **SEA COVE 24** [15]4-9-2 (44) P Hanagan 11/1: 6500-455: In tch wide halfway, drvn & onepace fnl 3f. *½* **44a**
1579 **DALON 35** [9]5-9-8 BL (50) D Allan(3) 40/1: 41614-06: b g Winds of Light - Dikte (Babant) Prom, no *3½* **45a**
extra over 1f out: tried blnks: ex-Polish, dual '03 wnr: seems suited by 9/10f on gd & soft, prob fibresand.
2162 **MOYNE PLEASURE 8** [6]6-9-3 p (45) L Fletcher(3) 25/1: 0231467: Prom & led over 4f out, sn hdd & wknd. *3* **36a**
1589 **MELOGRANO 35** [11]4-9-2 (44) D Nolan(3) 25/1: 60360-28: Led 4f out till over 1f out, wknd qckly. *½* **34a**
1342 **KENTUCKY BULLET 47** [16]8-9-3 (45) L Keniry(3) 10/1: 5-306369: Prom till over 1f out, eased: 7 wk abs. *1½* **33a**
1654 **RED MOOR 31** [1]4-9-6 (48) A Culhane 4/1 FAV: 5-261230: 10th: In tch till over 2f out, fin lame. *6* **28a**
1645 **KALANISHA 31** [13]4-9-0 (42) G Duffield 40/1: 000-060: 11th: Dwelt, sn outpcd & bhd: flattered 1358. *6* **14a**
2120 **ARJAY 9** [2]6-9-3 (45) J Carroll 14/1: 0-003530: 12th: Led 15f out, sn bhd & eased: btr 2120 & 1657. *1¼* **15a**
1645 **PIPSSALIO 31** [12]7-9-0 t (42) P Doe 5/1: 43-62620: 13th: Al in rear: btr 1645 & 666 (banded). *7* **3a**
2112 **CRACOW 10** [14]7-9-3 (45) P Makin(5) 11/1: 05300/-20: 14th: Chsd ldrs till 3f out, eased: see 2112. *9* **0a**
1992 **Kenny The Truth 16** [4]5-9-7 t(49) I Mongan 11/1:P 1564 **Eurolink Artemis 36** [8]7-8-13 p(41) N Callan 14/1:P
16 Ran Time 2m 44.08(9.78) Owned: 21st Century Racing Trained: Malton

Official Going FIRM (GOOD/FIRM IN PLACES)

2341 2.20 E B F Novice Median Auction Stakes 2yo (E)
£3328 £1024 £512 **6f str** Good/Firm 37 -15 Slow Stands side

1964 **SATCHEM 17** [5] D R Loder 2-8-12 T P Queally(3) 1/1 FAV: 21: Made all, rdn & hung left over 1f **89**
out but held on well: well bckd, confirmed debut promise: eff at 6f on fast grnd, 7f shld suit: see 1964.
CAPTAIN HURRICANE 0 [1] P W Chapple Hyam 2-8-12 J Quinn 6/5: 2: b c Desert Style - Ravine *½* **86**
(Indian Ridge) Trkd ldrs & keen, eff to chall from 2f out, hung left ins last & held cl-home: hvly bckd: 21,000gns
Feb first foal, dam a 6/7f wnr: eff at 6f on fast grnd: win similar.
1727* **HIGHLAND CASCADE 27** [2] J M P Eustace 2-8-11 S Sanders 10/1: 13: Chsd ldrs, rdn & kept on over *1½* **80**
1f out: op 16/1: prob ran to form of 1727 (C/D).
RIGHT TO ROAM 0 [3] A R Toller 2-8-12 Lisa Jones(3) 25/1: 4: b c Namid - Lloc (Absalom) *11* **48**
Dwelt, sn outpcd: March foal, 50,000gns purchase: half-brother to a 5f/1m scorer: dam 5f wnr.
2144 **PARSLEYS RETURN 8** [4]2-8-12 S W Kelly 100/1: 05: Sn outpcd: see 2144. *9* **21**
5 Ran Time 1m 13.53 (3.13) Owned: Lucayan Stud & Mr D D Clee Trained: Newmarket

YARMOUTH THURSDAY 10.06.04 Lefthand, Flat, Fair Track

2342 2.55 Racecourse Video Services Maiden Stakes Fillies 3yo (D)
£3419 £1052 £526 7f str Good/Firm 37 -08 Slow Stands side

1617 **KEYAKI 34** [2] C F Wall 3-8-11 S Sanders 9/2: 661: b f Shinko Forest - Woodie Dancer (Green Dancer) Trkd ldrs, rdn & led over 1f out, held on gamely, all out: op 13/2: eff at 7f, imprvd on fast ground today. 78
2092 **ZAMEYLA 11** [4] M A Jarvis 3-8-11 P Robinson 2/5 FAV: 022: Led/dsptd lead, went on halfway till over 1f out, ev ch ins last, just held: acts on firm & fast grnd: clr of rem: see 2092. *nk* 77
CHERTSEY 0 [1] C E Brittain 3-8-11 B Doyle 8/1: 3: ch f Medaaly - Cerisette (Polar Falcon) Chsd ldrs, rdn & no impress dist, position accepted in fin: op 5/1, debut. 5 67
1210 **SET ALIGHT 55** [5] Miss K B Boutflower 3-8-11 S Carson 33/1: 04: b f Forzando - Me Spede (Valiyar) Cl-up/dsptd lead till halfway, btn 2f out: 8 wk abs: bhd on debut prev: 7f/1m shld suit. 6 55
1651 **CROCOLAT 31** [3]3-8-11 A Mackay 33/1: 005: Outpcd, nvr a factor, drpd in trip. 3½ 48
2092 **MARY CARLETON 11** [6]3-8-11 M Fenton 80/1: 06: Led/dsptd lead till over 4f out, sn btn. 1½ 45
6 Ran Time 1m 25.75 (3.15) Owned: Hintlesham SPD Partners Trained: Newmarket

2343 3.25 Dimascio's Ice Creams Selling Stakes 2yo (G)
£2527 £722 £361 7f str Good/Firm 37 -37 Slow Stands side

1212 **LISA MONA LISA 55** [5] V Smith 2-8-11 J Quinn 15/8 FAV: 141: Made all, rdn & styd on strongly ins last: nicely bckd, bght in for 11,200gns: eff at 5f, apprec step up to 7f (dam styd 12f): acts on fast & gd/soft grnd: enjoys sell grade & goes well fresh: see 1212 & 929. 73
2115 **LAKESDALE 10** [6] C J Gray 2-8-6 K Darley 5/2: 022: Held up, prog from halfway, kept on but al held: nicely bckd tho' op 7/4: styd longer 7f trip, acts on fast & gd grnd: claimed for 7,000. 3 60
2183 **TONIGHT 7** [2] W M Brisbourne 2-8-11 B Swarbrick(5) 16/1: 343: Keen & prom, rdn & onepace over 1f out: op 20/1: longer 7f trip may yet suit, only mod form prev: see 1906. 2 61
2110 **GENERAL NUISANCE 10** [4] J S Moore 2-8-11 P Derek Nolan(7) 8/1: 26454: Chsd wnr & ch over 1f out, sn no extra: first time cheek pieces: handles fast & hvy grnd: see 1640. *nk* 60
LOUISE RAYNER 0 [1]2-8-6 J Mackay 3/1: 5: b f Vettori - Showery (Rainbow Quest) Dwelt, sn outpcd & nvr a factor: bckd, op 7/1: Jan foal, half-sister to a dual 1m juv wnr: dam a 6f 3yo scorer. 6 43
FAITHFUL FLASH 0 [3]2-8-6 T P Queally(3) 22/1: 6: b f Tipsy Creek - Tudorealm (Palace Music) Pushed along & chsd ldrs, no impress from halfway: Jan foal, half-sister to a hdle scorer. 1 41
6 Ran Time 1m 27.81 (5.21) Owned: Mr Stephen Dartnell Trained: Newmarket

2344 3.55 'one' Anglia Wherry Lines Handicap Stakes Fillies 3yo 0-70 (E) [77]
£3907 £1202 £601 1m str Good/Firm 37 -11 Slow Stands side

1822* **PERLE DOR 23** [4] W J Haggas 3-9-7 (70) K Darley 4/1 FAV: 450-11: In tch, rdn & hdwy to lead over 1f out, drvn out: nicely bckd on h'cap bow: eff at 7f, apprec step up to 1m & bred to apprec mid-dists: acts on fast grnd, gall/easy trk: type to prog with racing &/or over further: see 1822. 77
2011 **PRINCESS GALADRIEL 15** [7] J R Best 3-8-9 (58) N Pollard 11/2: 040-2132: Held up, hdwy for press 2f out, styd on well, just failed: styd longer 1m trip well: progressive & can win again after 2011 & 1730 (6f). *nk* 64
1956 **GABANA 17** [10] C F Wall 3-9-2 (65) S Sanders 9/2: 003-0603: br f Polish Precedent - Out West (Gone West) Held up in tch, rdn & styd on onepace fnl 2f: mdn plcd fnl '03 start (rtd 78, earlier AW unplcd, rtd 66a, mdn): eff around 1m on fast & gd grnd, gall/easy trk. 1½ 68
2134 **FAITH HEALER 9** [1] V Smith 3-8-6 BL (55) J Quinn 40/1: 460-0004: br f Key of Luck - Cindy's Star (Dancing Dissident) Led till over 1f out, no extra: first time blnks, imprvd run with forcing tactics: ex-Irish, eff over an easy 1m on fast & soft grnd in blnks. 2½ 53
1823 **BLAEBERRY 23** [2]3-8-8 (57) M Fenton 11/2: 00-0055: Chsd ldr, no impress dist: btr 1823. 1¾ 51
861 **LA PUCE 85** [3]3-9-3 (66) T P Queally(3) 7/1: 0-401146: Keen early, prom till ins last: 12 wk abs. ¾ 58
4808} **LADY BLADE 234** [6]3-9-1 (64) Lisa Jones(3) 12/1: 6360-7: b f Daggers Drawn - Singhana (Mouktar) Held up, eff 2f out, no impress: reapp: unplcd '03 (rtd 65, auct mdn): dam a 14f wnr. 2½ 51
2046 **TARDIS 13** [8]3-9-1 (64) J Mackay 9/1: 61524-08: Chsd ldrs till 2f out: see 2046. 18 15
1904 **PLEASURE SEEKER 20** [5]3-8-11 (60) S Carson 33/1: 00-009: Hld up & no impress: 'lost action on grnd'. *nk* 10
1798 **WELSH EMPRESS 24** [9]3-8-3 (52) R Miles(3) 10/1: 6603-030: 10th: Prom, rdn & btn 3f out: btr 1798. 2½ 0
10 Ran Time 1m 39.00 (3.9) Owned: The Perle d'Or Partnership Trained: Newmarket

2345 4.30 Weatherbys Insurance Handicap Stakes 3yo 0-70 (E) [74]
£3770 £1160 £580 1m6f17y Good/Firm 37 +08 Fast Inside

2130 **CONSIDINE 9** [1] J M P Eustace 3-9-7 (67) S Sanders 3/1 FAV: 045-0121: Made all, drvn & held on all out: bckd, op 7/2: best time of day: eff at 12f, imprvd of late at 14f: acts on fast & soft grnd, stiff or easy trks: likes to race with/force the pace: tough & progressive type: see 2130 & 1429. 76
2134 **ILWADOD 9** [2] M R Channon 3-8-10 (56) K Darley 100/30: 006-1222: Pushed along in rear, styd on well for press from over 1f out, just failed: bckd, op 4/1: styd longer 14f trip well: acts on fast & hvy grnd. *shd* 64
2134 **SIEGFRIEDS NIGHT 9** [7] M C Chapman 3-9-6 (66) L Vickers 8/1: 3362133: Chsd ldrs, kept on onepace. 3 69
2046 **VELVET WATERS 13** [4] R F Johnson Houghton 3-8-13 (59) S Carson 12/1: 600-364: Chsd wnr, ch 3f out, no extra dist: op 10/1: prob styd longer 14f trip: see 1790 (11f). 1¼ 60
1976 **EUIPPE 16** [3]3-9-2 (62) M Fenton 33/1: 456-05: Chsd wnr, no extra when hmpd dist: clr of rem: stays 14f on fast grnd: see 1976. *shd* 62
2134 **DANEFONIQUE 9** [6]3-8-11 (57) R Fitzpatrick 9/1: 0-032256: Held up & keen, rdn & btn 2f out: btr 1836. 9 43
1785 **CANNI THINKAAR 25** [5]3-9-6 e (66) N Pollard 33/1: 0406-607: b g Alhaarth - Cannikin (Lahib) Prom, lost place from halfway: op 20/1: eye-shield: unplcd '03 (rtd 71, mdn): half-brother to a 6/7f juv wnr. 18 25
1140 **FRANKIES WINGS 59** [8]3-9-0 (60) R Miles(3) 5/1: 0-068: Mid-div, btn 4f out: abs, h'cap bow, reportedly unsuited by this fast grnd: btr 1140 (gd). 5 11
1836 **CEASAR 23** [9]3-8-13 p (59) G Faulkner 6/1: 4-210139: Held up & struggling fnl 4f: 'lost action'. 25 0
9 Ran Time 3m 1.98 (4.18) Owned: Mr Elias Haloute Trained: Newmarket

---

2346 5.05 Rfc Bed-Down Excel Plus Handicap Stakes 3yo 35-55 (F) **[61]**
£3353 £958 £479　　1m3f101y　　Good/Firm 37　　+00 Fast　Inside

2014 **WINSLOW BOY** 15 [1] C F Wall 3-9-6 (53) J Quinn 7/2 FAV: 000-0461: Held up, short of room over 3f **59**
out, styd on for press to lead line, all out: nicely bckd: eff around 11.5f/12f: acts on fast grnd: first win today.
1947 **CUNNING PURSUIT** 17 [11] M L W Bell 3-8-10 (43) K Darley 4/1: 06562: b g Pursuit of Love - _shd_ **48**
Mistitled (Miswaki) In tch, prog to lead 2f out, rdn & hdd line: op 6/1: h'cap bow: imprvd for step up to 11.5f:
acts on fast grnd: only mod form at up to 1m prev, incl in banded company.
2014 **VRISAKI** 15 [7] Miss D Mountain 3-9-2 (49) A McCarthy 6/1: 0-204003: Prom & led over 3f out till _2½_ **50**
2f out, not pace of front pair ins last: clr of rem, op 8/1: stays 11.5f, acts on fast grnd & fibresand.
2205 **ANISETTE** 6 [4] Julian Poulton 3-9-2 (49) Lisa Jones(3) 20/1: 2-306064: In tch, rdn & no extra dist. _5_ **42**
2123 **ROYAL UPSTART** 9 [12]3-8-7 bl (40) B Swarbrick(5) 10/1: 00-03265: Held up in tch, prog/ch 2f out, wknd. _2½_ **29**
2019 **PRINCESS ISMENE** 15 [10]3-8-12 bl (45) G Faulkner 13/2: 3340546: V slow away & bhd, only mod prog. _3½_ **29**
2134 **HEARTBEAT** 9 [5]3-8-12 BL (45) T P Queally(3) 11/2: 0044507: Prom, ch over 2f out, wknd: blnks. _hd_ **28**
1612 **LA CONCHA** 34 [9]3-9-5 VIS (52) S W Kelly 33/1: 000008: b g Kahyasi - Trojan Crown (Trojan Fen) _5_ **27**
Led 1m, btn 2f out: unplcd prev at up to 14f.
1971 **BALLYBORO** 17 [6]3-9-7 VIS (54) P Robinson 16/1: 5-609: Chsd ldrs till 3f out: vis, op 9/1, h'cap _11_ **12**
bow, reportedly lost action & made a noise.
1610 **MARIA MARIA** 34 [2]3-9-1 (48) R Fitzpatrick 40/1: 0-0040: 10th: Bhd from halfway: unplcd at up _23_ **0**
to 1m prev, has tried cheek pieces: 'finished distressed'.
2065 **SIGNORA PANETTIERA** 12 [8]3-9-8 (55) B O'Neill(7) 20/1: 640-6060: 11th: Prom, struggling from halfway. _½_ **0**
11 Ran　Time 2m 27.15 (4.35)　Owned: Mrs J E Dobie　Trained: Newmarket

---

2347 5.35 Saffie Joseph & Sons Handicap Stakes 3yo+ 35-55 (F) **[57]**
£3451 £986 £493　　6f str　　Good/Firm 37　　-16 Slow　Stands side

2262 **GONENDUNNETT** 4 [3] Mrs C A Dunnett 5-9-7 vis (50) Lisa Jones(3) 8/1: 0000661: Made all, hung right **59**
but styd on well for press in last: qck reapp: suited by 5/6f on firm, fast & both AWs, sharp/undul or easy trk.
2080 **KENNINGTON** 12 [14] Mrs C A Dunnett 4-9-9 vis (52) Hayley Turner(5) 5/1: 4034002: Bhd, switched & _2½_ **54**
kept on late, not able to reach wnr: acts on fast, gd/soft & fibresand: spot on in similar at 7f.
2063 **ADANTINO** 12 [8] B R Millman 5-9-10 bl (53) K Darley 4/1 FAV: 3413363: Held up, kept on onepace. _hd_ **54**
2150 **FEAST OF ROMANCE** 8 [12] C N Allen 7-9-4 bl (47) B Reilly(3) 8/1: 1503064: Held up & prog halfway, _2_ **42**
kept on onepace: eff at 6f, ideally suited by 7f: see 1132 & 661.
1988 **MR UPPITY** 16 [1]5-8-11 e (40) N Pollard 16/1: 0245365: Rcd alone in centre, hung right & no _3½_ **24**
impress from over 1f out, eased nr fin: see 982.
1765 **AFRICAN SPUR** 26 [5]4-9-12 (55) R Fitzpatrick 6/1: 0000006: Prom till over 1f out: bckd, op _2½_ **31**
10/1: modest improve'ment: t-strap omitted: see 775 & 533.
1989 **CRUSTY LILY** 16 [4]8-8-6 (5oh)p (30) J Mackay 25/1: 0000-307: Held up & nvr a factor: see 1715. _½_ **9**
524 **KOMENA** 129 [7]6-9-4 (47) P Robinson 12/1: 240-5008: Chsd ldrs till over 1f out: btr 400. _1¼_ **17**
1046 **OFF HIRE** 66 [10]8-9-9 vis (52) M Fenton 25/1: 00-23409: Prom 4f: abs: btr 641 (5f, AW). _nk_ **21**
1368 **POLAR FORCE** 46 [6]4-9-12 (55) S Carson 9/1: 4003030: 10th: Prom till lost place after 2f, sn _9_ **0**
bhd, abs: new stable: btr 1368 & 897.
2262 **EMMERVALE** 4 [9]5-9-7 (50) B Doyle 14/1: 6100-500: 11th: Al outpcd & nvr a factor: qck reapp. _5_ **0**
653 **ON THE LEVEL** 115 [2]5-9-0 (43) P McCabe 50/1: 3255-000: 12th: ch f Beveled - Join The Clan _3½_ **0**
(Clantime) Keen & prom, btn halfway: recent jumps runner (mod, nov): C/D mdn rnr-up in '03: unplcd '02 (rtd 35,
mdn): eff at 5/6f on fast grnd & an easy trk: best without cheek pieces. 2 Sep'03 Yarm 6.0g/f 50-(40) D:
1989 **POLAR HAZE** 16 [11]7-8-8 vis (37) J Quinn 9/1: 0455040: 13th: Al outpcd: btr 1989 & 533 (AW). _shd_ **0**
13 Ran　Time 1m 13.61(3.21)　Owned: College Farm Thoroughbreds　Trained: Norwich

---

Official Going Good/Firm (Firm places)

2348 2.10 Rectangle Group Maiden Stakes Colts & Geldings 2yo (D)
£5272 £1622 £811　　6f8y　　Good/Firm 31　　-14 Slow　Centre

1760 **PERFECT CHOICE** 26 [3] B J Meehan 2-8-11 D Holland 4/1: 01: gr c Daylami - Fairy Contessa (Fairy **89**
King) Handy, hdwy to lead dist, hung right ins last but kept on, rdn out: May foal, cost 155,000gns: half-brother
to a useful 5f juv scorer: dam plcd over 6f: eff over a gall 6f on fast grnd: much imprvd for debut.
FINANCIAL TIMES [10] Saeed bin Suroor 2-8-11 L Dettori 3/1: 2: b c Awesome Again - Investabull _1¼_ **84**
(Holy Bull) In tch, eff to chall over 1f out, kept on same pace ins last on debut: March foal, cost $190,000: eff
over a gall 6f, 7f will suit: acts on fast grnd: learn from this, will be winning sn.
COUNCELLOR [11] R Hannon 2-8-11 R Hughes 5/2 FAV: 3: b c Gilded Time - Sudden Storm Bird _shd_ **84**
(Storm Bird) Led till over 1f out, onepace & sltly short of room ins last: hvly bckd on debut: well clr rem: Feb
foal, cost £140,000: half-brother to wnrs over 7/12f: eff at 6f, 7f sure to suit: acts on fast grnd: win sn.
ROYAL ORISSA [5] D Haydn Jones 2-8-11 Paul Eddery 33/1: 4: b c Royal Applause - Ling Lane _5_ **70**
(Slip Anchor) In tchd, edged left well over 1f out, no extra on debut: April foal, cost 9,000gns: half-brother to
a 10f wnr: bred to apprec 7f/1m in time.
TRAIANOS [6]2-8-11 T Quinn 16/1: 5: Cl-up, wknd well over 1f out on debut. _nk_ **69**
DREAM TONIC [7]2-8-11 S Hitchcott(3) 11/1: 6: Sn cl-up, wknd 2f out. _2_ **63**
1900 **MASTER JOSEPH** 20 [4]2-8-11 T E Durcan 14/1: 47: In tch, wknd 2f out: op 25/1. _½_ **61**
2071 **DOCTORS CAVE** 12 [2]2-8-11 E Ahern 25/1: 08: Al bhd. _¾_ **59**
WAVERTREE WARRIOR [12]2-8-11 W Supple 16/1: 9: Slow away, sn in tch, wknd 2f out. _½_ **57**
LIQUID LOVER [8]2-8-11 Dane O'Neill 20/1: 0: 10th: Slow away & al bhd. _shd_ **57**
WAATHEB [1]2-8-11 P Dobbs 33/1: 0: 11th: Al bhd on debut. _shd_ **57**
GO MO [9]2-8-11 J F Egan 33/1: 0: 12th: Al bhd on debut. _3_ **48**
12 Ran　Time 1m 14.31 (2.71)　Owned: Mrs Susan Roy　Trained: Upper Lambourn

2349 2.45 Renault Master Maiden Stakes Fillies 3yo (D)
£5785 £1780 £890 1m2f6y Good/Firm 31 +01 Fast Outside

4056} **NUZOOA 280** [9] M P Tregoning 3-8-11 R Hills 11/4: 2-1: b f A P Indy - Min Alhawa (Riverman) 95+
Handy, hdwy to lead 3f out, rdn clr over 1f out, readily: rnr-up in a mdn sole juv start: dam 7/10f scorer:
relished this step up to 10f, 12f shld suit: acts on firm & fast grnd, gall trks: useful, open to plenty of further
improvement & shld make up into List/group class. 2 Sep'03 Sali 7.0fm 84- D:
4871} **ASALEEB 230** [7] A C Stewart 3-8-11 W Supple 8/1: 32-2: b f Alhaarth - Gharam (Green Dancer) 5 84
Chsd ldr till over 5f out & again well over 1f out, kept on, not pace or wnr on reapp: plcd both '03 fills mdn
starts: half-sister to a decent stayer: stays 10f on fast grnd & on a gall trk: shld find similar.
2 Oct'03 Donc 8g/f 82- D:
1762 **SECRET FLAME 26** [8] W J Haggas 3-8-11 K Fallon 5/4 FAV: 5-33: Chsd ldrs, rdn & outpcd over 2f 1 82
out, rallied appr fnl 1f, no extra ins last: hvly bckd: prob stays 10f & clearly even btr expected after 1762.
4251} **GAME DAME 268** [10] B W Hills 3-8-11 M Hills 12/1: 33-4: ch f Nashwan - Gentle Dame (Kris) Held ½ 81+
up, sltly short of room over 2f out, some late gains, hands & heels on reapp: rtd 82 when 3rd both '03 starts (mdn):
dam 10f wnr & looks sure to apprec 12f: acts on firm & fast grnd: encouraging, just the type for 12f h'caps.
1904 **DARK RAIDER 20** [12]3-8-11 (63) D Corby(3) 100/1: 00-255: Bhd, eff 2f out, wknd: see 1610 (1m). 2½ 77
SILVER SASH [5]3-8-11 T Quinn 40/1: 6: Slow away & bhd, modest late gains on debut. hd 76
BURN [4]3-8-11 R Hughes 33/1: 7: Bhd, nvr a factor on debut. 4 70
1885 **STOCKING ISLAND 20** [2]3-8-11 (79) J Murtagh 8/1: 0238: Led after 1f till 3f out, wknd: see 1885. hd 69
ALENUSHKA [6]3-8-11 Dane O'Neill 33/1: 9: Slow away, al bhd. 2½ 65
4973} **WATERSHIP CRYSTAL 222** [3]3-8-11 L Dettori 16/1: 0-0: 10th: In tch, wknd 3f out. 3 60
1666 **NASSIRIA 30** [11]3-8-11 D Holland 25/1: 660: 11th: In tch, wknd 3f out. 6 50
11 Ran Time 2m 05.82 (3.02) Owned: Mr Hamdan Al Maktoum Trained: Lambourn

2350 3.15 Cantorodds Com Stakes Handicap 3yo+ 0-75 (E)
[75]
£4544 £1398 £699 1m str Good/Firm 31 -09 Slow Centre

2129 **OH BOY 9** [5] R Hannon 4-8-13 (60) R Smith 16/1: 040-0051: Handy, hdwy to lead appr fnl 1f, edged 68
left for press ins last but kept on, drvn out: first win: imprvd over this straight 1m on fast grnd & a gall trk.
2129 **SPIRITS AWAKENING 9** [3] J Akehurst 5-8-9 (56) C Catlin 6/1: 422-0632: Chsd ldrs, hdwy 2f out, ¾ 62
hung right under press ins last but kept on, not btn far: fin in front of this wnr in 2129: in gd form: see 1849.
1891 **HABSHAN 20** [10] N A Graham 4-9-8 (69) R Hughes 13/2: 52-043: Held up, hdwy to lead over 1f out, 2 71
sn hdd & onepcd when short of room in last: fair run: see 1891.
1082 **CUDDLES 64** [4] K O Cunningham Brown 5-8-13 (60) Dane O'Neill 20/1: 450-0504: Held up, some late ½ 60
gains, nvr dngrs: 2 mth abs & prev with C Brittain: needs further: see 876.
2116* **JUST TIM 10** [2]3-9-8 (6ex) (80) R L Moore 6/1: 2-414015: In tch, wknd appr fnl 1f: btr 2116. 1¼ 79
2057 **MAGIC AMOUR 13** [1]6-9-0 (61) D Holland 4/1 FAV: 12020-26: Led till over 1f out, wknd: btr 2057. 2 56
629 **ICED DIAMOND 117** [7]5-8-11 (58) T E Durcan 16/1: 6200-107: In tch, wknd 2f out: 4 mth abs: btr 558. 2 49
1915 **MUYASSIR 19** [9]9-9-2 (63) S Drowne 16/1: 100-0108: Al bhd: btr 406 (polytrack). 5 44
1909 **POP UP AGAIN 19** [8]4-10-0 (75) L Dettori 7/1: 20510-09: ch f Bahamian Bounty - Bellair (Beveled) 15 26
In tch, wknd well over 1f out: '03 h'cap wnr: suited by 7f on firm or fast grnd, gall or sharp trks.
2d Oct'03 Redc 7g/f 76-73 E: 1 Oct'03 Newc 7fm 74-67 D: 2 Sep'03 Redc 7fm 68-(70) D: 2 Jul'03 Carl 6.9g/f 71-(73) D:
2 Sep'02 York 6g/f 67- E:
1915 **BOUNDLESS PROSPECT 19** [6]5-9-9 (70) M Hills 9/2: 000-0000: 10th: b g Boundary - Cape (Mr dist 0
Prospector). Net muzzle caught in stalls & left well bhd, no ch after: unplcd in '03 (rtd 76): mdn & h'cap wnr in
'02: eff at 6/7.5f on firm, gd/soft & both AWs: has tried a visor, has suffered breathing problems.
2 Jun'02 Ches 7.5fm 88- D: 1 Jun'02 Leic 7gd 86-78 D: 1 Apr'02 Nott 6g/s 83- D:
10 Ran Time 1m 40.02 (3.22) Owned: Mr A F Merritt Trained: Marlborough

2351 3.45 Listed Lord Weinstock Memorial Stakes Registered As The Ballymacoll Stud Stakes fillies 3yo (A)
£17400 £6600 £3300 1m2f6y Good/Firm 31 -10 Slow Outside

1863 **INCHENI 21** [7] G Wragg 3-8-9 (101) S Drowne 9/2: 61-2031: Held up, hdwy 2f out, styd on to lead 103
appr fnl 1f, drvn out relished step up to 10f & acts on fast, gd & polytrack: useful, improve further over mid-dists.
1844* **HALICARDIA 22** [2] P W Harris 3-8-12 (106) D Holland 11/10 FAV: 311-312: Held up, hdwy over 2f ¾ 104
out, short of room over 1f out, kept on to chase wnr ins last, not her pace: hvly bckd: useful run conceding weight
& looks well worth a try with more positive tactics: ran green 1844, 1110.
1863 **CLASSICAL DANCER 21** [4] H Candy 3-8-9 (95) Dane O'Neill 9/4: 3-123: Chsd ldrs, hdwy to lead over nk 100
1f out, sn hdd & onepcd: styd this longer 10f trip & ran to form of 1863: useful & lightly rcd: see 1258.
2013 **SHUHEB 15** [3] C E Brittain 3-8-9 T E Durcan 100/1: 54: ch f Nashwan - Shimna (Mr Prospector) 2½ 96
Cl-up, led 3f out till over 1f out, wknd: mid-dist bred & this was a pleasing eff, tho' treat rating with caution.
1931 **SI SI AMIGA 19** [1]3-8-9 (92) M Hills 16/1: 1-445: In tch, wknd well over 1f out: see 1568. ½ 95
1568 **PROUD TRADITION 36** [6]3-8-9 (80) L Dettori 16/1: 1-06: b f Seeking The Gold - Family Tradition 13 77
(Sadler's Wells). Led till 3f out, wknd: won sole juv start (fills mdn): dam smart over 7/14f: stays a stiff 1m,
mid-dists shld suit: acts on fast grnd: has run well fresh: needs an ease in grade.
1 Sep'03 Newm 8g/f 79- D:
6 Ran Time 2m 06.87 (4.07) Owned: Mrs Emily Oppenheimer Turner Trained: Newmarket

2352 4.20 Renault Trafic Maiden Stakes 3yo (D)
£5961 £1834 £917 7f str Good/Firm 31 +12 Fast Centre

KEHAAR [8] M A Magnusson 3-9-0 E Ahern 13/2: 1: ch c Cadeaux Genereux - Lighthouse (Warning) 90+
Handy, hdwy over 1f out, styd on to lead ins last, pushed out on debut: gd time: cost 170,000gns: eff over a stiff
7f, 1m sure to suit: acts on fast & runs well fresh: not given a hard time, promising future.
2098 **PIZAZZ 10** [1] B J Meehan 3-9-0 (79) D Holland 10/11 FAV: 0-52522: With ldrs, led over 3f out, 1¼ 86
kept on till collared ins last, no extra: well bckd: deserves similar: see 2098, 1511.
DEUXIEME [4] R Charlton 3-8-9 S Drowne 8/1: 3: b f Second Empire - Kardelle (Kalaglow) Slow ¾ 79

away & bhd, hdwy over 2f out, onepace under hands & heels ins last: half-sister to a 7f/1m wnr: eff over a gall 7f, 1m shld suit: acts on fast grnd: clr of rem on debut, plenty to like about this & shld rate more highly.
CORKY [9] R Hannon 3-9-0 R L Moore 33/1: 4: b g Intikhab - Khamseh (Thatching) Slow away, bhd, some late gains, nvr dngrs on debut: cost 30,000gns: half-brother to useful sprinter Bonus: showed some promise here & shld apprec 1m: learn from this. *5* **74**
2031 **ALL QUIET 14** [7]3-8-9 (78) R Hughes 11/2: 000-3235: In tch, eff over 1f out, sn no extra: exposed. *¾* **67**
NAZZWAH [3]3-8-9 T E Durcan 25/1: 6: Bhd, modest late gains on debut: needs further. *nk* **66**
REVENIR [5]3-9-0 L Dettori 28/1: 7: In tch, wknd well over 1f out on debut. *1¼* **69**
1935 **CAYMAN CALYPSO 19** [10]3-9-0 K Fallon 16/1: 08: In tch, wknd well over 1f out. *¾* **67**
4952} **RICHIE BOY 223** [2]3-9-0 M Henry 50/1: 0-9: In tch, wknd 2f out. *3½* **60**
1929 **GENTLE RAINDROP 19** [13]3-8-9 J F Egan 16/1: 050: 10th: Slow away, nvr a factor. *hd* **54**
1514 **BLACK SABBETH 38** [11]3-9-0 C Catlin 100/1: 00: 11th: Al bhd. *4* **51**
4980} **SO DETERMINED 221** [12]3-9-0 J Fortune 66/1: 00-0: 12th: Led till over 3f out, wknd. *5* **41**
12 Ran Time 1m 25.66 (1.36) Owned: East Wind Racing Ltd Trained: Upper Lambourn

2353

4.50 Fortis Bank Stakes Handicap 3yo 0-85 (D) **[91]**
£5688 £1750 £875 **1m4f5y** **Good/Firm 31** **-04 Slow** Outside

2114 **PORTRAIT OF A LADY 10** [6] H R A Cecil 3-8-11 (74) L Dettori 7/4 FAV: 540-3131: Handy, hdwy to lead over 3f out, kept on well fnl 1f, pushed out: stays 12f well on fast & soft grnd, any trk: tough & progressive. **84**
1865 **OBAY 21** [1] E A L Dunlop 3-9-7 (84) K Fallon 2/1: 0-4142: Chsd ldr, kept on till not pace of wnr appr fnl 1f: proving tough & consistent: see 1213. *3* **88**
2225 **GJOVIC 6** [2] B J Meehan 3-8-12 (75) J F McDonald(3) 10/1: 2-250433: In tch, outpcd over 2f out, rallied over 1f out, no threat to front pair: qck reapp, shld stay 12f: see 2225, 1105. *3½* **75**
2024* **BOULE DOR 15** [5] R Ingram 3-9-4 (81) N Day 3/1: 1300-414: Held up, hdwy over 3f out, wknd well over 1f out: big step up in trip: see 2024 (9f). *1¾* **78**
2024 **MASTER MAHOGANY 15** [4]3-8-3 (66) J F Egan 25/1: 040065: b g Bandmaster - Impropriety (Law Society) Led till over 3f out, wknd: unplcd earlier. *14* **43**
2031 **FIRE FINCH 14** [3]3-8-6 (69) T E Durcan 16/1: 6606: Slow away, in tch till wknd qckly 4f out. *dist* **0**
6 Ran Time 2m 33.57 (4.27) Owned: Mr J Shack Trained: Newmarket

2354

5.25 Handicap Stakes For Gentleman Amateur Riders 4yo+ 0-75 (E) **[42]**
£3601 £1108 £554 **1m2f6y** **Good/Firm 31** **-33 Slow** Outside

1792 **SANGIOVESE 24** [7] H Morrison 5-11-11 (67) Mr J J Best(5) 5/1: 0335231: Handy, styd on to lead over 1f out, pushed out: joc received a 7-day careless riding ban: eff over 1m/10f on fast, gd & fibresand, handles polytrack: can front run: tough: see 195. **76**
1693 **EASTBOROUGH 29** [8] B G Powell 5-11-2 (58) Mr S Walker 8/1: 3434662: Held up, hdwy well over 2f out, kept on to go 2nd ins last, not pace of wnr: gd run: see 1098, 978. *1½* **63**
2170 **ICANNSHIFT 8** [13] S Dow 4-10-12 (54) Mr D Hutchison(5) 6/1: 2130363: Led till over 1f out, no extra: gd run: see 1357 (made virtually all), 1273. *½* **58**
2170 **GALEY RIVER 8** [4] J J Sheehan 5-9-13 (41) Mr J Pemberton(5) 20/1: 1623504: In tch, onepace. *1¾* **42**
2217* **RED FOREST 6** [5]5-11-2 (5ex)t (58) Mr Stephen Harrison(7) 5/2 FAV: 0-316115: In tch, outpcd over 2f out, rallied ins last: qck reapp, btr 2217 (12f). *4* **53**
2146 **BURGUNDY 8** [12]7-10-11 bl (53) Mr L Newnes(3) 9/1: 4200036: In tch, wide, mod late gains, nvr dngrs. *shd* **48**
2035 **NOBLE CALLING 14** [11]7-10-10 (52) Mr James White(3) 10/1: 0006-037: Bhd, hung right over 2f out, no impress: see 2035. *2½* **43**
1913 **BLUEGRASS BOY 19** [3]4-11-6 (62) Mr D H Dunsdon 16/1: 5300-308: Slow away & nvr a factor. *3½* **48**
2067 **LILLI MARLANE 12** [1]4-12-0 (70) Mr S Callaghan(3) 7/1: 350-2609: Slow away & bhd, no dngr. *1¼* **54**
2036 **NUZZLE 14** [9]4-10-4 (46) Mr S Dobson(3) 20/1: 0050260: 10th: Chsd ldr till 4f out, wknd: btr 1884. *5* **23**
2220 **SOMAYDA 6** [2]9-10-5 (47) Mr J Doyle(7) 50/1: 25000-00: 11th: b g Last Tycoon - Flame of Tara (Artaius) Al bhd: rnr-up in a h'cap in '03: eff at 1m/10f on gd/soft & hvy: has run well fresh & tried blnks/visor/t-strap. 2 Jul'03 Kemp 8g/f 52-52 E: *4* **18**
SEATTLE ART 1443 [10]10-9-10 (3oh) (35) Mr G Bartley(7) 100/1: 66/605///-0: 12th: Slow away & bhd. *19* **0**
12 Ran Time 2m 09.21(6.41) Owned: Kentisbeare Quartet Trained: East Ilsley

YORK FRIDAY 11.06.04 Lefthand, Flat, Galloping Track

Official Going GOOD/FIRM.

2355

2.15 Britessunglasses & Fox River Socks Rated Stakes Handicap 4yo+ 0-95 (C) **[94]**
£9965 £3066 £1533 **1m5f197y** **Good/Firm 36** **-02 Slow** Inside

1928 **STAR MEMBER 20** [2] A P Jarvis 5-9-5 (85) K McEvoy 4/1: 050-5141: Chsd ldrs, prog to lead 2f out, rdn clr fnl 1f: well bckd: eff at 10f, suited by 14f & prob stays 2m: acts on fast, gd/soft & polytrack, any trk, likes York: confirmed promise of 1928 & is v progressive, win again. **98**
1861 **ESCAYOLA 22** [6] W J Haggas 4-9-7 vis (87) T Quinn 9/2: 11211-02: Held up, prog 3f out, kept on to chsd wnr fnl 1f, no impress ins last: tchd 6/1: back to form, return to 2m will now suit: see 1861. *4* **92**
1637 **THEWHIRLINGDERVISH 34** [5] T D Easterby 6-8-12 (78) K Darley 9/1: 000-3403: Held up, short of room 2f out, styd on for press but no ch with wnr: not disgraced over an inadequate 14f, return to 2m+ will suit. *1¾* **81**
2085 **FLOTTA 13** [1] M R Channon 5-9-3 (83) A Culhane 10/3 FAV: 10-45044: Set pace till 2f out, no extra: well bckd: see 877 (AW). *nk* **85**
1861 **GOLD RING 22** [4]4-9-6 (86) R Havlin 6/1: 13-02365: Chsd ldrs, onepcd fnl 2f: see 1668 (soft). *3½* **83**
1569 **GRALMANO 37** [3]9-9-3 (83) N Callan 6/1: 3102-006: Trkd ldr, eff 3f out, wknd 2f out: see 695. *nk* **79**
2009* **TIYOUN 16** [7]6-9-2 (82) S Sanders 9/1: 025-2617: Chsd ldrs wide, btn over 2f out: btr 2009 (2m). *1¾* **76**
7 Ran Time 2m 58.76 (5.36) Owned: Jarvis Associates Trained: Twyford

2356	2.45 Batleys Charity Raceday Premier Claiming Stakes 3yo+ (D)				
	£6084 £1872 £936	1m2f88y	Good/Firm 36	-20 Slow	Inside

1552 **ETON** 38 [2] D Nicholls 8-9-3 (67) Alex Greaves 9/4: 310-3051: Made all, styd on v well fnl 1f,   **75**
rdn out: well bckd: eff at 10/12f on gd, loves fast & firm grnd: eff in claim grade & apprec uncontested lead.

1232 **MAKULU** 55 [1] B J Meehan 4-9-7 P (75) T Quinn 7/1: 2350-002: b g Alzao - Karinski (Palace Music)   *1½* **75**
Chsd ldrs, ch 2f out, kept on under press: 8 wk abs & tried cheek pieces (prev blnkd): won thrice on AW in '03 (2
h'caps & a clmr): eff at 10/11.6f on fast, gd/soft & polytrack: settled better today & back to form.
2 Apr'03 Wind 11.6g/f 81-75 E: 1 Mar'03 Ling 10ap 79a-73 D. 2 Feb'03 Ling 10ap 70a (76) D:
1 Feb'03 Ling 10ap 78a- D: 2 Jan'03 Ling 10ap 75a-74 E: 1 Jan'03 Ling 10ap 76a-66 E:

2197 **ILE MICHEL** 8 [5] J G M O'Shea 7-9-3 (82) A Culhane 15/8 FAV: 210-0043: Rear, prog 3f out, kept   *1¼* **69**
on for press but not pace to chall: well bckd, clr of rem: prob stays 10f: see 688.

2774} **TOMASINO** 337 [3] Mrs M Reveley 6-9-5 (93) K Darley 4/1: 23/00/66-4: br g Celtic Swing -   *10* **56**
Bustinetta (Bustino) Chsd ldrs btn 2f out on reapp: nicely bckd: well btn on both '03 starts (M Johnston): unplcd
both '02 starts (rtd 95, rtd h'cap): h'cap wnr in '01 (also plcd in 2 val h'cap, rtd 102): eff at 12f on firm & hvy
grnd: has gone well fresh, handles a gall trk: dropped in grade, has reportedly had plenty of probs.
2 Jun'01 Asco 12g/f 102-94 B: 2 May'01 Ches 12.3fm 97-90 C: 1 Apr'01 Ripo 12.2hvy 90-81 D:

1894 **AFRICAN SUNSET** 21 [4]4-9-3 R Winston 14/1: 0/-35: Trkd ldr, eff 2f out, sn wknd: see 1894.   *nk* **53**

1503} **CURATE** 394 [6]5-9-3 t (40) N Callan 40/1: 004040-6: ch g Unfuwain - Carniola (Rainbow Quest)   *dist* **8**
Keen in rear, btn over 3f out on reapp: h'cap 4th in '03 (rtd 44, J Parkes): mod form back in '01 for M P Tregoning
(rtd 58, mdn): stays 12f, handles fast grnd:
6 Ran   Time 2m 14.32 (7.02)   Owned: The McCauley Boys   Trained: Thirsk

2357	3.15 Sportingoptions Co Uk Rated Stakes Handicap 4yo+ 0-100 (B)					**[107]**
	£12444 £4712 £2356	6f3y str	Good/Firm 36	+05 Fast	Centre	

1703 **CIRCUIT DANCER** 29 [5] A Berry 4-8-13 (92) F Lynch 20/1: 316-3401: Dwelt, prog 2f out, led well   **98**
ins fnl 1f, all-out: surprise win, gd time: eff at 5/6f on firm & gd/soft, poss handles soft: handles a gall or
tight trk: prev best up with/forcing the pace, did well from bhnd here: see 1227.

2070 **MARSAD** 13 [9] J Akehurst 10-8-7 (86) P Doe 9/1: 203-0302: Rear, short of room 2f out, fin well &   *shd* **91**
only just failed: lkd unlucky, also 2nd in this race last year (2lbs higher): deserves to go one better, see 1703.

1703 **DAZZLING BAY** 29 [6] T D Easterby 4-9-7 (100) S Sanders 6/1: 0206-603: b g Mind Games - Adorable   *¾* **102**
Cherub (Halo) Trkd ldr, went on 2f out, hung right dist & caught cl home: clr of rem: completed hat-trick of h'cap
wins in 03: suited by 6f on firm & soft, runs well fresh: likes a stiff trk & has tried blnks: useful, back to form
here & may well have won if keeping a straight line.
2 Aug'03 Newm 6g/f 108-105 B: 1 Jun'03 Ripo 6g/f 108-92 C: 1 Jun'03 York 6.0fm 103-85 B:
1 May'03 Newm 6g/f 87-78 C: 2 Apr'03 Newm 6gd 89-73 C: 1 May'02 Hami 5sft 88- D: 2 Apr'02 Newc 5sft 79- D:

2076 **PIETER BRUEGHEL** 13 [8] D Nicholls 5-8-7 (4oh) (82) R Winston 12/1: 00000-04: Led till 2f out, no   *3* **79**
extra fnl 1f: better run, well h'capped for similar tactics at Chester: see 2076.

2186 **STEEL BLUE** 8 [11]4-8-12 (91) A Culhane 4/1 FAV: 0-50107: Chsd ldrs, drvn 2f out, sn onepcd: well bckd   *¾* **81**

1703 **HALMAHERA** 29 [1]9-9-7 bl (100) N Callan 10/1: 44-02466: Held up, mod late prog: top-weight.   *½* **89**

2082 **RIVER FALCON** 13 [7]4-8-7 (2oh) (84) K Darley 8/1: 00-50107: Mid-div, not pace to chall: btr 1683.   *nk* **74**

1977 **JOHNSTONS DIAMOND** 17 [10]6-8-11 (90) K McEvoy 9/2: 0104628: Chsd ldrs, btn 2f out.   *nk* **77**

2206 **FOREVER PHOENIX** 7 [3]4-8-13 (92) E Ahern 9/2: 21312R9: Chsd ldrs, wknd 2f out: nicely bckd.   *5* **64**

1926 **WILL HE WISH** 20 [2]8-8-13 (92) K Dalgleish 20/1: 0056000: 10th: Al rear, fin last.   *2½* **57**
10 Ran   Time 1m 11.30 (1.90)   Owned: Mr David Fish   Trained: Cockerham

2358	3.50 M&J Seafood Rous Selling Stakes 2yo (E)				
	£4014 £1235 £618	6f3y str	Good/Firm 36	-39 Slow	Centre

2183* **ISLAND SWING** 8 [7] J L Spearing 2-8-7 (1ow) S Sanders 11/4 FAV: 011: Broke well & made all, clr   **85+**
dist, readily: hvly bckd from 4/1, bght in for 28,000gns: suited by 6f & forcing tactics, acts on fast grnd & on a
flat or gall trk: btr than sell grade, interesting in nurseries: see 2183.

  GOLD QUAY [3] P C Haslam 2-8-6 G Faulkner 14/1: 2: b f Docksider - Viaticum (Scenic) Dwelt,   *3½* **73**
green & prog halfway, rdn & flicked tail dist, styd on well under hands-and-heels but no ch with wnr on debut: clmd
for N Shields for 12,000: Mar foal, half-sister to sev mid-dist performers: dam a 10f wnr, sire a top-class miler:
eff at 6f on fast, will relish further.

2194 **AMPHITHEATRE** 8 [2] R F Johnson Houghton 2-8-11 A Culhane 9/2: 503: Dwelt, prog when short of   *4* **66**
room halfway, styd on nicely under hands-and-heels riding fnl 1f: nicely bckd from 11/2: see 1880.

2083 **LITTLE BISCUIT** 13 [9] K R Burke 2-8-6 A Nicholls 11/2: 11254: Chsd ldrs, outpcd 1.5f out: btr 1634.   *1¾* **56**

  MAGIC GENIE [1]2-8-6 Dale Gibson 20/1: 5: b f Lujain - Haut Volee (Top Ville) Mid-div, nvr nr   *¾* **53**
to chall on debut: Mar foal, cost 12,000gns: half-sister to sev wnrs, incl 1m scorer Cat's Whisker.

1687 **SOWERBY** 30 [10]2-8-11 T Williams 25/1: 06: b c Grey Desire - Brief Star (Brief Truce) Trkd   *1¾* **53**
ldrs, btn 2f out: Mar first foal: sire a smart sprinter: with M Brittain.

1874 **DISHDASHA** 22 [12]2-8-11 D Allan(3) 33/1: 07: Slowly away, recovered to chase ldrs till halfway.   *1* **50**

2017 **DIATONIC** 16 [13]2-8-11 G Carter 25/1: 008: Nvr btr than mid-div.   *2½* **43**

1752 **ROKO** 27 [4]2-8-11 P Mulrennan(5) 12/1: 09: Mid-div, btn halfway.   *nk* **42**

2167 **DEN PERRY** 9 [6]2-8-11 P Bradley(5) 16/1: 60: 10th: Held up, al well bhd: see 2167.   *9* **17**

1968 **SHUCHBAA** 18 [8]2-8-6 P Fessey 10/1: 30: 11th: Slowly away, al bhd, t.o.: op 7/1: see 1968.   *6* **0**

1974 **MILL END CHATEAU** 17 [11]2-8-11 R Winston 14/1: 00: 12th: Chsd ldrs 3f, wknd qckly & eased, t.o.   *29* **0**

1968 **JOSHAR** 18 [5]2-8-6 K Darley 9/1: 0303340: 13th: Al bhd, t.o. in last: see 1869.   *2* **0**
13 Ran   Time 1m 13.95 (4.55)   Owned: Mr J Spearing   Trained: Kinnersley

---

2359   **4.25 Blacks - The People For Property Stakes Handicap 3yo+ 0-100 (C)**   [95]
£10329 £3178 £1589   **5f3y str**   **Good/Firm 36**   **-03 Slow**   Centre

2286 **PICCLED 3** [10] E J Alston 6-8-10 (77) D Allan(3) 33/1: 0-030001: Dwelt, mid-div, hdwy to lead   86
dist, rdn clr: qck reapp: 5f specialist, acts on firm, gd/soft & fibresand: best up with/forcing the pace, did
well from bhd here: on a decent mark & could follow up, see 834.
2286 **OBE ONE 3** [9] A Berry 4-8-2 (69) F Norton 10/1: 0006402: Held up, rdn to improve halfway, styd   1¾ 71
on late: qck reapp: another on a decent mark & turn shld not be far away: see 2084 & 1977.
2253 **HENRY HALL 6** [3] N Tinkler 8-9-13 (94) Kim Tinkler 10/1: 13-30303: Nvr far away, led briefly   shd 95
dist, kept on & just btn in a thrilling battle for 2nd: qck reapp, jt top-weight: most consistent, see 1653 (C/D).
2253 **ATLANTIC VIKING 6** [6] D Nicholls 9-9-13 (94) R Winston 16/1: 5060-004: Dwelt, hdwy dist, styd on   shd 95
well fnl 1f & nrst fin: jt top-weight, qck reapp: back to form here, likes Epsom: see 2253.
2253 **WATCHING 6** [7]7-9-4 (85) A Nicholls 8/1: 40-30255: Nvr far away, kept on fnl 1f: qck reapp.   nk 85
2084* **CATCH THE CAT 13** [13]5-8-5 bl (72) G Parkin 12/1: 0-302016: Chsd ldrs, onepcd fnl 1f: see 2084.   1½ 68
2084 **STRENSALL 13** [11]7-8-10 (77) R Fitzpatrick 14/1: 1420-027: Chsd ldrs, ev ch dist, not qckn fnl 1f.   ¾ 70
2279* **TOMMY SMITH 4** [2]6-8-7 (7ex)bl (74) Darren Williams 7/1: 0-000018: Qckly away & led till dist,   hd 67
fdd: op 5/1, qck reapp under 7lb pen: 3rd in this race from a 6lb higher mark last year: front-rnr, btr 2279.
2070 **ZARZU 13** [1]5-8-7 (74) J Bramhill 14/1: 5434309: Al mid-div: see 1103.   1 64
2082 **CONNECT 13** [4]7-9-6 bl (87) P Robinson 4/1 FAV: 6006-240: 10th: Held up, nvr troubled ldrs: well   shd 77
bckd: won this race from an 11lb lower mark last year: nvr got in contention here, see 2082 & 1917.
1217 **RECTANGLE 56** [14]4-8-10 (77) A Culhane 66/1: 2630-000: 11th: ch g Fayruz - Moona (Lear Fan)   ½ 66
Chsd ldrs, btn dist: 8 wk abs: plcd on 2 of 5 '03 h'cap starts: '02 mdn auct wnr: eff at 5/5.5f on fast & gd/soft
grnd: handles an easy or stiff trk: with D Nicholls.
2 Mar'03 Asco 5.5g/f 86-80 C: 1 Aug'02 Thir 5gd 81- E: 2 Jun'02 Donc 5.6g/f 68- D:
2279 **ONLINE INVESTOR 4** [8]5-8-2 (69) D R McCabe 14/1: 0520550: 12th: Dwelt, nvr nr ldrs: qck reapp.   ½ 57
2253 **MAGIC GLADE 6** [5]5-9-6 (87) R Thomas(5) 8/1: 0121300: 13th: Mid-div, btn 2f out: reportedly   1½ 71
broke a blood vessel for the 2nd time in 6 days & clrly needs a rest: see 2253 & 1120.
13 Ran   Time 58.75 (1.95)   Owned: The Pain and Heartache Partnership   Trained: Preston

---

2360   **5.00 Sportingoptions Co Uk Low Commission Maiden Auction Stakes 2yo (E)**
£5070 £1560 £780   **5f3y str**   **Good/Firm 36**   **-18 Slow**   Centre

2051 **DISTINCTLY GAME 14** [5] K A Ryan 2-8-10 N Callan 7/4 FAV: 2221: Prom, went on dist, collared ins   82
fnl 1f, rallied gamely to force head back in front on line: hvly bckd from 11/4: deserved win, rnr-up on prev 3
starts: eff at 5/6f on gd, fast grnd & fibresand: v consistent, see 2051 & 1503.
2056 **LADY DAN 14** [10] M W Easterby 2-8-4 T Lucas 10/1: 432: Chsd ldrs, imprvd to lead ins fnl 1f,   shd 75
caught on line in a most thrilling fin: eff at 5f on fast grnd, 6f will suit: shld find similar, see 2056.
1874 **MIMI MOUSE 22** [12] T D Easterby 2-8-6 P Robinson 12/1: 643: Prom, ev ch fnl 1f, just btn in a v   nk 76
tight fin: has shown enough to find similar, prob back over 6f: see 1874 & 1212.
     DISPOL ISLE 13 [13] T D Barron 2-8-3 P Fessey 50/1: 4: gr f Trans Island - Pictina (Petong)   2 67
Dwelt, mid-div, styd on fnl 1f & nrst fin on debut: cheaply bght Apr foal, dam unrcd, sire a high-class miler: eff
at 5f on fast grnd, 6f will suit: shd have to learn from this.
2056 **MELANDRE 14** [8]2-8-4 T Williams 33/1: 6045: Led till dist, no extra.   ½ 67
     BORDERLESCOTT [7]2-8-11 R Ffrench 25/1: 6: b c Compton Place - Jeewan (Touching Wood) Dwelt,   3½ 64
styd on late, nrst fin on debut: won 3,000gns Apr foal: half-brother to sev sprint wnrs: dam a mid-dist scorer.
     RANCHO CUCAMONGA [15]2-8-5 (1ow) K Darley 10/1: 7: ch f Raphane - Kunucu (Bluebird) Chsd ldrs,   shd 58
onepcd fnl 1f on racecourse bow: £10,000 Apr foal: half-sister to sprint juv wnr Hillside Girl: dam a 5f 2yo wnr.
     SKIDDAW WOLF [9]2-8-3 F Norton 33/1: 8: ch f Wolfhound - Stealthy (Kind of Hush) Dwelt, chsd   shd 56
ldrs, onepcd fnl 1.5f on debut: Mar foal, cost 2,200gns: half-sister to 6f juv wnr Stealthy Times: dam a 1m wnr.
1550 **LLAMADAS 38** [3]2-8-11 L Enstone(3) 8/1: 39: Chsd ldrs 3f, sn btn: btr 1550.   1¾ 59
1911 **MILL BY THE STREAM 20** [18]2-8-11 A Nicholls 50/1: 00: 10th: Rear, some late hdwy, nvr dngrs.   nk 58
2051 **ZANDO 14** [17]2-8-10 G Faulkner 40/1: 00: 11th: Bhd, modest late progress.   ½ 56
     KUDBEME [6]2-8-3 E Ahern 40/1: 0: 12th: Nvr btr than mid-div on debut.   2 43
     BUST [11]2-8-9 K Dalgleish 25/1: 0: 13th: Dwelt, al bhd on racecourse bow.   hd 49
1974 **RICH ALBI 17** [14]2-8-13 D Allan(3) 8/1: 0: 14th: Nvr btr than mid-div.   ½ 52
     STAR OF KILDARE [16]2-8-3 Kim Tinkler 50/1: 0: 15th: Al bhd on debut.   shd 42
     OPEN VERDICT [2]2-8-11 K McEvoy 16/1: 0: 16th: Slowly away, al bhd on racecourse bow.   ½ 49
     NEGAS [4]2-8-13 R Winston 9/1: 0: 17th: Dwelt, recovered to chase ldrs till halfway on debut.   ½ 50
     BEN CASEY [1]2-8-10 F Lynch 33/1: 0: 18th: Al bhd & hung right thr'out on debut.   2½ 40
18 Ran   Time 59.51(2.71)   Owned: Mr & Mrs Julian and Rosie Richer   Trained: Hambleton

---

SANDOWN   FRIDAY 11.06.04   Righthand, Galloping Track, Stiff Finish

---

Official Going Good/Firm (Good places)

2361   **2.00 Sharp Minds Betfair Claiming Stakes 3yo+ (E)**
£3653 £1124 £562   **5f6y str**   **Good 52**   **-01 Slow**   Far Side

2074 **WILLHEWIZ 13** [7] C A Dwyer 4-9-8 vis (78) J F Egan 2/1 FAV: 01-05601: Made virtually all, styd on   84
well over 1f out, rdn out: nicely bckd: enjoys dominating over 5/6f on firm, gd/soft & fibresand, any trk: enjoyed
return to clmg company: claimed for 15,000: wears a visor, tired blnks in 2074, see 1217.
1827 **KALLISTAS PRIDE 24** [8] M R Bosley 4-8-7 Joanna Badger 66/1: 0-00-02: b f Puissance - Clan Scotia   1½ 63
(Clantime) Handy, hdwy over 1f out, kept on ins last, no threat to wnr: best eff to date dropped back to 5f in
clmg grade on fast grnd: claimed for 5,000.
2161 **PROUD NATIVE 9** [4] D Nicholls 10-9-8 (83) D Holland 4/1: 105-0003: Trkd ldr, rdn over 1f out,   ¾ 76
onepace: won this race last term, not disgraced: see 2161.
2059 **ENDLESS SUMMER 14** [6] K R Burke 6-9-8 (78) R Hughes 9/4: 04-35504: In tch, onepcd over 1f out,   hd 75
nicely bckd on drop in class: claimed for 15,000: see 1970, 921.

2016* **BELLS BEACH 16** [3]6-8-10 (45) K Fallon 13/2: 6104415: In tch, wknd well over 1f out: stiff task.   3½   53$
2331 **ELA FIGURA 1** [5]4-8-11 (50) W Ryan 12/1: 020-60036: Al bhd: see 1371.   1¼   50
1788 **RIDICULE 25** [2]5-9-1 vis t (51) R L Moore 25/1: 0-000007: In tch, wknd 2f out: see 1788, 1103.   5   39
1806 **HERES HARRY 25** [1]4-9-0 L Keniry(3) 100/1: 08: b c Most Welcome - Nahla (Wassl) Al bhd: mod form.   19   0
8 Ran   Time 1m 02.24 (2.64)   Owned: Mrs C M Goode   Trained: Newmarket

---

2362   2.35 Sbj Group Classified Stakes 3yo 0-85 (C)
£9516 £2928 £1464   **7f16y rnd**   Good 52   -15 Slow   Inside

1919 **OASIS STAR 20** [2] P W Harris 3-8-12 (86) D Holland 8/13 FAV: 1-1151: Ol up, hdwy to lead over 2f   91
out, hdd over 1f out but rallied v gamely to get up again cl-home, drvn out: hvly bckd: prob stays 1m, enjoyed this
drop back to a stiff 7f: acts on firm & gd, stiff or sharp trks: prog, useful & v genuine: see 1583.
2212 **MISTER SAIF 7** [5] R Hannon 3-9-0 (85) R Hughes 9/2: 2-0U5042: Led,hdd over 2f out till led again   ¾   90
over 1f out, kept on for press till collared cl-home: ran to best & met a useful/v game filly: see 2212.
4420* **KING OF CASHEL 261** [4] R Hannon 3-9-3 (88) K Fallon 7/1: 5341-3: b c King of Kings - Jaya (Ela   2½   88
Mana Mou) Handy, hdwy & hung right 2f out, onepcd: won last of 4 '03 starts (mdn): eff over 7f/1m on firm, gd/soft
& on any trk: sharper for this.   1 Sep'03 Ches 7.0g/s 85-(91) D:
1813 **HATCH 24** [3] R M H Cowell 3-9-5 (90) J Murtagh 8/1: 2131304: Keen in tch, wknd dist: btr run.   ½   89
2136 **NEPHETRITI WAY 10** [1]3-8-13 (87) S Drowne 25/1: 212-055: Held up, btn 2f out: see 1419.   5   73
5 Ran   Time 1m 31.11 (4.71)   Owned: Mr R J Creese   Trained: Berkhamsted

---

2363   3.05 Sbj Group Handicap Stakes 3yo+ 0-90 (C)   [83]
£10244 £3152 £1576   **1m2f7y**   Good 52   +04 Fast   Inside

4989* **GROOMS AFFECTION 221** [8] P W Harris 4-9-10 (79) J Murtagh 10/1: 0/01-1: b c Groom Dancer - Love   87
And Affection (Exclusive Era) Keen, in tch, lost place over 3f out & lkd held over 2f out, strong run fnl 1f to get
up cl-home, going away: won last of 2 '03 starts (mdn, landed gamble): eff over a stiff 10f, 12f lks sure to suit:
acts on gd & soft: clrly runs v well fresh: lightly rcd, shld be more to come over further.
1 Nov'03 Redc 10sft 76- D:
2157 **SAY WHAT YOU SEE 9** [3] J W Hills 4-9-2 vis (71) M Hills 9/2: 4215422: Set gd pace, kept on for   1¼   75
press till collared cl-home: gd run: see 2157, 900.
2067 **STREET LIFE 13** [4] W J Musson 6-9-4 (73) K Fallon 13/2: 2523343: Held up, eff 2f out, onepcd.   ½   76
2099* **FAAYEJ 11** [2] Sir Michael Stoute 4-10-0 (5ex) (83) W Supple 2/1 FAV: 521-14: Handy, eff to chall   nk   85
2f out, hung right for press & no extra ins last: bckd: not disgraced but poss not straightforward.
1849 **MAD CAREW 23** [1]5-9-7 (76) R L Moore 11/1: 5104055: Held up, plenty to do 2f out, late gains.   1   76
2260 **QABAS 5** [5]4-9-0 (69) R Hughes 16/1: 2222-506: Slow away, nvr a factor: quick reapp, see 1913.   5   62
2090 **JUSTE POUR LAMOUR 12** [7]4-9-5 (74) D Holland 12/1: 4500-047: Chsd ldr till over 4f out, no   5   60
extra: big step up in trip, needs return to 7f as in 2090.
2067 **KARAOKE 13** [6]4-8-12 (67) J F Egan 9/2: 0554228: Held up, wknd over 2f out, eased: nicely bckd.   6   43
8 Ran   Time 2m 08.95 (4.85)   Owned: The Racing Grooms   Trained: Berkhamsted

---

2364   3.40 Sharp Minds Betfair European Breeders Fund Maiden Stakes 2yo (D)
£4758 £1464 £732   **5f6y str**   Good 52   -04 Slow   Far Side

1499 **SPREE 40** [2] R Hannon 2-8-9 R Hughes 5/1: 61: gr f Dansili - Ibiza (Linamix) Made all, pushed   94
clr dist, rdly: bckd: Feb 1st foal, cost £30,000: much imprvd from debut & eff at 5f on gd grnd: looks useful.
2109 **DRUM DANCE 11** [4] R F Johnson Houghton 2-9-0 S Carson 7/4 FAV: 22: Chsd wnr, outpcd over 1f   6   83
out: well bckd: prob caught a useful sort: eff at 5f on firm & gd grnd: must win a mdn.
2188 **PITCH UP 8** [3] T G Mills 2-9-0 S Drowne 7/2: 03: In tch, outpcd over 1f out: see 2188.   1¾   78
      ANNATALIA [5] B J Meehan 2-8-9 D Holland 12/1: 4: ch f Pivotal - See You Later (Emarati) In   1   70
tch, wknd over 1f out: op 20/1: Feb 1st foal, cost £50,000: dam useful 5f wnr, bred for speed.
      AFRICAN STORM [6]2-9-0 J F Egan 25/1: 5: b c Fasliyev - Out of Africa (Common Grounds) Dwelt,   4   63
sn in tch, wknd over 1f out: Feb 1st foal, cost E110,000: dam useful 6/7f juv scorer: bred for speed.
      HORNPIPE [1]2-9-0 K Fallon 3/1: 6: Ran green & al bhd on debut: nicely bckd.   6   45
6 Ran   Time 1m 02.39 (2.79)   Owned: Mr A F Merritt   Trained: Marlborough

---

2365   4.15 Mousetrap Challenge Cup Handicap Stakes 3yo 0-80 (D)   [84]
£5603 £1724 £862   **1m14y rnd**   Good 52   +01 Fast   Inside

1956 **HABANERO 18** [8] R Hannon 3-8-10 (66) D Holland 6/1 CO FAV: 21-00531: Led, rdn & hdd over 1f out,   73
sn rallied v gamely for press to get up again ins last, rdn out: suited by 1m on gd & fast grnd, any trk: enjoyed
front rng today: in-form & a most genuine eff: see 1647.
1956 **FOLEY PRINCE 18** [9] Mrs Stef Liddiard 3-9-0 (70) S Drowne 6/1 CO FAV: 6-030122: Chsd wnr, hdwy   nk   75
to lead over 1f out, sn rdn & hdd by wnr ins last, kept on, not btn far: fine run & clrly in gd heart.
1825 **GO SOLO 24** [5] B W Hills 3-9-7 (77) M Hills 7/1: 1516-033: Handy, eff to chall dist, no extra   ¾   80
cl-home: not btn far: see 1825.
1707 **APERITIF 29** [4] W J Haggas 3-9-3 (73) S W Kelly 10/1: 663-04: In tch, eff 2f out, kept on ins   nk   75
last, no threat to wnr: stays 1m on gd & polytrack, poss firm: shld find a race: see 1707.
869* **FIT TO FLY 85** [13]3-9-5 (71) J F Egan 20/1: 050-2515: Bhd, late gains, nvr dangerous: 3 month   shd   76
abs: styd this step up to 1m & acts on fast, gd & both AWs: poss more to come next time: see 869.
2072 **CHIGORIN 12** [3]3-9-0 (70) J Murtagh 12/1: 03-06: b g Pivotal - Belle Vue (Petong) Keen, held   1   69+
up, plenty to do over 2f out, late hdwy, nrst fin: 3rd in a mdn on last of 2 '03 starts (rtd 75+): dam 6f wnr:
stays 1m on fast & gd grnd: again shaped with promise and one to keep an eye on.
2098 **WHITGIFT ROCK 11** [10]3-9-5 (75) R L Moore 7/1: 31-12007: In tch, onepcd over 1f out: see 1163   ½   73
(tried visor), 341 (polytrack).
2259 **WYCHBURY 5** [3]3-9-4 (74) J Fortune 8/1: 532-5228: In tch, no extra over 1f out: quick reapp.   nk   71
1369 **SOUND BLASTER 47** [7]3-9-4 (74) L Keniry(3) 12/1: 041-59: Keen held up, hung dist, wknd.   nk   70
1983 **JOMUS 17** [2]3-8-7 (63) Lisa Jones(3) 20/1: 5-521200: 10th: Dwelt, keen, nvr a factor: see 1983, 855.   2½   54
1953* **SUNSET MIRAGE 18** [1]3-9-1 (71) W Supple 14/1: 0-2610: 11th: Keen, al bhd: won a fill h'cap in 1953.   3½   55

SANDOWN FRIDAY 11.06.04 Righthand, Galloping Track, Stiff Finish

2024 **THE WAY WE WERE 16** [11]3-9-2 (72) K Fallon 6/1 CO FAV: 31-650: 12th: In tch, wknd over 2f out. — 1¼ 53
2079 **GREEN FALCON 13** [6]3-8-4 VIS (60) N Day 14/1: 033000: 13th: Al bhd: tried visor: see 697, 566. — 1¾ 37
13 Ran Time 1m 43.11 (4.11) Owned: The Waney Racing Group Inc Trained: Marlborough

---

2366 4.50 Royal Star & Garter Home Handicap Stakes Fillies 3yo 0-75 (E) [82]
£3939 £1212 £606   1m2f7y   Good 52   -11 Slow   Inside

1756 **MOCCA 27** [7] D J Coakley 3-9-7 (75) D Holland 7/2 JT FAV: 4152-451: Cl-up, short of room over 1f 86
out but styd on well to lead nr fin: nicely bckd: stays 10f on fast & gd grnd, easy or gall trk: see 1192.
2046 **WEE DINNS 14** [6] S Kirk 3-9-2 (70) J F Egan 7/2 JT FAV: 000-0522: In tch, hdwy to lead 2f out, shd 80
rdn clr appr fnl 1f, rdn & collared on line: well bckd: fine run from the front & deserves similar: see 2046.
1791 **KYTHIA 25** [12] H Morrison 3-9-4 (72) S Drowne 8/1: 315-43: In tch, eff 2f out, onepace: gd run. 2½ 76
175 **BIENVENUE 184** [10] M P Tregoning 3-8-13 (67) W Supple 8/1: 235-4: In tch, lost place over 2f 2 70
out, some late gains: long abs & prob stays 10f: acts on gd & polytrack: see 21.
2103 **SAND AND STARS 11** [5]3-9-1 (69) F P Ferris(3) 10/1: 540-35: Keen, led 2f, lost plc 2f out, late gains. 2 69
1651 **ELLINA 3** [13]3-8-13 (67) R Price 40/1: 00-046: Held up, mod late gains: see 1651. ½ 66
1953 **NIGHT FROLIC 18** [4]3-8-12 (66) M Hills 8/1: 00-137: Led after 2f till 2f out, wknd: well bckd. shd 65
1617 **WYOMING 35** [2]3-8-6 (60) Lisa Jones(3) 10/1: 00-38: Held up, btn 2f out: longer trip, see 1617. ½ 58
1648 **VARUNI 32** [9]3-8-8 (62) R L Moore 25/1: 0-10209: Al bhd: see 1165, 626. hd 59
1791 **PRINCIPESSA 25** [1]3-8-13 (67) W Ryan 40/1: 3-5000: 10th: Trkd ldr after 3f till 2f out, wknd. 2 61
4392} **CAZISA STAR 263** [8]3-8-8 (62) S Carson 25/1: 036-0: 11th: ch f Mister Baileys - Placer Queen 3½ 51
(Habitat) Held up, btn 2f out on reapp: plcd in an auct mdn in '03 (rtd 65): half sister to wnrs btwn 5/12f.
2031 **GIRL WARRIOR 15** [3]3-9-1 (69) K Fallon 11/2: 3-640: 12th: In tch, eff 2f out, wknd & eased. 5 51
12 Ran Time 2m 10.43(6.33) Owned: Mocca Partnership Trained: West Ilsley

---

CHEPSTOW FRIDAY 11.06.04 Lefthand, Undulating, Galloping Track

Official Going GOOD/FIRM

2367 6.35 Knight Frank/E B F Novice Stakes 2yo (D)
£3517 £1082 £541   6f16y str   Good 48   -21 Slow   Stands side

2043* **DAHTEER 14** [1] M R Channon 2-9-2 K Fallon 4/5 FAV: 411: Handy, hdwy to lead over 1f out, kept 94
on well for press fnl 1f: well bckd: stays 6f, 7f looks sure to suit: acts on fast & gd, likes an undul trk:
in-form & imprvg: see 2043 & 1780.
1981 **EDGE FUND 17** [7] B R Millman 2-8-12 S Drowne 5/1: 3332: Led till over 1f out, sn no extra: eff 2½ 81
at 5/6f: another consistent run: see 1981 & 1001.
1077* **OBSERVER 65** [6] D R Loder 2-9-5 VIS T P Queally(3) 9/4: 13: With ldr, ev ch 2f out, no impress 2½ 80
ins fnl 1f: 9 wks abs, top weight: 1st time visor: shade btr 1077 (5f).
2194 **GAVIOLI 8** [4] J M Bradley 2-8-12 T B Swarbrick(5) 100/1: 504: b c Namid - Pamina (Perugino) 1¾ 68
Mid-div, outpcd over 2f out, kept on late: unplcd both earlier mdn starts: 1st time t-strap here: try 7f.
1786 **TROUBLESOME GERRI 25** [2]2-8-7 D Corby(3) 50/1: 635: In tch, btn fnl 4f: see 1786. 17 12
JUST BONNIE [5]2-8-12 R Miles(3) 40/1: 6: b c Lujain - Fairy Flight (Fairy King) Rear, t.o., 22 0
saddle slipped on debut: half brother to high-class sprinter Just James: dam 6f 2yo wnr.
6 Ran Time 1m 12.94 (4.14) Owned: Sheikh Ahmed Al Maktoum Trained: West Ilsley

---

2368 7.05 Grolsch Premium Lager Maiden Stakes Fillies 3yo (D)
£3634 £1118 £559   1m4f23y   Good 48   -19 Slow   Inside

1719 **GOSLAR 29** [3] H Candy 3-8-11 Dane O'Neill 9/4: 31: Rcd in 2nd till led 3f out, rdn over 1f out, 91
kept on well ins fnl 1f: stays 12f, acts on fast, gall/undul trk: improved from debut, see 1719.
1922 **IDEALISTIC 20** [7] L M Cumani 3-8-11 K Fallon 2/5 FAV: 022: Chsd ldrs, hdwy over 2f out, edged 1¾ 87
left & onepcd over 1f out: well clr of rem: stays 12f: btr expected after 1922.
1939 **OH SO HARDY 19** [1] M A Allen 3-8-11 D Corby(3) 50/1: 043: b f Fleetwood - Miss Hardy 21 55
(Formidable) Handy, wknd 3f out: mainly mod form to date, sell grade will suit.
2131 **DELFINIA 10** [2] H S Howe 3-8-11 S Drowne 100/1: 04: b f Kingsinger - Delvecchia (Glint of Gold) 6 46
Led to 3f out, sn no extra: well btn sole earlier mdn start.
2117 **NINA FONTENAIL 11** [4]3-8-11 (45) A Beech(3) 100/1: 06-0005: gr f Kaldounevees - Ninon Fontenail 8 34
(Turgeon) Bhd, nvr a factor: mdn unplcd in '03 (rtd 43): with N Hawke.
1790 **DORSET 25** [6]3-8-11 N Chalmers(5) 50/1: 006: Al bhd. 7 23
1259 **SINGITTA 53** [8]3-8-11 R Miles(3) 50/1: 07: Al bhd: 8 wk abs. ½ 22
1959 **PEARNICKITY 18** [5]3-8-11 I Mongan 100/1: 08: Rear, t.o. dist 0
8 Ran Time 2m 39.15 (8.05) Owned: Major M G Wyatt Trained: Wantage

---

2369 7.35 Sky Bet Astrac At Chepstow Claiming Stakes 3yo+ (F)
£3164 £904 £452   7f16y str   Good 48   -06 Slow   Stands side

1984 **A ONE 17** [13] B Palling 5-9-2 (51) S Sanders 7/1: 0000-431: Made all, styd on well for press ins 59
fnl 1f, claimed for 6,000: eff at 6f/1m on fast, likes soft, hvy, handles fibresand, any trk: see 1413.
2288 **CHEVRONNE 3** [16] L G Cottrell 4-9-6 (68) I Mongan 16/1: 0350-002: In tch, hdwy & ev ch fnl 1f, hd 60
kept on: quick reapp: eff at 7f/1m: not btn far, find similar based on this: see 2288.
1984 **IVY MOON 17** [11] B J Llewellyn 4-8-9 (45) A Daly 12/1: 0-360353: Rear, hdwy 2f out, kept on fnl 1f. 2½ 46
2149 **LORD CHAMBERLAIN 9** [8] J M Bradley 11-9-6 bl (55) Dane O'Neill 6/1: 0220344: Rear, hdwy 2f out, nk 56
kept on ins fnl 1f: ran to wng form of 379, see 311.
2129 **FEN GYPSY 10** [9]6-9-10 (60) S Donohoe(7) 4/1 FAV: 0021245: Bhd, hdwy 3f out, onepcd ins fnl 1f. ½ 59
2314 **ONE UPMANSHIP 2** [14]3-9-0 bl (66) K Fallon 15/2: 430-0006: ch g Bahamian Bounty - Magnolia 1¾ 55
(Petong) Chsd ldrs, wknd ins fnl 1f: quick reapp, clr of rem: rnr-up one of 9 '03 starts (nurs): stays 7f on

fast: has tried blnks & cheek pieces: with J Portman. 2 Sep'03 Ling 7g/f 67-65 E:

2032 **MOBO BACO 15** [1]7-9-2 (54) S Drowne 8/1: 30-44007: Rcd in centre, not pace to chall over 1f out. *6* **35**

1750 **IN TUNE 27** [5]4-9-3 T (40) D Corby(3) 66/1: 0/55-0008: b g Distinctly North - Lingering (Kind of Hush) Rear, hdwy fnl 1f, kept on & nrst fin: 5th both '03 starts (h'caps, rtd 60a): lightly rcd & unplcd in '02 (rtd 66a, mdn): stays a sharp 7f, handles polytrack: has tried blnks, tried a t-strap here. *1½* **33**

2161 **NEEDWOOD BUCOLIC 9** [12]6-9-2 R Miles(3) 33/1: 10/013/-09: br g Charnwood Forest - Greek Icon (Thatching) Rcd in 2nd, wknd over 1f out: p.u./fell both nov hdle starts in 03/04 (with R Shiels): with R Allan. *shd* **31**

338 **CURZON LODGE 156** [7]4-10-0 T T P Queally(3) 50/1: 0-00: 10th: Rear, late gains & nrst fin: t-strap. *½* **42**

2204 **GILLYS GENERAL 7** [10]4-9-2 (49) S Whitworth 20/1: 50-40160: 11th: Handy, wknd 2f out. *1½* **27**

2133 **DESERT DAISY 10** [15]3-7-13 VIS (59) B Swarbrick(5) 10/1: 200 0000: 12th: Chsd ldrs, wknd 2f out. *hd* **19**

1963* **RILEYS DREAM 18** [6]5-8-9 (43) R Havlin 9/1: 0-050010: 13th: Nvr btr than mid-div. *¾* **17**

1992 **OVER TO YOU BERT 17** [2]5-9-0 (42) M Savage(5) 40/1: 6514000: 14th: In tch & wide, switched after 2f, no impress fnl 1f: btr 831 (seller). *¾* **20**

1992 **Chickasaw Trail 17** [3]6-8-9 (43) Stephanie Hollinshead(5) 25/1:0

3824} **Variety Club 293** [4]3-8-4 T Block(4) 25/1:0

16 Ran Time 1m 23.58 (3.78) Owned: Mr Albert Yemm Trained: Cowbridge

2370

8.10 Sky Bet Astrac Record Breaker Handicap Stakes 3yo+ 0-80 (D) **[76]**
£5512 £1696 £848 **7f16y str** **Good 48** **+07 Fast** Stands side

2199 **GOODENOUGH MOVER 8** [5] J S King 8-9-8 (70) Hayley Turner(5) 4/1 FAV: 00-21221: Made all, rdn & kept on well ins fnl 1f: won this race in '00: eff at 6f, suited by 7f, stays 1m: acts on firm, soft & polytrack, likes Chepstow & Salisbury: v tough 8yo, in fine form: see 1723 & 1025. **84**

1606 **ASTRAC 35** [10] Mrs A L M King 13-8-0 (48) P M Quinn 33/1: 115-5002: Rear, hdwy into 2nd over 1f out, no impress ins fnl 1f: clr of rem: fine eff from another veteran: see 1127. *3* **52**

2063 **MISTRAL SKY 13** [7] Mrs Stef Liddiard 5-9-5 p (67) S Drowne 7/1: 0020433: Mid-div, hdwy 2f out, onepace *4* **65**

2116 **LEAPING BRAVE 11** [8] B R Millman 3-9-4 (76) A McCarthy 9/2: 0130-424: Handy, hdwy into 2nd 3f out, lost place over 1f out. *hd* **73**

2063 **LOGISTICAL 13** [4]4-9-0 (62) D Sweeney 12/1: 4560-005: Rear, hdwy 2f out, sn wknd: see 2063. *1¾* **55**

461 **COMPTON BANKER 141** [9]7-9-10 (72) S Sanders 8/1: 04115-06: Chsd ldrs, wknd fnl 1f: see 149. *hd* **64**

1849 **LOCKSTOCK 23** [11]6-9-10 p (72) R Miles(3) 8/1: 14-00107: Nvr a factor: btr 1542. *¾* **62**

2080 **BENEKING 13** [6]4-8-7 (55) H Fellows(7) 12/1: 4000-038: In tch, hdwy 2f out, sn wknd: see 2080. *3½* **38**

2258 **ALAFZAR 5** [1]6-8-11 vis t (59) K Fallon 5/1: 1313049: Handy, wknd over 2f out: qck reapp: see 761. *8* **26**

1215 **JACARANDA 56** [3]4-9-7 (69) Dane O'Neill 10/1: 4024-050: 10th: ch g Bahhare - Near Miracle (Be My Guest) Rear, nvr nr ldrs: 8 wk abs: won a h'cap in '03 (with B Meehan): mdn scorer in '02: eff at 7f on firm & gd, prob any trk: both wins from the front: with Mrs A King. *5* **26**

2 Sep'03 Warw 7.1g/f 70-(74) D: 2 Jun'03 Ling 7.6g/f 80-79 D: 1 Jun'03 Newb 7fm 81-70 E: 1 Aug'02 Epso 7g/f 87- E:

1755 **BENNANABAA 27** [2]5-8-0 t (48) J F McDonald(3) 66/1: 050000: 11th: Rcd in 2nd, wknd over 2f out. *½* **0**

11 Ran Time 1m 22.72 (2.92) Owned: D Goodenough Removals & Transport Trained: Swindon

2371

8.45 Sky Bet Press Red To Bet Now Handicap Stakes 3yo+ 0-70 (E) **[70]**
£3712 £1142 £571 **1m2f36y** **Good 48** **-12 Slow** Inside

2114+**TIDAL 11** [5] A W Carroll 5-9-5 (6ex) (61) R Thomas(5) 5/2 FAV: 6000-611: Rcd in 2nd till led 7f out, clr fnl 1f, rdly: landed double: eff at 10/12f, handles soft, likes firm & gd, likes Chepstow: thriving, taking advantage of handy mark, can land hat-trick: see 2114 & 1541. **83**

2157* **REALISM 9** [11] P W Hiatt 4-9-4 (60) R Miles(3) 7/2: 0503612: Led 3f, rcd in 2nd, no extra over 1f out. *8* **69**

2036 **BILLY BATHWICK 15** [9] J M Bradley 7-9-0 (56) Dane O'Neill 9/1: 6553-003: Mid-div, onepcd. *½* **64**

2036 **SKYLARKER 15** [8] W S Kittow 6-10-0 (70) M Savage(5) 13/2: 3300044: Rear, hdwy 4f out, wknd 2f out. *¾* **77**

2225 **HAZEWIND 7** [4]3-8-1 vis t (56) F P Ferris(3) 11/2: 1000025: Handy, hdwy over 4f out, no impress 2f out. *½* **62**

1348 **MILK AND SULTANA 48** [7]4-8-11 (53) S Drowne 50/1: 30000-06: b f Millkom - Premier Princess (Hard Fought) Rear, hdwy 2f out, not pace to chall: 7 wk abs: mdn scorer in '03 (with W Brisbourne): eff at 7f, shld stay further: acts on fibresand & a sharp trk: now with G Ham. 1 Jan'03 Wolv 7af 71a- D: *¾* **58**

2088 **GREYFIELD 12** [3]8-8-13 (55) A Daly 12/1: 2/0400//-57: Rear, nvr a factor: see 2088. *3½* **55**

2156 **LUNAR LORD 9** [1]8-8-11 (53) R Price 33/1: 00/5-0008: Al bhd: see 924. *2½* **49**

1992 **SEEJAY 17** [2]4-8-0 (42) P M Quinn 33/1: 600-3009: Rear, nvr a factor: see 1045. *2½* **34**

2226 **MARGARETS WISH 7** [6]4-8-1 (43) B Swarbrick(5) 20/1: 4001000: 10th: Rear, nvr nr ldrs: btr 1333. *3* **30**

1006 **MOUNT BENGER 72** [10]4-9-9 (65) S Sanders 16/1: 63/000-60: 11th: Handy, wknd 3f out: see 1006. *10* **37**

11 Ran Time 2m 10.1 (6.0) Owned: Mrs B Quinn Trained: Alcester

2372

9.15 Sofrydd Social Club Chairman's 30th Anniversary Maiden Handicap Stakes 3yo+ 0-70 (E) **[64]**
£3926 £1208 £604 **6f16y str** **Good 48** **-03 Slow** Stands side

3882} **MILLFIELDS DREAMS 291** [3] R Brotherton 5-8-11 (47) F P Ferris(3) 33/1: 404604-1: b g Dreams End - Millfields Lady (Sayf El Arab) Made all far side, clr over 1f out, eased nr fin: reapp: unplcd all '03 starts (mdns, h'caps, seller, rtd 60): improved at 6f on gd with forcing tactics: runs v well fresh. **62**

2055 **GO YELLOW 14** [2] P D Evans 3-9-10 (68) S Donohoe(7) 18/1: 626-0052: Rcd in 2nd far side, no impress on wnr 2f out: see 2055. *6* **68**

1825 **DANISH MONARCH 24** [20] A D W Pinder 3-9-8 (66) D Sweeney 14/1: 6224-003: b g Great Dane - Moly (Inchinor) Handy stands side, kept on for press ins fnl 1f: rnr-up 3 of 5 '03 starts (mdns, with J Dunlop): eff at 6/7.5f on fast: first home from those drawn high. *1½* **61**

2 Sep'03 Beve 7.5g/f 72-(77) E: 2 Sep'03 Folk 7g/f 78- F: 2 Jul'03 Sali 6g/f 76- D:

1078 **EIGHT ELLINGTON 65** [18] Miss Gay Kelleway 3-9-1 (59) I Mongan 16/1: 40000-04: b g Ali Royal - Where's Charlotte (Sure Blade) Rear stands side, hdwy 2f out, kept on: 9 wk abs: 3rd 1 of 6 '03 starts (mdn, debut, rtd 66, with R Johnson Houghton): eff at 6f on fast. *hd* **53**

1426 **LIGNE DEAU 44** [1]3-9-1 (59) S Drowne 33/1: 000-05: Mid-div far side, hdwy 2f out, onepcd fnl 1f. *shd* **52**

1876 **KENSINGTON 22** [17]3-9-8 (66) S Sanders 5/2 FAV: 064-6326: Held up stands side, hdwy over 1f out, wknd fnl 1f: see 1876. *2½* **51**

1902 **BLUE MOON HITMAN 21** [14]3-9-2 (60) S Whitworth 33/1: 54636-37: Led stands side, no extra fnl 1f. *shd* **44**

2314 **PICCLEYES 2** [15]3-9-5 bl (63) Dane O'Neill 10/1: 0353-008: With ldrs stands side, wknd ins fnl 1f. *nk* **46**

2288 **MY GIRL PEARL 3** [6]4-9-0 (50) R Miles(3) 8/1: 00-02429: Rear centre, not clr run over 2f out, *¾* **31**

CHEPSTOW FRIDAY 11.06.04 Lefthand, Undulating, Galloping Track

hdwy over 1f out, onepcd ins fnl 1f: qck reapp: see 2288.
1989 **TRAVELLERS JOY** 17 [13]4-7-13 (35) J F McDonald(3) 14/1: 0-003069: Handy stands side, wknd 2f out. ¾ 14
1787 **GENERAL FEELING** 25 [12]3-9-9 (67) P Dobbs 4/1: 3-330: 11th: Mid-div stands side, wknd ins fnl 1f. 2 40
1963 **ZAMBEZI RIVER** 18 [4]5-9-0 (50) B Swarbrick(5) 25/1: 00060: 12th: Handy far side, wknd 2f out. 6 5
2117 **Sweet Az** 11 [11]4-8-3 (39) S Righton 50/1:0
1320 **The Butterfly Boy** 49 [16]3-9-2 (60) N De Souza(5) 16/1:0
2232 **Ballinger Express** 6 [9]4-10-0 bl(64) N Chalmers(5) 12/1:0
1989 **Vlasta Weiner** 17 [10]4-7-13 bl(35) A McCarthy 50/1:0
4701‡ **Stagnite** 243 [7]4-9-9 (59) G Baker 20/1:0   1985 **Bold Wolf** 17 [5]3-8-6 (50) A Daly 33/1:0
2118 **Lyrical Lady** 11 [19]3-8-9 P(53) R Thomas(5) 40/1:0   1415 **Mahlstick** 45 [8]6-8-8 (44) R Havlin 50/1:0
20 Ran Time 1m 11.86(3.06) Owned: Mrs S S Chandler Trained: Pershore

GOODWOOD FRIDAY 11.06.04 Righthand, Sharpish, Undulating Track

Official Going GOOD

2373   6.20 E B F Charlie Newman - A Lifetime In Racing Median Auction Maiden Stakes Fillies 2yo (E)
£4667 £1436 £718   6f str   Good 52   -40 Slow   Stands side

TREMPJANE [4] R Hannon 2-8-11 R Hughes 1/1 FAV: 1: b f Lujain - Trempkate (Trempolino) In 80
tch, switched & led over 1f out, styd on strongly: Apr foal, half-sister to a 6f juv performer & subs 9f US wnr:
dam a 9f wnr abroad: eff at 6f, will get further: acts on gd grnd & a sharp/undul trk: goes well fresh: type to progress.
GEE BEE EM [1] M R Channon 2-8-11 S Hitchcott(3) 12/1: 2: b f Piccolo - Cibenze (Owington) 1½ 74
Chsd ldrs, styd on for press, not pace of wnr: Jan first foal: dam a 7f/1m performer: eff at 6f on gd grnd shld
stay further: will learn from this.
BINT IL SULTAN [2] E A L Dunlop 2-8-11 J Murtagh 6/1: 3: b f Xaar - Knight's Place (Hamas) 1¾ 69
Keen & prom, outpcd 2f out, kept on ins last: 115,000gns Feb first foal: dam plcd at 1m/9f as a 3yo & half-sister
to wnrs at 1m/12f: apprec further in time.
CLASSIC GUEST [3] M R Channon 2-8-11 C Catlin 6/1: 4: Led till over 1f out, not pace of front nk 68
pair: stablemate of rnr-up.
AUWITESWEETHEART [5]2-8-11 S W Kelly 12/1: 5: Chsd ldrs ch 2f out, no extra dist on debut. ½ 66
CASTEROSSA [6]2-8-11 Paul Eddery 4/1: 6: Sn outpcd & struggling on debut. 5 51
6 Ran Time 1m 15.54 (5.54) Owned: Mrs W H Gibson Fleming Trained: Marlborough

2374   6.50 Sun-X Uk Leaderboard Sports Classified Stakes 3yo+ 0-75 (D)
£5421 £1668 £834   7f rnd   Good 52   -15 Slow   Inside

2249 **LADY GEORGINA** 6 [8] J R Fanshawe 3-8-5 (1ow) (75) O Urbina 13/8 FAV: 00-36121: Trkd ldrs, 78+
switched & no room dist till ins last, squeezed thr' gap & styd on to lead line, val for more than winning margin:
eff at 7f/1m on firm & gd/soft grnd, sharp/undul or stiff trk: game & prog filly.
2256 **IDLE POWER** 6 [1] J R Boyle 4-9-5 p (77) J Murtagh 6/1: 0-001102: Keen & trkd ldrs, ev ch fnl 1f & shd 79
just btn in a thrill fin: qck reapp, in gd form: see 2045.
2122 **SAMUEL CHARLES** 10 [3] W M Brisbourne 6-9-3 (72) S W Kelly 9/1: 1231223: Led, rdn & strongly prsd nk 76
fnl 2f, just hdd & no extra nr line: loves to force the pace: see 2122, 1909 & 1823.
2076 **WHAT A DANCER** 13 [7] G A Swinbank 7-9-4 (76) T Quinn 3/1: 4314044: Held up, switched for eff nk 76
over 1f out, styd on for press & btn arnd 0.5L in a bunched fin: see 887.
2172 **TERRAQUIN** 9 [5]4-9-3 P (74) D Kinsella 25/1: 0400505: Rear, outpcd over 2f out, kept on late, no 1¼ 72
threat: fair run in first time cheek pieces: see 517.
2172 **QUANTUM LEAP** 9 [4]7-9-3 vis (72) D Holland 7/1: 0303166: Chsd ldrs, no extra dist: btr 2063. 2½ 67
2116 **OAKLEY RAMBO** 11 [2]5-9-8 (80) R Hughes 12/1: 5062067: Held up, eff 2f out, btn dist: btr 1624. 3½ 65
7 Ran Time 1m 29.24 (4.74) Owned: Byerley Turf Trained: Newmarket

2375   7.20 Southern Daily Echo Stakes Handicap 3yo 0-80 (D)
£5408 £1664 £832   6f str   Good 52   -04 Slow   Stands side   [84]

2155 **PRESTO SHINKO** 9 [3] R Hannon 3-9-7 (77) R Hughes 5/2 FAV: 33-16321: Rear, no room repeatedly 89+
halfway till switched & qcknd to lead ins last, v cosily: eff at 6f, acts on fast, gd & polytrack, gall or
sharp/undul trk: eff forcing the pace or held up: won with plenty in hand, thriving & one to follow: see 2155.
1949* **ESTIHLAL** 18 [2] E A L Dunlop 3-8-8 (64) W Supple 7/2: 60-0412: Trkd ldrs, switched to chall 2f 1¼ 70
out & sn led, hdd ins last & not pace to repel easy wnr: acts on firm & gd grnd: se 1949 (mdn).
1575* **EISTEDDFOD** 36 [8] P F I Cole 3-9-5 (75) T Quinn 9/2: 13: In tch, rdn & styd on fnl 1f, not pace hd 80
of wnr: acts on gd & soft grnd, stays a sharp 6f: h'cap bow after 1575 (debut, mdn, soft).
1881 **RED ROMEO** 21 [1] G A Swinbank 3-9-5 (75) J Murtagh 3/1: 2016-244: Led till over 2f out, outpcd ½ 78
sn after but kept on ins last: rest well covered, only btn around 2L: see 1881 & 1360.
1417 **HAYDN** 44 [6]3-9-3 (72) J F Egan 16/1: 000-5005: Trkd ldrs, no impress from dist: abs, gelded. 3½ 65
2215 **ARFINNIT** 7 [7]3-8-8 vis (64) S Hitchcott(3) 16/1: 3065166: Led till 2f out, sn btn: btr 1975 (clmr). shd 55
712 **POMPEY BLUE** 108 [4]3-8-10 (66) D Holland 10/1: 515-5507: Trkd ldrs, btn dist: abs: btr 3 (AW). 2½ 49
2048 **AVERLLINE** 14 [5]3-9-0 (70) D Kinsella 20/1: 32210-08: Mid-div, no impress dist: see 2048. 7 32
8 Ran Time 1m 13.41 (3.41) Owned: Major A M Everett Trained: Marlborough

2376
7.55 Sally Miller Mount Kilimanjaro Trek Maiden Handicap Stakes 3yo 0-75 (E)   [81]
£3770 £1160 £580   1m6f   Good 52   +09 Fast   Inside

2130 **HATHLEN** 10 [5] M R Channon 3-9-6 (73) S Hitchcott(3) 7/1: 2-066561: Mid-div, rdn & hdwy to press ldr over 2f out, drvn out: now suited by 14f, shapes as if 2m+ shld suit: acts on firm & gd grnd, gall or sharp/undul trks: see 1768, 1174.
　　80

1939 **SUNNY LADY** 19 [6] E A L Dunlop 3-9-7 (74) D Holland 11/4 FAV: 60-2222: Trkd ldrs, led 4f out, rdn & hdd bef dist, kept on: stays a sharp 14f: consistent: see 1939, 1768 & 1140.
1　78

1708 **GLIDE** 29 [7] H Charlton 3-9-3 VIS (70) R Hughes 13/2: 045-303. Held up, rdn & styd on fnl 2f, nrst fin: clr of rem: first time visor: stays 14f: see 1124.
hd　73

2130 **FU FIGHTER** 10 [3] J A Osborne 3-9-5 (72) J Murtagh 11/2: 54-054: Prom, chall over 3f out, wknd dist.
5　67

2175 **MUSTANG ALI** 9 [9]3-9-1 (68) J F Egan 9/2: 003-6035: Held up, eff 3f out, no extra fnl 2f: longer trip.
1¾　60

1864 **OLYMPIAS** 22 [4]3-8-7 (60) S W Kelly 14/1: 5006: Held up, switched for eff over 2f out, no impress: h'cap bow & longer trip: unplcd prev at up to 12f: see 980.
¾　51

2134 **DARN GOOD** 10 [2]3-8-13 bl (66) R L Moore 20/1: 0-003067: Trkd ldr, rdn & btn 2f out: btr 915.
hd　56

1384 **FLYING PATRIARCH** 46 [10]3-7-12 (4oh)bl (47) Lisa Jones(3) 33/1: 000-08: gr g Silver Patriarch - Flying Wind (Forzando) Trkd ldrs, btn 2f out: 6 wk abs: blnks reapplied: unplcd '03 (rtd 46, mdn, blnks).
13　21

2134 **WALTZING BEAU** 10 [1]3-8-6 VIS (59) T Quinn 25/1: 0-2009: Sn rdn & led, hdd 4f out, btn 2f out: visor.
1　27

1939 **AL BEEDAA** 19 [8]3-9-6 VIS (73) W Supple 4/1: 03-4330: 10th: Held up, rdn & btn 3f out: visor.
15　18

10 Ran　Time 3m 4.92 (6.12)　Owned: Sheikh Ahmed Al Maktoum　Trained: West Ilsley

2377
8.30 Crimbourne Stud Stakes Handicap 3yo 0-85 (D)   [90]
£6776 £2085 £1043   1m1f192y   Good 52   -03 Slow   Inside

2079* **GAVROCHE** 13 [3] C A Dwyer 3-9-2 (78) J P Guillambert(3) 5/1: 3522511: Dwelt, settled rear, hdwy 3f out & led ins last, all out, gamely: eff at 9/10f on fast, hvy & fibresand, sharp/undul or gall trk: tough, genuine & progressive: see 2079.
　　87

2066* **SWAINSON** 13 [4] P Mitchell 3-9-3 (79) D Holland 7/2 FAV: 3412: Trkd ldr & led 2f out, drvn & hdd ins last, rallied gamely, just denied: h'cap bow: handles gd, soft & polytrack: genuine & improving.
shd　87

1791 **SAILMAKER** 25 [8] R Charlton 3-8-13 T (75) R Hughes 5/1: 6-2303: Held up, kept on for press fnl 2f, not pace to front pair: first time t-strap: handles gd & hvy grnd, stays 10f: see 1791 & 1511 & 1101.
3½　78

1930 **MUHAYMIN** 20 [5] J L Dunlop 3-9-7 (83) W Supple 5/1: 031-004: Led, hdd 2f out, no extra: see 1930.
2½　82

2012 **WOU OODD** 16 [2]3-9-3 (79) S Hitchcott(3) 12/1: 0-435: Keen & in tch, rdn & no impress fnl 2f: see 1719.
1¾　75

1864* **SPRINGTIME ROMANCE** 22 [7]3-9-4 (80) J Murtagh 4/1: 3616: Trkd ldrs, rdn & btn 2f out: h'cap bow.
1　74

2024 **UNCLE JOHN** 16 [1]3-8-3 (65) J F Egan 10/1: 00105-07: Mid-div, rdn & btn over 1f out: 'lost action'.
4　53

1427 **RED SKELTON** 44 [6]3-9-1 T (77) T Quinn 14/1: 01-08: Sn strugg rear, nvr factor, abs, t-strap.
2½　61

8 Ran　Time 2m 9.7 (5.5)　Owned: Mr J L Guillambert　Trained: Newmarket

2378
9.00 Raughmere Maiden Stakes 3yo (D)
£5486 £1688 £844   1m rnd   Good 52   -05 Slow   Inside

1815 **GOLD MASK** 24 [6] J H M Gosden 3-9-0 VIS (78) D Holland 4/5 FAV: 0-621: Led after 1f, briefly rdn dist, styd on strongly under hand riding ins last: eff at 1m on fast & gd/soft: improved form front in a vis.
　　80

4611} **ADMIRAL COMPTON** 249 [9] A C Stewart 3-9-0 J Murtagh 10/1: 0-2: ch c Compton Place - Sunfleet (Red Sunset) Mid-div, shkn up from over 1f out & styd on well cl-home, not able to chall wnr: reapp: unplcd sole '03 start (mdn): related to wnrs at 5f/1m, dam styd 12f: styd this longer 1m trip well & shapes as if further could suit: acts on fast grnd, sharp/undul trk: shld win a race.
1½　76

1810 **TENNYS GOLD** 25 [3] B W Hills 3-8-9 (70) M Hills 3/1: 02-43: Prom & chsd wnr 3f out, rdn & no extra ins last: acts on fast, gd & polytrack: see 1810.
nk　70

2225 **LORD OF THE SEA** 7 [8] Jamie Poulton 3-9-0 (67) P Doe 10/1: 3340004: Mid-div, styd on onepcd for press, no threat to front trio: see 798, 568 & 514.
2½　70$

1763 **DESERT HAWK** 27 [2]3-9-0 J Egan 16/1: 005: b c Cape Cross - Milling (In The Wings) Mid-div, switched wide & kept on fn 2f, nvr threat: unplcd prev: type to apprec 10f & h'cap company now.
nk　69

1495 **MISS INKHA** 40 [4]3-8-9 R L Moore 25/1: 006: Mid-div, btn over 1f out: 6 wk abs: qual for h'caps.
nk　63

2072 **SHAABAN** 13 [7]3-9-0 C Catlin 12/1: 007: b c Woodman - Ashbilya (Nureyev) Held up, eff 2f out, btn dist: unplcd prev, mid-dist h'caps shld suit.
½　67

4066} **ROYAL STARLET** 280 [1]3-8-9 W Supple 50/1: 000-8: Mid-div, btn 2f out, reapp.
1½　59

1511 **HERIOT** 39 [5]3-9-0 BL T Quinn 20/1: 09: Led 1f, chsd wnr, btn 2f out, blnks.
20　24

5013} **LOLA LOLA** 218 [10]3-8-9 Paul Eddery 33/1: 000-0: 10th: Sn struggling rear, reapp.
7　5

10 Ran　Time 1m 41.97(4.57)　Owned: Mr W S Farish　Trained: Manton

Official Going Standard

2379
2.25 At The Races Is Back Claiming Stakes 3yo (F)
£2912 £832 £416   6f aw rnd   Going 73   +04 Fast   Inside

2055 **GARNOCK VENTURE** 14 [8] A Berry 3-9-5 bl (54) J Fanning 7/1: 0103001: Cl-up, led halfway trav well, rdn & styd on strongly ins last: gd time: eff at 5f, suited by 6/7f: acts on fibresand & gd/soft grnd, likes a sharp/turning trk: best in blnks & clmg/sell grade: imprvd form, see 1457 & 871.
　　74a

2215* **EL PALMAR** 7 [3] P A Blockley 3-9-1 (65) Dean McKeown 3/1 FAV: 62-33012: Prom, eff to press wnr 2f out, no extra bef dist: prev with T D Barron: nicely bckd: acts on fibresand but btr 2215 (7f, clmr, fast).
2　63a

2268 **INNCLASSIC** 4 [6] B J Meehan 3-8-10 BL (75) J F McDonald(3) 6/1: 03-003: Chsd ldrs, not pace to chall wnr over 1f out: 1st time blnks, qck reapp: handles both AWs: see 1732.
2　53a

1949 **WILLJOJO** 18 [5] R A Fahey 3-8-2 (55) P Hanagan 100/30: 3503-354: Chsd ldrs, outpcd halfway, kept
½　43a

on late, nvr a threat: see 995.
1842 **BOOKIESINDEXDOTCOM 23** [7]3-8-2 vis (41) G Gibbons 20/1: 3066055: Sn drvn & outpcd, nvr a factor. *5* **31a**
2102 **BEAMSLEY BEACON 11** [4]3-8-11 bl (59) N Pollard 16/1: 00-00406: Led till halfway, wknd qckly. *¾* **38a**
2118 **CREWES MISS ISLE 11** [2]3-8-10 (67) S Whitworth 7/2: 4615007: In tch till halfway: btr 1338. *3½* **28a**
1641 **ST GEORGES GIRL 32** [1]3-8-2 (25) J Jeffrey(5) 50/1: 000-008: Dwelt & sn outpcd: see 1641. *12* **0a**
8 Ran Time 1m 17.45 (4.15) Owned: Mr Robert Aird Trained: Cockerham

2380 **2.55 Sky 415 Ntl 908 Telewest 534 Handicap Stakes 3yo 0-70 (E)** **[76]**
£3406 £1048 £524 **5f aw str** **Going 73** **Inapplicable** Stands Side

1951 **BLUE POWER 18** [11] K R Burke 3-8-10 (58) D Sweeney 5/1: 3-003531: Trkd ldrs trav well, led over 1f out, rdn out: op 9/1: eff at 5f: acts on firm grnd, loves fibresand/Southwell: see 1951 & 169. **68a**
2034 **NANNA 15** [10] R Hollinshead 3-8-3 (51) G Duffield 9/2: 0302162: Al prom & ch over 1f out, drvn & not pace of wnr: remains in gd heart: see 1787. *1½* **56a**
1441 **SAHARA SILK 43** [6] D Shaw 3-9-6 vis (68) J F McDonald(3) 7/1: 1341203: Prom, drvn & ch over 1f out, no extra: 6 wk abs: see 1338 & 872. *1* **70a**
2219* **ICENASLICE 7** [9] J J Quinn 3-8-3 (51) P Hanagan 3/1 FAV: 346-014: Led, hung left & hdd over 1f out, no extra: reportedly hung LH'd closing stages: acts on fibresand, but much btr 2219 (fast). *¾* **51a**
2111 **WONKY DONKEY 11** [1]3-8-6 (54) Hayley Turner(2) 8/1: 0-34305: Mid-div, hung right under press from halfway, kept on, nvr able to chall: needs 6f+ in similar: see 1374 & 751. *½* **52a**
2202 **BRAVE CHIEF 7** [2]3-8-4 (1ow) (51) N Pollard 33/1: 002-0056: Outpcd, nvr able to chall: see 256. *¾* **48a**
835 **BARRAS 90** [4]3-8-9 vis (57) M Fenton 20/1: 1-003547: Badly bmpd start & nvr on terms: abs. *2½* **46a**
2326 **BOND SHAKIRA 2** [7]3-8-7 (55) D McGaffin 12/1: 5-3048: Sn outpcd: qck reapp: btr 2326 (g/s). *shd* **44a**
1054 **HEAD OF STATE 67** [5]3-8-12 vis (60) J Quinn 16/1: 0010309: Badly bmpd start & nvr on terms, abs. *nk* **48a**
1344 **EASTERN PEARL 48** [3]3-9-7 (69) S Whitworth 25/1: 2100-000: 10th: ch f Wolfhound - Wild Humour (Fayruz) Stumbled & hmpd start, in tch till over 1f out: 7 wk abs: h'cap wnr in '03: eff at 5f on firm & fast, enjoys soft & forcing tactics: loves a stiff trk. *1½* **53a**
1 Aug'03 Sand 5.0sft 76-67 D: 2 Aug'03 Carl 5fm 67-(54) F: 2 Aug'03 Sand 5.0g/f 68-(54) E:
1575 **VELVET TOUCH 36** [8]3-8-6 VIS (54) G Gibbons 12/1: 2-260650: 11th: Chsd ldrs, struggling halfway: tried visor, poor run: btr 1575 & 1441. *5* **26a**
11 Ran Time 58.83 () Owned: Mr F Jeffers Trained: Leyburn

2381 **3.25 At The Races 9am To 1am Every Day Amateur Riders' Selling Stakes 4yo+ (G)**
£2569 £734 £367 **1m4f** **Going 73** **-34 Slow** Inside

2200* **ROMIL STAR 7** [6] K R Burke 7-11-5 vis (65) Mr S Dobson(3) 2/5 FAV: 0021411: Sn handy trav well, went on over 5f out, cruised clr fnl 3f, any amount in hand: bckd at long odds-on: eff at 12/14.7f on gd, hvy & fibresand: loves sell/clmg grade: see 2200 & 1838. **60a+**
1840 **WESTERN COMMAND 23** [8] Mrs N Macauley 8-11-0 p (35) Mrs M Morris 20/1: 5335052: Held up, kept on to chase wnr fnl 3f, nvr any impress: see 456. *6* **35a**
2273 **COOLFORE JADE 4** [5] N E Berry 4-11-0 (49) Mr Joshua Harris(7) 9/2: 0500063: Cl-up 5f out, rdn & btn 3f out: qck reapp: see 505. *11* **22a**
2052 **BANNERS FLYING 14** [2] D W Chapman 4-11-0 (64) Miss Rachel Clark(7) 40/1: 245-004: Led after 1f till over 5f out, sn struggling: see 1195. *1½* **20a**
1838 **MORRIS DANCING 23** [3]5-11-0 vis (32) Mr E Dehdashti(3) 50/1: 0500035: Prom 7f: see 1838 & 784. *1¾* **18a**
1407 **KING PRIAM 45** [9]9-11-5 p (30) Miss Faye Bramley(5) 50/1: 6540066: Cl-up till 4f out: see 353. *nk* **22a**
1252 **PROTOCOL 53** [7]10-11-0 t p (27) Mr B King(5) 14/1: 0040-007: Dwelt, al bhd: see 1064. *10* **6a**
1714 **THE LAST MOHICAN 29** [1]5-11-5 (38) Miss F Guillambert(7) 12/1: 0032108: Led 1f, prom till 5f out. *hd* **10a**
SHAMELESS [4]7-11-0 t Miss Dawn Rankin(5) 50/1: 9: ch g Prince Daniel - Level Edge (Beveled) Slow away & al outpcd: jumps fit (no form): wears a t-strap: Flat debut today. *4* **0a**
9 Ran Time 2m 47.19 (12.89) Owned: Mrs Elaine M Burke Trained: Leyburn

2382 **4.00 At The Races Dedicated Racing Channel Maiden Stakes 2yo (D)**
£3838 £1181 £591 **6f aw rnd** **Going 73** **-03 Slow** Inside

1401 **AL QUDRA 45** [8] B J Meehan 2-9-0 J F McDonald(3) 15/8 FAV: 51: Made all & rdn clr over 1f out, easily: nicely bckd, op 9/4: 6 wk abs & AW bow: apprec step-up to 6f, 7f+ shld suit: handles gd grnd, relished fibresand today: goes well fresh: win again in this form: see 1401. **91a+**
1893 **AUNTY EURO 21** [6] E J O'Neill 2-8-9 J Carroll 8/1: 4332: Chsd ldrs, rdn & outpcd by wnr fnl 2f: prob handles fast & fibresand: consistent: see 1893 & 1084. *8* **68a**
HOMME DANGEREUX [11] C R Egerton 2-9-0 J Quinn 20/1: 3: b c Royal Applause - Happy Lady (Cadeaux Genereux) In tch, outpcd halfway, kept on late, nvr a threat: Mar foal, brother to a 6f juv wnr, dam plcd at 9f: eff at 6f, looks sure to apprec further: prob handles fibresand: improve. *1¾* **69a**
1367 **WEET YER TERN 47** [7] P A Blockley 2-9-0 P Hanagan 5/2: 424: Chsd ldrs, rdn & no impress fnl 2f: bckd: 7 wk abs, AW bow: btr 1367 & 1001 (5f, firm & fast). *½* **67a**
2228 **NO COMMISSION 7** [4]2-9-0 D Nolan(3) 12/1: 05405: Cl-up, ch over 2f out, wknd: see 1893. *1½* **64a**
1880 **OLDSTEAD FLYER 21** [10]2-9-0 D Tudhope(7) 33/1: 06: b c Foxhound - Princess Tycoon (Last Tycoon) Dwelt, chsd ldrs till over 2f out, AW bow: cheaply bought Apr foal, half brother to a 9f plcd 4yo. *6* **49a**
1439 **LORD CHALFONT 43** [9]2-9-0 G Duffield 100/1: 007: Drvn rear & nvr a factor: new yard, abs. *6* **34a**
1608 **MONASHEE MISS 35** [2]2-8-9 N Pollard 50/1: 48: Dwelt & sn outpcd, AW bow: btr 1608. *1¾* **25a**
1805 **MISTY PRINCESS 25** [5]2-8-9 G Gibbons 14/1: 05609: Cl-up till halfway, sn wknd, AW bow. *1½* **22a**
2177 **KRISTIKHAB 8** [1]2-9-0 J Fanning 11/2: 05420: 10th: Al outpcd & nvr factor, op 9/2: btr 2177 (gd). *27* **0a**
10 Ran Time 1m 17.84 (4.54) Owned: Abbott Racing Limited Trained: Upper Lambourn

SOUTHWELL   Fibresand   FRIDAY 11.06.04   Lefthand, Sharp, Oval Track

2383

4.35 At The Races On Ntl Ireland And Chorus Median Auction Maiden Stakes 3yo (E)
£3455 £1063 £532   1m aw rnd   Going 73   -03 Slow   Inside

1511 **PASS THE PORT 39** [6] J R Fanshawe 3-9-0 J D Smith 15/8: 51: ch g Docksider - One of The Family   79a
(Alzao) Pushed along chsg ldrs, led 2f out, sn rdn clr, rdly: AW bow, left debut bhd: eff at 1m, further shld
suit: relished fibresand today: lightly rcd & op to improvement.
     SENOR SET [10] P A Blockley 3-9-0 Stacey Renwick(7) 66/1: 2: b g Second Set - Shine Share (El   6   69a
Gran Senor) Slow away, styd on from halfway, took 2nd nr fin, nvr a threat: debut: stays 1m on fibresand, further
shld suit: shld learn plenty from this.
1580 **EXTRA COVER 36** [9] R Charlton 3-9-0 BL (74) D Sweeney 5/6 FAV: 5-2223: Chsd ldrs & led over 4f   1½   66a
out, hd carried high & hdd 2f out, sn btn: well bckd at odds-on in 1st time blnks: tricky ride.
1959 **MAGIC VERSE 18** [8] R Guest 3-8-9 C Lowther 66/1: 004: ch f Opening Verse - Festival Sister   5   52a
(Belmez) Prom, no impress over 2f out: AW bow: well held on turf prev: may improve in low grade mid-dist h'caps.
2012 **BLUE VIKING 16** [12] 3-9-0 P Hanagan 100/1: 4-05: Prom, lost place 5f out, no impress after: AW bow.   1¾   54a
1554 **CRATHES 38** [7] 3-8-9 M Fenton 9/1: 246: Led 3f, btn 2f out: btr 1070.   3   43a
102   **SILVER ISLAND 198** [11] 3-9-0 J Carroll 100/1: 00-7: Bhd halfway: 6 month abs, new yard.   2½   43a
     DREAM EASY [3] 3-9-0 G Duffield 40/1: 8: Slow away, sn rdn & nvr a factor on debut.   10   26a
     SWEET AT HEART [1] 3-8-9 Dean McKeown 66/1: 9: Slow away & sn outpcd on debut.   5   12a
1675 **MYSTIC PROMISE 31** [13] 3-9-0 t (32) N Pollard 100/1: 5034560: 10th: Chsd ldrs till 2f out.   5   8a
2148 **CRONKYVODDY 9** [4] 3-9-0 t J Quinn 11/1: 60: 11th: Chsd ldrs, btn 2f out: btr 2148 (firm).   nk   7a
1472 **ROCKY RAMBO 41** [5] 3-9-0 BL T Eaves(3) 50/1: 0-00: 12th: Held up & sn struggling, blnks, abs.   5   0a
     DESERT CORAL [2] 3-8-9 S Yourston(7) 66/1: 0: 13th: Slow away & sn bhd.   nk   0a
13 Ran   Time 1m 17.84 (4.54)   Owned: Lancen Farm Partnership   Trained: Newmarket

2384

5.10 At The Races Committed To Racing Handicap Stakes 3yo+ 35-55 (F)   [52]
£3038 £868 £434   7f aw rnd   Going 73   -02 Slow   Inside

4360} **TANCRED MISS 265** [8] D W Barker 5-8-11 (35) T Eaves(3) 33/1: 000000-1: b f Presidium -   42a
Mischievous Miss (Niniski) Chsd ldrs, rdn & ch over 2f out, short of room over 1f out but styd on for press to lead
cl-home: reapp: unplcd '03 (rtd 49a & 27, h'caps): h'cap wnr '02: eff at 6/7f, poss stays 1m & has tried 10f:
acts on firm, gd/soft & fibresand, likes a sharp trk & forcing tactics: goes well fresh.
2 Aug'02 Carl 6g/f 57-54 F: 1 Jul'02 Catt 6fm 55-48 E: 2 Jun'02 Carl 6g/f 50-47 E: 2 May'02 Catt 7g/f 52- F:
2 Jul'01 Sout 6af 73a- F:
1947 **TSARBUCK 18** [13] R M H Cowell 3-9-7 (55) J Carroll 8/1: 0-000152: Chsd ldrs, led 2f out, hung   ½   60a
left under press & hdd nr fin: back to form on return to sand: see 1842 (C/D banded).
2080 **ROCKY REPPIN 13** [9] J Balding 4-9-8 (46) K Pierrepont(7) 25/1: 40-00003: b g Rock City - Tino   1¾   47a
Reppin (Neltino) Prom, outpcd 2f out, kept on ins last: lightly rcd & unplcd '03 (rtd 67): eff around 7f, tried up
to 10f prev: acts on fibresand, best without blnks.
1954 **SHIFTY 18** [2] D Nicholls 5-9-10 (48) J Fanning 7/2 FAV: 0040524: Held up, keeping on when short   ¾   49a
of room over 1f out, not able to reach front trio: see 1954.
2215 **SALUT SAINT CLOUD 7** [14] 3-9-0 vis (48) N Pollard 25/1: 0045-605: Pushed along chsg ldrs, onepace.   ½   48a
1642* **EXTEMPORISE 32** [4] 4-10-0 (52) T G McLaughlin 13/2: 0-035116: Chsd ldrs, btn dist: btr 1642.   1½   49a
1839* **BRONX BOMBER 23** [7] 6-9-13 bl (51) C Lowther 12/1: 0/600-117: Led/dsptd lead 5f, wknd: op 8/1.   1   46a
4859} **BANDBOX 232** [5] 9-8-11 (35) M Fenton 25/1: 000600-8: Bhd & sn pushed along, mod prog, reapp.   nk   29a
2049 **DASAR 14** [11] 4-9-10 vis (48) M Lawson(5) 8/1: 6-640239: Led 2f, handy till 2f out: btr 1266.   2½   37a
2205 **DANTES DEVINE 7** [6] 3-9-4 (52) G Duffield 25/1: 5-065040: 10th: Dwelt, al outpcd: flattered 1086.   1½   38a
2149 **PEARTREE HOUSE 9** [15] 10-8-8 (5oh) (27) D Fentiman(7) 25/1: 0066600: 11th: Dwelt, eff wide to chase   ½   17a
ldrs 2f out, sn hung left & wknd.
2135 **RILEYS ROCKET 10** [12] 5-8-8 (32) J Quinn 33/1: 005-0000: 12th: Al bhd.   5   8a
1989 **GRUFF 17** [10] 5-8-8 (32) Dean McKeown 28/1: 0-00000: 13th: Mid-div, strug halfway: up in trip.   ½   7a
1755 **SAROS 27** [3] 3-9-7 (55) D McGaffin 4/1: 06-01160: 14th: Slow away & sn bhd: 'not face kick-back'.   14   6a
2049 **DUNCANBIL 14** [1] 3-9-2 (50) D Nolan(3) 25/1: 50066-00: 15th: Prom, drvn & lost pl 5f out, sn bhd.   17   0a
15 Ran   Time 1m 45.39 (5.99)   Owned: Mrs S J Barker   Trained: Richmond

SANDOWN   SATURDAY 12.06.04   Righthand, Galloping Track, Stiff Finish

Official Going Good/Firm (Good Places)

2385

1.00 Royalties Gold Handicap Stakes 3yo 0-90 (C)   [96]
£10322 £3176 £1588   1m1f   Good/Firm 31   -03 Slow   Inside

2247 **CIMYLA 7** [9] C F Wall 3-9-4 (86) G Baker 12/1: 41-30101: Mid-div, smooth hdwy to lead over 1f   98+
out & sn rdn clr, cosily: op 16/1: reportedly lost action when disapp latest, also reported earlier this term: well
suited by 1m/9f on polytrk, fast & soft: useful/progressive colt & prob one to keep on side: see 1741.
1930 **LETS ROLL 21** [10] C W Thornton 3-8-3 (71) T Williams 9/2: 251-2622: Rear, hdwy when no room over   2   76
2f out, swtchd & kept on well for press, no threat to wnr: nicely bckd: stays 9f, remains a likely type for similar.
2117 **RONDELET 12** [1] R M Beckett 3-8-8 (76) R L Moore 10/1: 064-2023: Rear, rdn 3f out, styd on well   nk   80
late: stays 9f on fast & gd/sft, sure to relish 10f+: see 1707.
2157 **CARTRONAGEERAGHLAD 10** [7] J A Osborne 3-8-9 (77) Dane O'Neill 25/1: 0000244: Dwelt, rear, rdn 3f   shd   81
out, styd on well fnl 1f, nrst fin: op 12/1: gd run, crying out for return to 10f+: see 1707.
2249 **BLUE DAZE 7** [6] 3-8-0 (68) R Smith 50/1: 01-005: b f Danzero - Sparkling (Kris) Trkd ldrs, kept   1½   69
on onepace for press fnl 3f: lightly rcd fills mdn wnr last term: winning form & at 6f, styd this longer 9f trip: acts
on fast & gall trk: can go well fresh: encouraging. 1 Jun'03 Nott 6.1g/f 72- E:
1813 **WOODY VALENTINE 25** [4] 3-8-12 (80) K Dalgleish 7/2 FAV: 00-42166: Led/dsptd lead till went on   ½   80
over 4f out, edged left & hdd 2f out, no extra dist: bckd, op 4/1: vet reported gelding lost a plate: see 1427.
1956* **BALEARIC STAR 19** [2] 3-8-1 (69) A McCarthy 9/1: 000-6017: Held up, eff over 2f out, btn dist.   ½   68
2079 **SUNISA 14** [3] 3-8-10 (78) P Robinson 13/2: 624-2138: Mid-div, efft wide 3f out, fdd fnl 2f: ½   76
jockey reported filly was unsuited by the ground: btr 2079, 1220.

2259 **OLIVANDER 6** [11]3-8-7 bl (75) S Sanders 16/1: 52U6-039: Rear, pushed along halfway, little prog.   *1*   **71**
1813 **ZWEIBRUCKEN 25** [8]3-9-1 (83) J Fortune 20/1: 32120-00: 10th: b f Alhaarth - Solar Attraction   *hd*   **78**
(Salt Dome). Keen & chsd ldrs, btn/hmpd over 2f out, sn fdd: h'cap wnr '03, subs h'cap rnr up: best efforts over a
stiff 7f, yet to convince over further: acts on fast & gd/sft ground, sharp/undul or stiff trk.
2 Sep'03 Asco 7g/f 84-80 B: 1 Aug'03 Sand 7.1g/s 83-75 D: 2 Aug'03 Folk 7g/f 81- D:
1924 **SHALAYA 21** [5]3-9-5 (87) D Holland 6/1: 16-50: 11th: Rear, efft over 2f out, wknd qckly from dist.   *½*   **81**
1844 **DERAASAAT 24** [12]3-9-7 (89) W Supple 20/1: 01-060: 12th: Led/dsptd lead till over 4f out, wknd 2f out.   *½*   **82**
12 Ran Time 1m 54.30 (3.1)   Owned: Mr Peter Botham   Trained: Newmarket

---

2386   1.35 32red Online Casino Maiden Stakes 3yo (D)
        £5668 £1744 £872   **1m2f7y**   **Good/Firm 31**   **-31 Slow**   Inside

1651 **TREW CLASS 33** [6] M H Tompkins 3-8-9 P Robinson 25/1: 001: ch f Inchinor - Inimitable (Polish   **79**
Precedent). Trkd ldrs, styd on for press to lead well ins last: left prev soft ground starts bhd: sister to useful 1m
performer Inverness & also a 1m/10f wnr, dam a 10f 3yo wnr: eff at 10f, shld get further: relished switch to fast
ground today & handles a stiff trk: entitled to progress.
4597} **MEISSEN 252** [7] A C Stewart 3-8-9 T Quinn 9/1: 60-2: ch f Amfortas - Musetta (Cadeaux Genereux)   *½*   **77+**
Chsd ldr, shkn up & outpcd 2f out, styd on strongly close home, not rch wnr: lightly rcd & unplcd in '03 (rtd 76,
highly tried, Lstd, C Brittain): styd longer 10f trip, looks sure to apprec 12f+: acts on fast ground & a stiff trk:
still green & expect improvement over further, interesting for h'caps.
4568} **DALISAY 253** [9] Sir Michael Stoute 3-8-9 J Fortune 7/1: 0-3: b f Sadler's Wells - Dabiliya   *½*   **76**
(Vayrann). Held up, efft to chse front pair 2f out, kept on well ins last, not pace to chall: op 5/1: unplcd sole '03
start (mdn, rtd 58): eff at 10f on fast ground: will relish 12f & shld improve.
1597 **LINE DRAWING 36** [2] B W Hills 3-9-0 S Sanders 9/4: 24: Led & arnd 4L clr halfway, rdn & hdd   *nk*   **78**
over 1f out, hdd & no extra ins last: hvly bckd: acts on fast & gd grnd: see 1597.
1166 **RAWDON 59** [3]3-9-0 VIS R Havlin 11/1: 05: b c Singspiel - Rebecca Sharp (Machiavellian) Slow   *½*   **79**
away & bhd, rdn & styd on fnl 2f, not able to chall: half brother to a 1m wnr & dam a high class 1m performer: styd
this longer 10f trip, may get further: acts on fast ground & eff in a stiff trk today: prob needs strong handling.
      MIJDAAF 0 [10]3-9-0 P McCabe 16/1: 6: Slow away & bhd, kept on well from over 1f out: debut.   *½*   **78**
2072 **ZUMA 14** [11]3-9-0 (80) D Holland 15/8 FAV: 00-037: Sn pushed along chasing ldrs, hmpd early,   *shd*   **78**
outpcd over 2f out, kept on ins last: well bckd: does not look entirely straightforward but 12f+ shld suit.
1935 **BOLD PHOENIX 21** [8]3-9-0 J McAuley 50/1: 08: In tch, btn 3f out: longer trip.   *14*   **58**
1961 **GREEK STAR 19** [5]3-9-0 P Makin(5) 50/1: 0-49: Held up & sn strugg rear.   *3½*   **53**
      JACOBIN 0 [4]3-9-0 S Whitworth 50/1: 0: 10th: Slow away & always bhd on debut.   *1¼*   **51**
10 Ran Time 2m 09.7 (5.6)   Owned: Russell Trew Roofing Ltd   Trained: Newmarket

---

2387   2.10 One Account Handicap Stakes 3yo 0-80 (D)   **[84]**
        £5408 £1664 £832   **5f6y**   **Good/Firm 31**   **-19 Slow**   Inside

2227 **BARON RHODES 8** [6] J S Wainwright 3-9-3 (73) T Eaves(3) 8/1: 42-22231: Trkd ldrs, qcknd to lead   **81**
ins last, all out to hold on: deserved success, plcd all 4 starts prev this term: suited by 5f on fast & soft ground,
stiff/undul or sharp trk: tough & genuine with a progressive profile: see 2227, 1973 & 1229.
1942 **INTRIGUING GLIMPSE 20** [7] Miss B Sanders 3-9-4 (74) S Sanders 3/1 FAV: 113-3222: Rear, hdwy over   *hd*   **82**
1f out, drvn & styd on strongly, just failed: hvly bckd: remains an obvious candidate for similar: see 1942, 1809.
1881 **TREASURE CAY 22** [2] P W D'Arcy 3-9-5 t (75) Paul Eddery 9/2: 1-5353: Dwelt, rear, swtchd & kept   *1½*   **78**
on well ins last, not able to apprec return to 6f: see 1881, 1477.
2121 **BORZOI MAESTRO 11** [4] J L Spearing 3-9-7 (77) A Daly 16/1: 00-23104: Led till 2f out, no extra dist.   *1¼*   **76**
2271* **SIMPSONS MOUNT 5** [3]3-8-12 (6ex) (68) R L Moore 8/1: 5305015: Handy & led 2f out, hdd ins last,   *hd*   **66**
wknd, 'hung': bckd: btr 2271 (6f).
1901 **MIRASOL PRINCESS 22** [9]3-9-6 (76) T Quinn 9/1: 100-0046: Chsd ldrs, no impress dist: see 1901.   *1¼*   **70**
1734 **AFTER THE SHOW 29** [8]3-8-11 (67) W Supple 13/2: 051-6067: Rear & al outpcd: bckd, op 9/1: btr 1116.   *hd*   **60**
1942 **DELLAGIO 20** [1]3-8-1 (57) J Quinn 12/1: 0-000048: Rear, little prog, 'hung left': btr 1942.   *nk*   **49**
2227 **BAYLAW STAR 8** [5]3-9-3 (73) D Holland 8/1: 03-63049: Mid-div, btn 2f out, 'hung left': btr 2227 (g/s).   *6*   **49**
9 Ran Time 1m 02.09 (2.49)   Owned: Mr I Barran & Mr P Rhodes   Trained: Malton

---

2388   2.40 Palletline Plc Maiden Stakes 2yo (D)
        £4953 £1524 £762   **7f16y**   **Good/Firm 31**   **-65 Slow**   Inside

      JALAMID 0 [13] J H M Gosden 2-9-0 T W Supple 5/1: 1: b c Danehill - Vignelaure (Royal Academy)   **82+**
Trkd ldrs, duelled with rnr up when narrow lead over 1f out, rdn out: nicley bckd: 300,000gns Mar foal: half brother
to a 1m 3yo wnr: eff over a stiff 7f, 1m sure to suit: acts on fast & a stiff trk: overcame greeness, sure to improve.
      CHAPTER 0 [5] R Hannon 2-9-0 J Fortune 8/1: 2: ch c Sinndar - Web of Intrigue (Machiavellian)   *hd*   **80**
Led, rdn & hdd over 1f out, duelled with wnr, always held: op 7/1: 100,000gns Mar foal: half brother to a placed
10/12f performer: stays a stiff 7f, 1m sure to suit: acts on fast ground & a stiff trk: v pleasing intro & bred to
progress over further, win sn.
2245 **MADAM CAVERSFIELD 7** [7] R Hannon 2-8-9 Dane O'Neill 12/1: 503: Chsd ldrs wide, shkn up &   *1½*   **72**
onepace over 2f out: op 10/1: imprvd for this step up to 7f & will get further: acts on fast grnd & stiff trk.
2228 **GROUP CAPTAIN 8** [3] S Kirk 2-9-0 R L Moore 4/1 FAV: 54: b c Dr Fong - Alusha (Soviet Star)   *nk*   **76**
Chsd ldrs, outpcd over 2f out, kept on well ins last: well bckd, op 8/1: confirmed promise of debut: half brother to
useful mid-dist performer Scheming & also a 1m wnr: dam related to mid-dist performers: stayed this stiff 7f on fast
ground, 1m+ looks sure to suit & appeals as the type to progress with racing.
      MELROSE AVENUE 0 [9]2-9-0 K Dalgleish 5/1: 5: b c Kris S - Sham Street (Sham) Chsd ldr, outpcd   *½*   **75**
over 2f out, kept on well ins last: well bckd: 80,000gns Apr foal: US pedigree, related to sev wnrs & 1m/10f shld suit in time:
acts on fast grnd & a stiff trk: not btn far on this intro & likely to improve.
1728 **PACIFIC STAR 29** [4]2-9-0 T Quinn 12/1: 06: Bhd, late gains, nrst fin: op 20/1.   *2*   **71**
1728 **GRYSKIRK 29** [10]2-9-0 Paul Eddery 14/1: 4637: Dwelt, rear, kept on late, no dngr: see 1077.   *1¾*   **68**
      TUVALU 0 [11]2-9-0 P Robinson 12/1: 8: Dwelt, keen, in tch, efft over 2f out, sn no impress.   *½*   **67**
      SOUTH OTHE BORDER 0 [1]2-9-0 S Sanders 12/1: 9: Bhd, no more prog for this intro: op 10/1.   *1¾*   **64**
      MOSHKIL 0 [12]2-9-0 A Daly 6/1: 10th: Keen & hmpd after 1f, mid-div, rdn over 2f out, no impress.   *nk*   **63**
      Pocketwood 0 [2]2-9-0 M O'Hara 66/1:0   **Kayf Aramis 0** [6]2-9-0 L Enstone(3) 50/1:0

12 Ran   Time 1m 33.14 (6.74)   Owned: Mr Hamdan Al Maktoum   Trained: Manton

2389   3.15 32red Com Handicap Stakes 3yo+ 0-100 (C)   [94]
£12325 £4675 £2338   7f16y   Good/Firm 31   -03 Slow   Inside

2272* **WATERSIDE** 5 [6] G L Moore 5-8-8 (6ex) (74) R L Moore 8/1: 0030311: Made all, clr 3f out, drvn out to hold on: suited by 6/7f on fm, soft & polytrack, any trk: imprvd lately for change of stable and forcing tactics, gd positive ride landed this: see 2272.   78

2223 **EPHESUS** 8 [8] Miss Gay Kelleway 4-8-12 vis (78) W Supple 10/1: 0006142: Held up, drvn & strong run his last, just failed: gd run: see 2223 & 1810.   hd   81

2282 **FLYING EXPRESS** 4 [3] B W Hills 4-9-5 (85) P Robinson 11/2: 44-60203: Chsd wnr, no extra fnl 1f.   1½   85

2082 **MOAYED** 14 [1] N P Littmoden 5-9-6 bl t (86) S Sanders 5/1: 2633104: V Slow away, rear, styd on for press, not able to chall: quirky type but prob not helped by v slow start today: see 1481.   ¾   85

2172 **DIGITAL** 10 [7]7-9-5 (85) Dane O'Neill 6/1: 4036005: Held up, nvr able to land blow: op 5/1: see 1598.   1   82

2096 **BINANTI** 12 [5]4-9-10 (90) J Quinn 12/1: 20140-06: b g Bin Ajwaad - Princess Rosananti (Shareef Dancer) Rear, efft 3f out, sn no impress: h'cap scorer '03: auct mdn & val auct stks wnr '02: eff at 7f/1m on firm, fast & fibresand, prob handles any trk.   nk   86
1 Aug'03 Warw 7.1g/f 91-(92) C: 1 Sep'02 Good 7fm 96- C: 1 Sep'02 Sout 8af 86a- F:

2096 **KING CARNIVAL** 12 [2]3-9-0 (90) R Smith 10/1: 5112-007: Chsd ldrs, no impress fnl 2f: op 8/1: see 2096.   4   78

2235 **BORREGO** 7 [4]4-8-12 (78) D Holland 7/4 FAV: 02112-28: Chsd ldrs, btn 2f out: hvly bckd, 'nvr trav'.   17   36
8 Ran   Time 1m 28.77 (2.37)   Owned: Mr Nigel Shields   Trained: Brighton

2390   3.50 Cbfm Conditions Stakes 3yo (C)
£9048 £3432 £1716   5f6y   Good/Firm 31   +07 Fast   Far Side

2327 **BENBAUN** 5 [1] M J Wallace 3-8-10 vis (93) D Corby(3) 5/4 FAV: 20-10121: Sn led & rdn clr over 1f out, won decisively in a good time: hvly bckd, qck reapp: suited by 5f on firm & fast ground, best forcing the pace: v speedy & useful: see 2327 & 1766.   100+

2121+ **ENCHANTMENT** 11 [3] J M Bradley 3-9-1 (85) R L Moore 2/1: 01-52112: Chsd ldrs, styd on for press, nvr any impress on wnr: well bckd: continues in fine form: see 2121.   2   97

1621 **ORO VERDE** 35 [4] R Hannon 3-8-13 (86) Dane O'Neill 16/1: 3402-063: Held up in tch, onepace.   ¾   93

2206 **INCISE** 8 [5] B J Meehan 3-8-5 (90) T Quinn 17/2: 201-6004: Held up in tch, nvr pace to chall: see 1400.   shd   85

4057] **CHANGARI** 282 [6]3-8-8 (90) J Fortune 16/1: 1255-5: b f Gulch - Danzari (Arazi) Sn outpcd & nvr factor on reapp: lightly rcd fills mdn wnr '03, subs Listed unplcd (rtd 90): eff at 5f, stays 6f: acts on firm & fast ground, sharp/turning or stiff trks: has gone well fresh.   6   70
2 Jul'03 Wind 6g/f 82- D: 1 Jun'03 Warw 5fm 81- D:

4347] **DALLAAH** 266 [2]3-8-8 (92) P Robinson 7/1: 1306-6: b f Green Desert - Saeedah (Bustino) Chsd wnr, no impress from halfway: bckd, op 8/1, reapp: lightly rcd mdn scorer '03, subs Gr 3 plcd (rtd 95): winning form at 6f, eff at 5f: acts on gd grnd, sharp/undul trks: has gone well fresh. 1 Jul'03 Ling 6gd 91- D: 5   56
6 Ran   Time 1m 00.8 (1.2)   Owned: Ransley Skidmore Birks   Trained: Newmarket

2391   4.25 32redpoker Com Handicap Stakes 3yo+ 0-80 (D)   [80]
£5486 £1688 £844   1m6f   Good/Firm 31   -24 Slow   Centre

2192 **MOSTARSIL** 9 [5] G L Moore 6-9-2 p (68) R L Moore 100/30 FAV: 06-06341: Chsd ldrs, drvn & hdwy to lead ins last, styd on strongly: bckd, op 4/1: prev eff at 10f, now seems best arnd 14f/2m on fast, gd & polytrk.   73

4079] **MR ED** 280 [2] P Bowen 6-9-8 (74) D Corby(3) 12/1: 026000-2: ch g In The Wings - Center Moriches (Magical Wonder) Bhd, styd on well for press fnl 2f, not rch wnr: reapp: dual h'cap wnr '03, subs disapp in blnks: h'cap wnr '02: eff at 12f, suited by 14f & stays 2m, tried further: acts on fast, gd/sft & any trk: fine return & should find similar, likes Salisbury. 2 Jul'03 Sand 14gd 79-75 C: 1 May'03 Nott 14.1g/s 77-72 D: ¾   77
1 May'03 Sali 14.1gd 74-67 C: 1 Aug'02 Good 12g/f 70-65 D: 2 Jul'02 Asco 16.2g/f 67-66 D:
2 Jun'02 Sali 14g/f 69-67 D: 1 Aug'01 Sali 10g/f 67-65 E: 2 Jul'01 Warw 11.6g/f 67-65 D:

2273* **CANTRIP** 5 [6] Miss B Sanders 4-7-12 (5ex) (50) J Quinn 9/1: 0-000013: Led till hdd ins last, no extra nr line: qck reapp, gd run under a pen: best up with/forcing the pace: see 2273 & 1693.   shd   53

2233 **DOVEDON HERO** 7 [4] P J McBride 4-9-12 bl (78) S Sanders 9/1: 16-00204: Mid-div trav well over 3f out, onepace for press fnl 2f: stays a stiff 14f but did not find as much as looked likely here, 12f poss stted.   2   78

2192 **ROME** 9 [3]5-9-0 (66) Dane O'Neill 10/1: 530-3035: Chsd ldrs, no impress over 1f out: btr 2192 (C/D).   2   63

2192 **MOON EMPEROR** 9 [9]7-9-9 (75) D Holland 5/1: 0-00466: Bhd, drvn & only mod prog: bckd: btr 2192.   1¾   70

2073 **SNOWS RIDE** 14 [8]4-9-3 (69) P Makin(5) 16/1: 11-00007: Bhd, rdn & little prog: blnks omitted: see 140.   1   63

2060 **GALANDORA** 15 [7]4-8-1 (53) Lucy Russell(7) 9/1: 5610128: Rear, no prog fnl 2f: btr 2060, 1793.   ½   46

2073 **HEAD TO KERRY** 14 [1]4-8-10 (62) T Quinn 10/1: 3513-009: b g Eagle Eyed - The Poachers Lady (Salmon Leap) Chsd ldrs 4f out, btn 2f out: mdn h'cap & h'cap wnr '03, AW h'cap rnr up: eff btwn 12f/2m on firm, fast & fbsnd: handles any trk, loves Goodwood: eff held up or forcing the pace: prog profile last term but yet to come to hand in '04. 1 Sep'03 Good 16fm 64-57 E: 1 Aug'03 Good 12fm 58-51 E: 2 Jul'03 Wolv 12af 56a-51 F: 1½   53

3212] **CEDAR MASTER** 320 [10]7-9-0 bl t (66) A Quinn(5) 25/1: 0/20050-0: 10th: Chsd ldr, btn 3f out, jmps fit.   3½   52

1990* **COURT ONE** 18 [11]6-7-12 (3oh) (47) R Miles 11/2: 00-00110: 11th: Dwelt, al bhd: 'nvr trav'.   15   15
11 Ran   Time 3m 02.65(7.65)   Owned: Mr G A Jackman   Trained: Brighton

Official Going Standard

2392
6.30 Arabian International Horse Festival Handicap Stakes 3yo+ 0-75 (E) [75]
£4280 £1317 £659 **1m2f aw** Going **Inapplicable** Inside

2242 **SILVALINE** 7 [3] T Keddy 5-9-2 (63) P Doe 7/1: 4550601: Dwelt, rear/wide, hdwy wide over 3f out & **72a**
led ins last, drvn out: all wins 10f, stays 12f: acts on fast, gd/soft & polytrk: eff held up or forcing the pace.
83 **GOLANO** 203 [6] C F Wall 4-9-13 (74) S Sanders 15/2: 343110-2: gr g Linamix - Dimakya (Dayjur) ½ **81a**
Mid-div, rdn & outpcd over 2f out, kept on well ins last: 7 month abs: dual AW h'cap wnr '03, turf h'cap plcd (rtd
81): eff at 10/12f, has shaped as if 14f will suit: acts on fast, hvy & polytrack, likes Lingfield.
1 Oct'03 Ling 12ap 76a-72 D: 1 Oct'03 Ling 10ap 73a-70 E: 2 Nov'02 Donc 7hvy 85- D: 2 Sep'02 Yarm 8g/f 82- D:
2220 **BANK ON HIM** 8 [12] G L Moore 9-9-1 (62) J Quinn 6/1: 2251343: Trkd ldr & led 3f out, rdn & hdd 1 **68a**
ins last, no extra: op 5/1: v tough, loves Lingfield: see 1695, 498.
1038 **FIDDLERS FORD** 70 [10] J Noseda 3-8-12 (72) P Robinson 14/1: 3226404: Trkd ldrs, outpcd over 2f nk **77a**
out, drvn & kept on ins last: 10 wk abs: eff at 10f, worth another try at 12f in similar: see 873, 817 & 473.
2067 **RASID** 14 [8]6-9-10 (71) D Holland 16/1: 0231005: Trkd ldrs, onepace fnl 2f: see 1397. 1¼ **74a**
2260 **LARA FALANA** 6 [5]6-9-0 (61) R L Moore 7/1: 0-025426: Held up, short of room over 2f out, onepace. ¾ **63a**
2038 **DANCE PARTY** 15 [4]4-9-1 p (62) N Chalmers(5) 25/1: 3300407: Mid-div, onepace & held fnl 2f: see 1082. 1¼ **62a**
SALTANGO 283 [7]5-9-11 (72) Dane O'Neill 20/1: 103222-8: b c Acatenango - Salde (Alkalde) Held 3½ **67a**
up, ridden wide under hand ride: reapp: ex German, '03 h'cap scorer: eff at 1m, prob suited by 9/10f: on gd &
soft grnd: not given a hard time, likely improver.
1748 **PHAROAHS GOLD** 29 [1]6-8-13 (60) W Supple 33/1: 0301009: Keen, rear, eff wide, btn over 1f out. ¾ **54a**
1613 **BRAVE DANE** 36 [2]6-9-13 (74) I Mongan 3/1 FAV: 1156120: 10th: Dwelt, rear, eff wide 3f out, no dngr. ½ **67a**
2260 **FOREST TUNE** 6 [9]6-9-1 (62) Lisa Jones(3) 25/1: 6-000600: 11th: Led 7f, fdd, qck reapp. ¾ **54a**
3216] **WELCOME SIGNAL** 320 [13]4-9-6 (67) O Urbina 20/1: 0/33035-0: 12th: Mid-div wide, rdn 2f out, sn nk **58a**
btn & eased ins last, reapp.
2099 **TRUE COMPANION** 12 [14]5-9-13 (74) J P Guillambert(3) 9/1: 3031420: 13th: Mid-div wide, btn 2f out. 5 **58a**
1972 **ARIES** 19 [11]4-9-7 (68) D Corby(3) 33/1: 32000-00: 14th: Dwelt, wide & al twds rear longer trip. 2½ **48a**
14 Ran Time 2m 08.87 (6.07) Owned: Mr Andrew Duffield Trained: Newmarket

---

2393
7.00 Aihf At Lingfield Park 13th June Median Auction Maiden Stakes 3-4yo (E)
£3582 £1102 £551 **1m4f aw** Going **Inapplicable** Inside

2175 **PEAK OF PERFECTION** 10 [14] M A Jarvis 3-8-9 (73) P Robinson 4/1: 00-5351: Made all, drvn & held **76a**
up on well ins last: eff around 12f, stays further: handles gd grnd & both AWs: enjoyed forcing tactics tonight.
1382 **CHAMPAGNE SHADOW** 47 [8] G L Moore 3-8-9 bl (64) R L Moore 10/1: 4-040202: Mid-div, rdn & styd on ½ **74a**
well from over 2f out, not able to reach wnr: 7 wk abs, back to form on sand: see 915 (C/D h'cap).
1725 **SHONGWENI** 29 [4] P J McBride 3-8-9 S Sanders 15/2: 43: Dwelt, rear, outpcd over 3f out, kept on 1¾ **72a**
wide for press fnl 2f, nrst fin: stays a sharp 12f, handles fast grnd & polytrack: crying out for 14f+: see 1725.
2196 **CHARLESTON** 9 [10] J H M Gosden 3-8-9 (73) J Fortune 9/4 FAV: 2224: Trkd wnr, no extra dist: nk **71a**
stays a sharp 12f: handles fast, hvy & polytrack: see 2196, 1790 & 1514.
1495 **VICAT COLE** 41 [13]3-8-9 I Mongan 100/1: 05: ch c Hector Protector - Dancing Spirit (Ahonoora) nk **70a**
Chsd wnr 3f out, hung left under press over 1f out & no extra ins last: AW bow, imprvd from debut: stays a sharp
12f, may get further: handles polytrack.
1904 **DELIGHTFULLY** 22 [3]3-8-4 (69) A Medeiros(5) 12/1: 0-0246: Trkd ldrs, rdn & no impress over 1f out. 1 **64a**
1502 **CROWN AGENT** 41 [5]4-9-10 (61) D Holland 15/2: 2U-05007: Held up, rapid hdwy wide halfway to trk ½ **68a**
wnr, fdd fnl 1f: 6 wk abs: mid-race manouevre prob not suit, could improve on this: see 918.
1581 **MUSLIN** 37 [7]3-8-5 (1ow) O Urbina 8/1: 038: Trkd ldrs, no impress fnl 2f: AW bow, longer trip: see 1581. 5 **57a**
1580 **MAXIMINUS** 37 [12]4-9-10 (59) G Baker 66/1: 0/00-49: Hld up wide, no impress: see 1580 (9f). 2 **58a**
2066 **BEE DEES LEGACY** 14 [15]3-8-9 R Brisland 100/1: 0-00: 10th: b g Atraf - Bee Dee Dancer 11 **45a**
(Ballacashtal) Dwelt, rear, nvr a factor: longer trip, unplcd sole '03 start for C Weedon: tried up to 10f prev.
PITTON MILL 0 [2]4-9-10 C Haddon(7) 66/1: 0: 11th: Sn pushed along in mid-div, btn 3f out on debut. nk **44a**
3497] **Fabranese** 308 [11]4-9-5 Lisa Jones(3) 100/1:0 1607 **Petrolina** 36 [9]3-8-4 J Mackay 100/1:0
1904 **Seagold** 22 [1]3-8-4 J Quinn 66/1:0 **Triggers Double** 0 [6]3-8-9 D R McCabe 33/1:0
15 Ran Time 2m 37.88 (8.68) Owned: HRH Sultan Ahmad Shah Trained: Newmarket

---

2394
7.30 Etihad Airways Classified Stakes 3yo+ 0-60 (F)
£3031 £866 £433 **1m aw rnd** Going **Inapplicable** Outside

1982 **DEIGN TO DANCE** 18 [5] J G Portman 3-8-5 (62) R L Moore 16/1: 20-50051: Rear, hdwy inner 3f out & **67a**
led dist, drvn out: first win: prev eff at 5.7f/7f, now stays a sharp 1m well: acts on firm, fast & fibresand,
sharp/undul trks: best without cheek pieces: see 1982.
MILLENIO 83 [3] D Flood 4-9-7 (64) O Urbina 11/2: 01-33362: ch c Big Shuffle - Molto In Forma ½ **70a**
(Surumu) Trkd ldrs, eff to chall dist, not pace of wnr: nicely bckd, 12 wk abs: Brit bow, ex German, dual '03
scorer: eff at 5f, wng from at 7/7.5f, stays 1m on gd & polytrack.
1982 **CHORUS BEAUTY** 18 [11] G Wragg 3-8-6 (63) F Norton 16/1: 01-0003: Rear, hdwy & drvn/chall dist, 1 **64a**
onepace ins last: stays a sharp 1m: see 260 (6f mdn).
1777 **FORTUNE POINT** 28 [10] A W Carroll 6-9-4 (61) I Mongan 14/1: 2132004: Trkd ldrs, led 2f out till 2 **61a**
dist, no extra: recent jumps rnr (p.u.): see 718 (10f, h'cap).
2018 **ROYAL ADVOCATE** 17 [1]4-9-6 (63) S Whitworth 12/1: 00654-45: Briefly led over 2f out, no extra dist. 1¾ **60a**
1822 **LITTLE EYE** 25 [7]3-8-9 (63) N Pollard 16/1: 34-40306: Drvn mid-div, not pace to chall: btr 670. nk **59a**
912 **RAHEEL** 80 [8]4-9-3 t (60) D Holland 11/2: 4061437: Dwelt, held up wide, no impress dist: see 757. shd **56a**
1297 **SECOND WARNING** 52 [6]3-8-8 (62) Dane O'Neill 25/1: 000-58: Slow away, towards rear, little prog. 1¼ **55a**
2018 **DIDNT TELL MY WIFE** 17 [4]5-9-6 (63) Lisa Jones(3) 4/1 FAV: 1021-669: No impress fnl 3f: 'nvr trav'. 1¾ **53a**
1537 **SWIFT ALCHEMIST** 39 [2]4-9-2 (62) G Baker 7/1: 000-0030: 10th: Chsd ldr, struggling from halfway. 1 **47a**
266 **FULVIO** 165 [9]4-9-6 (63) P Doe 25/1: 004000-0: 11th: b g Sword Dance - One Tuff Gal (Lac Ouimet) 5 **42a**
Chsd ldrs till over 1f out, eased: 5 month abs: dual AW h'cap wnr '03, also landed a clmr (with S Williams): stays
sharp 1m well: winning form at 6/7f: acts on both AWs & fast grnd, loves a sharp/undul trk: eff with/without

visor. 2 Apr'03 Brig 8.0g/f 72-(70) E: 1 Mar'03 Ling 7ap 74a-(67) F: 1 Feb'03 Ling 7ap 76a-68 E:
1 Jan'03 Wolv 6af 70a-60 F: 2 Dec'02 Wolv 7af 62a-61 E:

4949} **FLORIAN 226** [12]6-9-6 (63) R Miles(3) 5/1: 241133-0: 12th: Led till over 2f out, sn btn.	6	31a

12 Ran Time 1m 41.24 (5.04) Owned: Mrs S J Portman Trained: Compton

Official Going Good

2395	8.00 Terry West Memorial Median Auction Maiden Stakes Fillies 2yo (F)
	£3311 £946 £473 5f str Good Inapplicable Stands Side

1981 **KWAME 18** [6] Miss E C Lavelle 2-8-11   S W Kelly 7/2: 21: Trkd ldrs, short of room & switched **77**
dist, drvn to lead line, all out: op 11/4, comfirmed debut promise: eff at 5f, 6f shld suit: acts on fast & gd.
1170 **MISS CASSIA 59** [7] R Hannon 2-8-11   P Dobbs 15/8 FAV: 32: Trkd ldrs trav well & led over 1f out, *shd* **76**
drvn & hdd cl-home: 2 month abs, shld win a race: see 1170.
2171 **LILY LENAT 10** [2] J R Boyle 2-8-11   D Sweeney 8/1: 043: b f Josr Algarhoud - Rushing River *¾* **74**
(Irish River) Trkd ldrs, bmpd dist, kept on, not pace of front pair: 13,000gns Mar foal, dam a unrcd daughter of a
US wnr: sire smart at 7f/1m: eff at 5f on gd grnd & a sharp trk.
 RIGHT ANSWER 0 [3] A P Jarvis 2-8-11   J Quinn 6/1: 4: b f Lujain - Quiz Show (Primo Dominie) In *hd* **73+**
tch, short of room 2f out & again dist, kept on well cl-home: op 10/1: 25,000gns Mar foal, dam a 7f 3yo scorer:
eff at 5f on gd grnd: plenty of promise, likely improver over 6f.
2020 **TIGHT CIRCLE 17** [5]2-8-11   J Mackay 33/1: 05: b f Danzero - Tight Spin (High Top) Prom, drvn & *hd* **72**
chall dist, no extra ins last: left debut bhd: 7,000gns 2yo purchase, Apr foal: half-sister to a useful 10f wnr,
also 2 juv wnrs: dam unplcd sole start: eff at 5f on gd grnd & a sharp/undul trk.
 EPITOMISE 0 [4]2-8-11   S Sanders 14/1: 6: Bhd, late gains, nrst fin: apprec 6f+, improve. *½* **70+**
1170 **GAUDALPIN 59** [11]2-8-11   S Righton 14/1: 347: Led/dsptd lead till over 1f out, no extra: abs, new yard. *¾* **68$**
1760 **ABERDEEN PARK 28** [8]2-8-11   G Baker 25/1: 508: In tch, hmpd over 1f out, kept on late. *nk* **67**
 SAUCEPOT 0 [1]2-8-11   A Daly 20/1: 9: Bhd, kept on late, nvr a factor: only btn around 3L. *1¼* **63**
 APPLE OF MY EYE 0 [9]2-8-11   W Supple 20/1: 0: 10th: Dwelt, sn outpcd. *6* **46**
2151 **BEECHES THEATRE 10** [10]2-8-11   I Mongan 100/1: 00: 11th: Led 1f, sn lost pl & struggling. *6* **29**
11 Ran Time 59.64 (2.84) Owned: First Impressions Racing Group 2 Trained: Andover

2396	8.30 Hever Lakeside Theatre Handicap Stakes 3yo+ 35-55 (F)	[57]
	£3171 £906 £453 6f str Good Inapplicable Stands Side	

2269 **DOUBLE M 5** [8] Mrs L Richards 7-9-10 vis (53) R Thomas(5) 7/2 FAV: 0655321: Held up, hdwy from **63**
halfway & rdn to lead ins last, styd on strongly: bckd, op 9/2: qck reapp: eff at 5/6f, stays 7f: acts on fast,
gd & both AWs, loves Lingfield: see 902.
2269 **INDIAN BAZAAR 5** [4] N E Berry 8-9-7 (50) R Miles(3) 25/1: 3145-002: Led, hdd ins last & not pace *1¼* **55**
of wnr: qck reapp: fine front running eff, looks to have come to hand, loves Chepstow: see 2269.
1248 **NIGHT CAP 54** [16] T D McCarthy 5-9-0 (43) J P Guillambert(3) 14/1: 3-600203: Chsd ldrs, styd on late. *½* **46**
2201 **DAVIDS MARK 8** [14] J R Jenkins 4-9-8 (51) S Sanders 9/1: 30-03444: Trkd ldrs, onepce for press dist. *2* **48**
2187 **ATTORNEY 9** [3]6-9-6 vis (49) W Supple 16/1: 1203665: Held up, kept on late, nvr a factor: see 1241. *1* **43**
2262 **AINTNECESSARILYSO 6** [12]6-9-4 (47) M Savage(5) 9/1: 3322236: Dwelt, rear, kept on late, no threat. *hd* **40**
2266 **YORKIES BOY 5** [13]9-9-11 (54) R L Moore 8/1: 0400-547: Held up, eff when short of room dist, nvr *¾* **45**
pace to threaten: qck reapp: see 2266 & 1914.
2262 **TENDER 6** [19]4-9-12 P (55) F Norton 14/1: 0-350058: Trkd ldrs, rdn & no impress dist: btr 2262. *shd* **46**
2280 **LONG WEEKEND 5** [17]6-9-2 (45) J F McDonald(3) 25/1: 4606009: Sn rdn rear, mod late prog: qck reapp. *hd* **35**
2334 **BADOU 2** [9]4-9-0 vis (43) C Cogan 20/1: 0002400: 10th: Mid-div, nvr pace to threaten: qck reapp. *2* **27**
2262 **GUN SALUTE 6** [10]4-9-3 BL (46) J Fortune 12/1: 0460600: 11th: Chsd ldr 2f out, sn wknd: blnks. *½* **28**
2111 **DANAKIM 12** [7]7-9-7 (50) D Fentiman(7) 25/1: 0400150: 12th: Cl-up till 2f out, sn wknd: btr 1988. *1* **29**
2262 **MANNORA 6** [6]4-9-10 (53) J Mackay 25/1: 0430-400: 13th: Slow away & rear, no prog fnl 2f: qck reapp. *1½* **27**
2189 **MAYZIN 9** [18]4-9-8 p (51) D Sweeney 33/1: 3140000: 14th: Dwelt, al bhd: see 897. *nk* **24**
2201 **STAR LAD 8** [5]4-9-3 bl (46) I Mongan 33/1: 0145030: 15th: Mid-div, struggling fnl 2f: btr 2201 (fibresand). *½* **17**
2262 **RUN ON 6** [2]6-9-7 (50) S Righton 33/1: 466-0000: 16th: Sn outpcd & nvr a factor, qck reapp: see 1788. *¾* **19**
822 **ENJOY THE BUZZ 96** [15]5-9-2 (45) C Catlin 9/1: 2312420: 17th: Al bhd, abs: btr 822 & 667 (fibresand). *½* **12**
941 **SECOND MINISTER 77** [1]5-9-7 bl t (50) L Treadwell(7) 16/1: 032-3060: 18th: Sn struggling, t.o. *15* **0**
18 Ran Time 1m 11.01 (2.21) Owned: Mr Bryan Mathieson Trained: Chichester

2397	9.00 Find All Your Winners At Tips Tv Handicap Stakes 3yo+ 35-55 (F)	[55]
	£3164 £904 £452 7f str Good Inapplicable Stands Side	

2032 **ESPADA 16** [7] J A Osborne 8-9-7 bl (48) S W Kelly 12/1: 0000441: Made all, rdn clr from halfway & **54**
drvn/held on well ins last: winning form at 6f/1m, best at 7f: acts on firm, soft & polytrack, any trk: loves
forcing tactics & imprvd last twice for blnks: well h'capped: see 216.
2288* **SHIRLEY OAKS 4** [17] Miss Z C Davison 6-9-8 (6ex) (49) N Chalmers(5) 13/2: 2316312: Chsd ldrs, drvn *½* **53**
& styd on well ins last, not able to chall wnr: qck reapp & remains in gd form: see 2288 (amat clmr).
2258 **SCARROTTOO 6** [3] S C Williams 6-10-0 (55) A Daly 6/1: 0551403: Rear, styd on wide from press *nk* **58**
from over 1f out, nrst fin: see 1132.
2149 **BALERNO 14** [1] R Ingram 5-9-9 (50) N Day 8/1: 5052304: Mid-div, kept on for press, not able to chall. *shd* **53**
2034 **LILY OF THE GUILD 16** [16]5-9-12 (53) I Mongan 11/2 FAV: 2-002445: Mid-div, drvn & onepace fnl 2f. *1* **54**
2045 **SINGLE TRACK MIND 15** [11]6-9-3 p (44) A Daly(5) 40/1: 0235006: Mid-div, kept on late, not able to *1½* **42**
chall: imprvd eff with cheek pieces re-applied: see 1073, 846 & 708.
1579 **ROYAL RACER 37** [9]6-9-9 (50) N Pollard 20/1: 50/0-1367: Prom till over 1f out, sn no impress. *1* **46**
2369 **LORD CHAMBERLAIN 1** [20]11-9-12 bl (50) C J Davies(7) 10/1: 0235000: Dwelt, mod late prog, nvr threat. *hd* **48**
2063 **TREETOPS HOTEL 14** [8]5-9-13 (54) D Sweeney 20/1: 000-2009: Dwelt, mod late prog, nvr threat. *hd* **48**
2334 **KINSMAN 2** [6]7-9-12 bl (53) J P Guillambert(3) 14/1: 0-215460: 10th: Dwelt, held up, nvr able to chall. *shd* **47**
1989 **GRAND VIEW 18** [5]8-8-11 p (38) J Quinn 20/1: 0421000: 11th: Chsd ldrs till over 1f out: btr 1415 (6f). *¾* **30**

LINGFIELD Polytrack SATURDAY 12.06.04 Lefthand, Sharp, Undulating Track

2125	**CHANTRY FALLS 11** [1]4-9-4 BL (45) S Sanders 33/1: 463-0600: 12th: Rcd alone far side, nvr factor: blnks.2			33
2258	**LOCH LAIRD 6** [4]9-9-11 (52) G Baker 20/1: 0010500: 13th: Mid-div early, sn lost pl & struggling.		nk	39
2034	**ANNIJAZ 16** [19]7-10-0 (55) R L Moore 6/1: 60-22400: 14th: Dwelt & al bhd: btr 1660.		1	40
1989	**MOONGLADE 18** [18]4-8-8 bl (35) J McAuley 33/1: 00-00050: 15th: Dwelt, chsd wnr till over 1f out.		1	18

1963 **Dr Fox 19** [13]3-8-7 (1oh)p(44) R Thomas(5) 50/1:0   2064 **Mister Completely 14** [15]3-8-10 (47) C Catlin 33/1:0
17 Ran   Time 1m 24.22(3.82)   Owned: John Livock and Partners   Trained: Upper Lambourn

LEICESTER SATURDAY 12.06.04 Righthand, Stiff, Galloping Track

Official Going Good/Firm

2398   6.45 Mercury Race Night Handicap Stakes Fillies 3yo+ 0-75 (E)   [80]
£4163 £1281 £641   **6f str**   Good/Firm 38   -06 Slow   Stands Side

2268	**UNDER MY SPELL 5** [1] P D Evans 3-9-4 (70) S Donohoe(7) 11/1: 5-002251: Pushed along rear, hdwy halfway & led over 1f out, sn rdn & in command, eased cl-home, val 3L: qck reapp: eff at 5/6f on firm & soft grnd, likes a stiff/gall trk: progressive profile of late, win again on this evidence: see 1743.			80+
1540	**AMELIA 39** [5] W M Brisbourne 6-8-12 (56) B Swarbrick(5) 6/1: 5530132: Chsd ldrs, lost place early, short of room over 1f out, styd on for press fnl 2f, not pace to chall wnr: see 1465.		½	58
2326	**ACE MA VAHRA 3** [8] S R Bowring 6-7-13 bl (43) J Bramhill 40/1: 6000503: Held up, styd on fnl 2f, not threaten wnr: qck reapp: eff at 6f, apprec a return to 7f/1m: see 677.		1	42
2232	**BINT ROYAL 7** [9] Miss V Haigh 6-9-2 p (60) G Gibbons 16/1: 5503404: Chsd ldrs, outpcd halfway, kept on ins last: wants 7f, see 2093.		1½	54
2093*	**SILVER CHIME 13** [4]4-9-12 (70) M Fenton 9/2: 50-00415: Led 2f, onepace dist: see 2093 (made all).		½	62
2262	**TUSCAN TREATY 6** [11]4-8-9 vis (53) B Doyle 20/1: 00-00406: Dwelt, eff halfway, onepace: see 2262.		¾	43
4860}	**INCH BY INCH 233** [14]5-9-0 bl (58) G Duffield 25/1: 200300-7: b f Inchinor - Maid Welcome (Mummy's Pet) Prom & led over 4f out till over 1f out, lost action ins last when held, eased: reapp: class stks scorer '03, AW h'cap unplcd (rtd 43a): eff at 5f, suited by 6f: acts on firm, fast & polytrack, sharp/undul or gall trk: best blnkd & likes to race up with/force the pace.		hd	47

2 Aug'03 Folk 6g/f 59-(60) E: 1 Jul'03 Ling 6ap 51a-50 E:

1973	**SHAROURA 19** [6]8-9-2 (60) P Hanagan 15/2: 33505-58: Held up, no room over 1f out, nvr able to chall: closer with a clr run, kind ride, improve: see 1973.		hd	48+
2062	**BOAVISTA 14** [3]4-9-2 (60) R Havlin 16/1: 4422109: Prom, btn dist: btr 2034.		shd	48
2062	**REDWOOD STAR 14** [7]4-8-12 e (56) J F Egan 33/1: 1030-400: 10th: Chsd ldrs & ch over 1f out, wknd.		¾	42
2062	**TAMARELLA 14** [12]4-8-7 vis (51) A McCarthy 25/1: 0005000: 11th: Chsd ldrs, btn dist: see 767.		2	31
878	**BLONDE EN BLONDE 85** [15]4-8-11 bl (55) Steven Harrison(7) 16/1: 1203300: 12th: Held up, short of room over 1f out, sn no impress: 1st drawn, drop in trip.		nk	34
2098	**MISSUS LINKS 12** [10]3-9-5 (71) R Hughes 100/30 FAV: 1-5250: 13th: Stumbled start, chsd ldrs, btn/eased over 1f out: rider reported filly nvr trav after stumbling early: btr 1734.		2	44

2152 **Lady Justice 10** [13]4-9-2 BL(60) K Fallon 16/1:0   1983 **Disco Diva 18** [2]3-8-10 (62) Dale Gibson 25/1:0
15 Ran   Time 1m 12.43 (2.63)   Owned: Mr J R Salter   Trained: Abergavenny

2399   7.15 Sport On Monday Maiden Stakes Fillies 2yo (D)
£5616 £1728 £864   **6f str**   Good/Firm 38   -18 Slow   Stands Side

	SATIN KISS 0 [1] Saeed bin Suroor 2-8-11 K McEvoy 11/10 FAV: 1: b f Seeking The Gold - Satin Flower (Shadeed) Dsptd lead 4f, prn/briefly outpcd over 1f out, led ins last & styd on strongly under hand riding: well bckd: April foal, full sister to top-class 6f juv Lujain, half-sister to a 7f/12f scorer, dam useful at 7/10f: eff at 6f, 7f+ shld suit: acts on fast & a stiff/gall trk: goes well fresh: looks useful, more success beckons.			89+
	CODE ORANGE 0 [8] J H M Gosden 2-8-11 R Havlin 9/2: 2: b f Green Desert - Warning Belle (Warning) Al prom & led over 1f out, hdd ins last, kept on well: op 6/1, rest well covered: 150,000gns March foal, half-sister to a 7f juv wnr: eff at 6f, will get further: acts on fast grnd & a stiff trk: most pleasing start, win sn.		½	85
1669	**AZUREE 32** [5] R Hannon 2-8-11 R Hughes 5/2: 263: Trkd wnr, rdn & no extra from dist, eased nr fin: handles fast & gd/soft grnd: see 1499.		4	73
	NIGHT OF JOY 0 [2] M A Jarvis 2-8-11 N Callan 16/1: 4: b f King's Best - Gilah (Saddlers' Hall) Dwelt, eff 3f out, btn over 1f out: op 9/1: 70,000gns Feb first foal, dam uncrd, related to several wnrs.		3	64
	QAWAAFIL 0 [7]2-8-11 R Hills 14/1: 5: b f Intidab - Indihash (Gulch) Dwelt, chsd ldrs till outpcd fnl 2f: op 10/1: 7f foal, half-sister to a pair of 7f wnrs, dam a 7f juv wnr.		¾	62
	LIAMELISS 0 [3]2-8-11 R Ffrench 50/1: 6: Dwelt, sn handy, lost place from halfway.		4	50

6 Ran   Time 1m 13.13 (3.33)   Owned: Godolphin   Trained: Newmarket

2400   7.45 Leicester Mercury Handicap Stakes 3yo 0-90 (C)   [97]
£12412 £4708 £2354   **5f str**   Good/Firm 38   -00 Slow   Stands Side

4892}	**FICTIONAL 231** [9] B A McMahon 3-8-10 (79) G Gibbons 16/1: 203132-1: b c Fraam - Manon Lescaut (Then Again) Prom & led over 1f out, edged left, drvn out: op 20/1: reapp: auct mdn scorer '03, subs h'cap rnr-up: eff at 5/6f on fast & gd grnd, stiff/undul or sharp/turning trk: goes well fresh: most consistent & progressive last term, continued in that same vein tonight.			89

2 Oct'03 Newb 6.0gd 80-73 D: 1 Sep'03 Catt 6.0g/f 74-(71) F: 2 Jul'03 Pont 6g/f 77- E:

725*	**TONY THE TAP 108** [6] N A Callaghan 3-8-6 (75) K Fallon 4/1 JT FAV: 4-12: Held up, sn rdn, styd on well for press from over 1f out, not reach wnr: 4 mth abs, turf/h'cap bow: eff at 5f on polytrack & fast, stiff/gall or sharp/undul trk: fine eff & a likely type for similar soon, poss at 6f: see 725.		nk	85
2082	**GREEN MANALISHI 14** [5] D W P Arbuthnot 3-8-9 (88) T Quinn 4/1 JT FAV: 1-422103: Trkd ldrs, rdn & onepace from dist: found much less than lkd likely tonight, return to a sharp trk shld suit: see 1809.		1½	93
1917	**FOURSQUARE 21** [1] J Mackie 3-8-12 (90) N Callan 11/2: 100-1504: Led, hung right & hdd over 1f out.		1	92
2227	**ABELARD 8** [7]3-7-12 (2oh) (65) P Hanagan 10/1: 333-65: Outpcd, kept on late, not able to chall: bckd.		1¼	63
2121	**DIVINE SPIRIT 11** [2]3-8-11 (80) F Lynch 14/1: 61-00036: Slow away & bhd, late gains under kind		1	75+

ride: again shaped with promise, one to be with when cheekpieces are re-applied: see 2121.
2137 **FYODOR 11** [10]3-8-13 (82) J Murtagh 10/1: 2312-067: Chsd ldrs, not able to chall: see 2137 (6f). *shd* **77**
2121 **CELTIC THUNDER 11** [3]3-9-0 (83) J Fanning 12/1: 246-2058: Cl-up & ch over 1f out, wknd: see 1387. *shd* **77**
1918 **EMBASSY LORD 21** [12]3-8-11 bl (80) J D O'Reilly(7) 50/1: 1500-409: Dwelt, outpcd & nvr a factor. *2* **68**
2137 **HILITES 11** [15]3-8-13 (82) J F Egan 33/1: 004-3030: 10th: Held up, eff 2f out, no impress dist. *½* **68**
2121 **SILVER PRELUDE 11** [6]3-9-1 (84) A Culhane 33/1: 5250-000: 11th: Chsd ldrs till over 1f out: see 2121. *1* **67**
2195 **IMPERIUM 9** [16]3-8-5 (74) S Drowne 20/1: 0051130: 12th: Sn outpcd: btr 2195 (Brighton). *½* **55**
2266 **VIENNAS BOY 5** [14]3-9-0 (83) R Hughes 6/1: 0-446460: 13th: Chsd ldrs till 2f out: qk reapp: see 2137. *¾* **62**
2155 **LUALUA 10** [8]3-8-8 (77) P Makin(5) 11/2: 105-4230: 14th: Slow away, chsd ldrs till halfway: btr 2155. *¾* **54**
4947} **Bella Tutrice 220** [11]0 0 0 (77) G Duffield 40/1:0 1773 **Vermilliann 29** [13]3-9-5 (88) P Gallagher(7) 50/1:0
16 Ran Time 1m 0.19 (1.89) Owned: Mr J C Fretwell Trained: Tamworth

2401 **8.15 Sports Mercury Classified Stakes 3yo+ 0-70 (E)**
£5538 £1704 £852 **1m2f** **Good/Firm 38** **-22 Slow** Inside

1976 **FITTING GUEST 18** [2] G G Margarson 3-8-4 (69) G Duffield 9/4: 40-6221: Led after 1f & dictated pace, rdn & in command fnl 1f, eased cl-home: eff at 10f, shows plenty of pace & return to 1m may suit: acts on fast & gd/soft grnd: enjoyed an easy lead tonight, first win: see 1976 & 1834. **76**
1971 **BLUE MARINER 19** [4] P W Harris 4-9-3 (70) B Doyle 12/1: 2/0-032: b c Marju - Mazarine Blue (Bellypha) Chsd wnr, rdn & outpcd over 1f out, kept on ins last: missed '03: rnr-up sole start '02 (auct mdn): eff at 7f, now stays 10f well: acts on fast grnd, easy or stiff/gall trk. 2 Jul'02 Leic 7g/f 80- E: *2* **71**
2185 **FREELOADER 9** [3] J W Hills 4-9-6 (73) R Hills 7/4 FAV: 1260-043: Led 1f, remained keen early & trkd ldrs, trav well 2f out, rdn & found little bef dist: well bckd, op 5/2: see 2185. *1¾* **72**
1381 **COLOPHONY 47** [5] K A Morgan 4-9-8 t (75) J P Murtagh 9/1: 3216-04: ch g Distant View - Private Line (Private Account) Held up & keen, outpcd over 2f out, kept on late, nvr a threat: recent jumps runner (unplcd, amat nov): mdn scorer '03 for H Cecil, lightly rcd: eff at 1m/10.5f on firm & gd grnd, stiff/gall trks: eff in a t-strap & can force the pace. 1 Jul'03 Hayd 10.5g/f 80- D: 2 Jun'03 Newc 8gd 80- D: *shd* **74**
2129 **ANNA WALHAAN 11** [1]5-9-3 (70) T Quinn 3/1: 205-0025: Keen & prom, no impress bef dist: btr 2129. *4* **63**
5 Ran Time 2m 08.49 (5.99) Owned: Mr John Guest Trained: Newmarket

2402 **8.45 Harvey Gardiner Mercury Tipsters Table Champion Handicap Stakes 4yo+ 35-55 (F)** **[63]**
£4427 £1362 £681 **1m rnd** **Good/Firm 38** **Inapplicable** Inside

2149 **CLASSIC VISION 10** [1] W J Haggas 4-9-2 BL (51) R Hills 16/1: 1004501: Held up & switched inner rail, hdwy 2f out & switched/styd on for press to lead well ins last: eff at 6f, now stays 1m with waiting tactics: acts on fast, gd & both AWs, sharp/easy or stiff trks: tried cheek pieces latest, improved for blnks, in foal. **56**
2216 **CANLIS 8** [10] D W Thompson 5-8-10 (45) P Hanagan 33/1: 5/0000-02: b g Halling - Fajjoura (Fairy King) Prom & led over 1f out, hdd well ins last, just denied: lightly rcd & unplcd '03 (rtd 41, tried blnks, K Ryan): unplcd '02 (rtd 64 & 30a): eff around 1m on fast grnd. *hd* **50**
1960 **DUBONAI 19** [2] Andrew Turnell 4-9-0 (49) J P Murtagh 5/1: 3230-003: Prom & led over 2f out till over 1f out, no extra when short of room cl-home: op 9/1: eff at 1m/12f: see 1960. *1¾* **51**
2149 **NO CHANCE TO DANCE 10** [14] H J Collingridge 4-8-13 t (48) Dean McKeown 25/1: 050-004: Held up, styd on onepace fnl 2f, nvr a threat: eff at 1m on fast grnd: see 2149. *2½* **45**
2049 **HILARIOUS 15** [16]4-8-12 (47) A McCarthy 11/1: 3440-545: Prom & led over 3f out till over 2f out, wknd. *shd* **44**
2149 **POPPYLINE 10** [11]4-9-4 (53) P Makin(5) 13/2: 40-00U36: Mid-div, no impress over 1f out: btr 2149. *1¾* **47**
1635 **ZAMYATINA 35** [15]5-8-12 (47) J Bramhill 33/1: 4000-007: In tch & keen, no impress over 1f out. *shd* **41**
2159 **ENCOUNTER 10** [5]8-8-12 (47) D McGaffin 11/1: 0-003568: Dwelt, pulled hard, mid-div, no impress. *shd* **40**
1348 **VERMILION CREEK 49** [9]5-9-4 (53) Stephanie Hollinshead(5) 8/1: 5066629: Held up wide, no dngr. *3* **40**
2120* **ARCHIRONDEL 11** [3]6-9-5 (54) A Culhane 2/1 FAV: 0U00210: 10th: Mid-div wide halfway, hung right & btn over 1f out: well bckd: btr 2120. *3½* **34**
2204 **ENCORE ROYALE 8** [4]4-8-12 (47) B Doyle 40/1: 00-05600: 11th: V slow away & al bhd, lost ch start. *2* **23**
1992 **GEMINI LADY 18** [7]4-8-11 (46) G Duffield 10/1: 0420-020: 12th: Held up, hmpd after 3f, nvr a factor. *3* **16**
2335 **Niteowl Dream 2** [13]4-9-6 (55) J D O'Reilly(7) 40/1:0 2054 **Rocinante 15** [8]4-9-4 (53) M Fenton 11/1:0
14 Ran Time 1m 41.46 () Owned: The Chosen Few Partnership Trained: Newmarket

2403 **9.15 Sporting Blue Handicap Stakes 3yo 0-80 (D)** **[85]**
£7280 £2240 £1120 **7f str** **Good/Firm 38** **+07 Fast** Stands Side

2148+ **ROYAL PRINCE 10** [8] J R Fanshawe 3-9-7 (78) J Murtagh 8/11 FAV: 34-411: Trkd ldrs & led over 2f out, briefly rdn but readily pulled clr & eased cl-home: decisive wnr in a fast time: eff at 7f, will get 1m: acts on firm, gd/soft & polytrack: v progressive colt, more success looks imminent, keep on side: see 2148 & 1080. **95+**
2168* **RILEY BOYS 10** [5] J G Given 3-9-3 (74) M Fenton 5/1: 0-121212: Al prom, rdn & outpcd by wnr from 2f out: clr rem: v tough: prob ran to form of 2168 (made all, 8.5f). *5* **77**
1825 **SPIN KING 25** [6] M L W Bell 3-9-7 (78) K Fallon 7/2: 613-0403: Led 4f, no impress over 1f out: see 1496. *3* **75**
1977 **FIORE DI BOSCO 18** [2] T D Barron 3-9-5 (76) P Makin(5) 16/1: 3002-504: Chsd ldrs & ch over 2f out, sn no impress: see 1745. *½* **72**
1949 **BORIS THE SPIDER 19** [3]3-7-12 (55) P Hanagan 25/1: 000-2005: Held up, rdn & nvr a factor: btr 1426. *1¾* **48**
4713} **CHORISTAR 243** [4]3-8-3 (60) G Duffield 40/1: 060-6: ch g Inchinor - Star Tulip (Night Shift) Held up & keen, sn strugg: gelded, reapp/h'cap bow: lightly rcd & unplcd in '03 (rtd 67, mdn). *2* **49**
2199 **FIVE GOLD 9** [7]3-8-8 (65) S Drowne 25/1: 62410-07: Dwelt, sn prom till over 2f out: see 2199. *7* **42**
1570 **TICERO 38** [1]3-9-6 (77) B Doyle 33/1: 04-008: ch g First Trump - Lucky Flinders (Free State) Chsd ldrs, strugg halfway: reapp, gelded: unplcd '03 (lightly rcd, rtd 77, nov stks): related to smart 6f juv wnr Pomfret Lad, also a brother to a 10f/2m1f wnr. *26* **4**
8 Ran Time 1m 24.17(2.17) Owned: Mr Abdulla BuHaleeba Trained: Newmarket

Official Going GOOD/FIRM.

2404   1.50 Cadogan Silver Salver Handicap Stakes 3yo+ 0-105 (B)   **[100]**
£18281 £5625 £2813   **1m208y rnd**   **Good/Firm 29**   **+05 Fast**   Inside

1423 **KRUGERRAND** 45 [5] W J Musson 5-8-5 (77) G Carter 14/1: 40-00001: ch g Gulch - Nasers Pride (Al   87+
Nasr) Keen, hld up, plenty to do over 1f out but v strong run to lead well ins last, going away, v readily: abs: won
this race in '03 off a 2lb higher mark: class stks wnr in '02 for M Bell: well suited by 9f & loves fm & fast grnd,
poss handles gd/soft: has run well fresh with/without t-strap, loves York: fine turn of foot.
1 Jun'03 York 8.9fm 85-79 B: 1 Jul'02 Warw 7.1g/f 90- C: 2 Jun'02 Newm 8g/f 92- C: 1 Sep'01 Warw 7.1g/f 82- D:
2 Jul'01 Ling 6g/s 83- D:
2101 **JAMES CAIRD** 12 [6] M H Tompkins 4-8-12 (84) F P Ferris(3) 7/1: 1162-622: In tch, hdwy & short of   2½   88+
room sev times fnl 2f, styd on strongly ins last, nrst fin: poss a shade unlucky & remains on the up-grade: looks
sure to relish a rtn to 10f & a stiff fin: see 2101.
2101 **VICIOUS WARRIOR** 12 [11] R M Whitaker 5-9-0 (86) Dean McKeown 14/1: 020-2053: Keen, handy, eff   shd   90
over 1f out, styd on: useful & consistent, ran to best: see 2101, 1475.
2096 **OUR TEDDY** 12 [3] A M Balding 4-9-1 bl (87) K Darley 8/1: 00-40054: In tch, sltly outpcd 2f out,   shd   90
styd on ins last: needs further now? see 2096, 547.
1704 **MIDDLEMARCH** 30 [4]4-10-0 P (100) J F Egan 20/1: 016-0405: ch c Grand Lodge - Blanche Dubois   hd   102
(Nashwan) Led, hdd over 2f out, kept on same pace: with A O'Brien in '03, Curragh stks wnr, not btn far in Gr class,
rtd 112): eff over 1m/10f on fast & soft, tried blnks, visor & polytrack: useful run under big weight.
     POLYGONAL 58 [7]4-9-3 (89) R Hughes 14/1: 0020-136: b g Octagonal - Sectarine (Maelstrom Lake)   hd   90+
Stdd start, hld up, kept on nicely late, hands-and-heels: abs: French import, earlier won a stks at Longchamp: stays
10f well, poss 12f on fast & soft grnd: caught the eye under v kind ride here, must be kept in mind.
2101 **CRIPSEY BROOK** 12 [13]6-8-13 (85) Kim Tinkler 20/1: 330-6607: Bhd, late hdwy, nrst fin: needs 10f.   ½   85
2096 **CONSONANT** 12 [8]7-9-3 (89) A Culhane 12/1: 1111068: Cl-up, chsd ldr 4f out, wknd over 2f out.   hd   88
2101 **STRETTON** 12 [9]6-8-6 (78) J Fanning 10/1: 310-0609: Held up, some late gains, nst fin: nicely   ¾   75
bckd: back on a fair mark & likes York: see 1833.
2087* **SEA STORM** 14 [1]6-8-11 p (83) J Murtagh 12/1: 0503010: 10th: Cl up, wknd 3f out: btr 2087.   ¾   78
2159 **TOP DIRHAM** 10 [10]6-7-13 (71) Dale Gibson 13/2 FAV: 000-2320: 11th: Chsd ldrs, rdn & short of   nk   65
room over 1f out, no dngr: nicely bckd: btr 2159, 1036.
2242 **INTRICATE WEB** 7 [14]8-8-6 (78) G Duffield 14/1: 4601330: 12th: Al bhd: btr 2242, 1883.   1   70
2207 **DEFINITE GUEST** 8 [16]6-8-10 (82) P Hanagan 8/1: 13565-30: 13th: In tch, wknd dist: btr 2207.   ½   73
1354‡ **VICIOUS KNIGHT** 404 [15]6-10-0 (100) Alex Greaves 40/1: 0340/15-0: 14th: Handy, wide & keen,   1¾   87
chall 3f out, wknd over 1f out: apprec 7f, changed stable.
1877 **TEDSTALE** 23 [2]6-8-8 bl (80) K McEvoy 12/1: 604-0050: 15th: In tch, keen, hdwy & no room from   nk   66
over 2f out, jock accepted situation & eased: rnr-up in this race last term & this shld be forgiven: see 1877.
15 Ran   Time 1m 50.99 (2.19)   Owned: The Square Table II   Trained: Newmarket

2405   2.20 Queen Mother's Cup Lady Amateur Riders Handicap 3yo+ 0-95 (C)   **[81]**
£10920 £3360 £1680   **1m3f198y**   **Good/Firm 29**   **-10 Slow**   Inside

1759 **MEPHISTO** 28 [3] L M Cumani 5-10-5 (86) Mrs S Cumani 4/1: 3216-051: In tch, hdwy & edged left   95
over 1f out but styd on for press to lead nr line: nicely bckd: suited by 12f now on fast grnd & on a stiff/undul
trk: can carry big weights: useful & improving: see 1759.
1969 **COURT OF APPEAL** 19 [5] B Ellison 7-10-5 t (86) Miss L Ellison 15/2: 434-1132: Cl-up, led over 2f   hd   94
out, kept on till collared cl-home: v genuine & in grand heart: see 1599, 997.
1979 **STALLONE** 18 [1] N Wilson 7-9-6 (73) Mrs N Wilson(3) 12/1: 310-0343: Held up, hdwy & short of room   ¾   79
over 1f out, switched right & kept on, not btn far: fine run: see 1781.
1969 **SPORTING GESTURE** 19 [4] M W Easterby 7-9-8 (75) Miss S Brotherton 3/1 FAV: 2000-054: In tch, eff   nk   79
over 2f out, kept on same pace: won this race last term off a 6lb lower mark & ran well again: see 1969.
2157 **KYLKENNY** 10 [10]9-9-6 t (73) Mrs S Bosley 6/1: 04-30065: Chsd ldrs, hdwy to chall over 2f out, ev   ½   77
ch till onepcd ins last: rnr-up in this race last year (9lbs higher): see 856, 225.
1668 **KUSTER** 32 [9]8-10-10 bl (91) Miss F Cumani(6) 9/1: 10115-06: b g Indian Ridge - Ustka (Lomond)   2   92
Held up, short of room over 2f out, some late gains: '03 3 time h'cap scorer: 4th at best in '02: suited by 12f
now on firm or gd/soft, any trk: wears blnks: useful & tough.
1 Sep'03 Hayd 11.9fm 92-88 C: 1 Aug'03 Bath 11.7fm 89-85 C: 1 Jul'03 Hayd 11.9gd 88-83 E: 1 Jul'01 Good 9.8fm 88-81 B:
1569 **RAYSHAN** 38 [2]4-11-0 (95) Miss P Robson 20/1: 21356-07: b g Darshaan - Rayseka (Dancing Brave)   9   82
In tch, wknd over 2f out: juv nov hdle wnr last winter (rtd 130h, 2m, fast & gd): '03 Limerick mdn wnr for J Oxx,
Gr 3 plcd: eff over 12/14f on gd & gd/soft: been gelded. 1 Jun'03 Lime 12g/s 94- : 2 May'03 Leop 12g/s 90- :
2208 **DANELOR** 8 [6]6-10-4 (85) Miss V Tunnicliffe(3) 9/1: 220-4508: Sn clr ldr, hdd over 2f out, wknd: ½   71
prob went off too fast: see 2209, 836.
2284 **LAWOOD** 4 [7]4-9-8 (75) Miss N Carberry 10/1: 4012409: Held up, rdn & hmpd over 1f out, sn wknd.   5   53
1966 **NICHOLAS NICKELBY** 19 [8]4-8-10 (3oh) Miss Faye Bramley(3) 33/1: 622-0620: 10th: Chsd ldr,   dist   0
wknd over 4f out: btr 1966 (clmr), 115.
10 Ran   Time 2m 31.52 (4.72)   Owned: Mrs Angie Silver   Trained: Newmarket

2406   2.50 Daniel Prenn Royal Yorkshire Rated Stakes Handicap 3yo 0-100 (B)   **[104]**
£12342 £4682 £2341   **1m2f88y**   **Good/Firm 29**   **+01 Fast**   Inside

2079 **ETMAAM** 14 [5] M Johnston 3-8-8 (84) R Hills 4/1: 4-15121: Hld up, outpcd over 3f out, rallied   91+
well 2f out & styd on strongly to lead cl-home, going away: nicely bckd: stay 10f, looks to be crying out for 12f:
acts on fast & soft: runs well fresh on gall trks: plenty more to come over further, keep on side.
1959* **MOTIVE** 19 [2] Sir Michael Stoute 3-8-10 (86) K Fallon 7/2 FAV: 512: Cl-up, hdwy to lead & hung   hd   91
left 2f out, kept on well for press, collared cl home: hvly bckd: lost nothing in defeat: useful & progressive.
1813 **SEWNSO CHARACTER** 25 [3] M Blanshard 3-9-5 (95) P Hanagan 9/1: 6225-403: Handy, hdwy & short of   2½   96
room 2f out, onepcd: stays 10f: useful, conceded weight to front 2: see 1583.
2250 **SPRING GODDESS** 7 [8] A P Jarvis 3-8-6 (82) N Callan 11/1: 3160-304: Held up, hdwy 2f out, onepcd.   ½   82
1965* **SOUND OF FLEET** 19 [4]3-8-8 (84) K Darley 4/1: 2-4615: Chsd ldr, led 3f out till hdd & hmpd 2f   1¼   82
out, no extra: not disgraced: see 1965 (weaker h'cap).

4975} **LUNAR EXIT 224** [7]3-9-7 (97) J Murtagh 20/1: 315-6: gr g Exit To Nowhere - Moon Magic (Polish **4**   **89**
Precedent) Al bhd on reapp: '03 mdn wnr: stays 10f on fast grnd & a gall trk: useful.
1 Oct'03 Newm 8g/f 96- D:
1922* **NUNKI 21** [6]3-8-11 (87) W Ryan 8/1: 317: In tch, wknd 2f out: btr expected after 1922 (mdn).   *1*   **77**
1783* **AQUALUNG 27** [1]3-9-2 (92) R Hughes 5/1: 4-018: Keen, led 3f out, wknd: poss rcd too keenly but   *9*   **68**
much btr expected after 1783 (cmftble mdn wnr).
8 Ran   Time 2m 10.24 (2.94)   Owned: Mr Hamdan Al Maktoum   Trained: Middleham

---

2407   3.25 William Hill Trophy Heritage Handicap 3yo 0-105 (B)   **[107]**
£55000 £17117 £0550   6f3y str   Good/Firm 20   13 Slow   Centre

1766 **TWO STEP KID 28** [3] J Noseda 3-8-9 (88) S W Kelly 14/1: 1-641: Led over 2f out, styd on strongly   **101**
ins last, drvn out: relished rtn to 6f: acts on fast & polytrack, sharp or gall trks: lightly rcd & v useful.
2249* **DELPHIE QUEEN 7** [8] S Kirk 3-8-11 (90) J F Egan 16/1: 410-4312: In tch, rdn & sltly outpcd over   nk   **102+**
2f out, rallied well over 1f out, just failed: excellent run, thriving & must win sn with return to 7f.
2186* **TRAYTONIC 9** [16] J R Fanshawe 3-9-7 (100) J Murtagh 10/1: 410-5013: Sn rdn bhd, hdwy over 1f   1½   **108+**
out, fin well, nrst fin: promising run & progressed again, remains one to keep on your side when stepped up to 7f,
and/or back on easier grnd as in 2186 (easy wnr).
1829* **ALDERNEY RACE 25** [4] R Charlton 3-8-11 (90) S Drowne 15/2: 4-5214: Bhd, short of room & sltly   shd   **98**
outpcd halfway, hdwy 2f out, kept on ins last: lightly rcd, useful & progressive, another sure to relish 7f.
4953} **DOOHULLA 225** [18]3-8-10 (89) R Hughes 33/1: 3513-5: ch f Stravinsky - Viva Zapata (Affirmed)   nk   **96+**
Held up last, switched to stands rail & strong burst over 1f out, hung left ins last & no extra cl-home: '03 stks
wnr (first time blnks), List plcd: eff at 6f on fast, gd & polytrack: won (1st time blnks last term): plenty of
promise here, shld be winning sn when stable rtn to form & poss with blnks back on.
1 Oct'03 Ling 6ap 85a- D:
1918 **HIGH VOLTAGE 21** [6]3-9-6 t (99) Darren Williams 25/1: 2020-136: Led, hdd halfway, onepace: gd run.   1½   **101**
1572 **WANCHAI LAD 38** [12]3-8-9 (88) K Darley 8/1: 1160-37: In tch, eff 1f out, onepace: gd run.   1¾   **85**
1583 **GLARAMARA 37** [15]3-9-5 (98) K Fallon 10/1: 13-02038: Dwelt, bhd, hung left halfway, no impress.   ½   **93**
1933 **DANZIG RIVER 21** [11]3-9-3 (96) R Hills 16/1: 6115-209: Dwelt & bhd, modest late gains: btr 1154.   ¾   **89**
1175* **BONNE DE FLEUR 58** [13]3-9-4 (97) F Lynch 33/1: 11232-10: 10th: In tch, wknd 2f out: 2 month   2½   **83**
abs: much btr 1175 (List fill, gd, made all).
1460 **RYDAL 43** [5]3-8-8 bl (87) P Mulrennan(5) 100/1: 2221-040: 11th: Cl-up, wknd 2f out: see 1460.   1½   **69**
1933 **BIG BRADFORD 21** [17]3-8-11 vis (90) D Kinsella 12/1: 32420-20: 12th: Al bhd: btr 1933 (visor).   ½   **70**
1918 **FAST HEART 21** [14]3-9-4 t (97) A Culhane 40/1: 003-0040: 13th: In tch, hmpd & wknd over 1f out.   ¾   **75**
2137* **TIMES REVIEW 11** [20]3-8-6 (85) P Hanagan 7/1: 500-2510: 14th: In tch, wknd 2f out: btr 2137.   hd   **62**
1918 **NEROS RETURN 21** [2]3-9-7 (100) J Fanning 50/1: 11-6060: 15th: Nvr a factor: see 1113.   ¾   **75**
2121 **HARRY UP 11** [19]3-8-10 (89) M Fenton 20/1: 0-230340: 16th: In tch, wknd 2f out: see 2121, 1771.   1   **61**
1918 **LOCAL POET 21** [9]3-8-13 T (92) G Gibbons 33/1: 24-15050: 17th: In tch, wknd 2f out: btr 953 (gd).   shd   **63**
2055* **MIS CHICAF 15** [1]3-8-11 (90) R Winston 5/1 FAV: 501-2110: 18th: In tch, wknd 2f out: well bckd: 3   **52**
much btr expected after 7L win over this C/D in 2055.
4086} **LATIN REVIEW 280** [7]3-9-3 (96) K McEvoy 66/1: 41410-0: 19th: ch f Titus Livius - Law Review   3½   **48**
(Case Law) Al bhd on reapp: '03 mdn & stks wnr: stays 6f well on firm & fast grnd, likes a sharp trk, does handle
any: useful last term.   1 May'03 Good 5g/f 89- E:
1570 **FUN TO RIDE 38** [10]3-9-0 (93) M Hills 7/1: 22-120: 20th: Keen, handy, wknd & wandered 2f out,   3   **36**
eased: hvly bckd tho' op 11/2: surely something amiss: much btr 1570, 1191.
20 Ran   Time 1m 11.94 (2.54)   Owned: Hesmonds Stud   Trained: Newmarket

---

2408   4.00 Leonard Sainer E B F Maiden Stakes 2yo (D)
£5772 £1776 £888   6f3y str   Good/Firm 29   -52 Slow   Centre

BLUES AND ROYALS [9] Saeed bin Suroor 2-9-0 K McEvoy 2/1 FAV: 1: b c Honour And Glory -   **94+**
Dixieland Blues (Dixieland Band) Handy, hdwy to lead over 1f out, styd on well, rdn out: hvly bckd on debut: Apr
foal, cost $40,000: half-brother to a smart 12f scorer: eff at 6f, 7f+ sure to suit: runs well fresh on fast grnd &
a gall trk: v pleasing start, potentially smart & looks sure to win btr races.
WISE OWL [2] M Johnston 2-9-0 J Fanning 5/1: 2: b c Danehill - Mistle Thrush (Storm Bird)   1¾   **87+**
Cl-up, rdn to chall 2f out, kept on but not pace of wnr on debut: bckd: Mar foal, cost 200,000gns: half-brother to a
smart 12f scorer: dam 10f wnr: eff at 6f, bred to relish 7f/1m+ in time: acts on fast grnd: promising, will come
on plenty for this & type to win gd races.
THE DUKE OF DIXIE [7] P F I Cole 2-9-0 K Fallon 4/1: 3: b c Dixieland Band - Money Madam (A P   ½   **86+**
Indy) Sn bhd, styd on takingly late under the kind ride on debut: Mar foal, cost $150,000: dam wnr in US: eff at
6f, bred to relish 1m+ in time: bundles of promise here, will come on plenty for this & must be put in the notebook.
MALCHEEK [1] T D Easterby 2-9-0 J F Egan 25/1: 4: br c Lend A Hand - Russland (Surumu) Chsd   2   **78**
ldrs, onepace over 1f out: debut: Apr foal, cost £27,000: dam wnr in Germany: pleasing start, apprec minor trks.
VENETIAN KING [4]2-9-0 P Hanagan 5/1: 5: Stumbled start, sn in tch, no impress dbt on debut.   1¼   **74**
2158 **MISTY MILLER 10** [3]2-9-0 D Allan(3) 20/1: 506: Led till over 1f out, wknd.   2½   **67**
MOUNT BUTLER [6]2-9-0 M Fenton 25/1: 7: Al bhd.   5   **52**
1893 **TOSS THE CABER 22** [5]2-9-0 K Darley 10/1: 08: Unruly stalls, handy, wknd over 2f out.   12   **16**
8 Ran   Time 1m 14.3 (4.9)   Owned: Godolphin   Trained: Newmarket

---

2409   4.35 Charles Henry Memorial Handicap Stakes 3yo+ 0-80 (D)   **[80]**
£7963 £2450 £1225   6f3y str   Good/Firm 29   +01 Fast   Centre

699 **CLOUD DANCER 110** [16] K A Ryan 5-9-5 (71) G Parkin 20/1: 10-30221: Keen, held up, hdwy 2f out,   **80**
strong run ins last to lead cl-home, going away: long abs: winning form over 6f/1m, stays 8.5f & likes firm & fast
grnd, acts on both AWs & any trk: clrly runs well fresh: nicely turn of foot here, right back to turf best.
2256 **BLACKHEATH 7** [14] D Nicholls 8-9-11 (77) Alex Greaves 11/1: 3-044062: Chsd ldrs, gd hdwy 2f out,   1   **83**
carr it appr fnl 1f but led ins last, collared cl-home: fair run & looks poised to strike: gd run: see 1217.
2074 **MR MALARKEY 14** [17] Mrs C A Dunnett 4-9-10 bl (76) J Murtagh 12/1: 00-40463: Cl-up, led over 2f   ½   **80**
out, hung left & hdd ins last, no extra: has had steering probs this term but a tough & consistent sort: see 1726.
2256 **UNDETERRED 7** [6] T D Barron 8-9-7 vis (73) K Darley 10/1: 00-05004: Sn bhd, styd on late, nrst   1¾   **72**
fin: looks to be coming to hand & has drpd to a winning mark: keep in mind, likes Goodwood: see 1898.

YORK SATURDAY 12.06.04 Lefthand, Flat, Galloping Track

2059 **PADDYWACK 15** [15]7-8-12 bl (64) A Culhane 13/2 FAV: 00-04035: Chsd ldrs, onepace dist: bckd. *hd* **62**
1820 **FLYING EDGE 25** [18]4-8-7 (59) D Allan(3) 33/1: 0-020506: In tch, onepace over 1f out: see 585. *hd* **56**
2216 **AMANDAS LAD 8** [9]4-8-8 (60) S Drowne 40/1: 3550427: Cl-up, wknd 2f out: see 2216 (7f, mdn). *1½* **53**
2282 **UP TEMPO 4** [11]6-9-10 bl (76) N Callan 14/1: 1420058: Went left start, in tch, eff 2f out, onepace. *nk* **68**
2057 **PRIDE OF KINLOCH 15** [8]4-8-6 (58) W Ryan 33/1: 6040309: In tch, short of room 2f out, mod gains. *shd* **50**
1638 **MISTER SWEETS 35** [3]5-9-5 (71) R Fitzpatrick 33/1: 30000-60: 10th: Bhd, late gains: needs 7f. *¾* **61**
2084 **BALLYBUNION 14** [7]5-8-7 (59) P M Quinn 25/1: 100-0000: 11th: Went left start, nvr a factor: see 2084. *nk* **48**
2150 **TUSCAN FLYER 10** [13]6-8-10 (62) R Ffrench 14/1: 142-0030: 12th: Nvr a factor: btr 2150, see 1600. *1¼* **47**
1977 **BLYTHE SPIRIT 18** [1]5-9-8 p (74) T Hamilton(3) 14/1: 05045-50: 13th: Led till over 2f out, wknd. *½* **57**
2059 **VIEWFORTH 15** [4]6-9-5 bl (71) P Mulrennan(5) 10/1: 0-440000: 14th: In tch, wknd 2f out: see 1276. *2* **48**
1638 **QUANTICA 35** [20]5-8-10 (62) Kim Tinkler 66/1: 002-6000: 15th: Al bhd. *6* **21**
2282+**H HARRISON 4** [10]4-10-3 (7ex) (83) P Mathers(7) 12/1: 0645410: 16th: Al bhd: too sn? *1* **39**
2059 **WINTHORPE 15** [12]4-9-5 (71) Darren Williams 7/1: 0000040: 17th: Keen in tch, wknd over 2f out: *2½* **20**
well bckd, reportedly struck into: btr 2059, 482.
2187 **GREY COSSACK 9** [19]7-9-12 (78) J Carroll 33/1: 0-010050: 18th: Al bhd: btr 1145. *1¾* **22**
2214 **TALLY 8** [5]4-8-5 (57) J Fanning 9/1: 0603120: 19th: In tch, wknd 2f out: nicely bckd: see 2214. *¾* **0**
1523 **SIR DON 40** [2]5-8-9 vis (61) A Nicholls 16/1: 530-0000: 20th: Al bhd. *13* **0**
20 Ran Time 1m 12.5 (3.1) Owned: Mrs Gillian Quinn Trained: Hambleton

2410

5.05 Michael Sobell Maiden Stakes 3yo (D)
£6494 £1998 £999 **7f205y rnd** **Good/Firm 29** **-28 Slow** Inside

BINARY VISION [10] J H M Gosden 3-9-0 R Hughes 1/1 FAV: 1: ch c Distant View - Binary (Rainbow **94+**
Quest) Handy, hdwy to lead 2f out, qcknd clr appr fnl 1f, v easily: hvly bckd on debut: half-brother to smart
1m/10f wnr Binary File: dam 9/10f scorer: eff over a gall 1m, sure to relish 10f: runs well fresh on fast grnd:
most promising start, potentially smart & must be kept in mind when stepped up to List/Gr 3 class.
2092 **SHARAAB 13** [1] B Hanbury 3-9-0 t (70) R Hills 11/1: 30-6052: b c Erhaab - Ghashtah (Nijinsky) *7* **76$**
Led till 3f out, kept on but not pace of wnr: plcd in a mdn on first of 2 '03 starts: half-brother to wnrs over
1m/hdles: stays 1m on fast grnd in a t-strap.
1495 **MIKAO 41** [6] M H Tompkins 3-9-0 Saleem Golam(7) 13/2: 53: Held up, hdwy over 2f out, kept on ins *shd* **76**
last, nvr a threat: clrly crying out for 10f+ & sure to improve at that trip.
2066 **SUPAMACH 14** [7] P F I Cole 3-8-9 S Drowne 12/1: 34: In tch, onepcd fnl 2f: ran to form of 2066 *1* **69**
(10f): prob acts on fast & polytrack.
HUGS DESTINY [12]3-9-0 Dean McKeown 25/1: 5: b g Victory Note - Embracing (Reference Point) *½* **73**
In tch, outpcd over 2f out, some late gains: debut: half-brother to smart 12f/2m5f wnr Hugs Dancer: dam
12/14f wnr: will needs 10/12f+ & this was a pleasing start: sure fire improver when stepping up in trip.
1270 **NISTAKI 53** [2]3-9-0 K Darley 10/1: 46: In tch, hdwy to lead 3f out till 2f out, wknd: longer trip. *1* **71**
2131 **MY SUNSHINE 11** [11]3-8-9 M Hills 16/1: 00-07: In tch, wknd over 2f out. *2* **62**
TEAM PLAYER [9]3-9-0 N Mackay(3) 10/1: 8: Al bhd on debut. *¾* **65**
1628 **GALLAS 35** [4]3-9-0 (61) G Parkin 80/1: 55000-09: Al bhd. *4* **53**
1636 **ARRAN SCOUT 35** [3]3-9-0 (77) J Murtagh 10/1: 04-30: 10th: Handy, wknd over 2f out: see 1636. *1¼* **54**
TRINITY FAIR [8]3-8-9 J Fanning 50/1: 0: 11th: In tch, wknd over 3f out on debut. *5* **39**
2106 **SUPER KING 12** [13]3-9-0 (68) Darren Williams 50/1: 02-00: 12th: Al bhd. *1* **42**
12 Ran Time 1m 37.76(1.96) Owned: Mr K Abdulla Trained: Manton

BATH SATURDAY 12.06.04 Lefthand, Turning Track with Uphill Finish

Official Going FIRM (HARD places). All Times Slow

2411

2.15 E B F Mainline Employment Novice Stakes 2yo (D)
£4017 £1236 £618 **5f11y rnd** **Firm** **Slow** Far Side

2257* **SILVER WRAITH 6** [2] N A Callaghan 2-9-0 T P Queally(3) 10/3: 4211: Trkd ldrs, rdn & styd on **93**
strongly to lead cl-home: eff at 5f, stays 6f & a return to that trip will suit: acts on fast & firm grnd & on a
sharp/undul or stiffish trk: useful & continues to prog, see 2257 & 1848.
1950* **CARTE ROYALE 19** [1] M Johnston 2-9-2 S Chin 10/11 FAV: 12: Tried to make all, collared cl-home: *½* **93**
well bckd & far from disgraced under top-weight: useful sort, see 1950 (debut).
2213 **BIBURY FLYER 8** [3] M R Channon 2-8-7 S Hitchcott(2) 3/1: 2233: Trkd ldr, ev ch ent fnl 1f, prob *1¼* **79**
just held when short of room cl-home: another consistent run, acts on firm & hvy: shld find a small race.
MY DREAM [5] R Hannon 2-8-3 F Norton 12/1: 4: b f King's Theatre - Dream Chaser (Record Token) *10* **45**
Dwelt, al last on debut: tchd 20/1: March foal, sister to smart miler King's Ironbridge: dam a sprint wnr.
4 Ran Time 1m 02.53 (2.23) Owned: Mr M Tabor Trained: Newmarket

2412

2.45 Gerald & Freda Brown's Golden Wedding Selling Stakes 3yo+ (G)
£2576 £736 £368 **5f161y rnd** **Firm** **Slow** Far Side

1644* **FOLEY MILLENNIUM 33** [8] M Quinn 6-9-10 (49) F Norton 9/1: 0/0/6P-011: Made all, clr fnl 1f, **62**
decisively: bght in for 7,200gns: eff at 5/6f on firm & hvy grnd: likes to force the pace & gd weight-carrier.
1218 **JUWWI 56** [6] J M Bradley 10-9-4 (62) S Hitchcott(3) 8/1: 0044062: Held up, fin well into 2nd, not *2* **48**
reach wnr: 8 wk abs: 10yo now, came with customary late run on this return to sell grade: see 646 (AW seller).
1948 **DIAMOND RING 19** [4] Mrs J Candlish 5-8-13 (40) I Mongan 14/1: 5360-503: Mid-div, styd on late, *½* **42**
nrst fin: acts on firm & gd/soft: see 1336.
2118 **JINKSONTHEHOUSE 12** [10] M D I Usher 3-8-11 (60) Hayley Turner(5) 11/2: 00-40104: Mid-div, styd on *1¼* **44**
under press, nvr nrr: twice below 1902.
2161 **TAPPIT 10** [7]5-9-4 p (54) C Catlin 15/2: 0000305: Rear, late prog, nvr dngrs: btr 1963 (6f). *1¼* **39**
2125 **FRENCHMANS LODGE 11** [12]4-9-4 bl (40) B Swarbrick(5) 9/1: 0000256: Rear, modest late prog. *hd* **39**
2266 **DELEGATE 5** [11]11-9-4 (67) T P Queally(3) 7/2 FAV: 52330-07: Held up, nvr a factor: qck reapp. *1½* **35**
1948 **HENRY TUN 19** [13]6-9-10 p (41) M Savage(5) 12/1: 3020068: Prom 5f, wknd: jt top-weight. *½* **40**
2269 **NAUGHTY GIRL 5** [1]4-8-13 (60) Joanna Badger 10/1: 0000009: Prom 4f, wknd: qck reapp. *nk* **28**

2016 **KILMEENA STAR** 17 [2]6-9-10 bl (37) Derek Nolan(7) 25/1: 0412000: 10th: Slowly away, al bhd. | 8 | 15
641 **HAWK** 117 [3]6-9-4 (63) L Keniry(3) 11/1: 05-00000: 11th: Speed till halfway: long abs. | 6 | 0

11 Ran   Time 1m 12.16 (3.06)   Owned: Mrs S G Davies   Trained: Wantage

---

2413   3.20 Weatherbys Insurance Classified Stakes 3yo 0-70 (E)
£4251 £1308 £654   **1m3f144y**   **Firm**   **Slow**   Inside

2079 **ZAFFEU** 14 [6] N P Littmoden 3-8-11 (69) T P Queally(3) 11/4: 0662451: Held up, switched wide 2f   **72**
out, styd on well to lead cl-home, rdn out: drifted from 13/8: first success: eff around 12f on gd, firm,
polytrack & poss soft grnd: handles a stiffish trk: see 1429 & 1184.

1791 **DESERT IMAGE** 26 [5] C Tinkler 3-9-0 (73) S Hitchcott(3) 11/8 FAV: 2600332: Prom, led 3f out till   nk   **73**
cl-home, not btn far: clr of 3rd: consistent, acts on firm, gd & both AWs: stays 12f, see 1791 & 337 (AW).

645 **VENGEROV** 117 [3] M L W Bell 3-8-13 (72) I Mongan 4/1: 0340-163: Chsd ldrs, onepcd fnl 1.5f: 5   **64**
bckd from 7/1, long abs & has been gelded: longer 11.7f trip, best 553 (AW mdn, 1m).

1488 **WEST COUNTRY** 42 [2] M L W Bell 3-8-11 (70) S Chin 7/2: 32-43004: br c Gone West - Crystal Gazing   6   **53**
(El Gran Senor) Led till 3f out, grad wknd: op 5/1, 6 wk abs: plcd on all 3 juv mdn starts: eff at 7f, prob not
stay this longer 11.7f trip: acts on fast & firm grnd, handles a stiff/gall trk:
2 Oct'03 Donc 7g/f 75- D: 2 Sep'03 York 7.0g/f 84- D:

4 Ran   Time 2m 30.16 (5.16)   Owned: The Headquarters Partnership Ltd   Trained: Newmarket

---

2414   3.55 Toteplacepot Handicap Stakes Fillies 3yo+ 0-85 (D)   [74]
£6721 £2068 £1034   **1m5y rnd**   **Firm**   **Fair**   Inside

1775* **BRAZILIAN TERRACE** 28 [2] M L W Bell 4-9-13 (73) Hayley Turner(5) 11/4 FAV: 50-34011: Chsd ldrs,   **78**
imprvd to lead 2f out, held on well fnl 1f, rdn out: top-weight: 1m specialist, acts on firm, gd/soft & polytrack:
seems to handle any trk: in-form & gets on well with Hayley Turner: see 1775 & 800.

2032 **MARNIE** 16 [3] J Akehurst 7-8-5 (51) C Catlin 7/2: 0-013022: Held up, imprvd 2f out, styd on well   nk   **54**
& only just failed: deserves similar, see 2032 (C/D).

2354 **NUZZLE** 2 [1] M Quinn 4-8-0 vis (46) J F McDonald(3) 11/2: 0502603: Led till 2f out, onepcd when   2   **45**
sltly short of room cl-home: qck reappr, op 7/1: see 1884 (10f).

2174 **HERE TO ME** 10 [5] R Hannon 3-8-12 (69) P Dobbs 5/1: 502-5344: Trkd ldr, outpcd fnl 1.5f: see 1982.   2   **64**

2296 **OH SO ROSIE** 4 [4]4-8-12 (58) Derek Nolan(7) 10/3: 4330325: Held up, nvr nr ldrs: qck reappr: btr 2296.   1¾   **49**

4972} **STELLA MARAIS** 224 [6]3-8-10 (67) F Norton 12/1: 400-6: b f Second Empire - Karakapa (Subotica)   12   **33**
Slowly away, keen in rear, nvr dngrs: reappr: some mdn promise in 3 '03 starts (4th on debut, rtd 71 at best).

6 Ran   Time 1m 40.43 (2.13)   Owned: Mrs GRowland-Clark/MLWBell Racing   Trained: Newmarket

---

2415   4.30 Western Daily Press Raceclub Maiden Auction Stakes 2yo (E)
£3751 £1154 £577   **5f11y rnd**   **Firm**   **Slow**   Far Side

2109 **EMPIRES GHODHA** 12 [8] B J Meehan 2-8-11 bl J F McDonald(3) 15/8 FAV: 53231: Trkd ldr, went on 2f   **90**
out, styd on strongly fnl 1f, rdn out: well bckd & overdue win: eff at 5f on fast & firm grnd, handles a stiff/gall
or sharp trk: eff in blnks: deserved win, see 2109 & 1816.

2194 **ENCANTO** 9 [5] J S Moore 2-8-8 C Catlin 10/1: 062: ch f Bahhare - Born To Glamour (Ajdal) Rear,   1¼   **74**
hdwy to chase wnr fnl 1f, no impress cl-home: op 14/1: £10,000 Feb foal: half-sister to juv scorer Sailing Shoes &
a couple of other wnrs: dam a 6f juv scorer, sire a smart 1m/10f performer: eff at 5f on firm grnd.

1880 **BOLD MINSTREL** 22 [2] M Quinn 2-8-7 F Norton 14/1: 03: Nvr far away, onepcd fnl 1f: eff at 5f on fm.   1½   **75**

1752 **FORZEEN** 28 [3] J A Osborne 2-8-9 T P Queally(3) 9/2: 34: Al mid-div: handles fibresand & fm.   nk   **76**

PEOPLETON BROOK [4]2-8-7 P Dobbs 25/1: 5: b c Compton Place - Merch Rhyd Y Grug (Sabrehill)   2   **68**
Keen in rear, nvr a factor on debut: April foal, cost 9,500gns: dam modest, sire a top-class sprinter.

1601 **MISTER BELL** 36 [6]2-8-11 D Sweeney 5/1: 36: Led till after halfway, wknd: see 1601.   6   **54**

2171 **FEMINIST** 10 [7]2-8-9 S Hitchcott(3) 3/1: 537: Prom till halfway, wknd: much btr 2171.   1½   **48**

7 Ran   Time 1m 03.25 (2.95)   Owned: Clipper Group Holdings   Trained: Upper Lambourn

---

2416   5.00 Totequadpot Rated Stakes Handicap 3yo+ 0-85 (D)   [82]
£5990 £2272 £1136   **5f161y rnd**   **Firm**   **Fair**   Far Side

2199 **HIGH RIDGE** 9 [2] J M Bradley 5-8-6 (4oh)(60) C Catlin 12/1: 360-0151: Rdn in rear, styd on well   **74**
to lead ins fnl 1f, rdn clr: eff at 5.8/7f, has trnsd further: acts on fast & firm grnd, clearly likes Bath.

2266+ **DEVON FLAME** 5 [3] R J Hodges 5-8-13 (3ex) (71) J F McDonald(3) 8/11 FAV: 4111-212: Trkd ldr, ev ch   1½   **76**
after halfway, not pace of wnr cl-home: op 8/13: qck reapp under 3lb pen for 2266 (sharp trk).

2315 **ONE WAY TICKET** 3 [6] J M Bradley 4-8-6 (2oh)p (62) Hayley Turner(5) 6/1: 0003203: Led till   1¾   **64**
entering fnl 1f, no extra: tchd 9/1: qck reappr, see 2111.

3752} **PINTLE** 297 [1] J L Spearing 4-8-9 (67) S Carson 14/1: 215-4: b f Pivotal - Boozy (Absalom)   1¼   **63**
Prom, onepcd fnl 1.5f on reappr: won middle of 3 juv starts (Kempton mdn): eff at 5f on fast & firm grnd, handles a
fair trk: sharper next time. 1 Aug'03 Kemp 5g/f 61- D: 2 Jul'03 Leic 5.0fm 69- F:

1914* **DEVISE** 21 [5]4-9-9 (81) T G McLaughlin 4/1: 00-16015: Reared stalls, rcd wide & nvr a factor: ½   **76**
lost chance at the start today: btr 1914.

2044 **BYO** 15 [4]6-9-0 (72) S Hitchcott(3) 14/1: 0620106: Chsd ldrs 4f, sn wknd: well below 1886.   5   **52**

6 Ran   Time 1m 10.53 (1.43)   Owned: James Leisure Ltd   Trained: Chepstow

---

2417   5.30 Bathwick Tyres Lady Riders' Handicap Stakes 4yo+ 35-55 (F)   [40]
£3432 £1056 £528   **2m2f34y**   **Firm**   **No Standard Time**   Inside

3883} **HIGH DRAMA** 292 [12] P Bowen 7-9-8 (1oh) (34) Miss Gwen Morris(7) 8/1: 506/520-1: b g In The Wings   **43**
- Maestrale (Top Ville) Prom, led 3f out, held on well fnl 1f, rdn out: op 13/2: '03 h'cap rnr-up: h'cap hdle wnr
Mar '03 (eff arnd 2m6f on gd & firm, rtd 107h): dual '01 Flat h'cap wnr (W MUir): eff at 2m/2m2f on gd & fm,
handles gd/sft: likes a sharp/turning or stiff trk, best without blnks: runs well fresh for an inexp pilot.

BATH   SATURDAY 12.06.04   Lefthand, Turning Track with Uphill Finish

2 Aug'03 Thir 16g/s 35-35 F: 1 Sep'01 Catt 15.8g/f 42-35 F: 1 Sep'01 Warw 16.1g/f 42-35 F:

288   **HARIK** 161 [8] G L Moore 10-10-1 bl t (42) Miss H Grissell(5) 10/1: 04206-62: ch g Persian Bold -   ¾   **48**
Yaqut (Northern Dancer) Mid-div, hdwy to chall 2f out, just btn in a close fin: won a h'cap chase at Fontwell in
May '04 (rtd 118c, eff at 2m/2m4f on firm & soft): '03 AW h'cap rnr-up: '01 dual h'cap wnr: best around 2m on firm
& both AWs: handles a stiff or sharp trk, carries weight well: eff with/without blnks/t-strap.

2 Feb'03 Ling 16ap 78a-75 D: 2 Feb'02 Ling 16ap 81a-77 D: 1 Dec'01 Wolv 16.2af 75a-75 D: 2 Apr'01 Ling 13ap 74a-72 E:
1 Feb'01 Ling 16ap 74a-70 D:

2354   **NOBLE CALLING** 2 [11] R J Hodges 7-10-11 (52) Miss E Folkes(3) 5/1: 006-0303: Keen in rear, hdwy   ½   **57**
2f out, nrst fin: op 7/1 & qck reapp: see 2035 (here).

2156   **PURDEY** 10 [6] H Morrison 4-10-3 (45) Mrs S Moore(3) 7/1: 6004-054: Chsd ldrs, onepcd: longer trip.   2½   **47**
2198   **MOONSHINE BEACH** 9 [14]6-11-0 p (55) Mrs Marie King(5) 9/2: 5-406365: Prom, no extra fnl 1f.   nk   **56**
2035   **SARIBA** 16 [5]5-9-13 (40) Ms C Williams 7/2 FAV: 10-06156: Led till 3f out, no extra: op 5/1.   ½   **40**
2276   **VANBRUGH** 5 [7]4-10-3 t (45) Miss E J Jones 14/1: 6000007: Held up, nvr nr ldrs: op 10/1, qck reapp.   ¾   **52**
2276   **JOELY GREEN** 5 [15]7-10-7 bl (48) Mrs Emma Littmoden(3) 10/1: 6660208: Nvr btr than mid-div: qk reapp. 3   **44**
2147   **RIVER OF FIRE** 10 [3]6-9-8 (5oh)vis (80) Miss J Ellis(5) 16/1: 0-030409: Al mid-div.   5   **26**
2088   **FLETCHER** 13 [1]10-9-13 p (40) Miss G D Gracey Davison(5) 11/1: 4-051000: 10th: Held up, nvr nr ldrs.   12   **19**
4687}   **WOODSTOCK EXPRESS** 244 [4]4-9-6 (8oh) (28) Miss Jodie Hughes(5) 33/1: 060-0: 11th: b g Alflora -   nk   **12**
Young Tess (Teenoso) Keen & chsd ldrs till after halfway, sn btn on reapp: lightly rcd & mod '03 mdn form.
4802}   **CANTORIS** 238 [9]4-10-11 bl (53) Miss C Stucley(5) 25/1: 204605-0: 12th: Held up, al bhd: jumps fit.   4   **27**
2825}   **PERTEMPS SIA** 337 [2]4-9-9 (37) Miss J Pledge(7) 33/1: 506606-0: 13th: Reared start, v keen in   12   **0**
rear & jnd ldrs halfway, sn btn: reapp.
2200   **GORDYS JOY** 8 [13]4-9-12 (40) Miss Charmaine O'Neill 25/1: 064-030: 14th: Keen in rear, al bhd, t.o.   *dist*   **0**
14 Ran   Time 3m 51.93()   Owned: Mr P Bowen   Trained: Haverfordwest

SALISBURY   SUNDAY 13.06.04   Righthand, Galloping Track, Stiff Finish

Official Going Firm (Fast Places), Last 4f - Good/Firm (Firm Places)

2418   2.00 Autecnique Alfa Romeo Rated Stakes Handicap 3yo 0-95 (C)   [98]
£8969 £3402 £1701   **1m6f15y**   **Firm 08**   **-36 Slow**   No Stalls

2175   **LE TISS** 11 [1] M R Channon 3-8-9 (79) S Hitchcott(3) 100/30: 162-4021: Chsd ldrs, no room 2f out,   **91**
sn switched wide, kept on well to lead cl-home, all out: eff at 1m, stays slowly run 12f/14f: acts on firm & gd
grnd, likes Salisbury: in-form performer who is unexposed at staying dists: see 2175 & 947.
2318   **TUDOR BELL** 4 [5] J G M O'Shea 3-8-8 (78) D Sweeney 100/30: 0231162: Led 4f, led again 2f out,   shd **88**
sltly short of room when hdd cl-home: qck reapp: eff at 10/11.5f, stays slowly run 14f: acts on firm & hvy grnd:
apprec being able to dominate & was only just denied: see 2318 & 1807.
1807   **COVENTINA** 27 [2] J L Dunlop 3-8-12 (82) T Quinn 2/1 FAV: 310-0023: Cl-up, ev ch dist, kept on   nk **91**
ins fnl 1f, just denied: clr rem: suited 11.5f, stays slowly run 14f: acts on firm & fast: see 1807.
2021   **ABSOLUTELYTHEBEST** 18 [4] E A L Dunlop 3-8-12 VIS (82) J Murtagh 11/2: 04-12264: Keen rear, led   7   **81**
after 4f till 2f out, wknd: failed to settle in first time visor: see 2021 & btr 1708 (gd/soft, 12f).
2238   **ZOUAVE** 8 [6]3-9-3 BL (87) L Dettori 7/1: 103-005: Held up, nvr a factor: 1st time blnks: btr 1814.   2½ **87**
5 Ran   Time 3m 4.29 (6.29)   Owned: Mr P Trant   Trained: West Ilsley

2419   2.30 Chas H Baker Maiden Stakes Fillies 3yo (D)
£6136 £1888 £944   **1m str**   **Firm 08**   **-07 Slow**   Far side

1718   **DAWN SURPRISE** 31 [10] Saeed bin Suroor 3-8-11 T L Dettori 11/10 FAV: 3-21: Grabbed far rail &   **92+**
made all, pushed out fnl 2f, val 7L+: well bckd: stays 10f, enjoyed rtn to 1m: acts on firm & fast grnd,
stiff/gall trk: wears a t-strap: showed gd turn of foot & is improving with racing: see 1718.
2224   **POSTERITAS** 9 [7] H R A Cecil 3-8-11 R Hughes 7/2: 32: Mid-div, prog to chase wnr ins 1f, al   5   **80**
held: acts on firm & fast grnd: again ran with credit & looks in needs of further: see 2224 (debut).
2224   **NOUVEAU RICHE** 9 [6] H Morrison 3-8-11 R L Moore 8/1: 23: Slow away, sn mid-div, prog to chase   hd **79**
wnr ins fnl 2f, just caught for 2nd cl-home: clr rem: acts on firm & fast grnd: see 2224.
2291   **HUNTERS VALLEY** 5 [3] R Hannon 3-8-11 (78) P Dobbs 16/1: 0523-024: Handy, wknd dist: qck reapp.   5   **69**
2031   **GRAND APOLLO** 17 [12]3-8-11 J Fortune 6/1: 6-25: Nvr nrr than mid-div: btr 2031.   ¾   **67**
      SUDDEN IMPULSE [4]3-8-11 R Smith 150/1: 6: b f Silver Patriarch - Sanshang (Astronef) Slow   hd **66**
away, nvr nrr than mid-div: sire Gr 1 wnr at 12/14f: with A Charlton.
      MEDICA BOBA [11]3-8-11 J Fanning 66/1: 7: b f Dr Fong - Silly View (Scenic) Bhd, nvr a   3½ **59**
factor: debut: Apr foal: with H Morrison.
2072   **ZWADI** 15 [9]3-8-11 (75) Dane O'Neill 14/1: 34324-48: Cl-up 6f, sn wknd: btr 2072.   nk **58**
1846   **TIPSY LADY** 25 [1]3-8-11 T Quinn 33/1: 009: Al in rear.   1   **56**
2031   **KERRISTINA** 17 [5]3-8-11 S Carson 100/1: 000: 10th: Bhd, nvr a factor.   1   **54**
1718   **APRON** 31 [8]3-8-11 D Sweeney 50/1: 000: 11th: Handy 6f, sn fdd.   hd **53**
11 Ran   Time 1m 40.30 (1.20)   Owned: Godolphin   Trained: Newmarket

2420   3.05 Toteplacepot Handicap Stakes 3yo+ 0-85 (D)   [83]
£6916 £2128 £1064   **5f str**   **Firm 08**   **-04 Slow**   Far side

2266   **DANCING MYSTERY** 6 [9] E A Wheeler 10-9-11 (80) S Carson 22/1: 3500001: Chsd ldrs, trav well when   **90+**
no room 2f out till dist, flew home to lead cl home, going away: qck reapp: stays 6f, 5f specialist on firm & fast,
likes both AWs, gd/soft or soft: back to form with blnks left off: can follow up.
2084   **ROXANNE MILL** 15 [2] J M Bradley 6-9-6 (75) R L Moore 5/1 CO FAV: 20-32632: Handy, styd on to   hd **78**
lead dist, hdd cl-home: continues to run well & deserves to find similar: see 2084 & 1615.
2286   **WHISTLER** 5 [4] J M Bradley 7-9-12 p (81) M Hills 11/2: 0030103: Rear, prog to chase ldr ins fnl   hd **83**
1f, not btn far in 3rd: op 4/1 on qck reapp: back to form run: see 2189.
2266   **SEVEN NO TRUMPS** 6 [5] J M Bradley 7-9-8 p (77) L Dettori 13/2: 0003604: Held up, prog 2f out, no   ¾ **77**
impress well ins fnl 1f: qck reapp: see 2070 & 944.
2269   **PLAYTIME BLUE** 6 [1]4-8-6 (61) N Chalmers(5) 20/1: 1430605: Cl-up, led after 2f, hdd dist, no extra.   ½ **60**

SALISBURY   SUNDAY 13.06.04   Righthand, Galloping Track, Stiff Finish

2253 **KATHOLOGY** 8 [8]7-10-0 (83) T Quinn 5/1 CO FAV: 00530-06: Led 2f, styd prom, wknd fnl 1f. nk **81**
2266 **PORT ST CHARLES** 6 [7]7-8-8 (63) R Thomas(5) 7/1: 4004307: Bhd, prog when little room throughout nk **60+**
fnl 2f: qck reapp: lot closer with clr run & is well h'capped: see 2189.
2189 **NIVERNALS** 10 [3]5-9-8 (77) Dane O'Neill 5/1 CO FAV: 336-0008: Handy, wkng when short of room dist. 1½ **70**
2189 **TABOOR** 10 [6]6-8-1 h bl (56) Lisa Jones(3) 6/1: 5005029: Al bhd: btr expected after 2189 (t-strap). 1 **46**
9 Ran   Time 1m 0.43 (0.63)   Owned: Astrod TA Austin Stroud & Co   Trained: Pangbourne

2421   3.35 Listed Axminster Carpets Cathedral Stakes 3yo+ **(A)**
£20300 £7700 £3850   **6f str   Firm 08   +12 Fast**   Far side

1918+ **MOSS VALE** 22 [8] B W Hills 3-8-13 (112) M Hills 4/9 FAV: 163-4111: Cl-up, led 2f out, pushed out **114+**
ins fnl 1f, val bit more: well bckd at odds on: eff at 5/6f on firm & gd/soft grnd: in-form sprinter who easily
dealt with racing against older horses: open to more prog & can find a Group race: see 1918.
1732 **MAC LOVE** 30 [6] J Akehurst 3-8-9 (102) G Carter 8/1: 232-5422: Chsd ldrs, chsd wnr bef 1f out, ¾ **107**
styd on ins fnl 1f, al held: clr rem: smart run, met a high-class rival: see 1732.
2022 **KINGS POINT** 18 [4] R Hannon 3-8-9 (99) Dane O'Neill 12/1: 116-5053: Rear, prog bef 1f out, no 3½ **97**
impress on front 2: appreciated drop back to 6f & not disgraced at today's weights: see 1040.
2068 **BALI ROYAL** 15 [5] M S Saunders 6-8-12 (104) R Miles 8/1: 22124-64: Handy till dist, wknd: see 2068. 3 **83**
2256 **LITTLE EDWARD** 8 [2]6-9-3 (94) T Quinn 28/1: 5-505005: Keen rear, prog when short of room dist, ¾ **86**
not recover: shade closer with clr run: btr 1845 (h'cap).
2206 **REPERTORY** 9 [3]11-9-10 (102) T G McLaughlin 33/1: 10-00006: Led 4f, sn wknd: see 2206. 2 **87**
2068 **FROMSONG** 15 [9]6-9-3 (99) R Hughes 12/1: 0-244447: Mid-div over 4f, sn wknd: btr 2068. ½ **79**
      LIVE WIRE LUCY 151 [7]3-8-4 T P Queally 50/1: 3155-038: b f King of The Heap - Approach The 8 **52**
Bench (Majestic Light) Al in rear: long abs & Brit bow, ex American, earlier plcd (1m4f, firm): wnr at Calder in
late '03 (8.4f, firm): with C Tinkler.
8 Ran   Time 1m 11.85 (u 0.25)   Owned: Mr John C Grant   Trained: Lambourn

2422   4.10 Totesport Com 'city Bowl' Handicap Fillies 3yo+ 0-80 **(D)**
£7098 £2184 £1092   **1m4f   Firm 08   -02 Slow**   Stands side   **[91]**

2134+ **SELEBELA** 12 [3] L M Cumani 3-9-5 (82) J Murtagh 4/6 FAV: 605-0111: Made all, pushed clr ins fnl **98+**
2f, val 7L+: well bckd at odds on: eff around 12f on firm, gd grnd & prob soft: v progressive performer who likes
to dominate: fine eff out of own age group & fill List company may now suit: see 2134 & 1967.
2293 **ANYHOW** 5 [5] Miss K M George 7-8-13 (61) D Nolan(3) 9/2: 5421532: Rear, prog to chase ldr ins fnl 4 **67**
2f, kept on but al held: qck reapp: running well, met a most prog rival: see 2293.
2067 **DESERT ISLAND DISC** 15 [2] J J Bridger 7-9-11 (73) J F McDonald(3) 5/1: 30-04403: Keen handy, prog 2½ **74**
to chase wnr bef 1f out, no extra dist: op 7/2: clr rem: btr 1381.
1986 **RIBBONS AND BOWS** 19 [4] C A Cyzer 4-9-3 (65) L Dettori 8/1: 600-0604: Al in rear: see 1721. 7 **57**
      LATIN QUEEN 359 [1]4-8-7 (55) S Hitchcott(3) 50/1: 06/000-5: b f Desert Prince - Atlantic Dream 7 **37**
(Muscovite) Cl-up 9f, sn hung right & fdd: reapp & Brit bow: ex Irish, unplcd in all 5 starts to date.
5 Ran   Time 2m 33.31 (1.31)   Owned: Scuderia Rencati Srl   Trained: Newmarket

2423   4.40 Axminster Carpets Apprentice Handicap Stakes 3yo 0-70 **(E)**
£3744 £1152 £576   **1m str   Firm 08   -26 Slow**   Far side   **[77]**

1260 **ALFRIDINI** 55 [14] D R C Elsworth 3-9-7 (70) L Keniry 12/1: 0221401: Cl-up, led 2f out, rdn out **76**
to hold on: eff at 7/10f on firm grnd & polytrack: acts on a stiff/gall or sharp trk: see 817.
1511 **CAPTAIN MARRYAT** 41 [15] P W Harris 3-8-8 (57) T P Queally 6/1: 0-202: Chsd ldrs, short of room ½ **63+**
2f out, styd on to chase wnr ins fnl 1f, post came to sn: 6 wk abs & h'cap bow: eff at 1m on firm & gd/soft grnd:
prob wnr with clr run, unexposed 3yo who can find similar: see 1100.
2013 **FUEL CELL** 18 [7] R Hannon 3-9-2 (65) P Gallagher(5) 11/2: 0033: Rear, prog 3f out, styd on ins 1 **68**
fnl 1f: op 7/1, clr rem: eff at 1m on fast & firm, will apprec rtn to 9f: reportedly lost a shoe.
2127 **CHARLIE TANGO** 12 [4] M R Channon 3-8-13 (62) S Hitchcott 8/1: 3000304: Mid-div, no impress dist. 5 **56**
2261 **PREGNANT PAUSE** 7 [13]3-9-1 (64) J D Walsh(7) 16/1: 402-4045: Nvr nrr than mid-div: qck reapp. ¾ **56**
1976 **REDI** 19 [12]3-9-5 (68) N Mackay 4/1 FAV: 4054-046: Mid-div, no impress dist: btr 1976. ¾ **58**
2134 **THREE WELSHMEN** 12 [11]3-8-8 bl (57) A Beech 20/1: 0051307: Cl-up over 6f, sn wknd: btr 1577. nk **46**
1983 **JOY AND PAIN** 19 [5]3-9-4 (67) A Quinn(3) 11/2: 6016238: Prom over 6f, sn wknd: btr 1983. 3½ **49**
2098 **NINE RED** 13 [3]3-8-9 (58) K May(7) 14/1: 5550-009: Led 6f, sn fdd: see 2098. 2½ **35**
1940 **VENETIAN ROMANCE** 21 [10]3-7-12 (2oh)p (45) Hayley Turner(3) 33/1: 305-5000: 10th: Cl-up 6f, fdd. 3 **18**
783 **BIENHEUREUX** 103 [8]3-7-12 (7oh) (40) Lisa Jones 25/1: 00-0000: 11th: Mid-div till halfway, wknd. 1 **16**
2072 **COURT CHANCELLOR** 15 [2]3-8-1 VIS (50) B Swarbrick(5) 66/1: 000-00: 12th: Al bhd: 1st time visor. 1 **17**
1778 **LADY REDERA** 29 [6]3-8-6 (55) B O'Neill(7) 33/1: 5400-00: 13th: Bhd, nvr a factor. shd **21**
1982 **KITLEY** 19 [9]3-8-13 (62) R Miles 7/1: 643-0060: 14th: Chsd ldrs 6f, fdd: too keen. 4 **20**
14 Ran   Time 1m 41.82(2.72)   Owned: Mr A Heaney   Trained: Whitsbury

---

DONCASTER   SUNDAY 13.06.04   Lefthand, Flat, Galloping Track

Official Going FIRM (GOOD/FIRM IN PLACES)

2424   2.20 E B F Amateur Jockeys Association Charity Raceday Median Auction Maiden Stakes 2yo **(E)**
£3650 £1123 £562   **6f str   Good/Firm 40   -30 Slow**   Stands side

1687 **FIEFDOM** 32 [17] M Johnston 2-9-0 K Dalgleish 10/11 FAV: 541: Led after 2f, hung left under **86**
press ins fnl 2f, all out: well bckd: eff at 6f on fast & gd/soft grnd: acts on a gall trk: see 1687.
2158 **MOZAFIN** 11 [4] M R Channon 2-9-0 T E Durcan 16/1: 62: b c Zafonic - Bedara (Barathea) Handy, shd **85**
prog & ev ch ins fnl 1f, just held by wnr: March first foal, cost 58,000gns: dam wnr at 11f: sire Gr 1 wnr at 1m:
eff at 6f, will apprec further: stepped up on debut eff with a gd performance, find similar.

QUEUE UP 0 [14] J G Given 2-9-0 M Fenton 12/1: 3: b c Royal Applause - Faraway Lass (Distant   *3* **76**
Relative) Cl-up, no extra ins fnl 1f: debut: Feb foal, half-brother 5f wnr: dam won numerous times at 6f: sire
Gr 1 winning sprinter: eff at 6f on fast grnd: encouraging eff & can rate higher with experience.

GOLDEN FURY 0 [8] J L Dunlop 2-9-0 K Darley 13/2: 4: ch c Cadeaux Genereux - Galaxie Dust   *2½* **68**
(Blushing Groom) Rear, prog halfway, no impress dist: debut: Feb foal, half-brother to a 7/10f wnr: dam 6f wnr at
2: sire decent performer at sprint dists: sharper for today.

DOVER STREET 0 [12]2-9-0 Paul Eddery 14/1: 5: Rear, prog halfway, no impress fnl 2f: debut.   *3½* **57**

1795 **SKIPPIT JOHN 27** [5]2-9-0 Dean McKeown 25/1: 266: Handy till 2f out, sn no extra: btr 1632 (5f).   *nk* **56**

1987 **KANAD 19** [1]2-9-0 t R Hills 9/2: 327: Cl-up 4f, sn wknd: btr 1987 (5f).   *nk* **55**

2039 **FOREST VIKING 16** [9]2-9-0 T Eaves(3) 50/1: 58: Led 2f, fdd fnl 2f: see 2039.   *1* **52**

MR MAXIM 0 [7]2-9-0 V Halliday 50/1: 9: Mid-div, outpcd halfway, modest late gains on debut.   *nk* **51**

KING OF BLUES 0 [13]2-9-0 E Ahern 16/1: 0: 10th: Nvr nrr than mid-div.   *¾* **49**

2236 **SLATE GREY 8** [11]2-9-0 Darren Williams 66/1: 00: 11th: Al in rear.   *hd* **48**

1439 Danehill Angel 45 [10]2-8-9 G Gibbons 50/1:0   1780 **Northern Revoque 28** [6]2-8-9 P Mathers(7) 100/1:0

2178 Eminence Gift 10 [15]2-8-9 T Hamilton(3) 50/1:0   **Detroit Dancer 0** [16]2-9-0 N Callan 40/1:0

1779 Lady Indiana 28 [3]2-8-9 L Enstone(3) 100/1:0   1779 **La Bella Rosa 28** [2]2-8-9 A Reilly(7) 100/1:0

17 Ran Time 1m 15.02 (4.22) Owned: Sheikh Mohammed Trained: Middleham

---

2425 2.50 S P Bell Private Client Stockbrokers Rated Stakes Handicap 3yo+ 0-85 (D)   **[86]**
£5736 £1765 £883 **1m str** **Good/Firm 40** **+05 Fast** Stands side

2091+**ACE OF HEARTS 14** [8] C F Wall 5-9-11 (83) S Sanders 3/1: 2-050211: Handy, styd on to lead dist,   **93+**
pushed clr, val further: tchd 4/1: eff at 7f/1m, stays 10f well: acts on firm, soft grnd & both AWs: confidence
sky high at present & hat-trick surely awaits: see 2091.

2160 **DISTANT COUNTRY 11** [2] Mrs J R Ramsden 5-8-13 p (71) S Whitworth 13/2: 4-660252: Slow away, prog *3* **73**
3f out, chsd wnr ins fnl 1f, al held: not disgraced on return to 1m, but poss not straightforward: see 2010.

2057 **SARRAAF 16** [7] J S Goldie 8-8-13 (71) K Darley 12/1: 3250533: Mid-div, prog 2f out, nrst fin.   *½* **72**

2207 **JAY GEES CHOICE 9** [4] M R Channon 4-9-12 (84) T E Durcan 6/1: 0-600304: Handy till dist, no   *hd* **84**
extra: will apprec return to 7f: btr 2076.

1970* **ATLANTIC QUEST 20** [5]5-9-10 p (82) P Mulrennan(5) 11/4 FAV: 0-050015: Nvr nrr than mid-div: bckd *2½* **77**
tho' op 7/2: v disappointing on return to 1m: btr 1970 (7f).

2242 **NUIT SOMBRE 8** [6]4-9-4 (76) K Dalgleish 11/2: 600-0546: Led, hdd bef 1f out, sn fdd: disapp   *5* **61**
effort & poss went off too fast: ran with encouragement in 2242.

1927 **KEEPERS LODGE 22** [3]3-8-0 (9oh) F Norton 50/1: 0504-407: Al in rear: btr 1587.   *2½* **49**

2317 **JORDANS ELECT 4** [1]4-9-1 (73) T Eaves(3) 15/2: 0-510148: Handy 6f, sn fdd: qck reapp: btr 2179. *2* **49**

8 Ran Time 1m 39.32 (2.82) Owned: Lady Stuttaford & Mr W G Bovill Trained: Newmarket

---

2426 3.25 Arena Leisure Proud To Be At Doncaster Classified Stakes 3yo 0-70 (E)
£3582 £1102 £551 **1m2f60y** **Good/Firm 40** **-06 Slow** Outside

1769 **LA PERSIANA 29** [2] W Jarvis 3-9-0 (75) W Ryan 1/1 FAV: 40-521: Cl-up, led 3f out, rdn out: well   **85**
bckd: eff at 1m, imprvd for step up to 10f: acts on fast: going the right way: see 1769.

2040 **MY PARIS 16** [1] K A Ryan 3-9-1 (73) N Callan 6/1: 0-322252: Cl-up, kept on ins fnl 1f, not pace *1¼* **83**
of wnr: op 7/1 at 7/9f, imprvd on step up to 10f: see 1784.

2283 **MAGIC AMIGO 5** [3] J R Jenkins 3-8-13 (71) K Darley 7/2: 20-21023: Mid-div, prog 2f out, hung *1¾* **78**
left & onepcd fnl 1f: qck reapp: again did little wrong: just btr 2283.

2024 **BEAUCHAMP STAR 18** [5] G A Butler 3-8-11 (72) E Ahern 11/2: 03204: Sn mid-div, chsd wnr 3f out, *1* **74**
no extra dist: clr rem: just btr 1527 (1m, soft).

1707 **CERTIFIABLE 31** [6]3-8-12 (70) J F Egan 8/1: 411505: Led, hdd 3f out, sn fdd: btr 934.   *11* **58**

1283 KALUSH 54 [4]3-8-12 (61) Dean McKeown 50/1: 6336-006: b g Makbul - The Lady Vanishes (Robin des *dist* **8**
Pins) Al in rear: 8 wk abs: plcd 4 times in '03 (mdns & sellers, rtd 69): eff at 6/7f on firm & soft grnd.
2 Jul'03 Catt 7fm 68- F:

6 Ran Time 2m 11.23 (4.83) Owned: Plantation Stud Trained: Newmarket

---

2427 4.00 John Gordon Chemists Stakes Handicap 3yo 0-95 (C)   **[102]**
£9750 £3000 £1500 **7f str** **Good/Firm 40** **+04 Fast** Stands side

1825* **WARDEN COMPLEX 26** [4] J R Fanshawe 3-8-9 (83) O Urbina 13/8 FAV: 3-3211: Rear, prog when struck **90**
on hd by rivals whip 2f out, rdn out: well bckd: eff at 6/7f, 1m will suit: acts on fast,
gd/soft grnd & polytrack: progressive, more to come: see 1825.

1881 **FLIPANDO 23** [5] T D Barron 3-8-7 (77) P Hanagan 13/2: 310-422: Cl-up, led 3f out, hdd 1f out, *shd* **84**
kept on ins fnl 1f, just held: eff at 6f, enjoyed step up to 7f: game, deserves to find similar: see 1881.

2155 **PRIMO WAY 11** [1] B W Hills 3-8-7 (81) R Hills 10/1: 435-1363: Rear, prog halfway, ev ch dist, *½* **87**
kept on ins fnl 1f, just held: clr rem: eff at 6f, imprvd for step up to 7f: see 1734.

1933 **MOLCON 22** [7] N A Callaghan 3-8-9 (83) E Ahern 7/1: 50-51534: Handy, short of room 2f out, sn no *6* **77**
extra: op 5/1: below form on step up in trip: btr 1933 (6f).

1665 MRS MOH 33 [8]3-8-3 (77) D Allan(2) 33/1: 2032-005: b f Orpen - My Gray (Danehill) Keen in tch *nk* **70**
5f, sn wknd: fills auct mdn wnr first time out in '03 (also plcd 4 times): prev eff at 5f, stays a gall 7f well on
fast, gd grnd & fibresand: has gone well fresh.
2 Nov'03 Donc 7gd 83-85 D: 2 Sep'03 Donc 6gd 81-(72) B: 2 Sep'03 Donc 6.5gd 78-72 B: 1 Jun'03 Sout 5af 76a- F:

3513} BALTIC WAVE 308 [3]3-9-7 (95) P Makin(5) 18/1: 12144-6: b g Polish Precedent - Flourish (Selkirk) *½* **87**
Handy 5f, sn wknd: reapp: mdn i stks wnr in '03: eff at 5/6f on gd & fast grnd: has run well fresh & acts on a
gall or sharp trk: useful last term: gelded since last term: with H Morrison.
1 Jul'03 Donc 6gd 95- C: 2 Jun'03 Beve 5g/f 86- B: 1 Apr'03 Ripo 5g/f 78- D:

2040 **GRANSTON 16** [9]3-8-3 (77) C Catlin 8/1: 01-31667: Led, hdd 6f out, wknd fnl 2f: btr 1176.   *1¾* **66**

2212 **OVERDRAWN 9** [11]3-8-13 BL (87) G Duffield 7/1: 15-00008: Slow away, al bhd: first time blnks. *½* **75**

2166 **POPPYS FOOTPRINT 11** [10]3-8-2 (76) P Fessey 9/1: 0005349: Slow away, al bhd: btr 1879.   *3* **58**

2040 **INCHLOSS 16** [6]3-8-3 (77) G Gibbons 25/1: 041200: 10th: Led 6f out, hdd after 4f, fdd fnl 2f. *nk* **58**

DONCASTER SUNDAY 13.06.04 Lefthand, Flat, Galloping Track

10 Ran   Time 1m 25.75 (2.55)   Owned: Park Farm Racing   Trained: Newmarket

2428
4.30 Jobs@Pertemps Median Auction Maiden Stakes 3-4yo (E)
£3611 £1111 £556   **6f str**   **Good/Firm 40**   **-21 Slow**   Stands side

5032} **KHALIDIA 218** [6] M A Magnusson 3-8-13 E Ahern 9/2: 0-1: b c Boundary - Maniches Slew (Slew O'   73
Gold) Cl-up, rdn out to lead cl-home: op 7/2 on reapp: unplcd sole '03 start (rtd 63, mdn): eff at 6f, shld
apprec further: acts on fast grnd & a gall trk: goes well fresh.
2104 **FLYING BANTAM 13** [14] R A Fahey 3-8-13 (70) P Hanagan 4/5 FAV: 2503-222: Al hung left in lead,   hd   71
hdd under press cl home: another plcd effort & worth try in headgear: see 2104.
       BOLD BUNNY 0 [12] S C Williams 3-8-8 Dale Gibson 20/1: 3: b f Piccolo - Bold And Beautiful   2   61
(Bold Lady) Dwelt, prog after 2f, styd on ins fnl 1f: debut: eff at 6f, shld apprec further: acts on fast grnd.
2117 **CHATSHOW 13** [8] L A Dace 3-8-13 A Culhane 20/1: 6-004: Bhd, prog halfway, no impress fnl 1f.   2½   58
2237 **ROAN RAIDER 8** [3]4-9-7 P (49) L Fletcher(3) 8/1: 0340535: Handy till dist, sn no extra: see 2237.   1   55
5014} **COMIC TALES 220** [7]3-8-13 S Righton 50/1: 0-6: b g Mind Games - Glorious Aragon (Aragon) Slow   3   46
away, nvr nrr than mid-div on reapp: unplcd sole '03 start (rtd 14): with M Mullineaux.
3691} **WONDER WOLF 300** [13]3-8-8 T Hamilton(3) 20/1: 0-7: Nvr nrr than mid-div on reapp.   shd   40
1146 **AGUILERA 62** [15]3-8-8 L Enstone(3) 50/1: 00-08: Cl-up till dist, wknd.   ½   38
1216 **RAGAZZI 58** [9]3-8-13 K Darley 9/1: 09: Keen cl-up, sn outpcd, modest late gains.   1¾   38
2182 **DESIGNER CITY 10** [4]3-8-8 (50) P Bradley(5) 20/1: 4660-000: 10th: Handy till halfway, wknd.   1   30
1222 **Blue Emperor 57** [2]3-8-13 (52) G Parkin 25/1:0   2237 **Trinaree 8** [1]3-8-13 C Catlin 50/1:0
2169 **Cottam Karminski 11** [11]3-8-8 P M Quinn 33/1:0   4751} **Oniz Tiptoes 242** [5]3-8-13 T Eaves(3) 50/1:0
14 Ran   Time 1m 14.46 (3.66)   Owned: East Wind Racing Ltd   Trained: Upper Lambourn

2429
5.00 Littlewoods Bet Direct Stakes Handicap Fillies 3yo+ 0-85 (D)   **[85]**
£5574 £1715 £858   **5f str**   **Good/Firm 40**   **-06 Slow**   Stands side

2084 **FRASCATI 15** [11] A Berry 4-8-13 (70) F Lynch 6/1: 4102301: Handy, styd on to lead dist, rdn out: 81
eff at 5f on firm, gd/soft & fibresand: capable performer: see 1749 & 1627.
1867 **CERULEAN ROSE 24** [1] A W Carroll 5-8-10 (67) A Culhane 5/1: 1135-402: Rear, prog 2f out, styd on   1¼   73
ins fnl 1f, not pace of wnr: fine run: see 1615.
2062* **LADY PROTECTOR 15** [9] J Balding 5-7-12 (55) Dale Gibson 6/1: 3000113: Bhd, prog 2f out, onepcd   ½   59
when short of room ins fnl 1f: not disgraced on hat-trick bid: see 2062 & 1873.
2232 **COLLEGE QUEEN 8** [6] S Gollings 6-8-8 p (65) C Catlin 12/1: 400-0654: Handy, ev ch dist, sn no extra.   1   66
4304} **LE MERIDIEN 270** [3]6-7-12 (55) P M Quinn 33/1: 400000-5: ch f Magical Wonder - Dutch Queen   nk   55
(Ahonoora) Rear, prog 2f out, modest late gains: reapp: fills h'cap wnr in '03: appr h'cap wnr in '02: stays 6f,
suited by stiff 5f on firm & soft grnd: suited by visor or t-strap: on winning mark for Beverley.
1 Jun'03 Beve 5g/f 64-58 E: 2 Aug'02 Yarm 7fm 60-59 D: 2 Jun'02 Hami 5sft 60-58 E: 1 Jun'02 Beve 5g/f 61-58 F:
1 Aug'01 Beve 5g/f 58- D:
2214 **BETTYS PRIDE 9** [2]5-7-13 (56) P Hanagan 11/1: 600-0406: Slow away, nvr nrr than mid-div: btr 1973.   1¾   51
2240 **DANI RIDGE 8** [10]6-10-0 (85) E Ahern 7/1: 00030-47: Handy, short of room dist, sn wknd: btr 2240.   nk   79
2266 **LADY PEKAN 6** [7]5-8-5 bl (62) J Bramhill 14/1: 0035308: Led after 1f, hung right & hdd dist, sn fdd.   1¾   51
2093 **SAFRANINE 14** [4]7-8-6 p (63) Ann Stokell 25/1: 0000009: Handy, wknd bef 1f out.   nk   51
2082 **ROSES OF SPRING 15** [8]6-9-11 p (82) P Makin(5) 7/1: 100-0300: 10th: Handy over halfway, wknd: btr 1845.   55
10 Ran   Time 1m 0.54(2.34)   Owned: Lord Crawshaw   Trained: Cockerham

BRIGHTON MONDAY 14.06.04 Lefthand, V Sharp, Unulating Track

Official Going FIRM

2430
2.15 Llewellyn Rok Maiden Auction Stakes 2yo (F)
£2891 £826 £413   **5f59y rnd**   **Good/Firm**   **V Slow**   Inside

2257 **TALCEN GWYN 8** [2] M F Harris 2-8-10 J F Egan 100/30: 41: Made all, rcd centre over 1f out, kept   81
on, rdn out: imprvd from debut: eff at 5.3f on fast grnd & on a sharp/ undul trk: see 2257.
       CONNOTATION [4] P W D'Arcy 2-8-7 S Sanders 9/1: 2: b f Mujahid - Seven Wonders (Rahy) Handy,   1¾   72
eff to chase wnr over 1f out, onepace on debut: Feb first foal, cost 17,000: eff at 5.3f on fast: improve.
1981 **RIDE SAFARI 20** [5] P Winkworth 2-8-7 P Doe 9/4 FAV: 45-0: b g Fraam - Vocation (Royal Academy)   1½   73
Slow away & bhd, eff dist, no impress: Apr foal, cost 11,000gns: half-brother to a 5f juv wnr: dam 7f wnr.
2194 **HES A STAR 1** [1] R Hannon 2-8-11 R L Moore 100/30: 04: ch c Mark of Esteem - Sahara Belle   3½   62
(Sanglamore) Sn chsd wnr, wknd over 1f out: Jan foal, cost 10,000gns: bred to stay 6f+ in time.
2257 **QUEENS GLORY 8** [3]2-8-4 R Miles(3) 7/2: 6265: Handy, wknd well over 1f out: btr 1937, 1640.   1¾   50
5 Ran   Time 1m 04.09 (4.09)   Owned: Mr D K Watkins   Trained: Banbury

2431
2.45 Friends Of The Elderly Charity Selling Stakes 3yo+ (G)
£2541 £726 £363   **7f214y rnd**   **Good/Firm**   **Fair**   Inside

1899 **SENIOR MINISTER 24** [2] P W Hiatt 6-9-5 (62) R Miles(3) 12/1: 03000-01: Made all, hung right &   58
gained stands side over 1f out, kept on, rdn out: no bid: eff at 5f, suited by this 1m: likes firm & fast grnd,
prob any trk: relished drop to the lowest grade: see 1899.
2288 **MR BELVEDERE 6** [8] R Hannon 3-8-8 (61) Dane O'Neill 5/1: 30-00032: Chsd ldrs, eff over 1f out,   2   54
kept on, not pace of wnr: fair run with cheek pieces discarded: stays 1m in sell grade: see 2288.
1966 **KELSEAS KOLBY 21** [5] P A Blockley 4-9-10 vis (55) I Mongan 7/1: 20-00143: Held up, hdwy to chase   nk   58$
wnr over 2f out, no extra ins last: stays 1m: see 1966, 1827.
2133 **PAPEETE 13** [6] W J Haggas 3-8-4 (10w)BL (70) T Quinn 9/4 FAV: 33100-44: In tch, rcd centre over   1   47

732

2f out, onepace: clmd for 6,000, well bckd: tried blnks & best kept to this grade: see 2133.
2332 **MARGERY DAW 4** [1]4-9-0 (50) R L Moore 15/2: 0063005: In tch, wknd 2f out. *3½* **39**
2032 **BUCHANAN STREET 18** [4]3-8-8 (49) S Whitworth 33/1: 0206-06: b c Barathea - Please Believe Me *1¼* **42**
(Try My Best) Al bhd: rnr-up in a nov stks in '03: poss eff at 6f on fast grnd. 2 Jul'03 Newm 6g/f 53- D:
2052 **CAL MAC 17** [3]5-9-5 P (70) E Ahern 5/1: 0034-007: In tch, hung left & wknd dist: cheek pieces. *4* **34**
1193 **SMART BOY PRINCE 60** [7]3-8-13 (60) S W Kelly 8/1: 1105038: Handy, hmpd over 4f out, sn bhd: abs. *6* **27**
2088 **TRUSTED INSTINCT 15** [9]4-9-5 (62) J F Egan 14/1: 10-00009: Chsd wnr over 3f out till wknd qckly *5* **12**
over 2f out, eased: see 714.
9 Ran Time 1m 36.61 (4.61) Owned: Mr Phil Kelly Trained: Banbury

2432

3.15 Totesport Com Handicap Stakes Fillies 3yo+ 0-70 (E) **[67]**
£3546 £1091 £546 **7f214y rnd** **Good/Firm** **Fair** Inside

2258* **A WOMAN IN LOVE 8** [8] Miss B Sanders 5-10-2 (6ex) (69) S Sanders 2/1 FAV: 640-6111: Keen held up, **79**
hdwy to lead over 1f out, styd on well, rdn out: eff over 7f/1m & likes firm grnd, acts on gd & polytrack, loves
Brighton (4 crse wins): can carry big weights: thriving & genuine mare, see 2258, 1941.
2147 **DAMI 12** [1] C E Brittain 3-9-4 P (68) D Holland 13/2: 4400-552: Prom, led over 4f out till over *1¼* **75**
1f out, not pace of wnr: encouraging run in first time cheek pieces: shld find a modest race: see 1956.
1913 **CASTAWAY QUEEN 23** [6] W R Muir 5-9-7 bl (60) B Doyle 8/1: 620-2003: In tch, hdwy 2f out, sn wknd. *2½* **62**
2292 **EVEN EASIER 6** [4] G L Moore 3-8-5 bl (55) R L Moore 5/2: 0050644: Held up, hdwy 2f out, sn wknd. *2½* **52**
2220 **TARKWA 10** [2]5-8-1 (40) M Henry 16/1: 0-601005: Handy, lost pl over 3f out, modest late gains. *shd* **36**
2153 **SUSIEDIL 12** [5]3-8-7 (57) E Ahern 8/1: 140-0066: Chsd ldrs, wknd well over 1f out: see 2153. *6* **41**
2153 **COCONUT COOKIE 12** [7]3-9-1 (65) P Dobbs 33/1: 200-007: ch f Bahamian Bounty - Spicy Manner *13* **23**
(Cryptoclearance) Handy, wknd 2f out: rnr-up in a mdn fill on first of 3 '03 starts: eff over a sharp 6f on fast.
2 Jul'03 Wind 6g/f 73- D:
2146 **FIGURA 12** [3]6-8-6 VIS (45) N Day 12/1: 6665008: Led till 4f out, wknd: visor: see 520 (polytrk). *7* **0**
8 Ran Time 1m 36.19 (4.19) Owned: High & Dry Racing Trained: Epsom

2433

3.45 Hardings Bar & Catering Services Classified Stakes 3yo+ 0-60 (F)
£2905 £830 £415 **1m1f209y** **Good/Firm** **Fair** Outside

2146* **KERNEL DOWERY 12** [1] P W Harris 4-9-3 e (58) D Holland 2/1 FAV: 43-00211: In tch, rdn to lead ent **67**
fnl 1f, styd on strongly: eff at 10f on firm, fast grnd & polytrack: suited by an eye-shield, handles a stiff/gall
or sharp/undul trk, likes Brighton: in fine form, see 2146.
2135 **KIRKHAM ABBEY 13** [2] M A Jarvis 4-9-8 vis (65) M Henry 9/2: 1011-032: Nvr far away, led 4f out *1½* **69**
till ent fnl 1f, kept on but not pace of wnr: clr of rem, op 7/2: imprvd again in defeat: see 2135 & 1895.
2018 **REBATE 19** [3] R Hannon 4-9-5 (62) P Dobbs 7/1: 0500033: Trkd ldr, left bhd by front 2 fnl 1f: see 2018. *5* **58**
2120 **SCRIPTORIUM 13** [6] L M Cumani 3-8-6 (1ow) (61) S Sanders 11/4: 0-6024: Held up, not pace to *½* **57**
chall: drifted from 2/1: did not handle this trk?: btr 2120 (gall trk).
2134 **CANADIAN STORM 13** [5]3-8-4 (60) F P Ferris(3) 9/1: 050-5045: Chsd ldrs, btn dist. *7* **45**
2047 **CHOCOLATE BOY 17** [7]5-9-3 (60) R L Moore 10/1: 4410256: Al rear, eased when btn fnl 1f: tchd *14* **25**
14/1: reportedly lost his action: much btr 1692.
2260 **PRINCE VALENTINE 8** [4]3-8-4 bl (58) T Quinn 33/1: 0-003547: Led till 4f out, wknd & eased, t.o.: *13* **7**
reportedly lost a shoe: see 2260.
7 Ran Time 2m 02.52 (4.72) Owned: The Treasure Hunters Trained: Berkhamsted

2434

4.15 Barking Brickwork Company Maiden Handicap Stakes 3yo 0-70 (E) **[73]**
£3533 £1087 £544 **6f209y rnd** **Good/Firm** **Fair** Inside

2248 **ALBADI 9** [2] C E Brittain 3-8-4 bl (49) Dean Williams(7) 12/1: 0-0001: b c Green Desert - Lyrist **54**
(Cozzene) Prom, went on ent fnl 1f, held on gamely & just prevailed: has contested major trk mdns to date & apprec
this big drop in grade: eff over a sharp/undul 7f on fast grnd: seems suited by blnks.
2016 **BAHAMA REEF 19** [7] B Gubby 3-8-10 (55) S Carson 12/1: 400-0052: Trkd ldrs, imprvd to lead dist, *hd* **59**
collared ent fnl 1f, rallied & only just btn: stays a sharp/undul 7f: see 2016 (AW).
1359 **GROWLER 51** [4] J L Dunlop 3-8-11 (56) E Ahern 20/1: 0000-03: ch g Foxhound - Femme Femme *nk* **59**
(Lyphard) Chsd ldrs, ev ch fnl 1f & just btn in a 3-way photo: 7 wk abs: only modest form to date, has been gelded
since last term: eff over a sharp/undul 7f on fast grnd: could find a modest event.
2218 **ABLAJ 10** [8] E A L Dunlop 3-8-8 vis (53) Dane O'Neill 4/1: 400-044: Mid-div, onepcd fnl 1f: see 2218. *2½* **51**
2292 **TURNBERRY 6** [3]3-8-10 vis (55) T Quinn 15/8 FAV: 4-436225: Rear, nvr nr to chall: bckd from 9/4: *1¾* **49**
becoming frustrating, rcd much more prominently in 2292.
1539 **RICKY MARTAN 41** [6]3-8-8 (53) S Whitworth 33/1: 4-000006: Held up, nvr nr ldrs: 6 wk abs. *½* **46**
2155 **GET TO THE POINT 12** [1]3-9-7 (66) S Sanders 11/4: 0225007: Chsd ldrs, rdn & btn 2f out: top-weight. *4* **51**
2193 **BLAISE WOOD 11** [5]3-9-6 BL (65) R L Moore 8/1: 6-068: Led till dist, wknd & eased: too keen in blnks. *6* **38**
8 Ran Time 1m 23.69 (3.89) Owned: Mr Saeed Manana Trained: Newmarket

2435

4.45 Racecourse Video Services Handicap Stakes 3yo 35-55 (F) **[61]**
£2898 £828 £414 **5f213y rnd** **Good/Firm** **Slow** Inside

2268 **ALIZAR 7** [4] S Dow 3-9-8 (55) R L Moore 10/1: 2360601: Nvr far away, went on fnl 1f, held on all **61**
out: earlier in gd form on the AW, trained by M Polglase to win a seller: eff at 5/6f on gd, firm & both AWs:
likes to run up with/force the pace & loves a sharp/undul trk: see 495 (AW seller).
1978 **RED MONARCH 20** [3] P A Blockley 3-9-5 (52) I Mongan 3/1 FAV: 00062: Led 2f, remained prom & *shd* **58**
regained lead briefly dist, ev ch fnl 1f & just btn in a thrilling fin: clrly apprec this drop back to a sharp/undul
6f, has tried 1m: acts on fast grnd: see 1787.
1985 **MALUTI 20** [5] R Guest 3-9-1 (48) S Sanders 4/1: 0006-063: Trkd ldrs, kept on fnl 1f. *1¼* **50**
1694 **SAVERNAKE BRAVE 33** [1] Mrs H Sweeting 3-8-13 (46) G Baker 7/1: 500-5204: Led after 2f till *2* **42**
collared dist, no extra: twice below 1374 (AW).
2271 **SUSSEX STYLE 7** [10]3-9-3 t (50) P Dobbs 33/1: 0606005: Rear, late prog, nvr dngrs. *½* **44**
1312* **LITTLE FLUTE 53** [7]3-8-13 (46) P Doe 6/1: 4000016: Chsd ldrs, onepcd fnl 1.5f: 8 wk abs. *shd* **39**

BRIGHTON MONDAY 14.06.04 Lefthand, V Sharp, Unulating Track

1985 **PARDON MOI 20** [11]3-9-1 (48) Lisa Jones(3) 7/1: 0041047: Nvr btr than mid-div. ½ **39**
2292 **JOHNNY ALLJAYS 6** [2]3-8-9 bl (42) Derek Nolan(7) 25/1: 000-0008: Rear, nvr nr ldrs: qck reapp. ¾ **31**
2243 **ASHSTANZA 9** [8]3-9-8 BL (55) M Henry 14/1: 4-434009: Al bhd in first time blnks. 2 **38**
2195 **PASS GO 11** [12]3-9-8 BL t (55) R Miles(3) 16/1: 3-0000: 10th: Keen & prom 4.5f, wknd: tried blnks. ¾ **36**
2292 **I WISH I KNEW 6** [6]3-8-12 vis (45) Dane O'Neill 12/1: 00-60000: 11th: Mid-div, btn 2f out: qck reapp. 2 **20**
1985 **SCARLETT BREEZE 20** [9]3-9-1 (48) S Whitworth 16/1: 0065-000: 12th: Prom wide, btn halfway. ½ **21**
12 Ran Time 1m 11.81(4.01) Owned: The Pink Punters Trained: Epsom

WARWICK MONDAY 14.06.04 Lefthand, Sharp, Turning Track

Official Going FIRM (GOOD/FIRM IN PLACES)

2436

6.45 Juhannus Apprentice Handicap Stakes 4yo+ 35-55 (F) **[63]**
£3066 £876 £438 **1m2f188y** **Firm 16** **-07 Slow** Inside

2260 **SHORT CHANGE 8** [2] A W Carroll 5-8-12 (47) R Thomas(3) 7/2 FAV: 222-0451: Led till over 2f out, rallied to lead again ins fnl 1f, edged right but kept on: op 5/1: eff at 10/12f on fm & gd/soft, likes Windsor. **52**
2176 **TRUSTED MOLE 11** [9] W M Brisbourne 6-9-6 (55) B Swarbrick(3) 7/1: 353-5162: Trkd ldrs, eff over 1f out, edged left & kept on ins fnl 1f: ran to winning form of 2112, see 1830. *shd* **59**
2273 **VANDENBERGHE 7** [7] J A Osborne 5-8-13 (48) T P Queally 4/1: 35-15343: Chsd ldrs, short of room ins last, kept on: op 6/1: handles firm, fast & fibresand: poss unlucky, see 1657. *shd* **51**
2038 **HOLLY ROSE 17** [12] D E Cantillon 5-9-3 p (52) Hayley Turner(3) 11/1: 00-02404: Rcd in 2nd, led over 2f out, hdd ins fnl 1f & no extra: eff at 7/11f: see 1267. ¾ **54**
2112 **GLEN VALE WALK 14** [5]7-8-12 bl (47) N Mackay 7/1: 4034-635: Rear, hdwy 1f out, not pace to chall. 1¼ **47**
1954 **THEATRE LADY 21** [1]6-8-10 (45) D Tudhope(5) 13/2: 3043566: Mid-div, onepcd ins fnl 1f: see 539. *hd* **44**
1800 **BEN KENOBI 28** [4]6-8-6 (41) D Corby 16/1: 100-5227: Rear, nvr a factor: see 1676. 2½ **36**
1712 **RYANS BLISS 32** [3]4-8-9 (44) J P Guillambert 16/1: 0025328: Handy, onepcd fnl 1f: see 970. *shd* **38**
2157 **PRIVATE SEAL 12** [6]9-8-6 t (41) M Halford(7) 25/1: 0205009: Rear, nvr a factor: see 539. 1¾ **32**
1940 **FAIRLAND 22** [11]5-9-0 (49) L Smith(7) 10/1: 0/040-340: 10th: Bhd, some hdwy 3f out, wknd: see 1940. 1½ **38**
777 **MANIKATO 105** [10]10-8-1 (10oh) (25) Kirby Harris 66/1: 660-0000: 11th: b g Clever Trick - Pasampsi (Crow) Handy, wknd over 2f out: jumps fit (sell hdle, p.u.): rnr-up in a h'cap in '03 (with R Curtis): rnr-up in a h'cap in '02: eff at 7/12f on firm, gd/soft & fibresand, without visor: tried cheekpieces/t-strap. ¾ **24**
2 May'03 Brig 9.9g/f 34-31 F: 2 Apr'02 Brig 11.8fm 37-35 F:
REGAL FANTASY 331 [8]4-8-5 (40) Stacey Renwick(7) 20/1: 0050/00-0: 12th: b f King's Theatre - Threesome (Seattle Dancer) Rear, wknd 2f out: long abs, Brit bow: unplcd both '03 starts in native Ireland (h'caps): unplcd in '02 (mdns, nurs): with P Blockley. 6 **19**
12 Ran Time 2m 18.76 (2.56) Owned: Mr Dennis Deacon Trained: Alcester

2437

7.15 E B F Maiden Stakes Fillies 2yo (D)
£5470 £1683 £842 **5f rnd** **Firm 16** **-16 Slow** Inside

2061 **KISSING LIGHTS 16** [2] M L W Bell 2-8-11 K Fallon 10/11 FAV: 51: b f Machiavellian - Nasaieb (Fairy King) Rcd in 2nd, led over 1f out & went clr: bckd from 2/1: cost 110,000gns: first foal, dam 5f juv wnr: half-sister to smart 6/7f juv wnr Raise A Grand: improved from debut back at 5f on firm. **90**
BORN FOR DANCING 0 [1] B W Hills 2-8-11 M Hills 5/1: 2: b f Fasliyev - Fancy Boots (Salt Dome) Trkd ldrs & keen, hdwy into 2nd 1f out, sn onepcd on debut: clr of rem: speedily bred, 5th foal: cost E45,000: dam styd 1m: fair start, learn from this. 5 **75**
VONDOVA 0 [6] R Hannon 2-8-11 R Hughes 12/1: 3: b f Efisio - Well Proud (Sadler's Wells) In tch, hdwy over 1f out, not pace to chall on debut: 5th foal, half-sister to 7f 3yo wnr Michael Maher. 3 **66**
2132 **MISS COTSWOLD LADY 13** [5] A W Carroll 2-8-11 J Quinn 66/1: 54: Chsd ldrs, wknd ins fnl 1f. ¾ **64**
2097 **XEERAN 14** [4]2-8-11 P Robinson 2/1: 55: Led over 3f, no extra ins fnl 1f: see 2097. 2½ **56**
INAGH 0 [3]2-8-11 D Corby(3) 33/1: 6: Al bhd on debut. 6 **38**
6 Ran Time 58.91s (1.61) Owned: Mr M B Hawtin Trained: Newmarket

2438

7.45 Pricewaterhousecoopers Classified Stakes 3yo+ 0-80 (D)
£5616 £1728 £864 **7f26y rnd** **Firm 16** **-07 Slow** Inside

2184 **PAWAN 11** [1] Miss A Stokell 4-9-4 (63) Ann Stokell 13/8: 3530201: Rcd in 2nd till led over 1f out, hdd ins fnl 1f, rallied to lead again fnl stride: first win: eff btwn 6/7f on firm, soft & fibresand. **70**
2092 **BARONS SPY 15** [3] A W Carroll 3-8-8 (66) M Hills 1/1 FAV: 00-42: Handy, hdwy to lead ins fnl 1f, hdd fnl stride: clr of rem: stays 7f on firm: see 2092. *shd* **69**
2154 **SOPHRANO 12** [5] P A Blockley 4-9-4 (63) S Yourston(7) 9/1: 00620-53: Led over 5f, no extra fnl 1f. 5 **59**
2186 **TELEPATHIC 11** [4] A Berry 4-9-4 (59) P Bradley(5) 10/1: 0060004: Bhd, nvr a factor: see 1218. 2 **55**
4 Ran Time 1m 24.02 (1.62) Owned: Ms Caron Stokell Trained: Richmond

2439

8.15 Wragge & Co Handicap Stakes Fillies 3yo 35-55 (F) **[61]**
£3304 £944 £472 **6f21y rnd** **Firm 16** **+16 Fast** Inside

2181 **WENDYS GIRL 11** [1] R P Elliott 3-9-3 bl (50) S Chin 9/1: 052P401: With ldr, led over 2f out, rdn out ins fnl 1f: fast time: eff at 5/6f, tried 7f: acts on firm, gd & fibresand: first win: see 835. **63**
1985 **MISS JUDGEMENT 20** [11] W R Muir 3-9-6 (53) F Norton 13/2: 0006-532: Led till over 4f out, styd on ins fnl 1f: clr of rem: handles firm & fast: see 1985. 1¾ **61**
2292 **YAMATO PINK 6** [3] Mrs H Sweeting 3-9-5 (52) L Fletcher(3) 5/1: 60-01253: Outpcd & bhd, hdwy over 1f out, not pace to reach ldrs: qck reapp: see 1985 & 1453. 2½ **52**
2118 **DANIFAH 14** [2] P D Evans 3-9-0 (47) B Swarbrick(5) 7/1: 00-00004: Handy, no impress fnl 1f: see 2118. *shd* **46**
1798 **BREEZIT 28** [13]3-9-5 (52) J Bramhill 15/2: 0300-445: Chsd ldrs, onepcd over 1f out: see 1242. 1¾ **46**
2075 **OPEN MIND 16** [5]3-9-3 (50) T E Durcan 12/1: 040-4306: Rear, some late gains: see 1509. ½ **42**

1575 **INDIAN LILY 39** [8]3-9-8 (55) J Quinn 4/1 FAV: 5067: ch f Compton Place - Princess Lily   *shd* 46
(Blakeney) Handy, wknd over 1f out: h'cap bow: unplcd all earlier starts (mdns): reportedly did not handle bend.
2133 **RED ROCKY 13** [10]3-9-1 P (48) Stephanie Hollinshead(5) 40/1: 655-0058: Keen & handy, lost pl 4f   *1*   36
out, sn btn: first time cheek pieces: see 2133.
1963 **QUEEN OF BULGARIA 21** [9]3-9-3 (50) R Price 20/1: 02-00009: With ldrs, led over 4f out till over 2f out.   *1½* 33
901   **ZONNEBEKE 83** [12]3-9-3 (50) D Sweeney 14/1: 4520300: 10th: Nvr a factor: long abs: see 535.   *1¼* 29
4844} **BERRY RACER 236** [6]3-9-3 (50) T G McLaughlin 25/1: 00305-0: 11th: ch f Titus Livius - Opening   *1¾* 24
Day (Day Is Done) Handy, wknd over 1f out: abs: 3rd 1 of 5 '03 starts (mdn, rtd 55, with R Smith).
1374 **MOSCOW MARY 49** [4]3-9-8 (55) P Gallagher(7) 11/1: 3240-000: 12th: Rear, nvr nr ldrs: 7 wk abs.   *1¼* 25
1903 **JAILBIRD 24** [7]3-9-8 VIS (55) T P Queally(3) 40/1: 505-00: 13th: Al bhd: tried visor: see 1903.   *1½* 20
13 Ran   Time 1m 10.56 (u0.04)   Owned: Mr E Grayson   Trained: Formby

| **2440** | 8.45 Kpmg Handicap Stakes 3yo+ 35-55 (F) | | **[55]** |
| | £3822 £1092 £546   **1m22y rnd**   **Firm 16**   **-02 Slow**   Inside | |

4158} **HOLLYWOOD HENRY 278** [8] J Akehurst 4-9-13 P (54) J Quinn 12/1: 000000-1: b g Bahhare - Takeshi   58
(Cadeaux Genereux) Rear, hdwy over 1f out, rdn & kept on well ins fnl 1f to lead nr fin: reapp: unplcd in '03
(h'caps, rtd 63): mdn rnr-up in '02 (with B Hills): eff btwn 7f/1m on firm & soft, acts on a gall or sharp/turning
trk: tried blnks & t-strap, imprvd for fitting of cheek pieces: first win. 2 Jun'02 Newm 7fm 81- D:
2397 **TREETOPS HOTEL 2** [1] B R Johnson 5-9-13 (54) D Sweeney 12/1: 00-20002: Bhd, hdwy 3f out, ev ch   *hd* 57
ins fnl 1f, kept on nr fin: qck reapp: handles firm, gd/soft & polytrack: see 520.
1992 **TOJONESKI 20** [16] I W McInnes 5-9-4 p (45) J F McDonald(3) 12/1: 3422233: Chsd ldrs, led over 1f   *shd* 47
out, hdd nr fin: handles firm, hvy & fibresand: see 830.
1273 **PACIFIC OCEAN 55** [11] Mrs Stef Liddiard 5-9-11 t (52) F Norton 20/1: 4-233604: Rear, hdwy 1f out,   *¾*   52
kept on: 8 wk abs: handles firm & fibresand: see 509 & 199.
1927 **TUSCARORA 23** [15]5-9-11 (52) M Hills 7/1: 6406-005: Mid-div, hdwy & ev ch over 1f out, sn no extra.   *1¼* 49
669   **BALMACARA 117** [12]5-9-6 (47) T P Queally(3) 40/1: 0554-006: b f Lake Coniston - Diabaig   *2*   40
(Precocious) Rear, hdwy over 1f out, not pace to chall: long abs: rnr-up in a fill h'cap & an auct mdn in '03:
3rd in 2 h'caps in '02 (rtd 54 at best): eff at 5/6f, stays a sharp 1m: handles polytrack & fast, gall or sharp
trks: has tried blnks & cheek pieces: mdn. 2 Jun'03 Donc 7g/f 50-49 E: 2 Jan'03 Ling 8ap 60a- E:
2334* **LONDONER 4** [13]6-10-6 (6ex) (61) R Hughes 7/2 J FAV: 0032217: Chsd ldrs, no impress ins fnl 1f.   *nk* 53
2324 **SHAMWARI FIRE 5** [2]4-9-10 (51) L Vickers 16/1: 4600168: Handy, wknd fnl 1f: qck reapp.   *shd* 42
2402 **DUBONAI 2** [9]4-9-8 (49) K Fallon 7/2 J FAV: 230-0039: Bhd, hdwy 1f out, no extra ins fnl 1f: qck reapp.   *1½* 37
1535 **BOJANGLES 41** [3]5-9-7 (48) D Nolan(3) 9/2: 00-00130: 10th: Led till over 1f out, no extra ins fnl 1f.   *1½* 33
1262 **JAMESTOWN 56** [5]7-9-6 (47) L Fletcher(3) 33/1: 0000040: 11th: Al bhd: 8 wk abs: see 221.   *nk* 31
2120 **ASH LADDIE 13** [4]4-9-12 P (53) T E Durcan 40/1: 0/050-000: 12th: ch g Ashkalani - Lady Ellen   *3*   31
(Horage) Al bhd: h'cap/mdn unplcd in '03 (rtd 68): unplcd '02 (sole start, rtd 67, mdn): first time cheek pieces.
2402 **ZAMYATINA 2** [7]5-9-6 (47) J Bramhill 28/1: 000-0000: 13th: Handy, wknd over 1f out: qck reapp.   *1*   23
2369 **CHICKASAW TRAIL 3** [6]6-9-2 VIS (48) Stephanie Hollinshead(5) 25/1: 6510500: 14th: Al bhd: visor.   *1*   17
1778 **MADAME MARIE 30** [17]4-9-9 (50) W Ryan 16/1: 003-0020: 15th: Al bhd: see 1778.   *shd* 23
2201 **BLESSED PLACE 10** [10]4-9-4 (45) P McCabe 100/1: 0-000000: 16th: Keen in rear, hdwy 6f out, wkng   *15* 0
when not much room over 1f out: see 2201.
1972 **SOFT MIST 21** [14]4-9-10 (51) B Swarbrick(5) 33/1: 0-600000: 17th: Handy, wknd over 3f out.   *6*   0
17 Ran   Time 1m 38.28 (1.48)   Owned: Lonwin Partnership   Trained: Epsom

| **2441** | 9.15 Eversheds Maiden Stakes 3yo+ (D) | |
| | £3819 £1175 £588   **1m4f134y**   **Firm 16**   **-04 Slow**   Inside | |

2113 **HORNER 14** [5] P F I Cole 3-8-7 (80) J Quinn 11/10 FAV: 446-0421: Handy, hdwy to lead 5f out, clr   86
& eased ins fnl 1f: suited by 11.6/12.5f on fm & gd, acts on a sharp/ turning trk: shld stay further.
1384 **LEVITATOR 49** [4] Sir Michael Stoute 3-8-7 K Fallon 13/2: 0-02: b c Sadler's Wells - Cantilever   *7*   72
(Sanglamore) Chsd ldrs, outpcd by wnr 3f out: 7 wk abs: unplcd sole '03 start (mdn, rtd 73).
1936 **WATER TAXI 23** [2] R Charlton 3-8-7 R Hughes 15/8: 433: Led to 7f out, no extra 3f out: see 1936.   *shd* 71
4974} **FOUR PENCE 226** [3] B W Hills 3-8-7 M Hills 8/1: 40-4: b c Rainbow Quest - American Queen (Fairy   *9*   57
King) Bhd, nvr a factor: reapp: 4th 1 of 2 '03 starts (mdn, rtd 74 at best).
2217 **EAST RIDING 10** [1]4-9-5 (37) Ann Stokell 100/1: 6630005: Keen in 2nd pl, led 7f out till 5f out, no extra.   *dist* 2
5 Ran   Time 2m 41.85(2.55)   Owned: Sir George Meyrick   Trained: Whatcombe

Official Going Firm (Good/Firm Places)

| **2442** | 2.30 News & Star Novice Auction Stakes 2yo (E) | |
| | £3494 £1075 £538   **5f rnd**   **Firm**   **Slow**   Inside | |

2056 **KATIE BOO 17** [4] A Berry 2-8-4 F Norton 7/2: 321: Trkd ldrs, rdn to lead ins last, styd on   76
strongly: nicely bckd, op 4/1: eff at 5f on firm & gd grnd, stiff/gall or sharp trk: see 2056 & 1795.
2287* **EVANESCE 6** [7] M R Channon 2-8-10 S Hitchcott(3) 2/1 FAV: 2242212: Led, drvn & hdd ins last, not   *1½* 76
pace of wnr: bckd tho' op 7/4: clr of rem: qck reapp: gd run see 2287 (6f).
1652 **WISE WAGER 35** [3] R A Fahey 2-8-2 P Hanagan 11/4: 23: Slow away, hung badly left thr'out,   *4*   56
stands side from over 1f out, no impress ins last: hvly bckd, op 4/1: turf bow: looked a tricky ride.
1362 **ANGELOFTHENORTH 51** [2] J D Bethell 2-8-2 R Ffrench 25/1: 34: Rdn chasing ldrs halfway, hung   *½*   54
left & no impress last: 7 wk abs: see 1362.
1652* **RIGHTPRICE PREMIER 35** [5]2-8-10 N Callan 4/1: 3215: Sn outpcd, nvr on terms: op 11/4: btr 1652.   *2*   56
1764 **SERENE PEARL 30** [1]2-8-7 K Darley 40/1: 006: b f Night Shift - Shanjah (Darshaan) Cl-up,   *11* 22
struggling from halfway: 16,000gns Apr foal: sister to a 5f juv wnr: dam 10f wnr.
6 Ran   Time 1m 01.19 (1.69)   Owned: The Early Doors Partnership   Trained: Cockerham

CARLISLE   MONDAY 14.06.04   Righthand, Stiff Track, Uphill Finish

---

2443   3.00 Scotby Maiden Stakes 3yo   (D)
£5720 £1760 £880   1m1f61y rnd   Firm   Fast   Inside

4213} **LITTLE JIMBOB** 275 [7] R A Fahey 3-9-0 (70) P Hanagan 13/2: 432342-1: b g Desert Story - Artistic   **78**
Licence (High Top) Keen early chasing ldr, led 2f out, drvn & held on all out: reapp: dual h'cap rnr-up in '03,
consistent performer: eff at 7f/1m, now stays stiff 9f well: acts on firm & fast grnd, stiff/gall or sharp trk:
goes well fresh: tough, improved here. 2 Sep'03 Muss 8g/f 71-65 E: 2 Aug'03 Newc 7g/f 64-62 E:
1427 **JUST A FLUKE** 47 [2] M Johnston 3-9-0 (77) K Dalgleish 9/4: 22-402: Trkd ldr, eff to press wnr   hd   **77**
over 1f out, hung left under press but kept on well, just denied: bckd: 7 wk abs: t-strap omitted after latest:
acts on firm & gd/soft grnd: see 1019.
1130 **LEG SPINNER** 63 [6] M R Channon 3-9-0 K Darley 11/10 FAV: 33: Chsd ldrs, outpcd 4f out, kept on   3½   **70**
for press, no threat to front pair: clr of rem: hvly bckd: 2 month abs: styd longer 9f trip, shapes as if 10f+ may
suit: handles firm & fast grnd: see 1130.
2148 **STANLEY CRANE** 12 [5] B Hanbury 3-9-0 t (70) J Carroll 9/1: 435-054: br g Bahri - Grey Starling   11   **52**
(Pharly) Led & clr halfway, hdd 2f out, sn btn: plcd '03 (lightly rcd, AW mdn), rtd 76a: turf mdn unplcd, rtd 80):
eff at 6/7f, has tried 10f: handles fast grnd & polytrack, stiff/gall or sharp/undul trk: eff in a t-strap.
1768 **IM A DARK HORSE** 30 [4]3-9-0 N Callan 40/1: 05: Slow away & al rear, no ch 2f out.   2½   **47**
2081 **YOUNG WARRIOR** 16 [3]3-9-0 D R McCabe 66/1: 056: Al bhd, no ch fnl 3f.   10   **30**
3383} **THE RIP** 314 [1]3-9-0 (72) D Allan(3) 14/1: 004-7: Bhd, no ch fnl 3f on reapp.   2½   **25**
7 Ran   Time 1m 53.84 (u1.56)   Owned: Dale Scaffolding Co Ltd   Trained: Malton

---

2444   3.30 Black Sheep Brewery Handicap Stakes 3yo+ 0-80 (D)   **[77]**
£5538 £1704 £852   1m6f32y   Firm   Slow   Inside

1689 **SAHEM** 33 [8] D Eddy 7-9-10 (73) P Hanagan 6/1: 30-50401: Made all & dictated pace, rdn & qcknd   **81**
over 2f out, al in command from dist: acts at 10f, stays 14f well, tried 2m2f: acts on firm & gd/soft grnd, likes a
stiff/undul trk: suited by forcing tactics today under well judged ride: see 926.
3745} **MOST DEFINITELY** 299 [3] T D Easterby 4-8-13 (62) D Allan(3) 9/1: 322222-2: b g Definite Article -   3½   **64**
Unbidden Melody (Chieftain) Held up, styd on for press to chase wnr ins last, nvr any threat: bckd, op 12/1:
reapp: 4 times h'cap rnr-up '03, also mdn rnr-up, sand unplcd, rtd 14a, h'cap): unplcd '02 (rtd 64, mdn): eff at
14f, prob best at 2m/2m1f on firm & gd/soft grnd: likes a stiff trk: eff in blnks, gd run without today:
2 Aug'03 Carl 14.1fm 63-(62) D: 2 Aug'03 Newc 14.4g/f 63-59 E: 2 Jul'03 Beve 16.2gd 62-59 F:
2 Jul'03 Beve 16.2g/s 60-57 E: 2 Jun'03 Carl 17.2g/f 57-54 F:
2192 **GREENWICH MEANTIME** 11 [9] Mrs J R Ramsden 4-10-0 (77) L Goncalves 14/1: 21-03003: Held up, styd ½   **77**
on for press fnl 2f, not able to chall: handles firm & gd/soft grnd: see 1361.
2276 **TONI ALCALA** 7 [10] R F Fisher 5-9-4 (67) D Nolan(3) 5/1: 1613524: Mid-div, drvn & styd on onepace.   nk   **67**
965 **MAGIC COMBINATION** 77 [4]11-9-8 (71) W Dowling 16/1: 0//0110/-25: Held up, styd on for press fnl   shd   **71**
2f but nvr any threat: handles firm & soft grnd: see 965.
2035 **DELTA FORCE** 18 [6]5-8-1 (50) G Duffield 7/2 FAV: 1445326: Trkd wnr, outpcd from over 2f out.   1½   **48**
2009 **FREEDOM NOW** 19 [2]6-9-6 (69) A Culhane 12/1: 660-0067: Held up, rdn 3f out, no impress: see 1689.   hd   **66**
2180 **CLARADOTNET** 11 [7]4-9-1 (64) S Hitchcott(3) 9/1: 0-000638: Held up, rdn & no prog fnl 2f.   3   **57**
1478} **EBINZAYD** 1117 [1]8-10-0 (77) P Mulrennan(5) 8/1: 5345//0//-9: b g Tenby - Sharakawa (Darshaan)   ¾   **69**
Trkd ldrs, btn 2f out: long Flat abs, 7 wk jumps abs (h'cap hdle wnr, 2m2f, gd): unplcd sole start on the level
back in '01 (h'cap): '98 mdn wnr, winning form at 1m, mid-dists shld suit: acts on fast & gd grnd, stiff/gall trks.
1689 **BID FOR FAME** 33 [5]7-9-13 (76) K Darley 6/1: 621-0000: 10th: Sn bhd & no ch fnl 4f, t.o.: op   dist   **0**
9/2, cheek pieces omitted after latest: see 173 (AW).
10 Ran   Time 3m 07.05 (7.25)   Owned: Mr Robert Gray   Trained: Newcastle Upon Tyne

---

2445   4.00 Mitchell & Heap Handicap Stakes 3yo+ 0-70 (E)   **[68]**
£3851 £1185 £593   5f193y rnd   Firm   Slow   Inside

2214 **SILVER MASCOT** 10 [1] I Semple 5-8-10 (50) T Eaves(3) 25/1: 1423001: Sn trkd ldrs trav well, styd   **58**
on for press to lead well ins last: eff at 5f, suited by 6/7f on fibresand, firm & gd grnd, sharp/turning or stiff
trk: showed fine speed to overcome tricky low draw, could win again: see 825.
2315 **XANADU** 5 [12] Miss L A Perratt 8-8-11 p (51) R Ffrench 9/1: 0200062: Led after 2f till well ins last: op 15/2. ½   **55**
2086* **KIRKBYS TREASURE** 16 [4] A Berry 6-9-12 (66) K Darley 7/1: 005-1213: Chsd ldrs, rdn & kept on,   nk   **70**
not pace of wnr cl-home: apprec a return to 7f & Musselburgh: see 2086 (7f).
2080 **TEDSDALE MAC** 16 [6] N Bycroft 5-8-10 (50) N Callan 12/1: 43304-04: Rear, styd on for press   1   **51**
halfway, not reach front trio: imprvd eff: see 2080 (7f).
1820 **FLYING EDGE** 2 [9]4-9-5 (59) D Allan(3) 8/1: 0205065: Chsd ldrs halfway, no extra from dist: qck   1¼   **56**
reapp: acts on firm, gd/soft & fibresand: see 585.
2007 **HARTSHEAD** 19 [5]5-10-0 (68) P Mulrennan(5) 16/1: 4460-206: Held up wide, hdwy halfway, rdn & no   ½   **63**
prog dist: handles firm & gd grnd: back to form after latest but still just btr 1638.
1765 **CANDLERIGGS** 30 [15]8-9-9 (63) A Nicholls 16/1: 0650-007: Chsd ldrs, rdn & no impress dist.   ½   **56**
2280* **ALBASHOOSH** 7 [16]6-10-1 (6ex) (69) Alex Greaves 11/8 FAV: 06-65618: Trkd ldrs, prog 2f out, no   nk   **61**
extra dist: hvly bckd under a pen, qck reapp: btr 2280.
2204* **OLD BAILEY** 10 [3]4-8-6 vis (46) P Fessey 12/1: 6-605019: Towards rear, only mod prog: btr 2204 (7f).   4   **26**
1910 **GOLDEN SPECTRUM** 23 [2]5-9-4 (58) D R McCabe 33/1: 0000-350: 10th: Sn outpcd, nvr a factor.   1   **35**
2279 **JOHN OGROATS** 7 [13]6-9-6 (62) R Winston 25/1: 0000000: 11th: Mid-div, no prog 2f out: see 2027.   hd   **34**
1886 **QUICKS THE WORD** 24 [11]4-9-6 bl (60) Dean McKeown 33/1: 00-00400: 12th: Prom 4f, sn btn: btr 1532. 2   **30**

2111 **BABY BARRY** 14 [8]7-9-0 vis (54) G Duffield 33/1: 42300-00: 13th: b g Komaite - Malcesine (Auction   shd   **24**
Ring) Mid-div, struggling from halfway: AW h'cap in '03, turf unplcd (rtd 60, class stks): '02 h'cap wnr: eff at
5f, suited by 6f on firm & gd grnd, handles soft & fibresand: acts on firm, fast & fibresand, likes a sharp trk.
2 Oct'03 Ling 6ap 58a-58 F: 1 Jul'02 Pont 6g/f 75-71 C: 2 Jun'02 Donc 6g/f 72-68 D: 1 Sep'01 Good 6g/f 75-71 C:
1 Aug'01 Newc 6gd 75-67 E: 1 Jul'01 Pont 6g/f 68- E:
4722} **ANGEL ISA** 245 [7]4-8-10 (50) P Hanagan 25/1: 601060-0: 14th: b f Fayruz - Isa (Dance In Time)   3   **11**
Sn bhd & struggling on reapp: h'cap scorer '03, AW h'cap unplcd (rtd 42a): plcd fnl '02 start (mdn, rtd 54): eff at
5f, sole win at 7f: acts on firm, fast & fibresand, likes a sharp trk. 1 Aug'03 Muss 7.1g/f 52-49 E:
1988 **Travelling Times** 20 [14]5-8-5 bl(45) P M Quinn 25/1:0

736

CARLISLE   MONDAY 14.06.04   Righthand, Stiff Track, Uphill Finish

3926} **Whinhill House 292** [10]4-8-13 (53) L Enstone(3) 40/1:0
16 Ran   Time 1m 11.99 (1.29)   Owned: The Ipso Facto Syndicate   Trained: Carluke

---

2446	4.30 Linstock Handicap Stakes Fillies 3yo 0-70 (E)				[74]
	£3494 £1075 £538 **6f192y rnd Firm Slow** Inside				

2169 **NEQAAWI 12** [2] B Hanbury 3-8-13 t (59) K Darley 7/4 FAV: 00-51: Handy & led 2f out, rdn clr: **68**
well bckd, op 7/2: h'cap bow: eff at 7f, shld get 1m: acts on firm grnd & eff in a t-strap: see 2169.
1372 **FRIENDS HOPE 50** [1] P A Blockley 3-8-10 (56) G Duffield 4/1: 501-0152: Dwelt, sn led till 2f   5   **55**
out, not pace of wnr: op 5/2: 7 wk abs: back in trip: see 1280 (10f, held up).
2237 **FIREBIRD RISING 9** [5] T D Barron 3-9-7 (67) P Makin(5) 5/1: 3-503: In tch, eff 2f out, onepace.   1¾   **63**
4994} **MICKLEGATE 223** [3] J D Bethell 3-9-3 (63) P Hanagan 11/4: 06443-4: b f Dracula - Primulette   6   **49**
(Mummy's Pet) Held up, rdn & no impress fnl 2f: op 7/2, reapp: auct mdn plcd fnl '03 start (rtd 63): stays a
sharp 7f, handles fast & soft grnd.
1477 **ALICE BLACKTHORN 44** [4]3-9-4 (64) D McGaffin 8/1: 4510-005: Swerved badly left leaving stalls &   16   **22**
reluctant to race, sn well bhd: op 7/1, 6 wk abs: see 1477.
5 Ran   Time 1m 26.14 (2.24)   Owned: Mr Hamdan Al Maktoum   Trained: Newmarket

---

2447	5.00 Hayton Handicap Stakes 3yo+ 0-75 (E)				[75]
	£3754 £1155 £578 **1m rnd Firm Slow** Inside				

1635 **PEPPER ROAD 37** [10] R Bastiman 5-8-1 (48) R Ffrench 11/1: 1060-001: ch g Elmaamul - Floral Spark   **57**
(Forzando) Sn trkd ldrs, led ins last, drvn out: h'cap scorer '03: h'cap wnr '02: eff at 7f, suited by 1m: acts
on firm & gd grnd, prob any trk, likes Carlisle.
1 Sep'03 Thir 8fm 55-49 D: 2 Sep'03 Carl 6.9fm 50-49 F: 1 Jun'02 Muss 8g/f 58-54 F:
2324 **BEN HUR 5** [8] W M Brisbourne 5-9-1 (62) K Darley 5/1 FAV: 050-0102: Led, hdd ins last & no   1   **68**
extra: back to form, able to lead today: could win again after1966 (clmr).
2159 **WAHOO SAM 12** [6] T D Barron 4-8-12 (59) P Makin(5) 28/1: 0000-003: Trkd ldrs trav well 3f out, sn   ¾   **64+**
short of room, kept on ins last, not able to chall: shade closer with a clr run: acts on firm, fast & fibresand:
styd stiff 1m well: potentially well h'capped, keep in mind: see 2159.
1748 **GIFTED FLAME 31** [5] T D Barron 5-9-2 (63) P Hanagan 13/2: 4006-004: b g Revouke - Little Lady   ½   **66**
Leah (Shareef Dancer) Dwelt, mid-div, to press ldrs over 1f out, sn rdn & no extra: h'cap scorer '03 (I Semple):
h'cap wnr '02: eff at 7/8.4f on fm & gd, prob not hvy: likes a stiff fin: eff with/without cheek pieces.
1 Jun'03 Carl 7.9fm 72-65 E: 2 Jun'03 Thir 8g/f 68-64 E: 1 Sep'02 Beve 8.4g/f 66-60 E:
2235 **LOW CLOUD 9** [3]4-10-0 vis (75) J Carroll 7/1: 650-6035: Trkd ldrs & ch 2f out, sn rdn & onepace: 1¼   **76**
handles firm & gd grnd: see 2235.
1485 **ACTIVE ACCOUNT 44** [11]7-9-2 (63) A Culhane 7/1: 33-22566: Held up, mod gains, no threat: abs.   hd   **63**
1909 **WOOD DALLING 23** [12]6-8-8 (55) P Mathers(7) 7/1: 04305-07: b g Woodman - Cloelia (Lyphard) Held   1¼   **52**
up in tch, no prog fnl 2f: sell grade plcd '03, AW class stks unplcd (rtd 74a, C Dwyer): h'cap plcd '02 (rtd 85, H
Cecil): eff at 1m/10f on firm, fast & polytrack, prob handles any trk: eff in visor, winning form without.
2 Jul'01 Good 9.8fm 89-85 C: 1 Jun'01 Ripo 9g/f 89- D: 2 May'01 Good 8fm 90- D:
1972 **RYMERS RASCAL 21** [2]12-8-4 (51) G Duffield 8/1: 0302-328: Mid-div, hmpd over 1f out, sn no prog.   1   **46**
2027 **WALTZING WIZARD 18** [7]5-8-5 (52) P M Quinn 6/1: 5550549: Held up, eff over 2f out, sn no impress.   ½   **46**
1954 **LATE ARRIVAL 21** [1]7-7-12 (1oh)vis (44) Dale Gibson 25/1: 06/5-0000: 10th: Bhd, nvr a factor.   ¾   **38**
2324 **SMITH N ALLAN OILS 5** [4]5-8-10 p (57) L Enstone(3) 14/1: 1000000: 11th: Al towards rear: qck reapp.   1   **48**
2054 **Call Of The Wild 17** [13]4-8-4 p(51) T Hamilton 12/1:0
2102 **Time To Regret 14** [9]4-8-6 (1ow)(52) R Winston 14/1:0
13 Ran   Time 1m 37.89(1.9)   Owned: Mr Peter Julian   Trained: Wetherby

---

WINDSOR   MONDAY 14.06.04   Sharp, Fig 8 Track

Official Going Good/Firm (Firm Places)

2448	6.30 Chg-Meridian Handicap Stakes 3yo+ 0-75 (E)				[75]
	£3582 £1102 £551 **1m67y rnd Good/Firm 28 +11 Fast** Inside				

2220 **BEST BEFORE 10** [6] P D Evans 4-9-6 (67) S Donohoe(7) 4/1: 0122021: Mid-div, hdwy to lead dist,   **76**
rdn out: now suited by 1m/9f on fast, soft grnd & polytrack: can follow up: see 2220 & 1530.
2199 **PHRED 11** [1] R F Johnson Houghton 4-9-0 (61) S Carson 100/30 FAV: 0-646542: Cl-up, styd on ins   3   **62**
fnl 1f, al held by wnr: gd effort in defeat & is on a winning mark: see 1059.
2010 **ADOBE 19** [8] W M Brisbourne 9-9-6 (67) M Savage(5) 15/2: 0002-003: Handy, kept on ins fnl 1f,   hd   **67**
just held for 2nd: op 9/2: on a wng mark & will be of interest back at Bath: see 2010.
2265 **YEOMAN LAD 7** [2] A M Balding 4-9-11 vis (72) L Keniry(3) 12/1: 0000-004: b g Groom Dancer - First   nk   **71**
Amendment (Caerleon) Prcm, no extra dist: quick reapp: plcd once in '03 (class stks): med auct mdn wnr in '02:
eff at 6/7f, stays 1m on firm & gd/soft grnd, prob any trk: has tried visor: slipped to a fair mark.
2 Jul'02 Newb 6fm 85- D: 1 Jul'02 Chep 6g/s 88- E:
2397* **ESPADA 2** [5]8-8-7 (6ex)bl (54) S W Kelly 11/2: 0004415: Led, hdd dist, no extra: op 4/1 on quick   hd   **52**
reapp: will appreciate a return to 7f: btr 2397.
1821 **EVERY NOTE COUNTS 27** [3]4-9-1 (62) T Quinn 11/1: 520-0006: b g Bluegrass Prince - Miss Mirror   3½   **53**
(Magic Mirror) Mid-div, prog when short of room ins fnl 2f, sn onepcd: rnr-up 4 times in '03 (clmrs & h'cap, W
Jarvis): mdn wnr in late '02: stays 12f, 1o/11f poss ideal: acts on firm, gd/soft grnd & fibresand, gall or sharp trk.
2 Sep'03 Leic 10.0g/f 77-(75) D: 2 Jul'03 Hayd 10.5g/f 78-(77) D: 2 Jun'03 York 10.4g/f 75-(75) D:
2 May'03 Ling 10ap 75a-74 E: 1 Dec'02 Wolv 7af 74a- D:
118 **BACK IN ACTION 198** [4]4-10-0 t (75) E Ahern 14/1: 53/5000-7: b c Hector Protector - Lucca (Sure   1¾   **62**
Blade) Rear, nvr a factor: reapp: unplcd in '03 (rtd 68a & 55, mdns): plcd on 1 of 2 '02 starts (rtd 82): eff at
1m, shld be suited by polytrack, stays 8/4g on gd/soft grnd: eff in a t-strap.
2394 **RAHEEL 2** [7]4-8-10 t (57) D Holland 9/2: 0614308: Al bhd: back from 8/1 on quick reapp: btr 757.   ½   **43**
8 Ran   Time 1m 44.46 (1.46)   Owned: Waterline Racing Club   Trained: Abergavenny

2449   7.00 Kadooment Trophy Selling Stakes 2yo (G)
£2884 £824 £412   6f str   Good/Firm 28   -46 Slow   Inside

2109 **CLOANN** 14 [4] R Hannon 2-8-6   Dane O'Neill 2/1 FAV: 501: b f Danetime - Rustic Lawn (Rusticaro)   64
Cl-up, led 4f out, hung left & flashed tail ins fnl 1f, rdn out: well bckd: May foal, cost E7,000: half sisters
wnrs at 1m/10f: dam unrcd: sire decent performer at sprint dists: eff at 6f, 7f shld suit: acts on fast grnd & a
sharp trk: appreciated drop to sell grade.
2310 **DEBS BROUGHTON** 5 [2] W J Musson 2-8-6   G Carter 12/1: 002: b f Prince Sabo - Coy Debutante   ¾ 59
(Arehway) Chsd ldrs, styd on to chase wnr ins fnl 1f, kept on but al held: qk reapp: Feb 1st foal, cost 2,000 gns:
dam plcd at 10f on flat & 17f in bmpr grade: eff at 6f on fast: imprvd eff on drop in grade.
2270 **SONGGARIA** 7 [3] J R Best 2-8-6   N Pollard 7/2: 23: Cl-up, no extra ins fnl 1f: clr rem: quick   1 56
reapp: eff at 5/6f on fast grnd: see 2270.
2115 **GLASSON LODGE** 14 [7] P D Evans 2-8-7 (1ow)VIS D Holland 5/2: 45634: Led, hdd 4f out, outpcd 2f   3 48
out, rallied fnl 1f: well bckd in 1st time visor: see 2115 & btr 1256.
2033 **MUESTRA** 18 [6]2-8-6 R Havlin 33/1: 00005: ch f Raise A Grand - Iva's Flyer (Imperial Frontier)   2½ 40
Slow away, nvr nrr than mid-div: Apr foal, cost E5,000: half sister won at 5/6f: dam juv wnr at 5f.
2194 **ZACHY BOY** 11 [5]2-8-11 E Ahern 16/1: 605006: Handy over 4f, wknd dist: btr 1325.   ½ 44
2270 **SHISH** 7 [8]2-8-6 S W Kelly 14/1: 66437: Handy over 4f, sn wknd: quick reapp: btr 2270.   ½ 38
2294 **JOE NINETY** 6 [1]2-8-11 BL Derek Nolan(7) 14/1: 560038: Bhd, nvr a factor: qck reapp & 1st time blnks.   hd 42
8 Ran   Time 1m 14.76 (4.46)   Owned: Dr Michael Dunleavy   Trained: Marlborough

2450   7.30 Gold Cup Festival Trophy E B F Maiden Stakes 2yo (D)
£4316 £1328 £664   5f10y str   Good/Firm 28   -08 Slow   Inside

MARAJUANA 0 [11] A M Balding 2-8-9   N Chalmers(5) 8/1: 1: b f Robellino - Mara River (Efisio)   82
Made all, drvn out ins fnl 1f to hold on: debut: Mar foal, half sister to a 1m wnr: dam successful at 6f/1m: eff
at 5f, further will suit: acts on fast grnd & a sharp trk: goes well fresh: fine start.
1826 **MARCHING SONG** 27 [6] R Hannon 2-9-0   J Fortune 6/5 FAV: 532: Prom, ev ch dist, kept on ins fnl   ½ 84
1f, just held: v well bckd: continues to prog with racing & can lose mdn tag: see 1826.
DIAMOND JOSH 0 [9] P D Evans 2-9-0   R Havlin 33/1: 3: ch g Primo Dominie - Exit (Exbourne)   3½ 74
Travelling well in tch, outpcd after 3f, rallied despite hanging left ins fnl 1f: debut: Apr foal, cost 4,000 gns:
dam successful at 6f as a juv: eff at 5f, further will suit: acts on fast grnd: encouraging.
1510 **FIRST RULE** 42 [1] C F Wall 2-9-0   S Sanders 11/2: 04: ch c Primo Dominie - Tarsa (Ballad Rock)   1½ 70
Bhd, hdwy halfway, onepcd fnl 1f: 6 wk abs: Mar foal, cost 37,000 gns: brother/held brother to wnrs at 6/7f: dam
successful at 6f: sire decent performer as a juv: can rate higher.
1458 **CAMPEON** 45 [4]2-9-0 R L Moore 16/1: 0505: Bhd, prog ins fnl 2f, nrst fin: 6 wk abs: been gldd.   ½ 69
1981 **KEMPSEY** 20 [5]2-9-0 A Daly 46/1: 06: Chsd ldrs, no extra fnl 2f: see 1981.   ½ 68
PHI PHI 0 [7]2-8-9 L Dettori 4/1: 7: Dwelt, in tch till dist, sn edged left & no extra: debut.   shd 62
2083 **KNOCK BRIDGE** 16 [2]2-8-9 Joanna Badger 16/1: 428: Bhd, nvr a factor: btr 2083.   hd 61
FOLLOW MY LEAD 0 [3]2-8-9 E Ahern 10/1: 9: Slow away, al bhd: debut.   4 49
2171 **JOSEAR** 12 [10]2-9-0 A McCarthy 50/1: 400: 10th: Rear, hdwy when short of room dist, sn fdd.   5 39
2089 **LIGHTHORNE LAD** 15 [8]2-9-0 S W Kelly 66/1: 00: 11th: Handy 3f, sn fdd.   nk 38
11 Ran   Time 1m 0.80 (1.80)   Owned: Lady C S Cadbury   Trained: Kingsclere

2451   8.00 Gold Cup Triple Winner 'blast Of Storm' Handicap Stakes 3yo+ 0-80 (D)   [80]
£5720 £1760 £880   6f str   Good/Firm 28   -00 Slow   Inside

2289* **CAUSTIC WIT** 6 [10] M S Saunders 6-9-6 (6ex)p (72) R Miles(3) 4/1 FAV: 0-101111: Cl-up, led   90+
halfway, clr dist, eased cl home, val 5L+: qck reapp: eff at 5f, all wins have come at 6f: acts on firm, soft &
fibresand: suited by cheek pieces: v progressive sprinter who can win yet more prizes on this evidence: see 2289.
2416 **HIGH RIDGE** 2 [4] J M Bradley 5-9-0 (6ex)p (66) C Catlin 8/1: 60-015122: Rear, hdwy halfway, styd   3 71
on chase wnr dist, al held in fnl 1f: qck reapp: likes Bath: continues in gd form: see 2416.
2160 **FULL SPATE** 12 [18] J M Bradley 9-9-2 (68) R L Moore 8/1: 0546463: Handy, kept on ins fnl 2f, no   1 70
ch with front 2: enouraging eff & is h'capped to win sn: see 1354.
2289 **COMPLICATION** 6 [14] J A R Toller 4-8-9 bl (61) Lisa Jones(3) 6/1: 000-0624: Slow away, hdwy   ½ 62
halfway, nrst fin: qck reapp: lost chance today at start: btr 2289.
2232* **GLENCOE SOLAS** 9 [17]4-9-6 (72) M Fenton 8/1: 0-642215: Led 3f, styd cl-up till hung left & wknd dist.   1¾ 68
2034 **YOMALO** 18 [2]4-8-12 (64) S Sanders 16/1: 220-0056: Bhd, prog after 3f, no impress fnl 1f: btr 2034.   hd 59
2258 **WARLINGHAM** 8 [16]6-8-6 (58) J Fanning 16/1: 1501057: Handy over 4f, sn onepcd: btr 2258 (7f).   ½ 52
1806 **EFFECTIVE** 28 [8]4-8-12 (64) D Holland 11/1: 0501528: Nvr nrr than mid-div: btr 1806.   shd 57
2023 **FIREWORK** 19 [12]6-8-8 p (60) T Quinn 14/1: 0-000659: Handy over 4f, sn wknd: btr 2023.   2 47
2189 **MARGALITA** 11 [9]4-9-2 t (68) J F Egan 40/1: 00-60060: 10th: Nvr nrr than mid-div: btr 2189.   ¾ 53
2280 **BLUE PATRICK** 7 [6]4-9-9 p (75) J Mackay 16/1: 00-00020: 11th: Rear, nvr able to chall: qck reapp.   shd 59
2016 **MACS TALISMAN** 19 [11]4-8-8 (60) M Tebbutt 50/1: 2003-000: 12th: Bhd, mod prog when no room dist.   1¾ 40
1615 **MADRASEE** 38 [5]6-9-10 (76) C Cogan 25/1: 0045050: 13th: Bhd, nvr a factor: btr 1615.   ½ 55
2214 **TAPAU** 10 [13]6-9-0 (66) Dane O'Neill 20/1: 130-5000: 14th: Slow away, al bhd: btr 1269.   nk 44
45 **ESATTO** 210 [3]5-9-9 (75) S Righton 50/1: 050635-0: 15th: b g Puissance - Stoneydale (Tickled   shd 52
Pink) Dwelt, al bhd: reapp: h'cap wnr in '03 (P A Blockley): won 4 h'caps in '02: eff at 5/6f, has tried 7f:
acts on firm, gd/soft & both AWs: handles any trk, Brighton specialist who has had breathing probs.
2 Sep'03 Ayr 5g/f 76-73 D: 1 Aug'03 Brig 5.3fm 74-70 E: 1 Aug'02 Brig 5.2g/f 83-72 E: 1 Aug'02 Ripo 6gd 82-72 D:
1 Aug'02 Carl 5fm 80-72 D: 1 Aug'02 Brig 5.2g/f 74-66 E: 2 Aug'02 Ripo 5g/s 64-61 F: 2 Jun'01 Nott 5g/f 74- D:
2111 **SUPER SONG** 14 [1]4-8-13 t (65) Joanna Badger 66/1: 01-00000: 16th: Al bhd.   nk 41
2289 **THURLESTONE ROCK** 6 [15]4-9-11 (77) L Dettori 9/1: 1001-050: 17th: Cl-up till halfway, fdd.   10 28
17 Ran   Time 1m 12.00 (1.7)   Owned: Mrs Sandra Jones   Trained: Wells

WINDSOR MONDAY 14.06.04 Sharp, Fig 8 Track

2452 8.30 Crop Over Festival Trophy Handicap Stakes 3yo 0-75 (E) [82]
£4446 £1368 £684 1m2f7y Good/Firm 28 +02 Fast Inside

2127 **MR TAMBOURINE MAN 13** [14] P F I Cole 3-9-7 (75) T Quinn 5/1: 261-6001: Rear, plenty to do halfway, prog 3f out, drvn out to lead cl-home: eff at 1m, now stays 10f: acts on gd & firm grnd: lightly rcd. **83**
1505* **HAWKIT 43** [5] P D Evans 3-9-6 (74) S Donohoe(7) 12/1: 3-521012: Handy, styd on to lead bef 1f out, hdd cl-home: 6 wk abs & new stable: eff at 1m/9f, imprvd for step up to 10f: see 1505 (clmr, J A Osborne). *hd* **81**
843 **FOXILLA 92** [7] D R C Elsworth 3-7-12 (52) R Thomas(2) 50/1: 000-003: Held up, prog 5f out, hung left & onepcd dist: long abs: eff at 10f on fast grnd: gd eff today & unexposed in h'cap grade: see 843. *2½* **55**
1124 **PETITE COLLEEN 63** [11] D Haydn Jones 3-8-11 (65) D Kinsella 25/1: 0235-04: Cl-up, led bef 3f out, hdd bef 1f out, no extra: 9 wk abs: plcd in 2 of 3 '03 starts (rtd 75a & 68, mdns): eff at 1m, poss stays 10f: acts on firm, gd grnd & polytrack. *1½* **66**
2088 **GOBLIN 15** [2]3-9-2 (70) S Sanders 7/2 FAV: 0-415135: Bhd, short of room 6f out, kept on fnl 2f, nrst fin: could never get competitive on drop back to 10f: btr 2088. *2½* **67**
2024 **SMOOTHLY DOES IT 19** [8]3-8-13 (67) E Ahern 9/1: 020-0206: Handy, ev ch 2f out, sn wknd: btr 1647. *shd* **63**
2168 **AUROVILLE 12** [12]3-8-9 (63) I Mongan 9/1: 50-04057: Rear, nvr nrr than mid-div: btr 2168. *1¾* **56**
1953 **IVORY COAST 21** [10]3-8-7 (61) R Miles(3) 7/1: 004-4128: Cl-up 1m, sn wknd: btr 1953. *7* **44**
1790 **AUTUMN FLYER 28** [1]3-8-11 (65) R Smith 50/1: 000-09: ch g Salse - Autumn Fall (Sanglamore) Cl-up, not handle bend & lost pl after 3f, wknd 3f out: unplcd all 3 '02 starts (rtd 74 & 69a, mdns). *nk* **47**
1965 **ANDURIL 21** [6]3-8-13 P (67) J Mackay 11/1: 5-603640: 10th: Bhd, nvr a factor: cheek pieces: btr 1965. *nk* **48**
2098 **LA PROFESSORESSA 14** [3]3-8-8 (62) R Havlin 25/1: 3005-600: 11th: Mid-div 7f, sn wknd: btr 2031. *shd* **42**
98 **CORNISH GOLD 202** [4]3-8-11 (65) D Holland 16/1: 0056-0: 12th: b f Slip Anchor - Sans Diablo (Mac's Imp) Handy 7f, sn wknd: reapp: unplcd in '03 (rtd 71, mdn, D Haydn Jones): with N J Henderson. *5* **38**
2205* **INCISOR 10** [13]3-9-1 (69) P Dobbs 11/2: 56-51110: 13th: Al bhd: something amiss? see 2205. *2½* **38**
2216 **REGAL FLIGHT 10** [9]3-8-0 (1ow) (53) C Catlin 50/1: 505-60: 14th: b g King's Theatre - Green Belt (Tirol) Led, race keenly, hdd bef 3f out, sn fdd: unplcd in 3 '03 starts (rtd 61, I A Wood): has been gelded. *1* **21**
14 Ran Time 2m 8.67 (2.67) Owned: The Hon Mrs JMCorbett & Mr CWright Trained: Whatcombe

2453 9.00 Barbados Jazz Festival Maiden Stakes 3yo+ (D)
£4407 £1356 £678 1m2f7y Good/Firm 28 -07 Slow Inside

LITTLETON TELCHAR 13 [3] M J Ryan 4-9-11 B Doyle 50/1: 51: ch c Atticus - Miss Waikiki (Miswaki) Handy, styd on to lead bef 1f out, drvn out: Brit bow, 5th of 13 recent debut in Ireland (mdns): eff at 10f, further shld suit: acts on fast grnd & a sharp trk: op to more improvement. **78**
SUMMER SERENADE 0 [8] L M Cumani 3-8-7 L Dettori 2/1 FAV: 2: b f Sadler's Wells - Summer Sonnet (Baillamont) Mid-div, prog when short of room 2f out, kept on: debut: dam 12f wnr: eff at 10f, 12f will suit: acts on fast: encouraging start & sure to improve. *¾* **72**
2013 **MICHABO 19** [6] D R C Elsworth 3-8-12 T Quinn 10/1: 0-43: Keen cl-up over 1m, sn no extra: eff at 10f, further will suit: acts on fast grnd: now quals for h'caps: see 2013. *3½* **72**
1959 **DOUBLE DAGGER LADY 21** [12] J Noseda 3-8-7 E Ahern 9/2: 64: Cl-up, led 2f out, sn hdd & wknd. *2½* **63**
2131 **SHAMBAR 13** [2]5-9-11 J Murtagh 5/2: 4/-35: Led 1m, sn wknd & eased: btr 2131 (gd/soft). *1½* **66**
1719 **LEBENSTANZ 32** [7]4-9-6 S Sanders 16/1: 666: Nvr nrr than mid div under hands & heels: stable-mate of wnr: now quals for h 'caps. *5* **54**
2066 **SURFACE TO AIR 16** [5]3-8-12 R Havlin 66/1: 07: Bhd, nvr a factor. *¾* **57**
1885 **HEART SPRINGS 24** [10]4-9-6 A Daly 50/1: 00-08: Held up, nvr a factor. *2½* **48$**
1210 **MISS SHANGRI LA 59** [11]3-8-7 D Holland 10/1: 09: Chsd ldrs 7f, sn fdd. *1½* **46**
1810 **AGOUTI 28** [15]3-8-7 Dane O'Neill 66/1: 00: 10th: Bhd, nvr a factor. *3½* **41**
1384 **DORINGO 49** [9]3-8-12 S Carson 66/1: 0-000: 11th: Cl-up 6f, sn fdd. *5* **39**
1358 **LAKE OF DREAMS 51** [1]5-9-11 Lucy Russell(7) 66/1: 00/-00: 12th: Bhd, nvr a factor. *2½* **35**
BARANOOK 0 [14]3-8-12 I Mongan 10/1: 0: 13th: Slow away, al adrift. *dist* **10**
13 Ran Time 2m 9.52(3.52) Owned: Dr P O'Driscoll Trained: Newmarket

LEOPARDSTOWN WEDNESDAY 09.06.04 Lefthand, Galloping Track

Official Going Good/Firm

2454 6.30 Listed Rochestown Stakes 2yo ()
£21808 £6399 £3049 6f rnd Good/Firm

MAN O WORLD [2] D K Weld 2-9-0 P J Smullen 7/4: 3211: b c Spinning World - Rihan (Dayjur) Trkd ldr, led over 1f out, all out to hold on: earlier landed a Naas mdn: well suited by 6f, acts on fast & soft ground, stiff/gall trks: speedy & useful juvenile. **101**
1994 **JOYCE 18** [4] A P O'Brien 2-9-0 J P Spencer 13/8 FAV: 142: b c Danehill Dancer - Miss Kinabalu (Shirley Heights) Led till over 1f out, rallied gamely, just held: last of 4 in a recent Listed event, earlier landed a Tipperary mdn: eff at 5/6f on fast & hvy grnd. *hd* **100**
CLASH OF THE ASH [1] J S Bolger 2-9-0 K J Manning 2/1: 513: Ridden rear early, not pace to chall. *2* **94**
4 Ran Time 1m 14.10 () Owned: L W Heiligbrodt Trained: The Curragh

2455 7.00 Gr 3 Ballycorus Stakes 3yo+ ()
£30485 £8911 £4221 7f rnd Good/Firm

1811* **NAAHY 22** [3] M R Channon 4-9-7 (103) S Hitchcott 7/4 FAV: 050001-11: Made all & styd on strongly ins last: 7f specialist on firm & gd/sft grnd, any trk: best dominating & enjoyed another easy lead today: smart. **109+**
1299 **HAMAIRI** [2] J M Oxx 3-8-11 M J Kinane 13/2: 4212: Trkd ldrs, no room dist, rdn & styd on strongly ins last, closer with a clr run: recent Tipperary mdn wnr: eff at 7f/1m on fast & soft ground: lightly rcd, progressive & useful colt: shade unlucky, win similar: see 1299. *½* **106**

LEOPARDSTOWN WEDNESDAY 09.06.04 Lefthand, Galloping Track

1560 **LATINO MAGIC** [1] R J Osborne 4-9-7 R M Burke 4/1: 26-50243: Dwelt, held up in tch, hdwy to   ½ **105**
pressed ldrs over 1f out, no extra ins last: op 7/2: useful, see 1560.
2139 **ROCKETS N ROLLERS 13** [4] R Hannon 4-9-7 (106) Dane O'Neill 7/2: 333231454: Chsd ldrs, bumped   3 **99**
over 1f out & no extra when sn hmpd: op 3/1: see 1486.
6 Ran   Time 1m 25.90 () Owned: Kuwait Racing Syndicate   Trained: West Ilsley

2456   **8.30 Listed Silver Stakes 3yo+**   ()
      £21808 £6398 £3048   **1m2f**   **Good/Firm**

1700 **MEDICINAL 31** [2] D K Weld 3-8-8 Bl P J Smullen 4/1: 1-431: Held up & pulled hard, rdn/chall over   **109**
1f out, led well ins last, styd on strongly: op 100/30: now suited by 10f & shld get 12f+: acts on fast & soft
ground: highly tried by 1st time blnks today: lightly rcd & v useful colt: see 1700.
2022 **GRAND PASSION 14** [5] G Wragg 4-9-7 (103) J F Egan 6/1: 32-210042: Sn handy, led over 1f out, hdd   ½ **107**
well ins last: returned to 10f & back to best: see 693, 82.
    COBRA [10] A P O'Brien 3-8-8 J P Spencer 6/1: 3214D-3: b c Sadlers Wells - Pucks Castle   2 **104**
(Shirley Heights) Trkd ldrs, chall 2f out, no extra ins last: reapp: lightly rcd Leopardstown mdn wnr in '03: wng
form at 1m, stayed this longer 10f trip well: acts on fast & gd, likes a gall trk: entitled to progress.
10 Ran   Time 2m 03.00() Owned: Ballylinch Stud   Trained: The Curragh

---

CORK SATURDAY 12.06.04 Righthand, Galloping Track, Long Run In

Official Going Firm (Good/Firm Places)

2457   **8.00 Gr 3 Ballyogan Stakes (Fillies & Mares) 3yo+**   ()
      £34840 £10184 £4824   **6f**   **Firm**

2240 **GOLDEN NUN 7** T D Easterby 4-9-3 (100) R Winston 3/1: 05-023131: Rear, smooth prog to chall over   **102**
1f out, sn led, rdn out: suited by 6f, stays 7f: acts on firm & soft grnd: smart & thriving: see 1773, 1436.
2240 **SIMIANNA 7** A Berry 5-9-3 (90) D P McDonogh 16/1: 0-5520672: Rear, hdwy to chall over 1f out,   1½ **96**
rdn & kept on ins last, not pace of wnr: useful, back to best: see 1162.
2140 **TOPKAMP 15** M L W Bell 4-9-3 (104) J P Spencer 5/2 FAV: 011342323: Prom, onepace.   1 **93**
1620 **DOWAGER 35** R Hannon 3-8-9 (99) P Shanahan 6/1: 162461-54: Chsd ldrs, onepace.   ¾ **91**
2090 **ENCHANTED 13** 5-9-3 (95) M J Kinane 16/1: 0463-1177: Mid-div, not pace to chall fnl 2f: see 1925.   **0**
9 Ran   Time 1m 07.50() Owned: T G & Mrs E Holdcroft   Trained: Great Habton

---

CHANTILLY SUNDAY 13.06.04 Righthand, Galloping Track

Official Going Righthand, Galloping Track

2458   **2.10 Gr 3 Prix du Chemin de Fer du Nord 4yo+**   ()
      £25704 £10282 £7711   **1m rnd**   **Good/Soft**

993* **MY RISK** [1] J M Beguigne 5-9-1 C Soumillon 6/4 FAV: 1121-151: b c Take Risks - Miss Pat   **116**
(Vacarme) Sn handy, led over 1f out, held on gamely for press, all out: well suited by 1m on good/soft & soft
ground, likes a gall trk: v smart colt: see 993. 1 Mar'04 Sain 8sft 116- : 2 Oct'03 Long 8sft 116- A:
4804] **CHARMING GROOM** [4] F Head 5-8-12 O Peslier 16/1: 02-14642: Led early, ev ch fnl 1f, kept on.   hd **112**
    STAR VALLEY [7] J C Rouget 4-8-12 I Mendizabal 32/1: 1322-543: Rear, kept on late, no threat.   2½ **107**
1649* **PUTRA PEKAN 34** [6]6-8-12 bl (108) P Robinson 52/10: 10010-117: Led after 3f till over 1f out, sn   2 **103**
btn: jockey reported he prefers softer grnd: btr 1649 (soft), 1420.
10 Ran   Time 1m 36.10 () Owned: R Monnier   Trained: France

2459   **3.20 Gr 2 Grand Prix de Chantilly 4yo+**   ()
      £42148 £16268 £7764   **1m4f**   **Good/Soft**

4633} **POLICY MAKER** [2] E Lellouche 4-9-2 K Fallon 72./10: 12110-51: b c Sadler's Wells - Palmeraie   **123**
(Lear Fan) Mid-div, hdwy over 1f out, styd on strongly for press to lead close home: Gr 2 success among wins last
term (awarded race, fin 2nd), makes a Gr 3 & Listed wnr: well suited by 12f on good & soft ground: high class colt.
1 Aug'03 Deau 12.5sft 118- A: 2 Jun'03 Long 12gd 112- A:
1558 **FAIR MIX** [4] M Rolland 6-8-12 O Peslier 9/10 FAV: 655-1632: Prom, pulled hard early, led 3f   snk **118**
out, rdn & hdd close home: smart, see 1558.
1698* **SHORT PAUSE** [7] A Fabre 5-8-12 Gary Stevens 2/1: 4142-313: Always handy, rdn & styd on fnl 2f.   2 **115**
7 Ran   Time 2m 34.90 () Owned: Ecurie Wildenstein   Trained: France

2460   **4.35 Gr 1 Prix de Diane Hermes 3yo**   ()
      £201197 £80493 £40246   **1m 2f110y**   **Good/Soft**

1557* **LATICE** [18] J M Beguigne 3-9-0 C Soumillon 9/5 FAV: 11-11: Rear, hdwy wide 3f out, rdn/hung   **119**
right & led ins last, styd on strongly: eff at 9f, imprvd for this step up to 10.5f: acts on gd/sft & hvy grnd: high
class, unbeaten filly, win more Gr 1 races: see 1557 (Gr 3).
    MILLIONAIA [1] E Lellouche 3-9-0 T Thulliez 57/10: -2212: b f Peintre Celebre - Moonlight   ¾ **117**
Dance (Alysheba) Mid-div, efft to chall 2f out, styd on strongly but not pace of wnr ins last: recent stakes wnr
here at Chantilly: well suited by 10.5f on good & soft ground, gall trks: lightly rcd, progressive & clrly v smart.
1854 **GREY LILAS** [14] A Fabre 3-9-0 A Fabre 121/10: 62-1123: Trkd ldr, led over 2f out, hdd ins last   ½ **116**

CHANTILLY SUNDAY 13.06.04 Righthand, Galloping Track

& no extra: styd longer 12f trip well: see 1854 & 1432.
2005 **ALEXANDER GOLDRUN 21** [4] J S Bolger 3-9-0 K Manning 33/2: 01221-1124: Mid-div, kept on for ¾ **115**
press, not able to chall: styd longer 10.5f trip well: tough & progressive filly: see 2005 (1m).
2001 **AGATA** [13]3-9-0 D Boeuf 17/1: 323-2335: Rear, styd on wide fnl 3f, nrst fin: stays 10.5f. 1½ **113**
1850 **BARANCELLA** [10]3-9-0 D Bonilla 54/1: -136: Rear, kept on wide, nrst fin. 2½ **109**
1999* **MENHOUBAH 21** [15]3-9-0 (100) C E Brittain 18/1: 4-230210: 13th: Prom, btn over 1f out: btr 1999 (gd). 8 **97**
17 Ran   Time 2m 07.00()   Owned: E Ciampi   Trained: France

THIRSK TUESDAY 15.06.04 Lefthand, Flat, Oval Track

Official Going Firm ALL TIMES SLOW

2461 2.15 Esk Selling Stakes 2yo (E)
£3536 £1088 £544   **6f str**   Firm   Slow   Stands Side

2115 **PRINCELY VALE 15** [9] W G M Turner 2-8-11 P C Haddon(7) 7/2: 041: Sn led, drvn out ins last: **71**
bckd, op 9/2: bght in for 6,000gns: prob handles gd, gall/undul or easy trk: eff in sell
grade & suited by cheek pieces today: see 2115.
2183 **LOJO 12** [8] R P Elliott 2-8-6 S Chin 9/2: 032: Trkd ldrs trav well, drvn to press wnr dist, al nk **65**
just held but clr of rem: handles firm & fast grnd: stays 6f: see 2183 & 1869.
2321 **DANEHILL FAIRY 6** [4] Mrs A Duffield 2-8-6 vis G Duffield 9/1: 020633: Dsptd lead early, not pace 5 **50**
of front pair over 1f out: op 7/1, qck reapp: longer 6f trip may yet suit: prob btr 2321 (5f, g/s).
2321 **URABANDE 6** [7] Julian Poulton Lisa Jones(3) 13/2: 02064: Cl-up till outpcd fnl 2f: qck 2 **44**
reapp: also bhd today's 3rd 2321, btr 1439 (AW).
2321 **PROCRASTINATE 6** [11]2-8-11 P Robinson 3/1 FAV: 3065305: Slow away, sn handy, rdn & btn dist: 1¼ **45**
well bckd: btr 2177 (gd, 5f).
2158 **FORPETESAKE 13** [6]2-8-11 A Culhane 13/2: 06: ch g Primo Dominie - Showcase (Shareef Dancer) 4 **33**
Slow away & rear, little prog: 37,000gns Feb foal, half-brother to a plcd 1m 3yo, dam unplcd at up to 2m1f.
PARIS TAPIS [10]2-8-6 G Parkin 16/1: 7: gr f Paris House - Time of Night (Night Shift) Slow 1¼ **24**
away & wide, nvr on terms: cheaply bght Feb first foal, dam a multiple 7f/1m wnr.
XEIGHT EXPRESS [3]2-8-6 J Bramhill 16/1: 8: Sn struggling. 1¾ **19**
1968 **RUBY REBEL 22** [5]2-8-6 bl R Fitzpatrick 66/1: 0009: Slow away, in tch till halfway. 13 **0**
2183 **ETERNAL SUNSHINE 12** [2]2-8-6 T Hamilton(3) 66/1: 00: 10th: Slow away & sn bhd. 3 **0**
10 Ran   Time 1m 12.10 (2.6)   Owned: Vale Racing   Trained: Sherborne

2462 2.50 Middleham Median Auction Maiden Stakes 2yo (E)
£3702 £1139 £570   **7f rnd**   Firm   **V Slow**   Inside

2043 **STEDFAST MCSTAUNCH 18** [8] B J Meehan 2-9-0 L Keniry(3) 8/11 FAV: 4231: Cl-up & al trav well, led **83+**
2f out & readily asserted, handles firm & heels, val 4L+: well bckd at odds-on: relished step up to 7f, get further:
acts on firm & soft grnd: type to prog & h'cap company could suit: see 2043 & 1738.
1458 **FORFEITER 46** [2] T D Barron 2-9-0 BL P Hanagan 9/2: 262: Led, hdd 2f out, kept on, no ch with 2½ **75**
easy wnr: stays 7f, acts on firm & fast: eff in blnks & padd pick today, see 1091.
DRAX [5] D R Loder 2-9-0 D R McCabe 6/1: 3: b c Mark of Esteem - Tanasie (Cadeaux Genereux) 3½ **68**
Mid-div, rdn & outpcd 3f out, kept on for press, no threat to front pair: op 8/1: Feb foal, 35,000gns purchase:
half-brother to a 5f plcd juv, dam a wnr abroad: eff at 7f, looks likely to apprec 1m+: handles firm grnd.
KING HENRIK [11] A Crook 2-9-0 L Enstone(3) 20/1: 4: b c King of Kings - Ma Biche (Key To The 1½ **65**
Kingdom) Chsd ldrs, no impress over 2f out: 21,000gns 2yo purchase, Feb foal: half-brother to sev wnrs, dam a
top-class miler: this trip/1m likely to suit, prob sharper for this, an encouraging start.
2109 **TIT FOR TAT 15** [3]2-8-9 S Chin 16/1: 05: b f Diktat - Wenda (Priolo) Chsd ldrs, rdn & no prog 2 **56**
fnl 2f: E47,000 Feb foal, dam a 6f juv wnr & subs plcd at 9f.
1818 **KASHMAR FLIGHT 28** [7]2-8-9 A Mullen(7) 33/1: 006: Dwelt & held up, mod late prog, longer trip. ½ **55**
CAVA BIEN [10]2-9-0 M Fenton 20/1: 7: Dwelt, rear, carried right & hmpd over 2f out, nvr a 3 **54**
threat: scopey type but needed this & will improve in time.
BOLLIN RUTH [6]2-8-9 D Allan 25/1: 8: Slow away & al rear. nk **48**
2028 **WEB RACER 19** [1]2-8-9 D Fentiman(7) 33/1: 59: Mid-div, btn 3f out: btr 2028. 1 **46**
PARIS HEIGHTS [12]2-9-0 Dean McKeown 28/1: 0: Slow away & al bhd. 4 **43**
1974 **MIST OPPORTUNITY 21** [4]2-9-0 G Faulkner 50/1: 00: 11th: Rear whn hung right 3f out, sn btn. 2½ **38**
11 Ran   Time 1m 26.56 (3.66)   Owned: The Comic Strip Heroes   Trained: Upper Lambourn

2463 3.25 Go Racing In Yorkshire Maiden Stakes 3yo (D)
£5460 £1680 £840   **7f rnd**   Firm   Slow   Inside

2182 **MAJORCA 12** [9] J H M Gosden 3-9-0 (78) R Havlin 9/4: 0-3241: Held up, hdwy wide over 2f out & **83**
led over 1f out, sn asserted, rdn out: nicely bckd: eff at 6f, appeared to impr for step up to 7f & 1m could suit:
acts on firm & fast grnd, stiff/gall or easy trks: type to prog in h'cap company: see 2181, 1829 & 1191.
3989} **TAAQAAH 288** [6] M P Tregoning 3-9-0 A Daly 8/13 FAV: 62-2: ch g Grand Lodge - Belle Ile 1½ **79**
(Diesis) Led till 2f out, kept on for press but not pace of wnr: hvly bckd at odds-on, fit for reapp: rnr-up fnl
of just 2 '03 starts (mdn): half-brother to a 10f scorer: stays a stiff/undul 1m, return to that trip shld suit:
handles firm & fast grnd, gall or stiff/undul trk: type to impr over further in h'caps.
2 Sep'03 Hami 8.3g/f 76- D:
4789} **MISTRESS TWISTER 242** [11] T D Barron 3-8-9 P Hanagan 14/1: 03-3: b f Pivotal - Foreign Mistress 2½ **69**
(Darshaan) Trkd ldr, onepace for press fnl 2f: op 12/1, reapp: plcd 2nd of just 2 '03 starts (rtd 78, mdn): eff
at 6f, styd this easy 7f well: handles firm & fast grnd, gall or easy trk.
1971 **SWAINSWORLD 22** [4] T D Easterby 3-9-0 D Allan 20/1: 44: b g Swain - Highest Dream (Highest ¾ **72+**
Honor) Held up, prog whn no room over 1f out, kept on well cl-home, no threat: half-brother to a plcd 1m 3yo
performer: dam a multiple wnr abroad: eff at 7f, shaped as if 1m+ will suit: acts on firm & fast grnd: caught the
eye with late hdwy, clr of rem here: strong & scopey type, more to come.
1763 **THREE SHIPS 31** [3]3-9-0 P Robinson 11/1: 0-05: Dwelt, chsd ldrs till 2f out. 6 **60**

	ROSIE MAC [7]3-8-9 Suzanne France(7) 100/1: 6: Cl-up, btn 2f out: stamina laden pedigree.	nk	54
2104	BORODINSKY 15 [5]3-9-0 (45) T Eaves(3) 200/1: 000-57: Mid-div, no prog fnl 2f, longer trip.	1½	56$
1871	MILLY GOLIGHTLY 26 [2]3-8-9 L Enstone(3) 150/1: 068: Handy, btn over 1f out.	2	47
1473	TRYSTING GROVE 45 [1]3-8-9 G Parkin 66/1: 009: Mid-div, no impress fnl 3f, abs.	½	46
1539	PRINCE RENESIS 42 [8]3-9-0 Natalia Gemelova(7) 100/1: 00: 10th: Mid-div, btn 2f out, abs.	1¼	48
2325	KEY FACTOR 6 [10]3-8-9 P Mulrennan(5) 50/1: 400: 11th: Slow away & sn ran wide on bend, t.o.	dist	0

11 Ran   Time 1m 25.95 (3.05)   Owned: Sheikh Mohammed   Trained: Manton

---

2464   **4.00 Anthony Fawcett Memorial Handicap Stakes Fillies 3yo+ 0-90 (C)**   [91]
£9273 £2884 £1442   **1m rnd**   **Firm**   **Slow**   Inside

2031*	PEERESS 19 [7] Sir Michael Stoute 3-9-5 (82) B Doyle 13/8 FAV: 3-11: Held up trav well, qcknd to lead clr, rdn to assert ins last: hvly bckd on h'cap bow: suited by 1m on firm & gd: type to prog with racing.		93
1755	WATERPARK 31 [6] R Craggs 6-8-4 (56) P Fessey 16/1: 131-0102: Led, drvn & hdd dist, kept on well: op 20/1: back to form on turf & loves to force the pace: acts on firm, soft & fibresand: see 1660.	¾	63
1598	RAPHAEL 39 [2] T D Easterby 5-9-13 (79) Dale Gibson 3/1: 223-0103: Trkd ldrs, not pace of front pair over 1f out: see 1474 (7f).	2½	81
2296	SUMMER SHADES 7 [3] W M Brisbourne 6-9-6 (72) B Swarbrick(5) 11/2: 20-65244: Held up trav well, rdn & found little dist: often finds less than looks likely, poss of more interest if tried at 6/7f: see 1322.	3	68
2280	LINDENS LADY 8 [5]4-9-1 (67) M Fenton 50/1: 405-0605: Rear, mod prog fnl 3f: see 2280 (6f).	3½	56
2335	MARABAR 5 [4]6-8-9 bl (61) A Culhane 16/1: 0312266: Prom, btn 2f out: qck reapp: btr 2204.	½	49
2169	GRACEFUL AIR 13 [1]3-7-13 (62) P Hanagan 20/1: 3-452247: Dwelt, in tch till drpd rear halfway, no hdwy: btr 2169 & 1896 (prom).	2	46
2278	SCOTLAND THE BRAVE 8 [8]4-9-1 (67) M Robinson 5/1: 050-0358: Slow away, held up in tch, eff 3f out, sn btn: op 13/2: btr 2027.	1½	48

8 Ran   Time 1m 38.15 (2.75)   Owned: Cheveley Park Stud   Trained: Newmarket

---

2465   **4.35 White Swan Ampleforth Handicap Stakes 3yo+ 0-80 (D)**   [80]
£5356 £1648 £824   **1m4f**   **Firm**   **Slow**   Inside

2176*	PARTY PLOY 12 [1] K R Burke 6-8-8 (60) L Enstone(3) 5/1: 06-00211: Trkd ldrs, styd on for press to lead well ins last, gamely: suited by 12/14f on firm, soft & both AWs: tough & in great form: see 2176, 2105.		67
2217	BAKIRI 11 [4] Andrew Reid 6-8-8 (60) B Doyle 16/1: 0405232: Prom & drvn/led 2f out, hdd well ins last: clr of rem: bandaged: see 2217, 2163 & 1271.	nk	66
2217	FIELD SPARK 11 [2] J A Glover 4-8-7 p (59) G Duffield 9/2: 16-61523: Held up, drvn & kept on onepace fnl 2f, no threat: op 11/2: handles firm & gd: ahd of today's 2nd in 2217, see 1830.	3½	60
2078	CRATHORNE 17 [3] J D Bethell 4-10-0 p (80) P Robinson 3/1 FAV: 5030-434: Held up, rdn & kept on fnl 3f, not able to chall: nicely bckd: btr 2078 & 1668.	1	80
2284	COMPTON DRAGON 7 [9]5-9-8 vis (74) A Nicholls 7/1: 0505225: Held up, no impress fnl 2f: btr 2284.	2½	70
2041	MARITIME BLUES 18 [5]4-8-13 (65) M Fenton 7/1: 0-000106: Led till 2f out, sn btn: btr 1875.	3	57
1781	BOND MAY DAY 30 [6]4-9-4 (70) F Lynch 20/1: 00160-07: b f Among Men - State Romance (Free State) Cl-up, btn over 1f out: class stks & h'cap scorer '03, AW h'cap plcd (rtd 59a): h'cap rnr-up in '02: eff at 10/12f on firm, gd & fibresand, prob any trk.	3	58

1 Jul'03 Beve 9.9gd 74-66 E: 2 Apr'03 Beve 12.1fm 74-72 E: 1 Apr'03 Thir 12fm 71-(66) E: 2 Apr'03 Ripo 10g/f 70-65 E:
2 Mar'03 Sout 10g/f 67-65 F: 2 Aug'02 Ches 7g/f 69-69 C: 2 Aug'02 Bath 5.7fm 64- E:

1884	SIR NIGHT 25 [10]4-8-0 (52) P Hanagan 20/1: 4000-408: Bhd & no ch fnl 2f: btr 1821.	10	26
2147	MERRYMAKER 13 [7]4-8-3 vis (55) B Swarbrick(5) 9/1: 433-464P: Saddle slipped & p.u.: see 1693.		0

9 Ran   Time 2m 33.70 (3.9)   Owned: Mr Ian A McInnes   Trained: Leyburn

---

2466   **5.10 Barnard Handicap Stakes 3yo+ 0-70 (E)**   [68]
£3731 £1148 £574   **7f rnd**   **Firm**   **Slow**   Inside

2059	LORD OF THE EAST 18 [10] D Nicholls 5-9-13 (67) D R McCabe 14/1: 02-03201: Keen, made all, strongly pressed dist, all out: eff at 6/7f on firm & gd/soft, any trk, loves a sharp/easy one: see 1215.		77
2324	ALCHEMIST MASTER 6 [4] R M Whitaker 5-9-0 (54) Dean McKeown 5/2 FAV: 0000-622: Trkd ldrs & drvn to chall dist, just held cl-home: nicely bckd, op 7/2: acts on firm, gd/soft & both AWs: see 2324 & 1972.	nk	63
2280	BOLLIN EDWARD 8 [1] T D Easterby 5-9-7 (61) D Allan, 8/1: 0000-653: Chsd ldrs, drvn & kept on, not pace of front pair: stays 7f: acts on firm & gd grnd: see 2059.	1¾	66
2317	BORDER ARTIST 6 [8] D Nicholls 5-9-10 (64) A Nicholls 8/1: 0-001004: Held up, kept on for press, not pace to chall front pair: stablemate of wnr: acts on firm, gd & fibresand: see 1794.	shd	69
2280	DOWNLAND 8 [12]8-9-2 (56) Kim Tinkler 12/1: 00-02165: Chsd ldrs, kept on fnl 2f: see 1897.	2	57
2218	DARA MAC 11 [9]5-8-13 (53) Suzanne France(7) 33/1: 2005-026: Mid-div 3f out, onepace for press.	shd	54
2447	SMITH N ALLAN OILS 1 [6]5-9-3 p (57) L Enstone(3) 16/1: 10000007: Held up, mod late prog for press, unplcd yesterday.	1¼	55
1897	MR BOUNTIFUL 25 [5]6-8-13 p (53) P Hanagan 8/1: 300-0048: Mid-div, no prog fnl 2f: see 22 (AW).	hd	50
2235*	YORKSHIRE BLUE 10 [7]5-9-4 (58) N Mackay(3) 6/1: 00-00119: Rear, late prog: btr 2235 (gd).	nk	54
905	NOBLE PURSUIT 84 [13]7-8-13 (50) T Eaves(3) 50/1: 0035500: 10th: Mid-div, no impress fnl 2f: 12 wk abs: new yard: btr 811 & 502 (AW).	½	48
2218	LUKE AFTER ME 11 [2]4-9-0 (54) B Doyle 8/1: 3020430: 11th: Al rear: op 10/1.	3½	42
2214	DRURY LANE 11 [11]4-9-2 bl (56) A Culhane 14/1: 0000040: 12th: Chsd wnr, drvn & btn over 1f out.	¾	42

1972 Northern Games 22 [14]5-9-3 (57) P Fessey 33/1:0   2053 St Ivian 18 [3]4-9-6 vis(60) R Fitzpatrick 33/1:0

14 Ran   Time 1m 24.69(1.79)   Owned: The Wayward Lads   Trained: Thirsk

Official Going Good/Firm

2467	2.30 Gr2 Coventry Stakes 2yo (A)
	£40600　£15400　£7700　　6f str　　Good/Firm 30　　-19 Slow　Stands Side

1760* **ICEMAN 31** [11] J H M Gosden 2-8-12　K Fallon　5/1 JT FAV: 211: Held up, rdn 3f out, styd on &　112+
switched right over 1f out, led ins last, ran on well, drvn out: well bckd: v eff at 6f, 7f looks sure to suit (dam
1m/11f scorer): relished fast grnd last twice & a gall trk: v smart & progressive, genuine & shld win more Gr
races, esp over further: see 1760, 1538.

2158* **COUNCIL MEMBER 13** [5] Saeed bin Suroor 2-8-12　L Dettori　5/1 JT FAV: 12: With ldrs, hdwy to lead　½　110
over 1f out, flicked tail for press but styd on gamely till collared cl-home, just held: smart run stepped up in
class & clearly stays a stiff 6f well, shld stay further: acts on fast grnd: lightly rcd, must be winning in Gr class.

1934 **CAPABLE GUEST 24** [9] M R Channon 2-8-12　C Catlin　33/1: 333: Sn detached, still last 2f out,　1¾　105+
"flew home" fnl 1f, nrst fin: imprvd up in class & crying out for 7f+ now: win over further.

2039* **TONY JAMES 18** [7] C E Brittain 2-8-12　D Holland　13/2: 14: Made most till over 1f out, no extra　nk　104
ins last: nicely bckd: useful run, drop into Gr 3/List will suit: see 2039.

1510* **TURNKEY 43** [14]2-8-12　T E Durcan　7/1: 215: Dwelt, bhd, outer, hdwy well over 1f out, sn no　1¾　99
extra: bckd tho' op 11/2: form of race 1510 (5f) is working out well but that was on v testing grnd.

1014* **BERKHAMSTED 75** [8]2-8-12　J Murtagh　25/1: 16: In tch, outpcd well over 1f out, some late gains:　1½　95
11 wk abs: far from disgraced up in class & 6/7f will suit: acts on fast & gd/soft: lightly rcd, see 1014.

2003* **ORATORIO 23** [6]2-8-12　J P Spencer　6/1: 17: With ldrs, chall over 1f out, sn wknd: btr expected　hd　94
after making all in mdn company in 2003.

2039 **DARIO GEE GEE 18** [3]2-8-12　N Callan　33/1: 1228: In tch, no impress fnl 2f: stiff task, see 2039, 1149.　½　92
1738* **GOODRICKE 32** [4]2-8-12　T P Queally　14/1: 2119: Trkd ldrs, wknd well over 1f out: btr 1738 (stks, soft).　1　89
2144 **DANCE ANTHEM 13** [12]2-8-12　P McCabe　50/1: 120: 10th: In tch, wknd well over 1f out: see 2144.　2　83
2071* **BEAVER PATROL 17** [13]2-8-12　S Carson　20/1: 13210: 11th: With ldrs, wknd well over 1f out.　1　80
2188* **KINGS QUAY 12** [2]2-8-12　Dane O'Neill　6/1: 10: 12th: Slow away, sn in tch, wknd 2f out, eased:　1½　76
well bckd: up in class & trip but btr expected after 2188 (gd grnd, mdn auct).

2303 **CATWALK CLERIC 11** [1]2-8-12　K Darley　50/1: 4120: 13th: Al bhd, eased: stiff task: see 1571 (gd/soft). 7　55
13 Ran　Time 1m 14.83 (1.73)　Owned: Cheveley Park Stud　Trained: Manton

---

2468	3.05 Gr2 King's Stand Stakes 3yo+ (A)
	£81200　£30800　£15400　　5f str　　Good/Firm 30　　-13 Slow　Stands Side

2305 **THE TATLING 9** [5] J M Bradley 7-9-2　(112) D Holland　8/1: 340-2341: Held up, gd hdwy 2f out,　120
qcknd to lead ins last, rdn clr, readily: stays 6f, prob best over a stiff 5f & likes firm & gd, acts on soft & any
trk: best without t-strap: relishes a fast pace, career best here & thriving at 7yo, credit to connections: see 1856.

3985] **CAPE OF GOOD HOPE 51** [1] D Oughton 6-9-2 VIS T M J Kinane　13/2: 43-63222: ch g Inchinor - Cape　1½　116
Merino (Clantime)　In tch, rdn & hdwy 2f out, styd on to chall ins last, kept on well, not pace of wnr: earlier
rnr-up in Gr 1 sprint in Hong Kong, last win back in '02: trained by D Elsworth back in '01, Newmarket mdn wnr:
suited to 5/6f, stays 7f: handles gd/soft, likes fast grnd & wears visor/t-strap: v smart sprinter.
1 May'01 Newm 7g/f 94- D:

1479* **FRIZZANTE 45** [7] J R Fanshawe 5-8-13　(111) J Murtagh　9/2 FAV: 4611-213: Held up, hdwy & short of　nk　113+
room twice/lost momentum 2f out, switched left & styd on strongly ins last, nrst fin: nicely bckd: 6 wk abs: much
closer with a clr run & another v promising/smart eff from this progressive mare: has a nice turn of foot over a
stiff 5/6f, remains one to keep on your side: see 1479, 1187.

1996 **RINGMOOR DOWN 24** [2] D W P Arbuthnot 5-8-13　(103) Dane O'Neill　25/1: 243-6134: Slow away, held　nk　112
up, hdwy & short of room well over 1f out, switched right & kept on ins last, nrst fin: imprvd/smart eff & a shade
closer with clr run: shld win races, esp fillls List/Gr 3s: see 1400, 1207.

4680* **MAJESTIC MISSILE 248** [13]3-8-10　(116) K Fallon　5/1: 211161-5: b c Royal Applause - Tshusick　nk　114
(Dancing Brave)　In tch, hdwy 2f out, chall just ins last, kept on well, not pace of wnr: won 5 of 7 '03 starts
(mdn, stks & 2 Gr3s): v eff at 5f on firm & gd grnd, any trk: runs well fresh: v smart & a fine turn of foot last
term, gd return & shld be more to come.　1 Oct'03 Asco 5gd 118-(100) A:　1 Jul'03 Sand 5gd 112-(99) A:
1 Jul'03 Ches 5.1fm 102- B:　1 Jul'03 Kemp 5g/f 99- D:　2 Jun'03 Wind 5.0g/f 89- D:

2068* **BOOGIE STREET 17** [18]3-8-10　(107) R Hughes　12/1: 341-3216: Led, edged right stands rail over 2f　nk　113
out, hdd 1f out, onepace: v smart run under enterprising tactics: relish a drop into List/Gr 3 as in 2068.

1667 **BAHAMIAN PIRATE 35** [11]9-9-2　(105) Gary Stevens　50/1: 1442107: Slow away, bhd, hdwy over 1f out,　hd　111
kept on ins last, hands & heels, never dngr: ride: smart run & a v tough 9yo who looks poised to win again on soft.

1732 **NIGHTS CROSS 32** [16]3-8-10　(105) T E Durcan　50/1: 3212-438: Held up, late gains, nvr dngrs:　nk　111
encouraging, relish a return to List: see 1732, 1106.

LYDGATE 46 [19]4-9-2 T L Dettori　16/1: 0-244219: b c Pulpit - Mariuka (Danzig)　Held up, nvr a　1¼　106
factor: 6 wk abs: American raider, Gr 3 wnr there earlier: eff at 5/6.5f on gd & firm grnd.

2305 **THE TRADER 9** [17]6-9-2 bl (113) J P Spencer　10/1: 1426-130: 10th: Slow away, bhd, hdwy when short　nk　105
of room appr fnl 1f, nvr dngrs: in front of this wnr in 2305 & 1856.

2206 **DRAGON FLYER 11** [12]5-8-13　(98) J A Heffernan　100/1: 0-420000: 11th: Prom, wknd fnl 1f:　shd　101
overfaced: needs stks/List: see 1159, 883.

1958 **STORMONT 22** [8]4-9-5　J Quinn　66/1: 310-4000: 12th: Slow away, bhd, short of room over 1f out,　1½　103
no dngr: see 1958.

2206 **IF PARADISE 11** [10]3-8-10　(105) R L Moore　100/1: 205-1060: 13th: In tch, wknd well over 1f out:　1¼　97
btr 1106 (5f, soft).

2068 **LOCHRIDGE 17** [6]5-8-13　(106) K Darley　7/1: 61130-20: 14th: Al bhd: see 2068 (List, 5f).　nk　92
1479 **MORNIN RESERVES 45** [3]5-9-2　(107) R Winston　18/1: 13012-00: 15th: Handy, wknd well over 1f out.　1¼　91
2206 **COLONEL COTTON 11** [4]5-9-2 bl (103) E Ahern　33/1: 0-606550: 16th: Nvr a factor.　½　89
1594 **SMOKIN BEAU 39** [14]7-9-2 BL (97) T G McLaughlin　100/1: 00-62000: 17th: Handy, wknd well over 1f　shd　88
out: tried blnks: see 1594, 1137.

2206 **SPEED COP 11** [9]4-8-13　(99) M Hills　50/1: 410-2300: 18th: In tch, wknd over 2f out: see 1400, 883.　4　73
2206 **DUBAIAN GIFT 11** [15]5-9-2　(101) K McEvoy　66/1: 16-00000: 19th: Handy, wknd qckly 2f out, sadly　14　76
collapsed & died after race.
19 Ran　Time 1m 0.16 (1.16)　Owned: Dab Hand Racing　Trained: Chepstow

2469   3.45 Gr1 St James's Palace Stakes Colts 3yo (A)
£139896 £53064 £26532   1m rnd   Good/Firm 30   + 04 Fast   Inside

1995 **AZAMOUR 24** [1] John M Oxx 3-9-0 M J Kinane 9/2: 11-321: Handy, hdwy 2f out, styd on strongly to   123
lead ins last, drvn out, gamely: well bckd: plcd in Newmarket & Irish 2,000 Guineas prev: stays a stiff 1m well,
10f looks sure to suit: enjoys fast grnd, acts on gd/soft: high-class & genuine, imprvd today & shld win more Gr 1's.

1855 **DIAMOND GREEN FR 30** [8] A Fabre 3-9-0 Gary Stevens 10/1: 111-322: In tch, hdwy 2f out, styd on   nk   122
well to chall ins last, just held for press: excellent/imprvd eff & enjoyed this fast grnd, also acts on soft:
high-class, shld find a Gr 1 shortly: see 1855.

1855 **ANTONIUS PIUS 30** [10] A P O'Brien 3-9-0 T J P Spencer 7/1: 110-453: Hld up, hdwy trav well when   ¾   120
short of room 2f out, sn cruised up on bit but found little & no extra under press ins last: wore t-strap: bundles of
talent but unfortunately a v suspect temperament (threw away 2,000 Guineas in 1433 by veering sharply right
having hit lead): acts on fast & gd/soft: try headgear?

1480+ **HAAFHD 45** [6] B W Hills 3-9-0 [124] R Hills 6/4 FAV: 1133-114: Trkd ldr, led 2f out, styd on for   nk   119
press till collared ins last, no extra, not btn far: hvly bckd: reportedly shade below best on lead up to this race
& did not quite "fire" like when beating this wnr in 2,000 Guineas in 1480: worth another chance, see 1188.

1860* **BRUNEL 30** [4]3-9-0 [115] D Holland 14/1: 2215-115: Dwelt, sn in tch, eff 2f out, onepace: prob   1½   116
ran close to best & will apprec Gr 2/3 in Britain: see 1860 (German Guineas).

2248* **CASTLETON 10** [7]3-9-0 [100] K Fallon 66/1: 34-2316: Set pace, rdn & hdd 2f out, onepace & held   shd 115
when hmpd ins last, not recover: seemingly much imprvd on this big step up in class: shld be winning in List/Gr 3.

1995* **BACHELOR DUKE 24** [9]3-9-0 [120] S Sanders 6/1: 334-017: Keen in tch, rdn over 2f out, no   1¼   112
impress: beat this wnr 1L in Irish 2,000 Guineas in 1995 (much imprvd form), but failed to repeat that here.

1855 **BYRON 30** [3]3-9-0 T [111] L Dettori 20/1: 1341-38: In tch, wkng when short of room over 1f out,   1½   109
no extra: t-strap: see 1855.

2190* **MADID 12** [5]3-9-0 W Supple 12/1: 119: Dwelt, sn rdn bhd, btn 2f out: big step up in class: ½   108
shld stay 1m & worth another chance in List/Gr 3 class after 2190.

2307 **PEARL OF LOVE 9** [2]3-9-0 [114] K Darley 25/1: 111-00: 10th: In tch, wknd over 2f out: 3   102
reportedly bled from hoof after race: poss not trained on? see 2307.

1995 **NEWTON 24** [11]3-9-0 VIS Paul Scallan 100/1: 42-14660: 11th: Reluctant to race & left bhd start,   20   42
wknd over 2f out: tried visor: see 1063.

11 Ran   Time 1m 39.02 (0.52)   Owned: HH Aga Khan   Trained: Ireland

2470   4.20 Gr1 Queen Anne Stakes 4yo+ (A)
£145000 £55000 £27500   1m str   Good/Firm 30   + 05 Fast   Stands Side

1758 **REFUSE TO BEND 31** [1] Saeed bin Suroor 4-9-0 t [115] L Dettori 12/1: 0100-001: Trkd ldrs, hdwy 2f   123
out, strong run to lead cl-home, drvn out: well bckd, gd time, joc given 1-day whip ban: right back to v best,
suited by 1m, has tried 12f: acts on gd & fast grnd, stiff/gall trks: wears a t-strap: high-class miler at best.

1997* **SOVIET SONG 24** [3] J R Fanshawe 4-8-11 [114] J Murtagh 6/1: 245-2312: Nvr far away, went on   nk   119
entering fnl 1f, worn down cl-home: well bckd: tremendous run in a race in which filly has a poor record: deserves
another Gr 1 & the Falmouth stks at Newmarket shld be ideal: see 1997.

1758 **SALSELON 31** [9] L M Cumani 5-9-0 bl [118] D Holland 14/1: 2310-023: Unruly start, sn bhd,   ¾   119
switched wide & styd on v strongly under hands & heels fnl 1f, nrst fin: made a lot of late hdwy & well worth a try
at 10f now: high-class performer who shld benefit from more positive tactics: see 1758.

2002 **NEBRASKA TORNADO 23** [4] A Fabre 4-8-11 Gary Stevens 20/1: 11161-54: b f Storm Cat - Media Nox   1   115
(Lycius) Nvr far away, led halfway till entering fnl 1f, no extra: French challenger, won 4 times in '03, notably a
Gr 1 at Longchamp: winning form at 1m/10f on gd & v soft, handles fast grnd: likes to run up with the pace: v
smart filly who shld win more group races this term. 1 Jun'03 Chan 10.5gd 116- A:

4795} **TILLERMAN 241** [5]8-9-0 [117] R Hughes 7/1: D10330-5: b c In The Wings - Autumn Tint (Roberto)   1¼   115
Slowly away, hld up, no run several times from 3f out, styd on eye-catchingly under a kind ride: dual Gr 3 wnr in
'03, rnr-up in this race prev 2 seasons: '02 Gr 2 wnr: best btwn 7/9f: handles gd/soft, loves fast & firm grnd, also
Ascot: v smart & has a fine turn of foot, one to be with next time.
1 Jul'03 Asco 8g/f 118-(117) A: 2 Jun'03 Asco 8g/f 118-(117) A: 1 Apr'03 Leic 7.0gd 118-(117) A:
1 Aug'02 Good 8fm 118- A: 2 Jun'02 Asco 8gd 118- A: 1 Jun'02 Leic 7g/f 111- C:

2002 **SIX PERFECTIONS 23** [12]4-8-11 T Thulliez 5/2 FAV: 22211-26: Held up, switched wide & hdwy 2f   ¾   110
out, onepcd fnl 1f: hvly bckd: French challenger: below best on on grnd prob faster than ideal (connections
reported it too firm): high-class with a fine turn of foot at best: see 2002.

1859 **BOWMANS CROSSING 30** [6]5-9-0 VIS M J Kinane 33/1: 2-335437: b g Dolphin Street - Biraya   hd   112
(Valiyar) Mid-div, hmpd 2f out, not qckn fnl 1f: Hong Kong challenger, won at Sha Tin in Jan '03: winning form at
7/9f on gd & fast grnd: wears a visor: see 2002.

2252 **CHECKIT 10** [7]4-9-0 [112] T E Durcan 66/1: 3600348: Nvr btr than mid-div: see 2002.   1½   109

991 **MARTILLO 45** [10]4-9-0 W Mongil 14/1: 1310-519: b c Anabaa - Maltage (Affirmed) Held up, eff &   nk   108
no room 2f out, no impress: 6 wk abs: disapp run from this German challenger, recent Gr 2 wnr in France: dual Gr 2
wnr in '03, also sltly unlucky 3rd in Gr 1 St James's Palace here at Royal Ascot: suited by 1m on fast & soft grnd:
btr than this. 1 Jul'03 Hopp 8gd 112- A:

1758 **HURRICANE ALAN 31** [11]4-9-0 [114] P Dobbs 25/1: 205-3150: 10th: Held up, short of room 2f out,   2½   103
nvr nr ldrs: btr 1349.

1862* **ALKAADHEM 26** [8]4-9-0 [108] R Hills 9/1: 121-5410: 11th: Prom, wknd dist: up in grade after 1862.   1¾   99

1996 **ARAKAN 24** [17]4-9-0 [111] K Fallon 16/1: 263-1320: 12th: Held up, brief eff wide 2f out, sn btn: 5   89
moderately drawn: this is not his form, see 1996 & 1187 (6f).

1667 **JUST JAMES 35** [16]5-9-0 [113] E Ahern 33/1: 25201-00: 13th: Al rear.   1½   86

1758 **NORSE DANCER 31** [14]4-9-0 [117] T Quinn 10/1: 0360-430: 14th: Nvr trav mid-div, btn 2f out,   12   62
eased: well bckd: often finds less than expected under press but v smart at best & beat today's wnr in 1758.

2128 **LATEEN SAILS 14** [2]4-9-0 t [114] K McEvoy 33/1: 1/0141-00: 15th: Led till halfway, wknd & eased: 7   48
stablemate & prob pacemaker for wnr: see 1758.

2252 **BEAUCHAMP PILOT 10** [15]6-9-0 J P Spencer 66/1: 1/3020-60: 16th: Chsd ldrs 2f, wknd qckly, eased   24   0
& virtually p.u.: something clearly amiss & stable out of form: see 2252.

16 Ran   Time 1m 39.14 (0.44)   Owned: Godolphin   Trained: Newmarket

2471   4.55 Ascot Stakes Handicap 4yo+ 0-95 (C)   [98]
£23200 £8800 £4400   2m4f   Good/Firm 30   +05 Fast   Inside

2239 **DOUBLE OBSESSION 10** [24] M Johnston 4-9-2 vis (86) J F Egan 25/1: 000-0001: Prom, went on 2f out,   **98**
rdn well clr, decisively: gd time: right back to form & clearly apprec this big step up in trip, eff at 12f, stays
2m4f really well: acts on fast & gd/soft, handles firm: handles any trk: loves Ascot: apprec reapplication of vis.
1689 **PROMOTER 34** [28] J Noseda 4-9-1 (85) E Ahern 14/1: 1404-002: Keen & prom, went after wnr dist,   5   **92**
styd on well but no impress: stays a stiff/gall 2m4f, may drop back to 2m for the Northumberland Plate next time.
3508] **PENNY PICTURES 670** [15] M C Pipe 5-9-6 (87) Gary Stevens 25/1: 512234/-3: b g Theatrical -   6   **88**
Copper Creek (Habitat) Keen in rear, hdwy wide halfway, chsd ldrs 4f out, onepcd fnl 2f on Flat reapp: jumps fit,
April '04 h'cap hdle wnr (eff around 2m on gd & hvy, rtd 122h): missed '03 on the Flat, prev term won a h'cap for J
Given: eff at 12f, stays 2m4f: acts on firm & fast grnd, hvy over hdles: handles any trk.
2 Jul'02 Bath 11.6g/f 88- C: 2 Jun'02 Ches 12.3fm 88-85 D: 1 Jun'02 Ripo 12.2fm 87-77 D: 1 Aug'01 Catt 7g/f 85- D:
1232 **REDSPIN 59** [2] J S Moore 4-7-12 (68) D Kinsella 100/1: 502-3004: Held up, hdwy wide 3f out, fin   1   **68**
strongly but too late: 8 wk abs & fine run from this rank outsider: unproven prev beyond 10f, clearly stays
marathon trip: see 288 (AW).
1928* **LAND N STARS 24** [14]4-8-9 (79) P Doe 11/2 FAV: 0/422-015: Trkd ldrs, outpcd fnl 2f: hvly bckd: 1¼   **78**
reportedly failed to stay this longer 2m4f trip: impressive wnr over 2m here at Ascot in 1928.
1112 **TERESA 45** [11]4-8-8 (78) J Quinn 16/1: 3133-266: Trkd ldrs, left bhd fnl 2f: 6 wk abs: see 1112.   nk   **77**
2276 **RIYADH 8** [29]6-8-1 vis (68) R Ffrench 14/1: 0003037: Trkd ldrs, fdd fnl 2f, carried head high: 1½   **66**
won this race from a 20lb higher mark in '02 (with M Pipe): does not look an easy ride now, see 2276.
2198 **ALMIZAN 12** [13]4-8-12 (82) T E Durcan 33/1: 564-0048: Mid-div, nvr nr to chall: see 2198.   ½   **79**
1335] **STANCE 184** [16]5-8-10 (77) R L Moore 20/1: 005023-9: b g Salse - De Stael (Nijinsky) Rear, some   2   **72**
late hdwy, nvr dngrs: hdles fit, won last 3 starts (novs, eff at 2m/2m2f on gd & gd/soft, rtd 128h): plcd on the
Flat in Spain in '03, prev term won a mdn for H Cecil: unproven beyond 12f, shld stay further: acts on fast &
gd/soft, prob soft grnd: now with G L Moore & poss well h'capped on the Flat.
1 Jul'02 Newb 12g/f 84- D: 2 Jun'02 Warw 12.6gd 84- D:
1928 **DON FERNANDO 24** [27]5-8-9 (76) D Holland 12/1: 0000-050: 10th: Held up last, modest late hdwy: 1¼   **70**
7th from a 5lb higher mark when also unenterprisingly rdn in this race last yr: see 1928.
2114 **WASTED TALENT 15** [20]4-8-5 (75) Dane O'Neill 25/1: 2531-120: 11th: Trkd ldrs, btn 2f out.   ½   **68**
1928 **GOT ONE TOO 24** [25]7-8-6 (73) M J Kinane 11/1: 01///113-20: 12th: Led, clr halfway, hdd 2f out,   2   **64**
wknd qckly: prob failed to stay this longer 2m4f trip: btr 1928 (2m).
2355 **GRALMANO 4** [6]9-9-2 (83) N Callan 66/1: 102-0060: 13th: Chsd ldrs, wknd 2f out: qck reapp.   1¼   **73**
2198 **ESTABLISHMENT 12** [10]7-8-3 (70) K McEvoy 16/1: 15-00000: 14th: Nvr btr than mid-div: rnr-up in   2   **58**
this race from a 3lb higher mark 2 yrs ago & usually runs well here at Ascot: see 1484.
2276 **HERNANDITA 8** [23]6-7-12 (1oh) (64) J F McDonald(3) 66/1: 002/00/-40: 15th: Chsd ldrs, btn 2f out.   1¼   **52**
2293] **AMID THE CHAOS 24** [4]4-9-4 VIS T (88) P J Smullen 25/1: 6401-00: 16th: ch c Nashwan - Celebrity   3   **72**
Style (Seeking The Gold) Nvr btr than mid-div: Irish challenger, won fnl '03 start (mdn): unproven beyond 10f,
acts on gd grnd: wears a visor & t-strap: with D Weld.
1112 **HAWADETH 66** [22]9-8-12 p (79) K Darley 25/1: //06/0//-50: 17th: Held up, nvr nr ldrs: see 1112.   1¼   **62**
1689 **MANA DARGENT 34** [19]7-9-7 (88) J Fanning 33/1: 433-0500: 18th: Mid-div, sltly short of room 4f   1½   **69**
out, sn btn: shorter priced stablemate of wnr, well bckd: 3rd, 4th & 6th in this race in prev 3 yrs: loves Ascot &
will come gd here in July/Aug over 2m: see 1569.
2198 **KING FLYER 12** [7]8-9-0 (81) S Whitworth 25/1: 6-023020: 19th: Al bhd from modest draw: btr 2198.   1¼   **61**
2229* **GLORY QUEST 11** [21]7-8-8 (75) I Mongan 33/1: 2103410: 20th: Chsd ldrs, wknd qckly 3f out: btr 2229.   16   **39**
2239 **SENTRY 10** [1]4-9-2 (86) L Dettori 11/1: 31-14330: 21th: Rear, imprvd to chase ldrs 3f out, sn   2   **48**
btn: bckd from 14/1, poor draw: see 2239.
1923 **ONCE 24** [26]4-8-5 (75) S W Kelly 66/1: 3/2300-30: 22th: Chsd ldrs, wknd 4f out: see 1923 (14f).   ½   **36**
1569 **NUMITAS 41** [12]4-9-5 (89) S Sanders 12/1: 02010-00: 23th: Al bhd: 6 wk abs.   5   **45**
2486] **CHIMES AT MIDNIGHT 683** [18]7-10-0 bl (95) J A Heffernan 80/1: 005060/-0: 24th: Al bhd on reapp.   5   **46**
2198 **MALARKEY 12** [5]7-8-10 (77) K Fallon 16/1: 5121530: 25th: Mid-div, btn 4f out, t.o.: modest draw.   9   **19**
2244 **DOMENICO 16** [17]6-8-3 (70) W Supple 66/1: 6002-030: 26th: Mid-div, btn 4f out, t.o..   1½   **11**
2602] **CARLYS QUEST 710** [3]10-9-1 vis t (82) R Winston 50/1: 2/4320/0/-0: 27th: Al bhd, t.o.: jumps fit.   13   **10**

2192 **INVITATION 12** [9]6-8-7 (1ow) (73) R Hughes 66/1: 0642020: 28th: Slowly away, al bhd, t.o..   15   **0**
3193] **XELLANCE 685** [8]7-8-8 (75) J P Spencer 20/1: 020320/-0: 29th: Front rank, wknd qckly 5f out,   dist   **0**
t.o. in last: jumps fit.
29 Ran   Time 4m 20.99 (2.99)   Owned: RWHuggins RBHuckerby Atlantic Racing   Trained: Middleham

2472   5.30 Listed Windsor Castle Stakes 2yo (A)
£23200 £8800 £4400   5f str   Good/Firm 30   -39 Slow   Stands Side

1826* **CHATEAU ISTANA 28** [7] N P Littmoden 2-8-13   T P Queally 12/1: 611: Held up, gd hdwy dist, styd   **108**
on strongly to lead cl-home despite being hit by rival joc's whip, rdn out: eff over a stiff/gall 5f, will stay 6f:
acts on fast grnd: fast improving & v useful juv, see 1826 & 1256.
2167 **TOURNEDOS 13** [12] M R Channon 2-8-13   T E Durcan 12/1: 122: Held up, hdwy 2f out, ev ch fnl 1f &   ½   **106**
only just btn: eff at 5f on gd & fast grnd, 6f shld now suit: v useful juv, win more races: see 2167 & 1205.
2109* **SAFARI SUNSET 15** [1] P Winkworth 2-8-11   P Doe 4/2/1: 13: Nvr far away, led dist till ins fnl 1f,   ½   **102**
no extra: nicely bckd & only btn around 1L: acts on fast & firm grnd & confirmed debut promise of 2109.
2158 **JUANTORENA 13** [5] M L W Bell 2-8-11   D Holland 8/1: 224: Front rank, ev ch dist, not qckn   nk   **100**
cl-home: only btn around 1L & nailed on to find a mdn judged on this: see 2158 & 1934 (6f).
2094 **CELTIC SPA 15** [6]2-8-6   R L Moore 66/1: 0105: Mid-div, styd on under press fnl 1f, nrst fin: 1½   **92**
fine run from this rank outsider: see 1608 (soft grnd).
1717 **AGE OF KINGS 33** [3]2-8-11   J Murtagh 5/2 FAV: 36: Rear, eff when short of room dist, fin well   ½   **95+**
but too late: hvly bckd from 4/1, reportedly hung right: did not get the run of today's race, held in high regard &
must surely find at least a mdn: relish 6f: see 1717.
     DARK CHEETAH 18 [13]2-8-13   J P Spencer 9/2: 17: b c Storm Cat - Layoune (Mt Livermore) Led   hd   **96**
till dist, wkng when short of room ins fnl 1f: well bckd Irish challenger: Cork mdn wnr on sole prev start:
half-brother to a juv wnr in the US: eff at 5f on firm grnd: with A O'Brien.
2188 **ALPAGA LE JOMAGE 12** [10]2-8-11   P J Smullen 100/1: 332458: Speed 3.5f: see 2094 & 1573.   1   **91**
251 **ROYAL ISLAND 10** [14]2-8-13   K Darley 6/1: 1129: Front rank, wknd dist: had a hard race in 2251   2   **92**
(6f) & a return to further will suit.

2171 **SAFSOOF 13** [4]2-8-11 L Dettori 13/2: 20: 10th: Slowly away, nvr nr ldrs: showed more 2171. ¾ 87
2100* **BOLD MARC 15** [2]2-8-11 Darren Williams 20/1: 41210: 11th: Chsd ldrs, btn dist: up in grade. ¾ 81
2094 **NEXT TIME AROUND 15** [8]2-9-1 R Winston 33/1: 1350: 12th: Sn rdn & al bhd: reportedly unsuited ½ 83
by this v fast grnd: see 1149 & 920 (gd, debut).
2158 **PROSPECT COURT 13** [9]2-8-11 T Quinn 100/1: 030: 13th: Al towards rear: highly tried. 1¼ 77
1669 **ELSIE HART 35** [11]2-8-8 W Supple 33/1: 130: 14th: Al bhd: see 1669 (6f, soft). 6 72
2051 **IAM FOREVERBLOWING 18** [15]2-8-6 D Corby 200/1: 54500: 15th: Bhd halfway, fin last: v highly tried. 8 46
15 Ran   Time 1m 01.45(2.45)   Owned: Mr Ivan Allan   Trained: Newmarket

Official Going Good/Firm

2473   **2.20 Unit Median Auction Maiden Stakes Qualifier For Hamilton Park 2-Y-O Series Final 2yo (E)**
£3835 £1180 £590   **6f5y str**   **Good/Firm 32**   **-02 Slow**   Stands side

2236 **SACRED NUTS 11** [2] M L W Bell 2-9-0 J Mackay 3/1: 51: b c Sri Pekan - Sagrada (Primo Dominie) 84
Dwelt, prog after 3f, led dist, drvn out to hold on: op 2/1: Mar foal, cost 28,000 gns: half brother to wnrs at 2:
dam wnr abroad: sire decent performer as a juv: eff at 6f, further shld suit: acts on fast grnd & a stiff/undul trk.
2119 **JANE JUBILEE 15** [5] M Johnston 2-8-9 J Fanning 14/1: 352: Led, hdd dist, rallied ins fnl 1f, nk 77
just held: eff at 6f, 7f will suit: shld find a race: see 1658.
2109 **MELVINO 16** [3] T D Barron 2-9-0 P Makin(5) 12/1: 403: Handy, kept on ins fnl 1f, not btn far: 1¼ 78
clr rem: apprec return to 6f: acts on fast grnd: see 1744.
     DENNICK 0 [7] P C Haslam 2-9-0 G Faulkner 25/1: 4: b g Nicolotte - Branston Dancer 5 64
(Rudimentary) Prom till dist, wknd: debut: Feb 1st foal, cost 10,000 gns: dam unrcd.
2263 **MY PRINCESS 9** [6]2-8-9 G Duffield 8/11 FAV: 35: Handy over 4f, sn fdd: well bckd: v disapp 4 48
effort & failed to build on promise shown in 2263 (debut).
1950 **JERRYS GIRL 23** [1]2-8-9 J Carroll 7/1: 36: Slow away, al in rear: op 4/1: btr 1950. 11 18
1950 **BLACK COMBE LADY 23** [4]2-8-9 P Mathers(7) 100/1: 07: br f Indian Danehill - Florinda (Vice 8 0
Regent) Al in rear: Apr foal, cost £8,500: half sister to wnrs at 5/9f: sire decent performer around 10f.
7 Ran   Time 1m 11.88 (2.08)   Owned: Fitzroy Thoroughbreds   Trained: Newmarket

2474   **2.55 Health Matters For Men Classified Stakes 3yo 0-65 (E)**
£3933 £1210 £605   **1m65y rnd**   **Good/Firm 32**   **-05 Slow**   Inside

2046 **MUNAAWASHAT 19** [4] M Johnston 3-8-11 (68) J Fanning 9/4 FAV: 261-31: Made all, pushed out ins 73+
fnl 1f, val 4L+: tchd 11/4: eff at 7f/1m, has tried further: acts on fast & gd grnd: lightly rcd performer who is
op to more improvement: see 2046.
2243 **ON THE WATERFRONT 11** [1] J W Hills 3-8-12 (66) G Duffield 11/4: 5542042: Cl-up, ev ch 2f out, 3 66
kept on but al held ins fnl 1f: bckd from 5/1: another creditable eff: see 2243 & 1370.
2042 **FOUR KINGS 19** [3] J M P Eustace 3-8-11 t (63) J Carroll 14/1: 5033: Handy, outpcd halfway, ½ 64
rallied ins fnl 1f: eff at 6f, apprec step up to 1m & shaped as tho' further will suit: acts on fast grnd: see 2042.
2203 **AMANKILA 12** [5] M L W Bell 3-8-9 J Mackay 7/1: 03164: Keen prom over 6f, sn no extra: op 5/1. shd 61
2319* **HEARTHSTEAD DREAM 7** [6]3-9-3 bl (62) B Swarbrick(5) 14/1: 20-03215: Nvr nrr than mid-div: top-weight. 1¼ 67
1982 **BIG BAD BURT 22** [7]3-8-11 t p (63) Dean Williams(7) 11/1: 2230346: Mid-div, onepcd fnl 2f: btr 1778. nk 60
1953 **FAIRLIE 23** [2]3-8-8 (65) A Culhane 9/2: 41046-57: Slow away, al in rear: btr 1953. 1¼ 55
7 Ran   Time 1m 46.92 (3.12)   Owned: Mr Hamdan Al Maktoum   Trained: Middleham

2475   **3.30 Hamish Macsporran Handicap Stakes Fillies 3yo+ 0-70 (E)**   **[71]**
£3819 £1175 £588   **1m1f36y**   **Good/Firm 32**   **-09 Slow**   Inside

1810 **SHARP NEEDLE 30** [4] J Noseda 3-9-11 (68) S W Kelly 5/4 FAV: 0251: Cl-up, styd on to lead 1f out, 75
drvn out: op 7/4 on h'cap bow: eff at 9f, further shld suit: acts on fast & gd grnd, sharp & stiff/undul trk.
2168 **RABITATIT 14** [7] J G M O'Shea 3-9-5 (62) B Swarbrick(5) 17/2: 150-2402: Led, hdd 1f out, styd on shd 67
ins fnl 1f, just denied: op 6/1: eff at 1m/9f: shld find similar: see 1953 & 1099.
4922} **CYCLONIC STORM 232** [5] R A Fahey 5-10-0 (60) T Hamilton(3) 5/1: 230000-3: b f Catrail - Wheeler's ½ 64
Wonder (Sure Blade) Mid-div, prog 3f out, styd on ins fnl 1f, not btn far: tchd 7/1: reapp: h'cap wnr in '03:
won 2 h'caps in '02: suited by 1m/9f on fast & soft grnd: goes well fresh: likes Hamilton: tried cheek pieces:
fine eff on reapp & is on a winning mark.
2 Jun'03 Carl 9.3fm 72-72 D: 1 Jun'03 Hami 9.2gd 72-67 E: 2 May'03 Hami 8.3sft 69-67 C: 1 Jul'02 Sali 8g/f 70-60 E:
1 Jul'02 Carl 9.2gd 66-54 E: 2 May'02 Carl 9.2g/s 57-52 E:
4782} **ELLOVAMUL 243** [1] W M Brisbourne 4-9-6 (52) P Makin(5) 14/1: 611545-4: b f Elmaamul - Multi Sofft ¾ 54
(Northern State) Handy, onepcd dist: reapp: appr sell h'cap & clmg wnr in '03: sell wnr in late '02 (I A Wood,
earlier turf unplcd, rtd 63, auct mdn): eff at 1m/11.4f on firm, fast grnd & fibresand: tried blnks, best without.
1 Sep'03 Yarm 11.5g/f 54-(50) F: 1 Aug'03 Ripo 10g/f 51-47 F: 1 Dec'02 Wolv 8.4af 55a- G:
2147 **JOINT DESTINY 14** [8]3-8-6 (49) J Carroll 10/1: 0-502105: Slow away, prog 3f out, no impress fnl 1f. dht 51
2038 **INFIDELITY 19** [3]3-9-1 P (58) D Tudhope(7) 7/1: 6000606: Mid-div, hung right & onepcd fnl 2f. 1¼ 58
1661 **FOREST AIR 37** [6]4-9-1 (47) D McGaffin 14/1: 300-0107: Handy 5f, sn wknd: btr 1446 (1m, gd/soft). 7 36
2092 **KALAMANSI 17** [2]3-8-10 (53) G Duffield 12/1: 6008: In tch 6f, sn fdd: h'cap bow. 4 36
8 Ran   Time 1m 57.85 (3.75)   Owned: Mr Arashan Ali   Trained: Newmarket

2476 4.05 O2 Claiming Stakes 3yo+ (E)
£3494 £1075 £538 **5f4y str** **Good/Firm 32** **-01 Slow** Stands side

1797 **ROBWILLCALL 30** [4] A Berry 4-8-8 p (45) P Mathers(7) 16/1: 0000-051: Cl-up, styd on to lead cl-home, rdn out: eff at 5/6f on fast & gd/soft grnd: eff with cheek pieces & likes Hamilton: see 1797. **51**
2161* **SOAKED 14** [5] D W Chapman 11-8-12 bl (59) A Culhane 5/2: 2340412: Led, hdd under press cl-home: not disgraced on follow up bid: 11yo, just btr 2161. *1* **51**
2161 **BEST LEAD 14** [1] Ian Emmerson 5-9-2 bl (52) D Tudhope(7) 10/1: 4434333: Handy, eff when short of room dist & again ins fnl 1f, styd on cl-home: prob rnr-up with clr run: see 2161 & 1797. *½* **54+**
2161 **JOYCES CHOICE 14** [9] J S Wainwright 5-8-12 (52) G Parkin 16/1: 50-20R54: Handy, onepcd dist. *¾* **48**
2161 **AMERICAN COUSIN 14** [7]9-9-3 (62) A Nicholls 7/4 FAV: 0-101025: Rear, nvr nrr than mid-div: well bckd: won this race 12 months ago: btr 2161 & 1797. *1¼* **50**
2320 **VIJAY 7** [2]5-8-10 p (54) P Mulrennan(5) 7/1: 0602006: Cl-up 4f, wknd: quick reapp: btr 1797. *2½* **36**
2369 **NEEDWOOD BUCOLIC 5** [6]6-9-2 L Enstone(3) 50/1: 0/013/-007: Al in rear: quick reapp: see 2369. *1¼* **37**
2320 **NORTHERN SVENGALI 7** [3]8-8-12 t p (36) C Haddon(7) 100/1: 4000-008: b g Distinctly North - Trilby's Dream (Mansooj) Handy till halfway, wknd: quick reapp: unplcd in '03 (rtd 42, h'cap): AW plcd in early '02 (rtd 55a at best, h'cap): dual h'cap wnr in '01 for T D Baron: eff at 6f, suited by 5f: acts on firm, hvy grnd & fibresand: best without blnks, wears a t-strap: with D A Nolan. *½* **34**
1 Jun'01 Hami 5g/f 62-55 F: 1 Jun'01 Newc 5g/f 62-57 E:
1944 **BETTYS VALENTINE 23** [8]4-8-5 (25) T Williams 100/1: 00/-40009: Al in rear. *2½* **20**
4184} **BREVITY 279** [10]9-8-10 VIS (60) B Swarbrick(5) 10/1: 060400-0: 10th: b g Tenby - Rive (Riverman) Bhd, nvr a factor: 7/1: earlier jumps unplcd (rtd 38h, nov hdle): unplcd in '03 (h'caps, rtd 83, J M Bradley): plcd once in '02 (rtd 99): multiple scorer in '01: stays 10f, best around 6f on firm grnd, handles hvy & fibresand: eff with/without t-strap: tried blnks & cheek pieces: with J G M O'Shea. *13* **0**
2 Sep'01 Ayr 6g/f 104-96 B: 1 Jul'01 Asco 6g/f 98-90 C: 1 Jul'01 Epso 6fm 92-85 C: 1 Jun'01 Sali 6g/f 90-82 C: 1 Jun'01 Epso 6fm 93-76 C: 2 Jun'01 Ches 7fm 76-73 C: 1 Jun'01 Brig 7g/f 76-61 D: 1 May'01 Leic 6fm 85-62 E: 1 May'01 Brig 6fm 69-55 F: 1 May'01 Hami 6g/f 69- F:
10 Ran Time 59.75 (1.65) Owned: Mr William Burns Trained: Cockerham

2477 4.40 Raeburn Brick Handicap Stakes 3yo+ 0-80 (D) **[80]**
£6357 £1956 £978 **6f5y str** **Good/Firm 32** **+05 Fast** Stands side

2409 **SIR DON 4** [2] D Nicholls 5-8-9 vis (61) A Nicholls 12/1: 30-00001: b g Lake Coniston - New Sensitive (Wattlefield) Prom, sn switched to far side, led 2f out, pushed out ins fnl 1f, val 2L+: quick reapp: won 2 h'caps in '03 (also plcd 4 times): rcd mainly for J Eustace in '02, showed promise (mdn, rtd 66): eff at 6f/1m on gd & firm grnd: eff with a visor: back to form after some poor efforts. **69+**
1 Jul'03 York 6.0fm 69-61 C: 2 Jul'03 Catt 7g/f 63-(61) E: 2 Jun'03 Thir 7g/f 60-59 E: 1 Apr'03 Thir 8fm 63-58 F: 2 Sep'01 Nott 5gd 73- F: 2 Aug'01 Thir 5gd 76- E:
2315 **BUNDY 7** [1] M Dods 8-8-9 (61) S W Kelly 5/1: 50-00022: Cl-up, rcd alone stands side, kept on despite hanging right ins fnl 1f, not pace wnr: quick reapp: another gd eff & is h'capped to win bef long. *1¼* **64**
1873 **TANCRED TIMES 27** [7] D W Barker 9-8-3 (55) T Williams 12/1: 00-04403: Handy, kept on same pace from dist: encouraging run & has slipped to a wng mark: see 1046. *1* **55**
2320 **LEGAL SET 7** [12] Miss A Stokell 8-7-12 (5oh)t (45) D Fentiman(7) 50/1: 2000004: Mid-div, prog halfway, no impress fnl 1f: quick reapp: gd eff from out of h'cap: btr 1074 & 728. *nk* **49**
2320 **CHAIRMAN BOBBY 7** [4]6-9-4 (70) L Enstone(3) 100/30 FAV: 0032025: Led, hdd 2f out, sn no extra. *½* **68**
2459} **FONTHILL ROAD 355** [13]4-9-6 (72) T Hamilton(3) 8/1: 11612-6: ch g Royal Abjar - Hannah Huxtable (Master Willie) Nvr nrr than mid-div: reapp: won 3 of 5 starts in '03 (AW mdn, class stks & h'cap): eff at 5/7f on fast, soft grnd & fibresand: goes well fresh & acts on a sharp or gall trk: with R A Fahey. *1½* **66**
2 Jun'03 Wolv 7af 73a-71 D: 1 May'03 Hayd 6sft 73-65 D: 1 Mar'03 Catt 5g/f 65-(60) F: 1 Mar'03 Sout 6af 61a- D:
1627 **SHARP HAT 39** [5]10-8-10 (62) A Culhane 14/1: 0550007: Cl-up over 4f, wknd: btr 317. *1* **53**
976 **FORT MCHENRY 78** [8]4-9-6 (72) G Duffield 7/1: 41100-08: b g Danehill Dancer - Griqualand (Connaught) Handy 4f, sn wknd: amat class stks & h'cap wnr in '03: auct mdn scorer in '02: wng form at 5/7f: acts on fast & gd/soft grnd: likes to force the pace: with N A Callaghan. *¾* **61**
1 Aug'03 Sand 5.0g/s 76-70 D: 1 Jul'03 Redc 7g/f 73-(67) G: 1 Jul'02 Epso 7gd 81- E:
2160 **FRIAR TUCK 14** [10]9-8-5 (2ow) (55) J Carroll 8/1: 0014649: Al in rear: btr 1508. *½* **45**
4852} **HAULAGE MAN 238** [6]6-8-6 (58) J Fanning 6/1: 000040-0: 10th: Chsd ldrs 3f, sn wknd: op 8/1 on reapp. *3½* **37**
2409 **GREY COSSACK 4** [3]7-9-12 (78) M Lawson(5) 16/1: 0100500: 11th: Rear, nvr a factor: quick reapp. *1* **54**
11 Ran Time 1m 11.46 (1.66) Owned: Mrs Dian Plant Trained: Thirsk

2478 5.15 Dm Hall Rating Related Maiden Stakes 3-4yo 0-70 (E)
£3559 £1095 £548 **1m3f16y** **Good/Firm 32** **+00 Fast** Stands side

2117 **MASKED 16** [4] J W Hills 3-8-8 (70) G Duffield 15/8: 0041: Mid-div, outpcd 3f out, rallied to lead dist, rdn out: tchd 5/2: eff at 1m, apprec step up to 11f: acts on fast & gd: op to more improvement. **74**
2025 **LA PETITE CHINOISE 20** [3] R Guest 3-8-5 (66) J Carroll 16/1: 406-6042: Rear, gd prog & ev ch dist, styd on ins fnl 1f, not pace wnr: clr rem: prev eff at 5f, now suited by 9/11f: see 2025. *¾* **69**
1959 **LUCKY ARTHUR 23** [2] J G M O'Shea 3-8-5 (60) B Swarbrick(5) 20/1: 0503: Rear, hung left under press after 1m, styd on fnl 1f: h'caps will suit: see 1790. *5* **62**
2103 **SILVERHAY 16** [1] T D Barron 3-8-8 (69) P Makin(5) 4/5 FAV: 523-424: Keen prom, led trav well 3f out, hdd dist, wknd: v disapp & rcd far too keenly: btr 2103. *hd* **64**
1935 **VIOLA DA BRACCIO 25** [5]3-8-5 (65) J Fanning 16/1: 0-055: Cl-up, led briefly bef 3f out, sn wknd. *3½* **56**
2230 **DOUBLE TURN 12** [6]4-9-7 (70) S W Kelly 20/1: 5-506: Led, hdd bef 3f out, fdd: btr 1885. *3* **55**
1604 **SILVER RHYTHM 40** [7]3-8-5 (52) V Halliday 40/1: 0-357: Keen in tch 7f, sn wknd: btr 1275. *shd* **51**
7 Ran Time 2m 22.32 (3.52) Owned: The Phantom Partnership Trained: Lambourn

HAMILTON WEDNESDAY 16.06.04 Righthand, Undulating Track, Stiff Uphill Finish

---

2479 **5.50 Lanarkshire Chamber Of Commerce Apprentice Handicap Round 1 4yo+ 35-55** (F) [63]
£3010 £860 £430 **1m5f9y** Good/Firm 32 -14 Slow Stands side

2318* **MILLENNIUM HALL 7** [5] P Monteith 5-9-11 (6ex) (60) L Enstone 5/2 FAV: 0-063311: Mid-div, prog to **68+**
lead dist, pushed clr, eased cl-home, val 4L+: well bckd on quick reapp: eff btwn 1m & 13f on fast & hvy grnd:
likes a stiff/undul one, esp Hamilton: continues in fine form: see 2318 & 2176.
4664\} **ELLWAY HEIGHTS 251** [9] W M Brisbourne 7-9-2 (51) B Swarbrick(3) 6/1: 111020-2: b g Shirley 1\} 53
Heights - Amina (Brigadier Gerard) Led, rcd keenly, hdd dist, kept on, no ch with easy wnr: reapp: prog, amat &
normal h'cap wnr in '03: unplcd on sole '02 start (rtd 34, h'cap): plcd once in '01 (h'cap, rtd 57, I Balding): eff
at 12/13f on firm & gd grnd: acts on any trk & has gone well fresh: gd return.
2 Oct'03 Pont 12.0g/f 53-50 F: 1 Sep'03 Good 12g/f 50-45 E: 1 Sep'03 Carl 11.9fm 46-40 F:
1 Sep'03 Hami 12.1g/f 46-40 E:
2176 **COSMIC CASE 13** [3] J S Goldie 9-8-11 (46) P Mulrennan(3) 7/2: 5300-103: Rear, prog 4f out, onepcd. 1 46
2112 **TOM BELL 16** [6] J G M O'Shea 4-8-13 (48) P Mathers(5) 11/2: 005-2044: Chsd ldrs, no extra ins fnl 1f. \} 47
1991 **IPLEDGEALLEGIANCE 22** [2]8-8-0 (5oh)BL (30) D Fentiman(5) 16/1: 0055055: Nvr nrr than mid-div. 2\} 30
2276 **KRISTINEAU 9** [10]6-8-12 t (47) P Makin(3) 9/1: 0000//-506: In tch 12f, sn wknd: btr 2060. 2 39
2180 **HOWARDS DREAM 13** [8]6-8-0 (5oh)t (30) C Haddon(5) 33/1: 60-04067: Handy 12f, sn wknd: see 1450. 5 20
2200 **AVEIRO 12** [7]8-8-10 (45) Dean Williams(5) 10/1: 1200058: Prom, wknd fnl 3f: btr 937. 1\} 29
1939 **SALFORD ROCKET 24** [1]4-8-0 (5oh) (30) Rory Moore(5) 50/1: 0-0069: Cl-up 11f, sn fdd: see 1939. 18 0
CONGO MAN 2828 [4]11-9-6 (55) T Hamilton 33/1: 51////////-0: 10th: b g Rainbow Quest - African 6 4
Dance (El Gran Senor) Prom 6f, fdd: v long abs: unplcd sole hdle start in 00/01 (nov): mdn wnr one of only 2 Flat
starts in '96 (mdn, rtd 80, Sir M R Stoute): eff at 10f on fast grnd: has gone well fresh: with D W Whillans.
10 Ran Time 2m 51.52(6.02) Owned: Mrs Elizabeth Ferguson Trained: Rosewell

---

RIPON WEDNESDAY 16.06.04 Righthand, Sharpish Track

Official Going GOOD/FIRM.

2480 **6.50 Skybet Com Apprentice Selling Stakes 3-4yo** (F)
£3248 £928 £464 **6f str** Good/Firm 30 -17 Slow Stands Side

2102 **WEET WATCHERS 16** [5] D Nicholls 4-9-12 (55) M Halford 11/4: 1643051: Made all, rdn & pulled clr 64
over 1f out, rdly: op 9/4: sold for 8,600 gns, will reportedly join P Blockley: eff at 7f/1m on fast, soft &
fibresand: enjoys sell grade: see 555.
2186 **JALOUHAR 13** [2] B P J Baugh 4-9-7 (46) Jemma Marshall 10/1: 5020602: Trkd ldrs, eff to chase wnr 5 44
fnl 2f, al held: prob stays a sharpish 1m in sell grade: see 1368 & 65.
2295 **KILLOCH PLACE 8** [1] J A Glover 3-9-0 vis (42) J Roberts(5) 9/1: 00-00003: Prom, onepace dist. 1\} 39
2326 **EFIMAC 7** [6] N Bycroft 4-9-2 bl (40) Suzanne France 16/1: 500-0004: Handy, no extra over 1f out. 1 31
2102 **MATRIARCHAL 16** [3]4-9-2 (34) Janice Webster(5) 66/1: 00400-05: ch f Presidium - Mayor (Laxton) 5 16
Al bhd: plcd '03 (rtd 53, auct mdn): unplcd '02 (rtd 61, N Tinkler).
607 **INISTRAHULL ISLAND 126** [4]4-9-7 BL (56) M Stainton 2/1 FAV: 423-3606: Dwelt, sn rdn rear & no ch 8 0
2f out: poor display in 1st time blnks: well bckd, op 10/3: 4 month abs: much btr 471 (polytrack).
2337 **MISS NOTERIETY 6** [8]4-9-2 T P (25) C Ely(5) 66/1: 000/0-07: b f Victory Note - Mystic Maid 11 0
(Mujtahid) Dwelt, prom wide till 2f out: t-strap & cheek pieces, qck reapp: mod form, breathing probs prev.
1656 **QUEEN OF NIGHT 37** [7]4-9-2 (60) A Reilly 3/1: 15-0404R: Refused to race: op 9/4. 0
8 Ran Time 1n 12.85 (2.85) Owned: A A Bloodstock Ltd Trained: Thirsk

---

2481 **7.20 Sky Bet Just Press Red To Bet Novice Median Auction Stakes 2yo** (E)
£3692 £1136 £568 **5f str** Good/Firm 30 -02 Slow Stands Side

1955* **PIKE BISHOP 23** [4] R Charlton 2-9-6 D Holland 2/9 FAV: 11: Made all & al in command, val 5L+: **103+**
bckd at long odds-on: eff at 5f, will get 6f: acts on fast grnd, sharpish trks: looks useful & set for higher grade.
2213* **BECKERMET 12** [6] R F Fisher 2-9-10 P Bradley(5) 9/2: 3112: Trkd wnr, no impress on wnr over 1f 3 96
out & eased when clr 2nd well ins last: op 7/2: see 2213.
1503 **NEE LEMON LEFT 45** [2] A Berry 2-8-7 F Norton 22/1: 263: Chsd ldrs, drvn & outpcd halfway: abs. 2\} 72
1831 **OUR LOUIS 29** [1] J S Wainwright 2-8-7 P T Eaves(3) 100/1: 6054: Rdn in tch, no ch from halfway: 4 60
tried cheek pieces, highly tried: see 1831 (sell).
2119 **SPECTRUM OF LIGHT 15** [3]2-8-7 Dean McKeown 50/1: 05: b f Spectrum - Empress of Light (Emperor 1 57
Jones) Mid-div, drvn & strug fnl 2f: no form to date: sire high-class mid-dist performer, may get further in time.
5 Ran Time 59.44 (1.64) Owned: Mr Michael Pescod Trained: Beckhampton

---

2482 **7.50 Norman Wells Memorial Challenge Trophy Handicap Stakes 3yo 0-95** (C) [92]
£8607 £3265 £1632 **6f str** Good/Firm 30 -02 Slow Stands Side

2055 **BRIDGEWATER BOYS 19** [3] K A Ryan 3-8-9 bl (73) R Ffrench 13/2: 4131121: Held up stands side, prog 82
to lead ins fnl 1f, rdn out: eff at 5/6f on firm, gd grnd or fibresand: eff with blnks: prog performer: see 2055.
1745* **BO MCGINTY 33** [5] R A Fahey 3-9-7 (85) P Hanagan 6/1: 301-012: Prom stands side, led after 4f, 1\} 89
hdd ins fnl 1f, not pace wnr: imprvd in defeat today, see 1745 (gd).
2166 **NEON BLUE 14** [11] R M Whitaker 3-8-4 (68) Hayley Turner(5) 16/1: 040-5103: Handy far side, styd 1\} 68
on to lead far side group ins fnl 1f, not pace front 2 stands side: back to form on return to 6f: see 1876.
1933 **IMPERIAL ECHO 25** [1] T D Barron 3-9-2 (80) R Winston 6/1: 1433-004: Handy stands side, ev ch \} 79
dist, sn no extra: encouraging effort: see 1460.
1460 **RIVER TREAT 47** [6]3-9-5 (83) J F Egan 14/1: 524-165: In tch stands side, ev ch 1f out, no extra. nk 81
1766 **MR WOLF 32** [9]3-9-1 (79) T Eaves(3) 14/1: 0-221166: Led stands side group 4f, wknd dist: btr 1477. 1 74
2137 **DOLCE PICCATA 15** [4]3-9-4 (82) J Bramhill 14/1: 32-05457: Handy stands side 4f, sn wknd: btr 1809. \} 76
1771 **MAHMOOM 32** [12]3-9-6 VIS (84) A Culhane 17/2: 211-0068: Cl-up far side, led far side group dist, shd 78

748

RIPON   WEDNESDAY 16.06.04   Righthand, Sharpish Track

hdd ins fnl 1f & wknd: bckd from 14/1 in 1st time visor: btr 1771.

2271 **SNOW WOLF 9** [13]3-9-0 (78) D Holland 4/1 FAV: 023-0129: Led far side group till dist, fdd: btr 2271. *3* **63**
2212 **ISKANDER 12** [10]3-9-6 (84) N Callan 12/1: 154-6000: 10th: Rear far side, nvr a factor: btr 1665. *3½* **59**
1933 **Distant Times 25** [8]3-9-0 ViS(78) D Allan 20/1:0 2011 **Piccolo Prince 21** [7]3-8-5 (69) J Quinn 14/1:0
12 Ran Time 1m 11.96 (1.96) Owned: Bishopthorpe Racing Trained: Hambleton

---

| **2483** | **8.20 Pricewaterhousecoopers Handicap Stakes 3yo+ 0-85 (D)** | | | | **[82]** |
| | £5343 £1644 £822 **1m2f** **Good/Firm 30** **+06 Fast** Inside | | | | |

2323 **OLIVIA ROSE 7** [4] J Pearce 5-9-5 (73) J Quinn 9/2: 0131231: Mid-div, al trav well, prog to lead **81**
dist, rdn out: quick reapp: eff btwn 1m/12f on fast, hvy grnd & fibresand: in form 5yo: see 2323 & 1821.
2242 **GO TECH 11** [7] T D Easterby 4-9-8 (76) D Allan 14/1: 5-006062: b g Gothenberg - Bollin Sophie *1¾* **81**
(Efisio) Chsd ldrs, prog to lead briefly 1.5f out, no extra ins fnl 1f: op 9/1: unplcd in '03 (rtd 88, h'caps):
auct mdn & stks wnr in '02: eff at 7f/1m, stays 10f: acts on firm & gd: eff on stiff/gall trk: h'capped to win similar.
1 Sep'02 Ayr 7.2gd 94- C: 2 Sep'02 Donc 8fm 92-87 B: 2 Aug'02 Newc 8gd 91-85 B: 1 Aug'02 Newc 6gd 88- F:
1979 **MEGANS MAGIC 22** [11] W Storey 4-9-0 (68) J Bramhill 14/1: 2-612003: Bhd, prog 4f out, onepcd fnl 1f. *2* **69**
2179 **OSCAR PEPPER 13** [5] T D Barron 7-8-9 vis (63) R Winston 11/1: 04-50634: Rear, prog halfway, short *hd* **63**
of room 2f out, no impress fnl 1f: btr 2179.
1668 **DUNASKIN 36** [2]4-10-0 (82) D Holland 7/2 FAV: 053-0005: Led, hdd bef 1f out, no extra: *1½* **80**
disappointing effort under top weight: btr 1668.
1668 **INDIAN SOLITAIRE 36** [3]5-9-5 vis (73) P Hanagan 6/1: 0200-306: Rear, prog 4f out, short of room *¾* **70**
dist, styd on fnl 1f: op 8/1: just btr 918.
2284 **TROUBLE MOUNTAIN 8** [6]7-9-2 bl (70) R Hughes 11/2: 3352447: Nvr nrr than mid-div: btr 2284. *5* **59**
2120 **ARAWAN 15** [8]4-8-11 (65) Dale Gibson 33/1: 04-00008: b g Entrepreneur - Asmara (Lear Fan) Cl-up *½* **53**
1m, wknd: ex-Irish, mdn wnr at Roscommon on 1 of 3 '03 starts (7f, gd): with M W Easterby.
2264 **JOHANNIAN 9** [9]6-9-6 (74) R Ffrench 8/1: 05-00359: Mid div, prog & ev ch 2f out, wknd dist. *½* **61**
2185 **LA SYLPHIDE GB 13** [1]7-9-12 (80) K Dalgleish 11/1: 610-2560: 10th: Prom 1m, fdd: btr 1346. *11* **51**
2323 **HARAMBEE 7** [10]4-9-2 (80) T Eaves(3) 100/1: 0116-PU0: 11th: b f Robellino - Hymenee (Chief's *16* **26**
Crown) Cl-up 6f, fdd: qck reapp: won twice in native France in '03 (11f, soft & gd/soft): with B S Rothwell.
11 Ran Time 2m 05.74 (2.44) Owned: Mr A Watford Trained: Newmarket

---

| **2484** | **8.50 H & C Moore Maiden Stakes 3yo+ (D)** | | | | |
| | £4849 £1492 £746 **1m4f60y** **Good/Firm 30** **-05 Slow** Inside | | | | |

1390 **ACT OF THE PACE 51** [1] M Johnston 4-9-5 K Dalgleish 20/1: 5-41: Handy, hdwy to lead 2f out, **76**
kept on well for press ins fnl 1f: 7 wk abs, op 9/1: stays 12.5f on fast, acts on a sharp trk: imprvd for a step
up in trip, shld win more races: see 1390.
MANDATUM [3] L M Cumani 3-8-10 D Holland 5/2: 2: b g Mtoto - Reamur (Top Ville) Mid-div, *2* **77**
ouptcd 5f out, rallied over 2f out & kept on but no ch with wnr on debut: tchd 7/2: half-brother to smart mid-dist
stayer Boreas: stays 12.5f on fast: shown enough to find similar.
2230 **FARNE ISLE 12** [4] G A Harker 5-9-5 R Winston 20/1: 43: Bhd, hdwy 5f out, no impress ins fnl 1f. *2* **69**
2058 **FORCE OF NATURE 19** [2] H R A Cecil 4-9-5 (85) R Hughes 4/9 FAV: 2-024: Led to 2f out, no extra *6* **60**
fnl 1f, btn & eased nr fin: see 2058.
4 Ran Time 2m 37.89 (4.39) Owned: Mrs Joan Keaney Trained: Middleham

---

| **2485** | **9.20 Coverdale Maiden Stakes 3yo (D)** | | | | |
| | £4420 £1360 £680 **6f str** **Good/Firm 30** **-10 Slow** Stands Side | | | | |

DOITNOW [2] R A Fahey 3-9-0 P Hanagan 20/1: 1: b g Princely Heir - Tonys Gift (Midyan) Rear, **84**
hdwy over 1f out, led ins fnl 1f, rdn clr on debut: 2nd foal, dam a dual 7/8f wnr at 3, multiple wnr over hdles:
eff at 6f, shld stay further: acts on fast, sharp trk: runs well fresh: win more races.
2182 **SAN LORENZO 13** [7] M R Channon 3-8-9 A Culhane 11/4: 032: Made most till ins fnl 1f, no extra. *4* **67**
2182 **KENTUCKY EXPRESS 13** [5] T D Easterby 3-9-0 R Winston 15/8 FAV: 023: Trkd ldrs, ev ch bef fnl *1½* **68**
1f, no impress ins fnl 1f: see 2182.
5013} **TROODOS JET 223** [8] A Berry 3-9-0 (65) F Norton 16/1: 2464-4: b g Atraf - Costa Verde (King of *½* **67**
Spain) Handy, ev ch appr fnl 1f, no impress ins fnl 1f: reapp: rnr-up 1st of 4 '03 starts (mdn): eff at 5f on
gd/soft & soft. 2 May'03 Hayd 5sft 76- E:
4869} **HAMAASY 236** [4]3-9-0 (61) Alex Greaves 50/1: 0600-5: b g Machiavellian - Sakha (Wolfhound) *½* **67**
Handy, ev ch appr fnl 1f, fdd ins fnl 1f: reapp: unplcd all '03 starts (mdn, nurs, rtd 72, with J Dunlop): has
tried a t-strap: now with D Nicholls.
2075 **HARRINGTON BATES 18** [1]3-9-0 Dean McKeown 2/1: 46: Trkd ldrs & keen, wknd over 1f out. *shd* **66**
4454} **YORKES FOLLY 264** [6]3-8-9 K Dalgleish 100/1: 50-7: Rear, modest late gains on reapp. *1* **58**
BANK GAMES [3]3-9-0 Dale Gibson 100/1: 8: Nvr a factor on debut. *7* **43**
2309 **CHICA ROCA 7** [9]3-8-9 BL T (70) D Holland 20/1: 350-0069: Rear, t.o.: tried blnks & t-strap. *14* **3**
9 Ran Time 1m 12.41(2.41) Owned: Hi-Tech Racing Club Trained: Malton

---

ASCOT   WEDNESDAY 16.06.04   Righthand, Stiff, Galloping Track

---

Official Going Good/Firm (Firm places)

2486   2.30 Gr3 Jersey Stakes 3yo (A)
          £37700 £14300 £7150   7f str   Good/Firm 39   +00 Fast   Stands Side

4571} **KHELEYF 257** [1] Saeed bin Suroor 3-8-10 (108) L Dettori 6/1: 1210-1: b c Green Desert - Society   114+
Lady (Mr Prospector) Hld up, gd hdwy over 1f out, led dist, pushed clr, hands-and-heels, val further: bckd on reapp:
won 2 of 4 juv starts for D Loder (mdn & stks): stays a stiff 7f well, shld get further tho' not certain on breeding:
acts on fm & gd: clrly runs well fresh: v smart with a turn of foot, unexposed, win more Gr races.
1 Sep'03 Donc 6gd 109- C: 2 Jun'03 Asco 5g/f 108- A: 1 May'03 York 5.0fm 104- D:
1932* **FOKINE 25** [2] B W Hills 3-8-13 (113) M Hills 11/2 FAV: 620-2212: Held up, hdwy to lead over 1f   1¾   112
out, styd on despite hdd dist, not pace of wnr: well bckd: proving tough, smart & consistent: see 1932 (List).
1932 **CARTOGRAPHY 25** [6] Saeed bin Suroor 3-8-10 T (106) K McEvoy 8/1: 1310-33: Handy, hdwy to chall   ½   108
when sltly short of room over 1f out, kept on, not pace of wnr: useful, ran right up to best in first time t-strap.
1919 **BÁHIANO 25** [3] C E Brittain 3-8-10 (97) D Holland 50/1: 1236004: Sn well bhd, hdwy & not clr run   hd   106
well over 1f out, switched right & styd on ins last, nrst fin: shade closer with a clr run & a promising effort
stepped up in class: acts on fast & both AWs: see 885, 713.
1888 **MUKAFEH 26** [8]3-8-10 (105) R Hills 10/1: 13-025: Made most till over 1f out, wknd: up in class.   2½   102
4405} **FAVOURITE NATION 25** [5]3-8-10 P J Smullen 25/1: 212-06: ch c Cadeaux Genereux - Fernanda (Be   5   92
My Chief) In tch, wknd well over 1f out: '03 mdn wnr: eff over 6/7.5f on gd grnd. 2 Sep'03 Curr 6.3gd 98- :
1995 **LEITRIM HOUSE 25** [11]3-9-2 (114) M J Kinane 6/1: 16-1147: With ldr till 2f out, wknd: hvly bckd: 1½   95
btr expected despite carrying a pen: smart earlier: see 1995, 1559.
1688 **IMTALKINGGIBBERISH 35** [4]3-8-10 E Ahern 200/1: 058: b g Pursuit of Love - Royal Orchid   nk   88
(Shalford) In tch, wknd over 1f out: needs mdns.
1773 **SILCAS GIFT 32** [15]3-8-13 (109) T E Durcan 20/1: 000-1059: In tch, wknd over 1f out: best 1169.   1¼   88
1888 **PSYCHIATRIST 26** [10]3-8-10 (101) R Hughes 14/1: 412-3240: 10th: In tch, wknd 2f out: btr 1189 (List). 1½   82
1932 **SGT PEPPER 25** [9]3-8-13 (98) J Fortune 50/1: 31140-00: 11th: Al bhd: see 1932.   nk   84
1932 **AUDITORIUM 25** [12]3-8-13 (113) K Fallon 6/1: 01123-40: 12th: Nvr a factor: see 1932.   5   74
2407 **GLARAMARA 4** [14]3-8-10 (98) R Winston 40/1: 3-020300: 13th: Nvr a factor: see 1583, 1150.   shd   70
4797} **TASHKIL 242** [7]3-8-10 (106) W Supple 20/1: 4110-0: 14th: In tch, wknd qckly over 2f out.   8   54
1995 **GRAND REWARD 25** [13]3-8-10 J P Spencer 11/1: 1325-250: 15th: Handy, wknd qckly 2f out: btr 1559.   7   40
15 Ran   Time 1m 27.35 (1.35) Owned: Godolphin   Trained: Newmarket

2487   3.05 Gr2 Windsor Forest Stakes Fillies 4yo+ (A)
          £81200 £30800 £15400   1m str   Good/Firm 39   -02 Slow   Stands Side

4598} **FAVOURABLE TERMS 256** [4] Sir Michael Stoute 4-8-12 (108) K Fallon 13/2: 11215-1: b f Selkirk -   117
Fatefully (Private Account) Mid-div, imprvd 2f out, led dist & rdn clr: bckd from 10/1, reapp: '03 mdn (debut),
List & Gr 2 wnr: eff at 1m, stays 10f: acts on fast & gd/soft grnd, any trk: clrly goes v well fresh: smart return
& clearly thrived over winter, Gr 1 Falmouth Stks looks an ideal target.
1 Sep'03 Leop 8g/f 109- A: 2 Jul'03 Chep 10.2g/s 103- A: 1 Jul'03 Sand 8.1g/f 109- A: 1 May'03 Good 7g/f 90- D:
2143 **MONTURANI 16** [8] G Wragg 5-8-9 (104) D Holland 20/1: 3422-362: Chsd ldrs, imprvd to lead 2f our   2   110
till collared dist, kept on but not pace of wnr: v useful mare, may apprec a return to 10f: see 1115 & 57.
4598} **SOLDERA 256** [3] J R Fanshawe 4-8-9 (103) J Murtagh 25/1: 12/4140-3: b f Polish Numbers - La   3½   103
Pepite (Mr Prospector) Chsd ldrs, eff 2f out, onepace: reapp: '03 Listed wnr here at Ascot: '02 mdn wnr: eff at
7f/1m on gd & firm grnd: likes a stiff/gall trk: clrly runs well fresh: prob worth a try at 10f now & sharper next
time. 1 Jul'03 Asco 8gd 106-(98) A: 2 Oct'02 Newm 7fm 93- A: 1 Sep'02 Sali 6.9fm 89- E:
2143* **ACTRICE 16** [10] E Lellouche 4-8-12 O Peslier 12/1: 143-1614: Held up, some late hdwy, not pace   1   104
to chall: French chall, below form on grnd faster than ideal: beat today's 2nd in 2143 (gd/soft, 10f).
4841*}**MARBYE 14** [1]4-8-12 T T M Demuro 10/1: 1413-415: b f Marju - Hambye (Distant Relative) Held up,   1   100
late prog, nvr dngrs: Italian chall, recent Gr 2 wnr at San Siro: won 4 times in '03, incl a Gr 3: wng form at
6f/9f, acts on firm & gd/soft grnd: warrants a t-strap: with B Grizzetti. 1 Oct'03 San 12gd 105- :
1684* **CRIMSON PALACE 35** [6]5-8-9 (110) L Dettori 6/5 FAV: 01/4-1416: Chsd ldrs, rdn & btn over 1f out: 1¾   94
hvly bckd: something clry amiss on this drop back in trip: much btr judged on 1684 (10f, gd/soft grnd).
1863 **CHIC 27** [2]4-8-9 (97) Gary Stevens 16/1: 13621-67: Held up travelling strongly, poised to chall   1¼   91+
when clipped heels & nearly fell 2f out, no ch after: longer priced stable-mate of wnr: impress with the way she
was travelling bef incident & must be given another ch: see 1863.
1684 **BENEVENTA 35** [11]4-8-9 (110) S Sanders 7/1: 340-1128: Front rank, led bef halfway till 2f out,   1¼   90
wknd: most disapp, much btr 1684 (10f) & 1491.
2211* **GONFILIA 12** [9]4-8-9 1 (102) K McEvoy 8/1: 1-012119: Led till halfway, again briefly 2f out, wknd   shd   80
& eased: prob went off too fast, this was well below 2211 & 1683.
1925 **STARBECK 25** [5]6-8-10 (1ow) (88) P McCabe 100/1: 20-00540: 10th: Dwelt, keen in rear, nvr dngrs.   5   71
10 Ran   Time 1m 40.37 (1.67) Owned: Maktoum Al Maktoum   Trained: Newmarket

2488   3.45 Gr1 Prince Of Wales's Stakes 4yo+ (A)
          £203000 £77000 £38500   1m2f   Good/Firm 39   +10 Fast   Inside

4798* **RAKTI 185** [10] M A Jarvis 5-9-0 (121) P Robinson 3/1: 30/1212-1: b c Polish Precedent - Ragera   125
(Rainbow Quest) Keen, handy, styd on well to lead over 1f out, rdn clr, rdly: well bckd on reapp: '03 dual Gr1
wnr, rnr-up in this race: '03 Gr 1 Italian Derby wnr: v eff at 10f, stays 12f: eff on fast & gd/soft, runs well
fresh: top class, career best eff, take all the beating in similar Gr 1's this term.
1 Oct'03 Newm 10g/f 123-(121) A: 2 Jun'03 Asco 10gd 122-(115) A: 1 May'03 Capa 10gd 120- A:
1 Sep'02 Capa 10g/s 115- : 1 May'02 Capa 12g/f 119- :
2004* **POWERSCOURT 24** [5] A P O'Brien 4-9-0 J P Spencer 9/2: 2/6113-12: Handy, hdwy to chase wnr over   2   120
1f out, styd on, not pace wnr: ran right up to best & shld win more Gr1's when avoiding this wnr: see 2004.
2128 **IKHTYAR 15** [3] J H M Gosden 4-9-0 (113) R Hills 8/1: 210-3623: Held up rear, hdwy wide over 2f   ½   119
out, styd on well over 1f out, nrst fin: excellent/high-class run: must be wng Gr races on this evidence.
4916} **SULAMANI 235** [4] Saeed bin Suroor 5-9-0 (125) L Dettori 11/4 FAV: 142115-4: b c Hernando - Soul   1½   116
Dream (Alleged) Held up, brief eff over 2f out, no impress: hvly bckd on reapp: '03 3 time Gr 1 wnr, rnr-up in
King George: '02 French Derby wnr: eff at 10f, poss best at 12f: acts on firm & soft grnd: tough & high-class
sharper for this & capable of much btr.
1 Sep'03 Belm 12fm 123- A: 1 Aug'03 Arli 10gd 119- A: 2 Jul'03 Asco 12gd 124-(126) A: 1 Mar'03 Nad 12gd 127- A:

2 Oct'02 Long 12gd 127- : 1 Sep'02 Long 12g/f 115- : 1 Jun'02 Chan 12gd 122- :

2209	**SCOTTS VIEW** 12 [2]5-9-0 (115) S Chin 25/1: 1313305: Held up, eff 2f out, onepace: wants List/Gr3.	nk	115
4843*	**PHOENIX REACH** 241 [7]4-9-0 (115) D Holland 16/1: 2/1131-6: b c Alhaarth - Carroll's Canyon	¾	113

(Hatim) Trkd ldr till 3f out, no extra on reapp: won 3 of 4 '03 starts, mdn, Gr3 & Gr1 in Canada: suited by 12f, stays 14.6f on fast or soft grnd: eff with/without blnks: lightly rcd & v smart, capable of btr.

1 Oct'03 Wood 12sft 121- : 1 Jul'03 Good 12gd 113-(90) A: 1 Jul'03 Newb 12.0g/f 95- D: 2 Jun'02 Sali 6.9g/f 90- D:

2128	**COMFY** 15 [11]5-9-0 (113) K Fallon 16/1: 15//103-57: Hld up, brief eff 2f out, no impress/eased.	2½	108
2128	**KAIETEUR** 15 [9]5-9-0 (117) M J Kinane 16/1: 63230-68: In tch, wknd 2f out: yet to fire this term.	2½	103
2128+	**BANDARI** 15 [1]5-9-0 (114) W Supple 8/1: 42-01119: With ldrs, wknd 2f out: in front of this 3rd	3	97

in 2128 (Gr 3) & needs an ease in grade.

990	**LUNAR SOVEREIGN** 81 [8]5-9-0 T (110) K McEvoy 66/1: 0106-300: 10th: Led till over 1f out, wknd.	1¼	95

10 Ran   Time 2m 04.95 (0.95)   Owned: Mr Gary A Tanaka   Trained: Newmarket

---

2489 · 4.20 Royal Hunt Cup Heritage Handicap 3yo+ (B) [114]
£58000 £22000 £11000   1m str   Good/Firm 39   -08 Slow   Stands Side

1926+	**MINE** 25 [8] J D Bethell 6-9-5 vis (105) T Quinn 16/1: 406-2311: Mid-div stands side, gd hdwy		112

dist, styd on well under strong press to force head in front on line: v eff at 7f/1m & enjoys a gall trk, esp Ascot: acts on firm & soft grnd, eff with/without a visor: v smart h'capper who thrives off a strong pace/big field: has a fine run of placed form & can win in Gr company now: see 1926 & 1225.

1812	**ABLE BAKER CHARLIE** 29 [3] J R Fanshawe 5-8-5 (91) O Urbina 14/1: 25110-42: Mid-div stands side,	hd	97

strong run to lead well ins fnl 1f, caught on line: tremendous run tho' jockey lkd nowhere nr as strong as wnr: progressive, win a val prize, see 1812.

570	**ZONERGEM** 130 [23] Lady Herries 6-8-4 p (90) K McEvoy 33/1: 3603-063: Held up far side, weaved	shd	96

thro' dist, fin v strongly & just btn in a tremendous fin: jumps fnl, recent dual Huntingdon nov wnr (eff around 2m on fast & gd/soft, rtd 129h): best held up & clrly apprec this return to 1m: see 134.

1812	**AMANDUS** 29 [29] D R Loder 4-8-8 (94) T P Queally(3) 20/1: 214-0024: Prom far side, led that group	hd	99

ent fnl 1f, just btn in a fin of hds: excellent run, continues to progr: just in front of today's 2nd in 1812.

1926	**CAMP COMMANDER** 25 [31]5-8-9 t (95) Gary Stevens 8/1: 0034-045: Held up far side, short of room 2f	shd	99

out, fin strongly & just btn in a v tight fin: clrly loves big fields/fast run h'caps, rnr-up off a 3lb lower mark in this race last term: see 1926 (7f here).

1862	**LAGO DORTA** 27 [15]4-9-0 (100) J P Spencer 66/1: 21-64006: Held up stands side, hdwy over 1f out,	½	103+

fin best of all: fine fin burst but set too much to do: multiple wnr in '03 & shld be doing so again nr.

1512	**NORTON** 44 [9]7-8-5 (1ow) (90) M J Kinane 16/1: 00-05047: Led stands side till ins fnl 1f, btn	shd	93

under 1L: 6 wk abs: tremendous run from this 7yo, won this race from a 1lb higher mark in '02 & 1st home on the wrong side last year: clrly loves Ascot & overdue another win: see 1296.

1926	**AUDIENCE** 25 [30]4-8-4 p (90) R L Moore 33/1: 26-00008: Held up far side, hdwy to chall when	shd	92

drifted left fnl 1f, kept on & btn under 1L in a bunched fin: fine run, looks to be on a wng mark: see 1512.

2207	**IMPELLER** 12 [5]5-8-1 (87) J Quinn 16/1: 22-00269: Chsd ldrs stands side, kept on well fnl 1f &	hd	88

only btn around 1L in a bunched fin: loves big fields/fast run h'caps: see 2096.

1926	**VORTEX** 25 [6]5-8-12 e t (98) L Dettori 9/1: 1100130: 10th: Chsd ldrs stands side, kept on under	nk	98

press fnl 1f: another sound run, btn just over 1L: see 1926 & 1697 (AW).

2207+	**UHOOMAGOO** 12 [4]6-8-1 (7ex)bl (87) P Fessey 12/1: 1000110: 11th: Rear stands side, still last 2f	¾	85

out, fin well but too late: only btn around 2L: rtd higher 2207.

2010*	**LANGFORD** 21 [26]4-8-1 (7ex) (87) F P Ferris(3) 66/1: 3136-210: 12th: Led far side, no extra fnl 1f.	shd	84
2184	**EL COTO** 13 [13]4-9-2 (102) S Sanders 50/1: 0155000: 13th: Mid-div stands side, onepcd fnl 1f.	¾	97
2090	**WING COMMANDER** 17 [24]5-8-7 (90) P Hanagan 40/1: 233-4300: 14th: Front rank, no extra fnl 1f.	shd	87
2096*	**PUTRA KUANTAN** 16 [27]4-9-1 (7ex) (101) P Robinson 14/1: 200-6310: 15th: Dsptd lead far side, wknd	1	93

fnl 1f: nicely bckd: prev most prog, see 2096.

2096	**FINISHED ARTICLE** 16 [11]7-8-4 (90) Dane O'Neill 40/1: 204-0530: 16th: Chsd ldrs stands side, onepcd.	1½	79
2101	**ZERO TOLERANCE** 16 [1]4-8-4 (90) K Darley 16/1: 1304-140: 17th: Dsptd lead stands side 6f, no	¾	77

extra: well bckd: rtd higher over 10f in 2101 & 1104 (soft grnd).

1833+	**FLIGHTY FELLOW** 29 [10]4-8-8 (94) W Supple 66/1: 322-0610: 18th: Mid-div stands side, nvr nr ldrs.	hd	80
2096	**CALCUTTA** 16 [32]8-8-10 (96) M Hills 66/1: 14-00000: 19th: Chsd ldrs fnl 1f stands side.	¾	80
4599‡	**COURAGEOUS DUKE** 130 [2]5-8-8 (1ow) (93) O Peslier 50/1: 4060-350: 20th: b g Spinning World -	1¾	74

Araadh (Blushing Groom) Dwelt, nvr trbld ldrs stands side: long abs & has been gldd: '03 h'cap wnr: '02 mdn & rtd h'cap wnr: eff at 1m/10f on gd & firm grnd, prob handles gd/soft: likes a stiff/gall trk: with J Noseda.

2 Jul'03 Sand 10.0gd 96-93 B: 1 Jun'03 Newm 10g/f 99-87 C: 1 Oct'02 Newm 10fm 89-81 B: 1 Aug'02 Newc 8gd 80- D: 2 Aug'02 Newb 9g/f 83- D:

2404	**VICIOUS KNIGHT** 4 [16]9-9-0 (100) R Hughes 80/1: 340/15-00: 21th: b g Night Shift - Myth (Troy)	1	78

Dwelt, nvr dangerous stands side: quick reapp: twice rcd for L Cumani in '03, stks wnr on reapp: h'cap plcd in '02, '01 stks wnr: eff at 7f/1m on gd & firm grnd: acts on a sharp or stiff/gall trk: has run well fresh.

1 Apr'03 Warw 7.1fm 101-(102) B: 2 Jun'02 Leic 7g/f 105- C: 1 Jul'01 Sand 8fm 107- C:

3186‡	**WIZARD OF NOZ** 116 [22]4-9-4 (104) E Ahern 33/1: 33/40-260: 22th: b g Inchinor - Winning Girl	2½	77

(Green Desert) Chsd ldrs 6f far side: long abs & has been gldd: twice rcd in '03, 4th in Gr 3 Jersey at R Ascot (rtd 108) on reapp: '02 mdn wnr, plcd in Gr company: v eff at 7f, acts on firm & soft grnd: likes a gall trk, runs well fresh: with J Noseda. 1 Jul'03 Hayd 6gd 87- D:

2096	**CHINKARA** 16 [28]4-8-6 (92) T E Durcan 66/1: 4110-000: 23th: Held up far side, nvr dangerous.	nk	64
1624	**POLAR BEAR** 39 [20]4-8-4 (90) R Hills 9/1: 053/11-30: 24th: Chsd ldrs far side, btn 2f out: well	hd	61

bckd: prev most prog, see 1624 (

1686	**PENTECOST** 35 [16]5-8-10 (96) L Keniry(3) 25/1: 3240-060: 25th: Nvr dangerous stands side: 4th in	2½	62

this race from a 4lb lower mark in '03, won a val R Ascot h'cap in '02: see 1686.

2096	**HIGHLAND REEL** 16 [18]7-8-1 (87) Lisa Jones(3) 66/1: 0000-100: 26th: Front rank 5f stands side.	½	52
991	**EVOLVING TACTICS** 81 [21]4-9-10 VIS (110) P J Smullen 50/1: 0316-100: 27th: b c Machiavellian -	5	65

Token Gesture (Alzao) Chsd ldrs 5f far side: 12 wk abs, tried a visor: val h'cap wnr in Dubai this winter: '03 Gr 2 wnr in N America: wng form at 1m-9f on gd & firm grnd: with D Weld.

1686+	**AUTUMN GLORY** 35 [7]4-9-3 (103) K Fallon 11/2 FAV: 140-110: 28th: Chsd ldrs stands side, btn 2f	¾	56

out: reportedly lost action & did not handle this much faster grnd: prev most prog on easy grnd, see 1686 & 928.

2090	**KINGS COUNTY** 17 [14]6-8-9 (95) D Holland 16/1: 512-3030: 29th: Al bhd stands side.	3	42
2207	**CONVENT GIRL** 12 [12]4-8-8 (94) R Havlin 80/1: 26-00000: 30th: Chsd ldrs till halfway stands side.	½	40
2234	**SHAMROCK CITY** 11 [25]7-8-7 (93) R Winston 100/1: 02400-60: 31th: Al bhd far side, fin last.	2	35

31 Ran   Time 1m 40.85 (2.15)   Owned: Mr M J Dawson   Trained: Middleham

2490 **4.55 Gr2 Queen Mary Stakes Fillies 2yo (A)**
£40600 £15400 £7700 **5f str Good/Firm 39 -37 Slow** Stands Side

2328* **DAMSON 9** [15] D Wachman 2-8-10 J P Spencer 11/2 JT FAV: 111: Held up, hdwy when switched dist, qcknd to lead ins fnl 1f, rdn clr, impressive: well bckd: eff at 5/6f on fast & gd/soft, shld stay further: v smart juv filly, tremendous turn of foot here, win plenty more Gr races, must be followed. **117+**
2171* **SOAR 14** [16] J R Fanshawe 2-8-10 J Murtagh 11/2 JT FAV: 12: Held up, short of room halfway, prog & ev ch ent fnl 1f, kept on well but no ch with impress wnr: tchd 13/2: acts on gd & fast grnd: v useful filly, only 2nd start & shld win List/Gr races at 6f: see 2171. *3* **106+**
2132* **SHARPLAW STAR 15** [17] W J Haggas 2-8-10 M Hills 10/1: 13: Dwelt, chsd ldrs wide, ev ch ent fnl 1f, sn onepcd: acts on gd & fast grnd: useful eff on only 2nd start & shld be wng in Listed/Gr3 company: see 2132. *1¼* **102**
2094 **BUNDITTEN 16** [1] Andrew Reid 2-8-10 J F Egan 40/1: 134: Set fast pace, collared ent fnl 1f, no extra: decent front rng eff from this v speedy filly: see 2094 & 882. *1¼* **98**
1764 **BRIGHT MOLL 32** [13]2-8-10 I Mongan 40/1: 1225: Mid-div, kept on late, nrst fin: relish 6f. *1¼* **94**
2033* **DONT TELL MUM 20** [6]2-8-10 R Hughes 6/1: 16: Front rank, bmpd dist, sn onepcd: see 2033. *shd* **94**
1499* **LADY FILLY 45** [7]2-8-10 A Daly 14/1: 1117: Chsd ldr till dist, fdd: 6 wk abs: much faster grnd than prev encountered: see 1499 (gd/soft). *shd* **93**
1735* **SIENA GOLD 33** [3]2-8-10 L Dettori 13/2: 118: Prom 3.5f, no extra: btr 1735 & 1170 (gd grnd). *1* **90**
2165* **MISS MEGGY 14** [9]2-8-10 D Allan 10/1: 119: Nvr btr than mid-div: showed more 2165. *½* **89**
LADY ANN SUMMERS [12]2-8-10 J Fortune 66/1: 0: 10th: ch f Two Punch - Why Walk (Zilzal) Dwelt, mod late prog on debut: Feb 1st foal: dam unrcd, sire a decent sprint wnr: with B Meehan. *¾* **87**
2094* **POLLY PERKINS 16** [10]2-8-10 K Darley 11/1: 110: 11th: Outpcd, nvr a factor: fin strongly to win 2094. *½* **85**
1955 **HIGH CHART 23** [4]2-8-10 A McCarthy 100/1: 1440: 12th: Chsd ldrs, btn dist. *nk* **84**
2094 **INDIANNIE STAR 16** [2]2-8-10 T E Durcan 50/1: 2160: 13th: Chsd ldrs, wknd fnl 1f: see 1981. *¾* **82**
2151* **GLOVED HAND 14** [8]2-8-10 K Fallon 7/1: 10: 14th: Chsd ldrs, btn when sltly hmpd dist. *2½* **75**
1567 **TARA TARA 42** [14]2-8-10 R Winston 50/1: 100: 15th: Hmpd sn after start, al struggling: 6 wk abs. *1* **72**
2151 **CASTELLETTO 14** [11]2-8-10 G Gibbons 33/1: 320: 16th: Mid-div wide, short of rm halfway, sn btn. *shd* **72**
1786 **MAKE IT HAPPEN NOW 30** [5]2-8-10 L Keniry 150/1: 040: 17th: Hmpd start, al bhd & t.o. in last. *13* **33**
17 Ran Time 1m 01.81 (2.81) Owned: Mrs John Magnier & Mr M Tabor Trained: Ireland

2491 **5.30 Listed Sandringham Rated Stakes Handicapfillies 3yo 0-110 (A)** **[110]**
£29000 £11000 £5500 **1m str Good/Firm 39 -02 Slow** Stands Side

2026 **CELTIC HEROINE 20** [17] M A Jarvis 3-8-7 (1oh) (89) K Darley 11/1: 541-2121: Dwelt, held up, hdwy well over 2f out, hit by rivals whip 2f out, led dist, drvn out: eff at 1m/9f on fast, gd/soft & both AWs, stiff or sharp trks: v prog, useful & genuine: see 1602. **103**
2136 **COY 15** [2] Sir Michael Stoute 3-8-11 (94) K Fallon 11/2: 01-522: Cl-up, led 2f out till dist, styd on gamely, just held by wnr: apprec return to 1m & acts on gd & fast grnd, gall trk: lightly rcd, useful, win a nice prize shortly: see 1888. *½* **106**
ZOSIMA 235 [7] Saeed bin Suroor 3-9-7 T (104) L Dettori 11/2: 12115-3: b f Capote - Grafin (Miswaki) Hld up, hdwy & no room 2f out, styd on well ins last, not pace of front 2: well bckd on Brit debut: trained in America in '03, dual stks & a Gr3 scorer: stays a stiff 1m, could get further: acts on dirt & fast: wore a t-strap: v smart run under top weight, plenty more to come & shld be wng flls Gr races shortly. *2* **112+**
1882* **BRINDISI 26** [14] B W Hills 3-8-12 (95) M Hills 14/1: 2-3414: Held up, hdwy to chall over 1f out, onepace: useful eff up in class after mdn win in 1882. *2½* **98**
2312 **DANCLARE 7** [4]3-8-7 (6oh) (84) K McEvoy 11/1: 4210-065: Handy, onepcd fnl 2f: prob just stays 1m. *1¾* **89**
2211 **QASIRAH 12** [13]3-8-12 bl (95) P Robinson 16/1: 120-0536: Dwelt, held up, hmpd over 2f out, eff & short of room over 1f out, no threat: no luck in rng & well worth forgiving this: see 2211, 1568. *2½* **89**
1929 **RED TOP 25** [19]3-8-7 (6oh) (84) R Hughes 25/1: 3-2327: Held up, switched wide over 3f out, sn hdwy till no extra over 1f out: btr 1929, 1419. *nk* **83**
1110 **DOCTRINE 67** [20]3-9-2 (99) J Fortune 50/1: 62116-48: In tch, hdwy & short of room over 2f out, no impress: 2 month abs, see 1110. *1¾* **88**
1741 **CUSCO 33** [18]3-8-7 (1oh) (89) R L Moore 66/1: 1305-269: Bhd, hmpd 2f out, no danger: see 1513. *shd* **78**
1732 **CRAFTY FANCY 33** [6]3-8-10 (93) T Quinn 100/1: 655-2300: 10th: In tch, wknd 2f out: btr 1421 (6f). *nk* **80**
1666 **BAY TREE 36** [8]3-9-2 (99) T P Queally 25/1: 1100-630: 11th: In tch, wknd over 1f out: btr 1666. *1½* **83**
2250 **MYSTICAL GIRL 11** [1]3-8-11 (94) S Chin 7/2 FAV: 3312130: 12th: Led till hdd & wknd 2f out: hvly bckd: some of stable's rnrs have reportedly had coughing: cld pay to forgive this: see 2250, 2126. *8* **62**
4175} **BUZZ BUZZ 279** [5]3-8-7 (22oh) (68) Lisa Jones 100/1: 02040-0: 13th: b f Mtoto - Abuzz (Absalom) In tch, wknd 2f out on reapp: rnr-up in a nov fills in '03: prob stays 1m on firm & fast grnd. *shd* **57**
2 Jun'03 Pont 6g/f 72- D:
1844 **MADAEH 28** [10]3-8-10 (93) R Hills 25/1: 3115-40: 14th: Handy, wknd over 3f out: see 1844. *2* **56**
2136 **SURF THE NET 15** [3]3-8-9 (92) Dane O'Neill 12/1: 16-30: 15th: Dwelt, in tch, wknd over 2f out. *3* **49**
SAND N SEA 10 [12]3-8-7 (3oh) (87) W Supple 33/1: 00-00130: 16th: b f Desert Story - Poscimur (Prince Rupert) In tch, wknd over 2f out: earlier won a h'cap: '03 mdn & stks wnr: stays 10f on fast & gd/soft. *5* **37**
2136 **TOTALLY YOURS 15** [11]3-8-7 (1oh) (89) S Sanders 33/1: 2210-040: 17th: Al bhd: see 2136. *3½* **30**
2261* **ST FRANCIS WOOD 10** [16]3-8-7 (90) E Ahern 14/1: 2-0210: 18th: Keen with ldr, wknd over 2f out. *4* **22**
4743} **SUMMER SUNSET 7** [9]3-8-12 BL (95) P J Smullen 16/1: 5103-550: 19th: ch f Grand Lodge - Elegant Bloom (Be My Guest) Dwelt, in tch, wknd over 2f out: tried blnks: '03 mdn wnr: eff over 7f/1m on firm & gd/soft. *9* **9**
19 Ran Time 1m 40.41(1.71) Owned: Mr P D Savill Trained: Newmarket

Official Going STANDARD.

2492

2.10 Feast Of St Quiricus Maiden Auction Stakes Fillies 2yo (F)
£2940 £840 £420 **7f aw rnd** **Going 63** -30 Slow Inside

SIMPLY ST LUCIA [6] J R Weymes 2-8-2 C Catlin 20/1: 1: b f Charnwood Forest - Mubadara (Lahib) **69a**
Sn handy, led over 4f out, rdn clr ins last: op 25/1: cheaply bought Mar foal: dam a 6f juv mdn scorer, sire
high-class at 7f/1m: eff at 7f, 1m likely to suit: acts on fibresand & a sharp trk: goes well fresh.
1795 LADY HOPEFUL 30 [16] R P Elliott 2-8-6 Dean McKeown 5/1: 542: Led, hdd over 4f out, remained 3 **66a**
cl-up till rdn & no extra ins last: rest well covered, op 3/1: AW bow: styd longer 7f trip, acts on gd & fibresand.
1727 BE BOP ALOHA 33 [15] I A Wood 2-8-4 J F McDonald(3) 14/1: 063: b f Most Welcome - Just Julia 6 **54a**
(Natroun) Chsd ldrs, no impress fnl 2f: AW bow, op 10/1: cheaply bought Apr foal, sister to a multiple 1m 3yo
scorer: sire top class at 1m/12f: this longer 7f trip shld suit & will get further: prob handles f/sand.
SISTER GEE [12] R Hollinshead 2-8-4 Stephanie Hollinshead(5) 16/1: 4: Mid-div, kept on late, ½ **53a**
nrst fin on debut, clr of rem.
2056 LANAS TURN 19 [8]2-8-2 Paul Eddery 40/1: 05: Hmpd start, late prog: longer trip, AW bow. 6 **41a**
1874 SATIN ROSE 27 [11]2-8-8 A Mullen(7) 5/2 FAV: 56: Went left start & bhd, only mod prog: op 3/1. shd **47a**
1920 SUKUMA 25 [13]2-8-8 N Chalmers(5) 4/1: 07: Slow away, in tch 4f, AW bow. 3½ **41a**
2275 KALIKA 9 [7]2-8-4 S Righton 40/1: 608: Slow away & bhd, mod prog, longer trip. 2 **33a**
1687 LAUREN LOUISE 35 [3]2-8-6 t Kim Tinkler 25/1: 09: Dwelt, in tch 4f, AW bow. nk **34a**
1779 COIS NA TINE EILE 31 [1]2-8-2 D Kinsella 6/1: 30: 10th: Dwelt & sn outpcd, 'not face kickback'. 2½ **25a**
Fraambuoyant [5]2-8-2 R Ffrench 20/1:0 1727 Lady Suesanne 33 [2]2-8-6 F Norton 25/1:0
2132 Dancing Moonlight 15 [14]2-8-10 R Fitzpatrick 40/1:0 2336 Desert Fern 6 [4]2-8-6 N Callan 10/1:0
14 Ran Time 1m 33.08 (6.48) Owned: Sporting Occasions Racing No 6 Trained: Middleham

---

2493

2.45 St Madonna Of Carmine's Day Claiming Stakes 3yo (F)
£3269 £934 £467 **6f aw rnd** **Going 63** -03 Slow Inside

2227 OBE BOLD 12 [5] A Berry 3-8-4 (54) F Norton 11/8 FAV: 4302001: Made all, rdn clr fnl 2f, rdly: **72a**
nicely bckd, op 6/4: eff at 5/6f on firm, fast & fibresand, sharp or gall trk: enjoyed the switch to clmg grade &
forcing tactics: see 1975, 1441 & 1338.
2243 LA FONTEYNE 11 [8] C B B Booth 3-8-2 (55) J McAuley 25/1: 00-502: Chsd ldrs till outpcd bef 8 **52a**
halfway, kept on late, nvr a threat: op 16/1: prob handles fibresand: see 1659.
1902 ONLY IF I LAUGH 26 [6] P A Blockley 3-8-9 (68) Dean McKeown 9/4: 04-34023: Reared start, late ½ **57a+**
gains under a kind ride: prev with B Meehan: lost chance at the start: return to 5f could suit: see 1902.
2379 BEAMSLEY BEACON 5 [1] G M Moore 3-8-11 VIS (57) T Eaves(3) 14/1: 0-004064: Chsd ldrs, btn over 1f 3½ **50a**
out: visor: see 1949.
2215 KNIGHT TO REMEMBER 12 [9]3-8-5 (43) W Ryan 33/1: 3400505: Held up, nvr pace to threaten. nk **43a**
2202 BACK AT DE FRONT 12 [3]3-8-2 (55) R Miles(1) 11/2: 5600006: Dwelt, rear, little hdwy: op 4/1. 1½ **36a**
1787 PHILLY DEE 30 [4]3-8-0 (40) Hayley Turner(5) 16/1: 3000007: Chsd wnr, btn 2f out: btr 256 & 139 (5f). 4 **24a**
2380 VELVET TOUCH 5 [2]3-9-0 (54) S Whitworth 14/1: 2606508: Prom, no impress fnl 2f: btr 1575. 1 **36a**
670 EUNICE CHOICE 119 [7]3-8-5 J F McDonald(3) 66/1: 00-09: b g College Chapel - Aquiletta (Bairn) 24 **0a**
Prom early, sn struggling: 4 month abs: unplcd '03 (rtd 27 & 30a, AW mdns).
9 Ran Time 1m 17.25 (3.95) Owned: Mr Alan Berry Trained: Cockerham

---

2494

3.20 David Brookfield 40th Birthday Handicap Stakes 3yo+ 0-70 (E)
£3474 £1069 £535 **1m6f** **Going 63** -08 Slow Inside [67]

1407 BROUGHTONS FLUSH 50 [5] W J Musson 6-8-1 vis (40) F Norton 18/1: 150/-0051: Held up, hdwy to duel **50a**
with rnr-up 2f out, rdn & led ins last, all out: eff at 14f/2m on both AWs & gd, likes Southwell: see 733.
2105 NEXT FLIGHT 16 [7] R E Barr 5-8-6 (45) W Ryan 9/2: 3231432: Prom & led over 2f out, sn duelled hd **54a**
with wnr, hdd ins last but battled on gamely, just held: op 11/2: clr of rem & win again with similar attitude.
554 HIGH POLICY 132 [11] R Hollinshead 8-9-11 (64) Stephanie Hollinshead(5) 10/1: 30156-453: Held up, 6 **65a**
kept on fnl 3f, not pace of front pair: 4 month abs: see 554.
812 BROUGHTON MELODY 103 [4] W J Musson 5-8-1 (40) D R McCabe 14/1: 00//6-3044: ch f Alhijaz - 1½ **39a**
Broughton Singer (Common Grounds) Chsd ldrs, onepace for press over 2f out: 3 month abs, stable-mate of
wnr: stays 14f on fibresand: lightly rcd & mod prev.
1637* LUCKY JUDGE 39 [8]7-8-11 (50) Dale Gibson 5/1: 35/4/-4015: Drvn rear, late gains, nvr danger: ½ **48a**
reportedly not face kickback & nvr trav: btr 1637 (gd, 2m).
2203* QUEENS FANTASY 12 [12]3-8-7 vis (63) Paul Eddery 4/1 FAV: 0-040216: Dwelt, prog wide to lead 3½ **56a**
after 2f till over 2f out, fdd: btr 2203 (12f).
1421 AL MABROOK 765 [13]9-7-12 (7oh) (30) R Ffrench 10/1: 4/33060/-7: b g Rainbows For Life - Sky 14 **14a**
Lover (Ela Mana Mou) Mid-div, lost tch fnl 3f: op 7/1, new yard: jumps fit, recent h'cap hdle wnr (rtd 100h, 2m/
2m5f, firm & soft): AW h'cap plcd '02 (K Ryan, rtd 40a): stays 2m: acts on fast grnd & fibresand, likes a sharp trk.
1840 STAFF NURSE 28 [10]4-8-1 (40) Kim Tinkler 33/1: 353-0048: Bhd halfway: btr 1840. 19 **0a**
2417 VANBRUGH 4 [1]4-9-12 vis t (65) Darren Williams 9/1: 0000009: Chsd ldr, drvn & struggling 24 **0a**
halfway: qck reapp & reportedly ran flat.
2203 EQUUS 12 [6]3-8-6 (62) P Doe 40/1: 500-00: 10th: Chsd ldrs, struggling from halfway: see 2203. 19 **0a**
1681 TURTLE DANCER 35 [2]6-9-13 (66) T Eaves(3) 1/1: 22243//-20: 11th: In tch till halfway, sn well 19 **0a**
bhd: reportedly not face the kickback: much btr 1681 (10f, soft).
1047 Estuary 72 [3]9-8-11 BL(50) S Hitchcott(3) 40/1:0 3643*} Swain Davis 306 [9]4-9-10 (63) S Whitworth 10/1:0
13 Ran Time 3m 09.8 (10.0) Owned: Broughton Thermal Insulation Trained: Newmarket

---

2495	3.55 Scrubwomen Tea Party Day Handicap Stakes 3yo 0-75 (E)		[80]
	£3426 £1054 £527 1m aw rnd Going 63 -08 Slow Inside		

1976 **DISPOL VELETA 22** [8] T D Barron 3-9-1 (67) N Callan 4/1: 1413001: Held up, hdwy to lead 2f out, **75a**
sn asserted, hands & heels nr fin: 1m specialist, tried 10f: acts on firm, gd & fibresand, gall or sharp trk:
tough & genuine: see 1176, 1007 & 662.

1660 **ANNIE HARVEY 37** [3] B Smart 3-9-4 (70) F Lynch 18/1: 1D30-002: Led 6f, drvn & kept on: AW bow, 2½ **72a**
gd run with forcing tactics applied: stays 1m: acts on fast, gd/soft & fibresand: see 1660.

1707 **PLAY MASTER 34** [4] D Haydn Jones 3-9-7 (73) Paul Eddery 5/2: 2120103: Held up, rdn & kept on fnl 1 **73a**
2f, nvr a threat to wnr: see 1257.

1628 **MISSION AFFIRMED 39** [5] T P Tate 3-9-2 (68) Dale Gibson 7/4 FAV: 5-015104: Chsd ldr, rdn & no 3 **62a**
impress over 1f out: btr 1198 (C/D).

2168 **GLENDALE 14** [6]3-8-10 p (62) J D Smith 12/1: 0-100005: Outpcd, eff wide, nvr dngrs: see 651. 5 **47a**

1141 **COUNT DRACULA 65** [7]3-9-1 VIS (67) N Chalmers(5) 10/1: 020-106: Prom till lost place halfway: 2 **48a**
visor, 9 wk abs: much btr 841 (polytrack mdn).

1865 **GROUND PATROL 27** [2]3-9-4 VIS (70) W Ryan 10/1: 0-343607: Dwelt, sn handy, btn 3f out: visor, 10 **34a**
poor run: btr 676 (polytrack mdn).

2174 **JUST ONE LOOK 14** [1]3-8-13 (65) D Sweeney 14/1: 00-00008: b f Barathea - Western Sal (Salse) 9 **13a**
Chsd ldrs till halfway, sn bhd: op 10/1: nov hlfcap scorer in '03: wng form at 6f, prob stays sharp 7f: acts on
firm, gd & prob polytrack, gall or sharp/turning trk.
2 Aug'03 Hayd 6fm 84-(80) D: 1 Jul'03 Hayd 6gd 79- D: 2 Jun'03 Chep 6.1g/f 79- D:
8 Ran Time 1m 45.07 (5.67) Owned: Mr W B Imison Trained: Thirsk

---

2496	4.30 Woodchoppers Jamboree Classified Stakes 3yo+ 0-60 (F)		
	£2961 £846 £423 7f aw rnd Going 63 +04 Fast Inside		

2037 **COUNTYKAT 19** [10] K R Burke 4-9-7 vis (64) Darren Williams 10/1: 30-60021: Dwelt, hdwy halfway, **78a+**
led dist, eased nr fin, val 5L+: gd time: eff at 6/7f, poss stays slow run 10f: handles fast, gd/soft & likes
fibresand/Southwell: suited by reapp of visor, has tried cheek pieces: enjoys clmg grade, see 467.

2338 **TEEHEE 6** [12] B Palling 6-9-4 bl (61) R Miles(3) 50/1: 50-46002: Sn handy wide travelling well, 2½ **63a**
led over 2f till over 1f out, no ch with wnr: apprec drop to 7f: see 280.

1750+ **ROMAN EMPIRE 32** [5] K A Ryan 4-9-3 bl (57) N Callan 2/1: 000-0413: Sn pushed along rear, switched 1½ **59a**
wide & kept on fnl 2f, no threat to wnr: see 1750.

2063 **AZREME 18** [2] D K Ivory 4-9-8 (65) M Howard(7) 9/1: 006-1504: Prom, no extra dist: see 1537. 4 **56a**

2338* **TRE COLLINE 6** [3]5-9-9 (60) G Baker 6/4 FAV: 0000015: Rdn rear, only mod prog when short of room 1 **55a**
2f out, no threat: reportedly not face kickback: much btr 2338.

2338 **YORKER 6** [8]6-9-8 (65) C Catlin 20/1: 2200036: Chsd ldrs, btn 2f out: quick reapp: btr 2338. ¾ **53a**

1221 **ZAGALA 60** [9]4-9-5 t (65) F Norton 10/1: 213-2027: Led 1f, prom till 2f out: abs: btr 1221 (6f). 3½ **44a**

2216* **CARTE NOIRE 12** [6]3-8-6 (1ow) (60) S Hitchcott 25/1: 6030-518: Prom, hmpd when btn 2f out. 2 **36a**

2166 **EBORACUM 14** [11]3-8-7 (62) A Mullen(7) 50/1: 4520-09: Handy, lost pl halfway, sn btn: see 2166. 1¼ **34a**

872 **MEGABOND 90** [4]3-8-10 (62) F Lynch 10/1: 05230-50: 10th: Slow away & sn rdn, brief eff, nvr a ½ **36a**
factor & eased ins last: reportedly not face kickback: 3 month abs: see 872.

2445 **OLD BAILEY 2** [1]4-9-3 bl (59) T Eaves(3) 20/1: 6050100: 11th: Chsd ldrs till 3f out: btr 2204. ¾ **33a**

2243 **DESERT BATTLE 11** [7]3-8-8 bl (55) Dale Gibson 66/1: 000-0000: 12th: ch g Desert Sun - Papal 5 **24a**
(Selkirk) Dwelt, prog to lead after 1f till over 2f out, sn btn: auct mdn plcd in '03 (rtd 80): eff over a sharp
or stiff/gall 6f, tried up to 12f: handles fast grnd.
12 Ran Time 1m 30.75 (4.15) Owned: Bernard Bargh Jeff Hamer Steve Henshaw Trained: Leyburn

---

2497	5.05 Teletext Racing Hands And Heels Apprentice Handicap Stakes 3yo+ 35-55 (F)		[55]
	£2996 £856 £428 1m Going 63 -43 Slow Inside		

2052* **FRANKS QUEST 19** [13] P Burgoyne 4-9-12 (53) R J Killoran(5) 13/2: 6040211: Cl-up & led bef **65a+**
halfway, in command dist, val 5L+: suited by 1m, stays 11f well: acts on polytrack, fast & gd/soft grnd, loves
fibresand: see 2052 & 718.

2335* **DIAMOND SHANNON 6** [15] D Carroll 3-9-5 (7ex) (56) Danielle McCreery(5) 100/30 FAV: 2-00512: Keen & 3 **59a**
prom, styd on for press fnl 2f, no ch with wnr: quick reapp under a pen: stays 1m: see 2335 (7f).

1819 **ERUPT 29** [14] R E Barr 11-8-8 (5oh) (30) Laura Pike 25/1: 0060-503: b g Beveled - ½ **37a$**
Sparklingsovereign (Sparkler) Dwelt, rear, kept on late, not able to chall: h'cap plcd '03 (rtd 52, M Brittain):
sell wnr in '02: eff at 7/10f: acts on firm & f/sand, likes gd/soft & soft, any trk: best without a visor.
1 Oct'02 Ayr 9sft 53- F: 2 Aug'01 Thir 8gd 47-44 F:

2335 **LEYAALY 6** [7] B A Pearce 5-8-11 p (38) Liam Jones 8/1: 0-600124: Dwelt, chsd wnr halfway, no ½ **39a**
extra dist: see 2335 (7f).

2055 **KILLERBY NICKO 19** [12]3-9-1 (52) A Mullen 12/1: 00-60605: Led after 1f till 4f out, longer trip. 4 **46a**

2204 **KANZ WOOD 12** [9]8-9-4 vis (45) T Dean(5) 7/1: 0553436: Mid-div, not able to chall: btr 2204 (7f). 1 **37a**

2107 **BUCKENHAM STONE 16** [3]5-8-8 (5oh) (30) Kirsty Milczarek(5) 25/1: 00-007: ch f Wing Park - Walk 6 **17a**
That Walk (Hadeer) Led 1f, btn 3f out: h'cap bow: mod form at up to 10f prev.

2340 **MOYNE PLEASURE 6** [10]6-9-4 p (45) Steven Harrison 8/1: 2314608: Chsd ldrs till 2f out: btr 1943. nk **26a**

2102 **LIBRE 16** [6]4-10-0 bl (55) K May 10/1: 0-054009: Chsd ldrs, struggling fnl 3f: btr 1430 (10f). 6 **24a**

2338 **HOHS BACK 6** [2]5-9-7 p (48) Lucy Russell 6/1: 2060050: 10th: Slow away & al bhd, quick reapp. 2 **13a**

2248 **GLANWORTH 11** [4]3-7-12 (15oh)BL (30) Charlotte Kerton(5) 16/1: 0600: 11th: Sn strug: op 12/1, blnks. 2 **0a**

2080 **STONE CREST 18** [8]6-8-8 (5oh) (30) S Guryson 50/1: 660//-00: 12th: Al outpcd. 13 **0a**

2037 **HOLDERNESS GIRL 19** [5]11-8-8 (10oh) (25) Stacey Renwick 66/1: 000/////-60: 13th: Lost pl halfway. ½ **0a**
13 Ran Time 1m 47.9(8.5) Owned: Fun & Fantasy & Andrew Haynes Racing Ltd Trained: Marlborough

Official Going Standard

2498
2.20 Japanese Lily Festival Maiden Auction Stakes Fillies 2yo (F)
£3367 £1036 £518 **5f aw str** Going 70 Inapplicable Stands Side

1571 **CHILLY CRACKER 43** [1] R Hollinshead 2-8-2 Dale Gibson 8/1: 261: Made all, drvn & styd on **71a**
strongly ins last: abs AW bow: eff at 5f, further will sn: acts on gd & gd/soft, sharp/turning trk: goes well
fresh: likes to force the pace, entitled to progress: see 1123.
2151 **COLONIAL GIRL 15** [5] T D Easterby 2-8-6 D Allan 9/4: 432: Al prom, eff 2f out, onepace: bckd, 1¼ **70a**
op 3/1: AW bow: eff at 5f, 6f will suit: handles fast & fibresand: see 2151 & 1764.
1887 **MOON MISCHIEF 27** [2] N P Littmoden 2-8-6 J Bramhill 9/2: 03: b f Desert Sun - Moonlight Path nk **69a**
(Fairy King) Chsd ldrs, drvn & hdwy over 1f out, onepace ins last: op 7/2: AW bow: 15,000gns Feb foal, dam unrcd,
related to several sprint wnrs: eff at 5f, handles fibresand: left intro bhd.
2109 **BELLY DANCER 17** [7] P F I Cole 2-8-8 T P Queally(3) 13/8 FAV: 64: Sn handy trav well, rdn & no ½ **69a**
extra dist: nicely bckd, AW bow: handles firm grnd & fibresand: see 2109.
CLASSIC STYLE 0 [3]2-8-3 A Mullen(7) 16/1: 5: b f Desert Style - Classic Ring (Auction Ring) 8 **45a**
Slow away & al outpcd, nvr a factor: April foal, half-sister to 6/7f wnr Waterside, also useful sprint wnr Seven No
Trumps: dam a 7f juv wnr.
2056 **JUSTENJOY YOURSELF 20** [4]2-8-2 Hayley Turner(5) 28/1: 606: Prom till over 1f out, AW bow. ½ **37a**
SURREY DOWNS GIRL 0 [8]2-8-3 (1ow) R Price 33/1: 7: Outpcd, sn bhd, fin lame. 16 **0a**
7 Ran Time 59.61 () Owned: Mr John L Marriott Trained: Upper Longdon

2499
2.55 Procession Of The Golden Chariot Claiming Stakes 3yo+ (F)
£2968 £848 £424 **1m3f** Going 70 -06 Slow Inside

1681 **PURE MISCHIEF 36** [9] W M Brisbourne 5-9-12 (62) B Swarbrick(5) 11/2: 30/-31151: Held up, prog to **78a**
lead over 1f out, edged left, drvn out: clmd by C Dore for £14,000: eff at 10f, now stays 12f well, may get
further: acts on gd/soft, soft & both AWs, stiff or sharp trk: see 1609.
1668 **MANIATIS 37** [6] Andrew Reid 7-9-13 vis (73) I Mongan 9/4 FAV: 65/-61102: Held up in tch, smooth ½ **77a**
hdwy to lead 3f out, rdn & hdd over 1f out, kept on well: clr of rem, op 11/4: back to form on return to sand.
2381* **ROMIL STAR 6** [8] K R Burke 7-9-10 vis (65) D Sweeney 3/1: 0214113: Held up in tch, not pace of 6 **65a**
front pair fnl 2f: qck reapp: see 2381 (12f, seller).
2317 **BIG SMOKE 8** [10] J Howard Johnson 4-9-6 bl (74) P Mulrennan(5) 25/1: 20300-04: Handy, hung left & 1¾ **59a**
no extra from 2f out: ran well for a long way, big in trip suit.
1467 **PERUVIA 48** [5]4-9-3 VIS T (75) G Duffield 12/1: 0/4412-05: b f Perugino - Dane's Lane (Danehill) nk **55a**
Led/dsptd lead 1m, no extra: clr of rem: mod form over jumps in 03/04: mdn scorer on the level '03 (H Morrison): '02
plcd (rtd 83, R Hannon, auct mdn): prob suited by 9/10f on fast & gd/soft grnd, prob handles polytrack: tried vis &
t-strap here. 2 Oct'03 Ayr 10g/s 77-75 D: 1 Sep'03 Hami 9.2gd 77-(75) D:
1544↓ **AL AZHAR 398** [2]10-9-4 (68) D Allan 9/1: 150/453-6: b g Alzao - Upend (Main Reef) Chsd ldrs, 15 **36a**
btn 3f out: reapp: lightly rcd '03 (plcd, rtd 72, appr h'cap): won 2 h'caps & a class stks in '02: eff at 1m,
suited by a strong pace at 10/12f on firm & hvy, any trk: can go well fresh: 10yo.
1 Jun'02 Thir 12g/f 73-67 D: 2 Jun'02 Donc 12g/f 69-63 D: 1 May'02 Carl 11.9fm 67- E: 1 Apr'02 Ripo 12.2gd 63-57 E:
2 Jun'01 Thir 12gd 76-75 D: 2 Apr'01 Pont 10fhvy 76-72 E:
2050 **CASPIAN DUSK 20** [1]3-8-9 (65) C Haddon(7) 5/1: 2312137: In tch, btn 3f out: btr 2050 & 1754. 2 **37a**
3091 **WORTH A GAMBLE 692** [7]6-9-6 (35) J D O'Reilly(7) 100/1: 060000/-8: Chsd ldrs 1m, abs, gelded. 2 **32a**
1966 **IRISH CHAPEL 24** [4]8-9-8 M Savage(5) 100/1: 09: Led 3f, no ch fnl 5f, longer trip AW bow. 28 **0a**
1712 **MANDARAH 35** [3]5-9-6 VIS (40) N Callan 9/1: 000000: 10th: Held up & struggling fnl 3f: visor. ¾ **0a**
10 Ran Time 2m 29.64 (8.34) Owned: The Cartmel Syndicate Trained: Nesscliffe

2500
3.30 Battle Of Bunker Hill Handicap Stakes 3yo+ 0-70 (E) **[70]**
£3780 £1163 £582 **1m aw rnd** Going 70 -10 Slow Inside

2496 **TRE COLLINE 1** [10] N Tinkler 5-9-10 (6ex) (66) G Baker 7/2 FAV: 00000101: Held up, smooth hdwy **83a**
wide from halfway & led over 1f out, sn rdn & in command, eased cl-home: unplcd yesterday when reportedly not facing
kickback over 7f, seems suited by 1m: acts on firm, fast & fibresand: thriving, see 2338.
2147 **MIDSHIPMAN 15** [9] A W Carroll 6-8-13 vis t (55) I Mongan 9/1: 0003002: Prom & led over 3f out 4 **59a**
till over 1f out, no ch with wnr ins last: eff in blnks/visor & t-strap: wants further now: see 1430.
2338 **HAUNT THE ZOO 7** [6] John A Harris 9-9-3 (59) L Treadwell(7) 33/1: 2513-503: Chsd ldrs, kept on 2½ **58a**
onepace for press, no threat: see 1546.
2018 **QUIET READING 22** [7] M R Bosley 7-9-11 vis (67) Hayley Turner(5) 8/1: 6322004: Rear, late gains. ½ **65a**
1198 **BRANDY COVE 63** [14]7-9-6 (62) M Stainton(7) 28/1: 4523-405: Slow away, bhd, late prog: 2 mth abs. 2 **56a**
1960 **MCQUEEN 24** [11]4-10-0 (70) D Sweeney 9/1: 10-06006: Rdn rear, late gains, nrst fin: see 99. 1 **62a**
2018 **ESTIMATION 22** [15]4-9-5 (61) A Quinn(5) 16/1: 3500007: Chsd ldrs, btn over 1f out: see 255 (C/D). 2 **49a**
2324 **BAILIEBOROUGH 8** [7]5-9-11 vis (67) Alex Greaves 10/1: 0340138: Pushed along rear, nvr a factor. hd **54a**
2338 **CRUSOE 7** [5]7-8-9 bl (51) N Chalmers(5) 16/1: 0420029: Sn rdn & no impress halfway: qck reapp. 1¾ **35a**
2120 **MERDIFF 16** [12]5-9-8 (64) B Swarbrick(5) 12/1: 3201-000: 10th: Sn cl-up/dsptd lead, hdd 3f out, wknd. 3 **42a**
2497* **FRANKS QUEST 1** [8]4-8-11 (53) L Keniry(3) 7/1: 60402110: 11th: Mid-div, no impress from halfway: 2 **27a**
appr h'cap wnr yesterday: see 2497 (C/D).
1883 **BAND 27** [3]4-9-11 (67) S Whitworth 33/1: 0360-000: 12th: Prom, btn 3f out: see 1883. 5 **32a**
1825 **TRENCH COAT 30** [4]3-9-1 (67) G Duffield 33/1: 253-2000: 13th: Led/dsptd lead 3f, sn btn/eased, 8 **19a**
saddle slipped: see 814.
1024 **DIXIE DANCING 76** [13]5-9-2 (58) N Callan 20/1: 1/5030-50: 14th: Prom till 3f out: 10 wk abs: see 1024. 7 **0a**
2394 **MILLENIO 5** [1]4-9-8 (64) O Urbina 8/1: 1-333620: 15th: Reluctant to race, t.o. throughout: qck reapp. 4 **0a**
15 Ran Time 1m 45.83 (6.43) Owned: Peter Alderson Mike Gosse Adrian Mornin Trained: Malton

---

2501	4.05 St Harveys Day Selling Handicap Stakes 3yo+ 35-55 (G)				**[54]**
	£2639 £754 £377	7f aw rnd	Going 70	+06 Fast Inside	

2204 **TURN AROUND 13** [12] B W Hills 4-9-11 (51) I Mongan 3/1 FAV: 0-002151: Cl-up, led 3f out & sn rdn **68a**
clr, readily: bckd from 6/1: sold to P Blockley for 9,200gns: eff at 8.5f, suited by 7f on fibresand & gd/soft.
2204 **BULAWAYO 13** [9] Andrew Reid 7-9-8 bl (48) B Swarbrick(5) 9/1: 0610642: Dwelt, pushed along & chsd 7 **52a**
ldrs, kept on in last, no ch with easy wnr: see 956.
2258 **JONNY EBENEEZER 11** [16] R M H Cowell 5-9-13 (53) A Quinn(5) 6/1: 0202103: Chsd wnr 3f out, hung 1 **55a**
left & no impress fnl 2f: claimed for 6,000: see 1938.
2202 **INDIAN MUSIC 13** [6] A Berry 7-9-4 (44) G Carter 8/1: 5443324: Held up, eff from halfway, nvr dngrs. 3½ **39a**
2384 **BANDBOX 6** [10]9-8-9 (35) A Daly 14/1: 00600-05: ch g Imperial Frontier - Dublah (Private nk **29a**
Account) Dwelt, rear, late gains, nvr a threat: qck reapp: unplcd '03 (rtd 38a & 37, h'caps): unplcd '02 (rtd 48a
& 71, flattered, class stks): eff btwn 5/7f on firm, gd/soft & fibresand, with/without visor, tried t-strap: can go
well fresh. 2 Aug'01 Newb 6g/f 66-65 E: 2 Jul'01 Wind 6g/f 66-66 E: 2 Jun'01 Bath 5.7fm 67- E:
2202* **MALLIA 13** [11]11-9-6 (46) Laura Jayne Crawford(7) 9/1: 1406-416: Reared start & rear, late gains. nk **39a**
PRINCE OF ARAGON 1459 [15]8-9-3 (43) D Sweeney 50/1: 0400/0///-7: b g Aragon - Queens Welcome nk **35a**
(Northfields) Chsd ldrs, btn 7f out: v long abs: unplcd when last seen on the level back in '00: '99 mdn wnr:
winning form at 7f on gd grnd.
811 **LORD MELBOURNE 104** [13]5-9-10 (50) N Chalmers(5) 14/1: 4305168: Mid-div, hung left & btn 2f out. nk **41a**
890 **HEADLAND 87** [5]6-9-11 bl e (51) M Savage(5) 12/1: 2003039: Slow away, mid-div, btn 2f out: 3 mth abs. ½ **41a**
2497 **KANZ WOOD 1** [3]8-9-5 vis (45) R Thomas(5) 6/1: 05534360: 10th: Slow away, rear, little hdwy. ¾ **34a**
1635 **ZIETZIG 40** [8]7-9-0 (40) Alex Greaves 14/1: 2306-000: 11th: Led/dsptd lead 4f, sn btn: 6 wk abs. 3½ **22a**
2369 **GILLYS GENERAL 6** [7]4-9-8 P (48) S Whitworth 20/1: 0-401600: 12th: Led/dsptd lead till over 4f out. 6 **18a**
3778} **CUTE CAIT 300** [14]3-9-2 (51) G Duffield 25/1: 135000-0: 13th: Al rear, abs, new yard. 2 **17a**
495 **Magico 141** [1]3-8-10 (45) L Keniry(3) 50/1:0 1921 **My Little Sophia 26** [4]4-9-3 P(43) P Varley(7) 50/1:0
15 Ran Time 1m 31.07 (4.47) Owned: Gryffindor (wwwracingtourscouk) Trained: Lambourn

---

2502	4.40 Ludi Piscatari Classified Stakes 3yo+ 0-60 (F)				
	£3003 £858 £429	6f aw rnd	Going 70	+01 Fast Inside	

1533 **NEVER WITHOUT ME 44** [8] J F Coupland 4-9-2 (54) S Whitworth 14/1: 5210341: Chsd ldrs, hdwy & led **64a**
over 1f out, drvn out: abs, new yard: eff at 5/6f & loves fibresand: freshened up by new connections.
2111 **BRANTWOOD 17** [7] B A McMahon 4-9-2 t (58) L Keniry(3) 10/1: 0-000432: Cl-up & rdn/led over 1f out, ¾ **61a**
sn hdd, kept on for press: acts on firm, v soft grnd & fibresand: gd run: see 1774.
2496 **ROMAN EMPIRE 1** [12] K A Ryan 4-9-2 bl (57) N Callan 5/2 FAV: 000-04133: Dwelt, sn chsd ldrs, hd **60a**
outpcd briefly halfway, styd on well cl-home, nrst fin: plcd over 7f yesterday: see 1750.
2053 **GILDED COVE 20** [1] R Hollinshead 4-9-5 (63) Stephanie Hollinshead(5) 9/1: 3351144: Rear, late gains. 1½ **58a**
2496 **AZREME 1** [2]4-9-7 (65) M Howard(7) 9/1: 006-15045: Dwelt, rear, mod prog, no threat. 2½ **53a**
2201+**LARKYS LOB 13** [14]5-9-5 (63) J D O'Reilly(7) 9/2: 6312216: Led till over 1f out, wknd: see 2201 (5f). 2 **46a**
2337 **PAYS DAMOUR 7** [13]7-9-2 (57) Alex Greaves 5/1: 0-001037: In tch, no prog fnl 2f: btr 2337 & 1522. 3½ **34a**
2315 **CARIBE 8** [10]5-9-2 (60) G Carter 50/1: 046-6008: b c Octagonal - Caring Society (Caerleon) 2 **29a**
Mid-div at best: won 4 times in Spain 02/03: all wins at 6f on gd grnd.
3117} **HAZE BABYBEAR 329** [9]4-8-13 (56) G Parkin 28/1: 003310-9: b f Mujadil - River's Rising (Mendez) shd **26a**
Outpcd & nvr a factor: reapp: mdn scorer '03, AW h'cap plcd (rtd 55a): unplcd '02 (rtd 68): eff at 5f, stays 6f &
has tried 7f: acts on gd, gd/soft & fibresand. 1 Jul'03 Beve 5g/s 57-(56) D:
1982 **YASHIN 23** [4]3-8-9 (60) G Duffield 20/1: 050-00: 10th: b g Soviet Star - My Mariam (Salse) 2½ **22a**
Outpcd & nvr a factor: AW bow: unplcd '03 (lightly rcd, rtd 66, auct mdn): half-brother to a 1m wnr abroad, dam a
6f 2yo wnr: prob stays an easy 7f on gd grnd.
1743 **FREE WHEELIN 34** [6]4-9-7 (65) I Mongan 16/1: 000-0300: 11th: Dwelt, nvr able to chall ldrs: btr 1345. 1½ **23a**
2883} **WHITE LEDGER 339** [5]5-9-7 (65) Natalia Gemelova(7) 25/1: 0/00000-0: 12th: Mid-div, struggling shd **23a**
from halfway, reapp, new yard.
1837} **MORITAT 384** [11]4-9-2 (60) S Donohoe(7) 10/1: 6/0206-0: 13th: Chsd ldrs, no impress fnl 2f: op 16/1. shd **17a**
458 **SUGAR SNAP 147** [3]4-8-13 (55) M Halford(7) 100/1: 60/000-00: 14th: Al outpcd & struggling, 5 mth abs. 10 **0a**
14 Ran Time 1m 17.43 (4.13) Owned: Mr J F Coupland Trained: Grimsby

---

2503	5.15 Eat All Of Your Vegetables Day Handicap Stakes 3yo 35-55 (F)				**[59]**
	£3304 £944 £472	1m4f aw	Going 70	-23 Slow Inside	

2332 **JACKIE KIELY 7** [16] P S McEntee 3-9-5 (50) I Mongan 9/2: 2055421: Dwelt, sn handy & dsptd lead **57a**
from halfway, led over 2f out, wandered under press but styd on strongly, drvn out: first win: prev with T G Mills:
eff at 10f, now stays 12f well: acts on both AWs, firm & fast grnd: likes a sharp/undul trk: see 2332, 2014 & 676.
1785 **THE KING OF ROCK 32** [5] A G Newcombe 3-9-0 (45) S Whitworth 10/1: 00-05402: Held up, hdwy from 1¼ **49a**
halfway, outpcd over 2f out, kept on well ins last: stays 12f well, 14f+ shld suit: handles gd, soft & fibresand.
2299 **HOLLY WALK 9** [15] M Dods 3-9-1 P (46) D Sweeney 12/1: 4-025543: Handy & led halfway till over 2f ½ **49a**
out, kept on onepace: gd run in first time cheek pieces on AW bow: eff at 10/12f on firm, soft & fibresand.
2149 **RUBAIYAT 15** [8] G Wragg 3-9-7 (52) R Havlin 16/1: 06-004: b g Desert Story - Lovers' Parlour 1 **54a**
(Beldale Flutter) Held up, eff to chase wnr when hung left over 1f out, no extra: only btn around 3L on AW bow, clr
of rem: lightly rcd '03 (unplcd, rtd 68, mdn): stays 12f, acts on fibresand & a sharp trk.
2299 **PEARL OF YORK 9** [9]3-9-7 (52) L Keniry(3) 8/1: 000-0025: Chsd ldrs, no impress fnl 2f: btr 2299 (10f). 6 **46a**
2134 **TRUE TO YOURSELF 16** [6]3-8-12 (43) A Daly 15/2: 00-02106: Towards rear, late prog, nvr a threat. 5 **30a**
1978 **NODS STAR 23** [3]3-9-2 (47) G Parkin 12/1: 5007: ch f Starborough - Barsham (Be My Guest) Bhd, 5 **27a**
eff halfway, btn 3f out: AW/h'cap bow, longer trip: unplcd at up to 1m prev (rtd 56S).
2123 **QUAY WALLOPER 16** [7]3-9-1 (46) J Bramhill 33/1: U000-008: Sn outpcd & nvr a factor: see 2123. 19 **0a**
795 **KING OF MEZE 106** [11]3-8-9 (40) O Urbina 50/1: 0609: b g Croco Rouge - Cossack Princess (Lomond) 9 **0a**
Chsd ldrs, btn 4f out: h'cap bow: unplcd prev at up to 1m.
2163 **PRAIRIE SUN 15** [4]3-9-2 (47) G Duffield 4/1 FAV: 0-445100: 10th: Rear, nvr a factor: btr 1836 (fast). 3 **0a**
2050 **PEPE 20** [12]3-9-10 (55) Stephanie Hollinshead(5) 8/1: 6630140: 11th: Led, hdd halfway & sn struggling. 1¾ **0a**
2267 **FOX HOLLOW 10** [13]3-9-6 (51) M Savage(5) 20/1: 3262300: 12th: Chsd ldrs, btn 5f out: btr 1754 & 1324. shd **0a**

SOUTHWELL Fibresand THURSDAY 17.06.04 Lefthand, Sharp, Oval Track

1473 **THEATRE BELLE 47** [2]3-9-9 (54) D Allan 16/1: 00-000: 13th: Chsd ldrs 6f, 7 wk abs, longer trip.	5	0a
1976 **STRANGELY BROWN 23** [1]3-9-10 (55) G Carter 10/1: 00-00300: 14th: In tch till halfway: btr 1611.	2½	0a
1953 **DAME NOVA 24** [10]3-9-0 (45) G Faulkner 12/1: 000-060: 15th: Drvn rear & no ch from halfway: AW bow.	25	0a

15 Ran   Time 2m 45.47(11.17)   Owned: Mr P S J Croft   Trained: Newmarket

AYR THURSDAY 17.06.04 Lefthand, Galloping Track

Official Going GOOD (GOOD/FIRM IN PLACES)

2504   7.00 Serendipity Interactive Maiden Claiming Stakes 3-4yo (E)
£3504 £1078 £539   **1m rnd**   **Good 58**   **-07 Slow**   Inside

1129 **THE FUN MERCHANT 66** [7] W Jarvis 3-8-8 (1ow) (63) M Tebbutt 3/1 FAV: 60-01: b g Mind Games -   **67**
Sinking (Midyan) Handy, outpcd halfway, rallied despite edg left to lead well fnl 1f, rdn out: 9 wk abs, op
9/4: clmd for £8,000: unplcd both '03 starts (auct mdns, rtd 63): eff at 1m, further will suit: acts on gd grnd &
a gall trk: goes well fresh: lightly rcd performer who can rate higher.
2107 **ALI BRUCE 17** [4] D E Cantillon 4-9-8   Darren Williams 11/1: 52: Led till well ins fnl 1f, no   1½   **67**
extra: clr rem under top-weight: app drop back to 1m, acts on gd grnd: see 2107.
2285 **SUMMER SPECIAL 9** [1] D W Barker 4-9-1 p (47) L Enstone(3) 7/1: 5530503: Handy, wknd dist.   7   **46**
2133 **COMPASSION 16** [2] G C H Chung 3-8-0 p (53) D Fentiman(7) 50/1: 450-0004: In tch, prog 2f out, wknd.   2   **37**
2055 **SHINKO FEMME 20** [6]3-8-2 (55) Kim Tinkler 25/1: 630-0005: b f Shinko Forest - Kilshanny (Groom   ½   **38**
Dancer) Rear, hdwy 3f out, wknd 1f out: rnr-up once in '03 (mdn, with W Muir): prob stays 6f on firm & fast.
2 Aug'03 Brig 6.0fm 60-(58) E:
1778 **TOP ACHIEVER 33** [8]3-8-12 BL (59) R Winston 12/1: 5-0006: ch g Intikhab - Nancy Maloney (Persian   1¼   **45**
Bold) Cl up & fdd out: unplcd sole '03 start (mdn, rtd 54): tried 1st time blnks.
2081 **LUCKY LARGO 19** [11]4-9-6 bl (53) D McGaffin 16/1: 0-050047: Rear, nvr nr ldrs.   hd   **42**
HOLLYWOOD CRITIC 0 [10]3-9-0 T Hamilton(3) 66/1: 8: Rear, modest late gains on debut.   2½   **41**
CHARLIE GEORGE 0 [14]3-9-0 P Fessey 33/1: 9: Bhd, nvr a factor on debut.   ¾   **39**
2205 **PURPLE RAIN 13** [12]3-8-2 (50) J Mackay 14/1: 00650: 10th: Al bhd.   3½   **20**
2215 **DELUSION 13** [3]3-8-1 (56) R Ffrench 4/1: 4040-630: 11th: In tch 5f, sn wknd: see 2215.   ½   **18**
1935 **EIZAWINA DOCKLANDS 26** [13]3-8-7 t J Currie(7) 8/1: 0000: 12th: Al bhd.   7   **10**
2131 **GOOD ARTICLE 16** [16]3-8-7 T (35) D Corby(2) 100/1: 00-0B00: 13th: Al bhd: tried t-strap.   6   **0**
4923} **BISHOPS BOUNCE 233** [9]3-8-4 (60) R Fitzpatrick 50/1: 002000-0: 14th: Handy, wknd 3f out on reapp.   6   **0**
1798 **ARGENT 31** [15]3-8-7 P (50) J Carroll 33/1: 50-P0200: 15th: Rear, wknd 3f out: cheek pieces.   dist   **0**

15 Ran   Time 1m 41.8 (5.2)   Owned: Mr D J Hindmarsh   Trained: Newmarket

2505   7.30 Zoe Duff 30th Birthday Maiden Auction Stakes 2yo (E)
£3348 £1030 £515   **5f str**   **Good 58**   **-21 Slow**   Stands side

1795 **SWEET ROYALE 31** [6] Miss L A Perratt 2-8-6 (2ow) R Winston 13/2: 21: Handy, led dist, rdn clr   **80**
fnl 1f: op 7/2: eff at 5f, 6f will suit: acts on gd, gall trk: imprvd from debut, win again: see 1795.
1091 **BRUT 70** [8] D W Barker 2-8-8 L Enstone(3) 50/1: 062: b c Mind Games - Champenoise (Forzando)   6   **66**
Led, hdd dist, sn no extra: 10 wk abs: Mar foal, cost 9,000 gns: brother/half brother to wnrs at 5/6f: dam wnr at
1m: sire Group winner at sprint dists.
2083 **CHILALI 19** [3] A Berry 2-8-2 P Fessey 20/1: 5033: Cl up, outpcd 2f outr, rallied late.   1¼   **56**
2275 **SWEET MARGUERITE 10** [5] T D Easterby 2-8-3 R Ffrench 8/1: 544: Nvr nrr than mid div: clr rem.   1   **54**
2228 **ISITLOVEYOURAFTER 13** [2]2-8-2 T Hamilton 100/1: 05: b f Orpen - Pericolo (Kris) Al bhd, nvr a   5   **38**
factor: Feb foal, cost 6,000 euros: half-sister to wnrs at 5/6f: dam plcd at 7f: sire top class juv performer at 6f.
1974 **HIGH MINDED 23** [1]2-8-10 Darren Williams 16/1: 06: b c Mind Games - Pips Way (Pips Pride) Al   3½   **35**
in rear: May first foal, cost 21,000 gns: dam wnr at 6f/9f: sire Group wnr at sprint dists: with K R Burke.
2251 **VICTORIA PEEK 12** [7]2-8-5 J Carroll 15/2: 407: Prom 3f, sn hung left & fdd: btr 1571.   2½   **22**
2263 **SPACE MAKER 10** [4]2-8-10 J Mackay 4/6 FAV: 48: Handy 3f, hung left & sn wknd: well bckd: nk   **26**
disappointing effort, failed to build on promise shown in 2263.

8 Ran   Time 1m 0.59 (3.99)   Owned: Mrs Lucille Bone   Trained: Ayr

2506   8.00 Integrity Recruitment Group Classified Stakes 3yo 0-60 (F)
£3080 £880 £440   **7f50y**   **Good 58**   **-28 Slow**   Outside

1910* **SHES OUR LASS 26** [7] D Carroll 3-9-0 (63) R Fitzpatrick 9/4 FAV: 2-001311: Mid div, prog to lead   **73+**
bef 1f out, pushed out, val 5L+: stays 1m, suited by 7f on firm, soft & fibresand, acts on a sharp or a gall trk,
likes Ayr: improving 3yo who can land hatrick: see 1910.
2218* **MISS PORCIA 13** [2] P W Chapple Hyam 3-8-11 (59) J Mackay 7/2: 0060-12: Handy, outpcd 2f out,   3½   **61**
kept on late, no ch with wnr: ran to winning form of 2218 (mdn).
2243* **FUTOO 12** [3] G M Moore 3-9-1 (61) L Enstone(3) 13/2: 106-6513: Chsd ldrs, prog to lead 2f out, sn   shd   **65**
hdd & no extra: just btr 2243 (h'cap, 1m).
2231 **ACUZIO 13** [1] W M Brisbourne 3-9-5 (65) R Ffrench 16/1: 6604: b c Mon Tresor - Veni Vici   2   **64**
(Namaqualand) Nvr nrr than mid div: not disgraced under top-weight.
2464 **GRACEFUL AIR 2** [8]3-8-13 (62) M Tebbutt 16/1: 4522405: Led, hdd 2f out, sn wknd: qck reapp.   hd   **58**
2174 **UNITED SPIRIT 15** [4]3-8-11 (58) T P Queally(3) 9/2: 504-06: Cl up, fdd bef 1f out: see 2174.   3½   **49**
4693} **MR LEWIN 249** [5]3-9-0 (60) T Hamilton 25/1: 005-7: ch g Primo Dominie - Fighting Run (Runnett)   hd   **51**
Sn rear, prog 3f out, no impress dist: reapp: 5th 1 of 3 '03 starts (mdn, rtd 66): acts on firm.
995 **BLADES EDGE 78** [6]3-9-0 (59) R Winston 14/1: 04-05308: Prom 5f, sn wknd: 11 wk abs: btr 673.   2   **47**

8 Ran   Time 1m 32.82 (6.02)   Owned: We-Know Partnership   Trained: Warthilll

AYR THURSDAY 17.06.04 Lefthand, Galloping Track

2507 **8.30 Saffie Joseph Handicap Stakes 3yo+ 0-85 (D)** **[84]**
£5428 £1670 £835 **1m2f** **Good 58** **+07 Fast** Inside

2180 **KIDZPLAY 14** [6] J S Goldie 8-8-8 (64) T Eaves(3) 4/1: 64-03421: Led 1m, rallied to lead 1f out, drvn out: eff at 10/12f, stays 13f: likes gd/soft & hvy, handles firm, acts on any trk, likes Musselburgh & loves Ayr: game & tough performer: see 1389. **71**
1979 **OPENING CEREMONY 23** [1] R A Fahey 5-8-12 (68) T Hamilton(3) 6/1: 30531-62: Handy, led trav well 2f out, hung left & hdd 1f out, sn no extra: find similar on this evidence: see 1979. *1½* **72**
2317 **CHERISHED NUMBER 8** [4] I Semple 5-9-7 vis (77) R Winston 7/2 J FAV: 4-040633: Bhd, prog 3f out, onepcd fnl 1f: clr rem: now stays 10f: see 2317. *2* **78**
1885 **KELBROOK 27** [7] A Bailey 5-8-9 (65) L Enstone(3) 33/1: 2-504: b g Unfuwain - Pidona (Baillamont) Handy 7f, sn wknd: rnr-up sole '03 start (mdn). *16* **42**
2 Jul'03 Hayd 10.5g/f 57- D:
2067 **PRAIRIE WOLF 19** [3]8-9-6 (76) J Mackay 11/2: 20-00005: ch g Wolfhound - Bay Queen (Damister) Mid-div 7f, sn wknd: rnr-up 2 of 9 '03 starts (h'caps): won a h'cap in '02: suited by 1m/10f on firm, handles soft & fibresand: acts on any trk, loves Goodwood: has run well fresh: tough, well h'capped. *hd* **52**
2 Oct'03 York 10.4g/f 86-84 C: 2 Aug'03 Ripo 10gd 84-81 C: 1 Jul'02 Good 9.8fm 90-86 B: 1 Sep'01 Good 9g/f 92-88 C: 2 Jun'01 Pont 10gd 90- C:
2197 **ANGLO SAXON 14** [5]4-9-11 (81) T P Queally(3) 7/2 J FAV: 101-0036: Prom, fdd 3f out. *8* **45**
2179 **CHAMPAIN SANDS 14** [2]5-8-1 (57) R Ffrench 17/2: 62-34257: Prom 7f, fdd: btr 2030. *5* **13**
7 Ran Time 2m 9.55 (5.15) Owned: Mr Liam McGuigan Trained: Glasgow

2508 **9.00 Peter's Restaurant Handicap Stakes Fillies 3yo+ 0-70 (E)** **[65]**
£3426 £1054 £527 **7f50y** **Good 58** **-37 Slow** Outside

2315 **COLLEGE MAID 8** [5] J S Goldie 7-9-3 (54) J Currie(7) 5/1: 0600241: Cl up, styd on to lead dist, rdn out: eff at 5/7f on fast, likes gd & hvy, acts on a gall or sharp trk: made gd use of drop to to winning mark: was reportedly in season when 4th in 2315, see 1096. **62**
4126} **ROSACARA 283** [4] D J Daly 3-9-3 T (63) R Ffrench 14/1: 504-2: b f Green Desert - Rambling Rose (Cadeaux Genereux) In tch, ev ch 2f out, styd on fnl 1f, not pace wnr: reapp: 4th on 1 of 3 '03 starts (fills mdn, rtd 70, Sir M Stoute): eff at 7f on gd: eff with a t-strap: gd start for new yard, only lighty rcd & can find similar. *1½* **67**
2398 **BLONDE EN BLONDE 5** [1] N P Littmoden 4-9-4 bl (55) R Fitzpatrick 8/1: 2033003: Mid div, prog & ev ch dist, onepcd fnl 1f: qck reapp: on winning mark: see 562. *2½* **54**
1794 **BELLA BEGUINE 31** [2] A Bailey 5-8-13 vis (50) R Winston 9/1: 02-50204: Led, hdd dist, no extra. *¾* **47**
2159 **HULA BALLEW 15** [9]4-9-3 (54) Darren Williams 12/1: 66-05005: Rear, hdwy 2f out, wknd fnl 1f. *1½* **48**
2296 **CELTIC ROMANCE 9** [3]5-8-12 P (49) J Carroll 7/1: 0-000506: Bhd, nvr nr ldrs: tried cheek pieces. *4* **35**
1879 **CAPETOWN GIRL 28** [7]3-9-10 (70) L Enstone(3) 8/1: 025-1007: Handy, wknd 2f out: top-weight. *1¾* **52**
2384* **TANCRED MISS 6** [8]5-8-7 (6ex) (44) T Eaves(3) 6/1: 00000-18: Handy 5f, sn wknd: btr 2384. *1½* **23**
1448 **TANCRED ARMS 49** [6]8-8-3 (40) Dale Gibson 4/1 FAV: 1060-049: Keen & handy, wknd over 1f out. *1* **17**
9 Ran Time 1m 33.51 (6.71) Owned: Mrs S E Bruce Trained: Glasgow

2509 **9.30 Kidz Play Handicap Stakes 3yo 0-70 (E)** **[72]**
£3474 £1069 £535 **1m1f20y** **Good 58** **Inapplicable** Inside

2349 **DARK RAIDER 7** [2] A P Jones 3-9-5 (63) D Corby(3) 100/30 J FAV: 00-2551: Prom, led 3f out, rdn out: first win, h'cap bow: eff at 1m/9f, acts on gd & hvy grnd: acts on a gall trk: can rate higher: see 1610. **72**
2243 **CHARLOTTE VALE 12** [5] M D Hammond 3-9-7 (65) Darren Williams 7/2: 4246-652: Mid div, prog to chsd wnr fnl 1f, al held: stays 9f, further shld suit: not disgraced under top weight, see 1707. *2* **68**
2475 **INFIDELITY 1** [3] A Bailey 3-9-0 P (58) R Winston 100/30 J FAV: 60006063: Prom, ev ch 2f out, no extra ins fnl 1f: clr rem, unplcd yesterday: 1st time pieces: see 568. *1½* **58**
1747 **KINTORE 34** [6] J S Goldie 3-8-6 (50) R Ffrench 12/1: 000-64: Rear, mod late gains: see 1747. *8* **34**
2216 **INDI ANO STAR 13** [4]3-8-11 VIS (55) R Fitzpatrick 10/1: 666055: b g Indian Rocket - Audriano (Cyrano de Bergerac) Nvr nrr than mid-div: 1st time visor: mod prev form. *1½* **36**
1798* **SON OF THUNDER 31** [7]3-8-11 (55) L Enstone(3) 5/1: 00-616: Cl up 7f, fdd: btr 1798. *nk* **35**
1067 **SAAMEQ 72** [1]3-8-1 (45) P Fessey 12/1: 0-607: b g Bahhare - Tajawuz (Kris) Led, hdd 3f out, sn wknd: long abs: unplcd sole '03 start (mdn, rtd 46, with E Dunlop): with I Semple. *11* **3**
7 Ran Time 1m 58.62() Owned: Mr T G N Burrage Trained: Upper Lambourn

BEVERLEY THURSDAY 17.06.04 Righthand, Oval Track with Stiff, Uphill Finish

Official Going GOOD/FIRM

2510 **6.45 Stars Of The Future Apprentice Handicap Stakes Fillies 3yo+ 0-70 (E)** **[63]**
£3588 £1104 £552 **1m1f207y** **Good 46** **+03 Fast** Inside

2296 **WESTCOURT DREAM 9** [1] M W Easterby 4-8-11 (46) P Mulrennan 4/1: 0333-31: Handy, styd on to lead dist, pushed out, val 4L+: eff at 7f/1m, imprvd for step up to 10f: handles firm & gd/soft: unexposed at this trip. **54+**
1876 **FEED THE METER 28** [8] T T Clement 4-9-1 (50) Saleem Golam(5) 12/1: 00/0-02: b f Desert King - Watch The Clock (Mtoto) Handy, styd on to chase ldr ins fnl 1f, al held: unplcd sole '03 start (rtd 58, mdn, G C H Chung): unplcd both '02 starts (rtd 75, mdn): eff at 10f on gd grnd: lightly rcd. *2* **53**
2038 **GOT TO BE CASH 20** [9] W M Brisbourne 5-9-3 (52) B Swarbrick 100/30: 0-421053: Cl-up, led 2f out, hdd dist, no extra: 7lb higher since last win in 1579. *1¾* **52**
2278 **TRANSCENDANTALE 10** [2] Mrs S Lamyman 6-8-12 (47) R Thomas 11/2: 2356004: Handy 7f, sn no extra *4* **41**
1945* **LIFE IS BEAUTIFUL 24** [6]5-9-1 (50) D Tudhope(5) 2/1 FAV: 2010-615: Handy, no extra fnl 2f: op 11/4: disapp on drop back to 10f: btr 1945 (12f, banded). *2½* **40**
2217 **NORMA SPEAKMAN 13** [10]4-8-10 (45) A Mullen(5) 25/1: 0220/-06: Rear, nvr nrr than mid-div: see 2217. *1* **33**

2024} **LADY NETBETSPORTS 374** [3]5-10-0 (63) M Lawson(3) 25/1: 044000-7: b f In The Wings - Auntie   nk   **50**
Maureen (Roi Danzig) Nvr nrr than mid-div: earlier hdles wnr on 1 of 3 starts (rtd 90h, mares mdn, stays 2m3f on
fast grnd): plcd twice in '03 (rtd 65, h'caps): 4th at best in '02 (rtd 78, fill mdn): eff at 1m/14f on firm & hvy
grnd: tried visor: has been treated for an irregular heart beat.
2 Sep'01 Leic 8g/f 80- D: 2 Jun'01 Pont 6fm 68- D:
2296 **MISS OCEAN MONARCH 9** [5]4-8-5 (40) C Haddon(3) 12/1: 0000208: Played up start & u.r., led 1m, fdd. 1   **25**
1279 **BARTON FLOWER 58** [7]3-8-3 (50) P Mathers(3) 25/1: 00-009: Handy 7f, sn hung left & fdd: 8 wk abs.   8   **23**
521   **TAMARINA 138** [4]3-8-3 (50) P Makin 33/1: 004-0000: 10th: Al hung left in tch, fdd fnl 3f: long abs.   dist   **0**
10 Ran   Time 2m 6.66 (4.36)   Owned: Mr K Hodgson & Mrs J Hodgson   Trained: Sheriff Hutton

---

2511	7.15 Welcome To Our Works Night Out Maiden Auction Stakes 2yo (E)

£3666 £1128   £564   **7f100y**   **Good 46**   **-09 Slow**   Inside

2263 **BRIDGE PLACE 10** [3] B J Meehan 2-8-12 bl S Sanders 6/4 FAV: 0321: Made all, hung left under   **83**
press ins fnl 2f, rdn out: eff at 6f, imprvd for step up to 7.4f: acts on fast & gd grnd: imprvd for recent
fitting of blnks: see 2263 & 1937.
2316 **MCELDOWNEY 8** [9] M Johnston 2-8-10 K Dalgleish 15/8: 32: Slow away, prog halfway, chsd ldr from   1½   **77**
fnl 1f, no extra: imprvd for step up to 7.4f, acts on gd grnd: encouraging run & can be plcd to find similar.
1893 **MAC COIS NA TINE 27** [1] K A Ryan 2-8-10   N Callan 11/2: 023: Handy 5f, sn onepcd: tchd 7/1:   3   **71**
prob stays 7.4f on fast & gd grnd: see 1893.
2028 **ROYAL FLYNN 21** [7] M Dods 2-8-12   P Makin(5) 50/1: 64: b g Royal Applause - Shamriyna (Darshaan)   1½   **70**
In tch 5f, sn no extra: Mar foal, cost 26,000gns: dam unplcd: sire Gr 1 wnr at sprint dists.
2236 **SOUND AND VISION 12** [6]2-8-11 P Mulrennan(5) 12/1: 565: b c Fayruz - Lyrical Vision (Vision)   1¾   **65**
Handy, wknd dist: Apr foal, cost 22,000gns: half-brother to a couple of wnrs at 2: dam unrcd: with M Dods.
1574 **DUSTY DANE 42** [5]2-8-8 t C Haddon(7) 14/1: 56: b c Indian Danehill - Teer On Eer (Persian   ¾   **60**
Heights) Keen cl-up, wknd fnl 2f: 6 wk abs: Apr foal, cost 9,400gns: dam mdn: sire decent around 1m/12f.
2119 **WOLDS DANCER 16** [8]2-8-3   P M Quinn 11/1: 607: Al in rear: btr 2119.   9   **37**
2297 **COUNTRYWIDE DREAM 9** [2]2-8-9 P Mathers(7) 66/1: 008: Al in rear: modest form to date.   12   **19**
8 Ran   Time 1m 34.95 (4.15)   Owned: Mr Des O'Rourke & Gallagher Equine Ltd   Trained: Upper Lambourn

---

2512	7.45 Jaguar Centre Handicap Stakes 3yo+ 0-70 (E)	[70]

£7033 £2164   £1082   **5f str**   **Good 46**   **+08 Fast**   Inside

2315 **DIZZY IN THE HEAD 8** [19] Paul Johnson 5-9-6 bl (62) N Chalmers(5) 6/1: 00-01631: Made all, clr ins   76+
fnl 2f, pushed out, val 4L+: eff at 5/6f on firm & soft, poss hvy grnd: eff with blnks, visor or eye-shield: made
gd usef of fav'able high draw on only 2nd start for current stable, h'capped to follow-up: see 2315.
2279 **KARMINSKEY PARK 10** [8] T J Etherington 5-9-6 (62) R Havlin 12/1: 0-626532: Prom, styd on to   3   **66**
chase ldr ins fnl 1f, onepace: clr rem: continues to run well & winning turn shld not be far away: see 2279, 1532.
2359 **OBE ONE 6** [4] A Berry 4-9-13 (69) A Culhane 14/1: 0064023: Rear, prog halfway, kept on, no   3   **64**
impress on front 2 fnl 1f: encouraging again from poor draw, well h'capped.
1886 **VALIANT ROMEO 27** [15] R Bastiman 4-9-0 vis (56) S Sanders 5/1 J FAV: 000-5224: Handy 3f, onepcd.   ¾   **49**
2409 **BALLYBUNION 5** [7]5-9-3 (59) A Nicholls 16/1: 00-00005: Rear, swtchd & kept on fnl 2f, nrst fin: nk   **51+**
qck reapp: gd eff from poor low draw, has slipped to a winning mark & 8f suits: btr 2084.
1765 **SIR SANDROVITCH 33** [14]8-8-12 p (54) P Hanagan 5/1 J FAV: 6000-006: b g Polish Patriot - Old   shd   **45**
Downie (Be My Guest) Mid-div, prog ins fnl 2f, kept on late: won 3 h'caps in '03: h'cap wnr in '02: dual h'cap
wnr in '01: all wins at 5f, suited by gd, firm grnd & fibresand: eff with cheek pieces, tried blnks: likes to come
late off a decent gallop: on a winning mark. 1 Jun'03 Ches 5.1g/f 73-66 C: 1 Jun'03 Thir 5g/f 64-58 D:
1 Jun'03 Beve 5fm 69-58 F: 2 Jun'03 Beve 5g/f 60-58 E: 2 Jun'03 Wind 5.0g/f 59-56 E: 1 Jun'02 Ches 5fm 77-68 C:
1 Jul'01 Pont 5g/f 77-69 D: 1 Jun'01 Beve 5g/f 71-65 F: 2 Mar'01 Wolv 6af 68a-67 D:
2279 **FAR NOTE 10** [20]6-9-9 bl (65) J Bramhill 6/1: 6101447: Stumbled after start, prog when short of   ¾   **54**
room ins fnl 2f, nrst fin: lost all chance at start: btr 1142.
2280 **MIDNIGHT PARKES 10** [5]5-9-10 (66) M Henry 25/1: 4500-048: Nvr nrr than mid-div: btr 2280.   hd   **54**
2214 **BRIGADIER MONTY 13** [3]6-8-12 (54) R Thomas(5) 100/1: 000-0609: Rear, modest late gains: see 2214.   ¾   **40**
2201 **RED LEICESTER 13** [16]4-9-0 vis (56) N Callan 20/1: 0-305160: 10th: Handy 3f, sn no extra: btr 2152.   nk   **41**
2280 **LOUGHLORIEN 10** [1]5-8-11 vis (53) G Parkin 33/1: 0006-000: 11th: Al in rear: see 1886.   hd   **37**
2409 **TALLY 5** [9]4-9-1 (57) M Nem(7) 20/1: 6031200: 12th: Dwelt, al in rear: qck reapp: btr 2214 & 2160.   ¾   **39**
2016 **ILLUSIVE 22** [6]7-9-3 bl (59) W Ryan 25/1: 0226200: 13th: Al bhd: btr 1025.   ½   **39**
2084 **KANGARILLA ROAD 19** [12]5-9-12 (68) S Whitworth 12/1: 00-00200: 14th: Handy 3f, sn wknd: btr 2029.   nk   **47**
2445 **XANADU 3** [18]8-8-9 p (51) P Mulrennan(5) 13/2: 2000620: 15th: Handy 4f, wknd: qck reapp: btr 2445.   1   **27**
2445 John Ogroats 3 [10]6-9-6 VIS(62) F Lynch 33/1:0   453   Count Cougar 148 [13]4-9-4 (60) J McAuley 33/1:0
2016 Arctic Burst 22 [11]4-10-0 vis(70) L Vickers 40/1:0   2445 Whinhill House 3 [17]4-8-11 (53) K Dalgleish 25/1:0
19 Ran   Time 1m 3.21 (1.91)   Owned: P and Mrs D M Johnson   Trained: Stanley

---

2513	8.15 Les Hart Lifetime In Racing Novice Stakes 2yo (D)

£5509 £1695   £848   **5f str**   **Good 46**   **-03 Slow**   Inside

IMPERIAL SOUND 0 [7] T D Barron 2-8-8 S Sanders 5/1: 1: b c Efisio - Final Trick (Primo   94+
Dominie) Made all, clr dist, eased cl-home, val 5L+: debut: Mar first foal, cost 36,000gns: dam unplcd: sire
useful performer at 6f/1m: eff over a stiff 5f, further will suit: acts on gd grnd & goes well fresh: showed a gd
turn of foot & useful, must win more races.
2100 **MELALCHRIST 17** [6] J J Quinn 2-9-2 P Hanagan 7/2: 122: Keen cl-up, styd on ins fnl 1f, no ch   3½   **87**
with easy wnr: faced no easy task conceding 8lbs to wnr: can find similar: see 2100 & 1631.
2236* **SPACE SHUTTLE 12** [4] T D Easterby 2-9-2 bl D Allan 5/4 FAV: 3213: Dwelt, prog when badly short   ¾   **85**
of room bef 3f out, prog halfway, onepcd fnl 1f: clr rem: below best back in trip: btr 2236 (6f, 1st time blnks).
2109 **ALCHARINGA 17** [3] T J Etherington 2-8-12 R Havlin 25/1: 504: b g Ashkalani - Bird In Blue   5   **66**
(Bluebird) Handy 3f, sn no extra: Apr foal, cost E11,000: half-brother to & wnrs abroad: sire decent at 1m.
2281* **DORN DANCER 9** [5]2-9-0 F Lynch 7/2: 015: Handy till halfway, sn wknd: v disapp run: btr 2281.   2   **62**
PAULA JO 0 [1]2-8-3 P M Quinn 40/1: 6: b f Factual - Superstream (Superpower) Al in rear on   6   **33**
debut: May foal, half-sister to wnrs at 5/6f: dam unrcd: sire performer at 2: with J S Wainwright.

759

BEVERLEY THURSDAY 17.06.04 Righthand, Oval Track with Stiff, Uphill Finish

6 Ran   Time 1m 3.77 (2.47)   Owned: Mr J Stephenson   Trained: Thirsk

2514   8.45 Westwood Classified Stakes 3yo+ 0-70 (E)
£4108 £1264 £632   **1m100y rnd**   **Good 46**   **-10 Slow**   Inside

2447 **LOW CLOUD 3** [4] D Nicholls 4-9-9 vis (75) A Nicholls 5/1: 50-60351: Held up, prog halfway, kept   77
on fnl 1f to lead cl-home, rdn out: qck reapp: eff at 7f/8.4f, has tried 10f: acts on gd & fast: eff with visor.

2403 **RILEY BOYS 5** [7] J G Given 3-8-12 (74) M Fenton 10/11 FAV: 1212122: Led, under press ins fnl 2f,   hd   75
hdd cl-home: qck reapp: another fine run here at Beverley: see 2403 & 2168.

2157 **ASWAN 15** [5] S R Bowring 6-9-4 t (64) J Bramhill 25/1: 03440-53: Keen rear, prog when short of   nk   70
room 2f out, pushed & ev ch dist, styd on fnl 1f, just denied: lost little in defeat: see 2157.

2086 **RISKA KING 19** [3] R A Fahey 4-9-4 (66) P Hanagan 12/1: 0-000004: Handy, some late gains.   1½   67

2153 **CATHERINE HOWARD 15** [1]3-8-6 (71) A Culhane 3/1: 1-4045: In tch, shortt of room 2f out, no extra.   3   59

2120 **HELDERBERG 16** [6]4-9-1 (66) K Darley 16/1: 2210-056: Cl-up & short of room 2f out, sn wknd & eased.   5   48

6 Ran   Time 1m 48.63 (4.83)   Owned: Maxilead Limited   Trained: Thirsk

2515   9.15 Works Night Out Median Auction Maiden Stakes 3yo (E)
£3536 £1088 £544   **1m4f16y**   **Good 46**   **-57 Slow**   Inside

1241 **MOUNTAIN MEADOW 61** [7] Mrs A J Perrett 3-9-0   K Darley 1/2 FAV: 2-21: Led early, styd in tch,   85
prog to lead ins fnl 1f, rdn out: 9 wk abs: eff at 10f, apprec step up to 12f: acts on gd grnd: see 1241.

1604 **RECOGNISE 41** [8] M Johnston 3-9-0   K Dalgleish 9/2: 242: Led bef 11f out, edged left & hdd ins   1½   80
fnl 1f, no extra: clr rem: 6 wk abs: back to form on this gd grnd: see 1507.

1936 **HONEYMOONING 26** [2] H R A Cecil 3-8-9   W Ryan 4/1: 043: Cl-up, ev ch bef 2f out, sn no extra.   6   66

       CHESTALL 0 [6] R Hollinshead 3-9-0 R Kennemore(7) 50/1: 4: b c Polar Prince - Maradata   3   66
(Shardari) Chsd ldrs 9f, sn no extra: debut: dam wnr at mid-dists.

1894 **COLUMBIAN EMERALD 27** [1]3-9-0   R Havlin 40/1: 045: In tch over 1m, sn wknd: see 1894.   4   60

2123 **UPTHEDALE 16** [4]3-9-0 (35) P Hanagan 66/1: 043U506: Al in rear.   6   51$

1922 **TWILIGHT YEARS 26** [3]3-9-0   F Lynch 40/1: 07: Rear, nvr a factor.   2½   47

43   **WEET AN STORE 213** [5]3-9-0 t A Culhane 50/1: 00-8: gr c Spectrum - Karmisymixa (Linamix) Sn in   25   9
rear, t.o. ins fnl 2f: reapp: modest form to date: with R Hollinshead.

8 Ran   Time 2m 43.76(12.46)   Owned: Mr K Abdulla   Trained: Pulborough

---

ASCOT   THURSDAY 17.06.04   Righthand, Stiff, Galloping Track

Official Going Good/Firm (Firm places)

2516   2.30 Gr3 Norfolk Stakes 2yo (A)
£34800 £13200 £6600   **5f str**   **Good/Firm 37**   **-32 Slow**   Stands Side

1808* **BLUE DAKOTA 31** [5] J Noseda 2-8-12   E Ahern 5/4 FAV: 1111: Cl-up trav well & led over 1f out,   109
drvn to hold on: hvly bckd & remains unbeaten: well suited by 5f on fast & soft grnd, stiff or sharp trk: best up
with/forcing the pace: v speedy & useful sprinting juv, win more Gr races: see 1808, 1646 & 1190.

1517* **MYSTICAL LAND 45** [4] J H M Gosden 2-8-12   K Fallon 9/1: 212: Bmpd start & rdn chasing ldrs, drvn   nk   107
& styd on well ins last, just held: 6 wk abs: eff at 5f, 6f will suit: acts on fast & soft grnd, stiff/gall trks:
v useful & progressing, spot on in similar company at 6f: see 1517 & 1107.

2089* **SKYWARDS 18** [1] Saeed bin Suroor 2-8-12   L Dettori 4/1: 513: Broke fast from stalls & led till   1   104
over 1f out, kept on for press ins last: bckd: rest well covered: v speedy, win more races: see 2089.

       COUGAR CAT 28 [10] A P O'Brien 2-8-12   J P Spencer 11/2: 14: b c Storm Cat - Excellent Meeting   3   95
(General Meeting) Pushed along rear, hdwy to chase ldrs when hung right bef dist, no extra: Irish raider, mdn
scorer at Tipperary last month: March foal, dam a top-class 7f/1m performer: eff at 5f on fast.

2415* **EMPIRES GHODHA 5** [2]2-8-12 bl P J Smullen 66/1: 532315: Went right start, sn chsd ldrs, no extra   2   89
over 1f out: qck reapp: consistent, needs an ease in grade.

1567* **DANCE NIGHT 43** [9]2-8-12   G Gibbons 20/1: 2116: Mid-div & sn rdn, no impress over 1f out: 6 wk abs.   6   71

2051* **WINDY PROSPECT 20** [7]2-8-12   D Holland 66/1: 35217: Sn outpcd & bhd, nvr a factor: reportedly   shd   70
unsuited by this firm ground after 2051 (AW).

2194   **HOLBECK GHYLL 14** [12]2-8-12   K Darley 33/1: 38: Dwelt, mid-div, sn struggling: needs mdn company.   1½   66

2364* **SPREE 6** [8]2-8-9   R Hughes 7/1: 619: Went right start, sn chsd ldrs & no ch from halfway: 6   45
reportedly not suited by today's firm grnd: impressive 2364 (made all, gd).

9 Ran   Time 1m 01.97 (2.97)   Owned: Mr A F Nolan Mrs J M Ryan Mrs P Duffin   Trained: Newmarket

2517   3.05 Gr2 Ribblesdale Stakes Fillies 3yo (A)
£75400 £28600 £14300   **1m4f**   **Good/Firm 37**   **+08 Fast**   Inside

2210   **PUNCTILIOUS 13** [1] Saeed bin Suroor 3-8-11 t (110) L Dettori 9/2: 113-131: Sn cl-up & rdn to   113
chall fnl 2f, led ins last & gamely asserted for press fnl 100y: hvly bckd tho' op 7/2: reportedly struggled with
the undulations of Epsom latest: eff at 10/12f & could get further: acts on firm & soft grnd, enjoys a gall trk:
admirable battling qualities today & more Gr success awaits.

1733   **SAHOOL 34** [3] M P Tregoning 3-8-11 (103) R Hills 7/1: 61-222: Led, rdn & strongly pressed fnl   1½   109
2f, hdd dist, kept on, not pace wnr: nicely bckd: styd longer 12f trip well with forcing tactics: lightly rcd,
progressive & clearly smart, can find a List/Gr 3: see 1733 & 1494.

1718* **QUIFF 35** [5] Sir Michael Stoute 3-8-11 (84) K Fallon 7/2 FAV: 5-13: Rear, short of room over 2f   1½   106
out, switched wide & styd on for press ins last, nrst fin & nvr a threat: hvly bckd, op 9/2: stiff rise in grade
but a fine run: styd longer 12f trip & shaped as if further may suit: v useful, progressive & lightly rcd, win a Gr
race sn: see 1718.

1961* **NEW MORNING 24** [2] M A Jarvis 3-8-11   P Robinson 6/1: 4-214: Keen & sn handy, ch over 2f out, no   nk   106
extra ins last: hvly bckd: up in grade & improved: acts on fast & gd/soft: apprec Listed: see 1961.

1568* **HIDDEN HOPE** 43 [9]3-8-11 (106) T E Durcan 11/2: 00-215: Keen & trkd ldrs, onepace for press fnl   *1* **104**
2f: abs: stays 12f: acts on fast & gd/soft: not disgraced: see 1568.
2124* **FEAAT** 16 [8]3-8-11 W Supple 33/1: 316: Mid-div, no impress fnl 2f: see 2124 (10f mdn).   *6* **95**
1733 **CRYSTAL CURLING** 34 [6]3-8-11 (99) M Hills 20/1: 21-337: Keen rear, drvn & no prog fnl 2f: btr 1568.   nk **94**
2238 **MODESTA** 12 [7]3-8-11 (78) R Hughes 10/1: 4128: Rear, no ch fnl 3f: beat today's 4th in a mdn   *5* **87**
prev this term: much btr 2238 & 1725.
1733* **RAVE REVIEWS** 34 [4]3-8-11 (105) K Darley 6/1: 61-319: Trkd ldrs, wknd qckly from 3f out: 1½ **84**
trainer reported filly unsuited by the fast grnd: see 1733 (10f).
9 Ran Time 2m 30.12 (1.12) Owned: Godolphin Trained: Newmarket

---

2518

3.45 Gr1 Gold Cup 4yo+ (A)
£139896 £53064 £26532   **2m4f**   **Good/Firm 37**   **+03 Fast** Inside

2095+ **PAPINEAU** 17 [4] Saeed bin Suroor 4-9-0 t (111) L Dettori 5/1: 2115-111: Dwelt & held up, hdwy   **123+**
from 4f out & led dist, rdn & styd on strongly: relished this step up to 2m4f, eff at 12f: acts on fast & soft:
high-class, genuine & still unexposed at staying trips, plenty more Gr races to be won: see 2095.
2000 **WESTERNER** 25 [9] E Lellouche 5-9-2 G Mosse 13/2: 2211-122: Mid-div, smooth prog from 4f out &   1½ **121**
led 2f out till dist, not pace of wnr: well bckd: acts on fast grnd, thought to ideally prefer much softer conds:
high class, thorough stayer: see 2000 & 1431.
1993* **DARASIM** 26 [1] M Johnston 6-9-2 vis (114) J Fanning 28/1: 1130-613: Chsd ldrs & ch 2f out, kept   2½ **118**
on for press fnl 3f, not pace of front pair: clr of rem: moody customer but clearly in great heart at present:
stays a stiff 2m4f well: prev thought best when dominating, sure to win again in group company on this form.
2095 **ROYAL REBEL** 17 [2] M Johnston 8-9-2 (112) J Murtagh 10/1: 3/001/-504: Sn rdn in tch, styd on for   *5* **113**
press fnl 3f, not able to chall: dual wnr of this race prev, a v hard ride who reserves best for this race: see 1418.
2209 **BRIAN BORU** 13 [11]4-9-0 t J P Spencer 40/1: 213-1555: Held up, drvn & hdwy over 3f out, sn no   nk **113**
impress: big step up in trip & a return to around 14f shld suit: high-class at best, will enjoy easier grnd: see 994.
2095 **MR DINOS** 17 [3]5-9-2 (120) K Fallon 5/4 FAV: 1/116-426: Trkd ldrs & went cl-up from 7f out, led   1¼ **112**
3f out till 2f out, wknd qckly: last yr's clearcut wnr & v hvly bckd: connections puzzled by display: see 2095.
1705 **HIGHEST** 35 [14]5-9-2 T (115) T E Durcan 25/1: 10325-07: Mid-div, rdn & no impress over 2f out,   nk **112**
fin lame: tried a t-strap over this longer trip: see 1705.
2095 **MISTERNANDO** 17 [6]4-9-0 (105) S Hitchcott 25/1: 611-0268: Rear & sn rdn, late prog for press.   1¼ **111**
INGRANDIRE 46 [8]5-9-2 N Yokoyama 16/1: 1645-219: b c White Muzzle - Marilyn Momoko (Real   24 **87**
Shadai) Led till 3f out, wknd qckly fnl 2f: Japanese raider: multiple wnr prev, a Gr 1 wnr in native Japan this
yr: winning form at up to 2m on firm & muddy grnd.
2095 **NEW SOUTH WALES** 17 [13]4-9-0 t (105) K McEvoy 20/1: 1/6401-30: 10th: Chsd ldrs, struggling fnl 4f.   14 **73**
2471 **CHIMES AT MIDNIGHT** 2 [7]7-9-2 bl J A Heffernan 200/1: 05060/-00: 11th: Rear & no ch 5f out.   10 **63**
1993 **DUSKY WARBLER** 26 [10]5-9-2 (107) D Holland 66/1: 325-2200: 12th: Chsd ldrs, struggling from 4f   1¾ **61**
out: joc reported gelding unsuited by the v fast grnd: much btr 1005 (List).
1705 **ALCAZAR** 35 [12]9-9-2 (115) M Fenton 33/1: 1024-120: 13th: Rear, no ch fnl 4f, broke blood vessel.   *9* **52**
13 Ran Time 4m 20.9 (2.9) Owned: Godolphin Trained: Newmarket

---

2519

4.20 King George V Stakes Heritage Handicap 3yo 0-105 (B)   **[107]**
£29000 £11000 £5500   **1m4f**   **Good/Firm 37**   **-02 Slow** Inside

2238 **ADMIRAL** 12 [14] Sir Michael Stoute 3-8-3 (82) N Mackay(3) 9/1: 64-0131: Keen & led after 2f till   **90**
6f out, remained handy & led again over 1f out, drvn & held on all out: jock rec a 3 day careless riding ban: nicely
bckd: suited by 12f on fast & gd grnd, sharp/undul or stiff/gall trk: lightly rcd, progressive & genuine: see 2238.
1756 **MARAAHEL** 33 [4] Sir Michael Stoute 3-9-7 (100) R Hills 6/1 FAV: 414-22: Mid-div wide, hdwy over   nk **107+**
2f out & drvn/styd on strongly ins last, just denied: hvly bckd, top-weight: clearly stays stiff 12f & will get
further on this evidence: fine eff despite awkward wide passage under a big weight: open to further improvement, win
in Listed/Gr 3 sn: see 1756.
2406* **ETMAAM** 5 [13] M Johnston 3-8-12 (7ex) (91) D Holland 8/1: 4-151213: Hld up, hdwy & short of room   shd **98+**
sen times from 3f out, styd on strongly ins last, just failed, unlucky: qck reapp: well bckd: styd longer 12f trip
well, further will suit: most progressive & useful, wold have won this with any sort of run, must be kept on side.
2418* **LE TISS** 4 [6] M R Channon 3-8-7 (7ex) (86) S Hitchcott(2) 40/1: 62-40214: Rear, taken wide & styd   nk **92**
on well for press fnl 2f, nrst fin: excellent run & shld be wng again sn with a return to 14f as in 2418.
2130* **GOLDEN QUEST** 16 [8]3-8-3 (82) J Fanning 25/1: 0-11015: Mid-div, rdn to press wnr dist, no extra   *1* **86**
well ins last: progressive profile: see 2130.
1756 **SWAGGER STICK** 54 [16]3-8-11 (90) K Darley 13/2: 0014-116: Handy & ev ch 2f out, onepace: bckd: ½ **93**
8 wk abs: see 1355.
2127 **ANOUSA** 16 [3]3-8-2 (81) C Catlin 100/1: 01-01007: Wide & rear, styd on well fnl 2f, nrst fin &   ¾ **82**
nvr a dngr: imprvd on this return to a faster surface: visor omitted: stays stiff 12f: v encouraging giving up
plenty of grnd by racing so wide: see 1515 (9f).
2021 **DESTINATION DUBAI** 22 [15]3-8-13 vis (92) L Dettori 11/1: 22-138: Led/dsptd lead till over 1f out,   1¼ **92**
no extra: op 14/1: prob styd 12f, return to 10f in similar could suit: seems 14f (10.5f mdn).
2127* **ODIHAM** 16 [10]3-8-6 (85) R L Moore 10/1: 002-19: Mid-div, lost place 4f out & drpd rear, kept on   nk **84**
late, no threat: nicely bckd: longer 12f trip may yet suit: see 2127.
1708 **ASIATIC** 35 [17]3-8-7 (86) S Chin 14/1: 241-200: 10th: Mid-div, eff 3f out, no impress dist: see 1582.   1¾ **82**
2127 **SETTLEMENT CRAIC** 16 [11]3-8-7 (86) M J Kinane 14/1: 2-1430: 11th: Sn handy, wknd over 1f out.   nk **81**
1384 **GIRONDE** 52 [7]3-8-8 (87) K Fallon 14/1: 5-430: 12th: Slow away & bhd, only mod prog: 8 wk abs: 2½ **78**
h'cap bow: longer trip: see 1384 & 1148 (mdns).
1664 **WOODCRACKER** 37 [19]3-8-11 (90) T Quinn 11/1: 0-120: 13th: Mid-div, btn 2f out: bckd: btr 1664, 1241.   3 **77**
1924* **MUDAWIN** 26 [5]3-9-5 (98) W Supple 12/1: 5-01010: 14th: Rear, eff wide 4f out, btn 2f out: btr 1924.   2 **82**
2250 **OVER THE RAINBOW** 12 [20]3-8-6 (85) M Hills 25/1: 230-100: 15th: Bhd 4f out, no prog: btr 886.   3 **65**
2127 **KEELUNG** 16 [18]3-8-9 (88) P Robinson 20/1: 4221320: 16th: Slow away & rear, sn hanging badly   7 **58**
left & pulled hard to lead from halfway, hdd over 3f out & wknd qckly: lkd virtually unsteerable: see 2127, 1500.
1924 **GOLDEN GRACE** 26 [9]3-8-9 (88) P J Smullen 25/1: 631-0440: 17th: Held up, hdwy to chase ldrs 3f   nk **57**
out, wknd qckly: see 1924 & 1664 (10f).
17 Ran Time 2m 31.3 (2.3) Owned: Highclere Thoroughbred Racing XI Trained: Newmarket

2520 **4.55 Listed Hampton Court Stakes 3yo (A)**
£23200 £8800 £4400 **1m2f** **Good/Firm 37** **-22 Slow** Inside

2307 **MOSCOW BALLET 11** [11] A P O'Brien 3-8-11 J P Spencer 8/1: 125-661: Made all & dictated pace, drvn & al holding rivals from over 1f out, well judged ride: hvly bckd, op 10/1: eff at 1m, relished step up to 10f with forcing tactics, shld get 12f: acts on firm & gd grnd: smart colt: see 1685 (Gr 2). **113**
1814 **CROCODILE DUNDEE 30** [9] Jamie Poulton 3-8-11 (105) J F Egan 20/1: 05-06322: Handy & chsd wnr over 2f out, styd on strongly for press, al just held: clearly v useful around 10/11f on firm, fast & polytrack. *1½* **110**
1813 **MUTAFANEN 30** [13] E A L Dunlop 3-8-11 (99) R Hills 9/1: 331-1333: Rear, hdwy inner 3f out & chsd front pair over 1f out, kept on, al held: another gd run, had the ideal passage from the back: see 1813 & 923. *1½* **108**
4520*)**SIMPLE EXCHANGE 264** [7] D K Weld 3-9-2 P J Smullen 6/1: 1251-4: b c Danehill - Summer Trysting (Alleged) Mid-div, switched wide & kept on fnl 2f, not pace to chall wnr: hvly bckd Irish raider: reapp: mdn & List scorer in '03 (lightly rcd): eff at 6/7f, styd this stiff 10f well & could get further: acts on firm & gd grnd, stiff/gall trks: goes well fresh: fine return, smart run under a pen. *½* **112**
1 Sep'03 Cork 7fm 111- A: 2 Aug'03 Curr 6g/f 113- A:
2250* **LORD MAYOR 12** [8]3-8-11 (96) K Fallon 7/2 FAV: 631-315: Mid-div, staying on but hard rdn when short of room over 1f out, kept on well ins last, not able to chall: bckd: unexposed & worth a try over further: progressive, win again with a faster pace: see 2250 (h'cap). *nk* **106+**
2254 **GATWICK 12** [12]3-8-11 (104) T Quinn 5/1: 3-131106: Hld up, rdn 4f out, short of room when switched wide 2f out, nrst fin: hvly bckd: not disgraced, wld prefer a faster pace: see 2254, 1919. *1¾* **103**
2069 **LEICESTER SQUARE 19** [10]3-8-11 t (107) L Dettori 6/1: 1204-27: Chsd ldrs & smooth prog over 2f out, high hd carriage & no extra over 1f out: appeared not to see out this longer 10f trip tho' resolution must be questioned again after 2069 (1m, List). *1¾* **100**
1814 **HAPPY CRUSADER 30** [5]3-8-11 (104) D Holland 33/1: 1136-248: Chsd wnr 4f out, wknd fnl 2f: btr 1520. *1½* **97**
2142 **PRIVY SEAL 18** [2]3-9-2 VIS (109) J Murtagh 10/1: 55-12239: Pulled hard rear, short of room early, rdn & no prog fnl 3f: btr 2142 (Italian Derby). *nk* **101**
1707 **BARATHEA DREAMS 35** [1]3-8-11 (82) J Quinn 40/1: 114130: 10th: Keen, in tch, hdwy to go handy halfway, short of room 4f out & sn struggling: bckd at long odds but much btr 1707 & 1315 (1m). *1½* **93$**
2274* **WHITSBURY CROSS 10** [6]3-8-11 (77) Dane O'Neill 66/1: 0-5510: 11th: Dwelt, rear, no ch fnl 4f. *3½* **88**
1814 **MUTAHAYYA 30** [4]3-8-11 (105) W Supple 25/1: 4212-250: 12th: Chsd ldrs, wide, btn 2f out: btr 1113. *2* **85**
2193* **BUCKEYE WONDER 14** [3]3-8-11 (92) P Robinson 25/1: 24-210: 13th: Sn cl-up, stumbled badly on bend 3f out & qckly lost place: still held ev ch, this best forgiven: see 2193 (mdn). *10* **69**
13 Ran Time 2m 07.98 (3.98) Owned: Mr M Tabor & Mrs John Magnier Trained: Ireland

2521 **5.30 Britannia Stakes Heritage Handicap Colts & Geldings 3yo 0-105 (B)** **[111]**
£29000 £11000 £5500 **1m str** **Good/Firm 37** **-10 Slow** Stands Side. 2 Groups.

2212 **MANDOBI 13** [3] A C Stewart 3-8-12 (95) K Fallon 8/1: 2120-421: Held up stands side, hdwy over 2f out & led over 1f out, drvn & asserted ins last: eff at 7f, relished step up to 1m, stay further: acts on fast & gd grnd, stiff/gall or sharp/undul trks: v progressive colt, keep on the right side in List. **105+**
1978* **LUCAYAN LEGEND 23** [6] R Hannon 3-8-6 (89) D Holland 20/1: 6312: Bhd stands side, switched wide & styd on well for press fnl 1f, not pace of wnr: lightly rcd & fast improving: see 1978. *1* **97**
1664 **THYOLO 37** [13] C G Cox 3-8-12 (95) J P Spencer 9/1: 411-203: Dwelt & rear stands side, styd on well for press fnl 2f, nrst fin: nicely bckd, back to form on fav'd fast grnd: try 10f again. *½* **101**
2026* **FINE SILVER 21** [2] P F I Cole 3-8-5 (88) T Quinn 16/1: 146-4014: Rear stands side, short of room over 2f out, kept on well ins last, nrst fin: clearly progressing on a fast surface: useful, win again. *½* **94**
2212 **FREE TRIP 13** [17]3-8-2 (85) W Supple 25/1: 0-160255: Mid-div stands side, short of room over 2f out, sn hdwy to chall, no extra ins last: stays a stiff 1m, could prove spot on back at 7f: see 1983 & 955. *hd* **90**
1316 **FORTHRIGHT 55** [21]3-8-7 (90) K McEvoy 50/1: 60-10456: Trkd ldrs far side trav well, chall to lead that group dist, carried left, no impress on stands side ldrs fnl 100y: 8 wk abs: first home from far side group: eff at 7f/1m, stays sharp 10f well: useful gelding, keep on side for similar: see 325. *1½* **92+**
2247* **ALSHAWAMEQ 12** [28]3-8-3 (86) R Hills 14/1: 615-317: Trkd ldrs far side & rdn/led that group dist, sn hdd & not pace of ldrs far side: see 2247. *shd* **88**
1234 **JAZZ SCENE 61** [11]3-8-5 (88) C Catlin 33/1: 0102-08: b c Danehill Dancer - Dixie Jazz (Mtoto) Trkd ldrs stands side, no extra dist: 2 mth abs: val cond stks scorer in '03, subs h'cap rnr-up: best to date at 6f, prob stays a stiff 1m: handles firm & gd grnd, stiff/gall trks: drop to 7f might prove ideal. *2* **86**
2 Oct'03 York 6.0g/f 88-87 C: 1 Sep'03 Donc 6gd 87- B:
1847 **LORD LINKS 29** [5]3-8-2 (85) R L Moore 25/1: 13040-49: Rear stands side, short of room over 2f out, kept on late, nvr a threat: up in trip: see 1847 (7f). *nk* **82**
1763* **CREDIT 33** [24]3-8-5 (88) M J Kinane 25/1: 3310: 10th: Led/dsptd lead far side till dist, no extra. *nk* **84**
1919 **ZONUS 26** [14]3-8-7 (90) K Darley 11/2 FAV: 2-14230: 11th: Prom stands side, wknd over 1f out: bckd. *¾* **84**
1665* **STATE DILEMMA 37** [8]3-8-11 (94) M Hills 16/1: 3314-510: 12th: Mid-div stands side, no room over 2f out & again over 1f out, sn no impress: see 1665 (7f, soft). *2½* **83**
1154 **BENTLEYS BALL 65** [7]3-8-9 (92) R Hughes 20/1: 11432-60: 13th: b g Stravinsky - Slide By (Aragon) Chsd ldrs stands side, short of room 2f out, wknd: 2 mth abs: mdn & nursery h'cap scorer '03: winning form at 5/6f, stays stiff 7f well: acts on firm & gd grnd, likes a stiff/gall trk, handles a sharp one. *1½* **78**
2 Oct'03 Newm 6g/f 91-88 C: 1 Aug'03 Newm 6gd 87-82 B: 1 Jun'03 Sand 5.0g/f 85- D:
2401* **FITTING GUEST 5** [10]3-7-12 (5ex)(7oh) (74) A McCarthy 33/1: 40-62210: 14th: Led stands side till over 1f out, wknd: qck reapp: see 2401 (10f). *¾* **65**
2378* **GOLD MASK 6** [25]3-8-0 (5ex)BL (83) F Norton 14/1: 0-6210: 15th: Led far side till over 1f out, fdd: qck reapp in blnks: see 2378. *¾* **65**
KING JOCK 22 [22]3-8-9 (92) P J Smullen 7/1: 22-10: 16th: b c Ghazi - Glen Kate (Glenstal) Held up far side, eff 2f out, sn no extra: op 9/1: recent mdn scorer: eff at 7f/1m on fm & gd/soft. *hd* **73**
1860 **MOKABRA 32** [4]3-9-7 VIS (104) S Hitchcott(3) 50/1: 165-6300: 17th: Mid-div stands side, no room over 2f out, sn fdd under press: visor. *1* **83**
2212 **PARKVIEW LOVE 13** [1]3-9-0 (97) J Murtagh 33/1: 5-030000: 18th: Chsd ldrs stands side 5f. *¾* **74**
2250 **MASTER MARVEL 12** [23]3-8-6 (89) P Robinson 10/1: 21100: 19th: Held up far side, nvr a factor. *2½* **61**
1707* **ODDSMAKER 35** [26]3-8-2 (2ow) (83) Dean McKeown 20/1: 15-32510: 20th: Cl-up/dsptd lead far side 5f. *1* **55**
2212* **MAKFOOL 13** [9]3-9-1 (98) T E Durcan 16/1: 0340210: 21th: Cl-up stands side till 2f out: btr 2212 (7f). *1½* **65**
2166+**BURLEY FLAME 15** [19]3-7-12 (4oh) (77) N Mackay(3) 33/1: 0-43310: 22th: In tch far side 5f: see 2166. *1¾* **44**
1813 **NEVER WILL 30** [12]3-8-5 (88) S Chin 50/1: 5-22100: 23th: Cl-up/dsptd lead stands side 5f, wknd qckly. *nk* **50**
2352 **Pizazz 7** [18]3-7-13 (82) J F McDonald(3) 25/1:0

2212 **Ceilo 13** [15]3-7-12 (10h)(80) D Kinsella 40/1:0

2106 **Principal Witness 17** [20]3-7-13 (82) J Quinn 33/1:0   2069 **Resplendent One 19** [29]3-9-1 (98) R Miles(3) 33/1:0
27 Ran   Time 1m 40.85(2.15)   Owned: Sheikh Ahmed Al Maktoum   Trained: Newmarket

Official Going Good/Firm

2522   2.10 E B F Ladies' Day Maiden Stakes 2yo (D)
£5538 £1704 £852   **6f str**   Good/Firm 26   **-40 Slow**   Stands side

2188 **SPIRIT OF FRANCE 14** [5] M Johnston 2-9-0 K Dalgleish 4/5 FAV: 221: Made all, edged right ins   97+
fnl 1f, pushed out, val 3L+: well bckd, padd pick: eff at 5f, imprvd for step up to 6f: acts on fast & soft grnd,
sharp or gall trk: useful, win more races: see 2188 & 1274.
2077 **TOM FOREST 19** [2] A Crook 2-9-0 L Enstone(3) 9/1: 62: Cl-up, sn outpcd, prog ins fnl 2f, kept on   2   88
but not pace of wnr: op 13/2: eff at 6f on fast grnd: encouraging eff & can find similar: see 2077.
2228 **WASALAT 13** [7] M R Channon 2-8-9 A Culhane 5/2: 423: Prom, ev ch bef 1f out, sn no extra: well   ¾   81
bckd: clr rem: proving consistent: see 2228.
      JAZRAWY 0 [1] L M Cumani 2-9-0 S Sanders 20/1: 4: b c Dansili - Dalila di Mare (Bob Back) Sn   5   71
bhd, prog halfway, kept on fnl 1f: neat fir debut: Feb foal, cost 85,000gns: half-brother 2yo wnr abroad: dam
multiple wnr in Italy: sire decent performer at 1m: further will suit.
2178 **STRATHTAY 14** [9]2-8-9 G Faulkner 14/1: 305: Prom 4f, sn wknd: btr 1974 (5f).   shd 65
1687 **LOYALTY LODGE 36** [8]2-9-0 P Hanagan 100/1: 06: ch c Grand Lodge - Gaily Grecian (Ela Mana Mou)   1¾ 65
Handy 4f, sn wknd: April foal, cost 42,000gns: half-brother to wnrs at 6/11f: dam unrcd.
      TCHERINA 0 [4]2-8-9 F Lynch 100/1: 7: b f Danehill Dancer - Forget Paris (Broken Hearted) Al   ½   59
in rear: ndd race on debut: Jan foal, cost 54,000gns: half-sister plcd at 5/6f: dam unplcd.
2228 **WEDLOCK 13** [6]2-9-0 J Fortune 20/1: 48: Al in rear: btr 2228.   nk   63
      MERCARI 0 [3]2-8-9 T Eaves(3) 100/1: 9: Mid-div 4f, sn fdd: lkd burly on debut.   ½   57
9 Ran   Time 1m 14.01 (4.01)   Owned: Mr A D Spence   Trained: Middleham

2523   2.45 Adler & Allan Median Auction Maiden Stakes 3yo (E)
£3721 £1145 £573   **1m2f**   Good/Firm 26   **-02 Slow**   Inside

919   **GALVANISE 84** [7] B W Hills 3-9-0 A Culhane 11/8 FAV: 0-61: b c Run Softly - Shining Bright   89+
(Rainbow Quest) In tch, styd on to lead after 6f, pushed out: val 6L+: unplcd sole '03 start (rtd 86, mdn): imprvd
for step up to 10f, further shld suit: acts on a fast grnd & a sharp trk: goes well fresh: only lightly rcd.
1978 **MURBAAT 23** [3] A C Stewart 3-9-0 S Sanders 6/4: 32: In tch, prog & ev ch bef 2f out, kept on   4   82
fnl 1f, no ch with wnr: clr rem: eff at 1m/10f, further will suit: see 1978 (debut).
1784 **JALOUSIE DREAM 32** [1] G M Moore 3-8-9 T Eaves(3) 66/1: 053: b f Easycall - Forest Maid   25   42
(Thatching) Chsd ldrs 7f, sn fdd: modest form to date.
1763 **GOVERNMENT 33** [6] J H M Gosden 3-9-0 BL J Fortune 16/1: 04: Led 6f, sn wknd: first time blnks.   hd   46
1871 **ATLANTIC CITY 28** [2]3-9-0 P (71) S W Kelly 13/2: 622-25: Prom 7f, fdd: 1st time pieces.   1¾   43
1871 **ASTON LAD 28** [8]3-9-0 K Dalgleish 66/1: 46: Al in rear: btr 1871.   2   40
1390 **JORDANS SPARK 52** [5]3-9-0 P Hanagan 20/1: 57: Bhd, nvr a factor.   6   31
      RAYBERS MAGIC 0 [4]3-8-9 A Nicholls 50/1: 8: Slow away, al in rear: debut.   dist 1
8 Ran   Time 2m 6.17 (2.87)   Owned: Mr K Abdulla   Trained: Lambourn

2524   3.20 Total Butler Handicap Stakes 3yo+ 0-80 (D)   [75]
£5473 £1684 £842   **5f str**   Good/Firm 26   **+03 Fast**   Stands side

1555 **TORRENT 44** [6] D W Chapman 9-7-12 (5oh)bl (45) Lisa Jones(3) 20/1: 0010001: Made all stands rail,   56
rdn out fnl 1f: 6 wk abs: rider received a 2 day lang ban: landed this race 12 months ago off a 2lb lower mark:
eff at 5/6f on firm, soft grnd & both AWs: v tough: see 889 & 527.
2320 **KINGS COLLEGE BOY 8** [5] R A Fahey 4-8-6 bl (58) P Hanagan 11/2: 260-0032: Mid-div, prog halfway,   ½   60
kept on fnl 1f, not btn far: op 8/1: continues in gd form & h'capped to find similar: see 2320.
2409 **PADDYWACK 5** [1] D W Chapman 7-8-12 bl (64) A Culhane 5/1: 0-040353: Rear, prog halfway, styd on   ¾   64
fnl 1f, nrst fin: stablemate of wnr: qck reapp: not disgraced & h'capped to win sn: see 2059 & 1627.
2262 **BOANERGES 11** [2] W Bradley 7-8-3 (55) F P Ferris(3) 9/2 FAV: 05-05624: Rear, prog bef 1f out,   hd   54
nrst fin: apprec return to 6f: btr 2262.
2279 **BLUE MAEVE 10** [7] J Hetherton 4-7-12 (23oh) (27) S Righton 100/1: 6-404004: Prom, no extra fnl   dht 49
1f: gd eff from way out of h'cap: eff at 5f on fast grnd: see 663.
2266 **MUSICAL FAIR 10** [9]4-9-12 (78) J Fortune 8/1: 0002156: Handy till dist, wknd: btr 1973.   ¾   75
2359 **STRENSALL 6** [3]7-9-11 (77) F Lynch 9/1: 420-0207: In tch over 3f, sn no extra: qck reapp.   1   71
2007* **MERLINS DANCER 22** [12]4-10-0 (80) A Nicholls 5/1: 400-0518: Rcd alone far rail, nvr nrr than   1¾   69
mid-div: top-weight: padd pick: prob unsuited by racing on own & is worth another chance: btr 2007.
2266 **SUNLEY SENSE 10** [10]8-9-13 (79) B O'Neill(7) 14/1: 11000/-39: Bhd, nvr a factor: btr 2266.   1¼   64
1782 **BOLLIN JANET 32** [8]4-9-6 (72) S Sanders 25/1: 1500-000: 10th: b f Sheikh Albadou - Bollin Emily   nk   56
(Lochnager) Handy 3f, sn wknd: h'cap wnr in '03: won fnl of 3 '02 starts (mdn): eff at 5/6f on gd & fast grnd.
1 Jul'03 Hayd 6g/f 79-74 C: 1 Sep'02 Beve 5gd 79- D:
2266 **Mr Spliffy 10** [4]5-8-3 (55) S Carson 25/1:0
1476 **Beyond The Clouds 47** [11]8-9-13 (79) T Eaves(3) 14/1:0
12 Ran   Time 58.96 (1.16)   Owned: Mr David W Chapman   Trained: York

---

2525

3.55 Debenhams Harrogate Handicap Stakes 3yo 0-90   (C)   [95]
£8607 £3265 £1632   **1m rnd   Good/Firm 26   -02 Slow   Inside**

2314 **DISTANT CONNECTION 8** [1] A P Jarvis 3-8-7 (74) S Sanders 5/4 FAV: 0006121: Cl-up, styd on to   **81**
lead bef 1f out, drvn out to hold on: well bckd: stays 1m, seems best around 7f: acts on fast grnd & a sharp or
gall trk: showed battling qualities: see 2314 & 2098.
2231* **INVASIAN 13** [2] H R A Cecil 3-9-5 (86) W Ryan 7/2: 0-12: Led, rcd wide turning for home, hdd bef   hd   **91**
1f out, rallied in fnl 1f, just held: well bckd, padd pick: acts on fast & gd/soft grnd, sharp or gall trk: fine
eff on h'cap bow & can find similar: see 2231 (mdn).
4229} **HAVE FAITH 278** [4] B W Hills 3-9-4 (85) J Fortune 12/1: 6210-3: b f Machiavellian - Fatefully   1½   **87**
(Private Account) In tch, prog & ev ch bef 1f out, kept on same pace ins fnl 1f: reapp: fills mdn wnr on 1 of only
4 '03 starts: eff t 7f/1m on fast grnd: acts on a gall or sharp/undul trk: encouraging eff on reapp & can rate
higher. 1 Aug'03 Folk 7g/f 85- D: 2 Jul'03 Kemp 7g/f 82- D:
2127 **MOMTIC 16** [3] W Jarvis 3-8-13 (80) F Lynch 3/1: 21-33044: Rear, prog halfway, outpcd bef 1f out,   hd   **82**
rallied cl-home: bckd from 9/2: apprec stiffer trk or return to 9f+: see 2127 & 813.
1907* **WEST HIGHLAND WAY 26** [6]3-8-13 (80) T Eaves(3) 12/1: 22502-15: Chsd ldrs, outpcd after 5f,   1½   **79**
rallied fnl 1f: appears to be tho' further will suit: see 1907.
1496 **TAFAAHUM 46** [5]3-9-7 (88) K Dalgleish 14/1: 610-06: b c Erhaab - Makadir (Woodman) Short of   29   **42**
room after start, al in rear: 7 wk abs: mdn wnr in '03: eff at 7f, bred to apprec 1m+: acts on fast grnd & a gall
trk: reportedly made a noise last time out: with M Johnston.
1 Sep'03 Ayr 7.2g/f 89- D:
6 Ran   Time 1m 39.75 (2.25)   Owned: Mrs Ann Jarvis   Trained: Twyford

---

2526

4.30 Beaumont Robinson Ladies' Derby Handicap Stakes Lady Amateur Riders 3yo+ 0-70   (E)   [56]
£3858 £1187 £594   **1m4f60y   Good/Firm 26   -23 Slow   Inside**

4920} **LATALOMNE 233** [4] N Wilson 10-11-0 (70) Mrs N Wilson(5) 25/1: 00500///0-1: ch g Zilzal -   **78+**
Sanctuary (Welsh Pageant) Held up, prog 4f out, led well ins fnl 1f, pushed out, val 4L+: earlier rnr-up at best
over jumps in 03/04 (chase, rtd 148c, former smart 2m chaser, stays 2m5f on fast & gd/soft, B Ellison): unplcd sole
'03 Flat start (rtd 67): eff at 1m, imprvd for step up to 12f: acts on fast & gd, goes well fresh: well h'capped.
2285 **SUALDA 9** [11] R A Fahey 5-10-3 (59) Miss V Tunnicliffe(5) 9/2 FAV: 50500-52: Mid-div, prog to   2   **63**
lead dist, hdd well ins fnl 1f, no extra: bckd: gd run in defeat, h'capped to win: see 2285.
2285 **SARN 9** [3] M Mullineaux 5-8-13 (41) Miss M Mullineaux(7) 33/1: 0400403: Held up, prog 4f out,   shd   **44**
onepcd fnl 1f: eff at 7f/1m, now stays around 12f: see 894.
1991* **LITTLE TASK 23** [7] J S Wainwright 6-8-10 (1oh) (37) Miss Kelly Harrison(3) 14/1: 00/0/5-314:   2½   **37**
Mid-div, prog & ev ch bef 1f out, sn no extra: recent hdles plcd (sell h'cap, rtd 86h): see 1991 (10f, appr banded).
1830 **LAZZAZ 30** [14]6-9-5 (47) Mrs Marie King(5) 11/2: 3330205: Chsd ldrs, ev ch 2f out, sn wknd: btr 711.   1   **44**
1979 **JIMMY BYRNE 23** [5]4-10-12 P (68) Miss L Ellison(3) 16/1: 0-041056: Rear, nvr nrr than mid-div.   3   **61**
2088 **ROYAL AXMINSTER 18** [10]9-8-13 (41) Miss A Wallace(5) 10/1: 605-0527: Led, hdd 4f out, wknd dist.   ½   **33**
2771} **GOLDEN CHANCE 343** [2]7-9-7 (49) Miss S Brotherton 10/1: 330242-8: b g Unfuwain - Golden Digger   1   **39**
(Mr Prospector) In tch, ev ch 2f out, sn wknd: ndd race on reapp: plcd 4 times in '03 (h'caps, rtd 50): modest
form in 2 02/03 hdles starts (rtd 73h, nov hdle): unplcd in '02 (rtd 48, h'caps): suited by 10/14f, poss stays 2m:
acts on firm, gd/soft, gall or sharpish trk. 2 Jul'03 Donc 16.5g/f 50-46 E: 2 May'03 Catt 13.8fm 47-45 E:
2 Sep'01 Thir 12g/f 67-67 C: 2 Jul'01 Beve 10g/f 67-68 E: 1 Jun'01 Ripo 12.2g/f 69-63 E:
2285 **DICK THE TAXI 9** [8]10-10-11 (37) Miss E J Jones '8/1: 2132-339: Cl-up, led 2f out, hdd & wknd bef 1f out.1½   **54**
2088 **GRAFT 18** [1]5-10-6 bl (62) Mrs C Thompson(5) 14/1: 00-06200: 10th: Prom, led 4f out, hdd 2f out, fdd.   5   **42**
107 **FINAL DIVIDEND 204** [9]8-9-4 (46) Miss Joanna Rees(3) 8/1: 550643-0: 11th: Rear, wknd fnl 2f.   5   **19**
2088 **MICHAELS DREAM 18** [12]5-9-2 bl (44) Mrs S Bosley 9/1: 0-633040: 12th: Al bhd: btr 2217.   12   **0**
2217 **MAGIC CHARM 13** [6]6-8-10 (3oh) (35) Miss J Waring(7) 40/1: 0004060: 13th: Al rear, saddle slipped.   3   **0**
3750*} **Mischief 302** [13]8-8-10 (1oh)(37) Miss Joey Ellis(5) 25/1:0
1972 **Outward 24** [15]4-10-2 (58) Miss R Bastiman(5) 66/1:0
15 Ran   Time 2m 39.55 (6.05)   Owned: Alderclad Roofing/Mr K M Everitt   Trained: York

---

2527

5.05 Richmond Median Auction Maiden Stakes 3-4yo   (E)
£3809 £1172 £586   **6f str   Good/Firm 26   -21 Slow   Stands side**

1944 **SMART MINISTER 24** [8] J J Quinn 4-9-7 (46) K Dalgleish 5/1: 420-0001: gr g Muhtarram - She's   **68**
Smart (Absalom) Handy, prog & ev ch bef 1f out, led ins fnl 1f, drvn out to hold on: plcd twice in '03 (h'caps, rtd
56): unplcd in '02 (rtd 70, auct mdn): stays at 8.5f, imprvd for drop back to 6f: acts on firm & gd/soft grnd.
2 Sep'03 Beve 8.5g/s 56-51 E:
1822 **FLASH RAM 30** [7] T D Easterby 3-9-0 VIS (66) S Sanders 2/1 FAV: 333-642: Prom, led after 4f, hdd   nk   **66**
ins fnl 1f, kept on despite being short of room, just denied: eff at 5/6f: apprec fitting of first time visor: see 1002.
2409 **AMANDAS LAD 5** [1] M C Chapman 4-9-7 (60) L Vickers 9/2: 5504203: Led 4f, no extra dist: qck reapp.   5   **51**
2279 **DARK CHAMPION 10** [6] R E Barr 4-9-7 (62) P Hanagan 11/2: 4653004: Handy 4f, sn no extra: btr 1639. nk   **50**
2181 **AMBER FOX 14** [2]3-8-9 P (52) F Lynch 7/1: 6004-565: Prom 3f, fdd: cheek pieces: btr 1908.   10   **20**
2117 **LORD OF THE FENS 17** [4]4-9-7 S W Kelly 66/1: 006: Al in rear.   1   **22**
1667} **I SEE NO SHIPS 391** [3]4-9-2 S Righton 66/1: 000-7: Mid-div, fdd fnl 3f: reapp: modest form to date.   6   **1**
2102 **COMPTON PRINCESS 17** [5]4-9-2 S Carson 20/1: 0-360000: Short of room startt, al rear.   11   **0**
8 Ran   Time 1m 12.87 (2.87)   Owned: Mr B Shaw   Trained: Malton

---

2528

5.40 Levy Board Handicap Stakes 3yo 0-80   (D)   [83]
£5473 £1684 £842   **1m4f60y   Good/Firm 26   -02 Slow   Inside**

1355 **YOSHKA 54** [3] M Johnston 3-9-7 (76) K Dalgleish 11/4 FAV: 1-31: Handy, prog to lead despite   **85**
hanging right dist, drvn out: well bckd after 8 wk abs: eff at 9f, imprvd for step up to 12f: acts on firm & fast
grnd: goes well fresh & acts on a sharp or gall grnd: lightly rcd, see 1355.
2345 **ILWADOD 7** [5] M R Channon 3-8-5 VIS (60) A Culhane 7/2: 06-12222: Rear, under press 5f out, styd   1½   **66**
on well ins fnl 2f, nrst fin: qck reapp & first time visor: see 2345, 2134.

RIPON THURSDAY 17.06.04 Righthand, Sharpish Track

2164 **VICARIO 15** [7] M L W Bell 3-8-5 (60) F P Ferris(5) 11/2: 00-5133: Handy, prog & ev ch bef 1f out, sn onepcd: op 7/1: see 2164, 2014. ½ **65**
2164 **HAVETOAVIT 15** [1] J D Bethell 3-8-10 (65) P Hanagan 12/1: 400-5324: Led, hdd bef 1f out, wknd. 3½ **63**
2345 **SIEGFRIEDS NIGHT 7** [6]3-8-10 (65) Lisa Jones(3) 13/2: 3621335: In tch, ev ch bef 2f out, wknd dist. 1½ **63**
2164* **ZALDA 15** [2]3-8-11 (66) S W Kelly 6/1: 006-16: Cl-up over 10f, wknd: op 9/2: btr 2164. 3 **60**
2162 **MA YAHAB 15** [4]3-9-3 (72) S Sanders 13/2: 020-337: Rear, fdd ins fnl 2f, sn eased: v disapp eff: surely something amiss: btr 2162 (10f). *dist* **41**
7 Ran Time 2m 36.98(3.48) Owned: Mr Saeed Buhaleeba Trained: Middleham

NEWMARKET FRIDAY 18.06.04 Righthand, Stiff, Galloping Track

Official Going GOOD/FIRM

2529

6.30 Siemens Smart Home Technology Apprentice Handicap Stakes 3yo+ 0-70 (E) **[70]**
£3452 £1062 £531 **1m** **Good/Firm 29** **-08 Slow** Far side

2334 **PRIME OFFER 8** [8] J Jay 8-9-5 (61) C Haddon(3) 13/8 FAV: 0-024121: Made all, drvn out ins fnl 1f: suited by 7f/1m on firm, fast & both AWs, sharp or stiff/gall trks: in fine form: see 2149. **67**
2149 **HALCYON MAGIC 16** [9] Miss J Feilden 6-8-6 bl (48) Laura Pike(5) 10/1: 060-2002: Chsd ldrs, kept on ins fnl 1f but not pace of wnr: eff at 6f/7f, stayed this 1m: well h'capped: see 1267. 1¾ **48**
2148 **ARRAN 16** [6] V Smith 4-8-12 (54) Rory Moore(3) 8/1: U000-03: ch g Selkirk - Humble Pie (Known Fact) Rear, hdwy over 2f out, kept on ins fnl 1f: unplcd in '03 (mdns, with H Collingridge): eff at 1m on fast. ½ **53**
2397 **SINGLE TRACK MIND 6** [7] J R Boyle 6-8-2 p (44) Dean Williams(5) 12/1: 2350064: Rear, hdwy over 1f out, not pcd to chall: qck reapp: see 1073. *nk* **42**
2392 **WELCOME SIGNAL 6** [1]4-9-11 (67) Saleem Golam(5) 5/1: 33035-05: ch g Most Welcome - Glenfinlass (Lomond) Bhd, hdwy over 1f out, onepace: qck reapp: clr of rem: 3rd 3 of 5 '03 starts (h'cap, mdns, rtd 71a): unplcd sole '02 start (mdn, rtd 55): eff btwn 7/10f on fast & polytrack: mdn. ½ **64**
4871} **BROOKLANDS LODGE 238** [3]3-9-4 (70) G Edwards(7) 25/1: 450-6: ch f Grand Lodge - Princess Dixieland (Dixieland Band) Nvr a factor on reapp: unplcd all '03 starts (mdns, rtd 72, with J Harris & I Wood). 4 **59**
2010 **QUEEN CHARLOTTE 23** [5]5-9-10 (66) W Hogg(5) 5/1: 6/10-2007: Handy, wknd over 1f out. ¾ **53**
2146 **DENS JOY 16** [4]8-8-5 (47) Stephanie Hollinshead(3) 14/1: 56-00008: Bhd, wknd 2f out. 4 **26**
2296 **DALRIATH 10** [10]5-7-12 (1oh) (39) Charlotte Kerton(7) 8/1: 6421259: Rcd in 2nd over 5f, wknd. *10* **0**
9 Ran Time 1m 40.02 (3.0) Owned: Miss K A Bartlett Trained: Newmarket

2530

7.00 Vibe Fm Handicap Stakes 3yo+ 0-75 (E) **[74]**
£3445 £1060 £530 **1m4f** **Good/Firm 29** **-09 Slow** Stands side

1913 **SWELLMOVA 27** [6] J R Boyle 5-8-13 (59) K Darley 5/1: 1204/-21: Rear, hdwy over 3f out, led ins fnl 1f, drvn out: eff at 1m on fast & gd/soft, improved at 12f: genuine: see 1913. **69**
2322* **PRENUP 9** [8] L M Cumani 3-8-7 (5ex) (67) D Holland 1/2 FAV: 500-4112: Chsd ldrs, led over 8f out, trav best over 2f out, hdd ins fnl 1f, no extra: clr of rem, not disgraced: see 2322 (8lb lower mark). *1* **74**
2192 **THE VARLET 15** [10] B I Case 4-9-10 (70) D Corby(3) 50/1: 62605-03: Bhd, hdwy over 1f out, kept on onepace: top-weight: gd run on drop back to 12f but still a mdn: see 2192. 3½ **72**
1083 **JACK OF TRUMPS 72** [2] G Wragg 4-9-4 (64) S Sanders 8/1: 6/35-1004: Mid-div & keen, hdwy & ev ch over 1f out, no impress ins fnl 1f: 10 wk abs: shade btr 338 (mdn, 10f). *hd* **65**
2273 **SUMMER CHERRY 11** [7]7-7-12 (3oh)t (41) A McCarthy 12/1: 0/503-025: Keen & handy, ev ch over 1f out, no impress ins fnl 1f: see 2273. *nk* **44**
2079 **SAIDA LENASERA 20** [3]3-8-9 (69) W Ryan 25/1: 3140-066: Rear, hdwy 2f out, wknd 1f out: see 1708. 3 **64**
1729 **KING OF KNIGHT 35** [1]3-8-7 (67) B Reilly(3) 50/1: 000-4507: gr g Orpen - Peace Melody (Classic Music) Rear, hdwy over 3f out, no impress fnl 1f: fin unplcd all '03 starts (mdns, rtd 69): with G Prodromou. 4 **56**
3999} **LAHOB 291** [4]4-9-4 (64) K Dalgleish 25/1: 362326-8: ch c First Trump - Mystical Song (Mystiko) Sn led, hdd over 8f out, no extra over 1f out on reapp: rnr-up 2 of 7 '03 starts (mdns): poss stays 10/12f: has tried cheek pieces: with P Howling. *10* **38**
2 Aug'03 Ripo 12.3g/f 61-(60) D: 2 Aug'03 Hayd 10.5g/f 61-(60) D:
2311 **DUCS DREAM 9** [5]6-8-12 (58) D McGaffin 12/1: 00-00109: Handy, wknd over 3f out. 3½ **27**
1504 **LUNAR LEADER 47** [9]4-8-9 (55) B Doyle 50/1: 00-00000: 10th: Chsd ldrs, wknd 3f out: hdles fit (unplcd). *28* **0**
10 Ran Time 2m 32.85 (4.65) Owned: Mr Robert Allen Trained: Epsom

2531

7.30 Ngk Spark Plugs Maiden Stakes 2yo (D)
£4755 £1463 £732 **6f** **Good/Firm 29** **-18 Slow** Far side

STAGBURY HILL 0 [4] J W Hills 2-9-0 M Hills 16/1: 1: ch c Woodman - Shalabia (Fast Topaze) Rear, hdwy over 1f out, rdn ins fnl 1f to join wnr post on debut: Mar foal, cost $45,000: dam 7f wnr: eff at 6f, 7f sure to suit: acts on fast & a stiff trk: runs well fresh: will rate higher, esp over further. **96+**
ST ANDREWS STORM 0 [3] R Hannon 2-9-0 R Hughes 2/1: 1: b c Storm Creek - L'amour Toujours (Blushing Groom) Bhd, hdwy 5f out, led over 1f out, rdn/kept on ins fnl 1f but joined post on debut: Feb foal, cost 160,000gns: half brother to a 1m wnr: dam 10f wnr: eff at 6f, will stay further: acts on fast: runs well fresh, can rate higher & win more races. *dht* **94**
NORTHERN SPLENDOUR 0 [6] Saeed bin Suroor 2-9-0 L Dettori 5/4 FAV: 3: ch c Giant's Causeway - Ribbonwood (Diesis) Handy, ev ch over 1f out, onepcd ins fnl 1f on debut: Apr foal: half-brother to 7f wnr: dam 6f 2yo scorer: stays 6f, sure to get further: acts on fast: fair start, looks sure to improve. 1¼ **91**
COUP DETAT 0 [1] J L Dunlop 2-9-0 K Darley 8/1: 4: Trkd ldrs, rdn/1L 4th when short of room ins fnl 1f: debut: closer with a clr run. 1¼ **87**
2109 **MONASH LAD 18** [5]2-9-0 P Robinson 25/1: 05: Keen & handy, outpcd over 1f out, kept on ins fnl 1f. 1¼ **83**
2089 **LOWESTOFT PLAYBOY 19** [9]2-9-0 J Murtagh 20/1: 06: Led over 4f, no extra ins fnl 1f. 1¼ **79**
WILFORD MAVERICK 0 [8]2-9-0 S Righton 66/1: 7: In tch, wknd over 1f out on debut. 3 **70**
BELLALOU 0 [7]2-8-9 T P Queally(3) 20/1: 8: Al bhd on debut. 2½ **57**
2089 **HEDINGHAM KNIGHT 19** [2]2-9-0 Dane O'Neill 7/1: 69: Rear, nvr a factor. 1¼ **58**
9 Ran Time 1m 13.87 (2.87) Owned: Mr A T Macdonald Trained: Marlborough

---

2532

8.05 Portland Place Properties Rated Stakes Handicap 3yo+ 0-95 (C) [99]
£8694 £3298 £1649   **7f**   **Good/Firm 29**   **+16 Fast**   Far side

2172* **ETTRICK WATER** 16 [8] L M Cumani 5-9-7 vis (92) D Holland 11/4 FAV: 2113-511: Rcd in 2nd, led 2f **99**
out to 1f out, sn rallied, drvn ahead nr fin: landed double, fast time: suited by 7f/1m on firm, soft & any trk:
likes to dominate: tough & progressive, this was a v game effort: see 2172.

1919 **COLOUR WHEEL** 27 [9] R Charlton 3-8-8 (1ow)t (87) R Hughes 7/1: 0122-602: Bhd, hdwy to lead 1f   shd **94**
out, edged left ins fnl 1f, hdd nr fin: fine run back at 7f, v disapp 1o/w: see 1315.

1891 **LEOBALLERO** 28 [7] D J Daly 4-8-7 (1oh)t (87) Dane O'Neill 25/1: 52231-53: Bhd, hdwy trav well   hd **83**
over 2f out, ev ch ins fnl 1f, just held for press: gd run, improving: see 1891.

2427 **MOLCON** 5 [4] N A Callaghan 3-8-3 (4oh) (83) P Robinson 6/1: 0-515344: Handy, outpcd & not much   2 **84**
room 2f out, kept on ins fnl 1f: qck reapp, gd run from 4lbs out of the h'cap: see 1417.

2172 **KOOL** 16 [11]5-9-5 (90) S Sanders 5/1: 0/-305535: Bhd, hdwy trav well over 1f out, no extra.   hd **90**

2090 **VINDICATION GB** 19 [10]4-9-6 t (91) J Murtagh 100/30: 5110-066: Mid-div, no impress fnl 1f: see 2090.   1¾ **87**

2289 **TAHIRAH** 10 [2]4-9-4 (89) C Lowther 25/1: 40110-07: Bhd, hdwy over 1f out, no impress ins fnl 1f.   3½ **78**

2944 **AJEEL** 463 [3]5-8-9 (80) R Hills 12/1: 20/0500-8: b g Green Desert - Samheh (Private Account)   1½ **66**
Handy, not much room & wknd 2f out: reapp: missed '03: won 2 of 6 '02 starts (h'caps): suited by 1m, shld stay
further: acts on fast & soft, stiff or fair trks: runs well fresh: has tried blnks: on a fair mark.
2 Jul'02 Newm 8g/f 88-85 B: 1 Jul'02 Yarm 8g/f 86-78 D: 1 May'02 Newc 8gd 79-72 D: 2 Mar'02 Donc 7sft 78- D:

2235 **WARDEN WARREN** 13 [1]6-8-7 (5oh)p (73) B Reilly(3) 25/1: 1004109: Chsd ldrs to 5f out, no impress   6 **52**
over 2f out: stiff task at weights: btr 2122 (class stks).

4350} **FUNFAIR WANE** 272 [6]5-9-10 (95) K Dalgleish 20/1: 000000-0: 10th: b g Unfuwain - Ivory Bride   3½ **62**
(Domynsky) Led, hdd 2f out, no extra 1f on reapp: top-weight: won 1 of 9 '03 starts (cond stks): won Ayr '02
start (val Ayr Gold Cup h'cap, earlier with M Channon): relishes 6f, just stays 1m: acts on firm & gd/soft, can run
well fresh: likes forcing tactics: useful at best.
1 May'03 Beve 5gd 104-(105) C: 1 Sep'02 Ayr 6gd 108-100 B: 2 Aug'02 Ches 7.5fm 101- B: 2 Aug'02 Nott 5g/f 101- C:
1 Aug'01 Newb 7g/f 99- A: 1 Jun'01 Wind 6gd 93- D: 2 Jun'01 Newm 6fm 93- D:

1926 **CRAFTY CALLING** 27 [5]4-9-5 BL (90) K Darley 20/1: 1054-000: 11th: b c Crafty Prospector -   3 **51**
Glorious Calling (Nijinsky) Bhd, nvr nr ldrs: won 1 of 6 '03 starts (h'cap): won fnl '02 start (mdn): eff btwn
6/7f, acts on gd & fast, sharp or stiff trks: has tried a t-strap, tried blnks here: shld do better.
1 Jul'03 Sand 7.1g/f 99-94 D: 1 Aug'02 Wind 6gd 93- D:
11 Ran   Time 1m 24.87 (0.97)   Owned: Mrs E H Vestey   Trained: Newmarket

---

2533

8.40 Sharp Minds Betfair E B F Classified Stakes 3yo 0-90 (C)
£9841 £3028 £1514   **1m**   **Good/Firm 29**   **-12 Slow**   Far side

1919 **APPALACHIAN TRAIL** 27 [3] I Semple 3-9-0 (89) R Hughes 8/11 FAV: 5-312041: Trkd ldrs, hdwy to   **95**
lead over 1f out, drvn clr: eff at 1m on firm & gd/soft, acts on a gall or sharp trk: useful.

2212 **BETTALATETHANNEVER** 14 [1] S Dow 3-9-0 (87) Dane O'Neill 6/1: 61-14002: Bhd, hdwy over 1f out,   2½ **88**
onepcd ins fnl 1f: stays 1m, acts on gd & polytrack: see 360.

1460 **BESSEMER** 49 [4] M Johnston 3-9-0 (90) K Dalgleish 6/1: 310-53: Led till over 6f out, led again   2 **84**
over 1f out, sn hdd, no extra: 7 wk abs: longer trip: see 1460.

1844 **AL SIFAAT** 30 [2] Saeed bin Suroor 3-8-11 t (90) L Dettori 3/1: 21-04: Trkd ldrs & keen, hdwy to   2 **77**
lead over 6f out till hmpd over 1f out, no extra: see 1844.
4 Ran   Time 1m 40.52 (3.32)   Owned: G L S Partnership   Trained: Carluke

---

2534

9.10 Stuart Grant Breakfast Show Maiden Stakes 3yo (D)
£5551 £1708 £854   **1m2f**   **Good/Firm 29**   **-24 Slow**   Stands side

2131 **ELMUSTANSER** 17 [8] Saeed bin Suroor 3-9-0 t L Dettori 4/11 FAV: 21: Made all, pushed out ins fnl   **87**
1f: eff at 10f, further will suit: acts on fast & gd/soft, stiff/gall trk: imprvd from debut & shld continue to
rate higher: yard in tremendous form: see 2131.

FORTUNES PRINCESS 0 [7] M J Wallace 3-8-9   K Darley 25/1: 2: b f Desert Prince - Golden Fortune   1¼ **78**
(Forzando) Slowly away, sn handy, hdwy into 2nd over 2f out, kept on ins fnl 1f on debut: clr of rem: stays 10f,
12f shld suit on this evidence: acts on fast: gd start, learn from this intro & can find similar.

TASHREEFAT 0 [4] A C Stewart 3-8-9   R Hills 11/2: 3: b f Danehill - Aigue (High Top) Bhd, hdwy   5 **70**
over 2f out, wknd fnl 1f on debut: dam 1m wnr.

2248 **ZURI** 13 [1] L M Cumani 3-8-9   D Holland 10/1: 64: b f Kris S - Amizette (Forty Niner) Handy,   7 **59**
wknd over 1f out, eased: bred for mid-dists.

CONVICTION 0 [6]3-9-0   J Murtagh 8/1: 5: Bhd, sn handy, wknd 3f out on debut.   2½ **60**

CHAPELCO 0 [2]3-9-0   S Sanders 14/1: 6: Bhd, nvr a factor on debut.   shd **59**

4407} **HOLD UP** 269 [3]3-8-9   B Reilly(3) 28/1: 0-7: Rcd in 2nd till over 3f out, wknd: now with Miss J Feilden.   1½ **52**
7 Ran   Time 2m 7.21(5.31)   Owned: Godolphin   Trained: Newmarket

---

GOODWOOD   FRIDAY 18.06.04   Righthand, Sharpish, Undulating Track

Official Going GOOD

2535

6.15 Racing Uk Apprentice Stakes Handicap 3yo+ 0-70 (E) [70]
£3513 £1081 £541   **6f str**   **Good 57**   **-02 Slow**   Stands side

2396 **AINTNECESSARILYSO** 6 [9] N E Berry 6-8-5 (47) M Halford(5) 7/1: 3222361: Held up towards centre,   **56**
hdwy from halfway & led dist, held on all out: qck reapp: eff at 5/6f on firm, hvy & both AWs, any trk: v
consistent this: deserved this: see 2016, 1867 & 411.

2023 **STOKESIES WISH** 23 [8] J L Spearing 4-9-5 (61) Hayley Turner 20/1: 102-0002: Mid-div, switched   shd **68**
left & strong run for press ins last, just failed: likes Goodwood: see 1127.

2258 **WILLHECONQUERTOO** 12 [2] Andrew Reid 4-9-8 t (64) Derek Nolan(5) 20/1: 6500-003: Dwelt, sn in tch   2   66
trav well, hdwy to chall over 1f out, not pace of front pair fnl 100yds: well h'capped: see 1613.
2044 **BEYOND CALCULATION** 21 [6] J M Bradley 10-9-0 p (56) N Chalmers 11/1: 00-00004: Mid-div, styd on   shd   57
late, not able to chall: slipping down the weights: see 1886.
1817 **POLAR IMPACT** 31 [12]5-10-0 (70) A Quinn 7/2: 1011-105: br c Polar Falcon - Boozy (Absalom)   nk   70
Handy & briefly led over 1f out, onepace ins last: h'cap wnr for A Berry in '03 & multiple wnr in Spain last term:
suited by 5/6f, won at 7f in Spain: acts on good well fresh. 1 Oct'03 Newc 5gd 74-63 E:
2 Jul'03 Hami 5.0gd 70-67 D: 1 Apr'02 Newc 5sft 74- D: 2 Oct'01 Ling 5sft 79- D: 2 Aug'01 Newc 5gd 79- D:
2412 **JUWWI** 8 [5]10-9-6 (62) Hazel Boyd(7) 14/1: 0440626: Slow away & rear, mod late gains: qck reapp.   2½   54
2150 **SOMERSET WEST** 16 [10]4-9-10 (66) M Savage 16/1: 6001107: Led till over 2f out, sn btn: btr 1625.   ¾   56
2214 **TOPPLING** 14 [11]6-8-13 (55) B Swarbrick 10/1: 000-0008: Handy & led over 2f out till over 1f out, wknd.   hd   44
2199 **THREEZEDZZ** 15 [4]6-9-4 (60) S Donohoe(3) 7/1: 0000/-009: Sn outpcd & nvr factor: see 2199.   8   25
2396 **SECOND MINISTER** 6 [1]5-8-8 lol (50) J Tucker(7) 33/1: 32-30600: 10th: Al bhd: qck reapp: see 130.   5   0
2372* **MILLFIELDS DREAMS** 7 [7]5-8-12 (7ex) (54) P Makin 15/8 FAV: 04604-10: 11th: Led/dsptd lead till   19   0
halfway, wknd qckly: well bckd: 'lost action': see 2372.
11 Ran   Time 1m 13.57 (3.57)   Owned: Mrs Jan Adams   Trained: Earlswood

---

2536   **6.45 Taurus Waste Recycling Maiden Stakes 3yo+ (D)**
  £5564 £1712 £856   **1m1f**   **Good 57**   **-20 Slow**   Inside

4898} **GOODWOOD FINESSE** 237 [4] J L Dunlop 3-8-7 G Carter 7/1: 55-1: b f Revoque - Key To Paris   76
(Profit Key) Mid-div, eff over 1f out, strong run ins last to lead nr line: unplcd in '03 (rtd 73, lightly rcd,
mdns): eff at 1m, apprec step up to 9f, further shld suit: handles fast & gd grnd, stiff or sharp/undul trks: goes
well fresh: lightly rcd & a likely improver in h'cap company over further.
1210 **WOMAN IN WHITE** 63 [6] J H M Gosden 3-8-7 J Fortune 13/8 FAV: 02: gr f Daylami - Nicer (Pennine   hd   75
Walk) Dwelt, rear, hdwy over 2f out & rdn/led well ins last, hdd nr line: 2 month abs: left debut bhd:
half-sister to a 1m 3yo wnr, dam a 1m 1,000 Guineas wnr: styd longer 9f trip well, further shld suit: handles
gd grnd & a sharp/undul trk: clrly going the right way.
2224 **GWEN JOHN** 14 [9] H Morrison 3-8-7 S Drowne 7/4: 5-53: ch f Peintre Celebre - River Jig (Irish   nk   74
River) Trkd ldrs & led over 1f out, drvn & hdd well ins last, no extra nr line: unplcd '03 (sole stqart, rtd 74,
mdn): half-sister to a high-class 5f juv, dam a 9f wnr: eff at 9f on gd grnd & a sharp/undul trk: clr of rem.
5022} **SPRING ADIEU** 224 [1] Mrs A J Perrett 3-8-7 W Supple 11/1: 00-4: Led till over 1f out, no extra: reapp.   5   64
2193 **LAUGH N CRY** 15 [3]3-8-7 S Whitworth 25/1: 05: Keen & prom, no extra when hmpd over 1f out.   shd   63
2352 **NAZZWAH** 8 [8]3-8-7 C Catlin 6/1: 66: Trkd ldr, wknd qckly fnl 2f.   11   41
2309 **ROYAL LOGIC** 9 [7]3-8-7 A Daly 20/1: 07: Al rear & no ch fnl 2f, longer trip.   ¾   39
2393 **BEE DEES LEGACY** 6 [2]3-8-12 S Carson 50/1: 0-008: Al towards rear & bhd fnl 2f, qck reapp.   4   36
8 Ran   Time 1m 57.51 (7.01)   Owned: Goodwood Racehorse Owners Group (Nine)   Trained: Arundel

---

2537   **7.15 Midsummer Maiden Auction Stakes Fillies 2yo (E)**
  £4745 £1460 £730   **6f str**   **Good 57**   **-30 Slow**   Stands side

2245 **BENTLEYS BUSH** 13 [4] R Hannon 2-8-10 J Fortune 1/2 FAV: 521: Dwelt, held up in tch, switched &   82
drvn to lead well ins last, all out: eff at 6f on fast & gd, any trk: open to improvement.
2310 **SHOSOLOSA** 9 [3] B J Meehan 2-8-4 J F McDonald(3) 12/1: 02: b f Dansili - Hajat (Mujtahid) Sn   nk   75
handy & rdn/led over 1f out, hdd well ins last, just held: left debut well bhd: Feb foal, half-sister to a 7f juv
sell wnr, dam a 5f 3yo scorer: eff at 6f, shld get further: acts on gd: win a race.
  SWEET COINCIDENCE 0 [2] I A Wood 2-8-2 G Duffield 13/2: 3: b f Mujahid - Sibilant (Selkirk)   1¼   69+
Dwelt, rear, styd on well ins last, eye-catching: cheaply bght Mar foal, half-sister to a 6f juv wnr, dam plcd
abroad & related to a 6f/7f 2yo scorer: eff at 6f, 7f will suit: will improve.
  PHLAUNT 0 [7] R F Johnson Houghton 2-8-2 S Carson 25/1: 4: b f Faustus - Phlirty (Pharly) In   ¾   67
tch, hdwy to chall over 1f out, no extra ins last: cheaply bght Apr foal, half-sister to 7f wnr Pheckless, also a 5f
juv wnr Pheisty, a subs 10/12f scorer: dam unplcd: eff at 6f on gd/soft grnd: gave encouragement.
1524 **ELVINA HILLS** 46 [6]2-8-3 A Daly 20/1: 005: Led till over 1f out, no extra, abs.   ½   66
1874 **PIDDIES PRIDE** 29 [1]2-8-2 VIS B Swarbrick(5) 20/1: 566: Prom, no impress dist: tried visor.   ¾   63
  VICTORY HYMN 0 [8]2-8-3 C Catlin 10/1: 7: Mid-div, btn over 1f out.   7   43
  TRIPLE ZERO 0 [5]2-8-9 K McEvoy 11/1: 8: Mid-div, rdn & no impress over 1f out.   4   37
8 Ran   Time 1m 15.22 (5.22)   Owned: Off Trak Partnership   Trained: Marlborough

---

2538   **7.50 Renault Van Stakes Handicap 3yo+ 0-85 (D)**   **[85]**
  £6906 £2125 £1063   **1m4f**   **Good 57**   **+02 Fast**   Outside

1861 **WAIT FOR THE WILL** 29 [8] G L Moore 8-9-11 bl (82) A Quinn(5) 8/1: 426-0001: ch g Seeking The Gold   89+
- You'd Be Surprised (Blushing Groom) Hld up, prog halfway, led trav well ins fnl 1f, readily: nov hdle wnr in 03/04
(2m1f, fm & gd/soft, rtd 117h): won this race in '03 & '02: all 9 wins at 12f, stays 14f on fm, gd/soft & polytrack:
eff with/without blnks: loves Goodwood, well h'capped.
2 Sep'03 Kemp 12gd 89-(89) C: 2 Aug'03 Newm 12gd 91-(89) C: 1 Jun'03 Good 12g/f 90-86 C:
2 Aug'02 Epso 12g/f 89-87 C: 1 Jul'02 Asco 12g/f 89-82 C: 2 Jul'02 Asco 12gd 85-81 C:
1 Jun'02 Good 12gd 86-75 C: 1 Apr'02 Newm 12gd 81-70 E: 2 Apr'02 Ling 12ap 69a-68 C:
2067 **NORTHSIDE LODGE** 20 [2] P W Harris 6-9-5 (76) W Supple 6/1: 0300352: Mid-div, prog when short of   1¾   79
room 2f out, switched & kept on ins fnl 1f, no ch with wnr: stays 12f, all wins at 10f: see 1822.
1295 **SERGEANT CECIL** 58 [1] B R Millman 5-10-0 (85) S Drowne 33/1: 21020-03: ch g King's Signet -   hd   87
Jadidh (Touching Wood) In tch, prog to lead 2f out, hdd ins fnl 1f, no extra: 8 wk abs & top-weight: won 2 h'caps
in '03: plcd 5 times in '02 (h'caps, rtd 74): eff at 12f, both wins at 14f: acts on fm & gd/soft, any trk, likes
Sandown: tried cheek pieces. 2 Aug'03 Asco 12g/f 90-87 B: 1 Jul'03 Sand 14gd 87-82 C: 2 Jun'03 Sand 14fm 84-79 D:
1 May'03 Sand 14 g/f 84-76 D: 2 Apr'03 Wind 11.6g/f 77-73 D: 2 Oct'02 Wind 11.6g/s 74-71 D:
2 Oct'02 Bath 11.6gd 74-68 D: 2 Oct'02 Sali 14gd 71-65 E: 2 Aug'02 Chep 10.1gd 65-63 E:
2333* **MAN AT ARMS** 8 [4] R Hannon 3-8-3 (5ex) (74) R L Moore 5/2: 0003-414: Bhd, prog ins fnl 2f, nrst   ½   75
fin: not disgraced & shapes as for future: well h'capped: btr 2333.
2126 **WINNERS DELIGHT** 17 [7]3-8-9 (80) K McEvoy 9/1: 165-0055: Mid-div, no impress ins fnl 2f: eff   1½   79
at 7f/1m, poss stays 12f: see 2126.
2209 **SUNNY GLENN** 14 [9]6-9-12 (83) R Havlin 40/1: 25000-06: ch c Rock Hopper - La Ballerine   ½   81

(Lafontaine) Nvr nrr than mid-div: unplcd sole '03 Brit start (earlier listed plcd abroad, rtd 85): unplcd in '02 (rtd 94, listed, J Cullinen): eff at 9f on gd/soft & soft grnd. 2 Apr'01 Newm 9g/s 109- A:
2371* **TIDAL 7** [3]5-8-8 (5ex) (65) R Thomas(5) 7/4 FAV: 000-6117: Handy, led halfway, hdd 2f out, sn wknd: reapp: v disapp on hat-trick bid: btr 2371 (gall trk). 1¼ 61
2422 **DESERT ISLAND DISC 5** [10]7-9-2 (73) J F McDonald(3) 16/1: 0-044038: Nvr nrr than mid-div: qck reapp. 5 61
2293* **PRIVATE BENJAMIN 10** [5]4-7-13 (5ex)(1ow)(1oh) (54) C Catlin 16/1: 1063019: Mid-div 10f, wknd. 10 29
2267 **RAINBOW WORLD 11** [6]4-8-8 p (65) J F Egan 33/1: 0-030030: 10th: Cl-up 10f, fdd: btr 2267. 5 30
2233 **RICHEMAUR 13** [11]4-9-2 (73) G Duffield 14/1: 00-40040: 11th: Led till halfway, sn wknd: btr 2233. 23 3
11 Ran Time 2m 38.46 (6.66) Owned: RDM Racing Trained: Brighton

2539

8.25 Peters Plc Stakes Handicap Fillies 3yo+ 0-85 (D) **[82]**
£5382 £1656 £828 **7f rnd** **Good 57** **-08 Slow** Inside

1927 **IN THE PINK 27** [3] M R Channon 4-8-8 (62) C Catlin 9/1: 4351-001: gr f Indian Ridge - Norfolk Lavender (Ascot Knight) Held up, prog halfway, styd on to lead ins fnl 1f, rdn out: mdn wnr on fnl '03 start: eff at 7f, stays a sharp 1m: acts on firm or gd grnd, sharp/undul or fair trk: unexposed in h'cap grade, rate higher. 1 Oct'03 Yarm 7.0gd 67-(67) D: 69
2258 **CONCUBINE 12** [4] J R Boyle 5-8-6 (60) D Sweeney 4/1: 0300-302: Al trav well in tch, short of room bef 1f out, eventually got gap ins fnl 1f & kept on but not closing at fin: shade closer with clr run. 1¼ 63
2398 **BINT ROYAL 6** [2] Miss V Haigh 6-8-6 p (60) J Egan 3/1 FAV: 5034043: Cl-up, led dist, hdd ins fnl 1f, no extra: qck reapp: see 2150 & 2093. 1¾ 59
2397 **ANNIJAZ 6** [6] J M Bradley 7-8-1 (55) R L Moore 11/2: 0-224004: Rear, prog 2f out, no impress fnl 1f. ¾ 52
2062 **I WISH 20** [1]6-8-2 (56) A Daly 100/30: 0504155: Keen rear, nvr able to chall: btr 1806 (6f). 1½ 50
2312 **RIVA ROYALE 9** [5]4-10-0 (82) G Duffield 7/2: 01-00046: Led till dist, wknd: btr 2312. 4 68
6 Ran Time 1m 29.06 (4.56) Owned: Mrs D J Buckley Trained: West Ilsley

2540

8.55 Racing Uk On 425 Stakes Handicap 3yo+ 0-85 (D) **[82]**
£5564 £1712 £856 **1m rnd** **Good 57** **+06 Fast** Inside

2018 **OMAHA CITY 23** [3] B Gubby 10-9-1 (69) M Tebbutt 13/2: 600-0021: Held up, prog to lead dist, rdn out to assert: eff at 7f/sharp 1m on firm, gd/soft & any trk, loves Goodwood (5 crse wins): see 2018. 76
2389 **EPHESUS 6** [9] Miss Gay Kelleway 4-9-10 vis (78) W Supple 100/30: 0061422: Chsd ldrs, led bef 1f out, sn hdd, rallied fnl 1f, al held by wnr: qck reapp: remains in gd form: see 2389 & 2223. 1 82
2448+ **BEST BEFORE 4** [1] P D Evans 4-9-5 (6ex) (73) S Donohoe(7) 4/1: 1220213: Mid-div, prog ins fnl 2f, not btn far: qck reapp: clr rem: not disgraced under a 6lb pen: just btr 2448. ½ 76
2363 **MAD CAREW 7** [7] G L Moore 5-9-8 bl e (76) R L Moore 3/1 FAV: 1040554: Rear, prog 3f out, onepcd dist. 4 71
2272 **RECOUNT 11** [2]4-9-7 (75) N Pollard 25/1: 450-0065: Cl-up 6f, sn no extra: btr 1296. shd 69
2108* **MADAMOISELLE JONES 18** [6]4-9-0 (68) D Kinsella 15/2: 00-04516: Led, hdd dist, sn fdd: btr 2108 (fm). ¾ 60
1691 **DEEPER IN DEBT 37** [4]6-9-0 (68) G Carter 10/1: 2433507: Cl-up 5f, sn wknd: btr 1042. 4 52
2350 **MUYASSIR 8** [8]9-8-9 (63) S Drowne 12/1: 00-01008: Chsd ldrs over 6f, sn wknd: btr 406. 1½ 44
365 **COMPETITOR 160** [5]3-8-8 (72) C Catlin 16/1: 10-29: Al in rear: btr 365 (polytrack, 10f). 18 17
9 Ran Time 1m 41.51(4.11) Owned: Brian Gubby Ltd Trained: Bagshot

AYR FRIDAY 18.06.04 Lefthand, Galloping Track

Official Going Good (Good/Soft Places) HEAVY SHOWERS

2541

2.20 Peter's Restaurant Claiming Stakes 3yo (E)
£3387 £1042 £521 **6f str** **Good** **Inapplicable** Stands Side

2375 **ARFINNIT 7** [4] M R Channon 3-8-13 vis (63) A Culhane 4/5 FAV: 0651661: Made all, drvn & held on ins last, hvly bckd at odds on: eff at 5f, suited by 6f, tried 7f: acts on fast & soft grnd: apprec claim grade. 63
1842 **BEAVER DIVA 30** [5] W M Brisbourne 3-8-0 (23) D Fentiman(7) 100/1: 0-4002: Chsd ldr, drvn & styd on ins last, al just held: clr of rem: only mod form at up to 10f prev: eff at 6f on gd grnd in modest claim grade. ½ 47$
2215 **WARES HOME 14** [3] K R Burke 3-9-1 vis (65) Darren Williams 6/4: 6-060343: Keen & cl-up, went left under press & btn dist: bckd, gelded: btr 2215 & 1975 (fast). 5 48
1566 **VAUDEVIRE 44** [1] R P Elliott 3-8-5 bl (23) S Chin 66/1: 6-60304: Prom, no impress from over 2f out. 7 19
2380 **HEAD OF STATE 7** [2]3-9-1 vis (57) N Mackay(3) 8/1: 0103005: Cl-up, btn over 1f out & sn eased: qck reapp: jock rec a 4-day ban for easing down: btr 872 & 591 (AW). ½ 27
5 Ran Time 1m 13.52 (4.22) Owned: Mr Tim Corby Trained: West Ilsley

2542

2.55 U K Racing Here Today Handicap Stakes 3yo+ 0-80 (D) **[77]**
£5639 £1735 £868 **6f str** **Good** **Inapplicable** Stands Side

2160 **ULYSEES 16** [3] I Semple 5-9-7 (70) T Eaves(3) 11/2: 600-1031: Mid-div, switched rail & strong run well ins last for press, led cl-home, going away: eff at 6/7f on fast & soft: more in hand than wng margin, can win again: see 2160 & 1391. 78+
2477 **LEGAL SET 2** [1] Miss A Stokell 8-7-12 (2oh)t (45) Natalia Gemelova(6) 20/1: 0000042: Trkd ldr, rdn & narrow lead ins last till nr line: qck reapp: well h'capped for a modest event: see 2477, 1074 & 728. nk 52
2508* **COLLEGE MAID 1** [5] J S Goldie 7-8-11 (6ex) (60) J Currie(7) 13/2: 06002413: Trkd ldrs & narrow lead over 1f out till ins last, just held cl-home: op 11/2, 7f wnr here last night: see 2508, 2315 & 1096. hd 64
2320 **HIGHLAND WARRIOR 9** [7] J S Goldie 5-9-10 (73) N Mackay(3) 3/1 FAV: 3416004: Missed break & around 3L adrift early, in tch by halfway & hdwy wide to chall over 1f out, no extra: bckd, op 7/2: ran a fine race in circumstances but slow starts often a problem: win similar again with a level break: see 1898 (C/D). 2 71
2286 **PRINCE OF BLUES 10** [9]6-8-11 p (60) P Varley(7) 10/1: 4500335: Trkd ldrs, no impress dist: btr 2286. ½ 56
2315* **DESERT ARC 9** [8]6-9-0 (6ex) (63) S W Kelly 9/2: 600-0116: Trkd ldrs, outpcd from halfway: rcd nk 58

much handier than of late: btr 2315 & 2125 (came from well off the pace).

4466} **FAIR SPIN** 266 [10]4-9-2 (65) A Culhane 25/1: 004000-7: ch g Pivotal - Frankie Fair (Red Sunset)   hd   59
Held up & sn outpcd, nvr able to chall: reapp: unplcd in '03 (rtd 79, flattered, cond stks, rtd 69, unplcd, h'cap):
ex Italian wnr & rnr-up in a List contest '02: eff at 6f on gd/soft & hvy grnd.

2477 **FRIAR TUCK** 2 [11]9-8-6 (55) P Fessey 12/1: 0146408: Held up in tch, btn over 1f out: qck reapp.   ¾   47
2214 **PLAYFUL DANE** 14 [4]7-8-9 (58) L Enstone(3) 17/2: 3100-159: Led till over 1f out, wknd: btr 1824.   1¼   46
2396 **DANAKIM** 6 [6]7-8-1 (50) D Fentiman 25/1: 4001500: 10th: Chsd ldrs, btn 2f out: see 1988.   4   27
2554} **STRAWBERRY PATCH** 353 [2]5-9-1 p (64) J Carroll 50/1: 4/00600-0: 11th: b g Woodborough - Okino   18   0
(Strawberry Road) Outpcd & struggling halfway: reapp: unplcd '03 (rtd 66, h'cap, tried cheek pieces): dual h'cap
rnr-up in '02: eff at 5f/6f on firm & fast grnd, prob handles any trk, likes Musselburgh.
2 Sep'02 Kemp 6fm 76-74 C: 2 Jul'02 Newc 6g/f 70-69 C: 2 Aug'01 Redc 5g/f 82- E: 1 Aug'01 Muss 5g/f 80-71 D:
1 Jun'01 Muss 5g/f 72- E:
11 Ran   Time 1m 13.03 (3.73)   Owned: The Farmer Boys (Jock Danny & Ally)   Trained: Carluke

---

2543

3.30 Daily Record First For Scottish Racing Classified Stakes 3yo+ 0-75 (D)
£5639 £1735 £868   **1m rnd**   **Good/Soft**   Inapplicable Inside

2317 **TONY TIE** 9 [4] J S Goldie 8-9-6 (73) N Mackay(3) 11/4: 6225021: Trkd ldrs & smooth hdwy to lead   86+
over 1f out, readily asserted under hand riding: bckd: eff at 7/10f, 1m/9f ideal: acts on firm & hvy grnd, loves
galloping trks: tough & genuine 8yo: see 964.
1849 **STOIC LEADER** 30 [7] R F Fisher 4-9-10 (79) D Nolan(3) 8/1: 0111002: Mid-div, styd on for press to   6   81
take 2nd, nvr threat to wnr: had a short break & reported beforehand by trainer to likely just need this.
2374 **SAMUEL CHARLES** 7 [2] W M Brisbourne 6-9-6 (72) S W Kelly 5/1: 2312233: Led/dsptd lead till over   2   73
1f out, sn no impress on wnr: likes firm, fast & both AWs, handles gd/soft: see 2374, 1909 & 1823.
2323 **LAURO** 9 [10] Miss J A Camacho 4-9-5 (77) P Mulrennan(5) 5/2 FAV: 214-3244: Held up in tch, rdn &   shd   72
no impress def dist: well bckd: btr 2323 & 1602.
2133* **WESTERN ROOTS** 17 [3]3-8-13 (78) A Culhane 7/1: 2400615: Mid-div, nvr impress dist, new stable.   3   71
2438 **TELEPATHIC** 4 [8]4-9-6 (59) P Bradley(5) 50/1: 0600046: Held up, btn 2f out: qck reapp: see 1218.   3   63
2159 **FRANCIS FLUTE** 16 [9]6-9-6 (51) T Eaves(3) 33/1: 000-0247: Trkd ldrs, btn 2f out: see 1897 (7f).   1¾   60
2029 **PERCY DOUGLAS** 22 [11]4-9-6 (45) Ann Stokell 100/1: 3-000008: b c Elmaamul - Qualitair Dream   5   51
(Dreams To Reality) Rear/wide, nvr a factor: h'cap plcd '03 (AW h'cap, rtd 70a, List unplcd, rtd 78): late '02
auct mdn wnr on sand: winning form at 5f on fibresand, stays 6f: eff in cheek pieces/visor.
1 Dec'02 Wolv 5af 61a- F: 2 Dec'02 Wolv 5af 68a- D: 2 Nov'02 Wolv 5af 71a- F:
2159 **ANTHEMION** 16 [1]7-9-6 (58) W Dowling 50/1: 25-02009: Led/dsptd lead till 2f out: btr 1504.   1¼   48
2186 **ROSSELLI** 15 [5]8-9-6 (40) C Ely(7) 100/1: 044-0000: 10th: Led/dsptd lead, hdd 4f out, sn btn.   19   13
2428 **BLUE EMPEROR** 5 [12]3-8-10 (52) R Fitzpatrick 100/1: 6-005000: 11th: Al bhd, qck reapp.   9   0
2315 **UNSHAKEN** 9 [6]10-9-6 (57) J D O'Reilly(7) 50/1: 33430-00: 12th: Dwelt & sn struggling rear.   2   0
12 Ran   Time 1m 44.03 (7.43)   Owned: Mr Frank Brady   Trained: Glasgow

---

2544

4.05 Unbeatable Offer Selling Stakes 3yo+ (F)
£2975 £850 £425   **1m rnd**   **Good/Soft**   Inapplicable Inside

2447 **BEN HUR** 4 [2] W M Brisbourne 5-9-12 (62) S W Kelly 1/1 FAV: 50-01021: Trkd ldrs, hdwy & led over   65
1f out, hung right under press but asserted well in last: hvly bckd: no bid, qck reapp: eff btwn 1m/10f on firm,
soft & fibresand, any trk, gd weight carrier: v head strong & needs strong handling but well suited by claim/sells.
1446 **ROYAL WINDMILL** 50 [8] M D Hammond 5-9-7 p (45) D Fentiman 25/1: 206-0052: Keen in mid-div,   1¼   56
hdwy wide & led halfway, rdn clr over 2f out, hdd over 1f out, kept on well: clr of rem: 7 wk abs: see 1446.
2504 **SUMMER SPECIAL** 1 [5] D W Barker 4-9-7 p (47) L Enstone(3) 8/1: 55305033: Dwelt, held up in tch,   6   46
hdwy over 2f out, hung left & no impress def dist: op 10/1, fin 3rd here last night: see 1388 & 1052.
2146 **TINIAN** 16 [1] K R Burke 6-9-7 (53) Darren Williams 4/1: 0454324: Led 2f, wknd qckly from fnl 2f: bckd.   2   42
1897 **ANDREYEV** 28 [11]10-9-7 (39) J Currie(7) 50/1: 00-60005: ch g Presidium - Missish (Mummy's Pet)   5   34
Bhd, mod late prog, nvr factor: unplcd '03 (rtd 53, clmr): unplcd '02 (rtd 80, h'cap): former smart sprint
performer: prev best at 6f & stays 7f: acts on fast, likes soft/hvy & any trk: eff with/without blnks.
3990} **AMBUSHED** 291 [4]8-9-7 (59) T Eaves(3) 7/1: 0/42030-6: b g Indian Ridge - Surprise Move (Simply   ¾   33
Great) Keen, dsptd lead 2f, btn 2f out: Flat reapp, jumps fit (mod form, h'cap chase): Flat h'cap rnr-up '03: h'cap
scorer '02: eff at 1m/10f on fm & fibresand, likes gd/soft & hvy, any trk, with/without vis/blnks.
2 May'03 Ayr 10g/s 61-64 C: 2 Jul'02 Ayr 10g/s 69-69 E: 2 May'02 Hami 8.2gd 67-65 E: 1 May'02 Hami 8.2sft 69-59 E:
2 Apr'02 Ayr 8g/f 64-59 E: 1 May'01 Ayr 9g/f 63-58 E:
2202 **PLATTOCRAT** 14 [10]4-9-7 S Chin 50/1: 507: Mid-div, struggling from halfway.   7   22
4708} **SHERWOOD FOREST** 249 [7]4-9-7 vis (44) N Mackay(3) 16/1: 060500-8: Mid-div, rdn & btn 3f out: reapp.   nk   21
4395 **THWAAB** 625 [3]12-9-7 (43) P Mulrennan(5) 40/1: 020600/-9: Al bhd, long abs.   27   0
1553 **LIONS DOMANE** 45 [9]7-9-7 (52) J Carroll 25/1: 560P000: 10th: Led after 2f till halfway, sn btn: 6 wk abs. 5   0
10 Ran   Time 1m 46.35 (9.75)   Owned: D C Rutter & H Clewlow   Trained: Nesscliffe

---

2545

4.40 Kidzplay Handicap Stakes 4yo+ 35-55 (F)   [63]
£3178 £908 £454   **1m2f192y**   **Good/Soft**   Inapplicable Inside

1446 **SCURRA** 50 [2] A C Whillans 5-8-12 (47) P Mulrennan(5) 14/1: 320-6031: Trkd ldrs, led over 2f out,   58
joined & duelled with rnr-up ins last, all out: 1st win, abs: eff at 9/11f on fast, hvy & fibresand: goes well fresh.
2226 **INCHNADAMPH** 14 [14] T J Fitzgerald 4-9-1 t (50) A Culhane 5/1: 0/000-622: Mid-div, rdn & hdwy to   shd   60
chall from dist, drvn, carr head v high & lkd reluctant, just denied: blnks/visor could help, imprvd here for strong
handling but still looked a difficult ride: clr of rem: eff at 10.5f/11f: see 2226.
2226 **BORDER TERRIER** 14 [13] M D Hammond 6-8-10 BL (45) N Mackay(3) 14/1: 010-0003: Keen & held up,   10   44
kept on to take 3rd, no impress on front pair: see 1796.
2217 **ESCALADE** 14 [12] W M Brisbourne 7-9-6 p (55) S W Kelly 15/2: 50-04054: Held up, drvn 3f out, little prog. 5   48
2052 **MIKASA** 21 [9]4-8-5 (40) P Bradley(5) 33/1: 0003005: Keen & led till over 2f out, wknd: btr 1552.   2   30
2285 **GRADY** 10 [5]5-8-3 (38) D Fentiman(7) 25/1: 600-6606: Held up, rdn & no impress fnl 3f: btr 2008.   shd   28
1946 **MERLINS PROFIT** 25 [4]4-8-9 (44) L Enstone(3) 10/1: 003-5427: Cl-up, btn 2f out: btr 1946 (10f, fast).   1¾   32
2008 **FAIRY MONARCH** 23 [15]5-8-13 p (48) R Fitzpatrick 14/1: 50000-286: Wide & rear, nvr a factor: btr 2008.   4   31
1943 **OPTIMUM NIGHT** 25 [8]5-8-0 (5oh)p (30) P Fessey 16/1: 0-030459: Al bhd: bckd: see 1450.   2½   14
1980 **ROYAL MELBOURNE** 24 [3]4-9-5 (54) J Carroll 10/1: 0000-160: 10th: Trkd ldrs, btn 2f out: btr 1680.   1   32

AYR   FRIDAY 18.06.04   Lefthand, Galloping Track

2112 **SMARTER CHARTER** 18 [1]11-8-5 (40) Kristin Stubbs(7) 14/1: 5020650: 11th: Reared start, rider lost irons & not able to recover them: forgive this: see 1450. | 1 | 17
2340 **MELOGRANO** 8 [10]4-9-5 (54) D Nolan(3) 12/1: 0360-200: 12th: Dwelt & al bhd: btr 1589 (AW). | 4 | 26
1944 **GOOD TIMING** 25 [6]6-8-5 (40) Dale Gibson 50/1: 0/0-20000: 13th: Prom, wknd fnl 3f: jumps fit. | 12 | 0
2233 **REPULSE BAY** 13 [11]6-9-2 (51) J Currie(7) 4/1 FAV: 0-603050: 14th: Dwelt, al towards rear: btr 1793. | 6 | 0
1777 **BURLEY FIREBRAND** 34 [7]4-9-6 BL (55) Darren Williams 14/1: 2020-000: 15th: Mid-div, btn 3f out: blnks, no improvement: see 1777. | 12 | 0
15 Ran   Time 2m 55.55 (9.55)   Owned: Mrs L M Whillans   Trained: Hawick

2546   5.15 Racing Here Tomorrow Apprentice Maiden Handicap Stakes 3yo+ 0-70 (E)   [67]
£3474 £1069 £535   1m5f13y   Good/Soft   Inapplicable   Inside

2465 **MERRYMAKER** 3 [6] W M Brisbourne 4-9-2 (55) P Mathers 11/4 FAV: 33-464P1: Rear, in tch, rdn & hdwy to lead over 1f out, rdn out, jockey prob decisive in this close finish: first win: eff around 11.5f/14f on firm & gd/soft grnd, sharp/undul or gall trk: eff with/without visor, tried blnks: see 1693. | | 62
2164 **DUNLEA DANCER** 16 [7] M Johnston 3-7-13 (53) A Elliott(7) 7/2: 0500-342: Keen/handy, led over 2f out till over 1f out, rallied gamely cl-home, just held, poss wnr with stronger handling: clr of rem: bckd: eff at 10/13f on gd/soft & soft grnd: see 1306. | hd | 59
2081 **CAYMANS GIFT** 20 [1] A C Whillans 4-9-7 (60) A Reilly(5) 16/1: 4563: In tch, rdn to chall over 2f out, sn no extra: h'cap bow & longer trip: stays a slowly run 13f on gd/soft grnd: see 1507. | 5 | 60
2038 **ODABELLA** 21 [5] John Berry 4-10-0 T (67) J D O'Reilly(3) 7/2: 340-3004: In tch, hdwy & led over 3f out, hdd over 2f out, sn no impress: nicely bckd: t-strap: btr 1131 (1m, fast). | 10 | 55
2277 **GAIETY GIRL** 11 [8]3-8-10 (64) A Mullen(5) 7/1: 4430-065: Trkd ldrs, hung left & btn 3f out: see 2277. | 2½ | 48
2105 **MORVERN** 18 [4]4-8-6 (45) D Tudhope(3) 4/1: 004-4056: Led till over 3f out, sn btn: btr 2105 & 324. | 7 | 21
2299 **MR MOON** 10 [2]3-7-12 (17oh) (35) D Fentiman(3) 50/1: 00-66007: Cl-up & briefly led over 3f out, wknd. | 1½ | 26
7 Ran   Time 3m 03.41(18.81)   Owned: The Blacktoffee Partnership   Trained: Nesscliffe

REDCAR   FRIDAY 18.06.04   Lefthand, Flat, Galloping Track

Official Going Good (Good/Firm Places)

2547   2.10 Ings Maiden Stakes 2yo (D)
£3406 £1048 £524   5f str   Good   Slow   Centre

2165 **AFRICAN BREEZE** 16 [7] R M Whitaker 2-8-9 Dean McKeown 1/2 FAV: 041: Cl-up, styd on to lead dist, drvn out: eff at 5f, step up to 6f shld suit: acts on fast & gd grnd, stiff or gall trk: see 2165. | | 80
2241 **WONDERFUL MIND** 13 [4] T D Easterby 2-9-0 R Winston 8/1: 052: Led, hdd dist, not pace of wnr fnl 1f: eff at 5f on gd grnd: improving with racing & can find a mdn: see 2241. | 1¾ | 77
TRIM IMAGE 47 [6] Ms Joanna Morgan 2-8-9 R Lappin 11/2: 233: br f Averti - Altizaf (Zafonic) Cl up, outpcd after 3f, rallied fnl 1f: Irish raider, 7 wk abs: April foal, cost £25,000: dam unplcd: sire top-class performer at sprint dists: prev plcd both starts to date at Navan (mdns): eff at 5f on fast & gd/soft. | nk | 71
HILLSIDE HEATHER 0 [3] A Berry 2-8-9 F Norton 20/1: 4: ch f Tagula - Danzig Craft (Roi Danzig) Rear, onepcd ins fnl 1f: debut: March foal, cost 5,000gns: half-sister plcd at 5f: dam unrcd: sire decent performer at 6/7f: eff at 5f, bred to apprec further: acts on gd grnd. | hd | 70
2119 **KILMOVEE** 17 [1]2-8-9 S Sanders 12/1: 505: Handy, outpcd halfway, rallied late: clr rem: see 1780. | hd | 69
FOR NOWT 0 [2]2-9-0 G Faulkner 33/1: 6: b c Forzando - Angel Chimes (Most Welcome) Dwelt, al in rear: debut: March foal, cost 6,500gns: half-brother wnr at 1m: dam wnr at 5/7f: sire useful around 1m. | 12 | 44
2321 **TAKS GIRL** 9 [5]2-8-9 D Allan 100/1: 07: Dwelt, al in rear. | 7 | 19
7 Ran   Time 1m 2.30 (5.8)   Owned: Mr G F Pemberton   Trained: Scarcroft

2548   2.45 Newton Claiming Stakes 3yo+ (F)
£2968 £848 £424   1m2f   Good   Slow   Inside

2384 **SALUT SAINT CLOUD** 7 [9] Miss V Haigh 3-8-3 (46) F Norton 5/1: 045-6051: Mid-div, prog to lead dist, pushed clr, eased cl-home, val 7L+: clmd for 5,500, qck reapp: apprec step up to 10f: acts on gd grnd. | | 52+
1945 **CEZZARO** 25 [3] S R Bowring 6-9-1 (40) J Bramhill 9/1: 040-5602: Led, hdd dist, sn not pace of wnr. | 5 | 43
2332 **ERTE** 8 [1] M R Channon 3-8-6 (58) S Hitchcott(2) 9/2: 406-0663: Handy over 7f, sn outpcd, rallied late. | nk | 45
2008 **TURFTANZER** 23 [5] Don Enrico Incisa 5-9-1 t (30) Kim Tinkler 33/1: 4600004: Prom 1m, sn no extra. | 1 | 40
2146 **ROJABAA** 16 [7]5-10-0 (53) L Treadwell(7) 7/2: 53411-65: In tch, prog & ev ch bef 1f out, sn fdd. | 2½ | 49
1164 **FACE THE LIMELIGHT** 65 [2]5-9-4 (65) G Faulkner 11/4 FAV: 55050-06: b g Quest For Fame - Miss Boniface (Tap On Wood) Rear, nvr able to chall: bckd: recent hdles unplcd (rtd 58h, nov): h'cap wnr first time out in '03 (H Morrison): h'cap 2nd & 3rd in '02 (rtd 72): eff at 9.6f/12f on fast, soft & fibresand: handles any trk & has gone well fresh: with Jedd O'Keeffe. | hd | 38
1 Apr'03 Folk 9.7g/f 72-65 E: 2 Apr'02 Bath 10.2gd 70-67 E: 1 Nov'01 Donc 7sft 68-61 D: 2 Nov'01 Brig 8g/s 63-58 D:
4998} **ULTRA MARINE** 227 [8]4-9-4 bl (54) R Winston 7/1: 560004-7: b c Blues Traveller - The Aspecto Girl (Alzao) Al in rear: earlier hdles unplcd (rtd 82h, juv nov): unplcd on Flat in '03 (rtd 65, mdn): dual mdn rnr-up in '02: eff at 7.5f/1m on firm & gd/soft grnd: tried cheek pieces, wears blnks. | 5 | 31
2 Jul'02 Beve 7.4g/s 68- E: 2 Jun'02 Muss 7.1g/f 68- F:
2230 **GREY SAMURAI** 14 [6]4-9-10 D Allan 33/1: 608: Al in rear: see 2058. | 6 | 29
8 Ran   Time 2m 9.97 (7.67)   Owned: Miss V Haigh   Trained: Bawtry

2549 3.20 Staithes Maiden Stakes 3yo+ (D)
£3513 £1081 £541 **1m3f** **Good** **Fair** Inside

CARTE DIAMOND 0 [4] M Johnston 3-8-8 R Ffrench 6/1: 1: ch c Theatrical - Liteup My Life (Green Dancer) Mid-div, prog to lead 2f out, sn clr, eased well ins fnl 1f, val bit more: debut: half-brother to a wnr abroad: eff at 11f, further will suit: acts on gd grnd & a gall trk: goes well fresh: fine start. **93+**
2124 **ARRGATT 17** [2] M A Jarvis 3-8-8 (83) S Sanders 1/5 FAV: 0-322: Led 1f, styd cl-up, led 3f out, hdd 2f out, kept on, not pace of wnr: clr rem: bckd at long odds-on: eff at 10/11f on fast & gd: see 2124. *5* **84**
HIRAYNA 0 [3] W M Brisbourne 5-9-2 R Winston 33/1: 3: b f Doyoun - Himaya (Mouktar) Led 10f out, hdd 3f out, fdd: Flat debut, bmpr unplcd on sole 02/03 start: half-sister to useful Flat stayer Hirapour. *26* **39**
KING TOP 0 [1] T D Easterby 3-8-8 D Allan 25/1: 4: b g Inchinor - Panorama (Shirley Heights) Slow away, al well adrift: debut: bred to apprec mid-dists. *17* **19**
4 Ran Time 2m 22.14 (6.64) Owned: Mr & Mrs Heywood & Mr & Mrs Bovingdon Trained: Middleham

2550 3.55 Go Racing In Yorkshire Handicap Stakes 3yo+ 0-70 (E) **[68]**
£3877 £1193 £597 **1m str** **Good** **Slow** Centre

2317* **GOODBYE MR BOND 9** [3] E J Alston 4-9-7 (6ex) (61) F Norton 9/4 FAV: 3434111: In tch, prog to lead bef 1f out, sn pushed clr, val 5L+: eff around 1m/9f on fast, soft grnd & fibresand, handles any trk: in form 4yo who is progressing with racing, more h'caps await: see 2317 & 2159. **79+**
2466 **ALCHEMIST MASTER 3** [8] R M Whitaker 5-9-0 P (54) Dean McKeown 5/2: 000-6222: Handy, prog & ev ch dist, kept on, no ch with wnr: qck reapp: ran to form with cheek pieces fitted: well h'capped, see 2466 & 2324. *3½* **61**
2466 **DARA MAC 3** [2] N Bycroft 5-8-13 (53) Suzanne France(7) 20/1: 005-0263: Rear, prog 3f out, onepcd dist. *1½* **58**
2057 **MEHMAAS 21** [7] R E Barr 8-8-6 vis (46) R Winston 20/1: 00-00004: b g Distant Relative - Guest List (Be My Guest) Led, hdd bef 1f out, wknd: plcd 3 times in '03 (h'caps & class stks, rtd 64): h'cap wnr in '02: amat class stks wnr in '01: stays 1m, suited by around 7f: acts on firm, hvy grnd & fibresand: eff with/without blnks/visor & has gone well fresh: likes Redcar & Beverley: eff in cheek pieces. *1½* **48**
2 Jul'03 Redc 8gd 64-60 E: 2 May'03 Muss 8gd 64-(69) E: 2 Nov'02 Donc 8hvy 71-63 E: 2 Aug'02 Catt 7gd 65-63 E: 1 Jul'02 Beve 7.4g/s 63-59 E: 2 Jul'02 Beve 8.4g/s 60- D: 2 May'02 Redc 8fm 61-59 F: 2 Sep'01 Beve 7.4gd 66-62 E: 1 Jul'01 Redc 7fm 66- G: 2 Jul'01 Muss 8g/f 55-53 E:
2120 **APACHE POINT 17** [6]7-9-2 (56) Kim Tinkler 6/1: 24-00545: Chsd ldrs, outpcd halfway, mod late gains. *hd* **57**
2179 **MOUNT PEKAN 15** [4]4-8-6 (46) R Ffrench 16/1: 000-0306: Keen rear, nvr a factor: btr 1748. *5* **37**
2235 **CASHNEEM 13** [9]6-9-10 (64) D Allan 13/2: 00-46147: Keen cl-up 6f, fdd: btr 2150 (7f). *3* **49**
2086 **NIGHT WOLF 20** [5]4-9-12 (66) S Hitchcott(3) 8/1: 15-60038: Al in rear: v disapp run: btr 2086. *18* **19**
8 Ran Time 1m 42.53 (7.73) Owned: Mr Peter J Davies Trained: Preston

2551 4.30 Gribdale Handicap Stakes 3yo 0-80 (D) **[87]**
£5639 £1735 £868 **6f str** **Good** **Slow** Centre

2155 **KINGSMAITE 16** [2] S R Bowring 3-8-4 BL (63) J Bramhill 10/1: 12-04051: Prom, led 3f out, rdn out: stays 1m, enjoyed recent drop back to 6f: acts on fast, gd grnd & fibresand: apprec fitting of 1st time blnks. **72**
1881 **COMMANDO SCOTT 28** [5] A Berry 3-9-0 (73) F Lynch 6/1: 340-1002: Chsd ldrs, styd on to chase wnr ins fnl 1f, sn edged left & held: gd eff, see 1216. *1½* **77**
2155 **BRIGHT SUN 16** [4] N Tinkler 3-9-3 (76) Kim Tinkler 3/1: 00-00043: Sn in tch, hung left & onepcd dist. *2* **74**
2121 **TYNE 17** [3] T D Barron 3-9-7 (80) S Sanders 5/2 FAV: 216-064: Rear, prog halfway, no extra fnl 1f: well bckd under top-weight: has been gelded since 2121 (5f). *½* **77**
2055 **FOX COVERT 21** [6]3-8-0 vis (59) R Ffrench 7/2: 0-000235: Led 3f, wknd fnl 2f: btr 2055 & 1949. *5* **41**
2042 **WRENLANE 21** [1]3-8-9 (68) T Hamilton(3) 7/1: 30-26: Chsd ldrs 3f, sn hung left & wknd: op 5/1. *1½* **46**
6 Ran Time 1m 14.34 (5.44) Owned: Mr S R Bowring Trained: Edwinstowe

2552 5.05 'hand To Rouf' Lady Amateur Riders' Maiden Handicap Stakes 3yo+ 0-70 (G) **[52]**
£2639 £754 £377 **1m str** **Good** **Slow** Centre

416 **ZANJEER 155** [4] N Wilson 4-9-12 (50) Mrs N Wilson(5) 16/1: 4/40-01: b g Averti - Cloudslea (Chief's Crown) Made all, clr 2f out, eased cl-home, val 10L+: long abs: unplcd in 2 '03 starts (D Nicholls, rtd 67, mdn): 4th sole '02 start (mdn, rtd 67): eff at 1m on gd: goes well fresh: improved for forcing tactics. **68**
1910 **REGENTS SECRET 27** [12] J S Goldie 4-10-11 (63) Ms C Williams 4/1 JT FAV: 040-4002: Rear, prog to chase ldr 3f out, no impress bef 1f out: acts on firm & gd grnd: see 1092. *8* **65**
2335 **SHOTLEY DANCER 8** [5] N Bycroft 5-8-13 (37) Miss L Ellison(3) 8/1: 60-40043: Rear, prog 3f out, onepcd. *2½* **35**
2235 **NOBLE PENNY 13** [9] Mrs K Walton 5-9-11 (49) Miss Kelly Harrison(3) 9/1: 00-06204: Rear, prog halfway, onepcd fnl 2f: return to 7f will suit: btr 2080. *2½* **42**
2403 **BORIS THE SPIDER 6** [11]3-9-7 (55) Miss E J Jones 11/1: 00-20055: Cl-up 4f, sn outpcd, mod gains. *nk* **47**
2295 **ORION EXPRESS 10** [1]3-10-0 (62) Miss S Brotherton 4/1 JT FAV: 0-660046: In tch, outpcd halfway, modest late gains: well bckd: btr 2295. *1¼* **52**
2125 **ORANGINO 17** [8]6-9-2 (40) Miss R Davidson(5) 7/1: 0000-027: Cl-up 6f, sn wknd: btr 2125 (6f). *¾* **28**
4859} **KAMAS WHEEL 239** [6]5-9-0 (38) Mrs M Morris 33/1: 540D60-8: ch f Magic Ring - Tea And Scandals (Key To The Kingdom) Nvr nrr than mid-div on reapp: plcd twice in '03 (h'caps, rtd 39): rnr-up in '02 (sell h'cap): eff at 7f/1m on firm & gd/soft grnd: tried cheek pieces. 2 Aug'02 Yarm 8fm 40-38 G: *1¼* **24**
2218 **MIDDLEHAM PARK 14** [3]4-10-2 (54) Miss A Armitage(5) 16/1: 0060-209: Cl-up 6f, fdd: btr 677. *1½* **37**
2168 **ATHOLLBROSE 16** [7]3-9-5 (53) Miss A Elsey 6/1: 0-424540: 10th: Handy 5f, sn wknd: btr 1834. *1¼* **34**
2381 **BANNERS FLYING 7** [2]4-11-0 (66) Miss Rachel Clark(7) 50/1: 245-0040: 11th: Rear, nvr a factor. *6* **35**
2243 **CAMPBELLS LAD 13** [13]3-8-10 (2oh) (42) Miss Dawn Rankin(5) 28/1: 540-5400: 12th: Cl-up 4f, fdd. *shd* **12**
4550} **MANDINKA 261** [10]4-8-10 (2oh) (32) Miss Joey Ellis(5) 16/1: 000500-0: 13th: Mid-div 5f, fdd. *2* **0**
13 Ran Time 1m 43.10(8.3) Owned: Mr Malcom Wilson Trained: York

Official Going Firm

2553

2.30 Listed Albany Stakes Fillies 2yo (A)
£23200 £8800 £4400   **6f str**   **Good/Firm 30**   -40 Slow   Stands Side

2097* **JEWEL IN THE SAND** 18 [8] R Hannon 2-8-11 R Hughes 10/1: 11: In tch, lost place halfway, hdwy &   **109+**
squeezed through over 1f out, styd on well to lead 1f out, qcknd clr, cosily: eff at 5f, relished this step up to 6f
& shld get further: acts on fast grnd & stiff trks: smart & with a turn of foot, one to follow in Gr class.
1735 **SPIRIT OF CHESTER** 35 [1] Mrs P N Dutfield 2-8-9 R Havlin 40/1: 42: Held up, hdwy & short of   1½ **101+**
room over 2f out till over 1f out, kept on ins last to chase wnr, nrst fin: much imprvd from debut & styd this stiff
6f well, 7f sure to suit: acts on fast grnd: closer with a clr run & must be winning races shortly: see 1735.
1805* **SALSA BRAVA** 32 [17] N P Littmoden 2-8-11 J P Guillambert 14/1: 13: Dwelt, held up & sn rdn,   1 **100**
hdwy well over 1f out, kept on same pace: stays a stiff 6f & imprvd on recent mdn win: shld win more races.
2328 **UMNIYA** 11 [9] M R Channon 2-8-9 C Catlin 20/1: 321334: Handy, hdwy to lead well over 1f out, sn   nk **97**
hdd & onepace: consistent but needs an ease in grade: see 2328, 2071.
2245* **PARK ROMANCE** 13 [4]2-8-11 K Fallon 6/1: 215: Bhd, hdwy 2f out, sn bmpd & kept on same pace: 1½ **95**
ran to form of 2245 (fills mdn) on step up in class: stks company will suit.
2119 **ARABIAN DANCER** 17 [7]2-8-9 T E Durcan 14/1: 26: Dwelt, sn handy, onepace over 1f out: relish mdns. hd **92**
2275* **EXTREME BEAUTY** 11 [2]2-8-9 D Holland 33/1: 617: Bhd, hdwy & short of room over 2f out till over   1¼ **88**
1f out, onepace, saddle reportedly slipped: nothing went right here & looks sure to rate more highly: see 2275.
2297 **GOLDEN LEGACY** 10 [14]2-8-9 P Hanagan 20/1: 28: Cl-up, led briefly over 1f out, wknd: wants mdns. nk **87**
2061* **MASA** 20 [6]2-8-11 L Dettori 13/8 FAV: 19: Dwelt, sn in tch, short of room over 1f out but sn   ½ **87**
wknd: hvly bckd: clearly much btr expected but slow start did not help: expect btr, made all to land debut in 2061.
1728* **ALTA PETENS** 35 [13]2-8-9 J Mackay 16/1: 410: 10th: Keen with ldr, led halfway till over 1f out,   ¾ **83**
wknd: stiff task, see 1728 (mdn auct).
1964* **NUFOOS** 25 [5]2-8-11 R Hills 7/1: 310: 11th: Held up, hdwy & short of room over 2f out, well   ¾ **83**
held when not clr run ins last: type to do btr, see 1964 (made all).
1669* **JUSTAQUESTION** 38 [3]2-8-11 G Duffield 25/1: 0110: 12th: Nvr a factor: up in class, see 1669 (soft). nk **82**
2310 **COURS DE LA REINE** 9 [16]2-8-9 J Quinn 20/1: 30: 13th: Al bhd, reportedly hung right. nk **79**
    CHANTILLY BEAUTY 41 [12]2-8-9 P J Murtagh 25/1: 010: 14th: b f Josr Algarhoud - Lysabelle   1 **76**
(Lesotho) Keen, al bhd: tried cheek pieces: earlier won in the French Provinces (5.5f, gd).
2097 **TOUCH OF SILK** 18 [15]2-8-9 M Hills 40/1: 520: 15th: In tch, wknd well over 1f out: see 2097, 1805. ½ **74**
1640* **GOLDEN ANTHEM** 39 [11]2-8-9 T Quinn 40/1: 10: 16th: Bhd, eff well over 1f out, sn wknd: btr 1640 (hvy).2 **68**
2165 **SAPPHIRE DREAM** 16 [10]2-8-11 P Robinson 40/1: 22160: 17th: Led to halfway, wkng/hmpd over 1f out.6 **52**
17 Ran   Time 1m 16.13 (3.03)   Owned: Sand Associates   Trained: Marlborough

---

2554

3.05 Gr2 King Edward Vii Stakes Colts & Geldings 3yo (A)
£81238 £30814 £15407   **1m4f**   **Good/Firm 30**   -17 Slow   Inside

2308 **FIVE DYNASTIES** 12 [7] A P O'Brien 3-8-11 J P Spencer 11/4 FAV: 14-301: Handy trav well, led   **112**
over 1f out, edged right but styd on, rdn out: earlier 5L8th in French Derby: stays 12f well on firm & gd/soft:
smart, weak renewal of this event but confidence shld be high after this: see 1622.
2254 **ELSHADI** 13 [6] M P Tregoning 3-8-11 bl (96) W Supple 4/1: 114-02: Set pace, rdn & hdd over 1f   4 **105**
out, not pace of wnr: useful run back in blnks & styd 12f on fast grnd: drop in class will suit: see 2254.
2006 **BARATI** 26 [2] John M Oxx 3-8-11 M J Kinane 3/1: 143: Held up, rdn over 3f out, hdwy & short of   3 **100**
room 2f out, wknd appr fnl 1f: nicely bckd: shld stay 12f, poss wants easier grnd: see 2006.
2131* **HAADEF** 17 [3] J H M Gosden 3-8-11 R Hills 3/1: 314: With ldr, wknd 2f out: big step up in   hd **100**
class after mdn win in 2131.
1316 **GOLD HISTORY** 56 [4]3-8-11 (103) J Fanning 6/1: 110-2135: Held up, hdwy to chall 2f out, sn wknd: 3½ **95**
8 wk abs: see 1316, 1189 (9f).
5 Ran   Time 2m 32.26 (3.26)   Owned: Mrs John Magnier & Mr M Tabor   Trained: Ireland

---

2555

3.45 Gr1 Coronation Stakes Fillies 3yo (A)
£139823 £53037 £26518   **1m rnd**   **Good/Firm 30**   +10 Fast   Inside

2005* **ATTRACTION** 26 [10] M Johnston 3-9-0 (119) K Darley 6/4 FAV: 1111-111: Made all, qcknd clr 2f   **120**
out, flashed tail but styd on strongly, rdn out: hvly bckd: well suited by a stiff 1m & loves to dominate: likes
firm & fast grnd, handles gd/soft: top-class, tough, genuine & unbeaten filly, continues to improve & will take all
the beating in the Falmouth stks at Newmarket: see 2005.
2005 **MAJESTIC DESERT** 26 [5] M R Channon 3-9-0 (111) T E Durcan 25/1: 312-1002: Held up, hdwy & short 2½ **113**
of room over 2f out, styd on well to take 2nd ins last, no ch with wnr: further bhd this wnr in English & Irish
1,000 Guineas earlier but right back to best here with waiting tactics: win again in Gr 2/3 class: see 1233.
1492 **RED BLOOM** 47 [12] Sir Michael Stoute 3-9-0 (113) K Fallon 100/30: 311-43: Cl-up, hdwy to chase hd **112**
wnr over 2f out, not her pace over 1f out but kept on: well bckd: abs: another smart run, well worth a try at 10f.
1935* **MOON DAZZLE** 27 [6] W J Haggas 3-9-0 R Hills 25/1: 14: Dwelt, held up, hdwy well over 1f out,   3½ **105+**
kept on, nrst fin: v encouraging on only 2nd start: looks sure to relish further on this evidence & v interesting
in a Gr 3/List next time: see 1935.
2005 **KINNAIRD** 26 [1]3-9-0 M J Kinane 12/1: 15111-45: In tch, outpcd 2f out: see 2005.   3½ **98**
2069 **KELUCIA** 20 [8]3-9-0 (100) W Supple 100/1: 334-5056: ch f Grand Lodge - Karachi (Zino) In tch, 1 **96**
wknd 2f out: '03 auct & stks wnr: eff over 7f/1m on gd & firm grnd, gall trks: needs an ease in grade.
1 Sep'03 Ayr 8fm 91-(82) D: 2 Sep'03 Hayd 8.1gd 82-79 C: 1 Aug'03 Newc 8.0g/f 82- F: 2 Aug'03 Redc 7g/f 71- D:
1300* **ROYAL TIGRESS** 33 [11]3-9-0 J P Spencer 40/1: 2-3107: Cl-up, outpcd 2f out, hmpd ins last: nk **95**
unplcd in a Gr 1 in France since 1300 (soft).
1171* **RELAXED** 65 [3]3-9-0 (82) R Hughes 9/1: 2-18: Handy, wknd 2f out: 2 mth abs, step up in class &   1½ **92**
trip after 1171 (fills mdn, gd).
1854 **CAIRNS** 33 [7]3-9-0 (107) L Dettori 7/1: 11-069: Held up, btn over 2f out: see 1854.   hd **91**
2092* **ARICIA** 19 [2]3-9-0 J Murtagh 20/1: 010: 10th: Al bhd: see 2092 (mdn, 7f).   nk **90**
2005 **SECRET CHARM** 26 [9]3-9-0 (112) M Hills 14/1: 11-550: 11th: Prom, wknd over 2f out: see 1492.   5 **80**
11 Ran   Time 1m 38.54 (0.04)   Owned: Duke of Roxburghe   Trained: Middleham

2556 4.20 Listed Wolferton Rated Stakes Handicap 4yo+ 0-110 (A) [117]
£23200 £8800 £4400 **1m2f** **Good/Firm 30** **+10 Fast** Inside

1759 **RED FORT 34** [11] M A Jarvis 4-8-8 (97) P Robinson 6/1: 0140-131: Handy, hdwy to lead 2f out, pushed clr, v readily/impressive: well bckd: stays 12f, relished this return to 10f: acts on fast & gd/soft, likes gall trks: v smart run to demolish a useful field, looks Gr class & must take all the beating under an 8lb pen in John Smith H'cap at York: see 1346. **113+**
1478* **PROMOTION 48** [10] Sir Michael Stoute 4-8-7 (1oh) (95) K Fallon 2/1 FAV: 132-12: In tch, hdwy to chall over 2f out, kept on but cmftbly outpcd by wnr over 1f out: 7 wk abs, massive gamble: v useful & progressive but caught a tartar here: open to further improvement & shld win more nice prizes: see 1478. *8* **100**
2208 **BLYTHE KNIGHT 14** [9] E A L Dunlop 4-9-0 (103) L Dettori 10/1: 30-41463: Held up, hdwy over 2f out, kept on over 1f out, no ch with wnr: tough & consistent: see 1478, 1296. *1¼* **105**
2208* **PERSIAN LIGHTNING 14** [3] J L Dunlop 5-9-4 (107) M J Kinane 6/1: 200-4414: Held up rear, late gains, nrst fin: nicely bckd: set plenty to do & can rate higher: see 2208. *1¼* **107**
1746 **BONECRUSHER 35** [16]5-9-4 (107) T P Queally 16/1: 6405205: In tch, eff well over 2f out, onepace. *½* **106**
1862 **FOODBROKER FOUNDER 29** [14]4-8-11 (100) Dane O'Neill 25/1: 50200-06: Held up, eff well over 2f out, no impress: see 1862. *1* **96**
1862 **ANANI 29** [2]4-9-1 (104) J P Spencer 25/1: 0342067: Held up rear, late gains, nrst fin: set plenty to do. *1½* **98**
2101 **MILLAFONIC 18** [8]4-8-7 (1oh) (95) D Holland 8/1: 31150-68: Nvr a factor: showed more 2101. *2* **87**
1843 **CORRIOLANUS 30** [4]4-8-8 (97) Gary Stevens 33/1: 3-300069: Keen bhd, brief eff & short of room 2f out, eased: see 693. *1¼* **86**
2208 **COMPTON BOLTER 14** [13]7-9-7 (110) R Hughes 16/1: 0503250: 10th: In tch, wkng when hmpd over 1f out: reportedly unsuited by this fast grnd: stable out of form, see 1862. *2* **96**
1560 **AKSHAR 46** [12]5-9-4 BL (107) P J Smullen 12/1: 3130-030: 11th: Slow away & al bhd: abs, blnks. *½* **92**
2101 **ULUNDI 18** [6]9-8-7 (1oh) (95) T Quinn 25/1: 000-0000: 12th: With ldr, wknd 2f out: 9yo: see 1843. *6* **71**
2208 **SIR GEORGE TURNER 14** [5]5-8-9 VIS (98) J Fanning 50/1: 32/-00000: 13th: In tch, wknd over 2f out. *12* **61**
2141 **TUNING FORK 19** [1]4-8-7 (1oh)T (95) J Quinn 33/1: 650-0000: 14th: Led till 2f out, wknd qckly: tried t-strap, went off too fast: see 2141, 1843. *7* **47**
14 Ran Time 2m 04.0 (0.0) Owned: The Red Fort Partnership Trained: Newmarket

2557 4.55 Gr3 Queen's Vase 3yo (A)
£34800 £13200 £6600 **2m45y** **Good/Firm 30** **-09 Slow** Inside

1931 **DUKE OF VENICE 27** [6] Saeed bin Suroor 3-8-11 t (109) L Dettori 9/2: 310-121: In tch, smooth hdwy over 2f out, led over 1f out, pushed clr, v readily: nicely bckd: relished this step up to 2m, get further on this evidence: acts on fast & gd/soft, gall trks: smart stayer in the making, eye-catching here & looks gd value at a double figure price for St Leger later in yr: see 1520. **109+**
TWO MILES WEST 9 [8] A P O'Brien 3-8-11 J P Spencer 5/2 FAV: 12: b c Sadler's Wells - User Friendly (Slip Anchor) Handy, hdwy to lead over 2f out, hdd over 1f out, not pace of wnr: bckd: earlier won a Leopardstown mdn on debut: eff at 12f, stays 2m on fast & gall trks: open to further improvement, well clr rem. *6* **100**
2308 **TOP SEED 12** [1] M R Channon 3-8-11 (108) T E Durcan 11/2: 624-2403: In tch, sltly outpcd over 2f out, eff over 1f out, no impress: longer trip: see 1208 (10f, gd). *6* **94**
2130 **BUMPTIOUS 17** [7] M H Tompkins 3-8-11 BL (75) P Robinson 33/1: 46-33144: Held up, rdn over 4f out, kept on same pace: tried blnks & looks a dour stayer: much more interesting back in h'caps if running off around current mark (75): see 2130, 1507. *1¼* **93**
1885* **STRIKE 28** [10]3-8-11 VIS (82) J Murtagh 8/1: 2615: Slow away, bhd, btn over 2f out: visor: longer trip. *3* **90**
1814 **RED LANCER 31** [5]3-9-0 (110) R Miles 8/1: 2222136: Held up, outpcd over 2f out, hung right: prob not stay: see 1814, 1584 (12f). *1¾* **91**
2058* **TARANDOT 21** [3]3-8-8 (87) A McCarthy 11/1: 0-217: Cl-up, wknd 2f out: longer trip, see 2058 (12f, mdn). *1* **84**
2130 **NESSEN DORMA 17** [4]3-8-11 VIS (81) M Fenton 16/1: 5521338: In tch, wknd over 3f out: visor, see 2130. *½* **86$**
1999 **TAMARILLO 26** [9]3-8-8 (99) D Holland 8/1: 5-521659: Keen held up, wknd over 2f out: see 1999. *17* **67**
2418 **ZOUAVE 5** [2]3-8-11 bl (87) P J Smullen 50/1: 103-0050: 10th: Led till over 2f out, wknd: see 1814. *5* **65**
10 Ran Time 3m 29.14 (3.14) Owned: Godolphin Trained: Newmarket

2558 5.30 Buckingham Palace Stakes Handicap 3yo+ 0-105 (B) [103]
£23200 £8800 £4400 **7f str** **Good/Firm 30** **-10 Slow** Stands Side. 2 Groups.

2091 **UNSCRUPULOUS 19** [23] J R Fanshawe 5-8-5 (80) O Urbina 8/1: 4/0321-31: Held up far side, gd hdwy to lead 1f out, qcknd clr, v readily: eff over 7f/1m on firm & gd grnd: enjoys waiting tactics & relishes a fast pace: useful, clearly thriving & open to further improvement, win more races: see 2091. **97+**
2154 **MAGHANIM 16** [30] J L Dunlop 4-9-7 (96) R Hills 33/1: 210/0-532: Led far side till dist, not pace of wnr: fine run back at 7f, stays 1m: shld continue to give a gd account: see 2154, 1811. *5* **101**
2282 **TRUE NIGHT 10** [29] D Nicholls 7-8-2 (77) J Quinn 11/1: 0004233: Held up far side, hdwy 2f out, kept on ins last: tough, winning form in July/Aug last 2 seasons: see 2282, 2070. *nk* **81**
1420 **NEW SEEKER 51** [1] C G Cox 4-10-0 (103) J P Spencer 4/1 FAV: 21311-24: Led stands side, kept on well over 1f out, no ch with far side group: excellent eff on poss "wrong" side after a 7 wk abs: loves Ascot & dominating: tough, useful & clearly remains in fine heart: see 1420. *3* **101+**
1929* **PETER PAUL RUBENS 27** [20]3-8-6 (90) R L Moore 9/1: 0415: Cl-up centre, no extra fnl 1f: btr run than fin position indicates, can rate higher: see 1929. *hd* **87**
1962 **ST ANDREWS 25** [28]4-9-4 (93) P Robinson 16/1: 314/-26: Handy far side, wknd fnl 1f: see 1962. *shd* **89**
2076 **MANAAR 20** [26]4-8-8 (83) E Ahern 25/1: 2220-057: In tch far side, eff over 1f out, onepace: fair run. *½* **78**
2256 **LOYAL TYCOON 13** [10]6-8-5 (80) A Nicholls 40/1: 0-002508: Hld up stands side, gd late gains. *½* **74**
2190 **JACK SULLIVAN 15** [27]3-9-2 T (100) R Hughes 50/1: 615-2449: Nvr a factor far side: t-strap. *½* **93**
2010 **MYSTIC MAN 23** [5]6-8-13 (88) N Callan 10/1: 0000130: 10th: In tch stands side, eff 2f out, sn no extra: btr expected after 1877, see 611. *nk* **80**
2421 **KINGS POINT 5** [8]3-9-1 (99) Dane O'Neill 25/1: 16-50530: 11th: Held up stands side, short of room over 2f out, some late gains: see 2421 (6f), 1040. *hd* **90**
2357 **WILL HE WISH 7** [7]8-9-3 bl (92) I Mongan 66/1: 0560000: 12th: In tch stands side, no impress over 1f out. *1* **81**
2489 **UHOOMAGOO 2** [17]6-9-5 bl (94) M Fenton 16/1: 0001100: 13th: Nvr dngrs stands side: btr 2207. *shd* **82**
2090 **HURRICANE FLOYD 19** [21]6-8-8 (83) Gary Stevens 33/1: 003-0000: 14th: Nvr a factor far side: see 1512. *2½* **66**

ASCOT FRIDAY 18.06.04 Righthand, Stiff, Galloping Track

2207 **BLUE TROJAN 14** [25]4-8-9 (84) J F Egan 50/1: 2001400: 15th: In tch far side, wknd 2f out: 'hung left'. *nk* **66**
2207 **SAWWAAH 14** [16]7-8-9 (84) P Dobbs 50/1: 0-001340: 16th: Held up stands side, hmpd over 1f out, no impress: btr 1820. *¾* **64**
1898 **MACHINIST 28** [9]4-8-5 (80) R Miles(3) 40/1: 31/040-00: 17th: Held up stands side, short of room 2f out, no impress: see 1898. *½* **59**
2256 **BANJO BAY 13** [2]6-8-3 (78) P Doe 50/1: 00-00300: 18th: Handy stands side, wknd well over 1f out. *1½* **54**
2282 **MASTER ROBBIE 10** [18]5-9-3 (92) T E Durcan 16/1: 0000160: 19th: In tch, wknd 2f out: btr 2090. *1* **66**
4860} **SIR EDWIN LANDSEER 64** [4]4-8-7 (82) R Thomas(5) 66/1: 55600-00: 20th: Handy, wknd 2f out. *5* **46**
2057 **KAREEB 21** [13]7-8-1 (76) Lisa Jones(3) 16/1: 00-60040: 21th: In tch stands side, eff when hmpd over 1f out, no impress: btr 2057, 800. *nk* **39**
1926 **ATAVUS 27** [24]7-9-4 (93) J Mackay 20/1: 0104-060: 22th: Chsd ldr far side, wknd over 1f out: see 1926. *5* **46**
2409 **H HARRISON 6** [22]4-8-8 (7ex) (83) J F McDonald(3) 50/1: 6454100: 23th: In tch far side, wknd 3f out. *1¾* **32**
1926 **SELECTIVE 27** [12]5-9-8 (97) K Fallon 15/2: 2230-400: 24th: Held up stands side, no impress when hmpd over 1f out: well bckd: see 1225. *1* **44**
1883 **NAMROUD 28** [15]5-8-10 BL (85) P Hanagan 33/1: 210-0600: 25th: In tch stands side, wknd 3f out: blnks. *1* **30**
2076 **KING HARSON 20** [14]5-8-7 vis (82) J Fanning 66/1: 331-0200: 26th: Handy stands side, wknd 2f out. *½* **26**
2090 **OBRIGADO 19** [11]4-8-7 (82) P J Smullen 16/1: 4216-020: 27th: In tch stands side, wknd 2f out. *hd* **25**
1151 **ARCTIC DESERT 66** [19]4-8-13 (88) M Hills 50/1: 4352-000: 28th: Al bhd. *1½* **28**
28 Ran Time 1m 27.41(1.41) Owned: Unscrupulous Partners & Mr P Veitch Trained: Newmarket

REDCAR SATURDAY 19.06.04 Lefthand, Flat, Galloping Track

Official Going Good (Rain throughout afternoon)

2559 1.45 Tees Components Maiden Stakes 3yo+ (D)
£3474 £1069 £535 **6f str** **Good** **Slow** Centre

2445 **HARTSHEAD 5** [7] G A Swinbank 5-9-7 (68) P Mulrennan(5) 7/2: 460-2061: Prom, went on dist, styd on strongly fnl 1f, rdn out: nicely bckd, qck reapp, jt top-weight: eff at 6f/1m on gd & fm: see 1638. **75**
2214 **COMPTON PLUME 15** [3] W H Tinning 4-9-7 (55) Dale Gibson 4/1: 26-03D32: Rear, switched & hdwy to chall ent fnl 1f, not pace of wnr cl-home: tchd 11/2: jt top-weight: see 2214. *1* **71**
2463 **MISTRESS TWISTER 4** [4] T D Barron 3-8-9 P Fessey 11/4 FAV: 03-33: Chsd ldrs, sltly outpcd halfway, rallied fnl 1f: well bckd & qck reapp: btr 2463 (7f) & a rtn to that trip will suit. *½* **64**
2182 **BRAIN WASHED 16** [10] T D Easterby 3-8-9 D Allan 50/1: 04: b f Mind Games - Bollin Dorothy (Rambo Dancer) Held up, late hdwy, nvr dngrs: only 2nd start & sltly more encouragment: poss eff at 6f on gd. *1½* **60**
2125 **FRIMLEYS MATTERRY 18** [1]4-9-7 (42) M Lawson(5) 66/1: 0-606665: Prom, onepcd fnl 1.5f. *nk* **64$**
1971 **AKIRAMENAI 26** [6]4-9-2 (58) R Winston 16/1: 0406: Led till dist, wknd. *1* **56**
2174 **MAN CRAZY 17** [9]3-8-9 (60) G Duffield 9/1: 00-06007: Chsd ldrs, rdn & btn 2f out. *6* **38**
2428 **DESIGNER CITY 6** [8]3-8-9 (50) P Bradley(5) 33/1: 660-0008: Chsd ldrs till halfway, wknd. *3* **29**
2237 **URBAN CALM 14** [2]3-8-9 (63) S Hitchcott(3) 7/2: 4229: Prom, wknd qckly 2f out: nicely bckd, reportedly lost a shoe: much btr 2237 & 1575 (soft grnd, 5f). *1½* **25**
1682 **CASEYS HOUSE 38** [5]4-9-2 R Ffrench 100/1: 000: 10th: Al outpcd, fin last. *15* **0**
10 Ran Time 1m 15.11 (6.21) Owned: Miss Sally R Haynes Trained: Richmond

2560 2.20 Totepool Handicap Stakes 3yo+ 0-90 (C) [89]
£13585 £4180 £2090 **1m2f** **Good** **Fast** Inside

2404 **INTRICATE WEB 7** [9] E J Alston 8-9-3 (78) D Allan 11/1: 6013301: Held up, switched wide & strong run 1.5f out, led ent fnl 1f, held on drvn out: suited by 9.4f/10f on firm, soft grnd & fibresand: enjoys a fast pace: v tough & in great heart despite advancing years. **86**
2404 **CRIPSEY BROOK 7** [5] Don Enrico Incisa 6-9-9 (84) Kim Tinkler 11/2: 30-66002: Trkd ldrs, went after wnr fnl 1f, kept on & not btn far: bckd from 8/1: apprec this rtn to 10f: see 1704. *¾* **90**
2404 **STRETTON 7** [11] J D Bethell 6-9-3 (78) R Ffrench 7/1: 10-06003: Held up, short of room & hit by rival's whip dist, fin well & btn under 1L: won off this mark last year & likes York: see 1833. *nk* **83**
2323+**OLDENWAY 10** [10] R A Fahey 5-9-1 (76) T Hamilton(3) 15/2: 0224214: Trkd ldrs, imprvd to lead 2.5f out, collared ent fnl 1f, no extra: clr of rem: another gd run: see 2323. *2* **77**
2483 **OSCAR PEPPER 3** [1]7-8-2 vis (63) P Fessey 9/1: 4-506345: Chsd ldrs, onepcd fnl 2f: qck reapp. *5* **56**
2162 **WAHCHI 17** [8]5-8-6 (67) Dale Gibson 100/1: 40-00006: Rear, some late prog, nvr dngrs: see 2162. *¾* **59**
2313 **ARRY DASH 10** [4]4-9-8 (83) S Hitchcott(3) 13/2: 4020037: Chsd ldrs, btn 2f out. *½* **74**
2101 **TELEMACHUS 19** [12]4-10-0 (89) Dean McKeown 16/1: 30-61008: Chsd ldrs, wknd 2f out: top-weight. *2½* **76**
2363 **SAY WHAT YOU SEE 8** [6]4-8-11 vis (72) G Duffield 6/1: 2154229: Led till over 2f out, wknd: btr 2363. *4* **52**
2323 **BROADWAY SCORE 10** [3]6-9-5 (80) P Mulrennan(5) 20/1: 0-000000: 10th: Al rear: tumbling down h'cap. *¾* **59**
2197 **TRUENO 16** [2]5-9-9 (84) R Winston 5/1 FAV: 2524-120: 11th: Trkd ldrs, rdn & btn 2f out: qck reapp: something amiss? much btr 2197 & 1890. *5* **56**
2323 **GALA SUNDAY 10** [13]4-9-2 (77) T Lucas 33/1: 00-00000: 12th: Mid-div, btn 3f out. *11* **31**
2284 **MOVIE KING 11** [7]5-8-4 p (65) G Faulkner 33/1: 50-00200: 13th: Prom, wknd halfway: btr 2135. *3* **15**
13 Ran Time 2m 06.45 (4.15) Owned: Morris Oliver Pierce Trained: Preston

2561 2.50 Tetley's Smooth Handicap Stakes 3yo+ 0-90 (C) [84]
£13943 £4290 £2145 **6f str** **Good** **Fair** Centre

2187 **CD FLYER 16** [2] B Ellison 7-9-13 (83) P Mulrennan(5) 14/1: 0-520041: Dwelt, hdwy 2f out, strong run to lead nr line: stays 7f, best at 6f: acts on firm & polytrack, likes gd & hvy, handles hvy: best coming late. **90**
2409 **BLACKHEATH 7** [6] D Nicholls 8-9-9 (79) Alex Greaves 11/2 JT FAV: 0440622: Trkd ldrs, imprvd to lead ins fnl 1f, caught nr line: fine run, deserves a change of luck: see 2409. *hd* **84**
2512 **MIDNIGHT PARKES 2** [1] E J Alston 5-8-8 (64) D Allan 14/1: 500-0403: Prom, led dist till ins fnl 1f, no extra: qck reapp: best prev on fm & fast, handled gd/soft here: well h'capped. *¾* **67**
2409 **UNDETERRED 7** [10] T D Barron 8-9-2 vis (72) P Fessey 8/1: 0-050044: Rear, styd on fnl 1f, nrst fin: knocking on the door, likes Goodwood: see 2409. *1¾* **70**

2235 **SNOW BUNTING 14** [9]6-8-3 (59) G Duffield 14/1: 0030205: Rear, prog after halfway, nrst fin: btr 2160.   1½   53
880 **SKIP OF COLOUR 92** [4]4-9-5 (75) D Nolan(3) 20/1: 0-451206: Led till dist, no extra: 3 month abs.   1¼   65
2027 **JUST ONE SMILE 23** [5]4-8-4 (60) Dale Gibson 33/1: 42-03607: Chsd ldrs, rdn & btn dist: see 1878.   1¾   45
2512 **OBE ONE 2** [11]4-8-13 (69) P Mathers(7) 13/2: 0640238: Rear, modest late gains: qck reapp.   shd   53
2409 **BLYTHE SPIRIT 7** [7]5-9-2 (72) T Hamilton(3) 16/1: 5045-509: Chsd ldrs, rdn & btn dist: see 1977.   hd   55
2074* **HICCUPS 21** [13]4-9-12 p (82) R Winston 11/2 JT FAV: 30-20310: 10th: Slowly away, hdwy when   1   62
switched dist, nvr dngrs: bckd from 7/1: again slowly away, did not pick up on today's rain-softened grnd.
1767 **INTER VISION 35** [17]4-10-0 (84) A Beech(3) 8/1: 054-0050: 11th: Nvr btr than mid-div: top-weight.   4   52
2253 **SEAFIELD TOWERS 14** [3]4-9-5 p (75) D McGaffin 20/1: 0-003000: 12th: Prom 4f, wknd: wants gd/fm.   ½   41
2524 **PADDYWACK 2** [14]7-8-8 bl (64) D Fentiman(7) 8/1: 0403530: 13th: Slowly away, al bhd: qck reapp.   2½   23
2466 **DRURY LANE 4** [16]4-8-0 bl (56) P M Quinn 16/1: 0000400: 14th: Slowly away, al rear: qck reapp.   1¼   11
2084 **TWICE UPON A TIME 21** [8]5-9-1 (71) S Hitchcott(3) 25/1: 210-4400: 15th: Chsd ldrs, btn halfway.   shd   25
2429 **SAFRANINE 6** [15]7-8-7 p (63) Ann Stokell 40/1: 0000000: 16th: b f Dolphin Street - Webbiana   ¾   15
(African Sky) Al bhd: won 3 h'caps in '03, also plcd sev times: eff at 5/6f on firm, gd/soft grnd & fibresand:
handles a sharp or gall trk: wears cheek pieces: back on a winning mark.
1 Sep'03 Redc 6fm 77-73 D: 1 Jul'03 Warw 5.5g/f 73-53 D: 1 Jul'03 Warw 5.5g/f 53-48 E: 2 May'03 Redc 5g/f 51-50 D:
1 Jun'02 Hami 5sft 56-51 E: 1 Mar'02 Sout 5af 48a-40 E:
2409 **PRIDE OF KINLOCH 7** [12]4-8-1 (57) R Ffrench 25/1: 0403000: 17th: Chsd ldrs, btn halfway.   ½   7
17 Ran   Time 1m 12.97 (4.07)   Owned: Mr Keith Middleton   Trained: Malton

---

2562   3.25 Redcar Grandstand 'ruby Anniversary' Handicap Stakes 4yo+ 35-55 (F)   [61]
£3374 £964 £482   **1m6f19y**   **Good/Soft**   **Slow**   Inside

2060 **ASTROMANCER 22** [2] M H Tompkins 4-9-2 (49) Saleem Golam(7) 100/30 FAV: 0450031: Trkd ldrs, imprvd   54
to lead 3f out till 2f out, rallied well to regain lead cl-home, drvn out: nicely bckd: deserved first win: eff at
14f, prog stays 2m: acts on fast, gd/soft & polytrack: see 2060 & 11.
2479 **IPLEDGEALLEGIANCE 3** [5] D W Chapman 8-8-2 (5oh)bl (30) D Fentiman(7) 9/1: 0550552: Held up, hdwy   1   38
to lead 2f out, drifted left ent fnl 1f, tired & hdd cl-home: lkd all over the wnr entering fnl 1f but
did not quite last home over this longer 14f trip: see 353 (12f, AW).
1680 **EAST CAPE 38** [9] Don Enrico Incisa 7-8-10 (43) Kim Tinkler 13/2: 0100063: Held up, styd on well   nk   46
under press fnl 2f, nrst fin: op 11/2, clr of rem: see 724 (AW banded).
1923 **CIRCUS MAXIMUS 28** [3] Ian Williams 7-9-8 p (55) G Faulkner 8/1: 5/5020-04: Chsd ldrs, btn 2f out.   5   51
2340* **DASH OF MAGIC 9** [8]6-8-8 (41) T Hamilton(3) 4/1: 5106315: Held up, nvr nr ldrs: btr 2340 (12f, AW).   ½   36
2298 **BALALAIKA TUNE 11** [7]5-8-2 (35) P M Quinn 10/1: 6040046: Chsd ldrs, ev ch 3f out, sn btn: op 7/1.   ½   29
4265} **LADY STRATAGEM 634** [11]5-9-0 (47) P Mulrennan(5) 33/1: 0/60000/-7: gr f Mark of Esteem - Grey   11   27
Angel (Kenmare) Al bhd on Flat reapp: jumps fit, modest form: 4th in a 03/04 sell h'cap hdle (rtd 72h, eff on 2m
on firm): modest Flat form, incl when with R Hannon in '01: now with E Tuer.
2039} **OOPS 375** [1]5-8-12 (45) D Allan 7/1: 56/0042-8: b g In The Wings - Atsuko (Mtoto) Led till over   ½   24
3f out, wknd: op 9/1: rnr-up on fnl '03 start (clmr, with T Easterby): stays 2m, handles firm & fast grnd.
2 Jun'03 Redc 16.0fm 46-(56) F:
1449 **COPPLESTONE 51** [6]8-8-2 (2oh)p (33) Rory Moore(7) 12/1: 6565-069: b g Second Set - Queen of The   12   0
Brush (Averof) Mid-div, btn 4f out: jumps fit, dual sell h'cap wnr in 03/04 (rtd 99h, eff at 2m on gd & hvy,
handles fast): '03 h'cap rnr-up (reapp): '02 sell h'cap wnr: eff at 12f/2m on gd, firm & fibresand, prob any trk:
eff with/without visor or cheek pieces, tried t-strap.
2 Jun'03 Muss 14fm 40-39 F: 2 Jul'02 Redc 16g/f 54-56 E: 1 May'02 Newc 12.4g/f 59-54 G:
1128 **KINGS MOUNTAIN 68** [12]4-9-3 (50) G Duffield 20/1: 0/0600-00: 10th: Cl-up, btn sn after halfway.   ½   12
10 Ran   Time 3m 10.02 (12.22)   Owned: Mystic Meg Limited   Trained: Newmarket

---

2563   4.00 Best Dressed Elvis Competition Selling Stakes 2yo (G)
£2926 £836 £418   **7f str**   **Good/Soft**   **V Slow**   Inside

2461* **PRINCELY VALE 4** [6] W G M Turner 2-9-3 p C Haddon(7) 9/4 FAV: 0411: Prom, imprvd to lead dist,   65
held on well despite wandering fnl 1f, all out: well bckd, qck reapp, no bid, top- weight: eff at 6/7f on fm &
gd/soft: handles a gall or easy trk: suited by sell grade & cheek pieces, in fine form: see 2461.
2294 **RIVERWELD 11** [5] G M Moore 2-8-11   D Fentiman(7) 14/1: 642: Trkd ldrs, ev ch 2f out, just btn in   shd   58
a v tight fin: eff at 7f on gd/soft: see 1779.
2358 **DISHDASHA 8** [7] T D Easterby 2-8-11   D Allan 4/1: 003: b g Desert Prince - Counterplot (Last   1¾   54
Tycoon) Chsd ldrs, kept on under press fnl 1f: gambled from 16/1, clmd by- C Dore for 8,000: Mar foal,
half-brother to a mid-dist wnr abroad: dam a 10f wnr abroad, sire a top-class miler: eff over a gall 7f on gd grnd.
1869 **MOUNT EPHRAM 30** [2] R F Fisher 2-8-11   P Bradley(5) 7/2: 4564: Held up, hdwy when hung left dist,   shd   53
not pace to chall: op 5/2: btr 1677.
2294* **MAUREENS LOUGH 11** [4]2-8-12   P Fessey 11/4: 3615: Led till dist, wknd: op 2/1: see 2294 (fm).   4   46
1869 **FRANSISCAN 30** [8]2-8-11 VIS G Faulkner 25/1: 006: Chsd ldrs, wknd 2f out: tried a visor: see 1869.   2   41
2424 **LADY INDIANA 6** [1]2-8-7 (1ow) R Winston 28/1: 007: b f King's Theatre - Najeyba (Indian Ridge)   16   5
Slowly away, al bhd: qck reapp: £6,000 Mar first foal: dam a 6f wnr, sire a top-class mid-dist performer.
     KINFAYRE BOY [3]2-8-11   P Mathers(7) 50/1: 8: b g Grey Eagle - Amber Gambler (Nijin) Al bhd,   22   0
t.o. in last on debut: cheaply bght Apr foal: with K W Hogg.
8 Ran   Time 1m 30.48 (8.68)   Owned: Vale Racing   Trained: Sherborne

---

2564   4.35 Romfords Caterers Classified Stakes 3yo+ 0-70 (E)
£3377 £1039 £520   **7f str**   **Good/Soft**   **Slow**   Centre

1775 **MR VELOCITY 35** [1] A C Stewart 4-9-3 (70) R Ffrench 1/1 FAV: 3330-321: Trkd ldrs, prog to lead   76
dist, styd on strongly fnl 1f, rdn out: well bckd: deserved first win: eff at 7f/1m on firm, gd/soft & polytrack:
handles a sharp or stiff/gall trk: see 1775 & 1352.
2350 **BOUNDLESS PROSPECT 9** [2] J W Hills 5-9-3 (70) G Duffield 4/1: 00-00002: Slowly away, switched &   1¼   73
hdwy 2f out, styd on fnl 1f, nrst fin: op 3/1: back to form: see 2350.
2235 **EFIDIUM 14** [3] N Bycroft 6-9-3 (69) G Faulkner 4/1: 0423153: Nvr far away, led briefly 2f out, onepace.   shd   73
2040 **REIDIES CHOICE 22** [4] J G Given 3-8-12 (74) P Mulrennan(5) 7/1: 000-0204: Trkd ldrs, onepcd fnl 1f.   nk   76
1820 **IBERUS 32** [8]6-9-5 (72) S Hitchcott(3) 14/1: 505-0005: Prom, wknd dist: btr 1820.   3½   67
2464 **LINDENS LADY 4** [5]4-9-0 (63) T Hamilton(3) 20/1: 05-06056: Led till 2f out, wknd: qck reapp.   8   46

REDCAR **SATURDAY 19.06.04 Lefthand, Flat, Galloping Track**

6 Ran Time 1m 27.46 (5.66) Owned: Mr A M Pickering Trained: Newmarket

2565 **5.10 Bbc Radio Cleveland Handicap Stakes 3yo 0-75 (E)** **[78]**
£3533 £1087 £544 **1m1f** **Good/Soft** **Slow** Inside

2423 **CHARLIE TANGO 6** [6] M R Channon 3-8-12 (62) S Hitchcott(3) 5/1: 0003041: Held up, hdwy wide 2f out, led dist, held on drvn out despite drifting left: first success: eff at 9/10f on fast, gd/soft & polytrack. **69**
2299* **RICHTEE 11** [7] R A Fahey 3-8-11 (61) T Hamilton(3) 2/1 FAV: 060-12: Trkd ldrs, imprvd to lead 3f out till collared dist, rallied fnl 1f & not btn far: hvly bckd from 7/2: acts on firm & gd/soft: in fine form. *nk* **67**
1978 **GHANTOOT 25** [1] L M Cumani 3-8-12 VIS (62) R Winston 9/1: 00003: ch c Inchinor - Shall We Run (Hotfoot) Chsd ldrs, keeping on well when sltly short of room cl-home: clr of rem: imprvd form on h'cap bow & in first time visor: eff at 9f on gd/soft, 10f will suit: poss a shade unlucky, could find similar. *hd* **67**
2055 **GASPARINI 22** [3] T D Easterby 3-8-9 (59) D Allan 20/1: 2-0004: ch c Docksider - Tarjou (Marju) Chsd ldrs, ev ch halfway till onepcd fnl 1.5f: rnr-up on sole juv start (mdn): apprec this step up to 9f, prob handles gd & soft grnd: with T Easterby. 2 May'03 Ripo 6sft 73- D: *5* **54**
1427 **RIGONZA 52** [2]3-9-6 (70) G Faulkner 20/1: 4346-005: Slowly away, eff 2f out, sn no impress. *½* **64**
2231 **FOOLISH GROOM 15** [9]3-9-7 P (71) G Duffield 7/1: 3456: Prom, ev ch 2f out, sn wknd: cheekpieces. *5* **55**
2203 **PERFECT BALANCE 15** [10]3-8-7 (57) Kim Tinkler 10/1: 0165407: Nvr nr ldrs. *1¾* **38**
1976 **ALWAYS FLYING 25** [5]3-9-5 (69) R Ffrench 3/1: 5-152668: Led till 3f out, wknd: btr 923 (10f). *1¾* **46**
2277 **ROYAL DISTANT 12** [11]3-9-6 (70) Dale Gibson 18/1: 4-600009: Al towards rear. *1½* **44**
2338 **BOOK MATCHED 9** [4]3-9-1 (65) D McGaffin 16/1: 3-314060: 10th: Mid-div, btn 3f out. *nk* **38**
4561} **VENERDI TREDICI 261** [13]3-8-5 (55) S Yourston(7) 33/1: 0030-0: 11th: b f Desert Style - Stifen (Burslem) Al bhd, fin last on reapp: plcd on 1 of 4 '03 starts (4 rnr mdn): eff at 6f on firm. *7* **14**
11 Ran Time 1m 55.62(6.82) Owned: Mr P Trant Trained: West Ilsley

AYR **SATURDAY 19.06.04 Lefthand, Galloping Track**

Official Going Good (Good/Soft Places) ALL TIMES SLOW

2566 **1.50 Stanleybet Com Handicap Stakes 3yo 0-85 (D)** **[92]**
£6799 £2092 £1046 **5f str** **Good/Soft** **Slow** Stands Side

2400 **DIVINE SPIRIT 7** [2] M Dods 3-9-1 (79) A Culhane 10/1: 1-000361: Swtchd stands rail & bhd early, hdwy from halfway & swtchd/qcknd to lead well ins last, cosily: eyecatching last twice: stays 6f, best at 5f on firm & gd/soft grnd, with/without chkpcs: on a fair mark, qk follow-up likely: see 2121. **89+**
2295 **SWEET CANDO 11** [11] Miss L A Perratt 3-7-12 (3oh)P (59) N Mackay(3) 16/1: 0334-602: Trkd ldr stands rail, led over 1f out till well ins last, not pace of wnr: chkpcs, gd run: see 112. *½* **68**
2387* **BARON RHODES 7** [4] J S Wainwright 3-9-0 (78) T Eaves(3) 5/1 JT FAV: 2-222313: Pshd along chasing ldrs, styd on for press, not pace of front pair: most consistent: see 2387. *1¼* **80**
2400 **LUALUA 7** [6] T D Barron 3-8-13 (77) P Makin(5) 6/1: 05-42304: Handy, no extra from dist: btr 1766. *2½* **71**
2227* **CHAMPAGNE CRACKER 15** [10]3-8-2 (66) D Kinsella 7/1: 622-0315: Led/dsptd lead till over 1f out, no extra when short of room ins last: stablemate of rnr up: see 2227. *2* **54**
1360 **FOUR AMIGOS 56** [7]3-9-7 (85) S Chin 5/1 JT FAV: 102-5106: Chsd ldrs till over 1f out: abs: btr 1229. *1½* **68**
2029 **PETERS CHOICE 23** [8]3-8-2 (66) J Bramhill 25/1: 11-00507: Led/dsptd lead till over 1f out, fdd. *hd* **48**
2380* **BLUE POWER 8** [5]3-7-12 (4oh) (58) B Swarbrick(5) 10/1: 0035318: Held up in tch, btn dist: btr 2380 (AW). *shd* **44**
2493 **ONLY IF I LAUGH 3** [9]3-7-13 (63) Stacey Renwick(7) 16/1: 4-340239: Trkd ldrs, short of room 2f out & no impress dist: qck reapp, improve for stronger handling: see 1902, 1268. *shd* **44**
2387 **BAYLAW STAR 7** [12]3-8-7 P (71) J Edmunds 16/1: 3-630400: 10th: Cl up, btn over 1f out, chkpcs. *1¼* **48**
2227 **SIR ERNEST 15** [1]3-8-12 (76) Darren Williams 16/1: 00-06020: 11th: Reared start & went badly left, no chance after: see 2227. *6* **38**
2380 **SAHARA SILK 8** [3]3-7-12 vis (62) Hayley Turner(5) 16/1: 3412030: 12th: Sn strugg: btr 2380, 1338 (AW). *18* **0**
12 Ran Time 1m 01.62 (2.42) Owned: Mr A Mallen Trained: Darlington

2567 **2.25 Freephone Stanleybet Handicap Stakes 3yo+ 0-95 (C)** **[93]**
£9646 £2968 £1484 **1m5f13y** **Good/Soft** **Slow** Inside

2233* **TRANCE 14** [3] T D Barron 4-9-3 (82) P Makin(5) 6/1: 001-0411: Mid-div, rdn & hdwy to lead dist, rdn out: bckd, op 7/1: imprvd for 12/13f last twice: acts on fast, gd/sft & fibresand, loves a gall trk: unexposed at mid-dists & winning run could continue: see 2233. **88**
2444* **SAHEM 5** [9] D Eddy 7-9-0 (6ex) (79) D Kinsella 9/2: 0-504012: Led & dictated pace early, rdn & hdd dist, kept on: qck reapp under a pen: progressive, see 2444. *1¼* **82**
4330*]**MONOLITH 985** [5] L Lungo 6-9-3 (82) W Dowling 9/1: 4361//-3: b g Bigstone - Ancara (Dancing Brave) Trkd ldrs, onepace & held from dist: recent jmps wnr (duel intermediate hdle wnr, 2m4f/3m, rtd 139h+, firm & gd/sft): mdn scorer for Mrs A Perrett in '01: winning form at 10f, stays 13f, acts on good & hvy ground: gd Flat return, can be placed to find similar. 1 Oct'01 Wind 10hvy 83- D: *2½* **81**
2318 **COLORADO FALLS 10** [1] P Monteith 6-8-13 (78) L Enstone(3) 8/1: 5306/-154: Mid-div, onepace. *2½* **73**
2009 **GEORGE STUBBS 24** [4]6-7-12 (63) N Mackay(3) 7/1: 0313555: Trk ldr, no extra over 1f out: btr 1361. *¾* **57**
1721 **TAWNY WAY 37** [2]4-9-7 (86) A Culhane 4/1 FAV: 220-5126: Chsd ldrs, no impress fnl 1f: see 1721, 1381. *3½* **75**
1068 **PRINCE HOLING 74** [8]4-9-10 (89) T Eaves(3) 25/1: 2/4122-57: Held up, btn 2f out: 8 wk jmps abs (mod form, Miss V Williams): see 1068. *16* **57**
1814 **GRAHAM ISLAND 32** [6]3-8-5 (85) J Carroll 9/2: 05-1668: Mid-div wide, hdwy halfway, btn 2f out. *3½* **48**
1931*]**LORD DUNDEE 743** [7]6-9-6 (85) Darren Williams 33/1: 3/1/-9: ch c Polish Precedent - Easy To Copy (Affirmed) Rear, left bhd fnl 3f: long abs: missed '03, sole start mdn wnr in '02 for H Cecil: winning form at 14f on soft ground, handles fast: likes a gall trk & has run well fresh. 1 Jun'02 Hayd 14sft 87- D: *12* **34**
9 Ran Time 2m 58.93 (14.33) Owned: Mr Nigel Shields Trained: Thirsk

2568	**2.55 Stanleybet Handicap Stakes 3yo+ 0-90 (C)**					**[87]**
	£10277 £3162 £1581	**7f50y rnd**	**Good/Soft**	**Slow**	Inside	

2235 **BALAKIREF 14** [7] M Dods 5-8-5 (64) Hayley Turner(5) 16/1: 10222U1: Held up, rdn & hdwy wide 2f   **72**
out, led dist, drvn out: eff at 6/7f on fast & fbsnd, likes gd & hvy grnd: see 1052.
2389 **DIGITAL 7** [10] M R Channon 7-9-10 (83) A Culhane 11/2: 0360052: Held up, hdwy over 2f out & rdn   nk   **90**
to chall dist, drvn & al just held: clr rem: on a fair mark & likes easy grnd: see 945.
2425 **SARRAAF 6** [13] J S Goldie 8-8-11 (70) V Halliday 12/1: 2505333: Mid-div, onepace fnl 2f: qk reapp.   3½   **70**
2543 **SAMUEL CHARLES 1** [2] W M Brisbourne 6-8-13 (72) P Makin(5) 7/1: 23122334: Handy & led over 3f out   ½   **71**
till over 1f out, fdd: finished 3rd here yesterday: see 2543.
1393 **FAIR SHAKE 54** [12]4-8-7 p (66) D Kinsella 10/1: 600-0035: Mid-div, eff 2f out, no impress: abs.   2   **61**
2086 **BALLYHURRY 21** [4]7-8-12 (71) N Mackay(3) 4/1: 154-0646: Mid-div, efft over 2f out, btn dist: btr 2086.   1¾   **63**
2317 **WESSEX 10** [11]4-9-3 (76) J Carroll 33/1: 010-0607: Held up, efft 3f out, no impress: btr 1970.   ¾   **67**
1354 **TIDY 56** [5]4-9-7 (80) Darren Williams 20/1: 60-015U8: Mid-div, no hdwy over 2f out, abs: btr 1035 (hvy).   3½   **64**
2379 **EL PALMAR 8** [9]3-8-4 (72) J Bramhill 33/1: 2-330129: Sn handy wide, btn over 2f out: see 2379, 2215.   1¾   **53**
2116 **THE BONUS KING 19** [6]4-9-7 (80) S Chin 7/1: 0000240: 10th: Mid-div, rdn & no impress fnl 2f: btr 2027.   3   **55**
2542 **DESERT ARC 1** [3]6-8-6 (65) B Swarbrick(5) 11/1: 600-01160: 11th: Always bhd, unplcd yesterday.   ½   **39**
1909* **FLUR NA H ALBA 28** [1]5-9-10 p (83) T Eaves(3) 8/1: 62000-10: 12th: Led/dsptd lead till over 3f   4   **49**
out, sn wknd: much btr 1909 (C/D, fm).
2122 **BANDOS 18** [8]4-9-1 t (74) L Enstone(3) 20/1: 10220-30: 13th: Slow away & al bhd: btr 2122 (gd/fm).   7   **28**
13 Ran   Time 1m 34.61 (7.81)   Owned: Septimus Racing Group   Trained: Darlington

2569	**3.30 Stanleybet Com Maiden Auction Stakes 2yo (E)**					
	£4105 £1263 £632	**6f str**	**Good/Soft**	**Slow**	Stands Side	

LAMH EILE 0 [12] T D Barron 2-8-2 N Mackay(3) 12/1: 1: b f Lend A Hand - Mothers Footprints   **80+**
(Maelstrom Lake) Made all, hung left but rdn & pulled clr from over 1f out, easily: op 10/1: Mar foal: eff over a
gall 6f, 7f looks sure to suit: acts on gd/soft & a gall trk: goes well fresh & can force the pace: fine start, looks
sure to win more races.
2158 **HYMN OF VICTORY 17** [10] T J Etherington 2-8-7 T Eaves(3) 12/1: 052: b c Bluebird - Vaga Follia   7   **67**
(Alzao) Handy, kept on fnl 2f but no chance with wnr: cheaply bought Mar foal, dam a multple wnr btwn 7f/12f: prob
handles gd/soft: likely to get further than this trip, should prove suited to nurseries.
2360 **LLAMADAS 8** [5] M Dods 2-8-13 L Enstone(3) 8/1: 303: Mid-div, styd on onepace fnl 2f.   1¾   **68**
UNION JACK JACKSON 0 [11] J G Given 2-8-13 J Bramhill 11/1: 4: b c Daggers Drawn - Beechwood   1½   **64**
Quest (River Falls) Handy, shkn up & onepace fnl 2f: op 20/1: Jan foal, 12,000gns purchase: half brother to a 5f/1m
plcd juv: dam a dual 5f juv wnr.
1868 **REGAL LUSTRE 30** [8]2-8-5 P Makin(5) 33/1: 35: Trkd ldrs, no impress 2f: see 1868.   hd   **55**
1911 **FLY TO DUBAI 28** [4]2-8-10 J Carroll 7/2 JT FAV: 06: Mid-div, no impress over 2f out, op 4/1.   shd   **60**
IM SO LUCKY 0 [7]2-8-10 S Chin 9/2: 7: Chsd ldrs, sn rdn & nvr on terms: op 7/2.   1¼   **56**
2275 **WHATATODO 12** [1]2-8-2 Hayley Turner(5) 7/2 JT FAV: 038: Mid-div, no impress fnl 2f: btr 2275.   ½   **46**
1911 **ZENDARO 28** [3]2-8-10 B Swarbrick(5) 16/1: 469: Sn bhd, nvr factor, needs sells.   shd   **54**
ORPHAN 0 [9]2-8-7 Darren Williams 20/1: 0: 10th: Trkd ldr trav well, edged left & wknd qckly 2f out.   5   **38**
1905* **WILLINGBORN DANCER 26** [6]2-8-10 A Culhane 25/1: 00: 11th: Mid-div, btn 3f out, gelded.   10   **15**
11 Ran   Time 1m 15.13 (5.83)   Owned: Oghill House Stud   Trained: Thirsk

2570	**4.05 Freephone Stanleybet European Breeders Fund Maiden Stakes 2yo (D)**					
	£4183 £1287 £644	**7f50y rnd**	**Good/Soft**	**V Slow**	Inside	

BUDDY BROWN 0 [4] J Howard Johnson 2-9-0 D Kinsella 4/1: 1: b c Lujain - Rose Bay (Shareef   **76**
Dancer) Keen, held up in tch, drvn & styd on to lead nr line: 13,000gns Mar foal: dam a multiple wnr abroad, sire a
top class juv sprinter: eff at 7f on gd/soft ground & a gall trk, goes well fresh: can progress.
1893 **BALLYCROY GIRL 29** [8] A Bailey 2-8-9 N Mackay(3) 16/1: 62: ch f Pennekamp - Hulm (Mujtahid)   hd   **70**
Handy & led 2f out till well in last, just held: half sister to 6/7f multiple wnr Blonde En Blonde: dam a 6/7f plcd
juv: imprvd over longer 7f trip on gd/soft.
DANCERS SERENADE 0 [9] T P Tate 2-9-0 Darren Williams 25/1: 3: b c Almutawakel - Dance Serenade   1¼   **72**
(Marju) Dwelt, in tch, hdwy chall over 2f out, not pace of front pair from dist: 27,000E Mar foal: dam stayed
12f: learn from this & stay further.
2263 **MAKEPEACE 12** [5] M R Channon 2-9-0 A Culhane 6/1: 04: Prom, no impress fnl 2f, lngr trip.   1¾   **69**
2297 **SPEAGLE 11** [6]2-9-0 J Carroll 25/1: 05: Keen & led after 2f till 2f out, no extra, lngr trip.   1½   **66**
HAWKS TOR 0 [2]2-9-0 S Chin 11/10 FAV: 6: Led 2f, lost plce halfway & no impress after: bckd.   6   **56**
SPANISH LAW 0 [3]2-9-0 L Enstone(3) 25/1: 7: Chsd ldrs, no impress fnl 3f.   3   **51**
7 Ran   Time 1m 38.41 (11.6)   Owned: Andrea & Graham Wylie   Trained: Crook

2571	**4.40 Stanleybet Com Summer Handicap Stakes 3yo+ 0-80 (D)**					**[76]**
	£5486 £1688 £844	**1m1f20y rnd**	**Good**	**Slow**	Inside	

2030 **STING LIKE A BEE 23** [10] J S Goldie 5-8-0 (48) N Mackay(3) 7/2 FAV: 0244661: Rear, hdwy wide fnl   **57**
3f & led dist, rdn to assert: eff btwn 1m/11f on firm, hvy & fbsnd, any trk: likes to come late: see 746 & 464.
2504 **LUCKY LARGO 2** [6] Miss L A Perratt 4-8-5 bl (53) D Kinsella 16/1: 0500402: Handy wide & led 3f   1   **59**
out till dist, kept on for press: clr rem, qck reapp: mdn: see 1160 (sell).
2242 **HARRY POTTER 14** [2] K R Burke 5-9-7 bl (60) Darren Williams 7/1: 3010603: Handy & ch over 2f out,   6   **64**
sn no impress on front pair: btr 1214.
2392 **PHAROAHS GOLD 7** [5] D Shaw 6-8-5 (53) A Culhane 8/1: 3010004: Held up, some prog, nvr threat.   1½   **45**
2324 **EXTINGUISHER 10** [8]5-8-11 VIS (59) S Chin 14/1: 00-00005: Trkd ldrs, btn 2f out: vis: btr 1977.   5   **42**
2087 **MILLAGROS 21** [4]4-9-13 (75) T Eaves(3) 4/1: 410-0446: Mid-div, btn 2f out: btr 1895.   1   **56**
2317 **NEMO FUGAT 10** [1]5-8-11 (59) J Carroll 9/2: 00-00567: Held up, no prog fnl 2f: btr 2317 (fast).   1   **38**
1884 **LUXOR 29** [7]7-7-12 (6oh) (40) B Swarbrick(5) 20/1: 60000-08: Led 6f, sn btn: see 1884.   9   **10**
2120 **BUSCADOR 18** [9]5-8-2 (50) J Bramhill 12/1: 61-00009: Cl up, btn 3f out: btr 157 (AW).   30   **0**

AYR   SATURDAY 19.06.04   Lefthand, Galloping Track

1660 **PHARAOH HATSHEPSUT** 40 [3]6-7-12 (11oh) (35) Hayley Turner(5) 100/1: 00/-00000: 10th: b f Definite   4   0
Article - Maid of Mourne (Fairy King) V slow away, always t.o: abs: missed '03: unplcd '02 (rtd 38, h'cap, R
Fahey): eff at 6f, prob stays 7f: acts on gd/sft & hvy grnd, gall trk: 1 May'01 Thir 6g/s 67- E:
10 Ran   Time 2m 01.36(No Std Time)   Owned: Mrs C Brown   Trained: Glasgow

---

WARWICK   SATURDAY 19.06.04   Lefthand, Sharp, Turning Track

Official Going Good/Firm

2572   6.45 Peugeot Amateur Riders' Handicap Stakes 3yo+ 35-55 (F)   [34]
£3189 £911 £456   **1m22y rnd**   **Firm 10**   **-23 Slow**   Inside

1755 **NIGHT MARKET** 35 [2] N Wilson 6-10-13 (47) Mrs N Wilson(5) 12/1: 00600-01: Mid div, prog trav well   54
to lead 1f out, rdn out: recent jumps unplcd (rtd 67h): eff at 7f/10f on firm, fast grnd & fibresand: on fair mark.
2157 **FIRST MAITE** 17 [14] S R Bowring 11-11-2 (50) Mrs M Morris 11/1: 2-666432: Cl up, rcd wide   1½   53
turning in, kept on fnl 1f, not pace wnr: another gd eff & is on winning mark: see 2157 & btr 255.
2440 **BOJANGLES** 5 [5] R Brotherton 5-11-0 (48) Mr L Newnes(3) 13/2: 0-001303: Held up, prog 3f out,   shd   50
styd on fnl 1f, not btn far in 3rd: qck reapp: acts on firm & soft, poss hvy: see 1535.
2324 **WELL MEET AGAIN** 10 [13] M W Easterby 4-11-5 (53) Miss S Brotherton 10/1: 1065-304: Bhd, hdwy   shd   54
halfway, chsd ldr ins fnl 1f, no extra cl home: not disgraced: see 1954.
2440 **LONDONER** 5 [1]6-11-12 (60) Mr D Hutchison(5) 9/2 FAV: 0322105: Cl up, led bef 1f out, sn hdd & no   2½   56
extra: qck reapp: 5lbs higher than recent win in 2334 (7f).
2226 **PENSION FUND** 15 [12]10-11-1 (49) Miss J Coward(7) 16/1: 0000-556: Handy, outpcd 3f out, rallied late.   1   43
2369 **MOBO BACO** 8 [10]7-11-4 (52) Mr J J Best(3) 9/1: 0-440007: Nvr nrr than mid div: see 1402.   nk   45
1984 **CARGO** 25 [7]5-11-0 t p (48) Mr G Gallagher(5) 12/1: 4202328: Led, hdd bef 1f out, wknd: btr 1984 (7f).   nk   40
2397 **SHIRLEY OAKS** 7 [3]6-11-3 (51) Miss G D Gracey Davison(5) 9/1: 3163129: Cl up over 6f, sn wknd.   1½   40
2440 **SHAMWARI FIRE** 5 [9]4-11-2 (50) Mr M Seston(5) 14/1: 6001600: 10th: In tch 6f, sn wknd: qck reapp.   2½   34
2135 **LUCKY ARCHER** 18 [6]11-11-2 (50) Mrs S Bosley 16/1: 26000-00: 11th: Chsd ldrs 6f, sn fdd: see 2135.   1¼   31
1291 **OUR IMPERIAL BAY** 59 [4]5-11-3 p (51) Mr D Weekes(5) 14/1: 6-001030: 12th: Al bhd.   2   28
2220* **GRAN CLICQUOT** 15 [16]9-11-0 (48) Mr J Pemberton(5) 10/1: 0-002010: 13th: Mid div 5f, wknd: btr 2220. 1½   22
2032 Dark Shah 23 [11]4-11-2 t p(50) Mr B Evans(7) 25/1:0   4731} Didoe 249 [15]5-11-1 (49) Mrs Marie King(5) 33/1:0
1750 The Gambler 35 [17]4-11-3 p(51) Mr P Owens(5) 16/1:0
1625 Grumpyintmorning 42 [8]5-11-5 (53) Mrs C Thompson(5) 25/1:P
17 Ran   Time 1m 39.45 (2.65)   Owned: Mr J Watson   Trained: York

2573   7.15 Lee Beesley Maiden Auction Stakes 2yo (E)
£3656 £1125 £563   **5f rnd**   **Firm 10**   **-30 Slow**   Inside

1739 **THE CROOKED RING** 36 [4] P D Evans 2-8-7 VIS K Fallon 8/11 FAV: 52321: Mid div, prog ins fnl 2f,   75
led cl home, rdn out: eff at 5f/6f on firm & gd grnd: apprec visor: btr 1739 & 1571.
2415 **FORZEEN** 7 [6] J A Osborne 2-8-10 G Gibbons 6/1: 342: Cl up, led ins fnl 1f, hdd cl home: qck   nk   76
reapp: lost little in defeat & step up to 6f will suit: see 2415 & 1752.
1900 **AGILETE** 29 [7] L G Cottrell 2-8-13 S Drowne 8/1: 033: Handy 3f, sn outpcd, rallied ins fnl   nk   76
1f, just denied: eff at 5f, crying out for return to further: acts on firm grnd: see 1900.
1752 **COLEORTON DANCER** 35 [5] K A Ryan 2-8-7 N Callan 6/1: 0444: Led, hdd under press ins fnl 1f, no   1   69
extra: acts on firm & gd grnd: see 1550.
1826 **DOVE COTTAGE** 32 [3]2-8-10 I Mongan 8/1: 65: Keen bhd, nvr nrr than mid div: see 1826 (debut).   3½   62
      PAULINES PRINCE 0 [8]2-8-7 D Sweeney 33/1: 6: b c Polar Prince - Etma Rose (Fairy King) Al in   2½   52
rear: debut: Mar foal, cost 4,000 gns: dam unplcd: sire stayed around 10f in decent company: with R Hollinshead.
2257 **IVORY WOLF** 13 [2]2-8-7 R Miles(3) 33/1: 07: ch g Wolfhound - Ashkernazy (Salt Dome) Sn bhd, nvr   3   43
a factor: Mar foal, half-brother wnr at 5/6f: dam 5f wnr: sire top class performer at sprint dists: been gelded.
7 Ran   Time 59.32 (2.02)   Owned: Mr J R Salter   Trained: Abergavenny

2574   7.45 Listed Eternal Stakes Fillies 3yo (A)
£17400 £6600 £3300   **7f26y rnd**   **Firm 10**   **+21 Fast**   Inside

2136* **LUCKY SPIN** 18 [2] R Hannon 3-8-11 (97) K Fallon 2/1 FAV: 2111: Cl up, led dist, pushed out, val   107+
5L+: eff at 7f, 1m shld suit: acts on firm & gd/sft: v progressive & lightly rcd, broke course record: win in
fills Gr class: see 2136 & 1617.
1169 **LUCKY PIPIT** 66 [9] B W Hills 3-9-2 (102) M Hills 8/1: 01103-52: Led, hdd dist, no ch with easy   3   103
wnr: 9 wk abs: acts on firm & gd grnd: career best eff here, can return to winning ways: see 1169.
2211 **KUNDA** 15 [1] R Hannon 3-8-11 (96) R Hughes 7/1: 3152-623: Bhd, prog 2f out, nrst fin: 1¼   96
stablemate of wnr: creditable effort back in trip: just btr 2211.
1169 **SNOW GOOSE** 66 [8] J L Dunlop 3-8-11 (103) T Quinn 5/1: 41112-04: b f Polar Falcon - Bronzewing   ½   95
(Beldale Flutter) Mid div, prog 3f out, no impress fnl 1f: 9 wk abs: progressive in '03, winning 3 of 5 starts
(auct mdn, nov & h'cap, also Gr 2 rnr up): eff at 6f/7f, shld be suited by 1m: acts on firm & gd grnd, gall trk &
goes well fresh: more encouraging eff after fin lame last time out.
2 Oct'03 Newm 7g/f 104-(95) A: 1 Oct'03 Newm 7fm 97-85 B: 1 Aug'03 Redc 7g/f 87-(88) E: 1 Jul'03 Leic 6.0gd 84- E:
2190 **CATSTAR** 16 [3]3-8-11 (107) L Dettori 5/2: 12-155: In tch, prog halfway, onepcd fnl 1f: again   nk   94
disappointing: see 2190 & btr 599 (dirt).
4773} **DARK EMPRESS** 246 [5]3-8-11 BL (90) F Lynch 66/1: 155305-6: br f Second Empire - Good Reference   ½   93$
(Reference Point) Rear, nvr nrr than mid div: reapp: nov auct wnr in '03: eff at 6f/7f, tried 1m: acts on fast
grnd: eff on a sharp/undul trk, tried cheek pieces, blnks here: with R M Beckett.
1 Jul'03 Warw 7.1g/f 76- E: 2 Jun'03 Good 6g/f 75- E:
1933 **VALJARV** 28 [10]3-8-11 (93) J Fanning 16/1: 31-00007: Nvr nrr than mid div.   1   91
      MAPLE SYRPLE 332 [7]3-8-11 T K McEvoy 20/1: 112-8: b f American Chance - Sweet And Lowdown   1¼   89
(Stalwart) Cl up 5f, sn wknd: reapp & Brit bow: won 2 of only 3 '03 US starts (rnr up in Grade 2 fnl start): eff
at 5f/6f on dirt: t-strap fitted here: with Saeed Bin Suroor.

WARWICK   SATURDAY 19.06.04   Lefthand, Sharp, Turning Track

2259* **SWEET REPLY** 13 [6]3-8-11 (75) N Callan 66/1: 104-0519: Mid div 4f, sn no extra: see 2259.	1	**87$**
1400 **WITHORWITHOUTYOU** 53 [11]3-8-11 (80) G Gibbons 66/1: 054-6500: 10th: Handy 5f, wknd: 8 wk abs.	3	**81**
2042 **LASKA** 22 [4]3-8-11 D Corby 100/1: 440: 11th: Bhd, nvr a factor.	9	**64**

11 Ran   Time 1m 21.26 (u 0.80)   Owned: Mr George C Scudder   Trained: Marlborough

---

2575   8.20 Evening Telegraph Maiden Stakes 3yo+   (D)
£3835 £1180 £590   **7f26y rnd**   **Firm 10**   **+08 Fast**   Inside

2174 **KALI** 17 [1] R Charlton 3-8-9 (76) D Sweeney 8/11 FAV: 2-3321: In tch, led despite hanging left dist, rdn out: eff at 7f, will apprec return to 1m: acts on firm, gd grnd & polytrack: gd confidence boost.		**74**
2148 **RIVER NUREY** 17 [6] B W Hills 3-9-0 (72) M Hills 7/2: 60052-32: Chsd ldrs 3f, sn outpcd, rallied ins fnl 1f, al held by wnr: clr rem: gd run & can rate higher when stepped up to 1m: see 2148.	1½	**75**
2148 **KABEER** 17 [5] P S McEntee 6-9-9 P McCabe 10/1: 43: Led till dist, sn no extra: just btr 2148.	4	**67**
1377 **JARVO** 54 [8] N P Littmoden 3-9-0 T (66) J Fanning 16/1: 2230-254: Handy wide, no extra fnl 2f.	1	**65**
2072 **KARMA CHAMELIAN** 21 [4]3-8-9 T Quinn 33/1: 0-05: b f Diesis - Wild Rumour (Sadler's Wells) Chsd ldr 5f, sn fdd: unplcd sole '03 start (mdn, rtd 36): with J W Hills.	7	**47**
1544 **TOP PLACE** 46 [7]3-8-9 (35) R Miles(3) 100/1: 0005506: Prom, wknd bef 1f out: 7 wk abs & new stable.	5	**37$**
2092 **EIJAAZ** 20 [3]3-9-0 R Hills 11/2: 07: b c Green Desert - Kismah (Machiavellian) Played up start, al rear: brother wnr at 7f/1m: dam 1m wnr both starts: with A C Stewart.	3	**36**
2378 **HERIOT** 8 [2]3-9-0 VIS Dane O'Neill 66/1: 008: Al in rear: 1st time visor.	6	**25**

8 Ran   Time 1m 22.55 (0.15)   Owned: Miss M D Gordon-Watson   Trained: Beckhampton

---

2576   8.50 West Midlands Racing Club Handicap Stakes 3yo 0-70 (E)   **[77]**
£4290 £1320 £660   **1m2f188y**   **Firm 10**   **-06 Slow**   Inside

2452 **GOBLIN** 5 [1] D E Cantillon 3-9-7 (70) K Fallon 8/11 FAV: 4151351: Rear, prog after 5f, styd on to lead dist, rdn out: eff at 10f, poss stays 12f: acts on firm, gd & handles fibresand: gd performance under top-weight: see 2452 & 2088.		**77**
2014 **REGAL PERFORMER** 24 [6] S Kirk 3-8-8 (57) R Hughes 7/2: 00-0022: Bhd, prog 3f out, styd on to chase wnr fnl 1f, nd pace wnr: acts on firm & fast grnd: remains in gd form & shld find a race: see 2014.	1½	**61**
2393 **DELIGHTFULLY** 7 [4] B W Hills 3-9-4 (67) M Hills 15/2: 0-02463: Handy, led after 7f, hdd dist, sn no extra: qck reappr: eff at 8.4f, now stays 11f: acts on firm grnd & fibresand: see 1377.	½	**70**
1673 **SCORCHIO** 39 [3] M F Harris 3-7-12 (2oh) (45) J F McDonald(3) 28/1: 006-6254: Handy, rcd keenly, no room bef 1f out, sn onepcd: clr rem: eff at 10f/11f on firm grnd & polytrack: see 1454.	1	**48$**
290 **AFRICAN STAR** 168 [7]3-8-8 (57) Dane O'Neill 17/2: 05-65: b c Mtoto - Pass The Rose (Thatching) Handy 1m, sn wknd: long abs: unplcd in '03 (rtd 67a, mdn).	5	**51**
2066 **MAIDSTONE MIDAS** 21 [5]3-9-1 (64) I Mongan 25/1: 0456: In tch 1m, sn hung left & fdd: btr 2066.	1	**56**
2134 **VERASI** 18 [2]3-9-3 BL (66) S Drowne 12/1: 000-407: Led 7f, sn fdd: 1st time blnks: see 1514.	2½	**54**

7 Ran   Time 2m 17.98 (1.78)   Owned: Mrs E M Clarke   Trained: Newmarket

---

2577   9.20 Syd Mercer Memorial Handicap Stakes 3yo+ 0-70 (E)   **[89]**
£3981 £1225 £613   **2m3f13y**   **Firm 10**   **-36 Slow**   Inside

2376 **DARN GOOD** 8 [2] R Hannon 3-7-13 bl (60) J F McDonald(3) 16/1: 0030601: Mid div, prog when no room just ins fnl half mile, led cl home, rdn out: eff at 12f, apprec step up to 2m3f: acts on firm, fast grnd & polytrack: enjoyed today's severe stamina test for first win: see 915.		**67**
1252 **ACCEPTING** 61 [12] J Mackie 7-8-12 bl (51) N Callan 9/1: 0010-502: Handy, chsd wnr bef 3f out, led ins fnl 1f, hdd cl home: 9 wk abs: eff at 2m/2m3f: back to form: see 1069.	shd	**56**
2156 **CALIBAN** 17 [3] Ian Williams 6-8-6 (45) R Fitzpatrick 20/1: 4550-003: Keen bhd, prog 5f out, ev ch dist, kept on, just held in 3 way photo: eff at 2m/2m3f on firm grnd & fibresand: see 1654.	nk	**50**
2417 **MOONSHINE BEACH** 7 [5] P W Hiatt 6-9-0 (53) Dane O'Neill 100/30: 4063654: In tch, outpcd after 13f, short of room 3f out, kept on ins fnl 1f, nrst fin: qck reappr: see 1087.	2	**56**
1870 **DANCE LIGHT** 30 [9]5-9-9 (62) T G McLaughlin 25/1: 0600-005: Handy, led 4f out, hdd ins fnl 1f, wknd.	6	**59**
1990 **PROMOTE** 25 [11]8-8-13 (12ow) (40) P McCabe 40/1: 00/00-066: Nvr nrr than mid div.	6	**41**
1109 **DANCING PEARL** 70 [7]6-8-6 (45) D Corby(2) 6/1: 6/5-057: In tch when short of room 3f out, sn no extra.	½	**35**
2750 **PLAIN CHANT** 1067 [1] P W Harris 6-9-0 (35) A Medeiros(4) 25/1: 000/653//-8: b g Doyoun - Sing Softly (Luthier) Led, hdd after 2f, led again after 13f, hdd 4f out, sn wknd: recent jumps 2nd (nov h'cap chase, rtd 76c, stays 2m4.5f on fast, cheek pieces): mod form prev with P W Harris (rtd 41): has been gelded.	½	**26**
1840* **BERKELEY HEIGHTS** 31 [10]4-8-5 (45) A Daly 10/1: 0623419: Bhd, nvr a factor: btr 1840 (14f, banded).	¾	**32**
1252 **ULSHAW** 61 [4]7-9-2 (55) D Sweeney 25/1: 22000-00: 10th: Mid div, 1m, sn no impress.	shd	**42**
2417 **JOELY GREEN** 7 [6]7-8-6 bl (45) Steven Harrison(7) 16/1: 6602000: 11th: Rear, nvr a factor: qck reappr.	1¾	**31**
315} **QUICK** 532 [13]4-9-5 vis (59) K Fallon 11/8 FAV: 60/0-P: b g Kahyasi - Prompt (Old Vic) Led 17f out, still handy when badly short of room 3f out, sn wknd & eased, p.u. ins fnl 1f: recent hdles 2nd (rtd 133h, inter, stays 3m on firm & soft, visor): won 5 times in 03/04 (rtd 134h): gelded since mod Flat form prev (rtd 58a, R Cowell): disappointing though prob something amiss.		**0**

12 Ran   Time 4m 12.59(8.79)   Owned: Mr J E Garrett   Trained: Marlborough

---

ASCOT   SATURDAY 19.06.04   Righthand, Stiff, Galloping Track

Official Going FIRM.

2578   2.30 Listed Chesham Stakes 2yo   (A)
£23200 £8800 £4400   **7f str**   **Firm 20**   **-51 Slow**   Stands Side

2310* **WHAZZAT 10** [3] B W Hills 2-8-7   M Hills 7/1: 11: In tch, trav well & gd hdwy to lead over 1f   **107+**
out, qcknd clr, v readily: nicely bckd: relished step up to 7f, further sure to suit (dam styd 12f): acts on firm
& fast grnd: potentially smart, neat turn of foot displayed, shld be winning in Group class shortly: see 2310.

1937* **BRECON BEACON 27** [4] P F I Cole 2-9-0   K Fallon 7/1: 112: Led early, handy, switched right over   3½   **104**
1f out, sn chall, not pace of wnr in last: op 9/1: imprvd up in class & stays 7f on firm & fast, acts on soft:
useful & improving, reportedly fin lame here: see 1937.

2144* **WILKO 17** [12] J Noseda 2-9-0   E Ahern 16/1: 3013: Keen outer, switched left well over 3f out,   hd   **103**
switched right & hdwy over 1f out, kept on, nrst fin: imprvd up in class & stepped up to 7f, shaped like 1m is sure
to suit: win more races: see 2144.

1780* **HEARTHSTEAD WINGS 34** [5] M Johnston 2-9-0   J Fanning 4/1 JT FAV: 14: Set pace till over 1f out,   2   **99**
onepace: well bckd: not disgraced & shld stay 7f+: clearly even btr expected but up in class & on firmer grnd.

      IN EXCELSIS 58 [2]2-9-0   J P Spencer 4/1 JT FAV: 15: b c Fusaichi Pegasus - Lakeway (Seattle   5   **89**
Slew) Cl-up, wknd over 1f out: 8 wk abs: earlier won a Tipperary mdn: dam smart mid-dist US performer: eff at 5f
on hvy, bred to stay 7f+: shld do btr on easier grnd.

2167* **BOLTON HALL 17** [9]2-9-4   P Hanagan 10/1: 16: Keen cl-up, wknd 2f out: up in class, see 2167.   3   **87**

2228* **WHERE WITH ALL 15** [8]2-9-0   L Dettori 5/1: 17: Dwelt & bmpd start, handy, ev ch well over 1f   hd   **82**
out, sn wknd: up in class & trip: see 2228 (gd/soft).

2348* **PERFECT CHOICE 9** [10]2-9-0   D Holland 10/1: 018: With ldr, wkng when hmpd dist: btr 2348 (6f).   2½   **77**

      JOHN FORBES [1]2-8-12   Dane O'Neill 100/1: 9: b c High Estate - Mavourneen (Dynaformer) Slow   nk   **74**
away & al bhd on debut: March foal, cost 8,500gns: bred to need 7f/1m+ & a v stiff intro here.

1934   **DARKO KARIM 28** [6]2-8-12   T P Queally 12/1: 40: 10th: In tch, wknd over 2f out: see 1934.   1   **72**

      SWELL LAD [7]2-8-12   K Darley 40/1: 0: 11th: b c Sadler's Wells - Lydara (Alydar) Dwelt, ran   5   **62**
green & al bhd on debut: Feb foal: half-brother to 7f wnrs: bred to need 7f+ in time: stiff introduction.
11 Ran   Time 1m 29.55 (3.55)   Owned: Mr W J Gredley   Trained: Lambourn

2579   3.05 Gr2 Hardwicke Stakes 4yo+   (A)
£81200 £30800 £15400   **1m4f**   **Firm 20**   **+20 Fast**   Inside

2209   **DOYEN 15** [7] Saeed bin Suroor 4-8-9 (121) L Dettori 6/5 FAV: 11124-21: Held up, gd hdwy trav   **125+**
well & led on bit over 1f out, pushed clr, easily/impressive, val further: hvly bckd, crse rec time: stays 12f well
on firm & soft grnd, likes gall trks: top-class, improving & this was impressive, the one to beat back over this C/D
in the King George next month: see 2209.

2209   **HIGH ACCOLADE 15** [2] M P Tregoning 4-8-9 (116) W Supple 9/4: 26212-42: Chsd ldrs, rdn 4f out,   6   **115**
sltly outpcd over 2f out, rallied to take 2nd ins last, no ch with impressive wnr: hvly bckd: tough & smart, likes
this course but this wnr has progressed since 2209.

1843   **PERSIAN MAJESTY 31** [8] P W Harris 4-8-9 (113) J Murtagh 6/1: 1/1-633: Held up last, eff 3f out,   ½   **114**
onepace fnl 2f: acts on firm & fast: smart, prob ran to best & would apprec a return to List/Gr 3 class: see 1350.

1843   **SONGLARK 31** [6] Saeed bin Suroor 4-8-9 vis t (105) K McEvoy 25/1: 0452-524: Set gd pace till well   2   **111**
over 1f out, wknd: s/mate & prob pacemaker for wnr: in front of this 3rd in 1843.

2209   **SYSTEMATIC 15** [3]5-8-9   (113) K Darley 9/1: 55-32105: With ldr, wknd 2f out: needs an ease in class.   nk   **110**

1483   **MUSANID 49** [4]4-8-9 (107) R Hills 14/1: 33/1-36: Stumbled start, in tch, wknd 3f out: 7 wk abs.   18   **84**
6 Ran   Time 2m 26.53 (u2.47)   Owned: Godolphin   Trained: Newmarket

2580   3.45 Gr1 Golden Jubilee Stakes 3yo+   (A)
£145000 £55000 £27500   **6f str**   **Firm 20**   **-04 Slow**   Stands Side

1667   **FAYR JAG 39** [9] T D Easterby 5-9-4 (109) W Supple 12/1: 1510U-01: In tch, gd hdwy to lead 2f   **117**
out, edged right but styd on strongly ins last, drvn out: well bckd: Wokingham h'cap wnr at this meet last term:
eff at 5f, suited by 6f on firm or fast grnd, handles gd/soft: likes a gall trk, esp Ascot: v tough, high-class now
& career best/imprvd run on 26th career start, tribute to trainer: see 1667.

2139   **CRYSTAL CASTLE 23** [2] J E Hammond 6-9-4 t K Fallon 8/1: 0300-332: Hld up, hdwy & short of room   hd   **116**
well over 1f out, switched right ins last, styd on, just failed: plcd in a Gr 3 in '03: '02 Gr 2 & 3 wnr: suited by
6/7f on firm or soft grnd, loves Ascot: clrly eff in a t-strap now: v smart, prob career best eff here at fav crse &
shade unlucky, still well up to winning in Gr class: see 2139.

2468   **CAPE OF GOOD HOPE 4** [1] D Oughton 6-9-4 vis t M J Kinane 13/2: 3-662223: In tch, hdwy & sltly   hd   **115**
short of room dist, kept on for press appr fnl 1f, not btn far: qck reapp, proving tough & v smart: see 2468.

1958   **COUNTRY REEL 26** [12] Saeed bin Suroor 4-9-4 vis t (107) L Dettori 33/1: 4/205-044: Went right   ¾   **113**
start, sn cl-up, eff well over 1f out, kept on, not btn far: career best/imprvd run stepped up to Gr 1 class &
stable's runners have had an awesome R Ascot this yr: see 1667.

2305* **AVONBRIDGE 13** [3]4-9-4   (113) S Drowne 100/30 FAV: 1343-215: Cl-up, eff to chall appr fnl 1f, no   ¾   **111**
extra cl-home: hvly bckd: not disgraced but even btr expected after v smart runs in 2305 & 1479 (5f).

1667   **AIRWAVE 39** [7]4-9-1 (115) Dane O'Neill 9/2: 23360-66: Slow away, held up, hdwy over 1f out, kept   1½   **104**
on, nrst fin: nicely bckd: rnr-up in this race last term but proving shade hard to win with now: see 1667.

1958   **ASHDOWN EXPRESS 26** [14]5-9-4 (111) S Sanders 16/1: 410-3027: Held up, hdwy outer well over 1f   nk   **106**
out, wknd ins last: relish a return to List/Gr 3: see 1958, 1187.

2468   **BAHAMIAN PIRATE 4** [6]9-9-4 (105) Gary Stevens 40/1: 4421008: Held up, some late gains, nvr   1   **103**
dngrs: qk reapp: likes easier grnd: see 2468.

1667   **STEENBERG 39** [13]5-9-4 (113) R Hills 16/1: 401-2129: Slow away & hmpd start, held up, eff 2f   hd   **102**
out, sn wknd: reportedly needs easier grnd nowadays & smart eff in 1667 (soft), 1487.

2468   **NIGHTS CROSS 4** [4]3-8-11 (105) T E Durcan 40/1: 212-4300: 10th: Held up, rdn & short of room   nk   **101**
over 1f out, no impress: qk reapp: showed more 2468 (5f).

1958   **TWILIGHT BLUES 26** [11]5-9-4 (114) D Holland 33/1: 10000-50: 11th: Led till 2f out, wknd.   1   **98**

1667* **MONSIEUR BOND 39** [10]4-9-4 (117) F Lynch 6/1: 125-5110: 12th: Cl-up, wkng when short of room   5   **83**
over 1f out, eased: most progressive/high-class earlier on easier grnd & shld pay to forgive this with 'cut'.

2468   **LOCHRIDGE 4** [8]5-9-1 (106) K Darley 20/1: 1130-200: 13th: Prom, wknd dist: qk reapp: btr 2068.   1½   **76**

4878* **POLAR WAY 238** [5]5-9-4 (111) R Hughes 16/1: 360201-0: 14th: ch g Polar Falcon - Fetish (Dancing   hd   **78**
Brave) Prom, eff to chall over 2f out, wknd well over 1f out: '03 stks wnr, Gr 2 rnr-up: '02 mdn, 2 time class

stks & a Gr 3 wnr: eff at 6f, both wins at 7f: acts on firm & soft, prob any trk: has run well fresh.
1 Oct'03 Donc 7g/f 106-(113) B: 2 Sep'03 Asco 6fm 113-(113) A: 1 Sep'02 Curr 6g/f 112- : 1 Aug'02 Kemp 6fm 103- C: 1 Jul'02 Kemp 6g/f 99- D: 1 Jun'02 Newb 7sft 90- D:
14 Ran Time 1m 13.35 (0.25) Owned: Mr Jonathan Gill Trained: Malton

2581 **4.25 Wokingham Stakes Heritage Handicap 3yo+ 0-110 (B)** **[106]**
£46400 £17600 £8800 **6f str** **Firm 20** **-17 Slow** Stands Side

2256 **LAFI 14** [30] D Nicholls 5-8-13 (91) E Ahern 6/1 FAV: 4310-031: Trkd ldrs far side, imprvd to lead ent fnl 1f, rdn clr: hvly bckd: eff over a stiff/gall 6f, stays 7f/1m well: acts on firm & gd/soft: loves a stiff/gall trk: fast progressing sprinter who may reapp qckly & will be hard to beat under a pen: see 2256. **103+**
1162 **COCONUT PENANG 66** [7] P W Chapple Hyam 4-9-1 (93) S Whitworth 12/1: 6350-002: b c Night Shift - Play With Fire (Priolo) Prom stands side, styd on strongly to lead that group cl-home, no ch with wnr far side: 10 wk abs: trained by B Millman in '03, failed to win tho' plcd sev times: '02 mdn & stks wnr: eff at 6f on firm & v soft grnd, likes to run up with/force the pace: clearly runs well fresh: win sn for new trainer. *1½* **99+**
2 May'03 Hayd 6sft 101-97 A: 1 Jun'02 Kemp 6fm 99- C: 1 May'02 Ling 5gd 92- D: 2 Apr'02 Wind 5g/f 85- D:
1481 **HIGH REACH 49** [11] T G Mills 4-8-11 (89) K Fallon 10/1: 3144-363: Prom stands side, led that group dist, caught cl-home: tchd 14/1, 7 wk abs: another fine run from this tough & improving sprinter, Stewards Cup h'cap at Goodwood shld be an ideal target: see 1138. *nk* **94**
1490* **ROYAL STORM 48** [16] Mrs A J Perrett 5-9-6 (98) M J Kinane 16/1: 2126-014: Led far side till ent fnl 1f, kept on under press: 7 wk abs: fine front running eff, likes Newmarket & 7f: see 1490. *½* **101**
2357 **DAZZLING BAY 8** [25]4-9-8 (100) J F Egan 8/1: 206-6035: Prom far side, ev ch ent fnl 1f, kept on under press: hvly bckd: another fine run: see 2357. *hd* **102**
1207 **PIC UP STICKS 64** [26]5-9-4 (96) T E Durcan 12/1: 0P-31636: Held up far side, switched dist, styd on fnl 1f, nrst fin: 9 wk abs: fine run & turn shld not be far away: see 1207. *shd* **97**
2457 **SIMIANNA 7** [4]5-8-12 (90) F Norton 33/1: 5206027: Chsd ldrs stands side, not qckn fnl 1f: see 2457. *½* **89**
2187* **CARDINAL VENTURE 16** [2]6-8-12 (5ex) (90) G Parkin 20/1: 1-200018: Dwelt stands side, styd on strongly fnl 1f, nrst fin: usually front runs, lost any real ch at the start today: see 2187. *nk* **88**
2253 **BOSTON LODGE 14** [27]4-9-5 (97) T P Queally(3) 40/1: 3232409: Chsd ldrs far side, onepcd fnl 1f. *¾* **93**
2282 **DAME DE NOCHE 11** [21]4-8-10 (88) M Fenton 50/1: 00-60300: 10th: Front rank far side, ev ch ent fnl 1f, no extra: prefers 7f & best when able to dominate: see 1925. *½* **83**
2186 **INDIAN SPARK 16** [17]10-9-0 (92) Gary Stevens 50/1: 0-404460: 11th: Held up far side, hdwy when short of room dist, fin well but too late: game 10yo, set far too much to do today: well h'capped now, see 1917. *nk* **86+**
2289 **GAELIC PRINCESS 11** [15]4-8-7 (85) L Keniry(3) 66/1: 0-006000: 12th: Rear far side, styd on late. *½* **77**
1926 **GREENSLADES 28** [22]5-9-3 (95) S Sanders 13/2: 105-4420: 13th: Mid-div far side, nvr nr to chall. *shd* **86**
2253 **WHITBARROW 14** [28]5-9-4 (96) R L Moore 33/1: 5001000: 14th: Front rank far side, wknd fnl 1f. *nk* **86**
1683 **FANNYS FANCY 38** [18]4-8-12 (90) J Quinn 11/1: 1143-000: 15th: Slow away far side, nvr nr ldrs: well bckd: both wins at polytrack: see 1683. *nk* **79**
2357* **CIRCUIT DANCER 8** [19]4-9-8 (8ex) (100) F Lynch 50/1: 16-34010: 16th: Dwelt far side, late hdwy. *½* **87**
2070 **DANEHILL STROLLER 21** [8]4-8-10 p (88) K McEvoy 33/1: 01243-00: 17th: Chsd ldrs stands side, btn dist. *½* **73**
2256* **NATIVE TITLE 14** [24]6-8-13 (8ex) (91) P Hanagan 33/1: 010-4010: 18th: Prom far side, wknd fnl 1f: longer priced stablemate of wnr: see 2256. *hd* **75**
SHEER TENBY 12 [20]7-9-7 BL T (99) J Murtagh 33/1: 1022-140: 19th: b c Tenby - Take My Pledge (Ahonoora) Chsd ldrs far side, wknd dist: Irish challenger, earlier won a h'cap at Cork: '03 h'cap wnr: winning form at 6f/1m on fast & gd/soft grnd: with P Roche, wore blnks & a t-strap here. *½* **81**
2357 **HALMAHERA 8** [1]9-9-8 (100) K Darley 33/1: 4-024660: 20th: Prom stands side, wknd dist. *nk* **81**
1227 **FIRE UP THE BAND 63** [6]5-9-10 (102) D Holland 16/1: 23-00340: 21th: Led stands side till dist, wknd: 9 wk abs, stablemate of wnr: btr 1137. *nk* **82**
2357 **JOHNSTONS DIAMOND 8** [29]6-8-10 (88) W Supple 66/1: 1046200: 22th: Mid-div far side. *shd* **67**
2082 **SALVIATI 21** [12]7-8-9 (87) Dane O'Neill 66/1: 205-0000: 23th: Dwelt stands side, nvr a factor. *1¼* **65**
2253 **CORRIDOR CREEPER 14** [3]7-8-11 p (89) R Hills 20/1: 0-544260: 24th: Front rank till halfway stands side. *¾* **65**
1767 **CD EUROPE 35** [13]6-9-0 p (92) N Callan 33/1: 02021-00: 25th: ch g Royal Academy - Woodland Orchid (Woodman) Nvr nr ldrs stands side: dual h'cap wnr '03: failed to score in '02 (with M Channon): eff at 5f, best at 6f: acts on firm, likes gd/soft & soft grnd, has tried fibresand: handles any trk: eff in cheek pieces & a gd weight-carrier: best held up for a late run. 1 Nov'03 Redc 6sft 94-87 C: 2 Oct'03 York 6.0g/f 89-85 B: 2 Sep'03 Redc 6fm 85-83 D: 2 Jun'03 York 6.0fm 83-79 D: 1 Apr'03 Hami 6.0gd 83-72 E: 2 Aug'01 Chep 7g/f 102- C: *4* **56**
2253 **TEXAS GOLD 14** [14]6-8-12 (90) S Drowne 28/1: 0113-240: 26th: Front rank till halfway stands side. *2* **48**
2253 **TYCHY 14** [10]5-8-12 (90) J P Spencer 12/1: 2110-530: 27th: Chsd ldrs 4f stands side, wknd. *1¼* **44**
2068 **BOLEYN CASTLE 21** [23]7-9-4 (96) T G McLaughlin 66/1: 00000-00: 28th: Mid-div far side, btn 2f out. *2½* **43**
1917 **MATTY TUN 28** [9]5-9-0 (92) L Dettori 25/1: 00-05500: 29th: Al bhd stands side, fin last. *5* **24**
29 Ran Time 1m 14.15 (1.05) Owned: Alfi and Partners Trained: Thirsk

2582 **5.00 Duke Of Edinburgh Stakes Heritage Handicap 3yo+ 0-105 (B)** **[105]**
£29000 £11000 £5500 **1m4f** **Firm 20** **+02 Fast** Inside

2246* **WUNDERWOOD 14** [13] Lady Herries 5-9-1 (92) S Sanders 15/2: 014-0011: In tch, imprvd to lead dist, rdn clr, readily: well bckd: eff at 10/12f: likes firm, gd grnd & polytrack: handles a stiff or sharp trk, runs well fresh: fast improving & this was a v useful eff: impressed here, well worth try in Listed. **104+**
1484 **PAGAN DANCE 49** [8] Mrs A J Perrett 5-9-1 p (92) M J Kinane 8/1: 440-3422: Held up, gd hdwy 2f out, fin well into 2nd but no ch with wnr: nicely bckd, 7 wk abs: stable showing signs of a return to form. *3½* **97**
2255 **SWIFT TANGO 14** [6] E A L Dunlop 4-9-7 (98) L Dettori 9/2 FAV: 0234123: Held up, hdwy 2f out, kept on fnl 1f: well bckd: another fine run from this useful h'capper: see 2255 & 1759. *shd* **103**
1843 **HAMBLEDEN 31** [12] M A Jarvis 7-9-9 (100) N Callan 10/1: 5312-604: Chsd ldr, led over 2f out till dist, no extra: often runs well at York & a return to 14f/2m may suit: see 1585. *2* **102**
2246 **HIGHLAND GAMES 14** [17]4-8-10 (87) K Darley 20/1: 60-20245: Held up, hdwy when short of room 2f out, switched & short of room again dist, nrst fin: did not get the run of today's race & worth another ch. *hd* **88+**
2185 **BRIAREUS 16** [14]4-8-1 (78) J Quinn 22/1: 0002036: Chsd ldrs, wknd fnl 1f: see 2185 (10f). *1½* **76**
2255 **ANTICIPATING 14** [10]4-8-8 (85) K Fallon 11/2: 1460-047: Nvr btr than mid-div: see 2255. *hd* **82**
1916* **OCEAN AVENUE 28** [11]5-8-7 (84) D Holland 8/1: 0/2431-18: Led till 2f out, grad wknd: btr 1916. *1* **79**
1704 **PRINCE NUREYEV 37** [9]4-9-1 (92) S Drowne 16/1: 2440-009: Prom, wknd dist: see 1704. *5* **80**
2255 **TRUST RULE 14** [3]4-9-4 (95) M Hills 7/1: 102-0650: 10th: Chsd ldrs, struggling after halfway: reportedly unsuited by this firm grnd: see 2255 & likes York. *1¼* **81**
2208 **COUNSELS OPINION 15** [4]7-9-13 (104) J Murtagh 9/1: 0110-340: 11th: Al towards rear: reportedly *1* **88**

ASCOT SATURDAY 19.06.04 Righthand, Stiff, Galloping Track

unsuited by this firm grnd: top-weight, much btr 2208 & 1111 (10f, gd/soft).

2207 **OCEAN OF STORMS 15** [16]9-8-1 t (78) R Thomas(4) 50/1: 43R-2100: 12th: Reluctant to race & al bhd.	5	55
2250} **NOPEKAN 36** [1]4-9-3 (94) V Slattery 66/1: 0606-560: 13th: b g Sri Pekan - Giadamar (Be My Guest)	dist	0

Chsd ldrs till halfway, t.o.: prev trained in Ireland, dual h'cap wnr in '03: eff at 1m/10f on gd & gd/soft grnd.
13 Ran   Time 2m 28.74 (u0.26)   Owned: Mr Tony Perkins   Trained: Littlehampton

---

2583	**5.35 Queen Alexandra Stakes Conditions Race 4yo+ (B)** £20300 £7700 £3850 **2m6f34y** **Firm 20** **-45 Slow** Inside

CORRIB ECLIPSE [11] Jamie Poulton 5-9-0 J F Egan 25/1: 1: b g Double Eclipse - Last Night's		109

Fun (Law Society) Held up, rdn to impr 2f out, qcknd to lead dist, drvn out: rider reportedly given a 1-day whip ban: Flat debut, rcd in bmprs 3 mths ago, Sept '03 Worcester bmpr wnr (eff at 2m on gd grnd): stays 2m6f well & acts on firm grnd: runs v well fresh: clearly a thorough stayer, useful run over unique trip.

2239* **DANCING BAY 14** [5] N J Henderson 7-9-0 (100) K Fallon 11/2: 010/31/-12: Mid-div, prog when short	1½	107

of room 2f out, short of room again dist, styd on after wnr fnl 1f but nvr going to get there: stays a gall 2m6f well, acts on firm & hvy grnd: closer with clr run, useful: see 2239.

1861 **ROMANY PRINCE 30** [4] D R C Elsworth 5-9-0 (100) Dane O'Neill 6/1: 02330-33: Held up, styd on fnl	1¾	105

2f, not reach ldrs: stays a gall 2m6f judged on this: see 1861 (14f).

5012} **HOLY ORDERS 24** [1] W P Mullins 7-9-0 bl D J Condon 9/1: 316U0-44: b c Unblest - Shadowglow	3	102

(Shaadi) Mid-div, imprvd to lead briefly dist, wknd fnl 1f: Irish chall, op 7/1: v smart hdler, Gr 1 Irish Champion Stayers Hdle wnr at Punchestown in May '03 (rtd 154h, eff at 2m/3m on gd/soft): h'cap & List wnr on the Flat in '03: eff at 12/14f, poss not quite stay 2m6f: winning form on gd & soft, handles firm: wears blnks.
2 Mar'03 Leop 10gd 103- A: 2 Jun'02 Asco 12gd 105-99 B:

1569 **BIG MOMENT 45** [10]6-9-0 (99) M J Kinane 5/1 FAV: 20440-35: Chsd ldrs till lost place 2f out, no	1½	101

ch after: well bckd: btr expected after 1569 but prob not quite stay 2m6f here.

2471 **DON FERNANDO 4** [7]5-9-0 (76) Gary Stevens 25/1: 000-0506: Rear, eff 2f out, not rch ldrs: qck reapp.	¾	100$
2095 **SAVANNAH BAY 19** [12]5-9-0 bl (106) L Dettori 7/1: 355-0407: Held up, prog when short of room 2f	shd	100

out, nvr nr ldrs: see 1757.

2846} **DOUBLE HONOUR 343** [6]6-9-0 (102) D Holland 6/1: 0650/30-8: gr g Highest Honor - Silver Cobra	1	99

(Silver Hawk) Trkd ldr, went on 3f out till hdd dist, wknd: jumps fnl, won 3 nov chases in 03/04 (stays 3m, acts on firm & soft, rtd 139c): twice rcd on the Flat in '03, plcd in this race (rtd 104): '02 stks & List wnr for M Johnston: eff at 2m/2m6f on fast, hvy & any trk.
1 Jul'02 Hamb 16hvy 109- : 1 Mar'02 Donc 12sft 114- B: 1 Nov'01 Donc 14.6sft 105- C: 2 Aug'01 Donc 16g/f 116- A:
1 Jun'01 Hayd 12gd 106-92 B: 1 May'01 Donc 12g/f 102-86 C: 2 Apr'01 Newm 10g/s 88-82 C:

1843 **PUGIN 31** [8]6-9-0 (104) J P Spencer 9/1: 060-5509: Chsd ldrs, wknd qckly 2f out.	1½	97
2255 **GALLERY GOD 14** [2]8-9-0 (95) R L Moore 66/1: 0030-000: 10th: Held up, al bhd, t.o..	20	77
BLACKCHURCH MIST [9]7-8-9 t A Daly 100/1: 0: 11th: Chsd ldrs, wknd after 2m, t.o.: Flat bow.	25	47
2138* **WINDERMERE 24** [3]5-9-5 J Murtagh 6/1: 12/152-10: 12th: Led till 3f out, wknd qckly, eased & t.o.	6	51

12 Ran   Time 4m 57.41(9.91)   Owned: Mr M Ioannou   Trained: Lewes

---

LINGFIELD Polytrack SATURDAY 19.06.04 Lefthand, Sharp, Undulating Track

Official Going Good/Firm (Good Places)

2584	**6.30 Len Burdfield's Birthday Maiden Auction Stakes 2yo (E)** £3543 £1090 £545 **7f str** **Good/Firm** **Inapplicable** Stands Side	

2194 **LADY CHEF 16** [10] B R Millman 2-8-2 A McCarthy 10/1: 051: ch f Double Trigger - Dundeelin		74

(Dunbeath) Made all, held on well under hands riding ins last: cheaply bght Apr foal, sister to a 1m/11f plcd 3yo performer, dam a 5f juv wnr: apprec step up to 7f & shld get further in time: acts on fast grnd, sharp/undul trk: well suited by forcing tactics tonight: can rate higher.

PRIZE FIGHTER 0 [5] P W Chapple Hyam 2-8-10 J Quinn 5/2 FAV: 2: b g Desert Sun - Papal	hd	81

(Selkirk) Dwelt, mid-div, drvn to chall ins last, al just held: op 13/8 on debut: 17,000gns Mar foal, dam unrcd but related prolific wnr: sire smart at 6f/1m: eff at 7f on fast grnd & a sharp/undul trk: promising start.

2287 **BEE STINGER 11** [3] I A Wood 2-8-8 T P Queally(3) 33/1: 03: b c Almaty - Nest Egg (Prince Sabo)	nk	78

Handy, drvn & chall dist, not pace of front pair cl-home: left debut bhd (poorly drawn): cheaply bght May foal, dam unrcd, related to a 6f wnr: eff at 7f, stay further on this evidence: acts on a fast grnd & a sharp/ undul trk.

1887 **TIME FOR YOU 29** [9] P J McBride 2-8-2 K Jackson(7) 20/1: 04: Mid-div, rdn & styd on fnl 2f, not	1	70

able to chall: styd longer 7f trip on fast grnd, well clr of rem.

1727 **SILVER VISAGE 36** [12]2-8-10 B Reilly(3) 25/1: 555: Trkd wnr, btn over 1f out, longer trip.	5	67
1911 **SPACED 28** [17]2-8-13 P Dobbs 4/1: 06: Pushed along twds rear, late gains, nrst fin: op 11/2 on debut.	1½	69
PERSIAN CARPET 0 [1]2-8-2 R Thomas(5) 66/1: 7: Mid-div, no impress over 1f out.	1	56
2348 **MASTER JOSEPH 9** [4]2-8-12 T E Durcan 13/2: 408: Mid-div, rdn & no impress fnl 2f, longer trip.	nk	64
DAISY BUCKET 0 [16]2-8-2 F P Ferris(3) 16/1: 9: Dwelt, rcd green & bhd, late prog.	1½	52
PLAY UP POMPEY 0 [15]2-8-8 N Chalmers(5) 50/1: 0: 10th: Dwelt & outpcd, only mod prog.	1¼	55
2236 **FANTASY DEFENDER 14** [6]2-8-8 N Pollard 20/1: 0000: 11th: Chsd ldrs till over 2f out, longer trip.	nk	54
1744 **AHAZ 36** [2]2-8-9 S Sanders 50/1: 060: 12th: Prom, no impress fnl 2f, longer trip, gelded.	1¾	52
1739 **GRAND WELCOME 36** [11]2-8-8 E Ahern 9/1: 000: 13th: In tch till halfway, op 10/1, longer trip.	1¼	48

1161 **Victimised 66** [14]2-8-9 L Keniry(3) 33/1:0		2310 **Dara Girl 0** [8]2-8-5 (1ow) R Havlin 16/1:0	
Miss Cuisina 0 [7]2-8-4 Joanna Badger 100/1:0		**Chin Dancer 0** [13]2-8-2 R Smith 50/1:0	

17 Ran   Time 1m 26.33 (5.93)   Owned: Percys Country Hotel & Restaurant   Trained: Cullompton

LINGFIELD Polytrack SATURDAY 19.06.04 Lefthand, Sharp, Undulating Track

2585 **7.00 Ladbrokes Com Handicap Stakes 3yo+ 0-70 (E)** **[62]**
£3601 £1108 £554 **5f str** **Good/Firm** **Inapplicable** Stands Side

2396 **ENJOY THE BUZZ 7** [6] J M Bradley 5-8-9 (43) C Catlin 25/1: 3124201: Mid-div, drvn & styd on to lead cl-home: eff at 5/7f, tried 1m: acts on fast grnd & fibresand: see 582 (banded). **53**
2331 **INCHING 9** [9] R M H Cowell 4-8-12 (46) E Ahern 14/1: 0002602: Cl up, led 3f out, hdd under press cl-home: lost little in defeat & is h'capped to find similar: see 740 & 242. *nk* **54**
2396* **DOUBLE M 7** [14] Mrs L Richards 7-9-10 vis (58) R Thomas(5) 11/4 FAV: 6553213: Rear, switched & styd on for press ins last, nrst fin: qck reapp: app return to 6f: btr 2396 (6f). *1¼* **63**
2331* **AVIT 9** [10] P L Gilligan 4-8-5 (39) J F Egan 16/1: 2306014: Handy, drvn & onepcd from dist: see 2331. *½* **42**
4856} **FLAPDOODLE 241** [3]6-9-8 (56) T P Queally(3) 16/1: 063050-5: b f Superpower - My Concordia (Belfort) Led 2f, remained prom, no extra dist: reapp: fill h'cap scorer '03, AW unplcd (rtd 34a, h'cap): fill h'cap wnr '02 (first time blnks): suited by sharp/undul 5f, handles a gall trk: acts on fast, gd & fibresand, eff with/without blnks: with A W Carroll. *1½* **54**
2 Aug'03 Wind 5.0g/f 55-55 E: 1 Jun'03 Brig 5.3g/f 56-52 F: 1 Aug'02 Folk 5g/f 55-46 E: 2 Jul'02 Folk 5g/s 45-43 E: 2 Jan'01 Wolv 5af 57a-56 F: 1 Nov'00 Wolv 5af 56a- G:
2269 **LAW MAKER 12** [2]4-8-12 vis (46) D Holland 10/1: 4230436: Rcd alone far side, prom 4f: see 2269. *hd* **43**
2524 **BOANERGES 2** [7]7-9-10 (58) R L Moore 3/1: 5-056247: Chsd ldrs, not pace to chall: qck reapp. *1¼* **51**
2269 **TOMTHEVIC 12** [4]6-9-9 P (57) M Fenton 25/1: 0220-008: ch g Emarati - Madame Bovary (Ile de Bourbon) Dwelt, chsd ldrs till halfway: cheek pieces: h'cap scorer '03 for P R Chamings: h'cap wnr '02: loves to race with/force the pace at 5f, stay 6f: acts on firm & gd grnd, prob handles any trk. *shd* **50**
2 Aug'03 Newm 5fm 62-60 D: 2 Aug'03 Kemp 5fm 62-60 D: 1 Jul'03 Wind 5.0g/f 61-55 E: 2 Jun'03 Ling 5g/f 54-52 E: 2 Aug'02 Sand 5gd 61-56 E: 1 Aug'02 Newm 5fm 57-52 D: 2 Aug'02 Kemp 5fm 54-50 D: 2 Jun'02 Nott 6gd 55-53 F: 2 Aug'01 Donc 5gd 62-57 E:
2375 **POMPEY BLUE 8** [5]3-9-8 (62) S Sanders 20/1: 15-55009: Mid-div, no impress fnl 2f: see 105 & 3. *1* **52**
798 **FORZENUFF 107** [11]3-9-9 (63) V Venkaya 25/1: 03-50600: 10th: Pushed along, rear, nvr a factor. *nk* **52**
853 **CATCHTHEBATCH 95** [1]8-9-2 (50) Liam Jones(7) 50/1: 300-4300: 11th: Mid-div, no impress fnl 2f. *nk* **38**
2396 **INDIAN BAZAAR 7** [12]8-9-3 (51) L Keniry(3) 11/2: 145-0020: 12th: Dwelt, al outpcd: btr 2396. *1¼* **35**
2062 **MINIMUM BID 21** [8]3-9-2 (56) J Quinn 9/1: 063-00: 13th: Rdn to go handy, btn 2f out: see 2062. *½* **38**
2195 **ARDKEEL LASS 16** [13]3-9-8 (62) M Howard(7) 25/1: 12306-00: 14th: Rear, no room 2f out, nvr a factor. *½* **42**
14 Ran Time 59.55 (2.75) Owned: Miss F Fenley Trained: Chepstow

2586 **7.30 Veritas Dgc Services Maiden Stakes 3yo+ (D)**
£3799 £1169 £585 **6f str** **Good/Firm** **Inapplicable** Stands Side

2372 **PICCLEYES 8** [1] R Hannon 3-8-12 bl (59) R L Moore 8/1: 353-0001: b g Piccolo - Dark Eyed Lady (Exhibitioner) Pushed along bhd, hdwy & hung right over 1f out, sn led & clr, drvn to hold on: op 10/1: mdn rnr-up in '03, disapp in blnks: eff at 6f, stays 8.5f: acts on gd, gd/soft & fibresand, eff with/without blnks. **65**
2 Jul'03 Leic 6.0gd 69- D:
176 **RAGGED JACK 192** [8] G A Butler 3-8-12 (77) S W Kelly 11/2: 50U4-2: b g Cape Cross - Isticanna (Far North) Mid-div, short of room 2f out, strong run for press ins last, just failed: may have won this with a clr run: 6 month abs: unplcd '03 (lightly rcd, rtd 75, mdn): half-brother to a 7f juv & subs smart 10f wnr Chancellor: eff at 6f, tried 1m, rtn to further shld suit: handles fast grnd & polytrack, sharp/undul trks. *shd* **65**
2372 **LIGNE DEAU 8** [9] P D Evans 3-8-12 (57) R Havlin 8/1: 000-053: ch c Cadeaux Genereux - Miss Waterline (Rock City) Handy, drvn & kept on well ins last, just held: unplcd '03 (rtd 66, lightly rcd, mdn): eff at 6f on fast grnd & a sharp/undul trk. *hd* **64**
RACHELS VERDICT 0 [5] J R Fanshawe 3-8-7 O Urbina 5/1: 4: Mid-div, short of room 2f out, switched & kept on well cl-home: op 4/1 on debut: eff at 6f, 7f+ shld suit: handles fast grnd: rate higher. *¾* **57+**
2237 **SHIBUMI 14** [4]3-8-7 M Fenton 7/1: 0-55: Cl up, drvn & no extra dist. *2½* **49**
5015} **INNSTYLE 226** [7]3-8-7 (67) Lisa Jones(3) 4/1 FAV: 603440-6: Led till over 1f out, wknd, new yard. *3* **40**
2182 **BUNKHOUSE 16** [2]4-9-5 D Holland 15/2: 07: Chsd ldrs, no impress when hmpd over 1f out. *1¼* **41**
2309 **THEMESOFGREEN 10** [10]3-8-12 T O'Brien(7) 25/1: 0-008: Reared start & well bhd, late prog. *1* **38**
995} **ALBERTINE 437** [12]4-9-0 T P Queally(3) 33/1: 0-9: Bhd, nvr a factor, long abs, new yard. *¾* **31**
1148 **TRIFTI 67** [11]3-8-12 S Sanders 14/1: 400: 10th: Chsd ldrs, drvn & btn over 1f out: 9 wk abs: reportedly unsuited by today's fast grnd. *¾* **34**
Memory Man 0 [3]3-8-12 J Quinn 25/1:0 **Chems Legacy 0** [6]4-9-5 E Ahern 20/1:0
12 Ran Time 1m 12.84 (4.04) Owned: Mr Paul J Dixon Trained: Marlborough

2587 **8.05 Listen To The Band After Racing Rated Stakes Handicap 3yo+ 0-80 (D)** **[85]**
£5005 £1899 £949 **7f140y str** **Good/Firm** **Inapplicable** Stands Side

2432* **A WOMAN IN LOVE 5** [13] Miss B Sanders 5-9-1 (3ex) (72) S Sanders 7/2 JT FAV: 40-61111: Trkd ldrs & led over 1f out, rdn clr: nicely bckd tho' op 5/2: progressive mare, completed 4-timers: suited by 7f/1m on firm, gd & polytrack, loves sharp/undul trks: progressive 5yo: see 2432 & 2258. **84**
2099 **WELCOME STRANGER 19** [8] J M P Eustace 4-9-4 (75) L Fletcher(3) 10/1: 034-0002: Mid-div, styd on for press fnl 2f, not pace to chall wnr: imprvd eff dropped in trip: eff at 7.5f/1m: see 1057. *2½* **81**
1530 **FLEETWOOD BAY 47** [14] B R Millman 4-8-12 (69) G Baker 12/1: 020-0063: b g Fleetwood - Caviar And Candy (Soviet Star) Led/dsptd lead till over 1f out, onepace: abs, op 10/1: h'cap rnr-up '03: val cond stks wnr '02, AW unplcd (rtd 74a, auct mdn): eff at 6/7.5f on firm, soft & polytrack, any trk: nicely h'capped. *½* **74**
2 May'03 Bath 5.7g/f 78-75 E: 1 Sep'02 Donc 6fm 85- B: 2 Aug'02 Sali 6.9g/f 83- E: 2 May'02 Wind 6sft 89- E:
2374 **QUANTUM LEAP 8** [7] S Dow 7-9-0 vis (71) R L Moore 8/1: 3031664: Held up, switched & styd on ins last. *¾* **75**
2370 **MISTRAL SKY 8** [5]5-8-9 p (66) M Fenton 9/1: 0204335: Mid-div, kept on onepace fnl 2f: see 121. *nk* **69**
2018* **CLIMATE 24** [2]5-9-6 vis (77) J Murtagh 7/2 JT FAV: 0-540216: Held up, kept on late, nvr able to chall: op 6/1: clr of rem: see 2018 (1m, AW). *¾* **79**
2027 **ROMAN MAZE 23** [3]4-8-8 (65) S W Kelly 10/1: 5514-057: Dwelt, keen rear, btn 2f out: btr 2027. *7* **55**
2129 **INVADER 18** [11]8-9-7 bl t (78) E Ahern 14/1: 3-006008: Chsd ldrs, no impress fnl 2f: see 2129 & 234. *1* **66**
2173 **MR HULLABALOU 17** [12]3-8-6 (2oh) (73) M Henry 50/1: 004509: Led 2f, prom till over 1f out: btr 1497. *shd* **61**
2312 **AND TOTO TOO 10** [1]4-8-11 bl (68) F P Ferris(3) 15/2: 4424020: 10th: Drvn & bhd, nvr factor: op 6/1. *½* **55**
2288 **WOOD FERN 11** [6]4-8-8 (8oh) (57) C Catlin 25/1: 1-000050: 11th: Al bhd: btr 2288. *4* **44**

LINGFIELD   Polytrack   SATURDAY 19.06.04   Lefthand, Sharp, Undulating Track

1044 **King Of Diamonds 77** [10]3-8-10 (77) N Pollard 16/1:0
4579} **Kindlelight Debut 260** [4]4-9-8 (79) D Holland 16/1:0
13 Ran   Time 1m 32.12 (4.32)   Owned: High & Dry Racing   Trained: Epsom

LINGFIELD   Polytrack   SATURDAY 19.06.04   Lefthand, V Sharp Track

Official Going Standard

2588	8.35 Come Racing Here Again Next Saturday Selling Stakes 3yo+ (G)

£2618 £748 £374   **1m4f aw**   **Going Standard**   **Inapplicable**   Inside

1259 **JELLY BABY 61** [10] W J Haggas 3-8-3 BL J F Egan 16/1: 01: b f Marju - Daisy May (In The Wings)   **67a**
Dwelt, held up in tch, hdwy to lead 2f out & sn rdn clr, decisively: bght in for 9,800 gns: 2 month abs: AW bow:
apprec step up to 12f, 14f+ could suit: acts on polytrack & a sharp trk: goes well fresh: app fitting of blnks &
drop to sell grade: gd confidence boost.
2116 **TRESOR SECRET 19** [6] N A Callaghan 4-9-8 (72) T P Queally(3) 9/2: 010-0502: Held up, eff to chase   3   **67a**
wnr over 1f out, kept on, al held: clr of rem: AW bow: stays 12f in sell grade: acts on polytrack, gd & gd/soft.
1645 **NEPTUNE 40** [2] J C Fox 8-9-8 (35) M Fenton 12/1: 5002453: Bhd, prog wide 4f out, no threat to wnr.   5   **60a$**
1693 **MANDOOB 38** [7] B R Johnson 7-9-13 VIS (65) J P Guillambert(3) 3/1 FAV: 1100204: V slow away & well   ¾   **64a**
bhd, styd on for press fnl 2f, nrst fin: first time visor: prob handles both AWs, fast & soft grnd: lost any ch
here at start & is interesting for similar with a level break: see 634.
1986 **LIGHT BRIGADE 25** [4]5-9-8 vis (41) F P Ferris(3) 6/1: 6/03-6005: Chsd ldr 4f out, sn no impress.   7   **50a**
2200 **AMUSEMENT 15** [1]8-9-8 S Righton 16/1: 46: Chsd ldrs, rdn & btn 3f out: see 2200.   7   **41a$**
2397 **MISTER COMPLETELY 7** [11]3-8-8 (47) N Pollard 20/1: 6500007: Prom & led 4f out till 2f out, sn btn.   1   **40a**
2260 **SPRINGALONG 13** [9]4-9-8 (62) S Donohoe(7) 7/2: 0450008: Led 1f, cl-up till 3f out: btr 715.   9   **29a**
3738} **FLYOFF 304** [8]7-9-8 vis (46) P Doe 6/1: 0/01164-9: b g Mtoto - Flyleaf (Persian Bold) Chsd ldrs   5   **22a**
till 5f out: Flat reapp, 4 month jumpst abs (unplcd, h'cap, rtd 78h): clmr & h'cap wnr in '03, AW unplcd: eff at
11.4f/13f on firm & fast grnd: eff in visor, tried blnks: well suited by forcing tactics prev.
1 Jul'03 Yarm 11.5fm 45-29 E: 1 Jul'03 Leic 11.8g/f 46-(23) F:
1543 **JAVA DAWN 46** [3]4-9-3 (45) E Ahern 33/1: 20/000-00: 10th: Led till 5f out, wkng & hmpd 3f out.   14   **0a**
     YDRAVLIS 885 [5]6-9-3 S Whitworth 50/1: 0000/0/-0: 11th: Keen, tkn wide, mid-div, fdd half-way.   dist   **0a**
11 Ran   Time 2m 36.19 (6.99)   Owned: Mr B Haggas   Trained: Newmarket

2589	9.05 Play Golf & Come Racing Handicap Stakes 4yo+ 35-55 (F)	[61]

£3017 £862 £431   **1m2f aw**   **Going Standard**   **Inapplicable**   Inside

1712* **KINGSDON 37** [3] T J Fitzgerald 7-9-5 vis t (52) J F Egan 11/2: 1044111: Mid-div, rdn & hdwy 3f   **60a**
out & led ins last, drvn out: suited by 1m/10f on fast, soft & polytrack: loves Lingfield: see 1712.
2260 **FANTASY CRUSADER 13** [7] J A Gilbert 5-9-1 p (48) J Quinn 12/1: 0-033032: Prom & led over 1f out   1½   **53a**
till ins last, not pace of wnr: acts on firm, fast & fibresand: see 2260 & 1695.
1841 **CUMBRIAN PRINCESS 31** [4] M Blanshard 7-8-12 (45) R Thomas(5) 25/1: 0011363: Mid-div, prog when   2½   **46a**
short of room over 2f out, onepace from dist: stays a sharp 10f, 1m prob ideal: see 1185 (banded, 1m).
1541 **NAUTICAL 46** [14] A W Carroll 6-9-5 (52) M Fenton 7/1: 310/0-004: gr g Lion Cavern - Russian   ¾   **52a**
Royal (Nureyev) Rear, hdwy to press ldrs over 1f out, sn no extra: bckd, op 10/1: 6 wk abs: no form sole '03 Flat
start, no form over jumps 03/04: '02 wnr on the level in Dubai (10f h'cap, dirt): eff at 1m/10f on gd & polytrack.
1960* **DIAMOND ORCHID 26** [10]4-8-13 vis (46) J Murtagh 3/1 FAV: 3242215: Dwelt & held up, eff wide,   1   **45a**
onepace & held dist: slightly below form on switch to turf: see 1960.
2436 **FAIRLAND 5** [8]5-9-2 (49) L Smith(7) 25/1: 040-3406: V slow away & well bhd, eff wide from 3f out,   hd   **47a**
not pace to chall: lost ch start: qck reapp: remains one to note with stronger handling: see 1940 & 1712.
259 **WAVET 173** [1]4-9-0 (47) R Price 25/1: 0/6000-7: b f Pursuit of Love - Ballerina Bay (Myjinski)   1¾   **43a**
Handy, no impress over 1f out, 6 month abs: unplcd sole '03 turf start (61, mdn, AW unplcd, rtd 48a, C/D mdn):
unplcd sole '02 start (rtd 71): with J Pearce.
2146 **SAMMYS SHUFFLE 17** [6]9-8-13 bl (46) P Doe 10/1: 0400048: Hld up, prog/led 3f out, hdd/wknd dist.   5   **36a**
622   **MAGIC WARRIOR 126** [13]4-9-5 (52) P Dobbs 16/1: 505-3469: Mid-div, no impress fnl 2f: 4 month abs.   ½   **41a**
4209} **BLUE STREAK 281** [11]7-9-1 bl (48) E Ahern 12/1: 565220-0: 10th: Al bhd, nvr a factor.   6   **29a**
2354 **ICANNSHIFT 9** [9]4-9-8 (55) R L Moore 9/1: 1303630: 11th: Chsd ldr, briefly led 4f out, btn 2f out.   ½   **35a**
1827 **HAPPY CAMPER 32** [2]4-8-10 (43) S Whitworth 33/1: 0065300: 12th: Chsd ldrs, lost pl from halfway.   7   **14a**
2150 **HORIZONTAL 17** [5]4-9-6 N Day 20/1: 5-660050: 13th: Led 6f, sn btn, longer trip, new yard.   10   **11a**
2149 **MY LILLI 17** [12]4-9-7 (54) D Holland 14/1: 0641300: 14th: Sn handy, btn 3f out: much btr 1045 (1m).   26   **0a**
14 Ran   Time 2m 08.24(5.44)   Owned: Mr Mike Browne   Trained: Malton

NEWMARKET   SATURDAY 19.06.04   Righthand, Stiff, Galloping Track

Official Going GOOD/FIRM.

2590	1.35 Capital Sports Early Prices At 9 30 Handicap Stakes 3yo 0-80 (D)	[87]

£6955 £2140 £1070   **7f str**   **Firm 00**   **-00 Slow**   Stands Side

2249 **DUMNONI 14** [11] Julian Poulton 3-9-4 (77) N Callan 14/1: 1-063041: Handy, hdwy over 1f out to   **84**
lead ins last, edged left cl-home, drvn out: suited by 7f, stays 8.3f on firm/fast grnd, both AWs & prob gd/soft,
sharp or gall trks: genuine: see 36.
2048 **PLACE COWBOY 22** [13] J A Osborne 3-9-1 (74) S W Kelly 12/1: 2-152: With ldr, led over 2f out,   nk   **80**
hung left over 1f out & hdd ins last, just held for press: stays a gall 7f & acts on firm, gd & fibresand, sharp or
gall trks: lightly rcd & improving: see 999.
2174 **PICKLE 17** [12] S C Williams 3-8-2 (61) A McCarthy 7/1: 3041033: Held up, hdwy & not clr run   nk   **65+**
dist, sn hit by rival's whip, styd on well cl-home, just failed: lkd unlucky & acts on firm, soft & polytrack: shld
certainly win at least a fills h'cap: see 2174, 1577.

NEWMARKET SATURDAY 19.06.04 Righthand, Stiff, Galloping Track

1847 **DR THONG 31** [5] P F I Cole 3-9-6 (79) T Quinn 11/10 FAV: 5-4124: Keen with ldrs, chall over 1f out, no extra cl-home, not btn far: hvly bckd: proving tough & consistent: acts on firm & gd/soft: see 1847, 1518. ½ 82
2126 **COMPTONS ELEVEN 18** [2]3-9-7 (80) C Catlin 12/1: 33-00005: With ldrs, no extra fnl 1f: see 2126. 2½ 78
2271 **ASK THE CLERK 12** [10]3-8-13 (72) M Tebbutt 11/1: 1020346: Handy, short of room 2f out, wknd fnl 1f. 1¾ 66
2126 **STEVEDORE 18** [6]3-9-4 (77) L Keniry(3) 14/1: 0214-007: Led till over 2f out, wknd: see 2126. 4 63
2271 **WHOS WINNING 12** [3]3-8-7 (66) J F McDonald(3) 25/1: 436-0068: Keen held up, btn well over 1f out. 1 50
4899} **FLAME QUEEN 236** [7]3-9-1 (74) S Carson 25/1: 002-9: b f The West - Red Cloud (Taufan) Held up, short of room 2f out, sn wknd: rnr-up on last of 3 '03 starts (auct mdn, rtd 78): eff at 6f on firm grnd. ½ 57
2 Oct'03 Leic 6.0fm 78- F:
1496 **MOUNTCHARGE 48** [9]3-9-7 (80) I Mongan 25/1: 0613-00: 10th: With ldrs, wknd 2f out: 7 wk abs. nk 62
1358 **PATRIXTOO 56** [1]3-8-1 (60) M Henry 16/1: 00-050: 11th: gr c Linamix - Maradadi (Shadeed) Sn rdn & al bhd: 8 wk abs: unplcd all starts to date. 3½ 35
2314 **EPAMINONDAS 10** [4]3-8-11 (70) P Dobbs 25/1: 053-000: 12th: Handy, wknd over 2f out: see 1417. nk 44
2378 **LORD OF THE SEA 8** [8]3-8-5 (64) P Doe 14/1: 3400040: 13th: Held up, wknd over 1f out: see 798. shd 38
13 Ran Time 1m 23.93 (0.03) Owned: Meddler Bloodstock Trained: Newmarket

2591 2.05 Capital Sports Bet By Telephone 08000 288 233 Classified Stakes 3yo+ 0-80 (D)
£6773 £2084 £1042 6f str Firm 00 +03 Fast Stands Side

2361* **WILLHEWIZ 8** [4] R M Stronge 4-9-3 vis (78) S Carson 6/1: 1-056011: Made all, styd on v gamely for press ins last: another fine run up in class after claim win for C Dwyer in 2361: loves to dominate over 5/6f on firm & gd, acts on gd/soft & fibresand, any trk: wears a visor: tough & game: see 1217. 81
2074 **MILLION PERCENT 21** [6] K R Burke 5-9-4 (81) K Dalgleish 2/1 JT FAV: 430-0622: Cl-up, eff to chase wnr over 1f out, kept on: running well: see 2074, 1767. ¾ 79
2269 **BEAUVRAI 12** [7] V Smith 4-9-3 (67) M Tebbutt 16/1: 0-000053: Held up in tch, promising run when short of room dist, onepace cl-home: v encouraging at these weights tho' poss not straightforward: acts on firm & both AWs: also caught the eye 1914, see 567. 1¾ 74
1131 **GREY PEARL 44** [2] Miss Gay Kelleway 5-9-1 (81) I Mongan 6/1: 1364604: Dwelt, held up, eff 2f out, onepace: 6 wk abs: all 3 wins at 7f: see 518. 1½ 68
1583 **SKYHARBOR 44** [5]3-9-1 (85) W Ryan 12/1: 13100-05: b g Cyrano de Bergerac - Pea Green (Try My Best) Chsd wnr till well over 1f out, wknd: 6 wk abs: won 2 of 6 '03 starts, mdn auct & auct: eff over 5/6f on firm & gd/soft, likes stiff trks: more encouraging here, sharper for this. 3 66
1 Jun'03 Carl 5fm 92- E: 1 May'03 Hami 6.0g/s 83- E:
2289 **NAJEEBON 11** [3]5-9-5 (82) C Catlin 2/1 JT FAV: 50-00036: Sn rdn & bhd, no dngr: btr 2289. 2½ 56
2266 **ITS ECCO BOY 12** [8]6-9-3 (60) Lisa Jones(3) 28/1: 4100007: Hung right throughout, in tch 4f, wknd. 1 51
2718] **GARDEN SOCIETY 709** [1]7-9-3 (75) B Doyle 33/1: 300/U06/-8: ch g Caerleon - Eurobird (Ela Mana Mou) Held up, btn over 2f out: last rcd back in '02, unplcd for J Toller (rtd 85?): eff at 10/13f on fast & gd grnd: has run well fresh on any trk: now with W O'Gorman. 9 24
8 Ran Time 1m 10.82 (u0.18) Owned: Mr Tim Bostwick Trained: Newbury

2592 2.40 Bet Online At Capitalsports Com Handicap Stakes Fillies 3yo+ 0-90 (C)
£9412 £2896 £1448 1m2f Firm 00 -15 Slow Stands Side [90]

2191* **POLAR JEM 16** [8] G G Margarson 4-9-10 (86) A McCarthy 4/1: 1-341111: Made all, kept on strongly fnl 2f, rdn out: readily landed 4-timer: loves to dominate over 9/10f on firm or fast grnd, easy or stiff trk: v useful, continues to thrive & poss even more to come: see 2191. 96
2015 **FLING 24** [3] J R Fanshawe 3-8-6 (80) O Urbina 7/2: 152: Slow away, held up, hdwy 2f out, edged right over 1f out but kept on, no threat to wnr: stays 10f well on gd & firm, further shld suit: lightly rcd, progressing with each run & shld find similar shortly: see 1283. 1½ 86
2323 **GREY CLOUDS 10** [10] T D Easterby 4-9-2 (78) J Fortune 100/30 FAV: 0-420123: In tch, hdwy to chase wnr over 1f out, kept on, not her pace: proving consistent & handles firm & soft: see 2323, 2038. shd 84
2067 **WINDY BRITAIN 21** [7] L M Cumani 5-9-12 (88) P Robinson 4/1: 13131-04: Held up, switched left & hdwy over 1f out, sn no impress: not disgraced under top-weight: see 179, 82. 1½ 91
2078 **ASTROCHARM 21** [1]5-9-0 (76) T Quinn 10/1: 400-5105: Held up, hdwy over 3f out, no impress fnl 2f. 1¾ 75
1927 **STRATEGY 28** [5]4-9-4 (80) P Dobbs 12/1: 16123-06: br f Machiavellian - Island Story (Shirley Heights) Chsd wnr, no extra well over 1f out: '03 mdn & h'cap wnr for Sir M Stoute: eff over 10/12f on firm & gd grnd, stiff or sharp trks. nk 78
2 Aug'03 Sand 10.0g/f 83-80 D: 1 Aug'03 Nott 10.0gd 80-72 D: 1 Jun'03 Warw 10.9fm 74- D:
1233 **FRAGRANT STAR 63** [9]3-8-7 (81) B Doyle 25/1: 40105-07: gr f Soviet Star - Norfolk Lavender (Ascot Knight) Held up, eff well over 1f out, sn wknd: 2 mth abs: '03 nursery h'cap wnr: eff at 6f on fast grnd & on a stiff/undul trk: big step up in trip here (dam 1m wnr). 1 Jul'03 Pont 6g/f 80-76 D: 3 73
1651 **LADY PEACHES 40** [6]3-7-12 (5oh) (67) F P Ferris(3) 20/1: 0-038: In tch, short of room over 2f out, wknd over 1f out: 6 wk abs: see 1651 (both). ¾ 62
2284 **RANI TWO 11** [2]5-8-12 (74) N Chalmers(5) 25/1: 60410-09: In tch, wknd over 1f out: see 2284. ¾ 62
2191 **ISLAND RAPTURE 16** [4]4-8-12 (74) Lisa Jones(3) 12/1: 055-0040: 10th: Keen held up, wknd 2f out. 6 50
10 Ran Time 2m 03.45 (1.55) Owned: Norcroft Park Stud Trained: Newmarket

2593 3.15 Capital Sports Handicap Stakes 3yo 0-105 (B)
£13624 £4192 £2096 5f str Firm 00 +02 Fast Stands Side [105]

2400 **GREEN MANALISHI 7** [3] D W P Arbuthnot 3-8-12 (89) T Quinn 7/1: 4221031: In tch, hdwy over 1f out, styd on well to lead ins last, drvn out: well suited by 5f on firm, gd/soft & polytrack, sharp or stiff trks. 95
2400 **TONY THE TAP 7** [2] N A Callaghan 3-8-2 (79) Lisa Jones(3) 7/2 JT FAV: 4-122: In tch, hdwy over 1f out, styd on well ins last, just held: acts on firm & polytrack: in fine heart, worth a try at 6f now: see 2400. nk 84
2206 **AUTUMN PEARL 15** [5] M A Jarvis 3-9-7 (98) P Robinson 7/2 JT FAV: 151-123: Set pace, rdn & collared well ins last, kept on, just held in a blanket fin: useful run under a big weight: acts on firm, hvy & polytrack: lightly rcd & improving: see 2206, 1513. shd 102
1766 **PARADISE ISLE 35** [10] C F Wall 3-8-11 (88) G Baker 7/1: 22211-04: b f Bahamian Bounty - Merry Rous (Rousillon) Dwelt, held up, hdwy & short of room over 1f out, switched left & styd on well ins last, short of room again cl-home: won 2 (auct mdn & mdn) & rnr-up other 3 '03 starts: eff over 5/6f & likes fm & fast, poss handles gd/soft: progressive & useful, lkd unlucky here, stable right back to form & can find similar. shd 91+

785

1 Oct'03 Nott 6.1fm 90-(86) F: 1 Sep'03 Pont 5g/f 87- E: 2 Sep'03 York 6.0g/f 88- E: 2 Jul'03 Newc 6g/s 77- F: 2 Jul'03 Newm 6fm 89- D:

2407 **WANCHAI LAD 7** [8]3-8-9 (86) W Ryan 9/2: 1160-305: Chsd ldr, eff to chall over 1f out, no extra cl-home but not btn far: stays 6f, shld be plcd to win a h'cap: see 1572. ½ **87**

2407 **RYDAL 7** [6]3-8-6 bl (83) R Miles(3) 25/1: 221-0406: Held up, some late gains, nvr dngrs: on a fair mark & looks sure to go much closer over further when stable returns to form: see 1460. 2½ **77**

2407 **HIGH VOLTAGE 7** [7]3-9-7 t (98) K Dalgleish 13/2: 020-1367: In tch, wknd fnl 1f: btr 1360. 1½ **88**

2390 **ORO VERDE 7** [1]3-8-10 (87) P Dobbs 11/1: 402-0638: Held up, no impress over 1f out: see 176. 1¾ **73**

2121 **PROMENADE 18** [9]3-8-6 (83) J Mackay 20/1: 1161-509: Held up, wknd well over 1f out: see 1771. ¾ **67**

9 Ran Time 58.38 (u0.12) Owned: Mr Derrick C Broomfield Trained: Upper Lambourn

2594

3.50 Football Handicaps At Capital Sports Maiden Stakes 2yo (D)
£4755 £1463 £732 **7f str** **Firm 00** **-17 Slow** Stands Side

2221 **FOX 15** [1] C E Brittain 2-9-0 B Doyle 5/6 FAV: 21: Handy, styd on over 1f out to lead ins last, rdn clr: bckd: enjoyed step up to 7f & 1m will suit: acts on fm & gd: lightly rcd, improving, more to come. **97**

IN THE FAN [5] J L Dunlop 2-9-0 J Fortune 16/1: 2: b g Lear Fan - Dippers (Polish Numbers) Led, rdn & hdd ins last, kept on but not pace of wnr on debut: March first foal, dam 5f juv wnr: stays a stiff 7f well, 1m sure to suit: acts on firm grnd: well clr of rem & a useful debut, looks sure to prog & win races. ¾ **94**

RAZA CAB [6] C N Allen 2-9-0 I Mongan 40/1: 3: b g Intikhab - Laraissa (Machiavellian) In tch, eff 2f out, outpcd by front pair well over 1f out on debut: March first foal, cost 31,000gns: bred to apprec 7f/1m in time & shld learn plenty from this. 6 **82**

SRI LIPIS [9] P F I Cole 2-9-0 T Quinn 7/1: 4: ch c Cadeaux Genereux - Katrina (Ela Mana Mou) Slow away, sn in tch, hung left & wknd well over 1f out on debut: Jan first foal, cost 200,000gns: bred for 7f+. 1 **80**

GRAND MARQUE [4]2-9-0 P Dobbs 12/1: 5: Handy, outpcd halfway, modest late gains on debut. 2 **76**

BOBBIE LOVE [2]2-9-0 C Catlin 18/1: 6: Slow away, sn handy, wknd 2f out on debut. 7 **62**

1670 **BLUE KANDORA 39** [3]2-9-0 P Robinson 7/2: 47: Al bhd. 1½ **59**

ELIZABETHS CHOICE [8]2-8-9 M Henry 33/1: 8: Slow away, sn handy, wknd 2f out on debut. 1 **52**

ROBESON [7]2-9-0 R Mullen 33/1: 9: Sn rdn & al bhd. 2½ **52**

2341 **PARSLEYS RETURN 9** [10]2-9-0 W Ryan 50/1: 050: 10th: Al bhd. 15 **22**

10 Ran Time 1m 25.11 (1.21) Owned: Sheikh Marwan Al Maktoum Trained: Newmarket

2595

4.20 Capital Sports At The Centre Of Racing Maiden Stakes 3yo (D)
£5525 £1700 £850 **1m str** **Firm 00** **-20 Slow** Stands Side

NAMROC [2] A C Stewart 3-9-0 P Robinson 10/1: 1: b c Indian Ridge - Hesperia (Slip Anchor) In tch, hdwy & switched to stands rail over 1f out, styd on to lead ins last, rdn clr: cost 85,000gns: half-brother to a 1m wnr: stays a stiff 1m well, shld get further: acts on firm grnd & runs well fresh: v encouraging start. **85**

2248 **FLAMJICA 14** [1] J A R Toller 3-8-9 (70) Lisa Jones(3) 5/1: 35-42: Set pace, rdn & hdd ins last, not pace of wnr: stays a stiff 1m on firm & fast grnd: consistent, shld find a modest race: see 2248. 2 **74**

1978 **GRAND BUT ONE 25** [8] B W Hills 3-9-0 (87) I Mongan 8/11 FAV: 6223: Cl-up, eff to chall 2f out, hung left & onepace over 1f out: hvly bckd: much btr expected after 1978 & worth a try in headgear now. 2½ **74**

ARRJOOK [13] A C Stewart 3-9-0 J McAuley 33/1: 4: b c Intikhab - Chief Ornament (Chief's Crown) Slow away, held up, hung left & no dngr over 1f out: debut: stablemate of wnr: dam 1m/9f scorer: 1m/10f shld suit, shld come on for this. nk **73**

2383 **DREAM EASY 8** [10]3-9-0 R Price 50/1: 05: b g Pyramus - Hush Baby (Ballacashtal) In tch, eff 2f out, no impress: dam 12f wnr: bred to stay mid-dists. 1¼ **70**

1929 **NIKIFOROS 28** [9]3-9-0 J Fortune 33/1: 06: In tch, keen, no impress over 1f out. ¾ **68**

977 **NORTH SEA 81** [3]3-8-9 C Catlin 16/1: 0-07: Handy, no extra over 1f out: abs, op 9/1. hd **62**

4409} **SILK CRAVAT 270** [4]3-9-0 R Havlin 20/1: 0-8: In tch, wknd 2f out: reapp, gelded. 7 **53**

2092 **RAWALPINDI 20** [12]3-9-0 K Dalgleish 33/1: 0-009: Al bhd. 1 **51**

SPES BONA [5]3-9-0 S W Kelly 14/1: 0: 10th: Slow away, nvr a factor: op 10/1. 1¾ **47**

CAPITOLE [11]3-9-0 P McCabe 40/1: 0: 11th: Al bhd. 5 **37**

ARTIST RIFLE [6]3-9-0 T Quinn 12/1: 0: 12th: Slow away & al bhd. 4 **29**

ALJAFLIYAH [7]3-8-9 A Hamblett(7) 25/1: U: U.r. start on debut. **0**

13 Ran Time 1m 38.79 (1.59) Owned: Mr Bruce Corman Trained: Newmarket

2596

4.50 Capital Sports #20 Free Bet Handicap Stakes 4yo+ 0-85 (D) **[85]**
£5460 £1680 £840 **1m6f175y** **Firm 00** **-06 Slow** Stands Side

2239 **DOROTHYS FRIEND 14** [2] R Charlton 4-9-7 (78) J Fortune 9/4 FAV: 0/5111-01: Cl-up, hdwy to lead 3f out, kept on fnl 1f, rdn out: stays 2m well & likes firm & fast grnd, any trk: back to form & is v progressive (4 wins from last 5 starts), prob even more to come: see 2239. **87**

2073 **THEATRE 21** [4] Jamie Poulton 5-9-10 (81) P Doe 9/2: 004-0S22: Held up, hdwy to chall well over 1f out, not pace of wnr: another gd run: see 2073. 2 **86**

2298 **RED SCORPION 11** [9] W M Brisbourne 5-8-8 (65) S W Kelly 8/1: 5-165023: In tch, rdn & sltly short of room over 2f out, kept on same pace over 1f out: gd run: see 2298, 288. 1¼ **68**

2311 **CARROWDORE 10** [3] C N Allen 4-8-11 p (68) I Mongan 9/2: 220-2434: Held up, hdwy & short of room over 2f out, onepace: prob just stays 2m: 1 win from 25: see 2311, 2078. nk **71**

2246 **ARRESTING 14** [7]4-10-0 (85) O Urbina 12/1: 222-1065: Held up, eff over 2f out, sn no extra: prob not stay 2m: see 1516, 1016 (12f). 5 **82**

1003 **SIMONS SEAT 80** [6]5-8-8 (65) G Carter 16/1: 65030-66: ch g Woodman - Spire (Topsider) Slow away, al bhd: 12 wk abs: unplcd in 2 hdles last winter: plcd on 1 of 7 '03 Flat starts (h'cap, rtd 69): stays 2m on firm & fast grnd. 11 **51**

2233 **SOVEREIGN DREAMER 14** [5]4-9-5 t (76) C Catlin 20/1: 110-0607: Led till 3f out, wknd: see 1969. 1½ **61**

2196 **HASHID 16** [8]4-8-13 VIS (70) K Dalgleish 10/1: 53-638: Chsd ldr, wknd 2f out: see 2196. 14 **41**

2239 **PRAIRIE FALCON 14** [1]10-9-10 (81) A Medeiros(5) 15/2: 010-300P: Keen, handy, sadly broke leg & p.u. after 6f, sad loss to connections: see 1172. **0**

9 Ran Time 3m 06.5(1) Owned: Mountgrange Stud Trained: Beckhampton

WARWICK   SUNDAY 20.06.04   Lefthand, Sharp, Turning Track

Official Going Firm (Good/Firm Places)

2597   2.30 Evening Telegraph Celebration Maiden Stakes 2yo   (D)
£3851 £1185 £593   **7f26y rnd**   **Firm 03**   -04 Slow   Inside

2077 **COUNTRY RAMBLER 22** [6] B W Hills 2-9-0   R Hughes 5/2: 01: b c Red Ransom - Country Garden (Selkirk) Made all, al trav well, clr after halfway, eased ins fnl 1f, val 10L+: tchd 7/4: Feb first foal, cost $125,000: dam decent performer at 1m/10f: eff at 7f, shld apprec further: acts on firm grnd & a sharp trk: left poor debut eff bhd with v easy success & broke 2yo course record, can rate higher.   **93+**
2051 **LEAGUE OF NATIONS 23** [5] P F I Cole 2-9-0   S Drowne 9/2: 052: Al cl-up, kept on ins fnl 2f, no ch with easy wnr: op 7/1: eff at 7f on firm grnd: see 2051.   5   **80**
2144 **SIMPLIFY 18** [3] D R Loder 2-9-0   T P Queally(3) 1/1 FAV: 453: Rear, prog 4f out, onepace & hung left ins fnl 2f: well bckd: btr expected on step up to 7f: just btr 2144 (6f).   ¾   **78**
1573 **SHARP N FROSTY 46** [2] W M Brisbourne 2-9-0   S W Kelly 12/1: 404: Handy 4f, wknd: 7 wk abs.   8   **64**
1716 **DARTANIAN 38** [4]2-9-0   Joanna Badger 22/1: 05: b g Jurado - Blackpool Mamma's (Merdon Melody) Handy 4f, wknd: April first foal, dam wnr at 5/7f: sire decent performer at 1m/10f: with P D Evans.   nk   **63**
       ROBMANTRA [1]2-9-0   V Slattery 66/1: 6: b c Prince Sabo - Eliza Jane (Mistertopogigo) Al in rear: debut: Feb first foal, cost 2,800gns: dam unrcd: sire top-class juv performer: with B J Llewellyn.   14   **37**
6 Ran   Time 1m 22.90 (0.50)   Owned: Mr Ahmed BuHaleeba   Trained: Lambourn

2598   3.00 Evening Telegraph Property Guide Classified Stakes 3yo+ 0-70 (E)
£3705 £1140 £570   **6f21y rnd**   **Firm 03**   +18 Fast   Inside

2289 **PARKSIDE PURSUIT 12** [5] J M Bradley 6-9-2 (70) R L Moore 7/2: 0-011041: Held up, prog 2f out, styd on despite hanging left to lead cl-home: eff at 5/6f on firm, gd grnd: broke course record: see 2029.   **77**
2512+ **DIZZY IN THE HEAD 3** [3] Paul Johnson 5-9-8 bl (67) N Chalmers(5) 100/30 FAV: 0-016312: Led after 1f, hdd under press cl-home: qck reapp: lost little in defeat, 5lb higher than 2512.   ½   **80**
2269* **HARD TO CATCH 13** [2] D K Ivory 6-9-9 bl (77) M Savage(5) 7/2: 5500113: Handy, kept on ins fnl 1f, not btn far: not disgraced under top-weight: btr 2269 & 2044 (5f).   ½   **80**
2048 **SWEET PICKLE 23** [4] D J Coakley 3-8-6 (70) T P Queally(3) 4/1: 3010-24: Handy, onepcd from dist.   ¾   **68**
2370 **COMPTON BANKER 9** [1]7-9-2 vis (70) E Ahern 6/1: 4115-065: Rear, prog when short of room ins fnl 2f, sn no impress: tchd 8/1: btr 149 (polytrack).   1½   **67**
2416 **BYO 8** [6]6-9-3 (71) N Pollard 12/1: 6201066: Led, hdd 5f out, styd cl-up, wknd dist: btr 1886.   2   **62**
2186 **SPEEDFIT FREE 17** [7]7-9-2 (46) Ann Stokell 100/1: 0400607: Handy 4f, sn wknd: btr 1750.   8   **39**
7 Ran   Time 1m 09.68 (u 0.92)   Owned: Mr J M Bradley   Trained: Chepstow

2599   3.30 Evening Telegraph 1st For Jobs Handicap Stakes 3yo+ 0-75 (E)   [75]
£4274 £1315 £658   **5f rnd**   **Firm 03**   -25 Slow   Inside

2412* **FOLEY MILLENNIUM 8** [13] M Quinn 6-8-12 (59) N Pollard 7/1 JT FAV: 0/6P-0111: Cl-up, styd on to lead 1f out, drvn out to hold on: eff at 5/6f on firm & hvy grnd: in form performrer: see 2412 (sell) & 1644.   **65**
2585 **LAW MAKER 1** [15] M A Buckley 4-7-13 vis (46) J Bramhill 16/1: 42304362: Cl-up, styd on well ins fnl 1f, just held: fin 6th at Lingfield yesterday: acts on firm, gd grnd & polytrack: see 2429 & 2237.   hd   **50**
2440 **BLESSED PLACE 6** [2] D J S ffrench Davis 4-7-12 (45) J F McDonald(3) 66/1: 0000003: In tch, styd on ins fnl 1f, just held: qck reapp: acts on firm, fast & both AWs: encouraging run & well h'capped: see 2201.   shd   **48**
2269 **LOCH INCH 13** [3] J M Bradley 7-8-4 bl (51) E Ahern 25/1: 000-0004: Slow away, prog 3f out, nrst fin.   ¾   **52**
2269 **PULSE 13** [17]6-9-0 p (61) R L Moore 15/2: 0236645: Rear, prog 2f out, kept on fnl 1f: op 6/1.   hd   **61**
944   **JUSTALORD 85** [4]6-9-6 p (67) J Edmunds 8/1: 0212306: Led, hdd 1f out, sn no extra: 12 wk abs.   hd   **66**
2084 **IZMAIL 22** [6]5-9-5 (66) S Whitworth 9/1: 015-0007: Slow away, in tch halfway, onepcd fnl 1f.   hd   **64**
2561 **SAFRANINE 1** [8]7-9-2 p (63) Ann Stokell 25/1: 00000008: Sn short of room, nvr nrr than mid-div.   nk   **60**
2396 **YORKIES BOY 8** [10]9-8-6 (53) C Catlin 14/1: 400-5409: Rear, nvr nrr than mid-div: btr 2266 & 1914.   1   **47**
2044 **GUNS BLAZING 23** [14]5-9-5 bl (66) M Howard(7) 14/1: 0-001360: 10th: Handy 4f, no extra: btr 1867.   hd   **59**
2214 **INTELLIBET ONE 16** [5]4-8-10 (57) S Drowne 50/1: 00000-00: 11th: b f Compton Place - Safe House (Lyphard) Handy till dist, no extra: won 2 h'caps in '03: auct stks wnr in '02 (also h'cap rnr-up for P Monteith): eff at 5/6f on firm, soft grnd & polytrack: tried visor: with P D Evans.   ¾   **48**
2 Aug'03 Wind 5.0gd 63-62 D: 2 Aug'03 Wind 5.0g/f 62-62 E: 2 Jul'03 Folk 5g/f 62-60 F: 1 Jul'03 Ling 5g/f 57-54 F: 1 Jul'03 Catt 6.0g/f 56-50 E: 2 Sep'02 Hami 5.9g/f 75-73 D: 2 Apr'02 Ling 5ap 76a- D: 1 Mar'02 Donc 5sft 74- E:
2585 **INDIAN BAZAAR 1** [12]8-8-4 (51) N Chalmers(3) 16/1: 145-00200: 12th: Mid-div 4f, sn wknd.   nk   **41**
2429 **LADY PEKAN 7** [1]5-9-1 bl (62) T G McLaughlin 12/1: 0353000: 13th: Handy over 3f, wknd: qck reapp.   2   **46**
1824 **ONE LAST TIME 33** [9]4-9-0 (61) R Ffrench 7/1 JT FAV: 60-00020: 14th: Al in rear: tchd 9/1: never able to get competitive back at 5f: btr 1824 (6f).   nk   **44**
2279 **SHOLTO 13** [11]6-9-3 bl (64) J D O'Reilly(7) 9/1: 6000-020: 15th: In tch till dist, fdd: btr 2279.   nk   **36**
2326 **COLLEGE HIPPIE 11** [16]5-7-12 p (45) C Haddon(5) 40/1: 04060-00: 16th: b f Cosmonaut - Eccentric Dancer (Rambo Dancer) Al in rear: plcd twice in '03 (h'caps): auct mdn wnr in '02: eff at 5/5.5f on firm & gd/soft grnd: handles any trk: eff forcing the pace. 2 Jul'03 Warw 5.5g/f 58-55 E: 1 Jul'02 Leic 5g/f 62- E: 2 Jun'02 Donc 5fm 69- E: 2 Jul'01 Yarm 5.1g/f 74- C: 2 Jul'01 Beve 5g/f 76- D: 4   **5**
2286 **CHICO GUAPO 12** [7]4-9-12 BL (73) R Hughes 8/1: 0105000: 17th: Cl-up, sn lost position, wknd ins fnl 2f, sn eased: top-weight & first time blnks: btr 1476 & 692.   3½   **23**
17 Ran   Time 58.72 (1.42)   Owned: Mrs S G Davies   Trained: Wantage

2600   4.00 Evening Telegraph Cup Handicap Stakes 3yo+ 0-80 (D)   [80]
£5876 £1808 £904   **1m22y rnd**   **Firm 03**   -09 Slow   Inside

845   **WIND CHIME 98** [1] A G Newcombe 7-8-12 (64) L Keniry(3) 9/1: 000-0201: Cl-up, styd on to lead ins fnl 1f, rdn out: long abs: suited by 7f/8.5f on firm, gd/soft & both AWs: likes Warwick: goes well fresh, see 766.   **69**
2091 **TIBER TIGER 21** [7] N P Littmoden 4-10-0 bl (80) J P Guillambert(3) 8/1: 500-4102: Mid-div, prog ins fnl 2f, kept on, not pace of wnr: back to form today: see 1891 & 1059.   ¾   **82**
542   **ANSWERED PROMISE 137** [2] I A Wood 5-8-3 (1ow) (54) P Doe 20/1: 00-00623: Led after 1f, hdd under   hd   **56**

787

press ins fnl 1f, no extra: long abs: acts on firm, gd/soft & both AWs: decent eff on first start for new yard.

2448	**ADOBE** 6 [12] W M Brisbourne 9-9-1 (67) M Savage(5) 9/1: 002-0034: Rear, prog ins fnl 2f, nrst fin.					nk	67
1915	**ANALYZE** 29 [11]6-9-7 (73) R L Moore 15/2: 1506-235: Rear, prog & short of room dist, styd on ins fnl 1f: recent hdles unplcd (rtd 60h, mdn): btr 1691.					¾	71
2438*	**PAWAN** 6 [8]4-9-3 (6ex) (69) Ann Stokell 11/1: 5302016: Cl-up over 6f, sn no extra: qck reapp.					2½	62
2397	**BALERNO** 8 [10]5-7-13 (1ow) (60) C Catlin 9/1: 0523047: Nvr nrr than mid-div: btr 2397 & 1463.					¾	42
2223	**ZAFARSHAH** 16 [4]5-8-11 (63) S Drowne 9/2: 1462038: Handy 6f, sn wknd: btr 2223.					1	52
2032	**MUQTADI** 24 [13]6-7-12 (6oh) (44) K May(7) 18/1: 0454069: Al in rear: btr 1267 & 717.					nk	38
2324*	**PRINCE OF GOLD** 11 [6]4-9-1 p (67) R Hughes 4/1 FAV: 5006010: 10th: Led 1f, styd in tch, wknd fnl 2f: disapp run: btr 2324 (gd/soft).					¾	53
2497	**HOHS BACK** 4 [9]5-8-8 p (60) N Chalmers(5) 16/1: 0600500: 11th: Bhd, nvr a factor: qck reapp.					¾	44

11 Ran   Time 1m 37.78 (0.98)   Owned: Mr M K F Seymour   Trained: Barnstaple

---

2601

4.30 Evening Telegraph Drivetime Handicap Stakes 3yo+ 0-75 (E)   [75]
£4193 £1290 £645   1m4f134y   Firm 03   -18 Slow   Inside

2114	**COMPTON ECLAIRE** 20 [4] G A Butler 4-8-7 vis (54) E Ahern 10/1: 4-332461: Rear, prog 3f out, styd on to lead cl-home, rdn out: stays 15f: acts on firm & both AWs: eff with a visor: see 1654.						60
1375	**THEATRE TINKA** 55 [2] R Hollinshead 5-8-9 p (56) R Hughes 20/1: 5524052: Led, hdd 5f out, rallied to lead again 1f out, hdd cl-home: 8 wk abs: gd eff on return to turf & is weighted to find similar: see 679.					hd	60
2047	**BANNINGHAM BLAZE** 23 [6] A W Carroll 4-8-3 (50) R Thomas(2) 5/1: 0041223: Rear, prog ins fnl 2f, nrst fin: continues to run well: see 2047 & 1692 (seller).					1½	51
2465	**BAKIRI** 5 [3] Andrew Reid 6-8-13 (60) Rory Moore(7) 7/2 FAV: 4052324: Handy, styd on to lead bef 1f out, sn hdd & no extra: qck reapp: btr 2465.					½	60
2293	**MOST SAUCY** 24 [11]8-8-12 (59) T P Queally(3) 11/2: 6650345: Rear, prog 2f out, onepcd fnl 1f.					½	58
2041	**TASNEEF** 23 [8]5-8-13 (60) J P Guillambert(3) 22/1: 26140-06: Bhd, prog to lead 5f out, hdd bef 1f out, sn wknd: see 2041 (reapp).					1½	56
2284	**GALLANT BOY** 12 [1]5-9-11 vis t (72) S Donohoe(7) 7/1: 0040057: Cl-up, no extra dist: btr 2284.					½	67
2041	**RED RIVER REBEL** 23 [7]6-8-8 (55) F Norton 11/2: 6340-048: Prom 10f, sn wknd: btr 2041.					¾	48
2371	**MILK AND SULTANA** 9 [5]4-8-6 (53) S Drowne 25/1: 0000-069: Mid-div, wknd fnl 2f: btr 2371.					2	43
2135	**ARMS ACROSSTHESEA** 19 [9]5-9-0 (61) J Edmunds 9/1: 00-21140: 10th: Keen in rear, nvr a factor.					nk	50
3887}	**CELTIC STAR** 300 [10]6-9-2 p (63) D Nolan(3) 16/1: 006//116-0: 11th: b g Celtic Swing - Recherchee (Rainbow Quest) Bhd, nvr a factor: recent p.u. over fences: h'cap hdle wnr in 03/04 (rtd 114h, stays 2m2.5f on firm & soft grnd, eff with/without visor, N Williams): won first 2 of only 3 '03 Flat starts (amat h'cap & h'cap): eff around 12f on gd & gd/soft grnd: acts on a gall or undul trk: likes Chepstow.					3	47

1 Aug'03 Chep 12.1gd 64-57 F: 1 Jul'03 Chep 12.1g's 60-49 F:
11 Ran   Time 2m 41.99 (2.69)   Owned: Mr Erik Penser   Trained: Blewbury

---

2602

5.00 Coventry Citizen Maiden Stakes 3yo+ (D)
£3819 £1175 £588   1m2f188y   Firm 03   -06 Slow   Inside

2222	**ON EVERY STREET** 16 [2] H R A Cecil 3-8-13 vis t (72) W Ryan 5/1: 5-431: Cl-up, kept on under press to lead cl-home: tchd 7/1: eff at 11f, further shld suit: acts on firm grnd & a sharp trk: eff with visor, apprec fitting of a t-strap: see 2222 & 1892.						80
2426	**BEAUCHAMP STAR** 7 [5] G A Butler 3-8-8 BL (72) E Ahern 11/4: 032042: Led, hdd under press cl-home: qck reapp & first time blnks: prev eff at 7f/1m, now stays 11f: acts on firm & soft grnd: apprec fitting of blnks: can find similar now stable has started to hit form: see 1527.					¾	74
2386	**LINE DRAWING** 8 [4] B W Hills 3-8-13 R Hughes 5/6 FAV: 243: Rear, prog 4f out, rdn & sn flashed tail ins fnl 2f, no impress dist: well bckd: disapp on step up to 11f & does not looks a straightforward ride.					3	74
	DAFINA 233 [6] H Morrison 4-9-7 S Drowne 9/1: 23-4: b f Mtoto - Dafayna (Habitat) Cl-up, wknd 2f out: tchd 11/2 on reapp & Brit bow: plcd on both '03 starts in native Ireland (mdns): eff around 9/10f on gd & gd/soft grnd: sure to impr on today for shrewd stable.					5	62
1654	**CELTIC VISION** 41 [7]8-9-12 t p (45) S Righton 100/1: 6600465: Al bhd: recent hdles unplcd.					16	46

5 Ran   Time 2m 16.60(0.40)   Owned: Colin Davey Racing   Trained: Newmarket

---

Official Going Good/Firm

2603

2.20 E B F Betfred Com Maiden Stakes Div 1 Fillies 2yo (D)
£5434 £1672 £836   6f rnd   Good/Firm 29   -48 Slow   Inside

2119	**MISSPERON** 19 [1] K A Ryan 2-8-11 N Callan 13/8: 531: Made all, hung right under press from dist but al holding rivals: well bckd, op 15/8: eff at 6f on fast grnd, stiff/undul or gall trk: type to progress again.						80
	CONSIDER THIS 0 [9] W M Brisbourne 2-8-11 D Allan 16/1: 2: b f Josr Algarhoud - River of Fortune (Lahib) Mid-div, switched & styd on for press from over 1f out, not able to chall wnr: cheaply bght Apr foal: dam a 7f juv wnr: eff at 6f, get further: acts on fast: pleasing start, rate higher.					1¼	75
1805	**ORPEN ANNIE** 34 [4] Miss J Feilden 2-8-11 B Reilly(3) 20/1: 03: b f Orpen - Nisibis (In The Wings) Handy, outpcd halfway, rdn & kept on ins last: Apr foal: eff at 6f, 7f+ shld suit: handles fast grnd.					2½	67
2151	**FRANTIC** 18 [7] T D Easterby 2-8-11 T Quinn 12/1: 04: ch f Fraam - Carn Maire (Northern Prospect) Held up, rdn & kept on fnl 2f, nvr pace to threaten: imprvd from debut: Mar foal: half sister to wnrs at 5/7f: dam 5f wnr: eff over a stiff 6f on fast grnd: clr of rem, better run.					½	65
	E BRIDE 0 [11]2-8-11 M Fenton 8/1: 5: Chsd wnr halfway, rdn & fdd over 1f out: op 13/2.					5	51
	ENTERTAINING 0 [3]2-8-11 Dane O'Neill 11/8 FAV: 6: Chsd wnr, rdn & btn 2f out: well bckd, op 7/4.					3	42
	FINAL OVERTURE 0 [10]2-8-11 T Eaves(3) 20/1: 7: Slow away & al bhd.					19	0
	AGREAT DAYOUTWITHU 0 [6]2-8-11 R Fitzpatrick 50/1: 8: Prom till halfway, sn bhd.					20	0

8 Ran   Time 1m 18.73 (4.63)   Owned: Mrs Angie Bailey   Trained: Hambleton

---

2604

2.50 Skybet Handicap Stakes Fillies 3yo+ 0-75 (E)   **[63]**
£4115   £1266   £633   **1m rnd**   **Good/Firm 29**   **-39 Slow**   Inside

2108 **SHARP SECRET 20** [9] J A R Toller 6-9-6 (55) Lisa Jones(3) 9/2: 34265-51: Dwelt & held up,   **60**
switched wide & strong run for press to lead well ins last: op 7/2: eff at 7f, suited by 1m: acts on gd/soft, loves
firm/fast grnd, prob any trk: see 2018.
2149 **KINDNESS 18** [1] A D W Pinder 4-8-13 (48) Dane O'Neill 16/1: 003-6002: Led, rdn & hdd well ins   ¾   **51**
last, not pace of wnr: imprvd eff with forcing tactics applied: acts on firm & fast grnd: see 1045.
2296 **UNO MENTE 12** [3] Don Enrico Incisa 5-9-4 (53) Kim Tinkler 11/1: 50-00063: Chsd ldrs, drvn & kept   hd   **55**
on fnl 1f, not pace of wnr: on a winning mark: see 1602.
2153 **MAGICAL MIMI 18** [5] Jedd O'Keeffe 3-9-10 (69) Leanne Kershaw(7) 33/1: 130-0004: Mid-div, hdwy   hd   **70**
wide to chall ins last, no extra nr fin: stays a stiff 1m: see 2153.
2508 **HULA BALLEW 3** [4]4-9-5 P (54) Darren Williams 9/1: 6-050055: Prom, no extra dist: chkpcs.   1¼   **52**
2243 **MISS ELOISE 15** [7]3-8-12 (57) D Allan 9/2: 0052-626: Held up, eff 2f out, no extra when short of   ¾   **54**
room over 1f out: btr 2243 (gd).
2402* **CLASSIC VISION 8** [6]4-9-5 bl (54) R Hills 3/1 FAV: 0045017: Hld up, short of room 2f out, no impress.   3   **45**
2510 **TRANSCENDANTALE 3** [10]6-8-12 (47) K Fallon 9/2: 3560048: Trkd ldrs, btn over 1f out: qck reapp.   4   **30**
1348 **LARK IN THE PARK 57** [2]4-8-9 (44) K Darley 11/1: 1006-009: ch f Grand Lodge - Jarrayan   1¾   **24**
(Machiavellian) Chsd ldr, btn over 1f out, 8 wk abs: h'cap scorer '03: unplcd '02 (lightly rcd, rtd 57, mdns, M
Bell): eff at 7f/1m on firm & fast grnd, gall on turning trks. 1 Aug'03 Bath 8.0fm 51-46 F:
9 Ran   Time 1m 47.24 (5.44)   Owned: Mr John Drew   Trained: Newmarket

---

2605

3.20 Stanleybet Com Classified Stakes 3yo+ 0-90 (C)
£9025   £3423   £1712   **1m2f**   **Good/Firm 29**   **-05 Slow**   Inside

2012* **MUTASALLIL 25** [1] Saeed bin Suroor 4-9-3 t (87) L Dettori 5/2 FAV: 3-11: Made all, rdn & styd on   **101**
strongly: hvly bckd tho' op 15/8: eff at 10f, 12f shld suit: acts on fast & suited by forcing tactics today: lightly
rcd, useful & prog: win again: see 2012.
2234 **KINGSWORD 15** [2] Sir Michael Stoute 3-8-8 (93) K Fallon 11/4: 41-52: Chsd ldrs, eff to chase wnr   1¾   **100**
fnl 2f, kept on but al held: pulled clr of rem: bckd, op 4/1: stays a stiff 10f & will be plcd to effect: see 2234.
1833 **SPURADICH 33** [6] L M Cumani 4-9-6 (93) J Murtagh 11/2: 10110-03: Held up in tch, rdn & no   4   **94**
impress on front pair over 1f out: not disgraced bhd 2 prog scorers: see 1833.
2404 **OUR TEDDY 8** [4] A M Balding 4-9-3 bl (87) K Darley 8/1: 0-400544: Chsd ldrs, hdwy wide over 2f   2½   **87**
out, no impress over 1f out: btr 2404 7 2096.
2101 **CROW WOOD 20** [7]5-9-7 (94) M Fenton 11/4: 305-0335: Cl-up, btn 2f out: btr 2101 & 1586.   1½   **89**
2029 **PERCY DOUGLAS 24** [8]4-9-3 (45) L Fletcher(3) 200/1: 3-000006: Sn bhd: see 275.   21   **48**
2337 **EASTERN DAGGER 10** [3]4-9-3 (48) R Fitzpatrick 200/1: 4060-007: Dwelt, keen, chsd ldrs 6f: new yard.   2   **49**
7 Ran   Time 2m 11.5 (3.4)   Owned: Godolphin   Trained: Newmarket

---

2606

3.50 William Hill Rated Stakes Handicap 3yo+ 0-105 (B)   **[104]**
£12093   £4587   £2294   **1m rnd**   **Good/Firm 29**   **+12 Fast**   Inside

2425* **ACE OF HEARTS 7** [5] C F Wall 5-8-10 (3ex) (86) S Sanders 11/8 FAV: 0502111: Trkd ldrs, short of   **93**
room over 1f out, switched & strong run for press to lead nr fin, going away in a fast time: hvly bckd: stays 10f, 1m
suits: acts on soft & both AWs, loves fm/fast grnd, gall trks: thriving, can land 4-timer.
2489 **CALCUTTA 4** [4] B W Hills 8-9-5 (95) M Hills 11/2: 4-000002: Held up, hdwy wide & rdn/led ins   ½   **97**
last, hdd nr fin: op 13/2: qck reapp: back to form & on a handy mark: see 1926.
2234 **KINGS THOUGHT 15** [10] S Gollings 5-9-6 (96) K Dalgleish 16/1: 6046443: Led, drvn & hdd ins last,   1   **96**
kept on: gd run on drop to 1m: see 1296.
2101 **ALWAYS ESTEEMED 20** [9] G Wragg 4-9-5 (95) J F Egan 12/1: 000-2004: Pushed along chasing ldrs   ¾   **94**
halfway, kept on onepace: imprvd eff on drop to 1m: see 1351.
2405 **DANELOR 8** [1]6-8-9 (85) T Hamilton(3) 9/1: 20-45005: Held up, short of room over 1f out, kept on late.   1   **82**
2154 **NARRATIVE 18** [11]6-9-10 (100) R Hills 14/1: 4300-046: Trkd ldr wide, chall over 1f out, no extra dist.   ½   **96**
2404 **SEA STORM 8** [7]6-8-8 (2oh)p (82) P Mulrennan(5) 12/1: 5030107: Cl-up, btn 2f out: btr 2087.   3½   **73**
4172} **RUSSIAN DANCE 283** [3]3-8-12 (98) K Fallon 7/2: 2140-8: br f Nureyev - Population (General   30   **34**
Assembly) Rear & sn pushed along, drvn & btn over 1f out, eased: reapp: lightly rcd juv, fill nov scorer, subs Gr
3 4th (rtd 93 at best): eff at 6/7f, 1m shld suit this term: acts on fast grnd, sharp trk.
1 Jul'03 Wind 6g/f 86- D: 2 Jun'03 Newm 6g/f 90- D:
8 Ran   Time 1m 43.18 (1.38)   Owned: Lady Stuttaford & Mr W G Bovill   Trained: Newmarket

---

2607

4.20 Toteexacta Pontefract Cup Handicap 4yo+ 0-80 (D)   **[78]**
£6776   £2085   £1043   **2m2f**   **Good/Firm 29**   **-08 Slow**   Inside

2355 **THEWHIRLINGDERVISH 9** [10] T D Easterby 6-9-13 (77) T Quinn 7/2: 00-34031: Rear, smooth hdwy 3f   **84**
out & led over 1f out, asserted under hand riding: eff at 12/14f, suited by stiff 2m/2m2f: handles soft, loves firm
& fast grnd: goes v well for T Quinn (last 3 wins under this rider): see 1109.
2444 **MAGIC COMBINATION 6** [3] L Lungo 11-9-7 (71) W Dowling 16/1: 0110/-252: Mid-div, hdwy 5f out, sn   2   **75**
outpcd, switched & styd on well ins last, not pace to trouble wnr: styd stiff 2m2f well: tough 11yo.
2198 **OCEAN TIDE 17** [4] R Ford 7-9-8 BL (72) K Darley 14/1: 0-334403: Led, rdn & hdd over 2f out,   2½   **73**
rallied late for press to retake 3rd: fair run with forcing tactics in first time blnks: see 926 & 743.
2276* **STOOP TO CONQUER 13** [8] J L Dunlop 4-9-8 (73) K Fallon 5/4 FAV: 356-0014: Trkd ldrs, keen early,   1½   **72**
rdn & led over 2f out, hdd over 1f out & no extra: hvly bckd: btr 2276.
2444 **TONI ALCALA 6** [2]5-9-4 (68) J Fanning 15/2: 6135245: Trkd ldrs, onepace for press fnl 3f: qck reapp.   1½   **66**
2192 **TILLA 17** [11]4-9-2 (67) L Fletcher(3) 11/2: 62131-56: Held up, eff to chall over 2f out, no extra   1   **63**
dist: op 4/1: not quite see out this longer 2m2f trip, 2m may prove ideal: see 2192.
2073 **PEAK PARK 22** [9]4-7-12 (3oh)VIS (46) Lisa Jones(3) 25/1: 00360-07: Chsd ldrs, btn 3f out: tried visor.   14   **34**
2105 **GREEN N GOLD 20** [5]4-8-6 (57) Darren Williams 20/1: 00-10408: Al bhd: btr 1870.   9   **33**
2131 **INDIAN CHASE 19** [7]7-8-5 vis (55) Lucy Russell(7) 100/1: 2609: Keen, cl-up, wknd qckly 4f out: see 1291.   *dist*   **0**

PONTEFRACT   SUNDAY 20.06.04   Lefthand, Undulating Track, Stiff Uphill Finish

9 Ran   Time 3m 58.74 (6.74)   Owned: Major I C Straker   Trained: Malton

2608   4.50 Ladbrokes Maiden Stakes 3yo (D)
£5538 £1704 £852   1m4f   Good/Firm 29   -14 Slow   Inside

2175 SCHAPIRO 18 [4] J H M Gosden 3-9-0 bl (78) L Dettori 15/8 FAV: 045-0341: Handy & led 3f out, **86+**
readily pulled clr: val 10L+: eff at 11/12f on fast grnd, sharp or stiff/undul trk: now suited by blnks: found
this straightforward, could progress in h'cap company: see 1807.
1892 RACE THE ACE 30 [2] J L Dunlop 3-9-0 S Sanders 16/1: 452: Bhd, kept on to take 2nd, nvr threat   6   74
to wnr: clr of rem: stays 12f: handles fast & gd/soft: more interesting in h'caps, poss over further.
1768 SUNDAY CITY 36 [3] D R Loder 3-9-0 VIS K Fallon 9/4: 33: Stumbled start, chsd ldrs, rdn & no   6   65
impress fnl 2f: nicely bckd tho' op 13/8: first time visor: btr 1768.
2193 ZANGEAL 17 [5] C F Wall 3-9-0 J Quinn 2/1: 434: Dwelt, held up in tch & pulled hard, rdn & btn   2   62
3f out: well bckd, op 11/4: longer trip, needs to learn more restraint: btr 2193 & 759.
2230 MOLEHILL 16 [6]3-8-9 M Fenton 25/1: 05: b f Salse - Mountain Lodge (Blakeney) Chsd ldrs, no   hd   56
impress fnl 3f: half-sister to sev wnrs, incl smart mid-dist performer Compton Ace, dam a high-class stayer.
2428 ONIZ TIPTOES 7 [1]3-9-0 P T Eaves(3) 100/1: 00-06: ch g Russian Revival - Edionda (Magical   18   36
Strike) Led, hdd 3f out & sn btn: long trip, cheek pieces: unplcd '03 (rtd 26a & 19, W R Muir, mdns).
       BESEEKA RUNNIN FOX 0 [9]3-8-9 B Reilly(3) 100/1: 7: Al bhd & no ch 4f out.   27   0
       DEANGATE 0 [10]3-9-0 R Fitzpatrick 50/1: P: Sn struggling rear & t.o./p.u. 2f out, dismounted.   0
8 Ran   Time 2m 39.30 (5.2)   Owned: Sangster Family   Trained: Manton

2609   5.20 Bet Direct Handicap Stakes 3yo 0-85 (D)   **[92]**
£5499 £1692 £846   6f rnd   Good/Firm 29   -12 Slow   Inside

2375 RED ROMEO 9 [6] G A Swinbank 3-8-11 (75) K Fallon 2/1 JT FAV: 016-2441: Prom & led over 2f out, **91+**
rdn clr, easily: well bckd, op 9/4: eff at 6f, stays 7f well: acts on fast & gd/soft grnd: useful & impressed
here, can defy a pen: see 1881 & 1368.
1881 MIND ALERT 30 [8] T D Easterby 3-8-6 (70) D Allan 28/1: 21006-02: Held up in tch, styd on for   5   71
press, no ch with wnr: back to form: see 1881.
2400 BELLA TUTRICE 8 [4] I A Wood 3-8-8 (72) J Fanning 25/1: 30200-03: b f Woodborough - Institutrice   shd   73
(College Chapel) Led, hdd 2f out, kept on for press, no ch with wnr: auct mdn scorer '03 for current yard, subs
unplcd for J A Harris (rtd 57a, stks): best at 5f, 6f may yet suit: acts on fast & gd/soft.
2 Jun'03 Wind 5.0gd 83- E: 1 May'03 Muss 5g/f 86- E: 2 Apr'03 Wind 5.0g/s 80- F: 2 Apr'03 Wind 5.0g/f 78- E:
2 Mar'03 Kemp 5gd 80- D:
2403 FIORE DI BOSCO 8 [7] T D Barron 3-8-9 (73) P Makin(5) 12/1: 002-5044: Held up, rdn & kept on late.   hd   73
2237* RENE BARBIER 15 [10]3-8-5 (69) Dean McKeown 16/1: 0415: Bhd, mod prog, no dngr: h'cap bow.   1½   64
1163 SENOR BOND 67 [2]3-8-7 (3ow) (68) F Lynch 16/1: 400-6306: Bhd, nvr factor: abs: btr 1088 (soft).   shd   66
2482 BO MCGINTY 4 [5]3-9-7 (85) T Hamilton(3) 2/1 JT FAV: 301-0127: Cl-up, drvn & hung left over 1f   shd   79
out, sn btn: bckd, qck reapp: btr 2482 & 1745.
1881 LETS GET IT ON 30 [3]3-9-1 (79) R Winston 7/1: 2-005208: Sn rdn chasing ldrs, no impress 2f out.   nk   72
2482 IMPERIAL ECHO 4 [1]3-9-2 VIS (80) S Sanders 11/2: 433-0049: Cl-up, rdn & btn when hmpd over 1f   3½   62
out, eased: tried visor, qck reapp: btr 2482.
9 Ran   Time 1m 16.53 (2.43)   Owned: Mr J Yates   Trained: Richmond

2610   5.50 E B F Betfred Com Maiden Stakes Div 2 Fillies 2yo (D)
£5434 £1672 £836   6f rnd   Good/Firm 29   -46 Slow   Inside

       KRYNICA 0 [6] Sir Michael Stoute 2-8-11 K Fallon 11/2: 1: br f Danzig - Bionic (Zafonic)   **79+**
Handy, styd on for to lead well ins last, rdn out: mkt drifter, op 5/2: May foal, dam a 7f juv scorer on sole
start: eff at 6f, get further: acts on fast & goes well fresh: shld learn plenty from this & can rate higher.
       SECRET HISTORY 0 [8] M Johnston 2-8-11 J Fanning 6/1: 2: b f Bahri - Ravnina (Nureyev) Led,   hd   77
rdn & hdd well ins last, just held: op 5/1: 25,000gns Mar foal: high-class miler: eff at 6f, 7f will suit: acts on
fast grnd & a stiff/undul trk: sharp type who can find a race.
       BALLETTO 0 [3] K R Burke 2-8-11 Darren Williams 16/1: 3: b f Robellino - Denial (Sadler's   1   74
Wells) Prom & styd on from over 1f out, not able to chall: op 20/1: 27,000gns Feb first foal, dam a wnr
abroad: eff at 6f, 7f/1m+ likely to suit: handles fast grnd: promising type, win races.
2119 TARAS TREASURE 19 [4] J J Quinn 2-8-11 R Winston 5/2 FAV: 264: Keen & prom, short of room &   shd   74
lost pl halfway, no room over 1f out, switched & kept on late: no luck in running, closer with a clr passage: bckd,
op 7/2: can improve on this & find a race, poss in h'cap company: see 1818.
       LOTTIE DUNDASS 0 [1]2-8-11 J Murtagh 11/1: 5: Rear, no room & switched over 1f out, styd on well   ¾   72
fnl 1f, nrst fin: op 5/1: u.r. bef start, also unruly in stalls but eye-catching late hdwy & a likely improver.
2061 IMPERIAL MISS 22 [5]2-8-11 A Daly 25/1: 06: Cl-up, onepace & held dist.   ½   70
       PRINCEABLE LADY 0 [2]2-8-11 D Allan 18/1: 7: Bhd, kept on late, nvr a factor.   1   67
       ROCK FEVER 0 [10]2-8-11 K Darley 6/1: 8: Dwelt, chsd ldrs wide, no impress dist.   hd   66
2178 MAKE US FLUSH 17 [7]2-8-11 P Mathers(7) 16/1: 4049: Chsd ldrs till over 1f out: see 2178.   1   63
       SCISSORS 0 [9]2-8-11 B Reilly(3) 66/1: 0: 10th: Chsd ldrs, no impress from halfway.   1¼   59
10 Ran   Time 1m 18.61 (4.51)   Owned: Mr K Abdulla   Trained: Newmarket

790

Official Going Good/Firm (Firm Places)

2611 | 2.30 Racing Uk On Channel 425 Selling Stakes 2yo   (G)
£2877 £822 £411   5f str   Good/Firm 32   -23 Slow   Stands Side

2481 **OUR LOUIS** 5 [7] J S Wainwright 2-8-6   T Eaves(3) 16/1: 60541: Made all, held on well, drvn out: **60**
no bid: first win: cheek pieces omitted: eff at 5f on fast: apprec drop in grade & forcing tactics.
2358 **LITTLE BISCUIT** 10 [5] K R Burke 2-8-11   Darren Williams 6/5 FAV: 112542: Dwelt, trkd ldrs trav   nk   **64**
well, short of room halfway & again over 1f out: rider drpd whip ins last, not able to reach wnr: hvly bckd, op
11/8: prob unlucky, whip may have made the difference: acts on fast, soft & firesand: see 1634, 1224 & 938.
1950 **ALMATY EXPRESS** 28 [4] M Todhunter 2-8-11   R Winston 9/4: 3003: Held up, eff when no room over 1f   1½   **59**
out, switched & kept on late, nrst fin: eff at 5f, shapes as tho' a rtn to 6f in similar will suit: handles fast & soft.
2321 **FRISBY RIDGE** 12 [5] T D Easterby 2-8-6 bl   D Allan 16/1: 050554: Cl-up, outpcd fnl 2f: see 1303.   2   **48**
1869 **VOICE OF AN ANGEL** 32 [6]2-8-6   P Mathers(7) 20/1: 50505: Dwelt, in tch, outpcd over 1f out: see 1653.   ½   **46**
2083 **SHATIN LEADER** 23 [8]2-8-6   R Ffrench 40/1: P6: Went right start, chsd ldrs till over 1f out: see 2083.   ¾   **44**
2449 **SONGGARIA** 7 [3]2-8-7 (1ow) G Parkin 11/2: 237: Sn outpcd & struggling: mkt drifter, new yard.   5   **30**
1968 **BORACAY BEAUTY** 28 [1]2-8-6 BL J Carroll 66/1: 0008: b f Tipsy Creek - Grandads Dream (Never So   3   **20**
Bold) Cl-up, struggling halfway, modest form.
8 Ran   Time 1m 0.23 (2.73)   Owned: Whitestonecliffe Racing Partnership   Trained: Malton

2612 | 3.00 Watch Racing Uk Live Channel 425 Novice Auction Stakes 2yo   (E)
£3988 £1227 £614   7f30y rnd   Good/Firm 32   -18 Slow   Inside

2039 **SOCIETY MUSIC** 24 [5] M Dods 2-8-13   F Lynch 3/1: 131: Made all & dictated pace, qcknd tempo from   **81**
halfway, drvn & held on well ins last: eff at 5/6f, apprec step up to 7f: acts on fast & hvy grnd, stiff/undul or
sharp trk: well suited by forcing tactics today under a well judged ride: see 2039 & 1249.
2462 **FORFEITER** 6 [3] T D Barron 2-8-12 bl   R Winston 13/8 FAV: 2622: Trkd ldr, rdn to chall over 2f   1   **77**
out, no extra well ins last: nicely bckd, op 5/2: qck reapp: shown enough to find a race in mdn company.
2178 **SPINNAKERS GIRL** 18 [4] J R Weymes 2-8-7   D Fentiman(7) 12/1: 03: b f Bluegrass Prince - Brac   ½   **71**
Princess (Nicolotte) Trkd ldrs, onepace fnl 2f: left debut bhd: op 10/1: cheaply bght Mar first foal: stays a
sharp 7f, shld get further: handles fast grnd.
2039 **INDIBRAUN** 24 [1] P C Haslam 2-9-4   G Faulkner 7/4: 5144: Cl-up wide, rdn & hung left under press   14   **57**
from over 2f out, sn btn: well bckd: much btr 2039 & 1874.
2511 **COUNTRYWIDE DREAM** 4 [2]2-8-12 p J Carroll 66/1: 0005: Sn strugg rear, qck reapp, mod form.   25   **9**
5 Ran   Time 1m 28.45 (3.55)   Owned: Mr M J K Dods   Trained: Darlington

2613 | 3.30 Forth2 Handicap Stakes 3yo 35-55   (F)   [61]
£2968 £848 £424   1m rnd   Good/Firm 32   +02 Fast   Inside

2243 **COBALT BLUE** 16 [1] W J Haggas 3-9-3 bl (50) R Winston 9/4 FAV: 0000-061: Led, rdn & hdd over 2f   **57**
out, rallied for press to lead again ins last, gamely: hvly bckd, op 11/4: first win: eff at 1m on a sharp trk in
blnks: acts on fast & gd grnd: see 2243 & 1872.
2509 **SON OF THUNDER** 4 [2] M Dods 3-9-6 (53) Darren Williams 11/4: 00-6162: Trkd ldrs, no room over 1f   ¾   **58+**
out, switched & hmpd ins last, kept on late, winning ch had gone: qk reapp, likely wnr here with a clr run: acts on
fast & gd: normally raced much bigger, but 2nd below par ride of the afternoon: see 1798 (C/D).
1947* **ROMAN THE PARK** 28 [5] T D Easterby 3-8-9 (42) D Allan 11/4: 0-312313: Trkd ldr & led over 2f   hd   **46**
out, edged left under press & hdd ins last, no extra cl-home: nicely bckd: clr of rem: ran to form of 1947.
5014} **A MONK SWIMMING** 228 [6] John Berry 3-8-2 (35) R Ffrench 12/1: 060-4: br g Among Men - Sea Magic   7   **28**
(Distinctly North) Trkd ldrs, rdn & btn 2f out: reapp/h'cap bow: unplcd at up to 6f in '03 (lightly rcd, rtd 25, mdn).
2216 **POLAR GALAXY** 17 [4]3-9-3 (50) G Faulkner 25/1: 05400-05: br f Polar Falcon - June Brilly   3   **37**
(Fayruz) Held up, rdn & no impress fnl 2f: unplcd '03 (rtd 60, auct mdn).
2339 **PETRION** 11 [3]3-8-13 (46) C Lowther 8/1: 0036: Chsd ldrs, struggling fnl 3f: op 6/1, h'cap bow.   2½   **28**
1876 **QUINTILLION** 32 [7]3-8-11 (44) T Eaves(3) 20/1: 00-007: Bhd halfway, longer trip, modest.   16   **0**
7 Ran   Time 1m 39.88 (2.38)   Owned: Mr Peter S Jensen   Trained: Newmarket

2614 | 4.00 Racing Uk On Channel 425 Handicap Stakes Fillies 3yo+ 0-75   (E)   [68]
£4027 £1239 £620   5f str   Good/Firm 32   +01 Fast   Stands Side

2326 **PETANA** 12 [3] M Dods 4-7-12 (7oh)P (38) Natalia Gemelova(7) 20/1: 20-50401: Held up in tch, hdwy   **52**
to lead ins last, rdn out: eff at 5/6f on fast grnd: eff in blnks, imprvd in cheek pieces today: first win.
2195 **SCOTTISH EXILE** 18 [9] K R Burke 3-9-1 vis (68) Darren Williams 14/1: 4431002: Held up in tch,   1¼   **70**
styd on well cl-home, nrst fin: back to form, excuse latest & poorly drawn prev: stiffer trk shld suit: see 1509.
2420 **ROXANNE MILL** 8 [2] J M Bradley 6-10-0 (75) C J Davies(7) 1/1 FAV: 0-326323: Led, rdn & hung left   nk   **75**
dist, sn hdd & no extra: hvly bckd: just btr 2420 & 2084 (C/D).
2326 **MYSTERY PIPS** 12 [1] N Tinkler 4-8-0 vis (47) Kim Tinkler 12/1: 15-00004: Handy & ch 2f out, onepace.   nk   **46**
2476* **ROBWILLCALL** 5 [7]4-8-4 (6ex)p (51) P Mathers(7) 9/1: 000-0515: Handy, drvn & no extra dist: op 7/1.   ½   **49**
397 **STAR APPLAUSE** 159 [4]4-7-12 (11oh) (34) D Fentiman(7) 25/1: 6000-006: b f Royal Applause - Cominna   ½   **41$**
(Dominion) Chsd ldrs, edged left & no extra dist, dem: visor omitted: AW seller wnr '03 for J Balding, disapp in
cheek pieces, turf unplcd (rtd 44, h'cap): winning form over a sharp 5f on fibresand: eff forcing the pace.
2 Mar'03 Catt 5g/f 53-(54) F: 1 Feb'03 Wolv 5af 55a-(45) G:
2320 **PIRLIE HILL** 12 [8]4-8-8 (55) J Carroll 8/1: 0250167: Outpcd rear, hung right & little hdwy.   nk   **50**
2219 **GEMINI GIRL** 17 [6]3-7-12 (1oh) (50) P M Quinn 33/1: 5366-008: b f Petardia - Miss Sabre   5   **32**
(Sabrehill) Outpcd rear, nvr a factor: unplcd '03 (rtd 69, auct mdn).
2331 **INCHING** 2 [5]4-7-13 (46) Dale Gibson 5/1: 0026029: Cl-up, rdn & btn 2f out: bckd: qck reapp.   3   **19**
9 Ran   Time 59.04 (1.54)   Owned: The Four Aces   Trained: Darlington

MUSSELBURGH   MONDAY 21.06.04   Righthand, Sharp Track

2615   4.30 Rectangle Group Handicap Stakes 3yo+ 35-55 (F)   [55]
£3038 £868 £434   **7f30y rnd**   **Good/Firm 32**   -02 Slow   Inside

1943* SENNEN COVE 28 [9] R Bastiman 5-9-1 t (42) R Ffrench 20/1: 0636611: Held up, hdwy when no room & 48
forced to switch right over 1f out, styd on for press to lead line: would have been an unlucky loser: eff btwn
7f/9f on fast & fibresand: confidence seems boosted after 1943 (banded).

1277 THE OLD SOLDIER 62 [5] A Dickman 5-6-9 (50) A Beech(3) 12/1: 5200-002: Held up, styd on wide for shd 55
press to lead ins last, hdd line: bckd, op 14/1, 2 month abs: eff at 5f/6f, now stays a sharp 7f: see 1052.

2397 LORD CHAMBERLAIN 9 [12] J M Bradley 11-9-10 bl (51) C J Davies(3) 10/1: 2034403: Trkd ldrs, hdwy ½ 55
to lead over 1f out, edged left & hdd ins last, no extra cl-home: tricky ride, prob best delivered as late as poss.

2440 TOJONESKI 7 [6] I W McInnes 5-9-4 p (45) D Allan 9/2: 4222334: Chsd ldrs halfway, ch dist, onepace. shd 49

2347 AFRICAN SPUR 11 [10]4-9-10 (51) D Tudhope(7) 10/1: 0000065: Cl-up, drvn & no extra dist: see 2347. 2 51

2447 WALTZING WIZARD 7 [13]5-9-11 (52) F Lynch 4/1 FAV: 5505406: Chsd ldrs, chall 2f out, sn wknd. hd 51

2544 ROYAL WINDMILL 3 [9]5-9-4 p (45) D Fentiman(7) 10/1: 06-00527: Reared start, dwelt & bhd, late shd 44
prog, nrst fin: qck reapp: lost winning ch start from poor low draw, interesting in a sell h'cap.

2326 MICKLEDOR 12 [14]4-9-2 p (43) P Makin(5) 8/1: 034-0038: Mid-div, outpcd when short of room 2f out. ½ 41

2466 LUKE AFTER ME 6 [8]4-9-13 (54) R Winston 12/1: 0204309: Mid-div, no impress over 1f out: qck reapp. ½ 51

2216 LIEUDAY 17 [2]5-9-8 p (49) D Nolan(3) 20/1: 053-5030: 10th: Bhd, rdn & no room 2f out, sn btn. 1¼ 43

1661 HORMUZ 42 [11]8-9-4 (45) M Lawson(5) 33/1: 06040-00: 11th: b g Hamas - Balqis (Advocator) Led, 3 33
drvn & hdd 2f out, wknd: 6 wk abs: h'cap plcd '03 (rtd 61 & 50a, tried cheek pieces): won 4 h'caps in '02 (incl
with D Nicholls): eff btwn 7.5f/10f on gd/soft & both AWs, loves firm & fast grnd: can go well fresh on any trk.
2 Oct'02 Sout 8af 70a-69 E: 1 Sep'02 Sout 8af 70a-64 E: 2 Sep'02 Sout 8af 64a-63 F: 1 Aug'02 Beve 7.4g/f 66-66 E:
2 Jun'02 Ches 10.3fm 63- D: 2 May'02 Beve 8.4gd 75-70 D: 1 May'02 Ches 7.5fm 76-64 C: 2 May'02 Hami 9.1sft 64- E:
1 Apr'02 Ripo 8g/f 64-60 E: 2 Mar'02 Sout 8af 58a- F: 1 Sep'01 Ripo 9g/f 62-59 D: 1 Aug'01 Beve 8.4g/s 59-58 E:

1750 THE GAMBLER 2 [4]4-9-10 p (51) Natalia Gemelova(7) 20/1: 0002000: 12th: Al bhd, qck reapp: btr 1393. 3½ 32

1948 Proud Western 28 [3]6-8-13 (40) T Eaves(3) 16/1:0

4360} Always Daring 275 [7]5-8-13 (40) T Hamilton(3) 66/1:0

14 Ran   Time 1m 27.32 (2.42)   Owned: Border Rail & Plant Limited   Trained: Wetherby

---

2616   5.00 Watch Racing Uk Live On 425 Handicap Stakes 4yo+ 35-55 (F)   [63]
£2947 £842 £421   **1m4f**   **Good/Firm 32**   +01 Fast   Inside

2526 LITTLE TASK 4 [8] J S Wainwright 6-8-1 (36) R Ffrench 5/2 FAV: 0/0/5-3141: Held up, rdn to chall 44
over 1f out, led dist, rdn out: qck reapp, well bckd: eff at 1m/10f, now stays a sharp 12f well: acts on fast & gd.

2402 ARCHIRONDEL 9 [7] M D Hammond 6-9-5 (54) P Mulrennan(5) 5/1: U002102: Trkd ldrs trav well, smooth nk 61
prog to chall over 1f out, rdn & no extra well ins last, just held: nicely bckd: back to form after wide passage
when disapp latest: stays a sharp 12f well: remains on a fair mark for similar: see 2120 (9f).

2163 PLATINUM CHARMER 19 [5] K R Burke 4-9-6 p (55) Darren Williams 5/1: 2142403: Trkd ldrs, hdwy to 1¼ 60
lead over 2f out, drvn & hdd dist, no extra: see 1819 & 1552.

2545 SMARTER CHARTER 3 [2] Mrs L Stubbs 11-8-5 (40) Kristin Stubbs(7) 11/1: 0206504: Rear, eff 2f out, 2 42
no impress dist: qck reapp: see 1450 & 1287.

336 MINIVET 167 [1]9-9-6 bl (55) D Allan 10/1: 60054-05: b g Midyan - Bronzewing (Beldale Flutter) 3½ 52
Chsd ldrs, no impress fnl 2f: jumps fit (plcd, rtd 110h, h'cap hdle): unplcd '03 (rtd 58, h'cap): claim hdle wnr
03/04 (rtd 111h, 2m/2m6.5f, fast & soft): missed '02 on the level: eff at 9f/12f on fast & soft grnd, without blnks.

1945 HIBERNATE 28 [4]10-8-5 (40) T Hamilton(3) 33/1: 00265/-06: ch g Lahib - Ministra (Deputy 4 31
Minister) Led till over 2f out, sn btn: missed '03: clmr rnr-up for K Burke in '02 (AW unplcd, rtd 42a, clmr):
lady riders h'cap & clmr scorer back in '01: loves to dominate at 10/12f on firm & soft grnd, any trk.
2 Jul'02 Catt 11.9g/f 41- F: 1 Aug'01 Muss 12g/f 63- F: 1 Jun'01 York 11.8g/s 63-57 C: 2 Jun'01 Hami 12g/f 60-57 E:

2497 MOYNE PLEASURE 5 [6]6-8-3 p (38) Natalia Gemelova(7) 10/1: 3146007: Prom, rdn & btn over 2f out. 1 28

2285 SHALBEBLUE 13 [3]7-8-10 bl (45) T Eaves(3) 7/2: 0325-008: Stumbled start & held up, no impress: bckd. 9 23

8 Ran   Time 2m 34.36 (3.76)   Owned: Mr Keith Jackson   Trained: Malton

---

WINDSOR   MONDAY 21.06.04   Sharp Fig 8 Track

Official Going Good/Firm (Heavy rain after race 2619)

2617   6.40 Fortune Centre Of Riding Therapy Handicap Stakes Fillies 3yo 0-70 (E)   [77]
£3552 £1093 £547   **1m2f7y**   **Good**   Fair   Inside

2452 FOXILLA 7 [2] D R C Elsworth 3-8-3 (52) R Thomas(5) 9/2 FAV: 000-0031: Handy, hdwy to lead over 60
1f out, styd on well, rdn out: 1st win: enjoys this sharp 10f on fast or gd grnd: lightly rcd, gd confidence boost.

1835 HIGH SCHOOL 34 [6] D R Loder 3-9-5 (68) E Ahern 8/1: 2642: In tch, eff outer over 2f out, chall 1 74
ins last, no pace of wnr cl-home: op 13/2: imprvd on h'cap bow & stays a sharp 10f, shld get further: acts on gd
grnd, poss soft: shld find a race: see 980.

2046 BUBBLING FUN 24 [14] E A L Dunlop 3-9-1 (64) T E Durcan 11/2: 02-4043: Handy, hdwy & short of 1¼ 68
room over 2f out till over 1f out, onepace: shade closer with clr run: see 2046.

2344 BLAEBERRY 11 [8] P L Gilligan 3-8-6 (55) G Carter 11/1: 00-00554: Dwelt, bhd, hdwy over 2f out, 1¾ 55
wknd fnl 1f: just failed too see out this 10f trip? see 1823.

1907 QUEEN LUCIA 30 [11]3-8-9 (58) T Quinn 16/1: 4445: In tch, eff dist, sn no extra: lngr trip. 3½ 51

2344 FAITH HEALER 11 [9]3-8-3 bl (52) J Quinn 14/1: 60-00046: Handy, hdwy to lead 2f out, sn hdd & nk 44
wknd: longer trip, see 2344 (1m, blnks).

2452 IVORY COAST 7 [7]3-8-11 (60) R Mullen 6/1: 04-41207: Bhd, some late gains: btr 1953 (fm). shd 52

1982 DREAM OF DUBAI 27 [5]3-8-11 (60) R L Moore 33/1: 05-008: b f Vettori - Immortelle (Arazi) ¾ 50
Dwelt, bhd, nvr a factor: unplcd both '03 starts (rtd 55a): bred for mid-dists.

1784 SAHARAN SONG 36 [1]3-8-11 (62) I Mongan 25/1: 4-009: ch f Singspiel - Sahara Baladee (Shadeed) 3½ 45
Cl-up, wknd 2f out: 4th sole juv start (mdn, rtd 66a): eff at 7f on polytrack, bred to get mid-dists.

1941 ELSINORA 29 [13]3-8-4 VIS (53) J F McDonald(3) 33/1: 0300-000: 10th: Al bhd: visored: see 798. nk 35

3973} NABTAT SAIF 102 [12]3-9-7 (70) P Gallagher(7) 18/1: 240-0400: 11th: b f Compton Place - Bahawir hd 51

Pour (Green Dancer) Dwelt, al bhd: unplcd in Dubai over 3 months ago: rnr-up in a mdn in '03: eff at 7f on gd grnd, not bred for mid-dists. 2 Jul'03 Good 7gd 76- D:
2064 **DAYDREAM DANCER 23** [10]3-8-4 (53) P Robinson 10/1: 000-500: 12th: In tch, outpcd over 3f out. ½ **33**
2025 **NUKHBAH 25** [3]3-9-3 (66) S Sanders 8/1: 43-3450: 13th: Led till 2f out, wknd: btr 1258 (1m). 15 **16**
2174 **SNOW JOKE 19** [4]3-8-8 (57) R Havlin 25/1: 000-0400: 14th: Al bhd, eased: see 1912. 5 **0**
14 Ran Time 2m 09.54 (3.54) Owned: Mr J Wotherspoon Trained: Whitsbury

2618

7.10 Mll Telecom Maiden Auction Stakes 2yo (E)
£3630 £1117 £559 **6f rnd** **Good** **Slow** Inside

2194 **DON PELE 18** [6] S Kirk 2-8-9 J Fortune 7/2: 021: Made virtually all, styd on well over 1f out, rdn out: nicely bckd: eff at 6f on gd: nursery type. **94**
AMAZIN [7] R Hannon 2-8-9 R Hughes 9/1: 2: b c Primo Dominie - Aegean Blue (Warning) Dwelt, held up, hdwy outer over 2f out, kept on, no threat to wnr: Mar foal, cost 24,000 gns: eff over a sharp 6f, 7f will suit: acts on gd grnd: v pleasing start, will learn from this & shld be wng sn. 2 **87**
ARIODANTE [9] J M P Eustace 2-8-7 S Sanders 20/1: 3: b g Groom Dancer - Maestrale (Top Ville) Dwelt, well bhd, styd on late, nrst fin on debut: Jan foal, cost 9,000 gns: half brother to a pair of 1m wnrs: eff at 6f, 7f sure to suit: acts on gd: plenty to like about this, kind ride, shld be wng shortly. 1½ **81+**
2171 **TRANSVESTITE 19** [11] J W Hills 2-8-11 E Ahern 6/1: 54: b c Trans Island - Christoph's Girl (Efisio) Sn rdn in tch, onepcd fnl 2f: Mar foal, cost 27,000 gns: half brother to a pair of 5f scorers: eff at 6f on gd grnd: worth a try in head-gear. ½ **83**
2061 **ROSIELLA 23** [2]2-8-2 J Quinn 80/1: 05: b f Tagula - Queen of Silk (Brief Truce) In tch, eff dist, onepace: Jan foal, cost 5,000gns: half sister to a 1m wnr: dam 1m juv scorer: bred to apprec 7f/1m. 1¾ **69**
2194 **MUSICO 18** [15]2-9-0 S Drowne 3/1 FAV: 46: Cl-up, no extra dist: hvly bckd, btr 2194. 2 **75**
2430 **HES A STAR 7** [14]2-8-9 P Gallagher(7) 14/1: 047: Bhd, some late gains: see 2430. 1 **67$**
2424 **DOVER STREET 8** [8]2-8-11 Paul Eddery 10/1: 58: Sn rdn in tch, lost place 2f out, mod gains. ½ **67**
ARIANE STAR [10]2-8-4 P Robinson 12/1: 9: Nvr a factor. nk **59**
PEPPERMINT TEA [4]2-8-6 I Mongan 20/1: 0: 10th: Dwelt, in tch, wknd 2f out on debut. nk **60**
Picot De Say [18]2-8-7 R Mullen 66/1:0
Grand Place [1]2-8-9 R L Moore 25/1:0
Marians Maid [16]2-8-2 D Kinsella 66/1:0
Asteem [12]2-8-7 S Carson 40/1:0
Busaco [17]2-8-9 T Quinn 14/1:0
2251 **Blue Marble 16** [5]2-8-11 T E Durcan 12/1:0
Emeraude Du Cap [3]2-8-2 J Mackay 66/1:0
Mister Elegant [13]2-8-7 L Keniry(3) 66/1:0
18 Ran Time 1m 14.21 (3.91) Owned: Mr Pedro Rosas Trained: Upper Lambourn

2619

7.40 Kpmg Llp Uk Handicap Stakes 3yo 0-80 (D) **[82]**
£5590 £1720 £860 **6f rnd** **Good** **Slow** Inside

2268* **BOHOLA FLYER 14** [9] R Hannon 3-9-7 (75) R Hughes 13/8 FAV: 2-146411: Handy, hdwy & styd on well to lead just ins fnl 1f, kept on despite rider losing whip: hvly bckd: suited by 6f on fast, gd & polytrack, handles soft & any trk, likes Windsor: lightly rcd & imprvg: see 2268. **82**
2271 **CHEROKEE NATION 14** [5] P W D'Arcy 3-8-3 (57) T Quinn 17/2: 06-44102: Keen in tch, eff well over 1f out, styd on to chall ins last, just held: back to form: see 1985. nk **63**
1829 **HALF A HANDFUL 34** [10] M J Wallace 3-8-11 (65) K Fallon 15/2: 00063: Held up, hdwy outer over 1f out, styd on ins last, nrst fin, not btn far: imprvd run over this sharp 6f on gd grnd. ½ **69**
2372 **GENERAL FEELING 10** [8] S Kirk 3-8-11 (65) J Fortune 13/2: 3-3304: In tch, hdwy to chall over 1f out, kept on, just held ins last: gd run, see 1787, 1575. shd **68**
2268 **WHISTFUL 14** [4]3-9-1 (69) S Sanders 7/2: 542-3035: Sn led, hdd & no extra ins last, not btn far. nk **71$**
2155 **SHIELALIGH 19** [3]3-9-4 t P (72) I Mongan 12/1: 43-00306: Dwelt, sn prom, wknd & hmpd over 1f out, eased: cheek pieces: see 1901. 6 **56**
2314 **ROCKLEY BAY 12** [7]3-8-8 (62) J Quinn 20/1: 054-007: b c Mujadil - Kilkee Bay (Case Law) Al bhd: 5th at best in '03 (mdn, rtd 63). 3 **37**
1872 **SHEBAAN 32** [6]3-7-12 (2oh) (50) F P Ferris(3) 66/1: U050-008: Al bhd: btr 1171. 7 **6**
560 **KNIGHT ONTHE TILES 136** [2]3-9-7 bl (75) N Pollard 16/1: 1060-009: Handy, wknd 2f out: see 560. 21 **0**
9 Ran Time 1m 14.15 (3.85) Owned: Mr William Durkan Trained: Marlborough

2620

8.10 Fraser Miller Can't Believe Yogi's Only 50 Classified Stakes 3yo+ 0-75 (D)
£5688 £1750 £875 **1m67y rnd** **Good/Soft** **Fair** Inside

2126 **DIAMOND LODGE 20** [6] J Noseda 3-8-9 (80) E Ahern 4/5 FAV: 4121: Held up in tch, rdn & narrow lead over 1f out, held on gamely for press: eff around 1m/8.3f on fast & gd/soft grnd, stiff or sharp trk, likes Windsor: prog profile & showed a fine attitude tonight: see 2126, 1810. **86**
1890 **ULTIMATA 31** [8] J R Fanshawe 4-9-5 (80) O Urbina 20/1: 1-02: ch f Unfuwain - Last Look (Rainbow Quest) Rear, switched wide & eff to chall over 1f out, al just held: left reapp bhd: sole start mdn auct wnr '03: eff at 1m, tried 10f, shld suit: acts on gd & gd/soft grnd, stiff/gall or sharp trk: can go well fresh: fine return, open to improvement. 1 May'03 Leic 8.0gd 81- F: nk **85**
2587 **CLIMATE 2** [3] J R Boyle 5-9-5 vis (77) J Fortune 8/1: 5402163: Trkd ldrs, styd on for press late. 1¾ **81**
2099 **JOOLS 21** [7] D K Ivory 6-9-6 (78) T Quinn 14/1: 0153004: Chsd ldrs, chall 2f out, no extra fnl 1f. ¾ **80**
4946} **GRANDALEA 235** [2]3-8-7 (78) K Fallon 4/1: 0236-5: b f Grand Lodge - Red Azalea (Shirley Heights) Led & dictated pace till over 1f out, sn rdn & btn: reapp: lightly rcd '03, AW fills mdn rnr-up, turf mdn plcd (rtd 76): eff at 7f/1m on fast grnd & polytrack, gall or sharp trk. 2 Sep'03 Ling 7ap 85a- D: 5 **67**
2197 **SCOTTISH RIVER 18** [1]5-9-5 (77) W Ryan 25/1: 0561466: Reluctant to race, no impress on ldrs. 2½ **64**
2350 **JUST TIM 11** [5]3-8-12 (80) R Hughes 10/1: 4140157: Chsd ldr, hung left & btn over 2f out: reportedly not handle gd/soft grnd: btr 2116 (gd). 1½ **64**
2356 **ILE MICHEL 10** [4]7-9-6 (78) S Sanders 25/1: 10-00438: Mid-div, btn 2f out, eased: btr 2356. 13 **36**
8 Ran Time 1m 48.98 (5.98) Owned: Mrs J Harris Trained: Newmarket

---

2621 8.40 Sharp Minds Betfair Handicap Stakes 3yo 0-75 (E)   [82]
£4355 £1340 £670   1m3f135y   **Good/Soft**   **V Slow** Inside

2130 **BILL BENNETT 20** [11] J Jay 3-9-7 (75) O Urbina 6/1: 5112501: Mid-div, hdwy over 3f out & led **84**
over 1f out, cmftbly: eff at 9f, suited by 11/14f: acts on firm, likes gd, hvy & fibresand: see 1528.
2113 **BLAZE OF COLOUR 21** [15] Sir Michael Stoute 3-9-2 (70) T Quinn 13/2: 0-342: Led till over 1f out, 4 **73**
no impress on wnr from dist: h'cap bow: eff around 11.5f/12f on gd & gd/soft grnd: can find a race: see 2113.
4377} **CELLARMASTER 275** [5] A C Stewart 3-9-4 (72) J Fortune 14/1: 352-3: ch g Alhaarth - Cheeky Weeky ¾ **74**
(Cadeaux Genereux) Trkd ldrs, styd on onepace for press fnl 3f: gldd: 'cap bow: AW mdn rnr-up '03, turf unplcd (rtd
68): styd longer 11.5f trip, could get further: handles fibresand, gd/soft grnd & a sharp/turning trk.
2 Sep'03 Wolv 8.5af 73a- D:
1648 **BAKHTYAR 42** [4] R Charlton 3-8-4 BL (58) J Quinn 20/1: 005-004: gr g Daylami - Gentilesse ½ **59**
(Generous) Handy, rdn & no extra over 1f out: 1st time blnks, imprvd eff: unplcd '03 (lightly rcd, rtd 50a & 65,
mdns, subs gldd): stays sharp 11.5f on gd/soft grnd.
2134 **CHANFRON 20** [13]3-8-6 (60) A McCarthy 20/1: 0360-05: Mid-div, eff over 3f out, no impress dist. 2 **59**
2250 **IN DEEP 16** [6]3-9-2 (70) Paul Eddery 14/1: 5562-006: Trkd ldrs, no impress fnl 2f: longer trip. 5 **63**
2248 **GOLDEN DRIFT 16** [2]3-8-6 (60) S Drowne 16/1: 0-057: Held up, eff wide 3f out, only mod prog. 4 **49**
2353 **GJOVIC 11** [14]3-9-7 (75) J F McDonald(3) 8/1: 2504338: Chsd ldrs 10f: btr 2353 & 2225. 2½ **61**
2135* **PLANTERS PUNCH 20** [16]3-9-1 VIS (69) R Hughes 5/1 FAV: 00-00019: Dwelt, chsd ldrs, rdn & btn when 2 **53**
short of room over 1f out: 1st time visor, reportedly not handle gd/soft grnd: btr 2135 (gd, 10f).
2392 **FIDDLERS FORD 9** [3]3-9-4 (72) E Ahern 9/1: 2264040: 10th: Rear, eff 3f out, no impress: hung left. 4 **52**
4216} **TUNGSTEN STRIKE 282** [10]3-9-0 (68) S Carson 40/1: 400-0: 11th: Prom, btn over 2f out: 2 **46**
reapp/h'cap bow, longer trip: has been gldd.
2024 **WILD PITCH 26** [7]3-8-7 (61) R L Moore 10/1: 6-0030: 12th: Sn strug rear, no impress: btr 2024. shd **39**
1528 **DUKES VIEW 49** [1]3-8-12 (66) S Sanders 14/1: 006-00: 13th: Slow away & al bhd, 7 wk abs. 4 **40**
1390* **GOLDEN EMPIRE 56** [12]3-9-5 (73) T E Durcan 10/1: 32-22410: 14th: Chsd ldrs till 3f out: abs, gldd. 5 **42**
1647 Inchpast 42 [8]3-8-6 (60) F P Ferris(3) 20/1:0   2133 Cashema 20 [9]3-7-12 (5oh)(47) D Kinsella 100/1:0
16 Ran   Time 2m 40.43 (13.13)   Owned: Mr & Mrs Jonathan Jay   Trained: Newmarket

---

2622 9.10 Yogi Breisner 50th Birthday Maiden Stakes 3yo (D)
£4459 £1372 £686   1m67y rnd   **Good/Soft**   **Slow** Inside

4429} **TAKE A BOW 271** [14] P R Chamings 3-9-0 J Quinn 8/1: 02-1: b c Royal Applause - Giant Nipper **90**
(Nashwan) Keen & trkd ldr, led 4f out & clr over 2f out, easily, val further: reapp: lightly rcd '03, mdn rnr-up:
eff around sharp/undul 1m: acts on firm & gd/soft grnd: goes well fresh, decisive scorer, interesting type for
h'cap company. 2 Sep'03 Good 8g/f 85- D:
NOBLE MIND [3] P G Murphy 3-9-0 D Kinsella 50/1: 2: b g Mind Games - Lady Annabel (Alhijaz) 4 **79**
Rear, styd on well fnl 2f, nvr threat to wnr on debut: dam only mod at up to 1m: stays 1m, get further on this
evidence: handles gd/soft grnd: encouraging.
RAAKAAN [5] A C Stewart 3-9-0 J Fortune 10/1: 3: b c Halling - Glimpse (Night Shift) Dwelt, 1¼ **78**
in tch, late gains: debut: 72,000gns purchase, dam 6f juv wnr: eff at 1m, 10f+ likely to suit: acts on gd/soft.
1514 **ANATOLIAN QUEEN 49** [10] J M P Eustace 3-8-9 S Sanders 3/1 FAV: 34: Handy & chsd wnr over 2f hd **72**
out, no extra in last: 7 wk abs: handles gd/soft & hvy grnd: see 1514.
2106 **DIFFERENT PLANET 21** [13]3-9-0 T Quinn 9/2: 445: Chsd ldrs, onepace fnl 2f: see 2106 & 1763. 3½ **71**
472 **STAGE RIGHT 149** [12]3-9-0 L Keniry(3) 6/1: 46: Mid-div, drvn & btn 2f out: abs, turf bow. 7 **59**
HOMEBRED STAR [11]3-9-0 D Corby(3) 33/1: 7: Slow away & rear, no impress fnl 2f on debut. 1 **57**
WEDDING CAKE [1]3-8-9 O Urbina 4/1: 8: Mid-div, btn 3f out, debut. 4 **45**
2106 **DAN DI CANIO 21** [2]3-9-0 T E Durcan 12/1: 59: Chsd ldrs, struggling fnl 3f. 3½ **45**
4924} **ARGENTUM 237** [4]3-9-0 R L Moore 33/1: 00-0: 10th: Bhd, little hdwy on reapp. 1¾ **42**
Blaze The Trail [9]3-8-9 M Henry 50/1:0   2291 **Benny Bathwick 13** [6]3-9-0 S Drowne 25/1:0
Sayrianna [7]3-8-9 I Mongan 50/1:0   233 **Dont Let Go 184** [8]3-8-9 S Carson 50/1:0
14 Ran   Time 1m 50.42(7.42)   Owned: Mrs J E L Wright   Trained: Basingstoke

---

Official Going Good/Firm

2623 6.50 Velindre Hospital Race Night Maiden Stakes 3yo+ (D)
£3614 £1112 £556   1m4f23y   **Good/Firm 36**   **-25 Slow** Inside

1501 **LIGHT WIND 50** [2] Mrs A J Perrett 3-8-7 W Supple 15/8: 51: ch f Unfuwain - River Spey (Mill **80+**
Reef) Slow away, sn cl-up, led 2f out, pushed out, val 5L+: 7 wk abs: cost 55,000gns: half-sister to numerous
wnrs: dam plcd in List grade at 10f: eff at 12f, shapes as tho' further will suit: acts on fast grnd & a
gall/undul trk: goes well fresh, only lightly rcd & can rate higher.
JAYER GILLES 0 [3] H Candy 4-9-12 Dane O'Neill 16/1: 2: br g Busy Flight - Jadidh (Touching 2½ **79**
Wood) Slow away, prog after 1m, chsd wnr ins fnl 1f, al held: clr rem: debut: dam successful over hdles: eff at
12f on fast grnd: encouraging run, can improve & stay further.
1308 **AT YOUR REQUEST 60** [8] E A L Dunlop 3-8-12 M Hills 10/1: 333: Cl-up, led after 5f, hdd 2f out, 6 **71**
sn no extra: 9 wk abs: now quals for h'caps: see 1308 & 1067.
1885 **POPES HILL 31** [5] L M Cumani 3-8-12 L Dettori 4/5 FAV: 0-44: Rear, prog after 7f, wknd fnl 2f: 1¾ **68**
well bckd: btr expected after promising 4th in 1885.
2107 **UNCLE BATTY 21** [7]4-9-12 S Hitchcott(3) 50/1: 45: Rear, prog halfway, fdd 4f out: btr 2107. 19 **43**
2368 **DELFINIA 10** [1]3-8-7 T P Queally(3) 33/1: 046: Cl-up 1m, sn wknd: btr 2368. 10 **24**
939} **SHANNONS DREAM 1161** [6]8-9-7 (18) Lisa Jones(3) 100/1: 0000/00//-7: gr f Anshan - Jenny's Call 21 **0**
(Petong) Cl-up 5f, sn fdd: v modest turf & hdles form to date.

2052 **FREDS FIRST** 24 [4]3-8-12 C Catlin 100/1: 0-58: Led 5f, sn fdd: btr 2052.   13   0
8 Ran   Time 2m 38.48 (7.38)   Owned: Hesmonds Stud   Trained: Pulborough

---

2624   7.20 Eversheds Solicitors Stakes Handicap Fillies 3yo 0-75 (E)   **[82]**
                  £3897 £1199 £600   1m14y str   Good/Firm 36   +02 Fast   Stands side

2312 **HOT LIPS PAGE** 12 [10] R Hannon 3-9-1 (69) Dane O'Neill 7/1: 005-51: Mid-div, prog to lead ins   76+
fnl 1f, pushed out, val bit more: eff at 7f, apprec step up to 1m: acts on fast grnd & a gall/undul trk: unexposed.
2432 **DAMI** 7 [8] C E Brittain 3-9-0 p (68) B Doyle 100/30 FAV: 400-5522: Held up, prog 3f out, kept on   1¾   71
ins fnl 1f, not pace wnr: qck reapp: op 9/4: .another gd effort, worth a try over further: see 2432.
1088 **LA LANDONNE** 75 [2] P M Phelan 3-9-0 (68) S W Kelly 16/1: 351-43: Led, hdd under press ins fnl   nk   70
1f, no extra: 11 wk abs: eff at 6f/1m on fast grnd & polytrack: see 146.
2013 **YOUNG LOVE** 26 [4] Miss E C Lavelle 3-8-1 (55) C Catlin 16/1: 00-064: ch f Pursuit of Love -   1¾   53
Polar Fair (Polar Falcon) Cl-up till dist, no extra: unplcd both '03 starts (rtd 59a, mdn): eff at 1m on fast grnd.
2153 **PELLA** 19 [1]3-8-7 (61) F Norton 7/1: 00625: Cl-up over 6f, no extra: btr 2153.   hd   58
2365 **SUNSET MIRAGE** 10 [6]3-9-2 (70) W Supple 4/1: 0-26106: Nvr nrr than mid-div: btr 1953 (11.5f).   2   63
1894 **MISS ADELAIDE** 31 [7]3-9-1 (69) M Hills 9/2: 43-4427: Rear, prog halfway, fdd dist: op 11/2.   5   52
1740 **FARAWAY ECHO** 38 [9]3-7-12 (20h) Hayley Turner(5) 12/1: 500-0638: Al in rear: btr 1740 (soft).   3½   28
4066J **GONE LOCO** 290 [5]3-7-12 (20h) (50) Lisa Jones(3) 25/1: 060-9: b f Piccolo - Missed Again (High   5   18
Top) Keen cl-up 6f, fdd: reapp: unplcd in '03 (rtd 57, mdn): with H S Howe.
2169 **VAS Y CARLA** 19 [3]3-9-7 (75) T P Queally(3) 9/1: 626-020: 10th: Slow away, prog halfway, wknd 3f out.   shd   40
10 Ran   Time 1m 34.67 (2.77)   Owned: Mr Bob Lalemant   Trained: Marlborough

---

2625   7.50 Terry Jayne Scallops Selling Stakes 2yo (G)
                  £2562 £732 £366   5f16y str   Good/Firm 36   -64 Slow   Stands side

2115 **ROYAL COZYFIRE** 21 [2] B Palling 2-8-11 S Hitchcott(3) 9/2: 51: b g Revoque - Mystic Thoughts   67
(Shernazar) Cl-up, styd on to lead dist, rdn out: no bid: Mar foal, cost £2,000: half-brother wnr abroad: dam
unrcd: sire Gr 1 wnr as a juv: apprec drop back to 5f, shld stay further: acts on fast & an undul/gall trk.
2449 **GLASSON LODGE** 7 [10] P D Evans 2-8-6 N Callan 2/1 FAV: 456342: Led & hdd 4f out, styd cl-up,   ¾   59
kept on but not pace wnr ins fnl 1f: qck reapp: acts on fast, gd grnd & fibresand: visor left off: see 2449 & 1256.
      WITTY GIRL 0 [3] M D I Usher 2-8-6 Hayley Turner(5) 11/1: 3: b f Whittingham - Zando's Charm   1   56
(Forzando) Bhd, prog halfway, styd on well ins fnl 1f, nrst fin: debut: clmd for 6,000: Feb First foal, dam 7f
wnr at 2: sire speedily bred: eff at 5f, crying out for further: acts on fast grnd: may do better.
1987 **WIZZSKILAD** 27 [7] Mrs P N Dutfield 2-8-11 Lisa Jones(3) 9/4: 046304: Bhd, prog halfway, onepcd dist.   ½   60
2270 **SAPPHIRE PRINCESS** 14 [6]2-8-6 T P Queally(3) 9/1: 45: Cl-up 3f, sn outpcd, rallied late: see 2270.   hd   54
2449 **ZACHY BOY** 7 [9]2-8-11 P Derek Nolan(7) 12/1: 6050066: b g Inchinor - Ellway Dancer (Mujadil) Led   ¾   57
4f out, hdd dist, no extra: clr rem: qck reapp & cheek pieces: Feb foal, cost 3,000gns: dam unplcd.
      FIRE AT WILL 0 [8]2-8-11 W Supple 12/1: 7: Al in rear: debut.   5   42
2257 **SABO PRINCE** 15 [4]2-8-11 Dane O'Neill 25/1: 0508: Cl-up 3f, hung left & wknd: see 1937.   1   39
2257 **ANGELAS GIRL** 15 [5]2-8-6 C Catlin 25/1: 09: Al in rear.   16   0
9 Ran   Time 1m 1.80 (5.0)   Owned: Crosslee PLC   Trained: Cowbridge

---

2626   8.20 Betfred Sprint Series Handicap Stakes Qualifier 3yo+ 0-80 (D)   **[80]**
                  £5421 £1668 £834   6f16y str   Good/Firm 36   +03 Fast   Stands side

2416 **ONE WAY TICKET** 9 [3] J M Bradley 4-8-10 p (62) S W Kelly 6/1: 0032031: Sn grabbed stands rail &   73+
made all, pushed out, cmftbly: eff at 6f/7f on firm, gd/soft grnd & prob any trk: eff with cheek pieces: enjoyed
getting own way upfront & is weighted to win again: see 2416 & 2111.
2451 **FULL SPATE** 7 [10] J M Bradley 9-9-2 (68) C Catlin 7/2: 5464632: Rear, prog 2f out, kept on fnl   2½   69
1f, not pace wnr: shorter priced stablemate of wnr: continues to run well & winning turn shld not be far away.
2451 **GLENCOE SOLAS** 7 [7] S Kirk 4-9-6 (72) L Dettori 3/1 FAV: 6422153: Cl-up, onepcd from dist: qck   nk   73
reapp: 6lb higher than recent win in 2232.
2235 **SEWMUCH CHARACTER** 16 [9] M Blanshard 5-8-13 (65) N Callan 9/2: 304-4064: Mid-div, prog 2f out,   1¾   61
no impress on fnl 1f: clr rem: see 1345.
2289 **FORMALISE** 13 [1]4-8-10 (62) F Norton 9/1: 5060-005: Nvr nrr than mid-div: see 1914.   4   46
1383 **GOLDEN BOUNTY** 56 [5]5-9-9 (75) P Dobbs 16/1: 05000-06: b c Bahamian Bounty - Cumbrian Melody   nk   58
(Petong) Rear, modest late gains: 8 wk abs: rnr-up once in '03 (stks): h'cap wnr in '02, subs List rnr-up: eff
at 5f, stays 6f on gd & firm, likes a stiff/gall trk: with R Hannon.
2 Jun'03 Sand 5.0fm 91-(90) C: 2 May'02 Newb 6g/f 99- A: 1 Apr'02 Sand 5gd 101-90 B: 1 Sep'01 Pont 5fm 90- E:
2269 **AMONG FRIENDS** 14 [2]4-8-11 (63) Lisa Jones(3) 25/1: 036-6007: Cl-up 4f, sn wknd: see 1079.   ¾   44
2398 **BOAVISTA** 9 [8]4-8-7 (59) Joanna Badger 16/1: 4221008: Cl-up over 4f, wknd: btr 2034.   2   34
2320 **CURRENCY** 12 [4]7-9-10 (76) Dane O'Neill 9/1: 2400049: Al bhd: rdr reported mount lost action.   10   26
9 Ran   Time 1m 10.80 (2.0)   Owned: Saracen Racing   Trained: Chepstow

---

2627   8.50 Velindre Hospital Cancer Research Maiden Stakes Fillies 3yo (D)
                  £3731 £1148 £574   1m14y str   Good/Firm 36   -05 Slow   Stands side

2349 **GAME DAME** 11 [10] B W Hills 3-8-11 (78) M Hills 3/1: 33-41: Mid-div, prog to lead 1f out, drvn   81
out: eff at 1m, 10f+ lks sure to suit: acts on fm & fast: more to come.
2072 **POWERFUL PARRISH** 23 [11] P F I Cole 3-8-11 S Chin 20/1: 25-02: b f Quiet American - Parish   1   78
Business (Phone Trick) Mid-div, outpcd 3f out, styd on strongly cl-home, not reach wnr: rnr-up on sole '03 start
(fill stks): prev eff at 5f, now suited by 1m, shapes as tho' further will suit: acts on fast grnd: encouraging
run & can find similar. 2 May'03 Sali 5g/f 78- C:
2231 **CANTARNA** 17 [1] J Mackie 3-8-11 (76) N Callan 5/2: 555-23: Cl-up, ev ch bef 1f out, sn no extra: 1   76
acts on fast & gd/soft grnd: again ran well: see 2231 (debut).
4408J **STRAWBERRY FAIR** 272 [6] Saeed bin Suroor 3-8-11 L Dettori 7/4 FAV: 2-4: b f Kingmambo - Storm   nk   75
Song (Summer Squall) Led, hdd 1f out, no extra: bckd on reapp: rnr-up sole '03 start (mdn, D R Loder): stays 1m,
drop back to 6/7f might suit: acts on fast grnd. 2 Sep'03 Newm 8g/f 74- D:

1209 **CHERUBIM 66** [7]3-8-11 (78) T P Queally(3) 13/2: 32-55: ch f Sunday Silence - Curly Angel (Judge Angelucci) Cl-up, onepcd from dist: 9 wk abs: plcd on both '03 starts (rtd 82, fill mdn): eff 6f/1m on fast & gd grnd. 2 Jul'03 Yarm 7.0gd 82- D: *nk* **74**
2117 **COTTON EASTER 21** [2]3-8-11 F Norton 100/1: 006: Rear, nvr nrr than mid-div: now quals for h'caps. *8* **58**
2031 **PALABELLE 25** [9]3-8-11 B Doyle 25/1: 007: Rear, modest late gains. *5* **50**
2224 **PRELUDE 17** [3]3-8-11 S W Kelly 50/1: 508: Bhd, nvr a factor. *2½* **45**
1651 **HIGHLIGHT GIRL 42** [8]3-8-11 S Hitchcott(3) 100/1: 09: Mid-div 6f, wknd. *3½* **38**
2118 **NINAH 21** [4]3-8-11 (64) C Catlin 50/1: 2240-000: 10th: Keen cl-up 5f, fdd. *3½* **31**
WAY OUT 0 [5]3-8-11 M Tebbutt 66/1: 0: 11th: Al in rear on debut. *6* **19**
11 Ran Time 1m 35.20 (3.3) Owned: Maktoum Al Maktoum Trained: Lambourn

2628

9.20 Velindre Hospital Handicap Stakes 3yo+ 0-75 (E) **[73]**
£3751 £1154 £577 **1m2f36y** **Good/Firm 36** **-50 Slow** Inside

2371 **REALISM 10** [5] P W Hiatt 4-9-4 (63) Lisa Jones(3) 11/4 FAV: 5036121: Cl-up, styd on to lead 2f out, rdn out to hold on: eff at 1m/10f on fast, gd grnd & fibresand: in-form 4yo: see 2371 & 2157. **75**
2284* **FRONTIER 13** [6] B J Llewellyn 7-9-13 t (72) R Havlin 4/1: 0000-212: Cl-up, trav well & ev ch 1f out, not pace of wnr: clr rem: top-weight: 3lb higher than recent win in 2284. *¾* **82**
2371 **BILLY BATHWICK 10** [2] J M Bradley 7-8-11 (56) Dane O'Neill 5/1: 553-0033: Mid-div, eff 3f out, no extra dist: back on a winning mark: just btr 2371. *5* **59**
1884* **SMART JOHN 31** [9] W M Brisbourne 4-9-4 (63) S W Kelly 7/2: 3050-414: Rear, prog 4f out, no impress fnl 2f: only 3lb higher than recent win in 1884. *shd* **65**
1772 **SAHAAT 37** [1]6-10-0 (73) T P Queally(3) 14/1: 00-00005: b g Machiavellian - Tawaaded (Nashwan) Rear, prog after 6f, wknd 1f out: rnr-up once in '03 (AW stks): French, '02 wnr in the provinces: eff at 8.5f on gd, soft & fibresand: with J A Osborne. 2 Jan'03 Wolv 8.4af 96a- C: *½* **74**
2433 **REBATE 7** [8]4-9-3 (62) P Dobbs 6/1: 5000336: Led 1m, sn wknd: qck reapp: just btr 2433. *nk* **62**
1530 **MR DIP 49** [3]4-8-8 (53) C Haddon(7) 33/1: 050-0607: Al in rear: 7 wk abs. *4* **47**
4966} **ZULETA 233** [4]3-8-0 (57) F Norton 16/1: 000044-8: ch f Vettori - Victoria (Old Vic) Mid-div till halfway, sn wknd: reapp: unplcd in '03 (rtd 61, fill mdn): eff at 1m on fibresand. *12* **35**
8 Ran Time 2m 12.72(8.62) Owned: Miss Maria McKinney Trained: Banbury

NOTTINGHAM **MONDAY 21.06.04 Lefthand, Galloping Track**

Official Going GOOD/FIRM. All Time Slow.

2629

2.15 European Breeders Fund Maiden Stakes 2yo (D)
£5301 £1631 £816 **6f15y str** **Good/Firm** **Slow** Stands Side

2364 **HORNPIPE 10** [1] Sir Michael Stoute 2-9-0 K Fallon 13/8 FAV: 61: b c Danehill - Dance Sequence (Mr Prospector) Swerved start, led after 2f, sn clr, v easily: well bkcd: Mar foal, half-brother to wnrs over 5f/12f: dam high-class 6f juv: eff over a gall 6f on fast grnd: left debut bhd & deserves a step up in grade. **88+**
2367 **GAVIOLI 10** [7] J M Bradley 2-9-0 t R L Moore 10/1: 5042: Prom, chsd wnr from halfway, sn left bhd: op 14/1: caught a tartar here, see 2367. *5* **68**
BLAKESHALL HOPE [4] P D Evans 2-9-0 Dean McKeown 66/1: 3: ch g Piccolo - Elite Hope (Moment of Hope) Speed till halfway on debut: Mar foal, dam a 7f wnr: sire a high-class sprinter: sellers will suit. *2½* **61**
BADDAM [6] J L Dunlop 2-9-0 J Murtagh 8/1: 4: b c Mujahid - Aude La Belle (Ela Mana Mou) Slowly away, al bhd on debut: 15,000gns Mar foal: half-brother to a couple of wnrs abroad: dam 2m wnr. *5* **46**
ROWAN WARNING [5]2-9-0 T Quinn 13/2: 5: Slowly away, al bhd on debut. *1½* **42**
2089 **TOWN END TOM 22** [2]2-9-0 M Fenton 6/1: 56: Led 2f, wknd after halfway: op 9/1. *7* **22**
FACT AND FICTION [3]2-9-0 K Dalgleish 4/1: 7: b c Fasliyev - Flyleaf (Persian Bold) Prom 4f, wknd & eased on debut: drifter from 5/2: E70,000 Feb foal: half-brother to a juv wnr abroad: dam a wnr in France, sire a top-class juv sprinter: with M Johnston & much btr clrly expected. *11* **0**
7 Ran Time 1m 15.45 (4.65) Owned: Cheveley Park Stud Trained: Newmarket

2630

2.45 Pablo Picasso Handicap Stakes 3yo+ 35-55 (F) **[65]**
£3584 £1024 £512 **6f15y str** **Good/Firm** **Slow** Stands Side

2439 **MISS JUDGEMENT 7** [20] W R Muir 3-9-2 (53) F Norton 13/2 JT FAV: 006-5321: Chsd ldrs stands side, led ent fnl 1f, rdn well clr: suited by 6f, shld stay 7f: acts on fast & firm grnd & on a sharp/undul or gall trk: deserved first win, shld follow up under a pen: see 2439 & 1985. **67**
1897 **REDOUBTABLE 31** [4] D W Chapman 13-9-4 (48) A Culhane 16/1: 1001002: Chsd ldrs far side, led dist, kept on well but no ch with wnr stands side: 13yo who remains a credit to connections: see 1606 (C/D). *5* **51**
2599 **BLESSED PLACE 1** [6] D J S ffrench Davis 4-9-1 t (45) P McCabe 14/1: 00000033: Chsd ldrs far side, kept on under press fnl 1f: another fair eff, also 3rd at Warwick yesterday: see 2599. *shd* **48**
2535 **TOPPLING 3** [19] J M Bradley 6-9-11 (55) R L Moore 13/2 JT FAV: 00-00004: Led till dist stands side, no extra: qck reapp: see 2214. *shd* **58**
1938 **CAFE AMERICANO 29** [18]4-9-1 e (45) J Fortune 66/1: 05000-05: Swerved start, outpcd stands side, fin well but too late: eye-shield: got going too late & a rtn to 7f will suit judged on this: acts on gd & fast. *1* **45**
2370 **BENEKING 10** [9]4-9-10 (54) N Callan 14/1: 000-0306: Slow away far side, chsd ldrs 5f. *shd* **54**
2396 **TENDER 9** [1]4-9-9 p (53) S Drowne 10/1: 3500507: Chsd ldrs far side, onepcd fnl 1f: btr 2262. *1¾* **48**
2398 **TAMARELLA 9** [8]4-9-5 vis (49) A McCarthy 12/1: 0050008: Led 4f far side, wknd: see 2062. *2* **38**
2396 **MANNORA 9** [11]4-9-7 (51) K Fallon 17/2: 430-4009: Chsd ldrs stands side, btn fnl 1f: see 1730. *1* **37**
2347 **KOMENA 11** [14]6-9-1 BL (45) J Murtagh 20/1: 40-50000: 10th: Front rank 5f stands side, wknd: blnks. *nk* **30**
2201 **DISPOL VERITY 17** [2]4-9-1 (45) S W Kelly 100/1: 34000/-00: 11th: b f Averti - Fawley Mist (Suave Dancer) Al outpcd far side: missed '03: plcd sev times in juv sellers in '02: eff at 5/6f on firm & gd/soft, handles fibresand: handles a gall or sharp trk: with W Brisbourne. 2 May'02 Beve 5gd 59- F: *1¾* **25**
2428 **ROAN RAIDER 8** [10]4-9-5 p (49) L Fletcher(3) 33/1: 3405350: 12th: Chsd ldrs 4f stands side. *1* **26**
2398 **TUSCAN TREATY 9** [7]4-9-6 (50) J F McDonald(3) 16/1: 0-004060: 13th: Chsd ldrs far side, btn dist. *½* **26**
2262 **SERGEANT SLIPPER 15** [3]7-9-0 vis (44) R Fitzpatrick 28/1: 1201500: 14th: Slowly away, al bhd far side. *1½* **16**

92	**VINTAGE STYLE 209** [16]5-9-10 (54) K Darley 20/1: 404050-0: 15th: ch g Piccolo - Gibaltarik (Jareer) Al bhd stands side on reapp: class stks plcd & h'cap 4th in '03 (rtd 62 at best): '02 AW h'cap rnr-up for R Hannon: eff at 5/6f, prob stays 7f: acts on fast, soft grnd & prob both AWs: has tried blnks & cheek pieces. 2 Jan'02 Ling 5ap 73a-67 E: 1 Dec'01 Ling 6ap 70a-64 E:	hd	26
2396	**ATTORNEY 9** [17]6-9-4 vis (48) L Vickers 12/1: 2036650: 16th: Hmpd start stands side, al bhd.	7	0
2201	**MOLOTOV 17** [13]4-9-2 (46) K Dalgleish 33/1: 0000-100: 17th: Speed 4f stands side: upset prelims.	2½	0
1988	**FLYING FAISAL 27** [15]6-9-0 (44) C Catlin 33/1: 6100000: 18th: Al bhd stands side.	3	0
2080	**SUPER CANYON 23** [5]6-9-10 vis t (54) T Quinn 8/1: 32-42000: 19th: Dwelt far side, al bhd: op 12/1.	nk	0
2598	**SPEEDFIT FREE 1** [12]7-9-2 p (46) Ann Stokell 25/1: 04006070: 20th: Chsd ldrs 4f stands side, wknd.	5	0

20 Ran   Time 1m 15.15 (4.35)   Owned: Double D Partnership   Trained: Lambourn

---

2631   3.15 Midsummers Day Stakes Handicap 3yo 0-85 (D)   [90]
£5954 £1832 £916   **1m1f213y**   Good/Firm   V Slow   Inside

2283	**PENZANCE 13** [7] J R Fanshawe 3-9-2 (78) J Murtagh 5/2: 13-641: Nvr far away, went on dist, styd on strongly, rdn out: eff at 1m, stays 10f well: acts on fast & firm grnd, can run well fresh: half-brother to top-class miler Soviet Song & prob more to come: see 1515.		82
2314	**SWIFT SAILING 12** [2] B W Hills 3-8-7 (69) A Culhane 33/1: 015-0002: Chsd ldrs, sltly outpcd halfway, rallied strongly fnl 1f: stayed longer 10f trip, acts on fast & gd/soft grnd: see 1983.	1¼	69
1924	**INCURSION 30** [4] A King 3-9-7 (83) R Hughes 10/1: 063-103: Slowly away, hdwy 2f out, onepace: jt top-weight: acts on fast & soft grnd: see 1651 (reapp).	shd	83
4639*	**)KINGS EMPIRE 258** [8] D Carroll 3-9-7 (83) R Fitzpatrick 16/1: 31-4: b g Second Empire - Dancing Feather (Suave Dancer) Held up, rdn to imprvd 2f out, sn no impress: won fnl of 2 juv starts (AW mdn auct): eff at 1m on fast grnd & fibresand, shld stay 10f: can force the pace. 1 Oct'03 Sout 8af 83a- F:	1¼	81
2250	**MALIBU 16** [1]3-8-13 (75) R L Moore 9/2: 1500-465: Held up, not pace to chall.	1½	71
2168	**FOSSGATE 19** [3]3-8-9 (71) T Quinn 14/1: 05-2036: Led till halfway, lost pl 2f out, rallied fnl 1f.	1	65
2113	**SONG OF VALA 21** [5]3-9-2 (78) S Drowne 10/1: 042-057: Chsd ldr, led 2f out till dist, wknd: see 2113.	2	69
2036*	**NANTUCKET SOUND 25** [9]3-8-8 (70) K Fallon 9/4 FAV: 634-0418: Prom, led halfway till 2f out, wknd: well bckd: reportedly hung right & this is not his form: much btr judged 2036.	2	58

8 Ran   Time 2m 12.48 (10.18)   Owned: Elite Racing Club   Trained: Newmarket

---

2632   3.45 Midlands Racing - 9 Great Venues - Classified Stakes 4yo+ 0-60 (F)
£3178 £908 £454   **2m9y**   Good/Firm   Slow   Inside

2156	**SONOMA 19** [6] M L W Bell 4-8-11 (60) K Darley 9/2: 5-506001: Cl-up, styd on to lead 3f out, rdn out: op 11/2: eff at 14f/2m on fast grnd: acts on gall or sharp trk: see 1003.		67
2298*	**SPITTING IMAGE 13** [2] Mrs M Reveley 4-8-11 (58) A Culhane 10/3: 0302412: Cl-up, kept on under press fnl 2f, not pace wnr: clr rem: see 2298 (clmr).	2	64
2198*	**CALAMINTHA 18** [1] M C Pipe 4-9-2 (65) K Fallon 5/4 FAV: 501-2613: Led, hdd under press 3f out, sn wknd: v well bckd: disapp eff: btr 2198 (2m2f, h'cap).	11	59
2329	**SQUIRTLE TURTLE 11** [3] P F I Cole 4-9-0 (60) N De Souza(5) 33/1: 3-100454: Handy 12f, sn wknd.	nk	56
1469	**STARRY MARY 52** [4]6-8-11 (55) G Duffield 12/1: 006-2205: Rear, prog after 5f, wknd fnl 3f.	5	48
2391	**SNOWS RIDE 9** [5]4-9-5 (65) S Drowne 9/2: 4-000006: Al in rear: btr 140.	14	41

6 Ran   Time 3m 37.21 (13.01)   Owned: Mrs P D Gray   Trained: Newmarket

---

2633   4.15 Monet Maiden Stakes 3yo+ (D)
£4046 £1245 £623   **1m54y rnd**   Good/Firm   V Slow   Inside

2093	**FLASHING BLADE 22** [12] B A McMahon 4-9-2 t (70) G Gibbons 10/1: 5-000001: b f Inchinor - Finlaggan (Be My Chief) Keen in tch, led 2f out, hung left under press ins fnl 1f, drvn out: unplcd in 3 '03 starts (incl Gr 3, rtd 87): apprec step up to 1m: acts on fast grnd & a gall trk: eff with a t-strap: has had muscle probs, gd confidence boost & rate higher around this trip.		69
	ZATHONIA [10] R Charlton 3-8-6 S Drowne 14/1: 2: b f Zafonic - Danthonia (Northern Dancer) Slow away, prog ins fnl 2f, styd on well cl-home, post came too soon: op 8/1 on debut: sire Gr 1 wnr at 1m: eff at 1m, shapes as tho' 10f will suit: acts on fast grnd: encouraging start to career & can find similar.	½	67
4067}	**PENDING 290** [11] J R Fanshawe 3-8-11 J Murtagh 3/1: 05-3: b g Pennekamp - Dolcezza (Lichine) Cl-up, led after 2f, hdd 2f out, no extra dist: reapp: 5th of 18th on 1 of 2 '03 starts (mdn, rtd 81): half-brother to sev wnrs, incl 7f juv wnr Martin House: eff at 1m, shld apprec further: acts on fast grnd: has been gelded.	1¾	68
98	**JOLIZERO 209** [13] P W Chapple Hyam 3-8-11 A McCarthy 40/1: 000-4: br g Danzero - Jolis Absent (Primo Dominie) Rear, prog 3f out, kept on ins fnl 1f: reapp & new stable: modest form in 3 '03 starts (rtd 61, mdn, G Margarson): eff at 1m on fast grnd: imprvd eff since been gelded, can rate higher for v capable yard.	1¾	64$
2135	**LITTLE ENGLANDER 20** [6]4-9-7 (52) S Whitworth 33/1: 240-5005: Slow away, prog despite hanging left ins fnl 2f, mod late gains: needs modest h'caps: see 1430.	1½	61$
2231	**SUCCESSOR 17** [7]4-9-7 R Hughes 9/1: 2/-06: Led 2f, styd in tch till wknd dist: see 2231.	1¼	58
1978	**BLUETORIA 27** [1]3-8-6 Dean McKeown 12/1: 0-47: Nvr nrr than mid-div: rider reported mount was unsuited by loose ground: btr 1978.	1¾	49
2117	**MINORITY REPORT 21** [5]4-9-7 N Mackay(3) 15/8 FAV: 38: Slow away, cl-up halfway, wknd fnl 2f: well bckd: failed to build on promise shown in 2117 (debut).	1¼	51
1835	**RAINBOW COLOURS 34** [8]3-8-6 T G Duffield 28/1: 6-09: Cl-up till halfway, sn wknd.	3	40
1705}	**PRETTY KOOL 394** [4] 4-9-2 S Drowne 100/1: 0/00-0: 10th: Al in rear on reapp.	nk	39
2182	**LIGHT THE DAWN 18** [3]4-9-2 S W Kelly 100/1: 0-000: 11th: Keen mid-div, wknd fnl 3f.	14	14
	Super Boston [2]4-9-7 R Lappin 100/1:0 1810 **Torchlight 35** [9]4-9-2 BL T J Fortune 14/1:0		

13 Ran   Time 1m 48.34 (8.94)   Owned: Mr W D McClennon   Trained: Tamworth

NOTTINGHAM   MONDAY 21.06.04   Lefthand, Galloping Track

2634   4.45 Van Gogh Handicap Stakes 3yo 0-75 (E)   [79]
£3998 £1230 £615   **1m54y rnd**   **Good/Firm**   **V Slow**   Inside

2272 **SPRING JIM 14** [8] J R Fanshawe 3-9-5 (70) J Murtagh 9/1: 450-41: Rear, prog well ins fnl 2f,   79
qcknd for press to lead cl-home: eff at 7f, imprvd for step up to 1m: acts on fast grnd & stiff or sharp/undul or
gall trk: unexposed in h'cap grade: see 2272 (reapp).
2423 **CAPTAIN MARRYAT 8** [14] P W Harris 3-8-6 (57) R L Moore 4/1: 0-2022: Held up wide, prog to lead   nk   64
1f out, sn hung left under press, hdd cl-home: well bckd: gd run despite racing wide, can find similar: see 2423.
2365 **FOLEY PRINCE 10** [2] Mrs Stef Liddiard 3-9-7 (72) K Darley 4/1: 0301223: Led, hdd 3f out, styd   2   75
cl-up, onepcd ins fnl 1f: continues to run well: see 2365 & 1956.
2272 **BERTOCELLI 14** [5] G G Margarson 3-9-4 (69) A McCarthy 14/1: 610-0034: Cl-up, led after 5f, hdd   1   70
1f out, no extra: prob stays 1m, rtn to 7f shld suit: just btr 2272.
2205 **RAYSOOT 17** [11]3-8-9 (60) R Hughes 3/1 FAV: 000-025: Cl-up, rcd wide, trav best halfway, wknd   1   59
under press from dist: well bckd: acts on fast grnd & fibresand: task not helped by racing v wide: see 2205.
1896 **VIOLET AVENUE 31** [10]3-8-8 (59) M Fenton 66/1: 204-06: Slow away, prog/no room 2f out, onepcd.   1½   55
2032 **GO GREEN 25** [1]3-7-12 (49) Joanna Badger 25/1: 000057: Handy 6f, sn wknd: btr 2032.   3½   38
2166 **TROJAN FLIGHT 19** [6]3-8-12 (63) A Culhane 16/1: 00-45468: Dwelt, prog when no room 2f out, onepcd. hd   52
1763 **MY HOPE 37** [4]3-9-5 (70) S Drowne 14/1: 00-009: b f Danehill - Lady Elgar (Sadler's Wells)   hd   59
Cl-up 6f, sn wknd: unplcd both '03 starts (rtd 67 & 55a, mdns).
1647 **SOLO SOLE 42** [9]3-9-0 (65) N Mackay(3) 28/1: 6003-000: 10th: Cl-up, sn outpcd, prog halfway, wknd   2½   49
fnl 2f: 6 wk abs: has been gelded.
2314 **Molinia 12** [13]3-8-9 (60) G Duffield 25/1:0   2439 **Breezit 7** [7]3-8-1 (52) J Bramhill 25/1:0
1872 **Joshuas Gold 32** [12]3-8-5 (56) R Fitzpatrick 40/1:0   1257 **Desert Diplomat 63** [3]3-9-1 (66) K Fallon 14/1:0
14 Ran   Time 1m 48.45(9.05)   Owned: Andrew & Julia Turner   Trained: Newmarket

LONGCHAMP   THURSDAY 17.06.04   Righthand, Stiff, Galloping Track

Official Going Good/Soft

2635   2.20 Gr 3 La Coupe 4yo+ ()
£25704 £10282 £7711   **1m2f**   **Good/Soft**

AUBONNE [3] E Libaud 4-8-8 C Soumillon 2/1 FAV: 4353-141: ch f Monsun - Anna Maria (Night   113
Shift) Held up, hdwy to chse ldr over 1f out, led well ins last: earlier scored over C/D here at Longchamp: well
suited by 10f on gd & v soft ground: smart filly.
1079* **SOLDIER HOLLOW** [7] P Schiergen 4-8-11 A Suborics 42/1: /14-4202: Held up, styd on wide late.   1½   113
4275} **LOOK HONEY** [4] C Lerner 4-8-11 bl Y Lerner 88/10: 23155-03: Held up, styd on wide, nrst fin.   snk   112
1862 **BIG BAD BOB 28** [1] J L Dunlop 4-8-11 (112) O Peslier 43/10: 201110-34: Led & sn well clr, hdd   hd   111
well ins last & no extra: not disgraced: see 1862.
10 Ran   Time 2m 05.00()   Owned: Mme I Von Schubert   Trained: France

SAN SIRO   SUNDAY 20.06.04   Righthand, Stiff, Galloping Track

Official Going Good

2636   4.20 Gr 1 Gran Premio di Milano 3yo+ ()
£177042 £89120 £51901   **1m4f**   **Good**

1556 **SENEX 49** [1] H Blume 4-9-6 W Mongil 169/10: 226-3351: b c Pelder - Septima (Touching Wood)   119
Rear, hdwy 2f out & led dist, rdn & styd on strongly: Gr 2 rnr up last term: eff at 10/12f on good & soft ground:
smart colt. 2 Aug'03 Bade 10gd 110- A:
1705 **MAKTUB 38** [4] M A Jarvis 5-9-6 P Robinson 101/10: 1200-062: Led & qcknd tempo 4f out, hdd dist, 2½   115
kept on: back to form: see 1705 (Gr 2).
2573} **THE GREAT GATSBY** [5] J H M Gosden 4-9-6 J Fortune 24/10: 44/225-3: b c Sadler's Wells - Ionian 1   114
Sea (Slip Anchor) Trkd ldr, drvn & chall over 1f out, no extra: reapp: lightly rcd '03 for A P O'Brien, Epsom Derby
rnr up: Galway mdn wnr '02, also Gr 1 4th (rtd 105): eff at 1m/10f, stays 12f: acts on fm & gd/sft grnd: likes a
stiff/gall trk: smart performer, encouraging comeback, reportedly would have enjoyed softer ground.
2 Jun'03 Epso 12.0fm 120-0 A: 2 May'03 Leop 10g/s 116- A:
7 Ran   Time 2m 28.70()   Owned: Stall Meerbusch   Trained: Germany

DORTMUND   SUNDAY 20.06.04

Official Going Good

DORTMUND   SUNDAY 20.06.04

2637   **5.00 Gr 3 Grosser Preis der Wirtschaft 3yo+** ()
£22535 £9155 £4577   **1m1f65y rnd   Good**

2069* **TAHREEB 22** [8] M P Tregoning 3-8-2 (108) W Supple 18/10 FAV: 1344-4211: Chsd ldr, led over 2f   **111**
out, styd on strongly, rdn out: eff over 1m/10f on firm & gd/sft, any trk: smart, win more gd prizes: see 2069.
　　　　ANOLITAS [10] U Ostmann 4-8-13 bl I Ferguson 153/10: 2: Held up in tch, styd on late, no dngr.   1¼   **107**
　　　　MORBIDEZZA [3] M Trinker 4-8-11 L Hammer Hansen 171/10: 3: Mid-div, styd on late, nvr dngr to wnr.   1¼   **103**
　　　　11 Ran Time 1m 47.14() Owned: Sheikh Ahmed Al Maktoum Trained: Lambourn

CHANTILLY   MONDAY 21.06.04   Righthand, Galloping Track

Official Going Good/Soft

2638   **1.50 Listed Prix Hampton 3yo+** ()
£15845 £6338 £4754   **5f str   Good/Soft**

　　　　CHINEUR [3] M Delzangles 3-8-13 E Legrix : 1 : b c Fasliyev - Wardara (Sharpo) Just prevailed   **111**
in a tight finish, earlier 6th in a Gr 2 here behind Avonbridge: v eff at 5f on gd/soft: smart.
　　　　RUE LA FAYETTE [12] F Reuterskiold 4-9-2 O Doleuze : 2: Just denied in a tight finish.   nk   **107**
2206 **BISHOPS COURT 17** [11] Mrs J R Ramsden 10-9-5 (110) T Gillet : 153-12033: Trkd ldrs, styd on for   1½   **105**
press ins last, nrst fin: not disgraced, v tough 10yo: see 1626, 1207.
2421 **BALI ROYAL 8** [2]6-9-2 (104) I Mendizabal : 22124-648: Cl up, wknd over 1f out: see 2068.   1½   **97**
13 Ran Time 59.20 () Owned: Marquesa de Moratalla Trained: France

2639   **2.20 Gr 3 Prix de la Jonchere 3yo** ()
£25704 £10282 £7711   **1m rnd   Good/Soft**

　　　　ART MASTER [2] A Fabre 3-8-11 Gary Stevens 7/10 FAV: -111: b c Royal Academy - True Flare   **116+**
(Capote) Pshd along to lead early, in command under hands & heels ins last: earlier won a List: suited by 1m on
gd/sft & v soft: likes to force the pace: smart & improving, win more Gr races.
1060 **JOURSANVAULT** [1] A de Royer Dupre 3-8-11 C Soumillon 54/10: 15-12442: Trkd ldr, onepace.   3   **108**
1851 **CHARMO** [5] P Demercastel 3-8-11 S Pasquier 56/10: 6-420343: Held up, styd on late, nvr a threat.   ½   **107**
5 Ran Time 1m 38.00() Owned: K Abdulla Trained: France

BRIGHTON   TUESDAY 22.06.04   Lefthand, V Sharp, Undulating Track

Official Going FIRM.

2640   **2.30 Bet Direct On Attheraces Interactive Claiming Stakes 2yo** (F)
£2863 £818 £409   **6f209y rnd   Good/Firm 30   -53 Slow   Inside**

2461 **LOJO 7** [3] C A Dwyer 2-8-12 R Thomas(5) 10/3: 0321: Trkd ldrs, strong run to lead ent fnl 1f,   **69**
pushed clr: clmd for 11,000: prev trained by R Elliott & deserved first success here: apprec this step up to
sharp/undul 7f, acts on fast & firm grnd: suited by sell/claim grade: see 2461 & 1869.
2245 **JAY 17** [2] N A Callaghan 2-8-10 BL R L Moore 13/2: 002: ch f Bluebird - Welsh Dawn (Zafonic)   2½   **60**
Dwelt, recovered to press ldr, led halfway till dist, sn no extra: op 11/2: May foal, sire a top-class sprinter:
imprvd run in first time blnks on drop to sell grade: eff at 7f on fast grnd.
2330* **GOLDHILL PRINCE 12** [4] W G M Turner 2-9-3 p C Haddon(7) 4/7 FAV: 0211113: Keen & led till after   2½   **62**
halfway, remained prom till wknd ins fnl 1f: nicely bckd, top-weight: been busy of late, btr 2330 (6f here).
2275 **LARAS GIRL 15** [1] I A Wood 2-8-0 F P Ferris(3) 14/1: 04: b f Tipsy Creek - Joe's Dancer (Shareef   5   **35**
Dancer) Dwelt, al in rear: April first foal, cost 1,000gns: dam unrcd, sire a decent sprinter: modest so far.
4 Ran Time 1m 25.65 (5.85) Owned: Miss Lilo Blum Trained: Newmarket

2641   **3.00 Littlewoods Bet Direct Median Auction Maiden Stakes 3-4yo** (F)
£2870 £820 £410   **7f214y rnd   Good/Firm 30   -21 Slow   Inside**

2324 **ARAGONS BOY 13** [1] H Candy 4-9-6 (66) Dane O'Neill 5/1: 054-001: Made all, clr fnl 1.5f,   **71**
readily: suited by forcing tactics over 1m: acts on fast grnd & on a stiff or sharp/undul trk: see 2324.
2174 **ARCHERFIELD 20** [2] J W Hills 3-8-5 T (63) R L Moore 7/2: 5-223002: Keen & chsd ldrs, went after   2½   **60**
wnr dist, sn no impress: bckd from 6/1, clr of rem: tried a t-strap & back to form: see 734 (AW).
2342 **CHERTSEY 12** [5] C E Brittain 3-8-5 T E Durcan 2/1 FAV: 33: Dwelt, keen in rear, imprvd to chall   5   **50**
after halfway, btn dist: nicely bckd: showed more on debut in 2342.
2423 **PREGNANT PAUSE 9** [3] S Kirk 3-8-10 (64) J D Walsh(7) 12/1: 02-40454: Keen & prom, btn 2f out.   2½   **50**
102 **SUAVE QUARTET 209** [4]3-8-10 BL (78) E Ahern 11/4: 622-5: Keen & front rank, wknd sn after   17   **20**
halfway, t.o.: reapp, drifted from 7/4, tried blnks: has been gelded: reportedly not handle this trk, stable
struggling for form: see 102 (AW mdn).
5 Ran Time 1m 36.12 (4.12) Owned: Paul & Linda Dixon Trained: Wantage

---

2642   3.30 National Talking Newspaper Maiden Handicap Stakes 3yo+ 0-75 (E)   [75]
£3396 £1045 £523   1m3f196y   Good/Firm 30   +10 Fast   Outside

2376 **SUNNY LADY** 11 [2] E A L Dunlop 3-10-0 (75) L Dettori 4/7 FAV: 60-22221: Made all, held on well   **81**
fnl 1f, drvn out: well bckd, best time of day: top-weight: overdue win after 4 rnr-up effs: eff at 12/14f on gd &
fast grnd: likes a sharp/undul trk & apprec forcing tactics today: long overdue win, see 2376 & 1140.
2342 **CROCOLAT** 12 [3] N A Callaghan 3-8-8 (55) R L Moore 14/1: 0052: ch f Croco Rouge - Lamanka Lass   ½   **61**
(Woodman) Trkd ldrs, sltly outpcd 2.5f out, rallied to chall fnl 1f, just btn: clr of rem: h'cap bow: imprvd form
over this longer 12f trip, acts on fast grnd.
2576 **REGAL PERFORMER** 3 [4] S Kirk 3-8-10 (57) P Dobbs 11/4: 00-00223: Front rank, btn 2f out: op   8   **51**
9/4: qck reapp since 2576 (11f).
2366 **ELLINA** 11 [1] J Pearce 3-9-5 (66) S Sanders 14/1: 00-0464: Chsd ldrs, rdn & btn 2f out.   3½   **55**
2274 **LUCKY AGAIN** 15 [5]3-9-1 (62) G Carter 20/1: 0405: br g Be My Guest - Persian Fantasia (Alzao)   12   **33**
Chsd ldrs, wknd 3f out, eased & t.o.: seems modest.
5 Ran   Time 2m 30.65 (2.45)   Owned: Maktoum Al Maktoum   Trained: Newmarket

---

2643   4.00 Windmill Catering Claiming Stakes 3yo+ (F)
£2898 £828 £414   1m1f209y   Good/Firm 30   -11 Slow   Outside

1776 **ZEIS** 38 [8] H Morrison 4-9-11 t (68) L Fletcher(3) 7/2: 1/00-0001: Chsd ldrs, styd on for press to   **68**
lead ins last: eff at 1m, now stays a sharp 10f well in claim grade: acts on fast & soft grnd, sharp/undul or gall
trk: has broken blood vessels: apprec drop to claim grade: see 1776.
2431 **CAL MAC** 8 [6] R M H Cowell 5-9-1 (70) M Henry 11/1: 034-0002: Led after 3f, rdn & hdd ins last,   2   **53**
not pace of wnr: cheek pieces omitted: stays 10f in claim grade with forcing tactics: see 2052.
2436 **PRIVATE SEAL** 8 [3] Julian Poulton 9-9-1 t (41) N Callan 25/1: 2050003: Rear, drvn & kept on to   1½   **51$**
take 3rd ins last, no threat: see 707 & 539.
2146 **OUR DESTINY** 20 [1] A W Carroll 6-9-9 (55) I Mongan 9/4 FAV: 1243104: Held up, eff to press ldrs   1½   **57**
2f out, no extra dist: nicely bckd, op 3/1: clr of rem: see 1940 (C/D h'cap).
2548 **ROJABAA** 4 [4]5-9-13 p (53) L Treadwell(7) 13/2: 3411-655: Keen & prom, btn 2f out, qck reapp.   8   **49**
1273 **CORONADO FOREST** 63 [7]5-9-7 (49) S Whitworth 12/1: 2410006: Keen mid-div, btn 3f out: jmps fit.   7   **33**
2332 **BONTADINI** 12 [2]5-9-3 (42) S Sanders 11/1: 00-50037: Led 3f, cl-up till 2f out, eased.   shd   **29**
175 **SKATER BOY** 195 [9]3-8-9 N Chalmers(5) 25/1: 000-8: b g Wizard King - Makalu (Godswalk) Mid-div,   9   **19**
struggling fnl 3f: 6 mth abs: unplcd up to 1m prev (rtd 49, no sand form).
2267 **REGULATED** 15 [5]3-8-9 (67) Dane O'Neill 5/1: 0155169: Rear, struggling fnl 3f: lost action.   26   **0**
9 Ran   Time 2m 01.93 (4.13)   Owned: Mr D J Donner   Trained: East Ilsley

---

2644   4.30 Edgar's Cool Water Handicap Stakes 3yo+ 0-70 (E)   [64]
£3416 £1051 £526   6f209y rnd   Good/Firm 30   -11 Slow   Inside

2063 **FRANKSALOT** 24 [11] Miss B Sanders 4-10-0 (64) S Sanders 10/1: 21222-01: ch g Desert Story -   **73**
Rosie's Guest (Be My Guest) Held up, hdwy wide for press to lead ins last, styd on strongly: top-weight: C/D class
stks wnr '03: auct mdn rnr-up '02, AW unplcd (rtd 66a, h'cap): eff at 6f/1m, 7f suits: acts on firm & gd/soft grnd,
loves a sharp/undul trk, esp Brighton: gd weight-carrier.
2 Oct'03 Brig 8.0g/f 66-(64) E: 2 Sep'03 Epso 7gd 65-62 D: 1 Aug'03 Brig 7.0fm 62-(59) F:
2 Aug'03 Wind 6gd 60-59 F: 2 Jul'02 Folk 7g/s 72- F:
2149 **ZIET DALSACE** 20 [4] A W Carroll 4-9-0 (50) I Mongan 10/1: 54-02002: Handy, led over 1f out till   1¼   **55**
ins last, not pace of wnr: op 12/1: see 1938.
2572 **LONDONER** 3 [8] S Dow 6-9-10 (60) R L Moore 4/1: 3221053: Led/dsptd lead till over 2f out, hung   1¼   **62**
left & lost place, kept on late for press: op 5/1: made most, C/D.
2334 **MISTER CLINTON** 12 [6] D K Ivory 7-9-3 (53) Dane O'Neill 9/2: 0000634: Trkd ldrs, drvn & handy   ½   **54**
over 1f out, no extra ins last: op 6/1: rider given 1 day careless riding ban: just btr 2334 (C/D).
2451 **WARLINGHAM** 8 [1]6-9-7 (57) C Catlin 9/1: 5010505: Led after 2f till dist, no extra: see 1731.   shd   **58**
2262 **JAZZY MILLENNIUM** 16 [5]7-9-3 bl (53) N Callan 3/1 FAV: 1500-036: Cl-up, fdd dist: bckd: best   hd   **54**
when able to dominate: won this race last term off a 1lb higher mark: see 2262.
2334 **TEE JAY KASSIDY** 12 [9]4-8-4 (40) Lisa Jones(3) 12/1: 5204257: Rear, hmpd after 2f, nvr on terms.   2½   **36**
2262 **GOODWOOD PRINCE** 16 [2]4-9-2 (52) S Whitworth 20/1: 5000008: Slow away, eff wide, no impress.   3   **42**
2258 **ZINGING** 16 [3]5-8-0 (36) D Kinsella 20/1: 0065569: Stumbled star, no prog: prefers polytrk.   ½   **25**
2312 **MEDUSA** 13 [7]4-9-10 (60) M Tebbutt 50/1: 2300-000: 10th: b f Emperor Jones - Diebiedale   4   **41**
(Dominion) Chsd ldrs till 2f out: lightly rcd '03, fills mdn rnr-up: eff at 6f on fast grnd, stiff/undul trk.
2 Apr'03 Pont 6g/f 76- D:
2397 **KINSMAN** 10 [10]7-9-1 bl (51) J P Guillambert(3) 14/1: 2154600: 11th: Slow away & rear, brief eff   3½   **25**
wide 3f out, sn eased, saddle slipped: forgive this: btr 2334, 935.
11 Ran   Time 1m 22.70 (2.90)   Owned: Peter Crate Jane Byers Roger Knight   Trained: Epsom

---

2645   5.00 Alexander Catering Handicap Stakes 3yo+ 35-55 (F)   [64]
£2968 £848 £424   5f59y rnd   Good/Firm 30   -22 Slow   Inside

2435 **MALUTI** 8 [8] R Guest 3-8-12 (48) S Sanders 10/3: 006-0631: Mid-div, styd on for press to lead   **56**
well ins last: op 13/2, first win: eff at 5.3f/6f on fast grnd & a sharp/undul trk: type to prog: see 1985.
2044 **YORKIE** 25 [2] P A Blockley 5-9-10 (54) I Mongan 5/2 FAV: 0-100022: Rear, hdwy to lead over 1f   1   **58**
out, drvn & hdd well ins last: see 2044 & 819.
2398 **REDWOOD STAR** 10 [10] P L Gilligan 4-9-10 e (54) R Price 10/1: 030-4003: Rear, styd on wide for   ¾   **55**
press, nrst fin: op 7/1: see 1867.
2331 **LUCKY VALENTINE** 12 [9] G L Moore 4-9-3 bl (47) R L Moore 5/1: 00100-24: Handy, ch dist, no extra.   1¼   **44**
935 **BEENABOUTABIT** 88 [11]6-8-4 (4oh) (30) J F McDonald(3) 66/1: 0/000-005: b f Komaite - Tassagh   1¾   **26**
Bridge (Double Schwartz) Led/dsptd lead till over 1f out: 12 wk abs, cheek pieces omitted: lightly rcd & unplcd
'03 (rtd 33, t-strap): mdn h'cap plcd in '02 (rtd 48): eff at 6f on firm & gd/soft: best eff without headgear.
2397 **MOONGLADE** 10 [3]4-8-4 (1oh)bl (28) J McAuley 25/1: 0-000506: Rear, nvr on terms: btr 1989.   hd   **26**

BRIGHTON TUESDAY 22.06.04 Lefthand, V Sharp, Undulating Track

2435 **SAVERNAKE BRAVE 8** [6]3-8-10 (46) N Callan 12/1: 00-52047: Held up, nvr a factor. | hd | 38
2062 **RYANS QUEST 24** [1]5-8-12 (42) J P Guillambert(3) 20/1: 4405-008: b f Mukaddamah - Preponderance | 1¼ | 30
(Cyrano de Bergerac) In tch till dist: unplcd '03 (rtd 46a & 51): unplcd '02 (rtd 56a & 55, K Burke): has tried a hood. 2 Jul'01 Ripo 5g/f 70- F:
2331 **BAHAMIAN BELLE 12** [12]4-9-4 (48) Laura Pike(7) 16/1: 4000009: Chsd ldrs till over 1f out, sn btn. | 1¾ | 31
2331 **MUST BE SO 12** [5]3-7-13 (5oh)t (35) D Kinsella 16/1: 0006040: 10th: Mid-div, drvn & nvr on terms. | nk | 17
2435* **ALIZAR 8** [7]3-9-8 (6ex) (58) C Catlin 7/1: 3606010: 11th: Led/dsptd lead 3f, fdd: op 5/1: btr 2435. | shd | 40
2152 **CEDRIC COVERWELL 20** [4]4-9-5 (49) Dane O'Neill 25/1: 40000: 12th: ch g Charmer - Marsara (Never | 2½ | 24
So Bold) Led till over 3f out, sn struggling: unplcd & modest form up to 7f previously.
12 Ran Time 1m 02.80(2.80) Owned: Mrs Jane Poulter Trained: Newmarket

NEWBURY TUESDAY 22.06.04 Lefthand, Flat, Galloping Track

Official Going Good/Firm

2646 6.30 Stanjamesuk Com E B F Maiden Stakes 2yo (D)
£5538 £1704 £852 **5f34y str** **Firm 01** **-10 Slow** Stands Side

SOUTHERN AFRICA [4] G A Butler 2-9-0 T P Queally(3) 16/1: 1: b c Cape Town - Al Fahda (Be My | | 94
Chief) Chsd ldrs, gd hdwy over 1f out, styd on despite edging right to lead ins last, shade cosily: debut: Feb
foal, cost 52,000gns: dam 6/7f wnr: eff at 5f, 6f sure to suit: goes well fresh on firm grnd: plenty to like
about this, looks sure to rate more highly & win more races.
2310 **LADY LE QUESNE 13** [7] A M Balding 2-8-9 S Drowne 7/1: 62: Chsd ldr, led over 2f out, rdn & hdd | hd | 86
ins last, just btn: eff at 5f on firm, 6f will suit: imprvd for debut & shld find similar: see 2310.
BOUNTY QUEST [3] R Hannon 2-9-0 R Hughes 5/2: 3: b c Fasliyev - Just Dreams (Salse) Slow | 2 | 85
away, sn rdn in tch, hdwy well over 1f out, onepace ins last on debut: April first foal, cost E60,000: dam 12f wnr:
bred to apprec 6/7f in time & showed ability here, sharper for this.
MASTER COBBLER [6] G A Butler 2-9-0 E Ahern 14/1: 4: b c Alhaarth - Lady Joshua (Royal | ¾ | 83
Academy) Slow away, bhd, late gains, nrst fin: stablemate of wnr: April foal, cost E50,000: half-brother to wnrs
over sprint trips/hdles: dam styd 12f: sure to relish 6f+ & reportedly not enjoy this firm grnd, plenty of promise.
2472 **ALPAGA LE JOMAGE 7** [5]2-9-0 L Dettori 7/4 FAV: 3324505: Led till over 2f out, wknd ins last. | nk | 82
2373 **GUEST CELL 11** [8]2-8-9 T E Durcan 11/2: 46: In tch, wknd well over 1f out: see 2373. | 6 | 59
2450 **FOLLOW MY LEAD 8** [1]2-8-9 M Hills 20/1: 07: In tch, wknd 2f out. | 5 | 44
BEAUCHAMP TWIST [2]2-8-9 J Fortune 33/1: 8: Slow away & al bhd on debut. | 1¾ | 39
8 Ran Time 1m 0.87 (0.57) Owned: The International Carnival Partnership Trained: Blewbury

---

2647 7.00 Stan James Handicap Stakes 4yo+ 0-75 (E) [75]
£4420 £1360 £680 **1m str** **Firm 01** **-05 Slow** Centre

2350* **OH BOY 12** [3] R Hannon 4-9-3 (64) R Hughes 7/1: 40-00511: With ldrs, led over 1f out, hung left | | 73
but styd on ins last, pushed clr, cmftbly: relishes this straight 1m here at Newbury: acts on fm & fast, likes to
race up with the pace: high in confidence & improving, shld win again: see 2129.
2129 **SRI DIAMOND 21** [11] S Kirk 4-9-13 (74) L Dettori 7/1: 030-0062: Set pace till over 1f out, | 3 | 77
outpcd by wnr ins last: gd run: enjoys forcing tactics on firm & fast, acts on polytrack: on a fair mark, see 1812.
2540 **BEST BEFORE 4** [12] P D Evans 4-9-12 (6ex) (73) S Donohoe(7) 5/1 JT FAV: 2202133: Slow away, sn | shd | 76
handy, eff but hung right over 1f out, kept on late: qck reapp, in gd form: see 2448.
2129 **CRAIL 21** [7] C F Wall 4-9-9 (70) G Baker 5/1 JT FAV: 0010-304: Held up, short of room over 2f | 1 | 71
out, carried head awkwardly but kept on late, nrst fin: poss not straightforward but has ability: see 1423.
2220 **PARNASSIAN 18** [16]4-8-12 (59) R Thomas(5) 9/1: 0331305: Held up, hdwy when short of room over 1f | 1½ | 57
out, late gains, nvr a dngr: see 1891, 1778 (gd/soft, mdn h'cap).
2332 **LABELLED WITH LOVE 12** [10]4-8-5 (52) R Miles(3) 33/1: 0-256: Held up, eff over 2f out, sn wknd. | ¾ | 48
1890 **TE QUIERO GB 32** [4]6-10-0 t (75) S Drowne 12/1: 0220007: Held up, eff 2f out, no impress: see 1057. | 1¼ | 68
2036 **WANNA SHOUT 26** [6]6-8-9 (56) Lisa Jones(3) 16/1: 1212058: Bhd, btn dist: see 917 (polytrk). | nk | 48
2448 **PHRED 8** [2]4-9-0 (61) S Carson 8/1: 6465429: With ldrs, wknd dist: much btr 2448, see 1059. | 3 | 47
2394 **FORTUNE POINT 10** [14]6-8-13 (60) J Fortune 12/1: 1320040: 10th: Nvr a factor: see 2394, 718. | hd | 45
1823 **DUELLING BANJOS 35** [8]5-9-2 (63) E Ahern 10/1: 001-0400: 11th: In tch, wknd 2f out: likes cut. | 6 | 36
476 **HAVE SOME FUN 150** [15]4-8-12 (59) J Quinn 16/1: 6-320: 12th: In tch, wknd 2f out: abs, see 476. | ½ | 31
2057 **SPY GUN 25** [1]4-8-3 (50) N Chalmers(2) 33/1: 0406200: 13th: In tch, wknd 2f out: see 2057, 1755. | 1 | 20
13 Ran Time 1m 37.27 (0.47) Owned: Mr A F Merritt Trained: Marlborough

---

2648 7.30 Octagon Toyota Handicap Stakes Fillies 3yo+ 0-80 (D) [83]
£5746 £1768 £884 **6f8y str** **Firm 01** **+01 Fast** Stands Side

2075* **CATHERINE WHEEL 24** [6] J R Fanshawe 3-8-13 (68) J Murtagh 15/8 FAV: 211: Set pace, edged left & | | 78
hdd just ins last, rallied gamely to get up again cl-home, drvn out: hvly bckd: eff over 5/6f on firm & gd/soft,
gall or fair trks: typical lightly rcd, genuine & progressive 3yo for the stable: see 2075, 1216.
2249 **BEE MINOR 17** [5] R Hannon 3-9-0 (70) R Hughes 16/1: 53500-02: Trkd wnr, eff over 1f out, edged | nk | 78
left but styd on to lead ins last, collared cl-home: deserves a race: see 2249.
2539 **I WISH 4** [7] M Madgwick 6-8-9 (1ow) (56) G Baker 14/1: 5041553: Cl-up, eff dist, onepace ins last. | 1¾ | 60
2539 **CONCUBINE 4** [9] J R Boyle 5-8-10 P (58) J Fortune 13/2: 300-3024: Chsd ldrs, wknd fnl 1f: see 2539. | 2 | 55
2398 **AMELIA 10** [2]6-8-10 (58) B Swarbrick(5) 11/2: 5301325: Chsd ldrs, wknd dist: btr 2398 (fill h'cap). | 1 | 52
2249 **GO BETWEEN 17** [4]3-9-11 (80) S Drowne 10/1: 3210-206: Slow away & nvr a factor: btr 1761 (7f). | nk | 73
874 **PRIMA STELLA 95** [12]5-9-0 (62) Lisa Jones(3) 9/1: 1026607: In tch, wknd 2f out: 3 mth abs: best | 6 | 37
on fibresand: see 611, 386.
2429 **CERULEAN ROSE 9** [8]5-9-5 (67) L Dettori 11/4: 135-4028: Al bhd: something amiss? btr 2429 (5f). | 6 | 24
8 Ran Time 1m 11.56 (u0.04) Owned: Cheveley Park Stud Trained: Newmarket

NEWBURY TUESDAY 22.06.04 Lefthand, Flat, Galloping Track

2649 **8.00 Stan James 08000 383384 Maiden Stakes 3yo (D)**
£5564 £1712 £856 **5f34y str** **Firm 01** **+02 Fast** Stands Side

1 **TREGARRON 225** [1] R Hannon 3-9-0 (62) R L Moore 10/1: 426000-1: br c Efisio - Language of Love (Rock City) Prom, styd on to lead bef 1f out, rdn out to hold on: reapp: rnr-up twice in '03 (mdn & h'cap): eff at 5/6f on firm & rain-softened grnd: acts on a gall trk & goes well fresh: gd confidence boost. **73**
2 Sep'03 Hayd 6gd 74-(68) D: 2 Jul'03 Hayd 5g/f 67-66 D:
5031} **ROYAL CHALLENGE 227** [7] G A Butler 3-9-0 E Ahern 4/1: 0-2: b c Royal Applause - Anotheranniversary (Emarati) Chsd ldrs, prog & ev ch ins fnl 1f, just held: reapp: 10th of 15 on sole '03 start (mdn, rtd 59): eff at 5f, return to 6f shld suit: acts on firm grnd: only just denied today, can improve. *hd* **72**
2237 **MILLINSKY 17** [6] R Guest 3-8-9 S Sanders 6/1: 63: Rear, prog halfway, kept on ins fnl 1f, not btn far: eff at 5f, 6f will suit: acts on firm grnd: see 2237. *1½* **63$**
1659 **GREEN RIDGE 43** [9] P W D'Arcy 3-8-9 (68) Paul Eddery 6/1: 2506-24: Handy, no extra dist: 6 wk abs. *2½* **56**
2435 **SCARLETT BREEZE 8** [8]3-8-9 (48) M Hills 40/1: 065-0005: b f Shinko Forest - La Suquet (Puissance) Slow away, prog halfway, wknd dist: unplcd in '03 (rtd 68, mdn): with J W Hills. *shd* **55**
2372 **EIGHT ELLINGTON 11** [2]3-9-0 (58) I Mongan 10/1: 0000-046: Chsd ldrs, outpcd halfway, late gains. *shd* **60**
2182 **INDIANA BLUES 19** [5]3-8-9 BL (83) K Fallon 3/1 FAV: 040-407: Led, hdd bef 1f out, sn wknd: disappointing in first time blnks: btr 1846 (reapp). *¾* **53**
2309 **LOVEYOULONGTIME 13** [10]3-8-9 L Dettori 16/1: 08: Chsd ldrs till dist, fdd. *3* **44**
FIRENZE [3]3-8-9 J Murtagh 9/2: 9: Slow away, al in rear: debut. *1½* **40**
2309 **BATCHWORTH BEAU 13** [4]3-9-0 S Carson 50/1: 0000: 10th: Slow away, al in rear. *1* **42**
10 Ran Time 1m 0.22 (u.0.08) Owned: Mr J R Good Trained: Marlborough

2650 **8.30 Stan James Telebetting Handicap Stakes 3yo 0-70 (E)** **[77]**
£4446 £1368 £684 **7f str** **Firm 01** **+00 Fast** Stands Side

2314 **EVALUATOR 13** [19] T G Mills 3-9-7 (70) R Miles(3) 9/1: 36-43061: Held up, prog ins fnl 2f, rdn out to lead cl-home: eff at 7f/1m on firm & soft grnd: acts on a gall trk: see 1470 & 1136. **80**
2414 **HERE TO ME 10** [11] R Hannon 3-9-5 (68) R Hughes 14/1: 02-53442: Cl-up, led bef 1f out, hdd under press cl-home: acts on firm & gd/soft grnd: find similar on this evidence: see 2174 & 1982. *½* **76**
2174* **KRYSSA 20** [16] G L Moore 3-9-1 (64) R L Moore 5/1 FAV: 4133513: Held up, prog 3f out, kept on ins fnl 1f, not btn far: acts on firm, gd/soft grnd & polytrack: raised 5lb since recent win in 2174. *1* **70**
2372 **GO YELLOW 11** [3] P D Evans 3-9-5 (68) S Donohoe(7) 33/1: 26-00524: Handy, ev ch bef 1f out, sn onepcd: eff at 6f, imprvd for step up to 7f: acts on firm & fast grnd: see 2055. *½* **73**
1722 **MOSCOW TIMES 40** [14]3-9-7 (70) J Murtagh 8/1: 600-65: Mid-div, prog when short of room 2f out, styd on ins fnl 1f, nrst fin: 6 wk abs: eff at 7f, further shld suit: acts on firm grnd: closer with clr run. *1½* **72+**
1722 **DR SYNN 40** [7]3-9-2 (65) P Doe 7/1: 6-0636: Handy, ev ch bef 1f out, sn no extra: 6 wk abs. *½* **66**
2249 **SFORZANDO 17** [20]3-9-5 (68) Lisa Jones(3) 13/2: 6500-157: Slow away, prog 3f out, nrst fin: btr 1729. *1¾* **65**
2314 **BLUE JAVA 13** [12]3-9-0 (63) S Drowne 33/1: 040-08: ch g Bluegrass Prince - Java Bay (Statoblest) Handy over 5f, sn no extra: unplcd sole '03 start (rtd 61, mdn): with H Morrison. *½* **59**
2182 **TROIS ETOILES 19** [5]3-8-12 (61) M Hills 12/1: 00-59: Nvr nrr than mid-div: promise in 2181. *nk* **56**
182 **BURLINGTON PLACE 193** [4]3-9-0 (63) J Daly(7) 50/1: 040246-0: 10th: Handy 4f, sn outpcd, mod gains. *2½* **53**
2199* **MISTER TRICKSTER 19** [17]3-8-13 (62) S Righton 9/1: 50-60010: 11th: Handy 5f, wknd: btr 2199 (gd). *½* **51**
2295 **ADORATA 14** [10]3-9-1 (64) O Urbina 16/1: 000320: 12th: Led 4f, sn wknd: btr 2295. *¾* **51**
1080 **MUTASSEM 76** [13]3-9-6 (69) R Hills 16/1: 6-000: 13th: Dsptd lead, led 3f out, hdd dist, fdd. *2½* **51**
1982 **BEST DESERT 28** [8]3-9-3 (66) N Pollard 16/1: 5602-420: 14th: Handy 5f, fdd: btr 1982. *1¾* **44**
1879 **Nesnaas 33** [1]3-9-5 (68) W Supple 33/1:0
2117 **Total Force 22** [2]3-8-13 (62) P Dobbs 50/1:0
2314 **Off Beat 13** [9]3-9-2 bl(65) S Carson 40/1:0
1720* **Whiplash 40** [6]3-8-9 (58) C Catlin 33/1:0
2372 **Danish Monarch 11** [18]3-9-2 (65) Dane O'Neill 33/1:0
4869} **Scholarship 242** [15]3-9-4 (67) S Sanders 12/1:0
20 Ran Time 1m 24.37 (0.07) Owned: Mrs L M Askew Trained: Epsom

2651 **9.00 Stan James Online Handicap Stakes 3yo+ 0-75 (E)** **[75]**
£4388 £1350 £675 **1m5f61y** **Firm 01** **-97 Slow** Centre

2422 **ANYHOW 9** [8] Miss K M George 7-9-2 (63) J P Murtagh(3) 3/1 FAV: 4215321: Made all, pushed out hands & heels ins fnl 1f: suited by 12/13f on firm, soft grnd & both AWs: apprec switch to forcing tactics. **68**
2265 **STOLEN HOURS 15** [2] J Akehurst 4-8-11 (58) J Quinn 8/1: 34-00002: Chsd ldrs, kept on to chase wnr ins fnl 1f, al held: encouraging eff & has dropped to a fair mark: see 2265. *¾* **61**
2391 **HEAD TO KERRY 10** [14] D J S ffrench Davis 4-8-11 (58) E Ahern 10/1: 513-0003: Rear, prog after 5f, onepcd ins fnl 1f: not disgraced: see 2391. *1½* **58**
2311 **CLASSIC MILLENNIUM 13** [7] W J Musson 6-8-10 (57) Lisa Jones(3) 7/2: 5-022504: Bhd, prog 4f out, no impress dist: see 1342 & 1197. *1* **56**
1789 **BEECHY BANK 36** [13]6-9-7 (68) V Slattery 20/1: 1/431-005: Handy over 10f, sn no extra: see 342. *2½* **63**
2192 **PERSIAN KING 19** [4]7-9-4 (65) Dane O'Neill 20/1: 50-00006: Nvr nrr than mid-div: btr 2192. *hd* **60**
2601 **MOST SAUCY 2** [1]8-8-12 (59) T P Queally(3) 6/1: 6503457: Held up, prog 5f out, wknd fnl 2f: qck reapp. *¾* **53**
2293 **REMINISCENT 14** [11]5-8-10 vis (57) S Carson 9/2: 22-42458: Rear, prog 4f out, fdd bef 1f out. *½* **50**
1516 **DOLZAGO 50** [3]4-9-4 bl (65) R L Moore 10/1: 55-12309: Cl-up over 1m, sn wknd: recent wnr over hdles (nov, stays 2m2.5f on firm grnd, rtd 112h): btr 877 & 762. *11* **42**
DOMART 233 [9]4-9-12 (73) S Drowne 22/1: 116306-0: 10th: gr c Baby Bid - Dominet (Dixieland) Al in rear: reapp: Brit bow, ex-Polish, won 3 times in '03 (1m/11f, gd): with M Pitman. *2½* **46**
1736 **ROYAL TRIGGER 39** [10]4-9-9 t (70) C Catlin 50/1: 6020-000: 11th: Handy till halfway, sn wknd. *½* **42**
11 Ran Time 2m 58.18(13.08) Owned: Stableline Trained: Crediton

BEVERLEY TUESDAY 22.06.04 Righthand, Oval Track with Stiff, Uphill Finish

Official Going Good

2652

2.15 Paddock Bar Maiden Auction Stakes Fillies 2yo (E)
£3822 £1176 £588 **7f100y rnd** **Good 43** **-08 Slow** Inside

1818 **THREE PENNIES 35** [9] M Dods 2-8-11 F Lynch 25/1: 01: b f Pennekamp - Triple Zee (Zilzal) Keen, chsd ldrs, switched & rdn to lead well ins last: op 33/1: 25,000gns March foal, half-sister to a useful 7f juv & subs 1m 3yo scorer: apprec step up to 7.5f, get further: acts on gd grnd: entitled to progress. **77**
2097 **CHUTNEY MARY 22** [5] J G Portman 2-8-8 A Culhane 16/1: 062: b f Indian Danehill - Grade A Star (Alzao) Led till well ins last, no extra: op 20/1: E23,000 Jan foal, half-sister to a 6f Gr 3 wnr, also a 10f scorer: dam a 1m 2yo wnr: imprvd for forcing tactics over longer 7.5f trip, shld get further in time: acts on gd. *nk* **72**
2119 **LADY MISHA 21** [11] Jedd O'Keeffe 2-8-2 P Hanagan 7/1: 5503: b f Mister Baileys - Hakone (Alzao) Chsd ldrs, hung left & kept on onepace fnl 1f: op 9/1: cheaply bght Jan foal, half-sister to wnrs at 1m/10f, dam plcd at 1m: apprec step up to 7.5f, get further: handles gd grnd: low grade nurseries will suit. *1¼* **63**
2343 **LOUISE RAYNER 12** [8] M L W Bell 2-8-5 K Darley 16/1: 54: Mid-div, not pace to chall. *3½* **59**
2194 **BARNBROOK EMPIRE 19** [4]2-8-2 G Duffield 50/1: 05: Chsd ldrs till over 1f out, longer trip. *1¼* **53**
GOLDEN SQUAW 0 [6]2-8-2 D Allan 14/1: 6: Dwelt & bhd, late prog, no threat: op 10/1, clr of rem. *½* **52**
18[illegible] **MRS KEPPLE 35** [2]2-8-11 J Fanning 16/1: 407: Chsd ldrs till over 1f out, longer trip. *8* **46**
2492 **LANAS TURN 6** [10]2-8-2 P Robinson 20/1: 058: Slow away, rear, eff wide, no impress. *1¼* **34**
2360 **LADY DAN 11** [7]2-8-5 T Lucas 2/5 FAV: 4329: Pulled hard mid-div, btn 2f out: lngr trip, too keen. *2* **33**
1764 **AMANDERICA 38** [1]2-8-2 P Makin(5) 100/1: 00: 10th: Dwelt, rear, t.o. halfway. *dist* **0**
10 Ran Time 1m 34.6 (3.8) Owned: Mr W J P Jackson Trained: Darlington

2653

2.45 Westwood Claiming Stakes 4yo+ (F)
£3377 £1039 £520 **1m4f16y** **Good 43** **-21 Slow** Inside

2510 **LIFE IS BEAUTIFUL 5** [2] W H Tinning 5-8-12 (50) R Winston 15/8: 010-6151: Trkd ldr, led over 1f out, drvn out: nicely bckd: suited by 12f on fast & gd/soft, Beverley specialist: see 1945 (C/D, banded). **51**
2548 **CEZZARO 4** [5] S R Bowring 6-8-3 (40) J Bramhill 10/1: 40-56022: Led till over 1f out, not pace of wnr: rest well covered: stays 12f. see 1200. *3* **37**
2499 **AL AZHAR 5** [1] M Dods 10-8-5 (68) S W Kelly 7/2: 50/453-63: Trkd ldrs, hung right under press & no impress fnl 2f: reportedly better for race & has had physical probs: see 2599. *3½* **34**
2112 **PISTE BLEU 22** [4] R Ford 4-8-4 (54) P Hanagan 13/8 FAV: 5-000164: Held up, eff 3f out, no impress fnl 2f: bckd: btr 2008 (fast, sell h'cap). *2* **30**
2548 **TURFTANZER 4** [6]5-8-9 t (30) Kim Tinkler 25/1: 6000045: Held up in tch, btn 2f out: qck reapp: btr 2548. *5* **28**
1449 **JEZADIL 54** [3]6-8-12 (27) Kristin Stubbs(7) 40/1: 30-00306: Dwelt, hdwy & handy after 3f, wknd 2f out: abs. *9* **18**
6 Ran Time 2m 38.99 (7.69) Owned: W H & Mrs J A Tinning Trained: York

2654

3.15 Totequadpot Stakes Handicap 3yo+ 0-80 (D) **[78]**
£6809 £2095 £1048 **1m2f** **Good 43** **-43 Slow** Inside

2284 **ROTUMA 14** [3] M Dods 5-9-1 bl (65) S W Kelly 7/2: 0503161: Trkd ldrs wide, hung right but styd on for press fnl 2f to lead well ins last, going away: stays 11f, 10f specialist on fm & hvy grnd, any trk: suited by blnks: tough, progressive & stable right back to form: see 2162, 1254. **76**
1519 **LES ARCS 50** [1] R C Guest 4-9-6 P (70) J F Egan 100/30 JT FA: 210-002: br g Arch - La Sarto (Cormorant) Trkd front pair, keen early, led trav well over 1f out till ins last, no extra: hvly bckd tho' op 9/4: abs: lightly rcd '03, auct mdn scorer for J Gosden: eff at 10f on fast grnd, sharpish or stiff/turning trk: gd run in cheek pieces today. 1 Jun'03 Ripo 10g/f 84- E: 2 May'03 Bath 10.2g/f 71- E: *3* **75**
2015 **TIGHT SQUEEZE 27** [7] P W Hiatt 7-9-12 (76) A Culhane 100/30 JT FA: 1010063: Held up in tch, styd on onepace fnl 2f: top-weight: see 1027. *1¾* **79**
2170 **EXPECTED BONUS 20** [2] S C Williams 5-8-2 (52) J Bramhill 7/1: 00000-04: Led till over 1f out, no extra. *½* **54**
2217 **EASIBET DOT NET 18** [6]4-8-11 p (61) R Winston 8/1: 5-402305: Rear, hmpd 2f out, sn no impress. *3* **59**
2277 **VIBE 15** [5]3-8-10 (72) K Dalgleish 25/1: U00406: Rear, eff when hung right over 2f out, sn btn: btr 1832. *2* **67**
2483 **INDIAN SOLITAIRE 6** [4]5-9-9 vis (73) P Hanagan 9/2: 200-3067: Trkd ldrs, rdn & no impress when badly hmpd 2f out: qck reapp: btr 918. *hd* **67**
7 Ran Time 2m 06.44 (8.64) Owned: Denton Hall Racing Ltd Trained: Darlington

2655

3.45 Minster Enclosure Handicap Stakes 3yo+ 0-75 (E) **[68]**
£4719 £1452 £726 **7f100y rnd** **Good 43** **+01 Fast** Inside

2497 **LIBRE 6** [4] R C Guest 4-9-1 bl t (55) J F Egan 25/1: 0540001: Held up, switched wide & styd on for press to lead well ins last: eff at 7f/1m on firm & soft grnd: well h'capped: see 924. **63**
2445 **TEDSDALE MAC 8** [6] N Bycroft 5-8-10 (50) K McEvoy 11/1: 3304-042: Bhd, switched wide & styd on for press, not reach wnr: see 2445. *¾* **56**
2466 **BORDER ARTIST 7** [8] D Nicholls 5-9-10 (64) A Nicholls 6/1 JT FAV: 0010043: Chsd ldrs & led ins last, hdd well ins last, no extra: tough: see 1794 (Musselburgh). *½* **69**
2384 **SHIFTY 11** [1] D Nicholls 5-8-9 vis (49) J Fanning 12/1: 0405244: Mid-div, kept on onepace for press. *¾* **52**
2466 **SMITH N ALLAN OILS 7** [9]5-9-1 p (55) S W Kelly 12/1: 0000005: Chsd ldrs, hung left & onepace. *nk* **57**
996 **BLUNHAM 83** [3]4-8-8 (48) G Duffield 66/1: 00-45006: b g Danzig Connection - Relatively Sharp (Sharpen Up) Handy & led 2f out till ins last, no extra: 12 wk abs: imprvd eff with forcing tactics from poor low draw: auct mdn scorer '03: nov auct plcd '02 for C Fairhurst: eff at 7f/1m on fast & gd/soft grnd: likes to force the pace: keep in mind for a low grade event. 1 Sep'03 Catt 7g/f 59-(53) F: *½* **49**
2324 **JEDEYDD 13** [7]7-9-2 t (56) P Hanagan 7/1: 000-0047: Rear, keeping on but lkd held when short of room 2f out, not able to chall: see 2324. *shd* **57**
2324 **CRYFIELD 13** [11]7-9-2 (56) Kim Tinkler 8/1: 0062408: Mid-div, short of room over 2f out, no impress. *1¼* **54**
103 **MAUREEN ANN 209** [13]4-9-1 (55) P Mulrennan(5) 50/1: 010000-9: b f Elmaamul - Running Glimpse *½* **52+**

(Runnett) Reared start, bhd, late gains under hand ride: abs: '03 h'cap wnr for Miss B Sanders, no sand form: unplcd '02 (rtd 66, mdn): eff over a sharp/undul 7f, poss stays 1m: acts on fast & gd/soft grnd: eff in a hood, not worn today: tenderly handled, likely improver. 1 Jul'03 Epso 7gd 60-54 D:

2431* **SENIOR MINISTER 8** [15]6-10-0 (6ex) (68) A Culhane 12/1: 3000-010: 10th: Chsd ldrs, short of room when btn dist: btr 2431 (seller).			½	64
1366 **JAKEAL 59** [16]5-8-13 (53) Dean McKeown 8/1: 030-0400: 11th: Led till 2f out, wknd: abs: see 1214.			shd	49
2159 **MALLARD 20** [2]6-9-10 (64) M Fenton 8/1: 11101-30: 12th: Chsd ldrs, no impress over 1f out: see 2159.			4	52
2600 **HOHS BACK 2** [14]5-9-6 (60) J D O'Reilly(7) 16/1: 6005000: 13th: Chsd ldrs, btn/eased ins last.			9	32
1820 **BOND PLAYBOY 35** [12]4-9-8 (62) F Lynch 16/1: 0600000: 14th: Dwelt, bhd, eased dist.			3½	27
2315 **LOCOMBE HILL 13** [5]8-9-6 (60) J Carroll 25/1: 0-020050: 15th: Mid-div, lost place from 3f out, eased.			21	0
2480* **WEET WATCHERS 6** [10]4-9-1 (55) K Darley 6/1 JT FAV: 643051P: Chsd ldrs when wknd/eased over 2f out, p.u. & dismounted, broke a blood vessel: qck reapp, new yard.				0

16 Ran   Time 1m 33.94 (3.14)   Owned: Mr Willie McKay   Trained: Brancepeth

---

2656   4.15 St John Ambulance Maiden Stakes 3yo   (D)
£5688 £1750 £875   **1m100y rnd**   **Good 43**   -06 Slow   Inside

2463 **SWAINSWORLD 7** [11] T D Easterby 3-9-0 D Allan 11/2: 441: Trkd ldr trav well & led over 1f out, rdn clr, just held on cl-home: nicely bckd: apprec step up to 8.5f: acts on firm & gd grnd: clearly progressing & likely more to come in h'caps: see 2463 & 1971.				75
2325 **AWESOME LOVE 13** [10] M Johnston 3-9-0 (79) K Dalgleish 1/1 FAV: 2-3222: Led till over 1f out, sn outpcd by wnr but rallied well cl-home: nicely bckd: consistent, shown enough to find similar: see 2325, 2081.			½	74
1810 **LILLIANNA 36** [8] H R A Cecil 3-8-9 W Ryan 16/1: 403: Chsd ldrs, kept on onepace.			2½	62
2410 **NISTAKI 10** [6] T D Easterby 3-9-0 K Darley 9/2: 464: Chsd ldrs, not able to chall fnl 2f: shorter priced stablemate of wnr: now qual for h'caps: see 1260.			3	63
925 **STEPHANO 88** [1]3-9-0 (75) A Culhane 15/2: 50-05: ch g Efisio - Polo (Warning) Mid-div, kept on late, nvr a threat from awkward low draw: unplcd '03 (lightly rcd, rtd 79, mdn): dam a mid-dist wnr, sire smart at 6f/1m: expect improvement in 1m+ h'caps.			3½	56
2248 **PHONE TAPPING 17** [7]3-9-0 P Robinson 50/1: 06: b g Robellino - Miss Party Line (Phone Trick) Dwelt & bhd, mod late prog: cheaply retained gelding, a first foal, dam a wnr abroad.			1¼	53
2012 **BELSHAZZAR 27** [2]3-9-0 Dale Gibson 100/1: 047: Bhd, little hdwy: btr 2012.			3	47
2410 **GALLAS 10** [3]3-9-0 (61) G Parkin 100/1: 5000-008: Chsd ldrs, btn 2f out.			¾	46
1783 **DALMARNOCK 37** [9]3-9-0 F Lynch 100/1: 09: ch g Grand Lodge - Lochbelle (Robellino) Dwelt & nvr a factor: bhd on debut prev: 13,500gns 2yo, half-brother to a 5f juv wnr, dam a 10f 3yo scorer.			1½	43
2325 **SCOTT 13** [4]3-9-0 A Nicholls 50/1: 00: 10th: Dwelt & al bhd, t.o. fnl 3f.			10	26
2106 **FIFTH COLUMN 22** [5]3-9-0 G Duffield 14/1: 0-00: 11th: Chsd ldrs, hung right & btn 2f out, eased.			7	14

11 Ran   Time 1m 47.95 (4.15)   Owned: Bigwigs Bloodstock   Trained: Malton

---

2657   4.45 Racing Here Again On 2nd July Apprentice Handicap Stakes 3yo+ 35-55   (F)
£3640 £1120 £560   **5f str**   **Good 43**   +06 Fast   Inside   **[59]**

2279 **LAUREL DAWN 15** [17] I W McInnes 6-9-4 (49) W Hogg 6/1: 03-00001: Broke well, made all from fav high draw, readily: best time of day: eff at 5f, suited by 5f on firm, gd/soft & both AWs, likes Beverley: enjoyed return to forcing tactics & well h'capped: see 187.				61
2280 **FLYING TACKLE 15** [4] M Dods 6-9-3 p (48) D Tudhope 20/1: 03-00032: Dwelt & switched right from start, short of room 2f out, kept on eye-catchingly cl-home to take 2nd: gd run from poor low draw, well h'capped & stable enjoying purple patch, keep in mind: see 2161.			5	47+
2512 **BALLYBUNION 5** [16] D Nicholls 5-9-10 (55) M Halford 5/2 FAV: 0-000053: Dwelt, mid-div, kept on late, nvr a threat: nicely bckd, qck reapp: on a fair mark, caught the eye 2512: prob best at 6f.			1	51
2445 **TRAVELLING TIMES 8** [12] J S Wainwright 5-9-0 bl (45) M Howard 25/1: 00-56004: Chsd ldr, hung right & no impress over 1f out: see 94.			hd	38
2347 **OFF HIRE 12** [13]8-9-4 vis (49) Derek Nolan 20/1: 0-234005: Chsd wnr, no extra dist: see 508.			1	41
2326* **LYDIAS LOOK 13** [11]7-9-6 (51) A Mullen 8/1: 0554516: Mid-div, nvr pace to chall: see 2326 (C/D).			½	41
1948 **FAIRGAME MAN 29** [6]6-9-0 p (45) D Fentiman 14/1: 000-0027: Mid-div, kept on late, no threat: moderate draw last twice, well h'capped, likely improver for talented sprint trainer in modest company: see 1948.			nk	34
2007 **BLESSINGINDISGUISE 27** [20]11-9-0 bl (45) R Keogh 12/1: 22240-08: b g Kala Shikari - Blowing Bubbles (Native Admiral) Missed break & bhd, kept on late: 4 times h'cap rnr-up '03: h'cap wnr '02: stays 6f, all wins at 5f: likes fm & fast, speedy gd/soft & any trk: best blnkd & can go well fresh: likes to race with/force the pace. 2 Sep'03 Beve 5g/f 49-48 E: 2 Aug'03 Catt 5g/f 48-46 F: 2 Aug'03 Beve 5g/f 49-46 E: 2 May'03 Thir 6g/f 52-51 E: 1 May'02 Catt 5gd 61-58 D: 2 May'02 Thir 5g/s 61-58 D: 1 Jun'01 Newc 5fm 68-64 E:			nk	33
2512 **LOUGHLORIEN 5** [5]5-9-5 (50) J D O'Reilly 20/1: 006-0009: Held up, mod late prog from poor draw.			hd	37
2480 **EFIMAC 6** [18]4-8-9 VIS (40) Suzanne France 14/1: 00-0000: 10th: Mid-div, nvr a pace to threaten: vis.			¾	25
2524 **MR SPLIFFY 5** [19]5-9-6 (51) Andrew Webb 12/1: 0050000: 11th: Chsd ldrs till over 1f out: qck reapp.			¾	34
4712} **BOWLEGS BILLY 253** [14]4-9-7 (52) K Pierrepont(4) 33/1: 25000-0: 12th: gr g Raphane - Swallow Bay (Penmarric) Mid-div, no impress from halfway: reapp: lightly rcd '03, mdn rnr-up, no sand form (rtd 35a, unplcd): eff over a stiff 5f, tried 7f: handles gd/soft grnd. 2 Jul'03 Beve 5g/s 59- D:			1¼	31
2501 **ZIETZIG 5** [3]7-9-6 (51) B O'Neill 100/1: 306-0000: 13th: Wide, nvr a factor from poor draw.			nk	29
2398 **Ace Ma Vahra 10** [10]6-8-9 bl(40) Saleem Golam 25/1:0				
2599 **College Hippie 2** [15]5-9-0 p(45) Dean Williams 16/1:0				
2380 **Bond Shakira 11** [7]3-9-3 (54) M Stainton 50/1:0				
2429 **Le Meridien 9** [9]6-9-10 (55) A Reilly 14/1:0				
2214 **Rum Destiny 18** [2]5-9-5 vis(50) K Jackson 66/1:0				
2331 **Somethingabouther 12** [8]4-9-0 (45) Steven Harrison 40/1:0				

19 Ran   Time 1m 03.15(1.85)   Owned: Ivy House Racing   Trained: Catwick

Official Going GOOD.

2658

2.10 Approach Vauxhall E B F Maiden Stakes Fillies 2yo (D)
£5057 £1556 £778   5f str   Good 60   -08 Slow   Far Side. 2 Groups.

2395 **RIGHT ANSWER 11** [2] A P Jarvis 2-8-11 K Fallon 13/2: 41: Trkd ldrs stands side, imprvd to lead   **87**
2f out, styd on strongly, rdn out: tchd 9/1: caught the eye on recent debut & confirmed that promise today: eff at
5f on gd grnd, handles a gall trk: reportedly held in some regard & open to plenty more improvement: see 2395.
1816 **WITHERING LADY 36** [4] Mrs P N Dutfield 2-8-11 R Havlin 33/1: 3462: Chsd ldrs stands side, ev ch   1¾   **79**
dist, kept on but no pace of ready wnr: fine run from this outsider: eff at 5f on gd & fast: see 1123 (debut).
        PEEPTOE [3] J L Dunlop 2-8-11 T Quinn 12/1: 3: ch f Machiavellian - Alfaguara (Red Ransom)   nk   **78**
Waited with stands side, slightly outpcd dist, rallied well & only just btn for 2nd on debut: £150,000 Mar first
foal: eff at 5f on gd grnd, 6f+ will suit: plenty to like about this, relish further.
        CLOVE [12] B W Hills 2-8-11 R Hughes 4/1 FAV: 4: b f Distant View - Nidd (Known Fact) Dwelt,   2   **72**
sn prom far side, led that group fnl 1f, no ch with stands side on debut: well bckd: Mar foal, half sister to a 7f
2yo wnr: dam high-class over 7f, sire a top-class miler: not disgraced on the wrong side & worth another chance.
2411 **BIBURY FLYER 11** [1]2-8-11 T E Durcan 11/2: 22335: Led stands side till after halfway, no extra: hd   **71**
carried head to one side & does not look an easy ride: see 2411 & 2213.
2033 **ANGEL SPRINTS 27** [6]2-8-11 A Daly 8/1: 336: Prom, jmpd path far side halfway, sn led till 1f   hd   **71**
out, no ch with stands side: on the wrong side: nursery h'caps may now suit: see 2033 & 1716.
2033 **BRAG 27** [11]2-8-11 S Drowne 7/2: 247: Led till halfway far side: nicely bckd: on the wrong side.   1   **68**
2399 **AZUREE 11** [5]2-8-11 P Dobbs 14/1: 2638: Chsd ldrs till after halfway far side.   5   **53**
        THREE ACES [10]2-8-11 S Sanders 50/1: 9: ch f Raise A Grand - Fallacy (Selkirk) Slowly away,   2   **47**
al bhnd far side on debut: 8,500gns Apr foal: half sister to 6f juv wnr Bad Intentions: dam unrcd.
        RUBY MUJA [9]2-8-11 Dane O'Neill 25/1: 0: 10th: Slow away, at rear far side: debut.   3½   **37**
        GOLD MAJESTY [8]2-8-11 C Catlin 20/1: 0: 11th: Al outpcd far side on debut.   10   **7**
11 Ran   Time 1m 03.20 (3.40)   Owned: Mr Christopher Shankland   Trained: Twyford

---

2659

2.40 Smith & Williamson Maiden Stakes Fillies 3yo (D)
£5688 £1750 £875   6f212y str   Good 60   -00 Slow   Centre

        ALQWAH [3] Saeed bin Suroor 3-8-11 T L Dettori 5/1: b f Danehill - Delage (Bellypha) Made   **84**
all, styd on strongly fnl 1f, unchall: op 3/1, debut: eff with forcing tactics over a gall 7f on gd, 1m will suit:
runs well fresh, wears a t-strap: enterprisingly rdn & defied mkt weakness, rate higher.
2491 **RED TOP 7** [10] R Hannon 3-8-11 (84) R Hughes 1/1 FAV: 3-23202: Dwelt, prog when short of room 2f   2   **76**
out, chsd wnr fnl 1f, nvr going to get there: hvly bckd: encouraging but remains a mdn after 6 starts.
2174 **ELA PAPAROUNA 21** [2] H Candy 3-8-11 (70) S Whitworth 9/2: 543-3063: Mid-div, prog 2f out,   nk   **74**
onepace: tchd 8/1: again suggested that further may suit, although sprint bred: see 2174 & 1281.
1846 **SCRUNCH 35** [1] B J Meehan 3-8-11 K Fallon 20/1: 604: b f Royal Applause - Antonia's Folly   1   **72**
(Music Boy) Prom, chsd wnr 2f out till ins fnl 1f: imprvd run, eff at 7f on gd grnd.
        TETCOTT [5]3-8-11 D Holland 12/1: 5: ch f Definite Article - Charlene Lacy (Pips Pride) Rear,   2½   **67**
late prog, nvr dngrs on debut: dam 5f wnr: prob stays 7f & acts on gd grnd: modicum of debut promise.
276 **ANNA PANNA 175** [9]3-8-11 Dane O'Neill 20/1: 3-6: Chsd ldrs, wknd fnl 1f: op 14/1: see 276 (AW).   2½   **62**
2793} **DU PRE 349** [7]3-8-11 S Sanders 25/1: 30-7: Rear, nvr a factor on reapp.   shd   **62**
        GAY ROMANCE [6]3-8-11 M Hills 16/1: 8: ch f Singspiel - Gaijin (Caerleon) Al bhnd on debut: ¾   **60**
half sister to high-class miler Hawksley Hill: sire a top-class mid-dist performer: with B Hills.
        LIBERA 83 [8]3-8-11 P McCabe 25/1: 20-59: Chsd wnr 5f, keen & hung left: 8 wk abs.   2½   **55**
2169 **KHAFAYIF 21** [4]3-8-11 R Hills 16/1: 030: 10th: Chsd ldrs till halfway: btr 2169.   3   **49**
10 Ran   Time 1m 29.69 (4.19)   Owned: Godolphin   Trained: Newmarket

---

2660

3.10 Totetrifecta Bibury Cup Stakes Handicap 3yo 0-95 (C)   **[93]**
£15587 £5913 £2956   1m4f   Good 60   +07 Fast   Stands Side. Rcd Stands Side Str.

1980* **ALBINUS 29** [10] A M Balding 3-9-1 bl (80) D Holland 6/1: 03-0211: Front rank, went on 3f out,   **99+**
styd on strongly, pushed out: op time: eff at 1m/10f, suited by 12f now: acts on gd, fast grnd & polytrack: wears
blnks & likes to run up with/force the pace: fast improving, keep on side for a hat-trick.
2422* **SELEBELA 10** [2] L M Cumani 3-9-8 (5ex) (87) L Dettori 3/1: 05-01112: Prom, went after wnr 2f out,   1¾   **100**
kept on: nicely bckd under 5lbs pen: far from disgraced in this tougher h'cap company: see 2422 (fill h'cap).
1582* **LOCHBUIE 48** [7] G Wragg 3-9-7 (86) J F Egan 9/4 FAV: 640-4113: Keen in rear, hdwy 3f out, kept   1¼   **97**
on same pace: well bckd, clr of rem: fine run of late: useful: see 1582.
2250 **TIGER TIGER 18** [6] Jamie Poulton 3-9-5 (84) N Callan 14/1: 1312004: Dwelt, bhd, onepace fnl 3f.   5   **87**
2225 **PANGLOSS 19** [4]3-8-4 (7) R L Moore 25/1: 0300-305: Rear, some late gains: cheekpeices.   ¾   **71$**
2021 **WATAMU 28** [3]3-9-7 (86) S Sanders 6/1: 01-00126: Chsd ldrs, onepcd fnl 2f: btr on fast in 2021.   ½   **87**
1582 **RAREFIED 48** [9]3-9-3 (82) R Hughes 20/1: 62-0107: Keen & chsd ldrs, btn 2f out: 7 wk abs: btr 1382.   ¾   **80**
2413* **ZAFFEU 11** [1]3-8-6 (71) T P Queally(3) 25/1: 6624518: Rdn in rear, nvr dngrs: btr 2413 (fm).   nk   **70**
2175 **BUKIT FRASER 21** [8]3-9-4 (83) K Fallon 7/1: 34-1409: Led till 3f out, wknd: op 10/1.   3   **77**
2441* **HORNER 9** [5]3-9-6 (5ex) (85) J Quinn 11/1: 46-04210: 10th: Keen & chsd ldrs 1m, wknd: amiss?   23   **49**
10 Ran   Time 2m 38.71 (6.31)   Owned: Miss K Rausing   Trained: Kingsclere

---

2661

3.40 Goadsby & Harding Handicap Stakes Fillies 3yo 0-75 (E)   **[80]**
£4339 £1335 £668   6f str   Good 60   -36 Slow   Far Side. Rcd Stands Side Str.

2268 **RISE 16** [1] Andrew Reid 3-8-1 (2ow)bl (53) J F Egan 14/1: 0-006001: Front rank, led dist, styd on   **67**
strongly, rdn out: eff at 5/6f on gd, fast grnd & both AWs: suited by blnks: on a handy turf mark, see 494 (AW).
220 **SABRINA BROWN 189** [7] G B Balding 3-8-1 (55) R Thomas(5) 14/1: 006-2: br f Polar Falcon - So True   1½   **61**
(So Blessed) Mid-div, styd on late into 2nd, not rch wnr: reapp: some promise on sole '03 start (mdn): sister to
smart 1m/10f performer Bomb Alaska: eff at 6f, 7f/1m shld suit: acts on gd & runs well fresh: shld find similar.
1908 **WAVERTREE GIRL 32** [9] N P Littmoden 3-8-13 BL (67) T G McLaughlin 14/1: 4-305043: Slowly away,   1½   **69**

drvn to impr dist, nrst fin: tried in blnks, return to 7f shld suit: mdn, see 764 (AW).
2375 **ESTIHLAL 12** [2] E A L Dunlop 3-8-10 (64) R Hills 7/4 FAV: 60-04124: Dwelt, sn recovered & prom, ½ **65**
ev ch 2f out, onepcd fnl 1f: bckd from 5/2: rtd higher on fast/firm grnd in 2375 & 1949.
1903 **BARABELLA 33** [8]3-8-4 (58) R L Moore 14/1: 40-05045: Outpcd, styd on late, nvr dngrs: try 7f? *shd* **59**
2398 **MISSUS LINKS 11** [11]3-9-3 (71) R Hughes 11/2: 1-52506: Prom, wknd dist: op 9/2: see 1734. 3½ **62**
2268 **COMERAINCOMESHINE 16** [4]3-8-9 (63) R Miles(3) 9/2: 30-36427: Led till dist, wknd: btr 2268. ¾ **51**
2331 **BLACK OVAL 13** [10]3-7-12 (3oh) (49) Lisa Jones(3) 16/1: 5030058: Dwelt, nvr nr ldrs. 1¾ **36**
2118 **LA VIE EST BELLE 23** [3]3-9-2 (70) A McCarthy 10/1: 320-6049: Prom, short of room halfway, btn dist. 12 **18**
2173 **OUR GAMBLE 21** [5]3-9-7 (75) Dane O'Neill 25/1: 410-6000: 10th: Mid-div, btn 2f out. 1½ **19**
2309 **EVEN HOTTER 14** [6]3-8-0 (54) J Quinn 16/1: 0-050: 11th: Slowly away, al bhd. ½ **0**
11 Ran Time 1m 17.84 (5.74) Owned: Mr A S Reid Trained: Mill Hill London

2662 **4.10 Noel Cannon Memorial Trophy Rated Stakes Handicap 3yo+ 0-95 (C)** **[96]**
£9229 £3501 £1750 **1m str** **Good 60** **-09 Slow** Centre. Rcd Stands Side in Str.

1883 **FLOWERDRUM 33** [12] W J Haggas 4-9-1 (83) R Hills 7/1: 101-0141: Mid-div, imprvd 1.5f out, led **91**
cl-home, rdn out: op 11/2: eff at 7f/1m on gd, fast grnd & fibresand: handles a sharp or stiff/gall trk: runs well fresh: useful & improving filly, see 1131.
2404 **CONSONANT 11** [3] D G Bridgwater 7-9-7 (89) K Fallon 8/1: 1110602: Chsd ldrs, ev ch fnl 1f, just *hd* **95**
btn in a tight fin: tchd 11/1: sltly short of room cl-home, but that prob made little difference: see 758 (AW).
1617 **PRESUMPTIVE 47** [2] R Charlton 4-8-9 (77) S Drowne 8/1: 0/3-53: b c Danehill - Demure ½ **82**
(Machiavellian) Chsd ldrs, led dist, caught cl-home: clr of rem, 7 wk abs: mdn plcd on sole '03 start (J Noseda, rtd 93): eff at 7f/1m on gd: clearly runs well fresh: only lightly rcd & has shown enough to win similar.
2489 **HIGHLAND REEL 7** [7] D R C Elsworth 7-9-5 (87) T Quinn 12/1: 000-1004: Rear, prog 2f out, onepace. 4 **84**
1512 **CORNELIUS 51** [6]7-9-11 (93) S Sanders 20/1: 0410-005: b g Barathea - Rainbow Mountain (Rainbow *nk* **89**
Quest) Slowly away, styd on late, nvr dngrs: 7 wk abs: ended '03 with a stks win: Gr 2 wnr in '02: eff at 10f, prob best at 1m: acts on fast, prefers gd & hvy grnd: suited by a stiff/gall trk & runs well fresh: gd weight-carrier, smart at best & well h'capped now. 1 Nov'03 Nott 8.2sft 98-(100) C: 1 May'02 San 8gd 111- :
2 May'02 Sain 8gd 111- : 2 Nov'01 Sain 8hvy 113- : 1 Oct'01 York 8g/s 107-102 B: 1 Jul'01 Donc 8gd 106- C:
2247 **RED SPELL 18** [8]3-8-3 (81) J F Egan 5/1: 1-05126: Prom, led 2f out till dist, no extra: see 2247 (fast). *nk* **76**
2207 **ALRAFID 19** [13]5-9-6 (88) R L Moore 9/2: 26-05627: Rear, nvr troubled ldrs: btr 2207. 2½ **78**
2489 **NORTON 7** [4]7-9-8 VIS (90) R Miles(3) 7/2 FAV: 0-050408: Prom, ev ch 2f out, wknd fnl 1f: well 1½ **77**
bckd in first time visor: unable to dominate today, see 2489.
2242 **MEZUZAH 18** [11]4-8-12 (80) T E Durcan 16/1: 0406-059: Outpcd, nvr nr ldrs. *nk* **66**
2207 **IRONY 19** [1]5-9-3 (85) L Dettori 12/1: 63-00400: 10th: Led till 2f out, wknd. ½ **70**
1926 **CAPTAIN SAIF 32** [5]4-9-5 (87) R Hughes 33/1: 6635-000: 11th: b c Compton Place - Bahawir Pour 7 **58**
(Green Dancer) Nvr btr than mid-div: plcd in a class stks in '03 (rtd 99), also unsuccessfully tried blnks: mdn auct & dual stks wnr in '02: eff at 7.6f on fast & firm grnd, any trk: with R Hannon.
1 Sep'02 Asco 7g/f 101- C: 1 Sep'02 Kemp 7fm 98- C: 1 Aug'02 Ling 7.6g/f 84- F:
4977} **ZUCCHERO 235** [9]8-8-12 (80) Dane O'Neill 33/1: 000000-0: 12th: Slowly away, al outpcd on reapp. 4 **43**
2313 **STAR SENSATION 14** [10]4-9-2 (84) D Holland 16/1: 400-6560: 13th: Prom, wknd 3f out: reportedly 1¾ **44**
unsuited by this rain softened grnd: see 1231.
13 Ran Time 1m 44.58 (5.48) Owned: Mr J Caplan Trained: Newmarket

2663 **4.40 John S Gledhill & Associates Chartered Surveyors Classified Stakes 3yo 0-75 (D)**
£5707 £1756 £878 **1m1f198y** **Good 60** **-12 Slow** Inside

1834 **RED BIRR 36** [9] A M Balding 3-9-0 (75) D Holland 4/1: 043-041: Trkd ldrs, imprvd to lead 2f out, **84**
rdn clr fnl 1f: op 11/2: eff at 10f on gd & fast grnd: likes a gall trk: lightly rcd & improving, see 1834.
2274 **ANTIGIOTTO 16** [8] L M Cumani 3-9-1 (76) L Dettori 8/1: 00042: Mid-div, styd on well for press 5 **77**
fnl 1f to take 2nd cl home, no ch with wnr: 12f will suit judged on this: see 2274 (mdn auct).
2423* **ALFRIDINI 10** [7] D R C Elsworth 3-9-0 (70) L Keniry(3) 10/3: 2214013: Waited with, hdwy to chase ¾ **74**
wnr fnl 1f, caught for 2nd cl home: op 9/4: rtd higher over 1m on firm grnd in 2423.
2377 **SAILMAKER 12** [4] R Charlton 3-9-0 t (75) S Drowne 5/2 FAV: 6-23034: Trkd ldr, wknd fnl 1f: see 2377. 1¾ **72**
2283 **MOMMKIN 15** [5]3-8-11 (74) S Hitchcott(3) 6/1: 425-555: Led till 2f out, wknd. 1¾ **67**
977 **CONCERT HALL 85** [6]3-8-11 (75) R Hughes 8/1: 333-46: Keen in rear, eased when btn fnl 2f: too keen. 24 **37**
6 Ran Time 2m 11.67(7.17) Owned: John Nicholls (Banbury) Ltd Trained: Kingsclere

BATH WEDNESDAY 23.06.04 Lefthand, Turning Track With Uphill Finish

Official Going FIRM (GOOD/FIRM places).

2664 **6.45 Kleeneze European Handicap Stakes 3yo 35-55 (F)** **[63]**
£3539 £1011 £506 **1m2f46y** **Firm** **Inapplicable** Inside

2014 **DONASTRELA 28** [4] A M Balding 3-9-1 VIS (50) N Chalmers(5) 33/1: 0-6001: b f Tagula - David's Star **62**
(Welsh Saint) Chsd ldrs, prog ins fnl 2f, styd on to lead cl-home, rdn out: eff at 10f, tried further: acts on firm grnd: appr fitting of 1st time visor: stable in fine form at present.
2333 **OKTIS MORILIOUS 13** [6] A W Carroll 3-8-9 (44) D Holland 5/1: 1234262: Handy, led dist, hdd 1½ **53**
cl-home: clr of rem: acts on firm, fast grnd & polytrack: find similar on this evidence: see 2019.
2064 **SAUCY 25** [13] B J Meehan 3-8-13 bl (48) J F McDonald(3) 16/1: 0-66053: Led early, no extra dist. 5 **48**
1134* **FIDDLES MUSIC 72** [5] M R Channon 3-8-10 (45) B O'Neill(7) 6/1: 0-014: In tch, hung right & no 1 **45**
extra fnl 1f: 10 wk abs: btr 1134.
2013 **TELL THE TREES 28** [11]3-9-4 (53) M Tebbutt 33/1: 000-05: br f Tamure - Bluebell Copse ½ **52**
(Formidable) Handy, outpcd after 6f, rallied late: unplcd all 3 '03 starts (rtd 58, mdn).
2346 **VRISAKI 13** [1]3-9-0 (49) A McCarthy 3/1 FAV: 2040036: Keen & handy 1m, wknd: op 4/1: btr 2346. 1½ **45**
2299 **LARAD 15** [12]3-8-13 bl (48) Derek Nolan(7) 8/1: 3461067: Slow away, prog when no room dist, nrst fin. ½ **43**
2376 **WALTZING BEAU 12** [3]3-9-6 vis (55) T P Queally(3) 25/1: 0-20008: Handy over 7f, sn wknd: btr 438. *shd* **49**
2288 **THE FOOTBALLRESULT 15** [14]3-8-10 (45) Joanna Badger 25/1: 60-00509: Al in rear: btr 1720. 1¾ **37**

2064 **NAFFERTON GIRL 25** [8]3-9-1 (50) S Hitchcott(3) 14/1: 03-4000: 10th: Handy 7f, sn wknd: btr 1078. ½ 41
2031 **HSI WANG MU 27** [10]3-8-11 (46) S Whitworth 11/1: 0-250500: 11th: Al bhd: btr 1280. 5 30
1949 **JOEY PERHAPS 30** [9]3-9-6 (55) N Pollard 28/1: 0450-000: 12th: b g Danzig Connection - Realms of 17 17
Gold (Gulch) Led after 2f, hdd dist, fdd: unplcd in '03 (rtd 74, mdn): eff at 6f on fast grnd: with J R Best.
2222 **PURR 19** [2]3-9-5 VIS (54) Dane O'Neill 9/1: 0-060: 13th: Handy 6f, fdd: tried visor: btr 2222. 16
2503* **JACKIE KIELY 6** [7]3-9-7 (6ex) (56) T G McLaughlin 5/1: 0554210: 14th: Chsd ldrs 1m, sn fdd, eased 18
fnl 1f: op 7/2 on qck reapp: btr 2503 (12f, fibresand).
14 Ran   Time 2m 13.20 (7.2)   Owned: Guy Luck Rosemary de Rougemont Tom Cox   Trained: Kingsclere

---

2665 7.15 Skybet Press Red To Bet Now Handicap Stakes 3yo+ 0-85 (D) [81]
  £5720 £1760 £880 1m5y rnd Firm Inapplicable Inside

2208 **ST PANCRAS 19** [8] N A Callaghan 4-9-11 (78) D Holland 5/2 FAV: 6-000201: Sn handy, ran wide on 85
bend after 3f, rdn to chall over 1f out, narrow lead ins last, all out: op 4/1: eff at 7f, suited by 1m, tried 10f,
likely to suit in time: acts on firm & gd grnd, likes a stiff trk: see 2091 & 1478.
2207 **VOICE MAIL 19** [2] A M Balding 5-9-11 (78) T Block(7) 8/1: 0011302: Rear, strong run wide from nk 83
over 1f out, just failed: op 6/1: loves this trk: see 1899 (10f).
2414* **BRAZILIAN TERRACE 11** [5] M L W Bell 4-9-8 (75) Hayley Turner(5) 5/1: 0-340113: Rear, hdwy 2f out nk 79
& ev ch ins last, just held cl-home: op 7/2: see 2414 (C/D).
2600 **ADOBE 3** [1] W M Brisbourne 9-9-0 (67) M Savage(5) 7/1: 02-00344: Chsd ldrs, rdn/led over 1f out, 2 67
hdd ins last & no extra: op 5/1, qck reapp: see 2010.
2414 **MARNIE 11** [4]7-7-13 (52) J Quinn 13/2: 0130225: Mid-div, styd on for press, not pace of ldrs ins nk 51
last: op 5/1: see 2414, 2032.
887 **DANCE ON THE TOP 95** [7]6-10-0 t (81) T P Queally(3) 4/1: 320-1106: Led till dist, no extra, abs. shd 79
2414 **NUZZLE 11** [6]4-7-12 (6oh)vis (45) J F McDonald(3) 33/1: 5026037: Chsd ldrs, no impress dist: btr 2414. 1¼ 47
1792 **BISHOPSTONE MAN 37** [3]7-9-1 (68) Dane O'Neill 7/1: 240-0048: Rear, eff over 2f out, no impress. 1 62
8 Ran   Time 1m 41.79 (3.49)   Owned: Mr Michael Hill   Trained: Newmarket

---

2666 7.45 Withy King Solicitors Maiden Stakes 2yo (D)
  £3614 £1112 £556 5f161y rnd Firm Inapplicable Far side

2373 **GEE BEE EM 12** [5] M R Channon 2-8-9 T E Durcan 7/2: 21: Chsd ldrs, rdn/led over 1f out, in 79
command under hand riding nr fin: confirmed debut promise: eff at 5.8f/6f on firm & gd grnd: entitled to progress.
  MINNESOTA [8] H Candy 2-9-0 Dane O'Neill 15/2: 2: ch c Silver Hawk - Coco (Storm Bird) ½ 80
Mid-div, pushed along & hdwy halfway, styd on well ins last: Apr first foal, dam a 1m 3yo scorer: eff at 5.8f, 6f+
looks sure to suit: acts on firm grnd: most promising start, only just btn & can find similar.
1760 **RUSKY DUSKY 39** [4] R Hannon 2-9-0 P Dobbs 10/1: 03: b c Stravinsky - Celtic Shade (Lomond) shd 79
Chsd ldrs, eff to chase wnr over 1f out, rdn & al held ins last: left debut bhd: 38,000gns April foal, half-brother
to wnrs at 6f/1m, dam plcd abroad & related to high-class performers at 10/14f: eff at 5.8f, likely get 1m+ in time:
acts on firm grnd: showed ability & can find a race.
2395 **ABERDEEN PARK 11** [1] Mrs H Sweeting 2-8-9 G Baker 9/1: 5004: gr f Environment Friend - Michelee 2 68
(Merdon Melody) Led till over 3f out, no impress dist: May foal, dam a dual 6f juv AW wnr: eff at 5.8f on firm
grnd: low-grade nurseries could suit.
1911 **RIDDER 32** [9]2-9-0 D Holland 3/1 FAV: 45: Handy, led 3f out till dist, no extra ins last. ½ 72
  CORKER [2]2-9-0 T P Queally(3) 4/1: 6: Sn pushed along rear, late prog: likely improver. 2½ 65
  GOOD WEE GIRL [3]2-8-9 J F Egan 12/1: 7: Dwelt, bhd, late prog: know more next time. shd 59
  VOOM [6]2-8-9 B O'Neill(7) 14/1: 8: Bhd, nvr pace to threaten but late prog. nk 58
  RUSSIAN SERVANA [7]2-8-9 S Righton 40/1: 9: Dwelt, hung right on bend early, sn struggling. 10 33
2281 **DOUGHTY 15** [10]2-9-0 V Slattery 50/1: 00: 10th: Sn well bhd. 3½ 28
10 Ran   Time 1m 14.89 (5.79)   Owned: Phil Jen Racing   Trained: West Ilsley

---

2667 8.15 Bath Chronicle Selling Handicap Stakes 3yo 35-55 (G) [62]
  £2597 £742 £371 1m5y rnd Firm Inapplicable Inside

2588 **MISTER COMPLETELY 4** [3] J R Best 3-8-8 (42) N Pollard 8/1: 5000001: Mid-div, drvn & styd on to 48
lead well ins last: no bid, first win, qck reapp: eff at 6f, suited by 1m tonight in sell grade, has tried 12f:
acts on firm grnd & polytrack, sharp/undul or stiffish/turning trk: enjoyed sell grade: see 691.
2299 **DELCIENNE 15** [1] G G Margarson 3-8-8 (42) A McCarthy 7/1: 20-00302: Dwelt & bhd, styd on wide ¾ 46
for press ins last, not quite get there: handles firm, fast & polytrack: eff arnd 1m in low grade company.
2346 **HEARTBEAT 13** [2] P J McBride 3-8-7 bl T (41) J Quinn 13/2: 0445003: Rear, switched wide & styd on 1 43
from over 1f out, not rch wnr: imprvd eff in first time t-strap on drop to sell grade: eff at 1m/10f on firm &
gd/soft: eff in blnks: see 1976.
2052 **ROVING VIXEN 26** [6] J L Spearing 3-8-7 bl (41) Hayley Turner(5) 13/2: 0040334: Led, veered right ½ 42
over 1f out & hdd ins last, no extra: handles firm grnd & fibresand: see 1801 & 1565.
2064 **AVERTAINE 25** [10]3-9-2 BL (50) D Holland 9/2 FAV: 0052065: Chsd ldrs, no impress dist: blnks. 1¾ 47
2431 **BUCHANAN STREET 9** [13]3-9-1 (49) O Urbina 12/1: 0206-066: Bhd, mod late prog, nvr a factor. 2 42
1720 **LIVIA 41** [12]3-8-11 e (45) T E Durcan 20/1: 0406007: Bhd, little hdwy & nvr a dngr: abs: btr 1085. 1½ 39
2435 **JOHNNY ALLJAYS 9** [9]3-8-5 bl (39) S Whitworth 20/1: 00-00008: Chsd ldrs, btn 2f out: btr 2292 (7f). shd 28
1125 **SOUL PROVIDER 72** [11]3-9-4 (52) F P Ferris(3) 7/1: 5343249: Chsd ldrs, wknd qckly dist: new yard, abs. hd 40
2292 **CHARLIEISMYDARLING 15** [4]3-9-0 (48) T P Queally(3) 15/2: 0560-400: 10th: Chsd ldrs, btn 2f out. 4 28
2292 **CHASE THE RAINBOW 15** [7]3-9-4 (52) Derek Nolan(7) 12/1: 2-660600: 11th: Mid-div, btn 2f out. 1¼ 30
1270 **Diverted 64** [8]3-8-6 (40) E Stack 25/1:0 1655 **Lady Predominant 44** [5]3-8-13 (47) V Slattery 20/1:0
13 Ran   Time 1m 44.94 (6.64)   Owned: Eastwell Manor Racing Ltd   Trained: Maidstone

---

2668　8.45 M J Church Maiden Stakes 3yo+　(D)
£3497　£1076　£538　**1m3f144y**　**Firm**　**Inapplicable**　Inside

2443　**LEG SPINNER 9** [4] M R Channon 3-8-10　T E Durcan　6/4: 331: Led 1f & remained handy, led again　　80
over 1f out, in command ins last under hand riding: apprec step up to 11.5f, likely get further: acts on firm &
fast grnd: lightly rcd & appeals as likely improver in mid-dist/staying h'caps: see 2443, 1130.
4779*)**SEEKING A WAY 250** [5] J H M Gosden 3-8-5　R Havlin　5/4 FAV: 21-2: b f Seeking The Gold - Seattle　3½　68
Way (Seattle Slew) Keen, sn trkd ldr & led over 2f out till over 1f out, no extra: reapp: wnr of a private stks
match race in '03, earlier fills mdn rnr-up: eff at 1m, apprec step up to 11.5f, 12f+ may yet suit: handles firm &
fast grnd, stiff/gall trks: rest well covered tonight.　1 Oct'03 Newm 7g/f 1- G: 2 Sep'03 Nott 8.2g/f 66- D:
1398　**OPERA STAR 57** [2] B W Hills 3-8-6 (1ow) (63) D Holland　4/1: 0-503: Led after 1f till over 2f out,　4　63
sn no impress: clr of rem, 8 wk abs: unplcd prev up to 10f: low-grade h'caps may suit best.
　　　　LORD NELLSSON [6] J S King 8-9-10　Hayley Turner(5) 25/1: 4: b g Arctic Lord - Miss Petronella　11　52
(Petoski) Dwelt, bhd, nvr a factor: jumps fit (unplcd, mdn hdles).
　　　　CHELSEAS DIAMOND [1]4-9-5 BL　T G McLaughlin 33/1: 5: b f Man Among Men - Sharp Thistle (Sharpo) 6　39
Mid-div, struggling from 3f out: tried blnks on Flat debut, 6 wk jumps abs (bmpr unplcd).
2066　**BREAKING THE RULE 25** [3]3-8-5　S Whitworth 16/1: 06: Bhd, brief eff 4f out, sn btn.　5　32
6 Ran　Time 2m 33.45 (8.45)　Owned: Mr P D Savill　Trained: West Ilsley

---

2669　9.15 Oval Of Bath　Peugeot Classified Stakes 3yo+ 0-70　(E)
£3348　£1030　£515　**5f161y rnd**　**Firm**　**Inapplicable**　Far side

2412　**DELEGATE 11** [1] N A Callaghan 11-9-0 (63) O Urbina　16/1: 2330-001: Rear, hdwy halfway & led ins　　77
last, al holding rivals nr fin: suited by 5/6f, poss stays 7f: acts on firm or hvy, any trk, likes a stiff fin, Bath suits.
2289　**SPARKLING JEWEL 15** [9] R Hannon 4-9-1 BL (74) Dane O'Neill　3/1: 2/31-062: Mid-div, eff when　½　75
carried left over 2f out, kept on for press: first time blnks, gd run: acts on firm, fast & polytrack: see 2093.
2598+ **PARKSIDE PURSUIT 3** [2] J M Bradley 6-9-6 (70) D Holland　5/4 FAV: 0110413: In tch, hmpd halfway &　2　74+
again no room dist, switched & kept on, ch had gone:　much closer with a clr run, remains one to keep on side.
2286　**MELODY KING 15** [5] P D Evans 3-8-7 bl (66) T E Durcan　11/1: 40-03254: Chsd ldrs, narrow lead 2f　¾　66
out, hdd ins last & wknd: clr of rem: fair run, sharper trk may suit this speedy type: see 2195 & 1903.
1255　**LANDING STRIP 65** [3]4-9-4 (74) F P Ferris(3) 10/1: 4340-005: b g Dolphin Street - Funny Cut (Sure　6　54
Blade) Chsd ldrs, short of room over 1f out, sn btn: abs: dual turf h'cap wnr '03, also landed an AW h'cap: eff
at 5f/sharp 6f on firm, gd/soft & both AWs: enjoys forcing tactics: best without cheek pieces & loves a sharp/undul
trk.　1 Oct'03 Brig 5.3fm 76-70 E: 1 Oct'03 Ling 6ap 79a-64 E: 2 Jun'03 Muss 5fm 70-(70) E:
1 Jun'03 Catt 5g/f 71-65 F: 2 May'02 Sout 5af 66a- F:
4466}　**BAD INTENTIONS 271** [7]4-8-11 (70) A McCarthy　20/1: 056500-6: b f Victory Note - Fallacy　nk　46
(Selkirk) Chsd ldrs & led 2f out, sn hdd & btn: reapp: fills stks plcd '03 (270 89$): lightly rcd '02, fills mdn
wnr for G Chung: wng form at 6f, tried 1m: acts on fast grnd & a gall or easy trk: best up with/forcing the pace.
1 Sep'02 Redc 6g/f 79- D:
2598　**BYO 3** [6]6-9-1 (71) T P Queally(3) 8/1: 2010667: Led till 2f out, sn btn: qck reapp.　1½　46
1638　**MIMIC 46** [8]4-8-11 (70) R Mills(7) 8/1: 51140-08: Chsd ldrs, edged left & btn halfway, 6 wk abs.　1¼　38
8 Ran　Time 1m 14.10(5.0)　Owned: Mr N A Callaghan　Trained: Newmarket

---

Official Going Good (Good/Soft Places)

2670　2.20 Border Construction Maiden Auction Stakes 2yo　(E)
£5772　£1776　£888　**5f rnd**　**Good**　**Inapplicable**　Inside

1874　**BOND CITY 34** [5] B Smart 2-8-11　F Lynch　20/1: 01: Rdn rear, styd on for press to lead ins last,　　88+
drvn out: left debut bhd: 16,000gns April foal, half-brother to a 6f plcd juv: dam plcd at 5/6f: eff over a stiff 5f
on gd, 6f will suit: game, will rate higher.
2281　**GIFTED GAMBLE 15** [3] K A Ryan 2-8-9 bl R Winston　9/2: 03332: Dwelt & sn pushed along near, styd　shd　85
on well from halfway & narrow lead ins last, sn hdd, just held: well bckd: clr of rem, shld win a race.
2516　**HOLBECK GHYLL 6** [4] A M Balding 2-8-11　A Culhane　11/4 FAV: 303: Sn handy & ch dist, no extra　4　75
ins last: nicely bckd, op 4/1: apprec drop in grade: eff around 5/6f on gd grnd, stiff/gall trks: nursery type.
2089　**KOMAC 24** [8] B A McMahon 2-8-7　G Duffield　4/1: 624: Led till ins last, no extra: btr 2089 (firm).　½　69
　　　　BIG HASSLE 0 [1]2-8-9　G Faulkner 20/1: 5: Dwelt, held up, hdwy to chall over 1f out, sn no　hd　70
extra: 15,000gns April foal: eff over a stiff 5f on gd: learn from this.
1780　**TWICE NIGHTLY 38** [9]2-8-9　J Fanning　6/1: 336: Mid-div, not pace to chall: btr 1471.　shd　70
2360　**RANCHO CUCAMONGA 12** [12]2-8-4　K Darley 10/1: 07: Prom till over 1f out: op 8/1: see 2360.　½　63
2275　**LORNA DUNE 16** [7]2-8-4　L Goncalves 16/1: 368: Mid-div, nvr pace to threaten: see 1677.　shd　63
2100　**RYEDANE 23** [6]2-8-9　D Allan 20/1: 039: Twds rear, nvr a factor.　1¾　63
2360　**BORDERLESCOTT 12** [10]2-8-11　R Ffrench 16/1: 60: 10th: Mid-div, btn over 1f out: see 2360.　2½　57
1728　**MEGELL 40** [2]2-8-2　J Mackay 10/1: 620: 11th: Al outpcd rear: abs: btr 1728 (fast, 6f).　¾　46
2213　**OUTRAGEOUS FLIRT 19** [11]2-8-4　P Hanagan 80/1: 00: 12th: Prom, struggling from halfway.　13　13
2316　**ALEXIA ROSE 14** [13]2-8-6　F Norton 25/1: 60: 13th: Dwelt & sn bhd, t.o..　½　13
13 Ran　Time 1m 01.18 (1.68)　Owned: Mr R C Bond　Trained: Thirsk

CARLISLE WEDNESDAY 23.06.04 Righthand, Stiff Track, Uphill Finish

2671 2.50 Scottish & Newcastle Pub Enterprises Pennine Region E B F Maiden Stakes 2yo (D)
£5772 £1776 £888 **5f193y rnd** **Good** **Inapplicable** Inside

KING OF LOVE 0 [1] M Johnston 2-9-0 J Fanning 4/1: 1: b c King's Best - Fadaki Hawaki (Vice Regent) Sn handy, green on path after 1f, went on 2f out, rdn & styd on strongly: op 7/2: 46,000gns April foal, half-brother to 3yo+ wnrs at 7/10f: eff at 6f, get further: acts on gd grnd & a stiff/undul trk: goes well fresh: still green & will learn plenty, win more races. **79+**
2228 **NOODLES 19** [3] T D Easterby 2-9-0 VIS R Winston 10/1: 02: b c Mind Games - Salacious (Sallust) Sn handy, drvn to chall dist, not pace of wnr: left debut bhd in first time visor: 36,000gns Feb foal, brother to a 5f juv wnr & also a wnr on the Flat/hdles: dam List scorer: eff at 6f on gd: win a race. *1¼* **74**
2360 **SKIDDAW WOLF 12** [6] B Smart 2-8-9 F Lynch 9/2: 03: Led, hdd 2f out, hung right & no extra from dist: nicely bckd, op 11/2: eff at 6f on gd grnd: going the right way after 2360. *1¼* **65**
2071 **BANKNOTE 25** [5] A M Balding 2-9-0 K Darley 1/1 FAV: 44: Slow away & bhd, jmpd path after 1f, late gains for press, nvr threatened: well bckd but still v green, penny drpd late on, likely to prog with racing. *1¾* **65**
2424 **MR MAXIM 10** [2]2-9-0 V Halliday 20/1: 05: ch g Lake Coniston - White Hare (Indian Ridge) Mid-div, rdn & no impress fnl 2f: March foal, dam plcd at 1m as a 3yo, sire progressive/top-class sprinter. *1¼* **61**
1780 **FROGS GIFT 38** [7]2-8-9 T Eaves(3) 40/1: 06: Chsd ldrs, btn 2f out. *1½* **51**
ALLSTAR PRINCESS 0 [4]2-8-9 T Hamilton(3) 12/1: 7: Al rear & outpcd, op 8/1. *½* **49**
WOR KID 0 [8]2-8-9 K Dalgleish 20/1: 8: Mid-div, btn 2f out. *¾* **47**
2241 **TOLDO 18** [9]2-9-0 F Norton 33/1: 09: In tch, eff to chase ldrs halfway, sn wknd. *4* **40**
9 Ran Time 1m 14.98 (4.28) Owned: Mr M Doyle Trained: Middleham

2672 3.20 Carlisle Glass Carlisle Bell Handicap 3yo+ 0-80 (D) **[80]**
£17485 £5380 £2690 **7f200y rnd** **Good** **Inapplicable** Inside

2550* **GOODBYE MR BOND 5** [7] E J Alston 4-9-1 (5ex) (67) F Norton 5/1 JT FAV: 4341111: Mid-div, styd on for press to lead well ins last: nicely bckd under a 5lb pen, qck reapp: eff at 1m/9f on fast, soft & fibresand, any trk: v tough & progressive, fine advert for his talented trainer: see 2550, 2317 & 2159. **76**
2496* **COUNTYKAT 7** [1] K R Burke 4-9-3 (5ex)vis (69) Darren Williams 20/1: 0-600212: Handy & led halfway, drvn & hdd well ins last: qck reapp under a 5lb pen, confirmed AW improvement of latest: stays a stiff 1m well: win similar on turf if repeating: see 2496 & 467. *nk* **77**
2404 **TEDSTALE 11** [16] T D Easterby 6-10-0 bl (80) J Fanning 20/1: 04-00503: Held up, drvn & styd on strongly fnl 1f, not reach front pair: looks to have come to hand: see 1877. *½* **86**
2543 **STOIC LEADER 5** [6] R F Fisher 4-9-13 (79) L Fletcher(3) 33/1: 1110024: Al handy, drvn & no extra cl-home: qck reapp: v progressive profile & another fine run: see 2543, 1600. *¾* **84**
2317 **TAKES TUTU 14** [11]5-9-8 p (74) K Darley 20/1: 0002255: Trkd ldrs & chall over 1f out, just held when hmpd nr fin, poss 4th without interference: travels v well in races, see 2179, 2087. *shd* **79**
2600 **PAWAN 3** [15]4-9-2 (5ex) (68) Ann Stokell 66/1: 3020166: Mid-div, styd on for press, not able to chall. *1* **71**
2108 **BLONDE STREAK 23** [13]4-9-11 (77) P Hanagan 8/1: 3204-447: Handy, no extra dist: see 2010. *nk* **79**
2404 **TOP DIRHAM 11** [9]6-9-5 (71) Dale Gibson 15/2: 00-23208: Held up, eff fnl 3f, not able to chall. *shd* **73**
2445 **KIRKBYS TREASURE 9** [17]6-9-0 (66) F Lynch 14/1: 05-12139: Dwelt & held up, late gains, nvr threat. *hd* **67**
2507 **CHERISHED NUMBER 6** [3]5-9-10 vis (76) R Winston 12/1: 0406330: 10th: Chsd ldrs, btn dist: qck reapp. *nk* **76**
2558 **TRUE NIGHT 5** [10]7-9-11 (77) E Ahern 11/2: 0042330: 11th: Led till halfway, btn dist: best held up. *hd* **76**
2280 **NO GROUSE 16** [18]4-9-6 P (72) T Hamilton(3) 50/1: 5003000: 12th: Mid-div, no impress fnl 1f: chkpcs. *½* **70**
2600 **TIBER TIGER 3** [12]4-10-0 bl (80) J P Guillambert(3) 14/1: 00-41020: 13th: Mid-div, no impress fnl 2f. *shd* **78**
2284 **EVEREST 15** [4]7-9-12 (78) T Eaves(3) 11/1: 00-00000: 14th: Dwelt, rear & struggling halfway: see 928. *½* **75**
2067 **CAROUBIER 25** [14]4-9-8 (74) Dean McKeown 50/1: 2010000: 15th: Held up, eff over 2f out, sn btn. *nk* **70**
1915* **SALINOR 32** [5]4-10-0 (80) A Culhane 5/1 JT FAV: 1323-110: 16th: Mid-div, btn 2f out: much btr 1915. *3* **70**
1883 **QUALITAIR WINGS 33** [8]5-9-7 (73) D McGaffin 33/1: 1026-300: 17th: Dwelt, held up, struggling fnl 2f. *3* **57**
17 Ran Time 1m 40.53 (2.83) Owned: Mr Peter J Davies Trained: Preston

2673 3.50 Toteplacepot Cumberland Plate Handicap 3yo+ 0-80 (D) **[80]**
£17258 £5310 £2655 **1m3f206y** **Good** **Inapplicable** Outside.

2233 **LOVES TRAVELLING 18** [11] L M Cumani 4-10-0 (80) N Mackay(3) 15/2: 01123-21: Mid-div, hdwy to lead 2f out, held on all out, most gamely: confirmed promise of reapp: suited by 12f on firm, gd & polytrack, shld get further: handles any trk, enjoys a stiff fin: gd weight-carrier with a fine attitude, keep on side: see 2233. **87**
2244* **BUCKS 18** [17] D K Ivory 7-9-12 (78) M Howard(7) 11/1: 0302112: Held up, rdn & hdwy 3f out, joined wnr ins last, just denied: progressive profile, win again: see 2244, 1772. *hd* **84**
2392 **SALTANGO 11** [13] A M Hales 5-9-6 (72) P Makin(5) 33/1: 03222-03: Trkd ldrs & chall 2f out, not pace of front pair well ins last: imprvd on turf return over longer 12f trip: appeals for similar: see 2392. *¾* **77**
2405 **SPORTING GESTURE 11** [2] M W Easterby 7-9-9 (75) P Mulrennan(5) 11/1: 000-0544: Held up, rdn & styd on fnl 2f, not able to chall: tough & genuine, loves York: see 2405, 1969. *½* **79**
2285 **RAJAM 15** [18]6-9-7 vis (73) A Nicholls 33/1: 6013065: Held up, styd on for press, not able to chall. *nk* **76**
2391* **MOSTARSIL 11** [7]6-9-5 p (71) E Ahern 7/1: 6-063416: Mid-div, drvn & kept on, not pace to chall: nicely bckd, op 9/1: eff at 12f, 14f ideal nowadays: see 2391. *2½* **70**
2465* **PARTY PLOY 8** [3]6-8-13 (5ex) (65) Darren Williams 14/1: 6-002117: Handy & led over 3f out till 2f out, no extra when hmpd ins last: 5lb pen for latest: see 2465. *½* **63**
2185 **VICIOUS PRINCE 20** [20]5-9-6 (72) Dean McKeown 20/1: 0000-408: Mid-div, drvn & kept on onepace. *shd* **70**
2354 **RED FOREST 13** [5]5-8-13 t (65) Dale Gibson 20/1: 3161159: Held up, rdn & no impress 2f out: btr 2217. *½* **62**
1979 **ALERON 29** [12]6-9-6 (72) R Winston 7/1: 434-2120: 10th: Handy over 2f out, wknd dist: btr 1979, 1681. *shd* **69**
3621] **VALDESCO 673** [19]6-9-4 (70) L Enstone(3) 40/1: 201120/-0: 11th: ch g Bluebird - Allegheny River (Lear Fan) Held up, btn 2f out: gelded, abs: missed '03: progressive for G M Moore in '02, landed AW clmr for J Eyre & AW h'cap, dual turf class stks & turf h'cap wnr: eff btwn 1m/13f on firm & soft, loves fibresand & Southwell: suited by blnks, not worn today: best held up: prob sharper for this & more interesting with headgear reapplied. *2* **64**
2 Aug'02 Newc 14.4gd 71-71 E: 1 Jul'02 Ripo 12.2gd 74-69 D: 1 Jul'02 Hami 13sft 70-67 D: 2 Jun'02 Donc 12fm 69-68 D:
1 May'02 Hami 11gd 64- E: 1 May'02 Newc 10.1g/f 69- E: 1 Feb'02 Sout 8af 64a-57 F: 1 Jan'02 Sout 8af 58a- F:
2479* **MILLENNIUM HALL 7** [14]5-8-7 (59) P Fessey 5/1 FAV: 0633110: 12th: Rear, little prog for press: nicely bckd: much btr 2479. *3* **49**
2465 **FIELD SPARK 8** [15]4-8-7 p (59) G Duffield 16/1: 6-615230: 13th: Held up & keen, hung badly left *6* **40**

4f out & sn no impress: btr 2465 & 2217.
2444 **GREENWICH MEANTIME 9** [16]4-9-11 (77) A Culhane 12/1: 1-030030: 14th: Handy & ch 3f out, wknd. 3½ 53
1484 **MONTECRISTO 53** [9]11-9-8 (74) C Lowther 20/1: 35323-00: 15th: br g Warning - Sutosky (Great 1¾ 48
Nephew) Sn bhd, 8 wk abs: h'cap rnr-up in '03, AW h'cap unplcd (rtd 74a): appr h'cap & dual class stks scorer '02:
best at 12/14f on firm, likes gd/soft & hvy, handles fibresand & any trk, likes Epsom. 2 Aug'03 Pont 12.0fm 74-72 D:
1 Jul'02 Ayr 13gd 66- E: 1 Jul'02 Carl 11.9gd 74- E: 1 Jul'02 Epso 12g/s 75-70 E: 1 May'01 Sout 12g/f 86-79 D:
2162 **SILVERTOWN 21** [6]9-9-2 (68) P Hanagan 9/1: 03/11-000: 16th: Led till over 3f out, sn btn: won 2½ 38
this race last term off a 3lb lower mark: see 2162.
2318 **GRAN DANA 14** [10]4-9-7 (73) J Fanning 33/1: 210000: 17th: Trkd ldrs, btn 2f out: btr 1389. 5 36
2238 **MEKURIA 18** [8]3-9-0 (80) K Dalgleish 25/1: 241-00: 18th: Mid-div, struggling fnl 2f. nk 42
1759 **GENERAL GB 39** [4]7-9-4 bl (70) J P Guillambert(3) 25/1: 2052000: 19th: Dwelt & al bhd, t.o.: btr 1295. 18 8
19 Ran   Time 2m 31.98 (1.18)   Owned: Mr G Robotti   Trained: Newmarket

2674   4.20 European Breeders Fund Handicap Stakes Fillies 3yo+ 0-80 (D)   [80]
   £7053 £2170 £1085   **1m1f61y rnd**   **Good**   **Inapplicable**   Inside. Rcd Stands Side.

2015* **HENESEYS LEG 28** [4] John Berry 4-9-4 (70) A Culhane 7/4: 2645-111: Handy & led over 3f out, sn 80
rdn clr, decisively: hvly bckd: remains unbeaten from 3 starts this term: eff at 1m/12f on firm & soft grnd, prob
any trk: shows a fine attitude & winning run could continue: see 2015 & 1530.
1535 **ROUTE SIXTY SIX 50** [1] Jedd O'Keeffe 8-7-12 (7oh) (43) Dale Gibson 14/1: 3500-062: b f Brief 4 51
Truce - Lyphards Goddess (Lyphard's Special) Held up, eff to chase wnr over 1f out, onepace: 7 wk abs: h'cap
hdle plcd 03/04 (rtd 100h): h'cap plcd on the level '03 (rtd 48): fills h'cap wnr '02: eff btwn 7/9f on firm &
hvy, any trk: best without blnks & can go well fresh. 1 Jul'02 Carl 7g/s 56-50 E:
2076 **PENNY CROSS 25** [3] J G Given 4-10-0 (80) M Fenton 9/2: 33-00003: Handy & chsd wnr 3f out, btn 1½ 78
dist: prefers 7f/1m: see 2076.
2475 **CYCLONIC STORM 7** [2] R A Fahey 5-8-8 (60) P Hanagan 11/10 FAV: 30000-34: Dwelt & held up, rdn 3f 5 49
out & no impress: hvly bckd, op 11/8: more expected after 2475.
2441 **EAST RIDING 9** [5]4-7-12 (13oh) (37) D Fentiman(7) 33/1: 6300055: Led till over 3f out, sn btn: drop in trip. 1¾ 36
5 Ran   Time 1m 58.36 (2.96)   Owned: Mr Peter J Skinner   Trained: Newmarket

2675   4.50 Saffie Joseph & Sons Handicap Stakes 3yo 0-75 (E)   [82]
   £7313 £2250 £1125   **5f rnd**   **Good**   **Inapplicable**   Inside. Rcd Stands Side.

2387 **TREASURE CAY 11** [12] P W D'Arcy 3-9-7 e t (75) K Darley 11/4 FAV: 1-53531: Sn handy trav well, 83
drvn & duelled with rivals from dist, narrowly prevailed cl-home, all out: hvly bckd: stays 6f well, suited by a
stiff 5f, acts on fast, gd/soft & polytrack, sharp or stiff trk: can go well fresh: apprec reapp of eye-shield
today, also eff in t-strap & run well in blnks: lightly rcd & entitled to prog: see 2387,
2121 **TRUE MAGIC 22** [6] J D Bethell 3-8-12 (66) J Fanning 12/2: 306-5622: Trkd ldrs trav well, drvn to nk 73
chall ins last, just held: confirmed improvement of latest: win similar: see 2121 & 1876.
1572 **JADAN 49** [11] E J Alston 3-9-2 (70) E Ahern 8/1: 4501-003: b g Imperial Ballet - Sports Post 1½ 72
Lady (M Double M) Led till rdn & hdd ins last, no extra: 7 wk abs: mdn scorer fnl '03 start: stays a sharp 7f,
winning form at 5f on firm & fast grnd, handles a stiff/undul or sharp/turning trk. 1 Oct'03 Catt 5g/f 75-(72) D:
2195 **ALCHERA 20** [7] R F Johnson Houghton 3-8-12 bl (66) G Duffield 9/1: 10-00644: Chsd ldrs, onepace. 1¾ 63
2493* **OBE BOLD 7** [5]3-8-7 (7ex) (61) F Norton 9/1: 3020015: Handy, no extra dist: see 2493 (AW clmr). 1¼ 54
2609 **RENE BARBIER 3** [4]3-9-1 (69) Dean McKeown 12/1: 04156: Handy till over 1f out: qck reapp. hd 61
2566 **SWEET CANDO 4** [2]3-8-5 p (59) N Mackay(3) 100/30: 334-6027: Hmpd start & slow away, nvr a factor. 3½ 40
2326 **LEOPARD CREEK 14** [3]3-8-3 p (57) D Allan 9/1: 0-002028: Dwelt, chsd ldrs halfway, ch over 1f out, ½ 36
sn drifted badly right & btn: steering problems under press: btr 2326.
1639 **SUJOSISE 46** [1]3-7-12 (3oh) (49) P Hanagan 33/1: 000-09: b c Prince Sabo - Statuette (Statoblest) 3 22
Dwelt & al bhd: 6 wk abs: lightly rcd & unplcd '03 (rtd 66, mdn).
1344 **MULTIPLE CHOICE 60** [10]3-9-2 (70) J P Guillambert(3) 20/1: 004-0000: 10th: Prom, lost place halfway. ½ 38
10 Ran   Time 59.69(0.19)   Owned: Bigwigs Bloodstock IV   Trained: Newmarket

Official Going Good

2676   6.30 European Breeders Fund Maiden Stakes Fillies 2yo (D)
   £5311 £1634 £817   **7f Jub**   **Good/Soft 61**   **-50 Slow**   Inside

2310 **MAIDS CAUSEWAY 14** [3] B W Hills 2-8-11 M Hills 2/5 FAV: 21: Dwelt, sn chsd ldrs, hdwy to lead 98+
1f out, pushed clr ins last: well bckd at odds-on: apprec step up to 7f, 1m will suit in time: acts on fast &
gd/soft, gall or fair trks: looks useful & open to plenty of further improvement: see 2310.
PARK LAW [1] J H M Gosden 2-8-11 J Fortune 7/1: 2: b f Fasliyev - Blanche Dubois (Nashwan) 2½ 90
Dwelt, bhd, hdwy to lead over 2f out till dist, not pace of wnr: debut: March foal: half-brother to wnrs over
7f/1m: eff over a fair 7f on gd/soft: will come on for this & win similar.
LITTLE MISS GRACIE [8] P Burgoyne 2-8-11 D Corby(3) 25/1: 3: gr f Efisio - Circled (Cozzene) 1½ 87
In tch, eff well over 1f out, kept on same pace: debut: April foal, cost 9,000gns: full sister to a 1m wnr: dam 7f
juv scorer, styd 12f: eff at 7f, 1m sure to suit: handles gd/soft: gd start, shld find a race on this form.
DANEHILL DAZZLER [2] A P Jarvis 2-8-11 K Fallon 10/1: 4: b f Danehill Dancer - Finnegans 3 82
Dilemma (Marktingo) Dwelt, ran green bhd, some late gains, nvr dngrs on debut: Feb foal, cost £4,000:
dam bmpr scorer: looks sure to relish 1m+ & showed some promise here.
GWYNETH [6]2-8-11 S Sanders 14/1: 5: Dwelt, bhd, modest late gains on debut. 1¼ 80
MULBERRY WINE [7]2-8-11 N Callan 33/1: 6: Chsd ldrs till over 2f out, no extra on debut. 3 75
2437 **VONDOVA 9** [4]2-8-11 R Hughes 8/1: 37: Reluctant to enter stalls, led, clr halfway, hdd over 2f 6 65
out, wknd & eased: see 2437.
2061 **JUST BEWARE 25** [5]2-8-11 C Catlin 100/1: 08: In tch, wknd over 2f out. 16 35
8 Ran   Time 1m 31.92 (7.82)   Owned: Lady Richard Wellesley   Trained: Lambourn

2677 7.00 Williamhillradio Com Classified Stakes 3yo 0-80 (D)
£5421 £1668 £834 **6f str** **Good/Soft 61** **-03 Slow** Centre

2173+ **KIND 21** [7] R Charlton 3-8-10 (82) R Hughes 11/4 JT FAV: 34-3111: Handy trav well, hdwy to lead 1f out, pushed out, cosily: well bckd: landed hat-trick: best up with/forcing the pace at 6/7f: acts on firm & gd/soft: loves Kempton, also handles a gall trk: in grand form & improving, looks like even more to come. **90**

2400 **CELTIC THUNDER 11** [4] T J Etherington 3-8-13 (82) J Fortune 12/1: 46-20502: Held up trav well, hdwy & short of room over 1f out, styd on to chase wnr ins last, kept on but al held by cosy wnr: gd run: acts on fast & gd/soft, stiff or fair trks: see 1387. ½ **88**

2309 **FAREWELL GIFT 14** [3] R Hannon 3-8-11 (80) K Fallon 11/4 JT FAV: 0-432323: Chsd ldrs, eff appr fnl 1f, kept on, not btn far & clr of rem: tough & consistent, deserves a race: see 2400. hd **85**

4464*]THE JOBBER 271 [9] M Blanshard 3-8-13 (82) N Callan 20/1: 021-4: b g Foxhound - Clairification (Shernazar). Keen, led after 1f till dist, no extra: won last of 3 '03 starts (mdn): eff over a gall 6f on fast & gd/soft: shld be sharper for this. 1 Sep'03 Hayd 6g/s 76- D: 2 Sep'03 Sali 6g/f 84- D: 3½ **79**

2400 **VIENNAS BOY 11** [2]3-8-13 (82) R L Moore 11/2: 4464605: Keen held up, eff well over 1f out, sn wknd: bckd from 9/1: btr 2137, 1018. 1¾ **74**

2137 **CHANCE FOR ROMANCE 22** [6]3-8-11 (83) S Drowne 8/1: 06050-26: Cl-up, wknd well over 1f out: showed much more on reapp in 2137 (gd grnd). ½ **71**

2098 **LOVE TRIANGLE 23** [8]3-8-11 (80) L Keniry(3) 7/1: 14600-37: Cl-up, wknd dist: not handle gd/soft? 1 **69**

2482 **DOLCE PICCATA 7** [1]3-8-10 (82) T Quinn 20/1: 2-054508: In tch, wknd dist: btr 1809 (5f, fast). 3½ **60**

8 Ran Time 1m 14.94 (3.84) Owned: Mr K Abdulla Trained: Beckhampton

2678 7.30 Girls' Night Out Next Wednesday Maiden Stakes Fillies 3yo (D)
£5642 £1736 £868 **1m2f** **Good/Soft 61** **-30 Slow** Inside

TARTOUCHE [1] Lady Herries 3-8-11 S Sanders 33/1: 1: b f Pursuit of Love - Megan's Flight (Welsh Pageant). Held up, hdwy to lead 2f out, pushed clr, cmftbly on debut: well bckd: dam 14f/hdle scorer: eff over a fair 10f, sure to relish 12f+: runs well fresh on gd/soft: v pleasing start, open to plenty of further improvement, shld go on & win more races. **87+**

APSARA [7] H R A Cecil 3-8-11 VIS W Ryan 16/1: 2: br f Groom Dancer - Ayodhya (Astronef). Keen, chsd ldrs, rdn 2f out, late gains into 2nd: debut: dam 6/7f scorer: stays 10f, further shld suit on this evidence: acts on gd/soft: shade worrying that visor applied on debut but showed promise here. 5 **78**

2349 **SILVER SASH 13** [12] M L W Bell 3-8-11 R Hughes 10/1: 63: gr f Mark of Esteem - Salinova (Linamix). Led till 2f out, onepace: half-sister to a decent staying h'capper: prob stays 10f on gd/soft. shd **78**

4723} **WHOLE GRAIN 254** [8] Sir Michael Stoute 3-8-11 K Fallon 12/1: 0-4: b f Polish Precedent - Mill Line (Mill Reef). Handy, lost place over 3f out, rallied fnl 1f, nvr dngrs: well btn sole '03 start: dam 14f scorer: shaped like she needs 12f+ & may do btr once h'capped. 2 **75**

4070} **DARING AIM 292** [5]3-8-11 J Fortune 7/2: 4-5: Sn bhd, some late gains on reapp. ¾ **74**

2131 **MAID TO TREASURE 22** [4]3-8-11 T Quinn 2/1 FAV: 2-46: Handy, wknd well over 1f out: hvly bckd. 1¼ **72**

2113 **ON CLOUD NINE 23** [6]3-8-11 R Mullen 25/1: 267: Bhd, btn over 2f out: see 977. 3½ **67**

4868} **PERSIAN GENIE 243** [11]3-8-11 S Drowne 100/1: 0-8: In tch, wknd over 2f out. ½ **66**

2131 **SONG OF THE SEA 22** [2]3-8-11 M Hills 25/1: 0-09: Al bhd. ½ **63**

ARCTIC SILK [3]3-8-11 L Dettori 4/1: 0: 10th: Chsd ldrs till 2f out, wknd & eased: bckd, debut. 1 **63**

2182 PAINT THE LILY 20 [14]3-8-11 Lisa Jones(3) 100/1: 00: 11th: Al bhd. nk **63**

TANMEYA [10]3-8-11 R L Moore 16/1: 0: 12th: Dwelt, sn handy, wknd over 2f out. 8 **51**

1935 **SUSPICIOUS MINDS 32** [9]3-8-11 C Catlin 66/1: 0000: 13th: Al bhd. hd **50**

DISPARITY [13]3-8-11 J D Smith 16/1: 0: 14th: In tch, wknd over 2f out. 5 **43**

14 Ran Time 2m 11.47 (9.17) Owned: Lady Herries Trained: Littlehampton

2679 8.00 William Hill On 0800 44 40 40 Handicap Stakes 3yo+ 0-90 (C) [88]
£9601 £2954 £1477 **7f Jub** **Good/Soft 61** **+02 Fast** Inside

2172 **CHATEAU NICOL 21** [2] B G Powell 5-9-4 vis (78) T Quinn 10/1: 4133341: In tch, hdwy 2f out, styd on for press to lead cl-home: suited by 6/7f, stays 1m on fast, hvy & fibresand: like sharp trks, esp Lingfield: v tough & still improving 5yo: see 1079. **88**

2389* **WATERSIDE 11** [11] G L Moore 5-9-4 (78) R L Moore 7/1: 0303112: Set pace, rdn clr over 1f out, drvn & collared ins last, just btn: another fine eff from the front: progressive: see 2389, 2272. hd **86**

2172 **GIFT HORSE 21** [4] J R Fanshawe 4-9-10 (84) L Dettori 9/4 FAV: 216-023: Held up, hdwy & short of room over 2f out, sn switched left & hmpd, kept on late: clr of rem & even closer with a clr run: acts on firm & gd/soft: fin in front of this wnr in 2172 & shld win sn: see 1817. ¾ **90**

2070 **MARKER 25** [7] G B Balding 4-9-6 (80) R Thomas(5) 10/1: 0-600404: Held up, rdn 2f out, late gains. 4 **79**

2374 **TERRAQUIN 12** [6]4-8-10 p (70) D Kinsella 25/1: 4005055: Held up, eff 2f out, onepcd: see 2374. hd **68**

2096 **LIFTED WAY 23** [8]5-9-6 (80) S Drowne 14/1: 00-01106: Cl-up, wknd fnl 1f: twice below 1613. 1½ **75**

2172 **CRAIOVA 21** [12]5-9-10 (84) M Hills 10/1: 250-0007: Keen, handy, wknd over 1f out: see 2172. 2 **75**

2223 **FEARBY CROSS 19** [3]8-8-5 (65) Lisa Jones(3) 14/1: 00-60458: Held up, most late gains, no dngr. 2½ **52**

4660} **GREAT SCOTT 258** [9]3-9-4 (87) S Chin 20/1: 115005-9: b g Fasliyev - Arabis (Arazi). In tch, short of room when wkng 2f out: '03 stks & mdn auct wnr: eff at 5f, has tried 1m: acts on fast & soft, gall trks. 1½ **71**
1 Jun'03 Beve 5g/f 86- B: 1 May'03 Hayd 5sft 82- E: 2 Apr'03 Hami 5.0gd 80- E:

2532 **MOLCON 5** [13]3-9-0 (83) P Robinson 11/2: 5153440: 10th: Slow away, sn in tch, wknd over 1f out. 3 **62**

2425 **JAY GEES CHOICE 10** [10]4-9-10 (84) C Catlin 12/1: 6003040: 11th: Chsd ldr till 3f out: see 2425. nk **62**

1941 **TEMPER TANTRUM 31** [1]6-8-0 p (60) B Swarbrick(5) 20/1: 3-552040: 12th: Held up, wknd 2f out. shd **38**

12 Ran Time 1m 28.25 (4.15) Owned: Basingstoke Commercials Trained: Winchester

KEMPTON WEDNESDAY 23.06.04 Righthand, Flat, Fair Track

2680 **8.30 Williamhill Co Uk Handicap Stakes Fillies 3yo+ 0-80 (D)** **[73]**
£5473 £1684 £842 **1m1f** **Good/Soft 61** **-21 Slow** Inside

2170* **UNSUITED 21** [8] J E Long 5-9-2 (61) Natalia Gemelova(7) 11/4 JT FAV: 3264111: Held up, gd hdwy to lead over 1f out, hands & heels: eff over 9/10f on gd, hvy & fibresand, loves Kempton (3 recent wins here): thriving. **68**
2385 **SUNISA 11** [1] B W Hills 3-9-8 (78) M Hills 11/4 JT FAV: 24-21302: Handy trav well, hdwy to chase wnr over 1f out, kept on but al held: acts on fast, gd/soft & both AWs: back to best: see 2079, 1220. *1½* **82**
1515 **THIRTEEN TRICKS 51** [5] Mrs A J Perrett 3-9-5 (75) L Dettori 10/1: 034-03: b f Grand Slam - Talltalelady (Naskra) Handy, eff over 1f out, onepace: 7 wk abs: plcd in a mdn in '03 (rtd 77): prob stays 9f on fast, gd/soft & polytrack. *2½* **74**
2377 **SPRINGTIME ROMANCE 12** [2] E A L Dunlop 3-9-10 (80) K Fallon 11/2: 36164: Led till over 1f out, no extra: fills mdn wnr on fast grnd with more patient tactics in 1864. *1* **77**
2350 **CUDDLES 13** [6]5-9-0 (59) C Catlin 10/1: 50-05045: Slow away, held up, hdwy & short of room 2f out, sn rdn & no extra: see 2350, 876. *1½* **53**
1927 **FLORIDA HEART 32** [10]3-9-6 (76) L Keniry(3) 9/2: 54221-46: Held up, wknd dist: btr 1927 (fast). *½* **69**
2038 **ESTIMATE 26** [3]4-8-12 vis (57) Paul Eddery 33/1: 4-000107: Chsd ldr 7f, wknd: btr 1724 (fast). *4* **42**
1924 **GRETNA 32** [7]3-9-9 (79) T Quinn 16/1: 6-1008: Handy, wkng when hmpd over 2f out, eased: reportedly slipped coming out of stalls: best 977 (soft). *13* **38**
8 Ran Time 1m 57.35 (7.35) Owned: Amaroni Racing Trained: Woldingham

2681 **9.00 Williamhillcasino Com Handicap Stakes 3yo+ 0-85 (D)** **[85]**
£5330 £1640 £820 **1m4f** **Good/Soft 61** **+00 Fast** Inside

2354* **SANGIOVESE 13** [5] H Morrison 5-9-2 (73) S Drowne 7/2: 3352311: Cl-up, hdwy to lead over 1f out, styd on, rdn out: eff at 1m, stays 12f on fast, gd/soft & fibresand, handles polytrack: acts on a sharp or gall trk: progressing well: see 2354, 195. **77**
2244 **DANAKIL 18** [2] S Dow 9-9-3 (74) R L Moore 3/1: 0024122: Held up, hdwy to chase wnr over 1f out, onepace: in gd form: tough, see 1986. *1* **76**
1664 **WHISPERED PROMISES 43** [3] M Johnston 3-8-11 (82) S Chin 7/1: 4211-03: b c Real Quiet - Anna's Honor (Alleged) Chsd ldrs, sltly outpcd over 2f out, rallied fnl 1f, no threat to front 2: won last 2 of 4 '03 starts (auct mdn & h'cap): eff at 7.5f, stays 12f on fast & gd/soft, prob any trk: looks like more to come & shld stay further. 1 Aug'03 Beve 7.5g/f 83-77 E: 1 Jul'03 Catt 7g/f 78- E: 2 Jun'03 Thir 7g/f 75- E: *1½* **82**
2233 **MEXICAN PETE 18** [1] P W Hiatt 4-9-6 (77) K Fallon 11/4 FAV: 3-030204: Chsd ldrs, eff over 1f out, onepace: see 2078 (fast grnd), 1599. *hd* **77**
2311 **REVIEWER 14** [4]6-8-8 bl (65) C Catlin 10/1: 116/-0005: Chsd ldr after 4f till 2f out, wknd: see 2088. *1¼* **63**
2197* **SKI JUMP 20** [6]4-10-0 bl (85) R Hughes 5/1: 3/1601-16: Rdn to lead till over 1f out, wknd: 3 times below best at 12f, best at 10f as in 2197. *1¼* **81**
6 Ran Time 2m 37.39(7.39) Owned: Kentisbeare Quartet Trained: East Ilsley

NEWCASTLE THURSDAY 24.06.04 Lefthand, Galloping, Stiff Track

Official Going SOFT.

2682 **2.20 Tsg Sophos Maiden Auction Stakes 2yo (F)**
£3395 £970 £485 **6f str** **Soft 111** **-40 Slow** Stands Side. 2 Groups.

1950 **MONSIEUR MIRASOL 31** [10] K A Ryan 2-9-0 N Callan 9/2 FAV: 3351: Chsd ldrs far side, imprvd to lead dist, collared ins fnl 1f, rallied gamely to regain lead cl-home, drvn out: deserved win, eff at 5/6f on fast & soft grnd: handles a sharp or gall trk: battled on well today & clearly relishes soft conds: see 1458 & 1117. **81**
2336 **BRACE OF DOVES 14** [9] T D Barron 2-8-9 J F Egan 12/1: 052: b g Bahamian Bounty - Overcome (Belmez) Chsd ldrs far side, imprvd to lead ins fnl 1f, caught cl-home: 7,500gns Apr first foal: dam a 10f wnr abroad: sire a decent juv: eff at 6f, imprvd for soft grnd: could find a small race, poss in sell/claim grade. *1¼* **71**
PROPELLOR [14] A Dickman 2-9-0 A Beech(3) 25/1: 3: ch c Pivotal - Clunie (Inchinor) Chsd ldrs stands side, led that group halfway, kept on fnl 1f but no ch with front 2 far side: debut: March foal, cost 19,000gns: half-brother to 1m wnr Poker: dam a sprint wnr, sire a high-class sprinter: eff at 6f on soft grnd: first home on unfav'd side & a pleasing start. *2* **70+**
2297 **KAGGAMAGIC 16** [19] J R Norton 2-8-7 Darren Williams 7/1: 54: Chsd ldrs stands side, kept on under press fnl 1f: reportedly unsuited by this soft grnd, rcd on the wrong side here: see 2297. *1¾* **58**
ARTIC FOX [18]2-9-0 R Winston 16/1: 5: b g Robellino - Lets Be Fair (Efisio) Slowly away stands side, styd on late on debut: 21,000gns Feb foal: half-brother to juv wnrs Head Of State & Beauvrai: dam a dual 5f 2yo wnr, sire a high-class juv: with T Easterby & sure to learn from this encouraging first run. *½* **64**
2511 **SOUND AND VISION 7** [6]2-9-0 A Culhane 6/1: 5656: Chsd ldrs far side, onepcd fnl 1f. *1¾* **59**
2336 **GARDASEE 14** [5]2-8-9 J Edmunds 25/1: 07: gr g Dashing Blade - Gladstone Street (Waajib) Outpcd far side, styd on & nrst fin: E11,000 May foal: half-brother to a couple of wnrs abroad. *¾* **51**
HEYBROOK BOY [4]2-8-11 K Dalgleish 9/1: 8: Dwelt & bhd far side, some late hdwy on debut. *¾* **50**
2498 **CLASSIC STYLE 7** [20]2-8-6 K Darley 20/1: 59: Dwelt stands side, styd on late, nvr dngrs. *1* **42**
MORNING MAJOR [2]2-8-9 P Fessey 20/1: 0: 10th: Chsd ldrs far side, btn 2f out on debut. *2* **39**
2297 **MISTER BUZZ 16** [1]2-8-9 G Duffield 25/1: 00: 11th: Chsd ldrs far side 4f, wknd. *nk* **38**
XAARIST [17]2-8-11 Dale Gibson 10/1: 0: 12th: Al outpcd stands side on debut. *1¾* **35**
FILEY BUOY [15]2-8-7 Dean McKeown 33/1: 0: 13th: Slowly away, al bhd stands side on debut. *3* **22**
FLAXBY [16]2-8-9 T P Queally(3) 20/1: 0: 14th: Chsd ldrs till halfway stands side on debut. *½* **23**
KEYALZAO [8]2-8-6 T Eaves(2) 25/1: 0: 15th: Slowly away, al bhd far side on racecourse bow. *¾* **17**
2158 **DAVY CROCKETT 22** [13]2-8-7 L Goncalves 16/1: 00: 16th: Led till halfway stands side, wknd. *1* **15**
2505 **BRUT 7** [3]2-8-9 L Enstone(3) 8/1: 0620: 17th: Led till dist far side, wknd & eased: btr 2505. *1½* **13**
NORTON ROSE [11]2-8-4 E Ahern 25/1: 0: 18th: Dwelt, al bhd far side on debut. *2½* **1**
1632 **Niteowl Lad 47** [12]2-8-9 J D O'Reilly(4) 20/1:0 2228 **The Terminator 20** [7]2-8-9 J Carroll 50/1:0
20 Ran Time 1m 20.36 (9.06) Owned: Mrs M Forsyth & Mrs E Jamieson Trained: Hambleton

| **2683** | 2.50 Tsg Brice Associates Handicap Stakes 3yo 35-55 (F) | | | | [63] |

£3325 £950 £475   **6f str**   **Soft 111**   **-46 Slow**   Stands Side. 2 Groups.

2219 **SHAMROCK TEA 20** [2] R A Fahey 3-9-3 (52) T Hamilton(3) 6/1: 5000-051: Chsd ldr far side, led 2f   **62**
out, held on drvn out cl-home: eff at 6f, relishes soft grnd: right back to form & looks on a decent mark: see 2219.
2055 **MUSIOTAL 27** [3] J S Goldie 3-8-11 (46) N Mackay(3) 9/2 FAV: 50-05502: ch c Pivotal - Bemuse   ½   **55**
(Forzando) Bhd far side, imprvd halfway, sltly short of room & kept on fnl 1f, not btn far: tchd 13/2, clr of rem:
well btn both juv starts: 23,000gns brother to a 6f juv wnr: eff at 6f, seems to relish soft grnd: handles a gall trk.
1842 **SAM THE SORCERER 36** [12] J R Norton 3-8-10 (45) K Dalgleish 25/1: 000-0103: Made all stands   3½   **47+**
side, kept on fnl 1f but no ch with front 2 far side: first home on the wrong side: acts on soft & fibresand.
2463 **BORODINSKY 9** [5] R E Barr 3-8-10 (45) T Eaves(3) 50/1: 000-504: Chsd ldrs far side, outpcd   ½   **46**
halfway, rallied fnl 1f: flattered 2463 (7f), see 2104.
2339 **WESTBOROUGH 14** [8]3-9-4 (53) Kim Tinkler 14/1: 205-2505: Switched far side, in tch, wknd fnl 1f.   1¼   **51**
2326 **A BID IN TIME 15** [9]3-8-10 (45) Darren Williams 8/1: 0020666: Slowly away stands side, prog 2f   ¾   **41**
out, sn btn: on the wrong side: see 1268.
2055 **REVERSIONARY 27** [6]3-8-10 bl (45) K Darley 12/1: 0-005007: Dwelt, modest late gains, nvr dngrs.   1¾   **37**
1948 **SMART DANNY 31** [4]3-8-8 (43) R Winston 13/2: 40-05508: Chsd ldrs far side, short of room 2f out, wknd. 6   **21**
2218 **CARIBBEAN BLUE 20** [13]3-8-12 (47) Dean McKeown 25/1: 600-509: Chsd ldrs stands side 4f, wknd.   1¾   **22**
2125 **LORD WISHINGWELL 23** [10]3-8-2 vis (37) P Fessey 12/1: 000-0330: 10th: Chsd ldrs till halfway.   3½   **5**
2379* **GARNOCK VENTURE 13** [11]3-9-6 bl (55) A Culhane 7/1: 1030010: 11th: Chsd ldrs 4f stands side.   hd   **23**
2439+**WENDYS GIRL 10** [1]3-9-7 (6ex)bl (56) D Fentiman(7) 7/1: 52P4010: 12th: Led far side, clr halfway,   8   **8**
hdd 2f out & wknd qckly: op 11/2 under tpr wsght: disapp on this soft grnd, much btr judged 2439 (firm).
2497 **KILLERBY NICKO 8** [7]3-9-3 BL (52) Dale Gibson 10/1: 0-60605U: U.r. leaving stalls: tried blnks.   **0**
13 Ran   Time 1m 20.73 (9.43)   Owned: Keith Brown Properties (Hull) Ltd   Trained: Malton

| **2684** | 3.20 Tsg Seaton Delaval Trophy Handicap Stakes 3yo+ 0-100 (C) | | | | [94] |

£17400 £6600 £3300   **7f str**   **Soft 111**   **+09 Fast**   Stands Side - Hand Timed

2489 **POLAR BEAR 8** [1] W J Haggas 4-9-10 (90) A Culhane 9/4 FAV: 53/11-301: Held up far side, smooth   **108+**
prog 2f out, led ins fnl 1f, sprinted clr, easily: well bckd, gd time: eff at 7f/1m on firm & fibresand, clearly
relishes a soft surface: handles a sharp or gall trk, runs well fresh: most progressive & v useful, looks up to
Listed/Gr 3 under similar conditions: see 1624.
2568 **DIGITAL 5** [11] M R Channon 7-9-3 (83) S Hitchcott(3) 11/2: 3600522: Chsd ldr far side, went on 2f   5   **91**
out, collared ins fnl 1f & sn left bhd by easy wnr: qck reapp: in fine form, likes easy grnd & well h'capped.
2568 **TIDY 5** [4] M D Hammond 4-9-0 (80) Darren Williams 25/1: 0-015U03: Held up far side, short of   1½   **84**
room & switched 2f out, fin well but no ch with wnr: qck reapp: loves soft: see 1354 & 1035.
2558 **MYSTIC MAN 6** [3] K A Ryan 6-9-8 (88) N Callan 8/1: 0001304: Held up far side, eff 2f out, onepace.   ¾   **91**
2568 **SARRAAF 5** [5]8-8-4 (70) T Hamilton(3) 16/1: 5053335: Mid-div far side, not pace to chall: qck reapp.   nk   **72**
2543* **TONY TIE 6** [15]8-8-13 (6ex) (79) N Mackay(3) 12/1: 2250216: Chsd ldrs stands side, prog to lead   2   **77+**
that group ins fnl 1f, no ch with far side: qck reapp under 6lb pen: first home on the wrong side: see 2543.
1366+**HILLS OF GOLD 61** [6]5-8-5 (71) K Darley 8/1: 1400-417: Chsd ldrs far side, onepcd fnl 1.5f: abs.   1½   **66**
2542* **ULYSEES 6** [17]5-8-10 (6ex) (76) T Eaves(3) 16/1: 00-10318: Slowly away, chsd ldrs stands side,   shd   **71**
onepcd fnl 2f: another on the wrong side & qck reapp under 6lb pen: btr judged 2542.
2172 **SOYUZ 22** [14]4-9-7 (87) P Robinson 10/1: 00-23159: Rear stands side, hdwy to lead that group 2f   nk   **81**
out, collared ins fnl 1f & wknd: btr 1616.
1490 **ZILCH 53** [16]6-9-12 (92) T P Queally(3) 7/1: 3-122140: 10th: Rear stands side: abs, poor draw.   3   **80**
2863} **INCHDURA 348** [7]6-8-6 (72) Kim Tinkler 66/1: 000000-0: 11th: ch g Inchinor - Sunshine Coast   1   **58**
(Posse) Chsd ldrs far side, wknd fnl 1.5f on reapp: mainly out of form in '03, tumbled down the h'cap: progressive
in '02, won 2 rtd h'caps for R Charlton: stays 1m, best at 7f: acts on gd & firm grnd, any trk: eff wth/without a
t-strap: v well h'capped for N Tinkler, needs faster grnd. 2 Oct'02 York 7fm 96-95 B: 1 Sep'02 Good 7fm 96-92 B:
2 Aug'02 Ches 7g/f 95-91 B: 1 Aug'02 Newb 7fm 93-86 C: 1 Sep'01 Newb 8fm 84-80 C: 2 Sep'01 Ling 7.6gd 82-79 D:
1 Aug'01 Ling 7.6gd 81-72 E: 1 Jun'01 Sali 7g/f 77-64 F: 2 Jun'01 Newb 7g/f 74-64 E:
2350 **POP UP AGAIN 14** [13]4-8-7 (73) E Ahern 25/1: 0513-000: 12th: Chsd ldrs stands side, btn 2f out.   hd   **59**
2558 **SAWWAAH 6** [8]7-9-4 (84) J Carroll 33/1: 0013400: 13th: Held up far side, chsd ldrs halfway, btn dist.   1   **68**
2076 **HITS ONLY MONEY 26** [9]4-9-12 (92) Dean McKeown 33/1: 130-0000: 14th: Chsd ldr far side, ev ch 2f   3½   **69**
out, wknd & eased: prob not handle soft: see 1126.
2464 Raphael 9 [19]5-8-13 (79) R Winston 25/1:0   2315 Colemanstown 15 [18]4-7-12 (64) P Fessey 33/1:0
1703 Chappel Cresent 42 [10]4-10-0 (94) A Nicholls 20/1:0   2568 Bandos 5 [12]4-8-8 t(74) G Duffield 66/1:0
18 Ran   Time 1m 31.3 (7.2)   Owned: Mr B Haggas   Trained: Newmarket

| **2685** | 3.50 Tsg Ibm Handicap Stakes 3yo+ 0-75 (E) | | | | [71] |

£10316 £3174 £1587   **2m19y**   **Soft 111**   **-25 Slow**   Stands Side

2494 **LUCKY JUDGE 8** [6] G A Swinbank 7-9-3 (60) E Ahern 14/1: 5/4/-40151: Held up, imprvd halfway, led   **73**
dist, rdn clr: back to form on this return to turf: eff at 13f/2m on fast & hvy grnd: see 1637 & 1034.
2198 **QUEDEX 21** [9] R J Price 8-9-7 (64) B Swarbrick(5) 5/1: 65/06-152: Chsd ldrs, sltly outpcd 5f out,   2½   **73**
rallied well to take 2nd cl-home, not reach wnr: 7L clr 3rd: gd run: see 1298 & 2073.
2494 **NEXT FLIGHT 8** [12] R E Barr 5-8-7 (50) P Robinson 9/2: 2314323: Trkd ldrs, imprvd to lead 3f out   7   **53**
till dist, wknd: see 2494 (AW) & 2105 (14f).
4263} **ALRIDA 282** [8] R A Fahey 5-9-10 (67) T Hamilton(3) 8/1: 560050-4: b g Ali Royal - Ride Bold (J O   ½   **69**
Tobin) Held up, styd on late, nrst fin: hdles fit, won a nov 2 wks ago (eff at 2m1f on fast & gd/soft, rtd 116h):
trained by W Jarvis & failed to win in '03, tried cheek pieces: mdn & h'cap wnr in '02: stays 2m: acts on fast & soft grnd, likes a sharp/easy trk: can run well fresh: decent Flat reapp for new stable.
2 Aug'02 Thir 16gd 84-78 D: 1 Jul'02 Catt 15.8fm 81-75 E: 1 Jun'02 Yarm 14fm 77- D: 2 May'02 Pont 10gd 75-74 D:
173   **SIMPLE IDEALS 198** [13]10-7-12 (9oh) (32) Kim Tinkler 100/1: 650040-5: Mid-div, styd on late, nvr dngrs.   4   **39**
2105* **BEST PORT 24** [10]8-9-7 (64) M Lawson(5) 12/1: 54-01016: Held up, nvr nr ldrs: wants faster grnd.   1¾   **60**
3053} **HOPE SOUND 339** [2]4-9-5 p (62) T Eaves(3) 14/1: 200-7: b g Turtle Island - Lucky Pick (Auction   ¾   **57**
Ring) Slowly away, prog to chase ldrs halfway, not pace to chall fnl 2f: jumps fit, won a mdn hdle 3 wks ago (eff

at 2m/3m on gd & soft, rtd 106h, wears cheek pieces): thrice rcd on the Flat for J Noseda in '03, mdn rnr-up on debut: eff at 10f on gd/soft grnd, wears cheek pieces: now with B Ellison. 2 May'03 Newc 10.1g/s 68- E:
2345+ **CONSIDINE 14** [1]3-8-8 (71) A Culhane 11/4 FAV: 45-01218: Led till 3f out, wknd: bckd, btr 2345. *1¾* **64**
2176 **TANDAVA 21** [4]6-9-13 p (70) G Duffield 25/1: 00-10549: Chsd ldrs, wknd 2f out. *1¼* **62**
2276 **RED SUN 17** [11]7-9-3 t (60) N Callan 11/1: 244-1260: 10th: Chsd ldrs, wknd & eased fnl 1.5f: btr 2009. *15* **37**
2085 **GARGOYLE GIRL 26** [3]7-9-1 (58) N Mackay(3) 11/1: 0-051060: 11th: Al bhd, t.o.: much btr 1551. *dist* **5**
2444 **MOST DEFINITELY 10** [7]4-9-5 bl (62) R Winston 12/1: 22222-20: 12th: Keen mid-div, btn 2f out, t.o.: not stay longer trip on soft? btr 2444 (14f, firm grnd). *10* **0**
1629 **THE RING 47** [5]4-10-0 (71) K Darley 13/2: 431-0230: 13th: Trkd ldrs, lost place 3f out, eased: btr 1629. *1¾* **6**
13 Ran Time 3m 47.28 (21.78) Owned: Mrs I Gibson Trained: Richmond

2686

4.20 Tsg Pegasus Claiming Stakes 3yo+ (F)
£3248 £928 £464 **1m4f93y** **Soft 111** **-54 Slow** Inside - Hand Timed

2474 **HEARTHSTEAD DREAM 8** [3] J G M O'Shea 3-8-8 bl (63) B Swarbrick(5) 5/1: 0-032151: Trkd ldrs, ch 2f out, forged ahd cl-home: eff at 1m/12f in claim grade: acts on firm & soft grnd: suited by blnks now. **71**
2356* **ETON 13** [6] D Nicholls 8-10-0 (73) A Nicholls 6/1: 10-30512: Tried to make all, collared cl-home: gd run under top-weight on grnd that was reportedly too soft: see 2356. *nk* **75**
965 **PADDY MUL 87** [5] W Storey 7-9-4 t (40) Rory Moore(7) 8/1: 2143453: Held up, hdwy 2f out, onepcd fnl 1f: clr of rem, 3 mth abs: rider reportedly given a 1-day careless riding ban: see 965. *2½* **62$**
2298 **LORD LAMB 16** [1] Mrs M Reveley 12-9-4 (65) A Culhane 9/2: 2/5//014-34: Trkd ldrs, short of room 2f out, sn onepcd: op 3/1: see 2298. *6* **52**
2499 **ROMIL STAR 7** [7]7-9-10 vis (50) Darren Williams 11/4 FAV: 2141135: Keen & prom, wknd 1.5f out: prev in fine AW form: see 2499 & 2381. *3½* **52**
2356 **TOMASINO 13** [2]6-10-0 (83) K Darley 4/1: 3/00/66-46: Rear, prog halfway, wknd 2f out, eased & t.o.: jt top-weight: see 2356. *28* **21**
6 Ran Time 2m 58.2 (20.3) Owned: Mr Gary Roberts Trained: Westbury On Severn

2687

4.50 Tsg Microsoft Classified Stakes 3yo+ 0-75 (D)
£5876 £1808 £904 **1m2f32y** **Soft 111** **-09 Slow** Far Side

1108 **BURNING MOON 75** [7] J Noseda 3-8-10 (80) E Ahern 9/2: 50-51: b c Bering - Triple Green (Green Desert) Trkd ldrs, smooth hdwy to lead dist, pushed clr: abs: twice rcd in '03, plenty of mdn promise (rtd 77+): half-sister to a 10f Gr 2 wnr: apprec step up to 10f on soft: runs well fresh: unexposed, follow-up. **89+**
2284 **SUMMER BOUNTY 16** [6] F Jordan 8-9-4 (76) N Callan 5/1: 0-011032: Rear, prog when short of room 1.5f out, kept on for 2nd but no ch with wnr: clr of rem: caught an imprvd rival here: see 2284. *5* **76**
2443 **JUST A FLUKE 10** [2] M Johnston 3-8-7 (77) S Chin 9/2: 22-4023: Led till dist, wknd: op 7/2. *5* **70**
2483 **GO TECH 8** [3] T D Easterby 4-9-4 (76) R Winston 3/1 JT FAV: 0060624: Keen & prom, ev ch 3f out, wkng when short of room dist: nicely bckd: much btr 2483 (fast grnd). *4* **63**
1056 **INTERNATIONALGUEST 80** [8]5-9-3 bl (75) P Robinson 3/1 JT FAV: 0002005: Rdn in rear, nvr dngrs. *2½* **59**
2605 **EASTERN DAGGER 4** [5]4-9-3 (48) L Enstone(3) 100/1: 060-0006: Slowly away, recovered to chase ldrs 1m, wknd: qck reapp & highly tried: see 2337 (J Turner). *shd* **59$**
2030 **LEIGHTON 28** [1]4-9-8 p (80) T P Queally(3) 14/1: 403-0547: Trkd ldrs 1m, wknd. *19* **39**
1802} **JOHNS CHAMP 392** [4]4-9-3 (50) T Eaves(3) 100/1: 5/40620-8: b g Mujadil - Big Buyer (Quest For Fame) Al bhd, t.o. in last: reapp: '03 sell rnr-up for A Jarvis: eff around 9/10f on fibresand & polytrack: wears a visor, not today: now with R Barr. 2 Feb'03 Wolv 9.3af 52a- G: *dist* **0**
8 Ran Time 2m 18.59(12.09) Owned: Hesmonds Stud Trained: Newmarket

THIRSK THURSDAY 24.06.04 Lefthand, Flat, Oval Track

Official Going Good/Soft (Soft Places) HEAVY RAIN DURING MEETING

2688

2.30 Colin Hazelden Bbc Radio York Selling Stakes 4yo+ (E)
£3721 £1145 £573 **1m rnd** **Good/Soft** **Inapplicable** Inside

2550 **DARA MAC 6** [12] N Bycroft 5-8-11 (53) Suzanne France(7) 13/2: 05-02631: Bhd, hdwy wide over 2f out & led dist, rdn clr: no bid: first win on drop in class: qck reapp: eff at 7f/1m on fast & gd/soft. **63**
2466 **NOBLE PURSUIT 9** [10] R E Barr 7-8-11 (53) R Ffrench 20/1: 0355002: Mid-div, hdwy & rdn/led over 1f out, sn hdd & not pace of wnr: best kept to this grade: see 502. *2½* **57**
1132 **SENOR EDUARDO 73** [14] S Gollings 7-8-11 (51) N Pollard 50/1: 4305-003: Handy, rdn/chall 2f out, not pace of front pair: 10 wk abs: handles fast & gd/soft grnd: eff at 7.5f/1m: mdn, see 1132. *1¾* **54**
2431 **KELSEAS KOLBY 10** [6] P A Blockley 4-9-2 vis (55) M Fenton 12/1: 0-001434: Bhd, kept on late. *hd* **58**
1463 **MAGIC MAMMAS TOO 55** [5]4-8-11 p (50) P Makin(5) 14/1: 6-253405: Mid-div, styd on onepace: abs. *1½* **50**
2615 **ROYAL WINDMILL 3** [3]5-8-11 p (45) P Mulrennan(5) 7/1: 6-005206: Trkd ldrs trav well, led 2f out, sn hdd & found little: qck reapp: btr 2544. *nk* **49**
2445 **QUICKS THE WORD 10** [9]4-8-11 (60) J Fanning 20/1: 0-004007: Chsd ldrs, no impress dist: btr 1532. *1½* **46**
2447 **RYMERS RASCAL 10** [4]12-8-11 (51) W Supple 6/1: 302-3208: Dwelt, bhd, short of room 2f out, sn btn. *¾* **45**
2338 **ZARIN 14** [8]6-8-11 (57) Lisa Jones(3) 10/1: 023-0309: Dwelt, al bhd: btr 744 (AW). *2* **41**
1954 **ZOUCHE 31** [15]4-8-11 (45) T E Durcan 25/1: 06065-00: 10th: b g Zamindar - Al Corniche (Bluebird) Mid-div, no impress: clmr plcd in '03, AW unplcd (rtd 71a, flattered): unplcd sole '02 start (rtd 83, mdn, B Meehan): eff at 7f in claim grade, tried 9f: handles firm grnd & eff in cheek pieces, tried blnks. *¾* **40**
2615 **LORD CHAMBERLAIN 3** [13]11-8-11 bl (51) F Norton 11/2 FAV: 0344030: 11th: Chsd ldrs, btn over 1f out. *2* **36**
2653 **CEZZARO 2** [11]6-8-11 (40) J Bramhill 12/1: 0-560220: 12th: Led till halfway, sn btn, qck reapp. *3* **30**
2405 **NICHOLAS NICKELBY 12** [1]4-8-11 (60) G Gibbons 8/1: 22-06200: 13th: Led halfway till over 2f out, fdd. *20* **0**
2497 **Stone Crest 8** [16]6-8-6 (30) S Yourston(7) 100/1:0
2480 **Inistrahull Island 8** [17]4-8-11 (56) O Urbina 11/1:0
15 Ran Time 1m 43.21 (7.81) Owned: Mr N Bycroft Trained: Malton

---

2689 3.00 Sandie Dunleavy Bbc Radio York Median Auction Maiden Stakes 2yo (E)
£3702 £1139 £570 **6f str** **Good/Soft** **Inapplicable** Stands Side

SIR ANTHONY 0 [6] B Smart 2-9-0 F Lynch 6/1: 1: b c Danehill Dancer - Brief Fairy (Brief Truce) **85**
Mid-div, switched & styd on well for press to lead ins last: op 5/1: 39,000gns 2yo, April first foal: dam a dual
5/7f wnr: sire top-class sprinter: eff at 6f, get 7f: acts on gd/soft: scopey, rate higher.
2297 **TAKHMIN 16** [10] M Johnston 2-9-0 W Supple 5/2 FAV: 02: b c Almutawakel - Magdalene (College *1¼* **80**
Chapel) Went right start, sn trkd ldrs & led over 1f out, rdn & hdd ins last, not pace of wnr: bckd, op 4/1: left
debut bhd: 60,000gns April foal, half-brother to a 5/6f 2yo scorer: eff at 6f, stay further: acts on gd/soft grnd &
an easy trk: going the right way.
2263 **ROWAN LODGE 17** [2] M H Tompkins 2-9-0 J Fanning 14/1: 03: ch c Indian Lodge - Tirol Hope *1¼* **76**
(Tirol) Prom, rdn to chall over 1f out, kept on onepace: imprvd from intro: cheaply bght April foal, half-brother
to a plcd 7f juv, subs plcd over hdles: dam a 6/7f juv wnr: eff at 6f, get further: handles gd/soft: gd run.
2360 **RICH ALBI 13** [7] T D Easterby 2-9-0 VIS D Allan 7/1: 604: Handy, rdn & no extra over 1f out: op *1* **71**
11/2, better eff in first time visor: handles gd/soft grnd.
COMMENDABLE COUP 0 [11]2-9-0 G Gibbons 12/1: 5: Badly hmpd start, bhd, kept on late, nrst fin: *hd* **72+**
eyecatcher, closer without interference, scopey but needed this & will learn plenty, expect improvement.
EUKLEIA 0 [13]2-8-9 R Ffrench 7/1: 6: Led till over 2f out, no extra. *hd* **66**
DUCAL DIVA 0 [3]2-8-9 J Quinn 33/1: 7: Led/dsptd lead till over 1f out, wknd. *½* **64**
REGIS FLIGHT 0 [12]2-9-0 J Bramhill 25/1: 8: Hmpd start, rear, hdwy halfway, no extra distance. *1* **66**
IMPERIAL DYNASTY 0 [8]2-9-0 P Makin(5) 13/2: 9: Held up in tch, no impress over 1f out: bckd. *2* **60**
1752 **PEE JAYS DREAM 40** [9]2-9-0 P Mulrennan(5) 17/2: 60: 10th: Chsd ldrs till over 2f out, abs, turf bow. *1¾* **55**
HERENCIA 0 [4]2-9-0 M Fenton 20/1: 0: 11th: Al rear. *¾* **53**
2522 **WEDLOCK 7** [1]2-9-0 T E Durcan 10/1: 400: 12th: Sn outpcd & bhd: btr 2228 (debut). *3* **45**
2241 **FELLBECK FRED 19** [14]2-9-0 G Faulkner 50/1: 00: 13th: Chsd ldrs, struggling from halfway. *2* **39**
13 Ran Time 1m 14.26 (4.76) Owned: Mr Anthony D Gee Trained: Thirsk

---

2690 3.30 Jack Calvert Handicap Stakes 3yo+ 0-80 (D) **[79]**
£5590 £1720 £860 **5f str** **Good/Soft** **Inapplicable** Stands Side

2561 **PADDYWACK 5** [11] D W Chapman 7-8-13 bl (64) Lisa Jones(3) 13/2: 4035301: Trkd ldrs, switched & **72**
rdn/led dist, rdn out: qck reapp: stays 7f, best at 5f on firm, gd/soft & both AWs, handles soft, any trk: see 155.
2512 **TALLY 7** [7] M J Polglase 4-8-6 (57) G Gibbons 18/1: 0312002: Al prom & styd on well for press, *¾* **62**
not pace of wnr: op 20/1: back to form: acts on fast, gd/soft & both AWs: eff at 5/6f: see 2214 & 2160.
2524 **STRENSALL 7** [14] R E Barr 7-9-12 (77) P Mulrennan(5) 12/1: 20-02003: Al handy & led halfway till *shd* **82**
dist, drvn & kept on: likes Catterick: see 2084.
2512 **FAR NOTE 7** [13] S R Bowring 6-8-13 bl (64) J Bramhill 5/1: 1014404: Missed break, sn trkd ldrs, *hd* **68**
styd on well cl-home, nrst fin: has a tendency to miss break of late but likely type for similar, prob over stiff 5f.
2527 **AMANDAS LAD 7** [10]4-8-7 (58) D Fox(5) 14/1: 5042035: Led/dsptd lead till halfway, no extra when *1* **59**
hmpd dist: mdn after 49: see 2527 & 2216.
2286* **AWAKE 16** [4]7-9-13 (78) T E Durcan 9/2 JT FAV: 0-065016: Bhd, late gains under hands & heels, *shd* **79**
nvr a threat: padd pick: see 2286 (well drawn).
2320 **ELLIOTS CHOICE 15** [8]3-8-11 (68) D Tudhope(7) 16/1: 020-4407: Mid-div, no impress from halfway. *1¼* **65**
2232 **ROMAN MISTRESS 19** [9]4-9-0 bl (65) W Supple 7/1: 00-04638: Trkd ldrs, chall/rdn & keeping on for *shd* **62**
press when badly hmpd dist, no ch after: much closer with a clr run, on a handy mark: see 1873.
2657 **BALLYBUNION 2** [6]5-8-4 (55) P M Quinn 9/2 JT FAV: 0000539: Held up in tch, no impress dist. *nk* **51**
2361 **PROUD NATIVE 13** [12]10-9-9 (74) Alex Greaves 14/1: 05-00030: 10th: Rear, nvr a factor: btr 2361 (clmr). *1* **67**
1837 **MISS CEYLON 36** [3]4-7-12 (14oh) (3h) Hayley Turner(5) 80/1: 00000-00: 11th: Handy, btn over 1f out. *nk* **41$**
2585 **BOANERGES 5** [1]7-8-7 (58) F Norton 8/1: 0562400: 12th: Sn bhd: qck reapp: much btr 2262 (firm). *8* **30**
12 Ran Time 58.89 (1.89) Owned: Mr T S Redman Trained: York

2691 4.00 Skipton Handicap Stakes Fillies 3yo+ 0-70 (E) **[72]**
£3614 £1112 £556 **1m4f** **Good/Soft** **Inapplicable** Inside

2509 **CHARLOTTE VALE 7** [7] M D Hammond 3-9-7 (65) M Fenton 11/2: 246-6521: Held up, hdwy 4f out & styd **73**
on well for press to lead well ins last: first win: eff at 1m/9f, clearly enjoyed step up to 12f & could get
further: acts on fast & gd/soft, gall or easy trk: lightly rcd, appears to be progressing as she steps up in trip.
2366 **SAND AND STARS 13** [2] M H Tompkins 3-9-10 (68) J Fanning 5/1: 540-352: Led & dictated pace, drvn *hd* **75**
& hdd well ins last: eff at 11/12f on fast & gd/soft: enjoyed an easy lead today: see 2103.
2529 **DALRIATH 6** [8] M C Chapman 5-8-8 (38) D Fox(5) 25/1: 4212503: Rear, drvn to press ldrs over 1f *1½* **43**
out, no extra nr fin: qck reapp: stays 12f: acts on fast, gd/soft & fibresand: see 1593 (banded, AW).
1785 **CALOMERIA 39** [4] R M Beckett 3-9-2 (60) J Quinn 20/1: 00-0004: b f Groom Dancer - Calendula (Be *½* **64**
My Guest) Handy, sn niggled along, styd on for press fnl 3f, not pace of front pair nr fin: well clr of rem:
unplcd '03 (lightly rcd, rtd 43a & 51, mdns): imprvd for this step up to 12f on gd/soft grnd.
2340 **SEA COVE 14** [3]4-8-13 (43) R Ffrench 6/1: 500-4555: Sn handy, lost place from 3f out: op 9/1. *8* **38**
2503 **THEATRE BELLE 7** [5]3-8-10 (54) D Allan 33/1: 00-0006: b f King's Theatre - Cumbrian Rhapsody *5* **43**
(Sharrood) Mid-div, struggling fnl 3f, qck reapp: unplcd '03 (rtd 37a & 60, mdns): stoutly bred.
1967 **CANTEMERLE 31** [6]4-9-10 bl (54) T E Durcan 15/2: 0350-207: Chsd ldrs halfway, btn 3f out: btr 1680. *8* **34**
2510* **WESTCOURT DREAM 7** [9]4-9-1 (45) P Mulrennan(5) 5/4 FAV: 0333-318: Chsd ldrs, rdn & btn 3f out: *2½* **21**
connections unable to offer explanation: much btr 2510 (10f, gd).
8 Ran Time 2m 43.42 (13.62) Owned: Mr Peter J Davies Trained: Middleham

THIRSK   THURSDAY 24.06.04   Lefthand, Flat, Oval Track

2692   4.30 Jerry Scott Bbc Radio York Maiden Stakes 3yo+   (D)
£5486 £1688 £844   **7f rnd**   **Soft**   **Inapplicable**   Inside

POLAR MAGIC 0 [10] J R Fanshawe 3-9-0   O Urbina 5/4 FAV: 1: ch c Polar Falcon - Enchant (Lion   78
Cavern) Held up, rdn & hdwy to lead ins last, asserted under hands & heels, readily: debut, well bckd, op 6/4:
37,000gns purchase, half-brother to a 6f wnr abroad: eff at 7/10f: eff at 7f, 1m sure to suit: acts on
soft: goes well fresh: plenty more to come.t.
2527 **FLASH RAM** 7 [5] T D Easterby 3-9-0 bl (66) W Supple 11/2: 333-6422: Handy, led 3f out, drvn/hdd   1¾   71
ins last, not pace wnr: gelded, bckd: eff at 5/6f, now stays 7f: acts on fm & soft: consistent: see 1002 (h'cap).
2463 **ROSIE MAC** 9 [13] N Bycroft 3-8-9   Suzanne France(7) 50/1: 63: Mid-div, styd on wide for press,   1½   64
not pace of wnr from dist: imprvd from debut, eff at 7f, breeding suggests 1m+ will suit: acts on gd grnd.
5032] **EDGEHILL** 229 [9] C R Egerton 3-9-0   M Fenton 22/1: 00-4: b c Ali Royal - Elfin Queen (Fairy   3   64
King) Held up, eff 3f out, onepace: reapp: unplcd both '03 start (rtd 54a & 61, mdns): bred to apprec 1m+.
DANCER KING 0 [11]3-9-0   Dale Gibson 33/1: 5: b g King of Kings - Tigresa (Tejano) Chsd ldrs,   1   62
no impress fnl 2f on debut: $75,000 purchase, half-brother to a plcd US sprint performer, dam US sprint wnr.
ALPHA JULIET 0 [12]3-8-9   N Pollard 40/1: 6: b f Victory Note - Zara's Birthday (Waajib) Dwelt,   nk   56
bhd, styd on wide for press, nrst fin: encouragement on debut: stoutly bred, dam 2m wnr.
3891] **GRELE** 303 [3]3-8-9   J Fanning 50/1: 0-7: Trkd ldrs, fdd fnl 2f, reapp.   5   49
2485 **HARRINGTON BATES** 8 [7]3-9-0   V Halliday 16/1: 468: Keen & led till 3f out, fdd.   3½   49
1912 **TROPICAL STORM** 33 [2]3-9-0 (70) J Quinn 7/4: 24-39: Mid-div, btn 2f out: bckd: btr 1912 (fast).   1½   46
2182 **GRAND RAPIDE** 21 [8]3-8-9   Hayley Turner(5) 16/1: 60: 10th: Al rear.   nk   40
2339 **TOO KEEN** 14 [4]3-8-9   R Ffrench 40/1: 50: 11th: Keen, mid-div, struggling fnl 2f.   7   30
BLACKBURN MEADOWS 0 [14]7-9-4   Natalia Gemelova(7) 80/1: 0: 12th: Al bhd.   1¾   28
2342 **MARY CARLETON** 14 [6]3-8-9   Lisa Jones(3) 100/1: 060: 13th: Dwelt & al bhd.   3½   23
1549] **FUSILLADE** 405 [1]4-9-9   D McGaffin 100/1: 0/00-0: 14th: Dwelt, sn struggling in rear, long abs.   3   23
14 Ran   Time 1m 32.21 (9.31)   Owned: Mr R C Thompson   Trained: Newmarket

2693   5.00 Skelton Handicap Stakes 3yo 0-75 (E)   [80]
£3653 £1124 £562   **7f rnd**   **Soft**   **Inapplicable**   Inside

2166 **SNAP** 22 [9] M Johnston 3-9-7 (73) J Fanning 7/4 FAV: 2131: Keen & handy, led 3f out till 2f out,   79
led again ins last, all out: bckd: eff at 6f, now suited by 7/7.5f: acts on fast & soft, likes Thirsk: game.
2551 **COMMANDO SCOTT** 6 [8] A Berry 3-9-7 (73) T E Durcan 3/1: 40-10022: Handy, rdn to lead 2f out, hdd   nk   78
ins last, styd on well, just held: styd longer 7f trip well: acts on fast & soft grnd: see 2551 & 1216.
2296 **ACCA LARENTIA** 16 [6] R M Whitaker 3-7-12 (2oh) (48) Hayley Turner(5) 25/1: 0062-003: Chsd ldrs,   1¼   52
outprcd over 2f out, kept on late, not pace to chall: handles fast & soft grnd: see 2296.
355* **COTTINGHAM** 168 [4] M C Chapman 3-8-13 (65) Andrew Webb(7) 12/1: 00040-14: Held up, styd on   ¾   67
onepace/hung left from over 1f out: 5 mth abs: turf return: handles firm, soft & fibresand: return to 1m shld suit.
2384 **TSARBUCK** 13 [3]3-7-12 (1oh) (49) Lisa Jones(3) 3/1: 0001525: Chsd ldrs, onepace for press fnl 2f: ¾   51
handles fibresand & soft grnd: clr rem: see 2384 &1842 (banded).
1742] **PLUMPIE MAC** 394 [5]3-7-12 (1oh) (49) Suzanne France(7) 40/1: 060-6: b f Key of Luck - Petrine   5   44
(Petorius) Led till 3f out, fdd: reapp/h'cap bow: unplcd at up to 6f '03 (lightly rcd, rtd 52, debut).
4808] **CHICAGO BOND** 248 [7]3-8-13 (65) D McGaffin 20/1: 54360-7: b f Real Quiet - Shariyfa (Zayyani)   4   53
Held up in tch, rdn & no impress fnl 3f: ndd race: plcd '03 (auct mdn, rtd 73): half-sister to a wnr abroad: eff
at 6f, 7f/1m shld suit this term: handles firm grnd.
2295* **DARK DAY BLUES** 16 [1]3-9-1 (67) M Fenton 7/1: 30-00018: Rear, strugg fnl 3f, gelded: btr 2295 (firm).   ¾   54
8 Ran   Time 1m 32.02(9.12)   Owned: Duke of Devonshire   Trained: Middleham

SALISBURY   THURSDAY 24.06.04   Righthand, Galloping Track, Stiff Finish

Official Going Good (Good/Firm in loop)

2694   1.40 Levy Board Handicap Stakes 3yo+ 0-80 (D)   [80]
£5649 £1738 £869   **1m1f198y**   **Good 60**   **+11 Fast**   Inside

1736* **HAWRIDGE PRINCE** 41 [4] L G Cottrell 4-10-0 (80) L Dettori 8/11 FAV: 0312-11: Held up, hdwy to   92
lead 2f out, drew clr over 1f out, pushed out, v cmftbly: 6 wk abs: eff at 1m/10f on gd & fast grnd, sharp or gall
trk: won this in a fast time, makes it 2/2 here & most progressive, can land a qck hat-trick: see 1736.
2401 **BLUE MARINER** 12 [5] P W Harris 4-9-4 (70) B Doyle 13/2: 2/0-0322: Trkd ldr, eff to chall well   6   71
over 1f out, sn outpcd: running well & shld find a race: see 2401.
1650 **MY GALLIANO** 45 [3] B G Powell 8-9-2 (68) T Quinn 25/1: 60216-03: b g Muharib - Hogan Stand   ¾   68
(Buckskin) Led till 2f out, sn outpcd till rallied ins last: fit from hdlg: earlier won a h'cap chase (rtd 93c,
stays 2m3f on firm & soft): '03 Flat appr h'cap wnr: eff at 10/12f on fast grnd & polytrack, likes sharp trks.
1 Jul'03 Epso 10.1g/f 68-64 E: 2 Jul'03 Epso 10.1g/f 66-62 E: 2 Feb'03 Ling 12ap 67a- D: 2 Feb'03 Ling 12ap 65a- D:
2 Jan'03 Ling 10ap 64a- D:
2600 **ANALYZE** 4 [1] B G Powell 6-9-7 (73) R L Moore 4/1: 506-2354: In tch, eff 2f out, sn no impress.   2½   69
2448 **YEOMAN LAD** 10 [2]4-9-3 vis (69) L Keniry(3) 13/2: 000-0045: In tch, wknd 2f out: btr 2448 (1m).   12   47
5 Ran   Time 2m 09.43 (4.93)   Owned: Mr Eric Gadsden   Trained: Cullompton

2695   2.10 Herbert And Gwen Blagrave E B F Maiden Stakes Div 1 Colts & Geldings 2yo   (D)
£5532 £1702 £851   **6f212y str**   **Good 60**   **-36 Slow**   Centre

PERFECTPERFORMANCE [4] Saeed bin Suroor 2-8-11 L Dettori 4/1: 1: ch c Rahy - Balistroika   99+
(Nijinsky) In tch, hdwy to lead over 1f out, led over 1f out, styd on, rdn out: bg foal, cost $1,100,000:
half-brother to top-class miler Russian Rhythm: eff at 7f, sure to relish 1m: runs well fresh on gd grnd: useful
start, will learn plenty from this, rate more highly & win in btr class.

CAPE GREKO [5] A M Balding 2-8-11 J Fortune 25/1: 2: ro c Loup Sauvage - Onefortheditch (With Approval) Held up, hdwy over 2f out, led over 1f out, sn hdd but kept on for press, just held on debut: Apr foal, cost 35,000gns: half-brother to wnrs over 6/7f: dam 1m/10f scorer: eff over a stiff 7f, 1m sure to suit: acts on gd grnd: clr of rem, most promising start & must be winning races sn for in-form stable.   nk   96+

FLAG POINT [7] J L Dunlop 2-8-11 T Quinn 25/1: 3: b c Indian Danehill - Bianca Cappello (Glenstal) Held up, eff over 2f out, kept on same pace on debut: Apr foal, cost 18,000gns: half-brother to a useful 7f juv scorer: will learn plenty from this, shld apprec 1m & will be wng a less well contested mdn.   5   86

1760 MUSHAJER 40 [1] M P Tregoning 2-8-11 R Hills 1/2 FAV: 34: Handy, hdwy to lead over 2f out, hdd over 1f out, no extra: hvly bckd at odds on: did not progress from debut in 1760 (6f, fast grnd) as expected.   hd   85

2348 ROYAL ORISSA 14 [9]2-8-11 Paul Eddery 25/1: 45: Led till over 2f out, wknd dist: see 2348.   1   83

HAWRIDGE STAR [6]2-8-11 S Sanders 50/1: 6: Slow away & bhd, modest late gains on debut.   ¾   81

WORTH A GRAND [8]2-8-11 R Thomas(5) 66/1: 7: In tch, wkng when short of room over 1f out.   3   75

GOLDEN DYNASTY [3]2-8-11 R Hughes 7/1: 8: In tch, wknd over 2f out on debut.   7   61

8 Ran   Time 1m 32.22 (6.72)   Owned: Godolphin   Trained: Newmarket

---

2696 2.40 Herbert And Gwen Blagrave E B F Maiden Stakes Div 2 Colts & Geldings 2yo (D)
£5512 £1696 £848   6f212y str   Good 60   -65 Slow   Centre

PROPINQUITY [8] P W Harris 2-8-11 D Holland 4/1: 1: b c Primo Dominie - Lydia Maria (Dancing Brave) In tch, eff for press 2f out, short of room & switched left over 1f out, strong run ins last & qcknd to lead cl-home, going away: bckd from 7/1: Apr foal: half-brother to wnrs over 6f/hdles, incl Barolo: eff at 7f, 1m+ sure to suit: runs well fresh on gd: showed a neat turn of foot on debut, keep on your side.   86+

2388 CHAPTER 12 [3] R Hannon 2-8-11 R Hughes 5/2 FAV: 22: Cl-up, led over 2f out, hung left for press over 1f out but kept on ins last, collared last strides: well bckd: acts on fast & gd grnd: going the right way & can find similar shortly: see 2388.   nk   81

CELESTIAL ARC [4] P F I Cole 2-8-11 K Fallon 8/1: 3: b c Southern Halo - Perfect Arc (Brown Arc) Led till over 2f out, onepace ins last: Feb foal, half-brother to a 6f/1m scorer: dam 9f wnr: eff at 7f, 1m will suit: acts on gd grnd: pleasing start, learn from this & shld win shortly.   1¼   78

TOMBOLA [7] J L Dunlop 2-8-11 T Quinn 14/1: 4: In tch, kept on nicely late under hands & heels on debut: April foal: half-brother to a 7f juv wnr: dam 7f 2yo scorer: eff over a stiff 7f, 1m sure to suit: plenty to like about this educational start, will improve bundles & win races.   1   76+

2263 MERRYMADCAP 17 [2]2-8-11 Dane O'Neill 40/1: 05: Bhd, some late gains, nvr dngrs.   2   72

BENEDICT BAY [9]2-8-11 S Drowne 10/1: 6: Bhd, modest late gains, nvr dngrs on debut.   hd   71

SNOW TEMPEST [6]2-8-11 R Miles(3) 20/1: 7: Slow away & bhd, nvr a factor on debut.   ¾   69

RAWAABET [5]2-8-11 R Hills 10/1: 8: Held up, brief eff over 2f out, sn wknd.   ¾   67

MOLLZAM [1]2-8-11 L Dettori 3/1: 9: In tch, wknd 2f out on debut: op 9/4.   5   57

9 Ran   Time 1m 34.24 (8.74)   Owned: Mrs P W Harris   Trained: Berkhamsted

---

2697 3.10 Piper Heidsieck Champagne Auction Stakes Conditions Race 2yo (B)
£12600 £4780 £2390   6f str   Good 60   -11 Slow   Far Side

2302 POLLY ALEXANDER 20 [2] M J Wallace 2-8-11 R L Moore 13/2: 511321: Handy, hdwy to lead over 2f out, styd on gamely for press when pressed ins last, just held on, all out: eff over 5/6f on gd & soft grnd, any trk: useful, tough, genuine & progressive: see 2302, 1362.   93

2341 CAPTAIN HURRICANE 14 [6] P W Chapple Hyam 2-8-7 J Fortune 2/1 FAV: 22: Keen, held up, hdwy to chase wnr over 1f out, styd on to chall ins last, just held for press: useful run conceding this tough wnr weight: acts on gd & fast grnd: well clr of rem, will be winning v sn: see 2341.   hd   97

1955 ASIAN TIGER 31 [11] R Hannon 2-8-9 D Holland 12/1: 2253: In tch, hdwy & short of room over 2f out, rallied appr fnl 1f, no threat to front 2: stays 6f: back to form & must win a minor trk mdn: see 816, 1670.   4   87

1422 ALVARINHO LADY 57 [9] D Haydn Jones 2-8-3 Paul Eddery 33/1: 154: Chsd ldrs, sltly outpcd over 2f out, rallied late: 2 mth abs: stays 6f, shaped like 7f will suit: apprec nursery h'caps: see 1001.   2½   74

2511 DUSTY DANE 7 [1]2-8-4 A Daly 66/1: 565: Bhd, modest late gains, nvr a dngr: needs mdns.   ½   73

1816 DETONATE 37 [7]2-8-3 J F McDonald 33/1: 6406: In tch, wknd well over 1f out: see 1422.   2   66

2263* HAPPY EVENT 17 [10]2-8-6 (1ow) S Drowne 11/1: 17: Sn led till 3f out, wknd dist: btr 2263 (mdn).   3   60

2442 EVANESCE 10 [8]2-7-13 C Catlin 14/1: 2422128: In tch, hdwy to lead 3f out till 2f out, sn wknd.   1   50

2071 IM SPARTACUS 26 [4]2-8-6 D Kinsella 66/1: 021659: Al bhd: reportedly lost action: see 1367.   nk   56

2251 GORTUMBLO 19 [3]2-8-7 T Quinn 4/1: 130: 10th: In tch, wknd over 2f out: reportedly nvr trav.   5   42

10 Ran   Time 1m 16.35 (4.25)   Owned: Mrs T A Foreman   Trained: Newmarket

---

2698 3.40 Alderholt Sprint Handicap Stakes 3yo+ 0-85 (D)   [84]
£6942 £2136 £1068   5f str   Good 60   +00 Fast   Far Side

2420 WHISTLER 11 [3] J M Bradley 7-9-11 p (81) R L Moore 10/1: 0301031: Held up, hdwy 2f out, styd on strongly ins last to lead cl-home, drvn out: suited by 5f, stays 6f: acts on firm, soft & any trk: tough.   89

2286 DOMIRATI 16 [4] R Charlton 4-9-8 (78) S Drowne 11/2: 2234-042: Held up, hdwy over 2f out, led appr fnl 1f, kept on till collared cl-home, not btn far: ran right up to best & shld find another h'cap: see 2286.   ½   83

2266 FURTHER OUTLOOK 17 [9] D K Ivory 10-10-0 (84) Dane O'Neill 14/1: 3000423: Set pace, rdn & hdd appr fnl 1f, kept on, not btn far: tough 10yo: see 2266, 944.   ½   87

2286 ROMANY NIGHTS 16 [5] J W Unett 4-9-8 bl (78) D Holland 5/1 FAV: 4342224: In tch, hdwy & short of room over 1f out, switched left & kept on ins last, not btn far: often runs with promise from the rear: see 2286.   hd   80

2416 DEVISE 12 [1]5-9-10 (80) S Sanders 10/1: 0-160155: Switched right start, hdwy on bit 2f out, sn no room at any stage & lkd most unlucky: keep in mind next time: see 1914.   hd   81+

2585 DOUBLE M 5 [12]7-8-2 vis (58) R Thomas(5) 11/2: 5532136: Chsd ldrs, hdwy & short of room over 1f out, sn onepace: qck reapp: see 2585, 2396 (Lingfield).   hd   58

2420 KATHOLOGY 11 [11]7-9-13 (83) T Quinn 17/2: 0530-067: With ldr, wknd fnl 1f: see 2253.   1¾   78

2420 SEVEN NO TRUMPS 11 [7]7-9-5 p (75) L Dettori 15/2: 0036048: In tch, wknd well over 1f out.   ½   68

2289 HEY PRESTO 16 [8]4-8-13 (69) K Fallon 7/1: 0040-009: Held up, hdwy 2f out, trav well & no run fnl 1f, not recover: no run at crucial stage & this stiff trk: well h'capped & coming to hand.   nk   61

2524 SUNLEY SENSE 7 [2]8-9-9 (79) T Dean(7) 25/1: 1000/-300: 10th: In tch, wknd 2f out: btr 2266.   ¾   69

1371 ZARGUS 60 [10]5-8-6 (62) L Keniry(3) 16/1: 040-5000: 11th: In tch, wknd well over 1f out: 2 month abs, now with A Balding: well h'capped if showing a rtn to form: see 1371 (blnks), 1011.   ¾   50

1615 **OK PAL 48** [6]4-9-10 BL (80) R Miles(3) 14/1: 4-U30060: 12th: With ldrs outer, hung left 2f out,   nk   67
wknd: 8 wk abs, did not apprec first time blnks: see 834.
12 Ran   Time 1m 02.82 (3.02)   Owned: Mr Raymond Tooth   Trained: Chepstow

---

2699   **4.10 H S Lester Memorial Handicap Stakes 3yo+ 0-80 (D)**   [97]
£5551 £1708 £854   **1m6f15y**   **Good 60**   **-23 Slow**   Flag Start

2418 **TUDOR BELL 11** [5] J G M O'Shea 3-8-9 (78) K Fallon 3/1 FAV: 2311621: Made all, kept on gamely   87
for press ins last, just held on: stays 14f well on firm & hvy, any trk: loves to dominate, lightly rcd,
genuine & progressive this term: see 1807, 1604.
2233 **COALITION 19** [2] H Candy 5-9-9 (75) Dane O'Neill 14/1: 11162/-02: In tch, hdwy to chase wnr over   nk   84
2f out, chall but held head shade high ins last, just held: fine run on 2nd start after long abs, see 2233.
2471 **GLORY QUEST 9** [4] Miss Gay Kelleway 7-9-9 (75) D Holland 7/1: 1034103: Held up, hdwy trav well   3   79
over 2f out, no extra appr fnl 1f: back to form after 2471: see 2229.
2471 **REDSPIN 9** [9] J S Moore 4-9-2 (68) Derek Nolan(7) 9/1: 02-30044: In tch, eff 2f out, sn onepace.   ½   71
1889 **VALANCE 34** [6]4-9-10 (76) S Drowne 13/2: 04103-35: In tch, eff dist, sn no impress: fair run.   shd   79
2311 **DONALD 15** [3]4-8-3 (55) R L Moore 20/1: 6/124-306: Held up, eff over 2f out, sn no impress.   1¾   55
2311 **SILVER PROPHET 15** [10]5-9-3 (69) G Baker 10/1: 00-05557: Chsd ldr till 2f out, wknd: see 2311.   hd   69
2085 **SEA PLUME 26** [8]5-9-4 (70) S Sanders 12/1: 2000-508: Held up, eff & flashed tail over 2f out,   nk   69
hung right & no extra: mulish display, see 2085.
2311 **SAN HERNANDO 15** [7]4-9-5 (71) T Quinn 7/2: 0-640049: Held up, eff 2f out, wknd: see 1232.   5   63
2156 **FIGHT THE FEELING 22** [1]6-7-13 (1ow)(5oh) (45) C Catlin 40/1: 2005060: 10th: Held up, wknd 2f out.   3½   38
10 Ran   Time 3m 09.63 (11.63)   Owned: K W Bell & Son Ltd   Trained: Westbury On Severn

---

2700   **4.40 Catisfield Hinton & Stud Supporting The R N L I Maiden Stakes 3yo+ (D)**
£5805 £1786 £893   **1m1f198y**   **Good 60**   **-06 Slow**   Inside

1737 **DOUBLE ASPECT 41** [11] Sir Michael Stoute 3-8-10   K Fallon 4/7 FAV: 41: Handy, hdwy 2f out, styd   84+
on to lead ins last, rdn out but pdzd more in hand: 6 wk abs: eff at 10f, 12f sure to suit (dam smart over 12/14f):
acts on gd grnd & a stiff trk: looks plenty more to come esp over further in h'caps: see 1737.
2453 **MICHABO 10** [10] D R C Elsworth 3-8-10 T Quinn 14/1: 0-432: Set pace, rdn & kept on till   ¾   80
collared cl-home, not btn far: much imprvd bhd a potentially useful type: acts on fast & gd: can find similar.
2620} **DUNDRY 357** [14] G L Moore 3-8-10 R L Moore 25/1: 0-3: b g Bin Ajwaad - China's Pearl (Shirley   2½   75
Heights) Chsd ldrs, eff well over 1f out, onepace: rtd 71 when unplcd in '03 for R Hannon: half-brother to a 10f
wnr: eff at 10f on gd grnd: encouraging rtn for new stable.
2230 **HISTORIC PLACE 20** [7] G B Balding 4-9-8 S Drowne 11/1: 24: In tch, eff over 1f out, nrst fin,   1¾   72
no dngr: encouraging run but looks to be crying out for a rtn to 12f+: see 2230.
2386 **ZUMA 12** [5]3-8-10 VIS (79) D Holland 8/1: 00-0305: In tch, eff to chall 2f out, wknd fnl 1f: visor.   shd   71
2193 **WARNINGCAMP 21** [4]3-8-10 S Sanders 6/1: 46: In tch, eff over 2f out, sn no extra: see 2193.   1¼   69
2193 **MASTERMAN READY 21** [1]3-8-10 B Doyle 50/1: 6-07: b g Unfuwain - Maria Isabella (Young   hd   68
Generation) Bhd, nvr a factor: rtd 60a when unplcd sole '03 start: full brother to a 1m/12f scorer.
      TOPKAT [8]3-8-10 Dane O'Neill 16/1: 8: b g Simply Great - Kitty's Sister (Bustino) Slow away   1¼   66
& bhd, modest late gains on debut: cost E58,000: brother to wnrs over 7f/14f: bred to need 12f+.
4981} **GREY ADMIRAL 235** [12]3-8-10 N Chalmers(5) 25/1: 000-9: In tch, wknd over 2f out.   ½   65
2521} **LASSER LIGHT 361** [9]4-9-8 V Slattery 100/1: 0-0: 10th: Al bhd on reapp.   13   47
886   **PADDY BOY 96** [3]3-8-10 R Miles(3) 100/1: 300: 11th: In tch, wknd over 3f out.   4   41
      JUST DASHING [13]5-9-8 C Lowther 100/1: 0: 12th: Al bhd, t.o..   dist   0
2291 **TARTIRUGA 16** [6]3-8-10 L Keniry(3) 100/1: 00-00: 13th: Saddle slipped after 3f, t.o..   dist   0
13 Ran   Time 2m 11.07 (6.57)   Owned: The Celle Syndicate Incorporated   Trained: Newmarket

---

2701   **5.10 Teletext Racing 'hands And Heels' Apprentice Handicap Stakes 3yo 0-70 (E)**   [73]
£4241 £1305 £653   **1m**   **Good 60**   **-26 Slow**   Centre

2292 **KNICKYKNACKIENOO 16** [2] A G Newcombe 3-8-10 (55) M Halford 11/2: 0-422031: Slow away, held up,   64
hdwy & switched left 2f out, short of room dist but styd on to lead ins last, rdn clr: first win: apprec step up to
1m on fm & soft, prob any trk: did well to defy trouble in running, confidence high now, cld follow-up.
2344 **GABANA 14** [6] C F Wall 3-9-6 (65) S O'Hara(3) 4/1: 03-06032: In tch, hdwy & carried hd high just   1¾   69
ins last, not pace of wnr: gd run but remains a mdn: see 2344.
2064 **ASK THE DRIVER 26** [8] D J S ffrench Davis 3-8-9 (54) Liam Jones 6/1: 050-2433: Held up, hdwy   1¾   54
over 1f out, onepace fnl 1f: will apprec a return to 10f as in 2064.
2264 **CHASING THE DREAM 17** [5] A M Balding 3-9-6 (65) R J Killoran(3) 9/2: 126034: Handy, hdwy to lead   hd   64
over 2f out, hdd just ins last, no extra: see 2264, 322.
2432 **EVEN EASIER 10** [7]3-8-10 bl (55) Jemma Marshall(3) 15/2: 0506445: In tch, eff 2f out, sn no extra.   nk   53
2378 **MISS INKHA 13** [1]3-9-4 (63) R Mills(8) 16/1: 0066: b f Intikhab - Santi Sana (Formidable) Slow   1   59
away & nvr a factor: unplcd prev: poss stays 1m on gd grnd.
2506 **MISS PORCIA 7** [3]3-9-0 (59) B O'Neill 3/1 FAV: 0060-127: Led till over 2f out, wknd: btr 2506 (7f).   7   41
2174 **FIRST DAWN 22** [4]3-9-7 (66) L Harman(8) 16/1: 6-06-008: ch f Dr Fong - Delight of Dawn (Never So   ½   47
Bold) In tch, wknd 2f out: unplcd both '03 starts (rtd 71).
8 Ran   Time 1m 45.98 (6.88)   Owned: Mr A G Newcombe   Trained: Barnstaple

Official Going Good

2702   6.50 Mark Jarvis G-Ronn Handicap Stakes Lady Amateur Riders 3yo+ 0-70 (E)   [52]
£3582 £1102 £551   **5f2y str**   **Good 55**   **-02 Slow**   Stands side

2535 **SOMERSET WEST 6** [3] J R Best 4-11-0 (66) Miss J Ferguson(5) 20/1: 0011001: Bhd stands side, prog   73
after 2f, styd on to lead dist, rdn out: qck reapp: eff at 5/7f, has tried 1m: acts on fast, soft grnd &
polytrack: goes well for today's pilot: see 1625 & 1074.
2524* **TORRENT 7** [18] D W Chapman 9-10-0 (7ex)bl (52) Miss Lynsey Hanna 6/1 JT FAV: 0100012: Cl-up far   1½   53
side, styd on to lead dist, hdd ins fnl 1f, no extra: qck reapp: continues to run well: see 2524.
1988 **VALAZAR 30** [5] D W Chapman 5-9-7 (45) Miss Kelly Harrison(3) 6/1 JT FAV: 0002323: Cl-up stands   nk   45
side, ev ch dist, edged right under press & onepcd: acts on firm, gd grnd & fibresand: see 1988 & 1405.
2409 **TUSCAN FLYER 12** [15] R Bastiman 6-10-10 bl (62) Miss R Bastiman(5) 9/1: 42-00304: Bhd centre, prog   ¾   60
2f out, nrst fin: will appreciate return to 7f: btr 2150.
2566 **ONLY IF I LAUGH 5** [4]3-10-5 (63) Miss Faye Bramley(5) 20/1: 3402305: Rear stands side, prog 2f   nk   60
out, nrst fin: qck reapp: see 2493.
2372 **TRAVELLERS JOY 13** [14]4-8-10 (1oh) (33) Miss R D'Arcy(5) 33/1: 0030606: Mid-div centre, prog 2f   ½   30
out, no impress fnl 1f: see 1562.
2512 **SIR SANDROVITCH 7** [8]8-10-2 p (54) Miss V Tunnicliffe(5) 7/1: 000-0067: Sn bhd centre, prog ins   1¾   45
fnl 1f, nrst fin: op 5/1: qck reapp: see 2512.
2466 **ST IVIAN 9** [10]4-10-8 p (60) Mrs M Morris 40/1: 0200008: Handy centre, wknd bef 1f out: btr 1127.   2   45
2361 **KALLISTAS PRIDE 13** [16]4-10-6 (58) Miss K Manser(7) 14/1: 00-029: Nvr nrr than mid-div far side.   shd   42
825 **REPEAT 108** [11]4-9-7 (45) Miss M Britton(7) 33/1: 2044000: 10th: Rcd centre, led till bef 2f out, wknd.   nk   28
2412 **JINKSONTHEHOUSE 12** [19]3-10-0 (58) Miss A Wallace(5) 20/1: 0-401040: 11th: Handy far side 3f, wknd.   1   38
1914 **PRIME RECREATION 33** [17]7-10-10 (62) Miss S Brotherton 15/2: 6000300: 12th: Led far side group   ½   41
till bef 1f out, wknd: btr 1774 (gd/soft).
453 **OUR FRED 155** [13]7-10-5 bl (57) Miss M Sowerby(5) 14/1: 0306-600: 13th: Al in rear centre: long abs.   ½   35
2420 **PORT ST CHARLES 11** [1]7-10-10 (62) Miss E J Jones 7/1: 0043000: 14th: Al bhd stands side: btr 2189.   ½   39
2412 **DIAMOND RING 12** [9]5-9-2 (40) Miss Gwen Morris(5) 12/1: 360-5030: 15th: Handy centre 3f, sn wknd.   nk   16
2645 **BEENABOUTABIT 2** [6]6-8-13 (3ow)(4oh) (30) Miss L McIntosh 66/1: 000-0050: 16th: Al in rear: qck reapp.1   10
2599 **LADY PEKAN 4** [7]5-10-10 bl (42) Miss J C Duncan(5) 20/1: 3530000: 17th: Rcd centre, led bef 2f   shd   34
out, hdd bef 1f out, wknd: qck reapp: btr 2266.
2049 **Cloudless 27** [2]4-9-9 (47) Miss E Folkes(3) 33/1:0   2201 **Boisdale 20** [12]6-9-11 (49) Miss A L Turner(5) 16/1:0
19 Ran   Time 1m 1.17 (2.87)   Owned: Mr J P Ferguson   Trained: Maidstone

---

2703   7.20 Mark Jarvis See Andy Maiden Auction Stakes 2yo (E)
£4232 £1302 £651   **5f218y str**   **Good 55**   **+01 Fast**   Stands side

  INTOXICATING 0 [3] R F Johnson Houghton 2-8-9 G Duffield 14/1: 1: b c Mujahid - Salalah (Lion   90
Cavern) Slow away, sn in tch & rdn/led over 2f out, rdn out: 20,000gns April foal, dam a 7f 3yo scorer: eff at 6f,
get further: acts on gd grnd & a stiff/gall trk: goes well fresh: promising start & looks potentially useful.
931 **TRANSACTION 90** [5] J M P Eustace 2-8-9 S Sanders 5/1: 32: Al prom, rdn to chall over 1f out,   1½   84
not pace of wnr ins last: 3 mth abs & turf bow: acts on polytrack & gd: win a race.
2367 **EDGE FUND 13** [2] B R Millman 2-8-11 S Drowne 4/1: 33323: Prom, rdn & chall over 1f out, no   1½   82
extra ins last: op 10/3: consistent: see 2367.
  SCARLET INVADER 0 [4] J L Dunlop 2-8-11 K Darley 7/1: 4: b c Indian Ridge - Scarlet Plume   1½   78
(Warning) Dwelt, bhd, kept on late: op 6/1: 27,000gns Feb foal, half-brother to a 6f juv wnr, dam a high-class
filly abroad: learn from this & apprec 7f.
2316 **ARTHUR WARDLE 15** [9]2-8-11 D Holland 11/4 FAV: 25: Dwelt, sn chsd ldrs, rdn & no impress fnl   ¾   76
1f: bckd, op 10/3: handles fast & gd grnd: see 2316.
2151 **NELLA FANTASIA 22** [10]2-8-9 M Hills 20/1: 66: Chsd ldrs, no impress over 1f out.   hd   73
  HIGH DYKE 0 [1]2-8-7 Paul Eddery 66/1: 7: b c Mujahid - Gold Linnet (Nashwan) Held up, no   3   62
impress fnl 2f: 7,000gns 2yo purchase, April foal: half-brother to a 12f wnr: dam plcd at 10f.
1964 **TAIPAN TOMMY 31** [7]2-8-11 J F Egan 66/1: 668: Led 3f, btn dist.   5   52
  DAHLIYEV 0 [6]2-9-0 T Quinn 9/2: 9: Dwelt, in tch, btn 2f out.   nk   54
  TOBYS DREAM 0 [8]2-8-11 K Dalgleish 14/1: 0: 100th: Slow away & al outpcd: op 16/1.   6   35
10 Ran   Time 1m 13.05 (3.25)   Owned: Anthony Pye-Jeary And Mel Smith   Trained: Didcot

---

2704   7.50 Mark Jarvis Bunch O Moss Selling Stakes 3yo (G)
£3045 £870 £435   **7f9y str**   **Good 55**   **-09 Slow**   Stands side

2379 **WILLJOJO 13** [14] R A Fahey 3-8-9 vis (52) M Hills 11/2: 503-3541: Chsd ldr far side & led over 1f   57
out, in command ins last, rdn out: no bid: first win: eff at 5/6f, now stays stiff 7f well in sell grade: acts on
firm, gd/soft & fibresand: see 995.
2439 **RED ROCKY 10** [18] R Hollinshead 3-8-9 p (48) Stephanie Hollinshead(5) 25/1: 55-00502: Led far side   3   50
4f, kept on, not pace of wnr: stays a stiff 7f in sell grade on gd grnd, imprvd eff with cheek pieces omitted.
2439 **ZONNEBEKE 10** [17] K R Burke 3-8-9 VIS (50) K Dalgleish 11/1: 5203003: Prom, outpcd 2f out, kept   ½   49
on late to take 3rd: first time visor, gd run: eff at 7f, return to 1m could suit: acts on polytrack & gd: see 535.
1965 **CHUBBES 31** [12] M D Hammond 3-9-0 P (69) S Drowne 11/4 FAV: 4230-004: Rdn towards rear far side,   1¼   52
kept on late, not able to chall: first time cheek pieces, prev with M Pipe: see 54 (1m).
2292 **DAVIDS GIRL 16** [6]3-8-9 (38) J Mackay 8/1: 005-5665: Chsd ldrs stands side, led that group dist,   1½   44
not pace of ldrs far side: see 1416.
4021} **COCO REEF 296** [16]3-8-9 (57) S Sanders 11/1: 0330-6: b f Kingsinger - Highland Blue (Never So   1¾   40
Bold) Chsd ldrs far side, no impress dist, reapp: dual AW mdn plcd in '03 (rtd 58a, turf unplcd, rtd 32, lightly
rcd): eff at 6f, further could suit this term: handles fibresand.
2292 **JAOLINS 16** [11]3-9-0 (40) D Kinsella 25/1: 0500007: Slow away & held up, keen, no dngr.   ½   44
2339 **OSLA 14** [8]3-8-9 D Holland 20/1: 008: In tch stands side till 2f out: only mod form prev.   nk   38
2065 **MARKSGOLD 26** [15]3-9-0 (55) T Quinn 6/1: 0-366059: Rdn chasing ldrs far side, btn 2f out: btr 1539.   ¾   41
2219 **PEACE TREATY 20** [2]3-8-9 (30) J Bramhill 66/1: 0000060: 10th: Chsd ldrs stands side till 2f out.   4   28

819

2032 **EMPEROR CAT 28** [9]3-9-0 bl (50) Stacey Renwick(7) 40/1: 5-230000: 11th: Led stands side 4f, sn btn.   nk   **32**
2493 **LA FONTEYNE 8** [13]3-8-9 (55) J McAuley 14/1: 00-5020: 12th: Far side, prom till over 2f out: btr 2493.   5   **17**
2397 **DR FOX 12** [10]3-9-0 p (40) A Quinn(5) 25/1: 5-000000: 13th: Chsd ldrs 3f far side.   hd   **21**
2215 **Delta Lady 20** [7]3-8-9 (42) J F Egan 14/1:0   2428 **Trinaree 11** [5]3-9-0 N Pollard 66/1:0
4930} **Back In Fashion 240** [3]3-8-9 M Fenton 66/1:0   2428 **Ragazzi 11** [1]3-9-0 K Darley 10/1:0
17 Ran   Time 1m 26.50 (4.50)   Owned: The Yorkshire Lancashire Alliance   Trained: Malton

---

2705   8.20 Mark Jarvis It's Only Just Changed Handicap Stakes 3yo 0-85 (D)   [89]
£7222 £2222 £1111   **1m9y rnd**   **Good 55**   **Inapplicable**   Inside

1879* **KAMANDA LAUGH 35** [1] B W Hills 3-9-5 (80) M Hills 5/2-FAV: 60-1211: Keen early, in tch wide, led   **88**
dist, drnn out: eff at 6/7, styd stiff 1m well: acts on fast, soft & polytrack, likes a stiff/gall trk: clearly on upgrade.
2443* **LITTLE JIMBOB 10** [6] R A Fahey 3-9-0 (5ex) (75) T Hamilton(3) 10/1: 32342-12: Led till over 1f   1   **80**
out, no extra fnl 100y: acts on firm & gd grnd: loves forcing tactics: see 2443 (mdn).
2365 **WHITGIFT ROCK 13** [8] S Dow 3-8-12 (73) D Holland 10/1: 1-120003: Handy when short of room & rdn   hd   **77**
2f out, late rally for 3rd, no threat: see 341.
2117* **MAGIC MERLIN 24** [3] P W Harris 3-9-3 (78) B Doyle 7/2: 314: Held up, styd on late for press, no   shd   **81**
danger: only 3rd start & h'cap bow: btr 2117 (mdn, al prom).
2127 **RIO DE JUMEIRAH 23** [2]3-9-0 (75) T E Durcan 20/1: 035-3605: Chsd ldrs, onepcd fnl 1f: wants 10f.   nk   **77**
2427 **INCHLOSS 11** [9]3-9-2 (77) G Gibbons 20/1: 0412006: Held up, eff 2f out, no impress: btr 1707 (g/s).   5   **69**
2377 **MUHAYMIN 13** [7]3-9-7 (82) W Supple 10/1: 031-0047: Trkd ldrs trav well, found little dist.   shd   **73**
2247 **MR JACK DANIELLS 19** [5]3-9-0 (75) S Drowne 3/1: 100-3638: Trkd ldrs, stumbled badly & lost place   11   **48**
after 2f, no impress fnl 2f: this run best forgiven: see 2247 & 1526.
1625 **CARRIACOU 47** [4]3-8-9 (70) Paul Eddery 33/1: 002-6459: Rdn to chase ldr, btn 2f out: abs: btr 1625.   2½   **38**
9 Ran   Time 1m 41.96 ()   Owned: Mr John Sillett   Trained: Lambourn

---

2706   8.50 Jarvis Six Foot Injured Jockeys Fund Handicap Stakes 3yo 0-70 (E)   [76]
£7475 £2300 £1150   **1m1f218y**   **Good 55**   **+02 Fast**   Inside

2203 **JAKARMI 20** [2] B Palling 3-9-3 (65) R Miles(3) 15/2: 3222321: Held up, smooth hdwy wide halfway,   **76+**
led over 1f out, styd on strongly to assert ins last: fair time: stays 12f, seems suited by 1m/10f on firm, soft &
f/sand, prob any trk: v tough & consistent & a most deserved win, gave away grnd by racing wide rnd bend: win again.
2366 **PRINCIPESSA 13** [11] B Palling 3-9-3 (65) T Quinn 33/1: 3-50002: Chsd ldr, led after 2f till   1½   **72**
halfway, rallied fnl 1f & just snatched 2nd: stays 10f, acts on gd & soft: s/mate of wnr.
2365* **HABANERO 13** [8] R Hannon 3-9-7 (69) D Holland 6/1: 1-005313: Prom, led halfway till dist, no   shd   **73**
extra ins fnl 1f, eased fnl strides & caught for 2nd: enjoys forcing tactics, stays 10f.
2353 **MASTER MAHOGANY 14** [7] R J Hodges 3-9-2 (64) S Drowne 40/1: 0400654: Held up, styd on onepace   2½   **66**
for press fnl 3f: eff at 10f, tried 12f: acts on gd grnd: first placing tonight: see 2353.
2277 **CHARMATIC 17** [4]3-9-3 (65) Dean McKeown 7/1: 5221545: Trkd ldrs, onepace dist: btr 2277.   1   **65**
2338 **INMOM 14** [1]3-8-10 (58) J Bramhill 50/1: 50-3046: Held up in tch wide, onepace fnl 3f: see 1610.   ¾   **56**
2277 **ILE FACILE 17** [14]3-9-7 t (69) T G McLaughlin 8/1: 4241027: Held up, hmpd over 2f out, kept on   ¾   **65**
late, shade closer without interference: see 2277 & 706.
2366 **WYOMING 13** [12]3-8-11 (59) W Ryan 14/1: 00-308: Handy, edged right & wknd from dist, eased: not   nk   **54**
knocked about, ran well for a long way: see 1617.
1834 **LATE OPPOSITION 37** [19]3-9-7 (69) K Darley 9/1: 6-422209: Mid-div, no impress fnl 2f: btr 1648.   ¾   **62**
2243 **DAGOLA 19** [18]3-9-0 (62) R Smith 14/1: 0000-100: 10th: Chd ldrs, btn when no room over 1f out.   ½   **54**
1647 **MUSIC MIX 45** [15]3-8-11 e (59) T E Durcan 33/1: 466-00: 11th: Held up, no impress dist, abs: btr 102.   ½   **50**
2180* **MAGIC STING 21** [17]3-9-7 (69) J Mackay 5/1-FAV: 5-556110: 12th: Led 2f, btn over 1f out.   1¼   **58**
2338 **Munaawesh 14** [5]3-8-11 (59) G Duffield 66/1:0   2175 **Lawaaheb 22** [13]3-9-7 (69) W Supple 14/1:0
2452 **Petite Colleen 10** [6]3-9-3 (65) D Kinsella 33/1:0   2295 **Colloseum 16** [9]3-8-10 (58) Paul Eddery 50/1:0
2103 **Badr 24** [10]3-9-0 (62) K Dalgleish 14/1:0   1417 **Smokin Joe 57** [3]3-9-1 (63) N Pollard 33/1:0
18 Ran   Time 2m 7.85 (5.35)   Owned: Mrs M M Palling   Trained: Cowbridge

---

2707   9.20 Mark Jarvis I Know Mark Classified Stakes 3yo+ 0-65 (E)
£4202 £1293 £647   **1m3f183y**   **Good 55**   **-01 Slow**   Inside

2099 **TENDER FALCON 24** [6] R J Hodges 4-9-9 (67) J F McDonald(3) 7/1: 33214-51: Held up, hdwy 3f out &   **75**
styd on for press to lead line, all out: eff at 10/12f on firm & gd/soft grnd: tough & genuine: see 2099.
2318 **RUTTERS REBEL 15** [11] G A Swinbank 3-8-12 (70) B Doyle 10/1: 26-50402: Led 1f & remained prom,   shd   **76**
rdn & led over 1f out, hdd line: eff around 11/12f: see 2103, 1226.
1922 **MUNGO JERRY 33** [1] J G Given 3-8-12 (70) W Supple 20/1: 0-363: Held up, hung right over 2f out,   1   **74**
kept on for press ins last: stays 12f: prob handles fast & gd grnd: see 1489 (mdn).
2318 **ISAAF 15** [4] P W Hiatt 5-9-7 (65) P Makin(5) 5/2: 2110244: Handy till lost place after 1f,   ¾   **67**
remained in tch, kept on fnl 2f, not pace to chall: see 2176, 1469.
1718 **SANTA CATERINA 42** [8]3-8-8 (69) K Darley 9/4 FAV: 000-45: b f Daylami - Samara (Polish Patriot)   ½   **67**
Pulled hard & sn trkd ldr, led over 4f out till over 1f out, no extra: 6 wk abs: unplcd up to 1m in '03 (rtd 66,
mdn): eff at 10f, 12f will suit when learning more restraint: handles fast & gd grnd: fin well clr of rem.
2293 **TRAVELLERS TALE 16** [7]5-9-7 (64) D Kinsella 25/1: 4-006006: Held up, btn 2f out: btr 1098.   8   **54**
2157 **PERFECT PUNCH 22** [3]5-9-9 (67) R Mullen 5/1: 2540-207: Pulled hard & handy, btn 2f out: btr 1777.   ½   **55**
1807 **HOH NELSON 38** [2]3-8-12 (70) S Drowne 33/1: 000-308: Chsd ldrs, lost place fnl 4f: btr 1177 (1m).   nk   **57**
2230 **IMPERIAL ROYALE 20** [10]3-8-7 (65) J Bramhill 3/1: 30052-59: Held up, rdn & struggling fnl 2f.   15   **31**
2377 **RED SKELTON 13** [9]3-8-12 BL t (70) T Quinn 16/1: 01-000: 10th: Led after 1f till 4f out, blnks.   2½   **32**
10 Ran   Time 2m 35.07(6.77)   Owned: Mr P E Axon   Trained: Somerton

Official Going Good (Good/Soft Places)

2708   7.05 Diet Irn-Bru Lady Amateur Handicap Stakes 3yo+ 0-75 (E)   **[49]**
£3981 £1225 £613   **1m5f9y**   **Good 58**   **-82 Slow**   Stands side

2545 **INCHNADAMPH 6** [9] T J Fitzgerald 4-10-1 t (50) Miss A Elsey 3/1: 000-6221: Keen cl-up, led 3f   **62**
out, pushed clr: qck reapp: eff at 10.5f/11f, apprec step up to 13f: acts on gd & gd/soft grnd: imprvd for recent
fitting of t-strap: can be a difficult ride: unexposed around this trip: see 2545.
2526 **SARN 7** [7] M Mullineaux 5-9-5 (40) Miss M Mullineaux(7) 7/1: 4004032: Handy, kept on to chase wnr   3½   47
ins fnl 1f, al held: qck reapp: stays 13f: stays 13f: see 2526 & 894.
2510 **LADY NETBETSPORTS 7** [10] B S Rothwell 5-11-0 (63) Miss A Armitage(5) 25/1: 44000-03: Led, hdd 3f   3   66
out, sn no extra: qck reapp: mdn after 19: see 2510 (reapp).
2526* **LATALOMNE 7** [8] N Wilson 10-11-13 (6ex) (76) Mrs N Wilson(3) 2/1 FAV: 0500///0-14: Mid-div, outpcd   1¾   76
after 12f, rallied late: well bckd on qck reapp: prob unsuited by today's slow gallop: btr 2526.
2479 **COSMIC CASE 8** [3]9-9-11 (46) Ms C Williams 8/1: 300-1035: Held up, modest late gains: btr 2479.   hd   45
2176 **EXALTED 21** [6]11-10-2 (51) Miss H Cuthbert(5) 4/1: 200-5506: Mid-div, prog 3f out, onepcd dist.   shd   49
1238 **DARK CUT 68** [2]4-9-10 (45) Miss Dawn Rankin(5) 33/1: 100-0007: b g Ali Royal - Prima Nox   3   39
(Sabrehill) Handy over 10f, wknd: 10 wk abs: h'cap wnr in '03 (Mrs A M Naughton): unplcd in '02 (rtd 56): stays
around 9f on gd & gd/soft grnd: acts on a stiff/undul trk: with H Alexander.
1 May'03 Hami 9.2g/s 57-45 E: 2 May'03 Hami 9.2gd 52-(40) E:
7 Ran   Time 3m 3.76 (18.26)   Owned: Mr R N Cardwell   Trained: Malton

---

2709   7.35 Alona Hotels Maiden Stakes Fillies 3yo (D)
£5590 £1720 £860   **1m1f36y**   **Good 58**   **-68 Slow**   Inside

2349 **SECRET FLAME 14** [5] W J Haggas 3-8-11 (78) A Culhane 1/4 FAv: 5-331: Handy, led trav well 2f   80+
out, sn pushed clr, eased cl-home, val 7L+: eff at 1m/9f, prob stays 10f: acts on fast & gd grnd:
lightly rcd performer who can progress: see 2349 & 1762.
4721} **JUST DANCE ME 255** [3] W J Haggas 3-8-11 Dale Gibson 10/1: 0-2: gr f Linamix - Reine de La Ciel   5   71
(Conquistador Cielo) Led 6f, kept on but not pace of wnr ins fnl 2f: reapp: stablemate of wnr: 10th of 13 on sole
'03 start (fills mdn, rtd 63): prob stays 9f on gd grnd.
2349 **BURN 14** [2] M L W Bell 3-8-11 F Lynch 7/1: 03: Cl-up 7f, sn wknd: op 5/1.   3½   62
2504 **COMPASSION 7** [1] Miss L A Perratt 3-8-11 (53) J Carroll 66/1: 50-00004: Prom over 6f, sn fdd.   6   53
4 Ran   Time 2m 5.46 (11.36)   Owned: Cheveley Park Stud   Trained: Newmarket

---

2710   8.05 European Breeders Fund Conditions Stakes Fillies 3yo+ (C)
£10672 £4048 £2024   **1m65y rnd**   **Good 58**   **+02 Fast**   Inside

4603*}**ANTEDILUVIAN 264** [6] Sir Michael Stoute 3-8-2 N Mackay(3) 5/1: 1-1: b f Air Express - Divina Mia   104
(Dowsing) Handy, short of room 2f out, stayd on to lead dist, rdn out: reapp & new stable: fills mdn wnr on sole '03
start (J G Given): eff at 7f, imprvd for step up to 1m & further shld suit: acts on fast & gd grnd, gall or
stiff/undul trk: goes well fresh: got first run on unlucky second but useful & improving. 1 Oct'03 Redc 7g/f 86- D:
2491* **CELTIC HEROINE 8** [2] M A Jarvis 3-8-2 (89) M Henry 1/2 FAV: 41-21212: Cl-up, no room 2f out till   1½   101+
dist, switched & stvd on well ins last, wnr had flown: clr rem: prob wnr with a clr run: useful & tough, win again.
3144} **SHARPLAW VENTURE 335** [1] W J Haggas 4-8-9 (95) A Culhane 12/1: 16/5230-3: b f Polar Falcon -   9   79
Breakaway (Song) Cl-up, ev ch after 6f, sn no extra: reapp: rnr-up on 1 of 4 '03 starts (List h'cap): won 2 of 4
'02 starts (mdn & val auct race): eff around 1m on firm & gd grnd: has gone well fresh.
2 Jun'03 Asco 8fm 98-99 A: 1 Sep'02 Asco 6.5g/f 100- B: 2 Aug'02 Ches 6g/f 89- B: 1 Aug'02 Pont 5g/f 71- D:
2191 **PLAY THAT TUNE 21** [4] M Johnston 4-8-9 (93) J Fanning 7/1: 2033-054: Prom, led 3f out, hdd dist, fdd.   1¼   77
2475 **RABITATIT 8** [5]3-7-13 (62) Natalia Gemelova(7) 100/1: 50-24025: Led 5f, sn wknd: see 2475.   2   73$
2599 **SAFRANINE 4** [3]7-8-9 (63) Ann Stokell 200/1: 0000006: Handy 6f, fdd: qck reapp.   5   62
6 Ran   Time 1m 48.48 (4.68)   Owned: Lordship Stud   Trained: Newmarket

---

2711   8.35 Scottish Daily Mail Novice Auct Stakes Hamilton Park 2-Y-O Series Final 2yo (D)
£4823 £1484 £742   **6f5y str**   **Good 58**   **-21 Slow**   Stands side

2275 **TEQUILA SHEILA 17** [1] K R Burke 2-8-5 A Nicholls 16/1: 01: ch f Raise A Grand - Hever Rosina   83
(Efisio) Prom till halfway, sn outpcd, rallied ins fnl 1f, rdn out to lead cl-home: April foal, cost E13,000:
half-sister wnr at 5f, dam successful at 6f: sire decent performer at 2: eff at 6f, shaped as tho' 7f will suit:
acts on gd grnd & a stiff/undul trk: game & improved run.
2297* **LINCOLNEUROCRUISER 16** [4] J O'Reilly 2-9-1 J D O'Reilly(7) 15/2: 52312: Led, hdd under press   ½   91
cl-home: only just denied & lost little in defeat: see 2297 (firm).
2442* **KATIE BOO 10** [6] A Berry 2-8-10 F Norton 6/1: 3213: Prom, al hung right, ev ch dist, sn no   2   80
extra: eff at 5/6f: just btr 2442 (5f, firm).
2167 **MIDNIGHT TYCOON 22** [3] B Smart 2-9-1 F Lynch 13/8 FAV: 134: Keen, handy over 4f, no impress: 1   82
disapp on step up to 6f: btr 2167 (5f) & 1601.
2213 **SELKIRK STORM 20** [5]2-9-4 P Mulrennan(5) 4/1: 125: Cl-up 4f, fdd: v disapp: btr 2213 & 1677.   6   69
2411 **CARTE ROYALE 12** [2]2-9-6 S Chin 9/2: 126: Cl-up over halfway, sn wknd: v disapp: btr 2411 (5f, fm).   3   62
6 Ran   Time 1m 14.57 (4.77)   Owned: Mr Lee Westwood   Trained: Leyburn

---

2712	9.05 Totequadpot Sprint Handicap Stakes Fillies 3yo+ 0-85 (D)				[65]
	£6754 £2078 £1039 **5f4y str** **Good 58** -03 Slow Stands side				

2512 **KARMINSKEY PARK** 7 [5] T J Etherington 5-9-10 (61) J Fanning 11/8 FAV: 6265321: Prom, styd on to   69
lead dist, all out to hold on: qck reapp: best at 5f, stays 6f: acts on firm & both AWs, likes gd & soft grnd.
2320 **AAHGOWANGOWAN** 15 [4] M Dods 5-9-7 t (58) R Ffrench 100/30: 230-0052: Stall opened slightly late,   hd   66+
in tch, short of room & switched 1f out, styd on well for press & just failed: most unlucky on 2 counts & race should
surely have been voided: likes easy grnd, win again: see 1276.
2477 **TANCRED TIMES** 8 [7] D W Barker 9-9-4 (55) F Lynch 11/2: 0-044033: Led, hdd dist, rallied but no   1¾   58
ch with front 2 ins fnl 1f: see 2477 (6f).
2614 **PIRLIE HILL** 3 [8] Miss L A Perratt 4-9-4 (55) J Carroll 12/1: 2501604: Handy, ev ch 2f out, sn no extra.   3   49
2542 **COLLEGE MAID** 6 [6]7-9-9 (6ex) (60) J Currie(7) 6/1: 0024135: Prom till dist, wknd: qck reapp.   ½   53
2279 **SUGAR CUBE TREAT** 17 [3]8-7-12 (4oh) (31) S Righton 20/1: 0005006: Al in rear.   11   0
6 Ran   Time 1m 1.19 (3.09)   Owned: Wold House Partnership   Trained: Malton

---

2713	9.35 Flowerscene Handicap Stakes 4yo+ 0-75 (E)				[67]
	£3933 £1210 £605 **6f5y str** **Good 58** +00 Fast Stands side				

2542 **LEGAL SET** 6 [2] Miss A Stokell 8-8-6 t (45) Natalia Gemelova(7) 9/2: 0000421: Cl-up, styd on to   58
lead 1f out, pushed out: qck reapp: stays 1m, best btwn 5/7f on firm & gd/soft, likes polytrack: eff with t-strap.
2445* **SILVER MASCOT** 10 [8] I Semple 5-9-3 (6ex) (56) T Eaves(3) 3/1: 4230012: Keen cl-up, styd on ins   1¾   61
fnl 1f, not pace of wnr: another gd run: ran to form of 2445 under a 6lb pen.
2477 **BUNDY** 8 [9] M Dods 8-9-10 (63) R Winston 7/4 FAV: 0-000223: Rear, prog 2f out, nrst fin: see 2477.   ¾   67
1820 **MY BAYARD** 37 [7] J O'Reilly 5-9-4 (57) J D O'Reilly(7) 7/1: 6250104: Cl-up 3f, sn edged right & onepcd.   ¾   59
2280 **MARSHALLSPARK** 17 [6]5-9-8 (61) G Parkin 8/1: 600-0005: Cl-up, outpcd halfway, rallied late: btr 1749.   shd   62
4712} **MUTAYAM** 255 [4]4-8-0 t (39) C Haddon(2) 66/1: 5000000-6: b g Compton Place - Final Shot (Dalsaan)   2½   33
Led, hdd 1f out, wknd: reapp: rnr-up once in '03 (mdn, rtd 47): modest form in 3 '02 starts (M Channon, rtd 52):
eff at 5f on fast grnd: tried t-strap: with D A Nolan. 2 Jun'03 Muss 5g/f 47-(44) D:
2542 **FRIAR TUCK** 6 [5]9-9-2 (55) J Carroll 12/1: 1464007: Al in rear: qck reapp: btr 2160.   4   37
2315 **SAIF SAREEA** 15 [3]4-8-13 (52) P Mathers(7) 100/1: 56000/-08: Al adrift: see 2315.   3½   24
8 Ran   Time 1m 13.30(3.5)   Owned: Mr Paul Byrne   Trained: Richmond

---

Official Going GOOD/FIRM.

2714	2.30 Pilgrims Hospice Median Auction Maiden Stakes 2yo (F)			
	£3024 £864 £432 **7f str** **Firm 12** -20 Slow Stands Side			

   SKY CRUSADER [7] R Ingram 2-9-0   S Drowne 6/1: 1: b c Mujahid - Red Cloud (Taufan) Dwelt, sn   87+
chsd ldrs, imprvd to lead ins fnl 1f, readily: hvly bckd from 10/1, debut: 8,500gns May foal: dam stayed 7f: eff at
7f on fm grnd: runs well fresh: rate higher & win again.
1987 **LACONICOS** 31 [6] D R Loder 2-9-0   T P Queally(3) 4/1: 232: Led after 1f & tried to make rest, not   2½   80
pace to repel ready wnr fnl 1f: nicely bckd: stayed this longer 7f trip, acts on firm & gd/soft grnd: met a well
regarded rival today & deserves similar: see 1987 & 1014 (5f).
2077 **SAFENDONSEABISCUIT** 27 [9] S Kirk 2-9-0   J Fortune 13/8 FAV: 533: Led early, remained prom, not   ½   79
qckn fnl 1f: bckd from 2/1: stays 7f, acts on firm grnd: rtd higher 2077 (6f).
2430 **RIDE SAFARI** 11 [1] P Winkworth 2-9-0   P Doe 25/1: 634: Slow away, mid-div, styd on late for   ½   78
press, nvr nrr: again showed promise & clearly stays 7f: now qual for nursery h'caps: see 2430 & 1981.
2388 **PACIFIC STAR** 13 [10]2-9-0   T Quinn 12/1: 065: b c Tagula - Acidanthera (Alzao) Chsd ldrs,   2½   73
onepcd fnl 1f: E30,000 Apr foal: dam a 7f wnr, dam a top-class 2yo: with E Dunlop.
2310 **YOU FOUND ME** 16 [3]2-8-9   S Sanders 6/1: 06: b f Robellino - Hana Marie (Formidable) Chsd ldrs   shd   68
wide, btn fnl 1f: cost E36,000: Mar foal, half sister to sev wnrs: dam a useful sprinter, sire a high-class juv.
2531 **BELLALOU** 7 [5]2-8-9   W Ryan 20/1: 07: b f Vettori - Spinning Mouse (Bustino) Chsd ldrs,   2½   63
slightly outpcd halfway, not pace to chal: 10,000gns Apr foal: half sister to a 12f/hdles wnr: dam 13f wnr: bred
to apprec 1m+ given time: with N Callaghan.
2424 **KING OF BLUES** 12 [11]2-9-0   Dane O'Neill 25/1: 08: Rdn in rear, mod prog.   ¾   66
   REVIVALIST [14]2-8-9   J Mackay 16/1: 9: Prom 5f, wknd on debut.   6   49
1900 **SARAH BROWN** 35 [13]2-8-9 VIS   B Swarbrick(5) 100/1: 00: 10th: Slowly away, al bhnd: tried visor.   nk   48
   FANTASIAS FOREST [4]2-8-9   G Carter 33/1: 0: 11th: Green in rear, nvr dngrs on debut.   3   42
   ARDASNAILS [12]2-9-0   D Corby(3) 100/1: 0: 12th: Dwelt, al bhnd on debut.   nk   46
1717 Pie Corner 43 [8]2-9-0 L Keniry(3) 100/1:0   Bregaglia [2]2-8-9 B Doyle 100/1:0
14 Ran   Time 1m 26.47 (2.27)   Owned: Pillar To Post Racing (IV)   Trained: Epsom

---

2715	3.00 Mark Rake Claiming Stakes 3yo+ (F)			
	£2926 £836 £418 **6f str** **Firm 12** +06 Fast Stands Side			

2451 **FIREWORK** 11 [2] J Akehurst 6-9-2 p (60) T Quinn 9/4: 0006501: Prom, went on 2f out, clr ins fnl   64
1f, readily: nicely bckd: suited by 5.7/6f, stays 7f: acts on firm, soft & f/sand, any trk: eff with/without
cheek pieces: best in sell/claim grade, see 628 (AW h'cap).
1985 **JASMINE PEARL** 31 [4] T M Jones 3-8-0 (45) C Catlin 50/1: 3600402: Prom, ev ch 1f out, no extra &   2½   48
drifted left well ins fnl 1f: eff at 6f on firm grnd: see 389 (AW).
2059 **PEDRO JACK** 28 [7] M A Buckley 7-9-6 (62) S Drowne 9/1: 0-010003: Chsd ldrs, slightly outpcd   2½   55
halfway, rallied late on: op 12/1: see 1310 (AW claimer).
2532 **CRAFTY CALLING** 7 [3] P F I Cole 4-9-8 t (90) K Fallon 11/8 FAV: 054-0004: Chsd ldrs, ch 1f out,   nk   56

sn wknd: well bckd from 2/1: found less than expected on this drop to claim grade: see 2532.
2337 **POWER BIRD 15** [5]4-8-5 BL (52) N Pollard 25/1: 0-200005: Dwelt, nvr nr ldrs: tried blnks. *1* **36**
1867 **AROGANT PRINCE 36** [1]7-9-4 (59) J Quinn 14/1: 0001006: Keen & led till 2f out, wknd: op 9/1: btr 1267. *nk* **48**
6 Ran Time 1m 11.39 (0.39) Owned: The Grass is Greener Partnership III Trained: Epsom

2716

3.30 Guy Parker Median Auction Maiden Stakes 3-5yo (F)
£2989 £854 £427 **7f str** **Firm 12** **+14 Fast** Stands Side

1983 **MIDNIGHT BALLARD 31** [7] R F Johnson Houghton 3-8-12 (80) S Carson 6/4 FAV: 36-64201: Made all, clr ent fnl 1f, held on well rdn out: bckd from 5/2, gd time: overdue win: eff at 6/7f on gd & firm gnd, easy or gall trk: apprec this return to mdn company, see 1825 (h'cap) & 1639. **80**
2334 **IPHIGENIA 15** [8] P W Hiatt 3-8-7 (50) R Miles(3) 14/1: 000-0502: Chsd ldrs, went after 2nd 2f out, kept on well but not quite get there: op 20/1, clr of rem: offic rtd 50, ran well above that today: eff at 5/7f on firm & fibresand: see 1904. *1¼* **71$**
2342 **SET ALIGHT 15** [6] Miss K B Boutflower 3-8-7 T P Queally(3) 25/1: 043: Held up, mod late gains. *6* **57**
2274 **APPETINA 18** [3] J G Given 3-8-7 (73) M Fenton 11/2: 2303-554: Chsd wnr 5f, wknd: op 3/1. *2½* **54**
2309 **TRUMAN 16** [1]3-8-12 (72) S Sanders 9/4: 5-035: Slowly away, nvr dngrs: btr 2309 (6f). *1½* **56**
2291 **TROMP 17** [4]3-8-12 Dane O'Neill 8/1: 56: ch c Zilzal - Sulitelma (The Minstrel) Al rear: op 5/1: with D Coakley & little form so far. *shd* **56**
2049 **PRINCESS BANKES 28** [9]3-8-7 (45) S Drowne 33/1: 05-06007: Al bhnd. *1¼* **47**
2622 **DONT LET GO 4** [2]3-8-7 J Quinn 50/1: 00-08: b f Danzero - Il Doria (Mac's Imp) Keen & chsd ldrs wide, btn 2f out, t.o.: qck reapp & no form. *12* **22**
1715 **MRS BOZ 43** [5]4-9-2 (29) B Swarbrick(5) 150/1: 060-49: b f Superpower - Bar None (Rabdan) Prom till halfway, wknd & t.o.: 6 wk abs: no form. *2* **18**
9 Ran Time 1m 24.04 (u0.18) Owned: Mr C W Sumner Trained: Didcot

2717

4.00 John Atkins Maiden Stakes 3yo+ (D)
£3770 £1160 £580 **5f str** **Firm 12** **-00 Slow** Stands Side

2173 **SWINBROOK 23** [1] J A R Toller 3-9-0 (80) S Sanders 2/9 FAV: 52-0021: Trkd ldrs, short of room 2f out & squeezed thro', led ent fnl 1f, styd on well, drvn out: well bckd at odds-on: eff at 5/6f on gd & firm grnd: made hard work of this but will rate higher: see 2173. **75**
2075 **EX MILL LADY 27** [7] John Berry 3-8-9 (59) S Drowne 9/2: 5-422: Front rank, ev ch fnl 1f, kept on well but not quite pace of wnr: clr of rem: acts on fast & firm, handles soft: see 2075. *nk* **64**
1031 **LAKESIDE GUY 84** [4] P S McEntee 3-9-0 (55) T P Queally(3) 50/1: 0-00403: b c Revoque - Glen of Imaal (Common Grounds) Led till ent fnl 1f, no extra: 12 wk abs: eff with forcing tactics over an easy 5f, acts on firm grnd: off rtd 55 & treat this rating with caution. *2* **60$**
2148 **OTAGO 23** [3] J R Best 3-9-0 N Pollard 20/1: 304: Rear, styd on under press fnl 1f, nrst fin: has been gelded: prob not apprec this drop back to 5f on h'cap qual run: btr 2104 (6f debut). *½* **59**
2361 **ELA FIGURA 14** [6]4-9-1 p (49) B Swarbrick(5) 20/1: 0-600365: Keen & chsd ldrs, ev ch ent fnl 1f, no extra. *shd* **53$**
1867 **FIRE CAT 36** [5]5-9-6 (35) D Corby(3) 50/1: 0-000006: Keen & trkd ldrs till after halfway, wknd. *8* **28**
6 Ran Time 59.02 (0.62) Owned: Lady Sophia Topley Trained: Newmarket

2718

4.30 Martin Jordan Handicap Stakes 4yo+ 35-55 (F) **[63]**
£3052 £872 £436 **1m4f** **Firm 12** **-40 Slow** Outside

1357 **CRISTOFORO 62** [1] B J Curley 7-9-6 (55) T P Queally(3) 5/2 FAV: 2111/-101: Held up, smooth hdwy trav strongly to lead ent fnl 1f, sn clr, v easily: gamble from 4/1, 9 wk abs: eff at 9/13f on firm, soft grnd & both AWs: runs v well fresh: fast progressing & a decent gamble landed here: likely to win more races. **71**
2273 **ABSINTHER 18** [5] M R Bosley 7-8-10 (45) G Baker 16/1: 44000-02: Dwelt, imprvd to chase ldrs 3f out, styd on well into 2nd but no ch with easy wnr: acts on firm, soft grnd & fibresand: h'capped to win. *3* **49**
2545 **ESCALADE 7** [13] W M Brisbourne 7-9-6 p (55) B Swarbrick(5) 16/1: 0-040543: Chsd ldrs, kept on under press fnl 1f: slowly running into form: see 1777. *½* **58**
2220 **TINTAWN GOLD 21** [7] S Woodman 4-8-13 (48) D Sweeney 33/1: 2500-004: Keen mid-div, imprvd to lead briefly dist, onepcd fnl 1f: longer 12f trip & prob styd: see 2220. *¾* **50**
1960 **MAKE MY HAY 32** [9]5-9-0 (49) Dane O'Neill 11/2: 02-36125: Rear, bhd 2f out, styd on late, nvr nrr: set plenty to do & nvr lkd likely to be involved: prev in decent form, see 1960 & 1645. *¾* **50**
2526 **LAZZAZ 8** [12]6-8-12 (47) R Miles(3) 6/1: 3302056: Front rank, led after 4f till dist, no extra. *¾* **47**
2530 **SUMMER CHERRY 7** [15]7-8-10 t (45) P Doe 5/1: 503-0257: Dwelt, recovered to chase ldrs, ev ch 2f out, wknd fnl 1f: see 2273. *1½* **43**
1714 **RIPCORD 43** [16]6-8-0 (5oh) (30) J F McDonald(3) 16/1: 000/0-568: b g Diesis - Native Twine (Be My Native) Rear, brief eff 2f out, nvr dngrs: rnr-up in a nov hdle 12 days ago (rtd 109h, eff around 2m on firm): lightly rcd & modest form in recent seasons (prev with Lady Herries): eff at 1m on soft:+ now with B Johnson. *1½* **31**
PERIDA 45 [10]4-8-13 (48) S Whitworth 50/1: 00005-59: b f Perugino - Razida (Last Tycoon) Dwelt, hdwy from rear when short of room 3f out, btn fnl 1f: 4th in a nov hdle 10 days ago: ex-Irish, modest Flat form in native country: poss stays 12f & acts on firm grnd: with B Powell. *1¼* **42**
4209} **BURNT COPPER 287** [2]4-9-3 (52) N Pollard 20/1: 504250-0: 10th: b g College Chapel - Try My Rosie (Try My Best) Dwelt, nvr nr ldrs on reapp: '03 h'cap rnr-up: plcd in '02 (mdn): eff at 12f on fast grnd & polytrack: has tried cheek pieces: with J Best. 2 Aug'03 Folk 12g/f 55-56 F: *¾* **45**
2417 **RIVER OF FIRE 13** [11]6-8-0 (5oh)vis (30) Natalia Gemelova(7) 25/1: 0304000: 11th: Prom, wknd 3f out. *2* **25**
1714 **ADJIRAM 43** [4]8-8-4 (2ow)vis (37) W Ryan 14/1: 6/-354120: 12th: Chsd ldrs, wide, btn 2f out: 6 wk abs. *5* **21**
2088 **WIZARD OF THE WEST 26** [6]4-9-4 (53) N Chalmers(5) 33/1: 03600-00: 13th: Dwelt, al rear. *shd* **35**
2293 **AFRICAN DAWN 17** [14]6-9-3 t (52) L Keniry(3) 10/1: 2/4022-60: 14th: Led 4f, wknd 2f out. *3* **29**
1645 **Ersaal 46** [8]4-8-7 t(42) O Urbina 12/1:0 1990 **Watership Down 31** [3]7-8-5 (40) C Catlin 50/1:0
16 Ran Time 2m 37.71 (6.21) Owned: Mr P Byrne Trained: Newmarket

FOLKESTONE FRIDAY 25.06.04 Righthand, Sharpish, Undulating Track

---

2719

5.00 Mike White Handicap Stakes Fillies 3yo+ 0-70 (E)
£3523 £1084 £542   1m1f149y   Firm 12   -54 Slow   Outside   [68]

2354 **LILLI MARLANE 15** [12] N A Callaghan 4-10-0 (68) W Ryan 5/1: 50-26001: Held up, imprvd 2f out,   75
led ins fnl 1f, styd on well, rdn out: top-weight: eff at 1m/10f on firm & soft grnd: has tried blnks, btr without.
2604 **KINDNESS 5** [7] A D W Pinder 4-8-8 (48) Dane O'Neill 7/1: 03-60022: Led, clr 2f out, collared ins   1½   50
fnl 1f & no extra: see 2604 (1m).
2335 **JESSINCA 15** [9] A P Jones 8-8-0 (40) J Mackay 33/1: 60-00603: Keen in rear, prog 2f out, nrst fin.   1½   40
2392 **LARA FALANA 13** [6] Miss B Sanders 6-10-0 (68) S Sanders 4/1 FAV: 0254264: Trkd ldrs, onepcd fnl 2f.   nk   67
3048} **SCENIC LADY 340** [3]8-9-5 (59) D Sweeney 25/1: 056552-5: b f Scenic - Tu Tu Maori (Kings Lake)   3   53
Dwelt, eff 2f out, late prog but nvr dngrs on reapp: '03 h'cap wnr, also rnr-up: plcd numerous times in '02, dual
h'cap wnr in '01: eff at 9/12f on firm & soft: likes a sharp/undul or easy trk: best without blnks.
2 Jul'03 Brig 11.9g/f 56-56 E: 1 Apr'03 Yarm 11.5gd 63-58 E: 2 Aug'02 Good 9g/f 55-52 D: 2 Jul'02 Brig 11.8g/f 52-53 E:
2 Jun'02 Kemp 9sft 54-51 E: 2 May'02 Brig 10g/s 50-49 F: 2 Sep'01 Epso 12g/f 53-48 E: 1 Aug'01 Ling 10g/f 50-43 F:
1 Aug'01 Brig 11.8gd 42-35 G: 2 Jul'01 Wind 11.6g/f 35-33 F: 2 Jul'01 Brig 10fm 44- F:
1467 **SIENNA SUNSET 56** [8]5-9-3 (57) S Carson 9/1: 0200-066: Prom, wknd fnl 1f: 8 wk abs & new stable.   2½   47
2344 **PRINCESS GALADRIEL 15** [1]3-8-9 (61) N Pollard 9/2: 40-21327: Rear, prog wide 2f out, sn btn.   3½   46
2054 **SUERTE 28** [11]4-8-9 (49) B Doyle 10/1: 040-0008: Slowly away, keen & sn prom, btn 1.5f out: 1   32
bckd from 25/1: rcd too keenly today, btr clearly expected: see 1778.
2267 **PRINCESS MAGDALENA 18** [5]4-8-12 (52) L Keniry(3) 16/1: 0010-009: Nvr btr than mid-div.   ¾   34
2264 **LADY JEANNIE 18** [2]7-8-8 (48) R Miles(3) 50/1: 00400/00: 10th: Prom, wknd 2f out: see 2264.   ½   29
2510 **GOT TO BE CASH 8** [4]5-8-12 (52) B Swarbrick(5) 5/1: 4210530: 11th: Chsd ldrs 1m, wknd: btr 2510.   3   28
11 Ran   Time 2m 04.39(6.39)   Owned: Mrs T A Foreman   Trained: Newmarket

---

SOUTHWELL Fibresand FRIDAY 25.06.04 Lefthand, Sharp, Oval Track

Official Going Standard

2720

2.20 Feast Of The Optional Holiday Handicap Stakes 3yo+ 35-55 (F)
£3038 £868 £434   6f aw rnd   Going 50   -01 Slow   Inside   [57]

2502* **NEVER WITHOUT ME 8** [1] J F Coupland 4-10-3 (6ex) (60) M Savage(5) 5/1 FAV: 2103411: Led/dsptd lead   68a
thr'out, drvn & held on all out, gamely: eff at 5/6f & loves fibresand/Southwell: imprvd for new yard last twice.
1788 **JAGGED 39** [10] J R Jenkins 4-9-8 VIS (51) N Callan 10/1: 630-0002: Chsd ldrs, ev ch when edged   nk   58a
right over 1f out, kept on well for press, just held: 1st time visor, gd run: acts on fast, gd/soft & both AW's:
prev with Mrs H Sweeting: see 1533.
2501 **MALLIA 8** [15] T D Barron 11-9-3 (46) Laura Jayne Crawford(7) 14/1: 406-4163: Bhd, styd on wide   2½   46a
for press, nrst fin: see 2202 (sell).
2347 **MR UPPITY 15** [16] Julian Poulton 5-8-10 e (39) M Halford(7) 20/1: 2453654: Bhd & wide, kept on late.   ¾   37a
2204 **NEW OPTIONS 21** [3]7-9-5 bl (48) Lisa Jones(3) 25/1: 3030005: Chsd ldrs, no extra dist: see 902.   ½   44a
2501 **INDIAN MUSIC 8** [13]7-9-1 (44) F Lynch 12/1: 4433246: Bhd, late gains for press, no threat: see 982.   ¾   38a
2347 **KENNINGTON 15** [4]4-9-11 vis (54) Hayley Turner(5) 15/2: 0340027: Prom, fdd under dist: btr 2347.   shd   48a
2396 **STAR LAD 13** [8]4-9-2 bl (45) F Norton 33/1: 1450308: Chsd ldrs till 2f out: btr 2201.   3½   30a
2201 **LUCIUS VERRUS 21** [12]4-9-9 vis (52) Darren Williams 9/1: 3010529: Mid-div travelling well, no   ½   35a
impress fnl 2f: op 16/1: btr 2201 (5f).
2615 **AFRICAN SPUR 4** [9]4-9-8 P (51) D Tudhope(7) 6/1: 0000650: 10th: Sn prom wide, btn 2f out: quick   1¾   30a
reapp, cheek pieces: btr 2615.
1799* **LEVELLED 39** [11]10-9-4 (47) G Duffield 14/1: 5023310: 11th: Dwelt, nvr a factor: see 1799 (5f, bndd).   ½   24a
1750 **ALASTAIR SMELLIE 41** [2]8-9-4 (47) P McCabe 20/1: 0020100: 12th: Unruly start & al bhd, 6 wk abs.   ¾   22a
2080 **RATHMULLAN 27** [5]5-8-11 bl (40) Liam Jones(3) 20/1: 4313500: 13th: Well bhd & drvn, little hdwy.   hd   14a
2501* **TURN AROUND 8** [7]4-10-0 (6ex) (57) Dean McKeown 7/1: 0021510: 14th: Dwelt, mid-div, hung right &   1½   27a
btn over 2f out: new stable: btr 2501 (7f, gamble, sell).
2232 **PLAYFUL SPIRIT 20** [14]5-9-3 vis (46) J Edmunds 16/1: 0030000: 15th: Chsd ldrs wide, btn 2f out.   ¾   14a
1442 **SOUNDS LUCKY 57** [6]8-9-10 bl (53) I Mongan 33/1: 1260400: 16th: Chsd ldrs till halfway, eased.   9   0a
16 Ran   Time 1m 16.35 (3.05)   Owned: Mr J F Coupland   Trained: Grimsby

---

2721

2.50 Custer's Last Stand Selling Stakes 2yo (G)
£2548 £728 £364   7f aw rnd   Going 50   -44 Slow   Inside

2183 **DICTION 22** [3] K R Burke 2-8-6 Darren Williams 7/2: 051: Handy, led over 1f out, sn rdn clr &   68a
eased nr fin, val 7L+: op 4/1, no bid: 1st win on AW bow: apprec step up to 7f, get further: handles fibresand &
enjoys sell grade: win again with this company if repeating: see 1968.
2358 **DIATONIC 14** [6] W J Musson 2-8-11 Lisa Jones(3) 4/1: 0002: Chsd ldrs, outpcd halfway, kept on   4   59a
late for press, nvr threat to wnr: clr of rem: prob handles fibresand & stays 7f in sell grade: see 2017.
2382 **MONASHEE MISS 14** [1] J A Pickering 2-8-6 Dean McKeown 25/1: 403: Swerved right start, chsd ldrs   6   43a
& led over 4f out till over 1f out, sn btn: longer 7f trip: see 1608.
2145 **PETITE ELLE 23** [7] P J McBride 2-8-6 K Jackson(7) 5/1: 344: Chsd ldrs wide, btn 2f out: btr 2145.   3   37a
1968 **CONCERT TIME 32** [5]2-8-6 R Thomas(5) 5/2 FAV: 0365: Led till 4f out, btn 2f out: btr 1831 (5f, fast).   1¾   34a
1097 **PETITE NOIRE 78** [2]2-8-6 T S Hitchcott 14/1: 06: b f Lujain - Coffee Cream (Common Grounds)   3   28a
Dwelt, in tch, no impress fnl 2f: 11 wk abs, t-strap, AW bow: well btn on sole start prev, appears modest.
2183 **BOWLAND BRIDE 22** [4]2-8-12 P Mathers(7) 11/2: 5044017: Chsd ldrs, strug fnl 3f: btr 1968 (6f).   6   23a
7 Ran   Time 1m 33.16 (6.56)   Owned: Mr J C S Wilson   Trained: Leyburn

---

2722 3.20 St Eurosia's Day Maiden Stakes 3yo+ **(D)**
£3504 £1078 £539 **6f aw rnd** **Going 50** **-00 Slow** Inside

1723 **POINT CALIMERE 43** [5] C R Egerton 3-9-0 BL (70) N Callan 11/4: 30-04501: Al cl-up trav well, led **70a**
over 2f out & rdn clr, all out to hold closing rival: 6 wk abs, imprvd for 1st time blnks: eff at 5/6f on fast, gd
& f/sand, sharp/turning or easy trk: goes well fresh & travels well today in headgear: see 1023.
2231 **DESERT LEADER 21** [11] B A McMahon 3-9-0 G Gibbons 13/2: 002: b c Green Desert - Za Aamah (Mr *nk* **69a+**
Prospector) Rear/wide, styd on well from over 2f out under hand riding, just failed: AW bow, eff at 6f, unplcd at
1m prev: acts on fibresand: now qual for h'cap & could improve when return to 7f+.
3676} **SILENT STORM 672** [10] H J Cyzer 4-9-7 F Lynch 7/2: 5/-3: ch c Zafonic - Nanda (Nashwan) Held *2½* **62a**
up wide, outpcd halfway, kept on late, nrst fin: v long abs: missed '03: unplcd tho' promise sole '02 start (mdn,
H Cecil): dam a 10f 3yo mdn scorer: eff at 6f, return to 7f+ looks sure to suit: prob handles firm & fibresand:
not given hard time after long break, expect improvement.
2182 **IRUSAN 22** [8] Jedd O'Keeffe 4-9-7 (57) Leanne Kershaw(7) 12/1: 6004: Chsd ldrs, outpcd halfway, *shd* **62a**
hung left & kept on from over 1f out, no threat: AW bow: handles fibresand: see 1518.
2339 **WUNDERBRA 15** [1]3-8-9 I Mongan 9/4 FAV: 345: Led till over 2f out, fdd under press: bckd. *3½* **48a**
CLASSIC EXPRESSION [6]3-8-9 S Righton 14/1: 6: Dwelt & bhd/rdn, mod prog. *5* **36a**
2383 **SILVER ISLAND 14** [2]3-9-0 Lisa Jones(3) 33/1: 00-07: Chsd ldrs, lost place halfway, no impress. *½* **39a**
2485 **BANK GAMES 9** [7]3-9-0 Dale Gibson 40/1: 08: Chsd ldrs, btn 2f out. *¾* **37a**
2325 **NARCISO 16** [3]4-9-7 T Lucas 33/1: 009: Bhd/drvn, nvr factor. *1¾* **33a**
2339 **SAVANNAH SUE 15** [12]3-8-9 J Bramhill 66/1: 0-000: 10th: Chsd ldrs till halfway. *2½* **21a**
5022} **Lord Arthur 231** [4]3-9-0 P Mulrennan(5) 25/1:0 **Peters Ploy** [9]4-9-7 J P Guillambert(3) 33/1:0
12 Ran Time 1m 16.31 (3.01) Owned: Sangster Family & C R Egerton Trained: Chaddleworth

---

2723 3.50 Toteexacta Stakes Handicap 3yo 0-85 **(D)** **[88]**
£5395 £1660 £830 **7f aw rnd** **Going 50** **-00 Slow** Inside

1879 **COMMANDER BOND 36** [4] B Smart 3-8-7 (67) F Lynch 25/1: 004-001: b g Piccolo - Lonesome (Night **73a**
Shift) Cl-up/dsptd lead, narrow lead over 1f out, drvn & held on gamely: 1st win on AW bow: promise as a juv (rtd
73, 4th, mdn, subs gldd): eff at 6/7f on gd grnd & fibresand, stiff/gall or sharp/turning trk: enjoyed racing
with/forcing the pace today & showed a willing attitude.
2423 **NINE RED 12** [5] B W Hills 3-7-12 (58) R Ffrench 16/1: 550-0002: Chsd ldrs, drvn & styd on from *¾* **62a**
halfway, al just held: see 2098.
1707 **COTOSOL 43** [2] B A McMahon 3-9-2 (76) G Gibbons 4/1: 26-01503: Dwelt & outpcd early, styd on for *½* **79a**
press fnl 2f, not able to chall: 6 wk abs: see 1215.
2243 **ERMINE GREY 20** [1] D Haydn Jones 3-9-7 vis (81) Paul Eddery 8/1: 016-0034: Dwelt, sn in tch, drvn *hd* **83a**
to chall dist, no extra nr fin: see 2243 & 29.
2259 **GENEROUS GESTURE 19** [3]3-9-6 vis (80) I Mongan 6/1: 1561065: Dwelt, keen in tch, hdwy to chall *nk* **81a**
dist, no extra: only btn around 1L & clrly stays 7f, return to 6f in similar may suit: see 1441 (6f).
2365 **FIT TO FLY 14** [7]3-8-7 (67) F Norton 5/4 FAV: 50-25156: Trkd ldrs wide, drvn & onepcd fnl 2f: bckd. *shd* **68a**
2040 **WINGS OF MORNING 28** [8]3-8-6 BL (66) G Duffield 20/1: 2-156307: Led till dist, no extra: blnks. *3* **61a**
4709} **KEY OF GOLD 256** [6]3-9-5 (79) R Fitzpatrick 6/1: 30120-8: b g Key of Luck - Damaslin (Camden *5* **65a**
Town) Trkd ldrs wide, no impress over 2f out: reapp: auct mdn scorer '03, turf plcd (rtd 67, auct mdn, debut): eff
at 6/7f on fibresand, sharp/turning trk: can go well fresh.
2 Aug'03 Wolv 7af 81a-79 E: 1 Jul'03 Wolv 6af 81a- E:
8 Ran Time 1m 30.07 (3.47) Owned: Mr R C Bond Trained: Thirsk

---

2724 4.20 St Molaug's Day Claiming Stakes 4yo+ **(F)**
£2961 £846 £423 **1m4f aw** **Going 50** **-00 Slow** Inside

2499 **MANIATIS 8** [9] Andrew Reid 7-9-8 vis (73) I Mongan 6/5 FAV: 5/-611021: Held up, eff to chase ldrs **76a**
wide halfway, hung right under press dist & led line, all out: bckd, op 7/4: eff at 10/12f on fast, likes gd/soft &
fibresand: loves clmg grade: see 2499 & 1375.
2686 **ROMIL STAR 1** [5] K R Burke 7-9-0 vis (65) Darren Williams 5/1: 21411352: Handy & led after 4f *shd* **67a**
till 2f out, narrow lead again ins last, drvn & just denied line: unplcd yesterday: see 2686, 2499 & 2381.
2572 **OUR IMPERIAL BAY 6** [8] Mrs J Candlish 5-9-0 p (48) A Daly 16/1: 0010303: Rdn & bhd early, styd on *1¼* **65a$**
for press, not able to chall their top pair: return to 14f+ could suit: see 1291, 985.
2340 **HEATHERS GIRL 15** [6] D Haydn Jones 5-8-5 (52) Paul Eddery 7/2: 1624224: Unruly stalls, chsd ldrs *½* **55a**
& led 2f out till ins last, just outpcd cl-home: tough & consistent, deserves a race: see 1754, 862 & 633.
2499 **BIG SMOKE 8** [3]4-8-10 P (69) P Mulrennan(5) 12/1: 0300-045: gr g Perugino - Lightning Bug (Prince *1* **59a**
Bee) Chsd ldrs, drvn & kept on onepace fnl 2f: op 7/1: not btn far & well clr of rem: fair run in 1st time cheek
pieces: stays 12f in clmg grade: acts on fast, gd/soft & fibresand: see 2499 & 2317.
2 Jun'03 Sand 8.1g/f 78-75 D: 1 Jul'02 Sali 6g/s 86- D:
2381 **WESTERN COMMAND 14** [14]4-8-6 p (35) Hayley Turner(5) 20/1: 3350526: Mid-div, lost place fnl 4f. *20* **27a**
1061} **ART EXPERT 438** [7]6-8-6 R Fitzpatrick 66/1: 000/550-7: b g Pursuit of Love - Celtic Wing *1¼* **25a**
(Midyan) Chsd ldrs, no ch fnl 4f: reapp: unplcd '03 (rtd 27a, h'cap): mdn plcd in '02 (rtd 43a, turf unplcd, no
form): eff btwn 10/14f on fibresand, fast & hvy, handles any trk: eff with/without blnks or visor.
2 Oct'01 Sout 14af 54a-50 G:
2340 **SHATIN SPECIAL 15** [1]4-8-1 p (40) R Ffrench 14/1: 6660038: Chsd ldrs till 5f out: op 10/1: btr 2340. *shd* **20a**
2036 **BOWING 29** [2]4-8-8 (55) D Kinsella 28/1: 3-050009: b g Desert Prince - Introducing (Mtoto) Led *14* **9a**
4f, struggling fnl 4f: mdn & h'cap rnr-up for J Gosden in '03: mdn rnr-up '02: eff btwn 9/12f on fast & soft grnd,
prob any trk: has tried cheek pieces, best without.
2 Jul'03 Wind 10.0g/f 82-(82) D: 2 May'03 Good 11g/f 84-82 D: 2 Oct'02 Nott 9.9sft 82- D:
9 Ran Time 2m 40.27 (5.97) Owned: Mr Nigel Shields Trained: Mill Hill London

SOUTHWELL   Fibresand   FRIDAY 25.06.04   Lefthand, Sharp, Oval Track

2725
4.50 Festival Of Ranting And Vaporing Amateur Riders' Handicap Stakes 4yo+ 0-70 (G)   **[49]**
£3024 £864 £432   **1m aw rnd**   **Going 50**   -21 Slow   Inside

2204 **SUPER DOMINION 21** [10] R Hollinshead 7-9-8 p (43) Miss K Turbutt(7) 20/1: 30-51401: Chsd ldrs, led **49a**
when hung left over 1f out, just held on inexperienced rider: eff at 6f, best btwn 7/9f on fast, gd/soft &
likes fibresand: see 1801, 1564.

2288 **PASO DOBLE 17** [9] B R Millman 6-10-12 P (61) Mr J Millman(7) 10/1: 2620542: Led/dsptd lead till 4f   shd   **66a**
out, rallied well for press ins last, just denied: gd run in 1st time cheek pieces: see 747, 479 & 331.

2572 **FIRST MAITE 6** [15] S R Bowring 11-11-2 (65) Mrs M Morris 8/1: 6664323: Chsd ldrs wide, kept on   2½   **65a**
for press: op 13/2 & reapp: v tough veteran, well h'capped on turf: see 2572, 2157 & 255.

2572 **BOJANGLES 6** [14] R Brotherton 5-9-13 (48) Mr L Newnes(3) 3/1 FAV: 0013034: Mid-div, wide, short   ½   **47a**
of room over 1f out, kept on ins last: acts on firm, soft & fibresand, poss hvy: see 2572 & 1535.

2500 **BRANDY COVE 8** [12]7-10-13 (62) Mr J A Jenkins(3) 7/1: 523-4055: Slow away & bhd, late gains.   hd   **60a**

1681 **CHAPTER HOUSE 398** [8]5-11-7 bl (70) Mr O Greenall(7) 25/1: 10060/0-6: b g Pulpit - Lilian Bayliss   ½   **67a**
(Sadler's Wells) Rdn/bhd, late gains, nrst fin: 12 wk jumps abs (unplcd, rtd 97h, tried blnks, nov): unplcd for D
Nicholls in '03: '02 mdn scorer (J Gosden, disapp in a visor): eff at 7f/1m, tried 10f, may yet suit: acts on
fast, gd & prob f/sand, sharp or gall/undul trks: encouragement on AW bow.   1 Aug'02 Chep 7gd 79- D:

1590 **LITTLETON ZEPHIR 50** [4]5-9-13 (48) Mrs C Thompson(5) 12/1: 0200157: Trkd ldrs, led 3f out till   ¾   **44a**
over 1f out, wknd: abs: see 1451.

2500 **HAUNT THE ZOO 8** [11]9-10-8 (57) Miss Kelly Harrison(3) 8/1: 513-5038: Mid-div, outpcd 2f out,   ¾   **52a**
kept on late: clr rem.

2500 **QUIET READING 8** [13]7-11-4 vis (67) Ms C Williams 4/1: 3220049: Mid-div wide, btn 2f out: btr 2500.   7   **50a**

2500 **CRUSOE 8** [7]7-10-2 bl (51) Miss E J Jones 14/1: 4200200: 10th: Led/dsptd lead 5f, sn lost place.   ¾   **33a**

2220 **MUTARED 21** [2]6-10-6 (55) Mrs Emma Littmoden(3) 16/1: 0000-000: 11th: b g Marju - Shahaada   1¾   **34a**
(Private Account) Prom till halfway: amat h'cap plcd '03 (rtd 64, AW unplcd, rtd 74a): dual amat h'cap wnr in '02:
eff at 6f/1m, tried 12f: acts on fast, soft & polytrack, likes fibresand/sharp trks: gd weight carrier.
1 Dec'02 Wolv 6af 76a-70 E: 2 May'02 Bath 10.2g/s 75-69 F: 1 Apr'02 Wolv 8.4af 79a-67 E:
1 Nov'01 Sout 8af 67a-56 G: 2 Nov'01 Donc 8sft 58-53 E:

4832} **MADAAR 248** [1]5-9-3 (1oh) (37) Miss J Foster(5) 20/1: 003030-0: 12th: Chsd ldrs till 2f out, reapp.   2½   **12a**

1265 **KIMOE WARRIOR 67** [5]6-9-3 (8oh)p (30) Miss M Mullineaux(7) 33/1: 6050//0-50: 13th: Cl-up, lost pl   6   **2a**
3f out: jmps fit.

2394] **THE COPT 366** [3]5-9-8 T (43) Mr S Warren(7) 50/1: 000/000-0: 14th: Dwelt, al bhd, t-strap, reapp.   8   **0a**

1261 **EXPECTEDTOFLI 67** [6]6-10-0 (11ow)(8oh) (30) Mr L Edwards 50/1: 50000//-00: 15th: Rear & sn bhd, abs. dist **0a**
15 Ran   Time 1m 45.05(5.65)   Owned: Mrs Norman Hill   Trained: Upper Longdon

---

NEWCASTLE   FRIDAY 25.06.04   Lefthand, Galloping, Stiff Track

Official Going Soft

2726
6.55 Cantorodds Com Handicap Stakes For Gentleman Amateur Riders 4yo+ 0-75 (F)   **[40]**
£3426 £1054 £527   **1m2f32y**   **Good/Soft 65**   -65 Slow   Inside

2589* **KINGSDON 6** [10] T J Fitzgerald 7-11-3 (5ex)vis t (57) Mr Nicky Tinkler 6/1: 0441111: Chsd ldrs,   **62**
rdn over 2f out, led dist, drvn out: stays 1m/10f on fast, soft & polytrack: in great heart: see 2589.

2545* **SCURRA 7** [7] A C Whillans 5-10-12 (5ex) (52) Mr E Whillans(7) 9/1: 20-60312: Chsd ldrs & led 3f   1½   **54**
out till dist, kept on for press: confirmed improvement of latest: see 2545.

2499* **PURE MISCHIEF 8** [3] C R Dore 5-11-13 (5ex) (67) Mr S Walker 4/1: 0/-311513: Held up, eff to chall   hd   **69**
over 1f out, no extra nr fin: see 2499 (AW).

2507 **OPENING CEREMONY 8** [13] R A Fahey 5-12-0 P (68) Mr P Callaghan(5) 7/2 FAV: 0531-624: Keen, in tch, 4   **66**
hung left & no impress on front trio from dist: tried cheekpieces: see 1979.

2507* **KIDZPLAY 8** [12]8-12-1 (5ex) (69) Mr G Goldie(7) 7/1: 4-034215: Led till 3f out, btn dist: btr 2507.   ¾   **66**

2448 **EVERY NOTE COUNTS 11** [11]4-11-8 (62) Mr M Walford(5) 9/1: 20-00066: Held up, eff 2f out, no prog.   2½   **56**

2038 **UNTIDY DAUGHTER 28** [8]5-10-12 p (52) Mr E Dehdashti(3) 9/1: 0/00-5037: Rear, hdwy 5f out, rdn &   3½   **42**
btn 2f out: see 2038, 1307.

2544 **TINIAN 7** [2]6-10-13 (53) Mr S Dobson(3) 16/1: 4543248: Keen & prom, lost place fnl 3f: btr 2146 (firm).   26   **21**

4108} **MAFRUZ 292** [4]5-11-4 (58) Mr M J McAlister 33/1: 360060-9: ch g Hamas - Braari (Gulch) Chsd   4   **22**
ldrs, no ch fnl 3f: reapp: h'cap plcd '03 (rtd 66, 1st time blnks): mdn scorer in '02: wng form at 7f, stays 1m:
acts on fast & soft grnd, any trk: can go well fresh & eff in head-gear, not worn tonight.
1 Oct'02 Leic 7gd 72- D: 2 Mar'02 Donc 6sft 72- D:

2315 **ABLE MIND 16** [1]4-11-11 (65) Mr S Irving(7) 33/1: 23233-00: 10th: b g Mind Games - Chlo Jo   15   **17**
(Belmez) Keen & cl-up till 4f out, sn btn: plcd all starts '03, rnr-up thrice, incl h'cap & 2 class stks, AW plcd
(rtd 59a, h'cap, W J Haggas): plcd 3 of 4 mdn starts '02: eff btwn 6f & 7.5f, poss stays 8.5f: handles firm, gd &
fibresand: can go well fresh.   2 Jul'03 Ling 7.6gd 70-(75) F: 2 May'03 Ling 7sft 73-72 D:
2 May'03 Thir 6gd 72-(70) E: 2 Oct'02 Newc 7fm 72- F: 2 Sep'02 Warw 6g/f 66- E:

2616 **MOYNE PLEASURE 4** [9]6-9-12 p (38) Mr P Evans(5) 20/1: 146000R: Refused to race, quick reapp: see 1800.   **0**
11 Ran   Time 2m 19.78 (13.28)   Owned: Mr Mike Browne   Trained: Malton

---

2727
7.25 Northern Rock Gosforth Park Cup Rated Stakes Handicap 3yo+ 0-105 (B)   **[105]**
£17400 £6600 £3300   **5f str**   **Good/Soft 65**   +27 Fast   Stands Side

2253* **CARIBBEAN CORAL 20** [7] J J Quinn 5-9-5 (96) R Winston 5/1 FAV: 012-0211: Hld up, prog halfway,   **105+**
styd on to lead trav well ins fnl 1f, pushed out, cosily, val further: eff at 5/6f on fm & gd/soft: hold up performer
who has a gd turn of foot, thriving & can land hat-trick: see 2253.

2581 **CORRIDOR CREEPER 6** [11] J M Bradley 7-9-9 p (92) F Norton 12/1: 5442602: Prom, ev ch dist, styd   ¾   **96**
on, not pace wnr: quick reapp: rarely runs a bad race & deserves to find similar: see 2253, 2082 & 1594.

2357 **STEEL BLUE 14** [3] R M Whitaker 4-9-4 (95) A Culhane 8/1: 1001253: Led, hdd ins fnl 1f, no extra: ¾   **97**
imprvd eff in defeat: now 10lb higher than last win in 1977 but another gd run.

4672} **PHILHARMONIC 258** [9] R A Fahey 3-9-4 (101) P Hanagan 20/1: 2114-4: b g Victory Note - Lambast   ½   **101+**

(Relkino) Rear, prog & short of room 2f out, styd on well, kind ride: reapp: mdn & nov stks wnr in '03, 4th in
Listed: eff at 5f, relish a return to 6f: acts on fast & gd/soft, gd/or sharp trk: real eye-catcher in a gd sprint,
one to be on next time. 1 Sep'03 Ripo 6g/f 99- D: 1 Sep'03 York 6.0g/f 91- E: 2 Aug'03 Ripo 5gd 77- E:

2581	**HALMAHERA 6** [10]9-9-7 (98) N Callan 16/1: 0246605: Rear, prog 2f out, nrst fin: encouraging.		hd	97
2253	**PTARMIGAN RIDGE 20** [16]8-8-7 (84) N Mackay(3) 12/1: 1-001006: Handy till dist, no extra: btr 1594.		nk	82
2532	**FUNFAIR WANE 7** [8]5-9-4 (95) A Nicholls 33/1: 00000-07: Cl-up till dist, no extra: qck reapp.		½	91
2359	**ATLANTIC VIKING 14** [1]9-9-3 (94) E Ahern 12/1: 060-0048: In tch over 3f, sn onepcd: btr 2359.		shd	90
2581	**WHITBARROW 6** [6]5-9-6 (97) R Hills 11/2: 0010009: Nvr nrr than mid-div: quick reapp: btr 1845 (fast).		1¼	89
2581	**MATTY TUN 6** [5]5-9-1 (92) Dale Gibson 6/1: 0-055000: 10th: Handy 4f, no extra: qck reapp.		nk	83
2581	**INDIAN SPARK 6** [14]10-9-0 (91) T Eaves(3) 10/1: 4044600: 11th: Chsd ldrs 3f, no extra: qck reapp.		½	80
2581	**SALVIATI 6** [4]7-8-7 (84) Dean McKeown 16/1: 05-00000: 12th: Keen cl-up, wknd 1f out: qck reapp.		hd	72
2359	**ZARZU 14** [2]5-8-4 (9oh) (72) R Thomas(5) 25/1: 4343000: 13th: Al in rear: stiff task from out of h'cap.		nk	68
1703	**PROUD BOAST 43** [13]6-9-0 (91) K Darley 20/1: 60-01000: 14th: Bhd, nvr a factor: 6 wk abs: won		4	67
	this race in '02 off 2lb lower mark: btr 1162.			
2359*	**PICCLED 14** [15]6-8-6 (83) D Allan 16/1: 0300010: 15th: Al in rear: btr 2539 (fast).		13	23

15 Ran Time 1m 0.11 (1.91) Owned: Dawson Green Quinn Roberts Trained: Malton

---

2728   **7.55 Nitex Co Uk Maiden Stakes Fillies 3yo (D)**
£3751 £1154 £577   **6f str**   **Good/Soft 65**   **-10 Slow** Stands Side

	RAMPAGE 0 [3] W J Haggas 3-8-11 R Hills 11/10 FAV: 1: Mid-div, prog trav well to lead dist, sn			78+
	hung left, pushed clr, val 4L+: debut: related to sprint wnr J M W Turner: eff at 6f on gd/soft grnd: acts on a			
	stiff/gall trk & goes well fresh: sure to improve & rate higher.			
2559	**BRAIN WASHED 6** [5] T D Easterby 3-8-11 D Allan 12/1: 042: Prom, ev ch dist, styd on but not		2½	69
	pace easy wnr: quick reapp: improved on gd/soft: qual for h'caps: see 2559.			
1971	**ISLAND SPELL 32** [7] C Grant 3-8-11 (70) P Fessey 13/2: 3063-353: Prom, led 2f out, hdd dist, no extra.		2½	61
4965}	**KAMENKA 237** [6] R A Fahey 3-8-11 (73) P Hanagan 7/2: 63044-4: ch f Wolfhound - Aliuska (Fijar		shd	61
	Tango) Handy over 4f, no extra: reapp: 3rd of 6 once in '03 (rtd 71 at best, auct stks): eff at 5/6f on fast.			
2295	**SPEED RACER 17** [2]3-8-11 (57) Kim Tinkler 33/1: 305-05: b f Zieten - Sharenara (Vaguely Noble)		1¼	57$
	Led 4f, no extra: plcd on 1 of 3 '03 starts (M R Channon, rtd 67, mdns): eff at 6f on firm grnd.			
1146	**SCOOBY DOOBY DO 74** [1]3-8-11 (60) Dean McKeown 8/1: 60-56: Handy 4f, wknd: 10 wk abs.		1	54
	FESTIVE CHIMES 0 [4]3-8-11 R Winston 14/1: 7: b f Efisio - Delightful Chime (Alzao) Slow away,		5	40
	prog & cl-up halfway, fdd fnl 2f: debut: with J J Quinn.			

7 Ran Time 1m 15.80 (4.5) Owned: Cheveley Park Stud Trained: Newmarket

---

2729   **8.25 Champagne Lanson Median Auction Maiden Stakes 3-5yo (D)**
£6708 £2064 £1032   **1m rnd**   **Good/Soft 65**   **-42 Slow** Inside

2148	**MR MISTRAL 23** [1] G Wragg 5-9-7 K Darley 11/4: 21: Led, rcd keenly, rdn out fnl 1f: eff at 7f,			91
	imprvd for step to 1m: acts on firm & gd/soft grnd: eff on a stiff/gall trk: see 2148.			
1935	**LONG ROAD 34** [4] J Noseda 3-8-11 E Ahern 4/7 FAV: 222: Cl-up, travelled well & ev ch dist, styd		1	88
	on but not pace wnr: clr rem: acts on gd/soft grnd, prob apprec return to faster grnd: see 1935 & 1763.			
2325	**MASTER THEO 16** [2] H J Collingridge 3-8-11 (77) Dean McKeown 7/1: 335-0333: Cl-up 6f, sn wknd.		10	71
2231	**RICH CHIC 21** [3] M D Hammond 3-8-6 N Mackay(3) 40/1: 04: Handy over 5f, fdd: see 2231.		9	51

4 Ran Time 1m 45.57 (8.57) Owned: Howard Spooner and Partners (II) Trained: Newmarket

---

2730   **8.55 Cantor Odds Claiming Stakes 3yo+ (F)**
£3325 £950 £475   **6f str**   **Good/Soft 65**   **-00 Slow** Stands Side

2326	**MISS WIZZ 16** [7] W Storey 4-8-6 p (37) Rory Moore(7) 20/1: 4164451: Mid-div, prog halfway, rdn out			46
	to lead on line: eff at 5f, apprec return to 6f, styd 7f: acts on fast, gd/soft & fibresand: eff with cheekpieces.			
2477	**HAULAGE MAN 9** [13] D Eddy 6-9-7 (58) P Hanagan 12/1: 00040-02: ch g Komaite - Texita (Young		nk	61
	Generation) Cl-up, styd on to lead dist, hdd under press on line: rnr-up once in '03 (h'cap): h'cap wnr in early			
	'02, subs plcd 4 times: eff at 6f/1m on firm & gd/soft, stiff/gall or easy trk: has gone well fresh: tried cheek			
	pieces: apprec drop to clmg grade & can find similar.			
	2 Jun'03 Carl 5.9fm 69-66 E: 2 Oct'02 Newc 8fm 68-64 E: 2 Jul'02 Newc 6g/f 63-64 D: 2 May'02 Newc 8g/f 68-63 F:			
	1 May'02 Thir 6g/f 66-57 E: 1 Sep'01 Newc 6fm 54-48 F:			
2476	**BEST LEAD 9** [5] Ian Emmerson 5-9-0 bl (52) D Tudhope(7) 8/1: 4343333: Led, hdd dist, no extra.		3	46
2187	**TYPE ONE 22** [8] J J Quinn 6-9-4 (67) R Winston 7/2 FAV: 0002004: In tch, ev ch bef 1f out, sn no extra.		nk	49
2502	**PAYS DAMOUR 8** [15]7-9-0 (66) Alex Greaves 5/1: 0010305: Rear, prog 2f out, kept on cl-home: btr 2337.		2	39
2535	**JUWWI 7** [2]10-8-12 (58) Darren Williams 7/1: 4406266: Nvr nrr than mid-div: quick reapp: btr 2412.		1¾	32
2535	**BEYOND CALCULATION 7** [12]10-8-12 p (56) K Darley 7/1: 0-000047: Handy 4f, sn no extra: qck reapp.		hd	31
2476	**AMERICAN COUSIN 9** [10]9-9-0 (62) A Nicholls 15/2: 1010258: Nvr nrr than mid-div: btr 2161.		½	31
2182	**ALPHA ZETA 22** [4]3-8-9 Dean McKeown 66/1: 0-09: Bhd, mod late gains: mod form to date.		7	15
2480	**QUEEN OF NIGHT 9** [1]4-8-6 (60) A Culhane 10/1: 5-0404R0: 10th: Al in rear.		nk	4
1642	**Formeric 46** [11]8-8-12 vis(39) P Fessey 25/1:0			
2173}	**Nothing Daunted 376** [6]7-9-0 (55) M Lawson(5) 33/1:0			
2476	**Bettys Valentine 9** [17]4-8-6 (25) E Ahern 33/1:0 299 **Cayman Mischief 174** [3]4-8-8 T Eaves(3) 100/1:0			

14 Ran Time 1m 15.22 (3.92) Owned: Mr Tony McCormick Trained: Consett

---

2731   **9.25 Weatherbys Bank Handicap Stakes 3yo 0-75 (E)**   **[77]**
£5148 £1584 £792   **5f str**   **Good/Soft 65**   **-15 Slow** Stands Side

2380	**ICENASLICE 14** [8] J J Quinn 3-8-13 (62) D Tudhope(7) 11/2: 346-0141: Handy, styd on ins fnl 1f,			68
	rdn out to lead cl-home: eff at 5f, stays a stiff 7f: acts on fast & gd/soft grnd: see 2380 & 2219.			
2566	**BLUE POWER 6** [2] K R Burke 3-8-9 (58) Darren Williams 13/2: 0353102: Prom, styd on to lead 1f		hd	64
	out, sn edged left under press, hdd cl-home: quick reapp: acts on firm & gd/soft, loves fibresand: see 2380.			
818	**HELLO ROBERTO 109** [6] M J Polglase 3-9-2 (65) R Winston 6/1: 4-020253: Mid-div, prog ins fnl 2f,		nk	70

NEWCASTLE   FRIDAY 25.06.04   Lefthand, Galloping, Stiff Track

styd on ins fnl 1f, not btn far: long abs: encouraging run back on turf: see 217.

2055 VOLATICUS 28 [5] D Nicholls 3-8-9 VIS (58) A Nicholls 10/1: 0-2044: Keen cl-up, onepcd dist: not disgraced in 1st time visor: eff at 5f, return to 6f will suit: acts on gd & gd/soft grnd: btr 953.	1	61
2675 SWEET CANDO 2 [4]3-8-10 p (59) N Mackay(3) 9/4 FAV: 34-60205: Cl-up till dist, no extra: qck reapp.	hd	61
2675 JADAN 2 [7]3-9-7 (70) E Ahern 4/1: 501-0036: Led, hdd 1f out, no extra: quick reapp: btr 2675.	1	70
2227 SIR LOIN 21 [3]3-8-11 (60) Kim Tinkler 25/1: 20600-07: Handy over 4f, wknd: see 2227.	2½	53
1949 LORD BASKERVILLE 32 [1]3-8-8 (57) Rory Moore(7) 12/1: 0060308: Handy till halfway, wknd.	2½	43

8 Ran   Time 1m 02.21(4.01)   Owned: Miss D A Johnson   Trained: Malton

NEWMARKET   FRIDAY 25.06.04   Righthand, Stiff, Galloping Track

Official Going GOOD/FIRM.

2732   6.40 Newmarket Nights Claiming Stakes 3yo   (E)
£3393 £1044 £522   1m str   Good/Firm 20   -02 Slow   Far Side

2504* THE FUN MERCHANT 8 [6] D Carroll 3-8-4 (63) Lisa Jones(3) 7/2: 60-011: In tch, hdwy over 1f out to lead ins last, rdn clr: clmd for 11,000: prev with W Jarvis: v eff over a gall 1m on gd & gd/firm: lightly rcd, improving & making hay in claim grade: see 2504.		69
2238 ARKHOLME 20 [4] W J Haggas 3-9-4 BL (78) D Holland 13/2: 41-402: In tch, eff well over 1f out, kept on, not pace of wnr: relished drop into claim grade & first time blnks: acts on gd/firm & rain softened grnd.	1¼	79
2502 YASHIN 8 [10] M H Tompkins 3-8-7 (60) J Fanning 50/1: 050-003: Keen, sn led, rdn & collared ins last, no extra: imprvd eff drpd in class & with forcing tactics over this stiff 1m on gd/firm: see 2502.	1	66
1984* LADY PISTE 31 [5] G G Margarson 3-8-0 (61) A McCarthy 9/1: 2531014: With ldr, no extra fnl 1f: prev with P Evans, see 1984 (7f).	nk	58
2543 WESTERN ROOTS 7 [8]3-8-10 (78) L Dettori 11/2: 4006155: Held up, eff dist, nvr dngrs: btr 2133.	1½	65
2314 WIZARD LOOKING 16 [3]3-8-3 t (65) R L Moore 11/1: 526-6006: Held up, nvr a factor: see 1915.	½	57
2452 HAWKIT 11 [1]3-9-4 (74) K Fallon 2/1 FAV: 5210127: Sn bhd, mod late gains: reportedly fin lame.	shd	71
2504 EIZAWINA DOCKLANDS 8 [2]3-8-3 t J Quinn 50/1: 00008: Held up, nvr a factor: see 1762.	2½	51
2474 FOUR KINGS 9 [7]3-8-5 t (63) F P Ferris(3) 14/1: 50339: Dwelt, al bhd: btr 2474, 2042.	1¼	51
4412| SACCHARINE 276 [9]3-7-12 J Bramhill 50/1: 00-0: 10th: b f Whittingham - Sweet And Lucky (Lucky Wednesday) In tch, wknd over 2f out on reapp: modest.	9	26

10 Ran   Time 1m 39.0 (1.8)   Owned: Diamond Racing Ltd   Trained: Warthilll

2733   7.10 Mozart's Bistro E B F Maiden Stakes Fillies 2yo   (D)
£4745 £1460 £730   6f str   Good/Firm 20   -50 Slow   Far Side

BORTHWICK GIRL [6] B J Meehan 2-8-11 J Fortune 2/1 FAV: 1: b f Cape Cross - Shannon Dore (Turtle Island) Chsd ldr till led over 1f out, edged left but sn rdn clr, readily: Feb first foal, cost 35,000gns: dam 6f juv scorer: eff over a stiff 6f, 7f looks sure to suit: runs well fresh on gd/firm: v pleasing start, shld rate more highly & win more races.		88+
2437 MISS COTSWOLD LADY 11 [5] A W Carroll 2-8-11 J Quinn 20/1: 542: Led over 4f, rdn & short of room ins last but not pace of wnr: imprvd stepped up to 6f & with forcing tactics on this gd/firm: see 2132.	3	75
KEEP BACCKINHIT [8] G L Moore 2-8-11 R L Moore 9/1: 3: b f Raise A Grand - Taispeain (Petorius) Slow away, held up, eff 2f out, onepace on debut: March foal, cost £9,000: half-sister to a 5f juv scorer: dam 6f wnr: bred for speed & showed some promise here, shld do btr.	1¼	73
GENNIE BOND [3] R Hannon 2-8-11 R Hughes 9/4: 4: b f Pivotal - Miriam (Forzando) Dwelt, in tch, wknd over 1f out on debut: April foal, cost 37,000gns: half-sister to numerous 5f scorers: dam 5f wnr.	1¾	68
ROSAPENNA [7]2-8-11 R Mullen 12/1: 5: In tch, wknd fnl 1f on debut.	¾	66
NORDHOCK [2]2-8-11 A Mackay 14/1: 6: Al bhd on debut.	3½	56
SABBIOSA [4]2-8-11 T Quinn 5/1: 7: In tch, wknd over 2f out on debut.	2½	49

7 Ran   Time 1m 15.2 (4.2)   Owned: Mrs Wendy English   Trained: Upper Lambourn

2734   7.40 Siemens Smart Home Technology Handicap Stakes 3yo 0-85   (D)   [92]
£5434 £1672 £836   5f str   Good/Firm 20   +22 Fast   Far Side

2155 JIMMY RYAN 23 [7] T D McCarthy 3-9-3 (81) J P Guillambert(3) 20/1: 314-001: In tch far side, hdwy to lead over 1f out, hung right ins last but styd on, rdn out: back to best drpd to 5f, does stay 6f: likes gd/firm & a gall trk, handles a sharp one: reportedly got v warm in prelims on both wins to date: see 1734.		94
2593 TONY THE TAP 6 [10] N A Callaghan 3-9-1 (79) T Quinn 5/4 FAV: 4-1222: Switched to stands side over 4f out, led that pair, styd on well ins last: another fine rnr-up eff, deserves a nice prize: see 2593, 2400.	1¼	86
2400 SILVER PRELUDE 13 [4] D K Ivory 3-9-2 (80) D Holland 20/1: 250-0003: Led far side till over 3f out, ev ch till no extra ins last: back to form with fav'd forcing tactics: see 2121.	½	85
2390 INCISE 13 [2] B J Meehan 3-9-7 T (85) L Dettori 13/2: 01-60044: In tch far side, eff dist, onepace.	1½	84
2271 TRIBUTE 18 [11]3-8-13 VIS (77) T P Queally(3) 12/1: 261-0055: Switched to chase ldrs stands side over 4f out, eff over 1f out, onepace: tried a visor: see 1766.	1	75
1903 SIGNOR PANETTIERE 35 [1]3-8-6 (70) P Dobbs 10/1: 0005-026: In tch far side, onepace over 1f out.	nk	67
2566* DIVINE SPIRIT 6 [8]3-9-8 (7ex) (86) L Enstone(3) 11/2: 0003617: In tch far side, hung right & no extra over 1f out: btr expected after 2566.	hd	82
2227 TIZZYS LAW 21 [9]3-8-3 (67) J Bramhill 20/1: 0-16458: Led far side 3f out till dist, no extra.	shd	62
2566 SAHARA SILK 6 [5]3-7-12 vis (62) J F McDonald(3) 25/1: 4120309: Al bhd far side: see 2380, 1338.	2½	50
2268 PARTY PRINCESS 18 [3]3-8-0 (64) J Quinn 10/1: 53-00140: 10th: In tch far side, wknd 2f out.	1¼	48
2649 GREEN RIDGE 3 [6]3-8-4 (68) Paul Eddery 25/1: 2506-240: 11th: Slow away, al bhd far side: qck reapp.	1¾	47

11 Ran   Time 58.41 (u0.09)   Owned: Mr James Ryan   Trained: Godstone

NEWMARKET FRIDAY 25.06.04 Righthand, Stiff, Galloping Track

2735 8.10 Newmarketracecourses Co Uk Rated Stakes Handicap 3yo+ 0-85 (D) [83]
£4865 £1845 £923 1m2f Good/Firm 20 -12 Slow Centre

2265 **KENS DREAM 18** [6] Ms A E Embiricos 5-9-10 (79) P McCabe 9/1: 015/-0341: Held up, hdwy over 2f out, short of room over 1f out but styd on well to lead ins last, rdn out, going away: eff at 10/11f on fast or gd grnd, easy or gall trks: tough, 4 wins from 13 starts now: see 1890. 86
2153 **BAILEYS DANCER 23** [7] M Johnston 3-8-7 (3oh) (74) J Fanning 9/1: 40-04002: Led to halfway, led again 3f out, rdn & hung left ins last/collared ins last, not btn far: btr eff & stays 10f on gd & gd/firm. ¾ 77
2392 **RASID 13** [9] C A Dwyer 6-9-4 (73) D Holland 9/1: 2310053: Sn rdn, handy, hdwy & short of room over 1f out, styd on onepace cl home: right back to best: see 1397. nk 76
2405 **KYLKENNY 13** [5] H Morrison 9-9-3 t (72) S Drowne 7/2: 4-300653: In tch, eff to chall dist, no extra. dht 74
2363 **STREET LIFE 14** [3]6-9-4 (73) K Fallon 11/4 FAV: 5233435: In tch, rdn & short of room over 1f out, some late gains, no dngr: likes easier grnd: see 2067, 1650. ¾ 74
2099 **BLAZING THE TRAIL 25** [1]4-8-10 (65) M Hills 5/1: 5132306: Held up, eff 2f out, no extra dist. nk 65
2265 **GLIMMER OF LIGHT 18** [8]4-9-4 (73) I Mongan 14/1: 4150-607: b g Marju - Church Light (Caerleon) Chsd ldr till went on halfway till 3f out, wknd over 1f out: '03 mdn wnr: can force the pace over a fair 1m on firm. 1 May'03 Kemp 8fm 82- D: 1¾ 70
2318 **PIRI PIRI 16** [2]4-8-13 (68) S Whitworth 11/2: 660-6238: Slow away, eff over 1f out, wknd. 1¾ 62
8 Ran Time 2m 05.13 (3.23) Owned: Mr Michael Underwood Trained: Newmarket

2736 8.40 Vibefm Co Uk Conditions Stakes Fillies 3yo+ (C)
£8294 £3146 £1573 6f str Good/Firm 20 -43 Slow Far Side

2591 **GREY PEARL 6** [1] Miss Gay Kelleway 5-8-5 (81) M Fenton 20/1: 3646041: Set pace till 2f out, styd on ins last, drvn out: all 3 prev wins at 7f, clearly v eff at 6f & does stay 1m: acts on firm, fast & both AWs: best on a sharp or gall trk, likes Lingfield: useful, career best run: see 280. 93
2491 **CUSCO 9** [2] R Hannon 3-8-1 (89) R Smith 16/1: 305-2602: Led after 1f till 2f out, kept on for press ins last, just held: right back to best with a return to 6f, does stay 1m: useful, see 1513. ½ 93
2457 **TOPKAMP 13** [4] M L W Bell 4-8-6 (1ow) (104) K Fallon 1/2 FAV: 4235-233: Keen, handy, eff over 1f out, kept on ins last, not btn far: around a stone below best despite fin cl-up: see 2140. ½ 89
2574 **VALJARV 6** [6] N P Littmoden 3-8-1 BL (93) T P Queally 10/1: 1-000004: Held up, hdwy & short of room over 1f out, kept on ins last, no threat: tried blnks: shld find easier opportunities: see 1933. ½ 89
4057} **ANTHOS 295** [5]3-7-12 (93) C Catlin 11/2: 2614-5: b f Big Shuffle - Anemoni (Motley) Held up, eff 2f out, sn no extra on reapp: '03 7L mdn fills wnr, subs fin lame: suited by 6f on firm & gd grnd, has disapp on gd/soft: likes a sharp/undul trk. 1 Aug'03 Brig 6.0fm 85- F: 2 Jun'03 Wind 6gd 70- E: 4 74
1400 **TENTATIVE 59** [3]3-8-1 (90) J Quinn 9/1: 21103-06: ch f Distant View - Danzante (Danzig) Dwelt, held up, eff 2f out, sn wknd: 2 mth abs: won 3 of 7 '03 starts (mdn auct, stks & h'cap, rtd 90): v eff at 5f on firm or gd grnd, likes Doncaster: tough, genuine & progressive last term.
1 Jul'03 Donc 5g/f 88-81 D: 1 Jul'03 Donc 5gd 85- D: 2 Jun'03 Bath 5.0fm 83- D: 1 Jun'03 Bath 5.0fm 80- F: ½ 75
6 Ran Time 1m 14.76 (3.76) Owned: Andrea Wilkinson Gay Kelleway Trained: Newmarket

2737 9.10 Ltm Digital Rated Stakes Handicap 4yo+ 0-85 (D) [90]
£4849 £1839 £920 1m4f Good/Firm 20 -36 Slow Centre

2538* **WAIT FOR THE WILL 7** [7] G L Moore 8-9-9 (3ex)bl (85) R L Moore 15/8 FAV: 26-00011: Handy, hdwy & short of room over 1f out, styd on well ins last to lead cl-home, going away: bckd: all 10 wins at 12f, stays 14f on fm, gd/soft & polytrack: v tough (10 wins from 52 starts) & thriving, loves Goodwood: see 2538. 94
1216} **GENGHIS 426** [4] H Morrison 5-9-4 (80) J Fortune 11/2: 24/3-2: br g Persian Bold - Cindy's Baby (Bairn) Set pace, rdn & edged left 1f out, collared well ins last, not btn far: plcd in a mdn sole '03 start for P Webber (rtd 81): mdn rnr-up in '02: stays 12f well & can front run: acts on firm & fast grnd, gall trks: shown enough to win a race. 2 Jul'02 Newb 12g/f 80- D: ¾ 86
2355 **FLOTTA 14** [6] M R Channon 5-9-6 (82) S Hitchcott(3) 3/1: 0-450443: Held up, hdwy trav well when short of room over 1f out, sn hung left & no extra: see 877. 1½ 86
2220} **BENDARSHAAN 68** [2] M Johnston 4-9-7 (83) J Fanning 10/1: 323-0004: b c Darshaan - Calypso Run (Lycius) Chsd ldr, eff to chall over 1f out, sn no extra: prev with E Dunlop & recently unplcd in Dubai: plcd all 5 '03 starts (mdns): stays 12f on fast & gd/soft: needs to try headgear.
2 May'03 Chep 12.1g/s 81-(83) D: 2 May'03 Brig 9.9g/f 81- D: 2 Apr'03 Newm 8gd 74- D: 1 85
570 **TEAM MATE 139** [3]6-9-2 (78) B Reilly(3) 14/1: 61540-05: Held up, eff well over 1f out, sn no extra: long abs: see 570. 1¾ 77
2391 **DOVEDON HERO 13** [1]4-9-0 bl (76) S Sanders 9/2: 6-002046: Held up, eff well over 1f out, sn wknd. nk 75
1889 **SIR HAYDN 35** [5]4-8-5 VIS (67) Lisa Jones(3) 14/1: 33-36067: Dwelt, keen held up, wknd over 2f out: tried a visor: see 1006. 5 59
7 Ran Time 2m 34.91(6.71) Owned: RDM Racing Trained: Brighton

LINGFIELD Polytrack SATURDAY 26.06.04 Lefthand, Sharp, Undulating Track

Official Going Good (Good/Firm Places), AW - Standard

2738 6.35 European Breeders Fund Maiden Stakes 2yo (D)
£4134 £1272 £636 5f str Good/Firm 31 -26 Slow Stands side

2061 **TESARY 28** [4] E A L Dunlop 2-8-9 W Supple 5/6 FAV: 621: Handy, styd on to lead dist, pushed out, val 3L+: eff at 5/6f on fast grnd: acts on a sharp/undul trk: can progress: see 2061 & 1709. 77+
2364 **AFRICAN STORM 15** [1] S Kirk 2-9-0 P Dobbs 14/1: 52: Prom, ev ch dist, kept on, not pace wnr: eff at 5f, 6f shld suit: acts on fast grnd: imprvd on debut eff & can find similar: see 2364. 1½ 76
LOUPHOLE 0 [2] P J Makin 2-9-0 R Smith 33/1: 3: ch g Loup Sauvage - Goodwood Lass (Alzao) Slow shd 75

away, hdwy 2f out, kept on fnl 1f, nrst fin: debut: Apr foal, cost 2,500 gns: half-brother 7f wnr: dam won at 7f/12f: sire decent around 1m/10f: eff at 5f, will enjoy further: acts on fast grnd: encouraging run.
2450 **FIRST RULE 12** [3] C F Wall 2-9-0 R Havlin 5/2: 044: Led, hdd dist, no extra: eff at 5f on fast grnd. ¾ **73**
MULBERRY LAD 0 [7]2-9-0 D Kinsella 33/1: 5: b c Entrepreneur - Taisho (Namaqualand) Bhd, prog ins fnl 2f, nrst fin: debut: Jan first foal, cost 10,000 gns: dam wnr at 6f/7f: sire Group 1 wnr at a mile. 1½ **69**
COMTESSE LALANDE 0 [8]2-8-9 I Mongan 11/1: 6: ch f King of Kings - Beyond the Realm (Stop The Music) Handy over 3f, sn wknd: debut: Feb foal, cost 57,000 gns: sire Group 1 wnr at a mile: with M L W Bell. 1½ **61**
1805 **ROYAL ACCOLADE 40** [5]2-8-9 BL W Ryan 16/1: 007: Bhd, nvr a factor: 1st time blnks. 5 **46**
7 Ran Time 59.68 (2.88) Owned: Mr Khalifa Sultan Trained: Newmarket

LINGFIELD Polytrack SATURDAY 26.06.04 Lefthand, V Sharp Track

Official Going Good (Good/Firm Places), AW - Standard

2739

7.05 Dallas Kirkland Selling Stakes 3yo+ (G)
£2597 £742 £371 **1m4f aw** **Going 73** **-11 Slow** Inside

2576 **DELIGHTFULLY 7** [8] B W Hills 3-8-3 BL (67) R Mullen 15/8 FAV: 0-024631: Led 10f out, hdd under press ins fnl 1f, rallied to lead cl home, drvn out: 1st time blnks: sold for 8,000 gns: qck reapp: eff at 8.4f, now suited by 11/12f: acts on firm grnd & both AW's: appreciated fitting of blnks on drop to selling grade. **61a**
2588 **TRESOR SECRET 7** [4] P Butler 4-9-8 (65) R Thomas(5) 9/2: 10-05022: In tch, prog to lead trav well ins fnl 1f, sn found little under press & hdd, just held by wnr: clmd for 6,000: see 2588 (N A Callaghan). *hd* **65a**
2588 **JAVA DAWN 7** [1] T E Powell 4-9-3 (42) A Quinn(5) 66/1: 0/000-003: b f Fleetwood - Krakatoa (Shirley Heights) Slow away, prog in mid div when short of room 2f out, kept on from dist, no ch with front 2: qck reapp: unplcd in 3 '03 starts (rtd 35, h'cap): mdn rnr-up once in '02: stays 12f on polytrack: tried visor. 3 **56a**
2 Oct'02 Brig 6.9g/f 59- D:
2588 **MANDOOB 7** [3] B R Johnson 7-9-13 vis (60) Dane O'Neill 5/2: 1002044: Rear, prog 5f out, onepcd dist: qck reapp: again finished bhd today's 2nd & 3rd in 2588. *nk* **65a$**
2588 **NEPTUNE 7** [7]8-9-8 (45) P Dobbs 16/1: 0024535: Slow away, hdwy 3f out, no impress 1f out: qck reapp. 1 **58a$**
2267 **BLUE SAVANNA 19** [2]4-9-13 bl (45) R L Moore 10/1: 6421056: Handy & trav well after 9f, no extra dist. *shd* **62a$**
2419 **KERRISTINA 13** [6]3-8-3 VIS S Whitworth 40/1: 0007: b f So Factual - Arch Angel (Archway) Cl up 10f, sn fdd: 1st time visor: mod form to date. 9 **39a**
2381 **COOLFORE JADE 15** [5]4-9-8 (47) M Savage(5) 8/1: 5000638: Led, hdd 10f out, fdd fnl 3f: see 2381. 5 **37a**
8 Ran Time 2m 39.36 (10.16) Owned: Mr Stephen Crown Trained: Lambourn

2740

7.35 Mercedes Benz Direct Median Auction Maiden Stakes 3yo (F)
£2982 £852 £426 **1m2f aw** **Going 73** **+11 Fast** Inside

2106 **KENTMERE 26** [6] W J Haggas 3-9-0 BL (67) T P Queally(3) 7/1: 22500-61: In tch, prog to lead ins fnl 1f, drvn out: 1st time blnks: eff around 7f, imprvd for step up to 10f: acts on fast grnd & polytrack, v sharp trk: app fitting of blnks: see 2106 (reapp). **79a**
2410 **HUGS DESTINY 14** [4] J G Given 3-9-0 I Mongan 4/1: 52: Prom, styd on to lead dist, hdd ins fnl 1f, not pace wnr: clr rem: appreciated step up to 10f, further shld suit: acts on polytrack: ran with promise. 1½ **76a**
2393 **CHAMPAGNE SHADOW 14** [7] G L Moore 3-9-0 bl (69) R L Moore 3/1 JT FAV: 0402023: Handy over 7f, no extra fnl 1f. 6 **68a**
2344 **LADY BLADE 16** [5] B Hanbury 3-8-9 (61) Lisa Jones(3) 16/1: 6360-04: Mid div, outpcd after 1m, kept on despite hanging left from dist: see 2344. ¾ **61a**
2521 **PRINCIPAL WITNESS 9** [2]3-9-0 (82) S Drowne 3/1 JT FAV: 04205: Led, hdd bef 1f out, wknd: btr 2106. *nk* **65a**
2193 **SHAZANA 23** [12]3-8-9 P Dobbs 11/1: 606: Mid div, prog 3f out, onepcd fnl 2f: now qual for h'caps. *hd* **59a**
2419 **SUDDEN IMPULSE 13** [3]3-8-9 R Smith 14/1: 67: In tch 1m, sn wknd: btr 2419. 5 **52a**
1790 **STEPPENWOLF 40** [14]3-9-0 (37) C Haddon(7) 100/1: 6000008: Al bhd: 6 wk abs. *shd* **56a$**
2064 **CLARE GALWAY 28** [1]3-8-9 (49) R Thomas(5) 20/1: 050049: Cl up over 7f, sn wknd. 1½ **48a**
2423 **KITLEY 13** [13]3-9-0 (60) S Whitworth 20/1: 43-00600: 10th: Al in rear. 2½ **49a**
2092 **Electras Dream 27** [8]3-8-9 D Sweeney 66/1:0 **Explicit 0** [11]3-9-0 R Mullen 25/1:0
Little Gannet 0 [10]3-8-9 Dane O'Neill 50/1:0 2224 **Pine Bay 22** [9]3-8-9 W Supple 33/1:0
14 Ran Time 2m 9..08 (6.28) Owned: Mr & Mrs G Middlebrook Trained: Newmarket

2741

8.05 Mid-Market Handicap Stakes 3yo 35-55 (F) **[63]**
£3189 £911 £456 **1m4f aw** **Going 73** **-00 Slow** Inside

2588* **JELLY BABY 7** [12] W J Haggas 3-9-6 bl (55) T P Queally(3) 3/1 FAV: 011: Held up, gd hdwy to lead ins fnl 1f, rdn out: qck reapp: apprec recent step up to 12f, further shld suit: acts on polytrack & a v sharp trk, likes Lingfield: eff with blnks: lightly rcd performer who can progress & land hat-trick: see 2588 (sell). **67a**
2548 **ERTE 8** [8] M R Channon 3-8-13 (48) S Hitchcott(3) 12/1: 06-06632: Bhd, hdwy 4f out, ev ch dist, styd on but not pace wnr: eff at 7f/10f, imprvd for step up to 12f: acts on fast, gd grnd & polytrack: gd run. 1½ **57a**
2503 **RUBAIYAT 9** [9] G Wragg 3-9-3 (52) S Drowne 11/2: 06-0043: Cl up, styd on to lead bef 1f out, hdd ins fnl 1f, no extra: just btr 2503. 3½ **56a**
2065 **FRAMBO 28** [6] J G Portman 3-8-7 t (42) Lisa Jones(3) 14/1: 0050644: Mid div, outpcd after 1m, late gains. 1 **44a**
2434 **ABLAJ 12** [4]3-9-2 (51) R Mullen 9/1: 400-0445: Mid div, hdwy 3f out, onepcd dist: btr 2434 (7f). *nk* **52a**
1258 **GENUINELY 68** [10]3-8-5 (40) S Whitworth 20/1: 00-006: Slow away, nvr nrr than mid div: 10 wk abs. 1 **39a**
1713 **SHALATI PRINCESS 44** [11]3-8-8 (43) P Dobbs 12/1: 0604037: Nvr nrr than mid div: 6 wk abs, btr 1713. *nk* **41a**
2345 **DANEFONIQUE 16** [3]3-9-6 (55) D Tudhope(7) 7/1: 0322568: Al bhd: btr 1836. 3½ **48a**
1648 **SEMELLE DE VENT 47** [15]3-9-6 BL (55) R Havlin 12/1: 056-3309: Cl up, led after 1m, hdd bef 1f out, fdd: 1st time blnks: btr 1165. *nk* **47a**
1763 **FORGE LANE 42** [16]3-9-6 (55) R L Moore 4/1: 00000: 10th: Cl up 9f, sn wknd: 6 wk abs. *nk* **46a**
2131 **ALIANNA 25** [5]3-8-5 (40) R Smith 33/1: 00000: 11th: Al in rear. 1¾ **28a**
1376 **Tshukudu 61** [14]3-8-7 (42) D Sweeney 33/1:0

LINGFIELD Polytrack SATURDAY 26.06.04 Lefthand, V Sharp Track

1124 **Troubleinparadise 75** [1]3-9-5 (54) Dane O'Neill 25/1:0
2148 **Absolutely Fab 24** [2]3-8-0 (35) J McAuley 50/1:0 1444 **Miss Hoofbeats 58** [7]3-8-7 (42) B Reilly(3) 50/1:0
15 Ran Time 2m 38.02 (8.82) Owned: Mr B Haggas Trained: Newmarket

LINGFIELD Polytrack SATURDAY 26.06.04 Lefthand, Sharp, Undulating Track

Official Going Good (Good/Firm Places), AW - Standard

2742 **8.35 Weatherbys Bank Handicap Stakes Fillies 3yo 0-85 (D)** **[90]**
£5623 £1730 £865 **7f str** **Good/Firm 31** **-15 Slow** Stands side

2342* **KEYAKI 16** [3] C F Wall 3-8-13 (75) R Mullen 7/2: 6611: Dwelt, sn mid div, hdwy halfway, rdn out to lead cl home: eff at 7f, 1m+ will suit: acts on fast grnd: gd performance on h'cap bow, win again: see 2342. **81**
2312 **LORIEN HILL 17** [1] B W Hills 3-8-7 (69) W Supple 5/1: 34-65102: Prom, styd on to lead 2f out, hdd under press cl home: lost little in defeat & can find similar: see 2169. *½* **73**
2268 **VERKHOTINA 19** [5] R Charlton 3-9-4 (80) S Drowne 7/2: 550-6103: Bhd, prog ins fnl 2f, nrst fin: eff at 6f, now stays 7f: 8lb higher than earlier win in 2118 (6f) *2* **80**
2072* **CAPESTAR 28** [8] B G Powell 3-9-3 (79) D Sweeney 100/30 FAV: 6214: Prom till dist, sn no extra. *1¾* **75**
2419 **ZWADI 13** [2]3-8-11 (73) Dane O'Neill 12/1: 4324-405: Led 5f, sn no extra: btr 2072. *1½* **66**
1741 **GLEBE GARDEN 43** [6]3-9-7 (83) I Mongan 5/1: 310-556: Cl up ev ch 2f out, sn hung right & wknd. *3* **70**
2268 **PINK SUPREME 19** [7]3-8-3 t (65) F P Ferris(3) 22/1: 2-0007: Handy 5f, fdd: btr 2268. *4* **44**
4770} **ZARNEETA 254** [4]3-7-12 (5oh) (55) C Haddon(7) 50/1: 355000-8: b f Tragic Role - Compton Amber (Puissance) Cl up 3f, sn fdd: reapp & new stable: plcd once in '03 (rtd 66, mdn, I A Wood): eff at 6f on fast. *nk* **38**
8 Ran Time 1m 23.62 (3.22) Owned: Hintlesham SPD Partners Trained: Newmarket

2743 **9.05 Mercedes Benz Direct Handicap Stakes 3yo+ 0-75 (E)** **[75]**
£3780 £1163 £582 **5f str** **Good/Firm 31** **+15 Fast** Stands side

2599 **GUNS BLAZING 6** [8] D K Ivory 5-9-5 bl (66) M Howard(7) 11/1: 0013601: Made all, in command bef 1f out, rdn out: qck reapp: suited by around 5f on firm & soft grnd: eff with blnks: goes well for today's pilot. **73**
2599 **INDIAN BAZAAR 6** [1] N E Berry 8-8-4 (51) T P Queally(2) 14/1: 5-002002: Cl up, styd on ins fnl 1f, al held by wnr: qck reapp: gd run & is h'capped to win sn: see 2269. *2* **51**
2599 **PULSE 6** [12] J M Bradley 6-9-0 p (61) Dane O'Neill 5/2 FAV: 2366453: Cl up, kept on ins fnl 1f, just held for 2nd: qck reapp: fin ahead of today's front 2 in 2599, see 2269. *shd* **60**
2609 **BELLA TUTRICE 6** [2] I A Wood 3-9-5 (72) F P Ferris(3) 12/1: 0200-034: Mid div, prog after 3f, onepcd fnl 1f: qck reapp: btr 2609 (6f). *2* **65**
2614 **ROXANNE MILL 5** [11]6-10-1 P (76) R L Moore 9/2: 3263235: Prom till dist, no extra: cheekpieces. *1¼* **65**
2438} **ANOTHER VICTIM 366** [3]10-8-3 (50) D Kinsella 28/1: 1000/00-6: ch g Beveled - Ragtime Rose (Ragstone) Nvr nrr than mid div: reapp: unplcd both '03 starts (h'caps, rtd 48): won 2 h'caps in '02: eff at 6f, suited by 5f, acts on fast, likes hvy grnd & Windsor: with M R Bosley. 1 May'02 Ayr 5g/s 57-51 E: 1 May'02 Wind 5sft 59-45 E: 2 Oct'01 Newc 5hvy 50-46 E: 1 Jun'01 Wind 5gd 49-38 E: 2 May'01 Sout 6g/f 74- D: *¾* **37**
2347* **GONENDUNNETT 16** [4]5-8-10 vis (57) Lisa Jones(3) 9/2: 0006617: Cl up till dist, fdd: btr 2347 (6f). *¾* **42**
2698 **SEVEN NO TRUMPS 2** [10]7-10-1 p (76) C J Davies(7) 7/1: 0360408: Handy 3f, sn wknd: frustrating. *1¼* **57**
2614 **INCHING 5** [5]4-8-2 (49) R Mullen 14/1: 0260209: Al bhd: qck reapp: btr 2585. *hd* **29**
2286 **PERFECT SETTING 18** [9]4-9-2 (63) D Sweeney 10/1: 2/4000-60: 10th: Mid div, fdd 1f out: btr 2286. *½* **42**
2062 **EMPRESS JOSEPHINE 28** [6]4-8-6 vis (53) D Corby(3) 20/1: 4-125300: 11th: Al in rear: btr 1442. *1¼* **28**
2585 **FORZENUFF 7** [7]3-8-6 (59) V Venkaya 20/1: 3-506000: 12th: Bhd, nvr a factor: qck reapp. *hd* **33**
12 Ran Time 57.60(0.80) Owned: Mr R D Hartshorn Trained: Radlett

CHESTER SATURDAY 26.06.04 Lefthand, Very Tight Track

Official Going Good (Good/Soft Places) RAIN DURING MEETING

2744 **2.30 Warwick International E B F Novice Stakes 2yo (D)**
£4622 £1422 £711 **5f16y rnd** **Good/Soft** **Inapplicable** Inside

2481 **BECKERMET 10** [3] R F Fisher 2-9-9 R Ffrench 5/1: 31121: Trkd ldrs & led over 1f out, rdn clr, v readily under a big weight: made full use of low draw, well suited by 5f on fast & gd/sft, sharp/turning or gall trk: gd weight carrier: useful & improved, see 2481 **106+**
2144 **SPEED DIAL HARRY 24** [8] K R Burke 2-8-12 vis Darren Williams 16/1: 523132: Mid-div, styd on for press from over 1f out, no chance with wnr: fair run from awkward draw with vis reapp: eff at 5f, 6f cld suit. *5* **81**
2071 **DOCTOR HILARY 28** [2] M L W Bell 2-9-2 VIS M Hills 7/4 FAV: 4123: Missed break, slow into stride & bhd, taken wide 2f out & styd on strongly, nrst fin: nicely bckd: drop to 5f in vis, crying out for a return to 6f & prob a gall trk: see 2071, 1893. *nk* **84+**
2165 **NOVA TOR 24** [11] N P Littmoden 2-8-13 J P Guillambert(3) 25/1: 1104: Held up, swtchd wide & kept on, no dngr from poor draw: fair run: handles gd, fbsnd & gd/sft grnd: see 1634 & 1024. *1* **78**
2165 **HANDSOME LADY 24** [10]2-8-7 T Eaves(3) 14/1: 1605: Mid-div, rdn & not pace to chall: btr 1445. *nk* **71**
2395 **TIGHT CIRCLE 14** [5]2-8-7 S Chin 33/1: 056: Chsd ldrs till over 1f out: btr 2395. *hd* **70**
1987* **TOWN HOUSE 32** [1]2-8-7 R Miles(3) 7/2: 50217: Led till over 1f out, fdd, reportedly unsuited by ground. *1¼* **66**
2498 **MOON MISCHIEF 9** [6]2-8-7 J Bramhill 25/1: 038: Held up, no room over 1f out, nvr any threat. *1¼* **62**
1831* **MYTTONS DREAM 39** [9]2-8-9 D Allan 33/1: 6619: Slow into stride & al strugg: btr 1831 (gd/fm). *3½* **55**
2020* **ELISHA 31** [4]2-8-11 G Duffield 7/1: 4510: 10th: Cl up till over 1f out: btr 2020 (gd). *1¼* **53**
10 Ran Time 1m 03.92 (4.12) Owned: Bishopthorpe Racing Two Trained: Ulverston

2745   3.05 Edwards Homes Premier Claiming Stakes 3yo+ (D)
£5486 £1688 £844   1m2f75y   Good/Soft   Inapplicable   Outside

2544* **BEN HUR 8** [3] W M Brisbourne 5-9-2 (63) C Catlin 100/30: 0-010211: Handy & led after 3f, drvn   77
out ins last: nicely bckd, op 5/1: eff at 1m/10f, acts on firm, soft & fibresand: loves sells & clmrs, thriving.
1895 **JABAAR 36** [6] D Nicholls 6-9-12 (86) Alex Greaves 9/4 FAV: 20-03562: Held up, hdwy & rdn to chse   1   85
wnr over 2f out, kept on, al held: bckd, tho' op 13/8: clr rem, gd run: see 1519.
2170 **GIUNCHIGLIO 24** [2] W M Brisbourne 5-9-2 (64) Darren Williams 10/1: 600-3103: Chsd ldrs when lost   7   66
pl after 4f, rallied 2f out, onepace: op 8/1: see 1913.
2526 **DICK THE TAXI 9** [9] R J Smith 10-9-2 (67) R Miles(3) 6/1: 132-3304: Mid-div, eff 3f out, btn 2f out.   10   53
2265 **HIAWATHA 9** [5]5-9-2 (75) G Faulkner 7/1: 1300105: Chsd ldrs, btn 2f out: btr 2030 (gd/fm).   ½   52
2392 **FOREST TUNE 14** [1]6-9-2 (50) G Duffield 8/1: 0006006: Chsd ldrs till over 2f out: see 1083.   nk   51
2356 **MAKULU 15** [8]4-9-7 p (74) S Chin 7/1: 350-0027: Always rear: btr 2356 (fast).   6   48
4464} **BLUEBERRY JIM 274** [10]3-8-4 (39) D Allan 50/1: 06000-8: ch g First Trump - Short And Sharp   1½   41
(Sharpen Up) Dwelt & al rear: reapp: unplcd '03 at up to 6f (rtd 51, sell).
2242 **BUTHAINA 21** [4]4-8-11 (55) T Eaves(5) 50/1: 31-00009: Led till over 7f out, btn 3f out: see 1660.   4   31
9 Ran Time 2m 16.9 (8.4) Owned: D C Rutter & H Clewlow Trained: Nesscliffe

2746   3.40 Warwick International 25th Anniversary Handicap Stakes 3yo 0-85 (D)   [89]
£5486 £1688 £844   1m4f66y   Good/Soft   Inapplicable   Inside

2393* **PEAK OF PERFECTION 14** [4] M A Jarvis 3-8-12 (73) M Henry 4/1: 00-53511: Handy & led over 4f out,   85+
rdn clr ins last: suited by 12f on gd, gd/sft & both AWs: v prog, win again.
2238 **MASTER WELLS 21** [2] J D Bethell 3-9-4 (79) S Chin 8/1: 1002: Held up, styd on for press fnl 1f,   5   83
took 2nd from eased down rival on line, nvr threat: eff at 10/12f on gd/sft & soft ground: see 1428.
2519 **ANOUSA 9** [3] P Howling 3-9-6 (81) R Miles(3) 4/1: 1-010003: Mid-div, efft wide to chall wnr over   hd   84
2f out, held ins last, eased nr fin & lost 2nd line: jockey given 21 day ban for failing to ride out to the line
(would have been a clearcut 2nd): see 2519, 1515.
2377 **WOU OODD 15** [5] M R Channon 3-9-2 (77) C Catlin 14/1: 0-4354: Held up, efft over 3f out, sn rdn   2½   75
& no impress: not convince over longer trip today: see 2377, 2012.
FIRE DRAGON 46 [8]3-9-7 bl (82) G Duffield 5/1: 000-415: b g Sadler's Wells - Cattermole   2   78
(Roberto) Trkd ldrs, wknd over 1f out: 6 wk abs: ex-Irish, earlier landed a h'cap at Killarney (1st time blnks):
winning form at 12f on good/soft ground & a sharp trk: can go well fresh.
2283* **DAYTIME GIRL 18** [1]3-9-9 (78) M Hills 5/2 FAV: 51-3516: Trkd ldrs, lost pl qckly from 4f out: 9   63
connections unable to offer explanation: not handle gd/soft? much btr 2283 (10f, made all).
2131 **MIDSHIPMAN EASY 25** [9]3-9-0 (75) M Coumbe(7) 20/1: 0-3207: Slow away & al bhd: btr 1651, 1259 (10f).12   45
2050* **BOLD BLADE 29** [6]3-8-4 bl (65) R Ffrench 14/1: 3-250018: Led till over 4f out, btn 3f out: btr 2050 (AW).   20   9
8 Ran Time 2m 46.8 (10.4) Owned: HRH Sultan Ahmad Shah Trained: Newmarket

2747   4.15 Warwick International Handicap Stakes 3yo+ 0-95 (C)   [92]
£9737 £2996 £1498   5f16y rnd   Good/Soft   Inapplicable   Inside

2429* **FRASCATI 13** [5] A Berry 4-8-11 (75) P Mathers(7) 9/1: 1023011: Led early, sn forced to trkd ldrs,   82
led ins last, all out, gamely: bckd, op 16/1: suited by 5f on firm, gd/sft & fibresand, any trk: in gd form.
2253 **CAPE ROYAL 21** [3] Mrs J R Ramsden 4-9-7 (85) M Hills 7/2 JT FAV: 0610602: Hld up, hdwy &   nk   91
switched over 1f out, styd on, just held: another fine run: see 2253.
2007 **TIME N TIME AGAIN 31** [1] E J Alston 6-8-4 (68) D Allan 7/2 JT FAV: 5006303: Trkd ldrs, drvn to   hd   73
chall ins last, just held cl home: nicely bckd: back to form from fav draw on a track that suits.
2690 **TALLY 2** [9] M J Polglase 4-7-12 (6oh) (56) R Ffrench 20/1: 3120024: Held up, styd on fnl 1f, nrst   1¾   63
fin: qck reapp: in gd form: see 2690, 2214.
2561 **SKIP OF COLOUR 7** [2]4-8-9 (73) G Faulkner 13/2: 4512065: Led after 1f till over 1f out, fdd: btr 741.   nk   73
2698 **ROMANY NIGHTS 2** [7]4-9-0 bl (78) C Catlin 8/1: 3422046: Rear, kept on late, nvr in this from mod draw.   hd   77
2542 **PRINCE OF BLUES 8** [8]6-7-12 (2oh)p (60) P Varley(7) 25/1: 5003357: Mid-div, no impress fnl 1f: btr 453.   1½   57
2253 **MAKTAVISH 21** [6]5-9-5 p (83) T Eaves(3) 6/1: 1213008: Chsd ldrs 4f, not ideally drawn to lead.   1   75
2593 **WANCHAI LAD 7** [4]3-9-2 (86) Alex Greaves 11/2: 160-3059: Cl up, btn dist, 'hung right'.   5   66
2253 **BRAVE BURT 21** [10]7-9-5 (83) S Chin 16/1: 00013-00: 10th: Sn trk ldrs from wide draw, btn over   ½   61
1f out: poor draw & no better late in fin pos suggests: wnr at Newmarket's July meet in '02 & '01.
1745 **A LITTLE BIT YARIE 43** [12]3-8-7 vis (77) Darren Williams 25/1: 23-30400: 11th: Sn strugg rear: see 1229. 19   10
11 Ran Time 1m 04.01 (4.21) Owned: Lord Crawshaw Trained: Cockerham

2748   4.50 Warwick International Celebration Maiden Stakes 3yo (D)
£5447 £1676 £838   1m2f75y   Good/Soft   Inapplicable   Outside

2193 **GOLDEN ISLAND 23** [6] J W Hills 3-8-9 (85) M Hills 11/8 FAV: 0-321: Handy, led 4f out, readily   88+
pulled clr from dist: hvly bckd tho' op 5/6: eff at 9/10.3f on fast & gd/sft, stiff or sharp/turning trk: lightly
rcd, did this well & is potentially useful: see 2193, 1864.
2385 **RONDELET 14** [4] R M Beckett 3-9-0 (76) G Duffield 9/4: 64-20232: Trkd ldrs, effort to chse wnr   5   82
over 2f out, rdn & no impress from dist, well clr of rem: stays 10f: see 2385 (h'cap).
2283 **TURNER 18** [5] W M Brisbourne 3-9-0 (72) Darren Williams 6/1: 360-633: Held up, efft over 2f out,   11   68
sn no impress on front pair: btr 2283 (C/D, gd).
2678 **PAINT THE LILY 3** [2] J W Hills 3-8-9 M Henry 16/1: 004: b f Barathea - Chocolate Box (Most   6   55
Welcome) Dwelt & held up, no impress fnl 3f: op 25/1, qck reapp, longer priced stablemate of wnr: dam a
13f 3yo wnr & sister to high class stayer Arctic Owl: stoutly bred.
2378 **SHAABAN 15** [3]3-9-0 C Catlin 6/1: 0005: b c Woodman - Ashbilya (Nureyev) Led till 4f out, btn   6   52
2f out: unplcd prev at up to 1m: related to progressive 1m/7f fibresand specialist Najaaba.
5024} **POWER NAP 232** [1]3-8-9 t Kim Tinkler 20/1: 00-6: b f Acatenango - Dreams Are Free (Caerleon)   1¾   45
Bhd, rdn & no impress fnl 3f: reapp: unplcd both '03 mdn starts (rtd 45): dam a 10f 3yo wnr.
6 Ran Time 2m 17.73 (9.23) Owned: Mr D M Kerr and Mr N Brunskill Trained: Lambourn

CHESTER   SATURDAY 26.06.04   Lefthand, Very Tight Track

2749   5.25 Bryn Thomas Crane Hire Handicap Stakes 3yo 0-95 (C)   [99]
£9464 £2912 £1456   7f rnd   Good/Soft   inapplicable   Inside

2427 **MRS MOH 13** [4] T D Easterby 3-8-3 (74) D Allan 10/1: 032-0051: Mid-div, rdn when short of room   85
over 1f out, drvn to lead cl home, all out: eff at 7f on fast, gd/sft & fbsnd: acts on a gall or sharp/turning trk.
2521 **JAZZ SCENE 9** [3] M R Channon 3-9-2 (87) C Catlin 3/1: 0102-002: Rear, prog when no room over 1f   shd   97
out, styd on strongly for press cl home, just failed: op 7/2: eff at 7f, stays 1m: handles firm & gd/sft: see 2521.
2375 **EISTEDDFOD 15** [8] P F I Cole 3-8-4 (75) R Miles(3) 3/1: 133: Held up, smooth hdwy wide over 2f   shd 85+
out, led over 1f out going well, edged left & hdd under hand riding close home: bckd: styd this sharp 7f well despite
unhelpful wide passage: might have prevailed under stronger ride in closing stages, keep on side.
2427 **BALTIC WAVE 13** [1] T D Barron 3-9-7 (92) Darren Williams 11/2: 12144-64: Led till over 1f out, fdd.   4   95
1919 **CONVINCE 35** [2]3-8-13 (84) R Ffrench 11/1: 104-0005: Trkd ldrs, rdn & btn over 1f out: op 9/1: see 1665. ¾   86
2166 **MISARO 24** [5]3-8-2 (73) G Duffield 16/1: 351-056: Handy, wknd over 2f out: op 20/1: see 1627.   1¼   72
2212 **DESERT DREAMER 22** [7]3-9-5 (90) M Hills 11/4 FAV: 420-5067: Trkd ldr inner trav well, found   2½   84
little over 1f out: hvly bckd: caught the eye prev: btr 2212, 1813 & 1583.
7 Ran   Time 1m 03.71(3.91)   Owned: Salifix   Trained: Malton

DONCASTER   SATURDAY 26.06.04   Lefthand, Flat, Galloping Track

Official Going Good

2750   6.50 Doncaster-Racecourse Com E B F Maiden Stakes Fillies 2yo (D)
£4843 £1490 £745   6f str   Good 59   -59 Slow   Stands Side

DEEDAY BAY 0 [7] C F Wall 2-8-11   G Baker 16/1: 1: b f Brave Act - Skerries Bell (Taufan)   87
Led/dsptd lead stands rail, narrow lead 2f out & styd on strongly under hand riding: slow time: op 25/1: 22,000gns
Jan foal, half-sister to 5/6f winning sprinter Gone'N' Dunnett, dam plcd at 7f/1m & wnr abroad: eff at 6f, get
further: acts on gd: fine start, win more races.
TRYLKO 0 [1] J G Given 2-8-11   M Fenton 12/1: 2: ch f Diesis - Gossamer (Seattle Slew) Sn dsptd   ½   84+
lead, briefly outpcd 2f out, rdn & kept on well ins last: Apr foal, half-sister to Batchelor Duke (Irish 2,000
Guineas wnr: eff at 6f, relish 7f+: v pleasing start, will rate higher & win races.
SWAN NEBULA 0 [6] Saeed bin Suroor 2-8-11 T K McEvoy 11/4: 3: b f Seeking The Gold - Bright   hd   83
Tiara (Chief's Crown) Chsd ldrs, briefly outpcd halfway, hdwy to chall when hung left well ins last, just held
cl-home: eff at 6f, get further: acts on gd: gd start, win similar sn.
2132 **MOLLY MARIE 25** [5] T D Easterby 2-8-11   T Quinn 6/4 FAV: 24: Trkd ldrs, short of room when   1½   78
switched wide over 2f out, not pace to chall: well bckd: stronger gallop may have suited: just btr 2132.
GENEROUS OPTION 0 [2]2-8-11 S Chin 10/1: 5: Dwelt, sn handy, rdn & onepace from dist.   hd   77
MITRAILLETTE 0 [4]2-8-11 F Lynch 7/2: 6: Trkd ldrs, shkn up & no impress over 1f out: op 4/1.   4   65
2522 **TCHERINA 9** [8]2-8-11 J Carroll 33/1: 07: Keen & al bhd.   1½   60
NAN JAN 0 [3]2-8-11 N Day 25/1: 8: Dwelt, al rear: debut.   nk   59
8 Ran   Time 1m 17.86 (7.06)   Owned: Mr Peter Botham   Trained: Newmarket

2751   7.20 Go Racing In Yorkshire Maiden Stakes 3yo+ (D)
£5777 £1778 £889   1m2f60y   Good 59   -02 Slow   Inside

INTO THE DARK 0 [15] Saeed bin Suroor 3-8-11 VIS T K McEvoy 15/2: 1: Sn led from outpcd stall &   97+
briefly rdn over 2f out, sn in command, val 8L+: debut: wore a visor & t-strap: eff at 10.5f, will get
further on this evidence: acts on gd & a gall trk: enjoyed forcing tactics in headgear & looks potentially v useful.
2113 **FORGED 26** [14] L M Cumani 3-8-11 N Mackay(3) 12/1: 032: Mid-div, rdn for press, nvr threat   5   81
to wnr: eff at 10f, rtn to 12f will suit: now quals for h'caps, lightly improver in that sphere: see 2113.
2025 **LITTLE BOB 30** [7] J D Bethell 3-8-11 (69) T Quinn 14/1: 0-4423: Trkd ldrs & chsd ldr over 2f   shd   81
out, kept on onepace: longer 10.5f trip may yet suit: see 2025 & 1177.
OUNINPOHJA 0 [8] G A Swinbank 3-8-11 Dean McKeown 50/1: 4: Held up, kept on late for press,   2   78+
nrst fin: clr of rem: debut: half-brother to a 5f juv wnr & dam related to a winning hdler: eff at 10f, looks
sure to apprec 12f+: handles gd grnd: likely improver.
2180 **TEMPLET 23** [10]4-9-9 VIS (68) J Carroll 16/1: 4-2345: Handy 1m, no extra fnl 2f: 1st time visor.   8   68
4974} **MARAAKEB 238** [1]3-8-11 R Hills 8/13 FAV: 3-6: br c Linamix - Raheefa (Riverman) Chsd ldrs,   hd   67
switched for eff over 3f out, sn rdn & no impress: hvly bckd at odds on, reapp: plenty of promise sole '03 start
(plcd, mdn, rtd 89): half-brother to v useful 10f wnr Rawyaan, dam a 10f wnr: eff at 7f, bred for mid-dists: acts
on gd grnd & a stiff trk: disapp rtn: with J H M Gosden.
4974} **SINGLET 238** [9]3-8-11 M Fenton 50/1: 0-7: Held up, eff wide, nvr a threat: reapp.   1½   65
1719 **SPOT IN TIME 44** [12]4-9-4 Natalia Gemelova(7) 100/1: 008: Keen & prom, btn 3f out, abs.   3½   56
1166 **HILLTOP RHAPSODY 73** [4]3-8-6 A Nicholls 100/1: 09: Dwelt, al towards rear, 10 wk abs.   7   47
2230 **BRAVELY DOES IT 22** [13]4-9-9 G Baker 100/1: 00: 10th: Al bhd.   1   51
1737 **DUNE RAIDER 43** [6]3-8-11 F Lynch 5/1: 00: 11th: Mid-div, no impress fnl 3f, abs.   1¼   49
1284 **HOME BY SOCKS 67** [2]5-9-4 (40) L Vickers 100/1: 0060/0/-00: 12th: Chsd wnr till halfway, jmps fit. 1½   42
    Welkinos Boy 0 [11]3-8-11 Dale Gibson 66/1:0   2534 **Conviction 8** [16]3-8-11 E Ahern 25/1:0
    West End Wonder 0 [3]5-9-9 T E Durcan 50/1:0   2230 **Trofana Falcon 22** [5]4-9-9 J Quinn 66/1:0
16 Ran   Time 2m 12.72 (6.32)   Owned: Godolphin   Trained: Newmarket

2752

7.50 Finningley Handicap Stakes 3yo+ 0-80 (D)
£5840 £1797 £898   **6f str**   **Good 59**   +00 Fast   Stands Side   [80]

2535* **AINTNECESSARILYSO 8** [15] N E Berry 6-7-13 (51) M Halford(7) 10/1: 2223611: Towards rear stands **60**
side, hdwy when rider drpd whip over 1f out, styd on under hand riding to lead well ins last: eff at 5/6f on firm,
hvy & both AWs, any trk: v tough & consistent: see 2535, 501 & 379.

2466 **BOLLIN EDWARD 11** [12] T D Easterby 5-8-8 bl (60) D Allan 7/1: 000-6532: Prom, rdn to chall ins   nk **68**
last, not pace of wnr nr line: eff 6/7f: turn not far away: see 2466 & 2059.

2466* **LORD OF THE EAST 11** [9] D Nicholls 5-9-5 (71) Alex Greaves 12/1: 2-032013: Handy & led over 1f   nk **78**
out till well ins last: op 16/1: see 2466 & 1215.

2713* **LEGAL SET 2** [2] Miss A Stokell 8-8-5 (7ex)t (57) Natalia Gemelova(7) 12/1: 0004214: Chsd ldrs,   nk **63**
edged right & kept on for press, not able to chall: see 2713.

967 **SOBA JONES 89** [14]7-9-4 (70) J Edmunds 14/1: 2432565: Led over 3f out, hdd over 1f out, no extra.   ¾ **74**
2023 **A TEEN 31** [6]6-8-6 (58) R Hills 40/1: 0166006: Bhd, kept on late, nrst fin: see 740, 451.   1 **59**
2626 **FULL SPATE 5** [18]9-9-2 (68) K Dalgleish 6/1: 4646327: Dwelt, sn chsd ldrs, hung left & onepcd dist.   nk **68**
2690 **FAR NOTE 2** [11]6-8-11 bl (63) J Bramhill 9/1: 0144048: Dwelt, chsd ldrs, no extra dist: qck reapp.   1 **60**
2289 **CORANGLAIS 18** [8]4-8-9 P (61) R Winston 20/1: 50-00009: Chsd ldrs, hmpd 2f out, kept on, no dngr.   nk **57**
1977 **ARMAGNAC 32** [10]6-9-11 (77) J Quinn 11/1: 0003600: 10th: Held up in tch, hmpd 2f out, kept on   hd **72+**
late, ch had gone: much closer with a clr run: slipping to a handy mark & can improve on this, keep in mind.

1743+**ANTONIO CANOVA 43** [4]8-9-12 (78) T Williams 10/1: 00/0-0010: 11th: Chsd ldrs, fdd fnl 2f: abs.   1½ **68**
2535 **STOKESIES WISH 8** [17]4-8-12 (64) Hayley Turner(5) 14/1: 02-00020: 12th: Mid-div, no impress fnl 2f.   1½ **49**
1820 **OASES 39** [7]5-8-3 (55) T Hamilton(1) 33/1: 0206000: 13th: Dwelt, rear, no hdwy: see 940.   ½ **38**
2214 **TIME TO REMEMBER 22** [5]6-8-5 (57) J Carroll 25/1: R-000600: 14th: Led till over 3f out, sn fdd.   ¾ **38**
2409 **QUANTICA 14** [1]5-8-6 (58) Kim Tinkler 16/1: 02-60000: 15th: Rear & bhd halfway: see 1145.   5 **24**
2477* **SIR DON 10** [16]5-9-0 vis (66) A Nicholls 14/1: 0-000010: 16th: Handy 4f, sn wknd.   ½ **30**
1726* **PINCHBECK 43** [13]5-10-0 p (80) P Robinson 5/1 FAV: 033-0410: 17th: Mid-div & sn rdn, fdd fnl 2f &   1½ **40**
eased dist: v disappointing effort under top-weight: btr 1726.

2235 **COMPTON ARROW 21** [3]8-7-13 (51) S Righton 50/1: 00-00000: 18th: b g Petardia - Impressive Lady   1½ **6**
(Mr Fluorocarbon) Slow away & lkd reluctant to race, al bhd: h'cap wnr for D Nicholls in '03: dual h'cap wnr '02:
suited by 6/7f, stays 1m: acts on firm, soft & any trk: eff with/without t-strap, tried blnks & visor.
1 Oct'03 Catt 7g/f 64-59 E: 2 Aug'03 Catt 7fm 60-58 F: 1 Jul'02 Brig 6.9g/f 65-59 F: 1 Jun'02 Pont 6g/f 60-54 E:
2 Aug'01 Good 7g/s 72- D: 2 Nov'00 Ling 6ap 69a- E:
18 Ran   Time 1m 14.34 (3.54)   Owned: Mrs Jan Adams   Trained: Earlswood

2753

8.20 Ashgate Croft School Megan Pool Appeal Classified Stakes 3yo+ 0-80 (D)
£5699 £1754 £877   **1m rnd**   **Good 59**   -02 Slow   Outside

2521 **ODDSMAKER 9** [2] P D Evans 3-8-9 (83) Dean McKeown 9/1: 5-325101: Trkd ldrs, rdn to lead over 1f   **90**
out, styd on strongly: suited by 1m/10f, tried 12f: acts on fast, loves gd or softer: tough & progressive: see 1707.

2108 **DEVANT 26** [10] M A Jarvis 4-8-13 (79) P Robinson 12/1: 605-0402: Held up, styd on wide for   1½ **80**
press, not pace to chal: worth another try at 10f on this evidence: see 1877.

1481 **WINNING VENTURE 56** [13] A W Carroll 7-9-5 (83) M Fenton 20/1: 6305-603: Handy & led 5f out, clr   1 **84**
halfway, rdn & hdd over 1f out, no extra, flashed tail: op 16/1, 8 wk abs: likes easy grnd: see 1138.

1475 **CATS WHISKERS 56** [1] M W Easterby 5-9-3 (81) Dale Gibson 12/1: 0000-034: Handy 6f, sn onepcd.   ½ **81**
2560 **CRIPSEY BROOK 7** [7]6-9-9 (87) Kim Tinkler 14/1: 0-660025: Keen, prom, hmpd & lost pl after 3f,   1 **85**
keeping on when short of room ins last: closer without trouble in running: see 2560, 1704.

1351 **AFRICAN SAHARA 63** [6]5-9-2 t (80) G Carter 33/1: 1606006: Rear, eff 3f out, not able to chall, abs.   dht **78**
2091 **TOPTON 27** [1]10-9-2 bl (76) R Winston 16/1: 3100046: Rear, kept on late, nvr threat, ddhtd for 6th.   nk **77**
1351 **DUBROVSKY 63** [5]4-9-7 (85) E Ahern 13/8 FAV: 01/030-48: Eff 3f out, wknd: bckd, abs, btr 1351.   1¼ **79**
2558 **MACHINIST 8** [9]4-9-2 (77) Alex Greaves 16/1: 1/040-009: Trkd ldrs, prog wide 3f out, wknd fnl 2f.   1½ **71**
1598 **RETIREMENT 50** [14]5-9-4 (82) N Callan 7/2: 4212-130: 10th: Chsd ldrs, btn 2f out: abs: btr 1423.   7 **61**
2605 **PERCY DOUGLAS 6** [11]4-9-2 (45) Ann Stokell 100/1: 0000060: 11th: Led 3f, struggling fnl 3f, qck reapp.   7 **47$**
2543 **BLUE EMPEROR 8** [8]3-8-6 (45) R Fitzpatrick 100/1: 0050000: 12th: Sn bhd & struggling.   29 **0**
4329*)MURASHAH 281 [3]4-9-2 t (80) R Hills 11/2: 1-0: 13th: ch c Storm Cat - Shadayid (Shadeed) V slow   dist **0**
away & ref to race: reapp: sole start mdn wnr on debut '03: eff over a gall 1m on fast grnd, wears a t-strap: has
gone well fresh: worrying behaviour tonight: with Saeed Bin Suroor. 1 Sep'03 Nott 8.2g/f 78- D:
13 Ran   Time 1m 40.96 (4.86)   Owned: Mr D Maloney   Trained: Abergavenny

2754

8.50 Castle Working Men's Club Stayers' Handicap Stakes 4yo+ 0-80 (D)
£5512 £1696 £848   **1m6f132y**   **Good 59**   -29 Slow   Inside   [80]

2699 **GLORY QUEST 8** [8] Miss Gay Kelleway 7-9-7 (73) M Fenton 7/2: 0341031: Handy, led 5f out & rdn   **84**
clr 3f out, held on all out line: op 4/1: qck reapp: eff at 10f/2m on fast, hvy & loves fibresand: tough &
genuine, gvn a fine ride tonight by M Fenton: see 2229, 870 & 34.

1629* **DR SHARP 49** [3] T P Tate 4-9-10 (76) Dale Gibson 5/2 FAV: 0114-012: Chsd ldrs, rdn & outpcd over   shd **86**
2f out, drvn & styd on well ins last, just failed: nicely bckd, clr of rem: 7 wk abs: eff at 14f, rtn to 2m could
suit: fight little in defeat under top-weight: see 1629.

2239 **CLARINCH CLAYMORE 21** [6] J M Jefferson 8-9-5 (71) P Hanagan 7/2: 046-2053: Rear, prog 4f out, no   3½ **76**
impress dist: clr rem: appreciated return to staying trip: see 1772.

2233 **NIGHT SIGHT 21** [5] Mrs S Lamyman 7-9-4 (70) E Ahern 11/2: 004-0234: Held up, hdwy to chase ldrs   9 **64**
3f out, no impress fnl 2f: op 9/2: btr 2041 (12f, fast).

2699 **FIGHT THE FEELING 2** [1]6-7-12 (5oh) (45) D Fox(5) 20/1: 0050605: Led till 5f out, sn btn: qck reapp.   ¾ **43**
997 **BOLSHOI BALLET 87** [4]6-8-3 bl (55) J Fanning 9/1: 14/040-06: b g Dancing Spree - Broom Isle   ¾ **47**
(Damister) Chsd ldrs, btn 3f out: jumps fit (h'cap hdle wnr, rtd 115h, 2m, firm & gd/soft, blnks or cheek pieces):
AW h'cap plcd '03 (rtd 65a): auct mdn & h'cap wnr for T D Barron in '02, subs h'cap wnr for current yard: eff at
1m, suited by 11/14.7f on fast, soft & likes fibresand: with J Mackie.
1 May'02 Wolv 14.7af 63a-60 F: 1 Jan'02 Sout 12af 60a-54 E: 2 Jan'02 Sout 11af 53a-50 F: 1 Jan'02 Sout 11af 58a- F:
2 Dec'01 Sout 8af 53a-49 F:
2708 **LADY NETBETSPORTS 2** [7]5-8-9 (61) K Dalgleish 14/1: 4000-037: Mid-div, struggling fnl 3f, qck reapp.   14 **35**
2156 **DISTANT COUSIN 24** [2]7-8-8 vis (60) J Quinn 11/1: 56-05308: In tch, rdn & fdd fnl 4f: btr 1980.   19 **7**

DONCASTER SATURDAY 26.06.04 Lefthand, Flat, Galloping Track

8 Ran   Time 3m 15.94 (12.94)   Owned: WRB Racing 40 (wrbracingcom)   Trained: Newmarket

2755	9.20 Branton Handicap Stakes Fillies 3yo+ 0-70 (E)							[67]
	£3630 £1117 £559	**7f str**	**Good 59**	-24 Slow	Stands Side			

151 **GALLERY BREEZE** 203 [15] J L Spearing 5-9-11 (64) V Slattery 25/1: 041120-1: Mid-div, hdwy from **73**
halfway & led dist, drvn & held on all out: 7 month abs, op 33/1: eff at 5/6f, now suited by 7f: acts on firm,
gd/soft & polytrack, prob any trk: goes well fresh: see 55.

2539* **IN THE PINK** 8 [10] M R Channon 4-10-0 (67) C Catlin 3/1 FAV: 351-0012: Held up, hdwy when forced   nk   **76**+
to switch over 1f out, drvn & styd on well in last, just failed: well bckd, op 7/1: fine eff under top-weight, looks
to be on an upward curve & prob would have won this with a clr passage: see 2539.

4852} **PERTEMPS MAGUS** 248 [11] R A Fahey 4-9-4 (57) P Hanagan 6/1: P50000-3: b f Silver Wizard -   4   **58**
Brilliant Future (Welsh Saint) Trkd ldrs, styd on for press, not pace of front pair: reapp: unplcd '03 (rtd 69,
h'cap): fill mdn wnr '02: eff at 5f, stays 7f well: acts on gd & soft grnd, can go well fresh.
1 Apr'02 Warw 5g/s 71- E: 2 Mar'02 Donc 5sft 75- C:

2335 **JESSIE** 16 [18] Don Enrico Incisa 5-8-4 vis (43) Kim Tinkler 16/1: 2224054: Dwelt, rear, hdwy when   1¼   **41**
no room & switched over 1f out, nrst fin: closer with a clr run: acts on gd, gd/soft & fibresand.

2440 **ZAMYATINA** 12 [12]5-8-3 (42) M Halford(7) 16/1: 00-00005: Chsd ldrs, kept on onepace: see 1282.   ½   **39**

2539 **ANNIJAZ** 8 [14]7-9-0 (53) K Dalgleish 11/2: 2240046: Mid-div, chall over 1f out, no extra: op   2   **46**
7/1: won this last term of a 2lb lower mark: see 1540.

2080 **SPARK UP** 28 [8]4-9-7 bl (60) J Fanning 16/1: 4410607: Led/dsptd lead till 2f out, fdd: see 1322 (AW).   nk   **52**

2225 **FILLIEMOU** 22 [19]3-8-11 (59) M Fenton 16/1: 0400-008: Mid-div, no impress fnl 2f: see 2225.   1   **49**

2604 **HULA BALLEW** 6 [16]4-8-12 p (51) L Enstone(3) 9/1: 0500559: Cl-up, fdd fnl 2f: qck reapp: btr 2604.   1   **39**

1659* **EXTREMELY RARE** 47 [9]3-9-7 (69) D Allan 12/1: 2010: 10th: Led/dsptd lead till dist, fdd: 7 wk abs.   1   **55**

1983 **ONE ALONE** 32 [2]3-7-12 (10h) (45) D Fox(5) 50/1: 0000-000: 11th: b f Atraf - Songsheet (Dominion)   2   **28**
Al bhd: unplcd in '03 (rtd 63a, J G Given, also rtd 41): half-sister to a winning juv sprinter, dam a 5f wnr.

2215 **TRUE** 24 [4]3-9-3 (65) E Ahern 14/1: 43-0020: 12th: Chsd ldrs, btn 3f out: btr 2215.   shd   **47**

2451 **TAPAU** 12 [5]6-9-9 P (62) S Chin 25/1: 30-50000: 13th: Cl-up till halfway, sn bhd, cheek pieces.   4   **37**

2335 **MOONLIGHT SONG** 16 [6]7-8-5 (44) D Fentiman(7) 66/1: 60-30000: 14th: Al bhd & nvr a factor.   1¼   **16**

1678 **IMPULSIVE BID** 45 [13]3-9-1 (63) T E Durcan 12/1: 404-4020: 15th: Struggling halfway, 6 wk abs.   3   **29**

2674 **ROUTE SIXTY SIX** 3 [20]8-8-4 (43) Dale Gibson 8/1: 500-0620: 16th: Al rear, qck reapp: btr 2674.   3½   **2**

1660 **PARK STAR** 47 [7]4-9-2 (55) R Winston 20/1: 200U440: 17th: Al bhd, 7 wk abs: btr 1660 (soft).   2   **10**

2204 **TOKEWANNA** 22 [1]4-9-1 (54) B Swarbrick(5) 33/1: 64040-00: 18th: Cl-up till halfway, wknd qckly.   nk   **8**

18 Ran   Time 1m 28.99(5.79)   Owned: Appleby Lodge Stud   Trained: Kinnersley

---

WINDSOR SATURDAY 26.06.04 Sharp, Figure 8 Track

Official Going Good/Firm

2756	2.15 'at The Races:Dedicated To Racing' Maiden Stakes 3yo (D)					
	£4290 £1320 £660	**6f str**	**Firm -12**	-59 Slow	Inside	

2309 **KINGS CAPRICE** 17 [14] G B Balding 3-9-0 (85) S Carson 3/1 FAV: 523-0341: Trkd ldrs & smooth hdwy   **87**+
to lead over 1f out, easily: bckd, op 7/2: eff at 6f, get 7f: acts on firm or fast, gall or sharp trk: reportedly
saddled in the stables & has had temperament probs but looks potentially useful: see 1957.

4601} **STARGEM** 266 [11] J Pearce 3-8-9 R Price 100/30: 02-2: b f Compton Place - Holy Smoke   2½   **70**
(Statobiest) Led/dsptd lead till over 1f out, sn no ch with wnr: reapp: rnr-up 2nd of just 2 '03 starts (fill
mdn): eff over 6f, dam a 1m wnr: acts on firm grnd, sharp or stiff trk: now quals for h'caps.
2 Oct'03 Newm 6fm 87- D:

2352 **CORKY** 16 [15] R Hannon 3-9-0 R L Moore 4/1: 43: Chsd ldrs, rdn & styd on, no threat to wnr: shd   **75**
eff at 6/7f, rtn to further shld suit: prob handles firm & fast grnd: see 2352.

      KOSTAR 0 [9] C G Cox 3-9-0 R Smith 25/1: 4: ch g Komaite - Black And Amber (Weldnaas) Pushed   hd   **74**
along & bhd, kept on well from over 1f out, no threat: debut: dam a mdn, plcd at 6f as a 3yo & half-sister to a 5f
wnr & wnr over hdles: eff at 6f on fm, stay further: likely improver over 7f. .

2291 **CALLED UP** 18 [12]3-9-0 (64) D Sweeney 4/1: 4005: Led/dsptd lead till over 2f out, no extra bef   1   **69**
dist: rest well covered: prob handles firm & soft grnd: h'caps shld suit: see 1464.

2633} **ZAZOUS** 358 [10]3-9-0 V Slattery 14/1: 4: Zafonic - Confidentiality (Lyphard) Chsd ldrs   3½   **60**
till 2f out, reapp: plcd 2nd of just 2 '03 starts (mdn, rtd 74): eff over a stiff 6f on fast grnd.

2117 **RIDGE BOY** 26 [6]3-9-0 P Dobbs 12/1: 567: Mid-div, sn rdn, not pace to threaten, drop in trip.   3   **51**

      HIGHLAND LASS 0 [2]3-8-9 G Baker 25/1: 8: Went badly left start, bhd, no dngr.   nk   **45**

1876 **RADLETT LADY** 37 [7]3-8-9 B Doyle 33/1: 0009: Chsd ldrs till halfway.   2   **39**

1281 **BROWN DRAGON** 67 [3]3-9-0 (60) Paul Eddery 16/1: 00-62200: 10th: Sn outpcd & nvr a factor, op 12/1.   nk   **43**

4145} **PARADISE BREEZE** 291 [8]3-8-9 N Pollard 25/1: 0-0: 11th: Dwelt, rear, sn outpcd, reapp.   2½   **30**

1982 **Indian Edge** 32 [1]3-9-0 (63) M Halford(7) 16/1:0   2152 **Dane Rhapsody** 24 [5]3-8-9 P Doe 33/1:0

13 Ran   Time 1m 13.09 (2.79)   Owned: Miss B Swire   Trained: Andover

---

2757	2.50 Listed Totepool Midsummer Stakes 3yo+ (A)					
	£17400 £6600 £3300	**1m67y rnd**	**Firm -12**	+18 Fast	Inside	

2252 **GATEMAN** 21 [7] M Johnston 7-9-8 (113) K Dalgleish 5/2 FAV: 0212031: Led till over 2f out, drvn   **117**
to lead again cl-home, most gamely: well bckd, op 7/2: crse rec time: eff at 7/9f on firm & hvy, any trk: loves
to front-run: tough & v smart, as game as they come: see 2252, 1168.

2154* **SHOT TO FAME** 24 [5] P W Harris 5-9-3 (101) J Mongan 9/1: 00-50112: Handy & led over 2f out, drvn   hd   **111**
& hdd cl-home: loves to race with/force the pace: much improved of late, win a List on this form: see 2154.

2252 **VANDERLIN** 21 [6] A M Balding 5-9-3 (107) L Keniry 14/1: 040-3353: Trkd ldrs, chall dist, no   1½   **108**
extra well in last: stays 1m, poss best at 7f: see 2252, 2022 & 1043.

2470 **BEAUCHAMP PILOT** 11 [9] G A Butler 6-9-3 (111) N Pollard 12/1: 3020-604: Trkd ldrs, outpcd 2f   nk   **107**
out, kept on late, not able to chall: more encouraging, wants further: see 2252.

1486 **BABODANA 56** [3]4-9-6 (111) P Doe 8/1: 210-1635: Rear, eff wide from over 2f out, not able to chall: 8 wk abs: handles firm & fast, likes gd & soft grnd: see 951. ½ **109**
2410* **BINARY VISION 14** [2]3-8-7 R Havlin 5/1: 16: Hld up well off pace, some late gains: handles firm & fast grnd: up in class & a gd run under v unenterprising ride, improve with top jock up: see 2410. ¾ **105**
4570} **TARJMAN 267** [8]4-9-3 (111) R L Moore 5/1: 111234-7: b c Cadeaux Genereux - Dodo (Alzao) Chsd ldrs till 2f out: progressive '03, landed 2 val h'caps & a stks, subs Gr 3 plcd (rtd 112): mdn wnr in '02: eff at 6f, yet to convince at 1m, 7f suits best: acts on fm & gd: can go well fresh on any trk: smart at best, high head carraige here, poss something amiss? 2 Aug'03 Newb 7fm 110-(109) A: 1 Jul'03 Yarm 7.0gd 112-(102) C: 1 Jun'03 Epso 7g/f 109-96 C: 1 Apr'03 Newm 6gd 107-89 C: 1 Sep'02 Good 6fm 91- D: *3* **99**
3580*}**ALWAYS FIRST 318** [1]3-8-7 B Doyle 9/1: 1-8: b c Barathea - Pink Cristal (Dilum) Rear, rdn halfway, nvr a threat: op 7/1, reapp: sole start mdn wnr in '03: dam useful 7f/1m wnr: eff over a stiff 7f, shld get further: acts on fast grnd & can go well fresh. 1 Aug'03 Sand 7.1g/f 95- C: *nk* **98**
1649 **EXCELSIUS 47** [4]4-9-6 (103) W Ryan 25/1: 3301-039: Rear, rdn & btn 3f out: see 1649 & 108. *3½* **94**
9 Ran Time 1m 40.66 ((u2.32)C Rec) Owned: Kennet Valley Thoroughbreds V Trained: Middleham

2758

3.25 Royal Marbella Group Quality Homes Abroad Stakes Heritage Handicap 3yo+ 0-105 (B) **[105]**
£29000 £11000 £5500 **6f str** **Firm -12** **-34 Slow** Inside

2684 **ZILCH 2** [13] M L W Bell 6-9-1 (92) R Mullen 7/1: 1221401: Towards rear & sn pushed along, styd on well for press fnl 1f to lead well ins last: op 10/1, qck reapp: eff at 6/7f on firm, hvy & polytrack: see 1251. **101**
2451* **CAUSTIC WIT 12** [14] M S Saunders 6-8-6 p (83) P Makin(5) 5/2 FAV: 1011112: Sn handy & led over 1f out, rdn & hdd well ins last: nicely bckd: continues in grand form: see 2451. ¾ **89**
2184 **CRIMSON SILK 23** [17] D Haydn Jones 4-8-13 p (90) Paul Eddery 25/1: 3-000003: Rear, styd on for press, not able to chall: imprvd eff from fav'able high draw: see 2184. *nk* **95**
2468 **SMOKIN BEAU 11** [18] N P Littmoden 7-9-6 bl (97) T G McLaughlin 20/1: 0-620004: Led till over 1f out, no extra: imprvd eff, well drawn today: eff in blnks: see 1137. *1½* **97**
2593* **GREEN MANALISHI 7** [12]3-8-7 (91) P Dobbs 7/1: 2210315: Trkd ldrs, no extra dist: stays 6f, 5f suits. *1* **88**
2591 **MILLION PERCENT 7** [15]5-8-3 VIS (80) S Whitworth 10/1: 30-06226: Chsd ldrs, no impress dist: visor. *3* **68**
2359 **WATCHING 15** [9]7-8-8 (85) K Dalgleish 12/1: 0-302557: Chsd ldrs till over 1f out: btr 1683. *shd* **73**
1958 **MISS GEORGE 33** [7]6-8-5 (82) B Doyle 12/1: 1003068: Dwelt, bhd, some hdwy, nvr threat, mod draw. *1¼* **66**
1958 **BONUS 33** [10]4-9-11 T (102) R L Moore 20/1: 515-6009: Mid-div, no impress from halfway: t-strap. ¾ **84**
1703 **PIVOTAL POINT 44** [2]4-8-13 (90) D Sweeney 16/1: 21352-00: 10th: Rear, hdwy halfway, btn 2f out from poor draw: 6 wk abs: will likely do better: see 1703. *3½* **61**
2357 **MARSAD 15** [1]10-8-12 (89) P Doe 12/1: 03-03020: 11th: Sn rdn & hung badly right, al rear: poor draw. *6* **44**
2256 **MINE BEHIND 21** [8]4-8-4 (81) N Pollard 12/1: 1622000: 12th: Sn struggling: btr 1898. *3½* **25**
2591* **WILLHEWIZ 7** [6]4-8-4 vis (81) S Carson 14/1: 0560110: 13th: Chsd ldrs till 2f out from moderate draw. ¾ **23**
2558 **ARCTIC DESERT 8** [11]4-8-7 VIS (84) S Drowne 33/1: 352-0000: 14th: In tch till halfway, saddle slipped. ¾ **24**
2698 **Further Outlook 2** [5]10-8-7 (84) I Mongan 20/1:0 2407 **Danzig River 14** [4]3-8-11 (95) W Ryan 25/1:0
16 Ran Time 1m 11.61 (1.31) Owned: Mary Mayall Linda Redmond Julie Martin Trained: Newmarket

2759

4.00 Letheby & Christopher Handicap Stakes 3yo+ 0-95 (C) **[93]**
£17225 £5300 £2650 **1m3f135y** **Firm -12** **-00 Slow** Inside

1295 **VENGEANCE 66** [1] Mrs A J Perrett 4-9-11 (90) P Dobbs 13/2: 2105-031: Trkd ldrs & led over 1f out, rdn & styd on strongly: abs: eff at 11.5f/12f on firm & hvy grnd, any trk: runs well fresh: likes Windsor: progressive, stable finding its form: see 1295. **101**
695 **NAWAMEES 126** [10] G L Moore 6-9-5 P (84) K Dalgleish 20/1: 5236-422: Held up, short of room over 2f out, switched & kept on for press, nvr threaten wnr: 6 wk jumps abs, h'cap hdle wnr (2m/2m2.5f, fast & gd/soft, rtd 126h): acts on firm, soft & polytrack: 14f may prove ideal: see 605. *1¼* **91**
2628 **FRONTIER 5** [9] B J Llewellyn 7-8-7 t (72) S Whitworth 8/1: 000-2123: Rear, onepace: stays 11.5f. *1¾* **77**
2208 **DESERT QUEST 22** [4] A M Balding 4-9-13 bl (92) S Drowne 8/1: 1461-024: Rear, hdwy 3f out, onepace bef dist: acts on firm & soft grnd: see 1746. ½ **96**
2290 **CAMROSE 18** [8]3-8-8 (87) R L Moore 10/1: 321-4325: Chsd ldrs, outpcd 4f out, kept on late, no threat: looks worth a try at 12f+: see 1865, 1318. ½ **90**
2363* **GROOMS AFFECTION 15** [11]4-9-5 (84) I Mongan 9/4 FAV: 0/01-16: Dwelt, sn chsd ldrs, eff 2f out, no extra fnl 1f: clr of rem: well bckd: should stay 12f & prib wants easier grnd: see 2363. *nk* **86**
1746 **PERFECT STORM 43** [2]5-10-0 (93) D Sweeney 8/1: 12-00547: Held up in tch, eff to chase ldrs 2f out, sn btn: op 10/1, abs, top-weight: ideally suited by easier ground, connections reportedly pondered withdrawl. *6* **86**
2192* **SHREDDED 23** [12]4-9-1 (80) R Havlin 11/2: 3/54-0218: Chsd ldrs halfway & led over 2f out, hdd & fdd over 1f out: btr 2192 (14f). *nk* **72**
4056] **RANVILLE 652** [13]6-9-13 (92) B Doyle 33/1: 0/02024/-9: ch g Deploy - Kibitka (Baby Turk) Drpd towards rear early, mod late prog: v long abs: missed '03, dual h'cap rnr-up '02: v progressive '01, landed 5 h'caps: suited by 14f/2m: acts on firm & fast grnd, loves gd/soft & hvy, easy or gall trk: prev a progressive stayer & shld leave this bhd over 14f+.
2 Aug'02 Ches 18.6g/f 98-95 B:2 Jul'02 Sand 16.3g/s 97-90 C:1 Oct'01 Newb 16hvy 92-81 C:1 Oct'01 Newc 16g/s 84-73 E:
1 Sep'01 Ches 15.8g/s 74-68 D: 1 Aug'01 Hayd 14g/f 70-64 D: 1 Aug'01 Nott 14sft 66-58 E: 2 Jul'01 Yarm 14fm 59-54 E: *2* **81**
2392 **GOLANO 14** [3]4-9-1 (80) R Mullen 16/1: 43110-20: 10th: Mid-div, btn 3f out: 'struck into'. *2½* **65**
877 **GIG HARBOR 99** [6]5-9-3 (82) S Carson 25/1: 6-101560: 11th: Led till over 2f out, sn btn: jumps fit. *3½* **62**
2255 **HERODOTUS 21** [5]6-9-3 (82) N Pollard 100/1: 00050-00: 12th: b g Zafonic - Thalestria (Mill Reef) Sn handy, btn 4f out, t.o.: unplcd in '03 for C Brittain (rtd 98a & 89): '02 AW h'cap scorer, turf unplcd (rtd 101, cond stks): suited by a sharp 12f: acts on polytrack & hvy grnd, poss fast grnd: gd weight carrier who likes a sharp trk. 1 Feb'02 Ling 12ap 105a-98 C: 1 Apr'01 Kemp 8hvy 103- A: *dist* **0**
12 Ran Time 2m 25.83 (u1.47) Owned: Mr T Staplehurst Trained: Pulborough

WINDSOR   SATURDAY 26.06.04   Sharp, Figure 8 Track

2760   **4.35 Saracen-Promotions Co Uk Classified Stakes 3yo+ 0-70 (E)**
£3504 £1078 £539   **6f str**   **Firm -12**   **-48 Slow**   Inside

2535 **POLAR IMPACT 8** [10] G L Moore 5-9-3 (69) R L Moore 7/2 FAV: 011-1051: Trkd ldr, rdn to lead   **77**
dist, rdn out: op 4/1: suited by 5/6f, 7f wnr in Spain: acts on firm, soft & dirt: see 25
2189 **THE FISIO 23** [5] A M Balding 4-9-6 vis (73) S Drowne 12/1: 0204102: Led/dsptd lead till dist,   *1*   **76**
kept on: acts on firm, gd/soft & both AWs: see 1749, 1103 & 415.
2232 **INDIAN STEPPES 21** [3] Julian Poulton 5-9-0 (67) I Mongan 13/2: 003-6643: Dwelt & short of room   *1½*   **65**
early, eff to press ldrs halfway, onepcd from dist: acts on firm, soft & both AWs, loves fibresand: see 1773.
516 **INDIAN MAIDEN 147** [2] M S Saunders 4-9-2 (72) P Makin(5) 16/1: 10600-04: br f Indian Ridge -   *2½*   **59**
Jinsiyah (Housebuster) Rear, hung left from 2f out, kept on late: dual AW wnr '03, incl h'cap, subs turf h'cap
scorer: mdn plcd '02 (C/D, rtd 63): suited by 6f on fibresand & gd grnd, prob handles firm: likes a sharp/turning
trk. 1 Apr'03 Nott 6.1gd 77-73 E: 1 Mar'03 Wolv 6af 74a-68 E: 1 Jan'03 Wolv 6af 68a- D: 2 Nov'02 Wolv 6af 67a- D:
2359 **CATCH THE CAT 15** [8]5-9-5 bl (72) G Parkin 6/1: 3020165: Keen, led/dsptd lead 4f, fdd: btr 2084 (5f).   *3½*   **51**
2398 **SILVER CHIME 14** [4]4-9-0 (70) R Mullen 5/1: 0-004156: Sn rdn chasing ldrs, btn 2f out: likes to dominate.1½   **41**
1025 **CORMORANT WHARF 85** [6]4-9-3 P (70) A Quinn(5) 14/1: 6500507: Sn outpcd: abs, chkpcs, gelded.   *5*   **31**
1876 **ISAZ 37** [7]4-9-5 (72) D Sweeney 12/1: 25/4-5558: Dwelt, hmpd early, nvr on terms & eased dist.   *9*   **7**
2053 **ANOTHER GLIMPSE 29** [1]6-9-3 t (69) S Carson 9/2: 1002329: Bhd, eff 3f out, sn btn & eased.   *6*   **0**
9 Ran Time 1m 12.44 (2.14)   Owned: Mr N J Jones   Trained: Brighton

2761   **5.05 Royal Marbella Group Quality Homes Abroad Handicap Stakes Fillies 3yo+ 0-85 (D)**   **[85]**
£5525 £1700 £850   **1m2f7y**   **Firm -12**   **-18 Slow**   Inside

1927 **MISS PEBBLES 35** [4] B R Johnson 4-8-8 vis (65) N Pollard 7/1: 6-140051: Bmpd start & rear, smooth   **79+**
hdwy to chall dist, v cosily, val much further: eff at 1m/ sharp 10f on firm, soft & polytrack: well suited by
visor: win again, see 978.
2290* **MANGO MISCHIEF 18** [5] J L Dunlop 3-9-2 (85) R L Moore 3/1 FAV: 10-12: Keen, rear, hdwy to chall   *nk*   **94**
2f out, led over 1f out till ins last, no ch with cosy wnr: clr of rem: well bckd on h'cap bow: handles a
stiff/undul or sharp trk: lightly rcd & on the up-grade after 2290.
2265 **DORIS SOUTER 19** [8] R Hannon 4-8-11 (68) R Smith 11/1: 2050303: Led till over 1f out, no extra.   *6*   **68**
2483* **OLIVIA ROSE 10** [1] J Pearce 5-9-8 (79) R Thomas(5) 4/1: 1312314: Chsd ldrs, kept on, nvr threat.   *shd*   **79**
4185*]**BALLERINA SUPREMA 645** [10]4-10-0 (85) S Drowne 14/1: 31/-5: b f Sadler's Wells - Gravieres   *1¼*   **83**
(Saint Estephe) Mid-div, switched & some late gains: long abs: missed '03, lightly rcd mdn scorer for M Bell in
'02: eff at 1m on fast & gd grnd, mid-dist pedigree: acts on gall trks: not knocked about & showed promise.
1 Sep'02 Nott 8.2g/f 85- D:
2592 **RANI TWO 7** [2]5-9-1 (72) N Chalmers(5) 14/1: 0410-006: In tch, eff over 2f out, sn wknd: see 2284.   *¾*   **69**
1927 **DREAMING OF YOU 35** [6]3-8-4 (73) B Doyle 10/1: 0-107: Chsd ldrs, short of room when wkng 1f out.   *hd*   **69**
2592 **STRATEGY 7** [3]4-9-7 VIS (78) P Dobbs 14/1: 6123-068: Bmpd start, chsd ldrs till over 1f out, vis: btr 2592. *nk*   **73**
1986 **LARA BAY 32** [9]4-8-3 T (60) S Whitworth 40/1: 50/05-009: Rear, hmpd 2f out, no impress, t-strap.   *1½*   **53**
2265 **CZARINA WALTZ 19** [7]5-9-12 (83) R Mullen 7/2: 51040-20: 10th: Chsd ldrs, hung right & btn 2f out.   *1¾*   **74**
10 Ran Time 2m 06.56(0.56)   Owned: Mr A A Lyons   Trained: Epsom

NEWMARKET   SATURDAY 26.06.04   Righthand, Stiff, Galloping Track

Official Going GOOD/FIRM.

2762   **1.35 Listed Mcp Fred Archer Stakes 4yo+ (A)**
£17400 £6600 £3300   **1m4f**   **Good/Firm 29**   **-07 Slow**   Stands Side

1596 **FIRST CHARTER 50** [4] Sir Michael Stoute 5-8-11 (109) K Fallon 2/1 JT FAV: 31120-01: b c Polish   **114**
Precedent - By Charter (Shirley Heights) Trkd ldrs, went on well ins fnl 1f, drvn out & won going away: well bckd,
7 wk abs: dual '03 wnr (stks & List), also rnr-up in a Gr 3: '02 mdn & List wnr: eff at 12/14f on gd, firm grnd &
on any trk: runs well fresh: smart & Group success surely awaits. 2 Sep'03 Kemp 12g/f 112-(109) A:
1 Aug'03 Good 14fm 110-(109) A: 1 Jul'03 Newm 12g/f 110- C: 1 Aug'02 Good 14fm 110- A:
2 Jul'02 Good 12fm 110- A: 1 Apr'02 Leic 10g/f 96- D: 2 Nov'01 Newm 8gd 94- C:
4227} **WESTMORELAND ROAD 287** [1] Mrs A J Perrett 4-8-11 (112) K Darley 2/1 JT FAV: 2/11310-2: b c   *½*   **111**
Diesis - Tia Gigi (Assert) Keen in rear, gd hdwy to lead 2f out & sn kicked for home, worn down cl-home: well bckd
on reapp: won 3 times in '03 (mdn on reapp & 2 stks): eff at 11/12f, shld stay 14f: acts on gd & firm grnd, runs v
well fresh: fine reapp after racing a shade keenly & List/Gr 3 wins shld follow: smart colt.
1 Aug'03 Newm 12g/f 115-(108) B: 1 May'03 Newm 12g/f 109- C: 1 Apr'03 Newb 11.0g/f 98- D: 2 Sep'02 Good 8fm 79- D:
1862 **ISLAND HOUSE 37** [3] G Wragg 8-8-11 (109) S Drowne 13/2: 432-3053: Chsd ldrs, onepcd fnl 1f.   *2*   **108**
8yo, List company is ideal: ideally suited by softer grnd, see 1139.
2255 **TIZZY MAY 21** [6] R Hannon 4-8-11 (98) Dane O'Neill 12/1: 40-02504: Outpcd, late gains, nvr dngrs.   *¾*   **106**
4402*}**FRUHLINGSSTURM 279** [8]4-9-6 T E Durcan 6/1: 135151-5: b c Unfuwain - Fruhlingserwachen (Irish   *5*   **107**
River) Chsd ldr, ev ch till wknd dist: op 8/1: ex German, won 3 times in native country in '03, incl a Gr 2:
winning form at 1m/12f on gd & hvy grnd: now with M Jarvis. 1 Sep'03 Fran 10sft 112- A:
1310} **CALIBRE 420** [5]4-8-11 (98) R Hughes 12/1: 1/52-6: Led till 2f out, wknd on reapp.   *1½*   **96**
2538 **SUNNY GLENN 8** [7]6-8-11 (83) P McCabe 50/1: 5000-067: Keen in rear, nvr a factor: highly tried.   *5*   **86**
7 Ran Time 2m 32.59 (4.39)   Owned: Mr Saeed Suhail   Trained: Newmarket

2763

2.10 Listed Cheveley Park Stud Empress Stakes Fillies 2yo (A)
£14500 £5500 £2750 **6f str** **Good/Firm 29** **-16 Slow** Stands Side

SLIP DANCE 19 [8] E Tyrrell 2-8-11 K McEvoy 16/1: 3141: br f Celtic Swing - Hawala (Warning) **100**
Chsd ldrs, imprvd to lead 1f out, ran on strongly, rdn out: Irish chall, earlier scored at Ballinrobe (mdn auct): eff at 6f on fast & gd/soft grnd: handles a stiff/gall trk: v useful juv filly.
1739* **ROYAL ALCHEMIST 43** [9] M D I Usher 2-8-8 A Daly 7/1: 12: Slowly away, hdwy 2f out, sltly outpcd dist, ran on well cl-home & not btn far: 6 wk abs: acts on fast & soft grnd, longer 7f trip will suit: clrly runs well fresh & imprvd in defeat today, see 1739 (debut). *¾* **93**
2553 **GOLDEN ANTHEM 8** [2] J Pearce 2-8-8 T P Queally 50/1: 103: Held up, outpcd 2f out, styd on well fnl 1f, nrst fin: acts on fast & hvy grnd, crying out for 7f now: see 1640 (debut). *¾* **90+**
1866* **BALTIC DIP 37** [3] R Hannon 2-8-11 R Hughes 5/2 FAV: 14: Led till ent fnl 1f, no extra: well bckd: prob ran to winning debut form of 1866 (fill mdn). *nk* **92**
2553 **UMNIYA 8** [7]2-8-8 T E Durcan 9/2: 3213345: Chsd ldrs, ev ch till wknd fnl 1f: well bckd: btr 2553. *3* **80**
2437* **KISSING LIGHTS 12** [5]2-8-11 K Fallon 10/3: 516: Trkd ldr, ev ch till wknd fnl 1f: see 2437 (5f). *1½* **79**
1887* **HERES THE PLAN 36** [1]2-8-11 P McCabe 16/1: 17: Keen & prom, wknd dist: see 1887 (mdn, debut). *½* **78**
2490 **POLLY PERKINS 10** [4]2-9-1 K Darley 15/2: 1108: Dwelt, sn recovered & prom halfway, wknd dist. *1¾* **77**
2450* **MARAJUANA 12** [6]2-8-11 Dane O'Neill 7/1: 1W: Unruly stalls & withdrawn: see 2450 (debut). **0**
9 Ran Time 1m 13.70 (2.70) Owned: M McLoughlin Trained: Ireland

2764

2.40 Lancaster Rated Stakes Handicap 3yo 0-85 (D) **[89]**
£5509 £1695 £848 **6f str** **Good/Firm 29** **-07 Slow** Stands Side

2482 **MAHMOOM 10** [1] M R Channon 3-9-6 vis (81) T E Durcan 14/1: 11-00601: Held up, gd hdwy 1.5f out, led ins fnl 1f, styd on strongly, rdn out: eff at 6/7f, acts on fast grnd: can force the pace or come from bhd: suited by a visor now: back to useful best: see 1771. **93**
2428* **KHALIDIA 13** [5] M A Magnusson 3-8-10 (71) T P Queally(3) 8/1: 0-12: Tried to make all, collared cl-home: has been gelded: lightly rcd & in fine form, see 2428 (reapp, mdn auct). *¾* **79**
2309* **KSCHESSINKA 17** [7] W J Haggas 3-9-3 (78) K Fallon 10/11 FAV: 0-13: Keen in rear, prog when short of room dist, styd on ins last, ch had gone: hvly bckd: did not get the run of today's race & much closer with clr run: must be gvn another ch after 2309 (mdn). *1* **83+**
2182* **HAWAAJES 23** [6] B Hanbury 3-9-0 (75) W Supple 9/2: 0314: Chsd ldrs, sltly short of room dist, onepace. *1¼* **76**
2173 **INSTANT RECALL 24** [4]3-9-3 BL (78) K Darley 12/1: 3104545: Prom, sltly hmpd dist, no extra in blnks. *1* **76**
5034} **RISING SHADOW 231** [2]3-9-7 (82) T Hamilton(3) 12/1: 0135-6: b g Efisio - Jouet (Reprimand) *nk* **79**
Dwelt, sn prom, wknd fnl 1f: mkt drifter, top-weight, reapp: '03 mdn wnr (66/1 success): eff at 6f on gd grnd & polytrack, runs well fresh: with R Fahey. 1 Oct'03 Newc 6gd 79- D:
1983 **MISSION MAN 32** [3]3-9-6 (81) R Hughes 15/2: 24-42147: Front rank, wknd dist: see 1607 (sft). *½* **77**
7 Ran Time 1m 13.19 (2.19) Owned: Sheikh Ahmed Al Maktoum Trained: West Ilsley

2765

3.15 Gr3 Bango Criterion Stakes 3yo+ (A)
£29000 £11000 £5500 **7f str** **Good/Firm 29** **+13 Fast** Stands Side

2470 **ARAKAN 11** [2] Sir Michael Stoute 4-9-2 (111) K Fallon 7/4 FAV: 63-13201: Trkd ldrs, imprvd to lead ins fnl 1f, rdn out, shade more in hand: nicely bckd, gd time: eff at 6f, suited by 7f & stays 1m: acts on firm & soft grnd, gall or easy trk: smart, fine 2nd in Gr 2 Lennox Stks at Glorious Goodwood last term. **113**
2184 **DESERT DESTINY 23** [8] Saeed bin Suroor 4-9-2 T (105) K McEvoy 12/1: 15054-02: Front rank, sltly short of room & lost pl after 1f, prog when short of room dist, kept on but nvr going to get to wnr: visor omitted, but tried a t-strap: back to form, rtn to 1m shld suit: see 2184. *¾* **110**
1667 **TRADE FAIR 46** [1] R Charlton 4-9-2 (120) R Hughes 7/2: 11615-03: Trkd ldr, qcknd to lead 1f out, sn hdd & no extra: well bckd tho' op 11/4, 7 wk abs: won this race last year, much btr expected on fav'd fast grnd: high-class at best & better than this, see 1667. *2* **106**
2184 **COURT MASTERPIECE 23** [6] E A L Dunlop 4-9-2 (106) T E Durcan 12/1: 2301-354: Held up, prog 2f out, switched dist & no impress ins fnl 1f: needs stks/Listed: best 1811 (reapp). *nk* **105**
2558 **KINGS POINT 8** [4] R Hannon 3-8-7 (99) Dane O'Neill 25/1: 6-505304: Chsd ldrs, onepcd fnl 1.5f. *dht* **105$**
1686 **PRINCE TUM TUM 45** [3]4-9-2 (103) K Darley 12/1: 3311/1-06: Chsd ldrs, btn dist: op 25/1, 7 wk abs: yet to recapture best form after injury but clrly showing something at home: see 1686. *3½* **98**
2455* **NAAHY 17** [7]4-9-7 (106) S Hitchcott 11/2: 0001-117: Led till 1f out, no extra: op 7/1: 7f front running specialist, loves Goodwood: see 2455 & 1811. *1* **101**
1486 **POLAR BEN 56** [5]5-9-7 (112) W Supple 6/1: 3100-228: Held up, prog 2f out, btn fnl 1f: 8 wk abs. *1½* **98**
8 Ran Time 1m 25.04 (1.14) Owned: Niarchos Family Trained: Newmarket

2766

3.50 Bridgewell Securities Maiden Stakes 2yo (D)
£4774 £1469 £735 **7f str** **Good/Firm 29** **-38 Slow** Stands Side

SOLENT [1] R Hannon 2-9-0 Dane O'Neill 25/1: 1: b c Montjeu - Stylish (Anshan) Slowly away, outpcd rear, gd hdwy dist, fin strongly to lead cl-home, won going away: 60,000gns Mar foal: half-brother to 7f juv wnr Due Respect: dam unrcd, sire a top-class mid-dist performer: eff over a stiff/gall 7f on fast grnd, runs well fresh: plenty to like about this eye-catching debut & one to follow. **95+**
DANIEL THOMAS [11] Mrs A J Perrett 2-9-0 K Darley 7/2: 2: b c Dansili - Last Look (Rainbow Quest) Chsd ldrs, imprvd to lead dist, not pace to repel wnr cl-home: bckd from 6/1 on debut: Jan foal, half-brother to 1m11f wnrs: dam unrcd, sire a high-class miler: eff over a stiff/gall 7f on fast: useful start. *1¼* **87+**
EQDAAM [9] J H M Gosden 2-9-0 K Fallon 8/1: 3: b c Diesis - Awaamir (Green Desert) Nvr far away, ev ch ent fnl 1f, onepace on debut: Jan foal, dam 7f/1m winner: sire a top-class juv: eff over a stiff/gall 7f on fast grnd: sure to learn plenty from this & improve. *¾* **85**
2348 **COUNCELLOR 16** [10] R Hannon 2-9-0 R Hughes 7/4 FAV: 34: Led till over 1f out, no extra: well bckd: stays a gall 7f: see 2348 (debut). *1¼* **82**
SEYAADI [6]2-9-0 W Supple 14/1: 5: b c Intikhab - Sioux Chef (Be My Chief) Prom, onepcd fnl 1.5f on racecourse bow: 55,000gns Jan first foal: dam a 6f 2yo wnr: sure to learn from this. *½* **81**

SILVERLEAF [4]2-9-0 T E Durcan 16/1: 6: b c Lujain - Lovely Millie (Bluebird) Slowly away, 1¾ 78
late hdwy, nvr dngrs on racecourse bow: Apr foal, dam a high-class 6/7f winning 2yo: sire a top-class juv sprinter.
2348 DOCTORS CAVE 16 [14]2-9-0 S Hitchcott(3) 33/1: 007: Front rank, wknd fnl 1f. hd 77$
2245 CATCH A STAR 21 [2]2-8-9 A Mackay 10/1: 358: Dwelt, mid-div, nvr plcd to chall under a kind hd 71
ride: drifter from 7/1: rider reportedly gvn a 10 day ban for not taking all reasonable measures to win: now qual
for nursery h'caps, type to do better: see 2245 & 1887.
RED CHAIRMAN [3]2-9-0 T P Queally(3) 10/1: 9: Chsd ldrs, btn dist on debut. ½ 74
VELVET HEIGHTS [8]2-9-0 G Carter 33/1: 0: 10th: Slowly away, al outpcd on debut. nk 73
2071 BIBI HELEN 28 [5]2-8-9 D Fox(5) 40/1: 60: 11th: Slowly away, al bhd. 3 62
HIGH TREASON [12]2-9-0 Dean McKeown 20/1: 0: 12th: Mid-div, wknd 1.5f out on debut. ½ 66
RUDAKI [13]2-9-0 Nicol Polli(7) 8/1: 0: 13th: Chsd ldrs 5f, sn wknd on debut. 1½ 63
2382 OLDSTEAD FLYER 15 [7]2-9-0 D Tudhope(7) 100/1: 060: 14th: Prom till halfway. dist 33
14 Ran Time 1m 28.61 (4.71) Owned: Mrs J Wood Trained: Marlborough

---

2767 4.25 Landcom E B F Handicap Stakes Fillies 3yo+ 0-90 (C) [86]
£9529 £2932 £1466 1m str Good/Firm 29 -14 Slow Stands Side

2312 LITTLE VENICE 17 [6] C F Wall 4-9-4 (76) Lisa Jones(3) 6/1: 240-0531: Chsd ldrs stands side, left 90
in clr lead after halfway, pushed out fnl 1f, unchall: eff at 7f/1m on gd & firm grnd, handles soft: seems to
handle any trk, likes Newmarket: best up with/forcing the pace: career best run, see 1723.
2153* OUR JAFFA 24 [1] D J Daly 3-9-1 (83) K Fallon 3/1 FAV: 4112: Prom centre, joined stands side 7 85
halfway, chsd wnr fnl 1f but no impress: nicely bckd: wnr in another parish today, see 2153 & 1904.
2464 SUMMER SHADES 11 [10] W M Brisbourne 6-8-12 (70) B Swarbrick(5) 20/1: 0-652443: Chsd ldrs stands 1½ 69
side, onepcd fnl 2f: see 2108.
2491 DANCLARE 10 [2] J H M Gosden 3-9-3 (85) R Hughes 9/2: 210-0654: Set pace centre, switched stands 2 80
side halfway, btn fnl 1f: see 2312.
1733 PONT ALLAIRE 43 [5]3-8-11 (79) Dane O'Neill 13/2: 4-105: Chsd ldrs stands side, wknd 1.5f out: 2½ 69
6 wk abs: twice below 1468 (reapp, soft grnd).
2225 MRS PANKHURST 22 [9]3-8-5 (73) Dean McKeown 25/1: 010-5056: Held up stands side, nvr nr ldrs. 2 59
2278 ENCHANTED PRINCESS 19 [3]4-9-2 bl (74) W Supple 7/1: 01-05167: Rcd centre early, sn switched 9 42
stands side, nvr a factor: btr 1927.
2419 HUNTERS VALLEY 13 [8]3-8-2 (70) D Kinsella 25/1: 523-0248: Chsd ldrs 6f stands side: see 2291. ¾ 36
2191 SALAGAMA 23 [7]4-9-11 (83) T P Queally(3) 6/1: 1-439: Led stands side, rein broke halfway & 5 39
veered left, sn hdd & wknd: op 8/1 under top-weight: lost all ch when tack broke & this must be forgiven.
2592 FRAGRANT STAR 7 [4]3-8-10 (78) T E Durcan 25/1: 0105-000: 10th: Held up centre, switched stands 7 19
side halfway, btn 2f out, eased: see 2592.
10 Ran Time 1m 40.67 (3.47) Owned: Hintlesham SPD Partners Trained: Newmarket

---

2768 5.00 Bango Apprentice Handicap Stakes 3yo+ 0-70 (E) [68]
£3484 £1072 £536 7f str Good/Firm 29 -14 Slow Stands Side

2409 MISTER SWEETS 14 [7] D Carroll 5-10-0 (68) D Tudhope(5) 7/1: 0000-601: Chsd ldrs centre, imprvd 76
to lead 2f out, styd on well despite drifting left, drvn out: top-weight: eff btwn 6f & 1m, ideally suited by 7f:
acts on gd, firm & both AWs, prob any trk: tough & genuine: gd weight carrier: made most of decent h'cap mark.
2600 BALERNO 6 [2] R Ingram 5-8-10 (50) Rory Moore(5) 8/1: 5230402: Held up centre, prog to chall 2f nk 56
out, kept on fnl 1f & just btn in a tight fin: overdue a win: see 1463 & 408.
2214 PAGAN STORM 22 [8] Mrs L Stubbs 4-9-1 T (55) Kristin Stubbs(5) 33/1: 0050003: Held up centre, gd 1¼ 58
hdwy 2f out, kept on despite drifting left, nvr nrr: back to form in first time t-strap: tumbling down the h'cap.
1730 RANNY 43 [3] Dr J D Scargill 4-8-8 (48) D Corby 20/1: 0-422064: Held up centre, short of room 2f ¾ 49
out, styd on fnl 1f & nrst fin: 6 wk abs: rtn to 1m will suit judged on this: see 913.
2199 MIDDLETON GREY 23 [17]6-9-9 bl (63) L Keniry 6/1: 4-032035: Chsd ldrs centre, onepcd fnl 1f. nk 63
2655 JEDEYDD 4 [6]7-9-2 t (56) T P Queally 7/1: 00-00406: Trkd ldrs centre, onepcd fnl 1f: qck reapp. shd 56
2350 ICED DIAMOND 16 [5]5-9-1 (55) B Swarbrick(5) 16/1: 200-1007: Hld up, imprvd halfway, btn fnl 1f. ¾ 53
2679 FEARBY CROSS 3 [12]8-9-11 (65) Lisa Jones 7/1: 0-604508: Held up centre, styd on late, nvr shd 63
dngrs: qck reapp: won this race from a 3lb lower mark last term: see 698.
2199 CAERPHILLY GAL 23 [1]4-8-12 (52) D Fox(3) 25/1: 3040-009: b f Averti - Noble Lustre (Lyphard's 1¼ 47
Wish) Keen in rear centre, nvr dngrs: '03 h'cap wnr: eff at 7f on fast grnd: enjoys dominating on a gall/undul
trk: with P Gilligan. 1 Aug'03 Chep 7.1g/f 51-45 F.
2080* JUBILEE STREET 28 [14]5-9-4 (58) Saleem Golam(5) 9/2 FAV: 05-04310: 10th: Held up centre, nvr a nk 52
factor: bckd from 7/1: btr expected after 2082.
2370 LOGISTICAL 15 [16]4-9-5 (59) P Gallagher(5) 11/1: 560-0050: 11th: Slowly away, al bhd centre. 1½ 50
2150 DEXILEOS 43 [10]5-8-3 t (43) F P Ferris 40/1: 00-00000: 12th: Led early, wknd 1.5f out. 1 32
2591 ITS ECCO BOY 7 [9]6-9-6 (60) Hayley Turner(3) 33/1: 1000000: 13th: Chsd ldrs 5f centre, wknd. 1½ 46
2529 HALCYON MAGIC 8 [4]6-8-8 bl (48) Laura Pike(7) 20/1: 60-20020: 14th: Rcd alone & al bhd far side. ½ 33
1820 BRANSTON TIGER 39 [15]5-10-0 BL (68) S Hitchcott 14/1: 5000650: 15th: Led after 2f centre, hdd 2f 5 43
out, wknd: keen in first time blnks: see 1354.
2571 PHAROAHS GOLD 7 [18]6-8-12 vis (52) T Hamilton 20/1: 0100040: 16th: Slowly away, al bhd centre. 2 23
2434* ALBADI 12 [11]3-8-3 bl (52) Dean Williams(7) 12/1: 0-00010: 17th: Chsd ldrs 5f centre: btr 2434. 8 7
17 Ran Time 1m 26.96(3.06) Owned: Mr David Fravigar-Mr Alan Mann Trained: Warthilll

Official Going Soft (Heavy places)

2769
1.55 Gr3 Foster's Lager Chipchase Stakes 3yo+   (A)
£29000 £11000 £5500   **6f str**   **Good/Soft**   **Fast**   Stands Side

5037} **ROYAL MILLENNIUM 223** [4] M R Channon 6-9-2 (110) T Quinn 8/1: 221425-1: b g Royal Academy -   **114+**
Galatrix (Be My Guest) Cl-up far side, gd hdwy on bit over 1f out, only had to be niggled along to lead cl-home, v
cosily, val much further: sole '03 win in a h'cap, Gr1 rnr-up: '02 class stks wnr: v eff over 6/7f, does stay 1m:
acts on firm, likes soft: acts on any trk: runs well fresh: smart, win more Gr races.
2 Nov'03 Donc 6gd 110-(111) A: 1 Oct'03 Newb 6.0g/f 107-100 B: 2 Oct'03 Newm 6g/f 109-(100) A: 2 Oct'03 Long 7sft 115- :
2 Sep'02 Good 6fm 106- A: 2 Sep'02 York 6g/f 104-100 B: 1 Aug'02 Good 7fm 100- B: 2 Jul'02 Asco 6.5gd 90-87 C:
2 Aug'01 Good 7g/f 96-89 C: 2 Jul'01 Sand 7fm 91-85 C: 1 Jun'01 Sali 7g/f 92- D: 2 May'01 Good 7g/f 85- D:
1667 **SOMNUS 46** [3] T D Easterby 4-9-10 (117) P Robinson 5/1: 14210-02: Handy far side, led over 1f   nk   **119**
out, collared cl-home, just failed: hvly bckd after 6 wk abs: eff on firm, likes gd/soft: high-class eff
conceding lumps of weight, 7 wins from 15 career starts: see 1667.
2240 **RUBY ROCKET 21** [8] H Morrison 3-8-6 (105) M Fenton 14/1: 1314-523: Held up far side, hdwy &   ½   **106**
sltly short of room 2f out, styd on ins last, nrst fin, not btn far: acts on firm & gd/soft, shld certainly win a
fills Listed/Gr3: see 2240, 1233.
1996* **THE KIDDYKID 35** [6] P D Evans 4-9-6 (111) R Winston 9/1: 365-3014: Handy, eff over 1f out,   1   **111**
onepcd: gd run but even btr when able to dominate: see 1196.
2184 **QUITO 23** [7]7-9-2 bl (110) A Culhane 13/2: 5561065: Sn rdn bhd far side, late gains, nrst fin: ½   **106**
loves to come off a fast pace/big field, capable of rating more highly: see 1703.
1667 **WELSH EMPEROR 46** [2]5-9-2 bl (109) Dale Gibson 6/1: 2426-146: Led far side till appr fnl 1f,   ½   **104**
onepcd: 6 wk abs: fair run, likes easy grnd: see 1667, 1227.
2581 **SIMIANNA 7** [5]5-8-13 p (96) F Norton 33/1: 2060207: In tch far side, btn dist: see 2457, 1162.   1½   **98$**
1732* **SO WILL I 43** [1]3-8-9 (109) R Hills 4/1 FAV: 41-318: Handy far side, wknd over 1f out, nicely   nk   **100**
bckd after 6 wk abs: unproven on easy grnd, btr 1732 (gd).
1958* **CELTIC MILL 33** [9]6-9-2 (107) L Enstone 16/1: 0-140119: Led stands side, no ch with far side   9   **82**
group: jockey chose wrong side, ignore this: thriving earlier, see 1958 (fast grnd).
2580 **BAHAMIAN PIRATE 7** [11]9-9-2 (105) E Ahern 9/1: 4210000: 10th: In tch stands side, nvr   5   **72**
travelling: jockey chose wrong side: likes easy grnd, see 2468.
1667 **GOLDEVA 46** [10]5-8-13 (102) N Callan 20/1: 5620-150: 11th: Chsd stands side ldr, wknd 2f out.   11   **47**
11 Ran   Time 1m 13.03 (1.73)   Owned: Jackie & George Smith   Trained: West Ilsley

2770
2.25 Totesport Northern Sprint Handicap Stakes 3yo+ 0-95 (C)   [95]
£19036 £7220 £3610   **6f str**   **Good/Soft**   **Fair**   Stands Side

1782 **SIERRA VISTA 41** [10] D W Barker 4-8-9 (76) L Enstone(3) 33/1: 4-030051: Keen, handy, hdwy to lead   **84**
over 1f out, styd on, drvn out: eff over 5/6f on firm & gd/soft, any trk: sharper today with cheek pieces omitted.
2074 **ELLENS ACADEMY 28** [13] E J Alston 9-8-12 (79) F Norton 50/1: 6342442: Prom, hdwy over 1f out,   nk   **87**
styd on ins last, just held: 9yo, rng well & again suggested a win is imminent: see 386.
2357 **RIVER FALCON 15** [2] J S Goldie 4-9-3 (84) Gary Stevens 14/1: 0-501003: Led 2f, cl-up, kept on   1¼   **88**
ins last: fine run: see 1683, 927.
2256 **FANTASY BELIEVER 21** [6] J J Quinn 6-9-2 (83) R Winston 8/1: 1-000004: b g Sure Blade - Delicious   shd   **87**
(Dominion) In tch, eff over 1f out, kept on ins last, nrst fin: '03 dual h'cap & class stks scorer: unplcd in '02:
eff over 5/7f on any grnd or trk, likes an easy surface: back on a wng mark & will be wng again sn, v tough.
1 Oct'03 Newc 7gd 95-(91) C: 2 Aug'03 Good 6g/f 90-86 C: 1 Jul'03 Asco 6gd 88-82 C: 2 Jul'03 Pont 6g/f 87-78 D:
2 Jun'03 Good 6fm 81-78 C: 1 May'03 Ayr 6g/s 80-73 D: 1 Oct'01 Donc 5hvy 95-91 B: 1 Sep'01 Asco 6gd 91-87 B:
1 Aug'01 Ripo 6g/f 87-79 D: 1 Jul'01 Ling 6g/s 81-74 D: 2 Jul'01 Ripo 6g/f 80-74 D: 1 Jun'01 Kemp 6g/f 77-68 D:
1933 **BYGONE DAYS 35** [9]3-8-11 (85) T Quinn 13/2: 02-1345: Held up, eff over 1f out, some late gains,   ¾   **87**
no danger: fair run: see 1665, 946.
2542 **HIGHLAND WARRIOR 8** [7]5-8-6 (73) N Mackay(3) 16/1: 4160046: Dwelt, held up, hdwy & short of room   ½   **74**
over 2f out till ins last, kept on: again shaped with promise: see 2542, 1898.
2477 **SHARP HAT 10** [16]10-7-12 (6oh) (59) D Fentiman(7) 66/1: 5500007: Cl-up, eff over 1f out, no impress.   nk   **65$**
2256 **MUTAWAQED 21** [14]6-9-5 t (86) E Ahern 15/2: 630-0428: Held up, hdwy over 1f out, no extra ins   shd   **85**
last: won this race last term off an 8lb lower mark: see 2256, 2070.
2357 **PIETER BRUEGHEL 15** [17]5-9-1 (82) J Fanning 28/1: 0000-049: In tch, wknd over 1f out: see 2357.   ½   **80**
2568* **BALAKIREF 7** [11]5-8-2 (69) J Quinn 12/1: 0222U10: 10th: Bhd, some late gains, nvr dangerous: see 386.   ½   **66**
2477 **GREY COSSACK 10** [1]7-8-8 (75) R Fitzpatrick 14/1: 1005000: 11th: In tch, wknd 2f out: see 1145.   1   **70**
1481 **POLAR KINGDOM 56** [5]6-8-8 (75) R Hills 3/1 FAV: 3110030: 12th: Chsd ldrs, short of room halfway,   nk   **69**
no impress: hvly bckd: 8 wk abs & btr expected: see 611.
2561* **CD FLYER 7** [18]7-9-6 (87) P Mulrennan(5) 16/1: 5200410: 13th: Slow away, nvr a factor: likes easy grnd.   hd   **80**
1745 **GEORGE THE BEST 43** [4]3-7-13 (73) Dale Gibson 25/1: 000-0640: 14th: In tch, wknd dist: abs.   1½   **63**
2568 **FAIR SHAKE 7** [8]4-7-13 p (66) P Hanagan 9/1: 00-00350: 15th: Al bhd: btr 1393.   1¾   **52**
2581 **NATIVE TITLE 7** [12]6-9-7 (88) A Nicholls 25/1: 10-40100: 16th: Led 2f out till dist, wknd.   nk   **73**
2581 **CD EUROPE 7** [15]6-9-10 p (91) N Callan 20/1: 2021-000: 17th: Held up, btn 2f out: see 2581.   4   **68**
482 **SIR DESMOND 152** [3]6-8-13 p (80) P Robinson 20/1: 0034-300: 18th: In tch, wknd 2f out: long abs.   1   **55**
18 Ran   Time 1m 14.4 (3.1)   Owned: Mr David T J Metcalfe   Trained: Richmond

2771
3.00 John Smith's Northumberland Plate Heritage Handicap 3yo+   (B)   [111]
£104400 £39600 £19800   **2m19y**   **Good/Soft**   **Slow**   Stands Side

1093 **MIRJAN 79** [5] L Lungo 8-8-3 bl (86) P Hanagan 33/1: 2404////-31: In tch, hdwy over 2f out, styd   **96**
on to lead ins last, rdn out: recent h'cap hdle plcd (rtd 132h): stays 2m well on fast & soft grnd: apprec return
of blnks: lightly rcd & useful on the Flat: see 1093.
1998* **SWING WING 34** [7] P F I Cole 5-9-8 (105) J Fanning 20/1: 533-5012: Handy, hdwy to chall over 2f   hd   **114**
out, kept on over 1f out, just held: v smart eff conceding weight to those around him & likes easy grnd: see 1998.
1569* **ANAK PEKAN 52** [10] M A Jarvis 4-9-4 (101) P Robinson 5/2 FAV: 1222-113: Cl-up, led over 2f out   ¾   **109**
till ins last, kept on for press, not btn far: hvly bckd, 7 wk abs: most prog & type to be wng in List/Gr3 shortly.
1746+ **COLLIER HILL 43** [18] G A Swinbank 6-9-4 (101) R Winston 20/1: 0303-014: Held up, short of room   3   **106**

4f out till 2f out, kept on ins last, nrst fin: 6 wk abs: useful eff, even closer with a clr run: unexposed at 2m.

2085	**KRISTENSEN 28** [3]5-7-12 p (81) P Fessey 25/1: 33-50625: Cl-up, eff over 2f out, no extra fnl 1f.	*shd*	86
2582	**PAGAN DANCE 7** [19]5-8-9 p (92) A Culhane 25/1: 40-34226: Held up, eff 2f out, onepcd:	1¼	96

encouraging eff & prob styd this much longer 2m trip: see 1295, 695.

2246	**DEFINING 21** [8]5-8-12 (95) O Urbina 14/1: 0203-037: Held up, eff 2f out, sn onepcd: prob	*nk*	98

handles firm, gd/soft & both AWs: poss stays 2m: see 2246.

SELF DEFENSE 678 [2]7-9-3 (100) J F McDonald(3) 40/1: 46/1450/-8: b g Warning - Dansara (Dancing 1½ 101
Brave) Cl-up, wknd 2f out: won a stks on the Flat in France back in '02: stays 2m on gd & v soft on the Flat.

2471	**PROMOTER 11** [9]4-8-2 (85) E Ahern 15/2: 404-0029: Keen in tch, wknd over 2f out: had a hard	2½	83

race 11 days on much faster grnd in 2471.

2255	**ZIBELINE 21** [17]7-8-6 bl (89) F Norton 25/1: 30020-30: 10th: Keen held up, eff & short of room	*shd*	87

over 2f out, no impress: 4th in this race last term: see 2255 (firm).

2355	**ESCAVOLA 15** [20]4-8-4 bl (87) T Quinn 14/1: 1211-020: 11th: Keen held up, hung left & wknd 2f out.	3	82
2239	**DISTANT PROSPECT 21** [13]7-8-11 (94) R Hills 7/1: 0303-420: 12th: Al bhd: btr expected after 2239.	2½	86
4493+	**JAGGER 272** [12]4-9-0 (97) Gary Stevens 7/1: 416D11-0: 13th: apr c Linamix - Sweetness Herself	½	88

(Unfuwain) Held up, wknd 2f out: won 4 h'caps in '03: eff at 12/14f, 2m shld suit: acts on firm, gd & polytrack, any trk: v useful & prog last term, likely to do btr when stable returns to form.
1 Sep'03 Asco 12g/f 99-94 B: 1 Aug'03 York 13.9fm 96-86 B: 1 Jul'03 Good 14gd 89-76 C:
1 Jun'03 Ling 10ap 80a-68 E: 2 Apr'03 Thir 5fm 69- D:

2557	**RED LANCER 8** [14]3-8-7 (110) M Fenton 22/1: 2221360: 14th: Held up, btn 2f out: see 2557.	½	100
2246	**MAMCAZMA 21** [11]6-8-12 (95) M Tebbutt 66/1: 00002-00: 15th: gr g Terimon - Merryhill Maid (M	1½	83

Double M) Prom, wknd over 2f out: rnr-up sev times in '03 (incl Listed): '02 4 time h'cap wnr: eff over 14f/2m on firm, soft & fibresand: acts on any trk, loves Newmarket July: has run well fresh & best without blnks.
2 Nov'03 Donc 14.6gd 106-(91) C: 2 Jul'03 York 13.9fm 98-95 A: 2 Jun'03 York 13.9g/f 96-90 C:
2 May'03 Newm 12g/f 90-86 C: 1 Sep'02 York 13.8g/f 88-84 C: 1 Aug'02 Newm 14.7fm 85-78 C:
2 Aug'02 Newm 16.1sft 80-76 C: 1 Jul'02 Newm 14.7g/f 75-70 D: 1 Jul'02 Newm 14.7g/f 71-64 D:

2405	**RAYSHAN 14** [6]4-8-12 BL (95) P Mulrennan(5) 66/1: 1356-000: 16th: In tch, wknd 2f out: tried blnks.	3	80
1861*	**BAROLO 37** [16]5-9-10 (107) J Fortune 16/1: 3114-010: 17th: Held up, wknd over 2f out: unproven	5	87

on easy grnd but more expected after 1861 (fast).

2239	**JOROBADEN 21** [15]4-8-6 (89) J Quinn 28/1: 2161060: 18th: Nvr a factor: see 1516.	1¾	67
1389	**SPECTROMETER 61** [1]7-7-13 (82) J Mackay 33/1: 31030-00: 19th: Led till over 2f out, wknd.	20	40

19 Ran Time 3m 37.54 (12.04) Owned: Mrs Barbara Lungo Trained: Carrutherstown

---

2772 **3.30 Listed European Breeders Fund Hoppings Stakes Fillies 3yo+ (A)**
£17400 £6600 £3300 **1m2f32y** **Good/Soft** **Slow** Far Side

2278	**ICE PALACE 19** [5] J R Fanshawe 4-9-4 (96) E Ahern 2/1 FAV: 1140-321: Cl-up, hdwy when no run		98+

appr fnl 1f & sn switched, styd on strongly ins last to lead cl-home, going away: bckd tho' op 13/8: eff at 1m, apprec this step up to 10f: acts on firm & gd/soft, prob any trk: neat turn of foot to overcome trouble in rng, unexposed at this trip, rate higher: see 2278.

2211	**BLUE OASIS 22** [3] R Guest 3-8-6 (87) T Quinn 13/2: 152: Slow away, held up, hdwy over 1f out,	*nk*	93

styd on to lead ins last, kept on till collared cl-home: jockey received a 2 day whip ban: imprvd at 10f & acts on gd & gd/soft: useful, see 1636.

2278	**COTE QUEST 19** [6] S C Williams 4-9-4 (92) A Culhane 14/1: 3-400443: Prom, eff well over 1f out,	½	92

onepace: useful, stays 10f: see 1863, 1115.

2191	**SHAMARA 23** [8] C F Wall 4-9-4 (85) P Robinson 4/1: 1310-224: Keen cl-up, led briefly ins last,	*hd*	91

no extra: nicely bckd: see 2191.

2517	**CRYSTAL CURLING 9** [2]3-8-6 (99) R Hills 3/1: 21-3305: Set stdy pace till just ins last, wknd.	1¾	88
2015	**JUBILEE TREAT 31** [7]4-9-4 (74) F Norton 33/1: 5120-006: Keen cl-up, wknd 2f out: needs h'caps.	*dist*	0

6 Ran Time 2m 14.14 (7.64) Owned: Cheveley Park Stud Trained: Newmarket

---

2773 **4.05 Journal Good Morning Handicap Stakes 3yo 0-80 (D)**
£11971 £4541 £2270 **1m rnd** **Good/Soft** **Slow** Centre   [87]

2463*	**MAJORCA 11** [10] J H M Gosden 3-9-9 (82) J Fortune 4/1 FAV: 0-32411: Prom, gd hdwy to lead over		93

1f out, edged left but styd on ins last, rdn out: eff at 7f, enjoyed this step up to 1m: acts on firm & gd/soft, gall or easy trks: useful, v prog & landed nice tch from 7/1 here, win again: see 2463.

2247	**KIBRYAA 21** [2] M A Jarvis 3-9-3 (76) P Robinson 10/1: 021-62: Disptd lead till over 2f out, kept	1	83

on ins last, not pace of wnr: styd longer 1m trip: acts on firm & gd/soft: lightly rcd, win again: see 2247.

2385	**LETS ROLL 14** [11] C W Thornton 3-8-13 (72) P Mulrennan(5) 11/2: 51-26223: Held up, hdwy 2f out,	¾	78

kept on well ins last, no threat to front: plcd again: eff on fast & gd/soft: see 2385, 1176.

2168	**DOUBLE VODKA 24** [9] Mrs J R Ramsden 3-8-4 (63) F Norton 14/1: 035-0624: Held up, hdwy & short of	1½	66

room 2f out, kept on nicely ins last, no danger: handles fast & gd/soft: like so many of his stable-mates, showed promise from the rear having been held up: see 2168, 1769.

1663	**THIRD EMPIRE 47** [6]3-8-1 (60) P Fessey 50/1: 4050-305: Made most till over 1f out, onepace when	*nk*	62

hmpd/stumbled badly ins last, nvr recover: 7 wk abs: poss 3rd but for trouble: see 1144.

1427	**TYTHEKNOT 59** [12]3-9-2 (75) P Hanagan 16/1: 02-236: Held up, 2f out, sn onepcd: abs: see 1427.	¾	75
2365	**CHIGORIN 15** [7]3-8-11 (70) E Ahern 9/1: 03-067: Handy, wknd 2f out: keen, promise earlier on gd.	2½	66
1470	**CHARNOCK BATES ONE 57** [3]3-8-5 (64) R Winston 20/1: 3354-468: Slow away & nvr a factor: abs.	1	58
2604	**MISS ELOISE 6** [4]3-7-13 (1ow) (57) J Quinn 10/1: 052-6269: Held up, nvr factor: qck reapp.	*nk*	51
2325*	**LYCA BALLERINA 17** [5]3-9-2 (75) R Hills 7/1: 34-53410: 10th: In tch, wknd 2f out: btr 2325 (mdn).	¾	66
2116	**ALI DEO 26** [8]3-9-4 (77) T Quinn 12/1: 00-130: 11th: Nvr a factor: btr 2116 (gd), 1832.	2	65
2495*	**DISPOL VELETA 10** [1]3-8-9 (68) J Fanning 10/1: 4130010: 12th: Cl-up, wknd 2f out: btr 2495 (AW).	½	55
2474	**AMANKILA 10** [13]3-8-4 (63) J Mackay 11/1: 031640: 13th: Cl-up, wknd over 2f out: best 1581.	12	26

13 Ran Time 1m 45.14 (6.14) Owned: Sheikh Mohammed Trained: Manton

2774

4.40 Kronenbourg 1664 E B F Maiden Stakes 2yo (D)
£6825 £2100 £1050   **6f str**   **Good/Soft**   **V Slow**   Stands Side

2578 **JOHN FORBES 7** [3] B Ellison 2-9-0 P Mulrennan(5) 14/1: 01: Handy, rdn 2f out, kept on ins last to lead cl-home, rdn out: much imprvd for debut & step back to 6f: acts on gd/soft: shld be more to come. **86**

2241 **TURNAROUND 21** [7] Mrs J R Ramsden 2-9-0 A Culhane 5/2: 32: Keen cl-up, led halfway, kept on till collared cl-home, just btn: stays 6f on gd & gd/soft: can win a mdn shortly: see 2241. ½ **83**

TSAROXY [4] J Howard Johnson 2-9-0 P Hanagan 2/1 FAV: 3: b c Xaar - Belsay (Belmez) Cl-up, eff to chall ins last, no extra cl-home: hvly bckd on debut: Feb foal, cost E420,000: half brother to a 6f juv wnr: eff at 6f on gd/soft: clr of rem on debut, sharper for this & can win races. ¾ **81**

LODGICIAN [5] J J Quinn 2-9-0 R Winston 8/1: 4: b c Grand Lodge - Dundel (Machiavellian) Slow away, brief eff 2f out, no impress: op 9/2: Apr foal, cost 8,000gns: dam 7f wnr: bred to apprec 7f/1m. 6 **66**

MIDDLE EASTERN [6]2-9-0 N Callan 25/1: 5: b c Mujahid - Swissmatic (Petong) Keen cl-up, wknd over 2f out on debut: Mar foal, cost E9.000: half brother to a 5f juv wnr: speedily bred. 3½ **58**

HADRIAN [2]2-9-0 J Fanning 100/30: 6: Led till halfway, hung left & wknd 2f out. nk **57**

NOWADAY [1]2-9-0 Dale Gibson 33/1: 7: Went left start, in tch, wknd 2f out. 7 **41**

7 Ran   Time 1m 17.7 (6.4)   Owned: Mrs Claire Ellison   Trained: Malton

2775

5.10 Miller Uk Handicap Stakes 3yo+ 0-70 (E)   **[69]**
£4397 £1353 £677   **5f str**   **Good/Soft**   **Slow**   Stands Side

2476 **SOAKED 10** [2] D W Chapman 11-9-2 bl (57) A Culhane 7/2 FAV: 3404121: Made all far side, styd on well fnl 1f, rdn out: stays 6f, suited by 5f on firm, soft & both A/Ws: most tough (19th win from 151 starts) & a real credit to connections: see 335. **62**

2524 **BLUE MAEVE 9** [11] J Hetherton 4-8-9 (50) S Righton 25/1: 4040042: In tch, eff well over 1f out, onepcd ins last: acts on fast & gd/soft: shld find a mod event: see 2524, 663. 1¾ **50**

2409 **WINTHORPE 14** [1] J J Quinn 4-10-0 (69) P Mulrennan(5) 10/1: 0000403: Handy, sltly outpcd 2f out, rallied fnl 1f, nrst fin: encouraging & stable back to form: h'capped to win shortly: see 482. ½ **67**

2279 **MYND 19** [3] R M Whitaker 4-9-9 (64) V Halliday 7/1: 0210064: In tch, eff dist, onepcd ins last. 1¼ **58**

2657 **FAIRGAME MAN 4** [6]6-8-4 p (45) R Fitzpatrick 11/1: 00-00205: Held up, some late gains, nvr dangerous: quick reapp, see 1948 (gd/firm). 1 **36**

2720 **LEVELLED 1** [5]10-8-6 (47) D Fentiman(7) 22/1: 50233106: Handy, wknd dist: unplcd yesterday. ½ **37**

2657 **LE MERIDIEN 4** [4]6-8-12 vis (53) L Enstone(3) 11/1: 0000-507: In tch, wknd 2f out: needs Beverley. ½ **42**

2214 **HILLTIME 22** [8]4-9-3 (58) J Fanning 25/1: 550/0-008: Bhd, modest late gains: see 1638. 1½ **44**

2279 **TATWEER 19** [7]4-9-3 vis (58) R Winston 6/1: 000-5109: Al bhd: nicely bckd: btr 1682. ½ **43**

2476 **JOYCES CHOICE 10** [10]5-8-9 (50) D McGaffin 20/1: 0-20R540: 10th: Held up, wknd 1f out: see 1179. ½ **34**

2561 **OBE ONE 7** [14]4-9-13 (68) F Norton 16/1: 6402300: 11th: Handy, wknd when short of room dist. 1 **50**

2409 **VIEWFORTH 14** [17]6-10-0 (69) J Fortune 15/2: 4400000: 12th: Al bhd: see 1276. 1 **49**

2731 **LORD BASKERVILLE 1** [16]3-8-10 (57) P Fessey 50/1: 00603000: 13th: Slow away & al bhd. 2 **33**

2359 **ONLINE INVESTOR 15** [12]5-9-12 (67) L Treadwell(7) 10/1: 5205500: 14th: Slow away, nvr a factor. ¾ **41**

14 Ran   Time 1m 01.37(3.17)   Owned: Mr David W Chapman   Trained: York

Official Going GOOD/FIRM (GOOD IN PLACES)

2776

2.20 South Warwickshire Business Club Maiden Auction Stakes 2yo (E)
£3851 £1185 £593   **7f26y rnd**   **Firm 08**   **-17 Slow**   Inside

2263 **DRY ICE 20** [7] H Candy 2-8-9 Dane O'Neill 2/1: 51: Mid-div, hdwy over 2f out, edged left over 1f out, led ins fnl 1f, kept on: stays 7f on firm, acts on a sharp/turning trk: imprvd from debut, see 2263. **83**

2511 **MCELDOWNEY 10** [5] M Johnston 2-8-11 K Dalgleish 7/2: 322: Led 1f, remained with ldr, led again over 1f out, hdd ins fnl 1f & no extra: modest for under top-weight: acts on firm & gd: find similar sn. 1½ **80**

1687 **COLEORTON DANE 46** [6] K A Ryan 2-8-7 N Callan 15/8 FAV: 63: gr g Danehill Dancer - Cloudy Nine (Norton Challenger) Handy, not clr run dist, sn switched, no impress: op 3/1, 7 wk abs: unplcd prev on debut: 2nd foal, dam unrcd: sire a high-class sprinter: stays 7f on firm. 1¾ **72**

2584 **PERSIAN CARPET 8** [3] I A Wood 2-8-2 G Duffield 20/1: 04: b f Desert Style - Kuwah (Be My Guest) Led after 1f, hdd over 1f out, no extra: cost 3,000gns: dam a 12f wnr, sire a decent 7f performer: showed improvement from debut here. ½ **66**

1964 **HAWRIDGE KING 34** [8]2-8-7 M Fenton 16/1: 35: Handy, onepcd 2f out: op 11/1: see 1964. shd **70**

1874 **MIRAGE PRINCE 38** [1]2-8-9 B Swarbrick(5) 66/1: 606: ch g Desert Prince - Belle Bijou (Midyan) Rear, modest late gains: modest both earlier starts: cost 10,000gns: sire top-class miler, dam a 10f wnr. ¾ **70**

SKIDROW [4]2-8-9 I Mongan 4/1: 7: Bhd, nvr a factor on debut. 4 **62**

ANSELLS LEGACY [2]2-8-9 G Carter 25/1: 8: Al bhd on debut. 4 **54**

SEA MAP [9]2-8-9 E Ahern 16/1: 9: Al bhd on debut. 10 **34**

9 Ran   Time 1m 24.16 (1.76)   Owned: Simon Broke and Partners   Trained: Wantage

2777

2.50 European Breeders Fund Classified Stakes 3yo+ 0-90 (C)
£9999 £3793 £1896   **7f26y rnd**   **Firm 08**   **+18 Fast**   Inside

2223* **MATERIAL WITNESS 23** [1] W R Muir 7-9-4 (89) R Mullen 13/2: 0-002011: Made all, just held on under press: landed double in fast time: best at 6/7f, stays 1m: handles firm, soft & polytrack, loves a sharp trk: in fine form from the front, made use of gd draw here: see 2223 & 1817. **96**

2207 **MYSTERINCH 23** [10] Jedd O'Keeffe 4-9-5 (91) P Hanagan 14/1: 11/3-3002: Bhd, hdwy 2f out, kept on well ins fnl 1f but just failed: eff btwn 7f/1m: gd run on drop in trip: see 1225. shd **95**

2240 **LOOK HERES CAROL 22** [6] B A McMahon 4-9-1 (87) G Gibbons 9/1: 004-3363: Midfield, styd on well nk **91**

ins fnl 1f: see 1523.

2532 **KOOL 9** [11] P F I Cole 5-9-4 (89) T Quinn 7/2 J FAV: 3055354: Rear, hdwy 2f out, not clr run & switched right over 1f out, styd on ins fnl 1f: did not get the run of today's race: see 1126. ¾ 92

2558 **ATAVUS 9** [4]7-9-5 (91) J Mackay 6/1: 104-0605: Rcd in 2nd, ev ch 1f out, sn onepcd: see 1926. nk 92

2389 **BINANTI 15** [3]4-9-4 (88) J Quinn 7/1: 0140-066: Midfield, hdwy 2f out, no impress fnl 1f: clr rem. shd 90

2532 **VINDICATION GB 9** [12]4-9-4 t (89) E Ahern 7/2 J FAV: 110-0667: Rear, mod hdwy dist, sn no impress: nicely bckd: see 2090. 4 82

2543 **ROSSELLI 9** [9]8-9-4 (46) C Ely(7) 150/1: 44-00008: Handy, wknd over 1f out: see 1626. 5 72$

2543 **TELEPATHIC 9** [2]4-9-4 (57) P Mathers(7) 150/1: 6000469: Bhd early, sn handy, wknd over 1f out. 2 68$

2480 **JALOUHAR 11** [5]4-9-4 (46) M Tebbutt 100/1: 0206020: 10th: Al bhd: see 2480. 3 62$

2630 **SPEEDFIT FREE 6** [7]7-9-4 (46) Ann Stokell 200/1: 0060000: 11th: Al bhd: qck reapp: see 308. 1½ 59$

11 Ran   Time 1m 21.69 (u0.71)   Owned: Mr M J Caddy   Trained: Lambourn

---

2778   **3.25 Mercia Fm Claiming Stakes 3yo (E)**
£3445 £1060 £530   **6f21y rnd**   **Firm 08**   **+15 Fast**   Inside

2379 **INNCLASSIC 16** [8] B J Meehan 3-8-4 bl (67) J F McDonald(3) 9/1: 03-0031: Handy, hdwy to lead just over 1f out, drvn out ins fnl 1f: fast time, op 7/1: eff at 5/6f on firm & both AWs, acts on a sharp/turning trk: runs well in blnks: see 1732. 67

2590 **WHOS WINNING 8** [10] C A Dwyer 3-8-7 BL (63) E Ahern 5/1: 36-00602: Bhd, hdwy 3f out, ev ch ins fnl 1f, just btn in a tight fin: gd eff in first time blnks: see 2271. nk 69

2369 **ONE UPMANSHIP 16** [6] J G Portman 3-8-7 (61) N Callan 16/1: 30-00063: Midfield, lost pl 3f out till rallied over 1f out, kept on ins fnl 1f: op 10/1: stays 6/7f on firm & fast: see 2369. ¾ 67

2566 **SIR ERNEST 8** [1] M J Polglase 3-8-9 (76) G Duffield 7/2: 0-060204: Led till just over 1f out, no extra fnl 1f: op 9/4: see 2227. 1¼ 65

1956 **DREAMING WATERS 34** [4]3-8-4 (55) S Carson 16/1: 600-005: ch f Groom Dancer - Faraway Waters (Pharly) Bhd, hdwy over 1f out, no impress ins fnl 1f: mdn unplcd in '03 (rtd 66): prob eff at 6f on firm. 1¾ 55

2541* **ARFINNIT 9** [7]3-8-9 (61) S Hitchcott(3) 6/4 FAV: 6516616: Outpcd in rear, hdwy when not clr run & switched right over 1f out, no impress on ldrs: op 2/1: shade btr 2541 (similar). 1¼ 56

2575 **KARMA CHAMELIAN 8** [2]3-8-4 (44) T Quinn 16/1: 0-057: Bhd, hdwy over 3f out, no impress 1f out. 2½ 43

2152 **PARLIAMENT ACT 25** [3]3-8-7 t G Gibbons 33/1: 008: b g Mujadil - Law Student (Precocious) Handy, wknd over 1f out: mdn unplcd earlier: cost 44,000gns: with B McMahon. 2 40

1942 **MOUSEMAN 35** [9]3-8-7 bl (59) M Fenton 14/1: 30310-59: With ldr 3f, sn wknd: see 1942. 1½ 35

9 Ran   Time 1m 10.16 (u0.44)   Owned: The Inn Partnership   Trained: Upper Lambourn

---

2779   **4.00 St Mary's Lands Rated Stakes Handicap 3yo+ 0-85 (D)**
£6484 £2460 £1230   **5f110y rnd**   **Firm 08**   **Inapplicable**   Inside   [90]

2598 **DIZZY IN THE HEAD 7** [7] Paul Johnson 5-8-11 bl (73) N Chalmers(5) 6/1: 0163121: Made all, rdn/edged left dist, kept on fnl 1f in crse rec time: eff at 5/6f on firm & soft, poss hvy: ee 2512. 83

2053+ **CAPE ST VINCENT 30** [3] H Morrison 4-8-10 vis (72) M Fenton 11/2: 2024-012: Handy, chsd wnr fnl 1f, no impress cl home: stays 7f, best arnd 5.5/6f: acts on firm, fast & both AWs: see 2053. 1¼ 76

2451 **HIGH RIDGE 13** [1] J M Bradley 5-8-7 (1oh)p (68) S Hitchcott(3) 9/4 FAV: 0-015123: Handy, hdwy over 2f out, onepcd ins fnl 1f: op 9/2: shade below winning form of 2416. 1 70

2420* **DANCING MYSTERY 14** [5] E A Wheeler 10-9-7 (83) S Carson 11/1: 5000014: Rear, hdwy over 1f out, onepcd ins fnl 1f: op 7/1: shade btr 2420 (5f). nk 83

2561 **MIDNIGHT PARKES 8** [4]5-8-7 (4oh) (65) D Allan 7/2: 00-04035: In tch, outpcd over 3f out, rallied dist: see 2561 & 2280. shd 68

2361 **ENDLESS SUMMER 16** [8]6-8-12 (74) T Quinn 25/1: 4-355046: Rear, mod gains: now with A Carroll. hd 72

2698* **WHISTLER 3** [10]7-9-8 (3ex)p (84) Dane O'Neill 5/1: 3010317: Rear, nvr a factor: top-weight, qck reapp: poss came too qckly after winning in race 2698. 1½ 77

2561 **TWICE UPON A TIME 8** [2]5-8-7 (69) E Ahern 16/1: 10-44008: Nvr a factor: see 1749. hd 61

2710 **SAFRANINE 3** [6]7-8-7 (9oh)p (60) Ann Stokell 16/1: 0000069: Handy, no impress fnl 1f: qck reapp. ¾ 59

9 Ran   Time 1m 3.7 ()   Owned: P and Mrs D M Johnson   Trained: Stanley

---

2780   **4.35 Andrew Sykes Group Handicap Stakes 3yo 0-80 (D)**
£5876 £1808 £904   **1m2f188y**   **Firm 08**   **-18 Slow**   Inside   [83]

2238 **CAUSE CELEBRE 22** [2] B W Hills 3-9-7 (76) E Ahern 11/4: 0324-101: Led 2f, remained handy, led again dist, rdn & kept on well ins fnl 1f: eff at 1m/11f, has tried 12f: acts on firm, fast & likes a turning trk: made most of a drop in grade & a drop in trip: gd eff under top-weight: see 1790. 79

2203 **GENERAL FLUMPA 23** [4] C F Wall 3-8-10 (65) R Mullen 5/1: 0-63352: Handy, hdwy to lead over 2f out, hdd just over 1f out & no extra: stays 11/11.5f on firm & soft: see 1340. 1¾ 64

2576* **GOBLIN 8** [3] D E Cantillon 3-9-6 (75) T Quinn 5/2: 1513513: Bhd, hdwy over 1f out, ev ch just ins fnl 1f, sn onepcd: ran to winning form of 2576. shd 73

2413 **DESERT IMAGE 15** [1] C Tinkler 3-9-4 (73) D Corby(3) 2/1 FAV: 6003324: Handy, onepcd 2f out: op 5/2. 1¼ 69

2050 **SPECTESTED 30** [7]3-7-12 (3oh) (50) C Haddon(3) 20/1: 550-0025: Keen in rear, nvr a factor: op 12/1: now with A Carroll: see 2050. 5 41

1742 **BROUGH SUPREME 44** [5]3-9-3 (72) M Fenton 20/1: 0-546: Keen & led after 2f, hdd 2f out, wknd: op 10/1, 6 wk abs: see 1384. 1 58

6 Ran   Time 2m 19.08 (2.88)   Owned: The Hon Mrs J M Corbett & Mr C Wright   Trained: Lambourn

---

2781   **5.05 Weatherbys Insurance Maiden Stakes 3yo+ (D)**
£4251 £1308 £654   **2m2f**   **Firm 08**   **Inapplicable**   Inside

2621 **FIDDLERS FORD 6** [9] J Noseda 3-8-5 (72) E Ahern 5/1: 2640401: Rear, hdwy 2f out, led just over 1f out, kept on ins fnl 1f: qck reapp: eff btwn 10/12f, relished this step up to 2m2f, acts on firm & polytrack, sharp/turning trk: made most of drop in grade & a thorough stayer: see 367. 78

2515 **RECOGNISE 10** [4] M Johnston 3-8-5 (80) J Fanning 11/8 FAV: 2422: Led after 3f till just over 1f 3 73

out, no extra: clr of rem: stays 2m2f, acts on gd, poss firm: see 1507.

2376 **FU FIGHTER 16** [5] J A Osborne 3-8-5 (71) T Quinn 3/1: 54-0543: Keen & handy, hdwy into 2nd bef   *3* **70**
halfway, no impress fnl 1f: see 2130.

1945 **DORA CORBINO 34** [1] R Hollinshead 4-9-7 (39) G Duffield 20/1: 6324234: Led 3f, remained handy,   *5* **59$**
no impress over 1f out: off rtd 39, treat rating with caution: see 1547.

    MY TRUE LOVE [2]5-9-13 V Slattery 16/1: 5: b g Beneficial - Elfi (Le Moss) Bhd, hdwy 6f out,   *¾* **64**
no impress from 3f out: op 25/1, 6 wk NH abs (bmpr rnr-up, eff at 2m/2m1f on fast & gd): top-weight here.

2668 **OPERA STAR 4** [3]3-8-0 (43) P Hanagan 10/1: 0-5036: Handy, wknd over 1f out: op 13/2, qck reapp.   *4* **55**

2164 **VICTORY LAP 25** [8]3-8-4 (4ow) (65) S Hitchcott 8/1: 3-0657: Rear, nvr a factor: op 5/1: see 192.   *2½* **59**

2196 **PRIDEWOOD DOVE 24** [7]5-9-8 M Fenton 100/1: 0P: b f Alderbrook - Flighty Dove (Cruise Missile)   **0**
Bhd, t.o./p.u. over 4f out: hdles rnr in 04/05 (ran out sole start): with R Price.

8 Ran   Time 3m 56.49 ()   Owned: Mrs Susan Roy   Trained: Newmarket

---

2782   5.35 Hill Close Gardens Apprentice Handicap Stakes 3yo+ 0-70 (G)   [66]
£3122 £892 £446   **1m4f134y**   **Firm 08**   **-83 Slow**   Inside

2436 **TRUSTED MOLE 13** [4] W M Brisbourne 6-9-4 (56) D Fentiman 15/8 FAV: 53-51621: Midfield, hdwy into   **60**
2nd over 3f out, styd on well fnl 1f to lead nr fin: slow time: eff btwn 10/12.5f, prob stays slowly run 14f,
acts on firm, soft & polytrack, any trk: see 1830.

2436 **BEN KENOBI 13** [5] Mrs P Ford 6-7-13 (37) Dean Williams 5/1: 00-52202: Mid-div, hdwy to lead over   *½* **39**
6f out, hdd nr fin: eff at 7f in banded company, winning form at 12f: acts on firm, fast & fibresand.

2293 **SAXE COBURG 19** [1] G A Ham 7-9-8 (60) W Hogg 5/1: 5103303: Handy, outpcd 3f out, styd on ins fnl   *1¼* **60**
1f: suited by 10/11.5f, stays 12.5f: see 2156.

2465 **BOND MAY DAY 12** [6] B Smart 4-10-0 (66) M Stainton(8) 7/1: 0160-004: Led till over 6f out, outpcd   *1¾* **63**
3f out, kept on fnl fnl 1f: clr of rem: see 2465.

2196 **SILENCIO 24** [8]3-8-7 (60) B O'Neill(5) 9/2: 00005: b g Sillery - Flabbergasted (Sadler's Wells)   *3½* **52**
Handy, outpcd 3f out, rallied over 1f out, no impress ins fnl 1f: cost 7,000gns: dam 1m2f wnr: with A King.

1594} **PANCAKE ROLE 405** [7]4-7-12 (1oh) (35) M Halford(3) 28/1: 040/50-6: b g Tragic Role - My Foxy Lady   *1½* **26**
(Jalmood) Bhd, nvr a factor on reapp: well btn both '03 starts (clmr, mdn, rtd 31a, with D Hayden Jones): mdn &
nov/unplcd in '02 (rtd 61): now with A Carroll.

2319 **STYLISH SUNRISE 18** [2]3-8-3 t (56) J Tucker(3) 12/1: 36-04357: Handy to 6f out, btn: with I Wood.   *6* **37**

7 Ran   Time 2m 50.75(11.45)   Owned: Mr PG Evans & David Manning Associates   Trained: Nesscliffe

---

Official Going GOOD/FIRM Track reconfigured

2783   2.30 Reading Evening Post Novice Auction Stakes 2yo (E)
£3582 £1102 £551   **6f str**   **Firm**   **Inapplicable**   Inside

1911* **AASTRAL MAGIC 36** [2] R Hannon 2-8-8   R L Moore 6/4 J FAV: 11: Made all, pushed clr ins fnl 1f,   **87+**
val 4L+: eff at 6f, 7f+ shld suit: acts on fm & fast: progressing well, see 1911.

2341 **HIGHLAND CASCADE 17** [1] J M P Eustace 2-8-6 F P Ferris(3) 6/4 J FAV: 132: Cl-up, outpcd by wnr   *3* **76**
fnl 1f: well bckd: acts on firm & fast grnd: see 2341 & 1727.

    HIDDEN STAR 0 [6] F Jordan 2-8-12 J Fortune 13/2: 3: br c Lujain - Inimitable (Polish   *3½* **72**
Precedent) Slow away, hdwy halfway, onepcd bef 1f out: bckd from 14/1 on debut: Feb foal, cost 21,000gns:
half-brother to wnrs over 1m/10f: dam wnr at 9f: sire decent sprinter at 2: encouraging effort.

1981 **HALLUCINATE 33** [3] R Hannon 2-8-9 P Dobbs 11/1: 04: b c Spectrum - Swift Spring (Bluebird)   *6* **51**
Handy, hung left from halfway & no extra: Apr foal, cost 14,000gns: half-brother to wnrs at 12f+: dam styd 1m.

2597 **ROBMANTRA 7** [5]2-8-7 S Drowne 33/1: 65: Trkd ldrs over 3f, sn hung left & fdd: qck reapp: see 2597.   *5* **34**

2310 **SIRECE 18** [4]2-8-2 T P Queally 25/1: 06: b f Josr Algarhoud - Trading Aces (Be My Chief) Slow   *1* **26**
away, al in rear: Apr foal, cost 3,500gns: half-sister plcd at 1m/14f: dam wnr at 6/7f: sire useful at up to 1m.

6 Ran   Time 1m 12.2 (1.9)   Owned: Green Pastures Partnership   Trained: Marlborough

---

2784   3.05 Rectangle Group Handicap Stakes 3yo 0-70 (E)   [77]
£3552 £1093 £547   **5f10y str**   **Firm**   **Inapplicable**   Inside

2614 **SCOTTISH EXILE 6** [14] K R Burke 3-9-5 vis (68) Darren Williams 5/1: 4310021: Cl-up, led bef 2f   **73**
out, hung left under press ins fnl 1f, rdn out to hold on: qck reapp: eff at 5f, 6f shld suit: acts on firm,
gd/soft grnd & both AWs: eff with visor: see 2614 & 1509.

2585 **ARDKEEL LASS 8** [6] D K Ivory 3-8-8 (57) J Fortune 14/1: 2306-002: Slow away, hdwy halfway, styd   *nk* **61**
on well ins fnl 1f, post came too soon: acts on firm & fast grnd: worth another try over 6f: see 2195.

2372 **BLUE MOON HITMAN 16** [12] R Brotherton 3-8-9 (58) F Norton 8/1: 4636-303: Handy, prog & ev ch ins   *nk* **61**
fnl 1f, just held in 3-way photo: bckd from 11/1: mdn after 18: see 256.

2690 **ELLIOTS CHOICE 3** [10] D Carroll 3-9-5 (68) S Drowne 7/1: 20-44004: Bhd, prog ins fnl 2f, nrst   *1* **68**
fin: qck reapp: acts on firm & fast, handles soft: see 1299.

2434 **GET TO THE POINT 13** [1]3-8-13 BL (62) R L Moore 16/1: 2250005: Dwelt, prog 2f out, nrst fin: blnks.   *1* **59**

1902 **CUT AND DRIED 37** [2]3-9-4 (67) D Holland 9/1: 1160546: Held up, prog ins fnl 2f, nrst fin: op 6/1.   *hd* **63**

2734 **SIGNOR PANETTIERE 2** [16]3-9-7 (70) P Dobbs 12/1: 0005-0267: Led over 2f, hung left & wknd   *hd* **65**
dist: qck reapp, rider reported mount had lost a front shoe: btr 1903.

2237 **LACONIA 22** [13]3-9-5 (68) Derek Nolan(7) 11/1: 2626208: Cl-up 3f, sn hung left & wknd: btr 2152.   *1¾* **58**

1729 **ORCHESTRATION 44** [8]3-9-1 (64) S Whitworth 33/1: 26-4409: Handy over 3f, sn wknd: 6 wk abs.   *¾* **52**

2586 **INNSTYLE 8** [5]3-9-1 (64) Lisa Jones(3) 12/1: 03440-60: 10th: Handy wide 3f, sn hung left & wknd.   *5* **37**

1694 **MAXIS PRINCESS 46** [4]3-8-3 P (52) K McEvoy 20/1: 4000-600: 11th: Cl-up 3f, fdd: cheek pieces.   *2* **19**

2585 **Pompey Blue 8** [3]3-8-9 (58) T P Queally(3) 14/1:0   2092 **Tikitano 28** [7]3-8-8 (2ow)(55) F Lynch 25/1:0

13 Ran   Time 59.87s (0.87)   Owned: Mrs Melba Bryce   Trained: Leyburn

2785 **3.40 Totesport Com Rated Stakes Handicap 3yo 0-95 (B)** **[99]**
£12695 £4815 £2408 **1m2f7y** **Firm** **Inapplicable** Inside

2426* **LA PERSIANA 14** [10] W Jarvis 3-8-9 (80) W Ryan 10/1: 40-5211: Handy, styd on to lead dist, rdn clr: eff at 1m, apprec recent step up to 10f, 12f shld suit: acts on firm & fast grnd: lightly rcd & useful, more prizes await: see 2426. **91+**
2250 **ROYAL WARRANT 22** [2] A M Balding 3-9-3 (88) L Keniry(3) 9/2: 3613422: Held up, hdwy 3f out, staying on when short of room ins fnl 1f, al held by wnr: well bckd: consistent performer who did nothing wrong. *1¼* **95**
1500 **TORINMOOR 56** [5] Mrs A J Perrett 3-9-6 (91) R L Moore 10/1: 316-53: Dwelt, sn handy, chsd wnr ins fnl 2f, sn onepcd: 8 wk abs: eff at 7f, now stays 10f: encouraging run & is open to more improvement. *1¾* **94**
2377* **GAVROCHE 16** [4] C A Dwyer 3-8-13 (84) J P Guillambert(3) 7/1: 5225114: Held up, hdwy ins fnl 2f, no impress ins fnl 1f: 6lb higher than recent win in 2377. *2½* **84**
2196* **LOST SOLDIER THREE 24** [1]3-9-5 (90) D Holland 7/2 FAV: 615: Handy over 7f, sn onepcd: btr 2196. *dht* **90**
2238 **DUMFRIES 22** [8]3-8-7 VIS (78) J Fortune 10/1: 031-5365: Cl-up, led 2f out, hdd dist, wknd: visor. *nk* **77**
2222* **RESERVOIR 23** [12]3-8-11 (82) P Robinson 9/1: 043-217: Led 1m, sn wknd: btr 2222 (gd, mdn). *1¼* **79**
2406 **SOUND OF FLEET 15** [7]3-8-11 (82) P Dobbs 9/1: 2-46158: Al in rear: btr 1965. *shd* **78**
4306*}**RINJANI 283** [9]3-9-7 T (92) K McEvoy 10/1: 41-9: b c Gone West - Ringshaan (Darshaan) Keen in tch, short of room after 4f, sn no impress: reapp: mdn wnr on last of only 2 '03 starts (D R Loder): eff at 1m on gd grnd: with Saeed bin Suroor. 1 Sep'03 Yarm 8.0gd 98- D: *nk* **87**
1501 **IRISH BLADE 56** [3]3-8-8 (79) D Sweeney 20/1: 0-430: 10th: Bhd, nvr a factor: btr 1501. *¾* **70**
10 Ran Time 2m 5.42 (4.82) Owned: Plantation Stud Trained: Newmarket

2786 **4.10 Royal Marbella Group Quality Homes Abroad E B F Conditions Stakes Fillies 2yo (B)**
£12087 £4585 £2292 **5f10y** **Firm** **Inapplicable** Inside

2165 **MARY READ 25** [5] B Smart 2-8-8 F Lynch 5/2 FAV: 3131: Made all, drvn out ins fnl 2f, held on gamely: eff at 5f on firm & hvy grnd: loves to race with/force the pace: game performer: see 2165 & 1458. **95**
2658* **RIGHT ANSWER 4** [7] A P Jarvis 2-8-11 D Holland 11/4: 412: Prom, ev ch when dist, kept on but just held by wnr: clr rem: qck reapp: acts on firm & gd grnd: useful run. *hd* **97**
2472 **CELTIC SPA 12** [4] Mrs P N Dutfield 2-8-8 R L Moore 11/4: 01053: Cl-up, carr left bef 2f out, onepcd dist: well bckd: btr 1608 (soft). *4* **82**
2358 **GOLD QUAY 16** [1] N P Littmoden 2-8-8 D Sweeney 16/1: 24: Handy over 3f, sn no extra: see 2358. *1* **79**
2373* **TREMPJANE 16** [6]2-8-8 P Dobbs 5/1: 15: Al in rear: btr 2373 (mdn, 6f). *1½* **74**
2241* **PIPER LILY 22** [2]2-8-11 F Norton 9/1: 516: Bhd, nvr a factor: btr 2241 (gd). *1½* **72**
6 Ran Time 1m 1.24 (2.24) Owned: S J F Racing Trained: Thirsk

2787 **4.45 Royal Marbella Group Quality Homes Abroad Handicap Stakes 3yo+ 0-90 (C)** **[86]**
£9303 £3529 £1764 **1m67y rnd** **Firm** **Inapplicable** Inside

2369* **A ONE 16** [5] H J Manners 5-7-12 (4oh) (56) F P Ferris(3) 25/1: 000-4311: Made all, rdn clr ins fnl 2f, eased cl-home, val 4L+: new stable: eff at 6f/1m on firm & fast, soft & hvy, handles fibresand: improving performer who app fine ride from F P Ferris: see 2369 (B Palling). **72+**
1664 **BAYHIRR 47** [2] M A Jarvis 3-8-13 (85) P Robinson 5/2 FAV: 0-3152: Cl-up, onepace fnl 1f: well bckd: 7 wk abs: eff at 1m, will apprec rtn to 10f: acts on firm & soft grnd: see 1664 & 1358. *2* **92**
2404* **KRUGERRAND 15** [6] W J Musson 5-9-8 (84) G Carter 6/1: 0-000013: Slow away, rear, prog ins fnl 2f, nrst fin: clr rem: gd run: see 2404 (8.9f, York). *2½* **86**
2620 **JOOLS 6** [1] D K Ivory 6-9-2 (78) D Holland 7/1: 1530044: Nvr nrr than mid-div: qck reapp: btr 1351. *5* **70**
1919 **STAR PUPIL 36** [7]3-8-10 (82) L Keniry(3) 14/1: 02-42005: Al bhd: btr 1498 (6f). *¾* **72**
1812 **DESERT OPAL 40** [10]4-10-0 (90) J Fortune 4/1: 10-00506: Handy 6f, sn wknd: 6 wk abs & top-weight. *7* **66**
2672 **COUNTYKAT 4** [9]4-8-11 vis (73) Darren Williams 11/4: 6002127: Mid-div 6f, fdd: qck reapp: perhaps too sn after fine 2nd in 2672. *7* **35**
7 Ran Time 1m 41.05 (u1.95) Owned: Mr H J Manners Trained: Swindon

2788 **5.15 Gavin & Clare Engagement Celebration Median Auction Maiden Stakes 3-4yo (E)**
£3435 £1057 £529 **1m3f135y** **Firm** **Inapplicable** Inside

2366 **BIENVENUE 16** [10] M P Tregoning 3-8-2 (67) R L Moore 7/2 FAV: 235-41: Handy, prog to lead 2f out, sn switched to stands rail, rdn out: eff at 1m/10f, improvd for step up to 11.6f: acts on firm, gd & polytrack. **69**
701 **PONT NEUF 125** [17] J W Hills 4-9-2 t (55) S Whitworth 33/1: 200-0042: b f Revoque - Petite Maxine (Sharpo) Mid-div, hdwy 4f out, styd on ins fnl 1f, al held by wnr: long abs: rnr-up on 1 of 4 '03 starts (rtd related mdn): eff at 9/11.6f on firm & gd/soft grnd: eff with t-strap. *1¼* **64**
2 May'03 Ayr 9.1g/s 65-(68) E: 2 Sep'02 Sout 8af 70a- F: 2 Aug'02 Wind 8.3g/s 73- F:
2393 **SHONGWENI 15** [14] P J McBride 3-8-7 T P Queally(3) 13/2: 433: Handy, prog 3f out, hung left & onepcd dist: acts on firm grnd & polytrack: now quals for h'caps: see 2393. *¾* **67**
GARNETT 0 [7] A King 3-8-8 (1ow) D Holland 12/1: 4: b c Desert Story - In Behind (Entitled) Dwelt, prog ins fnl 4f, nrst fin: debut. *5* **61**
2196 **ROSSALL POINT 24** [8]3-8-7 S Drowne 9/1: 45: Rear, prog 4f out, no impress fnl 2f. *¾* **59**
2393 **MAXIMINUS 15** [16]4-9-7 (56) L Keniry(3) 14/1: 0/00-406: Nvr nrr than mid-div. *nk* **58$**
2392 **DANCE PARTY 15** [13]4-9-2 p (60) P Robinson 11/1: 3004007: Prom, ev ch 2f out, sn wknd: btr 1082. *½* **52**
2131 **SECRET JEWEL 26** [2]4-9-2 (72) K McEvoy 11/2: 0/0-68: Held up, nvr nrr than mid-div: btr 2131. *2* **49**
734 **LOOKOUTHEREICOME 122** [18]3-8-2 Lisa Jones(3) 66/1: 009: Slow away, nvr a factor: long abs. *3* **44**
2534 **HOLD UP 9** [6]3-8-3 (1ow) B Reilly 25/1: 0-00: 10th: Cl-up 7f, fdd. *10* **30**
2393 **CHARLESTON 15** [9]3-8-7 BL (73) J Fortune 4/1: 22240: 11th: Led till 2 out, fdd: disapp in blnks. *shd* **33**
2261 **FRANGIPANI 21** [1]3-8-2 (70) N De Souza(5) 8/1: 334-30: 12th: Handy 7f, fdd. *nk* **27**
SAMARIA 0 [5]3-8-2 F Norton 16/1: 0: 13th: Mid-div 1m, sn wknd. *5* **19**
1307 **Green Ocean 66** [3]4-9-2 (50) D Sweeney 50/1:0 2393 **Pitton Mill 15** [11]4-9-7 A Quinn(5) 100/1:0
2058 **Watchful Witness 30** [4]4-9-7 Lucy Russell(7) 33/1:0

2205 Rumour Mill 23 [15]3-8-7 (45) P Doe 66/1:0

17 Ran   Time 2m 30.88(3.58)   Owned: Mr Stanley J Sharp   Trained: Lambourn

PONTEFRACT   MONDAY 28.06.04   Lefthand, Undulating Track, Stiff Uphill Finish

Official Going GOOD/FIRM.

2789	2.15 Gerrard Financial Planning Services Maiden Auction Stakes 2yo (E)

£4784 £1472 £736   **5f rnd**   **Good/Firm 40**   **-13 Slow**   Inside

2360 **MIMI MOUSE 17** [2] T D Easterby 2-8-4   P Robinson 5/2: 6431: Made virtually all, hard prsd & hung   82
right to stands side fnl 1f but held on well for press: jockey received a 1 day whip ban: imprvd eff from the front
over this stiff/undul 5f on gd/firm: game eff, see 1212.

2165 **TAGULA SUNRISE 26** [1] R A Fahey 2-8-9   P Hanagan 2/5 FAV: 222: Trkd wnr, eff to chall dist, kept   hd   86
on, just held ins last: well bckd, jockey received a 2 day whip ban: clr of rem & shown enough to win a race.

2547 **HILLSIDE HEATHER 10** [3] A Berry 2-8-2   F Norton 16/1: 43: Prom, eff dist, sn wknd: see 2547.   3   70

PRO TEMPORE [4] Mrs J R Ramsden 2-8-4 L Goncalves 40/1: 4: b f Fraam - Record Time (Clantime)   2½   65
Keen, held up, btn over 2f out on debut: Jan 1st foal, cost 21,000 gns: dam 5f wnr: speedily bred.

1874 **HAMBURG SPRINGER 39** [6]2-8-7 J F McDonald(3) 100/1: 05: b g Charnwood Forest - Kyra Crown   16   20
(Astronef) Slow away & al bhd, t.o.: Mar foal, cost £10,000: half brother to wnrs over 5f/1m: bred to stay 7f/1m.

5 Ran   Time 1m 03.95 (2.65)   Owned: Mrs Jean P Connew   Trained: Malton

2790	2.45 Smeaton Selling Handicap Stakes 3yo 35-55 (F)	[64]

£3458 £1064 £532   **1m4f8y**   **Good/Firm 40**   **-13 Slow**   Inside

2299 **LET IT BE 20** [2] Mrs M Reveley 3-8-4 (40) P Hanagan 7/2 FAV: 00-25051: Chsd ldrs, hdwy to lead   47
over 2f out, clr dist, drvn to hold on ins last: well bckd, bought in for 6,600 gns: 1st win: imprvd for step up to
12f & acts on gd/firm & gd/soft, poss any trk: gd confidence boost & enjoyed drop in class: see 1363.

2423 **BIENHEUREUX 15** [4] W J Musson 3-8-4 (40) R Mullen 11/1: 00-00002: b g Bien Bien - Rochea (Rock   hd   46
City) Held up, hdwy over 2f out, chsd wnr ins last, kept on, just held: clr rem: clmd for 6,000: poor form prev &
imprvd for step up to 12f on fast grnd & drop to sell h'cap company: shld find similar.

326 **DEFANA 174** [11] M Dods 3-9-4 (54) L Enstone(3) 16/1: 0653-53: b g Defacto - Thalya (Crofthall)   5   53
Slow away, held up, eff 2f out, onepace: long abs: plcd fnl '03 start (sell, rtd 57): poss eff over a stiff/undul
12f on fast grnd in sell grade.

2123 **VALIANT AIR 27** [5] J R Weymes 3-8-4 BL (40) W Supple 5/1: 4524004: Led after 1f till 2f out, wknd.   nk   38

2691 **THEATRE BELLE 4** [3]3-9-1 VIS (51) D Allan 14/1: 00-00065: In tch, wknd over 2f out: tried visor.   1¼   47

2576 **SCORCHIO 9** [6]3-8-9 (45) E Ahern 4/1: 06-62546: Cl-up, wknd over 2f out: btr 2576.   shd   40

2346 **ROYAL UPSTART 18** [9]3-7-13 bl (35) B Swarbrick(5) 7/1: 0-032657: In tch, wknd 2f out: see 1675.   24   0

1836 **CIACOLE 41** [7]3-9-0 (50) Dean McKeown 12/1: 0403108: Handy, wknd over 2f out: twice below 1630.   7   1

1740 **WEAVER SPELL 45** [8]3-7-13 (35) F Norton 14/1: 006-5649: Hld up, btn over 3f out: abs, see 1312.   8   0

2123 **BAROQUE 27** [8]3-7-12 (14oh)BL (20) M Halford(6) 50/1: 000600: 10th: b c Merdon Melody - Dubitable   1¼   0
(Formidable) Cl-up, wknd over 2f out: blnks: mod form.

2125 **REEDSMAN 27** [10]3-8-6 (42) T Eaves(2) 9/1: 00-20000: 11th: Slow away & bhd, t.o./virtually p.u.   22   0
ins last: op 12/1: surely something amiss: see 2125, 495.

11 Ran   Time 2m 40.45 (6.35)   Owned: Mr A Frame   Trained: Saltburn

2791	3.15 E B F Gerrard Wealth Management Handicap Stakes Fillies 3yo+ 0-85 (D)	[84]

£10452 £3216 £1608   **6f rnd**   **Good/Firm 40**   **+07 Fast**   Inside

2398 **SHAROURA 16** [7] R A Fahey 8-8-3 (59) P Hanagan 10/1: 3505-501: Chsd ldrs, hdwy over 1f out, styd   68
on to lead ins last, drvn: gd time: confirmed promise of 2398 & suited by 6f, stays 7f on firm, soft & fibresand,
any trk: imprvd in gd form: see 1973.

2451 **COMPLICATION 14** [3] J A R Toller 4-8-9 bl (65) T P Queally(3) 9/2: 00-06242: Handy, hdwy over 1f   nk   73
out, styd on to chall ins last, just held: gd run: see 2289, 1726.

2409* **CLOUD DANCER 16** [9] K A Ryan 5-9-4 (76) N Callan 5/2 FAV: 0-302213: Slow away, held up, hdwy   1¼   80
over 2f out, kept on ins last, not reach front pair: in gd form: see 2409.

2429 **DANI RIDGE 15** [6] E J Alston 6-10-0 (84) J D O'Reilly(7) 11/1: 0030-404: Prom, hdwy to lead over   ½   86
1f out, hdd & no extra ins last: best eff: see 2240.

2429 **COLLEGE QUEEN 15** [10]6-8-3 bl (64) W Supple 16/1: 00-06545: Hld up, late gains, nvr dngrs.   ½   64

2057 **FAVOUR 31** [4]4-9-3 (73) J Murtagh 9/2: 0223-206: Held up, most late gains: btr 1878.   1   70

2566 **BARON RHODES 9** [1]3-9-1 (78) T Eaves(3) 12/1: 2223137: Led till over 1f out, wknd: btr 2566.   nk   74

2539 **BINT ROYAL 10** [11]6-8-2 p (58) M Halford(7) 10/1: 0340438: Chsd ldrs, edged left & wknd dist.   ¾   52

2055 **BOWLING ALONG 31** [5]3-7-13 (1ow)(8oh) (53) R Ffrench 100/1: 300-5009: Nvr a factor: see 1465.   1   53

2561 **JUST ONE SMILE 9** [8]4-8-1 BL (57) D Allan 16/1: 2-036000: 10th: Slow away & bhd, eff when badly   nk   47
hmpd ins last, no ch after: tried blnks & shade closer with clr run: see 1660, 22.

2464 **MARABAR 13** [2]6-8-3 bl (59) B Swarbrick(5) 20/1: 3122660: 11th: In tch, wknd 2f out: btr 2204, 1804.   hd   48

11 Ran   Time 1m 16.1 (2)   Owned: Manor House Partnership   Trained: Malton

2792	3.45 Spindrifter Conditions Stakes 2yo (C)

£7238 £2746 £1373   **6f rnd**   **Good/Firm 40**   **-07 Slow**   Inside

2028* **LEOS LUCKY STAR 32** [2] M Johnston 2-9-2   J Fanning 2/7 FAV: 11: Made all, clr fnl 1f, easily,   100+
val 5L+: well bckd under top-weight: eff at 6f on fast grnd, shld stay 7f+: likes to force the pace & proved a
class above these rivals, List/Gr 3 company shld now suit: see 2028.

2522 **TOM FOREST 11** [9] A Crook 2-8-10 L Enstone(3) 9/1: 622: Prom, went after wnr 2f out, sn no   3½   80
impress: clr of rem: sound run, caught a tartar today: has shown enough to find similar, see 2522.

BUNNY RABBIT [4] B J Meehan 2-8-7   K McEvoy 10/1: 3: b c Cherokee Run - Jane's The Name   5   64

PONTEFRACT   MONDAY 28.06.04   Lefthand, Undulating Track, Stiff Uphill Finish

(Trempolino) Dwelt, modest late hdwy, nvr dngrs on debut: Feb first foal, cost $150,000: dam unrcd.

2165 **TIVISKI** 26 [7] E J Alston 2-8-11 W Supple 9/1: 34104: Chsd ldrs, btn 2f out: btr 1573 (5f).		2	62
2165 **TANTIEN** 26 [3]2-8-5 T P Queally(3) 40/1: 5405: Chsd ldrs 4f, sn btn: highly tried.		½	54
THE PLAINSMAN [1]2-8-7 E Ahern 66/1: 6: b g Atraf - Mylania (Midyan) Dwelt, nvr a factor on debut: cheaply bght Mar first foal: dam stayed 1m sire a high-class sprinter: with P Hiatt.		10	26
2358 **DEN PERRY** 17 [6]2-8-10 F Lynch 100/1: 607: Chsd wnr till halfway, wknd qckly: see 2167.		3½	19

7 Ran   Time 1m 16.94 (2.84)   Owned: Mrs S J Brookhouse   Trained: Middleham

---

2793   **4.15 Wragby Maiden Stakes Fillies 3yo   (D)**
£5525 £1700 £850   **1m2f6y   Good/Firm 40   -01 Slow   Inside**

2419 **POSTERITAS** 15 [6] H R A Cecil 3-8-11 R Hughes 2/1: 321: Chsd ldrs, led dist, rdn clr: apprec this step up to 10f, acts on fast & firm grnd: handles a gall trk: consistent: see 2419 & 2224.			86
2534 **FORTUNES PRINCESS** 10 [1] M J Wallace 3-8-11 E Ahern 9/2: 22: Prom, led 3f out till dist, no extra: shld find a small race, see 2534.		3	81
2386 **DALISAY** 16 [3] Sir Michael Stoute 3-8-11 F Lynch 9/2: 0-33: Chsd ldrs, not pace to chall fnl 1f: clr of rem: now quals for h'caps & 12f+ shld suit: see 2386.		1¾	78
1666 **CHANTELOUP** 48 [2] J R Fanshawe 3-8-11 J Murtagh 15/8 FAV: 244: Led till 3f out, eased when btn fnl 1f: bckd from 9/4, 7 wk abs: much btr prev on soft grnd in 1666.		5	71
4408] **SIERRA** 279 [7]3-8-11 T P Queally(3) 33/1: 0-5: ch f Dr Fong - Warning Belle (Warning) Dwelt, nvr troubled ldrs on reapp: fin last on sole juv start: 18,000gns half-sister to a 7f juv wnr: dam unrcd.		1¼	69
2058 **DARING GAMES** 31 [5]3-8-11 R Ffrench 80/1: 56: Bhd, t.o. fnl 2f.		dist	0

6 Ran   Time 2m 12.17 (4.07)   Owned: Mr K Abdulla   Trained: Newmarket

---

2794   **4.45 Betfair Com Apprentice Series Round 3 Handicap Stakes 3yo+ 0-70 (E)**   **[70]**
£4173 £1284 £642   **1m2f6y   Good/Firm 40   -06 Slow   Inside**

2628* **REALISM** 7 [5] P W Hiatt 4-9-13 (6ex) (69) Steven Harrison(3) 11/2: 0361211: Chsd ldrs, led ins fnl 1f, styd on strongly, rdn out: op 4/1: eff at 1m/10f on gd, fast grnd & fibresand: in fine form, see 2628.			79
2628 **SMART JOHN** 7 [9] W M Brisbourne 4-9-7 (63) D Fentiman 15/2: 050-4142: Held up, gd hdwy to lead 2f out, collared ins fnl 1f, not btn far: 6L clr rem: gd run bhd an in-form rival: again bhd today's wnr in 2628.		1	72
4318] **VALEUREUX** 284 [8] J Hetherton 6-8-10 (52) M Halford 6/1: 433002-3: ch g Cadeaux Genereux - La Strada (Niniski) Held up, imprvd to chase ldrs 2f out, btn fnl 1f: 2 months jumps abs, won 2 nov hdles in 03/04 (rtd 128h, 2m1f, gd/soft & hvy): h'cap plcd in '03, unsuccessfully tried cheek pieces: h'cap plcd in '02, 01 mdn wnr: eff at 1m/10f on fast & hvy grnd, likes a gall trk. 2 Sep'03 Ayr 10.9g/f 54-52 E: 1 Mar'01 Nott 8.2hvy 84- D:		6	52
2323 **DERWENT** 19 [3] J D Bethell 5-10-0 bl (70) S Shaw(7) 20/1: 0/03-0004: b g Distant View - Nothing Sweeter (Darby Creek Road) Rear, styd on late under press, nvr dngrs: top-weight: twice rcd in '03, dist last of 3 (class stks): '02 mdn & dual h'cap wnr: eff at 10f, has tried 12f: acts on gd/soft, loves fast & firm grnd: likes a stiff/gall trk, esp Pontefract: can go well fresh & eff in blnks: dropped to a handy mark. 1 Sep'02 Pont 10fm 88-84 C: 1 Jul'02 Pont 10g/f 86-81 D: 1 Jun'02 Donc 10.2g/f 83- D:		shd	70
2572 **WELL MEET AGAIN** 9 [1]4-8-11 (53) D Tudhope 9/1: 065-3045: Chsd ldrs, onepcd fnl 2f.		2½	49
1214 **PENWELL HILL** 73 [2]5-8-12 (54) Laura Jayne Crawford 14/1: 5-102206: Led till 2f out, wknd: 10 wk abs.		8	38
1821 **MARKET AVENUE** 41 [7]5-9-6 (62) A Mullen(3) 7/4 FAV: 000006-67: Keen & prom, ev ch 2f out, sn btn: hvly bckd from 9/4, 6 wk abs: much btr expected, but rcd too keenly here: showed promise in 1821.		4	40
2168 **GIVEN A CHANCE** 26 [4]3-7-12 (6oh) (46) Dean Williams 50/1: 0534268: Chsd ldrs 1m, wknd: btr 1947.		6	20
2572* **NIGHT MARKET** 9 [10]6-8-10 (50) J D O'Reilly 7/1: 0600-019: Keen & prom, wknd 3f out, eased & t.o.: much too keen today, see 2572 (1m).		dist	0
50] **DRAGON PRINCE** 587 [6]4-9-12 (68) A Reilly(3) 20/1: 060/-0: 10th: b g Zamindar - Nawafell (Kris) Keen & al rear, t.o.: well btn in a nov hdle 3 month ago: missed '03, some mdn promise for M Jarvis in '02 (rtd 77), has since been gelded: now with R Guest & saddle slipped today.		1	0

10 Ran   Time 2m 12.66(4.56)   Owned: Miss Maria McKinney   Trained: Banbury

---

WINDSOR   MONDAY 28.06.04   Sharp, Figure 8 Track

Official Going GOOD (GOOD/SOFT IN PLACES). Times Suggest Much Faster.

2795   **6.40 Royal Marbella Group Quality Homes Abroad Median Auction Maiden Stakes Fillies 2yo (E)**
£3455 £1063 £532   **5f10y   Good/Firm   Fair   Inside**

2033 **ROODEYE** 32 [4] R F Johnson Houghton 2-8-11 K Fallon 9/4 FAV: 21: Made all, pushed out ins fnl 1f, val 3L: joc rec a 1 day whip ban: eff at 5f, shld get 6f, acts on firm & fast: going right way.			94
2490 **CASTELLETTO** 12 [3] B A McMahon 2-8-11 G Gibbons 4/1: 3202: Rcd in 2nd, kept on but no impress on wnr over 1f out: clr of rem: rider rec a 1 day whip ban: fair run: see 2151 & 1608.		1¾	87
NOORAIN 0 [8] M R Channon 2-8-11 S Hitchcott(3) 25/1: 3: ch f Kabool - Abeyr (Unfuwain) Handy, outpcd halfway, kept on again ins fnl 1f on debut: Apr foal: half sister to wnrs over 6/7f: dam 7f/1m wnr: sure to improve & apprec 6f.		3	78
MAGICAL ROMANCE 0 [5] B J Meehan 2-8-11 J Fortune 7/1: 4: b f Barathea - Shouk (Shirley Heights) Dwelt, sn handy, no impress over 1f out on debut: op 10/1: Feb foal, cost 125,000gns: half sister to wnrs over 7f/10f: dam 11f wnr: bred to need 1m+ in time.		½	76
2287 **MABELLA** 20 [9]2-8-11 S Drowne 50/1: 05: b f Brave Act - Wee Merkin (Thatching) Chsd ldrs, outpcd 2f out: Mar first foal, cost 15,000gns: half sister to wnrs over 7f/10f.		½	74
2395 **SAUCEPOT** 16 [7]2-8-11 A Daly 40/1: 06: Chsd ldrs, btn sn after halfway.		3	65
2097 **LIWAS LAKE** 28 [2]2-8-11 T L Dettori 11/4: 37: Chsd ldrs, fdd after halfway: tried t-strap.		10	35
2297 **BEAUTIFUL MOVER** 20 [1]2-8-11 R Hills 7/1: 238: Bhd, hdwy after 2f, fdd 2f out: see 2297.		3½	24
MIDNIGHT LACE 0 [6]2-8-11 R L Moore 16/1: 9: Bhd, t.o. on debut.		5	9

9 Ran   Time 1m 0.54 (1.54)   Owned: Mrs H Johnson Houghton   Trained: Didcot

---

2796   **7.10 Collyer Bristow Solicitors Handicap Stakes Fillies 3yo+ 0-75 (E)**   **[67]**
£4121 £1268 £634   1m3f135y   Good/Firm   Fast   Inside. Rcd Far Side in Str.

2510 **FEED THE METER 11** [8] T T Clement 4-8-13 (52) Saleem Golam(7) 10/1: 00/0-021: Rear, styd on over   58
1f out to lead nr fin, rdn out: first win: apprec first start at 11.5f on fast & gd: open to improvement.
2283 **KRISTALS DREAM 20** [3] J L Dunlop 3-9-7 (74) L Dettori 5/1: 031-3502: Led, chall fnl 1f, hdd nr   hd   78
fin: stayed longer 11.6f tripf: gd eff: see 1369.
2621 **BLAZE OF COLOUR 7** [7] Sir Michael Stoute 3-9-3 (70) K Fallon 9/4 FAV: 0-3423: Handy, hdwy & ev   ¾   74
ch ins fnl 1f, onepcd cl-home: bckd tho' op 6/4, qck reapp, clr of rem: handles fast & gd/soft: see 2621.
2617* **FOXILLA 7** [5] D R C Elsworth 3-8-8 (6ex) (61) R Thomas(5) 11/4: 00-00314: Handy, onepcd over 1f   4   59
out: qck reapp: not quite stay this longer trip?: shade btr 2617 (10f).
2117 **CHAMBRAY 28** [1]3-8-5 (58) N Chalmers(5) 12/1: 5-005: b f Barathea - Spurned (Robellino) Mid-div,   ½   55
onepcd over 2f out: h'cap bow: mdn unplcd sole '03 start (rtd 51): with A Balding.
1960 **VANILLA MOON 35** [2]4-8-9 vis (48) J Egan 13/2: 05-52436: Rcd in 2nd to 2f out, no extra: btr 1960.   5   37
4910} **BEAUCHAMP RIBBON 245** [6]4-10-0 (67) V Slattery 25/1: 113030-7: b f Vettori - Beauchamp Kate   dist   0
(Petoski) Slow away, sn in tch, wknd 3f out, t.o.: reapp, top-weight: won 2 sellers & a h'cap in '03 (with G
Butler): mdn unplcd in '02 (rtd 56a): suited by 10/11.7f: acts on firm & fast, poss any trk: eff in blnks, has
tried a t-strap: goes well in sell grade: now with A Chamberlain.
1 Sep'03 Chep 10.2g/f 69-60 F: 1 Aug'03 Brig 9.9fm 61-(58) G: 1 Aug'03 Bath 11.7fm 51-(58) G:
2 Jun'03 Chep 8.1g/f 57-53 E: 2 Jun'03 Wind 10.0g/f 56-53 E:
1973} **DONT MATTER 388** [4]4-9-6 (59) Joanna Badger 40/1: 5400/00-8: b f Petong - Cool Run (Deep Run)   ¾   0
Dwelt, rear, t.o.: reapp: unplcd both '03 starts (with B Palling): mdn & nurs unplcd in '02 (rtd 63).
8 Ran   Time 2m 29.28 (1.98)   Owned: Mr P Harper   Trained: Newmarket

---

2797   **7.40 Weatherbys Bank Rated Stakes Handicap 3yo 0-85 (D)**   **[92]**
£6136 £2328 £1164   6f   Good/Firm   Slow   Inside. 2 Groups.

2609* **RED ROMEO 8** [2] G A Swinbank 3-9-0 (3ex) (78) K Fallon 13/8 FAV: 16-24411: Mid-div, switched to   87
far side halfway, led that group 1f out & sn overall ldr, rdn out: nicely bckd: eff at 6f, stays 7f well: acts on
fast & gd/soft, any trk: fast improving, see 2609 & 1360.
2677 **VIENNAS BOY 5** [5] R Hannon 3-9-4 (82) Dane O'Neill 12/1: 4646052: Handy, switched far side & led   1¼   85
group halfway, hdd 1f out & onepace: qck reapp: back to form, likes Windsor: see 1018.
1901 **BATHWICK BILL 38** [9] B R Millman 3-9-3 (81) G Baker 6/1: 530-0623: Led near side, no extra &   nk   83
lost overall lead ins fnl 1f: gd run: see 1901.
2590 **ASK THE CLERK 9** [8] V Smith 3-8-7 (71) Rory Moore(7) 8/1: 0203464: Mid-div near side, hdwy into   hd   72
2nd halfway, kept on ins fnl 1f: op 12/1: shade btr 975 (soft).
2650 **DR SYNN 6** [6]3-8-4 (3oh) (65) J Quinn 8/1: 6-06365: Bhd near side, some late gains ins fnl 1f.   nk   68
2400* **FICTIONAL 16** [1]3-9-7 (85) G Gibbons 4/1: 03132-16: Mid-div, switched to far side halfway, no impress.   2½   77
1901 **TRICK CYCLIST 38** [4]3-8-12 (76) T Block(7) 20/1: 00-24067: Switched far side halfway, btn 2f out.   ¾   66
2587 **MR HULLABALOU 9** [3]3-8-6 (70) M Henry 50/1: 0045008: Bhd, switched far side halfway, nvr nr ldrs.   shd   59
2482 **RIVER TREAT 12** [7]3-9-4 (82) S Drowne 10/1: 524-1659: Rcd in 2nd, switched far side halfway, sn btn.   1½   66
9 Ran   Time 1m 13.24 (2.94)   Owned: Mr J Yates   Trained: Richmond

---

2798   **8.10 Royal Marbella Group Quality Homes Abroad Premier Claiming Stakes 3yo+ (D)**
£6949 £2138 £1069   1m2f7y   Good/Firm   Fast   Inside

2405 **KUSTER 16** [4] L M Cumani 8-9-12 bl (90) A Hamblett(7) 5/1: 0115-061: Rear, hdwy to lead/trav best   95
2f out, kept up to work ins fnl 1f, v cmftbly, val 5L+: suited by 10/12f on firm or gd/soft, acts on any trk:
useful, relished drop in grade, see 2405.
2265 **BARKING MAD 21** [3] M L W Bell 6-9-10 (82) K Fallon 4/6 FAV: 350-6432: Rcd in 2nd, led over 6f   3   85
out till 2f out, no extra: caught a useful sort & must win a claimer: see 1890.
2724* **MANIATIS 3** [7] Andrew Reid 7-9-4 vis (70) J F Egan 5/2: 6110213: Mid-div, hdwy into 2nd 4f out,   3½   75
lost plc over 2f out & sn no impress: qck reapp: shade below winning form of 2724 (fibresand).
2264 **CLOUDINGSWELL 21** [1] D L Williams 3-7-13 (57) N De Souza(3) 20/1: 006-0664: Led till over 4f out,   12   50
no extra over 2f out: see 1528.
4 Ran   Time 2m 6.74 (0.74)   Owned: Mrs Luca Cumani   Trained: Newmarket

---

2799   **8.40 Slough Estates Handicap Stakes 3yo+ 0-70 (E)**   **[70]**
£5447 £1676 £838   1m67y   Good/Firm   Fast   Inside. All bar one rcd Far Side.

4515} **FIREWIRE 273** [12] Miss B Sanders 6-9-3 (59) S Sanders 8/1: 212000-1: b g Blushing Flame - Bay   69
Risk (Risk Me) Bhd, hdwy 2f out, drvn out to lead well ins fnl 1f: reapp: won 1 of 7 '03 starts (h'cap): modest
for N Hamilton in '02 (h'caps, rtd 64): eff at 1m/10f on fast & gd, sharp or gall trks: runs well fresh.
2 Aug'03 Wind 8.3g/f 62-59 E: 1 Jul'03 Kemp 8g/f 62-53 E: 2 Jul'03 Kemp 9g/f 54-53 E: 2 Jul'01 Nott 10g/f 69-67 E:
1 Jun'01 Nott 10gd 68-62 E:
2063 **EL CHAPARRAL 30** [11] D K Ivory 4-9-6 (62) Dane O'Neill 25/1: 03/-06002: Bhd, hdwy over 2f out,   ¾   69+
plenty to do 1f out, 'flew home', nrst fin: stays 8.3f, well worth a try over further.
2634 **CAPTAIN MARRYAT 7** [10] P W Harris 3-8-7 (59) K Fallon 2/1 FAV: 0-20223: In tch, hwy 2f out,   ¾   64
onepcd over 1f out: qck reapp: consistent: see 2423.
2502 **AZREME 11** [8] D K Ivory 4-9-13 (69) M Howard(7) 9/1: 6-150454: Mid-div, hdwy to lead over 1f out,   hd   73
hdd nr fin & no extra: eff over 7f/8.5f on fast, hvy & both AWs: shade btr 1537 (class stks).
1541 **ESPERANCE 55** [1]4-8-3 (45) J Quinn 40/1: 0000-005: ch g Bluebird - Dioscorea (Pharly) Rcd in   nk   48
2nd, rcd alone near side down straight, no impress ins fnl 1f: 8 wk abs: rnr-up in a clmr in '03 (with M Tompkins):
3rd 1 of 2 '02 starts (mdn, rtd 74): eff at 7/11f on fast, soft & polytrack: has tried cheek pieces.
2 Jun'03 Hami 11.1g/f 64-(63) E:
2604 **CLASSIC VISION 8** [5]4-8-12 bl (54) R Hills 15/2: 0450106: Bhd, late gains, no impress.   1½   54
2170 **MYTHICAL CHARM 26** [7]5-8-9 (51) A Daly 20/1: 0633007: Led over 2f out, hdd over 1f out.   2   47
2394 **FLORIAN 16** [9]6-9-7 P (63) R Miles(3) 10/1: 41133-08: b g Young Ern - Murmuring (Kind of Hush)   3½   52

848

WINDSOR MONDAY 28.06.04 Sharp, Figure 8 Track

Led till over 2f out, no extra: won 2 h'caps in '03 (earlier with P Mitchell): mdn h'cap & appr h'cap rnr-up in
'02: eff at 7f/1m on fast & both AWs, sharp or easy trks: goes well fresh, with forcing tactics: tried cheek
pieces. 1 Aug'03 Kemp 8g/f 62-57 E: 1 May'03 Ling 8ap 63a-56 E: 2 Jan'03 Ling 7ap 57a-55 F:
2 Jan'02 Ling 7ap 55a-52 F: 2 Jan'02 Ling 8ap 55a-50 F:

2452	SMOOTHLY DOES IT 14 [4]3-9-0 (66) E Ahern 13/2: 20-02069: Handy, wknd over 2f out.						nk	54
2755	ONE ALONE 2 [6]3-7-12 (5oh) (45) D Fox(5) 66/1: 000-0000: 10th: Mid-div, no impress 4f out: qk reapp.						1¼	35
2260	MY MAITE 22 [3]5-8-5 vis t (47) N Day 9/1: 2400160: 11th: Bhd, nvr a factor: btr 1992.						½	31
917	COPPINGTON FLYER 96 [14]4-8-3 (45) C Catlin 12/1: 0-404040: 12th: In tch, no impress 2f out.						1½	26
1132	BELTANE 77 [13]6-8-4 (46) J F Egan 25/1: P-001200: 13th: Chsd ldrs, lost pl & btn 5f out: abs.						5	17
3506}	LADY WEST 323 [2]4-7-12 (2oh) (38) Lucy Russell(6) 66/1: 200/000-0: 14th: Rear, t.o. on reapp.						25	0

14 Ran Time 1m 44.01 (1.01) Owned: Miss Jennie Wisher Trained: Epsom

---

2800 9.10 At The Races : Dedicated To Racing Classified Stakes 3yo+ 0-65 (E)
£3621 £1114 £557 1m2f7y Good/Firm Fair Inside. Wnr rcd alone on stands side.

2277	HATCH A PLAN 21 [2] R M Beckett 3-8-6 (62) J Quinn 50/1: 000-0U01: Bhd, rcd alone near side down			73

straight, led fnl 1f, pushed clr, val 4L: eff at 10f on fast grnd: one of few jocks prepared to back his own judgement.

2761*	MISS PEBBLES 2 [4] B R Johnson 4-9-7 vis (65) N Pollard 9/4 FAV: 1400512: Keen bhd, hdwy to lead		3	70

main group ent fnl 1f, no impress on wnr: qck reapp: gd run: see 2761.

2267	COSI FAN TUTTE 21 [1] M C Pipe 6-9-4 vis t (65) R Miles(3) 10/1: 25410/-23: Handy, led main group		1¼	65

over 3f out till ent fnl 1f, no extra: see 2267.

4658}	MALAK AL MOULOUK 264 [7] J M P Eustace 4-9-4 (65) S Sanders 50/1: 425-4: ch g King of Kings -		nk	64

Honor To Her (Sir Ivor) Handy, hdwy to chall over 1f out, onepcd ins fnl 1f on reapp: rnr-up 1 of 3 '03 starts
(mdn): eff at 7f/1m on fast & fibresand: lightly rcd 4yo. 2 Sep'03 Sout 7af 64a- D:

2376	MUSTANG ALI 17 [11]3-8-9 (68) J F Egan 12/1: 03-60355: In tch, hdwy 2f out, onepcd fnl 1f: see 2175.		1½	65
2433	KIRKHAM ABBEY 14 [12]4-9-4 vis (65) J Fortune 7/2: 011-0326: Rear, hdwy 2f out, onepcd fnl 1f.		1½	60
2621	PLANTERS PUNCH 7 [5]3-8-10 vis (69) K Fallon 5/1: 0-000107: Bhd, hdwy 2f out, wknd: qck reapp.		¾	63
2265	SECLUDED 21 [6]4-9-8 (69) L Dettori 5/1: 4355-58: Made most till over 3f out, no extra 2f out: see 2265.		2	60
43*	ALMOND WILLOW 224 [10]3-8-6 (68) E Ahern 12/1: 060361-9: Mid-div, no impress over 1f out: abs.		2	53
2500	BAND 11 [3]4-9-4 (62) G Gibbons 50/1: 360-0000: 10th: Keen & handy, no impress over 2f out: see 1883.		nk	52
1484	ENVIRONMENT AUDIT 58 [8]5-9-4 vis (65) V Slattery 33/1: 0/0-00000: 11th: With ldr, ev ch 3f out,		1½	50

no impress over 2f out: 8 wk abs: see 979.

2540	COMPETITOR 10 [9]3-8-11 (70) C Catlin 20/1: 10-200: 12th: Keen in rear, nvr a factor.		8	43

12 Ran Time 2m 10.08(4.08) Owned: TGS Sijpesteijn and Deal Trained: Lambourn

---

SOUTHWELL Fibresand MONDAY 28.06.04 Lefthand, Sharp, Oval Track

Official Going Standard

2801 2.00 St Basilides Day Apprentice Claiming Stakes 4yo+ (G)
£2954 £844 £422 7f aw rnd Going 42 +04 Fast Inside

2504	ALI BRUCE 11 [9] D E Cantillon 4-9-5 Hayley Turner 11/4: 521: Dwelt, sn cl-up & led over 4f			60a

out, rdn clr over 2f out, drvn to hold on: best time of day: clmd by N Shields for 12,000: 1st win, AW bow: eff at
7f/1m, tried 10f: acts on gd & fibresand, sharp/turning or gall trk: likes to race with/force the pace in claim grade.

2451	MACS TALISMAN 14 [3] V Smith 4-9-3 (55) Rory Moore(3) 2/1 FAV: 003-0002: Dwelt, sn pushed along &		½	56a

rdn/styd on well from over 1f out, not reach wnr: bckd, apprec rtn to fibresand: see 1806.

1839	COUNTRYWIDE GIRL 40 [8] A Berry 5-8-2 (39) P Mathers(3) 16/1: 4332153: Chsd ldrs, hung left &		1	39a

kept on onepace fnl 2f: 6 wk abs: see 1676 (banded).

2688	NICHOLAS NICKELBY 4 [1] M J Polglase 4-9-1 P (62) M Savage 16/1: 2-062004: Handy, no extra over		2½	47a

1f out: cheek pieces: btr 1966.

2337*	ONLY ONE LEGEND 18 [7]6-8-11 bl (60) C Williams(7) 4/1: 0030315: Chsd ldrs till lost pl after 3f,		1¼	40a

no threat after: much btr 2337 (C/D).

2501	HEADLAND 11 [5]6-8-5 bl (49) D Fentiman(5) 10/1: 0030306: Led/dsptd lead 3f, btn over 1f out: btr 890.		5	25a
2501	BANDBOX 11 [2]9-8-5 (32) D Fox 20/1: 0600-057: Sn bhd & nvr factor: see 2501.		6	14a
2480	MATRIARCHAL 12 [9]4-8-7 (38) Janice Webster(3) 66/1: 0400-058: Dwelt, sn struggling rear: see 2480.		3	5a
1660	EAGER ANGEL 49 [4]6-8-10 p (56) M Nem(7) 12/1: 5103009: Dwelt & sn towards rear, no impress: abs.		1¾	10a

9 Ran Time 1m 29.28 (2.68) Owned: Mrs Edward Cantillon Trained: Newmarket

---

2802 2.30 European Breeders Fund Putney Maiden Stakes 2yo (D)
£4046 £1245 £623 7f aw rnd Going 42 -24 Slow Inside

2573	PAULINES PRINCE 9 [5] R Hollinshead 2-9-0 D Sweeney 12/1: 61: Led early, sn trkd ldrs trav			71a

well, led over 1f out, rdn out, decisively: AW bow: apprec step up to 7f & relished fibresand, will get further.

1631	MING VASE 51 [3] D Carroll 2-9-0 D Tudhope(7) 3/1: 62: b c Vettori - Minstrel's Dance (Pleasant		3	64a

Colony) Dwelt & held up in tch, hdwy over 2f out, styd on for press over 1f out: abs: 8,000gns Apr foal: apprec
step up to 7f, 1m+ looks likely to suit: handles fibresand, poss soft: win a race.

	KEYNES 0 [6] J H M Gosden 2-9-0 R Havlin 11/4 FAV: 3: ch c Gold Fever - Eternal Reve (Diesis)		3	58a

Handy, rdn & outpcd by wnr over 1f out: Apr foal, half-brother to sev wnrs btwn 6f/1m: dam smart over 6f/9f.

2236	ELLIS CAVE 23 [7] J J Quinn 2-9-0 VIS R Winston 7/1: 004: Slow away, sn handy, rdn & no extra 2f out.		1½	55a
1237	HIAMOVI 72 [9]2-9-0 B Doyle 4/1: 05: Missed break, sn cl-up & pulled hard, wknd over 1f out: bckd.		1¼	52a
2336	HIDDEN JEWEL 18 [8]2-9-0 G Gibbons 14/1: 066: Dwelt, sn handy, btn over 1f out, longer trip.		2½	47a
1728	UGLY SISTER 45 [10]2-8-9 S Whitworth 25/1: 07: In tch wide & keen, btn 2f out, abs/AW bow.		4	34a
2584	MISS CUISINA 9 [2]2-8-9 Joanna Badger 66/1: 08: Outpcd & nvr a factor.		8	20a
2382	LORD CHALFONT 17 [1]2-9-0 M Savage(5) 66/1: 0009: Dwelt & sn struggling, longer trip.		15	0a
	REACHING OUT 0 [4]2-9-0 S Sanders 7/1: 0: 10th: Slow away & al well bhd.		5	0a

10 Ran Time 1m 31.23 (4.63) Owned: Mr N Chapman Trained: Upper Longdon

2803	3.00 National Tapioca Day Selling Stakes 3yo+ (G)

£2653 £758 £379   5f aw str   Going 42   Inapplicable   Stands Side

2730 QUEEN OF NIGHT 3 [9] D W Chapman 4-9-0 (60) Darren Williams 12/1: 0404R01: Slow away, sn in tch   56a
& led over 1f out, in command when eased cl-home: no bid: qck reapp: suited by 5/6f, tried 7f: acts on firm,
gd/soft & likes fibresand: temperamental filly (refused to race earlier this term), apprec drop to sell grade: see 30.
2201 SCARY NIGHT 24 [2] J Balding 4-9-10 p (51) J Edmunds 16/1: 1600602: Chsd ldrs, outpcd over 2f   3   54a
out, kept on for press ins last, no threat: shld win a seller: see 793 (C/D clmr).
2326 RIVER LARK 19 [10] M A Buckley 5-9-0 BL (41) Hayley Turner(5) 16/1: 4606503: Al prom, onepace: blnks. hd   43a
2702 VALAZAR 4 [6] D W Chapman 5-9-5 (45) G Duffield 9/2 FAV: 0023234: Dwelt & outpcd, kept on late,   nk   47a
nvr threat: shorter priced stablemate of wnr: qck reapp: see 1988, 1199 & 587.
1442 THE LEATHER WEDGE 60 [4]5-9-5 p (45) P Mathers(7) 11/2: 0405255: Led/dsptd lead 3f, no extra dist.   nk   46a
2412 FRENCHMANS LODGE 16 [5]4-9-5 bl (39) P Doe 25/1: 0002566: Chsd ldrs, not pace to chall: acts on   ¾   44a
fast & both AWs: mdn: see 1963 & 1544.
2201 HAGLEY PARK 24 [14]5-9-5 (48) P Mulrennan(5) 10/1: 4303107: Chsd ldrs, no impress dist, 'hung left'.   hd   43a
1075 CONFUZED 83 [3]4-9-5 e (43) S Whitworth 20/1: 0360008: Mid-div, drvn & nvr pace to chall: 12 wk abs.   ½   41a
2630 ATTORNEY 7 [1]6-9-10 vis (54) L Vickers 12/1: 0366509: Chsd ldrs till dist: op 8/1: btr 1248 & 1199.   ½   44a
1806 TICKLE 42 [7]6-9-0 t (45) S Sanders 10/1: 4036600: 10th: Chsd ldrs, no impress ovr 1f out: 6 wk abs.   3   25a
2585 CATCHTHEBATCH 9 [11]8-9-5 (47) S Carson 14/1: 00-43000: 11th: Dwelt, outpcd & nvr factor: btr 619.   ½   28a
2402 NITEOWL DREAM 16 [8]4-9-0 (48) P M Quinn 33/1: 5/00-4000: 12th: Al outpcd: btr 1944.   ¾   21a
2412 HENRY TUN 16 [15]6-9-10 p (52) M Savage(5) 6/1: 0200600: 13th: Bhd & nvr factor: best dominating.   nk   30a
2730 JUWWI 3 [12]10-9-5 (55) C Catlin 7/1: 4062660: 14th: Slow away & al rear: qck reapp: btr 2412 (firm). nk   24a
2380 BRAVE CHIEF 17 [16]3-8-13 (48) N Pollard 20/1: 02-00500: 15th: Slowly away & sn struggling: btr 2380. 12   0a
15 Ran   Time 59.47 ()   Owned: Mr Michael Hill   Trained: York

2804	3.30 Battle Of Vicksburg Handicap Stakes 3yo 0-70 (E)	[74]

£3465 £1066 £533   1m4f aw   Going 42   -02 Slow   Inside

2203 ITS BLUE CHIP 24 [2] P W D'Arcy 3-9-0 e (60) Paul Eddery 6/1: 3014641: Rear, smooth hdwy wide   68a
from halfway, rdn over 2f out & styd on to lead line: eff around 11.5f/12f, tried 14f, may yet suit: likes
fibresand & gd/soft grnd, sharp trks: suited by eye-shield & waiting tactics: see 1260 & 438.
2503 HOLLY WALK 11 [6] M Dods 3-8-0 p (46) F P Ferris(3) 9/2: 0255432: Led/dsptd lead trav well, went   hd   53a
on over 1f out, rdn & hdd line: deserves similar: see 2503, 2299 & 1308.
2285 FLEETFOOT MAC 20 [4] P D Evans 3-9-3 (63) R Havlin 12/1: 06-11003: Led/dsptd lead, went on over   1½   68a
3f out till over 1f out, no extra ins last: imprvd eff with forcing tactics: acts on soft grnd & fibresand.
2642 CROCOLAT 6 [10] N A Callaghan 3-8-9 (55) D Fox(5) 9/2: 00524: Chsd ldrs, pushed along halfway,   nk   59a
rdn & kept on fnl 2f, not pace of wnr: acts on fast grnd & fibresand: encouraging AW bow: see 2642 (mdn h'cap).
2528 SIEGFRIEDS NIGHT 11 [11]3-9-4 (64) L Vickers 7/1: 6213355: Held up, chall 2f out, no extra: clr rem.   nk   67a
2203 ROCK LOBSTER 24 [8]3-9-7 (67) B Doyle 4/1 FAV: 14-05636: Trkd ldrs, fdd under press fnl 2f: btr 2203. 12   55a
2706 MUNAAWESH 4 [3]3-8-7 (53) G Duffield 16/1: 0000007: Held up, rdn & btn 3f out, qck reapp: see 1050.   5   34a
2041 COMMEMORATION DAY 31 [9]3-9-2 (62) S Sanders 7/1: 60-068: Prom, lost tch from 3f out, eased.   30   3a
2333 PERUVIAN BREEZE 18 [1]3-9-5 (65) T G McLaughlin 12/1: 66-56109: Led/dsptd lead 4f, btn 3f out.   17   0a
2383 BLUE VIKING 17 [7]3-8-9 (55) R Winston 40/1: 4-050: 10th: Held up, struggling fnl 3f, eased: btr 2383.   25   0a
1489 ROYAL APPROACH 58 [5]3-9-3 (63) D Sweeney 7/1: 60-050: 11th: b f Royal Applause - Passionelle   dist 0a
(Nashwan) Prom, struggling from halfway, abs, AW/h'cap bow: unplcd from 2 '03 starts (rtd 66, mdn).
11 Ran   Time 2m 39.57 (5.27)   Owned: Blue Chip Feed Ltd   Trained: Newmarket

2805	4.00 Signing Of The Treaty Of Versailles Handicap Stakes 3yo+ 35-55 (F)	[55]

£3003 £858 £429   1m aw rnd   Going 42   -07 Slow   Inside

2466 DOWNLAND 13 [2] N Tinkler 8-10-0 (55) Kim Tinkler 10/1: 0-021651: Mid-div trav well, rdn & led   66a
ins last, drvn out: eff at 6f/1m on firm, likes fibresand & hvy grnd: remains on a fair mark & could win again.
2500 MIDSHIPMAN 1 [5] A W Carroll 6-10-0 vis t (55) S Sanders 9/4 FAV: 0030022: Outpcd early & bhd,   ½   64a
hdwy inner halfway, drvn to chall ins last, just held: clr rem, nicely bckd: see 2500, 1430.
664   SUDRA 132 [4] D J Daly 7-9-12 (53) C Catlin 9/1: 3443143: Handy, outpcd bef halfway, kept on   5   53a
late, no threat: 4 month abs: see 639 (seller).
2383 MAGIC VERSE 17 [13] R Guest 3-9-2 (53) C Lowther 16/1: 0044: Chsd ldrs, outpcd halfway, kept on   ½   52a
late, no threat: h'cap bow, tried 12f: eff around 1m, rtn to 10f may suit: handles fibresand: see 2383.
2691 DALRIATH 4 [11]5-8-12 (39) D Fox(5) 7/1: 2125035: Trkd ldrs trav well, led 2f out till ins last, fdd.   ¾   37a
2340 KENNY THE TRUTH 18 [10]5-9-8 t (49) A Daly 14/1: 14330P6: Pushed along towards rear, late gains,   ¾   46a
no impress: see 850 (C/D, banded).
1379 DONEGAL SHORE 63 [6]5-9-7 vis t (48) N Chalmers(5) 12/1: 0 422437: Dwelt, rear, kept on late, abs.   4   38a
1943 SEA YA MAITE 35 [1]10-8-13 t (40) S Whitworth 20/1: 4502408: Mid-div when short of room over 3f   2   26a
out & again over 1f out, no impress: btr 905.
2339* MITZI CASPAR 18 [9]3-9-3 (54) R Price 14/1: 0003219: Sn prom, wknd fnl 2f: btr 2339 (7f, mdn).   1½   37a
2093 TATA NAKA 29 [3]4-8-13 T P (40) Hayley Turner(5) 33/1: 50-00500: 10th: Cl-up & led over 3f out   ¾   22a
till 2f out, fdd: t-strap & cheek pieces: see 757.
2445 BABY BARRY 14 [7]7-10-0 vis (55) G Duffield 20/1: 2300-000: 11th: Led 4f, btn dist: see 2445 (6f).   2½   32a
2447 CALL OF THE WILD 14 [15]4-9-10 vis (51) T Hamilton(3) 8/1: 3644200: 12th: Prom wide till halfway.   ½   27a
2501 Prince Of Aragon 11 [16]8-8-12 (39) D Sweeney 33/1:0 2218 Sonderborg 24 [12]3-9-1 (52) G Carter 14/1:0
2015) Melford Red 385 [8]4-9-2 (43) T G McLaughlin 50/1:0 457   Muqarrar 158 [14]5-9-8 bl e T(49) R Winston 14/1:0
16 Ran   Time 1m 43.34 (3.94)   Owned: Mr A Graham   Trained: Malton

SOUTHWELL Fibresand MONDAY 28.06.04 Lefthand, Sharp, Oval Track

2806 4.30 St Irenaeus' Day Handicap Stakes 3yo+ 35-55 (F) [57]
£3087 £882 £441 **6f aw rnd** **Going 42** **-01 Slow** Inside

2702 **BOISDALE** 4 [4] S L Keightley 6-9-9 (52) L Treadwell(7) 12/1: 0-616501: Trkd ldrs trav well, drvn **60a**
to lead line, all out: op 14/1, qck reapp: stay 7f, suited by 6f on firm, soft & f/sand, likes Southwell.
2720 **INDIAN MUSIC** 3 [1] A Berry 7-8-13 (42) P Mathers(7) 8/1: 4332462: Led/dsptd lead, rdn & went on hd **49a**
over 1f out, hdd line: qck reapp, in gd heart: see 982 (C/D).
2338 **SEMPER PARATUS** 18 [6] V Smith 5-9-10 bl (53) M Tebbutt 8/1: 0-400203: Outpcd, hdwy for press 2f 1½ **55a**
out & chs ins last, eased & held nr line: rest well covered: drop in trip & back to form with blnks reapplied.
2237 **SHIFTY NIGHT** 23 [9] Mrs C A Dunnett 3-8-6 (42) Hayley Turner(5) 33/1: 00-004: b f Night Shift - 3½ **35a**
Bean Island (Afleet) Prom when outpcd after 2f, late rally wide, no threat: unplcd '03 (rtd 26, mdn): has tried
7.5f prev: prob handles fibresand.
2720 **LUCIUS VERRUS** 3 [12]4-9-9 vis (52) Darren Williams 11/1: 0105205: Slow away & switched left/rear ½ **43a**
early, styd on late for press, nvr threat: qck reapp: poss best racing closer to the pace at 5f: btr 2201 (5f).
2657 **ACE MA VAHRA** 6 [10]6-9-3 bl (46) S Whitworth 12/1: 0050306: Prom, led over 2f out till dist. 2 **32a**
1799 **BACK IN SPIRIT** 42 [11]4-8-5 (1oh)t (33) F P Ferris(3) 33/1: 0/00-0007: Rear, mod prog: abs. 2 **15a**
2626* **ONE WAY TICKET** 7 [16]4-10-2 (7ex)p (59) C J Davies(7) 5/1 FAV: 0320318: Prom, hung left & btn over ½ **38a**
1f out: top-weight: btr 2626 (fast, made all).
2585* **ENJOY THE BUZZ** 9 [7]5-9-2 (45) C Catlin 7/1: 1242019: Held up, sn rdn & no impress: btr 2585. nk **23a**
1261 **SPY MASTER** 70 [8]6-8-5 (3oh)t p (31) G Duffield 16/1: 3250650: 10th: Cl-up till outpcd halfway: abs. hd **11a**
2125 **FIZZY LIZZY** 27 [5]4-8-7 (36) N Pollard 25/1: 50000-00: 11th: b f Cool Jazz - Formidable Liz ½ **11a**
(Formidable) Dwelt & held up, nvr on terms: h'cap plcd in '03 (rtd 43): unplcd '02 (rtd 63): stays a stiff 6f,
handles fast & gd grnd, sharp or gall trk: AW bow today.
385 **KISS THE RAIN** 168 [3]4-9-6 (49) Stacey Renwick(7) 14/1: 10334-60: 12th: Prom till halfway, abs. 1 **22a**
2476 **NEEDWOOD BUCOLIC** 12 [15]6-8-12 (41) R Winston 20/1: 013/-0000: 13th: Mid-div, no impress fnl 2f. 1 **12a**
2502 **HAZE BABYBEAR** 11 [14]4-9-11 (54) T Hamilton(3) 8/1: 03310-00: 14th: Dwelt & al outpcd. 2½ **18a**
313* **STRIKE LUCKY** 175 [2]4-9-10 (53) S Sanders 11/2: 400-10: 15th: Led, hdd 3f out, hung left/sn btn. ¾ **15a**
2335 **BRIGHT MIST** 18 [13]5-8-7 (36) D Sweeney 20/1: 000/-0400: 16th: Strug halfway: btr 2335 & 1799. 14 **0a**
16 Ran Time 1m 15.89(2.59) Owned: Ms S Gray & Mr M F Galvin Trained: Melton Mowbray

MUSSELBURGH MONDAY 28.06.04 Righthand, Sharp Track

Official Going GOOD (GOOD/FIRM places).

2807 6.25 Bollinger Champagne Challenge Handicap For Gentleman Amateur Riders 3yo+ 0-70 (E) [40]
£4017 £1236 £618 **2m** **Good/Firm 35** **-61 Slow** Stands side

2607 **TONI ALCALA** 8 [6] R F Fisher 5-12-0 (68) Mr M Seston(5) 9/4: 1352451: Cl-up, led bef 2f out, **76**
pushed out hands & heels: slow time: eff at 12f, suited by 13/14f, stays 2m1f: acts on firm, gd/soft & fibresand:
acts on any trk, likes Musselburgh: see 2276 & 1905.
2060 **WESTERN BLUEBIRD** 31 [2] Miss Kate Milligan 6-10-2 bl (42) Mr M J McAlister 9/1: 044/-6402: Led, 2½ **46**
hdd bef 2f out, kept on, not pace wnr: clr rem, op 12/1: has slipped to a fair mark: see 1793.
1521 **MUZIO SCEVOLA** 56 [1] M R Channon 3-10-5 (65) Mr L Newnes(3) 12/1: 25563: Rear, prog after 12f, no 8 **61**
impress fnl 2f: 8 wk abs: op 8/1: btr 873 (12f, polytrack, mdn).
2577 **ACCEPTING** 9 [4] J Mackie 7-11-0 bl (54) Mr Stephen Harrison(7) 2/1 FAV: 010-5024: Chsd ldrs over 1½ **49**
12f, sn no extra: see 2577 (19.1f, firm).
2200 **DESERT QUILL** 24 [5]4-11-3 (57) Mr C Davies(5) 10/1: 00030-25: Handy 12f, no extra: see 2200 (reapp). ½ **51**
3642] **WELSH DREAM** 647 [3]7-10-9 (49) Mr C Storey 6/1: 414016/-6: b g Mtoto - Morgannwg (Simply Great) 17 **28**
In tch, fdd fnl 4f: mdn hdle wnr on sole 03/04 start (rtd 109h, stays 2m1.5f on gd/soft grnd, goes well fresh): mdn
hdle rnr-up in early '02 (rtd 90h): won 3 h'caps over 2f/2m on firm, gd/soft &
both AWs: acts on any trk & has gone well fresh: with Miss S E Forster.
1 Jul'02 Muss 16g/s 50-45 F: 1 Mar'02 Ling 16ap 54a-48 E: 1 Feb'02 Wolv 16.2af 49a-45 F:
6 Ran Time 3m 37.93 (15.43) Owned: Mr Alan Willoughby Trained: Ulverston

2808 6.55 Wilkinsoncorr Com Selling Stakes 3yo (F)
£2877 £822 £411 **5f str** **Good/Firm 35** **-34 Slow** Stands side

2702 **JINKSONTHEHOUSE** 4 [4] M D I Usher 3-8-13 (58) K Dalgleish 5/2: 4010401: Prom, led bef 2f out, **55**
drvn out: no bid, qck reapp: eff arnd 5f on firm & gd grnd: likes sell/clmg grade: see 1902.
2541 **BEAVER DIVA** 10 [3] W M Brisbourne 3-8-8 (40) S W Kelly 10/1: 0-400022: Slow away, prog halfway, ¾ **47$**
ev ch ins fnl 1f, hung right & not pace wnr: op 6/1: eff at 5f, return to 6f will suit: acts on fast & gd: see 2541.
2702 **ONLY IF I LAUGH** 4 [1] P A Blockley 3-8-13 (59) Dean McKeown 11/10 FAV: 4023053: Led over 2f, 1½ **48**
styd cl-up, onepace dist: well bckd on quick reapp: see 2493 & 1902.
2541 **VAUDEVIRE** 10 [2] R P Elliott 3-8-13 bl (23) S Chin 40/1: 6-603044: Prom, ev ch 2f out, no extra dist. ¾ **46$**
1951 **LAVISH TIMES** 35 [5]3-8-13 bl (48) F Lynch 5/1: 0636065: Rear, prog halfway, onepcd fnl 1f. ½ **45**
637 **SALONIKA SKY** 134 [6]3-8-8 bl (40) J McAuley 25/1: 000-0606: ch f Pursuit of Love - Willisa (Polar 6 **23**
Falcon) Prom 3f, fdd: long abs: unplcd '03 (rtd 60, auct mdn, J W Weymes).
6 Ran Time 1m 0.99 (3.49) Owned: Midweek Racing Trained: Lambourn

2809 7.25 George Wimpey East Scotland Ltd Handicap Stakes 3yo+ 0-85 (D) [82]
£6747 £2076 £1038 **7f30y rnd** **Good/Firm 35** **-03 Slow** Outside

2672 **KIRKBYS TREASURE** 5 [2] A Berry 6-8-13 (67) F Lynch 7/2 JT FAV: 5-121301: Held up, prog when **77**
short of room ins fnl 3f, styd on to lead well ins fnl 1f, rdn out: quick reapp: eff btwn 6f/1m, 7f is ideal: acts
on firm, hvy & any trk, likes Musselburgh: enjoys being held up off a strong pace: see 2445 & 2086.
2672 **STOIC LEADER** 5 [3] R F Fisher 4-9-11 (79) L Fletcher(3) 7/2 JT FAV: 1100242: Handy, prog to lead 1¼ **85**

bef 1f out, hdd well ins fnl 1f, no extra: clr rem, well bckd, qck reapp: continues in gd form: see 2672 & 2543.
2672 **PAWAN 5** [8] Miss A Stokell 4-8-12 (66) Ann Stokell 7/1: 0201663: Cl-up, styd on to lead halfway, hdd bef 1f out, no extra: bckd from 10/1 on quick reapp: btr 2438. *4* **64**
2514* **LOW CLOUD 11** [9] D Nicholls 4-9-8 vis (76) A Nicholls 7/1: 0-603514: Handy 5f, sn onepcd: btr 2514. *hd* **73**
2086 **KILLALA 30** [7]4-8-10 (64) T Eaves(3) 8/1: 0436-355: Rear, prog halfway, no impress fnl 2f: btr 1794. *1¾* **59**
2533 **BESSEMER 10** [1]3-9-8 (85) J Fanning 8/1: 310-536: Slow away, nvr nrr than mid-div: btr 2533 (1m). *3* **75**
2558 **NAMROUD 10** [4]5-10-0 bl (82) P Hanagan 5/1: 10-06007: Handy 5f, wkng when no room bef 1f out. *nk* **71**
2102 **SILVER SEEKER 28** [10]4-8-6 (60) P Fessey 16/1: 0/0-50028: Led, rcd keenly, hdd halfway, sn fdd: prob went off too fast on first start for A R Dicken: btr 2102 (I Semple). *5* **39**
8 Ran Time 1m 27.6 (2.7) Owned: Kirkby Lonsdale Racing Trained: Cockerham

2810

7.55 Wilkinsoncorr Com Maiden Auction Stakes 2yo (F)
£3361 £1034 £517 **7f30y rnd** **Good/Firm 35** **-45 Slow** Outside

2563 **MOUNT EPHRAM 9** [5] R F Fisher 2-8-13 P P Hanagan 8/1: 45641: In tch, prog to lead dist, sn hung left, rdn out: eff around 7f, 1m will suit: acts on fast & gd/soft: apprec fitting of cheek pieces: see 2563. **73**
2492 **LADY HOPEFUL 12** [6] R P Elliott 2-8-4 S Chin 9/4 FAV: 5422: Led, hdd under press dist, kept on ins fnl 1f, just held: eff at 7f on fast, grnd & fibresand: continues to run well: see 2492. *hd* **62**
2462 **CAVA BIEN 13** [3] J G Given 2-8-7 M Fenton 11/2: 03: b c Bien Bien - Bebe de Cham (Tragic Role) Bhd, prog halfway, styd on despite hanging left ins fnl 2f, nrst fin: Feb 1st foal, cost 2,000 gns: dam wnr at 5/6f: sire decent performer in US: eff at 7f, shld apprec further: acts on fast grnd: ran green today. *¾* **63**
1911 **YOUNG THOMAS 37** [4] M L W Bell 2-8-11 F Lynch 5/1: 04: ch g Inchinor - Splicing (Sharpo) Cl-up, ev ch 2f out, sn no extra: Apr foal, cost 10,000 gns: half brother to a couple of wnrs at 2: dam successful at 5/6f: sire decent performer at 7f: eff at 7f on fast grnd. *1¾* **63**
2537 **VICTORY HYMN 10** [7]2-8-6 A Culhane 5/1: 05: b f Victory Note - Nordic Union (Nordico) Nvr nrr than mid-div: Apr foal, cost E12,000: half sister wnr at 11f: sire Gr1 wnr at 1m: with M R Channon. *1* **56**
2360 **BUST 17** [2]2-8-9 K Dalgleish 5/1: 06: Handy till halfway, sn wknd: see 2360. *2½* **54**
2473 **BLACK COMBE LADY 12** [1]2-8-4 J Fanning 66/1: 007: Bhd, nvr a factor. *dist* **19**
7 Ran Time 1m 30.50 (5.6) Owned: Great Head House Estates Limited Trained: Ulverston

2811

8.25 George Wimpey East Scotland Ltd Claiming Stakes 3yo+ (F)
£2947 £842 £421 **1m1f** **Good/Firm 35** **+16 Fast** Outside

2500 **BAILIEBOROUGH 11** [7] D Nicholls 5-9-11 vis (67) Alex Greaves 2/1: 3401301: Chsd ldrs, prog to lead bef 1f out, pushed clr fnl 1f, val 4L+: eff at 7/9f on firm & gd/soft: eff with a visor: enjoys clmg grade. **74+**
2565 **ALWAYS FLYING 9** [1] M Johnston 3-8-8 (67) J Fanning 7/4 FAV: 1526602: Led, hdd bef 1f out, not pace wnr: clr rem: gd eff on drop in grade & can find similar: see 923 & 438. *3* **65**
2544 **SHERWOOD FOREST 10** [5] Miss L A Perratt 4-9-3 vis (44) Leanne Kershaw(7) 33/1: 60500-03: ch g Fleetwood - Jay Gee Ell (Vaigly Great) Bhd, prog 3f out, no impress fnl 2f: h'cap wnr in '03: unplcd in '02 (rtd 32, mdns): eff at 1m/11f on gd grnd: eff with visor, tried cheek pieces & blnks. 1 Aug'03 Ayr 10.9gd 51-34 E: *5* **56$**
2544 **AMBUSHED 10** [2] P Monteith 8-9-5 (57) T Eaves(3) 14/1: 42030-64: Handy over 6f, sn onepcd: see 2544. *1¾* **55**
2265 **KYLE OF LOCHALSH 21** [8]4-9-4 BL (52) A McCarthy 13/2: 00-30005: In tch, hdwy after 6f, onepcd fnl 2f. *1½* **51**
2571 **PHARAOH HATSHEPSUT 9** [6]6-8-12 (32) F Lynch 100/1: 0/-000006: Prom 6f, wknd: see 2571. *7* **35$**
2674 **EAST RIDING 5** [10]4-9-0 (37) Ann Stokell 33/1: 3000557: Handy till halfway, sn wknd: qck reapp. *1¾* **35**
1897 **ENVIRONMENTALIST 38** [3]5-9-0 BL t (40) P Fessey 66/1: 006-0008: b c Danehill - Way O'Gold (Slew O' Gold) Bhd, nvr a factor: 1st time blnks: unplcd all 3 '03 starts (M A Jarvis, tried t-strap): reported to have a breathing problem: with D A Nolan. 2 Oct'02 Ling 8ap 73a- D: *7* **25**
1895 **DEVINE LIGHT 38** [4]4-9-6 (60) P Hanagan 10/1: 00501-09: b f Spectrum - Siskin (Royal Academy) Bhd, nvr a factor: mdn wnr on fnl '03 start: unplcd in '02 (rtd 67a, auct mdn, A P Jarvis): eff at 9f, has tried further: acts on gd grnd & polytrack: best without visor. 1 Oct'03 Muss 9gd 66-(45) D: *6* **23**
4712} **THE SPOOK 259** [9]4-9-5 (39) S W Kelly 20/1: 005300-0: 10th: b g Bin Ajwaad - Rose Mill (Puissance) Al in rear: reapp: h'cap plcd once in '03 (rtd 49, J F Goldie): eff at 5f on soft grnd: reported to have struck into himself. *dist* **0**
10 Ran Time 1m 52.49 (1.79) Owned: Middleham Park Racing XVIII Trained: Thirsk

2812

8.55 Wilkinsoncorr Com Handicap Stakes 3yo 35-55 (F) **[61]**
£2947 £842 £421 **7f30y rnd** **Good/Firm 35** **-21 Slow** Outside

2504 **SHINKO FEMME 11** [1] N Tinkler 3-9-1 (48) P Mulrennan(5) 10/1: 30-00051: Held up, prog when short of room 2f out, sn switched, rdn out to lead cl-home: now stays 7f on fast & firm: acts on a sharp trk: 1st win. **56**
2384 **SAROS 17** [4] B Smart 3-9-6 (53) F Lynch 11/2 CO FAV: 6-011602: Led, edged left under press from dist, hdd cl-home: clr rem: acts on fast grnd & fibresand: win similar on this evidence: see 1591. *shd* **59**
2683 **KILLERBY NICKO 4** [13] T D Easterby 3-9-3 bl (50) K Dalgleish 11/1: 60605U3: In tch, prog 3f out, no extra dist: quick reapp: 1st time blnks: see 2055. *6* **44**
2480 **KILLOCH PLACE 12** [6] J A Glover 3-8-7 vis (40) S W Kelly 11/2 CO FAV: 0-000034: Bhd, prog 3f out, no impress fnl 1f: showed more on 2480 (6f). *½* **33**
2586 **THEMESOFGREEN 9** [2]3-9-7 (54) A Culhane 8/1: 0-0005: ch g Botanic - Harmonia (Glint of Gold) Rear, prog halfway, no room sev times ins fnl 2f, closer with clr run: unplcd sole '03 start (rtd 43, nov stks): will apprec step up to 1m on a more gall trk. *¾* **45+**
2243 **SCHINKEN OTTO 23** [8]3-9-1 (48) P Hanagan 10/1: 060-06: ch c Shinko Forest - Athassel Rose (Reasonable) Handy 5f, sn no extra: unplcd all 3 starts in '03 (rtd 61, mdn). *nk* **38**
2683 **GARNOCK VENTURE 4** [9]3-9-8 bl (55) L Fletcher(3) 11/2 CO FAV: 0300107: Handy over 5f, sn wknd. *nk* **44**
2182 **LUKE SHARP 25** [11]3-8-2 (35) P Fessey 25/1: 000-08: gr g Muhtarram - Heaven Liegh Grey (Grey Desire) In tch, prog 3f out, wknd dist: mod form to date. *¾* **22**
1651 **ST TROPEZ 49** [12]3-9-3 (50) J Fanning 6/1: 00-009: Nvr nrr than mid-div: 7 wk abs: h'cap bow. *¾* **35**
2428 **AGUILERA 15** [7]3-8-12 P (45) L Enstone(3) 12/1: 00-000: Cl-up 5f, sn wknd. *¾* **28**
2181 **BE MY ALIBI 25** [10]3-8-2 (35) B Swarbrick(5) 12/1: 000-0500: 11th: Bhd, nvr a factor: btr 1803. *1¾* **14**
2565 **Venerdi Tredici 9** [3]3-9-5 (52) Dean McKeown 25/1:0 2326 **Grey Orchid 19** [5]3-8-12 (45) T Eaves(3) 66/1:0
13 Ran Time 1m 28.85 (3.95) Owned: The Penniless Partnership Trained: Malton

MUSSELBURGH   MONDAY 28.06.04   Righthand, Sharp Track

2813   9.25 Edinburgh Evening News Handicap Stakes 3yo+ 0-60 (F)   [60]
£2975 £850 £425   1m4f   Good/Firm 35   -13 Slow   Inside

2616 **ARCHIRONDEL** 7 [9] M D Hammond 6-9-8 (54) A Culhane 5/2 JT FAV: 0021021: Rear, prog halfway, led   62
trav well bef 1f out, pushed clr fnl 1f: quick reapp: eff over 1m/10f, stays a sharp 12f well: firm & fast grnd,
handles soft & any trk: remains on a fair mark & more prizes await: see 2616.
2479 **ELLWAY HEIGHTS** 12 [10] W M Brisbourne 7-9-7 (53) S W Kelly 5/2 JT FAV: 11020-22: Rear, prog   2½   56+
halfway, staying on when short of room dist, switched & kept on fnl 1f: closer with clr run, can find similar.
2509 **SAAMEQ** 11 [3] J Semple 3-7-12 (2oh) (42) P Fessey 20/1: 0-6003: ;Rear, prog 3f out, styd on ins   shd   46
fnl 1f: left mod form bhd on step up to 12f: acts on fast grnd: see 2509.
2616 **HIBERNATE** 7 [1] C J Teague 10-8-8 (40) T Eaves(3) 25/1: 0265/-064: Led, hdd bef 1f out, no extra.   hd   41
3521} **CHEVIN** 322 [8]5-8-10 (42) P Hanagan 7/1: 115450-5: ch f Danzig Connection - Starr Danias   1¾   40
(Sensitive Prince) Cl-up, ev ch 2f out, sn no extra: reapp: won 2 h'caps in '03: unplcd in '02 (mdns & h'caps),
rtd 44 at best): eff at 11/11f on firm & fast grnd: with R A Fahey.
1 Jun'03 Warw 10.9fm 49-43 G: 1 Jun'03 Carl 14.1fm 48-37 D:
2571 **LUCKY LARGO** 9 [4]4-9-12 bl (58) D McGaffin 12/1: 5004026: Nvr nrr than mid-div: btr 2571 (9f).   shd   55
2479 **HOWARDS DREAM** 2 [7]6-7-12 (2oh) (28) J McAuley 25/1: 0-040607: Handy over 1m: btr 2180.   2½   23
2526 **MAGIC CHARM** 11 [6]6-8-3 (35) Leanne Kershaw(7) 14/1: 0040608: Handy over 7f: btr 2217.   1¼   26
2545 **REPULSE BAY** 10 [2]6-9-5 (51) J Currie(7) 8/1: 6030509: Al in rear: see 1793.   9   29
2546 **CAYMANS GIFT** 10 [5]4-9-12 (58) P Mulrennan(5) 10/1: 45630: 10th: Chsd ldrs 9f, wknd: btr 2546.   1   34
10 Ran   Time 2m 36.46(5.86)   Owned: The Archi Partnership   Trained: Middleham

CHANTILLY   THURSDAY 24.06.04   Righthand, Galloping Track

Official Going Good/Soft

2814   2.50 Gr 3 Prix Chloe 3yo Fillies ()
£25704 £10282 £7711   1m1f   Good/Soft

1850 **LOVE AND BUBBLES** [4] R Collet 3-8-11 I Mendizabal 44/10: 2121-201: b f Loup Sauvage - Bubble   111+
Dream (Akarad) Held up, hdwy/swtched over 2f out & smooth prog to lead dist, readily: earlier rnr up in Gr 3
company: eff at 1m/11f on gd/sft & hvy grnd. 2 May'04 Sain 10.5sft 108- :
  CATTIVA GENEROSA [7] T Jarnet 3-8-11 T Jarnet 4/1: 51-5012: Led till dist, no chance with wnr ins last. 3   102
  CLOON [6] N Clement 3-8-11 bl C P Lemaire 11/2: 41-45213: Held up, styd on wide, not able to chall.   1½   99
7 Ran   Time 1m 51.10()   Owned: B P Hayes   Trained: France

CURRAGH   FRIDAY 25.06.04   Righthand, Galloping Track

Official Going Good

2815   7.30 The Goffs Challenge 2yo ()
£51389 £16549 £7839   6f63y str   Good

  KESTREL CROSS [3] K Prendergast 2-9-0 W Supple 14/1: 43211: b g Cape Cross - Lady Rachel   95
(Priolo) Held up, styd on for press fnl 2f & led line, all out: eff at 6/7f on firm & gd/sft grnd.
2415 **ENCANTO** 13 [8] J S Moore 2-8-9 J F Egan 20/1: 0622: Held up, hdwy to lead well ins last, hdd   shd   89$
line: stays 6.3f on firm & gd grnd: much improved, must be wng sn: see 2415.
  NEPRO [2] E J Creighton 2-9-0 K J Manning 10/1: 0113: Trkd ldrs wide, led over 1f out, hdd ins last.   1   91
2364 **ANNATALIA** 14 [14]2-8-9 F M Berry 16/1: 46: Chsd ldrs wide, not pace of ldrs ins last: stays 6.3f.   2¼   79
2310 **MISS MALONE** 16 [7]2-8-9 M J Kinane 4/1: 77: Cl up, led halfway, hdd 2f out, no extra.   hd   78
2553 **SPIRIT OF CHESTER** 7 [4]2-8-9 R Havlin 9/4 FAV: 429: Led/dpstd lead till halfway, sn lost place: 3½   67
poss too soon after 2553.
1744* **ALSU** 42 [5]2-8-9 J P Spencer 8/1: 310: 10th: Chsd ldrs, no impress fnl 2f: op 7/1: btr 1744.   4   55
2382 **KRISTIKHAB** 14 [10]2-9-0 W M Lordan 20/1: 054200: 12th: Sn bhd, t.o.   15   15
13 Ran   Time 1m 18.20 ()   Owned: N Ormiston   Trained: Friarstown

CURRAGH   SATURDAY 26.06.04   Righthand, Galloping Track

Official Going Good (Good/Firm Places)

2816   3.40 Gr 1 Pretty Polly Stakes Fillies ()
£104520 £33098 £15678   1m2f rnd   Good

2278* **CHORIST** 19 [1] W J Haggas 5-9-7 (111) D Holland 7/4: 211013-11: Made all, drvn & held on well   117
ins last: eff at 1m, suited by 10f, tried 12f: acts on firm & gd/sft, handles soft: well suited by forcing tactics
this term: v smart, tough & genuine, career best run: see 2278.
2460 **ALEXANDER GOLDRUN** 13 [2] J S Bolger 3-8-9 K J Manning 6/4 FAV: 01221-11242: Chsd ldrs, hdwy to   ½   116
chall over 1f out, kept on but always just held: clr rem: smart run: see 2460, 2005 & 1701.
  IVOWEN [3] D K Weld 4-9-7 P J Smullen 16/1: 1003-123: b f Theatrical - Shee Cat (Storm Cat)   6   106
Chsd ldrs, rdn & not pace of front pair from 2f out: Listed rnr up when beaten, earlier deadheated for 1st in a val h'cap
here at The Curragh: eff btwn 9/12f on fast & soft ground: v useful filly.
2487 **SOLDERA** 10 [5] J R Fanshawe 4-9-7 (103) J P Murtagh 11/2: /4140-34: Trkd ldrs, rdn & no impress   ¾   104

fnl 2f: not convince today over this longer 10f trip tho' should prove effective at this trip in a lower grade: see 2487.
1997 **HANAMI** 35 [4]4-9-7 (110) S Sanders 7/1: /56100-36: Held & strugg over 4f out: much btr 1997.   8   92
6 Ran   Time 2m 02.80 ()   Owned: Cheveley Park Stud   Trained: Newmarket

---

2817   4.45 Gr 3 Curragh Cup 3yo+   ()
     £32160 £10184 £4824   **1m6f**   **Good**

4406} **MKUZI** [2] J M Oxx 5-9-10   M J Kinane 7/1: 3-660511: ch c Halling - African Peace (Roberto)   114
Trkd ldrs, rdn to chall over 1f out, led ins last & styd on strongly: Listed wnr at Limerick last month: val h'cap &
Listed scorer '03: eff at 10/12f, enjoyed this step up to 14f: acts on firm & soft ground: smart performer.
2 Jun'03 Lime 12g/s 107- A: 2 Apr'03 Curr 10g/s 109- : 1 Aug'02 Leop 10gd 104-98 :
2209 **DUBAI SUCCESS** 22 [5] B W Hills 4-9-13 (113) J P Murtagh 100/30 JT FA: 05D3-1482: Trkd ldr, rdn &   ½   115
chance over 1f out, not pace of wnr: stays 14f well: see 1230.
3910*)**CRUZSPIEL** [4] J M Oxx 4-9-10 bl   F M Berry 20/1: 443316-3: Dwelt, sn led till ins last, just held cl home. 1   111
10*} **MIKADO** 231 [6] A P O'Brien 3-8-7   J P Spencer 4/1: 211-4: Trkd ldrs, rdn & kept on ins last, not   2   108
pace of wnr: reapp, styd longer 14f trip.
1757* **THE WHISTLING TEAL** 42 [1]8-9-10 (107) J F Egan 100/30 JT FA: 4452-0215: Chsd ldrs wide, onepace shd   108
for press over 2f out, al held: 6 wk abs: btn under 4L: not an ideal passage today & shld do better: see 1757 (13f).
7 Ran   Time 2m 59.70 ()   Owned: Sheikh Mohammed   Trained: Currabeg

---

Official Going Good/Firm

2818   2.05 Listed King Of Beers Stakes 3yo+   ()
     £43617 £12997 £6097   **5f str**   **Good/Firm**

2327* **OSTERHASE** 20 [6] J E Mulhern 5-9-7 bl (94) F M Berry 3/1: 261-0611: b g Flying Spur - Ostrusa   114+
(Rustan) Made all, rdn clr dist, easily in a course rec time: eff at 6f, suited by a stiff/gall 5f on fast & soft
ground: suited by blnks: likes to force the pace: v smart, keep on your side in Gr races: see 2327.
1 Jun'04 Naas 5g/f 105-94 : 2 Jun'03 Curr 5gd 110- A: 2 Apr'03 Cork 5g/f 113- : 2 Jul'02 Curr 5sft 100-94 :
1159* **MOON UNIT** 53 [1] H Rogers 3-8-12   D M Grant 6/1: 2050-132: Chsd wnr, kept on but no impress over   4   105
1f out: 8 wk abs: acts on fast & soft ground: useful, see 1159 (Listed).
1996 **ORIENTOR** 36 [5] J S Goldie 6-9-4 (109) K Fallon 5/1: 006-245953: Held up, efft wide over 1f out, onepace 1   102
1918 **MILLBAG** 36 [4]3-9-1 (107) T E Durcan 9/2: 31313-175: Chsd ldrs, kept on, not pace to threaten: see 1421½   3   103
6 Ran   Time 57.30 ()   Owned: Michael Rosenfeld   Trained: Curragh

---

2819   3.10 Gr 2 Railway Stakes 2yo   ()
     £52260 £16549 £7839   **6f str**   **Good/Firm**

     DEMOCRATIC DEFICIT [6] J S Bolger 2-9-0   K J Manning 7/1: 11: b c Soviet Star - Grandiose Idea   112
(Danehill) Chsd ldrs, rdn to chall when edged left over 1f out, led ins last, drvn out: op 6/1: 7 wk abs:
Leopardstown auct mdn wnr: suited by 6f on fast & gd/sft: goes well fresh: unbeaten & smart.
1994* **RUSSIAN BLUE** 36 [4] A P O'Brien 2-9-0   J P Spencer 1/2 FAV: 1112: Dwelt, held up in tch, swtchd   ¾   109
for effort over 1f out, not pace to rch wnr: lost unbeaten record here, stays 6f & looks ready for 7f after this.
1994 **LALTRO MONDO** 36 [3] M Halford 2-9-0   T P O'Shea 12/1: 4123: Trkd ldr, rdn/slightly hmpd over 1f   1   106
out, sn ev chance, drifted left & no extra in last: eff at 5/6f on fast & soft ground: also bhd today's 2nd in 1994.
7 Ran   Time 1m 11.60 ()   Owned: D H W Dobson   Trained: Coolcullen

---

2820   5.10 Listed Budweiser Celebration Stakes 3yo+   ()
     £43617 £12797 £6097   **1m rnd**   **Good/Firm**

2456 **GRAND PASSION** 18 [2] G Wragg 4-9-7 (103) J F Egan 9/2: 32-2100421: Mid-div, hdwy wide 2f out &   109
led dist, drvn out: suited by 1m/10f on firm, good & polytrk, prob any trk: v useful gelding: see 2456, 693 & 82.
1790} **SOLSKJAER** [6] A P O'Brien 4-9-7   J P Spencer 2/1 FAV: 0-12: b c Danehill - Lyndonville (Top   1   106
Ville) Sn led, rdn & hdd dist, pulled & kept on: op 5/2: recent easy wnr of a 4 rnr cond stks at Naas: unplcd
sole start last term: suited by 7f/1m on fast ground & a stiff/gall trk: lightly rcd & clearly v useful.
2455 **LATINO MAGIC** 18 [10] R J Osborne 4-9-10   J P Murtagh 4/1: 6-502433: Trkd ldrs, no room   ½   108+
repeatedly over 1f out till ins last, winning chance had gone: would surely have gone v close with a clr run.
2252 **DUCK ROW** 22 [9]9-9-7 (108) S Sanders 6/1: 14440-295: Trkd ldr, not pace of ldrs from over 2f   2½   100
out: might prefer the ground a shade easier nowadays: btr 1686 (g/s).
2404 **MIDDLEMARCH** 15 [4]4-9-7 p (100) K Fallon 14/1: 16-04056: Chsd ldrs leaders till 4f out, sn bhd & eased.   0
8 Ran   Time 1m 35.60 ()   Owned: Mr & Mrs H H Morriss   Trained: Newmarket

---

2821   5.45 EBF Waterford Crystal H'cap 3yo+   ()
     £34893 £10237 £4878   **1m4f**   **Good/Firm**   [109]

     THEME SONG [11] A Mullins 5-8-4 p (85) Catherine Gannon(3) 8/1: 1213-031: b g Singspiel -   97+
Glatisant (Rainbow Quest) Cl up & led over 1f out, readily asserted: recent h'cap placed: mdn & conditions stakes
wnr '03, also val h'cap plcd: eff btwn 12f/2m on fm & gd/sft, likes a gall trk: wears cheekpieces: progressive.
     DANELISSIMA [8] J S Bolger 3-8-7 (102) K J Manning 3/1: 52-54412: br f Danehill - Zavaleta   3½   107
(Kahyasi) Trkd ldrs, rdn & styd on fnl 2f, no chance with easy wnr: recent Gr 3 wnr at Naas (1st win): eff at 10f,
sole win at 12f: acts on fast ground & stiff/gall trk: lightly rcd & v useful filly.
4412} **MUTAKARRIM** [12] D K Weld 7-9-12 bl (107) J P Spencer 10/1: 0021-453: Chsd ldrs, hdwy 2f out,   ¾   111
kept on onepace ins last: op 12/1.

CURRAGH SUNDAY 27.06.04 Righthand, Galloping Track

12 Ran   Time 2m 29.90()   Owned: Brainwave Syndicate   Trained: Gowran

2822

3.50 Group 1 Budweiser Irish Derby 3yo ()
£493522 £168237 £81137   **1m4f**   **Good/Firm**

1995 **GREY SWALLOW 36** [6] D K Weld 3-9-0 P J Smullen 10/1: -1431: gr c Daylami - Style of Life (The   **123**
Minstrel) Trkd ldrs trav well, smooth prog & led ins last, drvn out: 2000 Guineas 4th & Irish 2000 Guineas 3rd,
clearly relished this step up to 12f: acts on fast & soft grnd: high-class, trav supremely well throughout race
today: more mid-dist Gr 1 success awaits judged on this evidence, see 1995, 1480 & 1301.
1 Apr'04 Leop 8sft 116- A: 1 Oct'03 Leop 7gd 118- :
2254+ **NORTH LIGHT 22** [10] Sir Michael Stoute 3-9-0 (115) K Fallon 8/11 FAV: 1-112: Trkd front pair,   ½   **122**
rdn & hdwy to lead dist, hdd ins last, kept on well but not pace of wnr: lost little in defeat, confirmed Derby form
with 2nd 3rd & 4th there: high-class mid-dist performer, King George at Ascot is on the agenda & a big run looks
assured: see 2254 (Epsom Derby).
4632} **TYCOON 266** [4] A P O'Brien 3-9-0 C O'Donoghue 150/1: 214D-3: b c Sadler's Wells - Fleeting   1½   **120**
Glimpse (Rainbow Quest) Rear, styd on well for press fnl 3f, nrst fin: excellent reapp, longest price of 5 A O'Brien
rnrs: v useful juv, mdn wnr, also List rnr-up & Gr 1 4th (subs disq): prev eff at 7f, stays a gall 12f well: acts on
fast & gd/soft grnd: v smart on this evidence, Gr success awaits. 2 Jun'03 Asco 7g/f 102-0 A:
2254 **RULE OF LAW 22** [1] Saeed bin Suroor 3-9-0 t (114) L Dettori 13/2: 3-224: Cl up, chall over 2f out, sn   2½   **116**
led, hdd dist & no extra ins last: drop to Gr 2/3 shld bring success: closer to today's 2nd in 2254.
2254 **LET THE LION ROAR 22** [11] 3-9-0 BL (110) M J Kinane 11/2: -1335: Chsd ldrs, eff over 2f out,   nk   **115**
onepace for press: swapped vis for blnks: also bhd today's 2nd & 4th last twice: 14f may now suit: see 2254, 1685.
BOOK OF KINGS 84 [9] 3-9-0 P Cosgrave 66/1: 16: b c Kingmambo - Honfleur (Sadler's Wells)   1½   **113**
Mid-div, styd on, not able to chall: abs: significant step up in grade after Curragh mdn win in early Apr: wng form
at 1m, strong mid-dist pedigree: acts on fast & soft: goes well fresh: lightly raced, appears smart.
2520* **MOSCOW BALLET 10** [7] 3-9-0 P J Scallan 50/1: -6617: Led till over 2f out, sn btn: btr 2520.   5   **105**
2554* **FIVE DYNASTIES 9** [3] 3-9-0 J A Heffernan 33/1: -3818: Al rear: see 2554 (Gr 2).   2½   **101**
2456 **COBRA 18** [2] 3-9-0 J P Spencer 25/1: 31-39: Mid-div, lost place halfway: see 2456 (List).   25   **71**
2254 **PERCUSSIONIST 22** [5] 3-9-0 (113) K Darley 10/1: -1140: 10th: Sn strugg & rear halfway, t.o.:   dist   **0**
reportedly unsuited by the fast ground: much btr 2254 & 1622.
10 Ran   Time 2m 28.70()   Owned: Trained: Co Kildare

SAN SIRO SUNDAY 27.06.04 Righthand, Stiff, Galloping Track

Official Going Good/Firm

2823

3.50 Gr 3 Primi Passi 2yo ()
£33891 £15631 £8731   **6f**   **Good/Firm**

SHIFTING PLACE R Menichetti 2-8-8 L Maniezzi 3.63/1: 1: Trkd ldrs, short of room over 1f out,   **89**
styd on strongly, just failed, finished 2nd, awarded race.
2251 **OBE GOLD 22** M R Channon 2-8-11 A Culhane 37/10: 3142D: Trkd ldrs, chall 2f out, hung left ins   hd   **92**
last, drvn/led well ins last: disq & plcd 2nd: eff at 5/6f: useful, improved run: see 2251, 1716.
2302* **TENDERLIT 23** R Menichetti 2-8-8 M Esposito 3.63/1: 13: Outpcd early, styd on late.   ¾   **87**
9 Ran   Time 1m 10.70()   Owned: Trained:

LONGCHAMP SUNDAY 27.06.04 Righthand, Stiff, Galloping Track

Official Going Good/Soft

2824

2.15 Gr 3 Prix du Lys 3yo ()
£25704 £10282 £7711   **1m4f**   **Good/Soft**

2308 **PROSPECT PARK 21** [5] C Laffon Parias 3-8-11 O Peslier 6/10 FAV: 33-11221: Held up, hdwy to trk   **118**
ldrs halfway, short of room when stumbled over 2f out, swtchd & led ins last, hands & heels close home: suited by
10/12f on gd/sft & soft: v smart colt who looks worth another try in Gr 1/Gr 2 company: see 2308.
LORD DARNLEY [6] A Fabre 3-8-11 Gary Stevens 39/10: 312: b c Darshaan - Ghariba (Final Straw)   1½   **115**
Chsd ldrs, rdn & led over 1f out, hdd ins last, no extra: recent 10f wnr at Saint Cloud: eff at 1m/10f, styd 12f well
today: acts on good/soft & soft grnd: only 3rd career start, clearly smart & a likely type for similar.
LYONELS GLORY [2] U Suter 3-8-11 T Jarnet 172/10: 233: Chsd ldrs, styd on onepace for press.   1½   **113**
6 Ran   Time 2m 29.20 ()   Owned: Wertheimer Et Frere   Trained: France

2825

2.50 Gr 1 Grand Prix de Paris 3yo ()
£201197 £80493 £40246   **1m2f**   **Good/Soft**

2307* **BAGO 21** [2] J E Pease 3-9-2 T Gillet 1/10 FAV: 1111-11: Rear, hdwy & rdn to chall dist,   **121**
narrowly asserted close home under hand riding: eff at 1m/10f on gd & v soft ground: likes a gall trk: high-class.
2307 **CACIQUE 21** [4] A Fabre 3-9-2 Gary Stevens 36/10: 1122: Trkd ldr, led over 2f out, rdn & hdd   ½   **118**
close home: clr rem: stays 10f: Gr 1 rnr up to this wnr last twice: see 2307.
ALNITAK [1] J E Pease 3-9-2 C P Lemaire 1/10 FAV: 2536-003: br c Nureyev - Very True (Proud   5   **111**
Truth) Led 2f, outpcd by front pair fnl 2f, bhd this wnr latest.
2520 **PRIVY SEAL 10** [3] J H M Gosden 3-9-2 (109) O Peslier 86/10: 5-122304: Held up in tch, led after   nk   **110**
2f till over 2f out, no impress over 1f out: see 2520, 2142.
4 Ran   Time 2m 05.60 ()   Owned: Niarchos Family   Trained: France

2826 4.35 Gr 3 Prix de la Porte Maillot 3yo+ ()
£25704 £10282 £7711   7f rnd   Good/Soft

2458 **CHARMING GROOM 14** [2] F Head 5-9-2 D Bonilla 14/10 FAV: 2-146421: gr c Kaldoun - Danagroom   112
(Groom Dancer) Led till 2f out, rallied for press to lead again ins last, all out: recent 1m Gr 3 rnr up: well
suited by 7f/1m on good/soft ground: smart colt.
2 Jun'04 Chan 8g/s 112- : 2 Nov'02 Sain 8hvy 111- :
2184 **MILLENNIUM FORCE 24** [1] M R Channon 6-9-2 (107) C Catlin 84/10: 230-0042: Trkd ldr, chall 3f out   shd 111
& led 2f out, hdd ins last, just denied: gd run, loves easy ground: smart, see 2184, 1486.
       SUNDAY DOUBT [6] Mme C Head Maarek 3-8-7 O Peslier 14/10 FAV: 3-061713: Just held ins last.   nse 110
2184* **SUGGESTIVE 24** [4] W J Haggas 6-9-2 bl (107) M Hills 31/10: 15-45214: In tch, efft to press ldrs   1½ 107
over 2f out, sn drvn & no extra ins last: beat today's rnr-up 2184.
6 Ran   Time 1m 20.70()   Owned: Wertheimer Et Frere   Trained: France

Official Going GOOD/SOFT (GOOD places). Heavy Rain Throughout Afternoon.

2827 2.20 Weatherbys Insurance Services Handicap Stakes 3yo 0-75 (E)   [82]
£3884 £1195 £598   1m4f17y   Good/Soft   Inapplicable   Stands Side

2546 **DUNLEA DANCER 11** [3] M Johnston 3-8-3 (57) J Fanning 11/4: 500-3421: Made all, rdn & in command   69
over 1f out, styd on strongly: first win, op 9/4: eff btwn 10/13f on gd/soft & soft grnd, poss handles fast:
enjoys forcing tactics: type to progress with racing: see 1306.
2163 **GOLD CARD 27** [5] J R Weymes 3-8-7 ViS (61) R Winston 6/1: 34-22552: Held up, eff to press wnr   6   64
over 2f out, kept on but no impress dist: first time visor, op 9/2: handles fast & gd/soft grnd: see 1604 & 983.
1429 **HABITUAL DANCER 62** [4] Jedd O'Keeffe 3-8-5 (59) G Duffield 9/4 JT FAV: 000-6123: Trkd wnr, rdn &   3   58
no impress over 2f out: op 3/1, 2 month abs: btr 1429 & 1051.
2621* **BILL BENNETT 8** [2] J Jay 3-9-13 (6ex) (81) O Urbina 9/4 JT FAV: 1125014: Held up, eff over 2f   ¾   79
out, no impress: bckd under a pen: btr 2621.
2709 **COMPASSION 5** [6]3-7-13 (1ow)(5oh) (47) R Ffrench 20/1: 0-000445: Chsd ldrs till 3f out: see 1339.   6   42
5 Ran   Time 2m 41.71 (9.91)   Owned: Mr K Towey   Trained: Middleham

2828 2.50 Hamilton Park Investors In People Classified Stakes 3yo+ 0-70 (E)
£3738 £1150 £575   1m65y rnd   Good/Soft   Inapplicable   Inside

2654 **LES ARCS 7** [3] R C Guest 4-9-3 (70) K Fallon 15/8 FAV: 210-0021: Held up, switched & hdwy to   82
lead distt, styd on strongly, rdn out: hvly bckd: eff at 1m/10f on fast & gd/soft grnd: settled better today &
confirmed imprvd form on 2654: could follow up.
2474* **MUNAAWASHAT 13** [5] M Johnston 3-8-5 (71) W Supple 11/4: 261-312: Led till over 1f out, kept on   1½ 76
for press: handles fast & gd/soft grnd: clr of rem here, can win again after 2474 (C/D).
2514 **RISKA KING 2** [2] R A Fahey 4-9-3 (66) T Hamilton(3) 25/1: 0000043: Dwelt, rear, eff over 3f out,   4   70
no impress 2f out: see 318.
2425 **JORDANS ELECT 16** [4] I Semple 4-9-6 (73) T Eaves(3) 4/1: 5101404: Trkd ldrs, btn 2f out: nicely bckd.   3   67
1736 **J R STEVENSON 6** [6]8-8-8 (75) S W Kelly 5/1: 51-20465: Trkd ldrs when hmpd over 2f out, no ch   1¼ 66
after: nicely bckd, 7 wk abs: needs things to go his way: btr 1736 & 1423.
2259 **CATALINI 23** [1]3-8-10 (73) A Culhane 10/1: 363-2556: Cl-up, btn 2f out: btr 934 & 841 (AW).   3   58
6 Ran   Time 1m 49.12 (5.32)   Owned: Mr Willie McKay   Trained: Brancepeth

2829 3.20 EBF Maiden Stakes A Qualifier For The Hamilton Park 2-Y-O Series Final 2yo (D)
£4765 £1466 £733   6f str   Good/Soft   Inapplicable   Stands Side

1866 **SHIVAREE 40** [2] M R Channon 2-8-9 A Culhane 6/4 FAV: 31: Handy, rdn & led dist, styd on   84
strongly: well bckd, 6 wk abs: eff at 6f, shld get further: acts on fast & gd/soft grnd, stiff or sharp/undul trk:
confirmed debut promise, see 1866.
       VALUE PLUS 33 [1] Ms Joanna Morgan 2-8-9 P Amy Parsons(7) 5/2: 2222: b f Mujadil - Brittas Blues   1¼ 79
(Blues Traveller) Keen & led/dsptd lead, hung right halfway & hdd dist, kept on under a kind ride: nicely bckd:
Irish raider, rnr-up on 3 prev starts, incl bhnd a subs Gr 2 wnr: eff at 5/6f on firm & gd/soft, stiff/gall or undul
trks: wears cheek pieces: shown enough to find a race, esp with stronger handling.
2610 **SECRET HISTORY 9** [4] M Johnston 2-8-9 J Fanning 9/4: 23: Handy, rdn & kept on, not pace of   ¾   77
front pair: nicely bckd: handles fast & gd/soft grnd: see 2610.
2382 **NO COMMISSION 18** [5] R F Fisher 2-9-0 R Winston 33/1: 054054: Pushed along rear early, kept on   nk 81$
late, nvr able to chall: stays a stiff 6f, prob handles fast & gd/soft grnd: see 1893.
2275 **SCORPIO SALLY 22** [3]2-8-9 Darren Williams 33/1: 05: b f Mujadil - Clear Procedure (The   3½ 65
Minstrel) Chsd ldrs, rdn & no extra halfway: highly tried after debut: 8,000gns Mar foal, dam a 1m wnr.
5 Ran   Time 1m 13.68 (2.38)   Owned: Sheikh Mohammed   Trained: West Ilsley

2830 3.50 Toteexacta Stakes Handicap 3yo+ 0-85 (D)   [80]
£8210 £2526 £1263   5f str   Good/Soft   Inapplicable   Stands Side

2712 **AAHGOWANGOWAN 5** [3] M Dods 5-8-6 t (58) R Ffrench 9/4 FAV: 30-00521: Broke well, made all, rdn/in   68
command fnl 1f: well bckd: lkd unlucky when stall opened late on prev start: best at 5f, stays a gall 7f: acts on
firm or soft grnd, any trk: best dominating: see 2712 & 127.
2524 **BEYOND THE CLOUDS 12** [7] J S Wainwright 8-9-10 (76) R Winston 8/1: 000-0002: b g Midhish -   1¾ 78

Tongabezi (Shernazar) Held up, styd on for press, nvr threatened wnr: thrice h'cap rnr-up in '03: dual h'cap wnr '02: stays 6f, 5f specialist: acts on gd/soft, loves firm & fast grnd, any trk: best without visor & a gd weight carrier: slipping to a fair mark & a rtn to a faster surface shld suit.   2 Jul'03 Asco 5g/s 88-87 B:
2 Jun'03 Newc 5g/f 90-80 B: 2 May'03 Wind 5.0g/f 82-77 B: 1 Sep'02 Donc 5fm 82-77 D: 1 Aug'02 Beve 5g/f 77-73 E:
2 Jul'02 Beve 5g/s 79-79 D: 2 Jun'02 York 6g/s 79-77 D: 1 Jun'01 Wind 5g/f 84-77 B: 1 May'01 Beve 5fm 81-69 E:

2524 **KINGS COLLEGE BOY 12** [9] R A Fahey 4-8-8 bl (60) T Hamilton(3) 9/2: 60-00323: Rear, styd on for   **hd**   **61**
press, nvr able to threaten: see 2524 & 2320.
2690 **STRENSALL 5** [1] R E Barr 7-9-10 (69) P Mulrennan(5) 13/2: 0-020034: Chsd ldrs, no impress dist.   **nk**   **76**
2476 **NORTHERN SVENGALI 13** [6]8-7-12 (14oh)t p (36) J McAuley 66/1: 000-0005: Reared start & bhd, mod   **1¾**   **45$**
late prog: stiff task: see 2476.
2558 **BANJO BAY 11** [4]6-9-10 (76) Alex Greaves 9/2: 0-003006: Trkd ldrs, short of room when no impress   **hd**   **70**
over 1f out: see 2074 & 1598.
2712* **KARMINSKEY PARK 5** [5]5-9-5 (7ex) (71) J Fanning 11/2: 2653217: Chsd ldrs, btn over 1f out: 7lb   **shd**   **65**
pen for fortunate win over today's wnr in 2712 (C/D).
2713 **MUTAYAM 5** [8]4-7-13 (1ow)(11oh)t (39) P Fessey 40/1: 20000-68: Cl-up, outpcd halfway: see 2713.   **3**   **37**
8 Ran   Time 1m 0.14 (2.04)   Owned: Mr D Vic Roper   Trained: Darlington

---

2831   4.20 Friends Of Scottish Racing Classified Stakes 3yo+ 0-65 (E)
£3559 £1095 £548   **6f str**   **Good/Soft**   **Inapplicable**   Stands Side

2477 **FONTHILL ROAD 13** [3] R A Fahey 4-9-8 (70) T Hamilton(3) 15/8: 11612-61: Trkd ldrs, rdn & hdwy to   **76**
lead dist, rdn out: eff at 5/7f on fast, likes gd/soft, soft & fibresand, prob any trk: see 2477.
2713 **BUNDY 5** [1] M Dods 8-9-3 (63) S W Kelly 13/8 FAV: 0002232: Led, hung right over 1f out & hdd   **½**   **68**
dist, railled well for press: qck reapp: normally best coming late off a strong pace: see 2477, 2315.
2445 **ALBASHOOSH 15** [4] D Nicholls 6-9-8 (70) Alex Greaves 5/2: 6-656103: Cl-up, rdn & wknd over 1f   **5**   **59**
out: op 2/1: twice well below 2280 (fast).
2713 **FRIAR TUCK 5** [2] Miss L A Perratt 9-9-3 (53) R Ffrench 14/1: 4640004: Cl-up, eff 2f out, no   **3½**   **43**
impress dist: qck reapp: see 1508 (C/D, h'cap).
4 Ran   Time 1m 13.33 (3.53)   Owned: Mrs Una Towell   Trained: Malton

---

2832   4.50 Supercounty Handicap Stakes A Qualifier For The Totepool Series Final 3yo+ 0-75 (E)   **[70]**
£3949 £1215 £608   **1m1f36y rnd**   **Good/Soft**   **Inapplicable**   Inside

2447 **WAHOO SAM 15** [8] T D Barron 4-9-3 (59) P Makin(5) 8/1: 000-0031: Cl-up/dsptd lead, went on 4f   **67**
out, edged left under press ins last, drvn & held on gamely: prev eff at 6/7f, now suited by 1m/9f: acts on firm,
gd/soft & fibresand, sharp/easy or stiff/undul trk: well h'capped & showed a fine attitude here, win again.
1776 **DOUBLE RANSOM 45** [1] Mrs L Stubbs 5-9-2 bl (58) G Duffield 9/2: 3142162: Rear, drvn & styd on   **¾**   **64**
well from over 1f out, not quite get there: well bckd, op 11/2: 6 wk abs: see 1504.
2402 **NO CHANCE TO DANCE 17** [6] H J Collingridge 4-8-4 t (46) Dean McKeown 16/1: 050-0043: Trkd ldrs   **¾**   **51**
trav well, styd on for press, not pace of wnr: clr rem: acts on fast, imprvd again on gd/soft today: can find a race.
2552 **REGENTS SECRET 11** [7] J S Goldie 4-9-7 (63) W Supple 10/1: 40-40024: Rear, switched & kept on   **5**   **59**
late, no threat: btr 2552.
5010} **DONNAS DOUBLE 237** [3]9-9-0 p (56) P Mulrennan(5) 10/1: 340555-5: ch g Weldnaas - Shadha (Shirley   **½**   **51**
Heights) Held up in tch, smooth hdwy 3f out, rdn & hdd bef 1f out: h'cap plcd in '03 (rtd 65), subs tumbled down
weights: landed hat-trick in '02 (clmr & 2 h'caps): eff at 1m/10f, stays 12f on firm, soft & any trk, likes
Newcastle: eff in cheek pieces, tried blnks, best held up: genuine, well h'capped & encouraging reapp.
1 Jun'02 Newc 8g/f 86-79 C: 1 Jun'02 York 10.3g/f 80- D: 1 Jun'02 Newc 10.1g/s 71-65 E:
1 Sep'01 Newc 10.1fm 71-67 D: 1 Jun'01 Ripo 10g/f 68-64 D: 2 Jun'01 Muss 8g/f 66- E:

2447 **WOOD DALLING 15** [5]6-8-11 (53) R Winston 9/1: 4305-006: Mid-div, eff 3f out, drvn & no extra dist.   **hd**   **47**
2284 **NEWCORP LAD 21** [12]4-9-6 (62) A Culhane 4/1: 26-04007: Mid-div, no impress dist: see 1397.   **1¼**   **53**
2325 **CHISEL 20** [2]3-8-7 (60) J Fanning 20/1: 0068: Chsd ldrs, btn 3f out: h'cap bow, longer trip.   **8**   **38**
2655* **LIBRE 7** [13]4-9-3 (6ex)bl t (59) K Fallon 11/4 FAV: 5400019: Dwelt, rear, rdn & no impress over   **2**   **33**
2f out: well bckd under a pen: btr 2655.
2543 **ANTHEMION 11** [10]7-8-13 (55) D McGaffin 28/1: 5-020000: 10th: Chsd ldrs, btn 2f out: btr 1504.   **3½**   **23**
2499 **PERUVIA 12** [11]4-10-0 vis t (70) F Lynch 12/1: 4412-050: 11th: Led till 4f out, sn btn: btr 2499.   **3**   **33**
2708 **DARK CUT 5** [9]4-8-3 (45) Amy Parsons(7) 50/1: 00-00000: 12th: Chsd ldrs, btn 3f out: qck reapp.   **1½**   **5**
12 Ran   Time 2m 0.46(6.36)   Owned: Mr C A Washbourn   Trained: Thirsk

---

Official Going Firm (Good/Firm Places)

2833   2.30 John Connor Press Associates Claiming Stakes 2yo (F)
£2905 £830 £415   **5f213y rnd**   **Firm**   **Inapplicable**   Inside

2563* **PRINCELY VALE 10** [3] W G M Turner 2-8-12 p C Haddon(7) 7/4: 04111: Handy, styd on to lead bef 1f   **76**
out, rdn clr, eased cl-home: well bckd: eff at 6/7f on firm & gd/soft grnd: acts on a gall & v sharp/undul trk:
eff in cheek pieces: thriving in sell/claim grade: see 2563 & 2461.
2330 **RONNIES LAD 19** [1] Andrew Reid 2-8-11 p J P Guillambert(3) 13/8 FAV: 50122: Led, hdd 5f out,   **4**   **63**
outpcd halfway, rallied ins fnl 1f, no ch with wnr: bckd: new stable: acts on firm & gd: see 2330 (G L Moore).
2343 **GENERAL NUISANCE 19** [4] J S Moore 2-8-8 p Derek Nolan(6) 8/1: 264543: Bhd, prog to chase wnr bef   **hd**   **59**
1f out, not extra cl-home: handles firm & hvy grnd: see 2343.
2625 **WITTY GIRL 8** [5] C A Dwyer 2-8-11 R Thomas(5) 9/2: 34: Dwelt, prog centre trk halfway, modest   **shd**   **61**
late gains: cmb for £5,000: see 2625 (debut, M D I Usher).
2584 **AHAZ 10** [2]2-8-6 BL T P Queally(3) 20/1: 0605: Led 5f out, sn clr, hdd bef 1f out, fdd: 1st time blnks.   **4**   **44**
5 Ran   Time 1m 12.61 (4.81)   Owned: Vale Racing   Trained: Sherborne

---

2834	3.00 Saltwell Signs Selling Stakes 3yo (G)
	£2562 £732 £366 7f214y rnd **Firm** **Inapplicable** Inside

2667 **DELCIENNE** 6 [4] G G Margarson 3-8-9 (42) A McCarthy 4/1 JT FAV: 0-003021: Held up, prog wide   **49+**
halfway, styd on to lead 1f out, pushed clr, val 6L+: qck reapp: bght in for 8,800gns: eff around 1m on firm, fast
grnd & polytrack: acts on sharp/undul trk: can win again in this grade: see 2667.
2434 **BLAISE WOOD** 15 [7] G L Moore 3-9-0 p (62) R L Moore 5/1: 6-0602: Rear, prog to lead bef 1f out,   4   **47**
sn hdd & no extra: blnks left off: prob stays 1m, drop to 6/7f shld suit: acts on firm grnd: see 2193.
2501 **MAGICO** 12 [9] P Burgoyne 3-9-0 BL (48) Derek Nolan(7) 25/1: 000-0003: Sn in tch, rdn keenly, led   1½   **44**
2f out, hung left & hdd bef 1f out, sn no extra: first time blnks: unplcd in 3 '03 starts (rtd 60, auct mdn).
2667 **JOHNNY ALLJAYS** 6 [1] J S Moore 3-9-0 P (38) J D Smith 33/1: 0-000004: Led 6f, sn no extra: qck reapp. 1¼   **42**
2664 **FIDDLES MUSIC** 6 [5]3-9-0 (45) T E Durcan 11/2: 0-0145: Cl-up, wknd bef 1f out: op 7/2 on qck reapp. 1½   **39**
4715} **MONASH GIRL** 260 [6]3-8-9 N Chalmers(5) 33/1: 00-6: b f General Monash - Maricica (Ahonoora)   5   **24**
Handy, wknd fnl 2f: reapp: unplcd in 2 '03 starts (rtd 31, seller): with B R Johnson.
1960 **ROAMING VAGABOND** 36 [2]3-9-0 (52) D Holland 15/2: 00-607: Stumbled start, al in rear: see 1604.   2½   **24**
2288 **MAC THE KNIFE** 21 [3]3-9-0 (60) P Dobbs 5/1: 20-00008: Chsd ldrs, wknd fnl 2f: tchd 7/1: see   2   **20**
1984.
2292 **SHARPLAW DESTINY** 21 [8]3-8-9 (47) T P Queally(3) 4/1 JT FAV: 004-5009: Keen cl-up, fdd 2f out.   2½   **10**
9 Ran   Time 1m 37.36 (5.36)   Owned: The Del Boys   Trained: Newmarket

---

2835	3.30 Brasserie Italian Restaurant At The Marina Maiden Stakes Fillies 3yo (D)
	£3455 £1063 £532 1m1f209y **Firm** **Inapplicable** Outside

2627 **CHERUBIM** 8 [3] D R Loder 3-8-11 (78) T P Queally(3) 7/2: 32-551: Sn dsptd lead, led after 5f, hdd   **75**
2f out, rallied to lead dist, drvn out to hold: eff at 6f/1m, now stays 10f: acts on firm & gd grnd: see 2627.
1810 **SEA OF GOLD** 43 [5] H J Cyzer 3-8-11 R L Moore 100/30 JT FA: 062: Mid-div, prog to lead 2f out,   1½   **72**
hdd dist, kept on, not pace wnr: 6 wk abs: imprvd for step up to 10f: acts on firm grnd.
1864 **MISS MONICA** 40 [6] H R A Cecil 3-8-11 W Ryan 100/30 JT FA: 643: Bhd, prog 3f out, kept on fnl   1½   **69**
1f: 6 wk abs: eff at 9/10f on firm & fast grnd: see 1864.
2277 **AL SHUUA** 22 [1] C E Brittain 3-8-11 (79) T E Durcan 7/2: 36-204: Led, hdd 9f out, styd cl-up,   1¼   **67**
onepcd bef 1f out: clr rem: twice below 1864 (reapp).
229 **KILMINCHY LADY** 192 [4]3-8-11 R Miles(3) 20/1: 006-5: b f Cape Cross - Lace Flower (Old Vic) Rcd   14   **47**
keenly, dsptd lead 5f, fdd fnl 3f: long abs: modest form to date.
2453 **MISS SHANGRI LA** 15 [2]3-8-11 D Holland 7/1: 006: Handy, wknd fnl 3f: op 10/1.   19   **21**
6 Ran   Time 2m 04.23 (6.43)   Owned: Sheikh Mohammed   Trained: Newmarket

---

2836	4.00 John Bloor Memorial Handicap For The Operatic Society Challenge Cup 3yo+ 0-70 (E) [58]
	£3367 £1036 £518 1m3f196y **Firm** **Inapplicable** Outside

2718 **ABSINTHER** 4 [6] M R Bosley 7-9-1 (45) G Baker 13/2: 4000-021: Held up, prog 5f out, styd on to   **53+**
lead 1f out, pushed out, val 3L+: qck reapp: eff at 11/12f on firm, soft grnd & fibresand: made gd use of drop
back to winning mark & can follow up: see 2718.
2601* **COMPTON ECLAIRE** 9 [7] G A Butler 4-10-2 (6ex)vis (60) T P Queally(3) 7/2: 3324612: Bhd, prog 3f   1½   **64**
out, styd on ins fnl 1f, no ch with wnr: 6lb higher than recent win in 2601.
2548* **SALUT SAINT CLOUD** 11 [1] G L Moore 3-8-8 (52) S Whitworth 3/1 FAV: 45-60513: Handy, onepcd dist   1   **54**
when saddle slipped: new stable: eff at 10/12f on firm & gd grnd: see 2548 (clmr, Miss V Haig).
2035 **NORTH POINT** 33 [5] R Curtis 6-9-4 bl (48) R Miles(3) 14/1: 0666-004: b g Definite Article -   2½   **46**
Friendly Song (Song) Led, hdd 2f out, no extra: unplcd in 4 '03 starts (rtd 56, h'caps): unplcd in 3 03/04 hdle
starts (rtd 94h, h'cap): won 2 nov hdles in 02/03 (rtd 112h, stays 2m on firm & gd): appr & amat h'cap wnr in '02:
eff at 9/10f on firm, gd/soft & fibresand: acts on any trk: tried visor, pieces & blnks: on fair mark.
1 Jul'02 Epso 10gd 68-62 E: 1 Jul'02 Kemp 9g/s 59-55 E: 1 Jun'01 Leic 10g/f 77-73 D: 2 May'01 Hami 9.1fm 79- D:
2538 **PRIVATE BENJAMIN** 11 [4]4-9-6 (50) P Doe 6/1: 0630105: Handy over 7f, sn outpcd, rallied ins fnl 2f.   hd   **47**
2601 **BANNINGHAM BLAZE** 9 [2]4-9-6 (50) D Holland 4/1: 0412236: Cl-up, led 2f out, hdd 1f out, sn wknd: ¾   **45**
op 11/4: below par eff: btr 2601, 1967 & 1692.
2718 **SUMMER CHERRY** 4 [3]7-9-1 t (45) I Mongan 9/1: 03-02507: Bhd, prog after 5f, no impress fnl 2f.   shd   **39**
7 Ran   Time 2m 35.54 (7.34)   Owned: Mrs Jean M O'Connor   Trained: Wantage

---

2837	4.30 University Of Sussex Natalie Naylor Memorial Stakes Handicap 3yo 0-75 (E) [77]
	£3396 £1045 £523 1m1f209y **Firm** **Inapplicable** Outside

2624 **DAMI** 8 [1] C E Brittain 3-9-7 p (70) D Holland 6/4 FAV: 00-55221: Cl-up, styd on to lead dist,   **76+**
pushed out, val bit more: bckd under top-weight: eff at 7f/1m, now stays 10f: acts on firm & gd grnd: eff with
cheek pieces: gd confidence boost: see 2624 & 2432.
1528 **RUSSALKA** 57 [2] Julian Poulton 3-8-3 (52) M Halford(7) 14/1: 22-00502: Rear, prog when no room   1½   **55**
bef 1f out, switchd & kept on ins fnl 1f, no ch with wnr: 8 wk abs: eff at 9.4f/10f on firm & fibresand.
2565* **CHARLIE TANGO** 10 [4] M R Channon 3-9-4 (67) S Hitchcott(3) 11/4: 0030413: Handy, rcd keenly, kept   shd   **68**
on ins fnl 1f, just held for 2nd: acts on firm, gd/soft grnd & polytrack: 5lb higher than recent win in 2565.
2631 **SWIFT SAILING** 8 [6] B W Hills 3-9-6 (69) T E Durcan 7/2: 15-00024: Led, hdd dist, sn no extra: ½   **70**
not helped by playing up at start: showed more in 2631.
2621 **DUKES VIEW** 8 [5]3-9-3 BL (66) Dane O'Neill 7/1: 006-005: b g Sadler's Wells - Igreja (Southern   nk   **66**
Halo) Handy, ev ch when hung left dist, sn no extra: op 10/1 on first time blnks: unplcd all 3 '03 starts (rtd 76, mdn).
5 Ran   Time 2m 6.24 (8.44)   Owned: Mr Saeed Manana   Trained: Newmarket

BRIGHTON   TUESDAY 29.06.04   Lefthand, V Sharp, Undulating Track

2838	5.00 Totesport Com Rated Stakes Handicap 3yo+ 0-80 (D)				[84]
	£4922 £1820 £910 5f59y rnd Firm Inapplicable Inside				

2669 **PARKSIDE PURSUIT 6** [2] J M Bradley 6-9-3 (3ex) (73) R L Moore 7/4 JT FAV: 1104131: Prom, styd on   77
to lead ins fnl 1f, rdn out: bckd on qck reapp: eff at 5/6f on firm & gd grnd: remains in gd form: see 2669 & 2598.
2598 **COMPTON BANKER 9** [3] G A Butler 7-9-0 (70) T P Queally(3) 5/1: 115-0652: Dwelt, sn mid-div, kept   1   70
on ins fnl 1f, al held by wnr: eff at 5.3f, apprec rtn to 6f+: has slipped to a fair mark & can find similar: see 2370.
2598 **HARD TO CATCH 9** [5] D K Ivory 6-9-7 bl (77) M Savage(5) 7/4 JT FAV: 5001133: Prom, styd on to lead   ½   76
bef 1f out, hdd ins fnl 1f, no extra: loves Brighton: ran to form of 2598 & 2269.
2752 **CORANGLAIS 3** [1] J M Bradley 4-8-5 bl (61) C Catlin 4/1: 0-000004: Led, hdd dist, sn no extra.   1¼   56
4 Ran   Time 1m 3.29(3.29)   Owned: Mr J M Bradley   Trained: Chepstow

---

LINGFIELD   Polytrack   WEDNESDAY 30.06.04   Lefthand, V Sharp Track

Official Going Standard

2839	2.10 Whips And Tees Maiden Auction Stakes 2yo (E)			
	£3406 £1048 £524 5f aw rnd Standard Inapplicable Outside			

2257 **RUSSIAN ROCKET 24** [8] Mrs C A Dunnett 2-8-7 Hayley Turner(5) 7/2: 0521: Chsd ldrs, rdn & wide on   81a
bend over 1f out, styd on for press to lead well ins last: AW bow: eff at 5f, shld get 6f: acts on firm, fast &
polytrack, sharp/undul trk: see 2257, 1981.
2430 **CONNOTATION 16** [1] P W D'Arcy 2-8-4 E Ahern 9/2: 22: Trkd ldrs, rdn to chall ins last, no extra   ½   75a
cl-home: AW bow: acts on fast grnd & polytrack: going the right way: see 2430.
2573 **FORZEEN 11** [7] J A Osborne 2-8-9 L Dettori 11/8 FAV: 3423: Led, edged right & hdd well ins   ¾   78a
last: handles firm & both AWs: see 2573, 2415 & 1752.
2450 **KEMPSEY 16** [5] J J Bridger 2-8-7 A Daly 20/1: 064: ch c Wolfhound - Mockingbird (Sharpo) Trkd   ½   74a
ldr, hung right from halfway, rdn/ch ins last but no extra when hmpd cl-home: AW bow: cheaply bought Apr foal, half
brother to a multiple sprint wnr Ridicule, dam a 6f juv wnr: eff at 5f on polytrack: clr rem here.
2287 **KINGSGATE BAY 22** [3]2-8-9 N Pollard 16/1: 05: b g Desert Sun - Selkirk Flyer (Selkirk) Slow   4   64a
away, bhd, late prog, op 12/1: AW bow: 21,000 gns Mar foal, dam uncrd, sire proved smart at 6f/1m.
2415 **PEOPLETON BROOK 18** [4]2-8-7 T Quinn 7/1: 56: Chsd ldrs, hmpd after 1f, btn 1f out, AW bow.   ½   60a
1727 **DUSTINI 47** [2]2-8-9 bl M Halford(7) 20/1: 35307: Sn outpcd & bhd, t.o.: 7 wk abs: btr 1538.   11   33a
7 Ran   Time 1m 0.51 (2.71)   Owned: Mrs Christine Dunnett   Trained: Norwich

---

2840	2.40 Formost Fabrications Summer Classified Stakes 3yo+ 0-70 (E)			
	£3393 £1044 £522 1m aw rnd Standard Inapplicable Outside			

2587 **INVADER 11** [2] C E Brittain 8-9-7 bl t (74) D Holland 14/1: 0060001: Mid-div, dropped rear   79a
halfway, strong run for press to lead at 1m/10f on firm, gd/soft & both AWs: see 234.
2655 **MALLARD 8** [6] J G Given 6-9-7 (74) M Fenton 9/1: 1101-302: Handy, rdn & led dist, edged right &   shd   78a
drvn/hdd line: back to form: loves a/w's: see 2159.
2592 **ISLAND RAPTURE 11** [8] J A R Toller 4-9-1 L Dettori 7/1: 55-00403: Dwelt, rear, hdwy wide to   1   70a
press ldr ins last, no extra cl-home: see 1891.
2500* **TRE COLLINE 13** [11] N Tinkler 5-9-8 (75) G Baker 7/1: 0001514: Rear, hdwy wide 3f out, drvn & no   2   73a
extra dist: acts on firm, fast & both AWs: just btr 2500 (fibresand).
1122 **FLYING TREATY 80** [9]7-9-6 (73) S Drowne 25/1: 0006005: Chsd ldrs wide till dist, abs, improved   nk   70a
effort & definitely of more interest now with new yard, prev a prolific fibresand wnr & well h'capped, keep in mind.
1877 **MORNING AFTER 41** [1]4-9-4 (74) J Murtagh 7/1: 122/43-06: b f Emperor Jones - Onefortheditch   nk   67a
(With Approval) Rear when switched over 1f out, strong run: lightly rcd '03, unplcd (rtd 76, class stks): fills
auct mdn rnr wnr in '02, fills nurs rnr-up: eff at 5.5f/7f, poss stays sharp 1m: acts on firm, fast & polytrack,
stiff or sharp trk. 2 Oct'02 Newm 6g/f 80- B: 2 Sep'02 Yarm 7fm 85-78 D: 1 Aug'02 Bath 5.7g/f 82- E:
1235 **SLALOM 74** [10]4-9-8 e (75) W Supple 10/1: 53-107: Dwelt, sn wide & handy, led over 1f out, sn hdd   2   67a
& wknd dist: abs: prob handles both AWs but btr 939 (fibresand, mdn).
798 **ATHBOY 118** [3]3-8-7 vis (70) K Fallon 13/2: 60-01108: Rear, switched & no prog dist: abs, gelded.   hd   61a
2665 **BRAZILIAN TERRACE 7** [5]4-9-5 (75) Hayley Turner(5) 5/1 FAV: 3401139: Trkd ldrs, no impress fnl 2f.   ½   62a
2116 **CERTAIN JUSTICE 30** [7]6-9-8 P (75) T Quinn 11/1: 040-0650: 10th: Led/dsptd lead, btn dist: btr 44.   1½   62a
2426 **CERTIFIABLE 17** [4]3-8-11 (74) S Carson 8/1: 4115050: 11th: Led 2f, btn 3f out: btr 1315 & 934.   3   55a
2540 **RECOUNT 12** [12]4-9-5 (72) N Pollard 33/1: 50-00650: 12th: led after 2f till over 1f out, wknd qckly.   1½   50a
12 Ran   Time 1m 40.82 (4.62)   Owned: Mr R J Swinbourne   Trained: Newmarket

---

2841	3.10 Energy & Power Consultants Handicap Stakes 3yo 0-85 (D)				[90]
	£5610 £1726 £863 6f aw rnd Standard Inapplicable Inside				

2764 **INSTANT RECALL 4** [5] B J Meehan 3-9-4 bl (80) J Fortune 6/1: 1045451: Trkd ldrs, led ins last,   90a
drvn out: qk reapp: eff at 6/7f on polytrack, gd & gd/soft, likes Lingfield: suited by blnks.
2271 **TAG TEAM 23** [1] A M Balding 3-9-1 (77) L Keniry(3) 9/2: 1305132: Chsd ldrs, rdn & hdwy to lead   ½   84a
ins last, sn hdd & no pace fnl cl-home: loves this trk, can win again: see 1903.
2314 **TORQUEMADA 21** [7] W Jarvis 3-7-12 (3oh) (57) F P Ferris(3) 20/1: 60-30003: Dwelt & rear, switched   1   64a
& kept on late, no threat: gd run, mdn: see 898 (C/D).
1116 **ECCENTRIC 81** [9] Andrew Reid 3-9-0 (76) S Sanders 14/1: 0-41104: Cl-up/dsptd lead, went on over   ¾   78a
2f out till ins last, no extra: 12 wk abs: eff at 6f, suited by dominating at 7f: see 933.
1901 **CATCH THE WIND 40** [3]3-9-0 (76) D Holland 25/1: 3140-055: Led/dsptd lead till dist: abs: stays   1   75a
sharp 6f, more convincing at 5f: acts on fast, soft & polytrack: see 1901 (5f).
2268 **SWEETEST REVENGE 23** [4]3-9-1 (77) Hayley Turner(5) 14/1: 04254-06: Mid-div, not pace to chall.   ½   74a
1881 **ACE CLUB 40** [10]3-8-8 (70) M Hills 10/1: 21-507: Chsd ldrs, no extra dist: abs: see 1570.   ½   65a

859

2586 **TRIFTI 11** [8]3-8-3 (65) E Ahern 33/1: 4008: Al rear, abs/h'cap bow. ½ 58a
2271 **EMTILAAK 23** [6]3-9-2 (78) W Supple 9/1: 23-23109: Led after 1f till over 2f out, sn btn: btr 2042 (mdn). 4 59a
2743 **BELLA TUTRICE 4** [11]3-8-10 (72) K Fallon 14/1: 200-0340: 10th: Rear/wide, no prog & eased dist. 2½ 45a
1933 **MORSE 39** [3]3-9-7 (83) L Dettori 6/4 FAV: 2231200: 11th: Rear & lost tch from halfway, t.o.: 19 4a
hvly bckd, op 9/4: reportedly resented kick back: much btr 1771 & 1621 (turf).
11 Ran   Time 1m 13.27 (2.87)   Owned: Mrs Susan Roy   Trained: Upper Lambourn

Official Going Good/Firm

2842 3.40 Ladbrokes Com Handicap Stakes Fillies 3yo 0-70 (E)   [74]
£3445 £1060 £530   **1m3f106y**   **Good/Firm**   **Inapplicable**   Inside

4575} **MAZUNA 271** [5] C E Brittain 3-8-13 (59) E Ahern 20/1: 04406-1: b f Cape Cross - Keswa (Kings 71
Lake) Trkd ldrs & led over 2f out, drvn out: 1st win: reapp: unplcd '03 (rtd 56a & 64, mdns): prev tried at up
to 7f, relished step up to 11.5f, could get further: acts on fast grnd & a sharp/undul trk: goes well fresh.
2478 **LA PETITE CHINOISE 14** [1] R Guest 3-9-6 (66) S Sanders 5/1: 06-60422: Mid-div, rdn & chall wnr 1¼ 75
2f out, rdn & chall dist, no extra well ins last: nicely bckd: eff at 9/11.5f: shown enough to find a race.
2617 **BUBBLING FUN 9** [10] E A L Dunlop 3-9-4 (64) K Fallon 4/1: 02-40433: Rear, drvn & kept on fnl 2f, 2½ 69
not threaten front pair: stays 11.5f: mdn, see 2046.
2592 **LADY PEACHES 11** [9] D Mullarkey 3-9-7 (67) J P Guillambert(3) 14/1: 0-0304: Dwelt, keen in rear, 2½ 68
eff wide from 3f out, no impress dist: prob handles fast & soft grnd, longer 11.5f trip may yet suit: see 1651.
1165 **MACCHIATO GB 77** [4]3-8-10 (56) S Carson 16/1: 00602-05: br f Inchinor - Tereyna (Terimon) Led 3 53
till over 2f out, fdd: 11 wk abs: h'cap rnr-up fnl '03 start: stays a gall 10f, dam a plcd 15f 3yo performer:
acts on fast grnd. 2 Sep'03 Nott 10.0g/f 57-53 E:
2719 **PRINCESS GALADRIEL 5** [3]3-9-1 (61) N Pollard 9/1: 0-213206: Keen in mid-div, rdn & btn over 1f ¾ 57
out: nicely bckd: quick reapp: btr 2344 & 2111 (1m/6f).
2642 **ELLINA 8** [11]3-9-6 (66) L Dettori 14/1: 00-04647: Keen, rear, eff wide, btn 2f out: see 1651. ¾ 61
1785 **ALALOOF 45** [6]3-9-6 (66) W Supple 4/1: 605-668: Held up in tch, rdn & btn 2f out: see 1403. nk 60
2163* **ILLEANA 28** [8]3-8-12 (58) D Holland 7/2 FAV: 00-40019: Mid-div, hdwy wide 5f out, wknd fnl 2f: bckd. 1 51
2617 **DAYDREAM DANCER 9** [7]3-8-7 (53) P Robinson 16/1: 000-5000: 10th: gr f Daylami - Dancing Wolf nk 45
(Wolfhound) Chsd ldr till 3f out, wknd: unplcd '03 (rtd 54, mdn).
1454 **OUT OF MY WAY 62** [2]3-7-12 (17oh) (27) F P Ferris(3) 66/1: 00-00040: 11th: Prom, wknd qckly 3f out, abs. 18 11
11 Ran   Time 2m 32.00 (8.6)   Owned: Mr Saeed Manana   Trained: Newmarket

2843 4.10 Henry Streeter Maiden Stakes 3yo+ (D)
£3877 £1193 £597   **1m2f**   **Good/Firm**   **Inapplicable**   Inside

3790} **ALPHECCA 313** [2] Sir Michael Stoute 3-8-12 K Fallon 2/1: 0-1: b c Kingmambo - Limbo (A P Indy) 88+
Led after 1f, shaken up & in command from dist, pushed out: well bckd on debut tho' op 6/4: eff at 10f, 12f should
suit: acts on fast: goes well fresh & well suited by forcing tactics: potentially useful, win more races.
2222 **GANYMEDE 26** [7] M L W Bell 3-8-12 VIS (81) D Holland 8/11 FAV: 63-23222: Sn chsd wnr, rdn & prsd 3 80
wnr over 2f out, hung left & no extra fnl 100yds: clr of rem: hvly bckd, op 11/10: prob ran to form in a visor.
   SAFIRAH 0 [4] M A Jarvis 3-8-7 P Robinson 10/1: 3: b f Singspiel - Princess Haifa (Mr 5 68
Prospector) Led 1f, sn chsd front pair, outpcd over 2f out: debut, op 7/1: half sister to an 11f 3yo scorer & subs
hdles wnr: dam a 1m 3yo wnr: gd mid-dist pedigree, 12f+ may suit.
   ST BARCHAN 0 [3] W Jarvis 3-8-12 T Quinn 33/1: 4: ch g Grand Lodge - Moon Tango (Last Tycoon) nk 72
Slow away & rear, outpcd over 3f out, some late gains: 40,000 gns purchase, dam a 6f 3yo scorer.
2222 **PORT N STARBOARD 26** [5]3-8-12 L Dettori 16/1: 45: Trkd ldrs, hung badly right from over 1f out, wknd. 2½ 68
2656 **SCOTT 8** [6]3-8-12 G Baker 66/1: 006: M bhd & drvn/btn 2f out: longer trip. ½ 67
6 Ran   Time 2m 10.48 (6.28)   Owned: Niarchos Family   Trained: Newmarket

2844 4.40 Don't Forget Ladies Evening 17th July Apprentice Handicap Stakes 4yo+ 35-55 (F)   [63]
£3031 £866 £433   **1m2f**   **Good/Firm**   **Inapplicable**   Inside

2643 **OUR DESTINY 8** [2] A W Carroll 6-9-6 (55) L Treadwell 10/1: 2431041: Rear, hdwy 3f out & led ins 61
last, rdn out: eff btwn 1m/11f on fast, soft & fibresand, any trk, likes a sharp one: see 1940.
2719 **JESSINCA 5** [11] A P Jones 8-8-5 (40) Liam Jones(5) 10/1: 0-006032: Al handy & led 2f out, hdd ins 1½ 43
last, kept on: op 9/1: stays a sharp 10f well nowadays: see 597.
805 **MOLLYS SECRET 118** [4] C G Cox 6-8-10 p (45) Ashleigh Horton(7) 16/1: 00-10003: Led, hdd 2f out, nk 47
kept on, not pace of wnr: 4 month abs: imprvd eff on turf return with forcing tactics applied: see 424.
2436 **HOLLY ROSE 16** [10] D E Cantillon 5-9-3 p (52) Laura Pike(5) 7/1: 0-024044: Dwelt, held up in tch, 1 53
eff wide from over 2f out, no extra dist: op 9/1: see 2436 & 1267.
2436 **VANDENBERGHE 16** [13]5-9-0 (49) R Keogh(5) 13/2: 5-153435: Trkd ldrs, no extra over 1f out. nk 49
2589 **NAUTICAL 11** [5]6-9-3 (52) W Hogg(3) 6/1: 10/0-0046: Dwelt, rear, eff wide, no prog over 1f out. 4 46
2529 **SINGLE TRACK MIND 12** [8]6-8-7 (42) Stephanie Hollinshead 14/1: 3500647: Rear, eff 2f out, no dngr. ½ 35
2644 **MISTER CLINTON 8** [3]7-9-4 (53) M Howard(3) 7/1: 0006348: Keen & prom, btn 2f out: see 2644, 2334. 1½ 44
2589 **FANTASY CRUSADER 11** [9]5-9-1 p (50) M Halford(3) 4/1 FAV: 0330329: Unruly stalls beforehand, in ½ 40
tch, btn 2f out: btr 2589, 2260.
2149 **MISS PEACHES 28** [1]6-8-11 (46) Kristin Stubbs 10/1: 1354650: 10th: Rear, no prog: btr 2149 & 648. ¾ 35
2129 **NIGHT DRIVER 29** [7]5-8-13 e (48) Jemma Marshall(5) 10/1: 05/0-0000: 11th: Mid-div, struggling fnl 3f. shd 37
1076 **ANTONY EBENEEZER 85** [12]5-8-0 (35) Dean Williams(3) 20/1: 3001500: 12th: Cl-up till 3f out, sn btn. 2 21
12 Ran   Time 2m 11.75(7.55)   Owned: Mr Dennis Deacon   Trained: Alcester

Official Going Good/Firm (Good Places)

2845   2.30 European Breeders Fund Zetland Median Auction Maiden Stakes 2yo   (E)
£4251 £1308 £654   7f rnd   Good/Firm 30   -05 Slow   Inside

2194 **AL GARHOUD BRIDGE 27** [3] M R Channon 2-9-0 T E Durcan 11/4 FAV: 501: Handy, short of room 2f **92**
out, styd on well ins fnl 1f, rdn out: op 7/2: padd pick: imprvd for step up to 7f: acts on fast grnd & an
undul/tight trk: back to form after disapp last time out in 2194, see 1760.
2473 **JANE JUBILEE 14** [10] M Johnston 2-8-9 K Dalgleish 7/2: 3522: Prom, led 2f out, hdd under press   nk **85**
well ins fnl 1f, just held: clr rem: eff at 6/7f on fast grnd: another gd eff & shld find a similar event: see 2473.
2610 **TARAS TREASURE 10** [6] J J Quinn 2-8-9 R Winston 7/2: 2643: Handy, ev ch bef 1f out, sn no   5 **75**
extra: below form on step up to 7f: btr 2610 (6f).
       LITTLE DALHAM 0 [7] P W Chapple Hyam 2-9-0 A McCarthy 4/1: 4: b c Diktat - Almost Amber (Mt   1¾ **76**
Livermore) Bhd & ran green, jmpd path after 2f, modest late gains: debut: Feb foal, cost 13,000gns: dam 5f wnr as
a juv: sire decent sprint performer: sure to improve for today's experience & can rate higher.
2462 **KASHMAR FLIGHT 15** [8]2-8-9 D Allan 66/1: 0065: b f Fraam - Evasive Step (Batshoof) Mid-div,   3 **65**
prog halfway, onepcd fnl 2f: Mar first foal: dam styd up to 1m: sire useful performer around 1m.
2462 **KING HENRIK 15** [1]2-9-0 K Darley 14/1: 46: Led 5f, wknd: btr 2462.   2½ **63**
2294 **DANS HEIR 22** [5]2-9-0 G Faulkner 33/1: 027: Nvr nrr than mid-div: btr 2294.   ½ **64**
2462 **DRAX 15** [11]2-9-0 T P Queally(3) 7/1: 38: Slow away, nvr a factor: tchd 9/1: btr 2462.   1¼ **62**
2569 **TILLINGBORN DANCER 11** [4]2-9-0 A Culhane 100/1: 009: Mid-div 4f, sn wknd: see 1950.   1¾ **58**
       HARRYS SIMMIE 0 [2]2-8-9 Dale Gibson 50/1: 0: 10th: ch f Spectrum - Minstrels Folly (The   3½ **46**
Minstrel) Slow away, nvr a factor: just ndd race on debut: May foal, cost E6,000: sister to a couple of wnrs:
dam 1m wnr: sire Gr 1 wnr at 1m/10f: with R Hollinshead.
10 Ran   Time 1m 25.51 (2.51)   Owned: Mr Jaber Abdullah   Trained: West Ilsley

---

2846   3.00 Project Management Scotland Handicap Stakes 3yo+ 0-75 (E)   [73]
£3543 £1090 £545   5f rnd   Good/Firm 30   +05 Fast   Inside

2286 **WICKED UNCLE 22** [3] S Gollings 5-10-0 vis (73) K Darley 11/1: 2320-001: Made all far rail, clr **89**
ins fnl 2f, unchall: eff at 5/6f on gd & firm grnd: eff with a visor & likes to dominate: fine eff under top-weight
& is h'capped to make a qk follow-up: see 2189 (reapp).
2512 **BRIGADIER MONTY 13** [1] Mrs S Lamyman 6-8-5 (50) D Fentiman(7) 16/1: 00-06002: Mid-div far side,   4 **55**
prog 2f out, kept on fnl 1f, no ch with wnr: eff at 5f, will apprec rtn to 6f: see 2214.
2770 **SHARP HAT 4** [13] D W Chapman 10-9-0 (59) A Culhane 10/1: 5000003: Dwelt far side, prog ins fnl   1 **61**
2f, nrst fin: another gd eff here at Catterick: slipped to a far mark: see 317 & btr 153.
2690 **AMANDAS LAD 6** [7] M C Chapman 4-8-11 (56) D Fox(5) 25/1: 0420354: Handy far side till dist, onepcd.   nk **57**
2657* **LAUREL DAWN 8** [14]6-8-4 (49) Natalia Gemelova(7) 4/1 FAV: 3-000015: Bhd, prog 2f out, onepcd ins   ¾ **48**
fnl 1f: below par on follow up bid: see 2657 (appr h'cap, made all).
2512 **COUNT COUGAR 13** [6]4-8-11 (56) Dale Gibson 100/1: 010-3006: Cl-up far side over 3f, sn no extra.   shd **54**
2645 **YORKIE 8** [9]5-8-9 (54) Dean McKeown 11/1: 1000227: Nvr nrr than mid-div far side: btr 2645.   nk **51**
2477 **CHAIRMAN BOBBY 14** [2]6-9-13 (72) T E Durcan 13/2: 0320258: Nvr nrr than mid-div far side: btr 2320.   nk **68**
2320* **MALAHIDE EXPRESS 21** [5]4-8-13 (58) J D O'Reilly(7) 15/2: 2055419: Handy far side over 3f, sn no extra. ½ **53**
2657 **MR SPLIFFY 8** [4]5-8-5 (50) G Duffield 16/1: 0500000: 10th: Cl-up far side 4f, wknd: btr 413.   shd **44**
2512 **VALIANT ROMEO 13** [10]4-8-10 va (55) R Ffrench 10/1: 00-52240: 11th: Handy over 3f, sn wknd: btr 1886. 1½ **45**
2599 **CHICO GUAPO 10** [12]4-10-0 bl (73) R Winston 20/1: 1050000: 12th: Rcd stands side, made all that   shd **62**
group, al well bhd far side: top-weight: btr 1476.
2775 **LORD BASKERVILLE 4** [8]3-8-6 (57) Rory Moore(7) 66/1: 6030000: 13th: Al in rear: qck reapp.   nk **45**
2512 **KANGARILLA ROAD 13** [17]5-9-7 (66) P Mulrennan(5) 15/2: 0-002000: 14th: Cl-up stands side till   hd **53**
dist, sn onepcd: broke blood vessel: btr 2029.
2059 **ZUHAIR 33** [16]11-9-8 (67) Alex Greaves 33/1: 00-00000: 15th: Al in rear stands side: btr 2059.   ¾ **52**
1973 **Vigorous 37** [15]4-9-9 (68) J Carroll 25/1:0   2779 **Safranine 3** [11]7-9-1 p(60) Ann Stokell 28/1:0
17 Ran   Time 58.59 (1.29)   Owned: Northern Bloodstock Racing   Trained: Louth

---

2847   3.30 European Breeders Fund Maiden Stakes Fillies 2yo (D)
£4160 £1280 £640   5f rnd   Good/Firm 30   -27 Slow   Inside

       OH DARA 0 [3] P A Blockley 2-8-11 Dean McKeown 100/30: 1: b f Aljabr - Sabaah Elfull (Kris)   **88+**
Made all, clr ins fnl 2f, pushed out, val 5L+: op 9/4 on debut: Jan foal, cost 9,000gns: half-sister won a couple
of times in Middle East: dam 5f wnr: sire high-class performer around 1m: eff at 5f, shld apprec 6f: acts on fast
grnd & an undul/tight trk: goes well fresh: decisive wnr, useful, win more races.
2658 **BIBURY FLYER 7** [7] M R Channon 2-8-11 T E Durcan 6/4 FAV: 223352: Handy, prog to chase ldr ins   3½ **74**
fnl 2f, al held: bckd on qck reapp: another solid eff but has started to become frustrating, try headgear?
2442 **ANGELOFTHENORTH 16** [10] J D Bethell 2-8-11 S Chin 16/1: 343: Handy over 3f, sn onepcd: see 2442. 1¼ **70**
2395 **EPITOMISE 18** [9] R M Beckett 2-8-11 G Duffield 11/2: 64: b f Mind Games - Yanomami (Slew O'   hd **69**
Gold) Handy till halfway, wknd late: op 9/2: Feb foal, cost 16,000gns: half-sister to a couple of
wnrs at 5f: dam successful at 6f: sire Group wnr at sprint dists.
2547 **KILMOVEE 12** [2]2-8-11 K Darley 8/1: 5055: Handy 2f, sn outpcd, rallied late: clr rem: see   nk **68**
2547.
2442 **SERENE PEARL 16** [6]2-8-11 T R Winston 66/1: 0066: Al in rear: first time t-strap.   5 **53**
2481 **NEE LEMON LEFT 14** [5]2-8-11 P Mathers(7) 11/2: 2637: Handy 3f, sn wknd: btr 2481.   3½ **44**
2321 **HUNIPOT 21** [1]2-8-11 R Ffrench 100/1: 0008: In tch till halfway, wknd.   11 **14**
8 Ran   Time 1m 0.19 (2.89)   Owned: Mrs Joanna Hughes   Trained: Southwell

2848 4.00 **Derby House Stabling Handicap Stakes** 4yo+ 0-80 (D) [80]
£5753 £1770 £885 **7f rnd** **Good/Firm 30** +09 Fast Inside

2550 **ALCHEMIST MASTER 12** [9] R M Whitaker 5-8-5 p (57) Dean McKeown 5/1: 00-62221: Cl-up, led bef 1f 72
out, rdn clr: padd pick: eff at 7f/1m on firm, gd/soft & both AWs: eff with cheek pieces: has been in gd form &
this was deserved: h'capped to follow up: see 2550 & 2466.

2655 **SMITH N ALLAN OILS 8** [7] M Dods 5-8-2 p (54) P Fessey 14/1: 0000052: Mid-div, prog when short of 5 59
room 3f out, styd on ins fnl 1f, no ch with wnr: encouraging eff & is back on a winning mark: btr 323.

2615 **WALTZING WIZARD 9** [13] A Berry 5-7-13 (51) F Norton 25/1: 5054063: Handy, kept on ins fnl 1f, hd 55
just held for 2nd: not disgraced, slipped down the weights: see 684.

2684 **RAPHAEL 6** [17] T D Easterby 5-9-13 (79) A Mullen(7) 20/1: 3-010304: Mid-div, prog 3f out, kept on 1 80
fnl 1f: qck reapp: not disgraced.

2324 **RONNIE FROM DONNY 21** [5]4-8-13 (65) A Culhane 11/1: 5500555: Handy over 5f, sn onepcd: see 2057. nk 65

2558 **KING HARSON 12** [6]5-10-0 vis (80) G Duffield 9/1: 31-02006: Led, hdd bef 1f out, sn no extra. hd 80

2672 **NO GROUSE 7** [11]4-9-6 p (72) T Hamilton(3) 12/1: 0030007: Mid-div, prog 3f out, onepcd fnl 1f. nk 71

2672 **QUALITAIR WINGS 7** [1]5-9-7 (73) D McGaffin 14/1: 026-3008: Held up, nvr nrr than mid-div: qck reapp. 1¼ 70

2374 **WHAT A DANCER 19** [7]9-9-9 (75) P Mulrennan(5) 9/2 FAV: 3140449: Chsd ldrs, no room 2f out, onepcd. hd 71

2466 **MR BOUNTIFUL 15** [10]6-7-13 p (51) R Ffrench 14/1: 00-00400: 10th: Held up, modest late gains. nk 46

2809 **PAWAN 2** [2]4-9-0 (66) Ann Stokell 12/1: 2016630: 11th: Rear, prog when short of room ins fnl 1f, 1 59
not recover: closer with clr passage: btr 2809.

2337 **SKYLARK 20** [16]7-8-5 (57) Kim Tinkler 66/1: 36204-00: 12th: Bhd, nvr a factor: see 2337. nk 49

2730 **PAYS DAMOUR 5** [12]7-9-0 (66) Alex Greaves 33/1: 0103050: 13th: Handy over 5f, sn fdd: qck reapp. hd 57

2571 **EXTINGUISHER 11** [8]5-8-5 vis (57) J Carroll 33/1: 0-000050: 14th: Al bhd: btr 2571. shd 47

2527* **SMART MINISTER 13** [4]4-8-12 (64) K Dalgleish 25/1: 20-00010: 15th: Bhd, nvr a factor. 1 52

2445 **FLYING EDGE 16** [18]4-8-5 (57) D Allan 16/1: 2050650: 16th: Bhd, nvr a factor. 1½ 42

2672 **TAKES TUTU 7** [15]5-9-8 bl (74) K Darley 7/1: 0022550: 17th: Chsd ldrs wide, hung v badly right & 1¼ 57
wknd from dist: tchd 8/1 on qck reapp: btr 2672 & 2179.

4659} **MARTIN HOUSE 265** [14]5-8-8 (60) R Winston 66/1: 400000-0: 18th: b g Mujadil - Dolcezza (Lichine) 6 31
Bhd, nvr a factor: ealrier jumps unplcd (nov h'cap, rtd 76h): unplcd on Flat in '03 (rtd 76, class stks, J D
Bethell): rnr-up at best in '02: winning h'cap hdle: handles fast & gd/soft grnd: gall trks.
2 Aug'02 Hayd 10.5g/s 85-88 C: 1 Jul'01 York 7g/f 88- D:
18 Ran Time 1m 24.53 (1.53) Owned: Mr T L Adams Trained: Scarcroft

2849 4.30 **We Race Again Next Wednesday Median Auction Maiden Stakes** 3-4yo (F)
£3017 £862 £431 **5f212y rnd** **Good/Firm 30** -08 Slow Inside

2559 **COMPTON PLUME 11** [2] W H Tinning 4-9-6 (55) Dale Gibson 9/2: 6-03D321: Handy, styd on to lead 72
halfway, rdn out: op 8/1: eff at 5/6f on firm, gd/soft & both AWs: first win at 25th attempt: see 2559 & 2214.

1761 **CYFRWYS 46** [12] B Palling 3-8-8 (75) A Culhane 5/1: 42524-02: b f Foxhound - Divine Elegance ¾ 65
(College Chapel) Handy, styd on ins fnl 1f, just held by wnr: 7 wk abs: rnr-up twice since '03 (rtd 80, auct
mdns): eff at 6f, has tried further: acts on fast & gd grnd.
2 Oct'03 Wind 6g/f 79-(78) D: 2 Jul'03 Leic 6.0gd 80- E:

2619 **HALF A HANDFUL 9** [5] M J Wallace 3-8-13 (65) K Darley 4/1: 000633: In tch, prog when hung badly ¾ 68
ins fnl 2f, styd on, no ch with front 2: padd pick: see 2619.

2428 **FLYING BANTAM 17** [1] R A Fahey 3-8-13 P (70) T Hamilton(3) 11/4 FAV: 503-2224: Led 5f out, hung ½ 67
right turning from home, hdd after 4f, sn onepcd: well bckd in 1st time cheek pieces: becoming frustrating.

2527 **DARK CHAMPION 13** [13]4-9-6 (59) R Winston 25/1: 6530045: Led, hdd 5f out, styd in tch, no extra dist. 1½ 63

2692 **FLASH RAM 6** [9]3-8-13 bl (64) D Allan 9/2: 33-64226: Handy 4f, sn no extra: qck reapp: btr 2692. ½ 62

1499} **HARRISONS FLYER 413** [14]3-8-13 G Parkin 20/1: 4-7: b g Imperial Ballet - Smart Pet (Petong) 2 56
Rear, nvr nrr than mid-div: fit on reapp: 4th of 5 of sole '03 start (mdn, rtd 74): with R A Fahey.

2551 **FOX COVERT 12** [7]3-8-13 (58) P Mulrennan(5) 10/1: 0002358: Handy 4f, sn no extra: btr 2055. ½ 55

2463 **PRINCE RENESIS 15** [3]3-8-13 R Ffrench 100/1: 009: Al in rear. 2 49

2811 **EAST RIDING 2** [10]4-9-1 P (37) Ann Stokell 100/1: 0005500: 10th: Al in rear: qck reapp, cheek pieces. ½ 43

2559 **Designer City 11** [6]3-8-8 (45) J Carroll 100/1:0 **Miss Chancelot 0** [8]3-8-8 R Lappin 66/1:0
12 Ran Time 1m 12.61 (2.31) Owned: Mr W H Tinning Trained: York

2850 5.00 **Stockton Handicap Stakes** 4yo+ 35-55 (F) [61]
£3073 £878 £439 **1m3f214y** **Good/Firm 30** -22 Slow Inside

4315} **SOVEREIGN STATE 642** [14] D W Thompson 7-8-8 p (41) F Norton 20/1: 040/000/-1: b g Soviet Lad - 49
Portree (Slip Anchor) Handy, styd on to lead dist, rdn out: earlier h'cap hdle wnr (rtd 108h, stays 2m1.5f on fast
& soft): won 4 times over hdles in 03/04: missed '03: mod form in 3 '02 Flat starts (rtd 35a, h'cap, Miss S E
Hall): eff at 1m, now stays 12f: acts on firm & gd grnd, eff with pieces: well h'capped.

2545 **FAIRY MONARCH 12** [12] P T Midgley 5-8-13 p (46) R Fitzpatrick 25/1: 0000-202: Mid-div, prog 4f ½ 52
out, styd on to chase ldr ins fnl 1f, just held: back to form & deserves to find similar on this evidence: see 2008.

2686 **PADDY MUL 6** [18] W Storey 7-8-7 t (46) Rory Moore(7) 8/1: 1434533: Rear, prog 3f out, kept on ins 1½ 43
fnl 1f, nrst fin: qck reapp: see 2686 & 357.

2718 **LAZZAZ 5** [9] P W Hiatt 6-8-13 P (46) P Makin(5) 5/1 FAV: 3020564: Led, hdd dist, sn no extra: qck reapp. 1 47

2296 **CRYPTOGAM 22** [15]4-8-8 (1ow) (40) D McGaffin 66/1: 0-000005: Held up, prog 3f out, kept on ins fnl 1f. 1½ 39

4790} **PRIZE RING 257** [16]5-9-5 (52) R Winston 12/1: 036410-6: ch g Bering - Spot Prize (Seattle ½ 49
Dancer) Chsd ldrs over 12f, sn onepcd: hdles fit, earlier won 2 h'caps (rtd 113h, stays 2m1f on fast & gd/soft):
won 2 nov hdles in 03/04 (rtd 108h at best): sell wnr on Flat in '03 (Mrs J R Ramsden): plcd twice in '02 (mdn &
clmr, rtd 77): stays around 12f, apprec 10f: acts on gd & firm grnd: suited by cheek pieces.
1 Aug'03 Newc 10.1g/f 53-(47) G: 2 Sep'02 Sali 12fm 74- D:

1946 **RIGHTLY HO 37** [10]10-8-12 (45) V Halliday 12/1: 200-1337: Cl-up 10f, sn wknd: btr 1946 & 1449. ¾ 40

4238* **MILLKOM ELEGANCE 289** [4]5-8-12 bl (45) G Parkin 10/1: 05/0501-8: b f Millkom - Premier Princess ½ 39
(Hard Fought) Cl-up, ev ch 2f out, wknd dist: recent jumps unplcd (rtd 55h, h'cap hdle): sell h'cap wnr in 03/04
(rtd 90h, eff around 2m on fast & gd/soft, eff with blnks): sell h'cap wnr on fnl '03 Flat start: h'cap rnr-up in
'02: eff at 10/12f on firm & gd/soft grnd: acts on a gall trk.

CATTERICK WEDNESDAY 30.06.04 Lefthand, Undulating, V Tight Track

1 Sep'03 Redc 10fm 45-40 G: 2 Apr'02 Nott 10g/s 49-45 F:

2120	**STEPASTRAY 29** [11]7-8-11 (44) D Allan 28/1: 0000-509: Handy 10f, sn wknd: btr 1821.	*1*	**36**
2436	**REGAL FANTASY 16** [13]4-8-3 (36) P Fessey 66/1: 050/00-00: 10th: Nvr nrr than mid-div.	*shd*	**27**
2562	**IPLEDGEALLEGIANCE 11** [2]8-8-2 bl (35) G Duffield 6/1: 5505520: 11th: Nvr nrr than mid-div: btr 2562.	*¾*	**24**
2545	**BORDER TERRIER 12** [20]6-8-7 bl (40) K Darley 12/1: 10-00030: 12th: Chsd ldrs, hung badly right on bend after 3f, fdd fnl 3f: btr 2545.	*shd*	**28**
2008	**BLUE VENTURE 35** [19]4-9-4 (51) G Faulkner 16/1: 00-00040: 13th: Al in rear: btr 2008.	*1½*	**36**
2616*	**LITTLE TASK 9** [5]6-8-11 (6ex) J R Ffrench 7/1: 0/5-31410: 14th: Nvr nrr than mid-div: btr 2616.	*1¼*	**27**
2298	**SEA OF HAPPINESS 22** [3]4-8-7 (40) T Hamilton(3) 100/1: 0404-000: 15th: Mid-div 6f, wknd.	*10*	**10**
2990]	**FREE WILL 709** [6]7-9-8 (55) Dean McKeown 14/1: 032046/-0: 16th: Nvr nrr than mid-div.	*1½*	**22**

2548	**Ultra Marine 12** [17]4-9-3 bl(50) L Enstone(3) 50/1:0
	2008 **Margold 35** [7]4-9-1 (48) A Culhane 12/1:0
557}	**Natmsky 510** [1]5-8-2 (35) D Fentiman(7) 66/1:0
2510	**Norma Speakman 13** [8]4-8-10 (43) P Mulrennan(5) 50/1:0

20 Ran   Time 2m 37.55(6.35)   Owned: Mr J Greenbank   Trained: Darlington

YARMOUTH WEDNESDAY 30.06.04 Lefthand, Flat, Fair Track

Official Going FIRM (GOOD/FIRM places). All Times Slow.

2851 6.25 European Breeders Fund Adios Maiden Stakes 2yo (D)
£4735 £1457 £729   **6f3y str**   **Good/Firm**   **Slow**   Stands Side

PERSONIFY [2] Saeed bin Suroor 2-9-0 K McEvoy 9/4: 1: ch c Zafonic - Dignify (Rainbow Quest) **89+**
Prom, led after halfway, collared dist, rallied well to regain lead cl-home, rdn out: nicely bckd, debut: 250,000 gns Mar foal: half brother to a 7f 2yo wnr, also top class juv hdler Made In Japan: dam 10f wnr: eff at 6f on fast, 7f/1m will suit given time: sure to win btr races.

SOVEREIGNTY [3] D R Loder 2-9-0 T P Queally(3) 11/1: 2: b c King's Best - Calando (Storm Cat) *nk* **87**
Keen & prom, went on dist, collared cl-home: fine debut: Apr foal, dam smart over 1m/10f: sire a top class miler: eff at 6f on fast grnd, 7f will suit: must sn go one btr.

MOTARASSED [5] J L Dunlop 2-9-0 R Hills 11/8 FAV: 3: b c Green Desert - Sayedati Eljamilah (Mr *2* **81**
Prospector) Chsd ldrs, onepcd fnl 1f on debut: well bckd from 2/1: Apr 1st foal: dam from a gd family, sire a top class sprint/miler: stables juvs usually learn from their 1st eff & improvement likely.

TANZANI [4] C E Brittain 2-9-0 D Holland 6/1: 4: b c Giant's Causeway - Aunt Pearl (Seattle *3* **72**
Slew) Chsd ldrs, sltly short of room halfway, no ch after: debut: Feb foal, cost $200,000: half brother to sev juv wnrs, notably decent performer Pearl Of Love: dam a 7f wnr in the US, sire a top-class 7/10f performer.

DRALION [6]2-9-0 S Sanders 7/1: 5: Led till after halfway, no extra on debut. *1¼* **68**
AFRICAN EMPEROR [7]2-9-0 M Tebbutt 28/1: 6: Speed till halfway, wknd & eased on debut. *20* **18**

6 Ran   Time 1m 14.38 (3.98)   Owned: Godolphin   Trained: Newmarket

2852 6.55 Happinose Selling Stakes 3yo (G)
£2583 £738 £369   **7f3y str**   **Good/Firm**   **Slow**   Stands Side. 2 Groups.

694	**MUGEBA 130** [2] W J Musson 3-8-9 (59) G Carter 11/4 FAV: 02-551: Held up centre, imprvd halfway, led ent fnl 1f, styd on strongly despite drifting right, drvn out: gamble from 8/1, long abs, bght by G Kelleway: eff at 6/7f on fast grnd & polytrack: clrly runs v well fresh: apprec this drop in grade, see 260 (AW mdn).		**52**
2288	**CITY GENERAL 22** [10] J S Moore 3-9-0 p (49) Derek Nolan(7) 11/1: 3343502: Led till after halfway stands side, styd on well fnl 1f despite drifting right, not btn far: apprec this return to sell grade: see 996.	*¾*	**54**
2541	**WARES HOME 12** [12] K R Burke 3-9-0 (50) Darren Williams 5/1: 0603433: Chsd ldrs stands side, styd on under press fnl 1f despite drifting left, nrst fin: op 3/1: vis discarded: see 2541.	*¾*	**52**
2704	**ZONNEBEKE 6** [5] K R Burke 3-8-9 vis (45) I Mongan 4/1: 2030034: Chsd ldrs centre, led that group halfway & sn overall ldr, clr dist, collared cl-home: well clr rem: acts on gd, fast grnd & polytrack: see 2704.	*hd*	**47**
2667	**SOUL PROVIDER 7** [9]3-8-9 (52) S Righton 3/1: 5: 3432405: Chsd ldrs stands side, wknd fnl 1f.	*6*	**35**
2379	**BOOKIESINDEXDOTCOM 19** [3]3-8-9 P (39) T P Queally(3) 20/1: 0660556: Chsd ldrs centre, btn 2f out: tried cheek pieces: see 617 (AW mdn).	*3*	**29**
2337	**MAYBE SOMEDAY 20** [6]3-9-0 bl (55) D Holland 12/1: 3302007: Led till halfway centre, wknd.	*1½*	**31**
2704	**DAVIDS GIRL 6** [1]3-8-9 (38) R Mullen 15/2: 05-56658: Rcd centre & al bhd.	*¾*	**24**
	TRIVIAL PURSUIT [7]3-9-0 M Tebbutt 10/1: 9: b c Mind Games - Chushan Venture (Pursuit of Love) Bhd halfway centre on debut: op 7/1: speedily bred, with W Jarvis.	*1½*	**26**
2260	**JUSTICE JONES 24** [11]3-9-0 (47) D Kinsella 40/1: 000000: 10th: Dwelt, sn prom centre, btn halfway.	*6*	**14**
2379	**ST GEORGES GIRL 19** [4]3-8-9 (25) S Whitworth 100/1: 000-0000: 11th: Slowly away, al bhd centre.	*16*	**0**

11 Ran   Time 1m 26.63 (4.03)   Owned: Billings & Broughton Thermal Insulation   Trained: Newmarket

2853 7.25 Aeropak Handicap Stakes 3yo+ 0-80 (D)
£5395 £1660 £830   **1m3y str**   **Good/Firm**   **Slow**   Stands Side   **[80]**

2587	**WELCOME STRANGER 11** [6] J M P Eustace 4-9-10 (76) L Fletcher(3) 10/3: 34-00021: Dwelt, imprvd halfway, led dist, styd on strongly, rdn out: well bckd: eff at 7.5f/1m on fast, firm grnd & polytrack: handles a stiff/gall or sharp trk, can run well fresh: in gd form: see 1057.		**86**
2753	**TOPTON 4** [4] P Howling 10-9-10 bl (76) S Sanders 9/2: 1000462: Held up, prog to chase wnr fnl 1f, kept on but nvr going to get there: op 11/2, qck reapp & well clr rem: prefers a stronger pace: see 714.	*1½*	**81**
2600	**ANSWERED PROMISE 10** [7] I A Wood 5-8-2 (54) C Haddon(7) 7/1: 0-006233: Front rank, led after halfway till dist, wknd: op 9/2: likes claimers: see 2600.	*5*	**49**
2558	**HURRICANE FLOYD 12** [2] D R Loder 6-10-0 (80) T P Queally(3) 6/1: 03-00004: Trkd ldrs, ev ch till wknd fnl 1f: top weight, op 8/1: see 1512.	*1*	**73**
2590	**MOUNTCHARGE 11** [3]3-9-1 (77) I Mongan 16/1: 0613-005: Prom till halfway: see 132 (AW).	*1½*	**67**
2389	**BORREGO 18** [5]4-9-12 (78) D Holland 9/4 FAV: 2112-206: Chsd ldrs, rdn & btn dist: bckd from 10/3.	*hd*	**68**
2350	**MAGIC AMOUR 20** [1]6-8-8 (60) C Catlin 12/1: 2020-267: Led till after halfway, wknd fnl 1f.	*½*	**49**

7 Ran   Time 1m 39.15 (4.05)   Owned: Mr H R Moszkowicz   Trained: Newmarket

2854

7.55 Diomed Developments Claiming Stakes 3yo+   (F)
£2947 £842 £421   1m3y str   **Good/Firm**   **Slow**   Stands Side

4244*]THE PRINCE 289 [5] Ian Williams 10-9-5 (85) C Catlin 15/8: 0://21031-1: b g Machiavellian -   75
Mohican Girl (Dancing Brave) Held up, prog 3f out, styd on to lead ins fnl 1f, rdn out: well bckd: p.u. sole 03/04
hdle start (h'cap): won 2 clmrs in '03: missed '02: plcd in '01 (val AW h'cap, rtd 93a): eff at 7.5/9f on firm,
gd/soft & both AWs: acts on any trk: eff with/without t-strap: goes well fresh: enjoys clmg grade.
1 Sep'03 Muss 9g/f 86-(85) E: 1 Aug'03 Galw 8.5g/s 86- : 2 Mar'03 Ling 8ap 88a-85 D:
2259 HEVERSHAM 24 [8] W J Haggas 3-9-0 (73) D Holland 13/8 FAV: 1200042: Led, hdd ins fnl 1f, kept   hd   78
on, just held: well bckd: acts on polytrack & fast grnd: gd run dropped in grade & can find similar: see 694.
2325 SOVIET SPIRIT 21 [3] J R Fanshawe 3-8-8 (63) O Urbina 10/3: 5053: Handy over 6f, sn no extra.   6   60
THE NIBBLER [4] G C H Chung 3-9-0 B Doyle 80/1: 4: b g General Monash - Spoilt Again (Mummy's   3   60
Pet) Slow away, prog when short of room & lost place 3f out, mod late gains: debut: mid-dist bred.
2412 NAUGHTY GIRL 18 [6]4-8-10 T (55) N Callan 20/1: 0000005: Rear, nvr nrr than mid-div: tried t-strap.   nk   45
1080 LOVE OF LIFE 84 [10]3-8-3 P Doe 100/1: 006: b f Spectrum - Night Over Day (Most Welcome) Cl-up   3½   41
over 6f, sn fdd: 12 wk abs, prev with M Quinlan: seems modest.
2667 ROVING VIXEN 7 [1]3-8-0 bl (41) J Mackay 12/1: 0403347: Keen cl-up 6f, fdd: quick reapp.   4   30
2586 ALBERTINE 11 [7]4-9-2 T P Queally(3) 66/1: 0-08: Slow away, cl-up over 5f, sn fdd: see 2586.   18   6
8 Ran   Time 1m 39.19 (4.09)   Owned: Mr Patrick Kelly   Trained: Alvechurch

2855

8.25 Bazuka Handicap Stakes 3yo+ 0-70 (E)   [77]
£3897 £1199 £600   6f3y str   **Good/Firm**   **Slow**   Stands Side

2619 CHEROKEE NATION 9 [9] P W D'Arcy 3-8-8 (57) D Holland 9/2 FAV: 6-441021: Rear, prog ins fnl 2f,   65
rdn out to lead cl-home: tried 10f, suited by around 6f: acts on fast, gd & poss handles firesand: see 2619.
2451 YOMALO 16 [1] R Guest 4-9-6 (62) S Sanders 5/1: 20-00562: Cl-up, styd on to lead dist, hdd   ½   66
cl-home: tchd 13/2: lost little in defeat & back on a wng mark: see 2034.
2743 GONENDUNNETT 4 [6] Mrs C A Dunnett 5-9-1 vis (57) T G McLaughlin 9/1: 0066103: Led, hdd dist,   shd   61
kept on despite hanging right, not btn far: quick reapp: 7lb higher than recent C/D win in 2347.
2512 ILLUSIVE 13 [3] M Wigham 7-9-2 bl (58) M Tebbutt 14/1: 2262004: Handy till dist, edged right & onepcd.   ½   61
1354 BOBS BUZZ 67 [11]4-9-13 (69) O Urbina 12/1: 0/3110-05: ch g Zilzal - Aethra (Trempolino) Handy   1   69
over 4f, sn outpcd, rallied late: 10 wk abs: won 2 of only 4 '03 starts (mdn & h'cap): eff at 5/7f on firm &
gd/soft grnd: return to further will suit: with S C Williams.
1 Aug'03 Yarm 7.0g/f 71-67 E: 1 Jul'03 Newc 5g/s 67- D:
2372 STAGNITE 19 [4]4-8-13 (55) Darren Williams 50/1: 00200-06: ch g Compton Place - Superspring   nk   54
(Superlative) Cl-up, ev ch ins fnl 2f, sn no extra: rnr-up 6 times in '03 (h'caps & clmrs, K R Burke): unplcd in
'02 (rtd 75, prob flattered, M D I Usher): eff at 6/7f on firm, gd/ grnd & polytrack: tried visor.
2 Aug'03 Brig 6.0fm 61-59 D: 2 Jul'03 Chep 6.1gd 60-57 E: 2 Jun'03 Folk 6fm 59-(57) F: 2 Jun'03 Brig 6.0fm 56-56 F:
2 Jun'03 Chep 6.1g/f 58-56 E: 2 May'03 Redc 6g/f 57-57 G:
1010 COLD CLIMATE 91 [12]9-9-0 (56) B Doyle 5/1: 1521-047: Mid-div, kept on ins fnl 2f, nrst fin.   nk   54
2644 WARLINGHAM 8 [13]6-9-0 (56) C Catlin 9/1: 0105058: Mid-div till halfway, sn outpcd, rallied late.   hd   53
2111 CHARLOTTEBUTTERFLY 30 [5]4-9-0 (56) J Mackay 14/1: 0353-049: Nvr nrr than mid-div: btr 2111.   hd   53
2237 MULTAHAB 25 [8]5-8-11 t (53) C Lowther 16/1: 2424000: 10th: Rear, prog halfway, ev ch dist, wknd.   ¾   47
2445 ANGEL ISA 16 [14]4-8-7 (1ow) (48) N Callan 20/1: 01060-00: 11th: Handy over halfway, sn wknd.   1¼   39
2428 CHATSHOW 17 [10]3-8-11 (60) P Doe 16/1: 6-0040: 12th: Al in rear: btr 2428.   4   38
2375 HAYDN 19 [2]3-9-7 (70) J Quinn 14/1: 00-50050: 13th: Cl-up 4f, fdd: op 10/1: btr 2375.   1½   44
2669 BAD INTENTIONS 7 [15]4-10-0 (70) A McCarthy 33/1: 56500-60: 14th: Handy 4f, sn fdd.   2½   37
14 Ran   Time 1m 12.93 (2.53)   Owned: Mr Walt Sylvester   Trained: Newmarket

2856

8.55 4head For Headaches Handicap Stakes 4yo+ 35-55 (F)   [61]
£3290 £940 £470   1m6f17y   **Good/Firm**   **Slow**   Inside

2589 DIAMOND ORCHID 11 [4] P D Evans 4-9-6 vis (53) S Donohoe(7) 9/2: 2422151: Held up, prog halfway,   58
styd on to lead 3f out, rdn out fnl 1f: suited by 9/12f, imprvd for step up to 14f: acts on fast, soft grnd & both
AWs: eff with visor or cheek pieces: unexposed at staying trips: see 1960.
2607 PEAK PARK 10 [8] J A R Toller 4-8-13 vis (46) S Sanders 7/1: 0360-002: Handy, kept on ins fnl 2f,   1¾   48
not pace wnr: eff at 14f/2m: can find a mod staying h'cap: see 2073.
2273 AMBERSONG 23 [3] A W Carroll 6-8-8 (41) I Mongan 7/2 JT FAV: 3306433: Cl-up, no extra fnl 1f.   nk   42
1990 ANNAKITA 36 [7] W J Musson 4-8-7 (40) G Carter 20/1: 060-0004: Mid-div, outpcd 4f out, rallied late.   2½   37
2616 SMARTER CHARTER 9 [1]11-8-7 (40) Kristin Stubbs(7) 10/1: 2065045: Nvr nrr than mid-div: btr 2616.   1¼   35
2311 LISSAHANELODGE 21 [6]5-8-9 P (42) S Whitworth 5/1: 0/-120666: Rear, prog trav well when stumbled   3   32
2f out, sn onepcd: fitted with cheek pieces: first try at 14f: btr 1373.
2562* ASTROMANCER 11 [9]4-9-3 (50) Saleem Golam(7) 7/2 JT FAV: 4500317: Mid-div 13f, wknd fnl 2f.   ¾   39
2273 FREE STYLE 23 [2]4-9-1 (48) Darren Williams 12/1: 5520458: Handy, fdd fnl 3f: btr 2273.   6   28
2088 LITTLE SKY 31 [5]7-8-7 e (40) J P Guillambert(1) 50/1: 2000-009: Led, hdd 3f out, sn wknd.   5   12
9 Ran   Time 3m 03.77(5.97)   Owned: Diamond Racing Ltd   Trained: Abergavenny

KEMPTON **WEDNESDAY 30.06.04 Righthand, Flat, Fair Track**

Official Going GOOD/FIRM (GOOD places).

2857

6.40 Handicap Stakes For Lady And Gentleman Amateur Riders 3yo+ 0-75 (E) **[50]**
£3582 £1102 £551 **1m1f** **Good/Firm 26** **-33 Slow** Inside

2526 **GRAFT 13** [7] Mrs P Townsley 5-10-10 bl (60) Mrs C Thompson(5) 25/1: 0-062001: In tch, hdwy & switched left over 1f out, strong run to lead cl-home on bit, going away: eff at 1m/12f on firm, soft & polytrack, likes easy trks, handles any: revitalised by switch to new trainer (prev with M W Easterby): see 1164. **66**

2572 **GRAN CLICQUOT 11** [12] G P Enright 9-9-12 (48) Mr J Pemberton(5) 16/1: 0020102: Chsd ldrs, hdwy 2f out, styd on to chall ins last, no extra cl-home: right back to best: see 2220, 1451. *1¼* **51**

2265 **TODLEA 23** [9] J A Osborne 4-11-7 (71) Mr J A Jenkins(3) 11/2 FAV: 0-644363: In tch, hdwy over 2f out, led dist, hdd & no extra cl-home: see 1736, 1352. *dht* **74**

2170 **PAS DE SURPRISE 28** [11] P D Evans 6-10-3 (53) Miss E Folkes(3) 10/1: 5540054: In tch, onepace fnl 2f. *2½* **51**

2725 **BOJANGLES 5** [1]5-9-12 (48) Mr L Newnes(3) 12/1: 0130345: Bhd, plenty to do over 2f out, styd on well late, nrst fin: can come from bhd or force the pace: see 2725, 1334. *½* **45**

2440 **MADAME MARIE 16** [2]4-10-0 (50) Mr D Hutchison(5) 25/1: 03-00206: In tch, kept on fnl 2f. *nk* **46**

2285 **RAINSTORM 22** [19]9-9-7 (1oh) (42) Mrs S Owen(3) 12/1: 00-65607: Slow away & bhd, some late gains. *hd* **38**

2220 **LIBERTY ROYAL 26** [18]5-11-0 p (64) Mr S Walker 13/2: 00-60638: Handy, led 2f out till dist, no extra. *1¼* **57**

2370 **JACARANDA 19** [13]4-11-3 (67) Ms C Williams 25/1: 024-0509: Bhd, some late gains: see 2370. *shd* **59**

2647 **PHRED 8** [6]4-10-10 (60) Miss E Johnson Houghton 14/1: 4654200: 10th: In tch, wknd over 1f out. *3½* **45**

2414 **OH SO ROSIE 18** [10]4-10-7 (57) Mrs S Moore(3) 14/1: 3303250: 11th: In tch, wknd 2f out. *nk* **41**

3216} **ARK ADMIRAL 338** [15]5-11-3 (67) Miss C Tizzard(3) 25/1: 0/60000-0: 12th: b g Inchinor - Kelimutu (Top Ville) Led 5f out till 4f out, wknd 2f out: fit from hdlg, earlier rnr-up in a sell (rtd 96h, with P Nicholls, 2m, fast grnd): unplcd in '03 for B Meehan: '02 rtd h'cap wnr: stays 10f on fast & gd/soft, sharp trk: tried blnks. 1 Aug'02 Wind 10g/s 80-76 D: 2 Jul'02 Wind 10g/f 78- D: *nk* **50**

2285 **HONEYSTREET 22** [3]4-10-2 (52) Miss S Brotherton 20/1: 51600-00: 13th: b f Woodborough - Ring of Kerry (Kenmare) In tch, wknd 2f out: '03 dual h'cap wnr: suited by 1m on firm or gd/soft, likes stiff trks & best in cheek pieces. 1 Jul'03 Sali 8g/s 56-50 E: 1 Jun'03 Bath 8.0fm 53-48 G: *1¼* **33**

2725 **PASO DOBLE 5** [16]6-10-7 p (57) Mr J Millman(7) 7/1: 6205420: 14th: Led till 5f out, wknd 2f out. *¾* **36**

2354 **SOMAYDA 20** [4]9-9-7 (3oh) (40) Mr J Doyle(7) 50/1: 5000-000: 15th: Al bhd: see 2354. *hd* **21**

2369 **CHEVRONNE 19** [17]4-10-9 (59) Mr L Jefford 7/1: 350-0020: 16th: Al bhd: btr 2369 (7f, clmr). *½* **36**

1792 **THE GAIKWAR 44** [20]5-11-1 bl (65) Mr Joshua Harris(7) 20/1: 5012U00: 17th: Led 4f out till 2f out, wknd. *1* **40**

2540 **DEEPER IN DEBT 12** [14]6-11-1 (65) Mr S Gascoyne(7) 25/1: 4335000: 18th: Nvr a factor: see 1042. *4* **32**

2551} **TITIAN FLAME 366** [8]4-10-8 (58) Miss A Wallace(5) 33/1: 043640-0: 19th: ch f Titus Livius - Golden Choice (Midyan) Nvr a factor: recent 4th in a mare's nov (rtd 82h, rnr-up in 03/04, 2m, soft): plcd in a h'cap in '03 (rtd 63): auct mdn wnr in '02: eff at 1m/12.6f on fast & gd/soft. 1 Aug'02 Wind 8.3g/s 74- F: *1¼* **23**

2497 **LEYAALY 14** [5]5-9-7 (5oh)p (38) Miss L J Harwood(3) 33/1: 6001240: 20th: Al bhd: btr 2335. *28* **0**

20 Ran Time 1m 55.28 (5.28) Owned: Mr Paul Townsley Trained: Godalming

2858

7.10 Girls Night Out Maiden Stakes 2yo (D)
£4797 £1476 £738 **5f str** **Good/Firm 26** **-01 Slow** Stands Side

NOTJUSTAPRETTYFACE [3] H Morrison 2-8-9 S Drowne 9/1: 1: b f Red Ransom - Maudie May (Gilded Time) Slow away & bhd, hdwy over 2f out, led ins last, pushed out, v cmftbly: Mar foal, cost $19,000: eff at 5f on gd/firm, 6f sure to suit: runs well fresh: v pleasing & useful start, just the type to go on & win more races. **87+**

2738 **AFRICAN STORM 4** [5] S Kirk 2-9-0 L Dettori 5/1: 522: Set pace, rdn & not pace of wnr ins last: quick reapp, find similar: see 2738. *2* **79**

2490 **LADY ANN SUMMERS 14** [8] B J Meehan 2-8-9 J Fortune 11/10 FAV: 03: In tch, eff over 1f out, no extra ins last: hvly bckd: clrly btr expected: see 2490. *1½* **70**

2618 **GRAND PLACE 9** [7] R Hannon 2-9-0 R L Moore 11/2: 04: b g Compton Place - Comme Ca (Cyrano de Bergerac) Slow away & bhd, eff over 1f out, no extra ins last: Mar foal, cost 15,000: half brother to a 6f wnr. *½* **73**

2531 **LOWESTOFT PLAYBOY 12** [2]2-9-0 J Murtagh 10/1: 065: ch g Pivotal - Red Typhoon (Belfort) In tch, wknd 2f out: Mar 1st foal, cost 4,500 gns: dam 6f juv wnr: speedily bred. *2* **67**

2703 **TAIPAN TOMMY 6** [9]2-9-0 Dane O'Neill 66/1: 6606: Reared in stalls, al bhd. *2½* **60**

LOOKING GREAT [6]2-9-0 S Carson 14/1: 7: Sn rdn & nvr factor on debut. *hd* **59**

1531 **NINAHS INTUITION 57** [4]2-9-0 S Hitchcott(3) 20/1: 448: In tch, wknd 2f out: abs: see 1325. *nk* **58**

8 Ran Time 59.63 (1.33) Owned: Loddington Bloodstock Trained: East Ilsley

2859

7.40 Williamhillpoker Com E B F Novice Stakes 2yo (D)
£5343 £1644 £822 **6f str** **Good/Firm 26** **-02 Slow** Stands Side

2618 **AMAZIN 9** [2] R Hannon 2-8-12 R Hughes 8/13 FAV: 21: Keen, in tch, gd hdwy to lead over 1f out, pushed clr, cmftbly: v eff at 6f, 7f sure to suit: acts on fast & gd grnd, easy trks: prog with racing, win again. **95+**

GOODWOOD SPIRIT [1] J L Dunlop 2-8-8 T Quinn 8/1: 2: b c Fraam - Rechanit (Local Suitor) Handy, eff & short of room over 1f out, switched right & styd on ins last, closer with a clr run: op 11/2 on debut: Mar foal, cost 28,000 gns: half brother to wnrs over 6/10f: dam 5/7f scorer: plenty to like about this, improve. *1¼* **82**

2573* **THE CROOKED RING 11** [3] P D Evans 2-9-2 K Fallon 100/30: 523213: Led till 3f out, led again 2f out till dist, no extra ins last: prob ran to form of 2573 & 1739 conceding weight & visor discarded. *½* **88**

2666* **GEE BEE EM 7** [4] M R Channon 2-9-0 S Hitchcott(3) 15/2: 214: With ldr, led 3f out till 2f out, wknd. *5* **71**

4 Ran Time 1m 12.78 (1.68) Owned: Mr K Panos Trained: Marlborough

2860

8.10 Clear Channel Handicap Stakes 3yo+ 0-90 (C) **[90]**
£9555 £2940 £1470 **1m1f** **Good/Firm 26** **-08 Slow** Inside

2313 **SPANISH DON 21** [3] D R C Elsworth 6-9-7 (83) T Quinn 8/1: 141-0051: Bhd, hdwy over 1f out, edged right ins fnl 1f, led last strides, won going away: eff over 1m/9f on fast & soft: useful, see 2313. **92**

2404 **JAMES CAIRD 18** [8] M H Tompkins 4-9-8 (84) J Murtagh 3/1 FAV: 162-6222: Chsd ldrs, hdwy to lead over 1f out, hdd/hard drvn last strides: eff at 9f, suited by 10f, tried 12f: gd run, improving: see 2101. *nk* **91**

KEMPTON   WEDNESDAY 30.06.04   Righthand, Flat, Fair Track

2208 **GUILDED FLYER 26** [2] W S Kittow 5-9-11 (87) W Supple 14/1: 500-0103: Handy, hdwy into 2nd after   1½   91
3f, led ins fnl 3f till over 1f out, no extra ins fnl 1f: tough (6 wins from 23): see 1586.
2489 **CHINKARA 14** [5] B J Meehan 4-10-0 (90) J F McDonald(3) 20/1: 110-0004: ch g Desert Prince - You   1   92
Make Me Real (Give Me Strength) Rear, hdwy 3f out, chall over 1f out, onepcd when not much room ins fnl 1f: won a
mdn & 2 h'caps in '03: 3rd 1 of 5 '02 starts (2yo stks, rtd 79 at best): eff over 1m/10.3f on fast, gd/soft &
polytrack, likes sharp trks: better run.
1 May'03 Good 9g/f 94-84 B: 1 May'03 Kemp 9g/f 88-80 D: 1 Mar'03 Ling 10ap 79a-(77) D:
2099 **BEST BE GOING 30** [4]4-9-0 (76) E Ahern 9/1: 3451-005: Led 1f, remained handy, onepcd when not   1½   75
much room ins fnl 1f, eased nr fin: see 2099.
2538 **DESERT ISLAND DISC 12** [10]7-8-9 (71) N Chalmers(5) 20/1: 0440306: Chsd ldrs, no impress fnl 1f.   1   68
2665 **VOICE MAIL 7** [7]5-9-2 (78) L Keniry(3) 9/1: 0113027: Bhd, nvr nr ldrs: qck reapp, btr 2665.   hd   74
1835* **PORTMANTEAU 43** [6]3-8-12 (85) K Fallon 11/2: 0-018: Bhd, nvr nr ldrs: 6 wk abs: btr 1835 (fill mdn).   5   71
2223 **GIOCOSO 26** [9]4-9-6 (82) S Hitchcott(3) 25/1: 12060-69: Rear, hdwy on inner when hmpd 2f out.   ½   67
2277 **TANNOOR 23** [12]3-8-5 (78) P Robinson 10/1: 033-3150: 10th: Al bhd: btr 1894.   1   61
2290 **PENRITH 22** [11]3-9-2 (89) J Fanning 6/1: 1-130: 11th: Chsd ldrs, wkng when hmpd rails ins fnl 2f.   1½   69
2489 **SHAMROCK CITY 14** [1]7-9-12 (88) S Drowne 66/1: 2400-600: 12th: Led after 1f till ins fnl 3f, no   8   52
extra when hmpd 2f out: see 2234.
12 Ran   Time 1m 53.11 (3.11)   Owned: Mr Richard J Cohen   Trained: Whitsbury

2861   8.40 Williamhillcasino Com Handicap Stakes 3yo+ 0-80 (D)   [78]
£5499 £1692 £846   **6f str**   **Good/Firm 26**   **+12 Fast**   Stands Side

1767 **PRINCE DAYJUR 46** [3] M J Wallace 5-9-10 VIS (74) K Fallon 14/1: 0/0000-01: b g Dayjur - Distinct   81
Beauty (Phone Trick) Made all, rdn & kept on well ins fnl 1f: 7 wk abs, gd time: unplcd all '03 starts
(h'caps/stks, rtd 74, D Nicholls): well btn both '02 starts: eff at 6f on firm & fast, sharp or stiff trks: imprvd
for fitting of first time visor & switch to forcing tactics., potentially well h'capped.
2 Jul'01 Good 6fm 102- A: 1 Jun'01 Sali 6g/f 103- B: 2 Jun'01 Sand 5g/f 98- D:
2416 **DEVON FLAME 18** [8] R J Hodges 5-9-11 (75) J F McDonald(3) 11/4: 111-2122: Rcd in 2nd, kept on fnl   ¾   78
1f but not pace of wnr: v tough & prog: ran to winning form of 2268.
2409 **MR MALARKEY 18** [1] Mrs C A Dunnett 4-9-13 (77) J Murtagh 5/2 FAV: 0-404633: Chsd ldrs, kept on   hd   79
ins fnl 1f but onepcd nr fin: top-weight: see 1354.
2370 **ASTRAC 19** [11] Mrs A L M King 13-7-13 (49) P M Quinn 16/1: 15-50024: Bhd, hdwy 2f out, onepcd.   nk   50
2698 **HEY PRESTO 6** [2]4-9-5 (69) P Robinson 7/2: 040-0005: Bhd, hdwy over 1f out, not pace of ldrs.   hd   69
2626 **CURRENCY 9** [9]7-9-12 (76) R L Moore 20/1: 4000406: Bhd, hdwy dist, not pace of ldrs: see 453.   1¼   72
2070 **CANTERLOUPE 32** [7]6-9-12 † (76) D Sweeney 14/1: 0516-007: Handy, wknd ins fnl 1f: see 41.   ½   75
2669 **SPARKLING JEWEL 7** [4]4-9-10 (74) Dane O'Neill 12/1: 2/31-0628: Bhd, mod late gains: qck reapp.   1½   63
2626 **FORMALISE 9** [10]4-8-12 (62) S Carson 20/1: 060-0059: Rear, hdwy halfway, no impress fnl 2f: see 1914.   4   39
2626 **GOLDEN BOUNTY 9** [5]5-9-11 (75) R Hughes 20/1: 5000-060: 10th: Chsd ldrs, fdd dist: see 2626.   nk   51
10 Ran   Time 1m 11.92 (0.82)   Owned: Lucayan Stud   Trained: Newmarket

2862   9.10 Book Now For Gala Night Maiden Stakes 3yo (D)
£5564 £1712 £856   **1m4f**   **Good/Firm 26**   **-24 Slow**   Inside

2622 **STAGE RIGHT 9** [2] D R C Elsworth 3-9-0   Dane O'Neill 25/1: 461: b c In The Wings - Spot Prize   88
(Seattle Dancer) Chsd ldrs, hdwy to lead over 1f out, kept on well for press fnl 1f, cmftbly: mdn unplcd prev:
half-brother to wnrs over 10/15f: dam 4th in Oaks: much imprvd on step up to 12f, will stay further: acts on fast
grnd: open toplenty of improvement in 12f+ h'caps.
2386 **MEISSEN 18** [7] A C Stewart 3-8-9 (75) T Quinn 5/1: 60-22: Handy & keen early, hdwy to chall over   1½   77
1f out, onepcd ins fnl 1f: clr of rem: stays 12f: shown enough to find similar: see 2386.
1737 **GIFT VOUCHER 47** [4] Sir Michael Stoute 3-9-0   K Fallon 1/1: 03: ch c Cadeaux Genereux - Highland   3   78
Gift (Generous) Bhd, hdwy over 1f out, kept on ins fnl 1f to go 3rd cl-home: 7 wk abs: mdn unplcd earlier debut:
half-brother to 2,000 Guineas/King George wnr George Golan: dam a 10f 3yo wnr: improve.
         DAHJEE 9 [9] Saeed bin Suroor 3-9-0 T L Dettori 13/8 FAV: 4: b c Seeking The Gold - Colorado   nk   78
Dancer (Shareef Dancer) Slowly away, sn mid-div, outpcd 3 out, kept on from 2 out, no impress well ins fnl 1f & lost
3rd cl-home: racecourse bow: full-brother to v smart 10f wnr Dubai Millennium: dam 13.5f wnr: tried a t-strap.
2012 **ROMAN FORUM 35** [6]3-9-0   R Hughes 14/1: 65: Led till 2f out, fdd over 1f out: see 2012.   3   74
2623 **POPES HILL 9** [5]3-9-0   J Murtagh 7/1: 0-446: Bhd, hdwy 3f out, no impress fnl 1f: see 2623.   nk   73
2393 **VICAT COLE 18** [3]3-9-0   J Fortune 33/1: 057: Rcd in 2nd, led 2f out till over 1f out, fdd.   ½   72
2193 **QUDRAAT 27** [8]3-9-0   W Supple 4/1: 58: Rear, nvr a factor: see 2193.   1   71
1961 **TOUT LES SOUS 37** [10]3-9-0   S W Kelly 100/1: 0-09: Bhd, t.o.   dist   0
9 Ran   Time 2m 36.01(6.01)   Owned: Mr J C Smith   Trained: Whitsbury

YARMOUTH   THURSDAY 01.07.04   Lefthand, Flat, Fair Track

Official Going Firm (Good/Firm Places) ALL TIME SLOW

2863   2.30 European Breeders Fund Maiden Stakes Fillies 2yo (D)
£4794 £1475 £738   **7f str**   **Firm**   **Slow**   Stands Side

         QUEEN OF POLAND 0 [9] D R Loder 2-8-11   N Pollard 16/1: 1: b f Halling - Polska (Danzig) Sn   87
prom, briefly rdn & led ins last, styd on strongly under hand riding fnl 100yds: Feb foal, half sister to a multiple
juv wnr Grizel, also 7f juv wnr White Hawk, dam a 6f wnr: eff at 7f, will stay 1m+: acts on firm grnd & an easy
trk: goes well fresh: plenty to like about this, potentially useful.
2151 **GREAT OPINIONS 29** [4] J H M Gosden 2-8-11   R Hills 16/1: 02: b f Rahy - Gracie Lady (Generous)   nk   86
Dwelt, sn trkd ldrs & led over 1f out, hdd ins last & not pace of wnr: op 25/1, left debut bhd: $180,000 Apr foal,
dam styd 7f: eff at 7f, stay 1m+: acts on firm: win similar.
         GLORIOUS STEP 0 [7] J H M Gosden 2-8-11   S Sanders 16/1: 3: b f Diesis - Bessie's Chips (Rakeen)   nk   85+
Dwelt, sn trkd ldrs, briefly outpcd 2f out, styd on well in last, nrst fin: $35,000 Apr 1st foal: eff at 7f, sure
to get 1m on this evidence: acts on fm: encouraging.

2399 **NIGHT OF JOY 19** [12] M A Jarvis 2-8-11 P Robinson 3/1: 44: Led 5f, shaken up & no extra from dist, reportedly hung left: well bckd, op 13/2: imprvd from intro: styd this easy 7f on firm grnd: see 2399. 1¾ **82**
THEAS DANCE 0 [2]2-8-11 T P Queally(3) 13/2: 5: Held up travelling well, eff over 1f out, no threat. 1¼ **79**
ECCENTRICITY 0 [1]2-8-11 W Ryan 9/2: 6: Dwelt, towards rear, late gains, nvr threat: op 10/3. 1¾ **76**
LUNAR SKY 0 [11]2-8-11 D Holland 12/1: 7: Chsd ldrs, no impress over 1f out. shd **76**
GEORGINA 0 [10]2-8-11 M Henry 28/1: 8: Prom till lost place after 2f, no impress after. ½ **75**
MEDITATION 0 [8]2-8-11 G Duffield 66/1: 9: Chsd ldr, btn/stumbled 2f out. 11 **58**
RIYMA 0 [6]2-8-11 K Fallon 5/2 FAV: 0: 10th: Dwelt & struggling halfway: op 9/4. 8 **45**
10 Ran Time 1m 26.18 (3.58) Owned: Sheikh Mohammed Trained: Newmarket

2864

3.00 Custom Kitchens Handicap Stakes Fillies 3yo+ 0-80 (D) **[75]**
£5577 £1716 £858 **7f str** **Firm** **Slow** Stands Side

2416 **PINTLE 19** [2] J L Spearing 4-9-4 (65) K McEvoy 16/1: 215-41: Made all & dictated pace, qcknd over 1f out & al holding rivals ins last under a well judged ride: improved for step up to 7f & forcing tactics: likes fm & fast: unexposed, see 2416. **75**
3994} **SEARCH MISSION 304** [4] Mrs A J Perrett 3-9-10 (79) P Robinson 16/1: 512-2: b f Red Ransom - Skimble (Lyphard) Trkd ldrs & keen early, kept on from over 1f out, not pace of wnr: reapp, op 14/1: lightly rcd fills mdn scorer in '03, subs h'cap rnr-up: suited by 7f on firm & fast grnd, sharp/undul or easy trks: can go well fresh. 2 Sep'03 Folk 7g/f 83-80 D: 1 Aug'03 Folk 7g/f 80- D: 1¼ **84**
2092 **MOON LEGEND 32** [1] W Jarvis 3-8-10 (65) S Sanders 66/1: 06-03: ch f Gulch - Highland Legend (Storm Bird) Held up & keen, styd on from over 1f out, nvr threatened wnr: h'cap bow: unplcd '03 (rtd 73, lightly rcd, fills mdn): dam useful at 10f: eff at 7f, 1m+ suit: handles fm: win over further. hd **70**
2587 **AND TOTO TOO 12** [12] P D Evans 4-9-6 bl (67) K Fallon 11/1: 4240204: In tch, onepace fnl 2f. nk **71**
2374* **LADY GEORGINA 20** [6]3-9-9 (78) O Urbina 15/8 FAV: 0-361215: Held up, keen, short of room over 1f out, nvr pace to threaten: nicely bckd: shade more expected after 2374. ½ **81**
2249 **CARA BELLA 26** [5]3-9-5 (74) T P Queally(3) 8/1: 4-0536: Prom, outpcd from over 1f out: btr 2249. nk **76**
2755 **ANNIJAZ 5** [11]7-8-6 (53) F P Ferris(3) 22/1: 2400467: Dwelt, rear, short of room over 2f out, no threat. ¾ **54**
2755 **TAPAU 5** [3]6-9-1 p (62) D Holland 33/1: 0-500008: Held up, no room 2f out, nvr a threat: quick reapp. ¾ **62**
2791 **BINT ROYAL 3** [9]6-8-11 p (58) R Mullen 14/1: 3404309: Chsd ldrs, btn dist: quick reapp: btr 2539. ¾ **57**
2755 **IN THE PINK 5** [8]4-9-6 (67) T E Durcan 5/2: 51-00120: 10th: Held up & no room 2f out, sn no impress: bckd: too sn? btr 2755 & 2539. shd **66**
1827 **WODHILL BE 44** [7]4-7-12 (1oh) (44) J Mackay 66/1: 5650030: 11th: Dwelt & held up, keen, btn 2f out. 2 **40**
2855 **ANGEL ISA 1** [10]4-8-1 (48) G Duffield 33/1: 01060-000: 12th: Cl-up 4f, btn over 1f out: unplcd last night. ¾ **42**
12 Ran Time 1m 26.26 (3.66) Owned: Mr Robert Heathcote Trained: Kinnersley

2865

3.30 Street Construction In Partnership With Northern Racing Selling Stakes 2yo (G)
£2541 £726 £363 **6f str** **Firm** **V Slow** Stands Side

2733 **NORDHOCK 6** [4] N A Callaghan 2-8-6 T P Queally(3) 3/1: 61: gr f Luhuk - Starlight Dreams (Black Tie Affair) Dwelt, sn handy, rdn to lead ins last, styd on well: bckd from 9/2: bought in for 10,400gns:: Mar 1st foal, dam: sire smart at 10/12f: eff at 6f, 7f will suit: acts on firm grnd & relished this drop to sell grade. **63**
2145 **ZIMBALI 29** [6] J M Bradley 2-8-11 D Holland 11/4 FAV: 5413422: Led, hdd ins last & not pace of wnr: rest al well covered: nicely bckd: stays an easy 7f well in sell grade, can find similar: see 2145, 1325. 1 **66**
2721 **PETITE ELLE 6** [3] P J McBride 2-8-6 R Mullen 14/1: 3443: Chsd ldrs, outpcd 2f out, kept on late, not threaten front pair: quick reapp: prob handles firm grnd & fibresand. 1¾ **56**
2666 **VOOM 8** [2] M R Channon 2-8-6 T E Durcan 11/2: 04: b f Fraam - Natalie Jay (Ballacashtal) Chsd ldrs, rdn & no impress bef dist: op 5/2: dam a wnr btwn 6f/1m. 1¾ **51**
2625 **ZACHY BOY 10** [1]2-8-11 p D Kinsella 33/1: 0500665: Unruly stalls, cl-up till over 1f out. ¾ **54**
2597 **DARTANIAN 11** [5]2-8-11 G Duffield 7/1: 056: Prom, struggling fnl 2f. 2½ **46**
2461 **URABANDE 16** [7]2-8-6 G Carter 15/2: 020647: Slow away & sn well bhd: bckd, op 12/1, longer trip. 23 **0**
TIGER HUNTER 0 [8]2-8-11 K Fallon 8/1: 8: Sn struggling on debut, op 5/1. 2½ **0**
8 Ran Time 1m 14.50 (4.1) Owned: Mrs J Doyle & Mrs P Shanahan Trained: Newmarket

2866

4.00 Street Construction Handicap Stakes 3yo+ 0-70 (E) **[69]**
£3936 £1211 £606 **1m2f21y** **Firm** **Slow** Inside

2628 **BILLY BATHWICK 10** [1] J M Bradley 7-9-1 (56) F P Ferris(3) 7/1: 53-00331: Handy, led ins last, drvn & just held on: suited by 10/12f: acts on soft, loves fm & fast: well h'capped. **63**
2596 **CARROWDORE 12** [8] C N Allen 4-9-13 (68) R Mullen 7/2: 20-24342: Rear, switched wide & strong run ins last, just failed: bckd op 4/1: apprec drop to 10f, poor strike rate but unlucky here & h'capped to win. hd **75**
2170 **EMBER DAYS 29** [2] J L Spearing 5-9-4 p (59) K McEvoy 7/1: 2-503023: Prom & led over 1f out till ins last, not pace of front pair: op 5/1: see 2170, 1542 & 178. 1¼ **64**
2285 **ADALAR 23** [6] P D Evans 4-9-5 (60) K Fallon 13/2: 0060004: Held up, eff to press ldrs over 1f out, no extra from dist: handles firm, gd & polytrack: worth a try back at 10f: see 903. 1¼ **63**
2589 **SAMMYS SHUFFLE 12** [7]9-8-4 bl (45) P Doe 16/1: 4000405: Held up, not able to chall: just btr 2146. 2½ **44**
1064 **NIAGARA 86** [3]7-9-11 (66) P Robinson 16/1: 010/06-06: b g Rainbows For Life - Highbrook (Alphabatim) Trkd ldrs & keen, outpcd over 1f out: 6 wk jumps abs (p.u., h'cap hdle): dual nov chase scorer in 03/04 (rtd 105c, 2m/2m4f, firm & gd): Flat unplcd '03 (rtd 52a & 64, h'caps): class stks wnr '02: eff at 9/12f on firm, hvy & any trk: enjoys forcing tactics. nk **64**
1 Sep'02 Folk 12gd 72- E: 2 Aug'02 Hami 9.1hvy 71-68 C: 1 Sep'01 Hami 9.1gd 72-67 B: 1 Jul'01 Wind 10g/f 69- E:
1 Jun'01 Ayr 9g/f 66-64 D: 2 Jun'01 Hami 9.1g/s 66-64 E:
2433* **KERNEL DOWERY 17** [5]4-9-9 e (64) D Holland 13/8 FAV: 3-002117: Trkd ldrs & led over 2f out till over 1f out, fdd: bckd: btr 2433. hd **61**
2366 **CAZISA STAR 20** [9]3-8-8 (60) N Pollard 33/1: 036-08: Led 7f, btn 2f out: see 2366. 10 **45**
1792 **DAIMAJIN 45** [4]5-8-11 (52) W Ryan 33/1: 0000009: Dwelt, held up, eff 3f out, sn btn: abs: see 362. 11 **24**
9 Ran Time 2m 07.76 (3.56) Owned: Ms A M Williams Trained: Chepstow

2867	4.30 Grosvenor Casino Great Yarmouth Maiden Stakes 3yo+ (D)

£3419 £1052 £526   **1m3f101y**   **Firm**   **V Slow**   Inside

2349 **ASALEEB 21** [2] A C Stewart 3-8-7 (80) R Hills 1/16 FAV: 32-21: Handy & led 3f out, asserted from   **70+**
dist & eased nr fin, val 6L+: v slow time: eff at 10/11.5f, 12f+ may suit: acts on firm & fast grnd, gall/easy
trk: found this straightforward & can rate higher: see 2349.
2148 **BOOGIE MAGIC 29** [1] C N Allen 4-9-5 (62) R Mullen 22/1: 00400-02: b f Wizard King - Dalby Dancer   **3½   56**
(Bustiki) Led till 3f out, no ch with wnr from dist: 4th at best in '03 (lightly rcd, rtd 71, fills mdn): stays a
sharp 1m on gd/soft grnd, prob handles firm: mid-dist may yet suit.
1742 **WODHILL HOPE 48** [4] D Morris 4-9-5 D McGaffin 20/1: 43: Dwelt, chsd ldrs, rdn & no impress fnl 2f.   **5   50**
3 Ran   Time 2m 32.05 (9.25)   Owned: Mr Hamdan Al Maktoum   Trained: Newmarket

2868	5.00 Roy & Joan Tanner Amateur Riders' Handicap Stakes 3yo+ 35-55 (F)	[34]

£3017 £862 £431   **1m3f101y**   **Firm**   **Slow**   Inside

2526 **GOLDEN CHANCE 14** [13] M W Easterby 7-11-0 (48) Miss S Brotherton 5/1 JT FAV: 30242-01: Cl up,   **56**
led over 1f out, drvn out: op 8/1: eff at 10/14f, poss stays 2m: acts on firm & gd/soft: well h'capped.
2616 **PLATINUM CHARMER 10** [4] K R Burke 4-11-7 p (55) Mr S Dobson(3) 13/2: 1424032: Held up, switched & ½   **61**
styd on despite hanging left ins last, not pace of wnr: acts on firm, soft & fibresand: see 1552 (clmr).
2664 **VRISAKI 8** [1] Miss D Mountain 3-10-3 (49) Mrs S Bosley 8/1: 0400363: Held up in tch, styd on   **2½   51**
onepace for press: acts on firm, fast & fibresand: see 2346, 284.
1307 **JADE STAR 70** [3] Miss Gay Kelleway 4-11-3 (51) Miss E J Jones 5/1 JT FAV: 4102644: Chsd ldrs,   **2   50**
hung left under press over 1f out & sn no extra: return to 1m/9f could suit: see 961 & 620 (fibresand).
2526 **FINAL DIVIDEND 14** [8]8-10-11 (45) Miss Joanna Rees(3) 8/1: 50643-05: Dwelt, sn handy, onepace.   **nk   43**
2576 **AFRICAN STAR 12** [10]3-10-9 (55) Miss L J Harwood(3) 14/1: 05-656: Led/dsptd lead till over 1f   **½   52**
out, no extra: prob stays 11.5f on firm grnd: see 2576.
563 **ROPPONGI DANCER 146** [7]5-10-1 (5oh)bl (30) Mrs M Morris 40/1: 00-53057: Led/dsptd lead till over   **1½   30**
2f out, wknd: jumps fit (mod, rtd 72h, sell h'cap): see 363.
2475 **ELLOVAMUL 15** [9]4-11-4 (52) Mr C Davies(5) 11/2: 11545-48: Held up, eff over 2f out, sn btn: btr 2475.   **1½   45**
2600} **ARCTIC BLUE 365** [6]4-11-4 (52) Mr S Walsh(5) 14/1: 00/0000-9: b g Polar Prince - Miss Sarajane   **6   37**
(Skyliner) Held up & keen, btn over 1f out: reapp: unplcd '03 (rtd 58, h'cap) & '02 unplcd (rtd 81 at best, stks).
554 **TOMMY CARSON 147** [2]9-10-6 (40) Mr E Dehdashti(3) 12/1: 20/26/5-30: 10th: Hmpd after 1f &   **3   21**
struggling rear halfway: 12 wk jumps abs: see 554.
2436 **THEATRE LADY 17** [12]6-10-10 vis (44) Miss E Folkes(3) 10/1: 0435660: 11th: Trkd ldrs & keen, btn 2f out.   **4   19**
2545 **GRADY 13** [5]5-10-1 (35) Mrs S Owen(3) 16/1: 00-66060: 12th: Slow away & sn struggling rear: btr 2008.   **1   9**
1033 **BID SPOTTER 90** [11]5-10-3 (2ow) (35) Mr N Pearce 25/1: 4/000-400: 13th: Led/dsptd lead 4f, wknd.   **8   0**
13 Ran   Time 2m 28.26(5.46)   Owned: Miss S Brotherton   Trained: Sheriff Hutton

Official Going GOOD/FIRM (GOOD places).

2869	6.25 Totequadpot Handicap Stakes 3yo+ 0-70 (E)	[70]

£4810 £1480 £740   **1m4f10y**   **Good/Firm 37**   **-15 Slow**   Centre

2718* **CRISTOFORO 6** [9] B J Curley 7-9-4 (5ex) (60) T P Queally(3) 8/11 FAV: 111/-1011: Held up, prog to   **77+**
chase ldr but still 4L 2nd dist, led on line under hands & heels: well bckd & qck reapp under pen: eff at 9.13f on
firm, soft grnd & both AWs: runs v well fresh: v confident ride, clrly prog & can win more races: see 2718 & 1090.
2651 **STOLEN HOURS 9** [8] J Akehurst 4-9-2 (58) J Quinn 7/2: 4-000022: Prom, led 3f out & clr dist,   **shd   71**
collared on line: nicely bckd, well clr 3rd: eff at 12/14f: enterprising tactics nearly paid off, see 2651 & 2265.
2651 **PERSIAN KING 9** [6] J A B Old 7-9-9 (65) V Slattery 20/1: 0-000063: Prom, lost place halfway,   **6   66**
rallied late into 3rd but no ch with front 2: usually runs well here at Epsom, poss stays 12f: see 2192.
2371 **LUNAR LORD 20** [7] D Burchell 8-8-8 (50) J D Smith 16/1: 0/5-00004: Led till 3f out, wknd: see 1402.   **1½   51**
2391 **ROME 19** [4]5-9-9 P (65) S Hitchcott(3) 10/1: 30-30355: Chsd ldrs, not handle switch-back trk, no   **3   61**
danger fnl 2f: tried cheek pieces: return to 14f & a more gall trk will suit, as in 2192.
2530 **THE VARLET 13** [1]4-10-0 (70) D Corby(3) 14/1: 2605-036: Slowly away, sn rear: top weight: btr 2530.   **8   54**
2719 **SCENIC LADY 6** [2]8-9-3 (59) D Sweeney 16/1: 56552-57: Dwelt & rear, nvr dngrs: see 2719.   **1¾   41**
2651 **DOLZAGO 9** [3]4-9-9 bl (65) A Quinn(5) 16/1: 5-123008: Prom, wknd 3f out, t.o. in last.   **12   29**
8 Ran   Time 2m 41.06 (6.26)   Owned: Mr P Byrne   Trained: Newmarket

2870	6.55 Mckeever St Lawrence E B F Median Auction Maiden Stakes 2yo (E)

£4254 £1309 £655   **7f rnd**   **Good/Firm 37**   **-37 Slow**   Inside

2144 **EMERALD PENANG 29** [1] P W Chapple Hyam 2-9-0 S Whitworth 9/2 JT FAV: 541: Prom, led halfway,   **78**
styd on strongly fnl 1f, rdn out: well bckd & made most of fav low draw: apprec this step up to 7f, acts on fast
grnd: handles a sharp/undul trk & likes to run up with/force the pace: see 2144.
2263 **FLYING PASS 24** [4] D J S ffrench Davis 2-9-0 T Quinn 13/2: 0302: Prom, ev ch 2f out, kept on   **1¼   73**
fnl 1f but not pace of wnr: stays a sharp/undul 7f, acts on fast grnd: decent low draw, see 1911.
2263 **DREEMON 24** [3] B R Millman 2-9-0 G Baker 8/1: 03: ch g Tipsy Creek - Prudence (Grundy) Chsd   **½   72**
ldrs, kept on under press fnl 1f: May foal, half brother to a 1m/12f wnr: dam styd mid-dists, sire a smart sprinter:
eff over a sharp/undul 7f on fast grnd.
2388 **MADAM CAVERSFIELD 19** [8] R Hannon 2-8-9 P Dobbs 8/1: 5034: Mid-div, styd on under press fnl 1f.   **1   65**
2388 **TUVALU 19** [11]2-9-0 L Keniry(3) 16/1: 05: ch c Dashing Blade - Tepana (Polish Precedent) Slowly   **nk   69+**
away, hdwy from rear when short of room 1.5f out, hung left & nrst fin: Apr foal, cost £30,000: dam a wnr abroad,
sire a high-class juv: eye-catching run from a poor high draw under a kind ride: one to keep in mind.
2537 **ELVINA HILLS 13** [2]2-8-9 A Beech(3) 20/1: 0056: ch f Bluebird - Women In Love (Danehill) Led   **1¼   61**

till after halfway, wknd fnl 1f: 10,000 gns Mar foal: dam a wng miler abroad, sire a top-class sprinter: prob failed to stay this longer 7f trip: with W G M Turner.
2373 **BINT IL SULTAN 20** [6]2-8-9 E Ahern 9/2 JT FAV: 37: Chsd ldrs, ch 2f out, wknd fnl 1f: nicely bckd tho' drifted from 3/1: more expected after encouraging debut in 2373 (sharp trk). *2½* **56**
2594 **BOBBIE LOVE 12** [10]2-9-0 S Hitchcott(3) 16/1: 68: Mid-div & wide, eff 2f out, btn fnl 1f: mod draw. *nk* **60**
2020 **CHEK OI 36** [12]2-9-0 J Quinn 33/1: 09: Chsd ldrs 5.5f, wknd: poor draw. *1¼* **57**
1848 **WISE DENNIS 43** [9]2-9-0 S Sanders 15/2: 00: 10th: Al bhd after 6 wk abs. *3½* **50**
2348 **LIQUID LOVER 21** [7]2-9-0 R Smith 33/1: 00: 11th: Al bhd, t.o. *11* **30**
COOL CRISTAL [13]2-8-9 B Doyle 33/1: 0: 12th: Slowly away, al detached on debut: poor draw. *¾* **23**
DIZZY LIZZY [5]2-8-9 B Reilly(3) 25/1: 0: 13th: Hmpd start & sn bhd, t.o. in last on debut. *nk* **22**
13 Ran Time 1m 25.32 (5.22) Owned: Mrs A K H Ooi Trained: Newmarket

2871

7.25 Toteexacta Handicap Stakes 3yo+ 0-90 (C) **[83]**
£9601 £2954 £1477 **6f rnd** **Good/Firm 37** **+19 Fast** Outside

2558 **LOYAL TYCOON 13** [4] D Nicholls 6-9-10 (79) L Treadwell(7) 5/1: 0025001: Trkd ldrs trav strongly, led dist, pushed well clr, v readily: fast time, top weight: eff at 6/7f on soft & hvy, loves fast & firm & both AWs: handles any trk, likes a sharp one: gd weight carrier, likes Epsom & made most of fav h'cap mark. **96**
2752 **LORD OF THE EAST 5** [1] D Nicholls 5-9-2 (71) Alex Greaves 9/2: 0320132: Led till dist, kept on but no ch with easy wnr: qck reapp, shorter priced stable-mate of wnr: continues in gd form, see 2752 & 2466 (7f). *5* **78**
2256 **JAYANJAY 26** [8] Miss B Sanders 5-9-8 (77) S Sanders 5/1: 02-04343: Chsd ldrs, sltly outpcd 2f out, kept on late but no ch with front 2: see 2044. *2* **78**
2679 **WATERSIDE 8** [2] G L Moore 5-9-9 (78) E Ahern 4/1: 3031124: Stumbled start, recovered to chase ldrs, btn fnl 1f: al struggling after slow start on this drop back to 6f: see 2679 & 2389 (7f). *1¾* **74**
2535 **WILLHECONQUERTOO 13** [9]4-8-8 t (63) J F Egan 12/1: 500-0035: Dwelt, sn prom, wknd fnl 1f. *½* **58**
2760 **SILVER CHIME 5** [6]4-9-1 (70) L Keniry(3) 25/1: 0041566: Front rank 4f, grad wknd: qck reapp. *½* **64**
2779 **CAPE ST VINCENT 4** [5]4-9-3 vis (72) T P Queally(3) 3/1 FAV: 024-0127: Dwelt, well bhd, mod prog but nvr dngrs: nicely bckd & qck reapp: al struggling after slow start, showed plenty of pace in 2779 (5f) & 2053. *2* **60**
2451 **MADRASEE 17** [7]6-9-4 (73) T Quinn 20/1: 0450508: Stumbled start, no ch after: lost all ch at start. *2½* **54**
2451 **ESATTO 17** [3]5-9-3 t (72) S Righton 33/1: 50635-09: Sn outpcd, fin last: see 2451. *2½* **46**
9 Ran Time 1m 08.91 (1.11) Owned: Michael A J Hall & Mrs Mandy Hall Trained: Thirsk

2872

7.55 Scottish Equitable/Jockeys Association Handicap Stakes 3yo+ 0-85 (D) **[84]**
£6939 £2135 £1068 **7f rnd** **Good/Firm 37** **-08 Slow** Inside

2264 **PANGO 24** [4] H Morrison 5-9-2 (72) P Dobbs 5/1: 0500-221: Handy, qcknd to lead ins fnl 1f, rdn out: stays 11f, imprvd for drop back to 7f: acts on fast, gd/soft & both AWs, likes Epsom: turn of foot here. **80**
2587 **QUANTUM LEAP 12** [3] S Dow 7-9-1 vis (71) T Quinn 15/2: 0316642: Led, hdd under press ins fnl 1f, not pace wnr: likes undul trks: see 2063 & 1849. *1¼* **74**
2558 **H HARRISON 13** [8] I W McInnes 4-9-11 (81) L Vickers 15/2: 4541003: Cl-up, ev ch bef 1f out, sn carried head high & hung right, just held for 2nd: 5lb higher than last win in 2282. *nk* **83**
2644* **FRANKSALOT 9** [1] Miss B Sanders 4-8-13 (5ex) (69) S Sanders 9/2 FAV: 1222-014: Chsd ldrs, kept on ins fnl 1f, not btn far in 4th: ran to form of win in 2644. *shd* **71**
2679 **TEMPER TANTRUM 8** [5]6-8-4 p (60) J F McDonald(3) 14/1: 5520405: Held up, prog 2f out, onepcd fnl 1f. *1* **60**
2587 **FLEETWOOD BAY 12** [2]4-8-13 (69) G Baker 6/1: 20-00636: Trkd ldrs over 5f, no extra: btr 2587. *1¼* **66**
2648 **CONCUBINE 9** [6]5-8-6 p (62) D Sweeney 15/2: 00-30247: Held up, prog when short of room 2f out till dist, again short of room 1f out: no luck in running, forgive this: btr 2539. *1¼* **56**
2684 **SAWWAAH 7** [7]7-9-12 (82) Alex Greaves 10/1: 0134008: Al in rear: quick reapp: btr 2207. *nk* **75**
2451 **MARGALITA 17** [9]4-8-9 t (65) J F Egan 20/1: 0-600609: Handy over 5f, sn wknd: btr 2189. *8* **42**
2684 **COLEMANSTOWN 7** [10]4-8-8 (64) E Ahern 8/1: 0000000: 10th: b g Charnwood Forest - Arme Fatale (Trempolino) Bhd, fdd ins fnl 3f: tchd 12/1 on qck reapp: unplcd in 3 '03 starts (h'caps & clas stks, rtd 75): ex-Irish, h'cap wnr at The Curragh in '03: eff at 6/7f on fast & gd/soft grnd. *11* **21**
10 Ran Time 1m 23.29 (3.19) Owned: Pangfield Partners Trained: East Ilsley

2873

8.25 Drivers Jonas Claiming Stakes 3yo+ (E)
£4154 £1278 £639 **1m114y rnd** **Good/Firm 37** **-13 Slow** Inside

2354 **BURGUNDY 21** [3] P Mitchell 7-9-2 bl (57) T P Queally(3) 11/2: 2000361: Dwelt, plenty to do turning in, prog ins fnl 2f, rdn out to lead cl-home: eff at 7f/10f on fast, soft & polytrack: apprec return to clmg grade. **60**
2615 **TOJONESKI 10** [7] I W McInnes 5-9-3 p (47) J F McDonald(3) 10/1: 2223342: Cl-up, styd on to lead dist, hdd cl-home: fine eff in defeat, tho' off rtd 47: see 2440 & 1642. *nk* **60$**
2641 **ARCHERFIELD 9** [8] J W Hills 3-8-4 t (63) E Ahern 15/2: 2230023: Mid-div, prog ins fnl 2f, styd on well ins fnl 1f, post came too sn: worth a try over further on this evidence: see 2641 & 734. *shd* **57**
2662 **CAPTAIN SAIF 8** [2] R Hannon 4-9-3 (87) P Dobbs 5/2: 635-0004: Handy, prog 2f out, no extra fnl 1f. *1½* **57**
2745* **BEN HUR 5** [6]5-9-5 (63) S W Kelly 7/4 FAV: 0102115: Led, hdd dist, sn no extra: quick reapp: below par run on hat-trick bid: btr 2745 & 2544. *1* **57**
3861} **GAMESETNMATCH 311** [1]3-8-7 (70) C Haddon(7) 16/1: 02065-6: b g Hector Protector - Tanasie (Cadeaux Genereux) Al rear: unplcd yesterday: rnr-up once in '03 (mdn): eff at 5f on fast grnd: eff with blnks, has tried cheek pieces: with W G M Turner. 2 Apr'03 Ripo 5g/f 77- D: *8* **40**
2844 **SINGLE TRACK MIND 1** [5]6-8-13 p (42) A Quinn(5) 33/1: 35006477: Slow away, al adrift: btr 2529. *8* **21**
2432 **FIGURA 17** [4]6-8-8 T (41) N Day 33/1: 6650008: Mid-div 6f, sn fdd: see 2520. *2½* **11**
8 Ran Time 1m 46.12 (4.32) Owned: Mr Nigel Shields Trained: Epsom

EPSOM THURSDAY 01.07.04 Lefthand, Very Sharp, Undulating Track

2874 **8.55 Lewis Silkin Classified Stakes 3yo+ 0-80 (D)**
£5330 £1640 £820 **1m2f18y** **Good/Firm 37** **-34 Slow** Inside

2385 **WOODY VALENTINE 19** [1] M Johnston 3-8-6 (80) S Chin 2/1 JT FAV: 0-421661: Cl-up, styd on to lead 1f out, drvn out to hold on: well bckd: eff at 10f, stays 12f: acts on firm & soft: in-form performer: see 1813. **84**
4716} **SILVER CITY 262** [2] Mrs A J Perrett 4-9-3 (80) P Dobbs 10/1: 4/32610-2: ro g Unfuwain - Madiyla (Darshaan) Led, hdd dist, rallied ins fnl 1f, just held: reapp: med auct mdn wnr in '03 (also plcd twice): showed mdn promise in '02 (rtd 80): eff at 1m/12f on firm & gd, prob soft grnd: has been gldd since last term. *nk* **83**
1 Jun'03 Beve 12.1g/f 78-(82) E: 2 May'03 Thir 12gd 82-(80) D:
2452* **MR TAMBOURINE MAN 17** [7] P F I Cole 3-8-7 (81) T Quinn 2/1 JT FAV: 61-60013: Mid-div, outpcd after 6f, rallied bef 1f out, not btn far in 3rd: see 2452. *½* **83**
2582 **OCEAN OF STORMS 12** [4] Christian Wroe 9-9-3 t (78) R Thomas(5) 20/1: 3R-21004: Slow away, sn handy, wknd fnl 2f: op 14/1: btr 2207. *5* **74**
2255 **DISSIDENT 26** [6]6-9-7 (84) J Tucker(7) 8/1: 2214565: Rear, nvr a factor: btr 1516 & 1484. *3* **73**
2560 **ARRY DASH 12** [5]4-9-3 (80) S Hitchcott(3) 10/3: 0200306: Bhd, nvr a factor: op 4/1: btr 2312. *4* **63**
6 Ran Time 2m 10.97(7.17) Owned: Favourites Racing Trained: Middleham

NEWBURY THURSDAY 01.07.04 Lefthand, Flat, Galloping Track

Official Going Good/Firm

2875 **6.40 Kerridge Computers Apprentice Handicap Stakes 4yo+ 0-75 (E)** **[73]**
£3640 £1120 £560 **1m3f5y** **Good/Firm 26** **-33 Slow** Centre

2078* **LUCKY LEO 33** [7] Ian Williams 4-9-9 (68) Dean Williams(5) 13/2: 0/300-011: Held up, prog halfway, styd on to lead 2f out, drvn out to hold on: eff at 11/12f on fast grnd: acts on a gall trk: imprvg 4yo: see 2078. **76**
2088 **MAN THE GATE 32** [5] P D Cundell 5-8-10 (55) N Chalmers 9/2 FAV: 0-250362: Held up, prog 5f out, ev ch ins fnl 1f, kept on but just held: another gd eff & is on a wng mark: likes Leicester. *½* **61**
2354 **EASTBOROUGH 21** [3] B G Powell 5-9-1 (60) M Savage 11/2: 4346623: Slow away, prog 4f out, onepcd. *1¾* **63**
2718 **ESCALADE 6** [4] W M Brisbourne 7-8-7 p (52) B Swarbrick 5/1: 0405434: Rear, prog ins fnl 3f, nrst fin. *2½* **51**
2354 **GALEY RIVER 21** [10]5-7-12 (3oh) (40) M Halford(5) 14/1: 6235045: Handy, ev ch bef 2f out, sn no extra. *3* **37**
2601 **TASNEEF 11** [8]5-9-1 (60) P Makin 7/1: 6140-066: In tch, styd on to lead 3f out, hdd 2f out, wknd. *1½* **51**
2601 **BAKIRI 11** [1]6-9-5 (64) Derek Nolan(5) 13/2: 0523247: Mid-div, prog trav well after 1m, wknd bef 1f out. *1¼* **53**
2354 **BLUEGRASS BOY 21** [9]4-9-2 (61) R Thomas 16/1: 300-3008: Handy, ev ch 3f out, sn wknd: btr 1098. *¾* **48**
2538 **RICHEMAUR 13** [2]4-9-11 (70) Saleem Golam(5) 11/1: 0-400409: Led 1m out, hdd 3f out, fdd: btr 2233. *½* **56**
2526 **ROYAL AXMINSTER 14** [6]9-7-12 (3oh) (40) Amy Baker(4) 16/1: 05-0520U: Led 3f, wkng & u.r. 3f out. **0**
10 Ran Time 2m 22.30 (6.5) Owned: B and S Vaughan Trained: Alvechurch

2876 **7.10 Choisir E B F Maiden Stakes 2yo (D)**
£5824 £1792 £896 **7f str** **Good/Firm 26** **-33 Slow** Centre

2594 **GRAND MARQUE 12** [3] R Hannon 2-9-0 K Fallon 9/2 FAV: 51: ch c Grand Lodge - Royal Fizz (Royal Academy) In tch, led after 3f, pushed out ins fnl 1f, val bit more: tchd 6/1: Feb foal, cost 50,000 gns: dam wnr as a juv: sire Gr1 wnr at 1m/10f: eff at 7f, will apprec further: acts on fast: open to improvement. **88+**
MASTMAN 0 [13] B J Meehan 2-9-0 J Fortune 12/1: 2: ch c Intikhab - Spanker (Suave Dancer) Handy, ev ch 2f out, kept on ins fnl 1f, al held under hands & heels: debut: Apr foal, cost 35,000 gns: half brother plcd up to 1m: dam eff at mid-dists: sire decent performer at 1m: eff at 7f, 1m+ will suit: acts on fast grnd: encouraging start & looks sure to improve with racing & can find similar. *2* **80**
TRANSGRESS 0 [11] R Hannon 2-9-0 Martin Dwyer 28/1: 3: b c Trans Island - Ned's Contessa (Persian Heights) Cl-up, kept on ins fnl 2f, not pace front 2: debut: Feb foal, cost 35,000 gns: half brother to a wnr at 6/8f: dam successful at 7f: sire decent performer around 1m: eff at 7f, will apprec further: acts on fast grnd: encouraging eff & can rate higher. *1¼* **78**
JONQUIL 0 [5] J H M Gosden 2-9-0 R Havlin 13/2: 4: ch c Machiavellian - Jumilla (El Gran Senor) Handy, prog & ev ch bef 2f out, no extra dist: debut: May foal, cost 130,000 gns: half brother won a couple of times around 10f: dam juv wnr at 6f: sire decent performer around 1m: eff at 7f, shld apprec further: acts on fast grnd: shld improve for today's experience. *1½* **75**
WANSDYKE LASS 0 [1]2-8-9 C Catlin 33/1: 5: Held up, prog halfway, onepcd fnl 1f: debut. *1¾* **66**
NORTH SHORE 0 [10]2-9-0 D Holland 5/1: 6: Slow away, prog halfway, mod late gains: debut. *hd* **70**
BALL BOY 0 [9]2-9-0 T O'Brien(7) 33/1: 7: Slow away, nvr nrr than mid-div: debut. *½* **69**
WORTH ABBEY 0 [8]2-9-0 R L Moore 33/1: 8: Led 3f, wknd dist: debut. *nk* **68**
SCALE THE HEIGHTS 0 [15]2-9-0 M Hills 8/1: 9: Nvr nrr than mid-div on debut. *hd* **67**
DUNMAGLASS 0 [2]2-9-0 S Drowne 20/1: 0: 10th: Chsd ldrs over 4f, sn wknd. *hd* **66**
GARANCE 0 [4]2-8-9 Dane O'Neill 16/1: 0: 11th: Slow away, nvr a factor. *nk* **60**
DISCOMANIA 0 [12]2-9-0 R Hughes 6/1: 0: 12th: Al bhd: op 4/1 on debut. *½* **64**
VOIR DIRE 0 [7]2-9-0 M Fenton 33/1: 0: 13th: Al in rear. *1½* **61**
1760 **BAKKE 47** [14]2-9-0 A Daly 8/1: 00: 14th: Keen cl-up 6f, fdd. *1¼* **59**
GUYANA 0 [6]2-9-0 J Murtagh 20/1: 0: 15th: Handy till halfway, fdd. *1¼* **57**
15 Ran Time 1m 28.49 (4.19) Owned: Noodles Racing Trained: Marlborough

2877 **7.40 Jurys Doyle Hotels Handicap Stakes 3yo 0-85 (D)** **[92]**
£6136 £1888 £944 **1m str** **Good/Firm 26** **-11 Slow** Centre

2025* **ANOTHER BOTTLE 35** [7] T P Tate 3-9-0 (78) Dale Gibson 11/2: 033-011: Keen rear, prog halfway, styd on to lead fnl 1f, drvn out, gamely: eff at 7f, suited by 1m/9f: acts on fast grnd & a gall trk: fine effort on h'cap bow: progressive & genuine: see 2025. **87**
2463 **TAAQAAH 16** [8] M P Tregoning 3-9-0 (78) Martin Dwyer 100/30 FAV: 62-22: Held up, rcd keenly, *¾* **85**

prog 3f out, styd on to chase wnr ins fnl 1f, kept on for press, just held: gd run with change of tactics.

2662 **RED SPELL 8** [2] R Hannon 3-9-3 (81) R Hughes 11/2: 1-051263: Handy, led bef 1f out, hung left & *1½* **85**
hdd ins fnl 1f, no extra: continues to run well: 4lb higher than last win in 1930.

2705 **MR JACK DANIELLS 7** [10] W R Muir 3-8-11 (75) S Drowne 8/1: 00-36304: Bhd, prog 3f out, no *2½* **74**
impress fnl 1f: quick reapp: showed more in 2247.

2166 **DOCTORATE 29** [4]3-9-6 (84) D Holland 7/1: 4-0125: Handy over 6f, wknd dist: disapp back at 1m. *1* **81**

2525 **HAVE FAITH 14** [5]3-9-7 (85) M Hills 12/1: 6210-36: Cl-up, wknd 2f out: btr 2525 (reapp). *2½* **77**

2520 **BARATHEA DREAMS 14** [13]3-8-7 (85) K Fallon 6/1: 1141307: Led, hdd bef 1f out, wknd: btr 1707 & 1315. *½* **76**

2290 **GELLER 23** [11]3-8-8 (72) R L Moore 25/1: 2204-548: Handy 6f, sn wknd: btr 2290. *3* **57**

2314 **SCIENTIST 22** [6]3-8-10 (74) J Fortune 9/1: 65-0039: Mid-div till halfway, sn wknd: btr 2314 (7f). *2* **55**

438 **BARONS SPY 17** [3]3-8-1 (65) C Catlin 20/1: 00-420: 10th: Chsd ldrs 5f, sn fdd: v disapp: btr 2438. *19* **11**
10 Ran   Time 1m 39.80 (3.0)   Owned: Mr J Hanson   Trained: Tadcaster

---

2878   8.10 Invesco Perpetual Rated Stakes Handicap 3yo+ 0-95 (C)   [98]
£9248 £3508 £1754   **6f8y str**   **Good/Firm 26**   **+23 Fast**   Centre

2770 **FANTASY BELIEVER 5** [5] J J Quinn 6-8-13 (83) D Holland 5/1: 0000041: Mid-div, prog to lead ins **96+**
fnl 1f, pushed clr, val 4L+: quick reapp: eff over 5/7f on any grnd or trk: can make a qk follow up.

2758 **CAUSTIC WIT 5** [8] M S Saunders 6-8-13 p (83) R Miles(3) 7/2: 0111122: Cl-up, led after 2f out, hdd *2½* **86**
ins fnl 1f, not pace wnr: quick reapp: continues in fine form: see 2758 & 2451.

2591 **NAJEEBON 12** [10] M R Channon 5-8-10 (80) C Catlin 10/1: 0-000363: Chsd ldrs, styd on from dist, *hd* **82**
just held for 2nd: encouraging eff & is on a fair mark: see 2289 & 1489.

4754} **KHABFAIR 260** [7] Mrs A J Perrett 3-9-1 (91) Dane O'Neill 16/1: 312-4: b c Intikhab - Ruby Affair *nk* **92**
(Night Shift) Held up, prog halfway, styd on ins fnl 1f for 4th: reapp & h'cap bow: mdn wnr on one of only 3 '03
starts: eff at 6f: shld be suited by 7f: acts on fast grnd & polytrack: eff on a v sharp or gall trk: gd eff after
long lay-off & up to 2 more improvement. 2 Oct'03 Ling 6ap 90a- D: 1 Oct'03 Ling 6ap 88a- D:

2679* **CHATEAU NICOL 8** [9]5-8-11 (3ex)vis (81) J Murtagh 15/2: 1333415: Rear, prog ins fnl 2f, onepcd. *¾* **80**

2420 **NIVERNAIS 18** [3]5-8-5 (75) N Chalmers(5) 16/1: 36-00006: Rear, prog when short of room bef 1f *½* **73**
out, hung left & onepace ins fnl 1f: btr 2023.

2581 **HIGH REACH 12** [1]4-9-7 (91) K Fallon 7/4 FAV: 144-3637: Bhd, prog 3f out, wknd dist: btr *shd* **88**
expected after fine 3rd in 2581 (val Wokingham h'cap).

2758 **WILLHEWIZ 5** [11]4-8-11 vis (81) S Carson 25/1: 5601108: Led, hdd ins fnl 2f, sn wknd: quick reapp. *5* **64**

2581 **DANEHILL STROLLER 12** [6]4-9-2 p (86) J Fortune 25/1: 1243-009: Al in rear: btr 2070. *hd* **68**

4776} **GOLDEN DIXIE 258** [2]5-8-12 (82) Martin Dwyer 25/1: 240000-0: 10th: ch g Dixieland Band - *1½* **60**
Beyrouth (Alleged) Cl-up 4f, sn wknd: reapp: rnr-up once in '03 (h'cap): mdn & class stks wnr on 2 of only 3 '02
starts: eff at 6f on firm & fast grnd: has gone well fresh.
2 Jul'03 Newb 6.0fm 88-85 C: 1 Aug'02 Newc 6g/f 88- D: 1 Jul'02 Sali 6g/f 84- D:

2581 **DAME DE NOCHE 12** [4]4-9-1 (85) M Fenton 20/1: 0-603000: 11th: Chsd ldrs 4f, sn fdd: btr 1925. *6* **47**
11 Ran   Time 1m 11.80 (0.20)   Owned: The Fantasy Fellowship B   Trained: Malton

---

2879   8.40 Hughie Cameron-Rose Memorial Maiden Stakes 3yo (D)
£5850 £1800 £900   **1m4f5y**   **Good/Firm 26**   **-15 Slow**   Centre

2254 **MASSIF CENTRALE 26** [1] D R C Elsworth 3-9-0 (100) Dane O'Neill 2/7 FAV: 0201: Led 10f out, **90+**
pushed clr ins fnl 2f, eased cl-home, val 11L+: eff at 10/12f on fast & gd: gd confidence boost.

2441 **FOUR PENCE 17** [6] B W Hills 3-9-0 (65) M Hills 20/1: 40-42: Mid-div, prog & ev 2f out, kept *7* **75$**
on but al held by v easy wnr: clr rem: eff at 12f on fast grnd: see 2441.

1959 **SHASTYE 38** [7] J H M Gosden 3-8-9 J Fortune 6/1: 03: Handy, prog after 1m, wknd fnl 2f: see 1959. *10* **56**

2678 **SONG OF THE SEA 8** [4] J W Hills 3-8-9 T R Hughes 25/1: 5-0-004: ch f Bering - Calypso Run (Lycius) *6* **47**
Nvr nrr than mid-div: 1st time t-strap: unplcd sole '03 start (rtd 61a, mdn).

1961 **DEVITO 38** [2]3-9-0 V Slattery 16/1: 0-25: Handy till halfway, sn wknd: btr 1961. *5* **45**

2622 **BLAZE THE TRAIL 10** [3]3-8-9 Martin Dwyer 100/1: 06: Led 10f out, styd cl-up till fdd fnl 4f. *7* **30**

2534 **CHAPELCO 13** [5]3-9-0 R L Moore 33/1: 67: Rear, al adrift: btr 2534. *5* **28**
7 Ran   Time 2m 34.33 (5.03)   Owned: Mr Raymond Tooth   Trained: Whitsbury

---

2880   9.10 Motor Neurone Disease Association Handicap Stakes 3yo+ 0-85 (D)   [84]
£5902 £1816 £908   **7f str**   **Good/Firm 26**   **+04 Fast**   Centre

2370* **GOODENOUGH MOVER 20** [4] J S Moore 8-9-7 (77) K Fallon 3/1 FAV: 0-212211: Made all, under press **85**
bef 1f out, drvn out: eff at 6f, suited by 7f, stays 1m: acts on firm, soft & polytrack, v tough.

2590 **COMPTONS ELEVEN 12** [6] M R Channon 3-9-0 (78) C Catlin 14/1: 3-000052: Handy, prog to chase wnr *½* **83**
ins fnl 1f, kept on, just held: eff at 5/6f, now stays 7f: gd run in defeat & h'capped to find similar: see 1847.

2564 **BOUNDLESS PROSPECT 12** [10] J W Hills 5-9-0 (70) R Hughes 12/1: 0-000023: Held up, prog ins fnl *nk* **74**
3f, styd on ins fnl 1f, not btn far in 3rd: in gd form: see 2564.

2108 **CRAIC SA CEILI 31** [12] M S Saunders 4-8-7 (63) R Miles(3) 25/1: 450-0004: Handy, prog & ev ch bef *½* **65**
1f out, onepcd ins fnl 1f: encouraging eff & is on a winning mark: see 1423.

4753} **POINT OF DISPUTE 260** [11]9-9-10 vis (80) J Fortune 25/1: 056302-5: b g Cyrano de Bergerac - *hd* **82**
Opuntia (Rousillon) Rear, prog 2f out, nrst fin: reapp: plcd twice in '03 (h'cap & clmr, rtd 86 at best): plcd in
'02 (val h'cap, rtd 94): suited by 6/7f, poss stays 1m: acts on fast, gd & both AWs, any trk: suited by visor & is
a gd weight carrier: sharper for today.
2 Oct'03 Ling 7ap 73a-(85) F: 1 Nov'01 Ling 7ap 96a-90 C: 2 Oct'01 Newm 7g/f 95-89 B: 1 Nov'00 Sout 7af 90a-84 D:

2451 **BLUE PATRICK 17** [5]4-9-5 p (75) L Fletcher(3) 14/1: 0-000206: Nvr nrr than mid-div: btr 2280. *1* **75**

2679 **TERRAQUIN 8** [7]4-9-0 p (70) A Daly 10/1: 0050557: Chsd ldrs over 5f, no extra dist: btr 2374. *½* **67**

2648 **BEE MINOR 9** [13]3-8-6 (70) R L Moore 13/2: 3500-028: Handy 5f, sn no extra: btr 2648 (6f). *2* **65**

3971} **INDIAN TRAIL 306** [2]4-9-13 (83) Dane O'Neill 16/1: 0/31100-9: ch g Indian Ridge - Take Heart *¾* **76**
(Electric) Mid-div, prog 3f out, fdd fnl 1f: reapp: mdn & class stks wnr in '03: mdn plcd in '02 (rtd 80): eff
at 6/7f on firm & soft grnd: has been gelded since last term.
1 Jun'03 Kemp 6fm 85-(80) D: 1 May'03 Good 7g/f 88-(76) D:

2679 **MARKER 8** [14]4-9-10 (80) R Havlin 6/1: 6004040: 10th: Rear, prog halfway, wknd fnl 2f: btr 2679. *1* **71**

2427 **PRIMO WAY 18** [9]3-9-4 (82) M Hills 11/2: 35-13630: 11th: Al in rear: btr 2427 & 1734. *1½* **70**

2173 **Handsome Cross 29** [1]3-9-3 (81) S Drowne 11/1:0

NEWBURY THURSDAY 01.07.04 Lefthand, Flat, Galloping Track

2550 Night Wolf 13 [8]4-8-10 (66) T Dean(7) 33/1.0

13 Ran   Time 1m 25.85(1.55)   Owned: D Goodenough Removals & Transport   Trained: Swindon

HAYDOCK THURSDAY 01.07.04 Lefthand, Flat, Galloping Track

Official Going Good (Good/Soft places)

2881 2.20 Victoria Park Handicap Stakes Fillies 3yo+ 0-80 (D) [76]
£5632 £1733 £867   1m3f200y   Good 40   -09 Slow   Outside

2592 **ASTROCHARM 12** [4] M H Tompkins 5-9-12 (74) L Dettori 3/1 FAV: 00-51051: Cl-up, led 2f out, 85
pushed clr, cmftbly: suited by 12f now & acts on any trk: eff on firm & gd, handles gd/soft: back to best.
2484* **ACT OF THE PACE 15** [7] M Johnston 4-10-0 (76) K Dalgleish 5/1: 5-412: Cl-up, led over 4f out, 2½ 81
hdd 2f out, not pace of wnr: gd run under a big weight: acts on fast & gd grnd: likely to win a h'cap, see 2484.
2217 **SWYNFORD PLEASURE 27** [2] J Hetherton 8-8-3 (51) Dale Gibson 9/2: 050-2543: Held up, hdwy 2f out, 1½ 53
onepace: well h'capped, comes gd at this time of year & shld be winning on fast grnd sn, likes Beverley: see 1875.
2604 **TRANSCENDANTALE 11** [3] Mrs S Lamyman 6-7-13 (47) F Norton 9/1: 5600404: Chsd ldrs, hdwy & not 4 43
clr run over 2f out, sn no impress: btr 1307, 1135.
2509 **INFIDELITY 14** [5]3-7-12 (2oh)VIS (57) Hayley Turner(5) 4/1: 0060635: Slow away, held up, eff & 1½ 53
switched right 3f out, hung left & no impress over 1f out: reportedly fin distressed: visor: see 2509, 568 (10f).
2691 **CANTEMERLE 7** [1]4-8-6 bl (54) K Darley 15/2: 350-2006: Slow away & al bhd: btr 1680 (soft). ½ 47
2807 **DESERT QUILL 3** [6]4-8-9 (57) W Supple 16/1: 0030-257: Led till over 4f out, wknd: see 2200. 13 32
2483 **HARAMBEE 15** [8]4-9-11 (73) R Winston 40/1: 116-PU08: Cl-up, wknd over 2f out: see 2483. 6 38
8 Ran   Time 2m 33.71 (5.91)   Owned: Mystic Meg Limited   Trained: Newmarket

2882 2.50 Dalkia & Land Securities Trillium Partnership Maiden Claiming Stakes 2yo (F)
£3206 £916 £458   6f str   Good 40   -59 Slow   Centre

2610 **MAKE US FLUSH 11** [8] A Berry 2-8-6 F Norton 5/1 JT FAV: 40401: Handy, hdwy to lead dist, styd 70
on, rdn out: eff at 6f on gd grnd & a gall trk: relished drop to v modest company: see 1343.
 AS HANDSOME DOES 0 [13] N Tinkler 2-9-0 T A Culhane 33/1: 2: ch g Handsome Ridge - Fast To Light 2½ 70
(Pharly) Slow away, bhd, styd on late, nrst fin on debut: June first foal: eff at 6f, 7f sure to suit: acts on gd.
2194 **ALZARMA 28** [6] Mrs L Williamson 2-8-10 T Eaves(3) 33/1: 03: b g Alzao - Skimra (Hernando) Led shd 66
till dist, no extra: clmd for 10,000: dam 12f wnr: eff at 6f, bred to apprec 7f+
in time: acts on gd grnd: may do btr.
2537 **PIDDIES PRIDE 13** [3] I A Wood 2-8-2 vis J Fanning 10/1: 5664: In tch, eff to chall over 1f out, onepace. nk 57
1728 **KERRYS BLADE 48** [10]2-9-0 G Faulkner 20/1: 05: ch g Daggers Drawn - Treasure (Treasure Kay) In 3 60
tch, hung right & onepace over 1f out: 7 wk abs: Apr foal, cost £9,000: dam styd 10f.
1739 **MISS GOOD TIME 48** [20]2-8-0 Dean McKeown 12/1: 0606: Cl-up, wknd appr fnl 1f. 2 40
1887 **LADRUCA 41** [4]2-8-8 R L Moore 8/1: 07: In tch, wknd appr fnl 1f. ½ 46
2358 **MAGIC GENIE 20** [1]2-8-7 Dale Gibson 16/1: 58: In tch, eff over 1f out, no extra: see 2358. shd 45
1869 **TURTLE MAGIC 42** [16]2-8-5 C Haddon(7) 5/1 JT FAV: 0236649: Al bhd: btr 1869. hd 42
 HOPELESSLY DEVOTED 0 [5]2-8-7 Rory Moore(7) 14/1: 0: 10th: Dwelt, in tch, wknd appr fnl 1f. 2½ 40
2358 **ROKO 20** [17]2-9-1 P Mulrennan(5) 33/1: 000: 11th: In tch, wknd over 2f out. 1¾ 40
2547 **FOR NOWT 13** [18]2-9-1 W Supple 25/1: 60: 12th: Went left start, al bhd. ½ 38
2461 **XEIGHT EXPRESS 16** [2]2-8-3 R Ffrench 50/1: 00: 13th: In tch, wknd well over 1f out. ½ 24
2183 **CASH TIME 28** [11]2-8-3 P M Quinn 50/1: 60: 14th: Dwelt, nvr a factor. 1 21
2119 **ELLIEBOW 30** [19]2-8-7 D Allan 14/1: 00: 15th: In tch, wknd over 2f out. 1¼ 21
 CARMANIA 0 [12]2-8-12 T Hamilton(3) 25/1: 0: 16th: Cl-up, wknd 2f out. 1 23
 WINTER MIST 0 [7]2-8-10 K Darley 14/1: 0: 17th: Al bhd. 3 12
 MISS TRENDSETTER 0 [14]2-8-10 N Callan 14/1: 0: 18th: In tch, wknd over 2f out. ¾ 10
2547 **TAKS GIRL 13** [9]2-8-4 R Fitzpatrick 66/1: 000: 19th: Al bhd. 5 0
2051 **MAS O MENOS 34** [15]2-8-8 I Mongan 25/1: 200: 20th: Cl-up, wknd over 2f out: see 1658. ¾ 0
20 Ran   Time 1m 17.24 (5.94)   Owned: The Bath Tub Boys   Trained: Cockerham

2883 3.20 European Breeders Fund Novice Stakes Fillies 2yo (D)
£4999 £1538 £769   6f str   Good 40   -41 Slow   Centre

2490 **BRIGHT MOLL 15** [2] M L W Bell 2-8-11 I Mongan 5/4 FAV: 12251: Cl-up, led over 1f out, edged 93
right but kept on ins last, rdn out: hvly bckd: 7L 5th in Queen Mary last time & relished step up to 6f: acts on
fast & soft, any trk: consistent & useful: see 974.
 ALL NIGHT DANCER 24 [5] D Wachman 2-9-2 L Dettori 9/4: 152: In tch, hdwy to go 2nd fnl 1f, not 3½ 86
pace of wnr: Apr foal: half-sister to a 6f juv wnr: earlier won a Navan mdn: eff at 5/6f on fast & gd grnd.
2178* **ROCKBURST 28** [4] K R Burke 2-8-13 Darren Williams 7/1: 5213: Led till over 1f out, no extra ins ¾ 81
last: gd run, nurs will suit: see 2178.
2547* **AFRICAN BREEZE 13** [3] R M Whitaker 2-9-2 Dean McKeown 15/2: 0414: Held up, eff over 2f out, nk 83
onepcd: prob ran to winning form of 2547 & stays 6f, see 2165.
 HOWARDS PRINCESS 0 [7]2-8-5 W Supple 33/1: 5: gr f Lujain - Grey Princess (Common Grounds) 1 69
Slow away, bhd, eff over 2f out, sn no extra: Feb first foal: dam 5/6f juv wnr: sharper for this.
2213 **MITCHELLAND 27** [1]2-9-2 T Eaves(3) 25/1: 41066: Held up, modest late gains, nvr a factor: see 1037. hd 79
2281 **MENNA 23** [6]2-8-9 A Culhane 33/1: 57: Keen cl-up, wknd over 2f out: see 2281. 3½ 62
7 Ran   Time 1m 16.14 (4.84)   Owned: A Buxton P Fenwick & Lostford Manor Stud   Trained: Newmarket

---

2884 3.50 Silver Cross Prams Handicap Stakes 3yo+ 0-80 (D) [80]
£6224 £1915 £958 **6f str** **Good 40** -18 Slow Centre

2070 **SAVILES DELIGHT** 33 [8] R Brotherton 5-9-4 (70) D Nolan(3) 11/2: 2431201: Made virtually all, hung 77
left over 1f out but kept on despite edging right, drvn out: stays 7f, best at 6f: acts on firm, hvy & both AWs,
any trk: tough & genuine, see 1533, 214.

2747 **TIME N TIME AGAIN** 5 [5] E J Alston 6-9-2 p (68) D Allan 8/1: 0063032: With ldrs, eff over 1f out, hd 73
kept on, just held: in fine form: see 2747.

2502 **BRANTWOOD** 14 [10] B A McMahon 4-8-7 t (59) G Gibbons 8/1: 0004323: Handy, hdwy well over 1f out, 1 61
styd on ins last: likes Haydock: see 2502, 174.

2655 **LOCOMBE HILL** 9 [4] D Nicholls 8-8-8 VIS (60) J Carroll 25/1: 0200504: Bhd, switched right over 2f shd 62
out, styd on ins last, nrst fin: pleasing run, h'capped to win: see 2315, 417.

2160 **WILLIAMS WELL** 29 [7]10-8-6 bl (58) P Mulrennan(3) 25/1: 020-0005: Cl-up, eff when hmpd ins last, ¾ 58
no extra cl-home: much closer with clr run: 10yo, but tough & looks still capable of winning a h'cap on fast grnd.

2770 **HIGHLAND WARRIOR** 5 [1]5-9-7 (73) W Supple 5/1: 1600466: Slow away, bhd, hdwy & poised to chall 1 70
when hmpd ins last, lost ch: yet again shaped with promise but seems to find trouble on every run: loves Ayr.

2752 **LEGAL SET** 5 [12]8-8-4 (6ex)t (56) Natalia Gemelova(7) 8/1: 0042147: In tch, onepace over 1f out. ½ 51

2280 **SMIRFYS PARTY** 24 [9]6-7-13 vis (51) P M Quinn 33/1: 0106-008: ch g Clantime - Party Scenes (Most 1 43
Welcome) Slow away, sn in tch, no extra appr fnl 1f: '03 h'cap wnr: back in '01 won a h'cap: suited by 6f on
firm, gd/soft & fibresand: enjoys forcing tactics in a visor & on gall trks. 1 Aug'03 Redc 6g/f 57-55 F:
2 Jun'02 Donc 7g/f 75-73 D: 1 Jul'01 Hayd 6gd 77-72 C: 2 Jun'01 Ches 5fm 73-70 D: 2 May'01 Nott 6g/s 71- E:

2779 **MIDNIGHT PARKES** 4 [11]5-8-13 (65) R Hughes 9/2 FAV: 0-040359: Dwelt, held up, no impress. 1¼ 53
2690 **BALLYBUNION** 7 [2]5-8-3 (55) J Fanning 10/1: 0005300: 10th: In tch, wknd fnl 1f: btr 2657, see 2084. ¾ 41
2723 **KEY OF GOLD** 6 [6]3-9-3 (75) L Dettori 16/1: 30120-00: 11th: Al bhd: see 2723. 5 46
2524 **BOLLIN JANET** 14 [13]4-9-3 (69) R Winston 20/1: 500-0000: 12th: Al bhd: see 2524. 2½ 33
2482 **MR WOLF** 15 [14]3-9-6 (78) K Darley 10/1: 2211660: 13th: With ldrs, wknd over 2f out: btr 1477 (gd/soft). 1¾ 37
13 Ran Time 1m 14.76 (3.46) Owned: Mr Roy Brotherton Trained: Pershore

---

2885 4.20 Xchanging Hr Services Maiden Stakes Div 1 3yo (D)
£5629 £1732 £866 **1m30y rnd** **Good 40** -06 Slow Inside

   BALAVISTA 0 [8] R Charlton 3-9-0 R Hughes 4/1: 1: br c Distant View - Balabina (Nijinsky) 88+
Handy & led over 2f out, rdn clr over 1f out, hands-and-heels ins last, readily, val 5L+: nicely bckd tho' op 3/1 on
debut: half-brothers to wnrs up to 12f, incl smart Bequeath & Binary: eff at 1m, relish further: acts on gd:
showed a useful turn of foot, keep on side.

1236 **NEWS SKY** 75 [5] B W Hills 3-9-0 W Supple 4/1: 02: b c Gone West - Dubian (High Line) Mid-div, 3 76
styd on for press fnl 2f, no ch with easy wnr: 11 wk abs: imprvd from debut: brother to a smart 1m performer &
half-brother to 1,000 Guineas wnr Sayyedati: eff at 1m on gd, will apprec further: clr of rem, win on.

   GO GARUDA 0 [10] D W P Arbuthnot 3-9-0 R L Moore 33/1: 3: b c Air Express - Free As A Bird 3 69
(Robellino) Held up, kept on late despite hanging left, nvr threat: debut: 10,000gns purchase, half-brother to a
useful sprinter, dam plcd at 7f as a 3yo: prob stays gall 1m.

2248 **MESAYAN** 26 [2] A C Stewart 3-9-0 t J McAuley 16/1: 04: Dwelt, mid-div, not pace to chall: op 25/1. 1¼ 66
2622 **DAN DI CANIO** 10 [4]3-9-0 I Mongan 10/1: 505: Mid-div, no impress fnl 2f. 2½ 60
4971} **KINKOZAN** 243 [6]3-9-0 J P Guillambert(3) 33/1: 06-6: Prom, btn over 1f out, reapp. 1½ 57
   JAVA DANCER 0 [7]3-9-0 D Allan 25/1: 7: Held up, rdn & btn 2f out on debut. nk 56
1747 **HOWARDS ROCKET** 84 [9]3-9-0 K Dalgleish 50/1: 08: Bhd, rdn & btn 2f out, 7 wk abs. hd 53
   ELTIHAAB 0 [3]3-8-9 L Dettori 5/4 FAV: 9: Led till over 2f out, sn btn: hvly bckd, op 7/4. 2 46
   CLASSIC LEASE 0 [1]3-9-0 N Callan 33/1: 0: 10th: Trkd ldrs, btn over 1f out. 1 49
4942} **TREASON TRIAL** 246 [11]3-9-0 A Culhane 12/1: 40-0: 11th: Bhd thr'out, op 10/1, reapp, new stable. dist 0
11 Ran Time 1m 44.21 (3.71) Owned: Mr K Abdulla Trained: Beckhampton

---

2886 4.50 Xchanging Hr Services Maiden Stakes Div 2 3yo (D)
£5629 £1732 £866 **1m30y rnd** **Good 40** +09 Fast Inside

1688 **NEW ORDER** 50 [5] B W Hills 3-8-9 R Hughes 5/4 FAV: 31: Led 1f, led again from 3f out, pressed 76
from over 1f out, rdn & al holding rival ins last: hvly bckd, op 11/8, 7 wk abs, imprvd from intro: apprec step up
to 1m, mid-dists shld suit: enjoyed gd grnd, handles gd/soft, likes a gall trk & goes well fresh: see 1688.

2352 **REVENIR** 21 [2] A C Stewart 3-9-0 L Dettori 13/2: 02: ch g Spectrum - Petite Liqueuerelle 1 77$
(Shernazar) Held up, hdwy & rdn to chall ins last, no extra fnl 100yds: rest well covered: imprvd run: 22,000gns
purchase, half-brother to numerous wnrs: eff at 1m on gd: shld find similar.

   CLIPPERDOWN 0 [6] P W Harris 3-9-0 R L Moore 11/2: 3: b c Green Desert - Maroussie (Saumarez) 2½ 71
Dwelt & held up, switched & kept on ins last, nvr threaten front pair: 70,000gns purchase, brother to a smart 9/12f
wnr: dam high-class at 10f abroad: eff at 1m, relish mid-dists: acts on gd: improve over further.

2325 **PREMIER ROUGE** 22 [7] A C Stewart 3-9-0 K Darley 9/2: 44: Trkd ldrs, rdn & no extra ins last: op 3/1. 1¾ 66
2627 **PALABELLE** 10 [4]3-8-9 I Mongan 20/1: 0005: b f Desert Prince - Moviegoer (Pharly) Mid-div, rdn ¾ 59
& not pace to chall fnl 2f: £80,000 purchase: related to wnrs at 6f/2m: dam a 7f 3yo scorer: apprec h'cap company.

2383 **CRONKYVODDY** 20 [10]3-9-0 t N Callan 25/1: 606: Mid-div, btn 2f out. 2½ 57
1473 **WARBRECK** 61 [8]3-9-0 J Fortune 25/1: 07: Held up, nvr a threat to ldrs, abs. 3 51
2595 **NIKIFOROS** 12 [9]3-9-0 P K Dalgleish 16/1: 068: Trkd ldrs, ch over 2f out, sn wknd & hmpd: op 12/1, abs.5 41
1688 **GUSTAVO** 50 [1]3-9-0 W Supple 25/1: 0009: Held up, rdn & btn 2f out, 7 wk abs. 3½ 34
2627 **WAY OUT** 10 [11]3-8-9 Darren Williams 100/1: 00: 10th: Mid-div, btn over 2f out. 18 0
2745 **BLUEBERRY JIM** 5 [3]3-9-0 (39) R Winston 100/1: 06000-00: 11th: Led after 1f, hdd 3f out & wknd. 6 0
11 Ran Time 1m 42.96 (2.46) Owned: Mr K Abdulla Trained: Lambourn

2887   5.20 Goose Green Handicap Stakes 3yo+ 0-80 (D)   **[80]**
£5649 £1738 £869   **1m6f**   **Good 40**   + 05 Fast   Inside

2754 **DR SHARP 5** [2] T P Tate 4-9-10 (76) J Edmunds 4/1: 114-0121: Trkd ldrs, rdn to lead over 1f out,   82
al holding rival ins last: bckd, op 7/2: qck reapp: eff at 14f/2m on gd & soft grnd: in gd heart: can win again.
2311* **MY LEGAL EAGLE 22** [3] R J Price 10-8-6 (58) Hayley Turner(5) 4/1: 1421112: In tch, rdn & hdwy to   ½   63
chall ins last, al just held: op 7/2: tough & thriving 10yo: see 2311.
2073 **SUDDEN FLIGHT 33** [5] P D Evans 7-9-1 (67) R Havlin 7/2 FAV: 0030043: Handy, rdn & edged left ins   1¼   70
last, not pace of front pair: nicely bckd: likes easy grnd: see 549.
2229 **NORTHERN NYMPH 27** [8] R Hollinshead 5-9-0 (66) Stephanie Hollinshead(5) 14/1: 0056234: Trkd ldrs,   nk   69
rdn & styd on onepace fnl 2f, not able to chall: 1 win in 24: see 743.
2737 **GENGHIS 6** [4]5-10-0 (80) J Fortune 11/2: 24/3-25: Keen & held up, eff when not room over 2f out,   3   79
switched & no hdwy ins last: nicely bckd: qck reapp: btr 2737 (12f).
2229 **NAKWA 27** [7]6-9-6 (72) D Allan 7/1: 5322126: Led till over 1f out, wknd: btr 2229 & 1923.   nk   71
2708 **SARN 7** [1]5-7-13 (1ow)(6oh) (44) R Ffrench 25/1: 0040327: Mid-div, lost pl from halfway, nvr a factor.   6   41$
2596 **RED SCORPION 12** [6]5-8-13 (65) K Darley 8/1: 1650238: Held up, rdn & no impress fnl 3f: btr 2596 (fm). 1   53
8 Ran   Time 3m 02.98(4.98)   Owned: The Ivy Syndicate   Trained: Tadcaster

Official Going GOOD/FIRM.

2888   6.45 European Breeders Fund Wellbeing Novice Stakes A Guaranteed Sweepstakes 2yo (D)
£4388 £1350 £675   **5f str**   **Good 56**   -47 Slow   Inside

2513 **MELALCHRIST 15** [4] J J Quinn 2-9-2 R Winston 7/2: 1221: Trkd ldrs, switched & hdwy to lead 1f   98
out, styd on strongly, rdn out: eff at 5f on fast & soft grnd, 6f shld suit: likes a stiff trk: tough & useful.
2513* **IMPERIAL SOUND 15** [5] T D Barron 2-9-5 S Sanders 2/5 FAV: 12: Sn hmpd & rear, hdwy to chall ent   1¼   98
fnl 1f, not pace of wnr cl-home: well bckd, clr of rem: beat today's wnr over C/D in 2513 (11lb worse today).
2670* **BOND CITY 9** [1] B Smart 2-9-2 F Lynch 7/1: 013: Chsd ldr, went on after halfway till ent fnl   3   86
1f, grad wknd: op 11/2: prob ran to form of 2670.
ZANDERIDO [3] B S Rothwell 2-8-8 Darren Williams 50/1: 4: b g Forzando - Triple Concerto   9   53
(Grand Lodge) Dwelt, al outpcd on debut: Mar 1st foal, dam lightly rcd: sire a tough 1m/9f performer.
2611* **OUR LOUIS 11** [2]2-8-7 T Eaves(3) 33/1: 605415: Led till after halfway, wknd & eased: see 2611 (sell).   2½   45
5 Ran   Time 1m 06.49 (5.19)   Owned: Mr T G S Wood   Trained: Malton

2889   7.15 Hull Mitsubishi Grandis Maiden Stakes 2yo (D)
£4687 £1442 £721   **5f str**   **Good 56**   -51 Slow   Inside

2547 **WONDERFUL MIND 14** [13] T D Easterby 2-9-0 R Winston 11/10 FAV: 0521: Chsd ldrs, went on dist,   76
styd on strongly, rdn out: well bckd & made most of fav high-draw: eff at 5f on gd, stiff/undul trk.
1237 **RASA SAYANG 76** [4] T D Barron 2-9-0 S Sanders 9/1: 02: b c Salt Lake - Annie Ruth (Gulch) Chsd   1¾   70
ldrs, kept on onepace fnl 1f, nrst fin: 11 wk abs: $20,000 Mar foal: dam a wnr in the US, sire a high-class
sprinter on dirt: eff over a stiff 5f on gd: gd run from poor draw.
CLARET AND AMBER [3] R A Fahey 2-9-0 R Ffrench 14/1: 3: b c Forzando - Artistic Licence (High   shd   70+
Top) Rear, styd on strongly fnl 1f, nrst fin on debut: 13,000 gns Feb foal: full brother to a 6/7f wnr: dam styd
12f: eff at 5f on gd, 6f will suit: v encouraging debut from a poor draw, keep in mind.
2358 **SOWERBY 21** [6] M Brittain 2-9-0 M Lawson(5) 40/1: 064: Prom, chsd wnr ent fnl 1f, sn no extra.   1   67
WAYWARD SHOT [2]2-9-0 Dale Gibson 40/1: 5: b g Desert Prince - Style Parade (Diesis) Slowly   ¾   64+
away, styd on fnl 1f, nrst fin on debut: op 8/1: 1,500 gns Mar 1st foal: dam stayed 12f: encouraging from poor low
draw, improve & apprec 6f+.
1874 **ZAROVA 43** [14]2-9-0 T Lucas 12/1: 06: gr c Zafonic - Estarova (Saint Estephe) Chsd ldrs, lost   1   61
pl halfway, rallied fnl 1f: 6 wk abs: Mar foal, cost 36,000gns: dam a mid-dist wnr in France, sire a top-class miler.
CHOREOGRAPHIC [7]2-9-0 T Hamilton(3) 8/1: 7: Slow away, late prog, nvr dngrs: debut, op 9/2.   shd   61
2513 **PAULA JO 15** [11]2-8-9 T Eaves(3) 20/1: 68: Chsd ldrs 3.5f, wknd.   nk   55
2505 **CHILALI 15** [8]2-8-9 F Lynch 7/2: 50339: Led till after halfway, wknd: gamble from 9/1: see 2505.   2   49
2360 **STAR OF KILDARE 21** [10]2-8-9 Kim Tinkler 25/1: 00: 10th: Chsd ldrs, wknd dist.   ½   48
1869 **SAMALAN 43** [5]2-9-0 G Duffield 66/1: 00: 11th: Al bhd after 6 wk abs.   6   38
CADOGEN SQUARE [12]2-8-9 Darren Williams 20/1: 0: 12th: Al bhd on debut.   2   27
EXPONENTIAL [9]2-9-0 BL e V Halliday 25/1: 0: 13th: Nvr nr ldrs on debut: wore   1½   28
blnks/eye-shield.
13 Ran   Time 1m 06.69 (5.39)   Owned: Mr T G & Mrs M E Holdcroft   Trained: Malton

2890   7.45 Aunt Bessie's Yorkshire Pudding Handicap Stakes 4yo+ 0-85 (D)   **[81]**
£6923 £2130 £1065   **1m100y rnd**   **Good 56**   + 04 Fast   Inside

2655 **CRYFIELD 10** [4] N Tinkler 7-8-3 (56) Kim Tinkler 12/1: 0624001: Went left start, hdwy from rear   66
1.5f out, strong run to lead cl-home, rdn out: gd time: eff at 6f/1m, stays 10f: likes gd & firm, acts on soft &
fibresand: handles any trk, eff with/without a visor: made most of fav h'cap mark: see 1214.
1253* **TORRID KENTAVR 74** [11] B Ellison 7-8-12 (65) R Winston 13/2: 2305-012: Held up, hdwy to chall   1   72
dist, ev ch till not pace to repel wnr cl-home: in gd form: plcd in a h'cap chase since 1253 (hvy).
2828* **LES ARCS 3** [8] R C Guest 4-9-9 (6ex) (76) J F Egan 2/1 FAV: 10-00213: Rear, hdwy to lead dist,   2½   78
collared ent fnl 1f, no extra: quick reapp & nicely bckd off 6lb pen: rtd higher on gd/soft in 2828.
2564 **IBERUS 13** [10] S Gollings 6-9-2 (69) T Eaves(3) 20/1: 05-00054: Trkd ldrs, ev ch when sltly short   nk   70
of room 2f out, held 1f out, rallied late: apprec this return to 1m, caught the eye in 1820.
2655 **TEDSDALE MAC 10** [7]5-7-12 (1oh) (50) R Ffrench 9/1: 304-0425: Chsd ldrs, led 2f out till dist, no extra.   1¼   49

2672 **TEDSTALE 9** [12]6-9-13 bl (80) S Sanders 9/2: 4-005036: Trkd ldrs, short of room 2f out , sn held.   nk   77
2768 **JUBILEE STREET 6** [9]5-8-5 (58) G Duffield 7/1: 5-043107: Keen & prom, wknd fnl 1f: qck reapp.   2   51
2087 **ATLANTIC ACE 34** [3]7-9-6 (73) F Lynch 14/1: 05-00068: Hmpd start, keen in rear, nvr dangerous: 4   58
likes to come late off a strong pace & often runs well at Goodwood: see 2087.
1748 **WUXI VENTURE 49** [2]9-8-12 (65) T Hamilton(3) 25/1: 2160-069: Hmpd start, nvr dangerous: won a   1¼   47
h'cap chase at Kelso 6 wks ago (eff at 2m/2m3f on firm & hvy, rtd 115c): see 1748.
2483 **ARAWAN 16** [5]4-8-9 (62) Dale Gibson 16/1: 4-000000: 10th: Led till 2f out, wknd: see 2483.   1½   41
2560 **BROADWAY SCORE 13** [6]9-6-8 (75) T Lucas 9/1: 0000000: 11th: Prom, led briefly 3f out, sn wknd.   2   50
2514 **ASWAN 15** [1]6-8-13 t (66) J Bramhill 20/1: 3440-530: 12th: Hmpd start, al bhd, fin last: btr 2514.   5   31
12 Ran   Time 1m 48.25 (4.45)   Owned: Mrs Andrea O'Grady   Trained: Malton

---

2891   **8.15 Westwood Barratt Homes Selling Handicap Stakes 3yo+ 35-55 (F)**   **[57]**
£3339   £954   £477   **7f100y rnd**   **Good 56**   **-05 Slow**   Inside

2630 **REDOUBTABLE 11** [8] D W Chapman 13-9-5 (48) A Culhane 7/1: 0010021: Held up, gd hdwy 2f out,   57
strong run to lead into fnl 1f, sprinted clr: no bid: eff at 6/7f, stays a sharp 1m well: acts on firm, soft & on
both AWs: 13yo, 4th success this year & clrly remains in tremendous heart: credit to connections, see 1447 & 541.
2655 **JAKEAL 10** [9] R M Whitaker 5-9-10 P (53) V Halliday 12/1: 30-04002: Tried to make all, clr 2f   2½   56
out, swamped by wnr cl-home: front rnr, back to form in cheek pieces: stays 7.5f, see 913.
2572 **SHAMWARI FIRE 13** [15] I W McInnes 4-9-7 (50) R ffrench 15/2: 0016003: Chsd ldrs, kept on under   2½   48
press but not pace to chall front 2: apprec this drop into sell grade: see 1944 (C/D, mdn clmr).
2688 **NOBLE PURSUIT 8** [13] R E Barr 7-9-6 (49) F Lynch 11/2: 3550024: Held up, styd on fnl 1f, nrst fin.   shd   47
2080 **OPEN HANDED 34** [16]4-9-12 t (55) T Eaves(3) 5/1 FAV: 6001055: Rear, rdn to improve 2f out, nrst   nk   52
fin: joint top weight, nicely bckd from 13/2: back to form of 1160 (gd/soft).
2080 **ALPINE HIDEAWAY 34** [14]11-9-4 p (47) T Hamilton(3) 14/1: 06140-06: b g Tirol - Arbour (Graustark)   ½   43
Chsd ldr, wknd fnl 1f: jumps fit, rnr-up in a sell h'cap hdle 7 days ago (rtd 91h, eff around 2m1f on firm & fast,
handles soft): '03 clmg wnr here in 2 starts: suited by 7f/1m on firm, gd/soft grnd &
fibresand: wears a cheek pieces, likes Beverley. 1 Aug'03 Beve 8.5gd 45-(36) E:
2508 **CELTIC ROMANCE 15** [4]5-9-3 (46) J Carroll 14/1: 0005067: Swerved start, hdwy wide 2f out, nvr nrr.   ½   41
2338 **DELIGHTFUL GIFT 22** [5]4-9-2 (45) M Lawson(5) 50/1: 0640-608: Nvr btr than mid-div: see 2338.   nk   39
2812 **KILLERBY NICKO 4** [2]3-8-13 bl (50) S Sanders 12/1: 0605U39: Chsd ldrs, btn dist: quick reapp.   ¾   42
2655 **MAUREEN ANN 10** [11]4-9-12 (51) J Bramhill 12/1: 10000-00: 10th: Chsd ldrs, btn 2f out: joint   hd   47
top weight: dropped in grade & more expected after 2655 (C/D).
2288 **CLANN A COUGAR 24** [12]4-9-12 bl (55) G Duffield 9/1: 4-006000: 11th: Slowly away, al bhd.   3   41
2402 **CANLIS 20** [1]5-9-4 (47) R Winston 12/1: 0000-020: 12th: Nvr btr than mid-div: btr 2402.   2   29
2755 **Moonlight Song 6** [10]7-9-1 BL(44) L Fletcher(3) 33/1:0
4136] **Splodger Mac 297** [7]5-9-0 (43) Suzanne France(7) 25/1:0
2384 **Dasar 21** [3]4-9-5 vis(48) Darren Williams 25/1:0   2687 **Eastern Dagger 8** [6]4-9-5 (48) R Fitzpatrick 28/1:0
16 Ran   Time 1m 35.41 (4.61)   Owned: Mr David W Chapman   Trained: York

---

2892   **8.45 Ferguson Fawsitt Arms Handicap Stakes 3yo+ 0-70 (E)**   **[66]**
£4550   £1400   £700   **1m4f16y**   **Good 56**   **-20 Slow**   Inside

2526 **SUALDA 15** [8] R A Fahey 5-9-10 (62) T Hamilton(3) 7/2 CO FAV: 0500-521: Trkd ldrs, imprvd to   69
chall dist, went on ent fnl 1f, held on well, drvn out: top weight: eff at 1m, suited by 10/12f: acts on gd &
firm, sharp/turning or gall trk: gd weight carrier, made most of fav h'cap mark: see 2526 & 2285.
2601 **RED RIVER REBEL 12** [4] J R Norton 6-9-3 (55) Darren Williams 7/2 CO FAV: 340-0402: Led till ent   nk   61
fnl 1f, rallied & only just btn: op 9/2, clr of rem: fine run at fav course, loves to front run & shld be wng sn.
2875 **ESCALADE 1** [10] W M Brisbourne 7-9-0 p (52) A Culhane 11/2: 04054343: Chsd ldrs, onepcd fnl 1f: 5   50
op 9/2: fin 4th at Newbury yesterday: see 2875 & 2718.
2850 **LITTLE TASK 2** [6] J S Wainwright 6-8-6 (6ex) (44) R ffrench 10/1: 5-314104: Held up, hdwy 3f out,   2   39
onepcd fnl 1.5f: quick reapp: see 2616.
2562 **EAST CAPE 13** [9]7-8-5 (43) Kim Tinkler 9/1: 1000635: Rear, prog 2f out, sn no impress.   ½   37
2653* **LIFE IS BEAUTIFUL 10** [2]5-9-4 (6ex) (56) R Winston 7/2 CO FAV: 10-61516: Chsd ldrs, btn dist: btr 2653.   3   45
534 **DUBAI DREAMS 150** [7]4-9-1 (53) J Bramhill 16/1: 40-42507: Chsd ldrs 9f, wknd: long abs & new stable.   1¼   40
2244 **CYBER SANTA 27** [1]6-8-7 (45) Dale Gibson 16/1: 32430/-68: Rear, imprvd halfway, btn 2f out.   6   23
2545 **ROYAL MELBOURNE 14** [3]4-9-2 (54) J Carroll 20/1: 000-1609: Slow away, prog to chall halfway, wknd.   23   2
9 Ran   Time 2m 40.50 (9.20)   Owned: Mr J H Tattersall   Trained: Malton

---

2893   **9.15 William Jackson Bakery Stakes Handicap Fillies 3yo 0-70 (E)**   **[75]**
£3770   £1160   £580   **1m1f207y**   **Good 56**   **-19 Slow**   Inside

2773 **MISS ELOISE 6** [12] T D Easterby 3-8-10 (57) A Mullen(7) 11/2: 52-62601: Chsd ldrs, prog 2f out,   66
led ins fnl 1f, drvn out: op 7/1: eff at 1m, styd this longer 10f trip well: acts on firm & soft, handles a stiff trk.
2706 **PRINCIPESSA 8** [9] B Palling 3-9-4 (65) A Culhane 5/2 FAV: 3-500022: Prom, led dist till ins fnl   nk   72
1f, rallied & only just btn: nicely bckd, clr of rem: knocking on the door, see 2706.
2314 **AESCULUS 23** [7] L M Cumani 3-9-4 (67) Dale Gibson 11/2: 51-05303: Trkd ldrs, onepcd fnl 1f: op   4   68
9/2: much longer 10f trip, see 2034 (5.5f).
2617 **QUEEN LUCIA 11** [10] J G Given 3-8-11 (58) Darren Williams 10/1: 44454: Led till dist, no extra.   2   56
1835 **ADEES DANCER 45** [6]3-8-11 (58) D McGaffin 33/1: 4-005: b f Danehill Dancer - Note (Reliance II)   2½   52
Rear, imprvd to chase ldrs 2f out, sn onepcd: 6 wk abs: h'cap bow: mdn 4th on sole '03 start.
2706 **INMOM 8** [2]3-8-11 (58) J Bramhill 25/1: 50-30466: Chsd ldrs wide, onepcd fnl 2f.   ½   51
2503 **NODS STAR 15** [8]3-7-12 (45) R ffrench 22/1: 50007: Rear, nvr nr ldrs.   1¾   36
2565 **ROYAL DISTANT 13** [5]3-9-7 (68) T Lucas 30/1: 4480008: Nvr a factor under top weight.   1¾   57
2536 **SPRING ADIEU 14** [11]3-9-5 (66) S Sanders 7/2: 00-49: b f Green Desert - Nanda (Nashwan) Chsd   shd   55
ldrs, btn 2f out on h'cap bow: unplcd both juv mdn starts: 75,000gns purchase, dam a 10f wnr: with Miss A Perrett.
2503 **PRAIRIE SUN 15** [13]3-8-10 VIS (57) G Duffield 8/1: 4451000: 10th: Nvr a factor in 1st time visor.   3   41
2693 **CHICAGO BOND 8** [3]3-9-4 (65) F Lynch 25/1: 54360-000: 11th: Keen & chsd ldrs wide, btn 4f out.   16   24
2169 **WEDOWANNAGIVEUTHAT 30** [4]3-8-8 (55) R Winston 20/1: 0060: 12th: Chsd ldrs 1m, wknd.   3½   9
12 Ran   Time 2m 09.82(7.52)   Owned: Slatch Farm Stud   Trained: Malton

Official Going GOOD/SOFT.

2894   2.05 Friends Of Jonathan Cooper Rated Stakes Handicap 3yo+ 0-95 (C)   [102]
£9651 £2970 £1485   5f6y str   Good/Soft 81   -06 Slow   Far Side

2779 **WHISTLER 5** [9] J M Bradley 7-8-10 (3ex)p (84) R Hills 13/2: 0103101: Held up, switched left 2f   95
out, styd on strongly to lead ins last, rdn, shade cosily: suited by 5f, stays 6f on firm, soft & any trk: v tough,
thriving this term & has a turn of foot from the rear: gets on v well wiht R Hills, see 2189.
2253 **TALBOT AVENUE 27** [3] M Mullineaux 6-8-7 (1oh) (80) P Dobbs 10/1: 00-05502: Held up, hdwy outer 2f   1¼   87
out, ev ch ins last, outpcd by wnr cl-home: continues to run well & acts on firm & gd/soft: likes York: see 1917.
2727 **CORRIDOR CREEPER 7** [2] J M Bradley 7-9-3 p (91) D Holland 5/1: 4426023: Handy, hdwy to lead   1¾   93
briefly just ins last, sn hdd & no extra: tough: see 2727, 1594.
2359 **CONNECT 21** [10] M H Tompkins 7-8-12 bl (86) P Robinson 5/1: 006-2404: Handy, onepace over 1f out.   2   83
2727 **MATTY TUN 7** [5]5-9-2 (90) R Hughes 8/1: 0550005: In tch, hdwy to lead 2f out, sn hung right, hdd   1   85
& wknd ins last: see 1479.
2082 **ABSENT FRIENDS 34** [11]7-9-4 (92) J Edmunds 20/1: 500-0606: Handy, led halfway till 2f out, wknd.   ½   86
2256 **MALAPROPISM 27** [6]4-8-10 (84) T E Durcan 12/1: 001-6007: Slow away & nvr a factor: see 1845.   1¼   75
2698 **KATHOLOGY 8** [7]7-8-8 (82) K Fallon 7/1: 530-0608: With ldrs, wknd 2f out: see 2253.   5   63
2421 **REPERTORY 19** [8]11-9-7 (95) T G McLaughlin 16/1: 0-000069: Led to halfway, wknd: 11yo.   nk   75
2359 **HENRY HALL 21** [12]8-9-6 (94) Kim Tinkler 8/1: 3-303030: 10th: Al bhd: something amiss? btr 2359.   5   64
2421 **LITTLE EDWARD 19** [1]6-9-4 (92) T Quinn 12/1: 5050050: 11th: Rcd alone stands side, al bhd: 8   46
strange tactics, far side usually favoured: best giving weight in small fields: see 1845.
11 Ran   Time 1m 03.96 (4.36)   Owned: Mr Raymond Tooth   Trained: Chepstow

2895   2.40 Listed Dragon Stakes 2yo (A)
£14875 £5500 £2750   5f6y str   Good/Soft 81   -27 Slow   Far Side

2763 **POLLY PERKINS 6** [1] N P Littmoden 2-9-0   J P Guillambert 8/1: 11001: Held up, gd hdwy 2f out,   106
led appr fnl 1f, drvn clr, readily: relished rtn to 5f & acts on fast & gd/soft: likes Sandown (gd turn of foot on
both starts to date here): v useful, see 2094.
2646* **SOUTHERN AFRICA 10** [3] G A Butler 2-8-12   R Hughes 9/4: 12: Handy, hdwy over 1f out, chsd wnr   8   88
ins last, no impress: well bckd: prob handles firm & gd/soft: more to come, see 2646.
2516 **EMPIRES GHODHA 15** [2] B J Meehan 2-8-12 bl   J Fortune 10/1: 5323153: Chsd ldrs, hdwy to lead over   1¾   84
1f out, sn hdd & no extra: tough, needs ease in grade: see 2516, 2415 (mdn auct, firm grnd).
2490 **BUNDITTEN 16** [4] Andrew Reid 2-8-10   J F Egan 3/1: 1344: Led till over 1f out, wknd: well bckd: 2   78
not handle easy ground: btr 2490, 2094 (fast grnd).
2490 **LADY FILLY 16** [5]2-8-10   A Daly 15/8 FAV: 11105: In tch, wknd over 2f out: well bckd: well   7   64
below best, handled gd/soft well earlier & surely capable of btr: see 2490, 1499 (made all).
5 Ran   Time 1m 05.0 (5.4)   Owned: Miss Vanessa Church   Trained: Newmarket

2896   3.15 Action Online Casino Summer Stakes Handicap 3yo+ 0-105 (B)   [102]
£17400 £6600 £3300   1m2f7y   Good/Soft 81   -07 Slow   Inside

2392* **SILVALINE 20** [1] T Keddy 5-8-0 (74) C Haddon(7) 7/1: 5506011: In tch, hdwy to lead over 2f out,   84
styd on strongly, rdn out: bckd: all wins at 10f, stays 12f on fast, gd/soft & polytrack: v tough & in fine heart.
2582 **PRINCE NUREYEV 13** [3] B R Millman 4-8-13 (87) K Fallon 7/1: 440-0002: Held up, hdwy to chase wnr   2½   93
2f out, not pace of wnr fnl 1f: much btr run & h'capped to win shortly: see 1704.
2208 **SHAHZAN HOUSE 28** [8] M A Jarvis 5-9-8 p (96) P Robinson 9/4 FAV: 410-3233: Set pace till over 2f   ¾   100
out, kept on same pace: well bckd: another consistent run: see 2208, 1296.
2560 **STRETTON 13** [11] J D Bethell 6-8-6 (80) T Quinn 5/1: 0-060034: Held up, eff dist, no impress.   ½   83
2246 **FINE PALETTE 27** [10]4-8-13 (87) W Ryan 11/2: 2-1155: Keen held up, eff & hung right over 1f out,   1½   88
sn no extra: nicely bckd: see 1828.
2556 **FOODBROKER FOUNDER 14** [7]4-9-10 (98) K Darley 16/1: 0200-066: Trkd ldr, wknd 2f out: see 1862.   ½   98
2407 **NEROS RETURN 20** [4]3-8-10 (95) K Dalgleish 25/1: 11-60607: Handy, wknd 2f out: see 1113 (1m).   shd   95
2556 **MILLAFONIC 14** [9]4-9-7 VIS (95) D Holland 6/1: 1150-608: In tch, wknd 2f out: tried a visor: btr 2101.   1¾   92
2404 **DEFINITE GUEST 20** [6]6-8-8 (82) Martin Dwyer 16/1: 3565-309: In tch, wknd 2f out: see 2207.   1¾   76
9 Ran   Time 2m 12.9 (8.8)   Owned: Mr Andrew Duffield   Trained: Newmarket

2897   3.45 European Breeders Fund Maiden Stakes 2yo (D)
£6357 £1956 £978   7f16y rnd   Good/Soft 81   -32 Slow   Inside

2388 **MELROSE AVENUE 20** [1] M Johnston 2-9-0   K Dalgleish 11/4 FAV: 51: Made all, clr 3f out, pushed   86
out, unchall: well bckd: enjoyed front running & stays 7f well, 1m sure to suit: acts on gd/soft: more to come.
GROUND RULES [5] B W Hills 2-9-0   R Hughes 3/1: 2: b c Boundary - Gombeen (Private Account)   6   73+
Held up, hdwy to chase wnr 2f out, too much to do, hands-and-heels: nicely bckd on debut: Mar foal: eff at 7f, 1m
will suit in time: prob handles gd/soft: nice intro but gave wnr too much rope, improve.
ROAD TO HEAVEN [4] E A L Dunlop 2-9-0   T Quinn 12/1: 3: ch c Southern Halo - Glory Way   8   59
(Woodman) Chsd ldrs, brief eff 2f out, no impress on debut: Mar first foal, cost $110,000: bred to stay 7f/1m.
OFF COLOUR [3] Mrs A J Perrett 2-9-0   K Darley 4/1: 4: b c Rainbow Quest - Air of Distinction   2   56
(Distinctly North) Chsd wnr, wknd 2f out on debut: Apr foal: brother to a 1m wnr: dam high-class 6f juv scorer.
ALMANSHOOD [7]2-9-0   R Hills 7/2: 5: Slow away & bhd, nvr a factor on debut.   ¾   54
SPILL A LITTLE [6]2-9-0   T E Durcan 16/1: 6: In tch, wknd over 2f out in debut.   2   51
TUMBLEWEED GALORE [2]2-9-0   J Fortune 20/1: 7: In tch, wknd 2f out on debut.   1¼   48
7 Ran   Time 1m 34.31 (7.91)   Owned: Sheikh Mohammed   Trained: Middleham

SANDOWN   FRIDAY 02.07.04   Righthand, Galloping Track, Stiff Finish

2898
4.20 Listed Champagne J Lassalle Imported By O W Loeb Gala Stakes 3yo+   (A)
£17400 £6600 £3300   1m2f7y   Good/Soft 81   +12 Fast   Inside

2520 **CROCODILE DUNDEE** 15 [3] Jamie Poulton 3-8-8 (105) J F Egan 7/1: 5-063221: Keen, in tch, gd hdwy   **112**
to lead over 1f out, styd on strongly ins last, drvn out: gd time: eff over 10/11f on fm, gd/soft & polytrack:
gradual improvement & smart now, gameness shld reap further success.

2143 **SILENCE IS GOLDEN** 32 [2] B J Meehan 5-9-0 (100) J Fortune 7/1: 325-1202: Held up, rcd wide, hdwy   nk **106**
over 2f out, chall dist, kept on for press, just held by most game wnr: in foal & in grand heart: win a mares List.

2128 **SUNSTRACH** 31 [5] L M Cumani 6-9-5 (112) J Murtagh 85/40 FAV: 103-3433: Led after 2f, rdn & hdd   3   **107**
over 1f out, no extra ins last: reportedly fin lame but far from disgraced: see 2128, 1350.

2470 **ALKAADHEM** 17 [8] M P Tregoning 4-9-8 (108) R Hills 100/30: 21-54104: Handy, eff 2f out, sn no   3   **106**
extra: bckd: prob prefers a sounder surface as in 1862 (gd/firm).

2252 **DUTCH GOLD** 27 [7]4-9-5 bl (110) D Holland 9/2: 0200525: Chsd ldr after 3f till 3f out, wknd over   1½ **101**
1f out: does not enjoy easy grnd & worth another ch on a sound surface after promising eff in 2252, see 1705.

2556 **COMPTON BOLTER** 14 [4]7-9-8 (109) R Hughes 7/1: 5032506: Led 2f, wknd over 2f out: reportedly   3½ **99**
unsuited by easy grnd & stable remain out of sorts: see 2556, 1862.

4760} **WEECANDOO** 260 [6]6-9-0 (90) G Carter 33/1: 133154-7: b f Turtle Island - Romantic Air (He Loves   25 **51**
Me) Al bhd, t.o. on reappr: '03 mdn & dual h'cap wnr: stays 12f, all 3 wins at 10f: likes fast & gd: handles both
AWs, any trk: has run well fresh: needs h'caps.

1 Aug'03 Asco 10g/f 83-75 C: 1 Jun'03 Sand 10ap g/f 66-60 C: 2 May'03 Ling 10ap 65a-62 E: 1 Jan'03 Ling 10ap 60a- D:
2 Dec'02 Ling 10ap 66a-63 E: 2 Sep'01 Sand 9gd 81- D:
7 Ran   Time 2m 10.99 (6.89)   Owned: Mr R W Huggins   Trained: Lewes

2899
4.50 Sundown At Sandown Handicap Stakes 3yo+ 0-90 (C)   **[89]**
£9750 £3000 £1500   1m6f   Good/Soft 81   -28 Slow   Centre

2685 **QUEDEX** 8 [7] R J Price 8-8-3 (64) J F McDonald(3) 4/1: 5/06-1521: Handy, hdwy to lead 2f out,   **74**
pushed clr fnl 1f, readily: bckd: eff over 2m/2m2f on firm or soft grnd, any trk: tough, revitalised this term by a
spell over timber & looks like more to come: see 2685.

2391 **MR ED** 20 [5] P Bowen 6-9-0 p (75) D Corby(3) 7/2 FAV: 26000-22: Dwelt, held up rear, plenty to do   7   **77**
over 2f out but hdwy well over 1f out, onepace fnl 1f & eased cl-home: well bckd: fine run: tough & in form (3m
h'cap hdle wnr 9 days ago): wld benefit from being rdn more positively: see 2391.

2596 **THEATRE** 13 [3] Jamie Poulton 5-9-8 (83) P Doe 9/1: 04-0S223: Dwelt, held up, hdwy over 2f out,   shd **85**
kept on same pace: proving consistent: handles firm, gd/soft & polytrack: see 2073 (2m).

2699 **REDSPIN** 8 [10] J S Moore 4-8-7 (68) Martin Dwyer 14/1: 2-300444: Cl-up, led 3f out till 2f out, wknd. 5   **65**

2538 **SERGEANT CECIL** 14 [6]5-9-11 (86) K Fallon 7/1: 1020-035: Keen, handy, wknd over 1f out: won   5   **78**
this race last term off a 4lb lower mark, prob pref faster grnd: see 2538.

1742* **TWOFAN** 49 [9]3-8-6 (82) S Chin 5/1: 2216: Led till 3f out, wknd over 1f out: shade more   nk **74**
expected after mdn win on soft grnd 7 wks ago: see 1742 (made all).

2737 **FLOTTA** 7 [2]5-9-7 (82) T E Durcan 6/1: 4504437: In tch, wknd over 2f out: btr 2737, 877 (AW).   10 **64**
7 Ran   Time 3m 10.31(15.31)   Owned: Fox and Cub Partnership   Trained: Hereford

HAYDOCK   FRIDAY 02.07.04   Lefthand, Flat, Galloping Track

Official Going GOOD

2900
7.00 Dave And Debbie Watkins Wedding Anniversary Apprentice Handicap Stakes 3yo+ 0-85 (E) [84]
£3471 £1068 £534   1m3f200y   Good 52   -15 Slow   Outside

2794 **SMART JOHN** 4 [8] W M Brisbourne 4-8-7 (63) B Swarbrick 5/2 J FAV: 50-41421: Held up, smooth hdwy   **72**
to lead over 1f out, sn rdn clr: quick reappr: eff at 10/12f on fast & gd/soft grnd, likes Haydock: improving.

2546* **MERRYMAKER** 14 [4] W M Brisbourne 4-8-4 (60) P Mathers(3) 6/1: 3-464P12: Held up, rdn & outpcd 3f   4   **62**
out, styd on well for press ins last, nearest fin: completed stable 1-2: apprec return to 13f+.

1000 **YANKEEDOODLEDANDY** 93 [9] P C Haslam 3-8-6 (75) Rory Moore(3) 5/2 J FAV: 1212123: Handy, outpcd 1¼   **75**
3f out, kept on onepace after: see 1000 & 796.

1389 **SPREE VISION** 67 [3] P Monteith 8-7-12 (1oh)vis (53) D Fentiman(3) 16/1: 0360/-604: Led/dsptd lead   nk **53**
till over 3f out, no extra dist: jumps fit (unplcd): see 1278.

2113* **ALWAYS WAINING** 32 [7]3-9-2 (85) W Hogg(5) 13/2: 3315: Saddle slipped early, led/dsptd lead till   nk **83**
over 1f out, eased when btn nr fin: jockey did well in circumstances, this best forgiven after 2113 (mdn).

2673 **MILLENNIUM HALL** 9 [2]5-8-12 (68) D Tudhope(3) 9/1: 6331106: Dwelt, held up in tch, smooth hdwy &   7   **55**
chall over 2f out, sn hung left & btn when no room ins last: twice well below 2479 (Hamilton).

2401 **COLOPHONY** 20 [5]4-9-4 t (74) P Makin 16/1: 3216-047: Chsd ldrs till 3f out: btr 2401.   1½ **59**

2567 **PRINCE HOLING** 13 [1]4-10-0 t (84) R Thomas 20/1: 4122-508: Led 1f, remained handy, btn 2f out.   21 **38**

2567 **LORD DUNDEE** 13 [6]6-9-8 T (78) A Reilly(5) 40/1: 3/1/-09: Held up & no ch fnl 3f: 1st time t-strap.   dist **0**
9 Ran   Time 2m 35.85 (8.05)   Owned: Mr & Mrs D J Smart   Trained: Nesscliffe

2901
7.30 Merchant Rentals Plc Claiming Stakes 3-4yo (D)
£7833 £2410 £1205   1m2f120y   Good 52   -26 Slow   Outside

2526 **JIMMY BYRNE** 15 [9] B Ellison 4-9-6 (67) S Drowne 5/1: 0410561: Handy & led over 1f out, rdn out: **58**
cheek pieces omitted after latest: suited to firm, gd, tried 12f latest: acts on firm & soft, handles hvy, gall trks.

534 **ALLIED VICTORY** 150 [5] E J Alston 4-10-0 (69) J Murtagh 10/1: 324-1002: Keen & handy, rdn & kept   1¼ **62**
on, not pace of wnr: 5 month abs: back to form dropped in class: see 334 (AW mdn).

2010 **TAGULA BLUE** 37 [1] J A Glover 4-9-7 BL t (78) Dean McKeown 16/1: 006-U0R3: Reluctant to race &   nk **54**
lost around 10L start, sn in tch racing keenly, hdwy to chall when bmpd over 2f out: carried head awkwardly & no
extra ins last: 1st time blnks, lkd a v hard ride: has ability but one to tread carefully with: see 2010 & 1525.

2706 **ILE FACILE 8** [8] N P Littmoden 3-8-10 (69) T P Queally(3) 5/2 J FAV: 2410204: Handy & led over 3f   nk   54
out till over 1f out, no extra: clr rem: btr 2277.
2365 **GO SOLO 21** [2]3-8-12 (77) M Hills 5/2 J FAV: 516-0335: Held up, no room over 3f out & badly hmpd   5   48+
over 2f out, no ch after: luckless run, closer with a clr passage: see 2365 & 1825 (1m).
2504 **CHARLIE GEORGE 15** [7]3-8-8 D Fentiman(7) 80/1: 06: Slow away, held up in tch, eff over 2f out, sn btn.   nk   43
2582 **NOPEKAN 13** [4]4-9-12 (89) P Makin(5) 9/2: 606-5607: Mid-div, rdn & btn 2f out: see 2582.   shd   48
2504 **HOLLYWOOD CRITIC 15** [10]3-8-8 G Faulkner 50/1: 08: Held up, btn 2f out.   nk   41
4164} **RED MOUNTAIN 296** [6]3-9-2 L Enstone(3) 50/1: 0-9: b c Unfuwain - Red Cascade (Danehill) Led   14   28
till over 3f out, sn struggling: unplcd sole '03 start (rtd 55, mdn).
9 Ran   Time 2m 18.22 (8.22)   Owned: Mr Keith Middleton   Trained: Malton

---

| **2902** | 8.00 Mtb Group Maiden Auction Stakes 2yo (E) | | | | |
| | £3809 £1172 £586 | **6f str** | **Good 52** | **-18 Slow** | Centre |

2281 **HARVEST WARRIOR 24** [12] T D Easterby 2-8-9 D Allan 100/30 J FAV: 221: Sn handy & led 2f out,   97+
rdn clr from dist, decisively: eff at 5f, imprvd for step up to 6f & shld stay further: potentially useful: see 2281.
2236 **MALINSA BLUE 27** [13] J A Glover 2-8-2 J Quinn 4/1: 622: Chsd ldrs, eff to chase wnr over 1f   5   75
out, no impress ins last: see 2236.
SAMBARINA 0 [6] C G Cox 2-8-6 R Smith 33/1: 3: b f Victory Note - Brazilia (Forzando) Sn trkd   2   73
ldrs, shaken up & kept on from over 1f out, no threat to wnr: encouraging intro: E46,000 Feb foal, half sister to a
multiple 7f h'cap wnr Santisima Trinidad: eff at 6f on gd, 7f will suit: improve.
2646 **BOUNTY QUEST 10** [3] R Hannon 2-8-9 Dane O'Neill 100/30 J FAV: 34: Chsd ldrs, no impress dist.   1   73
SEAMLESS 0 [9]2-8-11 M Hills 11/2: 5: b c Gold Away - Fallara (Tropular) Held up, eff 2f out,   1¼   71
not pace to chall: 40,000 gns 2yo purchase, a Mar 1st foal, dam a 15f wnr: need further.
1816 **SHUJUNE AL HAWAA 45** [10]2-8-6 S Hitchcott(3) 9/1: 56: Mid-div, outpcd halfway, kept on late, no dngr.   nk   65
2569 **UNION JACK JACKSON 13** [2]2-8-9 M Fenton 18/1: 47: Good speed & led till 2f out, no extra.   1   65
BLAISE HOLLOW 0 [5]2-8-9 S Drowne 20/1: 8: b c Woodman - Castellina (Danzig Connection) Slow   1½   60
away & bhd, late prog, nvr factor: weak in mkt: 25,000 gns Apr foal, half brother to a 1m juv wnr.
PETERS DELITE 0 [4]2-8-11 G Parkin 33/1: 9: Al outpcd & nvr factor.   nk   61
1458 **TIFFIN DEANO 63** [7]2-8-7 Rory Moore(7) 33/1: 500: 10th: Mid-div, outpcd from halfway.   ¾   55
2618 **PEPPERMINT TEA 11** [1]2-8-4 J Mackay 14/1: 00: 11th: Mid-div, no impress fnl 2f.   7   31
GALLEGO 0 [11]2-8-9 F Norton 66/1: 0: 12th: Slow away & sn outpcd.   14   0
12 Ran   Time 1m 15.5 (4.2)   Owned: Mr & Mrs W J Williams   Trained: Malton

---

| **2903** | 8.30 John Suffield Memorial Rated Stakes Handicap 3yo+ 0-95 (C) | | | | [110] |
| | £8857 £3359 £1680 | **1m30y rnd** | **Good 52** | **+09 Fast** | Inside |

4683} **PRIMUS INTER PARES 265** [10] J R Fanshawe 3-8-13 (95) J Murtagh 11/1: 312-1: b c Sadler's Wells -   104+
Life At The Top (Habitat) Mid-div wide, rdn & hdwy to lead ins last, rdn, going away: fast time:, reapp: mdn scorer
'03: eff at 7f/1m on fast, gd & polytrack, further will suit: goes well fresh: useful, lightly rcd & prog, one to
keep on your side. 2 Oct'03 Asco 7gd 95- C: 1 Sep'03 Newm 7g/f 95- D:
1664 **HELLO ITS ME 52** [5] H J Collingridge 3-8-3 (4oh) (85) J Quinn 16/1: 331-202: Handy, rdn/bmpd over   1½   88
1f out, drvn & kept on, not pace of wnr: eff at 1m/10f: back to best on sound surface: see 1192.
2662 **CONSONANT 9** [7] D G Bridgwater 7-9-2 (89) D Nolan(3) 6/1 J FAV: 1106023: Chsd ldrs & led over 1f   ½   91
out, hdd ins last, kept on: see 2662, 758.
2406 **SEWNSO CHARACTER 20** [4] M Blanshard 3-8-13 (95) F Norton 6/1 J FAV: 225-4034: Trkd ldrs, bmpd   1½   94
over 1f out, kept on ins last: see 2406, 1583.
2753* **ODDSMAKER 6** [13]3-8-4 (3ex)(3oh) (86) Dean McKeown 8/1: 3251015: Keen & led till over 1f out.   hd   84
2489 **FLIGHTY FELLOW 16** [9]4-9-7 bl (94) J Fortune 16/1: 22-06106: Held up, eff when short of room over   1   90
1f out, kept on late: no luck, rate higher: see 1833.
2777 **MYSTERINCH 5** [3]4-9-4 (91) J Fanning 8/1: 1/3-30027: Held up, no room over 2f out, mod late   ¾   85
prog, short of room when no impress well ins last: see 2777 & 1225.
2250 **ALEKHINE 27** [8]3-8-4 (3oh) (86) R L Moore 9/1: 16-2308: Mid-div, eff fnl 2f, not able to chall: btr 2040.   ½   79
2679 **CRAIOVA 9** [2]5-8-11 (84) M Hills 16/1: 50-00009: Mid-div, eff from over 2f out, no extra when   ½   76
short of room well ins last: see 2172.
2560* **INTRICATE WEB 13** [1]8-8-10 (83) D Allan 12/1: 0133010: 10th: Held up, no room over 2f out, no   1   73
impress: needs further: see 2560.
2853 **BORREGO 2** [12]4-8-7 (2oh) (78) T P Queally(3) 14/1: 112-2060: 11th: Mid-div, btn dist: btr 2235.   1¾   66
2487 **STARBECK 16** [11]6-8-13 (86) N Callan 25/1: 0-005400: 12th: Al bhd: see 1620.   3   66
452 **TRAVELLING BAND 163** [6]6-8-7 (80) L Keniry(3) 33/1: 0/0024-00: 13th: b g Blues Traveller - Kind   ¾   58
of Cute (Prince Sabo) Sn bhd & nvr factor: 03/04 nov hdle wnr (2m, gd/soft grnd, rtd 116h at best): class stks
rnr-up '03, sand unplcd (rtd 42a, h'cap): mdn & val h'cap wnr '02: eff at 1m on fast, gd/soft & a stiff/undul trk.
2 Apr'03 Wind 10.0g/s 80-(80) D: 1 Jun'02 Carl 8g/f 83-75 D: 1 Jun'02 Chep 8g/s 83- D:
2242* **BISHOPRIC 27** [14]4-9-7 VIS (94) Dane O'Neill 8/1: 41-010: 14th: Prom, ch 2f out, fdd: visor: btr 2242.   nk   71
14 Ran   Time 1m 43.97 (3.47)   Owned: Colin Davey Racing   Trained: Newmarket

---

| **2904** | 9.00 Ocs Handicap Stakes Fillies 3yo 0-80 (D) | | | | [83] |
| | £5951 £1831 £916 | **1m30y rnd** | **Good 52** | **-25 Slow** | Inside |

2425 **KEEPERS LODGE 19** [4] B A McMahon 3-8-11 (66) G Gibbons 20/1: 504-4001: ch f Grand Lodge -   72
Gembira (Alysheba) Chsd ldrs, drvn to lead well ins last: unplcd '03 (rtd 77, fill mdn): now suited by 1m on gd
grnd & a gall trk: first win tonight.
2496 **EBORACUM 16** [5] T D Easterby 3-8-5 (60) D Allan 22/1: 4520-002: Trkd ldrs, led over 2f out, rdn   ½   66
& hdd well ins last: acts on fast & gd grnd: see 2166.
2624 **PELLA 11** [3] M Blanshard 3-8-6 (61) F Norton 5/1: 006253: Held up, eff over 2f out, drvn & styd   2½   62
on, not pace to chall: acts on fast & gd grnd: see 2153.
2634 **VIOLET AVENUE 11** [6] J G Given 3-8-4 (59) M Fenton 20/1: 204-064: Keen in mid-div, styd on   nk   59
onepace for press fnl 2f: stays a gall 1m: see 1896.
2385 **BLUE DAZE 20** [1]3-8-13 (68) R Smith 8/1: 01-0055: Mid-div, onepace fnl 2f: just btr 2385.   2½   63
2366 **NIGHT FROLIC 21** [10]3-8-10 (65) M Hills 7/1: 00-1306: Led till 2f out, fdd: see 1953 & 1514.   2½   55
1515 **BAFFLE 60** [12]3-9-7 (76) J Murtagh 100/30 FAV: 026-157: Handy wide, wknd over 1f out: see 1108.   2½   61

HAYDOCK FRIDAY 02.07.04 Lefthand, Flat, Galloping Track

2546 **GAIETY GIRL 14** [11]3-8-5 (60) R Mullen 14/1: 430-0658: Trkd ldrs, btn 2f out: see 2277.	1	43
4229} **BEAUTY OF DREAMS 293** [9]3-9-5 (74) S Hitchcott(3) 20/1: 224150-9: b f Russian Revival - Giggleswick Girl (Full Extent) Mid-div, btn 2f out: reapp: mdn scorer '03: eff at 5/6f: acts on firm & gd/soft grnd, stiff/undul or gall trk. 1 Jul'03 Beve 5g's 70- D: 2 Jun'03 Pont 6g/f 75- D: 2 Jun'03 Newb 6.0fm 78- D:	1	55
1762*)**HI DARL 401** [2]3-8-1 (56) B Swarbrick(5) 33/1: 641-0: 10th: ch f Wolfhound - Sugar Token (Record Token) Mid-div, btn 2f out: reapp/h'cap bow: sell wnr in '03 (lightly rcd, J G Given, rtd 60 & 53a): winning form at 6f: acts on fast grnd: eff in sell grade. 1 May'03 Yarm 6.0g/f 62- G:	3	31
2590 **FLAME QUEEN 13** [8]3-9-2 (71) S Drowne 20/1: 002-00: 11th: Slow away & al bhd: longer trip.	shd	45
2427 **POPPYS FOOTPRINT 19** [7]3-9-6 (75) N Callan 5/1: 005340P: Unruly stalls, slow away & al bhd, p.u.		0
12 Ran Time 1m 46.7 (6.2) Owned: Mr W D McClennon Trained: Tamworth		

2905 9.30 Steve Vincent 30th Birthday Handicap Stakes 3yo 0-70 (E) [71]
£3757 £1156 £578 **1m6f** Good 52 -10 Slow Inside

2345 **EUIPPE 22** [6] J G Given 3-9-3 (60) M Fenton 33/1: 456-051: Trkd ldrs, rdn & led over 2f out, rdn clr & eased nr fin, val 5L+: first win: suited by 14f, shapes as a thorough stayer: handles fast grnd, reportedly relished gd grnd tonight: see 1976.		70
2346* **WINSLOW BOY 22** [5] C F Wall 3-9-1 (58) J Quinn 10/1: 00-04612: Mid-div, eff to chase wnr over 1f out, al well held: stays 14f: acts on fast & gd grnd: see 2346.	3½	62
1444 **PRINCESS KIOTTO 64** [18] T D Easterby 3-8-12 (55) D Allan 50/1: 000-523: Switched start & bhd, styd on for press fnl 3f, nrst fin: stays 14f: acts on fibresand & gd grnd: shapes as a thorough stayer, set plenty to do from difficult high draw & can be expected to improve: see 1444 & 1178.	2½	55+
1965 **PENNY STALL 39** [11] J L Dunlop 3-9-5 (62) R L Moore 11/1: 044-04: b f Silver Patriarch - Madiyla (Darshaan) Mid-div, drvn & styd on fnl 2f, no threat: dual mdn 4th in '03 (lightly rcd, rtd 67): apprec step up to 14f, 2m+ looks likely to suit: acts on gd & fast tho' reportedly unsuited by the latter: keep in mind over further.	1	60+
2528 **ZALDA 15** [14]3-9-7 (64) S Drowne 16/1: 006-165: Prom, btn over 1f out: btr 2164 (12f).	½	61
2827* **DUNLEA DANCER 3** [3]3-9-6 (6ex) (63) J Fanning 5/2 FAV: 00-34216: Led/dsptd lead till over 2f out, sn btn: qck reapp: btr 2827 (12f).	½	59
2528 **ILWADOD 15** [13]3-9-5 vis (62) S Hitchcott(3) 3/1: 6-122227: Dwelt, rear, mod prog: ahd of wnr.	hd	57
1872 **RESTART 43** [9]3-9-3 (60) Rory Moore(7) 50/1: 6030-08: Held up, eff 3f out, no impress: abs: see 1872.	7	44
2123 **BOLLIN ANNABEL 31** [1]3-8-10 (53) G Gibbons 20/1: 0-25049: Led after 2f till over 3f out, sn btn.	¾	36
2346 **CUNNING PURSUIT 22** [7]3-8-4 (47) R Mullen 20/1: 065620: 10th: Trkd ldrs, btn when no room 2f out.	4	24
2827 **HABITUAL DANCER 3** [17]3-9-2 (59) Dane O'Neill 12/1: 00-61230: 11th: Mid-div, btn 2f out: btr 2827.	2	33
1547 **TIMBUKTU 59** [4]3-8-1 (44) F Norton 33/1: 6-000200: 12th: Dwelt, btn 2f out: abs: btr 1449.	2	15
2393 **Muslin 20** [2]3-8-12 (55) J Murtagh 12/1:0		
2503 **Quay Walloper 15** [12]3-7-12 (1oh)VIS(40) B Swarbrick(5) 100/1:0		
2274 **Great Gidding 25** [8]3-9-2 (59) J Fortune 40/1:0		
1612* **Crackleando 56** [10]3-9-5 (62) T P Queally(3) 14/1:0		
2565 **Perfect Balance 13** [16]3-9-0 (57) G Baker 20/1:0 1768 **Dawn Air 48** [15]3-9-0 P(57) N Callan 33/1:0		
18 Ran Time 3m 6.74(8.74) Owned: Mr C G Rowles Nicholson Trained: Gainsborough		

WARWICK FRIDAY 02.07.04 Lefthand, Sharp, Turning Track

Official Going GOOD/FIRM.

2906 2.15 Yorkshire Bank Maiden Stakes 3yo+ (D)
£4466 £1374 £687 **6f21y rnd** Good/Firm Inapplicable Inside

2650 **HERE TO ME 10** [3] R Hannon 3-8-10 (68) R L Moore 11/8 FAV: 2-534421: Made all, strongly prsd fnl 1f, drvn & held on all out: op 7/4: stays a stiff 1m, likes 6/7f on firm & gd/soft grnd, prob any trk: deserved this: see 2650, 2174 & 1761.		75
2659 **ANNA PANNA 9** [1] H Candy 3-8-10 (--) Dane O'Neill 5/1: 3-62: Al cl-up & ev ch ins last, drvn & just held: eff at 6/7f, acts on fast grnd & prob handles fibresand: now qual for h'caps: see 2659 & 276.	hd	74
2586 **RAGGED JACK 13** [9] G A Butler 3-9-1 (72) S W Kelly 2/1: 50U4-23: Held up in tch, kept on, not pace front pair: see 2586.	2	73
2485 **TROODOS JET 16** [4] A Berry 3-9-1 (65) F Norton 20/1: 2464-44: Handy, rdn & no extra ins last: acts on fast & soft grnd: see 2485.	3½	62
2641 **CHERTSEY 10** [5]3-8-10 B Doyle 20/1: 335: Dwelt, keen, not pace to chall: see 2641, 2342.	¾	55
1070 **PICK A BERRY 87** [2]3-8-10 S Drowne 66/1: 0-006: b f Piccolo - Bonne de Berry (Habitat) Dwelt & held up, nvr on terms with ldrs: 12 wk abs, unplcd & only mod form prev.	shd	55
2649 **EIGHT ELLINGTON 10** [7]3-9-1 (58) I Mongan 12/1: 000-0467: Bhd, nvr pace to threaten: see 2372.	1	57
1825 **PERFECT HINDSIGHT 45** [8]3-9-1 (55) R Smith 50/1: 005-008: b g Spectrum - Vinicky (Kingmambo) Al bhd, b wk abs, unplcd '03 (rtd 63, auct mdn): sire high-class at 1m/10f.	hd	56
4868} **FLEET ANCHOR 252** [6]3-9-1 (--) C Catlin 40/1: 50-9: b c Fleetwood - Upping The Tempo (Dunbeath) Prom, btn over 1f out: reapp: lightly rcd & unplcd in '03 (rtd 70, mdn).	3½	45
9 Ran Time 1m 10.24 () Owned: Mrs D Joly Trained: Marlborough		

2907 2.50 Mcdonalds Service Celebration Maiden Stakes 3yo+ (D)
£4719 £1452 £726 **7f26y rnd** Good/Firm Inapplicable Inside

1191 **THREE SECRETS 78** [7] P W Chapple Hyam 3-8-8 (85) A McCarthy 9/4: 20-01: b f Danehill - Castilian Queen (Diesis) Handy, rdn to lead over 2f out, rdn out: op 15/8, 11 wk abs: debut rnr-up '03 (fills mdn, G Margarson), subs Gr 2 unplcd (rtd 89$): eff at 6/7f on fast & gd grnd, stiff or sharp/turning trk: likes to race with/force the pace: could progress. 2 Jul'03 Asco 6gd 73- D:		81
2378 **ADMIRAL COMPTON 21** [4] A C Stewart 3-8-13 S Drowne 2/1 FAV: 0-22: Chsd ldrs, rdn to chase wnr ins last, al held: eff at 7f, return to 1m+ could suit: handles fast & gd grnd: now qual for h'caps: see 2378.	2	76
MAJORS CAST [2] J Noseda 3-8-13 S W Kelly 16/1: 3: b c Victory Note - Ziffany (Taufan) Slow away & rear, styd on well from over 1f out under hand riding, no threat to front pair: op 10/1, debut: 190,000gns	3	75+

purchase, half brother to smart sprinter Jessicas Dream: dam a 7f wnr: stays 7f on fast grnd, looks likely to apprec 1m+: not knocked about & caught the eye, expect improvement.

2586	MEMORY MAN 13 [1] W R Muir 3-8-13 F Norton 66/1: 04: b g Primo Dominie - Surrealist (Night Shift) Chsd ldr, no impress ins last: 33,000gns purchase, half brother to a 5/6f juv wnr: eff over a sharp 7f on fast.		1¼	72
1473	MOORS MYTH 62 [10]3-8-13 (80) R Mullen 7/1: 0-365: Chsd ldrs, no impress dist, abs: handles fast & gd/soft grnd: see 1152.		½	71
2352	CAYMAN CALYPSO 22 [12]3-8-13 N Callan 20/1: 006: Mid-div, rdn & nvr pace to chall.		2	66
2622	NOBLE MIND 11 [5]3-8-13 D Kinsella 6/1: 27: Held up, only mod prog: btr 2622 (1m, gd/soft).		nk	66
2549	HIRAYNA 14 [8]5-9-2 G Baker 66/1: 38: Slow away, only mod prog: drop in trip.		1½	58
4181}	SCARPIA 295 [3]4-9-7 (39) R Smith 100/1: 50/0000-9: Held up, eff 3f out, sn btn: new yard.		2½	58$
2352	BLACK SABBETH 22 [9]3-8-13 D Sweeney 66/1: 000: 10th: Mid-div, btn over 1f out.		1¾	55
2575	KABEER 13 [13]6-9-7 N Pollard 10/1: 430: 11th: Led till over 2f out, sn btn: btr 2575 & 2148.		1¼	52
2291	PURE IMAGINATION 24 [14]3-8-13 R L Moore 25/1: 630: 12th: Dwelt & al bhd: btr 2291.		1½	49
2586	BUNKHOUSE 13 [11]4-9-7 M Fenton 50/1: 000: 13th: Sn rdn & al bhd.		13	27
	JIMMY HAY [6]3-8-13 L Keniry(3) 100/1: 0: 14th: Slow away & sn struggling.		nk	26

14 Ran Time 1m 22.30 () Owned: Norcroft Park Stud Trained: Newmarket

2908 3.25 Pyments Trophy Handicap Stakes 3yo+ 0-70 (E) [82]
£4622 £1422 £711 1m6f213y Good/Firm Inapplicable Inside

2577*	DARN GOOD 13 [11] R Hannon 3-8-10 bl (64) R L Moore 6/1: 0306011: Handy, rdn & hdwy to lead ins last, drvn out: eff at 12f, suited by 15f/2m3f last twice: acts on firm, fast & polytrack, likes Warwick: see 2577.		73
2417	NOBLE CALLING 20 [2] R J Hodges 7-9-1 (52) F Norton 6/1: 06-03032: Held up, short of room 3f out, switched & hdwy to lead dist, sn rdn & hdd, kept on well: shown enough to find similar: see 2035.	½	59
2333	PERSIAN DAGGER 22 [1] J L Dunlop 3-8-10 (64) S Drowne 8/1: 0-00653: b c Daylami - Persian Fantasy (Persian Bold) Held up, no room 3f out, styd on well fnl 1f, not rch front pair: stays 15f well, shapes like a thorough stayer: acts on fast grnd: hmpd at a crucial stage & merits close attention for similar staying h'caps.	3	68+
896	MAKARIM 101 [13] M R Bosley 8-8-6 p (43) Hayley Turner(5) 20/1: 3-003504: Bhd, styd on, nvr dngrs.	1¾	45
2651	HEAD TO KERRY 10 [9]4-9-7 (58) S Whitworth 5/1 FAV: 13-00035: Rear, hdwy & rdn/led over 2f out, hdd dist, sn btn: btr 2651.	2	58
2471	HERNANDITA 17 [3]6-9-10 (61) M Fenton 8/1: 02/00/-406: Led/dsptd lead, btn dist: btr 2276.	2	59
2267	REAL ESTATE 25 [8]10-8-11 (48) Lisa Jones(3) 66/1: 000//00/-07: b g High Estate - Haitienne (Green Dancer) In tch, no impress fnl 4f: missed '03: unplcd '02 (trk 43, appr h'cap): former jumps wnr who has broken blood vessels: prev eff at 10/12f, acts on firm, gd/soft & any trk.	1¼	45
2601	THEATRE TINKA 12 [5]5-9-5 p (56) Stephanie Hollinshead(5) 8/1: 5240528: Led & clr after 4f, hdd over 2f out, sn btn: btr 2601 (12f).	¾	52
2577	QUICK 13 [7]4-9-8 vis (59) P Makin(5) 7/1: 60/0-P9: Rear, eff from halfway, btn 4f out: see 2577.	1	54
2453	HEART SPRINGS 18 [4]4-8-8 (45) S Carson 40/1: 00-000: 10th: b f Parthian Springs - Metannee (The Brianstan) Chsd ldrs, btn 2f out: longer trip: unplcd '03 (rtd 56a & 42, mdns).	1¼	39
1543	WESTERN RIDGE 59 [10]7-8-13 (50) D Sweeney 16/1: 214/00-0P: Held up, btn 2f out, p.u. lame.		0
2577	MOONSHINE BEACH 13 [12]6-9-3 (54) Dane O'Neill 6/1: 063654P: In tch, p.u. 6f out, saddle slipped.		0

12 Ran Time 3m 13.80 () Owned: Mr J E Garrett Trained: Marlborough

2909 3.55 Calthorpe Estates Selling Handicap Stakes 3yo+ 35-55 (F) [53]
£3241 £926 £463 1m22y rnd Good/Firm Inapplicable Inside

2572	MOBO BACO 13 [3] R J Hodges 7-9-13 (52) R L Moore 6/1 FAV: 4400001: Towards rear, hdwy 3f out & drvn to lead well ins last: no bid: eff btwn 7/10f on firm, soft & fibresand, any trk: see 1402.		58
2688	LORD CHAMBERLAIN 8 [15] J M Bradley 11-9-12 bl (51) C J Davies(7) 8/1: 3440302: Held up, hdwy wide & rdn/led over 1f out, hdd ins last & not pace of wnr: see 2615, 379.	1¼	53
2369	OVER TO YOU BERT 21 [2] R J Hodges 5-9-1 (40) R Havlin 33/1: 5140003: Prom, ch over 1f out, styd on onepace: jumps fit (unplcd, rtd 71h): acts on fast, gd/soft & polytrack: see 831, 652.	¾	41
2369	IVY MOON 21 [5] B J Llewellyn 4-9-6 (45) S Donohoe(7) 7/1: 3603534: Dwelt, sn handy, switched & kept on ins last: see 398.	nk	45
2688	SENOR EDUARDO 8 [4]7-9-12 (51) I Mongan 8/1: 305-0035: Trkd ldrs, onepace dist: see 2688.	1	49
2702	REPEAT 8 [17]4-9-6 (45) M Savage(5) 20/1: 0440006: Handy, ch dist, no extra: see 298 (7f, AW).	nk	42
2572	DIDOE 13 [6]5-9-8 (47) Lisa Jones(3) 16/1: 03230-07: br f Son Pardo - My Diamond Ring (Sparkling Boy) Bhd, eff 2f out, little hdwy: sell & mdn h'cap plcd '03, AW mdn unplcd (rtd 55a & 50): unplcd '02 (rtd 59, mdn): eff around 7f/1m on firm grnd & a sharp or turning trk.	3½	37
2335	ENNA 22 [13]5-9-12 (51) S Drowne 20/1: 013-4608: Handy, led 3f out till dist, wknd: see 1284.	shd	41
2448	ESPADA 18 [9]3-9-13 bl (52) S W Kelly 13/2: 0044159: Mid-div, btn dist: btr 2397 (7f, made all).	¾	41
2600	MUQTADI 12 [1]6-9-5 (44) F Norton 25/1: 4540600: 10th: Dwelt, held up, no impress on ldrs: btr 2032.	2½	28
2572	LUCKY ARCHER 13 [10]11-9-9 (48) L Treadwell(7) 25/1: 6000-000: 11th: Held up, eff 3f out, no impress.	hd	31
2715	POWER BIRD 7 [9]4-9-13 bl (52) N Pollard 20/1: 2000050: 12th: Prom, btn over 1f out: see 450.	1½	32
2146	FIFE AND DRUM 30 [12]7-9-6 p (45) B Reilly(3) 25/1: 0-006000: 13th: Cl-up/dsptd lead till over 1f out: recent jumps rnr (well btn): see 1695.	½	24
1992	Benjamin 38 [11]6-9-3 bl t(42) R Mullen 14/1:0		
2205	Flying Spud 28 [16]3-9-2 (50) Dean McKeown 14/1:0		
2588	Light Brigade 13 [8]5-9-1 (40) S Carson 14/1:0		
2530	Lunar Leader 14 [14]4-9-6 VIS(45) M Fenton 25/1:0		

17 Ran Time 1m 38.68 () Owned: Frome Racing Trained: Somerton

2910 4.30 Shoosmiths Maiden Handicap Stakes 4yo+ 35-55 (F) [61]
£3458 £988 £494 1m2f188y Good/Firm Inapplicable Inside

4531}	TOCCATA ARIA 276 [4] J M Bradley 6-8-12 (45) R L Moore 25/1: 003006-1: b f Unfuwain - Distant Music (Darshaan) Held up, hdwy 2f out, styd on for press to lead well ins last: reapp: mdn plcd in '03 (rtd 66): h'cap unplcd '02: eff at 1m, stays sharp 11f: acts on gd/soft, gall/undul or sharp trk: can go well fresh.		50
2718	TINTAWN GOLD 7 [11] S Woodman 4-9-1 (48) D Sweeney 4/1 JT FAV: 500-0042: Held up, hdwy & rdn/led over 1f out, hdd nr fin: see 2718 & 2220.	¾	51
2440	PACIFIC OCEAN 18 [2] Mrs Stef Liddiard 5-9-6 t (53) S Drowne 4/1 JT FAV: 2336043: Handy, rdn &	nk	53

kept on onepace fnl 2f: handles firm, fast & fibresand: stays 11f in mdn h'cap company: see 2440, 509 & 199.
2036 **CASTAIGNE 36** [10] B W Duke 5-9-5 (52) R Havlin 10/1: 20-00604: Dwelt & held up, hdwy to press ldrs 2f out, no extra from dist: see 101. *2½* **50**
2628 **MR DIP 11** [3]4-9-6 (53) L Treadwell(7) 33/1: 50-06005: b g Reprimand - Scottish Lady (Dunbeath) Dwelt & held up, switched & kept on onepace fnl 2f, no threat: unplcd '03 (rtd 70, mdn). *1* **50**
4853} **EBORACUM LADY 254** [16]4-9-3 (50) C Catlin 16/1: 0346-6: b f Lure - Konvincha (Cormorant) Chsd ldr, led over 3f out till dist, wknd: reapp: unplcd '03 (rtd 72, mdn): half sister to a smart 1m/10f performer. *shd* **47**
1414 **DASH FOR GLORY 66** [5]5-8-0 (3oh) (30) Hayley Turner(5) 10/1: 000-0007: Chsd ldrs 1m: new yard. *¾* **29**
2422 **LATIN QUEEN 19** [13]4-9-3 (50) S Whitworth 20/1: 06/000-58: Bhd, eff 2f out, mod prog: see 2422. *5* **39**
2436 **RYANS BLISS 18** [14]4-8-11 (44) R Miles(3) 6/1: 0253209: Handy trav well, wknd qckly over 1f out. *1¾* **31**
2146 **ZALKANI 30** [7]4-9-2 (49) V Slattery 7/1: 3300050: 10th: Handy, fdd fnl 2f: btr 2146. *7* **27**
2572 **GRUMPYINTMORNING 13** [9]5-9-6 BL (53) M Savage(5) 40/1: 054-00P0: 11th: Dwelt, in tch till 2f out. *5* **24**
2548 **Grey Samurai 14** [8]4-8-2 P(35) F Norton 50/1:0 2688 **Zouche 8** [15]4-8-12 (45) S W Kelly 20/1:0
1990 **Dances With Angels 38** [12]4-8-2 (35) P M Quinn 14/1:P2204 **Puri 28** [1]5-9-3 BL(50) M Fenton 16/1:P
15 Ran Time 2m 17.57 () Owned: Mr Terry Warner Trained: Chepstow

2911 **5.00 Birmingham Garrick Club Median Auction Maiden Stakes 2yo (E)**
£3786 £1165 £583 **5f rnd** **Good/Firm** **Inapplicable** Inside

1805 **GODSEND 46** [7] R Hannon 2-8-9 Dane O'Neill 4/6 FAV: 21: Trkd ldrs, rdn & styd on to lead well ins last: nicely bckd at odds-on, 6 wk abs: confirmed debut promise: eff at 5f on fast grnd & a sharp/turning trk. **77**
2415 **BOLD MINSTREL 20** [1] M Quinn 2-9-0 F Norton 5/1: 032: Al prom & ev ch dist, rdn & not pace of wnr cl-home: acts on firm & fast grnd: can find a race: see 2415 & 1880. *1* **78**
2171 **ANFIELD DREAM 30** [4] J R Jenkins 2-9-0 J Mackay 16/1: 63: b c Lujain - Fifth Emerald (Formidable) Handy, rdn & edged right/led over 1f out, hdd well ins last: Mar foal, half brother to prog 9f h'cap wnr Goodbye Mr Bond: dam a 1m 3yo scorer: eff at 5f, get further: acts on fast grnd. *1½* **73**
2251 **NEXT TIME 27** [2] M J Polglase 2-8-9 G Gibbons 16/1: 45004: Led till dist, no extra ins last. *1¾* **63**
2703 **HIGH DYKE 8** [5]2-9-0 Paul Eddery 50/1: 05: Dwelt, nvr pace to chall: crying out for return to 6f+. *1½* **63**
2629 **TOWN END TOM 11** [11]2-9-0 C Catlin 50/1: 566: b c Entrepreneur - Prima Silk (Primo Dominie) Chsd ldrs, no impress dist: Apr foal, dam a 5/7f wnr, incl as a juv. *½* **61**
FADAEL [3]2-8-9 R L Moore 8/1: 7: Dwelt, in tch till over 1f out: op 16/1. *2½* **48**
1466 **OUR FUGITIVE 63** [10]2-9-0 I Mongan 25/1: 48: Dwelt, nvr on terms: 9 wk abs. *shd* **53**
2537 **PHLAUNT 14** [9]2-8-9 S Carson 12/1: 49: Sn outpcd: btr 2537 (gd). *shd* **47**
2646 **BEAUCHAMP TWIST 10** [8]2-8-9 S W Kelly 66/1: 00: 10th: Mid-div, btn over 1f out. *3½* **36**
ABSOLUT EDGE [6]2-9-0 D Sweeney 50/1: 0: 11th: V slow away & al bhd on debut. *11* **11**
11 Ran Time 58.90 () Owned: The Queen Trained: Marlborough

2912 **5.30 Bollinger Champagne Challenge Handicap Gentleman Amateur Riders 4yo+ 0-70 (F)** **[42]**
£3543 £1090 £545 **1m4f134y** **Good/Firm** **Inapplicable** Inside

2371 **SKYLARKER 21** [3] W S Kittow 6-11-13 (69) Mr L Jefford 5/1: 3000441: Handy/dsptd lead, went on over 5f out, rdn & held on well ins last: eff btwn 1m/12f on firm, gd/soft & both AWs: see 273. **78**
2088 **GREAT VIEW 33** [6] Mrs A L M King 5-11-6 vis (62) Mr S Walker 7/2: 1212402: Held up, rdn to chall ins last, just held: clr of rem: back to form & can win again: see 1830 & 1373. *nk* **70**
2293 **GIKO 24** [2] Jane Southcombe 10-9-12 (40) Mr Adam Jones 9/2: 3060623: In tch, rdn & no impress on front pair over 1f out: see 2293 & 707. *7* **38**
3135} **KARAKUM 343** [5] A J Chamberlain 5-10-2 (44) Mr G Tumelty(7) 66/1: 4/0000/0-4: b g Mtoto - Magongo (Be My Chief) Prom, no extra over 1f out: long abs: dual sell hdle rnr-up 03/04 (rtd 83h at best, sell): mod form on the Level '03 & '02, incl in blnks. *2* **39**
2782 **SAXE COBURG 5** [7]7-11-4 (60) Mr G Denvir(7) 9/1: 1033035: Held up, no impress from 3f out. *2* **52**
3881} **JAVELIN 312** [4]8-10-9 (51) Mr B Gallagher(7) 8/1: 20/4045-6: ch g Generous - Moss (Alzao) Held up, eff 3f out, btn dist: reapp: 03/04 h'cap hdle scorer (rtd 114h, 2m/2m4f on firm & gd/soft grnd): unplcd '03 (rtd 54, h'cap): dual '02 h'cap wnr: eff at 10/12f on firm, handles soft & any trk: can go well fresh. *½* **42**
2 Jul'02 Warw 12.6gd 61-56 E: 1 Jun'02 Warw 12.6fm 58-51 F: 1 May'02 Nott 9.9g/f 51-45 E:
2725 **CHAPTER HOUSE 7** [8]5-12-0 bl (70) Mr O Greenall(7) 25/1: 0060/0-67: Bhnd after 5f & nvr factor. *nk* **60**
2782* **TRUSTED MOLE 5** [9]6-11-0 (56) Mr C Davies(5) 5/2 FAV: 3-516218: In tch 9f: btr 2782 (C/D). *1* **45**
2267 **JACK DURRANCE 25** [1]4-10-3 (45) Mr E Dehdashti(3) 14/1: 100-0049: Prom till 2f out: btr 2267. *8* **22**
2381 **MORRIS DANCING 21** [10]5-9-10 (8oh)vis (30) Mr J Pemberton(5) 100/1: 5000350: 10th: Led till over 5f out, sn bhd: stiff task: btr 1838 (AW). *7* **5**
10 Ran Time 2m 42.56() Owned: Midd Shire Racing Trained: Cullompton

SANDOWN SATURDAY 03.07.04 Righthand, Galloping Track, Stiff Finish

Official Going GOOD/SOFT.

2913 **1.35 Gr3 Champagne Laurent-Perrier Sprint Stakes 3yo+ (A)**
£29000 £11000 £5500 **5f6y str** **Good/Soft 60** **+05 Fast** Far Side

2818 **ORIENTOR 6** [3] J S Goldie 6-9-3 (105) K Fallon 5/1: 2450531: Held up, gd hdwy to lead over 1f out, edged right but rdn clr ins last, readily: qck reapp: best held up over 6f, stays 7f: handles firm & gd, relishes gd/soft & hvy, gall trks: smart at best, right back to form on fav'd grnd: see 952. **114**
2468 **RINGMOOR DOWN 18** [1] D W P Arbuthnot 5-9-0 (106) T Quinn 7/1: 43-61342: Held up, hdwy 2f out, styd on to chase wnr appr fnl 1f, not his pace: well clr of rem & in-form, progressive & smart mare: acts on firm & gd & gd/soft: can win a Gr 3: see 2468, 1400. *2½* **105**
2468 **COLONEL COTTON 18** [9] N A Callaghan 5-9-3 (100) P Robinson 14/1: 6065503: Held up, hdwy & hung over 1f out but kept on to take 3rd on line: nicely bckd: needs things to fall right: see 2206, 1159. *4* **100**
2468 **BOOGIE STREET 18** [12] R Hannon 3-8-12 (111) R Hughes 7/2 FAV: 41-32164: Set pace, rdn & hdd over *shd* **100**

1f out, no extra: nicely bckd: prob not enjoy easy grnd, worth another ch on fast as in 2468 & 2068.
2580 **TWILIGHT BLUES 14** [6]5-9-3 P (105) E Ahern 25/1: 0000-505: Sn rdn in tch, eff dist, sn no extra. *nk* **99**
2769 **THE KIDDYKID 7** [11]4-9-7 (111) J P Spencer 7/1: 65-30146: In tch, wknd dist: best dominating. *¾* **101**
2468 **STORMONT 18** [7]4-9-9 VIS (104) J Quinn 25/1: 10-40007: Dwelt, bhd, nvr a factor: vis, see 1958. *½* **102**
2421 **FROMSONG 20** [2]6-9-3 (97) S Sanders 33/1: 2444408: Held up, wknd over 1f out: see 1957, 1004. *hd* **95**
2468* **THE TATLING 18** [10]7-9-9 (115) D Holland 4/1: 40-23419: Hld up, brief eff & short of rm 2f out, *1½* **99**
no extra: well bckd: won this last yr & enjoys faster grnd: Gr 2 wnr in 2468, this is prob best forgiven.
2206* **NIGHT PROSPECTOR 29** [8]4-9-9 (105) J Murtagh 25/1: 5100-010: 10th: With ldrs, wknd & eased fnl *6* **87**
1f: not enjoy softer grnd?: btr 2206.
2468 **MORNIN RESERVES 18** [5]5-9-3 (105) L Dettori 10/1: 3012-000: 11th: b g Atraf - Pusey Street Girl *¾* **79**
(Gildoran) With ldr, wknd qckly 2f out: '03 3 time h'cap scorer: '02 4 time h'cap wnr for D Nolan: loves to dominate at 5f & acts on firm & hvy grnd, any trk: eff with/without cheek pieces: v useful, yet to fire this term.
2 Sep'03 Newb 5.2fm 108-(102) A: 1 Aug'03 Sand 5.0g/s 105-95 B: 1 Jun'03 Newc 5g/f 98-85 B:
1 Jun'03 Hami 5.0g/f 88-77 D: 1 Jul'02 Ches 5fm 81-74 C: 1 Jun'02 Carl 5fm 78-68 E: 1 Jun'02 Ayr 5hvy 73-61 D:
1 May'02 Hami 5g/s 64-52 F:
2638 **BALI ROYAL 12** [4]6-9-0 (102) Dane O'Neill 20/1: 124-6400: 12th: Cl-up, wknd 2f out: reportedly *1½* **73**
rcd with only one front shoe: see 2068.
12 Ran Time 1m 02.38 (2.78) Owned: Mr S Bruce Trained: Glasgow

2914

2.05 Listed Addleshaw Goddard Stakes Registered As The Esher Stakes 4yo+ (A)
£17400 £6600 £3300 **2m78y** **Good/Soft 60** **-09 Slow** Inside

2583 **ROMANY PRINCE 14** [9] D R C Elsworth 5-8-12 (100) Dane O'Neill 6/1: 2330-331: Held up, gd hdwy to lead 3f out, edged right but styd on v gamely to hold on for press fnl 1f: eff btwn 12f/2m6f, prob best at 2m: likes gd/soft & soft, acts on firm & any trk: smart now & genuine, shld win more staying events: see 1861. **110**
2234 **SILVER GILT 28** [3] J H M Gosden 4-8-12 (100) L Dettori 7/2 FAV: 12/34-332: Cl-up, hdwy to chase wnr & sltly short of room dist, styd on to chall ins last, just held for press in a stiring duel: well bckd, clr rem: relished step up to 2m & a shade unlucky: lightly rcd & more to come over staying trips: win similar. *shd* **109**
2518 **MISTERNANDO 16** [4] M R Channon 4-9-1 VIS (109) S Hitchcott 5/1: 11-02603: Ran in snatches, held up, eff over 2f out, onepace over 1f out: not disgraced conceding weight in first time visor: tough & smart. *5* **108**
2518 **ROYAL REBEL 16** [7] M Johnston 8-8-12 (110) J Murtagh 5/1: 001/-5044: Sn drvn to keep cl-up, wknd over 2f out: hard ride: see 2518, 1418. *3½* **102**
1757 **GULF 49** [6]5-8-12 (105) K Fallon 13/2: 0606-035: Keen held up, short of room over 4f out, eff over 3f out, sn wknd: 7 wk abs: likes fast grnd: see 1757. *3* **99**
2583* **CORRIB ECLIPSE 14** [8]5-8-12 (105) J F Egan 6/1: 16: Sn rdn in tch, eff well over 3f out, sn wknd: 2m6f wnr on firm grnd in 2583 (stks). *6* **93**
1757 **GOLD MEDALLIST 49** [2]4-8-12 (102) T Quinn 10/1: 51603-67: ch g Zilzal - Spot Prize (Seattle Dancer) Led till 3f out, wknd: 7 wk abs: '03 mdn, h'cap & List scorer: stays 2m on firm & gd grnd, gall or fair trks: best up with or forcing the pace: prob needs faster grnd. *13* **80**
1 Jul'03 Newm 14.8g/f 104-(99) A: 1 Jun'03 Kemp 12fm 95-85 D: 1 May'03 Sali 12g/f 98-(85) D:
2 Apr'03 Kemp 11.1fm 86-(85) D: 2 Apr'03 Wind 10.0g/f 87-(81) D:
2762 **TIZZY MAY 7** [1]4-8-12 (98) R Hughes 16/1: 0-025048: In tch, wknd 3f out, t.o.: see 1478 (10f). *dist* **0**
8 Ran Time 3m 41.17 (11.37) Owned: Mr J C Smith Trained: Whitsbury

2915

2.40 Totescoop6 Stakes Heritage Handicap 3yo+ (B) **[112]**
£58000 £22000 £11000 **1m14y rnd** **Good/Soft 60** **+07 Fast** Inside

2489 **PENTECOST 17** [1] A M Balding 5-8-10 (94) L Dettori 20/1: 240-0601: Held up, strong hdwy 2f out, styd on well to lead ins last, rdn out: suited by a stiff 1m, prob stays 9f: acts on firm & gd/soft, does handle any trk, likes Ascot: loves to come late off a fast pace, right back to useful best: see 1686. **103**
2558 **ST ANDREWS 15** [8] M A Jarvis 4-8-8 (92) P Robinson 6/1: 314/-262: In tch, hdwy 2f out, styd on well to lead ins last, collared cl-home, just held for press: well bckd from 9/1: relished step up to a stiff 1m on gd/soft, acts on fast: lightly rcd, useful & improving, more to come: see 1962. *hd* **100**
1351* **UNSHAKABLE 70** [2] Bob Jones 5-8-10 (94) F Norton 11/2 FAV: 000-0013: Prom, eff to chall over 1f out, kept on till no extra cl-home: well bckd: 10 wk abs & another fine run over favourite C/D: see 1351. *1½* **100**
2637* **TAHREEB 13** [6] M P Tregoning 3-9-1 (108) Martin Dwyer 6/1: 44-42114: Trkd ldr, styd on to lead over 1f out, rdn & hdd ins last, no extra: not btn far: another fine run & continues on the up-grade, smart, win another List/Gr 3: see 2637, 2069. *nk* **113**
2489* **MINE 17** [3]6-9-10 vis (108) T Quinn 9/1: 06-23115: Held up, hdwy 2f out, no threat to front 2: ran right up to smart form of 2489 & loves a big field/strong pace. *shd* **112**
1962 **COLISAY 40** [14]5-9-3 (101) K Fallon 9/1: 0/4210-36: In tch, hdwy 2f out, onepace fnl 1f: useful. *nk* **104**
2489 **CAMP COMMANDER 17** [5]5-8-12 t (96) D Holland 14/1: 034-0457: Held up, hdwy over 1f out, kept on ins last, nrst fin: another encouraging run & handles fast, gd/soft & polytrack: see 1624. *shd* **99**
2581 **BOSTON LODGE 14** [11]4-8-12 bl (96) R Hughes 33/1: 2324008: Held up, eff over 1f out, no impress. *1* **97**
2606+ **ACE OF HEARTS 13** [13]5-8-7 (91) S Sanders 8/1: 5021119: In tch, eff to chall over 1f out, sn no extra: not disgraced but this was a tougher h'cap than in recent wins: see 2606 (fast grnd). *½* **91**
2489 **FINISHED ARTICLE 17** [4]7-8-6 (1ow) (89) Dane O'Neill 14/1: 04-05300: 10th: Dwelt, held up, some late gains, nvr dngrs: likes Goodwood: see 2096, 1812. *¾* **88**
2521 **THYOLO 16** [18]3-8-6 (99) J P Spencer 9/1: 411-2030: 11th: Led, styd far side/overall ldrs till over 1f out, no extra & eased: joc took wrng option: see 2521, 1664. *14* **77**
2606 **CALCUTTA 13** [16]8-8-13 (97) R Hills 20/1: 0000020: 12th: In tch, wknd 2f out: btr 2606 (g/f). *3½* **70**
1686 **PABLO 52** [17]5-9-2 (100) J Murtagh 12/1: 55-01000: 13th: Cl-up, wknd qckly over 1f out, 7 wk abs, something amiss?: does like easy grnd: btr 1126. *shd* **73**
2605 **OUR TEDDY 13** [12]4-8-3 bl (87) E Ahern 25/1: 4005440: 14th: Al bhd, t.o.: see 2096, 547. *5* **52**
2556 **TUNING FORK 15** [7]4-8-8 t (92) J Quinn 33/1: 50-00000: 15th: Keen cl-up, wknd over 2f out, t.o. *19* **27**
15 Ran Time 1m 43.25 (4.25) Owned: J C J R and S R Hitchins Trained: Kingsclere

---

2916 **3.15 Gr1 Coral-Eclipse Stakes 3yo+ (A)**
£237220 £89980 £44990 **1m2f7y** **Good/Soft 60** **+18 Fast** Inside

2470* **REFUSE TO BEND** 18 [9] Saeed bin Suroor 4-9-7 t L Dettori 15/2: 100-0011: Cl-up, gd hdwy to lead   **123**
over 1f out, styd on strongly/v gamely to hold off chall ins last: prev well suited by 1m, clrly stays a stiff 10f
well & acts on fast & gd/soft, gall/stiff trks: top-class, fully revitalised now & v game, more Gr 1's to be won.

2209+ **WARRSAN** 29 [6] C E Brittain 6-9-7 (118) D Holland 12/1: 333-5312: Handy, hdwy 2f out, styd on   hd **122**
well to chall ins last, just held in a thrilling fin, gamely: joc rec a 1 day careless riding ban, clr of rem:
high-class entire who continues to be underestimated in top events: clrly eff at 10f, prob best over 12f & does stay
14f: game, in fine heart & can win another Gr 1: see 2209.

2022+ **KALAMAN** 38 [3] Sir Michael Stoute 4-9-7 (116) K Fallon 12/1: 1202-213: Hld up rear, eff & hmpd   4 **117**
well over 2f out, hdwy over 1f out, hung left ins last but kept on, too late: closer with a clr run & stays 10f:
acts on firm & gd/soft: smart, encouraging & can surely win at least a Gr 3: see 2022, 1168.

2470 **NORSE DANCER** 18 [11] D R C Elsworth 4-9-7 BL (117) T Quinn 20/1: 360-4304: Hld up, short of room   ½ **116**
over 2f out, styd on over 1f out, no threat: smart run in blnks but tends to keep something for himself.

2488 **POWERSCOURT** 17 [10]4-9-7 J P Spencer 11/2: 6113-125: Cl-up, hdwy to lead 4f out & trav well   hd **116**
till hdd 3f out, ev ch till wknd qckly over 1f out: shade below best & poss prefers a sounder surface: see 2488.

2488 **IKHTYAR** 17 [7]4-9-7 (116) R Hills 8/1: 10-36236: Held up, brief eff over 2f out, no impress: 1¾ **114**
needs a drop into Gr 3: see 2488, 2128 & 1420.

2209 **IMPERIAL DANCER** 29 [4]6-9-7 (117) T E Durcan 25/1: 110-3607: Held up, btn 2f out: see 1230.   2 **111**

2488+ **RAKTI** 17 [12]5-9-7 (121) P Robinson 13/8 FAV: 0/1212-18: Slow away & pulled way too hard & sn   nk **110**
went prom, led 3f out trav well till over 1f out, fdd: hvly bckd: v talented but has his quirks & threw away eff
with sloppy start & racing much too fresh: top-class eff when landing 2488 (fast, not as keen as here).

2254 **SALFORD CITY** 28 [2]3-8-10 (115) J Murtagh 8/1: 1-1659: Hld up, eff over 2f out, sn no extra: nk **109**
needs a drop into Gr 3: see 2254, 1480.

1595* **AFRICAN DREAM** 57 [5]3-8-10 (113) J Quinn 8/1: 3111110: 10th: In tch, eff over 3f out, wknd over   2½ **105**
2f out: 8 wk abs: up in class but btr expected after 1595 & 1316 (Gr 3).

2636 **MAKTUB** 13 [1]5-9-7 (110) G Carter 100/1: 200-0620: 11th: Led to 4f out, wknd 2f out: see 2636.   2½ **101**

2128 **CHANCELLOR 32** [13]6-9-7 (110) S Sanders 66/1: 64-01000: 12th: Handy, wknd over 2f out, t.o.:   30 **71**
something amiss?: see 1350.

12 Ran Time 2m 08.31 (4.21) Owned: Godolphin Trained: Newmarket

---

2917 **3.50 Listed Pacemaker Distaff Stakes Fillies 3yo (A)**
£17400 £6600 £3300 **1m14y rnd** **Good/Soft 60** **-10 Slow** Inside

2710* **ANTEDILUVIAN** 9 [7] Sir Michael Stoute 3-8-11 K Fallon 9/4 FAV: 1-11: In tch, hdwy to chall 2f   **106**
out, kept on gamely for press & led/asserted ins last: stays 1m well, shld get further: acts on fast, gd/soft & on
stiff & undul trks: unbtn, genuine & useful filly, more to come: see 2710.

2574 **SNOW GOOSE** 14 [4] J L Dunlop 3-8-11 (100) T Quinn 8/1: 1112-042: Set pace, clr halfway, prsd 2f   ¾ **103**
out, kept on till collared ins last, not btn far: styd this stiff 1m well & acts on firm & gd/soft: game & useful.

1733 **ITHACA** 50 [3] H R A Cecil 3-8-11 (94) R Hughes 25/1: 120-3653: Trkd ldr, eff to chall 2f out, no   1½ **100**
extra ins last: clr of rem after 7 wk abs: useful run drpd back to 1m: see 1150.

2491 **BRINDISI** 17 [1] B W Hills 3-8-11 (95) Martin Dwyer 14/1: 2-34144: Keen, handy, wknd well over 1f   4 **93**
out: shade btr 2491 (h'cap), 1882 (mdn, fast grnd).

2555 **MOON DAZZLE** 15 [2]3-8-11 (106) R Hills 3/1: 145: Keen in tch, eff 2f out, sn no extra: well   ¾ **92**
bckd: btr expected after promising run in 2555 but poss not enjoy this easier grnd: see 1935 (fast).

2555 **KELUCIA** 15 [8]3-8-11 (98) J Murtagh 16/1: 34-50566: Held up, eff 2f out, sn btn: see 2555 (fast).   ¾ **91**

2574 **KUNDA** 14 [6]3-8-11 (96) L Dettori 7/1: 152-6237: Held up, wknd 2f out: see 2574, 2211 (fast grnd).   1½ **89**

1619 **DONNA VITA** 56 [5]3-8-11 (90) D Holland 33/1: 10-48: Keen, handy, wknd over 2f out: 8 wk abs,   7 **79**
now with P Chapple Hyam, see 1619.

1492 **NATALIYA** 62 [9]3-8-11 (110) S Sanders 11/2: 13-309: Held up, wknd over 2f out, reportedly lost   2½ **75**
action: hvly bckd: 2 month abs: stable not firing as usual at present: see 1492, 1233 (7f, gd).

9 Ran Time 1m 44.59 (5.59) Owned: Lordship Stud Trained: Newmarket

---

2918 **4.20 Woodhurst Construction Handicap Stakes 3yo 0-100 (C)**   **[99]**
£12528 £4752 £2376 **7f16y rnd** **Good/Soft 60** **-15 Slow** Inside

4337*)**SILK FAN** 288 [6] P W Harris 3-9-7 (92) Martin Dwyer 9/2: 2211-1: b f Unfuwain - Alikhlas (Lahib)   **101**
Hld up, gd hdwy to lead over 1f out, styd on well ins last, rdn out: won last 2 of 4 '03 starts (mdn & stks): v eff
over a stiff 7f on fm & gd/soft: can front run or come bhd: genuine, progressing with ev run, keep on your side.
1 Sep'03 Newb 7g/f 93-(92) B: 1 Sep'03 Sali 7.0fm 92- D: 2 Aug'03 Newm 7g/f 90- D: 2 Jun'03 Pont 6g/f 84- E:

2749 **JAZZ SCENE** 7 [11] M R Channon 3-9-7 (90) S Hitchcott(3) 9/1: 102-0022: Held up, hdwy dist, styd   ¾ **99**
on well ins last, not btn far: another encouraging run & looks sure to apprec a rtn to 1m now: see 2749, 2521.

2521 **ZONUS** 16 [13] B W Hills 3-9-5 (90) R Hills 3/1 FAV: 2-142303: Handy, hdwy to chall over 2f out,   shd **97**
hung over 1f out, late gains: hvly bckd: another gd plcd run: see 1919, 1583.

2590 **PLACE COWBOY** 14 [15] J A Osborne 3-8-5 (76) T Quinn 11/1: 2-1524: Held up, hdwy to chall well   shd **82**
over 1f out, sn onepace: acts on gd/soft & fibresand: in fine form: see 2590, 999.

2525* **DISTANT CONNECTION** 16 [9]3-8-10 (81) S Sanders 8/1: 0061215: Cl-up, led trav well over 2f out   1 **85**
till over 1f out, no extra: acts on fast & gd/soft, on the up-grade: see 2525, 2314.

2533* **APPALACHIAN TRAIL** 15 [3]3-9-5 (90) J Murtagh 11/2: 3120416: Keen held up, hdwy & short of room   ½ **93+**
over 2f out till ins last, not recover: much closer with any sort run & clrly in fine heart, keep in mind.

2756* **KINGS CAPRICE** 7 [7]3-9-0 (85) D Holland 14/1: 23-03417: Keen in tch, eff over 2f out, sn onepace   nk **87**
& held when short of room ins last: nicely bckd: prob stays 7f on firm & gd/soft: see 2756 (mdn).

2521 **BENTLEYS BALL** 16 [2]3-9-5 (90) Dane O'Neill 20/1: 1432-608: Held up, eff 2f out, sn no impress.   2½ **88**

2362 **KING OF CASHEL** 22 [8]3-9-7 (86) K Fallon 8/1: 5341-39: In tch, wknd 2f out: see 2362.   2 **80**

2679 **GREAT SCOTT** 10 [12]3-9-2 (82) S Chin 25/1: 15005-00: 10th: Led 1f, lost pl 3f out, wknd dist.   3 **76**

2677 **LOVE TRIANGLE** 10 [10]3-8-9 (80) J Quinn 20/1: 4600-300: 11th: Led after 1f till 2f out, wknd.   nk **68**

11 Ran Time 1m 31.66 (5.26) Owned: Harris Clark Swinburn & Harris Trained: Berkhamsted

SANDOWN SATURDAY 03.07.04 Righthand, Galloping Track, Stiff Finish

2919 4.55 Deborah Shailer Handicap Stakes 3yo 0-85 (D) **[91]**
£14203 £4370 £2185 **1m2f7y** **Good/Soft 60** **-13 Slow** Inside

2225 **HEZAAM 29** [14] J L Dunlop 3-8-11 (74) R Hills 12/1: 01-0501: Held up, hdwy over 2f out, styd on well for press to lead cl-home: eff at 7f, clrly stays 10f well & acts on fast & gd/soft, likes gall trks: unexposed at this trip, see 1769. **85**
2353 **BOULE DOR 23** [5] R Ingram 3-9-4 (81) N Day 9/1: 300-4142: In tch, hdwy to lead over 1f out, sn clr, tired & collared cl-home, not btn far: stays 10f on fast & gd/soft: poss hit the front a shade too sn but clrly in gd heart: see 2024, 1825. ½ **90**
2538 **WINNERS DELIGHT 15** [9] A P Jarvis 3-9-2 (79) K Fallon 4/1 FAV: 65-00553: Held up, short of room 3f out, hdwy over 2f out, onepace fnl 1f: well bckd: stays 10f: see 2538, 2126. 1¼ **86**
2520 **WHITSBURY CROSS 16** [3] D R C Elsworth 3-9-3 (80) T Quinn 14/1: 0-55104: In tch, eff over 2f out, sn no impress till kept on late: back in correct company & handles fast & gd/soft: try 12f. 2½ **83**
2385 **CARTRONAGEERAGHLAD 21** [8]3-9-0 (77) Dane O'Neill 12/1: 0002445: Held up, hdwy & short of room over 2f out, late gains, nvr dngrs: nicely bckd: again suggested even further will now suit: see 2385, 2157. ¾ **79**
923 **BAAWRAH 100** [1]3-8-2 (65) P Doe 25/1: 32-21406: Held up, eff dist, no impress: see 568, 473. shd **67**
2663* **RED BIRR 10** [4]3-9-5 (82) Martin Dwyer 15/2: 043-0417: Held up, hdwy & short of room over 1f out, kept on ins last, nrst fin: see 2663 (gd grnd). 2½ **80**
2314 **AMERICAN DUKE 24** [12]3-8-3 (66) S Chin 50/1: 4400-08: b g Cryptoclearance - Prologue (Theatrical) With ldrs, wknd over 1f out: 4th in 2 mdns in '03: eff at 7f, shld stay further: acts on firm grnd. shd **64**
1707 **BREATHING SUN 51** [7]3-8-13 t (76) G Carter 20/1: 3011-009: b c Bahhare - Zapata (Thatching) Dwelt, held up, short of room 3f out till over 2f out, some late gains: 7 wk abs: won fnl 2 '03 starts (nurs h'caps): v eff at 1m, shld stay further: acts on fast & rain-softened grnd, sharp or gall trks. 1¼ **72**
1 Sep'03 Donc 8gd 78-72 B: 1 Aug'03 Ripo 8g/f 72-66 D:
2519 **OVER THE RAINBOW 16** [11]3-9-5 BL (82) J Murtagh 12/1: 230-1000: 10th: Keen, led till over 2f out, wknd & eased: tried blnks: see 886 (polytrack). ¾ **76**
2631 **MALIBU 12** [13]3-8-12 (75) J Quinn 25/1: 500-4650: 11th: Cl-up, led 2f out till dist, wknd. ½ **68**
2197 **TOP SPEC 30** [16]3-9-3 (80) R Hughes 25/1: 161-0050: 12th: Dwelt, sn handy, wknd qckly dist. 3 **69**
2175* **PAGAN MAGIC 31** [2]3-8-13 (76) Lisa Jones(3) 5/1: 05-3010: 13th: In tch, wknd 2f out: btr 2175. 2½ **61**
2385 **BALEARIC STAR 21** [18]3-8-6 (69) S Hitchcott(3) 14/1: 00-60100: 14th: Handy, wknd over 2f out. ¾ **53**
2126 **HOH BLEU DEE 32** [15]3-9-5 (82) L Dettori 16/1: 1666-060: 15th: Bhd, rdn & short of room over 2f out, sn wknd: see 1847 (7f). shd **66**
2377 **SWAINSON 22** [6]3-9-7 (84) D Holland 8/1: 34120: 16th: Keen, wide, handy, wknd over 2f out: reportedly not handle easy grnd: much btr 2377 (gd), 2066. 3 **64**
16 Ran Time 2m 11.45(7.35) Owned: Mr Hamdan Al Maktoum Trained: Arundel

LEICESTER SATURDAY 03.07.04 Righthand, Stiff, Galloping Track

Official Going Good (Good/Firm Places)

2920 2.00 Vista Classified Stakes 3yo+ 0-70 (E)
£5512 £1696 £848 **7f str** **Good/Firm 31** **+07 Fast** Stands Side

4823* **}ALINDA 256** [9] P W Harris 3-8-5 (70) S Carson 12/1: 01-1: b f Revoque - Gratclo (Belfort) Dwelt, held up, hdwy halfway & rdn/led ins last, sn clr, v readily: op 11/1: AW mdn scorer on 2nd of just 2 '03 starts: eff at 6f, imprvd for step up to 7f, 1m will suit: acts on fast grnd & fbsnd: goes v well fresh on a sharp or stiff/undul trk: v promising effort, keep on side. 1 Oct'03 Sout 6af 72a- F: **84+**
2568 **SAMUEL CHARLES 14** [11] W M Brisbourne 6-9-3 (71) S W Kelly 9/2: 1223342: Raced along far side & always prom, styd on for press, no impress on wnr ins last: quirky type who prob enjoyed being able to race alone. 3½ **77**
2773 **LYCA BALLERINA 7** [10] B W Hills 3-8-8 (73) W Ryan 5/1: 4-534103: Held up stands side, styd on for press fnl 2f, no threat to wnr: op 4/1: back to form: see 2325 (mdn). ¾ **75**
2587 **MISTRAL SKY 14** [6] Mrs Stef Liddiard 5-9-2 bl (66) B Doyle 7/1: 2043354: Handy stands side & led over 2f out, hdd ins last & no extra: gd run on a trk that suits: see 2063, 1020 & 121. 1 **73**
730* **OVERRIDE 129** [5]4-9-7 (75) L Fletcher(3) 8/1: 20060-15: Dwelt, hled up, efft over 2f out, btn dist: abs. 3 **72**
2650 **GO YELLOW 11** [4]3-8-8 (69) Derek Nolan(6) 12/1: 6-005246: Cl up, wknd over 1f out: btr 2650 & 2372. 1¾ **64**
2264* **BAKER OF OZ 26** [8]3-8-10 (72) P Dobbs 7/2 FAV: 60-26417: In tch till 2f out, op 4/1: btr 2264 (1m). 1½ **63**
2634 **BERTOCELLI 12** [2]3-8-8 (68) A McCarthy 11/1: 10-00348: Led till over 5f out, sn strugg: btr 2272. 6 **49**
2363 **JUSTE POUR LAMOUR 22** [3]4-9-6 BL (74) R Price 10/1: 500-0409: Dwelt,sn cl up/dsptd lead till 5f.. 1¾ **50**
1345 **CROSS ASH 70** [7]4-9-4 (72) D Sweeney 40/1: 05100-00: 10th: ch g Ashkalani - Priorite (Kenmare) Held up, keen, btn 3f out, abs: auct mdn wnr '03, eff over a sharp 7f, acts on firm & fast grnd, likes a sharp trk. 5 **38**
1 May'03 Catt 7fm 76- F:
10 Ran Time 1m 23.66 (1.66) Owned: Mrs P W Harris & Mr E Jehu Trained: Berkhamsted

2921 2.30 Vista Selling Stakes 2yo (G)
£2912 £832 £416 **5f str** **Good/Firm 31** **-43 Slow** Stands Side

2336 **TIPSY LILLIE 23** [9] Julian Poulton 2-8-6 M Halford(7) 7/2: 50001: Chsd ldrs & led over 1f out, rdn & just held on: bckd, op 9/2: 1st win: unplcd prev, apprec drop to 5f on fast ground in sell grade. **58**
2666 **RUSSIAN SERVANA 10** [7] M J Attwater 2-8-6 F P Ferris(3) 20/1: 02: b f Rossini - Ring of Light (Auction Ring) Dwelt & hampd start, in tch, swtchd & styd on well close home, just denied: op 16/1: improvement from debut on this drop to sell grade: cheaply bought Apr foal: dam 5/6f wnr: eff at 5f on fast. hd **57**
2721 **CONCERT TIME 8** [5] C R Dore 2-8-6 R Thomas(5) 6/1: 03653: Led & rcd keenly, hdd over 1f out, no extra ins last: op 5/1: see 1831. 2½ **49**
2498 **JUSTENJOY YOURSELF 16** [3] C A Dwyer 2-8-6 B Reilly(3) 11/2: 6064: b f Tipsy Creek - Habibi (Alhijaz) Cl up, ch 2f out, wknd ins last: op 9/2: 5,000gns Apr 1st foal, dam a 6f juv wnr. 1½ **44**
2330 **STORY OF ONE 23** [2]2-9-2 B Doyle 11/4 FAV: 201355: Chsd ldrs till dist: op 9/4: btr 2145, 2017. 1 **51**
2321 **JONNY FOXS 24** [6]2-8-11 BL D Sweeney 8/1: 606: Hmpd start, trkd ldrs, btn dist: op 11/1. nk **45**
2689 **FELLBECK FRED 9** [8]2-8-11 S W Kelly 20/1: 007: Went left start, rear, nvr on terms. 1¾ **40**

2461 **ETERNAL SUNSHINE 18** [4]2-8-6 R Miles(3) 50/1: 008: Cl up till halfway. ½ 33
2336 **MERMAIDS CRY 23** [1]2-8-6 R Havlin 8/1: 2009: Held up, efft over 2f out, sn rdn & btn: btr 1968. 3 24
9 Ran Time 1m 01.98 (3.68) Owned: Mrs A C Guinle Trained: Newmarket

2922 **3.05 Vista Charity Handicap Stakes 3yo 0-80 (D)** **[86]**
£7300 £2246 £1123 **1m rnd** **Good/Firm 31** **-03 Slow** Inside

2590 **DR THONG 14** [3] P F I Cole 3-9-7 (79) N De Souza(5) 5/1: 5-41241: Keen & trk ldrs, led over 2f out, rdn & just held on close home: eff at 7f, now stays a stiff/undul 1m: acts on firm & gd/sft grnd, any trk: consistent & has a progressive profile: see 2590, 1847 & 1518. 86
2650* **EVALUATOR 11** [9] T G Mills 3-9-3 (75) R Miles(3) 9/2 FAV: 6-430612: Held up, no room & lost place over 2f out, swtchd & 'flew home', just failed, most unlucky: most prog & wld have won this easily with any sort of run, wnr without a pen, keep on side: see 2650. *hd* 82+
2521 **BURLEY FLAME 16** [5] J G Given 3-9-5 (77) B Doyle 13/2: 0-433103: Keen, mid-div, styd on onepace. *1¼* 81
2403 **SPIN KING 21** [8] M L W Bell 3-9-4 (76) Hayley Turner(5) 8/1: 13-04034: Handy, hung right over 1f out & no extra ins last: see 2403, 1496. ¾ 79
2650 **TROIS ETOILES 11** [10]3-8-2 (60) D Kinsella 14/1: 00-505: Rear, gd hdwy over 2f out, onepace & held ins last: caught the eye for the 2nd start time this season: stays 1m, 7f ideal?: -see 2650. ½ 60
2634 **FOLEY PRINCE 12** [11]3-9-0 (72) R Havlin 8/1: 3012236: Mid-div, rdn & no extra over 1f out: op 6/1. *2½* 69
545 **IFFY 150** [1]3-8-2 (60) C Catlin 16/1: 050-47: Dwelt, held up, efft over 2f out, no impress, abs: see 545. *nk* 56
2024 **PHLUKE 38** [2]3-9-0 (72) S Carson 9/1: 0512048: Mid-div, btn 2f out: btr 1359. ¾ 67
2370 **LEAPING BRAVE 22** [4]3-9-4 (76) A McCarthy 14/1: 130-4249: Led till over 2f out, sn wknd: btr 2116. 4 63
1270 **FLYING ADORED 74** [7]3-9-0 (72) S W Kelly 9/1: 040-30: 10th: Dwelt, always bhd: op 8/1: abs: btr 1270. 3 53
2173 **BINNION BAY 31** [12]3-9-6 (78) P Dobbs 33/1: 3100-00: 11th: Dwlt & al rear, up in trip: see 2173. *1* 57
2575 **JARVO 14** [6]3-8-8 (66) D Sweeney 16/1: 230-2540: 12th: Chsd ldrs, btn 3f out: btr 1283 (10f). *nk* 44
12 Ran Time 1m 40.89 (2.69) Owned: Mr Frank Stella Trained: Whatcombe

2923 **3.40 European Breeders Fund Handicap Stakes Fillies 3yo+ 0-85 (D)** **[87]**
£8093 £2490 £1245 **1m3f183y** **Good/Firm 31** Inside

2353* **PORTRAIT OF A LADY 23** [1] H R A Cecil 3-9-8 (81) W Ryan 1/1 FAV: 40-31311: Trkd ldr & led over 3f out, rdn & in command fnl 1f: bckd: suited by 12f on fast & soft: game & prog. 89
1165 **KEEP ON MOVIN 80** [2] T G Mills 3-8-13 (72) R Miles(3) 9/1: 6531-502: Trkd ldrs, rdn to chall over 2f out, edged right over 1f out, kept on: clr rem: op 7/1: 12 wk abs: stays a stiff 12f well: see 1017, 116. *1¼* 74
4677} **GAELIC ROULETTE 266** [3] P W Harris 4-9-10 (70) B Doyle 9/1: 311650-3: b f Turtle Island - Money Spinner (Teenoso) Led till over 3f out, sn no impress: reapp: dual h'cap wnr '03 (AW unplcd, rtd 42a, h'cap): suited by 12f on fast ground, handles a stiff/undul trk, likes an easy one. 5 67
1 Aug'03 Kemp 12g/f 72-68 E: 1 Aug'03 Thir 12g/f 70-64 E:
2836 **COMPTON ECLAIRE 4** [4] G A Butler 4-8-12 (58) C Catlin 100/30: 3246124: Dwelt, held up in tch, rdn & no impress fnl 3f: qck reapp: btr 2836, 2601. *2½* 51
1472* **KARAMEA 63** [5]3-9-9 (82) S W Kelly 5/1: 03-315: Chsd ldrs, btn 3f out: op 7/2: abs, h'cap bow: much btr 1472 (g/s, mdn) *11* 60
5 Ran Time () Owned: Mr J Shack Trained: Newmarket

2924 **4.15 Vista Claiming Stakes 3yo (E)**
£4115 £1266 £633 **1m1f218y** **Good/Firm 31** **-20 Slow** Inside

2433 **CANADIAN STORM 19** [2] M H Tompkins 3-8-13 (58) F P Ferris(3) 11/2: 50-50451: Led & clr after 2f, pressed over 2f out, rdn clr again fnl 2f, eased cl home, val 4L: 1st win, claimed by Miss V Williams for 10,000: eff at 10f, tried 12f: acts on fast & gd grnd: apprec drop to claiming grade: see 2134, 1554. 69
2590 **EPAMINONDAS 14** [4] R Hannon 3-9-3 (66) P Dobbs 9/2: 053-0002: Chsd ldrs, kept on fnl 3f, nvr threat: clr rem: stays 10f in claiming grade, acts on fast & gd grnd: see 1417. *2½* 66
1403 **SIMONOVSKI 67** [6] J A Osborne 3-9-3 (67) V Slattery 7/1: 55-003: Chsd ldrs, rdn & kept on, no threat. 6 57
2274 **LAURENS GIRL 26** [8] M G Quinlan 3-8-8 R Havlin 12/1: 064: b f Imperial Ballet - Tresor Vert (Storm Cat) Chsd wnr & ch over 2f out, hung left & fdd dist: did not appear to see out this 10f trip. ½ 47
2203 **HOUSE OF BLUES 29** [1]3-8-9 (57) S W Kelly 16/1: 000-005: Bhd, rdn over 3f out, only mod prog. ¾ 47
2332* **BOSCO 23** [3]3-8-7 T (52) W Ryan 7/1: 05-00016: Held up, mod late prog: t-strap, new stable: btr 2332. *nk* 44
2732 **EIZAWINA DOCKLANDS 8** [7]3-8-5 t (50) C Catlin 16/1: 000007: Rear, rdn & no impress: see 1762. *1¾* 40
2344 **TARDIS 23** [11]3-8-4 (61) Hayley Turner(5) 3/1 FAV: 1524-008: Chsd ldrs, btn over 1f out: bckd. *3½* 34
2346 **ANISETTE 23** [5]3-8-4 (46) M Halford(7) 9/1: 3060649: Slow away & always bhd: btr 126. *2½* 30
2704 **OSLA 9** [9]3-8-8 R Thomas(5) 50/1: 0000: 10th: Held up, strugg 4f out, longer trip, no form. 3 30
953 **FLY SO HIGH 98** [10]3-8-4 (2ow) S Whitworth 50/1: 0000: 11th: Sn bhd: abs, no form. *26* 0
11 Ran Time 2m 07.60 (5.1) Owned: P A & D G Sakal Trained: Newmarket

2925 **4.45 Vista Handicap Stakes Fillies 3yo 0-70 (E)** **[75]**
£5837 £1796 £898 **6f str** **Good/Firm 31** **-03 Slow** Stands Side

2661 **ESTIHLAL 10** [8] E A L Dunlop 3-9-3 (64) W Ryan 4/1: 0-041241: Dwelt & rear, hdwy from halfway & led over 1f out, easily drew clr: suited by 6f on fm & gd: impressed here, follow-up. 79
2661* **RISE 10** [12] Andrew Reid 3-9-3 bl (64) J F Egan 9/1: 0060012: Held up, rdn & kept on fnl 2f, no threat to wnr: confirmed improvement of latest when ahead of this wnr: see 2661. *2½* 68
2630* **MISS JUDGEMENT 12** [10] W R Muir 3-9-4 (65) F Norton 5/2 FAV: 06-53213: Handy when no room over 2f out & again over 1f out, hung right & kept on ins last: closer with clr run tho' would not have troubled wnr. *2½* 61
2195 **FAIR COMPTON 30** [11] R Hannon 3-9-1 (62) P Dobbs 20/1: 04-4654: Handy, ch over 1f out, onepce. ¾ 56
1803 **INDRANI 47** [1]3-7-12 (2oh) (43) R Thomas(1) 40/1: 0040205: Held up, smooth hdwy halfway, rdn & no extra dist: 7 wk abs: handles fibresand, fast, gd/sft & hvy grnd: interesting for 5f in modest company: see 1641. *hd* 38
2624 **LA LANDONNE 12** [5]3-9-7 (68) S W Kelly 12/1: 351-436: Outpcd, hung right & late hdwy: btr 2624 (1m). *nk* 60
2439 **INDIAN LILY 19** [13]3-8-6 (53) S Whitworth 12/1: 50607: Held up, hdwy & ch over 1f out, btn ins last. *1* 42
2268 **TURKISH DELIGHT 26** [3]3-8-12 (59) C Catlin 28/1: 430-5608: Held up, not able to chall: see 2055. *2* 42

LEICESTER SATURDAY 03.07.04 Righthand, Stiff, Galloping Track

4382} **ANNIE MILLER 285** [18]3-9-4 (65) D Corby(3) 20/1: 5305-9: b f Night Shift - Lost Dream (Niniski)   hd   47
Dwelt & outpcd, short of room ins last, late prog: unplcd '03 (rtd 70 & 39a): half sister to a plcd 1m performer.
2439 **DANIFAH 19** [6]3-7-12 (45) Joanna Badger 12/1: 0-000040: 10th: Chsd ldrs, no impress fnl 2f: btr 2439.   nk   26
2742 **PINK SUPREME 7** [16]3-8-13 t (60) Derek Nolan(7) 33/1: 2-00000: 11th: Held up, little hdwy: see 2268.   1¼   37
2291 **BAHAMA BELLE 25** [4]3-8-10 (57) D Kinsella. 33/1: 0000-040: 12th: Chsd ldrs till over 1f out: btr 2291.   1½   29
2734 **PARTY PRINCESS 8** [14]3-9-2 (63) B Doyle 8/1: 3-001400: 13th: Prom, briefly led over 1f out, sn   ½   33
hdd & wknd: btr 2268, 2011.
1102 **LIZHAR 86** [20]3-8-3 (50) M Henry 20/1: 4204600: 14th: Prom till over 1f out, 'lost action': new yard.   ½   18
2118 **MELAINA 33** [19]3-9-4 p (65) R Miles(3) 20/1: 0611050: 15th: Chsd ldrs & chance over 1f out, wknd/eased. ¾   31
2704 **RED ROCKY 9** [2]3-7-13 p (46) Stephanie Hollinshead(1) 20/1: 5-005020: 16th: Prom till over 1f out.   hd   11
712 **SMART STARPRINCESS 130** [9]3-9-0 (61) F P Ferris(3) 20/1: 1-112350: 17th: Led 3f, sn btn: op 25/1.   1   23
2435 **Pardon Moi 19** [17]3-8-1 (48) Hayley Turner(5) 25/1:0   1729   **Carla Moon 50** [15]3-8-13 (60) G Baker 20/1:0
19 Ran   Time 1m 11.86(2.06)   Owned: Mr Hamdan Al Maktoum   Trained: Newmarket

NOTTINGHAM SATURDAY 03.07.04 Lefthand, Galloping Track

Official Going Good HEAVY SHOWERS THROUGH EVENING

2926 6.50 Bet With The Bookies Median Auction Maiden Stakes 2yo (F)
£3360 £960 £480   5f str   Good   Inapplicable   Stands Side

2618 **BLUE MARBLE 12** [8] C E Brittain 2-9-0 J P Guillambert(3) 8/1: 4601: Al prom, rdn & led ins last,   78
styd on strongly: op 11/1: eff at 5f, tried 6f, rtn to that trip shld suit: acts on gd & a sharp/undul or gall trk.
       LUCKY EMERALD 0 [10] B Palling 2-8-9 K Darley 12/1: 2: b f Lend A Hand - Anita's Love (Anita's   1½   67
Prince) Dwelt, chsd ldrs, rdn/hung left but kept on ins last: Apr foal, half-sister to a 5f juv wnr: dam plcd at
6f as a juv: eff at 5f, get 6f: acts on gd grnd & a gall trk: pleasing start, rate higher.
2618 **TRANSVESTITE 12** [9] J W Hills 2-9-0 R L Moore 2/1: 543: Al prom & led over 1f out till ins last, wknd.   shd   72
2603 **FRANTIC 13** [2] T D Easterby 2-8-9 G Duffield 9/1: 044: Chsd ldrs, rdn & no extra from dist: op   1¼   63
10/1: handles fast & gd grnd: see 2603.
2658 **THREE ACES 10** [5]2-8-9 M Tebbutt 25/1: 05: Dwelt, sn rdn, kept on but not pace to chall.   nk   62
2670 **KOMAC 10** [1]2-9-0 S Sanders 13/8 FAV: 6246: Led till over 1f out, no extra: bckd: btr 2089.   3   59
       KATIE KILLANE 0 [6]2-8-9 A Daly 33/1: 7: ch f Komaite - Efficacy (Efisio) Slow away & al bhd: 9   31
Apr foal, half-sister to a mulitple 6f wnr effective, dam a multiple 6f wnr.
       STARLIGHT RIVER 0 [7]2-8-9 S Drowne 16/1: 8: Chsd ldrs till 2f out.   3½   21
       INDEPENDENT SPIRIT 0 [3]2-9-0 R Miles(3) 33/1: 9: Slow away & hung left, sn strugg twds centre.   3   18
9 Ran   Time 1m 04.51 (6.01)   Owned: HESheikh Rashid Bin Mohammed   Trained: Newmarket

2927 7.20 Saturday Night Racing Maiden Auction Stakes Fillies 2yo (E)
£4063 £1250 £625   6f str   Good   Inapplicable   Stands Side

2670 **RANCHO CUCAMONGA 10** [15] T D Barron 2-8-4 (2ow) K Darley 14/1: 001: Sn prom, switched & hdwy/rdn   77
to lead dist, rdn out: imprvd significantly for step up to 6f, get further: acts on gd.
2537 **SHOSOLOSA 15** [13] B J Meehan 2-8-7 (1ow) J Fortune 5/1: 022: Sn handy, rdn when short of room   2   74
dist, kept on for press, not pace of wnr: confirmed improvement of 253, win a race.
2310 **AGENT KENSINGTON 24** [1] R Hannon 2-8-2 R L Moore 4/1: 2253: Sn handy, rdn when short of room   shd   69
out, not pace of ldrs stands side ins last: eff around 5/6f, handles fast & soft grnd: likely to apprec h'caps.
2395 **GAUDALPIN 21** [11] M J Attwater 2-8-2 S Righton 25/1: 3404: Led till dist, no extra: stays 6f.   nk   68
2603 **CONSIDER THIS 13** [6]2-8-2 C Catlin 9/1: 25: Al handy far side, no extra: acts on fast & gd grnd.   3   60
2505 **SWEET MARGUERITE 16** [5]2-8-6 D Allan 16/1: 5446: Led far side 2f, btn dist: just btr 2275.   nk   63
       BEFORE THE DAWN 0 [16]2-8-2 F P Ferris(3) 33/1: 7: b f Lugana Beach - Chayanee's Arena (High   ¾   57
Estate) In tch, hung left & no impress dist: op 50/1: cheaply bght Feb first foal.
2537 **SWEET COINCIDENCE 15** [14]2-8-2 G Duffield 100/30 FAV: 38: Dwelt, in tch till dist: btr 2537.   ½   55
2343 **LAKESDALE 23** [17]2-8-2 Hayley Turner(5) 33/1: 0229: In tch, no prog over 1f out: btr 2343.   1¾   50
2618 **EMERAUDE DU CAP 12** [2]2-8-6 A Daly 100/1: 00: 10th: b f Tipsy Creek - High Typha (Dowsing)   ½   48
Dwelt, sn outpcd & nvr factor: cheaply bght Mar foal, half-sister to 5f juv wnr Tyne, dam a 7f 3yo scorer.
2618 **ARIANE STAR 12** [3]2-8-2 P Robinson 6/1: 00: 11th: Cl-up over 2f, btn over 1f out.   shd   52
2281 **OCEANICO DOT COM 25** [9]2-8-2 F Norton 33/1: 00: 12th: Chsd ldrs, btn 2f out.   3   40
2020 **CLINET 38** [7]2-8-3 (1ow) J F Egan 8/1: 0520: 13th: Dwelt, prom till over 1f out: btr 2020.   shd   41
2666 **Good Wee Girl 10** [8]2-8-2 R Miles 33/1:0   **Royal Abigail 0** [4]2-8-6 S Drowne 40/1:0
2652 **Lanas Turn 11** [12]2-8-2 Saleem Golam 66/1:0   **Pride Of London 0** [10]2-8-2 T P Queally 66/1:0
17 Ran   Time 1m 19.35 (8.35)   Owned: Mr P D Savill   Trained: Thirsk

2928 7.50 Letheby & Christopher Selling Handicap Stakes 3yo+ 35-55 (G) [59]
£2800 £800 £400   6f str   Good   Inapplicable   Stands Side

2615 **MICKLEDOR 12** [19] M Dods 4-8-12 p (43) D Tudhope(7) 10/1: 34-00301: Held up stands rail, hdwy 2f   53
out & rdn to lead well ins last: no bid: eff at 5/6f on fast & gd/soft grnd: imprvd of late in cheek pieces.
2801 **HEADLAND 5** [20] D W Chapman 6-9-4 bl e (49) S Sanders 12/1: 0303062: Handy & led over 1f out till   1¾   53
ins last, no extra: gd run back on turf: see 227.
1988 **SHADY DEAL 39** [4] J M Bradley 8-9-0 (45) F P Ferris(3) 16/1: 0003003: Dwelt, bhd far side, kept   ¾   47
on late, no threat: op 12/1: see 1662 & 775.
2730 **BEYOND CALCULATION 8** [6] J M Bradley 10-9-10 BL (55) R L Moore 12/1: 0000404: Prom far side, led   nk   56
that group 3f out, drvn & no extra cl-home: first time blnks, gd run: ideally suited by firm/fast grnd: see 1886.
2630 **KOMENA 12** [1]6-8-12 (43) G Duffield 12/1: 0-500005: Prom far side, onepcd from dist.   nk   43
2372 **MY GIRL PEARL 22** [18]4-9-2 (47) V Slattery 7/1: 0-024206: Mid-div, not pace to chall: op 12/1.   1   44
2572 **CARGO 14** [12]5-9-3 t p (48) R Miles(3) 12/1: 2023207: Sn led till over 1f out, no extra: btr 1588.   hd   44

2657 **ZIETZIG 11** [13]7-9-0 (45) P Dobbs 33/1: 06-00008: Bhd, late prog, nvr threat: see 1635. *1¼* **37**
2657 **LOUGHLORIEN 11** [16]5-9-1 vis (46) T Hamilton(3) 100/30 FAV: 06-00009: Chsd ldrs till over 1f out. *¾* **36**
2361 **BELLS BEACH 22** [5]6-9-0 (45) S Drowne 7/1: 1044150: 10th: Sn struggling, nvr factor: btr 2016 (AW). *5* **22**
1401} **OCTENNIAL 422** [17]5-9-5 (50) R Fitzpatrick 33/1: 40/2650-0: 11th: gr g Octagonal - Laune (Kenmare) Outpcd, nvr on terms: reapp: lightly rcd '03, seller rnr-up for P Blockley, AW unplcd (rtd 49a, clmr): late '01 AW mdn scorer for R Hannon: winning form at 6f, stays stiff 7f well: acts on fibresand & fast grnd, best without cheek pieces/visor. 2 Mar'03 Leic 7.0g/f 53-(65) G: 1 Dec'01 Wolv 6af 73a- D: *1¼* **23**
2369 **RILEYS DREAM 22** [9]5-8-12 (43) D Sweeney 16/1: 0500100: 12th: Dwelt, nvr factor: btr 1963. *hd* **15**
2542 **DANAKIM 15** [10]7-9-0 (45) C Catlin 9/1: 0015000: 13th: Prom 4f racing alone centre. *½* **15**
1806 **SABANA 47** [8]6-8-12 (43) F Norton 28/1: 3060000: 14th: Led far side till 3f out, sn btn: 7 wk abs. *1½* **8**
2720 **SOUNDS LUCKY 8** [14]8-9-0 bl (45) J F Egan 25/1: 2604000: 15th: Prom, struggling fnl 2f: btr 1012 (AW). *nk* **9**
2645 **CEDRIC COVERWELL 11** [3]4-9-0 (45) R Hughes 33/1: 400000: 16th: Far side & sn struggling. *¾* **7**
2361 **RIDICULE 22** [11]5-9-2 vis t (47) N Callan 10/1: 0000000: 17th: Mid-div, no prog 2f out. *1¾* **4**
2506 **BLADES EDGE 16** [15]3-9-4 BL (55) J Fortune 14/1: 4-053000: 18th: Struggling halfway: blnks: btr 953. *2* **6**
2630 **Vintage Style 12** [2]5-9-9 VIS(54) K Darley 40/1:0
1074 **Foolish Thought 88** [7]4-9-2 p(47) L Enstone(3) 33/1:0
20 Ran Time 1m 17.87 (7.07) Owned: Mr D B Stanley Trained: Darlington

2929

8.20 Search Consultancy's Grahame & Debbie Wedding Handicap Stakes 3yo+ 0-80 (D) **[80]**
£5883 £1810 £905 **1m2f** **Good/Soft** **Inapplicable** Inside

2735 **RASID 8** [5] C A Dwyer 6-9-7 (73) D Holland 4/1: 3100531: Led after 2f, rdn & al holding rivals from over 1f out: suited by 10/12f on fast & polytrack, loves soft: enjoyed forcing tactics tonight: see 1397. **80**
2654* **ROTUMA 11** [3] M Dods 5-9-6 bl (72) L Enstone(3) 4/1: 5031612: In tch, hmpd & lost pl early, rdn & hdwy from over 2f out, not able to chall wnr: shade closer with a kinder passage, would not have troubled wnr. *2* **76**
2447 **ACTIVE ACCOUNT 19** [8] Mrs H Dalton 7-8-9 (61) S Drowne 11/1: 3-225663: Led 2f, remained handy, no extra dist: acts on fast, gd/soft & both AWs: see 809 (8.5f). *½* **64**
2673 **MEKURIA 10** [2] M Johnston 3-8-12 (75) S Chin 9/1: 241-004: Dwelt, sn in tch, not pace to chall 1f out. *1¼* **76**
2737 **SIR HAYDN 8** [4]4-8-13 vis (65) T P Queally 16/1: 3-360605: Dwelt, held up in tch, no impress 1f out. *½* **65**
2687 **GO TECH 9** [6]4-9-10 (76) D Allan 8/1: 0606246: Keen & prom, btn dist: btr 2483. *3½* **71**
2719* **LILLI MARLANE 8** [1]4-9-6 (72) W Ryan 100/30 FAV: 0-260017: Rear, eff over 2f out, no impress: bckd. *7* **58**
2363 **KARAOKE 22** [7]4-9-1 (67) R L Moore 7/2: 5542208: Rear & struggling 2f out: much btr 2067, 803. *12* **38**
8 Ran Time 2m 17.12 (14.82) Owned: Mr David L Bowkett Trained: Newmarket

2930

8.50 Bdn Construction Classified Stakes 3yo 0-70 (E)
£3949 £1215 £608 **1m2f** **Good/Soft** **Inapplicable** Inside

2706* **JAKARMI 9** [11] B Palling 3-9-2 (72) R Miles(3) 6/5 FAV: 2223211: In tch wide, hdwy to lead over 1f out, rdn, cosily: suited by 1m/10f, stays 12f: acts on firm, soft & fibresand: v progressive. **78+**
2705 **WHITGIFT ROCK 9** [10] S Dow 3-9-3 (73) D Holland 13/2: 1200032: Led/dsptd lead, went on over 3f out till over 1f out, not pace of wnr: op 5/1: stays 10f: acts on polytrack, firm & gd/soft grnd: see 2705 & 341. *2* **73**
1983 **BAILAORA 39** [7] B W Duke 3-9-3 bl (73) R L Moore 20/1: 302-6063: Trkd ldrs, rdn & styd on onepace fnl 2f: handles firm & gd/soft grnd: stays 10f: see 1983. *1½* **71**
2773 **TYTHEKNOT 7** [1] Jedd O'Keeffe 3-9-4 (74) R Hughes 10/1: 02-2364: Led till over 3f out, no extra: op 8/1. *½* **71**
1365 **TRULLITTI 70** [6]3-9-2 (75) K Darley 7/2: 65-35: Rear, eff 2f out, not able to chall: abs: btr 1365. *½* **68**
2707 **IMPERIAL ROYALE 9** [9]3-9-0 (62) M Halford(7) 50/1: 0052-506: Held up, eff 3f out, btn dist: see 2230. *2½* **62**
2247 **THE VIOLIN PLAYER 28** [2]3-9-4 (74) T P Queally 12/1: 313-0007: Dwelt, mid-div, btn 2f out: btr 2247. *½* **65**
2515 **HONEYMOONING 16** [3]3-8-11 (68) W Ryan 12/1: 0438: Dwelt & al bhd: btr 2515, 1936. *nk* **57**
2723 **FIT TO FLY 8** [8]3-9-5 (75) J D Walsh(7) 14/1: 0-251569: Held up, eff 3f out, sn btn: see 869. *1* **64**
2413 **VENGEROV 21** [5]3-9-0 (70) Saleem Golam(7) 14/1: 340-1630: 10th: Chsd ldrs, btn 2f out: see 553. *3½* **54**
10 Ran Time 2m 17.66 (15.36) Owned: Mrs M M Palling Trained: Cowbridge

2931

9.20 Midlands Racing - 9 Great Venues - Handicap Stakes 3yo+ 0-75 (E) **[75]**
£4095 £1260 £630 **1m54y rnd** **Good/Soft** **Inapplicable** Inside

2633 **LITTLE ENGLANDER 12** [1] H Candy 4-8-8 (55) D Sweeney 12/1: 40-50051: Held up, hdwy to lead ins last, drvn out: first win: eff at 1m, prob stays 10f & has tried 12f: acts on fast & gd/soft: see 1430. **62**
2483 **JOHANNIAN 17** [11] J M Bradley 6-9-10 (71) R L Moore 12/1: 5-003502: Bhd, hdwy to chall ins last, not pace of wnr: op 9/1: h'capped to win: see 2087. *1¼* **74**
1036* **TROUSERS 91** [12] Andrew Reid 5-9-1 (62) J F Egan 2/1 FAV: 2136-013: Led/dsptd lead till ins last, no extra: bckd, op 3/1: in gd form: see 1036. *nk* **64**
2162 **DISABUSE 31** [6] M W Easterby 4-8-3 BL (50) G Duffield 9/2: 2134454: Dwelt, sn handy, rdn & no extra ins last: first time blnks, fair run: handles fast, gd/soft & fibresand: see 2162, 746 & 463. *½* **51**
2350 **HABSHAN 23** [9]4-9-7 (68) R Hughes 9/2: 52-0435: Held up, eff 2f out, onepcd: op 11/2: see 1891. *¾* **68**
2402 **VERMILION CREEK 21** [14]5-8-6 (53) Stephanie Hollinshead(5) 16/1: 0666206: Held up, eff over 2f out, rdn & no prog dist: see 1348, 1160 & 445. *1¾* **50**
2633* **FLASHING BLADE 12** [5]4-9-9 t (70) G Gibbons 7/1: 0000017: Mid-div, btn/eased ins last: btr 2633. *5* **58**
1883 **SHERIFFS DEPUTY 43** [13]4-9-9 (70) D Holland 6/1: 21042-08: Held up, strugg halfway: abs: see 1883. *6* **48**
2529 **BROOKLANDS LODGE 15** [7]3-8-11 (67) S Righton 40/1: 450-69: Chsd ldrs, struggling fnl 3f: see 2529. *2* **41**
2628 **SAHAAT 12** [4]6-9-11 BL (72) T P Queally 10/1: 0-000050: 10th: Held up, struggling 2f out: blnks. *3½* **39**
2626 **AMONG FRIENDS 12** [2]4-8-11 (58) Lisa Jones(3) 20/1: 36-60000: 11th: Keen & sn led till 3f out, sn btn. *3* **19**
2296 **AIMEES DELIGHT 25** [15]4-9-6 BL (67) S Sanders 16/1: 0060000: 12th: Al bhd, tried blnks, poor run. *2* **24**
12 Ran Time 1m 50.44(11.04) Owned: The Earl Cadogan Trained: Wantage

Official Going GOOD

2932   7.05 Azure Selling Stakes 3yo   (F)
£3094 £884 £442   7f200y   Good 59   -04 Slow   Inside

2683 **REVERSIONARY 9** [7] M W Easterby 3-8-12 bl (43) R Winston 8/1: 0050001: Handy, led over 1f out   53
till ins fnl 1f, bumped/led again nr fin: no bid: first win: eff at 1m on gd: enjoyed drop in grade.
2617 **ELSINORA 12** [5] H Morrison 3-8-7 P (50) M Fenton 5/1: 300-0002: Handy, not clr run over 1f out,   nk   47
hung badly right & led ins fnl 1f, hdd nr fin: eff at 5f/1m on firm & gd: tried cheekpieces.
2299 **BARGAIN HUNT 25** [1] W Storey 3-8-12 (46) J Bramhill 9/2: 03-02003: Rear, hdwy/ev ch 1f out, onepace. 2   48
2704 **CHUBBES 9** [8] M D Hammond 3-8-12 vis (60) A Culhane 1/1 FAV: 230-0044: Led till over 1f out, no extra. 1   46
2552 **CAMPBELLS LAD 15** [4]3-8-12 (40) P Bradley 16/1: 40-54005: Handy, outpaced over 1f out, kept on late. shd   45
2501 **CUTE CAIT 16** [2]3-8-7 (49) W Supple 12/1: 35000-06: b f Atraf - Clunk Click (Star Appeal)   10   20
Handy, wknd 2f out: won a sell stks in '03 (L Stubbs): eff at 5/6f on fast & gd, stiff/gall trks: enjoys sell
grade. 1 Jun'03 Hayd 6g/f 62- E: 2 May'03 Leic 5.0gd 55- F:
2493 **KNIGHT TO REMEMBER 17** [3]3-8-12 (40) T Eaves(3) 20/1: 4005057: Bhd, nvr a factor: see 613.   8   9
2523 **RAYBERS MAGIC 16** [6]3-8-7 J Fanning 33/1: 08: b f Magic Ring - Kirkadian (Norwick) Handy till   3½   0
over 2f out, wknd: mdn unplcd earlier debut: with J Weymes.
8 Ran   Time 1m 42.81 (5.11)   Owned: Mr A G Black & Mr A M Hedley   Trained: Sheriff Hutton

2933   7.35 Village Nightclub Maiden Auction Stakes 2yo   (E)
£3543 £1090 £545   5f   Good 59   -05 Slow   Inside

     STRAWBERRY DALE 0 [8] J D Bethell 2-8-6 J Fanning 18/1: 1: b f Bering - Manchaca (Highest   84
Honor) Handy, led 1f out, kept on: debut: Mar foal, cost 20,000gns: eff at 5f, 6f shld suit: acts on gd & a stiff
trk: runs well fresh: gd start, rate higher over further.
2670 **BIG HASSLE 10** [11] T D Easterby 2-8-9 W Supple 6/4 FAV: 52: Trkd ldrs, hdwy to chall 1f out, onepace. ½   84
     ON THE BRIGHT SIDE 0 [9] D Nicholls 2-8-4 P M Quinn 20/1: 3: b f Cyrano de Bergerac - Jade Pet   2   73
(Petong) Rear, hdwy 2f out, kept on well ins fnl 1f on debut: clr of rem: Mar foal, cost 13,000 gns: bred for
speed, dam won thrice over 5f (inc at 2), sire smart juv & sprinter: eff at 5f on gd: encouraging start.
2360 **DISPOL ISLE 22** [1] T D Barron 2-8-2 P Fessey 5/2: 44: Prom, fdd over 1f out: see 2360.   2½   63
2297 **DESERT BUZZ 25** [3]2-8-7 M Fenton 20/1: 0605: Bhd, some late gains: see 1987.   hd   67
2671 **SKIDDAW WOLF 10** [6]2-8-2 R Ffrench 6/1: 036: Led, hdd & no extra 1f out: see 2671.   hd   61
2178 **OCHIL HILLS DANCER 30** [2]2-8-6 V Halliday 14/1: 057: Handy, no impress fnl 2f: see 2178 & 2056.   1¼   61
2829 **NO COMMISSION 4** [4]2-8-11 A Culhane 8/1: 0540548: Handy, wknd 2f out: qck reapp, top-weight.   1   63
2671 **TOLDO 10** [7]2-8-9 F Lynch 50/1: 009: gr g Tagula - Mystic Belle (Thatching) In tch, wknd   6   43
halfway: mdn unplcd prev: May foal, cost £21,500: dam 7f wnr.
     DANCEINTHEVALLEY 0 [5]2-8-9 R Winston 16/1: 0: 10th: Al bhd on debut.   3   34
2077 **ROBURY 35** [10]2-8-7 Dean McKeown 100/1: 000: 11th: Handy till over 2f out, wknd.   1½   27
     TITUS ROCK 0 [12]2-8-2 J Bramhill 100/1: 0: 12th: Nvr a factor on debut.   3   13
12 Ran   Time 1m 2.71 (3.21)   Owned: Mr M J Dawson   Trained: Middleham

2934   8.05 Cranemakers Classified Stakes 3yo+ 0-70   (E)
£3624 £1115 £558   5f193y   Good 59   +09 Fast   Inside

2559* **HARTSHEAD 14** [4] G A Swinbank 5-9-3 (68) Dean McKeown 10/1: 60-20611: Trkd ldrs, led last 150   79
yds, readily: gd time: eff at 6f/1m on fm & gd: confidence high now, win again: see 2559 & 1638.
2884 **TIME N TIME AGAIN 2** [3] E J Alston 6-9-3 p (70) W Supple 7/4 FAV: 0630322: Led till over 2f out,   1½   72
no extra ins fnl 1f: qck reapp: in gd form: see 551.
2713 **MY BAYARD 9** [2] J O'Reilly 5-9-3 BL (56) J D O'Reilly(7) 20/1: 2501043: Handy till led over 2f   1½   67
out, hdd ins fnl 1f & no extra: tried blinks: btr 1319 (7f, fibresand).
2752 **SOBA JONES 7** [6] J Balding 7-9-3 (70) J Edmunds 3/1: 4325654: Chsd ldrs, wknd over 1f out.   2½   59
2684 **ULYSEES 9** [7]5-9-7 (74) T Eaves(3) 11/4: 0-103105: Rear, hdwy 3f out, no impress over 1f out.   1¾   58
2609 **FIORE DI BOSCO 13** [9]3-8-11 (73) P Makin(5) 8/1: 02-50446: Rear, nvr a factor: see 1745.   ½   52
6 Ran   Time 1m 13.71 (3.01)   Owned: Mr B Valentine   Trained: Richmond

2935   8.35 Carling Handicap Stakes 3yo+ 0-80   (D)   [80]
£6032 £1856 £928   6f192y   Good 59   -08 Slow   Inside

2087 **YOUNG MR GRACE 35** [1] T D Easterby 4-9-8 (74) A Mullen(7) 12/1: 0-034251: Made all, kept on well   82
for press to hold on ins fnl 1f: eff at 5f/1m on fm & soft: imprvd for a drop back to 7f: see 1142.
2809* **KIRKBYS TREASURE 5** [5] A Berry 6-9-7 (6ex) (73) F Lynch 9/2: 1213012: Handy, hdwy over 2f out,   ½   79
one paced nr fin: qck reapp: ran to wng form of 2809.
2828 **RISKA KING 4** [6] R A Fahey 4-9-0 (66) R Winston 11/1: 0000433: Mid-div, styd on fnl 1f: qck reapp.   hd   71
2848 **WALTZING WIZARD 3** [10] A Berry 5-7-13 (51) P Fessey 9/1: 0540634: Keen & handy, kept on fnl 1f.   ½   55
2564 **EFIDIUM 14** [8]6-9-3 (69) Dean McKeown 9/1: 4231535: Rear, hdwy over 2f out, onepaced fnl 1f.   1   71
2809 **STOIC LEADER 5** [7]4-9-13 (79) L Fletcher(3) 15/8 FAV: 1002426: Handy, fdd ins fnl 1f: qck reapp.   1½   78
2684 **TIDY 9** [9]4-10-0 (80) A Culhane 8/1: 015U037: Trkd ldrs, hmprd over 2f out, sn btn: top-weight.   1½   76
2102 **TANTRIC 33** [2]5-8-6 (58) J D O'Reilly 8/1: 000-0038: Rear, hdwy when not clr run 2f out, sn btn.   nk   53
2655 **SHIFTY 11** [3]5-7-12 (1oh)vis (49) P M Quinn 12/1: 4052449: Rear, hdwy over 1f out, not pace to chall.   1¼   42
2848 **FLYING EDGE 3** [4]4-8-5 (57) W Supple 14/1: 0506500: 10th: Keen in tch, not clr run over 2f out, sn btn.   ½   48
10 Ran   Time 1m 28.65 (4.75)   Owned: Mr Norman Jackson   Trained: Malton

2936   **9.05 Carlisle Brass Handicap Stakes 3yo 0-70 (E)**   [77]
£3673 £1130 £565   **6f192y**   **Good 59**   **-24 Slow**   Inside

2295   **MENAI STRAIGHTS 25** [6] R F Fisher 3-8-10 (59) R Ffrench 12/1: 3-606351: Handy, hdwy to lead appr   64
fnl 1f, kept on nr fin: eff at 7f/1m on fm & gd/soft, stiff trk: imprvd for omission of cheek pieces: see 2081.
2650   **ADORATA 11** [10] J Jay 3-9-1 (64) A Culhane 8/1: 0003202: In tch, hdwy & ev ch fnl 1f, just held.   nk   68
2565   **GASPARINI 14** [4] T D Easterby 3-8-8 (57) R Winston 7/1: 2-00043: Led after 1f till appr fnl 1f,   1   59
kept on: eff at 7f on gd, prob handles soft: see 2565.
2446   **MICKLEGATE 19** [5] J D Bethell 3-8-12 (61) J Fanning 14/1: 06443-44: Chsd ldrs, onepaced over 1f out.   1½   60
2755   **IMPULSIVE BID 7** [3]3-9-0 (63) Darren Williams 12/1: 04-40205: Led 1f, rem handy, no extra 1f out.   1   60
2446   **FIREBIRD RISING 19** [2]3-9-1 (64) P Makin(5) 12/1: 3-5036: Reared start, bhd, hdwy 2f out, styd on.   1½   58
2683   **BORODINSKY 9** [7]3-7-12 (3oh) (44) P Fessey 14/1: 000-5047: In tch, hdwy 2f out, not pace to chall.   1¼   38
2485   **YORKES FOLLY 17** [11]3-8-7 (56) Dean McKeown 16/1: 50-08: b f Stravinsky - Tommelise (Dayjur)   hd   46
Rear, hdwy & not clr run over 2f out, kept on: unplcd both '03 starts (nov stks, mdn rtd 39a): with C Fairhurst.
2723* **COMMANDER BOND 8** [1]3-9-8 (71) F Lynch 9/2: 004-0019: Handy, no impresss over 1f out.   1¼   58
2508   **CAPETOWN GIRL 16** [8]3-9-4 P (67) V Halliday 12/1: 25-10000: 10th: In tch, wknd fnl 1f: cheekpieces.   2½   49
2446* **NEQAAWI 19** [9]3-9-3 t (66) W Supple 15/8 FAV: 00-510: 11th: Trkd ldrs, hdwy 3f out, wknd 2f out: 3   42
something amiss? much btr over C/D in 2446 (frm).
11 Ran   Time 1m 29.74 (5.84)   Owned: Mr M Maclennan   Trained: Ulverston

2937   **9.35 Richmond Hotel Maiden Handicap Stakes 4yo+ 35-55 (F)**   [59]
£3066 £876 £438   **2m1f52y**   **Good 59**   **-43 Slow**   Inside

    THE KELT 11 [14] Eoin Doyle 7-8-4 t (35) W Supple 11/4 J FAV: 000/-31: b g Leading Counsel -   45
Casheral (Le Soleil) Slow away in rear, hdwy to lead over 3f out, styd on for press ins fnl 1f: Irish raider:
h'cap hdle wnr in 03/04 (eff at 2m5.5f on gd, t-strap, rtd 95h): missed '03: unplcd all Flat '02 starts (mdns,
clmr): eff at 2m1f on gd, stiff trk.
2479   **TOM BELL 17** [9] J G M O'Shea 4-9-2 (47) B Swarbrick(5) 11/2: 05-20442: Bhd, hdwy far side over 3f   4   50
out, one paced fnl 1f: clr of rem: eff at 12f/2m1f: see 2112 & 1064.
2577   **DANCING PEARL 14** [5] C J Price 6-8-12 (43) Darren Williams 6/1: 6/5-0503: Bhd, hdwy to lead 4f   6   40
out, sn hdd, no extra: see 1109.
1819   **PERCY VERANCE 46** [11] J J Quinn 6-8-9 (40) R Winston 16/1: 000///-54: Mid-div, hdwy over 3f out,   1   36
sn no impress: recent hdles unplcd (nov h'cap, rtd 79): see 1819.
2417   **PURDEY 21** [6]4-8-12 (43) M Fenton 11/4 J FAV: 004-0545: Rear, some late gains: see 1543.   ¾   38
1802   **TON CHEE 47** [2]5-8-0 (11oh) (20) P M Quinn 33/1: 0043-606: Keen & handy, hdwy over 3f out, no   13   13
impress over 1f out: recent hdles 4th (nov, rtd 86): see 824.
3387↓ **FLY KICKER 333** [13]7-8-0 (1oh)p (30) J Bramhill 14/1: 000/064-7: ch g High Kicker - Double   ¾   12
Birthday (Cavo Doro) In tch, wknd over 1f out: recent hdles unplcd (h'cap, rtd 92): unplcd in 3 '03 starts
(h'caps, rtd 35): mod form in '02 (rtd 43, E Alston): wears cheek pieces.
2298   **BULGARIA MOON 25** [8]4-8-3 (39) A Culhane 25/1: 0-0008: Handy, wknd over 1f out: see 2060.   nk   19
2479   **KRISTINEAU 17** [4]6-8-12 t P (43) P Mathers(7) 14/1: 000//-5069: Rear, hdwy/hmprd over 4f out, wknd   2½   20
over 1f out: tried cheek pieces: see 2060.
2545   **MIKASA 15** [1]4-8-5 (36) R Ffrench 16/1: 0030050: 10th: Trkd ldrs till wknd over 3f out.   1¼   12
2298   **DIVA DANCER 25** [12]4-8-2 bl (33) D Fentiman(7) 25/1: 00-00000: 11th: Led 5f, handy, wknd 3f out.   shd   8
3452   **WESTERNMOST 691** [10]6-8-9 (40) T Eaves(3) 8/1: 23/0002/-0: 12th: b g Most Welcome - Dakota Girl   nk   14
(Northern State) In tch, wknd over 3f out: recent hdles 5th (h'cap, rtd 92): missed '03: rnr-up fnl '02 start
(h'cap): eff at 12f/2m on fm, hvy & fibresand. 2 Aug'02 Thir 16gd 45-40 F: 2 Jul'01 Newc 12.4gd 46-48 E:
2 Jun'01 Sout 12af 58a-56 F: 2 Apr'01 Sout 12af 52a-53 F: 2 Mar'01 Muss 12hvy 52- F:
2562   **BALALAIKA TUNE 14** [3]5-8-1 (32) Rory Moore(7) 16/1: 0400460: 13th: Led after 5f to 4f out, wknd.   15   0
2850   **BLUE VENTURE 3** [7]4-9-6 (51) Mr G Bartley(7) 14/1: 0-000400: 14th: Al bhd: qck reapp.   ½   9
14 Ran   Time 3m 59.28(17.38)   Owned: J J P Murphy   Trained: Ireland

BEVERLEY   SATURDAY 03.07.04   Righthand, Oval Track with Stiff Uphill Finish

Official Going GOOD/SOFT.

2938   **1.45 Coachman Caravans Novice Stakes 2yo (D)**
£4622 £1422 £711   **7f100y rnd**   **Soft 105**   **-41 Slow**   Inside

    GYPSY JOHNNY [3] M L W Bell 2-8-8   I Mongan 9/4: 1: gr c Bachir - Gentle Gypsy (Junius) In   84
tch, hdwy 2f out, styd on to lead over 1f out, pushed clr, plenty in hand on debut: April foal, cost 16,000gns:
half-brother to a useful sprinter: stays a stiff/undul 7.5f well, further sure to suit: runs well fresh on soft
grnd: v pleasing start, plenty more juv staying events to be won.
    LOVE PALACE [2] M Johnston 2-8-8   K Dalgleish 9/4: 2: b c King's Best - Vijaya (Lear Fan)   4   76
Cl-up, rdn over 2f out, chall over 1f out, not pace of wnr on debut: March foal, cost E110,000: half-brother to a
5f/1m scorer: prob stays 7.5f on soft grnd: shld be sharper for this & win a race soon.
2652* **THREE PENNIES 11** [4] M Dods 2-8-11   F Lynch 2/1 FAV: 013: Set stdy pace, hdd & wknd over 1f out: ¾   75
prob ran close to form of 2652 (mdn fills, gd).
    EBORARRY [1] T D Easterby 2-8-8   D Allan 7/1: 4: b c Desert Sun - Aztec Princess (Indian King)   5   66
Slow away & al bhd on debut: March foal, cost E13,500gns: half-brother to wnrs over 6f/hdles.
4 Ran   Time 1m 41.77 (10.97)   Owned: HESheikh Rashid Bin Mohammed   Trained: Newmarket

BEVERLEY   SATURDAY 03.07.04   Righthand, Oval Track with Stiff Uphill Finish

---

2939   **2.15 Happy Birthday Robert Selling Stakes 2yo (F)**
£3161 £903 £452   **7f100y rnd**   **Soft 105**   **-50 Slow**   Inside

PON MY SOUL [2] M G Quinlan 2-8-11 R Fitzpatrick 8/1: 1: b g Imperial Ballet - Erin Anam Cara   59
(Exit To Nowhere) Held up, hdwy to lead 2f out, drvn & hung left ins last but kept on for press: bght in for
6,800gns on debut: March first foal: dam styd 10f: eff over a stiff/undul 7.5f on soft, shld get further: runs
well fresh in sell grade: prob more to come.
2611 **SONGGARIA** 12 [4] J S Wainwright 2-8-6 T Eaves(3) 15/2: 2302: Bhd, hdwy outer 2f out, hung right   ½   53
ins last but styd on to chall, just held: clmd for 6,000: stays 7.5f: acts on fast & gd/soft: see 2449, 2270.
2492 **COIS NA TINE EILE** 17 [8] K A Ryan 2-8-6 G Parkin 9/1: 303: Sn rdn bhd, kept on late, nrst fin: shd 53
clmd for 6,000: stays 7.5f on gd/soft: apprec drop in class: see 2492, 1779.
2563 **MAUREENS LOUGH** 14 [7] T D Barron 2-8-13 Darren Williams 5/1: 36154: In tch, eff over 1f out,   nk   59
onepace: stays 7.5f on firm & gd/soft: see 2294, 1224.
2563 **RIVERWELD** 14 [5]2-8-11 D Fentiman(7) 9/2 FAV: 6425: In tch, eff when short of room ins last,   nk   56
kept on, not btn far: see 2563, 1779.
2461 **FORPETESAKE** 18 [10]2-8-11 I Mongan 10/1: 066: Bhd, some late gains, nvr dngrs: clmd for 6,000:   ¾   54
prob stays 7.5f on gd/soft: see 2461.
2167 **LANE MARSHAL** 31 [16]2-8-11 BL G Faulkner 20/1: 65007: Led after 1f till 2f out, wknd: tried blnks.   4   47
2343 **FAITHFUL FLASH** 23 [6]2-8-6 T Hamilton(3) 33/1: 68: Chsd ldrs, wknd 2f out: see 2343.   1¼   39
2611 **FRISBY RIDGE** 12 [12]2-8-6 D Allan 13/2: 0505549: Led 1f, handy till wknd over 2f out.   1½   37
2321 **HOLLINGWOOD SOUL** 24 [9]2-8-6 Dean McKeown 20/1: 0000: 10th: Al bhd: see 2321.   ½   36
2321 **TIMMY** 24 [14]2-8-11 D McGaffin 33/1: 0000: 11th: In tch, wknd over 1f out: see 2321.   4   35
2358 **SHUCHBAA** 22 [15]2-8-6 R Ffrench 8/1: 300: 12th: Al bhd: twice below 1968 (debut, 6f, gd/firm).   8   18
TEWITFIELD LASS [3]2-8-6 L Enstone 33/1: 0: 13th: b f Bluegrass Prince - Madam Marash   3   14
(Astronef) Slow away & al bhd on debut: March foal, cheaply bought.
2652 **AMANDERICA** 11 [11]2-8-6 D Fox(5) 100/1: 000: 14th: Slow away & al bhd.   ¾   13
14 Ran   Time 1m 42.46 (11.66)   Owned: Archangels   Trained: Newmarket

---

2940   **2.50 Bp Saltend Handicap Stakes 3yo 0-85 (D)**   [85]
£5558 £1710 £855   **1m100y rnd**   **Soft 105**   **+08 Fast**   Inside

2773 **CHARNOCK BATES ONE** 7 [5] T D Easterby 3-8-6 (63) G Gibbons 7/1: 354-4601: Sn rdn in tch, hdwy &   75
hung right 2f out but styd on to lead ins last, drvn out: first win, gd time: stays a stiff 8.5f well on gd/soft,
handles fm: see 1163 (reapp).
2514 **RILEY BOYS** 16 [6] J G Given 3-9-3 (74) I Mongan 9/2 CO FAV: 2121222: Led early, led again 3f   hd   85
out, kept on till collared ins last, just held for press: well clr of rem & lost little in defeat: loves Beverley.
2127 **MAN OF LETTERS** 32 [2] M Johnston 3-9-7 (78) K Dalgleish 9/2 CO FAV: 3221253: Prom, sltly outpcd   8   77
over 2f out, eff & hmpd 2f out, kept on in tch, no threat: see 1965, 1554.
2705 **LITTLE JIMBOB** 9 [4] R A Fahey 3-9-6 (77) T Hamilton(3) 11/2: 2342-124: In tch, wknd over 2f out: 5   68
btr on gd grnd in 2705, 2443.
2495 **ANNIE HARVEY** 17 [1]3-8-11 (70) F Lynch 12/1: D30-0025: Led after 1f till 3f out, wknd: see 2495.   5   53
2693 **COTTINGHAM** 9 [3]3-8-8 (65) D Fox(5) 12/1: 0040-146: Al bhd: see 2693, 355.   hd   47
2474 **FAIRLIE** 17 [9]3-8-5 (62) R Ffrench 12/1: 1046-507: Held up, wknd over 2f out: see 1953.   1   42
2656* **SWAINSWORLD** 11 [8]3-9-7 (78) D Allan 9/2 CO FAV: 4418: Held up, eff & short of room 2f out, sn   shd 58
wknd: btr 2656 (gd grnd).
2277 **MOUNT VETTORE** 26 [7]3-9-4 (75) Dean McKeown 9/1: 1200009: In tch, hmpd & lost place after 2f,   3   51
eff over 2f out, sn wknd: see 955 (7f, gd), 481.
9 Ran   Time 1m 52.1 (8.3)   Owned: Charnock Bates   Trained: Malton

---

2941   **3.25 Eltherington Stakes Handicap 3yo+ 0-70 (E)**   [70]
£3900 £1200 £600   **2m35y**   **Soft 105**   **-56 Slow**   Inside

2562 **OOPS** 14 [3] J F Coupland 5-7-13 (41) Dean Williams(6) 6/1: 6/0042-01: Led till ran wide bend   46
after 6f, cl-up, kept on over 1f out to lead ins last, drvn out: stays 2m on firm & gd/soft: likes a gall trk:
confidence boosting first success: see 2562.
2754 **LADY NETBETSPORTS** 7 [6] B S Rothwell 5-9-5 (61) M Lawson(5) 11/1: 000-0302: Cl-up, led after 6f,   ½   65
kept on for press till collared ins last, not btn far: gd run & stays 2m but remains a mdn: see 2708, 2510.
2577 **DANCE LIGHT** 14 [7] T T Clement 5-9-4 (60) T G McLaughlin 3/1: 600-0053: b f Lycius - Embracing   ½   63
(Reference Point) Held up, hdwy to chall over 1f out, no extra ins last, not btn far: well btn both '03 starts:
won a mdn & 3 h'caps in '02: suited by 14f/2m on firm & gd grnd, handled gd/soft here, prob any trk: more
encouraging, clr of rem & has drpd to a handy mark.
1 Sep'02 Catt 15.8fm 66-64 F: 1 Aug'02 Chep 16.2gd 65-57 F: 1 Aug'02 Thir 16gd 59-53 F: 1 Jul'02 Catt 13.7fm 57- F:
4508] **GALLEON BEACH** 278 [4] B D Leavy 7-10-0 (70) L Vickers 16/1: 3110/06-4: b g Shirley Heights -   5   66
Music In My Life (Law Society) Hld up, eff 2f out, onepace: well btn both starts in '03 for W Brisbourne: '02 3 time
h'cap wnr for A Streeter: suited by 2m/2m2f on fm or hvy: tried blnks/visor/t-strap: broken blood vessels.
1 Oct'02 Pont 17.1fm 71-66 E: 1 Sep'02 Bath 17.1fm 66-61 D: 1 Jul'02 Chep 18gd 63-61 E: 2 Sep'01 Pont 18fm 76- C:
1768 **ASHTAROUTE** 49 [2]4-8-7 (49) D Fox(5) 16/1: 0050-605: b f Holy Bull - Beating The Buzz (Bluebird)   11   37
Hld up, wknd over 2f out: earlier rnr-up in a mdn hdle (rtd 96h, 2m6f, gd): rtd 75S when 3rd in a mdn in '03 (12f).
3733] **ONLY WORDS** 678 [5]7-7-13 (1ow)(6oh) (34) R Ffrench 9/1: 46/0000/-6: In tch, wknd over 4f out on   ½   28
comeback: jumps rumour.
2471 **RIYADH** 18 [1]6-9-9 vis (65) K Dalgleish 11/10 FAV: 0030307: In tch, lost place over 4f out, eff   8   45
over 2f out, sn wknd: hvly bckd: has own ideas about the game now: see 2471, 2276.
7 Ran   Time 3m 56.18 (25.88)   Owned: Mr J F Coupland   Trained: Grimsby

2942   3.55 Mondi Hypac Stakes Handicap 3yo+ 0-90 (C)   [90]
£13884 £4272 £2136   **5f str**   **Soft 105**   -12 Slow   Inside

2690* **PADDYWACK 9** [18] D W Chapman 7-8-6 bl (68) Rory Moore(7) 11/2: 0353011: Rear, switched wide & hdwy   **75**
halfway, strong run to lead cl-home: rider given a 2-day careless riding ban: stays 7f, best at 5f: acts on firm,
soft & both AWs, handles soft: handles any trk: in fine form, see 2690.
2775 **WINTHORPE 7** [14] J J Quinn 4-8-7 (69) K Dalgleish 6/1: 0004032: Hmpd start & rear, short of room   ½   **74+**
halfway & again dist, switched & hmpd again entering fnl 1f, fin strongly & only just failed: acts on fast, soft &
f/sand: no luck, most unfortunate & deserves similar, well h'capped: see 2775.
1490 **BOND BOY 62** [13] B Smart 7-10-0 (90) F Lynch 12/1: 0040603: Rear, styd on fnl 1f, nrst fin: 9   nk   **94**
wk abs, top-weight: loves easy grnd, poised to strike, see 1162 & 927.
2747 **TALLY 7** [16] M J Polglase 4-7-12 (1oh) (59) D Fox(5) 7/1: 1200244: Chsd ldrs, sltly short of room   1½   **60**
dist, kept on fnl 1f & not btn far: another consistent run, had the best of the draw: see 2690.
2846 **BRIGADIER MONTY 3** [9]6-7-12 (1o0h) (50) D Fentiman(7) 33/1: 0-060005: Held up, hdwy when short of   2   **56**
room dist, nrst fin: qck reapp: fine run from out of the h'cap: see 2846.
2561 **BLACKHEATH 14** [15]8-9-6 (82) Alex Greaves 4/1 FAV: 4406226: Trkd ldrs, ev ch till wknd ins fnl   ¾   **76**
1f: well bckd: had a decent high drawn: see 2561 & 2409.
2760 **CATCH THE CAT 7** [17]5-8-10 bl (72) G Parkin 6/1: 0201657: Broke well & led till ins fnl 1f, wknd.   shd   **65**
2830 **KINGS COLLEGE BOY 4** [8]4-7-12 VIS (60) J McAuley 20/1: 0-003238: Mid-div, keeping on when short   nk   **52**
of room entering fnl 1f: qck reapp, tried a visor: see 2830 & 2524.
2830 **BEYOND THE CLOUDS 4** [6]8-9-0 (76) D Allan 18/1: 00-00029: Prom till wknd dist: qck reapp,   2½   **63**
modest draw & unsuitably soft grnd: btr 2830.
2758 **WATCHING 7** [12]7-9-8 (84) A Nicholls 10/1: 3025500: 10th: Chsd ldrs, wknd fnl 1f.   ½   **70**
2702 **TUSCAN FLYER 9** [10]6-7-13 bl (61) R Ffrench 16/1: 2-003040: 11th: Nvr btr than mid-div.   1¾   **44**
2256 **VITA SPERICOLATA 28** [3]7-9-7 bl (83) T Eaves(3) 40/1: 0-003500: 12th: Speed 3.5f, wknd: poor draw.   5   **56**
2359 **RECTANGLE 22** [5]4-8-10 (72) I Mongan 66/1: 630-0000: 13th: Al rear from poor draw: see 2359.   1½   **42**
2779* **DIZZY IN THE HEAD 6** [7]5-9-10 (6ex)bl (86) N Chalmers(5) 12/1: 1631210: 14th: Speed till halfway,   hd   **55**
wknd: qck reapp under 6lb pen, poor draw: prev in fine form on firm grnd, see 2779 & 2598.
1683 **ARTIE 52** [1]5-9-7 (83) J Carroll 25/1: 0-002100: 15th: Dwelt, al bhd: 7 wk abs & poor draw.   1¾   **49**
15 Ran   Time 1m 07.19 (5.89)   Owned: Mr T S Redman   Trained: York

2943   4.30 Coachman Caravans Handicap Stakes 3yo+ 0-75 (E)   [75]
£3770 £1160 £580   **1m1f207y**   **Soft 105**   +06 Fast   Inside

2226* **SANTIBURI LAD 29** [1] N Wilson 7-8-10 (57) T Hamilton(3) 9/4 FAV: 460-3211: Made all, clr fnl   **67**
1.5f, easily: nicely bckd, gd time: poss stays 12f, suited by 10f: acts on firm, soft grnd & fibresand: loves
forcing tactics & clearly in fine form: can complete qck hat-trick, see 2226.
2465 **COMPTON DRAGON 18** [6] D Nicholls 5-10-0 vis (75) A Nicholls 7/2: 5052252: Keen & trkd ldrs, eff   8   **75**
when hmpd dist, kept on for 2nd but no ch with facile wnr: top-weight: see 2284 & 1519.
2726* **KINGSDON 8** [3] T J Fitzgerald 7-9-2 vis t (63) K Dalgleish 5/2: 4411113: Chsd ldrs, outpcd 4f   2   **60**
out, rallied fnl 2f but no ch with wnr: nicely bckd: see 2726 & 2589.
2782 **BOND MAY DAY 6** [5] B Smart 4-9-5 (66) F Lynch 11/2: 160-0044: Prom, wknd 2f out: not like soft?   hd   **63**
1253 **LUCAYAN DANCER 75** [4]4-8-13 (60) Alex Greaves 9/2: 0334-655: Chsd ldrs, btn 2f out: 11 wk abs.   3   **54**
5 Ran   Time 2m 12.2 (9.9)   Owned: Mrs Karan Ridley   Trained: York

2944   5.00 George Kilburn Memorial Stakes Maiden Div 1 3yo+ (D)
£3435 £1057 £529   **5f str**   **Soft 105**   -01 Slow   Inside

2649 **ROYAL CHALLENGE 11** [4] G A Butler 3-9-0 I Mongan 4/6 FAV: 0-21: Trkd ldrs, hdwy to lead 1.5f   **80**
out, styd on strongly, decisively: hvly bckd: eff at 5f, will stay 6f: acts on firm & soft grnd: improved.
2849 **HARRISONS FLYER 3** [11] R A Fahey 3-9-0 G Parkin 6/1: 4-02: Led till dist, no extra: qck reapp   3   **70**
& well clr rem: eff at 5f on soft grnd: could find a small race, see 2849.
2182 **RED HOT RUBY 30** [1] R A Fahey 3-8-9 T Hamilton(3) 25/1: 03: ch f Komaite - Gleam of Gold   8   **49**
(Crested Lark) Outpcd, late gains, no ch with front 2: longer-priced s/mate 2nd: stay further judged on this.
2775 **BLUE MAEVE 7** [8] J Hetherton 4-9-5 (51) S Righton 4/1: 40400424: Speed 3f, wknd: see 2775.   1¾   **50**
3368} **MECCAS MATE 334** [6]3-8-9 L Enstone(3) 50/1: 0-5: gr f Paris House - Clancassie (Clantime)   ½   **44**
Outpcd, nvr a factor on reapp: unplcd sole juv start: half-sister won over 6f: stumbled halfway today.
2428 **COTTAM KARMINSKI 20** [7]3-8-9 Rory Moore(7) 50/1: 0006: Al outpcd.   1½   **41**
2485 **HAMAASY 17** [5]3-9-0 (61) Alex Greaves 12/1: 0600-57: Chsd ldrs till halfway, wknd: flattered 2485.   1¾   **42**
2657 **BOWLEGS BILLY 11** [9]4-9-5 P (48) K Pierrepont(7) 16/1: 25000-08: Al bhd: first time cheek pieces.   1½   **39**
69 **BOND ROMEO 225** [3]3-9-0 (70) D McGaffin 11/1: 555020-9: ch g Titus Livius - At Amal (Astronef)   5   **29**
Prom wide, wknd 2f out on reapp: '03 mdn auct rnr-up (rtd 76$): eff at 5f on fast grnd, handles a gall trk.
2 Oct'03 Redc 5g/f 76-(57) F:
2730 **ALPHA ZETA 8** [10]3-9-0 Dean McKeown 66/1: 0-000: 10th: Al outpcd, fin last.   hd   **28**
10 Ran   Time 1m 06.59 (5.29)   Owned: Cheveley Park Stud   Trained: Blewbury

2945   5.30 George Kilburn Memorial Stakes Maiden Div 2 3yo+ (D)
£3426 £1054 £527   **5f str**   **Soft 105**   -34 Slow   Inside

3423} **CHIMALI 332** [6] J Noseda 3-9-0 A Nicholls 7/4 FAV: 4-1: b g Foxhound - Mari Ela (River Falls)   **64**
Made all, held on well fnl 1f, drvn out: reapp: mdn auct 4th (with J Nicol) on sole juv start, has subs been
gelded: 150,000gns Jan foal: eff at 5f on soft grnd, handles fast: likes to force the pace & runs well fresh.
2630 **ROAN RAIDER 12** [9] M J Polglase 4-9-5 vis (53) G Gibbons 14/1: 4053502: Nvr far away, chall fnl   nk   **62$**
1f & only just btn: eff btwn 5f & 1m on fast & soft grnd: see 2237.
2784 **ELLIOTS CHOICE 6** [7] D Carroll 3-9-0 (66) D Nolan(3) 2/1: 0-440043: Held up, styd on late, nrst fin.   1½   **59**
2152 **INTAVAC BOY 31** [8] C W Thornton 3-9-0 J Carroll 10/1: 664: ch g Emperor Fountain - Altaia   4   **51**
(Sicyos) Outpcd, keeping on when short of room dist: now qual for h'caps.
2846 **AMANDAS LAD 3** [1]4-9-5 (56) D Fox(5) 7/1: 4203545: Prom 3.5f, wknd: qck reapp.   hd   **50**

2182	**GREY GURKHA** 30 [2]3-9-0 R Fitzpatrick 33/1: 606: Dwelt, chsd ldrs 3f, sn btn.	10	30
2559	**AKIRAMENAI** 14 [5]4-9-0 (55) I Mongan 25/1: 04067: Chsd ldrs till halfway, sn btn.	nk	24
2237	**ESTOILLE** 28 [10]3-8-9 T D Fentiman(7) 50/1: 008: Al bhd in first time t-strap.	1	22
2938}	**IO CALLISTO** 352 [4]3-8-9 G Parkin 25/1: 60-9: br f Hector Protector - Queen Shirley (Fairy	25	0

King) Speed 3f, wknd & t.o. in last: well btn on both juv starts: cost 10,000gns: with R Fahey.
9 Ran   Time 1m 08.24(6.94) Owned: Mrs Susan Roy Trained: Newmarket

Official Going GOOD (GOOD/SOFT Places).

2946

1.50 Gr2 Bet365 Lancashire Oaks Fillies 3yo+ (A)
£58000 £22000 £11000   **1m3f200y**   **Good 47**   **+05 Fast**   Outside

1921* **PONGEE** 42 [6] L M Cumani 4-9-3 (96) J Fortune 9/2: 1110-311: Chsd ldrs, drvn 2f out, strong run **110**
to lead cl-home despite flashing tail: 6 wk abs, gd time: eff at 10f, suited by 12f: acts on firm, gd/soft &
polytrack: progressive & smart now, clearly runs well fresh & the 14f Park Hil is ideal target: see 1921.
2517 **SAHOOL** 16 [4] M P Tregoning 3-8-4 (107) W Supple 11/8 FAV: 61-2222: Nvr far away, led entering 1 **108**
fnl 1f, not pace to repel wnr cl-home: well bckd: another fine run in defeat, struck by rival's whip entering fnl
1f & that clearly did not help: shld win a Gr 3: see 2517 & 1494.
2821 **DANELISSIMA** 6 [8] J S Bolger 3-8-4 BL T P Queally 10/1: 2-544124: Held up, eff 2f out, fin nk **107**
strongly but too late: qck reapp in first time blnks: Irish challenger, 14f will suit judged on this, see 2821.
2517 **HIDDEN HOPE** 16 [1] G Wragg 3-8-5 (1ow) (106) S Drowne 13/2: 00-2154: Chsd ldrs, styd on under ¾ **107**
press fnl 1f, not pace to chall: needs List/Gr 3: see 1568.
2517 **NEW MORNING** 16 [5]3-8-5 (1ow) (104) N Callan 13/2: 4-2145: Led till ent fnl 1f, no extra: see 2517. ½ **106**
1684 **SUMMITVILLE** 17 [3]4-9-3 (107) M Fenton 7/1: 5302-326: Held up, prog 2f out, no impress fnl 1f: nk **105**
struggling to recapture last season's smart form, see 1684.
1921 **CHANTRESS** 42 [7]4-9-3 (92) J Fanning 66/1: 1413-037: Trkd ldrs, wknd 2f out: 6 wk abs: btr 1921. 12 **89**
2351 **SI SI AMIGA** 23 [2]3-8-4 (94) M Hills 50/1: 1-4458: Prom 10f, wknd. 3 **85**
8 Ran   Time 2m 32.9 (5.1) Owned: Fittocks Stud Trained: Newmarket

2947

2.25 Birchley Handicap Stakes 3yo+ 0-70 (E) [70]
£4069 £1252 £626   **1m30y rnd**   **Good 47**   **-16 Slow**   Inside

2647 **PARNASSIAN** 11 [4] G B Balding 4-9-2 (58) S Drowne 6/1: 3313051: Held up, switched & gd hdwy **65**
dist, led ins fnl 1f, pushed out: eff btwn 7f & 1m on gd & soft grnd, handles fast & firm: see 1778.
2688 **RYMERS RASCAL** 9 [11] E J Alston 12-8-7 (49) W Supple 25/1: 02-32002: Mid-div, hdwy to lead 1¼ **52**
briefly ins fnl 1f, kept on but not pace of wnr: this evergreen 12yo: see 1972 & 1425.
2542 **FAIR SPIN** 15 [9] M D Hammond 4-9-7 (63) A Culhane 11/1: 04000-03: Mid-div, hdwy when short of ½ **65**
room fnl 1f, not btn far: eff at 6f/1m on gd & hvy grnd: shade closer with a clr run, see 2542.
2394 **DIDNT TELL MY WIFE** 21 [17] C F Wall 5-9-7 (63) R Mullen 16/1: 021-6604: Mid-div, prog dist, hit nk **65**
by rival's whip & hmpd ins fnl 1f, nrst fin: did not get the run of today's race: see 12 (AW h'cap).
2550 **APACHE POINT** 15 [1]7-8-12 (54) Kim Tinkler 8/1: 4-005455: Mid-div, hdwy to chall entering fnl ½ **55**
1f, no extra cl-home: see 1776.
2840 **MALLARD** 3 [2]6-9-7 (63) M Fenton 4/1 FAV: 101-3026: Prom, ev ch till wknd ins fnl 1f: nicely bckd. nk **63**
2873 **TOJONESKI** 2 [8]5-8-4 p (46) J F McDonald(3) 11/2: 2233427: Chsd ldrs, onepcd when hmpd ins fnl 1f: hd **45**
nicely bckd: qck reapp, see 2873 (flattered).
2199 **BOUGHT DIRECT** 30 [3]5-8-13 (55) K McEvoy 10/1: 0065468: Rear, nvr nr ldrs: see 791. 1½ **51**
1748 **CRESKELD** 50 [13]5-10-0 (70) R Winston 20/1: 00-30009: Prom, led halfway till ins fnl 1f, wknd: abs. 3 **60**
2600 **PRINCE OF GOLD** 13 [7]4-9-11 p (67) N Callan 12/1: 0060100: 10th: Trkd ldrs, ev ch dist, wknd fnl 1f. ¾ **55**
2745 **BUTHAINA** 7 [6]4-8-8 (50) P Makin(5) 33/1: 1-000000: 11th: Rear, nvr nr ldrs. 1¾ **34**
2060 **THE LOOSE SCREW** 36 [18]6-7-12 P (40) B Swarbrick(5) 50/1: 00-00000: 12th: Prom 6f, wknd: chkpieces. ½ **23**
2402 **GEMINI LADY** 21 [15]4-8-4 (46) G Duffield 33/1: 420-0200: 13th: Nvr btr than mid-div: btr 1992. 8 **13**
700 Hows Things 131 [16]4-9-7 (63) Paul Eddery 20/1:0 1954* **Zawrak** 40 [10]5-9-4 (60) Natalia Gemelova(7) 12/1:0
1884 Iftikhar 43 [5]5-9-4 (60) N Pollard 25/1:0 2550 **Mount Pekan** 15 [12]4-8-2 (44) J Mackay 33/1:0
17 Ran   Time 1m 45.56 (5.06) Owned: Miss B Swire Trained: Andover

2948

2.55 Bet365 Old Newton Cup Heritage Handicap 3yo+ 0-110 (B) [107]
£40600 £15400 £7700   **1m3f200y**   **Good 47**   **+10 Fast**   Outside

2246 **ALKAASED** 28 [11] L M Cumani 4-9-1 (94) J Fortune 7/1: 4/2122-21: Trkd ldrs, smooth hdwy to lead **110+**
2f out, rdn clr, v impressive: val 6L+, best time of day: eff at 12/14f on gd & firm grnd: handles a sharpish or
stiff trk: smart, has a fine turn of foot & shld be followed in List/Gr 3: see 2246.
2605 **CROW WOOD** 13 [5] J G Given 5-9-1 (94) K McEvoy 33/1: 05-03352: Mid-div, hdwy when short of room 4 **99**
1.5f out, styd on into 2nd but no ch with wnr: stays a stiff 12f: met a fast improving & v well h'capped rival.
2234 **GRAMPIAN** 28 [17] J G Given 5-9-9 (102) M Fenton 33/1: 525/-2623: Rear, styd on fnl 1.5f, nrst nk **107**
fin: stablemate of rnr-up: v useful h'capper, another fine consistent run: see 2234 & 1364.
2582 **HAMBLEDEN** 14 [7] M A Jarvis 7-9-6 (99) N Callan 10/1: 312-6044: Led till 2f out, no extra: 1¼ **102**
front runner, far from disgraced: likes York & a return to 14f/2m shld suit: see 2582 & 1585.
1596 **ROYAL CAVALIER** 57 [14]7-9-5 (98) A Culhane 16/1: 206-0145: Mid-div, styd on fnl 1f, nrst fin: abs. shd **101**
2582 **SWIFT TANGO** 14 [6]4-9-7 (100) K Darley 10/1: 2341236: Held up, eff 2f out, nrst fin: see 2582. nk **102**
2560 **OLDENWAY** 14 [16]5-7-12 (1oh) (76) P Fessey 40/1: 2242147: Mid-div, not pace to chall: up in 1 **77**
grade, but not disgraced: see 2323.
2519 **SWAGGER STICK** 16 [1]3-7-12 (90) J Mackay 9/2 FAV: 014-1168: Prom, ev ch till wknd fnl 1f: ½ **89**
nicely bckd: stable not really firing at present: see 1355.
2582 **COUNSELS OPINION** 14 [3]7-9-10 (103) R Mullen 14/1: 110-3409: Dwelt, keen in mid-div, onepcd fnl shd **102**
1.5f: top-weight: 3rd from a 9lb lower mark in this race last yr: see 2582 & 1111.

1969* **BOURGEOIS 40** [12]7-9-5 (98) R Winston 14/1: 350-2310: 10th: Nvr btr than mid-div: 6 wk abs. nk 96
2582 **TRUST RULE 14** [8]4-9-1 (94) M Hills 9/1: 02-06500: 11th: Prom 10f, wknd. 1¼ 90
1668+ **BALKAN KNIGHT 53** [15]4-8-5 vis (84) T P Queally 7/1: 01/1-610: 12th: Held up, nvr nr ldrs: btr 1668. 6 71
1759 **TURBO 49** [2]5-9-0 p (93) S Drowne 8/1: 021-0040: 13th: Al bhd: 7 wk abs & reportedly nvr trav. 5 72
433 **SANTANDO 133** [9]4-9-4 vis (97) G Duffield 20/1: 06-53050: 14th: Trkd ldrs 10f, wknd: long abs. 4 70
2554 **HAADEF 15** [4]3-8-7 (99) W Supple 8/1: 3140: 15th: Hmpd after 2f & al bhd, fin last: reportedly 20 42
injured when hmpd & this must be forgiven: see 2554 & 2131.
15 Ran   Time 2m 32.3 (4.5)   Owned: Mr M R Charlton   Trained: Newmarket

2949   3.35 Thwaites Smooth Beer Conditions Stakes 3yo+   (C)
£8932 £3388 £1694   **6f str**   **Good 47**   **-39 Slow**   Centre

2769 **QUITO 7** [7] D W Chapman 7-8-10 bl (110) A Culhane 7/4 FAV: 5610651: Held up, gd hdwy dist, led 109
cl-home, rdn out: eff at 5f, best at 6/7f: acts on firm, loves gd/soft, soft & fibresand: handles any trk: loves
to come late in a big field/off a fast pace & more val prizes await, see 1703.
2581 **DAZZLING BAY 14** [6] T D Easterby 4-8-10 bl (102) W Supple 100/30: 06-60352: Keen & chsd ldrs, 1 104
imprvd to lead ins fnl 1f, not pace to repel wnr cl-home: nicely bckd: fine run, deserves a race: see 2357.
4080) **CONTINENT 301** [4] D Nicholls 7-8-10 (112) J Fortune 8/1: 0/00600-3: ch g Lake Coniston - Krisia 1¾ 99
(Kris) Slow away, hdwy to lead briefly ent fnl 1f, no extra cl-home: op 13/2, reapp: mainly below best in '03, 6th
in Gr 1 July Cup (rtd 112), subs tried a visor: '02 Gr 1 July Cup & Prix L'Abbaye wnr: stays 7f, suited by 5/6f on
firm, likes gd & soft, stiff trks: best held up & goes esp well for D Holland: top-class at best.
1 Oct'02 Long 5gd 120- : 1 Jul'02 Newm 6g/s 120- A: 2 Jun'02 Asco 5gd 115- A: 2 Apr'02 Newm 6g/f 111- A:
2 Apr'02 Kemp 6gd 109- C: 1 Sep'01 Ayr 6g/f 101-92 B:
2186 **TOM TUN 30** [9] J Balding 9-9-1 bl (93) M Fenton 12/1: 010-0204: Chsd ldrs, onepcd fnl 1f: see 1703. 1 101
2581 **CIRCUIT DANCER 14** [2]4-8-10 (96) K Darley 11/2: 6-340105: Led till 2f out, no extra: see 2357. nk 95
2457 **DOWAGER 21** [1]3-8-4 (97) R L Moore 7/1: 2461-546: Led 2f out till ent fnl 1f, wknd: clr rem. 4 83
2777 **JALOUHAR 6** [8]4-8-10 (46) T Woodley 125/1: 2060207: Prom 4f, wknd qckly: outclassed. 10 33
2777 **ROSSELLI 6** [5]8-8-10 (46) C Ely(7) 125/1: 4-000008: Prom till halfway, wknd: v highly tried. 12 0
8 Ran   Time 1m 16.48 (5.18)   Owned: Mr Michael Hill   Trained: York

2950   4.05 Duke Of Lancaster's Own Yeomanry Handicap Stakes 3yo 0-95 (C)   [101]
£10270 £3160 £1580   **6f str**   **Good 47**   **-32 Slow**   Centre

2427 **FLIPANDO 20** [5] T D Barron 3-8-6 (79) K Darley 3/1 FAV: 310-4221: Trkd ldrs, styd on under press 90
to lead dying strides: nicely bckd: eff at 6/7f on gd & firm grnd, prob handles soft: handles a sharpish or
stiff/gall trk: in fine form & deserved win, see 2427 & 1417.
2485* **DOITNOW 17** [9] R A Fahey 3-8-8 (81) R Winston 8/1: 12: Rear, hdwy to lead entering fnl 1f, worn hd 91
down fnl strides: fine run on only 2nd start, acts on gd & fast grnd: handles a sharpish or gall trk: plenty more
to come & shld develop into a useful sprinter: see 2485.
2566 **FOUR AMIGOS 14** [11] J G Given 3-8-10 (83) K McEvoy 11/1: 02-51063: Rear, hdwy dist, styd on fnl 3 84
1f & nrst fin, not ch front 2: stays a gall 6f: see 1229.
2619* **BOHOLA FLYER 12** [1] R Hannon 3-8-5 (78) R L Moore 7/1: 1464114: Rear, styd on fnl 1f, nrst fin: ¾ 77
continues in fine form: see 2619.
2609 **LETS GET IT ON 13** [2]3-8-4 (77) P Fessey 20/1: 0052005: Rear, switched & hdwy 1.5f out, nvr nrr. shd 76
2770 **GEORGE THE BEST 7** [10]3-7-12 (1oh) (70) B Swarbrick(5) 25/1: 00-06406: Prom, led briefly dist, wknd. 3½ 60
2677 **CELTIC THUNDER 10** [14]3-8-11 (84) J Fortune 7/1: 6-205027: Held up, late hdwy, nvr dngrs: btr 2677. 1 64
2407 **TIMES REVIEW 21** [7]3-8-11 (84) W Supple 20/1: 00-25108: Nvr btr than mid-div: twice below 2137. 1¾ 65
2482 **ISKANDER 17** [6]3-8-8 bl (81) N Callan 16/1: 54-60009: Al mid-div: see 1665. 1 59
2398* **UNDER MY SPELL 21** [16]3-8-3 (76) R Mullen 14/1: 0022510: 10th: Trkd ldrs, wknd dist: btr 2398. ¾ 52
2591 **SKYHARBOR 14** [12]3-8-7 (80) M Hills 16/1: 3100-050: 11th: Chsd ldrs 4f, wknd: see 2591. ½ 55
2400 **FOURSQUARE 21** [15]3-9-2 (89) A Culhane 10/1: 02-15040: 12th: Sn led, hdd dist, wknd. ½ 62
2407 **BONNE DE FLEUR 21** [13]3-9-7 (94) T P Queally 16/1: 1232-100: 13th: Early ldr, prom till dist, wknd. 4 55
2482 **Piccolo Prince 17** [4]3-7-12 (3oh) (68) J Bramhill 33/1:0 2609 **Mind Alert 13** [3]3-7-12 (1oh) (70) J Mackay 16/1:0
15 Ran   Time 1m 16.03 (4.73)   Owned: Mrs J Hazell   Trained: Thirsk

2951   4.40 Ellesmere Handicap Stakes 3yo+ 0-70 (E)   [69]
£3913 £1204 £602   **5f str**   **Good 47**   **-35 Slow**   Centre

2599* **FOLEY MILLENNIUM 13** [9] M Quinn 6-9-7 (62) N Pollard 9/2 FAV: 6P-01111: Made all, held on gamely 67
cl-home: nicely bckd to complete 4-timer: eff at 5/6f on firm & hvy grnd: handles a sharp or gall trk: remains in
terrific form & likes to run up with/force the pace: see 2599 & 1644.
2846 **LAUREL DAWN 3** [8] I W McInnes 6-9-4 (59) J F McDonald(3) 10/1: 0000152: Bmpd start, hdwy from shd 63
rear 1.5f out, fin strongly & only just failed: qck reapp & poss a shade unlucky: made all in 2657.
2599 **INTELLIBET ONE 13** [13] P D Evans 4-8-13 (54) N Callan 25/1: 0000-003: Chsd ldrs, styd on under nk 57
press fnl 1f, just btn in a tight fin: on a fair mark: see 2599.
2775 **VIEWFORTH 7** [7] J S Goldie 6-9-12 bl (67) W Supple 7/1: 4000004: Stumbled start, hdwy from rear ¾ 68
dist, nrst fin: only btn around 1L under top-weight: a fine run in the circumstances, well h'capped.
2630 **BLESSED PLACE 12** [12]4-8-6 p (47) T P Queally 14/1: 0000335: Chsd ldrs, not qckn fnl 1f: see 2630. nk 47
2029 **DUNN DEAL 37** [6]4-9-9 (64) B Swarbrick(5) 16/1: 0120506: Chsd ldrs, onepcd fnl 1f. ½ 62
2846 **SHARP HAT 3** [17]10-9-7 (62) A Culhane 7/1: 0000037: Mid-div, nvr nr to chall: qck reapp. 1 57
2053 **FULL PITCH 36** [10]8-9-13 (68) Kirby Harris(7) 33/1: 0061008: Dwelt, styd on late, nrst fin: btr 1532. ½ 61
2846 **MALAHIDE EXPRESS 3** [2]4-9-3 (58) J D O'Reilly(7) 10/1: 0554109: Prom till wknd ins fnl 1f: qck reapp. 1 48
2232 **CERTA CITO 28** [4]4-9-0 (55) J Fortune 25/1: 00-00500: 10th: Chsd ldrs, btn dist. ½ 43
2734 **GREEN RIDGE 8** [11]3-9-5 (65) Paul Eddery 12/1: 506-2400: 11th: Dwelt, recovered to chase ldrs ½ 51
till halfway, sn short of room & no ch after: see 2659 (reapp, reef & soft grnd).
2326 **BLUES PRINCESS 24** [5]4-8-8 (1ow)bl (48) R Winston 25/1: 00000-00: 12th: b f Bluebird - Queen 1¼ 31
Shirley (Fairy King) Dwelt, nvr a factor: out of form in '03: '02 juv fills auct mdn wnr for C Cox: suited by 5f
on gd & fast grnd: eff with/without blnks. 1 Sep'02 Bath 5gd 73- E:
2698 **ZARGUS 9** [15]5-9-2 (57) L Keniry(3) 15/2: 40-50000: 13th: Prom, wknd dist. ½ 37
2775 **MYND 7** [16]4-9-8 (63) D Tudhope(7) 7/1: 2100640: 14th: Chsd ldrs 3.5f, wknd. hd 42

HAYDOCK   SATURDAY 03.07.04   Lefthand, Flat, Galloping Track

2614 **Mystery Pips** 12 [19]4-8-5 vis(46) Kim Tinkler 20/1:0   2614 **Star Applause** 12 [18]4-8-1 (42) J Mackay 40/1:0
2657 **Blessingindisguise** 11 [20]11-8-2 bl(43) P Fessey 16/1:0
2753 **Percy Douglas** 7 [1]4-8-4 vis(45) Ann Stokell 40/1:0
18 Ran   Time 1m 02.92(4.12)   Owned: Mrs S G Davies   Trained: Wantage

BRIGHTON   SUNDAY 04.07.04   Lefthand, V Sharp, Undulating Track

Official Going GOOD/FIRM (FIRM IN PLACES)

2952
2.30 Stan James In-Running Maiden Auction Stakes 2yo (E)
£3702 £1139 £570   **6f209y rnd   Good 58   -27 Slow**   Inside

2287 **HES A DIAMOND** 26 [2] T G Mills 2-8-11   R Miles(3) 5/2: 51: Mid-div, hdwy to lead appr fnl 1f, all | | 80
out to hold on nr fin: eff at 7f on gd, acts on a sharp/undul trk: imprvd from debut: see 2287.
2450 **CAMPEON** 20 [7] M J Wallace 2-8-9   R L Moore 7/1: 05052: Prom, led after 3f till appr fnl 1f, | shd | 77
rallied cl home & only just btn: stays 7f on gd: see 1149.
2697 **DUSTY DANE** 10 [1] W G M Turner 2-8-8   A Daly 7/1: 5653: Mid-div, kept on fnl 1f but not pace | 1 | 74
of first 2: stays 7f on gd: see 2511.
2714 **SAFENDONSEABISCUIT** 9 [4] S Kirk 2-8-9   J Fortune 15/8 FAV: 5334: Led 3f, rem handy, fdd fnl 1f. | 1¾ | 71
2492 **BE BOP ALOHA** 18 [8]2-8-2 T P Queally 33/1: 0635: Keen in mid-div, no impress dist: see 2492. | 1¼ | 61
2714 **PACIFIC STAR** 9 [5]2-8-10 T E Durcan 7/1: 0656: Slowly away, sn handy, no impress over 1f out. | shd | 68
        TOP PURSUIT [9]2-8-7 S Drowne 33/1: 7: b g Pursuit of Love - Top of The Parkes | 3 | 59
(Mistertopogigo) Mid-div, sn outpcd on debut: cost 2,200gns, April first foal: dam plcd over 5/6f, sire high-class
at 6/8f: with J Spearing.
1728 **LORD NORMACOTE** 51 [6]2-8-9 S Sanders 20/1: 08: b g Loup Sauvage - Blessed Event (Kings Lake) | nk | 60
Al bhd: 7 wk abs: April foal, cost 14,000gns: dam smart mid-dist performer, sire top-class over 8/10f.
8 Ran   Time 1m 25.77 (5.97)   Owned: Ms Tracey Barker   Trained: Epsom

2953
3.00 Stan James Online Maiden Stakes 3yo (D)
£5473 £1684 £842   **7f214y rnd   Good 58   -05 Slow**   Inside

1904 **CARRY ON DOC** 44 [8] J W Hills 3-9-0 (73) S Whitworth 11/2: 5355-361: Bhd, hdwy when short of | | 80
room over 1f out, sn switched left, rdn & styd on to lead ins fnl 1f: 6 wk abs, op 9/1: eff at 7f/1m on fast, gd &
f/sand, sharp/undul trk: runs well fresh & eff with waiting tactics: see 1321.
2659 **DU PRE** 11 [4] Mrs A J Perrett 3-8-9 (74) S Sanders 6/1: 30-02: b f Singspiel - Child Prodigy | hd | 75
(Ballad Rock) Bhd, hdwy to lead dist, hdd ins fnl 1f, rallied & only just btn: op 4/1, clr of rem: 3rd 1 of 2 '03
starts (fills mdn, rtd 83): eff at 6f/1m on fast & gd: shld be plcd to find similar.
2649 **INDIANA BLUES** 12 [6] A M Balding 3-8-9 (75) L Keniry(3) 9/1: 040-4003: Keen & handy, ev ch over | 3 | 69
1f out, wknd ins fnl 1f: see 1846.
2575 **EIJAAZ** 15 [9] A C Stewart 3-9-0 R Hills 12/1: 004: Bhd, hdwy over 1f out, not pace to chall. | 1 | 72
2575 **RIVER NUREY** 15 [2]3-9-0 (72) D Holland 10/11 FAV: 0052-325: Led till dist, sn no extra. | 1½ | 69
2452 **REGAL FLIGHT** 20 [7]3-9-0 (50) R L Moore 33/1: 505-606: Keen & handy, wknd 2f out: see 2452. | 6 | 57$
        CEYLON ROUND [1]3-8-9 D Corby(3) 33/1: 7: b f Royal Applause - Tea Colony (Pleasant Colony) | 8 | 36
Trkd ldrs, wknd over 1f out on debut: cost 30,000gns: dam unrcd: with M Wallace.
2434 **BAHAMA REEF** 20 [5]3-9-0 P (57) S Carson 25/1: 00-00528: In tch, wknd 2f out: cheek pieces. | ¾ | 39
2536 **NAZZWAH** 16 [3]3-8-9 T E Durcan 16/1: 669: ch f Rahy - Baaderah (Cadeaux Genereux) Al bhd: dam | ¾ | 32
a 6f 2yo wnr, later a 6f 3yo wnr: with M Channon.
9 Ran   Time 1m 37.09 (5.09)   Owned: Stuart Whitehouse & Abbott Racing Partne   Trained: Lambourn

2954
3.30 Stan James Telebetting Handicap Stakes 3yo+ 0-75 (E)
£3721 £1145 £573   **7f214y rnd   Good 58   +03 Fast**   Inside   [72]

2844 **MISTER CLINTON** 4 [2] D K Ivory 7-8-9 (53) D Holland 13/2: 0063401: Bhd, hdwy & short of room 2f | | 66
out, led just ins fnl 1f, drvn out: qck reapp: eff btwn 6f/1m, stays 10f well: acts on firm & gd, sharp trks, loves
Brighton: won in a gd time: see 761.
2440 **TUSCARORA** 20 [8] A W Carroll 5-8-8 (52) I Mongan 5/1: 406-0052: Keen in rear, hdwy over 2f out, | 2½ | 58
ev ch over 1f out, not pace of wnr: well h'capped: see 1465.
2402 **POPPYLINE** 22 [4] W R Muir 4-8-9 (53) S Drowne 12/1: 0-00U363: Mid-div, ev ch dist, onepcd. | 1 | 57
2655 **BORDER ARTIST** 12 [9] D Nicholls 5-9-7 (65) A Nicholls 5/1: 0100434: Handy, hdd just ins fnl 1f, | hd | 68
edged left/no extra: clr of rem: see 1794.
2872 **FRANKSALOT** 3 [7]4-9-12 (70) S Sanders 11/4 FAV: 222-0145: Bhd & keen, hdwy 2f out, btn fnl 1f. | 6 | 61
2840 **FLYING TREATY** 4 [5]7-9-2 BL (60) J Mackay 12/1: 0060056: Trkd ldrs, wknd over 2f out: blnks. | 2 | 47
2641* **ARAGONS BOY** 12 [10]4-10-0 (72) D Sweeney 8/1: 054-0017: Led 3f, wknd fnl 1f: top-weight. | ½ | 58
2655 **SENIOR MINISTER** 12 [1]6-9-4 (62) R Miles(3) 12/1: 000-0108: Rcd in 2nd till led 4f out, hdd over | 1½ | 45
2f out, no extra: reportedly unsuited by this loose grnd: much btr 2431 (seller).
2587 **WOOD FERN** 15 [3]4-8-13 (57) S Hitchcott(3) 10/1: 0000509: Al bhd: op 20/1: reportedly unsuited | 7 | 26
by this loose grnd: much btr 263 (mdn).
969 **ESTRELLA LEVANTE** 97 [11]4-8-9 (53) T P Queally 33/1: 0530600: 10th: Al bhd: abs, new stable. | nk | 21
10 Ran   Time 1m 36.44 (4.44)   Owned: Mr J B Waterfall   Trained: Radlett

2955 | **4.00 Stanjamesuk Com Handicap Stakes 3yo 0-70 (E)** | **[77]**
£3770 £1160 £580   1m1f209y   Good 58   -05 Slow   Outside

2565 **GHANTOOT 15** [1] L M Cumani 3-9-3 vis (66) D Holland 5/2 FAV: 000031: In tch, hdwy 2f out, styd on well for press to lead nr fin: eff at 9/10f on gd & gd/soft, acts on a sharp/undul trk: runs well in a visor: see 2565.   **76**
2014 **LITTLESTAR 39** [10] J L Dunlop 3-7-13 (48) J Mackay 25/1: 00-00002: b c Robellino - Green Charter (Green Desert) Bhd, hdwy to lead appr fnl 1f, hdd/no extra nr fin: clr of rem: mdn unplcd in '03 (rtd 70): eff at 10f on gd: has tried blnks, imprvd here without.   nk   **57**
2333 **RESPLENDENT KING 24** [8] T G Mills 3-9-7 P (70) I Mongan 5/1: 3553233: Led till over 3f out, no extra ins fnl 1f: tried cheek pieces: see 2013.   4   **73**
2377 **UNCLE JOHN 23** [7] S Kirk 3-8-11 (60) J Fortune 9/1: 0105-004: Trkd ldrs, wknd fnl 1f: see 2024.   ¾   **62**
2837 **DUKES VIEW 5** [6]3-9-0 bl (63) S Sanders 12/1: 006-0055: In tch, hdwy to lead over 3f out, hdd appr fnl 1f, fdd: qck reapp: see 2837.   3   **60**
2621 **WILD PITCH 13** [11]3-8-11 (60) R L Moore 7/1: 6-00306: Al bhd: see 2024.   5   **49**
2701 **ASK THE DRIVER 10** [9]3-8-4 (53) S Whitworth 4/1: 50-24337: Al bhd: op 6/1: see 2064.   1¼   **40**
2423 **THREE WELSHMEN 21** [4]3-8-6 bl (55) R Miles(3) 14/1: 0513008: Keen in 2nd, wknd over 2f out.   17   **16**
2495 **GLENDALE 18** [5]3-8-3 vis (66) Lisa Jones(3) 10/1: 1000059: Keen & handy, wknd over 3f out.   2   **10**
9 Ran   Time 2m 4.11 (6.31)   Owned: Sheikh Mohammed Obaid Al Maktoum   Trained: Newmarket

2956 | **4.30 Stanjamesuk Com Classified Stakes 3yo+ 0-70 (E)** |
£3692 £1136 £568   1m3f196y   Good 58   +11 Fast   Outside

2860 **DESERT ISLAND DISC 4** [2] J J Bridger 7-9-1 (71) T P Queally 6/1: 4403061: Led till over 3f out, led again 1f out, kept up to work run-in: qck reapp, fast time: best at 12f, acts on fast, hvy, handles polytrack, acts on any trk, likes Kempton: imprvd for a return to fav'd trip: see 1381.   **75**
2366 **KYTHIA 23** [4] H Morrison 3-8-4 (73) R L Moore 15/8 FAV: 315-432: Bhd, hdwy 2f out, switched right 1f out, kept on ins fnl 1f but not pace of wnr: winning form at 7.5f, stays 12f, acts on firm & gd: see 1791.   1   **74**
2686 **ETON 10** [3] D Nicholls 8-9-6 (73) A Nicholls 8/1: 0-305123: Rcd in 2nd till led over 3f out, hdd 1f out, no extra ins fnl 1f: top-weight: ran to winning form of 2356.   1¼   **75**
2642 + **SUNNY LADY 12** [1] E A L Dunlop 3-8-11 (80) T E Durcan 7/2: 0-222214: In tch, onepcd fnl 1f.   4   **73**
2114 **STEALING BEAUTY 34** [5]4-9-5 (75) D Holland 9/4: 5/01-405: Rear, nvr a factor: op 3/1: see 1889.   ½   **67**
5 Ran   Time 2m 33.85 (5.65)   Owned: Mr W Wood   Trained: Liphook

2957 | **5.00 Stan James Handicap Stakes 3yo+ 0-75 (E)** | **[73]**
£3721 £1145 £573   5f59y rnd   Good 58   -06 Slow   Inside

2855 **GONENDUNNETT 4** [9] Mrs C A Dunnett 5-8-12 vis (57) Hayley Turner(5) 13/2: 0661031: Handy, hdwy to lead 1f out, kept on for press ins fnl 1f: op 8/1, qck reapp: suited by 5/6f on firm, gd & both AWs: see 35.   **62**
2262 **HARBOUR HOUSE 28** [4] J J Bridger 5-8-0 (45) A Daly 16/1: 0631302: Bhd, hdwy over 1f out, kept on ins fnl 1f: goes well back, gd run & worth a try over further: see 2262.   ½   **47**
2644 **JAZZY MILLENNIUM 12** [6] B R Millman 7-8-8 bl (53) S Drowne 7/1: 500-0363: Bhd, eff over 1f out, kept on ins fnl 1f: goes well back, gd run & worth a try over further: see 2262.   shd   **54**
2778 **ARFINNIT 7** [7] M R Channon 3-8-11 vis (61) S Hitchcott(3) 14/1: 5166164: Bhd, hdwy ins fnl 1f, kept on.   ¾   **60**
2690 **BOANERGES 10** [10]7-8-10 P (55) T E Durcan 12/1: 5624005: Led to 1f out, no extra: cheek pieces.   1   **51**
2420 **TABOOR 21** [1]7-8-11 h bl (56) D Holland 9/1: 0050206: Mid-div, rcd alone far side str, btn 2f out.   shd   **51**
2743 **PULSE 8** [3]6-9-3 p (62) R L Moore 100/30 FAV: 3664537: Handy, wknd just ins fnl 1f.   hd   **56**
2743 + **GUNS BLAZING 8** [5]5-10-0 bl (73) M Howard(7) 7/1: 0136018: Keen & handy, wknd over 1f out.   5   **52**
2599 **LOCH INCH 14** [8]7-8-6 bl (51) C Catlin 9/1: 00-00049: Keen & handy, wknd 2f out: see 1867.   1¼   **26**
2599 **IZMAIL 14** [11]5-9-7 (66) S Whitworth 7/1: 15-00000: 10th: In tch, wknd over 2f out: see 1293.   shd   **40**
2669 **LANDING STRIP 11** [2]4-9-13 (72) L Fletcher(3) 20/1: 340-0050: 11th: Al bhd: see 2669.   11   **13**
11 Ran   Time 1m 3.54(3.54)   Owned: College Farm Thoroughbreds   Trained: Norwich

Official Going Soft (Good/Soft Places) HEAVY SHOWERS

2958 | **2.20 Yankee Doodle Day Apprentice Handicap Stakes 3yo+ 0-75 (E)** | **[70]**
£3621 £1114 £557   1m str   Good/Soft   Inapplicable   Centre

1992 **PARISIAN PLAYBOY 40** [6] Jedd O'Keeffe 4-8-0 (42) Leanne Kershaw(5) 66/1: 03-00001: Hld up, prog/switched 3f out & styd on for press to lead well ins last: abs: first win: eff at 7f/1m on gd/soft & soft.   **49**
2560 **OSCAR PEPPER 15** [8] T D Barron 7-9-7 vis (63) P Makin(3) 6/1: 5063452: Mid-div, hdwy & led over 1f out, edged left & hdd well ins last: likes Redcar: see 1485.   nk   **69**
2324 **EASTERN HOPE 25** [4] Mrs L Stubbs 5-9-4 (60) Kristin Stubbs(5) 16/1: 0-003003: Dwelt & bhd, staying on for press when short of room well ins last: slipping down weights: see 1823.   1   **64**
2120 **BASINET 33** [7] J J Quinn 6-8-12 (54) D Tudhope(5) 12/1: 506-0004: Dwelt & held up, hdwy over 2f out, styd on onepace ins last: recent jumps plcd (rtd 98h, now): cheek pieces omitted today, nicely h'capped.   1   **56**
2529* **PRIME OFFER 16** [3]8-9-9 (65) C Haddon(5) 7/1: 0241215: Led till over 2f out, kept on: acts on gd/soft grnd, loves firm/fast: see 2529.   shd   **67**
2552* **ZANJEER 16** [10]4-9-10 (66) L Treadwell(5) 13/2: 4/40-016: Led/dsptd lead till over 1f out.   hd   **67**
2688* **DARA MAC 10** [1]5-8-13 (55) Suzanne France(5) 10/1: 5-026317: Bhd, kept on late for press, no dngr.   ¾   **55**
2402 **ENCOUNTER 22** [16]8-8-4 (46) D Fentiman(5) 14/1: 0035608: Rear, mod late prog, no danger.   1   **44**
2550 **CASHNEEM 16** [5]6-9-8 (64) D Allan 14/1: 0-461409: Mid-div, drvn & btn 2f out: btr 2150 (firm, 7f).   1½   **59**
2775 **HILLTIME 8** [11]4-8-11 (53) D Nolan 16/1: 50/0-0000: 10th: Chsd ldrs till over 1f out: see 1638.   1¾   **45**
2730 **HAULAGE MAN 9** [9]6-9-3 (59) T Eaves 14/1: 0040-020: 11th: Slow away, no room 3f out, sn btn.   1¼   **48**
2102* **SEDGE 34** [13]4-9-4 (60) L Enstone 20/1: 10: 12th: Trkd ldrs, btn over 1f out: see 2102 (7f, seller).   7   **37**

2550 **MEHMAAS** 16 [14]8-8-2 vis (44) B Swarbrick(3) 14/1: 0-000040: 13th: Led/dsptd lead 5f: btr 2550.   1¾   18
2713 **SAIF SAREEA** 10 [2]4-8-6 (48) P Mathers(5) 100/1: 6000/-000: 14th: Led/dsptd lead till over 3f out.   12   2
4140} **LONER** 299 [12]6-8-10 (52) T Hamilton 5/1 FAV: 042500-0: 15th: b g Magic Ring - Jolis Absent   2½   1
(Primo Dominie) Chsd ldrs, struggling from 3f out, eased: op 11/1, reapp: sell h'cap scorer for M Wighan in '03:
h'cap rnr-up '02, AW unplcd (rtd 45a): off at 7f/1m on firm & soft grnd, sharp/turning trks.
2 Aug'03 Yarm 7.0g/f 54-53 D: 1 Jul'03 Warw 8.1fm 51-46 G: 2 Sep'02 Beve 7.4g/f 44-43 E:
2559 **FRIMLEYS MATTERRY** 15 [15]4-8-8 (50) Natalia Gemelova(5) 66/1: 6066650: 16th: Sn bhd & eased dist.   2   0
16 Ran   Time 1m 41.3 (6.5)   Owned: Playboy Partnership   Trained: Leyburn

---

2959   2.50 European Breeders Fund Maiden Stakes 2yo (D)
£4498 £1384 £692   **7f str**   **Good/Soft**   **Inapplicable**   Centre

2531 **NORTHERN SPLENDOUR** 16 [10] Saeed bin Suroor 2-9-0 K McEvoy 8/11 FAV: 31: Mid-div, hdwy from   93
halfway, hung left & led ins last, rdn out: hvly bckd at odds-on & confirmed debut promise: eff at 6/7f, get 1m:
acts on fast & gd/soft grnd, gall trks: potentially useful: see 2531.
2061 **GONE FISHING** 36 [2] M A Jarvis 2-8-9 P Robinson 7/2: 02: ch f Cadeaux Genereux - Dabbing (Cure   1¾   84
The Blues) Sn prom & led over 2f out till ins last, no extra cl-home: imprvd from debut: £110,000 Feb foal, sister
to a 1m wnr:stays 7f on gd/soft: find a race on this evidence.
2676 **LITTLE MISS GRACIE** 11 [5] P Burgoyne 2-8-9 Derek Nolan(7) 14/1: 33: Trkd ldrs, switched & kept   ½   83
on fnl 2f, not pace of wnr: confirmed promise of debut: clr rem, win a race: see 2676.
2236 **AIRE DE MOUGINS** 29 [6] P C Haslam 2-9-0 G Faulkner 14/1: 044: Led till over 5f out, sn outpcd &   5   79+
sltly hmpd, rallied well ins last under hand riding: likely improver in h'caps.
2570 **DANCERS SERENADE** 15 [11]2-9-0 Dale Gibson 16/1: 35: Swerved right start, sn cl-up, outpcd fnl 2f.   1   77
2462 **PARIS HEIGHTS** 19 [4]2-9-0 Dean McKeown 100/1: 06: gr g Paris House - Petra Nova (First Trump)   1¼   72
Chsd ldrs, hung left & no impress 2f out: Feb first foal, dam 5f plcd juv.
    WOLF HAMMER 0 [1]2-9-0 R Winston 10/1: 7: ch c Diesis - Polly's Link (Phone Trick) Dwelt, sn   hd   73
cl-up & led over 5f out till over 3f out, fdd: op 8/1: 90,000gns 2yo purchase: May foal: dam 1m wnr.
2671 **MR MAXIM** 11 [9]2-9-0 V Halliday 100/1: 058: Sn outpcd & struggling.   6   64
2671 **WOR KID** 11 [7]2-8-9 T Hamilton(3) 100/1: 09: Bhd, swerved badly left after 3f, sn bhd.   12   39
2522 **LOYALTY LODGE** 17 [3]2-9-0 J Murtagh 40/1: 060: 10th: Struggling from halfway, longer trip.   6   35
10 Ran   Time 1m 28.56 (6.76)   Owned: Godolphin   Trained: Newmarket

---

2960   3.20 Formica Surfacing Your World Stakes Handicap 3yo 0-80 (D)   [87]
£14365 £4420 £2210   **1m3f**   **Good/Soft**   **Inapplicable**   Inside

2773 **LETS ROLL** 8 [6] C W Thornton 3-9-0 (73) Dean McKeown 11/2: 1-262231: Rear, rdn & hdwy wide 3f   83
out, styd on for press to lead well in last: eff around 1m/9f, enjoyed step up to 11f & shld get further: acts on
fast & gd/soft grnd, stiff/undul or sharpish trks: v tough, unexposed at this trip, win again: see 2773.
2530 **PRENUP** 16 [11] L M Cumani 3-9-0 (73) J Murtagh 100/30 FAV: 00-41122: Sn handy & led over 3f out,   ½   81
hung left & kept on ins last, kept on: nicely bckd & continues to prog: see 2530 & 2322.
2691* **CHARLOTTE VALE** 10 [13] M D Hammond 3-8-9 (68) A Culhane 10/1: 46-65213: Mid-div, styd on for   ¾   75
press fnl 2f, not pace of wnr: confirmed improvement of latest & enjoys rain softened grnd: see 2691.
2804 **MUNAAWESH** 6 [9] D W Chapman 3-7-12 (20h)BL (55) D Fentiman(7) 50/1: 0000004: Rear, styd on for   shd   64
press fnl 2f, much imprvd: stays 11f: interesting for similar if hdgr works again.
2565 **RICHTEE** 15 [2]3-8-6 (68) T Hamilton(3) 9/1: 060-125: Mid-div, outpcd 3f out, kept on late: stays 11f.   shd   71
2277 **MEADAAF** 27 [5]3-9-7 (80) K Darley 33/1: 045-1236: Chsd ldrs, onepace & not much room repeatedly   1½   84
from over 2f out, pos accepted: much closer with a clr passage: handles fast & gd/soft grnd.
2773 **DOUBLE VODKA** 8 [3]3-8-4 (63) K McEvoy 10/1: 35-06247: Trkd ldrs, repeatedly short of room from   hd   66+
over 2f out, not able to chall: again a luckless passage & this longer 11f trip looks likely to suit.
2322 **WING COLLAR** 25 [12]3-8-9 (68) W Supple 12/1: 40-03328: Mid-div, eff wide, btn/eased ins last.   3½   66
2319 **MANHATTAN JACK** 25 [7]3-8-10 (69) R Winston 7/1: 0529: Bhd, eff wide 4f out, no impress: abs.   2   64
2222 **SHARADI** 30 [4]3-8-11 (70) M Tebbutt 33/1: 0456-00: 10th: b c Desert Sun - Sharadiya (Akarad)   2   62
Mid-div, hung left & btn 2f out: was: ex-Irish mdn at up to 1m.
2528 **HAVETOAVIT** 17 [10]3-8-4 (63) S Chin 16/1: 00-53240: 11th: Led till 3f out, sn btn: btr 2528 & 2164.   1½   53
1663 **HERNANDOS BOY** 55 [1]3-8-0 (59) P Fessey 20/1: 000-5000: 12th: b g Hernando - Leave At Dawn (Slip   3½   44
Anchor) Dwelt, in tch, btn 2f out: 8 wk abs: unplcd '03 (rtd 63a, auct mdn) half-brother to a 1m wnr.
2565 **RIGONZA** 15 [8]3-8-9 VIS (68) D Allan 33/1: 346-0050: 13th: Unruly start, slow away & al bhd: tried vis.   1¼   52
13 Ran   Time 2m 24.93 (9.43)   Owned: A Crute and Partners   Trained: Leyburn

---

2961   3.50 'win A Holiday To Orlando' - Racecard Competition Handicap Stakes 3yo 0-70 (E)   [77]
£3936 £1211 £606   **5f str**   **Good/Soft**   **Inapplicable**   Centre

2380 **NANNA** 23 [18] R Hollinshead 3-8-9 (58) F Lynch 8/1: 3021621: Led/dsptd lead throughout, led ins   67
last, drvn out: suited by 5f, stays 6f: acts on fast, gd/soft & fibresand: see 1787.
1605* **SHORT CHORUS** 58 [3] J Balding 3-8-1 p (50) Dale Gibson 7/1: 00-04012: Al prom far side & led that   ¾   56
group over 1f out, no extra well ins last: 8 wk abs: see 1605.
2055 **FITZWARREN** 37 [4] N Bycroft 3-9-4 vis (67) Dean McKeown 16/1: 04402-03: b g Presidium - Coney   ½   71
Hills (Beverley Boy) Led far side till over 1f out, no extra: auct mdn wnr '03, subs h'cap rnr-up: eff at 5/6f on
firm & gd/soft grnd, stiff/gall trk: eff in a visor, tried t-strap: back to form.
2 Oct'03 Redc 6g/f 72-67 E: 1 Jun'03 Carl 5fm 74- E: 2 Jun'03 Pont 5g/f 75- F: 2 Apr'03 Beve 5fm 79- E:
2645* **MALUTI** 12 [1] R Guest 3-8-4 (53) K Darley 7/1 FAV: 06-06314: Chsd ldrs far side, hung right & no   ¾   55
extra ins last: nicely bckd: acts on fast & gd/soft grnd, sharp/undul or gall trk: see 2645.
2731 **SIR LOIN** 9 [14]3-8-6 (55) Kim Tinkler 25/1: 0600-005: Chsd ldrs stands side, drvn & kept on: shd   57
acts on gd & gd/soft grnd: see 2227.
2731 **JADAN** 9 [10]3-9-7 (70) W Supple 7/1: 01-00366: Held up stands side, hdwy when hit by rival's   nk   71
whip over 1f out, kept on under hand riding: not given a hard time, imprve on this: acts on firm & gd/soft grnd.
2755 **EXTREMELY RARE** 8 [13]3-9-5 (68) D Allan 10/1: 20107: Outpcd, kept on late, no threat: see 1659.   shd   69
2683 **SMART DANNY** 10 [8]3-7-12 (6oh) R Ffrench 14/1: 0-055008: Badly hmpd start & bhd, rdn & late   ½   46$
hdwy, ch had gone: fair run in circumstances & expect improvement upon this in modest company: see 1002.
2731 **HELLO ROBERTO** 9 [12]3-9-3 (66) R Winston 6/1: 0202539: Prom stands side, no impress: btr 673.   hd   64
2227 **HES A ROCKET** 30 [6]3-8-13 bl (62) Darren Williams 8/1: 5113600: 10th: Swerved right start, chsd   1½   56

896

ldrs till 2f out: btr 1605.
606   **ROYAL AWAKENING 144** [9]3-8-6 (55) T Eaves(1) 66/1: 30-00: 11th: b g Ali Royal - Morning Surprise   1½   45
(Tragic Role) Badly hmpd start, bhd, nvr a factor: 5 mth abs, prev with A P Jarvis: unplcd sole start '03 (rtd 64).
2614 **Gemini Girl 13** [2]3-7-12 (1oh)(46) P M Quinn 25/1:0
2075 **From The North 36** [11]3-8-5 vis(54) P Makin(3) 16/1:0
2722 **Savannah Sue 9** [7]3-7-12 (17oh)(30) D Fentiman(7) 66/2128 **Island Spell 9** [16]3-9-5 (68) P Fessey 25/1:0
15 Ran   Time 1m 0.6 (4.1)   Owned: Mrs G A Weetman   Trained: Upper Longdon

2962   4.20 Redcarracing Co Uk Classified Stakes 3yo+ 0-70 (E)
£3504 £1078 £539   1m1f rnd   Good/Soft   Inapplicable   Inside

2848 **PAWAN 4** [6] Miss A Stokell 4-9-3 (66) Ann Stokell 16/1: 0166301: Trkd ldrs, drvn & styd on to   74
lead well ins last: op 12/1, qck reapp: eff at 6f, now seems suited by 7/9f on firm, soft & fibresand: see 2438.
2726 **OPENING CEREMONY 9** [4] R A Fahey 5-9-0 (70) T Hamilton(3) 7/2: 531-6242: Held up, hdwy to chall   ½   70
when hung left over 1f out, not pace of wnr nr fin: nicely bckd: eff around 9/10f, drop to 7f/1m may suit as she
frequently finds less than looks likely for press: see 2507, 1979.
1810 **PINCHING 48** [5] H R A Cecil 3-8-9 vis(75) W Ryan 7/2: 4323: Led/dsptd lead, went on over 2f out,   nk   74
hdd well ins last & no extra: nicely bckd: 7 wk abs: stays 9f but a return to 1m could suit: acts on fast & gd/soft.
2673 **ALERON 11** [7] J J Quinn 6-9-5 (72) R Winston 6/4 FAV: 34-21204: Trkd ldrs, keen early, drvn/hung   2½   70
left & no impress dist, eased cl-home: hvly bckd, op 5/2: btr 1979 & 1681.
2767 **SUMMER SHADES 8** [3]6-9-0 (69) B Swarbrick(5) 9/1: 6524435: Held up, no impress fnl 2f: op 11/2.   2   62
2560 **GALA SUNDAY 15** [1]4-9-5 (72) Dale Gibson 14/1: 0-000006: Led till over 2f out, btn when hit rail   13   49
over 1f out, eased nr fin: op 10/1.
2179 **RIFLEMAN 31** [2]4-9-5 p (72) G Duffield 14/1: 340-0007: Trkd ldrs, lost place qckly over 2f out: see 2179.   5   42
7 Ran   Time 1m 58.39 (9.59)   Owned: Ms Caron Stokell   Trained: Richmond

2963   4.50 Car Boot Fairs Every Saturday And Sunday Handicap Stakes 3yo+ 0-75 (E)   [75]
£3780 £1163 £582   2m4y   Soft   Inapplicable   Inside

2685* **LUCKY JUDGE 10** [4] G A Swinbank 7-9-7 (68) Dale Gibson 2/1 FAV: 4/-401511: Trkd ldrs, short of   77
room over 3f out, styd on for press to lead well ins last: nicely bckd, op 5/2: eff at 13f, suited by 2m & shapes
as a thorough stayer: acts on fast, relished soft last twice & acts on hvy: see 2685, 1637 & 1034.
2607 **MAGIC COMBINATION 14** [11] L Lungo 11-9-11 (72) W Dowling 5/1: 110/-2522: Held up wide, hdwy &   ¾   80
led 3f out, hdd well ins last: thorough stayer who can find a race: see 2607 & 965.
2632 **SPITTING IMAGE 13** [8] Mrs M Reveley 4-8-11 (58) A Culhane 8/1: 3024123: Trkd ldrs & led over 3f   2   64
out, sn hdd & no extra ins last: acts on firm & soft grnd: see 2298 (C/D clmr).
2685 **SIMPLE IDEALS 10** [3] Don Enrico Incisa 10-7-12 (13oh) (32) Kim Tinkler 16/1: 50040-54: Rear, kept   1¼   50$
on for press, unable to chall: see 90.
2673 **VICIOUS PRINCE 11** [1]5-9-9 (70) Dean McKeown 6/1: 000-4005: Held up, switched wide for eff 4f   3   72
out, only mod prog: longer trip: likes Ripon: see 1226.
2685 **MOST DEFINITELY 10** [6]4-9-1 (62) D Allan 12/1: 2222-206: Trkd ldrs, btn over 1f out: btr 2444 (firm).   1   63
2444 **EBINZAYD 20** [7]8-10-0 (75) R Winston 20/1: 345//0//-07: Rear, eff 3f out, no impress: see 2444.   2   74
2686 **LORD LAMB 36** [5]12-8-13 (60) K Darley 12/1: 5//014-348: Trkd ldrs, hung right & btn 3f out: see 2298.   hd   59
2276 **PRINCE OF THE WOOD 27** [2]4-8-2 p (49) J Fanning 6/1: 4-214059: Led, hdd over 3f out, sn   14   37
struggling & eased over 1f out: bckd: btr 2060 & 1802.
9 Ran   Time 3m 40.6(15.8)   Owned: Mrs I Gibson   Trained: Richmond

MUSSELBURGH   MONDAY 05.07.04   Righthand, Sharp Track

Official Going Rnd Course - Gd, Str Course - Gd/Soft

2964   2.15 Peter Walker Group Stayers Handicap Stakes 4yo+ 35-55 (F)   [63]
£2954 £844 £422   2m   Good 46   -01 Slow   Inside

2850 **PADDY MUL 5** [4] W Storey 7-9-0 t (49) J Bramhill 10/1: 4345331: Held up, hdwy from halfway & led   54
3f out, rdn & held on well ins last: op 8/1, qck reapp: eff at 12f, suited by 14f/2m , a thorough stayer: acts on
fast, gd/soft & fibresand, any trk: joc gvn 2 day whip ban: see 357.
2813 **ELLWAY HEIGHTS 7** [3] W M Brisbourne 7-9-2 (51) B Swarbrick(5) 4/1: 1020-222: Held up, hdwy   ½   55
halfway, drvn & styd on fnl 2f, al held by wnr: nicely bckd: styd longer 2m trip well: tough & consistent.
2850 **IPLEDGEALLEGIANCE 5** [9] D W Chapman 8-8-0 bl (35) D Fentiman(7) 14/1: 5055203: Dwelt, rear, hdwy   nk   38
5f out & styd on for press fnl 2f, not able to chall wnr: stays an easy 2m: clr of rem here: see 2562, 353.
2685 **NEXT FLIGHT 11** [8] R E Barr 5-9-1 (50) D Holland 10/30 FAV: 3143234: Chsd ldrs, rdn & no   5   48
impress fnl 2f: yet to fully convince at 2m:: sees 2494, 1396 (14f).
4093 **BILLY TWO RIVERS 658** [12]5-8-0 (2oh)p (33) R Ffrench 16/1: 05500/-5: ch g Woodborough - Good   12   23
Visibility (Electric) Chsd ldrs, struggling fnl 3f: qck reapp: jumps fit (plcd, nov h'cap hdle): mod.
2060 **MR FORTYWINKS 38** [10]10-8-12 (47) T Eaves(3) 11/2: 406-0506: Led 3f, rdn & btn 3f out: btr 1551.   ½   34
2807 **WESTERN BLUEBIRD 7** [11]6-8-7 bl (42) P Fessey 16/1: 44/-64027: Chsd ldrs, struggling fnl 4f: btr 2807. 15   16
2607 **GREEN N GOLD 15** [2]4-9-6 (55) A Culhane 12/1: 0-104008: Mid-div, btn 4f out: btr 1681.   1   28
4261 **END OF AN ERROR 650** [1]5-8-0 (4oh) (31) Natalia Gemelova(7) 20/1: 050000/-9: b f Charmer -   1½   7
Needwood Poppy (Rolfe) Struggling halfway: jumps fit (unplcd, rtd 91h, h'cap), won 4 times in h'cap company 03/04
(rtd 101h, gd & gd/soft, 2m4f/3m): unplcd on the level '02 (M Chapman).
1 Sep'01 Leic 8g/f 56-51 G:
2937 **TON CHEE 2** [6]5-8-0 (15oh) (20) P M Quinn 33/1: 043-6060: 10th: Led after 3f till 3f out, wknd.   21   0
2060 **WASHINGTON PINK 38** [7]5-8-3 P (38) T Hamilton(3) 33/1: 0-004000: 11th: Struggling halfway: btr 1396.   24   0
2577 **BERKELEY HEIGHTS 16** [5]4-8-7 (42) R Winston 16/1: 6234100: 12th: Dwelt & al bhd: btr 1840 (AW).   dist   0
12 Ran   Time 3m 30.05 (7.55)   Owned: Gremlin Racing   Trained: Consett

2965 **2.45 European Breeders Fund Median Auction Maiden Stakes 2yo (E)**
£4362 £1342 £671 **5f str** **Good/Soft** **Inapplicable** Stands Side

2646 **ALPAGA LE JOMAGE 13** [6] B J Meehan 2-9-0 D Holland 1/1 FAV: 3245051: Made all, rdn & al holding rivals fnl 1f: hvly bckd: eff at 5f, 6f shld suit: acts on fast & gd/soft: best without blnks: improving. **88**
2281 **MADAME TOPFLIGHT 27** [3] Mrs G S Rees 2-8-9 N Mackay(3) 25/1: 02: b f Komaite - Jamarj (Tyrnavos) *1½* **77**
Handy, rdn & outpcd halfway, styd on for press ins last, not pace of wnr: left debut bhd: cheaply retained Feb foal: dam sprint/9f wnr: eff at 5f, wants 6f: acts on gd/soft: going the right way.
2547 **TRIM IMAGE 17** [4] W Jarvis 2-8-9 R Lappin 11/4: 2333: Chsd ldrs, switched & styd on, not pace to chall: bckd tho' op 9/4: prev trained in Ireland: see 2547. *1¼* **73**
2611 **ALMATY EXPRESS 14** [5] M Todhunter 2-9-0 R Winston 12/1: 30034: Chsd ldrs till over 1f out: see 2611. *3½* **67**
PREMIER TIMES 0 [1]2-9-0 A Culhane 50/1: 5: ch c Timeless Times - Lady Magician (Lord Bud) *1¾* **62**
Dwelt, bhd, mod late prog: Apr foal, dam unplcd at 9/12f, related to numerous wnrs.
2847 **NEE LEMON LEFT 5** [2]2-8-9 P P Mathers(7) 16/1: 26306: Prom till halfway: prob flattered 2481. *1¼* **53**
BOND PUCCINI 0 [7]2-9-0 F Lynch 11/2: 7: b c Piccolo - Baileys By Name (Nomination) Dwelt & sn bhd, nvr factor: 12,000gns Feb foal, brother to a 5/6f juv wnr, dam a multiple 6f juv scorer. *14* **18**
7 Ran Time () Owned: The Top Banana Partnership Trained: Upper Lambourn

2966 **3.15 Peter Walker Group Handicap Stakes Fillies 4yo+ 35-55 (F)** **[61]**
£3354 £1032 £516 **1m4f** **Good 46** **-30 Slow** Inside

2458] **WOODWIND DOWN 1095** [2] M Todhunter 7-8-12 (45) R Winston 10/1: 3250/20//-1: Made all & dictated pace, held on well for press fnl 2f: long Flat abs, jumps fit (plcd, h'cap hdle): last rcd on the level in '01, h'cap rnr-up: eff at 9f, now suited by a sharp 12f & forcing tactics: acts on fast & gd grnd: well judged ride. **50**
2708 **COSMIC CASE 11** [7] J S Goldie 9-8-12 (45) N Mackay(3) 9/4: 00-10352: Trkd ldrs, styd on for press, not able to chall wnr: tough 9yo, likes fast grnd: see 1905. *1¾* **49**
2937 **BALALAIKA TUNE 2** [6] W Storey 5-8-2 (3oh) (32) J Bramhill 12/1: 4004603: Rear, hdwy & switched 2f out, rdn & no extra dist: eff at up to 2m, handles firm & gd grnd: mdn, see 2298 & 852. *½* **38**
2868 **ELLOVAMUL 4** [1] W M Brisbourne 4-9-5 (52) P Makin(5) 11/2: 1545-404: Mid-div, rdn to press ldr over 1f out, no extra ins last: qck reapp: stays a sharp 12f: acts on firm, gd & fibresand: see 2475. *½* **54**
2788 **PONT NEUF 8** [3]4-9-8 t (55) K Darley 2/1 FAV: 00-00425: Held up, not pace to chall: see 2788. *¾* **56**
1592 **MISS FLEURIE 60** [4]4-8-2 (3oh) (32) P Fessey 11/1: 4/-00026: Chsd wnr, btn ove 2f out: abs: see 1592. *3* **32**
2510 **MISS OCEAN MONARCH 18** [5]4-8-6 BL e (39) A Culhane 20/1: 0002007: Keen & trkd ldr, btn 2f out. *12* **20**
7 Ran Time 2m 39.71 (9.11) Owned: Domino Racing Trained: Penrith

2967 **3.45 Ysc Scotland Selling Stakes 3yo+ (F)**
£2982 £852 £426 **1m rnd** **Good 46** **-00 Slow** Inside

1823 **ARTISTIC STYLE 48** [11] B Ellison 4-9-0 (63) T Eaves(3) 7/2 FAV: 23-06001: Chsd ldrs, drvn to lead well ins last: bght in for 5,200gns, nicely bckd: first win: eff at 5.5f, suited by 1m on fast & soft. **59**
2688 **QUICKS THE WORD 11** [6] C W Thornton 4-9-0 (54) K Darley 8/1: 0040002: Handy, rdn & led over 1f out, drvn & hdd nr fin: op 12/1: now stays a sharp 1m in sell grade: prev best at sprint trips: see 1532. *hd* **58**
2801 **MACS TALISMAN 7** [3] V Smith 4-9-0 (55) M Tebbutt 11/2: 03-00023: Held up, hdwy & rdn/short of room over 1f out, kept on ins last, not able to chall: stays a sharp 1m in sell grade: see 1806. *2½* **53**
2768 **JEDEYDD 9** [1] M Dods 7-9-0 t p (55) R Winston 9/2: 0-004064: Bhd, hdwy when short of room over 1f out, rdn & no extra ins last: cheek pieces reapplied: see 2324 & 2057. *1½* **50**
2475 **FOREST AIR 19** [10]4-9-0 (46) R Ffrench 33/1: 00-01005: Mid-div, eff wide over 2f out, not pace to chall. *nk* **49$**
2688 **ROYAL WINDMILL 11** [8]5-9-0 p (46) A Culhane 7/1: 0052066: Held up, smooth prog to chall 2f out, wknd. *¾* **48$**
2544 **SUMMER SPECIAL 17** [9]4-9-0 (44) L Enstone(3) 12/1: 3050337: Led/dsptd lead till over 1f out, wknd. *3½* **41**
2544 **LIONS DOMANE 17** [2]7-9-0 (47) F Lynch 33/: 60P0008: Led till over 2f out, sn btn: see 528. *hd* **40**
2497 **ERUPT 19** [4]11-9-0 (40) D Holland 16/1: 060-5039: Bhd, mod late prog: see 2497. *shd* **40**
2720 **AFRICAN SPUR 10** [12]4-9-0 (49) D Tudhope(7) 14/1: 0006500: 10th: Chsd ldrs, drvn & btn 2f out: bckd. *1* **38**
2726 **MAFRUZ 10** [13]5-9-0 (55) T Hamilton(3) 14/1: 60060-00: 11th: Sn rdn, al rear: see 2726. *18* **6**
1944 **Welcome Archie 42** [14]4-9-0 G Faulkner 100/1:0 **Crazy Like A Fool 0** [5]5-9-0 N Mackay(3) 100/1:0
13 Ran Time 1m 41.18 (3.68) Owned: Mr & Mrs D A Gamble Trained: Malton

2968 **4.15 Peter Walker Group Le Garcon D'or Stakes Handicap 3yo+ 0-80 (D)** **[80]**
£6786 £2088 £1044 **5f str** **Good/Soft** **Inapplicable** Stands Side

2727 **ZARZU 10** [4] C R Dore 5-9-6 (72) R Thomas(5) 9/2: 3430001: Trkd ldrs & qcknd to lead dist, sn in command, readily: eff at 5/7f on firm, gd/soft & both AWs, prob any trk: well h'capped, follow-up. **84+**
2747* **FRASCATI 9** [6] A Berry 4-9-12 (78) P Mathers(7) 7/1: 0230112: Handy & led over 1f out, sn hdd & not pace of wnr: in form sprinter: see 2747. *2½* **80**
2951 **VIEWFORTH 2** [3] J S Goldie 6-9-1 bl (67) N Mackay(3) 9/4 FAV: 0000043: Trkd ldrs, styd on for press, not pace to chall: qck reapp: well h'capped, likes a stiffer trk: see 1120. *nk* **68**
2712 **PIRLIE HILL 11** [7] Miss L A Perratt 4-8-1 (53) R Ffrench 16/1: 5016044: Short of room early, held up in tch, no room over 1f out & dist, not pace to chall: prefer a stiffer trk at this trip: see 2181. *1½* **50**
2830 **NORTHERN SVENGALI 6** [5]8-7-12 (14oh)t p (36) J McAuley 50/1: 00-00055: Held up, late gains, nrst fin. *1* **44$**
2830 **MUTAYAM 6** [10]4-7-12 (11oh)t (39) B Swarbrick(5) 100/1: 0000-606: Handy, btn dist: see 2713. *shd* **44$**
2830 **STRENSALL 6** [8]7-9-12 (78) R Fitzpatrick 10/1: 0200347: Cl-up, wknd dist: btr 2690. *1½* **69**
1948 **FINGER OF FATE 42** [2]4-7-12 (8oh)bl (42) P M Quinn 40/1: 0264608: Led till over 1f out, sn btn: abs. *1* **38**
2551 **TYNE 17** [9]3-9-6 (77) K Darley 7/1: 216-0649: Hmpd start, sn trkd ldrs, btn over 1f out, eased: op 12/1. *1¾* **61**
2542 **STRAWBERRY PATCH 17** [1]5-8-8 p (60) J Carroll 33/1: 00600-00: 10th: Al rear, eased ins last: see 2542. *½* **42**
10 Ran Time 1m 0.85 (3.35) Owned: Page Pickering Taylor Ward Marsh Trained: Spalding

MUSSELBURGH MONDAY 05.07.04 Righthand, Sharp Track

2969 **4.45 Matthew Mcleod Handicap Stakes 3yo 35-55 (F)** **[63]**
£3380 £1040 £520 **1m1f rnd** **Good 46** **+02 Fast** Inside

2503 **PEARL OF YORK 18** [8] R Guest 3-9-6 (55) K Darley 9/2: 00-00251: Rear, rdn & hdwy wide to lead over 1f out, sn clr, readily: nicely bckd: first win: eff at 9/10f, tried 12f, may yet suit: acts on firm & gd grnd. **66**
2960 **MUNAAWESH 1** [3] D W Chapman 3-9-6 bl (55) A Culhane 5/1: 00000022: Dwelt, bhd, switched & styd on for press fnl 2f, not pace of wnr: rnr-up yesterday in first time blnks, confirmed improvement: eff at 9/11f: see 1050. 4 **57**
2827 **COMPASSION 6** [2] Miss L A Perratt 3-8-12 p (47) R Winston 25/1: 0004453: Handy & led halfway, rdn clr over 2f out, hdd over 1f out & no extra: qck reapp: gd run with forcing tactics & cheek pieces reapplied. *1* **46**
2613 **ROMAN THE PARK 14** [10] T D Easterby 3-8-9 (44) A Mullen(7) 7/2 FAV: 3123134: Trkd ldrs, no extra. *2½* **38**
2664 **SAUCY 12** [6]3-8-12 (47) D Holland 9/2: 0-660535: Chsd ldrs, no impress over 1f out: btr 2664 (firm). *3* **35**
2932 **BARGAIN HUNT 2** [4]3-8-11 vis (46) B Swarbrick(5) 15/2: 3-020036: Trkd ldrs, btn over 1f out: qck reapp. *3* **28**
2124 **RIVER LINE 34** [9]3-9-1 (50) K Dalgleish 25/1: 000-47: Al rear: bckd at long odds: btr 2124. *shd* **32**
2299 **KOODOO 27** [1]3-9-3 P (52) L Enstone(3) 12/1: 000-0608: Dwelt & al bhd: cheek pieces, poor run. *7* **22**
2011 **SARATOGA SPLENDOUR 40** [5]3-8-10 (45) Darren Williams 50/1: 00-609: Chsd ldrs, no ch fnl 3f: abs. *6* **5**
2509 **KINTORE 18** [7]3-8-12 (47) N Mackay(3) 14/1: 000-640: 10th: Bhd halfway: see 2509. *16* **0**
2243 **STILETTO LADY 30** [11]3-9-6 BL (55) M Fenton 25/1: 040-4000: 11th: Dwelt, rdn to lead early, hdd halfway & sn btn: blnks: btr 1655. *4* **0**
11 Ran Time 1m 54.62(3.92) Owned: Mr N Elsass Trained: Newmarket

WINDSOR MONDAY 05.07.04 Sharp, Figure 8 Track

Official Going GOOD/FIRM

2970 **6.35 Great Ormond Street Hospital E B F Maiden Stakes Sponsored By Mrs John Magnier 2yo (D)**
£5421 £1668 £834 **6f** **Firm -3** **-62 Slow** Inside

STREET CRED 0 [7] A M Balding 2-9-0 Martin Dwyer 25/1: 1: ch c Bold Edge - Trump Street (First Trump) Handy, hdwy to lead 1f out, rdn & kept on well ins fnl 1f on debut: Feb first foal, cost 18,000gns: dam 6f wnr: stays 6f on firm, acts on a sharp trk: runs well fresh: fine start, rate higher. **82**
2666 **RUSKY DUSKY 12** [20] R Hannon 2-9-0 P Dobbs 6/1: 032: Made most till 1f out, kept on till held well ins fnl 1f: op 9/1: stays 6f: shld find similar: see 2666. *½* **79**
DANES CASTLE 0 [11] B J Meehan 2-9-0 L P Keniry(3) 33/1: 3: b g Danetime - Faypool (Fayruz) Slowly away in tch, hdwy over 2f out, hung left ins fnl 1f, kept on on debut: Mar foal, cost 8,500gns: half brother to wnrs at 6/7f: stays 6f on fm, 7f will suit: gd start, will improve. *1¼* **75**
2618 **MUSICO 14** [8] B R Millman 2-9-0 S Drowne 16/1: 464: Handy, onepcd fnl 1f: see 2194. *1¾* **70**
BLAZING VIEW 0 [6]2-8-9 W Supple 50/1: 5: b f Bahri - Dixie Eyes Blazing (Gone West) Bhd, kept on fnl 1f, nrst fin on debut: Mar foal, cost 75,000gns: half sister to a 1m wnr: relish 7f & shld improve. *shd* **64**
2364 **PITCH UP 24** [3]2-9-0 K Fallon 4/1: 036: Sn prom, hdwy & ch over 1f out, fdd ins fnl 1f: see 2188. *nk* **68**
JE SUIS BELLE 0 [1]2-8-9 A Medeiros(5) 50/1: 7: Slowly away, hdwy halfway, ch over 1f out, wknd. *hd* **62**
JACK THE GIANT 0 [2]2-9-0 M Hills 12/1: 8: Slowly away in rear, hdwy over 1f out, kept on: debut. *1* **64**
NAVAL FORCE 0 [12]2-9-0 R Hughes 12/1: 9: Handy, wkng when not clr run briefly 1f out, sn btn. *¾* **62**
2876 **WORTH ABBEY 4** [19]2-9-0 R L Moore 20/1: 00: 10th: Nvr btr than mid-div: qck reapp. *3* **53**
GYPSY ROYAL 0 [13]2-8-9 N Day 33/1: 0: 11th: Bhd, nvr nr ldrs on debut. *½* **46**
MAGGIE TULLIVER 0 [15]2-8-9 T Quinn 16/1: 0: 12th: Outpcd in rear, kept on over 1f out on debut. *½* **44**
2703 **ARTHUR WARDLE 11** [5]2-9-0 I Mongan 20/1: 250: 13th: Dwelt bhd, nvr nr ldrs: see 2703. *½* **47**
LAMA ALBARQ 0 [14]2-9-0 L Dettori 9/4 FAV: 0: 14th: With ldr over 3f, sn fdd on debut. *¾* **45**
1816 **IN DREAMS 48** [18]2-9-0 J F Egan 33/1: 00: 15th: Reared start, al bhd: 7 wk abs. *3* **36**
MICKEY PEARCE 0 [16]2-9-0 D Sweeney 33/1: 0: 16th: Outpcd bhd, modest late gains on debut. *½* **34**
GLOBAL BANKER 0 [10]2-9-0 O Urbina 50/1: 0: 17th: Slowly away in rear, nvr a factor on debut. *1* **31**
1911 **PIPS PEARL 44** [9]2-8-9 R Havlin 100/1: 00: 18th: Bhd, nvr a factor: 6 wk abs. *¾* **24**
2666 **DOUGHTY 12** [4]2-9-0 V Slattery 100/1: 000: 19th: Bhd, nvr a factor. *nk* **28**
CAVARADOSSI 0 [17]2-9-0 J Fortune 20/1: P: Slowly away in rear, p.u. bef 1f on debut. **0**
20 Ran Time 1m 13.87 (3.57) Owned: Young Guns Syndicate Trained: Kingsclere

2971 **7.05 Trinity Hospice Handicap Stakes Sponsored By Mrs Urs Schwarzenbach 3yo 0-70 (E)** **[74]**
£3640 £1120 £560 **1m67y** **Firm -3** **-11 Slow** Inside

2756 **RIDGE BOY 9** [1] R Hannon 3-9-7 (67) P Dobbs 40/1: 5601: b c Indian Ridge - Bold Tina (Persian Bold) Led, joined/went on over 3f out, hdd 2f out, rallied fnl 1f, edged left & led again fnl stride: eff around 1m on firm: first win & improved from the front. **72**
2508 **ROSACARA 18** [9] D J Daly 3-9-6 t (66) J Murtagh 8/1: 504-22: Rcd in 2nd till 5f out, led 2f out, hdd/hard rdn fnl stride: eff btwn 7f/1m: acts on firm & gd: find similar: see 2508. *shd* **70**
2706 **DAGOLA 11** [4] C G Cox 3-9-2 (62) J Fortune 14/1: 000-1003: Keen in tch, hdwy into 2nd 5f out, chall 3f out, ev ch nr fin, just failed: acts on firm & gd: ran to winning form of 1242. *shd* **65**
2394 **LITTLE EYE 23** [12] J R Best 3-9-2 VIS (62) N Pollard 33/1: 4-403064: Keen & handy, hdwy 2f out, onepace: acts on firm & both AWs: tried a visor: rtn to 9/10f shld suit: see 497. *1¾* **61**
2098 **KINBRACE 35** [14]3-9-0 (60) Martin Dwyer 7/1: 050-65: Keen in tch, modest late gains: see 2098. *¾* **57**
2590 **PICKLE 16** [7]3-9-3 (63) S Sanders 7/2: 0410336: Bhd, modest late gains: nicely bckd. *shd* **59**
2701* **KNICKYKNACKIENOO 11** [5]3-8-13 (59) S Whitworth 9/1: 4220317: Dwelt in rear, modest late gains. *1* **53**
2423 **FUEL CELL 22** [13]3-9-5 (65) R Hughes 100/30 FAV: 00338: Slowly away in rear, hdwy over 3f out, wkng when not clr run briefly 2f out: nicely bckd: btr 2423. *1½* **56**
1124 **KEEPERS KNIGHT 84** [6]3-9-5 (65) N De Souza(5) 40/1: 5-135009: Dwelt, in tch, nvr nr ldrs: abs. *hd* **55**
2365 **JOMUS 24** [8]3-9-1 (61) T Quinn 12/1: 5212000: 10th: Dwelt, some late prog: op 16/1. *2* **47**
2496 **CARTE NOIRE 19** [11]3-8-13 (59) E Ahern 33/1: 030-5100: 11th: Bhd, hdwy 2f out, no impress fnl 1f. *¾* **43**
2627 **COTTON EASTER 14** [2]3-8-13 (59) T E Durcan 50/1: 0060: 12th: b f Robellino - Pluck (Never So Bold) Dwelt in rear, nvr nr ldrs: h'cap bow: Feb foal, cost 1,800gns: dam fair 6f 2/3yo wnr: mdn unplcd prev. *1¼* **40**
1903 **NEBRASKA CITY 45** [3]3-8-13 (59) Dane O'Neill 40/1: 5050-060: 13th: Keen in tch, wknd 2f out: abs. *6* **28**

1722 **CORNWALLIS 53** [10]3-9-4 (64) K Fallon 5/1: 06-0120: 14th: Keen & handy, wknd over 2f out: 8 wk abs. *5* **23**
14 Ran   Time 1m 43.69 (0.69)   Owned: Mrs Chris Harrington   Trained: Marlborough

2972 7.35 Jobs @ Pertemps E B F Classified Stakes 3yo+ 0-80 (D)
£6890 £2120 £1060 **1m3f135y** Firm -3 **+21 Fast** Inside

2623* **LIGHT WIND 14** [1] Mrs A J Perrett 3-8-1 (79) R L Moore 9/4: 511: Dsptd lead, led 3f out, joined **88**
over 2f out, kept on well for press to assert ins fnl 1f: tchd 3/1: landed double in fast time: eff around
11.5f/12f, further shld suit: acts on firm & fast, sharp or gall/undul trks: improving & genuine.
2582 **ANTICIPATING 16** [6] A M Balding 4-9-7 (84) Martin Dwyer 2/1 FAV: 460-0402: Bhd, hdwy over 3f *3* **87**
out, ev ch till no impress ins fnl 1f: clr of rem: gd eff: win sn: see 877.
2353 **OBAY 25** [5] E A L Dunlop 3-8-8 BL (84) K Fallon 4/1: 0-41423: Dsptd lead to 3f out, no ch over 1f out. *5* **79**
2519 **ASIATIC 18** [2] M Johnston 3-8-9 (85) S Chin 7/2: 241-2004: Handy, outpcd over 2f out, kept on. *1¼* **78**
570 **DONT SIOUX ME 149** [3]6-9-6 (83) I Mongan 20/1: 40/00/4-05: b g Sadler's Wells - Commanche Belle *14* **55**
(Shirley Heights) Mid-div, wknd over 3f out: hdles fit (h'cap unplcd, rtd 109, eff at 2m/2m3.5f on fast & gd/soft,
any trk): well btn sole '03 start (cond stks, rtd 83): unplcd both '02 starts (rtd 92, h'cap, H Cecil): eff at
12f, has tried 14f: acts on gd & soft: has gone well fresh: has tried a t-strap.
2 Aug'01 Newm 12gd 97- C: 1 Jul'01 Newb 12g/f 86- D:
3816 **LITTLE FOX 676** [4]9-9-0 (45) A Daly 100/1: 504500/-6: br f Persian Bold - Dance Land (Nordance) *9* **35**
Mid-div, lost place 4f out & sn btn on reapp: missed '03: won a mdn & a fills h'cap in '02: eff btwn 1m/13f on
firm, fast & loves polytrack/Lingfield.
1 Feb'02 Ling 12ap 59a-54 E: 2 Dec'01 Ling 10ap 56a-53 F: 1 Nov'01 Ling 10ap 56a- D: 2 Oct'01 Bath 8g/f 49-48 F:
2 Aug'01 Ling 10g/f 49-46 F: 2 Jun'01 Ling 10ap 56m 46-43 E:
6 Ran   Time 2m 24.5 (u2.8)   Owned: Hesmonds Stud   Trained: Pulborough

2973 8.05 Tote Supports The G O S H C C And Trinity Hospice Handicap Stakes 3yo+ 0-85 (D) [79]
£5525 £1700 £850 **1m2f7y** Firm -3 **-31 Slow** Inside

2787* **A ONE 8** [8] H J Manners 5-8-11 (6ex) (62) F P Ferris(3) 2/1 FAV: 00-43111: Made all, pushed out **77**
fnl 1f, cmftbly: eff at 6f/10f on firm & fast, soft & hvy, handles fibresand: in fine heart at present & goes well
for this rider: see 2787.
2761 **DORIS SOUTER 9** [6] R Hannon 4-9-3 (68) R Hughes 4/1: 0503032: Handy, hdwy into 2nd over 1f out, *5* **71**
not pace of wnr: likes to dominate but unable to do so here: see 736.
2538 **RAINBOW WORLD 17** [1] Andrew Reid 4-8-8 p (59) J F Egan 14/1: 0300303: Rcd in 2nd, btn over 1f out. *1½* **60**
1736 **BEST FLIGHT 52** [7] B W Hills 4-9-5 (70) M Hills 10/1: 0341-004: gr g Sheikh Albadou - Bustling *1¾* **68**
Nelly (Bustino) Slowly away, in tch, no impress fnl 2f: 7 wk abs: won fnl '03 start (mdn h'cap): eff btwn 7/8.5f
on fibresand, acts on a sharp trk: runs well fresh: lightly rcd 4yo. 1 Sep'03 Wolv 8.5af 72a-66 E:
2687 **INTERNATIONALGUEST 11** [3]5-9-8 vis (73) S Sanders 8/1: 0020055: Trkd ldrs, wknd over 2f out. *1½* **69**
2601 **GALLANT BOY 15** [4]5-9-4 vis t (69) S Donohoe(7) 5/1: 0400506: Rear, nvr a factor. *½* **64**
2453* **LITTLETON TELCHAR 21** [5]4-9-13 (78) M Halford(7) 7/1: 517: Bhd, hdwy 3f out, fdd over 1f out. *10* **58**
743 **ROLEX FREE 130** [9]6-9-2 (67) R Smith 33/1: 06/40-068: ch g Friul - Karolera (Kaljerry) Bhd, *14* **26**
t.o.: long abs: 4th at best in '03 (stks, rtd 80a at best): ex-Argentian, '02 wnr in native land (10f, fast):
poss handles fibresand: now with D Flood.
8 Ran   Time 2m 3.48 (2.88)   Owned: Mr H J Manners   Trained: Swindon

2974 8.35 Sunley Maiden Stakes Fillies 3yo (D)
£4342 £1336 £668 **1m67y** Firm -3 **-10 Slow** Inside

2751 **HILLTOP RHAPSODY 9** [13] D J Daly 3-8-11 J Murtagh 50/1: 001: b f Bin Ajwaad - Saferjel **71**
(Elmaamul) Rcd in 2nd till led well over 2f out, rdn & kept on well for press fnl 1f: 1st foal: dam unplcd all
3 starts: much imprvd for forcing tactics today: gd confidence booster.
LIBERTY FLAG 0 [7] J H M Gosden 3-8-11 J Fortune 14/1: 2: b f Kingmambo - Banner Dancer *½* **69+**
(Danzig) Slowly away in rear, hdwy 2f out, kept on ins fnl 1f to go 2nd nr fin on debut: eff around 1m on firm,
further will suit: gd start, improve.
2633 **ZATHONIA 14** [14] R Charlton 3-8-11 R Hughes 9/4 J FAV: 23: Slowly away, sn handy, rcd in 2nd *¾* **67**
over 1f out, onepcd ins fnl 1f & lost 2nd nr fin: reputable, handles firm & fast: see 2633.
2410 **SUPAMACH 23** [4] P F I Cole 3-8-11 T Quinn 6/1: 344: Keen & handy, outpcd over 3f out, kept on *½* **66**
fnl 1f: apprec 10f h'caps: see 2066.
2453 **DOUBLE DAGGER LADY 21** [3]3-8-11 E Ahern 9/1: 645: b f Diesis - Darby Jane (Silver Deputy) Chsd *1¼* **63**
ldrs, outpcd over 3f out, onepcd 2f out: dam wnr of 3 US dirt sprints: with J Noseda.
2349 **ALENUSHKA 25** [12]3-8-11 Dane O'Neill 16/1: 06: In tch, kept on ins fnl 1f. *nk* **62**
2627 **STRAWBERRY FAIR 14** [2]3-8-11 T L Dettori A J FAV: 2-47: Led till well over 2f out, no extra: t-strap. *nk* **61**
2419 **MEDICA BOBA 22** [8]3-8-11 S Drowne 66/1: 08: Handy, outpcd halfway, onepcd & btn over 2f out. *2½* **56**
2534 **ZURI 17** [5]3-8-11 T E Durcan 25/1: 649: Bhd, nvr nr ldrs: see 2534. *¾* **54**
2659 **GAY ROMANCE 12** [10]3-8-11 M Hills 25/1: 00: 10th: Bhd, nvr nr ldrs. *1½* **51**
2709 **BURN 11** [6]3-8-11 I Mongan 25/1: 030: 11th: Rear, hdwy halfway, sn outpcd & btn. *¾* **49**
GOLD RELIC 0 [9]3-8-11 Martin Dwyer 14/1: 0: 12th: Bhd, nvr nr ldrs on debut. *½* **48**
PRIMESHADE PROMISE 0 [1]3-8-11 R Price 66/1: 0: 13th: Bhd, nvr nr ldrs on debut. *½* **47**
ROSINGS 0 [11]3-8-11 R L Moore 25/1: 0: 14th: Bhd, nvr a factor on debut. *½* **46**
14 Ran   Time 1m 43.67 (0.67)   Owned: Mr G Noble   Trained: Newmarket

2975 9.05 Claudia Swinburn Peter Pan Centenary Handicap Stakes 3yo+ 0-70 (E) [70]
£3601 £1108 £554 **6f** Firm -3 **-27 Slow** Inside

2871 **WILLHECONQUERTOO 4** [20] Andrew Reid 4-9-7 t (63) J F Egan 10/1: 00-00351: Made all, clr bef **72**
halfway, v cmftbly: qk reapp: eff btwn 5/7f, yet to convince at 1m: acts on firm, gd & polytrack, handles a gall trk,
loves a sharp/undul one: made full use of gd high-draw: see 1613.
2626 **SEWMUCH CHARACTER 14** [19] M Blanshard 5-9-7 (63) D Sweeney 8/1: 04-40642: Handy, hdwy *3½* **64**
into 2nd over 1f out, not pace of wnr: clr of rem: on a handy mark: see 1345.

2799 **MYTHICAL CHARM 7** [14] J J Bridger 5-8-9 t (51) A Daly 16/1: 6330003: Dwelt, hdwy & not clr run over 1f out, kept on ins fnl 1f to go 3rd nr fin: quick reapp: see 427. *3½* **41**
2951 **INTELLIBET ONE 2** [5] P D Evans 4-8-12 (54) N Callan 8/1: 000-0034: Handy, onepcd over 1f out. *¾* **42**
2752 **STOKESIES WISH 9** [16]4-9-8 (64) L Dettori 6/1 FAV: 2-000205: Rcd in 2nd, lost pl over 1f out, onepcd. *shd* **51**
2394 **ROYAL ADVOCATE 23** [17]4-9-4 (60) S Whitworth 14/1: 0654-456: Bhd, late gains: see 2018. *1½* **42**
2720 **KENNINGTON 10** [10]4-8-11 vis (53) Hayley Turner(5) 11/1: 3400207: Handy, fdd over 1f out. *½* **33**
2648 **PRIMA STELLA 13** [18]5-9-2 (58) Lisa Jones(3) 12/1: 0266008: In tch, onepcd fnl 2f. *nk* **37**
2314 **NIGHT WORKER 26** [9]3-8-5 (53) R Smith 25/1: 40-60009: Dwelt, hdwy over 2f out, not pace to chall. *½* **30**
2752 **A TEEN 9** [4]6-9-1 (57) K Fallon 10/1: 1660060: 10th: Bhd main group, hdwy over 2f out, btn 1f out. *¾* **32**
2586* **PICCLEYES 16** [15]3-9-1 bl (63) R L Moore 10/1: 53-00010: 11th: Mid-div, btn over 2f out: btr 2586. *1* **35**
2760 **ISAZ 9** [1]4-10-0 (70) Dane O'Neill 33/1: 5/4-55500: 12th: Bhd, nvr a factor under top weight. *1* **39**
2451 **SUPER SONG 21** [13]4-9-2 t (58) Joanna Badger 25/1: 1-000000: 13th: Mid-div, no impress 2f out. *3½* **16**
2262* **DOCTOR DENNIS 29** [12]7-8-10 vis (52) S Sanders 7/1: 6-516010: 14th: Al bhd: btr 2262 (Brighton). *1¼* **6**
2630 **TENDER 14** [11]4-8-9 VIS (51) S Drowne 18/1: 5005000: 15th: Handy, lost place halfway, fdd: visor. *1* **2**
2743 **INDIAN BAZAAR 9** [3]8-8-11 (53) M Halford(7) 12/1: 0020020: 16th: Al bhd: see 2269. *3* **0**
1452 **ONEFORTHEBOYS 67** [6]5-7-13 (1ow)(1oh) (39) C Catlin 33/1: 0030630: 17th: Reared stalls, al bhd, t.o. *18* **0**
17 Ran Time 1m 11.79(1.49) Owned: Mr A S Reid Trained: Mill Hill London

BATH MONDAY 05.07.04 Lefthand, Turning Track with Uphill Finish

Official Going FIRM.

2976

2.00 E B F /Sponsorship Raceday Event Maiden Stakes 2yo (D)
£4449 £1369 £685 **5f11y rnd** **Good/Firm 25** **+06 Fast** Far Side

2815 **ANNATALIA 10** [6] B J Meehan 2-8-9 L Dettori 8/11 FAV: 461: Broke well & made, clr fnl 1f, easily in a fast juv time: eff at 5f, stays 6f: acts on gd & fast grnd: speedy, likes to force the pace & lks useful, win more races: see 2815 & 2364. **84+**
2738 **MULBERRY LAD 9** [8] W R Muir 2-9-0 R Mullen 9/1: 52: Chsd wnr thr'out, no ch fnl 1f: eff at 5f on fast grnd: prob met an above rival here, see 2738. *6* **70**
2573 **DOVE COTTAGE 16** [5] W S Kittow 2-9-0 W Supple 16/1: 653: Rear, late prog, nvr dngrs: see 1826. *3½* **60**
DANZILI BAY [9] R M Beckett 2-9-0 T Quinn 9/1: 4: b c Dansili - Lady Bankes (Alzao) Swerved start, imprvd to chase ldrs after halfway, wknd fnl 1f on debut: Jan foal, cost 30,000gns: half-brother to 1m wnr Moten Swing: dam a 10f wnr, sire a high-class miler: shld learn from this. *shd* **60**
AVERTING [3]2-9-0 S Carson 5/1: 5: br c Averti - Sweet Compliance (Safawan) Rdn in rear, nvr dngrs on debut: 24,000gns Mar foal: dam a 7f juv wnr, sire a high-class sprinter, with R Johnson Houghton. *1¼* **55**
1900 **DOMINER 45** [4]2-9-0 R L Moore 66/1: 666: b c Desert Prince - Smart (Last Tycoon) Speed till halfway, 6 wk abs: 10,000gns Mar foal: dam mainly modest, sire a top-class miler: with J Bradley. *5* **40**
2188 **OUR NIGEL 32** [1]2-9-0 R Havlin 50/1: 07: Chsd ldrs, wknd halfway. *nk* **39**
7 Ran Time 1m 01.27 (0.97) Owned: Mrs Sheila Tucker Trained: Upper Lambourn

2977

2.30 Oval Of Bath Peugeot Selling Stakes 2yo (G)
£2527 £722 £361 **5f11y rnd** **Good/Firm 25** **-66 Slow** Far Side

2330 **STRAFFAN 25** [2] E J O'Neill 2-8-7 S Sanders 7/2: 6332541: Chsd ldrs, imprvd to lead ins fnl 1f, drvn out: bght by W Clifford for 8,500gns: slow time: acts on fast, soft & fibresand, eff at 5/6f. **59**
2625 **GLASSON LODGE 14** [4] P D Evans 2-8-8 (1ow) N Callan 11/4 FAV: 4563422: Chsd ldrs, kept on under press fnl 1f, took 2nd on line & not btn far: consistent in plating company, see 2625. *¾* **57**
2865 **VOOM 4** [1] M R Channon 2-8-7 S Hitchcott(1) 4/1: 043: Chsd ldrs, not qckn ins fnl 1f: qck reapp: not disgraced, btn under 1L: eff at 5f on fast grnd, see 2865. *nk* **55**
2865 **ZACHY BOY 4** [3] J S Moore 2-8-12 BL Derek Nolan(7) 14/1: 5006654: Broke well & led till ins fnl 1f, no extra: qck reapp & best run to date in first time blnks: btn under 1L, see 2625. *hd* **60**
2625 **SAPPHIRE PRINCESS 14** [5]2-8-7 T P Queally 7/1: 455: Chsd ldrs, keeping on when short of room ins fnl 1f, eased: rcd without advertised t-strap: see 2270. *1* **52**
1826 **TIP TOES 48** [7]2-8-7 T Dean(7) 16/1: 06: b f Bianconi - Tip Tap Toe (Pleasant Tap) Dwelt, mod hdwy, nvr dngrs: 7 wk abs: E2,000 Mar foal: dam unrcd, but from a decent family, sire a high-class sprinter. *1½* **48**
2625 **FIRE AT WILL 14** [6]2-8-12 W Supple 20/1: 07: b c Lugana Beach - Kahyasi Moll (Brief Truce) Slowly away, al outpcd: Apr foal, cost 17,000gns: dam modest, sire a smart sprinter: with A Carroll. *nk* **52**
1751 **NUTTY TIMES 51** [8]2-8-7 C Haddon(7) 5/1: 233008: Chsd ldrs, wknd 1.5f out: 7 wk abs: rider given 2 day ban (1-day careless, 1-day not riding to draw): see 1097 (C/D). *1* **44**
8 Ran Time 1m 04.87 (4.57) Owned: Mrs Melissa O'Neill Trained: Newmarket

2978

3.00 Lansdown Maiden Handicap Stakes 3yo 0-75 (E) **[75]**
£3692 £1136 £568 **1m3f144y** **Good/Firm 25** **-21 Slow** Inside

2345 **VELVET WATERS 25** [7] R F Johnson Houghton 3-8-10 (57) S Carson 7/2: 600-3641: Led till ins fnl 1f, rallied gamely to force head back in front on line: eff at 12f, prob stays 14f: acts on fast. **60**
2478 **LUCKY ARTHUR 19** [5] J G M O'Shea 3-8-12 (59) D Sweeney 7/1: 05032: Rear, prog wide 2f out, fin well & just btn in a fin of heads: sound run on h'cap bow, stays 12f well: acts on fast grnd: see 2478. *hd* **61**
2800 **MUSTANG ALI 7** [9] S Kirk 3-9-7 (68) L Dettori 3/1 FAV: 3-603553: Chsd ldrs, led briefly ins fnl 1f, just btn in a 3-way photo: top-weight: see 2175. *hd* **70**
2503 **THE KING OF ROCK 18** [2] A G Newcombe 3-8-9 (56) S Whitworth 6/1: 0-054024: Held up, imprvd 2f out, nrst fin: op 8/1: see 2503 (AW). *1¾* **54**
2322 **DHEHDAAH 26** [8]3-9-0 BL (61) W Supple 13/2: 600-035: Chsd ldrs, wknd ins fnl 1f: tried blnks. *½* **59**
1967 **SCIENCE ACADEMY 42** [10]3-8-7 (54) T Quinn 10/1: 500-056: Chsd wnr, wknd fnl 1f: 6 wk abs. *¾* **50**
2782 **SILENCIO 8** [4]3-8-13 (60) V Slattery 16/1: 000057: Keen & chsd ldrs, btn 2f out: see 2782. *5* **48**
2378 **ROYAL STARLET 24** [1]3-8-6 (53) P Dobbs 10/1: 000-08: b f Royal Applause - Legend (Belmez) Chsd ldrs 10f, wknd: well btn on 3 juv starts: longer 12f trip on h'cap bow today: with Mrs A Perrett. *1¼* **39**
2346 **SIGNORA PANETTIERA 25** [6]3-8-3 (50) C Catlin 50/1: 40-60609: Al bhd: see 1250. *3* **31**

BATH   MONDAY 05.07.04   Lefthand, Turning Track with Uphill Finish

1140 **ALMOST WELCOME 84** [3]3-8-8 (55) R L Moore 20/1: 0-003500: 10th: Al rear after 12f wk abs.   *hd*   **36**
10 Ran   Time 2m 30.42 (5.42)   Owned: Mr R Crutchley   Trained: Didcot

---

2979   3.30 Grosvenor Casinos Stakes Handicap 3yo+ 0-75 (E)   **[74]**
£4459 £1372 £686   **1m2f46y**   **Good/Firm 25**   **+02 Fast**   Inside

2866 **EMBER DAYS 4** [4] J L Spearing 5-8-13 p (59) E Ahern 4/1: 5030231: Mid-div, hdwy into 2nd 2f out,   **66**
drvn & kept on to lead fnl strides: qck reapp, fair time: wng form at 1m/10f: acts on firm, soft & polytrack.
2857 **TODLEA 5** [3] J A Osborne 4-9-11 (71) L Dettori 5/4 FAV: 6443622: Led after 1f till collared fnl   *shd*   **77**
strides: qck reapp: not disgraced under top-weight: see 1736.
2628 **REBATE 14** [5] R Hannon 4-9-0 (60) P Dobbs 5/1: 0003363: Bhd, hdwy 2f out, not qckn ins fnl 1f,.   *1¼*   **62**
1791 **MARIA BONITA 49** [1] R M Beckett 3-8-8 BL (65) R L Moore 16/1: 03-404: Keen & prom, onepcd for   *¾*   **65**
press fnl 1f: 3yo abs: tried blnks: poss stays 10f on fast grnd: see 1791.
2664 **OKTIS MORILIOUS 12** [2]3-7-12 (7oh) (48) C Haddon(7) 8/1: 2342625: Bhd, hdwy fnl 2f, not pace to chall. *hd*   **55$**
2601 **CELTIC STAR 15** [6]6-9-0 (60) D Nolan(3) 25/1: 06-/116: Led 1f, remained prom, wknd fnl 1f.   *3*   **55**
2707 **TRAVELLERS TALE 11** [7]5-9-1 (61) S Drowne 7/1: 0060067: Bhd, nvr nr to chall: tchd 12/1.   *2*   **53**
7 Ran   Time 2m 08.37 (2.37)   Owned: Mrs Carol J Welch   Trained: Kinnersley

---

2980   4.00 Weatherbys Bank Maiden Stakes 3yo (D)
£3536 £1088 £544   **1m2f46y**   **Good/Firm 25**   **-08 Slow**   Inside

2274 **VAMP 28** [5] R M Beckett 3-8-9 (73) S Sanders 11/4: 0231: Trkd ldrs, hdwy to lead 2f out, held on   **75**
well, rdn out: nicely bckd: stays 9.7/10f on firm & fast, acts on a sharp trk: see 2274.
1922 **MOUFTARI 44** [3] B W Hills 3-9-0 (84) L Dettori 5/1: 0-5452: Led till 2f out, kept on fnl 1f but   *1*   **78**
not pace of wnr: 6 wk abs: eff at 10f on fast grnd: see 1597.
2622 **WEDDING CAKE 14** [2] Sir Michael Stoute 3-8-9 E Ahern 7/1: 03: ch f Groom Dancer - Greektown   *1*   **71**
(Ela Mana Mou) Bhd, hdwy 2f out, not pace of first 2: clr of rem: dam a French Gr 3 wnr: fair run.
2627 **POWERFUL PARRISH 14** [6] P F I Cole 3-8-9 (78) T Quinn 15/8 FAV: 25-024: Chsd ldr, wknd fnl 1f.   *3½*   **66**
2608 **SUNDAY CITY 15** [1]3-9-0 vis T P Queally 4/1: 335: Handy, wknd over 2f out.   *3½*   **66**
WHENWILLITWIN [4]3-9-0 Derek Nolan(7) 100/1: 6: b g Bluegrass Prince - Madam Marash (Astronef)   *4*   **60**
Slowly away, al rear on debut: first foal: dam unplcd over 6/12f: with J Moore.
6 Ran   Time 2m 09.37 (3.37)   Owned: Mr A D G Oldrey   Trained: Lambourn

---

2981   4.30 Teletext Racing Hands And Heels Apprentice Handicap Stakes 3yo+ 35-55 (G)   **[60]**
£2653 £758 £379   **5f11y rnd**   **Good/Firm 25**   **-15 Slow**   Far Side

2657 **FLYING TACKLE 13** [14] M Dods 6-9-2 p (48) W Hogg 4/1 FAV: 3-000321: Mid-div, hdwy to lead ent fnl   **55**
1f, drifted left & all out to hold on: eff btwn 5/6f on fast & hvy: likes a gall trk, acts on a sharp one: see 2657.
2806 **ENJOY THE BUZZ 7** [13] J M Bradley 5-9-1 (47) M Halford 5/1: 2420102: Rear, hdwy over 2f out, fin   *hd*   **53**
strongly & just failed: op 9/1, qck reapp: ran to winning form of 2585.
2645 **LUCKY VALENTINE 13** [2] G L Moore 4-9-0 bl (46) Jemma Marshall(6) 9/1: 0100-243: Chsd ldrs, hdwy &   *shd*   **52**
led briefly ent fnl 1f, kept on & just btn in a thrilling fin: gd run: see 2331.
2951 **BLESSED PLACE 2** [9] D J S ffrench Davis 4-9-1 p (47) Derek Nolan 5/1: 0003354: With ldr till   *1½*   **49**
definite lead over 3f out, hdd 1f out, no extra ins fnl 1f: op 7/1, qck reapp: see 2599.
2630 **TAMARELLA 14** [8]4-9-1 BL (47) M Howard 12/1: 0500005: Slowly away, hdwy 2f out, not pace to rch ldrs.   *nk*   **48**
1540 **FIAMMA ROYALE 62** [4]6-8-13 (45) Steven Harrison 16/1: 00-40006: Handy, kept on late.   *hd*   **46**
2585 **TOMTHEVIC 16** [16]6-9-7 (53) Saleem Golam 20/1: 220-0007: Led till halfway, no extra: see 2585.   *1½*   **50**
2370 **BENNANABAA 24** [3]5-8-11 t (43) B O'Neill(3) 50/1: 0500008: Rear, modest late gains: see 713.   *hd*   **40**
2803 **HAGLEY PARK 7** [12]5-9-2 vis (48) K May 25/1: 3031009: Chsd ldrs, hmpd/wknd 1f out: qck reapp.   *hd*   **45**
1327 **XSYNNA 73** [6]8-8-5 (37) K Jackson(3) 33/1: 0-306030: 10th: Rear, mod gains: abs, new yard.   *1¼*   **30**
2957 **BOANERGES 1** [5]7-9-9 p (55) C J Davies(3) 7/1: 56240050: 11th: Mid-div, hdwy when not much room &   *shd*   **48**
sn no impress 1f out: 5th yesterday: see 1886.
2585 **FLAPDOODLE 16** [11]6-9-8 (54) R Lucey Butler 12/1: 63050-50: 12th: Handy, no impress over 1f out.   *1*   **44**
2925 **DANIFAH 2** [15]3-8-8 bl (45) R J Killoran(3) 20/1: 0000400: 13th: Slow away, mod gains: qck reapp.   *hd*   **35**
2657 **SOMETHINGABOUTHER 13** [7]4-8-11 (43) Frances Pickard(5) 50/1: 0502000: 14th: Nvr a factor.   *½*   **32**
2928 **SHADY DEAL 2** [17]8-8-13 (45) Dean Williams 10/1: 0030030: 15th: In tch on outer, sn btn: qck reapp.   *nk*   **33**
2412 **TAPPIT 23** [1]5-9-6 (52) Hazel Boyd(5) 20/1: 0003050: 16th: Nvr a factor.   *nk*   **39**
832 **DIAPHANOUS 118** [10]6-8-5 bl (37) Liam Jones(6) 33/1: 644-0000: 17th: Handy, wknd dist: long abs.   *2*   **18**
17 Ran   Time 1m 02.34(2.04)   Owned: Mr Neil Harrison   Trained: Darlington

---

RIPON   MONDAY 05.07.04   Righthand, Sahrpish Track

Official Going GOOD.

2982   6.50 Mary Dodds 90th Birthday Celebration Selling Stakes 3yo (F)
£3255 £930 £465   **1m2f**   **Good 49**   **-21 Slow**   Inside

1976 **BISCAR TWO 41** [5] R M Whitaker 3-8-12 BL (48) V Halliday 7/4 FAV: 4622201: Slow away & sn rdn,   **54**
bhd, hdwy to lead 2f out, rdn clr ins last: no bid: first win: stays 10f on gd & soft, 12f lks sure to suit: runs
well fresh: tried a visor, improved here in blnks drpd to the lowest class: see 490.
2667 **BUCHANAN STREET 12** [6] N A Callaghan 3-8-12 (49) P Robinson 3/1: 206-0662: In tch, rdn & sltly   *5*   **46**
outpcd over 2f out, rallied over 1f out, not pace of wnr: clmd for 6,000: stays 10f: see 2431.
1836 **BONJOUR BOND 48** [2] B Smart 3-8-12 bl (51) D McGaffin 6/1: 0-400303: In tch, led 4f out, trav   *1¾*   **44**
well till hdd 2f out, found little: 7 wk abs: see 1630.
2608 **ONIZ TIPTOES 15** [3] J S Wainwright 3-8-12 BL (35) G Parkin 20/1: 00-064: Held up, eff over 2f   *3½*   **39**
out, sn no impress: tried blnks: see 2608.
2790 **CIACOLE 7** [7]3-8-12 (50) Dean McKeown 6/1: 4031005: Dwelt, with ldrs, wknd 2f out: btr 1630.   *8*   **25**

2295 **LUPINE HOWL 27** [8]3-8-12 p (44) G Gibbons 7/1: 60-00006: b c Wolfhound - Classic Fan (Lear Fan)   nk   24
Held up, hmpd over 3f out, sn wknd: rtd 74$ when plcd in a mdn in '03: eff at 6f on gd/soft.
1832 **BALLIN ROUGE 48** [4]3-8-7 T D Allan 12/1: 00-07: ch f Dr Fong - Bogus John (Blushing John) Led   6   9
till 4f out, wknd: 7 wk abs, tried t-strap, poor form.
7 Ran   Time 2m 10.29 (6.99)   Owned: Mr M J O'Dwyer   Trained: Scarcroft

---

2983   7.20 Sky Bet Just Press Red To Bet Maiden Auction Stakes Fillies 2yo (F)
£4144 £1275 £638   **5f str**   **Good 49**   -42 Slow   Stands Side

2795 **CASTELLETTO 7** [3] B A McMahon 2-8-11   G Gibbons 8/15 FAV: 32021: With ldr, led over 1f out, styd   89
on to lead over 1f out, rdn, more in hand: hvly bckd: eff at 5f on gd/firm & gd, sharp trks: going the right way, gd
confidence boost & prob more to come in nurseries: see 1608.
2789 **HILLSIDE HEATHER 7** [9] A Berry 2-8-2 F Norton 16/1: 432: Held up, hdwy halfway, hung left but   1¾   72
chall dist, not pace of wnr ins last: consistent, shown enough to win a modest race: see 2547.
2442 **WISE WAGER 21** [6] R A Fahey 2-8-2   P Fessey 8/1: 233: Slow away, hdwy 2f out, no threat to wnr.   ½   70
2498 **COLONIAL GIRL 18** [5] T D Easterby 2-8-8   D Allan 9/2: 4324: Led till dist, wknd: see 2498, 2151.   1   73
   BAYMIST [12]2-8-5 Dale Gibson 100/1: 5: b f Mind Games - Milliscent (Primo Dominie) Dwelt,   6   52
nvr a factor: Jan foal, cost 5,200gns: speedily bred.
   DESERT PHOENIX [10]2-8-8 Natalia Gemelova(7) 50/1: 6: ch f Desert Story - Bird In My Hand   ½   53
(Bluebird) Slow away nvr a factor on debut: Feb foal, cost E15,000: half-brother to 5f juv wnr.
2670 **OUTRAGEOUS FLIRT 12** [1]2-8-5   A Beech(3) 33/1: 007: In tch, wknd 2f out: see 2213.   ½   48
2733 **MISS COTSWOLD LADY 10** [7]2-8-5 J Quinn 16/1: 5428: In tch, wknd 2f out: btr 2733, see 2132.   ½   46
   MISTY BAY [8]2-8-2 J Bramhill 100/1: 9: b f Namaqualand - Paris Mist (Paris House) Slow away   11   10
& al bhd: Mar foal, cost 140,000gns.
   ALESHANEE [4]2-8-8 J Fanning 16/1: 0: 10th: In tch, wknd 2f out.   nk   15
10 Ran   Time 1m 02.34 (4.54)   Owned: Mr J C Fretwell   Trained: Tamworth

---

2984   7.50 Ripon Land Rover Handicap Stakes 3yo 0-80 (D)   [87]
£6825 £2100 £1050   **1m4f60y**   **Good 49**   +07 Fast   Stands Side

2691 **SAND AND STARS 11** [10] M H Tompkins 3-8-11 (70) P Robinson 9/2: 540-3521: Made all, kept on fnl   83
2f, rdn clr fnl 1f, swished tail: first win: eff over 11/12f on fast & gd/soft: imprvd for forcing tactics last twice
& shld win again in this form: see 2691, 2366.
1403 **DR CERULLO 69** [7] C Tinkler 3-8-13 (72) J Quinn 33/1: 301-3302: Cl-up, eff over 1f out, kept on   5   77
but not pace of wnr: btr run after 10 wk abs: stays 12f on fast, gd & both AWs: see 238.
2804 **SIEGFRIEDS NIGHT 7** [2] M C Chapman 3-8-5 (64) D Fox(5) 11/1: 2133553: Cl-up, eff dist, onepace.   ¾   67
2707 **RUTTERS REBEL 11** [5] G A Swinbank 3-8-13 (72) K Darley 13/2: 6-504024: Slow away, sn in tch, no   1½   72
extra over 1f out: see 2707, 2103.
2478* **MASKED 19** [1]3-8-12 (71) Dale Gibson 5/1: 00415: Keen held up, eff 2f out, no impress: btr 2478.   nk   71
2238 **JOMACOMI 30** [6]3-9-5 (78) J Fanning 8/1: 13606: In tch, wknd 2f out: see 1382, 701.   3½   73
2746 **MASTER WELLS 9** [3]3-9-7 (80) N Chalmers(5) 11/1: 10027: Held up, btn 2f out: see 2746 (g/s).   hd   75
2538 **MAN AT ARMS 17** [4]3-9-5 VIS (78) D Holland 7/2 FAV: 003-4148: In tch, wknd 2f out, eased: vis.   11   57
2741* **JELLY BABY 9** [8]3-8-6 bl (65) A Culhane 7/1: 0119: In tch, wknd over 3f out, eased: surely   18   18
something amiss?: last 2 wins have come on polytrack: see 2741.
9 Ran   Time 2m 38.68 (5.18)   Owned: Pollards Stables   Trained: Newmarket

---

2985   8.20 Skybet Com Handicap Stakes 3yo 0-80 (D)   [83]
£10394 £3198 £1599   **6f str**   **Good 49**   -03 Slow   Stands Side

2855* **CHEROKEE NATION 5** [8] P W D'Arcy 3-8-9 (6ex) (64) D Holland 3/1 JT FAV: 4410211: Mid-div, keen   75
early, hdwy to lead trav well ins last, pushed clr, plenty in hand: suited by 6f on fast, gd & poss handles
fibresand: progressive & confidence is high, land hat-trick.
2693 **COMMANDO SCOTT 11** [10] A Berry 3-9-7 (76) F Lynch 7/1: 0-100222: Handy & narrow lead dist, sn   1¼   79
rdn & hdd, not pace of wnr: deserves similar: see 2693 & 2551.
2482 **NEON BLUE 19** [3] R M Whitaker 3-8-13 (68) A Culhane 3/1 JT FAV: 40-51033: Handy/dsptd lead till   1   68
dist, not pace of wnr from pair: see 2482, 1876.
2683* **SHAMROCK TEA 11** [6] R A Fahey 3-8-4 (59) T Hamilton(3) 8/1: 000-0514: Dwelt, held up in tch, hdwy   nk   58
over 2f out, onepace ins last: acts on gd, loves soft grnd: see 2683.
2717 **OTAGO 10** [4]3-8-2 (57) Dale Gibson 11/1: 3045: Sn pushed along mid-div, kept on, nvr threat: ¾   54
h'cap bow: handles firm & gd grnd: see 2717, 2104.
2945 **ELLIOTS CHOICE 2** [5]3-8-11 (66) J Fanning 12/1: 4400436: Trkd ldrs trav well, rdn & btn dist.   nk   62
2551 **BRIGHT SUN 17** [12]3-9-5 (74) Kim Tinkler 10/1: 0-000437: In tch, no impress dist: btr 2551, 2155.   2½   63
2675 **RENE BARBIER 12** [1]3-8-10 VIS (65) Dean McKeown 25/1: 041568: Led till 2f out, sn btn: btr 2237.   ¾   52
2961 **EXTREMELY RARE 1** [7]3-8-13 (69) D Allan 22/1: 201009: Cl-up, btn over 1f out: unplcd yesterday.   nk   54
2155 **LOUISIADE 33** [9]3-8-10 (65) K Darley 14/1: 000-0300: 10th: Al towards rear: btr 1745.   ½   49
2053 **XPRES DIGITAL 38** [11]3-9-3 t (72) J Bramhill 14/1: 10-04030: 11th: Dwelt, rear, nvr a factor: shd   55
see 1360.
11 Ran   Time 1m 13.14 (3.14)   Owned: Mr Walt Sylvester   Trained: Newmarket

---

2986   8.50 Dufell Roofing Handicap Stakes 3yo+ 0-70 (E)   [67]
£4232 £1302 £651   **1m rnd**   **Good 49**   -06 Slow   Stands Side

2848+ **ALCHEMIST MASTER 5** [7] R M Whitaker 5-9-10 (6ex)p (63) Dean McKeown 1/1 FAV: 0-622211: Trkd ldr,   76+
short of room & switched over 2f out, led over 1f out, pushed out, cmtfbly: qck reapp under a pen: eff at 7f/1m on
firm, gd/soft & both AWs: thriving, hat-trick on the cards: see 2848.
2655 **BLUNHAM 13** [4] M C Chapman 4-8-8 (47) D Holland 10/1: 0-450062: Led, hdd over 1f out, no impress   5   46
on wnr sn after: gd run: see 2655.
2755 **JESSIE 9** [3] Don Enrico Incisa 5-8-4 vis (43) Kim Tinkler 14/1: 2240543: Dwelt, bhd, styd on late   ½   41
for press, nrst fin: some promise but on a long losing run: see 2755.

RIPON   MONDAY 05.07.04   Righthand, Sahrpish Track

1872 **PREMIER DREAM 46** [1] M Johnston 3-9-8 (70) J Fanning 16/1: 663104: Mid-div, styd on onepace: 1¼ 65
abs: handles gd & hvy grnd: see 1534 (hvy, made all).
1991 **EDDIES JEWEL 41** [5]4-8-0 (2ow)(2oh) (35) R Ffrench 25/1: 00300-25: Prom, ch 2f out, onepce: new yard. shd 34
2552 **NOBLE PENNY 17** [10]5-8-10 P (49) G Duffield 16/1: 0-062046: Dwelt, eff 3f out, no impress.   shd 43
2447 **GIFTED FLAME 21** [6]5-9-10 (63) K Darley 6/1: 006-0047: Mid-div wide, eff 2f out, sn btn: btr 2447. hd 56
2799 **CLASSIC VISION 7** [2]4-9-1 bl (54) A Culhane 7/1: 4501068: Held up, no room 4f out & keeping on ¾ 45
when short of room ins last, nvr threat: see 2402.
2935 **SHIFTY 2** [9]5-8-10 (49) A Nicholls 10/1: 0524409: Held up, eff 3f out, btn when short of room ins last. 1¼ 37
2891 **SPLODGER MAC 3** [8]5-8-4 (43) J Quinn 50/1: 04306-00: 10th: b g Lahib - Little Love (Warrshan) ¾ 29
Trkd ldrs, struggling from halfway: qk reapp: lightly rcd '03, amat h'cap plcd: mod form '02: stays 8.5f on fast.
2216 **ESTEBAN 31** [11]4-8-13 (52) R Winston 20/1: 0450-040: 11th: Mid-div, hmpd 4f out, sn drpd rear. 8 22
11 Ran   Time 1m 41.87 (4.37)   Owned: Mr T L Adams   Trained: Scarcroft

2987   **9.20 Kirkgate Maiden Stakes 3yo+ (D)**
    £4833 £1487 £744   **1m rnd**   **Good 49**   **+01 Fast**   Stands Side

2595 **GRAND BUT ONE 16** [13] B W Hills 3-8-12 (87) D Holland 10/11 FAV: 62231: Made all, pushed out, v   87
cmftbly: eff at 1m on fast & gd grnd, enjoys forcing tactics: see 1978 & 1762.
4661} **TRIPLE JUMP 270** [7] T D Easterby 3-8-12 K Dalgleish 16/1: 4-2: ch g Inchinor - Meteoric (High 1 80
Line) Trkd ldrs, rdn & chsd wnr over 2f out, kept on, al held: reapp: unplcd sole '03 start (cond stks, rtd 55, M
Tregoning): eff at 1m, 10f will suit acts on gd: pleasing return.
2751 **OUNINPOHJA 9** [10] G A Swinbank 3-8-12 Dean McKeown 6/1: 43: Held up, hdwy & chsd front pair 2½ 75
over 1f out, kept on, al held but well clr of rem: acts on gd grnd: eff at 1m, rtn to 10f+ will suit: see 2751.
2595 **SPES BONA 16** [14] W J Haggas 3-8-12 A Culhane 14/1: 04: b c Rakeen - Novelette (Darshaan) Bhd, 10 55
short of room over 2f out, mod late prog, nvr threat to front trio: dam a French 1m wnr: imprvd from debut.
1495 **GLENCALVIE 64** [6]3-8-12 K Darley 9/1: 05: ch c Grand Lodge - Top of The Form (Masterclass) shd 55
Mid-div, eff 2f out, sn no impress: 2 month abs: 225,000gns purchase, dam a 5/6f wnr.
2656 **PHONE TAPPING 13** [8]3-8-12 P Robinson 5/1: 066: Mid-div, drvn & no prog fnl 2f. ¾ 53
2484 **FARNE ISLE 19** [9]5-9-2 R Winston 20/1: 437: Slow away, kept on late, no threat: btr 2484. 1½ 45
2729 **RICH CHIC 10** [11]3-8-7 Darren Williams 100/1: 048: Mid-div, eff 2f out: see 2729. ½ 44
2692 **DANCER KING 11** [1]3-8-12 Dale Gibson 7/1: 59: Keen & prom 6f, longer trip. nk 48
1688 **DEE EN AY 54** [15]3-8-12 D Allan 50/1: 00: 10th: Mid-div, btn 2f out, abs, longer trip. 2½ 43
3108} **ALETHEA GEE 347** [2]6-9-2 G Parkin 66/1: 0-0: 11th: Al bhd & nvr factor, reapp. shd 38
    HIGH CLASS PET [12]4-9-2 T Hamilton(3) 100/1: 0: 12th: Sn strug rear: 5 month jumps abs. 5 28
    Transkei [16]3-8-7 R Ffrench 66/1:0   **Rouge Et Noir** [3]6-9-7 J Fanning 20/1:0
2793 **Daring Games 7** [4]3-8-7 T Eaves(3) 100/1:0   **Wild Tide** [5]5-9-2 P Bradley 100/1:0
16 Ran   Time 1m 41.39(3.89)   Owned: Enton Thoroughbred Racing 2   Trained: Lambourn

PONTEFRACT   TUESDAY 06.07.04   Lefthand, Undulating Track, Stiff Uphill Finish

Official Going Good/Firm

2988   **2.05 Pontefract Ladies Handicap Stakes For Lady Amateur Riders 3yo+ 35-55 (F)**   [33]
    £5057 £1556 £778   **1m2f6y**   **Good/Firm 37**   **-34 Slow**   Inside

2718 **BURNT COPPER 11** [16] J R Best 4-11-3 (50) Miss K Manser(7) 20/1: 04250-01: Dwelt & well bhd, hmpd   56
over 3f out, strong run for press to lead line, all out: first win: eff at 10/12f on fast grnd & polytrack, any trk.
2794 **VALEUREUX 8** [3] J Hetherton 6-11-5 (52) Mrs S Bosley 100/30 FAV: 33002-32: Mid-div, hdwy over 2f shd 57
out, rdn & led well ins last, hdd line: nicely bckd, op 9/2: see 2794.
2850 **LAZZAZ 6** [7] P W Hiatt 6-10-12 (45) Mrs Marie King(5) 9/2: 0205643: Led, rdn clr over 1f out, hdd ¾ 49
well ins last & no extra: rest well covered, brave front running effort: see 711 & 330.
2572 **PENSION FUND 17** [12] M W Easterby 10-11-2 (49) Miss J Coward(7) 11/1: 000-5564: Mid-div, short of 3½ 48
room when keeping on onepace dist: 10yo: see 1633.
2725 **FIRST MAITE 11** [15]11-11-3 (50) Mrs M Morris 10/1: 6643235: Rear, hdwy wide over 3f out, btn dist. 5 42
2868 **FINAL DIVIDEND 5** [6]8-10-12 (45) Miss Joanna Rees(3) 17/2: 0643-056: Trkd ldrs, outpcd fnl 2f: see 2868.hd 36
2850 **STEPASTRAY 6** [1]7-10-11 (44) Miss S Brotherton 25/1: 000-5007: Trkd ldrs early, no impress fnl 2f. hd 34
2532} **HEALEY 372** [9]6-11-1 (48) Miss Kelly Harrison(3) 16/1: 06/4032-8: ch g Dr Devious - Bean Siamsa 1 37
(Solinus) Mid-div, btn 2f out: reapp: appr h'cap rnr-up '03, AW polytrack (rtd 15a, C Dwyer): unplcd '02 (rtd 54 &
26a): eff around 10/12f, handles fast & gd/soft grnd: best without cheek pieces, t-strap & blnks.
2 Jun'03 Time 10.0g/s 43-37 E:
2832 **DARK CUT 7** [13]4-10-9 (42) Miss Dawn Rankin(5) 50/1: 0-000009: Dwelt & held up, only mod prog. nk 30
2562 **LADY STRATAGEM 17** [19]5-10-12 (45) Miss M Sowerby(5) 50/1: 60000/-00: 10th: Bhd, mod late prog. ¾ 32
2857 **RAINSTORM 6** [11]9-10-9 (42) Mrs S Owen(3) 7/1: 0-656000: 11th: Chsd ldrs 4f out, wknd over 1f out. 1½ 27
2545 **MELOGRANO 18** [10]4-11-3 (50) Miss A Goschen 33/1: 360-2000: 12th: Mid-div, struggling fnl 2f. shd 35
2891 **Noble Pursuit 4** [14]7-11-3 (50) Miss V Barr(7) 25/1:0   2794 **Penwell Hill 8** [8]5-11-7 (54) Ms C Williams 14/1:0
2526 **Outward 19** [5]4-11-3 (50) Miss R Bastiman(5) 50/1:0
2725 **Mutared 11** [2]6-10-13 p(46) Mrs Emma Littmoden(3) 33/1:0
2654 **Expected Bonus 14** [18]5-11-4 (51) Miss E Folkes(3) 14/1:0
2937 **Kristineau 3** [4]6-10-10 t(43) Miss Beverley Kendall(5) 25/1:0
18 Ran   Time 2m 15.24 (7.14)   Owned: Mr R Blake   Trained: Maidstone

---

2989   2.35 Dianne Nursery Handicap Stakes 2yo (D)   [96]
£7241 £2228 £1114   **6f rnd**   Good/Firm 37   **-31 Slow**   Inside

2472 **PROSPECT COURT 21** [2] J D Bethell 2-8-8 (76) T Quinn 8/1: 0301: Trkd ldrs & rdn to chase wnr   **83+**
over 1f out, styd on under hand riding to prevail line, gamely: h'cap bow: first win: eff at 5f, imprvd for step up
to 6f & 7f shld suit: acts on fast grnd, stiff/undul trk: appeals as the type to progress in similar company: see 2158.
2522* **SPIRIT OF FRANCE 19** [9] M Johnston 2-9-7 (89) K Dalgleish 5/4 FAV: 2212: Led/dsptd lead, went on   shd   96
over 2f out, drvn & hdd line: hvly bckd on h'cap bow, rest well covered: useful run under a big weight.
2682 **BRACE OF DOVES 12** [8] T D Barron 2-8-0 (68) P Fessey 9/1: 0523: Held up, drvn & styd on fnl 2f,   2½   67
no threat to front pair: acts on fast & soft grnd: see 2682.
2744 **MYTTONS DREAM 10** [7] A Bailey 2-7-12 (3oh) (66) D Fox(5) 25/1: 66104: Rear, drvn & mod late gains.   3   56
2670 **RYEDANE 13** [1]2-8-2 (70) C Catlin 25/1: 0305: Led/dsptd lead 4f, sn btn: btr 2100.   1½   55
2569 **HYMN OF VICTORY 17** [3]2-8-6 (74) R Havlin 16/1: 0526: Chsd ldrs, btn 2f out: btr 2569 (g/s).   1¾   54
2336* **SNOOKERED AGAIN 26** [6]2-8-4 (72) Dale Gibson 10/1: 517: Bhd & drvn, nvr a factor: btr 2336 (AW).   ¾   50
2682* **MONSIEUR MIRASOL 12** [4]2-8-9 (77) N Callan 4/1: 33518: Sn rdn rear, no impress: btr 2682 (soft).   nk   54
2744 **MOON MISCHIEF 10** [5]2-8-1 (69) J Bramhill 12/1: 0309: Chsd ldrs till rdn & btn 2f out, eased: btr 2498.   12   14
9 Ran   Time 1m 18.16 (4.06)   Owned: Mr John E Lund   Trained: Middleham

---

2990   3.10 St Giles Handicap Stakes 3yo+ 0-85 (D)   [84]
£14235 £4380 £2190   **6f rnd**   Good/Firm 37   **-06 Slow**   Inside

2791 **COMPLICATION 8** [12] J A R Toller 4-8-9 bl (65) Lisa Jones(3) 8/1: 0-062421: Mid-div, styd on for   74
press to lead well ins last: op 6/1: eff at 6f on fm & fast grnd, stiff or easy trk: see 1726.
2884 **LEGAL SET 5** [15] Miss A Stokell 8-8-3 t (59) D Fox(5) 28/1: 0421402: Al prom & ch dist, not pace of wnr.   1¾   63
2884 **MIDNIGHT PARKES 5** [16] E J Alston 5-8-9 p (65) M Henry 14/1: 0403503: Led till well ins last, no   shd   69
extra: qck reapp: on a handy mark: see 2561, 2280.
2561 **UNDETERRED 17** [10] T D Barron 8-9-1 vis (71) S Sanders 13/2 FAV: 0500444: Held up, styd on for   ¾   73
press, not able to chall: see 1898.
2752* **AINTNECESSARILYSO 10** [4]6-8-0 (56) M Halford(7) 12/1: 2236115: Towards rear, styd on for press.   hd   57
2561 **HICCUPS 17** [14]4-9-11 p (81) T Quinn 9/1: 0-203106: Mid-div, rdn & no extra dist: see 2074.   1¾   77
2752 **BOLLIN EDWARD 10** [8]5-8-8 vis (64) J Carroll 7/1: 00-65327: Bhd, late prog, nvr a threat: btr 2752.   ¾   58
2831 **BUNDY 7** [6]8-8-7 (63) S W Kelly 12/1: 0022328: Dwelt & bhd, late gains: btr 2315.   1   54
2256 **PAX 31** [2]7-9-13 (83) Alex Greaves 7/1: 0-660109: Mid-div, no prog from dist: btr 2059.   nk   73
2770 **PIETER BRUEGHEL 10** [11]5-9-10 (80) R Winston 7/1: 000-0400: 10th: Chsd ldrs, btn over 1f out.   nk   69
2846 **CHAIRMAN BOBBY 6** [13]6-9-2 (72) L Enstone(3) 33/1: 3202500: 11th: Cl-up till over 1f out: btr 2320.   shd   61
2561 **BLYTHE SPIRIT 17** [1]5-8-13 (69) Natalia Gemelova(7) 16/1: 045-5000: 12th: Mid-div, no prog dist.   1½   53
2791* **SHAROURA 8** [17]8-8-10 (7ex) (66) G Parkin 25/1: 505-5010: 13th: Chsd ldrs till over 1f out: btr 2791.   shd   50
2855 **ILLUSIVE 6** [5]7-8-2 bl (58) F Norton 20/1: 2620040: 14th: Prom, wknd over 1f out: qck reapp: btr 2855.   ½   40
2684 **POP UP AGAIN 12** [3]4-9-1 (71) Dean McKeown 33/1: 513-0000: 15th: Mid-div, no impress from 2f out.   2½   45
2747 **ROMANY NIGHTS 10** [9]4-9-8 bl (70) S Hitchcott(3) 9/1: 4222460: 16th: Chsd ldrs, drvn & btn 2f out.   hd   51
2848 **RONNIE FROM DONNY 6** [7]4-8-9 (65) T Eaves(3) 16/1: 5005550: 17th: Sn bhd, eased dist, t.o.   27   0
17 Ran   Time 1m 16.7 (2.6)   Owned: Miss Julia Staughton   Trained: Newmarket

---

2991   3.45 Wilfred Underwood Memorial Maiden Stakes 3yo+ (D)
£5811 £1788 £894   **1m2f6y**   Good/Firm 37   **+01 Fast**   Inside

2678 **APSARA 13** [1] H R A Cecil 3-8-5 vis W Ryan 4/1: 21: Made all, rdn & styd on strongly ins last,   **87+**
won decisively in a fast time: eff at 10f, stay further: acts on fast & gd/soft grnd, easy or stiff trk: suited by
visor: impressed here with forcing tactics on a circuit which rarely suits front runners, worth following.
2386 **MIJDAAF 24** [10] A C Stewart 3-8-10 S Sanders 4/1: 62: b c Mtoto - Zobaida (Green Desert) Chsd   3   86
ldrs & chsd wnr from 4f out, rdn & kept on, al held: imprvd from intro: dam a 7f AW mdn wnr & related to a 14f
scorer: eff at 10f & shld stay 12f: acts on fast grnd & a stiff/undul trk: can find similar.
4975) **HILLS SPITFIRE 248** [5] P W Harris 3-8-10   T Quinn 10/11 FAV: 24-3: b c Kahyasi - Questina   1¼   84
(Rainbow Quest) Dwelt, sn mid-div, rdn from halfway, onepace: well clr of rem: nicely bckd on reapp: mdn rnr-up
'03, subs Lst 4th (rtd 98+): strong mid/dist pedigree & looks sure to apprec 12f+: looked useful last
term & shld do btr over further. 2 Oct'03 Newm 8g/f 94- D:
2595 **CAPITOLE 17** [7] A C Stewart 3-8-10 R Winston 50/1: 04: b g Imperial Ballet - Blue Glass   10   69
(Ardkinglass) Slow away & bhd, hdwy over 4f out, no prog fnl 2f: longer 10f trip: £100,000 first foal: dam 1m wnr.
2627 **CANTARNA 15** [9]3-8-5 (76) Dale Gibson 15/2: 555-235: Chsd wnr, btn 2f out: btr 2627, 2231 (1m).   6   55
2751 **BRAVELY DOES IT 10** [3]4-9-7 S W Kelly 100/1: 006: Mid-div, no impress fnl 3f.   2½   56
1894 **SHARABAD 17** [2]6-9-7 L Vickers 100/1: 507: Dwelt & rear, btn 4f out.   ½   55
2725 **MADAAR 11** [4]5-9-7 (46) R Ffrench 100/1: 03030-08: Al towards rear & no ch fnl 4f.   8   44
522 **GIUST IN TEMP 155** [6]5-9-7 (36) Lisa Jones(3) 100/1: 50-42069: Keen, chsd ldrs till halfway: see 399.   3½   39$
   SHYSHIYRA 0 [11]3-8-5 G Parkin 50/1: 0: 10th: Slow away & al bhd on debut.   1½   32
396 **SVENSON 174** [8]3-8-10 P M Quinn 150/1: 0-000: 11th: Dwelt & sn strugg, t.o./eased dist, abs.   dist   0
11 Ran   Time 2m 11.13 (3.03)   Owned: Dr Catherine Wills   Trained: Newmarket

---

2992   4.20 Bradley Maiden Stakes 3yo+ (D)
£5577 £1716 £858   **1m4f8y**   Good/Firm 37   **-11 Slow**   Inside

2737 **BENDARSHAAN 11** [3] M Johnston 4-9-7 (81) K Dalgleish 6/4 FAV: 23-00041: Held up, hdwy over 3f   84
out & rdn/led over 1f out, styd on strongly: well bckd, op 2/1: eff at 12f on fast & gd/soft grnd: see 2737.
2623 **JAYER GILLES 15** [9] H Candy 4-9-7 D Sweeney 7/4: 22: Handy & led 3f out till over 1f out, no   2½   79
pace of wnr: nicely bckd & clr of rem: likely to find a race: see 2623.
2193 **ENCOMPASS 33** [1] H R A Cecil 3-8-4 (1ow) W Ryan 11/2: 03: b f Sadler's Wells - Totality (Dancing   5   68
Brave) Chsd ldrs, kept on fnl 2f, no impress on front pair: op 7/2: half-sister to wnrs at 10/12f, dam a 14f 3yo
scorer: mid-dists shld suit.
2608 **MOLEHILL 16** [4] J G Given 3-8-3 J Bramhill 16/1: 054: Sn handy & ch 3f out, no extra over 1f   2½   63

out: ran well for a long way, could impr in mid-dist/staying h'caps (stoutly bred): see 2608.
2751 **WELKINOS BOY 10** [2]3-8-8 Dale Gibson 100/1: 05: ch g Most Welcome - Khadino (Relkino) Rear, drvn & late prog, no threat: well clr of rem: imprvd from debut: brother to a 1m wnr, dam modest. *1¼* **66**
ALL BLEEVABLE 1548 [10]7-9-7 L Vickers 25/1: 00///-6: Led till 3f out, sn btn, 6 wk jumps abs. *11* **53**
2222 **STYLISH DANCER 32** [6]3-8-3 F Norton 16/1: 057: Sn towards rear & struggling 4f out, eased. *23* **14**
546 **JOEY THE SCHNOZE 153** [11]6-9-7 Derek Nolan(7) 100/1: 00//-08: Prom, wknd qckly 5f out, eased: new yard, qck reapp. *dist* **0**
2193 **CHARNWOOD PRIDE 33** [8]3-8-8 t N Callan 25/1: 009: Al rear & struggling from halfway, virtually p.u. *dist* **0**
9 Ran Time 2m 39.82 (5.72) Owned: Mr Malih L Al Basti Trained: Middleham

2993

4.55 King Richard Iii Stakes Handicap Fillies 3yo+ 0-70 (E) **[67]**
£4914 £1512 £756 **1m rnd** **Good/Firm 37** **-16 Slow** Inside

2755 **HULA BALLEW 10** [4] M Dods 4-8-12 p (51) S W Kelly 8/1: 5005501: Mid-div trav well, smooth hdwy to lead dist, rdn clr, readily: eff at 1m/10f on fast & gd/soft grnd, stiff/undul or sharp trk: ridden with more restraint today & much imprvd, win again if repeating this: well h'capped: see 1366. **68+**
2680 **ESTIMATE 13** [5] John A Harris 4-8-13 vis (52) Dean McKeown 25/1: 0001002: Handy & hmpd after 2f, drvn & kept on fnl 2f, no ch with easy wnr: see 1724 & 489. *6* **56**
2665 **NUZZLE 13** [8] M Quinn 4-8-6 vis (45) F Norton 9/1: 0260303: Led till dist, no ch with wnr: see 2032 & 845. *½* **47**
2506 **GRACEFUL AIR 19** [13] J R Weymes 3-8-11 p (59) R Winston 22/1: 5224054: Held up, kept on late. *¾* **61**
2604 **LARK IN THE PARK 16** [11]4-8-3 T (42) B Swarbrick(5) 33/1: 006-0005: Held up, mod gains for press. *1¼* **41**
2755 **SPARK UP 10** [10]4-9-6 (59) S Hitchcott(3) 16/1: 4106006: Dwelt, rear, mod gains for press: btr 1322. *¾* **57**
2604 **UNO MENTE 16** [12]5-9-0 (53) Kim Tinkler 17/2: 0-000637: Rear, prog/no room over 1f out, onepce. *2* **47**
2604* **SHARP SECRET 16** [1]6-9-4 (57) Lisa Jones(3) 2/1 FAV: 4265-518: Rear, late gains for press, nvr a factor: well bckd: btr 2604 (C/D). *½* **50**
2931 **AIMEES DELIGHT 3** [14]4-10-0 (67) M Fenton 14/1: 0600009: Cl-up, wknd over 1f out: qck reapp. *2* **56**
2674 **CYCLONIC STORM 13** [7]5-9-7 BL (60) G Parkin 9/1: 0000-340: 10th: Slow away & held up, eff over 3f out, sn btn: blnks: btr 2475. *1¼* **46**
2326 **CUT RIDGE 27** [2]5-8-2 (1ow) (40) P Bradley 33/1: 020-0000: 11th: b f Indian Ridge - Cutting Ground (Common Grounds) Keen & cl-up, hung right on bend after 2f, btn over 1f out: '03 mdn h'cap scorer: h'cap plcd '02 (rtd 57, earlier mdn plcd, rtd 72, J J Quinn): eff at 5/6f on fast & gd/soft grnd, sharp or stiff trk. *1* **25**
2 Sep'03 Catt 7g/s 47-46 F: 1 Jul'03 Ripo 6g/f 47-42 E:
2440 **BALMACARA 22** [6]5-8-6 (45) S Carson 9/1: 554-0060: 12th: Prom, btn 2f out: btr 2440. *3½* **22**
2857 **OH SO ROSIE 6** [3]4-9-4 (57) Derek Nolan(7) 8/1: 3032500: 13th: Dwelt & held up, rdn & btn 2f out. *3½* **27**
4886} **HUM 255** [9]3-8-8 (56) N Callan 25/1: 600-0: 14th: ch f Cadeaux Genereux - Ensorceleuse (Fabulous Dancer) Dwelt, in tch, btn 2f out: reapp/h'cap bow: unplcd from 3 '03 starts (rtd 71$, mdn, A Stewart). *1* **26**
14 Ran Time 1m 46.01 (4.21) Owned: Mrs J W Hutchinson & Mrs P A Knox Trained: Darlington

2994

5.25 Monkhill Classified Stakes 3yo 0-75 (D)
£5408 £1664 £832 **1m2f6y** **Good/Firm 37** **-18 Slow** Inside

2386* **TREW CLASS 24** [7] M H Tompkins 3-8-12 (76) T Quinn 11/2: 0011: Handy & led over 2f out till over 1f out, rallied gamely for press to lead again ins last, styd on strongly: eff at 10f, stay further: acts on fast grnd & a stiff/undul trk: progressing with racing, can win again: see 2386. **80**
2426 **MY PARIS 23** [5] K A Ryan 3-9-3 (78) N Callan 6/1: 3222522: Trkd ldrs & led over 1f out, hdd ins last & no extra cl-home: consistent type who deserves a race: see 2426, 1784. *½* **85**
1664 **NIGHTSPOT 56** [4] R Charlton 3-9-5 (80) R Winston 3/1 JT FAV: 5515-63: Held up in tch, eff to chase front pair 2f out, al held: 8 wk abs, nicely bckd: stays a stiff 10f: see 1664. *2½* **83**
2919 **CARTRONAGEERAGHLAD 3** [2] J A Osborne 3-9-2 (77) S W Kelly 3/1 JT FAV: 0024454: Hld up, prog when briefly short of room 2f out, not pace to chall: qk reapp: consistent, again suggested further will suit. *1¼* **78**
2854 **HEVERSHAM 6** [3]3-9-0 (73) M Tebbutt 16/1: 2000425: Led, hung right & hdd over 2f out, sn btn: qck reapp for new yard: btr 2854 (1m, clmr). *4* **70**
2656 **AWESOME LOVE 14** [1]3-9-2 (77) K Dalgleish 4/1: 2-32226: Trkd ldrs, rdn & btn over 1f out: btr 2656. *5* **65**
2283 **YAAHOMM 28** [6]3-9-2 VIS (77) D Nolan(3) 12/1: 3107: Held up in tch, rdn & btn 2f out: visor: disapp since narrow success over today's rnr-up in 1784. *1¼* **63**
7 Ran Time 2m 13.63(5.53) Owned: Russell Trew Roofing Ltd Trained: Newmarket

SOUTHWELL Fibresand TUESDAY 06.07.04 Lefthand, Sharp, Oval Track

Official Going STANDARD.

2995

6.30 St Maria Goretti's Day Maiden Auction Stakes 2yo (E)
£3455 £1063 £532 **7f aw rnd** **Going 33** **-25 Slow** Inside

2584 **PRIZE FIGHTER 17** [7] P W Chapple Hyam 2-8-9 A McCarthy 4/5 FAV: 21: In tch, went on dist, rdn clr: bckd: eff at 7f, 1m will suit: acts on fast & fibresand: interesting for nursery h'caps. **84a**
2652 **CHUTNEY MARY 14** [11] J G Portman 2-8-5 T P Queally 11/1: 0622: Front rank, led halfway till dist, kept on but not pace of wnr: clr rem: acts on gd & fibresand: *3* **73a**
UNCLE BULGARIA [10] G C Bravery 2-8-8 S Sanders 11/2: 3: b c Alhaarth - Istibshar (Mr Prospector) Held up, prog halfway, no impress fnl 1.5f on debut: 7,500 gns May foal: half-brother to a couple of mid-dist wnrs: dam 6f wnr: may do btr on turf. *8* **60a**
2569 **LLAMADAS 17** [2] M Dods 2-8-10 P L Enstone(3) 12/1: 3034: Rdn in mid-div, nvr nr ldrs: cheekpieces. *1½* **59a**

2802 **MING VASE 8** [1]2-8-8 D Tudhope(7) 6/1: 625: Bhd, nvr troubled ldrs: much btr 2802 (C/D). *1¾* **54a**
2682 **GARDASEE 12** [8]2-8-8 Dale Gibson 66/1: 006: Al outpcd: see 2682. *1* **52a**
2682 **CLASSIC STYLE 12** [5]2-8-6 D Allan 40/1: 507: Chsd ldrs till halfway, wknd: see 2498 (5f here). *1¼* **47a**
1911 **MISTER AZIZ 45** [12]2-8-9 D Holland 20/1: 08: b c Mister Baileys - Aziz Presenting (Charnwood Forest) Prom 5f, wknd: 6 wk abs, AW bow: 8,700 gns Apr 1st foal: dam a 5f juv wnr, sire a high-class miler. *½* **49a**
2766 **OLDSTEAD FLYER 10** [6]2-8-7 F Lynch 80/1: 0609: Led till halfway, wknd qckly, t.o. *20* **7a**

2721 **MONASHEE MISS 11** [3]2-8-2 D Kinsella 100/1: 4030: 10th: Prom till halfway, wknd qckly, t.o. — 19 — 0a
1161 **WELCOME DREAM 83** [9]2-8-2 J Quinn 25/1: 00: 11th: ch f Most Welcome - Sweet Dreams (Selkirk) — hd — 0a
Al bhd, t.o.: 12 wk abs: Feb foal, dam a 1m wnr: sire a top class 1m/12f performer: with Mrs A Duffield.
11 Ran Time 1m 30.71 (4.11) Owned: Diamond Racing Ltd Trained: Newmarket

2996	7.00 National Pickle Festival Selling Handicap Stakes 3yo+ 35-55 (G)			**[48]**
	£2597 £742 £371 **1m aw rnd** **Going 33** -14 Slow Inside			

2501 **BULAWAYO 19** [5] Andrew Reid 7-9-13 bl (47) B Swarbrick(5) 10/3 FAV: 6106421: Keen & prom, went on — 54a
after halfway, styd on well despite drifting left, rdn out: bought in for 3,200 gns: eff at 7f/1m on gd, fast grnd &
fibresand, loves W'hampton: eff with/without blnks/visor: gd weight carrier: see 2501 & 956.
2447 **LATE ARRIVAL 22** [3] M D Hammond 7-9-2 vis (36) Darren Williams 8/1: 6/5-00002: Slowly away, — 3 — 36a
imprvd halfway, styd on late into 2nd, no ch with wnr: btr run, see 1954.
2508 **TANCRED MISS 19** [6] D W Barker 5-9-6 (40) T Eaves(3) 12/1: 0000-103: Prom, onepcd fnl 1f: clr rem. — ½ — 39a
2801 **COUNTRYWIDE GIRL 8** [7] A Berry 5-9-5 (39) F Lynch 11/2: 3321534: Led till after halfway, wknd. — 6 — 26a
2552 **SHOTLEY DANCER 18** [8]5-9-2 (36) Suzanne France(7) 13/2: 0-400435: Slow away, nvr nr ldrs: op 5/1. — 3 — 17a
2667* **MISTER COMPLETELY 13** [4]3-9-7 (50) N Pollard 6/1: 0000016: Prom 6f, sn wknd: btr 2667 (turf). — 2½ — 26a
2805 **SEA YA MAITE 8** [10]10-9-6 t (40) J Bramhill 16/1: 5024007: Chsd ldrs 6f, wknd. — 2½ — 11a
2958 **MEHMAAS 2** [2]8-9-9 vis (43) R Ffrench 15/2: 0000408: Prom till halfway, sn wknd: quick reapp. — 10 — 0a
2181 **FOREST QUEEN 33** [1]7-8-7 (7oh) (20) P Mathers(7) 66/1: 0/00-0009: Slow away, al bhd, t.o.: see 1801. — 25 — 0a
9 Ran Time 1m 43.17 (3.77) Owned: Mr A S Reid Trained: Mill Hill London

2997	7.30 Music For Life Median Auction Maiden Stakes 3-4yo (F)			
	£2919 £834 £417 **1m aw rnd** **Going 33** -04 Slow Inside			

3308} **RUMOUR 340** [2] J R Fanshawe 4-9-2 O Urbina 13/8 FAV: 3-1: b f Lion Cavern - Thea (Marju) Trkd — 85a
ldr trav well, went on dist, pushed clr under hands & heels, val 8L+: well bckd from 9/4, reapp: plcd on sole '03
start: eff at 1m on gd & f/sand: handles a sharp trk, runs well fresh: intersting for h'caps.
2249 **TELEFONICA 31** [3] Sir Michael Stoute 3-8-7 (74) F Lynch 11/2: 42-402: Led till dist, sn left bhd — 5 — 72a
by easy wnr: drifted from 3/1, clr of rem & AW bow: see 1063.
2602 **DAFINA 16** [9] H Morrison 4-9-2 D Holland 5/2: 23-43: Prom, outpcd halfway, rallied fnl 1f: op 2/1. — 4 — 63a
2393 **PETROLINA 24** [7] M Morrison 3-8-7 J Quinn 50/1: 004: b f Petardia - Arbitration (Bigstone) — 2 — 56a
Front rank, wknd dist: has tried a variety of trips, prob bred to apprec 7f/1m: now quals for h'caps.
2339 **GO FREE 26** [4]3-8-12 (56) A Nicholls 12/1: 0-00-25: Chsd ldrs 6f, grad wknd: btr 2339. — 2½ — 56a
2478 **VIOLA DA BRACCIO 20** [6]3-8-7 (63) R Ffrench 14/1: 0-0556: Slowly away, al bhd. — 2 — 47a
2410 **SUPER KING 24** [5]3-8-12 (65) Suzanne France(7) 33/1: 02-007: b g Kingsinger - Super Sisters (Call — ¾ — 50a
Report) Slow away, nvr nr ldrs: AW bow: rnr-up on fnl of 2 '03 starts (mdn auct): eff at 7f on fast & firm.
2 Oct'03 Newc 7fm 76- E:
2692 **TOO KEEN 12** [8]3-8-7 T Eaves(3) 40/1: 508: Bhd from halfway. — 12 — 20a
2474 **BIG BAD BURT 20** [1]3-8-12 t p (66) Dean Williams(7) 8/1: 2303469: Slow away, al bhd, t.o.: new yard. — 15 — 0a
1130 **HELLO TIGER 85** [10]3-8-12 Rory Moore(7) 100/1: 000: 10th: Chsd ldrs till halfway, wknd, t.o. — 26 — 0a
10 Ran Time 1m 42.39 (2.99) Owned: T & J Vestey Trained: Newmarket

2998	8.00 Crowning Of Richard The Lionheart Handicap Stakes 3yo+ 0-75 (E)			**[88]**
	£3335 £1026 £513 **1m4f aw** **Going 33** +07 Fast Inside			

120 **ELUSIVE DREAM 220** [9] Sir Mark Prescott 3-8-1 (61) J Mackay 4/1: 0000-1: b c Rainbow Quest - — 74a
Dance A Dream (Sadler's Wells) Dwelt, hdwy halfway, hung right 2f out, led & hung right ins fnl 1f, rdn clr clr home:
op 5/2, abs, 1st win in h'cap bow: rider given a 2-day careless riding ban: mdn unplcd in '03 (rtd 62a): apprec
this step up to 12f, acts on a sharp trk & f/sand: runs well fresh: typical stable improver & will win more races.
2805 **MIDSHIPMAN 8** [2] A W Carroll 6-8-8 vis t (55) I Mongan 13/8 FAV: 0300222: Slowly away, hdwy — 5 — 61a
halfway, ev ch when carried right 2f out, sn led, hdd/badly hmpd fnl 1f, nvr recover: bckd from 5/2: still held
ev ch, prob wld have fin 2nd: see 2500.
2673 **RED FOREST 13** [7] J Mackie 5-9-2 t (63) Dale Gibson 3/1: 1611503: Rear, hdwy bef halfway, onepcd — 2½ — 65a
from 2f out: just btr 2217.
2277 **ALPINE SPECIAL 29** [4] P C Haslam 3-8-9 (69) G Faulkner 14/1: 3210-604: Keen & handy, no impress — 1½ — 69a
fnl 1f: well clr of rem: see 2277.
1841 **MEXICAN 48** [10]5-7-12 (8oh)p (37) Lisa Jones(3) 25/1: 500-0035: Rear, hdwy 3f out, sn no impress: — 8 — 33a
7 wk abs: has been gelded: stiff task at weights: see 1841.
2672 **CAROUBIER 13** [6]4-10-0 (75) Saleem Golam(7) 16/1: 0100006: Rear, hdwy 3f out, no impress fnl 2f. — ½ — 62a
2197 **DANCE WORLD 33** [8]4-10-0 (75) B Reilly(3) 9/1: 24-10307: Nvr nr to chall: op 7/1. — 8 — 50a
2426 **MAGIC AMIGO 23** [1]3-9-0 (74) D Holland 20/1: 0-210238: Handy, led halfway till 4f out, wknd. — 4 — 43a
2500 **MCQUEEN 19** [5]4-9-7 (68) D Sweeney 16/1: 0-060069: Nvr a factor: btr 99 (1m). — 11 — 21a
232 **MIDMAAR 199** [3]3-8-3 (63) F Norton 40/1: 531000-0: 10th: b c Cape Cross - Khazinat El Dar (Slew — dist — 0a
O' Gold) Led 5f, wknd 5f out, t.o.: '03 juv wnr in native France (6f, gd with F Head): eff at 6f on gd.
10 Ran Time 2m 37.53 (3.23) Owned: Cheveley Park Stud Trained: Newmarket

2999	8.30 Beatrix Potter Classified Stakes 3yo+ 0-60 (F)			
	£2961 £846 £423 **7f aw rnd** **Going 33** -02 Slow Inside			

2394 **CHORUS BEAUTY 24** [8] G Wragg 3-8-13 (63) F Norton 7/1: 01-00031: Rear, hdwy 4f out, led well ins — 65a
fnl 1f, kept on well for press: eff at 6f/1m on both AWs, acts on a sharp trk: gd run, see 260.
2500 **MERDIFF 19** [14] W M Brisbourne 5-9-9 (62) S W Kelly 16/1: 201-0002: Handy & wide, ev ch ins fnl — ½ — 65a
1f, kept on & only just btn: eff at 7/9f: see 39.
2496 **TEEHEE 20** [3] B Palling 6-9-7 bl (60) R Miles(3) 4/1: 0-460023: Handy, led on bit over 2f out, hdd — ½ — 62a
& no extra well ins fnl 1f: op 13/2, btn 1L: see 280.
2018 **SPINDOR 41** [11] J A Osborne 5-9-7 bl (60) D Holland 20/1: 0336004: Rear & wide, hdwy over 2f out, — 2 — 58a
onepcd fnl 1f: 6 wk abs.
1223+ **DANGER BIRD 80** [10]4-9-4 (57) D Sweeney 12/1: 3024415: Bhd, late hdwy: abs, clr rem. — 2½ — 50a

907

SOUTHWELL Fibresand TUESDAY 06.07.04 Lefthand, Sharp, Oval Track

2722 **IRUSAN** 11 [4]4-9-10 (63) Leanne Kershaw(7) 33/1: 60046: Handy, hung left 2f out, wknd fnl 1f. | 3 | 50a
2688 **ZARIN** 12 [12]6-9-10 BL (63) Lisa Jones(3) 25/1: 23-03007: Slow away, nvr nr ldrs in first time blnks. | shd | 50a
2496 **ZAGALA** 20 [9]4-9-8 t (64) L Treadwell(7) 10/1: 13-20208: Rear, nvr nr ldrs. | ½ | 47a
2496 **OLD BAILEY** 20 [7]4-9-7 vis (59) R Winston 14/1: 0501009: Handy, no impress over 2f out. | 1½ | 43a
2609 **SENOR BOND** 16 [13]3-9-4 (65) F Lynch 16/1: 00-63060: 10th: Led over 2f, wknd over 1f out. | ½ | 47a
2502 **WHITE LEDGER** 19 [5]5-9-7 (60) T Hamilton(3) 33/1: 00000-00: 11th: ch g Ali Royal - Boranwood | 1¼ | 39a
(Exhibitioner) Rear, nvr a factor: h'cap unplcd in '03 (rtd 47, with I Wood): won 2 h'caps for T Mils in '02, plcd
numerous times (rtd 73 at best): eff with/without visor: well h'capped. 1 Sep'02 Sand 5g/f 67-61 D: 1 Jun'02 Wolv 5af 66a-67 E:
2 May'02 Brig 5.2g/s 68-66 E: 2 Feb'02 Sout 5af 65a- D: 2 Feb'02 Ling 5ap 70a-65 E:
2713 **SILVER MASCOT** 12 [15]5-9-7 (60) T Eaves(3) 11/2: 2300120: 12th: Wide & keen, nvr a factor. | ¾ | 37a
2801 **ONLY ONE LEGEND** 8 [6]6-9-7 bl (60) R Ffrench 12/1: 0303150: 13th: Al bhd. | hd | 37a
2497 **DIAMOND SHANNON** 20 [2]3-8-10 (59) D Tudhope(7) 10/3 FAV: 2-005120: 14th: Led 3f out-2f out, wknd. | 3 | 28a
2347 **FEAST OF ROMANCE** 26 [1]7-9-7 (56) I Mongan 16/1: 5030640: 15th: Led briefly halfway, wknd. | 3½ | 24a
15 Ran Time 1m 20.09 (2.49) Owned: Mrs Claude Lilley Trained: Newmarket

---

3000
9.00 Festival Of Buddha's Eye Tooth Handicap Stakes 3yo+ 35-55 (F)   **[58]**
£3024 £864 £432   **6f aw rnd**   **Going 33**   **-26 Slow**   Inside

2501 **JONNY EBENEEZER** 19 [14] D Flood 5-9-7 bl (51) R Smith 11/2: 2021031: Handy, hdwy to lead halfway, | | 61a
rdn out: tchd 7/1: eff btwn 5/7f, stays a stiff 1m: acts on firm, soft & fibresand, any trk: gd start for new
stable (prev with R Cowell): see 1938.
2720 **MALLIA** 11 [16] T D Barron 11-9-1 (45) Laura Jayne Crawford(7) 13/2: 06-41632: In tch, hdwy over | 2 | 48a
1f out, kept on ins fnl 1f but not rch wnr: op 5/1: just below winning form of 2202 (seller).
2806 **ACE MA VAHRA** 8 [11] S R Bowring 6-9-2 bl (46) J Bramhill 20/1: 0503063: Handy, kept on fnl 1f. | ¾ | 46a
2334 **AGUILA LOCO** 26 [10] Mrs Stef Liddiard 5-9-8 p (52) F Norton 12/1: 0360004: Led 3f, wknd fnl 1f. | ¾ | 49a
2775 **LEVELLED** 10 [8]10-9-1 (45) Lisa Jones(3) 18/1: 2331065: Chsd ldrs, onepcd fnl 1f. | shd | 42a
2806 **LUCIUS VERRUS** 8 [9]4-9-6 vis (50) Darren Williams 7/1: 1052056: Dwelt, rear, hdwy over 1f out, | ½ | 46a
nrst fin: op 11/1: worth a try over 7f? btr 1320 (mdn clmr).
2806 **INDIAN MUSIC** 8 [1]7-8-10 (40) F Lynch 7/2 FAV: 3324627: Rear, hdwy over 1f out, fin well. | 1 | 33a
2803 **ATTORNEY** 8 [12]6-9-10 e (54) D Holland 12/1: 3665008: Chsd ldrs, outpcd 3f out, kept on fnl 1f. | nk | 46a
2806* **BOISDALE** 8 [6]6-10-0 (6ex) (58) L Treadwell(7) 4/1: 6165019: Chsd ldrs, no impress fnl 1f. | ½ | 49a
2720 **ALASTAIR SMELLIE** 11 [4]8-9-3 vis (47) L Keniry(3) 33/1: 0221000: 10th: Slow away, in tch 4f. | 3½ | 28a
1989* **SOTONIAN** 42 [5]11-8-8 (38) Stephanie Hollinshead(5) 33/1: 5334510: 11th: Handy, wknd 2f out: abs. | 1¾ | 14a
2704 **COCO REEF** 12 [13]3-9-5 (55) D Sweeney 20/1: 0330-60: 12th: Prom, wknd 2f out: see 2704. | ½ | 30a
1954 **NIFTY ROY** 43 [7]4-8-5 (35) A Daly 50/1: 6560/-000: 13th: b g Royal Applause - Nifty Fifty | 1¾ | 5a
(Runnett) Outpcd in rear, nvr a factor: 6 wk abs: missed '03: rnr-up first '02 starts (mdn, with A Berry): with
K Hogg. 2 Jun'02 Hami 6sft 67- D:
2777 **SPEEDFIT FREE** 9 [2]7-8-13 vis (43) Ann Stokell 25/1: 0600000: 14th: Al bhd: see 308. | 3½ | 3a
2725 **THE COPT** 11 [3]5-8-8 t (38) V Halliday 66/1: 00/000-00: 15th: b g Charmer - Coptic Dancer (Sayf | 3½ | 0a
El Arab) Dwelt, al bhd: h'cap unplcd in '03: plcd in '02 (rtd 52a & 72, J Eustace): wears a t-strap.
15 Ran Time 1m 16.85(3.55) Owned: Mrs Ruth M Serrell Trained: Hungerford

---

NEWMARKET TUESDAY 06.07.04 Righthand, Stiff, Galloping Track

Official Going Good/Firm

3001
1.20 H & K Commissions Bookmakers Handicap Stakes 3yo+ 0-90 (C)   **[90]**
£14014 £4312 £2156   **1m**   **Firm 01**   **-10 Slow**   Far Side

2672 **EVEREST** 13 [8] B Ellison 7-9-0 (76) Dane O'Neill 6/1: 0-000001: Held up far side, plenty to do | | 89
till strong run over 1f out to lead ins last, drvn out: suited by 1m, stays a sharp 9f on firm or hvy, any trk:
just tchd off in this race last term: expertly trained to peak & land a gamble here: on a handy mark, see 928.
2489 **AUDIENCE** 20 [15] J Akehurst 4-10-0 p (90) J Quinn 16/1: 6-000002: Handy stands side, led that | shd | 100
group over 2f out, styd on well ins last, just held by far side wnr: v useful/game run under a big weight: acts on
firm & gd: shld find similar shortly: see 2489, 1512.
2672 **TRUE NIGHT** 13 [19] D Nicholls 7-9-2 (78) E Ahern 16/1: 0423303: Held up stands side, hdwy over | shd | 88
1f out, kept on ins last, not btn far: fine run, comes gd at this time of year & on a fair mark: see 2558.
2558 **BLUE TROJAN** 18 [3] S Kirk 4-9-7 (83) J F Egan 33/1: 0014004: Handy far side, hdwy to lead that | shd | 92
group just ins last, kept on till hdd nr line: right back to useful best: see 1883, 294.
2665* **ST PANCRAS** 13 [9]4-9-4 (80) D Holland 15/2: 0002015: Led far side group over 2f out, hdd & no | 1¼ | 86
extra ins last: fine run: see 2665.
2853 **TOPTON** 6 [20]10-9-0 bl (76) M Hills 20/1: 0004626: Dwelt, held up, hdwy over 1f out, onepace. | ¾ | 80
4776} **RAFFERTY** 263 [7]5-9-6 bl (82) T E Durcan 40/1: 465000-7: ch g Lion Cavern - Badawi (Diesis) Held | hd | 85
up far side, eff & short of room over 2f out, kept on late: '03 stks wnr: '02 mdn & h'cap scorer: suited by around
1m, yet to convince at 10f: acts on firm, gd/soft & both AWs, any trk: goes well fresh & eff with/without blnks:
gelded since last term: gd return, on a handy mark now.
1 Mar'03 Wolv 7af 93a-82 D: 1 May'02 Ches 7.5fm 89-82 C: 1 Apr'02 Warw 7.1g/s 83- D:
2679 **GIFT HORSE** 13 [4]4-9-11 (87) J Murtagh 4/1 FAV: 216-0238: Held up far side, kept on late, nrst | hd | 89+
fin: again late gains & shaped like even further will suit: see 2679, 1817.
2753 **AFRICAN SAHARA** 10 [17]5-9-3 t (79) G Carter 33/1: 6060069: In tch stands side, onepace over 1f out. | ½ | 80
2223 **HARRISON POINT** 32 [16]4-9-8 (84) J Fortune 20/1: 30-11220: 10th: Held up stands side, late gains. | ½ | 84
2767* **LITTLE VENICE** 10 [6]4-9-10 (86) S Sanders 20/1: 40-05310: 11th: In tch far side, no impress over | hd | 85
1f out: clear cut fills h'cap wnr here in 2767 (10lb higher here).
2540* **OMAHA CITY** 18 [11]10-8-12 (74) M Tebbutt 50/1: 00-00210: 12th: Held up far side, short of room | ½ | 72
over 2f out, no impress: likes Goodwood, see 2540.
2662 **PRESUMPTIVE** 13 [14]4-9-2 (78) S Drowne 12/1: 0/3-530: 13th: Held up far side, btn over 1f out. | ½ | 75
2753 **DEVANT** 10 [18]4-9-3 (79) P Robinson 14/1: 05-04020: 14th: In tch stands side, wknd well over 1f | 1 | 74
out: won at this meeting last term, much btr 2753, 1877 (gd/firm).
2489 **LANGFORD** 20 [2]4-9-9 (85) L Dettori 10/1: 136-2100: 15th: Led far side, wknd 2f out: best 2010. | ½ | 79
2425 **ATLANTIC QUEST** 23 [12]5-9-6 vis (82) P Mulrennan(5) 40/1: 0500150: 16th: In tch far side, wknd | 2 | 72

over 1f out: twice below 1970.

2647* **OH BOY** 14 [5]4-8-10 (72) R Hughes 10/1: 0-005110: 17th: In tch far side, wkng when short of room   **1**   **60**
over 1f out: progressive earlier, see 2647.

2540   **EPHESUS** 18 [10]4-9-5 vis (81) W Supple 33/1: 0614220: 18th: In tch far side, wknd well over 1f out.   ½   **68**

2672   **TIBER TIGER** 13 [1]4-9-4 bl (80) J P Guillambert(3) 33/1: 0-410200: 19th: In tch, wknd over 2f out.   12   **43**

2767   **SALAGAMA** 10 [13]4-9-7 BL (83) K Fallon 20/1: 1-4300: 20th: Dwelt, sn led stands side, hdd over 2f   14   **18**
out, wknd: blnks: see 2767, 2191.

20 Ran   Time 1m 38.13 (0.93)   Owned: Mr I S Sandhu and Partners   Trained: Malton

---

3002   1.50 Totesport Rated Stakes Handicap 3yo 0-105 (B)   [112]
£34800 £13200 £6600   **6f str**   **Firm 01**   +01 Fast   Far Side

2407   **ALDERNEY RACE** 24 [17] R Charlton 3-8-7 (91) S Drowne 13/2: 4-52141: Prom stands side, hdwy to   **103**
lead ins last, styd on strongly, drvn out: eff at 6f on firm & gd/soft, has disapp on polytrack: useful, improving
& will apprec further in time, win more gd sprint races: see 1829.

2764* **MAHMOOM** 10 [13] M R Channon 3-8-5 (89) T E Durcan 14/1: 1-006012: Held up stands side, hdwy over ¾   **98**
1f out, styd on well ins last, not btn far: useful & improving, loves Newmarket: acts on fm & fast.

2407* **TWO STEP KID** 24 [5] J Noseda 3-8-11 (95) E Ahern 5/1 FAV: 1-6413: Chsd ldr far side, hdwy to   nk   **103**
lead that group 1f out, styd on well: nicely bckd: acts on firm & polytrack: useful & improving.

2736   **VALJARV** 11 [15] N P Littmoden 3-8-6 bl (90) T P Queally 40/1: 0000044: Dwelt, sn rdn stands side,   nk   **97**
hdwy well over 1f out, kept on: encouraging: see 1933.

2212   **SPANISH ACE** 32 [10]3-8-4 vis (88) Martin Dwyer 40/1: 60-00005: Led till dist far side, onepace.   ½   **93**

2421   **MAC LOVE** 23 [1]3-9-7 (105) G Carter 14/1: 32-54226: Held up far side, eff over 1f out, kept on.   ¾   **108**

2407   **DOOHULLA** 24 [11]3-8-5 (89) R Hughes 9/1: 3513-57: In tch far side, eff over 1f out, onepace: shd   **91**
may do btr when stable starts to fire: see 2407.

2407   **TRAYTONIC** 24 [3]3-9-3 (101) J Murtagh 7/1: 10-50138: Held up far side, short of room well over   hd   **102+**
1f out, late gains, nrst fin: set plenty to do & again shaped with promise: sure to relish 7f, keep in mind.

2212   **FANCY FOXTROT** 32 [12]3-8-5 (89) K McEvoy 14/1: 26-10039: Handy stands side, no extra dist.   1   **87**

2727   **PHILHARMONIC** 11 [14]3-9-3 (101) T Hamilton(3) 9/1: 2114-40: 10th: Handy stands side, wknd over 1f   ¾   **97**
out: much btr expected after promising return in 2727.

2749   **BALTIC WAVE** 10 [7]3-8-6 (90) K Darley 33/1: 2144-640: 11th: In tch far side, btn dist: see 2427.   ¾   **84**

1933   **SPLIFF** 45 [16]3-8-10 (94) Dane O'Neill 14/1: 021-100: 12th: Slow away stands side, nvr a factor.   shd   **87**

2069   **BARBAJUAN** 38 [9]3-9-2 BL (100) D Holland 20/1: 43-50000: 13th: In tch far side, wknd 2f out: blnks.   hd   **92**

2407   **FUN TO RIDE** 24 [4]3-8-9 (93) M Hills 12/1: 22-1200: 14th: In tch 4f far side: see 1570.   nk   **84**

1932   **MOONLIGHT MAN** 45 [19]3-9-5 (103) R L Moore 40/1: 113-2200: 15th: Handy, wknd over 1f out: abs.   shd   **93**

2407   **BIG BRADFORD** 24 [8]3-8-6 vis (90) D Kinsella 33/1: 2420-200: 16th: In tch far side, wknd dist.   ¾   **78**

2593   **HIGH VOLTAGE** 17 [18]3-8-12 t (96) Darren Williams 25/1: 20-13600: 17th: Led stands side till hdd   ½   **83**
& wknd fnl 1f: see 1360.

2407   **LOCAL POET** 24 [2]3-8-5 t (89) G Gibbons 50/1: 4-150500: 18th: In tch far side, wknd 2f out: see 953.   shd   **75**

2155* **CORPS DE BALLET** 34 [6]3-8-4 (88) J Quinn 16/1: 5431-010: 19th: In tch far side, wknd 2f out.   5   **59**

19 Ran   Time 1m 11.02 (0.02)   Owned: Britton House Stud Ltd   Trained: Beckhampton

---

3003   2.20 Gr2 Chippenham Lodge Stud Cherry Hinton Stakes Fillies 2yo (A)
£40600 £15400 £7700   **6f str**   **Firm 01**   -08 Slow   Far Side

2553* **JEWEL IN THE SAND** 18 [8] R Hannon 2-8-9   R Hughes 2/1 FAV: 111: Handy, hdwy & short of room 2f   **106+**
out, switched left & styd on to lead over 1f out, styd on strongly, rdn out: hvly bckd: eff at 6f, 7f will suit:
acts on firm & fast grnd, stiff trks: smart filly with a turn of foot, unbeaten & more Gr races to be won.

2553   **SALSA BRAVA** 18 [9] N P Littmoden 2-8-9   J P Guillambert 11/2: 132: Slow away, held up, hdwy &   hd   **105+**
hung right over 1f out, styd on strongly ins last, just held: acts on firm & fast grnd: fin wnk clr of rem & this
was another imprvd/v useful effort: shld be winning Gr races shortly: see 2553, 1805.

2553   **EXTREME BEAUTY** 18 [3] C E Brittain 2-8-9   D Holland 25/1: 6103: Held up, eff over 1f out, kept   5   **90**
on without troubling front 2: also bhd this pair in 2553: needs an ease in grade: see 2275.

2829* **SHIVAREE** 7 [1] M R Channon 2-8-9   C Catlin 33/1: 314: Sn bhd, some late gains, nrst fin: step up   ½   **88**
in class & well worth a try over 7f now: see 2829.

2553   **ARABIAN DANCER** 18 [2]2-8-9   T E Durcan 16/1: 265: In tch, hdwy to lead dist, sn hdd & wknd.   1½   **84**

2490   **MISS MEGGY** 20 [4]2-8-9   D Allan 33/1: 1106: Sn rdn bhd, eff 2f out, sn wknd: see 2165 (5f).   dht   **84**

2553   **MASA** 18 [7]2-8-9   L Dettori 7/2: 107: With ldrs, led halfway till dist, wknd: bckd: see 2553.   2½   **77**

2553   **NUFOOS** 18 [6]2-8-9   R Hills 11/2: 3108: With ldrs, wknd appr fnl 1f: see 1964 (mdn).   1   **74**

2697* **POLLY ALEXANDER** 12 [10]2-8-9   K Darley 7/1: 5113219: In tch, wknd over 1f out: see 2697, 2302.   1   **71**

2399* **SATIN KISS** 24 [5]2-8-9   K McEvoy 12/1: 10: 10th: Led to halfway, wkng/short of room fnl 1f.   1   **68**

10 Ran   Time 1m 11.55 (0.55)   Owned: Sand Associates   Trained: Marlborough

---

3004   2.55 Gr1 Uae Equestrian And Racing Federation Falmouth Stakes Fillies 3yo+ (A)
£116000 £44000 £22000   **1m str**   **Firm 01**   +14 Fast   Far Side

2470   **SOVIET SONG** 21 [3] J R Fanshawe 4-9-1 (114) J Murtagh 11/4: 45-23121: Held up, gd hdwy 2f out,   **122**
led over 1f out, rdn clr, going away: fast time: eff at 7f/1m on firm & soft grnd, any trk: v smart filly with a
turn of foot, career best here & clearly thriving, win more Gr 1s: see 2470, 1997.

2555+ **ATTRACTION** 18 [4] M Johnston 3-8-6 (119) K Darley 4/5 FAV: 111-1112: Set pace, rdn & hdd over 1f   2½   **117**
out, not pace of wnr ins last: hvly bckd: lost unbeaten record but another v smart run & clr of rem: can continue
to give a strong account in fillies Gr 1's: see 2555.

2306* **BAQAH** 30 [6] F Head 3-8-6 T D Bonilla 25/1: 2-312113: In tch, rdn over 2f out, not pace of front   2½   **112**
pair: wore t-strap: prob handles firm, likes soft grnd: smart, apprec a drop in class: see 2306.

2487   **MONTURANI** 20 [5] G Wragg 5-9-1 (104) D Holland 50/1: 422-3624: Chsd ldr over 6f, no extra: ¾   **110**
needs List/Gr 3: see 2487.

2005   **ILLUSTRIOUS MISS** 44 [1]3-8-6 (112) T P Queally 14/1: 1135: Keen handy, wknd well over 1f out: 6   7   **96**
wk abs: needs an ease in grade, see 2005, 1620.

2487* **FAVOURABLE TERMS** 20 [7]4-9-1 (108) K Fallon 6/1: 11215-16: Held up, eff well over 2f out, sn   1½   **93**
wknd: needs an ease in grade, see 2487.

2211   **TIZDUBAI** 32 [2]3-8-6 t K McEvoy 100/1: 11-67: In tch, wknd 2f out: see 2211.   3½   **86**

7 Ran   Time 1m 36.11 (u1.09)   Owned: Elite Racing Club   Trained: Newmarket

3005   3.30 Strutt & Parker Maiden Stakes 2yo (D)
£8444 £2598 £1299   7f str   Firm 01   -33 Slow   Far Side

BELENUS [5] Saeed bin Suroor 2-9-0 L Dettori 13/8 FAV: 1: ch c Dubai Millennium - Ajhiba   97+
(Barathea) Trkd ldrs, hdwy to lead over 1f out, readily asserted under hand riding: hvly bckd: March foal, dam a
1m/10f 3yo scorer: sire top-class at 1m/10f on turf & dirt: eff at 7f, relish further: acts on firm & goes well
fresh: most promising intro, looks well up to Gr class, must be kept on side.

FRITH [7] B W Hills 2-9-0 M Hills 9/1: 2: b c Benny The Dip - Melodist (The Minstrel) Chsd   1½   89+
ldr, kept on under hands & heels ins last, no threat to wnr: op 7/1: half-brother to wnrs btwn 1m/hdles: dam a
mutliple Oaks wnr: eff at 7f, strong mid-dist pedigree & sure to relish 1m/10f+: acts on fm: most pleasing start,
type to win plenty of good races.

LESCAPADE [1] A M Balding 2-9-0 Martin Dwyer 25/1: 3: ch c Grand Lodge - Brief Escapade (Brief   2½   84+
Truce) Dwelt, sn handy, styd on well fnl 1f under hand riding, not pace to chall: 3,000gns May foal, dam a 1m 3yo
scorer: eff at 7f, 1m sure to suit: improve for this promising start, win races.

2594 **SRI LIPIS** 17 [10] P F I Cole 2-9-0 K Fallon 7/2: 44: Held up, eff when hung left over 2f out,   nk   83
kept on for press: well bckd, op 5/1: imprvd from intro: will find a race: see 2594.

2766 **RED CHAIRMAN** 10 [11]2-9-0 T P Queally 18/1: 05: br c Red Ransom - Chine (Inchinor) Chsd ldrs &   1   81
led 5f out till over 1f out, hung left & no extra ins last: imprvd from debut: $150,000 April first foal, dam a 10f
3yo scorer abroad: handles firm grnd: apprec 1m+.

KING FOREVER [12]2-9-0 E Ahern 8/1: 6: b c King's Best - Elude (Slip Anchor) Dwelt, sn   ¾   79
mid-div, trav well when short of room over 2f out, again over 1f out, no impress: shade closer with a clr run: op
13/2: 65,000gns purchase, half-brother to a 1m 3yo scorer, dam unrcd but well related: shld apprec 1m in time.

NORTHERN SECRET [15]2-8-9 R Mullen 33/1: 7: Held up, eff over 2f out, not pace to threaten.   2½   69
RIVER BISCUIT [8]2-9-0 R L Moore 14/1: 8: Prom, hmpd over 2f out, sn no extra.   hd   73
FOLLOWING FLOW [6]2-9-0 K Darley 40/1: 9: Pushed along towards rear, nrst fin.   nk   72
CAPE QUEST [13]2-9-0 R Hughes 16/1: 0: 10th: Held up, eff over 1f out, no impress ins last.   hd   71
2316 **LOVE BEAUTY** 27 [3]2-9-0 J Fanning 16/1: 40: 11th: Led 2f, wknd over 1f out: see 2316.   hd   70
2845 **DRAX** 6 [2]2-9-0 A Beech(3) 33/1: 300: 12th: Al bhd: see 2462.   1   68
YOUNG MICK [9]2-9-0 A McCarthy 40/1: 0: 13th: Chsd ldrs, lost place from 4f out.   ½   67
GURRUN [14]2-9-0 A Mackay 66/1: 0: 14th: Dwelt, nvr factor in rear.   1½   64
KANDIDATE [4]2-9-0 D Holland 20/1: 0: 15th: Dwelt, keen & sn handy, struggling from halfway.   2½   59
15 Ran   Time 1m 26.3 (2.4)   Owned: Godolphin   Trained: Newmarket

3006   4.05 Racingpost Co Uk Rated Stakes Handicapfillies 3yo 0-100 (B)   [110]
£12081 £4583 £2291   7f str   Firm 01   +01 Fast   Far Side

2464* **PEERESS** 21 [8] Sir Michael Stoute 3-8-6 (88) K Fallon 2/1 FAV: 3-111: In tch, styd on to lead   100
dist, edged left & drvn out: hvly bckd, completed hat-trick: suited by 7f/1m on firm & gd grnd, stiff/gall or easy
trks: progressive filly with a fine turn of foot, likely to make her mark in List/Gr 3 company: see 2464.

2362* **OASIS STAR** 25 [9] P W Harris 3-8-5 (87) Martin Dwyer 7/2: 1-11512: Held up, drvn & styd on well   1¼   93
ins last, not reach wnr: most pleasing & progressive: see 2362.

2240 **MALVERN LIGHT** 31 [10] W J Haggas 3-9-0 (96) R Hills 25/1: 41-4003: Dwelt, held up, switched &   1   101
kept on ins last, no threat to front pair: back to form: acts on firm & gd/soft grnd: fine run.

1930 **SOLAR POWER** 45 [1] J R Fanshawe 3-8-2 (84) E Ahern 9/2: 1-2444: Trkd ldrs & ch dist, no extra   ¾   87
ins last: 6 wk abs: just btr 1930.

2419* **DAWN SURPRISE** 23 [4]3-8-8 t (90) L Dettori 11/4 3-215: Led till dist, no pace of front pair: see 2419.   shd   93
2400 **HILITES** 10 [6]3-8-0 (2oh) (80) N Mackay(3) 50/1: 4-303006: Dwelt, in tch, not pace to chall.   2   81
2212 **FIRST CANDLELIGHT** 32 [7]3-8-0 (82) J Quinn 50/1: 21-007: b f First Trump - No Candles Tonight   ¾   79
(Star Appeal) Cl-up/dsptd lead till over 1f out, sn no extra: lightly rcd mdn scorer '03: eff at 6f, winning form
at 7f: acts on gd & gd/soft grnd, stiff/gall trks. 1 Oct'03 Newc 7.1g/f 78-73 D: 2 Sep'03 Hayd 6g/s 85- D:

2574 **WITHORWITHOUTYOU** 17 [2]3-8-0 (2oh) (80) J Mackay 40/1: 54-65008: b f Danehill - Morningsurprice   2½   74
(Future Storm) Held up, rdn & btn over 1f out: '03 nursery h'cap wnr, subs Gr 2 5th (rtd 95, prob flattered):
winning form at 7f: acts on firm & fast grnd, sharp/stiff or turning trks.
1 Sep'03 Warw 7.1g/f 78-73 D: 2 Aug'03 Bath 5.0fm 71- D: 2 Aug'03 Beve 5g/f 76- D:

2736 **CUSCO** 11 [5]3-8-6 (88) R L Moore 20/1: 05-26029: Chsd ldrs, outpcd fnl 2f: see 2736.   nk   79
9 Ran   Time 1m 23.95 (0.05)   Owned: Cheveley Park Stud   Trained: Newmarket

3007   4.40 Robin Parke Memorial Maiden Stakes 3yo (D)
£8346 £2568 £1284   1m2f   Firm 01   -46 Slow   Stands Side

2729 **LONG ROAD** 11 [3] J Noseda 3-9-0 (85) E Ahern 11/4 FAV: 2221: Dwelt, sn in tch trkg ldrs,   88
squeezed through gap ins last & rdn clr, going away: hvly bckd, op 10/3: eff at 1m, apprec step up to 10f, further
shld suit: acts on firm & gd/soft grnd, stiff/gall trks: tough & useful.

2410 **MIKAO** 24 [8] M H Tompkins 3-9-0 P Robinson 10/1: 532: Led after 2f, hdd over 1f out, not pace   3½   80
of wnr: stays 10f on firm & fast grnd: win a race: see 2410 & 1495.

930 **FLAMBOYANT LAD** 102 [4] B W Hills 3-9-0 M Hills 9/2: 2-33: Held up, switched for eff over 2f   ¾   78
out, not pace of wnr from dist: nicely bckd, abs: handles firm & soft: qual for h'caps, shld find a race.

ARTICULATION [5] H R A Cecil 3-9-0 R Hughes 13/2: 4: b c Machiavellian - Stiletta (Dancing   ½   77
Brave) Trkd ldrs, rdn & led over 1f out, hdd ins last & no extra: nicely bckd tho' op 11/2: half-brother to a plcd
7f/1m 3yo performer, dam a full sister to a Derby wnr: eff at 10f on firm grnd & a stiff/gall trk: pleasing intro.

STREAM OF GOLD [9]3-9-0 K Fallon 7/2: 5: b c Rainbow Quest - River Dancer (Irish River) Keen   1¾   73
& handy, no extra over 1f out: debut, nicely bckd tho' op 11/4: superbly bred, full brother to top-class 10f
performer Spectrum: eff at 10f, may get further: acts on firm grnd: not btn far, can improve.

2386 **BOLD PHOENIX** 24 [6]3-9-0 Martin Dwyer 66/1: 006: b c Dr Fong - Subya (Night Shift) Led, hdd   ¾   71
after 2f, remained cl-up till no extra ins last: significant improvement from prev: half-brother to a 10/12f List
wnr, also a 10f 3yo wnr: dam a smart 10f wnr: now qual for h'caps.

2788 **HOLD UP** 9 [7]3-8-9 B Reilly(3) 100/1: 0-007: Keen & handy, wknd over 1f out.   2   62$
1236 **OGILVY** 80 [1]3-9-0 J Fortune 100/30: 08: Held up & keen early, rdn & btn 2f out: abs, nicely bckd.   2   63
8 Ran   Time 2m 06.64(4.74)   Owned: Mr Syd Belzberg   Trained: Newmarket

CHANTILLY MONDAY 28.06.04 Righthand, Galloping Track

Official Going Good

3008 1.50 Gr 3 Prix du Bois 2yo ()
£25704 £10282 £7711 **5f str** **Good**

DIVINE PROPORTIONS [2] P Bary 2-8-8 C P Lemaire 46/10: 11: b f Kingmambo - Myth To Reality 107+
(Sadler's Wells) Trkd ldrs, rdn to lead over 1f out, sn clr, easily: remains unbeaten after an earlier success at
Maisons Laffitte: both wins at 5f on good & gd/sft: v smart, win more Gr races.
GREAT BLOOD [1] X Thomas Demeaulte 2-8-8 Gary Stevens 4/5 FAV: 1112: Led, strongly pressed 4 92
from halfway, led over 2f out, hdd over 1f out, kept on but no ch with easy wnr, rest well covered.
SALUT THOMAS [6] R Collet 2-8-11 bl C Soumillon 39/10: 5421313: Cl up, wknd 1f out. 2½ 87
2490 **INDIANNIE STAR 12** [3]2-8-8 T Durcan 163/10: 21605: Mid-div, outpcd fnl 2f: see 1981. ¼ 83
7 Ran Time 58.70() Owned: Niarchos Family Trained: Niarchos Family

HAMBURG SATURDAY 3.07.04

Official Going Heavy

3009 4.20 Gr 3 Holsten Trophy 3yo+ ()
£42254 £14789 £7746 **6f rnd** **Heavy**

2140* **LUCKY STRIKE** [7] A Trybuhl 6-9-3 A de Vries 17/10 FAV: 40-21115311: Sn mid-div, hdwy to lead 116
dist, hung right, drvn out: eff at 6/7f on soft & hvy grnd: v smart sprinter: see 2140.
3551* **FIEPES SHUFFLE** [3] M Hofer 4-9-3 J P Carvalho 23/1: 2: Sn handy, led over 2f out till dist, kept on. 1¾ 112
AREIAS [5] A Schultz 6-9-1 A Starke 76/10: 3: Outpcd, styd on from over 2f out, nvr threat. 1 108
2769 **WELSH EMPEROR 7** [14]5-9-1 bl (109) Dale Gibson 39/10: 2426-1465: Dwelt, mid-div, swtchd & kept on 1¾ 105
onepace, no threat: usually best up with/forcing the pace: see 1227.
13 Ran Time 1m 15.07 () Owned: Stall Lucky Stables International Trained: Germany

HAMBURG SUNDAY 4.07.04

Official Going Heavy

3010 4.15 Gr1 German Derby 3yo ()
£223944 £74648 £44789 **1m4f** **Heavy**

SHIROCCO [7] A Schutz 3-9-2 A Suborics 5/1: -2131: Cl up & led over 2f out, drvn clr, 116
decisively: eff at 11/12f on soft & hvy: well regarded & clearly v smart.
MALINAS [8] P Schiergen 3-9-2 W Mongil 4/1: -31212: In tch, eff 2f out, onepace. 4 109
OMIKRON [13] M Hofer 3-9-2 A de Vries 234/10: 15-4523: In tch, swtchd 2f out, onepace. 6 102
18 Ran Time 2m 39.64() Owned: Baron G Von Ullmann Trained: Germany

LEOPARDSTOWN SATURDAY 3.07.04 Lefthand, Galloping Track

Official Going Good/Yielding

3011 7.15 Gr 3 EBF Brownstown Stakes Fillies & Mares 3yo+ ()
£39195 £11457 £5427 **7f rnd** **Good/Yielding**

TROPICAL LADY 6 [5] J S Bolger 4-9-5 K J Manning 11/4: 6-1111: b f Sri Pekan - Tropical Lake 111
(Lomond) Chsd ldrs, rdn & styd on strongly to lead close home: most progressive filly, earlier this landed 3 h'caps,
incl 2 val events at The Curragh: eff at 7f, return to 1m should suit: acts on fast & gd/sft ground: v smart.
2555 **MAJESTIC DESERT 15** [1] M R Channon 3-9-0 (111) T E Durcan 11/10 FAV: -10722: Trkd ldrs, chall 2f nk 113
out, led dist, rdn & hdd nr line: acts on fm & easy grnd: apprec a return to 1m: see 2555.
4010} **RED FEATHER 15** [8] E Lynam 3-8-11 N G McCullagh 10/1: 20-213: Led, rdn & hdd dist, onepace. 2 106
8 Ran Time 1m 29.20() Owned: J S Bolger Trained: Coolcullen

SAINT CLOUD SUNDAY 4.07.04 Lefthand, Galloping Track

Official Going Good/Soft

3012 3.25 Gr 1 Grand Prix de Saint Cloud 3yo+ ()
£140838 £56345 £28173 **1m4f** **Good/Soft**

1493* **GAMUT 63** [6] Sir Michael Stoute 5-9-9 (117) K Fallon 22/10: 13123-211: Sn trkd ldr, led over 2f 122
out & rdn clr, readily: eff at 11/14f on fast or gd/sft: career best run & now a strong King George candidate.
2459* **POLICY MAKER 21** [3] E Lellouche 4-9-9 T Thulliez 18/10 FAV: 2110-512: Chsd ldrs, chsd wnr over 3 117
1f out, always held: gd run: high-class: see 2459 (Gr 2).

SAINT CLOUD SUNDAY 4.07.04 Lefthand, Galloping Track

2143 **VISORAMA 34** [2] A Fabre 4-9-6 E Legrix 22/1: 3211-523: Mid-div, eff 2f out, onepace: stays 12f. *½* **113**
2459 **SHORT PAUSE 21** [5] A Fabre 5-9-9 T Gillet 21/10: 142-3134: Held up, styd on late, nvr a threat. *nk* **115**
2143 **PRIDE 34** [4]4-9-6 (80) D Bonilla 26/1: 210-4135: Mid-div, no impress fnl 2f: see 2143,1699. *shd* **112**
2488 **PHOENIX REACH 18** [1]4-9-9 (115) Martin Dwyer 87/10: 2/1131-66: Trkd front pair, no impress. *¾* **114**
1558 **POLISH SUMMER 63** [9]7-9-9 Gary Stevens 21/10: 2512-1157: Hld up, btn 2f out: 'lost plate'. *1½* **112**
10 Ran Time 2m 36.10 () Owned: Mrs G Smith Trained: France

3013 **2.50 Gr 2 Prix de Malleret 3yo Fillies ()**
£42148 £16268 £7764 **1m4f** **Good/Soft**

LUNE DOR 21 [4] R Gibson 3-8-9 T Jarnet 42/10: 2-311: b f Green Tune - Luth d'Or (Noit Et Or) **112**
Rear, hdwy over 1f out & drvn to lead cl home: earlier landed a 10f event at Chantilly: eff at 10f, apprec step up to 12f: acts on gd/sft & soft ground: lightly raced, smart & progressive filly.
BUOYANT 12 [7] F Head 3-8-9 D Bonilla 16/1: 312: Led & qcknd over 2f out, drvn & hdd cl home. *nk* **111**
DREAM PLAY 33 [1] A Fabre 3-8-9 Gary Stevens 4/1: 2313: Trkd ldr, rdn & onepace fnl 2f. *1½* **109**
7 Ran Time 2m 42.60() Owned: Mme P de Moussac Trained: France

CATTERICK WEDNESDAY 07.07.04 Lefthand, Undulating, Very Tight Track

Official Going Good/Firm

3014 **2.30 John Church Selling Stakes 2yo (G)**
£2891 £826 £413 **5f rnd** **Good/Firm 37** **-53 Slow** Inside

2965 **ALMATY EXPRESS 2** [4] M Todhunter 2-8-11 R Winston 4/5 FAV: 300341: Trkd ldrs, briefly outpcd & switched over 1f out, styd on for press to lead line: quick reapp: Apr foal, half sister to a 5f juv wnr, dam a 5f juv scorer: eff at 5f on fast & soft grnd in sell grade: see 2611, 1274. **64**
DISPOL IN MIND 0 [7] P T Midgley 2-8-6 R Fitzpatrick 14/1: 2: b f Mind Games - Sans Diablo (Mac's Imp) Prom & rdn/led over 1f out, hdd line: clmd for I Wood for È6,000: op 8/1: cheaply bought Feb foal, half sister to a 5f juv wnr, dam unrcd, sister to a smart sprinter abroad: eff at 5f on fast gnrd & a sharp trk. *hd* **58**
2461 **DANEHILL FAIRY 22** [3] Mrs A Duffield 2-8-6 vis J Carroll 2/1: 0206333: Led till over 1f out, no extra: bckd: handles firm & gd/soft grnd: see 2461, 2321. *2½* **50**
2882 **CASH TIME 6** [6] J O'Reilly 2-8-6 P M Quinn 25/1: 604: Dwelt, bhd, al outpcd, quick reapp: see 2183. *1* **47**
2721 **BOWLAND BRIDE 12** [2]2-8-6 BL P Mathers(7) 12/1: 0441005: Slow away, in tch till halfway, blnks. *3½* **36**
2847 **HUNIPOT 7** [5]2-8-6 BL R Ffrench 40/1: 00006: Cl-up, wknd qckly over 1f out: blnks: mod form. *3½* **25**
6 Ran Time 1m 01.79 (4.49) Owned: Abbadis Racing Club Trained: Penrith

3015 **3.05 Dragon Troop Turmeric Handicap Stakes 3yo+ 0-85 (D)** **[104]**
£5444 £1675 £838 **1m7f177y** **Good/Firm 37** **+04 Fast** Inside

2528* **YOSHKA 20** [3] M Johnston 3-8-5 (81) R Ffrench 1/1 FAV: 1-311: Chsd ldrs & hdwy to lead 2f out, drifted right, drvn out: eff at 12f, improve again for step up to sharp 2m: likes firm & fast grnd: see 2528, 1355. **92**
2355 **TIYOUN 26** [5] Jedd O'Keeffe 6-9-10 (81) Darren Williams 14/1: 25-26102: Held up in tch, rdn & outpcd over 2f out, styd on for press ins last, not able to reach wnr: gd run: see 2009, 997. *¾* **90**
2699* **TUDOR BELL 13** [6] J G M O'Shea 3-8-7 (83) D Sweeney 2/1: 3116213: Led, rdn & hdd 2f out, no extra: nicely bckd: poss not quite see out this longer 2m trip: btr 2699. *5* **85**
2685 **HOPE SOUND 13** [2] B Ellison 4-8-3 p (60) T Hamilton(3) 16/1: 200-04: Held up in tch, eff over 2f out, no impress over 1f out: longer 2m trip: see 2685. *3½* **61**
2607 **OCEAN TIDE 17** [4]7-8-13 bl (70) B Swarbrick(5) 6/1: 3344035: Cl-up, btn 3f out: btr 2607. *2½* **69**
2276 **VICARS DESTINY 30** [1]6-8-8 (65) R Winston 20/1: 6-220006: Held up, eff from 4f out, no impress. *hd* **63**
6 Ran Time 3m 25.89 (5.09) Owned: Mr Saeed Buhaleeba Trained: Middleham

3016 **3.40 5th Regiment Royal Artillery Handicap Stakes 3yo 0-75 (E)** **[80]**
£3533 £1087 £544 **7f rnd** **Good/Firm 37** **+03 Fast** Inside

2704* **WILLJOJO 13** [1] R A Fahey 3-8-1 vis (53) R Ffrench 5/1: 03-35411: Prom, led dist, rdn out: bckd, op 11/1: eff at 5/6f, now suited by 7f: acts on firm, gd/soft & fibresand: likes to race with/force the pace. **60**
2564 **REIDIES CHOICE 18** [3] J G Given 3-9-7 (73) M Fenton 7/2 FAV: 00-02042: Dwelt, rear, hdwy when short of room 2f out & badly bmpd over 1f out, styd on well cl-home, lkd unlucky: find similar. *1¼* **76+**
2755 **TRUE 11** [7] Mrs S Lamyman 3-8-11 (63) R Winston 25/1: 43-00203: Dwelt & rear, hdwy & short of room sev times fnl 2f, hung left but kept on under hands & heels, nrst fin: perhaps not entirely staightforward but shows ability & headgear may help: see 2215 (clmr). *½* **65**
2791 **BOWLING ALONG 9** [5] M E Sowersby 3-8-1 (53) T Hamilton(3) 16/1: 00-50004: Led/dsptd lead till dist, no extra: see 1465. *nk* **54**
4611} **CHRISTINAS DREAM 275** [4]3-9-7 (73) Dean McKeown 9/2: 334-5: b f Spectrum - Christine Daae (Sadler's Wells) Mid-div, short of room & checked over 2f out, switched over 1f out, sn no prog: nicely bckd tho' op 3/1: reapp/h'cap bow: mdn promise in '03 (lightly rcd, plcd, rtd 73): eff at 6f, breeding suggests further will suit: handles firm & fast grnd, stiff/undul or sharp trk. *1½* **71**
4803} **MIDNIGHT PRINCE 263** [2]3-8-1 (53) Dale Gibson 66/1: 040006-6: b c Dracula - Phylian (Glint of Gold) Prom early, sn dropped rear, late gains under kind ride, eyecatching reapp: unplcd '03 (rtd 70a): dam a 10/11f 3yo scorer & sure to relish 1m+, one to note over further. *1* **49+**
2812 **SAROS 9** [9]3-8-1 (53) M Stainton(7) 5/1: 0116027: Chsd ldrs, btn over 1f out: op 3/1: btr 2812. *nk* **48**
2559 **MISTRESS TWISTER 18** [10]3-9-4 (70) P Makin(5) 8/1: 03-338: Mid-div, btn dist: see 2559 & 2463. *hd* **64**
2812* **SHINKO FEMME 9** [6]3-8-2 (6ex) (54) Kim Tinkler 12/1: 0-000519: Dwelt, al rear: btr 2812. *1* **46**
1971 **MISTER REGENT 44** [8]3-8-12 BL (64) N Callan 10/1: 3000: 10th: Chsd ldrs, hung left & btn when hmpd over 1f out: blnks, op 7/1: 6 wk abs & h'cap bow: btr 1216 (gd/soft, debut, 6f). *6* **46**
10 Ran Time 1m 25.39 (2.39) Owned: The Yorkshire Lancashire Alliance Trained: Malton

3017   **4.15 Louisburg Classified Stakes 3yo+ 0-65 (E)**
£3445 £1060 £530   **7f rnd   Good/Firm 37   -07 Slow**   Inside

2451 **EFFECTIVE 23** [7] A P Jarvis 4-9-3 (63) N Callan 11/2: 5015201: Al prom & led 2f out, drvn out: 70
eff at 6f/7f on both AWs, fast & gd grnd: likes a sharp/turning trk, handles any: eff with/without visor: see 1025.
2848 **SMITH N ALLAN OILS 7** [3] M Dods 5-9-3 p (54) L Enstone(3) 4/1: 0000522: Mid-div when hmpd early,   1¾ 65
hdwy from 2f out & chsd wnr ins last, al held: gd run: see 2848, 323.
2752 **SIR DON 11** [11] D Nicholls 5-9-4 vis (66) Alex Greaves 9/1: 0000103: Chsd ldrs, styd on onepace.   1¾ 63
2464 **SCOTLAND THE BRAVE 22** [1] J D Bethell 4-9-1 (66) D Sweeney 9/2 FAV: 50-03504: Chsd ldrs, no   nk 59
impress from dist: see 2027.
1635* **TAP 60** [4]7-9-3 p (58) D Fentiman(7) 13/2: 2000-115: Cl-up early, sn mid-div, kept on onepace: abs.   1¾ 58
2712 **COLLEGE MAID 13** [10]7-9-0 (62) J Currie(7) 7/1: 0241356: Rear, late gains for press, no threat.   1 53
2848 **NO GROUSE 7** [9]4-9-8 p (70) T Hamilton(3) 7/1: 0300007: Mid-div, efft 3f out, no hdwy under min press.   1 59
1823 **GIVE HIM CREDIT 50** [2]4-9-3 P (60) J Carroll 40/1: 0400-508: Led 5f, btn dist: abs: see 1194.   hd 53
2935 **TANTRIC 4** [12]5-9-3 (58) J D O'Reilly(7) 12/1: 00-00309: In tch, eff 2f out, no impress: quick reapp.   2 49
2446 **ALICE BLACKTHORN 23** [6]3-8-6 (64) M Stainton(3) 20/1: 510-0050: 10th: Slow away & bhd, little prog.   3½ 39
2512 Arctic Burst 20 [5]4-9-3 vis(63) Darren Williams 40/1:0 2794 **Dragon Prince 9** [8]4-9-6 (68) T Eaves(3) 33/1:0
12 Ran   Time 1m 26.06 (3.06)   Owned: Eurostrait Ltd   Trained: Twyford

3018   **4.50 Sphinx & Workshops Handicap Stakes 3yo 0-70 (E)**   [73]
£3552 £1093 £547   **6f rnd   Good/Firm 37   -11 Slow**   Inside

2683 **WENDYS GIRL 13** [6] R P Elliott 3-8-11 bl (56) T Hamilton(3) 12/1: 2P40101: Led/dsptd lead, led   66
after 2f & rdn clr over 1f out, held on well: eff at 5/6f on firm, gd & fibresand: loves forcing tactics on a
sharp/turning trk: apprec blnks of late: see 2439.
2846 **LORD BASKERVILLE 7** [2] W Storey 3-8-8 (53) J Bramhill 40/1: 0300002: Mid-div, styd on for press   1½ 57
fnl 2f, no threat to wnr: imprvd run, has been gelded: see 1509.
2295 **UHURU PEAK 29** [10] M W Easterby 3-8-9 (54) Dale Gibson 25/1: 305003: Pushed along rear, styd on   ¾ 56+
late, nrst fin: eff at 6f, worth another try at 7f on this evidence: handles firm, fast & fibresand: see 2295 & 742.
1951 **THORNABY GREEN 44** [5] T D Barron 3-9-2 (61) P Makin(5) 10/1: 15600-44: Chsd ldrs, outpcd halfway,   nk 62
kept on late, no threat; 6 wk abs: prob stays a sharp 6f: see 1951.
2011 **GAME FLORA 42** [14]3-8-11 (56) T Eaves(3) 25/1: 000-1405: Chsd ldrs, no extra over 1f out: 6 wk abs.   2 51
1882 **CALCULAITE 47** [13]3-8-5 (50) M Fenton 50/1: 000-06: b g Komaite - Miss Calculate (Mummy's Game)   hd 44
Mid-div, outpcd over 2f out, kept on late: 7 wk abs: unplcd at up to 1m prev.
2734 **SAHARA SILK 12** [4]3-8-13 vis (58) Darren Williams 25/1: 1203007: Mid-div, chsd wnr over 1f out, wknd.   hd 51
2683 **A BID IN TIME 13** [12]3-8-0 (45) B Swarbrick(5) 20/1: 0206668: Slow away & bhd, mod prog for press.   hd 37
2566 **CHAMPAGNE CRACKER 18** [1]3-9-7 (64) R Ffrench 12/1: 22-03159: Mid-div, drvn/btn 2f out: btr 2227.   ¾ 56
2985* **CHEROKEE NATION 2** [9]3-9-5 (6ex) (64) R Winston 5/6 FAV: 4102110: 10th: Slow away in rear, short   hd 53
of room 2f out, sn no impress: well bckd under a 6lb pen, quick reapp: much btr 2985.
2675 **SUJOSISE 14** [3]3-8-2 VIS (47) P Fessey 25/1: 000-000: 11th: Held up, eff over 2f out, sn btn: vis.   1¼ 32
2731 **VOLATICUS 12** [7]3-8-13 vis (58) Alex Greaves 4/1: 0-20440: 12th: Dwelt & held up, btn 2f out: bckd.   2 37
1975 **MAUNBY GREEN 8** [8]3-9-4 VIS (63) G Faulkner 14/1: 1215-040: 13th: Led 2f, sn chsd wnr, btn 2f out.   1¾ 37
2728 **SPEED RACER 12** [11]3-8-12 (57) Kim Tinkler 66/1: 305-050: 14th: Sn struggling rear: flattered 2728.   3 22
14 Ran   Time 1m 13.26 (2.96)   Owned: Mr E Grayson   Trained: Formby

3019   **5.20 Sanna's Post Median Auction Maiden Stakes 3-4yo (F)**
£2891 £826 £413   **1m5f175y   Good/Firm 37   -12 Slow**   Inside

2678 **SILVER SASH 14** [2] M L W Bell 3-8-6 M Fenton 1/5 FAV: 631: Mid-div, smooth hdwy to lead over 3f   77
out & rdly drew clr, any amount in hand: styd this longer 14f trip in mod mdn company: acts on fast & gd/soft grnd:
found this v str-forward: see 2678 & 2349.
2384 **DUNCANBIL 26** [3] R F Fisher 3-8-6 (45) R Ffrench 25/1: 0066-002: b f Turtle Island - Saintly   15 47
Guest (What A Guest) Keen & trkd ldrs, took a remort 2nd ins last, no threat to easy wnr: unplcd '03 (rtd 57,
debut): prev tried at up to 7f.
4987J **BIEN GOOD 24** [5] Mrs M Reveley 3-8-6 T Eaves(3) 50/1: 0-3: b f Bien Bien - Southern Sky (Comedy   1½ 45
Star) Held up, eff from 3f out, no impress fnl 2f: reapp: unplcd sole '03 start (mdn, D Nicholls).
2515 **TWILIGHT YEARS 20** [6] T D Easterby 3-8-11 G Gibbons 33/1: 004: Held up, left bhd fnl 3f.   2½ 46
KYBER 0 [4]3-8-11   R Winston 10/1: 5: Rear, over 3f out, no threat: debut.   5 39
2523 **ASTON LAD 20** [1]3-8-11 Darren Williams 25/1: 466: Cl-up, hung badly right on bend after 5f, sn   21 9
led till over 3f out, wknd.
2443 **IM A DARK HORSE 23** [7]3-8-11 N Callan 20/1: 057: Led, hung right on bend after 5f & sn hdd, wknd.   16 0
7 Ran   Time 3m 02.14(6.74)   Owned: Baron F C Oppenheim   Trained: Newmarket

Official Going GOOD/FIRM (FIRM IN PLACES)

3020   **1.40 Come Evening Racing On 17th July Maiden Auction Stakes Div 1 2yo (E)**
£3435 £1057 £529   **6f str   Good 53   -25 Slow**   Stands side

2584 **TIME FOR YOU 18** [8] P J McBride 2-8-2 R Mullen 100/30: 041: Chsd ldrs, rdn to lead over 1f out,   70
styd on strongly: op 11/4: eff at 6f, stays a sharp 7f: acts on fast & gd: improving.
TYBALT 0 [7] P W Harris 2-8-7 I Mongan 10/1: 2: b c Polar Falcon - Once Removed (Distant   ¾ 71+
Relative) Slow away & bhd, hdwy from halfway & took 2nd ins last, no threat to wnr: op 8/1: cheaply bought Mar 1st
foal, dam plcd over 5f: eff at 6f, 7f+ shld suit: acts on gd grnd: green, expect improvement.

LINGFIELD Polytrack WEDNESDAY 07.07.04 Lefthand, Sharp, Undulating Track

TRACKATTACK 0 [2] J A Osborne 2-8-13 S W Kelly 14/1: 3: ch c Atraf - Verbena (Don't Forget Me) *nk* **76**
Dwelt & bhd, hdwy from halfway, styd on well ins last despite hanging, nrst fin: op 20/1: May foal, 15,000 gns purchase: half brother to a 5f juv wnr, dam a wnr abroad: eff at 6f, apprec 7f: green, improve.

BAMZOOKI 0 [5] J R Fanshawe 2-8-5 O Urbina 4/5 FAV: 4: b f Zilzal - Cavernista (Lion Cavern) *shd* **67+**
Dwelt, sn trkd ldrs, short of room & switched wide over 2f out, kept on late, nrst fin: nicely bckd at odds-on: Feb foal, half sister to a 6f 3yo scorer, dam plcd at 1m: eff at 6f, shaped as if 7f+ will suit: handles gd grnd: reportedly unsuited by the ground today, can improve.

AVERTIGO 0 [9]2-8-8 (1ow) S Sanders 25/1: 5: Led till over 1f out, no extra. *½* **68**

2618 **MARIANS MAID 16** [3]2-8-3 (1ow) J F Egan 8/1: 06: Cl-up, btn when hmpd ins last, op 10/1. *3* **54**

COOMBE CENTENARY 0 [1]2-8-2 C Catlin 50/1: 7: Chsd ldrs 4f. *5* **38**

2640 **LARAS GIRL 15** [6]2-8-2 J F McDonald(3) 33/1: 048: Cl-up, struggling from halfway. *1¾* **33**

2492 **DANCING MOONLIGHT 21** [4]2-8-8 Joanna Badger 100/1: 609: Prom till halfway, sn bhd. *5* **24**

9 Ran Time 1m 13.5 (4.7) Owned: Saracen Racing Trained: Newmarket

3021

2.10 Come Evening Racing On 17th July Maiden Auction Stakes Div 2 2yo (E)
£3426 £1054 £527 **6f** **Good 53** **-02 Slow** Stands side

2618 **ARIODANTE 16** [4] J M P Eustace 2-8-10 S Sanders 11/8 FAV: 31: Al prom styd on for press to assert ins last: hvly bckd: confirmed debut promise: eff at 6f, 7f will suit: acts on gd: nursery type. **86**

2584 **BEE STINGER 18** [7] I A Wood 2-8-7 I Mongan 9/1: 032: Led till ins last, not pace of wnr fnl 100yds: eff at 6/7f on fast & gd grnd: confirmed improvement of 2584. *1* **78**

2531 **MONASH LAD 19** [6] M H Tompkins 2-8-10 F P Ferris(3) 5/1: 053: ch c General Monash - Story Time (Mansooj) Keen & prom, ch dist, no extra: Mar foal: dam unrcd: eff at 6f on fast & gd. *½* **79**

2738 **LOUPHOLE 11** [5] P J Makin 2-8-7 R Smith 9/2: 34: Cl-up & briefly led 2f out, no extra well ins last: longer trip, btr 2738. *¾* **74**

SUNNY TIMES 0 [8]2-8-2 Lisa Jones(3) 25/1: 5: b f Raise A Grand - Dragon Star (Rudimentary) *1½* **65**
Chsd ldrs, not able to chall: cheaply bought Apr 1st foal.

2287 **ZOLASH 29** [2]2-8-10 Derek Nolan(7) 50/1: 506: Dwelt, chsd ldrs, not able to chall. *hd* **72**

THE KEEP 0 [3]2-8-5 J F Egan 4/1: 7: Dwelt, sn chsd ldrs, no prog bef dist: nicely bckd. *1½* **62**

2584 **PLAY UP POMPEY 18** [9]2-8-7 N Chalmers(5) 50/1: 08: Dwelt, held up, no impress. *½* **62**

8 Ran Time 1m 12.14 (3.34) Owned: The MacDougall Partnership Trained: Newmarket

3022

2.40 Rydon Group Nursery Handicap Stakes 2yo (E) **[87]**
£4134 £1272 £636 **6f** **Good 53** **-29 Slow** Stands side

1652 **LATERAL THINKER 58** [6] J A Osborne 2-8-8 (67) S W Kelly 7/1: 22341: Made all & dictated pace, drvn & held on gamely: 1st win, 2 month abs: eff at 5f, apprec step up to 6f: acts on polytrack, gd & gd/soft, sharp/undul trks: goes well fresh: well suited by forcing tactics today under a well judged ride: see 1380. **73**

2597 **SIMPLIFY 17** [3] D R Loder 2-9-2 BL (75) N Pollard 7/1: 4532: Keen & handy, drvn & chall ins last, held cl-home: op 5/1: gd run in blnks: handles firm & gd grnd: see 2597, 1205. *hd* **80**

2119* **ABERDOVEY 36** [7] M L W Bell 2-9-5 (78) I Mongan 3/1: 513: Dwelt, held up in tch, switched & drvn/kept on fnl 1f, not pace to reach front pair: op 9/2: wants 7f? see 2119. *1* **80**

2738* **TESARY 11** [8] E A L Dunlop 2-9-0 (73) W Supple 9/4 FAV: 6214: Keen & trkd ldrs, short of room over 1f out, sn onepace: bckd tho' op 7/4: see 2738. *¾* **73**

2430 **QUEENS GLORY 23** [5]2-8-13 (72) R Mullen 20/1: 62655: Keen, trkd ldrs, no impress dist: see 1937. *½* **70**

1531* **EARL OF LINKS 64** [4]2-9-7 (80) P Dobbs 4/1: 316: Keen, cl-up till over 1f out, abs: btr 1531 (hvy). *2½* **70**

6 Ran Time 1m 13.75 (4.95) Owned: Mrs Patricia Hughes Trained: Upper Lambourn

3023

3.15 Silks Suite Median Auction Maiden Stakes 3-4yo (F)
£2884 £824 £412 **5f** **Good 53** **+02 Fast** Stands side

2717 **EX MILL LADY 12** [1] John Berry 3-8-9 (59) B Doyle 1/2 FAV: 5-4221: Handy, rdn & led dist, drvn out: hvly bckd: eff at 5f, tried 6f: acts on firm, gd & handles soft, gall or sharp/undul trk: see 2717, 2075. **60**

SOKOKE 0 [3] R M Beckett 3-9-0 J Mackay 16/1: 2: ch g Compton Place - Sally Green (Common Grounds) Pushed along chsg ldrs, kept on ins last, al held on debut: op 12/1: eff at 5f, 6f shld suit: acts on gd grnd: still green, shld learn from this & can rate higher. *½* **62**

2784 **BLUE MOON HITMAN 10** [7] R Brotherton 3-9-0 (58) D Nolan(3) 11/4: 636-3033: Led/dsptd lead till dist, onepace: bckd: clr of rem: see 1902. *1½* **57**

2649 **LOVEYOULONGTIME 15** [5] A M Balding 3-8-9 N Chalmers(5) 14/1: 004: Handy & chsd ldr 3f out till over 1f out, wknd qckly. *5* **37**

2928 **CEDRIC COVERWELL 4** [6]4-9-5 (45) J F Egan 33/1: 4000005: Led till 3f out, sn btn, quick reapp. *nk* **41**

PANFIELD BELLE 0 [2]3-8-9 W Supple 33/1: 6: Dwelt, sn bhd on debut. *6* **18**

6 Ran Time 59.38s (2.58) Owned: Mrs Rosemary Moszkowicz Trained: Newmarket

3024

3.50 Furlongs And Fairways At Lingfield Park Handicap Stakes 3yo 35-55 (F) **[61]**
£3017 £862 £431 **7f** **Good 53** **-51 Slow** Stands side

2617 **BLAEBERRY 16** [8] P L Gilligan 3-9-8 BL (55) J F Egan 11/2 FAV: 0-005541: Made all & rdn clr from halfway, styd on well for press: 1st win: apprec drop back to 7f & blnks, prob stays 1m: acts on fast & gd grnd: suited by forcing tactics: see 1823. **66**

2403 **CHORISTAR 25** [14] W R Muir 3-9-8 (55) R Mullen 25/1: 060-62: Rear, switched & styd on well from over 1f out, nrst fin: eff at 7f, shaped as if 1m in similar will suit: acts on gd grnd: lightly rcd, encouraging. *2* **59**

2506 **UNITED SPIRIT 20** [11] M A Magnusson 3-9-8 P (55) S Hitchcott(3) 16/1: 504-063: Prom in chsg group & chsd wnr over 1f out, no extra ins last: eff at 7f on gd grnd: see 2174. *shd* **58**

2586 **SHIBUMI 18** [1] H Morrison 3-9-6 (53) L Fletcher(3) 10/1: 0-554: Held up, drvn & styd on fnl 2f, nrst fin: h'cap bow: stays a sharp 7f: handles fast & gd grnd: enjoy further now: see 2586, 2237. *½* **55+**

2314 **BEAUTIFUL NOISE 28** [2]3-9-7 (54) W Supple 9/1: 506-0655: Mid-div, kept on onepace, no threat. *1½* **53**

2975 **NIGHT WORKER 2** [6]3-9-6 (53) P Dobbs 20/1: 0-600006: Mid-div, not pace to chall: quick reapp. *¾* **50**

2292* **ACCENDERE 29** [4]3-9-8 (55) S Sanders 6/1: 005017: Dwelt & rear, hdwy over 2f out, no extra dist. *1* **50**

2387	**DELLAGIO 25** [3]3-9-6 (53) B Reilly(3) 20/1: 0000408: Held up, rdn & some hdwy, nvr threat: btr 1942.	½	47
2634	**JOSHUAS GOLD 16** [10]3-9-7 (54) D Tudhope(7) 9/1: 55-23609: Prom chsg group, btn over 1f out.	3½	41
1454*	**DIAL SQUARE 69** [16]3-9-7 (54) C Catlin 9/1: 3231110: 10th: Bhd, little prog: op 6/1: btr 1454.	¾	39
2380	**BARRAS 26** [7]3-9-8 vis (55) M Savage(5) 25/1: 0035400: 11th: Chsd wnr, rdn & fdd dist: flattered 835.	nk	39
2743	**FORZENUFF 11** [5]3-9-8 T (55) V Venkaya 33/1: 5060000: 12th: Prom in chsg group 5f, t-strap.	¾	37
975	**AVERAMI 99** [15]3-9-8 vis (55) R J Killoran(7) 40/1: 654-0500: 13th: Prom in chsg group till over 1f out.	½	36
2624	**YOUNG LOVE 16** [13]3-9-7 (54) L Keniry(3) 9/1: 00-0640: 14th: Prom chsg group, btn/eased over 1f out: reportedly unsuited by rain-softened grnd: btr 2624 (fast).	3½	28
	NEWTOWN CHIEF 336 [9]3-9-7 (54) Steven Harrison(7) 40/1: 0600-0: 15th: Sn bhd on reapp/Brit bow.	3	22
2380	**WONKY DONKEY 26** [12]3-9-7 (54) O Urbina 12/1: 0-343050: 16th: Al bhd & t.o, broke blood vessel.	*dist*	0

16 Ran   Time 1m 27.7 (7.3)   Owned: Lady Bland   Trained: Newmarket

Official Going STANDARD

3025   4.25 Seaholme Marquees Selling Stakes 3yo+   (G)
£2576   £736   £368   **1m2f**   Going 71   +01 Fast   Inside

2873*	**BURGUNDY 6** [6] P Mitchell 7-9-12 bl (58) I Mongan 3/1 J FAV: 0003611: Pushed along early, sn mid-div & hdwy to lead over 2f out, rdn clr, decisively: no bid: quick reapp: eff at 7/10f on fast, soft & polytrack: enjoys sell/clmg grade, quirky type, in great heart at present: see 2873 & 145.		63a
1841	**BRETTON 49** [12] B A Pearce 3-8-9 (35) B Reilly(3) 33/1: 6444302: Rear, styd on for press fnl 2f, nvr threat to wnr: eff at 9/10f on both AWs: see 351.	5	47a
2047	**PIQUET 40** [13] J J Bridger 6-9-7 (47) G Baker 12/1: 6600063: Rear, smooth hdwy 4f out, chsd wnr over 2f out, no impress dist: 6 wk abs: see 538 (1m, banded).	hd	47a
2799	**ONE ALONE 9** [11] Jean Rene Auvray 3-8-4 VIS (45) W Supple 33/1: 00-00004: Rear, eff 3f out, wknd.	5	33a
2643	**REGULATED 15** [5]3-9-1 (65) J P Guillambert(3) 4/1: 1551605: Rear, eff 4f out, little prog: btr 2107.	5	36a
4183}	**FRIXOS 300** [8]4-9-6 bl (70) V Slattery 14/1: 1260P0-6: ch g Barathea - Local Lass (Local Suitor) Mid-div, no impress fnl 3f: 2 month jumps abs (unplcd): '03 AW h'cap wnr for P Cole, turf unplcd (rtd 56, h'cap): eff at 9f on fibresand & a sharp trk: sole win came in 1st time blnks.	1¾	27a
	2 May'03 Sout 12af 71a-65 F: 1 Apr'03 Wolv 9.4af 72a-59 F:		
2497	**BUCKENHAM STONE 21** [4]5-9-1 (30) R Price 66/1: 00-0007: Trkd ldrs till lost place 5f out: see 2497.	1	20a
2694	**YEOMAN LAD 13** [9]4-9-6 vis (69) L Keniry 3/1 J FAV: 00-00458: Mid-div, btn 3f out: 'nvr travelling'.	8	13a
665	**LILIAN 141** [1]4-9-1 (37) M Savage(4) 12/1: 022-6569: b f First Trump - Lillibella (Reprimand) Chsd ldrs till 5f out, t.o.: eye-shield omitted: thrice rnr-up '03, incl sell h'cap, AW unplcd (rtd 46a): eff btwn 1m/10f on firm & fast grnd, stiff/turning or sharp trk: eff in a visor.	7	0a
	2 Oct'03 Leic 10.0g/f 47-(46) G: 2 Sep'03 Wind 10.0g/f 47-(43) G: 2 Jun'03 Bath 8.0fm 48-46 G:		
2643	**CORONADO FOREST 15** [10]5-9-12 BL (59) S Sanders 9/1: 4100060: 10th: Led over 4f out till 2f out.	¾	7a
2967	**AFRICAN SPUR 2** [14]4-9-6 (49) D Tudhope(7) 16/1: 0065000: 11th: Led after 1f till over 4f out, wknd.	1¼	0a
2588	**AMUSEMENT 18** [2]8-9-6 S Righton 25/1: 460: 12th: Led 1f, struggling after 4f, t.o.	1¾	0a
707	**BOOM OR BUST 135** [3]5-9-6 p (35) D Nolan(3) 16/1: 3200-000: 13th: Mid-div, btn 2f out, t.o.: jumps fit.	¾	0a

13 Ran   Time 2m 9.83 (7.03)   Owned: Mr Nigel Shields   Trained: Epsom

3026   5.00 Ladbrokes Com Handicap Stakes Fillies 3yo+ 0-70 (E)
£3455   £1063   £532   **1m4f**   Going 71   -02 Slow   Inside   [68]

3152}	**NADESZHDA 348** [4] Sir Mark Prescott 4-9-12 (66) S Sanders 4/7 FAV: 000/112-1: ch f Nashwan - Ninotchka (Nijinsky) Trkd ldrs & led over 3f out, pushed out, cmftbky: hvly bckd at odds-on: reapp: lightly rcd '03, landed 2 h'caps, incl a fills h'cap, also AW h'cap rnr-up: unplcd '02: all wins around 12f, stays sharp 2m: acts on both AWs, firm & fast: plenty more to come.		80a
	2 Jul'03 Wolv 16.2af 66a-59 G: 1 Jul'03 Brig 11.9g/f 77-59 E: 1 Jul'03 Catt 12.0fm 66-53 E:		
803	**REGAL GALLERY 125** [3] C A Horgan 6-9-11 (65) Paul Eddery 10/1: 41-11342: Rear, in tch, hdwy to chase wnr 2f out, styd on for press, al held: clr rem: 4 month abs: loves this trk, can win again: see 736 & 624.	¾	73a
2842	**ILLEANA 7** [5] W R Muir 3-8-5 (58) R Mullen 33/1: 0-400103: Rear, drvn & styd on for press, no threat to front pair: acts on fast & polytrack: see 2163.	5	58a
1789	**FLEETING MOON 51** [2] A M Balding 4-9-9 (63) L Keniry(3) 9/1: 0-221324: Mid-div, outpcd over 2f out, kept on late: +needs further: 7 wk abs: see 1789, 813 (2m).	1¾	60a
1990	**ROYALE PEARL 43** [1]4-8-2 (42) C Catlin 16/1: 0-004145: Handy, outpcd fnl 3f: 6 wk abs: btr	1	37a
2647	**WANNA SHOUT 15** [8]6-9-4 (58) Joanna Badger 33/1: 2120506: Cl-up, wknd fnl 2f: best at 1m/10f.	3½	48a
801	**DISPOL EVITA 125** [7]5-8-13 (53) I Mongan 16/1: 00-0427: Dwelt, rear, btn 2f out: abs: btr 801 & 736.	3½	38a
2651*	**ANYHOW 15** [6]7-10-0 (68) D Nolan(3) 4/1: 2153218: Led till 3f out, sn lost place & eased over 1f out: rider reported mare ran flat: normally v tough & consistent: see 2651.	5	45a

8 Ran   Time 2m 37.98(8.78)   Owned: Miss K Rausing   Trained: Newmarket

Official Going Good/Firm (Strong Headwind, times slow)

3027   1.20 Listed Bahrain Trophy 3yo (A)
£17850   £6600   £3300   **1m6f175y**   Good/Firm 32   -50 Slow   Stands Side

2746	**ANOUSA 11** [3] P Howling 3-8-11 (82) K Fallon 13/2: 0100031: Handy, hdwy trav well & led over 1f out, pushed clr, cmftbly: prev eff at up to 12f, relished step up to 14.8f: has tried a visor: acts on firm & hvy: useful now, unexposed over staying trips, win again: see 2519, 1515.		98
2557	**TOP SEED 19** [2] M R Channon 3-8-11 (108) T E Durcan 10/11 FAV: 24-24032: Chsd ldr till led over 2f out, rdn & hdd over 1f out, not pace of cmftble wnr: nicely bckd: prob stays 14.8f: ran to form of 2557.	3½	92

915

2557 **BUMPTIOUS 19** [1] M H Tompkins 3-8-11 bl (90) P Robinson 4/1: 6-331443: In tch, eff 2f out,   ¾   **91**
onepcd: again shaped as a dour stayer & 2m+ prob ndd: see 2557.
1584 **ISIDORE BONHEUR 62** [4] B W Hills 3-8-11 (98) D Holland 4/1: 14-4444: Set stdy pace till over 2f   16   **75**
out, hmpd & wknd over 1f out: 2 month abs: longer trip, see 1189.
4 Ran   Time 3m 17.83 (12.33)   Owned: Arkland International (UK) Ltd   Trained: Newmarket

---

3028	**1.50 Gr2 Tnt July Stakes Colts & Geldings 2yo** (A)				
	£40600 £15400 £7700	**6f str**	**Good/Firm 32**	**-09 Slow**	Far Side

2697 **CAPTAIN HURRICANE 13** [6] P W Chapple Hyam 2-8-10 J Fortune 10/1: 221: Held up, hdwy over 1f   **111**
out, styd on for press to lead cl-home, drvn out: bckd from 16/1: v eff over a stiff 6f on firm & gd: smart now,
genuine & progressing with each run: see 2341.
2467 **COUNCIL MEMBER 22** [5] Saeed bin Suroor 2-8-10 L Dettori 7/4 FAV: 122: Set pace, rdn & edged   shd **110**
right ins last, kept on till collared cl-home, just held: hvly bckd, another fine run in Gr 2 class & acts on firm &
fast: shld be wng a Gr race shortly: see 2467, 2158.
2516 **MYSTICAL LAND 20** [4] J H M Gosden 2-8-10 K Fallon 15/8: 2123: Handy, eff well over 1f out,   1¼ **106**
0.75L 3rd, rdn & prob held when hmpd cl-home: well bckd: stays 6f: useful, Listed/Gr3 will suit: see 2516, 1517.
2531* **ST ANDREWS STORM 19** [2] R Hannon 2-8-10 R Hughes 14/1: 14: Slow away, outpcd over 2f   1½ **101**
out, late gains, nvr dngrs: useful & imprvd from debut: will relish a step up to 7f.
2467 **TONY JAMES 22** [7]2-8-10 D Holland 10/1: 145: Cl-up, wknd fnl 1f: need Listed: see 2039.   shd **100**
2094 **MOSCOW MUSIC 37** [1]2-8-10 R L Moore 33/1: 2126: Held up, wknd dist: btr 2094 (5f, List).   4   **88**
2472* **CHATEAU ISTANA 22** [3]2-8-10 T P Queally 7/1: 6117: Chsd ldr, wknd over 1f out: btr expected on   5   **73**
step up in class after 2472 (5f, Listed).
7 Ran   Time 1m 13.61 (2.61)   Owned: The Comic Strip Heroes   Trained: Newmarket

---

3029	**2.20 Joss Collins Stakes Heritage Handicap 3yo 0-105** (B)				**[104]**
	£29000 £11000 £5500	**1m2f**	**Good/Firm 32**	**-34 Slow**	Stands Side

2519 **WOODCRACKER 20** [9] M L W Bell 3-9-0 (90) D Holland 10/1: 0-1201: Handy, hdwy & short of room 2f   **100**
out, switched & led over 1f out, held on gamely for press ins last: right back to form with return to 10f, tried 12f
last time: acts on firm & soft: lightly rcd, useful & genuine: see 1664, 1241.
2785 **ROYAL WARRANT 10** [7] A M Balding 3-8-12 (88) Martin Dwyer 5/1: 6134222: Handy, hdwy to chall   shd **97**
over 1f out, sn short of room but styd on ins last, just held in a stirring duel.
2785 **TORINMOOR 10** [8] Mrs A J Perrett 3-9-1 (91) J Murtagh 12/1: 316-533: Slow away, held up, hdwy   4   **93**
over 1f out, onepace fnl 1f: gd run, also bhd this rnr-up in 2785.
2250 **SILENT HAWK 32** [13] Saeed bin Suroor 3-8-13 vis t (89) L Dettori 12/1: 2-4104: Held up, eff to   3½ **86**
chall over 1f out, sn wknd: now twice below 1892 (mdn, gd).
2710 **CELTIC HEROINE 13** [5]3-9-7 (97) K Darley 7/2: 1-212125: Held up, eff well over 1f out, sn hmpd   ¾   **93**
but wknd: well bckd, top-weight: btr expected after 2710 & 2491.
2491 **MYSTICAL GIRL 21** [2]3-9-4 (94) S Chin 16/1: 3121306: Sn clr ldr, hdd & wknd 2f: went off too fast.   3   **86**
2523* **GALVANISE 20** [14]3-8-11 (87) R Hughes 17/2: 0-617: Cl-up, wandered & wkng when hmpd over 1f out: 2½ **75**
up in class after auct mdn win in 2523.
2406 **MOTIVE 25** [6]3-9-0 (90) K Fallon 9/4 FAV: 5128: Held up, hdwy to chase ldr over 3f out, poss   3½ **73**
just held when hmpd over 1f out, lost all ch: hvly bckd: lkd useful earlier & prob worth another ch: see 2406.
2557 **TARANDOT 19** [3]3-8-11 (87) A McCarthy 28/1: 0-2109: In tch, wknd 2f out: see 2558.   16   **48**
4328*)**QUARTINO 22** [11]3-8-13 (89) J Fortune 22/1: 521-0: 10th: b c Dynaformer - Qirmazi (Riverman)   2½ **46**
Held up, btn over 2f out: '03 mdn scorer: eff at 1m, shld stay further: acts on firm & fast grnd, gall or fair trk.
1 Sep'03 Nott 8.2g/f 85- D: 2 Sep'03 Kemp 8g/f 83- D:
2406 **LUNAR EXIT 25** [1]3-9-4 (94) K McEvoy 40/1: 315-60: 11th: Al bhd: reportedly unsuited by grnd.   11   **33**
11 Ran   Time 2m 08.51 (6.61)   Owned: Sir Thomas Pilkington   Trained: Newmarket

---

3030	**2.55 Gr2 Princess Of Wales's Cantorodds Com Stakes 3yo+** (A)				
	£58000 £22000 £11000	**1m4f**	**Good/Firm 32**	**-07 Slow**	Stands Side

2488 **BANDARI 21** [8] M Johnston 5-9-2 (117) R Hills 12/1: 2-011101: Held up, hdwy 2f out, led appr fnl   **120**
1f, styd on well, drvn out: close 2nd in this race last term: v eff over 10/12f, just stays 14f: acts on firm, soft
& any trk: thriving, career best: see 2128.
2488 **SULAMANI 21** [7] Saeed bin Suroor 5-9-7 T (125) L Dettori 11/8 FAV: 42115-42: Held up, gd hdwy &   ½   **125**
switched left over 2f out, hung right but chall over 1f out, styd on ins last, just held: hvly bckd: not completely
str-forward but ran close to top-class best conceding weight to smart rivals & clrly eff in a t-strap: tough, more
Gr1's to be won on this evidence: see 2488.
2579 **HIGH ACCOLADE 18** [2] M P Tregoning 4-9-2 (116) Martin Dwyer 6/1: 6212-423: Handy, hdwy to lead   2½ **116**
over 2f out till over 1f out, kept on same pace: v tough, consistent & smart, Gr 3 suit: see 2579, 2209.
2209 **MAGISTRETTI 33** [5] N A Callaghan 4-9-2 (121) D Holland 100/30: 11022-64: Held up, eff over 2f   3½ **111**
out, btn 2f out: hvly bckd: btr expected after pleasing reapp in 2209 but yet to prove fully eff over 12f.
2579 **PERSIAN MAJESTY 18** [6]4-9-2 (113) J Murtagh 8/1: 1/1-6335: Handy, eff to chall over 2f out, sn   hd   **110**
hung left & wknd: needs Listed/Gr3: see 2579.
2579 **SYSTEMATIC 18** [1]5-9-2 (113) K Darley 20/1: 5-321056: Held up, wknd 2f out: s/mate wnr.   3   **106**
2636 **THE GREAT GATSBY 17** [4]4-9-2 (119) J Fortune 10/1: 44/225-37: Chsd ldr till 3f out, wknd 2f out: 12   **89**
much btr than this tho' may need an easier surface: see 2636.
2004 **NAHEEF 45** [3]5-9-2 vis t (111) K McEvoy 66/1: 3125-358: Sn clr ldr, hdd & wknd 2f out: see 2004.   dist **0**
8 Ran   Time 2m 32.9 (4.7)   Owned: Mr Hamdan Al Maktoum   Trained: Middleham

---

3031	**3.30 Capannelle Racecourse E B F Novice Stakes 2yo** (D)
	£8860 £2726 £1363 **6f str** **Good/Firm 32** -24 Slow Far Side

STETCHWORTH PRINCE [6] D R Loder 2-8-8   T P Queally 9/2: 1: b c Cadeaux Genereux - Elfin   97
Laughter (Alzao) Handy, hdwy to lead over 1f out, styd on well, drvn out: Jan foal, cost 120,000: half brother to
useful 1m wnr Smirk: dam 7f/1m juv scorer: eff over a stiff 6f, 7f/1m sure to suit in time: runs well fresh on
firm grnd: v useful start, plenty more to come & shld be wng decent prizes.
  ARMY OF ANGELS [7] Saeed bin Suroor 2-8-8 T L Dettori 7/2: 2: ch c King's Best - Angelic Sounds   1¾   90+
(The Noble Player) Held up, eff over 1f out, kept on to chase wnr ins last, hands & heels: Apr foal, cost E250,000:
half brother to sev wnrs over 5f/11f: eff over a stiff 6f, 7f shld suit in time: acts on firm grnd: v useful
start, sure to improve & must win a mdn sn.
  PAPER TALK 0 [1] B W Hills 2-8-8   D Holland 11/8 FAV: 3: br c Unbridled's Song - Journalist   nk   89+
(Night Shift) Handy, eff & short of room over 1f out, styd on ins last on debut, hands & heels: Mar 1st foal: dam
6f juv wnr eff at 6f, 7f shld suit: acts on firm grnd: v encouraging start, type to win races.
  LOVE ANGEL [4] M Johnston 2-8-8   J Fanning 16/1: 4: b c Woodman - Omnia (Green Dancer) With   1   86
ldr, onepcd over 1f out on debut: Jan foal, cost $37,000: bred to apprec 7f/1m in time & showed ability here.
2786 **TREMPJANE 10** [3]2-8-11 R Hughes 8/1: 155: Set pace till dist, wknd: see 2373 (auct mdn, gd).   2½   82
  SIGN WRITER [8]2-8-8   E Ahern 9/1: 6: Swerved right start, keen, held up, btn over 1f out.   ½   77
6 Ran   Time 1m 14.35 (3.35)   Owned: Lucayan Stud   Trained: Newmarket

---

3032	**4.05 Rolls Royce Handicap Stakes 4yo+ 0-95** (C)	[91]
	£10166 £3128 £1564 **2m24y** **Good/Firm 32** -25 Slow Stands Side	

2699 **VALANCE 13** [10] C R Egerton 4-8-12 (75) J Murtagh 9/2 JT FAV: 4103-351: Cl-up, hdwy to lead &   83
hung right over 1f out, styd on ins last, drvn out: apprec step up to 2m & acts on firm & polytrack: unexposed.
2583 **DON FERNANDO 18** [9] M C Pipe 5-9-3 (80) K Fallon 9/1: 00-05062: Held up, hdwy & short of room   1¾   85
over 1f out, kept on ins last: btr run: on a fair mark: see 2471, 1928.
4796] **TEN CARAT 263** [11] Mrs A J Perrett 4-10-0 (91) R Hughes 9/2 JT FAV: 0/41110-3: ch c Grand Lodge   1¾   95+
- Emerald (El Gran Senor) Handy, lost place over 3f out, hdwy & no room over 1f out, styd on ins last, nrst fin:
well bckd: mdn & dual h'cap wnr in '03: eff at 14f, clrly stays 2m on firm or gd/soft, likes gall trks: has run
well fresh: useful, remains on the upgrade & a fine return, keep in mind for similar.
 1 Oct'03 Newm 14fm 93-86 C: 1 Aug'03 Beve 16.2gd 90-82 D: 1 May'03 Nott 14.1g/s 90- D:
2471 **LAND N STARS 22** [2] Jamie Poulton 4-9-2 (79) P Doe 5/1: 422-0154: Held up, eff over 2f out, kept   ½   82
on same pace: gd run: see 2471, 1928.
2685 **THE RING 13** [3]4-8-7 (70) K Darley 20/1: 31-02305: Held up, eff 2f out, onepace dist: see 1003.   shd   73
2073 **HIGH POINT 39** [13]6-9-3 (80) Dane O'Neill 7/1: 0023336: Keen held up, eff 2f out, wknd dist.   2½   80
2471 **TERESA 22** [12]4-9-0 (77) J Quinn 15/2: 133-2667: In tch, wknd over 1f out: see 1112.   1   76
2156 **MADIBA 35** [6]5-7-12 (2oh) (59) A McCarthy 66/1: 2022008: Prom, hdwy to lead & edged right over 2f   3   57
out, hdd over 1f out, wknd: see 1753, 1637.
2471 **KING FLYER 22** [7]8-9-3 (80) S Whitworth 9/1: 0230209: Held up, btn over 2f out: btr 2198, 813.   ¾   75
2887 **NAKWA 6** [5]6-8-9 (72) D Allan 20/1: 3221260: 10th: Handy, wknd 2f out: qck reapp: see 2229.   3   64
2567 **GEORGE STUBBS 18** [1]4-10-3 (62) R Thomas 20/1: 3135550: 11th: Set pace till over 2f out, wknd.   9   45
2899 **REDSPIN 5** [4]4-8-4 (67) Martin Dwyer 12/1: 3004440: 12th: Held up, wknd 2f out: qck reapp.   3   47
12 Ran   Time 3m 31.74 (9.24)   Owned: M Haynes A & J Allison J Weatherby   Trained: Chaddleworth

---

3033	**4.40 Ngk Spark Plugs Rated Stakes Handicap 3yo+ 0-85** (D)	[95]
	£10249 £3154 £1577 **5f str** **Good/Firm 32** +18 Fast Far Side	

2734 **SILVER PRELUDE 12** [11] D K Ivory 3-8-13 (80) P Robinson 25/1: 50-00031: Led far side group   86
early, led again dist, hung left but kept on well, drvn out: loves to dominate over 5f on firm or fast.
2690 **AWAKE 13** [12] D Nicholls 7-9-2 (78) A Nicholls 14/1: 0650162: Held up far side, hdwy over 1f   nk   83
out, styd on ins last, just held: in gd form: see 2286, 1251.
2861 **CURRENCY 7** [19] J M Bradley 7-9-0 P (76) R L Moore 20/1: 0004063: In tch, stands side, eff &   nk   80
short of room over 1f out, styd on strongly ins last: sharpened up by cheekpieces, shade unfortunate.
2698 **DEVISE 13** [7] M S Saunders 5-9-4 (80) K McEvoy 6/1: 1601554: Handy far side, hdwy over 1f out,   ½   82
kept on, btn 1L: gd run: lkd unlucky 2698, see 1914.
2727 **PICCLED 12** [18]6-9-7 (83) D Allan 16/1: 3000105: Slow away stands side, held up, hdwy over 1f   ½   83
out, kept on late: another gd run: see 2359.
516 **SEMENOVSKII 158** [9]4-8-10 (72) R Hills 12/1: 00600-36: In tch far side, eff dist, onepcd: abs.   nk   71
2698 **DOMIRATI 13** [1]4-9-1 (78) S Drowne 8/1: 234-0427: Cl-up far side, kept on same pace fnl 1f.   nk   77
2070 **MR MALARKEY 7** [4]4-9-1 bl (77) P Doe 7/1: 4046338: With ldr far side, wknd fnl 1f: tough: see 2861.   ½   73
2861 **TURIBIUS 39** [3]5-9-2 (78) R Hughes 33/1: 1-613009: Held up far side, some late gains: see 755.   nk   73
2677 **THE JOBBER 14** [16]3-9-1 (82) F Norton 25/1: 021-40: 10th: In tch stands side, wknd over 1f out.   ½   75
2861+**PRINCE DAYJUR 7** [14]5-9-1 (3ex)vis (77) K Fallon 9/1: 0000-010: 11th: Led stands side group till   ¾   68
ins last, wknd: nicely bckd: made all in 1st time visor in 2861 (6f).
2758 **MISS GEORGE 11** [15]6-9-6 (82) S Chin 14/1: 0030600: 12th: In tch stands side, hung left & btn 1f out.   ½   71
2591 **BEAUVRAI 13** [17]4-8-11 (73) M Tebbutt 18/1: 0000530: 13th: In tch stands side, wknd over 1f out.   hd   61
2747 **BRAVE BURT 11** [10]7-9-6 (82) E Ahern 10/1: 0013-000: 14th: Led 4f out far side, hdd early, wknd.   ½   68
2727 **SALVIATI 12** [5]7-9-4 (80) R Thomas(5) 14/1: 5-000000: 15th: Dwelt, al bhd far side.   1   63
2942 **WINTHORPE 4** [6]4-8-7 (69) D Holland 100/30 FAV: 0040320: 16th: In tch far side, wknd 2f out: 1¾   47
well bckd: something amiss? quick reapp, much btr 2942 (soft).
16 Ran   Time 59.2(0.7)   Owned: Mrs A Shone   Trained: Radlett

Official Going GOOD/FIRM.

3034   6.30 Betfred 'the Bonus King' Girl Apprentice Handicap Stakes 3yo+ 0-75 (E)   [73]
£4183 £1287 £644   7f jub   Good/Firm 38   -03 Slow   Inside

2369 **FEN GYPSY 26** [5] P D Evans 6-9-0 (59) Donna Bashton 6/1: 0212451: Trkd ldrs, went on fnl 1f,   65
styd on, pushed out: unplcd in a nov hdle 2 wks ago: eff btwn 7f & 1m, has tried 12f: acts on firm, gd/soft grnd &
prob polytrack: handles a sharp or gall trk: runs well for an inexperienced rider, see 1536 & 1284.
2272 **BI POLAR 30** [3] D R C Elsworth 4-10-0 (73) Natalia Gemelova 5/1: 020-0022: Trkd ldrs, ev ch   ½ 77
halfway, led 2f out till ent fnl 1f, kept on & not btn far: gd run under top-weight, deserves similar: see 2272.
2600* **WIND CHIME 17** [6] A G Newcombe 7-9-7 (66) Lisa Jones 4/1 FAV: 00-02013: Rear, styd on well fnl   ½ 69
1f, just failed: gd run over this inadequate 7f, rtn to 1m will suit as in 2600: likes Warwick.
2909 **ESPADA 5** [9] J A Osborne 8-8-7 bl (52) Danielle Deverson(5) 14/1: 0441504: Led till 2f out, onepace.   nk 54
2975 **MYTHICAL CHARM 2** [7]5-8-6 t (51) Lucy Russell 10/1: 3300035: Chsd ldrs, onepcd fnl 1f: qck reapp.   ½ 51
2768 **HALCYON MAGIC 11** [1]6-8-3 bl (48) Laura Pike 16/1: 0-200206: Mid-div, styd on late, nvr dngrs.   nk 47
2852 **CITY GENERAL 7** [12]3-7-12 (20h)p (49) Laura Reynolds(5) 20/1: 3435027: Chsd ldrs, onepcd fnl 1f.   nk 49
2768 **PAGAN STORM 11** [4]4-8-11 t (56) Kristin Stubbs 8/1: 0500038: Pushed in rear, late prog, nvr dngrs.   hd 53
2529 **ARRAN 19** [10]4-8-8 (53) Stephanie Hollinshead 8/1: U000-039: Slowly away, nvr a factor: see 2529.   ¾ 48
2644 **ZIET DALSACE 15** [13]4-8-8 (53) Leanne Kershaw 12/1: 4-020020: 10th: Slowly away, nvr nr ldrs.   ½ 47
2985 **OTAGO 2** [2]3-8-4 (57) Hayley Turner 8/1: 30450: 11th: Al bhd: qck reapp.   5 41
2500 **Franks Quest 20** [14]4-8-10 (55) Victoria Hill(5) 14/1:0   2394 **Fulvio 25** [11]4-9-1 (60) Jemma Marshall 16/1:0
13 Ran   Time 1m 27.02 (2.92)   Owned: Mr P D Evans   Trained: Abergavenny

3035   7.00 European Breeders Fund Maiden Stakes Fillies 2yo (D)
£4940 £1520 £760   7f jub   Good/Firm 38   -29 Slow   Inside

2676 **PARK LAW 14** [7] J H M Gosden 2-8-11 J Fortune 1/1 FAV: 21: Broke well & made all, styd on well   85
fnl 1f, pushed out: well bckd: confirmed debut promise & put that experience to gd use here: eff at 7f on fast &
gd/soft grnd, likes a flat trk: useful & improving: see 2676 (C/D).
    ARBELLA [1] P W Harris 2-8-11 N Mackay 12/1: 2: ch f Primo Dominie - Kristal Bridge (Kris)   1¼ 82+
Dwelt, prog halfway, fin strongly but too late on debut: op 8/1: Apr foal, half-sister to an 11f wnr: styd styd
11f: eff at 7f, 1m sure to suit: acts on fast & runs well fresh: most promising debut, will improve & win races.
    SHARABY [5] E A L Dunlop 2-8-11 W Supple 25/1: 3: b f Cadeaux Genereux - Shawanni (Shareef   ¾ 79
Dancer) Chsd ldrs, went after wnr fnl 1f, caught for 2nd cl-home on debut: Mar foal, half-sister to juv wnrs
Twilight (5f) & Shandy Star (10f): dam a 7f juv wnr: eff at 7f on fast: sure to learn from this, find similar.
    HEAT OF THE NIGHT [8] J L Dunlop 2-8-11 S Sanders 25/1: 4: b f Lear Fan - Hot Thong (Jarraar)   nk 78
Trkd ldrs, on rail when short of room 2f out, kept on under hands-&-heels on debut: May foal, dam a decent 7f wnr
abroad: sire a top-class miler: eff at 7f on gd grnd, 1m will suit: will learn plenty from this encouraging run.
    AUTUMN MELODY [12]2-8-11 T L Dettori 7/2: 5: b f Kingmambo - Dance of Leaves (Sadler's Wells)   ½ 77
Chsd ldrs, went after wnr 2f out, not qckn fnl 1f on debut: Mar foal, half-sister to sev wnrs, notably smart 7f/1m
performer Charnwood Forest: dam unrcd but from a decent family, sire a top-class miler: wears a t-strap.
2310 **SPINNING COIN 28** [16]2-8-11 Lisa Jones(3) 33/1: 06: b f Mujahid - Cointosser (Nordico) Chsd   3 71
ldrs, styd on late, not pace to disput fnl 1f on debut: Mar foal, cost 4,600gns: half-sister to a 5f juv wnr: dam a 7f/hdls wnr.
    HIDDEN CHANCE [2]2-8-11 Dane O'Neill 20/1: 7: Slowly away, late hdwy, nvr dngrs on debut.   ½ 70
2610 **IMPERIAL MISS 17** [15]2-8-11 A Daly 33/1: 068: Prom till after halfway, wknd fnl 1f.   hd 70
    TAKE IT THERE [3]2-8-11 P Dobbs 20/1: 9: Rear, prog when short of room 2f out, sn eased on debut.   ½ 69
    PAR JEU [6]2-8-11 B Doyle 11/2: 0: 10th: Chsd ldrs 5.5f, wknd on debut: op 7/1.   shd 69
    SHES MY OUTSIDER [13]2-8-11 T P Queally 33/1: 0: 11th: Slowly away, nvr a factor on debut.   ½ 68
    ENTERTAIN [11]2-8-11 J Mackay 25/1: 0: 12th: Rear, prog when short of room 1.5f out, eased.   nk 67
    Magic Tree [4]2-8-11 T E Durcan 20/1:0   2537 **Triple Zero 19** [10]2-8-11 E Stack 50/1:0
2399 **Liameliss 25** [5]2-8-11 C Catlin 50/1:0   **Big Hoo Hah** [14]2-8-11 S Whitworth 33/1:0
16 Ran   Time 1m 28.82 (4.72)   Owned: Sangster Family   Trained: Manton

3036   7.30 Betfred 'we Pay Double Result' Handicap Stakes 3yo 0-75 (E)   [80]
£4115 £1266 £633   5f str   Good/Firm 38   +14 Fast   Centre - 1st & 3rd rcd Far Side

1722 **RED SOVEREIGN 55** [11] I A Wood 3-9-2 (68) S Sanders 14/1: 1366-001: b f Danzig Connection - Ruby   78
Princess (Mac's Imp) Trkd ldr far side, went on strt, clr fnl 1f under hands-and-heels: 8 wk abs, fast time, val
3L+: '03 mdn auct wnr (subs plcd in a nurs h'cap): acts on fast grnd, prob handles polytrack & soft: runs
well fresh, handles a flat or stiff/gall trk: enterprisingly rdn.
1 Aug'03 Newc 6g/f 79- F: 2 Jul'03 Sali 6g/s 71- D:
2585 **MINIMUM BID 18** [1] Miss B Sanders 3-8-2 (54) J Quinn 10/1: 063-002: Rear, hdwy 1.5f out, fin   2 55
well to lead centre group cl-home, no ch with wnr far side: acts on fast grnd, again suggested a rtn to 6f will suit.
2669 **MELODY KING 14** [12] P D Evans 3-9-1 bl (67) J Fortune 6/1: 032-032543: Led duo far side, hdd dist,   1 65
no extra: front rnr, prob rcd on fastest grnd: see 2269.
2784 **CUT AND DRIED 10** [2] D M Simcock 3-9-1 (67) Martin Dwyer 7/1: 1605464: Chsd ldrs centre, onepcd.   ½ 64
2717 **LAKESIDE GUY 12** [7]3-8-6 (58) T P Queally 10/1: 0-004035: Led centre till dist: flattered 2717.   hd 55
2387 **MIRASOL PRINCESS 25** [9]3-9-7 (73) D Holland 6/1: 00-00466: Chsd ldrs centre, onepcd fnl 1f.   hd 70
2400 **IMPERIUM 25** [6]3-9-7 (73) S Drowne 8/1: 0511307: Chsd ldrs centre, btn fnl 1f: jt top-weight.   ¾ 67
2649 **SCARLETT BREEZE 15** [4]3-7-12 (3oh) (47) J F McDonald(3) 12/1: 65-00058: Chsd ldrs, outpcd fnl 1f.   nk 43
2841 **SWEETEST REVENGE 7** [8]3-9-6 (72) A Daly 14/1: 4254-069: Stdd start, nvr a factor centre group.   ½ 64
2675 **ALCHERA 14** [5]3-8-12 bl (64) S Carson 11/2 FAV: 0-006440: 10th: Chsd ldrs centre, btn dist.   1¼ 52
2268 **SWORN TO SECRECY 30** [3]3-8-7 (59) R L Moore 14/1: 0000060: 11th: Al outpcd centre.   ½ 46
2372 **THE BUTTERFLY BOY 26** [10]3-8-3 (55) N De Souza(5) 14/1: 6-0300: 12th: Chsd ldrs centre, wknd 2f out. 11 12
12 Ran   Time 59.52 (1.22)   Owned: Miss Jacqueline Goodearl   Trained: Upper Lambourn

3037

8.00 Hh Associates Handicap Stakes 3yo+ 0-80 (D) [94]
£8093 £2490 £1245 **1m6f92y** **Good/Firm 38** **-18 Slow** Inside

2621 **TUNGSTEN STRIKE 16** [7] Mrs A J Perrett 3-8-0 (1ow) (66) Martin Dwyer 20/1: 400-01: ch g Smart Strike - Bathilde (Generous) Held up, prog to lead 2f out, pushed clr fnl 1f under hands-&-heels: mdn 4th on first of 3 juv starts (rtd 74), gelded since: 52,000gns half-brother to a 7f juv wnr: dam won over 10f: apprec this step up to 14f, 2m shld suit: acts on fast grnd & on a flat trk: unexposed over staying dists, can follow up. **79+**

2441 **LEVITATOR 23** [4] Sir Michael Stoute 3-8-3 (70) N Mackay(3) 7/2: 0-022: Keen & prom, styd on for 2nd fnl 1f, no ch with wnr: seems to stay 14f & acts on fast grnd: see 2441. *5* **72**

2912 **SAXE COBURG 5** [8] G A Ham 7-8-8 (60) J F McDonald(3) 8/1: 0330353: Held up, prog 2f out, kept on under press but not pace to chall: qck reapp: see 2156. *¾* **60**

2973 **GALLANT BOY 2** [6] P D Evans 5-9-3 t (69) F P Ferris(3) 14/1: 4005064: Held up, prog 2f out, no dngr. *shd* **69**

2673 **BUCKS 14** [1]7-10-0 (80) D Holland 13/8 FAV: 3021125: Prom, led 4f out till 2f out, no extra: well bckd, top-weight, clr of rem: prev in fine form, see 2673 & 2244 (12f). *shd* **80**

2146 **URSA MAJOR 35** [3]10-7-12 (2oh) (48) Lisa Jones(3) 25/1: 0000/-006: Chsd ldrs, wknd 2f out, eased. *23* **20**

2673 **MOSTARSIL 14** [2]6-9-4 p (70) R L Moore 3/1: 0634167: Led till 4f out, wknd & eased: tchd 4/1: something clrly amiss, much btr 2391. *15* **20**

7 Ran Time 3m 10.96 (8.16) Owned: Mr John Connolly Trained: Pulborough

3038

8.30 Platinum Security Maiden Stakes Fillies 3yo (D)
£5590 £1720 £860 **1m2f** **Good/Firm 38** **-13 Slow** Inside

2230 **ANNA PALLIDA 33** [6] P W Harris 3-8-11 (80) D Holland 7/2: 02231: Trkd ldrs, sltly hmpd & slipped 3f out, qcknd to lead dist, styd on strongly under hands-&-heels: nicely bckd, deserved win: eff at 10f, shld stay 12f: acts on gd & fast, prob handles gd/soft: acts on a flat or a stiff/gall trk: overdue win, see 1892 & 1719. **84**

AUTUMN WEALTH [15] Mrs A J Perrett 3-8-11 K Darley 5/1: 2: ch f Cadeaux Genereux - Prickwillow (Nureyev) Chsd ldrs, styd on fnl 1f under hands-and-heels, nrst fin on encouraging debut: 170,000gns purchase: eff at 10f on fast grnd, 12f will suit judged on this: sure to learn plenty from this & win similar. *2* **79+**

2453 **SUMMER SERENADE 23** [5] L M Cumani 3-8-11 L Dettori 6/4 FAV: 23: Prom, led 3f out till dist, kept on under hands-and-heels: well bckd: see 2453. *½* **78**

4479} **CASTAGNA 284** [1] H R A Cecil 3-8-11 W Ryan 16/1: 0-4: ch f Horse Chestnut - Thrilling Day (Groom Dancer) Held up, prog when short of room 3f out, kept on cl-home on reapp: unplcd on sole juv start: half-sister to juv wnr In Space: dam a smart miler: eff at 10f on fast grnd: sharper next time. *1½* **76**

WAIT FOR SPRING [9]3-8-11 R Havlin 25/1: 5: b f Seeking The Gold - Polish Spring (Polish Precedent) Chsd ldrs, short of room 3f out, onepcd fnl 1f on debut: eff at 10f on fast grnd, 12f shld suit. *1¼* **74**

2536 **WOMAN IN WHITE 19** [13]3-8-11 J Fortune 13/2: 026: Chsd ldrs, wknd fnl 1f: btr 2536 (gd grnd). *2½* **71**

NIOBES WAY [10]3-8-11 S Drowne 33/1: 7: b f Singspiel - Arietta's Way (Darshaan) Chsd ldrs, wknd fnl 1f on debut: mid-dist bred, with P Chamings. *¾* **70**

2678 **PERSIAN GENIE 14** [8]3-8-11 S Carson 50/1: 0-08: Chsd ldrs 1m, wknd on h'cap qual run. *2½* **67**

100 **GLIDING BY 224** [12]3-8-11 J Quinn 50/1: 00-9: Held up, nvr a factor on reapp/h'cap qual run. *2½* **64**

1810 **LADY TAVERNER 51** [3]3-8-11 Dane O'Neill 50/1: 00: 10th: Al towards rear: 7 wk abs. *1¾* **62**

2622 **SAYRIANNA 16** [11]3-8-11 T P Queally 50/1: 00: 11th: Chsd ldrs 1m, wknd. *1¾* **60**

Under My Skin [4]3-8-11 T J Murtagh 14/1:0 2410 **Trinity Fair 25** [2]3-8-11 I Mongan 33/1:0

13 Ran Time 2m 07.49 (5.19) Owned: Aboobaker Harris & Taylor Trained: Berkhamsted

3039

9.00 'book Now For Gala Night' Handicap Stakes 3yo+ 0-80 (D) [90]
£6955 £2140 £1070 **1m1f** **Good/Firm 38** **-11 Slow** Inside

2525 **MOMTIC 20** [11] W Jarvis 3-9-4 (80) K Darley 8/1: 1-330441: Trkd ldrs, rdn to le'nad ent fnl 1f, held on drvn out: apprec this rtn to 9f & deserved win: eff at 1m, has tried 10f & that trip shld suit: acts on gd & firm grnd, handles gd/soft: likes a flat or easy trk: see 2525 & 1141 (C/D). **90**

2634* **SPRING JIM 16** [2] J R Fanshawe 3-8-13 (75) J Murtagh 7/2 FAV: 450-412: Held up, prog when switched 1.5f out, fin strongly but just failed: nicely bckd: eff at 7/9f: continues in fine form, see 2634. *hd* **84**

2647 **BEST BEFORE 15** [3] P D Evans 4-9-8 (74) S Donohoe(7) 9/1: 2021333: Rear, prog when hmpd 2f out, switched & fin well, ch had gone: poss unlucky, must be gvn another ch: see 2647 & 2448. *2½* **78**

2759 **GIG HARBOR 11** [1] Miss E C Lavelle 5-10-0 (80) T P Queally 33/1: 1015604: Chsd ldrs, ev ch halfway till not qckn ins fnl 1f: top-weight: ddhtd for 4th: rtn to 12f will suit, as in 570 (AW). *dht* **83**

2378 **DESERT HAWK 26** [10] R Hannon 3-8-7 (69) R L Moore 12/1: 0054: Chsd ldrs, ev ch ent fnl 1f, sn no extra on h'cap bow: stays 9f on fast grnd, 10f shld suit: see 2378. *nk* **72**

2787 **JOOLS 10** [9]6-9-11 (77) D Holland 14/1: 5300446: Led till ent fnl 1f, no extra. *1¼* **78**

2880 **TERRAQUIN 6** [8]4-9-3 p (69) A Daly 20/1: 0505507: Chsd ldrs, onepcd fnl 1f: qck reapp. *¾* **69**

2401 **FREELOADER 25** [7]4-9-6 (72) E Ahern 7/1: 260-0438: Mid-div, hdwy on rail when hmpd fnl 2f, fin full of running: no luck today, see 2401. *nk* **71+**

2929 **KARAOKE 4** [5]4-9-1 (67) L Dettori 10/1: 5422009: Rear, prog to chase ldrs 2f out, btn fnl 1f. *¾* **65**

1723 **RESONATE 55** [4]6-9-6 (72) Dane O'Neill 9/1: 52006-40: 10th: Held up, prog on rails when hmpd 2f out, no room thr'out fnl 1f, fin on the bridle: 8 wk abs: no room at any stage & will do better. *nk* **69+**

1979 **STATEROOM 43** [15]6-9-6 bl (72) Lisa Jones(3) 12/1: 0154-530: 11th: Held up, prog when short of room 2f out, nvr a factor: 6 wk abs: see 1979. *1¼* **67**

2170 **CATCH THE FOX 35** [14]4-7-12 (8oh) (42) Lucy Russell(7) 25/1: 0-020040: 12th: Chsd ldrs 7f, wknd. *2½* **41**

2170 **MUST BE MAGIC 35** [6]7-8-6 vis (58) W Supple 12/1: 0-450000: 13th: Chsd ldrs 7f, wknd. *5* **41**

2694 **BLUE MARINER 13** [12]4-9-4 (70) B Doyle 14/1: 2/0-03220: 14th: Speed to halfway, sn btn: something amiss, prev consistent: see 2694 & 2401. *¾* **52**

2220 **LEARNED LAD 33** [13]6-8-1 (53) P Doe 25/1: 2500000: 15th: Al towards rear. *6* **26**

2799* **FIREWIRE 9** [16]6-8-13 (6ex) (65) S Sanders 6/1: 12000-10: 16th: Al bhd & fin last: btr 2799. *4* **32**

16 Ran Time 1m 54.48(4.48) Owned: Heath Keenan & Verrier Trained: Newmarket

Official Going GOOD/SOFT.

3040   6.25 Eprocurement Apprentice Handicap Stakes 3yo+ 0-70 (E)   [70]
£4027 £1239 £620   1m4f10y   Good/Soft 70   -07 Slow   Centre

2875 **MAN THE GATE** 7 [8] P D Cundell 5-8-13 (55) N Chalmers(3) 7/2: 2503621: Held up, prog to lead   61
dist, hung to far rail fnl 1f, drvn out: eff at 10/12f on firm, soft grnd & polytrack: handles a sharp/undul or gall
trk, likes Leicester: runs well for N Chalmers, see 2875 & 979.
2333 **GARSTON STAR** 28 [6] J S Moore 3-8-0 (55) Rory Moore(5) 10/1: 006-3122: Tried to make all,   2   60
collared entering fnl 1f, kept on but not pace of wnr: well clr rem: another consistent run from this in-form sort,
acts on firm & gd/soft grnd: see 2333 & 2019 (sell h'cap).
2869 **STOLEN HOURS** 7 [1] J Akehurst 4-9-4 (60) J P Guillambert 11/4: 0000223: Dwelt, chsd ldrs, ev ch   7   55
2f out, wknd fnl 1f: btr 2869 (fast grnd).
2988 **VALEUREUX** 2 [5] J Hetherton 6-8-10 (52) Natalia Gemelova(5) 2/1 FAV: 3002-324: Chsd ldr, wknd 2f   2   44
out: well bckd: qck reapp & not stay this longer 12f trip? see 2988 & 2794.
2673 **GENERAL GB** 15 [4]7-10-0 (70) Steven Harrison(7) 8/1: 0520005: Chsd ldrs 9f, wknd: top-weight.   ½   61
2856 **SMARTER CHARTER** 8 [3]11-7-12 (2oh) (38) Kristin Stubbs(1) 20/1: 0650456: Nvr nr ldrs.   1¾   29
1307 **HALF INCH** 77 [2]4-9-2 p (58) D Corby 16/1: 024-0407: Chsd ldrs till halfway, wknd: 4th in a nov   2   44
hdle 3 wks ago (rtd 100h, eff around 2m on gd & firm): see 1083 & 912.
7 Ran   Time 2m 44.13 (9.33)   Owned: Mr John G Morley   Trained: Compton

---

3041   6.55 Ehrm Maiden Auction Stakes 2yo (E)
£4066 £1251 £626   6f rnd   Good/Soft 70   -06 Slow   Outside

2646 **LADY LE QUESNE** 16 [6] A M Balding 2-8-6 S Drowne 9/4: 621: Made all, styd on strongly fnl 1f,   85
pushed out: well bckd: eff at 5/6f on firm & gd/soft: enjoyed switch to forcing tactics: see 2646.
2815 **ENCANTO** 13 [2] J S Moore 2-8-4 J F Egan 7/4 FAV: 06222: Nvr far away, ev ch when sltly short of   1¾   75
room 2f out, kept on fnl 1f but not pace of wnr: clr of rem: handles firm & gd/soft: prob flattered 2815.
2310 **GUINEA A MINUTE** 29 [4] M L W Bell 2-8-9 K Fallon 4/1: 03: ch f Raise A Grand - Repique (Sharpen   5   68
Up) Chsd ldrs, onepcd fnl 1.5f: 20,000gns Feb foal: half-brother to a couple of 5f wnrs: dam 5f scorer: faster
grnd may suit, again bhd today's wnr in 2310 (debut).
2109 **SASTRE** 38 [3] P M Phelan 2-8-9 N Chalmers(4) 40/1: 04: b f Bluebird - No Rehearsal (Baillamont)   1¼   65
Slowly away, chsd ldrs 4f, wknd: March foal, cost 20,000gns: sister to a winning sprinter in France, half-sister to
mid-dist wnr Jelani: dam a mid-dist wnr in France, sire a top-class sprinter: sellers will suit.
2618 **ASTEEM** 17 [1]2-8-9 A Nicholls 25/1: 05: b g Mark of Esteem - Amidst (Midyan) Keen in rear, nvr   2½   59
nr ldrs: 9,000gns April foal: half-brother to 7f wnr Aploy & 1m scorer Ago: dam a 6f winning juv.
1805 **MAURO** 52 [5]2-8-4 J Quinn 7/1: 4246: Sn outpcd, al bhd: 7 wk abs: btr 1466 (5f).   4   44
6 Ran   Time 1m 12.39 (4.59)   Owned: Coriolan Partnership V   Trained: Kingsclere

---

3042   7.25 Extended Finance Handicap Stakes 3yo+ 0-85 (D)   [80]
£8112 £2496 £1248   1m114y rnd   Good/Soft 70   -32 Slow   Inside

1423 **NIMELLO** 71 [7] A G Newcombe 8-9-9 (75) L Dettori 9/2: 21-00101: Made all, clr halfway, held on   83
well fnl 1f, rdn out: 10 wk abs: eff at 6f, suited by 7/9f: acts on firm, prefers gd/soft, hvy & loves
fibresand/W'hampton: gd weight-carrier, well h'capped on turf: runs well fresh, see 1219.
2848 **QUALITAIR WINGS** 8 [2] J Hetherton 5-9-5 (71) K Fallon 7/2: 26-30002: Rear, imprvd to chase wnr   1¼   75
1.5f out, kept on but nvr going to get there: tchd 9/2: see 1474.
2026 **MBOSI** 42 [6] M Johnston 3-9-8 (84) S Chin 13/2: 15-33: Chsd wnr, lost place halfway, rallied fnl   1   86
1f: 6 wk abs: not disgraced against his elders: see 2026.
2540 **MADAMOISELLE JONES** 20 [4] H S Howe 4-9-1 (67) S Drowne 8/1: 0-045164: Chsd ldrs, onepcd fnl 1.5f. 1¼   66
2809 **LOW CLOUD** 10 [9]4-9-10 vis (76) A Nicholls 5/1: 6035145: Slowly away, keen, some hdwy halfway,   15   53
btn 2f out & eased: top-weight: rcd much too keenly, btr 2514.
2440* **HOLLYWOOD HENRY** 24 [1]4-8-4 p (56) J Quinn 9/2 FAV: 00000-16: Chsd ldrs 6f, wknd: btr 2440 (fm).   2   29
6 Ran   Time 1m 50.53 (8.73)   Owned: Ms Gerardine P O'Reilly   Trained: Barnstaple

---

3043   7.55 Collaborative Planning Conditions Stakes 4yo+ (C)
£8932 £3388 £1694   1m2f18y   Good/Soft 70   -00 Slow   Inside

2762 **FRUHLINGSSTURM** 12 [3] M A Jarvis 4-9-4 (111) P Robinson 9/2: 35151-51: Rcd in 2nd, hdwy over 2f   115
out, led ins fnl 1f, all out to hold on nr fin: top-weight: tchd 6/1: wng form at 1m/12f on gd & hvy, acts on a
sharp/undul trk: gd weight-carrier: apprec drop in grade & v smart run, see 2762.
2022 **IMTIYAZ** 43 [2] Saeed bin Suroor 5-8-12 t (109) L Dettori 5/6 FAV: 10631-22: Led & clr over 5f   shd   108
out, hdd ins fnl 1f, rallied & only just btn: 6 wk abs, well bckd, clr of rem: smart & consistent, see 2022.
2453 **SHAMBAR** 24 [6] P R Chamings 5-8-12 R L Moore 66/1: 4/-353: Slowly away, handy over 2f out, kept   6   99
on over 1f out but not pace of first 2: career best run, see 2131.
1350 **BUSTAN** 75 [5] M P Tregoning 5-8-12 (107) R Hills 6/1: 442-3204: Handy, no impress over 2f out: 3   94
long abs: not handle gd/soft in race 1350, see 1139.
2556 **BONECRUSHER** 20 [1]5-8-12 (105) K Fallon 4/1: 4052055: Rear, nvr a factor.   9   80
785 **MANTEL MINI** 128 [4]5-8-7 P J F Egan 200/1: 06: b f Reprimand - Foretell (Tirol) Slowly away,   dist   40
rear, t.o.: long abs: well btn sole National Hunt start in 03/04 (bmpr): well btn both 02/03 starts (bmprs):
tried cheek pieces & v highly tried here: with B Pearce.
6 Ran   Time 2m 10.84 (7.04)   Owned: Mr Gary A Tanaka   Trained: Newmarket

---

EPSOM   THURSDAY 08.07.04   Lefthand, Very Sharp, Undulating Track

3044	8.25 Portals Handicap Stakes 3yo+ 0-75 (E)				[75]
	£4784 £1472 £736	1m2f118y	Good/Soft 70	-25 Slow Inside	

2620 **SCOTTISH RIVER** 17 [8] M D I Usher 5-10-0 (75) Hayley Turner(5) 9/2: 5614661: Slowly away, hdwy to lead over 2f out, rdn out ins fnl 1f: top-weight, bckd from 7/1: eff at 1m/10f on firm, soft & both AWs, poss handles hvy, any trk, likes a sharp one: gd weight-carrier: see 1650. .... **86**

2857 **JACARANDA** 8 [7] Mrs A L M King 4-9-6 (67) S Drowne 8/1: 24-05002: Rear, hdwy into 2nd over 1f out, not pace of wnr: clr of rem, op 6/1: eff btwn 7/10f on firm & gd/soft: see 2370. .... 2½ **73**

2589 **ICANNSHIFT** 19 [6] S Dow 4-8-8 (55) R L Moore 5/2 FAV: 3036303: Led till appr fnl 2f, no extra. 3½ **56**

2371 **MOUNT BENGER** 27 [2] R M Beckett 4-9-1 P (62) S Sanders 12/1: 3/000-604: Rear, hdwy over 2f out, hmpd ins fnl 2f, no ch after: first time cheek pieces: see 1006. .... 3½ **58**

2799 **ESPERANCE** 10 [1]4-7-13 (1ow) (45) J Quinn 6/1: 000-0055: Rear, hdwy 2f out, not pace to chall. 2½ **38**

2694 **MY GALLIANO** 14 [4]8-9-7 (68) K Fallon 7/2: 0216-036: Handy, fdd 2f out: op 5/2. .... shd **60**

2643 **CAL MAC** 16 [10]5-8-12 (59) M Henry 12/1: 34-00027: Rcd in 2nd, wknd 3f out: op 9/1. .... 4 **45**

2909 **LUNAR LEADER** 6 [3]4-7-12 (45) Natalia Gemelova(6) 25/1: 000000U: Chsd ldrs, fdd over 4f out, btn when stumbled & u.r. fnl 1f out: qck reapp: see 1286. .... **0**

8 Ran   Time 2m 13.37 (9.57)   Owned: Mr M D I Usher   Trained: Lambourn

3045	8.55 Cedar Open Accounts Handicap Stakes 3yo+ 0-80 (D)				[79]
	£5421 £1668 £834	6f rnd	Good/Soft 70	+11 Fast Outside	

2871 **JAYANJAY** 7 [3] Miss B Sanders 5-9-12 (77) S Sanders 4/1: 2-043431: Rear, hdwy 3f out, hard drvn ins fnl 1f to lead post: qck reapp, gd time: eff at 5/6f on firm, soft & both AWs, loves a sharp/undul trk: gd run after recent consistent plcd effs: see 149. .... **82**

2626 **GLENCOE SOLAS** 17 [9] S Kirk 4-9-7 (72) J F Egan 8/1: 4221532: Tried to make all, collared on line: acts on firm & gd/soft, prob handles soft: ran above winning form of 2232. .... shd **76**

2871 **LORD OF THE EAST** 7 [4] D Nicholls 5-9-9 (74) Alex Greaves 7/2: 3201323: Rcd in 2nd, kept on fnl 1f, btn under 1L: qck reapp: ran to winning form of 2466. .... ½ **76**

2872 **QUANTUM LEAP** 7 [5] S Dow 7-9-6 vis (71) R L Moore 8/1: 3166424: Chsd ldrs, onepcd ins fnl 1f. .... nk **72**

2070 **KINGSCROSS** 40 [8]6-9-13 (78) D Sweeney 5/2 FAV: 00-42105: Rear, hdwy 2f out, not pace to chall. 5 **67**

3000 **ATTORNEY** 2 [1]6-7-12 (3oh)vis (46) Hayley Turner(5) 20/1: 6650006: Rear, mod late gains: qck reapp. .... nk **37**

2838 **COMPTON BANKER** 9 [7]7-9-3 (68) D Nolan(3) 11/1: 15-06527: Slow away, hdwy 3f out, onepcd fnl 2f. .... ¾ **53**

956 **SOCIAL CONTRACT** 101 [10]7-7-12 (1oh) (48) Lisa Jones(3) 25/1: 0620008: Handy, wknd 2f out: abs. 2 **29**

2715* **FIREWORK** 13 [2]6-8-13 p (64) J Quinn 14/1: 0065019: Handy, rcd alone far side, no ch with stands side over 1f out: rider took wrong option. 3 **37**

2775 **TATWEER** 12 [6]4-8-5 vis (56) S Whitworth 16/1: 00-51000: 10th: Slowly away, nvr a factor. 1 **27**

10 Ran   Time 1m 11.38(3.58)   Owned: Mr Peter Crate   Trained: Epsom

FOLKESTONE   THURSDAY 08.07.04   Righthand, Sharpish, Undulating Track

Official Going Good/Soft

3046	2.10 European Breeders Fund Median Auction Maiden Stakes Div 1 2yo (F)				
	£3101 £886 £443	7f str	Good/Soft 71	-13 Slow Stands Side	

MONTGOMERYS ARCH 0 [1] P W Chapple Hyam 2-9-0 J Quinn 6/4 FAV: 1: b c Arch - Inny River (Seattle Slew) Trkd ldrs, qcknd to lead over 1f out, sn in command, readily: Jan foal, 20,000gns 2yo: half-brother to a 2yo US wnr, dam plcd in US: sire high-class dirt performer: eff at 7f, 1m shld suit: acts on gd/soft grnd & a sharp/undul trk: goes well fresh: potentially useful, should be followed. .... **92+**

2610 **LOTTIE DUNDASS** 18 [6] P W Harris 2-8-9 B Doyle 2/1: 52: ch f Polar Falcon - Sand Grouse (Arctic Tern) Cl-up & led 3f out till over 1f out, sn outpcd by wnr: op 7/4: March foal, 42,000gns purchase: half-sister to a dual 1m List wnr abroad, dam a 3yo French wnr: eff at 7f, gd: 1m: acts on gd/soft grnd & a sharp/undul trk. 2½ **75**

JAMAAROON 0 [7] R Hannon 2-9-0 R L Moore 10/1: 3: ch c Bachir - Kentmere (Galetto) Cl-up, outpcd 2f out, kept on ins last: op 12/1: 30,000gns March foal, half-brother to a 6f juv wnr, also a 13f 3yo scorer: dam a 1m juv wnr abroad: eff at 7f, apprec 1m+: acts on gd/soft grnd: type to prog over further. 1¾ **79**

2310 **BAZELLE** 29 [9] P W D'Arcy 2-8-9 Paul Eddery 33/1: 04: ch f Ashkalani - Dona Royale (Darshaan) Trkd ldrs, not pace of front pair fnl 2f: £35,000 March foal, half-sister to plcd performers abroad, dam dns as a 3yo: sire a top-class miler: likely to apprec 1m, imprvd from debut & h'caps could suit in time. 1½ **71**

MERCHANT 0 [8]2-9-0 J Mongan 8/1: 5: ch c Tagula - Easy Pop (Shernazar) Dwelt, trkd ldrs, np impress from over 1f out: 17,000gns 2yo, March foal: dam uncrd. 1½ **73**

2696 **MERRYMADCAP** 14 [3]2-9-0 D Sweeney 16/1: 056: Pushed along rear, no impress fnl 2f, op 20/1. .... 1¼ **70**

CHAIRMAN RICK 0 [2]2-9-0 N Pollard 7/1: 7: Held up in tch, outpcd fnl 2f, op 9/1. .... ½ **69**

2610 **SCISSORS** 18 [10]2-8-9 B Reilly(3) 40/1: 08: Led 4f, fdd. .... ½ **63**

RHAPSODY IN SILVER 0 [4]2-9-0 M Tebbutt 66/1: 9: Sn bhd, 'hanging throughout'. 7 **55**

2573 **IVORY WOLF** 19 [5]2-9-0 P S Carson 66/1: 000: 10th: Prom, struggling fnl 2f, t.o., cheek pieces. 25 **8**

10 Ran   Time 1m 30.09 (5.89)   Owned: Franconson Partners   Trained: Newmarket

3047	2.40 European Breeders Fund Median Auction Maiden Stakes Div 2 2yo (F)				
	£3101 £886 £443	7f str	Good/Soft 71	-08 Slow Stands Side	

2584 **SPACED** 19 [3] R Hannon 2-9-0 R L Moore 11/1: 061: b c Indian Rocket - Tolomena (Tolomeo) Led/dsptd lead, went on over 2f out, rdn out: op 14/1: 3,000gns April foal, half-brother to a 7f/1m juv wnr, dam plcd at 12f/2m as a 3yo: eff at 7f, looks sure to apprec 1m+ in time: prob handles fast grnd, imprvd on gd/soft today: likes a sharp/undul trk: clearly progressing & interesting for nurseries. **90**

2028 **SUNSET STRIP** 42 [4] M R Channon 2-9-0 C Catlin 4/5 FAV: 22: Led till over 2f out, not pace of wnr fnl 1f: nicely bckd, op 11/10: 6 wk abs: styd longer 7f trip, acts on fast & gd/soft grnd: see 2028. .... 1½ **85**

	FAIRMILE 0 [2] P W Harris 2-9-0 I Mongan 3/1: 3: b c Spectrum - Juno Marlowe (Danehill) Dwelt,				¾	84

FAIRMILE 0 [2] P W Harris 2-9-0 I Mongan 3/1: 3: b c Spectrum - Juno Marlowe (Danehill) Dwelt,   ¾   84
sn trkd ldrs towards centre, outpcd 2f out, but kept on ins last: op 2/1: March first foal, dam a 7f wnr: eff at
7f, relish 1m+: handles gd/soft: promising intro.
2676 MULBERRY WINE 15 [1] M Blanshard 2-8-9   D Sweeney 50/1: 64: b f Benny The Dip - Top Berry (High   2   75
Top) Handy & ch 2f out, edged right & sn no extra: mid-dist pedigree, dam 1m scorer: apprec further.
2310 MARIANIS 29 [7]2-8-9 S Carson 16/1: 405: Pushed along rear, mod prog, op 12/1.   3½   68
2603 ORPEN ANNIE 18 [8]2-8-9 J McAuley 14/1: 036: Cl-up, btn over 1f out: btr 2603.   ½   67
1739 COUNTRYWIDE SUN 55 [9]2-9-0 BL J P Guillambert(3) 33/1: 007: Mid-div, rdn/jumped right over 2f   4   64
out, wknd: has been gelded: abs, blnks & longer trip.
PRECIOUS SAMMI 0 [5]2-9-0 J F Egan 7/1: 8: Chsd ldrs till over 2f out.   2½   59
OLIVIA TWIST 0 [6]2-8-9 A Beech(3) 33/1: 9: Sn rdn, al rear.   ¾   53
9 Ran   Time 1m 29.7 (5.5)   Owned: De La Warr Racing   Trained: Marlborough

---

3048   3.15 Come Evening Racing On 22nd July Maiden Stakes 3yo   (D)
£3494 £1075 £538   **7f str**   **Good/Soft 71**   +04 Fast   Stands Side

2756 CORKY 12 [3] R Hannon 3-9-0   R L Moore 3/1: 431: Trkd ldr, led over 1f out & rdn clr,   79
decisively: op 2/1 on firm & fast grnd, imprvd here on gd/soft: see 2756, 2352.
VIOLET PARK 0 [9] B J Meehan 3-8-9   C Catlin 12/1: 2: Dwelt, rear, rdn & bhd halfway, styd on   5   67
strongly from over 1f out, nrst fin: dropped, op 16/1: half-sister to a multiple 6/10f wnr, dam a 7f 3yo scorer: eff
at 7f, likely to apprec 1m + on this evidence: penny drpd late on, expect improvement.
2352 DEUXIEME 28 [1] R Charlton 3-8-9   D Sweeney 4/7 FAV: 33: Led till over 1f out, stride shortened   2½   62
& wknd qckly ins last: well bckd at odds-on: much btr 2352 (fast).
CAZENOVE 92 [6] M G Quinlan 3-9-0   J F Egan 12/1: 04: Trkd ldrs halfway, no impress fnl 2f: 6   57
bckd at long odds, op 33/1: Brit bow, 3 mth abs, earlier well btn sole start in Italy.
2622 ARGENTUM 17 [2]3-9-0 J Quinn 33/1: 00-05: Pushed along & well bhd halfway, late gains under   5   49+
hand riding, no dngr: lightly rcd & unplcd '03 (rtd 74, debut): improve in mid-dist h'caps.
886 PRESTON HALL 110 [7]3-9-0 S Carson 66/1: 006: Chsd ldrs till lost place from 3f out, 4 mth abs.   5   41
2622 HOMEBRED STAR 17 [4]3-9-0 D Corby(7) 25/1: 07: Dwelt, chsd ldrs till 3f out, gelded.   3   36
4926} SIXTILSIX 254 [11]3-9-0 R Lappin 25/1: 60000-8: Cl-up, wknd qckly fnl 3f: reapp, new yard.   2   32
2756 PARADISE BREEZE 12 [5]3-8-9 Paul Eddery 50/1: 0-09: Pushed along & sn bhd, eased over 1f out.   3   22
428 TILL THERE WAS YOU 173 [10]3-8-9 A Beech(3) 66/1: 00: 10th: Cl-up 3f, sn bhd, abs, new yard.   5   14
1130 NATIVE TURK 87 [8]3-9-0 B W Ryan 25/1: 0-00: 11th: Sn rdn & bhd, t.o. in first time blnks, abs.   dist   19
11 Ran   Time 1m 28.88 (4.68)   Owned: Robert Whitworth & Jane Whitworth   Trained: Marlborough

---

3049   3.50 Ladies Evening On The 5th August Handicap Stakes 4yo+ 35-55 (F)   [58]
£2996 £856 £428   **2m93y**   **Good/Soft 71**   -47 Slow   Inside

2718 RIVER OF FIRE 13 [2] C N Kellett 6-8-0 (2oh)vis (30) Natalia Gemelova(7) 14/1: 3040001: Led after   40
3f, rdn clr 2f out & al holding rivals ins last: won this race last term off a 4lb higher mark: suited by 14f/2m on
firm, soft & fibresand: likes to force the pace & given a well judged ride under an improving mdget: see 1563.
2417* HIGH DRAMA 26 [11] P Bowen 7-8-6 (38) D Corby(1) 4/1: 06/520-12: Led 3f, trkd wnr, rdn & styd on,   5   40
al held fnl 2f: op 5/1: recent stks runner (p.u., nov chase): acts on firm & gd/soft grnd: see 2417.
2391 GALANDORA 26 [4] Dr J R J Naylor 4-9-6 (52) Lucy Russell(7) 12/1: 6101203: Rear, onepace fnl 2f.   1½   53
2937 TOM BELL 5 [13] J G M O'Shea 4-9-1 (47) P Mathers(7) 3/1 FAV: 5-204424: Trkd ldrs, no impress fnl 2f.   3½   45
2036 MR WHIZZ 42 [1]7-8-4 (36) D Kinsella 25/1: 4432205: Rear, late gains, nvr a factor: jumps fit   nk   33
(unplcd, rtd 82c, nov chase): cheek pieces omitted today: see 1643, 1332 & 442 (1m/10f).
2739 JAVA DAWN 12 [10]4-8-10 (42) J F Egan 20/1: 000-0036: Keen rear, eff 3f out, mod prog.   4   35
2417 HARIK 26 [12]10-8-11 bl t (43) R L Moore 8/1: 4206-627: Mid-div inner, btn over 1f out: recent jmps rnr.   nk   36
2908 REAL ESTATE 6 [16]10-9-2 (48) Hayley Turner(5) 33/1: 00//00/-008: Mid-div, no impress fnl 2f.   4   37
2718 WIZARD OF THE WEST 13 [8]4-9-3 (49) N Chalmers(5) 40/1: 3600-009: b g Wizard King - Rose Burton   6   32
(Lucky Wednesday) Cl-up till 4f out, sn btn: unplcd '03 (rtd 52a, mdn, first time blnks): AW mdn rnr-up late '02:
eff around 1m/9f on fibresand, best without blnks. 2 Nov'02 Wolv 9.3af 71a- D:
2856 PEAK PARK 8 [5]4-8-13 vis (45) Lisa Jones(5) 8/1: 360-0020: 10th: Trkd ldrs till 5f out, sn btn: btr 2956.   3½   25
2340 DALON 28 [3]5-9-0 bl (46) M Tebbutt 16/1: 1614-060: 11th: Keen in mid-div, btn 3f out: see 2340.   hd   26
2562 CIRCUS MAXIMUS 19 [9]7-9-4 bl (50) C Catlin 8/1: 5020-400: 12th: Rear & rdn early, nvr a factor.   2½   28
733 STOPWATCH 133 [15]9-8-0 (7oh)p (25) M Henry 50/1: 00/0-0050: 13th: Dwelt & al bhd: see 733.   19   0
978 El Hamra 100 [7]6-8-4 (36) A Daly 33/1:0   2577 Joely Green 19 [6]7-8-8 bl(40) I Mongan 14/1:0
15 Ran   Time 3m 49.51 (18.21)   Owned: Mr J E Titley   Trained: Burton-On-Trent

---

3050   4.25 Faversham Handicap Stakes 3yo+ 0-70 (E)   [66]
£3445 £1060 £530   **5f str**   **Good/Soft 71**   +05 Fast   Stands Side

2981 ENJOY THE BUZZ 3 [2] J M Bradley 5-8-9 (47) R L Moore 1/1 FAV: 4201021: Rear & sn pushed along,   54
hdwy for press over 1f out to lead well ins last, cmftbly: hvly bckd: eff at 5/7f on fast, gd/soft & fibresand.
2791 COLLEGE QUEEN 10 [1] S Gollings 6-9-12 bl (64) I Mongan 7/2: 0-065452: Led, rdn & hdd well ins   1½   65
last: likes this trk & forcing tactics, handles gd/soft, ideally suited by sound surface: see 1873.
2016 LAKE VERDI 43 [5] B Hanbury 5-9-2 t (54) W Ryan 3/1: 0006-043: Held up, eff from 2f out, not pace   ¾   53
to chall: 6 wk abs, op 4/1: handles firm, gd/soft & polytrack: see 2016 & 1806.
2559 URBAN CALM 19 [3] R M H Cowell 3-9-6 (63) M Henry 8/1: 42204: Chsd ldr, btn dist & eased: btr 2237.   7   45
2645 BAHAMIAN BELLE 16 [4]4-8-7 (45) J Quinn 20/1: 0000005: Keen trkg ldrs, btn over 1f out: see 1179.   4   17
5 Ran   Time 1m01.68 (3.28)   Owned: Miss F Fenley   Trained: Chepstow

FOLKESTONE

THURSDAY 08.07.04   Righthand, Sharpish, Undulating Track

3051   **5.00 Hythe Festival Handicap Stakes 3yo 0-70 (E)**   **[68]**
£4316 £1328 £664   **1m4f**   **Good/Soft 71**   **-52 Slow**   Inside

2998* **ELUSIVE DREAM** 2 [9] Sir Mark Prescott 3-9-13 (6ex) (67) S Sanders 4/6 FAV: 0000-11: Handy & led   **89+**
3f out, shaken up & readily pulled clr fnl 2f, val 7L+: well bckd at odds-on, qck reapp under a pen: suited by 12f,
get further: acts on fibresand & gd/soft, sharp/undul trks: gd weight-carrier: more success awaits, keep on side.
2528 **VICARIO** 21 [7] M L W Bell 3-9-7 (61) I Mongan 6/1: 00-51332: Mid-div, eff to chase wnr 2f out,   5   66
no impress: clr rem, consistent type who caught a tartar today: acts on fast & gd/soft grnd.
2014 **RINNEEN** 43 [1] R Hannon 3-8-9 vis (49) R L Moore 8/1: 00-0053: Trkd ldr halfway, no impress fnl 2f.   4   48
2642 **REGAL PERFORMER** 16 [8] S Kirk 3-9-4 (58) J F Egan 14/1: 0-002234: Trkd ldrs 3f out, no hdwy dist.   1   56
2366 **VARUNI** 27 [11]3-9-6 (60) Lisa Jones(3) 9/1: 0-102005: In tch, no impress fnl 2f: op 16/1: btr 1165.   1½   56
2834 **FIDDLES MUSIC** 9 [10]3-8-5 (45) C Catlin 33/1: 0-01456: Led 2f, lost place qckly 4f out: new yard.   16   21
2706 **WYOMING** 14 [5]3-9-5 (59) W Ryan 12/1: 00-3007: Held up, rdn & btn 2f out: flattered 1617 (7f).   ½   34
2345 **FRANKIES WINGS** 28 [2]3-9-6 BL (60) B Doyle 14/1: 0-0608: Dwelt, hard prog to lead after 2f, hdd   3½   31
3f out, wknd qckly: op 20/1, first time blnks: btr 1140.
2536 **BEE DEES LEGACY** 20 [3]3-9-5 BL (59) R Brisland 50/1: 0-0009: Al bhd: blnks.   11   17
2231 **HIGH VIEW** 34 [4]3-9-4 (58) J Quinn 14/1: 00000: 10th: ch c Distant View - Disco Doll (Diesis)   dist   0
Keen & held up, no ch halfway: no form.
10 Ran   Time 2m 46.23 (14.73)   Owned: Cheveley Park Stud   Trained: Newmarket

---

3052   **5.30 Folkestone Handicap Stakes Fillies 3yo+ 0-70 (E)**   **[69]**
£3504 £1078 £539   **1m1f149y rnd**   **Good/Soft 71**   **-45 Slow**   Inside

2910* **TOCCATA ARIA** 6 [14] J M Bradley 6-8-10 (6ex) (51) R L Moore 7/1: 03006-11: Trkd ldrs, led over 1f   56
out, drvn out: qck reapp: eff at 1m, now suited by 9.7f/sharp 11f on fast & gd/soft grnd, likes sharp trks.
2844 **HOLLY ROSE** 8 [2] D E Cantillon 5-8-11 p (52) Hayley Turner(5) 9/1: 0240442: Dwelt & held up, hdwy   ½   55
wide 4f out & chall dist, not pace of wnr when jinked left cl-home: acts on firm & gd/soft grnd: consistent type.
2979* **EMBER DAYS** 3 [5] J L Spearing 5-9-10 (6ex)p (65) S Carson 9/2 JT FAV: 0302313: Rear, styd on for   ¾   67
press, not reach ldrs: qck reapp: reportedly best delivered late as poss, tactics generally not suited to this trk.
2910 **CASTAIGNE** 6 [9] B W Duke 5-8-11 (52) R Havlin 16/1: 0-006044: Mid-div, short of room over 1f   1   52
out, kept on late, nrst fin: acts on fast, gd/soft & polytrack: see 101.
2710 **RABITATIT** 14 [12]3-8-11 (63) P Mathers(7) 14/1: 0-240255: Led/dsptd lead till over 1f out: see 2475.   1   61
2323 **MAXILLA** 29 [10]4-10-0 (69) A Hamblett(7) 10/1: 241-4056: Rear, late gains, no threat: see 1467.   ¾   66
2857 **MADAME MARIE** 8 [1]4-8-9 (50) Lisa Jones(3) 8/1: 3-002067: Dwelt, rear, eff wide, not pace to chall.   hd   46
2725 **LITTLETON ZEPHIR** 13 [11]5-8-7 (48) Joanna Badger 25/1: 2001508: Rear, short of room 3f out, no dngr.1½   41
2844 **JESSINCA** 8 [6]8-7-12 (39) D Kinsella 9/2 JT FAV: 0060329: Mid-div, hdwy 5f out, btn 2f out: btr 2844.   1   30
2624 **SUNSET MIRAGE** 17 [8]3-9-3 (69) S Sanders 11/1: 0-261060: 10th: Mid-div, btn over 1f out: btr 1953.   1½   57
2719 **LADY JEANNIE** 13 [4]7-8-2 (43) C Catlin 50/1: 0400/-000: 11th: Sn prom, wknd fnl 2f: see 2264.   hd   30
2678 **ON CLOUD NINE** 15 [3]3-9-0 (66) I Mongan 50/1: 2600: 12th: Rear, eff 3f out, no impress: h'cap bow.   7   41
1913 **HAVANTADOUBT** 47 [7]4-9-0 p (55) D Sweeney 16/1: 3000-000: 13th: Sn prom, wknd qckly 2f out: abs.   13   7
2868 **JADE STAR** 7 [13]4-8-10 p (51) Rachel Costello(7) 7/1: 1026440: 14th: Led till 5f out, wknd qckly, fnl 3f.   1   1
14 Ran   Time 2m 09.27(11.27)   Owned: Mr Terry Warner   Trained: Chepstow

---

WARWICK

THURSDAY 08.07.04   Lefthand, Sharp, Turning Track

Official Going GOOD

3053   **2.30 Dla Novice Auction Stakes 2yo (E)**
£3868 £1190 £595   **7f26y rnd**   **Good 52**   **-12 Slow**   Inside

2569 **IM SO LUCKY** 19 [3] M Johnston 2-8-6 J Ffrench 8/1: 01: b c Zilzal - City of Angels (Woodman)   86
Handy, hdwy to lead ins fnl 1f, drvn out: mdn unplcd earlier debut: March foal, cost 10,000gns: half-brother to a
1m 2yo wnr: dam unrcd, sire smart miler at 3: eff at 7f on gd: improved for debut.
2388 **GROUP CAPTAIN** 26 [1] S Kirk 2-8-6 J D Smith 9/4 J FAV: 542: Slowly away, sn handy, led just   shd   85
over 1f out, hdd/edged left ins fnl 1f, kept on, just held: clr rem: acts on fast & gd: win a mdn.
2553 **JUSTAQUESTION** 20 [2] I A Wood 2-8-13 F Norton 9/4 J FAV: 01103: Handy, not much room & switched3½   85
over 1f out, no impress fnl 1f: tchd 7/2, top-weight: closer with a clr run: see 1669 (6f).
2810 **YOUNG THOMAS** 10 [9] M L W Bell 2-8-6 M Fenton 16/1: 044: With ldr till definite advantage well   1¼   75
over 1f out, sn hdd, btn when not much room ins fnl 1f: see 2810.
     BLACKCOMB MOUNTAIN 0 [11]2-8-1 F P Ferris(3) 40/1: 5: b f Royal Anthem - Ski Racer (Ski Chief)   ¾   68
Rear, hdwy 3f out, kept on ins fnl 1f on debut: cost $25,000, April foal: dam 13f wnr.
1097* **TREAT ME WILD** 91 [6]2-8-5 R Smith 11/2: 16: Rear, hdwy over 1f out, not pace to chall: long   hd   71
abs: longer trip: btr 1097 (5f, gd/soft).
2682 **KAGGAMAGIC** 14 [5]2-8-6 Darren Williams 16/1: 547: In tch, no impress over 1f out: see 2297.   1½   69
2876 **SCALE THE HEIGHTS** 7 [4]2-8-12 Dean McKeown 12/1: 08: b g Spectrum - Decrescendo (Polish   7   61
Precedent) Slowly away, al bhd: op 9/1, qck reapp: mdn unplcd earlier debut: cost 30,000gns, Jan foal: half
brother to wnrs over 10f/2m.
2178 **DIXIE QUEEN** 35 [8]2-8-4 Dale Gibson 14/1: 509: Led till over 1f out, sn no extra.   ½   52
2584 **CHIN DANCER** 19 [10]2-8-1 A McCarthy 66/1: 00: 10th: Handy, wknd over 3f out.   6   37
1911 **AMALGAM** 47 [1]2-8-1 J F McDonald(3) 50/1: 000: 11th: Slowly away, al bhd: 7 wk abs.   2   33
11 Ran   Time 1m 26.92 (4.52)   Owned: Mrs S J Brookhouse   Trained: Middleham

3054 **3.05 Barratt Mercia Handicap Stakes Fillies 3yo+ 0-70 (E)** **[70]**
£4095 £1260 £630 **5f110y rnd** **Good 52** **Inapplicable** Inside

1730 **COME AWAY WITH ME 55** [15] M A Buckley 4-8-13 (55) V Slattery 4/1 FAV: 012-21: Al handy, hdwy to lead over 1f out, rdn out ins fnl 1f: 8 wk abs: eff at 5.5/7f, has tried 1m: acts on fast, gd & fibresand, sharp/turning or easy trks: imprvd on gd reapp eff: see 1730. **63**
2626 **BOAVISTA 17** [12] P D Evans 4-9-2 (58) S Donohoe(7) 11/1: 2210002: Slowly away in rear, hdwy 2f out, ev ch ins fnl 1f, kept on: back to form: see 2034. *hd* **65**
2648 **AMELIA 16** [14] W M Brisbourne 6-9-1 (57) B Swarbrick(5) 5/1: 3013253: Keen in tch, hdwy 2f out, ev ch over 1f out, sn onepcd: ran to winning form of 1465. *1½* **59**
2975 **TENDER 3** [8] Mrs Stef Liddiard 4-8-9 p (51) S W Kelly 10/1: 0050004: Dsptd lead, ev ch over 1f out, no impress ins fnl 1f: qck reapp: see 1096. *1¾* **48**
2512 **RED LEICESTER 21** [9]4-8-9 vis (51) Dean McKeown 12/1: 3051605: Led till over 1f out, no extra ins last. *nk* **47**
2429 **BETTYS PRIDE 25** [13]5-8-11 (53) Darren Williams 5/1: 00-04066: Rear, hdwy 2f out, onepcd fnl 1f. *¾* **47**
2775 **LE MERIDIEN 12** [3]6-8-9 vis (51) R Ffrench 14/1: 000-5007: Mid-div, not much room/bmpd after 1f, no impress fnl 1f: see 2429. *¾* **43**
2702 **TRAVELLERS JOY 14** [7]4-7-12 (8oh) (32) J F McDonald(3) 14/1: 0306068: Slowly away, nvr a factor. *¾* **30**
2508 **BLONDE EN BLONDE 21** [4]4-8-11 bl (53) J Bramhill 10/1: 0330039: In tch, bmpd after 1f, sn bhd. *1¼* **39**
2855 **BAD INTENTIONS 8** [2]4-10-0 (70) Saleem Golam(7) 25/1: 6500-600: 10th: In tch, bmpd after 1f, sn rear. *nk* **55**
2619 **WHISTFUL 17** [19]3-9-7 (69) M Fenton 8/1: 42-30350: 11th: Mid-div, no impress over 2f out. *7* **33**
11 Ran Time 1m 7.34 () Owned: Mr C C Buckley Trained: Stamford

3055 **3.40 Churchill Office Solutions Selling Stakes 3yo (G)**
£3136 £896 £448 **1m2f188y** **Good 52** **+08 Fast** Inside

2979 **OKTIS MORILIOUS 3** [2] A W Carroll 3-9-4 (48) L Treadwell(7) 5/2 J FAV: 3426251: Handy, hdwy to lead over 1f out, rdn out ins fnl 1f: tchd 9/2, qck reapp: eff at 10/11f on firm, gd & polytrack: sharp or sharp/turning trks: made most of a drop in grade: see 831. **55**
2664 **WALTZING BEAU 15** [3] B G Powell 3-8-13 (53) G Baker 5/1: 0-200002: Rcd in 2nd, ev ch over 1f out, not pace of wnr: clr of rem: stays 9.4/11f on gd & fibresand: see 438. *1½* **48**
2790 **DEFANA 10** [1] M Dods 3-8-13 (54) L Enstone(3) 5/2 J FAV: 0653-533: Handy, onepcd from 2f out. *3½* **43**
2798 **CLOUDINGSWELL 10** [4] D L Williams 3-8-8 VIS (57) N De Souza(5) 13/2: 06-06644: Led till over 1f out, no extra ins fnl 1f: tried a visor: see 1528. *¾* **37**
2065 **COME WHAT JULY 40** [10]3-9-4 bl (60) C Lowther 5/1: 2566035: Rear, hdwy 3f out, wknd fnl 1f. *17* **21**
2924 **OSLA 5** [9]3-8-8 R Thomas(5) 40/1: 00006: Bhd, nvr nr ldrs: qck reapp: see 2924. *5* **3**
759 **SAINT ZITA 131** [5]3-8-8 BL J F McDonald(3) 20/1: 007: b f Desert Sun - Chatelsong (Seattle Song) Slowly away & keen in rear, nvr a factor: op 11/1, long abs: mdn unplcd prev: tried blnks here: with B Meehan. *8* **0**
2152 **BARHOLM CHARLIE 36** [6]3-8-13 V Slattery 40/1: 008: b g Atraf - Lady H (Never So Bold) Keen early, in tch, t.o. from 4f out: mdn unplcd prev: with M Buckley. *14* **0**
8 Ran Time 2m 21.13 (4.93) Owned: Mr Dennis Deacon Trained: Alcester

3056 **4.15 Bryant Homes Handicap Stakes 4yo+ 35-55 (F)** **[61]**
£3430 £980 £490 **1m4f134y** **Good 52** **-02 Slow** Inside

2135 **DANEBANK 37** [9] J Mackie 4-9-0 (47) Dale Gibson 8/1: 4600-051: Rcd in 2nd, hdwy to lead well over 1f out, drvn out ins fnl 1f: op 25/1: stays a sharp 12/12.5f on firm & gd, sharp/undul or turning trks: imprvd for a step up in trip & first win. 2135. **55**
2892 **RED RIVER REBEL 6** [2] J R Norton 6-9-4 (51) Darren Williams 9/4 FAV: 40-04022: Led till well over 1f out, still ev ch ins fnl 1f, kept on: nicely bckd tho' op 7/4, qck reapp: likes Beverley: see 1830. *½* **57**
2857 **BOJANGLES 8** [7] R Brotherton 5-9-1 (48) D Nolan(3) 11/2: 1303453: Rear, hdwy over 1f out, kept on ins fnl 1f: stays 12.5f: see 2725, ran to winning form of 1334. *¾* **53**
2850* **SOVEREIGN STATE 8** [4] D W Thompson 7-9-0 (6ex)p (47) F Norton 9/1: 40/000/-14: Handy, outpcd over 2f out, kept on ins fnl 1f: op 6/1: ran to winning form of 2850. *½* **51**
2718 **MAKE MY HAY 13** [8]5-9-2 (49) B Swarbrick(5) 11/2: 2-361255: Mid-div, outpcd 3f out, kept on fnl 1f. *nk* **51**
2080 **BOING BOING 40** [12]4-9-7 (54) J F McDonald(3) 20/1: 05001-06: b g King's Theatre - Limerick Princess (Polish Patriot) Handy, no impress over 1f out: 6 wk abs: won fnl '03 start (seller, with J Hills): mdn unplcd in '02 (rtd 67a): eff at 7f, stays 1m: acts on fast, stiff/gall trk: has tried a visor, btr without. *6* **48**
1 Sep'03 Leic 7.0g/f 58-(56) G:
2844* **OUR DESTINY 8** [6]6-9-8 (55) L Treadwell(7) 8/1: 4310417: Bhd, nvr nr ldrs: btr 2844. *1¼* **47**
2601 **MILK AND SULTANA 18** [5]4-9-4 (51) R Smith 25/1: 000-0608: Mid-div, lost place & btn over 3f out. *½* **42**
2718 **AFRICAN DAWN 13** [11]6-9-3 t (50) F P Ferris(3) 14/1: 4022-609: In tch, no impress over 1f out. *½* **40**
1753 **MIGRATION 54** [10]8-9-3 (50) L Vickers 25/1: 62////4-000: 10th: In tch, rcd wide bend bef straight, sn wknd: 8 wk abs: now with Mrs S Lamyman: see 1753. *5* **32**
4809+**DENISE BEST 262** [1]6-9-4 (51) V Slattery 16/1: 30/0501-0: 11th: ch f Goldmark - Titchwell Lass (Lead On Time) Slowly away, al bhd: reapp: won fnl '03 start for M Johnston in '03 (h'cap, earlier with Miss K George): rnr-up 1 of 5 '02 starts (fills h'cap): eff btwn 1m/12f on fast, soft & fibresand: stiff/undul trk: has tried blnks & cheek pieces: 1 Oct'03 Pont 10.0g/f 54-45 E: 2 May'02 Leic 11.8g/s 36-35 E: *10* **18**
2856 **FREE STYLE 8** [3]4-9-1 (48) G Baker 25/1: 5204500: 12th: Al bhd: see 1373. *12* **0**
2850 **ULTRA MARINE 8** [13]4-9-3 (50) L Fletcher(3) 40/1: 0004-000: 13th: Bhd, nvr a factor: see 2548. *3½* **0**
13 Ran Time 2m 46.13 (6.83) Owned: Ms L A Machin Trained: Church Broughton

3057 **4.50 Three A's Pertemps Handicap Stakes 3yo+ 0-75 (E)** **[73]**
£4349 £1338 £669 **2m39y** **Good 52** **-11 Slow** Inside

2908 **MOONSHINE BEACH 6** [8] P W Hiatt 6-8-9 (54) Darren Williams 11/4: 63654P1: Rcd in 2nd till led over 8f out, rdn clr over 3f out, eased ins fnl 1f, cmftbly, val 5L+: op 9/2, qck reapp: stays 2m/2m2f well on fast, gd & polytrack, sharp/turning or a gall trk: given a gd ride: made up for misfortune in 2908, see 1087. **71**
2908* **DARN GOOD 6** [5] R Hannon 3-8-6 (6ex)bl (70) J F McDonald(3) 5/2 FAV: 3060112: Bhd, hdwy over 6f *1* **81**

out, kept on fnl 1f but not reach wnr: qck reapp, well clr of rem: remains in gd form: acts on firm, gd & polytrack.
2651 **BEECHY BANK 16** [2] Mrs Mary Hambro 6-9-6 (65) V Slattery 12/1: 431-0053: Rear, hdwy over 6f out,   **10** **66**
no impress over 1f out: not stay 2m? see 342.
2035 **HENRY ISLAND 42** [7] Mrs A J Bowlby 11-9-6 (65) F Norton 7/2: 4443-504: ch g Sharp Victor -   **6** **60**
Monterana (Sallust) Handy, hdwy into 2nd over 7f out, no impress over 1f out: 6 wk abs: won 3 of 14 '03 starts
(h'caps): won a sell h'cap in '02: suited by 14f/2m3f on firm, soft & fibresand, loves Warwick: has gone well
fresh: gd weight-carrier: veteran.
1 Aug'03 Warw 16.2fm 73-64 E: 1 Jul'03 Warw 15.0fm 64-56 E: 1 Jun'03 Warw 19.1g/f 58-49 E:
2 Jun'03 Bath 17.2fm 49-47 E: 2 Jun'02 Warw 16.1gd 60-58 F: 1 Jun'02 Nott 14gd 58-52 G:
1 Nov'01 Muss 12gd 63-57 E: 2 Feb'01 Sout 12af 74a-71 E: 1 Feb'01 Sout 12af 71a- E:
2621 **CHANFRON 17** [3]3-7-12 (4oh) (58) A McCarthy 8/1: 0360-055: Handy, wknd 2f out: see 2134.   **7** **50**
2137 **THREE EAGLES 752** [4]7-7-12 (12oh)bl (31) B Swarbrick(5) 11/1: 50000/6/-6: ch g Eagle Eyed -   **nk** **30**
Tertiary (Vaguely Noble) Led till over 8f out, no extra 7f out: op 20/1: jumps fit (h'cap chase rnr-up in 04/05,
rtd 115c, eff btwn 2m4f/3m on firm & gd/soft, handles hvy, any trk, visor): missed '03: 6th sole '02 start (h'cap,
rtd 22, with A Bailey): eff around a sharp 2m on fast: eff with/without blnks: now with M Scudamore.
1 May'01 Warw 16.1g/f 40-37 E:
1109 **LILLEBROR 89** [6]6-9-3 (62) S W Kelly 12/1: 40000-07: b c Top Waltz - Lady Soliciti (Solicitor)   **1½** **47**
Bhd, nvr a factor: op 9/1, long abs: h'cap & class/cond stks unplcd in '03 (rtd 87): ex-German, won 2 h'caps in
'02 (11 & 12f, gd): eff btwn 11/12f on gd.
7 Ran   Time 3m 37.58 (10.08)   Owned: Mr Ken Read   Trained: Banbury

3058   **5.20 Hall Bros Handicap Stakes 3yo 0-70 (E)**   **[76]**
£3981 £1225 £613   **1m22y rnd**   **Good 52**   **+04 Fast**   Inside

2371 **HAZEWIND 27** [15] P D Evans 3-8-9 t (57) F P Ferris(3) 9/2: 0000251: Dsptd lead, led 1f out, kept   **65**
on ins fnl 1f: bckd from 15/2: eff at 1m, stays 10f: acts on fast, gd & polytrack, sharp/turning trk.
2955 **THREE WELSHMEN 4** [13] B R Millman 3-8-7 P (55) S W Kelly 12/1: 5130002: Led to 1f out, kept on   **hd** **62**
ins fnl 1f: qck reapp: handles gd, soft & polytrack: tried cheek pieces: just below winning form of 1529.
2701 **GABANA 14** [11] C F Wall 3-9-3 (65) G Baker 9/2: 3-060323: Rear, hdwy over 1f out, kept on: clr rem.   **nk** **71**
2716 **IPHIGENIA 13** [16] P W Hiatt 3-9-3 (60) P Makin(5) 9/1: 00-05024: Rear, hdwy 1f out, no pace to chall.   **4** **63**
2904 **BLUE DAZE 6** [7]3-9-6 BL (68) R Smith 8/1: 01-00555: Handy, no impress over 1f out: blnks.   **4** **58**
2794 **GIVEN A CHANCE 10** [2]3-7-12 (46) S Righton 12/1: 5342606: Handy, no impress over 1f out.   **hd** **35**
3931} **TEXT 315** [12]3-9-1 (63) F Norton 20/1: 6320-7: b g Atraf - Idle Chat (Assert) Rear, nvr nr ldrs   **5** **42**
on reapp: rnr-up 1 of 4 '03 starts (mdn, with J White): stays 5f, bred to relish further: acts on polytrack: has
tried blnks: now with Mrs S Liddiard.   2 Jul'03 Brig 6.0fm 64- E:
2613 **SON OF THUNDER 17** [4]3-8-9 (57) L Enstone(3) 3/1 FAV: 00-61628: Rear, nvr nr ldrs.   **shd** **35**
2619 **ROCKLEY BAY 17** [10]3-8-10 BL (58) M Fenton 25/1: 054-0009: Bhd, nvr a factor in first time blnks.   **10** **16**
2133 **KINGS ROCK 37** [3]3-8-10 (58) Donna Caldwell(7) 10/1: 2600630: 10th: Al bhd.   **3½** **9**
2617 **SNOW JOKE 17** [8]3-8-5 (53) B Swarbrick(5) 16/1: 00-04000: 11th: Rear, hmpd over 3f out, t.o..   **dist** **0**
843 **TONTO 116** [6]3-9-6 p (68) Saleem Golam(7) 22/1: 00-03260F: Rear, broke leg & fell over 3f out, sadly died.   **0**
2199 **DON ARGENTO 35** [5]3-7-12 (6oh) (40) D Fox(5) 33/1: 000-000U: Slow away, rear, hmpd & u.r. over 3f out.   **0**
13 Ran   Time 1m 40.65(3.85)   Owned: Waterline Racing Club   Trained: Abergavenny

Official Going GOOD/SOFT.

3059   **1.20 Venture Lifestyle Photography Handicap Stakes 3yo 0-100 (C)**   **[105]**
£13884 £4272 £2136   **1m str**   **Good/Firm 28**   **+10 Fast**   Far Side

2352+ **KEHAAR 28** [1] M A Magnusson 3-8-9 (86) E Ahern 10/1: 11: In tch far side, hdwy 2f out, styd on   **97**
strongly ins last, led cl-home, drvn out: fast time: apprec step up to 1m & acts on fast grnd & a gall trk:
useful, progressive, won this in a gd time, lightly rcd & plenty more to come: see 2352.
2640* **MISTER MONET 370** [8] M Johnston 3-9-1 (92) K Dalgleish 12/1: 31-2: b c Peintre Celebre - Breyani   **shd** **102**
(Commanche Run) Overall ldr far side, clr dist, rdn & collared cl-home: won 2nd of 2 '03 starts (mdn): eff at 7f,
stays a stiff 1m on fast & gd grnd, gall trks: lightly rcd, useful & v progressive.
1 Jul'03 Sand 7.1gd 88- D:
2365 **APERITIF 27** [4] W J Haggas 3-7-12 (2oh) (73) N Mackay(3) 14/1: 663-043: Early to post, hld up far   **1¾** **81$**
side, styd on late, nrst fin: poss fm: prob not straightforward but plenty of ability.
2521 **RESPLENDENT ONE 21** [9] T G Mills 3-9-7 (98) J Murtagh 50/1: 01-604: Keen, chsd ldr far side, eff   **1¼** **101**
well over 1f out, sn no extra: right back to form: see 2069.
2521 **ALSHAWAMEQ 21** [7]3-8-9 (86) R Hills 11/1: 615-3105: Bhd far side, some late gains, nvr dngrs: **3** **83**
see 2521, 2247.
1931 **REHEARSAL 47** [10]3-9-5 (96) J Fortune 12/2: 2156: Keen far side, cl-up till wknd dist: nicely bckd.   **1¼** **90**
2521 **CREDIT 21** [6]3-8-10 (87) K Fallon 14/1: 33107: In tch far side, wknd dist: btr 1763 (mdn).   **1** **79**
2521 **STATE DILEMMA 21** [2]3-9-3 (94) M Hills 14/1: 314-5108: Nvr a factor far side: btr 1665 (mdn, sft).   **1½** **83**
2247 **SECRETARY GENERAL 33** [11]3-8-11 (88) K Darley 16/1: 41-02059: Cl-up stands side, no ch with far   **nk** **76**
side group: best to forgive this: see 1919, 1741.
1930 **SWEET INDULGENCE 47** [12]3-8-7 (84) K McEvoy 10/1: 13-00: 10th: Keen stands side, no ch with far   **½** **71**
side group over 1f out: abs, see 1930.
2491 **QASIRAH 22** [13]3-9-4 bl (95) P Robinson 16/1: 20-05360: 11th: Al bhd stands side: btr 2491.   **½** **81**
2212 **TARUSKIN 34** [5]3-8-8 (85) D Holland 25/1: 31-31300: 12th: Al bhd far side: btr 1370.   **shd** **70**
2740 **PRINCIPAL WITNESS 12** [3]3-8-3 (80) Martin Dwyer 66/1: 042050: 13th: Handy far side, wknd dist.   **shd** **64**
4205} **HUNTING LODGE 300** [14]3-9-5 (96) T P Queally 25/1: 110-0: 14th: ch c Grand Lodge - Vijaya (Lear   **3½** **73**
Fan) Al bhd stands side: won 2 of 3 '03 starts (nov stks): stays 1m on fast & gd grnd, gall trks: has run well
fresh & in a visor.   1 Aug'03 Nott 8.2g/f 98- D: 1 Apr'03 Newm 5gd 93- C:
2773* **MAJORCA 12** [16]3-8-10 (87) L Dettori 4/1 FAV: 0-324110: 15th: Led stands side till wknd 2f out: **¾** **62**
nicely bckd: showed much more 2773 (prom).
2903+ **PRIMUS INTER PARES 6** [17]3-9-9 (5ex) (100) Alex Greaves 7/1: 312-10: 16th: Handy trav well stands   **nk** **74**
side, no ch with far side group fnl 2f: qck reapp, showed much more 2903: now with D Nicholls.
16 Ran   Time 1m 38.65 (1.45)   Owned: East Wind Racing Ltd   Trained: Upper Lambourn

NEWMARKET THURSDAY 08.07.04 Righthand, Stiff Galloping Track

3060 1.50 Gr3 Weatherbys Superlative Stakes 2yo (A)
£23200 £8800 £4400 7f str Good/Firm 28 -09 Slow Far Side

2221* **DUBAWI 34** [12] Saeed bin Suroor 2-8-11 L Dettori 15/8 FAV: 11: Hld up, hdwy well over 1f out, styd on to lead ins last, rdn out: bckd: eff at 6f, relished step up to 7f & 1m+ suit: acts on fast & gd, prob any trk: potentially high-class & type to prog with racing/stepped up in trip, win plenty more Gr races. **107+**
1848* **HENRIK 50** [9] M R Channon 2-8-11 T E Durcan 14/1: 12: Handy, hdwy to lead over 1f out, kept on till collared cl-home, just btn: 7 wk abs: fine run stepped up in class & stays 7f well: win a List/Gr 3: see 1848. *½* **105**
2578 **WILKO 19** [1] J Noseda 2-8-11 E Ahern 11/1: 30133: Held up, hdwy 2f out, kept on ins last, not btn far: another useful eff stepped up in class: looks sure to apprec 1m & shld find another stks/List. *nk* **104**
2594* **FOX 19** [11] C E Brittain 2-8-11 D Holland 10/1: 214: Slow away, held up, hdwy over 1f out, kept on, no dngr: plenty to like about this stepped up in class: shld be plcd to win more race & apprec 1m. *1½* **101**
1687* **PIVOTAL FLAME 57** [3]2-8-11 S Sanders 11/2: 15: Held up, hdwy well over 1f out, onepace: 8 wk abs: stays 7f on fast & gd/soft: win again with an ease in class: see 1687. *1½* **98**
2578 **HEARTHSTEAD WINGS 19** [6]2-8-11 J Fanning 14/1: 146: Handy, led 2f out till dist, no extra. *¾* **96**
2597* **COUNTRY RAMBLER 18** [5]2-8-11 R Hughes 10/1: 017: Keen handy, eff & hmpd 2f out, onepace. *½* **95**
ROWAN TREE 12 [7]2-8-11 J P Spencer 7/1: 18: b c Singspiel - Dashing Water (Dashing Blade) In tch, no impress fnl 2f: nicely bckd: March foal, cost 200,000gns: half-brother to a 10/12f wnr: dam 7f juv scorer: recent Curragh mdn wnr: eff at 6f, shld stay 7f+, acts on gd grnd: prob capable of btr. *nk* **94**
1934* **DESTINATE 47** [2]2-8-11 P Dobbs 20/1: 019: Held up, switched left over 1f out, nvr dngrs: joc received a 2-day careless riding ban: 7 wk abs: see 1934. *shd* **93**
2774* **JOHN FORBES 12** [4]2-8-11 R Winston 50/1: 010: 10th: In tch, hmpd & lost place 2f out, no dngr. *2* **89**
2388* **JALAMID 26** [10]2-8-11 t R Hills 16/1: 10: 11th: Led over 2f out, sn hdd & wknd: see 2388 (mdn). *3½* **82**
2382* **AL QUDRA 27** [8]2-8-11 J Fortune 50/1: 510: 12th: Keen, led till 2f out, wkng when hmpd dist. *11* **60**
12 Ran Time 1m 26.48 (2.58) Owned: Godolphin Trained: Newmarket

3061 2.20 Ladbrokes Bunbury Cup Heritage Handicap 3yo+ 0-105 (B) **[105]**
£45500 £14000 £7000 7f str Good/Firm 28 -05 Slow Far Side

2777+ **MATERIAL WITNESS 11** [6] W R Muir 7-9-3 (5ex) (94) Martin Dwyer 25/1: 0020111: Made all far side, styd on gamely for press to hold on ins last: well suited by 7f, stays 1m: acts on firm, soft & polytrack, any trk: loves to dominate: v useful, career best run on 53rd start: see 2777. **102**
2765 **COURT MASTERPIECE 12** [5] E A L Dunlop 4-10-0 (105) K Fallon 10/1: 301-3542: Dwelt, held up, hdwy & short of room 2f out till 1f out, styd on strongly ins last, just failed: lkd unlucky: nice turn of foot from rear & an excellent run under a big weight, win another List in this form: see 1811. *shd* **112+**
2581 **GREENSLADES 19** [10] P J Makin 5-9-4 (95) S Sanders 8/1 JT FAV: 05-44203: In tch, hdwy well over 1f out, styd on well till no extra just ins last: fine run on return to 7f: see 1926, 1151. *1½* **99**
2489 **EL COTO 22** [17] B A McMahon 4-9-9 BL (100) L Dettori 14/1: 1550004: Bhd stands side, gd hdwy over 1f out, fin well, no ch with far side group: caught the eye on unfav'd side & clearly enjoyed first time blnks: useful, capable of further success if headgear works next time: see 1231. *nk* **103+**
4977} **GRIZEDALE 250** [16]5-9-3 t (94) R Hughes 25/1: 010020-5: ch g Lake Coniston - Zabeta (Diesis) Held up far side, hdwy well over 1f out, onepace ins last on reapp: '03 h'cap wnr: rnr-up in this race back in '02 for E Dunlop: stays 1m, suited by 7f on firm or hvy grnd, any trk: suited by a t-strap & a gd weight-carrier: useful, fine return. 2 Sep'03 Asco 7fm 95-92 B: 1 May'03 Good 7g/f 97-87 C: 2 Jul'02 Newm 7g/s 95-91 B: 2 May'02 Newm 7g/f 92-89 C: 1 Jul'01 Newm 6g/f 87- E: *¾* **95**
2581 **ROYAL STORM 19** [9]5-9-8 (99) M J Kinane 9/1: 126-0146: Chsd far side ldr till no extra 1f out. *shd* **99**
2489 **AMANDUS 22** [12]4-9-4 (95) T P Queally 14/1: 14-00247: In tch far side, wknd dist: see 2489. *hd* **94**
2521 **MAKFOOL 21** [1]3-8-13 (98) T E Durcan 14/1: 3402108: Handy far side, wknd fnl 1f: btr 2212. *2½* **92**
2558 **MASTER ROBBIE 20** [11]5-9-0 (91) S Hitchcott(3) 33/1: 0001609: Slow away, bhd far side, some late gains, no dngr: btr up with the pace: see 2090, 1926. *½* **84**
2558 **MAGHANIM 20** [14]4-9-7 (98) R Hills 12/1: 10/0-5320: 10th: Led stands side group, wknd 2f out. *hd* **90**
2758* **ZILCH 12** [2]6-9-7 (98) R Mullen 17/2: 2214010: 11th: Slow away, in tch halfway, wknd 2f out. *hd* **89**
2489 **VICIOUS KNIGHT 22** [3]6-9-7 (98) Alex Greaves 33/1: 40/15-000: 12th: With ldrs, wknd over 1f out. *½* **88**
2765 **KINGS POINT 12** [15]3-9-1 (100) Dane O'Neill 25/1: 5053040: 13th: Handy stands side, wknd 2f out. *1½* **87**
1490 **CHOOKIE HEITON 67** [13]6-9-11 (102) R Winston 50/1: 0010-450: 14th: In tch far side, wknd dist. *1½* **86**
2777 **ATAVUS 11** [7]7-9-0 (91) J Mackay 33/1: 04-06050: 15th: Handy far side, wknd qckly fnl 1f: see 1926. *hd* **74**
2581 **CARDINAL VENTURE 19** [4]6-9-4 (95) N Callan 8/1 JT FAV: 2000100: 16th: Handy far side, wknd & eased over 1f out: see 2581, 2187. *1¾* **74**
1926 **GOLDEN CHALICE 47** [8]5-9-0 (91) J Murtagh 10/1: 5600100: 17th: In tch, eff over 2f out, sn wknd & eased: 7 wk abs: best 1624 (7f, soft). *nk* **69**
2581 **COCONUT PENANG 19** [19]4-9-5 (96) S Whitworth 11/1: 350-0020: 18th: Handy stands side, wknd over 2f out: much btr over 6f in 2581. *2½* **69**
1420 **HERETIC 71** [20]6-10-0 (105) O Urbina 16/1: 1000-140: 19th: Al bhd stands side: see 1225 (1m, sft). *11* **56**
19 Ran Time 1m 26.2 (2.3) Owned: Mr M J Caddy Trained: Lambourn

3062 2.55 Gr1 Darley July Cup 3yo+ (A)
£145000 £55000 £27500 6f str Good/Firm 28 +20 Fast Far Side

2468 **FRIZZANTE 23** [18] J R Fanshawe 5-9-2 (111) J Murtagh 14/1: 611-2131: Slow away, held up, hdwy & hung left over 1f out but strong run to lead ins last, rdn out: v eff over 5/6f on firm & gd grnd, loves a gall trk, esp Newmarket: best held up & has a fine turn of foot: thriving & now top-class filly, career best run: see 2468. **117**
2580 **ASHDOWN EXPRESS 19** [11] C F Wall 5-9-5 (111) S Sanders 100/1: 10-30202: Hld up, hdwy & short of room briefly over 1f out, styd on well ins last, just held: much imprvd/high-class eff stepped up to the highest class & a shade unlucky: has a turn of foot off a fast pace & must be wng Gr races with a repeat. *nk* **119**
4797} **BALMONT 264** [16] J Noseda 3-8-13 (115) E Ahern 25/1: 211110-3: b c Stravinsky - Aldebaran Light (Seattle Slew) Handy, hdwy to lead just ins last, sn hdd & not pace of front 2: won 3 of 6 '03 starts (mdn, stks & Gr 2), also subs awarded Gr 1 Middle Park: v eff at 6f on firm & fast grnd, gall trks: best up with/forcing the pace: excellent/v smart return, deserves further success. 2 Oct'03 Newm 6fm 113-(100) A: 1 Aug'03 York 6.0fm 111-(100) A: 1 Jul'03 Newm 6g/f 100- D: 1 Jul'03 Donc 6g/f 94- D: 2 Jun'03 Newm 6fm 89- D: *2* **113**
2580 **CAPE OF GOOD HOPE 19** [20] D Oughton 6-9-5 vis t M J Kinane 20/1: 6322234: Held up, hdwy over 1f *nk* **112**

out, styd on well ins last: proving tough & smart, needs a drop into Gr 3: see 2580.

2769 **SOMNUS 12** [17]4-9-5 (117) T E Durcan 12/1: 4210-025: In tch, hdwy over 1f out, kept on ins last, nvr dngrs: not disgraced but shld apprec easier grnd: see 2769, 1667.	hd	111
2580 **MONSIEUR BOND 19** [14]4-9-5 (117) F Lynch 14/1: 25-51106: In tch, rdn well over 2f out, kept on same pace: much more interesting on easier grnd: lkd high-class in 1667 (gd).	nk	110
2469 **ANTONIUS PIUS 23** [5]3-8-13 t J P Spencer 5/1: 110-4537: Handy, eff 2f out, onepace: quirky, drpd right back in trip & well worth a try in headgear: see 2469 (1m).	nk	109
2305 **PORLEZZA 32** [13]5-9-2 O Peslier 33/1: 1D15-128: Held up, short of room over 1f out, late gains.	hd	105
2580 **AIRWAVE 19** [15]4-9-2 (115) Dane O'Neill 20/1: 3360-669: Held up, short of room well over 1f out, some late gains, nvr dngrs: no run at any stage, yet to fire this term: see 2580, 1667.	nk	104
1856 **PATAVELLIAN 53** [12]6-9-5 bl (115) S Drowne 7/1: 15111-30: 10th: With ldr, led over 1f out, sn hdd & wknd: capable of much btr & front pair poss went off a shade too qck: could pay to forgive this, see 1856.	shd	107
2580 **COUNTRY REEL 19** [4]4-9-5 vis t (104) R Hills 25/1: 205-0440: 11th: In tch, eff 1f out, onepace.	1¼	103
SEEKING THE DIA 60 [1]3-8-13 Y Take 50/1: 51-11100: 12th: b c Storm Cat - Seeking The Pearl (Seeking The Gold) In tch, eff dist, wknd: HK raider, earlier won a Gr 3 & Gr 2: stays 1m well on firm.	hd	102
2580* **FAYR JAG 19** [10]5-9-5 (109) W Supple 25/1: 510U-010: 13th: Held up, rdn & short of room over 1f out, no impress: btr expected after v smart run in 2580.	shd	101
2486* **KHELEYF 22** [8]3-8-13 (108) L Dettori 8/1: 1210-10: 14th: Held up, short of room 2f out, late gains, nvr dngrs: nicely bckd: plenty more to come with a return to 7f, this is best forgiven: see 2486 (Gr 3, 7f).	shd	100
2949 **CONTINENT 5** [19]7-9-5 (112) J Fortune 50/1: 00600-30: 15th: Slow away & bhd, nvr a factor: former wnr of this race, 7yo, see 2949.	nk	99
991 **NAYYIR 103** [7]6-9-5 R Hughes 12/1: 1/6102-30: 16th: Slow away, held up, hdwy over 2f out, rdn when hmpd over 1f out, sn wknd: 3 mth abs: btr over 7f/1m & capable of much btr: see 991.	nk	98
2769 **BAHAMIAN PIRATE 12** [9]9-9-5 (105) K Darley 66/1: 2100000: 17th: Slow away & al bhd: see 2769.	1	95
2580 **STEENBERG 19** [6]5-9-5 (113) P Robinson 22/1: 01-21200: 18th: In tch, wknd dist: btr 1667.	¾	93
EXCEED AND EXCEL 124 [3]4-9-5 T K McEvoy 4/1 FAV: 1116-110: 19th: b c Danehill - Patrona (Lomond) Set pace till over 1f out, wknd: hvly bckd: Australian raider, Gr 2 & Gr 1 h'cap wnr earlier: multiple wnr in Australia in '03: eff over 6/7f on gd & gd/soft: wears a t-strap: top-class in home country, clearly btr expected here but poss went off too fast.	1	90
2421 + **MOSS VALE 25** [2]3-8-13 (112) M Hills 14/1: 63-41110: 20th: In tch, wknd fnl 1f: nicely bckd.	1	87

20 Ran   Time 1m 11.51 (0.51)   Owned: Mrs Jan Hopper & Mrs Elizabeth Grundy   Trained: Newmarket

---

3063   3.30 Michael Powles Bentley Maiden Stakes Div 1 Fillies 2yo (D)
£8093 £2490 £1245   6f str   Good/Firm 28   -48 Slow   Far Side

WINDS OF TIME [11] Mrs A J Perrett 2-8-11 M J Kinane 9/1: 1: b f Danehill - Windmill (Ezzoud) Dwelt, rear, hdwy over 1f out, led ins last, rdn out: 350,000 gns Mar first foal, dam 14f scorer: eff at 6f, stoutly bred on dam's side & 7f+ could suit in time: acts on fast: open to plenty of improvement.		88+
1735 **UNREAL 55** [3] B W Hills 2-8-11 R Hughes 9/2: 62: Led, rdn & hdd well ins last, joc given 2-day careless riding ban: nicely bckd, 8 wk abs, left debut bhd: apprec step up to 6f with forcing tactics, stay further: acts on fast grnd & a stiff trk: can find a race: see 1735.	nk	86
2766 **CATCH A STAR 12** [4] N A Callaghan 2-8-11 J Murtagh 5/1: 3503: Keen rear, hdwy from over 1f out & staying on but just held when hmpd wl ins last cl-home: nicely bckd, op 6/1: eff at 6f, return to 7f+ likely to suit.	¾	84
SATIN FINISH [7] M R Channon 2-8-11 T E Durcan 7/1: 4: b f Kingmambo - Shimaal (Sadler's Wells) Cl-up, rdn & outpcd over 1f out, kept on well cl-home: nicely bckd, op 8/1: Feb first foal, dam 1m wnr: eff at 6f, sure to relish 7f+: acts on fast grnd & a stiff trk: encouraging start & expect improvement over further.	nk	83
PAPALITY [10]2-8-11 Martin Dwyer 4/1 FAV: 5: b f Giant's Causeway - Papabile (Chief's Crown) Cl-up, keen, rdn & no extra ins last: well bckd, op 6/1: 100,000gns Feb first foal, dam a multiple 1m wnr.	2½	76
DELLA SALUTE [8]2-8-11 L Keniry(3) 33/1: 6: Held up, not pace to chall, op 25/1.	½	74
MADHAVI [1]2-8-11 P Dobbs 16/1: 7: Mid-div, rdn & no impress dist, op 10/1.	½	72
LADY HEN [6]2-8-11 K Fallon 8/1: 8: Chsd ldrs, no impress fnl 2f.	1¾	67
VELVETEEN RABBIT [2]2-8-11 L Dettori 6/1: 9: Mid-div, pushed along/hmpd 2f out, sn no impress.	shd	66
CAPTAIN MARGARET [5]2-8-11 K Darley 50/1: 0: 10th: Chsd ldr till halfway, t.o./eased.	dist	0

10 Ran   Time 1m 15.58 (4.58)   Owned: Mr & Mrs R Scott   Trained: Pulborough

---

3064   4.05 Michael Powles Bentley Maiden Stakes Div 2 Fillies 2yo (D)
£8093 £2490 £1245   6f str   Good/Firm 28   -39 Slow   Far Side

2676 **VONDOVA 15** [6] R Hannon 2-8-11 Dane O'Neill 20/1: 301: Keen & led after 1f, hung left under press but held on gamely cl-home: eff at 6f, tried 7f, may suit in time: acts on fast grnd & a stiff trk: enjoyed forcing tactics: still green & ndd strong handling, can win again: see 2437.		86
ALMANSOORA [5] Saeed bin Suroor 2-8-11 L Dettori 5/2: 2: b f Bahri - Bashayer (Mr Prospector) In tch, eff to chase wnr over 1f out, rdn & just failed: hvly bckd: related to wnrs btwn 6f/14f, dam a 1m juv wnr: eff at 6f, 7f sure to suit: acts on fast grnd & a stiff trk: most promising start, win similar soon.	shd	85+
AHDAAF [2] J L Dunlop 2-8-11 R Hills 2/1 FAV: 3: b f Bahri - Ashraakat (Danzig) Trkd ldrs, eff 2f out, onepace: rest well covered: hvly bckd, op 11/4: Feb foal, half-sister to a 1m wnr: dam a multiple 6/7f wnr: eff at 6f on fast grnd: gd start, shld find a race.	1¼	81
INDIENA [4] B J Meehan 2-8-11 J Fortune 8/1: 4: ch f Indian Ridge - Aliena (Grand Lodge) Led 1f, no impress from dist: nicely bckd tho' op 6/1: 75,000gns Jan first foal, dam a dual French 2yo scorer: subs List US wnr: eff at 6f, handles fast grnd: ran well for a long way, likely improver.	3	72
RINGAROOMA [1]2-8-11 P Robinson 20/1: 5: Dwelt & held up, kept on late, nvr pace to threaten.	1	69
CEREBUS [9]2-8-11 E Ahern 28/1: 6: Held up, rdn & no impress fnl 2f.	shd	69
YELDHAM LADY [7]2-8-11 R Price 50/1: 7: Held up & sn pushed along, nvr on terms.	1½	65
SILENT SPRING [8]2-8-11 M Hills 9/2: 8: Held up in tch, btn over 1f out: well bckd.	nk	64
NEVER AWAY [10]2-8-11 J Murtagh 16/1: 9: Reared over herf start, dwelt, nvr on terms.	½	62
1974 **SAFFA GARDEN 44** [3]2-8-11 D Holland 14/1: 00: 10th: Chsd ldrs, btn fnl 2f, op 12/1, abs.	nk	61

10 Ran   Time 1m 15.0 (4)   Owned: Mr W J Gredley   Trained: Marlborough

NEWMARKET THURSDAY 08.07.04 Righthand, Stiff Galloping Track

3065 **4.40 Newmarketracecourses Co Uk Nursery Handicap Stakes 2yo (C)** **[95]**
£10238 £3150 £1575 **7f str** **Good/Firm 28** **-05 Slow** Far Side

2341* **SATCHEM 28** [13] D R Loder 2-9-6 (87) T P Queally 7/2 FAV: 211: Bmpd start, held up in tch, hdwy to lead ins last, rdn out: well bckd: eff at 6f, imprvd for step up to 7f: acts on fast grnd, stiff/gall or easy trk: lightly rcd & v progressive: see 2341, 1964. **104**
1808 **SEA HUNTER 52** [2] M R Channon 2-9-0 (81) S Hitchcott(3) 14/1: 0142: Led till ins last, kept on well: 8 wk abs, styd longer 7f trip well with forcing tactics: acts on fast & gd grnd: find similar: see 1503. *¾* **95**
2411* **SILVER WRAITH 26** [10] N A Callaghan 2-9-7 (88) J Murtagh 10/1: 42113: Trkd ldrs, hung left but styd on from over 1f out, not pace of wnr: nicely bckd: styd longer 7f trip well, continues on the upgrade. *½* **101**
2450 **MARCHING SONG 24** [9] R Hannon 2-9-2 (83) R Hughes 13/2: 5324: Cl-up, ch ins last, no extra nr fin: nicely bckd: styd longer 7f trip well: see 2450 & 1826. *nk* **95**
2697 **ASIAN TIGER 14** [5]2-9-5 (86) D Holland 8/1: 22535: Cl-up, no impress fnl 1f: longer trip: see 1816. *3½* **91**
2697 **IM SPARTACUS 14** [8]2-8-3 (70) C Haddon(7) 40/1: 0216506: Chsd ldrs, edged left & btn dist: btr 1367. *hd* **74**
2511 **MAC COIS NA TINE 21** [6]2-8-6 (1ow) (72) N Callan 33/1: 0237: Chsd ldrs, no impress fnl 1f: see 2511. *hd* **76**
2388 **GRYSKIRK 26** [11]2-8-1 (68) Martin Dwyer 10/1: 46308: Rear, rdn & hdwy 2f out, no prog dist: op 16/1. *nk* **70**
1631 **LANGSTON BOY 61** [3]2-8-6 (73) R Mullen 25/1: 4239: Dwelt, nvr a factor: abs: btr 1631, 1353. *2* **71**
2343* **LISA MONA LISA 28** [12]2-8-5 (72) K Fallon 9/1: 1410: 10th: Went right start, cl-up till dist. *½* **69**
2358 **AMPHITHEATRE 27** [4]2-7-13 (66) M Halford(7) 33/1: 5030: 11th: Mid-div, rdn & btn over 2f out. *shd* **62**
2251 **ADORATION 33** [7]2-8-13 (80) K Darley 5/1: 3250: 12th: Held up in tch, btn 2f out: well bckd. *½* **75**
1517 **APOLOGIES 66** [1]2-8-11 (78) G Gibbons 12/1: 0140: 13th: Cl-up, btn 2f out, eased dist, abs: btr 1517. *12* **49**
13 Ran Time 1m 26.37 (2.47) Owned: Lucayan Stud & Mr D D Clee Trained: Newmarket

3066 **5.10 Dullingham Handicap Stakes 3yo+ 0-90 (C)** **[88]**
£13858 £4264 £2132 **1m4f** **Good/Firm 28** **-11 Slow** Stands Side

2405* **MEPHISTO 26** [11] L M Cumani 5-10-0 (88) D Holland 8/1: 216-0511: Al handy & dsptd lead from 5f out, rdn & led ins last, drvn & held on most gamely: suited by 12f on fast: game, useful & improving. **101**
2881* **ASTROCHARM 7** [2] M H Tompkins 5-9-6 (6ex) (80) N Callan 16/1: 0-510512: Held up, drvn & styd on fnl 2f, not pace of wnr cl-home: in fine form: see 2881. *½* **91**
2900 **ALWAYS WAINING 6** [15] M Johnston 3-8-12 (85) J Fanning 16/1: 33153: Led, rdn & hdd ins last, no extra nr fin: lightly rcd & on the upgrade: see 2900, 2113. *1½* **93**
2735 **STREET LIFE 13** [7] W J Musson 6-8-13 (73) K Fallon 6/1: 2334354: Held up, styd on for press, not able to chall: well bckd & clr of rem: see 391. *1¼* **79**
2737 **TEAM MATE 13** [14]6-9-2 (76) B Reilly(3) 50/1: 1540-055: In tch, eff over 2f out, no prog dist. *6* **73**
2530* **SWELLMOVA 20** [10]5-8-7 (1ow) (66) J Fortune 7/1: 1204/-216: Chsd ldr, btn over 1f out: btr 2530. *nk* **63**
2681* **SANGIOVESE 15** [8]5-9-4 (78) S Drowne 9/1: 3523117: Prom, wknd over 1f out: btr 2681. *nk* **74**
2681 **WHISPERED PROMISES 15** [12]3-8-9 (82) K Dalgleish 14/1: 4211-038: Chsd ldrs, no impress fnl 2f. *2½* **74**
2875* **LUCKY LEO 7** [4]4-8-8 (68) R Hughes 7/1: 300-0119: Held up, eff over 3f out, no impress: bckd. *1¾* **56**
1756 **ANOTHER CHOICE 54** [6]3-8-5 t (78) R Mullen 33/1: 00-31100: 10th: Held up, rdn & btn 2f out: abs. *hd* **66**
2538 **NORTHSIDE LODGE 20** [5]6-9-4 (78) Martin Dwyer 14/1: 3003520: 11th: Held up & keen, btn 2f out. *7* **56**
2737 **DOVEDON HERO 13** [3]4-9-1 bl (75) M Hills 33/1: 0020460: 12th: Held up & strug fnl 2f: btr 2391. *3* **49**
2465 **CRATHORNE 23** [13]4-9-5 p (79) J Murtagh 9/1: 030-4340: 13th: Held up, btn 2f out: see 1668. *1¾* **49**
2448 **BACK IN ACTION 24** [1]4-8-10 t (70) Dane O'Neill 50/1: 3/5000-00: 14th: Slow away, btn 2f out. *5* **32**
2687* **BURNING MOON 14** [9]3-8-13 (86) E Ahern 9/2 FAV: 50-510: 15th: Held up, rdn & btn 2f out: bckd. *1¼* **46**
15 Ran Time 2m 32.91(4.71) Owned: Mrs Angie Silver Trained: Newmarket

ASCOT FRIDAY 09.07.04 Righthand, Stiff, Galloping Track

Official Going GOOD (GOOD/SOFT places).

3067 **2.15 Sony Claiming Stakes 3yo (D)**
£10238 £3150 £1575 **1m rnd** **Good 60** **-00 Slow** Inside

2732 **ARKHOLME 14** [7] W J Haggas 3-9-0 bl (76) D Holland 7/2: 41-4021: Held up, prog wide 2f out, led dist, drvn out: bckd from 9/2: claimed for 22,000: eff at 1m, has tried 10f+: acts on gd & fast: wears blnks. **82**
2919 **HOH BLEU DEE 6** [4] S Kirk 3-9-0 (82) J F Egan 12/1: 666-0602: Mid-div, eff 2f out, styd on under press but not pace of wnr: apprec drop to claim grade, stays 1m: acts on gd & fast grnd: see 1847. *3* **76**
2247 **TOPARUDI 34** [2] M H Tompkins 3-9-3 (73) F P Ferris(3) 12/1: 330-0103: Chsd ldrs, slightly outpcd 2f out, rallied late: op 16/1: back to form on drop to claim company: see 1359. *1¾* **75**
2247 **TRANQUIL SKY 34** [10] N A Callaghan 3-9-2 (85) L Dettori 11/4 FAV: 0-005204: Chsd ldrs, ev ch 2f out, wknd ins fnl 1f: well bckd tho' op 2/1: better expected on this drop in grade: see 2040. *½* **73**
2930 **FIT TO FLY 6** [9]3-8-12 (75) S Whitworth 14/1: 2515605: Held up, mod late gains: claimed for 14,000. *2* **65**
2174 **LADY MO 37** [1]3-8-8 (60) A McCarthy 33/1: 1012306: Trkd ldr, led 2f out till dist, wknd: not disgraced at today's weights: see 1720 (7f, K Ryan). *hd* **61**
2650 **MOSCOW TIMES 17** [5]3-9-7 (70) J Murtagh 7/1: 600-657: Held up, nvr nr ldrs: see 2650. *¾* **72**
2924 **EPAMINONDAS 6** [3]3-8-12 (66) R L Moore 12/1: 53-00028: Chsd ldrs wide, btn 2f out: 'hung left'. *1¼* **60**
2922 **BINNION BAY 6** [6]3-9-0 (78) Dane O'Neill 33/1: 3100-009: Mid-div wide, btn 2f out: see 2173. *nk* **61**
213 **QUEENSTOWN 205** [8]3-9-1 bl (88) J Fortune 6/1: 244122-0: 10th: Led till 2f out, wknd: op 9/2, long abs: reportedly too keen & did not stay: see 213 (2yo nov, AW). *13* **37**
10 Ran Time 1m 43.31 (4.81) Owned: Mr & Mrs G Middlebrook Trained: Newmarket

ASCOT   FRIDAY 09.07.04   Righthand, Stiff, Galloping Track

3068   2.45 Woodcote Stud Handicap Stakes 3yo+ 0-90 (C)   [89]
£14144 £4352 £2176   7f str   Good 60   -08 Slow   Stands Side

3001 **TRUE NIGHT 3** [9] D Nicholls 7-9-3 (78) D Holland 7/2 FAV: 4233031: Prom, went on after halfway, held on v gamely: well bckd, qck reapp: eff at 7f/1m on firm & gd/soft grnd: handles any trk: made most of fav h'cap mark & usually comes gd in July/Aug: see 3001 & 1909. 88

2558 **MANAAR 21** [7] J Noseda 4-9-6 (81) L Dettori 7/1: 220-0502: Held up, prog 2f out, chall strongly fnl 1f, just btn: bckd from 12/1: eff at 5/7f on gd & firm: likes a stiff/gall trk: fine run: see 2558. nk 88

2799 **AZREME 11** [3] D K Ivory 4-8-8 (69) I Mongan 11/1: 1504543: Rear, prog to chall dist, just held. ½ 75

2587* **A WOMAN IN LOVE 20** [13] Miss B Sanders 5-9-4 (79) S Sanders 10/1: 0-611114: Rear, styd on fnl 1f, nvr nrr: fair run, best on a sharp/undul trk & loves Brighton: see 2587. 1½ 82

3039 **JOOLS 2** [14]6-9-2 (77) Dane O'Neill 33/1: 3004465: Held up, prog wide & ch 1.5f out, wknd ins fnl 1f. shd 80

2878 **CHATEAU NICOL 8** [6]5-9-9 vis (84) J Fortune 12/1: 3334156: Mid-div, prog 2f out, onepcd fnl 1f. 1½ 84

2427* **WARDEN COMPLEX 26** [8]3-9-3 (86) J Murtagh 4/1: 3-32117: Rear, nvr nr ldrs: well bckd, btr 2427. ¾ 84

2090 **TARANAKI 40** [4]6-9-13 (88) Lisa Jones 3) 16/1: 4140158: Trkd ldrs, ev ch 1.5f out, wknd fnl 1f: abs. 1¼ 83

2903 **CRAIOVA 7** [12]5-9-5 (80) C Catlin 12/1: 0-000009: Rear, prog & ch 2f out, sn wknd. ¾ 73

2312* **MUSIC MAID 30** [2]6-8-4 (65) T P Queally 20/1: 5115-010: 10th: Chsd ldrs, wknd dist: btr 2312. 3½ 51

2532 **COLOUR WHEEL 21** [10]3-9-7 t (90) R Hughes 11/1: 122-6020: 11th: Chsd ldrs, wknd 2f out: amiss? 5 66

2647 **TE QUIERO GB 12** [1]6-8-11 e t (72) S Hitchcott(3) 33/1: 2200000: 12th: Led till halfway, wknd qckly. nk 47

2212 **SECRET PLACE 35** [5]3-9-7 (90) W Ryan 14/1: 1130100: 13th: Chsd ldrs 5.5f, wknd: btr 1847. 7 50

13 Ran   Time 1m 30.80 (4.80)   Owned: Benton and Partners   Trained: Thirsk

3069   3.15 Rendezvous Casino Rated Stakes Handicap 3yo+ 0-90 (C)   [93]
£8733 £3313 £1656   6f110y str   Good 60   -02 Slow   Stands Side

2256 **PRINCE AARON 34** [5] C N Allen 4-9-2 (81) G Carter 11/2: 6213151: Chsd ldrs, qcknd to lead ins fnl 1f, pushed clr: nicely bckd: poorly drawn last time: suited by 6/6.5f on gd, firm & polytrack: handles a stiff/gall or easy trk, likes Lingfield: progressive, win again: see 2256 & 2070. 95

2752 **ARMAGNAC 13** [9] M A Buckley 6-8-10 (75) Dane O'Neill 12/1: 0036002: Rear, lost action briefly halfway, switched wide & fin fast but too late, nrst fin: v promising, h'capped to win sn, likes Haydock. 1½ 83+

2374 **IDLE POWER 28** [10] J R Boyle 6-8-12 p (77) J Murtagh 12/1: 0011023: Mid-div, kept on under press. hd 83

2861 **DEVON FLAME 9** [4] R J Hodges 5-8-10 (75) J F McDonald(3) 12/1: 11-21224: Led till ins fnl 1f, no extra: gd front running effort & continues in fine form: see 2861 & 2266. 1 78

2903 **STARBECK 7** [7]6-9-7 (78) T G McLaughlin 33/1: 0054005: Rear, styd on late, nvr dngrs. ¾ 86

2841 **MORSE 9** [1]3-9-3 (90) L Dettori 14/1: 2312006: Trkd ldrs, onepcd fnl 1f. shd 90

2878 **NAJEEBON 8** [6]5-9-1 (80) S Hitchcott(3) 8/1: 0003637: Mid-div, drvn & ch 1.5f out, wknd ins fnl 1f. 1¼ 76

2871+ **LOYAL TYCOON 8** [2]6-9-3 (3ex) (82) J Fortune 5/1: 0250018: Mid-div, no room fnl 2f, eased: well bckd: no run at any stage & this is best forgiven: see 2871. 2½ 71

2282 **BANDIT QUEEN 31** [3]4-9-7 (80) Lisa Jones(3) 12/1: 500-3429: Trkd ldrs, wknd dist: btr 2282. 5 60

2878+ **FANTASY BELIEVER 8** [11]6-9-8 (3ex) (87) D Holland 11/4 FAV: 0000410: 10th: Unruly stalls, rear, prog wide to chase ldrs halfway, btn fnl 1f: top-weight, well bckd from 7/2: prob lost chance at the start today (returned with cuts to his head): see 2878. 2 55

2362 **MISTER SAIF 28** [8]3-9-0 (87) R Hughes 20/1: 0U50420: 11th: Prom, wknd halfway, eased: rider given a 1-day ban for not riding to draw: btr 2362. 5 40

11 Ran   Time 1m 23.54 (4.04)   Owned: Black Star Racing   Trained: Newmarket

3070   3.50 Sony Wega Handicap Stakes 3yo+ 0-90 (C)   [87]
£9783 £3010 £1505   1m4f   Good 60   +12 Fast   Inside

2899 **SERGEANT CECIL 7** [8] B R Millman 5-9-13 (86) J Fortune 16/1: 020-0351: Held up, qcknd to lead over 1f out, just held cl-home: top-weight, best time of day: eff at 12/14f, acts on fm & gd/soft: handles any trk, likes Sandown: gd weight-carrier, showed a good turn of foot today: see 2538. 96

1865 **CUTTING CREW 50** [10] P W Harris 3-9-4 (90) D Holland 4/1: 402-3162: Trkd ldrs, sltly outpcd over 1f out, fin strongly & just tchd off: well bckd, 7 wk abs: fine run against his elders, 14f will now suit. shd 99

2250 **FORT 34** [2] M Johnston 3-9-1 (87) S Chin 11/1: 13-303: Led till dist, no extra: stays 12f, gd run. 1¼ 93

2681 **MEXICAN PETE 16** [9] P W Hiatt 4-9-4 (87) J F Egan 25/1: 0302044: Chsd ldrs, kept on fnl 1f. shd 82

2318 **ZEITGEIST 30** [3]3-9-1 (87) L Dettori 9/4 FAV: 01-4125: Held up, prog wide 2f out, not pace to chall: bckd from 3/1, clr of rem: ran to form of 2318 & 2103. hd 91

2099 **BARRY ISLAND 39** [6]5-9-3 (76) S Sanders 20/1: 4300306: Mid-div, nvr nr ldrs. 4 75

2582 **BRIAREUS 20** [7]4-9-4 (77) R L Moore 7/1: 0020367: Prom till wknd fnl 1f: bckd from 10/1. 1¾ 74

2896* **SILVALINE 7** [12]5-9-6 (5ex) (79) C Haddon(7) 10/1: 5060118: Keen in rear, prog wide over 2f out, sn wknd: taken v wide by inexperienced joc, all wins at 10f: see 2896. ¾ 75

2707* **TENDER FALCON 15** [4]4-8-10 (69) J F McDonald(3) 14/1: 3214-519: Mid-div, btn 2f out: btr 2707. shd 65

2631* **PENZANCE 18** [5]3-8-10 (82) J Murtagh 7/1: 13-6410: 10th: Nvr nr ldrs: op 9/2: btr 2631 (10f). shd 78

2796* **FEED THE METER 11** [1]4-7-12 (5ex) (57) F P Ferris(3) 20/1: 00/0-0210: 11th: Mid-div wide, btn 2f out. 3 48

11 Ran   Time 2m 34.86 (5.86)   Owned: Mr Terry Cooper   Trained: Cullompton

3071   4.25 Woodcote Stud Maiden Stakes Fillies 2yo (D)
£5538 £1704 £852   6f str   Good 60   -29 Slow   Stands Side

VALENTIN [1] R Hannon 2-8-11 Dane O'Neill 10/1: 1: ch f King of Kings - Slip Ashore (Slip Anchor) Dwelt, keen in rear, prog 2f out, led ins fnl 1f, won going away: £20,000 April foal, half-sister to several wnrs: dam unrcd, sire a top-class miler: eff at 6f, 7f will suit: runs well fresh: overcame greenness to win today, potentially useful & shld improve. 95+

DANCE FLOWER [6] M R Channon 2-8-11 C Catlin 10/1: 2: b f Cape Cross - Ninth Wonder (Forty Niner) Trkd ldr, led 2f out till ins fnl 1f, battled on for 2nd but no ch with wnr: debut: 58,000gns Feb foal: dam unrcd, sire a high-class miler: eff at 6f on gd grnd, 7f shld suit: showed decent battling qualities here. 3½ 81

2733 **GENNIE BOND 14** [4] R Hannon 2-8-11 R Hughes 4/1 JT FAV: 43: Chsd ldrs, outpcd over 1f out, styd ¾ 78

929

ASCOT   FRIDAY 09.07.04   Righthand, Stiff, Galloping Track

on late: bckd from 4/1 & shorter priced stablemate of wnr: 7f shld now suit: see 2733.

2858 **LADY ANN SUMMERS 9** [2] B J Meehan 2-8-11 J Fortune 9/2: 034: Chsd ldrs, ev ch over 1f out, onepcd.	hd	77

SUBYAN DREAMS [3]2-8-11   A McCarthy 7/1: 5: b f Spectrum - Subya (Night Shift) Chsd ldrs, wknd ¾ 75
fnl 1f on debut: Feb foal, cost 45,000gns: half-sister to a mid-dist wnr abroad: dam a useful 1m/10f performer,
sire top-class over 1m/10f: with P Chapple-Hyam & sure to improve.

TAMORA [7]2-8-11   D Holland 10/1: 6: ch f Dr Fong - Tahara (Caerleon) Dwelt & outpcd, nvr nr 4 63
ldrs on debut: op 16/1: 10,000gns April foal: half-sister to a couple of wnrs abroad: ran v green today.

2228 **AFRICAN GIFT 35** [5]2-8-11   S Sanders 13/2: 37: Led till 2f out, wknd: see 2228. nk 62
2863 **THEAS DANCE 8** [8]2-8-11   T P Queally 4/1 JT FAV: 58: Dwelt, chsd ldrs 4f, wknd & eased: well 15 17
bckd tho' op 5/2: with D Loder & more expected, reportedly became upset in stalls.

8 Ran   Time 1m 18.47 (5.37)   Owned: Mrs Valerie Hubbard & Mr A J Ilsley   Trained: Marlborough

3072   5.00 Sodexho Handicap Stakes Fillies 3yo+ 0-90 (C) [101]
£9393 £2890 £1445   1m2f   Good 60   -06 Slow   Inside

2678* **TARTOUCHE 16** [6] Lady Herries 3-9-0 (87) S Sanders 5/2 FAV: 11: Trkd ldrs, chall entering fnl 94
1f, forced head in front on line: well bckd: eff at 10f, 12f will suit: acts on gd & gd/soft grnd: handles a flat
or gall trk: remains unbeaten, battled v well today & sure to win more races: see 2678.
2592 **WINDY BRITAIN 20** [5] L M Cumani 5-9-11   (87) D Holland 11/2: 3131-042: Held up, short of room 2f shd 93
out, strong run to lead ins fnl 1f, idled & caught on line: op 7/2, top-weight: threw this away in closing stages.
2406 **SPRING GODDESS 27** [3] A P Jarvis 3-8-8 (81) A McCarthy 8/1: 160-3043: Held up, prog to lead ½ 85
dist, collared ins fnl 1f, kept on & not btn far: op 13/2: lkd likely wnr 1f out, see 1924 (C/D).
2013* **HASAIYDA 44** [4] Sir Michael Stoute 3-8-2 (75) Lisa Jones(3) 11/4: 14: Trkd ldrs, outpcd over 1f 1½ 76
out, rallied late: nicely bckd, 6 wk abs: ran green, 12f &/or a faster pace looks sure to suit: see 2013.
2748* **GOLDEN ISLAND 13** [1]3-8-12 (85) R L Moore 5/1: 0-3215: Keen & prom, led briefly 1.5f out, no extra. 1¼ 83
2098 **PINK SAPPHIRE 39** [2]3-8-0 (73) C Catlin 8/1: 510-0246: Led till 1.5f out, no extra: see 2098. ¾ 69

6 Ran   Time 2m 10.60(6.60)   Owned: Lady Herries   Trained: Littlehampton

YORK   FRIDAY 09.07.04   Lefthand, Flat, Galloping Track

Official Going GOOD/SOFT.

3073   2.00 Grampian Country Food Group Stakes Handicap 3yo+ 0-95 (C) [95]
£10602 £3262 £1631   5f str   Good/Soft 60   -30 Slow   Centre

2942 **ARTIE 6** [10] T D Easterby 5-9-2   (83) R Winston 12/1: 0021001: Led early, handy, styd on well fnl 89
1f to lead ins last, drvn out: qck reappr: eff over 5/6f on firm, likes soft grnd & any trk: enjoys York: best up
with/forcing the pace: tough, right back to form: see 1627, 1145.
2743 **SEVEN NO TRUMPS 13** [5] J M Bradley 7-8-8 p (75) K Darley 12/1: 3604002: With ldrs, led over 1f ½ 79
out, hdd & no extra ins last, not btn far: btr run, v well h'capped on best form: see 944.
2942 **TALLY 6** [11] M J Polglase 4-7-12 (6oh) (59) P M Quinn(5) 14/1: 2002443: Sn rdn bhd, plenty to do nk 69$
over 1f out, styd on well ins last, nrst fin: prefers a stiffer fin: see 2690, 2214.
2942 **BLACKHEATH 6** [6] D Nicholls 8-9-1 (82) Alex Greaves 9/1: 4062264: Chsd ldrs, eff over 1f out, ½ 84
onepace ins last: qck reappr: see 2561, 2409.
2727 **PTARMIGAN RIDGE 14** [2]8-9-2 (83) N Mackay(3) 5/1: 0010065: In tch, eff to chall dist, no extra. 1 83
2775 **OBE ONE 20** [3]4-8-1 (68) F Norton 11/2: 6402306: Sn rdn in tch, eff dist, no dngr: see 2512. hd 67
2942 **CATCH THE CAT 6** [8]5-8-5 vis (72) Rory Moore(7) 10/1: 2016507: Sn led, hdd dist, wknd: see 2084. 2 66
2747 **CAPE ROYAL 13** [1]4-9-6 (87) M Hills 6/1: 6106028: In tch, wknd fnl 1f: btr 2747, 2253. 1 78
2942 **BEYOND THE CLOUDS 6** [9]8-8-9 (76) D Allan 8/1: 0-000209: Outpcd, nvr a factor: likes faster grnd. ¾ 65
2894 **ABSENT FRIENDS 7** [4]7-9-11 (92) J Edmunds 25/1: 00-06060: 10th: In tch, wknd over 1f out, 2½ 74
reportedly broke a blood vessel: see 1626.
2942 **WATCHING 6** [12]7-9-3 (84) W Supple 9/1: 0255000: 11th: In tch, wknd 2f out: see 1683. hd 65
2698 **SUNLEY SENSE 15** [7]8-8-10 (77) T E Durcan 25/1: 000/-3000: 12th: Sn bhd: see 2266. 2½ 51

12 Ran   Time 1m 01.32 (4.52)   Owned: Mr A Arton   Trained: Malton

3074   2.35 Hearthstead Homes Stakes Handicap 3yo+ 0-85 (D) [83]
£5980 £1840 £920   7f205y rnd   Good/Soft 60   +05 Fast   Inside

2672 **BLONDE STREAK 16** [9] T D Barron 4-9-6 (75) K Darley 8/1: 204-4401: Set pace, kept on gamely for 82
press over 1f out, just held on: gd time: eff at 7f, all 3 wins at 1m: acts on firm & gd/soft, prob any trk:
genuine, right back to form best with switch to forcing tactics: see 2010.
2890 **TEDSDALE MAC 7** [8] N Bycroft 5-8-0 (2ow) (53) F Norton 25/1: 04-04252: Held up, plenty to do over nk 61
2f out, styd on well over 1f out, nrst fin, just held: hard to come from way back here & a shade unfortunate.
2684 **HILLS OF GOLD 15** [10] M W Easterby 5-9-2 (71) P Mulrennan(5) 8/1: 400-4103: In tch, eff 2f out, 1 75
kept on fnl 1f, no threat to wnr: back to form at 1m: tough: see 1366, 1142.
2986* **ALCHEMIST MASTER 4** [7] R M Whitaker 5-8-8 (6ex)p (63) Dean McKeown 2/1 FAV: 6222114: In tch, eff 1½ 63
trav well well over 1f out, wknd ins last: well bckd: been busy & thriving of late: see 2986.
1769 **HONEST INJUN 55** [2]3-8-12 (76) M Hills 8/1: 02-14405: In tch, onepcd fnl 2f: 8 wk abs: see 1515. 1 74
2890* **CRYFIELD 7** [5]7-8-6 (6ex) (61) Kim Tinkler 14/1: 6240016: Held up, eff & short of room over 2f 1½ 56
out till over 1f out, no impress: see 2890.
2929 **GO TECH 6** [6]4-9-7 (76) W Supple 11/1: 6062467: Keen bhd, brief eff over 2f out, sn wknd. 3½ 64
2606 **DANELOR 19** [3]6-10-0 (83) T Hamilton(3) 8/1: 0-450058: In tch, wknd over 2f out: see 2209, 836. 1½ 68
2962* **PAWAN 5** [1]4-9-3 (6ex) (72) Ann Stokell 25/1: 1663019: Chsd wnr, wknd dist: qck reappr, btr 2962. 1½ 54
2753 **RETIREMENT 13** [4]5-9-13 (82) J Fanning 11/2: 212-1300: 10th: In tch, wknd well over 1f out, 10 44
eased: surely something amiss? btr 1598, 1423.

10 Ran   Time 1m 40.24 (4.44)   Owned: Mrs Liz Jones   Trained: Thirsk

3075   3.05 Gr3 Cuisine De France Summer Stakes Fillies 3yo+   (A)
£29000 £11000 £5500   6f str   Good/Soft 60   -04 Slow   Centre

2240+ **TANTE ROSE 34** [1] R Charlton 4-9-0 (107) R Hills 11/4 FAV: 03040-11: Held up, trav well & short   **116+**
of room over 2f out till over 1f out, qcknd to lead just ins last, readily drew clr, impressive: well bckd tho' op
9/4: suited by 6/7f on any trk & acts on firm & gd/soft: thriving this term, smart now & has a fine turn of foot,
must be followed: see 2240.
2769 **RUBY ROCKET 13** [7] H Morrison 3-8-8 (105) M Fenton 3/1: 314-5232: Trkd ldr, hung left but led   2½   108
over 1f out, hdd just ins last, not pace of wnr: ran to useful/consistent best, wants stks/List: see 2769, 2240.
2580 **LOCHRIDGE 20** [5] A M Balding 5-9-0 (103) Dean McKeown 13/2: 130-2003: Set pace till over 1f out,   1½   104
no extra: needs fillies List/stks class: poss handles gd/soft, likes firm & fast: see 2068.
2913 **RINGMOOR DOWN 6** [9] D W P Arbuthnot 5-9-0 (106) K Darley 4/1: 3-613424: In tch, eff for press 2f   nk   103
out, onepace: nicely bckd: shade more expected after useful run against colts in 2913, see 2468.
2769 **GOLDEVA 13** [2]5-9-0 T (101) N Callan 25/1: 620-1505: In tch, onepace dist: btr run in a t-strap.   1½   100
2736 **TOPKAMP 14** [10]4-9-0 (102) R Mullen 25/1: 235-2336: In tch, no impress over 1f out: see 2140.   shd   100
2457* **GOLDEN NUN 27** [3]4-9-4 bl (101) R Winston 8/1: 0231317: Reared start, nvr a factor: nicely bckd.   shd   103
2942 **VITA SPERICOLATA 6** [6]7-9-0 (83) G Parkin 100/1: 0035008: Keen in tch, wknd dist: wants h'caps.   nk   98
2486 **SILCAS GIFT 23** [11]3-8-12 (107) T E Durcan 14/1: 00-10509: Held up, eff over 2f out, sn wknd.   1½   99
9 Ran   Time 1m 13.26 (3.86)   Owned: Mr B E Nielsen   Trained: Beckhampton

3076   3.40 John West Tuna Stakes Rated Stakes Handicap 3yo+ 0-100 (B)   **[115]**
£12911 £4897 £2449   1m3f198y   Good/Soft 60   -01 Slow   Inside

2549* **CARTE DIAMOND 21** [10] M Johnston 3-8-3 (90) J Fanning 8/1: 11: Prom, hdwy to lead over 2f out,   101
hung left & hdd dist, styd on gamely for press to get up again cl-home: unbeaten in 2 starts, useful, genuine & improving, more to come:
unbeaten in 2 starts, useful, genuine & improving, more to come: see 2549.
2673* **LOVES TRAVELLING 16** [1] L M Cumani 4-8-11 (83) N Mackay(3) 9/2: 1123-212: Held up, hdwy trav well   nk   93
to lead 1f out, sn drvn & hung badly left ins last, rider drpd reins & hdd nr fin: useful & most progressive
gelding, promising appr joc prob to blame for defeat: win more races: see 2673, 2233.
2355 **GOLD RING 28** [4] G B Balding 4-8-11 (85) S Drowne 4/1: 3-023653: Handy, eff over 2f out, kept on   1¾   92
same pace over 1f out: well bckd: back to form: see 1668, 1172.
1921 **DESERT ROYALTY 23** [3] E A L Dunlop 4-9-4 (92) W Supple 12/1: 23-21244: Handy, eff over 2f out,   2½   95
wknd ins last: useful, gd run: see 1921, 1721.
2759* **VENGEANCE 13** [7]4-9-10 (98) P Dobbs 5/1: 105-0315: Held up, rdn & no impress over 2f out, late   hd   100
gains: do btr, esp if rcd more positively: see 2759, 1295.
2483 **DUNASKIN 23** [9]4-8-11 (4oh) P Mulrennan(5) 40/1: 53-00056: Handy, eff but hung right over 2f   1   85
out, no extra: best dominating: see 1668.
2519 **DESTINATION DUBAI 22** [2]3-8-5 T (92) K McEvoy 13/2: 22-1307: Hung right, led till 2f out, no extra.   nk   92
2560 **TELEMACHUS 20** [6]4-8-13 (87) M Fenton 20/1: 0-610008: In tch, btn 2f out: see 1519.   2½   83
2246 **UROWELLS 34** [8]4-9-4 (92) T E Durcan 40/1: 6/41-09: b g Sadler's Wells - Highest Accolade   1½   84
(Shirley Heights) Bhd, hung left, nvr a factor: won 2nd of 2 '03 starts (mdn): stays 10f on gd grnd.
1 May'03 Newb 10.0gd 91- D:
4796} **FOURTH DIMENSION 265** [11]5-8-12 (86) Alex Greaves 50/1: 313000-0: 10th: b g Entrepreneur - Isle   shd   80
of Spice (Diesis) In tch, wknd 2f out: '03 h'cap wnr: 3 time h'cap scorer in '02: all 4 wins at 14f & likes gd &
firm grnd & Yarmouth: has run well fresh: with A Stewart last term, now gelded.
1 Jul'03 Sand 14gd 88-80 D: 2 Sep'02 Sand 14gd 78-77 D: 1 Jul'02 Yarm 14g/f 74-69 E: 1 Jun'02 Yarm 14fm 74-63 E:
1 Jun'02 Yarm 14fm 66-50 E: 2 Jun'02 Redc 14fm 59-50 F: 2 May'02 Pont 12gd 55-55 D:
3719} **CONQUERING LOVE 325** [5]6-8-11 (2oh) (83) T Hamilton(3) 33/1: 124110-0: 11th: b g Pursuit of Love -   11   65
Susquehanna Days (Chief's Crown) Slow away, sn well bhd on reapp: '03 2 time h'cap wnr & a class stks: '02 dual
h'cap wnr: eff at 10/12f, stays 14f on firm & gd/soft, any trk: tough & genuine.
1 Aug'03 Thir 12fm 85-(83) D: 1 Jul'03 Ripo 12.3g/f 85-80 D: 2 May'03 Muss 12g/f 83-76 D: 1 May'03 Muss 12gd 77-70 D:
2 Apr'03 Muss 14g/f 72-65 E: 1 Jul'02 Beve 12gd 66-60 E: 2 Jun'02 Epso 12gd 60-59 E: 2 Jun'02 Muss 12g/f 56-54 E:
1 May'02 Muss 12gd 54-49 F: 2 Jul'01 Asco 12g/f 59-60 D: 1 Jul'01 Brig 11.8g/f 62- F: 2 Jul'01 Warw 10.8g/f 58-55 F:
3761} **LODGER 323** [12]4-9-4 (92) K Darley 17/2: 323214-0: 12th: In tch, wknd well over 2f out on reapp.   5   65
4838} **ASTRONOMIC 264** [13]4-9-11 (99) R Winston 16/1: 342413-0: 13th: In tch, wknd over 2f out, t.o.   6   63
13 Ran   Time 2m 34.15 (7.35)   Owned: Mr & Mrs Heywood & Mr & Mrs Bovington   Trained: Middleham

3077   4.15 Tulip Bacon Rated Stakes Handicap 3yo+ 0-100 (B)   **[107]**
£12853 £4875 £2438   7f205y rnd   Good/Soft 60   +08 Fast   Inside

1512 **ST PETERSBURG 67** [7] M H Tompkins 4-9-0 (93) K Darley 7/2: 15-21021: Handy, hdwy to lead 2f out,   101
styd on well for press ins last: 10 wk abs, gd time: stays 1m well on fast & polytrack, likes gd/soft & hvy, any
trk: runs well fresh: useful, more to come, see 1066.
2903 **FLIGHTY FELLOW 7** [1] T D Easterby 4-9-1 (94) W Supple 11/2: 2-061062: Held up rear, eff & short   1½   97
of room over 2f out, switched & styd on well over 1f out, nrst fin: hard to make up a lot of grnd here at York &
again shaped with plenty of promise, win again with a stiffer tst: see 2903, 1833.
2710 **PLAY THAT TUNE 15** [2] M Johnston 4-8-10 (89) J Fanning 9/1: 033-0543: Held up, hdwy over 2f out,   ½   92
no extra fnl 1f: see 1686.
1895 **BLUE SKY THINKING 49** [5] K R Burke 5-9-0 (93) Darren Williams 6/1: 4-156034: In tch, eff over 2f   1¼   93
out, sn no extra: 7 wk abs: see 1895, 519.
2489 **WIZARD OF NOZ 23** [6]4-9-7 (100) M Hills 10/1: 3/40-2605: Held up, brief eff 2f out, no impress.   ¾   98
2489 **PUTRA KUANTAN 23** [4]4-9-7 (100) N Callan 11/4 FAV: 00-63106: Set pace till 2f out, wknd: hvly   5   88
bckd: prefers faster grnd: much btr 2096.
2903 **MYSTERINCH 7** [3]4-8-12 (91) T E Durcan 7/1: 3-300207: In tch, sn rdn, eff over 2f out, sn wknd.   2½   74
7 Ran   Time 1m 40.0 (4.2)   Owned: Mr P Heath   Trained: Newmarket

3078   4.50 Ramesys Maiden Stakes 2yo   (D)
£5255 £1617 £809   6f217y rnd   Good/Soft 60   -30 Slow   Inside

ELLIOTS WORLD [2] M Johnston 2-9-0 J Fanning 7/2: 1: b c King's Best - Morning Welcome (Be My   97+
Guest) Handy, hdwy to lead over 2f out, sn pushed clr & drifted left, v readily on debut: May foal, cost £75,000:
half-brother to Irish & French 2,000gns wnr Bachir: dam styd 12f: eff at 7f, sure to relish 1m+: runs well fresh
on gd/soft: looks v promising & potentially high-class, win in much stronger company.
2766 **SEYAADI 13** [3] E A L Dunlop 2-9-0 R Hills 2/1 FAV: 52: Handy, led over 3f out till over 2f out,   6   82
not pace of impressive wnr: imprvd from debut & eff at 7f on gd/soft: potentially caught a v smart type.
2774 **LODGICIAN 13** [4] J J Quinn 2-9-0 Darren Williams 14/1: 43: In tch, eff 2f out, no impress: 5   74
wants minor trks.
JACKADANDY [9] J Howard Johnson 2-9-0 P Mulrennan(5) 11/1: 4: b g Lear Fan - Chandra (Morning   2½   70
Bob) Slow away, bhd, modest late gains on debut: May foal, cost 30,000gns: bred to apprec 1m+ in time.
2570 **BALLYCROY GIRL 20** [5]2-8-9 N Mackay(3) 11/1: 625: In tch, wknd over 3f out: see 2570.   1¼   63
ZORIPP [8]2-9-0 M Fenton 22/1: 6: b c Spectrum - Allspice (Alzao) Al bhd on debut: Jan first   2   65
foal, cost 9,000gns: dam styd: bred to apprec 7f/1m.
MASQUERADER [1]2-9-0 K McEvoy 11/4: 7: In tch, hung left over 2f out, wknd on debut: bckd.   nk   64
BAHAMIAN BAY [6]2-8-9 G Parkin 50/1: 8: Swerved right start, led till 3f out, wknd & eased.   24   19
8 Ran   Time 1m 27.63(6.33)   Owned: Atlantic Racing Limited   Trained: Middleham

Official Going GOOD

3079   6.50 Claims Uk Maiden Stakes Fillies 3yo+   (D)
£5382 £1656 £828   7f122y rnd   Good/Firm 22   +08 Fast   Inside

2659 **RED TOP 16** [1] R Hannon 3-8-12 (82) F Norton 4/9 FAV: 3-232021: Trkd ldr & led 2f out, readily   84
pulled clr, val 7L+: well bckd at odds on: best time of night: eff btwn 7f/1m on fast & soft grnd, stiff/gall or
sharp/turning trk: found this straightforward task: see 2659, 1929 & 1171.
2224 **HEARTS DESIRE 35** [7] B W Hills 3-8-12 (77) M Hills 5/2: 52-62: b f Royal Applause - Touch And   3½   72
Love (Green Desert) Led, rdn & hdd 2f out, sn no ch with wnr, rest well covered: lightly rcd mdn rnr-up '03: h eff
around 7f, handles fast & soft. 2 Oct'03 Yarm 7.0sft 80- D:
2755 **TOKEWANNA 13** [4] W M Brisbourne 4-9-7 T (50) R Winston 40/1: 4040-003: Sn trkd ldrs, flashed tail   3½   65$
under press & no prog over 1f out: first time t-strap: see 2204.
2907 **HIRAYNA 7** [2] W M Brisbourne 5-9-7 D Allan 12/1: 304: Keen & trkd ldrs, rdn & btn 2f out: op 20/1.   1¼   62
2692 **GRELE 15** [3]3-8-12 J Carroll 50/1: 0-05: gr f Loup Sauvage - Fiveblushingroses (Runaway Groom)   1   60
Rear & sn pushed along, little hdwy: unplcd sole '03 start (mdn, rtd 59): dam a multiple US wnr.
REEM TWO 0 [6]3-8-12 L Enstone(3) 50/1: 6: b f Mtoto - Jamrat Samya (Sadler's Wells) Bhd, no   2½   55
impress & eased fnl 1f: debut: cheaply bght, related to a plcd bmpr performer & a hurdles wnr.
1425 **LETS PARTY 72** [5]4-9-7 t (45) J P Guillambert(3) 50/1: 0400-007: Sn bhd, 10 wk abs.   20   15
7 Ran   Time 1m 33.51 (1.11)   Owned: Mr William Durkan   Trained: Marlborough

3080   7.20 Kathleen B Corbett Memorial Handicap Stakes 3yo 0-95   (C)   [96]
£9510 £2926 £1463   5f16y rnd   Good/Firm 22   +02 Fast   Inside

2961 **HELLO ROBERTO 5** [3] M J Polglase 3-7-12 (3oh) (66) J Mackay 8/1: 2025301: Held up in tch,   76
switched & hdwy to lead ins last, styd on well under hand riding cl-home: joc gvn 2 day careless riding ban: qck
reapp: eff at 5/6f on fast, gd/soft & both AWs: seems best held up off a strong pace: see 2731.
2778 **SIR ERNEST 12** [1] M J Polglase 3-8-5 (76) R Ffrench 7/1: 0602042: Led, rdn & hdd well ins last: gd run.   ¾   79
2734 **DIVINE SPIRIT 14** [4] M Dods 3-9-0 (85) R Winston 9/2: 0036103: Trkd ldrs, rdn to chall ins last,   nk   87
not pace of wnr: just btr 2566 (g/s).
2390 **ENCHANTMENT 27** [5] J M Bradley 3-9-7 (92) M Hills 7/2 FAV: 1-521124: Prom, ch ins last no extra.   hd   93
2758 **GREEN MANALISHI 13** [9]3-9-6 (91) P Dobbs 6/1: 2103155: Mid-div, eff when hmpd over 1f out,   shd   91+
switched wide & kept on, fine run from poor draw: crucially denied the same gap as wnr, keep on side: see 2758.
3036 **MELODY KING 2** [2]3-7-12 (2oh)bl (67) T Quinn(5) 7/1: 0325406: Chsd ldrs, onepace distt: qck reapp.   ¾   67
2950 **FOUR AMIGOS 6** [8]3-8-12 (83) J Fanning 9/2: 2-510637: Bhd, rdn & only mod prog: qck reapp.   4   69
1766 **MOLLY MOON 55** [7]3-9-1 (86) F Norton 25/1: 13164-08: gr f Primo Dominie - Snowing (Tate Gallery)   nk   71
Bhd, nvr on terms, mod draw: mdn & nov stks scorer '03: both wins at 5f: acts on fast & gd.
1 Aug'03 Ling 5g/f 85-(82) D: 1 Jun'03 Ling 5g/f 82- D: 2 May'03 Newb 5.2g/f 82- D: 2 May'03 Warw 5g/f 76- D:
2884 **MR WOLF 8** [10]3-8-7 (78) L Enstone(3) 25/1: 2116609: Prom till over 1f out from poor high draw.   2   57
4203* **)DVINSKY 301** [11]3-9-5 T (90) R Hughes 10/1: 61-0: 10th: b c Stravinsky - Festive Season (Lypheor)   hd   68
Sn towards rear from poor high draw: reapp/h'cap bow in first time t-strap: lightly rcd mdn scorer in '03: winning
form at 6f, half-brother to 6f wnr: acts on fast grnd & sharp/undul trk.
1 Sep'03 Good 6g/f 88- D:
10 Ran   Time 1m 0.83 (1.03)   Owned: G A Lucas and I Buckley   Trained: Newark

3081   7.50 Nexus Gsa Conditions Stakes 2yo   (B)
£10301 £3907 £1954   5f16y rnd   Good/Firm 22   -01 Slow   Inside

2744* **BECKERMET 13** [2] R F Fisher 2-9-3 R Ffrench 5/4 FAV: 311211: Handy & led over 1f out, rdn clr: 106+
suited by 5f on fast & gd/soft grnd, loves Chester: v useful, again blessed by fav'able low draw: smart.
2859* **AMAZIN 9** [1] R Hannon 2-9-0 R Hughes 5/2: 212: Missed break, sn pushed along chasing ldrs,   2½   95
switched & kept on, wnr had been favoured: poss closer with a smart start: eff at 5f, rtn to 6f+ suit: see 2859.
2847* **OH DARA 9** [7] P A Blockley 2-8-9 Dean McKeown 15/2: 13: Led till over 1f out, no extra well ins   1   87
last but clr of rem: not disgraced from awkward draw: win again after 2847 (gamble, impressive).

CHESTER FRIDAY 09.07.04 Lefthand, Very Tight Track

2859 **THE CROOKED RING 9** [4] P D Evans 2-8-11 E Ahern 12/1: 5232134: Outpcd, only mod prog. *5* **74**
2792 **TIVISKI 11** [3]2-8-9 W Supple 9/1: 341045: Chsd ldrs when short of room after 2f, sn outpcd: btr 1573. *nk* **71**
2786 **GOLD QUAY 12** [5]2-8-6 J Fanning 25/1: 246: Rear, nvr on terms: see 2358. *1½* **64**
2792 **DEN PERRY 11** [6]2-8-11 C Ely 100/1: 6007: Sn struggling: needs sell grade: see 2167. *7* **48**
2167 **BIGALOS BANDIT 37** [9]2-9-0 R Winston 10/1: 1248: Chsd ldrs till 2f out: poor high drawm, btr 2167. *3* **42**
8 Ran Time 1m 0.95 (1.15) Owned: Bishopthorpe Racing Two Trained: Ulverston

3082 **8.20 New Vauxhall Tigra Nursery Handicap Stakes 2yo (D)** **[93]**
£4745 £1460 £730 **5f16y rnd** **Good/Firm 22** **-27 Slow** Inside

2744 **NOVA TOR 13** [2] N P Littmoden 2-8-12 (77) I Mongan 7/2 FAV: 11041: Broke well & dictated pace from fav low draw, qcknd clr dist, readily: eff at 5f on fast, gd/soft & fibresand, sharp/turning or easy trks: enjoyed forcing the pace under a well judged ride: see 2744, 1634 & 1029. **86**
1981 **IM AIMEE 45** [8] P D Evans 2-8-9 (74) E Ahern 11/1: 2630402: Cl-up, ch over 1f out, sn outpcd by wnr: 6 wk abs, gd run from awkward high draw: showed useful tactical speed & shld find a race if repeating. *1¾* **76**
2697 **DETONATE 15** [1] I A Wood 2-8-11 (76) R Hughes 9/2: 64063: Keen early, trkd ldrs trav well, shkn up & onepace from dist: fav'able draw, handles fast & soft grnd: see 1422. *shd* **77**
2430* **TALCEN GWYN 25** [3] M F Harris 2-9-2 (81) W Supple 9/2: 414: Mid-div when short of room over 1f out, not pace to threaten: see 2430 (made all, mdn auct). *nk* **81**
2711 **KATIE BOO 15** [5]2-9-0 (79) J Carroll 9/2: 32135: Trkd ldrs till lost pl after 3f, mod late rally: see 2711. *½* **77**
2611 **LITTLE BISCUIT 18** [9]2-7-12 (2oh) (63) B Swarbrick(5) 10/1: 1125426: Held up, nvr pace to chall. *nk* **60**
2573 **COLEORTON DANCER 20** [7]2-8-3 (68) P Fessey 11/1: 04447: Held up, nvr dngr, mod draw. *¾* **63**
2786 **PIPER LILY 12** [6]2-9-7 (86) F Norton 10/1: 5168: Trkd ldrs till over 1f out: moderate draw: btr 2241. *3* **72**
8 Ran Time 1m 2.25 (2.45) Owned: Mr Nigel Shields Trained: Newmarket

3083 **8.50 Ethel Austin Property Group Classified Stakes 4yo+ 0-80 (D)**
£5382 £1656 £828 **1m2f75y** **Good/Firm 22** **-03 Slow** Outside

2798 **BARKING MAD 11** [5] M L W Bell 6-9-0 (82) I Mongan 100/30: 50-64321: Made all, joined from dist, drvn & held on all out: suited by 10f on firm & gd grnd, handles soft & any trk, loves a sharp one & forcing tactics: another well judged ride by I Mongan: see 1890. **87**
2592 **GREY CLOUDS 20** [4] T D Easterby 4-8-9 (79) W Supple 5/4 FAV: 4201232: Trkd ldrs, switched & rdn to join wnr dist, duelled & just denied: fine run: see 2592, 2323 & 2038. *shd* **81**
2860 **VOICE MAIL 9** [3] A M Balding 5-8-12 (79) L Keniry(3) 13/2: 1130203: Trkd ldrs, not pace of front pair bef dist: fair run, Bath specialist: see 2665 & 1899. *2½* **80**
2873 **BEN HUR 8** [9] W M Brisbourne 5-8-12 (73) E Ahern 5/1: 1021154: Keen early trkg ldr, no extra over 1f out: see 2745 (C/D clmr). *½* **78**
2935 **STOIC LEADER 6** [6]4-8-12 (79) R Winston 8/1: 0024265: Chsd ldrs, rdn & no prog dist: btr 2809 (7f). *6* **70**
774 **PHOENIX NIGHTS 131** [2]4-8-12 (52) C Ely(7) 40/1: 30-05006: Dwelt, rear, nvr mount chall: see 423. *shd* **69$**
2747 **PRINCE OF BLUES 13** [8]6-8-12 (59) P Dobbs 33/1: 0033507: Al bhd: btr 2286 (5f). *3* **64**
2571 **BUSCADOR 20** [7]5-8-12 (47) B Swarbrick(5) 50/1: 1-000008: Keen, wide, in tch till 3f out: see 157 (AW). *19* **35**
8 Ran Time 2m 11.21 (2.71) Owned: Mr Christopher Wright Trained: Newmarket

3084 **9.20 Aspects Beauty Company Cheshire Yeomanry Handicap Stakes 3yo 0-85 (D)** **[91]**
£5421 £1668 £834 **1m2f75y** **Good/Firm 22** **-10 Slow** Outside

2785 **GAVROCHE 12** [4] C A Dwyer 3-9-7 (84) J P Guillambert(3) 100/30: 2251141: Bhd early, hdwy 4f out & rdn/led over 1f out, drvn out: eff at 9/10f on firm, hvy & fibresand, prob any trk: most tough & genuine: see 2377. **94**
2800* **HATCH A PLAN 11** [1] R M Beckett 3-8-5 (6ex) (68) J Quinn 3/1 J FAV: 00-0U012: Held up, briefly short of room 2f out, rdn to chase wnr dist, al just held: confirmed improvment of latest: see 2800. *1* **75**
2706 **MAGIC STING 15** [3] M L W Bell 3-8-5 (68) J Mackay 3/1 J FAV: 5561103: Chsd ldrs, led over 3f out, hdd over 1f out & no extra: acts on fast & soft grnd: see 2180. *2½* **71**
2631 **KINGS EMPIRE 18** [2] D Carroll 3-9-6 (83) D Tudhope(7) 5/1: 31-44: Led early & chsd ldr, wknd 2f out. *4* **80**
2700 **ZUMA 15** [5]3-8-13 BL (76) R Hughes 11/2: 00-03055: Rdn to lead after 1f, hdd over 3f out, sn btn: plenty of effort to obtain early lead here may have taken its toll: visor omitted, tried blnks: see 2386 (mdn). *1½* **71**
1587. **PRELUDE 18** [6]3-8-0 (63) B Swarbrick(5) 22/1: 5006: Held up, no impress fnl 2f, longer trip: see 1587. *hd* **57**
6 Ran Time 2m 11.93(3.43) Owned: Mr J L Guillambert Trained: Newmarket

CHEPSTOW FRIDAY 09.07.04 Lefthand, Undulating, Galloping Track

Official Going GOOD

3085 **6.35 Medinet Apprentice Handicap Stakes 3yo+ 0-70 (E)** **[63]**
£3374 £1038 £519 **1m4f23y** **Good/Soft 63** **-14 Slow** Inside

1736 **DICKIE DEADEYE 56** [7] G B Balding 7-9-8 (57) Derek Nolan(3) 9/2 FAV: 0-652231: Made all, clr 5f out, cmftbly: 8 wk abs: acts on gd & hvy: imprvd for step up to 12f & front-rng. **73**
2910 **MR DIP 7** [12] A W Carroll 4-9-1 (50) W Hogg(3) 8/1: 0-060052: Dwelt, hld up, hdwy over 2f out, took 2nd ins fnl 1f but no ch with easy wnr: op 10/1, qck reapp, clr of rem: see 2910. *11* **53**
2978 **LUCKY ARTHUR 4** [5] J G M O'Shea 3-8-11 (59) M Lawson 5/1: 050323: Rear, hdwy into 2nd 4f out, no ch with wnr & lost 2nd ins fnl 1f: qck reapp: see 2978. (fast). *5* **54**
1695 **SHOLAY 58** [9] P Mitchell 5-8-10 (45) Crystal Caetano(5) 66/1: 00-00004: Rear, hdwy over 3f out, saddle slipped over 2f out, no impress: 8 wk abs: see 842. *1¾* **37**
2892 **ESCALADE 7** [10]7-9-6 p (55) P Mathers 6/1: 0543435: Keen & handy, no impress fnl 1f: qck reapp. *nk* **46**
4931} **DIAMONDS WILL DO 255** [4]7-9-7 (56) L Treadwell 12/1: 0/205/20-6: b f Bigstone - Clear Ability (Be My Guest) Handy, no impress 2f out on reapp: won a h'cap hdle in 03/04 (eff at 2m/2m4f on fast & soft, rtd 101h): rnr-up 1 of 2 '03 starts (h'cap): ex Irish, rnr-up first of 3 '02 starts (mdn): eff at 12/13f, on firm & *nk* **46**

soft. 2 Sep'03 Asco 12g/f 57-54 D:
2868 **GRADY 8** [2]5-8-0 (35) D Fentiman 25/1: 0-660607: Slowly away, hdwy over 3f out, no impress fnl 1f. 1½ 23
2782 **BEN KENOBI 12** [3]6-8-2 (37) Dean Williams(3) 6/1: 0-522028: Dwelt, hdwy 4f out, no impress fnl 1f. ¾ 24
1780] **BARCELONA 769** [8]7-10-0 bl (63) H Poulton(3) 6/1: 00003/5/-9: b g Barathea - Pipitina (Bustino) 6 41
In tch, hdwy over 4f out, no impress over 2f out: hdles fit (h'cap 5th, eff at 2m2f/2m6.5f on firm & soft, any trk, rtd 107h in blnks): missed '03: 5th sole '02 start (h'cap, rtd 62): tried 2m, suited by 14f on firm & soft, acts on a sharp or gall trk: best in a t-strap, wears blnks: tried cheek pieces over timber.
2700 **GREY ADMIRAL 15** [1]3-9-6 (68) T Block(5) 16/1: 000-00: 10th: gr g Cozzene - Remarkable Style 11 29
(Danzig) Al bhd: mdn unplcd in '02 (rtd 81): with A Balding.
2700 **TARTIRUGA 15** [6]3-7-13 (47) Stephanie Hollinshead 40/1: 00-000: 11th: Keen in 2nd, lost pl over nk 7
5f out, no impress over 3f out.
1163} **STAGE DIRECTION 444** [11]7-8-8 (43) P Gallagher 14/1: 06214/0-0: 12th: Dwelt, nvr a factor on reapp. 4 0
12 Ran Time 2m 40.37 (9.27) Owned: Miss B Swire Trained: Andover

3086

7.05 European Breeders Fund Novice Stakes 2yo (D)
£5652 £1739 £870 **5f16y str** **Good/Soft 63** **-34 Slow** Stands side

3008 **INDIANNIE STAR 11** [5] M R Channon 2-8-9 S Hitchcott(3) 11/4: 216051: Dsptd lead till led just 84
over 2f out, rdn out fnl 1f: eff at 5f on fast & gd/soft, acts on a gall or sharp/undul trk: apprec this drop in grade: useful 2yo: ran to winning form of 1981.
2395* **KWAME 27** [1] Miss E C Lavelle 2-8-9 S W Kelly 6/1: 212: Handy, ev ch ins fnl 1f, kept on: acts nk 83
on fast & gd/soft: remains in gd form & imprvd in defeat: see 2395.
2783 **ROBMANTRA 12** [4] B J Llewellyn 2-8-12 S Whitworth 66/1: 653: Rear, not much room over 1f out, 1¾ 81
kept on: much improved on gd/soft: eff at 5f: see 2597.
2472 **SAFARI SUNSET 24** [2] P Winkworth 2-9-2 P Doe 8/13 FAV: 134: Led till just over 2f out, no extra 1½ 81
ins fnl 1f: top-weight: not handle gd/soft? much btr 2472 (fast).
2870 **DIZZY LIZZY 8** [3]2-8-7 M Henry 50/1: 05: gr f Sendawar - Black Velvet (Black Tie Affair) 18 18
Handy, no impress over 2f out: mdn unplcd earlier debut: Mar foal, cost 8,000gns: dam an 1m wnr.
5 Ran Time 1m 1.69 (4.89) Owned: Timberhill Racing Partnership Trained: West Ilsley

3087

7.35 Bet365 08000 322365 Selling Handicap Stakes 3yo+ 35-55 (G) **[56]**
£2653 £758 £379 **1m14y str** **Good/Soft 63** **-08 Slow** Stands side

2032 **CHANDELIER 43** [17] M S Saunders 4-9-0 (42) Dane O'Neill 10/1: 3603201: Cl-up, hdwy to lead over 56
3f out, rdn clr over 1f out, cmftbly: bght in for 7,000gns: 6 wk abs: eff btwn 7f/1m on gd/soft & both AWs, sharp or a gall/undul trk: made gd use of fav'able high draw: see 440.
2634 **GO GREEN 18** [8] P D Evans 3-8-9 T (46) F P Ferris(3) 16/1: 0000502: Slowly away, hdwy over 2f out, 5 48
not pace of wnr: tried a t-strap: acts on fm & gd/soft: see 2032.
2909 **OVER TO YOU BERT 7** [14] R J Hodges 5-8-12 (40) R Havlin 13/2: 1400033: Handy, ev ch 2f out, onepcd. 2½ 37
2909 **ENNA 7** [13] Mrs Stef Liddiard 5-9-9 (51) S Drowne 20/1: 13-46004: Bhd, switched to stands rail nk 47
over 2f out, hdwy over 1f out, not pace of chall: qck reapp: see 1284.
2909* **MOBO BACO 7** [12]7-10-2 (6ex) (58) J Fortune 7/1: 4000015: In tch, hdwy 2f out, onepcd fnl 1f. 1 52
2332 **LEITRIM ROCK 29** [4]4-9-2 (44) S Whitworth 16/1: 000-0046: Slowly away, switched to stands side 1½ 35
early, hdwy 2f out, wknd fnl 1f: see 2032.
2909 **LORD CHAMBERLAIN 7** [16]11-9-9 bl (51) C J Davies(7) 9/2 FAV: 4403027: Mid-div, eff 2f out, no impress. ½ 41
2667 **AVERTAINE 16** [2]3-8-12 bl (49) R L Moore 9/1: 0520658: Led far side, eased when no ch ins fnl 1f. 3 33
1348 **ZAHUNDA 76** [20]5-8-10 (38) S W Kelly 15/2: 4633649: Rear, hdwy 3f out, no impress over 1f out. ¾ 20
2369 **IN TUNE 28** [18]4-8-12 t (40) G Baker 25/1: 55-00000: 10th: Led over 4f, no extra over 2f out. 1½ 19
2910 **ZALKANI 7** [11]4-9-7 (49) A Hindley(7) 20/1: 3000500: 11th: Slow away, sn handy, no impress 2f out. 2 24
4590} **SOUTHAMPTON JOE 279** [7]4-9-9 (51) P Mathers(7) 16/1: 000000-0: 12th: ch g Just A Cat - Maple Hill 6 14
Jill (Executive Pride) Handy far side, no impress over 2f out: hdles fit (u.r., h'cap): h'cap unplcd in '03 (rtd 50, with A Balding): won 2 nurs h'caps for I Balding in '02, also plcd sev times: eff at 6/sharp 7f on fast & soft, prob any trk: has tried cheek pieces: now with J O'Shea.
1 Sep'02 Ling 7sft 72-65 E: 2 Aug'02 Nott 6g/f 68-62 E: 1 Aug'02 Chep 6gd 64-58 D:
2909 **MUQTADI 7** [19]6-9-2 (44) N Pollard 12/1: 5406000: 13th: Slow away, sn handy, no impress 2f out. 2½ 2
2369 **VARIETY CLUB 28** [6]3-9-4 VIS (55) T Block(7) 33/1: 000-00: 14th: b g Royal Applause - Starfida 2½ 8
(Soviet Star) Cl-up far side, wknd 3f out: mdn unplcd in '03 (rtd 67): tried a visor here: with A Balding.
2371 **MARGARETS WISH 28** [5]4-9-0 (42) S Sanders 20/1: 0010000: 15th: Cl-up far side, wknd over 3f out. shd 0
2476 **BREVITY 23** [15]9-9-13 (55) V Slattery 33/1: 60400-00: 16th: Al bhd: see 2476. 2½ 2
2220 **YOUNG DYNASTY 35** [3]4-8-12 bl (40) Liam Jones(7) 50/1: 0550500: 17th: Cl-up far side, wknd bef halfway 1½ 0
17 Ran Time 1m 37.63 (5.73) Owned: Chris Scott & Peter Hall Trained: Wells

3088

8.05 S E T Office Supplies Handicap Stakes 3yo+ 0-85 (D) **[85]**
£16796 £5168 £2584 **7f16y str** **Good/Soft 63** **+06 Fast** Stands side

2872* **PANGO 8** [17] H Morrison 5-9-6 (5ex) (77) L Fletcher(3) 9/2: 500-2211: Mid-div, switched left 2f 86
out, hard rdn ins fnl 1f, led fnl stride: landed double: eff btwn 7/11f on fast, gd/soft & both AWs, prob any trk, likes Epsom: made full use of gd high draw: thriving, see 2872.
3001 **BLUE TROJAN 3** [9] S Kirk 4-9-12 (83) J F Egan 11/1: 0140042: Chsd ldrs, hdwy to lead ins fnl 1f, shd 90
hdd fnl stride: qck reapp: eff at 7f, suited by 1m, stays a sharp 10f: in decent form: see 1883.
2590* **DUMNONI 20** [20] Julian Poulton 3-9-1 (80) N Callan 9/1: 0630413: Handy, hdwy over 2f out, kept 2 84
on ins fnl 1f: acts on firm, gd/soft & both AWs: shade btr 2590 (firm).
1512 **HURRICANE COAST 67** [10] D Flood 5-9-2 bl (73) R Smith 20/1: 4101664: Cl-up, ev ch 2f out, onepcd. hd 76
2880* **GOODENOUGH MOVER 8** [2]8-9-11 (5ex) (82) Hayley Turner(5) 8/1: 2122115: Switched to stands side ¾ 83
after 1f & sn handy, led over 2f out, hdd ins fnl 1f & no extra: just btr 2880.
2954 **TUSCARORA 5** [7]5-7-12 (3oh) (52) D Fentiman(7) 16/1: 06-00526: Rear, hdwy 1f out, nrst fin. hd 55
2864 **ANNIJAZ 8** [18]7-7-12 (3oh) (52) D Kinsella 25/1: 4004607: Slow away in rear, hdwy fnl 1f, nrst fin. shd 54
2973* **A ONE 4** [8]5-8-4 (5ex) (61) F P Ferris(3) 4/1 FAV: 0-431118: Led till over 2f out, no extra 1f out. ½ 59
2872 **FLEETWOOD BAY 8** [19]4-8-12 (69) G Baker 20/1: 0-006369: Handy, no impress over 1f out. 1 65
2880 **MARKER 8** [5]4-9-8 vis (79) S Drowne 20/1: 0040400: 10th: Switched to stands side after 1f, no impress. ¾ 73
2600 **ZAFARSHAH 19** [16]5-8-5 (62) N Pollard 16/1: 4620300: 11th: Nvr a factor. ½ 55

CHEPSTOW FRIDAY 09.07.04 Lefthand, Undulating, Galloping Track

2535 **MILLFIELDS DREAMS** 21 [6]5-8-3 (60) R Thomas(5) 20/1: 4604-100: 12th: Led far side, no extra ins fnl 1f. *hd* **52**
2172 **JUST FLY** 37 [12]4-9-7 (78) J Fortune 20/1: 2220300: 13th: Al bhd: see 1817. *1¼* **67**
2958 **CASHNEEM** 5 [3]6-8-7 (64) S W Kelly 50/1: 4614000: 14th: Rcd in 2nd far side, no impress ins fnl 1f. *shd* **52**
2172 **CHEESE N BISCUITS** 37 [14]4-9-2 p (73) R L Moore 33/1: 5-002000: 15th: Al bhd. *3½* **54**
2857 **CHEVRONNE** 9 [13]4-8-2 (59) J F McDonald(3) 50/1: 50-00200: 16th: In tch, lost pl & wknd 2f out. *hd* **39**
2857 **THE GAIKWAR** 9 [11]5-8-8 bl (65) Dane O'Neill 50/1: 012U000: 17th: Slowly away, nvr a factor. *½* **44**
2758 **ARCTIC DESERT** 13 [1]4-9-11 vis (82) K Darley 25/1: 52 00000: 18th: b g Desert Prince - Thamud *1¾* **58**
(Lahib): Dwelt far side, sn handy, no impress over 1f out: won first '03 start (mdn): plcd in '02 (rtd 77, l
Balding): eff at 7f on firm, polytrack & prob gd/soft, acts on a sharp trk: goes well fresh: wearing a visor now,
has tried a t-strap. 2 Oct'03 York 7.0g/f 91-89 B: 1 Apr'03 Ling 7ap 87a- D:
2684 **SOYUZ** 15 [15]4-10-0 (85) M Henry 12/1: 0-231500: 19th: Al bhd under top-weight. *3* **55**
2864 **TAPAU** 8 [4]6-8-2 p (59) C Catlin 50/1: 5000000: 20th: Rcd far side in tch, wknd 2f out: see 1269. *4* **21**
20 Ran   Time 1m 23.83 (4.03)   Owned: Pangfield Partners   Trained: East Ilsley

3089 8.35 Gr3 Oakgrove Stud Golden Daffodil Stakes Fillies 3yo+ (A)
£29000 £11000 £5500   1m2f36y   Good/Soft 63   +09 Fast   Inside

1921 **FELICITY** 48 [6] J H M Gosden 4-9-2 (94) J Fortune 12/1: 535-0341: Rcd in 2nd, hdwy to lead over **108**
2f out, hdd 1f out, rallied to lead again well ins fnl 1f, all out to hold on nr fin: gd time: 7 wk abs: eff at
10f, has tried 12f: acts on fast, much improved on gd/soft here: smart run, see 1857.
2555 **KINNAIRD** 21 [10] P C Haslam 3-8-5 (110) K Darley 7/4 FAV: 5111-452: Rear, hdwy 3f out, led 1f *nk* **107**
out till well ins fnl 1f, no extra nr fin: well clr of rem: eff btwn 1m/10f: smart, back to form of 2005.
2538 **TIDAL** 21 [1] A W Carroll 5-9-2 (74) T P Queally 20/1: 00-61103: Led till over 2f out, no extra. *7* **96$**
2351* **INCHENI** 29 [11] G Wragg 3-8-5 (102) S Drowne 3/1: 61-20314: Rear, hdwy 2f out, not pace to *2* **93**
chall: not handle gd/soft? see 2351.
2491 **DOCTRINE** 23 [4]3-8-5 (96) R Havlin 20/1: 2116-405: Bhd, brief eff over 1f out, not dngrs: see 1110. *1* **91**
2772 **COTE QUEST** 13 [2]4-9-2 (92) R L Moore 25/1: 4004436: Chsd ldrs, no impress 2f out. *3½* **86**
2772 **SHAMARA** 13 [3]4-9-2 (90) S Sanders 14/1: 310-2247: Rear, brief eff out, no impress over 1f out. *1* **84**
2351 **CLASSICAL DANCER** 29 [8]3-8-5 (99) Dane O'Neill 7/2: 3-1238: Bhd, nvr a factor: btr 2351. *1½* **82**
2432 **CASTAWAY QUEEN** 25 [7]5-9-2 (59) J F Egan 100/1: 20-20039: Rear, nvr nr ldrs. *1* **80$**
2557 **TAMARILLO** 21 [9]3-8-5 (99) T E Durcan 16/1: 5216500: 10th: Bmpd start, bhd, nvr a factor. *12* **62**
10 Ran   Time 2m 9.5 (5.4)   Owned: Mr George Strawbridge   Trained: Manton

3090 9.05 Medinet Handicap Stakes Fillies 3yo 0-70 (E) [74]
£6851 £2108 £1054   1m14y str   Good/Soft 63   -07 Slow   Stands side

2650 **KRYSSA** 17 [4] G L Moore 3-9-6 (66) R L Moore 9/4 FAV: 1335131: Mid-div, hdwy 3f out, led 1f out, **77**
kept on ins fnl 1f: eff at 5f, suited by 6f/1m: acts on firm, gd/soft & polytrack: prog.
2661 **SABRINA BROWN** 16 [1] G B Balding 3-9-0 (60) R Thomas(5) 11/2: 006-22: Cl-up, led over 5f out till *¾* **68**
over 1f out, no extra: clr of rem: stayed longer 1m trip on gd & gd/soft: see 2661.
2842 **DAYDREAM DANCER** 9 [10] C G Cox 3-8-4 BL (50) R Smith 33/1: 00-50003: Led over 3f, no extra over *3* **52**
2f out: tried blnks: see 2842.
1655 **KESHYA** 60 [7] D J Coakley 3-9-3 (63) Dane O'Neill 5/1: 062-3424: Prom, onepcd over 2f out: 9 wk abs. *½* **64**
2755 **FILLIEMOU** 13 [9]3-8-11 (57) N Callan 22/1: 400-0005: Bmpd start, in tch, nvr nrr: see 2225. *2* **54**
2495 **JUST ONE LOOK** 23 [13]3-9-1 (61) D Sweeney 16/1: 0-000006: Rear, hdwy over 1f out, not pace to chall. *nk* **57**
2423 **VENETIAN ROMANCE** 26 [3]3-7-12 (4oh) (40) Hayley Turner(5) 33/1: 05-50007: Slowly away, al bhd. *1¼* **37**
2634 **MY HOPE** 18 [2]3-9-7 (67) S Sanders 16/1: 00-0008: In tch, hdwy over 2f out, sn no impress. *2½* **55**
2299 **THE STICK** 31 [5]3-8-6 (52) C Catlin 20/1: 6-000009: Rear, some modest late gains: see 901. *2½* **35**
2394* **DEIGN TO DANCE** 27 [12]3-9-5 (65) T P Queally 15/2: 0-500510: 10th: In tch, no impress over 1f out. *1½* **45**
2272 **FIZZY LADY** 32 [8]3-9-4 t (64) M Savage(5) 25/1: 54-44100: 11th: Chsd ldrs, wknd over 2f out. *hd* **43**
2617 **DREAM OF DUBAI** 18 [14]3-9-0 (60) J Fortune 20/1: 05-0000: 12th: In tch, no impress 2f out: see 2617. *nk* **38**
2352 **GENTLE RAINDROP** 29 [11]3-9-5 (65) J F Egan 20/1: 0500: 13th: b f College Chapel - Dream Chaser *2½* **38**
(Record Token): Bhd, switched left over 2f out, not clr run 2f out, btn/eased ins fnl 1f: h'cap bow: mdn unplcd
prev: Mar foal: dam a dual 6f wnr: with S Kirk.
2617 **NUKHBAH** 18 [6]3-9-5 (65) S Whitworth 12/1: 43-34500: 14th: Handy, lost pl after 5f, fin t.o. *15* **8**
14 Ran   Time 1m 37.5(5.6)   Owned: Mr D J Deer   Trained: Brighton

SOUTHWELL Fibresand FRIDAY 09.07.04 Lefthand, Sharp, Oval Track

Official Going STANDARD.

3091 2.25 1st Wimbledon Final Claiming Stakes 3yo (F)
£2912 £832 £416   1m aw rnd   Going 53   -39 Slow   Inside

3055 **COME WHAT JULY** 1 [9] R Guest 3-8-10 bl (70) C Lowther 3/1: 25660351: Bhd early, hdwy halfway, **62a**
shkn up to lead cl-home, cheekily, val 2L: clmd for 6,500, unplcd yesterday: eff btwn 7f/10f, unconvincing at 12f
to date: acts on firm & both AWs, likes a sharp trk: see 601.
2675 **MULTIPLE CHOICE** 16 [7] N Littmoden 3-9-3 e T (65) J P Guillambert(3) 10/1: 04-00002: Cl-up & *shd* **67a**
rdn/led dist, hung right & hdd cl-home: op 8/1, gd run in first time t-strap: styd longer 1m trip in claim grade.
1495 **HINODE** 68 [10] J A R Toller 3-9-5 M Tebbutt 4/1: 003: ch c Vettori - Juvenilia (Masterclass) *1¼* **66a**
Chsd ldrs halfway, drvn & kept on, no pace of wnr: 10 wk abs, AW bow: eff around 1m on fibresand in claim
grade: unplcd & mdn form prev.
2590 **STEVEDORE** 20 [1] B J Meehan 3-8-13 BL (74) L Keniry(3) 9/4 FAV: 214-0004: Led, hdd 4f out, no *2* **56a**
extra dist: bckd in first time blnks: AW bow: stays a sharp 1m in claim grade, handles firm, fast & fibresand:
unplcd & mdn form prev.
2855 **CHATSHOW** 9 [5]3-9-7 (62) P Makin(5) 20/1: 6-00405: br g Distant View - Galanty Show (Danehill) *3* **58a**
Led/dsptd lead till dist: AW bow: unplcd prev on turf.
2704 **JAOLINS** 15 [4]3-8-0 (52) D Kinsella 14/1: 5000006: Slow away, bhd, only mod prog. *2½* **32a**
1740 **BROTHER CADFAEL** 56 [6]3-8-7 p (47) Paul Eddery 16/1: 3266607: Chsd ldrs, no impress from halfway. *3* **33a**
2299 **SNOW CHANCE** 31 [11]3-8-0 (34) B Swarbrick(5) 40/1: 0040-08: Chsd ldrs till till halfway. *2* **22a**

1339	**ZULOAGO 76** [3]3-8-10 (55) O Urbina 12/1: 532009: Sn struggling rear: abs: btr 839.	9	16a
2741	**ABSOLUTELY FAB 13** [2]3-8-12 (31) Hayley Turner(5) 66/1: 0000-000: 10th: Sn bhd: drpd in trip.	4	11a
2346	**MARIA MARIA 29** [8]3-8-6 (45) R Fitzpatrick 66/1: 0-00400: 11th: Slowly away & sn struggling.	3½	0a

11 Ran   Time 1m 46.76 (7.36)   Owned: The Storm Again Syndicate   Trained: Newmarket

---

3092

2.55 St Veronica Guiliani Handicap Stakes 3yo 0-70 (E)
£3458 £1064 £532   6f aw rnd   Going 53   +04 Fast   Inside   [72]

2806	**SHIFTY NIGHT 11** [6] Mrs C A Dunnett 3-7-12 (1oh) (42) Hayley Turner(5) 14/1: 00-0041: Sn handy wide, led 2f out, rdn out: op 11/1, first win: eff at 6f, tried further: acts on fibresand: see 2806.		51a
2693	**TSARBUCK 15** [4] R M H Cowell 3-8-13 (58) G Faulkner 5/2 FAV: 0015252: Led/dsptd lead 4f, drvn & kept on, not pace of wnr: eff at 6f, 7f prob ideal: see 1842 (banded, 7f).	1¾	60a
2936	**ADORATA 6** [3] J Jay 3-9-5 (64) O Urbina 7/2: 0032023: Trkd ldrs, styd on onepace for press: acts on firm, gd & fibresand: see 2936, 2295.	1½	61a
2496	**MEGABOND 23** [2] B Smart 3-9-0 (59) F Lynch 8/1: 5230-504: Rdn rear, late gains, no threat.	1	53a
2812	**GARNOCK VENTURE 11** [1]3-9-3 bl (62) Dale Gibson 11/2: 3001005: Pushed along & chsd ldrs, no impress dist: best dominating: see 2379 (C/D clmr).	1¼	52a
2756	**BROWN DRAGON 13** [7]3-9-4 (63) Paul Eddery 8/1: 0-622006: Dwelt & held up, nvr on terms: btr 863.	4	42a
2181	**NOBLE MOUNT 36** [8]3-9-0 (59) J Quinn 12/1: 50037: Chsd ldrs till halfway: btr 2181 (5f).	3	30a
2985	**ELLIOTS CHOICE 4** [5]3-9-7 (66) D Nolan(3) 7/1: 4004368: Chsd ldrs, strugg over 1f out: qck reapp.	1½	32a

8 Ran   Time 1m 16.25 (2.95)   Owned: Mr G R Price   Trained: Norwich

---

3093

3.30 Tom Hanks Birthday Selling Stakes 2yo (G)
£2520 £720 £360   5f aw str   Going 53   -63 Slow   Stands Side

2330	**ETERNALLY 29** [2] R M H Cowell 2-8-11 p B Doyle 2/5 FAV: 03531: Cl-up & led halfway, hung left but in command dist: eff at 5f, tried 6f: acts on fibresand, prob handles firm grnd, sharp trk: eff in cheek pieces & enjoys sell grade: see 1439.		54a
2330	**ITSA MONKEY 29** [3] M J Polglase 2-8-11 K Ghunowa(7) 10/1: 062: Dwelt, chsd ldrs, outpcd bef halfway, kept on ins last, nvr threat: new yard, handles fibresand: see 2330.	3	44a
2921	**ETERNAL SUNSHINE 6** [4] R P Elliott 2-8-6 VIS R Fitzpatrick 20/1: 0003: b f Rossini - Sweet As A Nut (Pips Pride) Led till halfway, btn dist: qck reapp in first time visor: cheaply bght Apr foal, half-sister to a modest mdn juv, dam a useful sprinter.	1¾	34a
2921	**FELLBECK FRED 6** [1] C W Thornton 2-8-11 T Eaves(3) 10/1: 0004: gr c Paris House - Wyse Folly (Colmore Row) Dwelt, chsd ldrs till halfway, qck reapp: AW bow: little form to date: Mar foal, half-brother to 2 mdn performers, dam modest.	1¾	34a
2424	**NORTHERN REVOQUE 26** [6]2-8-6 P Bradley 6/1: 5005: Chsd ldrs 3f, sn btn, AW bow.	8	9a
2911	**ABSOLUT EDGE 7** [5]2-8-11 D Sweeney 20/1: 06: Dwelt, sn outpcd & hung, nvr factor, AW bow.	3	5a

6 Ran   Time 1m 03.1 (5.8)   Owned: Bottisham Heath Stud   Trained: Newmarket

---

3094

4.00 Lobster Carnival Maiden Handicap Stakes Fillies 3yo+ 35-55 (F)
£3038 £868 £434   1m aw rnd   Going 53   -26 Slow   Inside   [60]

2617	**FAITH HEALER 18** [10] V Smith 3-9-4 bl (50) J Quinn 9/2 FAV: 0-000461: Made all & in command dist, rdn out: first win: eff around 1m, tried 12f: acts on fast, soft & fibresand: dift in blnks: enjoyed forcing tactics on AW bow: see 2344.		61a
2589	**WAVET 20** [1] J Pearce 4-9-9 (46) R Price 14/1: 0/6000-02: Prom when hmpd & lost pl after 3f, late rally, no threat: prob closer without interence: handles fibresand: eff at 1m, rtn to 10f may suit: see 2589.	3	50a
2335	**ESSEX STAR 29** [6] Miss J Feilden 3-9-3 (49) J McAuley 5/1: 0000-033: Chsd ldrs, styd on onepace: prob stays 1m: see 2335.	2	49a
2805	**MAGIC VERSE 11** [12] R Guest 3-9-7 (53) C Lowther 5/1: 00444: Chsd ldrs, onepace: see 2805.	shd	53a
2910	**EBORACUM LADY 7** [5]4-9-13 (50) O Urbina 7/1: 0346-65: Rear, hdwy halfway, no prog fnl 2f.	2½	45a
2402	**HILARIOUS 27** [2]4-9-8 (45) Lucy Russell(7) 15/2: 440-5456: Bhd, late prog, nrst fin: new yard.	3½	33a
1289	**CANDY ANCHOR 79** [8]5-9-4 bl (41) V Slattery 14/1: 0306-207: Dwelt, bhd, nrst fin: see 1072 (10f).	1½	26a
2378	**LOLA LOLA 28** [15]3-8-13 (45) D Kinsella 22/1: 000-08: b f Piccolo - French Gift (Cadeaux Genereux) Chsd ldrs till over 2f out: AW/h'cap bow: unplcd '03 (rtd 42, mdns).	1	28a
1576	**CHIQITITA 64** [7]3-9-0 (49) P Makin(5) 20/1: 00-00009: Prom, btn 2f out: 2 mnth abs, new yard.	2	28a
1943	**DIVINA 46** [14]3-8-6 (1oh)vis (38) A Daly 11/1: 0432200: 10th: Prom, strug fnl 3f: abs: btr 1713.	1¼	14a
2630	**DISPOL VERITY 18** [11]4-9-5 (42) B Swarbrick(5) 20/1: 4000/-000: 11th: Held up & strug halfway.	4	11a
2893	Wedowannagiveuthat 7 [3]3-9-9 (55) F Lynch 20/1:0 2719 Suerte 14 [9]4-9-6 (43) B Doyle 14/1:0		

13 Ran   Time 1m 45.68 (6.28)   Owned: Mr V Smith   Trained: Newmarket

---

3095

4.35 Every Breath You Take At Number 1 Maiden Stakes 3yo (D)
£3341 £1028 £514   6f aw rnd   Going 53   -04 Slow   Inside

2383	**EXTRA COVER 28** [4] R Charlton 3-9-0 bl (69) D Sweeney 2/1: 5-22231: b g Danehill Dancer - Ballycurrane (Elbio) In tch, smooth prog to lead ins last, readily asserted, val 5L+: bckd, op 3/1: stays 10f but apprec drop to 6f today: acts on both AWs, gd & soft grnd, likes a sharp trk: now suited for blnks: tidy success, has ability & could strike again in h'caps.		77a+
	2 May'04 Folk 9.7sft 72-(75) F: 2 Apr'04 Wind 10.0g/s 77- D: 2 Apr'04 Ling 8ap 73a- F:		
2849	**CYFRWYS 9** [1] B Palling 3-8-9 (75) J Quinn 15/8 FAV: 2524-022: Led/dsptd lead, went on after 2f till hdd ins last, no ch with wnr: acts on fast, gd & fibresand: see 2849.	4	63a
2659	**SCRUNCH 16** [2] B J Meehan 3-8-9 (68) L Keniry(3) 2/1: 6043: Cl-up, hung right & no extra over 1f out: eff at 6/7f, handles gd grnd & fibresand: type to apprec h'caps.	2	57a
2722	**LORD ARTHUR 14** [6] M W Easterby 3-9-0 (53) Dale Gibson 50/1: 00-04: b g Mind Games - Flower O'Cannie (Mujadil) Bhd, mod late prog, nvr factor: unplcd '03 (rtd 62 & 18a, mdns, lightly rcd).	2½	54a
2704	**LA FONTEYNE 15** [5]3-8-9 (50) T Eaves(3) 25/1: 00-50205: Chsd ldrs, strug halfway: btr 2493.	1½	44a
1659	**PALVIC MOON 60** [3]3-8-9 (60) R Fitzpatrick 14/1: 6066-536: Led, hdd after 2f, short of room when	3½	33a

struggling halfway: 9 wk abs: btr 1659 (soft).
6 Ran Time 1m 16.69 (3.39) Owned: John Livock Bloodstock Limited Trained: Beckhampton

---

| **3096** | 5.10 Run A Mile For Sport Relief Tomorrow Handicap Stakes 4yo+ 35-55 (F) | | | | [63] |
| | £2975 £850 £425 **1m6f aw** **Going 53** -01 Slow Inside | | | | |

3750} **MAGIC RED 324** [9] M J Ryan 4-8-5 (40) R Price 33/1: 0/00000-1: ch g Magic Ring - Jacquelina   **51a**
(Private Account) Cl-up & led halfway, rdn & styd on strongly fnl 2f: op 20/1: 2 month jumps abs, 03/04 juv nov
rnr-up (rtd 100h, 2m, fast): unplcd in '03 (rtd 35 & 33a, h'caps, tried blnks & cheek pieces): mdn rnr-up '02:
stays 14f, 2m cld suit: acts on f/sand & fast grnd: goes well fresh. 2 Jul'02 Yarm 6g/f 75- D:
1802 **MERCURIOUS 53** [10] J Mackie 4-8-7 (42) Dale Gibson 9/2: 34-41542: Prom & ch 2f out, no extra fnl   3   **49a**
1f: 8 wk abs, well clr of rem: see 1263.
2340 **KALANISHA 29** [4] N A Graham 4-8-3 (2ow)BL (36) Paul Eddery 33/1: 000-0603: Prom, rdn & btn 2f   13   **34a**
out: first time blnks: see 1645.
2691 **SEA COVE 15** [1] J M Jefferson 4-8-6 (41) T Eaves(2) 7/1: 00-45554: Chsd ldrs, struggling fnl 3f.   6   **31a**
2453 **LAKE OF DREAMS 25** [7]5-8-5 (40) Lucy Russell(7) 40/1: 00/-005: b g Polish Precedent - Rainbow   nk   **29a**
Lake (Rainbow Quest) Held up, eff 5f out, no impress fnl 3f: lightly rcd & only mod form '03, no form '02.
2724 **OUR IMPERIAL BAY 14** [6]5-9-6 p (55) A Daly 5/1: 0103036: Bhd after 5f: btr 2724 & 1291.   7   **37a**
2724 **WESTERN COMMAND 14** [2]8-8-0 (35) Joanna Badger 14/1: 3505267: Held up, strugg fnl 5f: see 2381. 6   **11a**
3061} **HEARTBREAKER 354** [3]4-8-4 (39) S Carson 33/1: 04/00-8: Led 6f, bhd fnl 4f, long abs.   10   **7a**
2937* **THE KELT 6** [8]7-8-6 (6ex)t (41) J Quinn 13/8 FAV: 000/-319: Slow away, bhd when p.u. 5f out, lame.   **0a**
2562 **DASH OF MAGIC 20** [5]6-8-10 (45) M Tebbutt 13/2: 106315W: Unruly stalls, withdrawn: see 2340.   **0a**
10 Ran Time 3m 07.39(7.59) Owned: Mr M J Ryan Trained: Newmarket

---

Official Going Good - Re Configured Track, Times Suggest Gd/Firm.

| **3097** | 2.25 Mercedes-Benz Of North Wales Maiden Auction Stakes 2yo (E) | | | |
| | £3377 £1039 £520 **5f rnd** **Good/Firm** **Inapplicable** Inside | | | |

2911 **BOLD MINSTREL 8** [7] M Quinn 2-8-7 F Norton 15/8 FAV: 0321: Al cl up & led dist, drvn & just   **72**
held on, all out: hvly bckd: eff at 5f on firm & fast grnd: likes a sharp/turning trk: showed gd early speed to
overcome awkward draw: see 2911, 2415.
SOUND THAT ALARM 0 [4] G A Butler 2-8-11 S W Kelly 100/30: 2: b c Groom Dancer - Warning Star   shd **75***
(Warning) Sn trkd ldrs, swtchd & styd on strongly from dist, just denied: bckd, tho' op 9/4: Jan foal, cost
29,000gns: half brother to juv wnrs abroad: dam a 5/6f juv wnr: eff at 5f, 6f shld suit: acts on fast grnd & a sharp
trk: promising start under a kind ride, likely to progress.
2889 **CHILALI 8** [1] A Berry 2-8-2 S Righton 10/1: 503303: Led till dist, no extra: gd run from low draw.   2   **60**
2360 **OPEN VERDICT 29** [5] A P Jarvis 2-8-9 E Stack 12/1: 04: b c Mujadil - Law Review (Case Law) Sn   2½ **59**
outpcd, rdn & kept on late, no threat: Apr foal, half brother to a plcd 5/6f juv wnr, dam plcd as a 3yo: looks likely
need to 6f+, handles fast ground & posted some improvement today.
2882 **CARMANIA 9** [8]2-8-7 W Supple 50/1: 05: In tch, no impress dist, mod draw.   nk   **56**
1367 **LEONALTO 76** [3]2-8-7 bl J Fortune 9/2: 0536: Trkd ldrs early, lost pl fnl 2f, abs: btr 1367.   ¾   **54**
2810 **LADY HOPEFUL 12** [9]2-8-2 D Fentiman(7) 13/2: 54227: Outpcd, effort over 1f out, hung right & sn btn.   ½ **47**
SWALLOW FALLS 0 [2]2-8-2 A Nicholls 20/1: 8: Dwelt & al outpcd: bckd, op 25/1.   5   **32**
2882 **XEIGHT EXPRESS 9** [6]2-8-2 C Catlin 66/1: 009: Sn strugg   6   **14**
9 Ran Time 1m 01.61 (4.81) Owned: The Boys from the Shed Partnership Trained: Wantage

---

| **3098** | 3.00 Mercedes-Benz Of Liverpool Conditions Stakes 3yo+ (B) | | | |
| | £12383 £4697 £2349 **7f rnd** **Good/Firm** **Inapplicable** Inside | | | |

2757 **VANDERLIN 14** [6] A M Balding 5-9-2 (107) L Keniry 100/30: 40-33531: Held up, hdwy to lead ins   **109**
last, rdn out: eff at 6f, stays 8.5f, suited by 7f: acts on firm, gd/sft & polytrk: tough & smart.
2184 **MAKHLAB 37** [5] B W Hills 4-9-2 BL (108) W Supple 2/1: 01-55422: Chsd ldrs, rdn & kept on fnl 2f,   1¾ **106**
not pace of wnr: nicely bckd, op 7/2: 1st time blnks & a gd run, reportedly lost a shoe: ideally suited by more give.
2826 **MILLENNIUM FORCE 13** [4] M R Channon 6-8-13 (107) C Catlin 7/4 FAV: 30-00423: Handy & led over 1f ½ **102**
out, hdd ins last, no extra: nicely bckd, tho' op 5/4: btr 2826 (g/s).
2486 **GLARAMARA 24** [3] A Bailey 3-8-7 (2ow) (97) J Fortune 6/1: 0203004: Outpcd, late gains: op 4/1.   1½ **101$**
2777 **TELEPATHIC 13** [2]4-8-13 (57) P Mathers 50/1: 0004605: Trkd ldrs, wknd over 1f out: off rtd 57.   3½ **92$**
2949 **JALOUHAR 7** [1]4-8-13 (46) T Woodley 66/1: 0602006: Led till over 1f out, sn btn: see 2480.   6   **80$**
6 Ran Time 1m 25.36 (.36) Owned: J C J R and S R Hitchins Trained: Kingsclere

---

| **3099** | 3.35 Mercedes-Benz Of Southport Handicap Stakes 4yo+ 0-80 (D) | | | | [80] |
| | £5512 £1696 £848 **1m2f75y** **Good/Firm** **Inapplicable** Outside | | | | |

2962 **OPENING CEREMONY 6** [8] R A Fahey 5-9-4 (70) L Vickers 9/1: 31-62421: Held up, prog/no room over   **79**
1f out, swtchd & qcknd to lead well ins last: qck reapp: eff at 9/10.3f on fast & gd/sft grnd, sharp or gall trks:
prev flattered to deceive, enjoyed being produced late: see 2962, 1979.
2285 **YENALED 32** [12] K A Ryan 7-9-2 (68) Donna Caldwell(7) 8/1: 0451122: Dwelt & bhd, hdwy wide over   ½   **75**
1f out & styd on for press, not pace of wnr: in fine form: see 2285, 1755.
2962 **ALÉRON 6** [7] J J Quinn 6-9-6 p (72) L Keniry(3) 8/1: 4-212043: Chsd ldrs, rdn & led dist, hdd &   ½   **78**
onepace ins last: qck reapp: also bhd today's wnr latest: chkpcs reapp: see 1681.
3042 **LOW CLOUD 2** [6] D Nicholls 4-9-10 (76) F Norton 14/1: 0351454: Mid-div, styd on onepace: qck   ¾   **80**
reapp: stays sharp 10f: see 2514 (8.5f).
2761 **RANI TWO 14** [1]5-9-5 (71) C Catlin 6/1: 410-0065: Chsd ldrs, no room over 1f out, kept on onepace.   hd **75**
2745 **GIUNCHIGLIO 14** [5]5-8-12 (64) S W Kelly 16/1: 00-31036: Mid-div, hdwy over 1f out, no extra.   shd **68**

CHESTER SATURDAY 10.07.04 Lefthand, Very Tight Track

2571 **LUXOR 21** [14]7-7-12 (13oh) (37) D Fentiman(7) 33/1: 0000-007: Led till dist, no extra: see 1884. hd **53$**
3037 **GALLANT BOY 3** [3]5-9-3 vis t (69) F P Ferris(3) 8/1: 0050648: Held up, hdwy when no room 1¼ **70+**
repeatedly fnl 1f, pos accepted, closer with a clr run: well h'capped & now in better form, keep in mind: see 549.
2265* **WAR OWL 33** [15]7-9-7 (73) A Beech(3) 10/1: 1135019: Mid-div,efft over 1f out, sn no impress: btr 2265. shd **74**
2687 **SUMMER BOUNTY 16** [10]8-9-10 (76) J Fortune 7/1: 0110320: 10th: Mid-div, no room 2f out, lost ch. hd **76**
2993 **NUZZLE 4** [4]4-7-12 (5oh) (45) R Brisland 20/1: 2603030: 11th: Chsd ldr, btn dist: qck reapp: prefer 1m. 1½ **48**
2943 Compton Dragon 7 [16]5-9-8 vis(74) A Nicholls 12/1:0 2285 Lennel 32 [2]6-8-12 bl(64) Joanna Badger 12/1:0
2947 Prince Of Gold 7 [9]4-9-0 p(66) W Supple 25/1:0   2753 Cats Whiskers 14 [13]5-10-0 (80) L Fletcher(3) 11/1:0
15 Ran   Time 2m 11.65 (3.15)   Owned: Mr H Hurst   Trained: Malton

3100 4.10 Listed Mercedes-Benz Of Chester City Wall Stakes 3yo+ (A)
£17400 £6600 £3300   5f16y rnd   Good/Firm   Inapplicable   Inside

2581 **FIRE UP THE BAND 21** [2] D Nicholls 5-9-0 (99) A Nicholls 7/2: 3-003401: Sn led from fav low **105**
draw, held on all out close home: eff at 5/6f, stays 7f: acts on firm & gd, handles polytrk, gd/sft: smart.
2894 **TALBOT AVENUE 8** [5] M Mullineaux 6-9-0 (80) S Righton 16/1: 0-055022: Keen chasing ldrs, swtchd shd **104$**
& styd on strongly for press ins last, just failed: off rtd 83, in fine form & interesting if reappearing qckly in a h'cap.
2468 **DRAGON FLYER 25** [3] M Quinn 5-8-9 (98) F Norton 4/1: 4200003: Cl up, ch ins last, no extra close 1¼ **94**
home: op 7/2: rnr up in this race '02 & '03: consistent: see 883.
       DORUBAKO 48 [1] Hideyuki Mori 3-8-9 S W Kelly 6/1: 2212214: b c Danzig - Spring Pitch (Storm 1¼ **94+**
Cat) Dwelt & outpcd early, hdwy inner 2f out & poised to chall when no room ins last, not able to recover, would
prob have gone very close: Japanese raider, 7 wk abs: dual wnr in Japan earlier this year, rnr up 4 times: eff at 5f,
both wins at 6f: acts on firm & fast ground.
1400 **CURFEW 74** [6]5-8-9 (94) P Makin 10/1: 04/505-45: Held up, short of room after 2f, nvr pace to threaten. 1¾ **84**
2791 **DANI RIDGE 12** [4]6-8-9 (84) W Supple 20/1: 030-4046: Trkd ldr, no impress from dist: btr 2240. 3 **75**
2638 **BISHOPS COURT 19** [9]10-9-0 (107) J Fortune 5/2 FAV: 3-120337: Held up, nvr able to chall: well shd **80**
bckd, tho' op 2/1: wnr of this race previous 2 seasons but reportedly broke blood vessel.
       STEVES CHAMP 9 [8]4-9-4 T S Fernando Diaz 16/1: 15-06218: b c Foxhound - Emigracion (Semenenko) ½ **82**
Prom, outpcd & lost pl fnl 2f: wore t-strap: Norwegian raider, Listed wnr: eff at 6/7.5f on fast & gd/sft.
2942 **DIZZY IN THE HEAD 7** [7]5-9-0 bl (80) F P Ferris 20/1: 6312109: Led early, prom wide 3f: see 2779 (h'cap).14 **38**
9 Ran   Time 59.74 (u0.06)   Owned: Mr P Crane Mr A Barker & Mr S Short   Trained: Thirsk

3101 4.45 Mercedes-Benz Of Wirral Handicap Stakes 3yo+ 0-80 (D)
£5447 £1676 £838   1m7f195y   Good/Firm   Inapplicable   Inside   [79]

2887 **SUDDEN FLIGHT 9** [4] P D Evans 7-9-2 (67) F P Ferris(3) 5/4 FAV: 0300431: Led after 1f & dictated **73**
pace, rdn over 1f out, in command from dist: hvly bckd: eff at 12f/sharp 2m on gd, soft & both AWs, any trk, likes a
sharp one: best dominating: see 549.
2009 **WEET FOR ME 45** [2] R Hollinshead 8-9-10 (75) W Supple 12/1: 1033//-002: Led 1f, trkd ldr, rdn & 4 **75**
no impress on wnr fnl 1ft: abs: well h'capped & btr wnr: see 2009.
2198 **GRAND FROMAGE 37** [1] A King 6-8-9 (60) F Norton 3/1: 521P/-003: Trkd ldrs, outpcd over 3f out, 2½ **57**
kept on late: see 2198.
2887 **SARN 9** [6] M Mullineaux 5-7-12 (6oh) (43) S Righton 12/1: 0403204: Held up, outpcd 3f out, mod prog. shd **46$**
2156 **HERNE BAY 38** [3]4-8-9 p (60) A Beech(3) 7/2: 0140-105: Trkd wnr halfway, wknd over 1f out: btr 1753. 5 **52**
2088 **KING HALLING 41** [5]5-8-11 P (62) Joanna Badger 14/1: 16400/-06: Held up, btn over 2f out: abs. 5 **49**
6 Ran   Time 3m 27.11 (No Std Time)   Owned: Norbury Ten   Trained: Abergavenny

3102 5.15 Mercedes-Benz Of Warrington Apprentice Handicap Stakes 3yo+ 0-70 (E)
£3572 £1099 £550   7f122y rnd   Good/Firm   Inapplicable   Inside   [66]

2999 **MERDIFF 4** [13] W M Brisbourne 5-9-3 (55) P Mathers(3) 11/1: 01-00021: Broke well from wide draw & **65**
swtcd to trk ldrs, led ins last, rdn out: qck reapp: eff at 7/9f on fast & fbsnd, loves a sharp/turning trk: eff
with/without t-strap: another fine ride from an apprentice to keep on side: see 39.
3034* **FEN GYPSY 3** [11] P D Evans 6-9-13 (6ex) (65) Donna Bashton(7) 13/2: 2124512: Mid-div, rdn to chall 1¾ **70**
over 1f out, not pace of wnr: qck reapp under a pen: in fine form: see 3034.
2805 **BABY BARRY 12** [14] Mrs G S Rees 7-8-9 (47) A Beech 25/1: 300-0003: Chsd ldr, rdn & led over 1f shd **52**
out, hdd ins last, no extra: more encouraging, stays 7.5f, prev best at sprint trips: v well h'capped: see 2445.
2857 **PAS DE SURPRISE 10** [1] P D Evans 6-9-1 (53) F P Ferris 4/1 FAV: 5400544: Mid div, styd on onepace. hd **57**
2615 **PROUD WESTERN 19** [3]6-8-2 t (40) Natalia Gemelova(3) 16/1: 40-00005: b g Gone West - Proud Lou 1¾ **40+**
(Proud Clarion) Hled up, prog/short of room over 1f out, kept on, nrst fin: closer with a clr run: mdn wnr '03:
unplcd '02: winning form at 5f, stays sharp 7.5f: acts on fast grnd & fibresand: handles a sharp or gall trk: eff in
a t-strap, tried blnks & chkpcs: imprvd effort today.
1 Sep'03 Newc 5g/f 54-(38) D: 2 Jun'03 Leic 5.0g/f 38-38 E: 2 Nov'01 Sout 8af 73a- D:
2891* **REDOUBTABLE 8** [4]13-9-2 (54) D Fentiman(5) 7/1: 0100216: Twds rear, late prog for press, no dngr. ½ **53**
2768 **ICED DIAMOND 14** [2]5-9-2 (54) P Gallagher(5) 7/1: 00-10007: MidOdiv, no impress: see 558. hd **52**
2947 **MALLARD 7** [5]6-9-10 (62) A Quinn 7/2: 01-30268: Held up, efft over 3f out, sn no impress: btr 2840. 1¾ **57**
2755 **ZAMYATINA 14** [10]5-8-3 (41) C Haddon(3) 16/1: 0-000059: Mid-div, btn dist: see 1282. ½ **35**
4093} **RISK FREE 308** [7]7-9-7 bl (59) S Donohoe(5) 10/1: 010535-0: 10th: ch g Risk Me - Princess Lily 1 **51**
(Blakeney) Led till over 1f out, wknd: reapp: AW clmr & h'cap wnr '03, also turf class stks scorer: eff btwn 6/8.5f
on firm, fast & both AWs, loves a sharp trk & likes to race with/force the pace.
1 Jul'03 Wolv 8.5af 68a-(72) F: 1 May'03 Catt 7fm 61-(62) F: 1 May'03 Wolv 6af 74a-67 E: 2 Apr'03 Wolv 7af 71a-(67) G:
2 Apr'03 Wolv 6af 67a-62 E: 1 Nov'01 Ling 7ap 80a-73 E: 2 Nov'01 Ling 8ap 75a-73 E: 2 Oct'01 Wolv 7af 75a- F:
1 Aug'01 Wolv 6af 73a- G: 1 Feb'01 Ling 8ap 86a-79 D: 2 Dec'00 Ling 7ap 81a- F:
2615 **HORMUZ 19** [12]8-8-4 (42) Stephanie Hollinshead(3) 20/1: 6040-000: 11th: Mid-div, btn over 1f out. 2 **30**
2928 Blades Edge 7 [9]3-8-6 bl(53) Dawn Watson(7) 25/1:0   2630 Beneking 19 [8]4-9-1 p(53) H Fellows(7) 12/1:0
2655 Hohs Back 18 [6]5-9-5 p(57) Leanne Kershaw(5) 20/1:0 1401 Midnight Arrow 881 [15]6-8-12 (50) C Ely(7) 33/1:0
15 Ran   Time 1m 34.17(1.77)   Owned: Team Racing   Trained: Nesscliffe

NOTTINGHAM SATURDAY 10.07.04 Lefthand, Galloping Track

Official Going Good (Good/Soft Places)

3103 **2.15 European Breeders Fund Maiden Stakes Fillies 2yo (D)**
£6042 £1859 £930 **6f str** **Good 59** **-51 Slow** Far Side

2750 **GENEROUS OPTION 14** [2] M Johnston 2-8-11 R Ffrench 7/2: 51: ch f Cadeaux Genereux - Easy Option (Prince Sabo) Handy far side & led that group over 1f out, rdn clr, decisively: op 9/2: Feb foal, half-sister to a smart sprinter, also useful 6f/1m performer Court Masterpiece: dam a smart juv/sprint performer: eff at 6f, stay further: acts on gd grnd & a gall trk: left debut bhd, potentially useful. **88**
2658 **PEEPTOE 17** [15] J L Dunlop 2-8-11 G Carter 6/4 FAV: 32: Reared start, sn in tch stands side, rdn & led that group over 1f out, hung left but kept on, no ch with wnr far side: hvly bckd, op 5/2: confirmed debut promise & well clr rem stands side: eff at 5/6f: can find similar: see 2658. *3* **77+**
2119 **BURTON ASH 39** [4] J G Given 2-8-11 M Fenton 12/1: 043: Led far side 4f, sn no ch with wnr: acts on fast & gd grnd: again ran with credit: see 2119. *1¼* **73**
AUTHENTICATE 0 [3] B A McMahon 2-8-11 G Gibbons 20/1: 4: b f Dansili - Exact Replica (Darshaan) Slow away, far side, in tch when short of room over 2f out, kept on: 24,000gns April foal, half-sister to a 3yo wnr abroad, dam unrcd, related to a high-class 1m performer: eff at 6f, stay further: acts on gd grnd & a gall trk: encouraging intro, can rate higher. *1* **70**
RAPID ROMANCE 0 [6]2-8-11 O Urbina 28/1: 5: b f Theatrical - Fast Nellie (Ack Ack) Chsd ldrs far side, hung right & btn dist: May foal, half-sister to a high-class 5f juv Raphane, also a 6f juv wnr: dam unrcd, related to a high-class US 3yo performer. *2* **64**
ICING 0 [16]2-8-11 B Doyle 8/1: 6: In tch stands side, btn over 1f out, op 4/1 on debut. *3* **55**
RESISTANCE HEROINE 0 [8]2-8-11 W Ryan 14/1: 7: Slow away, stands side, late gains. *1¼* **51**
2297 **ROYAL PARDON 32** [9]2-8-11 J Mackay 14/1: 08: Mid-div stands side, edged left & btn over 1f out. *nk* **50**
2795 **MIDNIGHT LACE 12** [5]2-8-11 A Daly 50/1: 09: Prom far side till over 1f out. *1¾* **45**
2610 **PRINCEABLE LADY 20** [1]2-8-11 D Allan 20/1: 00: 10th: Cl-up far side, btn over 1f out. *nk* **44**
MONTJEU BABY 0 [12]2-8-11 J Carroll 25/1: 0: 11th: Stands side, outpcd, nvr on terms. *shd* **44**
2522 **MERCARI 23** [13]2-8-11 R Fitzpatrick 80/1: 00: 12th: Prom stands side, hung left & btn over 1f out. *3* **35**
2382 **MISTY PRINCESS 29** [14]2-8-11 M Tebbutt 50/1: 056000: 13th: Led stands side, hung left & wknd fnl 2f. *3* **26**
2733 **ROSAPENNA 15** [10]2-8-11 R Mullen 12/1: 50: 14th: Prom stands side 4f, op 10/1. *shd* **26**
Mina Alsalaam 0 [7]2-8-11 R Lappin 28/1:0 1524 **Mrs Willy Nilly 68** [11]2-8-11 P S Whitworth 100/1:0
16 Ran Time 1m 17.40 (6.6) Owned: Maktoum Al Maktoum Trained: Middleham

3104 **2.50 Nottinghamshire Lifeboats Selling Stakes 3yo+ (G)**
£2902 £829 £415 **6f str** **Good 59** **-35 Slow** Far Side

2928 **SABANA 7** [6] J M Bradley 6-9-10 P (41) R Mullen 33/1: 0600001: Chsd ldrs far side, styd on for press to lead well ins last: eff at 6f, stays a sharp 1m well: acts on firm, gd & both AWs, any trk: eff with/without blnks, apprec fitting of cheek pieces today: enjoys sell grade: see 646, 448. **50**
2806 **BACK IN SPIRIT 12** [3] B A McMahon 4-9-4 t (30) G Carter 50/1: 00-00002: Far side & led/dsptd lead, led over 2f out till well ins last: eff at 6f on fibresand & gd grnd: see 1799. *1¼* **39**
2801 **NICHOLAS NICKELBY 12** [4] M J Polglase 4-9-4 p (58) M Fenton 15/2: 0620043: Led far side 3f, not pace of wnr dist: acts on fast, gd & fibresand: see 1966. *2* **33**
2928 **BEYOND CALCULATION 7** [5] J M Bradley 10-9-4 bl (54) S Whitworth 4/1 FAV: 0004044: Chsd ldrs far side, kept on onepace: qck reapp: see 1886. *hd* **32**
2928 **ZIETZIG 7** [18]7-9-4 (42) J Carroll 16/1: 6-000005: Led stands side, no ch with ldr far side fnl 1f: 1st home from stands side group: see 1635. *½* **30**
2805 **DONEGAL SHORE 12** [9]5-9-4 vis t (46) A Daly 25/1: 4224306: Dwelt, outpcd far side, nrst fin: see 373. *1¼* **26**
3000* **JONNY EBENEEZER 4** [11]5-9-10 bl (56) T J Murphy 9/2: 0210317: Cl-up stands side trav well, btn dist. *1¾* **27**
2981 **SHADY DEAL 5** [17]8-9-4 (45) D Corby(3) 9/1: 0300308: Chsd ldrs stands side till dist, wknd: qck reapp. *2½* **13**
1606* **KING NICHOLAS 64** [14]5-9-10 BL (53) M Lawson(5) 6/1: 0-010419: Prom stands side 4f: blnks. *½* **17**
1803 **NITEOWL EXPRESS 54** [16]3-8-7 (36) V Halliday 20/1: 0-06540: 10th: Dwelt, stands side, in tch till over 1f out: abs: see 1803, 1203. *nk* **5**
2806 **SPY MASTER 12** [15]6-9-4 bl t (31) D Allan 33/1: 2506500: 11th: Held up stands side, nvr on terms. *nk* **9**
2384 **Gruff 29** [19]5-9-4 (32) J Bramhill 50/1:0 2928 **Octennial 7** [10]5-9-4 (50) R Fitzpatrick 33/1:0
2909 **Repeat 8** [12]4-9-10 (42) M Savage(5) 14/1:0 2975 **Onefortheboys 5** [7]5-9-4 (39) L Treadwell(6) 16/1:0
2852 **Justice Jones 10** [2]3-8-12 BL(43) D Kinsella 40/1:0 2803 **River Lark 12** [8]5-8-13 bl(41) Hayley Turner(5) 12/1:0
2052 **My Country Club 43** [13]7-9-4 BL(47) V Slattery 33/1:0 2397 **Grand View 28** [1]8-9-10 p(36) M Tebbutt 25/1:0
19 Ran Time 1m 16.43 (5.63) Owned: Mr E A Hayward Trained: Chepstow

3105 **3.25 Les Stone Memorial Handicap Stakes 3yo+ 0-75 (E)** **[73]**
£3965 £1220 £610 **1m6f15y** **Good 59** **-09 Slow** Inside

2707 **ISAAF 16** [13] P W Hiatt 5-9-5 (64) Hayley Turner(5) 100/30: 1102441: Chsd ldrs, prog to lead over 3f out, drvn & held on all out cl-home: eff btwn 11/15.4f on firm, soft & fibresand, any trk: tough 5yo. **71**
2869 **LUNAR LORD 9** [3] D Burchell 8-7-13 (44) J Bramhill 7/1: 5-000042: Held up & keen, rdn & hdwy to chase wnr when hung left over 1f out, short of room ins last, styd on well just failed: find similar: see 924. *hd* **50**
2608 **RACE THE ACE 20** [9] J L Dunlop 3-8-8 (68) G Carter 3/1 FAV: 4523: Trkd ldr & keen, ch over 2f out, onepace when hmpd over 1f out, kept on: bckd, op 8/1: styd longer 14f trip, shaped as a thorough stayer, 2m+ will suit & can find similar: see 2608 (mdn). *2* **72**
2632* **SONOMA 19** [1] M L W Bell 4-9-3 (62) M Fenton 9/2: 5060014: Chsd ldrs, rdn & onepace fnl 3f: eff at 14f, return to 2m shld suit: acts on fast & gd grnd: see 2632 (2m). *1¼* **65**
2931 **DISABUSE 7** [8]4-8-4 (49) R Mullen 13/2: 1344545: Held up, styd on onepace fnl 2f, no threat: blnks omitted: prob stays 14f: see 2931, 2162, 746 & 463. *hd* **51**
1259 **MAJESTIC VISION 82** [12]3-8-7 (67) D Corby(3) 12/1: 34-06: ch g Desert King - Triste Oeil (Raise A *1¼* **68**

Cup) Led 10f, btn dist: h'cap bow: plcd sole '03 start (rtd 71, mdn): prob styd this longer 14f trip, drop to 12f could suit: handles fast & gd grnd, gall trk: with P W Harris.

2349 **STOCKING ISLAND** 30 [6]3-8-13 (73) J Carroll 9/1: 02307: Held up, kept on late, no threat: see 1885.	1	73
2780 **BROUGH SUPREME** 13 [5]3-8-7 (67) J Mackay 14/1: 0-5468: Held up, eff over 3f out, no impress fnl 2f.	¾	66
3976] **WELSH MAIN** 671 [7]7-9-11 (70) G Baker 25/1: 034060/-9: br g Zafonic - Welsh Daylight (Welsh Pageant) Held up & al bhd: long Flat abs, 7 wk jumps abs (h'cap hdle rnr-up 03/04, rtd 114h, 2m, gd): missed '03 on the level: plcd '02 (clmr, rtd 78): eff btwn 9/12f on fast & gd grnd: has tried visor.	4	65
2691 **CALOMERIA** 16 [2]3-7-13 (59) R Thomas(3) 11/1: 00-00040: 10th: Mid-div early, lost place from halfway & no impress fnl 3f under a v kind ride: surprising no stewards inquiry after much btr 2691.	13	44
1232 **Stolen Song** 84 [4]4-9-0 (59) B Doyle 12/1:0 221| **King Spinner** 936 [11]7-8-10 (55) V Slattery 33/1:0		

12 Ran   Time 3m 07.77 (9.47)   Owned: Miss Maria McKinney   Trained: Banbury

3106   4.00 Rectangle Group Handicap Stakes Fillies 3yo+ 0-90 (C)   **[89]**
£10569 £3252 £1626   **5f str**   **Good 59**   **+08 Fast**   Far Side

1957 **FRUIT OF GLORY** 47 [2] J R Jenkins 5-10-0 (89) W Ryan 5/1: 4430421: Cl-up, went on halfway, rdn & styd on strongly fnl 1f: op 7/2, best time of day: 7 wk abs: eff btwn 5/7f & stays 1m: acts on firm & gd, handles soft & polytrack, any trk: gd weight-carrier, tough & genuine: see 1137.		98
2593 **PARADISE ISLE** 21 [8] C F Wall 3-9-8 (88) G Baker 9/4 FAV: 2211-042: Held up, prog when hung right 2f out, hung left ins last, not reach wnr: will relish a return to 6f: see 2593.	½	94
1782 **DISPOL KATIE** 55 [4] T D Barron 3-9-1 (81) M Fenton 12/1: 1022-063: Chsd ldrs, outpcd 2f out, kept on ins last: 8 wk abs: acts on firm & gd grnd: spot on over a stiff 5f: see 1782.	1¼	83
2779 **TWICE UPON A TIME** 13 [7] B Smart 5-8-6 (67) R Mullen 10/1: 0-440004: Dwelt & held up, hdwy halfway, onepace for press dist: won this race in '03 off a 4lb lower mark: see 1749.	½	67
2690 **ROMAN MISTRESS** 16 [6]4-8-4 bl (65) D Allan 8/1: 0-046305: Held up, onepcd & hung left ins last.	nk	64
2743 **ROXANNE MILL** 14 [3]6-9-0 p (75) R Thomas(5) 9/1: 2632356: Dwelt & held up, no room when onepcd.	½	72
2830 **KARMINSKEY PARK** 11 [5]5-8-4 (65) D Kinsella 9/1: 6532107: Trkd ldrs, short of room over 1f out, no extra when hmpd ins last: closer with a clr run without troubling this wnr: see 2712.	1	59
2968 **FRASCATI** 5 [9]4-9-3 (78) J Carroll 4/1: 2301128: Chsd ldrs, btn when hmpd ins last: qck reapp.	1½	67
2884 **BOLLIN JANET** 9 [1]4-8-4 bl (65) J Mackay 33/1: 00-00009: Led till halfway, sn btn: see 2524.	3½	43

9 Ran   Time 1m 01.04 (2.54)   Owned: Mr R B Hill   Trained: Royston

3107   4.35 Letheby & Christopher Classified Stakes 3yo+ 0-70 (E)
£3819 £1175 £588   **1m54y rnd**   **Good 59**   **-27 Slow**   Inside

2705 **INCHLOSS** 16 [3] B A McMahon 3-8-12 (74) W Ryan 12/1: 4120061: Trkd ldrs when short of room & lost place over 2f out, rdn & styd on to lead well ins last: prev when at 6f, long suited by 1m: enjoys gd & soft grnd, gall trks, loves Nottingham: lightly rcd, type to prog in similar: see 1707 & 1464.		80
2940 **RILEY BOYS** 7 [1] J G Given 3-9-3 P (79) M Fenton 11/4 JT FAV: 1212222: Trkd ldrs, rdn to lead ins last, sn hdd & not pace of wnr nr line: v tough & consistent: see 2940, 2168.	nk	84
2662 **ZUCCHERO** 17 [5] D W P Arbuthnot 8-9-8 P (75) A Daly 16/1: 00000-03: br g Dilum - Legal Sound (Legal Eagle) Trkd ldrs, short of room over 2f out, kept on onepace ins last: reapp bhd in first time cheek pieces: well btn all '03 starts (rtd 86, val h'cap): won first of 2 '02 starts (Lincoln h'cap): suited by 7f/1m on firm & soft grnd: tried visor, eff with/without blnks: can go well fresh: on fair mark.	1½	77
1 Mar'02 Donc 8sft 97-91 B: 1 Jul'01 Newb 8fm 90-84 B: 2 May'01 Ling 7g/f 86-83 B:		
2672 **CHERISHED NUMBER** 17 [9] I Semple 5-9-8 vis (75) J Carroll 11/2: 4063304: In tch, hdwy to lead over 1f out, hdd ins last & no extra: see 2317.	¾	76
2840 **SLALOM** 10 [2]4-9-7 P (74) M Savage(5) 14/1: 53-1005: Dwelt & held up, not pace to chall: op 11/1: cheek pieces reapplied: acts on gd, gd/soft & fibresand: see 939.	½	74
2840 **TRE COLLINE** 10 [6]5-9-6 (73) G Baker 7/1: 0015146: Held up, not pace to chall: handles firm, gd & both AWs: only btn around 4L: see 2840.	1½	70
2314 **MOTU** 31 [4]3-8-8 (70) G Carter 11/2: 10-00007: Held up, hung left & not pace to chall: see 1930.	2	63
2633 **PENDING** 19 [10]3-8-13 (75) O Urbina 11/4 JT FAV: 05-38: Held up & keen, eff 2f out, btn dist: op 5/1: too free in the early stages: btr 2633 (C/D mdn).	nk	67
LIZARAZU 244 [7]5-9-8 (75) B Doyle 16/1: 562252-9: b c Second Set - Lilly (Motley) Trkd ldr, led over 2f out till over 1f out, sn btn: reapp: Brit bow, ex-German, thrice rnr-up in '03: dual '02 wnr: eff btwn 6.5f/10f on gd & soft grnd: with F Jordan.	5	58
2866 **DAIMAJIN** 9 [8]5-9-3 (47) J McAuley 100/1: 0000000: 10th: Led 5f, btn 2f out: btr 362 (AW, sell).	6	43

10 Ran   Time 1m 46.42 (7.02)   Owned: Mr R Thornhill   Trained: Tamworth

3108   5.10 Nottingham Evening Post Family Day Handicap Stakes 3yo 0-75 (E)   **[82]**
£4193 £1290 £645   **1m2f**   **Good 59**   **-25 Slow**   Inside

2621 **CELLARMASTER** 19 [3] A C Stewart 3-9-4 (72) B Doyle 8/1: 352-31: Chsd ldrs & led over 3f out, rdn clr, decisively: op 10/1: first win: eff at 10/11.5f, could get further: acts on gd, gd/soft & fibresand: win again.		81
2707 **SANTA CATERINA** 16 [2] J L Dunlop 3-9-2 (70) G Carter 12/1: 000-452: Dwelt, rdn & styd on fnl 3f, no threat to wnr: encouraging effort: see 2707, 1718.	3½	71
2706 **LATE OPPOSITION** 16 [14] E A L Dunlop 3-9-0 VIS (68) O Urbina 16/1: 4222003: Held up, eff to chase wnr over 2f out, hung left & no extra ins last: imprvd eff in first time visor: see 1648, 1382.	½	68
2345 **CANNI THINKAAR** 30 [8] P W Harris 3-8-9 (63) J Carroll 33/1: 406-6004: Chsd ldr, btn over 1f out: drpd in trip & imprvd eff: handles gd grnd: see 2345.	3	59
2613* **COBALT BLUE** 19 [9]3-8-0 bl (54) J Bramhill 16/1: 000-0615: Prom, btn over 1f out: see 2613 (1m).	1½	48
2780 **GENERAL FLUMPA** 13 [13]3-8-11 (65) R Mullen 7/2: 0-633526: Chsd ldrs, btn 2f out: btr 2780.	1¼	57
2452 **AUROVILLE** 26 [7]3-8-8 VIS (62) Hayley Turner(5) 16/1: 0-040507: Held up, eff over 1f out, mod prog: first time visor: again shaped as if 12f+ will suit: see 2452 & 2168.	½	53
2893* **MISS ELOISE** 8 [16]3-8-9 (63) A Mullen(7) 11/1: 2-626018: Mid-div, btn over 1f out: btr 2893.	nk	53
2633 **JOLIZERO** 19 [5]3-8-4 (58) M Henry 5/1: 000-49: Chsd ldrs, sn pushed along & losing place after 3f, rdn/stumbled over 1f out: h'cap bow: btr 2633 (1m, mdn).	nk	47
120 **ABBEYGATE** 224 [10]3-8-10 (64) M Tebbutt 9/1: 006-0: 10th: b c Unfuwain - Ayunli (Chief Singer) Hld up wide, rdn & little hdwy fnl 3f: reapp/h'cap bow: unplcd in '03 (rtd 62 & 67a): dam a wnr at up to 15f.	3½	48

NOTTINGHAM SATURDAY 10.07.04 Lefthand, Galloping Track

1681 **TRILEMMA 59** [1]3-8-9 (63) J Mackay 10/1: 0006-00: 11th: b f Slip Anchor - Thracian (Green Desert) Led till over 3f out, btn 2f out: 2 mth abs: unplcd '03 (rtd 9a & 65, mdns): mid-dist pedigree. — 1 — 46
2322 **SNOWED UNDER 31** [6]3-8-6 (60) D Allan 25/1: 0-5550: 12th: Dwelt & held up, hmpd halfway & al bhd. — ¾ — 42
2746 **WOU OODD 14** [12]3-9-7 (75) R Lappin 16/1: 0-43540: 13th: Al bhd. — 8 — 47
2930* **JAKARMI 7** [11]3-9-8 (76) L Treadwell(7) 2/1 FAV: 2232110: 14th: Held up, hdwy 4f out, btn 2f out: rider reported gelding ran flat: prev v tough & progressive: btr 2930 (C/D). — 7 — 39
2804 **COMMEMORATION DAY 12** [15]3-8-6 (60) M Fenton 25/1: 60-0600: 15th: Prom wide till 4f out. — 5 — 16
15 Ran Time 2m 10.67(8.3) Owned: Hill-Smith Fine Goddard Sangster Trained: Newmarket

SALISBURY SATURDAY 10.07.04 Righthand, Galloping Track, Stiff Finish

Official Going Good (Good/Firm Places)

3109 6.35 Carnarvon Amateur Riders' Handicap Stakes 3yo+ 0-75 (E) [58]
£3575 £1100 £550 6f str Good/Soft 69 -22 Slow Far Side

2702 **KALLISTAS PRIDE 16** [12] J R Best 4-10-0 (58) Miss K Manser(5) 14/1: 00-0201: Handy, styd on for press to lead nr line: eff at 5/6f on gd/soft grnd, stiff trks: 1st win: see 2361. — 62
2312 **CALUSA LADY 31** [11] G B Balding 4-9-8 (52) Miss J Hannaford(7) 11/1: 0005-502: ch f Titus Livius - Solas Abu (Red Sunset) Dwelt, sn mid-div, hdwy to briefly lead ins last, just held: plcd '03 (rtd 58, fills h'cap): mdn plcd '02 (rtd 65): eff at 6f on firm & soft grnd, best without t-strap & visor: dropped to fair mark. — nk — 55
2857 **SOMAYDA 10** [1] Miss Jacqueline S Doyle 9-8-10 P (40) Mr J Doyle(7) 66/1: 000-0003: Trkd ldr & ev ch dist, no extra cl-home: imprvd eff in first time cheek pieces: eff btwn 6/10f: see 2354. — ½ — 41
2559 **MAN CRAZY 21** [7] R M Beckett 3-9-5 bl (55) Mr R V Moore(7) 25/1: 0-060004: Hmpd start, keen & held up, hdwy to lead over 1f out, hdd well ins last, no extra: handles firm & gd/soft grnd: well h'capped: see 901. — shd — 56
2861 **FORMALISE 10** [3]4-10-0 (58) Miss K Cuthbertson(7) 14/1: 60-00505: Led till over 1f out, onepace: acts on firm & gd/soft grnd: see 1914. — ½ — 57
2760 **CORMORANT WHARF 14** [2]4-10-0 VIS (68) Miss J Powell(7) 14/1: 5005006: Rear, keeping on when hmpd ins last, not able to chall: first time visor, cheek pieces omitted: handles fast, gd/soft & polytrack. — ½ — 65
2702* **SOMERSET WEST 16** [9]4-11-0 (72) Miss L Baldwin(7) 13/2: 0110017: Keen rear, prog 2f out, nrst fin: stable-mate of wnr: btr 2702 (5f). — hd — 68
2397 **LILY OF THE GUILD 28** [8]5-9-8 (52) Mrs S Bosley 5/1 FAV: 0024458: Slow away, held up, keeping on when no room ins last, not btn far & would of gone close with clr run: see 761 & 270. — hd — 47+
1028 **SECAM 99** [10]5-9-1 (45) Mrs C Thompson(4) 14/1: 1321-039: Chsd ldrs, onepace fnl 2f: abs: see 1028. — nk — 39
2857 **ARK ADMIRAL 10** [6]5-10-5 t (63) Miss C Tizzard(3) 14/1: 60000-00: 10th: Keen & held up, btn dist. — ½ — 55
474 **EMERALD FIRE 168** [4]5-10-8 (66) Miss M Sowerby(5) 11/2: 0005-600: 11th: b f Pivotal - Four Legged Friend (Aragon) Held up, btn 2f out: abs: fills AW h'cap wnr '03, subs turf plcd (rtd 77, h'cap): h'cap rnr-up '02: eff at 6f on firm, hvy & polytrack, any trk: has gone well fresh: best without visor. — 3½ — 49
1 Mar'03 Ling 6ap 79a-75 E: 2 May'02 Hayd 6g/s 76-74 D: 1 Oct'01 Newm 6gd 75-69 C: 2 Jul'01 Bath 5.7fm 68- E:
3160} **SAINTLY PLACE 351** [13]3-9-13 (63) Mr L Newnes(3) 14/1: 060-0: 12th: ch g Compton Place - Always On A Sunday (Star Appeal) Slow away, in tch till 2f out: gelded, reapp/h'cap bow: unplcd in '03 (rtd 66). — 4 — 36
2568 **DESERT ARC 21** [5]6-10-7 (65) Mr S Walker 11/2: 0-011600: 13th: Keen, in tch, fdd 3f out, sn eased. — 8 — 18
13 Ran Time 1m 17.58 (5.48) Owned: G G Racing Trained: Maidstone

3110 7.05 Peter & Sarah Grubb Wedding Anniversary Novice Auction Stakes 2yo (F)
£3523 £1084 £542 6f str Good/Soft 69 -08 Slow Far Side

1538* **JOHNNY JUMPUP 67** [7] R M Beckett 2-9-3 S Sanders 13/8 FAV: 11: Hld up, short of room 2f out, hdwy & switched & rdn to lead ins last, readily: nicely bckd, 2 mth abs: eff at 5f, apprec step up to 6f, 7f sure to suit: likes gd/soft & soft, stiff trks: win more races. — 96+
2845 **LITTLE DALHAM 10** [6] P W Chapple Hyam 2-8-9 J Fortune 9/1: 42: Handy & led over 2f out, hdd well ins last, no extra: acts on fast & gd/soft grnd: eff at 6/7f: left debut bhd, can find a race sn: see 2845. — ¾ — 83
2703* **INTOXICATING 16** [8] R F Johnson Houghton 2-9-4 S Carson 5/2: 13: Handy & ch dist, no extra ins last: op 2/1: acts on gd & gd/soft grnd: gd run conceding weight all round: see 2703. — 1½ — 88
2750* **DEEDAY BAY 14** [5] C F Wall 2-9-1 J Quinn 8/1: 14: 7th: rdn/short of room over 2f out, kept on ins last, not pace of wnr: handles gd & gd/soft grnd: will rate higher: see 2750. — 1¼ — 82
2695 **WORTH A GRAND 16** [9]2-8-7 P Doe 33/1: 05: br g Raise A Grand - Ballykelt Pride (Indian Ridge) Handy, rdn & no extra dist: cheaply bght March first foal, dam plcd at 10f as a 3yo: eff at 6f, return to 7f+ shld suit in time: handles gd/soft grnd: with J W Mullins. — 1¼ — 71
2287 **PENNESTAMP 32** [3]2-8-9 R Havlin 66/1: 066: Led, hung right & hdd over 2f out, hung right & btn dist. — 5 — 61
2666 **RIDDER 17** [11]2-8-12 Martin Dwyer 16/1: 457: Chsd ldrs, not pace to chall fnl 2f: btr 2666 & 1911. — ½ — 62
2970 **PIPS PEARL 5** [2]2-8-4 (2ow) N Pollard 80/1: 008: b f Lil's Boy - Penka (Don't Forget Me) Bhd, nvr on terms: qck reapp: cheaply bght April foal, half-sister to wnrs at 6f/9f: dam a 6f juv wnr. — 2½ — 47
2584 **DARA GIRL 21** [1]2-8-4 T J F Egan 66/1: 009: br f Key of Luck - Tavildara (Kahyasi) Al rear in first time t-strap: £12,000 March foal, half-sister to a plcd 6/7f juv: dam related to a multiple wnr abroad, sire high-class 1m/10f dirt performer: with Mrs P N Dutfield. — 3 — 40
2629 **GAVIOLI 19** [4]2-8-9 t R L Moore 16/1: 50420: 10th: Prom, hung right & wknd 2f out: btr 2629. — 1¼ — 42
DAVIDS SYMPHONY 0 [10]2-8-12 Dane O'Neill 10/1: 0: 11th: Swerved right start & sn bhd. — 7 — 28
11 Ran Time 1m 16.7 (4.6) Owned: Mr & Mrs A Briars Trained: Lambourn

3111 7.35 George Smith Horseboxes E B F Maiden Stakes 2yo (D)
£6078 £1870 £935 7f str Good/Soft 69 -17 Slow Far Side

LIAKOURA 0 [15] Mrs A J Perrett 2-9-0 S Sanders 4/1: 1: b c Royal Academy - Lady Member (Saint Estephe) Trkd ldrs, rdn & led over 1f out, styd on strongly: op 5/2: 38,000 Feb foal, half-brother to a 1m juv wnr & subs multiple 7f/1m scorer: dam a US/French wnr: eff at 7f, stay 1m: acts on gd/soft grnd & a stiff/undul trk: goes well fresh: looks potentially useful & will reportedly enjoy a faster surface. — 92+
WOODSLEY HOUSE 0 [1] Mrs P N Dutfield 2-9-0 N Pollard 66/1: 0: b c Orpen - Flame And Shadow (Turtle Island) Led, hdd over 1f out, kept on well: cheaply bght March first foal, dam an unrcd half-sister to a — ¾ — 89

multiple French wnr: eff at 7f, stay 1m: acts on gd/soft grnd & a stiff/undul trk: most promising start, rest well covered, find a race on this evidence.

BAY HAWK 0 [7] A M Balding 2-9-0 Martin Dwyer 25/1: 3: b c Alhaarth - Fleeting Vision (Vision) 3½ 82
Mid-div, rdn & kept on fnl 2f, no threat to front pair: cheaply bght Jan foal, half-brother to a 2m 3yo scorer, dam a multiple wnr at 12f/2m2f: eff at 7f, stout pedigree & shld relish mid-staying dists in time: handles gd/soft grnd.

DESERT COMMANDER 0 [8] Saeed bin Suroor 2-9-0 L Dettori 4/1: 4: b c Green Desert - Meadow Pipit 1½ 79
(Meadowlake) Trkd ldrs trav well, shaken up & no impress fnl 1f under min press: op 5/2: March foal, half-brother to a dual 7f juv wnr: dam a multiple wnr btwn 7/12f: handles gd/soft grnd: not knocked about & a likely improver.

MISTER GENEPI 0 [4]2-9-0 J Quinn 25/1: 5: b c Mister Baileys - Ring Queen (Fairy King) Bhd, ½ 78
styd on late, nrst fin: 40,000gns March foal, dam unrcd half-sister to a multiple French/US wnr: eff at 7f, shaped as if 1m+ will suit, likely improver: with W R Muir.

CHINESE PUZZLE 0 [5]2-9-0 T R Hughes 11/1: 6: Prom, no extra dist, t-strap. nk 77
KAMAKIRI 0 [11]2-9-0 P Dobbs 50/1: 7: Rear, switched & late gains under kind ride, improve. 1 75
2876 **TRANSGRESS 9** [2]2-9-0 Dane O'Neill 100/30 FAV: 38: Prom, btn 2f out: btr 2876. 5 65
2696 **SNOW TEMPEST 16** [13]2-9-0 R L Moore 16/1: 09: Towards rear, nvr a factor. 1¾ 62
2696 **BENEDICT BAY 16** [10]2-9-0 S Carson 33/1: 60: 10th: Nvr a factor. ½ 61
2696 **CELESTIAL ARC 16** [14]2-9-0 S Drowne 8/1: 30: 11th: Cl-up, btn over 1f out: btr 2696. ¾ 60
2696 **MOLLZAM 16** [6]2-9-0 S Whitworth 20/1: 00: 12th: Went right start, keen in tch, btn over 1f out. hd 59
STORM FURY 0 [12]2-9-0 R Havlin 20/1: 0: 13th: Mid-div, no impress from halfway, op 14/1. 1 57
HAPPY BANKER 0 [9]2-9-0 T O'Brien(7) 20/1: 0: 14th: Mid-div, rdn & btn 3f out. 6 47
RUM CREEK 0 [3]2-9-0 J F Egan 66/1: 0: 15th: Prom, btn 2f out. nk 46
NORTHANGER ABBEY 0 [16]2-9-0 J Fortune 10/1: 0: 16th: Sn struggling. 1 44
16 Ran Time 1m31.51 (6.01) Owned: Mr Mark Tracey Trained: Pulborough

3112

8.05 Jacksons Group Mercedes-Benz Rated Stakes Handicap 3yo 0-85 (D) [92]
£7270 £2237 £1118 **1m str** **Good/Soft 69** **-14 Slow** Far Side

2622* **TAKE A BOW 19** [2] P R Chamings 3-9-6 (84) J Quinn 5/1: 02-11: Trkd ldrs, switched & rdn to lead 97
ins last, styd on strongly: h'cap bow: eff over a stiff or sharp/undul 1m on firm & gd/soft grnd: lightly rcd, progressive & useful, shows a willing attitude & more to come: see 2622.
2922 **EVALUATOR 7** [6] T G Mills 3-9-0 (78) R L Moore 6/4 FAV: 4306122: Chsd ldrs, rdn & styd on well ½ 89
ins last, not pace of wnr cl-home: nicely bckd & rest well covered: remains on the upgrade: see 2922 & 2650.
2247 **APEX 35** [7] E A L Dunlop 3-9-0 (78) L Dettori 8/1: 030-1503: Led, carried hd awkwardly, hdd 3 83
dist, not pace of front pair: imprvd eff with forcing tactics applied: acts on fast, enjoys gd/soft & soft.
2595* **NAMROC 21** [3] A C Stewart 3-9-7 (85) Martin Dwyer 4/1: 14: Held up, switched & kept on fnl 2f, 1 88
not pace to chall: op 2/1, h'cap bow: joc reported colt still green: handles firm & gd/soft grnd: can progress.
2663 **ALFRIDINI 17** [9]3-8-9 (73) L Keniry(3) 12/1: 2140135: Cl-up, bmpd over 1f out when no extra: see 2663. 1¾ 73
2212 **FLIP FLOP AND FLY 36** [4]3-9-7 (85) J F Egan 10/1: 00-00106: Rear, no impress fnl 2f: btr 1983 (fast). 1¾ 82
2259 **I WONT DANCE 34** [8]3-9-0 (78) P Dobbs 20/1: 012-007: Dwelt, held up in tch, btn 2f out: see 1734. 3 69
2650 **BEST DESERT 18** [11]3-8-4 (2oh) (66) N Pollard 33/1: 602-4208: Al bhd, nvr a factor: btr 1982 (fast). 1 57
2918 **LOVE TRIANGLE 7** [1]3-9-1 (79) Dane O'Neill 20/1: 600-3009: Trkd ldrs, btn 2f out: btr 2098 (7f, fast). shd 68
9 Ran Time 1m 45.7 (6.6) Owned: Mrs J E L Wright Trained: Basingstoke

3113

8.35 E B F Ladies Evening Classified Stakes 3yo 0-95 (B)
£14935 £5665 £2833 **7f str** **Good/Soft 69** **+04 Fast** Far Side

2407 **DELPHIE QUEEN 28** [2] S Kirk 3-8-11 (95) J F Egan 15/8 FAV: 10-43121: Held up in tch, switched & 106+
rdn to lead over 1f out, sn clr, going away: gd time: well bckd: relished step up to 7f, 1m will suit: acts on fast & gd/soft, loves a gall trk: v useful & progressive, keep on side: see 2407 & 2249.
1847 **JEDBURGH 52** [6] J L Dunlop 3-9-2 (97) T Quinn 3/1: 111-0332: Trkd ldrs, eff to chall when bmpd 5 100
by wnr over 1f out, sn no impress: op 7/2, 8 wk abs: acts on firm & gd/soft grnd: see 1847, 1496 & 1206.
1480 **GOLDEN SAHARA 70** [3] Saeed bin Suroor 3-9-1 vis t (96) L Dettori 4/1: 122-03: b c Green Desert - 1¾ 96
Golden Digger (Mr Prospector) Held up, eff over 1f out, no impress dist: lightly rcd juv, debut scorer (mdn), subs cond stks rnr-up: eff at 6/7f on fast grnd, prob handles gd/soft, stiff/gall or easy trk: eff in a t-strap & visor.
2 Oct'03 York 7.0g/f 99- B: 2 Sep'03 Donc 6gd 98- C: 1 Aug'03 Yarm 6.0g/f 80- D:
2486 **SGT PEPPER 24** [5] R Hannon 3-9-0 (95) P Dobbs 12/1: 1140-004: Led till over 1f out, sn btn: op 16/1. 1½ 92
2291* **CAMBERWELL 32** [7]3-9-0 (90) J Fortune 8/1: 15: Went right start, sn pushed along & onepcd fnl 2f. ½ 87
4844*}**POLONIUS 262** [1]3-9-0 (91) Dane O'Neill 13/2: 131-6: b g Great Dane - Bridge Pool (First Trump) 3½ 84
Keen & trk ldr, btn over 1f out: op 11/2, reapp: lightly rcd & progressive juv, landed an auct mdn & nov event: eff at 6/7f on fast grnd, gall/undul trk: can go well fresh: with H Candy.
1 Oct'03 Nott 6.1g/f 92-(88) F: 1 Sep'03 Chep 7.1g/f 86- F:
6 Ran Time 1m 30.04 (4.54) Owned: Mr N Hartery Trained: Upper Lambourn

3114

9.05 Ftx Logistics Handicap Stakes 3yo+ 0-75 (E) [75]
£3523 £1084 £542 **1m4f** **Good/Soft 69** **+05 Fast** Inside

2530 **JACK OF TRUMPS 22** [6] G Wragg 4-9-3 (64) D Holland 5/1: 35-10041: Mid-div, rdn & hdwy to lead 76
over 1f out, rdn out: fair time: eff at 10/12f, may get further: acts on fast, gd/soft & polytrack, see 2530.
2293 **AONINCH 32** [4] Mrs P N Dutfield 4-8-9 (56) N Pollard 14/1: 6050602: Rear, staying on for press ½ 66
when forced to switch ins last, not reach wnr: would have gone close: acts on firm, gd/soft & polytrack: worth another try at 14f in similar: see 801.
2130 **TURNSTILE 39** [1] R Hannon 3-8-12 (72) R Hughes 15/2: 4-4203: Prom, onepcd dist: tchd 10/1: 3 78
acts on fast & gd/soft grnd: see 1936 & 1211.
2735 **KYLKENNY 15** [14] H Morrison 9-9-11 t (72) L Fletcher(3) 4/1 FAV: 3006534: Handy when left in lead hd 77
7f out, hdd over 1f out & no extra: usually best when obtaining more cover: see 225.
2681 **REVIEWER 17** [3]6-9-2 (63) R Havlin 12/1: 16/-00055: Prom, no extra dist: see 2088. 1½ 66
2700 **MASTERMAN READY 16** [8]3-8-10 (70) R L Moore 9/1: 6-006: Mid-div, not able to chall. 2½ 69
5033} **FLAMENCO BRIDE 245** [2]4-9-8 (69) S Sanders 20/1: 234500-7: b f Hernando - Premier Night (Old 3 64
Vic) Held up, eff 2f out, no impress dist: reapp, op 16/1: mdn scorer '03, subs h'cap rnr-up & disapp in a t-strap: eff at 12f, suited by 14f & has tried 2m: acts on fast grnd, stiff/undul trks.
2 Jul'03 Sand 14g/f 73-66 D: 1 Jul'03 Sali 14.1g/f 68- D:

SALISBURY   SATURDAY 10.07.04   Righthand, Galloping Track, Stiff Finish

2607 **INDIAN CHASE 20** [5]7-7-12 (45) Lucy Russell(7) 33/1: 26008: Held up, eff over 3f out, no impress.   1½   38

ONWARD TO GLORY 397 [9]4-9-12 (73) L Dettori 6/1: 5/60-9: b c Zabeel - Landaria (Sadler's Wells)   ¾   65
Mid-div, struggling fnl 2f: reapp/h'cap bow: Brit bow, ex-French: unplcd at up to 1m in '03 (lightly rcd).
2836 **PRIVATE BENJAMIN 11** [7]4-8-3 (1ow) (49) P Doe 15/2: 6301050: 10th: Al rear: btr 2293 (firm).   3   38
743 **WESTERN 135** [12]4-9-13 (74) T Quinn 20/1: 641-2000: 11th: Rear, brief eff 2f out, sn btn: abs.   15   42
2596 **HASHID 21** [11]4-9-9 (70) Martin Dwyer 25/1: 53-6300: 12th: Led 1f, struggling fnl 5f: btr 2196 (10f).   2½   34
2759 **HERODOTUS 14** [10]6-10-0 t (75) J F Egan 40/1: 0050-000: 13th: Held up & no ch fnl 3f, eased.   20   9
2311 **NICK THE SILVER 31** [13]3-8-0 (60) R Thomas(4) 25/1: 030-060R: Led 11f out, ran out bend 7f out, u.r.   0
14 Ran   Time 2m 40.1(7.7)   Owned: Mollers Racing   Trained: Newmarket

---

YORK   SATURDAY 10.07.04   Lefthand, Flat, Galloping Track

Official Going GOOD (GOOD/SOFT places).

3115   2.05 John Smith's 'ave It' Stakes Nursery Handicap 2yo (C)   [102]
£8697 £2676 £1338   5f str   Good 40   -26 Slow   Centre

2110* **KEY SECRET 40** [6] M L W Bell 2-7-13 (73) A McCarthy 7/1: 111: Handy, hdwy to lead appr fnl 1f,   83
styd on well, rdn out: 6 wk abs: v eff at 5f on firm, gd & fibresand, sharp or gall trks: unbeaten, genuine & progressing with each run: prev with M Usher, see 3115.
2786 **RIGHT ANSWER 13** [2] A P Jarvis 2-9-7 (95) K Fallon 5/1: 4122: Set pace, rdn & hdd appr fnl 1f,   1¼   100
kept on but not pace of wnr: useful run under top-weight: see 2786, 2658.
2603* **MISSPERON 20** [8] K A Ryan 2-8-3 (77) P Fessey 11/1: 5313: In tch, eff dist, onepace ins last: 1   79
joc received a 1-day whip ban: proving consistent, shld apprec a return to 6f as in 2603 (mdn fills, made all).
2895 **EMPIRES GHODHA 8** [10] B J Meehan 2-9-0 bl (88) T E Durcan 10/1: 3231534: Bhd, hung left & eff   shd   89
over 1f out, kept on ins last: worth a try at 6f: see 2895, 2415.
2889* **WONDERFUL MIND 8** [7]2-7-13 (73) P M Quinn 13/2: 05215: Cl-up, eff dist, no extra ins last.   nk   73
2652 **LADY DAN 18** [1]2-7-13 (73) J F McDonald(3) 4/1 FAV: 43206: Chsd ldrs, wknd fnl 1f: see 2652, 2360.   1   70
2926* **BLUE MARBLE 7** [3]2-8-4 (78) N Mackay(3) 15/2: 46017: Bhd, late gains: try further: see 2926.   1¾   70
2513 **DORN DANCER 23** [4]2-8-10 (84) L Enstone(3) 16/1: 0158: Sn rdn & al bhd: twice below 2281 (mdn).   ½   74
1764 **WORLD AT MY FEET 56** [5]2-8-13 (87) Suzanne France(7) 13/2: 2139: Cl-up, wknd over 2f out: abs.   nk   76
2889 **SOWERBY 8** [9]2-7-12 (8oh) (72) B Swarbrick(5) 33/1: 0640: 10th: Al bhd: see 2358.   ¾   59
10 Ran   Time 1m 0.2 (3.32)   Owned: Joy and Valentine Feerick   Trained: Newmarket

3116   2.40 John Smith's Extra Cold Handicap Stakes 3yo+ 0-90 (C)   [90]
£10738 £3304 £1652   6f str   Good 40   -08 Slow   Centre

2990 **PIETER BRUEGHEL 4** [1] D Nicholls 5-9-4 (80) R Winston 13/2: 00-04001: Made all, kept on gamely   89
fnl 1f, drvn out: well bckd: eff over 6/7f on firm & gd, any trk, likes Chester: loves to dominate, well h'capped & back to useful best with money down here: see 2076.
2770 **ELLENS ACADEMY 14** [6] E J Alston 9-9-7 (83) S Sanders 13/2: 3424422: Hmpd start, bhd, hdwy &   ½   90
switched left over 1f out, styd on well ins last, just held: tough & in-form 9yo: see 2770.
2770 **NATIVE TITLE 7** [7] D Nicholls 6-9-11 (87) Alex Greaves 11/1: 0-401003: Handy trav well, gd hdwy   1¾   88
over 1f out, no extra ins last: btr run: see 2256.
2990 **LEGAL SET 4** [3] Miss A Stokell 8-7-12 (2oh)t (58) Catherine Gannon(3) 14/1: 4214024: Cl-up, rdn &   ¾   60
sltly outpcd over 2f out, kept on ins last: qck reapp: see 2990.
2791 **CLOUD DANCER 12** [5]5-9-1 (77) N Callan 5/1 FAV: 3022135: Hmpd start & bhd, eff well over 1f out,   shd   76
no impress: consistent: see 2791, 2409.
2770* **SIERRA VISTA 14** [10]4-9-5 (81) L Enstone(3) 8/1: 0300516: Handy, eff over 1f out, no impress.   1¼   76
2942* **PADDYWACK 7** [11]7-8-11 bl (73) Rory Moore(7) 6/1: 3530117: In tch, wknd dist: 5f specialist.   3½   58
2942 **BOND BOY 7** [4]7-10-2 (92) F Lynch 13/2: 0406038: Went right start, al bhd: big weight but much   5   62
btr expected after 2942, something amiss?
4810} **MITSUKI 264** [12]5-8-4 (66) P Robinson 33/1: 500400-9: b f Puissance - Surrealist (Night Shift)   2   30
Al bhd: '03 fills h'cap wnr: 4th at best in '02: eff over 5/6f on fm & gd, any trk, all 3 wins at Thirsk: tried a vis.
1 Jun'03 Thir 5g/f 75-69 D: 1 Aug'01 Thir 5fm 73-66 C: 2 Jun'01 York 6g/f 69- E: 1 Jun'01 Thir 6fm 64- E:
2727 **INDIAN SPARK 15** [2]10-10-0 (90) K Fallon 6/1: 0446000: 10th: In tch, wknd halfway: something amiss? 7   33
10 Ran   Time 1m 12.3 (2.9)   Owned: Mr David Faulkner   Trained: Thirsk

3117   3.15 John Smith's Cask Handicap Stakes 3yo+ 0-90 (C)   [89]
£10693 £3290 £1645   6f217y rnd   Good 40   -25 Slow   Inside

2777 **LOOK HERES CAROL 13** [14] B A McMahon 4-9-12 (87) D Holland 13/2: 04-33631: Cl-up, hdwy to lead   97
over 1f out, kept on gamely for press when pressed ins last: suited by 7f & acts on firm, likes gd & soft grnd, prob any trk: tough & useful, career best here & a game run: see 1523.
2684 **DIGITAL 16** [13] M R Channon 7-9-12 (87) S Hitchcott(3) 6/1: 6005222: In tch, hdwy 2f out, styd on   hd   96
to chall dist, just held for press ins last: another fine run: see 2684, 945.
2918 **DISTANT CONNECTION 7** [9] A P Jarvis 3-8-12 (81) K Fallon 6/1: 0612153: Sn led, hdd over 1f out,   ¾   88
rallied for press ins last, not btn far: in fine heart: see 2918, 2525 (1m).
2770 **CD FLYER 14** [6] B Ellison 7-9-12 (87) P Mulrennan(5) 16/1: 2004104: Held up, eff well over 1f   ¾   92
out, onepace fnl 1f: poss just best at 6f as in 2561.
2768* **MISTER SWEETS 14** [7]5-8-12 (73) D Tudhope(7) 9/1: 000-6015: In tch, eff over 1f out, onepace: nk   77
ran to winning form of 2768 (fast grnd).
2558 **KAREEB 22** [10]7-9-0 (75) A Rutter(7) 14/1: 0-600406: In tch, short of room 2f out, onepace under   1½   76
kind ride: won this race last term off a 3lb lower mark & shld do btr: see 800.
2587 **ROMAN MAZE 21** [1]4-8-2 (63) B Swarbrick(5) 20/1: 514-0507: Keen, hdwy & short of room over 2f   ½   63
out, some late gains, nvr dngrs: do better: see 2027, 721. -
2848 **RAPHAEL 10** [2]5-9-2 (77) R Winston 11/1: 0103048: Chsd ldrs, onepace over 1f out: see 1474.   shd   76
2770 **BALAKIREF 14** [8]5-8-8 (69) F Lynch 10/1: 222U109: Hmpd start & bhd, eff 2f out, sn short of room   hd   67
again, no impress: best to forgive this: see 2568.

2770 **CD EUROPE 14** [15]6-10-0 BL (89) N Callan 25/1: 021-0000: 10th: Keen in tch, wknd over 1f out. *1¼* **84**
2564* **MR VELOCITY 21** [3]4-8-11 (72) K Darley 11/2 FAV: 330-3210: 11th: In tch, wknd over 1f out. *shd* **66**
MOBANE FLYER 273 [5]4-8-9 (70) G Parkin 66/1: 010050-0: 12th: b g Groom Dancer - Enchant (Lion Cavern) Keen & hmpd after 1f, al bhd: ex-Irish, Cork mdn wnr in '03: eff over 6/7f on gd & firm grnd. *1¾* **60**
2558 **WILL HE WISH 22** [11]8-9-12 bl (87) T P Queally 16/1: 5600000: 13th: In tch, hung left & wknd dist. *½* **76**
2684 **INCHDURA 16** [16]6-8-11 (72) Kim Tinkler 50/1: 00000-00: 14th: Al bhd: see 2684. *¾* **59**
2935 **TIDY 7** [4]4-9-5 (80) Darren Williams 16/1: 15U0300: 15th: Al bhd: btr 2684. *2½* **62**
15 Ran Time 1m 25.82 (4.52) Owned: Mr S L Edwards Trained: Tamworth

3118 **3.50 45th John Smith's Cup Heritage Handicap 3yo+ 0-110 (B)** **[107]**
£91000 £28000 £14000 **1m2f88y** **Good 40** **+14 Fast** Inside

1895+**ARCALIS 50** [18] J Howard Johnson 4-9-2 (95) R Winston 20/1: 32412-11: In tch, hdwy to chall over 1f out, styd on well despite rider dropping whip ins last, pushed out to hold on: 7 wk abs, fast time: v eff at 10f, stays 12f on firm & gd/soft: loves a strong pace & goes esp well fresh on gall trks: has a neat turn of foot, v useful now & type to prog into List class: see 1895. **107**
2556 **PROMOTION 22** [9] Sir Michael Stoute 4-9-2 (95) K Fallon 7/2 FAV: 132-122: In tch, hdwy over 2f out, strong run to lead over 1f out, hung left ins last, drvn & collared cl-home: well bckd: v useful & another fine run: shld continue to give a gd account: see 2556, 1478. *hd* **106**
2255* **STARRY LODGE 35** [1] L M Cumani 4-9-2 (95) D Holland 8/1: 64121-13: In tch, hdwy 2f out, styd on over 1f out, not pace of front 2: most tough & progressive, useful & more to come, esp at 12f+: see 2255. *2½* **102**
2556+**RED FORT 22** [16] M A Jarvis 4-9-12 (8ex) (105) P Robinson 15/2: 140-1314: In tch, hdwy to chall over 2f out, ev ch till onepcd fnl 1f: excellent/smart run under a big weight & from a v poor draw: keep on your side in List/Gr 3 class: see 2556. *shd* **111+**
2745 **JABAAR 14** [12]6-8-7 vis (86) T Eaves(3) 50/1: 0-035625: In tch, rdn & sltly outpcd 2f out, rallied appr fnl 1f, nvr dngrs: v encouraging, shld win shortly on this evidence: see 2745, 1519. *1* **90**
2592* **POLAR JEM 21** [3]4-9-1 (8ex) (94) A McCarthy 14/1: 3411116: Set pace till over 1f out, onepace: another tough & useful eff stepped up in class: thriving front runner, see 2592 (firm grnd). *¾* **96**
2404 **VICIOUS WARRIOR 28** [21]5-8-7 (86) Dean McKeown 50/1: 20-20537: Prom, onepace fnl 2f: gd run. *nk* **87**
2489 **WING COMMANDER 24** [4]5-8-13 (92) G Parkin 25/1: 33-43008: Bhd, eff 2f out, nvr dngrs: btr run. *2½* **89**
2185* **IONIAN SPRING 37** [6]9-9-2 (95) R Smith 25/1: 530-1019: Slow away, some late gains, nvr dngrs. *1¾* **89**
2101+**BLUE SPINNAKER 40** [8]5-9-9 (102) P Mulrennan(5) 13/2: 04-01410: 10th: In tch, outpcd well over 2f out, no impress: shade more expected after val h'cap win in 2101. *3* **92**
2759 **DESERT QUEST 14** [5]4-8-13 bl (92) F Lynch 12/1: 461-0240: 11th: Slow away, nvr a factor: btr 2759. *1¼* **80**
2489 **ZERO TOLERANCE 24** [20]4-8-13 (92) K Darley 20/1: 304-1400: 12th: Cl-up, wknd 2f out: btr 2101. *2½* **76**
1168 **EASTERN BREEZE 87** [14]6-9-9 e (102) Paul Eddery 50/1: 6-412050: 13th: Bhd, nvr a factor: abs. *1* **84**
2903 **CONSONANT 8** [2]7-8-10 (89) D Nolan(3) 25/1: 1060230: 14th: In tch, wknd 2f out: btr 2903, 2662. *1* **69**
2556 **BLYTHE KNIGHT 22** [17]4-9-10 (103) K McEvoy 33/1: 0-414630: 15th: Al bhd: btr 2556. *1½* **80**
4465} **COAT OF HONOUR 288** [13]4-8-13 bl (92) S Sanders 9/1: 251132-0: 16th: gr g Mark of Esteem - Ballymac Girl (Niniski) In tch, wknd over 2f out: well bckd: '03 dual h'cap wnr: eff over 10/12f on fast & gd/soft, any trk: best in blnks & has run well fresh: capable of better. 2 Sep'03 Hayd 10.5g/s 94-87 C: 1 Jul'03 Brig 9.9g/f 85-81 D: 1 Jun'03 Pont 10.0g/f 86-75 D: 2 May'03 Newc 8.0gd 78-71 E: *hd* **68**
2101 **BOURGAINVILLE 40** [10]6-9-6 (99) N Chalmers(5) 50/1: 0455000: 17th: Al bhd: see 1350, 884. *¾* **74**
2606 **NARRATIVE 20** [11]6-9-7 (100) T P Queally 50/1: 300-0460: 18th: Al bhd: see 2154. *¾* **74**
2404 **POLYGONAL 28** [22]4-8-10 (89) T E Durcan 25/1: 020-1360: 19th: Slow away & al bhd: btr 2404. *¾* **62**
2520 **MUTAFANEN 23** [15]3-8-9 (99) R Hills 12/1: 31-13330: 20th: Slow away & al bhd: btr 2520, 1813. *1¾* **69**
1231 **LUNDYS LANE 84** [19]4-9-7 (100) J P Guillambert(3) 66/1: 600-4000: 21st: Al bhd: 3 mth abs: see 360. *15* **46**
21 Ran Time 2m 10.01 (2.71) Owned: Andrea & Graham Wylie Trained: Crook

3119 **4.25 Listed John Smith's Extra Smooth Silver Cup Rated Stakes Handicap 4yo+ 0-110 (A)** **[112]**
£17400 £6600 £3300 **1m5f197y** **Good 40** **+04 Fast** Inside

1757 **DISTINCTION 56** [1] Sir Michael Stoute 5-9-7 (105) K Fallon 11/2 JT FAV: 4015-051: Held up, hdwy over 2f out, led dist, styd on well, gamely, drvn out: well bckd after 8 wk abs: suited by 14f now, stays 2m on firm & gd/soft, prob any trk: runs well fresh: smart eff & career best run: see 1757. **114**
2355* **STAR MEMBER 29** [12] A P Jarvis 5-8-8 (92) K McEvoy 6/1: 50-51412: Hld up, gd hdwy to lead over 1f out, sn hdd but kept on gamely, just held: clr rem: most progressive, land another val prize. *½* **99**
2771 **COLLIER HILL 14** [6] G A Swinbank 6-9-6 (104) Dean McKeown 6/1: 303-0143: Held up, hdwy to lead over 2f out, hdd over 1f out, not pace of front 2: running well: useful: see 2771, 1746. *5* **105**
2771 **MAMCAZMA 14** [14] D Morris 6-8-8 (92) T E Durcan 16/1: 0002-004: In tch, eff over 2f out, kept on same pace: rnr-up in this race last term off a 3lb lower mark: clearly coming to hand, will relish faster grnd & a return to the Newmarket July crse: see 2771. *1½* **91**
2239 **PRINS WILLEM 35** [5]5-8-7 (1oh) (90) T P Queally 8/1: 610-2345: Held up, eff over 2f out, onepace. *¾* **89**
2798* **KUSTER 12** [3]8-8-7 (1oh)bl (90) N Mackay 12/1: 115-0616: Slow away & held up, some late gains. *shd* **89**
2239 **MORSON BOY 35** [4]4-8-13 (97) S Chin 25/1: 1151-007: b g Lear Fan - Esprit d'Escalier (Diesis) Chsd ldr, hung left when chall over 2f out, sn wknd: won 3 of 4 '03 starts, all h'caps: loves to dominate over 12/14.6f on firm & gd, likes gall trks: runs well fresh: btr than this. *4* **90**
1 Jul'03 York 11.9fm 99-91 B: 1 May'03 Donc 14.6gd 99-81 D: 1 Apr'03 Pont 12.0g/f 87-76 D:
2948 **SANTANDO 7** [8]4-8-10 vis (94) D Holland 20/1: 6-530508: In tch, eff 2f out, sn btn: see 433. *½* **86**
2948 **ROYAL CAVALIER 7** [7]7-9-0 (98) N Callan 12/1: 06-01459: In tch, wknd 2f out: see 2948, 950. *¾* **89**
2759 **RANVILLE 14** [10]6-8-7 (1oh) (90) P Robinson 14/1: 02024/-00: 10th: In tch, wknd 2f out: see 2759. *3* **78**
2821* **THEME SONG 13** [11]5-8-11 P (95) Catherine Gannon 11/2 JT FAV: 213-0310: 11th: Trkd ldr, led over 6f out till over 2f out, wknd: tried cheek pieces, see 2821 (fast grnd). *¾* **81**
2948 **BOURGEOIS 7** [13]7-9-0 (98) R Winston 11/1: 50-23100: 12th: In tch, wknd over 2f out: btr 1969. *5* **77**
4572} **MONTMARTRE 281** [2]4-8-8 (92) P Mulrennan 33/1: 223110-0: 13th: br f Grand Lodge - French Quarter (Ile de Bourbon) In tch, hmpd over 4f out, sn wknd: class stks & dual h'cap wnr for N Callaghan in '03: fills mdn wnr in '02: suited by 10/12f now on fast & gd grnd, acts on gd/soft: best up with/forcing the pace on any trk. *dist* **0**
1 Sep'03 Asco 12g/f 94-86 D: 1 Sep'03 Yarm 10.1g/f 88-81 C: 2 Aug'03 Newm 10fm 83-76 C: 2 Aug'03 Newb 9fm 77-(77) D: 1 Jul'03 Epso 10.1gd 75-(78) D: 2 Jul'03 Beve 9.9g/s 77-75 E: 2 May'03 Hami 9.2g/s 77-75 E: 1 Jul'02 Yarm 7fm 74- D:
2762 **CALIBRE 14** [9]4-9-0 (98) K Darley 20/1: 1/52-60: 14th: b c Lear Fan - Carya (Northern Dancer) Led till over 6f out, wknd 4f out, t.o.: '03 rnr-up in a stks: '02 mdn wnr on sole start: stays 12f on fast grnd & on a gall trk: has run well fresh: clearly something amiss & does not look easy to train but useful at best. *dist* **0**
2 May'03 Newm 12g/f 97- C: 1 Oct'02 Newm 8g/f 92- D:

14 Ran   Time 2m 58.44 (5.04)   Owned: Highclere Thoroughbred Racing Ltd   Trained: Newmarket

3120   5.00 John Smith's Heron & Brearley Median Auction Maiden Stakes Div 1 2yo (E)
£6906 £2125 £1063   6f str   Good 40   -37 Slow   Centre

VISIONIST [2] J A Osborne 2-9-0 D Holland 7/1: 1: b c Orpen - Lady Taufan (Taufan) Handy, **91+**
hdwy to lead just ins last, styd on well, hands & heels: Apr foal, cost E52,000: half-brother to wnrs over 5/7f: eff at 6f, 7f sure to suit: runs well fresh on gd: fine start, plenty more to come, win more races.

YAJBILL [8] M R Channon 2-9-0 T E Durcan 8/1: 2: b c Royal Applause - Tee Cee (Lion Cavern) **1** **84**
Hmpd start, sn in tch, hdwy to lead over 1f out, hdd ins last, not pace of wnr on debut: Feb first foal, cost 140,000gns: dam 7f wnr: eff at 6f, 7f sure to suit: acts on gd grnd: clr of rem, fine start, win races.

2348 **WAVERTREE WARRIOR 30** [5] N P Littmoden 2-9-0 J P Guillambert(3) 20/1: 03: br c Indian Lodge - **3** **75**
Karamana (Habitat) In tch, eff well over 1f out, no extra ins last: May foal, cost 30,000gns: half-brother to smart wnrs over 5/12f: much sharper for debut & eff at 6f on gd grnd: minor trks will suit.

BAHAMIAN MAGIC [12] D R Loder 2-9-0 T P Queally 9/2: 4: b c Royal Applause - Out Like Magic **hd** **74**
(Magic Ring) Sn in tch, eff over 1f out, onepace: debut: March foal, cost 65,000gns: dam 5f juv wnr.

2889 **CLARET AND AMBER 8** [9]2-9-0 K Fallon 3/1 FAV: 35: In tch, eff over 1f out, kept on under hands **3** **65**
& heels: well bckd: recently gelded: see 2889.

2689 **REGIS FLIGHT 16** [6]2-9-0 Dean McKeown 50/1: 06: In tch, onepace over 1f out. **hd** **64**
2689 **COMMENDABLE COUP 16** [3]2-9-0 G Gibbons 12/1: 57: Keen in tch, stumbled path after 1f, no impress.**hd** **63**
JEUNE LOUP [1]2-9-0 G Faulkner 66/1: 8: Nvr a factor on debut. **1¾** **59**
SPENCE APPEAL [10]2-9-0 N Callan 25/1: 9: Slow away & al bhd on debut. **¾** **57**
MOSTANAD [4]2-9-0 R Hills 12/1: 0: 10th: With ldrs, wkng when hmpd over 1f out on debut. **4** **45**
2889 **PAULA JO 8** [7]2-8-9 T Eaves(3) 66/1: 600: 11th: Led till 2f out, wknd: see 2513. **1** **37**
2682 **ARTIC FOX 16** [11]2-9-0 P Robinson 6/1: 50: 12th: In tch, wknd 2f out: nicely bckd, see 2682. **¾** **40**
2882 **AS HANDSOME DOES 9** [13]2-9-0 t K Darley 15/2: 20: 13th: Slow away & al bhd: btr 2882 (debut). **3½** **30**
13 Ran   Time 1m 14.01 (4.61)   Owned: Pat Eddery Racing (Alvaro)   Trained: Upper Lambourn

3121   5.30 John Smith's No Nonsense Racing Maiden Stakes Fillies 3yo (D)
£5616 £1728 £864   6f217y rnd   Good 40   -45 Slow   Inside

2622 **ANATOLIAN QUEEN 19** [4] J M P Eustace 3-8-11 K Darley 11/2: 341: In tch, hdwy 2f out, styd on to **75**
lead ins last, drvn out: imprvd with a return to 7f on this gd grnd, enjoys gall trks: see 1514.

1846 **NOORA 52** [6] M P Tregoning 3-8-11 (80) R Hills 11/4: 0-202: Led, kept on till collared just ins **1** **72**
last, not pace of wnr: nicely bckd after 7 wk abs: ran to form of 1587 & shld win similar.

LAKE CHARLOTTE [2] D R Loder 3-8-11 T P Queally 1/1 FAV: 3: b f Danzig - Quinpool (Alydar) In **1** **70**
tch, eff to chall over 1f out, sltly short of room & wknd ins last: hvly bckd on debut: clr of rem: eff at 7f, shld get further: acts on gd grnd: clearly even btr expected but far from disgraced.

2692 **ROSIE MAC 16** [7] N Bycroft 3-8-11 Suzanne France(7) 25/1: 634: In tch, wknd dist: see 2692. **5** **60$**
3770) **MISS PROCURER 324** [9]3-8-11 S Chin 20/1: 65-5: b f Entrepreneur - Kariyh (Shadeed) Switched **½** **59**
left start, held up, wknd well over 1f out on reapp: rtd 78 when 6th on debut in '03: eff at 6f on firm grnd.

2944 **MECCAS MATE 7** [8]3-8-11 F Lynch 100/1: 0-56: In tch, onepace over 2f out: apprec mod h'caps. **2½** **54**
LOTTIE [3]3-8-11 A McCarthy 50/1: 7: b f Robellino - Montserrat (Aragon) In tch, wknd over 2f **5** **44**
out on debut: bred to apprec 7f+.

2595 **ALJAFLIYAH 21** [5]3-8-11 N Mackay(3) 20/1: U8: Slow away & al bhd. **1½** **41**
2748 **POWER NAP 14** [1]3-8-11 t (48) T Eaves(3) 66/1: 00-69: In tch, wknd over 3f out. **1** **39**
9 Ran   Time 1m 27.24 (5.94)   Owned: Mr Y Gelgin   Trained: Newmarket

3122   6.00 John Smith's Heron & Brearley Median Auction Maiden Stakes Div 2 2yo (E)
£6890 £2120 £1060   6f str   Good 40   -39 Slow   Centre

2703 **TRANSACTION 16** [9] J M P Eustace 2-9-0 T E Durcan 11/2: 321: In tch, eff 2f out, styd on to **91**
lead ins last, rdn out: suited by 6f on gd & polytrack, gall trks: see 1514.

2531 **COUP DETAT 22** [3] J L Dunlop 2-9-0 K Darley 9/4 FAV: 42: b c Diktat - Megdale (Waajib) With **½** **88**
ldrs, slt lead over 1f out, hdd & no extra c-home: nicely bckd: March foal, half-brother to wnrs over 7/12f: dam styd 2m: eff at 6f, 7f+ sure to suit: acts on gd grnd: plenty more to come, shld win races.

FOR LIFE [8] A P Jarvis 2-9-0 K Fallon 11/2: 3: b c Bachir - Zest (Zilzal) In tch, sltly **hd** **87+**
outpcd 2f out, rallied fnl 1f, nrst fin, not btn far: Feb foal, cost 15,000gns: eff at 6f, 7f sure to suit: acts on gd grnd: v pleasing start, shld impr plenty for this & be winning soon, esp at 7f.

QUERIDO [2] Saeed bin Suroor 2-9-0 K McEvoy 11/2: 4: b c Spectrum - Polent (Polish Precedent) **¾** **85**
With ldrs, eff to chall appr fnl 1f, onepace on debut: March foal: half-brother to wnrs over 12/14f: dam 13/15f scorer: bred to relish 7f/1m+ in time & shld come on for this.

LUBECK [4]2-9-0 T P Queally 9/1: 5: In tch, keen, eff well over 1f out, onepace. **¾** **83**
REQQA [6]2-9-0 R Hills 9/2: 6: Set pace till over 1f out, onepace. **shd** **82**
SUPERSTITIOUS [12]2-9-0 G Gibbons 25/1: 7: Slow away, bhd, no impression. **6** **64**
2682 **MISTER BUZZ 16** [11]2-9-0 F Lynch 100/1: 008: In tch, wknd 2f out. **shd** **63**
LAST PIONEER [10]2-9-0 J Edmunds 100/1: 9: Swerved left start, hdwy halfway, wknd 2f out. **1½** **60**
TIFFIN BROWN [5]2-9-0 G Faulkner 66/1: 0: 10th: Slow away & al bhd. **1½** **56**
2671 **ALLSTAR PRINCESS 17** [5]2-8-9 P M Quinn 66/1: 00: 11th: In tch, wknd over 2f out. **1¾** **46**
2888 **ZANDERIDO 8** [7]2-9-0 T Eaves(3) 100/1: 40: 12th: Sn rdn & al bhd. **12** **15**
12 Ran   Time 1m 14.12(4.72)   Owned: Mr George Darling   Trained: Newmarket

ASCOT SATURDAY 10.07.04 Righthand, Stiff, Galloping Track

Official Going GOOD (GOOD/SOFT places).

3123 1.30 Millennium & Copthorne Hotels Handicap Stakes 3yo+ 0-100 (C) [97]
£10646 £4038 £2019 **5f str** **Good 57** **-16 Slow** Stands Side

2758 **PIVOTAL POINT 14** [6] P J Makin 4-9-5 (88) L Dettori 5/1 CO FAV: 1352-001: Broke well & made all, **102**
styd on well fnl 1f, rdn out: eff at 5/6f on gd & firm: handles a sharp or stiff/gall trk: useful, win again.
2734+**JIMMY RYAN 15** [8] T D McCarthy 3-8-12 (86) T Quinn 11/2: 314-0012: Front rank, ev ch fnl 1f, not *1* **95**
pace of wnr cl-home: swtg: acts on gd & fast grnd, continues in fine form: see 2734.
2770 **SIR DESMOND 14** [1] R Guest 6-8-8 p (77) E Ahern 14/1: 034-3003: Held up, switched wide & prog *1* **83+**
dist, short of room ins fnl 1f, fin well but too late: did not get the run of today's race, would have gone v close
if doing so: one to keep in mind: see 292 (AW).
2894* **WHISTLER 8** [2] J M Bradley 7-9-8 p (91) Dane O'Neill 6/1: 1031014: Hld up, eff 2f out, no impress. *1¼* **93**
2779 **DANCING MYSTERY 13** [4]10-8-13 (82) S Carson 5/1 CO FAV: 0000145: Held up, prog over 1f out, sn *¾* **81**
stumbled & no impress: btr 2420.
2581 **TEXAS GOLD 21** [7]6-9-6 (89) Martin Dwyer 5/1 CO FAV: 113-2406: Keen & prom, wknd fnl 1f: *½* **87**
reportedly unsuited by this rain-softened grnd, has run well on gd/soft prev but all best form on fast & firm.
2913 **FROMSONG 7** [9]6-10-0 (97) J Murtagh 10/1: 4444007: Prom, fdd fnl 1f under top-weight. *dht* **92**
2727 **WHITBARROW 15** [3]5-9-13 (96) R L Moore 13/2: 0100008: Front rank, wknd 1.5f out. *9* **69**
8 Ran Time 1m 02.66 (3.66) Owned: Mr R A Bernard Trained: Marlborough

3124 2.00 Gr3 Michael Page International Silver Trophy Stakes 4yo+ (A)
£31900 £12100 £6050 **1m rnd** **Good 57** **+08 Fast** Inside

2757 **SHOT TO FAME 14** [10] P W Harris 5-8-13 (107) L Dettori 6/1: 0-501121: Trkd ldr, ev ch ent fnl **114**
1f, forged ahd cl-home, drvn: bckd: suited by 1m, acts on firm & hvy grnd: loves to run-up with/force the pace:
improving with every run & a smart performer now: v tough, see 2757 & 2154.
2757+**GATEMAN 14** [4] M Johnston 7-9-2 (113) J Fanning 13/2: 2120312: Tried to make all, just btn in a *hd* **116**
thrilling fin: fin run conceding improving wnr 3lb, tho' just beat this rival in 2757: most game.
2470 **HURRICANE ALAN 25** [5] R Hannon 4-9-4 (114) P Dobbs 16/1: 05-31503: Held up, prog 2f out, styd on *¾* **116**
fnl 1f & nrst fin: set plenty to do under top-weight & back to smart best: see 1349.
2915* **PENTECOST 7** [7] A M Balding 5-8-13 (94) Martin Dwyer 20/1: 40-06014: Held up, styd on strongly *shd* **111**
fnl 1f, nrst fin: set too much to do & another fine run: loves Ascot/strong pace.
2757 **BABODANA 14** [8]4-8-13 (110) T Quinn 16/1: 10-16355: Trkd ldrs, onepcd fnl 1f: see 1486 (7f). *½* **110**
2470 **BOWMANS CROSSING 25** [6]5-8-13 M J Kinane 6/1: 3354306: Al mid-div: op 9/1: see 2470 (C/D). *1* **108**
2470 **SALSELON 25** [2]5-9-2 bl (118) J Murtagh 7/4 FAV: 310-0237: Trkd ldrs, eff & found little fnl 1f: *1¼* **108**
hvly bckd: rdn more prominently today & found less than expected under press: fin strongly over C/D in 2470.
2558 **NEW SEEKER 22** [3]4-8-13 (103) J Quinn 7/1: 1311-248: Prom, ev ch till wknd fnl 1f: well bckd: *nk* **104**
found this btr grade much tougher: see 2558 (7f h'cap here).
2898 **DUTCH GOLD 8** [9]4-8-13 bl (110) E Ahern 33/1: 2005259: Held up, nvr nr ldrs: unsuited by this *5* **94**
rtn to 1m & rain-softened grnd: remains one to keep in mind over 10f on a fast surface: beat today's 2nd in 2252.
2826 **SUGGESTIVE 13** [1]6-8-13 bl (109) M Hills 25/1: 5-452140: 10th: Keen in mid-div, btn fnl 1f: *2½* **89**
suited by 7f & rcd much too keenly today: btr 2184.
10 Ran Time 1m 42.49 (3.99) Owned: The Conquistadors Trained: Berkhamsted

3125 2.30 Totesport Stakes Heritage Handicap 3yo+ 0-105 (B) [100]
£37700 £14300 £7150 **2m45y** **Good 57** **-05 Slow** Inside

2596* **DOROTHYS FRIEND 21** [6] R Charlton 4-8-13 (85) S Drowne 5/1 FAV: 5111-011: Mid-div, prog 2f out, **91**
styd on strongly to lead cl-home, drvn out: well bckd: eff at 2m, shld stay further: acts on gd & fm, any trk:
most prog & more to come, keep on side & a real Cesarewitch type.
2239 **RANDOM QUEST 35** [4] B J Llewellyn 6-8-12 (84) R L Moore 22/1: 250-0002: Held up, fin strongly *nk* **89**
wide fnl 1f, ev ch cl-home & only just btn: fine run from this well h'capped gelding: shld find similar: see 1232.
2607* **THEWHIRLINGDERVISH 20** [2] T D Easterby 6-8-10 (82) T Quinn 14/1: 0-340313: Led early, remained *nk* **86**
prom, regained lead ins fnl 1f, collared cl-home: 2nd from a 4lbs lower mark in this race in '03: in gd form.
2771 **PROMOTER 14** [13] J Noseda 4-9-2 (88) E Ahern 12/1: 04-00204: Keen in rear, hdwy 2f out to chall *nk* **91**
fnl 1f, no extra cl-home, carried head high: seems to enjoy Ascot, see 2471 (2m4f here).
2471* **DOUBLE OBSESSION 25** [8]4-9-9 vis (95) J F Egan 8/1: 00-00015: Led, clr ent straight, collared *¾* **97**
well ins fnl 1f: gallant front running effort, loves Ascot & a thorough stayer: see 2471 (2m4f here).
2771 **SELF DEFENSE 14** [9]7-10-0 (100) J Murtagh 25/1: 6/1450/-06: Prom, lost pl halfway, styd on again *2* **99**
late but ch had gone: top-weight: gd run in the circumstances, could find a decent prize: see 2771.
2471 **SENTRY 25** [11]4-8-13 (85) Dane O'Neill 20/1: 1-143307: Trkd ldrs, lost pl after halfway, *1½* **82**
rallying when short of room 2f out, styd on: did not get the run of today's race: see 2239.
1519 **HIGH ACTION 68** [1]4-8-13 T (85) P Dobbs 50/1: 1106-008: ch g Theatrical - Secret Imperatrice *½* **81**
(Secretariat) Chsd ldrs, fdd fnl 1f: tried a t-strap: jumps fit, recent h'cap hdle wnr (rtd 98h, eff at 2m on gd):
trained by Sir M Stoute to win a mdn & 2 h'caps in '03, has since been gelded: eff at 1m/12f on fast & firm grnd,
likes to force the pace: handles an undul/stiff or sharp/undul trk: now with Ian Williams.
1 Aug'03 Pont 12.0g/f 95-89 C: 1 Aug'03 Pont 12.0fm 88-85 D: 1 Jul'03 Brig 8.0g/f 80-(86) D: 2 Jun'03 Carl 9.3fm 86- D:
2 May'03 Ling 9.2g/f 82- D:
2887* **DR SHARP 9** [16]4-8-8 (80) Dale Gibson 9/1: 14-01219: Keen & prom, wknd fnl 1f: see 2287 (14f). *1¼* **74**
2771 **KRISTENSEN 14** [7]5-8-10 (82) M J Kinane 14/1: 3-506250: 10th: Prom, wknd 1.5f out. *5* **70**
2471 **MANA DARGENT 25** [3]7-9-0 (86) J Fanning 8/1: 33-05000: 11th: Rear, some prog when short of room *½* **73**
3f out, no impress: crse specialist, won this race from a 2lb lower mark last term: yet to fire this term, see 2471.
2771 **DISTANT PROSPECT 14** [14]7-9-7 (93) Martin Dwyer 14/1: 303-4200: 12th: Rear, hmpd 4f out, no ch *1¼* **78**
after: forgive this: btr 2239.
2771 **PAGAN DANCE 14** [10]5-9-8 p (94) L Dettori 11/2: 0-342260: 13th: Rear, some prog when short of *6* **73**
room 3f out, sn ch after: well bckd: forgive this, stable rtng to form: see 2582 & 1484 (12f).
ALMAH 343 [15]6-9-9 (95) Lisa Jones(3) 100/1: 344630-0: 14th: b f Al Mufti - Jazz Champion *¾* **73**
(Dancing Champ) Al rear on reapp: ex South African, Gr 2 wnr in '03: eff at 10/14f, prob stays 2m: acts on gd
grnd, has worn blnks: now with Miss V Williams.

2899 **THEATRE 8** [5]5-8-10 (82) P Doe 22/1: 4-0S2230: 15th: Dwelt, rdn in rear, nvr nr ldrs: bckd at long odds. 2½ 57
2771 **ESCAYOLA 14** [17]4-9-1 bl (87) M Hills 10/1: 211-0200: 16th: Keen mid-div, short of room 3f out & hd 61
again 2f out, wknd qckly: btr 2355 (14f).
2567 **SAHEM 21** [12]7-8-10 (82) R Hughes 33/1: 5040120: 17th: Rear, gd prog halfway, btn 3f out. 3 53
17 Ran   Time 3m 35.97 (9.97)   Owned: Mountgrange Stud   Trained: Beckhampton

3126 **3.05 Alfred Franks & Bartlett Sunglasses Novice Stakes 2yo (D)**
£5564 £1712 £856   **7f str**   Stands Side

2695 **CAPE GREKO 16** [3] A M Balding 2-8-12   Martin Dwyer 7/2: 21: Keen in rear, prog 1.5f out, qcknd 104+
to lead ins fnl 1f, hands & heels: well bckd: eff at 7f, 1m will suit: acts on gd grnd & on a stiff/gall trk:
useful, did this well, win more races: see 2695.
2467 **BERKHAMSTED 25** [4] J A Osborne 2-9-0   L Dettori 11/4 FAV: 162: Trkd ldrs, imprvd to lead dist, ¾ 101
collared ins fnl 1f, kept on but not pace of wnr: well bckd, rider reportedly gvn a 1 day whip ban: stays a gall
7f: continues to progress: see 2467 & 1014.
2696* **PROPINQUITY 16** [9] P W Harris 2-9-5   J Murtagh 4/1: 13: Led till dist, rallied cl-home but not 1¾ 104
pace of front 2: op 6/1: looks sure to relish 1m: see 2696.
     KHARISH [8] J Noseda 2-8-8   E Ahern 7/1: 4: b c Desert Prince - Moy Water (Tirol) Slowly away, 1¼ 89
prog wide 2f out, not qckn fnl 1f on debut: op 9/2: £300,000 Mar foal: half-brother to 5f juv wnr Mona Em & 1m wnr
Mandhoor: dam a winning miler, sire a top-class miler: with J Noseda & sure to learn from this.
1848 **CHALISON 52** [1]2-8-12   R Hughes 5/1: 235: Mid-div, onepcd fnl 1f: 7 wk abs. 2½ 90
2714* **SKY CRUSADER 15** [2]2-9-0   S Drowne 8/1: 16: Prom, ev ch till wknd fnl 1f: btr 2714 (debut). ½ 85
     ZABEEL PALACE [7]2-8-8   N Pollard 16/1: 7: b c Grand Lodge - Applecross (Glint of Gold) Trkd nk 80
ldrs 5f, wknd: Feb foal, half-brother to sev wnrs, notably 1m/12f scorer Inchrory.
     CLASP [6]2-8-8   I Mongan 66/1: 8: ch c Singspiel - Embrace Me (Nashwan) Dwelt, recovered to 1¼ 79
chase ldrs 5f, wknd: ran green: 75,000gns Mar first foal: dam lightly rcd, sire a top-class mid-dist performer.
     PATRONOFCONFUCIUS [5]2-8-8   T Quinn 50/1: 9: b g Imperial Ballet - Shefoog (Kefaah) Slowly 11 59
away, al bhd, fin last on debut: £10,000 Apr foal: half-brother to 1m wnr Imperialistic: dam a 7f wnr.
9 Ran   Time 1m 32.99 (6.99)   Owned: Holistic Racing Ltd   Trained: Kingsclere

3127 **3.40 Michael Page International Nursery Handicap Stakes 2yo (D)** [96]
£5369 £1652 £826   **6f str**   Good 57   -26 Slow   Stands Side

2473* **SACRED NUTS 24** [6] M L W Bell 2-9-1 (83) L Dettori 3/1 FAV: 511: Mid-div, prog 1.5f out, styd on 95+
well to lead cl-home, drvn out: well bckd: eff at 6f, apprec 7f: acts on gd & fast grnd, stiff/undul or gall trk:
lightly rcd & fast improving, more to come: see 2473.
2424* **FIEFDOM 27** [3] M Johnston 2-9-7 (89) J Fanning 10/3: 5412: Broke well & tried to make all, nk 99
collared cl-home: well bckd & fine run under top-weight: imprvd in defeat, see 2424.
2537* **BENTLEYS BUSH 22** [1] R Hannon 2-9-1 (83) R Hughes 11/2: 5213: Chsd ldrs, onepace fnl 1f: bckd. 2½ 86
1567 **CANTON 66** [5] R Hannon 2-9-5 (87) R L Moore 13/2: 6144: Mid-div, kept on under press fnl 1f: abs. ½ 89
2927 **CLINET 7** [4]2-7-12 (1oh) (66) J Quinn 33/1: 05205: Slowly away & sn well bckd, styd on late, nvr 1¼ 64
dngrs: 7f will suit judged on this: see 2020.
2815 **ALSU 15** [9]2-8-6 (74) Martin Dwyer 12/1: 3106: Chsd ldrs wide, btn fnl 1f: btr 1744. ¾ 69
2367 **OBSERVER 29** [8]2-9-4 (86) N Pollard 8/1: 137: Rear, sltly short of room 1.5f out, nvr dngrs. 2 75
1738 **NORCROFT 57** [2]2-9-3 (85) J Murtagh 14/1: 21608: Al rear: 8 wk abs & has been gelded: btr 1237. ¾ 71
2395 **LILY LENAT 28** [7]2-8-5 (73) E Ahern 12/1: 0439: Chsd ldr 4f, wkng when hmpd dist: reportedly 1¼ 55
hung right & lost action halfway: see 2395.
9 Ran   Time 1m 18.12 (5.02)   Owned: Fitzroy Thoroughbreds   Trained: Newmarket

3128 **4.15 Mitsubishi Electric Classified Stakes 3yo 0-80 (D)**
£5499 £1692 £846   **1m rnd**   Good 57   -04 Slow   Inside

2127 **DUBOIS 39** [7] Saeed bin Suroor 3-8-13 vis t (82) L Dettori 9/2 CO FAV: 25-101: Made all, rcd far 95
rail to halfway clr 3f out, unchall: well bckd: back to form, suited by gd & fast grnd: eff at 7f/1m & forcing
tactics: handles a sharp/undul or stiff/gall trk: runs well fresh: great ride, see 1815.
2126 **SAFFRON FOX 39** [3] J G Portman 3-8-9 (81) E Ahern 9/1: 120-4042: Chsd ldrs, styd on into 2nd fnl 3 83
1f, no ch with wnr: acts on gd & soft grnd, once again suggested another try at 10f will suit: see 2126 & 1105.
1419 **DESERT CRISTAL 73** [6] J R Boyle 3-8-8 (80) Martin Dwyer 14/1: 25-263: Chsd wnr, caught for 2nd ¾ 80
ins fnl 1f: 10 wk abs: has shown enough to win a mdn, see 1297.
2764 **MISSION MAN 14** [10] R Hannon 3-8-11 (80) R L Moore 20/1: 4-421404: Rear, prog 2f out, nrst fin. nk 82
2081* **MARBUSH 42** [9]3-9-2 (85) M J Kinane 9/2 CO FAV: 3215: Held up, imprvd 2f out, btn fnl 1f: well 2 83
bckd, 6 wk abs: see 2081 (firm grnd).
2383* **PASS THE PORT 29** [5]3-8-11 (80) J Murtagh 7/1: 516: Rear, late hdwy, nvr dngrs: see 2383 (AW). 3 72
2521 **LORD LINKS 23** [8]3-9-1 (84) R Hughes 10/1: 3040-407: Rear, no ch when hmpd dist: see 1847. ½ 75
2742 **VERKHOTINA 14** [11]3-8-8 (80) S Drowne 6/1: 50-61038: Held up, nvr nr ldrs: btr 2742 & 2118 (6f). 2 64
2919 **BOULE DOR 7** [1]3-9-2 (85) N Day 9/2 CO FAV: 00-41429: Chsd ldrs 6.5f, wknd: well bckd: not ½ 71
apprec this drop back in trip, btr 2912 (10f).
2767 **FRAGRANT STAR 14** [2]3-8-8 (74) J Quinn 50/1: 105-0000: 10th: Chsd ldrs 6f, wknd: see 2592. 1¾ 59
2742 **GLEBE GARDEN 14** [4]3-8-9 (81) I Mongan 25/1: 310-5560: 11th: Dwelt, al bhd & fin last. ½ 59
11 Ran   Time 1m 43.44 (4.94)   Owned: Godolphin   Trained: Newmarket

Official Going GOOD

3129   6.50 Saturday Nights Are Back Apprentice Riders Stakes Round 2 Handicap 3yo+ 0-70 (E)   [65]
£4030 £1240 £620   6f5y   Good 44   -16 Slow   Stands side

2928* **MICKLEDOR** 7 [3] M Dods 4-8-13 p (50) M Howard 8/1: 4-003011: Rear stands side, hdwy & switched   55
left over 1f out, led ins fnl 1f, kept on well for press nr fin: landed double, qck reapp: eff at 5/6f on fast &
gd/soft, prob acts on any trk: in fine form: see 2928 (seller) & 2326.
2552 **ORANGINO** 22 [14] J S Haldane 6-8-3 (40) R Kennemore(7) 10/1: 000-0202: Switched to stands side   hd   45
after 2f & handy, led over 1f out till ins fnl 1f, styd on: joc 2 day careless riding ban: btr run back at 6f: see 2521.
2990 **SHAROURA** 4 [13] R A Fahey 8-9-13 (64) Dean Williams 4/1 J FAV: 05-50103: Handy far side, ev ch   1¼   65
over 1f out, no impress ins fnl 1f: qck reapp: back to form of 2791.
2990 **BUNDY** 4 [1] M Dods 8-9-13 (64) W Hogg 4/1 J FAV: 0223204: Bhd stands side, hdwy 1f out, kept on.   ½   63
2999 **OLD BAILEY** 4 [10]4-8-8 P (45) J D O'Reilly 8/1: 5010005: Switched stands side after 2f & cl-up,   1½   39
onepcd fnl 1f: qck reapp: first time cheek pieces: see 2204.
2968 **NORTHERN SVENGALI** 5 [12]8-8-7 t p (44) B O'Neill(5) 16/1: 0-000556: Handy far side, no impress fnl 1f.   hd   37
532* **MASSEY** 158 [6]8-9-6 (57) Laura Jayne Crawford 7/1: 000-1017: Led stands side till over 1f out, no extra.   ½   48
2730 **BEST LEAD** 15 [9]5-9-3 bl (54) K Jackson(5) 12/1: 3433338: Handy stands side, outpcd & btn over 1f out.   ½   43
2806 **NEEDWOOD BUCOLIC** 12 [2]6-8-3 (40) M Stainton(5) 33/1: 13/-00009: Mid-div, outpcd & btn 3f out.   ½   27
2512 **XANADU** 23 [5]8-9-2 p (53) Jemma Marshall(5) 10/1: 0006200: 10th: Chsd ldrs stands side, no impress.   1½   35
3000 **NIFTY ROY** 4 [7]4-7-12 (35) S Yourston(3) 66/1: 560/-0000: 11th: Slow away, nvr a factor: qck reapp.   2½   9
2657 **TRAVELLING TIMES** 18 [4]5-8-4 vis (41) A Reilly(3) 12/1: 0-560040: 12th: Handy stands side, wknd 2f out.   ½   13
3000 **SPEEDFIT FREE** 4 [8]7-8-6 vis (43) R Keogh(4) 33/1: 6000000: 13th: Bhd stands side, btn over 2f out.   3   6
2476 **VIJAY** 24 [11]5-9-1 p (52) G Bartley(7) 20/1: 6020060: 14th: Switched stands side group after 2f,   5   0
cl-up, no impress 2f out: see 1797.
14 Ran   Time 1m 13.45 (3.65)   Owned: Mr D B Stanley   Trained: Darlington

3130   7.20 Joe Punter Novice Auction Stakes A Qualifier For The Hamilton Park 2-Y-O Series Final 2yo (F)
£2940 £840 £420   5f4y   Good 44   -28 Slow   Stands side

2744 **SPEED DIAL HARRY** 14 [5] K R Burke 2-8-10 vis Darren Williams 7/4: 5231321: Made all, pushed clr   81
over 1f out: eff at 5/6f on firm, soft & fibresand, sharp or stiff/undul trks: consistent, deserved win: see 1143.
2569 **REGAL LUSTRE** 21 [4] J R Weymes 2-8-6   B Swarbrick(5) 25/1: 352: Handy, onepace fnl 2f.   7   56
1818 **UNDERTHEMISTLETOE** 53 [2] B Smart 2-8-6   D McGaffin 8/1: 63: b f Lujain - Christmas Kiss (Taufan)   hd   55
Rcd in 2nd, no impress & flashed tail ins fnl 1f: op 16/1, 8 wk abs: mdn unplcd earlier debut: Mar foal, cost
9,200gns: half-sister to a 5f 2yo wnr: dam plcd over 6f at 2, later fair 5/6f wnr: sire top-class juv sprinter.
2933 **TOLDO** 7 [3] A Berry 2-8-11 BL P Bradley 50/1: 0004: Cl-up, no impress 2f out: first time blnks.   4   48
2505* **SWEET ROYALE** 23 [1]2-8-11 R Winston 8/11 FAV: 215: In tch, hung right, wknd over 3f out: 9   23
top-weight: reportedly hung thr'out race & prob something amiss.
5 Ran   Time 1m 1.71 (3.61)   Owned: Mr Nigel Shields   Trained: Leyburn

3131   7.50 Mailsport Weekly Classified Stakes 3yo 0-75 (D)
£6162 £1896 £948   6f5y   Good 44   +08 Fast   Stands side

2880 **COMPTONS ELEVEN** 9 [5] M R Channon 3-9-5 (80) C Catlin 9/4: 0000521: Rcd in 2nd, hdwy to lead ins   91
fnl 1f, rdn clr: eff at 5/7f best at 6f on fast & gd, any trk: win again, see 1847.
2609 **IMPERIAL ECHO** 20 [1] T D Barron 3-9-3 (78) P Makin(5) 13/2: 33-00402: Led, hung right 3f out, hdd   3   78
ins fnl 1f, no extra: clr of rem: back to form without visor: see 1460.
2950 **LETS GET IT ON** 7 [3] J J Quinn 3-8-12 (76) R Winston 11/4: 0520053: Rear, nvr nr ldrs: qck reapp.   4   61
2675 **OBE BOLD** 14 [4] A Berry 3-8-11 (57) P Bradley 33/1: 2001504: Handy, outpcd 2f out.   1½   55
2482* **BRIDGEWATER BOYS** 24 [2]3-9-5 bl (80) R Ffrench 7/4 FAV: 1311215: Handy, no impress over 2f out: v   4   51
tough & prog earlier, something amiss?
5 Ran   Time 1m 11.96 (2.16)   Owned: PCM Racing   Trained: West Ilsley

3132   8.20 Sports Relief Handicap Stakes A Qualifier For The Totepool Series Final 3yo+ 0-75 (E)   [69]
£4176 £1285 £643   1m1f36y   Good 44   -01 Slow   Inside

2832* **WAHOO SAM** 11 [8] T D Barron 4-9-9 (64) P Makin(5) 2/1 FAV: 00-00311: Made all, kept on well for   71
press to hold on ins fnl 1f: nicely bckd: prev eff at 6/7f, now suited by 1m/9f: acts on firm,
gd/soft & fibresand, any trk, likes Hamilton: in fine form at present, see 2832 (C/D).
2947 **APACHE POINT** 7 [1] N Tinkler 7-8-12 (53) Kim Tinkler 11/4: 0054552: Mid-div, hdwy over 3f out,   ¾   57
kept on ins fnl 1f: op 4/1, qck reapp: see 1776.
1910 **COUSTOU** 49 [4] A R Dicken 4-9-4 (59) S W Kelly 16/1: 5-600433: Trkd ldrs, kept on ins fnl 1f: nk   62
hdles fit (nov hdle 4th, rtd 89h): stays 9f: see 1910 & 1094.
2832 **NEWCORP LAD** 11 [5] Mrs G S Rees 4-9-5 (60) B Swarbrick(5) 12/1: 6-040004: Cl-up, onepcd over 1f out.   1¾   59
2794 **MARKET AVENUE** 12 [2]5-9-7 (62) A Nicholls 4/1: 0006-605: Bhd, hdwy 2f out, wknd fnl 1f: see 1821.   1   59
c2832 **DONNAS DOUBLE** 11 [9]9-9-1 p (56) P Mulrennan(5) 7/1: 40555-56: Mid-div, wknd 2f out.   1½   50
2706 **BADR** 16 [6]3-8-8 (59) R Ffrench 12/1: 20-60507: Handy, wknd 3f out: see 2103.   5   43
4621¦ **KRISTIANSAND** 278 [7]4-9-10 (65) L Enstone(3) 20/1: 010505-8: b g Halling - Zonda (Fabulous   8   33
Dancer). Keen & prom, wknd over 2f out on reapp: won 1 of 10 '03 starts (appr h'cap, with M Channon): stays 9/10f
on fast, sharp/undul trks: can force the pace: now with P Monteith.
1 Aug'03 Folk 9.7g/f 70-65 F: 2 Jul'03 Ling 10.3g/f 69- D:
2338 **RARE COINCIDENCE** 30 [3]3-9-2 p (67) R Winston 14/1: 6044409: Handy, fdd after halfway.   22   0
9 Ran   Time 1m 58.2 (4.1)   Owned: Mr C A Washbourn   Trained: Thirsk

948

HAMILTON   SATURDAY 10.07.04   Righthand, Undulating Track, Stiff Uphill Finish

3133
8.50 Sunday Mail Median Auction Maiden Stakes 3yo (E)
£3786 £1165 £583   5f4y   Good 44   -30 Slow   Stands side

2906 **RAGGED JACK** 8 [4] G A Butler 3-9-0 BL (72) S W Kelly 2/7 FAV: 50U4-231: Rcd in 2nd, hdwy to lead 2f out, drvn out ins fnl 1f: eff at 5/6f, has tried 1m: acts on fast, gd & polytrack, sharp or stiff/undul trks: imprvd for a drop in trip & first time blnks in a poor run: see 2586.   **66**

2683 **WESTBOROUGH** 16 [1] N Tinkler 3-9-0 (51) Kim Tinkler 9/2: 05-25052: Keen & handy, styd on ins fnl 1f but no impress nr fin: clr of rem: see 1682.   1½   60

2944 **RED HOT RUBY** 7 [2] R A Fahey 3-8-9 G Parkin 8/1: 033: Bhd, nvr a factor: qck reapp.   5   40

2812 **AGUILERA** 12 [3] M Dods 3-8-9 p (43) L Enstone(3) 20/1: 00-0004: ch f Wolfhound - Mockingbird (Sharpo) Led, hdd & hung right 2f out, no extra: mdn unplcd in '03 (rtd 45): wears cheek pieces.   7   19

4 Ran   Time 1m 1.8 (3.7)   Owned: Mrs W W Fleming   Trained: Blewbury

3134
9.20 Support Velvet Fair Friday Handicap Stakes 3yo+ 0-75 (E)   [72]
£4144 £1275 £638   1m5f9y   Good 44   -08 Slow   Stands side

2708* **INCHNADAMPH** 16 [4] T J Fitzgerald 4-9-0 t (58) R Winston 11/4 FAV: 00-622211: Mid-div, hdwy over 2f out, led over 1f out, kept on well for press ins fnl 1f: landed double: eff at 10.5f/11f, relishing 13f at present: acts on gd & gd/soft, likes Hamilton: improving: see 2708.   **66**

2892* **SUALDA** 8 [5] R A Fahey 5-9-10 (68) G Parkin 5/1: 500-5212: Trkd ldrs, not clr run over 2f out, kept on ins fnl 1f, not pace of wnr: top-weight: eff at 1m, suited by 10/12f, stays 13f: in gd form: see 2892.   1   73

2966 **COSMIC CASE** 5 [2] J S Goldie 9-8-1 (45) A Nicholls 6/1: 0-103523: Led till over 1f out, no extra.   1½   48

2726 **SCURRA** 15 [7] A C Whillans 5-8-11 (55) P Mulrennan(5) 8/1: 0-603124: Nvr btr than mid-div.   1   55

2964 **ELLWAY HEIGHTS** 5 [3]7-8-9 (53) B Swarbrick(5) 3/1: 020-2225: Keen & handy, not much room over 2f out, no impress over 1f out: qck reapp: see 2964.   shd   53

2900 **MILLENNIUM HALL** 8 [6]5-9-4 (62) L Enstone(3) 7/2: 3311066: Bhd, hdwy over 3f out, wknd over 1f out.   6   53

2813 **HOWARDS DREAM** 12 [1]6-7-12 (17oh) (25) Kim Tinkler 50/1: 0406007: Keen & prom, wknd 2f out.   5   25

7 Ran   Time 2m 52.36(6.86)   Owned: Mr R N Cardwell   Trained: Malton

HAYDOCK   SUNDAY 11.07.04   Lefthand, Flat, Galloping Track

Official Going GOOD/SOFT (SOFT places).

3135
2.10 Paddy Power Nspcc Handicap Stakes 3yo 0-80 (D)   [87]
£6971 £2145 £1073   5f str   Good/Soft 84   -02 Slow   Centre

2961 **JADAN** 7 [1] E J Alston 3-8-11 (70) W Supple 7/1: 1-003661: Played up stalls, bhd, prog 2f out, rdn out to lead nr fin: qck reapp: eff at 5f on firm & gd/soft grnd: gd confidence boost: see 2961.   **76**

2593 **RYDAL** 22 [2] G A Butler 3-9-7 bl (80) T P Queally 14/1: 21-04062: Prom, led dist, sn edged right, hdd nr fin: clr rem: eff at 5f, stays 1m: acts on fast, gd/soft & polytrack: gd eff & is on fair mark.   nk   84

2566 **LUALUA** 22 [10] T D Barron 3-9-3 (76) K Fallon 5/1: 5-423043: Rear, prog halfway, kept on fnl 1f.   3½   70

2945* **CHIMALI** 8 J Noseda 3-8-8 (67) E Ahern 13/2: 4-14: Cl-up till dist, no extra: h'cap bow: failed to build on win in 2945 (mdn, soft).   1¼   57

2791 **BARON RHODES** 13 [8]3-9-4 (77) T Eaves(3) 8/1: 2231305: Cl-up over 3f, sn wknd: btr 2566 & 2387.   2½   62

2841 **CATCH THE WIND** 11 [5]3-9-0 (73) L Enstone(3) 16/1: 140-0556: Led over 3f, sn wknd: btr 2841.   hd   57

1734 **PERUVIAN STYLE** 58 [3]3-9-0 (73) E Ahern 12/1: 1-110507: Chsd ldrs 3f, no extra: 8 wk abs.   1¼   53

3033+ **SILVER PRELUDE** 4 [7]3-9-13 (6ex) (86) P Robinson 5/1: 0-000318: Cl-up 4f, fdd: op 4/1 on qck reapp: disapp on today's softer surface: btr 3033 (fast).   hd   65

2675* **TREASURE CAY** 18 [9]3-9-6 e t (79) K Darley 9/2 FAV: 1-535319: Chsd ldrs till dist, fdd: bckd tho' op 7/2: disappointing on today's rain softened grnd: btr 2675 (gd).   nk   57

2961 **FITZWARREN** 7 3-8-8 vis (67) Dean McKeown 20/1: 4402-030: 10th: Handy 3f, sn wknd: qck reapp.   1   42

10 Ran   Time 1m 3.12 (4.32)   Owned: Mr Derrick Mossop   Trained: Preston

3136
2.40 Paddy Power Bet In-Running Handicap Stakes 4yo+ 0-85 (D)   [82]
£7183 £2210 £1105   6f str   Good/Soft 84   -18 Slow   Centre

2752 **PINCHBECK** 15 [7] M A Jarvis 5-9-12 p (80) P Robinson 9/2 CO FAV: 33-04101: Keen held up, prog to lead ins fnl 1f, pushed out, val 2L+: bckd under jt top-weight: eff around 6f on firm & gd/soft grnd: apprec recent fitting of cheek pieces & left poor eff in 2752 well bhd: see 1726 & 1523.   **90+**

2878 **GOLDEN DIXIE** 10 [4] A M Balding 5-9-12 (80) K Fallon 5/1: 40000-02: Cl-up, led 3f out, hdd ins fnl 1f, not pace of wnr: bckd from 7/1 under jt top-weight: acts on firm & gd/soft grnd: h'capped to find similar.   1¼   84

2934 **TIME N TIME AGAIN** 8 [6] E J Alston 6-9-2 p (70) D Allan 9/2 CO FAV: 6303223: Cl-up till dist, no extra.   2   68

2884 **LOCOMBE HILL** 10 D Nicholls 8-8-6 (60) J Carroll 8/1: 2005044: Handy 3f, sn outpcd, rallied late.   nk   57

2770 **GREY COSSACK** 15 [2]7-9-5 (73) R Fitzpatrick 9/1: 0050005: Mid-div, prog halfway, no extra dist.   1¾   65

2758 **MILLION PERCENT** 15 [9]5-9-11 (79) Darren Williams 9/2 CO FAV: 0-062266: Mid-div, prog halfway, wknd dist, sn eased: op 7/2: btr 2591 (firm).   2½   64

2561 **INTER VISION** 22 [1]4-10-0 (82) A Beech(3) 16/1: 54-00507: Chsd ldrs over 4f, sn wknd: btr 1767.   nk   66

2074 **SMIRFYS SYSTEMS** 43 [5]5-9-8 (76) T G McLaughlin 12/1: 012-0058: Slow away, nvr a factor: abs.   1¼   56

2846 **ZUHAIR** 8 [8]11-8-12 (66) Alex Greaves 25/1: 0-000009: Rear, nvr a factor.   2   40

2838 **HARD TO CATCH** 12 [3]6-9-11 bl (79) M Howard(7) 11/1: 0011330: 10th: Led 3f, fdd fnl 2f: btr 2838.   10   26

10 Ran   Time 1m 17.43 (6.13)   Owned: Mr T G Warner   Trained: Newmarket

3137 **3.10 Paddy Power Handicap Stakes 4yo+ 0-70 (E)** **[70]**
£5720 £1760 £880 **7f30y rnd** **Good/Soft 84** **-08 Slow** Inside

2884* **SAVILES DELIGHT 10** [4] R Brotherton 5-10-4 (74) D Nolan(3) 11/2: 4312011: Cl-up, led after 2f, wandered under press ins fnl 2f, rnd out: eff at 6/7f on firm, hvy grnd & both AW's: likes Haydock: see 2884. **82**
2768 **MIDDLETON GREY 15** [3] A G Newcombe 6-9-7 bl (63) L Keniry(3) 11/2: 0320352: Mid-div, prog 3f out, kept on ins fnl 1f, just held by wnr: another sound eff & is h'capped to find similar: see 2199 & 840. *½* **68**
2831* **FONTHILL ROAD 12** [2] R A Fahey 4-10-0 (70) T Hamilton(3) 9/4 FAV: 1612-613: Slow away, prog halfway, ev ch dist, kept on fnl 1f, not btn far in 3rd: just below form of win in 2831. *nk* **74**
2935 **EFIDIUM 8** [7] N Bycroft 6-9-13 (69) Dean McKeown 10/1: 2315354: Bhd, prog 3f out, onepcd fnl 1f. *2½* **68**
2864 **BINT ROYAL 10** 6-8-13 p (55) P Robinson 16/1: 4043005: Led 2f, styd in tch, wknd dist: btr 2539. *¾* **52**
2726 **ABLE MIND 16** [5]4-9-6 (62) T Eaves(3) 40/1: 3233-006: Nvr nrr than mid-div: see 2726. *5* **49**
2768 **BRANSTON TIGER 15** [9]5-9-9 (65) M Fenton 9/1: 0006507: Rear, modest late gains: btr 1820. *¾* **50**
2947 **CRESKELD 8** [8]5-9-11 (67) F Lynch 11/1: 0-300008: Cl-up 5f, sn wknd: btr 1214. *1½* **49**
2890 **ASWAN 9** [6]6-9-9 t (65) K Fallon 8/1: 440-5309: Mid-div over 5f, sn wknd: btr 2514. *5* **37**
2752 **FAR NOTE 15** [10]6-9-9 bl (65) K Darley 10/1: 1440400: 10th: Prom 5f, sn fdd, eased ins fnl 1f. *18* **5**
10 Ran Time 1m 33.64 (6.54) Owned: Mr Roy Brotherton Trained: Pershore

3138 **3.40 Paddypower Com Handicap Stakes 3yo 0-70 (E)** **[76]**
£5655 £1740 £870 **1m30y rnd** **Good/Soft 84** **-22 Slow** Inside

2478 **SILVERHAY 25** [5] T D Barron 3-9-4 (66) K Fallon 13/8 FAV: 523-4241: Made all, rdn out to hold on: well bckd: stays 11f, suited by a return to around 1m: acts on fast & soft grnd: see 2103 & 1628. **70**
2800 **ALMOND WILLOW 13** [2] J Noseda 3-9-4 (66) E Ahern 12/1: 60361-02: Rear, prog 2f out, sn rdn & flashed tail, kept on fnl 1f, not pace of wnr: acts on fast, gd/soft grnd & fibresand: only lightly rcd: see 423. *¾* **67**
2565 **FOOLISH GROOM 22** [10] R Hollinshead 3-9-7 T p (69) W Supple 12/1: 34563: Mid-div, prog 3f out, ev ch 1f out, sn onepcd: first time t-strap: see 1882. *½* **69**
2552 **ORION EXPRESS 23** [7] M W Easterby 3-9-0 (62) P Mulrennan(5) 9/1: 6600464: Mid-div, prog 2f out, nrst fin: worth another try at 9f+: just btr 2295. *¾* **60**
2656 **BELSHAZZAR 19** [8]3-9-7 (69) J Edmunds 33/1: 0405: Bhd, hdwy ins fnl 2f, nrst fin: see 2012. *nk* **66**
2258 **MORAG 35** [3]3-9-2 (64) T P Queally 20/1: 50-40006: Handy over 6f, sn no extra: btr 1359. *shd* **60**
2722 **DESERT LEADER 16** [4]3-9-7 (69) G Gibbons 4/1: 0027: Handy, short of room 2f out, sn no extra, eased cl-home: well bckd: showed more in 2722. *2* **61**
2506 **ACUZIO 24** [6]3-9-1 (63) K Darley 25/1: 66048: Cl-up, ev ch bef 1f out, sn fdd: btr 2506 (7f). *¾* **53**
2773 **DISPOL VELETA 15** [9]3-9-5 (67) N Mackay(3) 7/1: 1300109: Handy, eff when no room fnl 2f, wknd. *hd* **56**
2495 **MISSION AFFIRMED 25** [1]3-9-4 (66) Dale Gibson 14/1: 0151040: 10th: Al in rear: btr 1198. *nk* **54**
10 Ran Time 1m 48.99 (8.49) Owned: D C Rutter P J Huntbach Trained: Thirsk

3139 **4.10 Paddy Power Dial-A-Bet Handicap Stakes 3yo+ 0-70 (E)** **[70]**
£5785 £1780 £890 **1m2f120y** **Good/Soft 84** **-06 Slow** Inside

2901* **JIMMY BYRNE 9** [1] B Ellison 4-10-0 (70) T Eaves(3) 6/1: 4105611: Cl-up, led trav well ins fnl 1f, drvn out to assert: suited by 10f, has tried 12f: acts on firm & soft grnd, handles hvy: likes Haydock, see 2901. **79**
2943* **SANTIBURI LAD 8** [10] N Wilson 7-9-10 (66) K Fallon 6/4 FAV: 60-32112: Led 2f, styd on to lead again 2f out, hdd ins fnl 1f, no extra & sn short of room: lost little in defeat on hat-trick bid: see 2943. *1¾* **72**
2654 **EASIBET DOT NET 19** [9] I Semple 4-9-4 p (60) P Fessey 12/1: 4023053: Cl-up 1m, sn outpcd, rallied late. *¾* **64**
2800 **BAND 13** B A McMahon 4-9-2 (58) G Gibbons 33/1: 60-00004: Rear, prog after 5f, no impress dist. *2* **57**
3099 **OPENING CEREMONY 1** [4]5-10-0 (70) T Hamilton(3) 9/2: 31-624215: Rear, prog 2f out, onepcd fnl 1f: op 7/2: perhaps came too sn after win yesterday in 3099. *1¼* **69**
3099 **LENNEL 1** [8]6-9-8 bl (64) T P Queally 12/1: 50400406: Bhd, mod late gains: unplcd yesterday. *1¼* **61**
2673 **VALDESCO 18** [3]6-9-11 P (67) L Enstone(3) 16/1: 01120/-07: Led over 1m out, hdd 2f out, wknd. *1* **62**
2901 **ALLIED VICTORY 9** [7]4-10-5 (75) W Supple 16/1: 24-10028: Chsd ldrs, fdd fnl 3f: btr 2901. *8* **59**
2929 **ACTIVE ACCOUNT 8** [5]7-9-5 (61) K Darley 12/1: 2256639: Handy over 6f, sn wknd. *6* **37**
1884 **MI ODDS 51** [6]8-9-11 (67) J Fanning 25/1: 2-150000: 10th: Al in rear: 7 wk abs. *26* **3**
10 Ran Time 2m 19.49 (9.49) Owned: Mr Keith Middleton Trained: Malton

3140 **4.40 Paddy Power Football Furlong Handicap Stakes 3yo+ 0-75 (E)** **[75]**
£5590 £1720 £860 **1m6f** **Good/Soft 84** **+14 Fast** Inside

2963 **MAGIC COMBINATION 7** [7] L Lungo 11-9-11 (72) P Mulrennan(5) 9/4 FAV: 10/-25221: Bhd, prog 3f out, led trav well ins fnl 1f, pushed out, val 5L+: well bckd, qck reapp, gd time: eff at 10f/2m2f on fast & soft grnd: enjoyed return to staying trip & this was a deserved success: see 2963 & 2607. **85+**
2850 **PRIZE RING 11** [3] G M Moore 5-8-3 (50) R Ffrench 9/1: 36410-62: Handy, styd on to lead 2f out, hdd ins fnl 1f, sn no extra: tchd 9/1: eff at 10/12f, now stays 14f: acts on firm & gd/soft grnd. *3* **55**
2900* **SMART JOHN 9** [6] W M Brisbourne 4-9-9 (70) B Swarbrick(5) 11/4: 0-414213: Rear, prog 4f out, no impress when jinked badly right well ins fnl 1f: btr 2900 (12f, gd). *6* **71**
2085 **PERESTROIKA 43** [8] B Ellison 6-8-8 (55) T Eaves(3) 14/1: 50/-00404: Nvr nrr than mid-div: 6 wk abs. *1½* **54**
2041 **BRAMANTINO 44** [2]4-8-9 bl (56) T Hamilton(3) 12/1: 3102505: Handy, led briefly 2f out, wknd dist. *¾* **54**
BUSHIDO 774 [1]5-8-12 (59) L Enstone(3) 9/1: 60/3500/-6: br g Brief Truce - Pheopotstown (Henbit) *nk* **56**
Cl-up, led 3f out, hdd bef 2f out, wkng when short of room dist & again ins fnl 1f: op 6/1: 6 wk jumps abs, earlier h'cap wnr (rtd 120h, stays 2m3f on gd & gd/soft grnd): won 2 juv nov hdles in 02/03 (rtd 107h): ex-Irish mdn on the Flat: with Mrs S J Smith.
2887 **NORTHERN NYMPH 10** [4]5-9-5 (66) Stephanie Hollinshead(5) 13/2: 0562347: Chsd ldrs over 12f. *6* **57**
2941 **LADY NETBETSPORTS 8** [5]5-9-1 (62) M Lawson(5) 16/1: 00-03028: Led, hdd 3f out, fdd: btr 2941. *20* **35**
8 Ran Time 3m 7.84(9.84) Owned: SW Transport (Swindon) Ltd & R J Gilbert Trained: Carrutherstown

BATH SUNDAY 11.07.04 Lefthand, Turning Track With Stiff Uphill Finish

Official Going Good (Good/Firm Places)

3141 **2.20 Haven Holidays At Devoncliffs Median Auction Maiden Stakes Fillies 2yo (F)**
£3353 £958 £479 **5f161y rnd** **Good 57** **-50 Slow** Inside

BRIDGE TTHE STARS 0 [11] R F Johnson Houghton 2-8-11 S Carson 50/1: 1: b f Josr Algarhoud - Petra's Star (Rock City) Bhd & short of room over 4f out, prog to lead 1f out, rdn out: debut: Feb foal, cost 800gns: half-sisters plcd at 6/9f: dam unplcd: sire useful performer at around 1m: eff at 5.7f, bred to apprec further: acts on gd grnd & goes well fresh: can rate higher. **76**
SCROOBY BABY 0 [1] J A Osborne 2-8-11 S W Kelly 12/1: 2: b f Mind Games - Lunar Music (Komaite) Slow away, sn mid-div, styd on to lead dist, sn hdd, kept on ins fnl 1f, just held by wnr: debut: March foal, cost 100,000gns: half-brother to Gr 1 7f juv wnr Milk It Mick: dam successful at 5f: sire Gr wnr at sprint dists: eff at 5.7f, 6f+ will suit: acts on gd grnd: encouraging effort, improve & win races. ½ **73**
2188 **GEISHA LADY 38** [6] R M Beckett 2-8-11 Martin Dwyer 16/1: 63: Slow away, prog 2f out, kept on ins fnl 1f: eff at 5.7f, will apprec further: acts on gd grnd: see 2188. ¾ **71**
2795 **NOORAIN 13** [3] M R Channon 2-8-11 S Hitchcott(3) 11/4 JT FAV: 34: Handy, styd on to lead 2f out, hdd dist, no extra: acts on fast & gd grnd: see 2795 (debut). ¾ **69**
2257 **RUBYS DREAM 35** [2]2-8-11 C Catlin 10/1: 423435: Handy, ev ch dist, sn wknd: see 2257 & 1805. 1½ **65**
1987 **DREAMERS LASS 47** [10]2-8-11 S Drowne 50/1: 206: Rcd wide, nvr nrr than mid-div: 7 wk abs. 2½ **58**
MISS PATRICIA 0 [13]2-8-11 N Callan 33/1: 7: b f Mister Baileys - Zoena (Emarati) Slow away, rear when short of room over 4f out, modest late gains: debut: March first foal, dam 5f wnr: sire Gr 1 wnr at 1m. ½ **57**
2783 **SIRCE 14** [12]2-8-11 Dane O'Neill 80/1: 068: Rear when hmpd over 4f out, sn fdd: see 2783. *20* **22**
2281 **GLORIA NIMBUS 33** [9]2-8-11 S Righton 80/1: 0069: Led, hdd 2f out, sn fdd: btr 2281. 1¾ **17**
2733 **KEEP BACCKINHIT 16** [8]2-8-11 R L Moore 13/2: 30: 10th: Hmpd over 4f out & sn eased: op 9/1: worth another ch: btr 2733 (debut). *dist* **0**
2829 **VALUE PLUS 12** [5]2-8-11 D Holland 11/4 JT FAV: 2222B: B.d. bef 4f out: worth another ch: btr 2829. **0**
2395 **MISS CASSIA 29** [7]2-8-11 P Dobbs 4/1: 32S: Cl-up when slipped up bend over 4f out: worth another ch. **0**
12 Ran Time 1m 15.22 (6.12) Owned: Mrs Zara Campbell-Harris Trained: Didcot

3142 **2.50 Be Hopeful Handicap Stakes 3yo+ 0-75 (E)** **[69]**
£4479 £1378 £689 **1m5y rnd** **Good 57** **-01 Slow** Inside

2909 **OVER TO YOU BERT 9** [8] R J Hodges 5-7-12 (3oh) (39) J F McDonald(3) 7/1: 1400031: Handy, styd on to lead cl-home, rdn out: bckd from 20/1: eff around 1m on fast, gd/soft & polytrack: see 2909 & 831. **48**
2665 **ADOBE 18** [7] W M Brisbourne 9-9-8 (66) M Savage(5) 11/2 CO FAV: 2-003442: Mid-div, prog to lead 1f out, hdd cl-home: op 4/1: won this prize 12 mths ago off a 3lb higher mark: see 2665 & 2010. ½ **70**
2931 **SHERIFFS DEPUTY 8** [2] J W Unett 4-9-10 (68) S Hitchcott(3) 14/1: 1042-003: Rear, prog halfway, styd on ins fnl 1f, nvr getting to ldrs: encouraging eff & is back on a fair mark: see 1883. 1¾ **68**
2844 **NAUTICAL 11** [5] A W Carroll 6-8-6 (50) R L Moore 7/1: 0/0-00464: Slow away, prog halfway, onepace. *1* **48**
2665 **MARNIE 18** [1]7-8-7 (51) J Mackay 6/1: 1302255: Chsd ldrs over 6f, sn onepcd: btr 2414 & 2032. *hd* **48**
2665 **BISHOPSTONE MAN 18** [9]7-9-8 (66) Dane O'Neill 11/2 CO FAV: 40-00406: Led, hdd 1f out, sn wknd. *nk* **62**
2866 **ADALAR 10** [3]4-9-2 (60) N Callan 11/2 CO FAV: 0600047: Chsd ldrs over 6f, sn wknd: btr 2866 (10f). ¾ **54**
2853 **ANSWERED PROMISE 11** [11]5-8-10 (54) S Sanders 8/1: 0062338: Cl-up till dist, fdd: btr 2853 & 2600. *5* **38**
2740 **STEPPENWOLF 15** [4]3-7-12 (14oh) (37) C Haddon(7) 100/1: 0000009: Al in rear: see 696. *4* **27**
2540 **MUYASSIR 23** [6]9-9-2 (60) S Drowne 16/1: 0-010000: 10th: Rear, nvr a factor: btr 406. ¾ **34**
2647 **HAVE SOME FUN 19** [10]4-8-11 (55) J Quinn 14/1: 6-3200: 11th: Keen cl-up 6f, fdd: btr 476 (polytrack). 3½ **22**
11 Ran Time 1m 43.01 (4.71) Owned: Mr R J Hodges Trained: Somerton

3143 **3.20 Devoncliffs Buy A Caravan Here! Classified Stakes 3yo+ 0-60 (F)**
£3318 £948 £474 **5f11y rnd** **Good 57** **-04 Slow** Far side

2838 **CORANGLAIS 12** [6] J M Bradley 4-9-3 p (58) R L Moore 15/2: 0000041: Mid-div, prog 2f out, drvn out to lead cl-home: eff at 5/7f on fast & gd/soft grnd: eff with cheek pieces: gd confidence boost: see 2023. **65**
3054 **BOAVISTA 3** [7] P D Evans 4-9-0 (58) N Callan 3/1 FAV: 2100022: Chsd ldrs, styd on to lead after 3f, hdd cl-home: op 4/1 on qck reapp: clr rem: another gd eff here at Bath: see 2034 & 1787. ¾ **59**
2702 **DIAMOND RING 17** [11] Mrs J Candlish 5-9-0 (40) A Daly 33/1: 60-50303: Held up, prog ins fnl 2f, nrst fin: closer with a more positive ride: see 2412 & 1336. *5* **44+**
2784 **ARDKEEL LASS 14** [13] D Haydn Jones 3-8-9 (59) Paul Eddery 12/1: 306-0024: Keen bhd, hdwy halfway, onepace dist: op 8/1: btr 2784 (firm). ½ **43**
2396 **RUN ON 29** [9]6-9-3 (46) S Righton 40/1: 66-00005: Rear, nvr nrr than mid-div: see 1788. ¾ **44**
2975 **INDIAN BAZAAR 6** [10]8-9-3 (53) M Halford(7) 16/1: 0200206: Cl-up, short of room 4f out, no extra. *nk* **43**
2062 **ERRACHT 43** [3]6-9-3 (63) N Chalmers(5) 8/1: 0516007: Cl-up 3f, sn no extra: 6 wk abs. *nk* **42**
2957 **ARFINNIT 7** [2]3-8-12 vis (60) S Hitchcott(3) 6/1: 1661648: Chsd ldrs over 3f, wknd dist: qck reapp. *nk* **41**
2743 **PERFECT SETTING 15** [12]4-9-3 (60) S Sanders 16/1: 4000-609: Mid-div till dist, fdd: btr 2286. *2* **35**
1625 **GIVERAND 64** [5]5-9-0 (42) J F Egan 25/1: 0/0030-00: 10th: Al in rear: 9 wk abs. *4* **21**
2803 **JUWWI 13** [14]10-9-3 (50) C Catlin 16/1: 0626600: 11th: Rear, nvr a factor. ¾ **22**
2951* **FOLEY MILLENNIUM 8** [15]6-9-9 (66) N Pollard 4/1: P-011110: 12th: Led 3f, sn fdd: amiss? *shd* **27**
2661 **BARABELLA 18** [1]3-8-9 (58) S Drowne 20/1: 0-050450: 13th: Cl-up 3f, sn fdd: btr 2661 & 1903. *2* **12**
13 Ran Time 1m 3.36 (3.06) Owned: Mr John Brookman Trained: Chepstow

3144 **3.50 Favourites Racing Classified Stakes 3yo+ 0-60 (F)**
£3626 £1036 £518 **1m2f46y** **Good 57** **+01 Fast** Inside

2032* **DOCTORED 45** [6] P D Evans 3-8-6 bl (60) N Callan 10/1: 4611011: Chsd ldrs, styd on to lead 3f out, hdd 2f out, sn hung right, rallied to lead ins fnl 1f, rdn out: op 16/1: new stable: eff at 7f/1m, now stays 10f: acts on firm, gd/soft & fibresand: likes Bath: see 2032 (B A Pearce). **68**
2875 **EASTBOROUGH 10** [5] B G Powell 5-9-3 (60) M Savage(5) 4/1 JT FAV: 3466232: Mid-div, prog trav well to lead 2f out, hdd dist, under press & just held when short of room dist: op 5/1: see 2354 & 1098. 1½ **65**

2680 **CUDDLES 18** [8] K O Cunningham Brown 5-9-0 (59) Dane O'Neill 7/1: 0-050453: Rear, prog 3f out,   *hd*   **61**
styd on to lead dist, sn hung left & hdd ins fnl 1f, no extra: op 9/1: back on a winning mark: see 876.
2664* **DONASTRELA 18** [4] A M Balding 3-8-3 vis (57) N Chalmers(3) 9/1: 0-60014: Rear, prog 4f out, no   *1½*   **58**
impress dist: clr rem: btr 2664 (firm, C/D, visor).
2947 **ZAWRAK 8** [13]5-9-3 (60) Natalia Gemelova(7) 16/1: 3-630105: Mid-div, prog 4f out, wknd fnl 2f.   *6*   **52**
2706 **MASTER MAHOGANY 17** [1]3-8-10 (64) S Drowne 11/1: 4006546: Led 5f out till hdd 3f out.   *5*   **49**
2866* **BILLY BATHWICK 10** [10]7-9-3 (59) R L Moore 11/2: 3-003317: Handy 1m, sn wknd: btr 2866.   *3*   **41**
2372 **SWEET AZ 30** [11]4-9-0 P (37) S Righton 100/1: 0500-008: Mid-div 6f, sn wknd: cheek pieces.   *1½*   **35**
757 **SO SURE 134** [2]4-9-3 bl (60) D Sweeney 25/1: 5101-469: Handy 7f, sn fdd.   *3*   **34**
4302} **OPTIMAL 298** [12]3-8-5 (62) S Sanders 4/1 JT FAV: 400-0: 10th: grf Green Desert - On Call   *5*   **26**
(Alleged) Mid-div, wknd fnl 2f: bckd on reapp: unplcd in 3 '03 starts (rtd 59, mdn): with Sir M Prescott.
2617 **IVORY COAST 20** [3]3-8-3 (59) Martin Dwyer 8/1: 4-412000: 11th: Keen cl-up 6f, sn fdd.   *5*   **17**
2742 **Zarneeta 15** [7]3-8-3 (55) C Haddon(7) 100/1:0   2842 **Macchiato Gb 11** [14]3-8-3 (54) S Carson 25/1:0
13 Ran   Time 2m 11.43 (5.43)   Owned: Treble Chance Partnership   Trained: Abergavenny

---

3145   4.20 Bathwick Tyres Lady Riders' Handicap Stakes 4yo+ 35-55 (F)   [41]
£3419 £1052 £526   **1m3f144y**   **Good 57**   **-26 Slow**   Inside

2868 **THEATRE LADY 10** [17] P D Evans 6-10-0 (41) Miss E Folkes(3) 16/1: 4356601: Mid-div, prog 4f out,   **49**
styd on to lead dist, sn no extra: eff btwn 7/12f on firm, hvy & polytrack: see 539.
3056 **MILK AND SULTANA 3** [13] G A Ham 4-10-10 (51) Mrs S Owen(5) 20/1: 00-06002: Rear, prog 4f out,   *1½*   **56**
styd on to chase wnr from dist, al held: qck reapp: eff at 7f, now stays 11.6f: acts on gd grnd & fibresand:
slipped down h'cap & this was encouraging: see 2371.
2739 **NEPTUNE 15** [9] J C Fox 8-9-8 (35) Miss Sarah Jane Durman(5) 20/1: 0245353: Bhd, prog ins fnl 2f,   *2*   **37**
nrst fin: acts on gd grnd & both AWs: see 1180.
2988 **LAZZAZ 5** [12] P W Hiatt 6-10-4 (45) Mrs C Thompson(5) 5/1 JT FAV: 2056434: Cl-up, led 1m out, hdd   *1¾*   **44**
2f out, sn no extra: qck reapp: just btr 2988.
1954 **HEATHYARDS PRIDE 48** [14]4-10-9 (50) Miss S Sharratt(5) 10/1: 4-1045: Handy, styd on to lead bef   *¾*   **47**
2f out, sn hdd, no extra dist: 7 wk abs: btr 1954 & 299.
2844 **VANDENBERGHE 11** [11]5-10-7 (48) Miss S Beddoes 9/1: 1534356: Nvr nrr than mid-div: btr 2436.   *shd*   **44**
2891 **CLANN A COUGAR 9** [16]4-10-12 p (53) Miss M Sowerby(5) 25/1: 0060607: Nvr nrr than mid-div: btr 1542.   *nk*   **48**
2988* **BURNT COPPER 5** [7]4-11-0 (5ex) (55) Miss K Manser(5) 7/1: 4250-018: Slow away, modest late gains.   *2*   **47**
1986 **COMPTON AVIATOR 47** [5]8-10-1 t (51) Miss Joanna Rees(3) 12/1: 244-6059: Mid-div 1m, sn no extra.   *3*   **39**
2912 **KARAKUM 9** [3]5-10-1 (42) Miss E J Tuck(7) 33/1: 0000/0-40: 10th: Handy 7f, sn no extra: btr 1912.   *1½*   **27**
2856 **AMBERSONG 11** [10]6-10-0 (41) Mrs S Bosley 5/1 JT FAV: 3064330: 11th: Rear, prog 7f out, fdd fnl 2f.   *hd*   **25**
2311 **DEFERLANT 32** [4]7-10-9 P (50) Miss Joey Ellis(7) 20/1: 311/5//-000: 12th: Rcd keenly, al in rear.   *1¾*   **31**
2653 **PISTE BLEU 19** [6]4-10-11 (52) Miss E J Jones 10/1: 0001640: 13th: Mid-div, prog 4f out, fdd fnl 2f.   *4*   **27**
2651 **REMINISCENT 19** [15]5-11-0 vis (55) Ms C Williams 7/1: 2-424500: 14th: Slow away, nvr a factor.   *10*   **16**
2909 **BENJAMIN 9** [1]6-9-12 t (39) Miss Kelly Harrison(3) 33/1: 6-225000: 15th: Led, hdd 1m out, fdd fnl 3f.   *9*   **0**
86   **WATERLINE SPIRIT 230** [8]4-10-2 (43) Miss A Wallace(5) 50/1: 000/000-0: 16th: Handy 1m, sn fdd.   *7*   **0**
2527 **I SEE NO SHIPS 24** [2]4-9-11 (38) Miss M Mullineaux(7) 50/1: 000-00: 17th: Cl-up 7f, fdd.   *15*   **0**
17 Ran   Time 2m 34.73 (9.73)   Owned: Waterline Racing Club   Trained: Abergavenny

---

3146   4.50 Totesport Com Handicap Stakes 3yo+ 0-85 (D)   [80]
£6864 £2112 £1056   **5f161y rnd**   **Good 57**   **-01 Slow**   Inside

2758 **MINE BEHIND 15** [3] J R Best 4-9-13 (79) M Savage(5) 8/1: 6220001: Handy, styd on to lead 2f out,   **86**
drvn out to hold on: eff at 5/7/6f, does stay 1m: acts on firm, gd/soft & polytrack: tried cheek pieces, best
without: goes well for today's pilot: see 1898 & 1255.
2990 **ROMANY NIGHTS 5** [10] J W Unett 4-9-12 bl (78) S Hitchcott(3) 14/1: 2224602: Rear, prog 2f out, ev   *shd*   **84**
ch ins fnl 1f, just held by wnr: qck reapp: on a fair mark & deserves to find similar: see 2286 & 2187.
2990 **AINTNECESSARILYSO 5** [5] N E Berry 6-8-3 (55) M Halford(7) 8/1: 2361153: Mid-div, prog wide 2f   *1¾*   **56**
out, onepcd ins fnl 1f: qck reapp: just btr 2752.
2779 **HIGH RIDGE 14** [4] J M Bradley 5-9-3 p (69) C Catlin 11/2: 0151234: Held up, prog 2f out, nrst fin.   *1¾*   **65**
2951 **LAUREL DAWN 8** [1]6-8-9 (61) J F McDonald(3) 8/1: 0001555: Rear, prog 3f out, no impress dist.   *nk*   **56**
3045 **GLENCOE SOLAS 3** [6]4-9-6 (72) J F Egan 5/1 FAV: 2215326: Handy over 4f, sn no extra: qck reapp.   *3*   **58**
2806 **ONE WAY TICKET 13** [11]4-9-3 p (69) R L Moore 10/1: 3203107: Cl-up till dist, sn wknd: btr 2626.   *½*   **54**
3033 **SALVIATI 4** [8]7-10-0 P (80) C J Davies(7) 16/1: 0000008: Chsd ldrs 4f, fdd: cheek pieces.   *2*   **59**
3109 **SOMERSET WEST 1** [7]4-9-6 (72) N Pollard 10/1: 01100109: Chsd ldrs, wknd dist: unplcd yesterday.   *½*   **50**
1734* **WYATT EARP 58** [12]3-9-4 (76) S Sanders 11/2: 046-010: 10th: Al in rear: 8 wk abs: btr 1734.   *¾*   **52**
2760 **INDIAN MAIDEN 15** [9]4-9-4 (70) S Carson 20/1: 0600-040: 11th: Led, hdd 2f out, fdd: btr 2760.   *5*   **32**
2669 **BYO 18** [2]6-9-4 (70) S Drowne 20/1: 0106600: 12th: Chsd ldrs over 3f, fdd: btr 2598.   *10*   **6**
12 Ran   Time 1m 12.45 (3.35)   Owned: M Folan R Lees R Crampton   Trained: Maidstone

---

3147   5.20 Buy Here! Improve Your Lifestyle With Devoncliffs Handicap Stakes 4yo+ 35-55 (F)   [63]
£3601 £1108 £554   **2m1f34y**   **Good 57**   **-31 Slow**   Inside

3057* **MOONSHINE BEACH 3** [13] P W Hiatt 6-9-10 (5ex) (59) Dane O'Neill 2/1 FAV: 3654P11: Cl-up, styd on   **65**
to lead 2f out, rdn out to hold on: qck reapp: stays 2m/2m2f on fast, gd & polytrack: remains in gd form.
3049 **CIRCUS MAXIMUS 3** [10] Ian Williams 7-9-1 p (50) S Sanders 20/1: 020-0402: Bhd, prog 7f out, ev ch   *nk*   **54**
ins fnl 1f, just held by wnr: qck reapp: eff at 14/17f on fast & gd grnd: on a fair mark & can find similar: see 1923.
3049 **GALANDORA 3** [5] Dr J R J Naylor 4-9-3 (52) Lucy Russell(7) 10/1: 1012033: Cl-up, no extra dist.   *2½*   **54**
2156 **COOL BATHWICK 39** [4] B R Millman 5-8-9 (44) S W Kelly 20/1: 6000004: Rear, prog 6f out, onepcd.   *nk*   **45**
2417 **PERTEMPS SIA 29** [8]4-8-2 (37) C Haddon(7) 50/1: 06006-05: b c Distinctly North - Shamrock Dancer   *1¾*   **36**
(Dance of Life) Rear, prog halfway, no impress bef 1f out: unplcd in '03 (h'caps, rtd 37): has tried a t-strap.
2293 **TOP TREES 33** [20]6-8-10 (45) N Callan 22/1: 50010-06: Mid-div, prog & ev ch bef 1f out, sn wknd.   *hd*   **43**
2156 **SNINFIA 39** [14]4-9-4 (53) A Daly 20/1: 00-00047: Slow away, prog 5f out, fdd dist: btr 2156.   *2*   **49**
821 **KNIGHT OF SILVER 1198** [18]7-8-10 (45) M Halford(7) 33/1: 3000//0//-8: gr g Presidium - Misty   *1*   **40**
Rocket (Roan Rocket) Nvr nrr than mid-div: jumps fit, earlier claim hdle wnr (rtd 90h), stays 2m5f on firm & gd
grnd): claim hdle wnr in 03/04 for R Williams (rtd 79h): modest Flat form previously.

BATH   SUNDAY 11.07.04   Lefthand, Turning Track With Stiff Uphill Finish

2311	**POLANSKI MILL 32** [7]5-9-6 (55) Paul Eddery 25/1: 0000-P09: Rear, modest late gains.	hd	49
2912	**JACK DURRANCE 9** [16]4-8-7 (42) J F McDonald(3) 25/1: 00-00400: 10th: Nvr nrr than mid-div.	2½	34
2912	**GIKO 9** [11]10-8-3 (38) Lisa Jones(3) 8/1: 0606230: 11th: Cl-up 14f, fdd: btr 2912 & 2293.	9	21
3049	**REAL ESTATE 3** [3]10-8-8 (43) Martin Dwyer 16/1: 0//00/-0000: 12th: Handy over 14f, sn fdd.	2	24
2699	**DONALD 17** [19]4-9-3 (52) S Drowne 13/2: 124-3060: 13th: Chsd ldrs 13f, fdd.	shd	32
2908	**MAKARIM 9** [12]8-8-8 p (43) G Baker 12/1: 0035040: 14th: Handy 13f, sn fdd.	nk	22
2651	**ROYAL TRIGGER 19** [17]4-9-6 BL t (55) C Catlin 12/1: 020-0000: 15th: Cl-up, led 4f out, hdd 2f out, wknd.	nk	33
2577	**ULSHAW 22** [1]7-8-10 (45) D Sweeney 25/1: 2000-000: 16th: Led, hdd 4f out, sn fdd.	½	22
	DEO GRATIAS 284 [6]4-9-0 (49) J F Egan 22/1: 633163-0: 17th: Rear, nvr a factor.	½	25
666	**PORT MORENO 145** [9]4-8-5 vis (40) R Havlin 20/1: 0060-500: 18th: Chsd ldrs, wknd fnl 4f.	1¼	15
2718	**PERIDA 16** [2]4-8-10 (45) S Whitworth 10/1: 0005-500: 19th: Mid-div 12f, sn fdd.	9	12

19 Ran   Time 3m 55.99(15.09)   Owned: Mr Ken Read   Trained: Banbury

AYR   MONDAY 12.07.04   Lefthand, Galloping Track

Official Going Good (Good/Firm Places)

3148   2.15 European Breeders Fund Maiden Stakes 2yo   (D)
£5447 £1676 £838   **6f str**   **Good 46**   +07 Fast   Stands Side

SHAMARDAL 0 [5] M Johnston 2-9-0 J Fanning 11/10 FAV: 1: b c Giant's Causeway - Helsinki (Machiavellian) Made all & qcknd clr over 1f out, val 10L+, most impressive in a fast time: hvly bckd: 50,000gns March foal, half-brother to a 7f 3yo scorer: dam a wnr abroad: eff at 6f, 7f will suit: acts on gd grnd & a gall trk: goes well fresh: useful, well regarded & looks a Gr wnr in the making.   **101+**

2933 **NO COMMISSION 9** [6] R F Fisher 2-9-0 F Norton 50/1: 5405402: Chsd ldrs, rdn & kept on fnl 1f, nvr a threat to easy wnr: more encouraging bhd a msrat sort: see 2829, 1893.   8   77

2774 **TSAROXY 16** [2] J Howard Johnson 2-9-0 R Winston 9/4: 33: Trkd ldrs, eff to chase wnr over 1f out, no impress fnl 1f: nicely bckd: prob handles gd grnd, just btr 2774 (g/s, debut).   1½   72

TARTAN SPECIAL 0 [4] K R Burke 2-9-0 Darren Williams 66/1: 4: b c Fasliyev - Colchica (Machiavellian) Dwelt & held up, kept on late, nvr a threat: April foal, 20,000gns 2yo purchase: speedily bred.   3   63

GEOJIMALI 0 [3]2-9-0 T Eaves(3) 150/1: 5: ch c Compton Place - Harrken Heights (Belmez) Held up, outpcd from halfway: March foal, half-brother to a plcd 7f 4yo, dam plcd at 1m as a 3yo.   3½   52

2666 **CORKER 19** [1]2-9-0 K Darley 20/1: 66: Cl-up, btn 2f out.   6   34

STRETFORD END 0 [7]2-9-0 F Lynch 7/2: F: Keen, chasing ldrs when edged right & hit rail over 4f out, stumbled badly & fell: hvly bckd on debut: emerged unscathed..   0

7 Ran   Time 1m 11.63 (2.33)   Owned: Mr Abdulla BuHaleeba   Trained: Middleham

3149   2.45 Garry Owen Handicap Stakes 3yo+ 0-70 (E)
£3624 £1115 £558   **1m2f192y**   **Good 46**   -32 Slow   Inside   [69]

2673 **PARTY PLOY 19** [5] K R Burke 6-9-8 (63) Darren Williams 7/4 FAV: 0021101: Dictated pace, rdn & pressed over 2f out, styd on strongly ins last, drvn out: nicely bckd: eff at 11/14f on firm, soft & both AWs: likes to race with/force the pace: see 2465 & 2176.   71

2900 **SPREE VISION 10** [3] P Monteith 8-8-9 vis (50) L Enstone(2) 10/1: 360/-6042: Handy & rdn to chall over 2f out, not pace of wnr fnl 1f: acts on gd & hvy grnd, handles fast: likes Ayr & Hamilton.   1   55

2751 **TEMPLET 9** [2] I Semple 4-9-10 BL (66) J Carroll 10/1: 4-23453: Chsd ldrs, rdn 2f out, kept on fnl 1f: imprvd eff in first time blnks, wore visor latest: mdn: see 1390 & 1038.   hd   68

2850 **BORDER TERRIER 12** [6] M D Hammond 6-7-12 (2oh)bl (37) R Ffrench 8/1: 0-000304: Trkd ldrs, not pace to chall fnl 2f: see 1796.   1¾   41

2571* **STING LIKE A BEE 23** [1]5-9-0 (55) N Mackay(3) 4/1: 2446615: Keen early, held up in tch, no impress fnl 2f: btr 2571 (9f).   2½   53

2811 **SHERWOOD FOREST 14** [4]4-8-3 vis (44) Leanne Kershaw(7) 7/1: 0500-036: Trkd ldrs wide, keen early, btn over 1f out: flattered 2811.   1¾   40

2813 **LUCKY LARGO 14** [7]4-9-2 bl (57) P Mulrennan(5) 11/1: 0040267: Rear, in tch, no impress fnl 2f.   1¾   51

7 Ran   Time 2m 24.59 (8.59)   Owned: Mr Ian A McInnes   Trained: Leyburn

3150   3.15 Toteexacta Stakes Handicap 3yo+ 0-95 (C)
£10927 £4145 £2072   **5f str**   **Good 46**   -02 Slow   Stands Side   [92]

3073 **PTARMIGAN RIDGE 3** [7] Miss L A Perratt 8-9-5 (83) M Fenton 12/1: 0100651: Rear, no room & switched 2f out, hdwy to lead ins last, rdn out: eff at 5f on fast, likes gd & hvy grnd, any trk: see 1594.   90

2727 **PROUD BOAST 17** [5] D Nicholls 6-9-11 (89) K Darley 16/1: 0-010002: Pushed along in tch, poised to chall when no room over 2f out till well ins last, no time to reach wnr: lkd unlucky, keepin mind.   1   92+

2950 **FOURSQUARE 9** [2] J Mackie 3-9-5 (88) Dale Gibson 12/1: 2-150403: Handy, eff 1f out, onepace.   shd   91

2747 **MAKTAVISH 16** [9] I Semple 5-9-3 p (81) T Eaves(3) 7/1: 2130004: Led/dsptd lead till over 1f out, no extra: op 10/1: see 1594, 1217.   nk   83

2830* **AAHGOWANGOWAN 13** [3]5-7-13 t (63) R Ffrench 5/1: 0-005215: Led/dsptd lead till ins last, no extra.   hd   64

2894 **MALAPROPISM 10** [6]4-9-4 (82) C Catlin 9/1: 01-60006: Pushed along, kept on onepace, no threat.   shd   83

3073 **OBE ONE 3** [10]4-8-4 (68) F Norton 9/2 JT FAV: 4023067: Trkd ldrs, poised to chall trav well from halfway, no room at any stage & must surely have gone close in a messy race.   ½   67

2968 **VIEWFORTH 7** [8]6-8-3 bl (67) N Mackay(3) 9/2 JT FAV: 0000438: Trkd ldrs, no room repeatedly fnl 2f, much closer with a clr run: well bckd tho' op 7/2: see 2968 & 2951.   ½   64+

2561 **SEAFIELD TOWERS 23** [4]4-8-9 p (73) J Fanning 18/1: 0030009: Chsd ldrs, onepace when hmpd dist.   6   54

2524 **MUSICAL FAIR 25** [1]4-8-13 VIS (77) R Winston 12/1: 0021560: 10th: Rcd towards centre & hung left throughout, struggling fnl 2f: not enjoy visor?   9   33

10 Ran   Time 59.01 (2.41)   Owned: The Hon Miss Heather Galbraith   Trained: Ayr

---

3151   3.45 Kidzplay Claiming Stakes 3yo+   (E)
   £3507 £1079 £540   1m2f   **Good 46**   **-04 Slow**   Inside

2827 **GOLD CARD 13** [4] J R Weymes 3-8-9 vis (60) R Winston 8/1: 4-225521: Chsd ldrs, rdn & led over 1f out, drvn out: clmd by J Best for 10,000: eff at 1m, suited by 10/12f on fast & gd/soft grnd, now suited by visor: apprec drop to claim grade, first career win: see 2827, 1604 & 983.		62
2967 **FOREST AIR 7** [2] Miss L A Perratt 4-8-10 P (46) R Ffrench 25/1: 0-010052: Held up, styd on for press, not pace to reach wnr: imprvd eff in first time cheek pieces: eff at 1m/10f: see 1446 (seller).	½	50$
2726 **KIDZPLAY 17** [6] J S Goldie 8-9-8 (69) T Eaves(3) 5/2: 0342153: Led/dsptd lead till over 2f out, onepace.	1	61
2837 **CHARLIE TANGO 13** [8] M R Channon 3-8-9 (68) C Catlin 9/4 FAV: 0304134: Rear, smooth prog wide over 2f out, rdn & found less than lkd likely dist: clmd for 10,000: stays 10f, apprec drop to 1m/9f.	nk	58
1552 **MINSTREL HALL 69** [3]5-9-6 (50) L Enstone(3) 50/1: 60310/-45: Cl-up/dsptd lead till went on over 2f out till over 1f out, no extra ins last: 10 wk abs: see 1552.	1	57
2811+ **BAILIEBOROUGH 14** [5]5-9-11 vis (70) Alex Greaves 3/1: 4013016: Held up in tch, wknd 2f out.	¾	61
2686 **TOMASINO 18** [7]6-9-11 T (76) K Darley 16/1: 00/66-467: Handy when short of room & lost place 2f out.	3	57
2811 **AMBUSHED 14** [1]8-9-4 (52) P Mulrennan(5) 25/1: 2030-648: Chsd ldrs, btn 2f out: see 2544.	1¾	48
8 Ran Time 2m 09.36 (4.96) Owned: Mrs R L Heaton Trained: Middleham		

3152   4.15 Dawn Group Classified Stakes 3yo+ 0-80   (D)
   £5377 £1654 £827   1m rnd   **Good 46**   **-18 Slow**   Inside

2684 **TONY TIE 18** [5] J S Goldie 8-9-6 (83) N Mackay(3) 5/2: 2502161: Trkd ldrs, led over 1f out, drvn & held on all out: eff at 7f/10f, 1m/9f ideal: acts on firm & hvy, loves gall trks: most tough, see 2543.		86
3083 **STOIC LEADER 3** [6] R F Fisher 4-9-6 (83) R Winston 12/1: 0242652: Chsd ldrs, short of room over 2f out, switched & styd on well ins last, just failed: op 9/1: qck reapp: most tough & genuine, win again.	shd	85
2877* **ANOTHER BOTTLE 11** [1] T P Tate 3-8-11 (83) Dale Gibson 1/1 FAV: 033-0113: Keen & chsd ldrs, rdn & outpcd over 1f out, kept on ins last: worth a try over further now: btr 2877.	2	81
2313* **BRIEF GOODBYE 33** [3] John Berry 4-9-4 (81) M Fenton 9/2: 63-14014: Led, hdd over 1f out, fdd.	3½	72
2832 **ANTHEMION 13** [4]7-9-3 (50) R Ffrench 150/1: 0200005: Cl-up, btn over 1f out: btr 1504.	nk	70
3098 **TELEPATHIC 2** [2]4-9-3 (57) P Bradley 100/1: 0046056: Al rear & no ch fnl 3f: qck reapp: see 1218.	8	57
6 Ran Time 1m 41.71 (5.11) Owned: Mr Frank Brady Trained: Glasgow		

3153   4.45 Scottish Racing Handicap Stakes 3yo 0-70   (E)
   £3643 £1121 £561   7f50y rnd   **Good 46**   **Inapplicable**   Inside

[72]

2683 **MUSIOTAL 18** [6] J S Goldie 3-8-8 (52) N Mackay(3) 11/2: 0-055021: Held up in tch, rdn over 1f out, styd on well for press to lead cl-home: eff at 5/6f, imprvd for return to 7f & may get further: acts on gd & soft grnd, stiff/gall trks: first win today, shld serve as a confidence boost: see 2683.		58
2849 **HALF A HANDFUL 12** [2] M J Wallace 3-9-7 (65) K Darley 11/4 JT FAV: 0006332: Chsd ldrs, rdn & hung left over 2f out, hdwy & led over 1f out, hdd cl-home: nicely bckd: styd longer 7f trip well: running well.	½	69
2936* **MENAI STRAIGHTS 9** [1] R F Fisher 3-9-6 (64) P Mulrennan(5) 4/1: 6063513: Trkd ldrs, switched & onepace over 1f out: bckd: see 2936.	¾	67
2295 **HANA DEE 34** [7] M R Channon 3-9-1 (59) C Catlin 14/1: 0-006004: Held up in tch, outpcd over 2f out, late prog, nrst fin: worth another try at 1m on this evidence: handles fast & gd grnd: see 1761.	1¾	59
3016* **WILLJOJO 5** [3]3-9-1 (6ex)vis (59) T Hamilton(3) 11/4 JT FAV: 3-354115: Handy & led 2f out till over 1f out, no extra, fin lame: qck reapp under a pen, nicely bckd: see 3016.	nk	58
2969 **COMPASSION 7** [5]3-8-3 p (47) R Ffrench 8/1: 0044536: Led till over 2f out, sn btn: op 11/1: btr 2969.	1½	43
2961 **GEMINI GIRL 8** [4]3-8-2 (46) P M Quinn 33/1: 66-00007: Held up, eff over 2f out, no impress: see 2614.	6	32
7 Ran Time 1m 34.21(No Std Time) Owned: Mr Frank Brady Trained: Glasgow		

Official Going STANDARD.

3154   6.10 St John Gualbert's Day Classified Claiming Stakes 3yo+ 0-60   (F)
   £2940 £840 £420   1m4f aw   **Going 38**   **-16 Slow**   Inside

2804 **CROCOLAT 14** [6] N A Callaghan 3-8-12 (57) N Callan 8/15 FAV: 005241: Handy, led trav well 3f out, sn clr, eased cl-home, val 8L+: acts at odds-on, clmd for 10,000: eff arnd 12f on fast grnd & fibresand: made gd use of drop in grade & can follow up: see 2804 & 2642.		64a+
985 **THINK QUICK 104** [9] R Hollinshead 4-9-4 (20) H Fellows(7) 100/1: 4030062: Handy, slightly outpcd 4f out, rallied ins fnl 1f, al held by v easy wnr: clr rem, long abs: see 689.	2½	47a
2726 **TINIAN 17** [10] K R Burke 6-9-9 (45) G Faulkner 17/2: 5432403: Mid-div, btn 2f out: op 7/1.	15	30a
2552 **BANNERS FLYING 24** [2] D W Chapman 4-9-10 (55) A Culhane 20/1: 45-00404: Led 1f, in tch, fdd 3f out.	hd	30a
2340 **KENTUCKY BULLET 32** [5]8-9-9 (42) L Keniry(3) 13/2: 3063605: Rear, prog to chase wnr 4f out, sn wknd.	¾	27a
INVOGUE 56 [4]4-9-6 (40) G Parkin 28/1: 00-006: b f Bin Ajwaad - Wenda (Priolo) Led early, led again 5f out till 3f out, fdd: 8 wk abs & Brit bow: ex-Irish, modest form to date.	3	20a
1197 **SPANISH STAR 88** [8]7-9-9 (47) Sarah Sayer(7) 20/1: 6133007: Slow away, al in rear: long abs.	3	19a
3096 **WESTERN COMMAND 3** [3]8-9-10 p (35) Joanna Badger 22/1: 5052608: Led after 2f, hdd 5f out, sn fdd.	12	4a
526] **COSMIC RANGER 891** [7]6-9-7 bl t (32) R Keogh(5) 100/1: 005/00/-9: b g Magic Ring - Lismore (Relkino) Al in rear: jumps fit (earlier rtd 68h, sell hdle, t-strap & blnks): rnr-up once in 03/04 (rtd 60h, sell h'cap hdle, stays 2m1.5f on gd): unplcd in 4 '03 Flat starts (rtd 66, mdn, T P McGovern): has been gelded.	10	0a
2623 **FREDS FIRST 21** [1]3-8-10 (35) S Sanders 66/1: 0-500: 10th: Cl-up 5f, sn wknd: btr 2052.	2	0a
DANTES BATTLE 739 [11]12-9-8 (60) Dean McKeown 16/1: 3/31/0/5/-0: 11th: b g Phardante - Via Battle (Khalkis) Slow away, al in rear: jumps fit, earlier won clmg hdle (rtd 103h, stays 2m5f on firm & gd grnd): won 3 times in 03/04 (rtd 101h, sells & sell h'cap): ex-Irish, mdn Flat wnr in '00 (14f, gd): with Miss K Marks.	14	0a

11 Ran   Time 2m 40.78 (6.48)   Owned: Lord Clinton   Trained: Newmarket

3155   6.40 Doctor In The House Handicap Stakes 3yo+ 0-70 (E)   [70]
£3387 £1042 £521   **7f aw rnd**   **Going 38**   + 06 Fast   Inside

2805* **DOWNLAND** 14 [4] N Tinkler 8-9-5 (61) Kim Tinkler 9/2: 0216511: Held up, prog halfway, styd on **75a**
despite hanging left to lead ins fnl 1f, rdn clr: fair time: eff at 6f/1m on firm, likes fibresand & hvy grnd: in
gd form at present & is h'capped to land hat-trick: see 2466.
3103* **MERDIFF** 2 [11] W M Brisbourne 5-9-6 (62) S W Kelly 5/2 FAV: 1-000212: Handy, led after 3f, hdd   3½   **66a**
ins fnl 1f, no extra: qck reapp: lost little in defeat on return to AW: see 3102.
3092 **TSARBUCK** 3 [5] R M H Cowell 3-8-8 (58) G Faulkner 5/1: 0152523: Cl-up, no extra dist: qck reapp.   2   **58a**
2999 **TEEHEE** 6 [9] B Palling 6-9-4 bl (60) S Sanders 13/2: 4600234: Prom over 5f, no extra: qck reapp.   hd   **59a**
2502 **ROMAN EMPIRE** 25 [12]4-9-2 bl (58) N Callan 6/1: 0-041335: Dwelt, prog wide ins fnl 2f, nrst fin.   2½   **52a**
2704 **EMPEROR CAT** 18 [7]3-7-12 (48) S Yourston(5) 80/1: 2300006: Rear, prog 4f out, fdd fnl 2f: btr 851.   2½   **37a**
2702 **ST IVIAN** 18 [1]4-9-10 p (66) R Fitzpatrick 33/1: 2000007: Nvr nrr than mid-div.   1½   **53a**
2335 **SANDORRA** 32 [13]6-8-5 (47) Dean McKeown 25/1: 6001608: Cl-up till halfway, sn wknd: btr 1590.   1   **32a**
2630 **SUPER CANYON** 21 [3]6-9-9 t (65) A Culhane 25/1: 2-420009: Slow away, al in rear: btr 1010.   nk   **49a**
2502 **CARIBE** 25 [10]5-8-8 (50) P Mathers(7) 100/1: 46-60000: 10th: Cl-up early, sn wknd: btr 1909.   nk   **33a**
2615 **ALWAYS DARING** 21 [8]5-7-12 (5oh) (35) Natalia Gemelova(7) 100/1: 0000/0-00: 11th: Led 1f, fdd 3f out.   11   **3a**
2715 **Arogant Prince** 17 [6]7-9-1 bl(57) D Holland 18/1:0
2891 **Moonlight Song** 10 [2]7-7-12 (10oh) (30) D Fentiman(7) 100/1:0
13 Ran   Time 1m 28.85 (2.25)   Owned: Mr A Graham   Trained: Malton

3156   7.10 Rain Of Frogs Selling Stakes 3-4yo (G)
£2534 £724 £362   **5f aw str**   **Going 38**   -01 Slow   Outside

2803* **QUEEN OF NIGHT** 14 [4] D W Chapman 4-9-5 (55) A Culhane 7/4 FAV: 404R011: Cl-up, drvn out to lead **58a**
cl-home: suited by 5/6f, has tried 7f: acts on firm, gd/soft & likes fibresand: enjoys sell grade: see 2803.
2778+ **INNCLASSIC** 15 [1] B J Meehan 3-9-0 bl (65) L Keniry(3) 2/1: 03-00312: Led, edged right under press   hd   **56a**
ins fnl 1f, hdd cl-home: clr rem, clmd for 6,000: continues in gd form: see 2778 (clmr).
2968 **FINGER OF FATE** 7 [6] M J Polglase 4-9-5 (38) L Fletcher(3) 10/1: 2646003: Rear, prog when short   5   **41a**
of room after 2f, switched & styd on, no ch with front 2: qck reapp: btr 1408.
2657 **BOND SHAKIRA** 20 [9] B Smart 3-8-9 (52) D McGaffin 9/1: 5-304004: Slow away, prog 3f out, fdd dist.   3   **27a**
2803 **BRAVE CHIEF** 14 [2]3-9-0 (46) R Havlin 33/1: 2-005605: Handy 3f, sn wknd: btr 256.   nk   **31a**
2806 **HAZE BABYBEAR** 14 [7]4-9-0 BL (52) G Parkin 9/1: 3310-006: Slow away, nvr nrr than mid-div: blnks.   2½   **19a**
2808 **LAVISH TIMES** 14 [10]3-9-0 P (45) P Mathers(7) 22/1: 6360657: Handy till halfway, wknd: cheek pieces.   7   **6a**
MISTBLACK [3]4-9-0   Dean McKeown 66/1: 8: Slow away, nvr a factor: debut.   1½   **0a**
2219 **SHANGHAI SURPRISE** 38 [8]3-9-0 bl (40) S Sanders 22/1: 00-50009: Handy 3f, fdd: see 1440.   4   **0a**
2480 **MISS NOTERIETY** 26 [5]4-9-0 BL t (23) Natalia Gemelova(7) 100/1: 000/0-000: 10th: Slow away, al bhd.   3½   **0a**
10 Ran   Time 59.26 (1.96)   Owned: Mr Michael Hill   Trained: York

3157   7.40 Julius Caesar Maiden Auction Stakes 2yo (E)
£3416 £1051 £526   **6f aw rnd**   **Going 38**   -21 Slow   Inside

COMIC STRIP [2] Sir Mark Prescott 2-8-13 S Sanders 11/4: 1: b g Marju - Comic (Be My Chief)   **89a+**
Slow away, styd on to lead 1f out, rdn clr: May foal, cost 26,000gns: dam a mid-dist wnr, sire a
decent 1m/12f performer: eff at 6f, will apprec 7f+: acts on fibresand & a sharp trk: goes well fresh:
authoritative success & looks sure to rate higher.
2970 **DANES CASTLE** 7 [3] B J Meehan 2-8-9 L Keniry(3) 5/2 FAV: 32: Cl-up, styd on to lead dist, sn   4   **73a**
hdd, no extra fnl 1f: qck reapp: AW bow: acts on firm grnd & fibresand: another encouraging effort: see 2970.
2492 **SISTER GEE** 26 [1] R Hollinshead 2-8-2 J Bramhill 25/1: 43: b f Desert Story - My Gloria (Saint   2½   **59a**
Estephe) Led, hdd dist, sn wknd: April foal, cost £5,000: dam unrcd: sire decent performer around 10f.
2336 **CAITLIN** 32 [9] B Smart 2-8-7 (1ow) D McGaffin 10/1: 624: Bhd, prog ins fnl 2f, nrst fin: see 2336.   ½   **63a**
3020 **TRACKATTACK** 5 [8]2-8-9 S W Kelly 4/1: 35: Cl-up 4f, no extra: op 3/1, qck reapp, AW bow.   ½   **64a**
1795 **NAMKING** 56 [6]2-8-7 Dean McKeown 33/1: 006: Cl-up till halfway, sn wknd: 8 wk abs, gelded.   5   **48a**
2802 **ELLIS CAVE** 14 [10]2-8-11 K Dalgleish 16/1: 0047: Al in rear: btr 2802.   shd   **51a**
2629 **BLAKESHALL HOPE** 21 [4]2-8-9 (2ow) A Culhane 11/1: 38: Handy till halfway, fdd: btr 2629 (fast).   1   **46a**
2531 **WILFORD MAVERICK** 24 [7]2-8-7 N Callan 15/2: 09: b c Fasliyev - Lioness (Lion Cavern) Chsd   1½   **40a**
ldrs, fdd fnl 2f: Apr first foal, cost £4,000: dam 9f wnr: sire high class juv performer: with M J Attwater.
9 Ran   Time 1m 16.88 (3.58)   Owned: Neil Greig - Osborne House   Trained: Newmarket

3158   8.10 Holding Back The Years Handicap Stakes 4yo+ 35-55 (F)   [63]
£2933 £838 £419   **1m6f aw**   **Going 38**   -06 Slow   Inside

3096* **MAGIC RED** 3 [2] M J Ryan 4-8-12 (7ex) (47) R Price 4/1: 00000-11: Made all, pushed clr ins fnl **61a+**
2f, eased cl-home, val 8L+: qck reapp & 7lb pen: imprvd for step up to 14f, further shld suit: acts on fibresand &
fast grnd, likes Southwell: unexposed at staying dists & can win again: see 3096.
2964 **IPLEDGEALLEGIANCE** 7 [11] D W Chapman 8-8-0 (5oh)bl (30) D Fentiman(7) 13/2: 0552032: Rear, prog   6   **37a**
to chase wnr 4f out, kept on fnl 2f, al hw: qck reapp: btr 2964 & 2562.
3096 **OUR IMPERIAL BAY** 3 [1] Mrs J Candlish 5-9-6 p (55) N Callan 11/1: 1030363: Handy over 10f, no extra.   8   **49a**
2964* **PADDY MUL** 7 [5] W Storey 7-9-0 (7ex)t (49) J Bramhill 11/2: 3453314: Bhd, prog 5f out, onepcd fnl 2f.   1   **42a**
2494 **BROUGHTON MELODY** 26 [8]5-8-5 (40) Dean McKeown 9/1: 0//6-30445: Nvr nrr than mid-div: btr 2494.   1   **32a**
2964 **NEXT FLIGHT** 7 [9]5-9-1 (50) R Fitzpatrick 3/1 FAV: 1432346: Rear, mod late gains: nicely bckd,   5   **37a**
reportedly nvr trav: btr 2685 & 2494.
2781 **DORA CORBINO** 15 [6]4-8-5 (40) Stephanie Hollinshead(5) 16/1: 3242347: Cl-up over 10f, sn wknd.   3½   **24a**
2963 **SIMPLE IDEALS** 8 [3]10-8-0 (8oh) (27) Kim Tinkler 9/1: 0040-548: Cl-up, fdd 3f out: see 90.   9   **11a**
2008 **KARYON** 47 [7]4-8-3 (38) A Nicholls 16/1: 60003-59: Handy, sn wknd: 7 wk abs: btr 2008.   10   **5a**
2787} **EASTWELL VIOLET** 368 [10]4-8-9 (44) S Sanders 16/1: 04406-0: 10th: b f Danzig Connection -   dist   **0a**
Kinchenjunga (Darshaan) Keen rear, fdd after 1m: reportedly nvr trav: unplcd sole 03/04 hdles start (rtd 22h, juv

mdn hdle): unplcd on Flat in '03 (rtd 56a, mdn, S Dow).
10 Ran   Time 3m 6.06 (6.26)   Owned: Mr M J Ryan   Trained: Newmarket

3159   8.40 Josiah Wedgewood Handicap Stakes 3yo+ 35-55 (F)   **[65]**
£3017 £862 £431   **1m aw rnd   Going 38   -15 Slow   Inside**

845   **MASAFI 120** [13] Sir Mark Prescott 3-9-2 (53) S Sanders 11/8 FAV: 000-21: Cl-up, styd on to lead   **67a+**
dist, sn pushed clr, val 6L+: apprec recent step up to 1m, shld get further: acts on both AWs & goes well fresh:
open to more improvement for shrewd yard & is worth following: see 845.
2998   **MEXICAN 6** [6] M D Hammond 5-8-9 vis (37) K Dalgleish 16/1: 00-00352: Led after 1f, hdd dist, no   4   40a
extra: qck reapp: eff at 1m, best prev efforts around 11/11.5f: acts on firm, gd grnd & fibresand: see 1841.
3000   **ACE MA VAHRA 6** [15] S R Bowring 6-9-3 (45) J Bramhill 20/1: 5030633: Rear, prog 3f out, onepcd fnl 1f. ¾   46a
2384   **ROCKY REPPIN 31** [8] J Balding 4-9-4 (46) K Pierrepont(7) 20/1: 0-000034: Handy till halfway, sn   2   43a
outpcd, rallied late: see 2384.
2805   **KENNY THE TRUTH 14** [9]5-9-6 t (48) A Daly 14/1: 4330P65: Bhd, prog ins fnl 2f, nrst fin: see 850.   1   43a
2996   **LATE ARRIVAL 6** [3]7-8-9 (1ow)bl (36) A Culhane 11/1: 5-000026: Slow away, nvr nrr than mid-div.   hd   31a
2805   **DONEGAL SHORE 2** [10]5-9-4 vis t (46) N Callan 16/1: 2243067: Cl-up over 6f, sn wknd: qck reapp.   2   36a
2996*   **BULAWAYO 6** [7]7-9-2 (bl) (54) B Swarbrick(5) 3/1: 1064218: Prom 2f, no extra fnl half-mile: 3   38a
qck reapp: btr expected after recent win in 2996.
2337   **AIR OF ESTEEM 32** [5]8-8-13 P (41) A Nicholls 14/1: 5602459: Al in rear: cheek pieces: btr 1200.   1½   22a
2725*   **SUPER DOMINION 17** [4]7-9-5 p (47) Stephanie Hollinshead(5) 14/1: 0-514010: 10th: Handy 5f, wknd.   hd   27a
2106   **KNIGHT OF HEARTS 42** [2]3-8-8 (45) Dean McKeown 66/1: 5500: 11th: Al in rear: 6 wk abs.   ¾   23a
2725   **HAUNT THE ZOO 13** [1]9-9-13 (55) L Fletcher(3) 20/1: 13-50300: 12th: Handy 5f, wknd: btr 2500.   2   29a
2440   **ASH LADDIE 28** [16]4-9-7 p (49) D Allan 66/1: 050-0000: 13th: In tch 6f, sn wknd: btr 1518.   nk   22a
2848   **SKYLARK 12** [11]7-9-10 (52) Kim Tinkler 33/1: 6204-000: 14th: Bhd, nvr a factor.   7   11a
3766]   **MAGIC BOX 1044** [14]6-9-6 p (48) G Faulkner 50/1: 000030//-0: 15th: b g Magic Ring - Princess   1   5a
Poquito (Hard Fought) Slow away, al in rear: recent jumps unplcd (sell hdle, rtd 55h): rnr-up in 03/04 (rtd 76h,
sell h'cap, stays stiff 2m on fast or gd): plcd once on Flat in '01 (clmr, A P Jarvis, rtd 73 at best, tried visor):
eff at 1m on fast grnd: with Miss Kate Milligan.
267   **ICECAP 195** [12]4-9-9 (51) P Makin(5) 20/1: 665002-0: 16th: Led 1f, fdd halfway: long abs.   19   0a
16 Ran   Time 1m 43.68(4.28)   Owned: Mr G D Waters   Trained: Newmarket

Official Going Good/Soft (Good places)

3160   6.30 C I Traders Ltd E B F Median Auction Maiden Stakes 2yo (E)
£3465 £1066 £533   **5f10y str   Good   Slow   Inside**

    SUNDANCE [6] H J Collingridge 2-9-0 J Quinn 14/1: 1: ch c Namid - Titchwell Lass (Lead On   96+
Time) With ldr, led over 2f out, pushed clr dist, eased & impress: Apr foal, cost £17,500: half-brother to a 5f
juv wnr: dam 10f scorer: v eff at 5f on gd grnd, 6f sure to suit: runs well fresh: v useful start, win btr races.
    DANCING ROSE [1] C G Cox 2-8-9 P Robinson 7/1: 2: b f Danehill Dancer - Shinkoh Rose (Warning)   4   76
In tch, eff to chall 2f out, not pace of wnr fnl 1f on debut: April foal, cost 32,000gns: half-sister to a 6/7f
juv scorer: eff at 5f on gd grnd: gd start, shld find similar.
    GREAT BELIEF [7] T D McCarthy 2-9-0 J P Guillambert(3) 20/1: 3: b c Namid - Fairy Lore (Fairy   2   75+
King) Slow away & bhd, hdwy late, nrst fin on debut: April foal, cost 12,000gns: dam 1m wnr: lost all ch at start
& v encouraging, learn plenty from this, relish 6f & looks sure to be winning soon.
    NINJA STORM [9] G L Moore 2-9-0 R L Moore 11/4 FAV: 4: b c Namid - Swan Lake (Waajib) Keen,   1   72
dwelt, sn in tch, onepace fnl 2f: well bckd on debut: March first foal, cost £15,000: dam plcd over 5f.
2573   **AGILETE 23** [5]2-9-0 S Drowne 4/1: 0335: In tch, no impress fnl 2f: see 2573.   shd   72
1071   **IL PRANZO 97** [8]2-9-0 J F Egan 20/1: 06: In tch, wknd well over 1f out: 3 mth abs.   shd   71
2926   **LUCKY EMERALD 9** [11]2-8-9 T Quinn 3/1: 27: In tch, wknd 2f out: bckd, see 2926.   1¼   62
2658   **RUBY MUJA 19** [2]2-8-9 Dane O'Neill 12/1: 08: Led till over 2f out, wknd: see 2926.   hd   61
    CHAMPAGNE ROSSINI [4]2-9-0 T P Queally 20/1: 9: Dwelt, al bhd on debut.   5   51
    A QUI LE TOUR [3]2-9-0 S Whitworth 66/1: 0: 10th: Sn rdn & al bhd.   4   39
    LITTLE INDY [10]2-9-0 D Nolan(3) 20/1: 0: 11th: Dwelt, al bhd on debut.   1   36
11 Ran   Time 1m 01.27 (2.27)   Owned: Mr Richard Farquhar   Trained: Newmarket

3161   7.00 Bdo Stoy Hayward Handicap Stakes 3yo 0-85 (D)   **[92]**
£5688 £1750 £875   **1m3f135y   Good   Fair   Inside**

2519   **SETTLEMENT CRAIC 25** [4] T G Mills 3-9-7 (85) J Fortune 4/1: 2-14301: Held up, hdwy over 2f out,   92
styd on to lead just ins last, drvn out: suited by 12f & acts on fast, gd/soft & polytrack, any trk, likes a sharp
one: genuine & useful: see 2519, 873.
2788*   **BIENVENUE 15** [2] M P Tregoning 3-8-5 (69) Martin Dwyer 7/1: 235-412: Handy, hdwy to lead 2f out   ½   76
till ins last, kept on, just held: imprvd again stepped up to h'cap class & going the right way: see 2788.
2519   **GIRONDE 25** [7] Sir Michael Stoute 3-9-7 (85) K Fallon 2/1 FAV: 5-4303: Dwelt, in tch, eff dist,   ¾   91
kept on ins last, not pace of front 2: well bckd: imprvd in this lesser h'cap & stays 12f on gd: win a race.
2804   **FLEETFOOT MAC 14** [8] P D Evans 3-8-1 (65) F P Ferris(3) 12/1: 6-110034: Led till 2f out, onepace.   1¾   68
2418   **ABSOLUTELYTHEBEST 29** [6]3-9-2 (80) E Ahern 16/1: 4-122645: Held up, eff 2f out, sn onepace.   1¼   81
2706   **PETITE COLLEEN 18** [9]3-7-12 P (62) D Kinsella 50/1: 235-0406: Handy, eff & switched left over 2f   nk   63
out, wkng when short of room over 1f out: tried cheek pieces, see 2452 (10f).
2631   **INCURSION 21** [1]3-9-6 (84) R Hughes 7/1: 063-1037: Handy, wknd well over 1f out: not stay 12f?   nk   84
2631   **NANTUCKET SOUND 21** [10]3-8-6 (70) R L Moore 12/1: 34-04108: Dwelt, in tch, outpcd bef halfway,   6   61
no impress: now twice well below form of 2036 (10f).
2780   **SPECTESTED 15** [12]3-7-12 (16oh)p (46) M Halford(6) 66/1: 50-00259: In tch, wknd 2f out: see 2780.   ½   52
2804*   **ITS BLUE CHIP 14** [5]3-8-2 (1ow)e (65) Paul Eddery 16/1: 0146410: 10th: Dwelt, al bhd: btr 2804 (AW).   4   50
1815   **STARMIX 55** [3]3-8-5 (69) T Quinn 14/1: 0040: 11th: Bhd, btn 2f out: h'cap bow, see 1815 (1m).   8   41

2984 **MAN AT ARMS 7** [11]3-9-0 (78) J Quinn 20/1: 03-41400: 12th: Al bhd: see 2984 (visor), btr 2333. *1½* **48**
12 Ran Time 2m 29.32 (2.03) Owned: Buxted Partnership Trained: Epsom

3162 **7.30 Barclays Capital Handicap Stakes Fillies 3yo+ 0-85 (D)** **[75]**
£5509 £1695 £848 **1m67y rnd** **Good** **Fair** Inside

3088 **TUSCARORA 3** [1] A W Carroll 5-8-5 (52) T P Queally 7/2 JT FAV: 6-005261: Held up, hdwy 2f out, rdn to lead over 1f out, just held on for press: eff at 6f, suited by 1m now on firm, gd & polytrack, sharp or gall trks: right back to best: see 1465. **61**
2249 **RED SAHARA 37** [8] W J Haggas 3-9-7 (77) P Robinson 9/2: 01-1662: Held up, hdwy over 2f out, strong chall ins last, just held: nicely bckd: well clr of rem & stays 1m: shld find another h'cap: see 1761. *hd* **83**
2620 **GRANDALEA 21** [4] Sir Michael Stoute 3-9-5 (75) K Fallon 4/1: 0236-53: Set gd pace till over 1f out, no extra: not disgraced, see 2620. *4* **75**
2854 **NAUGHTY GIRL 12** [6] P D Evans 4-8-3 vis t (50) F P Ferris(3) 16/1: 0000054: In tch, no impress fnl 1.5f. *¾* **48**
2881 **TRANSCENDANTALE 11** [2]6-7-12 (3oh) (42) M Halford(4) 12/1: 6004045: Al bhd: see 1307, 1135. *3* **37**
2249 **DRY WIT 37** [7]3-8-6 (62) J Quinn 16/1: 24260-06: In tch, wknd 2f out: see 2249. *1¾* **50**
2650 **SFORZANDO 20** [3]3-8-11 (67) Lisa Jones(3) 7/2 JT FAV: 500-1507: In tch, wknd 2f out: best 1729 (7f). *1* **53**
2680 **SPRINGTIME ROMANCE 19** [5]3-9-10 VIS (80) T E Durcan 7/1: 361648: Chsd ldr, wknd & eased over 1f out: not enjoy visor? see 2580, 1864. *22* **22**
8 Ran Time 1m 44.38 (1.38) Owned: Pursuit Media Trained: Alcester

3163 **8.00 Choisir Maiden Stakes 2yo (D)**
£5382 £1656 £828 **6f rnd** **Good** **Slow** Inside

1716 **GALEOTA 60** [6] R Hannon 2-9-0 R L Moore 7/2 JT FAV: 41: Nvr far away, went on ins fnl 1f, rdn clr cl-home: well bckd, 9 wk abs: eff at 5/6f on gd & fast grnd: runs well fresh: useful. **95**
2109 **LOADERFUN 42** [10] H Candy 2-9-0 Dane O'Neill 7/2 JT FAV: 42: Tried to make all, collared ins fnl 1f: 6 wk abs, nicely bckd: eff at 5/6f on gd & firm, handles a sharp or stiff trk: win similar, see 2109. *1¼* **90**
2695 **ROYAL ORISSA 18** [5] D Haydn Jones 2-9-0 Paul Eddery 25/1: 453: Chsd ldrs, onepcd fnl 1f. *1½* **86**
2851 **SOVEREIGNTY 12** [9] D R Loder 2-9-0 T P Queally 9/2: 24: Keen & chsd ldrs, onepcd fnl 1f: drifted from 3/1: acts on gd & fast grnd, 7f shld now suit: see 2851 (debut). *½* **84**
DISGUISE [1]2-9-0 R Hughes 8/1: 5: b c Pursuit of Love - Nullarbor (Green Desert) Chsd ldrs, onepcd fnl 1f on debut: April foal, half-brother to 6f/1m wnr Desert Opal: shld do better. *½* **82**
EMBOSSED [15]2-9-0 P Dobbs 14/1: 6: b c Mark of Esteem - L Way First (Vision) Slow away, switched centre & prog 2f out, nrst fin under a kind ride: op 25/1 on debut & longer priced s/mate of wnr: 20,000gsn March foal: half-brother to a 5f juv wnr: dam styd 2m: gd start, relish 7f+ & will improve. *2½* **75+**
1934 **ARC OF LIGHT 51** [14]2-9-0 M Hills 20/1: 57: b c Spectrum - Siwaayib (Green Desert) Mid-div, nvr nr ldrs: 7 wk abs: May foal, half-brother to a couple of useful 12f wnr: dam 6f scorer. *1¾* **70**
VIKING SPIRIT [12]2-9-0 T Quinn 7/1: 8: b c Mind Games - Dane Dancing (Danehill) Nvr btr than mid-div on debut: op 9/1: Feb first foal, cost 15,000gns: dam a 9f wnr, sire a high-class sprinter. *shd* **70**
LOOK AT THE STARS [8]2-9-0 P Robinson 33/1: 9: b c Bachir - Pizzazz (Unfuwain) Slowly away, nvr a factor on debut: E30,000 April foal: half-brother to 5f/1m wnr Creskeld: sire a high-class miler. *1¾* **65**
GRANDMAS GIRL [13]2-8-9 C Lowther 66/1: 0: 10th: Outpcd, nvr dngrs on debut. *1¼* **56**
VALIOS [3]2-9-0 T E Durcan 33/1: 0: 11th: Slowly away, nvr nr ldrs on debut. *¾* **59**
DANGER ZONE [4]2-9-0 E Ahern 12/1: 0: 12th: Dwelt, al bhd on debut: op 8/1. *1* **56**
YOUNG BOLDRIC [7]2-9-0 D Corby(3) 100/1: 0: 13th: Slowly away, al bhd on racecourse bow. *6* **38**
2858 **Looking Great 12** [2]2-9-0 S Carson 33/1:0 1717 **Kenwyn 60** [11]2-9-0 D Sweeney 66/1:0
15 Ran Time 1m 13.85 (3.55) Owned: Mr J A Lazzari Trained: Marlborough

3164 **8.30 Royal Windsor Welcomes Back Talksport Radio Selling Stakes 3-4yo (E)**
£3435 £1057 £529 **1m3f135y** **Good** **Slow** Inside

2966 **PONT NEUF 7** [3] J W Hills 4-9-3 t (65) S Whitworth 5/2 FAV: 0-004251: Hld up, hdwy to lead dist, rdn clr: well bckd, sold for 7,000gns: eff at 9/11.6f on fm & gd/soft: wears a t-strap: first win. **64**
306 **WHITE PARK BAY 190** [9] Miss Suzy Smith 4-9-3 (48) M Halford(7) 14/1: 30330-52: Held up, hmpd halfway, hdwy to chall 1.5f out, kept on but not pace of wnr: long abs & new stable (prev with J Gallagher). *3½* **57**
2867 **BOOGIE MAGIC 11** [7] C N Allen 4-9-3 (62) R Mullen 7/2: 0400-023: Led till dist, no extra: op 5/2. *2½* **56**
2739 **BLUE SAVANNA 16** [5] J G Portman 4-9-13 bl (40) R L Moore 10/1: 4210564: Chsd ldrs, ev ch 2f out, wknd fnl 1f: top-weight, tchd 14/1: offic rtd 40, treat this rating with caution: see 916 (AW). *2½* **62$**
2050 **SIR FRANK GIBSON 45** [1]3-8-9 (50) D Sweeney 25/1: 4230555: Chsd ldrs 10f, wknd: 6 wk abs. *½* **56**
2980 **WHENWILLITWIN 7** [6]3-8-9 Derek Nolan(7) 16/1: 66: Keen & chsd ldrs, btn 2f out: see 2980 (mdn). *nk* **56**
2719 **PRINCESS MAGDALENA 17** [8]4-9-3 (50) I Mongan 8/1: 010-0007: ch f Pennekamp - Reason To Dance (Damister) Chsd ldrs, wknd 3f out: op 6/1: '03 sell wnr: eff at 7/10f on gd & fast grnd: likes a sharp trk & sell grade: more expected here. 1 Sep'03 Wind 10.0g/f 56-(57) G: 2 Sep'02 Chep 7gd 79- D: *6* **42**
2924 **BOSCO 9** [4]3-9-0 t (52) K Fallon 7/2: 5-000168: Mid-div, nvr a factor: tchd 5/1: see 2924. *4* **46**
2019 **ALTARES 47** [2]3-8-9 (35) M Hills 33/1: 00-00009: Al bhd, t.o. in last: 7 wk abs. *17* **15**
9 Ran Time 2m 32.96 (5.66) Owned: Mr J W Hills Trained: Lambourn

3165 **9.00 Ladbrokes Com Handicap Stakes 3yo+ 0-70 (E)** **[69]**
£3494 £1075 £538 **5f10y str** **Good** **Slow** Inside

2981 **BLESSED PLACE 7** [13] D J S ffrench Davis 4-8-6 t (47) T Quinn 13/2: 0033541: Nvr far away, went on ent fnl 1f, held on well under hands & heels: eff at 5/6f on gd, fm & both AWs: eff with/without cheek pieces. **55**
3000* **JONNY EBENEEZER 2** [15] D Flood 5-9-7 (6ex)bl (62) R Smith 13/2: 2103102: Slowly away, hdwy when short of room dist, fin strongly & just failed: bckd from 9/1: qck reapp: fine run, poss a shade unlucky. *½* **68+**
2420 **PLAYTIME BLUE 29** [2] Mrs H Sweeting 4-9-4 (59) G Baker 16/1: 4306053: Nvr far away, kept on under press fnl 1f & only btn 1L: gd run from a poor low draw, see 749 (AW, with K Burke). *½* **63**
2957 **LOCH INCH 8** [12] J M Bradley 7-8-10 bl (51) Dane O'Neill 14/1: 0-000404: Dwelt, prog 2f out, no dngr. *shd* **55**

WINDSOR   MONDAY 12.07.04   Sharp, Fig 8 Track

2942 **BRIGADIER MONTY 9** [3]6-8-12 (53) K Fallon 5/1 FAV: 0600255: Mid-div, imprvd 2f out, onepcd fnl 1f.   ½   55
2951 **DUNN DEAL 9** [10]4-9-8 (63) T E Durcan 12/1: 1205066: Mid-div, short of room halfway, styd on late.   ¾   63
2975 **INTELLIBET ONE 7** [7]4-9-1 (56) F P Ferris(3) 13/2: 00-00347: Dwelt, nvr btr than mid-div: op 5/1.   1   53
2717 **ELA FIGURA 17** [5]4-8-8 p (49) T P Queally 33/1: 6003658: Rear, nvr nr ldrs.   1   43
2975* **WILLHECONQUERTOO 7** [1]4-9-13 (6ex)f (68) J F Egan 7/1: 0-003519: Front rank, led halfway till   ¾   60
dist, wknd: top-weight, poor low draw: 6lb pen for 2975 (6f, firm, made all).
117 **MONTANA 226** [4]4-9-10 (65) K McEvoy 25/1: 223000-0: 10th: b c Puissance - Mistral's Dancer   hd   56
(Shareef Dancer) Chsd ldrs till halfway: long abs: plcd on 3 of 4 '03 starts (mdns, with R Hannon): eff at 6f on
fast & firm grnd, runs well fresh: handles a sharp or gall trk: now with J Spearing, poor draw here.
2 Jun'03 Ling 6g/f 74-(75) D: 2 Jun'03 Newb 6.0fm 76- D:
2957 **PULSE 8** [9]6-9-7 p (62) R L Moore 9/1: 6645300: 11th: Nvr nr ldrs: btr 2743.   nk   52
2945 **ROAN RAIDER 9** [11]4-8-12 vis (63) K Ghunowa(7) 25/1: 0535020: 12th: Al towards rear.   1¼   39
1625 **GIVERAND 65** [8]5-8-1 (42) J Quinn 50/1: 0/0030-00: 13th: Slowly away, nvr a factor: 9 wk abs.   nk   27
2981 Diaphanous 7 [14]6-7-12 (2oh)bl(37) Liam Jones(5) 40/12743 Another Victim 16 [6]10-8-5 (46) D Sweeney 14/1:0
15 Ran   Time 1m 0.59(1.59)   Owned: Mr S J Edwards   Trained: Lambourn

HOPPEGARTEN   SUNDAY 11.07.04

Official Going GOOD.

3166   3.40 Gr 2 Berlin Brandenburg Trophy 3yo+   ()
      £44366 £15493 £7746   **1m rnd   Good**

2470 **MARTILLO 26** [2] R Suerland 4-9-6 W Mongil 7/10 FAV: 1310-5191: Trkd ldrs, short of room &   115
swtchd dist, styd on well to lead on line: also won this last term: suited by 1m on fast & soft grnd: v smart colt.
1860 **ASSIUN 56** [1] P Schiergen 3-8-9 A Suborics 29/10: 132: b c Monsun - Assia (Royal Academy) Held   shd   112
up in tch, hdwy to chall over 1f out, hdd line: abs: earlier landed a Gr 3 & 3rd in Gr 2 German 2000 Guineas: eff
at 1m/9f on gd grnd: smart run.
2470 **CHECKIT 26** [6] M R Channon 4-9-6 (112) A Culhane 47/10: 36003483: Trkd ldr, chall over 1f out,   hd   113
hdd close home: clr rem: gd run, just in front of today's wnr in 2470, see 1758.
6 Ran   Time 1m 39.40()   Owned: Gestut Hony-Hof   Trained: Germany

DEAUVILLE   SATURDAY 10.07.04   Righthand, Galloping Track

Official Going Soft

3167   3.20 Gr 3 Prix de Ris-Orangis 3yo+   ()
      £25704 £10282 £7711   **6f str   Soft**

2468 **THE TRADER 25** [2] M Blanshard 6-9-4 bl (113) D Sweeney 21/10 FAV: 1426-1301: Held up, hdwy over   115
1f out, led ins last, rdn & styd on strongly: eff at 5/6f on any ground: v smart sprinter: see 1856.
4472} **SWEDISH SHAVE** [11] R Gibson 6-9-0 T Jarnet 7/1: 086-2202: ch c Midyan - Shavya (Shavian) Led   2   106
after 1f & rdn clr 2f out, hdd ins last & no extra: dual Listed rnr up earlier this term: dual Listed scorer '03,
also landed a Gr 3: suited by 5/6f, stays 7f: acts on fast & hvy ground. 2 Aug'02 Deau 6sft 111- :
3544} **VASYWAIT** [7] D Boeuf 5-9-0 D Boeuf 7/2: 03-22143: Trkd ldr, rdn & hung left over 1f out, onepace.   2   100
12 Ran   Time 1m 10.70 ()   Owned: Mrs C J Ward   Trained: Upper Lambourn

DEAUVILLE   SUNDAY 11.07.04   Righthand, Galloping Track

Official Going V Soft

3168   2.30 Gr 3 Prix Messidor 3yo+   ()
      £25704 £10282 £7711   **1m   Soft**

4748* }**RYONO** [6] P Lautner 5-9-2 T Castanheira 125/10: 10210-11: ch c Mountain Cat - Racing Blue   120+
(Reference Point) Rear, hdwy to lead over 1f out, readily asserted: Listed wnr in '03: eff at 1m on gd, relishes
soft ground: smart & improving. 1 Oct'03 Long 8sft 102- :
2469 **DIAMOND GREEN FR 26** [7] A Fabre 3-8-7 Gary Stevens 4/5 FAV: 111-3222: Cl up, led over 1f out,   2½   115
hdd over 1f out, no extra: much btr expected after Royal Ascot Gr 1 2nd in 2469 (fast).
4626* }**SPECIAL KALDOUN** [4] D Smaga 5-9-2 D Boeuf 43/10: 0100-003: Trkd ldrs, kept on samepace.   ½   114
6 Ran   Time 1m39.60 ()   Owned: Frau H Focke   Trained: Germany

3169   1.30 Listed Prix Roland de Chambure 2yo   ()
      £15845 £6338 £4754   **7f str   Soft**

INHABITANT [6] Mme C Head Maarek 2-9-0 O Doleuze : 1: ch c Zafonic - Infringe (Warning)   105
Decisive success on step up to Listed company: remains unbeaten after an earlier success at Maisons Laffitte: eff at
6f, apprec step up to 7f, stay 1m: acts on gd & v soft grnd: well regarded & clearly useful.
KAPPELMANN [7] R Collet 2-9-0 T Jarnet : 2: Styd on for 2nd, no impress on wnr in cl home.   1½   101
ROYAL MISTRESS [5] R Gibson 2-8-11 O Peslier : 3: Finished 3rd.   ½   97
2367* **DAHTEER 30** [3]2-9-0 T E Durcan : 4116: Dsptd lead after 1f, hdd over 1f out, sn btn, fin 6th: 1¾   97
shld stay 7f: see 2367 (gd), 2043.

DEAUVILLE   SUNDAY 11.07.04   Righthand, Galloping Track

8 Ran   Time 1m 28.20()   Owned: K Abdulla   Trained: France

NAPLES   SUNDAY 11.07.04

Official Going GOOD/FIRM.

3170   10.00 Gr 3 Gran Premio Citta Di Napoli 3yo+   ()
£34194 £15821 £8857   5f   Good/Firm

4428] **T E LAWRENCE** [10] A Renzoni 4-8-12 (83) O Fancera 193/10: 1: b c Charnwood Forest - Only Gossip   **107**
(Trempolino) Trkd ldrs, led ins last, held on all out: eff at 5f on fast: useful. 1 Jul'02 Brig 5.9g/f 83- E:
       REGINA SAURA [13] M Ciciarelli 6-8-8 bl L Maniezzi 34/10: 2: ch m Wolfhound - Reine Maid (Mr   hd   **102**
Prospector) Rear, styd on strongly ins last, just failed: eff at 5f on fast grnd: useful mare.
2390* **BENBAUN** 29 [5] M J Wallace 3-8-7 (93) D Corby 16/10 FAV: 20-101213: Missed break, fin strongly &   hd   **105**
just btn in a 3-way photo: prev best best dominating: reapp of vis will suit, omitted here: see 2390.
15 Ran   Time 56.57()   Owned: Scuderia Jerome   Trained: Italy

BRIGHTON   TUESDAY 13.07.04   Lefthand, V Sharp, Undulating Track

Official Going Good/Firm (Good Places)

3171   2.30 Andrex Puppy Dash/E B F Median Auction Maiden Stakes 2yo (E)
£3359 £1034 £517   6f rnd   Good/Firm 36   -29 Slow   Inside

2689 **ROWAN LODGE** 19 [1] M H Tompkins 2-9-0 L Dettori 9/4: 031: Cl-up & led over 2f out, rdn out: **84**
bckd, op 3/1: eff at 6f, get further: acts on fast & gd/soft, easy or sharp/undul trks: progressive, nursery type.
2927 **GOOD WEE GIRL** 10 [2] S Kirk 2-8-9 J F Egan 66/1: 002: b f Tagula - Auriga (Belmez) Chsd ldrs,   1½   **73**
switched & hdwy to chall over 1f out, sn onepace for press: 8,000gns March foal, half-sister to multiple sprint wnr
Morse, dam a 6f plcd juv: eff at 6f on fast grnd: imprvd eff, h'cap company shld suit.
3020 **AVERTIGO** 6 [5] W R Muir 2-9-0 R Mullen 8/1: 53: b c Averti - Green Run (Green Dancer) Slow   ½   **76**
into stride & rdn rear, late gains, nrst fin: op 10/1, qck reapp: May first foal, 5,000gns purchase: dam a 1m wnr
in France: eff at 6f, looks in need of 7f: handles fast & gd grnd, sharp/undul trks.
2952 **CAMPEON** 9 [6] M J Wallace 2-9-0 J Fortune 11/8 FAV: 050524: Led till over 2f out, rdn & btn bef   1¾   **71**
dist: well bckd: btr 2952 (7f, gd).
2245 **TOP FORM** 38 [3]2-8-9 W Supple 9/2: 05: Rdn chasing ldrs halfway, btn over 1f out: op 11/4.   2½   **58**
2858 **TAIPAN TOMMY** 13 [4]2-9-0 R L Moore 20/1: 66066: In tch, wide over 2f out, sn btn.   5   **48**
6 Ran   Time 1m 11.69 (3.89)   Owned: The Rowan Stud and Clique Partnership   Trained: Newmarket

3172   3.00 Rendezvous Casino At The Marina Selling Stakes 2yo (G)
£2551 £729 £364   6f rnd   Good/Firm 36   -42 Slow   Inside

2882 **PIDDIES PRIDE** 12 [7] I A Wood 2-8-6 S Sanders 5/2: 56641: Trkd ldrs & led 2f out, rdn clr over   **68**
1f out, decisively: slow time: sold for 9,200gns: first win: visor omitted: eff at 6f, get 7f: acts on fast &
gd grnd, gall or sharp/undul trk: eff with/without visor: improved run: see 2882, 1471.
2833 **GENERAL NUISANCE** 14 [6] J S Moore 2-8-11 p Derek Nolan(7) 9/1: 2645432: Mid-div, rdn & kept on   3½   **60**
fnl 2f, no threat to wnr: see 2833 (C/D clmr).
2714 **BELLALOU** 18 [8] N A Callaghan 2-8-6 R L Moore 7/4 FAV: 003: Chsd ldrs wide, onepace over 1f   shd   **55**
out: nicely bckd, op 9/4: drop in grade: bred to relish 1m+ in time: see 2714 (7f).
2939 **FAITHFUL FLASH** 10 [5] C A Dwyer 2-8-6 E Ahern 25/1: 604: Rdn rear, hung left & no impress dist.   1¾   **50**
2584 **VICTIMISED** 24 [2]2-8-11 L Keniry(3) 50/1: 005: b g Victory Note - Eurolink Virago (Charmer) Led   1   **52**
till 2f out, sn btn: cheaply bght April foal, related to a 9f wnr & a sprint wnr abroad: dam uncrd.
2977 **GLASSON LODGE** 8 [3]2-8-6 F P Ferris(3) 7/2: 5634226: Cl-up & ch 2f out, no extra dist: btr 2977.   nk   **46**
2977 **TIP TOES** 8 [4]2-8-6 C Catlin 14/1: 067: Bhd, no hdwy: see 2977.   7   **28**
2115 **KENTUCKY BANKES** 43 [1]2-8-11 BL A Daly 33/1: 068: b c Bluegrass Prince - Countess Bankes (Son   3   **24**
Pardo) Dwelt, rdn chasing ldrs, btn 2f out: bred: April first foal, dam a 5f juv wnr.
8 Ran   Time 1m 12.45 (4.65)   Owned: Mrs Sue Pidcock   Trained: Upper Lambourn

3173   3.30 Kimberly-Clark Professional Classified Stakes 3yo+ 0-60 (F)
£2947 £842 £421   1m3f196y   Good/Firm 36   +10 Fast   Inside

3051* **ELUSIVE DREAM** 5 [2] Sir Mark Prescott 3-8-12 (61) S Sanders 1/3 FAV: 0000-111: Led 4f, led again   **84+**
6f out, rdn clr fnl 1f, going away: well bckd, qk reapp: eff at 12f, sure to get further: acts on fibresand, fast &
gd/soft, sharp trks: taking advantage of lenient h'cap mark & plenty more to come: see 3051.
2955 **UNCLE JOHN** 9 [5] S Kirk 3-8-5 (60) J F Egan 25/1: 105-0042: Chsd ldrs, hdwy to join wnr 3f out,   5   **63**
onepcd over 1f out: bred to relish 1m+ in time: acts on fast & fibresand: see 2024.
2912 **GREAT VIEW** 11 [6] Mrs A L M King 5-9-9 vis (65) S Drowne 7/1: 2124023: In tch, hdwy 4f out, ev ch   ¾   **67**
over 2f out, sn onepcd: see 1373.
2440 **TREETOPS HOTEL** 29 [1] B R Johnson 5-9-4 (55) Dane O'Neill 33/1: 0-200024: Rear, hdwy 3f out,   2½   **58**
hung left fnl 2f & sn onepcd: not stay 12f? see 2440 (1m) & 520.
2842 **LADY PEACHES** 13 [4]3-8-7 (65) R L Moore 25/1: 0-03045: Handy, wknd over 3f out: rider reported   13   **42**
mount did not handle this fast ground: see 2842.
2099 **KIROV KING** 43 [7]4-9-9 (65) L Dettori 20/1: 60-00006: Rear, nvr nr ldrs: 6 wk abs: see 1516.   6   **37**
2800 **COSI FAN TUTTE** 15 [3]6-9-9 vis t (65) W Supple 12/1: 5410/-237: Pressed ldr, led after 4f to 6f   22   **8**
out, fdd over 2f out: something amiss? btr see 2800, 2267.
7 Ran   Time 2m 31.28 (3.08)   Owned: Cheveley Park Stud   Trained: Newmarket

---

3174 4.00 Totesport Com Handicap Stakes 3yo+ 0-80 (D) [89]
£5352 £1647 £823 1m rnd Good/Firm 36 -12 Slow Inside

2919 **MALIBU 10** [6] S Dow 3-8-12 (73) R L Moore 7/2: 00-46501: Made all, drvn out ins fnl 1f: eff at 78
7/9f on fast & gd, sharp/undul trk: imprvd for a drop in trip & for forcing tactics: game eff: see 1141.
2840 **ISLAND RAPTURE 13** [3] J A R Toller 4-9-5 (71) L Dettori 7/2: 5-004032: Chsd ldrs, hdwy over 2f 2½ 72
out, hung left over 1f out, sn onepcd: top-weight: fair run: see 1891.
3142 **NAUTICAL 2** [8] A W Carroll 6-7-12 (50) M Halford(6) 7/2: 0-004643: Keen in rear, hdwy over 2f ½ 50
out, onepcd over 1f out: op 5/1, qck reapp: see 2589.
2872 **TEMPER TANTRUM 12** [7] Andrew Reid 6-8-6 p (58) J F Egan 9/4 FAV: 5204054: Mid-div, hdwy over 2f nk 57
out, no impress fnl 1f: see 151.
2362 **NEPHETRITI WAY 32** [5]3-9-3 (78) S Drowne 10/1: 212-0555: Bhd, nvr nr ldrs: op 7/1: see 1419. 8 63
2153 **SKY GALAXY 41** [4]3-9-0 VIS (75) J Fortune 16/1: 5000-006: Keen in 2nd, no impress 2f out: visor. 1½ 57
3034 **FULVIO 6** [1]4-8-8 vis (60) P Doe 25/1: 4000-007: Keen & handy, wknd over 2f out: qck reapp: see 2394. 4 34
7 Ran Time 1m 35.83 (3.83) Owned: John Robinson and Derek Stubbs Trained: Epsom

---

3175 4.30 Andrex With Aloe Vera Handicap Stakes 3yo+ 35-55 (F) [66]
£3045 £870 £435 1m1f209y Good/Firm 36 -25 Slow Inside

2664 **JACKIE KIELY 20** [15] P S McEntee 3-9-3 T (55) L Dettori 9/1: 5542101: In tch, hdwy & led 2f out, 64
drvn out: eff at 10f, stays 12f well: acts on both AWs, fm & fast: back to form in t-strap.
2244 **BHUTAN 38** [8] G B Balding 9-9-5 (46) R Thomas(5) 20/1: 15130-02: b g Polish Patriot - Bustinetta 2½ 49
(Bustino) Mid-div, hdwy on bit 2f out, onepace fnl 1f: won 3 h'caps in '03 (with G Moore): rnr-up 2 of 9 '02
starts (h'caps, with Mrs M Reveley): eff at 10/14f on firm, soft & fibresand, acts on any trk: best without visor:
likes W'hampton: well h'capped 9yo, wants further.
1 Feb'03 Ling 12ap 65a-58 F: 1 Feb'03 Wolv 12af 61a-53 F: 1 Feb'03 Wolv 12af 53a-47 F: 2 Jan'03 Sout 12af 50a-47 G:
2 Jan'03 Sout 12af 49a-44 E: 2 Jan'03 Sout 11af 49a-44 G: 2 Jun'02 Warw 12.6fm 47-45 F: 2 Jun'02 Redc 14fm 47-45 F:
2 Sep'01 Muss 12g/f 65- E: 2 Jun'01 Muss 16g/f 67-68 D:
3058 **DON ARGENTO 5** [12] Mrs A J Bowlby 3-8-2 (6oh) (40) D Kinsella 66/1: 00-000U3: Bhd, hdwy 3f out, hd 43
kept on: qck reapp: stays 10f on fast, try 12f: gd run from 6lb out of the h'cap: see 1940.
2741 **FORGE LANE 17** [13] G L Moore 3-9-3 (55) S Sanders 16/1: 000004: b g Desert Style - March shd 58
Fourteenth (Tricky Creek) Bhd, hdwy & not clr run over 2f out till over 1f out, styd on well ins fnl 1f: h'cap & mdn
unplcd prev (earlier with C Weedon): lightly rcd, prob rnr up with a clr run here.
3145* **THEATRE LADY 2** [6]6-9-6 (6ex) (47) F P Ferris(3) 6/1: 3566015: Mid-div, hdwy & ev ch 2f out, sn shd 49
onepcd: op 4/1, qck reapp: joc 1 day careless riding ban: in gd form: see 3145.
2837 **RUSSALKA 14** [11]3-9-1 (53) M Halford(7) 10/1: 2-005026: Bhd, hdwy over 2f out, staying on when 1 54
not clr run nr fin: op 7/1, tchd 12/1: shade closer with a clr run: see 2837.
2701 **EVEN EASIER 19** [7]3-9-1 bl (53) R L Moore 8/1: 5064457: Dwelt, sn in tch, hdwy over 2f out, onepcd. nk 53
2719 **KINDNESS 18** [14]4-9-7 (48) Dane O'Neill 15/2: 3-600228: In tch, hdwy 4f out, onepcd over 1f out. 2 45
2909 **DIDOE 11** [16]5-9-4 (45) E Ahern 20/1: 3230-009: Chsd ldrs, hdwy to lead 3f out to 2f out, no extra. 2 39
3044 **ICANNSHIFT 5** [1]4-10-0 (55) J Fortune 4/1 FAV: 0363030: 10th: Led to 3f out, wkng 4th when not 2 46
much room over 1f out: op 5/1, qck reapp, top-weight: see 1273.
3052 **CASTAIGNE 5** [3]5-9-9 (50) R Havlin 12/1: 0060440: 11th: Handy, onepcd 2f out: qck reapp: see 3052. 2 38
2910 **DANCES WITH ANGELS 11** [9]4-8-8 (35) S Drowne 25/1: 00300P0: 12th: In tch, not much room 5f out, ¾ 22
sn outpcd: see 1547.
2836 **SUMMER CHERRY 14** [10]7-8-13 t (40) P Doe 8/1: 3-025000: 13th: Handy, wknd over 2f out. 3½ 22
2782 **PANCAKE ROLE 16** [2]4-8-8 (3oh) (32) C Haddon(7) 50/1: 040/50-60: 14th: Handy, wknd bef halfway. 7 8
414 **BRIERY MEC 180** [5]9-8-8 (4oh) (37) J F Egan 50/1: 0000-060: 15th: b g Ron's Victory - Briery 16 0
Fille (Sayyaf) Al bhd: 7 wk hdles abs (p.u., nov): h'cap unplcd in '03 (trd 32a): rnr-up in a h'cap in '02: eff
at 10/12f on fast, soft & polytrack: has run well fresh on any trk: gd weight-carrier, tried cheek pieces.
2 Aug'02 Newm 10sft 44-47 E: 1 Aug'01 Wind 10gd 59-52 E: 1 Jul'01 Pont 10gd 59-46 F: 2 Nov'00 Ling 12ap 49a-49 G:
2805 **SONDERBORG 15** [4]3-9-3 (55) G Carter 33/1: 2002600: 16th: Rear, nvr a factor. 24 0
16 Ran Time 2m 03.92 (6.12) Owned: Mr P S J Croft Trained: Newmarket

---

3176 5.00 Wharton Slaney Ltd Rails Bookmakers Handicap Stakes 3yo+ 35-55 (F) [55]
£3038 £868 £434 7f rnd Good/Firm 36 -10 Slow Inside

3034 **ZIET DALSACE 6** [2] A W Carroll 4-9-12 (53) R L Moore 8/1: 0200201: Trkd ldrs, hdwy to lead ins 63
fnl 1f, rdn clr: op 10/1, qck reapp: stays eff at 6f/1m, winning form at 7f on firm, fast & polytrack, prob handles any
trk, likes Yarmouth & sell grade: back to form: see 1938.
2954* **MISTER CLINTON 9** [11] D K Ivory 7-10-3 (6ex) (58) J Fortune 7/1: 0634012: Bhd, hdwy fnl 2f, kept 3 62
on ins fnl 1f to go 2nd nr fin: top-weight: remains in gd form, return to further will suit: see 2954.
2957 **JAZZY MILLENNIUM 9** [5] B R Millman 7-9-12 bl (53) S Drowne 3/1 FAV: 00-03633: Rcd in 2nd, ev ch ½ 56
over 1f out, sn onepcd: nicely bckd: likes Brighton: see 2262.
2397 **LOCH LAIRD 31** [3] M Madgwick 9-9-8 (49) G Baker 25/1: 0105004: Mid-div, kept on fnl 1f. shd 52
2928 **MY GIRL PEARL 10** [1]4-9-4 (45) Dane O'Neill 16/1: 0242065: Led till ins fnl 1f, sn no extra. 1 46
2975 **DOCTOR DENNIS 8** [6]7-9-11 vis (52) S Sanders 11/1: 5160106: Bhd, hdwy 3f out, onepcd ins fnl 1f. ¾ 52
2334 **DUE TO ME 33** [12]4-9-4 p (45) S Whitworth 10/1: 5146347: Bhd, hdwy over 1f out, not pace to chall. ¾ 44
3045 **SOCIAL CONTRACT 5** [4]7-9-7 (48) C Catlin 40/1: 6200008: Handy, lost place over 3f out, mod gains. 1¼ 44
2630 **CAFE AMERICANO 22** [17]4-9-3 e (44) A Daly 33/1: 5000-059: Slow away, rear, hdwy 2f out, no impress. ¾ 39
2954 **POPPYLINE 9** [10]4-9-12 (53) R Mullen 12/1: 00U3630: 10th: Nvr btr than mid-div. hd 47
2572 **SHIRLEY OAKS 24** [8]6-9-10 (51) L Dettori 6/1: 1631200: 11th: Bhd, nvr nr ldrs. 2½ 40
3087 **ENNA 4** [14]5-9-7 (48) E Ahern 14/1: 3-460040: 12th: Bhd, nvr a factor: op 20/1, qck reapp: see 1284. ½ 36
2432 **SUSIEDIL 29** [18]3-9-3 VIS (52) J Fortune 20/1: 40-00660: 13th: Handy, wide, wknd over 2f out: visor. ½ 39
2273 **SILISTRA 36** [13]5-9-5 p (46) J F McDonald(3) 100/1: 000-0000: 14th: gr g Sadler's Wells - Dundel 1¼ 30
(Machiavellian) In tch, no impress over 2f out: mdn, h'cap & class stks unplcd in '03 (trd 35a): h'cap rnr-up in
'02 (Sir M Stoute, first visor): eff around 10/11f on firm & hvy: tried blnks, visor & a hood, wears cheek pieces.
2 Jun'02 Redc 11fm 73-72 D:
1463 **PEREGIAN 74** [9]6-9-7 (48) J F Egan 20/1: 005-5300: 15th: Handy, wknd over 1f out: long abs. 6 22
2928 **KOMENA 10** [16]6-9-1 (42) G Carter 20/1: 5000050: 16th: Al bhd: see 30. 1 14

BRIGHTON TUESDAY 13.07.04 Lefthand, V Sharp, Undulating Track

2799 **COPPINGTON FLYER 15** [7]4-9-1 (42) R Havlin 25/1: 4040400: 17th: Handy, wknd over 2f out: see 917. *7* **2**
17 Ran Time 1m 23.03(3.23) Owned: Mr Dennis Deacon Trained: Alcester

BEVERLEY TUESDAY 13.07.04 Righthand, Oval Track With Stiff Uphill Finish

Official Going GOOD/SOFT (GOOD places).

3177 **2.15 Dave Drew Is Our Plumber Claiming Stakes 3yo (E)**
£3523 £1084 £542 **7f100y rnd** **Good/Soft 60** **+06 Fast** Inside

2940 **FAIRLIE 10** [4] Mrs J R Ramsden 3-8-3 (59) L Goncalves 10/1: 046-5001: Held up, prog to lead dist, pushed clr, val 5L+: clmd for 9,000, fair time: eff at 6/7.4f, has tried further: acts on fast & gd/soft grnd, stiff/undul trk: fine eff from poor low draw, apprec drop to claim grade: see 1953. **64+**
2656 **GALLAS 21** [11] J S Wainwright 3-8-4 vis (57) R Ffrench 25/1: 000-0002: b c Charnwood Forest - Nellie's Away (Magical Strike) Mid-div, prog 3f out, short of room dist, kept on to chase wnr fnl 1f, al held: unplcd in '03 (rtd 79, med auct mdn): eff at 6/7.4f on fast & gd/soft grnd: eff with a visor. *3½* **56**
1944 **HEATHYARDS JOY 50** [2] R Hollinshead 3-7-13 (32) J Bramhill 40/1: 4255603: Mid-div, prog & ev ch bef 2f out, no impress fnl 1f: 7 wk abs: poor low draw: see 1330. *2½* **46**
2215 **TURF PRINCESS 39** [1] Ian Emmerson 3-8-4 (56) D Fentiman(7) 12/1: 1245304: Led, hdd dist, wknd. *1¾* **47**
2463 **TRYSTING GROVE 28** [14]3-8-4 P Fessey 12/1: 0005: Stumbled start, prog halfway, nrst fin. *¾* **45**
2925 **PINK SUPREME 10** [5]3-8-2 (58) T P Queally 10/1: 2-000006: Handy, ev ch 2f out, fdd dist: btr 2268. *2½* **38**
2811 **ALWAYS FLYING 15** [9]3-9-5 (64) P Mulrennan(5) 5/1: 5266027: In tch over 5f, sn no extra: tchd 4/1: new stable: btr 2811 (fast, M Johnston). *1½* **52**
2852 **SOUL PROVIDER 13** [6]3-8-0 (50) S Righton 16/1: 4324058: Mid-div 5f, onepcd fnl 2f: btr 1125. *2½* **28**
95 **SKELTHWAITE 231** [8]3-9-1 M Nem(7) 100/1: 000-9: b g Desert Story - Skip To Somerfield (Shavian) Handy till halfway, sn wknd: long abs & new stable: modest form to date. *1¼* **41$**
2693 **ACCA LARENTIA 19** [3]3-8-4 (50) Hayley Turner(5) 7/1: 062-0030: 10th: Al in rear: btr 2693. *½* **29**
2693 **PLUMPIE MAC 19** [12]3-8-9 (49) Suzanne France(7) 66/1: 060-60: 11th: Prom 4f, wknd: btr 2693. *nk* **33**
2936 **MICKLEGATE 10** [13]3-8-5 (60) T Quinn 5/2 FAV: 6443-440: 12th: In tch, prog 3f out, under press & wkng when short of room dist: btr expected on drop in grade: btr 2446. *3* **23**
2932 **RAYBERS MAGIC 10** [7]3-7-12 J Quinn 100/1: 000: 13th: Slow away, nvr a factor. *12* **0**
2619 **KNIGHT ONTHE TILES 22** [10]3-8-7 bl (72) N Pollard 10/1: 060-0000: 14th: Rear, nvr a factor. *14* **0**
14 Ran Time 1m 34.80 (4.0) Owned: Mr L C Sigsworth Trained: Thirsk

3178 **2.45 Bamboo Bistro Maiden Auction Stakes 2yo (E)**
£4154 £1278 £639 **5f str** **Good/Soft 60** **-30 Slow** Inside

2933 **BIG HASSLE 10** [14] T D Easterby 2-8-7 T Quinn 4/7 FAV: 521: Made all, al trav well, clr fnl 2f, eased cl-home, val 6L+: bckd at odds-on: eff over a stiff 5f on gd & gd/soft grnd: made gd use of fav'ble high draw with easy success: deserves a step up in grade, see 2670. **87+**
BREAKING SHADOW [11] R A Fahey 2-8-7 K Darley 10/1: 2: br c Danehill Dancer - Crimbourne (Mummy's Pet) Handy, styd on to chase wnr dist, kept on but al held: clr rem on debut: May foal, cost 12,000gns: half-brother to wnrs at sprint dists: sire useful performer at sprint dists: eff at 5f, 6f will suit: acts on gd/soft grnd: promising start to career & can improve. *3½* **72**
2670 **BORDERLESCOTT 20** [12] R Bastiman 2-8-10 R Ffrench 33/1: 603: Handy, prog & short of room dist, sn onepcd: now quals for h'caps: see 2360. *5* **62**
2882 **ROKO 12** [15] M W Easterby 2-8-7 P Mulrennan(5) 40/1: 0004: b g Komaite - Robert's Daughter (Robellino) Handy over 3f, sn no extra: April foal, cost 800gns: dam unplcd: sire successful at 7f. *nk* **58**
2424 **DETROIT DANCER 30** [16]2-8-7 Dean McKeown 25/1: 05: b c Makbul - First Play (Primo Dominie) Handy over 3f, sn no extra: Feb foal, cost 2,500gns: half-brother to wnrs abroad: dam successful at 6f. *2½* **51**
2983 **BAYMIST 8** [7]2-8-2 Dale Gibson 50/1: 56: Sn short of room in rear, late gains: see 2983. *½* **45**
2882 **ALZARMA 12** [10]2-8-7 R Winston 10/1: 037: Dwelt, prog when no room dist, switched & kept on cl-home: new stable: btr 2882 (6f, Mrs L Williamson). *¾* **48**
SUMMER SILKS [4]2-8-2 P Fessey 50/1: 8: Slow away, nvr nrr than mid-div: poor draw, debut. *½* **42**
2167 **WAGGLEDANCE 41** [3]2-8-7 G Parkin 33/1: 59: Prom till dist, fdd: poor draw: btr 2167. *shd* **46**
TIGER BOND [8]2-8-7 D McGaffin 20/1: 0: 10th: Al in rear on debut. *1* **43**
BREEDERS FOLLY [6]2-8-5 A Reilly(7) 66/1: 0: 11th: Slow away, nvr a factor. *½* **40**
DIAMOND HERITAGE [13]2-8-10 M Fenton 16/1: 0: 12th: Slow away, al bhd. *3½* **35**
PEACEFUL FRONTIER [5]2-8-5 (3ow) R Fitzpatrick 66/1: 0: 13th: Mid-div 3f, fdd. *2½* **23**
2077 **MIGHTY EMPIRE 45** [2]2-8-7 P Robinson 8/1: 00: 14th: Sn handy, hung right & wknd fnl 2f: 7 wk abs. *5* **12**
MARLENES GIRL [9]2-8-5 F Norton 33/1: 0: 15th: Handy 3f, fdd. *1½* **6**
15 Ran Time 1m 05.80 (4.5) Owned: Lee Connolly and Jason Jones Trained: Malton

3179 **3.15 Totejackpot Stakes Handicap 3yo 0-85 (D)** **[90]**
£6776 £2085 £1043 **7f100y rnd** **Good/Soft 60** **+01 Fast** Inside

2922 **BURLEY FLAME 10** [13] J G Given 3-9-1 (77) M Fenton 9/2: 4331031: Handy, grad prog to lead dist, rdn out: tchd 6/1: eff at 7f/1m on fast & gd/soft grnd: likes Beverley: see 2922 & 2166. **82**
2773 **KIBRYAA 17** [11] M A Jarvis 3-9-2 (78) P Robinson 2/1 FAV: 021-622: Handy, eff 3f out, bmpd dist, kept on well ins fnl 1f, just held by wnr: bckd from 11/4: another creditable effort: see 2773 & 2247. *½* **81**
1983 **ST SAVARIN 49** [6] J R Best 3-8-10 (72) N Pollard 16/1: 2531003: Dictated pace, hdd dist, kept on & not btn far in 3rd: 7 wk abs: acts on gd/soft & soft, best form on polytrack at Lingfield: btr 545. *nk* **74**
3016 **TRUE 6** [12] Mrs S Lamyman 3-8-1 (63) J Quinn 12/1: 3-002034: Chsd ldrs, prog & ev ch dist, onepcd cl-home: qck reapp: see 3016. *nk* **64**
2551 **WRENLANE 25** [4]3-8-2 (64) P Fessey 33/1: 30-265: Rear, sn short of room, prog halfway, kept on well ins fnl 1f, nrst fin: eff at 6/7f on fast & gd/soft grnd: see 2042. *shd* **64**
2985 **COMMANDO SCOTT 8** [1]3-9-0 (76) P P Mathers(7) 16/1: 1002226: Handy wide 6f, no extra: btr 2985. *2* **72**
2506 **FUTOO 26** [8]3-7-13 (61) R Ffrench 11/1: 06-65137: Rear, kept on fnl 1f, nrst fin: btr 2243. *1* **55**
2997 **SUPER KING 7** [2]3-8-3 (65) Dean McKeown 100/1: 02-0008: Sn short of room, nvr nrr than mid-div. *½* **58**

BEVERLEY TUESDAY 13.07.04 Righthand, Oval Track With Stiff Uphill Finish

2936 **GASPARINI 10** [9]3-7-12 (1oh) (59) J Mackay 25/1: 2-000439: Mid-div 5f, sn wknd: btr 2936. *2½* **48**
2574 **SWEET REPLY 24** [10]3-8-13 (75) T P Queally 14/1: 04-05100: 10th: Handy over 5f, wknd: btr 2259. *¾* **61**
2922* **DR THONG 10** [5]3-9-7 (83) K Darley 9/2: 5-412410: 11th: Keen handy, rcd wide, dsptd lead 3f out, *1½* **66**
wknd dist: op 7/2: rcd far too wide for a long way: btr 2922.
2944 **Harrisons Flyer 10** [7]3-8-5 (67) T Hamilton(3) 14/1:0
2950 **George The Best 10** [3]3-8-6 (68) Darren Williams 28/1:0
13 Ran Time 1m 35.20 (4.4) Owned: Burley Appliances Ltd Trained: Gainsborough

3180

3.45 Hall Golden Anniversary Handicap Guaranteed Sweepstakes 3yo+ 35-55 (F) **[60]**
£3250 £1000 £500 **5f str** **Good/Soft 60** **-19 Slow** Inside

2775 **FAIRGAME MAN 17** [4] J S Wainwright 6-8-11 p (43) G Parkin 33/1: 0-002051: Mid-div, prog ins fnl **50**
2f, rdn out to lead cl-home: eff at 5/6f on firm, gd/soft & any trk: eff with cheek pieces: fine eff from poor low draw to end long losing run: h'capped to win again on this evidence: see 1948.
2502 **LARKYS LOB 26** [16] J O'Reilly 5-8-13 (45) J D O'Reilly(7) 8/1: 3122162: Led, edged left under *nk* **50**
press ins fnl 1f, hdd cl-home: acts on gd/soft grnd & fibresand: see 2201 & 1405.
2337 **ON THE TRAIL 33** [8] D W Chapman 7-8-13 (45) J Mackay 33/1: 3121343: Bhd, prog wide ins fnl 2f, *nk* **49**
styd on well cl-home, not btn far: eff at 5/6f on gd/soft grnd & both AWs: gd run from mod draw: see 1443 & 1032.
2508 **BELLA BEGUINE 26** [7] A Bailey 5-9-2 (48) R Winston 33/1: 2-502044: Bhd, prog when short of room *¾* **50**
just ins fnl 1f, switched & styd on well cl-home: eff at 5f, apprec return to 6/7f: see 2508 & 27.
2846 **VALIANT ROMEO 13** [14]4-9-8 vis (54) R Ffrench 9/1: 0-522405: In tch, styd on from dist, not btn far. *½* **55**
3054 **LE MERIDIEN 5** [19]6-9-5 vis (51) L Fletcher(3) 13/2: 00-50006: Cl-up, onepcd dist: qck reapp. *hd* **51**
2702 **TORRENT 19** [18]9-9-8 bl (54) Lisa Jones(3) 6/1: 1000127: Prom, no extra fnl 1f: just btr 2702 & 2524. *¾* **52**
2951 **MYSTERY PIPS 10** [9]4-8-13 vis (45) Kim Tinkler 50/1: 0000408: Prom till dist, no extra: btr 2614. *hd* **42**
2884 **BALLYBUNION 12** [1]5-9-6 (52) A Nicholls 40/1: 0053009: Slow away, nvr nrr than mid-div: btr 2657. *½* **48**
2320 **ROSIES RESULT 34** [10]4-8-13 (45) P Mulrennan(5) 33/1: 0000-000: 10th: Chsd ldrs 3f, sn no extra. *½* **40**
2657 **OFF HIRE 21** [2]8-9-0 vis (46) R Fitzpatrick 66/1: 2340050: 11th: Handy wide till dist, wknd: btr 2657. *1* **38**
2775 **JOYCES CHOICE 17** [20]5-9-2 (48) P Mathers(7) 12/1: 20R5400: 12th: Cl-up over 3f, wknd: btr 1179. *nk* **39**
2657 **LYDIAS LOOK 21** [6]7-9-4 (50) T Eaves(3) 50/1: 5545160: 13th: Nvr nrr than mid-div: btr 2326. *¾* **39**
3000 **LEVELLED 7** [5]10-8-13 (45) J Quinn 50/1: 3310650: 14th: Bhd, nvr a factor: qck reapp. *hd* **33**
2981* **FLYING TACKLE 8** [15]6-9-2 p (48) D Tudhope(7) 5/2 FAV: 0003210: 15th: Dwelt, sn mid-div, prog when *1½* **32**
short of room bef 1f out, sn btn: well bckd: nvr able to get competitive: btr 2981.
2675 **LEOPARD CREEK 20** [13]3-9-4 p (55) D Allan 20/1: 0020200: 16th: Chsd ldrs 3f, sn wknd: btr 2326. *1¾* **36**
2219 **BURKEES GRAW 39** [12]3-8-10 (47) D Fentiman(7) 66/1: 0-000020: 17th: Rear, nvr a factor. *shd* **27**
2512 **JOHN OGROATS 26** [17]6-9-9 p (55) S W Kelly 9/1: 0000000: 18th: Mid-div 3f, sn wknd: tchd 12/1. *1½* **31**
2279 **Smirfys Night 36** [11]5-9-9 (55) J Fanning 50/1:0 2657 **Rum Destiny 21** [3]5-9-1 vis(47) L Enstone(3) 80/1:0
20 Ran Time 1m 05.25 (3.95) Owned: Mrs P Wake Trained: Malton

3181

4.15 119th Year Of The Watt Memorial Handicap Stakes 3yo+ 0-85 (D) **[85]**
£5587 £1719 £860 **2m35y** **Good/Soft 60** **-16 Slow** Inside

2754 **CLARINCH CLAYMORE 17** [6] J M Jefferson 8-9-0 (71) T Eaves(3) 7/2 JT FAV: 46-20531: Held up trav **76**
well, smooth prog & led dist, sn rdn & held on well: bckd: won this race last term off a 1lb lower mark: eff at 12f, suited by 14f/2m on fast, fibresand & likes gd/soft & soft grnd, handles any trk: v tough & genuine: see 1772.
3015 **OCEAN TIDE 6** [4] R Ford 7-8-13 vis (70) K Darley 11/2: 3440352: Sn handy & led after 2f, hdd *¾* **73**
dist, kept on for press: qck reapp: see 743.
3850} **CELTIC BLAZE 324** [9] B S Rothwell 5-7-13 t p (56) J Quinn 25/1: 613060-3: b f Charente River - *hd* **58**
Firdaunt (Tanfirion) Rear, hdwy when no room dist, switched & styd on: 8 wk jumps abs (h'cap hdle plcd, rtd 101h, eff at 2m on gd & soft, t-strap/chkpcs): h'cap scorer '03, AW rnr-up (rtd 57a, mdn): eff at 12/14f, stays stiff 2m well: acts on firm, gd/sft & fbsnd, any trk: poss a shade unlucky here.
1 Mar'03 Catt 13.8g/f 60-55 D: 2 Feb'03 Wolv 12af 57a- D:
3015 **VICARS DESTINY 6** [2] Mrs S Lamyman 6-8-8 (65) R Winston 11/1: 2200064: Dwelt, chsd ldrs wide, *½* **66**
chall 2f out, no extra cl-home: acts on firm & gd, enjoys give: did not get the run of today's race, see 1069.
1772 **ASTYANAX 59** [8]4-9-2 (73) J Mackay 8/1: 13241-05: b c Hector Protector - Craigmill (Slip Anchor) *shd* **73**
Trkd ldrs, drvn & no extra fnl 1f: 2 mth abs, op 5/1: AW h'cap & turf h'cap scorer in '03: unplcd '02 (rtd 57): winning form at 12f/14f, stays 2m well: acts on fast, gd/soft & fibresand, prob handles any trk & can go well fresh.
1 Aug'03 Yarm 14.1g/f 74-66 F: 2 May'03 Nott 14.1g/f 68-61 E: 1 May'03 Sout 12af 76a-55 F:
1581} **CONTACT DANCER 234** [3]5-10-0 (85) J Fanning 5/1: 3012/56-6: b g Sadler's Wells - Rain Queen *3½* **82**
(Rainbow Quest) Trkd ldr, rdn to chall over 2f out, no extra dist: reapp: unplcd '03, incl List race abroad (rtd 73, h'cap): progressive '02, landed 2 h'caps: eff at 14f/2m2f on fast, enjoys gd/soft & hvy grnd: acts on a gall or stiff/undul trk: prev with J L Dunlop.
2 Nov'02 Donc 16.5hvy 78-77 C: 1 Oct'02 Pont 17.9g/s 76-67 E: 1 May'02 Nott 14gd 67-58 E:
2673 **GREENWICH MEANTIME 20** [5]4-9-4 (75) L Goncalves 11/1: 0300307: Rear, hdwy 3f out, no prog dist. *nk* **70**
2941 **GALLEON BEACH 10** [1]7-8-9 (66) R Ffrench 50/1: 110/06-48: Handy, rdn & btn 2f out: btr 2941. *7* **55**
2557 **NESSEN DORMA 25** [7]3-8-7 (83) M Fenton 7/2 JT FAV: 5213309: Led 2f, lost place after 5f & no ch *1¾* **71**
4f out: reportedly lost a front shoe: see 2130 & 1708.
9 Ran Time 3m 42.46 (12.1) Owned: Mr John Donald Trained: Malton

3182

4.45 19 July Is Medieval Night Apprentice Handicap Stakes 3yo 35-55 (F) **[60]**
£3353 £958 £479 **1m100y rnd** **Good/Soft 60** **-04 Slow** Inside

4874} **BOPPYS PRINCESS 263** [1] R A Fahey 3-8-6 (38) T Hamilton 40/1: 060000-1: b f Wizard King - Laurel **46**
Queen (Viking) Rear, hdwy when no room over 1f out, switched & styd on strongly to lead well ins last: reapp: first success, unplcd in '03 (rtd 40, J S Wainwright, disapp in a visor): eff at 8.5f, could get further: acts on gd/soft grnd & goes well fresh: fine eff from difficult low draw.
2909 **FLYING SPUD 11** [13] J L Spearing 3-9-2 (48) D Nolan 8/1: 4510002: Handy, eff to chase ldr 3f *1* **53**
out, rdn & led over 1f out, hdd well ins last: eff around 1m/8.5f on soft & gd/soft grnd: see 1740 (sell h'cap).
3058 **GIVEN A CHANCE 5** [12] Mrs S Lamyman 3-9-0 (46) D Fentiman(5) 8/1: 3426063: Led & clr halfway, hdd *2½* **46**
over 1f out, kept on for press: qck reapp: see 1947, 1534 & 1250.
2552 **BORIS THE SPIDER 25** [14] M D Hammond 3-9-6 (52) Lisa Jones 13/2: 0-200554: Mid-div, nvr pace to *2½* **47**

BEVERLEY   TUESDAY 13.07.04   Righthand, Oval Track With Stiff Uphill Finish

chall: poss stays a stiff 8.5f, see 1426 (6f).

2834* **DELCIENNE 14** [11]3-9-2 (48) A Beech 6/1: 0030215: Rear, eff wide, late gains, nrst fin: btr 2834 (fm). ½ 42
2664 **JOEY PERHAPS 20** [2]3-9-4 (50) M Savage(3) 16/1: 450-0006: Reared & hmpd start, bhd, late gains ½ 43
for press, nrst fin: not disgraced from poor low draw: see 2664.
2812 **SCHINKEN OTTO 15** [4]3-9-0 (46) T Eaves 25/1: 060-067: Chsd ldr, btn over 1f out: see 2812. ¾ 37
2812 **KILLOCH PLACE 15** [5]3-8-8 vis (40) D Allan 12/1: 0000348: Mid-div, nvr able to chall: see 1395. 1 29
2932* **REVERSIONARY 10** [15]3-9-5 bl (51) P Mulrennan(3) 5/1 JT FAV: 0500019: Chsd ldrs, drvn & btn 2f out. 4 32
2982 **BONJOUR BOND 8** [7]3-9-5 bl (51) M Stainton(5) 14/1: 4003030: 10th: Mid-div, btn 3f out: btr 1630. 1¾ 28
1947 **A BIT OF FUN 50** [16]3-8-8 (40) D Tudhope(5) 5/1 JT FAV: 0-520100: 11th: Al bhd, op 8/1, abs: btr 1675. 5 7
2552 **ATHOLLBROSE 25** [3]3-9-6 BL (52) A Mullen(5) 10/1: 4245400: 12th: Went left start, mid-div, btn 2f 4 11
out: tried blnks: much btr 1834.
1591 **AIREDALE LAD 68** [9]3-8-1 (1oh) (32) Dean Williams(5) 66/1: 0-6450: 13th: Al rear: 10 wk abs. 1¼ 0
2944 **Cottam Karminski 10** [8]3-8-8 (40) L Enstone 50/1:0   1713 **Lenwade 61** [6]3-8-6 (38) P Makin(3) 20/1:0
15 Ran   Time 1m 49.20(5.4)   Owned: Mrs S Bond   Trained: Malton

KEMPTON   WEDNESDAY 14.07.04   Righthand, Flat, Fair Track

Official Going GOOD/FIRM (GOOD places).

3183	6.25 City & Suburban E B F Median Auction Maiden Stakes Fillies 2yo (E)				
	£4280 £1317 £659	6f str	Good 43	+02 Fast	Centre

2795 **MAGICAL ROMANCE 16** [1] B J Meehan 2-8-11 J Fortune 3/1 FAV: 41: Chsd ldrs stands side, imprvd 86
to lead that group 2f out & overall dist, styd on strongly, rdn out: well bckd, fast juv time: eff at 6f, 7f/1m
will suit given time: acts on gd grnd & on a flat trk: reportedly held in some regard, see 2795.
2815 **MISS MALONE 19** [12] R Hannon 2-8-11 R L Moore 11/2: 002: b f Daggers Drawn - Queen Molly 2½ 77
(Emarati) Chsd ldr far side, led 2f out till dist, kept on well but no ch with stands side wnr: tchd 7/1: £15,000
Feb first foal: sire a high-class juv: eff at 6f on gd grnd, handles a flat trk: shld find similar.
      WEDDING PARTY 4 [4] Mrs A J Perrett 2-8-11 K Fallon 4/1: 3: ch f Groom Dancer - Ceanothus 1¾ 72
(Bluebird) Chsd ldrs stands side, onepcd fnl 1f on debut: March foal, half-sister to 1m wnr Prince Hector: dam
stayed 12f: eff at 6f on grd gnrd, 7f will now suit: ran green today, encouraging first effort.
2658 **AZUREE 21** [13] R Hannon 2-8-11 BL R Hughes 14/1: 26304: Led far side till 2f out, no extra: shd 72
tried blnks & longer priced stablemate of rnr-up: twice below 2399 (fast grnd).
      CROCODILE KISS [5]2-8-11 L Dettori 9/1: 5: b f Rossini - Pipe Opener (Prince Sabo) Bmpd shd 72
start, recovered to chase ldrs stands side, not qckn fnl 1f on debut: op 6/1: £40,000 March foal: half sister to
wnrs over 5f/1m: dam stayed 7f: sire a high-class juv: with J Osborne.
      TOFFEE VODKA [10]2-8-11 M Hills 20/1: 6: b f Danehill Dancer - Vieux Carre (Pas de Seul) 2 66
Slowly away stands side, styd on late, nvr dngrs on debut: April foal, cost £9,000: half-sister to wnrs over 5/7f:
sire a smart sprinter: with J Hills.
2795 **MABELLA 16** [2]2-8-11 S Drowne 20/1: 057: Front rank stands side, wknd 1.5f out. 5 51
2658 **GOLD MAJESTY 21** [14]2-8-11 C Catlin 50/1: 08: Al outpcd far side. 2 45
      MOLLY DANCER [3]2-8-11 T E Durcan 13/2: 9: Led stands side till bef halfway, wknd: bckd. shd 45
2587 **ELIZABETHS CHOICE 25** [7]2-8-11 P Robinson 20/1: 00: 10th: Chsd ldrs 4f stands side. 1 42
      ROCKYS GIRL [9]2-8-11 D Bolye 50/1: 0: 11th: Led early stands side, sn lost pl & bhd on debut. 1½ 38
2870 **Bint II Sultan 13** [6]2-8-11 E Ahern 20/1:0   2310 **Mystery Maid 35** [11]2-8-11 D Kinsella 66/1:0
13 Ran   Time 1m 13.59 (2.49)   Owned: Mr F C T Wilson   Trained: Upper Lambourn

3184	6.55 Newton Investment Management Handicap Stakes 3yo+ 0-70 (E)				[70]
	£4280 £1317 £659	7f Jub	Good 43	-04 Slow	Inside

2768 **BALERNO 18** [13] R Ingram 5-8-12 (54) N Day 12/1: 2304021: Mid-div, hdwy to lead dist, ran on 63
strongly, drvn out: deserved win, plcd several times recently: eff at 7/10f on gd, fast grnd & on both AWs:
handles any trk, has tried a selection of headgear: see 2768 & 408.
3165 **JONNY EBENEEZER 2** [8] D Flood 5-9-6 (6ex)bl (62) R Smith 9/2 CO FAV: 1031022: Mid-div, prog 2f 1¼ 57
out, styd on well fnl 1f but not quite reach wnr: bckd from 7/1: 4th run in 9 days & remains in fine form.
2752 **OASES 18** [4] D Shaw 5-8-12 vis (54) S Whitworth 40/1: 2060003: Dwelt, hdwy from rear 2f out, ¾ 56
switched & fin strongly, nvr btr: fine run from this outsider, on a fair mark now: see 976 & 940.
3102 **FEN GYPSY 4** [10] P D Evans 6-9-3 (59) F P Ferris(3) 9/2 CO FAV: 1245124: Held up, imprvd halfway, 1 60
onepcd fnl 1f: nicely bckd, rckd reapp: btr 3102 & 3034.
2855 **COLD CLIMATE 14** [16]9-8-13 (55) O Urbina 11/1: 521-0405: Front rank, led 2f out till dist, no ½ 55
extra: op 8/1: reportedly wants easier grnd: see 1010 (AW).
2975 **SUPER SONG 9** [17]4-9-2 (58) R Mullen 50/1: 0000006: Chsd ldrs, wknd fnl 1f. 1 55
2920 **MISTRAL SKY 11** [1]5-9-10 vis (66) S Drowne 14/1: 0433547: Chsd ldrs, wknd dist: btr 2920. hd 64
2855 **CHARLOTTEBUTTERFLY 14** [2]4-8-13 (55) J F McDonald(3) 25/1: 353-0408: Held up, no prog, nvr dngrs. 1¾ 49
3102 **ICED DIAMOND 4** [11]5-8-12 (54) T E Durcan 16/1: 0-100009: Chsd ldrs, no room dist, no ch after: ½ 47
qck reapp: worth forgiving this, see 558 (AW).
1282 **ARTISTRY 85** [6]4-9-4 (60) J Fortune 14/1: 540-1500: 10th: Chsd ldrs, wknd 1.5f out: 12 wk abs. nk 52
2799 **EL CHAPARRAL 16** [9]4-9-7 (63) Dane O'Neill 10/1: 3/-060020: 11th: Nvr btr than mid-div: 'too keen'. ½ 54
2394 **SWIFT ALCHEMIST 32** [12]4-9-3 (59) G Baker 14/1: 00-00300: 12th: Chsd ldrs 5.5f: btr 1537 (hvy). 4 42
2799 **FLORIAN 16** [15]6-9-5 p (61) K Fallon 9/2 CO FAV: 1133-000: 13th: Led 2f out, eased & eased: ½ 43
well bckd: much btr expected, see 2799.
1131 **SISTER SOPHIA 93** [14]4-9-9 (65) G Carter 33/1: 20060-00: 14th: b f Deputy Commander - Sophia's 5 37
Choice (Clev Er Tell) Slowly away, al bhd: 3 mth abs: failed to win in '03, plcd 3 times in early season mdns (G
Wragg): eff at 6/7f on gd, firm grnd & polytrack: has tried cheek pieces, btr without:
2 May'03 Ches 7.0fm 73- D: 2 Nov'02 Ling 6ap 77a- D:
2768 **Logistical 18** [7]4-9-0 T(56) D Sweeney 20/1:0   2880 **Night Wolf 13** [5]4-9-9 (65) L Harman(7) 33/1:0
16 Ran   Time 1m 27.52 (3.32)   Owned: The Three Amigos   Trained: Epsom

KEMPTON WEDNESDAY 14.07.04 Righthand, Flat, Fair Track

3185 7.25 Toteexacta Stakes Handicap 3yo+ 0-90 (C) [90]
£9737 £2996 £1498 1m2f Good 43 -03 Slow Inside

2860* **SPANISH DON 14** [8] D R C Elsworth 6-9-12 (88) L Keniry(3) 6/1: 41-00511: Held up, imprvd 2f out, short of room ent fnl 1f, switched & fin well, led cl-home, going away: nicely bckd: eff at 1m/9f on fast & soft grnd: in fine form, clearly loves Kempton, has a turn of foot & can complete hat-trick. **100**
2694+ **HAWRIDGE PRINCE 20** [10] L G Cottrell 4-10-0 (90) L Dettori 9/4 FAV: 0312-112: Rear, imprvd to chall dist, led ent fnl 1f till caught cl-home: hvly bckd, jt top-weight, clr of rem: fine run on hat-trick bid. *nk* **99**
3039 **KARAOKE 7** [12] S Kirk 4-8-5 (67) R L Moore 20/1: 4220003: Rear, imprvd to chase ldrs when short of room 2f out, sn lost place, rallied cl-home but ch had gone: hinted at a return to form here, see 2067 (10f here). *5* **68**
2560 **SAY WHAT YOU SEE 25** [6] J W Hills 4-8-10 vis (72) M Hills 14/1: 1542204: Nvr far away, led 2f out till dist, no extra: see 2363. *nk* **72**
2185 **OFARABY 41** [7]4-10-0 (90) P Robinson 8/1: 4-316425: Keen & chsd ldrs, btn fnl 1f: 6 wk abs, jt top-weight: just btr 2185 (10f, gd/soft). *¾* **88**
2787 **KRUGERRAND 17** [4]5-9-8 (84) G Carter 12/1: 0000136: Chsd ldrs wide, btn 2f out: btr 2404. *4* **76**
2185 **LIQUID FORM 41** [5]4-9-7 (83) R Hughes 10/1: 4013-007: Dwelt, hdwy from rear when short of room 2f out, sn btn: 6 wk abs: see 2185. *1* **73**
2860 **GUILDED FLYER 14** [11]5-9-11 (87) W Supple 9/1: 00-01038: Chsd ldrs, led 3f out till 2f out, wkng when hmpd dist: tchd 12/1: btr 2860. *1¾* **74**
2860 **GIOCOSO 14** [2]4-9-4 (80) K Darley 25/1: 2060-609: Led till 3f out, wknd: see 2223. *1½* **65**
2840* **INVADER 14** [1]8-9-2 bl t (78) S Sanders 20/1: 0600010: 10th: Nvr a factor: btr 2840 (AW). *3* **58**
2874 **ARRY DASH 13** [3]4-9-3 (79) T E Durcan 16/1: 2003060: 11th: Al bhd. *1¾* **57**
2099 **DREAM MAGIC 44** [9]6-8-13 (75) B Doyle 8/1: 44-40500: 12th: Chsd ldrs till halfway, sn btn & t.o. *dist* **18**
12 Ran Time 2m 06.90 (4.60) Owned: Mr Richard J Cohen Trained: Whitsbury

3186 7.55 Royal British Legion Maiden Stakes 3yo (D)
£5707 £1756 £878 1m2f Good 43 -07 Slow Inside

DEEP PURPLE [10] M P Tregoning 3-9-0 Martin Dwyer 12/1: 1: b g Halling - Seal Indigo (Glenstal) Slow away, prog halfway, styd on to lead ins fnl 1f, pushed out to hold on despite edging right: debut: cost 40,000gns: dam mid-dist wnr: eff at 10f, 12f+ shld suit: acts on gd grnd & goes well fresh. **86**
1959 **PLUMMET 51** [9] J H M Gosden 3-8-9 R Hughes 3/1: 42: Cl-up, styd on to lead 2f out, hdd ins fnl 1f, kept on, just held by wnr: 7 wk abs: bckd from 9/2: eff at 10f, worth a try over further: acts on fast & gd grnd: shown enough to find similar & a game run here: see 1959. *hd* **80**
2700 **DUNDRY 20** [3] G L Moore 3-9-0 R L Moore 14/1: 0-33: Handy, kept on ins fnl 2f, no ch with front 2: encourgaging eff & now quals for h'caps: see 2700. *3½* **80**
2534 **TASHREEFAT 26** [15] A C Stewart 3-8-9 R Hills 7/1: 34: Handy over 1m, sn no extra: see 2534. *3½* **70**
2843 **SAFIRAH 14** [13]3-8-9 P Robinson 14/1: 35: Rear, prog ins fnl 3f, nrst fin: see 2843. *1¾* **68**
2700 **MICHABO 20** [2]3-9-0 (80) T Quinn 11/4 FAV: 0-4326: Led 1m, sn wknd: bckd from 4/1: better expected after promise shown in 2700 & 2453. *2* **70**
3038 **PERSIAN GENIE 7** [14]3-8-9 S Drowne 25/1: 0-007: Rear, prog after 6f, wknd dist: qck reapp. *½* **64**
2751 **SINGLET 18** [11]3-9-0 M Fenton 14/1: 0-08: ch c Singspiel - Ball Gown (Jalmood) In tch over 7f, sn wknd: op 25/1: unplcd sole '03 start (rtd 70, mdn, H J Collingridge). *nk* **68**
2013 **SAFA PARK 49** [4]3-9-0 T L Dettori 8/1: 09: Handy 7f, sn wknd: 7 wk abs & t-strap. *nk* **67**
CUGINA NICOLA [7]3-8-9 R Havlin 66/1: 0: 10th: b f Nicolotte - Cugina (Distant Relative) In rear when jmpd path at halfway, nvr a factor: debut: with G Balding. *2½* **58**
CHARMED BY FIRE [6]3-9-0 K Darley 12/1: 0: 11th: b c Silver Charm - Mama Dean (Woodman) Mid-div, prog after halfway, fdd 2f out: op 8/1 on debut. *¾* **62**
ANNA GAYLE [5]3-8-9 Dane O'Neill 33/1: 0: 12th: Slow away, nvr nrr than mid-div. *12* **39**
ORATION [8]3-9-0 K Fallon 12/1: 0: 13th: Rear, nvr a factor: op 8/1 on debut. *dist* **0**
13 Ran Time 2m 07.32 (5.02) Owned: Byculla Thoroughbreds Trained: Lambourn

3187 8.25 Leonard Curtis 'floating Charge' Handicap Stakes 3yo+ 0-75 (E) [74]
£4261 £1311 £656 1m1f Good 43 -02 Slow Outside

3039 **FREELOADER 7** [2] J W Hills 4-9-12 (72) R Hills 7/2: 60-04301: Held up, prog halfway, styd on to lead dist, rdn out: tchd 11/2 on qck reapp: suited by around 9/10f on fast, gd/soft & polytrack: see 3039 & 2401. **81**
2904 **PELLA 12** [7] M Blanshard 3-8-4 (60) F Norton 9/1: 0062532: Sn short of room, prog when short of room again 3f out, styd on well ins fnl 1f, post came too sn: eff at 1m/9f, worth another try over further: gd run in defeat & is worth keeping in mind for similar: see 2904. *1* **66**
2979 **TODLEA 9** [13] J A Osborne 4-9-11 (71) L Dettori 11/4 FAV: 4436223: Led, hdd dist, kept on, just held for 2nd: op 9/2: continues to peform with credit: see 2979 & 2067. *hd* **77**
2799 **MY MAITE 16** [12] R Ingram 5-8-0 t p (46) C Catlin 33/1: 4001604: Slow away, prog fnl 2f, nrst fin. *1½* **50**
3102 **PAS DE SURPRISE 4** [15]6-8-7 (53) F P Ferris(3) 7/1: 4005445: Handy, onepcd from dist: qck reapp. *nk* **56**
1013 **INDIAN BLAZE 105** [6]10-8-4 (50) T P Queally 33/1: 1203606: Held up, prog 3f out, kept on fnl 1f. *hd* **52**
2973 **RAINBOW WORLD 9** [3]4-8-13 p (59) J F Egan 20/1: 3003037: In tch, no extra dist: btr 2973 (fm). *1½* **58**
4789] **LAWRENCE OF ARABIA 620** [9]4-8-12 (58) S Sanders 10/1: 004/-8: b g Desert King - Cumbres (Kahyasi) Slow away, nvr nrr than mid-div: op 11/2 on reapp: missed '03: unplcd in 3 '02 starts (rtd 67 & 43a, mdns): shld do better over further for shrewd stable. *nk* **56**
2931 **JOHANNIAN 11** [8]6-9-12 (72) R L Moore 10/1: 0035029: Held up, prog 4f out, no impress fnl 2f. *½* **69**
3099 **GIUNCHIGLIO 4** [14]5-9-4 (64) K Fallon 9/1: 0-310360: 10th: Mid-div, prog 4f out, onepcd dist. *nk* **60**
2840 **RECOUNT 14** [16]4-9-10 (70) N Pollard 33/1: 0-006500: 11th: Handy 7f, sn wknd: btr 1296. *2½* **62**
2971* **RIDGE BOY 9** [11]3-9-3 (6ex) (73) P Dobbs 14/1: 56010: 12th: In tch when short of room over 4f out, short of room again & lost place 2f out, modest late gains: not get run of race: btr 2971. *1½* **62**
2857 **Deeper In Debt 14** [17]6-9-2 (62) G Carter 25/1:0 922} **Polish Spirit 470** [4]9-9-5 (65) T Quinn 33/1:0
3039 **Learned Lad 7** [1]6-8-7 (53) P Doe 50/1:0
1938 **Costa Del Sol 52** [10]3-7-12 (14oh)(40) J F McDonald(3) 66/1:0
16 Ran Time 1m 54.11 (4.11) Owned: Scott Hardy Partnership Trained: Lambourn

KEMPTON   WEDNESDAY 14.07.04   Righthand, Flat, Fair Track

3188   8.55 Firework Finale Classified Stakes 3yo 0-80 (D)
£5421 £1668 £834   **6f str**   **Good 43**   +06 Fast   Centre

2797* **RED ROMEO** 16 [1] G A Swinbank 3-9-4 (84) K Fallon 11/4 FAV: 6-244111: Held up, prog halfway, **93**
styd on to lead dist, drvn out: well bckd: eff at 6f, stays 7f well: acts on fast & gd/soft grnd: progressive.
2841* **INSTANT RECALL** 14 [10] B J Meehan 3-9-0 bl (78) J Fortune 10/1: 0454512: Chsd ldrs, styd on to   1¼   **83**
chase wnr ins fnl 1f, kept on but al held: continues to run well: btr 2841 (polytrack).
2387 **BORZOI MAESTRO** 32 [3] J L Spearing 3-9-0 p (76) Lisa Jones(3) 33/1: 0-231043: Led till dist, no extra.   1¾   **78**
2950 **CELTIC THUNDER** 11 [7] T J Etherington 3-9-4 (84) E Ahern 16/1: 2050204: Nvr nrr than mid div.   1½   **78**
2797 **VIENNAS BOY** 16 [4]3-9-3 (83) Dane O'Neill 14/1: 6460525: Handy, outpcd halfway, rallied late.   1   **74**
3033 **THE JOBBER** 7 [9]3-9-2 (82) F Norton 11/2: 021-406: Handy till dist, sn wknd: qck reapp: btr 2677.   ½   **72**
1933+ **BUY ON THE RED** 53 [5]3-9-4 (84) R Mullen 5/1: 24-22117: Slow away, nvr nrr than mid-div: 8 wk   ½   **73**
abs: disapp on bid for hat-trick: btr 1933 & 1690.
2797 **BATHWICK BILL** 16 [2]3-9-1 (81) G Baker 12/1: 30-06238: Handy 4f, sn wknd: btr 2797 & 1901.   3½   **60**
2482 **SNOW WOLF** 28 [6]3-9-1 (81) R L Moore 25/1: 23-01209: Mid-div till halfway, sn wknd.   2½   **53**
2877 **TAAQAAH** 13 [8]3-9-1 (81) Martin Dwyer 7/2: 62-220: 10th: Handy 4f, fdd: well bckd: v   7   **33**
disappointing on drop to 6f: btr 2877 (1m) & 2463 (7f).
10 Ran   Time 1m 13.37(2.27)   Owned: Mr J Yates   Trained: Richmond

---

CATTERICK   WEDNESDAY 14.07.04   Lefthand, Undulating, Very Tight Track

Official Going Good/Firm

3189   2.30 Middleham Suite Novice Auction Stakes 2yo (F)
£3455 £1063 £532   **7f rnd**   **Good/Firm 40**   -02 Slow   Inside

2569* **LAMH EILE** 25 [7] T D Barron 2-8-7 N Mackay(3) 1/1 FAV: 11: In tch, gd hdwy to lead over 1f out,   **91+**
qcknd clr, v readily: bckd: stays a sharp 7f well, 1m sure to suit: acts on fast, gd/soft & prob any trk:
potentially smart & one to keep on your side at present: see 2569.
2776 **COLEORTON DANE** 17 [2] K A Ryan 2-8-6 N Callan 9/4: 632: Made most till appr fnl 1f, not pace of   5   **75**
impressive wnr: well bckd: rangy, padd pick: encouraging run, caught a decent sort & shld find at least a mdn.
2612* **SOCIETY MUSIC** 23 [6] M Dods 2-9-1 L Enstone(3) 4/1: 1313: With ldr, eff to chall over 1f out,   2   **78**
hung right dist, no extra: prob ran to form of 2612 having to concede plenty of weight here.
2810* **MOUNT EPHRAM** 16 [9] R F Fisher 2-8-12 BL R Winston 16/1: 456414: Slow away, sn in tch, hung left   shd   **75**
& onepace over 1f out: up in class & tried blnks: see 2810 (cheek pieces, mdn auct).
2100 **UREDALE** 44 [1]2-8-8 M Tebbutt 66/1: 5065: Sn bhd, nvr a factor: 6 wk abs, see 2100.   3½   **61**
2275 **HARBOUR LEGEND** 37 [5]2-8-1 J Bramhill 66/1: 06: b f Dansili - English Harbour (Sabrehill) Al   7   **34**
bhd: lkd burly: March first foal, cost £8,000: dam 10f scorer.
2682 **FILEY BUOY** 20 [3]2-8-6 Dean McKeown 66/1: 07: b g Factual - Tugra (Baby Turk) Al bhd: btr for   1½   **35**
race: May foal, cheaply bght: dam plcd over hdles: bred to need 1m+.
7 Ran   Time 1m 25.98 (2.98)   Owned: Oghill House Stud   Trained: Thirsk

3190   3.00 Malton Suite Claiming Stakes 3yo+ (F)
£3484 £1072 £536   **1m3f214y**   **Good/Firm 40**   -26 Slow   Inside

3490} **PETERS IMP** 340 [12] A Berry 9-10-0 (25) P Mathers(7) 33/1: 560/000-1: Hld up, gd hdwy to lead   **55**
appr fnl 1f, styd on, rdn out: 03/04 sell h'cap hdle wnr (rtd 80h, 2m1f/2m6f on fast & gd): mod Flat form last term,
rnr-up in '02: stays 12f on fm & fast, handles soft & fibresand: eff with/without blnks: runs well fresh.
2966 **BALALAIKA TUNE** 9 [10] W Storey 5-8-13 T (28) J Bramhill 9/1: 0046032: Chsd ldrs, hdwy to lead 2f   1¼   **37**
out, rdn & hdd appr fnl 1f, not pace of wnr: fair run in first time t-strap but remains a mdn after 19: see 2966.
2653 **AL AZHAR** 22 [2] M Dods 10-9-8 (60) S W Kelly 7/1: 0/453-633: Held up, eff 2f out, sn onepcd.   ¾   **45**
2891 **CELTIC ROMANCE** 12 [8] Mrs M Reveley 5-9-1 (44) J Carroll 7/1: 0050604: Held up, eff over 1f out,   2½   **34**
sn no extra: see 2508, 1348.
2963 **LORD LAMB** 10 [5]12-9-10 (60) Neil Brown(7) 7/1: 014-3405: Slow away, sn handy, wknd over 3f out.   7   **33**
2850 **RIGHTY HO** 14 [11]10-9-8 (44) R Winston 4/1 FAV: 00-13306: In tch, wknd 2f out: btr 1946, 1449.   nk   **30**
2548 **FACE THE LIMELIGHT** 26 [9]5-9-8 (62) G Faulkner 9/2: 5050-067: In tch, wknd 2f out: see 2548.   ¾   **29**
3564} **MARTON MERE** 336 [1]8-9-6 (36) A Mullen(7) 33/1: 4060/40-8: ch g Cadeaux Genereux - Hyatti   nk   **26**
(Habitat) In tch, wknd over 2f out: well btn both '03 starts: rnr-up in a sell h'cap back in '01: stays 8.5f on
fast & gd grnd, likes Beverley.   2 Jul'01 Beve 7.4g/f 48-45 F:
2850 **NATMSKY** 14 [3]5-9-4 (30) P Mulrennan(5) 66/1: 00/000-09: b g Shadeed - Cockney Lass (Camden Town)5   **17**
Nvr a factor: well btn sole '03 start: poor form prev in blnks & a visor.
2 Dec'01 Sout 6af 68a-68 D: 2 Dec'01 Wolv 7af 69a- F:
2813 **HIBERNATE** 16 [4]10-9-10 (39) T Eaves(3) 6/1: 265/-0640: 10th: With ldr, led 2f out, sn hdd & wknd.   ¾   **22**
2937 **MIKASA** 11 [6]4-9-6 (30) D Nolan(3) 50/1: 0300500: 11th: Slt lead till 2f out, wknd: went off too fast?   4   **12**
11 Ran   Time 2m 39.16 (7.96)   Owned: Ian & Arthur Bolland   Trained: Cockerham

3191   3.30 Luncheon Suite Selling Stakes 3yo+ (G)
£2996 £856 £428   **5f212y rnd**   **Good/Firm 40**   +09 Fast   Inside

2712 **TANCRED TIMES** 20 [4] D W Barker 9-8-9 (55) L Enstone(3) 11/4 FAV: 0440331: Made virtually all,   **51**
edged right just ins last but kept on well, drvn out: well bckd, no bid: stays 7f, suited by forcing tactics at
5/6f: likes firm & fast grnd, handles hvy & fibresand, any trk: v tough, relished drop into lowest grade.
2852 **WARES HOME** 14 [3] K R Burke 3-8-8 (55) Darren Williams 6/1: 6034332: Cl-up, eff to chall over 1f   shd   **55**
out, kept on ins last, just held: could find a sell h'cap: see 2852 (7f), 2541.
2928 **LOUGHLORIEN** 11 [2] R A Fahey 5-9-0 (44) T Hamilton(3) 7/1: 6-000003: Chsd ldrs, hdwy & short of   ¾   **53**
room appr fnl 1f, kept on ins last, not btn far: more encouraging drpd in class & will apprec sell h'caps.

CATTERICK   WEDNESDAY 14.07.04   Lefthand, Undulating, Very Tight Track

2702	**PORT ST CHARLES** 20 [13] C R Dore 7-9-0 (60) R Thomas(5) 6/1: 0430004: Chsd ldrs, onepace.	2	46
3129	**OLD BAILEY** 4 [6]4-9-6 bl (45) P Makin(5) 12/1: 0100055: Chsd ldrs, onepace dist: see 3129, 2204.	1¾	48
3104	**ZIETZIG** 4 [14]7-9-0 (42) Alex Greaves 8/1: 0000056: In tch, eff 2f out, sn no extra: see 3104.	nk	41
2214	**MISTER MAL** 40 [1]8-9-6 bl e (54) T Eaves(3) 9/1: 53-06107: Slow away, sn in tch, wknd dist: abs.	2½	40
2999	**ONLY ONE LEGEND** 8 [8]6-9-6 bl (52) N Callan 12/1: 3031508: Held up, wknd 2f out: see 2337 (a/w).	nk	39
2928	**DANAKIM** 11 [11]7-9-6 bl e (42) D Fentiman(7) 33/1: 0150009: Keen held up, wknd 2f out: see 1988.	hd	38
2969	**BARGAIN HUNT** 9 [12]3-8-8 vis (46) J Bramhill 50/1: 0200360: 10th: Bhd, no impress.	1¼	28
3017	**GIVE HIM CREDIT** 7 [5]4-9-0 p (60) M Tebbutt 14/1: 400-5000: 11th: In tch, wknd 2f out: see 3017.	1½	28
3000	**INDIAN MUSIC** 8 [7]7-9-6 (46) P Mathers(7) 25/1: 3246200: 12th: Al bhd: see 2806, 982.	2	24
3133	**AGUILERA** 4 [10]3-8-5 (2ow) (43) S W Kelly 40/1: 00-00040: 13th: Cl-up, wknd 2f out: see 3133.	1¼	11
2808	**SALONIKA SKY** 16 [9]3-8-3 (35) J McAuley 100/1: 00-06060: 14th: Al bhd: see 2808.	nk	8

14 Ran   Time 1m 12.19 (1.89)   Owned: Mr D W Barker   Trained: Richmond

---

3192   4.00 Book Your Raceday Hospitality On 01777 247103 Handicap Stakes 3yo 0-70 (E)   [77]
£4193 £1290 £645   1m3f214y   Good/Firm 40   -07 Slow   Inside

2901	**ILE FACILE** 12 [4] N P Littmoden 3-9-5 t (68) J Fanning 7/1: 4102041: Made all, held on well for press fnl 2f: prev eff at 6f, now suited by 10/12f: acts on both AWs, fast & gd grnd, sharp/undul or stiff trk: suited by reapp of t-strap today & enjoyed forcing the pace: tough & genuine: see 2901, 2277 & 706.		76
4530}	**OUR EMMY LOU** 288 [1] Sir Mark Prescott 3-8-10 (59) J Mackay 6/1: 066-2: ch f Mark of Esteem – Regent's Folly (Touching Wood) Handy & chsd wnr 4f out, drvn & kept on, al held: h'cap bow, lkd fit on reapp, bckd tho' op 4/1: unplcd up to 1m in '03 (rtd 68, mdn): stays 12f, further may suit: handles fast grnd: cld find similar.	¾	65
2322	**SAVANNAH RIVER** 35 [5] C W Thornton 3-7-12 (5oh)t (42) J McAuley 33/1: 0-032543: Mid-div, rdn & styd on fnl 2f, not pace to chall: stays 12f, worth another try at 14f+: acts on fast & soft grnd: see 1528, 1240.	2	50
2621	**INCHPACE** 23 [10] M H Tompkins 3-8-6 BL (55) N Callan 25/1: 050-004: ch c Inchinor – Victor Ludorum (Rainbow Quest) Mid-div & keen, eff 3f out, kept on onepace: first time blnks: unplcd prev, incl '03 (rtd 57 & 69a, mdn): prob stays a sharp 12f on fast grnd: imprvd in headgear.	nk	57
2842	**LA PETITE CHINOISE** 14 [3]3-9-7 (70) J Carroll 6/1: 6-604225: Held up in tch, drvn & kept on, nvr pace to threaten: bckd, op 8/1: worth a try at 14f+: see 2842 & 2478.	1½	70
3051	**VICARIO** 6 [9]3-8-12 (61) Hayley Turner(5) 11/4 FAV: 0-513326: Held up, eff 2f out, hung badly left under press & no prog dist: btr 3051, 2528 & 2164.	2½	57
2984	**SIEGFRIEDS NIGHT** 9 [14]3-9-2 (65) C Haddon(7) 8/1: 1335537: Mid-div, btn 2f out: btr 2984.	3½	56
2124	**BAY SOLITAIRE** 43 [7]3-7-13 (48) P M Quinn 50/1: 000-68: b g Charnwood Forest – Golden Wings (Devil's Bag) Slow away & bhd, nvr a factor: abs: unplcd up to 1m in '03 (rtd 47, mdn): dam a smart 10f wnr.	5	32
2299	**EGO TRIP** 36 [12]3-8-5 (54) Dale Gibson 9/1: 000-0139: Slow away & sn pushed along, al rear.	12	20
2930	**IMPERIAL ROYALE** 11 [13]3-8-13 (62) M Halford(7) 33/1: 052-5060: 10th: Chsd ldrs, wknd qckly 2f out.	2	25
2510	**BARTON FLOWER** 27 [11]3-7-12 (47) P Fessey 66/1: 00-0000: 11th: Al bhd, longer trip.	3	6
2523	**JALOUSIE DREAM** 27 [6]3-7-13 (1ow) (47) R Ffrench 40/1: 0530: 12th: Prom till halfway: h'cap bow.	3½	2
2804	**HOLLY WALK** 16 [8]3-8-1 p (50) A Nicholls 9/1: 2554320: 13th: Cl-up, rdn & lost place from 4f out, eased ins last: consistent prev: see 2804, 2503 & 2299.	nk	3
2353	**FIRE FINCH** 34 [2]3-9-6 (69) A Culhane 20/1: 66060: 14th: Mid-div, btn 3f out: flattered 1733.	7	12

14 Ran   Time 2m 36.89 (5.69)   Owned: Mr Paul J Dixon   Trained: Newmarket

---

3193   4.30 Richmond Suite Handicap Stakes 3yo 0-75 (E)   [78]
£4183 £1287 £644   5f rnd   Good/Firm 40   -14 Slow   Inside

2961*	**NANNA** 10 [2] R Hollinshead 3-9-0 (6ex) (64) A Culhane 4/1 FAV: 0216211: Made all, held on well for press: nicely bckd, op 5/1: stays 6f, 5f specialist on fast, gd/soft & fibresand, prob any trk: loves to force the pace: tough & genuine, progressive profile: see 2961, 1787.		71
2961	**SIR LOIN** 10 [3] N Tinkler 3-8-5 (55) Kim Tinkler 12/1: 600-0052: Al handy, rdn & chall dist, edged right & not pace of wnr: acts on fast & gd/soft grnd, imprvd of late & could find a race: see 2961 & 2227.	¾	60
3131	**OBE BOLD** 4 [6] A Berry 3-8-7 (57) P Mathers(7) 9/1: 0015043: Dwelt, held up in tch, switched & styd on for press, not able to chall: qck reapp: see 2493 (6f, AW clmr).	nk	61
2961	**SHORT CHORUS** 10 [8] J Balding 3-8-0 p (50) Dale Gibson 5/1: 0-040124: Chsd ldrs, onepace: also bhd today's wnr in 2961, see 1605.	½	52
2692	**HARRINGTON BATES** 20 [1]3-9-0 (64) Dean McKeown 9/2: 4605: Chsd ldrs, onepace dist: h'cap bow.	½	64
3018*	**WENDYS GIRL** 7 [7]3-8-12 (6ex)bl (62) T Hamilton(3) 10/1: P401016: Dwelt & held up, kept on late, not pace to chall: return to 6f & forcing tactics shld suit: see 3018.	shd	61
2029	**SEA FERN** 48 [9]3-8-0 (50) P Fessey 40/1: 000-507: Dwelt & rear, kept on late for press: abs.	3½	39
2731*	**ICENASLICE** 19 [13]3-9-2 (66) P Mulrennan(5) 13/2: 46-01418: Chsd ldrs, btn dist: btr 2731.	½	53
5015}	**FIRST ECLIPSE** 251 [10]3-8-3 (53) J Edmunds 50/1: 154600-9: b f Fayruz – Naked Poser (Night Shift) Mid-div, no impress halfway: reapp: '03 auct mdn scorer, subs disapp in blnks: eff over a sharp 5f on firm. 1 Jun'03 Muss 5fm 66- E:	nk	39
2961	**ISLAND SPELL** 10 [5]3-9-4 (68) A Mullen(7) 20/1: 63-35300: 10th: Sn rdn rear, no prog: see 2728.	¾	52
2784*	**SCOTTISH EXILE** 17 [12]3-9-7 (71) Darren Williams 8/1: 3100210: 11th: Reluctant to enter stalls, dwelt, mid-div, btn dist: much btr 2784.	1½	51
2778	**MOUSEMAN** 17 [4]3-8-5 (55) S W Kelly 40/1: 0310-500: 12th: Sn bhd, eased dist: see 1942.	14	7

12 Ran   Time 1m 0.00 (2.7)   Owned: Mrs G A Weetman   Trained: Upper Longdon

---

3194   5.00 Paddock Suite Median Auction Maiden Stakes 3yo (F)
£3455 £1063 £532   7f rnd   Good/Firm 40   -14 Slow   Inside

3663}	**LISTEN TO REASON** 333 [5] J G Given 3-9-0 A Culhane 9/2: 50-1: b c Mukaddamah – Tenalist (Tenby) Led/dsptd lead throughout, narrowly asserted ins last, drvn out, gamely: reapp: lightly rcd & mdn unplcd '03 (rtd 66, debut): apprec step up to 7f, fm could suit: acts on fast grnd & a sharp/turning trk: goes well fresh.		65
2778	**ONE UPMANSHIP** 17 [7] J G Portman 3-9-0 (64) N Callan 15/8: 0-000632: Al cl-up/dsptd lead, rdn & ev ch ins last, just held: nicely bckd: confirmed prog of 2778 (clmr).	nk	64
2728	**FESTIVE CHIMES** 19 [1] J Quinn 3-8-9 R Winston 14/1: 03: In tch, eff to chase front pair 2f out, al held: op 11/1, still ndd this, clr of rem: stays 7f on fast, 1m may suit: going the right way.	1¾	55
2961	**ROYAL AWAKENING** 10 [3] R E Barr 3-9-0 (55) T Eaves(3) 20/1: 30-004: Drvn rear, mod prog, no dngr.	5	50
2728	**BRAIN WASHED** 19 [9]3-8-9 (72) D Allan 7/4 FAV: 0425: Chsd ldrs, outpcd 2f out: nicely bckd.	1	43

966

CATTERICK WEDNESDAY 14.07.04 Lefthand, Undulating, Very Tight Track

2428 **COMIC TALES 31** [2]3-9-0 S Righton 14/1: 0-66: b g Mind Games - Glorious Aragon (Aragon) Rear,   nk   47
rdn & btn 2f out: lightly rcd & mod form to date.
4707} **RUSTY BOY 275** [1]3-9-0 L Enstone(3) 40/1: 60-7: b g Defacto - Berl's Gift (Prince Sabo) Trkd   6   35
ldrs, btn 2f out: reapp: unplcd both '03 starts (rtd 44, mdn).
7 Ran   Time 1m 26.78(3.78)   Owned: Mike Beadle and John Furness   Trained: Gainsborough

LINGFIELD Polytrack WEDNESDAY 14.07.04 Lefthand, V Sharp Track

Official Going Standard

3195
1.50 Dormansland Median Auction Maiden Stakes Div 1 3-4yo (F)
£2919 £834 £417   **1m aw rnd**   **Going 38**   **-01 Slow**   Outside

2231 **NORDWIND 40** [6] P W Harris 3-8-12 T Quinn 11/8: 341: Chsd ldrs, rdn to chase ldr over 2f out,   82a+
led over 1f out, going away: op 7/4: abs: eff at 1m, further shld suit: acts on fast, gd/soft & polytrack, gall or
sharp trk: more to come in h'caps: see 2231.
2886 **REVENIR 13** [1] A C Stewart 3-8-12 L Dettori 10/11 FAV: 022: Led, hdd over 1f out & no extra: 3½   71a
nicely bckd at odds-on on AW bow: handles gd & polytrack: see 2886 (gd).
2650 **SCHOLARSHIP 22** [4] C F Wall 3-8-12 L Dettori 16/1: 40450-03: b g College Chapel - Royal   ½   70a
Bracelet (Night Shift) Mid-div, eff to chase front pair over 2f out, kept on, al held: clr rem: plcd '03 (debut, B
Meehan, rtd 80 & 66a): stays 1m on fast, gd & prob both AWs: tried blnks.
2323} **FRENCH GIGOLO 389** [5] C N Allen 4-9-7 (59) G Carter 50/1: 300/000-4: ch g Pursuit of Love -   7   56a
French Mist (Mystiko) Keen & held up, mod late prog, nvr a threat: reapp: unplcd '03 (rtd 54, h'cap): mdn plcd in
'02 (rtd 81): eff around 1m on fast grnd, stiff/gall trk.
2079} **FISBY 398** [7]3-8-12 J F Egan 40/1: 0-5: ch g Efisio - Trilby (In The Wings) Slow away, sn   7   42a
handy, wknd 3f out: reapp: no form sole '03 start (rtd 20, mdn, subs gelded).
2854 **THE NIBBLER 14** [9]3-8-12 B Doyle 40/1: 46: Al rear, no ch fnl 2f, AW bow.   nk   41a
     COCO POINT BREEZE 0 [3]3-8-7 M Fenton 25/1: 7: Chsd ldr till over 2f out, wknd: breathing problem.   1   34a
288 **ALBERTINE 14** [8]4-9-2 T J P Guillambert(3) 66/1: 0-008: Al bhd, t-strap.   6   24a
     THE PALLETMAN 0 [2]4-9-7 S Drowne 100/1: 9: Dwelt, sn rdn & struggling, Flat debut, 9 mth jumps abs. 1¾   26a
9 Ran   Time 1m 39.3 (3.1)   Owned: Mrs P W Harris   Trained: Berkhamsted

3196
2.20 European Breeders Fund Maiden Stakes 2yo (D)
£4303 £1324 £662   **6f aw rnd**   **Going 38**   **+10 Fast**   Inside

     AFRASHAD 0 [6] Saeed bin Suroor 2-9-0 L Dettori 1/2 FAV: 1: ch c Smoke Glacken - Flo White   110a+
(Whitesbury) Broke well & sn in clr lead, shaken up & styd on strongly, unchall: fast time: hvly bckd at odds-on:
$15,500 April foal, half brother to several US wnrs, dam a US sprint 3yo wnr: eff at 6f, showed plenty of pace
& drop to 5f may suit: acts on a sharp trk & polytrack: impressive, one to follow.
     WAZIR 0 [5] J H M Gosden 2-9-0 K Fallon 3/1: 2: b c Pulpit - Top Order (Dayjur) Dwelt, sn chsd   5   90a+
wnr, some hdwy 2f out, al held but rest well covered: nicely bckd: Feb first foal, dam a 5f 2yo scorer: eff at 6f
on polytrack & a sharp trk: showed plenty of ability bhd a useful sort & shld rate higher.
     SANT JORDI 0 [1] B J Meehan 2-9-0 J Fortune 20/1: 3: b c Cape Cross - Foresta Verde (Green   4   78a
Forest) Chsd wnr early, no impress on front pair from halfway: op 16/1: 25,000gns purchase, March foal:
half-brother to several mdn performers, dam a well related mdn: 7f/1m could suit in time.
     HYPNOTIC 0 [3] Sir Mark Prescott 2-9-0 S Sanders 14/1: 4: Sn outpcd & nvr able to chall, op 10/1.   ¾   76a
     VALE DE LOBO 0 [2]2-8-9 S Archer(7) 40/1: 5: Outpcd mid-div, no impression.   5   56a
3046 **CHAIRMAN RICK 6** [4]2-9-0 T P Queally 14/1: 06: Slow away & sn bhd, nvr a factor.   1   58a
2870 **CHEK OI 13** [7]2-9-0 S Drowne 40/1: 007: Sn bhd on AW bow.   ½   56a
7 Ran   Time 1m 12.1 (1.7)   Owned: Godolphin   Trained: Newmarket

3197
2.50 Dormansland Median Auction Maiden Stakes Div 2 3-4yo (F)
£2919 £834 £417   **1m aw rnd**   **Going 38**   **-22 Slow**   Outside

     KOMOTO 0 [2] G A Butler 3-8-12 T P Queally 6/1: 1: b g Mtoto - Imperial Scholar (Royal Academy)   74a+
Outpcd early, rdn/hdwy over 2f out & styd on for press to lead line, all out: debut: eff at 1m, 10f+ looks sure to
suit: acts on polytrack & a sharp trk: goes well fresh: fine start, improve.
     CASHBAR 0 [4] J R Fanshawe 3-8-7 O Urbina 11/2: 2: b f Bishop of Cashel - Barford Sovereign   shd   68a
(Unfuwain) Mid-div inner, hdwy to lead ins last, shaken up & hdd line: op 9/2: prob would have held on with
stronger handling: eff at 1m, relish further: acts on polytrack: encouraging, rate higher.
2907 **MEMORY MAN 12** [5] W R Muir 3-8-12 F Norton 8/1: 043: Led 1f & remained cl-up, went on 2f out   1½   70a
till ins last, not pace of front pair cl-home: AW bow: stays a sharp 1m, handles fast grnd & polytrack: see 2907.
2841 **TRIFTI 14** [6] C A Cyzer 3-8-12 (62) L Dettori 6/1: 40004: Trkd ldrs & chall going well 2f out,   1¾   67a
rdn & no extra from dist: stays a sharp 1m but a return to 6/7f may suit: handles polytrack: see 2841 & 1021.
2443 **STANLEY CRANE 30** [9]3-8-12 t (66) Dane O'Neill 11/4 FAV: 435-0545: Dwelt, sn handy & led after 2f   4   59a
till 2f out, wknd: bckd, op 9/2: see 2148.
     PORT SODRICK 0 [1]3-8-12 A Daly 33/1: 6: Slow away & bhd, late prog, nrst fin on debut.   2   55a
     IN EVERY STREET 0 [7]3-8-7 E Ahern 5/1: 7: Held up, wide, rdn & no impress 3f out, debut, op 10/3.   2½   45a
2907 **BUNKHOUSE 12** [3]4-9-7 S Drowne 33/1: 0008: Chsd ldrs, btn 3f out, longer trip, AW bow.   8   35a
2647 **LABELLED WITH LOVE 22** [8]4-9-7 (50) L Treadwell(7) 12/1: 0-2569: Dwelt, led early, cl-up till 3f out.   11   15a
9 Ran   Time 1m 40.99 (4.77)   Owned: Mr & Mrs Michael C Kwee   Trained: Blewbury

3198

3.20 Bellway Stakes Handicap 3yo 0-75 (E) [82]
£4277 £1316 £658 6f aw rnd Going 38 -10 Slow Inside

2648* **CATHERINE WHEEL** 22 [1] J R Fanshawe 3-9-5 (73) L Dettori 11/8 FAV: 2111: Held up, hdwy 2f out & 76a
led ins last, rdn out: completed hat-trick on AW bow, well bckd: eff at 5/6f on fm, gd/soft & polytrack: progressive.
2841 **ECCENTRIC** 14 [4] Andrew Reid 3-9-7 (75) J F Egan 9/2: 0-411042: Led, edged right under press ½ 75a
from over 1f out & hdd ins last, kept on: gd run, likes Lingfield: see 2841, 933.
2841 **BELLA TUTRICE** 14 [7] I A Wood 3-9-1 (69) K Fallon 14/1: 00-03403: Sn cl-up & ch 2f out, no extra ¾ 67a
from dist: stays a sharp 6f, more convincing prev at 5f: acts on fast, gd/soft & polytrack: see 2609.
621 **PURE FOLLY** 151 [3] Sir Mark Prescott 3-8-3 (57) T P Queally 10/1: 4-344: Trkd ldrs, drvn & nk 54a
onepace from dist: op 8/1: h'cap bow, 5 mth abs: eff at 5/6f on polytrack: see 621 & 572.
3036 **CUT AND DRIED** 7 [6]3-8-12 (66) Martin Dwyer 6/1: 6054645: Keen trkg ldrs, no extra dist: op nk 62a
10/1: stays a sharp 6f, best to date at 5f: handles firm, fast & polytrack: see 3036 & 712 (5f).
3036 **MIRASOL PRINCESS** 7 [9]3-9-5 (73) I Mongan 25/1: 0-004666: Chsd ldrs wide, drvn & edged left, ¾ 67a+
kept on: not beaten far from a poor wide passage: stays a sharp 6f, all wins at 5f: now well h'capped & one to note.
2650 **BURLINGTON PLACE** 22 [2]3-8-11 (65) E Ahern 20/1: 40246-07: Dwelt, rear, no impress: btr 51 (C/D). 2½ 51a
2925 **MISS JUDGEMENT** 11 [10]3-8-11 (65) F Norton 6/1: 6-532138: Cl-up wide till over 2f out: btr 2925. 1 48a
2645 **ALIZAR** 22 [11]3-8-5 (59) R L Moore 16/1: 6060109: Rear & wide early, only mod prog: btr 2435. ½ 40a
3036 **IMPERIUM** 7 [8]3-9-4 (72) S Drowne 33/1: 5113000: 10th: Slow away wide & al bhd: much btr 2195 (5f). ¾ 51a
2403 **TICERO** 32 [12]3-9-4 BL (72) J P Guillambert(3) 50/1: 04-0000: 11th: Dwelt, keen rear & wide, btn 2f out. 5 37a
11 Ran Time 1m 13.3 (2.9) Owned: Cheveley Park Stud Trained: Newmarket

3199

3.50 E B F Paul Kelleway Memorial Classified Stakes 3yo+ 0-90 (C)
£8572 £3252 £1626 1m aw rnd Going 38 +04 Fast Outside

2606 **ALWAYS ESTEEMED** 24 [4] G Wragg 4-9-7 (94) Martin Dwyer 6/1: 00-20041: Chsd ldrs, rdn 3f out, 100a
hdwy to lead over 1f out, drvn out: suited by 1m, unconvincing at 10f: acts on fast, gd/soft & polytrack: useful.
2091 **FIVEOCLOCK EXPRESS** 45 [1] Miss Gay Kelleway 4-9-3 p (90) I Mongan 10/1: 0-420052: Trkd ldr 2f 1½ 92a
out, rdn & ch dist, not pace of wnr ins last: 6 wk abs: stays a sharp 1m, prob best at 7f: see 887.
1317 **WARRAD** 82 [10] G A Butler 3-8-8 (88) S Sanders 9/1: 1-43: Rear/wide, styd on for press late: 12 ½ 91a+
wk abs: AW bow: stays a sharp 1m well, further shld suit: acts on fast & polytrack: much more encouraging, lightly
rcd & one to keep in mind: see 1317.
2558 **SELECTIVE** 26 [7] A C Stewart 5-9-7 (94) K Fallon 7/1: 230-4004: b g Selkirk - Portelet (Night 1¼ 92a
Shift) Mid-div, eff 2f out, onepace: AW bow: thrice rnr-up in val h'caps in '03, List plcd (rtd 107 at best):
mdn, class stks & val h'cap wnr '02: eff at 7f/1m on fast, gd/soft & polytrack, any trk: AW bow today.
2 Apr'03 Asco 7gd 106-99 B: 2 Apr'03 Newm 7gd 101-97 B: 2 Mar'03 Donc 8gd 101-94 B: 1 Sep'02 Sand 8gd 96-89 C:
1 Jul'02 Kemp 8g/s 90- D: 2 May'02 Good 7g 93-85- D: 2 Oct'01 Newc 8g/s 88- D:
2665 **DANCE ON THE TOP** 21 [2]6-9-7 t (94) D Sweeney 6/1: 20-11065: Led/dsptd lead till went on 3f out, ½ 91a
hdd over 1f out & no extra: fair run in a decent race: see 547 (C/D).
2533 **BETTALATETHANNEVER** 26 [12]3-8-13 (95) Dane O'Neill 6/1: 1-140026: Dwelt, rear, mod late prog. nk 91a
3002 **FANCY FOXTROT** 8 [3]3-8-8 (90) J Fortune 4/1 FAV: 6-100307: Keen mid-div, btn over 1f out: btr 2212. 1¼ 83a
2710 **SHARPLAW VENTURE** 20 [6]4-9-0 (90) R Hills 12/1: 6/5230-38: Mid-div when badly hmpd inner over 2f 4 73a
out, no ch after: closer without interference: see 2710.
2777 **BINANTI** 17 [11]4-9-3 (88) J Quinn 20/1: 140-0669: Rear, eff 2f out, no impress: btr 2777 & 2389 (7f). 3 70a
3001 **EPHESUS** 8 [5]4-9-3 vis (81) W Supple 20/1: 6142200: 10th: Held up wide, no ch fnl 2f: btr 2389. 1 68a
2362 **HATCH** 33 [9]3-8-8 (88) L Dettori 10/1: 1313040: 11th: Led/dsptd lead, wide early, btn 2f out: btr 1460. hd 67a
OUTSIDE INVESTOR 272 [8]4-9-3 (75) E Ahern 66/1: 302232-0: 12th: b g Cadeaux Genereux - Desert 19 32a
Ease (Green Desert) Al bhd & t.o. 3f out: reportedly not face kickback on AW bow: 6 mth jumps abs (unplcd, nov):
ex-Irish, dual '03 mdn rnr-up: styd up to 12f, handles fast & soft grnd.
12 Ran Time 1m 39.22 (3.02) Owned: Mollers Racing Trained: Newmarket

Official Going Good (Good/Firm Places)

3200

4.20 Ladies Night This Saturday Handicap Stakes 3yo+ 0-75 (E) [93]
£4251 £1308 £654 2m Good Inapplicable Inside

3037* **TUNGSTEN STRIKE** 7 [7] Mrs A J Perrett 3-8-6 (5ex) (71) Martin Dwyer 15/8 FAV: 400-011: Trkd ldr, 86+
led over 2f out, rdn clr, v readily: nicely bckd: stayed this step up to 2m well, further will suit: acts on fast &
gd, flat or sharp/undul trks: lightly rcd & progressive, one to keep on your side.
1082* **BELLE ROUGE** 98 [4] C A Horgan 6-8-13 (59) L Dettori 6/1: 022/-2212: Trkd ldrs, smooth prog to 4 65
press wnr over 2f out, sn outpcd to wnr: 3 mth abs: see 1082.
4689} **BOW STRADA** 977 [5] P J Hobbs 7-9-10 (70) E Ahern 8/1: 0/00510//-3: ch g Rainbow Quest - La 1 75
Strada (Niniski) Handy, drvn & onepace fnl 3f: op 11/1, jumps fit (unplcd, h'cap hdle): dual nov chase wnr 02/03,
ability over hdles (rtd 130h, stays 3m): last rcd on the level in '01, h'cap wnr for P Harris: eff at 14f/2m, shld
get further: acts on gd & gd/soft grnd & can go well fresh. 1 Oct'01 York 13.8g/s 70-66 D:
2699 **SAN HERNANDO** 20 [9] D R C Elsworth 4-9-10 (70) Dane O'Neill 10/1: 6400404: Hld up, some late gains. shd 75
565} **MARREL** 523 [6]6-7-13 (1ow)(5oh)vis (39) J Quinn 5/1: 603/333-5: b g Shareef Dancer - Upper Caen 1¾ 48
(High Top) Mid-div, hung under press & onepace fnl 2f: long Flat abs, jumps fit, recent h'cap hdle wnr (2m/2m4f,
fast & gd, rtd 120h): AW h'cap plcd '03 (rtd 32a, sell h'cap): plcd '02 (rtd 46a, h'cap): best btwn 12f/2m on fast
grnd & fibresand, tried blnks, eff in visor. 1 Jul'01 Beve 16.1g/f 51-48 F:
3101* **SUDDEN FLIGHT** 4 [12]7-9-12 (5ex) (72) S Donohoe(7) 8/1: 3004316: Led till over 2f out, fdd: op 5/1. 3½ 72
2391 **CEDAR MASTER** 32 [1]7-9-5 bl t (65) A Quinn(5) 100/1: 20050-07: Mid-div, no prog over 1f out. ¾ 64
2391 **MOON EMPEROR** 32 [11]7-10-0 (74) J Fortune 11/1: 0604668: Rear, rdn & btn 3f out: btr 1689. 4 69
4120} **DEAR SIR** 310 [10]4-8-3 (49) C Catlin 50/1: 05026-9: Rear, no ch 5f out, reapp. 13 34
2577 **PROMOTE** 25 [2]8-7-12 (4oh) (40) A McCarthy 33/1: 0/00-0660: 10th: Wknd 3f out: breathing prob. 9 21
3032 **MADIBA** 7 [3]5-8-13 (59) K Fallon 12/1: 022000P: Sn bhd & t.o., p.u. halfway: reportedly unsuited by grnd. 0

LINGFIELD Polytrack   WEDNESDAY 14.07.04   Lefthand, Sharp, Undulating Track

11 Ran   Time 3m 35.92 (10.72)   Owned: Mr John Connolly   Trained: Pulborough

3201   4.50 Come Racing Here On Saturday Night Classified Stakes 3yo 0-60 (F)
£3038 £868 £434   1m2f   Good   Inapplicable   Inside

3144* **DOCTORED** 3 [1] P D Evans 3-9-6 bl (60) S Donohoe(6) 7/2: 6110111: Mid-div, switched & rdn to lead ins last, drvn out: bckd: eff at 7f/1m, imprvd last twice at 10f: acts on firm, gd/soft & fbsd: thriving.   74

2621 **GOLDEN DRIFT** 23 [2] G Wragg 3-8-11 (58) S Drowne 14/1: 0-0502: ch f Inchinor - Carpet of Leaves (Green Forest) Trkd ldrs, hdwy to lead over 1f out, hdd ins last, kept on: clr of rem: op 12/1: eff at 10f, worth another try at 11f+: acts on gd grnd: often rnr, unplcd previously.   ½   63

1648 **POLAR DANCER** 65 [9] Mrs A J Perrett 3-8-11 (59) Dane O'Neill 8/1: 063-03: Dwelt & rear, kept on late, no threat to front pair: set plenty to do, worth another try at 11f+ on this evidence: see 120.   5   56

1956 **RAJAYOGA** 51 [8] M H Tompkins 3-9-0 (60) F P Ferris(3) 16/1: 440-004: Trkd ldrs wide, no extra dist: 8 wk abs: longer trip: handles gd grnd: see 1956 (1m).   ¾   58

2922 **TROIS ETOILES** 11 [6]3-8-11 (58) R Hills 3/1 FAV: 00-5055: Trkd ldrs, short of room over 2f out & again over 1f out, no extra: op 9/2: btr 2922 & 2182 (6f/1m).   1¼   53

KALIMENTA 68 [13]3-9-2 (65) J F Egan 33/1: 4266: ch f Rahy - Toujours Elle (Lyphard) Bolted bef start, led to post, rear, eff wide 3f out, mod prog under kind ride: 10 wk abs, Brit bow: ex-French, rnr-up in the provinces earlier: eff at 1m, shaped as if 10f will suit: handles gd grnd.   1¼   56

2907 **CAYMAN CALYPSO** 12 [12]3-9-5 (65) M Henry 16/1: 0067: Chsd wnr 4f out, ch 2f out, wknd.   3   55

2452 **AUTUMN FLYER** 30 [5]3-9-2 (62) R Smith 50/1: 000-008: Led, hung right & hdd over 1f out, no extra.   shd   52

2886 **PALABELLE** 13 [3]3-8-11 (60) Martin Dwyer 5/1: 00059: Keen trkg ldr, btn 2f out.   nk   46

2656 **LILLIANNA** 22 [7]3-9-2 (65) W Ryan 6/1: 4030: 10th: Mid-div, btn over 2f out: btr 2656 (1m).   2½   47

3051 **FRANKIES WINGS** 6 [10]3-9-0 bl (60) B Doyle 20/1: 0-06000: 11th: Rear, no ch 3f out, qck reapp.   nk   44

11 Ran   Time 2m 10.54(6.34)   Owned: Treble Chance Partnership   Trained: Abergavenny

HAMILTON   THURSDAY 15.07.04   Righthand, Undulating Track, Stiff Uphill Finish

Official Going GOOD/FIRM (GOOD IN PLACES)

3202   2.20 Shopmobility Maiden Auction Stakes A Qualifier For Hamilton Park 2-Y-O Series Final 2yo (D)
£4843 £1490 £745   6f5y   Good/Firm 21   -16 Slow   Stands side

2682 **PROPELLOR** 21 [5] A Dickman 2-8-10 A Beech(3) 7/2: 31: Made all, pushed out ins fnl 2f, val bit more: eff at 6f, 7f shld suit: acts on fast & soft, stiff/undul trk: only lightly rcd & there shld be more to come.   89+

SPY KING 0 [4] M Johnston 2-8-11 K Darley 6/1: 2: ch c Distant View - Regal Princess (Royal And Regal) Handy, outpcd halfway, rallied fnl 1f, al held by wnr: op 4/1 on debut: Feb foal, cost $35,000: half-brother American 2yo wnr: dam successful in US: sire decent performer around 1m: eff at 6f, further will suit: acts on fast grnd: encouraging start & can rate higher with experience.   2½   81

3021 **MONASH LAD** 8 [3] M H Tompkins 2-8-8 K Fallon 8/13 FAV: 0533: Badly hmpd after start, sn cl-up, hung left & onepcd fnl 1f: well bckd: disapp run & did not seem to relish a battle: showed more in 3021.   ¾   76

INVERTIEL 0 [6] J Semple 2-8-10 R Winston 20/1: 4: br c Royal Academy - Intriguing (Deputy Minister) Prom over 4f, no extra: debut: Apr foal, cost $17,000: half-brother to a couple of wnrs abroad: dam plcd abroad: sire decent performer up to 1m.   3   69

2275 **PATXARAN** 38 [1]2-8-3 D Fentiman(7) 50/1: 05: b f Revoque - Stargard (Polish Precedent) Badly short of room after start, sn mid-div, hung right & onepcd 2f out: Mar foal, cost £10,000: half-sister plcd at 7f: dam plcd abroad: sire Gr 1 wnr at 1m: with P C Haslam.   ½   60

ARABIAN ANA 0 [2]2-8-10 F Lynch 14/1: 6: Slow away, al in rear: op 8/1 on debut.   1¼   63

6 Ran   Time 1m 12.06 (2.26)   Owned: The Marooned Crew   Trained: Sandhuthon

3203   2.50 Arthur Balding Stakes Handicap 3yo 0-70 (E)   [77]
£4436 £1365 £683   6f5y   Good/Firm 21   -09 Slow   Stands side

3018 **THORNABY GREEN** 8 [9] T D Barron 3-8-12 (61) P Makin(5) 6/1: 5600-441: In tch far side, styd on to lead ins fnl 1f, drvn out: eff at 5/6f on fast & gd grnd: made gd use of drop down weights: see 3018.   67

3018 **LORD BASKERVILLE** 8 [7] W Storey 3-8-3 (52) J Bramhill 11/2: 3000022: Rcd far side, bhd, prog when short of room dist, kept on ins fnl 1f, just held by wnr: has imprvd recently for being gelded.   ½   56

2925 **TURKISH DELIGHT** 12 [1] J Balding 3-8-8 (57) J Edmunds 12/1: 30-56003: Rcd stands side, bhd, prog to lead stands side group dist, kept on, not btn far: bckd from 20/1: see 1441.   hd   60

2849 **FOX COVERT** 15 [10] D W Barker 3-8-8 vis (57) R Winston 11/2: 0023504: Rcd far side, led that group over 5f, no extra: see 2055 & btr 1949.   1¼   56

2961 **SMART DANNY** 11 [6]3-7-12 (6oh) (41) B Swarbrick(5) 5/1 FAV: 0550005: In tch far side 4f, sn onepcd.   2   40

3018 **CALCULAITE** 8 [5]3-8-1 (50) P Fessey 14/1: 000-066: Rcd stands side, led that group till dist, no extra.   shd   42

2849 **FLYING BANTAM** 15 [3]3-9-7 (70) T Hamilton(3) 8/1: 03-22247: Handy stands side till dist, wknd.   3½   51

2731 **SWEET CANDO** 20 [8]3-9-1 p (64) K Darley 6/1: 4-602058: Handy far side over 4f, wknd: op 4/1.   3½   34

2925 **INDRANI** 12 [4]3-7-12 (4oh) (43) D Fentiman(7) 14/1: 0402059: Rcd stands side, prom till dist, fdd.   ¾   15

2936 **YORKES FOLLY** 12 [2]3-8-5 (54) G Faulkner 33/1: 50-000: 10th: Rcd stands side, chsd ldrs over 4f, fdd.   1¼   18

10 Ran   Time 1m 11.63 (1.83)   Owned: Thornaby Racing Club   Trained: Thirsk

3204   3.20 Daily Record Conditions Stakes 3yo (C)
£9582 £3400 £1700   1m1f36y   Good/Firm 21   +00 Fast   Inside

3059 **MISTER MONET** 7 [1] M Johnston 3-8-12 (92) K Dalgleish 4/7 FAV: 31-21: Made all, clr bef 1f out, eased cl-home, val 6L+: bckd, qck reapp: eff at 7f/9f on fast & gd: lightly rcd & useful.   110+

2757 **ALWAYS FIRST** 19 [3] Sir Michael Stoute 3-9-3 (95) K Fallon 11/8: 1-02: Al cl-up, kept on fnl 1f, al held by easy wnr: clr rem: useful, only lightly rcd & can rate higher: just btr 2757.   4   105

BANANA GROVE 0 [2] A Berry 3-8-9 P Mathers(7) 100/1: 3: b g Sesaro - Megan's Dream (Fayruz)   10   77

Mid-div, no impress fnl 3f: debut: already gelded.
2993 **GRACEFUL AIR** 9 [4] J R Weymes 3-8-7 (59) R Winston 100/1: 2240544: Handy over 6f, wknd: stiff task. *1¼* **70**
4 Ran   Time 1m 56.04 (1.94)   Owned: Syndicate 2002   Trained: Middleham

3205 — 3.55 Rectangle Group Classified Stakes 3yo+ 0-80 (D)
£5818 £1790 £895   **1m65y**   **Good/Firm 21**   **+08 Fast**   Inside

3001 **LANGFORD** 9 [4] M H Tompkins 4-9-8 (85) K Fallon 6/4 J FAV: 36-21001: Cl-up, styd on to lead 1f   **90+**
out, eased cl-home, val bit more: well bckd: suited by 1m/10f on firm & gd: best up with/forcing pace.
2874* **WOODY VALENTINE** 14 [6] M Johnston 3-8-10 (82) S Chin 6/4 J FAV: 4216612: Handy, outpcd halfway, *nk* **85**
rallied ins fnl 1f, al held by wnr: well bckd: eff around 1m, crying out for return to 10f: see 2874.
3152 **ANTHEMION** 3 [2] Mrs J C McGregor 7-9-3 (50) D McGaffin 100/1: 2000053: Led, sn clr, hdd 1f out, *1* **81$**
kept on, not pace front 2: qck reapp: prob flattered: see 1504.
2890 **TEDSTALE** 13 [5] T D Easterby 6-9-4 bl (81) K Darley 3/1: 0050364: Chsd ldrs, hung right under *nk* **81**
press dist, clr rem: just btr 2672.
3152 **TELEPATHIC** 3 [3]4-9-3 (57) P Mathers(7) 100/1: 0460565: Cl-up 6f, fdd: qck reapp. *11* **58**
3714*]**ELSUNDUS** 1050 [1]6-9-8 (85) R Winston 16/1: 1//-6: b g Gone West - Aljawza (Riverman) Slow *24* **15**
away, nvr a factor: reapp: missed '03 & '02: mdn wnr on sole '01 start (mdn, J H Gosden): eff at 1m on fast grnd:
acts on a stiff/gall trk & has gone well fresh: gelded since last term: with K A Morgan.
1 Aug'01 Sali 8g/f 91- D:
6 Ran   Time 1m 44.94 (1.14)   Owned: Marlborough Electronics   Trained: Newmarket

3206 — 4.30 Famous Grouse Premier Claiming Stakes 3yo+ (D)
£5590 £1720 £860   **1m1f36y**   **Good/Firm 21**   **-02 Slow**   Inside

2948 **OLDENWAY** 12 [6] R A Fahey 5-9-12 (76) T Hamilton(3) 4/6 FAV: 2421401: Made all, edged left ins **81**
fnl 2f, pushed out: bckd, bt for 30,000: suited by 9/12f on firm & gd/soft: see 2323.
2687 **LEIGHTON** 21 [5] J D Bethell 4-9-10 (78) S Chin 9/2: 03-05402: Handy, outpcd 4f out, rallied ins *½* **76**
fnl 1f, al held by wnr: clr rem: claimed for 25,000: btr 2030.
2571 **MILLAGROS** 26 [3] I Semple 4-9-7 (74) T Eaves(3) 3/1: 10-04463: Cl-up, ev ch 2f out, no extra dist. *4* **65**
2440 **JAMESTOWN** 31 [4] M J Polglase 7-9-4 (45) A Culhane 20/1: 0000404: Chsd ldrs 6f, fdd: see 1262. *9* **44**
2988 **STEPASTRAY** 9 [1]7-9-4 (41) P Fessey 66/1: 00-50005: Mid-div 6f, fdd: btr 1821. *shd* **43**
5 Ran   Time 1m 56.2 (2.1)   Owned: Mr J J Staunton   Trained: Malton

3207 — 5.00 Saffie Joseph & Sons Handicap Stakes 3yo+ 0-70 (E)   **[69]**
£4225 £1300 £650   **1m3f16y**   **Good/Firm 21**   **-11 Slow**   Stands side

4188] **TIGER FROG** 664 [4] J Mackie 5-9-0 bl (55) T Eaves(3) 7/1: 30020/-1: b g French Deputy - **68+**
Woodyoubelieveit (Woodman) Cl-up, styd on to lead dist, pushed clr, val 7L+: hdles fit, earlier h'cap wnr (rtd 101h
best, eff around 2m/2m1.5f on fast & hvy grnd): plcd on level in '02 (rtd 65, h'cap, J H M Gosden): eff at 10/11f
on fast & gd grnd: eff with blnks & acts on a sharp or stiff/undul trk: gelded since last Flat run.
2 Aug'02 Ripo 10gd 65-63 E:
2686* **HEARTHSTEAD DREAM** 21 [6] J D Bethell 3-9-1 bl (68) B Swarbrick(5) 10/1: 0321512: Chsd ldrs, kept *5* **71**
on fnl 2f, no ch with easy wnr: gd run: see 2686 (clmr).
3134 **SUALDA** 5 [5] R A Fahey 5-9-13 (68) T Hamilton(3) 6/4 FAV: 00-52123: Led, hdd dist, sn no extra: *nk* **70**
well bckd on qck reapp:fair run: see btr 3134 & 2892.
2813 **SAAMEQ** 17 [8] I Semple 3-7-12 (8oh) (43) P Fessey 20/1: 0-60034: Dwelt, prog 3f out, onepcd fnl 1f. *1* **51**
2813* **ARCHIRONDEL** 17 [1]6-9-5 (60) A Culhane 7/2: 0210215: In tch over 1m, sn no extra: btr 2813. *2½* **56**
2892 **LITTLE TASK** 13 [7]6-7-12 (39) D Fentiman(7) 7/1: 3141046: Rear, nvr a factor: btr 2616. *shd* **54**
658* **TURKS AND CAICOS** 149 [2]3-8-5 (58) G Faulkner 16/1: 040-2217: Prom, ev ch 4f out, wknd fnl 2f. *1½* **51**
3149 **SHERWOOD FOREST** 3 [3]4-8-3 vis (44) Leanne Kershaw(7) 25/1: 500-0368: Rear, nvr a factor: qck reapp. *½* **36**
8 Ran   Time 2m 22.37(3.57)   Owned: Fools Who Dream   Trained: Church Broughton

Official Going GOOD/FIRM (GOOD places).

3208 — 2.10 Racecourse Sponsorship And Advertising Median Auction Maiden Stakes 3-4yo (F)
£3552 £1093 £547   **1m1f218y**   **Good/Firm 25**   **-32 Slow**   Inside

2622 **RAAKAAN** 24 [6] A C Stewart 3-8-9 S Drowne 6/4 FAV: 31: Handy, hdwy to lead over 1f out, edged **82**
right ins last & styd on, rdn out: bckd: apprec step up to 10f & acts on fast & gd/soft: type to prog again.
2663 **ANTIGIOTTO** 22 [1] L M Cumani 3-8-9 (76) D Holland 5/2: 000422: Led 3f, led over 2f out till over *2* **77**
1f out, no extra: shown enough to win a race: see 2663, 2274.
2700 **WARNINGCAMP** 21 [9] Lady Herries 3-8-9 S Sanders 7/2: 463: Dwelt, held up, hdwy 2f out, onepace: *1* **75**
fair run: clr rem, see 2193.
2678 **DISPARITY** 22 [7] J R Fanshawe 3-8-5 (1ow)T O Urbina 14/1: 04: b f Distant View - Eternity (Suave *5* **62**
Dancer) In tch, wknd over 1f out: btr eff in t-strap.
2113 **BAYOU PRINCESS** 45 [10]3-8-4 A McCarthy 100/1: 005: ch f Bluegrass Prince - Josifina (Master *1¾* **58**
Willie) Led 7f out till over 2f out, wknd: 6 wk abs.
2992 **WELKINOS BOY** 9 [13]3-8-9 Dale Gibson 25/1: 056: Handy, wknd 2f out: see 2992. *3* **58**
   THROUGH THE SLIPS [2]3-8-4 J Mackay 25/1: 7: ch f Boundary - Fast Selection (Talinum) Slow *4* **46**
away, sn handy, wknd well over 1f out on debut: bred to appear around 1m.
   BLUE TRACK [11]3-8-9 S Righton 66/1: 8: Slow away, al bhd on debut. *5* **42**
2740 **ELECTRAS DREAM** 19 [5]3-8-4 Hayley Turner(5) 100/1: 009: Keen, handy, wknd over 2f out. *shd* **37**
2722 **PETERS PLOY** 20 [8]4-9-6 J P Guillambert(3) 66/1: 00: 10th: In tch, wknd over 2f out. *17* **12**
   CROMARTY BAY [3]3-8-4 J Quinn 66/1: 0: 11th: Slow away & al bhd. *19* **0**

11 Ran   Time 2m 08.23 (5.73)   Owned: Sheikh Ahmed Al Maktoum   Trained: Newmarket

3209   2.40 Raceday Hospitality Selling Stakes 2yo (G)
£2898 £828 £414   **5f2y str**   **Good/Firm 25**   **-30 Slow** Stands Side

1048 **MARCELA ZABALA 101** [6] J G Given 2-8-6 M Fenton 10/1: 01: b f Zaha - Bay Bianca (Law Society)   58
Swerved right start, sn chsd ldr, led over 1f out, styd on, drvn out: joc received a 1-day whip ban: 3 mth abs: March
foal, cost 8,000gns: half-sister to wnrs over 5/8f: dam 6f scorer: eff at 5f on fast: goes well fresh.
2977* **STRAFFAN 10** [5] E J O'Neill 2-8-11 S Sanders 9/4 JT FAV: 3325412: Set pace till over 1f out,   nk   62
kept on, just held: ran to form of 2977.
2882 **TURTLE MAGIC 14** [1] W G M Turner 2-8-6 BL C Haddon(7) 9/4 JT FAV: 2366403: Sn rdn bhd, hdwy over shd   57
1f out, not go past ins last: back to form in first time blnks but poss lacks will to win: acts on fast & gd/soft.
2921* **TIPSY LILLIE 12** [2] Julian Poulton 2-8-11 M Halford(7) 5/2: 500014: In tch, eff 2f out, sn onepace.   2   56
3053 **AMALGAM 7** [4]2-8-6 R Havlin 40/1: 0005: ch f Namid - Carhue Gold (Bob Back) Chsd ldr, no extra   1½   47
over 1f out: Feb foal, cost E7,500: dam styd 1m.
2939 **LANE MARSHAL 12** [3]2-8-11 bl R Ffrench 11/1: 650006: Chsd ldrs, wknd dist: see 2939, 1424.   3½   42
6 Ran   Time 1m 01.04 (2.74)   Owned: Zaha Racing Syndicate   Trained: Gainsborough

3210   3.10 Totepool Handicap Stakes 3yo+ 0-80 (D)   [80]
£7066 £2174 £1087   **7f9y str**   **Good/Firm 25**   **+02 Fast** Stands Side

2864* **PINTLE 14** [1] J L Spearing 4-9-3 (69) K McEvoy 8/1: 215-411: With ldrs, rcd alone stands side,   79
hung right but led over 1f out, rdn out: stays 7f well & best up with/forcing the pace: likes firm & fast grnd:
lightly rcd & improving filly, more to come: see 2864.
2848 **TAKES TUTU 15** [3] K R Burke 5-9-8 bl (74) S Sanders 8/1: 0225502: Held up, hdwy well over 1f out,   ¾   81
kept on ins last, not btn far: back to form: see 2672, 2179.
3001 **ST PANCRAS 9** [7] N A Callaghan 4-10-0 (80) D Holland 5/2 FAV: 0020153: Handy, eff to chall over   ¾   85
1f out, kept on same pace ins last: well bckd: gd run under a big weight: see 2665 (1m).
2853 **MAGIC AMOUR 15** [4] Ian Williams 6-8-6 (58) P Robinson 25/1: 020-2604: Led till dist, wknd.   2   59
2532 **LEOBALLERO 27** [6]4-10-0 t (80) Dane O'Neill 11/2: 2231-535: Held up centre, hdwy dist, onepace.   ½   80
3074 **ALCHEMIST MASTER 6** [11]5-9-8 (6ex)p (74) Dean McKeown 5/1: 2221146: Held up centre, eff over 1f   1¾   70
out, sn wknd: been busy: see 2074, 2986.
3117 **ROMAN MAZE 5** [10]4-8-11 (63) S W Kelly 9/1: 14-05007: Slow away centre, held up, nvr a factor.   nk   58
2716+ **MIDNIGHT BALLARD 20** [9]3-9-6 (80) S Carson 14/1: 6-642018: With ldrs centre, wknd over 1f out: 1¼   72
made all in mdn company in 2716.
2861 **ASTRAC 15** [2]13-7-12 (1oh) (49) P M Quinn 25/1: 5-500249: Held up, nvr a factor: 13yo: see 2370.   1½   39
2884 **BRANTWOOD 14** [5]4-8-7 t (59) W Supple 11/1: 0043230: 10th: In tch, wknd 2f out: see 2884, 2502.   1¼   45
2568 **THE BONUS KING 26** [8]4-9-12 (78) O Urbina 25/1: 0002400: 11th: Nvr a factor: now with J Jay.   2   60
11 Ran   Time 1m 23.6 (1.6)   Owned: Mr Robert Heathcote   Trained: Kinnersley

3211   3.45 Barnsdale Hall Hotel County Air Ambulance Claiming Stakes 4yo+ (F)
£4076 £1254 £627   **1m3f183y**   **Good/Firm 25**   **-21 Slow** Inside

2643* **ZEIS 23** [7] H Morrison 4-9-7 t (68) L Fletcher(3) 100/30: 00-00011: In tch, hdwy to lead dist,   68
kept on, rdn out: clmd for 12,000: eff at 10f, styd this first try at 12f well & acts on fast & soft, any trk: has
broken blood vessels: see 2643.
2107 **RELATIVE HERO 45** [6] Miss S J Wilton 4-8-9 p (57) A Quinn(5) 80/1: 1650-002: ch g Entrepeneur -   2½   52
Aunty (Riverman) In tch, eff to chall over 1f out, not pace of wnr: 6 wk abs: '03 sell & claim wnr: eff at 7f,
stays 12f on firm & gd grnd, loves Leicester: wears cheek pieces at present, best form last term in blnks.
1 Jul'03 Leic 7.0gd 64-(63) F: 1 Jun'03 Leic 7.0g/f 68-(64) G:
4659) **FORBEARING 280** [4] M C Pipe 7-9-3 (73) D Holland 10/11 FAV: 101610-3: b g Bering - For Example   nk   59
(Northern Baby) In tch, eff 2f out, sn no extra: hdles fit, won 3 h'cap hdles in 03/04 (rtd 116h, 2m1f, fast &
soft, visor): '03 3 time claim wnr (Sir M Prescott): eff at 1m, suited by 12f now on firm, hvy & fibresand.
1 Aug'03 Catt 12.0fm 74-(75) F: 1 Jul'03 Carl 11.9g/f 73-(78) F: 1 Jun'03 York 10.4g/f 76-(87) D: 2 Jul'02 Donc 12gd 88- D
2340 **CRACOW 35** [5] A M Hales 7-8-7 (46) A McCarthy 16/1: 5300/-204: Unruly in stalls, chsd ldr till   1¼   47
led 3f out till over 1f out, no extra: see 2112.
2836 **BANNINGHAM BLAZE 16** [9]4-8-8 (50) T P Queally 11/2: 4122365: Held up, short of room 3f out, no   3½   43
impress: see 2601, 2047.
      BENS REVENGE [8]4-8-9 V Slattery 80/1: 6: b g Emperor Jones - Bumble Boogie (Bluebird) Slow   1½   42
away, nvr a factor on Flat debut: modest form in recent bmprs.
2668 **LORD NELLSSON 22** [2]8-9-7 Hayley Turner(5) 33/1: 47: Slow away & al bhd: see 2668.   2   51
3025 **LILIAN 8** [3]4-8-0 vis (46) J Quinn 40/1: 22-65608: Al bhd: see 3025.   shd   30
2244 **JAZIL 40** [10]9-8-5 t (50) Dean McKeown 50/1: 3/0///-609: In tch, wknd 2f out: see 1754.   ½   34
2588 **FLYOFF 26** [1]7-8-5 vis (45) R Thomas(5) 14/1: 01164-00: 10th: Sn clr ldr till hdd & wknd 2f out.   1½   32
10 Ran   Time 2m 33.87 (5.57)   Owned: Mr D J Donner   Trained: East Ilsley

3212   4.20 Introduction To Sponsorship Nursery Handicap Stakes 2yo (E)   [94]
£5629 £1732 £866   **5f218y str**   **Good/Firm 25**   **-13 Slow** Stands Side

2043 **COLONEL BILKO 48** [1] B R Millman 2-7-13 (1ow) (65) F Norton 16/1: 2061: With ldrs, hdwy over 1f   68
out, styd on to lead ins last, rdn out: 7 wk abs: eff at 6f on fast & gd grnd, stiff or sharp/undul trks: imprvd
for lay-off & discarded blnks: see 2043, 974.
2952 **SAFENDONSEABISCUIT 11** [12] S Kirk 2-8-10 (77) K McEvoy 8/1: 53342: In tch, hdwy to lead dist,   1½   75
hdd ins last, not pace of wnr: gd run: shld find a race: see 2714, 2077.
2833* **PRINCELY VALE 16** [15] W G M Turner 2-8-7 p (74) C Haddon(7) 14/1: 041113: Slow away, sn handy, led ½   70
halfway till hung left & hdd dist, onepace: joc received a 2-day careless riding ban: gd run up in class.
1795 **LORD JOHN 59** [8] M W Easterby 2-7-12 (3oh) (65) Dale Gibson 25/1: 0404: In tch, eff over 1f out,   nk   60$
onepace: 2 mth abs: eff at 6f on fast grnd: see 1161.
3022 **SIMPLIFY 8** [13]2-8-8 bl (75) T P Queally 5/1 CO FAV: 45325: Slow away, held up, hdwy over 2f out,   nk   69

LEICESTER   THURSDAY 15.07.04   Righthand, Stiff, Galloping Track

not clr run just ins last, kept on: shade closer with a clr run: see 1937.
2110	**HAROLDINI 45** [14]2-8-3 (70) S Carson 16/1: 0426: In tch, lost plc 4f out, late gains: abs, btr 2110.		1½	60
3022	**QUEENS GLORY 8** [7]2-8-5 (72) R Mullen 25/1: 626557: Handy, onepace when short of room 1f out.		½	60
2061	**IVANA ILLYICH 47** [2]2-8-5 (72) J F Egan 13/2: 5048: In tch, wknd dist: 7 wk abs: see 2061.		½	58
3110	**GAVIOLI 5** [11]2-8-3 t (70) S Whitworth 20/1: 504209: Held up, wknd over 1f out: see 2629, 2367.		2	50
2498*	**CHILLY CRACKER 28** [9]2-8-5 (72) Dean McKeown 14/1: 2610: 10th: Led to halfway, no extra: btr 2498.		2½	45
2115*	**DONT TELL TRIGGER 45** [6]2-7-13 (66) J Quinn 16/1: 0610: 11th: In tch, wknd 2f out: 6 wk abs.		½	37
2711	**LINCOLNEUROCRUISER 21** [10]2-9-7 (88) D Allan 5/1 CO FAV: 523120: 12th: Handy, wknd over 2f out.		2	53
2927	**GAUDALPIN 12** [5]2-8-0 (67) S Righton 20/1: 34040: 13th: Keen, handy, wknd over 1f out.		2½	25
2297	**ENGLISH FELLOW 37** [3]2-8-12 (79) W Supple 5/1 CO FAV: 3440: 14th: Slow away & al bhd: bckd from 8/1: something amiss? much btr 2297, 1950.		8	13

14 Ran   Time 1m 12.11 (2.31)   Owned: Ray Gudge Colin Lewis Malcolm Calvert   Trained: Cullompton

3213   4.50 Leicester Racecourse Conference Centre Handicap Stakes 3yo+ 0-75 (E)   [75]
£5850 £1800 £900   5f21 8y str   Good/Firm 25   +10 Fast   Stands Side

2713	**MARSHALLSPARK 21** [4] R A Fahey 5-8-13 (60) G Parkin 7/1: 00-00051: Handy, hdwy to lead dist, just held on for press ins last: eff over 6/7f on firm, gd/soft & fibresand, any trk: right back to form: see 1749.			70
2720*	**NEVER WITHOUT ME 20** [1] J F Coupland 4-8-9 (56) S Whitworth 13/2: 1034112: In tch, hdwy & short of room dist, switched left & kept on ins last, just held: loves fibresand, acts on fast grnd & any trk: see 2720.		shd	65
3016	**BOWLING ALONG 8** [13] M E Sowersby 3-8-0 (53) N Mackay(3) 14/1: 0-500043: Handy, eff to chall over 1f out, no extra ins last: gd run: see 1465.		2	56
2975	**STOKESIES WISH 10** [8] J L Spearing 4-9-3 (64) K McEvoy 10/1: 0002054: With ldrs, led over 1f out, sn hdd & onepace: see 2535, 1127.		hd	66
1607}	**ASBO 423** [10]4-8-13 (60) C Lowther 40/1: 00/00-5: b f Abou Zouz - Star (Most Welcome) With ldrs, wknd over 1f out: modest form prev: eff at 6f on fast grnd.		hd	61
2861	**HEY PRESTO 15** [11]4-9-8 (69) P Robinson 3/1 FAV: 40-00056: In tch, eff & short of room dist, no dngr.		¾	68
1050	**CHICKADO 101** [15]3-8-9 (62) Paul Eddery 22/1: 0613-367: Held up, btn dist: over 3 mth abs.		1½	57
3146	**ONE WAY TICKET 4** [3]4-9-8 p (69) R Mullen 6/1: 2031008: Cl-up, led 2f out till dist, no extra.		nk	63
2752	**FULL SPATE 19** [9]9-9-7 (68) Dane O'Neill 7/1: 6463209: Slow away & nvr a factor: see 2626, 2451.		nk	61
2975	**A TEEN 10** [6]6-8-10 (57) D Kinsella 14/1: 6600600: 10th: Al bhd: see 740, 451.		½	48
2791	**JUST ONE SMILE 17** [12]4-8-8 (55) W Supple 16/1: 0360000: 11th: Al bhd: see 2791, 1660.		½	44
2925	**SMART STARPRINCESS 12** [7]3-8-7 (60) S Righton 40/1: 1123500: 12th: Led 3f till wknd over 1f out.		3½	40
2384	**BRONX BOMBER 34** [2]6-8-4 (51) J Quinn 12/1: 600-1100: 13th: In tch, wknd 2f out: btr 1839 (bndd).		hd	30
2768	**ITS ECCO BOY 19** [14]6-8-11 (58) J Mackay 25/1: 0000000: 14th: In tch, wknd 2f out: see 500 (aw).		8	13

14 Ran   Time 1m 10.71(0.91)   Owned: Mr J J Staunton   Trained: Malton

---

EPSOM   THURSDAY 15.07.04   Lefthand, Very Sharp, Undulating Track

Official Going GOOD.

3214   6.25 Fts E B F Median Auction Maiden Stakes 2yo (E)
£4849 £1492 £746   7f rnd   Good 58   -16 Slow   Inside

2594	**IN THE FAN 26** [1] J L Dunlop 2-9-0 T Quinn 8/11 FAV: 21: Broke well & made all, styd on strongly despite running green, hands & heels: well bckd: eff at 7f, will stay 1m: acts on gd & firm grnd, stiff/gall or sharp/undul trk: likes to force the pace: can rate higher & win in btr grade, see 2594.			94+
	KISWAHILI [6] Sir Mark Prescott 2-8-9 S Sanders 8/1: 2: ch f Selkirk - Kiliniski (Niniski) Trkd ldrs, eff 2f out, kept on well fnl 1f: op 13/2, debut: Feb foal, half-sister to sev wnrs, incl 9/11f scorer Robe Chinoise: dam 12f wnr: eff at 7f, relish 1m+ will suit: acts on gd: v promising, win races.		1¼	84+
1677	**SECRET PACT 64** [7] M Johnston 2-9-0 R Ffrench 5/2: 423: Chsd wnr, wknd fnl 1f: bckd from 4/1, 9 wk abs: longer trip & not disgraced: see 1677 (soft).		3	83
2876	**DISCOMANIA 14** [3] R Charlton 2-9-0 R Hughes 20/1: 04: b c Pursuit of Love - Discomatic (Roberto) Chsd ldrs, outpcd 1.5f out, rallied late under a kind ride: April foal, half-brother to 7/10f performer Clog Dance, half-brother to a couple of mid-dist/staying wnrs: dam a wnr in France: improve.		hd	83
2876	**BALL BOY 14** [5]2-9-0 C Catlin 20/1: 05: b c Xaar - Tanz (Sadler's Wells) Slowly away, late prog, nvr dngrs: clr of rem: £80,000 Jan foal: half-brother to several wnrs: dam 12f wnr: relish 1m+.		hd	83
2570	**SPEAGLE 26** [4]2-9-0 J Fortune 40/1: 056: Prom, fdd fnl 1f.		4	75
	YARDSTICK [2]2-9-0 R L Moore 20/1: 7: Slowly away, al towards rear on debut.		9	57
	MICKEHAHA [8]2-9-0 P Doe 50/1: 8: Swerved left, al bhd, fin last on debut.		½	56

8 Ran   Time 1m 25.31 (5.21)   Owned: Mr Oliver Murphy (Ireland)   Trained: Arundel

---

EPSOM   THURSDAY 15.07.04   Lefthand, Very Sharp, Undulating Track

Official Going GOOD.

3215   6.55 Pinnacle Insurance Claiming Stakes 3yo+ (E)
£4066 £1251 £626   7f rnd   Good 58   +03 Fast   Inside

3067	**LADY MO 6** [7] G G Margarson 3-8-7 (60) S Sanders 12/1: 0123061: Trkd ldrs, imprvd to chall 2f out, went on dist, styd on strongly, rdn out: op 16/1, best time of evening: suited by 7f/1m on gd, firm & both AWs, poss gd/soft: likes a sharp trk & suited for sell/claim grade: see 1222 (AW seller).			69
3045	**LORD OF THE EAST 7** [4] D Nicholls 5-9-10 (73) Alex Greaves 5/4 FAV: 2013232: Keen & led early, regained lead halfway till collared dist, no extra cl-home: well bckd: another consistent run, likes Epsom.		2	73
2873	**CAPTAIN SAIF 14** [10] R Hannon 4-9-0 T (75) R L Moore 9/2: 35-00043: Prom, ev ch dist, not qckn cl-home: bckd from 11/2, tried a t-strap, clmd for 8,000: acts on gd & firm grnd: see 2662.		nk	62

1111 **ARABIE 96** [1] Ian Williams 6-9-2 (86) Martin Dwyer 8/1: 05-00004: b g Polish Precedent - Always **hd** **63**
Friendly (High Line) Chsd ldrs, onepcd fnl 1f: unplcd in a nov hdle 9 days ago: lightly rcd for M Johnston in '03,
prev term trained by H Cecil & rnr-up twice in val h'caps: eff over a stiff 12f, both wins at 10f: acts on fast &
soft, any trk: now with I Williams. 2 Jun'02 Asco 10g/f 104-99 A: 2 May'02 Wind 10sft 102-96 B:
1 Aug'01 Yarm 10gd 97- C: 1 Jun'01 Wind 10g/f 90-80 C: 2 May'01 Thir 12g/f 89- D:
2840 **CERTAIN JUSTICE 15** [5]6-9-12 (70) T Quinn 8/1: 40-06505: Held up, styd on late, nvr dngrs: op **2½** **68**
6/1, top-weight: did not look at home on this unique trk, see 44 (AW).
3034 **ESPADA 8** [6]8-8-12 bl (52) S W Kelly 11/1: 4415046: Led till halfway, sn wknd: op 8/1. **2** **50**
2768 **DEXILEOS 19** [3]5-9-0 t (40) N Chalmers(5) 66/1: 0000007: Prom, wknd 2f out. **½** **51$**
3176 **SOCIAL CONTRACT 2** [9]7-8-12 (48) C Catlin 40/1: 2000008: Al towards rear: qck reapp. **2** **45**
2975 **PICCLEYES 10** [8]3-8-8 bl (63) R Hughes 16/1: 3-000109: Held up wide, nvr nr ldrs: btr 2586 (6f). **¾** **47**
9 Ran   Time 1m 24.01 (3.91)   Owned: The Gunnicks Partnership   Trained: Newmarket

---

3216   **7.25 Pinnacle Direct & Affinity Marketing Classified Stakes 3yo+ 0-75 (D)**
£6906 £2125 £1063   **1m2f18y**   **Good 58**   **-01 Slow**   Inside

2748 **RONDELET 19** [7] R M Beckett 3-8-7 (76) S Sanders 5/1: 4-202321: Held up, hdwy wide to lead dist, **84**
rdn clr cl-home: bckd from 9/1: overdue first success: eff at 1m/10f on fast & gd/soft, any trk.
3044* **SCOTTISH RIVER 7** [4] M D I Usher 5-9-9 (75) Hayley Turner(5) 10/1: 6146612: Held up, hdwy wide 2f **1¼** **85**
out, styd on into 2nd but not reach wnr: remains in fine form, see 3044 (C/D).
1877 **KENTUCKY KING 56** [16] P W Hiatt 4-9-7 (79) J Fortune 40/1: 1030003: Mid-div, hdwy to chall dist, **hd** **83**
no extra cl-home: 8 wk abs: gd run from modest high draw & rapid back to form: stays a sharp 10f: see 1057 & 800.
3089 **TIDAL 6** [15] A W Carroll 5-9-0 (74) R Hughes 4/1 FAV: 0-611034: Made most till dist, no extra: **nk** **75**
well bckd tho' drifted from 5/2, clr of rem: prob flattered 3089 (Gr 3), see 2371.
2956 **ETON 11** [14]8-9-3 (73) Alex Greaves 20/1: 3051235: Keen & prom, wknd fnl 1f: see 2956 & 2356. **5** **70**
2903 **TRAVELLING BAND 13** [3]6-9-5 (77) T Block(7) 33/1: 0024-006: Held up, prog 2f out, sn no impress. **1½** **70**
2225* **WAZIRI 41** [10]3-8-8 (77) S Drowne 5/1: 464-17: Nvr btr than mid-div: 6 wk abs: btr 2225. **nk** **69**
2317 **ACOMB 36** [11]4-9-5 (77) J Murtagh 9/1: 0601108: Prom 1m, grad wknd: btr 2129. **2½** **65**
519 **RYANS FUTURE 166** [1]4-9-7 (79) C Catlin 25/1: 1415-509: Held up, nvr a factor: abs: see 174 (AW). **nk** **66**
2930 **WHITGIFT ROCK 12** [6]3-8-6 (73) Martin Dwyer 12/1: 2000320: 10th: Led early, prom, wknd 2f out. **1¾** **60**
2694 **ANALYZE 21** [5]6-9-3 (72) R L Moore 25/1: 06-23540: 11th: Nvr a factor in rear. **2** **57**
2264 **KATIYPOUR 38** [9]7-9-3 (75) Lisa Jones(3) 9/1: 3120140: 12th: Trkd ldrs, wknd 2f out: btr 1691 (1m, fm). **1** **55**
2687 **JUST A FLUKE 21** [2]3-8-8 (77) R Ffrench 12/1: 22-40230: 13th: Held up, al strug: btr 2687 & 2443. **3½** **52**
2929 **LILLI MARLANE 12** [13]4-9-0 (72) W Ryan 16/1: 2600100: 14th: Held up, al rear: btr 2719 (fm). **1¾** **45**
625 **PERFIDIOUS 152** [12]6-9-3 (73) D Sweeney 20/1: 01-32530: 15th: Chsd ldrs, lost place 3f out, eased. **10** **33**
15 Ran   Time 2m 09.77 (5.97)   Owned: Mr Richard A Pegum & Mrs Richard Aykroyd   Trained: Lambourn

---

3217   **7.55 Pinnacle Warranty Services Handicap Stakes 3yo+ 0-75 (E)**   **[75]**
£5460 £1680 £840   **1m4f10y**   **Good 58**   **-00 Slow**   Centre

2329* **FLYING SPIRIT 35** [3] G L Moore 5-9-8 (69) R L Moore 10/3: 3102-111: Trkd ldr, qcknd to lead 3f **79**
out, rdn clr fnl 1f: op 9/4: completed hat-trick, suited by 12f on firm & gd/soft: loves a sharp/undul trk, esp
Brighton & Epsom: continues in terrific form, see 2329 & 1693.
2673 **RAJAM 22** [7] D Nicholls 6-9-12 vis (73) Alex Greaves 10/1: 0130652: Chsd ldrs, went after wnr 2f **2½** **77**
out, no impress fnl 1f under top-weight: another consistent run, see 1796.
2329 **PAY THE SILVER 35** [5] I A Wood 6-9-4 p (65) T P Queally 7/1: 0402033: Rear, styd on late into **2** **65**
3rd, nvr dngrs: tchd 10/1: usually runs well here at Epsom, often gets himself too far bhd early on: see 1986.
2651 **MOST SAUCY 23** [8] I A Wood 8-8-10 (57) Hayley Turner(5) 4/1: 5034504: Held up, styd on late, nvr **¾** **57**
dngrs: op 13/2 & shorter priced stablemate of 3rd: slipped to a handy mark.
3040* **MAN THE GATE 7** [6]5-8-10 (57) S Sanders 3/1 FAV: 5036215: Held up, prog when short of room 3f **¾** **56**
out, hmpd 2f out, chsd ldrs fnl 1f, wknd cl-home: did not get the run of today's race & reportedly hung left.
3105* **ISAAF 5** [1]5-9-9 (6ex) (70) L Keniry(3) 8/1: 1024416: Led till 3f out, grad wknd: qck reapp, op 11/2. **3½** **64**
2923 **KEEP ON MOVIN 12** [9]3-9-1 (75) J Fortune 10/1: 531-5027: Trkd ldrs, rdn & btn 2f out: btr 2923. **3** **64**
4071§ **SIR ALFRED 314** [2]5-8-11 (58) E Ahern 25/1: 200630-8: b g Royal Academy - Magnificent Star **dist** **7**
(Silver Hawk) Chsd ldrs, wknd 3f out, eased & virtually p.u. on reapp: h'cap plcd in '03: '03 juv nov hdle wnr
(rtd 101h, eff at 2m on firm): '02 h'cap wnr (with B Millman): eff at 10/13f on firm & fast grnd: likes a
sharp/undul trk, can run well fresh: reportedly lost action today.
2 Jun'03 Bath 10.2fm 65-64 E: 1 Apr'02 Brig 10fm 73-66 E:
8 Ran   Time 2m 41.76 (6.96)   Owned: Richard Green (Fine Paintings)   Trained: Brighton

---

3218   **8.25 Pinnacle Creditor Handicap Stakes 3yo 0-80 (D)**   **[87]**
£8327 £2562 £1281   **7f rnd**   **Good 58**   **-02 Slow**   Inside

2971 **PICKLE 10** [7] S C Williams 3-8-4 (63) Martin Dwyer 5/1: 4103361: Trkd ldrs, imprvd to lead dist, **73**
styd on strongly under hands & heels: eff at 6/7f on firm, soft & polytrk: likes a sharp/undul trk: see 2590 & 1577.
2732 **YASHIN 20** [4] M H Tompkins 3-8-0 (59) F P Ferris(3) 16/1: 050-0032: Led till dist, kept on but **1¾** **64**
not pace of wnr: eff at 7f/1m on gd & fast: lightly rcd front runner, see 2732 (clmr).
2906* **HERE TO ME 13** [6] R Hannon 3-8-13 (72) R L Moore 8/1: 5344213: Prom, ev ch till no extra cl-home. **½** **74**
1577 **HEAD BOY 70** [8] S Dow 3-7-12 (4oh) (53) Lisa Jones(3) 33/1: 4005654: Held up, well bhd till styd **¾** **59**
on strongly fnl 1f, nrst fin: 10 wk abs: does not look an easy ride, but has ability for this grade: see 1054.
2734 **TONY THE TAP 20** [5]3-9-7 (80) T Quinn 10/3: 4-12225: Held up, prog wide 2f out, nvr dngrs: **¾** **80**
top-weight, op 9/4: prev in fine form over 5f: see 2734 & 2593.
2918 **PLACE COWBOY 12** [3]3-9-4 (77) E Ahern 9/4 FAV: 2-15246: Held up, nvr on terms: well bckd **1¾** **74**
reportedly unsuited by this gd grnd, did not seem at home on this unique trk: btr 2590 (firm).
2797 **MR HULLABALOU 17** [9]3-8-6 (65) M Henry 33/1: 0450007: Trkd ldrs, wknd dist. **½** **61**
4947§ **DARLA 259** [1]3-8-11 (70) J Murtagh 16/1: 42306-8: b f Night Shift - Darbela (Doyoun) Chsd ldrs **3½** **59**
5.5f, grad wknd on reapp: dual mdn plcd in '03: eff at 5f on gd & firm, handles a sharp or gall trk: with J Payne.
2 Jul'03 Warw 5fm 67- E:
2634 **RAYSOOT 24** [2]3-7-13 (58) J McAuley 11/2: 000-0259: Sn well bhd, fin last: bckd: btr 2205 (AW). **5** **37**
9 Ran   Time 1m 24.32 (4.22)   Owned: Mr S P Tindall   Trained: Newmarket

EPSOM THURSDAY 15.07.04 Lefthand, Very Sharp, Undulating Track

3219 **8.55 Pinnacle Investments Maiden Handicap Stakes 3yo 0-70 (E)** **[77]**
£4290 £1320 £660 **1m114y rnd** **Good 58** **-10 Slow** Inside

875 **DESERT REIGN 118** [13] A P Jarvis 3-9-2 (65) T P Queally 6/1: 000-51: ch g Desert King - Moondance (Siberian Express) Trkd ldrs trav well, eff & wandered 1.5f out, led ins fnl 1f, held on drvn out: long abs & has been gelded, gamble from 33/1: lightly rcd & mod mdn form in '03: eff over a sharp/undul 8.5f on gd grnd, clearly runs well fresh: benefitted from first try in h'cap company & landed a decent gamble. **73**
1690 **QUARRYMOUNT 64** [15] Sir Mark Prescott 3-8-6 (55) S Sanders 7/1: 000-02: b g Polar Falcon - Quilt (Terimon) Mid-div, prog wide 2f out, fin well but just failed: 9 wk abs: lightly rcd & some mdn promise in '03: apprec this step up to 8.5f & h'cap company, 10f will suit: acts on gd grnd, runs well fresh: will find similar. *nk* **62+**
2873 **ARCHERFIELD 14** [12] J W Hills 3-8-10 t (59) E Ahern 14/1: 2300233: Mid-div, prog wide 2f out, ev ch fnl 1f & just btn in a tight fin: another consistent run: see 2873 & 2641. *nk* **65**
2922 **IFFY 12** [9] P D Cundell 3-8-9 (58) S Carson 9/1: 050-404: Held up, imprvd 2f out, styd on & nrst fin: only btn around 1L & clr of rem: worth a try over 10f now, handles gd grnd & polytrack: see 545. *¾* **62**
3058 **IPHIGENIA 7** [16]3-9-2 (65) R L Moore 16/1: 0-050245: Front rank, led 2f out & kicked for home, collared entering fnl 1f, wknd: did not stay this sharp 8.5f: see 2716 (7f mdn). *3½* **62**
2885 **TREASON TRIAL 14** [10]3-8-13 (62) G Baker 33/1: 40-06: b g Peintre Celebre - Pampabella (High Estate) Hmpd start, styd on fnl 1f, nrst fin on h'cap bow: twice rcd for J Fanshawe in '03, mdn 4th (rtd 71$): eff at 7f on fast grnd, 10f shld suit: encouraging effort. *1½* **56**
2971 **LITTLE EYE 10** [11]3-8-13 vis (62) N Pollard 16/1: 4030647: Chsd ldrs, onepcd fnl 1f. *nk* **55**
2877 **GELLER 14** [2]3-9-5 (68) R Hughes 20/1: 204-5408: Led early, regained lead 3f out till 2f out, wknd. *1¾* **58**
3092 **ADORATA 6** [5]3-9-5 (68) O Urbina 12/1: 0320239: Held up, nvr nr ldrs: btr 2936. *½* **57**
2922 **JARVO 12** [6]3-8-13 t (62) Steven Harrison(7) 33/1: 30-25400: 10th: Prom, wkng when badly hmpd dist. *3½* **44**
2434 **GROWLER 31** [1]3-8-8 (57) T Quinn 12/1: 0000-030: 11th: Prom, wknd 2f out: btr 2434. *6* **27**
2650 **BLUE JAVA 23** [4]3-8-12 (61) S Drowne 11/1: 040-000: 12th: Dwelt, nvr nr ldrs: see 2650. *nk* **30**
2955 **RESPLENDENT KING 11** [14]3-9-7 bl (70) J Fortune 7/1: 5532330: 13th: Made most till 3f out, wknd: bckd from 10/1, top-weight & btr expected: prev consistent, see 2955 & 2333 (12f). *7* **25**
2993 **HUM 9** [7]3-8-7 P (56) Hayley Turner(5) 66/1: 600-00: 14th: Al bhd: tried cheek pieces: see 2993. *8* **0**
2971 **ROSACARA 10** [3]3-9-3 t (66) J Murtagh 11/4 FAV: 504-220: 15th: Mid-div, wknd 3f out, eased considerably: joc looking down & something prob amiss: well bckd & much btr 2971. *4* **0**
1078 **TURTLE PATRIARCH 99** [8]3-8-13 (62) Martin Dwyer 14/1: 60-00: 16th: b c Turtle Island - La Doyenne (Masterclass) Stumbled start, al bhd & t.o.: long abs: mdn promise on first of 2 '03 starts (rtd 69+): with Mrs A Perrett, lost all ch at the start today & allowed to come home in own time. *dist* **0**
16 Ran Time 1m 47.63(5.83) Owned: Mr Allen B Pope Trained: Twyford

DONCASTER THURSDAY 15.07.04 Lefthand, Flat, Galloping Track

Official Going Good/Soft

3220 **6.40 St Johns Ambulance Apprentice Handicap Stakes 3yo+ 35-55 (F)** **[58]**
£3708 £1141 £571 **5f str** **Good/Soft 83** **-06 Slow** Stands side

3180 **ROSIES RESULT 2** [19] M Todhunter 4-9-1 (45) Jemma Marshall(3) 12/1: 000-0001: Rcd centre, prog halfway, rdn out to lead cl-home: qck reapp: eff at 5f on firm & gd/soft grnd: back to form, see 2320. **52**
3165 **ROAN RAIDER 3** [10] M J Polglase 4-9-9 vis (53) K Ghunowa(3) 16/1: 5350202: Rcd centre, al cl-up, styd on to lead bef 1f out, hdd under press cl-home: qck reapp: only just denied & deserves to lose mdn tag. *hd* **58**
3180 **LARKYS LOB 2** [13] J O'Reilly 5-9-1 (45) H Fellows(5) 7/2 FAV: 1221623: Rcd centre, up front & ev ch bef 1f out, no extra ins fnl 1f: qck reapp: not disgraced but unable to make running as in 3180. *1¾* **45**
2975 **KENNINGTON 10** [9] Mrs C A Dunnett 4-9-9 BL (53) Laura Pike(3) 20/1: 4002004: Rcd centre, led, hdd bef 1f out, sn no extra: first time blnks: eff at 5f, return to 6/7f will suit: see 2347. *½* **52**
3180 **LE MERIDIEN 2** [20]6-9-7 p (51) Donna Caldwell(3) 6/1: 0-500065: Rcd stands side, prom & ev ch bef 1f out, no extra fnl 1f: qck reapp: btr 2429. *1½* **46**
3180 **LEVELLED 2** [18]10-9-1 (45) R Keogh(3) 16/1: 3106506: Chsd ldrs till dist, no extra: qck reapp. *¾* **38**
2951 **PERCY DOUGLAS 12** [17]4-8-13 T (43) M Stainton(3) 25/1: 0006007: Bhd, prog halfway, kept on ins fnl 1f. *shd* **35**
2784 **POMPEY BLUE 18** [3]3-9-5 (54) K Jackson(6) 33/1: 5500008: Rcd far side, styd on to lead stands side group after 3f, no extra fnl 1f: btr 3. *½* **45**
3180 **BALLYBUNION 2** [1]5-9-8 (52) P J Benson(5) 9/1: 0530009: Dwelt far side, prog halfway, onepcd fnl 1f. *hd* **42**
3180 **JOYCES CHOICE 2** [15]5-9-4 BL (48) B O'Neill(3) 20/1: 0R54000: 10th: Slow away, nvr nrr than mid-div: first time blnks & qck reapp: btr 1179. *nk* **37**
3045 **ATTORNEY 7** [2]6-9-2 vis (46) Lucy Russell(3) 12/1: 6500060: 11th: Handy far side 3f, sn no extra. *hd* **34**
1948 **SO SOBER 52** [6]6-8-10 (40) Stacey Renwick(3) 20/1: 4004300: 12th: In tch centre 3f, no extra. *½* **27**
3180 **RUM DESTINY 2** [11]5-9-3 vis (47) A Reilly(3) 40/1: 000-0000: 13th: Rcd centre, handy 3f, wknd. *½* **33**
2657 **COLLEGE HIPPIE 23** [5]5-9-1 BL (45) S Yourston(3) 40/1: 060-0000: 14th: In tch till halfway, wknd. *1¾* **26**
2981 **BOANERGES 10** [7]7-9-11 p (55) C J Davies(6) 16/1: 2400500: 15th: Bhd, nvr a factor. *nk* **35**
3054 **RED LEICESTER 7** [4]4-9-7 vis (51) J Roberts(8) 15/2: 0516050: 16th: Led far side group 3f, fdd. *1* **28**
3143 **JUWWI 4** [14]10-9-6 (50) Hazel Boyd(8) 16/1: 6266000: 17th: Rear, nvr a factor: qck reapp. *¾* **25**
2803 **Scary Night 17** [8]4-9-7 p(51) K Pierrepont(8) 16/1:0 2690 **Miss Ceylon 21** [16]4-8-11 (41) A Rutter(3) 25/1:0
19 Ran Time 1m 2.65 (4.45) Owned: Mrs J Mandle Trained: Penrith

3221 **7.10 Rectangle Group Novice Stakes 2yo (D)**
£4946 £1522 £761 **6f str** **Good/Soft 83** **-02 Slow** Stands side

2316* **ABRAXAS ANTELOPE 36** [5] J Howard Johnson 2-9-4 R Winston 7/2: 11: Prom 3f, slightly outpcd, switched wide & styd on to lead ins fnl 1f, rdn out, more in hand: eff at 6f, 7f looks sure to suit: acts on fast & gd/soft grnd, stiff/undul or gall trk: useful run conceding weight all round & well up to List/Gr grade. **109+**
2467 **DARIO GEE GEE 30** [2] K A Ryan 2-9-1 N Callan 3/1: 12202: Prom, styd on to lead dist, hdd ins fnl 1f, not pace of wnr: clr rem: op 11/2: useful eff on drop in grade & can find similar: see 2039. *1¾* **99**

2689* SIR ANTHONY 21 [7] B Smart 2-9-1   F Lynch 14/1: 13: Slow away, prog over 2f out, no impress   5   **84**
dist: up in class & ran to form of win in 2689 (med auct mdn).
2610* KRYNICA 25 [3] Sir Michael Stoute 2-8-13   K Fallon 6/1: 14: Prom, ev ch bef 1f out, sn no extra: nk   **81**
op 9/2: ran to form of debut win in 2610 (mdn, fast).
2902* HARVEST WARRIOR 13 [1]2-9-1   D Allan 9/4 FAV: 2215: Led, hdd & lkd held when hmpd dist, not   4   **71**
recover: much closer without troubling front 2 without interference: see 2902.
1401* ELGIN MARBLES 79 [4]2-8-13   Dane O'Neill 8/1: 16: In tch 4f, fdd, eased ins fnl 1f: abs, btr 1401.   22   **29**
2889 CADOGEN SQUARE 13 [6]2-8-6   Darren Williams 200/1: 07: ch f Takhlid - Mount Park (Colonel   2½   **15**
Collins) In tch 4f, sn wknd, eased ins fnl 1f: March first foal, dam successful at 5f: sire decent performer up to 1m.
7 Ran   Time 1m 15.93 (5.13)   Owned: Andrea & Graham Wylie   Trained: Crook

---

3222   **7.40 Rascal Uk Com Vip Hospitality Stakes Handicap 3yo+ 0-80 (D)**   **[79]**
     £5652 £1739 £870   **1m4f**   **Good/Soft 83**   **-24 Slow**   Inside

3085* DICKIE DEADEYE 6 [1] G B Balding 7-8-6   (57) R Thomas(5) 4/6 FAV: 6522311: Made all, clr after   **66**+
halfway, rdn out ins fnl 2f, eased cl home, val 5L+: bckd at odds-on: qck reapp: eff at 10f, apprec recent step up
to 12f with front running tactics: loves gd & hvy: thriving, land hat-trick: see 3085.
2673 FIELD SPARK 22 [4] J A Glover 4-8-6 p (57) F Norton 10/1: 6152302: Bhd, prog 5f out, kept on ins   2½   **59**
fnl 2f, al held by wnr: handles firm & gd/soft grnd: see 2465 & 2217.
2465 MARITIME BLUES 30 [8] J G Given 4-8-13   (64) B Doyle 16/1: 0001063: Mid-div, prog to chase wnr 3f   ½   **64**
out, no impress dist: clr rem: acts on firm, gd/soft & fibresand: 6lb higher than last win in 1875.
2754 NIGHT SIGHT 19 [2] Mrs S Lamyman 7-9-4   (69) K Fallon 7/2: 04-02344: Trkd ldrs, prog to chase wnr   20   **43**
after 6f, fdd 3f out: loves Doncaster but wants faster grnd: see 2233.
2788 SECRET JEWEL 18 [3]4-9-6   (71) K McEvoy 12/1: 0/0-605: b f Hernando - Opalette (Sharrood) Rear,   7   **35**
nvr a factor: op 9/1: unplcd sole '03 start (mdn, rtd 72): with Lady Herries.
2746 MIDSHIPMAN EASY 19 [6]3-8-10   (74) M Fenton 20/1: 0-32006: Bhd, nvr a factor: btr 1651.   7   **28**
2217 ZAN LO 41 [7]4-8-4   (55) J Quinn 66/1: 16-00607: In tch 7f, sn fdd: 6 wk abs: btr 1681.   26   **0**
2900 PRINCE HOLING 13 [5]4-9-10   (75) R Winston 22/1: 122-5008: Prom 7f, fdd: btr 1068.   dist   **0**
8 Ran   Time 2m 42.67 (12.87)   Owned: Miss B Swire   Trained: Andover

---

3223   **8.10 Real Radio 'winners' Handicap Stakes Fillies 3yo+ 0-95 (C)**   **[89]**
     £9646 £2968 £1484   **7f str**   **Good/Soft 83**   **-13 Slow**   Stands side

3017 SCOTLAND THE BRAVE 8 [5] J D Bethell 4-8-5 P (66) K McEvoy 12/1: 0-035041: Led, hdd bef 1f out,   **72**
rallied to lead fnl 1f, rdn out despite edging right: winning form at 7f, has tried 1m: acts on fast & gd/soft
grnd: apprec fitting of first time cheek pieces & is h'capped to win again: see 2022
3117 RAPHAEL 5 [4] T D Easterby 5-9-2   (77) R Winston 5/1: 10340042: In tch, prog & ev ch dist, kept on   ¾   **82**
but held by wnr when short of room cl-home: qck reapp: solid run & has shown enough to find similar.
3077 PLAY THAT TUNE 6 [9] M Johnston 4-10-0   (89) J Fanning 5/2 FAV: 33-05433: Prom, styd on to lead   nk   **93**
bef 1f out, hdd ins fnl 1f, no extra when short of room cl-home: qck reapp: clr rem: another gd eff: see 3077.
3069 STARBECK 6 [7] P Howling 6-9-7   (82) P McCabe 9/2: 0540054: Dwelt, prog & short of room 2f out,   3   **80**
switched & kept on fnl 1f, nrst fin: qck reapp: see 1620.
2491 TOTALLY YOURS 29 [2]3-9-6   (89) R Mullen 20/1: 210-0405: Mid-div, prog 3f out, no impress fnl 1f.   ½   **86**
2931 FLASHING BLADE 12 [11]4-8-7 t (68) W Supple 9/1: 0000106: Chsd ldrs over 5f, no extra: btr 2633 (fast).   shd   **64**
2791 FAVOUR 17 [3]4-8-10   (71) K Fallon 13/2: 223-2067: Rear, prog when short of room 2f out, sn btn.   1½   **64**
3137 BINT ROYAL 4 [6]6-7-13 (1ow)(4oh)p (55) J Quinn 20/1: 0430058: Handy 5f, wknd: qck reapp.   1½   **50**
1066 STRONG HAND 100 [1]4-9-3   (78) P Mulrennan(5) 6/1: 5110-639: In tch 5f, wknd: long abs: btr 1066.   shd   **67**
2491 SURF THE NET 29 [10]3-9-9   (92) Dane O'Neill 11/1: 16-300: 10th: Prom till halfway, wknd: btr 2136.   3½   **74**
2421 LIVE WIRE LUCY 32 [8]3-9-10   (93) J F Egan 50/1: 155-0300: 11th: Bhd, nvr a factor: btr 2421.   17   **44**
11 Ran   Time 1m 29.98 (6.78)   Owned: Mr Robert Gibbons   Trained: Middleham

---

3224   **8.40 Sasha Lyons Memorial Trophy E B F Novice Stakes Fillies 2yo (D)**
     £4732 £1456 £728   **5f str**   **Good/Soft 83**   **-25 Slow**   Stands side

1173* WORD PERFECT 91 [1] M W Easterby 2-9-2   Dale Gibson 5/6 FAV: 311: Made all, pushed out fnl 1f,   **93**+
val bit more: long abs: eff at 5f, 6f will suit: acts on gd & soft grnd, sharp or gall trk: goes well fresh:
improving with every start & can rate higher: see 1173.
2847 BIBURY FLYER 15 [3] M R Channon 2-8-9   T E Durcan 100/30: 2233522: Cl-up, ev ch bef 1f out, styd   1½   **81**
on ins fnl 1f, not pace wnr: clr rem: gd run but has yet to get head in front & headgear may suit, see 2847.
PIVOTALS PRINCESS 0 [2] B A McMahon 2-8-5   W Supple 9/4: 3: ch f Pivotal - Art Princess (Fairy   4   **65**
King) Slow away, prog 2f out, wknd fnl 1f: debut: Feb foal, cost 11,000gns: half-sister wnr in Scandinavia: sire
decent performer at sprint dists: ran green here.
2933 OCHIL HILLS DANCER 12 [4] A Crook 2-8-9   V Halliday 16/1: 0504: Handy 3f, wknd: btr 2056.   9   **45**
4 Ran   Time 1m 3.64 (5.44)   Owned: Mrs Jean Turpin   Trained: Sheriff Hutton

---

3225   **9.10 'doncaster Chamber Sponsorship Preview' Handicap Stakes 3yo+ 0-85 (D)**   **[80]**
     £5652 £1739 £870   **1m str**   **Good/Soft 83**   **+07 Fast**   Stands side

2947* PARNASSIAN 12 [6] G B Balding 4-8-9   (61) R Thomas(5) 5/1: 3130511: Rear, gd prog to lead bef 1f   **77**+
out, sn hung right, pushed clr, val 8L+: eff btwn 7f/1m on fm & fast, loves gd & gd/soft: confidence high, win again.
3074 HILLS OF GOLD 6 [9] M W Easterby 5-9-5   (71) P Mulrennan(5) 4/1: 00-41032: Handy, kept on bef 1f   5   **77**
out, al held by easy wnr: qck reapp: another creditable effort: see 3074 & 1366.
3001 AFRICAN SAHARA 9 [2] Miss D Mountain 5-9-13 t (79) G Carter 9/1: 00-00603: Trkd ldrs, no extra dist.   ¾   **83**
2931 TROUSERS 12 [1] Andrew Reid 5-8-10   (62) J F Egan 3/1 FAV: 136-0134: Led, hdd bef 1f out, wknd.   1¼   **64**
3001 TOPTON 9 [3]10-9-13 bl (79) K Fallon 6/1: 0046265: Held up, nvr nrr than mid-div: jt top-weight: nk   **80**
won this race 12 mths ago off a 1lb higher mark: btr 2853 & 714.
2935* YOUNG MR GRACE 12 [5]4-9-10   (76) A Mullen(7) 11/1: 0342516: Cl-up over 6f, sn wknd: btr 2935.   ¾   **75**
2891 OPEN HANDED 13 [4]4-8-1 t (53) J Quinn 22/1: 0010557: Bhd, nvr a factor: btr 2891.   8   **38**
3042 MBOSI 7 [8]3-9-9   (84) J Fanning 6/1: 15-338: Handy 5f, fdd: qck reapp: v disapp: btr 3042.   10   **51**

2890　**ATLANTIC ACE 13** [7]7-9-4　(70)　F Lynch　18/1: 5-000609: Al bhd: btr 2087.　　　　　*8*　　**23**
9 Ran　Time 1m 42.64(6.14)　Owned: Miss B Swire　Trained: Andover

---

Official Going GOOD/FIRM (FIRM places).

3226	**2.10 Cubby Construction Limited Claiming Stakes 3yo+** (F)
	£3052 £872 £436　**1m3f206y**　**Good/Firm 20**　**-16 Slow**　Outside

3151　**TOMASINO 4** [3]　Mrs M Reveley 6-9-12 t (76)　K Darley　12/1: 0/66-4601: Made virtually all, pushed　　**73**
clr fnl 1f under hands & heels: top-weight, qck reapp: eff at 12f on firm & hvy grnd: handles a gall trk: back to
form with forcing tactics: has had plenty of probs but a class above these rivals: see 2356.
3149　**SPREE VISION 4** [2]　P Monteith 8-9-7 vis (50)　G Baker　5/2: 60/-60422: Held up, hdwy to chase wnr　　*5*　　**58**
2f out, kept on but no ch with wnr: well bckd, clr of rem: acts on fast & hvy grnd: gd run, see 3148.
2724　**BIG SMOKE 21** [7]　J Howard Johnson 4-9-3 p (60)　P Mulrennan(5) 5/1: 300-0453: Led early, chsd ldrs　　*5*　　**46**
till wknd fnl 1f: rtd higher 2724 (AW).
2900　**LORD DUNDEE 14** [1]　R C Guest 6-9-2 t (65)　Dean McKeown　20/1: 3/1/-004: Rear, mod late gains:　　*nk*　　**44**
dropped in grade: return to 14f will suit judged on this: see 2567.
2868　**PLATINUM CHARMER 15** [6]4-9-9 p (57)　Darren Williams　1/1 FAV: 4240325: Keen & prom, wknd dist:　　*2*　　**48**
well bckd from 7/4: better expected on this drop to claim company, a stronger pace suits: see 2868 (h'cap).
2811　**DEVINE LIGHT 18** [4]4-9-1 P (60)　R Winston　16/1: 0501-006: Keen & prom, wknd 2f out: cheekpieces.　　*14*　　**20**
3194　**RUSTY BOY 2** [5]3-8-5　V Halliday　100/1: 60-07: b g Defacto - Berl's Gift (Prince Sabo) Keen &　　*dist*　　**0**
trkd ldrs 1m, wknd & eased, t.o.: qck reapp & much longer trip: lightly rcd & modest form for A Crook.
7 Ran　Time 2m 35.21 (4.41)　Owned: Mr P D Savill　Trained: Saltburn

3227	**2.45 Border Construction Ltd Maiden Auction Stakes 2yo** (E)
	£3608 £1110 £555　**5f rnd**　**Good/Firm 20**　**-11 Slow**　Inside

2789　**PRO TEMPORE 18** [10]　Mrs J R Ramsden 2-8-6 (1ow)　A Culhane　9/2: 41: Led till halfway, remained　　**68**
prom & regained lead ins fnl 1f, held on drvn out: drifted from 7/2: eff at 5f on fast grnd, handles a stiff trk.
2682　**NITEOWL LAD 22** [6]　J O'Reilly 2-8-7　D Allan　14/1: 002: ch g Tagula - Mareha (Cadeaux Genereux)　　*nk*　　**67**
Front rank, led halfway till worn down cl-home: has recently been gldd & much imprvd form: £20,000 Apr foal: half
brother to a couple of wnr abroad: eff at 5f, imprvd for fast grnd today: could find a small race.
2611　**SHATIN LEADER 25** [8]　Miss L A Perratt 2-8-2　R Ffrench　25/1: P63: Chsd ldrs, sltly outpcd　　*nk*　　**61**
halfway, rallied strongly fnl 1f & just btn in a cl-fin: clr of rem: eff over a stiff 5f on fast grnd: see 2083.
　　　　HANSOMELLE [9]　B Mactaggart 2-8-4 (2ow)　P Mulrennan　20/1: 4: b f Titus Livius - Handsome Anna　　*2½*　　**56**
(Bigstone) Slowly away, styd on late, nvr dangerous on debut: 2,500 gns Mar 1st foal: dam styd 7f, sire a
high-class sprinter: eff at 5f on fast grnd, 6f will suit: some encouragement here.
　　　　TAHLAL [3]2-8-10　S Sanders　7/1: 5: b c Dr Fong - Chatterberry (Aragon) Chsd ldrs, outpcd　　*shd*　　**62**
halfway, rallied late on debut: op 10/1: Mar foal, cost 12,000 gns: half brother to 5/7f juv wnrs: dam a 5f juv
wnr, sire a top class miler: with Mrs A Duffield.
2670　**LORNA DUNE 23** [7]2-8-2　P Fessey　10/3 FAV: 3606: Sn outpcd, mod late prog, nvr dangerous:　　*1¼*　　**50**
shorter priced stable-mate of wnr: return to 6f will suit: see 1677 (debut, soft grnd).
2815　**KRISTIKHAB 21** [5]2-8-10　F Lynch　9/2: 0542007: Slowly away, nvr a factor: nicely bckd: btr 2177.　　*1½*　　**54**
2424　**SLATE GREY 33** [2]2-8-7　Darren Williams　12/1: 008: Slow away, prog when hmpd dist, sn eased.　　*1*　　**48**
2933　**DANCEINTHEVALLEY 13** [1]2-8-7　Dean McKeown　11/1: 09: Chsd ldrs, btn halfway: reportedly　　*1*　　**45**
unsuited by this fast grnd & was struck into.
2360　**NEGAS 35** [4]2-8-10　R Winston　9/1: 00: 10th: Dwelt, al bhd: unsuited by this fast grnd.　　*1¾*　　**43**
10 Ran　Time 1m 01.06 (1.56)　Owned: Mr P R C Morrison　Trained: Thirsk

3228	**3.15 Kingmoor Park Handicap Stakes 3yo+ 0-70** (E)	**[69]**
	£7898 £2430 £1215　**5f rnd**　**Good/Firm 20**　**+04 Fast**　Inside	

2957　**IZMAIL 12** [11]　D Nicholls 5-9-11　(66)　L Treadwell(7) 25/1: 5-000001: Nvr far away, kept on　　**72**
strongly to lead cl-home despite being hit by rivals whip: fair time: suited by 5f & gd or firm grnd: gd weight
carrier who made most of fav h'cap mark: see 1293.
2566　**PETERS CHOICE 27** [13]　I Semple 3-9-4 BL (63)　T Eaves(3) 33/1: 1-005002: Tried to make all,　　*nk*　　**67**
collared cl-home: imprvd form in 1st time blnks: fine front rng eff, ideally suited by a sharp trk: rider given a
3-day careless riding ban & 1-day for hitting rival with whip: see 69 (AW).
3165　**PLAYTIME BLUE 4** [9]　Mrs H Sweeting 4-9-4　(59)　G Baker　10/1: 3060533: Chsd ldr, kept on under　　*¾*　　**60**
press fnl 1f, btn around 1L: quick reapp: acts on gd form, see 3165.
2942　**TUSCAN FLYER 13** [16]　R Bastiman 6-9-5 bl (60)　R Ffrench　12/1: 0030404: Chsd ldrs, keeping on when　　*shd*　　**61**
short of room cl-home: op 16/1: see 2702.
2775*　**SOAKED 20** [2]11-9-8 bl (63)　A Culhane　10/1: 4041215: Held up, keeping on when short of room ins　　*hd*　　**63**
fnl 1f, nrst fin: change of tactics, usually front runs: see 2775.
3129　**XANADU 6** [7]8-8-12 p (53)　J Carroll　25/1: 0062006: Mid-div, styd on late, nrst fin: see 2445 & 1508.　　*1*　　**50**
2934　**MY BAYARD 13** [10]5-9-5 bl (60)　D Allan　16/1: 5010437: Prom, ev ch when short of room dist, onepace.　　*shd*　　**57**
3180*　**FAIRGAME MAN 3** [19]6-8-8 (6ex)p (49)　G Parkin　7/1: 0020518: Rear, late hdwy, nvr dngrs: qck reapp.　　*nk*　　**45**
3180　**FLYING TACKLE 3** [18]6-8-7 p (48)　Darren Williams　15/2: 0032109: Mid-div, keeping on when short of　　*hd*　　**44**
room cl-home: op 9/1, quick reapp: twice below 2981.
3080*　**HELLO ROBERTO 7** [1]3-9-13 (6ex) (72)　K Ghunowa(7) 16/1: 0253010: 10th: Rear, late prog.　　*½*　　**67**
2968　**PIRLIE HILL 11** [4]4-8-12　(53)　K Darley　25/1: 0160440: 11th: Rear, nvr nr ldrs.　　*hd*　　**48**
2849　**DARK CHAMPION 16** [3]4-9-4 p (59)　R Winston　50/1: 5300450: 12th: Nvr btr than mid-div: see 2849.　　*nk*　　**53**
3054　**BETTYS PRIDE 8** [6]5-8-12 P (53)　L Enstone(3) 20/1: 0-040660: 13th: Chsd ldrs till halfway: cheekpieces.　　*shd*　　**47**
2730　**AMERICAN COUSIN 21** [8]9-9-3　(58)　A Nicholls　25/1: 0102500: 14th: Rear, nvr nr ldrs: s/mate wnr.　　*¾*　　**49**
3150　**VIEWFORTH 4** [15]6-9-12 bl (67)　S Sanders　5/1: 0004300: 15th: Trkd ldrs, wknd & eased fnl 1f:　　*½*　　**57**
nicely bckd, quick reapp: showed much more 3150.
3073　**TALLY 7** [17]4-9-4　(59)　L Fletcher(3) 9/2 FAV: 0024430: 16th: Slowly away, nvr nr ldrs.　　*shd*　　**49**

CARLISLE   FRIDAY 16.07.04   Righthand, Stiff Track, Uphill Finish

2775 **Online Investor 20** [5]5-9-9 VIS(64) Alex Greaves 16/1:02320 **Feu Duty 37** [20]3-9-8 BL e(67) D McGaffin 20/1:0
18 Ran   Time 1m 00.31 (0.81)   Owned: Mr G M McGuinness   Trained: Thirsk

3229	3.45 Ken Hope Ltd Handicap Stakes 3yo+ 0-70 (E)					[69]
	£3851 £1185 £593	6f192y rnd	Good/Firm 20	-04 Slow	Inside	

2832 **WOOD DALLING 17** [15] I Semple 6-8-11 (52) R Winston 10/1: 305-0061: Mid-div, imprvd 2f out, styd **58**
on strongly to lead cl-home, pushed out, going away: gamble: eff at 7/10f on fm, fast & polytrack: win again.
2447* **PEPPER ROAD 32** [13] R Bastiman 5-8-10 (51) R Ffrench 4/1 FAV: 060-0012: Chsd ldrs, went on ent   nk   **55**
fnl 1f, caught cl-home: bckd from 7/1: eff at 7f/1m: in fine form & clrly loves Carlisle: see 2447 (1m here).
2958 **ZANJEER 12** [3] N Wilson 4-9-11 (66) P Mulrennan(5) 8/1: 4/40-0163: Chsd ldrs, led briefly dist,   hd   **70**
kept on & just btn in a cl-fin: remains in fine form, eff at 7f/1m on gd & fast grnd: see 2552.
3017 **SMITH N ALLAN OILS 9** [10] M Dods 5-8-13 p (54) L Enstone(3) 9/2: 0005224: Held up, some late gains.   2½   **53**
2954 **BORDER ARTIST 12** [8]5-9-10 (65) A Nicholls 13/2: 1004345: Rear, prog wide 2f out, nrst fin: see 2665.   hd   **64**
2809 **SILVER SEEKER 18** [6]4-9-1 (56) P Fessey 50/1: 0-500206: Chsd ldrs, onepcd fnl 1f: btr 2102.   2½   **50**
2752 **TIME TO REMEMBER 20** [1]6-9-2 (57) S Sanders 25/1: 0006007: Slowly away, prog halfway, btn dist.   1½   **48**
3102 **REDOUBTABLE 6** [11]13-8-13 (54) A Culhane 14/1: 1002168: Chsd ldrs, wknd dist: qck reappr.   nk   **44**
3153 **MENAI STRAIGHTS 4** [4]3-9-2 (64) J Fanning 8/1: 0635139: Chsd ldrs, wknd dist: quick reappr.   2   **50**
2967 **JEDEYDD 11** [14]7-9-0 t (55) S W Kelly 12/1: 0040640: 10th: Held up, nvr a factor: see 2967.   1¼   **38**
3136 **LOCOMBE HILL 5** [2]8-9-5 vis (60) J Carroll 14/1: 0050440: 11th: Led till dist, wknd: qck reappr.   ¾   **41**
2832 **LIBRE 17** [12]4-9-5 bl t (60) Dean McKeown 16/1: 4000100: 14th: Slow away, al bhd: twice below 2655.   ½   **40**
2935 **Waltzing Wizard 13** [9]5-8-10 (51) F Lynch 12/1:0   3017 **Dragon Prince 9** [7]4-9-13 (68) P Aspell(3) 100/1:0
14 Ran   Time 1m 25.28 (1.68)   Owned: Mr William Laird   Trained: Carluke

3230	4.20 Baines Wilson Maiden Stakes 3yo+ (D)				
	£5824 £1792 £896	6f192y rnd	Good/Firm 20	-10 Slow	Inside

2849 **FLASH RAM 16** [3] T D Easterby 3-9-0 bl (64) S Sanders 8/1: 3-642261: Front rank, went on dist,   **70**
just held on: deserved win & career best run: eff at 6/7f on firm & soft grnd in blnks/visor: see 2692.
2987 **OUNINPOHJA 11** [7] G A Swinbank 3-9-0 Dean McKeown 4/1: 432: Chsd ldrs, eff 2f out, fin strongly   shd   **69**
& just failed: clr rem: eff at 7f, return to 1m/10f will suit: acts on gd & fast: wld have won in another stride.
3059 **APERITIF 8** [1] W J Haggas 3-9-0 (73) S W Kelly 1/3 FAV: 663-0433: Mid-div, kept on late under   5   **59**
press, nvr dngrs: hvly bckd: return to 1m/10f will suit: proving costly to follow, see 3059 (val h'cap).
2200 **GOOD TIME BOBBY 42** [4] J O'Reilly 7-9-7 D Nolan(3) 25/1: 304: Led till dist, wknd: 6 wk abs,   2½   **54**
clr of rem: back in trip, see 2037 (debut).
        MINSTRELS DOUBLE [10]3-9-0 P Bradley 50/1: 5: ch g Jumbo Hirt - Hand On Heart (Taufan) Slowly   7   **40**
away, nvr a factor on debut: half brother to a winning hurdler: with F Murtagh.
2325 **SONEARSOFAR 37** [9]4-9-7 M Lawson(5) 66/1: 06: b g General Monash - Not Too Near (Nashamaa)   5   **30**
Rear, mod late gains: no form yet, with J Parkes.
2751 **SPOT IN TIME 20** [2]4-9-2 L Fletcher(3) 50/1: 0007: b f Mtoto - Kelimutu (Top Ville) Chsd ldrs,   4   **17**
btn over 2f out: modest form to date.
2987 **ALETHEA GEE 11** [8]6-9-2 T Eaves(3) 50/1: 0-08: Held up, nvr dngrs.   1   **15**
        LUMBACK [5]5-9-7 T Aspell(3) 50/1: 9: Slowly away, al bhnd on debut: t-strap.   ½   **19**
2722 **NARCISO 21** [6]4-9-7 P Mulrennan(5) 50/1: 0000: 10th: Chsd ldrs till halfway.   2½   **14**
10 Ran   Time 1m 26.06 (2.16)   Owned: Mr Lee Connolly   Trained: Malton

3231	4.50 Lorne Stewart Plc Handicap Stakes 3yo 0-70 (E)					[76]
	£3754 £1155 £578	1m1f61y	Good/Firm 20	+20 Fast	Inside	

3159* **MASAFI 4** [2] Sir Mark Prescott 3-8-11 (6ex) (59) S Sanders 8/15 FAV: 000-211: Trkd ldrs, wanderes   **70+**
2f out, styd on strongly to lead cl home, won going away: hvly bckd, qck reappr, fast time: eff at 1m/9f, 10f will
suit: acts on fast grnd & both AW's: handles a sharp or stiff trk: typically tough & progressive, win more races.
2773 **THIRD EMPIRE 20** [5] C Grant 3-8-12 (60) R Winston 14/1: 050-3052: Tried to make all, worn down   1   **66**
cl home: clr of rem: eff at 9/10f on fast & soft grnd: met a most progressive rival: see 2773 & 1144.
2969* **PEARL OF YORK 11** [3] R Guest 3-8-13 (6ex) (61) K Darley 5/2: 0-002513: Trkd ldrs, onepcd fnl 1f: 6   **55**
bckd from 4/1: btr 2969 (gd grnd).
1872 **DANCE TO MY TUNE 57** [6] M W Easterby 3-8-12 (60) P Mulrennan(5) 16/1: 606-6104: Held up, hdwy 2f   1   **52**
out, nvr nr to chall: 8 wk abs: btr 1679 (soft grnd).
2604 **MAGICAL MIMI 26** [4]3-9-7 (69) Leanne Kershaw(7) 16/1: 30-00045: Front rank, wknd dist.   shd   **61**
2634 **TROJAN FLIGHT 25** [1]3-8-12 (60) J Fanning 16/1: 0-454606: Rear, eff 3f out, sn btn & eased.   9   **37**
6 Ran   Time 1m 55.36(u0.04)   Owned: Mr G D Waters   Trained: Newmarket

NEWMARKET   FRIDAY 16.07.04   Righthand, Stiff, Galloping Track

Official Going Good

3232	6.00 Vibe Fm Sales Babes Handicap Stakes 4yo+ 0-75 (E)					[74]
	£4251 £1308 £654	1m str	Good/Firm 26	-11 Slow	Far Side	

3039 **BEST BEFORE 9** [2] P D Evans 4-10-0 (74) F P Ferris(3) 7/1: 0213331: Chsd ldrs far side, rdn & led   **83**
dist, styd on strongly: suited by 1m/9f on fast, soft & polytrack, any trk: prog profile: see 3039, 2647 & 2448.
2967 **QUICKS THE WORD 11** [20] C W Thornton 4-8-8 (54) T Quinn 14/1: 0400022: Led stands side, rdn &   2   **58**
kept on, not pace of wnr far side: in gd form & shld find similar: see 2967.
2947 **DIDNT TELL MY WIFE 13** [15] C F Wall 5-9-3 (63) Lisa Jones(3) 11/2: 21-66043: Held up stands side,   nk   **66**
styd on from over 1f out, not pace of wnr far side: looks to have come to hand: see 2947.

1736 **HUXLEY 63** [13] M G Quinlan 5-9-10 (70) J Murtagh 5/1 FAV: 10-00004: Chsd ldrs stands side, rdn &   hd   72
kept on ins last: nicely bckd: 2 month abs: well h'casppped on Irish form: see 1423.
1006 **MAMORE GAP 107** [18]6-9-10 (70) P Gallagher(7) 25/1: 050-0005: Held up stands side, short of room   2½   67
over 1f out, not able to reach ldrs: 3 month abs.
2832 **NO CHANCE TO DANCE 17** [14]4-8-3 (1ow)t (48) K McEvoy 12/1: 50-00436: In tch stands side, onepcd.   1   44
2986 **GIFTED FLAME 11** [9]5-9-3 p (63) K Fallon 10/1: 06-00407: Held up far side, switched & prog to   nk   57
lead 2f out, hdd dist & no extra: op 8/1: btr 2447.
3107 **SLALOM 6** [17]4-10-0 p (74) M Fenton 20/1: 53-10058: Dwelt & held up stands side, late gains.   hd   67
2397 **ROYAL RACER 34** [1]6-8-4 (1ow)VIS (49) E Ahern 50/1: 0/0-13609: Chsd ldrs till over 1f out: vis.   ½   42
2920 **JUSTE POUR LAMOUR 13** [4]4-9-12 (72) J F Egan 20/1: 00-04000: 10th: Led far side 6f, btn dist.   ½   63
2986 **CLASSIC VISION 11** [19]4-8-7 bl (53) R Hills 12/1: 5010600: 11th: Chsd ldrs stands side till dist: see 2402. ½   43
3034 **HALCYON MAGIC 9** [11]6-8-2 bl (48) Hayley Turner(5) 25/1: 2002060: 12th: Mid-div far side, no impress.   1   36
2630 **TUSCAN TREATY 25** [3]4-8-1 vis (47) J Mackay 50/1: 0040600: 13th: Far side, nvr on terms with ldrs.   3½   28
2800 **SECLUDED 18** [6]4-9-7 (67) L Dettori 9/1: 4355-500: 14th: Chsd ldrs far side 6f: see 2265 (10f).   4   40
2967 **MACS TALISMAN 11** [10]4-8-10 (56) M Tebbutt 20/1: 3-000230: 15th: Held up far side, no impress.   2   25
2958 **EASTERN HOPE 12** [7]5-9-0 (60) Kristin Stubbs(7) 20/1: 0030030: 16th: Dwelt, bhd far side, nvr factor.   nk   28
2844 **Fantasy Crusader 16** [16]5-8-4 p(50) W Ryan 16/1:0
    Night Dance 250 [5]12-7-12 (19oh)(25) Frances Pickard(7) 50/1:0
4699] Were Stonybroke 45 [8]5-8-11 (57) C Lowther 25/1:0   344   **Pirouettes 191** [12]4-8-7 (53) Paul Eddery 50/1:0
20 Ran   Time 1m 40.13 (2.93)   Owned: Waterline Racing Club   Trained: Abergavenny

---

3233   6.30 Vibe Fm News Team Conditions Stakes 3yo+   (C)
    £8503 £3225 £1613   **1m4f**   **Good/Firm 26**   **+11 Fast**   Centre

3118 **EASTERN BREEZE 6** [5] P W D'Arcy 6-9-1 e (102) Paul Eddery 16/1: 4120501: Chsd ldrs & led over 4f   106
out, rdn & edged left ins last, held on well for press: fast time: quick reapp: eff at 9/12f on firm, hvy & both
AWs, any trk: improved here & a smart run+: see 433.
2762 **WESTMORELAND ROAD 20** [7] Mrs A J Perrett 4-9-4 (112) J Murtagh 6/5 FAV: 11310-22: Held up, hdwy ¾   107
to chall over 2f out, rdn & not pace of wnr ins last: hvly bckd, op 6/4: ran close to smart best: see 2762.
2762 **ISLAND HOUSE 20** [3] G Wragg 8-9-1 (106) D Holland 8/1: 32-30533: Held up, eff over 1f out, kept   1   103
on: v tough & useful: see 2762 & 1139.
1418 **SUPREMACY 79** [2] Sir Michael Stoute 5-9-4 (104) K Fallon 9/1: 1/0021-04: ch g Vettori - High   ½   105
Tern (High Line) Held up, hdwy 4f out, onepace fnl 2f: 11 wk abs: lightly rcd '03, Listed wnr (4 rnr race): eff at
13f, looks sure to apprec a return to 2m: acts on firm & gd grnd, prob any trk: smart.
1 Sep'03 Asco 16.2g/f 99-(107) A: 2 Aug'03 Ches 13.4fm 107-104 A: 1 Aug'02 Ches 13.4fm 105-99 A:
1 Jun'02 Wind 11.6g/f 97- C: 1 May'02 Newc 10.1g/f 95- E:
1757 **DELSARTE 62** [1]4-9-1 t (111) L Dettori 5/2: 2034-025: Chsd ldr, onepace fnl 2f: not disgraced.   hd   101
1844 **CARINI 58** [4]3-7-12 (94) C Catlin 14/1: 11-36: Mid-div, eff 3f out, sn no impress: see 1844.   4   90
2255 **PUTRA SANDHURST 41** [9]6-9-9 (102) P Robinson 9/1: 025-1007: Led 1f, cl-up till over 1f out: abs.   1   102$
2700 **HISTORIC PLACE 22** [6]4-9-1 S Drowne 100/1: 248: Held up, rdn & btn 2f out: see 2700 & 2230 (mdns). 5   87$
2781 **MY TRUE LOVE 19** [8]5-9-1 E Ahern 200/1: 59: Slow away, sn led till over 4f out, sn btn: see 2781.   20   57
9 Ran   Time 2m 30.01 (1.81)   Owned: Colin Cage and Peter Lupson   Trained: Newmarket

---

3234   7.00 Vibe Fm Production Kings Maiden Stakes 2yo   (D)
    £5031 £1548 £774   **7f str**   **Good/Firm 26**   **-32 Slow**   Far Side

    LIBRETTIST 0 [1] Saeed bin Suroor 2-9-0 L Dettori 7/2: 1: b c Danzig - Mysterial (Alleged)   97+
Slow away & held up, hdwy to lead ins last shaken up, cftbly: nicely bckd: Apr foal, half brother to top class
miler Dubai Destination: eff at 7f, 1m sure to suit: acts on fast grnd & a stiff/gall trk: goes well fresh:
decisive success, win List/Gr races.
    BARADORE 0 [11] M G Quinlan 2-8-9 R L Moore 6/1: 2: ch f Barathea - High Flying Adored (In The   2½   83
Wings) Sn handy & chsd ldr from halfway, led over 1f out till ins last, not pace of wnr: 28,000 gns Mar foal, half
sister to a 1m juv wnr: dam an 11f/12f 3yo scorer: eff at 7f, 1m+ sure to suit: acts on fast: v pleasing intro.
    ROAD RAGE 0 [5] E A L Dunlop 2-8-9 E Ahern 10/1: 3: b f Giant's Causeway - Endorsement   1½   80+
(Warning) Chsd ldrs, rdn & kept on fnl 2f, not pace of front pair: Jan 1st foal, dam a 12f/2m 3yo scorer: eff at
7f, likely to apprec mid/staying dists in time: acts on fast grnd: will improve over 1m+.
    ETAAR 0 [2] N A Graham 2-9-0 D Holland 10/1: 4: Chsd ldrs, onepace over 1f out, op 14/1.   hd   84
    HOME AFFAIRS 0 [7]2-9-0 K Fallon 5/2 FAV: 5: Held up, eff over 2f out, not pace to chall: nicely bckd.   ½   83
2348 **TRAIANOS 36** [3]2-9-0 T Quinn 9/1: 56: Led 5f, no extra dist.   2½   78$
    WUJOOD 0 [8]2-9-0 R Hills 9/1: 7: Held up, nvr pace to threaten: op 8/1.   1½   75
    THE COIRES 0 [9]2-9-0 Dane O'Neill 20/1: 8: Slow away & held up, no impress fnl 2f.   2½   70
3005 **GURRUN 10** [6]2-9-0 W Ryan 50/1: 09: Chsd ldr early, btn over 2f out.   2½   65
    RHOSLAN 0 [4]2-9-0 J Murtagh 14/1: 0: 10th: Held up, no impress fnl 3f.   1   63
    PENALTY KICK 0 [10]2-9-0 O Urbina 33/1: 0: 11th: Held up in tch, btn 2f out.   6   52
11 Ran   Time 1m 27.98 (4.08)   Owned: Godolphin   Trained: Newmarket

---

3235   7.30 Vibe Fm Rated Stakes Handicapfillies 3yo+ 0-95   (C)
    £8477 £3216 £1608   **6f str**   **Good/Firm 26**   **-14 Slow**   Far Side   **[101]**

2677* **KIND 23** [8] R Charlton 3-8-13 (86) R Hughes 3/1 CO FAV: 34-31111: Trkd ldrs, rdn & led ins last,   93
held on all out: eff at 6/7f on firm & gd/soft: most prog, useful & genuine: see 2677.
3002 **VALJARV 10** [4] N P Littmoden 3-9-3 bl (90) T P Queally 7/1: 0000442: Held up, short of room over   shd   95
1f out, rider dropped reins ins last, strong run cl-home, just failed: well suited by blnks of late, shade unlucky.
2581 **FANNYS FANCY 27** [6] C F Wall 4-9-6 T (88) J Fortune 3/1 CO FAV: 143-0003: Held up, kept on for   ¾   92
press fnl 2f, not pace of front pair: gd run in 1st time t-strap: see 1683.
3106+ **FRUIT OF GLORY 6** [1] J R Jenkins 5-9-10 (3ex) (92) D Holland 3/1 CO FAV: 4304214: Led till ins   hd   95
last, no extra: quick reapp: not btn far, see 3106.
2950 **BOHOLA FLYER 13** [5]3-8-5 (78) R L Moore 12/1: 4641145: Saddle slipped leaving stalls, cl-up, no   1   78
extra ins last & held when eased cl-home: gd run in circumstances: see 2619.
4462*)**CHANTERELLE 294** [2]3-9-0 (87) T Quinn 20/1: 441-6: ch f Indian Ridge - Chantereine (Trempolino)   shd   87

Chsd ldrs, onepace dist: reapp: lightly rcd mdn wnr in '03: eff at 6f on firm & gd/soft grnd, stiff/gall trks: eff forcing the pace. 1 Sep'03 Hayd 6g/s 90- D:
2760 **INDIAN STEPPES 20** [3]5-8-4 (6oh) (66) M Halford(7) 25/1: 03-66437: Trkd ldrs & keen, short of room when onepace ins last: see 1773. *hd* **71$**
2736 **ANTHOS 21** [7]3-9-3 (90) J Murtagh 20/1: 2614-58: Held up, btn over 1f out: see 2736. *3½* **78**
8 Ran Time 1m 13.41 (2.41) Owned: Mr K Abdulla Trained: Beckhampton

3236 **8.00 Vibe Fm Vibe Tribe Rated Stakes Handicap 3yo 0-95 (C)** **[97]**
£8565 £3249 £1624 **1m2f rnd** **Good/Firm 26** **+09 Fast** Centre

2751* **INTO THE DARK 20** [4] Saeed bin Suroor 3-9-7 vis t (90) L Dettori 100/30 FAV: 11: Made all, rdn & styd on strongly ins last, shade cmftbly: fast time: eff at 10f, 12f will suit: acts on fast & gd grnd, stiff/gall trks: loves to force the pace: lightly rcd, useful & prog colt, keep on side: see 2751. **107+**
5028} **ART TRADER 252** [2] Mrs A J Perrett 3-9-5 (88) J Murtagh 6/1: 14-2: b c Arch - Math (Devil's Bag) Hld up, hdwy & switched over 1f out, chall ins last, not pace of wnr: reapp: h'cap bow: lightly rcd mdn scorer '03: styd longer 10f trip well, 12f shld suit: acts on fast & gd, stiff/gall trks: goes well fresh: lightly rcd & useful, win more races. 1 Oct'03 Newm 8g/f 88- D: *1½* **100**
1259 **NOTABLE GUEST 88** [3] Sir Michael Stoute 3-9-1 (84) K Fallon 7/1: 22-53: Held up, hdwy/edged right over 1f out, kept on, not pace of wnr: 12 wk abs: now stays a stiff 10f well: win a race. *1¼* **94**
2785 **LOST SOLDIER THREE 19** [7] L M Cumani 3-9-5 (88) D Holland 11/2: 6154: Handy & chsd wnr from 3f out, hung left & no extra dist: prob handles firm & gd grnd: see 2785 & 2196 (mdn). *2* **95**
2793* **POSTERITAS 18** [1]3-9-1 (84) R Hughes 12/1: 3215: Held up, eff when hung right over 1f out, not pace to chall: h'cap bow: see 2793 (mdn). *1¼* **88**
2903 **ALEKHINE 14** [6]3-9-1 (84) R L Moore 14/1: 16-23006: Held up, eff over 1f out, short of room when no extra dist: see 2040 & 1770. *hd* **88**
2919 **WINNERS DELIGHT 13** [5]3-8-12 (81) K McEvoy 10/1: 5-005537: Held up, eff 2f out, no extra dist. *1¾* **81**
2843 **GANYMEDE 16** [9]3-8-11 (80) M Fenton 16/1: 3-232228: Keen, prom, hmpd after 2f, rdn & btn dist. *4* **76**
2940 **MAN OF LETTERS 13** [8]3-8-9 (78) A McCarthy 25/1: 2212539: Chsd ldrs, btn 2f out: btr 2940 (1m, soft). *3* **70**
2948 **SWAGGER STICK 13** [11]3-9-7 (90) T Quinn 11/2: 14-11600: 10th: Chsd wnr 7f, btn/hmpd over 1f out. *2* **79**
3066 **ANOTHER CHOICE 8** [10]3-8-9 t (78) T P Queally 33/1: 0-311000: 11th: Chsd ldrs, no impress fnl 2f. *1¾* **65**
11 Ran Time 2m 03.59 (1.69) Owned: Godolphin Trained: Newmarket

3237 **8.30 Hugo And The Huguenotes Maiden Stakes 3yo (D)**
£5590 £1720 £860 **1m str** **Good/Firm 26** **-17 Slow** Far Side

HERMITAGE COURT 0 [12] B J Meehan 3-9-0 K McEvoy 25/1: 1: ch g Out of Place - Russian Act (Siberian Express) Chsd ldrs stands side, rdn & led ins last, just prevailed: debut: $100,000 2yo purchase, 1st foal: eff at 1m, mid-dists shld suit: acts on fast grnd & a stiff/gall trk: goes well fresh: open to improvement. **86**
1136 **KAURI FOREST 95** [18] J R Fanshawe 3-9-0 J Murtagh 11/4 FAV: 32: Trkd ldrs stands side, rdn to chall ins last, just held: 3 month abs: imprvd over longer 1m trip: acts on fast & gd grnd: can find similar. *hd* **85**
2678 **ARCTIC SILK 23** [15] Saeed bin Suroor 3-8-9 T L Dettori 8/1: 03: ch f Selkirk - Cape Verdi (Caerleon) Stands side & led till rdn & hdd ins last, just held cl-home: clr rem: 1st time t-strap: dam 1000 Guineas wnr: apprec drop to 1m tho' 10f+ may suit in time: acts on fast & a stiff/gall trk. *½* **79**
GENTLEMANS DEAL 0 [2] E A L Dunlop 3-9-0 R Hughes 16/1: 4: b c Danehill - Sleepytime (Royal Academy) Trkd ldrs far side, switched right & hung right from over 2f out, no impress dist: debut: 460,000 gns purchase, dam a high-class 1m performer: eff at 1m on fast grnd & a stiff/gall trk: likely improver. *3½* **77**
SEA NYMPH 0 [20]3-8-9 K Fallon 12/1: 5: b f Spectrum - Sea Picture (Royal Academy) Held up stands side, kept on fnl 2f, not pace to threaten: debut: 1st foal: dam stayed 7f: gd start. *nk* **71**
COUNTRYWIDE LUCK 0 [19]3-9-0 T P Queally 66/1: 6: Held up, prob/stumbled dist, no dngr. *hd* **75**
2886 **CLIPPERDOWN 15** [4]3-9-0 R L Moore 7/2: 37: Led far side over 3f out, wknd ins last. *1¾* **72**
DANZE ROMANCE 0 [11]3-8-9 T Quinn 33/1: 8: Held up stands side, nvr on terms, debut. *½* **66**
ONE SO MARVELLOUS 0 [13]3-8-9 D Holland 12/1: 9: Held up stands side, late prog on debut. *shd* **66**
TADAWUL 0 [10]3-8-9 R Hills 25/1: 0: 10th: Held up far side, late prob, nrst fin, debut. *hd* **65**
ROYAL LUSTRE 0 [14]3-9-0 J Fortune 6/1: 0: 11th: Held up stands side, no impress on debut. *nk* **69**
4973} **RADISH 258** [1]3-8-9 P Robinson 25/1: 0-0: 12th: Mid-div far side, btn over 1f out, abs. *¾* **63**
2962 **PINCHING 12** [6]3-8-9 vis (75) W Ryan 9/1: 43230: 13th: Chsd ldrs far side & ch over 1f out, btn dist. *nk* **62**
INVITING 0 [16]3-8-9 S Drowne 20/1: 0: 14th: Chsd ldrs stands side 6f, sn btn. *hd* **61**
2987 **GLENCALVIE 11** [17]3-9-0 E Ahern 40/1: 050: 15th: Chsd ldrs 6f stands side. *¾* **65**
2248 **HOOPS AND BLADES 41** [5]3-9-0 t T G McLaughlin 100/1: 000: 16th: Dwelt, al rear far side, 6 wk abs. *5* **56**
1846 **BONNETTS 58** [3]3-8-9 Dane O'Neill 80/1: 00: 17th: Led far side 4f, btn over 1f out, abs. *½* **50**
ALFHALA 0 [7]3-8-9 Laura Wells(7) 100/1: 0: 18th: Dwelt, far side, al rear. *1¾* **47**
Zak Attack 0 [8]3-9-0 C Catlin 40/1:0 **Southburgh 0** [9]3-9-0 Hayley Turner(5) 100/1:0
20 Ran Time 1m 40.63 (3.43) Owned: Gallagher Equine Ltd Trained: Upper Lambourn

3238 **9.00 Vibe Fm Admin Hunnies Handicap Stakes 3yo+ 0-70 (E)** **[79]**
£4261 £1311 £656 **1m2f** **Good/Firm 26** **-09 Slow** Centre

3175* **JACKIE KIELY 3** [2] P S McEntee 3-8-10 (6ex)t (61) L Dettori 9/2 FAV: 5421011: Held up, prog when no room dist: styd on for press to lead well ins last: quick reapp under a pen: stays 12f well, imprvd of late at 10f: acts on both AWs, firm & fast grnd, prob any trk: best in a t-strap: see 3175 & 2503. **60**
3052 **EMBER DAYS 8** [16] J L Spearing 5-9-10 (6ex)p (65) E Ahern 15/2: 3023132: Chsd ldrs, rdn & led ins last, sn hdd, kept on: in gd heart, can win again: see 3052 & 2979. *¾* **62**
2955* **GHANTOOT 12** [1] L M Cumani 3-9-7 (6ex)vis (72) D Holland 6/1: 0000313: Held up, styd on fnl 2f, not pace to chall: acts on fast & gd/soft grnd: in gd form: see 2955. *1* **68**
2745 **FOREST TUNE 20** [17] B Hanbury 6-8-9 (50) T E Durcan 12/1: 0060064: Handy, chsd ldr 3f out & led over 1f out, edged left & hdd ins last, no extra: see 1083. *nk* **44**
2529 **WELCOME SIGNAL 28** [12]4-9-10 P (65) J Murtagh 8/1: 3035-055: Held up, prog 3f out, rdn & onepace. *nk* **59**
PRAIRIE LAW 160 [15]4-8-1 (42) Lisa Jones(3) 16/1: 352-1006: b g Law Society - Prairie Charm (Thatching) Held up, eff 2f out, hung right & no extra dist: 5 month abs, Brit bow: ex-German, Jan '04 wnr: sole win at 11.5f on AW: prob handles fast & gd/soft grnd. *1¾* **34**

NEWMARKET FRIDAY 16.07.04 Righthand, Stiff, Galloping Track

805	**KALOU 134** [7]6-8-7 (48) T P Queally 13/2: 0/6503-37: Mid-div, rdn & btn dist: 2 month jumps abs.	nk	39
3037	**URSA MAJOR 9** [14]10-8-7 (48) K McEvoy 25/1: 000/-0068: Led 1m, btn dist: see 2146.	1¼	37
2800	**PLANTERS PUNCH 18** [4]3-9-3 vis (68) K Fallon 8/1: 0001009: Held up, eff over 2f out, btn/eased ins last.	3½	52
3070	**FEED THE METER 7** [11]4-9-0 (55) G Carter 16/1: 0/0-02100: 10th: Held up & keen, no impress fnl 2f.	3½	34
2875	**GALEY RIVER 15** [10]5-7-13 (40) A McCarthy 12/1: 2350450: 11th: Chsd ldrs till over 1f out: btr 2354.	5	12
1254	**SINJAREE 88** [6]6-8-1 (42) S Righton 33/1: 0-051060: 12th: Chsd ldrs 6f, sn btn, abs: btr 821 (AW).	3½	9
3164	**BOSCO 4** [9]3-8-1 t (52) F P Ferris(3) 25/1: 0001600: 13th: Dwelt, sn rdn & al rear, qck reapp: btr 2332.	2	16
	BIRCHALL 75 [13]5-8-13 (54) C Catlin 25/1: 50-00200: 14th: Held up, rdn & al bhd.	2½	14
1712	**MR FLEMING 64** [3]5-7-13 bl (40) M Halford(7) 66/1: 0044-300: 15th: Chsd ldrs till over 2f out, abs.	3½	0
2866	**Niagara 15** [8]7-9-9 (64) P Robinson 16/1:0	3056 **Migration 8** [5]8-8-9 (50) M Tebbutt 50/1:0	

17 Ran   Time 2m 05.39(3.49)   Owned: Mr P S J Croft   Trained: Newmarket

---

PONTEFRACT FRIDAY 16.07.04 Lefthand, Undulating Track, Stiff Uphill Finish

Official Going GOOD/FIRM (GOOD IN PLACES)

3239   6.40 Betfred Com Maiden Auction Stakes 2yo (E)
£4241 £1305 £653   6f rnd   Good 58   -35 Slow   Inside

EL REY ROYALE [4] M D Hammond 2-8-7   N Mackay(3) 33/1: 1: b g Royal Applause - Spanish Serenade · **78**
(Nashwan) Mid-div, hdwy halfway & styd on strongly ins last to lead nr fin: cheaply bght Mar foal: half-brother to
a 7f juv wnr: dam a 7/11f scorer: eff at 6f, looks sure to get further: acts on gd grnd & a stiff/undul trk: goes
well fresh: set to rate higher over 7f+.

2776	**PERSIAN CARPET 19** [8] I A Wood 2-8-2 F Norton 9/2: 042: Led, rdn & hdd over 1f out, sn led	¾	70
	again till well ins last: acts on firm & gd grnd: see 2776.		

GOOD INVESTMENT [1] P C Haslam 2-8-7   G Faulkner 22/1: 3: b g Silver Patriarch - Bundled Up · ½ · **73**
(Sharpen Up) Held up, hdwy & switched over 1f out, kept on well cl-home: op 25/1: 12,500gns Mar foal, half-brother
to numerous wnrs, incl a 2yo scorer: dam a 2yo French wnr: eff at 6f, looks sure to apprec further: acts on gd
grnd & a stiff/undul trk: most encouraging start, one to note at 7f+.

2682	**HEYBROOK BOY 22** [10] M Johnston 2-8-9 R Ffrench 11/2: 04: ch c Woodman - Liberada (Spend A	shd	74
	Buck) Chsd ldrs, rdn & kept on onepace: Feb foal, half-brother to 3 US wnrs: dam a multiple US wnr: eff at 6f,		
	imprvd on gd grnd today: acts on a stiff trk.		
2682	**DAVY CROCKETT 22** [5]2-8-7 S Whitworth 22/1: 005: Mid-div, short of room dist, switched & kept on.	2	66
2783	**HIDDEN STAR 19** [11]2-8-11 (2ow) K Dalgleish 2/1 FAV: 36: Handy & led over 1f out, sn hdd & no	¾	68
	extra: nicely bckd: btr 2783 (firm).		
	ALONG THE NILE [9]2-9-0 L Goncalves 16/1: 7: Dwelt, bhd, kept on wide, nrst fin, improve.	nk	70
2671	**NOODLES 23** [12]2-8-11 vis W Supple 5/1: 028: Chsd ldrs till over 1f out: btr 2671.	¾	65
	LIGHTENING FIRE [2]2-8-7 D Kinsella 33/1: 9: Dwelt & bhd, late prog.	½	59
2511	**ROYAL FLYNN 29** [14]2-8-11 V Halliday 12/1: 640: 10th: Mid-div, btn 2f out: btr 2511.	nk	62
	COMICAL ERRORS [13]2-8-9 G Bartley(7) 40/1: 0: 11th: Dwelt & bhd, mod late prog.	1¼	56
	TIDAL FURY [3]2-8-11 G Baker 12/1: 0: 12th: Wide & al bhd.	¾	56
	HOWS THAT [7]2-8-2 R Mullen 40/1: 0: 13th: Dwelt, in tch till 2f out.	½	45
2275	**LIVE IN HOPE 39** [6]2-8-2 Dale Gibson 66/1: 000: 14th: Chsd ldrs till halfway, sn btn.	8	21
2889	**ZAROVA 14** [15]2-9-0 T Lucas 18/1: 060: 15th: Cl-up, struggling halfway, eased.	2½	25

15 Ran   Time 1m 19.71 (5.61)   Owned: Mr A Walker   Trained: Middleham

3240   7.10 Totequadpot Handicap Stakes Fillies 3yo+ 0-70 (E)
£5538 £1704 £852   1m4f8y   Good 58   +00 Fast   Inside   **[79]**

CHARLOTTE VALE 12 [3] M D Hammond 3-9-3 (68) A Culhane 9/2: 6-652131: Trkd ldrs, prog & chsd ldr · **78**
dist, duelled with rnr-up ins last, prevailed line, all out: suited by 12f: acts on fast & gd/soft grnd: tough,
progressive profile: see 2960 & 2691.

2984*	**SAND AND STARS 11** [6] M H Tompkins 3-9-11 (6ex) (76) M Henry 7/2 FAV: 40-35212: Trkd ldr, led 3f	shd	83
	out, drvn & strongly prsd dist, just denied on line: clr rem & lost nothing in defeat: keep on side: see 2984.		
2996	**SHOTLEY DANCER 10** [13] N Bycroft 5-8-0 (2ow)(1oh) (36) F Norton 33/1: 4004353: Rear, kept on late	7	37
	for press, nvr threatened front pair: see 677.		
2376	**OLYMPIAS 35** [2] H Morrison 3-8-7 (58) J Carroll 18/1: 50064: Mid-div, no impress fnl 2f: see 2376.	3	51
2494	**STAFF NURSE 30** [10]4-7-12 (2oh) (35) Kim Tinkler 25/1: 53-00405: Bhd, rdn & mod prog: see 1840.	2	27
2453	**LEBENSTANZ 32** [14]4-10-0 (67) N Mackay(3) 10/1: 6666: b f Singspiel - Reamur (Top Ville) Rear,	½	56
	only mod prog, nvr factor: h'cap bow: unplcd prev up to 10f.		
2966	**MISS FLEURIE 11** [8]4-7-12 (5oh) (32) D Kinsella 50/1: 4/-000267: Led till 3f out, sn btn: see 1592.	4	20
2740	**LADY BLADE 20** [1]3-8-9 (60) W Supple 20/1: 6360-048: Chsd ldrs, btn 2f out: btr 2740.	½	42
3052*	**TOCCATA ARIA 8** [7]6-9-0 (6ex) (53) R Thomas(5) 8/1: 3006-119: Trkd ldrs, btn 2f out: btr 3052..	3	30
2748	**PAINT THE LILY 20** [9]3-8-7 (58) S Whitworth 25/1: 0040: 10th: Al bhd on h'cap bow: longer trip.	1¾	32
2850	**CRYPTOGAM 16** [4]4-8-0 (39) R Ffrench 33/1: 0000050: 11th: Mid-div, btn 3f out.	7	2
2349	**Nassiria 36** [12]3-9-4 (69) J P Guillambert(3) 16/1:0	2422 **Ribbons And Bows 33** [11]4-9-9 (62) F Lynch 12/1:0	

13 Ran   Time 2m 41.08 (6.98)   Owned: Mr Peter J Davies   Trained: Middleham

3241   7.40 Antonia Deuters Rated Stakes Handicap 3yo+ 0-80 (D)
£9303 £3529 £1764   5f rnd   Good 58   +07 Fast   Inside   **[87]**

MIDNIGHT PARKES 10 [4] E J Alston 5-8-8 p (67) M Henry 10/1: 4035031: Led/dsptd lead thr'out, · **73**
went on over 1f out, drvn & held on gamely: eff at 5/6f on firm & fast grnd, prob not an easy surface: likes to
race with/force the pace: imprvd last twice back in cheek pieces: see 2990 & 2280.

2934	**SOBA JONES 13** [2] J Balding 7-8-10 (69) J Edmunds 33/1: 3256542: Trkd ldrs, eff to chase wnr	nk	74
	dist, just held cl-home: see 349.		
3116	**PADDYWACK 6** [7] D W Chapman 7-9-0 bl (73) A Culhane 12/1: 5301103: Chsd ldrs, short of room over	1¼	74

1f out, kept on, not able to chall: see 2942.

3150 **OBE ONE 4** [8] A Berry 4-8-9 (68) F Norton 6/1 FAV: 0230604: Chsd ldrs, styd on for press, not ¾ 67
able to chall: qck reapp: see 3150, 1977.

3033 **WINTHORPE 9** [13]4-8-13 (72) T Hamilton(3) 14/1: 0403205: Held up, kept on fnl 2f, nrst fin. ½ 69

2968* **ZARZU 11** [11]5-9-2 (3ex) (75) R Thomas(5) 7/1: 4300016: Held up, kept on late, nrst fin: see 2968. ¾ 70

3106 **KARMINSKEY PARK 6** [9]5-8-7 (1oh) (65) D Kinsella 22/1: 5321007: Chsd ldrs, drvn & onepcd dist. 1½ 56

3146 **LAUREL DAWN 5** [14]6-8-7 (5oh) (61) J F McDonald(3) 16/1: 0015258: Bhd, switched & late prog. shd 55

3033 **AWAKE 9** [17]7-9-5 (78) W Supple 9/1: 6501629: Held up, only mod prog: btr 2286. hd 66

3073 **CATCH THE CAT 7** [16]5-8-12 p (71) G Parkin 33/1: 0165000: 10th: Mid-div, no impress fnl 2f. nk 58

2524 **MERLINS DANCER 29** [6]4-9-7 (80) Alex Greaves 13/2: 00-05100: 11th: Led till over 1f out, sn btn. ½ 65

3146 **SALVIATI 5** [5]7-9-7 p (80) L Fletcher(3) 16/1: 0000000: 12th: Dwelt & bhd, late prog: qck reapp. ½ 63

4714} **SION HILL 277** [12]3-9-1 (78) F Lynch 10/1: 202-0: 13th: b g Desert Prince - Mobilia (Last 1¾ 56
Tycoon) Switched left start, al bhd: reapp/h'cap bow: dual mdn rnr-up '03: eff at 5/6f on fast grnd, sharp trks.
2 Oct'03 Wind 6g/f 83- D: 2 Jun'03 Ches 5.1g/f 75- D:

3106 **Twice Upon A Time 6** [10]5-8-8 (67) R Mullen 14/1:0   2838* **Parkside Pursuit 17** [18]6-9-3 (76) R Ffrench 12/1:0
2359 **Tommy Smith 35** [15]6-8-13 bl(72) K Dalgleish 25/1:0   3080 **Sir Ernest 7** [3]3-8-9 (72) K Ghunowa(7) 20/1:0
17 Ran   Time 1m 3.85 (2.55)   Owned: Mr Joseph Heler   Trained: Preston

---

3242   8.10 Weatherbys Injured Jockeys Fund Handicap Stakes 3yo+ 0-70 (E)   [70]
£4378 £1347 £674   **1m4y rnd**   **Good 58**   **-08 Slow**   Inside

2447 **TIME TO REGRET 32** [6] J S Wainwright 4-8-8 (50) T Hamilton(3) 25/1: 35-62401: Made all, drvn out 54
ins fnl 1f to hold on: eff btwn 7/9.3f on fast or gd grnd: improved on switch to new yard to record first win.

3144 **ZAWRAK 5** [1] I W McInnes 4-9-4 VIS (60) J F McDonald(3) 20/1: 6301052: Mid-div, prog & short of hd 63+
room 2f out, switched & short of room again dist, styd on well ins fnl 1f, post came too sn: qck reapp: responded
well to visor: likely wnr with a clr run & can land comp: see 1954.

2891 **SHAMWARI FIRE 14** [5] I W McInnes 4-8-8 (50) R Ffrench 16/1: 0160033: In tch, prog 2f out, kept 1 51
on ins fnl 1f, not btn far: stablemate of rnr-up: see 2891 & 1944.

3132 **NEWCORP LAD 6** [14] Mrs G S Rees 4-9-4 (60) W Supple 10/1: 0400044: In tch, prog & ev ch bef 1f hd 60
out, kept on, just held for 3rd: qck reapp: btr 2284 & 1397.

2993* **HULA BALLEW 10** [4]4-9-1 (6ex)p (57) S W Kelly 11/4 FAV: 0055015: Held up, prog over halfway, kept hd 56
on ins fnl 1f, nrst fin: rtd much higher when C/D wnr in 2993.

2901 **TAGULA BLUE 14** [10]4-10-0 (70) Dean McKeown 12/1: 06-U0R36: Rear, prog wide 3f out, kept on. hd 68

2947 **FAIR SPIN 13** [16]4-9-7 (63) A Culhane 5/1: 4000-037: Chsd ldrs, onepcd ins fnl 1f: btr 2947. hd 60

2958 **BASINET 12** [9]6-8-12 (54) K Dalgleish 10/1: 06-00048: Rear, prog 3f out, kept on ins fnl 1f. hd 50

2993 **UNO MENTE 10** [11]5-8-11 (53) Kim Tinkler 20/1: 0006309: Rear, modest late gains: btr 2604. 1¾ 45

2892 **DUBAI DREAMS 14** [13]4-8-8 (50) B Swarbrick(5) 25/1: 0-425000: 10th: Handy, wkng when no room dist. 3½ 36

2988 **PENWELL HILL 10** [18]5-8-12 (54) N Mackay(3) 12/1: 0220600: 11th: Prom, wkng when short of room dist. 1½ 36

2988 **HEALEY 10** [15]6-8-6 (48) V Halliday 40/1: 6/4032-00: 12th: Mid-div 5f, sn no extra: see 2988. ¾ 28

2958 **Dara Mac 12** [19]5-8-13 (55) Suzanne France(7) 21/1:0   1896 **Kalishka 56** [2]3-8-13 (63) J Carroll 14/1:0
2445 **Golden Spectrum 32** [17]5-9-1 (57) Alex Greaves 25/1:0   2958 **Sedge 12** [20]4-9-4 (60) G Parkin 33/1:0
3107 **Daimajin 6** [7]5-9-0 (9ow)(47) D Nolan 50/1:0   3137 **Aswan 5** [12]6-9-9 t(65) S Whitworth 25/1:0
18 Ran   Time 1m 47.09 (5.29)   Owned: Denison Arms   Trained: Malton

---

3243   8.40 Tenerife Holiday Maiden Stakes 3yo (D)
£7280 £2240 £1120   **1m2f6y**   **Good 58**   **-23 Slow**   Inside

2793 **FORTUNES PRINCESS 18** [4] M J Wallace 3-8-9 S W Kelly 3/1: 221: In tch, short of room bend after 76
3f, prog 4f out, kept on to lead ins fnl 1f, rdn out: eff at 10f, 12f shld suit: acts on fast & gd grnd: continues
to progress, see 2793 & 2534.

2484 **MANDATUM 30** [7] L M Cumani 3-9-0 N Mackay(3) 6/1: 22: Rear, prog 3f out, kept on fnl 1f, not btn ¾ 78
far: eff at 10f, will apprec rtn to 12f: acts on fast & gd grnd: shld sn go one better, see 2484.

1153 **TURN N BURN 94** [5] C A Cyzer 3-9-0 (73) Dean McKeown 14/1: 53-03: b c Unfuwain - Seasonal ½ 77
Splendour (Prince Rupert) Rear, prog 3f out, onepcd ins fnl 1f: plcd on 1 of 2 '03 starts (rtd 73a, mdn): stays
10f, further shld suit: acts on gd & polytrack.

2879 **SHASTYE 15** [2] J H M Gosden 3-8-9 R Havlin 12/1: 034: Cl-up, led 2f out till ins fnl 1f, no extra. nk 71

BARATHEA BLUE [6]3-9-0 Dale Gibson 16/1: 5: ch c Barathea - Empty Purse (Pennine Walk) Sn 2 73
bhd, prog fnl 2f, nrst fin: debut: cost 52,000gns: trained by P W Harris.

2793 **SIERRA 18** [3]3-8-9 J P Guillambert(3) 33/1: 0-56: Handy 6f, wknd fnl 2f. 15 45

2453 **BARANOOK 32** [10]3-9-0 R Mullen 33/1: 07: Bhd, nvr a factor. 2 47

2862 **GIFT VOUCHER 16** [1]3-9-0 F Lynch 13/8 FAV: 038: In tch, short of room & hung after 4f, mod gains. 2 44

2410 **SHARAAB 34** [8]3-9-0 t (73) W Supple 7/1: 30-60529: Handy, short of room after 4f, wknd fnl 3f. 12 26

2740 **EXPLICIT 20** [9]3-9-0 S Whitworth 50/1: 00: 10th: Led, hdd bef 2f out, fdd: see 2740. 30 0
10 Ran   Time 2m 16.29 (8.19)   Owned: Lucayan Stud   Trained: Newmarket

---

3244   9.10 Injured Jockeys Classified Stakes 3yo+ 0-65 (E)
£4927 £1516 £758   **6f rnd**   **Good 58**   **-14 Slow**   Inside

3146 **HIGH RIDGE 5** [9] J M Bradley 5-9-4 p (69) Dean McKeown 11/4 J FAV: 1512341: Held up, prog 74
halfway, styd on to lead well ins fnl 1f, rdn out: qck reapp: eff at 5f/6f/7f, tried further: acts on firm & fast
grnd: eff with cheek pieces: continues in gd form: see 2779 & 2416.

2942 **RECTANGLE 5** [5] D Nicholls 4-9-3 (68) Alex Greaves 12/1: 30-00002: Cl-up, trav well & led dist, ½ 70
hdd well ins fnl 1f, just held by wnr: eff at 5/6f: gd effort & slipped to a fair mark, see 2359.

3017 **TANTRIC 9** [3] J O'Reilly 5-9-0 (58) A Culhane 8/1: 0-003003: Rear, prog halfway, onepcd fnl 1f. 2 61

3129 **BUNDY 6** [2] M Dods 8-9-0 (64) S W Kelly 3/1: 2232044: In tch over 4f, sn no extra: qck reapp. 3 52

2564 **LINDENS LADY 27** [1]4-8-11 BL e (60) D Fentiman(7) 12/1: 5-060565: Led till dist, wknd: blnks. nk 48

PONTEFRACT   FRIDAY 16.07.04   Lefthand, Undulating Track, Stiff Uphill Finish

2848 **SMART MINISTER 16** [4]4-9-0 (64) K Dalgleish 12/1: 0-000106: Cl-up over 4f, fdd: btr 2527.   2½   43
2975 **SEWMUCH CHARACTER 11** [6]5-9-0 (63) D Sweeney 11/4 J FAV: 4-406427: Mid-div, prog 2f out, fdd   2   37
dist: v disappointing effort: btr 2975.
7 Ran   Time 1m 18.45(4.35)   Owned: James Leisure Ltd   Trained: Chepstow

HAMILTON   FRIDAY 16.07.04   Righthand, Undulating Track, Stiff Uphill Finish

Official Going GOOD/FIRM.

3245
6.50 John Banks Nursery Handicap Stakes 2yo (D)   [87]
£6832 £2102 £1051   **6f5y str**   **Firm 10**   -29 Slow   Stands Side

3148 **NO COMMISSION 4** [2] R F Fisher 2-8-11 (70) R Winston 7/2: 4054021: Held up, switched right over   75
2f out, led over 1f out, rdn out: first win: stays a stiff 6f on fm & prob gd/soft: confidence boost.
2776 **MCELDOWNEY 19** [3] M Johnston 2-9-6 (79) J Fanning 5/2 FAV: 3222: Handy, short of room over 2f   ½   82
out, hdwy to chase wnr appr fnl 1f, kept on ins last, not btn far: clr rem: back in trip: consistent & prog.
2847 **ANGELOFTHENORTH 16** [1] J D Bethell 2-8-11 (70) S Chin 14/1: 3433: With ldrs, wknd fnl 1f: see 1362. 5   58
2473 **MELVINO 30** [5] T D Barron 2-9-5 VIS (78) P Makin(5) 7/2: 4034: Dsptd lead till wknd dist: visor.   2½   59
3097 **LADY HOPEFUL 6** [4]2-8-7 VIS (66) T Eaves(3) 20/1: 542205: Dwelt, sn in tch, eff & hmpd over 1f   1¾   42
out, wknd: tried visor: see 2810 (7f), 2492.
2711* **TEQUILA SHEILA 22** [6]2-9-7 (80) Darren Williams 3/1: 016: Led, hdd & badly hmpd over 1f out, not   3½   46
recover: top-weight: much closer with clr run: see 2711.
6 Ran   Time 1m 12.17 (2.37)   Owned: Great Head House Estates Limited   Trained: Ulverston

3246
7.20 Velvet Fair Friday Maiden Stakes 3yo+ (D)
£7007 £2156 £1078   **1m65y rnd**   **Firm 10**   -06 Slow   Inside

2549 **ARRGATT 28** [8] M A Jarvis 3-8-13 (83) N Callan 1/9 FAV: 0-3221: Keen with ldr, led after 3f,   77
styd on strongly fnl 2f, cmftbly: eff at 1m/9f on firm & gd grnd: found a weak mdn & a confidence boost: see 2549.
1661 **ISLANDS FAREWELL 67** [6] D Nicholls 4-9-7 A Nicholls 50/1: 000-002: b g Emarati - Chief Island   3½   65
(Be My Chief) In tch, eff well over 1f out, kept on without threatening wnr: clr of rem after 11 wk abs: prev with
Mrs M Reveley & mod form: eff at 8.3f on firm grnd.
1768 **AWWAL MARRA 62** [1] E W Tuer 4-9-2 P Fessey 33/1: 2/-03: In tch, wknd over 2f out: 2 month abs. 7   46
      BIJOU DAN [7] I Semple 3-8-13 R Winston 16/1: 4: ch g Bijou d'Inde - Cal Norma's Lady   1¼   48
(Lyphard's Special) Dwelt, bhd, modest late gains: half-brother to wnrs up to 9f.
2901 **HOLLYWOOD CRITIC 14** [4]3-8-13 L Enstone(3) 25/1: 005: b g Theatrical - Lyphard's Starlite   ¾   46
(Lyphard) Led 3f, handy till wknd over 2f out: with P Monteith.
2885 **HOWARDS ROCKET 15** [2]3-8-13 P Mulrennan(5) 66/1: 006: Al bhd.   ¾   44
2987 **ROUGE ET NOIR 11** [5]6-9-7 T Eaves(3) 20/1: 07: Al bhd.   1   42
      DALKEYS LASS [3]3-8-8 S Chin 80/1: 8: In tch, wknd over 2f out on debut.   8   21
8 Ran   Time 1m 45.11 (1.31)   Owned: Sheikh Ahmed Al Maktoum   Trained: Newmarket

3247
7.50 EBF Maiden Stakes A Qualifier For The Hamilton Park 2-Y-O Series Final 2yo (D)
£5473 £1684 £842   **5f4y str**   **Firm 10**   -28 Slow   Stands Side

      ANDRONIKOS 4 [4] P F I Cole 2-9-0 K Darley 13/8: 1: ch c Dr Fong - Arctic Air (Polar Falcon)   94
With ldr, led over 1f out, rdn clr ins last on debut: Mar foal, cost 57,000gns: dam 7f juv wnr: eff over a
stiff/undul 5f on fm, 6f will suit: runs well fresh: gd start, can rate more highly & win more races.
2670 **GIFTED GAMBLE 23** [1] K A Ryan 2-9-0 bl N Callan 5/2: 033322: Led till over 1f out, onepace: 2   87
acts on firm & gd: proving consistent: see 1880, 1386.
      COUNTDOWN 6 [6] Sir Mark Prescott 2-9-0 S Sanders 11/8 FAV: 3: ch c Pivotal - Quiz Time (Efisio)   ½   85
In tch, outpcd over 1f out, some late gains: well bckd on debut: Mar foal, cost 170,000gns: dam 5f juv wnr: prob
eff at 5f on firm, shld be more to come.
3 Ran   Time 1m 0.01 (1.91)   Owned: Mr C Shiacolas   Trained: Whatcombe

3248
8.20 Tennents Scottish Stewards Cup Handicap Stakes 3yo+ 0-105 (B)   [102]
£18479 £7009 £3505   **6f5y str**   **Firm 10**   +08 Fast   Stands Side

3073 **BLACKHEATH 7** [11] D Nicholls 8-8-8 (82) P Makin(5) 8/1: 0622641: Made all far side, rdn clr fnl   95
1f: ideally suited by 5f & likes firm & fast grnd, handles gd/soft: acts on any trk: v tough, clrly in
fine heart & enjoyed front-running today: see 1217.
2949 **TOM TUN 13** [1] J Balding 9-9-8 bl (96) J Fanning 10/1: 10-02042: Handy stands side, hdwy over 1f   2½   101
out, carr right ins last, kept on, no ch with far side wnr: fine run on unsuitably firm grnd: tough & useful.
3116* **PIETER BRUEGHEL 6** [2] D Nicholls 5-8-12 (6ex) (86) R Winston 4/1 FAV: 0-040013: Led stands side   ½   89
group, hung right just ins last, hdd & no extra ins last: qck reapp, in fine form: see 3116.
2769 **SIMIANNA 20** [13] A Berry 5-9-5 p (93) P Mathers(7) 10/1: 0602004: Cl-up far side, onepcd dist.   ½   94
3069 **LOYAL TYCOON 7** [4]6-9-2 (90) A Nicholls 9/2: 2500105: In tch stands side, eff dist, onepace.   ½   89
3117 **CD EUROPE 6** [8]6-9-1 bl (89) N Callan 16/1: 21-00006: Switched far side, wknd dist: see 2581.   ½   86
3150 **SEAFIELD TOWERS 4** [6]4-7-13 p (73) Leanne Kershaw(7) 20/1: 0300007: Bhd stands side, hung right & 1¾   69
outpcd halfway, modest late gains: see 1917.
2990 **PAX 10** [12]7-8-9 (83) K Darley 16/1: 6601008: In tch, wknd well over 1f out: best 2059.   nk   78
2581 **JOHNSTONS DIAMOND 7** [3]6-9-1 (89) D Allan 16/1: 0462009: Cl-up stands side, wknd over 1f out.   3   75
3116 **LEGAL SET 6** [5]8-7-12 (14oh)t (58) Catherine Gannon(3) 33/1: 2140240: 10th: In tch, wknd 2f out.   3   49
3061 **CHOOKIE HEITON 8** [7]6-10-0 (102) T Eaves(3) 6/1: 010-4500: 11th: Handy stands side, wknd dist.   ¾   77
11 Ran   Time 1m 09.92 (0.12)   Owned: Middleham Park Racing XX & Streamhill   Trained: Thirsk

---

3249 8.50 Velvet Handicap Stakes For The Tennent Trophy 3yo+ 0-80 (D) [91]
£11060 £3403 £1702 **1m5f9y**   **Firm 10**   **+06 Fast** Stands Side

3173+ **ELUSIVE DREAM 3** [2] Sir Mark Prescott 3-8-4 (6ex) (67) S Sanders 4/9 FAV: 000-1111: Cl-up, hdwy   79
to lead 2f out, styd on well, cmftbly: 4-timer landed: stays 13f well, further sure to suit: acts on fm, gd/soft,
fibresand & prob any trk: exploiting v fav'able h'cap mark, plenty more to come as he steps up in trip.
2785 **SOUND OF FLEET 19** [6] P F I Cole 3-9-3 (80) J Fanning 25/1: 2-461502: In tch, hdwy 2f out, hung   1¼   87
left over 1f out & kept on but not pace of wnr: well clr of rem bhd a well h'capped sort: stays 13f: see 1965.
2998 **RED FOREST 10** [10] J Mackie 5-8-13 t (63) R Winston 12/1: 6115033: Prom, eased over 1f out: 5   63
fair run: 9lb higher than when winning 2217.
3158 **PADDY MUL 4** [3] W Storey 7-7-12 (6ex)t (48) P M Quinn 25/1: 4533144: Held up, some late gains,   1¾   45
nvr dngrs: qck reapp: crying out for rtn to 2m as in 2964
2685 **TANDAVA 22** [7]6-9-6 p (70) N Callan 50/1: 0-105405: Led till 2f out, wknd: best 1118.   nk   66
2881 **ACT OF THE PACE 15** [5]4-10-0 (78) W Hogg(7) 7/1: 5-4126: Keen, prom, wknd 2f out: btr 2881 (gd).   1¾   71
3134 **COSMIC CASE 6** [8]9-8-0 (2ow)(3oh) (45) A Nicholls 25/1: 1035237: Held up, nvr a factor: qck reapp.   ½   42
2567 **COLORADO FALLS 27** [4]6-10-0 (78) L Enstone(3) 25/1: 306/-1548:   1½   68
3032 **THE RING 9** [1]4-9-6 (70) K Darley 14/1: 1-023059: Held up, wknd over 2f out: see 1003 (2m).   2   57
3032 **NAKWA 9** [11]6-9-6 (70) D Allan 33/1: 2212600: 10th: In tch, wknd over 2f out: btr 2229, 1923.   ½   56
10 Ran Time 2m 46.04 (0.54) Owned: Cheveley Park Stud Trained: Newmarket

---

3250 9.20 Scottish Racing Your Best Bet Handicap Stakes 3yo+ 0-70 (E) [65]
£4323 £1330 £665 **1m1f36y**   **Firm 10**   **-10 Slow** Stands Side

3152 **ANTHEMION 4** [5] Mrs J C McGregor 7-8-13 (50) D McGaffin 8/1: 2000051: Made all, rdn clr over 1f   62
out, eased down: eff at 7f/9f on firm, gd/soft & fibresand, any trk: slipped down the weights & right back to form:
follow up under a pen, see 1504.
2958 **ENCOUNTER 12** [6] J Hetherton 8-8-9 (46) D Allan 12/1: 0356002: Keen in tch, hdwy well over 1f   6   46
out, not pace of wnr over 1f out: looks to be coming to hand & h'capped to win: see 1388.
3132 **DONNAS DOUBLE 6** [8] D Eddy 9-9-5 p (56) P Mulrennan(5) 6/1: 0555-563: Keen, handy, onepace.   ½   55
2958 **OSCAR PEPPER 12** [7] T D Barron 7-9-12 vis (63) P Makin(5) 100/30: 0634524: In tch, wknd dist.   ¾   60
2800 **KIRKHAM ABBEY 18** [1]4-10-0 vis (65) K Darley 3/1 FAV: 11-03265: Cl-up, wknd 2f out: btr 2433 (10f).   shd   62
3132 **KRISTIANSAND 6** [9]4-10-0 (65) L Enstone(3) 20/1: 10505-06: Dwelt, keen bhd, nvr a factor: see 3132.   ¾   60
3132 **COUSTOU 6** [4]4-9-8 p (59) T Eaves(3) 5/1: 6004337: Cl-up, wknd 2f out: qck reapp: see 3132 (9f).   ¾   52
1748 **ACE COMING 63** [3]3-9-10 (70) P Fessey 10/1: 0-031108: In tch, wknd 2f out: abs, not handle fm?   21   21
8 Ran Time 1m 55.95(1.85) Owned: On The Level Trained: Milnathort

---

Official Going GOOD (GOOD/FIRM places).

3251 2.00 E B F Starlight Maiden Stakes Fillies 2yo (D)
£7605 £2340 £1170 **6f8y str**   **Good/Firm 20**   **-29 Slow** Centre

FREE LIFT [8] R Charlton 2-8-11 S Drowne 33/1: 1: ch f Cadeaux Genereux - Step Aloft (Shirley   91+
Heights) Held up, prog halfway, pushed out to lead well ins fnl 1f: debut: Apr foal, half sister to a couple of
wnrs at 7f: dam successful at 10f: sire decent performer at sprint dists: eff at 6f, 7f+ will suit: acts on fast
grnd & a gall trk: goes well fresh: showed a gd turn of foot to land this & has a bright future.
QUICKFIRE [6] Sir Michael Stoute 2-8-11 K Fallon 4/9 FAV: 2: b f Dubai Millennium - Daring   ¾   85+
Miss (Sadler's Wells) Handy, styd on to lead dist, hdd well ins fnl 1f, no extra: Feb 1st foal: dam a
decent mid-dist performer, sire top-class over 1m/10f: eff at 6f, will apprec 7f/1m+: acts on fast grnd: pleasing
intro & looks sure to improve for today, esp over further.
3063 **MADHAVI 8** [4] R Hannon 2-8-11 R Hughes 33/1: 03: gr f Diktat - Grey Galava (Generous) In tch,   1   82$
kept on ins fnl 1f, not pace front 2: Jan foal, cost 24,000 gns: half sister successful at 9f: dam 14f wnr, sire
decent sprint performer: eff at 6f, further looks sure to suit: acts on fast grnd: can find similar.
MISS LAUGEVAL [10] G Wragg 2-8-11 T E Durcan 25/1: 4: b f Zilzal - Miss Sancerre (Last Tycoon)   nk   81
Slow away, prog ins fnl 2f, nrst fin: debut: Mar foal, sister successful at 1m: dam 7f wnr: sire top-class
performer at 1m: eff at 6f, 7f+ will suit: acts on fast grnd: promising run & looks sure to rate higher.
3064 **INDIENA 8** [5]2-8-11 J Fortune 10/1: 45: Led, hdd dist, no extra: see 3064.   1   78
1709 **ALEXANDER CAPETOWN 64** [3]2-8-11 Martin Dwyer 25/1: 256: Cl-up till dist, no extra: 9 wk abs.   1½   74
BOUNTIFUL [1]2-8-11 D Sweeney 40/1: 7: Chsd ldrs over 4f, wknd dist: debut.   1¾   69
CABIN FEVER [11]2-8-11 R Smith 100/1: 8: Slow away, mod late gains on debut.   1¼   65
MODRAJ [2]2-8-11 R Hills 14/1: 9: Handy over 4f, sn wknd: debut.   ½   64
EVASIVE QUALITY [12]2-8-11 T P Queally 7/1: 0: 10th: Handy 4f, wknd: tchd 9/1 on debut.   nk   63
Divine Diva [9]2-8-11 Dane O'Neill 33/1:0   **Midcap** [7]2-8-11 M Hills 25/1:0
12 Ran Time 1m 14.56 (2.96) Owned: The Queen Trained: Beckhampton

3252 2.35 Mountgrange Stud Maiden Stakes Fillies 2yo (D)
£7573 £2330 £1165 **7f str**   **Good/Firm 20**   **-08 Slow** Centre

WINDSCREAMER [10] J W Hills 2-8-11 M Hills 12/1: 1: b f Josr Algarhoud - St James's Antigua   93+
(Law Society) Held up, prog to lead dist, pushed clr fnl 1f, val 4L+: debut: Apr foal, cost 10,000 gns: half
sister to numerous wnrs: dam successful at 1m: sire useful miler: eff at 7f, will apprec 1m: acts on fast grnd &
a gall trk: goes well fresh: much to like about today's performance & looks sure to prog with experience.
PROUD SCHOLAR [11] Mrs A J Perrett 2-8-11 R Hughes 7/1: 2: br f Royal Academy - Proud Fact   2½   85
(Known Fact) Slow away, in tch halfway, styd on to chase ldr dist, styd on ins fnl 1f, al held: op 9/2 on debut:

Feb foal, half sister plcd at 6f, also successful over hdles: dam 7f wnr: sire Gr wnr at 6f/1m: eff at 7f, shaped as tho' 1m will suit: acts on fast grnd: decent enough from start to career & can find a race.

DUBAI SURPRISE [7] D R Loder 2-8-11 T P Queally 7/1: 3: b f King's Best - Toujours Irish 2½ 80
(Irish River) Cl-up, onepcd from dist: op 11/2 on debut: Mar foal, cost 220,000 gns: half sister to a wnr at 1m: dam unrcd: sire Gr1 wnr at 1m: eff at 7f, 1m will suit: acts on fast grnd: encouraging effort.

SOMETHING EXCITING [12] D R C Elsworth 2-8-11 N Pollard 40/1: 4: ch f Halling - Faraway Waters hd 79
(Pharly) Al handy, onepcd fnl 1f: debut: Mar foal, cost 20,000 gns: dam a smart 110f performer, sire multiple Gr 1 wnr at 10f: improve for today's experience & rate higher with a step up in trip.

2750 **SWAN NEBULA** 20 [6]2-8-11 t L Dettori 5/4 FAV: 35: Led, hdd dist, sn wknd: well bckd: v disapp 1 77
on step up to 7f: btr 2750 (6f, debut).

CASSYDORA [1]2-8-11 T Quinn 16/1: 6: Slow away, styd on fnl 1f, nrst fin: debut. 1¼ 75
KALMINI [9]2-8-11 C Catlin 40/1: 7: Chsd ldrs over 5f, sn no extra: debut. hd 74
SADIE THOMPSON [4]2-8-11 T E Durcan 16/1: 8: Nvr nrr than mid-div on debut. ¾ 72
SILVER HIGHLIGHT [8]2-8-11 Martin Dwyer 20/1: 9: Al in rear: debut. 1½ 69
3035 **TAKE IT THERE** 9 [5]2-8-11 Dane O'Neill 12/1: 00: 10th: Handy over 5f, wknd: see 3035. nk 68
MUSICAL DAY [2]2-8-11 J Fortune 40/1: 0: 11th: Al in rear. 1 66
Corniche Dancer [13]2-8-11 S Hitchcott(3) 66/1:0 **Ushindi** [3]2-8-11 K Fallon 12/1:0
13 Ran Time 1m 26.28 (1.98) Owned: Mrs Stevie Richards Trained: Lambourn

---

3253 **3.05 Tattersalls Conditions Stakes 3yo+ (B)**
£13050 £4950 £2475 **7f str** **Good/Firm 20** **+26 Fast** Centre

FONGS THONG 349 [3] B J Meehan 3-8-7 J Fortune 25/1: 321-1: ch c Dr Fong - Bacinella (El Gran 114+
Senor) Cl-up, imprvd to lead dist, rdn clr, impress: reapp & Brit bow, fast time: ex US, mdn wnr on last of only 3 '03 starts (1m, dirt): eff at 7f, apprec return to 1m: acts on fast grnd & a gall trk: goes well fresh: v impress & smart Brit bow, well up to Group company & looks one to follow.

3002 **MOONLIGHT MAN** 10 [6] R Hannon 3-8-7 Dane O'Neill 50/1: 13-22002: Handy, styd on to chase 3½ 106
wnr fnl 1f, al held: back to form, met a smart rival: see 1421.

2580 **POLAR WAY** 27 [7] Mrs A J Perrett 5-9-0 (110) R Hughes 9/2: 60201-03: Slow away, prog 3f out, shd 105
kept on ins fnl 1f, just held for 2nd: op 10/3: see 2580 (reapp).

2765 **PRINCE TUM TUM** 20 [5] J L Dunlop 4-8-11 (101) T Quinn 20/1: 311/1-064: In tch, wknd dist. 2½ 97
2765 **DESERT DESTINY** 20 [8]4-8-11 t (110) L Dettori 10/11 FAV: 5054-025: Held up, prog 3f out, wknd ins nk 96
fnl 1f: well bckd: v disapp on drop in grade: showed more in 2765 (Gr3).

2486 **PSYCHIATRIST** 30 [2]3-8-7 (100) K Fallon 12/1: 12-32406: Handy 5f, sn wknd: btr 1888 & 1189. 3½ 92
2069 **ORCADIAN** 48 [1]3-8-4 (103) R Hills 9/2: 31220-37: Led till dist, wknd: 7 wk abs: btr 2069. ½ 88
2913 **STORMONT** 13 [4]4-9-7 (104) T E Durcan 22/1: 0-400008: Slow away, al in rear: btr 1958. nk 97
8 Ran Time 1m 23.88 (u 0.42) Owned: Mr Joe L Allbritton Trained: Upper Lambourn

---

3254 **3.35 Listed Nayef Rose Bowl Stakes 2yo (A)**
£14500 £5500 £2750 **6f8y str** **Good/Firm 20** **-05 Slow** Centre

2618* **DON PELE** 25 [5] S Kirk 2-8-11 J Fortune 5/1: 0211: Made all, edged badly right ins fnl 1f, rdn 106
out: op 13/2: eff at 6f on fast & gd grnd: progressing with racing: useful, see 2618 (auct mdn).

1717* **BLACK VELVET** 64 [7] M P Tregoning 2-8-11 Martin Dwyer 13/8 FAV: 12: Handy, chsd wnr halfway, no 2 99
impress ins fnl 1f: bckd, 9 wk abs: eff at 5f, apprec step up to 6f: gd eff in defeat, see 1717.

3086* **INDIANNIE STAR** 7 [6] M R Channon 2 8 6 T E Durcan 25/1: 2160513: Keen rear, prog dist, no 3½ 84
impress ins fnl 1f: quick reapp: btr 3086 (5f).

3028 **ST ANDREWS STORM** 9 [8] R Hannon 2-8-11 R Hughes 11/4: 144: Held up, prog halfway, no impress nk 88
dist: well bckd: disapp on this drop in grade, btr 3028 (Gr 3) & 2531.

3060 **AL QUDRA** 8 [5]2-8-11 R L Moore 40/1: 5105: Handy over 4f, sn no extra: btr 2382. shd 87
2467 **BEAVER PATROL** 31 [4]2-9-0 S Carson 14/1: 132106: Chsd ldrs over 4f, sn wknd: btr 2071. 1¼ 86
2851 **TANZANI** 16 [1]2-8-11 M Hills 33/1: 47: Handy 4f, wknd: see 2851 (reapp). 1¼ 79
2970* **STREET CRED** 11 [2]2-8-11 K Fallon 6/1: 18: Cl-up halfway, fdd fnl 2f: failed to build on 2970. 2½ 72
8 Ran Time 1m 13.15 (1.55) Owned: Mr Pedro Rosas Trained: Upper Lambourn

---

3255 **4.10 Baileys Horse Feeds Handicap Stakes Fillies 3yo 0-80 (D)** [87]
£6032 £1856 £928 **1m2f6y** **Good/Firm 20** **-20 Slow** Outside

2366 **WEE DINNS** 35 [10] S Kirk 3-9-2 (75) J F Egan 9/2: 00-05221: Held up, prog halfway, led 2f out, 85
drvn out fnl 1f: eff at 1m: suited by arnd 10f: acts on fast & soft grnd: has been rng well & this was a deserved success: see 2366 & 2046.

2842* **MAZUNA** 16 [7] C E Brittain 3-8-8 (67) R L Moore 7/1: 04406-12: Handy, prog & styd on to chase 3 71
ldr ins fnl 1f, al held: eff at 10f, apprec return to 11.5f: see 2842.

1835 **TREE TOPS** 59 [11] J H M Gosden 3-8-13 (72) J Fortune 13/2: 5233: In tch, prog to lead bef 2f 1 74
out, sn hdd & no extra: bckd from 11/1, 8 wk abs: back to form in h'cap bow: see 1835 & 1468.

2680 **THIRTEEN TRICKS** 23 [2] Mrs A J Perrett 3-9-2 (75) J Murtagh 8/1: 034-034: Al handy, no extra dist. 2 74
2536* **GOODWOOD FINESSE** 28 [12]3-9-2 (75) G Carter 4/1 FAV: 55-15: Rear, prog bef 1f out, no impress on 5 67
ldrs: based from h'cap bow: showed more in 2536.

2780* **CAUSE CELEBRE** 19 [9]3-9-7 (80) M Hills 9/1: 324-1016: Al cl-up, led 4f out till 2f out, wknd. 1 70
1089 **LAND OF NOD** 100 [6]3-8-4 (63) E Ahern 14/1: 00-47: In tch, under press when short of room 2f 1 51
out, sn wknd: long abs & h'cap bow: see 1089.

2621 **IN DEEP** 25 [1]3-8-6 (65) Martin Dwyer 22/1: 562-0068: Rear, mod late gains: see 2250. 1½ 50
2893 **PRINCIPESSA** 14 [3]3-8-11 (70) T E Durcan 11/1: 5000229: Led 6f, sn wknd: btr 2893 & 2706. nk 54
2509* **DARK RAIDER** 29 [5]3-8-11 (70) D Corby(3) 14/1: 00-25510: 10th: In tch, wkng under press when nk 53
short of room 2f out: btr 2509.

2536 **GWEN JOHN** 28 [4]3-9-1 (74) S Drowne 10/1: 5-530: 11th: Bhd, nvr a factor: op 7/1: btr 2536 (mdn). hd 56
2980 **POWERFUL PARRISH** 11 [8]3-9-5 (78) K Fallon 16/1: 25-0240: 12th: Handy 7f, sn fdd: reportedly 2½ 56
lost action: btr 2627.
12 Ran Time 2m 6.86 (4.06) Owned: F B O T Racing Trained: Upper Lambourn

---

3256   **4.40 Windsor Plc Handicap Stakes 3yo+ 0-85 (D)**   **[85]**
£5850 £1800 £900   **1m3f5y**   **Good/Firm 20**   -15 Slow   Outside

3076 **GOLD RING** 7 [7] G B Balding 4-10-0 (85) S Carson 3/1 FAV: 0236531: In tch, prog to lead well   93
over 1f out, drvn out: well bckd on qck reapp: suited by 11/13.3f on firm & soft grnd: rarely runs a bad race &
this was deserved under top weight: see 3076 & 1668.
2887 **GENGHIS** 15 [10] H Morrison 5-9-9 (80) J Fortune 6/1: 24/3-252: Led after 1f, hdd well over 1f   2½   82
out, sn edged left & not pace wnr: only lightly rcd in h'cap grade & this was another gd eff: see 2737.
2680* **UNSUITED** 23 [6] J E Long 5-8-12 (69) Natalia Gemelova(7) 8/1: 2641113: Chsd ldrs, ev ch dist, no   1½   70
extra fnl 1f: op 5/1: eff at 9/11f on fast, hvy & fibresand: 8lbs higher than win in 2680.
2735* **KENS DREAM** 21 [8] Ms A E Embiricos 5-9-11 (82) P McCabe 5/1: 15/-03414: Keen bhd, prog 3f out,   ½   82
no impress ins fnl 1f: 3lb higher than win in 2735.
2874 **OCEAN OF STORMS** 15 [4] 9-9-7 t (78) R Thomas(5) 25/1: R-210045: Slow away, prog 4f out, onepcd   3½   73
3070 **BRIAREUS** 7 [9] 4-9-6 (77) Martin Dwyer 9/2: 0203606: Handy 1m, sn wknd: qck reapp: well bckd.   5   65
2874 **SILVER CITY** 15 [11] 4-9-10 (81) P Dobbs 8/1: 32610-27: Cl-up 1m, sn wknd: btr 2874.   1   67
2255 **FINANCIAL FUTURE** 41 [5] 4-10-0 (85) Brigitte Renk 33/1: 110-0008: b g Barathea - In Perpetuity   ½   70
(Great Nephew) Handy 7f, sn wknd: top weight: mdn & Swiss Derby wnr in '03: eff at 10/12f on fast & soft grnd:
acts on a gall, stiff or sharp trk: can force the pace.
1 Jun'03 Frau 12gd 100- : 1 Jun'03 Hayd 11.9g/f 99-(84) D: 2 May'03 Yarm 11.5gd 84-(85) D:
2 Apr'03 Newm 10gd 90-(85) D: 2 Mar'03 Kemp 9gd 86-(85) D:
2265 **VICTORY VENTURE** 39 [1] 4-9-3 t (78) J Fortune 50/1: 10030-09: Rear, nvr a factor.   11   44
   DAWTON 656 [3] 6-9-7 (78) R L Moore 7/1: 113422/-0: 10th: br c Greinton - Da Wega (Who Knows)   ½   47
Handy 1m, sn fdd: recent hdles unplcd (rtd 69h, mdn): ex-Polish, 7 times wnr in native country (1m/12f).
1087 **VIN DU PAYS** 100 [2] 4-7-12 (55) A McCarthy 40/1: 55116-00: 11th: Rear, nvr a factor: abs: btr 7.   4   18
11 Ran   Time 2m 19.67 (3.87)   Owned: Miss B Swire   Trained: Andover

---

3257   **5.10 Ladbrokes Com Handicap Stakes 3yo+ 0-80 (D)**   **[80]**
£6032 £1856 £928   **7f str**   **Good/Firm 20**   +02 Fast   Centre

2880 **BOUNDLESS PROSPECT** 15 [6] J W Hills 5-9-5 (71) M Hills 12/1: 0000231: Held up, prog halfway,   80
styd on to lead dist, rdn out: eff at 6/7.5f on firm, gd/soft & both AWs: gd confidence boost after long losing run
& is h'capped to win again: see 2880 & 2564.
2880 **POINT OF DISPUTE** 15 [4] P J Makin 9-10-0 vis (80) Martin Dwyer 14/1: 56302-52: Held up, prog 3f   1½   83
out, ev ch dist, styd on, not pace wnr: eff under top weight: see 2880.
52* **STAR OF LIGHT** 241 [8] B J Meehan 3-9-3 (76) J Fortune 50/1: 0621-3: Led, hdd 5f out, styd cl-up   ¾   78
& ev ch bef 1f out, sn no extra: long abs: acts on fast grnd & polytrack: gd eff after long lay-off: see 52.
2864 **AND TOTO TOO** 15 [2] P D Evans 4-9-1 bl (67) R L Moore 9/2: 2402044: Slow away, hdwy halfway, no   nk   68
impress ins fnl 1f: see 2864 & btr 2312.
2466 **YORKSHIRE BLUE** 31 [16] 5-8-6 (58) T E Durcan 11/1: 0-001105: In tch, short of room & outpcd after   1¾   55
5f, rallied ins fnl 1f, not reach ldrs: closer with clr passage: just btr 2235 & 2027.
3087* **CHANDELIER** 7 [7] 4-7-12 (6ex)(2oh) (48) A McCarthy 20/1: 6032016: Handy, styd on to lead well over   1   45
1f out, hdd dist, wknd: quick reapp: btr 3087.
2878 **NIVERNAIS** 15 [3] 5-9-7 t (73) N Chalmers(5) 12/1: 6-000067: In tch, ev ch dist, sn wknd: btr 2023.   2½   63
3088 **JUST FLY** 7 [15] 4-9-12 (78) J Daly(7) 25/1: 2203008: Handy over 5f, sn no extra: quick reapp.   nk   67
3162* **TUSCARORA** 4 [17] 5-8-6 (6ex) (58) T P Queally 8/1: 0052619: Nvr nrr than mid-div: quick reapp.   1½   44
2617 **NABTAT SAIF** 25 [10] 3-8-8 t (67) P Dobbs 50/1: 40-04000: 10th: Rear, hdwy when short of room ins   nk   52
fnl 3f, sn no impress: 1st time t-strap: see 2617.
2755* **GALLERY BREEZE** 20 [9] 5-9-4 (70) V Slattery 12/1: 41120-10: 11th: Handy, outpcd 3f out, late gains.   hd   54
3068 **AZREME** 7 [14] 4-9-4-30 (69) I Mongan 6/1 JT FAV: 5045430: 12th: In tch, ev ch 2f out, sn wknd.   ¾   51
3034 **BI POLAR** 9 [11] 4-9-7 (73) L Keniry(3) 7/1: 20-00220: 13th: Led 5f out, hdd 3f out, wknd.   1½   52
3090 **SABRINA BROWN** 7 [12] 3-8-1 (60) R Thomas(5) 6/1 JT FAV: 006-220: 14th: In tch, led 2f out, hdd   ½   38
over 1f out, fdd: quick reapp: btr 3090.
2954 **WOOD FERN** 12 [5] 4-8-5 VIS (57) S Hitchcott 33/1: 0005000: 15th: Handy 5f, wknd: 1st time visor.   3½   28
3001 **OH BOY** 10 [13] 4-9-6 (72) R Hughes 7/1: 0051100: 16th: Cl-up, led 3f out, hdd 2f out, wknd.   1¾   39
2587 **KINDLELIGHT DEBUT** 27 [1] 4-9-11 (77) M Howard(7) 40/1: 23100-00: 17th: b f Groom Dancer - Dancing   4   36
Debut (Polar Falcon) Handy 5f, fdd: h'cap wnr in '03: unplcd in '02 (rtd 70a, mdn): eff at 7f/1m on fast & gd
grnd: acts on a stiff/gall trk: with D K Ivory.
1 Aug'03 Newm 7fm 80-75 C: 2 Aug'03 Newm 7gd 75-72 D:
1 Jun'03 Sali 7.0g/f 72-65 F: 2 May'03 Yarm 8.0g/f 67-65 E: 2 May'03 Yarm 7.0gd 67-(65) E:
17 Ran   Time 1m 25.58(1.28)   Owned: M Wauchope Sir Simon Dunning R Cottam   Trained: Lambourn

---

Official Going Soft

3258   **2.05 E B F Sarah Anne Daniels 80th Birthday Maiden Stakes Fillies 2yo (D)**
£5398 £1661 £830   **5f str**   **Good/Soft 88**   -01 Slow   Stands side

3063 **SATIN FINISH** 9 [6] M R Channon 2-8-11 A Culhane 6/4 FAV: 41: Prom, styd on to lead dist, pushed   81+
out, val 6L+: well bckd: eff at 5f, return to 6f will suit: acts on fast, enjoyed this gd/soft grnd & a sharpish
trk: impressed here, win more races: see 3063.
2883 **HOWARDS PRINCESS** 16 [1] J S Goldie 2-8-11 T Eaves(3) 14/1: 52: In tch, prog when no room ins fnl   4   70
2f, kept on ins fnl 1f, not pace wnr: eff at 5f, return to 6f will suit: acts on gd/soft grnd: see 2883.
   PEDLAR OF DREAMS 0 [4] T D Barron 2-8-11 M Fenton 25/1: 3: b f Fayruz - Beautyofthepeace   ½   69
(Exactly Sharp) Prom, ev ch halfway, no extra dist: debut: Apr foal, half sister to wnrs at 6f/9f: dam uncrd:
sire useful juv performer: improve on today.
3141 **RUBYS DREAM** 6 [5] J M Bradley 2-8-11 S W Kelly 20/1: 4234354: Handy over 3f, sn onepcd: qck reapp.   nk   68
2132 **ELSIE WAGG** 46 [3] 2-8-11 N Callan 12/1: 345: Led, hdd dist, wknd: 7 wk abs: see 2132 & 2020.   ½   67
2750 **MOLLY MARIE** 21 [9] 2-8-11 D Allan 4/1: 246: Bhd, nvr nrr than mid div: btr 2750 (gd) & 2132.   hd   66

RIPON   SATURDAY 17.07.04   **Righthand, Sharpish Track**

2983 **HILLSIDE HEATHER** 12 [10]2-8-11 F Norton 10/1: 4327: Chsd ldrs over 3f, sn no extra: see 2983.   2   60
  ALGORITHM 0 [2]2-8-11 R Winston 33/1: 8: b f Danehill Dancer - Dominelle (Domynsky) Bhd, nvr a   ½   59
factor on debut: Mar first foal, dam won at 5f/7f: sire useful at sprint dists: with T D Easterby.
  NIGHT OUT 0 [7]2-8-11 J Fanning 33/1: 9: In tch till halfway, wknd: debut.   hd   58
  JASMINE HILL 0 [11]2-8-11 Dean McKeown 80/1: 0: 10th: Bhd, nvr a factor: debut.   8   37
  MATCH BALL 0 [8]2-8-11 J Carroll 4/1: 0: 11th: b f Grand Slam - Glitters (Glitterman) Handy   7   19
3f, fdd: op 3/1 on debut: May first foal, cost $160,000: dam plcd in US: sire decent at 6f/1m: with Saeed Bin Suroor.
11 Ran   Time 1m 2.28 (4.48)   Owned: Sheikh Mohammed   Trained: West Ilsley

3259   2.40 Alexandre Savile Row Selling Guaranteed Sweepstakes 2yo (E)
  £3250 £1000 £500   **6f str**   **Good/Soft 88**   **-66 Slow**   Stands side

2965 **PREMIER TIMES** 12 [3] M D Hammond 2-8-11 A Culhane 11/8 FAV: 51: Sn bhd, prog 3f out, styd on to   62
lead dist, rdn out: well bckd: bought in for 8,000 gns: eff at 6f on gd/soft grnd: lightly rcd juvenile who
appreciated drop to sell grade: see 2965.
3014 **DANEHILL FAIRY** 10 [2] Mrs A Duffield 2-8-6 bl J Fanning 11/2: 2063332: Up front, led 2f out, hdd   2½   47
dist, no extra fnl 1f: proving consistent: see 3014 & 2461.
2294 **SINGHALONGTASVEER** 39 [5] W Storey 2-8-11 S W Kelly 25/1: 053: b g Namaqualand - Felinwen   ¾   50
(White Mill) Dwelt, sn handy, onepcd bef 1f out: May foal, cost 500 gns: half brother to a wnr at 2m: dam unrcd:
sire smart around 1m: eff at 6f on gd/soft grnd.
3172 **TIP TOES** 4 [1] M R Channon 2-8-6 B O'Neill(7) 8/1: 0604: Rear, prog 3f out, nrst fin: qck   nk   44
reapp: eff at 6f on gd/soft grnd in sell grade: see 2321.
2939 **TIMMY** 14 [6]2-8-11 BL T Eaves(3) 40/1: 00005: Led 4f, sn wknd: 1st time blnks: see 2321.   1¾   44
2882 **MISS GOOD TIME** 16 [7]2-8-6 M Fenton 9/4: 06066: gr f Timeless Times - Fort Vally (Belfort)   ½   38
Dwelt, sn mid div, no impress 2f: Feb foal, cost 2,200 gns: sister successful at 7f: dam wnr at 1m/9f.
3093 **NORTHERN REVOQUE** 8 [4]2-8-6 BL R Winston 20/1: 50057: Handy 3f, fdd: 1st time blnks.   14   10
7 Ran   Time 1m 19.28 (9.28)   Owned: Pentland Times Partnership   Trained: Middleham

3260   3.15 Leeds Hospital Fund Handicap Guaranteed Sweepstakes 3yo+ 0-80 (D)   [80]
  £5850 £1800 £900   **1m2f**   **Good/Soft 88**   **-02 Slow**   Inside

2761 **OLIVIA ROSE** 21 [7] J Pearce 5-9-13 (79) N Callan 13/2: 3123141: In tch, prog 4f out, styd on to   88
lead dist, rdn out: eff btwn 1m/12f on fast, hvy grnd & fibresand: fine form & this was 4th success of year.
2010 **NEVADA DESERT** 52 [10] R M Whitaker 4-9-5 (71) Dean McKeown 11/2: 3425-452: Led, rcd keenly, hung 1½   77
left & hdd dist, kept on, not pace wnr: 7 wk abs: gd run but 1 win in 18: see 1781 (reapp).
3074 **TEDSDALE MAC** 8 [6] N Bycroft 5-8-5 (57) F Norton 7/1: 4-042523: Chsd ldrs, onepcd: poss stays 10f.   2½   59
2079 **STRIDER** 49 [1] Sir Michael Stoute 3-9-1 (77) R Winston 7/2 FAV: 00-244: Prom 1m, sn no extra: 7 wk abs.1¾   77
2929 **ROTUMA** 14 [3]5-9-7 bl (73) L Enstone(3) 9/2: 0316125: Handy, no extra ins fnl 2f: op 11/2: btr 2929.   1½   70
2483 **MEGANS MAGIC** 31 [2]4-9-2 (68) S W Kelly 9/2: 6120036: Dwelt, nvr nrr than mid div: btr 2483 (fast).   3   61
1978 **FANLING LADY** 53 [8]3-8-11 (73) A Nicholls 33/1: 03032-07: gr f Highest Honor - Pain Perdu   8   55
(Waajib) Bhd, nvr a factor: 7 wk abs: plcd 3 times in '03 (A P Jarvis, rtd 74, h'caps): eff at 7f/10f on firm &
gd grnd: with D Nicholls. 2 Oct'03 Pont 10.0g/f 74-(74) D:
2890 **BROADWAY SCORE** 15 [5]6-9-4 BL (70) P Mulrennan(5) 14/1: 0000008: Cl up, over 7f, sn wknd: blnks.   5   45
2507 **CHAMPAIN SANDS** 30 [4]5-8-3 (55) B Swarbrick(5) 16/1: 2-342509: Mid div, prog halfway, fdd 3f out.   ¾   28
9 Ran   Time 2m 12.32 (9.02)   Owned: Mr A Watford   Trained: Newmarket

3261   3.45 Ripon Bell-Ringer Stakes Handicap 3yo+ 0-85 (D)   [97]
  £13780 £4240 £2120   **1m4f60y**   **Good/Soft 88**   **+14 Fast**   Inside

2960* **LETS ROLL** 13 [6] C W Thornton 3-8-7 (76) Dean McKeown 3/1 FAV: 2622311: Held up, prog 4f out,   87+
led trav well, cmftbly, val 4L+: well bckd: eff around 1m/9f, imprvd for recent step up to 11/12f on fast & gd/soft
grnd: progressing with racing & can land hat-trick: see 2960.
3149* **PARTY PLOY** 5 [4] K R Burke 6-8-11 (5ex) (68) L Enstone(3) 7/1: 0211012: Prom, led over 3f out, hdd   2   76
dist, kept on, not pace wnr: tchd 9/1, clr rem: ran to form under 5lb pen of win in 3149.
3076 **DUNASKIN** 8 [7] D Eddy 4-9-10 (81) P Mulrennan(5) 8/1: 3-000563: Led, hdd over 3f out, sn no extra.   7   79
2673 **SPORTING GESTURE** 24 [8] M W Easterby 7-9-4 (75) Dale Gibson 10/1: 00-05444: Handy 9f, sn no extra.½   72
3099 **ALERON** 7 [2]6-9-1 p (72) N Callan 7/1: 2120435: In tch 10f, sn wknd: qck reapp: btr 3099.   3   65
2405 **STALLONE** 35 [10]7-9-2 (73) T Eaves(3) 14/1: 10-03436: Rear, nvr nrr than mid div: btr 2405.   2½   62
3066 **NORTHSIDE LODGE** 9 [9]6-9-5 (76) M Fenton 12/1: 0035207: Bhd, nvr a factor: btr 2538 (gd).   7   55
1783 **MAGNETIC POLE** 62 [1]3-9-2 (85) R Winston 9/2: 3-238: Dwelt, sn in tch, wknd 2f out: btr 1789 (9f).   1½   61
2984 **RUTTERS REBEL** 12 [5]3-8-3 (72) B Swarbrick(5) 20/1: 5040249: Chsd ldrs, fdd 3f out: btr 2707.   ½   47
2735 **BAILEYS DANCER** 22 [3]3-8-6 BL (75) J Fanning 10/1: 0-040020: 10th: Handy 1m, sn wknd: blnks.   dist 20
10 Ran   Time 2m 42.71 (9.21)   Owned: A Crute and Partners   Trained: Leyburn

3262   4.20 Heuston Hospitality Maiden Handicap Guaranteed Sweepstakes 3yo+ 0-70 (E)   [70]
  £4225 £1300 £650   **6f str**   **Good/Soft 88**   **-13 Slow**   Stands side

2435 **RED MONARCH** 33 [8] P A Blockley 3-8-13 (55) N Callan 6/1: 000621: Rcd stands side, made all, rdn   64
out fnl 1f: eff at 6f, tried 1m: acts on fast & gd/soft grnd: gd confidence boost: see 2435 & 1787.
3018 **UHURU PEAK** 10 [10] M W Easterby 3-8-12 (54) P Mulrennan(5) 12/1: 3050032: In tch stands side,   2   56
prog to chase wnr ins fnl 1f, styd on but al wknd: eff on firm, gd/soft & fibresand: another gd effort: see 3018.
2561 **PRIDE OF KINLOCH** 28 [12] J Hetherton 4-9-4 (55) F Norton 7/1: 4030003: Handy stands side, kept   hd   56
on ins fnl 1f, just held for 2nd: eff at 6f/7f on fast & gd/soft grnd: see 385.
3203 **LORD BASKERVILLE** 2 [20] W Storey 3-8-12 (54) M Lawson(5) 5/1 FAV: 0000224: Rcd far side, styd on   ¾   53
to lead that side 2f out, styd on far side, not pace stands side: well bckd: won race on far side: see 3203.
2891 **KILLERBY NICKO** 15 [19]3-8-4 (1ow)bl (46) J Carroll 8/1: 605U305: Rcd far side, al cl up, styd on   ½   44
ins fnl 1f, not pace stands side: see 2812.
2907 **PURE IMAGINATION** 15 [5]3-9-8 (64) Dean McKeown 16/1: 6306: Rcd stands side, prom, no extra dist.   hd   61
2906 **FLEET ANCHOR** 15 [18]3-9-4 (60) R Ffrench 25/1: 50-07: Handy far side, onepcd bef 1f out: see 2906.   1¾   52

986

RIPON SATURDAY 17.07.04 Righthand, Sharpish Track

2806 **FIZZY LIZZY 19** [7]4-7-12 (1oh) (34) Leanne Kershaw(7) 25/1: 0000-008: In tch stands side 4f, sn no extra. ½ 26
2936 **FIREBIRD RISING 14** [4]3-9-5 (61) M Fenton 8/1: 3-50369: Bhd stands side, nvr nrr than mid div. ¾ 50
3094 **DISPOL VERITY 8** [3]4-8-3 (40) P M Quinn 28/1: 000/-0000: 10th: Handy stands side 4f, sn wknd. nk 28
4136} **RUE DE PARIS 312** [13]4-8-5 (42) T Eaves(1) 66/1: 000000-0: 11th: br g Paris House - Innocent ½ 29
Abroad (Viking) Led stands side group 4f, fdd: new stable & reapp: plcd once in '03 (rtd 65, N Bycroft): unplcd
in '02 (rtd 65, mdn): eff at 6f on fast grnd: tried t-strap: with J A Harris.
3095 **PALVIC MOON 8** [1]3-9-4 (60) J Fanning 16/1: 066-5360: 12th: Prom stands side 4f, sn wknd: btr 1659. 1¼ 43
3018 **SUJOSISE 10** [17]3-8-0 (42) P Fessey 25/1: 000-0000: 13th: In tch far side 4f, fdd. ½ 24
1473 **ICE PLANET 77** [9]3-9-13 (69) R Winston 8/1: 0350: 14th: Handy stands side till halfway, wknd. ½ 50
2728 **SCOOBY DOOBY DO 22** [16]3-9-4 (60) V Halliday 20/1: 60-560: 15th: Handy far side 4f, wknd: btr 2728. nk 40
2808 **BEAVER DIVA 19** [15]3-7-12 (40) B Swarbrick(5) 11/2: 0-400220: 16th: Bhd far side, prog when short 1 17
of room 2f out, wknd: disappointing effort: btr 2808 (5f, fast).
1052 **TANAFFUS 103** [11]4-8-10 BL (47) A Culhane 50/1: 56-00000: 17th: Al rear stands side: 1st time blnks. 17 0
17 Ran Time 1m 16.08 (6.08) Owned: Bigwigs Bloodstock III Trained: Southwell

3263 4.55 Dobson Gaskets C & J Anniversary Median Auction Maiden Guaranteed Sweepstakes 3yo (F)
£4225 £1300 £650 1m1f Good/Soft 88 -11 Slow Inside

2994 **MY PARIS 11** [4] K A Ryan 3-9-0 (80) N Callan 10/11 FAV: 2225221: Prom, led halfway, sn clr, 80+
pushed out, val 7L+; well bckd: eff at 7f/10f on fast gd/soft grnd: in gd form & this was deserved: see 2994.
3019 **ASTON LAD 10** [3] M D Hammond 3-9-0 (45) P Mulrennan(5) 66/1: 4662: Rear, prog halfway, kept on 5 70$
fnl 2f, not pace wnr: clr rem: seemingly improved run: see 3019 & 1871.
2960 **RIGONZA 13** [7] T D Easterby 3-9-0 (65) D Allan 25/1: 46-00503: Handy, chsd wnr 4f out, wknd ins fnl 2f. 8 59
1725 **VAMOSE 64** [5] Miss Gay Kelleway 3-9-0 (66) M Fenton 10/1: 0230-404: Led till halfway, sn wknd. 5 52
3019 **BIEN GOOD 10** [8]3-8-9 T Eaves(3) 20/1: 0-35: Slow away, nvr a factor: btr 3019. 13 30
2893 **CHICAGO BOND 15** [1]3-8-9 (63) D McGaffin 50/1: 4360-006: Rear, nvr a factor. 1¾ 27
2751 **LITTLE BOB 21** [6]3-9-0 (75) J Fanning 6/4: 0-44237: Chsd ldrs, cocked jaw & ran v wide turning dist 2
in, sn eased: well bckd: not not impress with attitude & might need to race left-handed: btr 2751.
7 Ran Time 1m 58.98(8.98) Owned: J and A Spensley Trained: Hambleton

NEWBURY SATURDAY 17.07.04 Lefthand, Flat, Galloping Track

Official Going Good (Good/Firm places in back str)

3264 1.50 Listed Cantorodds Com Steventon Stakes 3yo+ (A)
£17400 £6600 £3300 1m2f6y Good/Firm 20 +07 Fast Outside

2234+ **MUQBIL 42** [4] J L Dunlop 4-9-3 (113) R Hills 11/4: 0234-011: Held up, gd hdwy 3f out, styd on 116
for press to lead in last, drvn out: 6 wk abs: well suited by 10f now on firm or gd grnd, any trk, loves Newbury:
thriving, v smart now & can win again in Gr class: see 2234.
2252 **VESPONE 42** [3] Saeed bin Suroor 4-9-3 vis t (118) L Dettori 6/1: 10-22202: Sn clr ldr, kept on ¾ 114
till rdn & hdd just ins last, joc lost whip cch frame, not btn far: abs, clr rem: enjoyed drop in class & ran to smart
best from the front: eff with/without a vis, wears t-strap: acts on fast, prob even btr on gd or hvy.
2579 **MUSANID 28** [1] Sir Michael Stoute 4-9-3 (107) K Fallon 11/1: 33/1-363: Held up, eff over 2f out, 6 105
no threat to forge 2f: back to useful best & worth another try over 12f: see 1483.
3030 **MAGISTRETTI 10** [2] N A Callaghan 4-9-3 (121) D Holland 15/8 FAV: 1022-644: In tch, nvr trav 1½ 103
well, wknd over 2f out: nicely bckd: back in trip but again failed to fire: see 3030, 2209.
2488 **KAIETEUR 31** [6]5-9-3 BL (114) J Fortune 10/1: 3230-605: Handy, rdn over 3f out, sn btn: no 3 99
improvement tried in blnks: formerly v smart, on easier grnd: see 2128.
2554 **ELSHADI 29** [5]3-8-7 bl (104) Martin Dwyer 11/1: 114-026: Chsd ldr till wknd 3f out: see 2554 (Gr 2). 2 96
4703* **TREE CHOPPER 279** [7]3-8-2 R L Moore 12/1: 1-7: ch f Woodman - Gazayil (Irish River) Slow away, dist 0
al bhd, t.o.: reapp: won sole '03 start (mdn): eff at 1m, bred to stay further: acts on firm grnd & has run well
fresh in a t-strap: poss been difficult to train: with M P Tregoning. 1 Oct'03 Bath 8.0fm 83- D:
7 Ran Time 2m 04.12 (1.32) Owned: Mr Hamdan Al Maktoum Trained: Arundel

3265 2.25 Ladbrokes Com Handicap Stakes 3yo+ 0-105 (B) [102]
£23200 £8800 £4400 1m str Good/Firm 20 +04 Fast Centre

3001* **EVEREST 11** [15] B Ellison 7-8-6 (80) K Fallon 11/2: 0000011: Held up, hdwy over 2f out, strong 90
run to lead appr fnl 1f, drvn to hold on: suited by 1m, stays a while fnl furlong, any trk: 3rd in this race
last term off a 5lb higher mark, thriving at present & taking advantage of lenient h'capping: see 3001.
2489 **VORTEX 31** [8] Miss Gay Kelleway 5-9-10 e t (98) L Dettori 14/1: 1001302: Held up, hdwy & short of shd 107
room well over 1f out, styd on strongly ins last, just failed: another excellent run & holds v strong claims in the
7f Tote international h'cap at Ascot next weekend, has a fine turn of foot: see 1926 (Victoria Cup).
5020} **BATTLE CHANT 254** [14] Mrs A J Perrett 4-10-0 (102) R L Moore 14/1: 504030-3: b g Coronado's 1½ 106
Quest - Appointed One (Danzig) Held up, hdwy to chall over 1f out, kept on same pace in last: been gelded: plcd in
a stks in '03 (with E Dunlop, rtd 107): '02 mdn & List wnr: stays 8.5f on firm & gd/soft: has run well fresh on
gall & undul trks: tried a t-strap: fine start for new stable under a big weight, win another Listed event.
1 Oct'02 Pont 8g/s 103- A: 1 Sep'02 Chep 7gd 93- D:
3001 **AUDIENCE 11** [4] J Akehurst 4-9-5 p (93) J Quinn 12/1: 0000024: Held up, hdwy 2f out, kept on same 1 97
pace in last: useful, another fine run: see 3001, 2489.
2489 **IMPELLER 31** [18]5-8-13 (87) S Drowne 20/1: 2-002605: Held up, hdwy & short of room 2f out, late 1 89
gains, no impress on front 2: see 2489, 2096.
2489 **LAGO DORTA 31** [5]4-9-12 (100) J Fortune 10/1: 1-640066: Slow away & held up, styd on late, nrst 1 100
fin: ran similar race in 2489 & clearly in gd heart: see 1168.
2860 **JAMES CAIRD 17** [7]4-8-13 (87) R Hills 10/1: 62-62227: Handy, wknd appr fnl 1f: shade btr 2860, 2101. 1 85
2489 **ABLE BAKER CHARLIE 31** [16]5-9-5 (93) O Urbina 9/2 FAV: 5110-428: Held up, hdwy over 2f out, wknd 1½ 88
dist: well bckd: better expected after fine 2nd in 2489 (Royal Hunt Cup H'cap).
2662 **HIGHLAND REEL 24** [13]7-8-12 (86) L Keniry(3) 33/1: 10-10049: In tch, eff over 1f out, no dngr. ¾ 79

987

3107 **ZUCCHERO 7** [12]8-8-1 p (75) A Daly 20/1: 0000-030: 10th: In tch, hdwy to lead dist, sn hdd & wknd. — 1¼ — 65

3088 **BLUE TROJAN 8** [17]4-8-12 (86) J F Egan 10/1: 1400420: 11th: Held up, btn 2f out: see 3088. — ½ — 75

REBEL LEADER 530 [9]7-9-2 (90) Martin Dwyer 50/1: 3105/50-0: 12th: br g Ezzoud - Haitienne — 1 — 77
(Green Dancer) In tch, hdwy & short of room 2f out, sn wknd: prev rcd in Hong Kong, unplcd in '03, dual h'cap wnr
in '02: stays 9f well on gd & fast grnd: with W R Muir.

3039 **GIG HARBOR 10** [11]5-8-6 (80) S Whitworth 40/1: 0156040: 13th: Led till over 1f out, wknd: see 3039. — 1½ — 64

2489 **KINGS COUNTY 31** [6]6-9-7 (95) D Holland 12/1: 12-30300: 14th: In tch, wknd qckly over 1f out: — 1¾ — 75
reportedly hung left: btr 2090, 1231.

2896 **DEFINITE GUEST 15** [10]6-8-6 (80) T Hamilton(3) 20/1: 565-3000: 15th: In tch, wknd 2f out: won — 3 — 54
this race last term off a 3lb lower mark, not in that form at present: see 2207.

2554 **GOLD HISTORY 29** [1]3-9-7 (103) K Dalgleish 25/1: 10-21350: 16th: In tch, wknd 2f out: much btr 1189. — 1 — 75

2915 **CAMP COMMANDER 14** [3]5-9-7 t (95) T E Durcan 14/1: 34-04500: 17th: Slow away, nvr a factor: btr 2915.5 — 57

1231 **SERIEUX 91** [2]5-9-2 (90) R Hughes 16/1: 00-00020: 18th: In tch, wknd 2f out, reportedly fin tired. — 9 — 34
18 Ran   Time 1m 38.1 (1.3)   Owned: Mr I S Sandhu and Partners   Trained: Malton

---

3266   3.00 Weatherbys Super Sprint 2yo (B)
£78300 £29700 £14850   5f34y str   Good/Firm 20   -20 Slow   Centre

2490 **SIENA GOLD 31** [9] B J Meehan 2-8-1 J F McDonald 11/2: 1101: Made virtually all, drvn to hold on — 92
ins last: v eff at 5f on fast & gd grnd, best up with/forcing the pace: right back to v useful best & clearly a
genuine & v speedy filly who likes Newbury: see 1735.

2490 **DONT TELL MUM 31** [5] R Hannon 2-8-2 R L Moore 9/2 FAV: 162: With wnr, chall & carried left just — ¾ — 90
ins last, not pace of wnr cl-home: acts on firm & fast grnd: v useful & improving: win again, see 2033.

2888 **BOND CITY 15** [1] B Smart 2-8-8 F Lynch 33/1: 0133: Handy, eff over 1f out, kept on, not pace of — ¾ — 94
front 2: much imprvd & clearly acts well on fast grnd: v useful, win more races: see 2670.

2965* **ALPAGA LE JOMAGE 12** [3] B J Meehan 2-8-5 J F Egan 33/1: 2450514: In tch, eff over 1f out, — 1 — 88
onepace: fine run up in class: see 2965.

3127 **CANTON 7** [19]2-8-13 Dane O'Neill 25/1: 61445: In tch, onepace fnl 2f: fine run up in class & — hd — 95
acts on fast, gd & polytrack: see 1567, 1041.

3224 **BIBURY FLYER 2** [4]2-8-10 S Hitchcott 33/1: 2335226: In tch, styd on late, nrst fin: much — 1¼ — 88
imprvd up in class: shld win a mdn in this form: see 3224.

2658 **WITHERING LADY 24** [18]2-8-0 D Kinsella 66/1: 34627: In tch, eff well over 1f out, onepace: see 2658. — hd — 77

2472 **TOURNEDOS 32** [2]2-8-10 T E Durcan 5/1: 1228: In tch, no impress fnl 1f: shade more expected. — hd — 86

1826 **CHISELLED 60** [16]2-8-9 Darren Williams 33/1: 4229: With ldrs, wknd fnl 1f: 2 mth abs: gd run. — nk — 84

2888 **IMPERIAL SOUND 15** [14]2-9-2 D Holland 14/1: 120: 10th: In tch, wknd when short of room just ins last. — ½ — 89

2697 **EVANESCE 23** [11]2-7-13 C Catlin 33/1: 4221200: 11th: In tch, wknd appr fnl 1f: see 2442, 2287. — ¾ — 70

2553 **ALTA PETENS 29** [20]2-7-12 A McCarthy 12/1: 4100: 12th: With ldrs, wknd fnl 1f: twice below 1728. — nk — 68

2786 **CELTIC SPA 20** [8]2-7-13 J Quinn 25/1: 010530: 13th: At rear: rider reported mount hung right. — ¾ — 67

THE QUIET WOMAN 22 [21]2-8-1 Martin Dwyer 14/1: 32540: 14th: b f Barathea - Tajawuz (Kris) Sn — nk — 68
bhd, modest late gains: Irish raider, plcd in mdns earlier: eff at 5/6.5f on gd & gd/soft: dam 10f wnr.

2789 **TAGULA SUNRISE 19** [22]2-8-10 T Hamilton 25/1: 2220: 15th: In tch, wknd over 1f out: see 2789. — ¾ — 75

3022* **LATERAL THINKER 10** [7]2-7-12 R Thomas 50/1: 223410: 16th: With ldrs, wknd over 1f out: see 3022. — 1¼ — 59

1744 **EXIT SMILING 64** [10]2-8-11 K Dalgleish 40/1: 230: 17th: Slow away, nvr a factor: 2 mth abs. — 1¾ — 67

2839 **PEOPLETON BROOK 17** [17]2-8-5 L Keniry 100/1: 560: 18th: Al bhd. — hd — 60

2697 **HAPPY EVENT 23** [6]2-8-7 S Drowne 50/1: 100: 19th: Slow away & al bhd: see 2263 (6f, fast). — nk — 61

2020 **GRAND OPTION 52** [13]2-8-5 BL A Daly 40/1: 0323250: 20th: Handy, wknd 2f out: tried blnks. — ½ — 57

2976* **ANNATALIA 12** [23]2-8-10 L Dettori 13/2: 4610: 21st: In tch, wknd 2f out: btr 2976 (made all, mdn). — shd — 62

2703 **EDGE FUND 23** [24]2-9-0 P J Fortune 50/1: 333230: 22nd: Sn rdn & al bhd: tried cheek pieces. — 1 — 64

2858 **GRAND PLACE 17** [15]2-8-7 K Fallon 20/1: 040: 23rd: Slow away & al bhd: see 2858. — 1 — 55

3022 **EARL OF LINKS 10** [12]2-8-10 R Hughes 25/1: 3160: 24th: In tch, wknd 2f out: twice below 1531. — 3½ — 48
24 Ran   Time 1m 01.89 (1.59)   Owned: Mr N Attenborough & Mrs L Mann   Trained: Upper Lambourn

---

3267   3.30 Cantorodds Com Conditions Stakes 2yo (C)
£7482 £2838 £1419   7f str   Good/Firm 20   -17 Slow   Centre

2876* **GRAND MARQUE 16** [3] R Hannon 2-8-13 K Fallon 7/2: 511: Set pace, hdd appr fnl 1f, rallied most — 101
gamely to get up again well ins last, drvn out: v eff here at Newbury at 7f, 1m sure to suit: acts on fast grnd: v
useful & genuine, win more races: see 2876.

2408* **BLUES AND ROYALS 35** [4] Saeed bin Suroor 2-8-13 L Dettori 9/4 FAV: 12: In tch, gd hdwy to lead — nk — 100
trav best appr fnl 1f, rdn & hdd ins last, just held: stays 7f: useful, more to come: see 2408.

3005 **KANDIDATE 11** [1] C E Brittain 2-8-13 R L Moore 40/1: 03: b c Kabool - Valleyrose (Royal — 1 — 94
Academy) Handy, eff to chall appr fnl 1f, onepace ins last: April foal, cost 26,000gns: half-brother to a useful
1m wnr: dam 1m/9f scorer: much imprvd from debut & stays 7f well on fast grnd, 1m will suit: well clr of rem,
useful, must win a mdn sn: see 3005.

2823 **OBE GOLD 20** [6] M R Channon 2-8-13 T E Durcan 4/1: 31424: In tch, eff over 2f out, sn no extra. — 6 — 85

2876 **MASTMAN 16** [8]2-8-10 J Fortune 13/2: 25: With wnr, wknd over 1f out: needs mdns: see 2876. — ¾ — 80

WILLIAM TELL 0 [7]2-8-7 S Hitchcott(3) 25/1: 6: b c Rossini - Livry (Lyphard) Bhd, hung badly — 3 — 71
left & wknd over 2f out on debut: April foal, cost £20,000: half-brother to wnrs over 6/7f: speedily bred.

2876 **VOIR DIRE 16** [2]2-8-10 R Havlin 66/1: 07: b c Vettori - Bobbie Dee (Blakeney) In tch, wknd & — 1½ — 71
hung left 2f out: May foal, cheaply bght: half-brother to plcd performers over 1m/hdles: dam styd 10f.

JUST A TRY 0 [5]2-8-7 R Hughes 20/1: 8: ch c Lure - Boubasis (Diesis) Slow away & al bhd on — 13 — 42
debut: Feb first foal, cost $27,000: bred to apprec 7f/1m: with R Hannon.
8 Ran   Time 1m 26.92 (2.62)   Owned: Noodles Racing   Trained: Marlborough

---

3268   4.05 Listed Racing Uk Stakes Registered As The Hackwood Stakes 3yo+ (A)
£17400 £6600 £3300   6f8y str   Good/Firm 20   -02 Slow   Centre

2190 **PASTORAL PURSUITS 44** [1] H Morrison 3-8-12 (110) S Drowne 15/8 FAV: 2111-21: Slow away, held up, — 111
hdwy 2f out, styd on well to lead ins last, drvn out: abs: all 4 wins at 6f, stays 7f on fm & gd/soft, sharp or gall
trks: runs well fresh: smart, game & has a decent turn of foot: yet to run a below par race: see 2190.

2486 **CARTOGRAPHY 31** [6] Saeed bin Suroor 3-8-12 t (106) L Dettori 11/4: 1310-332: Trkd ldr, led over — hd — 109

1f out, rdn & hdd just ins last, kept on, just held: ran right up to smart best back at 6f: deserves a List: see 2486.
2949 **DOWAGER 14** [7] R Hannon 3-8-7 (96) Dane O'Neill 50/1: 461-5463: Held up, hdwy when short of room appr fnl 1f, strong run ins last, just failed: right back to useful best with more patient tactics: well worth another try at 7f now: see 1620. *nk* **103+**
2769 **SO WILL I 21** [9] M P Tregoning 3-9-2 (109) R Hills 15/2: 41-3104: In tch, eff over 1f out, onepace: smart, ran well conceding weight to the 3 in front: see 1732. *1¼* **108**
1233 **PHANTOM WIND 91** [5]3-8-7 (98) R Hughes 7/1: 01-65: b f Storm Cat - Ryafan (Lear Fan) In tch, eff over 1f out, sn no extra: 3 mth abs: won last of 2 '03 starts (mdn): eff over a gall 6f, 7f shld suit (dam top-class at 1m): acts on fast grnd & a stiff trk: has tried a t-strap: useful. 1 Oct'03 Newm 6g/f 98- D: *¾* **97**
3002 **MAC LOVE 11** [3]3-8-12 (105) G Carter 16/1: 2-542266: In tch, eff over 1f out, wknd ins last. *1¼* **98**
2580 **NIGHTS CROSS 28** [12]3-8-12 (107) T E Durcan 11/1: 12-43007: In tch, wknd fnl 1f: see 2468. *hd* **97**
2913 **THE KIDDYKID 14** [11]4-9-10 (110) D Holland 16/1: 5-301468: Led till over 1f out, wknd: btr 2769. *shd* **103**
1932 **IQTE SAAB 56** [13]3-8-12 (104) Martin Dwyer 14/1: 12-169: Bhd, brief eff over 1f out, no extra: 8 wk abs: twice below 1150 (reapp, 7f, gd/soft). *nk* **95**
2913 **COLONEL COTTON 14** [4]5-9-7 (100) R L Moore 25/1: 0655030: 10th: In tch, wknd 2f out: see 2913. *shd* **99**
2758 **CRIMSON SILK 21** [8]4-9-3 p (92) Paul Eddery 33/1: 0000030: 11th: Al bhd: see 2758, 1137. *5* **80**
11 Ran Time 1m 12.1 (1.31) Owned: The Pursuits Partnership Trained: East Ilsley

3269

4.40 Doric Signs Rated Stakes Handicap 3yo+ 0-90 (C) **[93]**
£8756 £3321 £1661 **6f8y str** **Good/Firm 20** **-02 Slow** Centre

2880 **INDIAN TRAIL 16** [9] D R C Elsworth 4-9-4 (83) Dane O'Neill 14/1: 31100-01: Held up, hdwy & switched to stands side over 1f out, strong run to lead ins last, rdn out: eff over 6/7f on firm & fast grnd, handles soft: acts on any trk: right back to form, looks useful: see 2880. **92**
2950 **DOITNOW 14** [6] R A Fahey 3-9-3 (87) T Hamilton(3) 6/1 JT FAV: 122: Held up, gd hdwy over 1f out, styd on to chall ins last, flashed tail but kept on: lightly rcd, useful & improving: win again, see 2950. *¾* **93**
3069 **ARMAGNAC 8** [12] M A Buckley 6-8-12 (77) S Drowne 13/2: 0360023: Held up, gd hdwy over 1f out, styd on to lead just ins last, hdd cl-home, not btn far: clearly in fine heart & h'capped to win: likes Haydock. *shd* **83**
2878 **DANEHILL STROLLER 16** [10] R M Beckett 4-9-4 p (83) F Lynch 16/1: 243-0004: Held up, hdwy & switched right over 1f out, kept on ins last, nrst fin: on a fair mark, keep in mind: see 2070. *1¼* **85+**
3002 **SPANISH ACE 11** [15]3-9-4 vis (88) Martin Dwyer 8/1: 0-000055: Set pace, rdn & hdd just ins last, no extra: showed a lot of pace & return to minimum trip will suit: btr 3002. *1¼* **86**
3068 **CHATEAU NICOL 8** [14]5-9-4 vis (83) K Fallon 10/1: 3341566: In tch, eff to chall just ins last, no extra. *shd* **81**
2861 **CANTERLOUPE 17** [2]6-8-8 (73) R Smith 25/1: 516-0007: Chsd ldrs, wknd fnl 1f: see 41. *1* **68**
3069 **IDLE POWER 8** [11]6-9-0 p (79) J Fortune 12/1: 0110238: In tch, wknd over 1f out: btr 2374, 2045. *nk* **73**
2878 **CAUSTIC WIT 16** [13]6-9-7 p (86) P Makin(5) 6/1 JT FAV: 1111229: In tch, wknd over 1f out: btr 2878. *½* **78**
3069 **DEVON FLAME 8** [16]5-8-11 (76) J F McDonald(3) 15/2: 1-212240: 10th: In tch, wknd over 1f out. *1* **65**
3088 **MILLFIELDS DREAMS 8** [4]5-8-4 (10oh) (59) J F Egan 50/1: 604-1000: 11th: With ldr, wknd over 1f out. *1* **55**
3069 **NAJEEBON 8** [5]5-9-1 (80) S Hitchcott(3) 10/1: 0036300: 12th: Bhd, nvr a factor: see 2878. *nk* **65**
2558 **SIR EDWIN LANDSEER 29** [8]4-9-0 (79) R Thomas(5) 33/1: 5600-000: 13th: gr c Lit de Justice - Wildcat Blue (Cure The Blues) In tch, wknd over 1f out: rcd once in '03 (stks, rtd 102, P Cole): '02 mdn, stks & List wnr: eff at 5/6f, poss stays 7f: acts on firm & gd/soft, any trk: best up with/forcing the pace: with C Wroe. 1 Sep'02 Kemp 6fm 105- A: 2 Aug'02 Good 5g/f 103- A: 1 Jun'02 Donc 5g/f 102- C: 1 May'02 Newb 5.1g/s 89- D: 2 May'02 Good 5g/f 78- D: *3½* **54**
3069 **MORSE 8** [1]3-9-5 (89) L Fletcher(3) 25/1: 3120060: 14th: With ldrs, wknd well over 1f out: see 2841. *2* **58**
3100 **DANI RIDGE 7** [7]6-9-5 (84) T E Durcan 25/1: 30-40460: 15th: In tch, wknd 2f out: see 2791, 2240. *1¼* **49**
2880 **BEE MINOR 16** [3]3-8-4 (74) R L Moore 25/1: 500-0200: 16th: Al bhd: btr 2648, see 2249. *1¼* **35**
16 Ran Time 1m 12.96 (1.36) Owned: The Trail Blazers Trained: Whitsbury

3270

5.10 Cistm Racing Club Apprentice Handicap Stakes 3yo+ 0-75 (E) **[75]**
£4193 £1290 £645 **1m4f5y** **Good/Firm 20** **-28 Slow** Outside

2900 **MERRYMAKER 15** [8] W M Brisbourne 4-9-1 (62) P Mathers 11/2: 464P121: Slow away, hld up, hdwy over 2f out, styd on to lead ins last, drvn out: eff over 12/14f on fm & gd/soft: in fine heart, front two well clr. **69**
2984 **MASKED 12** [5] J W Hills 3-8-12 (71) Derek Nolan(3) 4/1: 004152: Trkd ldr, styd on to lead over 1f out, hdd ins last, just held: fine run & well clr of rem: stays 12f: see 2478. *nk* **77**
2908 **HEAD TO KERRY 15** [2] D J S ffrench Davis 4-8-10 T (57) P Gallagher 4/1: 3-000353: Set pace till over 1f out, no extra: fair run in t-strap: see 2651, 2391. *5* **56**
3037 **SAXE COBURG 10** [6] G A Ham 7-8-11 (58) W Hogg(3) 11/2: 3303534: Bhd, no extra over 1f out. *3* **53**
3056 **MAKE MY HAY 9** [1]5-8-2 (49) Natalia Gemelova 13/2: 3612555: In tch, wknd over 2f out: see 2718. *5* **37**
2371 **GREYFIELD 36** [3]8-8-6 (53) M Howard(3) 16/1: 0400//-506: Slow away & nvr a factor: see 2088. *6* **32**
2794* **REALISM 19** [7]4-9-13 (74) Steven Harrison(5) 7/2 FAV: 3612117: Keen in tch, wknd over 2f out: btr 2794. *2* **50**
2293 **ENCHANTED OCEAN 39** [4]5-8-8 (55) T Block(5) 14/1: 40//-008: Al bhd: see 2293. *12* **13**
8 Ran Time 2m 35.12(5.82) Owned: The Blacktoffee Partnership Trained: Nesscliffe

HAYDOCK SATURDAY 17.07.04 Lefthand, Flat, Galloping Track

Official Going Soft

3271

6.40 Haydock Park Pony Club Nursery Handicap Stakes 2yo (E) **[95]**
£3588 £1104 £552 **5f str** **Soft 101** **-11 Slow** Centre

2882* **MAKE US FLUSH 16** [5] A Berry 2-8-3 (70) F Norton 12/1: 404011: Chsd ldrs far side, styd on for press to lead well ins last, all out: eff at 6f on gd & soft grnd, likes Haydock: progressive: see 2882, 1343. **77**
3082 **IM AIMEE 8** [6] P D Evans 2-8-6 (73) K Fallon 4/1 CO FAV: 6304022: Far side & led overall till well ins last, just held: nicely bckd: eff at 5f on fast, soft & polytrack, prob any trk: speedy, can find a race. *shd* **79**
2883 **MITCHELLAND 16** [2] James Moffatt 2-8-7 (74) R Winston 9/1: 410663: Held up far side, styd on from over 1f out & clr of rem: acts on gd, best efforts to date on soft/hvy grnd: see 1037 & 920. *1½* **77**
3082 **LITTLE BISCUIT 8** [8] K R Burke 2-7-12 (5oh) (65) B Swarbrick(5) 9/1: 1254264: Sn handy stands side *5* **58**

& led that group over 1f out, no ch with ldrs far side ins last: first home from unfav'd stands side group: see 2611.
2682 **BRUT 23** [1]2-8-1 (68) R Ffrench 25/1: 06205: Sn handy far side, no extra dist: btr 2505 (gd). *1½* **58**
3065 **APOLOGIES 9** [4]2-8-11 (78) R L Moore 11/2: 01406: Sn bhd far side, nvr a factor: op 7/1: btr 1107. *2* **64**
2744 **TOWN HOUSE 21** [7]2-8-6 (73) J F Egan 14/1: 502107: Led stands side till over 1f out, sn btn: btr 1987. *nk* **58**
2467 **DANCE ANTHEM 32** [3]2-9-7 (88) P McCabe 4/1 CO FAV: 1208: Keen, sn rear far side & no ch from halfway: bckd: much btr 2144 & 1550 (firm & gd). *14* **45**
2711 **MIDNIGHT TYCOON 23** [9]2-9-7 (88) F Lynch 4/1 CO FAV: 1349: Chsd ldrs stands side till halfway, sn bhd: much btr 2167 & 1601. *9* **27**
9 Ran Time 1m 04.40 (5.6) Owned: The Bath Tub Boys Trained: Cockerham

3272

7.10 Mercedes-Benz Direct Birthday E B F Maiden Stakes 2yo (D)
£5311 £1634 £817 **6f str** **Soft 101** **-25 Slow** Centre

JOSH 0 [2] M A Jarvis 2-9-0 P Robinson 11/2: 1: b c Josr Algarhoud - Charlie Girl (Puissance) **97**
Keen & handy, rdn to lead ins last, styd on strongly: debut: 36,000gns April foal, half-brother to a 7f juv wnr, dam a 5f juv wnr: eff at 6f, get further: enjoyed soft grnd & a gall trk: goes well fresh: well regarded, useful.
THROW THE DICE 0 [11] K A Ryan 2-9-0 N Callan 11/1: 2: b c Lujain - Euridice (Woodman) Dwelt & held up, hdwy to lead 2f out, hung left & hdd ins last, not pace of wnr: debut: 13,000gns March foal, half-brother to useful 10f 3yo wnr Hazy View, also a 1m juv scorer: dam a 9f 3yo wnr: eff at 6f, get further: acts on soft grnd & a gall trk: promising start, shld be wng sn. *2½* **88**
SACRANUN 13 [14] L M Cumani 2-9-0 D Holland 5/1: 23: ch c Pivotal - Spanish Craft (Jareer) Sn handy & ch over 1f out, onepace ins last: clr of rem: op 11/4: Brit bow, rnr-up at San Siro earlier this mth: half brother to a 9f wnr, dam a placed miler: eff at 6f on gd & soft grnd. *hd* **87**
2424 **MOZAFIN 34** [1] M R Channon 2-9-0 A Culhane 9/4 FAV: 624: Cl-up, rdn when hmpd over 1f out, no dngr: well bckd: much btr on fast grnd in 2424. *5* **77**
2569 **ORPHAN 28** [10]2-9-0 Darren Williams 50/1: 05: b c Orpen - Ballinlee (Skyliner) Mid-div, rdn & no impress over 1f out: well bhd debut prev: cheaply bght Feb foal, half-brother to wnrs over 7f/10f. *¾* **76**
LOVE AND LAUGHTER 0 [8]2-8-9 J F Egan 16/1: 6: Slow away & bhd, late gains, no threat. *1¼* **68**
CHIEF SCOUT 0 [4]2-9-0 K Fallon 11/2: 7: Mid-div & sn pushed along, nvr on terms, op 8/1. *1* **71**
WIZARDMICKTEE 0 [5]2-9-0 R Winston 40/1: 8: Dwelt, mid-div, no impress fnl 2f. *2½* **66**
SYDNEYROUGHDIAMOND 0 [13]2-9-0 S Righton 66/1: 9: Dwelt & al bhd. *¾* **65**
2051 **MYTTONS BELL 50** [12]2-8-9 V Slattery 10/1: 230: 10th: Led till 2f out, btn when hmpd over 1f out: abs. *hd* **59**
Mickledo 0 [7]2-9-0 R L Moore 33/1:0 **Allizam 0** [9]2-9-0 W Supple 25/1:0
12 Ran Time 1m 18.88 (7.58) Owned: Mr T G & Mrs M E Holdcroft Trained: Newmarket

3273

7.40 Knights Pharmacy Rated Stakes Handicap 3yo 0-85 (D) **[89]**
£5165 £1959 £980 **6f str** **Soft 101** **+03 Fast** Centre

3179 **COMMANDO SCOTT 4** [4] A Berry 3-9-3 (78) F Lynch 6/1: 0022261: Trkd ldr & led 2f out, won decisively: eff at 6/7f on fast, likes soft grnd, prob any trk: tough & genuine: see 2985, 2693 & 1216. **95**
2764 **RISING SHADOW 21** [9] R A Fahey 3-9-7 (82) D Holland 14/1: 0135-62: Went right start, mid-div, rdn & kept on despite hanging left over 1f out, al held: op 11/1: handles gd, soft & polytrack: see 2764. *3* **90**
2985 **NEON BLUE 12** [2] R M Whitaker 3-8-7 (68) K Fallon 4/1 FAV: 0-510333: Chsd ldrs, outpcd halfway, kept on ins last: op 6/1: acts on fast & soft grnd: worth a try at 7f: see 2985. *2½* **71**
3135 **RYDAL 6** [14] G A Butler 3-9-5 bl (80) S W Kelly 9/2: 1-040624: Slow away & rear, kept on from halfway, not able to chall: acts on fast, soft & polytrack: see 3135, 1460. *½* **82**
2482 **DISTANT TIMES 31** [5]3-9-1 vis (76) D Allan 12/1: 3-513005: Trkd ldrs, edged right & no extra bef dist. *2* **74**
2950 **ISKANDER 14** [7]3-9-2 bl (77) J Carroll 33/1: 4-600006: Led till 2f out, sn btn: see 1665. *nk* **74**
2925 **RISE 14** [6]3-8-4 bl (65) J F Egan 7/1: 0600127: Mid-div when short of room over 2f out, switched & no room again over 1f out, kept on late: shade closer with a clr passage: see 2925 & 2661. *nk* **61**
2904* **KEEPERS LODGE 15** [10]3-8-9 (70) R L Moore 14/1: 04-40018: Held up, nvr land a blow: op 11/1. *shd* **66**
3080 **FOUR AMIGOS 8** [8]3-9-7 (82) J Fanning 11/1: 5106309: Chsd ldrs till over 1f out: btr 2950. *1¼* **75**
2904 **BEAUTY OF DREAMS 15** [1]3-8-10 (71) A Culhane 25/1: 24150-00: 10th: Mid-div, struggling 1f out. *½* **63**
3179 **George The Best 4** [11]3-8-7 (68) Darren Williams 14/1:0 2764 **Hawaajes 21** [13]3-9-0 (75) W Supple 9/1:0
12 Ran Time 1m 17.16 (5.86) Owned: Mrs Ann Morris Trained: Cockerham

3274

8.10 Listed H2o Stakes Registered As The July Trophy Colts & Geldings 3yo (A)
£17400 £6600 £3300 **1m3f200y** **Soft 101** **+03 Fast** Outside

2238+ **FRANK SONATA 42** [6] M G Quinlan 3-8-10 (101) R L Moore 100/30: 00-61311: In tch, hdwy & rdn to lead dist, held on gamely for press: well bckd tho' op 11/4: 6 wk abs: eff at 10f, suited by 12f last twice: acts on fast, likes gd & soft grnd, gall trks: goes well fresh: v tough, useful & progressive. **109**
2254 **PUKKA 42** [4] L M Cumani 3-8-10 (105) D Holland 9/4 JT FAV: 0431-102: Sn handy, rdn & styd on well fnl 2f, just held: 6 wk abs: useful run back in suitable class: stays 12f well: see 1756. *nk* **108**
2660* **ALBINUS 24** [7] A M Balding 3-8-10 bl (90) Martin Dwyer 5/1: 03-02113: Led till dist, no extra nr line: clr of rem: acts on fast, soft & polytrack: progressing with every run, win again: see 2660. *shd* **108**
2230* **PROTECTIVE 43** [2] J G Given 3-8-10 (88) W Supple 50/1: 4014: Rear, no impress fnl 2f: 6 wk abs. *10* **98$**
2520 **LORD MAYOR 30** [3]3-8-10 (103) K Fallon 9/4 JT FAV: 631-3155: Keen & prom, btn over 1f out: nicely bckd: longer trip & softer grnd: btr 2520. *shd* **98**
2771 **RED LANCER 21** [1]3-9-3 (108) M Fenton 12/1: 2213606: In tch, btn 2f out: btr 1814. *8* **97**
3027* **ANOUSA 10** [5]3-9-0 (82) R Winston 25/1: 1000317: Held up, rdn & btn 2f out: btr 3027 (fast grnd). *1½* **92**
7 Ran Time 2m 39.53 (11.73) Owned: Adams Flynn Arnold Trained: Newmarket

---

3275 8.40 Mick Sherwood 50th Birthday Handicap Stakes 3yo+ 0-75 (E) [73]
£3575 £1100 £550 **2m45y** **Soft 101** -07 Slow Inside

2899* **QUEDEX 15** [8] R J Price 8-9-11 (70) L Treadwell(7) 9/4 FAV: 06-15211: Held up, hdwy 5f out, rdn & 75
led 2f out, styd on strongly: hvly bckd: eff at 2m/2m2f on firm or soft grnd, any trk: thriving.
2905 **PENNY STALL 15** [5] J L Dunlop 3-8-0 (62) D Kinsella 11/2: 044-042: Chsd ldrs, prog to lead over *1* 65
4f out, hdd 2f out, not pace of wnr: op 9/2: acts on fast & gd, imprvd tonight on soft grnd: find similar: see 2905.
3105 **CALOMERIA 7** [4] R M Beckett 3-7-13 (1ow)(3oh)BL (57) F Norton 33/1: 0-000403: Led 7f, remained *1* 63
handy, flashed tail under press fnl 3f, kept on: imprvd eff in first time blnks tho' does show signs of temperament:
styd longer 2m trip well: acts on gd/soft & soft grnd: see 2691.
2905* **EUIPPE 15** [1] J G Given 3-8-8 (70) M Fenton 4/1: 456-0514: Held up, hdwy to chall over 2f out, *3½* 68
onepace: clr of rem: shade btr 2905 (14f, gd).
3181 **OCEAN TIDE 4** [6]7-9-9 (68) Martin Dwyer 9/2: 4403525: Chsd ldrs, btn 4f out: qck reapp: see 2607. *19* 51
2941* **OOPS 14** [7]5-8-0 (45) Dean Williams(7) 11/2: 0042-016: Wide & prom, led halfway till over 5f out, sn btn. *6* 23
2881 **CANTEMERLE 16** [3]4-8-5 bl (50) B Swarbrick(5) 33/1: 50-20067: Al rear: btr 1680 (12f). *3½* 25
2479 **CONGO MAN 31** [10]11-8-0 (45) R Ffrench 66/1: 1//////-08: Al bhd: see 2479. *4* 16
1069 **ALLEZ MOUSSON 102** [9]6-8-7 bl (52) W Supple 8/1: 6030-009: b g Hernando - Rynechra (Blakeney) *5* 18
Handy & led after 7f till halfway, btn 4f out: 3 mth abs: lightly rcd & unplcd '03 (rtd 61, h'caps): '02 h'cap
scorer: eff at 2m/2m2f on fast, likes gd/soft grnd: best without blnks or chkpcs: handles any trk
1 Jun'02 Bath 17.1g/s 70-65 D: 2 Nov'01 Donc 16.5sft 75-71 C: 1 Oct'01 Pont 17.1g/s 73-68 E:
1 Sep'01 Ayr 17.4gd 70-64 D: 2 Aug'01 Hayd 16.2sft 64-68 E: 1 Jul'01 Chep 16.2g/f 68-65 E:
3140 **LADY NETBETSPORTS 6** [2]5-9-3 (62) R Winston 25/1: 0-030200: 10th: Sn handy & led over 5f out *23* 9
till over 4f out, sn btn & eased: btr 2941.
10 Ran Time 3m 44.46 (17.46) Owned: Fox and Cub Partnership Trained: Hereford

---

3276 9.10 Rectangle Group Handicap Stakes 3yo+ 0-70 (E) [70]
£3692 £1136 £568 **1m2f120y** **Soft 101** -21 Slow Outside

3044 **MOUNT BENGER 9** [7] R M Beckett 4-9-4 p (60) F Lynch 8/1: 000-6041: Rear, edged right but styd on 67
for press from over 1f out to lead line, all out: eff at 7f, now suited by 10f well: acts on fibresand & enjoyed
soft grnd tonight, handles gd/soft: now suited by cheek pieces on a sharp or gall trk: see 1006.
2726 **PURE MISCHIEF 22** [9] C R Dore 5-10-0 (70) R Thomas(5) 5/1: 3115132: Held up, hdwy/hung left & led *shd* 76
well ins last, hdd line: op 15/2: remains in gd heart: see 2726 & 2499.
3139* **JIMMY BYRNE 6** [11] B Ellison 4-10-6 (6ex) (76) P Mulrennan(5) 9/4 FAV: 1056113: Trkd ldrs trav *hd* 81
well, rdn & led dist, hung left & hdd well ins last: well bckd under a 6lb pen, qck reapp: progressive.
3139 **LENNEL 6** [10] A Bailey 6-9-8 bl (64) V Slattery 16/1: 4004064: Dwelt & held up, styd on late, not *1¼* 67
pace to threaten: op 12/1, qck reapp: see 1388, 1128.
4475! **MR MIDAZ 648** [12]5-8-3 (45) R Ffrench 41/1: 504000/-5: ch g Danzig Connection - Marmy (Midyan) *¾* 47
Mid-div, rdn & ch over 1f out, no extra dist: long Flat abs, jumps fit (rnr-up, rtd 93h, h'cap hdle, 2m on gd/soft &
fast): last rcd on the level in '02 (unplcd, rtd 57, h'cap, first time blnks, J O'Keeffe): stays 10f, handles fast
& soft grnd. 2 Sep'01 Redc 7g/f 66-63 E:
3085 **MR DIP 8** [15]4-8-8 (50) P Makin(5) 11/2: 0600526: Mid-div, prog to lead over 1f out, sn hdd & no extra. *1½* 51
2719 **GOT TO BE CASH 22** [2]5-8-10 (52) B Swarbrick(5) 12/1: 2105307: Mid-div, rdn & onepace fnl 2f. *¾* 52
3139 **BAND 6** [5]4-9-2 (58) W Supple 9/1: 0-000048: Dwelt, mid-div, rdn & no extra when short of room ins last. *1½* 57
2848 **MARTIN HOUSE 17** [6]5-8-13 (55) J Fanning 33/1: 00000-09: In tch, btn over 1f out: see 2848. *8* 46
2340 **ARJAY 37** [13]6-8-5 (47) J Carroll 25/1: 0035300: 10th: Held up, rdn & btn 2f out: btr 2120. *3* 35
THE ROUNDSILLS 2478 [8]10-7-12 (40) S Righton 100/1: 040//////-0: 11th: ch g Handsome Sailor - *3* 25
Eye Sight (Roscoe Blake) Led till over 1f out, sn btn: v long abs: back in '97 landed a 12f h'cap on fast grnd.
3159 **KENNY THE TRUTH 5** [4]5-8-0 t (42) P W Burns 25/1: 330P650: 12th: Mid-div, no impress fnl 3f. *½* 26
3220} **Saddlers Quest 355** [3]7-9-7 (63) Darren Williams 25/1:29847 **Iftikhar 14** [14]5-9-1 (57) S W Kelly 33/1:0
3142 **Sheriffs Deputy 6** [16]4-9-12 (68) R Winston 16/1:0
3624] **Gablesea 697** [17]10-7-12 (16oh)(24) Dean Williams(4) 100/1:0
16 Ran Time 2m 22.89(12.89) Owned: Young Guns Syndicate Trained: Lambourn

---

Official Going GOOD

3277 2.10 Newmarket Trophy A Rated Stakes Handicap 3yo 0-100 (B) [102]
£17400 £6600 £3300 **1m str** **Good/Firm 22** -16 Slow Stands side

2620* **DIAMOND LODGE 26** [3] J Noseda 3-8-7 (2oh) (81) E Ahern 12/1: 41211: In tch, hdwy to lead just ins 92
last, styd on strongly, drvn out: eff around 1m/8.3f on fast & gd/soft, sharp or stiff trks: useful, genuine & prog.
2521 **FINE SILVER 30** [1] P F I Cole 3-9-1 (91) T Quinn 6/1: 46-40142: Handy, hdwy to lead over 1f out, *¾* 97
hdd ins last but kept on, not btn far: useful, continues to progress well: see 2521, 2026.
2903 **ODDSMAKER 15** [10] P D Evans 3-8-11 (87) J Mongan 20/1: 2510153: Held up, hdwy 2f out, kept on *¾* 91
ins last, not btn far: ran right up to useful best: see 2753.
2903 **SEWNSO CHARACTER 15** [13] M Blanshard 3-9-5 (95) D Sweeney 12/1: 25-40344: Slow away, in tch, *1¼* 96
hdwy over 4f out, onepace over 1f out: useful & consistent: see 2903, 2406.
3059 **SWEET INDULGENCE 9** [7]3-8-8 (84) T P Queally 16/1: 13-005: Held up, sltly outpcd over 2f out, *2* 81
some late gains: see 1930.
2918 **APPALACHIAN TRAIL 14** [2]3-9-0 (90) K Darley 11/2 FAV: 1204166: Held up, wknd fnl 1f: see 2918. *½* 86
2918 **ZONUS 14** [11]3-9-1 (91) M Hills 6/1: 1423037: Held up, nvr a factor: see 2918. *nk* 86
2525 **INVASIAN 30** [8]3-8-12 (88) W Ryan 8/1: 0-128: Cl-up, led over 2f out till over 1f out, no extra: btr 2525. *1* 80
1498 **ENFORD PRINCESS 76** [9]3-8-12 (88) S Sanders 50/1: 1100-49: Held up, nvr a factor: 11 wk abs. *1¾* 77
3002 **BARBAJUAN 11** [5]3-9-7 b (97) J Murtagh 33/1: 3-500000: 10th: Led over 5f, wknd over 1f out: see 3002. *7* 72
2787 **BAYHIRR 20** [4]3-8-10 (86) P Robinson 7/1: 0-31520: 11th: In tch, wknd 2f out: btr 2787. *nk* 60

3128* **DUBOIS** 7 [1]3-9-0 vis t (90) K McEvoy 15/2: 25-1010: 12th: ln tch, wknd 2f out: btr 3128.　hd　63
2521　**FORTHRIGHT** 30 [12]3-9-0 p (90) J P Guillambert(3) 14/1: 0-104560: 13th: ln tch, wknd over 2f out.　5　53
13 Ran　Time 1m 40.3 (3.1)　Owned: Mrs J Harris　Trained: Newmarket

3278　2.45 Listed Aphrodite Stakes Fillies 3yo+　(A)
£17400　£6600　£3300　**1m4f**　**Good/Firm 22**　**+19 Fast**　Stands side

2487　**BENEVENTA** 31 [9] J L Dunlop 4-9-7 (110) S Sanders 7/2: 40-11201: ln tch, hdwy to lead over 2f　109
out, styd on well ins last, rdn clr: fast time: relished step up to 12f, eff at 1m: acts on firm & gd/soft, easy
or gall trks: smart performer, relished drop in class: see 1491.
2660　**SELEBELA** 24 [4] L M Cumani 3-8-4 (93) T P Queally 4/1: 5-011122: Led till over 2f out, hung left　3½　96
over 1f out, kept on same pace: ran to useful best bhd a smart sort stepped up in class: see 2422.
2923* **PORTRAIT OF A LADY** 14 [3] H R A Cecil 3-8-4 (87) W Ryan 9/1: 0-313113: Held up, short of room　1½　94
over 2f out, eff over 1f out, not pace of front 2: imprvd again stepped up in class: proving tough & useful.
2368* **GOSLAR** 36 [6] H Candy 3-8-4 (87) T Quinn 12/1: 314: Held up, eff 2f out, sn no extra:　up in class.　2　91
2349* **NUZOOA** 37 [5]3-8-4 (92) W Supple 9/4 FAV: 2-15: Held up, eff over 2f out, sn no extra: well　¾　90
bckd: clrly btr expected but this was a step up in class after 2349 (lkd impressive in a mdn fill win, 10f).
2517　**FEAAT** 30 [2]3-8-4 (94) K McEvoy 9/1: 3166: ln tch, wknd over 1f out: see 2124 (mdn, 10f).　1　88
2567 13**TAWNY WAY** 28 [8]4-9-2 (86) P Robinson 33/1: 20-51267: ln tch, wknd well over 1f out: see 1721.　nk　87$
1005　**QUDRAH** 108 [7]4-9-2 (85) J Murtagh 50/1: 50-00548: Held up, wknd over 2f out: see 758.　25　49
3076　**DESERT ROYALTY** 8 [1]4-9-2 (92) R Mullen 14/1: 3-212449: Held up, wknd over 2f out: btr 3076 (h'cap).　1¼　47
9 Ran　Time 2m 28.57 (0.37)　Owned: Exors of the Late R N Khan　Trained: Arundel

3279　3.20 Glemsford Handicap Stakes 3yo+ 0-100　(C)　[96]
£9490　£2920　£1460　**5f str**　**Good/Firm 22**　**+04 Fast**　Stands side

2894　**CONNECT** 15 [10] M H Tompkins 7-9-3 bl (85) P Robinson 11/2: 06-24041: Chsd ldrs, fin strongly to　92
lead nr line: gd time: loves to come late over a stiff 5f, stays a sharp 6f well: acts on gd, firm grnd &
polytrack, poss fibresand: eff with/without blnks: deserved win, see 2359 & 1917.
3206] **FIRST ORDER** 355 [5] Sir Mark Prescott 3-10-0 (100) S Sanders 13/2: 312113-2: b g Primo Dominie -　nk　105
Unconditional Love (Polish Patriot) Keen & prom, led ins fnl 1f, caught on line: reapp & top-weight: won a mdn
auct, nurs h'cap & nov in '03, has since been gelded: eff at 5/6f on fast & firm grnd, handles gd/soft: gd weight
carrier who is a v useful sprinter: worth a try in List/Gr 3 company now & sure to win more races.
1 Jul'03 Bath 5.0g/f 101- D:　1 Jul'03 York 5.0fm 101-86 C:　2 Jul'03 Beve 5g/s 82- D:　1 Jun'03 Ripo 5g/f 88- E:
3073　**CAPE ROYAL** 8 [6] Mrs J R Ramsden 4-9-5 (87) J Murtagh 7/1: 1060203: Chsd ldrs, ev ch ins fnl 1f,　shd　91
just btn in a thrilling fin: see 2747.
2702　**PRIME RECREATION** 23 [3] P S Felgate 7-7-12 (5oh) (61) Lisa Jones(3) 25/1: 0003004: Tried to make　hd　69$
all, caught cl-home: just btn in a bunched fin & fin run from out of the h'cap: see 1774.
3123　**SIR DESMOND** 7 [1]6-8-9 p (77) E Ahern 11/2: 34-30035: Held up, eff halfway, fin strongly & btn　nk　79
under 1L in a bunched fin: op 9/2: see 3123.
3123　**TEXAS GOLD** 7 [11]6-9-6 (88) R Mullen 5/1 FAV: 13-24066: Held up, short of room dist, switched &　nk　89
fin well, not btn far: did not get the run of their race: see 1845 & 106, despite h'cap mark.
2758　**FURTHER OUTLOOK** 21 [7]10-9-2 (84) T Quinn 25/1: 0042307: Prom, sltly outpcd dist, kept on.　nk　84
2894　**HENRY HALL** 15 [4]8-9-11 (93) Kim Tinkler 12/1: 3030308: Chsd ldrs, ev ch till no extra cl-home.　shd　92
2779　**ENDLESS SUMMER** 20 [9]7-8-5 (73) P Doe 20/1: 3550469: Held up, styd on fnl 1f: btn arnd 1L.　hd　71
2429　**ROSES OF SPRING** 34 [2]6-8-12 p (80) A Quinn(5) 20/1: 00-03000: 10th: Dwelt, onepcd fnl 1f: see 1845.　1　75
3002　**SPLIFF** 11 [8]3-9-7 BL (93) D Sweeney 10/1: 021-1000: 11th: Held up, nvr nr ldrs in first time blnks.　nk　87
3033　**BEAUVRAI** 10 [12]4-8-4 P (72) T P Queally 11/1: 0005300: 12th: Slow away, al bhd: cheek pieces.　3½　55
12 Ran　Time 59.43s (0.93)　Owned: Mrs P R Bowring　Trained: Newmarket

3280　3.55 Invesco Perpetual Maiden Stakes 2yo　(D)
£4888　£1504　£752　**6f str**　**Good/Firm 22**　**-40 Slow**　Stands side

　CAMACHO [11] H R A Cecil 2-9-0　W Ryan 2/1 FAV: 1: b c Danehill - Arabesque (Zafonic) Nvr far　90+
away, went on 2f out, held on well, rdn out: well bckd on debut: Feb first foal: dam a 6f wnr, sire a top-class
sprinter/miler: eff over a gall 6f on fast grnd, runs well fresh: clrly held in some regard, shld win more races.
3031　**SIGN WRITER** 10 [6] J Noseda 2-9-0　E Ahern 5/1: 62: b c Quiet American - Mata Cara (Storm Bird)　½　87
Chsd ldrs, sltly short of room dist, styd on well fnl 1f & only just btn: op 13/2: Mar foal, half-brother to a 12f
wnr: dam 7f wnr: eff over a gall 6f on fast grnd, 7f will suit: much imprvd from debut, can find similar.
　FONGTASTIC [3] B J Meehan 2-9-0　W Supple 10/1: 3: ch c Dr Fong - Kelso Magic (Distant View)　nk　86
Nvr far away, kept on under press fnl 1f & btn under 1L on debut: 30,000gns Apr first foal: dam a 5f juv wnr, sire
a top-class miler: eff over a gall 6f on fast grnd: will learn from this & find similar.
　DIAMONDS AND DUST [9] M H Tompkins 2-9-0　P Robinson 33/1: 4: b c Mister Baileys - Dusty Shoes　1¼　82
(Shareef Dancer) Chsd ldrs, kept on under press fnl 1f on debut: 8,000gns Feb first foal: dam styd mid-dists, sire
a high-class miler: eff at 6f on fast grnd, 7f shld suit: sure to learn from this.
　DESERT DEMON [8]2-9-0　M Hills 10/1: 5: b c Unfuwain - Baldemosa (Lead On Time) Slowly away,　hd　81
styd on late, nrst fin on debut: op 16/1: Mar foal, half-brother to a mile sprint wnr Caustic Wit: dam a 1m wnr
in France, sire a top-class mid dist performer: eff over a gall 6f on fast grnd, 7f shld suit: will learn plenty from this.
　PIANOFORTE [1]2-9-0　T P Queally 8/1: 6: Led till 2f out, grad wknd o debut.　¾　79
　REBEL REBEL [2]2-9-0　R Mullen 40/1: 7: Slowly away, nvr nr ldrs on debut.　2½　71
　BASIC SYSTEM [12]2-9-0　B Doyle 14/1: 8: Dwelt, nvr a factor on racecourse bow.　nk　70
　SHRINE MOUNTAIN [7]2-9-0　J P Guillambert(3) 12/1: 9: Front rank till halfway, wknd on debut.　¾　68
3064　**NEVER AWAY** 9 [10]2-8-9　J Murtagh 16/1: 00: 10th: Chsd ldrs, wknd 1.5f out.　¾　61
　FIGHTING TOM CAT [4]2-9-0 T K McEvoy 5/1: 0: 11th: Prom, wknd 2f out on debut: t-strap.　7　45
　ROYAL MOUGINS [5]2-9-0　S Sanders 25/1: 0: 12th: Slowly away, al bhd & fin last on debut.　9　18
12 Ran　Time 1m 14.72 (3.72)　Owned: Mr K Abdulla　Trained: Newmarket

NEWMARKET SATURDAY 17.07.04 Righthand, Stiff, Galloping Track

3281 **4.30 Dodson And Horrell Handicap Stakes 4yo+ 0-85 (D)** **[85]**
£5395 £1660 £830 **1m6f175y Good/Firm 22 -25 Slow** Stands side

2992* **BENDARSHAAN 11** [5] M Johnston 4-9-12 (83) S Chin 100/30: 3-000411: Handy, styd on to lead 3f out, rdn out: well bckd: eff at 12f, imprvd for step up to 15f: acts on fast & gd/soft grnd: fine eff under jt top-weight & is unexposed at staying dists: see 2992 (12f, mdn). **91**
1861 **CARA FANTASY 58** [6] J L Dunlop 4-9-8 (79) T Quinn 4/1: 1661-402: Mid-div, trav well when short of room dist, switched & kept on ins fnl 1f, post came too sn: bckd after 8 wk abs: eff arnd 12f, now stays 15f: wld have gone v close with a trouble free passage, see 1109. *1¼* **84+**
2948 **BALKAN KNIGHT 14** [1] D R Loder 4-9-12 vis (83) T P Queally 4/1: 01/1-6103: Cl-up, ev ch dist, onepcd ins fnl 1f: jt top-weight: eff at 10/12f, stays 15f: see 1668. *½* **87**
1112 **BOBSLEIGH 98** [3] Mrs A J Perrett 5-9-1 (72) K Darley 3/1 FAV: 3040-604: Cl-up, no extra from dist: long abs: prob unsuited by today's slow run race, likes Yarmouth: just btr 926. *3* **73**
3099 **GALLANT BOY 7** [7]5-8-11 vis t (68) F P Ferris(3) 7/1: 0506405: Rear, prog 4f out, wknd dist: qck reapp: prob failed to stay this longer 15f trip: caught the eye in 3099 (10f). *1¼* **68**
2530 **LAHOB 29** [4]4-8-4 (61) R Mullen 33/1: 62326-06: Led, hdd 3f out, grad wknd: see 2530. *7* **54**
1295 **MUSKATSTURM 87** [2]5-8-13 (70) W Ryan 14/1: 4/000-007: b g Lecroix - Myrthe (Konigsstuhl) Keen rear, nvr a factor: long abs: plcd on 1 of 4 03/04 hdles start (rtd 88h, nov): lightly rcd & unplcd in '03 (rtd 81, List): ex German, won 3 times in '02: wng form at 1m/12f on gd & hvy grnd: tried blnks. *5* **58**
7 Ran Time 3m 12.68 (7.18) Owned: Mr Malih L Al Basti Trained: Middleham

3282 **5.05 De Niro's Niteclub Lord's Taverners Maiden Stakes 3yo (D)**
£5434 £1672 £836 **7f str Good/Firm 22 -26 Slow** Stands side

SURREPTITIOUS [7] D R Loder 3-8-9 T P Queally 7/2: 1: ch f Machiavellian - Nadma (Northern Dancer) Cl-up, styd on to lead dist, rdn out to hold on: bckd on debut: half-sister to wnrs at 7/10f: dam successful at 10f: eff at 7f, further looks sure to suit: acts on fast grnd & a stiff/gall trk: goes well fresh. **68**
3048 **VIOLET PARK 9** [4] B J Meehan 3-8-9 K McEvoy 5/2 FAV: 22: Keen in tch, prog when short of room dist, switched & styd on well ins fnl 1f, just held: well bckd: acts on fast & gd/soft grnd: poss unlucky. *nk* **66+**
2092 **POLAR SUN 48** [1] J R Fanshawe 3-9-0 J Murtagh 5/1: 63: Handy, prog & ev ch dist, kept on ins fnl 1f despite edging left, not btn far: op 4/1 after 7 wk abs: eff at 7f on fast, 1m will suit. *½* **70**
2595 **DREAM EASY 28** [3] P L Gilligan 3-9-0 R Price 12/1: 054: Led, hdd dist, no extra ins fnl 1f: eff at 7f, rtn to 1m shld suit: see 2595. *½* **69**
MUJAWER [2]3-9-0 W Supple 3/1: 5: b g Gulch - Good Cents (Deputy Minister) Rear, prog 2f out, ev ch dist, no extra ins fnl 1f: tchd 9/2 on debut: cost $350,000: half-brother to sprint performers abroad: dam unrcd: eff at 7f on fast grnd: with M P Tregoning. *nk* **68**
3048 **CAZENOVE 9** [6]3-9-0 K Darley 25/1: 046: Cl-up, no extra bef 1f out: see 3048. *1¾* **64**
3121 **ALJAFLIYAH 7** [8]3-8-9 A Hamblett(7) 33/1: U07: Slow away, nvr a factor: qck reapp. *5* **49**
TIDES [9]3-8-9 Lisa Jones(3) 28/1: 8: Slow away, sn cl-up, wknd fnl 2f on debut. *3* **43**
3770} **PAINTED MOON 331** [5]3-8-9 J P Guillambert(3) 16/1: 0-9: ch f Gone West - Crimson Conquest (Diesis) Cl-up till halfway, sn fdd: reapp & new stable: unplcd sole '03 start (D R Loder, rtd 63). *24* **0**
9 Ran Time 1m 27.29 (3.39) Owned: Sheikh Mohammed Trained: Newmarket

3283 **5.35 Gunite Eastern Ltd Lord's Taverners Handicap Stakes 3yo 0-80 (D)** **[86]**
£5733 £1764 £882 **7f str Good/Firm 22 -09 Slow** Stands side

3058* **HAZEWIND 9** [4] P D Evans 3-8-1 vis t (59) F P Ferris(3) 7/1: 0002511: Cl-up, styd on to lead 2f out, drvn clr, eased cl-home, val 3L+: eff at 1m/10f, apprec drop back to 7f: acts on fast, gd & polytrack: eff with t-strap & visor: continues in gd vein of form & hat-trick awaits: see 3058. **70+**
2314+**PANSHIR 27** [10] C F Wall 3-9-7 (79) R Mullen 7/2 FAV: 5030162: Rear, prog when short of room bef 1f out, styd on ins fnl 1f, no ch with easy wnr: closer with clr passage & can sn rtn to winning ways: see 2314. *1¾* **84**
2797 **ASK THE CLERK 19** [5] V Smith 3-8-13 (71) M Tebbutt 14/1: 2034643: Handy, onepcd fnl 1f: see 2797. *1½* **73**
2634 **MOLINIA 26** [1] R M Beckett 3-7-12 (56) N Mackay(3) 25/1: 50-0P404: Slow away, prog & short of room ins fnl 2f, sn no impress: eff at 7f on fast grnd: see 2314. *¾* **56**
2705 **CARRIACOU 23** [8]3-8-9 (67) T Quinn 20/1: 02-64505: Rear, prog 3f out, onepcd dist: btr 192. *1¼* **64**
2940 **MOUNT VETTORE 14** [6]3-9-0 (72) J Murtagh 9/1: 2000006: Led, hdd 2f out, sn no extra. *nk* **68**
2922 **SPIN KING 14** [2]3-9-3 (75) K Darley 4/1: 3-040347: Cl-up, ev ch dist, sn wknd: btr 2403. *hd* **70**
2742 **LORIEN HILL 21** [11]3-9-1 (73) M Hills 11/2: 4-651028: Rear, modest late gains: btr 2742. *¾* **66**
2797 **DR SYNN 19** [3]3-8-9 (67) K McEvoy 7/1: 6-063659: Handy 5f, wkng when short of room ins fnl 1f. *hd* **59**
3094* **FAITH HEALER 8** [9]3-7-13 bl (57) D Fentiman(7) 7/1: 0004610: 10th: In tch 5f, sn hung right & wknd. *¾* **47**
1865 **CARLBURG 58** [7]3-8-10 (68) J P Guillambert(3) 33/1: 00200-00: 11th: Cl-up, wknd when short of room ins fnl 1f: 8 wk abs: see 1865. *1½* **55**
11 Ran Time 1m 26.08(2.18) Owned: Waterline Racing Club Trained: Abergavenny

LINGFIELD Polytrack SATURDAY 17.07.04 Lefthand, Sharp, Undulating Track

Official Going Good

3284 **6.25 Independent Catering Nursery Handicap Stakes 2yo (E)** **[89]**
£3484 £1072 £536 **5f str Good Inapplicable** Stands Side

2839 **FORZEEN 17** [2] J A Osborne 2-8-13 (74) E Ahern 6/1: 34231: Mid-div, rdn & hdwy to lead dist, asserted ins last: op 8/1, first win: eff at 5f, 6f shld suit: acts on firm, gd & both AWs: likes a sharp/undul trk: most consistent, type to win again: see 2839 & 1752. **87**
2839* **RUSSIAN ROCKET 17** [3] Mrs C A Dunnett 2-9-2 (77) Hayley Turner(5) 9/1: 05212: Mid-div, rdn to chall over 1f out, not pace of wnr fnl 1f: just ahd of today's wnr latest: acts on firm, gd & polytrack: see 2839. *1¾* **82**

LINGFIELD **Polytrack SATURDAY 17.07.04 Lefthand, Sharp, Undulating Track**

3022 **TESARY 10** [12] E A L Dunlop 2-9-0 (75) L Dettori 2/1 FAV: 62143: Mid-div when short of room briefly 2f out, hanging over 1f out but kept on ins last: acts on fast & gd grnd: see 2738. *2* **74**
2839 **KEMPSEY 17** [11] J J Bridger 2-8-10 (71) A Daly 20/1: 0644: Chsd ldrs, outpcd 2f out, kept on late: handles polytrack & gd grnd, step up to 6f in similar could suit: acts on polytrack & gd grnd: see 2839. *¾* **68**
2213 **SMIDDY HILL 43** [6]2-9-7 (82) J Quinn 4/1: 324145: Rcd freely & led till dist, no extra: 6 wk abs. *shd* **79**
2744 **ELISHA 21** [7]2-8-12 (73) C Catlin 20/1: 45106: Chsd ldrs, btn dist: btr 2020. *½* **68**
3082 **TALCEN GWYN 8** [9]2-9-5 (80) I Mongan 12/1: 4147: Dwelt, rear, only mod prog: btr 2430. *1¾* **70**
2738 **FIRST RULE 21** [5]2-8-11 (72) S Sanders 8/1: 0448: Chsd ldrs till over 1f out: btr 2738, 2450. *½* **60**
2270* **KERESFORTH 40** [1]2-8-4 (65) P Doe 20/1: 00219: Sn outpcd, nvr any dngr, abs: btr 2270. *½* **51**
1981 **MAJESTICAL 53** [4]2-8-1 (62) A McCarthy 20/1: 3400: 10th: Held up, hung right 2f out, sn btn. *hd* **47**
2033 **MS POLLY GARTER 51** [10]2-7-12 (5oh) (59) M Halford(7) 33/1: 4060: 11th: Slow away & well bhd. *3½* **33**
1887 **BAILEYS APPLAUSE 57** [8]2-8-6 BL (67) R Havlin 16/1: 5360: 12th: Chsd ldrs, btn/hmpd over 1f out. *3½* **30**
12 Ran Time 58.73 (1.93) Owned: Cavendish Racing Trained: Upper Lambourn

3285 **6.55 European Breeders Fund Maiden Stakes 2yo (D)**
£4459 £1372 £686 **7f str Good Inapplicable** Stands Side

2666 **MINNESOTA 24** [6] H Candy 2-9-0 Dane O'Neill 3/1: 21: Made all, pressed over 1f out, styd on strongly to assert ins last: nicely bckd tho' op 9/4: confirmed debut promise: eff at 5.7f, apprec step up to 7f & will get further: acts on firm & gd grnd: see 2666. **82**
2020 **RAGGED GLORY 52** [4] R Hannon 2-9-0 R Smith 14/1: 462: Trkd ldrs, outpcd 2f out, kept on well ins last, no threat to wnr: 8 wk abs: styd longer 7f trip well, prob get further: acts on fast & gd grnd: see 1816. *1¾* **78**
2703 **DAHLIYEV 23** [1] P W Harris 2-9-0 E Ahern 12/1: 03: b c Fasliyev - Thaidah (Vice Regent) Mid-div, eff to press wnr over 1f out, no extra ins last: E55,000 May foal, half-brother to a 6f juv wnr & wnrs up to 12f, dam a dual 5/6f scorer as a juv: eff at 7f, drop to 6f may suit: acts on gd grnd: can find a race. *shd* **78**
CREATIVE CHARACTER 0 [9] P F I Cole 2-9-0 N De Souza(3) 28/1: 4: b c Theatrical - Shannkara (Akarad) Handy, styd on for press, not pace of wnr: May foal, related to US sprinters, dam a smart 1m performer abroad: eff at 7f, prob get further: acts on gd grnd & a sharp/undul trk. *½* **77**
2902 **BLAISE HOLLOW 15** [11]2-9-0 S Drowne 16/1: 05: U.r. bef start, mid-div, kept on from over 1f out, no threat: imprvd from debut: handles gd grnd & stays 7f: see 2902. *1¼* **74**
ZALAAL 0 [14]2-9-0 L Dettori 9/4 FAV: 6: b c A P Indy - Scoot Yer Boots (Seeking The Gold) Held up, rdn 2f out, no prog dist: bckd: Apr foal, dam plcd in US: looks likely to apprec 1m+. *hd* **73**
2876 **DUNMAGLASS 16** [8]2-9-0 S Sanders 25/1: 07: Chsd ldrs, onepace fnl 2f. *shd* **73**
2870 **DREEMON 16** [3]2-9-0 G Baker 9/1: 038: U.r. bef start, chsd wnr till over 2f out. *nk* **72**
KARLU 0 [5]2-9-0 R Hughes 14/1: 9: Dwelt, rdn & bhd, late prog, improve. *shd* **72**
ASAATEEL 0 [13]2-9-0 R Hills 4/1: 0: 10th: Held up, eff over 2f out, sn no impress. *¾* **71**
LADY LUISA 0 [12]2-8-9 S Whitworth 66/1: 0: 11th: Dwelt & al bhd. *1¾* **63**
Blue Spectrum 0 [16]2-9-0 J D Smith 50/1:0 2870 **Liquid Lover 16** [2]2-9-0 P Gallagher(7) 50/1:0
3111 **Snow Tempest 7** [10]2-9-0 I Mongan 25/1:0 **Pralin Star 0** [7]2-9-0 N Chalmers(5) 66/1:0
15 Ran Time 1m 25.71 (5.31) Owned: Mr Philip Newton Trained: Wantage

LINGFIELD **Polytrack SATURDAY 17.07.04 Lefthand, V Sharp Track**

Official Going Standard

3286 **7.25 Aneela Rose Boutique The Lanes Brighton Claiming Stakes 3-5yo (F)**
£3003 £858 £429 **1m aw rnd Standard Inapplicable** Outside

3107 **TRE COLLINE 7** [6] N Tinkler 5-9-13 (75) L Dettori 7/4 FAV: 0151461: Rear, hdwy to chase ldr over 1f out & led cl-home, all out: suited by 1m on firm, fast & both AWs: apprec drop to claim grade: see 2500. **82a**
4201} **ZARIANO 309** [3] S L Keightley 4-9-8 (90) R Havlin 12/1: 025160-2: b g Emperor Jones - Douce Maison (Fools Holme) Led & clr halfway, hdd well ins last, just held: reapp: auct mdn wnr '03, AW unplcd (rtd 93a, cond stks, poss flattered): plcd sole '02 start (rtd 91, mdn): eff at 1m: acts on fast, gd/soft & polytrack, gall or sharp trk: goes well fresh: can be placed to win similar. *nk* **76a**
1 Jun'03 Ayr 8g/f 83-(100) E: 2 Mar'03 Donc 8gd 100- C:
3067 **QUEENSTOWN 8** [10] B J Meehan 3-9-3 bl (84) J F McDonald(3) 5/2: 44122-03: Chsd ldr, no extra dist. *3½* **72a**
2500 **DIXIE DANCING 30** [1] C A Cyzer 5-9-0 (56) S Sanders 12/1: 5030-504: Chsd ldrs, onepace fnl 2f. *1¼* **58a$**
3174 **FULVIO 4** [7]4-9-3 vis (58) P Doe 16/1: 000-0005: Held up to chase ldrs over 2f out, wknd, qck reapp. *2½* **56a**
2650 **WHIPLASH 25** [12]3-8-7 (55) C Catlin 14/1: 0-040106: Rear, well bhd halfway, mod late prog: see 1720. *1* **52a**
2732 **WIZARD LOOKING 22** [4]3-8-6 BL t (60) Dane O'Neill 9/2: 26-60067: Mid-div, btn 2f out: blnks. *3½* **44a**
2924 **ANISETTE 14** [2]3-8-1 (45) M Halford(7) 16/1: 0606408: Dwelt, sn chsd ldrs, btn 2f out: btr 2346. *1* **37a**
2741 **TSHUKUDU 21** [9]3-8-2 (38) J Quinn 66/1: 5000-009: Sn well bhd halfway, nvr a factor. *1* **36a**
2644 **ZINGING 25** [11]5-9-0 (45) T P Queally 14/1: 0655600: 10th: Mid div over 5f, sn wknd. *2½* **35a**
1451 **SINGULARITY 79** [8]4-8-12 p (37) A McCarthy 66/1: 3055-000: 11th: b g Rudimentary - Lyrical Bid (Lyphard) Slow away & rear, no ch fnl 3f: jumps fit (unplcd, mod form): auct mdn plcd in '03, W R Muir, disapp in cheek pieces & blnks): auct mdn plcd '02 (rtd 68, subs clmr & sell rnr-up on sand): best eff at 5/6f on both AWs, firm & gd grnd, sharp trks: with K F Clutterbuck. 2 Dec'02 Wolv 6af 55a- G: 2 Nov'02 Sout 6af 59a- F: *1¼* **30a**
3043 **MANTEL MINI 9** [5]5-8-12 p G Baker 100/1: 060: 12th: Dwelt & rear, bhd from halfway. *nk* **29a**
12 Ran Time 1m 40.71 (4.51) Owned: Peter Alderson Mike Gosse Adrian Mornin Trained: Malton

3287 **7.55 Rectangle Group Handicap Stakes Fillies 3yo+ 0-85 (D)** **[85]**
£5444 £1675 £838 **1m2f aw Standard Inapplicable** Inside

2719 **LARA FALANA 22** [6] Miss B Sanders 6-8-4 (61) J Quinn 9/4: 2542641: Held up in tch, styd on for press to lead ins last: eff at 1m, 10f suits: acts on firm, gd & polytrack: see 799. **69a**
2835* **CHERUBIM 18** [1] D R Loder 3-8-8 (75) T P Queally 6/1: 32-5512: Dictated pace, hdd ins last, not pace of wnr: acts on firm, gd & polytrack: enjoyed forcing the pace last twice: see 2835 (fill mdn). *1¼* **80a**

LINGFIELD Polytrack SATURDAY 17.07.04 Lefthand, V Sharp Track

3026 **WANNA SHOUT 10** [5] R Dickin 6-7-12 (55) Joanna Badger 14/1: 1205063: Sn cl up, no extra. *2* **57a**
3026 **DISPOL EVITA 10** [4] Jamie Poulton 5-7-12 (3oh) (52) A McCarthy 14/1: 20-04204: Rear, mod prog. *2½* **53a**
2674* **HENESEYS LEG 24** [3]4-9-2 (73) Lisa Jones(3) 100/30: 645-1115: Held up, eff 2f out, btn dist: op 9/4: v disappointing on switch to all weather: btr 2674 (gd). *½* **70a**
2761 **CZARINA WALTZ 21** [2]5-10-0 (85) R Mullen 7/4 FAV: 1040-206: Trkd ldrs, btn 2f out: see 2265. *2* **79a**
2837* **DAMI 18** [7]3-8-7 p (74) S Sanders 9/2: 0-55221W: Withdrawn, bolted bef start; btr 2837. **0a**
7 Ran Time 2m 08.12 (5.32) Owned: Exors of the Late R Lamb Trained: Epsom

3288

8.25 Nutfield Priory Sponsors Of The Best Hat Selling Stakes 3yo+ (G)
£2632 £752 £376 **1m2f aw Standard Inapplicable** Inside

3025* **BURGUNDY 10** [2] P Mitchell 7-9-11 bl (58) I Mongan 5/6 FAV: 0036111: Dwelt & rdn early, hdwy halfway & led over 2f out, rdn clr: bght in for 10,000gns: well bckd: eff at 7/10f on fast, soft & polytrack, loves claim/sell grade & can win again: see 3025. **68a**
2643 **PRIVATE SEAL 25** [1] Julian Poulton 9-9-5 t (45) M Halford(7) 16/1: 0500032: Rear, kept on late, nvr a threat to wnr: see 2643, 707 & 539. *7* **51a**
2782 **STYLISH SUNRISE 20** [9] I A Wood 3-8-9 t (56) S Sanders 12/1: 6-043503: Mid-div wide, styd on onepace fnl 3f: handles firm, fast & polytrack: see 2107. *shd* **51a**
3176 **ENNA 4** [6] Mrs Stef Liddiard 5-9-0 (45) S Drowne 12/1: 4600404: Rear, kept on late for press, no threat. *nk* **45a**
2873 **FIGURA 16** [4]6-9-0 (54) N Day 4/1: 6500005: Held up, eff 4f out, rdn & no impress fnl 2f. *1¾* **43a**
1645] **ZELOSO 783** [8]6-9-5 vis A Daly 14/1: 046/000/-6: b g Alzao - Silk Petal (Petorius) Trkd ldrs, lost pl over 2f out & sn no impress: reapp, long abs: missed '03: unplcd '02 (rtd 54 & 0a, h'caps): mdn wnr back in '00 for R Charlton: best efforts at 6/7f, poss stays 10f: acts on fast & gd/soft grnd, stiff/gall trk: best without blnks or visor: with M F Harris. *1½* **46a**
539} **RAGASAH 530** [14]6-9-0 Lisa Jones(3) 66/1: 00060/0-7: b f Glory of Dancer - Slight Risk (Risk Me) Cl-up & led over 4f out till over 2f out, sn struggling: reapp/long abs: unplcd '03 (AW h'cap): unplcd '02 (rtd 33 & 46a, h'caps): late '02 AW mdn scorer (Miss G Kelleway): eff at 11f on fibresand. *½* **40a$**
1 Dec'01 Sout 11af 48a- F:
2973 **ROLEX FREE 12** [13]6-9-5 bl t (60) R Smith 20/1: 6/40-0608: Sn handy, btn 3f out. *9* **34a**
3164 **SIR FRANK GIBSON 5** [3]3-8-9 P (40) D Sweeney 28/1: 2305559: Chsd ldrs till halfway. *5* **27a**
3044 **CAL MAC 9** [5]5-9-5 (57) M Henry 9/1: 4-000200: 10th: Led till over 4f out, btn over 2f out: btr 2643. *10* **15a**
3087 **IN TUNE 8** [10]4-9-5 t (42) G Baker 50/1: 5-000000: 11th: Slow away & al bhd, t.o. *11* **1a**
4962} **Russian Icon 260** [12]3-8-4 C Catlin 100/1:0
1213] **Father Seamus 807** [7]6-9-5 P(20) R Lucey Butler(6) 66/1:0
13 Ran Time 2m 08.59 (5.79) Owned: Mr Nigel Shields Trained: Epsom

LINGFIELD Polytrack SATURDAY 17.07.04 Lefthand, Sharp, Undulating Track

Official Going Good

3289

8.55 Dp Caruana Wonga Handicap Stakes 3yo+ 35-55 (F) **[59]**
£3136 £896 £448 **6f str Good Inapplicable** Stands Side

2347 **ADANTINO 37** [12] B R Millman 5-9-9 bl (54) R Hughes 6/1: 4133631: Bhd, hdwy when short of room halfway, hdwy over 1f out & styd on strongly for press to lead cl-home: op 8/1: eff at 6/7f, stays 1m well: acts on fast, soft & both AWs: gd confidence boost: see 536. **60**
2855 **STAGNITE 17** [2] Mrs H Sweeting 4-9-9 P (54) N Chalmers(5) 25/1: 0200-062: Led till cl-home. *nk* **60**
2720 **JAGGED 22** [15] J R Jenkins 4-9-10 BL (55) L Dettori 11/2: 30-00023: Led/dsptd lead till cl-home: only just denied in first time blnks: see 2720. *nk* **59**
2561 **DRURY LANE 28** [14] D W Chapman 4-9-8 bl (53) E Ahern 7/1: 0004004: Dwelt & rear, switched & styd on well from over 1f out, nrst fin: well h'capped, could find similar: see 2214. *¾* **56**
3024 **CHORISTAR 10** [6]3-9-5 (55) R Mullen 12/1: 060-625: Held up, short of room 2f out, nrst fin: eff at 6f, crying out for rtn to 7f+: see 3024 (7f). *nk* **57**
3104* **SABANA 7** [11]6-9-3 p (48) Lisa Jones(3) 8/1: 6000016: Mid-div, not pace to chall: see 3104. *1¼* **46**
3050* **ENJOY THE BUZZ 9** [10]5-9-6 (51) C Catlin 4/1 FAV: 2010217: Chsd ldrs, drvn & btn ins last: op 6/1. *¾* **47**
2806 **STRIKE LUCKY 19** [4]4-9-6 P (51) D Sweeney 20/1: 400-108: Chsd ldrs, no impress bef dist, chkpcs. *shd* **47**
3036 **MINIMUM BID 10** [8]3-9-5 (55) J Quinn 7/1: 063-0029: Bhd, short of room 2f out, modest prog. *nk* **50**
3109 **MAN CRAZY 7** [16]3-9-5 bl (55) S Sanders 7/1: 0600040: 10th: Chsd ldrs till over 1f out: btr 3109. *1¼* **46**
2630 **Mannora 26** [7]4-9-5 (50) S Drowne 33/1:0 2599 **Yorkies Boy 27** [1]9-9-6 (51) M Savage(5) 14/1:0
2630 **Toppling 26** [5]6-9-10 (55) C J Davies(7) 12/1:0 2945 **Akiramenai 14** [9]4-9-8 (53) S Whitworth 66/1:0
14 Ran Time 1m 11.62(2.82) Owned: Tarka Two Racing Trained: Cullompton

WINDSOR MONDAY 19.07.04 Sharp, Figure 8 Track

Official Going GOOD/FIRM

3290

6.20 European Breeders Fund Maiden Stakes Fillies 2yo (D)
£5265 £1620 £810 **6f Firm 9 -30 Slow** Inside

2658 **ANGEL SPRINTS 26** [5] L G Cottrell 2-8-11 A Daly 7/2 FAV: 3361: Made all, drvn out fnl 1f: eff at 5f, imprvd for step up to 6f: acts on firm & fast, sharp trk: game eff on switch to forcing tactics: see 1716. **89**
3071 **GENNIE BOND 10** [1] R Hannon 2-8-11 R L Moore 9/2: 432: Rcd in 2nd, chall 3f out, onepcd ins fnl 1f: well bckd tho' op 7/2: stays 6f on firm: find similar sn: see 2733. *1¼* **81**
3141 **KEEP BACCKINHIT 8** [9] G L Moore 2-8-11 A Quinn(5) 14/1: 303: Chsd ldrs, onepcd 2f out: clr of rem: stays 6f on firm: see 2733. *1½* **78**

2395 **APPLE OF MY EYE 37** [6] J R Jenkins 2-8-11 W Ryan 40/1: 04: b f Fraam - Fresh Fruit Daily 3½ 67
(Reprimand) Outpcd, hdwy 2f out, not pace to chall: mdn unplcd earlier racecourse bow: Apr foal: half sister to
wnrs over 6f/1m: dam 10/12f wnr.

LILTING PROSE 0 [3]2-8-11 L Dettori 9/2: 5: ch f Indian Ridge - Kirkwood (Selkirk) Handy, no ½ 65
impress over 1f out on debut: Mar first foal, cost 45,000gns: dam a 6f 3yo wnr in France.

3041 **GUINEA A MINUTE 11** [7]2-8-11 I Mongan 7/1: 036: Rear, modest late gains: see 3041. 2 59

SEVERELY 0 [10]2-8-11 M Hills 5/1: 7: b f Cape Cross - Sevres (Lyphard's Wish) Keen in rear, ¾ 57
nvr a factor on debut: Mar foal, cost 34,000gns: dam unrcd, sire v smart miler at 4 & 5: with B Hills.

SHARP AS A TACK 0 [4]2-8-11 J F McDonald(3) 12/1: 8: Slow away, hdwy 3f out, hung left 2f out, wknd. 1½ 53

WINTER MOON 0 [2]2-8-11 S Drowne 16/1: 9: Slow away, hdwy 3f out, wknd on debut. 1¾ 48

2847 **EPITOMISE 19** [8]2-8-11 M Tebbutt 16/1: 640: 10th: Nvr a factor: see 2847. ¾ 46

10 Ran   Time 1m 12.64 (2.34)   Owned: Mrs Lucy Halloran   Trained: Cullompton

---

3291   6.50 Countryside Alliance Handicap Stakes Fillies 3yo 0-75 (E) [82]
£3591 £1105 £553   **1m67y**   **Firm 9**   **-08 Slow**   Inside

2953 **DU PRE 15** [11] Mrs A J Perrett 3-9-1 (69) S Drowne 100/30: 30-021: Rcd in 2nd, hdwy to lead ins 75
fnl 2f, drvn out fnl 1f: suited by 8.4f on fm & gd: first win, op to improvement.

3090 **FILLIEMOU 10** [13] A W Carroll 3-8-0 (54) F P Ferris(3) 10/1: 00-00052: Led till ins fnl 2f, kept 1 57
on well for 2nd ins fnl 1f but no ch with wnr: tchd 14/1: eff around 1m on firm: see 2225.

3090 **DEIGN TO DANCE 10** [8] J G Portman 3-8-7 (61) T E Durcan 8/1: 5005103: Rear, hdwy ins fnl 2f, 2 60
styd on well ins fnl 1f to go 3rd cl home: gd run: worth a try over further.

2624* **HOT LIPS PAGE 28** [1] R Hannon 3-9-7 (75) R L Moore 3/1 FAV: 005-514: Bhd, hdwy over 2f out, no nk 73
impress ins fnl 1f: top-weight: continues in gd form, see 2624.

2854 **SOVIET SPIRIT 19** [9]3-8-5 (59) M Halford(7) 12/1: 50535: Handy, onepcd fnl 1f: now with C Dwyer. nk 56

2835 **SEA OF GOLD 20** [10]3-9-4 (72) L Dettori 6/1: 0626: Chsd ldrs, onepcd 2f out. ¾ 67

3007 **HOLD UP 13** [6]3-8-6 (60) S Whitworth 20/1: 0-0007: ch f Daggers Drawn - Select Sale (Auction 2½ 50
Ring) Chsd ldrs, no impress over 1f out: mdn unplcd sole '03 start (rtd 55, with E Dunlop): lightly rcd.

4930} **GREAT BLASKET 265** [4]3-8-0 (54) J Quinn 25/1: 030004-8: b f Petardia - Alexander Goddess (Alzao) shd 43
Handy, hdwy to chall over 3f out, wknd fnl 1f on reapp: won 1 of 8 '03 starts (seller): eff at 7f on fast, gall
trk. 1 Jun'03 Redc 7g/f 62- G:

2904 **FLAME QUEEN 17** [5]3-9-1 (69) T P Queally 20/1: 002-009: Chsd ldrs, rcd wide bend 6f out & over 1½ 55
4f out, no impress over 2f out: see 2590.

3058 **SNOW JOKE 11** [7]3-7-13 (53) J F McDonald(3) 14/1: 0-040000: 10th: Rear, nvr a factor: op 20/1. 3 33

355 **PAPPY 193** [3]3-7-12 (2oh) (50) S Righton 33/1: 03500-40: 11th: b f Petardia - Impressive Lady (Mr 2 28
Fluorocarbon) Handy & keen, wide bend 6f out & over 4f out, no impress 3f out: long abs: 3rd one of 6 '03 starts
(mdn, rtd 63, with J Given): eff at 6f, shld stay further: has tried blnks: now with A Carroll.

2974 **BURN 14** [2]3-8-10 (64) I Mongan 16/1: 0300: 12th: Cl-up, wide bend 6f out & over 4f out, wknd 2f out. 9 22

12 Ran   Time 1m 44.45 (1.45)   Owned: Mr R A Grossman   Trained: Pulborough

---

3292   7.20 Rutland Maiden Stakes 3yo (D)
£4368 £1344 £672   **1m2f7y**   **Firm 9**   **+07 Fast**   Inside

1398 **MOTORWAY 83** [16] R Charlton 3-9-0 S Drowne 7/2: 61: Handy, led just ins fnl 2f, flashed tail 79
for 1 smack, hands & heels in last: abs: eff at 10f on fm, shld stay further: runs well fresh: imprvd from debut &
prob more to come: see 1398.

2885 **NEWS SKY 18** [14] B W Hills 3-9-0 M Hills 9/2: 022: Cl-up, hdwy into 2nd ins fnl 2f, chall ins ¾ 76
fnl 1f, no impress nr fin: clr of rem: eff at 1m/10f on firm & gd: shld find similar: see 2885.

DAY OF RECKONING 0 [5] Sir Michael Stoute 3-8-9 B Doyle 8/1: 3: b f Daylami - Trying For Gold 3½ 66+
(Northern Baby) Bhd, hdwy 3f out, styd on well under hands & heels ins fnl 1f to go 3rd nr fin: op 9/2, debut: dam
12f 3yo wnr: sure to improve for this, esp over further.

2608 **ZANGEAL 29** [4] C F Wall 3-9-0 T (79) R Mullen 100/30 FAV: 4344: Rcd in 2nd, led over 3f out till 1½ 69
ins fnl 2f, no extra: op 11/2: tried t-strap: see 2193.

2274 **KILINDINI 42** [6]3-9-0 L Keniry(3) 33/1: 6U5: gr g Silver Patriarch - Newlands Corner (Forzando) 1½ 67
Mid-div, onepcd 2f out: 6 wk abs: first foal, dam modest 6f 3/4yo wnr: with Miss E Lavelle.

4750} **HAT TRICK MAN 278** [11]3-9-0 R L Moore 20/1: 00-6: gr c Daylami - Silver Kristal (Kris) Rear, shd 66
modest late gains on reapp: mdn unplcd both '03 starts (rtd 68): with J Akehurst.

ASPIRED 0 [8]3-8-9 O Urbina 14/1: 7: In tch, hung left & green over 1f out, sn wknd on debut. 3½ 56

2788 **ROSSALL POINT 22** [17]3-9-0 T Quinn 8/1: 458: Slow away, modest late gains. 5 53

2907 **NOBLE MIND 17** [3]3-9-0 D Kinsella 14/1: 209: Chsd ldrs, wknd over 2f out: see 2622. 1¾ 50

2453 **SURFACE TO AIR 35** [15]3-9-0 R Havlin 66/1: 000: 10th: Slow away, al bhd. 3½ 45

2974 **PRIMESHADE PROMISE 14** [13]3-8-9 R Price 100/1: 00: 11th: Rear, nvr a factor. 2 37

3048 **SIXTILSIX 11** [2]3-9-0 (40) M Tebbutt 66/1: 60000-00: 12th: Sn led till over 3f out, no extra. 7 31

3038 **GLIDING BY 12** [7]3-8-9 J Quinn 33/1: 00-00: 13th: Chsd ldrs, wknd over 2f out. 5 18

2879 **BLAZE THE TRAIL 18** [1]3-8-9 T P Queally 100/1: 060: 14th: Handy, wknd bef halfway. 3 13

START OF AUTHORITY 0 [9]3-9-0 T E Durcan 28/1: 0: 15th: Al bhd on debut. 10 3

15 Ran   Time 2m 6.29 (0.29)   Owned: Mountgrange Stud   Trained: Beckhampton

---

3293   7.50 Catlin Group Classified Stakes 3yo 0-80 (D)
£6871 £2114 £1057   **6f**   **Firm 9**   **-29 Slow**   Inside

2749 **EISTEDDFOD 23** [3] P F I Cole 3-9-0 (80) N De Souza(5) 9/1: 1331: Trkd ldrs, hdwy to lead just ins 89
fnl 1f, drvn out: eff btwn 6/7f, acts on firm & soft, sharp trks: lightly rcd, consistent & useful: see 1575.

3235 **BOHOLA FLYER 3** [7] R Hannon 3-8-11 (78) L Dettori 9/2: 6411452: Trkd ldrs, outpcd over 2f out, 1 80
kept on again ins fnl 1f to go 2nd but no ch with wnr: qck reapp: handles firm & soft: see 2619.

2375* **PRESTO SHINKO 38** [2] R Hannon 3-9-3 (83) R L Moore 11/4: 3-163213: Bhd, hdwy/switched left 1f ½ 85
out, kept on but not pace of first 2: handles firm, acts on fast, gd & polytrack: btr 2375.

2918 **KINGS CAPRICE 16** [1] G B Balding 3-9-5 (85) S Carson 14/1: 3-034104: Mid-div, hdwy to lead well shd 86
over 1f out, hdd just ins fnl 1f, no extra: top-weight: see 2918 & 2756.

2677 **CHANCE FOR ROMANCE 26** [5]3-8-13 (82) R Mullen 25/1: 6050-265: Led till well over 1f out, no extra. 2½ 72

2764 **KSCHESSINKA 23** [4]3-8-12 (81) M Hills 5/4 FAV: 0-136: Keen & trkd ldrs, hdwy to chall over 2f 1¾ 66

WINDSOR   MONDAY 19.07.04   Sharp, Figure 8 Track

out, wknd ins fnl 1f: hvly bckd: btr expected after 2764 (fast).
3080 **MOLLY MOON 10** [6]3-8-13 (82) S Drowne 25/1: 3164-007: Nvr a factor: see 3080.   3½   56
7 Ran   Time 1m 12.62 (2.32)   Owned: Elite Racing Club   Trained: Whatcombe

---

3294	8.20 Countryside Alliance Selling Stakes 3yo+ (E)

£3435 £1057   £529   **1m3f135y**   **Firm 9**   **-04 Slow**   Inside

3145 **AMBERSONG 8** [8] A W Carroll 6-9-7 (41) I Mongan 4/1 J FAV: 0643301: Slow away, hdwy 4f out, led   48
ins fnl 2f, rdn out: no bid: eff at 1m/14.8f on firm, gd & both AWs, sharp trks: made most of drop in grade.
2804 **PERUVIAN BREEZE 21** [10] J Gallagher 3-9-0 (58) T E Durcan 13/2: 6-561002: Chsd ldrs, chall 2f   3   47
out, not pace of wnr fnl 1f: clr of rem: clmd for 6,000: new stable (prev with N Littmoden): see 2065.
4591} **MISS WOODPIGEON 289** [9] J D Frost 8-9-2 S Carson 16/1: 000-3: b f Landyap - Pigeon Loft   4   31
(Bellypha) Sn led till after 2f, led again 5f out till ins fnl 2f, no extra: reapp, long hdles abs (sell h'cap
unplcd, rtd 66h, stays 2m1f on fast & gd): unplcd all 3 '03 starts (mdns, clmr, rtd 52): lightly rcd 8yo.
3164 **BLUE SAVANNA 7** [4] J G Portman 4-9-12 bl (40) T J Murphy 6/1: 2105644: Pressed ldrs, hdwy & ev ch   3½   36
over 2f out, no impress over 1f out: qck reapp, top-weight: see 916.
2905 **GREAT GIDDING 17** [3]3-8-9 (55) S Drowne 4/1 J FAV: 03005: Handy to 4f out, sn btn.   ¾   30
1402 **DEVOTE 83** [6]6-9-7 bl S Whitworth 33/1: 506//-06: Slow away, hdwy & slt lead after 2f to 5f out,   ½   29
no extra 2f out: long abs: see 1402.
3168} **LIGHTNING STAR 1078** [1]9-9-7 bl R L Moore 9/2: /40/060//-7: b g El Gran Senor - Cuz's Star   ½   28
(Galaxy Libra) Cl-up, wknd over 4f out: reapp, hdles fit (h'cap rnr-up, rtd 106h, eff btwn 2m/2m2.5f, stays 2m5f,
acts on firm & soft, loves hvy, acts on any trk): missed '03 & '02: unplcd all 3 '01 starts (h'caps, rtd 54, with T
McGovern): eff at 10f, best on gd/soft & soft: wears blnks: with G Moore.
2700 **PADDY BOY 25** [5]3-8-9 (48) T Quinn 6/1: 3008: Keen & handy, wknd over 4f out.   6   19
2205 **KELTIC RAINBOW 45** [7]3-8-4 P (50) Paul Eddery 16/1: 033-4609: b f Spectrum - Secrets of Honour   3½   9
(Belmez) Al bhd: 6 wk abs: 3rd 2 of 4 '03 starts (mdns, rtd 65a): eff at 8.4f, further shld suit: acts on
fibresand: has tried a visor, tried cheek pieces here.
9 Ran   Time 2m 28.81 (1.51)   Owned: Pursuit Media   Trained: Alcester

---

3295	8.50 Sharon Burrows 40th Birthday Celebration Handicap Stakes 3yo+ 0-70 (E)	[69]

£3572 £1099   £550   **1m2f7y**   **Firm 9**   **+04 Fast**   Inside

3185 **KARAOKE 5** [2] S Kirk 4-9-10 (65) R L Moore 15/8 FAV: 2200031: In tch, hdwy to lead appr fnl 1f,   69
drvn out ins fnl 1f: qk reapp, top-weight: suited by 1m/10f on fm, gd & both AWs, prob any trk, likes Nottingham.
2800 **MALAK AL MOULOUK 21** [11] J M P Eustace 4-9-10 (65) L Fletcher(3) 6/1: 425-42: Mid-div, hdwy over   nk   67
3f out, chall 2f out, no impress nr fin: eff btwn 7/10f on firm, fast & fibresand: find similar: see 2800.
2929 **SIR HAYDN 16** [12] J R Jenkins 4-9-9 bl (64) T E Durcan 8/1: 3606053: Bhd, hdwy over 2f out, kept   1¼   64
on ins fnl 1f but not pace of first 2: see 1006.
3094 **HILARIOUS 10** [13] Dr J R J Naylor 4-8-3 (44) Lucy Russell(7) 11/1: 40-54564: Chsd ldrs, chall   ¾   42
over 2f out, ev ch 1f out, outpcd ins fnl 1f: see 2049.
2910 **LATIN QUEEN 17** [10]4-8-4 (45) F P Ferris(3) 16/1: 6/000-505: Chsd ldrs, hdwy to lead ins fnl 3f   ¾   43
till appr fnl 1f, sn no extra: see 2422.
3105 **STOLEN SONG 9** [5]4-9-0 (55) S Whitworth 16/1: 2-416006: Bhd, hdwy 3f out, sn chall, no impress fnl 1f. 1¼   51
3187 **RAINBOW WORLD 5** [7]4-9-3 p (58) J F Egan 5/1: 0030307: Rear, nvr nr ldrs: qck reapp, clr of rem.   2½   50
2954 **FLYING TREATY 15** [3]7-9-3 P (56) S Drowne 12/1: 0600568: Chsd ldrs, wknd 4f out: cheek pieces.   14   29
4457} **CURRAGH GOLD 297** [4]4-8-13 (54) Amy Baker(7) 25/1: 061300-9: b f Flying Spur - Go Indigo (Cyrano   nk   24
de Bergerac) Al bhd: reapp: long hdles abs (p.u., nov h'cap, eff at 2m3.5f on firm, rtd 89h): won 1 of 6 '03
starts (seller): mdn unplcd in native Ireland in '02: eff at 7f on slow fibresand, acts on a sharp trk: best in
sell grade, eff blnkd & has tried cheek pieces. 1 Feb'03 Sout 7af 56a-(55) G:
1913 **MAJOR BLADE 58** [9]6-8-13 (54) T Quinn 25/1: 3/006-000: 10th: b g Dashing Blade - Misniniski   nk   23
(Niniski) Chsd ldrs, wknd 3f out: 8 wk abs: h'cap unplcd in '03 (rtd 57): hdles unplcd in 02/03 (rtd 103h, nov).
1406 **SPIDERS WEB 83** [8]4-7-12 (10oh)bl (29) M Henry 50/1: B230000: 11th: Handy, wknd over 3f out: abs.   3½   3
2954 **SENIOR MINISTER 15** [1]6-9-5 (60) L Treadwell(7) 16/1: 00-01000: 12th: Led till ins fnl 3f, fdd.   13   4
12 Ran   Time 2m 6.58(0.58)   Owned: Speedlith Group   Trained: Upper Lambourn

---

BRIGHTON   MONDAY 19.07.04   Lefthand, V Sharp, Undulating Track

Official Going GOOD/FIRM.

3296	2.30 3663 First For Food Service Median Auction Maiden Stakes 2yo (F)

£2905 £830   £415   **5f59y rnd**   **Good/Firm 37**   **-14 Slow**   Inside

3021 **LOUPHOLE 12** [1] P J Makin 2-9-0 S Sanders 9/4 CO FAV: 341: Led early, led again appr fnl 1f,   82
rdn clr ins last: imprvd back at 5.3f on fast grnd & a sharp/undul trk: shld give a gd account in nurs: see 2738.
3157 **DANES CASTLE 7** [7] B J Meehan 2-9-0 L Dettori 9/4 CO FAV: 322: Led after 1f, rcd alone stands   2½   75
rail over 3f out, hdd appr appr 1f, not pace of wnr: eff over 5.3f/6f: shown enough to win a race: see 3157, 2970.
3141 **MISS CASSIA 8** [2] R Hannon 2-8-9 R Smith 9/4 CO FAV: 32S3: In tch, eff over 1f out, onepace.   2   64
2976 **MULBERRY LAD 14** [5] W R Muir 2-9-0 R Mullen 8/1: 524: Sn rdn in tch, onepace dist: see 2976.   ½   67
1574 **ARTADI 74** [6]2-8-9 J Quinn 33/1: 035: Slow away & al bhd: 11 wk abs: see 1574.   6   44
2926 **THREE ACES 16** [3]2-8-9 M Tebbutt 20/1: 056: Sn outpcd: btr 2926, 2658.   8   20
6 Ran   Time 1m 02.72 (2.72)   Owned: Ten of Hearts   Trained: Marlborough

---

3297 3.00 Commercial Catering Supplies Nursery Handicap Stakes 2yo (E) **[87]**
£3437 £1058 £529 **6f209y rnd** **Good/Firm 37** **-26 Slow** Inside

2569 **WHATATODO** 30 [4] M L W Bell 2-8-4 (63) J Quinn 8/1: 0301: Keen, made all, hung right appr fnl 1f   **69**
but kept on, rdn out: first win: imprvd for step up to 7f & acts on fast grnd & a sharp or stiff/undul trk.
2522 **WASALAT** 32 [9] M R Channon 2-9-7 (80) T E Durcan 6/1: 4232: Cl-up, chsd wnr over 2f out, not   1½ **82**
pace of wnr ins last: stays 7f & has shown enough to win a race: see 2522, 2228.
2952* **HES A DIAMOND** 15 [3] T G Mills 2-9-6 (79) L Dettori 2/1 FAV: 513: Chsd ldrs, eff over 1f out,   nk **80**
kept on, rdn out: acts on fast & gd grnd: gd run, see 2952 (C/D, mdn auct).
2927 **LAKESDALE** 16 [5] Mrs C A Dunnett 2-8-4 (63) Hayley Turner(5) 33/1: 02204: In tch, onepace over 1f   ½ **62**
out: back to form of 2343 (seller).
3053 **TREAT ME WILD** 11 [8]2-8-12 (71) R L Moore 10/1: 165: Bhd, eff 2f out, onepcd: see 3053, 1097 (5f).   2½ **65**
2865* **NORDHOCK** 18 [7]2-8-4 (63) T P Queally 9/2: 616: In tch, wknd 1.5f out: up in class, see 2865 (6f).   2½ **52**
3065 **GRYSKIRK** 11 [1]2-8-9 (68) Paul Eddery 7/1: 463007: V slow away, bhd, brief eff 2f out, stumbled   1½ **54**
over 1f out, eased & btn: see 1077.
2833 **RONNIES LAD** 20 [6]2-8-6 p (65) J F Egan 14/1: 501228: Handy, wknd 2f out: btr 2833 (6f), 2330.   1 **53**
2382 **AUNTY EURO** 38 [2]2-8-11 (70) S Sanders 16/1: 43329: In tch, wknd 2f out: btr 2382 (6f, f/sand).   1 **52**
9 Ran Time 1m 24.19 (4.39) Owned: Mr M Talbot-Ponsonby & Partners Trained: Newmarket

---

3298 3.30 Stowells Of Chelsea Selling Stakes 3-5yo (G)
£2607 £745 £372 **6f209y rnd** **Good/Firm 37** **-12 Slow** Inside

935 **MAJHOOL** 115 [4] T G Mills 5-9-5 (60) L Dettori 100/30 JT FA: 010-0451: Made all, kept on for   **52**
press fnl 2f: no bid, 4 month ago: eff over 6/7f & a sharp/undul trk, likes Lingfield: acts on firm & fast, enjoys
polytrack: prev with G L Moore, apprec switch to new connections, clrly goes well fresh in sell grade: see 730.
2928 **CARGO** 16 [6] B A Pearce 5-9-5 t p (46) L Treadwell(7) 10/1: 0232002: Chsd wnr, slightly outpcd   hd **51**
dist, rallied strongly & only just failed: gd run: see 1413, 709.
2953 **BAHAMA REEF** 15 [10] B Gubby 3-8-12 (57) M Tebbutt 10/1: 0-005203: Chsd ldrs, rdn 2f out, kept on   shd **51**
ins last, just failed: cheek pieces discarded & a btr run with drop to sell grade: best kept to this company.
3143 **BARABELLA** 8 [2] R J Hodges 3-8-7 (58) J F McDonald(3) 8/1: 0504504: In tch, eff over 1f out, kept   ½ **45**
on same pace ins last: btr run: see 1404.
2928 **RILEYS DREAM** 16 [9]5-9-6 P (40) S Whitworth 20/1: 5001005: Bhd, eff over 1f out, onepace: blnks.   1¼ **48$**
3067 **BINNION BAY** 10 [11]3-8-12 (67) R L Moore 100/30 JT FA: 100-0006: Held up, some late gains.   hd **46**
2854 **LOVE OF LIFE** 19 [7]3-8-7 (38) P Doe 50/1: 0067: Bhd, nvr a factor: see 2854.   3½ **34**
2909 **IVY MOON** 17 [3]4-9-0 (44) A Daly 6/1: 6035348: Al bhd: see 398.   ½ **33**
3667} **ANOTHER DEAL** 337 [8]5-9-5 (67) S Drowne 8/1: 603040-9: ch g Barathea - Mill Rainbow (Rainbow   ½ **37**
Quest) Nvr a factor on reapp: plcd in a mdn in '03 (rtd 75): prob stays 11.6f on firm.
2720 **RATHMULLAN** 24 [5]5-9-11 bl (36) Liam Jones(7) 33/1: 3135000: 10th: In tch, wknd dist: see 1710.   1½ **40**
3104 **REPEAT** 9 [1]4-9-11 (40) S Sanders 20/1: 4000600: 11th: In tch, wknd over 2f out: see 298, 66.   ¾ **38**
11 Ran Time 1m 23.21 (3.41) Owned: Mr T G Mills Trained: Epsom

---

3299 4.00 Blakes Butchers Handicap Stakes Fillies 3yo+ 0-75 (E) **[85]**
£3383 £1041 £520 **1m3f196y** **Good/Firm 37** **-27 Slow** Outside

2796 **BLAZE OF COLOUR** 21 [3] Sir Michael Stoute 3-9-0 VIS (71) B Doyle 6/1: 0-34231: Trkd ldr, led   **78**
dist, rdn clr: eff at 12f, shld stay 14f: acts on fast & gd/soft: handles a gall, likes a sharp/undul trk: enjoyed
visor & can progress further as she steps up in trip, see 2796 & 1428.
2842 **BUBBLING FUN** 19 [8] E A L Dunlop 3-8-9 (66) L Dettori 6/1: 2-404332: Held up, imprvd to chase   3 **69**
ldrs 3f out, onepcd fnl 1f: eff at 10/12f on gd & fast grnd: see 2842 & 2046 (10f here).
3211 **BANNINGHAM BLAZE** 4 [5] A W Carroll 4-8-5 vis (50) R L Moore 10/1: 1223653: Held up, prog 2f out,   hd **53**
nrst fin: op 14/1, qck reapp: interesting in sell h'caps: see 2601 & 2047.
3192 **OUR EMMY LOU** 5 [1] Sir Mark Prescott 3-8-2 (59) J Quinn 5/2 FAV: 066-24: Led till dist, no   1 **60**
extra: well bckd tho' op 7/4: qck reapp & btr clrly expected after 3192.
2956+ **DESERT ISLAND DISC** 15 [7]7-10-0 (73) G Baker 8/1: 4030615: Chsd ldrs, btn 2f out: op 6/1, clr   2½ **70**
of rem, top-weight: btr 2956 (gd grnd).
2617 **HIGH SCHOOL** 28 [4]3-9-1 (72) T P Queally 8/1: 26426: Al towards rear: btr 2617 & 1835.   8 **57**
2956 **KYTHIA** 5 [6]3-9-2 (73) S Drowne 3/1: 315-4327: Chsd ldrs till halfway, sn bhd: btr 2956.   6 **48**
291 **ARMENTIERES** 198 [2]3-8-1 P (58) Hayley Turner(5) 50/1: 43530-68: Al bhd, fin last: tried cheek pieces.   ½ **32**
8 Ran Time 2m 29.38 (1.18) Owned: Maktoum Al Maktoum Trained: Newmarket

---

3300 4.30 Brakes Handicap Stakes 3yo 35-55 (F) **[63]**
£2975 £850 £425 **1m1f209y** **Good/Firm 37** **-01 Slow** Outside

3231+ **MASAFI** 3 [1] Sir Mark Prescott 3-9-10 (6ex) (59) S Sanders 8/13 FAV: 000-2111: Nvr far away, went   **76+**
on 1.5f out, pushed well clr, easily: well bckd & top-weight: completed qck hat-trick, eff at 1m/10f, shld stay
further: acts on fast & both AWs: handles a sharp or stiff trk: tough & typically prog Sir M Prescott rnr.
3175 **FORGE LANE** 6 [11] G L Moore 3-9-6 P (55) S Whitworth 7/1: 0000042: Held up, imprvd 2f out, styd   7 **56**
on into 2nd fnl 1f, no ch with wnr: tried cheek pieces: caught a prog rival, cld find similar.
3055 **WALTZING BEAU** 11 [2] B G Powell 3-8-12 (47) G Baker 20/1: 2000023: Chsd ldrs, onepcd fnl 1.5f: ½ **47**
clr of rem: acts on gd, fast grnd & fibresand: see 3055.
2433 **PRINCE VALENTINE** 35 [5] D B Feek 3-9-6 (55) J P Guillambert(3) 50/1: 0035404: Rear, some late gains.   5 **47**
3025 **BRETTON** 12 [12]3-8-8 (43) T P Queally 33/1: 4443025: Nvr nrr than mid-div: btr 3025 (AW).   hd **34**
2924 **ANISETTE** 2 [7]3-8-10 (45) P Doe 66/1: 6064006: Led till dist, wknd: qck reapp.   5 **28**
3175 **RUSSALKA** 6 [3]3-9-4 (53) M Halford(7) 16/1: 0050267: Nvr btr than mid-div: btr 2837.   shd **36**
77 **ALLODARLIN** 240 [6]3-9-4 (53) N De Souza(5) 40/1: 50060-8: b f Cape Cross - Sharp Circle (Sure   1½ **34**
Blade) Chsd ldrs 1m, sn btn on reapp: lightly rcd in '03, mdn 5th on debut (rtd 65): half-sister to a 7f juv wnr.
3055+ **OKTIS MORILIOUS** 11 [9]3-9-6 (55) L Treadwell(7) 15/2: 4262519: Chsd ldrs 1m, wknd: btr 3055.   ¾ **34**
3175 **DON ARGENTO** 6 [10]3-8-5 (40) D Kinsella 20/1: 0-000U30: 10th: Slowly away, nvr a factor, fin lame.   2 **16**

BRIGHTON MONDAY 19.07.04 Lefthand, V Sharp, Undulating Track

2741 **ERTE 23** [8]3-9-2 (51) T E Durcan 9/1: 6-066320: 11th: Held up, al bhd: btr 2741 (12f, AW).		5	19
2739 **KERRISTINA 23** [4]3-8-0 (5oh)vis (30) J Quinn 25/1: 00000: 12th: b f So Factual - Arch Angel		23	0

(Archway) Trkd ldrs till halfway, wknd & eased, t.o.: stiff task, wears a visor: only modest form.
12 Ran   Time 2m 01.63 (3.83)   Owned: Mr G D Waters   Trained: Newmarket

---

3301   5.00 Gourmet Express Maiden Hcap To Be Ridden By NH Jockeys 3yo+ 35-55 (F)   [25]
£2975 £850 £425   **5f213y rnd**   **Good/Firm 37**   **-18 Slow**   Inside

3176 **MY GIRL PEARL 6** [8] M S Saunders 4-11-6 (45) S Durack 9/2 FAV: 2420641: Chsd ldrs, went on dist,		50
held on well cl-home, drvn out: op 7/2, qck reapp: deserved first win, eff at 6/7f on gd, firm grnd & fibresand.		
2720 **MR UPPITY 24** [6] Julian Poulton 5-10-13 e (38) A Procter 6/1: 4536542: Held up, imprvd 2f out,	nk	42
fin strongly & only just btn: op 8/1: again suggested a rtn to 7f will suit: may not be an easy ride, see 1837.		
3215 **DEXILEOS 4** [2] A D W Pinder 5-11-1 t (40) J Mogford 9/1: 0000003: Mid-div, hdwy & ev ch fnl 1f,	¾	42
no extra cl-home: tchd 12/1, qck reapp & only btn arnd 1L: mdn after 21: see 1273.		
2803 **CONFUZED 21** [5] D Flood 4-11-4 BL (43) D R Dennis 16/1: 3600004: Held up, gd hdwy to chall dist,	2	39
no extra fnl 1f: tried blnks: see 737.		
2715 **JASMINE PEARL 24** [4]3-11-4 (48) L Aspell 11/2: 6004025: Rear, imprvd 2f out, btn fnl 1f: btr 2715.	1¼	40
3187 **COSTA DEL SOL 5** [3]3-10-10 bl (40) B Hitchcott 33/1: 0004006: Nvr nr ldrs: qck reapp.	1½	28
3050 **BAHAMIAN BELLE 11** [10]4-11-1 (40) J A McCarthy 12/1: 0000057: Held up, nvr a factor.	½	26
3091 **CHATSHOW 10** [12]3-11-11 (55) P Flynn 8/1: 6-004058: Prom 4f, grad wknd: btr 3091 (AW).	½	39
2372 **BOLD WOLF 38** [7]3-11-3 P (47) J M Maguire 14/1: 0-444009: Led till 2f out, wknd: cheek pieces.	1¼	27
2645 **SAVERNAKE BRAVE 27** [11]3-10-13 (43) R Greene 8/1: 0-520400: 10th: Slow away, bhd: btr 2435.	½	21
2834 **BLAISE WOOD 20** [9]3-11-8 p (52) P Hide 7/1: 6-06020: 11th: Al rear: btr 2834 (1m).	nk	29
2645 **MOONGLADE 27** [1]4-10-6 bl (31) M Batchelor 20/1: 0005060: 12th: Mid-div, btn 2f out.	7	0

12 Ran   Time 1m 11.12(3.32)   Owned: Mr T A Godbert   Trained: Wells

---

AYR   MONDAY 19.07.04   Lefthand, Galloping Track

Official Going Good/Firm

3302   2.15 Fergie's 50th European Breeders Fund Maiden Stakes 2yo (D)
£5525 £1700 £850   **7f50y rnd**   **Good/Firm 24**   **-68 Slow**   Inside

3078 **BALLYCROY GIRL 10** [1] A Bailey 2-8-9 E Ahern 20/1: 6251: Chsd ldrs, led over 1f out, rdn & styd		78
on strongly: eff at 7f, will get 1m: acts on fast & gd/soft grnd, gall trk: see 2570 & 1893.		
2408 **VENETIAN KING 37** [5] J Howard Johnson 2-9-0 R Winston 11/4: 52: b g King of Kings - Vena	2	78
(Danehill) Keen trkg ldrs, smooth prog & led over 1f out, sn hdd, kept on, not pace of wnr: bckd: Feb foal, cost		
8,000 gns: dam 9f wnr: eff at 7f, will get further: acts on fast grnd: win a race.		
2902 **SHUJUNE AL HAWAA 17** [3] M R Channon 2-8-9 A Culhane 7/1: 563: Held up in tch, rdn over 2f out,	1¾	70
styd on, not pace to chall: styd longer 7f trip, already needs 1m on this evidence: acts on fast grnd: see 1816.		
HIGHEST RETURN 0 [6] M Johnston 2-9-0 J Fanning 11/4: 4: b c Theatrical - Hasene (Akarad) Trkd	nk	74
ldrs, briefly led 2f out, no impress from dist: Feb foal, dam a 5f 3yo scorer, subs a 1m/10f wnr: eff over 7f, shld		
get 1m+: acts on fast grnd & a gall trk.		
2792 **TOM FOREST 21** [7]2-9-0 D Holland 2/1 FAV: 6225: Led 3f, wknd 2f out: bckd, lngr trip.	1¾	71
3148 **GEOJIMALI 7** [4]2-9-0 N Mackay(3) 66/1: 66: Held up, no impress fnl 2f: see 3148.	5	61
2845 **KING HENRIK 19** [2]2-9-0 K Darley 33/1: 467: Keen & dsptd lead, went on after 3f till 2f out, sn wknd.	4	53

7 Ran   Time 1m 33.49 (6.69)   Owned: Mr R T Collins   Trained: Tarporley

---

3303   2.45 Kwik Keg 0800 3280508 Nursery Handicap Stakes 2yo (C)   [92]
£8060 £2480 £1240   **6f str**   **Good/Firm 24**   **-21 Slow**   Stands Side

3081 **THE CROOKED RING 10** [6] P D Evans 2-8-8 (77) R Winston 8/1: 2321341: Chsd ldrs, led over 1f out,		86
rdn out: eff at 5/6f on firm & soft grnd, prob any trk: eff with/without visor: tough, prog profile, see 2859 & 2573.		
2744 **DOCTOR HILARY 23** [4] M L W Bell 2-9-7 (90) K Fallon 7/2 JT FAV: 41232: Trkd ldrs travelling	1	95
well, rdn to chase wnr ins last, always held: useful: see 2744, 2071 & 1893.		
3103* **GENEROUS OPTION 9** [1] M Johnston 2-9-3 (86) J Fanning 4/1: 513: Gd speed & sn led, hdd over 1f	¾	89
out, onepace: clr rem & had a tricky task trying to dominate from low draw, creditable eff: acts on fast & gd.		
3202 **MONASH LAD 4** [7] M H Tompkins 2-8-10 (79) P Robinson 7/2: 05334: Chsd ldrs, outpaced fnl 2f.	3	73
3082* **NOVA TOR 10** [5]2-8-12 (81) E Ahern 10/1: 110415: Trkd ldrs, short of room over 2f out till dist,	2	69
sn no impress: btr 3082 (5f, well drawn).		
2472 **BOLD MARC 34** [3]2-9-7 (90) Darren Williams 10/1: 412106: Chsd ldrs, btn dist: btr 2100 (5f).	2	72
3130* **SPEED DIAL HARRY 9** [2]2-9-2 vis (85) K Dalgleish 16/1: 2313217: Cl-up, wknd 2f out: btr 3130 (5f).	5	52
2927* **RANCHO CUCAMONGA 16** [8]2-8-5 (74) K Darley 7/2 JT FAV: 0018: Held up, rdn/hmpd halfway & no	6	23
impress fnl 2f: bckd: much btr 2927 (mdn).		

8 Ran   Time 1m 11.97 (2.67)   Owned: Mr J R Salter   Trained: Abergavenny

---

3304   3.15 Listed Land O'burns Stakes Fillies 3yo+ (A)
£17400 £6600 £3300   **5f str**   **Good/Firm 24**   **+06 Fast**   Stands Side

3062 **AIRWAVE 11** [2] H Candy 4-8-13 (110) D Holland 4/6 FAV: 360-6601: Sn handy & led over 1f out rdly		107+
asserted, val 2L+: hvly bckd: eff at 5/6f on fm & fast, handles soft, likes a gall trk: high-class sprinter at best,		
relished drop in class & a gd confidence boost with more positive tactics: can rate higher in Gr company: see 1667.		
2357 **FOREVER PHOENIX 38** [6] R M H Cowell 4-8-13 (92) E Ahern 16/1: 1312R02: Held up, eff to chase wnr	1¼	97
ins last, kept on, al held: right back to useful best: see 1615.		
3150 **PROUD BOAST 7** [3] D Nicholls 6-8-13 (89) K Darley 16/1: 0100023: Chsd ldrs, kept on onepace:	1¼	95
confirmed improvement of 3150.		
3100 **DRAGON FLYER 9** [11] M Quinn 5-8-13 (98) R Winston 20/1: 2000034: Trkd ldr, onepace for press.	nk	94

999

2878 **DAME DE NOCHE 18** [8]4-8-13 (82) A Culhane 50/1: 6030005: Trkd ldrs, bumped 2f out, onepace over   hd   **93$**
1f out: gd run at 5f, wng form btwn 6f/1m: well h'capped & interesting with a high draw at Glorious Goodwood (won
over 7f in '03): see 1115.
2593 **AUTUMN PEARL 30** [5]3-8-9 (98) P Robinson 9/2: 151-1236: Led till over 1f out: btr 2206 & 1513.   shd   **93**
2240 **NEEDLES AND PINS 44** [10]3-8-9 (92) K Fallon 12/1: 125-4057: Held up in tch, no room over 2f out,   hd   **92**
kept on late, closer with a clr passage: 6 wk abs: see 1175.
3100 **CURFEW 9** [4]5-8-13 (92) W Supple 16/1: 4/505-458: Dwelt & held up, repeatedly no room from   1   **89+**
halfway & no prog: luckless passage, best forgiven: see 1400.
2913 **BALI ROYAL 16** [9]6-8-13 (98) J Fanning 20/1: 24-64009: Chsd ldrs, no impress over 1f out: see 2068.   1   **86**
4649} **BLUE CRUSH 42** [1]3-8-9 Darren Williams 100/1: 112-0000: 10th: ch f Entrepreneur - Prosaic Star   5   **72**
(Common Grounds) Cl-up, btn when hmpd dist: ex-Irish, 6 wk abs: unplcd in Listed/Gr3 company prev this term: '03
cond stks & h'cap wnr: both wins at 5f on gd grnd at Tipperary. 2 Oct'03 Tipp 5g/f 91- :
10 Ran   Time 57.49 (0.89)   Owned: Henry Candy & Partners   Trained: Wantage

---

3305	**3.45 Giles Insurance Stakes Handicap 3yo+ 0-95 (C)**				**[90]**
	£9510 £2926 £1463 **1m rnd** **Good/Firm 24** **-17 Slow** Inside				

2672 **TOP DIRHAM 26** [3] M W Easterby 6-8-8 (70) K Fallon 3/1 FAV: 0-232001: Chsd ldrs, qcknd & led   **77**
dist, al holding rivals under hand riding ins last: nicely bckd: eff at 6/7f, on firm & hvy grnd, loves a
stiff/gall trk: back on a handy mark & interesting with similar top jock aboard: see 1036.
3118 **VICIOUS WARRIOR 9** [6] R M Whitaker 5-9-10 (86) Dean McKeown 5/1: 0-205302: Handy & led 2f out   hd   **91**
till dist, late rally, al just held: bckd, op 13/2: true run: see 1475.
2860 **PENRITH 19** [2] M Johnston 3-9-4 (88) J Fanning 10/1: 1-1303: Held up, short of room over 1f out,   ¾   **92**
kept on ins last: op 7/1: imprvd eff with waiting tactics: clr rem, keep in mind over further: see 2040.
3107 **CHERISHED NUMBER 9** [7] I Semple 5-8-12 vis (74) D Holland 9/2: 0633044: Held up, eff over 2f out,   4   **70**
sn no impress: op 11/2: likes Ayr: see 2317.
3152 **STOIC LEADER 7** [4]4-9-7 (83) R Winston 8/1: 2426525: Held up, short of room over 2f out, rdn &   hd   **78**
no impress from dist: btr 3152.
2606 **SEA STORM 29** [9]6-9-5 (81) T Hamilton(3) 20/1: 0301006: Led/dsptd lead 6f, wknd.   shd   **76**
2787 **COUNTYKAT 22** [5]4-8-10 vis (72) Darren Williams 10/1: 0021207: Chsd ldrs, no impress fnl 2f: btr 2672.   2½   **62**
2568 **BALLYHURRY 30** [1]7-8-7 (69) N Mackay(3) 8/1: 54-06468: Held up, btn over 1f out: btr 2086 (7f).   shd   **59**
2684 **SARRAAF 25** [8]8-8-7 (69) W Supple 14/1: 0533359: Led till over 2f out, sn btn: prob best held up.   nk   **58**
9 Ran   Time 1m 39.85 (3.25)   Owned: Mr Steve Hull   Trained: Sheriff Hutton

---

3306	**4.15 Gr2 Daily Record Scottish Derby 3yo+ (A)**				
	£58000 £22000 £11000 **1m2f** **Good/Firm 24** **+19 Fast** Inside				

2916 **KALAMAN 16** [4] Sir Michael Stoute 4-9-2 (116) K Fallon 5/6 FAV: 202-2131: Chsd ldr, shaken up &   **119**
hdwy to lead over 1f out, edged left al prob holding rival ins last: hvly bckd: fast time: eff at 1m/10f on firm or
gd grnd: v smart colt, sn proved to give a gd account: see 2916, 2022.
3124 **GATEMAN 9** [6] M Johnston 7-9-2 (113) K Dalgleish 8/1: 1203122: Led & sn clr, rdn & hdd over 1f   1   **117**
out, sn short of room, rallied, prob al just held: smart, tough & often rallies most gamely when hdd, shld find
another Gr race: see 3124 & 2757.
2916 **IKHTYAR 16** [5] J H M Gosden 4-9-2 VIS (106) R Hills 7/2: 0-362363: Trkd ldrs, eff 2f out, not   1¼   **115**
able to chall: fair run in first time visor: wants List/Gr 3: see 2488, 2128.
3166 **CHECKIT 8** [2] M R Channon 4-9-2 (112) A Culhane 16/1: 0034034: Held up, styd on for press late,   nk   **114**
no threat: clr rem: prob stays 10f, drop to Listed/Gr3 company will suit: see 1349.
2488 **SCOTTS VIEW 33** [7]5-9-2 (115) S Chin 9/2: 3133055: Held up, eff over 2f out, no prog: op 5/1.   7   **104**
2917 **KELUCIA 16** [8]3-8-3 (97) W Supple 100/1: 4-505666: Held up, rdn & btn 2f out: see 2555.   2½   **97**
3043* **FRUHLINGSSTURM 11** [1]4-9-5 (112) P Robinson 11/1: 5151-517: Chsd ldrs, btn 2f out: btr 3043 (soft).   ¾   **102**
7 Ran   Time 2m 04.90 (0.5)   Owned: HH Aga Khan   Trained: Newmarket

---

3307	**4.45 Giles Insurance Rated Stakes Handicap 3yo+ 0-80 (D)**				**[84]**
	£7038 £2166 £1083 **6f str** **Good/Firm 24** **+14 Fast** Stands Side				

2753 **MACHINIST 23** [6] D Nicholls 4-9-5 (75) Alex Greaves 7/1: 040-0001: Trkd ldrs, led ins last & rdn   **90+**
clr, decisively in a gd time: eff at 6/7f, tried further: acts on fast, gd & polytrack, sharp or gall trk: more to follow.
3143 **FOLEY MILLENNIUM 8** [7] M Quinn 6-8-10 (66) R Winston 10/1: 0111102: Led till ins last, sn outpcd   3   **70**
by ready wnr: op 8/1: stays 6f, prob best at 5f: tough & remains on the upgrade: see 2951 (5f).
2884 **HIGHLAND WARRIOR 18** [2] J S Goldie 5-9-2 (72) W Supple 9/2 JT FAV: 6004663: Dwelt, rear, short   ½   **74**
of room over 2f out, styd on onepace ins last: continues to hamper chances with slow starts: see 2884, 2542 & 1898.
3129 **SHAROURA 9** [1] R A Fahey 4-8-8 (64) T Hamilton(3) 6/1: 5-501034: Trkd ldrs, short of room   ¾   **64**
halfway, onepace for press dist: bckd tho' op 9/2: see 3129 & 2791.
3017 **SIR DON 12** [3]5-8-10 vis (66) A Nicholls 8/1: 0001035: Handy, outpcd fnl 2f, op 12/1: see 2477.   2   **60**
3017 **COLLEGE MAID 12** [4]7-8-7 (2oh) (61) J Currie(7) 20/1: 2413566: Held up in tch, no impress dist, op 14/1. shd   **57**
3033 **PRINCE DAYJUR 12** [5]5-9-7 vis (77) K Fallon 9/2 JT FAV: 000-0107: Cl-up, btn over 1f out: btr 2861.   2   **65**
3248 **SEAFIELD TOWERS 3** [9]4-9-3 p (73) D Holland 5/1: 3000008: Dwelt, keen rear, hmpd halfway, sn btn.   nk   **60**
2950 **UNDER MY SPELL 16** [1]3-9-1 (76) J Fortune 9/1: 0225109: Chsd ldrs, btn over 1f out: btr 2398.   5   **48**
9 Ran   Time 1m 09.88(0.58)   Owned: Mr M J Pipe   Trained: Thirsk

BEVERLEY MONDAY 19.07.04 Righthand, Oval Track With Stiff Uphill Finish

Official Going GOOD/SOFT (GOOD places).

3308 **6.35 Old Gravel Pits Allerthorpe Claiming Stakes 2yo (F)**
£3297 £942 £471 **5f str** **Good 46** **-29 Slow** Inside

3178 **BAYMIST 6** [6] M W Easterby 2-8-11 T Lucas 9/2: 561: Cl-up, styd on to lead halfway, rdn out: bckd from 8/1: eff at 5f on gd grnd: acts on a stiff trk: apprec drop to claim grade: see 2983. **69**
2461 **PROCRASTINATE 34** [8] R F Fisher 2-8-6 R Ffrench 9/2: 0653052: Handy, kept on ins fnl 1f, not pace wnr: op 7/2: eff at 5f on gd grnd: see 2177 & 1037. *1½* **58**
3178 **ROKO 6** [5] M W Easterby 2-8-11 BL P Mulrennan(5) 17/2: 00043: In tch, styd on ins fnl 1f, just held for 2nd: qck reapp & first time blnks: eff at 5f, further shld suit: acts on gd grnd: eff with blnks. *hd* **62**
2321* **VON WESSEX 40** [9] W G M Turner 2-8-13 C Haddon(7) 6/4 FAV: 5163314: Led, hdd halfway, no extra dist: well bckd after 6 wk abs: disapp conceding weight all round: showed more in 2321 (C/D). *2* **58**
1869 **FOLD WALK 60** [4]2-8-2 P Fessey 40/1: 04U05: Slow away, nvr nrr than mid-div: 9 wk abs: see 1303. *1¼* **43**
2882 **HOPELESSLY DEVOTED 18** [7]2-8-10 G Faulkner 8/1: 06: b f Compton Place - Alpi Dora (Valiyar) Handy till halfway, sn hung left & no extra: Apr foal, cost 4,800gns: half-sister to a 6f wnr: dam successful abroad: sire decent performer at sprint dists: with P C Haslam. *1* **48**
2882 **MAGIC GENIE 18** [3]2-8-8 Dale Gibson 13/2: 507: Handy 3f, wknd: btr 2358. *3½* **36**
7 Ran Time 1m 5.06 (3.76) Owned: Mrs M E Curtis Trained: Sheriff Hutton

3309 **7.05 I J Blakey Haulage Handicap Stakes 3yo 0-75 (E)** **[80]**
£4992 £1536 £768 **1m1f207y** **Good 46** **-07 Slow** Inside

3179 **FUTOO 6** [7] G M Moore 3-8-9 (2ow) (61) F Lynch 7/1: 6-651301: Led, clr 2f out, rdn out to hold on cl-home: qck reapp: eff at 6f/1m, imprvd for step up to 10f: acts on fast & gd/soft grnd: apprec rtn to forcing tactics & is unexposed around this trip: see 2506 & 2243. **70**
1953 **PAY ATTENTION 56** [13] T D Easterby 3-8-3 (57) D Allan 13/2: 00-40202: In tch, outpcd when short of room 3f out, switched & kept on ins fnl 1f, post came too sn: 8 wk abs: apprec rtn to 10f: can find similar. *½* **64**
3182 **JOEY PERHAPS 6** [6] J R Best 3-7-12 (2oh) (50) R Thomas(2) 16/1: 50-00063: Chsd ldrs, styd on fnl 1f, no ch with front 2: qck reapp: eff at 6f, now stays 10f: acts on fast & gd: encouraging eff, see 2664. *1¼* **57**
2998 **MAGIC AMIGO 13** [1] J R Jenkins 3-9-7 (75) K Darley 9/1: 2102304: Handy over 1m, sn no extra. *2½* **76**
3179 **SUPER KING 6** [11]3-8-5 (59) Dean McKeown 12/1: 02-00005: Dwelt, rcd wide, prog fnl 2f, nrst fin. *1* **58**
3138 **ORION EXPRESS 8** [8]3-8-8 (62) P Mulrennan(5) 6/1 FAV: 6004646: Rear, mod late gains: btr 3138. *nk* **60**
3091* **COME WHAT JULY 10** [9]3-8-1 bl (55) Lisa Jones(3) 9/1: 6603517: Bhd, prog 3f out, short of room dist, sn no impress: btr 3091 (1m, fibresand). *hd* **52**
2969 **MUNAAWESH 14** [2]3-8-2 bl (56) J Bramhill 7/1: 0000428: Bhd, rcd keenly, nvr nrr than mid-div. *hd* **52**
2936 **IMPULSIVE BID 16** [10]3-8-8 (62) M Fenton 22/1: 4-402059: Keen mid-div, nvr able to chall: btr 1678. *¾* **56**
2832 **CHISEL 20** [12]3-8-3 (57) R Ffrench 16/1: 00600: 10th: Mid-div, prog after halfway, wknd fnl 2f. *1¾* **48**
3108 **MISS ELOISE 9** [5]3-8-9 (63) A Mullen(7) 15/2: 6260100: 11th: Chsd ldrs 1m, wknd: btr 2893. *3½* **49**
2969 **River Line 14** [4]3-7-12 (5oh)(47) D Fentiman(7) 33/1:0 1984 **Farnborough 55** [3]3-8-1 (55) B Swarbrick(5) 14/1:0
13 Ran Time 2m 7.63 (5.33) Owned: Mr M K Roddis Trained: Middleham

3310 **7.35 Mkm Building Supplies Handicap Stakes 3yo+ 0-80 (D)** **[76]**
£6851 £2108 £1054 **7f100y rnd** **Good 46** **+05 Fast** Inside

3229 **ZANJEER 3** [2] N Wilson 4-9-4 (66) P Mulrennan(5) 5/1: 40-01631: Cl-up, styd on to lead 1f out, rdn out: qck reapp: eff at 7f/1m on gd & fast grnd: has been in gd form & this was deserved: see 3229 & 2552. **75**
3225 **YOUNG MR GRACE 4** [6] T D Easterby 4-10-0 (76) A Mullen(7) 5/1: 3425162: Mid-div, prog when short of room dist, switched & kept on ins fnl 1f, not btn far: qck reapp: gd eff on return to 7f: see 2935. *½* **84**
3179 **ST SAVARIN 6** [9] J R Best 3-9-3 (72) N Pollard 9/2 JT FAV: 5310033: Led, hdd 1f out, no extra when short of room ins fnl 1f: qck reapp: showed a little more in 3179. *¾* **78**
2986 **EDDIES JEWEL 14** [5] J S Wainwright 4-7-12 (11oh) (35) D Fentiman(7) 40/1: 0300-254: Rear, styd on fnl 1.5f, nrst fin: eff at 7f, rtn to 1m/10f will suit: gd eff from way out of h'cap: see 1991. *1* **50$**
2204 **CARLTON 45** [7]10-8-11 (59) R Thomas(5) 10/1: 5222005: Handy, short of room ins fnl 1f, sn onepcd. *nk* **62**
2935 **RISKA KING 16** [3]4-9-5 (67) G Parkin 11/2: 0004336: Keen in tch 5f, sn wknd & eased. *2* **66**
3242* **TIME TO REGRET 3** [1]4-8-8 (6ex) (56) T Eaves(3) 10/1: 5-624017: Handy over 5f, sn wknd: qck reapp: btr expected after recent win in 3242. *1½* **52**
1976 **PEARL PRIDE 55** [4]3-8-13 (68) R Ffrench 20/1: 6420-008: Al bhd: 8 wk abs: see 1663. *3* **58**
3042 **QUALITAIR WINGS 11** [8]5-9-10 BL (72) K Darley 9/2 JT FAV: 6-300029: Reluctant to start, rear, prog when short of room after 5f, sn btn: disapp run in first time blnks: showed more in 3042 & 1474. *¾* **60**
9 Ran Time 1m 33.86 (3.06) Owned: Mr Malcom Wilson Trained: York

3311 **8.05 European Breeders Fund Ubc Novice Stakes 2yo (D)**
£4953 £1524 £762 **7f100y rnd** **Good 46** **+08 Fast** Inside

2578 **WHERE WITH ALL 30** [4] Saeed bin Suroor 2-9-5 K McEvoy 5/2: 101: Handy, styd on to lead 1f out, sn pushed clr, val 8L+: eff at 6f, now suited by around 7.4f, acts on gd & gd/soft, disapp on firm: enjoyed today's drop in grade & rtn to easier surface: won with ease in a fast time, worth another try in List/Group grade. **106+**
BLUE PRINCE [7] R Charlton 2-8-8 D Sweeney 10/1: 2: ch c Dixieland Band - Tussle (Kris S) Chsd ldrs, prog to lead dist, sn hdd & no extra: debut, clr rem: Mar first foal, dam unplcd: sire successful abroad: eff at 7.4f, shld apprec further: acts on gd grnd: sure to improve for today's experience. *6* **80**
3053 **BLACKCOMB MOUNTAIN 11** [8] M F Harris 2-8-7 B Swarbrick(5) 50/1: 53: Keen in tch 5f, wknd. *3* **73**
3157* **COMIC STRIP 7** [2] Sir Mark Prescott 2-9-2 S Sanders 5/4 FAV: 14: Bhd, prog wide after 3f, no impress fnl 2f: qck reapp: btr expected on turf bow: showed more in 3157 (debut, 6f, fibresand). *3* **76**
2776* **DRY ICE 22** [6]2-9-2 Dane O'Neill 100/30: 515: Led, hdd dist, wknd: btr 2776 (firm). *¾* **74**
2774 **NOWADAY 23** [3]2-8-12 Dale Gibson 100/1: 06: b g Dashing Blade - Notre Dame (Acatenango) Al in rear: Mar first foal, cost £20,000: dam won numerous times abroad: sire Gr 1 wnr: with T P Tate. *2* **66**

2766 **DOCTORS CAVE 23** [1]2-8-12 K Darley 20/1: 0007: b c Night Shift - Periquitum (Dilum) In tch, ev   *shd* **65**
ch halfway, wknd fnl 2f: Apr foal, cost 25,000gns: dam unplcd: sire speedily bred: with C E Brittain.
    MOONFLEET [5]2-8-3 C Catlin 100/1: 8: Al in rear: debut: with M F Harris.   **25** **16**
8 Ran Time 1m 33.65 (2.85) Owned: Godolphin Trained: Newmarket

3312	8.35 Sailors Families Society Maiden Handicap Guaranteed Sweepstakes 3yo 35-55 (F)	[63]
	£3150 £900 £450 **2m35y** Good 46 -08 Slow Inside	

2905 **PRINCESS KIOTTO 17** [15] T D Easterby 3-9-6 (55) D Allan 11/2 FAV: 000-5231: Rear, prog 4f out,   **71**
rdn out to lead cl-home: eff at 12/14f, improvd for step up to 2m: acts on gd grnd & fibresand: thorough stayer
who is unexposed around this trip & can follow up: see 2905 & 1444.
2503 **STRANGELY BROWN 32** [7] S C Williams 3-9-6 (55) P Makin(5) 28/1: 0-003002: Mid-div, prog 5f out,   *nk* **69**
styd on to lead dist, hdd under press cl-home: well clr of rem: eff at 10f, imprvd for step up to 2m: acts on gd &
hvy grnd: fin well clr of rem & can find similar: see 1611.
2123 **SPRING BREEZE 48** [14] M Dods 3-9-6 p (55) S W Kelly 7/1: 030-6023: Rear, prog 5f out, no impress dist. *9* **60**
1021 **HABITUAL 108** [12] Sir Mark Prescott 3-9-1 (50) S Sanders 8/1: 00-004: b g Kahyasi - Kick The   *1¾* **53**
Habit (Habitat) Handy, styd on to lead 2f out, hdd dist, wknd: long abs: appeared not to stay on h'cap bow.
2664 **TELL THE TREES 26** [5]3-9-3 (52) F Lynch 14/1: 000-055: Held up, prog ins fnl 3f, no impress fnl 2f.   *4* **51**
3192 **SAVANNAH RIVER 5** [1]3-8-7 t (42) Dean McKeown 9/1: 0325436: In tch 14f, wknd: qck reapp: btr 3192. *1½* **40**
2123 **ROMEOS DAY 48** [17]3-9-1 (50) C Catlin 16/1: 0-024307: Nvr nrr than mid-div: 7 wk abs: btr 2014. *3* **45**
2893 **ADEES DANCER 17** [13]3-9-6 (55) M Stainton(7) 40/1: 4-0058: Handy, outpcd after 10f, rallied late. *1¼* **49**
1183 **MORNING HAWK 95** [6]3-8-7 (42) Derek Nolan(5) 10/1: 00-04569: Rear, modest late gains: long abs. *2½* **34**
2267 **INTRODUCTION 42** [11]3-8-6 (1ow) (40) M Fenton 14/1: 000-000: 10th: Nvr nrr than mid-div: 6 wk abs. *2½* **31**
2123 **NORTHERN SPIRIT 48** [3]3-8-13 p (48) N Callan 11/1: 50-06030: 11th: Cl-up, led 6f out-2f out, wknd. *½* **37**
2905 **BOLLIN ANNABEL 17** [4]3-9-1 (50) K McEvoy 14/1: 0-250400: 12th: Handy 12f, wknd: btr 2123. *3* **36**
2879 **Devito 18** [2]3-9-4 (53) V Slattery 25/1:0   3192 **Barton Flower 5** [19]3-8-12 (47) T Lucas 50/1:0
2905 **Dawn Air 17** [10]3-9-3 (52) G Parkin 33/1:0   1612 **Over The Years 73** [18]3-8-2 (37) Dale Gibson 14/1:0
2339 **Flying With Eagles 39** [9]3-8-7 (42) Dane O'Neill 11/1:0
2123 **Nafferton Heights 48** [20]3-8-11 (46) P Mulrennan(5) 20/1:0
1742 **Pattern Man 66** [16]3-9-1 (50) J Bramhill 66/1:P   3019 **Duncanbil 12** [8]3-8-10 (45) R Ffrench 33/1:P
20 Ran Time 3m 39.05 (8.75) Owned: Mr Roy Matthews Trained: Malton

3313	9.05 C D Bramall Beverley Ford Classified Stakes 3yo+ 0-70 (E)
	£3861 £1188 £594 **1m1f207y** Good 46 -26 Slow Inside

2507 **PRAIRIE WOLF 32** [6] M L W Bell 8-9-7 (74) M Fenton 6/1: 0-000051: Made all, went 2L clr 3f out,   **79**
rdn out to hold on ins fnl 1f: suited by 1m/10f on firm & gd, handles soft & fibresand: apprec gd tactical ride
from M Fenton & is on a fair mark, likes Goodwood: see 2507.
3225 **HILLS OF GOLD 4** [5] M W Easterby 5-9-4 (71) P Mulrennan(5) 7/4 FAV: 0-410322: Rear, prog to chase   *hd* **76**
ldr dist, ev ch ins fnl 1f, just held: qck reapp: eff at 7f/1m, now stays 10f: remains in gd form: see 3225.
1174 **MESSE DE MINUIT 95** [1] R Charlton 3-8-12 (75) D Sweeney 11/1: 31-03: In tch, prog ins fnl 2f,   *2½* **76**
onepcd fnl 1f: long abs: eff at 1m/10f on gd grnd & polytrack: only lightly rcd: see 102.
3044 **JACARANDA 11** [2] M A L M Kings 4-9-3 (68) Dane O'Neill 9/2: 4-050024: Rear, prog 4f out, onepcd dist. *shd* **70**
2973 **INTERNATIONALGUEST 14** [4]5-9-4 bl (71) S Sanders 4/1: 0200555: Cl-up over 1m, sn wknd: see 404. *3½* **66**
2794 **DERWENT 21** [3]5-9-3 bl (69) K McEvoy 13/2: 03-00046: Al in rear: btr 2794. *2½* **61**
6 Ran Time 2m 9.57(7.27) Owned: Mr B J Warren Trained: Newmarket

Official Going Good/Yielding

3314	7.30 Listed Silver Flash Stakes 2yo ()
	£21809 £6399 £3049 **6f rnd** Good/Yielding

    SILK AND SCARLET 35 [10] A P O'Brien 2-8-11 J P Spencer 7/2 FAV: 21: b f Sadler's Wells -   **106**
Danilova (Lyphard) Rear, hdwy to chall ins last, led ins last & won going away: 1st win, earlier rnr up on debut in
mdn company: half sister to a smart 6/7f French performer, dam placed once: eff at 6f, stays 7f well & a return to
that trip will suit: acts on gd/sft ground, galt trk: useful filly, likes to progress over 7f+.
    ALEXANDER ICEQUEEN 46 [8] D K Weld 2-8-11 P J Smullen 6/1: 12: b f Soviet Star - Regal   *1½* **100**
Revolution (Hamas) Mid-div, hdwy to lead ins last, hdd well ins last & not pace of wnr: 6 wk abs: earlier landed a
Limerick 7f mdn: eff at 7f on firm & gd/sft ground: clr of rem here & this useful filly should win similar soon.
    LA MAITRESSE 9 [6] M Halford 2-8-11 T P O'Shea 10/1: 52013: Rear, kept on late, nrst fin.   *4½* **86**
12 Ran Time 1m 15.70 () Owned: Mrs John Magnier Trained: Ballydoyle

3315	9.00 Listed Challenge Stakes 3yo+ ()
	£21809 £6399 £3049 **1m6f** Good/Yielding

2771 **BAROLO 18** [3] P W Harris 5-9-9 (107) J P Murtagh 4/1: 114-0101: Led, rdn & styd on strongly fnl   **108**
2f: best at 14f this term: acts on fm or gd, stiff or sharp trks: enjoyed forcing tactics tonight, smart & remains
one to keep on side: see 1861.
2557 **TWO MILES WEST 26** [4] J P Spencer 3-8-8 J P Spencer 5/4 FAV: 122: Chsd ldrs, efft to chse wnr   *1½* **106**
fnl 2f, kept on, al held: op 6/4: eff at 14f/2m on fast & gd/sft grnd: see 2557 (Gr3).
    VALENTINA GUEST 21 [7] P Casey 3-8-5 Catherine Gannon 9/1: 20-21513: b f Be My Guest -   *1* **102**
Karamiyna (Shernazar) Held up, hdwy over 2f out, hmpd over 1f out, kept on, not able to chall: dual h'cap wnr prev

LEOPARDSTOWN WEDNESDAY 14.07.04 Lefthand, Galloping Track

this term: mdn scorer '03: both wins this term at 10f, styd this longer 14f trip well: acts on fast & gd/sft ground.
9 Ran   Time 3m 03.70()   Owned: Mrs P W Harris   Trained: Ringshall

MAISONS LAFFITTE WEDNESDAY 14.07.04 Left & Righthand, Sharpish Track

Official Going Soft

3316 **2.20 Gr 2 Prix Eugene Adam 3yo** ()
£42148 £16268 £7764   **1m2f**   **Soft**

2308 **VALIXIR 38** [3] A Fabre 3-8-11 E Legrix 6/10 FAV: 112-1331: b c Tremolino - Vadlamixa (Linamix)   **121+**
Made all & dictated pace, readily asserted from over 1f out: Gr 1 French Derby plcd last month: well suited by 10/12f
on gd & soft ground, enjoyed forcing tactics today: v smart, see 2308, 1853.
2 Sep'03 Long 8gd 99- A:
1696* **DELFOS 70** [4] C Laffon Parias 3-8-11 M Blancpain 54/10: 211102: Chsd ldr, kept on fnl 2f, not   3   **116**
pace of wnr: well bhd today's wnr in French Derby last month: see 1696 (Gr 3).
2254 **HAZYVIEW 39** [2] N A Callaghan 3-8-11 I Mendizabal 8/1: 21112103: Trkd ldr, outpcd over 2f   ½   **115**
out, kept on for press ins last: acts on fast & soft ground: tough & smart: see 1931 (Listed).
2916 **AFRICAN DREAM 11** [5] P W Chapple Hyam 3-8-11 (113) O Doleuze 59/10: 31111104: Held up, efft over 2½   **111**
2f out, no impress bef dist: see 1595 (Gr 3).
6 Ran   Time 2m 07.90 ()   Owned: Lagardere Family   Trained: France

MAISONS LAFFITTE SATURDAY 17.07.04 Left & Righthand, Sharpish Track

Official Going Good

3317 **3.20 Gr 2 Prix Maurice de Nieuil 4yo+** ()
£44736 £16268 £7764   **1m7f**   **Good**

2000* **FORESTIER 55** [1] E Danel 4-9-2 C P Lemaire 16/10 FAV: 151-1211: Made all, rdn & styd on well   **118**
fnl 2f: best arnd 14f/2m on gd & soft grnd: goes well fresh: v smart & improving stayer: see 2000.
5004*}**ROYAL FANTASY 258** [4] H Steinmetz 4-8-13 W Mongil 11/2: -1111282: ch f Monsun - Rudolfina   2   **111**
(Pleasant Colony) Unruly start, chsd wnr, kept on for press: Gr 2 German St Leger wnr in '03, also landed a Gr 3
contest: suited by 11/15f on gd & soft ground: smart stayer.
1 Nov'03 Fran 10.8sft 106- : 1 Nov'03 Fran 106- :
2000 **CLEAR THINKING** [5] A Fabre 4-8-12 C Soumillon 22/10: 3-153333: Prom, outpcd 2f out, late rally.   shd   **110**
2095 **RISK SEEKER 47** [3] E Lellouche 4-9-2 O Peslier 17/10: 120-2144: Rear, not able to chall fnl 2f: 1½   **112**
7 wk abs: v smart eff came on soft in 1418.
4 Ran   Time 3m 26.60()   Owned: Mme R J Wattinne   Trained: France

CURRAGH SATURDAY 17.07.04 Righthand, Galloping Track

Official Going Good

3318 **4.00 Gr 3 International Stakes 3yo** ()
£32445 £9598 £4572   **1m rnd**   **Good**

3011 **RED FEATHER 14** [7] E Lynam 3-8-11 t N G McCullagh 8/1: 320-2131: b f Marju - Galyph (Lyphard)   **108**
Led & dictated pace, rdn clr over 1f out, styd on strongly: earlier this term landed a cond stks event at Limerick:
Limerick mdn wnr '03: loves to take the pace at 7f/1m on firm & gd grnd: smart, well rdn.
2 Aug'03 Curr 7g/f 107- A:
TREFFLICH 21 [5] J M Oxx 3-9-0 M J Kinane 7/1: 12: Trkd ldr, onepace fnl 2f: stays 1m.   2½   **105**
1063 **WATHAB 104** [3] D K Weld 3-9-0 t P J Smullen 6/1: 26412-43: Chsd ldrs, rdn & onepace fnl 2f.   2   **101**
2918 **JAZZ SCENE 14** [4] M R Channon 3-9-0 (92) K J Manning 10/1: 02-00224: Trkd ldrs, rdn & no impress   1   **99**
over 1f out, op 8/1: longer trip: see 2918, 2749 (7f, h'caps).
1480 **ONE COOL CAT 77** [2]3-9-7 J P Spencer 1/2 FAV: 41111-05: Rear, eff over 2f out, rdn & no prog   ¾   **105**
bef dist: 10 wk abs: yet to replicate last year's top class juvenile efforts & may be retired.
7 Ran   Time 1m 41.00 ()   Owned: Lady O'Reilly   Trained: Dunshaughlin

CURRAGH SUNDAY 18.07.04 Righthand, Galloping Track

Official Going Good

3319 **2.40 Gr 3 Dubai Duty Free Anglesey Stakes 2yo** ()
£32712 £9597 £4572   **6f63y str**   **Good**

2467 **ORATORIO 33** [4] A P O'Brien 2-9-0 J A Heffernan 9/1: 101: Al handy & led 2f out, rdn clr over   **112**
1f out: well suited by 6/6.3f on fast & gd grnd, likes a gall trk: v useful juvenile.
2516 **COUGAR CAT 31** [3] A P O'Brien 2-9-0 J P Spencer 9/2: 142: Rear, hdwy over 1f out, kept on, no   1   **108**
threat: op 3/1: stays 6f, acts on fast & gd: shld win a List/Gr race: see 1931 (Listed).
INDESATCHEL 23 [5] D Wachman 2-9-0 K Fallon 2/1 FAV: 413: b c Danehill Dancer - Floria   nk   **107**

(Petorius) Held up, hdwy to chse wnr dist, onepace: recent mdn wnr: eff at 6f, winning form at 7f, a return to that trip shld suit: acts on gd grnd & a gall trk: useful, see 1510.

2467 **TURNKEY 33** [8] M R Channon 2-9-0 T E Durcan 7/2: 2154: Trkd ldrs, onepace fnl 2f: see 2467.	1½	102
2516 **DANCE NIGHT 31** [1]2-9-0 L Dettori 14/1: 21167: Chsd ldrs till 2f out: btr 1567 (5f).	3½	91

8 Ran   Time 1m 15.70 ()   Owned: Mrs John Magnier   Trained: Ballydoyle

---

3320   **3.40 Gr 3 Emirates Airline Minstrel Stakes 4yo+** ()
£34840 £10184 £4824   **7f str**   **Good**

2765 **TRADE FAIR 22** [6] R Charlton 4-9-0 (120) R Hughes 13/8 FAV: 1615-031: Trkd ldrs, hdwy to lead dist, styd on strongly, readily: op 2/1: all wins at 7f on firm & gd grnd: back to smart best & has a gd turn of foot, keep in mind for further Gr success: see 1667.	116
3186} **ONE MORE ROUND 84** [3] D K Weld 6-9-0 (106) P J Smullen 10/1: 0-220062: b c Ghazi - Life of The Party (Pleasant Colony) Chsd ldrs, hdwy to chall dist, sn outpcd by wnr: 12 wk abs: dual Gr 3 & also a val h'cap rnr up in '03: '02 val h'cap wnr: suited by 7f/1m on fast & gd/sft ground, loves a stiff/gall trk. 2 Jul'03 Asco 7gd 110-106 B: 2 Jun'03 Leop 7g/s 111- A: 2 Apr'03 Curr 7gd 111- :	1½ 109
3098 **MILLENNIUM FORCE 8** [5] M R Channon 6-9-0 (107) T E Durcan 9/1: 0-004233: In tch, some late gains, no dngr: smart: see 3098 & 2826.	½ 108
2765 **NAAHY 22** [4] M R Channon 4-9-3 (106) M R Channon 8/1: 001-1104: Led til dist, no extra: see 2455.	1 109
2184 **TOUT SEUL 45** [9]4-9-0 (110) S Carson 10/1: 605-1006: Held up, no impress fnl 3f: abs: btr 1356 (List).	0

9 Ran   Time 1m 21.50 ()   Owned: K Abdulla   Trained: Beckhampton

---

3321   **4.15 Gr 1 Irish Oaks 3yo Fillies** ()
£158924 £51724 £24924   **12f**   **Good/Firm**

2210+**OUIJA BOARD 44** [4] E A L Dunlop 3-9-0 (110) K Fallon 4/7 FAV: 313-111: Dwelt & held up, hdwy & rdn to lead over 1f out, styd on strongly & in command when eased cl home, val 2L: well suited by 12f on fm & gd: goes well fresh: top class filly who remains unbeaten this term after completing English/Irish Oaks double.	114
2517+**PUNCTILIOUS 31** [6] Saeed bin Suroor 3-9-0 t (110) L Dettori 5/1: 113-1312: Chsd ldrs, hdwy to lead 2f out, sn hdd, kept on but not pace of wnr: smart & in fine form: win more Gr races.	1 110
1857* **HAZARISTA 65** [5] J M Oxx 3-9-0 M J Kinane 20/1: 0-4113: Held up, styd on for press fnl 2f, not pace of wnr but well clr of rem: 2 mth abs: styd longer 12f trip well: lightly rcd & prog & smart, win another Gr race.	¾ 109
2210 **ALL TOO BEAUTIFUL 44** [7] A P O'Brien 3-9-0 J P Spencer 4/1: 1124: Led/dsptd lead till wknd qckly 2f out: 6 wk abs: fin 2nd to this wnr in Epsom Oaks in 2210.	7 99
MARINNETTE 23 [1]3-9-0 J A Heffernan 200/1: 23-5045: ch f Be My Guest - Al Cairo (Vayrann) Held up, no impress fnl 3f: mdn.	4 93
2946 **DANELISSIMA 15** [3]3-9-0 b (102) K J Manning 16/1: -5441236: Handy & led after 4f, sn clr, hdd over 2f out & wknd qckly: btr 2946 & 2821 (Gr 2 & val h'cap).	4 87

7 Ran   Time 2m 28.20 ()   Owned: Lord Derby   Trained: Newmarket

---

3322   **4.50 Listed Kilboy Estate Stakes Fillies & Mares 3yo+** ()
£26170 £7679 £3658   **1m1f rnd**   **Good/Firm**

3011* **TROPICAL LADY 15** [12] J S Bolger 4-9-11 K J Manning 4/5 FAV: 06-11111: Held up, hdwy 2f out & led ins last, rdn clr & in command when went right close home: completed a 5-timer & remains unbeaten this term: eff btwn 7f/9f on fast & gd/sft grnd, loves a gall trk: v tough, progressive & smart, well placed by connections.	111
NOAHS ARK 46 [2] D K Weld 3-8-11 P J Smullen 8/1: 14-42522: b f Charnwood Forest - Abstraction (Rainbow Quest) Led/dsptd lead till ins last, not pace of wnr: 6 wk abs: h'cap rnr up last month: auct mdn & cond stks wnr '03: winning form at 7f/1m, stays 9f well: acts on firm & gd/sft ground.	1½ 102
2210 **KISSES FOR ME 44** [8] A P O'Brien 3-8-11 J P Spencer 9/1: 1-5003: Handy, efft when slightly hampered over 1f out, kept on, not pace to chall: 6 wk abs.	½ 101
3838} **CALDY DANCER 329** [1]3-8-11 (96) T E Durcan 10/1: 11005250: 11th: ch f Soviet Star - Smile Awhile (Woodman) Always rear: reapp: auct mdn & cond stks wnr for A Berry '03, subs Gr 3 rnr up for current yard: both wins at 5f, stays 7f well: acts on firm & fast ground. 2 Aug'03 Curr 7g/f 102- A: 1 May'03 Ches 5.1fm 87-0 B: 1 Apr'03 Hayd 5g/f 80-0 E:	0

11 Ran   Time 1m 50.40()   Owned: George J Kent   Trained: Coolcullen

---

Official Going GOOD/FIRM.

3323   **2.15 Sharp Minds Winners Welcome Median Auction Maiden Stakes 2yo** **(E)**
£3565 £1097 £549   **6f str**   **Good 51**   **-02 Slow**   **Stands side**

2965 **MADAME TOPFLIGHT 15** [5] Mrs G S Rees 2-8-9 N Mackay(3) 12/1: 021: Grabbed stands rail & made all, pushed out ins fnl 1f, val bit more: eff at 5f, apprec step up to 6f: acts on gd & gd/soft grnd: see 2965.		84+
2646 **MASTER COBBLER 28** [1] G A Butler 2-9-0 K Darley 13/8: 42: Keen in tch, styd on ins fnl 2f, al held by wnr: eff at 5f, apprec step up to 6f: acts on gd grnd: has shown enough to find similar: see 2646.	1½	83
3031 **LOVE ANGEL 13** [4] M Johnston 2-9-0 J Fanning 6/4 FAV: 43: Al prom, styd on ins fnl 1f, just held for 2nd: well bckd: eff at 6f, looks in need of 7f+: acts on gd grnd: rtd higher in 3031 (debut).	shd	82
2473 **JERRYS GIRL 34** [6] Miss L A Perratt 2-8-9 P Hanagan 16/1: 364: Chsd ldrs 4f, no extra: btr 1950.	5	62
BESPOKE [2]2-9-0 S Sanders 10/1: 5: ch g Pivotal - Immaculate (Mark of Esteem) Dwelt, al in rear: op 7/1 on debut: Feb foal: dam unrcd: sire decent performer at sprint dists: with Sir Mark Prescott.	6	49
QUICK GRAND [7]2-8-9 R Ffrench 66/1: 6: br f Raise A Grand - Rose 'n Reason (Reasonable) Al bhd: debut: Mar foal, cost £5,000: half-sister to a wnr at 6f: sire decent 7f performer at 2.	¾	42
COMPTON CLASSIC [3]2-9-0 W Supple 33/1: 7: b c Compton Place - Ayr Classic (Local Suitor) Handy 4f, fdd: debut: Mar foal, cost 16,000gns: half-brother to wnrs at 5/8f: dam wnr at 5/6f.	6	31

1004

7 Ran   Time 1m 12.52 (3.22)   Owned: Mr P Bamford   Trained: Preston

3324

2.45 Sharp Minds Betfair Selling Stakes 3yo+ **(F)**
£3439 £1058 £529   **7f50y rnd**   **Good 51**   **-23 Slow**   Inside

1897 **ZHITOMIR** 60 [2] M Dods 6-9-11 (49) S W Kelly 13/2: 000-1661: Cl-up, short of room dist, switched   **54**
& styd on to lead ins fnl 1f, rdn out: 9 wk abs, no bid: eff at 6/7f on firm & soft grnd: goes well fresh: apprec
return to sell grade: fine win conceding weight all round: see 996.
3087 **ZAHUNDA** 11 [8] W M Brisbourne 5-9-0 (37) K Fallon 11/1: 6336402: Led, hdd under press ins fnl   ½   **41**
1f, kept on, just denied: op 8/1: eff at 7f/8.5f on gd grnd & fibresand: see 894 & 699.
3191 **WARES HOME** 6 [5] K R Burke 3-8-12 (55) Darren Williams 7/2 FAV: 0343323: Keen prom, ev ch when   1¼   **44**
hung left dist, sn no extra: well bckd on qck reapp: does not convince with attitude, see 3191 & 2852.
3162 **NAUGHTY GIRL** 8 [3] P D Evans 4-9-0 vis t (50) E Ahern 7/1: 0000544: Prom, ev ch dist, no extra.   1   **37**
2947 **MOUNT PEKAN** 17 [13]4-9-5 (41) W Supple 25/1: 0-030605: Held up, prog 2f out, hung left & onepcd.   nk   **41**
2999 **ZARIN** 14 [14]6-9-5 (54) A Culhane 8/1: 3-030006: Rear, prog ins fnl 2f, nrst fin: op 13/2: btr 195.   2½   **36**
2864 **ANGEL ISA** 19 [12]4-9-0 (44) P Hanagan 12/1: 060-0007: Nvr nrr than mid-div: see 2445.   1¼   **29**
1095 **SANDY BAY** 103 [10]5-9-5 (37) P Fessey 33/1: 400-008: b g Spectrum - Karinski (Palace Music)   ¾   **32**
Dwelt, mod late gains: long abs: unplcd in '03 (rtd 45, h'cap, R Allan, prev with M W Easterby): unplcd in '02
(rtd 69, mdn): has tried blnks: with A R Dicken.
2543 **FRANCIS FLUTE** 32 [7]6-9-5 (51) P Mulrennan(5) 4/1: 00-02409: Mid-div wide, no impress fnl 2f.   1   **30**
2811 **PHARAOH HATSHEPSUT** 22 [9]6-9-0 (32) R Ffrench 100/1: 0000060: 10th: Prom 5f, sn fdd: jumps fit.   1¾   **21**
3191 Bargain Hunt 6 [6]3-8-12 vis(44) J Bramhill 33/1:0   3102 Blades Edge 10 [4]3-8-12 bl(50) R L Moore 25/1:0
3129 Needwood Bucolic 10 [1]6-9-5 (37) T Eaves(3) 66/1:0   2967 Lions Domane 15 [11]7-9-5 (44) P Mathers(7) 25/1:0
14 Ran   Time 1m 32.16 (5.36)   Owned: Mr M J K Dods   Trained: Darlington

3325

3.15 Sharp Minds Betfair : Best Odds Handicap Stakes 3yo+ 0-70 (E)   **[70]**
£3692 £1136 £568   **1m2f**   **Good 51**   **+08 Fast**   Inside

3276 **LENNEL** 3 [5] A Bailey 6-9-8 bl (64) R L Moore 11/2: 0040641: Rear, prog to lead dist, rdn clr: **75**
qck reapp: suited by 10/11f on fast & gd/soft: enjoyed today's decent gallop & can follow up under a pen, see 3276.
2078 **JEEPSTAR** 52 [6] T D Easterby 4-10-0 (70) W Supple 7/2 FAV: 253-0062: Led, hdd dist, styd on, not   2   **74**
pace of wnr: 7 wk abs: fine eff in defeat under top-weight & is h'capped to find similar: see 2078.
3132 **APACHE POINT** 10 [7] N Tinkler 7-8-12 (54) Kim Tinkler 6/1: 0545523: Chsd ldrs, styd on ins fnl   ½   **57**
1f, just held for 2nd: eff at 1m/10f: see 3132 & 1776.
3260 **MEGANS MAGIC** 3 [10] W Storey 4-9-12 (68) J Bramhill 12/1: 1200364: Slow away, prog 5f out, short   hd   **70**
of room 2f out, switched & styd on fnl 1f: task not helped by bolting bef start: see 2483 & btr 1366.
3207 **SHERWOOD FOREST** 5 [11]4-8-2 vis (44) Leanne Kershaw(7) 50/1: 00-03605: Rear, prog 3f out, onepcd.   ¾   **44**
3151 **FOREST AIR** 8 [4]4-8-4 p (46) R Ffrench 11/1: 0100526: Handy, ev ch 2f out, no extra: btr 3151 (clmr).   3   **42**
3151 **MINSTREL HALL** 8 [1]5-8-8 (50) T Eaves(3) 20/1: 0310/-457: Rear, prog when no room 2f out, sn btn.   ½   **45**
3132* **WAHOO SAM** 10 [3]4-9-11 (67) P Makin(5) 8/1: 0-00318: Keen in tch, ev ch 3f out, hung right &   nk   **61**
wknd ins fnl 2f: disapp on hat-trick bid: btr 3132 & 2832 (9.2f).
2120 **WILSON BLUEBOTTLE** 49 [13]5-8-1 bl (43) Dale Gibson 25/1: 0220009: Cl-up wide 7f, wknd: 7 wk abs.   5   **30**
3149 **LUCKY LARGO** 8 [12]4-9-1 bl (57) P Mulrennan(5) 33/1: 0402600: 10th: Al bhd: btr 2571.   ¾   **42**
3099 **LUXOR** 10 [9]7-8-5 (47) D Fentiman(7) 33/1: 000-0000: 11th: Cl-up 6f, sn wknd: see 1884.   4   **26**
2813 **REPULSE BAY** 22 [2]6-8-7 (46) J Currie(7) 33/1: 0305000: 12th: Al in rear: first time blnks.   5   **21**
3149 **TEMPLET** 8 [8]4-9-9 bl (65) K Fallon 5/1: 4-234530: 13th: In tch, wknd 2f out, fdd: see 3149 (blnks).   9   **25**
13 Ran   Time 2m 08.77 (4.37)   Owned: Mr A Bailey   Trained: Tarporley

3326

3.45 Sharp Minds Betfair : Back And Lay Classified Stakes 3yo+ 0-80 (D)
£5343 £1644 £822   **7f50y rnd**   **Good 51**   **-15 Slow**   Inside

2558 **OBRIGADO** 32 [6] W J Haggas 4-9-3 (81) D Holland 11/2: 216-0201: Led after 2f till 2f out, sn   **84**
hung, styd on well to lead nr line despite flashing tail, drvn out: eff at 7f/1m, 10f shld suit: acts on firm & gd
grnd: did not look keen, but battled well in the end under a fine D Holland ride: see 2090.
2753 **WINNING VENTURE** 24 [4] A W Carroll 7-9-4 (82) R L Moore 3/1: 305-6032: Chsd ldrs, styd on to   nk   **84**
lead 2f out, sn went 2L clr, hung left ins fnl 1f, hdd nr line: remains in gd form: see 2753 & 1138.
2568 **FLUR NA H ALBA** 31 [3] I Semple 5-9-5 p (83) T Eaves(3) 11/1: 2000-103: Handy, outpcd 2f out,   1¾   **81**
rallied ins fnl 1f: clr rem: just btr 1909 (h'cap).
3205 **TELEPATHIC** 5 [8] A Berry 4-9-2 T (57) P Mathers(7) 150/1: 4605654: Chsd ldrs, hmpd halfway, wknd.   17   **43**
3001 **ATLANTIC QUEST** 14 [5]5-9-2 p (80) K Darley 8/1: 500150B: Slow away, sn mid-div, b.d. after 3f.   0
3068 **MANAAR** 11 [2]4-9-5 (83) E Ahern 1/1 FAV: 20-0502B: In tch when b.d. after 3f: well bckd: btr 3068.   0
2949 **ROSSELLI** 17 [1]8-9-2 (46) C Ely(7) 200/1: 000000F: Cl-up when fell after 3f, broke leg & sadly died.   0
7 Ran   Time 1m 31.42 (4.62)   Owned: Mr B Haggas   Trained: Newmarket

3327

4.15 Sharp Minds Phone 0870 90 80 121 Handicap Stakes 4yo+ 35-55 (F)   **[63]**
£3380 £1040 £520   **1m7f**   **Good 51**   **-18 Slow**   Inside

2705‡ **GONE TOO FAR** 379 [2] P Monteith 6-8-11 vis (46) K Darley 6/1: 00/4033-1: b g Reprimand - Blue   **55+**
Nile (Bluebird) Cl-up, led 9f out, pushed out fnl 1f, val 4L+: recent wnr over fences (h'cap, rtd 123c, eff arnd 2m
on firm & gd/soft grnd): plcd on 4 '03 starts (clmrs, rtd 46, M Dods): h'cap wnr in '02: suited by arnd 12f/2m on
fast & gd/soft grnd: eff with blnks or visor: has gone well fresh: remains on fair mark.
1 Apr'02 Nott 14g/s 57-51 E:
1875 **LIBERTY SEEKER** 61 [8] P D Niven 5-9-6 (55) P Hanagan 9/2 JT FAV: 0000-002: Cl-up, styd on to   2½   **61**
chase wnr fnl 2f, edged left ins fnl 1f, al held: well bckd, 9 wk abs: recent wnr of 2 nov chases (rtd 125c, eff at
2m1.5f on firm & gd): prev eff at 1m, now stays 15f: acts on gd, soft grnd & fibresand: see 1875.
3249 **COSMIC CASE** 4 [6] J S Goldie 9-8-10 (45) N Mackay 7/1: 0352303: Rear, prog 3f out, onepcd fnl 1f.   1   **50**
2963 **PRINCE OF THE WOOD** 16 [5] A Bailey 4-8-10 BL (45) D Holland 9/2 JT FAV: 2140504: Keen prom, hung   nk   **49**

left & no extra dist: first time blnks: btr 2060.
3049* **RIVER OF FIRE 12** [1]6-8-3 vis (38) Natalia Gemelova(7) 6/1: 0400015: Rear, nvr nrr than mid-div. *5* **37**
2937 **FLY KICKER 17** [3]7-8-0 (8oh)p (27) J Bramhill 20/1: 00/064-06: Bhd, modest late gains: see 2937. *½* **33**
3158 **IPLEDGEALLEGIANCE 8** [7]8-8-0 (5oh)bl (30) D Fentiman(7) 5/1: 5520327: Al rear: btr 3158 & 2964. *4* **29**
2966* **WOODWIND DOWN 15** [9]7-9-0 (49) P Mulrennan(5) 10/1: 250/20//-18: Cl-up over 12f, sn wknd: *1¾* **41**
appeared not to stay on first try at 15f: btr 2966 (12f).
3190 **MIKASA 6** [4]4-8-0 (5oh) (30) R Ffrench 50/1: 3005009: Led 6f, wknd fnl 3f: qck reapp. *8* **20**
9 Ran Time 3m 20.27 (10.47) Owned: Mr D A Johnson Trained: Rosewell

3328 **4.45 Sharp Minds Betfair : Bet In Running Handicap Stakes 3yo+ 0-80 (D)** **[74]**
£5512 £1696 £848 **1m rnd** **Good 51** **-07 Slow** Inside

2571 **HARRY POTTER 31** [5] K R Burke 5-9-9 vis (69) Darren Williams 20/1: 0106031: Al cl-up, styd on to **82+**
lead dist, sn clr, eased cl-home, val 10L+: eff at 7f/1m on gd & soft grnd: appreciated refitting of a visor:
could not have won much easier & can follow up: see 2571 & 1214.
2958* **PARISIAN PLAYBOY 16** [11] Jedd O'Keeffe 4-7-13 (45) Leanne Kershaw(7) 20/1: 3-000012: Rear, prog *6* **49**
4f out, styd on ins fnl 2f, not pace of wnr: acts on gd & soft grnd: see 2958.
3250* **ANTHEMION 4** [2] Mrs J C McGregor 7-8-10 (6ex) (56) D McGaffin 7/2 FAV: 0005313: Led, hdd dist, sn *hd* **59**
no extra: well bckd on qck reapp: not disgraced under pen: btr 3250 (9f).
3187 **PAS DE SURPRISE 6** [8] P D Evans 6-8-7 (53) E Ahern 8/1: 0054454: Rear, prog 3f out, onepcd dist. *nk* **55**
2568 **WESSEX 31** [6]4-9-12 (72) T Eaves(3) 33/1: 10-06005: Bhd, nvr nrr than mid-div: btr 1970. *2* **70**
3229* **WOOD DALLING 4** [3]6-8-12 (6ex) (58) P Mulrennan(5) 6/1: 05-00616: Cl-up 6f, no extra: qck reapp. *nk* **55**
3132 **MARKET AVENUE 10** [9]5-9-1 (61) P Hanagan 8/1: 006-6057: Nvr nrr than mid-div: see 1821. *hd* **57**
2504 **ARGENT 33** [4]3-7-12 (2oh)p (50) R Ffrench 66/1: 0-P02008: Cl-up over 6f, wknd: btr 1630. *nk* **47**
3142 **ADOBE 9** [12]9-9-6 (66) B Swarbrick(5) 10/1: 0034429: Al in rear: btr 3142. *½* **60**
2890 **ARAWAN 18** [7]4-8-11 BL (57) Dale Gibson 9/2: 0000000: 10th: Keen in mid-div, prog 3f out, hung *1* **49**
left & wknd fnl 2f: morning gamble with blnks refitted: btr 2483.
2832 **REGENTS SECRET 21** [1]4-9-1 (61) W Supple 10/1: 0-400240: 11th: Mid-div when no room 3f out. *4* **45**
2994 **AWESOME LOVE 14** [10]3-9-6 BL (74) J Fanning 16/1: 2-322260: 12th: Handy 5f, sn fdd: tried blnks. *13* **34**
12 Ran Time 1m 41.31(4.71) Owned: Mr F Jeffers Trained: Leyburn

LINGFIELD Polytrack WEDNESDAY 21.07.04 Lefthand, V Sharp Track

Official Going Turf - Good/Firm, AW - Standard

3329 **2.00 Jap Kitchen Contracts Median Auction Maiden Stakes Div 1 2yo (E)**
£3513 £1081 £541 **7f aw rnd** **Going 49** **-15 Slow** Inside

2594 **RAZA CAB 32** [6] C N Allen 2-9-0 K Fallon 5/1: 31: Cl-up, styd on to lead bef 1f out, pushed **94a+**
out, val 4L+: op 2/1: eff at 7f, further will suit: acts on polytrack & a v sharp trk: can rate higher, see 2594.
RUSSIAN CONSORT 0 [4] A King 2-9-0 J D Smith 40/1: 2: ch c Groom Dancer - Ukraine Venture (Slip *2½* **85a+**
Anchor) Slow away, prog v wide 3f out, styd on to chase wnr ins fnl 1f, al held: debut: Jan foal, cost 52,000 gns:
half brother successful at 6f: dam smart performer around mid-dists: sire decent performer around 10f: eff at 7f,
further will suit: acts on polytrack: fine start, win over 1m sn.
3005 **FOLLOWING FLOW 15** [3] W Jarvis 2-9-0 K Darley 16/1: 03: b c King of Kings - Sign Here (Private *1* **83a**
Terms) Prom over 5f, sn outpcd, rallied late: Mar 1st foal, dam successful at sprint dist: sire Gr1 wnr at 1m:
eff at 7f, crying out for 1m+: acts on polytrack: open to improvement.
2970 **NAVAL FORCE 16** [13] H Morrison 2-9-0 T S Drowne 10/1: 04: b c Forzando - Barsham (Be My Guest) *nk* **82a**
Cl-up, ev ch bef 1f out, sn no extra: op 20/1: Mar foal, cost 22,000 gns: brother wnr at 5f, half brother to
numerous wnrs: dam successful at 10f: sire useful performer around 1m: eff at 7f on polytrack.
3078 **SEYAADI 12** [8]2-9-0 R Hills 5/2 FAV: 525: In tch when short of room 2f out, sn no extra: bckd: *¾* **80a**
disapp on AW bow: showed more in 3078 (gd/soft).
CUPIDS GLORY 0 [5]2-9-0 S Sanders 9/2: 6: b c Pursuit of Love - Doctor's Glory (Elmaamul) *shd* **79a**
Mid-div, hdwy wide bef 1f out, no extra ins fnl 1f: bckd from 12/1 on debut: Apr foal, cost 48,000 gns:
brother/half brother to wnrs at 7/8f: dam successful at 5/6f: sire decent performer at 6f/1m.
1728 **FONG SHUI 68** [9]2-9-0 D Sweeney 33/1: 47: Dwelt, sn mid-div, short of room 2f out & again dist, *hd* **78a+**
staying on when no room again cl-home: 10 wk abs: abs: much closer with a clr run: see 1728.
3065 **ASIAN TIGER 13** [12]2-9-0 D Holland 7/2: 225358: Led, hdd bef 1f out, wknd: tchd 9/2: btr 2697. *1¼* **76a**
3021 **PLAY UP POMPEY 14** [2]2-9-0 A Daly 66/1: 009: Bhd, nvr a factor. *4* **68a**
2870 **ELVINA HILLS 20** [10]2-8-9 C Haddon(7) 50/1: 00560: 10th: Keen cl-up, ev ch 2f out, sn wknd: btr 2537. *½* **62a**
2802 **KEYNES 23** [11]2-9-0 J Fortune 18/1: 30: 11th: Keen cl-up when no room 2f out, short of room *1* **65a**
again dist, wknd: see 2802 (debut).
2911 **Beauchamp Twist 19** [7]2-8-9 S W Kelly 66/1:0 **Eastwell Magic 0** [1]2-8-9 B Doyle 66/1:0
13 Ran Time 1m 27.31 (4.51) Owned: Alan Brazil Racing Club Trained: Newmarket

3330 **2.30 Jap Kitchen Contracts Median Auction Maiden Stakes Div 2 2yo (E)**
£3513 £1081 £541 **7f aw rnd** **Going 49** **-17 Slow** Inside

3196 **HYPNOTIC 7** [13] Sir Mark Prescott 2-9-0 S Sanders 100/30 FAV: 41: ch c Lomitas - Hypnotize **91a+**
(Machiavellian) In tch, led 3f out, pushed clr ins fnl 2f, val 7L+: tchd 9/2 on quick reapp: Mar 1st foal, dam 7f
wnr at 2: sire high-class performer around mid-dists: eff at 7f, will apprec further: acts on polytrack & a v sharp
trk: left debut eff bhd with authoritive success: can improve with racing.
2870 **FLYING PASS 20** [6] D J S ffrench Davis 2-9-0 Dane O'Neill 7/2: 03022: Held up, styd on to chase *5* **79a**
wnr ins fnl 2f, al held: AW bow: acts on fast grnd & polytrack: see 2870.
SAADIGG 0 [2] M A Jarvis 2-9-0 P Robinson 6/1: 3: b c Indian Danehill - White Caps (Shirley *1¼* **77a+**
Heights) Handy, outpcd 3f out, rallied ins fnl 1f: tchd 8/1 on debut: Apr foal, half brother 11f Flat wnr, also
won numerous times over fences: dam plcd at best at 7f: sire decent performer at mid-dists: sure to improve for
today's experience & will relish 1m+: encouraging.

2714 **KING OF BLUES 26** [12] M A Magnusson 2-9-0 T E Ahern 33/1: 004: ch c Bluebird - Highly Respected (High Estate) Bhd, hdwy 3f out, no impress dist: 1st time t-strap: Feb foal, cost E80,000: half brother successful at 7/10f: dam unplcd: sire decent performer at sprint dists: now quals for h'caps. *nk* **76a**

SAMSON QUEST 0 [3]2-9-0 Martin Dwyer 12/1: 5: Handy, prog 3f out, no extra 1f out: debut. *nk* **75a**

MYSTERY LOT 0 [11]2-8-9 J D Smith 33/1: 6: Slow away, hdwy after 4f, nrst fin: debut. *½* **69a**

2863 **MEDITATION 20** [8]2-8-9 K Darley 25/1: 07: Cl-up, wknd ins fnl 2f: see 2863. *1¼* **67a**

RESPLENDENT PRINCE 0 [1]2-9-0 D Holland 5/1: 8: Handy 5f, no extra when short of room dist: op 8/1 on debut: rider reported mount ran too free & did not face the kickback. *¾* **70a**

1717 **INCHCAPE ROCK 69** [10]2-9-0 S Drowne 20/1: 09: Dwelt, al in rear: 'did not face the kickback'. *11* **46a**

WELSH GALAXY 0 [9]2-8-9 R Price 50/1: 0: 10th: Bhd, nvr a factor. *6* **29a**

2902 **GALLEGO 19** [4]2-9-0 BL R Havlin 66/1: 00: 11th: Handy 4f, fdd. *nk* **33a**

3041 **SASTRE 13** [5]2-8-9 J F Egan 14/1: 040: 12th: In tch & hmpd 6f out, styd cl-up, fdd bef 2f out. *3½* **21a**

2569 **FLY TO DUBAI 32** [7]2-9-0 K Fallon 11/2: 060: 13th: Led 4f, sn fdd: jock rec 4 day careless riding ban. *8* **12a**

13 Ran Time 1m 27.45 (4.65) Owned: Cheveley Park Stud Trained: Newmarket

3331

3.00 Rational Classified Stakes 3yo 0-70 (E)
£3504 £1078 £539 **7f aw rnd** **Going 49** **+05 Fast** Inside

3162 **GRANDALEA 9** [10] Sir Michael Stoute 3-9-0 (75) K Fallon 11/4: 0236-531: Cl-up, ev ch dist, drvn out to lead cl-home: tchd 4/1: stays around 1m, apprec drop back to 7f: acts on fast, gd grnd & polytrack. **79a**

3198 **ECCENTRIC 7** [11] Andrew Reid 3-9-3 (75) J F Egan 9/4 FAV: 4110422: Led 5f out, drew clr with wnr bef 1f out, hdd cl-home: clr rem: op 3/1 on quick reapp: another gd run here at Lingfield: see 3198 & 933. *nk* **81a**

3036 **SWEETEST REVENGE 14** [5] M D I Usher 3-8-13 (74) A Daly 14/1: 254-0603: Rcd keenly bhd, outpcd after 4f, rallied ins fnl 1f, no ch with front 2: btr 135. *7* **63a**

2886 **NIKIFOROS 20** [6] J W Hills 3-8-12 (67) S Whitworth 66/1: 0604: Bhd, outpcd halfway, rallied late. *1¼* **60a**

3133* **RAGGED JACK 11** [2]3-9-0 (72) S W Kelly 12/1: 0U4-2315: Cl-up over 5f, no extra: btr 3133 (5f, gd). *hd* **61a**

2925 **LA LANDONNE 18** [1]3-8-9 (68) S Sanders 12/1: 351-4366: Nvr nrr than mid-div: btr 2624. *1½* **53a**

2055 **FOOLS ENTIRE 54** [8]3-8-12 (67) F P Ferris(3) 33/1: 0360007: Cl-up over 5f, sn wknd: 8 wk abs. *shd* **55a**

3016 **CHRISTINAS DREAM 14** [9]3-8-11 (72) D Holland 6/1: 334-58: Mid-div 5f, wknd: op 9/2: btr 3016 (turf). *5* **44a**

2174 **THARAA 49** [7]3-8-9 (69) S Drowne 10/1: 0-2059: Dwelt, hdwy 3f out, fdd dist: 7 wk abs: btr 2174. *1½* **39a**

2661 **WAVERTREE GIRL 28** [3]3-8-9 bl (68) K Darley 10/1: 3050430: 10th: Slow away, al rear: btr 2661 (6f, gd). *8* **25a**

2756 **CALLED UP 25** [4]3-8-12 (68) Dane O'Neill 20/1: 40050: 11th: Led hdd 5f out, fdd halfway: btr 2756. *6* **17a**

11 Ran Time 1m 25.91 (3.11) Owned: Cheveley Park Stud Trained: Newmarket

3332

3.30 Winterhalter Handicap Stakes Fillies 3yo+ 35-55 (F) **[61]**
£2912 £832 £416 **5f aw rnd** **Going 49** **-03 Slow** Outside

3054 **TENDER 13** [6] Mrs Stef Liddiard 4-9-2 p (49) S Drowne 11/2: 0500041: Made all, hung left ins fnl 2f, rdn out to hold on: eff at 5/6f on firm, gd grnd & polytrack: likes a sharp trk & cheek pieces: on a wng mark. **56a**

3289 **MINIMUM BID 4** [8] Miss B Sanders 3-9-4 (55) S Sanders 7/1: 63-00202: Held up, hdwy wide over 2f out, styd on well ins fnl 1f, post came too sn: quick reapp: AW bow: eff at 5f, worth another try at 6f on this evidence: acts on fast grnd & polytrack: shown enough to find similar: see 3036. *nk* **61a**

2981 **LUCKY VALENTINE 16** [5] G L Moore 4-9-2 p (49) R L Moore 11/4 FAV: 100-2433: Handy, ev ch ins fnl 1f, kept on, just held in 3-way photo: op 7/2: continues to run well: see 2981 & 2331. *shd* **54a**

2398 **INCH BY INCH 39** [10] P J Makin 5-9-1 bl (48) D Holland 9/2: 00300-04: In tch, prog & ev ch ins fnl 1f, onepace cl-home: tchd 11/2: see 2398. *1* **50a**

3143 **ERRACHT 10** [3]6-9-4 (51) G Baker 6/1: 5160005: Cl-up till dist, no extra: btr 1371. *1¼* **49a**

3024 **AVERAMI 14** [9]3-9-4 vis (55) R J Killoran(7) 22/1: 54-05006: Rear, outpcd 2f out, rallied late. *1¼* **49a**

2614* **PETANA 30** [7]4-9-2 p (49) Natalia Gemelova(7) 10/1: 0-504017: Slow away, gd prog halfway, wknd dist. *¾* **41a**

2398 **LADY JUSTICE 39** [4]4-9-8 (55) K Fallon 8/1: 6/50-0408: Rear, nvr nrr than mid-div: tchd 11/1. *shd* **46a**

3289 **MANNORA 4** [2]4-9-3 (50) K Darley 16/1: 0-400009: Slow away, nvr a factor: quick reapp: see 1730. *1¼* **37a**

2784 **TIKITANO 24** [1]3-9-1 (52) M Howard(7) 50/1: 6-0000: 10th: b f Dr Fong - Asterita (Rainbow Quest) Handy 3f, fdd: 6 of 19 on sole '03 start (rtd 66, mdn): with D K Ivory. *9* **14a**

10 Ran Time 1m 0.43 (2.63) Owned: Mrs Felicity Ashfield Trained: Hungerford

3333

4.00 Letheby & Christopher Handicap Stakes 3yo+ 0-70 (E) **[67]**
£3523 £1084 £542 **6f aw rnd** **Going 49** **-03 Slow** Inside

902 **WOODBURY 120** [1] Mrs H Sweeting 5-9-0 (53) G Baker 14/1: D260-041: Made all, rdn out to hold on ins fnl 1f: long abs: suited by 6f, acts on firm, fast grnd & polytrack, handles gd/soft: goes well fresh: back to form on first start for new stable & is well h'capped: see 760 (K R Burke). **62a**

1691 **SALON PRIVE 70** [2] C A Cyzer 4-9-10 (63) K Fallon 10/1: 0232-002: Al cl-up, ev ch 1f out, styd on, not pace wnr: 10 wk abs: blnks left off: only lightly rcd & can find similar: see 23. *1* **68a**

3135 **CHIMALI 10** [4] J Noseda 3-9-9 (67) E Ahern 4/1: 4-143: Al cl-up, ev ch 1f out, kept on, just held for 2nd: AW bow: acts on polytrack & soft grnd: see 2945. *nk* **71a**

3109 **CORMORANT WHARF 11** [6] T E Powell 4-10-0 BL (67) J F Egan 9/1: 0050064: Dwelt, prog fnl 2f, nrst fin. *1¼* **68a**

2990 **ILLUSIVE 15** [8]7-9-5 bl (58) J Fortune 14/1: 6200405: In tch wide over 4f, sn no extra: btr 2855. *1¼* **56a**

2698 **DOUBLE M 27** [7]7-9-8 vis (61) R Thomas(5) 7/2 FAV: 5321366: Nvr nrr than mi-div: btr 2585 & 2396. *½* **58a**

2841 **TORQUEMADA 21** [11]3-9-2 (60) F P Ferris(3) 5/1: 0-300037: Handy over 4f, no extra: op 7/1: btr 2841. *nk* **56a**

4031} **THE BARONESS 323** [9]4-9-4 (57) S Sanders 25/1: 020545-8: b f Blues Traveller - Wicken Wonder (Distant Relative) Bhd, prog halfway, fdd dist: reapp: claim & sell wnr in '03 (J R Best): well btn both '02 starts (rtd 25, debut): eff at 5/6f on firm, fast grnd & both AWs: with E R Oertel. *3* **44a**

2 Jun'03 Warw 6.1fm 63-60 F: 1 Apr'03 Folk 5g/f 60-(55) F: 2 Feb'03 Ling 6ap 56a- G: 1 Jan'03 Ling 5ap 57a- F:

2999 **ZAGALA 15** [5]4-9-9 t (62) P Robinson 7/1: 3-202009: Handy over 4f, sn wknd: btr 1221. *½* **48a**

2873 **GAMESETNMATCH 20** [12]3-9-9 bl (67) C Haddon(7) 50/1: 02065-60: 10th: Bhd, nvr a factor: see 2873. *5* **38a**

2535 **SECOND MINISTER 33** [3]5-9-2 bl (55) D Holland 16/1: 2-306000: 11th: Slow away, al in rear: btr 802. *3½* **17a**

11 Ran Time 1m 13.52 (3.12) Owned: Mr P Sweeting Trained: Marlborough

LINGFIELD **Polytrack** **WEDNESDAY 21.07.04** **Lefthand, Sharp, Undulating Track**

Official Going Turf - Good/Firm, AW - Standard

3334

4.30 Emh International Handicap Stakes 3yo 0-75 (E) **[80]**
£4355 £1340 £670 **1m3f106y** **Good 56** **-02 Slow** Outside

2842 **ELLINA 21** [9] J Pearce 3-8-11 (63) K Fallon 14/1: 0-046401: Handy, styd on to lead ins fnl 1f, rdn out: eff at 10/11.5f on gd, handles soft grnd on a sharp/undul trk: first win: see 1651. **69**
2978* **VELVET WATERS 16** [6] R F Johnson Houghton 3-8-7 (59) S Carson 9/2: 00-36412: Cl-up, styd on to lead bef 1f out, hdd ins fnl 1f, kept on, not btn far: eff at 11/5f, rtn to 12f+ will suit: acts on fast & gd grnd. *½* **63**
2862 **POPES HILL 21** [1] L M Cumani 3-9-7 (73) D Holland 6/1: 0-4463: Sn bhd, hdwy 3f out, onepcd ins fnl 1f: op 8/1: h'cap bow: eff at 11.5f on gd grnd: see 2623 & 1885. *2* **74**
3192* **ILE FACILE 7** [3] N P Littmoden 3-9-9 (7ex)t (75) K Darley 5/1: 1020414: In tch, prog to 2f out, no extra fnl 1f: qck reapp: just btr 3192. *1¼* **74**
2978 **MUSTANG ALI 16** [7]3-9-3 (69) J F Egan 7/2 FAV: 6035535: Held up, prog 3f out, no impress fnl 1f. *½* **67**
3144 **OPTIMAL 10** [2]3-8-10 (62) S Sanders 8/1: 400-06: Led, hdd bef 1f out, wknd: h'cap bow: see 3144. *1½* **57**
2431 **PAPEETE 37** [10]3-8-8 (60) S Drowne 14/1: 3100-447: Al in rear: btr 2133. *3½* **50**
2621 **GOLDEN EMPIRE 30** [8]3-9-6 (72) T E Durcan 16/1: 2-224108: Handy 9f, sn hung right & wknd: btr 1390. *hd* **61**
2780 **DESERT IMAGE 24** [5]3-9-6 (72) D Corby(3) 7/1: 0033249: Handy, wknd 2f out: btr 2413 & 1791. *4* **55**
TEAM TACTICS 299 [4]3-8-7 (59) S Whitworth 50/1: 0005-0: 10th: b f Son of Sharp Shot - Sportin' Notion (Sportin' Life) Slow away, al bhd: reapp & Brit bow: ex Irish, unplcd in all 4 starts to date. *8* **31**
10 Ran Time 2m 30.18 (6.78) Owned: The Exclusive Two Partnership Trained: Newmarket

3335

5.00 Come Racing Here On Saturday Evening Maiden Stakes 3yo+ (D)
£3572 £1099 £550 **1m3f106y** **Good 56** **+01 Fast** Outside

2058 **LIGHT OF MORN 54** [10] R Guest 3-8-8 S Sanders 6/1: 231: Mid-div, prog 4f out, styd on to lead dist, pushed clr, val 5L+: 8 wk abs: eff at 11.5/12f, further will suit: acts on fast & soft grnd: lightly rcd performer who is improving with ev start: see 2058 & 1272. **89+**
2368 **IDEALISTIC 40** [2] L M Cumani 3-8-8 (82) D Holland 7/4 JT FAV: 0222: Handy, prog & ev ch dist, kept on, not pace wnr: tchd 5/2: continues to run well: see 2368 & 1922. *3½* **82**
3038 **WOMAN IN WHITE 14** [12] J H M Gosden 3-8-8 (73) J Fortune 12/1: 0263: Led 9f out, hdd bef 1f out, wknd: op 8/1: appeared not to stay on step up in trip: btr 2536 (9f). *5* **75**
2980 **WEDDING CAKE 16** [4] Sir Michael Stoute 3-8-8 K Fallon 7/4 JT FAV: 034: In tch, struggled to handle bend over 4f out, onepcd ins fnl 2f: looked unsuited by today's undul trk: showed more in 2980. *1¼* **73**
CEMGRAFT 0 [1]3-8-8 S Drowne 33/1: 5: b f In The Wings - Soviet Maid (Soviet Star) Slow away, bhd, outpcd after 6f, rallied late: debut: with Miss E C Lavelle. *3½* **68**
2992 **ENCOMPASS 15** [7]3-8-8 W Ryan 12/1: 036: In tch 9f, sn wknd: see 2992. *shd* **67**
2131 **ENHANCER 50** [9]6-9-10 J F Egan 33/1: 07: Sn cl-up, ev ch bef 3f out, sn wknd: 7 wk abs. *shd* **71**
MAGICAL QUEST 0 [13]4-9-10 K Darley 16/1: 8: b c Rainbow Quest - Apogee (Shirley Heights) Slow away, modest late gains: debut: brother 12f List wnr in France: dam useful performer around 12f. *1¼* **69**
DUAL PURPOSE 0 [3]9-9-10 L Vickers 100/1: 9: Led, hdd 9f out, styd in tch, fdd ins fnl 4f. *hd* **68**
3211 **LORD NELLSSON 6** [5]8-9-10 Hayley Turner(5) 100/1: 400: 10th: Dwelt, nvr nrr than mid-div: qck reapp. *1¾* **65**
Armatore 280 [8]4-9-10 S Whitworth 33/1:0 2763} **Whispering Valley 378** [11]4-9-5 R L Moore 33/1:0
2668 **Chelseas Diamond 28** [14]4-9-5 bl R Price 100/1:0 2740 **Little Gannet 25** [6]3-8-8 Dane O'Neill 100/1:0
14 Ran Time 2m 30.35(6.95) Owned: Matthews Breeding and Racing Trained: Newmarket

SANDOWN **WEDNESDAY 21.07.04** **Righthand, Galloping Track, Stiff Finish**

Official Going GOOD/FIRM (GOOD places).

3336

6.10 Panmure Gordon Equities Apprentice Handicap Stakes 3yo+ 0-75 (E) **[74]**
£5060 £1557 £779 **1m2f7y** **Good/Firm 31** **-16 Slow** Inside

3088 **A ONE 12** [9] H J Manners 5-9-13 (73) F P Ferris 9/2: 4311101: Set pace, rdn but kept on over 1f out, held on for press ins last: suited by 1m/10f now on firm or hvy grnd, handles fibresand: acts on a sharp or stiff trk: loves to dominate: genuine, thriving this term: see 2973, 2787. **84**
3187 **RECOUNT 7** [8] J R Best 4-9-10 (70) M Savage(3) 14/1: 0065002: Keen in tch, hdwy to chase wnr over 1f out, styd on to chall ins last, just held: back to form & clr of rem: on a fair mark & sn be wng over 12f shortly. *shd* **80**
2875 **BLUEGRASS BOY 20** [2] G B Balding 4-9-0 (60) R Thomas(3) 12/1: 00-30003: Held up, hdwy 2f out, sn no danger: mdn after 14: see 1098. *7* **59**
3070 **BARRY ISLAND 12** [4] D R C Elsworth 5-10-0 (74) L Keniry 7/2 FAV: 3003064: Chsd ldrs, eff well over 1f out, sn wknd: well bckd: top weight: all 3 wins on polytrack at Lingfield: see 429. *hd* **73**
2979 **REBATE 16** [6]4-9-0 (60) P Gallagher(5) 4/1: 0033635: Chsd ldrs, onepace dist: see 2018, 903. *1½* **56**
2560 **MOVIE KING 32** [7]5-9-3 (63) J P Guillambert 12/1: 0-002006: Chsd wnr, wknd 2f out: best dominating. *1¼* **57**
2260* **FACTUAL LAD 45** [1]6-9-12 (72) A Beech 8/1: 110-0017: Held up, btn over 2f out: abs, btr 2260. *1¾* **63**
1485 **COOL TEMPER 81** [10]8-9-6 (66) N De Souza(3) 8/1: 336-5308: Bhd, wknd 2f out: abs: see 1485. *½* **56**
2735 **GLIMMER OF LIGHT 26** [5]4-9-10 (70) M Coumbe(7) 14/1: 150-6009: Al bhd: see 2735. *8* **48**
1313] **JALONS STAR 1164** [3]6-8-13 (59) B O'Neill(7) 16/1: 651250//-0: 10th: b g Eagle Eyed - Regina St Cyr (Doulab) Bhd, nvr a factor: rnr-up in a nov chase in 03/04, nov h'cap wnr in 01/02 (poss stays 2m5f on fast, soft & sharp/undul trks): '01 Flat h'cap wnr: eff over a gall 10f on gd/soft & hvy. *nk* **36**
2 Apr'01 Wind 11.6g/s 56-60 E: 1 Apr'01 Nott 10hvy 64-55 F:
10 Ran Time 2m 08.76 (4.66) Owned: Mr H J Manners Trained: Swindon

SANDOWN WEDNESDAY 21.07.04 Righthand, Galloping Track, Stiff Finish

3337 **6.40 Panmure Gordon Investment Trust E B F Maiden Stakes 2yo (D)**
£5304 £1632 £816 **7f16y rnd** **Good/Firm 31** **-25 Slow** Inside

3163 **EMBOSSED 9** [15] R Hannon 2-9-0 R L Moore 7/2 FAV: 61: Chsd wnr, hdwy to lead over 2f out, clr over 1f out, v cmftbly: bckd: enjoyed step up to 7f, further sure to suit: acts on fast grnd: imprvd from debut as expected, looks useful, plenty more decent races to be won: see 163. **101+**
3111 **WOODSLEY HOUSE 11** [3] Mrs P N Dutfield 2-9-0 R Havlin 5/1: 22: Led till over 2f out, not pace of wnr: acts on fast & gd/soft: prob caught a useful sort & can win a minor trk mdn sn: see 3111. *4* **89**
SURWAKI [13] C G Cox 2-9-0 P Robinson 33/1: 3: b c Miswaki - Quinella (Generous) Cl-up, eff well over 1f out, onepace when jumped path ins last on debut: Apr foal, cost E90,000: half brother to a 7f as a juv: eff over a stiff 7f, shld stay 1m in time: acts on fast grnd: encouraging start, win a race on this form. *1¼* **86**
WINDSOR KNOT [1] J H M Gosden 2-9-0 J Fortune 14/1: 4: ch c Pivotal - Triple Tie (The Minstrel) Held up, eff well over 1f out, no threat to ldrs on debut: Mar foal, cost E260,000: dam 14f scorer: looks sure to relish 1m+, will be much sharper for this, v encouraging. *1* **84+**
FIRST ROW [2]2-9-0 S Sanders 20/1: 5: b c Daylami - Ballet Society (Sadler's Wells) U.r. & bolted to start, in tch, some late gains, nvr dangerous on debut: Feb foal, cost 220,000 gns, half brother to wnrs over 9/11f: bred to apprec 1m+ & showed promise here, esp after pre-race antics: improve. *1¾* **80**
KINGSHOLM [14]2-9-0 K Fallon 10/1: 6: U.r. & bolted to start, bhd, late gains, nvr dngrs. *1¼* **78**
2766 **VELVET HEIGHTS 25** [5]2-9-0 S Drowne 16/1: 07: Bhd, some late gains, nvr dangerous. *3* **72**
2897 **ROAD TO HEAVEN 19** [10]2-9-0 D Holland 11/2: 38: In tch, wknd well over 1f out: see 2897. *1¼* **70**
2876 **GUYANA 20** [4]2-9-0 J F Egan 50/1: 09: In tch, wknd 2f out. *nk* **69**
2897 **OFF COLOUR 19** [7]2-9-0 K Darley 10/1: 40: 10th: Slow away & al bhd. *1½* **66**
2696 **RAWAABET 27** [11]2-9-0 Dane O'Neill 33/1: 00: 11th: In tch, wknd over 2f out. *hd* **65**
SHAHAMA [9]2-9-0 A Daly 20/1: 0: 12th: Al bhd. *shd* **64**
3111 **NORTHANGER ABBEY 11** [6]2-9-0 K McEvoy 33/1: 00: 13th: Slow away & al bhd. *½* **63**
SENDEED [12]2-9-0 T R Hills 6/1: 0: 14th: Al bhd. *½* **62**
2578 **SWELL LAD 32** [8]2-9-0 S W Kelly 25/1: 00: 15th: In tch, wide bend over 3f out, btn. *3* **56**
15 Ran Time 1m 30.35 (3.95) Owned: Ms R Z Stephenson Trained: Marlborough

3338 **7.10 Lord Mcgowan Handicap Stakes 3yo 0-90 (C)** **[97]**
£10348 £3184 £1592 **7f16y rnd** **Good/Firm 31** **+04 Fast** Inside

2558 **PETER PAUL RUBENS 33** [8] P F I Cole 3-9-7 (90) D Holland 15/8 FAV: 04151: Made all, pushed clr well over 1f out, v cmftbly: hvly bckd: stays a stiff 7f well on fast grnd: built on promise of 2558 & clrly relishes front rng: looks v useful & up to Listed/Gr3 on this evidence: prob more to come: see 1929. **106**
3112 **FLIP FLOP AND FLY 11** [4] S Kirk 3-9-1 (84) J F Egan 12/1: 0-001062: Held up, hdwy & switched left & hung over 1f out, styd on ins last, no threat to easy wnr: back to form at 7f on fast grnd & caught a tartar. *6* **87**
2918 **BENTLEYS BALL 18** [6] R Hannon 3-9-5 (88) R L Moore 20/1: 432-6003: Handy, hdwy & short of room over 1f out, kept on to chase wnr ins last, sn no extra: fair run: see 2521. *nk* **90**
2247 **GRANATO 46** [3] A C Stewart 3-9-2 (85) K Fallon 6/1: 221-0044: Keen in tch, eff 2f out, no dngr: abs. *½* **86**
3068 **WARDEN COMPLEX 12** [7]3-9-3 (86) O Urbina 9/4: 3-321105: Chsd ldrs, eff to chase wnr over 1f out, sn wknd: well bckd: shade more expected but now twice below 2427. *1½* **84**
4490} **GO BANANAS 297** [1]3-9-4 (87) J Fortune 16/1: 613516-6: b g Primo Dominie - Amsicora (Cadeaux Genereux) Slow away, bhd, some late gains, no danger: '03 mdn & nurs h'cap wnr: stays 7f on firm & gd, poss handles gd/soft, sharp or gall trks: gldd since last term. 1 Sep'03 Donc 7gd 88-80 D: 1 Jul'03 Wind 6g/f 84- D: *½* **84**
3068 **COLOUR WHEEL 12** [9]3-9-7 t (90) S Drowne 11/1: 22-60207: In tch, wknd 2f out: twice below 2532. *½* **86**
2922 **LEAPING BRAVE 18** [5]3-8-5 (74) S W Kelly 66/1: 30-42408: Chsd ldr, wknd qckly dist: see 2116. *1¼* **68**
3113 **CAMBERWELL 11** [2]3-9-5 (88) S Sanders 16/1: 159: Slow away & al bhd: btr 2291. *6* **70**
9 Ran Time 1m 28.31 (1.91) Owned: Richard Green (Fine Paintings) Trained: Whatcombe

3339 **7.45 Panmure Gordon Classified Stakes 3yo 0-75 (D)**
£6858 £2110 £1055 **1m14y rnd** **Good/Firm 31** **-17 Slow** Inside

2877 **MR JACK DANIELLS 20** [9] W R Muir 3-9-0 (74) J Fortune 7/1: 0-363041: Handy, styd on to lead ins fnl 1f, all out: tchd 10/1: eff at 7f/1m, shapes as tho' further will suit: acts on fast & soft grnd: has not had best of luck this term & this was gd confidence boost: see 2705 & 2247. **80**
4094*}**STRAW BEAR 319** [1] Sir Mark Prescott 3-9-2 (77) S Sanders 11/2: 5231-2: ch c Diesis - Highland Ceilidh (Scottish Reel) Sn cl-up, led bef 1f out, rider sn dropped whip & hdd ins fnl 1f, kept on, just held by wnr: op 7/2: reapp: class stks wnr on fnl '03 start: prev eff at 6f, now suited by 8/8.5f, further shld suit: acts on fast grnd & fibresand: prob wnr but for rider dropping whip at vital stage & can find compensation. 1 Sep'03 Wolv 8.5af 82a-(76) F: 2 Jun'03 Wolv 6af 80a- D: *nk* **82**
2706 **HABANERO 27** [6] R Hannon 3-9-0 (72) D Holland 6/1: 0053133: Led 7f out, hdd under press bef 1f out, sn edgd left, kept on, just btn in 3-way photo: appreciated drop back to 1m: see 2706 & 2365. *hd* **79**
3179 **KIBRYAA 8** [7] M A Jarvis 3-9-3 P (78) P Robinson 7/2: 021-6224: Rcd keenly & led 1f, styd in tch, short of room dist, switched & kept on ins fnl 1f, not btn far: well bckd: ran to form with fitting of cheek pieces. *1* **80**
3128 **MISSION MAN 11** [3]3-9-5 (80) R L Moore 12/1: 4214045: Held up, prog 2f out, no impress ins last. *¾* **80**
2631 **SONG OF VALA 30** [8]3-9-0 T (75) S Drowne 20/1: 042-0506: Mid-div, prog bef 1f out, keeping on when badly short of room ins fnl 1f: acts on fast & soft grnd: sure to have gone close with a clr passage. *shd* **74+**
2587 **KING OF DIAMONDS 32** [5]3-9-0 (74) M Savage(5) 50/1: 26207: Bhd, prog when no room dist, onepcd. *1* **72**
3128 **GLEBE GARDEN 11** [2]3-8-11 (75) K Darley 50/1: 10-55608: Al in rear: btr 1419. *1¼* **66**
2709* **SECRET FLAME 27** [10]3-9-0 (78) K Fallon 5/2 FAV: 5-3319: Handy over 6f, sn no extra: well bckd: showed more in 2709 (9f, fills mdn). *1¾* **65**
2974 **STRAWBERRY FAIR 16** [4]3-8-11 t (73) K McEvoy 20/1: 2-400: 10th: Al in rear: btr 2627 (reapp). *5* **52**
10 Ran Time 1m 42.85 (3.85) Owned: Mr Martin P Graham Trained: Lambourn

SANDOWN WEDNESDAY 21.07.04 Righthand, Galloping Track, Stiff Finish

3340 8.15 Panmure Gordon Corporate Finance Handicap Stakes 4yo+ 0-80 (D) [75]
£6858 £2110 £1055 **1m6f** **Good/Firm 31** **-48 Slow** Centre

3147 **TOP TREES 10** [6] W S Kittow 6-7-12 (4oh) (45) N Mackay(3) 20/1: 0010-061: Held up, prog wide ins fnl 2f, rdn out to lead cl-home: eff at 9/13f, now stays 14f: acts on fast grnd & fibresand, gall or sharp trks: fine eff from out of h'cap & unexposed around this trip: see 2292. **56**
2699 **COALITION 27** [11] H Candy 5-9-13 (78) Dane O'Neill 7/2 JT FAV: 1162/-022: Chsd ldrs, prog when short of room bef 1f out, styd on to lead ins fnl 1f, hdd cl-home: fine run in defeat under top weight: see 2699. ½ **83**
3057 **LILLEBROR 13** [5] B J Curley 6-8-5 (56) S W Kelly 14/1: 0000-003: Held up, prog 4f out, kept on ins fnl 1f under hands & heels: eff at 11/12f, now stays 14f: acts on fast & gd grnd: has been gelded since last start & this was encouraging: has slipped dramtically down h'cap: see 3057. 1¾ **58**
2869 **ROME 20** [3] G P Enright 5-8-13 (64) K Fallon 6/1: 0-303554: Handy, styd on to lead dist, hdd ins fnl 1f, hung left & no extra: cheek pieces left off: just btr 2192. ½ **65**
2673 **SALTANGO 28** [12]5-9-8 (73) L Keniry(3) 8/1: 3222-035: Rear, prog when no room 2f out, onepcd fnl 1f. *hd* **74**
2088 **LARKING ABOUT 52** [8]4-8-1 (52) Lisa Jones(3) 25/1: 420-0006: Rear, prog wide 3f out, kept on fnl 1f. ½ **52**
3057 **HENRY ISLAND 13** [7]11-8-10 (61) S Drowne 14/1: 443-5047: Rear, prog 4f out, no impress fnl 2f. ¾ **60**
2923 **GAELIC ROULETTE 18** [9]4-9-5 (70) D Holland 6/1: 11650-38: Handy, short of room 2f out, sn no extra. *hd* **69**
2699 **SEA PLUME 27** [1]5-9-2 BL (67) J Fortune 16/1: 000-5009: Cl-up, styd on to lead 2f out, hdd dist, wknd. *1* **65**
2607 **TILLA 31** [10]4-9-1 (66) L Fletcher(3) 7/2 JT FAV: 2131-560: 10th: Rear, prog over 2f out, sev positions, no room, eased well ins fnl 1f: received luckless passage & is worth another ch: see 2607. *nk* **63+**
3114 **ONWARD TO GLORY 11** [4]4-9-5 (70) K McEvoy 16/1: 5/60-00: 11th: Led till 2f out, wknd: see 3114. 1¾ **65**
11 Ran Time 3m 06.03 (11.03) Owned: Mrs P E Hawkings Trained: Cullompton

3341 8.45 Harry Panmure Gordon Handicap Stakes 4yo+ 0-80 (D) [80]
£7036 £2165 £1083 **5f6y str** **Good/Firm 31** **+12 Fast** Far Side

3184 **JONNY EBENEEZER 7** [8] D Flood 5-8-4 bl (56) N Mackay(3) 4/1 FAV: 0310221: Held up, prog ins fnl 2f, styd on to lead cl-home, pushed out, val 2L+: eff btwn 5/7f, stays a stiff 1m: acts on firm, soft & fibresand: eff with blnks: has been in gd form & on fav mark: see 3184, 3000 & 1938. **68+**
3033 **DOMIRATI 14** [13] R Charlton 4-9-13 (79) S Drowne 11/2: 34-04202: Chsd ldrs, prog & ev ch ins fnl 1f, kept on, not pace wnr: continues to run well: see 2698 & 2286. 1½ **84**
2894 **KATHOLOGY 19** [12] D R C Elsworth 7-9-13 (79) L Keniry(3) 20/1: 30-06003: Handy, styd on to lead 1f out, hdd well ins fnl 1f, no extra: encouraging eff & is on a wng mark: see 2253. *1* **81**
2760* **POLAR IMPACT 25** [10] G L Moore 5-9-9 (75) J Fortune 9/1: 11-10514: Rear, prog 2f out, kept on ins fnl 1f: gd eff back at 5f, just btr 2760 (6f). ½ **75**
3045+**JAYANJAY 13** [2]5-10-0 (80) S Sanders 12/1: 0434315: Rear, prog fnl 2f, nrst fin: not disgraced. *shd* **80**
3146 **AINTNECESSARILYSO 10** [3]6-8-3 (55) M Halford(7) 20/1: 3611536: Rear, prog fnl 2f, nrst fin. ½ **53**
2957 **GUNS BLAZING 17** [15]5-9-6 bl (72) M Howard(7) 20/1: 1360107: Led, hdd 1f out, no extra: btr 2743. *nk* **69**
3073 **SEVEN NO TRUMPS 12** [7]7-9-11 p (77) S W Kelly 20/1: 6040028: Handy over 3f, no extra: btr 3073. ¾ **72**
3033 **CURRENCY 14** [14]7-9-11 p (77) R L Moore 6/1: 0040639: Rear, nvr nrr than mid-div: btr 3033. *nk* **71**
2599 **LAW MAKER 31** [11]4-7-12 (2oh)vis (48) J Bramhill 33/1: 3043620: 10th: Handy 4f, wknd: btr 2599. *1* **41**
2957 **TABOOR 17** [5]6-8-3 h bl (55) Lisa Jones(3) 25/1: 0502060: 11th: Al bhd: btr 2189. 1½ **42**
3033 **TURIBIUS 14** [9]5-9-11 (77) K Fallon 7/1: 6130000: 12th: Rear, nvr a factor: won this race in '03. *hd* **63**
3165 **ELA FIGURA 9** [4]4-7-12 (1oh)p (49) F P Ferris(3) 33/1: 0036500: 13th: Rear, nvr a factor: btr 2361. *hd* **35**
2760 **The Fisio 25** [18]4-9-9 vis(75) K Darley 12/1:0
4964} **Flaran 264** [16]4-8-9 (61) Laura Wells(7) 33/1:0
2872 **Margalita 20** [1]4-8-11 t(63) J F Egan 50/1:0
567 **Strathclyde 165** [17]5-9-13 (79) Dane O'Neill 25/1:0
17 Ran Time 1m 0.55(0.95) Owned: Mrs Ruth M Serrell Trained: Hungerford

LEICESTER WEDNESDAY 21.07.04 Righthand, Stiff, Galloping Track

Official Going GOOD/FIRM (GOOD places).

3342 6.25 Priscilla Brown Debenhams Ladies Night Vip Maiden Auction Stakes 2yo (E)
£4475 £1377 £689 **7f9y str** **Good/Firm 26** **-22 Slow** Stands Side

LUCKY RED PEPPER [4] P W Chapple Hyam 2-8-8 J Quinn 12/1: 1: b c Barathea - Mutige (Warning) Chsd ldrs stands side, went on dist, styd on strongly, rdn out on debut: op 8/1: 30,000gns Mar 1st foal: dam a mid-dist wnr abroad, sire a top class miler: eff over a gall 7f, will stay 1m: acts on fast & runs well fresh. **80**
2783 **HALLUCINATE 24** [2] R Hannon 2-8-5 R Mullen 28/1: 042: Chsd ldrs stands side, ev ch ent fnl 1f, kept on well but not quite pace of wnr: imprvd for this step up to 7f, shld stay 1m: acts on fast grnd. ¾ **74**
2897 **TUMBLEWEED GALORE 19** [12] B J Meehan 2-8-8 J F McDonald(3) 100/1: 03: b g Bluebird - Mary Hinge (Dowsing) Led stands side 2f, remained prom & ev ch ent fnl 1f, kept on & btn under 1L: 30,000 gns Feb foal: half brother to sprint wnr Compton Banker: dam a sprint wnr, sire a top class sprinter: eff over a stiff/gall 7f, much imprvd on this fast surface: could win a small race. *nk* **76**
3178 **MIGHTY EMPIRE 8** [10] M H Tompkins 2-8-3 P Doe 12/1: 004: Nvr far away stands side, ev ch ins fnl 1f, btn around 1L: eff over a stiff/gall 7f on fast grnd: see 2077 (debut). *hd* **71**
CHANTACO [14]2-8-5 Martin Dwyer 16/1: 5: b c Bahri - Dominant Dancer (Primo Dominie) Dwelt stands side, sn recovered & prom, led after 2f till dist, no extra on debut: 12,000 gns Mar 1st foal: dam a 6f juv wnr, sire a top class miler: eff at 7f on fast grnd: ran well for a long way, spot on next time. *2* **69**
2911 **HIGH DYKE 19** [13]2-8-4 Paul Eddery 15/2: 056: Trkd ldrs far side, led that group dist, styd on well but no ch with stands side: prob stays 7f on fast grnd: 1st home on far side, see 2911 & 2703. *nk* **67**
PENNY ISLAND [17]2-8-8 (1ow) J D Smith 25/1: 7: b c Trans Island - Sparklingsovereign (Sparkler) Slowly away far side, styd on late, nrst fin on debut: E20,000 Feb foal: half brother to mid-dist wnr Golden Rule: sire a high-class miler: encouraging start. *shd* **71**
2703 **SCARLET INVADER 27** [19]2-8-8 T Quinn 15/8 FAV: 48: Front rank far side, led 2f out till dist, wknd & eased: well bckd: much btr expected after encouraging debut in 2703 (6f, gd grnd, here). 1½ **68**

2652 **LOUISE RAYNER** 29 [11]2-7-13 A Nicholls 16/1: 549: Slowly away stands side, styd on late, nvr   1¾   55
dangerous: now quals for nurs h'caps: see 2343.
2776 **SEA MAP** 24 [15]2-8-5 W Supple 100/1: 00: 10th: Chsd ldrs 5f stands side.   nk   60
     DAYGAR [5]2-8-4 Joanna Badger 25/1: 0: 11th: Prom, wknd 2f out stands side on debut.   nk   58
     IFIT [8]2-8-4 C Catlin 16/1: 0: 12th: Nvr btr than mid-div stands side on debut.   1½   55
3064 **YELDHAM LADY** 13 [9]2-7-12 D Kinsella 9/1: 00: 13th: Dwelt stands side, nvr a factor: op 13/2.   ¾   47
2287 **MISSED A BEAT** 43 [20]2-7-13 F Norton 9/1: 040: 14th: Chsd ldrs far side, wknd dist: 6 wk abs.   ½   47
     Dudley Docker [6]2-8-5 N Pollard 100/1:0   3110 **Davids Symphony 11** [18]2-8-6 R Smith 66/1:0
     Southern Tide [16]2-8-9 D Sweeney 33/1:0   **Reference** [7]2-8-8 P Dobbs 20/1:0
18 Ran   Time 1m 25.40 (3.40)   Owned: Foreneish Racing   Trained: Newmarket

---

3343
6.55 Debenhams Leicester Ladies Night Nursery Handicap Stakes 2yo (D)   [80]
£4771 £1468 £734   **5f2y str**   **Good/Firm 26**   **+03 Fast**   Stands Side

2658 **BRAG** 28 [6] R Charlton 2-9-7 (73) D Sweeney 1/1 FAV: 2401: Trkd ldrs, styd on well under press   84
to lead well ins fnl 1f, drvn out: well bckd, fast juv time, top weight: eff at 5f on fast grnd, will stay 6f:
handles a stiff/gall trk & likes to run up with the pace: fine run under a big weight, see 1717 (debut).
3209 **STRAFFAN** 6 [1] D Nicholls 2-8-5 (59) A Nicholls 6/1: 3254122: Tried to make all, clr halfway,   1   63
collared cl-home: clr rem: enterprising ride on 1st start for new stable (prev E O'Neill): see 2309 (C/D, sell).
3127 **ALSU** 11 [7] A M Balding 2-9-6 (72) Martin Dwyer 11/2: 31063: Prom, onepcd fnl 1f: clr of rem.   2½   71
2911 **NEXT TIME** 19 [4] M J Polglase 2-8-9 (63) T Quinn 13/2: 450044: Front rank till halfway: op 8/1.   5   45
3097 **LEONALTO** 11 [5]2-8-9 bl (63) J F McDonald(3) 12/1: 05365: Prom till halfway, grad wknd: see 1367.   1   42
1751 **MISSED TURN** 67 [2]2-8-2 (56) F Norton 14/1: 5446: Al rear, nvr dangerous on h'cap bow: 9 wk abs   2½   28
& new stable (prev with K Ryan): see 1751 (AW sell).
2321 **COMINTRUE** 42 [3]2-8-6 (60) J Quinn 20/1: 00027: Speed till halfway: abs: btr 2321 (clmr, g/s).   3   23
7 Ran   Time 59.48 (1.18)   Owned: Lady Rothschild   Trained: Beckhampton

---

3344
7.25 Fred Archer 1885 Selling Stakes 3yo (G)   £2940 £840 £420   **1m9y rnd**   **Good/Firm 26**   **-13 Slow**   Inside

3058 **KINGS ROCK** 13 [14] K A Ryan 3-8-11 BL (55) N Callan 7/1: 6006301: Keen & prom, went on dist, styd   53
on strongly, rdn out: apprec blnks & 1st success: eff around 1m on gd, fast grnd & fibresand: likes a stiff/gall
trk, handles a sharp one: suited by sell grade, see 2133 (C/D & fast) (AW).
2834 **MAGICO** 22 [13] P Burgoyne 3-8-11 bl (44) Martin Dwyer 20/1: 00-00032: Keen & prom, kept on under   ½   48
press fnl 1f despite wandering, not btn far: eff over a stiff/gall 1m on fast grnd: see 2834.
2925 **RED ROCKY** 18 [11] R Hollinshead 3-8-6 p (46) Stephanie Hollinshead(5) 16/1: 0050203: Led till   ½   44
dist, kept on under press & only btn 1L: stays a stiff 1m, acts on gd & fast grnd: see 2704 (7f here).
3219 **TREASON TRIAL** 6 [4] N Tinkler 3-8-11 (62) Kim Tinkler 9/2 CO FAV: 40-064: Hmpd start, hdwy when   1   47
short of room 2f out, nrst fin: qck reapp: eff at 1m on fast grnd: apprec drop to sell grade & poss a shade unlucky.
3034 **CITY GENERAL** 14 [6]3-8-11 p (50) Derek Nolan(7) 9/1: 4350205: Held up, imprvd 2f out, onepcd fnl 1f.   ¾   45
2932 **ELSINORA** 18 [7]3-8-6 p (45) T P Queally 9/2 CO FAV: 00-00026: Slowly away, styd on under press   1¾   36
fnl 2f, nvr nrr: btr 2932.
3286 **WIZARD LOOKING** 4 [10]3-8-11 (55) R Smith 11/2: 6-600607: Chsd ldrs, onepcd fnl 2f: quick reapp.   1   39
2788 **RUMOUR MILL** 24 [8]3-8-11 BL (40) S Hitchcott(3) 66/1: 0-500008: Held up, nvr nr ldrs: tried blnks.   nk   38
2997 **GO FREE** 15 [12]3-8-11 (54) A Nicholls 16/1: 00-259: Prom, wknd dist: reportedly hung right   5   28
thr'out: op 2339 (7f, AW).
3286 **TSHUKUDU** 4 [5]3-8-6 (38) J Quinn 100/1: 000-0000: 10th: ch f Fleetwood - Pab's Choice (Telsmoss)   hd   23
Held up, nvr a factor: quick reapp & reportedly not handle bend: no form yet.
3055 **DEFANA** 9 [9]3-8-11 (52) J Fanning 9/2 CO FAV: 653-5330: 11th: Chsd ldrs, wknd 2f out: gambled   6   16
from 9/1, but reportedly lost action: big drop in trip, see 3055 (11f) & 2790 (12f).
2510 **TAMARINA** 34 [1]3-8-6 p (45) P Doe 100/1: 04-00000: 12th: Al outpcd.   2½   6
2835 **KILMINCHY LADY** 22 [3]3-8-6 (45) R Mullen 20/1: 006-50: 13th: Rdn in rear, al bhd: see 2835.   7   0
3055 **OSLA** 13 [2]3-8-6 BL (30) C Catlin 50/1: 000060: 14th: Al outpcd: blnks: breathing probs.   6   0
14 Ran   Time 1m 41.35 (3.15)   Owned: Miss Claire King and Mr Peter McBride   Trained: Hambleton

---

3345
8.00 Graham Percival Paddock Talk Vip Winner Handicap Stakes 3yo+ 0-85 (D)   [81]
£6871 £2114 £1057   **1m3f183y**   **Good/Firm 26**   **-50 Slow**   Inside

3261 **PARTY PLOY** 4 [6] K R Burke 6-9-1 (5ex) (68) Darren Williams 2/1 FAV: 2110121: Made all, all out   75
to hold on nr fin: well bckd, quick reapp: eff at 11/14f on firm, soft & both AWs: loves to race with/force the
pace: in gd form this term: see 2176.
3070 **TENDER FALCON** 12 [4] R J Hodges 4-9-2 (69) J F McDonald(3) 9/1: 214-5102: Rcd in 2nd, chall 4f   shd   76
out, kept on for press ins fnl 1f: op 7/1, tchd 10/1: back to form of 2707.
3070 **MEXICAN PETE** 12 [5] P W Hiatt 4-9-10 (77) E Ahern 9/2: 3020443: Chsd ldrs, ev ch ins fnl 1f,   ¾   82
onepcd nr fin: top weight: see 1599.
2860 **BEST BE GOING** 21 [3] P W Harris 4-9-9 (76) T Quinn 5/1: 451-0054: Mid-div & keen, short of room   ¾   78
2f out till ins fnl 1f, kept on onepaced: eff at 1m/12f on firm & fast: shade closer with a clr run: see 2099.
3207* **TIGER FROG** 6 [1]5-8-7 (5ex)bl (60) T Eaves(3) 7/2: 30020/-15: Cl-up, stumbled 5f out, kept on fnl   shd   63
1f: quick reapp: eff btwn 10/12f, acts on fast grnd: btr 3207.
3114 **AONINCH** 11 [2]4-8-8 (61) N Pollard 8/1: 0506026: Slow away & keen, hdwy/hung right dist, wknd.   4   58
6 Ran   Time 2m 37.42 (9.12)   Owned: Mr Ian A McInnes   Trained: Leyburn

3346   8.30 Some Robbie Some Day Handicap Stakes Fillies 3yo 0-80 (D)   [86]
£7261 £2234 £1117   7f9y str   Good/Firm 26   +04 Fast   Stands Side

3218* PICKLE 6 [9] S C Williams 3-8-11 (6ex) (69) Martin Dwyer 3/1 FAV: 1033611: Cl-up, outpcd over 2f   79
out, rallied dist & led fnl 1f, rdn out: bckd from 9/2, qck reappn: eff at 6/7f on firm, soft & polytrack:
likes a sharp/undul trk, acts on a gall one: tough: in fine form, see 3218.
2659 ELA PAPAROUNA 28 [13] H Candy 3-8-12 (70) D Sweeney 5/1: 43-30632: Chsd ldrs till led over 2f   1¾   75
out, hdd ins fnl 1f & no extra: stays 6/7f: shld be plcd to win sn: see 1281.
2249 SCARLETT ROSE 46 [12] Dr J D Scargill 3-8-7 (65) C Lowther 33/1: 360-603: b f Royal Applause -   1   68
Billie Blue (Ballad Rock) Chsd ldrs, ev ch over 1f out, no impress fnl 1f: 7 wk abs: 3rd 1st of 3 '03 starts
(auct mdn, rtd 72): eff over 6/7f on fast: fair run here.
1729 HASAYIS 68 [3] J L Dunlop 3-8-10 (68) W Supple 14/1: 00-104: Rear, hdwy over 1f out, not pace to   nk   70
chall: 9 wk abs: back to form of 1086.
3024* BLAEBERRY 14 [11]3-8-2 bl (60) A Nicholls 8/1: 0055415: Led 4f out till over 2f out, no extra.   1¾   58
2648 GO BETWEEN 29 [2]3-9-7 (79) E Ahern 11/1: 210-2066: Rear, hdwy 3f out, trav best when no run   ¾   75+
over 2f out till dist, not recover: top weight: no luck today, keep in mind: see 1761.
3273 BEAUTY OF DREAMS 4 [4]3-8-13 (71) L Harman(7) 66/1: 4150-007: Slow away, late gains: qck reappn.   2½   62
2344 LA PUCE 41 [5]3-8-7 (1ow) (64) F Lynch 16/1: 4011468: Chsd ldrs, no impress dist: 6 wk abs.   1¾   52
2864 MOON LEGEND 20 [1]3-8-8 (66) T Quinn 11/2: 06-039: Slow away, nvr a factor.   ½   52
3198 MISS JUDGEMENT 7 [10]3-8-6 (64) F Norton 8/1: 5321300: 10th: Rear, hdwy 2f out, no impress fnl 1f.   ½   49
3058 BLUE DAZE 13 [6]3-8-7 (65) R Mullen 16/1: 1-005550: 11th: Led 3f, wknd dist: see 2385.   1½   47
3179 TRUE 8 [8]3-8-5 (63) J Quinn 11/1: 0020340: 12th: Dwelt, sn cl-up, wknd over 2f out.   ½   44
2904 HI DARL 19 [7]3-7-12 (2oh) (54) B Swarbrick(5) 80/1: 641-00: 13th: Cl-up, wknd halfway: see 2904.   5   27
13 Ran   Time 1m 23.55 (1.55)   Owned: Mr S P Tindall   Trained: Newmarket

3347   9.00 Weatherbys Insurance Services Median Auction Maiden Stakes 3yo (F)
£3406 £1048 £524   5f2y str   Good/Firm 26   -00 Slow   Stands Side

2675 TRUE MAGIC 28 [1] J D Bethell 3-8-9 (69) T Quinn 1/1 FAV: 06-56221: Made all, pushed clr fnl 1f,   70
eased cl home, val 2L: well bckd: eff at 5/6f on fast & gd, acts on a gall trk: deserved win: see 1876.
3179 HARRISONS FLYER 8 [3] R A Fahey 3-9-0 BL (67) P Hanagan 15/2: 4-0202: Chsd ldrs, hdwy over 1f   ¾   67
out, kept on: handles fast & soft: tried blnks: see 3179.
3023 SOKOKE 14 [9] R M Beckett 3-9-0   J Quinn 10/3: 23: Bmpd start, cl-up, onepcd ins fnl 1f: tchd   1   64
4/1: acts on fast & gd: imprvd from debut: see 3023.
2075 FISHLAKE FLYER 53 [4] J G Given 3-8-9 (64) J Fanning 8/1: 0432-434: Hmpd start, handy, onepcd   hd   59
fnl 1f: op 6/1, 8 wk abs: see 1146.
3024 NIGHT WORKER 14 [7]3-9-0 (50) R Smith 12/1: 6000065: Outpcd, hdwy over 1f out, nvr dngrs.   1¾   58$
3036 LAKESIDE GUY 14 [8]3-9-0 (56) T P Queally 25/1: 0040356: Dsptd lead over 3f, wknd fnl 1f.   ½   56
3133 WESTBOROUGH 11 [5]3-9-0 (55) Miss Tinkler 22/1: 5-250527: Slow away & bmpd start, nvr a factor.   1¾   50
802 VITTORIOSO 139 [6]3-9-0 bl (54) F Lynch 20/1: 0-533208: Dsptd lead till over 2f out, wknd 1f out.   3½   40
904 MIND THE TIME 120 [10]3-9-0 (35) M Tebbutt 50/1: 0-0649: b g Mind Games - Rare Indigo (Timeless   8   15
Times) Rear, nvr a factor: long abs: unplcd sole '03 start (mdn).
9 Ran   Time 59.60(1.30)   Owned: Mr T R Lock   Trained: Middleham

Official Going GOOD/FIRM.

3348   2.20 Levy Board Maiden Stakes 2yo (D)
£3848 £1184 £592   6f rnd   Good/Firm   -28 Slow   Inside

2553 GOLDEN LEGACY 33 [3] R A Fahey 2-8-9   P Hanagan 4/9 FAV: 201: Trkd ldrs trav well, led over 1f   82+
out, rdn & rdly asserted, val 4L+: eff at 6f, stays 7f: acts on firm & fast grnd, sharp or gall trks: potentially
useful & can win again: see 2297.
2889 RASA SAYANG 19 [7] T D Barron 2-9-0 P Makin(5) 4/1: 022: Sn handy, eff to press wnr over 1f out,   2½   72
kept on but not pace of wnr ins last: styd longer 6f trip, acts on fast & gd grnd: see 2889.
2889 CHOREOGRAPHIC 19 [6] R A Fahey 2-9-0   T Hamilton(3) 16/1: 03: b c Komaite - Lambast (Relkino) In   2½   64
tch, kept on late, nvr threat to front pair: longer priced s/mate of wnr: 35,000gns Apr foal, half brother to a 1m
& subs hdles wnr, also useful 6f juv wnr Philharmonic: eff at 6f, can prog at 7f+: handles fast grnd.
3122 MISTER BUZZ 11 [8] M D Hammond 2-9-0   A Culhane 40/1: 0004: b c Mind Games - Compact Disc   ½   62
(Royal Academy) Chsd ldrs, no impress fnl 2f: 11,000gns Mar foal, brother to a 6f juv wnr: dam a 7f juv scorer.
MARY GRAY 5 [2]2-8-9   J Fanning 8/1: 5: Slow away, mod late prog under hand ride: 9,000gns Mar   shd   57
foal, half sister to sev wnrs, incl 2 sprinters: scopey filly who needed this.
3122 ZANDERIDO 11 [4]2-9-0   Darren Williams 100/1: 406: Led till over 1f out, fdd: see 2888.   2   56
THORNBER COURT [1]2-8-9   F Lynch 50/1: 7: Dwelt & al outpcd rear.   1   48
SO INDEPENDENT [1]2-8-9   R Winston 66/1: 8: Al rear on debut.   3½   37
8 Ran   Time 1m 14.24 (3.94)   Owned: Mr P N Devlin   Trained: Malton

3349   2.50 Halifax Selling Stakes 2yo (G)
£2618 £748 £374   7f rnd   Good/Firm 38   -16 Slow   Inside

3189 UREDALE 7 [1] Mrs A Duffield 2-8-11   A Culhane 5/1: 50651: Made all, drvn & styd on strongly fnl   65
1f: 1st win, bght in for 9,000gns: imprvd for forcing tactics over a sharp 7f, get 1m+: acts on fast grnd: apprec
drop to sell grade: see 2100.
3189 MOUNT EPHRAM 7 [8] R F Fisher 2-9-3 bl   P Hanagan 5/2 FAV: 4564142: Trkd ldrs, rdn & chsd wnr   1½   67
over 1f out, kept on, al held: bckd tho' op 2/1, clr of rem: ahead of today's wnr in 3189 (C/D).

2865 **DARTANIAN 20** [3] P D Evans 2-8-11 R Winston 6/1: 0563: Handy, drvn & outpcd fnl 2f: see 2597. *4* **53**
2939 **MAUREENS LOUGH 18** [10] T D Barron 2-8-12 P Makin(5) 7/2: 361544: Handy, fdd under press over 1f out: op 9/2: see 2939 & 2294. *1½* **51**
2939 **TEWITFIELD LASS 18** [13]2-8-6 D Fentiman(7) 66/1: 05: Mid-div, nvr pace to threaten: see 2939. *3* **39**
2343 **TONIGHT 41** [11]2-8-11 B Swarbrick(5) 10/1: 3436: Prom, drvn & btn 2f out: abs: see 1906. *½* **43**
3259 **NORTHERN REVOQUE 4** [2]2-8-6 bl P Mathers(5) 25/1: 500507: Chsd ldrs 5f: quick reapp: see 1517. *1½* **35**
2882 **MISS TRENDSETTER 20** [7]2-8-6 G Parkin 16/1: 08: b f Desert Style - Chummy's Friend (Be My Guest) Drvn mid-div, no prog fnl 2f: longer trip: Feb foal, cost E9,000: half sister to a 5/6f wnr. *4* **27**
2882 **TAKS GIRL 20** [12]2-8-6 R Fitzpatrick 66/1: 0009: ch f Takhlid - Sans Rivale (Elmaamul) Al towards rear: mod form: Apr foal, dam a 5f 2/3yo wnr. *1½* **24**
3020 **LARAS GIRL 14** [6]2-8-6 T P Queally 20/1: 0400: 10th: Sn struggling rear. *2* **20**
SPECIALISE [9]2-8-6 R Ffrench 12/1: 0: 11th: Slow away & al bhd: op 14/1, debut. *½* **19**
2939 **Hollingwood Soul 18** [4]2-8-6 Dean McKeown 33/1:0 2810 **Black Combe Lady 23** [5]2-8-6 P Bradley 100/1:0
13 Ran Time 1m 27.50 (4.5) Owned: Miss B Duxbury & Mrs A Duffield Trained: Leyburn

3350

3.20 Goodbye & Good Luck Tracey Stakes Handicap 3yo+ 0-85 (D) **[80]**
£5590 £1720 £860 **5f rnd** **Good/Firm** **-01 Slow** Inside

2599 **JUSTALORD 31** [2] J Balding 6-9-1 BL (67) J Edmunds 11/2: 2123061: Led/dsptd lead, drvn & asserted ins last, held on all out: eff at 6f, all wins at 5f: acts on firm, gd & loves both AWs, sharp trks: eff in cheek pieces, enjoyed blnks today: well h'capped on turf, could win again: see 567 (AW). **75**
2951 **SHARP HAT 18** [1] D W Chapman 10-8-8 (60) A Culhane 5/1 JT FAV: 0000302: Rdn & chsd ldrs, styd on well for press cl-home, just failed: tough veteran, on a handy mark & loves this trk: see 2846 & 70. *nk* **67**
2201 **MAROMITO 47** [15] R Bastiman 7-8-3 (55) R Ffrench 33/1: 0311003: Cl-up, no extra dist: 7 wk abs: showed excellent speed from awkward wide draw, could soon be winning: see 1408. *1¼* **57**
3241 **SALVIATI 5** [4] J M Bradley 7-9-11 p (77) C J Davies(7) 15/2: 0000004: Slow away, styd on well halfway, nrst fin: won this race last term off a 6lb higher mark, looks to be coming to hand. *hd* **79**
2968 **STRENSALL 16** [3]7-9-11 (77) T Eaves(3) 7/1: 2003405: Chsd ldrs, no extra dist: see 2690, 2084 & 124. *nk* **78**
2945 **AMANDAS LAD 18** [7]4-8-3 (55) T P Queally 25/1: 2035456: Mid-div, not pace to chall: see 2216, 487. *1* **53**
3146 **ROMANY NIGHTS 10** [5]4-9-11 bl (77) S Hitchcott(3) 5/1 JT FAV: 2246027: Held up, kept on for press, no threat: see 2286, 1354 & 807. *nk* **74**
3143 **BOAVISTA 10** [8]4-8-10 (62) Dean McKeown 8/1: 1000228: Dwelt, mid-div, not pace to threaten. *½* **57**
2990 **CHAIRMAN BOBBY 15** [12]6-9-3 (69) P Mulrennan(5) 14/1: 2025009: Mid-div, no impress halfway. *5* **49**
2999 **SILVER MASCOT 15** [14]5-8-7 (1ow) (58) R Winston 10/1: 3001200: 10th: Dwelt, nvr on terms: op 10/1. *1¼* **35**
2846 **MR SPLIFFY 21** [11]5-7-12 (4oh) (46) P Hanagan 28/1: 5000000: 11th: Chsd ldrs, btn 2f out: see 413. *shd* **26**
3100 **Dizzy In The Head 11** [13]5-9-13 bl(79) N Chalmers(5) 16/1:0 2445 **Candleriggs 37** [6]8-8-8 (60) A Nicholls 14/1:0
13 Ran Time 59.23 (1.93) Owned: Mr T H Heckingbottom Trained: Doncaster

3351

3.50 Darlington Operatic Society Guys And Dolls Nursery Handicap Stakes 2yo (D) **[85]**
£4940 £1520 £760 **7f rnd** **Good/Firm** **-22 Slow** Inside

2845 **JANE JUBILEE 21** [7] M Johnston 2-9-6 (77) J Fanning 7/4 FAV: 35221: Cl-up & led 2f out, rdn well clr & eased down nr fin: val 10L+: hvly bckd, op 2/1: eff at 6/7f, stay further: acts on fast grnd & a sharp/turning or stiff/undul trk: useful performance, win again, keep on side. **93+**
2845 **DANS HEIR 21** [1] P C Haslam 2-7-13 p (56) D Fentiman(7) 16/1: 0202: Mid-div, styd on for press, nvr a threat to wnr: imprvd eff with cheek pieces reapplied: acts on firm & fast grnd: see 2294 (sell). *5* **60**
2989 **BRACE OF DOVES 15** [2] T D Barron 2-8-12 (69) P Makin(5) 9/2: 05233: Held up, late gains for press, nvr a threat to easy wnr: longer 7f trip shld suit: see 2989 & 2682. *3* **67**
2597 **SHARP N FROSTY 31** [3] W M Brisbourne 2-8-10 (67) B Swarbrick(5) 25/1: 4044: Dwelt & bhd, kept on late, nvr a threat: see 1237. *1¼* **62**
2670 **TWICE NIGHTLY 28** [6]2-9-2 (73) T Hamilton(3) 12/1: 3365: Rear, hung right on bend halfway, kept on late: bolied over in paddock: 7f shld suit, appeared to struggle on this sharp/turning trk. *2½* **63**
3130 **REGAL LUSTRE 11** [4]2-8-3 (61) P Hanagan 25/1: 3526: Mid-div, btn when hmpd 2f out: btr 3130 (5f). *nk* **49**
1950 **PARIS BELL 58** [8]2-8-10 (67) D Allan 28/1: 3507: Keen & trkd ldrs, wknd fnl 2f: abs: btr 1143. *shd* **56**
2275 **CANARY DANCER 44** [9]2-8-6 (63) G Faulkner 10/1: 0428: Chsd ldrs, edged right & fdd fnl 2f, abs. *½* **51**
2640 **JAY 29** [10]2-7-12 bl (55) P M Quinn 16/1: 0029: V slow away & well bhd, mod prog: lost ch at start. *1½* **40**
2714 **LACONICOS 26** [12]2-9-7 VIS (78) T P Queally 6/1: 2320: 10th: Led 5f, wknd: visor, op 9/2: btr 2714. *¾* **62**
3245* **NO COMMISSION 5** [11]2-9-5 (6ex) (76) R Winston 13/2: 0540210: 11th: Mid-div, drvn & btn 2f out. *1¾* **57**
3093 **ITSA MONKEY 12** [5]2-7-12 (6oh) (55) R Ffrench 66/1: 0620: 12th: Pushed along & al rear: btr 3093. *2* **32**
12 Ran Time 1m 27.22 (4.22) Owned: Mrs Sheila Ramsden Trained: Middleham

3352

4.20 Bradford Handicap Stakes 3yo+ 0-70 (E) **[69]**
£3562 £1096 £548 **6f rnd** **Good/Firm** **-00 Slow** Inside

2466 **NORTHERN GAMES 36** [4] K A Ryan 5-8-12 bl (53) G Parkin 25/1: 0204-001: b g Mind Games - Northern Sal (Aragon) Reared start & bhd, pushed wide & styd on well for press from over 1f out, led nr fin: h'cap plcd '03 (rtd 64), class stks rnr-up: eff at 6/7f on fast, gd & fibresand, likes a sharp/turning trk: eff in cheek pieces, suited by reapp of blnks today. **63**
2 Sep'03 Nott 6.1g/f 60-(58) F: 1 Jul'02 Warw 6gd 72- D: 2 Jun'02 Wolv 6af 76a- D:
2571 **NEMO FUGAT 32** [10] D Nicholls 5-9-3 VIS (58) J Fanning 12/1: 0-005602: Trkd ldrs travelling well, ev ch over 1f out, not pace of wnr well ins last, 1st time visor, gd run: see 2317, 2159. *1¼* **64**
2942 **KINGS COLLEGE BOY 18** [14] R A Fahey 4-9-5 bl (60) P Hanagan 16/1: 0032303: Mid-div, styd on for press, not pace of wnr: fair run from moderate draw: see 2320. *1* **63**
3191+**TANCRED TIMES 7** [6] D W Barker 9-9-6 (6ex) (61) F Lynch 12/1: 4403314: Led till well ins last, short of room & eased cl home, lost 3rd nr line: jockey given 10 day ban for failing to ride out to the line. *shd* **64**
3220 **BALLYBUNION 6** [3]5-8-11 (52) P M Quinn 4/1 FAV: 5300005: Towards rear, late gains, nvr threat. *1¼* **51**
2848 **MR BOUNTIFUL 21** [12]6-8-9 T p (50) R Winston 14/1: 0-004006: Held up, wide, mod prog: t-strap. *1½* **44**
2849* **COMPTON PLUME 21** [1]4-10-0 (69) Dale Gibson 8/1: 03D3217: Mid-div, no impress fnl 2f: see 2849. *1¼* **59**
3307 **SIR DON 2** [7]5-9-11 BL (66) Alex Greaves 10/1: 0010358: Handy, no extra dist: blnks: btr 3017. *¾* **54**

3165 INTELLIBET ONE 9 [13]4-9-1 (56) N Callan 12/1: 0-003409: Mid-div, no impress fnl 2f: btr 2951.	1	41
2990 RONNIE FROM DONNY 15 [9]4-9-8 (63) T Eaves(3) 20/1: 0055500: 10th: Rear, no impress: see 241.	hd	47
3289 TOPPLING 4 [11]6-9-0 P (55) Dean McKeown 25/1: 0000400: 11th: Cl-up 5f: qck reapp, cheek pieces.	½	37
3129 MASSEY 11 [2]8-9-0 (55) P Makin(5) 7/1: 00-10100: 12th: Mid-div, btn 2f out: best dominating.	nk	36
3129* MICKLEDOR 11 [8]4-8-13 p (54) P Mulrennan(5) 12/1: 0030110: 13th: Sn struggling rear: btr 3129.	nk	34
3289 DRURY LANE 4 [5]4-8-12 bl (53) A Culhane 9/2: 0040040: 14th: Rear early & nvr factor.	1¾	28

14 Ran Time 1m 12.58 (2.28) Owned: Mr R E Robinson Trained: Hambleton

---

3353 4.50 Batley Claiming Stakes 3yo+ (F)
£2996 £856 £428 **5f rnd** **Good/Firm** +02 Fast Inside

3106 ROXANNE MILL 11 [9] J M Bradley 4-8-13 p (74) P Hanagan 11/10 FAV: 6323561: Handy & led halfway, rdn & al holding rivals from dist.: claimed for 12,000: v eff at 5f on firm, soft & fibresand, likes to dominate: eff with/without cheek pieces: apprec dropped to clmg grade: see 1269.		67
3156* QUEEN OF NIGHT 9 [2] D W Chapman 4-8-10 (55) A Culhane 5/1: 04R0112: Led till halfway, rallied late for press, not able to chall: see 3156 (AW sell).	1¼	59
3191 LOUGHLORIEN 7 [6] R A Fahey 5-8-12 (44) T Hamilton(3) 7/1: 0000033: Held up, kept on late for press, no threat: see 3191, 1886.	1¼	55
2981 TOMTHEVIC 16 [1] Mrs P Sly 6-8-12 (50) Dale Gibson 12/1: 20-00004: Dwelt, chsd ldrs till dist.	2	51
3104 BEYOND CALCULATION 11 [11]10-8-11 bl (53) Dean McKeown 14/1: 0040445: Rear, mod hdwy for press.	nk	49
3102 RISK FREE 11 [7]7-9-0 vis (59) P Mulrennan(5) 16/1: 10535-06: Rear, rdn & no impress: see 3102.	3½	41
3025 AFRICAN SPUR 14 [3]4-9-0 (47) M Lawson(5) 50/1: 0650007: Rear, rdn & no prog: see 775, 461.	1½	36
3129 VIJAY 11 [8]5-8-10 bl (49) R Winston 33/1: 0200608: Chsd ldrs, struggling halfway: see 748.	1½	27
2803 THE LEATHER WEDGE 23 [5]5-9-0 BL (40) P Mathers(5) 33/1: 4052559: Cl-up, wknd qckly 1f out, blnks.	½	29

9 Ran Time 59.09 (1.79) Owned: Dab Hand Racing Trained: Chepstow

---

3354 5.20 Willie Carson - Pinker's Pond Apprentice Handicap Stakes 3yo+ 35-55 (F) [67]
£3010 £860 £430 **1m3f214y** **Good/Firm** -18 Slow Inside

2790* LET IT BE 23 [8] Mrs M Reveley 3-8-7 (1oh) (46) Neil Brown 12/1: 0-250511: Trkd ldrs inner & led over 2f out, rdly asserted under hand riding: suited by 12f, get further: acts on fast & gd/soft, stiff/undul or sharp trk: on the upgrade, hat-trick on the cards: see 2790 & 1363.		58+
2805 DALRIATH 23 [9] M C Chapman 5-8-11 (38) P Varley 18/1: 1250352: Held up, hdwy wide from halfway & chsd wnr over 1f out, al held: recent jumps rnr (unplcd): see 2691 & 1593.	5	40
2937 BLUE VENTURE 18 [19] P C Haslam 4-9-7 (48) G Bartley 50/1: 0004003: Mid-div, styd on for press, not able to chall: stays 12f: see 2008.	½	49
2741 DANEFONIQUE 25 [4] D Carroll 3-9-2 (55) Danielle McCreery 16/1: 3225604: Mid-div, bmpd after 4f, kept on late, no threat: see 1836.	1½	54
3056 SOVEREIGN STATE 13 [12]7-9-6 p (47) P J Benson 8/1: 0/000/-145: Held up, hdwy over 5f out, not able to chall: see 3056 & 2850.	hd	45
2893 PRAIRIE SUN 19 [2]3-9-2 P (55) S Archer 16/1: 4510006: Dwelt, late prog, no threat, cheek pieces.	1¾	51
2844 MOLLYS SECRET 21 [16]6-9-4 p (45) Ashleigh Horton 8/1: 0-100037: Held up when short of room after 3f, late gains, no threat: see 2844 (10f).	1	40
3040 VALEUREUX 13 [7]6-10-0 (57) K Pierrepont 15/2: 002-3248: Trkd ldrs, onepcd fnl 3f: bckd.	¾	49
3238* JACKIE KIELY 5 [14]3-9-8 (6ex)t [21] J G Brennan 9/4 FAV: 4210119: Chsd ldrs, eff wide 3f out, btn dist: nicely bckd under a 6lb pen, qck reapp: awkward wide passage over this longer 12f trip.	¾	54
2552 MIDDLEHAM PARK 33 [1]4-9-10 (51) D Wakenshaw 25/1: 060-2000: 10th: Chsd ldrs, btn 2f out.	shd	44
711] DEEKAZZ 509 [11]5-8-12 (39) T O'Brien 40/1: 45/0406-0: 11th: b f Definite Article - Lyric Junction (Classic Secret) Rear, only mod late prog: long abs: unplcd '03 (rtd 35a, AW h'cap, K Ryan): appr sell h'cap rnr-up in '02: stays 10f, handles fast grnd: tried visor. 2 Aug'02 Ripo 10g/f 42-40 F:	1	31
2905 QUAY WALLOPER 19 [18]3-7-12 (12oh)vis (35) T Dean 66/1: 00-00000: 12th: Mid-div, no prog fnl 3f.	1¾	27
3190 HIBERNATE 7 [13]10-8-12 (39) Janice Webster 40/1: 65/-06400: 13th: Led till over 2f out, fdd.	nk	28
2813 CHEVIN 23 [6]5-9-1 (42) A Elliott 7/1: 15450-50: 14th: V slow away, little prog: see 2813.	¾	30
2688 CEZZARO 27 [5]6-8-12 (39) M Nem 25/1: 5602200: 15th: Cl-up, ch 2f out, wknd: btr 2653.	hd	26
3240 CRYPTOGAM 5 [10]4-8-12 (39) S Shaw 50/1: 0000500: 16th: Mid-div, hmpd 2f out, sn btn: qck reapp.	2	23

2850 Margold 21 [3]4-9-6 (47) H Fellows 20/1:0   3240 **Miss Fleurie** 5 [17]4-8-8 (3oh)(32) S Bushby 50/1:0
2692 Fusillade 27 [15]4-8-13 (40) Susannah Wileman 50/1:0 2244 **Iloveturtle** 46 [20]4-9-9 (50) C Ely 25/1:U

20 Ran Time 2m 37.9(6.7) Owned: Mr A Frame Trained: Saltburn

Official Going GOOD/FIRM.

3355 2.10 Keith Parker 'sun-Ice Air-Conditioning' Maiden Auction Stakes 2yo (E)
£4163 £1281 £641 **5f6y str** **Good/Firm 39** -03 Slow Far Side

2970 PITCH UP 8 [8] T G Mills 2-9-0 K Fallon 7/2: 0361: Made all, kept on well over 1f out, rdn out, shade cmftbly: nicely bckd: imprvd for forcing tactics & eff over a stiff 5f on fast grnd: see 2188.		89
2927 AGENT KENSINGTON 19 [5] R Hannon 2-8-2 R L Moore 7/2: 22532: Held up, hdwy 2f out, kept on ins last, al just held by wnr: back in trip: consistent: see 2927.	½	74
CUSOON [7] G L Moore 2-8-7 J Fortune 33/1: 3: b c Dansili - Charming Life (Habitat) Slow away & bhd, styd on late, nrst fin under kind on debut: April foal, cost £8,500: half-brother to useful wnrs over sprint trip/11f: dam 7f scorer: encouraging start, looks sure to relish 6f+ & will come on plenty for this.	1¼	75+
3110 PENNESTAMP 12 [2] Mrs P N Dutfield 2-8-7 R Havlin 33/1: 0664: Went left start, sn chsd ldr, wknd fnl 1f: eff at 5f on fast grnd: btr eff, see 2287.	nk	74
2995 MISTER AZIZ 16 [1]2-8-7 S Sanders 50/1: 005: Sn rdn in tch, onepace dist: btr run at 5f on fast.	½	72
3097 SOUND THAT ALARM 12 [3]2-8-11 S W Kelly 11/10 FAV: 26: In tch, wknd fnl 1f: bckd, btr 3097.	3	67

MONASHEE ROSE [9]2-8-2 E Ahern 40/1: 7: br f Monashee Mountain - Thorn Tree (Zafonic) Slow 2 52
away & al bhd on debut: Feb first foal, cheaply bght: speedily bred.
2382 HOMME DANGEREUX 41 [6]2-8-9 P Robinson 20/1: 38: In tch, hmpd 2f out, sn wknd: abs: see 2382. 3½ 49
FLOOSIE [4]2-8-4 T P Queally 12/1: 9: b f Night Shift - German Lady (Mon Tresor) Al bhd on 5 29
debut: April first foal, cost 15,000gns: dam 7f/1m scorer: wore a t-strap.
9 Ran Time 1m 01.72 (2.12) Owned: Mr B G Chamley Trained: Epsom

---

3356 2.45 Sungard Securities Finance Handicap Stakes 3yo 0-85 (D) [92]
£6971 £2145 £1073 5f 6y str Good/Firm 39 +22 Fast Far Side

2944* ROYAL CHALLENGE 19 [2] G A Butler 3-8-11 (75) S Sanders 100/30 FAV: 0-211: Handy, hdwy to lead 83
dist, styd on, drvn out: best time of day: v eff over a stiff 5f, shld stay 6f: acts on firm & soft grnd: lightly
rcd, genuine & progressive: see 2944.
3188 BUY ON THE RED 8 [10] W R Muir 3-9-6 (84) R Hughes 11/2: 4-221102: In tch, hdwy to chall appr ½ 90
fnl 1f, kept on ins last, just held: useful, right back to form & continues to prog: shld apprec a return to 6f.
3135 TREASURE CAY 11 [8] P W D'Arcy 3-9-1 e t (79) K Darley 11/2: 5353103: With ldr, led 2f out till ½ 83
dist, kept on, not btn far: back to best: see 2675.
2649* TREGARRON 30 [6] R Hannon 3-8-6 (70) R L Moore 8/1: 26000-14: In tch, onepace over 1f out: nk 73
another gd run raised in class: see 2649.
3135* JADAN 11 [5]3-8-11 (6ex) (75) W Supple 7/1: 0036615: In tch, onepace dist: gd run, see 3135. hd 77
3080 DIVINE SPIRIT 13 [1]3-9-7 (85) A Culhane 10/1: 0361036: Held up, hdwy & short of room dist, not ¾ 85
clr run ins last, not recover/no run at crucial stage: joc received a 2-day careless riding ban: wld have gone close.
3103] MORGAN LEWIS 364 [4]3-7-13 (63) R Thomas(5) 14/1: 400-7: b g Orpen - Party Piece (Thatch) Bhd, nk 62
eff when hmpd dist, not recover: reapp: unplcd all 3 '03 starts: eff at 5f, further shld suit: acts on fast grnd:
much closer with any sort of run, interesting return.
3188 BORZOI MAESTRO 8 [9]3-8-12 p (76) K McEvoy 10/1: 2310438: Led till 2f out, wknd fnl 1f: see 2048 (6f). 3½ 65
2677 DOLCE PICCATA 29 [7]3-8-13 bl (77) J Fortune 20/1: 0545009: Slow away & bhd, eff & badly hmpd 1 63
dist, not recover: another who would have fin closer in a messy race: see 1809.
3241 SION HILL 6 [11]3-9-0 VIS (78) K Fallon 12/1: 202-00: 10th: Hung right & al bhd: tried a visor & 14 22
looks to have temperament problems: see 3241.
10 Ran Time 1m 0.45 (0.85) Owned: Cheveley Park Stud Trained: Blewbury

---

3357 3.15 Listed Star Stakes Fillies 2yo (A)
£17400 £6600 £3300 7f 16y rnd Good/Firm 39 -08 Slow Inside

2863* QUEEN OF POLAND 21 [7] D R Loder 2-8-9 T P Queally 13/2: 11: Chsd ldrs, hdwy to chall & led 104
well ins last, rdn out: stays 7f well, 1m sure to suit: acts on firm & fast grnd: genuine, more to come.
2676* MAIDS CAUSEWAY 29 [10] B W Hills 2-8-9 K Fallon 5/2 FAV: 212: In tch, hdwy to lead dist, kept hd 103
on ins last, collared cl-home: hvly bckd, clr of rem: imprvd on step up in class, shld win a fills List: see 2676.
3127 BENTLEYS BUSH 12 [1] R Hannon 2-8-9 R Hughes 16/1: 52133: Held up, hdwy well over 1f out, 3½ 96
onepace ins last: stays 7f: gd run: see 2537 (mdn auct).
2733* BORTHWICK GIRL 27 [2] B J Meehan 2-8-9 K Darley 16/1: 14: Chsd ldr, outpcd well over 1f out, shd 95
rallied ins last: stays 7f & an encouraging run up in class after 2733 (mdn).
3035* PARK LAW 15 [5]2-8-9 J Fortune 3/1: 215: Led till just ins last, wknd: see 3035 (mdn). ¾ 93
2763 GOLDEN ANTHEM 26 [9]2-8-9 J Quinn 9/1: 1036: Keen in tch, eff dist, sn no extra: see 2763. ½ 92
3003 SHIVAREE 16 [8]2-8-9 T E Durcan 5/1: 3147: In tch, wknd well over 1f out: see 3003, 2829. 1¾ 88
3064* VONDOVA 14 [3]2-8-9 Dane O'Neill 20/1: 3018: Bhd, nvr a factor: see 3064 (6f, mdn). shd 87
LADY PILOT 33/1: 9: b f Dansili - Mighty Flyer (Mujtahid) Slow away & al ½ 84
bhd: Apr foal, cost 40,000gns: half-sister to a 10f wnr: dam styd 10f: bred to need further.
9 Ran Time 1m 29.67 (3.27) Owned: Sheikh Mohammed Trained: Newmarket

---

3358 3.50 Sandown Park Racing Plus Handicap Stakes 3yo+ 0-90 (C) [86]
£10192 £3136 £1568 1m2f7y Good/Firm 39 -11 Slow Inside

4831+ SKY QUEST GB 275 [4] P W Harris 6-9-10 t p (82) R L Moore 8/1: 226P21-1: b g Spectrum - Rose 88
Vibert (Caerleon) Rear, hdwy over 1f out & rdn to lead well ins last: nicely bckd: reapp: dual h'cap scorer in
'03: h'cap wnr '02: stays 12f, suited to gd on firm, gd/soft & polytrack, any trk: eff in t-strap/cheek pieces:
gd wght carrier who goes well fresh: tough, genuine & prog.
1 Oct'03 Yarm 10.1gd 83-78 D: 2 Oct'03 Redc 10g/f 82-74 D: 2 Jul'03 Leic 10.0gd 74-70 D: 2 Jul'03 Sand 10.0g/f 74-70 C:
1 Jun'03 Bath 10.2fm 74-66 D: 2 May'03 Sand 10.0g/f 70-66 D: 2 Apr'03 Ripo 12.3g/f 68-66 E: 2 Feb'03 Ling 10ap 67a- E:
1 Jul'02 Yarm 11.4g/f 71-65 E: 2 May'02 Hayd 8.1g/s 68- D:
2277* ADAIKALI 45 [3] Sir Michael Stoute 3-9-4 (86) K Fallon 10/11 FAV: 0-0212: Trkd ldr & led 3f out, nk 91
hdd well ins last: hvly bckd, 6 wk abs: useful, another gd run: see 2277.
2919 WHITSBURY CROSS 19 [1] D R C Elsworth 3-8-12 (80) Dane O'Neill 7/1: 0-551043: Held up in tch, nk 84
eff to press ldr over 1f out, not pace of wnr fnl 100y: clr rem, fine run: see 2919 & 2274.
2896 STRETTON 20 [2] J D Bethell 6-9-8 P (80) P Robinson 11/4: 0600344: Trkd ldr 2f out, rdn & no 6 74
extra bef dist: nicely bckd: cheek pieces: btr 2896 & 2560.
2918 GREAT SCOTT 19 [5]3-9-2 (84) S Chin 20/1: 5005-005: Led & clr halfway, hdd 3f out & sn btn: see 2679. 2 75
1525 SAN ANTONIO 80 [6]4-9-7 (79) A Culhane 50/1: 22000-06: Held up in tch, btn 2f out: abs, new yard. 7 58
6 Ran Time 2m 09.11 (5.01) Owned: Colourful Band Trained: Berkhamsted

---

3359 4.25 Sharp Minds Betfair Handicap Stakes 3yo 0-85 (D) [92]
£6971 £2145 £1073 1m6f Good/Firm 39 -25 Slow Far Side

2746* PEAK OF PERFECTION 26 [5] M A Jarvis 3-9-4 (82) P Robinson 8/1: 0-535111: Led 4f, rcd keenly & 87
sn trkd ldr, rdn to chall fnl 3f, gamely prevailed well ins last, all out: eff at 12f, imprvd for step up to 14f &
will stay 2m: acts on fast, gd/soft & both AWs: loves to race with/force the pace: v tough, genuine & progressive.
2685 CONSIDINE 28 [9] J M P Eustace 3-8-7 (71) S Sanders 9/2 CO FAV: 5-012102: Trkd ldrs & chall from nk 74
3f out, narrow lead 2f out, drvn & hdd well ins last: hvly bckd, op 11/2: back to form after disapp on soft.

SANDOWN THURSDAY 22.07.04 Righthand, Galloping Track, Stiff Finish

2418 **COVENTINA 39** [4] J L Dunlop 3-9-7 (85) K Darley 9/1: 10-00233: Rear, styd on well from over 2f *shd* **89**
out, just held: looks a tricky ride but remains a likely type for similar: see 2418 & 1807.
3161 **MAN AT ARMS 10** [6] R Hannon 3-9-0 (78) R L Moore 20/1: 3-414004: Mid-div, rdn & kept on onepace *1* **80**
fnl 2f: styd longer 14f trip: see 2538 & 2333.
2376+**NATHLEN 41** [2]3-8-12 (76) T E Durcan 10/1: 0665615: Rear, styd on, not able to chall, abs. *½* **77**
3161 **BIENVENUE 10** [10]3-8-5 (69) W Supple 9/2 CO FAV: 235-4126: Chsd ldrs, no extra from dist: well *hd* **69**
bckd tho' op 7/2: styd longer 14f trip, just btr 3161 & 2788 (11.6f).
3037 **LEVITATOR 15** [8]3-8-6 (70) K Fallon 9/2 CO FAV: 0-0227: Trkd ldrs, led 3f out till 2f out, no extra. *1¾* **68**
2788 **SHONGWENI 25** [11]3-8-3 BL (67) J Quinn 9/1: 4338: Mid-div, onepace fnl 3f: blnks, h'cap bow. *hd* **64**
2660 **BUKIT FRASER 29** [3]3-9-3 (81) A Culhane 16/1: 34-14009: Rear, little prog: flattered 1756. *1* **77**
1462 **SALAMBA 83** [12]3-8-8 (72) M Henry 25/1: 53-50: 10th: Rear, eff 3f out, no impress: gelded, abs. *¾* **66**
2984 **MASTER WELLS 17** [13]3-9-0 (78) K McEvoy 16/1: 100200: 11th: Al bhd: twice below 2746 (g/s). *¾* **71**
3040 **GARSTON STAR 14** [1]3-7-12 (2oh) (60) B Swarbrick(5) 25/1: 06-31220: 12th: Keen & led after 4f till *3* **51**
3f out, wknd qckly: btr 3040, 2333 & 2019 (11/12f).
12 Ran   Time 3m 03.92 (8.92)   Owned: HRH Sultan Ahmad Shah   Trained: Newmarket

3360	5.00 Sharp Minds Betfair Maiden Stakes 3-4yo (D)		
	£5577 £1716 £858	1m14y rnd Good/Firm 39 -23 Slow Inside	

2072 **SERRE CHEVALIER 54** [1] P W Harris 3-8-13 E Ahern 4/7 FAV: 21: Trkd ldr & rdn to chall over 1f **79**
out, styd on for press to narrowly assert ins last: hvly bckd at odds-on: 8 wk abs, confirmed debut promise: eff
at 1m on firm & fast grnd, easy or stiff/gall trks: can go well fresh: lightly rcd, entitled to progress.
2633 **MINORITY REPORT 31** [2] L M Cumani 4-9-7 N Mackay(3) 7/2: 302: Trkd ldrs, drvn & narrow lead 2f *hd* **78**
out till ins last, just held: back to form after disapp latest: acts on fast & gd grnd: rest well covered & shld
find a race, poss in h'cap company: see 2117.
2722 **SILENT STORM 27** [6] H J Cyzer 4-9-7 F Lynch 9/2: 5/-33: Led till 2f out, no impress on front *5* **68**
pair from dist: op 6/1: longer trip: see 2722 (AW).
2586 **CHEMS LEGACY 33** [3] W R Muir 4-9-7 S Chin 50/1: 04: Chsd ldrs, rdn & btn 2f out: longer trip. *9* **50**
2369 **CURZON LODGE 41** [5]4-9-7 J Quinn 50/1: 0-00P: Sn bhd & t.o./p.u. lame from 2f out, abs. **0**
5 Ran   Time 1m 44.0(5)   Owned: Mrs P W Harris   Trained: Berkhamsted

YARMOUTH THURSDAY 22.07.04 Lefthand, Flat, Fair Track

Official Going Good (Good/Firm Places)

3361	2.00 Britannia Pier Theatre Summer Season Maiden Stakes 2yo (D)		
	£3354 £1032 £516	5f43y str Good 41 -25 Slow Stands Side	

1955 **RUBYANNE 59** [5] M J Wallace 2-8-9 D Holland 1/3 FAV: 61: Trkd ldrs, smooth hdwy to lead over 1f **85+**
out, readily pulled clr, val 5L+: hvly bckd at odds-on, 2 mth abs, confirmed debut promise: eff at 5f, stays 6f:
acts on fast & gd grnd, sharp/easy trks: goes well fresh: well regarded & looks potentially useful, rate higher.
DANEHILL WILLY 0 [6] N A Callaghan 2-9-0 R Mullen 10/1: 2: b c Danehill Dancer - Lowtown *4* **72**
(Camden Town) Dwelt, sn pushed along, kept on well from over 1f out, no ch with easy wnr: op 12/1: 35,000gns Mar
foal, half-brother to a 7f juv wnr, dam a dual hdles scorer: eff at 5f, looks sure to apprec 6f+: acts on gd grnd.
3160 **IL PRANZO 10** [1] S Kirk 2-9-0 M Fenton 20/1: 10-: b c Piccolo - St Helena (Monsanto) Led till *¾* **70**
over 1f out, no extra ins last: cheaply bght Mar foal, half-brother to 5 juv wnrs, dam a multiple wnr abroad.
3196 **CHAIRMAN RICK 8** [3] D R Loder 2-9-0 R Pollard 28/1: 064: b c Danehill Dancer - Come Together *2* **64**
(Mtoto) Dwelt & pushed along rear, no prog: 86,000gns purchase, Mar first foal: dam an 11f 3yo scorer.
2851 **DRALION 22** [2]2-9-0 M Hills 6/1: 55: Cl-up 4f, btn dist: op 9/2. *1¾* **59**
IN RHUBARB 0 [4]2-9-0 T Natalia Gemelova(7) 50/1: 6: Slow into stride & al bhd, t-strap on debut. *6* **41**
6 Ran   Time 1m 03.6 (3.5)   Owned: HESheikh Rashid Bin Mohammed   Trained: Newmarket

3362	2.35 Pettitts Animal Adventure Park At Reedham Selling Stakes 3yo+ (G)		
	£2562 £732 £366	1m2f21y Good 41 -11 Slow Inside	

2909 **SENOR EDUARDO 20** [3] S Gollings 7-9-5 (48) N Pollard 5/1 CO FAV: 05-00351: Trkd ldrs trav well, **57**
led over 2f out & rdn clr, decisively: bght in for 6,000gns: first win: eff at 7.5f/1m, imprvd for step up to 10f,
has tried 12f: acts on fast & gd/soft grnd, enjoys sell grade: see 2688 & 1132.
2805 **TATA NAKA 24** [5] Mrs C A Dunnett 4-9-1 (1ow) (37) T G McLaughlin 33/1: 0-005002: Held up, keeping *4* **46$**
on when short of room ins last, nvr threat to wnr: stays 10f in sell grade, acts on gd grnd: imprvd eff with t-strap
& cheek pieces omitted, earlier tried visor: see 757.
3052 **JADE STAR 14** [7] Miss Gay Kelleway 4-9-6 (50) M Fenton 5/1 CO FAV: 0264403: Led till over 2f *½* **50**
out, drvn & kept on onepace: claimed for 6,000: cheek pieces omitted, imprvd eff: see 620, 456.
2064 **MYSTIC MOON 54** [8] J R Jenkins 3-8-4 (51) R Mullen 16/1: 0604004: Trkd ldrs, ch 2f out, onepace: abs. *1½* **42**
2811 **KYLE OF LOCHALSH 24** [4]4-9-5 (49) A McCarthy 13/2: 0-300055: Mid-div, not able to chall: no blnks. *shd* **47**
2588 **SPRINGALONG 33** [9]4-9-5 (56) N Callan 5/1 CO FAV: 4500006: Cl-up, fdd fnl 2f: op 8/1: recent *1½* **45**
jumps runner (unplcd): see 715.
3164 **WHENWILLITWIN 10** [11]3-8-9 Derek Nolan(7) 12/1: 667: Held up, hdwy wide over 3f out, no prog fnl 2f. *hd* **44**
3025 **BUCKENHAM STONE 15** [2]5-9-0 (30) R Price 100/1: 00-00008: Chsd ldrs, outpcd fnl 3f: see 2497. *1* **38$**
2997 **BIG BAD BURT 16** [1]3-8-9 (62) Dean Williams(7) 12/1: 3034609: Slow away & rear, no prog fnl 3f. *hd* **42**
2707 **RED SKELTON 28** [10]3-8-9 bl t (67) D Holland 11/2: 01-0000: 10th: Dwelt, bhd, no ch fnl 3f: see 1427. *2* **39**
2107 **FITZ THE BILL 52** [6]4-9-0 bl (42) J Mackay 12/1: 0-003300: 11th: Dwelt, sn mid-div, btn 3f out: abs. *8* **22**
11 Ran   Time 2m 09.45 (5.25)   Owned: Mr R L Houlton   Trained: Louth

3363 3.05 Wellington Pier & Winter Gardens Handicap Stakes Fillies 3yo+ 0-70 (E) [63]
£3799 £1169 £585 1m str Good 41 -16 Slow Stands Side

2993 **OH SO ROSIE 16** [8] J S Moore 4-9-4 p (53) Derek Nolan(7) 12/1: 0325001: Mid-div, rdn & hdwy to 61
chall over 1f out, duelled with rnr-up, drvn & narrowly asserted nr fin: eff btwn 7/9f on fast & gd/soft, disapp on
both AWs: suited by reapp of cheek pieces today: see 1020.
2893 **AESCULUS 20** [10] L M Cumani 3-9-10 (67) D Holland 13/2: 1-053032: Sn handy & led over 2f out, hd 74
drvn & hdd well in last: versatile as regards trip, could win again: see 2893, 2034 & 49 (6f).
3058 **GABANA 14** [13] C F Wall 3-9-8 (65) R Mullen 9/2 JT FAV: 0603233: Held up, styd on fnl 2f despite ½ 71
carrying hd high: looks a tricky ride: see 2344 (C/D).
2768 **RANNY 26** [6] Dr J D Scargill 4-8-13 (48) P Makin(5) 9/2 JT FAV: 4220644: Chsd ldrs, drvn & no 2½ 49
extra from dist: acts on fast, gd & polytrack: see 2768, 799 & 669.
2993 **BALMACARA 16** [14]5-8-6 (41) N Pollard 16/1: 54-00605: Mid-div, drvn & onepace: see 2440. 2 38
3138 **MORAG 11** [7]3-9-7 P (64) J D Smith 18/1: 0-400066: Held up, eff 3f out, only mod prog: cheekpieces. ½ 60
2552 **KAMAS WHEEL 34** [4]5-8-0 (35) D Fentiman(7) 50/1: 40D60-07: Chsd ldrs, btn 3f out: see 2552. 5 22
3223 **BINT ROYAL 7** [11]6-9-6 (55) A McCarthy 12/1: 4300508: Chsd ldrs, btn 3f out: chkpieces omitted. 5 33
2906 **CHERTSEY 20** [9]3-9-5 (62) M Hills 14/1: 3359: Led till over 2f out, sn hung left & btn. shd 40
2146 **ACOLA 50** [12]4-9-3 VIS (52) O Urbina 40/1: 00-00000: 10th: Keen rear, struggling fnl 3f: tried vis, abs. 1½ 27
2924 **TARDIS 19** [5]3-8-12 (55) J Mackay 33/1: 524-0000: 11th: Chsd ldrs, wknd qckly 3f out: see 2046. 5 21
3324 **NAUGHTY GIRL 2** [1]4-9-1 vis t (50) N Callan 9/1: 0005440: 12th: Chsd far side ldr, struggling halfway. 10 0
2864 **WODHILL BE 21** [2]4-8-8 (43) S Carson 40/1: 6500300: 13th: Sn bhd & struggling, t.o.: btr 1827. ½ 0
3232 **CLASSIC VISION 6** [3]4-9-4 bl (53) R Hills 5/1: 0106000: 14th: Led overall far side, clr till 2½ 0
halfway, hdd 2f out, sn t.o/eased: op 7/1, qck reapp: best prev held up, prob best forgiven: see 2402.
14 Ran Time 1m 39.69 (4.59) Owned: Mr J S Moore Trained: Hungerford

3364 3.40 Stanley M Treadwell Memorial Handicap Stakes 3yo+ 0-85 (D) [85]
£5798 £1784 £892 7f str Good 41 +02 Fast Stands Side

3117 **WILL HE WISH 12** [10] S Gollings 8-9-13 bl (84) I Mongan 16/1: 6000001: Rear, rdn & hdwy over 2f 92
out, led dist, drvn out: suited by 7f on firm & gd/soft: prob handles any trk: see 1043.
3257 **AND TOTO TOO 6** [1] P D Evans 4-8-10 bl (67) N Callan 12/1: 4020442: Mid-div, eff over 1f out, 1½ 71
kept on: qck reapp: tough, gd run: see 270.
2855 **BOBS BUZZ 22** [3] S C Williams 4-8-11 (68) R Mullen 4/1: 3110-053: Keen rear, hung left but kept ¾ 71
on from over 1f out, no threat to wnr: apprec return to 7f: see 2855.
2313 **PRINCE HECTOR 43** [5] W J Haggas 5-9-9 (80) R Hills 3/1 FAV: 10-02624: Rear, hung left from ½ 82
halfway but kept on, nvr a threat to wnr: op 4/1, 6 wk abs: see 1726 & 1255.
3001 **RAFFERTY 16** [11]5-9-11 bl (82) D Holland 9/2: 65000-05: Pulled hard mid-div, smooth hdwy to lead hd 83
over 1f out, sn hung left & no extra: impr on this if settling better: see 3001.
2840 **MORNING AFTER 22** [4]4-9-1 (72) O Urbina 12/1: 22/43-066: Chsd ldrs, no impress over 1f out. 2½ 68
1927 **MICHELLE MA BELLE 61** [6]4-9-2 BL (73) M Hills 25/1: 5-022007: Keen trkg ldrs, led over 2f out, ¾ 68
hdd & carried left over 1f out, wknd: first time blnks, 2 mth abs: trav well for a long way, drop to a stiff 6f suit.
3176* **ZIET DALSACE 9** [8]4-8-1 (6ex) (58) A McCarthy 9/1: 2002018: Trkd ldrs & ch over 2f out, btn/hmpd dist. nk 52
2539 **RIVA ROYALE 34** [2]4-9-9 P (80) J D Smith 28/1: 1-000469: Cl-up, wknd qckly from 2f out, eased in 7 63
last: tried cheek pieces: btr 2312.
2662 **STAR SENSATION 29** [7]4-9-11 (82) S Carson 20/1: 00-65600: 10th: Chsd ldrs, wknd qckly fnl 3f. 5 56
2920 **SAMUEL CHARLES 19** [9]6-9-0 (71) N Pollard 8/1: 2233420: 11th: Led till over 2f out, sn hung left & btn. 16 17
11 Ran Time 1m 25.33 (2.73) Owned: Mrs D Dukes Trained: Louth

3365 4.15 European Breeders Fund Carlsberg Tetley Conditions Stakes Fillies 3yo (C)
£8978 £3406 £1703 7f str Good 41 +05 Fast Stands Side

2574 **LUCKY PIPIT 33** [1] B W Hills 3-8-9 (102) M Hills 4/9 FAV: 1103-521: Made all, readily pulled clr 102+
from over 1f out, easily: hvly bckd at odds-on, best time of day: eff at 7f/1m on firm & gd grnd: enjoys forcing
tactics: useful filly, found this straightforward & could make her mark in List/Gr 3 company: see 2574.
2907* **THREE SECRETS 20** [2] P W Chapple Hyam 3-8-13 (85) A McCarthy 9/4: 20-012: Chsd ldr, rdn & no 8 85
impress over 1f out: caught a useful sort: see 2907 (mdn).
3223 **SURF THE NET 7** [3] R Hannon 3-8-9 (92) D Holland 14/1: 16-3003: Pushed along chasing ldrs, no 1½ 78
impress fnl 2f: see 2136.
TREGENNA 0 [5] R M H Cowell 3-8-6 O Urbina 100/1: 4: b f Forzando - Nineteenth of May (Homing) 13 49
Sn struggling rear & no ch over 2f out: sister to useful AW performer Zanay.
3121 **LOTTIE 12** [6]3-8-9 N Pollard 200/1: 05: Sn bhd & t.o. halfway: well held on debut prev: see 3121. 21 10
5 Ran Time 1m 25.14 (2.54) Owned: Maktoum Al Maktoum Trained: Lambourn

3366 4.50 Jardine Lloyd Thompson Corporate Risk Maiden Stakes 3yo (D)
£3374 £1038 £519 7f str Good 41 -21 Slow Stands Side

2920 **GO YELLOW 19** [5] P D Evans 3-9-0 (69) N Callan 14/1: 0052461: Keen, held up in tch, rdn & led 69
over 1f out, drvn out: op 8/1: eff at 6/7f on firm & gd grnd: see 2650, 2372 & 2055.
3121 **LAKE CHARLOTTE 12** [6] D R Loder 3-8-9 N Pollard 5/4: 32: Keen, held up in tch, drvn to chall 1 63
ins last, al just held: well bckd: btr 3121 (debut).
4568‡ **MENEEF 293** [4] M P Tregoning 3-9-0 R Hills 5/6 FAV: 4-3: b c Kingmambo - Black Penny (Private 2 64
Account) Handy & led over 3f out, hdd over 1f out & not pace of wnr: bckd: reapp: promise sole '03 start (4th,
mdn, rtd 83): eff at 7f, needs 1m+ on this evidence: handles fm & gd.
1464 **PRIVATE JESSICA 83** [3] J R Fanshawe 3-8-9 O Urbina 50/1: 004: ch f Cadeaux Genereux - Rose Bay 5 49
(Shareef Dancer) Handy & led halfway till over 1f out: btn over 1f out: 12 wk abs: 35,000gns purchase: dam mdn.
2997 **HELLO TIGER 16** [2]3-9-0 P P Gallagher(7) 250/1: 0005: Led till halfway, sn struggling, t.o., chkpcs. dist 0
5 Ran Time 1m 26.94 (4.34) Owned: Mr G R Price Trained: Abergavenny

---

3367	**5.20 South Pier Leisure Complex Lowestoft Handicap Stakes 3yo+ 35-55 (F)**		**[65]**
	£3409 £974 £487 **1m3f101y** **Good 41** **+02 Fast** Inside		

3192 **INCHPAST 8** [1] M H Tompkins 3-9-4 bl (55) N Callan 7/2: 050-0041: Handy & led 2f out, rdn & styd on strongly: first win: eff around 11.5f/12f on fast & gd grnd, sharp/easy trk: imprvd in blnks last twice. **63**

2905 **MUSLIN 20** [6] J R Fanshawe 3-9-1 (52) O Urbina 11/1: 03002: Handy & chsd wnr 2f out, kept on, al held: op 7/1: eff arnd an easy 11.5f, tried 14f latest: handles gd grnd. **2½ 55**

2741 **GENUINELY 26** [5] W J Musson 3-8-2 (6oh)VIS (39) J Mackay 14/1: 00-0063: b f Entrepreneur - Fearless (Groom Dancer) Mid-div, drvn & styd on onepace fnl 2f: imprvd eff in first time visor: unplcd in '03 (rtd 48, mdn): stays an easy 11.5f on gd grnd. **1 41**

2796 **VANILLA MOON 24** [3] J R Jenkins 4-9-6 vis (46) N Pollard 10/1: 5-524364: Led/dsptd lead till 2f out, onepace: acts on fast, gd & polytrack: see 1960 & 409. **1 47**

2530 **DUCS DREAM 34** [11]6-10-0 (54) R Mullen 100/30 FAV: 0-001005: Led/dsptd lead till 4f out, no extra. **shd 55**

3145 **COMPTON AVIATOR 11** [10]8-9-11 t (51) L Fletcher(3) 10/1: 44-60506: Mid-div, short of room 3f out, sn no impress: see 1986. **shd 51**

3242 **DAIMAJIN 6** [2]5-9-7 (47) L Vickers 50/1: 0000007: Keen, held up, drvn & no prog fnl 2f, qck reapp. **1¾ 45**

2966 **ELLOVAMUL 17** [4]4-9-10 (50) P Makin(5) 7/1: 545-4048: Chsd ldrs, no impress over 1f out: btr 2966. **½ 47**

3147 **PERIDA 11** [9]4-9-5 (45) A Hindley(7) 25/1: 005-5009: Dwelt, rear, drvn & no prog 3f out: see 2718. **1½ 40**

3354 **JACKIE KIELY 1** [8]3-9-10 (6ex)t (61) I Mongan 9/2: 42101100: 10th: Dwelt, bhd, hdwy wide 2f out, no extra when hmpd ins last, eased right down: unplcd yesterday: see 3238. **14 36**

3175 **PANCAKE ROLE 9** [7]4-8-8 (2oh) (32) A McCarthy 40/1: 40/50-600: 11th: V slow away, al bhd. **25 0**

11 Ran Time 2m 27.23(4.43) Owned: Marcoe Racing Welwyn Trained: Newmarket

---

Official Going Good/Firm (Firm Places)

3368	**2.20 Fish Brothers Renault Median Auction Maiden Stakes 2yo (F)**	
	£3164 £904 £452 **5f161y rnd** **Good/Firm 40** **-17 Slow** Far side	

2744 **TIGHT CIRCLE 26** [11] Mrs G Harvey 2-8-9 F Norton 16/1: 0561: Made all, drvn out ins fnl 1f: eff at 5/5.8f on fast & gd grnd: acts on a stiff/turning trk: gd confidence boost: see 2395. **80**

2859 **GOODWOOD SPIRIT 22** [9] J L Dunlop 2-9-0 T Quinn 1/2 FAV: 22: Handy, styd on ins fnl 2f, not pace of wnr: bckd at odds-on: eff at 5.8/6f, 7f shld suit: shade btr expected after 2859 (debut). **1½ 79**

1053 **CUMMISKEY 108** [7] J A Osborne 2-9-0 S Drowne 5/1: 53: b c Orpen - Ansariya (Shahrastani) Al cl-up, no extra fnl 1f: long abs: Feb foal, cost £180,000: half-brother to wnrs at 1m/9f: dam successful at 1m: sire top-class sprint performer at 2: eff at 5.8f, further shld suit: acts on fast grnd: left debut eff bhd. **1 76**

TASHYRA 0 [3] A M Balding 2-8-9 Martin Dwyer 10/1: 4: b f Tagula - Shiyra (Darshaan) Dwelt, prog halfway, no impress ins fnl 1f: debut: May foal, cost £65,000: dam successful up to 10f: sire decent performer at sprint dists: eff at 5.8f on fast grnd: will improve. **1 68**

TASKS MUPPET 0 [13]2-8-9 J F McDonald(3) 50/1: 5: ch f Raise A Grand - Highland Crumpet (First Trump) Rear, prog halfway, no impress dist: debut: Mar foal, cost £6,500: half-sister to a 5f wnr. **¾ 66**

WATCHMYEYES 0 [5]2-9-0 J P Guillambert(3) 16/1: 6: Slow away, handy halfway, no extra fnl 1f. **shd 70**

3157 **TRACKATTACK 10** [12]2-9-0 R Smith 20/1: 357: Slow away, nvr nrr than mid-div: btr 3020. **2 64**

MAKES PERFECT 0 [14]2-8-9 J F Egan 25/1: 8: Rear, modest late gains: debut. **¾ 57**

3183 **GOLD MAJESTY 8** [10]2-8-9 C Catlin 40/1: 009: Al in rear: btr 3183. **6 39**

THEFLYINGSCOTTIE 0 [8]2-9-0 V Slattery 66/1: 0: 10th: Slow away, nvr a factor. **hd 43**

2970 **DOUGHTY 17** [1]2-9-0 T Joanna Badger 100/1: 0000: 11th: Cl-up over 3f, fdd: first time t-strap. **4 31**

Slite 0 [2]2-8-9 R Keogh(6) 66/1:0 2714 **Pie Corner 27** [6]2-9-0 G Baker 100/1:0

13 Ran Time 1m 12.43 (3.33) Owned: Mr S A Cochrane Trained: Kingston Lisle

---

3369	**2.55 City Motors Renault/E B F Novice Stakes 2yo (D)**	
	£4332 £1333 £667 **5f11y rnd** **Good/Firm 40** **-27 Slow** Far side	

3041* **LADY LE QUESNE 14** [3] A M Balding 2-8-11 S Drowne 4/6 FAV: 6211: Cl-up, led 1f out, hdd ins fnl 1f, rallied to lead cl-home, drvn out: bckd at odds-on: eff at 5f, will apprec return to 6f: acts on firm & gd/soft grnd: likes to front run: game & tough performer, see 3041. **84**

3097* **BOLD MINSTREL 12** [1] M Quinn 2-9-2 F Norton 100/30: 03212: Al cl-up, styd on to lead ins fnl 1f, hdd cl home: lost rhythm in defeat conceding weight all round & an improved run: see 3097. **hd 86**

1048* **WESTBROOK BLUE 108** [4] W G M Turner 2-9-0 C Haddon(7) 5/1: 313: Led, hdd 1f out, kept on, just held by front 2: long abs: acts on fast, gd grnd & fibresand: decent eff: see 1048. **½ 83**

2859 **GEE BEE EM 22** [2] M R Channon 2-9-0 C Catlin 14/1: 2144: Mid-div, prog halfway, onepcd ins fnl 1f. **1¼ 79**

4 Ran Time 1m 3.69 (3.39) Owned: Coriolan Partnership V Trained: Kingsclere

---

3370	**3.25 A K S Yeovil Renault Selling Stakes 4yo+ (G)**	
	£2583 £738 £369 **1m2f46y** **Good/Firm 40** **-09 Slow** Inside	

3175 **DIDOE 9** [6] P W Hiatt 5-8-11 (45) P Doe 8/1: 230-0001: Cl-up, styd on to lead 3f out, rdn out to hold on: no bid: eff at 7f/1m, now stays 10f: acts on firm & fast grnd: apprec drop to sell grade: see 2909. **53**

3211 **FORBEARING 7** [4] M C Pipe 7-9-2 vis (73) C Catlin 2/5 FAV: 01610-32: Rear, prog 3f out, kept on ins fnl 1f, not pace of wnr: bckd at odds-on on qck reapp: clmd for 6,000: visor refitted: btr 3211. **1 56**

3288 **ROLEX FREE 5** [1] D Flood 6-9-2 VIS (60) S Whitworth 25/1: 40-06003: Led 7f, no extra ins fnl 2f: vis. **3 51**

2991 **GIUST IN TEMP 16** [2] P W Hiatt 5-9-2 (36) G Baker 33/1: 0-420604: Held up, prog 3f out, wknd dist. **shd 50$**

2643 **ROJABAA 30** [8]5-9-2 (51) A Daly 9/1: 411-6555: Cl-up, wknd ins fnl 1f: btr 2146. **shd 49**

3087 **SOUTHAMPTON JOE 13** [7]4-9-2 VIS (48) V Slattery 28/1: 00000-06: Al in rear: recent hdles unplcd **8 37**

BATH   THURSDAY 22.07.04   Lefthand, Turning Track With Stiff Uphill Finish

(rtd 72h, cheek pieces): see 3087.
2909 **LUCKY ARCHER 20** [5]11-9-2 (45) P Dobbs 12/1: 000-0007: Rear, prog after 3f, wknd 3f out: btr 2135.   3½   32
      SAPOSCAT 671 [3]4-9-2 T R Smith 66/1: 00-/8: b g Groom Dancer - Dance of Joy (Shareef Dancer)   3½   27
Rear, nvr a factor: recently p.u. over hdles (nov): ex-Irish, unplcd both '02 Flat starts in native country (mdn & clmr).
8 Ran   Time 2m 10.93 (4.93)   Owned: Mrs Marion Wickham   Trained: Banbury

3371   4.00 Westward Renault Bath Handicap Stakes 3yo 0-75 (E)   [80]
£4134 £1272 £636   **5f11y rnd**   **Good/Firm 40**   +00 Fast   Far side

3135 **CATCH THE WIND 11** [3] I A Wood 3-9-7 P (73) F Norton 9/1: 40-05561: Al cl-up, styd on to lead   84+
dist, sn clr, eased cl home, val 4L+: stays sharp 6f, acts on fast, soft & polytrack: authorative
wnr under top-weight, appreciated fitting of cheek pieces: see 2841.
2961 **MALUTI 18** [1] R Guest 3-8-1 (53) C Catlin 6/4 FAV: 6-063142: In tch, styd on ins fnl 1f, al held   2½   57
by wnr: well bckd: continues in gd form: see 2961 & 2645.
2331 **REHIA 42** [5] J W Hills 3-8-0 (52) R Smith 16/1: 4403503: Cl-up till dist, sn no extra: 6 wk abs.   nk   55
3198 **MIRASOL PRINCESS 8** [7] D K Ivory 3-9-5 (71) M Howard(7) 5/1: 0046664: Mid-div, eff halfway,   1   71
onepcd bef 1f out: btr expected after encourging eff in 3198.
3080 **MELODY KING 13** [4]3-9-1 bl (67) Hayley Turner(5) 4/1: 3254365: Held up, nvr nrr than mid-div: btr 3036. 1   64
3135 **PERUVIAN STYLE 11** [2]3-9-7 BL (73) J P Guillambert(3) 5/1: 1105006: Led till dist, wknd: tchd 7/1   nk   69
in first time blnks: btr 914 & 818 (polytrack).
2925 **BAHAMA BELLE 19** [6]3-8-3 BL (55) Martin Dwyer 25/1: 000-0407: Rear, nvr a factor: 1st time blnks.   1¼   47
7 Ran   Time 1m 2.31 (2.01)   Owned: Mr C S Tateson   Trained: Upper Lambourn

3372   4.35 Renault Master Claiming Stakes 3yo+ (F)
£3115 £890 £445   **5f11y rnd**   **Good/Firm 40**   -04 Slow   Far side

3146 **BYO 11** [8] M Quinn 6-9-9 (70) F Norton 9/1: 1066001: Made all, drvn out ins fnl 1f: eff at   73
5/5.7f, likes fast grnd, acts on fast & polytrack: enjoyed drop to claim grade: see 1886.
2784 **SIGNOR PANETTIERE 25** [7] R Hannon 3-9-3 (69) P Dobbs 7/2: 05-02602: Mid-div, prog 2f out,   1   67
staying on when hit on hd by wnr's joc ins fnl 1f: clmd for 9,000: gd effort dropped in grade & can find similar.
3045 **COMPTON BANKER 14** [10] G A Butler 7-9-3 vis (69) T Quinn 5/2 FAV: 5-065203: Slow away, prog 2f   ½   62
out, styd on ins fnl 1f: clmd for 7,000: just btr 2838.
2808* **JINKSONTHEHOUSE 24** [9] M D I Usher 3-8-10 (56) Hayley Turner(5) 9/1: 0104014: Al cl-up, ev ch   ½   58
dist, sn no extra: op 12/1: see 2808.
2981 **BENNANABAA 17** [2]5-9-9 t (40) B O'Neill(7) 66/1: 5000005: Slow away, prog halfway, onepcd fnl 1f.   1¾   62$
3143 **DIAMOND RING 11** [3]5-9-0 (40) N Chalmers(5) 20/1: 0-503036: Nvr nrr than mid-div: see 3143.   hd   52$
2981 **FIAMMA ROYALE 17** [5]6-9-0 (44) J F Egan 8/1: 0-400067: Handy over 3f, no extra: op 16/1: btr 385.   ½   51$
3156 **INNCLASSIC 10** [1]3-9-2 bl (65) V Slattery 7/1: 3-003128: Cl-up till dist, wknd: btr 3156 & 2778.   shd   56
3050 **LAKE VERDI 14** [4]5-9-5 t (53) Martin Dwyer 7/1: 006-0439: Bhd, prog when short of room halfway, wknd. 1   52
1371 **CAPTAIN CLOUDY 88** [11]4-9-5 (57) G Baker 25/1: 00-56600: 10th: Cl-up 4f, fdd: long abs.   ½   51
3048 **TILL THERE WAS YOU 14** [6]3-8-10 C Haddon(7) 100/1: 000: 11th: Al bhd: modest form to date.   1½   42
11 Ran   Time 1m 2.52 (2.22)   Owned: Mr J G Dooley   Trained: Wantage

3373   5.10 Renault Trafic Handicap Stakes Fillies 3yo+ 0-70 (E)   [75]
£3721 £1145 £573   **1m2f46y**   **Good/Firm 40**   +04 Fast   Inside

3144 **DONASTRELA 11** [8] A M Balding 3-8-10 vis (57) N Chalmers(5) 6/1: 0-600141: Rear, prog to lead 2f   69+
out, pushed clr ins fnl 1f, val 5L+: eff at 10f, has tried further: acts on firm & fast grnd: imprvd for recent
fitting of visor & likes Bath: improving, shld make qk follow-up: see 2664.
2719 **SIENNA SUNSET 27** [2] W M Brisbourne 5-9-4 (55) G Baker 20/1: 200-0662: Rear, short of room 3f   2½   59
out, styd on to chase wnr ins fnl 1f, al held: clr rem: encouraging eff & is on a fair mark: see 1348.
3090 **MY HOPE 13** [1] R Charlton 3-9-3 (64) S Drowne 14/1: 00-00003: Mid-div, prog & ev ch over 2f out,   3½   63
sn no extra: first try at 10f: see 2634.
3238 **EMBER DAYS 6** [9] J L Spearing 5-10-0 p (65) T Quinn 2/1 FAV: 0231324: Rear, prog after 6f, wknd   1   62
dist: qck reapp & top-weight: btr 3238 & 2979.
3052 **JESSINCA 14** [5]8-8-2 (39) Hayley Turner(5) 10/1: 0603205: Rear, prog 3f out, fdd fnl 1f: btr 2844.   3   32
3087 **MARGARETS WISH 13** [10]4-8-5 BL (42) C Catlin 50/1: 0100006: Led 1m, wknd: first time blnks: btr 1333. 3   31
3201 **KALIMENTA 8** [6]3-9-4 (65) J F Egan 13/2: 42667: Hit rider in face twice after start, al bhd.   1¼   52
2943 **BOND MAY DAY 19** [3]4-9-2 (63) Martin Dwyer 8/1: 60-00448: Keen cl-up 1m, wknd: btr 2943.   3   46
3099 **NUZZLE 12** [4]4-8-7 (44) F Norton 5/1: 6030309: Handy over 1m, wknd: tchd 15/2: btr 2993.   ½   26
403   **LYRICAL GIRL 190** [11]3-8-12 (59) S Whitworth 14/1: 0031-150: 10th: Cl-up over 7f, wknd: long abs.   10   27
2423 **LADY REDERA 39** [7]3-8-1 BL (48) D Kinsella 66/1: 5400-000: 11th: In rear: first time blnks.   2½   12
11 Ran   Time 2m 9.67(3.67)   Owned: Guy Luck Rosemary de Rougemont Tom Cox   Trained: Kingsclere

DONCASTER   THURSDAY 22.07.04   Lefthand, Flat, Galloping Track

Official Going GOOD - Rain Through Evening

3374   6.30 Galaxy 105 & Out In Publishing Nursery Handicap Stakes 2yo (E)   [82]
£4087 £1258 £629   **5f str**   **Good/Firm**   Slow   Stands Side

3266 **BIBURY FLYER 5** [4] M R Channon 2-9-7 (75) S Hitchcott(3) 11/4: 3352261: Held up, hdwy wide   85
halfway, styd on well to lead ins fnl 1f, rdn out: op 9/4, qck reapp: deserved first success, plcd many times prev,
6th in val super sprint last time: v eff at 5f, shld stay 6f: acts on firm & hvy: tough & useful.
3271 **IM AIMEE 5** [1] P D Evans 2-9-5 (73) F P Ferris(3) 4/1: 3040222: Chsd ldrs wide, ev ch fnl 1f, not   1   79
pace of wnr cl-home: qck reapp: another fine run, deserves similar: see 3271.
2989 **RYEDANE 16** [6] T D Easterby 2-8-12 (66) D Allan 20/1: 03053: Held up, outpcd 2f out, styd on late.   1½   68

1019

3284* **FORZEEN** 5 [8] J A Osborne 2-9-12 (6ex) (80) D Holland 7/4 FAV: 342314: Held up, prog when hmpd   *nk* **81**
entering fnl 1f, nvr nrr: hvly bckd: top-weight: no luck today & must be given another chance, 6lb pen for 3284.
2933 **SKIDDAW WOLF** 19 [3]2-8-9 (63) R Winston 12/1: 0365: Prom, led dist till ins fnl 1f, no extra.   *shd* **64**
3097 **CHILALI** 12 [7]2-8-9 (63) P Mathers(5) 14/1: 5033036: Prom, wandered & wknd fnl 1f.   *3* **55**
2888 **OUR LOUIS** 20 [2]2-8-2 (56) R Ffrench 20/1: 6054157: Led till dist, wknd: twice below 2611.   *½* **47**
3093* **ETERNALLY** 13 [5]2-7-13 p (53) Lisa Jones(3) 14/1: 035318: Prom 3.5f, wknd: btr 3093 (AW seller).   *6* **29**
8 Ran   Time 1m 01.21 (3.01)   Owned: Ridgeway Downs Racing   Trained: West Ilsley

---

3375   **7.00 Grolsch Classified Stakes 3yo+ 0-75 (D)**
   £5655 £1740 £870   **6f str**   **Good/Firm**   **Fair**   Stands Side

3215 **LORD OF THE EAST** 7 [4] D Nicholls 5-9-1 (75) J Fanning 9/1: 0132321: Broke well & made all, clr   **82**
dist, rdn out: eff at 6/7f on firm & gd/soft grnd, handles any trk: tough & in-form.
3269 **ARMAGNAC** 5 [11] M A Buckley 6-9-3 (77) D Holland 3/1: 3600232: Held up, prog & short of room   *¾* **81**
dist, styd on, nvr nrr: well bckd: qck reapp: deserves similar: see 3269.
2990 **HICCUPS** 16 [7] Mrs J R Ramsden 4-9-6 p (80) R Winston 8/1: 2031063: Held up, hdwy dist, nrst fin.   *2* **77**
2934+ **HARTSHEAD** 19 [8] G A Swinbank 5-9-1 (72) Dean McKeon 15/8 FAV: 0-206114: Trkd ldrs, no extra fnl   *½* **70**
1f: well bckd: not disgraced on hat-trick bid, tho' rtd higher 2934.
3241 **SOBA JONES** 6 [1]7-9-1 (69) J Edmunds 12/1: 2565425: Prom, ev ch till wknd fnl 1f: qck reapp.   *2½* **63**
3241 **PADDYWACK** 6 [2]7-9-1 bl (73) Lisa Jones(3) 10/1: 3011036: Chsd ldrs wide, btn fnl 1f: btr 2942 (5f).   *2½* **56**
3098 **JALOUHAR** 12 [9]4-9-1 (46) T Woodley 100/1: 6020067: Chsd ldrs 4.5f, wknd: v stiff task.   *4* **44**
2830 **BANJO BAY** 23 [10]6-9-1 (73) A Nicholls 12/1: 0030068: Front rank, wknd 1.5f out: s/mate of wnr.   *4* **32**
3136 **SMIRFYS SYSTEMS** 11 [6]5-9-2 (76) D Allan 20/1: 12-00509: Al rear: op 14/1.   *nk* **32**
3136 **GREY COSSACK** 11 [5]7-9-1 (73) R Fitzpatrick 16/1: 0500050: 10th: Dwelt, imprvd to chase ldrs   *nk* **30**
halfway, sn btn: mainly out of form since 1145 (soft grnd).
3326 **TELEPATHIC** 2 [3]4-9-1 t (57) P Mathers(5) 100/1: 6056540: 11th: Chsd ldrs, wknd 2f out: qck reapp.   *8* **6**
11 Ran   Time 1m 13.08 (2.28)   Owned: The Wayward Lads   Trained: Thirsk

---

3376   **7.30 Dc Training & Development Services Maiden Auction Stakes 2yo (E)**
   £3699 £1138 £569   **6f str**   **Good/Soft**   **Slow**   Stands Side

1107 **CAMMIES FUTURE** 103 [5] P W Chapple Hyam 2-8-12 W Ryan 13/8 FAV: 31: Chsd ldrs, imprvd to lead   **87+**
dist, hands & heels, cmftbly: hvly bckd, 3 mth abs: apprec step up to 6f, acts on gd/soft & soft grnd: handles a
gall trk, clearly runs well fresh: did this well, real nursery type: see 1107.
ABLE CHARLIE [16] Mrs J R Ramsden 2-8-11 R Winston 25/1: 2: ch g Lomitas - Alula (Monsun)   *1* **80+**
Held up, imprvd after halfway, switched & styd on fnl 1f, nrst fin: E28,000 Feb first foal: eff at 6f on gd/soft,
will relish 7f/1m+: v encouraging, win races.
3046 **MERCHANT** 14 [18] M L W Bell 2-8-11 A Nicholls 9/2: 53: Chsd ldrs, kept on under press fnl 1f,   *nk* **79**
not btn far: op 11/2, clr of rem: eff over a gall 6f, return to 7f shld suit: acts on gd/soft grnd: see 3046.
METHODICAL [14] I A Wood 2-8-3 G Gibbons 33/1: 4: ch g Lujain - Simple Logic (Aragon) Rear,   *3½* **61**
impvd 2f out, nrst fin on debut: 3,000gns Apr foal: dam a 6f juv wnr, sire a high-class juv: 7f shld suit, handles
gd/soft grnd: will learn from this.
3020 **TYBALT** 15 [12]2-8-9 D Holland 10/3: 25: Chsd ldrs, kept on fnl 1f, nrst fin: well bckd: more   *1½* **63**
expected after highly encouraging debut in 3020 & prob worth another chance back on faster grnd.
BRIANNSTA [15]2-8-9 S Hitchcott(3) 20/1: 6: b c Bluebird - Nacote (Mtoto) Rear, styd on late,   *shd* **63**
nrst fin on racecourse bow: E5,000 Apr foal: half-brother to several wnrs, incl 6f juv scorer Sineogron.
2221 **WATERLINE LOVER** 48 [8]2-8-6 F P Ferris(3) 25/1: 60047: Led till dist, wknd: 7 wk abs.   *¾* **57**
ADMITTANCE [10]2-8-6 L Goncalves 66/1: 8: b f Red Ransom - Quittance (Riverman) Mid-div,   *3½* **47**
outpcd bef halfway, rallied late on debut: longer priced stablemate of rnr-up: E24,000 Feb foal: dam 1m wnr.
2933 **DESERT BUZZ** 19 [7]2-8-8 M Tebbutt 25/1: 06059: Front rank, wknd dist.   *hd* **49**
2618 **DOVER STREET** 31 [11]2-8-11 Paul Eddery 25/1: 500: 10th: Nvr btr than mid-div: has been gelded.   *1* **49**
2652 **GOLDEN SQUAW** 30 [1]2-8-3 D Allan 33/1: 60: 11th: Prom wide, wknd 2f out.   *shd* **41**
2275 **FRENCH KISSES** 45 [6]2-8-4 Dean McKeown 100/1: 00: 12th: Nvr a factor: 6 wk abs.   *nk* **41**
3157 **WILFORD MAVERICK** 10 [2]2-8-8 J Fanning 33/1: 000: 13th: Al rear.   *1¼* **41**
2983 **DESERT PHOENIX** 17 [9]2-8-5 P Hanagan 25/1: 60: 14th: Nvr nr ldrs: see 2983.   *3* **29**
SHEKAN STAR [17]2-8-7 J Edmunds 20/1: 0: 15th: Al bhd on debut.   *½* **30**
CALA FONS [3]2-8-5 Kim Tinkler 100/1: 0: 16th: Slowly away, al rear on racecourse bow.   *shd* **28**
PLENTY CRIED WOLF [13]2-8-10 T Hamilton(3) 66/1: 0: 17th: Al rear on debut.   *hd* **33**
ORPEN WIDE [4]2-8-9 Lisa Jones(3) 66/1: 0: 18th: Slowly away, al bhd & fin last on debut.   *12* **0**
18 Ran   Time 1m 15.44 (4.64)   Owned: Collins Deal Harrison-Allan Chapple-Hyam   Trained: Newmarket

---

3377   **8.00 Carling Extra Cold Handicap Stakes Fillies 3yo 0-85 (D)**   [84]
   £5525 £1700 £820   **1m2f60y**   **Good/Soft**   **Slow**   Inside

2705 **RIO DE JUMEIRAH** 28 [1] C E Brittain 3-9-5 (75) K Fallon 4/1: 35-36051: Prom, styd on under press   **88+**
to lead ins fnl 2f, pushed clr, val 5L+: eff at 7f, now stays around 10f: acts on fast & gd/soft grnd: gd
confidence boost & can progress: see 1924 & 1619.
2904 **EBORACUM** 20 [3] T D Easterby 3-8-7 (63) D Allan 10/3: 520-0022: Bhd, prog after 6f, kept on ins   *3½* **66**
fnl 1f, al held by easy wnr: nicely bckd: eff at 1m, apprec step up to 10f: acts on fast & gd/soft grnd: see 2166.
2994* **TREW CLASS** 16 [2] M H Tompkins 3-9-7 (77) D Holland 11/4 FAV: 00113: Led after 2f, hdd under   *1½* **78**
press just ins fnl 2f, no extra: just below form on hat-trick bid: btr 2994 & 2386 (fast).
2716 **APPETINA** 27 [5] J G Given 3-8-9 (65) J Fanning 8/1: 303-5544: Led, hdd after 2f, styd prom, fdd dist.   *3* **61**
1209 **SERRAMANNA** 97 [4]3-9-6 (76) W Ryan 3/1: 62-65: ch f Grand Lodge - Spry (Suave Dancer) Mid-div   *14* **52**
7f, sn wknd: long abs: rnr-up on last of 2 '03 starts (mdn, rtd 79): eff at 1m, bred to apprec mid-dists: acts
on fast grnd: better expected today: with H R A Cecil. 2 Aug'03 Chep 8.1g/f 79- D:
5 Ran   Time 2m 15.29 (8.89)   Owned: Abdullah Saeed BelHab   Trained: Newmarket

DONCASTER THURSDAY 22.07.04 Lefthand, Flat, Galloping Track

3378 8.30 Eastside Magazine Handicap Stakes 3yo 0-80 (D) [87]
£5736 £1765 £883 1m str Good/Soft Fair Stands Side

2960 **DOUBLE VODKA** 18 [1] Mrs J R Ramsden 3-8-4 (63) P Hanagan 3/1: 5-062401: Held up, prog bef 1f 70
out, styd on well to lead cl-home: tchd 4/1: prob stays 11f, eff at 1m: acts on fast & gd/soft: confirmed promise
of 2960 & more to come.
2940+**CHARNOCK BATES ONE** 19 [7] T D Easterby 3-8-11 (70) R Winston 4/1: 54-46012: Handy, styd on to hd 75
lead bef 1f out, hdd under press cl-home: op 3/1: remains in gd form: see 2940 & 1163.
2985 **BRIGHT SUN** 17 [8] N Tinkler 3-8-13 (72) Kim Tinkler 12/1: 0004303: In tch, rcd keenly, prog & ev hd 77
ch ins fnl 1f, kept on, just held in 3-way photo: eff at 6f, ran to form on first try at 1m: see 2155.
3074 **HONEST INJUN** 13 [6] B W Hills 3-9-1 (74) D Holland 5/2 FAV: 2-144054: Mid-div, prog when no room 2 74+
bef 1f out, switched & styd on ins fnl 1f, ch had gone: bckd from 7/2: wld have gone close with a clr passage.
3138 **FOOLISH GROOM** 11 [4]3-8-10 t p (69) A Culhane 13/2: 345635: Mid-div, prog & ev ch bef 1f out, wknd. ¾ 67
2940 **COTTINGHAM** 19 [9]3-8-4 (63) Lisa Jones(3) 14/1: 040-1466: Prom till dist, fdd: btr 355. 9 43
2994 **HEVERSHAM** 16 [2]3-9-0 (73) M Tebbutt 12/1: 0004257: Led bef 6f out, hdd bef 1f out, fdd: see 2854. ½ 52
1822 **TYZACK** 65 [3]3-8-6 (65) J Edmunds 16/1: 5240-508: Al bhd: 9 wk abs, new stable, btr 1088 (J Given). 1½ 41
1822 **SPARTAN SPEAR** 65 [10]3-8-4 P (63) J Bramhill 25/1: 04-009: b g Sure Blade - Confection dist 0
(Formidable): Led, hdd bef 6f out, wkng & under press when badly short of room 4f out, sn eased: first time cheek
pieces: 4th of 18 on 1 of only 2 '03 starts (mdn, rtd 77): eff at 7f, bred to apprec further: acts on fast grnd.
9 Ran Time 1m 41.51 (5.01) Owned: Mrs Alison Iles Trained: Thirsk

3379 9.00 Doncaster Racecourse Sponsorship Club Handicap Stakes 3yo 0-85 (D) [91]
£5671 £1745 £873 6f str Good/Soft Fair Stands Side

3273* **COMMANDO SCOTT** 5 [5] A Berry 3-9-7 (6ex) (84) F Lynch 7/2 FAV: 0222611: Made all, went clr ins 95
fnl 2f, rdn clr: nicely bckd on qck reapp: eff at 6/7f on fast, likes soft: tough & genuine sprinter: see 3273.
3188* **RED ROMEO** 8 [7] G A Swinbank 3-9-13 (6ex) (90) K Fallon 9/2: 2441112: In tch, rcd keenly, styd on 2½ 93
to chase wnr ins fnl 1f, sn hung right & al held by wnr: op 3/1: fine run under top-weight & remains in form.
3018 **CHEROKEE NATION** 5 [8] P W D'Arcy 3-8-7 (70) D Holland 5/1: 1021103: Rear, prog halfway, late gains.1 70
3188 **INSTANT RECALL** 8 [12] B J Meehan 3-9-1 bl (78) J Fortune 4/1: 4545124: Chsd ldrs, no extra when ¾ 75
short of room ins fnl 1f: tchd 5/1: btr 3188 & 2841.
3262 **ICE PLANET** 5 [4]3-8-6 (69) R Winston 25/1: 03505: Dwelt & short of room sn after start, prog ½ 65
after halfway, nrst fin: qck reapp: acts on gd/soft & soft grnd: encouraging effort: see 1228.
2586 **LIGNE DEAU** 33 [9]3-7-13 (62) F P Ferris(3) 10/1: 000-0536: Handy over 4f, no extra: btr 2586. 2½ 51
1020 **SOLINIKI** 112 [11]3-9-2 (79) V Slattery 25/1: 1-07: b g Danzero - Pride of My Heart (Lion Cavern) 4 56
1 Aug'03 Asco 6g/f 73- D: Nvr nrr than mid-div: long abs: auct mdn wnr on sole '03 start: eff at 6f on fast grnd: has gone well fresh.
1933 **KABREET** 61 [1]3-9-1 (78) W Ryan 16/1: 01-31008: Prom over 4f, fdd: 9 wk abs: btr 494. 2 49
2295 **COMPTON MICKY** 44 [10]3-7-12 (5oh)p (56) J Bramhill 66/1: 0-000568: Handy 4f, fdd: 6 wk abs. nk 31
2400 **ABELARD** 40 [3]3-8-2 (65) P Hanagan 13/2: 333-650: 10th: Bhd, nvr a factor: btr 2227. ½ 34
4584} **MARYSIENKA** 292 [6]3-8-13 (76) J Edmunds 50/1: 620264-0: 11th: b f Primo Dominie - Polish Romance 5 30
(Danzig) Chsd ldrs 4f, fdd: reapp: rnr-up twice in '03 (h'caps, R Hannon): eff around 5f on fast & gd grnd.
2 Aug'03 Chep 5.1gd 80-78 D: 2 Jul'03 Ling 5g/f 76-74 E:
11 Ran Time 1m 14.47(3.67) Owned: Mrs Ann Morris Trained: Cockerham

FOLKESTONE THURSDAY 22.07.04 Righthand, Sharpish, Undulating Track

Official Going GOOD/FIRM (GOOD IN PLACES)

3380 6.15 Evening Racing At Folkestone Racecourse Apprentice Handicap Stakes 3yo 0-70 (F) [76]
£3059 £874 £437 6f Good 55 +10 Fast Stands side

4887} **DAVE** 271 [3] J R Best 3-8-7 (55) N De Souza(3) 20/1: 0050-1: b g Danzero - Paradise News (Sure 65
Blade) Reared start, rcd stands rail, made all, rdn out fnl 1f: fast time: first win, reapp: unplcd all '03
starts (mdns, nurs, rtd 67): eff at 6f on gd, sharp/undul trk: runs well fresh: improved since last term.
2852* **MUGEBA** 22 [12] Miss Gay Kelleway 3-8-11 T (59) Rachel Costello(5) 8/1: 02-5512: Prom far side, 3 60
hdwy to lead that group over 1f out, kept on but no ch with near side wnr: gd run for new stable (prev with W Musson)
in first time t-strap: see 2852.
3153 **HALF A HANDFUL** 10 [7] M J Wallace 3-9-3 VIS (65) D Corby 5/1: 0063323: Trkd near side ldrs, hdwy nk 65
1f out, sn wknd: tried a visor: consistent in defeat: see 3153.
2971 **NEBRASKA CITY** 17 [6] P Mitchell 3-8-7 T (55) L Keniry 33/1: 050-0604: Mid-div near side, kept on ¾ 53
fnl 1f & nrst fin: first time t-strap: worth a try at 7f on this evidence: see 3153.
2379 **CREWES MISS ISLE** 41 [10]3-9-0 (62) B Reilly 12/1: 6150005: In tch far side, hdwy 1f out, sn onepcd. 1½ 55
3301 **JASMINE PEARL** 3 [4]3-8-0 (48) M Halford(5) 6/1: 0040256: Chsd wnr near side, lost pl & wknd 1f out. hd 40
1690 **GENEROUS SPIRIT** 71 [5]3-9-0 (62) A Beech 8/1: 00067: ch c Cadeaux Genereux - Miss Rossi ¾ 52
(Artaius) Reared start, near near side, modest late gains: op 12/1, long abs: h'cap bow: mdn unplcd earlier.
3143 **ARFINNIT** 11 [8]3-8-12 vis (60) T Dean(7) 6/1: 6616408: Slow away, sn handy far side, wknd fnl 1f. 1 47
3198 **BELLA TUTRICE** 8 [2]3-9-7 (69) T P Queally 4/1 FAV: 0-034039: Cl-up near side, no impress fnl 1f. nk 55
2048 **KURINGAI** 55 [11]3-9-3 (65) D Fox(3) 16/1: 0430000: 10th: Led far side group till halfway, no extra. 2½ 43
2439 **QUEEN OF BULGARIA** 38 [7]3-7-12 (1oh) (45) R Thomas(1) 16/1: 2-000000: 11th: Near side, al bhd. 1¼ 20
2706 **SMOKIN JOE** 28 [9]3-8-12 VIS (60) M Savage(2) 12/1: 6-405000: 12th: Cl-up far side, hdwy to lead 3 25
group halfway till over 1f out, fdd: tried a visor: see 2586.
12 Ran Time 1m 13.71 (2.71) Owned: MFolan AWarner DGiles CDennison Trained: Maidstone

3381
6.45 European Breeders Fund Maiden Stakes Fillies 2yo (D)
£5408 £1664 £832   7f   Good 55   -21 Slow   Stands side

3035 **HIDDEN CHANCE 15** [12] R Hannon 2-8-11   R Thomas(5) 5/1: 01: ch f Hernando - Catch (Blushing   **71**
Groom) Dwelt, gd hdwy 2f out, drvn ins fnl 1f & led fnl stride: Feb foal, cost 15,000gns: half-sister to US wnrs:
sire high-class at 12f: stays 7f, further will suit: acts on gd: fine start.

  SWEET LORRAINE 0 [14] T G Mills 2-8-11   N de Souza(5) 16/1: 2: b f Dashing Blade - Royal Future   hd   **69**
(Royal Academy) Rcd in 2nd till led 3f out, hdd fnl stride on debut: op 12/1: Mar foal, cost 3,000gns: half
sister to a 10f wnr: dam unrcd: eff at 7f on gd: fine start, just caught nr fin & entitled to improve next time.

3063 **VELVETEEN RABBIT 14** [7] Saeed bin Suroor 2-8-11   L Dettori 5/2 FAV: 03: b f Singspiel - Velvet   ½   **68**
Lady (Nashwan) Cl-up, hdwy into 2nd over 2f out, kept on again ins fnl 1f: Jan first foal: dam 1m wnr: eff at 7f on
gd, will relish 1m: win a race.

  BONGOALI 0 [3] M R Channon 2-8-11   T Dean(7) 40/1: 4: Dwelt, sn mid-div, kept on well from 2f   nk   **67**
out, not pace to chall on debut: eff at 7f on gd: fine start.

  FLAUNTING IT 0 [9]2-8-11   D Sweeney 50/1: 5: Trkd ldrs to 3f out, pushed along/kept on ins fnl   hd   **66+**
1f on debut: relish further: v pleasing.

3035 **IMPERIAL MISS 15** [13]2-8-11   M Halford(7) 25/1: 0606: Trkd ldrs, onepcd 1f out: eff at 7f on gd.   nk   **65**

  KRUMPET 0 [11]2-8-11   A Beech(3) 66/1: 7: Dwelt, rear, some late gains on debut.   ½   **64**

2061 **ROMANTIC GIFT 54** [4]2-8-11   L Keniry(3) 20/1: 008: Dwelt, bhd, hdwy 2f out, onepcd over 1f out.   shd   **63**

  ISSY BLUE 0 [8]2-8-11   S W Kelly 33/1: 9: Trkd ldrs, onepcd fnl 1f on debut.   1   **61**

2733 **SABBIOSA 27** [10]2-8-11   B Doyle 33/1: 00: 10th: Rear, green, hdwy 2f out, not clr run ins fnl 1f   1¼   **58**
& eased: closer with a clr run, not btn far and capable of btr.

  FANTAISISTE 0 [6]2-8-11   S Sanders 3/1: 0: 11th: Bhd, nvr nr ldrs on debut: op 5/1.   3   **52**

3103 **RESISTANCE HEROINE 12** [2]2-8-11   B Reilly(3) 25/1: 00: 12th: In tch, wknd 2f out.   shd   **51**

3035 **ENTERTAIN 15** [1]2-8-11   M Savage(1) 12/1: 00: 13th: Mid-div, eff over 3f out, ran green & no impress.   6   **39**

2863 **GEORGINA 21** [5]2-8-11   D Corby(3) 8/1: 00: 14th: Trkd ldrs, no impress 3f out: op 6/1.   4   **31**

  FRENCH SCHOOL 0 [15]2-8-11   T P Queally 1/1: 0: 15th: Made most to 3f out, fdd, t.o. on debut.   25   **0**
15 Ran   Time 1m 29.56 (5.36)   Owned: Mr Nicholas R Hodges   Trained: Marlborough

3382
7.15 Kent Air Ambulance Trust Selling Stakes 2yo (G)
£2863 £818 £409   5f   Good 55   -10 Slow   Stands side

3172* **PIDDIES PRIDE 9** [5] P S McEntee 2-8-12   L Dettori 5/4 FAV: 566411: Dsptd lead till led halfway,   **72**
flashed tail for a smack 1f out but sn cmfbrbly, readily: bt in for 13,500gns: in gd form in sellers: new stable.

3284 **KERESFORTH 5** [4] I A Wood 2-9-3 bl   S Sanders 2/1: 002102: Led to halfway, remained in 2nd, no ch   5   **65**
with wnr fnl 1f: qck reapp, top-weight: btr 2270.

882 **HIS MAJESTY 124** [1] N P Littmoden 2-8-12   Steven Harrison(7) 22/1: 03: ch c Case Law - Eternal   5   **45**
Triangle (Barachois) Mid-div, wknd 2f out: long abs: Mar foal, half-brother to wnrs over 5f/10f: dam 2yo sprint wnr.

1041 **CUBIC CONFESSIONS 110** [2] J A Osborne 2-8-7   S W Kelly 5/2: 444: b f Cape Cross - Debinnair   9   **13**
(Wolfhound) Slow away, cl-up, wknd over 1f out: tchd 4/1, long abs: Mar foal, cost £34,000: sister to a dual
French 2yo mile wnr: dam a sprint wnr in France at 2.
4 Ran   Time 1m 1.67 (3.27)   Owned: Mrs B A McEntee   Trained: Newmarket

3383
7.45 Come Back On Ladies Night Handicap Stakes 3yo 35-55 (F)   [63]
£3080 £880 £440   1m4f   Good 55   -26 Slow   Outside

2790 **BIENHEUREUX 24** [13] Miss Gay Kelleway 3-8-10 (45) M Fenton 10/1: 0-000021: Dwelt, bhd, hdwy 3f   **53**
out, plenty to do 2f out, drvn & styd on well fnl 1f to lead fnl stride: first win: eff at 12f on fast & gd, acts on
a sharp/undul trk: gd start for new stable (prev with W Musson): see 2790.

2978 **SCIENCE ACADEMY 17** [10] P F I Cole 3-9-2 (51) N De Souza(5) 14/1: 500-0562: Led, chall 3f out,   hd   **58**
went clr over 1f out, hdd fnl stride: stays 12f: shld find a race: see 1648.

2613 **A MONK SWIMMING 31** [4] John Berry 3-8-0 (3oh) (32) N Mackay(3) 9/1: 060-43: Rcd in 2nd, lost pl 4f   1¾   **39**
out tho' remained cl-up, hdwy 2f out, onepcd fnl 1f: stays 12f on gd: gd eff from 3lb out of the h'cap: see 2613.

3051 **RINNEEN 14** [5] R Hannon 3-8-11 vis (46) R L Moore 7/1: 00-00534: In tch, hdwy 2f out, not pace to chall.   hd   **49**

3051 **REGAL PERFORMER 14** [14]3-9-6 (55) L Dettori 11/2: 0022345: Trkd ldrs, onepcd 2f out, wknd qckly.   4   **52**

2978 **THE KING OF ROCK 17** [9]3-9-6 (55) L Keniry(3) 5/1: 0540246: Keen in tch, hdwy into 2nd after 1m,   3   **47**
lost pl 2f out & wknd: see 2503.

3090 **VENETIAN ROMANCE 13** [1]3-8-5 (40) R Thomas(5) 33/1: 5-500007: Dwelt bhd, modest late gains.   3   **27**

1193 **JANGO MALFOY 98** [8]3-9-3 t (52) A Daly 80/1: 050-0008: ch g Russian Revival - Sialia (Bluebird)   6   **30**
Bhd, some late gains: abs: unplcd all 5 '03 starts (mdns, nov, nurs, rtd 66a): has tried blnks, wears a t-strap.

2866 **CAZISA STAR 21** [7]3-9-6 (55) E Ahern 25/1: 036-009: Nvr btr than mid-div: see 2366.   hd   **32**

617 **MRS BROWN 160** [12]3-9-6 (55) S Sanders 11/4 FAV: 3560: 10th: Cl-up, wknd over 1f out, eased.   5   **24**

2868 **VRISAKI 21** [2]3-8-13 (48) D Fox(5) 8/1: 4003630: 11th: Keen & trkd ldrs, wknd 2f out, eased fnl 1f.   3½   **12**

2843 **SCOTT 22** [3]3-9-6 (55) T E Durcan 20/1: 0060: 12th: In tch, lost pl 5f out, sn btn: see 2325.   13   **0**

3024 **NEWTOWN CHIEF 15** [11]3-9-6 (55) Steven Harrison(7) 66/1: 0600-00: 13th: b g So Factual - Polish   nk   **0**
Descent (Danehill) Keen & handy, lost pl halfway, no ch 3f out: mdn & nurs unplcd in '03 in native Ireland.

2131 **OCEAN ROCK 51** [6]3-9-6 (55) Dane O'Neill 10/1: 0-0000: 14th: b c Perugino - Polistatic (Free   11   **0**
State) Dwelt in rear, t.o.: 7 wk abs: well btn sole '03 start (mdn, rtd 50): with C Horgan.
14 Ran   Time 2m 41.3 (9.8)   Owned: Countrywide Classics Limited   Trained: Newmarket

3384
8.15 Gerald Lukehurst & Son Furnishers Handicap Stakes 3yo 0-80 (D)   [84]
£5509 £1695 £848   1m1f149y   Good 55   -01 Slow   Outside

3300* **MASAFI 3** [2] Sir Mark Prescott 3-8-3 (6ex) (59) S Sanders 2/9 FAV: 00-21111: In tch, hdwy to lead   **85+**
7f out, trav best 2f out, pushed out ins fnl 1f, val 5L+: landed 4-timer: op 1/3, qck reapp: eff at 1m/10f, shld
stay further: acts on fast, gd & both AWs, sharp/undul or stiff trks: v tough, can land 5-timer: see 3300.

3219 **LITTLE EYE 7** [3] J R Best 3-8-5 vis (61) T P Queally 25/1: 0306402: Rear, hdwy 3f out, chsd wnr   3   **68**
from 2f out but not his pace: qck reapp: acts on firm, gd & both AWs: caught a tartar: mdn: see 497.

FOLKESTONE THURSDAY 22.07.04 Righthand, Sharpish, Undulating Track

2971 **KEEPERS KNIGHT 17** [6] P F I Cole 3-8-6 (62) N De Souza(5) 33/1: 1350003: Bhd, hdwy 3f out, onepace. *1¾* **65**
2663 **MOMMKIN 29** [7] M R Channon 3-9-1 (71) T E Durcan 14/1: 425-5554: Trkd ldrs, no impress 2f out. *13* **48**
3112 **ALFRIDINI 12** [1]3-9-3 (73) L Keniry(3) 9/1: 1401355: Trkd ldrs, hdwy over 2f out, sn no impress. *1¼* **47**
2860 **TANNOOR 22** [5]3-9-7 (77) P Robinson 16/1: 33-31506: Led to 7f out, remained in 2nd, no extra 2f out. *3½* **44**
2930 **BAILAORA 19** [4]3-9-2 bl (72) R L Moore 20/1: 02-60637: Trkd ldrs till over 2f out, sn btn. *4* **31**
7 Ran Time 2m 3.32 (5.32) Owned: Mr G D Waters Trained: Newmarket

3385

8.45 Come Evening Racing Again On August 5th Median Auction Maiden Stakes 3-4yo (F)
£2961 £846 £423 **1m1f149y** **Good 55** **-25 Slow** Outside

2971 **FUEL CELL 17** [7] R Hannon 3-8-11 (65) R L Moore 15/8 FAV: 003301: Rcd in 2nd till led 3f out, pushed out fnl 1f: eff at 1m/9.5f on firm & gd, sharp/undul trk: imprvd for a step up in trip: see 2013. **75**
2700 **TOPKAT 28** [5] D R C Elsworth 3-8-11 L Keniry(3) 4/1: 02: Slow away in rear, hdwy 2f out, kept on ins fnl 1f but not pace of wnr: well clr of rem: eff at 9.5f on gd: see 2700. *2* **69**
2225 **SCARRABUS 48** [4] B G Powell 3-8-11 (69) L Dettori 3/1: 560-4063: Handy, hdwy over 1f out, sn onepcd. *7* **55**
3038 **SAYRIANNA 15** [1] I A Wood 3-8-6 T P Queally 33/1: 004: br f Sayaarr - Arianna Aldini (Habitat) *4* **42**
Led to 3f out, remained in 2nd to 1f out, no extra: Mar foal: half-sister to sev wnrs, incl smart 6f 2yo Green's Bid: dam unrcd: shown little thus far.
3048 **PRESTON HALL 14** [6]3-8-11 (50) R Thomas(5) 66/1: 0065: b g Accordion - Little Preston (Pennine *1¼* **44**
Walk) Trkd ldrs, fdd over 1f out: Apr foal: dam poor mdn, styd 10f.
WITCHING 0 [3]3-8-6 E Ahern 7/2: 6: b f Hector Protector - Charming Life (Habitat) Slow away, *9* **21**
nvr a factor on debut: Jan foal: half-sister to a 10/11f wnr: dam a 7f 4yo wnr.
5018} **TIZ MOLLY 259** [2]3-8-6 T E Durcan 20/1: 00-P: Chsd ldrs, p.u. 7f out, broke down: reapp. **0**
7 Ran Time 2m 5.6(7.6) Owned: A F M (Holdings) Ltd Trained: Marlborough

ASCOT FRIDAY 23.07.04 Righthand, Stiff, Galloping Track

Official Going Good/Firm (Good places)

3386

2.15 Brunswick Maiden Stakes Fillies 2yo (D)
£5395 £1660 £830 **6f str** **Good/Firm 39** **-18 Slow** Stands Side

SHOHRAH 0 [3] M P Tregoning 2-8-11 R Hills 7/2: 1: ch f Giant's Causeway - Taqreem (Nashwan) **97+**
Chsd ldrs, gd hdwy to lead over 1f out, rdn clr, shade readily: well bckd on debut: Feb foal: half-sister to useful wnrs over 7/10f: dam styd mid-dists: v eff at 6f, sure to relish 7f+ in time: goes well fresh on gd/firm: v useful start, expect plenty of further improvement & looks a ready made List/Gr wnr.
EPIPHANY 0 [7] E A L Dunlop 2-8-11 L Dettori 13/2: 2: br f Zafonic - Galette (Caerleon) Slow *2½* **87+**
away & hmpd start, held up, hdwy 2f out, kept on, not pace of wnr: clr of rem, bckd on debut: Apr first foal: dam 12f wnr: eff over a stiff 6f, will relish 7f/1m+ in time: acts on fast grnd: v pleasing start, win races.
3071 **DANCE FLOWER 14** [2] M R Channon 2-8-11 T E Durcan 11/4 FAV: 23: In tch, hdwy & short of room *3½* **77**
over 2f out, onepace over 1f out: ran to form of 3071: acts on fast & gd: shld win a minor trk mdn.
3183 **MISS MALONE 9** [5] R Hannon 2-8-11 R Hughes : 0024: Cl-up, led briefly 2f out, onepace: prob *nk* **76**
ran to form of 3183: acts on gd & fast grnd: shld win a minor trk mdn.
2829 **SECRET HISTORY 24** [1]2-8-11 J Fanning 7/1: 235: Led till 2f out, wknd over 1f out: needs minor trks. *1* **73**
GHASIBA 0 [6]2-8-11 D Holland 16/1: 6: gr f Daylami - Night Owl (Night Shift) Went right *1¼* **69**
start, bhd, no dngr on debut: Mar foal, cost 54,000gns: dam plcd over 6f: bred to apprec 7f/1m in time.
2610 **BALLETTO 33** [8]2-8-11 Darren Williams 12/1: 37: Held up, nvr a factor: see 2610. *1½* **64**
CAONA 0 [4]2-8-11 E Ahern 8/1: 8: Cl-up, wknd over 1f out: debut. *2* **58**
8 Ran Time 1m 16.53 (3.43) Owned: Mr Hamdan Al Maktoum Trained: Lambourn

3387

2.45 John Guest Brown Jack Stakes Handicap 3yo+ 0-85 (D) **[85]**
£9532 £2933 £1467 **2m45y** **Good/Firm 39** **-28 Slow** Inside

3125 **MANA DARGENT 13** [14] M Johnston 7-9-13 (84) J Fanning 11/2: 3-050001: b g Ela Mana Mou - Petite D Argent (Noalto) Handy, hdwy over 2f out, styd on to lead over 1f out, kept on, rdn out: well bckd: right back to form at beloved Ascot (6th crse win): '03 h'cap wnr: '02 3-time h'cap wnr: suited by 2m on firm, hvy & fibresand, Ascot specialist (6 wins): back on a handy mark, win again here. 1 Jul'03 Asco 16.2g/f 90-84 B: **91**
1 Sep'02 Asco 16.2g/f 92-88 C: 1 Aug'02 Asco 16.2g/s 93-86 B: 1 Jul'02 Asco 16.2gd 86-78 B:
2 May'02 York 11.8g/f 79-77 C: 2 Oct'01 Donc 12hvy 83-80 C: 2 Aug'01 Asco 12gd 91-87 B: 2 Jul'01 Asco 12fm 89-87 C:
2941 **RIYADH 20** [8] M Johnston 6-8-5 vis (62) K Darley 9/1: 0303002: Slow away, held up, hdwy 2f out, *shd* **68**
styd on to chase wnr ins last, held head high, just held: fine run but v hard to put his head in front nowadays.
2238 **AKRITAS 48** [4] P F I Cole 3-8-10 (84) T Quinn 9/2: 1P0-4453: Cl-up, gd hdwy to lead trav best 2f *¾* **89**
out, onepace fnl 1f: up in trip & styd 2m after 7 wk abs: unexposed over staying trips, win again: see 1582.
3032* **VALANCE 16** [3] C R Egerton 4-9-9 (80) J Murtagh 7/2 FAV: 103-3514: Cl-up, led over 3f out till *2½* **82**
2f out, onepace for press: well bckd: prob ran to form of 3032.
3057 **BEECHY BANK 15** [12]6-8-7 (1ow) (63) D Holland 25/1: 31-00535: Held up, hdwy over 1f out, late *1¼* **65**
gains, nvr dngrs: prob styd this stiff 2m & has slipped down the weights: see 342.
2887 **RED SCORPION 22** [13]5-8-7 (64) S W Kelly 25/1: 6502306: Held up, eff over 2f out, no impress. *hd* **64**
3114 **FLAMENCO BRIDE 13** [11]4-8-12 (69) R Hughes 16/1: 34500-07: In tch, wknd over 1f out: see 3114. *1½* **67**
2471 **ESTABLISHMENT 38** [1]7-8-10 (67) Martin Dwyer 11/1: 5-000008: Nvr a factor: see 2471, 1484. *1¼* **63**
3181 **ASTYANAX 10** [6]4-9-2 (73) J Mackay 11/1: 3241-059: In tch, wknd well over 1f out: see 3181. *2½* **66**
2471 **ONCE 38** [2]4-9-2 (73) E Ahern 66/1: 2300-300: 10th: Al bhd: twice below 1923. *6* **60**
2973 **BEST FLIGHT 18** [7]4-8-11 (68) M Hills 25/1: 341-0040: 11th: Al bhd: see 2973. *¾* **54**
3032 **HIGH POINT 16** [5]6-9-8 (79) K Fallon 9/1: 0233360: 12th: In tch, hdwy to lead after 3f till over *shd* **65**
3f out, wknd: change of tactics, see 2073.
3147* **MOONSHINE BEACH 12** [9]6-8-9 (4ex) (66) Dane O'Neill 10/1: 654P110: 13th: Led till over 3f out, *8* **44**
wknd: up in class after 3147 (weak h'cap).
13 Ran Time 3m 36.94 (10.94) Owned: Mr Daniel A Couper Trained: Middleham

3388   3.20 Ladbrokes Rated Stakes Handicap 3yo+ 0-95 (C)   **[103]**
£8441 £3202 £1601   **6f str**   **Good/Firm 39**   +10 Fast   Stands Side

2878 **KHABFAIR 22** [2] Mrs A J Perrett 3-9-2 (91) J Murtagh 7/4 FAV: 312-41: Handy, hdwy to lead on bit   **98**
dist, rdn out: well bckd: v eff at 6f, acts on fast & polytrack, sharp or gall trks: lightly rcd, useful & improving.
2282 **ONLYTIME WILL TELL 45** [6] D Nicholls 6-9-7 (91) J Fanning 4/1: 00-00542: Held up, hdwy to chase   1¼   **94**
wnr dist, not his pace: clr of rem after 6 wk abs: useful eff: see 888.
3346} **THE LORD 356** [7] W G M Turner 4-9-3 (87) C Haddon(7) 20/1: 206000-3: b g Averti - Lady Longmead   4   **78**
(Crimson Beau) Keen, led till dist, no extra: reapp: below best in '03 (rnr-up in a List): dual h'cap scorer in
'02: well suited by 5f, stays 6f on firm & soft, prob any trk: likes to dominate & has run well fresh: been
gelded: showed gd pace here, slipped down the weights & a rtn to 5f will suit, esp at Chester.
2 Apr'03 Hayd 5g/f 96-(103) A: 2 Oct'02 Newb 6sft 104-100 B: 1 Jul'02 Ches 5fm 102-96 D: 1 May'02 Ches 5fm 98- B:
1 Mar'02 Donc 5sft 96- C:
3248+**BLACKHEATH 7** [3] D Nicholls 8-9-1 (3ex) (85) A Nicholls 2/1: 6226414: Handy, wknd over 1f out: btr 3248nk   **75**
2896 **NEROS RETURN 21** [5]3-9-4 BL (93) K Dalgleish 6/1: 1-606005: Handy, wknd over 1f out: blnks.   1   **80**
5 Ran   Time 1m 14.87 (1.77)   Owned: Star Pointe Ltd & Arlington Bloodstock   Trained: Pulborough

3389   3.50 Listed Weatherbys European Breeders Fund Valiant Stakes Fillies 3yo+   (A)
£17400 £6600 £3300   **1m rnd**   **Good/Firm 39**   +09 Fast   Inside

2491 **COY 37** [3] Sir Michael Stoute 3-8-6 (1ow) (100) K Fallon 6/4 FAV: 01-5221: Sn rdn bhd, lkd held   **107**
over 2f out, sn strong run & squeezed thr' ins last to lead cl-home, drvn out: hvly bckd: stays a stiff 1m well on
fast & gd grnd: v useful, genuine & improving, a typical example of why K Fallon is a multiple champion: see 2491.
3029 **CELTIC HEROINE 16** [1] M A Jarvis 3-8-9 (97) K Darley 5/1: 2121252: Held up, hdwy over 2f out,   nk   **108**
styd on to lead ins last, rdn & collared cl-home: career best stepped up in class & dropped back to 1m.
2917 **SNOW GOOSE 20** [2] J L Dunlop 3-8-5 (103) T Quinn 5/1: 112-0423: Keen, set gd pace till rdn &   ½   **103**
collared ins last, kept on, not btn far: confirmed useful eff of 2917, see 2574.
2917 **NATALIYA 20** [7] J L Dunlop 3-8-5 (108) Martin Dwyer 8/1: 13-3004: Cl-up, chall over 1f out, no   1¾   **99**
extra ins last: bckd from 16/1: now twice below 1492, see 1233.
2917 **MOON DAZZLE 20** [5]3-8-5 (106) R Hills 4/1: 1455: In tch, brief eff 2f out, no impress: well   ¾   **97**
bckd: twice below promising 4th in Gr 1 class in 2555.
2917 **BRINDISI 20** [4]3-8-5 (103) K Fallon 2-341446: In tch, no extra over 1f out: see 2491 (h'cap), 1882.   ½   **96**
2917 **KUNDA 20** [8]3-8-5 (96) Dane O'Neill 25/1: 52-62307: Slow away, sn in tch, wknd over 2f out: btr 2574.   3½   **89**
7 Ran   Time 1m 40.92 (2.42)   Owned: Cheveley Park Stud   Trained: Newmarket

3390   4.25 European Breeders Fund Maiden Stakes 2yo (D)
£5551 £1708 £854   **7f str**   **Good/Firm 39**   -20 Slow   Stands Side

3111 **KAMAKIRI 13** [4] R Hannon 2-9-0 R Hughes 10/1: 01: b c Trans Island - Alpine Flair (Tirol) Held   **101+**
up, hdwy to lead over 2f out, led over 1f out, pushed clr, cmftbly: Feb foal, cost 35,000gns: much imprvd for
debut & stays a stiff 7f on fast grnd, 1m will suit: useful, more to come.
2467 **CAPABLE GUEST 38** [5] M R Channon 2-9-0 T E Durcan 1/2 FAV: 3332: Cl-up, eff to chall over 1f   2   **95**
out, outpcd by wnr ins last: shown more than enough to win a mdn but hvly bckd here after Gr 2 o3rd in 2467 (6f).
2689 **TAKHMIN 29** [6] M Johnston 2-9-0 R Hills 7/1: 023: With ldr, led 2f out till over 1f out,   1¾   **89**
onepcd: prob stays 7f on fast & gd/soft: minor trk mdns will suit: see 2689.
      BAYEUX DE MOI 0 [1] Mrs A J Perrett 2-9-0 J Murtagh 9/1: 4: b c Barathea - Rivana (Green   1   **89**
Desert) In tch, wknd over 1f out: debut: Feb foal, dam styd 9f: need to come 1m+ in time.
3005 **RIVER BISCUIT 17** [2]2-9-0 R L Moore 16/1: 05: ch c Diesis - Elle Est Revenue (Night Shift)   6   **77**
Dsptd lead till 2f out, wknd: Feb foal, cost £90,000: half-brother to a useful 1m wnr: dam smart of 6f as a juv.
      REGAL ATTIRE 0 [3]2-9-0 Martin Dwyer 14/1: 6: Slow away, sn in tch, wknd over 2f out on debut.   nk   **76**
6 Ran   Time 1m 30.13 (4.13)   Owned: Mr Michael Pescod   Trained: Marlborough

3391   5.00 Newsmith Capital October Club Handicap Stakes 3yo 0-80 (D)   **[84]**
£5447 £1676 £838   **1m2f**   **Good/Firm 39**   -35 Slow   Inside

3219 **IFFY 8** [8] P D Cundell 3-8-2 (58) C Catlin 9/2: 050-4041: Made all, styd on well for press when   **66**
pressed fnl 1f, drvn out: well bckd, first win: relished step up to 10f & acts on fast, gd & polytack, prob any
trk: apprec switch to forcing tactics, well rdn & game here: see 545.
2692 **EDGEHILL 29** [7] C R Egerton 3-8-4 (60) T Quinn 5/1: 00-42: In tch, eff to chase wnr over 1f out,   nk   **67**
chall ins last, just held: apprec step up to 10f on this fast grnd: shld win a modest race: see 2692.
2796 **FOXILLA 25** [3] D R C Elsworth 3-8-2 (58) R Thomas(5) 13/2: 0-003143: Held up, eff over 1f out, no dngr.   2½   **61**
3067 **EPAMINONDAS 14** [6] R Hannon 3-8-10 (66) R Smith 20/1: 3-000204: In tch, eff over 1f out, sn onepace.   ¾   **68**
2980* **VAMP 18** [4]3-9-7 (77) Martin Dwyer 7/2 JT FAV: 02315: In tch, wknd well over 1f out: bckd, btr 2980.7   2½   **75**
2773 **ALI DEO 27** [1]3-9-6 (76) R Hills 10/1: 00-1306: Held up, no impress over 1f out: see 2116, 1832.   ¾   **73**
3039 **DESERT HAWK 16** [5]3-8-13 (69) R L Moore 7/2 JT FAV: 00-0547: Cl-up, wknd well over 2f out: well bckd.   ½   **65**
2748 **TURNER 27** [2]3-9-2 (72) S W Kelly 16/1: 360-6338: Dwelt, keen held up, btn 7f out: see 2283, 1885.   ½   **67**
8 Ran   Time 2m 11.43(7.43)   Owned: Mr Nigel Johnson-Hill   Trained: Compton

Official Going Standard

3392 2.25 St Bridget's Day Claiming Stakes 3yo+ (F)
£2975 £850 £425 **1m aw rnd** **Going 58** **-21 Slow** Inside

2565 **BOOK MATCHED 34** [10] B Smart 3-9-1 (67) F Norton 14/1: 3140601: Led/dsptd lead, went on 3f out, **76a**
rdn & styd on strongly: suited by 1m/8.5f on fibresand: apprec drop to clmg grade: see 751.
2931 **SAHAAT 20** [11] M J Polglase 6-9-13 (70) L Fletcher(3) 5/1: 0000502: Al prom, eff 2f out, onepace 2½ **74a**
3040 **GENERAL GB 15** [1] N P Littmoden 7-9-11 (65) G Gibbons 9/1: 5200053: Held up, short of room 3 **66a**
halfway, kept on for press, nvr threatened wnr: clmd for 11,000: see 1295, 856 & 811.
3091 **MULTIPLE CHOICE 14** [14] N P Littmoden 3-9-1 e t (65) J P Guillambert(3) 11/2: 4-000024: Led/dsptd hd **63a**
lead till 3f out, no extra bef dist: see 3091 & 1011.
3091 **JAOLINS 14** [9]3-8-0 (49) D Kinsella 33/1: 0000065: Rdn chsg ldrs, kept on onepace. ¾ **47a**
2647 **FORTUNE POINT 31** [6]6-9-9 (61) I Mongan 11/1: 3200406: Led/dsptd lead early, rdn & no impress dist. 1 **60a**
3215 **CERTAIN JUSTICE 8** [7]6-9-13 (70) J Quinn 7/2: 0-065057: Held up, drvn & no impress fnl 3f: claimed. 1 **62a**
848 **KUSTOM KIT FOR HER 131** [5]4-8-10 t (45) J Bramhill 50/1: 2322408: Chsd ldrs till over 1f out: abs. 4 **37a**
2857 **TITIAN FLAME 23** [8]4-9-0 (55) R Havlin 33/1: 43640-09: In tch, no impress fnl 3f: see 2857. 5 **32a**
3154 **INVOGUE 11** [13]4-8-8 (40) T Hamilton(3) 40/1: 00-0060: 10th: Dwelt, al rear: see 3154. 9 **10a**
3215 **ARABIE 8** [4]6-9-9 S Sanders 100/30 FAV: 5-000040: 11th: Bhd, nvr a factor: AW bow: btr 3215 (gd). hd **24a**
710 **COLNE VALLEY AMY 151** [12]7-8-6 (39) P Mathers(5) 33/1: 60-42000: 13th: Sn strugg rear: new yard. 8 **0a**
630 **Pups Pride 160** [3]7-8-11 vis(53) Lisa Jones(3) 20/1:0 2920 **Cross Ash 20** [2]4-9-13 H(66) Dale Gibson 33/1:0
14 Ran Time 1m 45.71 (6.31) Owned: Mr Paul Darling Trained: Thirsk

---

3393 2.55 Ladbrokes Com Nursery Handicap Stakes 2yo (E) [79]
£3721 £1145 £573 **6f aw rnd** **Going 58** **-24 Slow** Inside

2721* **DICTION 28** [7] K R Burke 2-8-9 (60) M Fenton 100/30 FAV: 0511: Led/dsptd lead, narrow lead fnl **70a**
2f, drvn out, gamely: h'cap bow: eff at 6/7f on fibresand, likes Southwell: see 2721 (7f, sell).
3212 **HAROLDINI 8** [5] Mrs P N Dutfield 2-9-5 (70) R Havlin 11/1: 04262: Al prom & drvn/ch fnl 2f, not ½ **77a**
pace of wnr nr fin: op 9/1: AW bow: eff at 5/6f on firm, fast & fibresand: rest well covered, can find a race.
3065 **AMPHITHEATRE 15** [9] R F Johnson Houghton 2-9-1 (66) S Carson 14/1: 50303: Towards rear 3 **65a**
travelling well, hdwy from halfway, drvn & onepace over 1f out: AW bow: handles fast grnd & fibresand.
3065 **LISA MONA LISA 15** [4] V Smith 2-9-7 (72) J Quinn 7/1: 14104: Chsd ldrs, no impress over 1f out. 3½ **62a**
2178 **CHICAGO NIGHTS 50** [11]2-7-12 (49) Lisa Jones(3) 20/1: 4005: Chsd ldrs till 2f out: abs, AW/h'cap bow. 2½ **32a**
2640 **GOLDHILL PRINCE 31** [1]2-9-5 p (70) L Treadwell(5) 15/2: 2111136: Chsd ldrs, btn 2f out: h'cap bow. 1 **51a**
2183 **DANES ROCK 50** [8]2-9-0 (65) Rory Moore(7) 8/1: 40627: In tch, hung right & btn from halfway: abs. 1½ **42a**
3047 **ORPEN ANNIE 15** [6]2-9-4 (66) J McAuley 16/1: 0368: Sn rdn & al rear: AW/h'cap bow: btr 2603 (fast). shd **43a**
3212 **LORD JOHN 8** [10]2-8-11 (62) Dale Gibson 7/2: 04049: Sn struggling towards rear: AW bow. ¾ **37a**
3157 **ELLIS CAVE 11** [3]2-8-4 vis (53) T Hamilton(3) 10/1: 00400: 10th: Slow away & al bhd: much btr 2802. 6 **15a**
3212 **QUEENS GLORY 8** [2]2-9-5 (70) S Sanders 12/1: 6265500: 11th: Mid-div, struggling halfway: AW bow. 8 **10a**
11 Ran Time 1m 18.20 (4.9) Owned: Mr J C S Wilson Trained: Leyburn

---

3394 3.30 Fiesta De Santiago Selling Stakes Fillies 2yo (G)
£2618 £748 £374 **7f aw rnd** **Going 58** **-36 Slow** Inside

3196 **VALE DE LOBO 9** [7] Sir Mark Prescott 2-8-8 S Sanders 2/5 FAV: 51: b f Loup Sauvage - Frog **79a+**
(Akarad) Led/dsptd lead, went on over 2f out & rdn clr, easily, val 8L+: hvly bckd at odds-on, sold to A Carroll
for 20,000 gns: Mar foal, half sister to a dual 9f juv wnr, also multiple staying wnr Froglet, dam a multiple 9/12f
scorer: eff at 7f, bred to relish 1m+: acts on fibresand: better than this grade.
  KUMALA OCEAN 0 [11] P A Blockley 2-8-8 I Mongan 10/1: 2: ch f Blue Ocean - Kumala (Simply 6 **57a**
Great) Sn pushed along chsg ldrs, kept on fnl 2f, nvr ch with easy wnr: op 7/1: cheaply bought Apr foal, dam a mod
mdn, related to a wng juv: sire 6f juv wnr: prob handles fibresand: caught a fair sort.
2449 **MUESTRA 39** [8] Mrs P N Dutfield 2-8-8 P Makin(5) 25/1: 00003: Held up in tch, kept on late, no dngr. nk **56a**
2461 **PARIS TAPIS 38** [1] K A Ryan 2-8-8 N Callan 14/1: 04: Led/dsptd lead 5f, sn btn, AW bow. 2 **52a**
  POLESWORTH 0 [9]2-8-8 M Halford(7) 14/1: 5: Slow away & bhd, late gains, nrst fin on debut: op 11/1. 5 **43a**
3065 **CHIN DANCER 15** [5]2-8-8 BL T F Norton 25/1: 006: Sn struggling rear, late prog, blnks & t-strap. 1½ **40a**
3209 **AMALGAM 8** [12]2-8-8 R Havlin 50/1: 00057: Chsd ldrs till over 1f out: AW bow. 1¾ **37a**
2462 **WEB RACER 38** [10]2-8-8 BL D Fentiman(7) 20/1: 508: Sn bhd & nvr factor, blnks, AW bow. ¾ **36a**
1818 **FANTASTIC STAR 66** [6]2-8-8 M Fenton 14/1: 009: Chsd ldrs 4f, sn bhd, AW bow. 1¾ **33a**
3014 **BOWLAND BRIDE 16** [13]2-9-0 bl P Mathers(5) 11/1: 4410050: 10th: Slow away & al towards rear. 6 **28a**
3349 **BLACK COMBE LADY 2** [2]2-8-8 P Bradley 50/1: 00000: 11th: Led/dsptd lead early, strugg halfway. 5 **13a**
2995 **MONASHEE MISS 17** [3]2-8-8 Rory Moore(7) 25/1: 4030P: Chsd ldrs, btn when p.u. over 2f out, lame. **0a**
12 Ran Time 1m 33.18 (6.58) Owned: Mr B Haggas Trained: Newmarket

---

3395 4.00 Ladbrokes Com Handicap Stakes 3yo+ 0-75 (E) [79]
£3780 £1163 £582 **1m aw rnd** **Going 58** **+02 Fast** Inside

3384* **MASAFI 1** [2] Sir Mark Prescott 3-8-8 (6ex) S Sanders 2/7 FAV: 00-211111: Sn handy & led over **73a**
1f out, drvn out: hvly bckd under a 6lb pen, a wnr last night: eff btwn 1m/10f on fast & both AWs, sharp/undul
trks: superbly handled by connections, more to follow: see 3384, 3300.
3034 **ARRAN 16** [7] V Smith 4-8-9 (52) J Quinn 40/1: 000-0302: Held up, hdwy & led 2f out, sn drvn & 1½ **61a**
hdd, kept on: rest well covered: eff around 1m on fast grnd & fibresand: see 2529.
3155* **DOWNLAND 11** [5] N Tinkler 8-9-10 (6ex) (67) Kim Tinkler 5/1: 2165113: Held up racing keenly, kept 3 **70a**
on onepace for press fnl 3f: stays 1m, poss 7f ideal: see 3155 (7f).
2998 **MIDSHIPMAN 17** [1] A W Carroll 6-9-3 vis t (60) M Fenton 7/1: 3002224: Sn bhd & switched wide, 2½ **58a**
styd on from halfway, nvr a threat: see 2998, 2500 & 1430.
2725 **BRANDY COVE 28** [4]7-9-4 (61) F Lynch 40/1: 23-40555: Slow away & held up, nvr a threat: btr 2725. 3½ **52a**

SOUTHWELL Fibresand FRIDAY 23.07.04 Lefthand, Sharp, Oval Track

1322 **AIR MAIL 91** [8]7-9-10 (67) R Fitzpatrick 50/1: 0004606: Led/dsptd lead 6f, fdd under press: abs: see 513.3 **52a**
2601 **ARMS ACROSSTHESEA 33** [6]5-9-4 (61) J Edmunds 40/1: 0-211407: Towards rear & nvr land a blow. 1¾ **43a**
2999 **DANGER BIRD 17** [10]4-9-0 (57) Dale Gibson 40/1: 0244158: Pushed along to go handy, btn 3f out. 8 **25a**
2998 **MIDMAAR 17** [3]3-8-9 (60) F Norton 100/1: 31000-09: Led, hdd over 6f out, btn 2f out: see 2998. 5 **19a**
2746 **BOLD BLADE 27** [9]3-9-7 bl (72) G Gibbons 50/1: 2500100: 10th: Unruly stalls, led/dsptd lead till 6 **20a**
halfway, sn btn: much btr 2050 (12f, made all, clmr).
10 Ran   Time 1m 42.75 (3.35)   Owned: Mr G D Waters   Trained: Newmarket

3396   4.35 Ernst & Young Median Auction Maiden Stakes 3yo   (F)
£3283 £938 £469   6f aw rnd   Going 58   -02 Slow   Inside

2649 **FIRENZE 31** [1] J R Fanshawe 3-8-9   O Urbina 2/1: 01: ch f Efisio - Juliet Bravo (Glow) Slow **71a**
away & held up, rdn & hdwy 2f out, styd on to lead well ins last: wll bckd: AW bow, left debut bhd: apprec step up
to 6f, 7f+ shld suit: acts on fibresand & a sharp trk: going the right way.
2756 **STARGEM 27** [8] J Pearce 3-8-9 (75) J Quinn 4/6 FAV: 02-22: Prom & rdn/led over 1f out, edged ¾ **68a**
left, hdd well ins last: hvly bckd, op 5/4: AW bow: acts on firm grnd & fibresand: see 2756.
2704 **RAGAZZI 29** [3] T D Barron 3-9-0   P Makin(5) 20/1: 0003: Held up, hdwy/hung right over 3f out & 1¾ **68a**
hung left under press over 1f out: AW bow: eff at 6f, return to 7f could suit: acts on fibresand.
2906 **TROODOS JET 21** [6] A Berry 3-9-0 (65) F Norton 5/1: 2464-444: Led after 2f till over 1f out, no ½ **66a**
extra: eff at 5/6f on fast, soft & fibresand: see 2906 & 2485.
3000 **COCO REEF 17** [9]3-8-9 (50) M Fenton 16/1: 0330-605: Led 2f, rdn & btn dist: see 2704. 3 **52a**
2722 **BANK GAMES 28** [4]3-9-0 Dale Gibson 40/1: 006: Chsd ldrs till halfway: low grade h'caps shld suit. 3½ **46a**
3194 **FESTIVE CHIMES 9** [2]3-8-9   T Hamilton(3) 12/1: 037: Dwelt, sn handy, btn 2f out: AW bow: see 3194. 2 **35a**
2812 **LUKE SHARP 25** [7]3-9-0 bl (33) G Parkin 66/1: 000-008: Sn struggling rear, AW bow: see 2812. dist **0a**
TANNE BLIXEN 0 [5]3-8-9   L Keniry(3) 33/1: 9: Slow away & sn outpcd on debut. 24 **0a**
9 Ran   Time 1m 16.92 (3.62)   Owned: Mrs Jan Hopper   Trained: Newmarket

3397   5.10 Ladbrokes Com Apprentice Handicap Stakes 4yo+ 35-55   (G)   [57]
£2891 £826 £413   2m aw   Going 58   -56 Slow   Inside

3096 **MERCURIOUS 14** [2] J Mackie 4-9-2 (45) Derek Nolan(5) 13/8 FAV: 4-415421: Handy & chsd ldr over 3f **53a**
out, rdn & led over 1f out, styd on strongly to assert ins last: op 15/8: eff at 14f, suited by 2m: acts on both
AWs, loves fibresand & a sharp trk: see 1263, 1076.
1990 **DOCTOR JOHN 59** [1] Andrew Turnell 7-9-0 (43) P Makin(3) 7/4: 2162202: Held up, rdn & kept on 5 **45a**
onepace fnl 3f: 2 month abs: gd run with cheek pieces omitted: see 690.
3025 **AMUSEMENT 16** [6] D G Bridgwater 8-9-1 (44) A Beech 16/1: 4603: Led, rdn & hdd over 1f out, no 1½ **44a**
extra: clr of rem: h'cap bow: stays a slowly run 2m on fibresand: see 2200.
3056 **AFRICAN DAWN 15** [5] L G Cottrell 6-9-3 t P (46) L Keniry 9/2: 022-6004: Chsd ldr 5f out, rdn & 7 **39a**
btn over 2f out: cheek pieces & longer trip: see 2293.
1753 **MYRTUS 69** [4]5-8-11 (40) D Fentiman(5) 16/1: 0/0-305: Chsd ldrs, struggling fnl 4f: see 1323. 1 **32a**
1197 **WELSH AND WYLDE 99** [3]4-9-6 p (49) J P Guillambert 16/1: 20600-06: b g Anita's Prince - Waikiki dist **0a**
(Zampano) Chsd ldr, btn 5f out: 11 wk jumps abs (plcd, rtd 97h, sell, 2m, gd & gd/soft): sell rnr-up on the Level
'03: mdn rnr-up in '02 (flattered): eff around a sharp 8.5f on gd & fibresand: eff in sell grade & blnks.
2 Jan'03 Wolv 8.4af 62a- G: 2 Jun'02 Nott 6gd 85- D:
6 Ran   Time 3m 44.31 (8.31)   Owned: Gwen K DotCom   Trained: Church Broughton

CHEPSTOW   FRIDAY 23.07.04 Lefthand, Undulating, Galloping Track

Official Going GOOD/FIRM

3398   6.30 Tintern Amateur Riders' Handicap Stakes 3yo+ 0-70 (F)   [56]
£3101 £886 £443   1m4f23y   Good 45   -15 Slow   Inside

3175 **THEATRE LADY 10** [9] P D Evans 6-9-4 (5ex) (46) Miss E Folkes(3) 8/1: 5660151: Rear, hdwy over 2f **53**
out, rdn to lead well ins fnl 1f: eff btwn 7/12f on firm, hvy & polytrack, any trk: in gd form, consistent: see 539.
3145 **LAZZAZ 12** [17] P W Hiatt 6-9-5 (47) Mrs Marie King(5) 8/1: 0564342: Led till well ins fnl 1f, no 1½ **50**
extra: running well, likes W'hampton: see 711 & 330.
3145 **VANDENBERGHE 12** [3] J A Osborne 5-9-6 (48) Miss S Beddoes 16/1: 5343563: Rear, hdwy 4f out, not 1½ **49+**
clr run & switched right over 1f out, kept on: handles firm, gd & fibresand: poss 2nd with clr run.
3270 **HEAD TO KERRY 6** [16] D J S ffrench Davis 4-10-1 (57) Miss A Hockley(7) 15/2 FAV: 0003534: Keen & 1 **56**
cl-up, wknd fnl 1f: qck reapp: see 2391.
2988 **FINAL DIVIDEND 17** [5]8-9-2 (44) Miss Joanna Rees 16/1: 643-0565: Cl-up, onepcd fnl 1f: see 107. nk **42**
3114 **HASHID 13** [19]4-10-0 (65) Mr David Turner(5) 66/1: 53-63006: Cl-up, hung left over 3f out, no impress. ½ **62**
3101 **SARN 13** [13]5-8-13 (41) Miss M Mullineaux(7) 16/1: 4032047: Rear, hdwy from 2f out, nrst fin. 5 **30**
338 **WIZARD OF EDGE 198** [12]4-11-0 (70) Mr James White(3) 14/1: 25/3-68: b g Wizard King - Forever ½ **58**
Shineing (Glint of Gold) Rear, hdwy wknd fnl 1f: hdles wnr since race 338 (nov h'cap, eff at 2m1f/2m3f
on gd, sharp or stiff/undul trk, rtd 112h, with G Balding): 3rd sole Flat '03 start (mdn, rtd 68, G Balding):
promise both '02 starts (rtd 73a & 67): eff at 1m on fast & fibresand, poss handles soft: now with R Hodges.
2 Oct'02 Sout 8af 73a- F:
3145 **BURNT COPPER 12** [8]4-9-12 (54) Miss K Manser(5) 9/1: 250-0109: Slow away in rear, modest late shd **41**
gains.
683 **CRITICAL STAGE 155** [6]5-10-10 (66) Miss S Brotherton 12/1: 335-3130: 10th: Cl-up, no impress fnl 1¼ **51**
1f: long abs: now with J Frost: see 595.
3145 **MILK AND SULTANA 12** [1]4-9-7 (49) Mrs S Owen(3) 8/1: 0-060020: 11th: Al bhd. nk **33**
4918} **EIGHT 269** [2]8-9-5 (47) Ms T Dzieciolowska(4) 10/1: 5/03200-0: 12th: ch g Thatching - Up To You 1½ **29**
(Sallust) Nvr btr than mid-div on reapp: hdles plcd in 03/04 (plcd once, nov h'cap, rtd 84h, C Cox): rnr-up 2 of 6
Flat '03 starts (amat h'caps): rnr-up 1 of 5 '02 starts (amat h'cap): eff at 9f, suited by 12/14f on firm, gd/soft
& polytrack, has disapp on fibresand: eff with/without visor, any trk: now with M Channon.
2 Jul'03 Chep 12.1g/s 51-49 F: 2 Feb'03 Ling 12ap 40a-36 F: 2 Jul'02 Chep 12.1gd 51-50 F: 1 Jul'01 Chep 12.1g/f 53-52 F:

4615} **BLACK SWAN** 291 [7]4-8-12 (40) Mrs S Moore(3) 66/1: 0/50-0: 13th: b g Nashwan - Sea Spray (Royal   2½   18
Academy) In tch, btn fnl 4f: reapp: hdles rnr 4 months ago, '04 (unplcd, rtd 66h, nov): mdn unplcd both '03
starts: unplcd sole '02 start (mdn, rtd 74, M Tregoning): lightly rcd on the Flat.
3101 **KING HALLING** 13 [10]5-10-4 (60) Miss E J Jones 33/1: 6400/-060: 14th: With ldr, lost pl after   nk   37
6f, no impress 2f out: see 2088.
3109 **SOMAYDA** 13 [18]9-8-12 p (40) Mr J Doyle(7) 33/1: 00-00030: 15th: Mid-div, nvr nr ldrs.   3   12
2699 **SILVER PROPHET** 29 [14]5-10-10 P (66) Mrs S Bosley 8/1: 0-055500: 16th: Nvr a factor: cheekpieces.   7   27
1463} **KEEP THE PEACE** 438 [11]6-9-8 t P (50) Miss H M Lewis(7) 66/1: 0/5020//0-0: 17th: In tch, rear &   6   2
btn 5f out: tried cheek pieces, jumps fit (sell hdle unplcd, rtd 41h).
2955 **DUKES VIEW** 19 [4]3-9-8 bl (62) Miss L J Harwood(3) 16/1: 06-00550: 18th: Al bhd.   shd   13
2796 **BEAUCHAMP RIBBON** 25 [15]4-10-7 P (63) Mr G Tumelty(7) 33/1: 13030-00: 19th: Rear, t.o.: cheekpieces. 21   0
19 Ran   Time 2m 38.37 (7.27)   Owned: Waterline Racing Club   Trained: Abergavenny

---

3399   7.00 Letheby & Christopher Maiden Auction Stakes 2yo (E)
£3582   £1102   £551   **6f16y**   **Good 45**   **-37 Slow**   Stands side

2927 **SWEET COINCIDENCE** 20 [12] I A Wood 2-8-2 P Doe 9/1: 301: Slow away, sn cl-up, hdwy to lead just   81
over 1f out, rdn out fnl 1f: eff at 6f, 7f shld suit: acts on gd, gall/undul trk: back to debut form: see 2537.
3141 **GEISHA LADY** 12 [14] R M Beckett 2-8-2 N Chalmers(1) 8/1: 632: Cl-up, carr left over 4f out, ev   2   73
ch over 1f out, onepcd ins fnl 1f: shld find a race: see 3141.
2652 **BARNBROOK EMPIRE** 31 [3] I A Wood 2-8-2 D Fox(5) 66/1: 053: b f Second Empire - Home Comforts   shd   72
(Most Welcome) Led till just over 1f out, no extra: Mar foal, cost £2,500: half-sister to a 2/3yo wnr: dam a mdn,
sire 1m Gr 1 wnr at 2: stays 6f on gd grnd: improve effort.
3251 **DIVINE DIVA** 7 [10] R Hannon 2-8-4 R L Moore 20/1: 04: b f Diktat - Maid To Dance (Pyramus)   ½   72
Outpcd, in tch, hdwy fnl 1f, kept on: qck reappr: Mar first foal, cost 17,500gns: dam unplcd in 3 2yo starts: sire
top-class older sprinter: stays 6f on gd: imprvd from debut, yard shld find a suitable opening, poss over further.
2310 **KAPAJE** 44 [5]2-8-2 Joanna Badger 66/1: 05: b f Lake Coniston - Reina (Homeboy) In tch, hdwy   shd   69
over 1f out, kept on: 6 wk abs: cost 3,000gns, Apr foal: half-sister to sev wnrs, incl 2yo wnrs over 5f/1m: stays
6f on gd: now with P Evans.
2287 **POLAR DAWN** 45 [4]2-8-2 A McCarthy 100/30 FAV: 26: Slow away, sn cl-up, carr left over 4f out,   ½   67
onepcd fnl 1f: 6 wk abs, clr of rem: btr 2287.
GOLDEN APPLAUSE 0 [15]2-8-4 J F McDonald(3) 25/1: 7: In tch, nvr nrr on debut.   3   60
2927 **BEFORE THE DAWN** 20 [13]2-8-2 D Kinsella 20/1: 08: Nvr btr than mid-div.   1   55
GUILDENSTERN 0 [16]2-8-7 S Drowne 9/2: 9: Cl-up, hung left over 4f out, wknd 1f out: saddle slipped.   ¾   58
2953 **MICKEY PEARCE** 18 [1]2-8-7 S Righton 100/1: 00: 10th: Al outpcd.   5   43
LORD OF DREAMS 0 [9]2-8-9 S Carson 9/1: 0: 11th: Nvr a factor on debut.   nk   44
2415 **MISTER BELL** 41 [8]2-8-9 D Sweeney 25/1: 360: 12th: Dsptd lead, wknd 2f out: 6 wk abs.   1¼   40
ARTHURS DREAM 0 [11]2-9-0 S Whitworth 50/1: 0: 13th: Slow away, al bhd on debut.   ¾   43
13 Ran   Time 1m 13.73 (4.93)   Owned: Mr S A Douch   Trained: Upper Lambourn

---

3400   7.30 Piercefield Claiming Stakes 3yo+ (F)
£2961   £846   £423   **2m49y**   **Good 45**   **-31 Slow**   Inside

837 **TEORBAN** 132 [15] M Pitman 5-9-10 (58) R L Moore 100/30 FAV: 21010-61: Mid-div, hdwy to lead over   61
2f out, rdn out: clmd for £7,000: h'cap hdle plcd 6 wks ago (rtd 93h, stays 2m5.5f on firm): suited by 2m on gd &
fibresand, gall/undul trk, likes W'hampton: made most of this drop into claim grade: see 837 (h'cap).
2924 **SIMONOVSKI** 20 [10] J A Osborne 3-8-10 (63) V Slattery 9/2: 55-0032: Rear, hdwy halfway, 2nd over   5   61
1f out, not pace of wnr: clmd for 10,000: clr of rem: stays 2m on gd: see 1403.
3190 **LORD LAMB** 9 [5] Mrs M Reveley 12-9-7 (55) J Fortune 4/1: 14-34053: Rcd in 2nd, led 10f out, hdd   3½   51
over 3f out, no extra fnl 1f: see 2298.
3114 **INDIAN CHASE** 13 [11] Dr J R J Naylor 7-9-9 (40) Lucy Russell(7) 20/1: 260004: Keen in tch, hdwy   2½   50
after 5f, no impress over 1f out: see 1291.
2982 **BUCHANAN STREET** 18 [3]3-8-10 (44) D Sweeney 16/1: 06-06625: Rear, hdwy 4f out, no impress over   1¾   52
1f out: now with J O'Shea: much longer trip: see 2982 (10f).
3025 **FRIXOS** 16 [4]4-9-6 bl (53) S Whitworth 33/1: 260P0-66: Keen & led early, remained cl-up, led   hd   44
again over 3f out till over 2f out, sn no extra: see 3025.
3158 **OUR IMPERIAL BAY** 11 [8]5-9-13 p (52) A Daly 12/1: 0303637: Cl-up till after 2f, rear 6f out, late gains.   2   49
2881 **DESERT QUILL** 22 [12]4-9-4 (63) S W Kelly 12/1: 030-2508: Cl-up, no impress 2f out.   1¼   39
3211 **JAZIL** 8 [6]9-9-6 vis t (50) G Baker 20/1: /0////-6009: Led to 10f out, no extra 2f out: see 1754.   1¼   40
3147 **ULSHAW** 12 [3]7-9-8 (45) S Donohoe(7) 15/2: 000-0000: 10th: ch g Salse - Kintail (Kris) Nvr a   8   34
factor: hdles unplcd in 03/04 (rtd 85h, eff at 2m1f on firm, stiff/undul trk, P Hobbs): won 2 of 11 '03 starts (h'caps):
suited by 2m/2m2f, a thorough stayer: acts on firm, hvy & fibresand: goes well fresh: loves W'hampton: best
without visor. 2 Jul'03 Ches 15.9fm 58-55 D: 2 Jun'03 Warw 19.1g/f 56-54 E: 1 Jun'03 Chep 18g/f 55-49 D:
1 Feb'03 Wolv 16.2af 52a-47 F: 2 Jan'03 Wolv 16.2af 45a-43 F: 1 Jul'02 Wolv 16.2af 43a-37 G:
1 Jul'01 Ling 16g/s 47-40 E: 1 Feb'01 Wolv 16.2af 43a-38 F: 1 Feb'01 Wolv 16.2af 36a-31 G:
SOMEWIN 0 [13]4-9-6 P A McCarthy 40/1: 0: 11th: b f Goldmark - Janet Oliphant (Red Sunset) Slow   shd   31
away, al bhd on Flat debut: hdles fit (p.u., mdn, rtd 50h at best, stays 2m on fast & gd, sharp trk).
2417 **GORDYS JOY** 41 [14]4-9-3 (40) J F McDonald 33/1: 064-300: 12th: Rear, hdwy 6f out, sn wknd, t.o.   22   6
4968} **FATTAAN** 265 [2]4-9-9 (63) R Havlin 25/1: 0/05U60-0: 13th: b g Danehill - Bintalshaati (Kris)   2½   9
Rear, t.o.: saddle slipped: reapp: won a mdn hdle in 03/04 (rtd 85h, eff at 2m1f on firm, stiff/undul trk, P
Hobbs): lightly rcd Flat rnr in '03 (mdn 5th, rtd 73, with H M Tregoning): well btn sole '02 start (mdn, rtd 0).
2200 **REGAL REPOSE** 49 [9]4-9-1 (40) Hayley Turner(5) 66/1: 200-0060: 14th: Keen, cl-up till after 6f, t.o.   8   0
BRAZIL NUT 0 [1]3-8-8 P Doe 40/1: 0: 15th: Rear, t.o. on debut.   10   0
15 Ran   Time 3m 40.11 (12.31)   Owned: Something In The City Partnership   Trained: Upper Lambourn

3401   **8.00 Totesport Handicap Stakes 3yo+ 0-70 (E)**   **[68]**
£4664 £1435 £718   **7f16y**   **Good 45**   **+01 Fast**   Stands side

2535 **THREEZEDZZ 35** [6] P D Evans 6-9-4 T (58) F P Ferris(3) 25/1: 000/-0001: Made all far side, drvn out ins fnl 1f: eff at 5/7f on firm & gd, any trk: imprvd for fitting of t-strap: fine eff from unfav low draw: see 2199.			67
3142 **BISHOPSTONE MAN 12** [8] H Candy 7-9-12 (66) J Fortune 8/1: 0-004062: Bhd, hdwy 2f out, kept on.		nk	74
3219 **IPHIGENIA 8** [16] P W Hiatt 3-9-3 (64) Hayley Turner(5) 10/1: 0502453: Cl-up, asked for effort over 1f out, kept on: handles firm, gd & fibresand: see 2716.		½	71
3088 **THE GAIKWAR 14** [15] N E Berry 5-9-7 bl (61) M Savage(5) 20/1: 12U0004: Cl-up, led stands side & hung left over 1f out, onepcd nr fin: eff at 7f, suited by 1m, tried 10f: rtn to further will suit: see 1298.		½	67
3184 **OASES 9** [4]5-9-0 vis (54) S Whitworth 20/1: 0600035: Dwelt, switched to stands side group, hdwy over 1f out, kept on: see 940.		1½	57
3095 **CYFRWYS 14** [14]3-9-4 (65) D Kinsella 9/2 FAV: 524-0226: Led stands side over 5f, no extra ins fnl 1f.		hd	67
434 **GOLD GUEST 188** [17]5-9-12 (66) S Donohoe(7) 9/1: 0441-107: In trch, hdwy 2f out, no impress fnl 1f.		½	67
3142* **OVER TO YOU BERT 12** [9]5-8-5 (6ex) J F McDonald(3) 8/1: 0003318: Handy, no impress fnl 1f.		nk	45
2149 **BALLARE 51** [2]5-8-7 vis (47) R Thomas(5) 33/1: 4610409: Rcd in 2nd far side, no impress over 1f out.		1¾	43
3102 **BABY BARRY 13** [3]7-8-7 (47) A McCarthy 14/1: 00-00030: 10th: Rcd far side, nvr a factor.		nk	42
3213 **FULL SPATE 8** [20]9-10-0 (68) C J Davies(7) 12/1: 4632000: 11th: Slow away in rear, hdwy 4f out, no impress over 1f out: see 2626, 2451.		shd	62
2971 **COTTON EASTER 18** [13]3-8-8 (55) Paul Eddery 33/1: 00600: 12th: Slow away, nvr a factor: see 2971.		1¾	45
3109 **LILY OF THE GUILD 13** [10]5-8-11 (51) S Drowne 9/1: 0244500: 13th: Slow away, nvr a factor.		1½	38
3088 **ANNIJAZ 14** [19]7-8-12 (52) R L Moore 6/1: 0046000: 14th: Al bhd: see 1540.		1½	36
2752 **COMPTON ARROW 27** [12]8-8-11 (51) S Righton 25/1: 0-000000: 15th: Nvr a factor: see 2752.		nk	34
2129 **MEELUP 52** [7]4-9-4 p (58) V Slattery 33/1: 0002200: 16th: Cl-up, wknd 2f out: 7 wk abs.		3	35
2907 **SCARPIA 11** [18]4-8-5 (45) R Smith 50/1: 0/0000-00: 17th: ch g Rudimentary - Floria Tosca (Petong) Cl-up over 4f, wknd: fin unplcd all '03 starts (seller, h'cap, mdns, rtd 32, with E James).		2	18
1901} **VERTEDANZ 417** [5]4-8-9 (49) N Chalmers(5) 66/1: 0/56000-0: 18th: b f Sesaro - Blade of Grass (Kris) Al bhd on reapp: p.u. sole jumps 03/04 start (nov hdle): 5th at best in '03 (h'cap, rtd 59a): tried a vis.		½	21
2650 **DANISH MONARCH 31** [11]3-9-3 (64) D Sweeney 33/1: 24-00300: 19th: Cl-up, wknd over 2f out.		2½	31
19 Ran Time 1m 22.92 (3.12) Owned: Mr Steve Evans Trained: Abergavenny			

3402   **8.30 European Breeders Fund Classified Stakes 3yo+ 0-75 (D)**
£6682 £2056 £1028   **7f16y**   **Good 45**   **+06 Fast**   Stands side

2920* **ALINDA 20** [2] P W Harris 3-8-6 (75) R L Moore 10/11 FAV: 01-11: Rear, hdwy 2f out, rdn ins fnl 1f & led cl-home: landed double: eff at 6f, imprvd of late for 7f, 1m shld suit: acts on fast, gd & fibresand: prob acts on any trk: lightly rcd, in fine form this term & can win more races: see 2920.			79
3088 **GOODENOUGH MOVER 14** [5] J S King 8-9-7 (80) Hayley Turner(5) 3/1: 1221152: Cl-up, hdwy to lead over 1f out, hdd cl-home: clr of rem: remains in gd form: see 2880.		hd	85
3006 **HILITES 17** [4] J S Moore 3-8-10 (79) S Whitworth 16/1: 3030063: Rear, hdwy 2f out, wknd fnl 1f.		3	75
3137* **SAVILES DELIGHT 12** [1] R Brotherton 5-9-8 (74) J Fortune 5/1: 3120114: Dsptd lead till led over 2f out, hdd over 1f out, no extra: see 3137.		nk	79
1354 **ELIDORE 90** [7]4-8-13 (74) J F Egan 33/1: 0/3000-05: b f Danetime - Beveled Edge (Beveled) Led till over 2f out, no extra 1f out: long abs: unplcd all '03 starts (h'caps, fill cond stks, rtd 84): fill mdn & fill stks wnr '02, also List 4th (rtd 94): eff at 6/7f on fast, handles hvy & any trk: with B Palling. 1 Jul'02 Wind 6g/f 89- C: 1 Jun'02 Kemp 7g/f 88- D: 2 Jun'02 Chep 6hvy 94- D:		2	66
1513 **BREAD OF HEAVEN 81** [3]3-8-8 BL (77) S Drowne 12/1: 3221-06: b f Machiavellian - Khubza (Green Desert) Cl-up, lost pl halfway, sn btn: long abs: won fnl '03 start (fill mdn): stays 6f, shld appr further: acts on firm & gd, gall trk: tried blnks here. 1 Oct'03 Redc 6g/f 83-(84) D: 2 Aug'03 Good 6g/f 82- D: 2 Aug'03 Newb 6.0fm 85- D:		5	58
4038} **GIN N FONIC 324** [6]4-9-2 (70) R Havlin 50/1: 564100-7: ch g Zafonic - Crepe Ginger (Sadler's Wells) Nvr a factor: hdles fit (nov rnr-up, rtd 101h, eff at 2m1f on gd): won 1 of 7 '03 starts (seller, H Cyzer, earlier with J Fanshawe): eff around 12f, further may suit: acts on fibresand, firm & gd, sharp trk: has run well in cheek pieces: now with J Frost. 1 Aug'03 Wolv 12af 71a-(78) G:		8	43
7 Ran Time 1m 22.56 (2.76) Owned: Mrs P W Harris & Mr E Jehu Trained: Berkhamsted			

3403   **9.00 Dents Originals Fine Art Gallery Opens Tonight Handicap Stakes 3yo+ 0-70 (E)**   **[69]**
£3868 £1190 £595   **5f16y**   **Good 45**   **-07 Slow**   Stands side

3289 **STAGNITE 6** [16] Mrs H Sweeting 4-8-13 p (54) N Chalmers(5) 13/2: 200-0621: Dsptd lead till led stands side over 2f out, rdn to take overall lead well ins fnl 1f, rdn out: qck reapp: eff btwn 5/7f on firm, gd & polytrack, gall/undul trk: made full use of gd high draw: first win on 32nd start: see 2855.			60
3165 **LOCH INCH 11** [14] J M Bradley 7-8-10 bl (51) C Catlin 8/1: 0004042: Rear, hdwy 2f out, kept on.		1¼	53
2648 **CERULEAN ROSE 31** [9] A W Carroll 5-9-13 (68) L Fletcher(5) 7/1: 35-40203: Chsd ldrs, hdwy over 1f out, kept on ins fnl 1f, saddle slipped: v unfortunate, rider reported that he could not ride mount out.		hd	69
3213 **ONE WAY TICKET 8** [4] J M Bradley 4-10-0 p (69) S W Kelly 12/1: 0310004: Led far side, overall ldr over 1f out, hdd well ins fnl 1f: top-weight: first home from the far side: eff at 5/7f: back to form of 2626.		hd	69
2585 **AVIT 34** [11]4-7-12 (39) A McCarthy 14/1: 3060145: Cl-up, onepcd fnl 1f.		1¼	35
2502 **MORITAT 36** [6]4-8-12 (53) F P Ferris(3) 10/1: 6/0206-06: b g Night Shift - Aunty Eileen (Ahonoora) Held up far side, hdwy over 2f out, no impress ins fnl 1f: rnr-up at 5/7f (mdn, with P McEntee): stays 5f on fast, has disapp on firm: has tried a t-strap. 2 May'03 Folk 5g/f 64- D:		shd	48
3176 **JAZZY MILLENNIUM 10** [10]7-8-13 bl (54) S Drowne 14/1: 0-036337: Rear, hdwy 2f out, not pace to chall.		¾	47
3289 **YORKIES BOY 6** [17]9-8-10 p (51) R Thomas(5) 16/1: 0-540008: Rear, modest late gains: qck reapp.		shd	43
3220 **SO SOBER 8** [7]6-7-13 (40) Hayley Turner(5) 33/1: 0043009: Held up far side, modest late gains.		1	29
2063 **OLD HARRY 55** [1]4-8-6 T (47) D Sweeney 66/1: 54000-00: 10th: b g Case Law - Supreme Thought (Emarati) Cl-up far side, wknd over 1f out: 8 wk abs: mdn & h'cap unplcd '03 (rtd 61, L Cottrell): 4th 1 of 2 02 starts (mdn, rtd 68): has tried a visor, tried a t-strap here.		1	33
2931 **FLAPDOODLE 18** [13]6-8-10 (51) P Doe 14/1: 3050-500: 11th: Led stands side, hung left over 2f out & sn hdd, no extra: see 2585.		½	35
3143* **CORANGLAIS 12** [5]4-9-10 (7ex)p (65) R L Moore 11/2 JFAV: 0000410: 12th: Al bhd far side.		shd	48

CHEPSTOW   FRIDAY 23.07.04   Lefthand, Undulating, Galloping Track

3143 **INDIAN BAZAAR 12** [8]8-8-12 (53) M Savage(5) 25/1: 2002060: 13th: Dsptd lead far side, wknd 1f out.   1½   31
3017 **ARCTIC BURST 16** [12]4-9-0 vis (55) S Whitworth 66/1: 0000000: 14th: Al bhd: see 2016.   nk   32
2661 **COMERAINCOMESHINE 30** [15]3-9-4 (63) J Fortune 11/2 J FAV: 0-364200: 15th: Cl-up, lost   5   25
action/eased over 1f out: see 2268.
15 Ran   Time 59.44s(2.64)   Owned: Mr P Sweeting   Trained: Marlborough

NEWMARKET   FRIDAY 23.07.04   Righthand, Stiff, Galloping Track

Official Going GOOD/FIRM

3404   5.50 Bollinger Champagne Challenge Amat Rdrs Handicap 3yo+ 0-75 (E)   [44]
£3374 £1038 £519   1m2f   Firm 3   -50 Slow   Stands side

3313 **JACARANDA 4** [4] Mrs A L M King 4-11-10 (68) Mr S Walker 7/1: 0500241: Rear, rdn & hdwy when   72
forced to switch over 1f out, styd on for press to lead cl-home: quick reapp: slow time: eff at 7f, now suited by
10f: acts on firm, gd/soft & any trk: gd weight carrier: eff held up or forcing the pace: see 2370.
2900 **YANKEEDOODLEDANDY 21** [9] P C Haslam 3-11-7 P (75) Mr B Haslam(5) 4/1: 2121232: Handy & led over nk   78
6f out, drvn & hdd cl-home: gd run in 1st time cheek pieces: acts on firm, gd & both AWs: see 2900.
3238 **KALOU 7** [7] B J Curley 6-10-4 (48) Mr D Queally(7) 7/2 FAV: 6503-303: Rear, travelled well, styd   1¼   48+
on well but too late, gvn too much to do by inexperienced rider: acts on firm & both AWs: clrly stays a stiff 12f.
3114 **KYLKENNY 13** [10] H Morrison 9-12-0 t (72) Mr J Rees 13/2: 0065344: Cl-up, no extra dist: see 3114.   1½   71
3238 **FOREST TUNE 7** [2]6-10-6 (50) Mr E Dehdashti(3) 5/1: 0600645: Cl-up, onepace for press fnl 2f: see 1083. 1½   47
3288 **PRIVATE SEAL 6** [6]9-10-1 t (45) Mr A Chahal(7) 20/1: 5000326: Held up, not able to chall fnl 2f.   ¾   41
1701} **DRAMATIC QUEST 426** [8]7-11-12 p (70) Mr Michael Murphy(5) 14/1: 00/0224-7: b g Zafonic - Ultra   2   63
Finesse (Rahy) Chsd ldrs, rdn & btn over 1f out: long abs: AW class stks rnr-up in '03, turf h'cap plcd (amat
h'cap, rtd 65): unplcd '02 (rtd 87, h'cap): suited by 12f for fm, gd & polytrack, prob any trk: eff with/without
cheek pieces. 2 Mar'03 Ling 12ap 69a-(65) F: 2 Mar'03 Ling 12ap 44a-(80) F: 1 May'01 Newb 10gd 106- C:
2979 **MARIA BONITA 18** [5]3-10-11 bl (65) Mr R V Moore(7) 14/1: 03-4048: Keen, rear, no prog fnl 2f: btr 2979. 2½   54
2857 **PASO DOBLE 23** [1]6-10-13 (57) Mr J Millman(7) 14/1: 2054209: Bhd, rdn & btn 2f out, eased: btr 2725.   2   43
2741 **MISS HOOFBEATS 27** [11]3-9-10 (8oh) (42) Mr S Rees(5) 33/1: 030-0000: 10th: Led 3f, sn bhd.   dist   0
10 Ran   Time 2m 7.23 (5.33)   Owned: Touchwood Racing   Trained: Stratford-On-Avon

3405   6.15 Ngk Spark Plugs Maiden Stakes 3yo (D)
£5512 £1696 £848   1m4f   Firm 3   -11 Slow   Stands side

2678 **DARING AIM 30** [2] Sir Michael Stoute 3-8-9   K Fallon 3/1: 4-51: b f Daylami - Phantom Gold   82
(Machiavellian) Flashed tail early, sn led & dictated pace, rdn & al holding rivals fnl 2f under a well judged ride:
promise sole '03 start (fills cond stks, rtd 83): strong mid-dist pedigree: apprec step up to 12f, shld get
further: handles firm & fast grnd, stiff/easy trks: suited by forcing tactics.
3007 **ARTICULATION 17** [4] H R A Cecil 3-9-0 R Hughes 8/11 FAV: 42: Chsd ldr & chall 2f out, no extra   ¾   84
fnl 1f: styd longer 12f trip, rest well covered: see 3007.
2788 **GARNETT 26** [6] A King 3-9-0 D Holland 8/1: 43: Chsd ldrs, outpcd by front pair fnl 2f: better run.   5   76
3084 **ZUMA 14** [9] R Hannon 3-9-0 (74) E Ahern 14/1: 0-030554: Chsd ldrs, rdn & no impress fnl 3f: 2   73
headgear omitted: see 3084, 2700 & 2386.
1597 **PATRIXPRIAL 77** [1]3-9-0 P Robinson 10/1: 0-55: Mid-div, rdn & btn 3f out, t.o.: longer trip, see 1597.   15   51
      FFIZZAMO GO 0 [8]3-9-0 BL J Mackay 50/1: 6: b g Forzando - Lady Lacey (Kampala) Sn struggling   22   18
rear & no ch fnl 3f, t.o. on debut: wore blnks: full brother to a hdles scorer: dam a 7f/10f wnr.
3208 **BLUE TRACK 8** [7]3-9-0 T G McLaughlin 66/1: 07: b c Woodborough - Aryaah (Green Desert) Bhd &   7   7
drvn 5f out, t.o.
7 Ran   Time 2m 29.91 (1.71)   Owned: The Queen   Trained: Newmarket

3406   6.45 Cfx Forex E B F Novice Stakes 2yo (D)
£4667 £1436 £718   6f   Firm 3   -32 Slow   Stands side

2077* **CRIMSON SUN 55** [4] Saeed bin Suroor 2-9-5 L Dettori 13/8 FAV: 211: Led travelling well,   103
narrowly hdd ins last, rdn & led again cl-home: eff at 6f on fm & gd/soft: game & useful.
2467 **KINGS QUAY 38** [1] R Hannon 2-9-2 Dane O'Neill 5/2: 102: Held up, rdn to lead ins last, edged   hd   99
left & just hdd line: stays a stiff 6f: acts on firm & gd grnd: back to former alltr latest: see 2188.
3120 **YAJBILL 13** [2] M R Channon 2-8-12 K Fallon 15/8: 23: Cl-up, rdn & not pace of front pair from   2   89
dist: handles firm & gd grnd, apprec 7f: see 3120.
3005 **RED CHAIRMAN 17** [3] D R Loder 2-8-12 T P Queally 14/1: 054: Held up in tch, not pace to chall   1   86
from over 1f out: apprec return to 7f+: see 3005.
4 Ran   Time 1m 13.13 (2.13)   Owned: Godolphin   Trained: Newmarket

3407   7.15 Portland Place Properties Nursery Handicap Stakes 2yo (D)   [97]
£4833 £1487 £744   7f   Firm 3   -23 Slow   Stands side

3065 **SILVER WRAITH 15** [4] N A Callaghan 2-9-7 (90) J Murtagh 7/2 J FAV: 421131: Mid-div, drvn to lead   97
well ins last, all out: prev eff at 5f, now suited by 7f & shld get 1m on this evidence: acts on firm & fast grnd,
sharp or stiff trk: tough, useful & most progressive: see 3065, 2411.
3297* **WHATATODO 4** [7] M L W Bell 2-7-12 (6ex) (68) J Mackay 10/1: 03012: Led, drvn & hdd cl-home: nk   73
quick reapp under a pen: acts on firm & fast grnd: on the upgrade: see 3297.
3065 **SEA HUNTER 16** [6] M R Channon 2-9-1 (84) S Hitchcott(3) 7/2 J FAV: 01423: Handy, drvn to press   ¾   88
wnr ins last, drvn & just held when short of room cl-home: acts on firm & gd grnd: see 3065 & 1503.
2870 **MADAM CAVERSFIELD 22** [11] R Hannon 2-8-1 (70) F Norton 16/1: 50344: Mid-div, styd on for press,   ½   73
not able to chall: acts on firm & fast grnd: see 2870, 2388.
2043 **ALRIGHT MY SON 56** [9]2-8-6 (75) R Mullen 10/1: 0245: Drvn rear, no prog till strong run ins   hd   77+

last, nrst fin: h'cap bow, 8 wk abs: caught the eye late on, styd longer 7f trip well, 1m looks sure to suit: acts on firm & soft grnd: keep in mind: see 2043 & 1646.
2763 **HERES THE PLAN 27** [10]2-8-12 (81) L Dettori 4/1: 106: Keen, rear, styd on onepace fnl 2f: *1½* **80**
longer 7f trip shld suit: handles firm & gd grnd: see 1887 (6f, debut).
3212 **DONT TELL TRIGGER 8** [3]2-7-12 (1oh) (68) Lisa Jones(3) 20/1: 06107: Prom, rdn & no extra over 1f out. *nk* **65**
3302* **BALLYCROY GIRL 4** [8]2-8-4 (6ex) (73) E Ahern 7/1: 62518: Held up in tch, eff when hung left over *shd* **70**
1f out, no impress: quick reapp: btr 3302.
3297 **LAKESDALE 4** [2]2-7-12 (6oh) (68) M Halford(7) 50/1: 022049: Chsd ldrs, rdn & btn over 1f out. *7* **50**
3127 **CLINET 13** [5]2-7-13 (1ow)(4oh) (68) J Quinn 25/1: 052050: 10th: Reared start & slow away, sn keen *1½* **48**
& prom, btn over 1f out: btr 2020 (5f).
3020* **TIME FOR YOU 16** [1]2-8-2 (71) P Robinson 12/1: 0410: 11th: Rcd alone centre early, no impress fnl 2f. *1¾* **47**
11 Ran Time 1m 25.76 (1.86) Owned: Mr M Tabor Trained: Newmarket

3408

7.45 Corporate Fx Foreign Currency Handicap Stakes 3yo+ 0-90 (C) **[81]**
£9432 £2902 £1451 **6f** **Firm 3** **-03 Slow** Stands side

3341+**JONNY EBENEEZER 2** [11] D Flood 5-8-10 (7ex)bl (63) L Dettori 2/1 FAV: 3102211: Held up, prog **78+**
halfway, led trav well ins fnl 1f, pushed out, val 3L+: quick reapp: eff btwn 5/7f, stays stiff 1m: acts on firm, soft & fibresand: eff with blnks: inform 5yo who remains well treated & can land quick fire hat- trick: see 3341.
3218 **TONY THE TAP 8** [13] N A Callaghan 3-9-8 (80) D Holland 9/2: 4-122252: Al prom, styd on to lead *1¾* **87**
dist, hdd ins fnl 1f, kept on, no ch with easy wnr: eff at 5/6f: another gd eff in h'cap company: see 2734 & 2593.
2090 **PRINCE CYRANO 54** [4] W J Musson 5-9-5 (72) R Mullen 20/1: 0-000603: Held up, prog ins fnl 2f, *2½* **71**
nrst fin: 8 wk abs: encouraging eff & has slipped down weights: see 1481.
3232 **JUSTE POUR LAMOUR 7** [2] P L Gilligan 4-9-5 (72) J Murtagh 14/1: 0-040004: Held up, hdwy ins fnl *nk* **70**
2f, nrst fin: quick reapp: see 2090.
3136 **GOLDEN DIXIE 12** [9]5-9-13 (80) K Fallon 13/2: 0000-025: Cl-up, ev ch dist, sn no extra: btr 3136. *hd* **77**
3235 **INDIAN STEPPES 7** [10]5-8-13 (66) M Halford(7) 8/1: 3-664306: Slow away, nvr nrr than mid-div. *2* **57**
2752 **ANTONIO CANOVA 27** [8]8-9-11 (78) F Norton 16/1: 0/0-00107: Rear, mod late gains: btr 1743 (soft). *1¼* **65**
2871 **CAPE ST VINCENT 22** [3]4-9-7 vis (74) R Hughes 11/1: 24-01208: Bhd, eff when short of room ins fnl *1½* **56**
2f, sn no impress: btr 2779 & 2053.
179 **BARRANTES 226** [1]7-10-0 (81) Derek Nolan(7) 20/1: 236000-9: b f Distant Relative - Try The *1* **60**
Duchess (Try My Best) Led, hdd bef 1f out, fdd: reapp: won 2 h'caps in '03 (also rnr-up 5 times): class stks & lady's h'cap wnr in '02: eff btwn 5f/7f on fast & gd/soft, handles firm: best up with/forcing the pace & likes Lingfield. 2 Aug'03 Wind 6g/f 80-77 C: 1 Jul'03 Kemp 6g/f 77-73 D: 1 Jun'03 Ling 5g/f 72-65 E:
2 Jun'03 Wind 6g/f 68-65 D: 2 Jun'03 Donc 6fm 67-63 D: 2 Jun'03 Sand 5.0gd 66-63 D: 2 May'03 Ling 7gd 65-63 E:
2 Sep'02 Sali 5g/f 67-66 E: 1 Aug'02 Folk 6gd 67- E: 2 Aug'02 Newm 6gd 66-62 D: 2 Jul'02 Wind 6gd 61-60 E:
2669 **MIMIC 30** [5]4-9-1 (68) R Mills(7) 66/1: 1140-000: 10th: Cl-up till dist, fdd: btr 1638. *nk* **46**
3033 **SEMENOVSKII 16** [7]4-9-4 (71) S Sanders 6/1: 0600-360: 11th: Handy over 4f, wknd: btr 516. *shd* **48**
11 Ran Time 1m 11.41 (0.41) Owned: Mrs Ruth M Serrell Trained: Hungerford

3409

8.15 Vibe Fm Conditions Stakes 3yo+ (C)
£8416 £3192 £1596 **5f** **Firm 3** **+14 Fast** Stands side

3062 **BAHAMIAN PIRATE 15** [3] D Nicholls 9-9-9 (105) K Fallon 6/1: 1000001: Bhd, prog ins fnl 2f, drvn **117**
out to lead cl-home: fast time: eff at 5/6f on firm & fibresand, loves gd/soft & hvy: smart performer: see 2468.
3062 **BALMONT 15** [4] J Noseda 3-9-1 (115) E Ahern 2/5 FAV: 11110-32: Held up, prog ins fnl 2f, ev ch *nk* **112**
cl-home, just held by wnr: sltly disapp at odds-on: shade below 3rd in 3062 (Gr1 July Cup).
3304 **DRAGON FLYER 4** [5] M Quinn 5-8-3 (98) F Norton 7/1: 0000343: Prom, styd on to lead dist, hdd *1¼* **92**
cl-home: quick reapp: another gd run but without a win since '02: see 3100 & 883.
2727 **FUNFAIR WANE 28** [2] D Nicholls 5-8-8 (93) A Nicholls 25/1: 0000-004: Prom, ev ch dist, sn no extra. *1¼* **93**
3075 **VITA SPERICOLATA 14** [6]7-8-3 (81) J Mackay 33/1: 0350005: Led, hdd dist, sn hung left & wknd. *2* **82**
3268 **COLONEL COTTON 6** [1]5-8-13 (100) W Ryan 14/1: 6550306: Rear, mod late gains: qk reapp: btr 2913. *1* **89**
2581 **BOLEYN CASTLE 34** [7]7-8-8 P (89) T P Queally 50/1: 0000-007: Cl-up till halfway, fdd: cheek pieces. *6* **66**
7 Ran Time 57.94s (u0.56) Owned: Lucayan Stud Trained: Thirsk

3410

8.45 Corporate Fx Overseas Property Handicap Stakes 3yo 0-75 (E) **[80]**
£4241 £1305 £653 **1m** **Firm 3** **-33 Slow** Stands side

3346* **PICKLE 2** [3] S C Williams 3-9-3 (6ex) (69) S Sanders 15/8 FAV: 0336111: Mid-div, prog travelling **82+**
well to lead 1f out, sn pushed clr, val 4L+: quick reapp: eff at 6/7f, now stays 1m: acts on firm, soft & polytrack: thriving with racing & may not be at end of wng run: see 3346 & 3218.
2732* **THE FUN MERCHANT 28** [5] J Pearce 3-8-13 (65) J Quinn 9/2: 60-0112: Handy, styd on to lead 2f *2½* **71**
out, hdd 1f out, kept on but not pace easy wnr: lost little in defeat on bid for hat-trick: see 2732 (clmr).
2985 **LOUISIADE 18** [12] T D Easterby 3-8-11 (63) T E Durcan 20/1: 00-03003: Rear, prog 3f out, outpcd *4* **61**
bef 1f out, rallied cl-home: worth trying at 10f: btr 1745.
750 **BRIGHT FIRE 147** [8] W J Musson 3-8-0 (52) Lisa Jones(3) 12/1: 06-54: Cl-up, ev ch bef 1f out, sn wknd. *½* **49**
2885 **DAN DI CANIO 22** [9]3-8-13 T (65) D Holland 10/1: 5055: Rear, prog 3f out, hung left & lost action *shd* **61**
bef 1f out, kept on well ins fnl 1f: 1st time t-strap: see 2106.
3201 **CAYMAN CALYPSO 9** [2]3-8-13 (65) P Robinson 25/1: 00606: Al cl-up, wknd ins fnl 1f: btr 2907. *½* **60**
2920 **BERTOCELLI 20** [6]3-8-13 (65) J Mackay 14/1: 0-003407: Led 6f, wknd: btr 2272. *1* **58**
2773 **CHIGORIN 27** [4]3-9-2 (68) J Murtagh 13/2: 03-0608: Al in rear: btr 2365. *1¾* **57**
3177 **GALLAS 10** [13]3-8-3 vis (55) F Norton 25/1: 00-00029: Bhd, nvr a factor: showed more in 3177 (gd/soft). *3½* **37**
2974 **SUPAMACH 18** [7]3-9-0 (66) K Fallon 13/2: 3440: 10th: Prom, wknd 2f out: btr 2974 & 2110. *1½* **45**
3121 **Miss Procurer 13** [14]3-9-3 T(69) N De Souza(5) 20/1:0
3472} **Broughton Bounty 350** [10]3-9-2 (68) R Mullen 33/1:0
12 Ran Time 1m 40.15(2.95) Owned: Mr S P Tindall Trained: Newmarket

Official Going Good/Firm

3411 **2.05 European Breeders Fund July Maiden Stakes Fillies 2yo** (D)
£6253 £1924 £962 **6f str** **Good/Firm 32** **+03 Fast** stands side

3171 **TOP FORM 10** [3] E A L Dunlop 2-8-11 R Ffrench 16/1: 051: b f Almutawakel - Top of The Form **81**
(Masterclass) Made all, drvn out ins fnl 1f: Mar foal, cost 40,000 gns: fast time: dam successful at sprint dists:
eff at 6f, will apprec further: acts on fast grnd: imprvd eff with front rng tactics.
HONEY RYDER 0 [7] D R Loder 2-8-11 T P Queally 7/2: 2: b f Compton Place - Urania (Most shd **80+**
Welcome) In tch, prog & ev ch dist, kept on ins fnl 1f, just held by wnr: op 9/4 on debut: Feb foal, cost 42,000
gns: half sister to wnrs at 5/7f: dam plcd up to 10f: sire Gr1 wnr at sprint dists: eff at 6f, shaped as tho' 7f
will suit: acts on fast grnd: fine eff on intro despite rng green, improve for experience & go one btr.
2927 **CONSIDER THIS 20** [13] W M Brisbourne 2-8-11 P Hanagan 5/2 FAV: 253: Prom, ev ch 1f out, sn shd **79**
edged left under press, just held in 3-way photo: clr rem: well bckd: lost little in defeat: see 2603.
3064 **CEREBUS 15** [10] N P Littmoden 2-8-11 S Chin 7/2: 64: b f Wolfhound - Bring On The Choir (Chief 5 **64**
Singer) Handy over 4f, sn onepcd: op 5/1: Feb foal, cost 3,500 gns: half sister successful at 7f: dam 5f wnr.
IGNITION 0 [9]2-8-11 B Swarbrick(5) 50/1: 5: Slow away, prog halfway, kept on fnl 1f: debut. 2 **58**
3258 **ALGORITHM 6** [5]2-8-11 R Winston 14/1: 06: In tch wide 4f, sn hung right & no extra: see 3258. 1¾ **52**
THE PEN 0 [2]2-8-11 G Faulkner 50/1: 7: Slow away, nvr nrr than mid-div: debut. ½ **51**
2671 **FROGS GIFT 30** [12]2-8-11 T Eaves(3) 50/1: 068: Prom 4f, sn short of room & wknd. 1½ **47**
3183 **MOLLY DANCER 9** [1]2-8-11 A Culhane 7/1: 09: Dwelt, prog when short of room after 4f, sn btn. 1¼ **44**
CALAMARI 0 [8]2-8-11 M Tebbutt 33/1: 0: 10th: Chsd ldrs 4f, fdd. 1 **41**
2833 **Witty Girl 24** [4]2-8-11 K Ghunowa(7) 25/1:0 3103 **Princeable Lady 13** [6]2-8-11 D Allan 25/1:0
12 Ran Time 1m 11.29 (1.79) Owned: ORS Woods Weatherby Davies and Stone Trained: Newmarket

---

3412 **2.35 Harrogate Novice Stakes 2yo** (D)
£5681 £1748 £874 **7f rnd** **Good/Firm 32** **-43 Slow** Inside

2933* **STRAWBERRY DALE 20** [4] J D Bethell 2-8-11 W Supple 7/2: 11: In tch, rcd keenly, styd on to lead **91+**
dist, pushed out, val 5L+: eff at 5f, improved for step up to 7f: acts on fast & gd grnd: shown a gd turn of foot
to land this, can rate higher & win again: see 2933.
3141 **NOORAIN 12** [5] M R Channon 2-8-7 A Culhane 14/1: 342: Handy, styd on to lead after 4f, hdd 3 **80**
dist, kept on, not pace easy wnr: eff at 5/7f: continues to run with credit & now quals for h'caps: see 3141 & 2795.
THUNDERWING 0 [2] K R Burke 2-8-8 P Hanagan 40/1: 3: b c Indian Danehill - Scandisk (Kenmare) 1 **79**
Mid-div, prog 3f out, kept on ins fnl 1f: debut: May foal, cost £12,000: half brother plcd as a juv: dam
successful abroad at 2: sire decent performer at 1m/10f: eff at 7f, will apprec further: acts on fast: gd start.
3127 **FIEFDOM 13** [7] M Johnston 2-9-2 R Ffrench 4/9 FAV: 54124: Led 4f, sn no extra: well bckd at 2 **83**
odds-on: v disapp on step up to 7f & surely something amiss: btr 3127 & 2424 (6f).
3126 **ZABEEL PALACE 13** [6]2-8-12 T P Queally 14/1: 05: Bhd, nvr a factor: see 3126. 2½ **74**
DANCING SHIRL 0 [1]2-8-3 G Faulkner 125/1: 6: b f Dancing Spree - Shirl (Shirley Heights) In 4 **57**
tch 4f, wknd: debut: Feb foal, half sister successful at 6f: dam successful at 12f.
2028 **GENERAL MAX 57** [3]2-8-12 R Winston 20/1: 37: Bhd, prog halfway, wknd 2f out: 8 wk abs: btr 2028. 1¾ **62**
7 Ran Time 1m 28.15 (5.25) Owned: Mr M J Dawson Trained: Middleham

---

3413 **3.05 Michael J Wood - Chantry Chemicals Maiden Stakes 3yo** (D)
£5564 £1712 £856 **7f rnd** **Good/Firm 32** **-36 Slow** Inside

2365 **WYCHBURY 42** [7] M J Wallace 3-9-0 (75) D Corby(3) 4/6 FAV: 32-52201: Prom, led 3f out, pushed clr **66+**
ins fnl 1f, val bit more: well bckd after 6 wk abs: eff at 5/6f, now suited by 7f: acts on firm & fast grnd: has
been gelded since last run & this was a gd confidence boost: see 2259 & 1971.
2936 **BORODINSKY 20** [6] R E Barr 3-9-0 (44) T Eaves(3) 80/1: 00-50402: Handy, prog to chase wnr bef 1f 2 **59**
out, kept on ins fnl 1f, al held: eff at 7f on fast grnd: improved run: see 2104.
3179 **GASPARINI 10** [5] T D Easterby 3-9-0 (59) D Allan 13/2: 0004303: Led 4f, no extra bef 1f out: 1½ **56**
acts on fast & gd, prob handles soft: see 2936.
2683 **LORD WISHINGWELL 29** [4] J S Wainwright 3-9-0 vis (34) M Lawson(5) 100/1: 00-03304: Handy 5f. shd **55$**
2885 **CLASSIC LEASE 22** [8]3-9-0 A Culhane 66/1: 05: Rear, prog halfway, hung left & onepcd dist: see 2885. ¾ **53**
3121 **ROSIE MAC 13** [3]3-8-9 (62) Suzanne France(7) 10/1: 6346: Bhd, prog wide 3f out, styd on cl-home. shd **47**
4874† **DIUM MAC 273** [9]3-9-0 Dean McKeown 9/2: 24-7: b g Presidium - Efipetite (Efisio) Handy 5f, ¾ **50**
wkng when short of room dist: tchd 6/1 on reapp: nvr one of only 2 '03 starts (auct mdn): eff at 7f, shld
apprec further: acts on firm grnd & a stiff/gall trk: with N Bycroft. 2 Oct'03 Newc 7fm 70- E:
2231 **PURE VINTAGE 49** [1]3-9-0 P Hanagan 20/1: 068: Held up, prog halfway, staying on when short of 2½ **45**
room over 1f out, position sn accepted: 7 wk abs: see 1971 (debut).
2987 **DANCER KING 18** [2]3-9-0 R Winston 40/1: 509: Bhd, nvr a factor: btr 2692. ¾ **43**
9 Ran Time 1m 27.66 (4.76) Owned: Favourites Racing Trained: Newmarket

---

3414 **3.40 Humber Selling Handicap Stakes 3yo 35-55** (F) **[58]**
£3478 £1070 £535 **1m rnd** **Good/Firm 32** **-45 Slow** Inside

2852 **ZONNEBEKE 23** [3] K R Burke 3-9-1 (45) R Winston 9/2 JT FAV: 0300341: Chsd ldrs, prog 2f out, **52**
drvn out to lead cl-home: bought in for 5,200 gns: visor left off: eff at 7f, apprec return to 1m: acts on fast,
gd grnd & polytrack: 1st win: see 2704 & 535.
3177 **HEATHYARDS JOY 10** [8] R Hollinshead 3-8-2 (32) Stephanie Hollinshead(4) 9/2 JT FAV: 2556032: hd **37**
Prom, led 5f out, hdd under press cl-home: eff at 7f/1m on fast & gd/soft: rider's 1lb overweight proved costly.
2205 **WEET AN HAUL 49** [9] P A Blockley 3-9-5 VIS (49) P Hanagan 10/1: 0120-003: Handy, styd on ins fnl 1¼ **52**
1f, not btn far: 7 wk abs: eff at 7f/1m on fast grnd & fibresand: back to form with fitting of visor: see 203.
3324 **BARGAIN HUNT 3** [17] W Storey 3-9-0 (44) M Lawson(5) 16/1: 0036004: Mid-div, prog & ev ch bef 1f ¾ **45**
out, sn no extra: quick reapp: btr 1505.

2624 **FARAWAY ECHO 32** [11]3-9-5 vis (49) N Mackay(3) 12/1: 00-06305: Dwelt, prog when short of room bef halfway, kept on ins fnl 2f, nrst fin: op 6/1: just btr 1740 (soft). ½ **49**
2546 **MR MOON 35** [5]3-8-2 VIS (32) P M Quinn 25/1: 0-660006: Dwelt, prog halfway, no impress fnl 2f. 1½ **29**
2932 **CHUBBES 20** [13]3-9-6 BL (50) P Mulrennan(5) 11/2: 30-00447: Held up, prog 3f out, nrst fin: blnks. hd **46**
2704 **DELTA LADY 29** [10]3-8-12 (42) R Ffrench 20/1: 0-060508: Handy 6f, sn wknd: see 1591. 3 **32**
1798 **ABROGATE 67** [14]3-9-3 P (47) G Faulkner 10/1: 03-02459: Cl-up 6f, wknd: 1st time pieces & jumps fit. ½ **36**
2944 **ALPHA ZETA 20** [16]3-8-10 (40) Dean McKeown 50/1: 0-0000: 10th: Al bhd: see 2730. ¾ **27**
2991 **SVENSON 17** [12]3-8-0 (30) P Fessey 66/1: 0-0000: 11th: Al bhd. 1¾ **13**
3094 **WEDOWANNAGIVEUTHAT 14** [1]3-9-5 (49) D Allan 16/1: 006000: 12th: Chsd ldrs 5f, wknd. nk **31**
2932 **KNIGHT TO REMEMBER 20** [15]3-8-8 (38) T Eaves(3) 25/1: 0050500: 13th: Bhd, nvr a factor. 1½ **17**
3182 **COTTAM KARMINSKI 10** [7]3-8-10 (40) T Lucas 33/1: 000600: 14th: Al bhd. 3 **13**
3153 **GEMINI GIRL 11** [4]3-8-12 (42) A Culhane 14/1: 6-000000: 15th: Slow away, nvr a factor. shd **14**
2704 **TRINAREE 29** [2]3-8-8 (38) N Pollard 25/1: 0-0000: 16th: Led, hdd 5f out, sn fdd: btr 2237. 4 **2**
16 Ran Time 1m 41.63 (6.23) Owned: Mr John A Duffy Trained: Leyburn

3415

4.10 Adrian Tate Handicap Stakes 3yo 0-80 (D) **[86]**
£5564 £1712 £856 **1m4f** **Good/Firm 32** **-18 Slow** Inside

2751 **FORGED 27** [5] L M Cumani 3-9-7 (79) N Mackay(3) 13/8 FAV: 0321: Mid-div, prog to lead travelling well 2f out, sn pushed clr, eased cl-home, val 12L+: well bckd on h'cap bow: eff at 10f, enjoyed return to 12f: acts on fast & gd grnd: could not have been more impress & can follow up under a pen: see 2751 & 2113. **97+**
1785 **CLASSIC EVENT 68** [3] T D Easterby 3-8-5 (1ow) (62) R Winston 33/1: 0350-002: Slow away, prog over 3f out, no impress on easy wnr ins fnl 2f: 10 wk abs: signs of encouragement & 14f may suit: see 1000. 9 **66**
5024} **MARKET LEADER 259** [2] Mrs A J Perrett 3-9-0 (72) W Supple 6/1: 502-3: b f Marju - I Will Lead (Seattle Slew) Cl-up, ev ch bef 2f out, sn short of room, no extra fnl 2f: tchd 9/2 on reapp: rnr-up on last of only 3 '03 starts (auct mdn): eff at 1m, bred to apprec mid-dists: acts on gd grnd. 2 Nov'03 Donc 8gd 74- E: 1½ **72**
2960 **HAVETOAVIT 19** [6] J D Bethell 3-8-2 (60) S Chin 11/2: 0-532404: Led, hdd when hmpd 2f out, wknd. 1 **58**
2796 **KRISTALS DREAM 25** [4]3-9-4 (76) T P Queally 2/1: 31-35025: In tch over 9f, sn wknd: bckd, btr 2796. 1¾ **71**
3108 **AUROVILLE 13** [1]3-8-2 vis (60) R Ffrench 16/1: 0405006: Chsd ldrs 1m, sn fdd: btr 2168. 6 **47**
6 Ran Time 2m 35.86 (6.06) Owned: Mr G Callanan Trained: Newmarket

3416

4.45 Stanland Warwick Dryer Handicap Stakes Fillies 3yo+ 0-80 (D) **[73]**
£5577 £1716 £858 **6f str** **Good/Firm 32** **-03 Slow** Stands side

3220 **LE MERIDIEN 8** [3] J S Wainwright 6-8-3 p (48) R Ffrench 20/1: 5000651: Cl-up wide, styd on to lead bef 1f out, drvn out to hold on: eff at 5/6f on firm & soft grnd: eff with visor, t-strap & now cheek pieces: on a fair mark & this was a gd confidence boost: see 3220 & 2429. **56**
3307 **SHAROURA 4** [7] R A Fahey 8-9-5 (64) P Hanagan 7/1: 5010342: In tch, prog 2f out ev ch ins fnl 1f, just held: quick reapp: won this race 12 months ago off a 12lb lower mark: continues to run well. shd **70**
3054 **AMELIA 15** [4] W M Brisbourne 6-8-13 (58) B Swarbrick(5) 12/1: 0132533: In tch wide, prog & ev ch dist, kept on ins fnl 1f, not btn far: op 8/1: generally consistent performer: see 3054 & 1465. ½ **63**
2925* **ESTIHLAL 20** [5] E A L Dunlop 3-9-8 (72) W Supple 5/2 FAV: 0412414: Short of room after start, prog halfway, ev ch ins fnl 1f, onepace cl-home: well bckd: prob ran shade btr than bare form would indicate. ½ **76**
3116 **MITSUKI 13** [1]5-9-4 (63) S Chin 14/1: 00400-05: Bhd, prog halfway, kept on fnl 1f: see 3116. 1¾ **62**
3307 **COLLEGE MAID 4** [12]7-9-2 bl (61) J Currie(7) 14/1: 4135666: Rear, sn short of room, some late gains. ¾ **58**
3106 **ROMAN MISTRESS 13** [13]4-9-5 bl (64) D Allan 15/2: 0463057: Handy over 4f, onepace dist: btr 2232. ½ **60**
3213 **STOKESIES WISH 8** [2]4-9-4 (63) A Culhane 14/1: 0020548: Rcd alone on far rail, al in tch, onepcd. 1½ **55**
3193 **ISLAND SPELL 9** [10]3-9-0 P (64) P Fessey 80/1: 3-353009: Prom 4f, sn wknd: cheek pieces: btr 2728. shd **55**
3092* **SHIFTY NIGHT 14** [15]3-7-13 (49) N Mackay(3) 10/1': 00-00410: 10th: Rear, mod late gains: btr 3092. ½ **39**
3050 **COLLEGE QUEEN 15** [6]6-9-5 bl (64) N Pollard 15/2: 0654520: 11th: Prom, led 3f out, hdd bef 1f out, wknd: better expected after 2nd in 3050 (gd/soft). ¾ **52**
2936 **CAPETOWN GIRL 20** [11]3-8-12 VIS (62) V Halliday 25/1: 5-100000: 12th: Slow away, nvr a factor. 1¾ **45**
2232 **MAGIC MUSIC 48** [9]5-9-10 (69) R Winston 14/1: 1402-000: 13th: Chsd ldrs 4f, fdd. 4 **40**
2846 **SAFRANINE 23** [8]7-9-2 (61) Ann Stokell 33/1: 0006000: 14th: Led 3f, sn fdd: btr 2710. hd **31**
14 Ran Time 1m 11.06 (2.1) Owned: Miss S L Iggulden Trained: Malton

3417

5.20 Levy Board Apprentice Handicap Stakes 3yo+ 0-75 (E) **[67]**
£4183 £1287 £644 **5f str** **Good/Firm 32** **+18 Fast** Stands side

2542 **PLAYFUL DANE 35** [9] W S Cunningham 7-9-4 (57) K Pierrepont(5) 10/1: 100-1501: Cl-up, styd on to lead just ins fnl 2f, pushed clr, val 5L+: fast time: eff at 7f, apprec drop back to 5f: acts on fast & gd. **71+**
3228 **SOAKED 7** [3] D W Chapman 11-9-10 bl (63) B O'Neill 6/1: 0412152: Led, hdd under press ins fnl 2f, not pace wnr: quick reapp: gd eff under top weight: see 2775. 3½ **66**
3350 **AMANDAS LAD 2** [14] M C Chapman 4-9-2 (55) Liam Jones 9/1: 0354563: Dwelt, mid-div halfway, kept on ins fnl 1f: op 7/1: quick reapp: btr 2216. 1 **55**
3180 **MYSTERY PIPS 10** [11] N Tinkler 4-8-6 vis (45) R Keogh 10/1: 0004004: Mid-div, prog 3f out, onepcd. ¾ **43**
3180 **BELLA BEGUINE 10** [4]5-8-9 bl (48) Natalie Hassall(8) 10/1: 5020445: Handy over 3f, sn onepcd: btr 3180. ¾ **44**
3228 **AMERICAN COUSIN 7** [12]9-9-5 (58) P J Benson(5) 9/1: 1025006: Dwelt, prog ins fnl 2f, nrst fin. hd **53**
3191 **DANAKIM 9** [13]7-8-3 (42) Donna Caldwell 20/1: 1500007: Handy over 3f, sn no extra: btr 1988. shd **36**
3350 **MR SPLIFFY 2** [6]5-8-7 (46) M Stainton 16/1: 0000008: Rear, nvr nrr than mid-div: quick reapp. 1½ **36**
3220* **ROSIES RESULT 8** [8]4-8-12 (6ex) (51) Jemma Marshall 5/1: 00-00019: Chsd ldrs over 3f, wknd: btr 3220. ¾ **39**
2219 **CELLINO 49** [10]3-8-2 (45) K Jackson 33/1: 0050-040: 10th: Al in rear: 7 wk abs: btr 2219. hd **32**
2801 **MATRIARCHAL 25** [1]4-7-12 (7oh) (30) Janice Webster 100/1: 400-0500: 11th: Mid-div till halfway, wknd. 5 **11**
3220 **KENNINGTON 8** [7]4-8-13 bl (52) Laura Pike 9/2 FAV: 0020040: 12th: Al in rear: disapp eff: btr 3220. ¾ **24**
2951 **STAR APPLAUSE 20** [2]4-8-1 (40) J Currie(3) 66/1: 00-00600: 13th: Handy wide 3f, wknd. nk **11**
2029 **BLUEBERRY RHYME 57** [5]5-9-5 vis (58) Stacey Renwick(3) 12/1: 2101500: 14th: Handy 3f, fdd. 1½ **25**
14 Ran Time 57.71(0.71) Owned: Ann and David Bell Trained: Yarm

Official Going Good/Firm ALL TIMES SLOW

3418   2.30 City Life Magazine Maiden Stakes Fillies 2yo (D)
£4947 £1522 £761   6f15yds str   Good/Firm   Slow   Stands Side

3041 **ENCANTO 16** [4] J S Moore 2-8-11 Derek Nolan(7) 7/2: 062221: Sn cl up & led over 1f out, rdn out: **85**
eff at 6f on firm & gd/sft grnd, prob any trk: most tough & consistent, deserved this: see 3041, 2815, 2415.
3290 **SHARP AS A TACK 5** [6] B J Meehan 2-8-11 J F McDonald(3) 50/1: 02: b f Zafonic - Pretty Sharp 1½ **80**
(Interrex) Dwelt & held up, rdn/flashed tail but styd on well from over 1f out, not pace to chall: left debut bhd:
35,000gns Jan foal: half sister to smart sprinter Twilight Blues: dam a maiden: eff at 6f, 7f may suit: acts on fast
ground & gall trk: well related filly, clearly going the right way.
3064 **AHDAAF 16** [2] J L Dunlop 2-8-11 W Supple 10/11 FAV: 33: Cl up, led 2f out, rdn & hdd over 1f 1¼ **76**
out, no extra fnl 1f: well bckd: more expected after 3064.
2373 **CASTEROSSA 43** [10] D Haydn Jones 2-8-11 Paul Eddery 33/1: 64: ch f Rossini - First Musical nk **75**
(First Trump) Dwelt & outpcd early, rdn & hung left over 2f out, kept on well ins last, nvr dngrs: left debut bhd:
Feb 1st foal, 52,000gns purchase: dam a 5/6f juv wnr: eff at 6f on fast ground: still green but shows ability.
2750 **MITRAILLETTE 28** [8]2-8-11 B Doyle 12/1: 65: ch f Miswaki - Crockadore (Nijinsky) In tch, hdwy hd **74**
to chse front pair over 2f out, rdn/edged left & no extra ins last: op 9/1: Feb foal, half sister to a 7f/1m juv wnr,
also a modest 14f 3yo wnr: dam a 1m 3yo wnr: handles fast ground: likely to need further in time.
3103 **RAPID ROMANCE 14** [9]2-8-11 R Mullen 16/1: 56: Held up, rdn & nvr threatened ldrs: see 3105. 3½ **63**
3141 **SCROOBY BABY 13** [7]2-8-11 S W Kelly 5/1: 27: Chsd ldrs, no impress fnl 2f, op 6/1. 1 **60**
2689 **EUKLEIA 30** [1]2-8-11 P Makin(5) 40/1: 68: Led, rdn & hung left over 2f out, sn hdd & fdd. shd **60**
     SHAMROCK BAY 0 [3]2-8-11 M Fenton 20/1: 9: Chsd ldr, hung left halfway & sn no impress, op 14/1. 14 **20**
3221 **CADOGEN SQUARE 9** [5]2-8-11 Darren Williams 150/1: 000: 10th: Dwelt, cl up till halfway. 21 **0**
10 Ran   Time 1m 17.7 (6.9)   Owned: Cistm Racing Club Ltd   Trained: Hungerford

3419   3.00 Happy Birthday Mark Bemrose Handicap Stakes 3yo 0-70 (E)   [75]
£4160 £1280 £640   1m2f   Good/Firm   Slow   Inside

2804 **ROCK LOBSTER 26** [12] J G Given 3-8-13 (60) M Fenton 6/1: 4-056361: Held up, hdwy to lead over 1f **66**
out, drvn out: op 9/1: stays 12f, apprec drop to 10f: acts on fbsnd & fast grnd, sharp or gall trk: see 2203, 1144.
2433 **SCRIPTORIUM 40** [6] L M Cumani 3-9-0 (61) N Mackay(3) 100/30: 0-60242: Dwelt, sn trkd ldrs, rdn & 1 **65**
led over 2f out, hdd over 1f out, not pace of wnr: op 5/2, 6 wk abs: eff at 9/10f: see 2120.
3187 **PELLA 10** [9] M Blanshard 3-9-2 (63) D Sweeney 2/1 FAV: 0625323: Mid-div, rdn & hdwy to chall ½ **66**
dist, no extra ins last: nicely bckd, op 5/2: stays 10f: see 3187, 2904.
2046 **MAMBINA 57** [8] M R Channon 3-9-2 (63) S Hitchcott(3) 12/1: 0-044504: Chsd ldrs, efft over 2f out, 2½ **61**
onepace for press: abs: handles fast & soft ground: see 1648.
1619 **CHARA 77** [3]3-9-4 (65) R Mullen 16/1: 45-31055: Held up, prog/no room dist, kept on ins last, no 1½ **62**
threat: 11 wk abs: acts on fast, gd/sft & polytrk: see 1165.
2494 **QUEENS FANTASY 38** [16]3-9-1 vis (62) Paul Eddery 10/1: 0402166: Handy, rdn & led over 3f out, hdd hd **58**
over 2f out, hung left & btn dist: just btr 2203 (12f, AW).
3108 **SNOWED UNDER 14** [5]3-8-11 (58) T Quinn 18/1: 0-55507: Led till over 3f out, sn btn: see 2322. 1¾ **52**
3192 **IMPERIAL ROYALE 10** [13]3-8-12 P (59) M Tebbutt 28/1: 52-50608: Chsd ldrs, btn 2f out: chkpcs. hd **52**
2931 **BROOKLANDS LODGE 21** [1]3-9-2 (63) I Mongan 33/1: 450-609: Mid-div, hmpd & lost plce over 3f out, 1 **55**
keeping on late when no room dist, nvr threat: closer with a clr run: longer 10f trip may suit: see 2529.
3108 **CANNI THINKAAR 14** [14]3-9-1 (62) J Carroll 20/1: 06-60040: 10th: Mid-div, btn 3f out: btr 3108. ½ **53**
3242 **KALISHKA 8** [4]3-8-13 (60) W Supple 25/1: 000-6500: 11th: b c Fasliyev - Andromaque (Woodman) 2 **48**
Chsd ldrs, btn over 2f out: unplcd '03 (rtd 73, mdn).
1163 **Cheverak Forest 101** [15]3-9-3 (64) Kim Tinkler 25/1:0
3231 **Magical Mimi 8** [2]3-9-7 (68) Leanne Kershaw(7) 25/1:0
13 Ran   Time 2m 10.2 (7.9)   Owned: Mr A Clarke   Trained: Gainsborough

3420   3.35 John Watkins Celebration Selling Handicap Stakes 4yo+ 35-55 (G)   [61]
£2765 £790 £395   1m6f15y   Good/Firm   Slow   Inside

3299 **BANNINGHAM BLAZE 5** [11] A W Carroll 4-8-13 vis (46) I Mongan 3/1: 2236531: Held up, hdwy 3f out, **51**
led dist, drvn out: nicely bckd: eff at 12f, now stays a gall 14f well in sell grade: acts on firm, fast & polytrk.
3105 **LUNAR LORD 14** [5] D Burchell 8-9-2 (49) J Bramhill 100/30: 0000422: Keen early, trk ldr, led 1¾ **51**
over 3f out, hdd over 2f out, kept on for press: op 9/4: acts on fast, ideally suited by more give: see 924.
3147 **PERTEMPS SIA 13** [9] A D Smith 4-8-3 (36) W Supple 13/2: 6606-053: Chsd ldrs, rdn/outpcd over 2f 1 **37**
out, styd on for press late: op 14/1: eff at 14f/2m11f on fast & gd grnd: confirmed improv of 3147.
3149 **BORDER TERRIER 12** [10] M D Hammond 6-8-6 bl (39) N Mackay(3) 5/1: 0003044: Mid-div, lost pl 1½ **38**
halfway, styd on onepace for press fnl 3f: stays 14f: see 1796.
3211 **CRACOW 9** [6]7-8-13 P (46) P Makin(5) 14/1: 300/-2045: Mid-div, smooth hdwy 3f out, rdn & fnd 1¼ **43**
little dist: 1st time chkpcs: poss not see out this longer 14f trip: see 2112.
2813 **MAGIC CHARM 26** [8]6-8-0 (3oh) (30) Leanne Kershaw(7) 20/1: 0406006: Held up, efft 3f out, sn held. 3 **26**
3154 **THINK QUICK 12** [4]4-8-2 (35) R Kennemore(7) 9/1: 0300627: Held up, efft wide fnl 3f, llittle prog. ½ **27**
2910 **GREY SAMURAI 22** [7]4-8-0 (3oh) (30) Dean Williams(7) 100/1: 60008: Pulled hard tracking ldr, btn 2f out. 12 **9**
2279] **BURNING TRUTH 763** [3]10-9-6 (53) V Slattery 66/1: 040/640/-9: ch g Known Fact - Galega (Sure shd **29**
Blade) Led 10f, sn btn, long Flat abs, 3 mth jmps abs, 03/04 beginners chse wnr (2m/2m4f, firm & gd, rtd 109c):
unplcd '02 (rtd 40a, Mrs A Duffield, sell): prev eff btwn 1m/12f on firm, gd/sft & both AWs, sharp trks.
1 Mar'01 Wolv 12af 74a- D: 1 Dec'00 Wolv 9.3af 73a-68 E: 1 Nov'00 Ling 10ap 70a-64 E:
3147 **JACK DURRANCE 13** [1]4-8-6 (39) J F McDonald(3) 12/1: 0-004000: 10th: Handy, btn 2f out: btr 2267. 2 **12**
3211 **Lilian 9** [12]4-8-9 vis(42) M Fenton 20/1:0   2344] **Crispin House 398** [2]4-8-1 (34) Kim Tinkler 66/1:0
12 Ran   Time 3m 07.1 (8.8)   Owned: Mr Dennis Deacon   Trained: Alcester

3421 4.05 Letheby & Christopher Rated Stakes Handicap 3yo 0-90 (C)
£9605 £3643 £1822 1m54y rnd Good/Firm Slow Centre [96]

3059 **SECRETARY GENERAL** 16 [3] P F I Cole 3-9-6 (88) T Quinn 5/2 FAV: 1-020501: Handy & led over 2f 97
out, drvn out: bckd, op 100/30: eff at 7f/1m on fast & soft ground: likes a gall trk: see 1741.
3107* **INCHLOSS** 14 [8] B A McMahon 3-8-9 (77) W Supple 8/1: 1200612: Settled rear, swtchd & hdwy to ½ 84
chall dist, no reach wnr: op 9/1: acts on fast & soft: did not get the run of the race, prog, more to come.
2940 **LITTLE JIMBOB** 21 [4] R A Fahey 3-8-7 (75) G Parkin 9/1: 342-1243: Dwelt, keen, trkd ldrs, short 1 80
of room over 1f out, onepace ins last: see 2705 & 2443.
1888 **NAADDEY** 64 [1] M R Channon 3-9-6 (88) S Hitchcott(3) 25/1: 4353-064: Dwelt, sn trk ldrs, onepace ¾ 92
when short of room ins last: 2 mth abs: see 1888.
2903 **HELLO ITS ME** 22 [2]3-9-5 (87) M Tebbutt 9/2: 331-2025: Led till over 2f out, no extra: see 2903, 1192. ¾ 90
3179* **BURLEY FLAME** 11 [6]3-8-12 (80) M Fenton 7/1: 3310316: Held up, efft wide 3f out, sn btn: btr 3179. 2 79
3006 **OASIS STAR** 18 [7]3-9-7 (89) J Carroll 4/1: 1-115127: Held up, hdwy wide 3f out, sn chall but ½ 87
onepace & held when hmpd ins last: nicely bckd: closer without interference tho' not placed: see 3006, 2362 (7f).
2126 **ATTUNE** 53 [5]3-8-12 (80) J F McDonald(3) 25/1: 4-40108: Chsd ldrs, btn 2f out: abs: btr 1770. 3 72
8 Ran Time 1m 46.15 (6.75) Owned: The Blenheim Partnership Trained: Whatcombe

3422 4.35 Racing Uk Maiden Stakes Fillies 3yo (D)
£5005 £1540 £770 1m2f Good/Firm Slow Inside

3038 **CASTAGNA** 17 [9] H R A Cecil 3-8-11 T Quinn 11/4: 0-41: Chsd ldr & led 2f out, rdn clr: op 9/4: 81
eff at 10f, shld stay 12f: acts on fast ground, gall or easy trk: lightly rcd & progressing, fillies h'caps should suit.
3038 **AUTUMN WEALTH** 17 [10] Mrs A J Perrett 3-8-11 W Supple 8/11 FAV: 22: Trkd front pair, drvn & no 8 68
impress fnl 2f: well bckd at odds on: more expected after finishing ahead of this wnr in 3038.
2668 **SEEKING A WAY** 31 [8] J H M Gosden 3-8-11 R Havlin 11/2: 21-23: Led 1m, sn no impress: op 4/1. 2 65
SOVIETTA 0 [3] R M Beckett 3-8-11 M Tebbutt 33/1: 4: b f Soviet Star - La Riveraine (Riverman) 2 62
Dwelt & held up, hdwy 3f out, no prog 1f out: clr of rem on debut: half sister to wnrs at 1m/9f, dam 11f wnr.
2668 **BREAKING THE RULE** 31 [6]3-8-11 J Carroll 66/1: 065: ch f King of Kings - Thirtysomething 8 48
(Thirty Six Red) Dwelt & always bhd, no ch fnl 2f: mod form to date, including when well behind today's 3rd latest.
3197 **IN EVERY STREET** 10 [4]3-8-11 I Mongan 25/1: 06: Chsd ldr early, btn 2f out, op 16/1: turf bow. hd 49
KIKIS GIRLS 0 [5]3-8-11 P Makin(5) 80/1: 7: Dwelt & always bhd on debut. dist 0
7 Ran Time 1m 44.48 (5.08) Owned: Bloomsbury Stud Trained: Newmarket

3423 5.10 Midlands Racing - 9 Great Venues Classified Stakes 3yo+ 0-70 (E)
£3673 £1130 £565 1m54y rnd Good/Firm Slow Centre

3328* **HARRY POTTER** 4 [5] K R Burke 5-10-0 vis (69) Darren Williams 5/2 FAV: 1060311: Rear, swtchd & 80
prog 2f out, drvn to lead close home, all out: qck reapp, nicely bckd: eff at 7f, suited by 1m on fast & soft ground,
gall or easy trks: progressive profile: see 3328.
2840 **BRAZILIAN TERRACE** 24 [1] M L W Bell 4-9-10 (75) Hayley Turner(5) 3/1: 4011302: Trkd ldrs, rdn to hd 76
lead dist, edged left & hdd close home: back to best on turf: see 2414.
1049* **NEARLY A FOOL** 110 [2] G G Margarson 6-9-9 vis (71) N Mackay(3) 11/2: 1021013: Chsd ldrs, short of 1¼ 72+
room & swtchd over 1f out, short of room ins last till nr fin: op 10/1, 4 mth abs: would have gone close with a clr
run: stays a gall 1m well: see 1049.
2954 **ARAGONS BOY** 20 [8] H Candy 4-9-8 (70) D Sweeney 20/1: 54-00104: Led till dist, onepace: see 2641. ½ 70
3242 **TAGULA BLUE** 8 [6]4-9-8 (69) M Tebbutt 12/1: 6-U0R365: Held up, efft over 2f out, sn btn: btr 2901. 6 58
2962 **SUMMER SHADES** 20 [3]6-9-5 (67) T Quinn 9/1: 5244356: Chsd ldr halfway, btn over 1f out: btr 2767. ½ 54
3328 **ADOBE** 4 [7]9-9-8 (67) R Mullen 14/1: 0344207: Hld up, short of room over 2f out, no impress: qk reapp. shd 57
3232 **HUXLEY** 8 [9]5-9-8 t (70) P McCabe 4/1: 0-000048: Held up & keen, rdn & no impress fnl 2f: btr 3232. 2 53
2732 **WESTERN ROOTS** 29 [4]3-9-6 (75) W Supple 40/1: 0061559: Held up, left bhd fnl 2f: btr 2133 (clmr). 19 20
9 Ran Time 1m 44.48 (5.08) Owned: Mr F Jeffers Trained: Leyburn

Official Going Good (Good/Firm Places)

3424 1.00 Betfred Sprint Series Final Handicap Stakes 3yo+ (B)
£11945 £4531 £2265 6f str Good 44 -02 Slow Centre. 2 Groups. [91]

3069 **FANTASY BELIEVER** 15 [15] J J Quinn 6-10-0 (91) T Hamilton(3) 7/1: 0004101: Al handy stands side, 97
led that group dist & styd on for press to lead overall nr fin: op 9/2: eff at 5/7f on any grnd or trk: fien run
under a big weight & can race of this mark in Stewards Cup next week: see 2878, 2770.
2770 **FAIR SHAKE** 28 [9] D Eddy 4-8-2 VIS (65) P Fessey 33/1: 0-003502: Pushed along rear stands side, nk 70
briefly short of room & switched over 1f out, strong run ins last, just denied: cheek pieces omitted, fine run in
first time visor: loves this trk: acts on gd & soft grnd, handles firm: win similar if able to repeat: see 1393.
2561 **SNOW BUNTING** 35 [1] Jedd O'Keeffe 6-7-12 (3oh) (58) D Fentiman(7) 12/1: 0302053: Held up far side, ½ 64+
hdwy & led overall over 1f out, hdd well ins last: comfortable wnr on far side, could find similar: see 1020.
3136* **PINCHBECK** 13 [6] M A Jarvis 5-9-10 p (87) N Callan 9/2 FAV: 3-041014: Stands side, held up, styd 1¾ 85
on late, nrst fin: op 6/1: see 3136.
2855 **YOMALO** 24 [13]4-8-1 (64) M Halford(7) 11/2: 0-005625: Held up stands side, hdwy & briefly led nk 61
that group over 1f out, not pace of front pair ins last: nicely bckd: see 2855.
3033 **MR MALARKEY** 17 [14]4-9-1 bl (78) T G McLaughlin 11/1: 0463306: Led/dsptd lead stands side till dist. nk 74
3228 **TALLY** 8 [5]4-8-3 (66) R Thomas(5) 12/1: 0244307: Prom far side, no impress from dist: btr 3073 & 2942. nk 61
2957* **GONENDUNNETT** 20 [4]5-7-12 (1oh)vis (60) B Swarbrick(5) 11/1: 6610318: Cl-up far side till over 1f out. ¾ 54
2831 **FRIAR TUCK** 25 [10]9-7-12 (10oh) (51) R Ffrench 50/1: 6400049: Chsd ldrs stands side, no impress dist. ¾ 52$

3213 **A TEEN 9** [8]6-7-12 (7oh) (54) D Kinsella 33/1: 6006000: 10th: Held up stands side, no impress fnl 2f. nk **51**
3248 **LEGAL SET 8** [3]8-7-12 (1oh)t (60) D Fox(5) 20/1: 1402400: 11th: Led far side till over 1f out, sn struggling. 1½ **46**
3146 **GLENCOE SOLAS 13** [12]4-8-11 (74) K Dalgleish 12/1: 2153260: 12th: Led/dsptd lead stands side hd **58**
till over 1f out, wknd qckly: btr 3045 & 2626.
2884 **WILLIAMS WELL 23** [7]10-7-12 (3oh)bl (58) Dale Gibson 16/1: 20-00050: 13th: Chsd ldrs stands side 5f. nk **44**
2934 **ULYSEES 21** [2]5-8-11 (74) T Eaves(3) 10/1: 1031050: 14th: Trkd ldrs far side, wknd 2f out: btr 2542. ½ **55**
3307 **HIGHLAND WARRIOR 5** [11]5-8-9 (72) V Halliday 8/1: 0046630: 15th: Slow away, in tch stands side 4f. 7 **35**
15 Ran Time 1m 14.06 (2.76) Owned: The Fantasy Fellowship B Trained: Malton

3425

1.35 Appleby Group Limited Maiden Auction Stakes Div 1 2yo (F)
£3290 £940 £470 **7f str** **Good 44** **-24 Slow** Centre

2776 **SKIDROW 27** [7] M L W Bell 2-8-11 D Kinsella 12/1: 01: b c Bachir - Flourishing (Trojan Fen) **90**
Held up, prog/switched over 2f out, led dist & rdn clr, readily: left debut bhd: 14,000gns May foal, half-brother to a 5f juv wnr, dam a 7f juv wnr: eff over a stiff 7f, 1m will suit: just the type for a nursery.
3021 **BEE STINGER 17** [8] I A Wood 2-8-7 N Callan 4/5 FAV: 0322: Keen, led/dsptd lead till over 1f 4 **75**
out, no ch with wnr ins last: hvly bckd: ran to form of 3021.
COCONUT SQUEAK 0 [3] J G Given 2-8-4 S Chin 25/1: 3: b f Bahamian Bounty - Creeking (Persian ½ **71**
Bold) Handy, shaken up & kept on fnl 1f: 7,000gns May foal, half-sister to dual 1m 3yo wnr Yalla, dam plcd at 6f/1m: eff at 7f, 1m sure to suit: encouraging start, rate higher.
3120 **JEUNE LOUP 14** [6] P C Haslam 2-8-13 G Faulkner 12/1: 04: b g Loup Sauvage - Secret Waters 1¾ **77**
(Pharly) Trkd ldrs, no extra bef dist: 22,000gns Apr foal, half-brother to a 7f/1m juv wnr, also a 10f 3yo scorer: dam a multiple wnr at 12/14f: imprvd over this longer 7f trip, mid-dists likely to suit in time: handles gd grnd.
2995 **CLASSIC STYLE 18** [5]2-8-6 A Mullen(5) 40/1: 5005: Cl-up, no impress bef dist. 1 **68**
2829 **SCORPIO SALLY 25** [9]2-8-4 R Ffrench 20/1: 056: Mid-div, no impress fnl 2f, longer trip. 4 **58**
3122 **ALLSTAR PRINCESS 14** [2]2-8-2 T Hamilton(1) 50/1: 007: Held up, hdwy over 2f out, no prog bef dist. ½ **55**
2682 **MORNING MAJOR 30** [11]2-8-9 P Fessey 25/1: 08: Pushed along rear, only mod prog, longer trip. 3 **56**
2959 **DANCERS SERENADE 20** [12]2-8-13 Dale Gibson 11/2: 359: Cl-up, fdd fnl 2f: btr 2570. 1 **58**
2995 **LLAMADAS 18** [1]2-8-11 p L Enstone(3) 11/1: 30340: 10th: Held up, rdn & no impress fnl 2f: btr 2569. 1¼ **53**
3227 **Negas 8** [4]2-8-13 T Eaves(3) 20/1:0 **Trigony 0** [10]2-8-11 K Dalgleish 20/1:0
12 Ran Time 1m 28.83 (4.73) Owned: Mr Raymond Tooth & Miss Debbie Dove Trained: Newmarket

3426

2.10 Pimms Apprentice Claiming Stakes 3yo+ (G)
£2660 £760 £380 **7f str** **Good 44** **-18 Slow** Centre

2996 **MEHMAAS 18** [6] R E Barr 8-9-0 vis (43) Steven Harrison(3) 25/1: 0004001: Led/dsptd lead far side, **58**
went on 3f out, held on well for press ins last: stays 1m, suited by 7f on firm, hvy & fibresand: likes to race with/force the pace: apprec drop to claim grade: see 2550.
2809 **KILLALA 26** [3] I Semple 4-9-2 (62) W Hogg 11/4 FAV: 436-3552: Trkd ldrs far side, chall from 2f nk **60**
out, al just held ins last: nicely bckd: see 1794.
2988 **NOBLE PURSUIT 18** [1] R E Barr 7-9-0 (50) Laura Pike(5) 14/1: 5002403: Chsd ldrs far side, onepace. 2½ **53**
3250 **DONNAS DOUBLE 8** [9] D Eddy 9-9-3 p (54) A Mullen 9/2: 555-5634: Held up stands side, kept on fnl 5 **46**
2f, no ch with ldrs far side: first home from stands side group: return to 1m+ in similar shld suit: see 2832.
3151 **BAILIEBOROUGH 12** [11]5-9-10 vis (70) P J Benson(7) 9/2: 0130165: Cl-up stands side & led that 1¾ **50**
group 3f out, no ch fnl 2f: btr 2811.
3191 **GIVE HIM CREDIT 10** [15]4-9-1 p (52) H Poulton 33/1: 00-50006: Prom stands side 5f, sn no impress. 9 **25**
3286* **TRE COLLINE 7** [8]5-10-1 (70) M Howard 5/1: 1514617: Stands side & prom, struggling over 2f out. ½ **38**
3324 **MOUNT PEKAN 4** [2]4-9-1 (41) J Currie(5) 25/1: 0306058: Slow away & al bhd far side: qck reapp. 2½ **19**
3104 **NITEOWL EXPRESS 14** [5]3-8-5 (36) A Reilly(3) 66/1: 0-065409: Led far side till 3f out, sn struggling. 1¾ **13**
2996 **COUNTRYWIDE GIRL 18** [12]5-8-11 (39) K Pierrepont(7) 20/1: 3215340: 10th: Keen, prom stands side 4f. 2 **8**
967 **STORMVILLE 117** [14]7-9-3 (57) J D O'Reilly 40/1: 1500/0-00: 11th: b g Catrail - Haut Volee (Top 4 **6**
Ville) Led stands side 1f, prom 5f: 4 mth abs: unplcd '03 (rtd 42 & 36a, h'caps): dual '02 h'cap wnr: eff at 6f/9.4f, 7f poss ideal: acts on firm, gd/soft & fibresand, prob any trk, likes Newcastle: can go well fresh.
1 Aug'02 Newc 6g/s 64-59 F: 1 Aug'02 Newc 7gd 58-53 D: 2 Aug'01 Newc 7g/s 50-50 D:
2508 **TANCRED ARMS 37** [13]8-8-8 (38) Donna Caldwell(5) 22/1: 060-0400: 12th: Dsptd lead stands side 4f. shd **0**
2967 **SUMMER SPECIAL 19** [10]4-9-1 p (44) M Halford 20/1: 0503300: 13th: Mid-div stands side, no ch fnl 3f. 6 **0**
3156 **Finger Of Fate 12** [4]4-9-2 bl(42) K Ghunowa(3) 14/1:0
3180 **Leopard Creek 11** [7]3-8-6 VIS(53) A Hamblett(5) 14/1:0
15 Ran Time 1m 28.44 (4.34) Owned: Cloughton Racing Partnership Trained: Middlesbrough

3427

2.45 Pimms Summer Classic Handicap Stakes 3yo+ 0-85 (D) **[83]**
£7001 £2154 £1077 **5f str** **Good 44** **+03 Fast** Centre. 2 Groups.

3241 **AWAKE 8** [1] D Nicholls 7-9-10 (79) K Dalgleish 5/1 JT FAV: 5016201: Held up in tch far side, **87**
switched & rdn to lead ins last, going away: fair time: eff at 6f, suited by 5f on fm & hvy, any trk: see 2286 & 1251.
3131 **IMPERIAL ECHO 14** [3] T D Barron 3-9-5 vis (78) N Callan 10/1: 3-004022: Keen, trkd ldr far side, 1½ **81**
styd on for press, not pace of wnr: op 8/1: gd run with visor reapplied: eff btwn 5/7f: see 3131 & 1460.
3073 **BEYOND THE CLOUDS 15** [2] J S Wainwright 8-9-6 (75) T Eaves(3) 7/1: 0002003: Al prom far side & ½ **76**
led over 1f out till ins last, onepace: see 2830.
3241 **WINTHORPE 8** [8] J J Quinn 4-9-2 (71) T Hamilton(3) 5/1 JT FAV: 4032054: Held up far side, late gains. 1¾ **67**
2968 **STRAWBERRY PATCH 19** [7]5-8-0 p (55) P Fessey 25/1: 0600-005: Handy far side, styd on onepace. nk **50**
3228 **PIRLIE HILL 8** [6]4-7-12 (2oh) (51) D Kinsella 25/1: 1604406: Held up far side, mod prog, nvr dngrs. hd **47**
3352 **KINGS COLLEGE BOY 3** [10]4-8-5 bl (60) Dale Gibson 11/2: 0323037: Trkd ldrs stands side, led that nk **53+**
group over 1f out, no impress on ldrs far side: qck reapp: 1st home on stands side, gd run: most consistent.
3228 **VIEWFORTH 8** [13]6-8-11 bl (66) V Halliday 10/1: 0043008: Chsd ldrs stands side, kept on onepace. ¾ **57**
3150 **AAHGOWANGOWAN 12** [4]5-8-8 t (63) R Ffrench 11/2: 0052159: Led far side till over 1f out, wknd. ¾ **52**
1635 **TRINITY 77** [9]8-7-12 (5oh) (48) P M Quinn 33/1: 0040-000: 10th: Cl-up stands side till over 1f out, abs. 1½ **37**
3350 **STRENSALL 3** [12]7-9-8 (77) L Enstone(3) 9/1: 0034050: 11th: Led stands side till over 1f out, ½ **59**
wknd: won this race in '03 off a 6lb lower mark: see 124.
3244 **LINDENS LADY 8** [5]4-8-2 bl e (57) D Fentiman(7) 33/1: 0605650: 12th: Keen & cl-up far side 4f. 6 **23**

12 Ran   Time 1m 0.26 (2.06)   Owned: Lucayan Stud & D Nicholls   Trained: Thirsk

---

3428   3.15 Tsg Beeswing Rated Stakes Handicap 3yo+ 0-85 (D)   [88]
£12208 £4631 £2315   7f str   Good 44   -01 Slow   Centre. 2 Groups.

3068* **TRUE NIGHT** 15 [13] D Nicholls 7-9-7 (81) T Eaves(3) 9/2 CO FAV: 2330311: Hld up, prog/short of   **90**
room 2f out, led dist, drvn out: op 7/2: eff at 1m, loves a stiff 7f: acts on fm & gd/soft: thrives in July/Aug.

3223 **RAPHAEL** 9 [8] T D Easterby 5-9-5 (79) A Mullen(7) 12/1: 0304022: Al handy & chall dist, just held.   nk   **87**

2693* **SNAP** 30 [6] M Johnston 3-8-11 (78) R Ffrench 9/2 CO FAV: 21313: Held up, rdn & styd on from over   nk   **85**
1f out, not pace of wnr: improving: see 2693.

3117 **TIDY** 14 [3] M D Hammond 4-9-4 (78) K Dalgleish 25/1: 5U03004: Held up, styd on for press, not   shd   **85**
able to chall wnr: likes this trk: see 2684 & 1035.

3305 **SEA STORM** 5 [11]6-9-7 p (81) P Doe 20/1: 3010065: Chsd ldrs, led 2f out till dist, onepace: qck   1¼   **85**
reapp & gd run with cheek pieces reapplied: see 2087.

3305* **TOP DIRHAM** 5 [9]6-8-13 (3ex) (73) Dale Gibson 9/2 CO FAV: 2320016: Held up, hmpd over 1f out,   shd   **77+**
kept on late, nrst fin: closer with a clr passage: qck reapp: see 3305.

1624 **OUT FOR A STROLL** 77 [10]5-9-1 (75) P Fessey 7/1: 0110-007: Held up, rdn & no extra ins last: abs.   2½   **74**

3117 **BALAKIREF** 14 [5]5-8-9 (69) N Callan 8/1: 22U1008: Dwelt & held up, little prog: op 10/1: btr 2568.   1¾   **65**

3116 **SIERRA VISTA** 14 [12]4-9-7 (81) L Enstone(3) 14/1: 3005169: Cl-up till over 1f out: btr 2770.   5   **68**

3117 **MOBANE FLYER** 14 [4]4-8-7 (67) T Hamilton(3) 40/1: 10050-00: 10th: Mid-div, no prog over 1f out.   1   **52**

2848 **KING HARSON** 24 [7]5-9-5 vis (79) B Swarbrick(5) 16/1: 1-020060: 11th: Led till 2f out, sn btn: btr 2848.   2   **60**

3223 **FAVOUR** 9 [1]4-8-9 (69) L Goncalves 12/1: 23-20600: 12th: Keen, mid-div, struggling from halfway.   2   **46**

2935 **KIRKBYS TREASURE** 21 [2]6-9-0 (74) S Chin 14/1: 2130120: 13th: Chsd ldrs till over 2f out: btr 2935.   2   **47**

13 Ran   Time 1m 27.26 (3.16)   Owned: Benton and Partners   Trained: Thirsk

---

3429   3.50 Appleby Group Limited Maiden Auction Stakes Div 2 2yo (F)
£3283 £938 £469   7f str   Good 44   -35 Slow   Centre

3202 **ARABIAN ANA** 9 [6] B Smart 2-8-13 D McGaffin 6/1: 61: b c Night Shift - Al Shaqrah (Sir Ivor)   **81+**
Dwelt, sn mid-div, hdwy & led over 1f out, edged left but styd on well, pushed out: left debut bhd: Apr foal,
17,000gns 2yo purchase: half-brother to multiple wnrs abroad, dam plcd at 12/15f as a 3yo: apprec step up to 7f & 1m+
likely to suit: acts gd grnd & a stiff trk: open to further improvement.

2612 **SPINNAKERS GIRL** 33 [4] J R Weymes 2-8-2 D Fentiman(7) 5/2 FAV: 032: Handy & led over 2f out till   1½   **66**
over 1f out, short of room ins last when not pace of wnr: well bckd: acts on fast & gd, h'cap company shld suit.

3053 **DIXIE QUEEN** 16 [9] M Dods 2-8-6 N Callan 7/1: 5003: Mid-div, rdn & styd on fnl 2f, not pace to   1½   **67**
chall: op 6/1: stays 7f, acts on gd grnd: h'cap company will suit: see 1631.

3178 **SUMMER SILKS** 11 [11] R A Fahey 2-8-2 T Hamilton(3) 9/1: 04: ch f Bahamian Bounty - Sadler's Song   shd   **63**
(Saddlers' Hall) Held up, rdn & styd on from over 1f out, not able to chall: cheaply bght Mar first foal, dam
unplcd btwn 5f/2m, subs hdles plcd: sire top-class 6f juv: eff over a stiff 7f, shaped as if 1m+ will suit.

ASKWITH 0 [7]2-8-11 B Swarbrick(5) 12/1: 5: b g Marju - Hayward (Indian Ridge) Dwelt & bhd,   hd   **71**
kept on well fnl 2f, nrst fin: 15,000gns Apr foal, half-brother to a plcd 10/13f performer, dam a 9f 3yo wnr: sure
to apprec 1m+ & improve.

2360 **ZANDO** 43 [1]2-8-9 G Faulkner 7/1: 006: Chsd ldrs, btn 2f out: 6 wk abs.   2½   **64**

2275 **TRICKSHOT** 47 [5]2-8-2 P M Quinn 9/2: 207: Rdn mid-div, no impress fnl 2f, 7 wk abs: op 6/1: btr 1744.   3   **51**

2462 **MIST OPPORTUNITY** 39 [8]2-8-11 Rory Moore(7) 50/1: 008: Sn bhd & pushed along, nvr a factor.   3   **54**

2882 **FOR NOWT** 23 [2]2-8-9 A Mullen(7) 14/1: 609: Keen, chsd ldrs till halfway, longer trip, op 25/1.   2½   **47**

2845 **TILLINGBORN DANCER** 24 [10]2-8-11 K Dalgleish 25/1: 0000: 10th: Led/dsptd lead 5f, sn wknd.   4   **41**

2682 **XAARIST** 30 [3]2-8-11 Dale Gibson 12/1: 00: 11th: Keen & led 2f, struggling fnl 3f, longer trip.   5   **31**

11 Ran   Time 1m 29.62 (5.52)   Owned: HESheikh Rashid Bin Mohammed   Trained: Thirsk

---

3430   4.20 Bellway Homes Classified Stakes 3yo+ 0-80 (D)
£5746 £1768 £884   1m2f32y   Good 44   -25 Slow   Far Side

3261 **DUNASKIN** 7 [6] D Eddy 4-9-5 (80) D Kinsella 3/1: 0005631: Dictated pace till over 2f out,   **88**
rallied gamely for press to lead again ins last, styd on strongly: stays a sharp 12f, best dominating at 1m/10f on
fast & gd/soft, prob any trk: v genuine effort here, see 1668.

3225 **MBOSI** 9 [1] M Johnston 3-8-12 (83) R Ffrench 13/2: 15-3302: Trkd ldr & led over 2f out till ins   ¾   **89**
last, held cl-home: op see 3042 & 2026.

3260* **OLIVIA ROSE** 7 [4] J Pearce 5-9-5 (83) N Callan 7/4 FAV: 1231413: Trkd ldrs, hdwy to chall ins   shd   **86**
last, just held nr fin: remains in fine form: see 3260.

3216 **SCOTTISH RIVER** 9 [5] M D I Usher 5-9-7 (82) B Swarbrick(5) 5/2: 1466124: Slow away, held up   1¼   **86**
racing keenly, kept on for press, nvr able to chall: bckd, op 7/2: see 3044.

3074 **PAWAN** 15 [3]4-9-5 (73) Ann Stokell 20/1: 6630105: Held up, no ch fnl 2f: btr 2962 (9f).   11   **71**

4807] **AXFORD LORD** 626 [2]4-9-5 (60) T Eaves(3) 40/1: 100204/-6: gr g Petong - Bellyphax (Bellypha)   dist   **0**
Chsd ldrs, lost tch fnl 3f: long abs: missed '03: '02 seller wnr, AW unplcd (rtd 53a, seller): eff at 5/6f on
firm & soft grnd: handles any trk: suited by a visor.
2 Oct'02 Redc 7sft 62- F: 1 Aug'02 Ripo 6gd 66- F: 2 Jun'02 Carl 5g/s 73- E: 2 Jun'02 Redc 5fm 71- E:

6 Ran   Time 2m 13.55 (7.05)   Owned: Mrs I Battla   Trained: Newcastle Upon Tyne

YORK **SATURDAY 24.07.04 Lefthand, Flat, Galloping Track**

Official Going Good/Firm (Firm Places)

3431 **1.50 Pickerings Lifts 150th Anniversary Maiden Auction Stakes 2yo (E)**
£8619 £2652 £1326 **6f str** **Good/Firm 27** **-16 Slow** Centre

3110 **LITTLE DALHAM 14** [10] P W Chapple Hyam 2-8-9 A McCarthy 4/5 FAV: 421: Al prom & led over 1f out, pushed out, readily: hvly bckd at odds on: eff at 6f, stays a sharp 7f: acts on fast & gd/soft grnd, stiff/undul or sharp trks: did this well, type for a nursery: see 3110. **84**
3163 **VIKING SPIRIT 12** [1] P W Harris 2-8-9 R L Moore 8/1: 02: Trkd ldrs, rdn & kept on fnl 2f, not pace of wnr: imprvd from intro: eff at 6f, 7f shld suit: acts on fast: win a race: see 3163. *2* **75**
3171 **CAMPEON 11** [2] M J Wallace 2-8-10 K Darley 14/1: 0505243: Led till over 1f out, kept on: eff at 6/7f on fast & gd grnd: handles a gall or sharp/undul trk: see 2952. *shd* **76**
WIGWAM WILLIE 0 [13] M J Wallace 2-8-10 D Corby(3) 20/1: 4: b c Indian Rocket - Sweet Nature (Classic Secret) Chsd ldrs, outpcd 2f out, rdn & kept on late: 20,000gns Feb foal, half-brother to a 6f juv wnr, dam a 6f juv wnr: eff at 6f on fast grnd: gd start, improve. *½* **74**
3120 **CLARET AND AMBER 14** [11]2-8-9 P Hanagan 13/2: 355: Held up, short of room over 2f out, switched & styd on strongly ins last: nrst fin: handles fast & gd grnd: gd late prog, interesting for 7f nurseries. *¾* **71+**
SWIFT OSCAR 0 [4]2-8-8 E Ahern 13/2: 6: b c Mark of Esteem - Surf Bird (Shareef Dancer) Rear, switched & styd on from over 1f out: 6,000gns Mar foal, half-brother to a 1m/9f wnr, dam a mdn. *¾* **68**
ETOILE RUSSE 0 [5]2-8-9 Dean McKeown 66/1: 7: b c Soviet Star - To The Skies (Sky Classic) Mid-div, short of room 2f out, kept on ins last: shade closer with a clr run: dam a 10f 3yo scorer: will apprec 7f+. *1¾* **64**
BLUSHING RUSSIAN 0 [9]2-8-8 N Pollard 25/1: 8: Held up, nvr pace to threaten. *2½* **55**
KOOL OVATION 0 [8]2-8-9 A Beech 33/1: 9: Dwelt, mid-div, no prog fnl 2f. *1¼* **52**
3130 **UNDERTHEMISTLETOE 14** [7]2-8-3 F Norton 40/1: 630: 10th: Chsd ldrs till halfway: btr 3130 (5f). *2½* **38**
2424 **FOREST VIKING 41** [6]2-8-8 R Winston 66/1: 500: 11th: Chsd ldrs, rdn & struggling fnl 2f: abs. *1¼* **39**
2360 **Mill By The Stream 43** [3]2-8-9 T P Queally 40/1:0 3078 **Bahamian Bay 15** [12]2-8-3 (1ow) D Allan 100/1:0
13 Ran Time 1m 11.99 (2.59) Owned: Collins Deal Harrison-Allan Chapple-Hyam Trained: Newmarket

3432 **2.20 Skybet Press Red To Bet On Channel Four Stakes Nursery Handicap 2yo (C)** **[94]**
£10433 £3210 £1605 **5f str** **Good/Firm 27** **-08 Slow** Centre

2789* **MIMI MOUSE 26** [6] T D Easterby 2-9-3 (83) K Darley 4/1: 64311: Made all, rdn & styd on strongly fnl 1f: eff at 5f on fast grnd, stiff/undul or gall trks: steering problems corrected, useful & improving. **93**
3082 **KATIE BOO 15** [7] A Berry 2-8-13 (79) P Mathers(5) 13/2: 321352: Trkd ldrs, rdn & styd on fnl 2f: eff at 5f, worth another try at 6f in similar: see 2711 & 2442. *1½* **84**
2983 **WISE WAGER 19** [8] R A Fahey 2-8-3 (69) P Hanagan 4/1: 2333: Chsd ldrs, rdn & kept on fnl 2f, not able to chall: acts on fibresand, firm & gd grnd: see 2983 & 2442 & 1652. *1* **71**
3303 **NOVA TOR 5** [3] N P Littmoden 2-9-3 (83) T P Queally 13/2: 1104154: Chsd ldrs, onepace dist: qk reapp. *shd* **85**
3271 **BRUT 7** [5]2-8-0 (1ow) (65) F Norton 20/1: 062055: Chsd ldrs, onepace over 1f out: btr 2505. *¾* **66**
3115 **WONDERFUL MIND 14** [1]2-8-9 (75) R Winston 100/30 FAV: 052156: Led/dsptd lead till over 1f out. *nk* **74**
2711 **SELKIRK STORM 30** [4]2-9-7 (86) P Mulrennan(5) 6/1: 1257: Dwelt, sn struggling rear & no ch dist. *8* **65**
7 Ran Time 58.54 (1.74) Owned: Mrs Jean P Connew Trained: Malton

3433 **2.50 Skybet Interactive Betting On Channel Four Stakes Handicap 3yo 0-90 (C)** **[95]**
£11018 £3390 £1695 **7f rnd** **Good/Firm 27** **-05 Slow** Inside

3273 **NEON BLUE 7** [4] R M Whitaker 3-8-1 (68) Hayley Turner(5) 10/1: 5103331: Chsd ldrs, drvn to lead cl-home, gamely: eff at 6f, now suited by a gall 7f: acts on fast & soft grnd, sharpish or gall trk: tough. **78**
3117 **DISTANT CONNECTION 14** [3] A P Jarvis 3-9-1 (82) T P Queally 100/30 FAV: 6121532: Led & rdn clr over 1f out, hdd cl-home: well bckd: tough & genuine: see 3117, 2525. *nk* **91**
2749* **MRS MOH 28** [7] T D Easterby 3-8-13 (80) D Allan 6/1: 32-00513: Chsd ldrs, styd on onepace fnl 2f. *1½* **86**
3273 **RISING SHADOW 7** [9] R A Fahey 3-9-3 (84) P Hanagan 7/1: 0135-624: Held up, kept on wide for press, nrst fin: handles fast, soft & polytrack: stays a gall 7f: see 3273 & 2764. *2* **86**
2953* **CARRY ON DOC 20** [2]3-8-8 (75) S Whitworth 15/2: 355-3615: Rear, short of room over 2f out, switched & kept on onepace: rtn to 1m shld suit: see 2953 (1m mdn). *1¼* **74**
2693 **DARK DAY BLUES 30** [8]3-8-0 (67) F Norton 33/1: 0-000106: Chsd ldrs, rdn & btn dist: see 2295. *nk* **65**
3277 **ODDSMAKER 7** [5]3-9-7 (88) Dean McKeown 5/1: 5101537: Handy, outpcd when hmpd 2f out, sn no impress: well bckd: btr 3277 & 2753 (1m). *2* **82**
3024 **JOSHUAS GOLD 17** [6]3-7-12 (14oh) (51) Danielle McCreery(7) 100/1: 5-236008: Dwelt, held up, no dngr. *1½* **56**
3016 **REIDIES CHOICE 17** [1]3-8-7 (74) A Culhane 6/1: 0-020429: Rear, hdwy over 2f out, no prog over 1f out. *1¾* **62**
1745 **VADEMECUM 71** [10]3-8-10 (77) F Lynch 16/1: 0413-600: 11th: Keen & cl-up, btn over 1f out: abs. *10* **45**
3092 **ELLIOTS CHOICE 15** [11]3-7-13 (66) J Mackay 40/1: 0043600: 11th: Chsd ldrs, rdn & btn 2f out. *1¾* **31**
11 Ran Time 1m 23.54 (2.24) Owned: Country Lane Partnership Trained: Scarcroft

3434 **3.25 Skybet Dash Heritage Handicap 3yo+ 0-105 (B)** **[100]**
£32500 £10000 £5000 **6f str** **Good/Firm 27** **+18 Fast** Centre

2770 **MUTAWAQED 28** [8] M A Magnusson 6-8-13 t (85) R L Moore 13/2: 30-04201: Held up, prog 2f out & rdn/led ins last, hung right under press but styd on strongly to assert in a fast time: suited by 6f, has won at 1m: acts on fast & rain softened grnd, both AWs & any trk: progressive, big Stewards Cup rnr under 5lb pen. **94**
3307+ **MACHINIST 5** [15] D Nicholls 4-8-10 (7ex) (82) Alex Greaves 11/2: 40-00012: Held up, hdwy & rdn to chall ins last, not pace of wnr nr fin: qck reapp under a pen, remains unexposed: see 3307. *1* **87**
3116 **ELLENS ACADEMY 14** [9] E J Alston 9-9-0 (86) F Norton 13/2: 4244223: Held up, rdn & hdwy to chall dist, not pace of wnr when hmpd ins last: well bckd: in gd form: see 3116 & 2770. *½* **89**
3002 **TWO STEP KID 18** [5] J Noseda 3-9-7 (98) E Ahern 100/30 FAV: 1-64134: Chsd ldr, led 2f out, rdn & onepace when badly bmpd ins last: hvly bckd: prob plcd without intererence: see 3002 & 2407. *shd* **101**
3248 **LOYAL TYCOON 8** [7]6-9-3 (89) L Treadwell(5) 12/1: 5001055: Mid-div, styd on onepace: see 2871. *1* **89**

YORK   SATURDAY 24.07.04   Lefthand, Flat, Galloping Track

3248 **SIMIANNA** 8 [4]5-9-6 (92) P Mathers(5) 20/1: 6020046: Trkd ldrs, shkn up & not able to chall dist. ¾ 90
3100 **TALBOT AVENUE** 14 [12]6-9-6 (82) S Righton 12/1: 0550227: Chsd ldrs trav well, no extra dist: wants 5f. 1½ 85
2609 **BO MCGINTY** 34 [2]3-8-10 (87) P Hanagan 16/1: 01-01208: Chsd ldrs, btn over 1f out: btr 2482 & 1745. 1 77
3116 **INDIAN SPARK** 14 [10]10-9-1 (87) P Mulrennan(5) 33/1: 4460009: Mid-div, outpcd from halfway. 1 74
3375* **LORD OF THE EAST** 2 [1]5-8-10 (7ex) (82) S Whitworth 16/1: 1323210: 10th: Led till 2f out, sn btn. ¾ 67
2770 **RIVER FALCON** 28 [3]4-8-13 (85) T P Queally 20/1: 5010030: 11th: Chsd ldrs, btn 2f out: btr 2770 (g/s). 3 61
3146* **MINE BEHIND** 13 [11]4-8-12 (84) M Savage(5) 25/1: 2200010: 12th: Rear, nvr nrly a blow: btr 3146. ½ 58
3307 **SEAFIELD TOWERS** 5 [6]4-7-12 p (70) J Mackay 40/1: 0000000: 13th: Dwelt, in tch 4f, qck reapp. nk 43
3117 **MISTER SWEETS** 14 [13]5-8-3 (2ow) (73) R Fitzpatrick 33/1: 00-60150: 14th: Al outpcd rear: btr 2768 (7f). 2 42
2068 **BORDER SUBJECT** 56 [14]7-10-0 (100) K Darley 14/1: 4100-600: 15th: Prom, btn over 1f out: 8 wk abs. 14 30
15 Ran   Time 1m 09.95 (0.55)   Owned: East Wind Racing Ltd   Trained: Upper Lambourn

3435   4.00 Hovis E B F Handicap Stakes Fillies 3yo+ 0-95 (C)   [105]
£10286 £3165 £1583   **1m2f88y**   **Good/Firm 27**   -06 Slow   Inside

2785* **LA PERSIANA** 27 [1] W Jarvis 3-8-10 (87) K Darley 11/8 FAV: 40-52111: Made all, shkn up & in 98+
command over 1f out, val 5L: well bckd tho' op 6/5, completed hat-trick: suited by 10f, stay further: acts on firm
& fast grnd, sharp or gall trks: likes to race with/force the pace: useful & progressive filly, well plcd by connections.
3083 **GREY CLOUDS** 15 [4] T D Easterby 4-8-12 (79) D Allan 2/1: 2012322: Trkd wnr, rdn & no impress bef 3½ 82
dist: nicely bckd, op 5/2: caught a real improver: see 3083, 2592.
4327 **RAINBOW QUEEN** 665 [3] Sir Michael Stoute 4-10-0 (95) F Lynch 100/30: 10/-3: Held up, eff 3f out, 10 83
no impress & position accepted over 1f out: nicely bckd: reapp/long abs: missed '03: fill mdn wnr on debut '02,
subs well btn sole start (Gr 1): eff at 7f, 1m+ shld suit: acts on fast grnd & a sharp/turning trk: has gone well fresh.
3099 **RANI TWO** 14 [2] W M Brisbourne 5-8-4 (71) S Whitworth 10/1: 10-00654: Held up, rdn & btn 3f out. 8 47
4 Ran   Time 2m 10.71 (3.41)   Owned: Plantation Stud   Trained: Newmarket

3436   4.45 Mr Kipling Exceedingly Good Claiming Stakes 3yo+ (D)
£5720 £1760 £880   **6f str**   **Good/Firm 27**   -15 Slow   Centre

3352 **TANCRED TIMES** 3 [5] D W Barker 9-8-3 (55) F Norton 11/4: 4033141: Made all, rdn & in command 60
dist, styd on strongly: qck reapp: clmd for 5,000: stays 7f, suited by forcing tactics & 5/6f: likes firm & fast
grnd, handles hvy & fibresand, any trk: suited by sell/claim grade: see 3191.
2958 **HAULAGE MAN** 20 [6] D Eddy 4-9-4 p (57) P Hanagan 8/1: 040-0202: Trkd ldrs trav well, styd on 1½ 69$
onepace from dist: back to form with cheek pieces reapp: win a claimer: see 2730.
2848 **PAYS DAMOUR** 24 [4] D Nicholls 7-8-11 (62) S Whitworth 7/1: 1030503: Held up, styd on onepace fnl 2f. 1 59
3353 **AFRICAN SPUR** 3 [8] D Carroll 4-8-12 VIS (47) D Tudhope(7) 33/1: 6500004: Cl-up till over 1f out: vis. 1½ 55$
3229 **BORDER ARTIST** 8 [2]5-9-1 (64) Alex Greaves 4/1: 0043455: Trkd ldrs trav well, rdn & no impress dist. ½ 56
3017* **EFFECTIVE** 17 [1]4-9-4 (67) K Darley 9/4 FAV: 0152016: Chsd ldrs, btn over 1f out: bckd, 'lost action'. 1¾ 54
3269 **MILLFIELDS DREAMS** 7 [3]5-9-3 (59) M Savage(5) 16/1: 04-10007: Chsd ldrs, struggling from halfway. 5 38
7 Ran   Time 1m 11.93 (2.53)   Owned: Mr D W Barker   Trained: Richmond

3437   5.20 Duncan Wiltshire Memorial Rated Stakes Handicap 4yo+ 0-80 (D)   [82]
£5600 £1723 £862   **1m3f198y**   **Good/Firm 27**   -01 Slow   Inside

3114* **JACK OF TRUMPS** 14 [5] G Wragg 4-9-2 (70) F Norton 8/1: 5-100411: Trkd ldrs, hdwy to lead 2f out, 76
duelled with rnr-up ins last, prevailed all out: eff at 10f, imprvd of late at 12f: acts on fast, gd/soft &
polytrack, sharp or stiff/gall trk: progressive & genuine: see 3114 & 2530.
3217 **RAJAM** 9 [7] D Nicholls 6-9-7 vis (75) Alex Greaves 33/1: 1306522: Al prom & ev ch over 1f out, hd 80
duelled with wnr, just held: in gd form: see 3217, 1796.
3261 **SPORTING GESTURE** 7 [6] M W Easterby 7-9-6 (74) P Mulrennan(5) 11/2: 0-054443: Mid-div, switched & shd 79
styd on well for press from over 1f out, just failed: loves this trk: see 1969.
2681 **DANAKIL** 31 [1] S Dow 9-9-7 (75) T P Queally 10/1: 0241224: Chsd ldrs, outpcd 2f out, kept on ¾ 79
late: remains in gd heart: see 2681 & 1986.
3134* **INCHNADAMPH** 14 [8]4-8-9 t (63) R Winston 8/1: 0-622115: Held up, rdn & kept on onepace fnl 3f. 1¾ 65
3187 **LAWRENCE OF ARABIA** 10 [9]4-8-4 (58) J Mackay 2/1 FAV: 004/-06: Held up & wide over 3f out, rdn & ½ 59
kept on, nvr threat: hvly bckd: longer 12f trip, shapes as if further will suit: handles fast, might want more give.
3260 **NEVADA DESERT** 7 [3]4-9-3 (71) Dean McKeown 14/1: 425-4527: Led till over 2f out, fdd: see 1781 (10f). 1 71
3261 **STALLONE** 7 [13]7-9-4 (72) P Hanagan 16/1: 0-034368: Dwelt, rear, eff 3f out, mod prog: see 1781 (10f). ½ 71
3226* **TOMASINO** 8 [2]6-9-7 t (75) K Darley 16/1: 66-46019: Held up, eff over 2f out, sn btn: btr 3226 (clmr). 6 65
1897} **TIMBER ICE** 418 [10]4-9-7 (75) D Allan 20/1: 0/43-0: 10th: b f Woodman - Salchow (Nijinsky) 2½ 61
Cl-up till over 2f out, fdd: reapp/h'cap bow: plcd 2nd of just 2 '03 starts (mdn, rtd 77): unplcd sole juv start
'02 (mdn, rtd 54): eff around 11.5f/12f on fast & gd grnd, stiff/gall or easy trks.
3270* **MERRYMAKER** 7 [11]4-8-13 (67) P Mathers(5) 12/1: 64P1210: 11th: Rear, wide over 3f out, sn btn. 2½ 49
3222 **Maritime Blues** 9 [4]4-8-10 (64) A Culhane 16/1:0   2987 **Farne Isle** 19 [12]5-9-2 (70) F Lynch 12/1:0
13 Ran   Time 2m 30.11 (3.31)   Owned: Mollers Racing   Trained: Newmarket

ASCOT   SATURDAY 24.07.04   Righthand, Stiff, Galloping Track

Official Going GOOD/FIRM.

3438   2.00 European Breeders Fund Crocker Bulteel Maiden Stakes Colts & Geldings 2yo (D)
£6734 £2072 £1036   **6f str**   **Good/Firm 32**   **-50 Slow**   Stands Side

NIGHTFALL [5] Saeed bin Suroor 2-8-11 T L Dettori 4/1: 1: b c Rahy - Quality Gift (Last Tycoon)   86+
U.r. & ran loose bef start, made virtually all, styd on well over 1f out, rdn out to hold on on debut: Mar 2nd
foal: half-brother to a 1m wnr: dam plcd over 1m: eff over a stiff 6f, 7f sure to suit: goes well fresh on
gd/firm & wears a t-strap: useful/fine start, plenty more to come, win more races.

MOTH BALL [4] J A Osborne 2-8-11   D Holland 11/2: 2: b c Royal Applause - Chrysalis (Soviet   shd 86+
Star) In tch, eff dist, kept on to chall ins last, just held: bckd on debut: Apr foal, cost 110,000gns:
half-brother to wnrs over 5/6f: dam styd 7f: eff over a stiff 6f on fast grnd: useful start, plenty more to come.

HALLHOO [1] M R Channon 2-8-11   T E Durcan 7/1: 3: gr c Indian Ridge - Nuit Chaud (Woodman)   1½ 82
Held up, eff & hung right over 1f out, sltly short of room dist, kept on ins last on debut: Mar foal, cost
210,000gns: eff at 6f, 7f will suit: acts on fast grnd: learn plenty from this & can win similar soon.

PRINCE SAMOS [8] R Hannon 2-8-11   K Fallon 7/2 FAV: 4: b c Mujadil - Sabaniya (Lashkari) Slow   ½ 80
away, sn cl-up, onepcd over 1f out on debut: Apr foal, cost E65,000: full brother to a 5f juv wnr, dam bmpr scorer:
eff at 6f, 7f sure to suit: acts on fast grnd: v pleasing start, learn from this & win races.

TAJ INDIA [6]2-8-11   J Fanning 5/1: 5: With wnr, wknd fnl 1f on debut.   2 74
EDGE OF BLUE [3]2-8-11   Dane O'Neill 7/1: 6: Dwelt, bhd, no impress over 1f out on debut.   hd 73
ANTONIO STRADIVARI [7]2-8-11   Martin Dwyer 12/1: 7: Slow away, nvr a factor on debut.   3 64
SAN DENG [9]2-8-11   S Drowne 25/1: 8: Slow away, in tch, wknd over 1f out on debut.   5 49
8 Ran   Time 1m 18.0 (4.9)   Owned: Godolphin   Trained: Newmarket

3439   2.35 Solitare Diamond Rated Stakes Handicap 3yo+ 0-105 (B)   [118]
£17400 £6600 £3300   **1m2f**   **Good/Firm 32**   **-01 Slow**   Inside

3204* **MISTER MONET** 9 [5] M Johnston 3-8-8 (98) J Fanning 11/8 FAV: 31-211: Cl-up, hdwy & not clr run   111+
over 2f out till switched right over 1f out, qcknd to lead, rdn clr, v readily: hvly bckd: stays 10f well on fast &
gd, gall trks: lightly rcd, v smart & showed a fine turn of foot here, must be kept on side in Gr class.

2489 **COURAGEOUS DUKE** 38 [9] J Noseda 5-8-12 (92) K Fallon 5/1: 600-3502: Chsd ldrs, eff to chall over   2 99
1f out, not pace of impressive wnr: coming to hand & loves a gall trk: see 2489.

2896 **FINE PALETTE** 22 [2] H R A Cecil 4-8-8 (2oh) (86) W Ryan 16/1: 2-11553: Slow away, keen, handy,   ¾ 93
hdwy to lead over 1f out, sn hdd & onepace: fine run: see 1828.

2948 **SWIFT TANGO** 21 [6] E A L Dunlop 4-9-6 (100) L Dettori 5/1: 3412364: Dwelt, held up, eff over 1f   3½ 99
out, onepace: bckd: tough & useful: needs a return to 12f: see 2582, 2255.

3118 **POLYGONAL** 14 [8]4-8-10 (2ow)(1oh) (87) O Peslier 10/1: 20-13605: Held up, short of room over 2f   ½ 88
out, some late gains, no dngr: see 2404.

2605 **SPURADICH** 34 [4]4-8-11 (91) J Murtagh 15/2: 0110-036: In tch, wknd 2f out: bckd: see 1833.   6 79
3277 **FORTHRIGHT** 7 [1]3-7-13 p (89) C Catlin 20/1: 1045607: Keen, with ldr, wknd 2f out: btr 2521.   1½ 75
3233 **PUTRA SANDHURST** 8 [3]6-9-8 (102) P Robinson 25/1: 25-10008: Led till dist, wknd: best 1364.   5 80
2898 **WEECANDOO** 22 [7]6-8-10 (90) G Carter 25/1: 33154-09: Al bhd: see 2898.   1¾ 65
9 Ran   Time 2m 07.31 (3.31)   Owned: Syndicate 2002   Trained: Middleham

3440   3.10 Gr3 Princess Margaret Stakes Fillies 2yo (A)
£26100 £9900 £4950   **6f str**   **Good/Firm 32**   **-10 Slow**   Stands Side

2490 **SOAR** 38 [4] J R Fanshawe 2-8-9   J Murtagh 1/1 FAV: 121: In tch, gd hdwy to lead dist, rdn clr,   109+
readily: hvly bckd: styd longer 6f trip well, 7f looks sure to suit: acts on fast & gd grnd, clearly likes Ascot:
v smart filly with a turn of foot, win more Group races: see 2490, 2171.

3071* **VALENTIN** 15 [1] R Hannon 2-8-9   Dane O'Neill 9/2: 12: Dwelt, hld up, hdwy 2f out, kept on ins   1¾ 101
last, not pace of wnr: bckd: acts on gd & fast: fine run stepped up in class & will apprec List.

2763 **KISSING LIGHTS** 28 [5] M L W Bell 2-8-9   D Holland 25/1: 5163: Led over 4f out till over 1f out,   nk 100
kept on: stays 6f on firm & fast grnd: back to useful best: see 2437.

3258* **SATIN FINISH** 7 [3] M R Channon 2-8-9   T E Durcan 8/1: 414: Cl-up, hdwy to lead over 1f out, sn   1½ 96
hdd & no extra: shld stay 6f & up in class here: see 3258 (mdn, 5f, gd/soft).

3115 **RIGHT ANSWER** 14 [2]2-8-9   K Fallon 9/2: 41225: Handy, eff dist, sn no extra: see 3115, 2786.   hd 95
3183* **MAGICAL ROMANCE** 10 [6]2-8-9   J Fortune 12/1: 416: Led till 4f out, wknd 2f out: best 3183 (gd).   9 68
6 Ran   Time 1m 15.6 (2.5)   Owned: Cheveley Park Stud   Trained: Newmarket

3441   3.45 Totesport International Stakes Heritage Handicap 3yo+ (B)   [117]
£87000 £33000 £16500   **7f str**   **Good/Firm 32**   **+10 Fast**   Stands Side

3061 **COURT MASTERPIECE** 16 [6] E A L Dunlop 4-9-2 (105) K Fallon 7/1: 01-35421: Held up, gd hdwy &   113
short of room over 1f out, styd on strongly to lead ins last, drvn out: confirmed most promising run of 3061: eff
at 7f/1m on fast grnd & any trk: v smart colt with a turn of foot, looks well up to winning in Gr 3 now.

3253 **POLAR WAY** 8 [9] Mrs A J Perrett 5-9-7 (110) Gary Stevens 20/1: 0201-032: In tch, hdwy & switched   nk 115
right halfway, styd on well to lead over 1f out, collared ins last but kept on, just held: high-class effort in this
competitive h'cap under top-weight: stable in fine heart now & likes 7f: acts on gd & fast: running well with following in Gr class.

2558 **UHOOMAGOO** 36 [23] K A Ryan 6-8-3 bl (92) J F Egan 33/1: 0011003: Dwelt, held up, hdwy & switched   1 96
right over 2f out, sn strong run, nrst fin: right back to form & has a neat turn of foot: excellent effort from draw.

3265 **VORTEX** 7 [6] Miss Gay Kelleway 5-8-9 e t (98) L Dettori 4/1 FAV: 0013024: Dwelt, held up, hdwy &   1½ 99
short of room over 2f out, styd on to chall dist, onepace: hvly bckd: a shade closer with clr run & another v
useful run, well clr of rem: tough & has a fine turn of foot: see 3265.

2915 **ST ANDREWS** 21 [11]4-8-3 (92) P Robinson 10/1: 314/-2625: In tch, eff 1.5f out, no extra: btr 2915.   3½ 86
3124 **NEW SEEKER** 14 [18]4-9-0 BL (103) J P Spencer 7/1: 311-2406: In tch, eff to chall over 1f out,   hd 96
wknd ins last: well bckd: tried blinks: won this race last term off an 8lb lower mark: see 2558.

3117 **DIGITAL** 14 [16]7-7-12 (87) T Dean(7) 25/1: 0052227: Held up, eff over 2f out, no impress: likes easier grnd.   1¼ 78
2532 **TAHIRAH** 36 [15]4-7-12 (1oh) (86) M Henry 40/1: 0110-008: Keen held up, eff & short of room over   ½ 77
2f out, some late gains: see 2289.

ASCOT SATURDAY 24.07.04 Righthand, Stiff, Galloping Track

3061 **ROYAL STORM 16** [20]5-8-10 (99) J Murtagh 12/1: 26-01469: Made most till over 1f out, wknd. *1¾* **85**

2532+ **ETTRICK WATER 36** [4]5-8-6 vis (95) D Holland 9/1: 113-5110: 10th: In tch, btn 2f out: btr 2532. *1½* **78**

2140 **CAPRICHO 57** [12]7-9-1 (104) J Fortune 25/1: 4140-040: 11th: Held up, eff dist, sn wknd: abs. *3½* **80**

3061 **MASTER ROBBIE 16** [21]5-8-2 (91) C Catlin 25/1: 0016000: 12th: Al bhd: see 2090, 1926. *½* **66**

3061 **VICIOUS KNIGHT 16** [26]6-8-9 (98) A Nicholls 25/1: 0/15-0000: 13th: Held up, eff 2f out, no extra. *¾* **71**

3061 **GREENSLADES 16** [8]5-8-6 (95) Martin Dwyer 20/1: 5-442030: 14th: With ldr, wknd 2f out: see 3061. *1* **66**

3068 **TARANAKI 15** [1]6-7-13 (88) Lisa Jones(3) 25/1: 1401500: 15th: In tch, wknd dist: see 1817. *2* **55**

2489 **AUTUMN GLORY 38** [13]4-9-0 (103) S Drowne 20/1: 140-1100: 16th: In tch, hmpd & wknd over 1f out. *1½* **67**

3199 **BINANTI 10** [14]4-7-13 VIS (88) C Haddon(7) 66/1: 40-06600: 17th: With ldrs, wknd 2f out: vis. *1¾* **48**

2090 **MARSHMAN 55** [22]5-8-0 (89) F P Ferris(3) 50/1: 34-03000: 18th: Al bhd. *¾* **47**

2486 **BAHIANO 38** [27]3-8-9 (105) O Peslier 25/1: 2360040: 19th: Nvr a factor: see 2486, 885. *1¼* **60**

3061 **EL COTO 16** [24]4-8-11 bl (100) S Sanders 14/1: 5500040: 20th: Al bhd, hung & btn 2f out: see 3061. *13* **29**

3061 **GRIZEDALE 16** [17]5-8-5 t (94) J Quinn 14/1: 10020-50: 21th: Al bhd: see 3061. *3½* **16**

21 Ran Time 1m 27.54 (1.54) Owned: Maktoum Al Maktoum Trained: Newmarket

3442

4.25 Gr1 King George Vi And Queen Elizabeth Diamond Stakes 3yo+ (A)
£435000 £165000 £82500 1m4f Good/Firm 32 -03 Slow Inside

2579+ **DOYEN 35** [5] Saeed bin Suroor 4-9-7 (124) L Dettori 11/10 FAV: 1124-211: In tch, gd hdwy to lead trav well over 1f out, qcknd clr, v readily: bckd: stays 12f well on fm & soft, likes gall trks, esp Ascot: progressing with every start & a Champion mid-dist colt now, v hard to oppose at present. **130**

990 **HARD BUCK 21** [6] Kenneth G McPeek 5-9-7 Gary Stevens 33/1: 1-412252: b c Spend A Buck - Social Secret (Secreto) Keen cl-up, led briefly 2f out, kept on for press, not pace of wnr: 2nd & 3rd in America since Dubai Gr 1 2nd: multiple wnr prev incl in Gr 1: stays 12f well on firm & gd/soft: looks a high-class & game entire. 2 Mar'04 Nad 12g/f 118- : *3* **125**

3030 **SULAMANI 17** [7] Saeed bin Suroor 5-9-7 t (125) K McEvoy 7/1: 2115-423: Held up, plenty to do over 2f out, styd on late, nrst fin: longer priced stablemate of wnr, v encouraging, fin 2nd in this race last term (rtd 124): shld enjoy sltly easier grnd: see 3030. *hd* **125**

3012* **GAMUT 20** [11] Sir Michael Stoute 5-9-7 t (117) K Fallon 12/1: 123-2114: Hmpd early, in tch, hdwy over 2f out, onepace over 1f out: ran to high-class best & shld apprec sltly easier grnd: see 3012, 1493. *1¾* **122**

2209 **VALLEE ENCHANTEE 50** [4]4-9-4 O Peslier 6/1: 1411-435: In tch, hdwy over 2f out, sn onepace: well bckd, 7 wk abs: prob ran to smart best & another who may prefer a sltly easier surface: see 2209. *1* **117**

2822 **TYCOON 27** [3]3-8-9 J P Spencer 16/1: 3215-36: Held up, plenty to do 3f out, gd hdwy when hmpd 2f out, switchd & not recover: not given ch to show best & proves form of 2822 was no fluke: remains of interest. *¾* **119**

3030* **BANDARI 17** [2]5-9-7 (117) R Hills 12/1: 0111017: Held up, hdwy over 2f out, onepace: needs Gr 2. *nk* **119**

3030 **HIGH ACCOLADE 17** [10]4-9-7 (116) J Murtagh 25/1: 212-4238: Hld up, btn 3f out: see 3030, 2579. *2* **116**

2916 **WARRSAN 21** [9]6-9-7 (120) D Holland 13/2: 33-53129: Handy, wknd well over 1f out: well bckd: v tough & a rare off-day for this top-class performer: see 2916. *1¼* **114**

3012 **PHOENIX REACH 20** [1]4-9-7 VIS (115) Martin Dwyer 33/1: 1131-660: 10th: Keen, in tch, wknd 2f out: tried a visor, reportedly broke a blood vessel: see 2488. *2½* **110**

2488 **LUNAR SOVEREIGN 38** [8]5-9-7 t (110) T E Durcan 100/1: 106-3000: 11th: Set stdy pace till 2f out. *dist* **10**

11 Ran Time 2m 33.18 (4.18) Owned: Godolphin Trained: Newmarket

3443

5.00 Star Of South Africa Diamond Handicap Stakes Ladies Race 3yo+ 0-90 (C) **[69]**
£10351 £3185 £1593 7f str Good/Firm 32 -35 Slow Stands Side

3213 **HEY PRESTO 9** [8] C G Cox 4-10-0 (69) Miss N Forde(5) 20/1: 0-000561: In tch, hdwy to lead dist, just held on: enjoyed step up to 7f & acts on firm & gd grnd, prob any trk: took advantage of handy mark under tender handling & may be more to come at this trip: see 2698. **75**

3173 **TREETOPS HOTEL 11** [3] B R Johnson 5-9-0 p (55) Miss Joey Ellis(5) 33/1: 2000242: Held up, hdwy 2f out, kept on ins last, just failed: enjoyed drop back to 7f, 1m poss ideal: see 2440, 520. *shd* **60**

2872 **SAWWAAH 23** [19] D Nicholls 7-10-11 (80) Miss Kelly Harrison(3) 33/1: 1340003: Held up, eff well over 1f out, kept on, not btn far: see 1820. *¾* **83**

2350 **SPIRITS AWAKENING 44** [24] J Akehurst 5-9-3 (58) Miss A Elsey 20/1: 22-06324: Cl-up, led over 2f out til dist, onepace: 6 wk abs: see 2350, 2129. *½* **60**

2425 **DISTANT COUNTRY 41** [20]5-10-2 p (71) Miss L Hourigan(3) 9/1: 6602525: Bhd, kept on late, nrst fin. *1¼* **70**

2848 **WHAT A DANCER 24** [7]7-10-6 (75) Miss S Brotherton 16/1: 1404406: In tch, eff dist, kept on. *shd* **73**

3269 **CHATEAU NICOL 7** [12]5-10-13 (82) Mrs R Powell(5) 12/1: 3415667: Held up, eff 2f out, sn wknd. *nk* **79**

1891 **LYGETON LAD 64** [14]6-10-1 t (70) Miss E J Jones 14/1: 6510008: In tch, eff dist, onepace: abs. *nk* **66**

3087 **MOBO BACO 15** [21]7-9-0 (55) Miss Lynsey Hanna 40/1: 0000159: Dwelt, bhd, eff dist, onepace. *¾* **49**

2392 **BRAVE DANE 42** [17]6-10-5 (74) Mrs S Bosley 25/1: 1561200: 10th: Bhd, late gains, nrst fin: abs. *hd* **67**

3088 **ARCTIC DESERT 15** [6]4-10-9 (78) Miss M Sowerby(5) 33/1: 2-000000: 11th: In tch, eff dist, wknd. *1* **69**

1919 **CAPPED FOR VICTORY 63** [9]3-10-10 (86) Mrs S Eddery(5) 7/1 CO FAV: 232-200: 12th: Dwelt, in tch, eff & short of room over 1f out, no extra: 2 mth abs: see 1636. *1¼* **74**

2857* **GRAFT 24** [23]5-9-8 bl (63) Mrs C Thompson(5) 20/1: 0620010: 13th: In tch, hung left 2f out, wknd. *¾* **49**

2872 **COLEMANSTOWN 23** [5]4-9-5 (60) Miss L Ellison(3) 33/1: 0000000: 14th: Led till over 2f out, wknd. *shd* **45**

2581 **GAELIC PRINCESS 35** [15]4-10-10 (79) Miss C Hannaford 10/1: 0060000: 15th: Bhd, btn over 1f out. *nk* **63**

3199 **FIVEOCLOCK EXPRESS 10** [2]4-10-9 p (78) Ms C Williams 14/1: 4200520: 16th: Held up, short of room over 2f out, sn no extra: see 3199, 887. *hd* **61**

3116 **CLOUD DANCER 14** [25]5-10-8 (77) Miss N Carberry(3) 7/2 CO FAV: 0221350: 17th: Held up, eff over 2f out, sn wknd: see 2791, 2409 (6f). *1¼* **57**

3210 **MAGIC AMOUR 9** [10]6-9-2 (57) Miss S Beddoes 33/1: 20-26040: 18th: In tch, wknd well over 1f out. *hd* **36**

3363 **BINT ROYAL 2** [4]6-9-0 (2oh) (53) Miss Faye Bramley(4) 25/1: 3005000: 19th: In tch, wknd dist. *2½* **29**

3210 **TAKES TUTU 9** [22]5-10-7 bl (76) Mrs M Morris 11/1: 2255020: 20th: Dwelt, with ldrs, wknd dist. *3* **44**

4897} **GEMS BOND 112** [18]4-10-11 (80) Mrs S Moore(3) 40/1: 10-00000: 21th: Al bhd: now with J Moore. *5* **38**

3045 **QUANTUM LEAP 16** [11]7-10-3 vis (72) Miss Charmaine O'Neill 25/1: 1664240: 22th: In tch, wknd qckly over 1f out: btr 2872, 2063. *½* **29**

2988 **RAINSTORM 18** [16]9-9-0 (15oh) (40) Mrs S Owen(3) 100/1: 6560000: 23th: With ldrs, wknd 2f out. *nk* **11**

2495 **PLAY MASTER 38** [13]3-9-11 (73) Miss J Foster(5) 40/1: 1201030: 24th: With ldrs, wknd over 2f out. *7* **15**

2729* **MR MISTRAL 29** [1]5-11-4 (87) Mrs M Cowdrey 7/1 CO FAV: 210: 25th: Keen held up, wknd & eased over 2f out: well bckd: too keen but poss something amiss: much btr 2729 (mdn, gd/soft). *10* **9**

25 Ran Time 1m 30.68 (4.68) Owned: The Beechdown Flyers Trained: Hungerford

3444   5.35 South Africa Anniversary Diamond Rated Stakes Handicap 3yo+ 0-95 (C)   [110]
£10776 £4088 £2044   1m4f   Good/Firm 32   +06 Fast   Inside

3066 **ALWAYS WAINING** 16 [2] M Johnston 3-8-4 (86) J Fanning 11/2: 331531: Cl-up, led over 2f out, sn   99+
rdn clr, v readily: eff at 12f now, further shld suit: acts on fast & gd grnd, gall & undul trks: v useful &
progressive, impressed here & just the type to go on & win plenty more races: see 2113.
3070 **FORT 15** [7] M Johnston 3-8-5 (87) R Hills 9/2 JT FAV: 13-3032: In tch, hdwy to chase wnr over 1f   5   89
out, kept on but not his pace: stays 12f well: shorter priced s/mate of wnr: see 2250, 1741.
1068 **ARGONAUT 109** [3] Sir Michael Stoute 4-9-4 (88) K Fallon 9/2 JT FAV: 31-63: Held up, hdwy over 1f   ¾   88
out, kept on ins last, no threat: encouraging run after over 3 mth abs & clearly stays 12f well: lightly rcd, shld
stay further & prob more to come: see 1068.
1703} **ITS THE LIMIT 427** [6] M A J Perrett 5-9-8 (92) S Sanders 8/1: 0/131/42-4: b g Boundary -   ½   91
Beside (Sportin' Life) In tch, eff over 2f out, onepace: rnr-up in a class stks on 2nd of only 2 '03 starts: '02
mdn & class stks wnr: eff at 12/13.5f on fast grnd & on gall or fair trks: been gelded & an encouraging return.
2 May'03 Newm 12g/f 92-(90) C: 1 Sep'02 Kemp 12g/f 92- C: 1 Jul'02 Newm 12g/f 92- D:
4759} **MUHAREB 282** [5]5-9-10 (94) D Holland 20/1: 303004-5: ch g Thunder Gulch - Queen of Spirit   hd   93
(Deputy Minister) In tch, hdwy well over 1f out, sn onepace on reapp: '03 h'cap wnr: won 4 h'caps in '02: suited
by 12f, stays 14f & likes firm & gd grnd, acts on gd/soft & both AWs, any trk: best up with/forcing the pace & eff
with/without t-strap: tough & useful, gd return, been gelded.
1 May'03 York 11.9fm 99-92 C: 1 Sep'02 York 11.8g/f 94-87 B: 1 Aug'02 Ripo 12.2fm 88-82 C:
1 May'02 Good 12g/s 84-79 C: 1 Jan'02 Wolv 9.3af 79a-73 E: 2 Jan'02 Sout 8af 68a- F:
3076 **LODGER 15** [1]4-9-8 (92) W Ryan 16/1: 23214-06: ch c Grand Lodge - Light River (Irish River)   1¾   88
Dwelt, held up, some late gains, no threat: '03 mdn wnr: suited by 10/12f on firm & gd, gall or fair trks: useful.
1 Jul'03 Newc 12.4g/s 93-(88) D: 2 Jul'03 Kemp 12g/f 90-(88) D: 2 May'03 Newm 10fm 81- D:
2759 **GROOMS AFFECTION 28** [10]4-9-0 (84) J Murtagh 6/1: 0/01-167: Slow away, sn in tch, eff over 1f   nk   79
out, no impress: btr 2363.
3037 **BUCKS 17** [4]7-8-10 (80) P Robinson 9/1: 0211258: Held up, eff & hmpd dist, no extra: see 2673.   1¼   72
2583 **GALLERY GOD 35** [8]8-9-6 (90) J F Egan 25/1: 030-0009: Led till over 2f out, sn wknd.   9   68
2405 **COURT OF APPEAL 42** [9]7-9-3 t (87) K McEvoy 11/2: 34-11320: 10th: Handy, wknd dist: btr 2405.   2   62
10 Ran   Time 2m 32.09(3.09)   Owned: The Always Trying Partnership   Trained: Middleham

Official Going GOOD/FIRM

3445   6.05 Premier Pensions Management Maiden Auction Stakes 2yo (F)
£3297 £942 £471   5f str   Good 48   -01 Slow   Centre

3247 **GIFTED GAMBLE 8** [8] K A Ryan 2-8-8 bl P Dobbs 4/5 FAV: 0333221: Prom, hdwy to lead 2f out,   80
rdn out fnl 1f: nicely bckd: eff at 5f on firm & gd, sharp/undul trk: well deserved win: see 1386.
2795 **SAUCEPOT 26** [4] M D I Usher 2-8-3 A Daly 20/1: 062: ch f Bold Edge - Apple Sauce (Prince Sabo)   1½   68
Mid-div, hdwy ins fnl 1f, not pace of wnr: op 14/1: Feb foal, cost 6,500gns: half-sister to a dual 5f 3yo wnr: dam
a 5f wnr at 3, sire progressed into a top-class sprinter: eff at 5f on gd: consistent & now qual for h'caps.
3014 **DISPOL IN MIND 17** [3] I A Wood 2-8-3 G Gibbons 11/1: 23: Slow away, prog over 2f out, kept on   hd   67
fnl 1f: handles fast & gd: new stable (prev with P Midgley): see 3014.
2241 **NE OUBLIE 49** [6] J Mackie 2-8-8 E Ahern 16/1: 64: Cl-up, ev ch over 1f out, sn onepcd: 7 wk   hd   71
abs, op 33/1: stays 5f on gd: see 2241.
1652 **DOCKLANDS GRACE 75** [1]2-8-4 R L Moore 12/1: 55: Outpcd bhd, some late gains: long abs.   nk   66
   JOHN ROBIE 0 [5]2-8-11 S W Kelly 11/4: 6: ch c Rahy - Diamond Flower (Fly So Free) Slow away,   1¾   68
sn cl-up, wknd dist on debut: Apr first foal, cost $14,000: dam US turf wnr, sire high-class 2yo, later smart dirt
miler: with G Butler & entitled to come on for this.
2858 **LOWESTOFT PLAYBOY 24** [2]2-8-8 N Chalmers(5) 9/1: 0657: Led, hdd bef 2f out, no extra fnl 2f.   1   62
   MANIC 0 [7]2-8-2 A Nicholls 33/1: 8: br f Polar Falcon - Gentle Irony (Mazilier) Nvr a factor   shd   55
on debut: Apr foal, cost 2,800gns: half-sister to modest wnrs over 5/8f, incl one at 2: dam won 7 times btwn
6/10f, incl at 2, sire top-class btwn 6/8f: with A Reid.
8 Ran   Time 59.28s (2.48)   Owned: Margaret's Partnership   Trained: Hambleton

3446   6.35 Sharp Minds Winners Welcome Median Auction Maiden Stakes 3-5yo (F)
£3003 £858 £429   7f str   Good 48   -02 Slow   Centre

3128 **DESERT CRISTAL 14** [11] J R Boyle 3-8-9 (79) L Dettori 4/6 FAV: 25-2631: Made all, rdn out to   77
hold on fnl 1f: nicely bckd: eff at 7f, stays a sharp 1m: acts on gd & hvy, sharp/undul trk: deserved win: see 1297.
3058 **TEXT 16** [5] Mrs Stef Liddiard 3-9-0 (60) A Daly 25/1: 6320-02: Mid-div, outpcd 3f out, rallied   1½   77$
ins fnl 1f but no ch with wnr: stays 7f, acts on gd & polytrack: find similar in this form: see 3058.
1022 **WITCHES BROOM 113** [8] C A Cyzer 3-8-9 E Ahern 66/1: 03: b f Fraam - Carte Blanche (Cadeaux   1½   69
Genereux) RckKeen & cl-up, no extraonepcd fnl 1f: long abs: Mar foal, cost 2,000gns: dam unplcd at 2 & 3, twice
wnr over 1m at 4: left debut well behind with encouraging effort.
4895} **RESIDENTIAL 273** [10] Mrs A J Perrett 3-9-0 R L Moore 2/1: 5-4: ch c Zilzal - House Hunting   shd   73$
(Zafonic) Slow away, sn handy, onepcd fnl 1f: reapp: 5th sole '03 start (mdn, rtd 77): eff at 7f on gd grnd.
2925 **FAIR COMPTON 21** [9]3-8-9 (60) P Dobbs 14/1: 04-46545: Keen & dsptd lead, wknd fnl 1f: clr of rem.   1   66$
3380 **NEBRASKA CITY 2** [4]3-9-0 t (55) N Pollard 20/1: 50-06046: Chsd ldrs, no extra bef 1f out: qck reapp.   3   65$
3461} **ASSOON 351** [2]5-9-7 R Brisland 20/1: 23-7: b g Ezzoud - Handy Dancer (Green God) Slow away,   3   59
nvr a factor on reapp: won a bmpr in 03/04 (eff at 2m/2m3.5f on fast, sharp or a gall trk, also nov hdle rnr-up, rtd
108h): rnr-up 1st of 2 '03 starts (mdn): with G Moore. 2 Jul'03 Warw 18g/f 66- D:
3360 **CHEMS LEGACY 2** [7]4-9-7 J P Guillambert(3) 66/1: 048: Keen in mid-div, wknd over 3f out.   1¾   55
1270 **LADY FRANPALM 95** [1]4-9-2 (52) C Haddon(7) 66/1: 5440-009: Handy 4f, sn wknd.   ½   49
2756 **HIGHLAND LASS 28** [6]3-8-9 N Chalmers(5) 25/1: 00: 10th: In tch, no impress over 1f out.   5   39
10 Ran   Time 1m 23.94 (3.54)   Owned: John Hopkins (T/A South Hatch Racing)   Trained: Epsom

LINGFIELD Polytrack SATURDAY 24.07.04 Lefthand, Sharp, Undulating Track

3447 **7.05 Sharp Minds Betfair Handicap Stakes 3yo 0-85 (D)** **[91]**
£5541 £1705 £853 **7f str** **Good 48** **+03 Fast** Centre

2679 **MOLCON 31** [7] N A Callaghan 3-9-4 (81) J F Egan 9/2: 1534401: Bhd, prog 2f out, drvn out to lead nr line: tchd 13/2: eff at 5/7f on firm & soft, reportedly suited by the latter: likes a stiff trk, acts on a sharp/undul one: back to form: see 1417. **89**
3112 **APEX 14** [1] E A L Dunlop 3-9-1 (78) K Fallon 5/2 FAV: 30-15032: Mid-div, hdwy to lead 2f out, hdd under press nr fin: lost little in defeat: see 3112. *hd* **85**
2521 **PIZAZZ 37** [6] B J Meehan 3-9-5 (82) L Dettori 100/30: 5252203: Mid-div, hdwy & ev ch dist, kept on, not btn far in 3rd: see 2352 & 2098. *½* **88**
3112 **I WONT DANCE 14** [2] R Hannon 3-8-12 (75) R L Moore 10/1: 012-0004: Cl-up 6f, sn no extra: clr rem. *2½* **75**
3112 **BEST DESERT 14** [4]3-8-4 (2ow) (65) N Pollard 16/1: 02-42005: Rcd stands side & led, sn hdd, styd cl-up till dist, no extra: btr 1729. *3½* **61**
2749 **CONVINCE 28** [3]3-9-5 P (82) S W Kelly 8/1: 04-00056: Rcd stands side, sn led, hdd 2f out, no extra. *shd* **75**
1933 **SARISTAR 63** [9]3-9-7 T (84) D Holland 6/1: 1010-107: Bhd, nvr a factor: tried a t-strap. *2½* **72**
3177 **KNIGHT ONTHE TILES 11** [8]3-7-13 bl (62) C Haddon(7) 33/1: 60-00008: Keen in rear, nvr a factor. *10* **30**
933 **SACHIN 120** [5]3-8-4 (67) E Ahern 20/1: 4340-069: Al in rearr: long abs: see 735. *5* **25**
9 Ran Time 1m 23.57 (3.17) Owned: Mr Mark Venus Trained: Newmarket

3448 **7.35 Sharp Minds Betfair: Best Odds Classified Stakes 3yo+ 0-60 (F)**
£3087 £882 £441 **7f140y str** **Good 48** **-01 Slow** Centre

2195 **MISS MADAME 51** [2] R Guest 3-8-6 (58) E Ahern 22/1: 060-3361: Prom, led 3f out, drvn out: 7 wk abs: eff at 5.5/7.5f on fast, gd & fibresand, sharp/undul trk: up in trip: first win: see 1376. **68**
3215* **LADY MO 9** [1] G G Margarson 3-8-12 (66) S Sanders 11/4 FAV: 1230612: Cl-up, hdwy into 2nd 2f out, not pace of wnr: remains in gd form, shade btr 3215 (clmr). *2½* **67**
3289 **CHORISTAR 7** [7] W R Muir 3-8-9 (55) J P Guillambert(3) 14/1: 060-6253: Mid-div, styd on fnl 1f. *1¼* **61**
2971 **JOMUS 19** [4] L Montague Hall 3-8-9 (59) P Dobbs 33/1: 2120004: Outpcd bhd, hdwy 1f out, kept on. *½* **60**
2644 **LONDONER 32** [10]6-9-3 (60) R L Moore 6/1: 2210535: Led to 3f out, no extra over 1f out. *1* **58**
3194 **ONE UPMANSHIP 10** [8]3-8-13 (64) D Holland 8/1: 0006326: Bhd, hdwy 2f out, sn onepcd. *hd* **61**
2904 **VIOLET AVENUE 22** [5]3-8-8 (2ow) (58) M Fenton 14/1: 204-0647: In tch, no impress over 1f out. *nk* **55**
3144 **CUDDLES 13** [12]5-9-0 (57) A Nicholls 7/1: 0504538: Slow away, modest late gains. *¾* **51**
2906 **PICK A BERRY 22** [6]3-8-6 (57) J F Egan 25/1: 0-0069: Keen in mid-div, no impress 2f out. *¾* **49**
3176 **MISTER CLINTON 11** [9]7-9-3 (59) A Daly 7/1: 6340120: 10th: Keen cl-up 5f, sn wknd. *2* **48**
3109 **SECAM 14** [3]5-9-3 (44) N Chalmers(5) 50/1: 321-0300: 11th: Keen in rear, nvr a factor. *6* **36**
2872 **CONCUBINE 23** [11]5-9-0 (60) K Fallon 7/2: 0-302400: 12th: Trkd ldrs, no impress 2f out, eased. *3* **27**
12 Ran Time 1m 31.53 (3.73) Owned: Cosmic Greyhound Racing Partnership III Trained: Newmarket

LINGFIELD Polytrack SATURDAY 24.07.04 Lefthand, V Sharp Track

Official Going STANDARD

3449 **8.05 Sharp Minds Betfair: Back And Lay Handicap Stakes 3yo 35-55 (E)** **[63]**
£3017 £862 £431 **1m2f aw** **Going 85** **+05 Fast** Inside

3219 **QUARRYMOUNT 9** [5] Sir Mark Prescott 3-9-10 (59) S Sanders 1/1 FAV: 000-021: Cl-up, rdn out to lead cl home: first win: nicely bckd, top-weight: eff at 8.5f, imprvd for a step up to 10f: acts on gd & polytrack, v sharp trk: gd weight carrier: lightly rcd, can improve further: see 3219. **67a**
2741 **RUBAIYAT 28** [9] G Wragg 3-9-1 (50) J F Egan 8/1: 06-00432: Led, hdd 1m out, led again 5f out, hdd cl home: stays 10/12f, acts on both AWs: in decent form, consistent & shld find a race: see 2503. *shd* **57a**
2064 **WILLHEGO 56** [13] J R Best 3-9-5 (54) N Pollard 14/1: 000-0023: Slow away, prog 2f out, kept on well fnl 1f, just failed: 8 wk abs, clr of rem: lost little in defeat: see 2064. *shd* **60a**
2868 **AFRICAN STAR 23** [4] Mrs A J Perrett 3-9-4 (53) R L Moore 8/1: 05-6564: Cl-up, ev ch bef 1f out, wknd. *5* **51a**
3108 **COBALT BLUE 14** [11]3-9-3 bl (52) D Holland 8/1: 00-06155: Bhd, prog 3f out, onepcd. *1¼* **48a**
2992 **STYLISH DANCER 18** [2]3-9-0 (49) I Mongan 50/1: 0506: In tch, hdwy over 2f out, no impress 1f out. *5* **37a**
2893 **QUEEN LUCIA 22** [10]3-9-6 (55) M Fenton 20/1: 444547: Handy, 1m, sn wknd. *5* **35a**
2503 **FOX HOLLOW 37** [1]3-9-1 (50) L Dettori 16/1: 2623008: Led after 2f till 5f out, sn no extra. *2½* **26a**
3144 **MACCHIATO GB 13** [8]3-9-3 (52) E Ahern 33/1: 602-0509: Nvr btr than mid-div: see 2842. *hd* **27a**
3286 **WHIPLASH 7** [7]3-9-3 (52) A Nicholls 40/1: 0401060: 10th: Al bhd: qck reapp. *2½* **23a**
3383 **NEWTOWN CHIEF 2** [12]3-9-0 P (49) G Gibbons 40/1: 0600-000: 11th: Mid-div, nvr nr ldrs: cheek pieces. *nk* **19a**
2885 **KINKOZAN 23** [14]3-9-5 (54) J P Guillambert(3) 33/1: 06-60: 12th: ch c Peintre Celebre - Classic Design (Busted) Nvr a factor: 6th 1 of 2 '03 starts (mdn, rtd 57): has had a breathing prob: with N Littmoden. *25* **0a**
2955 **ASK THE DRIVER 20** [3]3-9-4 (53) K Fallon 7/1: 0-243300: 13th: Al bhd: see 2064. *6* **0a**
2435 **PASS GO 40** [6]3-9-6 t (55) S W Kelly 33/1: 3-00000: 14th: Rear, eased over 1f out, t.o.: 6 wk abs. *23* **0a**
14 Ran Time 2m 10.85 (8.05) Owned: Lady Fairhaven Trained: Newmarket

3450 **8.35 Sharp Minds Phone 0870 90 80 121 Handicap Stakes 3yo+ 0-70 (E)** **[66]**
£3494 £1075 £538 **2m aw** **Going 85** **-05 Slow** Inside

3200 **BELLE ROUGE 10** [11] C A Horgan 6-9-8 (60) L Dettori 13/8 FAV: 22/-22121: Led after 2f, rdn out fnl 1f: eff btwn 12f/2m on both AWs, gd & hvy, prob any trk: in fine form this term & v consistent: see 768. **69a**
2923 **COMPTON ECLAIRE 21** [5] G A Butler 4-9-0 vis (52) E Ahern 4/1: 2461242: Mid-div, hdwy bef halfway, not pace of wnr fnl 1f: clr of rem: suited by 12/14f, stays 2m: remains in decent form: see 2601. *¾* **59a**
3217 **MOST SAUCY 9** [9] I A Wood 8-9-3 (55) K Fallon 4/1: 0345043: Mid-div, hdwy 3f out, onepcd fnl 1f. *4* **58a**
2908 **HEART SPRINGS 22** [12] Dr J R J Naylor 4-8-7 (45) A Daly 50/1: 00-0004: Bhd, hdwy 3f out, mod gains. *3* **45a**
2621 **BAKHTYAR 33** [8]3-8-3 bl (58) J F Egan 11/1: 005-0045: Nvr btr than mid-div: op 8/1: see 2621. *1¼* **57a**

LINGFIELD Polytrack SATURDAY 24.07.04 Lefthand, V Sharp Track

2471 **DOMENICO 39** [3]6-9-13 (65) D Holland 9/1: 002-0306: Keen, mid-div, wknd 4f out: hdles fit. | 2 | 62a
148 **BETTERWARE BOY 231** [6]4-10-0 (66) M Howard(7) 33/1: 545-7: ch g Barathea - Crystal Drop (Cadeaux | 3 | 60a
Genereux) Bhd, hdwy over 4f out, no impress over 1f out: hdles unplcd in 03/04 (novs, mdn, rtd 95h): 4th 1 of 2
'03 starts (mdn, rtd 78 at best, with Mrs A Perrett): with P Phelan.
3052 **LADY JEANNIE 16** [7]7-8-2 (40) C Haddon(7) 50/1: 400/-0008: Keen & handy, no extra over 2f out. | 1¼ | 33a
3217 **PAY THE SILVER 9** [2]6-9-7 p (59) I Mongan 7/1: 4020339: Al bhd: see 1530. | 4 | 48a
2868 **ARCTIC BLUE 23** [1]4-8-12 P (50) Derek Nolan(7) 40/1: 0/0000-00: 10th: Led 2f, remained cl-up, no | 5 | 34a
extra 3f out: first time cheek pieces: see 2868.
2788 **WATCHFUL WITNESS 27** [4]4-9-3 VIS (55) L Vickers 20/1: 0-3400: 11th: Chsd ldrs 10f, fdd: visor. | 2½ | 36a
11 Ran Time 3m 34.54(14.54) Owned: Mrs B Woodford Trained: Ogbourne Maizey

SALISBURY SATURDAY 24.07.04 Righthand, Galloping Track, Stiff Finish

Official Going GOOD/FIRM (FIRM places).

3451 6.20 Saffie Joseph & Sons Maiden Stakes 2yo (D)
£5844 £1798 £899 6f str Good 53 -04 Slow Far side

2851 **MOTARASSED 24** [8] J L Dunlop 2-9-0 J Fortune 5/2: 31: Handy, styd on to lead well ins fnl 1f, | | 91
rdn out, val bit more: op 15/8: eff at 6f, further will suit: acts on fast & gd grnd, stiff/gall trk: can rate higher.
3065 **MARCHING SONG 16** [5] R Hannon 2-9-0 Martin Dwyer 5/4 FAV: 53242: Cl-up, styd on to lead 1f out, | 1½ | 85
hdd well ins fnl 1f, no extra: bckd from 7/4: acts on fast & gd: another gd run, see 3065.
3047 **SUNSET STRIP 16** [2] M R Channon 2-9-0 T E Durcan 5/1: 223: In tch, prog when short of room 2f | 2 | 79
out, sn switched, carried head high & onepcd dist: op 13/2: return to 7f will suit: see 3047.
PALATINATE [6] H Candy 2-9-0 Dane O'Neill 11/1: 4: br c Desert Prince - Dead Certain (Absalom) | ½ | 78+
Slow away, styd on fnl 2f, nrst fin under hands & heels: debut: Mar foal, half-brother to a couple of wnrs at 2:
dam decent sprint performer, sire Group 1 miler: ran green & sure to improve.
LUCIFEROUS [4]2-8-9 Lisa Jones(3) 33/1: 46: Chsd ldrs 4f, wknd: debut: Feb foal, cost 10,000gns: | 1½ | 69
Led, hdd 1f out, wknd: debut: Feb foal, cost 10,000gns: dam unrcd: sire high-class performer abroad.
2089 **DIAMOND HOMBRE 55** [7]2-9-0 M Hills 7/1: 46: Chsd ldrs 4f, wknd: op 12/1, 8 wk abs: see 2089. | nk | 73
3111 **CELESTIAL ARC 14** [3]2-9-0 S Drowne 20/1: 307: Al in rear: btr 2696. | 1 | 70
KOLYMA [1]2-8-9 C Catlin 33/1: 8: ch f Grand Lodge - Koniya (Doyoun) Dwelt, al in rear: | 10 | 40
debut: April foal, half-sister successful at 10f: dam wnr at 3: sire Gr 1 wnr at 1m/10f: with J L Dunlop.
8 Ran Time 1m 15.56 (3.46) Owned: Mr Hamdan Al Maktoum Trained: Arundel

3452 6.50 Fonthill Stud Maiden Stakes 3yo+ (D)
£5707 £1756 £878 6f str Good 53 -01 Slow Far side

2756 **KOSTAR 28** [9] C G Cox 3-8-12 R Smith 3/1: 41: Dwelt, sn in tch, ev ch fnl 1f, rdn out to | | 77
lead cl-home: op 4/1: eff at 6f, further will suit: acts on firm & gd grnd: progressing well: see 2756 (debut).
3269 **BEE MINOR 7** [2] R Hannon 3-8-7 (73) M Hills 6/1: 00-02002: Held up, prog wide halfway, ev ch ins | hd | 70
fnl 1f, just held by wnr: op 4/1 on qck reappr: gd run, see 2648 (fills h'cap).
FIREBIRD [4] H Candy 3-8-7 L Keniry(3) 16/1: 3: b f Soviet Star - Al Corniche (Bluebird) Rear, | 1¼ | 66
prog 2f out, kept on ins fnl 1f, nrst fin: debut: cost 28,000gns: half-sister to wnrs at 6f/9f: dam 5f wnr as a
juv: eff & bred to apprec further: acts on gd grnd: promising start & looks sure to impr for today.
4952} **AVESSIA 267** [6] G L Moore 3-8-7 J Fortune 12/2: 0-4: b f Averti - Alessia (Caerleon) Handy, | hd | 65
onepcd ins fnl 1f: reappr: unplcd on sole '03 start (mdn, rtd 56): eff at 6f on gd grnd.
2906 **ANNA PANNA 22** [10]3-8-7 (71) Dane O'Neill 11/8 FAV: 3-625: Led, hdd dist, sn no extra: well | nk | 64
bckd: better expected after gd 2nd in 2906.
2907 **BLACK SABBETH 22** [7]3-8-12 C Catlin 80/1: 0006: Al cl-up, ev ch dist, sn no extra: see 2907. | 1½ | 65
2575 **HERIOT 35** [8]3-8-12 bl S Carson 80/1: 0007: Dwelt, onepcd in mid-div when no room ins fnl 1f. | 1 | 62
MISS MONZA [3]3-8-7 T E Durcan 33/1: 8: b f Hazaaf - Monstrosa (Monsanto) Al bhd on debut. | hd | 56
INESCAPABLE [1]3-8-12 S Drowne 25/1: 9: Mid-div 4f, wknd: debut. | 5 | 46
CONJUROR [5]3-8-12 Martin Dwyer 7/1: U: Slow away, refused to race & unshipped rider sn after | | 0
start: tchd 10/1 on debut: with A M Balding.
10 Ran Time 1m 15.35 (3.25) Owned: Mrs P Scott-Dunn And Mrs F J Ryan Trained: Hungerford

3453 7.20 Manor Farm Meats Premier Claiming Stakes 3-4yo (D)
£5512 £1696 £848 1m str Good 53 +00 Fast Far side

3067 **HOH BLEU DEE 15** [9] S Kirk 3-8-9 BL (75) Dane O'Neill 6/4 FAV: 66-06021: Keen mid-div, prog to | | 76
lead 1f out, drvn out to hold on: prev eff at 5/6f, now suited by around 1m: acts on gd & fast grnd: apprec first
time blnks: see 3067 & 1847.
2919 **TOP SPEC 21** [8] R Hannon 3-8-11 (77) R Smith 3/1: 61-00502: Slow away, prog 3f out, ev ch ins | ½ | 76
fnl 1f, just held by wnr: apprec drop back to 1m on first try in claim grade: see 1924.
888 **ATAHUELPA 126** [7] A King 4-9-5 (77) Martin Dwyer 11/1: 310-0003: In tch, styd on to lead after | 1¼ | 74
5f, hdd 1f out, no extra: earlier jumps unplcd (rtd 44h, mdn hdle): see 888.
3112 **LOVE TRIANGLE 14** [2] D R C Elsworth 3-9-4 (76) L Keniry(3) 11/1: 00-30004: Bhd, rcd keenly, nvr | 2½ | 76
nrr than mid-div: btr 2098 (7f, h'cap).
3286 **QUEENSTOWN 7** [1]3-8-7 bl (80) J Fortune 7/2: 4122-035: Led 5f, sn wknd: tchd 9/2 on qck reappr. | 4 | 57
3052 **RABITATIT 16** [2]3-8-5 (62) S Drowne 8/1: 2402556: Cl-up 6f, sn wknd: btr 2475. | 1 | 53
2197 **AWARDING 51** [4]4-9-0 (70) Lucy Russell(7) 28/1: 6-500007: Chsd ldr 6f, fdd: 7 wk abs. | 20 | 18
7 Ran Time 1m 43.34 (4.24) Owned: Mr D F Allport Trained: Upper Lambourn

SALISBURY SATURDAY 24.07.04 Righthand, Galloping Track, Stiff Finish

3454 7.50 Approach Vauxhall Handicap Stakes 3yo+ 0-70 (E) **[70]**
£3627 £1116 £558 **1m6f15y** **Good 53** **-16 Slow** Flag Start

2869 **THE VARLET 23** [3] B I Case 4-9-12 P (68) S Hitchcott(3) 22/1: 605-0361: Held up, prog & short of room 2f out, switched & styd on to lead 1f out, drvn out: eff at 12/14f on fast & gd grnd: eff in a visor, apprec today's cheek pieces: first win: see 2530. **71**
3200 **SAN HERNANDO 10** [11] D R C Elsworth 4-10-0 (70) Dane O'Neill 7/1: 4004042: Mid-div, prog to lead 2f out, hdd 1f out, styd on ins fnl 1f, not btn far: lost little in defeat under top-weight: see 2311 & 1232. *½* **71**
2444 **CLARADOTNET 40** [13] M R Channon 4-9-6 (62) T E Durcan 20/1: 0006303: Cl-up 9f, sn outpcd, rallying when short of room ins fnl 1f: op 12/1: eff at 11.7f, now stays 14f: acts on fast & gd: see 2180. *1¾* **61**
3217 **SIR ALFRED 9** [14] A King 5-8-13 (55) C Catlin 16/1: 00630-04: Reluctant at start, whipped round & lost around 12L, prog 3f out, kept on ins fnl 1f: gd eff in circumstances but looks one to avoid: see 3217. *1½* **52**
3147 **COOL BATHWICK 13** [7]5-8-2 T (44) Lisa Jones(3) 10/1: 0000045: Bhd, prog & ev ch dist, sn no extra. *¾* **41**
2905 **WINSLOW BOY 22** [12]3-8-4 (60) J Quinn 100/30: 0-046126: Held up, prog when short of room 3f out, sn no impress: btr expected after promising eff in 2905. *1* **56**
3270 **GREYFIELD 7** [10]8-8-8 (50) N de Souza(5) 25/1: 400//-5067: Cl-up 12f, sn wknd: btr 2088. *1¼* **45**
3114 **MASTERMAN READY 14** [5]3-8-11 (67) J Fortune 11/1: 6-0068: Mid-div, prog & ev ch 3f out, wknd. *1¼* **61**
3147 **SNINFIA 13** [2]4-8-8 (50) J F McDonald(3) 14/1: 0-000409: Dsptd lead, led after 1m, hdd 2f out, wknd. *10* **34**
2491] **ASH HAB 1084** [9]6-9-4 (60) L Keniry(3) 33/1: 013000//-0: 10th: b g A P Indy - Histoire (Riverman) Mid-div 10f, wknd: long jumps abs, mod form in Ireland: h'cap wnr in '01 (J L Dunlop, 1st time blnks): eff at 2m on firm grnd: has been gelded: with P Burgoyne. 1 Jun'01 Thir 16fm 64-60 F: *1¼* **43**
3114 **NICK THE SILVER 14** [8]3-8-4 (60) S Carson 25/1: 30-060r0: 11th: Rcd keenly, dsptd lead 1m, wknd. *nk* **42**
2856* **DIAMOND ORCHID 24** [4]4-9-0 vis (56) F P Ferris(3) 11/4 FAV: 4221510: 12th: Bhd, btn when eased dist: bckd from 4/1: nvr dngrs & something clearly amiss, btr 2856. *6* **32**
2905 **ZALDA 22** [6]3-8-5 (61) S Drowne 11/2: 006-1650: 13th: Baulked & left nrly 1f bhd at start, nvr a factor: has own ideas about game & is one to avoid: btr 2164. *dist* **7**
13 Ran Time 3m 7.70 (9.7) Owned: Mrs A D Bourne Trained: Banbury

3455 8.20 Western Daily Press Handicap Stakes 3yo 0-70 (E) **[77]**
£3679 £1132 £566 **1m str** **Good 53** **-19 Slow** Far side

3067 **MOSCOW TIMES 15** [6] D R C Elsworth 3-9-7 (70) L Keniry(3) 7/1: 600-6501: Held up, prog 3f out, styd on to lead dist, rdn out: eff at 7f, now suited by 1m: acts on firm & gd: unexposed in h'cap grade: see 2650. **76**
2365 **THE WAY WE WERE 43** [2] T G Mills 3-9-6 (69) J Fortune 5/1: 31-6502D: Led after 1f, hdd 2f out, rallied & ev ch ins fnl 1f, edged right under press, just held by wnr: fin 2nd, disqual & plcd 3rd: 6 wk abs: acts on gd grnd & polytrack: encouraging eff & can be plcd to find similar: see 2024. *½* **73**
2971 **KNICKYKNACKIENOO 19** [3] A G Newcombe 3-8-10 (59) S Drowne 11/4 FAV: 2203102: Held up, hdwy when short of room 2f out, staying on when short of room again ins fnl 1f, fin 3rd, promoted to 2nd: bckd from 5/1: btn just over 1L & poss a shade unlucky: see 2701. *¾* **61+**
2971 **DAGOLA 19** [11] C G Cox 3-9-1 (64) R Smith 5/1: 00-10034: Cl-up, sltly outpcd & short of room bef 1f out, rallied cl-home: worth another try at 10f: see 2971 & 1242. *1* **64**
3153 **HANA DEE 12** [9]3-8-8 (57) T E Durcan 9/1: 0060045: Cl-up, styd on to lead 2f out, hdd dist, no extra when short of room ins fnl 1f: btr 3153. *¾* **55**
2919 **BALEARIC STAR 21** [10]3-9-5 (68) G Baker 6/1: 0-601006: Mid-div, led briefly 2f out, sn hdd. *4* **58**
3161 **STARMIX 12** [12]3-9-5 BL (68) N De Souza(5) 8/1: 00407: Nvr nrr than mid-div: first time blnks. *¾* **56**
3219 **TURTLE PATRIARCH 9** [1]3-8-13 (62) S Hitchcott(3) 16/1: 60-008: Nvr nrr than mid-div: see 3219. *shd* **49**
4368} **RUMBLING BRIDGE 308** [4]3-8-12 (61) Dane O'Neill 16/1: 546-9: ch g Air Express - Rushing River (Irish River) Slow away, al in rear: reapp: unplcd in all 3 '03 starts (mdns, rtd 62); has been gelded. *4* **40**
3144 **MASTER MAHOGANY 13** [8]3-8-13 (62) J F McDonald(3) 12/1: 0065460: 10th: Led early, sn bhnd. *6* **30**
495 **INTITNICE 178** [5]3-7-13 p (48) J Quinn 66/1: 0000-000: 11th: Cl-up over 5f, wknd: long abs. *29* **0**
11 Ran Time 1m 44.86 (5.76) Owned: Mr M Tabor Trained: Whitsbury

3456 8.50 City Cabs Salisbury Rated Stakes Handicapfillies 3yo+ 0-80 (D) **[80]**
£6214 £2357 £1179 **6f212y str** **Good 53** **+04 Fast** Centre

3364 **AND TOTO TOO 2** [3] P D Evans 4-9-1 bl (67) F P Ferris(3) 11/4: 0204421: Rear, prog 2f out, styd on to lead ins fnl 1f, rdn out: op 4/1: qck reapp: eff at 6/7f, has tried 1m: acts on firm, gd/soft & both AWs: eff with blnks: has been in gd form this term & this was a deserved success: see 3257 & 2312. **73**
2864 **IN THE PINK 23** [8] M R Channon 4-9-6 (72) S Hitchcott(3) 7/1: 1-001202: Dwelt, prog 3f out, ev ch 1f out, styd on & not btn far: op 5/1: ran to form on win in 2755. *¾* **75**
3257 **KINDLELIGHT DEBUT 8** [7] D K Ivory 4-9-8 (74) J Quinn 20/1: 3100-003: Handy, prog & ev ch dist, kept on ins fnl 1f, just held for 2nd: left recent effs bhd with encouraging run & is on a winning mark: see 3257. *shd* **76**
3072 **PINK SAPPHIRE 15** [9] D R C Elsworth 3-8-13 (72) Dane O'Neill 11/2: 10-02464: Cl-up, styd on to lead 2f out, hdd dist, sn no extra: btr 2098. *¾* **72**
2953 **INDIANA BLUES 20** [1]3-8-9 (68) L P Keniry(3) 8/1: 40-40035: Nvr nrr than mid-div: btr 2953. *1½* **65**
3176 **SHIRLEY OAKS 11** [5]6-8-5 (8oh) (49) J F McDonald(3) 25/1: 6312006: Dwelt, rear, prog when short of room dist, sn no impress: btr 2397. *½* **53$**
3068 **MUSIC MAID 15** [4]6-8-13 (65) S Drowne 5/1: 115-0107: Dwelt, nvr a factor: bckd from 10/1: btr 2312. *3½* **54**
2852} **BAYONET 378** [6]8-8-5 (17oh) (40) Lisa Jones(3) 66/1: 000000-8: b f Then Again - Lambay (Lorenzaccio) Led, hdd 2f out, wknd: reapp: unplcd in '03 (rtd 39, clmr): unplcd in '02 (rtd 22, h'cap): h'cap wnr in '00: eff at 6/7f on fast & gd/soft grnd: likes to race with/force the pace. 2 Sep'01 Chep 7g/f 56-53 F: 2 Aug'01 Ling 7gd 53-51 F: 2 Jul'01 Ling 6g/f 52-49 E: *3* **40**
2864 **SEARCH MISSION 23** [2]3-9-7 (80) J Fortune 2/1 FAV: 512-29: Handy, fdd 2f out, eased ins fnl 1f: v disapp & surely something amiss: showed more in 2864. *dist* **33**
9 Ran Time 1m 28.93(3.43) Owned: Mrs S J Lawrence Trained: Abergavenny

Official Going GOOD/FIRM

3457   **2.15 Tolent Construction Maiden Stakes 2yo   (D)**
£5577 £1716 £858   **5f rnd**   **Good 50**   **-03 Slow**   Inside

2089 **WITCHRY 56** [6] M A Jarvis 2-9-0 P Robinson 1/4 FAV: 431: Prom, styd on to lead dist, pushed   **91 +**
clr, val 6L+: well bckd, 8 wk abs: eff at 5f on gd, stiff/undul trk: goes well fresh, back to form after being gelded.
     GRAZE ON 0 [10] J J Quinn 2-9-0 R Winston 25/1: 2: b c Factual - Queens Check (Komaite)   4   76
Rear, prog 2f out, styd on fnl 1f, no ch with wnr: debut: Mar foal, cost 1,200gns: dam a 5f 2yo wnr, also a 5f wnr
at 3: sire speedily bred & was a smart 2yo: eff at 5f on gd: fair start, entitled to impr for this experience.
     ZOMERLUST 0 [2] J J Quinn 2-9-0 J Fanning 14/1: 3: b c Josr Algarhoud - Passiflora (Night   2½   68
Shift) Cl up over 3f, sn no extra on debut: Jan foal, cost 10,000gns: dam a 6f 2yo wnr, sire v smart 2yo.
     HARRYS HOUSE 0 [5] J J Quinn 2-9-0 P Hanagan 25/1: 4: gr c Paris House - Rum Lass (Distant   ½   66
Relative) Mid div, kept on fnl 1f on debut: Feb first foal: dam a poor mdn at 5/7f, sire a fast 2yo.
3227 **NITEOWL LAD 9** [3]2-9-0 J D O'Reilly(7) 11/1: 0025: Sn led, hung right over 1f out & sn hdd, no extra.   nk   65
     ASADARA 0 [1]2-8-9 Suzanne France(7) 100/1: 6: Slow away, kept on over 1f out on debut.   1¾   55
     TYRONE SAM 0 [4]2-9-0 N Callan 12/1: 7: In tch, nvr nearer on debut.   1   57
3178 **WAGGLEDANCE 8** [8]2-9-0 G Parkin 33/1: 508: Handy, wknd 1f out: rider reported bit had slipped.   3½   46
1780 **ESKDALE 70** [9]2-9-0 S Righton 66/1: 09: In tch, outpcd & btn halfway: long abs.   3½   35
     APETITE 0 [7]2-9-0 A Reilly(7) 100/1: 0: 10th: Slow away, nvr a factor on debut.   2   29
10 Ran   Time 1m 4.16 (2.66)   Owned: Sheikh Mohammed   Trained: Newmarket

---

3458   **2.50 L & J Windows Classified Stakes 3yo+ 0-80   (D)**
£5421 £1668 £834   **1m4f8y**   **Good 50**   **-07 Slow**   Inside

3066 **ASTROCHARM 17** [5] M H Tompkins 5-9-5 (83) P Robinson 6/4 FAV: 5105121: Mid-div, gd prog to lead   **92 +**
over 1f out, sn clr, eased cl home, val 7L+: well bckd: suited by 12f on firm & gd, handles any trk: gd form
continues, improving at present: win more races in this form: see 1461.
3281* **BENDARSHAAN 8** [1] M Johnston 4-9-12 (87) R Ffrench 2/1: 0004112: Trkd ldrs, hdwy to lead 3f out,   4   91
hdd over 1f out, no extra: well clr of rem, top-weight: gd eff on bid for treble: remains in gd form: see 3281.
2660 **HORNER 32** [6] P F I Cole 3-8-9 BL (82) N De Souza 15/2: 6-042103: Led to 3f out, sn wknd.   9   72
3076 **FOURTH DIMENSION 16** [2] D Nicholls 5-9-8 (83) Alex Greaves 7/1: 13000-04: Prom, ev ch 4f out, wknd. 14   52
3278 **QUDRAH 8** [3]4-9-7 (85) J Carroll 25/1: 0-005405: In tchMid-div, wknd over 5f out: op 14/1: see 758.   dist   1
3076 **CONQUERING LOVE 16** [4]6-9-8 (83) T Hamilton(3) 10/1: 24110-0R: Ref to race sn after start: see 3076.   0
6 Ran   Time 2m 41.04 (6.94)   Owned: Mystic Meg Limited   Trained: Newmarket

---

3459   **3.20 Graham Rock Memorial Handicap Stakes 3yo 0-85   (D)**   [88]
£6825 £2100 £1050   **1m2f6y**   **Good 50**   **-31 Slow**   Inside

2874 **MR TAMBOURINE MAN 24** [3] P F I Cole 3-9-7 (81) N De Souza(5) 6/4 FAV: 1-600131: Led, hdd bef 1f   87
out, rallied to lead again well ins fnl 1f, drvn out: eff at 1m/10f on firm & gd, prob acts on any trk: v game.
2893 **ROYAL DISTANT 23** [1] M W Easterby 3-8-5 (65) Dale Gibson 16/1: 0000002: Mid-div, hdwy 2f out,   hd   70
kept on well ins fnl 1f but hdd ins fnl 1m, no stays 10f: see 1108.
2930 **TYTHEKNOT 22** [5] Jedd O'Keeffe 3-8-12 (72) P Hanagan 5/1: 02-23643: Cl up, hdwy to lead bef 1f   shd   76
out, hdd well ins fnl 1f, now stays 10f: see 1108.
3231 **THIRD EMPIRE 9** [4] C Grant 3-8-7 (67) R Winston 7/1: 50-30524: Handy 7f, sn wknd.   8   59
3066 **WHISPERED PROMISES 17** [2]3-9-6 BL (80) R Ffrench 5/2: 211-0305: Handy over 5f, sn fdd: v   7   61
disappointing in 1st time blnks: btr 2681.
5 Ran   Time 2m 16.28 (8.18)   Owned: Mr CWright & The Hon Mrs JMCorbett   Trained: Whatcombe

---

3460   **3.55 Pomfret Rated Stakes Handicap 3yo+ 0-100   (B)**   [107]
£12070 £4578 £2289   **1m4y rnd**   **Good 50**   **+07 Fast**   Inside

3118 **WING COMMANDER 15** [5] R A Fahey 5-8-11 (90) P Hanagan 11/2: 3-430001: In tch, prog trav well to   **99 +**
lead ins fnl 1f, rdn clr, readily: bckd from 12/1: eff at 1m/10f on firm, gd & any trk: improving, 5yo who apprec
this drop back to 1m: must hold decent chance in William Hill H'cap at Goodwood under a pen: see 951.
3305 **VICIOUS WARRIOR 6** [10] R M Whitaker 5-8-7 (86) Dean McKeown 8/1: 2053022: Cl up wide, hdwy to   3   90
lead 2f out, hdd ins fnl 1f, no extra: qck reappr: continues in decent form: see 1475.
2915 **CALCUTTA 22** [2] B W Hills 8-9-4 (97) P Robinson 9/1: 0000203: Mid-div, hdwy & not clr run 2f   ¾   99
out, kept on ins fnl 1f: op 12/1: on a winning mark: see 1926.
3077 **FLIGHTY FELLOW 16** [6] T D Easterby 4-9-1 (94) D Allan 10/1: 0610624: Rear, hdwy 3f out, onepcd dist. 2   92
3305 **PENRITH 6** [7]3-8-1 (6oh) (88) J Fanning 100/30: 1-13035: Bhd, prog & not clr run bef 2f out &   nk   85
again dist, kept on late: qck reappr: nvr could get competitive: btr 2040.
2753 **CRIPSEY BROOK 29** [1]6-8-8 (87) Kim Tinkler 20/1: 6600256: Rear, prog 2f out, mod gains.   1¾   80
3265* **EVEREST 8** [8]7-8-7 (86) T Eaves(3) 5/2 FAV: 0000117: Bhd, prog when no room bef 2f out, sn wknd: 2   75
nicely bckd tho' op 9/4: better expected on hatrick bid: btr 3265.
2941 **ROSKILDE 374** [9]4-9-7 (100) A Culhane 14/1: 303002-8: b g Danehill - Melisendra (Highest Honor)   6   77
Chsd ldrs, no impress 2f out: op 11/1, reapp, top-weight: rnr-up fnl '03 start (cond stks): '02 mdn & stks wnr:
eff over 1m/10f & likes firm & fast, handles soft, acts on a gall trk: has been gelded.
2 Jul'03 Hami 9.2g/f 100-(100) C: 1 Sep'02 Sali 8g/f 101- D: 1 Jul'02 Redc 7g/f 86- D: 2 Jun'02 Good 6sft 84- D:
3001 **LITTLE VENICE 19** [3]4-8-7 (86) Lisa Jones 28/1: 0-053109: Led to 2f out, no extra.   3   57
1475 **TOUGH LOVE 85** [4]5-8-7 (86) R Winston 12/1: 30-00000: 10th: Bhd, nvr nr ldrs: long abs: see 1151. 13   31
10 Ran   Time 1m 45.3 (3.5)   Owned: Mr Steve Ryan   Trained: Malton

3461   4.30 Toteplacepot Handicap Stakes 3yo+ 0-90 (C)   **[90]**
£9326 £3538 £1769   **6f rnd**   **Good 50**   **+03 Fast**   Inside

2990 **UNDETERRED 19** [8] T D Barron 8-8-8 (70) N Callan 5/1: 5004441: In tch, prog to lead 1f out, rdn   78
out to hold on fnl 1f: best at 6f, stays 7f: acts on firm & gd, handles soft & gd, handles soft & any trk,
likes Goodwood: well h'capped 8yo: keep in mind if at Goodwood: see 1898.

3424 **LEGAL SET 1** [2] Miss A Stokell 8-7-12 t (60) D Fox(5) 20/1: 14024002: Trkd ldrs, not clr run &   ½   65
switched right 1f out, styd on ins fnl 1f: ran yesterday (unplcd): see 2713.

3117 **CD FLYER 15** [1] B Ellison 7-9-11 (87) P Mulrennan(5) 6/1: 0041043: Rear, prog 2f out, nrst fin.   1¼   88

3213 **NEVER WITHOUT ME 10** [4] J F Coupland 4-7-13 (61) J F McDonald(3) 5/1: 0341124: Prom, led 2f out,   1¼   58
hdd 1f out, sn no extra: btr 3213 & 2720..

2872 **H HARRISON 24** [3]4-9-5 (81) R Ffrench 10/1: 5410035: Led 4f, sn no extra: op 6/1: btr 2872.   2½   70

3136 **TIME N TIME AGAIN 14** [6]6-8-7 p (69) D Allan 5/1: 3032236: Slow away, mod late gains: btr 3136.   nk   57

2684 **HITS ONLY MONEY 31** [7]4-10-0 (90) Dean McKeown 4/1 FAV: 30-00007: Prom, wknd 2f out: op 10/1.   5   63

3213 + **MARSHALLSPARK 10** [5]5-8-4 (66) P Hanagan 5/1: 0-000518: Trkd ldrs, wknd over 1f out.   ½   37

8 Ran   Time 1m 16.96 (2.86)   Owned: Mr P D Savill   Trained: Thirsk

---

3462   5.05 Sunday Funday Maiden Stakes 3yo   (D)
£5460 £1680 £840   **1m4y rnd**   **Good 50**   **-12 Slow**   Inside

1358 **CHOIR LEADER 92** [7] W J Haggas 3-9-0   S W Kelly 10/11 FAV: 01: b c Sadler's Wells - Choir   87+
Mistress (Chief Singer) Made all, clr 2f out, eased cl home, val 12L+: well bckd: cost 80,000gns:
half-brother to high- class 10f filly Chorist: dam unrcd: stays 1m on gd, acts on a stiff/undul trk.

2072 **KILLMOREY 57** [6] S C Williams 3-9-0 R Ffrench 4/1: 002: ch g Nashwan - Zarma (Machiavellian)   9   66
Handy, not pace to go with wnr from 2f out: 8 wk abs, clr of rem: dam smart 10f French performer: needs to improve.

3018 **SPEED RACER 18** [9] Don Enrico Incisa 3-8-9 (55) Kim Tinkler 25/1: 305-0503: In tch 5f, sn no extra.   4   53

3019 **KYBER 18** [1] R F Fisher 3-9-0 R Winston 25/1: 54: ch g First Trump - Mahbob Dancer (Groom   ½   57
Dancer) Rear, hdwy 3f out, kept on: cost £14,000: half-brother to a 6f 2yo debut/hdles wnr: dam unrcd.

2656 **DALMARNOCK 33** [8]3-9-0 F Lynch 20/1: 005: Chsd ldrs, onepcd fnl 2f.   shd   56

        MOUNT COTTAGE 0 [2]3-8-9 A Culhane 13/2: 6: Mid-div, wknd 2f out: op 4/1, debut.   4   43

3204 **BANANA GROVE 10** [3]3-9-0 P Mathers(5) 7/1: 37: Al bhd: see 3204.   26   0

2426 **KALUSH 24** [5]3-9-0 N Callan 16/1: 336-0068: Rcd in 2nd, wknd 3f out: 6 wk abs.   dist   0

        MARDONICDECLARE 0 [4]3-9-0 G Parkin 40/1: 9: Outpcd in rear, nvr a factor on debut.   20   0

9 Ran   Time 1m 46.8 (5.0)   Owned: Cheveley Park Stud   Trained: Newmarket

---

3463   5.40 Family Day Handicap Stakes 3yo+ 0-70 (E)   **[70]**
£4261 £1311 £656   **5f rnd**   **Good 50**   **+08 Fast**   Inside

3352 **BALLYBUNION 4** [5] D Nicholls 5-8-7 (49) J Fanning 7/2 FAV: 3000051: Handy, prog fnl 2f, rdn out   59
to lead nr fin: tchd 6/1, qck reapp: eff at 5f, prob best at 6f: acts on firm & gd, prob any trk, likes Catterick:
imprvd for a drop back to the minimum trip: on fair mark & this was a gd confidence boost: see 2084.

2944 **BLUE MAEVE 22** [4] J Hetherton 4-8-9 (51) S Righton 16/1: 4004242: Led till over 2f out, led   ½   57
again over 1f out, drvn ins fnl 1f & hdd & no extra nr fin: running well, can find a similar contest: see 2775.

3244 **TANTRIC 9** [2] J O'Reilly 5-8-13 (55) J D O'Reilly(5) 14/1: 0030033: Mid-div, hdwy 2f out, not   ¾   59
much room over 1f out, kept on ins fnl 1f & nrst fin: eff at 5f, wng form btwn 7/9.4f: return to further will suit.

2630 **MOLOTOV 34** [13] I W McInnes 4-8-3 (45) Natalia Gemelova(7) 40/1: 000-1004: Prom, led over 2f out   ½   47
till over 1f out, no extra ins fnl 1f: acts on fast, gd & fibresand: back to winning form of 1948.

3165* **BLESSED PLACE 13** [7]4-8-9 t (51) P Hanagan 8/1: 0335415: Handy, btn when carried right ins fnl 1f.   nk   52

3241 **LAUREL DAWN 9** [6]6-9-5 (61) J F McDonald(3) 15/2: 0152506: Mid-div, hdwy & not much room over 1f   ½   60
out, switched right entering fnl 1f, kept on: see 2846.

3191 **PORT ST CHARLES 11** [10]7-9-2 (58) R Thomas(5) 25/1: 4300047: Bhd, hdwy over 1f out, nrst finish.   1   54

3416 **LE MERIDIEN 2** [3]6-8-7 p (49) R Winston 9/1: 50006518: In rear, hdwy over 1f out, nrst finish.   ½   43

3228 **FAIRGAME MAN 9** [15]6-8-5 p (47) G Parkin 10/1: 0205109: Mid-div, onepcd fnl 1f.   hd   40

3165 **BRIGADIER MONTY 13** [8]6-8-11 (53) A Culhane 10/1: 6002550: 10th: Rear, modest late gains.   2   40

3244 **RECTANGLE 9** [17]4-9-11 (67) Alex Greaves 11/1: 0000020: 11th: Cl-up, wknd 2f out.   ½   52

3403 **ARCTIC BURST 2** [1]4-8-13 vis (55) N Callan 50/1: 00000000: 12th: Rear, hdwy over 2f out, wknd fnl 1f.   1¾   35

2599 **ONE LAST TIME 35** [12]4-9-4 (60) R Ffrench 20/1: 0-000200: 13th: Al bhd: see 1824.   2   34

3203 **FOX COVERT 10** [18]3-8-10 (56) F Lynch 33/1: 0235040: 14th: Mid-div, no impress 2f out.   hd   29

3341 **LAW MAKER 4** [9]4-8-6 vis (48) J Bramhill 33/1: 0436200: 15th: Mid-div, wknd 2f out: qck reapp.   shd   20

3018 **GAME FLORA 18** [16]3-8-8 (54) T Eaves(3) 66/1: 00-10450: 16th: Mid-div, wknd 2f out.   3½   15

3228 **FLYING TACKLE 9** [14]6-8-9 p (51) S W Kelly 20/1: 0321000: 17th: Al bhd: thrice below 2981.   ¾   10

3228* **IZMAIL 9** [11]5-10-0 (70) L Treadwell(5) 11/1: 0000010: 18th: Cl-up, wknd 2f out: reportedly ran 'flat'.   3½   18

18 Ran   Time 1m 3.41(2.11)   Owned: Mr I Blakey Mr M Gosse Mr D Nicholls   Trained: Thirsk

---

ASCOT   SUNDAY 25.07.04 Righthand, Stiff, Galloping Track

Official Going GOOD/FIRM.

3464   2.00 Fullerton Trophy Ed Stakes 3yo+ 0-95 (B)
£11710 £4442 £2221   **1m2f**   **Good 47**   **-04 Slow**   Inside

2582* **WUNDERWOOD 36** [1] Lady Herries 5-9-7 (99) S Sanders 7/4 FAV: 14-00111: In tch, styd on to lead   106
dist, sn wandered under press, held on drvn out: well bckd: eff at 10/12f: likes firm, gd & polytrack: in-form 5yo
who likes Ascot & deserves step up to List/Group company: see 2582 & 2246.

2605* **MUTASALLIL 35** [5] Saeed bin Suroor 4-9-6 t (98) R Hills 4/1: 3-112: Led till dist, rallied fnl 1f   ¾   102
& not btn far: acts on fast & gd grnd: lost little in defeat, see 2605 & 2012.

2843* **ALPHECCA 25** [6] Sir Michael Stoute 3-8-7 (93) K Fallon 7/2: 0-13: In tch, kept on fnl 2f, al held by front 2: imprvd eff on only 3rd start & shapes as if 12f will suit: see 2843 (mdn).   1¼   97

2948 **COUNSELS OPINION 22** [7] C F Wall 7-9-8 (100) R Mullen 7/1: 10-34004: Held up, prog trav well 2f out, onepcd dist: btr 2208 & 1111.   1   100

3076 **VENGEANCE 16** [2]4-9-6 (98) P Dobbs 10/1: 05-03155: Sn rdn along in tch, no extra bef 1f out.   1¼   96

2556 **CORRIOLANUS 37** [4]4-9-3 (94) D Holland 33/1: 3000606: Cl-up 1m, sn wknd: btr 693.   1   91

3118 **BOURGAINVILLE 15** [3]6-9-3 P (94) J Fortune 12/1: 4550007: Slow away, al adrift: cheek pieces.   16   68

7 Ran   Time 2m 9.15 (5.15)   Owned: Mr Tony Perkins   Trained: Littlehampton

---

| **3465** | 2.30 Cathay Pacific Handicap Stakes 3yo+ 0-90 (C) | | | | [97] |
| | £9783 £3010 £1505   **1m rnd**   **Good 47**   -19 Slow   Inside | | | | |

3285*)**PRINCE OF THEBES 360** [7] A M Balding 3-9-4 (87) R Mullen 20/1: 031-1: b c Desert Prince - Persian Walk (Persian Bold) Keen cl-up, went on dist, held on rnd out on reapp: mdn wnr on last of only 3 '03 starts: eff at 7f, apprec stiff up to 1m: acts on fast or gd grnd, stiff/gall or sharp/undul trk: likes to force the pace & goes well fresh: fine effort after long absence due to stress fracture of pelvis.   97
1 Jul'03 Epso 7g/f 88- D:

2853* **WELCOME STRANGER 25** [9] J M P Eustace 4-9-6 (81) L Fletcher(3) 8/1: 4-000212: In tch, prog to chase wnr fnl 1f, kept on, post came too sn: continues in gd form, see 2853.   hd   89

2672* **GOODBYE MR BOND 32** [5] E J Alston 4-8-10 (71) F Norton 100/30 FAV: 3411113: Mid-div, styd on ins fnl 2f, not btn far in 3rd: well bckd: gd eff on bid for 5-timer: just btr 2672 & 2550.   1   77

3225 **AFRICAN SAHARA 10** [6] Miss D Mountain 5-9-3 t (78) G Carter 8/1: 6006034: Rear, hdwy fnl 2f, nrst fin: not too much to do: see 3225.   hd   83

2679 **LIFTED WAY 32** [4]5-9-4 (79) S Drowne 10/1: 0-011065: Led, hdd dist, no extra: bckd from 16/1.   ¾   82

3232* **BEST BEFORE 9** [10]4-9-5 (80) S Donohoe(7) 7/2: 2133316: Handy over 6f, sn no extra: btr 3232.   2   79

3068 **A WOMAN IN LOVE 16** [1]5-9-4 (79) S Sanders 4/1: 6111147: Al in rear: bckd: btr 2587 & 2432.   1   76

2828 **J R STEVENSON 26** [8]8-8-11 (72) J Fortune 20/1: 1-204658: Held up, nvr able to chall: btr 1423.   nk   68

3068 **JOOLS 16** [2]6-9-1 (76) M Howard(7) 11/1: 0044659: Mid-div over 6f, sn wknd: btr 1351.   8   57

9 Ran   Time 1m 43.80 (5.3)   Owned: Mr N H Harris/Dr E Harris/Miss M Green   Trained: Kingsclere

---

| **3466** | 3.00 Hong Kong Jockey Club Sprint Heritage Handicap Stakes 3yo+ (B) | | | | [111] |
| | £40600 £15400 £7700   **5f str**   **Good 47**   -06 Slow   Stands side | | | | |

1958 **BALTIC KING 62** [21] H Morrison 4-9-4 t (101) J Fortune 9/1: 3100-601: Rear far side, prog 2f out, kept on to lead cl-home, rdn out: well bckd after 9 wk abs: eff at 5/6f on gd & firm grnd, poss handles soft: eff in a t-strap & goes well fresh: worth another try in List/Group company on this evidence: see 1479 (reapp).   111

3123* **PIVOTAL POINT 15** [26] P J Makin 4-8-13 (8ex) (96) J Murtagh 16/1: 352-0012: Dsptd lead far side, led overall 1f out, hdd cl-home: fine run under 8lbs pen: useful, see 3123.   nk   104

3304 **FOREVER PHOENIX 6** [3] R M H Cowell 4-8-9 (92) B Doyle 9/1: 312R023: In tch trav well stands side, led that group ins fnl 1f, kept on, just held by ldrs far side: op 7/1, qck reapp, rider given 1-day whip ban: fine run, 1st home on stands side: just btr 3304.   1¼   97

3279* **CONNECT 8** [23] M H Tompkins 7-8-11 (8ex)bl (94) P Doe 33/1: 6-240414: Handy far side, styd on ins fnl 1f, not btn far: gd run under 8lb pen, see 3279.   hd   98

3388 **BLACKHEATH 2** [13]8-8-7 (8ex) (90) P Dobbs 33/1: 62264145: Held up stands side, hdwy fnl 2f, nrst fin: qck reapp: fin strongly & a gd run, see 3248.   ¾   92

2894 **CORRIDOR CREEPER 23** [5]7-8-12 p (95) D Holland 14/1: 4260236: Led till ins fnl 1f stands side, no extra: hit by a rivals whip twice in fnl 1f: 3rd in this race from a 10lbs lower mark last term: see 2894.   shd   96

3241 **MERLINS DANCER 9** 4-7-12 (1oh) (80) M Halford(6) 40/1: 0-051007: Dsptd lead far side, hung left & onepcd dist: last few wins have come at 6f: btr 2007.   nk   81

2581 **PIC UP STICKS 36** [4]5-8-13 (96) T E Durcan 7/1 FAV: P-316368: Held up stands side, prog & trav well when no room from 2f out till ins fnl 1f, switched & fin fast, ch had gone: no luck, eye-catching run & turn may not be far away: see 1207 & 790.   nk   95+

3123 **WHITBARROW 15** [11]5-8-13 P (96) R L Moore 33/1: 1000009: Rcd centre, handy till dist, sn wknd.   ½   94

3248 **PAX 9** [7]7-8-0 (83) P M Quinn 40/1: 6010000: 10th: Slow away, bhd stands side, kept on ins fnl 1f.   nk   80

2581 **TYCHY 36** [9]5-8-9 (92) S Drowne 16/1: 110-5300: 11th: Cl-up stands side till dist, wknd: btr 2253.   nk   88

3150 **MALAPROPISM 13** [15]4-8-1 (84) C Catlin 50/1: 1-600060: 12th: In tch stands side 3f, sn onepcd.   hd   79

2758 **DANZIG RIVER 29** [2]3-8-6 (93) Dane O'Neill 66/1: 15-20000: 13th: Nvr nrr than mid-div stands side.   ½   87

2758 **SMOKIN BEAU 29** [14]7-8-13 bl (96) T G McLaughlin 33/1: 6200040: 14th: Nvr nrr than mid-div.   ½   89

3123 **WHISTLER 15** [16]7-8-9 (8ex)p (92) R Hills 33/1: 0310140: 15th: Nvr nrr than mid-div far side.   shd   84

2727 **ATLANTIC VIKING 30** [22]9-8-10 (93) M Henry 33/1: 60-00400: 16th: In tch far side till dist.   nk   84

3268 **NIGHTS CROSS 8** [8]3-8-6 (107) S Hitchcott(3) 33/1: 2-430000: 17th: Cl-up stands side 3f, wknd.   hd   97

3304 **PROUD BOAST 6** [1]6-8-6 (89) K Darley 10/1: 1000230: 18th: Handy stands side, wkng when short of room dist: qck reapp: btr 3304 & 3150.   1   76

3409 **FUNFAIR WANE 2** [10]5-8-10 (93) S Whitworth 28/1: 0000-00040: 19th: Al rear stands side: qck reapp.   1   77

3080 **GREEN MANALISHI 16** [12]3-8-4 (91) J F Egan 16/1: 1031550: 20th: Cl-up, wknd dist stand side.   ½   74

2253 **PLATEAU 50** [18]5-8-1 (84) A Nicholls 9/1: 000-6020: 21th: Al bhd far side: 7 wk abs.   1¾   62

3279 **FIRST ORDER 8** [17]3-8-13 (100) S Sanders 8/1: 12113-20: 22th: Al bhd far side: drifted from 5/1: poss too sn after comeback in 3279 (reapp).   3   69

2894 **Little Edward 23** [24]6-8-9 (92) A Hindley(7) 33/1:0   3033 **Piccled 18** [19]6-8-0 (83) F Norton 20/1:0

24 Ran   Time 1m 1.66 (2.66)   Owned: Thurloe Thoroughbreds VIII   Trained: East IIsley

---

| **3467** | 3.35 Hong Kong International Sale Auction Stakes Trophy Conditions Race 2yo (C) | | | | |
| | £7772 £2948 £1474   **7f str**   **Good 47**   -20 Slow   Stands side | | | | |

2895 **SOUTHERN AFRICA 23** [4] G A Butler 2-8-13 J Fortune 11/2: 121: Keen cl-up, led dist, rdn out: tchd 7/1, top-weight: eff at 5f, apprec step up to 7f: acts on firm & gd/soft grnd: see 2646.   97

3053 **GROUP CAPTAIN 17** [7] S Kirk 2-8-7 R L Moore 7/1: 5422: Mid-div, hdwy over 2f out, ev ch ins fnl 1f, not pace wnr: tchd 10/1: gd run in defeat & deserves to lose mdn tag: see 3053.   1   88

3127* **SACRED NUTS 15** [1] M L W Bell 2-8-8 D Holland 10/11 FAV: 5113: Handy, short of room 2f out till ins fnl 1f, styd on well, post came too sn: well bckd under top-weight: likely wnr with clr run.   shd   88+

ASCOT   SUNDAY 25.07.04   Righthand, Stiff, Galloping Track

3021* **ARIODANTE** 18 [8] J M P Eustace 2-8-7 S Sanders 9/2: 314: Cl-up, ev ch 1f out, wknd: prob   **4**   **79**
failed to see out the 7f trip: btr 3021 (6f).
3065 **IM SPARTACUS** 17 [3]2-8-7 F Norton 25/1: 2165065: Handy over 5f, wknd: btr 1367.   **1**   **77**
3285 **LADY LUISA** 8 [2]2-8-2 Martin Dwyer 66/1: 06: b f Lujain - Lady of Dreams (Prince Rupert) Al in   **dht** **72**
rear: Feb foal, cost £4,700: half-sister to wnrs at 7/8f: dam successful at 10f: sire decent sprinter performer.
3111 **BENEDICT BAY** 15 [6]2-8-7 S Drowne 66/1: 607: Bhd, nvr a factor: see 2696.   **1¼** **75**
3060 **JOHN FORBES** 17 [5]2-8-7 Dane O'Neill 10/1: 0108: Led till dist, fdd: btr 2774 (6f, g/s).   **1**   **73**
8 Ran Time 1m 30.71 (4.71) Owned: The International Carnival Partnership Trained: Blewbury

---

3468   4.10 Cathay Pacific Hong Kong International Races Handicap Stakes 3yo 0-85 (D)   [91]
£5551 £1708 £854   **1m14f**   **Good**   **+09 Fast**   Inside

1756 **VINANDO** 71 [5] C R Egerton 3-9-7 T (84) S Drowne 8/1: 5-101: Bhd, prog under press to lead dist,   **99**
drvn out: tchd 12/1, 10 wk abs, gd time: eff at 10f, apprec step up to 12f: acts on gd & gd/soft grnd, gall/sharp
trk: goes well fresh: apprec today's t-strap & more h'caps await: see 1259.
4962* **SOULACROIX** 268 [2] Mrs A J Perrett 3-9-7 (84) S Drowne 11/4: 3221-2: b c Kylian - California   **5**   **90**
Dreamin (Slip Anchor) Led, hdd under press 2f out, ev ch bef 1f out, sn no extra: well bckd on reapp: mdn wnr on
fnl '03 start: eff at 7/10f, prob stays 12f: acts on gd & gd/soft grnd: encouraging effort.
1 Oct'03 Brig 9.9g/s 87-(84) D: 2 Sep'03 Wind 8.3g/f 85- D: 2 Sep'03 Warw 7.1g/f 87- D:
3255 **MAZUNA** 9 [1] C E Brittain 3-8-5   (68) R L Moore 2/1 FAV: 4406-123: Cl-up, styd on to lead 2f out,   **½**   **73**
hdd dist, no extra: well bckd: just btr 3255 & 2842.
3173 **UNCLE JOHN** 12 [3] S Kirk 3-7-12 (61) C Catlin 5/1: 05-00424: Chsd ldrs 10f, wknd: btr 3173.   **5**   **58**
2919 **SWAINSON** 22 [4]3-9-7 (84) D Holland 7/2: 341205: Dwelt, nvr trav, fdd 4f out: btr 2377.   **dist** **51**
5 Ran Time 2m 33.57 (4.57) Owned: Mrs Evelyn Hankinson Trained: Chaddleworth

---

3469   4.45 Owen Brown Maiden Stakes Fillies 3yo (D)
£5460 £1680 £840   **1m rnd**   **Good 47**   **+18 Fast**   Inside

TARFAH [2] G A Butler 3-8-11 S Sanders 5/1: 1: b f Kingmambo - Fickle (Danehill) Held up,   **85+**
prog wide to lead ins fnl 1f, pushed out, val 2L+: tchd 8/1, fast time: dam a smart 10f performer, sire aGr 1 wng
miler: eff at 1m, 10f shld suit: acts on gd grnd & a stiff/gall trk: goes well fresh: defied greeness to win well.
3237 **ARCTIC SILK** 9 [9] Saeed bin Suroor 3-8-11 T T E Durcan 11/4: 032: Led, hdd ins fnl 1f, not pace   **¾**   **79**
easy wnr: op 7/4: clr rem: acts on fast & gd grnd: can find a mdn: see 3237.
2224 **MERWAHA** 51 [5] M P Tregoning 3-8-11 R Hills 11/8 FAV: 43: Bhd, hdwy to chase ldr ins fnl 2f,   **5**   **69**
wknd ins fnl 1f: well bckd, 7 wk abs: failed to build on promising eff in 2224 (debut).
3038 **NIOBES WAY** 18 [6] P R Chamings 3-8-11 S Drowne 16/1: 04: Cl-up over 6f, wknd: btr 3038.   **4**   **61**
3038 **LADY TAVERNER** 18 [7]3-8-11 J F Egan 33/1: 005: Prom 6f, wknd: btr 3038.   **1¼** **55**
PAINTBOX [1]3-8-11 R L Moore 12/1: 6: b f Peintre Celebre - Photogenic (Midyan) Chsd ldrs   **1½** **56**
wide 5f, wknd: debut: dam wnr at 6/7f: sire top-class at mid-dists: with Mrs A J Perrett.
1008 **SYLVA ROYAL** 116 [4]3-8-11 D Holland 8/1: 4W: Withdrawn at start: btr 1008.   **0**
7 Ran Time 1m 43.76(5.26) Owned: Mr Abdulla Al Khalifa Trained: Blewbury

---

NEWMARKET   SUNDAY 25.07.04   Righthand, Stiff, Galloping Track

Official Going GOOD.

3470   2.40 Nspcc E B F Maiden Stakes 2yo (D)
£4888 £1504 £752   **7f str**   **Good/Firm 32**   **-29 Slow**   Far Side

OUDE [8] Saeed bin Suroor 2-9-0 L Dettori 6/4 JT FAV: 1: b c Dubai Millennium - Chosen Lady   **98+**
(Secretariat) Chsd ldrs, qcknd to lead well ins fnl 1f, rdn, more in hand: hvly bckd tho' drifted from 4/5, debut:
Mar foal, half brother to top-class Well Chosen: eff at 7f, will enjoy 1m: acts on fast & on a stiff/gall trk, runs
well fresh: reportedly held in high regard, will win better races.
SHANNON SPRINGS [12] B W Hills 2-9-0 M Hills 11/2: 2: b c Darshaan - Our Queen of Kings   **nk** **95+**
(Arazi) Chsd ldrs, went on 2f out, not pace to repel wnr cl-home: clr of rem, bckd from 12/1 on debut: 30,000gns
Mar foal: dam unrcd but from a decent family: sire a top-class mid-dist performer: eff over a stiff/gall 7f on
fast grnd: met a potentially smart rival today, looks nailed on for similar.
3126 **KHARISH** 15 [2] J Noseda 2-9-0 E Ahern 6/4 JT FAV: 43: Front rank, ev ch till no extra ins fnl   **3**   **85**
1f: well bckd: eff over a stiff/gall 7f on gd & fast grnd: shld find a less well contested mdn, see 3126.
DAHMAN [5] Saeed bin Suroor 2-9-0 K McEvoy 25/1: 4: b c Darshaan - Nuriva (Woodman) Slow   **1½** **82**
away, styd on fnl 1f, nrst fin on debut: longer priced s/mate of wnr: Apr foal, half-brother to 7f wnr State
Dilemma: dam a smart 5/6f performer, sire a top-class mid-dist wnr: eff at 7f on fast grnd, 1m will suit: improve.
MUTAMAASEK [11]2-9-0 W Supple 20/1: 5: b c Swain - Tamgeed (Woodman) Mid-div, kept on fnl 1f   **2**   **77**
on debut: Mar foal, brother to a 7f juv scorer: sire a top-class mid-dist performer: relish 1m+.
ELTIZAAM [9]2-9-0 N Pollard 33/1: 6: b c Bahri - Saffaanh (Shareef Dancer) Slowly away, nvr   **hd** **76**
nr to chall on debut: Apr foal, brother to high-class miler Harayir: dam a mid-dist scorer, sire a top-class
miler: with E Dunlop & sure to learn from this.
SAND REPEAL [6]2-9-0 B Reilly(3) 100/1: 7: Chsd ldrs, ev ch till wknd fnl 1f on debut.   **3**   **68**
3280 **REBEL REBEL** 8 [4]2-9-0 W Ryan 28/1: 08: Held up, nvr nr ldrs.   **1¼** **65**
FU MANCHU [7]2-9-0 T P Queally 20/1: 9: Held up, nvr a factor on debut.   **hd** **64**
FURL AWAY [3]2-9-0 J Quinn 100/1: 0: 10th: Keen & chsd ldrs 5f, wknd on racecourse bow.   **½**   **62**
3160 **LITTLE INDY** 13 [1]2-9-0 I Mongan 100/1: 00: 11th: Led till 2f out, wknd.   **3**   **54**
ONESHOTTWOLIONS [10]2-9-0 M Tebbutt 33/1: 0: 12th: Slowly away, al bhd & fin last on debut.   **nk** **53**
12 Ran Time 1m 28.22 (4.32) Owned: Godolphin Trained: Newmarket

---

3471

3.10 Rectangle Group Classified Stakes 3yo 0-70 (E)
£4105 £1263 £632 **1m2f** **Good/Firm 32** -20 Slow Centre

3201* **DOCTORED** 11 [8] P D Evans 3-9-1 bl (71) K Fallon 3/1 JT FAV: 1101111: Held up, hdwy to chall dist, styd on well to lead cl-home despite drifting right, drvn out: well bckd: 6th success of this term, 3 from 3 for current trainer: eff at 7/10f on firm, gd/soft & fibresand: handles a sharp/ undul or stiff/gall trk: eff in blnks/cheek pieces: thriving & game here: see 3201 & 1081.   76

3084 **HATCH A PLAN** 16 [7] R M Beckett 3-9-2 (72) J Quinn 9/2: 0-0U0122: Held up, prog when short of room dist, switched & led ins fnl 1f, caught cl-home: well clr rem: in fine form, see 3084 & 2800.   hd 76

3309 **MAGIC AMIGO** 6 [1] J R Jenkins 3-9-5 (75) L Dettori 7/1: 1023043: Nvr far away, led dist till ins fnl 1f when hmpd, no ch after: top-weight, qck reapp: prob just held but wld have fin closer, gd run.   4 72

2147 **FORT CHURCHILL** 53 [2] M H Tompkins 3-9-2 (72) M Hills 11/2: 00-534: Led till 3f out, no extra fnl 1f: op 7/1, 8 wk abs: rtn to 12f will suit judged on this, see 2147.   1½ 67

3384 **BAILAORA** 3 [2]3-9-2 bl (72) K McEvoy 25/1: 2-606005: Front rank, led 3f out till dist, wknd: qck reapp.   1½ 65

2855 **HAYDN** 25 [5]3-9-0 (65) I Mongan 25/1: 0-500506: Keen in rear, btn 2f out: new stable (prev with P Chapple-Hyam): big step up from sprint dists here: see 532 (AW).   6 54

1398 **BELISCO** 89 [6]3-9-2 (73) W Supple 14/1: 50-07: b c Royal Academy - A Mean Fit (Fit To Fight) Chsd ldrs, btn 1.5f out: 3 month abs: twice rcd juv, mdn 5th on debut (rtd 72): $85,000 half-brother to a 1m wnr in the US: sire a top-class sprinter/miler: with Mrs A Perrett.   3½ 52

2828 **MUNAAWASHAT** 26 [4]3-8-12 (71) Darren Williams 3/1 JT FAV: 261-3128: Keen & trkd ldrs, btn dist: well bckd on first start for new stable (prev with M Johnston): lngr trip: btr 2828 & 2474 (1m).   1¾ 44

8 Ran Time 2m 07.11 (5.21) Owned: Treble Chance Partnership Trained: Abergavenny

---

3472

3.45 Atos Origins Handicap Stakes 3yo 0-90 (C)
£9205 £3491 £1746 **1m str** **Good/Firm 32** -07 Slow Far Side [93]

2106* **TABLEAU** 55 [5] B W Hills 3-9-5 (84) M Hills 10/1: 5-311: Made all, held on well cl-home, drvn out: 8 wk abs: fine h'cap bow, eff at 7f/1m on gd & firm grnd, shld stay 10f: likes a stiff/gall trk, forcing tactics & runs well fresh: can continue to improve, see 2106 (mdn).   90

3039* **MOMTIC** 18 [6] W Jarvis 3-9-6 (85) L Dettori 5/1: 3304412: Chsd wnr thr'out, edged right fnl 1f, kept on well & only just btn in a v tight fin: tough, consistent & in fine form: see 3039.   shd 91

3059 **ALSHAWAMEQ** 17 [2] J L Dunlop 3-9-7 (86) W Supple 3/1: 15-31053: Held up, prog when hmpd dist, short of room ins fnl 1f, fin well: top-weight & little luck today, may well have won with a clr run: see 2247 (C/D).   ¾ 90

2127 **MACLEAN** 54 [4] Sir Michael Stoute 3-8-12 VIS (77) K Fallon 15/8 FAV: 2-21364D: Held up, prog when hung left dist, did not find as much as expected fnl 1f: went bckd from 11/4 in first time visor, 8 wk abs: fin 4th, subs demoted to 5th: does not look an easy ride, see 1930 & 1462.   ½ 79

2723 **ERMINE GREY** 30 [3] D Haydn Jones 3-8-6 vis (71) Paul Eddery 25/1: 16-00344: Chsd ldrs, hmpd dist, keeping on when short of room again cl-home, fin 5th, subs plcd 4th: little luck today & shld be gvn another ch.   hd 73

3283* **HAZEWIND** 8 [1]3-8-0 vis t (65) Hayley Turner(5) 7/2: 0025116: Chsd ldrs, onepcd fnl 1f: btr 3283.   hd 66

6 Ran Time 1m 40.32 (3.12) Owned: Mr K Abdulla Trained: Lambourn

---

3473

4.20 Ballygallon Stud Median Auction Maiden Stakes 2yo (E)
£4193 £1290 £645 **6f str** **Good/Firm 32** -30 Slow Far Side

3122 **LUBECK** 15 [8] D R Loder 2-9-0 T P Queally 7/2: 51: b c Lujain - Milling (In The Wings) Made all, held on well fnl 1f, rdn out: 15,000 gns Jan foal: dam 9f wnr: sire a top-class sprinter: eff over a stiff/gall 6f, shld stay 7f: acts on fast grnd: game effort here.   84

3163 **DISGUISE** 13 [2] B W Hills 2-9-0 K Fallon 4/5 FAV: 52: Chsd wnr thr'out, kept on well fnl 1f, just btn in a close fin: hvly bckd: eff over a stiff/gall 6f on fast, 7f will suit: win a minor trk mdn.   nk 82

SALINJA [3] Mrs A J Perrett 2-9-0 W Supple 7/1: 3: b c Boundary - Lasha (Rahy) Chsd ldrs, kept on under press fnl 1f, just btn in a 3-way fin: gamble from 20/1 on debut: $85,000 Mar foal: half-brother to a wnr in the US: dam won in the US, sire a smart sprinter: eff at 6f on fast grnd, 7f shld suit: will learn from this.   nk 81

MANEKI NEKO [9] M H Tompkins 2-9-0 L Dettori 11/1: 4: b c Rudimentary - Ardbess (Balla Cove) Mid-div, kept on fnl 1f but not pace of front 3 on debut: op 7/1, clr of rem: E15,000 Feb foal: dam unrcd but from a decent family, sire a high-class miler: sure to learn from this & will find easier races.   2½ 74

EASY MOVER [4]2-8-9 J Quinn 25/1: 5: ch f Bluebird - Top Brex (Top Ville) Outpcd, nvr a factor on debut: Feb foal, cost 13,000gns: dam a mid-dist wnr in France, sire a top-class sprinter: with R Guest.   6 51

3323 **BESPOKE** 5 [5]2-9-0 J Mackay 12/1: 56: Slowly away, nvr a factor: qck reapp after 3323.   2½ 49

LOLA SAPOLA [3]2-8-9 W Ryan 25/1: 7: All outpcd on racecourse bow.   2½ 37

MAMBAZO [1]2-9-0 E Ahern 33/1: 8: Slowly away, nvr nr ldrs on debut.   3½ 32

8 Ran Time 1m 14.77 (3.77) Owned: Sheikh Mohammed Trained: Newmarket

---

3474

4.55 Nspcc Family Race Day Rated Stakes Handicap 3yo+ 0-95 (C)
£12203 £4629 £2314 **1m2f** **Good/Firm 32** +04 Fast Centre [108]

1192 **KING OF DREAMS** 101 [1] M Johnston 3-8-9 (89) S Chin 16/1: 42-101: Nvr far away, went on dist, styd on strongly, rdn out: long day, fair time: eff around 10f, shld stay 12f: acts on gd, fast grnd & on a stiff/gall trk: runs v well fresh & suited by racing up with/forcing the pace: back to form here, see 930.   98

3038* **ANNA PALLIDA** 18 [6] P W Harris 3-8-0 (80) W Supple 5/1: 022312: Held up, hdwy to chall dist, not qckn cl-home: another gd run: see 3038.   1¾ 84

3118 **POLAR JEM** 15 [2] G G Margarson 4-9-8 (92) A McCarthy 5/2: 4111163: Sn led & made most till collared dist, no extra cl-home: well bckd: game, tough & useful: see 3118.   ½ 96

3059 **CREDIT** 17 [8] R Hannon 3-8-5 (85) J Quinn 14/1: 331004: Chsd ldrs, onepcd fnl 1f: longer 10f trip.   ¾ 87

2700* **DOUBLE ASPECT** 31 [5]3-8-8 (88) K Fallon 9/4 FAV: 415: Chsd ldrs, onepcd fnl 1f: well bckd on h'cap bow, well clr of rem: shade btr expected after 2700 (mdn).   ½ 89

3083* **BARKING MAD** 16 [4]6-9-0 (84) I Mongan 15/2: 0-643216: Early ldr, remained prom, wknd 2f out: op 10/1: won this race from a 2lb lower mark last term, something clrly amiss here: much btr 3083.   29 40

3118 **ZERO TOLERANCE** 15 [7]4-9-6 (90) E Ahern 6/1: 04-14007: Held up, al well bhd, eased & t.o.:   dist 1

---

saddle reportedly slipped: see 2489.
7 Ran   Time 2m 04.77 (2.87)   Owned: Mr Saeed Buhaleeba   Trained: Middleham

---

3475	**5.25 Richard Waddington & Sainsbury's Handicap Stakes 3yo+ 0-85 (D)**	**[85]**
	£6760 £2080 £1040 **1m6f175y** Good/Firm 32 +04 Fast Centre	

3125   **HIGH ACTION** 15 [5] Ian Williams 4-9-11 t (82) K Fallon   9/4 FAV: 106-0001: Chsd ldrs, led trav   **93**
well 2f out, pushed clr, easily: well bckd, gd time: styd this stiff 15f well & unexposed over staying dists: acts
on fast & firm grnd, likes to run up with/force the pace: well h'capped, follow-up.
3066   **DOVEDON HERO** 17 [6] P J McBride 4-9-1 bl (72) M Hills   8/1: 0204602: Held up, prog 2f out, no   5   **74**
impress fnl 1f: prob stays 15f, met a well h'capped rival here: see 2391.
2239   **SKYES FOLLY** 50 [3] J G Given 4-9-1 (72) K McEvoy   14/1: 515-0003: b g Kris S - Bittersweet Hour   nk   **73**
(Seattle Slew) Chsd ldrs, onepcd fnl 1.5f: 7 wk abs: won a mdn & h'cap for Mrs A Perrett in '03: eff at 12f/2m
on firm, fast & poss polytrack: handles a sharp or gall trk: well h'capped on last year's form & sharper next time.
1 Sep'03 Nott 16.0g/f 80-75 D: 1 Aug'03 Bath 11.7fm 73-(77) D:
2899   **TWOFAN** 23 [2] M Johnston 3-8-8 (80) S Chin   4/1: 22164: Led till 2f out, grad wknd: see 1742.   nk   **80**
3249   **THE RING** 9 [7]4-8-11 (68) L Dettori   3/1: 0230505: Held up, nvr nr ldrs: btr 3032.   8   **58**
3101   **WEET FOR ME** 15 [4]8-9-3 (74) W Supple   11/1: 033//-0026: Front rank, wknd qckly 1.5f out: btr 3101.   9   **54**
3032   **KING FLYER** 18 [1]8-9-6 bl (77) S Whitworth   6/1: 2302007: Held up, btn 2f out.   nk   **56**
7 Ran   Time 3m 09.72(4.22)   Owned: Mr C N Barnes   Trained: Alvechurch

---

WINDSOR   MONDAY 26.07.04   Sharp, Fig 8 Track

Official Going GOOD/FIRM.

3476	**6.15 Cannons Stoke Poges Maiden Stakes 2yo (D)**	
	£5161 £1588 £794 **5f10y rnd** Firm 04 -22 Slow Inside	

2658   **CLOVE** 33 [2] B W Hills 2-8-9 M Hills   4/5 FAV: 41: Cl-up, hdwy to lead over 1f out, styd on   **75**
well, rdn out: hvly bckd: eff at 5f on firm grnd: clrly going the right way, nurs type: see 2658.
  MIDDLE EARTH [3] A M Balding 2-9-0 Martin Dwyer   11/4: 2: ch c Dixieland Band - Lite Twilight   ¾   **77**
(Twilight Agenda) Slow away, sn in tch, eff over 1f out, kept on ins last, nt pace of wnr on debut: Feb first
foal, cost $100,000: dam sprinter: eff at 5f on firm grnd: encouraging start, sharper for this, win sn.
2911   **OUR FUGITIVE** 24 [6] A W Carroll 2-9-0 J Fortune   50/1: 403: Led till over 1f out, kept on: much   nk   **76**
imprvd with forcing tactics & eff at 5f on firm grnd: win a race in this form: see 1466.
3368   **CUMMISKEY** 4 [9] J A Osborne 2-9-0 S Drowne   10/1: 534: In tch, hdwy & short of room sev times   nk   **75**
fnl 2f, not recover: lkd unlucky & interesting for a nurs over 6f: acts on firm: see 3368.
3160   **NINJA STORM** 14 [7]2-9-0 R L Moore   9/1: 45: Dwelt, sn in tch, eff over 1f out, onepace ins last: hd   **74**
eff at 5f on firm: see 3160.
3160   **GREAT BELIEF** 14 [4]2-9-0 T Quinn   12/1: 36: Keen, chsd ldr till 2f out, wknd: btr 3160 (debut).   3   **65**
  REGAL DREAM [1]2-9-0 E Ahern   25/1: 7: b c Namid - Lovely Me (Vision) In tch, wknd over 1f out   5   **50**
on debut: May foal, cost 26,000gns: half-brother to a 5f juv wnr, dam styd 7f.
1780   **WHISTLING ALONG** 71 [8]2-9-0 Dane O'Neill   66/1: 0608: Al bhd: 10 wk abs: see 1466.   5   **35**
2367   **JUST BONNIE** 45 [10]2-9-0 T P Queally   66/1: 69: Al bhd: 6 wk abs.   2   **29**
  EDEN STAR [5]2-8-9 D Holland   50/1: 0: 10th: Al bhd on debut.   2½   **17**
10 Ran   Time 1m 0.29 (1.29)   Owned: Mr K Abdulla   Trained: Lambourn

---

3477	**6.45 Windsor-Racecourse Co Uk Handicap Stakes 3yo+ 0-75 (E)**	**[75]**
	£3621 £1114 £557 **1m2f7y** Firm 04 +09 Fast Inside	

3336* **A ONE** 5 [14] H J Manners 5-9-12 (73) F P Ferris(3)   2/1 FAV: 3111011: Made all, clr over 3f out,   **86**
won unchall, eased down, val 4L+: well bckd: suited by 10f now on firm or hvy, handles fibresand & any trk: loves to
dominate, genuine & thriving this term, looks like even more to come: see 3336.
3184   **EL CHAPARRAL** 12 [3] D K Ivory 4-9-2 (63) Dane O'Neill   12/1: 0600202: Dwelt, hld up, hdwy over 2f   2   **70**
out, chsd wnr over 1f out, kept on: imprvd for step up to 10f & acts on fm grnd: likes Windsor: win a race.
3336   **RECOUNT** 5 [4] J R Best 4-9-7 (65) M Savage(5)   7/1: 0650023: Keen, held up, in tch, kept on late,   nk   **75**
u.r. after line: on a fair mark & will relish a rtn to 12f: see 3336.
3281   **GALLANT BOY** 9 [6] P D Evans 5-9-5 vis t (66) J Fortune   6/1: 5064054: Slow away, held up, plenty   3½   **67**
to do over 2f out, late gains: see 3281.
3056   **OUR DESTINY** 18 [12]6-8-11 (58) R L Moore   14/1: 3104105: In tch, onepace fnl 2f: best 2844.   shd   **58**
2910   **PACIFIC OCEAN** 24 [11]5-8-6 t (53) F Norton   16/1: 3360436: Keen, held up, no extra over 1f out.   ¾   **58**
3173   **COSI FAN TUTTE** 13 [17]6-9-2 vis t (63) D Holland   8/1: 410/-2307: Held up, eff & short of room   3½   **57**
over 2f out, sn no extra: see 2800, 2267.
3206   **LEIGHTON** 11 [9]4-10-0 (75) S Carson   16/1: 3-054028: Cl-up, wknd well over 1f out: chnged stable.   hd   **68**
3295   **RAINBOW WORLD** 7 [8]4-8-10 T p (57) J F Egan   16/1: 0303009: Cl-up, wknd 2f out: btr 2267, 816.   ¾   **49**
4705]   **EFRHINA** 288 [13]4-9-4 (55) S Drowne   25/1: 002-0: 10th: ch f Woodman - Eshq Albahr (Riverman) In   ½   **56**
tch, hmpd bend 6f out, wknd over 3f out: p.u. over hdles 2 months ago: rnr-up on last of 3 '03 Flat starts (mdn):
stays 10f on firm grnd: prev with A Stewart, now with Mrs S Liddiard. 2 Oct'03 Bath 10.2fm 70- D:
  ICARUS DREAM 34 [2]3-8-13 (70) N Chalmers(5)   33/1: 462020: 11th: ch g Intikhab - Nymphs Echo   1   **59**
(Mujtahid) Al bhd: ex Irish, rnr-up in mdns earlier: styd 9f on gd & firm grnd.
3025   **PIQUET** 19 [18]6-7-12 (3oh) (42) J Mackay   33/1: 6000630: 12th: held up, lost tch 3f out, late gains.   hd   **33**
3256   **VICTORY VENTURE** 10 [7]4-9-8 (69) T Quinn   33/1: 0030-000: 13th: b g Victory Note - Shirley   6   **47**
Venture (Be My Chief) In tch, wknd over 2f out: '03 mdn wnr: stays 12f on fast & gd grnd.
1 Aug'03 Catt 12.0g/f 71- D: 2 Aug'03 Ayr 8gd 70- D:
3257   **NABTAT SAIF** 10 [15]3-8-6 (63) P Dobbs   33/1: 0-040000: 14th: Al bhd: see 3257, 2617.   1¼   **39**
2979   **CELTIC STAR** 21 [5]6-8-11 BL (58) J Murtagh   25/1: 6//116-060: 15th: Chsd wnr till hung left 4f   ½   **33**
out, no extra: tried blnks: see 2601.
3199   **OUTSIDE INVESTOR** 12 [10]4-10-0 (75) T P Queally   33/1: 02232-00: 16th: Handy, eff to chase wnr 4f   10   **35**
out till 3f out, wknd qckly: see 3199.

3373 **EMBER DAYS 4** [1]5-9-6 p (67) E Ahern 12/1: 2313240: 17th: Handy, wknd & lost action over 1f out. *8* **15**

17 Ran Time 2m 05.45 (u0.55) Owned: Mr H J Manners Trained: Swindon

3478

7.15 Tri Hospitality Consulting Maiden Stakes 2yo (D)
£5369 £1652 £826 **6f rnd** **Firm 04** **-40 Slow** Inside

954 **PERSIAN ROCK 121** [9] J A Osborne 2-9-0 D Holland 7/4 FAV: 21: With ldr, hdwy to lead over 1f out, styd on, drvn out: well bckd, 4 month abs: eff at 5/6f on firm & gd grnd: goes well fresh: prob more to come. **90**

2089 **COOL PANIC 57** [6] M L W Bell 2-9-0 J Murtagh 8/1: 02: b c Brave Act - Geht Schnell (Fairy King) Handy, hdwy to chase wnr fnl 1f, just held: 2 month abs: Mar foal, cost E26,000: half-brothers to wnrs over 6f/1m: eff at 6f on firm grnd: win a race with a repeat of this. *½* **88**

3005 **CAPE QUEST 20** [13] R Hannon 2-9-0 P Dobbs 5/1: 03: b c Piccolo - Belle Vue (Petong) Made most till over 1f out, onepace: nicely bckd: Mar foal, cost 28,000gns: half-brother to a 7f wnr: dam 6f juv scorer: eff at 6f on firm grnd: shld win a race. *1¼* **84**

ENFORCER [2] W R Muir 2-9-0 S Drowne 33/1: 4: b c Efisio - Tarneem (Zilzal) Dwelt, bhd, some late gains, nrst fin on debut: Apr foal, cost 12,000gns: full brother to a 5f juv wnr: dam 1m wnr: encouraging start, looks sure to apprec 7f & rate higher. *½* **82**

POLLITO [8]2-9-0 J Fortune 20/1: 5: Handy, onepace over 1f out on debut. *shd* **81**

RED RUDY [4]2-9-0 K Fallon 5/1: 6: In tch, eff 2f out, onepace: bckd. *½* **76**

LADY LONDRA [11]2-8-9 M Howard(5) 66/1: 7: Dwelt, in tch, some late gains on debut. *nk* **73**

3111 **RUM CREEK 16** [5]2-9-0 J F Egan 50/1: 08: In tch, wknd 2f out. *2* **72**

2578 **DARKO KARIM 37** [10]2-9-0 T P Queally 4/1: 409: Bhd, rdn halfway, no impress: try headgear? *hd* **71**

3020 **COOMBE CENTENARY 19** [12]2-8-9 Dane O'Neill 100/1: 00: 10th: Dwelt, al bhd. *3½* **56**

SONNTAG BLUE [1]2-9-0 T Quinn 33/1: 0: 11th: Al bhd. *3½* **51**

PADDYS TERN [7]2-9-0 D Corby(3) 100/1: 0: 12th: Al bhd. *8* **27**

MOON BIRD [3]2-8-9 E Ahern 16/1: 0: 13th: Al bhd. *½* **20**

13 Ran Time 1m 12.93 (2.63) Owned: Waney Racing Group Inc & Karmaa Racing Trained: Upper Lambourn

3479

7.45 Totesport Handicap Stakes Fillies 3yo+ 0-80 (D) **[85]**
£7202 £2216 £1108 **6f rnd** **Firm 04** **-15 Slow** Inside

2722 **WUNDERBRA 31** [8] M L W Bell 3-7-12 T (55) J Mackay 20/1: 3451: Cl-up, led over 1f out, styd on, rdn out: first win: imprvd back on turf at 6f on fm in first time t-strap. **66**

2372 **BALLINGER EXPRESS 45** [9] A M Balding 4-8-10 bl (62) Martin Dwyer 16/1: 0532002: Set pace till over 1f out, onepace: btr run after 6 wk abs: acts on firm & polytrack: see 1822, 1022. *1¼* **68**

3033 **MISS GEORGE 19** [6] D K Ivory 6-10-0 (80) D Holland 11/2: 0306003: Slow away, held up, hdwy over 2f out, onepace: see 1383, 879. *nk* **85**

2232 **MADDIES A JEM 51** [4] J R Jenkins 4-9-7 (73) K Fallon 7/1: 0-113564: In tch, eff dist, onepace. *nk* **77**

3218 **DARLA 11** [12]3-8-11 (68) J Murtagh 16/1: 42306-05: Keen in tch, onepace over 1f out: stays 6f. *¾* **70**

3416 **STOKESIES WISH 3** [7]4-8-12 (64) K McEvoy 6/1: 0205406: In tch, no impress dist: well bckd. *1* **63**

2742 **ZWADI 30** [11]3-9-0 (71) Dane O'Neill 14/1: 324-4057: Held up, late gains, no dngr: see 2072. *hd* **69**

3307 **UNDER MY SPELL 7** [5]3-9-5 (76) S Donohoe(7) 16/1: 2251008: In tch, wknd over 1f out: see 2398. *¾* **72**

2981 **HAGLEY PARK 21** [13]5-7-12 (5oh) (45) F P Ferris(3) 25/1: 0310009: In tch, wknd over 1f out: now with Miss K George: best 1562 (fibresand, banded). *¾* **44**

2232 **OFFICERS PINK 51** [3]4-9-2 t (68) N De Souza(5) 33/1: 4135-000: 10th: Al bhd: see 1878. *½* **60**

3293 **BOHOLA FLYER 7** [2]3-9-7 (78) R L Moore 4/1 FAV: 4114520: 11th: Nvr a factor: hvly bckd: btr 3293. *shd* **70**

3109* **KALLISTAS PRIDE 16** [10]4-8-9 (61) N Pollard 10/1: 00-02010: 12th: Dwelt, in tch, wknd dist. *shd* **52**

2648 **I WISH 34** [14]6-8-5 (57) L Keniry(1) 11/2: 0415530: 13th: In tch, wknd 2f out: see 1806 (clmr). *nk* **47**

13 Ran Time 1m 11.46 (1.16) Owned: Fitzroy Thoroughbreds Trained: Newmarket

3480

8.15 Come Racing Next Monday-Ladies Night Maiden Stakes 3yo (D)
£4264 £1312 £656 **1m67y rnd** **Firm 04** **-01 Slow** Inside

2419 **NOUVEAU RICHE 43** [12] H Morrison 3-8-9 R L Moore 11/4: 231: Front rank, led after 2f till collared dist, regained lead ins fnl 1f, styd on well, rdn out: nicely bckd: 6 wk abs: eff around 1m on gd & firm grnd, handles a gall or sharpish trk, runs well fresh: op to further improvement, see 2419 & 2224. **79**

3237 **SEA NYMPH 10** [18] Sir Michael Stoute 3-8-9 K Fallon 5/2 FAV: 52: Nvr far away, imprvd to lead dist, collared cl-home: imprvd eff & clrly benefited for recent debut: eff over a sharpish 1m on firm grnd. *¾* **75**

3282 **VIOLET PARK 9** [9] B J Meehan 3-8-9 J Fortune 11/4: 223: Keen & trkd ldrs, eff & hung left 1.5f out, styd on cl-home: did not look an easy ride today, easier grnd may suit: stays a sharp 1m, see 3282. *2* **71**

2974 **ALENUSHKA 21** [7] H Candy 3-8-9 Dane O'Neill 14/1: 064: b f Soviet Star - National Portrait (Royal Academy) Prom, onepcd fnl 1f: 47,000gns first foal: dam styd 1m in France, sire a high-class miler: eff over a sharpish 1m on firm grnd, shld stay further. *½* **70**

3195 **FISBY 12** [2]3-9-0 J F Egan 66/1: 0-55: Held up, hdwy wide 2f out, chsd ldrs fnl 1f & sn onepcd: now qual for h'caps & likely to be much btr suited by 10f+ in that sphere: with S Kirk, see 3195. *2½* **70**

2352 **RICHIE BOY 46** [6]3-9-0 M Henry 40/1: 0-06: b c Dr Fong - Alathezal (Zilzal) Chsd ldrs, outpcd 3f out, styd on again late: 7 wk abs: unplcd sole juv start (mdn): cost 16,000gns. *nk* **69**

2953 **CEYLON ROUND 22** [17]3-8-9 D Corby(3) 66/1: 07: Trkd ldrs, outpcd 2f out: see 2953. *¾* **62**

3085 **TARTIRUGA 17** [8]3-9-0 (45) F Norton 66/1: 00-0008: Led 2f, front rank till wknd dist. *nk* **66$**

2692 **GRAND RAPIDE 32** [11]3-8-9 K McEvoy 33/1: 609: ch f Grand Lodge - Vax Rapide (Sharpo) Nvr btr than mid-div: dam a 5f juv wnr, sire a high-class miler: with J Spearing. *2½* **56**

CONSTRUCTOR [3]3-9-0 T P Queally 50/1: 0: 10th: Chsd ldrs 6f, wknd on debut. *¾* **59**

2834 **MONASH GIRL 27** [14]3-8-9 (30) N Chalmers(5) 66/1: 00-60: 11th: Slowly away, nvr nr ldrs. *½* **53$**

2885 **GO GARUDA 25** [4]3-9-0 T Quinn 7/1: 30: 12th: Al bhd: btr 2885. *1¼* **55**

2974 **MEDICA BOBA 21** [5]3-8-9 S Drowne 50/1: 000: 13th: Held up, nvr a factor: stablemate of wnr. *¾* **48**

3186 **Anna Gayle 12** [13]3-8-9 S Carson 50/1:0 2291 **Crimson Star 48** [15]3-8-9 E Ahern 66/1:0

5022} **Ballet Ruse 262** [10]3-8-9 J Mackay 33/1:0 1912 **Sylvaticus 65** [1]3-9-0 P Dobbs 66/1:0

17 Ran Time 1m 43.47 (0.47) Owned: Mr Nicholas Cooper Trained: East Ilsley

3481   8.45 Veritas Handicap Stakes 3yo+ 0-70 (E)   [67]
£3660 £1126 £563   1m3f135y   Firm 04   +08 Fast   Inside

3164* **PONT NEUF** 14 [8] P D Evans 4-9-7 t (60) S Donohoe(7) 11/2: 0042511: Held up, gd hdwy to lead ent   **68**
fn 1f, styd on strongly, rdn clr: gd time: eff at 9/12f on firm & gd/soft grnd: improving, see 3164 (C/D, seller).
3398 **MILK AND SULTANA** 3 [2] G A Ham 4-9-0 (53) E Ahern 20/1: 0600202: Mid-div, hdwy to lead 2f out,   2   **57**
collared ent fnl 1f, kept on but not pace of wnr: qck reapp: acts on gd, firm grnd & fibresand: see 3145.
3295 **STOLEN SONG** 7 [12] M J Ryan 4-9-2 (55) S Whitworth 14/1: 4160063: Held up, prog wide 3f out,   nk   **59**
took 3rd cl-home, nrst fin: rtn to 14f/2m will suit: see 491 (2m, AW).
2836* **ABSINTHER** 27 [16] M R Bosley 7-8-11 (50) G Baker 7/1: 000-0214: Held up, hdwy wide 3f out, nrst fin.   1¼   **52**
3026 **ANYHOW** 19 [9]7-10-0 (67) J Murtagh 10/1: 1532105: Mid-div, went after ldrs 2f out, no impress   4   **63**
fnl 1f under top-weight: btr 2651 (13f).
2979 **TRAVELLERS TALE** 21 [10]5-9-6 (59) S Drowne 25/1: 0600606: Rear, eff 2f out, btn fnl 1f.   2½   **51**
196 **SMOOTHIE** 224 [1]6-9-10 (63) R L Moore 14/1: 166104-7: Trkd ldrs 10f, wknd: recent nov h'cap   shd   **55**
hdle plcd (rtd 60h): see 6 (AW).
2875 **TASNEEF** 25 [14]5-9-4 b (57) T P Queally 14/1: 140-0668: Keen & sn led, clr halfway, hdd 2f out, wknd.   ¾   **48**
2875 **BAKIRI** 25 [5]6-9-7 (60) J F Egan 18/1: 5232409: Chsd ldrs, hmpd 2f out, no ch after: btr 2465.   1   **49**
3367 **DUCS DREAM** 4 [15]6-9-1 (54) D Holland 5/1: 0010050: 10th: Prom, btn 2f out: qck reapp.   ½   **42**
3295 **SIR HAYDN** 7 [6]4-9-11 vis (64) K Fallon 9/2 FAV: 6060530: 11th: Held up, nvr dngrs: btr 3295.   1¼   **50**
3161 **PETITE COLLEEN** 14 [4]3-8-11 p (62) F Norton 14/1: 35-04060: 12th: Nvr btr than mid-div.   3½   **43**
2788 **MAXIMINUS** 29 [7]4-9-2 (55) L Keniry(3) 12/1: 0/00-4060: 13th: Mid-div, btn after halfway.   1¾   **33**
2788 **Frangipani** 29 [11]3-9-0 T(65) T Quinn 20/1:0   4946}   **Veneziana** 270 [3]3-8-12 (63) N De Souza(5) 25/1:0
15 Ran   Time 2m 256.83(u0.47)   Owned Mrs S J Lawrence   Trained: Abergavenny

Official Going Standard

3482   2.45 At The Races Committed To Racing Claiming Stakes 3yo+ (F)
£3073 £878 £439   6f aw rnd   Going 41   +02 Fast   Inside

3137 **BRANSTON TIGER** 15 [10] J G Given 5-9-4 bl (62) S Sanders 4/1 FAV: 0065001: Mid-div wide, hdwy to   **66a**
lead dist, styd on for press: clmd for 8,000: suited by 6/7f on firm, soft & fibresand, any trk: back in blnks.
3129 **TRAVELLING TIMES** 16 [11] J S Wainwright 5-9-0 vis (40) D Allan 50/1: 5600402: Sn prom, drvn &   1   **58a$**
chall dist, not pace of wnr fnl 100yds: inconsistent but capable when in the mood as in 94 (C/D h'cap).
3180 **ON THE TRAIL** 13 [12] D W Chapman 7-9-0 (56) A Culhane 9/2: 1213433: Mid-div wide, rdn to chall   1   **55a**
dist, no extra: see 1443 (C/D seller, made all).
3000 **MALLIA** 20 [9] T D Barron 11-8-8 (46) P Makin(5) 5/1: 6-416324: Dwelt, rdn mid-div, kept on onepace.   nk   **48a**
3156 **BOND SHAKIRA** 14 [5]3-8-4 (49) F Norton 20/1: 3040045: Led dist, no extra: see 2326.   1¾   **44a**
3325 **WILSON BLUEBOTTLE** 6 [13]5-8-12 bl (48) Dale Gibson 20/1: 2200006: Rear, nrst fin: needs 7f+.   ¾   **45a**
2971 **CORNWALLIS** 21 [8]3-8-9 (57) Hayley Turner(5) 11/2: 06-01207: Rdn chasing ldrs, btn dist: clmd.   nk   **46a**
3104 **SPY MASTER** 16 [2]6-8-8 t p (31) D Tudhope(5) 66/1: 5065008: Rear, eff halfway, no impress: see 637.   3½   **29a**
487 **HIGH ESTEEM** 181 [4]8-8-12 VIS T (53) V Slattery 33/1: 0000-409: Cl-up, wknd over 1f out: visor & t-strap.   ½   **31a**
3213 **ITS ECCO BOY** 11 [6]6-8-12 (55) R Winston 9/1: 0000000: 10th: Mid-div, no impress from halfway.   shd   **31a**
3301 **CONFUZED** 7 [7]4-8-12 e (43) S Whitworth 20/1: 6000040: 11th: Slow away & al rear: btr 3301.   ½   **29a**
2715 **PEDRO JACK** 31 [3]7-9-8 (70) P Mulrennan(5) 8/1: 0100030: 12th: Dwelt, al bhd: btr 2715.   ½   **37a**
3333 **SECOND MINISTER** 5 [1]5-9-12 bl (55) L Keniry(3) 25/1: 3060000: 13th: Dwelt, al bhd: qck reapp.   2½   **33a**
13 Ran   Time 1m 15.64 (2.34)   Owned: Mr J David Abell   Trained: Gainsborough

3483   3.15 At The Races From 9am Nursery Handicap Stakes 2yo (E)   [92]
£3819 £1175 £588   7f aw rnd   Going 41   -05 Slow   Inside

3157 **CAITLIN** 14 [8] B Smart 2-8-1 (65) F Norton 14/1: 6241: Chsd ldrs trav well, drvn to lead line,   **72a**
all out: first win on h'cap bow: eff at 6f, imprvd for step up to 7f & shld stay 1m+: acts on fibresand: prog.
2995* **PRIZE FIGHTER** 20 [6] P W Chapple Hyam 2-9-7 (85) A McCarthy 2/5 FAV: 212: Trkd ldrs & led 2f   hd   **91a**
out, sn pressed & hung left, drvn & hdd line: v hvly bckd on h'cap bow under topweight: win similar.
2989 **SNOOKERED AGAIN** 20 [4] M W Easterby 2-8-10 (74) P Mulrennan(5) 14/1: 5103: Dwelt, rdn rear, styd   2   **76a**
on for press fnl 2f, nrst fin: styd longer 7f trip, 1m shld suit: see 2336 (6f).
2802* **PAULINES PRINCE** 28 [5] R Hollinshead 2-8-8 (72) D Sweeney 9/1: 614: Keen, in tch, onepace.   ¾   **73a**
2995 **CHUTNEY MARY** 20 [2]2-8-8 (72) S Sanders 8/1: 06225: Led till 2f out, no extra when sltly hmpd dist.   nk   **72a**
3297 **AUNTY EURO** 7 [7]2-8-6 (70) J Carroll 66/1: 433206: Prom, btn over 1f out: just btr 2382 (6f).   3½   **63a**
2213 **UNLIMITED** 52 [9]2-9-1 (79) A Culhane 20/1: 21257: Outpcd & nvr a factor, 8 wk abs: much btr 2213.   9   **56a**
2612 **INDIBRAUN** 35 [3]2-9-4 (82) G Faulkner 12/1: 51448: Dwelt, mid-div till over 2f out: btr 2039 & 1874.   nk   **58a**
2952 **DUSTY DANE** 22 [1]2-8-8 (72) P Makin(5) 16/1: 56539: Mid-div, struggling from halfway: btr 2952 (gd).   2½   **43a**
2563 **DISHDASHA** 37 [10]2-7-12 (5oh) (62) J Bramhill 66/1: 0030: 10th: Mid-div, bhd fnl 3f: h'cap/AW   12   **12a**
bow: new yard: btr 2563 (seller, gd).
10 Ran   Time 1m 29.81 (3.21)   Owned: EKOS Pinnacle Partnership   Trained: Thirsk

3484   3.45 European Breeders Fund Maiden Stakes 2yo (D)
£4160 £1280 £640   5f aw str   Going 41   -09 Slow   Stands Side

2472 **SAFSOOF** 41 [2] Saeed bin Suroor 2-9-0 L Dettori 1/10 FAV: 201: Made all & readily pulled clr   **90a+**
over 1f out, any amount in hand: 6 wk abs, AW bow: eff at 5f, 6f will suit: acts on gd grnd & fibresand, easy trks:
goes well fresh: found this straightforward, rate higher in stronger company: see 2472 & 2171.
3157 **SISTER GEE** 14 [6] R Hollinshead 2-8-9 J Bramhill 11/1: 432: Trkd front pair, chsd wnr from   8   **61a**

halfway, nvr any impression, just held on for 2nd: acts on fibresand: h'cap company could suit: see 3157 & 2492.
GAME LAD 0 [1] T D Easterby 2-9-0   D Allan 12/1: 3: b c Mind Games - Catch Me (Rudimentary)   shd   66a
Dwelt, rdn chasing ldrs, kept on late, just failed to snatch 2nd: op 14/1: Apr foal, half-brother to a plcd 10f 3yo
mdn, dam a 7f juv wnr: looks sure to apprec 6f+, prob handles fibresand.
2847 SERENE PEARL 26 [3] G M Moore 2-8-9 t T Eaves(3) 40/1: 00664: Cl-up till halfway, fdd: see 2442.   1½   56a
3355 HOMME DANGEREUX 4 [7]2-9-0 N De Souza(5) 12/1: 305: Slow away & sn well bhd, mod late gains.   3   52a
ALL A DREAM 0 [5]2-8-9 S Sanders 16/1: 6: br f Desert Story - Alioli (Nishapour) Dwelt, in tch   hd   46a
till halfway: Jan foal, sister to a plcd 7f juv performer, dam a modest performer btwn 7/12f.
6 Ran   Time 59.81 (2.51)   Owned: Godolphin   Trained: Newmarket

---

3485   4.15 Sky 415 Ntl 908 Telewest 534 Handicap Stakes 3yo+ 0-75 (E)   [70]
£3721 £1145 £573   6f aw rnd   Going 41   +07 Fast   Inside

3424 TALLY 2 [5] M J Polglase 4-9-3 (59) L Fletcher(3) 10/1: 2443001: Al handy & led over 1f out, hung   70a
left but styd on strongly, drvn out: gd time: qck reapp: suited by 6f on fast, soft & both AWs, prob any trk: tough.
2928 HEADLAND 23 [4] D W Chapman 6-8-9 bl e (51) A Culhane 16/1: 3030622: Led till over 1f out, onepace   1½   56a
3155 TSARBUCK 14 [1] R M H Cowell 3-8-12 VIS (59) G Faulkner 12/1: 1525233: Trkd ldrs, drvn & onepace   ½   62a
from dist: first time visor, gd run: see 3092 & 1842 (banded, 7f).
3408* JONNY EBENEEZER 3 [2] D Flood 5-9-10 (6ex)bl (66) L Dettori 10/11 FAV: 1022114: Dwelt, sn   1¾   64a
mid-div, rdn & onepace fnl 2f: well bckd under a 6lb pen, qck reapp: btr 3408 (firm).
2999 IRUSAN 20 [6]4-9-5 (61) P Hanagan 33/1: 600465: Rear, late prog for press, no threat: see 2722.   2   53a
3095* EXTRA COVER 17 [7]3-10-0 bl (75) D Sweeney 7/2: 5-222316: Slow away & rear, carried head high &   1   64a
little prog fnl 3f: btr 3095 (mdn).
3155 ST IVIAN 14 [8]4-9-8 vis (64) R Fitzpatrick 33/1: 0000007: Sn prom, btn 2f out: btr 864 & 245.   ¾   51a
2936 COMMANDER BOND 23 [9]3-9-10 (71) F Lynch 10/1: 04-00108: Chsd ldrs, btn over 1f out: btr 2723.   1½   53a
3095 LORD ARTHUR 17 [3]3-8-9 (56) Dale Gibson 33/1: 00-049: Cl-up, btn 2f out: btr 3095 (mdn).   1   35a
9 Ran   Time 1m 15.34 (2.04)   Owned: General Sir Geoffrey Howlett   Trained: Newark

---

3486   4.45 At The Races Dedicated Racing Channel Handicap Stakes 3yo+ 35-55 (F)   [55]
£3094 £884 £442   1m4f aw   Going 41   -03 Slow   Inside

3370 ROLEX FREE 4 [13] D Flood 6-9-12 vis (53) L Dettori 11/2: 0-060031: Rdn to lead after 1f from   62a
wide draw, hdd 3f out drvn & led again over 1f out, gamely prevailed under an outstanding ride to land a gamble: op
8/1: eff around 12f, tried 2m: acts on fibresand: eff in visor, has tried cheek pieces, blnks & t-strap: see 2973.
2844 ANTONY EBENEEZER 26 [11] C R Dore 5-8-8 (35) Hayley Turner(5) 11/2: 0015002: Keen, in tch, rdn &   1   42a
hdwy to chsd wnr 1f out, not pace of wnr ins last: recent improv rnr (unplcd, h'cap hdle): gd run: see 867.
2836 SALUT SAINT CLOUD 27 [1] G L Moore 9-9-0 (53) S Whitworth 6/1: 5-605133: Mid-div, outpcd 4f out,   shd   60a
styd on for press from over 1f out, not reach wnr: acts on firm, gd & fibresand: see 2836, 2548.
2340 ELA RE 46 [10] C R Dore 5-9-2 (43) J Bramhill 5/1: 06/0-4044: Mid-div, smooth hdwy to lead 3f   1   49a
out, hdd over 1f out & no extra: well clr of rem: op 13/2: jumps fit (unplcd, h'cap hdle): rtd 99h): eff around
12f on fibresand, drop to 10f may not go amiss: see 421.
3154 KENTUCKY BULLET 14 [4]8-8-10 P (37) L Keniry(3) 8/1: 0636055: Led 1f, trkd ldrs, btn 2f out: cheekpieces.11   28a
3154 WESTERN COMMAND 14 [8]8-8-8 (10oh)p (25) Joanna Badger 50/1: 0526006: Mid-div, no impress fnl 3f.¾   25a
3294 PADDY BOY 7 [14]3-8-9 (48) D Sweeney 20/1: 30007: Dwelt, trkd ldrs, rdn & no extra fnl 2f: see 526.   shd   38a
3105 DISABUSE 16 [5]4-10-0 bl (55) P Mulrennan(5) 9/2 FAV: 3445458: Trkd ldrs, lost pl from 4f out: btr 3105.   6   38a
3354 CEZZARO 5 [12]6-8-8 (5oh)T (30) B Swarbrick(5) 20/1: 6022009: Bhd, only mod hdwy: qck reapp, t-strap.   5   12a
3154 SPANISH STAR 14 [6]7-9-2 (43) Sarah Sayer(7) 20/1: 1330000: 10th: Rear & little prog: sells/clmrs ideal.   shd   20a
2008 Seraph 61 [3]4-8-13 p(40) S Sanders 12/1:0   3164 White Park Bay 14 [7]4-9-13 (54) L Treadwell(5) 12/1:0
3154 Banners Flying 14 [9]4-9-9 (50) A Culhane 33/1:0   2032 Legion Of Honour 60 [2]5-9-9 (50) A Quinn(5) 66/1:0
14 Ran   Time 2m 39.54 (5.24)   Owned: Mrs Ruth M Serrell   Trained: Hungerford

---

3487   5.15 At The Races On Ntl Ireland Handicap Stakes 3yo+ 35-55 (F)   [55]
£3178 £908 £454   1m aw rnd   Going 41   -04 Slow   Inside

3395 ARRAN 8 [8] V Smith 4-9-11 (52) S Sanders 1/1 FAV: 00-03021: Mid-div trav well, hdwy over 2f   62a
out, rdn to lead ins last, drvn out: qck reapp & confirmed improvement of 3395: eff at 1m on fast & fibresand.
597 MISS GLORY BE 167 [5] E R Oertel 6-9-8 p (49) A Nicholls 14/1: 006-0352: Mid-div, hdwy & ch over   1½   55a
1f out, not pace of wnr ins last: modest AW bow, gd run: well h'capped: see 564.
3182 REVERSIONARY 13 [2] M W Easterby 3-9-0 bl (49) Dale Gibson 10/1: 5000103: Trkd ldrs & rdn/ch 2f   2½   50a
out, hung left under press & no extra ins last: encouraging AW bow: acts on gd & fibresand: see 2932 (seller).
3159 BULAWAYO 14 [4] Andrew Reid 7-9-11 bl (52) B Swarbrick(5) 10/1: 0642104: Led/dsptd lead, went on   nk   52a
halfway till ins last, no extra: see 2996 (C/D, sell h'cap).
2149 DESERT FURY 54 [1]7-9-2 (43) P Mulrennan(5) 9/1: 000-0065: Rear inner, late gains, nvr landed   1½   40a+
blow: 8 wk abs: caught the eye late on, well h'capped for similar: see 1750.
2402 ROCINANTE 44 [14]4-9-10 (51) R Winston 16/1: 3011006: Chsd ldrs till 3f out, mod late rally: btr 1661.   ¾   47a
1379 QOBTAAN 91 [3]5-9-12 (53) G Baker 25/1: 6110007: Chsd ldrs 3f out, sn rdn & no extra: 3 mth abs.   1½   46a
2997 PETROLINA 20 [11]3-9-6 (55) L Fletcher(3) 14/1: 0048: Prom, rdn & btn 2f out: h'cap bow: btr 2997.   ¾   43a
2440 DUBONAI 42 [16]4-9-12 (53) J Carroll 14/1: 30-00309: Held up, eff wide halfway, no prog 2f out: gelded.   2   41a
3159 ROCKY REPPIN 14 [13]4-9-4 (45) K Pierrepont(7) 16/1: 0000340: 10th: Rear, rdn & little prog: btr 3159.   hd   32a
3109 SECAM 2 [10]5-9-3 bl (44) A Culhane 33/1: 21-03000: 11th: Held up, wide, no ch fnl 3f: btr 1028 (C/D).   1½   28a
3159 SUPER DOMINION 14 [12]3-9-6 p (47) D Sweeney 20/1: 5140100: 12th: Sn rdn & al towards rear: btr 2725. 4   23a
3430} WARREN PLACE 354 [6]4-9-2 (43) S Righton 50/1: 000000-0: 13th: ch g Presidium - Coney Hills   1¾   16a
(Beverley Boy) Led till halfway, sn btn: long abs: AW bow: unplcd '03 (rtd 54, prob flattered, auct mdn): clmr &
dual mdn rnr-up '02: best efforts at 5f on fast & gd/soft grnd: eff with/without blnks, tried visor: prev with N
Bycroft. 2 Aug'02 Pont 5g/f 70- D: 2 Jul'02 Beve 5g/s 69- F: 2 Jul'02 Beve 5g/s 73- D:
2893 INMOM 24 [12]3-9-6 T (55) J Bramhill 20/1: 0-304660: 14th: Mid-div early, lost pl bef halfway: 2   24a
declared t-strap appeared to be omitted bef start: btr 2338 (C/D).
3362 Jade Star 4 [15]4-9-12 (53) D Fox(5) 12/1:0   2244 Amethyst Rock 51 [7]6-8-13 (40) F Lynch 25/1:0

16 Ran   Time 1m 43.0(3.6)   Owned: The Three Amigos   Trained: Newmarket

YARMOUTH   **MONDAY 26.07.04**   **Lefthand, Flat, Fair Track**

Official Going Good (Good/Firm Places)

3488   **6.00 Mills & Reeve Novice Auction Stakes Fillies 2yo** (E)
£3478 £1070 £535   **5f43y str**   **Good 58**   **-09 Slow**   Stands side

3284 **SMIDDY HILL 9** [2] R Bastiman 2-8-6 R Ffrench 6/4 FAV: 3241451: Made all, went clr ins fnl 2f,   **85**
rdn out: op 2/1: eff at 5f on fast & gd/soft grnd: improved run: see 2056.
  FARTHING 0 [7] G C Bravery 2-8-8 W Supple 1/1: 2: b f Mujadil - Neat Shilling (Bob Back)   3   **77**
Cl-up, kept on ins fnl 1f, al held by wnr: tchd 8/1 on debut: Apr foal, cost 21,000gns: half-sister successful at
6/7f: sire speedy performer as a juv: eff at 5f, will apprec further: fine start, win a race.
2490 **HIGH CHART 40** [4] G G Margarson 2-8-6 C Catlin 3/1: 14403: Prom till dist, no extra: 6 wk abs.   3½   **65**
3266 **EVANESCE 9** [1] M R Channon 2-8-8 S Hitchcott(3) 4/1: 2212004: Bhd, modest late gains: btr 2442 (firm) 3   **58**
2927 **ARIANE STAR 8** [5]2-8-5 P Robinson 8/1: 005: b f Marju - Northgate Raver (Absalom) Cl-up 3f,   ½   **54**
wknd: Mar foal, cost E20,000: half-sister to a number of wnrs abroad: dam unplcd.
1987 **SHERBOURNE 62** [3]2-8-2 Paul Eddery 100/1: 006: b f Tipsy Creek - Margarets First (Puissance)   ½   **50**
Al in rear: Mar foal, cost 1,200gns: sire Gr 3 winning sprinter as a juv: with M G Quinlan.
6 Ran   Time 1m 3.48 (3.38)   Owned: Mr I B Barker   Trained: Wetherby

---

3489   **6.30 Pertwee & Back Ford Drive For Value Maiden Auction Stakes 2yo** (F)
£2961 £846 £423   **7f3y str**   **Good 58**   **-24 Slow**   Stands side

1727 **ACTIVE ASSET 73** [4] M R Channon 2-8-10 T E Durcan 2/1: 21: Stumbled sn after start, sn in tch,   **85**
ev ch ins fnl 2f, rdn out to lead cl-home: 10 wk abs: eff at 6f, apprec step up to 7f: acts on fast or gd grnd:
likes Yarmouth & goes well fresh: still showed greeness & can improve: see 1727.
  DOUBLE KUDOS 0 [7] J G Given 2-8-10 I Mongan 14/1: 2: gr c Highest Honor - Black Tulip   shd **81+**
(Fabulous Dancer) Slow away, prog after halfway, styd on to lead ins fnl 1f, hdd cl-home: Apr foal, cost E30,000:
half-brother to high-class mid-dist performers: dam smart over mid-dists: eff at 7f, relish 1m+: improve.
2584 **DAISY BUCKET 37** [8] D M Simcock 2-8-2 R Ffrench 25/1: 03: b f Lujain - Masrora (Woodman)   1½   **72**
Handy, styd on to lead 2f out, hdd ins fnl 1f, no extra: Feb first foal, dam plcd at mid-dists: sire Group wng
sprinter as a juv: eff at 7f on gd grnd: left debut eff bhd with promising run & improve with more experience.
  CALL ME MAX 0 [1] E A L Dunlop 2-8-10 W Supple 14/1: 4: b c Vettori - Always Vigilant (Lear   nk   **79**
Fan) Rear, prog 3f out, styd on ins fnl 1f: debut: Mar first foal, cost 20,000gns: dam success at 1m: sire
high-class performer at 1m: eff at 7f, will apprec further: acts on gd grnd: gd start to career & can rate higher.
3063 **CAPTAIN MARGARET 18** [10]2-8-5 T J Quinn 40/1: 05: Slow away, prog after 5f, no impress ins fnl 1f.   ¾   **72$**
2911 **FADAEL 24** [13]2-8-5 Paul Eddery 18/1: 06: Keen in rear, prog & short of room ins fnl 2f, nrst   nk   **71+**
fin under hands & heels: not given hard time & will be seen to better effect over further.
3252 **MUSICAL DAY 10** [12]2-8-6 (1ow) N Callan 15/2: 07: Mid-div, prog when no room bef 1f out, sn onepcd.   1   **70**
2927 **PRIDE OF LONDON 23** [6]2-8-2 D Kinsella 100/1: 08: Led 3f, no extra ins fnl 2f: see 2927.   1¼   **64**
3064 **RINGAROOMA 18** [14]2-8-2 P Robinson 9/4 FAV: 59: Keen mid-div over 5f, sn wknd: bckd: not settle.   3½   **57**
3035 **LIAMELISS 19** [2]2-8-2 M Halford(7) 80/1: 600: 10th: Al in rear.   1¼   **55**
2952 **BE BOP ALOHA 22** [3]2-8-2 J F McDonald(3) 16/1: 06350: 11th: Keen cl-up, led 4f out, hdd 2f out, wknd. 1¾   **51**
  GIBRALTAR BAY 0 [5]2-8-5 C Catlin 40/1: 0: 12th: Al in rear on debut.   shd   **53**
3020 **Marians Maid 19** [11]2-8-2 R Mullen 25/1:0   **Prophets Calling 0** [9]2-8-7 J P Guillambert(3) 100/1:0
14 Ran   Time 1m 28.38 (5.78)   Owned: aAlM Racing Syndicate   Trained: West Ilsley

---

3490   **7.00 Halls Group Handicap Stakes 3yo+ 0-70** (E)   [70]
£3946 £1214 £607   **7f3y str**   **Good 58**   **-06 Slow**   Stands side

1691 **CONCER ETO 75** [9] S C Williams 5-9-13 p (69) W Supple 7/2 FAV: 0-002341: Rcd centre, prog ins fnl   **75**
2f, rdn out to lead cl-home: op 5/1: 11 wk abs: eff at 7/10f & likes fast, acts on gd/soft & both AWs: goes well
fresh & eff with cheek pieces: likes Yarmouth: see 1691 & 932.
3184* **BALERNO 12** [2] R Ingram 5-9-3 (59) N Day 5/1: 3040212: Mid-div centre, prog to lead 1f out, hdd   ½   **63**
cl-home: gd run in defeat: ran to form of 3184.
3184 **SISTER SOPHIA 12** [6] W J Musson 4-9-6 (62) R Mullen 40/1: 0060-003: Slow away centre, prog ins   1½   **63**
fn 2f, nrst fin: left prev efforts bhd from this term with an encouraging run & has slipped down weights: see 3184.
3184 **ICED DIAMOND 12** [11] W M Brisbourne 5-8-10 (52) C Catlin 8/1: 1000004: Held up centre, prog ins   ½   **52**
fnl 2f, kept on cl-home: op 13/2: btr 558 (fibresand).
3184 **ARTISTRY 12** [7]4-9-2 (58) J F McDonald(3) 25/1: 40-15005: Cl-up centre, led after 4f, hdd 1f out, wknd. ½   **57**
3229 **SMITH N ALLAN OILS 10** [4]5-8-12 p (54) S W Kelly 5/1: 0052246: In tch centre, ev ch dist, sn no extra. nk   **52**
3229 **JEDEYDD 10** [5]7-8-11 t (53) L Enstone(3) 14/1: 0406407: Handy centre over 5f, sn no extra: btr 2967. 1½   **48**
2855 **WARLINGHAM 26** [12]6-9-0 (56) Paul Eddery 12/1: 1050508: Rcd alone on stands side, in tch till   5   **41**
dist, sn edged left & wknd: btr 1731.
4294‡ **KIND EMPEROR 313** [3]7-9-8 (64) A Mackay 12/1: 115150-9: br g Emperor Jones - Kind Lady (Kind of   4   **41**
Hush) Rcd centre & led, hdd 3f out, sn wknd: reapp: won 2 h'caps & a class stks event here at Yarmouth last term:
h'capped plcd in '02 (rtd 53): loves to force the pace btwn 7f & 10f on firm, gd/soft & fibresand: loves Yarmouth:
2 Jul'01 Yarm 7fm 53-51 E: 1 May'03 Yarm 10.1g/f 66-60) F: 1 May'03 Yarm 10.1g/f 62-56 F: 1 Apr'03 Yarm 7.0gd 57-53 F:
1 May'01 Yarm 8gd 53-50 E:
3218 **YASHIN 11** [10]3-8-11 (60) P Robinson 9/2: 50-00320: 10th: Mid-div centre over 5f, wknd: tchd 6/1.   1¼   **35**
1723 **Kew The Music 74** [8]4-9-3 (59) T E Durcan 40/1:0   2768 **Albadi 30** [1]3-8-1 bl(50) J Quinn 20/1:0
12 Ran   Time 1m 27.08 (4.48)   Owned: Bainey Racing Partnership   Trained: Newmarket

---

3491 **7.30 Pertwee & Back Ford Streetka Selling Stakes 2yo (G)**
£2541 £726 £363   **6f3y str**   **Good 58**   **-61 Slow**   Stands side

3209 **TIPSY LILLIE 11** [1] Julian Poulton 2-8-11 N Callan 7/1: 5000141: Handy centre, styd on to lead   **59**
dist, hdd ins fnl 1f, rallied to lead cl-home: eff at 5/6f on fast & gd grnd: likes sell grade: game eff.
3351 **JAY 5** [4] N A Callaghan 2-8-6 P Robinson 7/2: 00202: Slow away centre, prog to lead ins fnl 1f,   *shd* **52**
hdd cl-home: qck reapp: op 9/2: eff at 6/7f on fast & gd grnd: see 2640.
3172 **GENERAL NUISANCE 13** [7] J S Moore 2-8-11 BL Derek Nolan(7) 5/2 FAV: 6454323: Keen cl-up centre, *1¾* **53**
led halfway, had no extra: op 4/1 in first time blnks: see 3172 & 2833.
2833 **AHAZ 27** [6] I A Wood 2-8-11 bl I Mongan 20/1: 06054: Mid-div centre, prog ins fnl 2f, sn onepcd.   *nk* **52**
3259 **TIP TOES 9** [5]2-8-6 T Dean(7) 14/1: 06045: Rcd centre, hdd after 2f, sn outpcd, rallied late.   *nk* **46**
2977 **SAPPHIRE PRINCESS 21** [2]2-8-6 P Doe 8/1: 4556: Keen cl-up centre, outpcd after 2f, mod late gains. *1¾* **41**
2689 **HERENCIA 32** [8]2-8-11 Dean McKeown 8/1: 07: b c Victory Note - Originality (Godswalk) Rcd   *nk* **45**
stands side, cl-up 4f, sn wknd: Apr foal, cost 9,500gns: half-brother to wnrs at 5/14f: dam unplcd.
3382 **KERESFORTH 4** [9]2-9-2 bl L Enstone(3) 9/2: 0021028: Rcd stands side, sn led that group, wknd bef   *1*   **47**
1f out: op 7/2: too sn after 3382?
8 Ran   Time 1m 17.55 (7.15)   Owned: Mrs A C Guinle   Trained: Newmarket

3492 **8.00 Cockrill Glass Handicap Stakes Fillies 3yo+ 0-70 (E)**   **[64]**
£3819 £1175 £588   **1m2f21y**   **Good 58**   **+14 Fast**   Inside

3367 **ELLOVAMUL 4** [9] W M Brisbourne 4-9-0 (50) P Makin(5) 6/1: 45-40401: Held up, prog 4f out, styd on   **57**
to lead bef 1f out, rdn out to hold on: fast time: eff at 1m, stays a sharp 12f: acts on firm, gd & firesand.
2993 **ESTIMATE 20** [10] John A Harris 4-9-2 vis (52) Dean McKeown 5/1 FAV: 0010022: Rear, prog ins fnl   *¾*   **57**
2f, styd on ins fnl 1f, just held by wnr: continues in gd form: see 2993 & 1724.
3283 **CARRIACOU 9** [6] P W D'Arcy 3-9-4 (64) P Robinson 13/2: 2-645053: Slow away, hdwy 2f out, no   *½*   **68**
impress ins fnl 1f: eff around 1m, now stays 10f: see 192.
3052 **SUNSET MIRAGE 18** [3] E A L Dunlop 3-9-8 VIS (68) T E Durcan 10/1: 2610604: Handy, styd on lead 3f *¾*   **70**
out, hdd bef 1f out, no extra when short of room ins fnl 1f: first time visor: see 1953.
3242 **HULA BALLEW 10** [13]4-9-10 p (60) S W Kelly 11/2: 0550155: Rear, prog 4f out, ev ch dist, sn no extra. *3* **58**
477 **LEGALITY 184** [14]4-9-1 (51) M Halford(7) 40/1: 00006-06: b f Polar Falcon - Lady Barrister (Law   *2*   **46**
Society) Rear, nvr nrr than mid-div: long abs: unplcd in '03 (P Mitchell, led 58a, class stks): auct mdn wnr in
'02 (M Bell): eff around 1m on gd/soft & firesand: acts on a sharp or stiff trk.
1 Sep'02 Sout 8af 73a- F: 2 Aug'02 Newc 8g/s 58- F:
3240 **NASSIRIA 10** [8]3-9-5 (65) J P Guillambert(3) 33/1: 66007: Al cl-up, wknd fnl 2f: see 1495.   *5*   **53**
2475 **JOINT DESTINY 40** [5]3-8-3 (49) Lisa Jones(3) 10/1: 5021048: Prom, ev ch bef 2f out, sn wknd: 6 wk abs. *½* **36**
1648 **ABSOLUTELY SOAKED 7** [1]3-8-13 (59) C Lowther 11/1: 30-5609: Keen mid-div, prog 2f out, wknd.   *¾*   **44**
3094 **EBORACUM LADY 17** [4]4-8-12 (48) C Catlin 10/1: 0346-650: 10th: Handy, wkng/no room ins fnl 2f.   *½*   **32**
3162 **DRY WIT 14** [11]3-8-13 (59) J Quinn 20/1: 4260-060: 11th: Handy, wknd 3f out.   *11* **29**
2925 **CARLA MOON 23** [12]3-9-0 (60) R Mullen 40/1: 600-000: 12th: Mid-div over 6f, wknd.   *1*   **28**
3164 **BOOGIE MAGIC 14** [7]4-9-10 (60) I Mongan 10/1: 400-0230: 13th: Led, hdd 3f out, wknd: btr 3164.   *15* **7**
13 Ran   Time 2m 8.67 (4.47)   Owned: Clayfields Racing   Trained: Nesscliffe

3493 **8.30 Littlewoods Bet Direct Handicap Stakes 4yo+ 35-55 (F)**   **[63]**
£3297 £942 £471   **2m**   **Good 58**   **-13 Slow**   Inside

2856 **ANNAKITA 26** [6] W J Musson 4-8-2 (37) Lisa Jones(3) 4/1: 60-00041: Rear, gd prog to lead 2f out,   **43**
rdn out to hold on to 2m: acts on gd grnd: first win: see 1064.
3275 **OOPS 9** [5] J F Coupland 5-8-8 (43) W Supple 8/1: 042-0162: Cl-up, kept on ins fnl 2f, just held   *½*   **47**
by wnr: back to form of 2941 (soft).
3147 **CIRCUS MAXIMUS 15** [8] Ian Williams 7-9-4 p (53) T E Durcan 3/1 FAV: 20-04023: Cl-up 9f, sn   *1*   **56**
outpcd, rallied late: ran to form of 2nd in 3147.
     SUPER FELLOW 1390 [10] C N Kellett 10-8-0 (35) M Halford(6) 10/1: 0///00///-3: b g Shy Groom -   *dht* **38**
Killough (Lord Gayle) Slow away, sn pushed along, gd prog ins fnl 2f, nrst fin: jumps fit, earlier h'cap chase wnr
(rtd 118c, stays 3m2.5f on gd & soft, eff with t-strap & blnks): plcd once in 03/04 (h'cap, rtd 115c): ex Irish,
won 2 nov chases in 02/03: modest prev Flat form: eff at 2m, shaped as tho' further will suit: acts on gd grnd.
3026 **ROYALE PEARL 19** [11]4-8-5 (40) C Catlin 8/1: 0041455: Rear, prog 4f out, no impress fnl 1f: btr 1456. *1¾* **42**
3327 **RIVER OF FIRE 6** [7]6-8-3 vis (38) Natalia Gemelova(7) 13/2: 4000156: Led, hdd 2f out, wknd: qck reapp. *4* **36**
3147 **GALANDORA 15** [4]4-9-3 (52) Lucy Russell(7) 6/1: 0120337: Cl-up 14f, wknd: btr 3147 & 3049.   *1*   **49**
2494 **VANBRUGH 40** [1]4-8-7 t (42) M Nem(7) 20/1: 0000008: Handy, wknd 3f out: 6 wk abs.   *19* **21**
3362 **FITZ THE BILL 4** [2]4-8-7 T (42) Derek Nolan(7) 66/1: 0033009: Handy over 12f, wknd: 1st time t-strap. *9* **13**
3147 **POLANSKI MILL 15** [9]5-9-3 (52) Paul Eddery 16/1: 000-P000: 10th: Al in rear.   *2½* **21**
3200 **Promote 12** [3]8-8-5 t(40) J Quinn 33/1:0   2112 **Lord Lahar 56** [12]5-8-5 (40) T Dean(7) 66/1:0
12 Ran   Time 3m 34.67(11.37)   Owned: Mr N A Rooney   Trained: Newmarket

LEOPARDSTOWN   SATURDAY 24.07.04   Lefthand, Galloping Track

Official Going Good/Firm (Good Places)

LEOPARDSTOWN SATURDAY 24.07.04 Lefthand, Galloping Track

3494
6.45 Listed Tyros Stakes 2yo ()
£21809 £6399 £3048   7f rnd   Good/Firm

ELUSIVE DOUBLE [6] D K Weld 2-9-0 P Shanahan 11/2: 11: ch c Grand Lodge - Lady Luck (Kris)   **106**
Rear, efft wide from over 2f out, drvn to lead ins last, styd on strongly: 6 wk abs: remains unbeaten after an
earlier Tipperary mdn success: eff at 7/7.5f, sure to relish 1m+: acts on fast ground & a gall trk: overcame a v
awkward passage to prevail, looks v useful & can rate higher.
LOCK AND KEY [7] E Lynam 2-8-11 Catheirne Gannon 10/1: 35112: b f Key Of Luck - Lock's Heath   *1* **100**
(Topsider) Dwelt & held up in tch, drvn to chall dist, not pace of wnr ins last: op 8/1: earlier landed a Sligo auct
mdn & a h'cap at The Curragh: eff at 6f, now stays a gall 7f well: acts on fast & gd grnd: progressive juvenile.
2300* **AMSTERDAM 52** [1] A P O'Brien 2-9-0 J P Spencer 7/4 FAV: 513: Led, hdd ins last & no extra: 8 wk   *hd* **102**
abs: eff at 6/7f on fast & gd/sft grnd: see 2300.
7 Ran   Time 1m 29.10 ()   Owned: Moyglare Stud Farm   Trained: The Curragh

3495
7.15 Listed EBF Sweet Mimosa Stakes Fillies 3yo+ ()
£30532 £8958 £4268   6f rnd   Good/Firm

3545} **ULFAH 27** [6] K Prendergast 3-8-11 D P McDonogh 4/1: 221-0611: b f Danzig - Sayedat Alhadh (Mr   **104**
Prospector) Led, drvn & strongly pressed over 1f out, hdd dist, rallied gamely to lead close home, all out: op 7/2:
recent wnr of a Curragh h'cap: eff at 6/6.5f on fast ground, likes a stiff/gall trk: v useful filly who displayed
battling qualities to prevail. 2 Aug'03 Curr 6gd 91-:
4321} **SHERSHA 27** [4] S J Treacy 5-9-2 (87) N G McCullagh 9/1: -3432232: Held up, hdwy to lead dist,   *hd* **103**
edged left & hdd close home.
3075 **RUBY ROCKET 15** [1] H Morrison 3-9-0 (105) M J Kinane 8/15 FAV: 14-52323: Trkd ldr, swtchd to   *hd* **105**
chall over 1f out, ev ch ins last, drvn & just held close home: poss prefers more give nowadays: see 3075, 2769.
7 Ran   Time 1m 13.60 ()   Owned: Hamdan Al Maktoum   Trained: Friarstown

3496
7.45 Gr 3 Meld Stakes 3yo+ ()
£30485 £8911 £4221   10f   Good/Firm

2820 **LATINO MAGIC 6** [4] R J Osborne 4-9-7 R M Burke 6/1: 50243351: ch c Lion Cavern - Tansy (Shareef   **110**
Dancer) Rear, rdn to chall dist, drvn to lead line, all out, most game: eff at 1m/10f on firm & gd/sft: see 2820,
1560. 2 May'04 Curr 10g/s 105-: 2 Oct'03 Tipp 7.5g/f 101-: 2 Aug'03 Leop 8g/f 101- A:
2820 **SOLSKJAER 27** [2] A P O'Brien 4-9-7 J P Spencer 5/1: 0-122: Chsd clr ldr, rdn to lead over 1f   *shd* **110**
out, drvn & hdd line: stays a gall 10f well: see 2820.
1857 **CACHE CREEK 10** [5] P Hughes 6-9-4 (89) F M Berry 100/30: 04254113: Held up rear, kept on late,   *4* **101**
nvr threat to front pair: op 5/2.
2456* **MEDICINAL 45** [3] D K Weld 3-8-11 bl P Shanahan 9/4 JT FAV: 1-4314: Chsd ldrs, rdn & no impress   *2* **101**
over 1f out: btr expected after 2456 (List).
2635 **BIG BAD BOB 37** [1]4-9-10 (112) M J Kinane 9/4 JT FAV: 1110-345: Led & sn well clr, hdd over 1f   *3½* **99**
out, wknd: capable of better: see 1862 (Listed).
8 Ran   Time 2m 05.70()   Owned: Mrs P D Osborne   Trained: Naas

DUSSELDORF SUNDAY 25.07.04

Official Going Soft

3497
3.45 Gr 1 West LB Deutschlandpreis 3yo+ ()
£63380 £24648 £11972   12f   Soft

4934} **ALBANOVA 273** [6] Sir Mark Prescott 5-9-2 (111) T Hellier 114/10: /115-10261: gr f Alzao -   **116**
Alouette (Darshaan) Trkd ldrs, drvn to lead well ins last: reapp: Listed wnr on reapp '03, subs Gr 2 rnr up: '02
class stks & List wnr: eff at 10f/12f, tried 2m: acts on gd & hvy grnd: goes v well fresh: loves a stiff/gall trk: v
smart mare, superbly placed to land a 1st Group success.
2 Sep'03 Colo 12sft 112- A: 1 May'03 Hayd 11.9sft 114-111 A: 1 Jul'02 Chep 10.1gd 109- A: 1 Jul'02 Pont 10g/s 89- D:
1 Sep'01 Hayd 7.1hvy 73- D:
2142 **DAYANO** [4] A Wohler 3-8-6 A Starke 59/10: 2-11202: Always handy, styd on for press, nrst fin: see 2142.*nk* **117**
2141 **ROTTECK** [1] H Steguweit 4-9-6 J Palik 42/10: 510-1213: Led till well ins last.   *¾* **118**
2518 **BRIAN BORU 38** [7]4-9-6 J P Spencer 11/10 FAV: 13-15555: Cl up, btn over 1f out: btr 994.   *5* **112**
7 Ran   Time 2m 33.29()   Owned: Miss K Rausing   Trained: Newmarket

MAISONS LAFFITTE SUNDAY 25.07.04 Left & Righthand, Sharpish Track

Official Going Good

3498
2.15 Gr 2 Prix Robert Papin 2yo ()
£42148 £16268 £7764   5f110yds   Good

3008* **DIVINE PROPORTIONS 27** [4] P Bary 2-8-13 C P Lemaire 9/10 FAV: 111: b f Kingmambo - Myth To   **112**
Reality (Sadler's Wells) Handy, rdn to lead ins last, pushed out close home: remains unbeaten: eff at 5f/5.5f on
good & good/soft ground: likes a gall trk: v smart & improving filly. 1 Jun'04 Chan 5gd 107-:
2823* **SHIFTING PLACE 28** [6] R Menichetti 2-8-13 D Vargiu 13/1: 421312: Led, rdn & hung right over 1f   *1* **108**

out, hdd ins last, not pace of wnr: acts on fast & gd grnd: see 2823.

PORTRAYAL 13 [7] A Fabre 2-8-13 Gary Stevens 29/10: 313: Trkd wnr, rdn over 1f out, kept on.   ¾   **106**
8 Ran   Time 1m 04.80()   Owned: Niarchos Family   Trained: France

BEVERLEY   TUESDAY 27.07.04   Righthand, Oval Track with Stiff, Uphill Finish

Official Going Good/Firm

3499   2.20 National Festival Circus Selling Handicap Stakes 3yo 35-55 (F)   [61]
£3416 £1051 £526   1m4f16y   Good/Firm 37   -41 Slow   Inside

3312 **NORTHERN SPIRIT 8** [9] K A Ryan 3-9-1 BL (48) N Callan 2/1 FAV: 0-060301: Chsd ldr, styd on for   **53**
press to lead well ins last: bckd, op 11/4: first win, sold for 6,200gns: stays 14f, tried 2m, apprec drop to 12f
in sell grade: acts on fast grnd: eff in cheek pieces, suited by blnks today: see 2123 & 1612.
2982 **ONIZ TIPTOES 22** [6] J S Wainwright 3-8-2 VIS (35) C Catlin 12/1: 00-0642: Keen, sn led, drvn &   nk   **39**
hdd well ins last: fair run with forcing tactics applied in first time visor, blnks omitted: stays 12f on fast grnd.
2932 **CAMPBELLS LAD 24** [4] A Berry 3-8-7 (40) F Norton 7/1: 0-540053: Held up, eff wide from over 2f   2½   **40**
out, no impress from dist: prob styd longer 12f trip in sell grade: handles fast grnd: see 1320.
2741 **FRAMBO 31** [7] J G Portman 3-8-7 t p (40) Lisa Jones(3) 15/2: 0506444: Chsd ldrs, no impress fnl 2f.   2½   **36**
3182 **BONJOUR BOND 14** [8]3-9-0 VIS (47) D McGaffin 10/1: 0030305: Mid-div, rdn & btn over 1f out: visor.   1¼   **41**
3312 **NAFFERTON HEIGHTS 8** [3]3-8-13 BL (46) T Lucas 14/1: 0-050006: Chsd ldr, fdd under press over 1f   1   **39**
out: tried blnks: btr 1836.
3300 **ERTE 8** [2]3-9-4 (51) A Culhane 9/2: 0663207: Rear, only mod prog for press: clmd for 6,000.   1¾   **42**
2790 **ROYAL UPSTART 29** [1]3-7-12 (1oh) (30) D Fentiman(7) 14/1: 0326508: Bhd, little hdwy: btr 2346.   3½   **17**
2503 **DAME NOVA 40** [10]3-8-9 (42) Rory Moore(7) 25/1: 000-0609: Slow away & al bhd: op 16/1, jumps fit.   9   **16**
1785 **TANCRED IMP 72** [5]3-8-8 (41) P Hanagan 14/1: 03-05300: 10th: Chsd ldrs, btn 3f out: 10 wk abs.   5   **9**
10 Ran   Time 2m 40.66 (9.36)   Owned: Mr Ralph Murray   Trained: Hambleton

---

3500   2.55 European Breeders Fund Holderness Pony Club Maiden Stakes 2yo (D)
£4940 £1520 £760   7f100y rnd   Good/Firm 37   -23 Slow   Inside

2671 **BANKNOTE 34** [4] A M Balding 2-9-0 K Darley 4/1: 441: Chsd ldrs, rdn & hdwy 2f out, led ins   **79**
last, rdn out: op 6/1: significant improvement for step up to 7.5f, get further: acts on fast grnd: going the
right way, interesting for nurs: see 2671 & 2071.
3214 **BALL BOY 12** [9] M R Channon 2-9-0 A Culhane 7/2: 052: Trkd ldrs, rdn & led dist, hdd ins last &   ¾   **77**
not pace of wnr: stays 7.5f, sure to apprec 1m+: acts on fast & gd grnd, sharp/undul or stiffish trk: find a race.
3342 **TUMBLEWEED GALORE 6** [7] B J Meehan 2-9-0 J F McDonald(3) 16/1: 033: Held up in tch, switched &   ¾   **76**
kept on for press, not able to reach front bar: stay 7.5f: confirmed imrpovement of 3342.
2077 **MISS ROSIE 59** [10] T D Easterby 2-8-9 D Allan 12/1: 44: Led till dist, no extra: op 4/1, 2 month abs.   1½   **68**
2776 **MIRAGE PRINCE 30** [5]2-9-0 B Swarbrick(5) 66/1: 6065: Chsd ldr, btn over 1f out: see 2776.   1   **71**
3111 **CHINESE PUZZLE 17** [8]2-9-0 t W Ryan 2/1 FAV: 66: ch g Loup Solitaire - Whoops (Shernazar) Held up,   2½   **66**
eff over 2f out, no impress dist: bckd: Mar first foal, dam 1m 3yo scorer & plcd in List company.
FENRIR 0 [6]2-9-0 G Hind 100/1: 7: ch c Loup Solitaire - Solitaire (Storm Bird) Dwelt, bhd, late   2   **62**
prog: Mar first foal, dam a lightly rcd mdn at 7f/1m: entitled to progress.
2939 **FORPETESAKE 24** [11]2-9-0 F Norton 66/1: 0668: Held up, eff over 2f out, no prog.   nk   **61**
3078 **LODGICIAN 18** [2]2-9-0 P Hanagan 12/1: 439: Chsd ldrs wide, hung right & btn over 1f out: see 3078.   3½   **54**
2938 **EBORARRY 24** [12]2-9-0 J Quinn 50/1: 40: 10th: Dwelt, al towards rear: btr 2938.   shd   **54**
TERMINATE 0 [1]2-9-0 J Mackay 10/1: 0: 11th: ch g Acatenango - Taghareed (Shadeed) Dwelt, held   1   **52**
up in tch wide, no impress fnl 3f: hvly bckd: £90,000 Mar foal, half-brothers to wnrs btwn 6f/1m, dam a 6f juv wnr.
11 Ran   Time 1m 35.27 (4.47)   Owned: The Queen   Trained: Kingsclere

---

3501   3.30 Toteexacta Handicap Stakes 3yo+ 0-80 (D)   [67]
£6939 £2135 £1068   1m100y rnd   Good/Firm 37   -08 Slow   Inside

2986 **SPLODGER MAC 22** [8] N Bycroft 5-7-13 (1ow)(12oh) (38) J Quinn 66/1: 4306-001: Dictated pace &   **57**
qcknd from over 2f out, held on well for press under a superbly judged ride, first win: eff around 8.5f on fast grnd.
3260 **TEDSDALE MAC 10** [10] N Bycroft 5-8-5 (57) F Norton 3/1 FAV: 0425232: Trkd ldrs, rdn & styd on   nk   **62**
fnl 1f, just failed: op 9/2, shorter priced stablemate of wnr: see 2890.
3232 **GIFTED FLAME 11** [3] T D Barron 5-8-9 (61) Darren Williams 4/1: 6-004003: Mid-div inner, switched   shd   **66**
& rdn/styd on ins last, just failed: op 6/1, clr of rem: on fair mark, likes a stiff trk: see 2447.
3074 **CRYFIELD 18** [7] N Tinkler 7-8-10 (62) Kim Tinkler 11/2: 2400164: Chsd ldr, fdd dist: btr 2890.   4   **59**
3205 **TEDSTALE 12** [4]6-10-0 (80) K Darley 6/1: 0503645: Held up, rdn & mod prog fnl 2f.   nk   **76**
1530 **FIRST DYNASTY 85** [9]4-9-11 (77) A Quinn(5) 14/1: 2/023-106: Chsd ldrs, no impress fnl 2f: 10 wk   nk   **72**
jumps abs: see 1340 (AW mdn).
3242 **SEDGE 11** [2]4-8-5 (57) R Fitzpatrick 33/1: 1007: Rear, no impress fnl 2f: btr 2102 (seller, 7f).   3   **46**
3099 **PRINCE OF GOLD 17** [5]4-9-0 p (66) N Callan 8/1: 6010008: Mid-div, eff over 2f out, sn btn: btr 2324.   ¾   **54**
3179 **WRENLANE 14** [1]3-8-4 (64) P Hanagan 7/1: 30-2659: Bmpd start, rear, no prog: op 9/2: btr 3179.   nk   **51**
3326 **ATLANTIC QUEST 7** [6]5-10-0 (80) P Mulrennan(5) 14/1: 00150B0: 10th: Chsd ldrs wide, btn 2f out.   3½   **60**
10 Ran   Time 1m 46.76 (3.8)   Owned: Mr N Bycroft   Trained: Malton

---

3502   4.05 Geo Houltons 125th Anniversary Handicap Stakes 3yo+ 0-70 (E)   [63]
£3848 £1184 £592   1m4f16y   Good/Firm 37   -31 Slow   Inside

3240 **SHOTLEY DANCER 11** [5] N Bycroft 5-7-13 (1ow)(6oh) (34) F Norton 20/1: 0043531: Mid-div, hdwy &   **44**
handy from haflway, led over 3f out, drvn & held on gamely: first win: eff at 1m/12f on firm, gd/soft & fibresand.
2892 **EAST CAPE 25** [2] Don Enrico Incisa 7-8-0 (42) Kim Tinkler 12/1: 0006352: Rear, switched & styd   ¾   **43**
on well for press ins last, nrst fin: see 724 (banded).

BEVERLEY TUESDAY 27.07.04 Righthand, Oval Track with Stiff, Uphill Finish

2988 **LADY STRATAGEM 21** [7] E W Tuer 5-8-0 (42) P Fessey 50/1: 0000/-003: Trkd ldrs, rdn to chall over 1f out, drvn & no extra nr fin: eff at 12f on fast grnd: mdn: see 2562. *1* **42**
3056 **RED RIVER REBEL 19** [6] J R Norton 6-8-13 (55) Darren Williams 4/5 FAV: 0-040224: Trkd ldrs, rdn & onepace from over 1f out: well bckd, op 11/10: won this race in '03 off today's mark: best when dominating. *nk* **54**
3310 **EDDIES JEWEL 8** [10]4-7-13 (1ow)(5oh) (35) C Catlin 14/1: 300-2545: Mid-div, eff over 2f out, onepcd for press dist: prob stays 12f: handles fast & gd grnd: see 1991. *½* **39**
3354 **ILOVETURTLE 6** [12]4-8-8 (50) Lisa Jones(3) 20/1: 00-035U6: Rear, styd on late, nvr rchd ldrs: see 1407. *½* **47**
3222 **ZAN LO 12** [9]4-8-9 (51) P Mulrennan(5) 66/1: 6-006007: Mid-div, onepace fnl 3f: btr 2038. *½* **47**
605 **TURN OF PHRASE 167** [8]5-9-3 bl (59) P Hanagan 11/1: 3/5213-08: b g Cadeaux Genereux - Token Gesture (Alzao) Mid-div, eff over 2f out, no impress: jumps fit (p.u., h'cap hdle): '03 appr class stks wnr, AW h'cap rnr-up: eff at 12/13f on firm, gd & polytrack, eff in blnks. *1¾* **53**
1 Jun'03 Newc 12.4fm 61-(58) G: 2 Feb'03 Ling 10ap 55a-54 F:
3161 **FLEETFOOT MAC 15** [1]3-8-12 (66) N Callan 9/1: 1100349: Rdn to lead early, hdd over 2f out & fdd. *½* **59**
3354 **DALRIATH 6** [4]5-7-12 (2oh) (38) D Fox(5) 16/1: 2503520: 10th: Dwelt & al bhd: btr 3354. *¾* **32**
3207 **LITTLE TASK 12** [11]6-7-12 (5oh) (35) A Reilly(3) 20/1: 1410460: 11th: Al rear: btr 2892. *12* **17**
2229 **Sadlers Pride 53** [13]4-10-0 (70) J Carroll 14/1:0
2966 **Miss Ocean Monarch 22** [3]4-7-12 (5oh)bl e(35) D Fentiman(7) 66/1:0
13 Ran Time 2m 39.45 (8.15) Owned: Mr J A Swinburne Trained: Malton

3503

4.40 Ladies Day Here On 11th August Classified Stakes 3yo+ 0-70 (E)
£3786 £1165 £583 **5f str** **Good/Firm 37** **+08 Fast** Inside

3273 **DISTANT TIMES 10** [10] T D Easterby 3-9-2 (74) D Allan 5/1: 5130051: Chsd ldrs, led ins last, drvn out: visor omitted: eff at 5/6f on fast & soft grnd: made full use of fav'able high draw: see 1088. **79**
2797 **TRICK CYCLIST 29** [6] A M Balding 3-9-0 (72) T Block(7) 10/1: 0-240602: Mid-div, hdwy to chall ins last, just held: gd run, can find similar: see 818. *nk* **76**
3350 **BOAVISTA 6** [4] P D Evans 4-8-13 (62) N Callan 14/1: 0002203: Bolted bef start, led, hdd dist, no extra: op 8/1: gd run in circumstances from awkward low draw: see 2034. *2½* **63**
3427 **WINTHORPE 3** [7] J J Quinn 4-9-3 (71) T Hamilton(3) 3/1 FAV: 0320544: Handy, no extra for press dist: op 5/2: qck reapp: best when covered up for a late run: see 2942 & 2775. *¾* **65**
3220 **PERCY DOUGLAS 12** [9]4-9-2 t (40) Ann Stokell 50/1: 0060005: Went left start, chsd ldrs till over 1f out. *1½* **59$**
3073 **SUNLEY SENSE 18** [5]8-9-6 vis (74) A Culhane 9/2: 00/-30006: Chsd ldrs, no impress fn 2f: op 10/1. *1¾* **59**
3220 **MISS CEYLON 12** [3]4-8-13 BL (39) J McAuley 66/1: 000-0007: Outpcd & struggling halfway: tried blnks. *9* **28**
3241 **TOMMY SMITH 11** [8]6-9-3 bl (71) Darren Williams 100/30: 0001008: Went right & bmpd start, rider lost iron & no ch after: well bckd: best forgiven: see 2279. *12* **0**
3341 **THE FISIO 6** [1]4-9-7 vis (75) K Darley 15/2: 0410209: Blindfold still on when stalls opened, v slow away & al rear: op 6/1: qck reapp: forgive this: see 2760. *1¾* **0**
2214 **GENERAL SMITH 53** [2]5-9-2 (50) P Mulrennan(5) 50/1: 55-0000R0: 10th: Reared start & got stuck in stalls, took no part, abs. **0**
10 Ran Time 1m 02.76 (1.46) Owned: Times of Wigan Trained: Malton

3504

5.15 Ken Magee Lifetime In Racing Maiden Auction Stakes Fillies 2yo (F)
£3396 £1045 £523 **5f str** **Good/Firm 37** **-12 Slow** Inside

3266 **WITHERING LADY 10** [8] Mrs P N Dutfield 2-8-5 R Havlin 4/9 FAV: 346201: Trkd ldrs, hdwy to lead 2f out, rdn & flashed tail ins fnl 1f, kept on: well bckd: eff at 5f on fast & gd, stiff trk: down in grade: see 1123. **79**
3258 **HILLSIDE HEATHER 10** [4] A Berry 2-8-2 F Norton 6/1: 43202: Cl-up, hdwy into 2nd just ins fnl 1f, edged right, styd on: clr of rem: acts on fast & gd: shld find a small race: see 2547. *1¾* **71**
2927 **EMERAUDE DU CAP 24** [9] M L W Bell 2-8-2 J Mackay 25/1: 003: Rear, hdwy 2f out, onepcd fnl 1f. *6* **53**
RAINBOW IRIS 0 [1] B Smart 2-8-9 D McGaffin 20/1: 4: b f Mister Baileys - Kastaway (Distant Relative) Prom, onepcd over 1f out: op 14/1 on debut: Feb foal, cost 14,000gns: half-sister to a fair 5f 2yo wnr: dam fair 4-time 5f 2yo wnr, sire a high-class 2yo, later 2,000 Guineas scorer: shld rate higher as a juv. *¾* **58**
2921 **RUSSIAN SERVANA 24** [6]2-8-2 J Quinn 12/1: 025: Nvr btr than mid-div: now with J Pearce. *nk* **50**
3258 **JASMINE HILL 10** [10]2-8-2 C Catlin 16/1: 06: ch f Timeless Times - Coney Hills (Beverley Boy) Prom, lost pl halfway, edged left ins fnl 1f, no impress: op 20/1: Apr foal, cost 1,600gns: half-sister to a 5f 2yo wnr: dam plcd over 7f at 4, sire a prolific 2yo wnr: some improvement from debut here. *hd* **49**
3021 **SUNNY TIMES 20** [2]2-8-2 Lisa Jones(3) 20/1: 57: Mid-div wide, nvr nrr: see 3021. *1* **46**
2889 **STAR OF KILDARE 25** [11]2-8-2 Kim Tinkler 50/1: 008: b f Raphane - Lady Fleetsin (Double Schwartz) Led to 2f out, no extra & in rear when hmpd ins fnl 1f: May foal, cost E2,000: half-sister to a 5f 2yo wnr, also dual 5/6f 2yo wnr Cable Media Boy: dam unrcd, sire a high-class 2yo sprinter: with N Tinkler. *7* **25**
BLISSPHILLY 0 [5]2-8-9 P Hanagan 25/1: 9: Slow away, al bhd on debut. *21* **0**
3178 **PEACEFUL FRONTIER 14** [7]2-8-3 (1ow) R Fitzpatrick 100/1: 0B: Bhd, btn when hmpd & b.d. ins fnl 1f. **0**
10 Ran Time 1m 03.74 (2.44) Owned: Salter Wilson and Oakes Trained: Seaton

3505

5.50 Dorothy Laird Memorial Trophy Ladies Race A Handicap Stakes 3yo+ 0-75 (E) **[55]**
£3991 £1228 £614 **1m1f207y** **Good/Firm 37** **-09 Slow** Inside

3250 **OSCAR PEPPER 11** [16] T D Barron 7-10-9 vis (64) Alex Greaves 8/1: 6345241: Mid-div, hdwy 3f out, led over 1f out, rdn out: suited by 7/10f on firm, gd/soft & fibresand, prob any trk: slipped to a wng mark. **72**
3443 **RAINSTORM 3** [12] W M Brisbourne 9-8-13 (40) Mrs S Owen 12/1: 5600002: Rear, hdwy 2f out, kept on ins fnl 1f: qck reapp: see 1379. *3* **43**
3309 **COME WHAT JULY 8** [19] Mrs N Macauley 3-9-4 bl (55) Mrs M Morris 16/1: 6035103: Bhd, hdwy after 6f, styd on fnl 1f: back to form of 3091. *nk* **57**
3099 **YENALED 17** [18] K A Ryan 7-11-0 (69) Miss N Carberry 11/4 FAV: 4511224: Bhd, hdwy 3f out, kept on. *nk* **70**
3102 **BENEKING 17** [8]4-9-10 (51) Stephanie Hollinshead 50/1: 0-030605: In tch, hdwy after 6f, onepcd fnl 1f. *½* **51**
3398 **LAZZAZ 4** [9]6-9-6 (47) Mrs Marie King(5) 6/1: 5643426: Prom, wknd over 1f out: qck reapp. *2½* **43**
3159 **LATE ARRIVAL 15** [17]7-8-13 bl (40) Lisa Jones 12/1: 0000267: Bhd, hdwy 2f out, not pace to chall. *1* **35**
2616 **SHALBEBLUE 36** [11]7-9-1 bl (42) Miss L Ellison 33/1: 325-0008: Handy, wknd 2f out: see 2285. *¾* **36**
3242 **UNO MENTE 11** [6]5-9-10 (51) Kim Tinkler 25/1: 0063009: Rear, hdwy 3f out, kept on onepace. *½* **44**
3398* **THEATRE LADY 4** [4]6-9-11 (5ex) (52) Miss E Folkes 12/1: 6601510: 10th: Rear, some late gains: qk reapp. *1* **44**
3052 **LITTLETON ZEPHIR 19** [1]5-9-6 (47) Mrs C Thompson(5) 40/1: 0015000: 11th: Mid-div wide, wknd 2f out. *½* **38**

BEVERLEY TUESDAY 27.07.04 Righthand, Oval Track with Stiff, Uphill Finish

4767} **EMPERORS WELL 285** [15]5-10-2 bl (57) Miss S Brotherton 40/1: 204146-0: 12th: ch g First Trump - Catherines Well (Junius) Led till over 1f out, no extra on reapp: won 1 of 9 '03 starts (sell h'cap): 5th at best in '02 (h'cap, rtd 49): suited by forcing the pace at 1m/8.5f on fast & gd, stiff/undul trk: eff in blnks. ½ **47**
1 Sep'03 Pont 8.0g/f 54-45 F: 2 Aug'03 Beve 8.5gd 54-(39) E:
3398 **EIGHT 4** [3]8-9-6 (47) Ms T Dzieciolowska(5) 50/1: 03200-00: 13th: Mid-div, wknd over 2f out: qck reapp. 2½ **33**
3246 **AWWAL MARRA 11** [14]4-9-4 (45) Ms C Williams 22/1: 2/-030: 14th: Al bhd: see 1768. ¾ **30**
3354 **DEEKAZZ 6** [13]5-9-0 (2ow) (39) Miss Victoria Casey 66/1: 5/0406-00: 15th: In tch, wknd over 3f out. nk **25**
3052 **HOLLY ROSE 19** [10]5-9-12 VIS (53) Hayley Turner 10/1: 2404420: 16th: In tch, rear & btn halfway: visor. 1¼ **35**
3139 **SANTIBURI LAD 16** [2]7-10-13 (68) Mrs N Wilson 8/1: 0-321120: 17th: Trkd ldrs, wknd over 1f out. 1¼ **48**
2890 **WUXI VENTURE 25** [7]9-10-8 (63) Miss V Tunnicliffe(5) 20/1: 160-0600: 18th: Al bhd: chase fit (h'cap 3rd, rtd 116c): see 1748. 3½ **38**
2134 **CADEAUX ROUGE 56** [5]3-9-4 (55) Miss A Wallace(5) 50/1: 560-4000: 19th: Prom, fdd over 3f out. 27 **0**
19 Ran Time 2m 06.92(4.62) Owned: Mr Ian Armitage Trained: Thirsk

GOODWOOD TUESDAY 27.07.04 Righthand, Sharpish, Undulating Track

Official Going Good (Good/Firm Places Rnd Course)

3506

2.05 Sterling Insurance Summer Stakes Heritage Handicap 4yo+ (B) **[108]**
£29000 £11000 £5500 **1m1f192y Good/Firm 23 -01 Slow** Inside

3118 **COAT OF HONOUR 17** [11] Sir Mark Prescott 4-8-12 (92) S Sanders 10/1: 51132-01: Rcd in 2nd, hdwy to lead 2f out, edged left over 1f out and again entering fnl 1f, drvn out: eff over 10/12f on fast & gd/soft, acts on any trk: runs well with/without blnks: imprvd from reapp, yard in excellent form & can win more races. **101**
3265 **IMPELLER 10** [16] W R Muir 5-8-6 (86) S Drowne 9/1: 0026052: In tch, hdwy & switched left 2f out, strong run ins last but not go past cl home: suited by 1m/9f, stays 10f: fine run but hard to put his head in front. nk **93**
3043 **BONECRUSHER 19** [14] D R Loder 5-9-10 vis (104) T P Queally 25/1: 0520553: Dwelt bhd, eff when hmpd 2f out, switched left & styd on strongly ins last, nrst fin: top-weight & a fine effort: lkd unlucky. ½ **110+**
2556 **ANANI 39** [13] E A L Dunlop 4-9-8 (102) T Quinn 25/1: 3420604: Cl-up, hdwy into 2nd over 1f out, lost pl ins fnl 1f, onepcd: gd run: see 884. 1 **106**
3185* **SPANISH DON 13** [8]6-9-1 (95) L Keniry(3) 11/2: 1-005115: Keen in tch, onepcd over 1f out, kept on ins fnl 1f: nicely bckd, tchd 15/2: eff at 1m/10f: remains in gd form, see 3185. hd **98**
3072 **WINDY BRITAIN 18** [4]5-8-8 (88) D Holland 7/1: 131-0426: Bhd, hdwy & switched to innerover 1f out, predictably no room till ins last, styd on well: rare tactical error by D Holland & a promising run, much closer with a clr run: progressive, see 179. nk **90**
2556 **SIR GEORGE TURNER 39** [10]5-9-1 (95) K Dalgleish 50/1: 2/-000007: Bhd, hdwy over 2f out, not clr run over 1f out, kept on ins fnl 1f: back to form, closer with a clr run: looks to be on a fair mark: see 2101. nk **95**
2249+ **FANTASTIC LOVE 404** [15]4-9-8 T (102) L Dettori 9/2 FAV: 22121-8: b g Peintre Celebre - Moon Flower (Sadler's Wells) Cl-up, hdwy to chall over 2f out, no extra fnl 1f: nicely bckd on reapp: won 2 of 5 '03 starts (h'cap, mdn, with M Johnston): eff at 1m, suited by 11/12f & may get further: acts on fast & gd, stiff or undul trks: tried a t-strap here: lightly rcd & a rtn to further will suit: now with Saeed bin Suroor. 1¾ **100**
1 Jun'03 Asco 12g/f 102-90 B: 2 May'03 Wind 11.6g/f 89-(90) C: 1 Apr'03 Hami 11.1gd 80- D: 2 Apr'03 Ripo 8g/f 88- D: 2 Apr'03 Ripo 8g/f 90- D:
3313* **PRAIRIE WOLF 8** [1]8-7-12 (4ex) (78) N Mackay(3) 12/1: 0000519: Trkd ldrs, rdn along when short of room 2f out, wknd: likes it here & is on a fair mark: see 3313. nk **75**
2860 **CHINKARA 27** [9]4-8-10 (90) J Fortune 10/1: 10-00040: 10th: In tch, hdwy wide over 2f out, no impress. ¾ **85**
3185 **KRUGERRAND 13** [17]5-8-4 (84) G Carter 25/1: 0001360: 11th: Dwelt bhd, hdwy when not clr run 2f out, kept on for hands & heels fnl 1f: forgive this, closer with a clr run. hd **78**
2662 **ALRAFID 34** [7]5-8-6 (86) R L Moore 12/1: 6-056200: 12th: Bhd, hdwy when not clr run 2f out, switched left well over 1f out, onepcd. nk **79**
3118 **BLYTHE KNIGHT 17** [5]4-9-9 (103) K Fallon 12/1: 4146300: 13th: Bhd, shkn up when hmpd 2f out, not recover, eased: forgive this. 1¼ **94**
3076 **TELEMACHUS 18** [12]4-8-6 BL (86) M Fenton 22/1: 6100000: 14th: Led till 2f out, no extra: tried blnks. 1 **75**
2896 **FOODBROKER FOUNDER 25** [6]4-9-3 (97) Dane O'Neill 33/1: 200-0660: 15th: Trkd ldrs, wknd over 3f out. 2 **83**
15 Ran Time 2m 06.61 (2.41) Owned: E B Rimmer-Osborne House Trained: Newmarket

3507

2.40 Gr3 Abn Amro Stakes Registered As The Gordon Stakes 3yo (A)
£29000 £11000 £5500 **1m4f Good/Firm 23 -12 Slow** Outside

2519 **MARAAHEL 40** [8] Sir Michael Stoute 3-8-10 (103) R Hills 9/4: 414-221: Trkd ldrs, gd hdwy to lead over 2f out, styd on well, rdn out: hvly bckd, 6 wk abs: stays 12f well, further could suit: acts on fast & soft, stiff or sharp/undul trks: smart & progressive, win more Gr races: see 2519. **117**
1706 **GO FOR GOLD 75** [7] A P O'Brien 3-8-10 K Fallon 25/1: 1-32: Bhd, hdwy 3f out, not pace of wnr ins fnl 1f but kept on: long abs: prev eff at 7f, imprvd for this step up to 12f: acts on fast & gd: win a Listed. 1½ **113**
1737* **REMAADD 74** [6] M P Tregoning 3-8-10 (100) Martin Dwyer 5/1: 13: Led for 2f, remained cl-up, outpcd over 2f out, kept on again ins fnl 1f: long abs: stays 12f on fast & gd, lks sure to relish 14f: lightly rcd & progressive, more to come, win Gr races sn: see 1737 (mdn). 1½ **110+**
2817 **MIKADO 31** [3] A P O'Brien 3-8-10 J Murtagh 11/1: 211-44: b c Sadler's Wells - Free At Last (Shirley Heights) Led after 2f, hdd over 2f out, no extra: clr of rem: won 2 of 3 '03 starts in native Ireland (mdn, List, 1m/9f, gd): stays 14f well: acts on fast & gd: shorter priced stablemate of rnr-up. nk **109**
1 Nov'03 Leop 9gd 109- :
2557* **DUKE OF VENICE 39** [4]3-8-13 t (114) L Dettori 13/8 FAV: 310-1215: Mid-div, hdwy into 2nd briefly over 1f out, sn wknd: hvly bckd, top-weight: joc reported mount did not handle trk & much better expected after 2557 (2m): further & a gall trk will suit. 3½ **107**
2824 **LYONELS GLORY 30** [1]3-8-10 D Holland 20/1: 2336: Bhd, hdwy wide over 2f out, not pace to chall. ¾ **102**
2879* **MASSIF CENTRALE 26** [2]3-8-10 (100) Dane O'Neill 14/1: 02017: Dsptd lead after 2f till over 2f out, wknd. 4 **96**
2308 **MANYANA 51** [5]3-8-10 t (106) W Supple 16/1: 1-5108: Keen in rear, nvr a factor: 7 wk abs. ¾ **94**
8 Ran Time 2m 36.01 (4.21) Owned: Mr Hamdan Al Maktoum Trained: Newmarket

3508   3.15 Gr2 Betfair Cup Registered As The Lennox Stakes 3yo+ (A)
£58000 £22000 £11000   7f rnd   Good/Firm 23   +07 Fast   Inside

2469 **BYRON** 42 [5] Saeed bin Suroor 3-8-7 t (111) K McEvoy 16/1: 1341-301: In tch, qcknd to lead dist, 117+
rdn out, val further: 6 wk abs: stays 1m, apprec rtn to 7f: acts on firm & gd grnd: goes well fresh & acts on any
trk: eff with a t-strap: lightly rcd & v smart, has a turn of foot & can continue to run well: see 2469.

3124 **SUGGESTIVE** 17 [1] W J Haggas 6-9-0 bl (109) M Hills 25/1: 4521402: Mid-div, lkd held over 1f out ¾ 113
till styd on well ins last, nrst fin: fin 4th in this race last year: fine run on drop back to 7f: smart, see 2826.

3062 **KHELEYF** 19 [7] Saeed bin Suroor 3-8-7 (112) L Dettori 9/4 FAV: 1210-103: Mid-div, prog to chase ¾ 111
wnr ins fnl 1f, kept on, not pace front 2: well bckd stablemate of wnr: apprec rtn to 7f but twice below 2486.

3320 **NAAHY** 9 [8] M R Channon 4-9-0 (106) S Hitchcott 14/1: 01-11044: Led, hdd dist, no extra: ran to 1½ 108
best on a trk that clearly suits, needs List/Gr 3: see 2765 & 2455.

2580 **CRYSTAL CASTLE** 38 [6]6-9-0 t K Fallon 11/4: 300-3325: Bhd, nvr lkd happy, prog after halfway, hd 107
onepcd bef 1f out: well bckd: lkd unsuited by today's undul trk: worth another ch on a more conventional one.

3320* **TRADE FAIR** 9 [2]4-9-0 (117) S Drowne 7/2: 615-0316: Handy, ev ch bef 1f out, no extra well ins nk 106
fnl 1f: unpredictable: btr expected after success in 3320 (Gr 3).

3268 **SO WILL I** 10 [3]3-8-7 (108) R Hills 16/1: 41-31047: Held up, prog well when short of room bef 1f hd 105
out, sn switched wide, no impress: btr 3268 & 1732.

3098* **VANDERLIN** 17 [4]5-9-0 (109) Martin Dwyer 8/1: 0-335318: Cl-up over 5f, sn wknd: showed more in 3098. 1 103
8 Ran   Time 1m 25.66 (1.16)   Owned: Godolphin   Trained: Newmarket

3509   3.50 Gr3 Betfair Molecomb Stakes 2yo (A)
£23200 £8800 £4400   5f str   Good/Firm   Fair   Stands side

3266 **TOURNEDOS** 10 [1] M R Channon 2-8-12 T E Durcan 14/1: 12201: Held up, prog when short of room 106+
halfway till dist, switched wide & flew ins fnl 1f, led cl home, going away: eff at 5f on fast & gd, 6f shld suit:
acts on any trk: useful, fine turn of foot here from near impossible position: see 2472 & 2167.

2786* **MARY READ** 30 [13] B Smart 2-8-9 F Lynch 25/1: 31312: Handy, styd on to lead 1f out, sn edged nk 100
left under press, hdd cl-home: fine run in defeat & is worth bearing in mind for similar: see 2786 & 2165.

3086 **SAFARI SUNSET** 18 [9] P Winkworth 2-8-12 P Doe 66/1: 1343: Cl-up, led 2f out, hdd 1f out, prom 2 97
when short of room snatched up well ins fnl 1f, just held on for 3rd: useful effort on return to fast grnd: see 2472.

3081 **BIGALOS BANDIT** 18 [10] J J Quinn 2-8-12 R Winston 66/1: 12404: In tch, under press when short shd 97
of room bef 1f out, styd on ins fn 1f, just held for 3rd: useful eff on step up in grade: see 2167 & 1517.

2795* **ROODEYE** 29 [6]2-8-9 K Fallon 11/2: 215: Mid-div, prog after halfway, staying on when hmpd 1f 1 90
out, kept on: op 7/1: shade closer with clr passage: see 2795.

3319 **DANCE NIGHT** 9 [3]2-8-12 G Gibbons 66/1: 211606: Mid-div, eff ins fnl 2f, no impress ins fnl 1f. shd 92

2516 **SKYWARDS** 40 [11]2-8-12 L Dettori 5/2 FAV: 5137: In tch wide trav well, rdn dist, sn hung press hd 91
& onepcd: well bckd after 6 wk abs: btr expected after decent 3rd in 2516 (Gr 3 Norfolk Stks).

3266* **SIENA GOLD** 10 [2]2-8-9 J Fortune 6/1: 11018: Bhd, prog & short of room when forced to switch hd 87
ins fnl 1f, nvr a dngr: change of tactics, fine all-the-way win in 3266 (Wetherby Super Sprint).

3081* **BECKERMET** 18 [4]2-8-12 R Ffrench 3/1: 3112119: Hit side of stalls start, rear, stumbled after nk 89+
2f, hdd when short of room 2f out, hmpd bef 1f out, kept on ins fnl 1f, ch had gone: well bckd: had a nightmare
passage & is worth another ch: btr 3081 & 2744.

2083* **THEATRE OF DREAMS** 59 [5]2-8-12 A Nicholls 50/1: 5410: 10th: Led 3f, no extra/short of room fnl 1f. 1½ 85
2472 **MARINO LAND** 42 [12]2-8-12 J Fanning 14/1: 11200: 11th: In tch wide 3f, sn no extra: 6 wk abs. 4 73
2516 **SPREE** 40 [7]2-8-9 R L Moore 10/1: 6100: 12th: Mid-div 3f, wknd: 6 wk abs: btr 2364. 2½ 63
3086 **KWAME** 18 [14]2-8-9 S W Kelly 50/1: 2120: 13th: Dwelt, in tch wide 3f, wknd: btr 3086. 5 50
13 Ran   Time 58.54 (1.84)   Owned: Ridgeway Downs Racing   Trained: West Ilsley

3510   4.25 Tatler Summer Season Stakes Heritage Handicap 3yo+ 0-105 (B)   [102]
£29000 £11000 £5500   1m6f   Good/Firm 23   +05 Fast   Inside

3066* **MEPHISTO** 19 [16] L M Cumani 5-9-4 (92) D Holland 7/2 FAV: 16-05111: Mid-div, short of room 2f 102+
out till dist, fin v strongly to lead cl-home, val 3L+: well bckd: eff at 12f, apprec step up to 14f: acts on fast
grnd & a stiff/gall or sharp/undul trk: prog 5yo who must have a major chance in the Ebor H'cap: see 3066.

3070+ **SERGEANT CECIL** 18 [3] B R Millman 5-9-1 (89) J Fortune 16/1: 20-03512: Held up, prog trav well ½ 96
to lead dist & sn clr, hdd cl-home: fine run, has a turn of foot & a return to 12f will suit.

2771 **JAGGER** 31 [9] G A Butler 4-9-9 (97) E Ahern 9/2: 16D11-03: Mid-div, prog when hmpd 2f out & lost ½ 103+
pl, switched wide & flew cl home: well bckd: no luck, most eye-catching: won at this meeting 12 months ago & clrly
likes Goodwood: most unlucky & strong comp claims in the Ebor, see 2771.

3119 **SANTANDO** 17 [4] C E Brittain 4-9-2 vis (90) K Fallon 25/1: 5305004: Bhd, hdwy 4f out, styd on to ½ 95
chase ldr 1f out, onepcd cl-home: back to form after sltly disapp on last 2 starts, can find a race off this mark.

3125 **SELF DEFENSE** 17 [1]7-9-1 (100) J Murtagh 25/1: 1450/-065: Held up, short of room after 9f, ¾ 104
short of again 2f out till dist, switched & kept on fnl 1f, nrst fin: eff at 14f, will apprec rtn to 2m: acts on
fast & good grnd: closer with clr passage: see 3125.

2583 **BIG MOMENT** 38 [6]6-9-9 (97) L Dettori 12/1: 0440-356: Bhd, hdwy 4f out, hung right & onepcd dist. 2½ 99
3458 **FOURTH DIMENSION** 2 [10]5-8-9 (83) A Nicholls 50/1: 3000-047: Rear, prog wide 4f out, onepcd dist. ½ 84
3125* **DOROTHYS FRIEND** 17 [13]4-9-0 (88) S Drowne 11/2: 111-0118: In tch, onepace when short of room ¾ 88
bef 1f out: well bckd tho' op 4/1: below par run on hat-trick bid but prob needs rtn to 2m: btr 3125.

3458 **BENDARSHAAN** 2 [8]4-8-13 (87) K Dalgleish 14/1: 0041129: Held up, hdwy when short of room 2f out nk 86
till dist, found daylight but ch had gone: qck reapp: did not get run of race: btr 3458 & 3281.

2759 **NAWAMEES** 31 [2]6-9-2 p (90) R L Moore 33/1: 236-4220: 10th: Handy, styd on to lead 2f out, hdd shd 88
bef 1f out, wknd: has been gelded: btr 2759.

3119 **MAMCAZMA** 17 [11]6-9-2 (90) M Tebbutt 25/1: 002-0040: 11th: Chsd ldrs, sltly outpcd 4f out, prog ½ 87
when short of room dist, sn no impress & eased: btr 3119.

3125 **ALMAH** 17 [15]6-9-2 (90) R Winston 100/1: 44630-00: 12th: Chsd ldrs over 11f, sn wknd: see 3125. 1½ 85
2948 **HAMBLEDEN** 24 [5]7-9-10 (98) P Robinson 11/1: 12-60440: 13th: Led, hdd & fdd 2f out: well bckd. 12 81
2972 **ANTICIPATING** 22 [14]4-8-11 (85) Martin Dwyer 14/1: 60-04020: 14th: Mid-div, wkng when short of 9 59
room dist, sn eased: btr 2972.

3119 **MORSON BOY** 17 [12]4-9-4 (92) J Fanning 7/1: 151-0000: 15th: Cl-up 11f, fdd, saddle slipped. 6 60

15 Ran   Time 3m 1.35 (2.55)   Owned: Mrs Angie Silver   Trained: Newmarket

3511   5.00 Evening Standard E B F Maiden Stakes Colts & Geldings 2yo (D)
£8249 £2538 £1269   **6f str**   **Good/Firm**   **Fair**   Stands side

3311 **DOCTORS CAVE 8** [8] C E Brittain 2-8-11   S Sanders 50/1: 00001: Cl-up, led 4f out, hdd 2f out, 90
rallied well to lead cl-home, rdn out: eff at 6f, has tried 7f: acts on fast grnd & a sharp/undul trk: game
performer who left prev efforts well bhd for a surprise win: see 3311.

RAJWA 0 [10] Saeed bin Suroor 2-8-11 T L Dettori 1/1 FAV: 2: ch c Dubai Millennium - Zelanda   nk 88
(Night Shift) Handy, gd prog to lead 2f out, hdd under press cl-home: debut: well bckd: Jan foal, half-brother to
wnrs at 5/6f: dam a sprint wnr, sire high-class 1m/10f performer: eff at 6f, will apprec further: acts on fast grnd
& eff with a t-strap: held in high regard & shld win similar.

3245 **MCELDOWNEY 11** [2] M Johnston 2-8-11   K Dalgleish 6/1: 32223: Led, hdd 4f out, styd handy, onepcd   2 82
fnl 1f: continues to run well but is starting to look exposed: see 3245 & 2776.

2766 **COUNCELLOR 31** [5] R Hannon 2-8-11 K Fallon 6/1: 344: Mid-div, prog ins fnl 2f, onepace fnl 1f.   1¼ 78

ONE PUTRA 0 [9]2-8-11 P Robinson 16/1: 5: b c Indian Ridge - Triomphale (Nureyev) In tch, prog   nk 77
2f out, no extra ins fnl 1f: debut: Mar foal, cost 200,000gns: half-brother successful at 10f: dam successful at
6f: sire decent performer at sprint dists: with M Jarvis.

OCEAN GIFT 0 [7]2-8-11 Dane O'Neill 28/1: 6: b c Cadeaux Genereux - Sea Drift (Warning) Slow   3½ 67
away, prog wide 3f out, onepace fnl 2f: debut: Feb first foal, cost 56,000gns: dam successful at 7f: sire
high-class performer at sprint dists: ran green here & looks sure to improve with experience.

TOSHI 0 [3]2-8-11 J Fanning 11/2: 7: b c Kingmambo - Majestic Role (Theatrical) Cl-up over 4f,   3½ 57
wknd: bckd from 12/1 on debut: May foal, cost 200,000gns: half-brother to a 10f Group wnr abroad: dam a smart 7f
juv wnr, sire a high-class miler: with M Johnston.

GRIGOROVITCH 0 [6]2-8-11 M Hills 16/1: 8: Slow away, sn keen in tch, wknd fnl 2f.   5 43

WEMBURY POINT 0 [1]2-8-11 S Whitworth 50/1: 9: Slow away, at rear.   1¾ 38

3122 **SUPERSTITIOUS 17** [4]2-8-11 G Gibbons 33/1: 00: 10th: Handy over 3f, sn short of room & wknd.   nk 37

10 Ran   Time 1m 12.38 (2.38)   Owned: Mr A J Richards   Trained: Newmarket

3512   5.35 Darnley Stakes Handicap 3yo+ 0-85 (D)   [85]
£8561 £2634 £1317   **1m rnd**   **Good/Firm 23**   **+01 Fast**   Inside

3088* **PANGO 18** [17] H Morrison 5-9-10 (81) L Fletcher(3) 5/1 JT FAV: 00-22111: Cl-up, prog trav well to   88
lead dist, drvn out to hold on: well bckd, gd time: eff btwn 7/11f on fast, gd/soft & both AWs: prog 5yo who made
gd use of fav'able high draw: see 3088 & 2872.

2250 **RINGSIDER 52** [19] G A Butler 3-8-12 (77) T P Queally 16/1: 01-002: Mid-div, hdwy 2f out, styd on   ½ 82
to chase wnr ins fnl 1f, just held: 7 wk abs: eff at 7f/1m on firm & fast grnd: unexposed in h'cap grade & can find
similar now yard has hit form: see 2250.

3265 **HIGHLAND REEL 10** [9] D R C Elsworth 7-10-0 (85) T Quinn 20/1: 0-100403: Held up, prog 2f out,   shd 89
styd on well ins fnl 1f, nrst fin: likes it here at Goodwood: won a similar contest over C/D in 1812.

3187* **FREELOADER 18** [18] J W Hills 4-9-6 (77) R Hills 5/1 JT FAV: 0-043014: In tch, prog to chase wnr   ½ 80
dist, kept on, not btn far in 4th: eff at 1m, rtn to 9/10f will suit: 5lb higher than recent win in 3187.

3443 **WHAT A DANCER 3** [11]7-9-4 (75) K Fallon 8/1: 4044065: Mid-div, hdwy 2f out, onepcd ins fnl 1f.   ¾ 76

3210* **PINTLE 12** [16]4-9-3 (74) K McEvoy 8/1: 215-4116: Prom, no extra dist: not disgraced on   nk 74
hat-trick bid: prob stays 1m, rtn to 7f will suit: btr 3210 & 2864 (7f).

3326 **WINNING VENTURE 7** [14]7-9-11 (82) D Holland 14/1: 05-60327: Led, hdd under press dist, no extra.   hd 81

3112 **EVALUATOR 17** [3]3-9-4 (83) J Fortune 12/1: 3061228: Held up, prog wide 3f out, kept on ins fnl   ½ 81
1f: not disgraced from poor low draw: btr 3112 & 2922.

3336 **REBATE 6** [13]4-8-3 T (60) R Smith 33/1: 0336359: In tch, prog 3f out, onepcd dist: qck reapp.   1¼ 55

3001 **OMAHA CITY 21** [10]10-9-2 (73) M Tebbutt 16/1: 0-002100: 10th: Held up, eff when short of room 2f   nk 67
out, sn hung left & onepcd: shade btr expected from this crse specialist: btr 2540.

3225 **ATLANTIC ACE 12** [7]7-8-8 (65) F Lynch 25/1: 0006000: 11th: Dwelt, nvr nrr than mid-div.   nk 58

3199 **EPHESUS 13** [2]4-9-9 vis (80) W Supple 50/1: 1422000: 12th: Bhd, no impress when short of room dist.   2½ 68

3328 **PAS DE SURPRISE 7** [15]6-7-12 (20h) (53) F P Ferris(3) 20/1: 0544540: 13th: Cl-up 6f, sn wknd.   nk 42

2620 **JUST TIM 36** [8]3-8-13 T (78) R L Moore 40/1: 1401500: 14th: Cl-up 6f, wknd: btr 2116.   nk 64

3034 **MYTHICAL CHARM 20** [5]5-7-12 (60h)t (49) Natalia Gemelova(7) 33/1: 3000350: 15th: Keen bhd.   hd 40

2943 **LUCAYAN DANCER 24** [4]4-8-1 (58) A Nicholls 50/1: 334-6550: 16th: Rear, nvr a factor: btr 1253.   2 39

249* **COMPTON DRAKE 214** [6]5-8-9 (66) L Dettori 10/1: 502110-0: 17th: Held up, nvr a factor: abs.   shd 46

3187 **Learned Lad 13** [1]6-7-12 (7oh)(48) D Kinsella 100/1:0 3039 **Terraquin 20** [12]4-8-10 p(67) G Baker 33/1:0

19 Ran   Time 1m 39.22(1.82)   Owned: Pangfield Partners   Trained: East Ilsley

Official Going Good (Good/Firm Places)

3513   6.20 E B F Crimebeat Charity Racenight Maiden Stakes 2yo (D)
£5447 £1676 £838   **5f218y str**   **Good/Firm 32**   **+12 Fast**   Stands side

3031 **ARMY OF ANGELS 21** [6] Saeed bin Suroor 2-9-0 t K McEvoy 2/13 FAV: 21: Al cl-up, led 2f out,   98+
pushed clr ins fnl 1f, v cmftbly: fast time: eff over a stiff 6f, 7f will suit: acts on firm & fast grnd: useful,
could not have won this any easier, win better races: see 3031 (debut).

3171 **AVERTIGO 15** [4] W R Muir 2-9-0   K Darley 15/2: 532: Led 4f, sn outpcd by easy wnr: op 13/2:   8 73
caught a useful sort: see 3171.

3111 **STORM FURY 18** [2] P W Chapple Hyam 2-9-0   A McCarthy 20/1: 03: b g Storm Creek - Danseuse du   1½ 69
Nord (Kahyasi) Handy over 4f, sn onepcd: clr rem: 3rd foal, cost 29,000gns: half-brother successful abroad as a
3yo: dam decent performer abroad: still ran green & sure to improve with experience.

3272 **ALLIZAM 11** [5] B A McMahon 2-9-0   G Carter 80/1: 04: b c Tragic Role - Mazilla (Mazilier) Slow   5 55
away, cl-up after 2f, wknd ins fnl 2f: Feb first foal, dam wnr 7f/hdls wnr: sire wnr at 1m4f.

BEAU MARCHE 0 [1]2-9-0 I Mongan 33/1: 5: b g My Best Valentine - Beau Dada (Pine Circle) Al in   1¾ **50**
rear: debut: May foal, cost 3,200gns: half-brother to smart sprint performer Smokin Beau: dam successful at 6f.
LAYED BACK ROCKY 0 [3]2-9-0 S Righton 66/1: 6: Slow away, al bhd on debut.   5 **37**
6 Ran   Time 1m 11.04 (1.24)   Owned: Godolphin   Trained: Newmarket

---

3514   6.50 Samworth Brothers Handicap Stakes 3yo+ 0-80 (D)   [78]
£6968 £2144 £1072   **1m1f218y**   **Good/Firm 32**   +01 Fast   Inside

3270 **REALISM 11** [2] P W Hiatt 4-9-10 (74) Darren Williams 5/1: 6121101: Cl-up, styd on to lead 2f   **84**+
out, rdn clr, eased cl-home: val 7L+: relished return to 10f: acts on gd, fast grnd & fibresand: v tough &
progressive, win again: see 2794 & 2628.
3243* **FORTUNES PRINCESS 12** [7] M J Wallace 3-9-3 (77) K Darley 3/1 FAV: 2212: Rear, prog 4f out, ev ch   5 **79**
dist, sn no extra: h'cap bow: gd eff on first try against older rivals: see 3243 (mdn).
4551} **ROYAL BATHWICK 301** [1] B R Millman 4-9-9 (73) G Baker 14/1: 040106-3: b f King's Theatre - Ring   nk **74**
of Light (Auction Ring) Slow away, prog ins fnl 2f, nrst fin: reapp: fill mdn & h'cap wnr in '03: eff at 1m/1f:
acts on fast grnd & sharp/turning trk, likes Warwick: just sharper for today.
1 Jul'03 Warw 10.9g/f 76-72 D: 1 May'03 Warw 8.1g/f 71- D:
2485} **YOUNG ROONEY 396** [5] M Mullineaux 4-9-5 (69) T P Queally 28/1: 204324-4: b c Danzig Connection -   ½ **69**
Lady Broker (Petorius) Led, hdd 2f out, sn no extra: reapp: rnr-up 3 times in '03 (mdn & h'caps): eff around
1m/9.1f on fast, gd/soft & fibresand: not disgraced & sure to improve for today.
2 Jun'03 Ayr 9.1g/f 69-66 E: 2 Apr'03 Wolv 9.4af 60a-61 F: 2 Apr'03 Wolv 8.5af 63a- D:
3099 **SUMMER BOUNTY 18** [3]8-9-12 (76) S W Kelly 7/2: 1103205: Rear, prog 3f out, wknd dist: tchd 9/2.   ½ **75**
2900 **COLOPHONY 26** [8]4-9-7 t (71) M Fenton 11/1: 216-0406: Slow away, prog 4f out, hung right & wknd fnl 2f.*1* **68**
3211* **ZEIS 13** [4]4-9-4 t (68) J F Egan 7/2: 0-000117: Handy 1m, wknd: new stable: gelded since last   ¾ **63**
start: below form on hat-trick bid: btr 3211 & 2643 (H Morrison, claimers).
3139 **ACTIVE ACCOUNT 17** [6]7-8-10 (60) I Mongan 8/1: 2566308: Cl-up 7f, wknd when short of room 2f out.   ¾ **53**
8 Ran   Time 2m 5.64 (3.14)   Owned: Miss Maria McKinney   Trained: Banbury

---

3515   7.20 Everards Brewery Claiming Stakes 3yo (E)
£3552 £1093 £547   **7f9y str**   **Good/Firm 32**   -06 Slow   Stands side

3091 **STEVEDORE 19** [11] John A Harris 3-9-3 (70) G Baker 5/1: 14-00041: Handy, styd on to lead 2f out,   **71**
rdn clr: tchd 8/1, clmd for 10,000: eff at 6/7f, stays sharp 1m in claiming grade: acts on fm & fibresand.
3219 **BLUE JAVA 13** [15] H Morrison 3-8-13 (59) M Fenton 9/2 FAV: 040-0002: Slow away, prog to lead bef   1½ **63**
3f out, hdd 2f out, styd cl-up & ev ch dist, not pace wnr well ins fnl 1f: eff at 7f on fast grnd: more encouraging.
3344 **ELSINORA 7** [2] H Morrison 3-8-0 BL (43) D Kinsella 10/1: 0-000263: In tch, ev ch 2f out, sn no   1¾ **46**
extra: first time blnks & qck reapp: see 2932.
3410 **MISS PROCURER 5** [5] P F I Cole 3-8-12 (69) J Quinn 14/1: 65-504: Slow away, prog 2f out, no   hd **57**
impress ins fnl 1f: t-strap left off: eff at 6/7f on firm & fast grnd: see 3121.
3344 **RED ROCKY 7** [4]3-8-4 p (46) Stephanie Hollinshead(5) 9/1: 0502035: Led, hdd bef 3f out, wknd fnl 1f.   1¾ **45**
3373 **LYRICAL GIRL 6** [7]3-8-12 (58) D Fox(5) 12/1: 031-1506: Bhd, nvr nrr than mid-div: qck reapp.   1½ **50**
3094 **CHIQITITA 19** [9]3-8-2 (51) Hayley Turner(5) 100/1: 0-000007: Mid-div over 5f, sn onepcd: see 1576.   nk **39**
2334 **PERERIN 48** [3]3-8-5 b (46) T P Queally 20/1: 00-01008: Cl-up over 5f, wknd: 7 wk abs: btr 1549.   shd **41**
3016 **SHINKO FEMME 21** [13]3-8-8 (53) Kim Tinkler 9/1: 0005109: Mid-div 5f, wknd: btr 2812.   nk **43**
2982 **LUPINE HOWL 23** [8]3-9-3 p (44) G Gibbons 66/1: 0-000060: 10th: Handy 5f, fdd.   5 **42**
3036 **SWORN TO SECRECY 21** [1]3-8-4 bl (57) K McEvoy 11/2: 0000060: 11th: Al in rear: see 1339.   6 **17**
3090 **FIZZY LADY 19** [12]3-8-8 t (60) R Smith 25/1: 4-441000: 12th: Cl-up 5f, fdd: btr 613.   4 **13**
3291 **SOVIET SPIRIT 9** [14]3-9-0 (59) M Halford(7) 10/1: 505350: 13th: Cl-up till halfway, wknd.   8 **5**
2852 **MAYBE SOMEDAY 28** [6]3-8-9 bl (52) I Mongan 50/1: 3020000: 14th: Al in rear.   8 **0**
2504 **DELUSION 41** [10]3-8-5 (1ow) (53) K Darley 9/1: 040-6300: 15th: Rear, nvr a factor: 6 wk abs.   8 **0**
15 Ran   Time 1m 24.66 (2.66)   Owned: Cleartherm Ltd   Trained: Melton Mowbray

---

3516   7.50 Next Handicap Stakes 3yo 0-70 (E)   [77]
£7300 £2246 £1123   **1m9y rnd**   **Good/Firm 32**   -08 Slow   Inside

2506* **SHES OUR LASS 41** [4] D Carroll 3-9-6 (69) K McEvoy 7/1: 0013111: Rear, prog 3f out, styd on to   **74**+
lead ins fnl 1f, pushed clr, going away: 6 wk abs: eff at 7f/1m on firm, soft & fibresand: v progressive.
3198 **BURLINGTON PLACE 14** [12] S Kirk 3-8-11 (60) J F Egan 25/1: 0246-002: Cl-up, led after 2f, hdd   2 **59**
ins fnl 1f, not pace wnr: eff at 6f/1m on fast grnd & polytrack: see 51.
3410 **LOUISIADE 5** [13] T D Easterby 3-9-0 (63) M Fenton 12/1: 0-030033: Cl-up, hung right under press   nk **61**
ins fnl 2f, just held for 2nd: qck reapp: another gd run: see 3410.
3197 **STANLEY CRANE 14** [5] B Hanbury 3-8-10 t (59) B Doyle 16/1: 35-05454: Bhd, prog when short of room   2 **53**
3f out, sn switched, kept on ins fnl 1f: see 2443.
3455 **KNICKYKNACKIENOO 4** [11]3-8-10 (59) S Whitworth 9/2: 2031025: Slow away, rcd keen, prog halfway,   ¾ **51**
edged right & onepcd fnl 1f: qck reapp: would have benefited from stronger gallop: lkd a shade unlucky in 3455.
2922 **PHLUKE 25** [14]3-9-7 (70) S Carson 16/1: 5120406: Led 2f, styd in tchd, wknd ins fnl 2f: btr 2024.   1½ **60**
3410 **THE FUN MERCHANT 5** [2]3-9-2 (65) J Quinn 7/4 FAV: 60-01127: Rear, prog halfway, hung right &   1 **53**
wknd dist: qck reapp: btr expected after 3410 & 2701.
2650 **MISTER TRICKSTER 36** [9]3-8-13 (62) S Righton 16/1: 0-600108: Keen cl-up 6f, wknd: jumps fit.   2 **46**
3197* **KOMOTO 14** [6]3-9-7 (70) T P Queally 9/1: 19: Slow away, al bhd: h'cap & turf bow: btr 3197 (mdn, aw).   5 **44**
2431 **MR BELVEDERE 44** [8]3-8-7 (56) J Mackay 25/1: 0-000320: 10th: Handy 6f, wknd: btr 2431 (sell).   6 **18**
3380 **HALF A HANDFUL 6** [7]3-9-3 vis (66) K Darley 12/1: 0633230: 11th: Mid-div when short of room after   1¼ **26**
3f, wknd ins fnl 2f: qck reapp: btr 3380 (6f) & 3153.
11 Ran   Time 1m 41.41 (3.21)   Owned: We-Know Partnership   Trained: Warthilll

3517
8.20 E B F High Sheriffs' Median Auction Maiden Stakes Fillies 2yo (E)
£4212 £1296 £648 5f218y str Good/Firm 32 -17 Slow Stands side

3171 **GOOD WEE GIRL 15** [12] S Kirk 2-8-11 J F Egan 12/1: 0021: In tch, gd prog to lead 1f out, rdn **80**
out: eff at 6f on fast grnd: improving: see 3171.

3411 **CEREBUS 5** [13] N P Littmoden 2-8-11 I Mongan 10/1: 642: Al handy, kept on ins fnl 2f, not pace 1 **76**
wnr: qck reapp: eff at 6f, shld apprec 7f: acts on fast grnd: see 3411.

3071 **SUBYAN DREAMS 19** [1] P W Chapple Hyam 2-8-11 A McCarthy 7/4 FAV: 53: Trkd ldrs, kept on ins fnl ½ **75**
1f, just held for 2nd: eff at 6f, looks in need of further: acts on fast grnd: see 3071.

HEARTSONFIRE 77 [11] P W D'Arcy 2-8-11 M Fenton 20/1: 3304: bl f Bold Fact - Jazirah (Main 2½ **68**
Reef) Led, hdd 1f out, sn no extra: 11 wk abs & Brit bow: Mar foal, cost E7,000: half-sister to wnrs at 7/13f.

2902 **SAMBARINA 26** [15]2-8-11 R Smith 3/1: 35: Sn cl-up, no extra fnl 1f: btr 2902. shd **67**

3063 **LADY HEN 20** [8]2-8-11 K Darley 9/2: 06: b f Efisio - Royale Rose (Bering) Mid-div over 4f, sn 2½ **60**
onepcd: Apr foal, cost 20,000gns: half-sister to wnrs at 9/16f: dam successful miler.

LAKE WAKATIPU 0 [4]2-8-11 S Righton 80/1: 7: Slow away, modest late gains: debut. hd **59**

3258 **RUBYS DREAM 11** [14]2-8-11 Dean McKeown 12/1: 2343548: Handy 4f, sn no extra: btr 3258. 1½ **55**

SUCCESSION 0 [5]2-8-11 J Mackay 25/1: 9: ch f Groom Dancer - Pitcroy (Unfuwain) Slow away, al 4 **43**
bhd on debut: Mar foal, half-sister 10f listed wnr: dam also 10f wnr: sire decent performer at 10f.

3355 **FLOOSIE 6** [2]2-8-11 t J P Guillambert(3) 33/1: 00: 10th: In tch 4f, wknd. 11 **13**

Frida 0 [6]2-8-11 S Whitworth 40/1:0   2926 **Katie Killane 25** [9]2-8-11 V Slattery 100/1:0
Isle Of Light 0 [3]2-8-11 J Quinn 66/1:0   **Little Waltham 0** [10]2-8-11 S Carson 100/1:0

14 Ran Time 1m 12.77 (2.97) Owned: E Power & M Kavanagh Trained: Upper Lambourn

3518
8.50 Crimebeat Charity Racenight Classified Stakes 3yo+ 0-70 (E)
£4037 £1242 £621 5f218y str Good/Firm 32 -06 Slow Stands side

3184 **MISTRAL SKY 14** [4] Mrs Stef Liddiard 5-9-2 vis (64) J F Egan 7/2: 4335401: Rear, prog halfway, **74**
drvn to lead cl-home: eff at 6/7f, stays 1m: acts on firm, gd & polytrack: likes Leicester & Lingfield.

3244* **HIGH RIDGE 12** [1] J M Bradley 5-9-2 p (69) Dean McKeown 15/8 FAV: 5123412: Handy, styd on to lead shd **72**
1f out, hdd under press cl-home: continues to run well: btr 3244.

3083 **PRINCE OF BLUES 19** [5] M Mullineaux 6-9-2 bl (59) S Righton 40/1: 0335003: Led, hdd 1f out, no extra. 3 **63**

3366* **GO YELLOW 6** [2] P D Evans 3-9-3 (69) I Mongan 11/2: 0524614: In tch, prog & ev ch dist, sn wknd: 1 **66**
qck reapp: showed more in 3366 (7f, mdn).

3379 **CHEROKEE NATION 6** [6]3-8-11 (70) K Darley 11/4: 0211036: Keen rear, nvr nrr than mid-div: qck reapp. 1¾ **56**

2723 **GENEROUS GESTURE 33** [3]3-8-11 vis (73) M Fenton 8/1: 5610656: Rear, prog halfway, wknd dist. ½ **55**

2981 **XSYNNA 23** [7]8-9-2 (34) Hayley Turner(5) 100/1: 3060307: Handy 4f, wknd: see 1327. 4 **43**

7 Ran Time 1m 12.12(2.32) Owned: Shefford Valley Stud Trained: Hungerford

Official Going GOOD/FIRM.

3519
6.05 Sharp Minds Betfair Apprentice Handicap Stakes 3yo+ 0-75 (E) [73]
£4037 £1242 £621 1m4f Good/Firm 27 -22 Slow Inside

3299 **DESERT ISLAND DISC 9** [5] J J Bridger 7-10-0 (73) A Beech 7/1: 0306151: Chsd ldrs, led over 1f **81**
out, rdn & in command ins last: eff around 12f on fast, hvy & handles polytrack, any trk: likes Kempton: see 2956.

3398 **HEAD TO KERRY 5** [3] D J S ffrench Davis 4-8-10 t (55) P Gallagher(3) 11/2: 0035342: Led & sn clr, 1¾ **57**
hdd over 1f out, kept on: quick reapp: t-strap reapplied, gd run with forcing tactics: eff btwn 10f/2m: see 2391.

3450 **MOST SAUCY 4** [6] I A Wood 8-8-10 (55) F P Ferris 4/1: 3450433: Trkd ldrs, styd on for press fnl 2f. hd **56**

3477 **RECOUNT 2** [2] J R Best 4-9-9 (68) M Savage 2/1 FAV: 6500234: Rear, eff over 3f out, no impress 1½ **66**
dist: nicely bckd tho' op 7/4: quick reapp: btr 3477, 3336.

3200 **SUDDEN FLIGHT 14** [7]7-9-11 (70) S Donohoe(3) 9/1: 0043165: Mid-div, rdn & no impress fnl 2f. 2½ **64**

3085 **ESCALADE 19** [1]7-8-2 p (47) Dean Williams(5) 12/1: 5434356: Rear, rdn & btn over 2f out: btr 2892. 4 **35**

3173 **GREAT VIEW 15** [4]5-9-6 vis (65) L Keniry 7/1: 1240237: Mid-div, rdn & btn over 2f out: btr 3173 & 2912. 1½ **51**

7 Ran Time 2m 35.88 (5.88) Owned: Mr W Wood Trained: Liphook

3520
6.35 European Breeders Fund Maiden Stakes Fillies 2yo (D)
£4971 £1530 £765 7f jub Good/Firm 27 -27 Slow Inside

HACHITA [8] H R A Cecil 2-8-11 W Ryan 12/1: 1: ch f Gone West - Choice Spirit (Danzig) Rear, **87+**
hdwy wide over 2f out, led ins last: op 10/1: Jan 1st foal, dam a 1m Listed wnr: eff at 7f, 1m will suit:
acts on fast grnd & an easy trk: goes well fresh: plenty more to come.

INNOCENT SPLENDOUR [2] E A L Dunlop 2-8-11 E Ahern 25/1: 2: b f Mtoto - Maureena (Grand Lodge) 1¼ **81**
Mid-div, rdn & hdwy to chall ins last, not pace of wnr: Jan 1st foal, 18,000 gns purchase: dam unrcd, eff at 7f,
1m+ could suit: handles fast grnd: fine start, rate higher.

3035 **SHES MY OUTSIDER 21** [5] I A Wood 2-8-11 F Norton 40/1: 03: b f Docksider - Solar Flare ¾ **79**
(Danehill) Keen in mid-div, rdn & kept on from over 1f out, not pace to chall: left debut bhd: Feb 1st foal, dam
unplcd sole start, related to 2 juv 1m wnrs: eff at 7f, 1m will suit: acts on fast: find a race on this evidence.

3035 **ARBELLA 21** [7] P W Harris 2-8-11 D Holland 11/4: 24: Rear, hdwy & little room over 2f out till hd **79+**
late on, prob gone close with a clr run: op 2/1: not gvn a hard time & will improve: win sn.

3047 **MULBERRY WINE 20** [1]2-8-11 D Sweeney 33/1: 645: Led till ins last, no extra: h'cap shld suit. 1¾ **73**

3035 **AUTUMN MELODY 21** [1]2-8-11 t L Dettori 11/2: 56: Cl-up, wknd over 1f out: btr 3035. 1¾ **71**

3035 **SPINNING COIN 21** [10]2-8-11 Dane O'Neill 50/1: 067: Slow away & rear, late gains, no threat. ½ **70**

BALLETOMAINE [12]2-8-11 K May(7) 33/1: 8: Chsd ldrs, btn when hmpd dist on debut. 1¼ 67
3035 HEAT OF THE NIGHT 21 [3]2-8-11 T Quinn 9/2: 49: Fly jump start, sn trkd ldrs, btn over 1f out. 3 61
2863 GREAT OPINIONS 27 [11]2-8-11 K Fallon 9/4 FAV: 020: 10th: Dwelt, chsd ldrs till 2f out: bckd. ½ 60
3381 IMPERIAL MISS 6 [4]2-8-11 A Daly 50/1: 06060: 11th: Trkd ldrs, btn 2f out, quick reapp. ¾ 58
Alpine Gold [6]2-8-11 S Drowne 40/1:0 2810 Victory Hymn 30 [9]2-8-11 C Catlin 50/1:0
13 Ran Time 1m 27.93 (3.83) Owned: Mr K Abdulla Trained: Newmarket

3521 **7.05 Shangri-La Hotel Singapore Nursery Handicap Stakes 2yo (E)** **[90]**
£4173 £1284 £642 **6f str** **Good/Firm 27** **+07 Fast** Centre

3303* **THE CROOKED RING 9** [5] P D Evans 2-9-8 (6ex) (84) S Donohoe(7) 5/1: 3213411: Held up, prog ins fnl 2f, styd on to lead cl-home, drvn out: fast time: eff at 5/6f on firm & soft grnd: prob any trk: tough performer who did well to defy a 7lb penalty: progressing with racing: see 3303 & 3081. **96**
3110 **RIDDER 18** [6] D J Coakley 2-8-9 (71) E Ahern 20/1: 4502: Mid-div, prog to lead ins fnl 1f, hdd cl-home: eff at 6f, further shld suit: only just denied on h'cap bow & can find similar: see 1911. ½ **81**
3382* **PIDDIES PRIDE 6** [3] P S McEntee 2-8-7 (6ex) (69) F P Ferris(3) 7/1: 5664113: Bhd, prog 2f out, kept on ins fnl 1f: quick reapp: gd run on hat-trick bid under 6lb pen: ran to form of win in 3382 (sell). ¾ **76**
2358* **ISLAND SWING 47** [4] J L Spearing 2-9-7 (83) L Dettori 9/2 JT FAV: 0114: Rcd stands side, ev ch dist, sn no extra: 7 wk abs: btr 2358 (sell). 1½ **86**
3266 **LATERAL THINKER 11** [2]2-8-8 (70) S Drowne 10/1: 2234105: In tch stands side till dist, sn wknd. ½ **72**
2970 **ARTHUR WARDLE 23** [11]2-8-10 (72) D Holland 7/1: 2506: Slow away, sn mid-div, wknd 1f out: btr 2316. ¾ **71**
3266 **GRAND OPTION 11** [10]2-9-0 (76) A Daly 20/1: 3232507: Rcd far side, led/dsptd overall lead till hdd ins fnl 1f, wknd: longer trip: btr 1716 (5f). nk **72**
3163 **ROYAL ORISSA 16** [8]2-9-2 (78) Paul Eddery 9/2 JT FAV: 4538: Held up, prog & ev ch bef 1f out, wknd. nk **75**
3369 **GEE BEE EM 6** [7]2-9-0 (76) C Catlin 16/1: 21449: Handy 4f, sn wknd: quick reapp. 2 **67**
3212* **COLONEL BILKO 13** [9]2-8-10 (72) F Norton 9/1: 20610: 10th: Rcd far side, cl-up till led briefly 3f out, wknd fnl 2f: op 6/1: has been gldd since last start: btr 3212. ½ **62**
10 Ran Time 1m 12.35 (1.25) Owned: Mr J R Salter Trained: Abergavenny

3522 **7.35 Commitments Live Here Next Wednesday Rated Stakes Handicap 3yo 0-85 (D)** **[89]**
£7276 £2760 £1380 **7f jub** **Good/Firm 27** **-01 Slow** Inside

3447 **PIZAZZ 4** [3] B J Meehan 3-9-7 BL (82) J Fortune 6/1: 2522031: Made all, went clr ins fnl 2f, eased cl-home, val 7L+: op 4/1 on quick reapp: eff at 7f/1m on fast & hvy grnd: has been in gd form this term & this was deserved: impvd for fitting of 1st time blnks: can follow up under a pen: see 3447. **93+**
3088 **DUMNONI 19** [4] Julian Poulton 3-9-5 (80) N Callan 9/2: 6304132: Al cl-up, not pace of wnr fnl 1f. 5 **83**
2677 **FAREWELL GIFT 35** [2] R Hannon 3-9-7 (82) K Fallon 3/1: 4323233: Mid-div, prog after halfway, no impress bef 1f out: well bckd: just appreciate drop back to 6f: just btr 2677. 1¾ **81**
2797 **RIVER TREAT 30** [7] G Wragg 3-9-5 (80) D Holland 10/1: 24-16504: Rear, prog 3f out, mod late gains. ½ **78**
3447 **CONVINCE 4** [5]3-9-7 (82) S Drowne 20/1: 4-000565: Al in rear: quick reapp: see 1665. 1¼ **77**
3283 **PANSHIR 11** [1]3-9-6 (81) R Mullen 15/8 FAV: 0301626: Slow away, prog halfway, no impress fnl 2f: well bckd: v disapp run: btr 3283 & 2314. 1½ **73**
3197 **MEMORY MAN 14** [6]3-8-6 (67) F Norton 20/1: 0437: Cl-up 5f, sn wknd, eased ins fnl 1f: btr 3917. 22 **19**
7 Ran Time 1m 26.08 (1.98) Owned: Mrs Susan Roy Trained: Upper Lambourn

3523 **8.05 'surrey Herald' Classified Stakes 3yo+ 0-80 (D)**
£6809 £2095 £1048 **1m jub** **Good/Firm 27** **-05 Slow** Inside

3465 **WELCOME STRANGER 3** [3] J M P Eustace 4-9-4 (81) L Fletcher(3) 7/4: 0002121: Mid-div, hdwy into 2nd over 2f out, led over 1f out, v cmftbly: qck reapp, op 5/4: eff at 7.5f/1m on firm, fast & polytrack, stiff/gall or sharp trks: tough, in gd form of late & improving: win more races: see 2853. **95**
3067* **ARKHOLME 19** [1] P Winkworth 3-8-9 bl (80) S Drowne 7/2: 41-40212: Rcd in 2nd till led 3f out, hdd over 1f out, no extra: new stable (prev with W Haggas): remains in gd form: see 3067 (clmr). 3½ **84**
3277 **SWEET INDULGENCE 11** [5] Dr J D Scargill 3-8-12 (83) K Fallon 13/8 FAV: 13-0053: Keen in mid-div, onepcd over 1f out: bckd from 5/2: see 1930. 1¾ **83**
3188 **VIENNAS BOY 14** [4] R Hannon 3-8-12 (83) Dane O'Neill 12/1: 4605254: Rear, hdwy 2f out, not pace to chall: not stay 1m?: btr 1018 (6f). shd **83**
3216 **RYANS FUTURE 13** [2]4-9-3 (79) C Catlin 16/1: 415-5005: Led to 3f out, sn no extra: btr 174. 9 **62**
5 Ran Time 1m 39.36 (2.56) Owned: Mr H R Moszkowicz Trained: Newmarket

3524 **8.35 Sharp Minds Betfair Handicap Stakes 3yo+ 0-75 (E)** **[75]**
£4232 £1302 £651 **1m jub** **Good/Firm 27** **-21 Slow** Inside

3187 **TODLEA 14** [7] J A Osborne 4-9-12 (73) L Dettori 5/2 FAV: 4362231: Cl-up, hdwy 2f out & sn led, rdn out: nicely bckd, top-weight: eff at 1m/10f on firm & gd, sharp/undul or fair trks: gd weight carrier. **79**
3088 **FLEETWOOD BAY 19** [12] B R Millman 4-9-6 T (67) J Fortune 12/1: 0063602: Led after 1f till over 1f out, not pace to go with wnr: stays 1m in a t-strap: see 2587. 1½ **68**
3401 **THE GAIKWAR 5** [1] N E Berry 5-9-0 bl (61) M Savage(5) 14/1: 2U00043: Bhd, hdwy over 2f out, kept on but not pace of first 2: qck reapp: see 3401. ½ **61**
3088 **ZAFARSHAH 19** [11] P D Evans 5-8-13 vis (60) K Fallon 9/2: 6203004: Keen in mid-div, kept on fnl 1f but not reach ldrs: op 6/1: back to winning form of 565. shd **60**
3187 **MY MAITE 14** [3]5-7-13 t p (46) C Catlin 8/1: 0016045: Bhd, some late gains: see 1992. 2½ **41**
3107 **PENDING 18** [6]3-9-3 P (72) J Murtagh 11/2: 05-306: Cl-up, wknd over 1f out: tried cheek pieces. ½ **66**
2931* **LITTLE ENGLANDER 25** [4]4-8-11 (58) Dane O'Neill 8/1: 0-500517: Bhd, some late gains. shd **52**
3044 **ESPERANCE 20** [8]4-7-12 (1oh) (44) F P Ferris(3) 33/1: 00-00558: Led for 1f, rem in 2nd, lost pl 2f out, sn no extra: see 2799. ½ **38**
3042 **HOLLYWOOD HENRY 20** [2]4-8-9 p (56) A Daly 10/1: 0000-169: Nvr a factor: btr 2440. ¾ **47**
3336 **COOL TEMPER 7** [9]8-9-5 BL (66) N De Souza(5) 20/1: 36-53000: 10th: In tch, wknd 2f out: blnks. ½ **56**

KEMPTON   WEDNESDAY 28.07.04   Righthand, Flat, Fair Track

3174 **NAUTICAL 15** [5]6-8-3 (50) R Mullen 10/1: 0046430: 11th: Slow away, nvr a factor. *shd* **40**
3295 **SENIOR MINISTER 9** [10]6-8-13 (60) E Ahern 33/1: 0-010000: 12th: Handy, fdd over 3f out, t.o., lame. *dist* **5**
12 Ran   Time 1m 40.68(3.88)   Owned: Lynn Wilson Giles Wilson Martin Landau   Trained: Upper Lambourn

MUSSELBURGH   WEDNESDAY 28.07.04   Righthand, Sharp Track

Official Going Good/Firm (Firm Places)

3525   2.30 European Breeders Fund Median Auction Maiden Stakes Fillies 2yo (E)
£4352 £1339 £670 **5f str** **Good/Firm 24** -48 Slow Stands Side

3323 **JERRYS GIRL 8** [6] Miss L A Perratt 2-8-11 S Sanders 11/4: 3641: Pushed along chsg ldrs, styd on **71**
for press to lead well ins last: nicely bckd, op 7/2: slow time: eff at 5f, return to 6f+ shld suit: acts on firm
& fast grnd, handles gd, stiff or sharp trk: see 3323 and 1950.
2689 **DUCAL DIVA 34** [1] J R Weymes 2-8-11 D Fentiman(7) 5/2 FAV: 02: b f Bahamian Bounty - Lucky Thing ¾ **67**
(Green Desert) Al handy, rdn & led over 1f out, edged right & hdd well ins last: hvly bckd: cheaply bought May
foal, half sister to a 7f juv wnr & subs hdles scorer: eff at 5f on fast.
  FOLGA 0 [2] R P Elliott 2-8-11 Dean McKeown 5/1: 3: b f Atraf - Desert Dawn (Belfort) Handy, 1¾ **62**
edged left early, rdn/ch over 1f out, not pace of front pair: Mar foal, half sister to numerous wnrs, incl a 1m 3yo
Listed scorer: dam a smart juv/sprint: eff at 5f on fast grnd.
  BOND BABE 0 [4] B Smart 2-8-11 F Lynch 3/1: 4: b f Forzando - Lindfield Belle (Fairy King) ¾ **60**
Bmpd start, outpcd, late gains: 14,000 gns Mar foal, half sister to useful 5/6f wnr: dam 5f juv wnr.
  ONE OF EACH 0 [7]2-8-11 D Tudhope(7) 14/1: 5: Led, hdd 2f out, no extra under press. 1 **57**
3323 **QUICK GRAND 8** [3]2-8-11 R Winston 14/1: 66: Went rght start, al outpcd, op 6/1. ½ **55**
6 Ran   Time 1m 01.08 (3.58)   Owned: Mr Jerry Ryan   Trained: Ayr

3526   3.00 Links Handicap Stakes 3yo+ 35-55 (F)   [64]
£2996 £856 £428 **1m rnd** **Good/Firm 24** -25 Slow Outside

3058 **SON OF THUNDER 20** [4] M Dods 3-9-5 (55) L Enstone(3) 9/1: 0-616201: Rear, switched wide & hdwy **65**
over 2f out, led ins last, rdn out: suited by 1m on fast & gd, loves Musselburgh: see 2613, 1798.
2958 **LONER 24** [9] R A Fahey 6-9-8 p (50) T Hamilton(3) 6/1: 42500-02: Slow into stride & sn rdn, 2 **55**
switched & hdwy over 2f out, led over 1f out, hdd ins last: bckd: btr run with cheek pieces reapplied.
3242 **PENWELL HILL 12** [12] T D Barron 5-9-9 (51) P Makin(5) 10/1: 2206003: Chsd ldrs, drvn & styd on 2½ **51**
onepace: well h'capped on turf: acts on fast grnd, loves fibresand: see 632 & 318.
3034 **OTAGO 21** [5] J R Best 3-9-5 (55) B Swarbrick(5) 14/1: 304504: Held up, hdwy 3f out, styd on onepace. 1 **53**
3246 **ISLANDS FAREWELL 12** [3]4-9-11 (53) Alex Greaves 12/1: 000-0025: Chsd ldrs, no extra over 1f out. ½ **50**
2324 **MON SECRET 4** [10]6-9-9 (51) F Lynch 16/1: 3-400606: Rear, no room 2f out, onepce, abs. ¾ **47**
3102 **HOHS BACK 18** [8]5-9-12 p (54) Natalia Gemelova(7) 25/1: 0500007: Mid-div, rdn & btn over 1f out. hd **49**
3242 **SHAMWARI FIRE 12** [14]4-9-7 (49) D Allan 6/1: 1600338: Chsd ldrs, fdd under press fnl 2f: btr 3242. ½ **43**
2988 **EXPECTED BONUS 22** [7]5-9-5 bl (47) Dale Gibson 5/1: R540004: Led till 2f out, sn btn: bckd. 2½ **36**
3310 **TIME TO REGRET 9** [6]4-9-11 (53) P Mulrennan(5) 10/1: 6240100: 10th: Chsd ldrs, rdn & no impress. nk **41**
1972 **SCRAMBLE 65** [13]6-9-8 t p (50) G Parkin 12/1: 3464-600: 11th: Al bhd: abs: chkpcs reapp. ¾ **37**
2891 **CANLIS 26** [2]5-9-5 (47) R Winston 16/1: 000-0200: 12th: Cl-up/dspted lead 6f, sn wknd: btr 2402. ½ **33**
2986 **SHIFTY 23** [11]5-9-5 (47) D Fentiman(7) 6/1: 5244000: 13th: Mid-div, btn over 2f out: btr 1954 & 86. 7 **21**
13 Ran   Time 1m 39.97 (2.47)   Owned: Mr Russ Mould   Trained: Darlington

3527   3.35 Stewarts Turf Selling Stakes 3yo+ (E)
£3465 £1066 £533 **5f str** **Good/Firm 24** -10 Slow Stands Side

3228 **BETTYS PRIDE 12** [1] M Dods 5-8-9 (49) R Winston 5/1: 0406601: Rear, switched & rdn/hdwy to lead **48**
ins last: rdn out: no bid: nicely bckd, op 8/1: chkpcs omitted: suited by 5/6f on firm & gd: apprec drop to sell.
3220 **JOYCES CHOICE 13** [3] J S Wainwright 5-9-0 p (45) M Lawson(5) 25/1: R540002: Trkd ldrs, switched to ½ **50**
chall over 1f out, not pace of wnr ins last: cheek pieces reapplied, imprvd eff: see 1179.
3417 **SOAKED 5** [8] D W Chapman 11-9-5 bl (63) S Sanders 1/1 FAV: 4121523: Sn handy & ch over 1f out, 2 **49**
briefly led dist, not pace of wnr ins last: rdn reapp: btr 3417 & 2775 (dominated).
3417 **DANAKIM 5** [4] J R Weymes 7-9-5 (40) D Fentiman(7) 33/1: 5000004: Handy, drvn & onepace when short nk **48$**
of room over 1f out: quick reapp: see 1988.
3193 **WENDYS GIRL 14** [6]3-8-10 bl (63) T Hamilton(3) 100/30: 4010165: Cl-up, rdn & btn dist: btr 3018 (6f). 1 **40**
3417 **AMERICAN COUSIN 5** [2]9-9-5 (55) Alex Greaves 13/2: 0250066: Rear, nvr pace to chall: qck reapp. shd **45**
5006} **ALFIE LEE 266** [7]7-9-0 t p (43) J McAuley 50/1: 000400-7: ch g Case Law - Nordic Living (Nordico) 1 **37**
Led/dspted lead till over 1f out, sn btn: reapp: apprec h'cap plcd '03 (rtd 45): unplcd '02 (rtd 47): eff at 5f
on fast, gd & fibresand, likes a sharp/undul trk: eff in t-strap & cheek pieces, tried blnks.
4709} **LOUIS PRIMA 289** [5]3-8-10 bl (38) D McGaffin 100/1: 600000-8: gr c Paris House - Chanson d'Amour 15 **0**
(High Estate) Sn rdn mid-div, btn 2f out: unplcd '03 (rtd 41, tried vis, blnks & cheek pieces)
8 Ran   Time 59.21 (1.71)   Owned: Betty's Brigade   Trained: Darlington

3528   4.10 Gerrard Wealth Management Handicap Stakes Fillies 3yo+ 0-80 (D)   [79]
£6708 £2064 £1032 **7f30y rnd** **Good/Firm 24** Inapplicable Outside

3346 **GO BETWEEN 7** [4] E A L Dunlop 3-10-0 (79) S Sanders 5/2 FAV: 10-20661: Dwelt & held up, switched **89**
& hdwy to lead dist, going away: hvly bckd tho' op 7/4: eff at 6/7f on fast & gd grnd: see 1761.
3443 **BINT ROYAL 4** [5] Miss V Haigh 6-8-9 (53) P Makin(5) 11/2: 0050002: Led/dspted lead till over 1f 1¾ **57**
out, kept on: quick reapp: back to form: see 2093 & 1337.
2993 **CUT RIDGE 22** [3] J S Wainwright 5-7-12 (4oh) (38) P Fessey 12/1: 20-00003: Trkd ldrs, rdn & led shd **46$**
over 1f out, sn hdd & not pace of wnr: op 25/1: stays a sharp 7f, spot on back at 6f in similar: see 2993.
3324 **ZAHUNDA 8** [1] W M Brisbourne 5-7-12 (5oh) (37) B Swarbrick(5) 5/1: 3364024: Led till halfway, rdn 3 **40**

& no extra over 1f out: needs sellers: see 3324 & 699.

3204	**GRACEFUL AIR 13** [6]3-8-6 (57) G Hind 9/1: 2405445: Rear, only mod prog: see 1896, 1554.	nk	54
3416	**COLLEGE MAID 5** [8]7-9-3 (61) J Currie(7) 11/2: 1356666: Chsd ldrs, btn 2f out: quick reapp: btr 2508.	nk	57
3079	**TOKEWANNA 19** [2]4-8-8 (52) R Winston 9/1: 040-0037: Keen, chsd ldrs wide, btn 2f out: btr 3079.	1¾	45
3017	**ALICE BLACKTHORN 21** [7]3-8-8 (59) D McGaffin 16/1: 10-00508: Dwelt, held up wide, btn 2f out.	3	46

8 Ran   Time 1m 28.46 (No Std Time)   Owned: Mr Ahmed BuHaleeba   Trained: Newmarket

---

3529   **4.45 Edinburgh Evening News Handicap Stakes 3yo 0-75 (E)**   [76]
£5424 £1669 £835   1m1f rnd   Good/Firm 24   +10 Fast   Outside

3395*	**MASAFI 5** [1] Sir Mark Prescott 3-9-13 (6ex) (75) S Sanders 4/9 FAV: 2111111: Made all & well clr over 1f out, val 10L: useful performance in a fast time: hvly bckd at odds-on, completed a 6-timer: eff at 1m/10f on fast & both AWs, sharp/undul trks: plenty more to come: see 3395 3384 & 3300.		96+
3309	**JOEY PERHAPS 9** [3] J R Best 3-8-0 (48) B Swarbrick(5) 9/2: 0-000632: Held up, hdwy to chase wnr 2f out, nvr any impress: see 3309 & 2664.	7	53
3151	**CHARLIE TANGO 16** [5] N Tinkler 3-9-6 (68) P Mulrennan(5) 11/1: 3041343: Chsd ldrs, onepace for press over 2f out: prev with M Channon: see 3151, 2565.	2	69
3309	**MUNAAWESH 9** [6] D W Chapman 3-8-8 bl (56) D Fentiman(7) 20/1: 0004204: Handy, wknd 2f out.	nk	56
3138	**MISSION AFFIRMED 17** [4]3-9-1 (63) Dale Gibson 25/1: 1510405: Chsd wnr, rdn & btn 3f out: btr 2495.	5	53
2732	**FOUR KINGS 33** [2]3-9-1 t (63) R Winston 33/1: 503306: Sn struggling & bhd halfway: new yard.	24	10

6 Ran   Time 1m 51.95 (1.25)   Owned: Mr G D Waters   Trained: Newmarket

---

3530   **5.20 Rectangle Group Apprentice Handicap Stakes 4yo+ 35-55 (F)**   [63]
£2968 £848 £424   1m5f   Good/Firm 24   Inapplicable   Inside

3327	**COSMIC CASE 8** [5] J S Goldie 9-8-9 (44) P Mulrennan(3) 7/4 FAV: 3523031: Trkd ldrs, rdn & led over 1f out, rdn out: nicely bckd, op 2/1: eff at 12f/2m on firm & gd grnd, handles gd/soft & any trk: eff with/without a visor & best held up: v tough & on a fair mark: see 1905.		52
3354	**SOVEREIGN STATE 7** [2] D W Thompson 7-8-12 p (47) L Enstone 4/1: 000/-1452: Rear travelling well when short of room 2f out, styd on ins last, wnr had 1st run: bckd, op 6/1: clr rem, shade unlucky.	¾	53
3134	**ELLWAY HEIGHTS 18** [1] W M Brisbourne 7-9-4 (53) B Swarbrick(3) 11/4: 20-22253: Held up, rdn & onepace fnl 2f: nicely bckd: btr 2964 & 2813.	5	52
3040	**SMARTER CHARTER 20** [3] Mrs L Stubbs 11-8-2 (37) Kristin Stubbs(5) 12/1: 6504564: Keen & held up, rapid prog to lead halfway, hdd 2f out & sn outpcd: op 9/1: see 1287.	2½	32
3354	**HIBERNATE 7** [7]10-8-2 (37) T Hamilton 20/1: 5/-064005: Dictated pace, hdd halfway, rdn & btn 3f out.	1½	30
3367	**DAIMAJIN 6** [6]5-8-12 P (47) D Tudhope(5) 20/1: 0000006: Prom, rdn & btn 2f out: qk reapp, cheekpieces.	1	39
3327	**IPLEDGEALLEGIANCE 8** [4]8-7-12 (3oh)bl (30) D Fentiman(5) 7/1: 5203207: Rdn early, bhd, rapid prog halfway, wide on bend over 3f out, sn btn: btr 2562 & 353.	5	18

7 Ran   Time 2m 51.10(No Std Time)   Owned: The Cosmic Cases   Trained: Glasgow

---

Official Going Good (Good/Firm places)

3531   **2.05 Goodwood Stakes Handicap 3yo+ 0-95 (C)**   [95]
£23640 £8800 £4400   2m5f   Firm 16   Inapplicable   Flip Start

2685	**ALRIDA 34** [9] R A Fahey 5-7-12 (65) P Hanagan 11/2: 60050-41: Cl-up, trav well, led 3f out, hard pressed fnl but kept on gamely for press: recent val h'cap hdle wnr (rtd 128h): eff at 14f, relished this step up to 2m5f: likes firm & fast grnd, acts on soft & enjoys easy/sharp trks: v well h'capped & thriving at present.		75
2471	**STANCE 43** [1] G L Moore 5-8-8 P (75) R L Moore 14/1: 05023-02: Held up, hdwy over 2f out, styd on to chall ins last, just held: 6 wk abs: sharper for first time cheek pieces & clrly stays 2m5f well on firm, gd/soft & prob soft: deserves a staying h'cap: see 2471.	nk	82
3125	**DISTANT PROSPECT 18** [2] A M Balding 7-9-9 (90) Martin Dwyer 25/1: 03-42003: Handy, lost pl over 5f out & short of room over 4f out, rallied 3f out, kept on well ins last: tough, right back to useful best & is a former Cesarewitch wnr, an ideal target again: thorough stayer, see 1569.	1¾	96
2471	**ALMIZAN 43** [8] M R Channon 4-8-13 VIS (80) T E Durcan 33/1: 64-00404: In tch, hdwy well over 3f out, chall over 1f out, no extra well ins last: 6 wk abs & much sharper for first time visor & having been gelding: stays 2m5f on firm & gd: on a handy mark: see 2198.	shd	86
3387*	**MANA DARGENT 5** [6]7-9-6 (3ex) (87) J Fanning 12/1: 0500015: Held up, hdwy over 3f out, ch over 1f out, sn no extra: ran well in this race prev seasons but reserves best for beloved Ascot as in 3387.	1	92
3281	**BOBSLEIGH 11** [11]5-8-4 (71) P Robinson 16/1: 040-6046: Led 5f, cl-up, lost pl over 3f out, some late gains: stays 2m5f: see 926.	½	75
3125	**KRISTENSEN 18** [16]5-8-13 p (80) D Holland 18/1: 5062507: Led after 5f till 7f out, sn lost pl, no impress.	5	79
3387	**VALANCE 5** [4]4-8-13 (80) J Murtagh 20/1: 03-35148: Keen held up, eff over 2f out, no impress.	3	75
3275*	**QUEDEX 11** [5]8-8-9 (76) J F McDonald(3) 14/1: 6-152119: Held up, outpcd over 4f out: btr around 2m & enjoys easier grnd: see 3275.	3½	67
3015	**TIYOUN 21** [19]6-9-4 (85) J P Spencer 33/1: 5-261020: 10th: Held up, wknd 4f out: btr 3015 (2m).	4	75
3032	**TERESA 21** [3]4-8-8 (75) M J Kinane 20/1: 33-26600: 11th: In tch, wknd over 3f out: see 1112.	2	60
3032	**REDSPIN 21** [17]4-7-12 (65) C Catlin 25/1: 0044400: 12th: Slow away & bhd: see 2471, 288.	¾	49
3032	**TEN CARAT 21** [7]4-10-0 (95) L Dettori 9/2 FAV: 41110-30: 13th: Handy, wknd over 3f out: well bckd: much btr expected after promising reapp in 3032 (2m).	4	75
3181	**GALLEON BEACH 15** [18]7-7-12 (5oh) (60) N Mackay(3) 66/1: 10/06-400: 14th: Slow away & al bhd.	1	44
5002}	**ALBANOV 249** [15]4-10-0 BL (95) K Dalgleish 16/1: 134522-0: 15th: b g Sadler's Wells - Love For Ever (Darshaan) Led 7f out till 6f out, wknd over 4f out: '03 mdn wnr, List rnr-up: stays 2m on firm & soft: prev with J Dunlop, now with M Johnston & tried blnks here.	shd	74

2 Oct'03 Sain 15.5sft 95- : 1 May'03 Chep 12.1g/s 83-(83) D: 2 May'03 Brig 11.9g/s 83-(83) D: 2 Nov'02 Donc 8hvy 81- C:

3387	**RIYADH 5** [14]6-7-12 (3oh)vis (62) R Ffrench 8/1: 3030020: 16th: Slow away, sn in tch, wknd 5f out.	½	43
3220}	**ONE FOR ME 366** [10]6-7-12 (26oh) (39) Lisa Jones(3) 100/1: 0010/00-0: 17th: br f Tragic Role -	3½	39

GOODWOOD   WEDNESDAY 28.07.04   Righthand, Sharpish, Undulating Track

Chantallee's Pride (Mansooj) Al bhd: recent modest nov chase form: back in '02 won a mdn h'cap on the Flat: stays 8.5f on fibresand: has tried a t-strap.
1 Jul'02 Wolv 8.4af 51a-45 F: 2 Dec'01 Wolv 8.4af 49a- D: 2 Nov'01 Wolv 9.3af 42a- D:

3125 **PROMOTER 18** [12]4-9-8 (89) E Ahern 13/2: 4-002040: 18th: Keen in tch, hdwy to lead to lead 6f out till 3f out, wknd qckly: sometime amiss?: btr 3125, styd 2m4f in 2471.   11   52

2941 **DANCE LIGHT 25** [13]5-7-12 (7oh) (58) J Quinn 66/1: 00-00530: 19th: Al bhd: see 2941.   dist   0

19 Ran   Time 4m 32.1 ()   Owned: Mark Russell & Friends   Trained: Malton

---

3532

2.40 Gr2 Veuve Clicquot Vintage Stakes 2yo   (A)
£40600 £15400 £7700   **7f rnd**   **Firm 16**   **-25 Slow**   Inside

3148* **SHAMARDAL 16** [10] M Johnston 2-8-11 J Fanning 8/13 FAV: 11: Made all, rdn clr over 1f out, v readily: hvly bckd: relished step up to 7f, 1m sure to suit: acts on gd grnd, prob any trk: v smart & already worthy 2,000 Guineas fav for next term, looks a ready made Gr 1 wnr: see 3148.   114+

3060 **WILKO 20** [7] J Noseda 2-8-11 E Ahern 7/1: 301332: Handy, eff to chase wnr over 1f out, kept on but no impress: well bckd: useful & consistent, relish a rtn to List/Gr 3: see 3060.   2½   105

3060 **FOX 20** [3] C E Brittain 2-8-11 K Fallon 10/1: 2143: Keen held up, hdwy 2f out, kept on to go 3rd ins last, no threat: useful, will relish a step up to 1m & drop back to List/Gr 3: see 3060, 2594.   1¼   102

3060 **DESTINATE 20** [4] R Hannon 2-8-11 P Dobbs 66/1: 0104: Bhd, outpcd over 2f out, some late gains: stay 7f on firm & fast grnd: useful, needs an ease in grade: see 1934.   shd   101

3126 **BERKHAMSTED 18** [9]2-8-11 L Dettori 14/1: 1625: Slow away, sn in tch, lost tch over 2f out, some late gains: sure to relish a step up to 1m now: see 3126.   hd   100

2531* **STAGBURY HILL 40** [8]2-8-11 M Hills 25/1: 16: Held up, eff dist, onepace: 6 wk abs: stays 7f.   hd   99

3060 **ROWAN TREE 20** [5]2-8-11 J P Spencer 20/1: 107: Chsd wnr till 2f out, no extra: see 3060.   ¾   97

3254 **BLACK VELVET 12** [1]2-8-11 BL Martin Dwyer 14/1: 128: Cl-up, wknd dist: tried blnks, see 3254.   1   95

2766* **SOLENT 32** [6]2-8-11 Dane O'Neill 16/1: 19: Held up, rdn & btn 2f out: btr expected after 2766.   3   89

3169 **DAHTEER 17** [2]2-8-11 VIS T E Durcan 50/1: 41160: 10th: Held up, wknd over 2f out: tried visor.   2   85

10 Ran   Time 1m 27.41 (2.91)   Owned: Mr Abdulla BuHaleeba   Trained: Middleham

---

3533

3.15 Gr1 Cantor Odds Sussex Stakes 3yo+   (A)
£174000 £66000 £33000   **1m rnd**   **Firm 16**   **+21 Fast**   Inside

3004+ **SOVIET SONG 22** [5] J R Fanshawe 4-9-4 (115) J Murtagh 3/1: 5-231211: In tch, hdwy & short of room over 2f out, led & qcknd over 1f out, held on for press ins last, gamely: hvly bckd: fast time: well suited by 1m now on fm or soft, any trk: top-class fill with a turn of foot, proving tough & genuine, win more Gr 1s.   120

3062 **NAYYIR 20** [11] G A Butler 6-9-7 M J Kinane 12/1: 6102-302: Held up, hdwy & short of room over 1f out, styd on strongly to chall just ins last styd on well, just held: career best run & a shade unlucky, enjoyed rtn to 1m: stable clrly right back to form now: tough & high-class gelding, find a Gr 1 with a repeat of this.   nk   122

4747*]LE VIE DEI COLORI 73 [7] L M Cumani 4-9-7 D Holland 12/1: 1121-143: b c Efisio - Mystic Tempo (El Gran Senor) Handy, hdwy to lead 2f out till just over 1f out, not pace of front pair: prev trained in Italy by R Brogi, last rcd 10 wk abs: earlier won a List: '03 Gr 1 scorer: well suited by 1m on firm or hvy grnd, likes gall trks: v smart, fine first run for new stable, more to come. 1 Oct'03 San 8g/f 117- : 1 Apr'03 Capa 8gd 110- : 2 Oct'02 Long 7gd 115- : 1 Sep'02 Long 7g/f 114- : 1 Jun'02 San fm 98- :   2   118

2916 **NORSE DANCER 25** [1] D R C Elsworth 4-9-7 bl (116) T Quinn 20/1: 60-43044: Held up, eff well over 1f out, no extra ins last: hard to win with, needs drop to List/Gr 3: see 2916, 2470.   2   113

3062 **ANTONIUS PIUS 20** [10]3-8-11 VIS t J P Spencer 8/1: 10-45305: Handy trav well, short of room over 2f out till over 1f out, no extra: tried a visor but again failed to show promise of earlier runs: see 3062, 2469.   nk   112

2470 **TILLERMAN 43** [6]8-9-7 (117) O Peslier 20/1: 10330-56: Held up, eff 2f out, onepace: 6 wk abs: not up to Gr 1 class, relish a rtn to Gr 3/2 at Ascot/Goodwood: see 2470.   shd   111

3124 **HURRICANE ALAN 18** [3]4-9-7 (114) K Fallon 40/1: 5-315037: Dwelt, held up, eff & short of room 2f out, onepace: not up to Gr 1 class: needs ease in grade, see 3124.   2   107

3306 **CHECKIT 9** [2]4-9-7 (112) A Culhane 100/1: 0340348: Held up, short of room over 2f out, staying on when badly hmpd just ins last, not recover: closer without threatening front pair with a clr run: see 3306.   2   103

2469 **HAAFHD 43** [8]3-8-13 (122) R Hills 9/2: 133-1149: Cl-up, wknd well over 1f out, hmpd ins last: hvly bckd: reportedly lost action & was re-shod bef the start: 6 wk abs: much btr 2469, 1480.   ¾   101

2252* **PASSING GLANCE 43** [4]5-9-7 (118) Martin Dwyer 16/1: 12160-10: 10th: Sn led till 3f out, wknd & hmpd 2f out: 7 wk abs: up in class but btr expected after 2252 (Gr 3, made all).   2   97

2916+ **REFUSE TO BEND 25** [9]4-9-7 t (121) L Dettori 11/4 FAV: 00-00110: 11th: Cl-up, led over 3f out till 2f out, wknd when badly hmpd ins last: hvly bckd: surely something amiss: high-class on gall trks earlier.   6   85

11 Ran   Time 1m 36.98 (u0.42)   Owned: Elite Racing Club   Trained: Newmarket

---

3534

3.50 Cantorodds Com Stakes Heritage Handicap 3yo 0-105   (B)
£49300 £18700 £9350   **1m4f**   **Firm 16**   **-17 Slow**   Outside   [112]

3070 **CUTTING CREW 19** [14] P W Harris 3-8-8 (92) D Holland 12/1: 02-31621: Made all, rdn clr dist, kept on well for press ins last: stays 12f well, further would suit: acts on firm, gd/soft & polytrack, any trk: v useful & improving, relished rtn to forcing tactics (both wins this term making all): see 3070, 1708.   101

1936* **LARKWING 67** [8] G Wragg 3-8-0 (84) F Norton 20/1: 4-2312: In tch, hdwy well over 1f out, styd on to chase wnr ins last, al just held: 10 wk abs & a fine/useful nun stepped up in class: lightly rcd, will stay further & looks just the sort to win h'caps: see 1936.   ¾   90

3204 **ALWAYS FIRST 13** [9] Sir Michael Stoute 3-8-11 (95) K Fallon 8/1: 1-023: Hld up, short of room 2f out, late gains: stays 12f on fm & fast, further will suit: lightly rcd, plenty more to come, esp on a gall trk, keep in mind: see 3204, 2757.   ¾   100+

2519 **ODIHAM 41** [3] H Morrison 3-8-1 (85) J F Egan 11/1: 002-104: In tch, hdwy to chase wnr till over 1f out, no impress: stays 1m4f on firm, gd/soft & polytrack: see 2127.   ½   89

2862* **STAGE RIGHT 28** [16]3-8-21 (85) Martin Dwyer 33/1: 4615: In tch, sltly outpcd over 2f out & short of room, kept on ins last, no dngr: encouraging run stepped up in class & acts on firm & fast.   1¼   86

3444* **ALWAYS WAINING 4** [6]3-8-9 (7ex) (93) J Fanning 4/1 FAV: 3315316: Cl-up, chsd wnr over 2f out, sn onepcd for press: hvly bckd: poss a shade too qck after impressive win in 3444.   ¾   93

3274 **RED LANCER 11** [10]3-9-7 (105) L Treadwell 5) 66/1: 2136067: Held up, outpcd 3f out, nrst fin.   2½   101

2250 **PRIME POWERED 53** [13]3-8-4 P (88) R L Moore 25/1: 021-558: In tch, wknd 2f out: cheek pieces.   ½   83

3070 **ZEITGEIST** 19 [4]3-8-3 (87) T P Queally 12/1: 01-41259: Held up, wknd 2f out: see 2318, 2103.   ½ 81
3444 **FORT** 4 [5]3-8-3 (87) R Ffrench 16/1: 13-30320: 10th: Chsd wnr till 2f out, wknd: too sn after 3444?   ½ 80
2519* **ADMIRAL** 41 [1]3-8-2 (86) N Mackay(3) 7/1: 64-01310: 11th: Keen, handy, wknd over 1f out: 6 wk   1 77
abs: btr expected after 2519.
2519 **LE TISS** 41 [12]3-8-5 (89) S Hitchcott(3) 10/1: 2-402140: 12th: Held up, wknd over 1f out: well   ¾ 79
bckd: 6 wk abs, btr expected after 2519.
3161* **SETTLEMENT CRAIC** 16 [7]3-8-7 (91) J Fortune 20/1: 2-143010: 13th: Al bhd: btr 3161 (gd).   3 77
3468 **SWAINSON** 3 [2]3-8-0 (84) J Quinn 100/1: 3412050: 14th: Slow away & al bhd: qck reapp.   hd 74
2519 **ETMAAM** 41 [11]3-8-10 (94) R Hills 9/2: 1512130: 15th: Held up, rdn & btn over 4f out: 6 wk abs: 3½ 74
v disapp after most promising eff in 2519 (wnr & 4th also disapp in this race).
3274 **PROTECTIVE** 11 [15]3-8-4 (88) W Supple 66/1: 40140: 16th: In tch, wknd qckly 2f out: see 2230 (g/s).   15 46
16 Ran   Time 2m 35.72 (3.92)   Owned: Mrs P W Harris   Trained: Berkhamsted

---

| 3535 | 4.25 Weatherbys Bank Rated Stakes Handicap fillies 3yo+ 0-90 (C) | | | | [93] |

£9251 £3509 £1755   **1m1f**   **Firm 16**   **-42 Slow**   Inside

3277* **DIAMOND LODGE** 11 [2] J Noseda 3-9-8 (87) E Ahern 11/4 FAV: 412111: Keen & prom, went on 2f out,   96
held on cl-home, drvn out: hvly bckd: eff around 1m/9f on firm & gd/soft grnd: handles a sharp or stiff trk:
won 4 of 6 starts this term, v progressive & game filly: see 3277 & 1810.
3255* **WEE DINNS** 12 [6] S Kirk 3-9-3 (82) J F Egan 3/1: 0-052212: Mid-div, short of room & switched   ½ 89
wide 3f out, hdwy to chall fnl 1f, just btn: hvly bckd: fine run in defeat, met a most prog rival: see 3255.
3072 **SPRING GODDESS** 19 [7] A P Jarvis 3-9-2 (81) K Fallon 9/2: 60-30433: Mid-div, prog to chall dist,   1½ 85
no extra ins fnl 1f: bckd from 11/2: consistency deserves reward, but does not look the most straightforward ride.
4234] **PETROSA** 317 [5] D R C Elsworth 4-9-0 (70) T Quinn 33/1: 340323-4: ch f Grand Lodge - Top Brex   2½ 69
(Top Ville) Held up, drvn to improve 2f out, not pace to chall on reapp: plcd on 4 of 6 '03 starts (mdns): eff at
1m/10f on fast & firm grnd: handles a gall or sharp/undul trk: sharper next time.
2 Aug'03 Sali 8g/f 69-(73) D:
3257 **TUSCARORA** 12 [9]5-8-7 (7oh) (56) T P Queally 20/1: 0526105: Dwelt, keen in rear, hdwy to chase   ¾ 60
ldrs when short of room 2f out till ent fnl 1f, no ch after: did not get the run of today's race.
1110 **WHY DUBAI** 109 [10]3-9-10 (89) R L Moore 12/1: 0102-06: br f Kris S - Highest Goal (Slew O' Gold)   1½ 83
Prom, ev ch till fdd dist: long abs: '03 fill mdn wnr, subs nurs h'cap rnr-up: eff at 7f on firm grnd: sharper
next time & a drop back to 1m shld suit.
2 Oct'03 Newm 7fm 91-82 B: 1 Aug'03 Newm 7fm 80- D:
4686* **TAMINOULA** 290 [11]3-9-1 (80) Dane O'Neill 7/1: 0311-7: b f Tagula - Taormina (Ela Mana Mou)   1¼ 71
Trkd ldrs, wkng when short of room 2f out: nicely bckd, reapp: won fnl 2 '03 starts, fill mdn auct & nurs h'cap:
eff at 7f, shld stay further: acts on firm grnd & a sharp/undul trk: runs well fresh, with Mrs A Perrett.
1 Oct'03 Good 7fm 83-76 D: 1 Aug'03 Brig 7.0fm 75- E:
3287* **LARA FALANA** 11 [8]6-8-12 (68) J Quinn 14/1: 5426418: Led till 2f out, wknd: see 3287 (AW).   1½ 56
3402 **HILITES** 5 [3]3-9-0 (79) S Whitworth 33/1: 0300639: Dwelt, al towards rear: qck reapp.   2½ 62
2091 **HONORINE** 59 [4]4-9-10 (80) P Robinson 16/1: 21243-60: 10th: Keen in rear, nvr a factor: 8 wk abs.   hd 62
3223 **TOTALLY YOURS** 13 [12]3-9-8 (87) Martin Dwyer 33/1: 10-04050: 11th: Mid-div, wknd dist.   3 63
3255 **DARK RAIDER** 12 [1]3-8-5 (2oh) (70) D Corby 33/1: 0-255100: 12th: Chsd ldrs 6f, sn wknd: btr 2509.   1 44
12 Ran   Time 1m 55.75 (5.25)   Owned: Mrs J Harris   Trained: Newmarket

---

| 3536 | 5.00 Findon Maiden Stakes Fillies 2yo (D) | | |

£10433 £3210 £1605   **6f str**   **Firm 16**   **+00 Fast**   Stands Side

SUEZ [3] M A Jarvis 2-8-11   P Robinson 9/2: 1: b f Green Desert - Repeat Warning (Warning) Led   98+
early, remained prom & regained lead after halfway, rdn clr fnl 1f on debut: bckd from 6/1: Feb foal, cost
480,000gns: dam styd 1m & from a high-class family, sire a top-class sprinter/miler: eff over a sharp/undul 6f on fm,
7f shld suit: runs well fresh: impressive debut in fast time, win better races.
CLEAR IMPRESSION [7] P W Chapple Hyam 2-8-11 J Fortune 7/4 FAV: 2: b f Danehill - Shining Hour   2½ 88
(Red Ransom) Chsd ldrs, went after wnr dist, kept on but nvr any impression: hvly bckd, well clr rem, debut: Jan
first foal, dam a smart 6f juv wnr: sire a top-class sprinter/miler: eff at 6f on firm grnd, 7f shld suit: handles
a sharp/undul trk, sure to learn from this & will be plcd to win similar.
3183 **TOFFEE VODKA** 14 [6] J W Hills 2-8-11 R Hills 16/1: 63: Short of room start, styd on nicely into   4 76
3rd, no ch with front 2: bckd at long odds: acts on gd & firm grnd, 7f will now suit: again showed promise.
1826 **ON THE WATERLINE** 71 [8] P D Evans 2-8-11 N Callan 40/1: 2304: Prom, onepcd fnl 1.5f: 10 wk abs.   ½ 74
3251 **MADHAVI** 12 [5]2-8-11 P Dobbs 7/1: 035: Outpcd, late gains, nvr dngrs: nicely bckd: btr 3251.   shd 74
3063 **UNREAL** 20 [2]2-8-11 M Hills 9/4: 626: Trkd ldrs, btn dist: hvly bckd: much btr 3063.   ½ 72
2926 **STARLIGHT RIVER** 25 [4]2-8-11 Martin Dwyer 100/1: 07: b f Spectrum - Prosaic Star (Common   5 57
Grounds) Led after 1f till after halfway, sn wknd: Feb foal, cost E42,000: half-sister to 5f juv wnrs Barringer,
Lupine & Blue Crush: dam won over 1m as a juv, sire a top-class 1m/10f performer: with W Muir, too keen today.
3252 **CORNICHE DANCER** 12 [9]2-8-11 S Hitchcott 100/1: 08: b f Marju - Sellette (Selkirk) Slowly   3 48
away, al rear: 22,000gns purchase: dam a 1m wnr, sire top-class mid-dist performer: with M Channon.
8 Ran   Time 1m 10.99 (0.99)   Owned: Sheikh Mohammed   Trained: Newmarket

---

| 3537 | 5.35 Zuhair Stakes Handicap Previously Known As The Charlton Stakes 4yo+ 0-80 (D) | | | [80] |

£10985 £3380 £1690   **5f str**   **Firm 16**   **-03 Slow**   Stands Side

3333 **DOUBLE M** 7 [10] Mrs L Richards 7-8-6 vis (58) R Thomas(5) 28/1: 3213661: Trkd stands side ldrs,   71
imprvd to lead dist, sn clr, cmftbly: eff at 5/6f, stays 7f: acts on gd, firm grnd & both AWs: likes a sharp trk,
esp Lingfield: wears a visor & career best run today, see 2396 & 902.
3229 **TIME TO REMEMBER** 12 [6] D Nicholls 4-8-3 (55) W Supple 25/1: 0060002: Mid-div stands side,   2 61
switched wide & gd prog dist, fin strongly into 2nd but no ch with wnr: eff at 5f, rtn to 6f will suit judged on
this: h'capped to win similar, see 1910.
2429 **LADY PROTECTOR** 45 [11] J Balding 5-8-3 (55) J Fanning 25/1: 0001133: Front rank stands side, led   shd 60
briefly dist, caught for 2nd cl-home: 6 wk abs: continues in fine form, see 2429 & 2062.
3466 **MERLINS DANCER** 3 [7] D Nicholls 4-9-13 (79) A Nicholls 13/2: 0510004: Front rank far side, led   ¾ 83
that group ins fnl 1f, no ch with stands side: hvly bckd, s/mate of rnr-up: first home on far side, all wins at 6f.
3350 **SALVIATI** 7 [21]7-9-9 p (75) C J Davies(7) 11/2 FAV: 0000045: Slowly away, bhd far side, fin v   shd 78+

strongly, nvr nrr: well bckd, rider gvn a 1 day careless riding ban: well h'capped now, poised to strike.

3279 **ROSES OF SPRING 11** [13]6-9-12 p (78) A Quinn(5) 16/1: 0-030006: Chsd ldrs far side, kept on under press fnl 1f: hinted at rtn to form here, see 1845 (C/D). ½ 79

3033 **DEVISE 21** [4]5-10-0 (80) T E Durcan 16/1: 6015547: Held up stands side, styd on late, nvr nrr. shd 80

3403* **STAGNITE 5** [22]4-8-10 (7ex)p (62) N Chalmers(5) 10/1: 00-06218: Chsd ldrs far side, kept on under press fnl 1f: qck reapp & 7lb pen for 3403. ½ 60

3228 **PLAYTIME BLUE 12** [12]4-8-8 (60) D Corby(3) 16/1: 0605339: Chsd ldrs far side, onepcd fnl 1f. hd 57

2266 **POLISH EMPEROR 51** [18]4-9-11 e (77) N Callan 10/1: 5031000: 10th: Front rank far side, wknd fnl 1f: 7 wk abs: best when able to dominate, see 1765. hd 73

3228 **ONLINE INVESTOR 12** [16]5-8-12 (64) A Culhane 10/1: 0550000: 11th: Outpcd far side, prog when short of room dist, nvr nrr: stablemate of 2nd & 4th: hinted at a rtn to form here: tried a visor in 3228. shd 59

3341 **GUNS BLAZING 7** [20]5-9-6 bl (72) M Howard(7) 16/1: 3601000: 12th: Led far side till ent fn 1f, wknd. shd 66

3463 **BLESSED PLACE 3** [8]4-7-13 t (51) J F McDonald(3) 33/1: 3354150: 13th: Front rank stands side, led halfway till dist, wknd: ddhtd for 12th: qck reapp, see 3165. dht 45

3341 **ELA FIGURA 7** [5]4-7-12 (2oh) (48) Lisa Jones(3) 100/1: 0365000: 14th: Chsd ldrs stands side, btn dist. ¾ 42

3403 **CERULEAN ROSE 5** [2]5-9-2 (68) R L Moore 9/1: 5-402030: 15th: Outpcd stands side, nvr a factor: bckd from 12/1, qck reapp: won this race from a 17lb lower mark last term: btr clrly expected after 3403. hd 59

2878 **WILLHEWIZ 27** [15]4-9-13 vis (79) K Dalgleish 25/1: 6011000: 16th: Front rank far side, wknd dist. hd 69

2645 **REDWOOD STAR 36** [17]4-8-3 (1ow)e (54) R Price 9/1: 30-40030: 17th: Sn bhd far side, nvr a factor. dht 45

2871 **MADRASEE 27** [9]6-9-4 (70) P Dobbs 25/1: 4505000: 18th: Nvr nr ldrs stands side: rnr-up in this race from a 4lb lower mark last term: see 1615. shd 59

3332 **Inch By Inch 7** [7]5-8-4 bl(56) Martin Dwyer 50/1:0

3269 **Sir Edwin Landseer 11** [19]4-9-9 (75) V Halliday 33/1:0

3352 **Intellibet One 7** [3]4-8-3 (55) P Hanagan 50/1:0   3184 **Super Song 14** [1]4-8-1 t(53) Joanna Badger 100/1:0

22 Ran   Time 57.64(0.94)   Owned: Mr Bryan Mathieson   Trained: Chichester

---

Official Going GOOD/FIRM.

3538   6.05 Betfred 'the Bonus King' Apprentice Handicap Stakes 3yo+ 0-75 (E) [75]
£4716 £1451 £726   1m2f18y   Firm 19   -09 Slow   Inside

2869* **CRISTOFORO 28** [3] B J Curley 7-9-5 (66) T P Queally 7/4 FAV: 11/-10111: Dwelt, rear, hdwy cver 2f out, rdn & styd on to lead ins last: well bckd, op 2/1: completed hat-trick: eff at 9/13f on firm, soft & both AW's: likes Epsom: most progressive, see 2869 & 2718. 77

3288* **BURGUNDY 12** [7] P Mitchell 7-8-12 bl (59) L Keniry 3/1: 0361112: Slow away, rear, styd on late for press, not reach wnr: acts on firm, soft & polytrack: remains in gd form: see 3288. 1¼ 66

3216 **KATIYPOUR 14** [8] Miss B Sanders 7-10-0 (75) Lisa Jones 7/1: 1201403: Keen & handy, led over 1f out till ins last, no extra: see 1691, 1042 & 932. 2½ 78

3175 **ICANNSHIFT 16** [4] S Dow 4-8-6 (53) R Miles 7/2: 3630304: Led till over 1f out, sn btn: op 9/2. 2 53

3044 **MY GALLIANO 21** [6]8-9-5 (66) A Hindley(5) 9/1: 216-0365: Handy, briefly led 3f out, btn dist. 3½ 61

595 **KINGSTON TOWN 170** [2]4-9-2 bl (63) J P Guillambert 20/1: 21-00406: Mid-div, no impress fnl 2f: 6 mth abs: btr 530 (AW). 6 49

3336 **JALONS STAR 8** [9]6-8-13 (60) T O'Brien(7) 25/1: 51250//-07: Mid-div, struggling fnl 2f: see 336. 3 41

2862 **VICAT COLE 29** [1]3-8-13 (70) A Quinn 20/1: 0508: Mid-div, btn 3f out: h'cap bow, new yard: btr 2393. 9 37

3398 **BEAUCHAMP RIBBON 6** [5]4-9-2 bl (63) F P Ferris 33/1: 3030-009: Mid-div, strug fnl 2f: qck reapp. 5 22

9 Ran   Time 2m 06.66 (2.86)   Owned: Mr P Byrne   Trained: Newmarket

3539   6.35 London Focus E B F Maiden Stakes 2yo (D)
£6841 £2105 £1053   7f rnd   Firm 19   +02 Fast   Inside - Juv Track Record

RED PEONY [1] Sir Mark Prescott 2-8-9 T Queally 4/1 JT FAV: 1: b f Montjeu - Red Azalea (Shirley Heights) Made all, in command & styd on strongly under hand riding fnl 2f: bckd from 8/1: Mar foal, dam a 7f juv wnr & subs 10f scorer: eff at 7f on firm, 1m+ will suit: enjoyed forcing tactics & scored in a fast time (juv crse rec), looks useful. 94+

2774 **HADRIAN 33** [6] M Johnston 2-9-0 K Dalgleish 8/1: 62: b c King's Best - Wanton (Kris) Chsd wnr, rdn & kept on fnl 2f, al foal: Mar foal, 90,000gns purchase: half-brother to sev wnrs, incl Irish 1,000 Guineas wnr Classic Park: dam a 5f juv wnr: apprec step up to 7f & firm grnd, acts on a sharp/undul trk: can find similar. 3½ 89

2902 **BOUNTY QUEST 27** [5] R Hannon 2-9-0 P Dobbs 13/2: 343: Mid-div, kept on fnl 2f, not able to chall: imprvd eff, styd longer 7f trip: acts on firm grnd & sharp/undul or gall trk: qual for h'caps: see 2646. 1½ 86

3267 **MASTMAN 12** [8] B J Meehan 2-9-0 T J Fortune 5/1: 254: Held up, eff & mod prog fnl 3f: t-strap: handles firm & fast grnd: wants 1m+ h'caps: see 3267, 2876. 2 82

3280 **BASIC SYSTEM 12** [7]2-9-0 B Doyle 6/1: 05: b c Belong To Me - Foible (Riverman) Keen, mid-div, rdn & no impress fnl 2f: Apr foal, dam a 12f 3yo scorer: shd show imprin time. 1¼ 79

3214 **DISCOMANIA 14** [3]2-9-0 S Drowne 4/1: 046: Rear, little hdwy under hand riding fnl 3f: stewards looked into run, joc reported colt was not to be shown the whip: kind ride, likely improver, h'caps will suit. hd 78+

3021 **ZOLASH 22** [4]2-9-0 Derek Nolan(7) 40/1: 5067: Outpcd early, al towards rear. 1 75

3063 **DELLA SALUTE 21** [9]2-8-9 L Keniry(3) 16/1: 68: Keen, chsd ldr, btn 2f out: btr 3063. 1½ 67

3297 **WASALAT 10** [2]2-8-9 C Catlin 4/1 JT FAV: 42329: Reared start & lost many lengths, allowed to come home in own time: this best forgiven after 3297 & 2522. 16 37

9 Ran   Time 1m 21.30 (1.20)   Owned: Cheveley Park Stud   Trained: Newmarket

3540   7.05 Betfred 'we Pay Double Result' Handicap Stakes Fillies 3yo+ 0-80 (D)   [78]
£8132 £2502 £1251   1m114y rnd   Firm 19   -03 Slow   Inside

3287 **DAMI 30** [5] C E Brittain 3-9-10 p (74) S Sanders 4/1: 0-552211: Chall over 1f out, led dist, all   82
out: eff at 7f/10f on firm & gd grnd, sharp/undul trk: gd weight-carrier: see 2837.
3175 **KINDNESS 16** [2] A D W Pinder 4-8-7 (48) C Catlin 12/1: 6002202: Led, hdd dist, rallied well   nk   53
cl-home, just held: op 10/1: apprec drop to 1m & enjoys forcing tactics: see 2604 & 1045.
3090* **KRYSSA 20** [6] G L Moore 3-9-8 (72) J Fortune 1/1 FAV: 3351313: In tch wide, no impress on front   3   73
pair fnl 2f: hvly bckd: see 3090.
3219 **ARCHERFIELD 14** [3] J W Hills 3-8-12 (62) S Drowne 6/1: 3002334: Held up, not pace to chall fnl 2f.   1½   60
3142 **MARNIE 18** [1]7-8-8 (49) J Quinn 7/1: 3022555: Chsd ldrs, btn 2f out: btr 2414.   4   39
3492 **JOINT DESTINY 3** [4]3-7-13 (49) N Mackay(3) 14/1: 0210406: Rear, no impress fnl 2f: qck reapp.   ¾   37
6 Ran Time 1m 43.66 (1.86)   Owned: Mr Saeed Manana   Trained: Newmarket

3541   7.35 Rubbing House Claiming Stakes 3yo+   (E)
£4726 £1454 £727   7f rnd   Firm 19   -03 Slow   Inside

2397 **SCARROTTOO 47** [11] S C Williams 6-9-2 (55) R L Moore 11/4: 5514031: Rear, switched & hdwy wide   60
2f out, styd on for press to lead well ins last: nicely bckd tho' op 2/1: 7 wk abs: eff at 6/7f on firm, gd & both
AWs, any trk, likes a sharp/undul one: can go well fresh: apprec drop to claim grade: see 1132 & 544.
3448 **LADY MO 5** [12] G G Margarson 3-8-10 (66) S Sanders 2/1 FAV: 2306122: In tch wide, rdn to lead   ½   59
over 1f out, hdd well ins last: rest well covered, nicely bckd tho' op 11/10: qck reapp: remains in fine form.
2199 **INSTINCT 56** [9] R Hannon 3-8-10 (59) P Dobbs 5/1: 5030003: Slow away & rear, kept on late, no   3   53
threat to front pair: 8 wk abs: eff at 6/7f on firm & soft grnd: see 975 & 670.
3333 **GAMESETNMATCH 8** [6] W G M Turner 3-8-8 p (67) A Daly 10/1: 2065-604: Handy & led over 2f out till   nk   50
over 1f out, no extra: clr rem: handles firm & fast grnd: stays a sharp 7f: see 2873.
     LA CALERA 123 [1]3-8-3 VIS C Catlin 25/1: 60-31005: ch f Big Shuffle - La Luce (Niniski) Chsd   5   35
ldrs till over 1f out: visor: recent jumps runner (unplcd, nov): ex-French, Feb '04 wnr: wng form at 7.5f on AW.
3054 **BAD INTENTIONS 21** [5]4-9-0 (65) G Carter 20/1: 500-6006: Chsd ldrs, btn 2f out: see 2669.   nk   38
1710 **NEWCORR 77** [2]5-8-13 P (32) T P Queally 33/1: 0063247: Mid-div, no impress fnl 2f: abs, chkpieces.   2   31
2288 **MUTABARI 51** [8]10-8-10 (30) Amy Myatt(7) 66/1: 0000008: Rear & no impress 3f out: abs: see 1341.   3½   23
3335 **CHELSEAS DIAMOND 8** [10]4-8-12 P V Slattery 33/1: 509: Slow away, al rear: chkpcs, drpd in trip.   1   23
2501 **GILLYS GENERAL 42** [3]4-8-12 (44) S Whitworth 33/1: 4016000: 10th: Led till over 2f out, sn btn.   2   19
3298* **MAJHOOL 10** [7]5-8-11 (60) R Miles(3) 9/4: 10-04510: 11th: Dwelt, sn chsd ldrs, wknd qckly 2f out,   20   0
eased: bckd, op 4/1: clmd by I W McInnes for 4,000: much btr 3298.
11 Ran Time 1m 21.64 (1.54)   Owned: Mr Michael Peacock   Trained: Newmarket

3542   8.05 Rectangle Group Handicap Stakes 3yo 0-80 (D)   [86]
£8093 £2490 £1245   1m114y rnd   Firm 19   +06 Fast   Inside

3339 **HABANERO 8** [5] R Hannon 3-9-0 (72) R L Moore 3/1: 0531331: Made all, strongly pressed dist, held   80
on gamely, all out: gd time: well bckd from 5/1: stays 10f, suited by 1m/8.5f on firm & gd grnd, any trk: loves
to force the pace: most genuine & tough: see 3339, 2706 & 2365.
3410* **PICKLE 6** [4] S C Williams 3-9-2 (6ex) (74) S Sanders 11/8 FAV: 3361112: Held up, switched & hdwy   ½   80
to chall ins last, just held cl-home: qck reapp: clr rem, continues in fine form: see 3410.
2901 **GO SOLO 27** [6] B W Hills 3-9-5 (77) M Hills 7/1: 16-03353: Chsd wnr 5f out, onepace & held over   5   73
1f out: see 2901, 2365 & 1825.
3535 **HILITES 1** [1] J S Moore 3-9-7 (79) Derek Nolan(7) 25/1: 03006394: Slow away, in tch, outpcd fnl   3   69
3f: unplcd yesterday.
3174* **MALIBU 16** [3]3-9-6 (78) K Fallon 3/1: 0-465015: Chsd ldr 3f, btn 2f out: btr 3174 (made all).   1   66
2877 **SCIENTIST 28** [7]3-9-0 (72) J Fortune 14/1: 65-00306: Mid-div, btn 2f out: much btr 2314.   6   48
3448 **JOMUS 5** [2]3-8-1 (59) N Mackay(3) 20/1: 1200047: Dwelt, rear, lost tch fnl 3f: btr 3448 & 798   9   17
(AW).
7 Ran Time 1m 42.88 (1.08)   Owned: The Waney Racing Group Inc   Trained: Marlborough

3543   8.35 Better Business Handicap Stakes 3yo 0-80 (D)   [87]
£8190 £2520 £1260   6f rnd   Firm 19   -01 Slow   Outside

3408 **TONY THE TAP 6** [10] N A Callaghan 3-9-7 (80) K Fallon 11/8 FAV: 1222521: Rear/wide, hdwy over 1f   87
out & drvn to lead well ins last: well bckd, qck reapp: eff at 5/6f, stays a sharp 7f: acts on firm, gd &
polytrack, prob any trk: gd weight-carrier, tough & remains on an upward curve: see 3408, 2734 & 2593.
3356 **TREGARRON 7** [1] R Hannon 3-8-11 (70) R L Moore 5/1: 6000-142: Led till over 2f out, rdn & led   nk   74
again ins last, hdd well ins last: acts on a sharp/undul or gall trk: apprec forcing tactics tonight, gd run.
3283 **ASK THE CLERK 12** [4] V Smith 3-8-12 (71) M Tebbutt 8/1: 0346433: Trkd ldrs, rdn & chall ins   ¾   72
last, just held cl-home: acts on firm & fast grnd, loves soft: see 1417, 975.
2841 **EMTILAAK 29** [5] B Hanbury 3-9-3 (76) W Supple 10/1: 3-231004: Rear, hdwy when briefly short of   nk   76
room over 1f out, kept on onepace ins last: acts on firm, gd & polytrack: see 2042.
3371 **PERUVIAN STYLE 7** [9]3-8-11 (70) T P Queally 16/1: 1050065: Mid-div, hdwy to chall ins last, no   nk   69
extra nr fin: blnks omitted: stays a sharp 6f, best to date over a sharp 5f: see 914 (AW).
3198 **IMPERIUM 15** [3]3-8-12 (71) S Drowne 16/1: 1130006: Mid-div, prog & led 2f out till ins last, no extra.   1½   66
2387 **INTRIGUING GLIMPSE 47** [6]3-9-5 (78) S Sanders 7/2: 13-32227: Held up, eff 2f out, no impress   ¾   70
from dist: abs: btr 2387 (5f).
2661 **BLACK OVAL 36** [2]3-7-12 (8oh) (49) Lisa Jones(3) 33/1: 0300508: Chsd ldrs, btn dist: see 1268.   1¼   45
3198 **ALIZAR 15** [7]3-7-13 (58) C Catlin 33/1: 0601009: Chsd ldrs, wknd qckly halfway: btr 2435.   9   21
9 Ran Time 1m 09.02(1.22)   Owned: Mr K J Mercer   Trained: Newmarket

CARLISLE THURSDAY 29.07.04 Righthand, Stiff Track, Uphill Finish

Official Going GOOD/FIRM (FIRM places).

3544

2.15 Viacom Maiden Auction Stakes 2yo (E)
£3835 £1180 £590 **5f193y rnd** **Firm 14** **-40 Slow** Inside

2703 **TOBYS DREAM 35** [4] M Johnston 2-8-11 S Chin 33/1: 01: b c Mujadil - Islandagore (Indian Ridge) **85**
Made all, drvn & held on well ins last: Apr first foal, 24,000gns purchase: dam a 7f 3yo scorer: eff at 6f, get further: acts on firm grnd & a stiff trk: enjoyed forcing tactics today & much imprvd from debut.
3376 **MERCHANT 7** [13] M L W Bell 2-8-9 J Mackay 13/8 FAV: 532: Dwelt, sn trkd ldrs, rdn & styd on, al held by wnr: well bckd, op 5/2: acts on firm & gd/soft grnd: qual for h'caps, can find a race: see 3376 & 3046. ¾ **80**
3329 **NAVAL FORCE 8** [5] H Morrison 2-8-11 t S Sanders 9/2: 043: Mid-div, rdn & outpcd 2f out, switched & kept on well ins last, not pace of wnr: op 6/1: eff at 6f, return to 7f+ will suit: acts on firm & polytrack, stiff or sharp trk: eff in a t-strap: see 3329. *nk* **81**
RAINBOW RISING [3] J Howard Johnson 2-9-0 R Winston 9/2: 4: b c Desert King - Fantastic Bid (Auction Ring) Keen & trkd ldrs, kept on onepace: op 7/2: 36,000gns Mar foal, half-brother to a 7f 3yo wnr, also a winning hdler: dam a 1m List wnr abroad: eff at 6f, stay further: handles firm grnd. *1* **81**
3183 **CROCODILE KISS 15** [1]2-8-6 S W Kelly 9/2: 55: Chsd ldrs, no extra dist: op 3/1: btr 3183. *nk* **72**
3239 **DAVY CROCKETT 13** [2]2-8-7 A Culhane 10/1: 0056: b g Polar Prince - Sing With The Band (Chief Singer) Held up, late prog, nrst fin: cheaply bght Feb first foal, dam a dual 5f 3yo wnr. *1¼* **69**
NASSEEM DUBAI [6]2-9-0 G Hind 33/1: 7: Dwelt, outpcd early, late gains, nrst fin. *shd* **76**
1631 **FAVOURING 82** [9]2-8-7 P Hanagan 25/1: 408: Bhd, only mod late prog: op 33/1, abs: see 1091. *1½* **64**
HANNAHS TRIBE [8]2-8-2 A McCarthy 25/1: 9: Sn outpcd rear, nvr a factor. ¾ **57**
2336 **LOVELORN 49** [10]2-8-7 T Lucas 20/1: 30: 10th: Keen & led/dsptd lead till halfway, wknd: abs. *1¼* **58**
3348 **So Independent 8** [7]2-8-2 T Hamilton 100/1:0 3130 **Toldo 19** [11]2-8-7 bl J Carroll 100/1:0
12 Ran Time 1m 13.91 (3.21) Owned: Mr Lawrence Wosskow Trained: Middleham

3545

2.50 Tote Neil Wyatt Groundstaff Award Claiming Stakes 3yo+ (F)
£3220 £920 £460 **5f193y rnd** **Firm 14** **-31 Slow** Inside

3262 **FIZZY LIZZY 12** [7] Jedd O'Keeffe 4-8-3 (32) Leanne Kershaw(7) 11/1: 000-0001: Rear, hdwy to lead 2f out, rdn & held on well: op 14/1: first win: clmd by G Ham for 2,500: eff over a stiff 6f on firm & gd grnd, stiff/gall or sharp trk: apprec drop to claim grade: see 2806. **43**
3353 **VIJAY 8** [9] I Semple 5-8-9 (49) R Winston 9/2: 2006002: Held up, styd on from halfway, not pace of wnr: gd run with blnks omitted: see 1797 & 748. *1* **45**
3324 **ANGEL ISA 9** [5] R A Fahey 4-8-10 (44) P Hanagan 5/1: 60-00003: Trkd ldrs & ch dist, no extra. *hd* **45**
3352 **MR BOUNTIFUL 8** [3] M Dods 6-9-7 t p (50) S W Kelly 7/2: 0040064: Held up, eff to chase ldrs over 1f out, no extra ins last: op 2/1: btr 50 & 22 (polytrack). *nk* **55**
1837 **PILGRIM PRINCESS 71** [10]6-8-8 (40) D Allan 100/30 FAV: 4600045: Cl-up, no impress dist: abs. *4* **32**
2730 **CAYMAN MISCHIEF 34** [8]4-8-10 (25) J Bramhill 66/1: 00-006: b f Cayman Kai - Tribal Mischief (Be My Chief) Bhd, late gains, nvr a factor: unplcd '03 (rtd 20, no sand form). ¾ **32$**
2987 **WILD TIDE 24** [12]5-8-3 T Hamilton(1) 50/1: 07: Bhd, al outpcd: no form. *hd* **24**
2504 **BISHOPS BOUNCE 42** [11]3-8-6 (55) Dale Gibson 7/1: 02000-08: Mid-div, btn 2f out: 6 wk abs. *1¼* **28**
3155 **ALWAYS DARING 17** [1]5-8-4 P (31) Natalia Gemelova(7) 50/1: 000/0-009: Led till 2f out, sn struggling: tried cheek pieces & no improvement. *5* **8**
2888] **JUMBOS FLYER 742** [6]7-8-11 P Mulrennan(5) 50/1: 00/0/000/-0: 10th: Cl-up till halfway, long abs. *2½* **8**
10 Ran Time 1m 13.33 (2.63) Owned: Only For Fun Partnership Trained: Leyburn

3546

3.25 St James Security Classified Stakes 3yo+ 0-70 (E)
£3559 £1095 £548 **1m1f61y** **Firm 14** **+27 Fast** Inside

3529* **MASAFI 1** [3] Sir Mark Prescott 3-9-0 (69) S Sanders 4/6 FAV: 21111111: Keen early, made all, rdn & styd on strongly fnl 2f to win in a v fast time: hvly bckd: record 7th win in 17 days: eff btwn 1m/10f on firm, fast & both AWs, prob any trk: tough & v progressive, typically plcd to perfection by Sir M Prescott: see 3395. **88**
3465 **GOODBYE MR BOND 4** [5] E J Alston 4-9-4 (71) D Allan 11/4: 4111132: Pushed along rear, hdwy to chase wnr ins last, al well held: op 7/2, qck reapp: met a v prog rival, see 3465, 2672. *2½* **77**
3206 **MILLAGROS 14** [9] I Semple 4-9-2 VIS (72) D McGaffin 25/1: 0-044633: Trkd ldrs, styd on onepace for press in first time visor: bckd at long odds: see 1895. ½ **74**
2631 **FOSSGATE 38** [8] J D Bethell 3-8-8 P (70) B Swarbrick(5) 40/1: 05-20364: Chsd wnr, btn over 1f out: cheek pieces: see 2168 & 1178. ½ **74**
3216 **JUST A FLUKE 14** [6]3-8-13 (75) S Chin 9/1: 2-402305: In tch, edged right & no extra over 1f out. ¾ **78**
3099 **COMPTON DRAGON 19** [1]5-9-7 vis (74) Alex Greaves 25/1: 5225206: Held up, lost tch fnl 2f: btr 2943. *10* **61**
2962 **GALA SUNDAY 25** [7]4-9-3 (70) Dale Gibson 50/1: 0000067: In tch till 3f out: see 2323. *5* **48**
3255 **GWEN JOHN 13** [2]3-8-7 BL (72) A Culhane 28/1: 5-5308: Chsd ldrs, btn 2f out: trkd blnks: btr 2536. *1¼* **44**
3328 **WESSEX 9** [4]4-9-5 (72) R Winston 33/1: 0-060059: Mid-div, btn 3f out: btr 3328. *2* **43**
9 Ran Time 1m 54.15 (u1.25) Owned: Mr G D Waters Trained: Newmarket

3547

4.00 Phil Cook 70th Birthday Handicap Stakes 3yo 35-55 (F) **[65]**
£3290 £940 £470 **7f200y rnd** **Firm 14** **-09 Slow** Inside

3433 **JOSHUAS GOLD 5** [2] D Carroll 3-9-0 (51) D Tudhope(7) 14/1: 2360001: Broke well & sn handy, led over 2f out, held on well for press: qck reapp: first win: eff at 7f/1m on firm, gd & polytrack, sharp/undul or stiff trk: overcame awkward low draw in fine style, could follow up in similar: see 1554 & 815. **59**
3182* **BOPPYS PRINCESS 16** [7] R A Fahey 3-8-6 (43) P Hanagan 6/1: 60000-12: Mid-div, rdn/short of room over 2f out, styd on well cl-home, just failed: met trouble at a crucial stage & prob unlucky: acts on firm & gd/soft grnd: confirmed improvement of 3182. *nk* **50+**
2969 **ROMAN THE PARK 24** [17] T D Easterby 3-8-5 (42) D Allan 5/1: 1231343: Trkd ldrs, ch over 1f out, styd on onepace: acts on firm, fast & fibresand: see 1947. ¾ **48**

CARLISLE   THURSDAY 29.07.04   Righthand, Stiff Track, Uphill Finish

3024 **SHIBUMI 22** [18] H Morrison 3-9-1 (52) A Culhane 4/1 FAV: 0-5544: Handy & led over 3f out till over 2f out, styd on onepace for press: acts on firm & gd grnd: stays a stiff 1m: see 3024.	hd	57
3016 **MIDNIGHT PRINCE 22** [15]3-9-0 (51) P Mulrennan(5) 15/2: 40006-65: Trkd ldrs, rdn & onepace fnl 2f: styd this longer 1m trip: handles firm grnd: eye-catching 3016.	2½	51
3079 **GRELE 20** [9]3-8-10 (47) P Makin(5) 20/1: 0-056: Held up, kept on late, not able to chall: h'cap bow.	½	46
3182 **DELCIENNE 16** [3]3-8-9 (46) A McCarthy 9/1: 0302157: Dwelt, mid-div, no extra dist: btr 2834 (sell).	shd	45
3262 **LORD BASKERVILLE 12** [14]3-9-3 (54) J Bramhill 10/1: 0002248: Keen & cl-up, btn over 1f out.	2½	48
3414 **ALPHA ZETA 6** [13]3-8-3 (40) Dale Gibson 25/1: 0-00009: b g Primo Dominie - Preening (Persian Bold) Held up, switched 2f out, little prog: qck reappr: no form sole '03 start (mdn).	1	32
2292 **DALIDA 51** [12]3-8-10 (47) G Faulkner 25/1: 00-U5500: 10th: Mid-div, strug fnl 2f: 7 wk abs.	nk	38
2434 **RICKY MARTAN 45** [10]3-8-12 (49) J Mackay 33/1: 0000060: 11th: Bhd, rdn & little hdwy: 6 wk abs.	½	39
2613 **POLAR GALAXY 38** [6]3-8-8 (45) S W Kelly 50/1: 5400-050: 12th: Mid-div, strug fnl 2f: btr 2613.	1½	32
2969 **KOODOO 24** [16]3-8-9 (46) R Winston 10/1: 00-06000: 13th: Slow away, al towards rear, gelded.	nk	32
3410 **GALLAS 6** [5]3-9-2 vis (53) T Hamilton(3) 25/1: 0-000200: 14th: Al bhd: qck reappr: btr 3177.	shd	39
3177 **TRYSTING GROVE 16** [11]3-8-6 (43) G Parkin 12/1: 00005: 15th: Sn rdn & bhd, nvr a factor.	3½	22
3177 **PLUMPIE MAC 16** [4]3-8-7 (44) D Kinsella 33/1: 060-600: 16th: Led till over 3f out, wknd: see 2693.	2	19
3309 **Farnborough 10** [1]3-9-4 (55) B Swarbrick(3) 20/1:0 3414 **Gemini Girl 6** [8]3-8-3 (40) P M Quinn 40/1:0		
18 Ran Time 1m 39.51 (1.81) Owned: K H Taylor Limited Trained: Warthilll		

3548	4.35 Mccallum Builders Handicap Stakes Fillies 3yo+ 0-75 (E) £3689 £1135 £568 6f192y rnd Firm 14 -17 Slow Inside	[75]
3528 **BINT ROYAL 1** [9] Miss V Haigh 6-8-6 (53) P Mathers(5) 5/1: 00500021: Trkd ldr, styd on for press to lead cl-home: rnr-up yesterday: suited by 6/7f on firm, soft & polytrack, loves fibresand: see 1337.		62
3528 **CUT RIDGE 1** [1] J S Wainwright 5-7-12 (7oh) (38) D Fentiman(7) 8/1: 20-000032: Keen & handy, led 3f out till well ins last: just bhd today's wnr again yesterday: stays a stiff 7f: acts on firm & gd/soft grnd.	½	53
3016 **MISTRESS TWISTER 22** [6] T D Barron 3-8-13 (67) P Makin(5) 8/1: 03-3303: Held up, styd on well for press fnl 2f, just held in a tight fin: eff at 6/7f on firm & fast grnd: see 2559 & 2463 (mdns).	hd	74
3416 **SHAROURA 6** [11] R A Fahey 8-9-3 (64) P Hanagan 7/4 FAV: 0103424: Trkd ldrs, rdn/struck by rival's whip over 2f out, kept on onepace ins last: nicely bckd, op 2/1: qck reappr: see 2791.	nk	70
3054 **BLONDE EN BLONDE 21** [5]4-8-5 bl (52) J Bramhill 11/2: 3300305: Rdn rear, kept on late, flashed tail, nvr a threat: see 499 (first time blnks).	2	54
2205 **SPRING DANCER 55** [8]3-7-12 (2oh)T (50) A McCarthy 16/1: 0-000536: Rear, eff over 1f out, only mod prog: new stable (prev with B Powell), 8 wk abs, t-strap: see 2205.	nk	51
2657 **EFIMAC 37** [2]4-7-12 (7oh) (38) D Kinsella 16/1: 0-000407: Bhd, hdwy over 2f out, no prog dist.	1	44
3102 **MIDNIGHT ARROW 19** [3]6-7-12 (45) R Thomas(1) 66/1: 00/300/-08: b f Robellino - Princess Oberon (Fairy King) Rear, rdn & no impress fnl 3f: sole win came back in '00 (mdn): winning form at 5f on gd grnd.	3½	37
3324 **PHARAOH HATSHEPSUT 9** [12]6-7-12 (13oh)BL (32) Dale Gibson 66/1: 0000609: Led/dsptd lead till halfway, sn btn: tried blnks, stiff task.	2½	32
2904 **GAIETY GIRL 27** [4]3-8-3 BL (57) D Allan 14/1: 30-06500: 10th: Keen & cl-up till 2f out: tried blnks.	9	29
3226 **Devine Light 13** [7]4-8-9 p(56) T Hamilton(3) 33/1:0 218 **Perfect Love 225** [10]4-10-0 (75) S W Kelly 11/1:0		
12 Ran Time 1m 26.03 (2.13) Owned: Miss V Haigh Trained: Bawtry		

3549	5.10 Tom Connors 'lifetime In Racing' Apprentice Handicap Stakes 4yo+ 35-55 (F) £3248 £928 £464 1m6f32y Firm 14 -34 Slow Inside	[60]
1469 **LITTLE TOBIAS 90** [7] Andrew Turnell 5-9-4 (50) R Thomas 11/1: 1010-601: Sn handy & led dist, rdn & styd on well: 3 mth abs: eff at 14f/2m on firm & gd/soft, stiff/gall or sharp trk: goes well fresh: see 1285.		57
2991 **BRAVELY DOES IT 23** [10] W M Brisbourne 4-9-6 (52) B Swarbrick 10/1: 0062: gr g Holy Bull - Vigors Destiny (Vigors) Led till dist, kept on for press: unplcd prev: apprec longer 14f trip & h'cap bow: acts on firm grnd & a stiff trk.	¾	57
3398 **VANDENBERGHE 6** [4] J A Osborne 5-9-0 (46) R Keogh(5) 3/1: 3435633: Held up, hdwy to chall over 1f out, no extra ins last: op 5/2, qck reappr: stays 14f: see 3398, 1657.	3	47
2417 **FLETCHER 47** [1] H Morrison 10-8-6 p (38) T Block(5) 8/1: 0510004: Cl-up, no extra dist: 7 wk abs.	1½	37
3276 **MR MIDAZ 12** [5]5-8-13 (45) A Mullen(5) 10/1: 04000/-55: Rear, late prog, no threat: see 3276.	1	43
3140 **PRIZE RING 18** [9]5-9-6 (52) M Lawson(3) 9/4 FAV: 6410-626: Mid-div, rdn, op 3/1.	¾	49
2391 **COURT ONE 47** [2]6-9-1 (47) L Treadwell(3) 6/1: 0-001107: Held up, no impress dist: abs.	1¾	42
3454 **SNINFIA 5** [8]4-9-4 (50) W Hogg(5) 11/1: 0004008: Keen in trk, btn 3f out: qck reappr: btr 2156.	8	33
2629} **CAPER 391** [6]4-8-13 (45) H Fellows(7) 25/1: 060/060-9: Keen, held up, no impress fnl 3f: unplcd '03 (lightly rcd, rtd 48, mdn h'cap, W M Brisbourne): unplaced '02 (mdn, M Bell).	13	11
3158 **KARYON 17** [3]4-8-3 (35) Rory Moore(3) 20/1: 0003-500: 10th: Chsd ldrs till 3f out: btr 2008.	2½	0
10 Ran Time 3m 06.61(6.81) Owned: Mrs Claire Hollowood Trained: Malton		

GOODWOOD   THURSDAY 29.07.04   Righthand, Sharpish, Undulating Track

Official Going GOOD/FIRM (GOOD places).

3550	2.05 Albert Stakes Handicap 3yo 0-100 (C) £26100 £9900 £4950 7f rnd Firm 12 +00 Fast Inside	[104]
3338* **PETER PAUL RUBENS 8** [8] P F I Cole 3-9-6 (6ex) (96) R L Moore 3/1: 041511: Made all, styd on strongly fnl 1f, rdn out: well bckd: eff at 7f, has tried 1m & shld suit: acts on fast & firm grnd & a stiff/gall or sharp/undul trk: prog performer who defied 6lb pen & low draw with a bit in hand: can rate higher & make presence felt in List/Gr company: see 3338 & 1929.		109+
3131+ **COMPTONS ELEVEN 19** [6] M R Channon 3-8-10 (86) S Hitchcott(3) 20/1: 0005212: Keen cl-up, went clr with wnr fnl 2f, just held ins fnl 1f: tchd 33/1: gd performance from poor low draw: see 3131 & 2880.	1½	94
3006* **PEERESS 23** [18] Sir Michael Stoute 3-9-4 (94) K Fallon 9/4 FAV: 3-1113: Mid-div, trav well	1	100

halfway, kept on fnl 2f, not rch front 2: gd run on hat-trick bid, will apprec return to 1m, see 3006.

3112* **TAKE A BOW** 19 [4] P R Chamings 3-9-0 (90) J Quinn 16/1: 02-114: Held up wide, prog 2f out, styd on ins fnl 1f, nrst fin: ran with credit from poor low draw & will apprec return to 1m: btr 3112 (1m). — 2½ — 91

2521 **FREE TRIP** 42 [16]3-8-13 (89) L Dettori 5/1: 1602555: Mid-div, prog 3f out, onepcd dist: morning gamble: 11lb higher than last win: see 1983. — hd — 89

3002 **MAHMOOM** 23 [17]3-9-2 (92) T E Durcan 10/1: 0060126: Chsd ldrs, no extra dist: btr 3002 & 2764 (6f). — ½ — 91

3199 **BETTALATETHANNEVER** 15 [12]3-8-9 (85) Dane O'Neill 50/1: 1400267: Bhd when short of room after 1f, late prog, nrst fin: btr 2533 (1m). — nk — 83

3113 **JEDBURGH** 19 [3]3-9-7 (97) T Quinn 25/1: 11-03328: Nvr nrr than mid-div: btr 3113 & 1847. — nk — 94

3199 **FANCY FOXTROT** 15 [1]3-8-13 (89) J Fortune 50/1: 1003009: Held up, nvr nrr than mid-div. — 1¼ — 84

3433 **DISTANT CONNECTION** 5 [14]3-8-6 (82) K McEvoy 12/1: 1215320: 10th: Handy 5f, wknd: qck reapp. — ½ — 76

2749 **DESERT DREAMER** 33 [11]3-8-12 (88) M Hills 33/1: 20-50600: 11th: Dwelt, al in rear: op 20/1. — ¾ — 80

3069 **MISTER SAIF** 20 [5]3-8-11 (87) P Dobbs 66/1: U504200: 12th: Handy 5f, wknd: btr 2362. — 3½ — 72

3331 **ECCENTRIC** 8 [9]3-7-13 (1ow) (74) F Norton 33/1: 1104220: 13th: Cl-up 5f, wknd: btr 3331 & 3198. — nk — 59

3080 **Dvinsky** 20 [2]3-8-12 BL(88) J Murtagh 28/1:0   3277 **Invasian** 12 [10]3-8-11 (87) W Ryan 33/1:0

2521 **Parkview Love** 42 [4]3-9-4 (94) K Dalgleish 25/1:0   3128 **Lord Links** 19 [7]3-8-6 (82) Martin Dwyer 33/1:0

17 Ran Time 1m 25.40 (0.90) Owned: Richard Green (Fine Paintings) Trained: Whatcombe

---

3551 2.40 Gr3 King George Stakes 3yo+ (A)
£29000 £11000 £5500 **5f str** **Firm 12** **+12 Fast** Stands side

3075 **RINGMOOR DOWN** 20 [12] D W P Arbuthnot 5-8-11 (106) T Quinn 10/1: 6134241: Held up, hdwy halfway, styd on well to get up on line, rdn out: fast time: eff over a fast run 5f/6f on firm, gd & gd/soft grnd: acts on a gall or sharp/undul trk: useful hold up performer who enjoyed today's strong pace: see 2913 & 2468. — — 111

2913 **BOOGIE STREET** 26 [9] R Hannon 3-8-10 t (110) J Fortune 15/2: 1-321642: Cl-up, led halfway, hung right under press ins fnl 1f, hdd cl-home: op 13/2: apprec return of t-strap: continues to run well in Group company & deserves to find similar: see 2468 & 2068. — hd — 112

2913 **THE TATLING** 26 [7] J M Bradley 7-9-8 (115) R L Moore 8/1: 0-234103: Held up, prog halfway, styd on well fnl 1f, just held: won this race in '03: fine eff under a penalty, shld give a gd account in the Gr 1 Nunthorpe next, see 2468 & 2305. — ¾ — 118

2580 **AVONBRIDGE** 40 [8] R Charlton 4-9-8 (114) S Drowne 13/2: 343-2154: Mid-div, prog to chase wnr fnl 2f, onepcd ins fnl 1f: 6 wk abs: not disgraced under jt top-weight: see 2580 & 2305. — 1 — 115

3466 **TYCHY** 4 [10]5-8-11 (92) Martin Dwyer 50/1: 10-53005: Led, hdd halfway, sn outpcd, rallied ins fnl 1f: qck reapp: flattered on step up in grade: see 2253 (h'cap). — ½ — 103$

3466+ **BAHAMIAN PIRATE** 6 [6]9-9-0 (105) E Ahern 14/1: 0000016: Mid-div, outpcd after halfway, rallied ins fnl 1f: prefers softer grnd: showed more in 3409 (stiff/gall trk). — nk — 105

2769 **CELTIC MILL** 33 [3]6-9-0 (107) L Enstone 9/1: 1401107: Cl-up over 3f, sn no extra: prob unsuited by drop back to minimum trip: btr 1958 (6f). — ½ — 104

2468 **MAJESTIC MISSILE** 44 [13]3-8-10 (116) K Fallon 2/1 FAV: 11161-58: Mid-div, prog halfway, hung right & onepcd dist: v well bckd after 6 wk abs: failed to build on reapp 5th in 2468 (Gr 2). — nk — 103

2468 **IF PARADISE** 44 [5]3-8-10 (102) Dane O'Neill 66/1: 05-10609: Handy over 3f, sn wknd: 6 wk abs. — 1¼ — 100

3100 **BISHOPS COURT** 19 [1]10-9-0 (107) L Dettori 12/1: 1203300: 10th: Held up, nvr a factor: tchd 20/1: fin 5th in this race 12 mths ago & 4th in '01: btr 2638 & 2206. — hd — 99

3409 **DRAGON FLYER** 6 [4]5-8-11 (98) F Norton 50/1: 0003430: 11th: Handy 3f, sn wknd: qck reapp: fin close 2nd in this race 12 mths ago: btr 3409. — nk — 95

3100* **FIRE UP THE BAND** 19 [2]5-9-0 (99) A Nicholls 20/1: 0034010: 12th: Cl-up till halfway, sn wknd. — 5 — 83

3304 **AUTUMN PEARL** 10 [11]3-8-7 (98) P Robinson 33/1: 51-12360: 13th: Cl-up wide 3f, fdd: rider reported mount was unsuited by grnd: btr 2593 & 2206. — ¾ — 78

13 Ran Time 56.73 (0.03) Owned: Prof C D Green Trained: Upper Lambourn

---

3552 3.15 Gr2 Lady O Goodwood Cup 3yo+ (A)
£58000 £22000 £11000 **2m** **Firm 12** **-04 Slow** Inside

2518 **DARASIM** 42 [8] M Johnston 6-9-4 vis (115) J Fanning 11/8 FAV: 130-6131: Made all, qcknd tempo fnl half-mile, styd on strongly, rdn out: v well bckd, 6 wk abs: prev eff at 12/14f, now suited by 2m/2m4f: acts on firm & gd/soft grnd: eff with a visor & loves to dominate: likes Goodwood (won at this meeting 3 yrs in a row): tough, smart & in-form 6yo: see 2518. — — 117+

2914 **ROYAL REBEL** 26 [1] M Johnston 8-9-4 vis (110) J Murtagh 14/1: 01/-50442: Bhd, hdwy 3f out, styd on to chase wnr fnl 1f, al held: longer priced s/mate of wnr & won this race back in '00: see 2518 & 1418. — 2½ — 112

2914 **MISTERNANDO** 26 [5] M R Channon 4-9-4 vis (108) S Hitchcott 11/1: 1-026033: Mid-div, hdwy & ch 2f out, no impress fnl 1f: decent eff & can be plcd to find a Group race: see 2914 & 1569. — ¾ — 111

3125 **DOUBLE OBSESSION** 19 [4] M Johnston 4-9-4 vis (95) J F Egan 12/1: 0-000154: Handy, styd on to chase wnr 3f out, onepcd ins fnl 1f: stablemate of first 2: see 2471 (h'cap). — 1 — 110$

2914* **ROMANY PRINCE** 26 [9]5-9-4 (110) Dane O'Neill 11/1: 330-3325: Slow away, still trav well in rear 4f out, kept on fnl 2f, nvr rch principals: set plenty to do in a tactical race btr 2914. — ½ — 109

2914 **SILVER GILT** 26 [7]4-9-4 (110) L Dettori 15/2: 2/34-3316: Keen in tch, onepcd when short of room dist. — nk — 108

3233 **SUPREMACY** 13 [6]5-9-4 (104) K Fallon 8/1: 0021-047: Mid-div over 11f, sn outpcd, rallied late. — ½ — 107

2771 **ANAK PEKAN** 33 [2]4-9-4 (105) P Robinson 7/1: 222-1138: Cl-up over 13f, sn wknd: rider reported mount was unsuited by grnd: btr 2771 (gd/soft, h'cap) & 1569 (h'cap). — 8 — 99

2095 **HILBRE ISLAND** 59 [3]4-9-4 (110) M Hills 16/1: 10-30P59: Held up, nvr a factor: 8 wk abs: trainer reported 4yo was unsuited by trk: btr 1005. — 7 — 92

9 Ran Time 3m 26.93 (2.63) Owned: Mr Markus Graff Trained: Middleham

3553 3.50 Ladbrokes Com Stakes Handicap 3yo 0-110 (B)   [111]
£43500 £16500 £8250   1m1f192y   Firm 12   +01 Fast   Inside

3236 **ART TRADER** 13 [11] Mrs A J Perrett 3-8-10 (93) J Murtagh 7/2 FAV: 14-21: Handy, hdwy trav well   **105+**
to lead 2f out, rdn out fnl 1f: well bckd: eff at 10f, 12f shld suit: acts on firm & gd grnd: eff on a stiff/gall
or sharp/undul trk: lightly rcd & fast improving, List company will now suit, see 3236 (reapp, h'cap bow).
3277 **FINE SILVER** 12 [7] P F I Cole 3-8-10 (93) T Quinn 12/1: 6-401422: Mid-div, hdwy to chase wnr fnl   1¼ **100**
1f, nvr going to get there: eff at 7f/1m, ran to form on step up to 10f: hung right & a return to a more gall trk
shld suit, see 3277 & 2521 (1m).
2660 **WATAMU** 36 [14] P J Makin 3-8-1 VIS (84) J Quinn 14/1: 1-001263: Held up, prog when short of room   1½ **88+**
2f out till dist, switched & kept on well ins fnl 1f: gd run in first time visor: eff at 10f, return to 11/12f will
suit: enjoys firm & fast grnd: did not get run of race fnl 2f, see 2021 & 1865.
3118 **MUTAFANEN** 19 [6] E A L Dunlop 3-9-6 (103) R Hills 12/1: 1-133304: Held up, prog wide 4f out,   shd **106**
hung right under press ins fnl 2f, just held on for 4th: v encouraging effort: see 2520 & 1813.
3199 **WARRAD** 15 [15]3-8-7 (93) E Ahern 9/1: 1-435: Cl-up, prog to lead 3f out, hdd 2f out, no extra   hd **90**
ins fnl 1f: op 7/1: h'cap bow: stays 10f, return to 1m suit: acts on firm, fast grnd & polytrack: promising
eff on only 4th ever start & can rate higher: see 3199.
3029 **ROYAL WARRANT** 22 [5]3-8-10 (93) Martin Dwyer 10/1: 1342226: Cl-up, under press when short of   3 **91**
room bef 1f out, sn no extra: poor low draw: btr 3029 & 2785.
3205 **WOODY VALENTINE** 14 [4]3-7-13 (82) R Ffrench 14/1: 2166127: Cl-up, ev ch bef 1f out, sn wknd.   ¾ **78**
2520 **GATWICK** 42 [3]3-9-7 (104) S Hitchcott(3) 8/1: 1311068: Nvr nrr than mid-div: 6 wk abs,   hd **99**
top-weight: poor low draw: 9lb higher than last h'cap success in 1919.
3084* **GAVROCHE** 20 [2]3-8-6 (89) J P Guillambert(3) 20/1: 2511419: Bhd, hdwy 3f out, wknd dist: btr 3084.   1¼ **82**
3265 **GOLD HISTORY** 12 [8]3-9-3 (100) J Fanning 40/1: 0-213500: 10th: Nvr nrr than mid-div: btr 3116.   5 **86**
2250 **DANCING LYRA** 54 [1]3-8-7 (90) M Hills 12/1: 0-611240: 11th: Cl-up over 7f, wkng when short of   hd **75**
room 2f out: 8 wk abs: poor low draw: btr 2250 & 1813.
1500 **SENESCHAL** 88 [10]3-8-4 (87) T Dean(7) 66/1: 21-000: 12th: Led, sn clr, hdd 3f out, sn wknd: 12   3 **68**
wk abs & went off too fast: has been gelded: see 1206.
3433 **ODDSMAKER** 5 [13] 3-8-5 (88) Dean McKeown 33/1: 1015300: 13th: Al bhd: qck reapp: btr 3277.   5 **62**
2605 **KINGSWORD** 39 [16]3-9-0 (97) K Fallon 9/1: 41-520: 14th: Mid-div, no impress when eased ins fnl   1¼ **69**
2f: bckd: disapp run: btr 2605.
2521 **LUCAYAN LEGEND** 42 [9]3-8-11 (94) L Dettori 9/1: 63120: 15th: Al in rear: 6 wk abs: rider   shd **65**
reported mount was unsuited by trk & grnd: btr 2521.
1595 **MUTAWASSEL** 83 [12]3-9-3 BL (100) W Supple 40/1: 01-430: 16th: Keen mid-div 6f: blnks, abs.   8 **60**
16 Ran   Time 2m 05.31 (1.11)   Owned: Matthew Green & Oliver Simmons   Trained: Pulborough

3554 4.25 European Breeders Fund New Ham Maiden Stakes Fillies 2yo (D)
£10465 £3220 £1610   7f rnd   Firm 12   -44 Slow   Inside

3251 **MISS LAUGEVAL** 13 [9] G Wragg 2-8-11 K Darley 100/30 FAV: 41: Handy, styd on despite wandering   **79**
under press to lead ins fnl 1f, rdn out to hold on: well bckd: eff at 6f, apprec step up to 7f: acts on firm &
fast grnd, sharp/undul trk: only lightly rcd & can rate higher: see 3251 (debut).
3252 **KALMINI** 13 [6] M R Channon 2-8-11 T E Durcan 16/1: 02: b f Rahy - Kilma (Silver Hawk) In tch,   ½ **77**
prog ins fnl 2f, kept on, ddhtd for 2nd: Apr foal, dam successful at mid-dists: sire decent juv performer: eff at
7f on form, further will suit in time: can find similar.
     LOVE AFFAIR [12] R Hannon 2-8-11 R L Moore 7/1: 2: b f Tagula - Changing Partners (Rainbow   dht **77**
Quest) Mid-div, prog 3f out, kept on well ins fnl 1f, just held: bckd from 16/1 on debut: Apr foal, cost
26,000gns: half-sister to wnrs abroad: dam successful at 12f, sire smart 6f juv wnr: eff at 7f, 1m will suit on
this evidence: acts on firm grnd: sure to impr for this experience & find similar.
     MISS SHARAPOVA [10] G A Butler 2-8-11 K Fallon 9/2: 4: b f Almutawakel - Dolcezza (Lichine)   hd **76**
Keen mid-div, outpcd over 2f out, rallied ins fnl 1f, not btn far in 4th: op 3/1 on debut: Apr foal, cost £15,000:
half-sister to numerous wnrs: dam unrcd: sire high-class performer at mid-dists: eff at 7f, 1m+ will suit: acts
on firm grnd: impr for today's experience & rate higher.
     ELLENS PRINCESS [2]2-8-11 P Dobbs 33/1: 5: b f Desert Prince - Lady Ellen (Horage) Held up,   shd **75**
hdwy 3f out, kept on ins fnl 1f: debut: Feb foal, half-sister to numerous wnrs at sprint dists: dam successful at
7f: sire a decent performer at 1m: eff at 7f, will apprec further: acts on firm grnd.
3251 **MIDCAP** 13 [4]2-8-11 M Hills 33/1: 06: Cl-up, led 2f out, hdd ins fnl 1f, no extra: see 3251.   1 **73**
     RUMBALARA [13]2-8-11 J Fortune 10/1: 7: Mid-div, prog when short of room dist, sn flashed tail   hd **72**
under press & fly-jmpd ins fnl 1f: debut.
     CEIRIOG VALLEY [7]2-8-11 R Hills 33/1: 8: Bhd, prog 3f out, kept on late: debut.   1 **70**
2676 **GWYNETH** 36 [11]2-8-11 T Quinn 12/1: 59: Handy over 5f, sn wknd: see 2676.   nk **69**
3252 **SOMETHING EXCITING** 13 [3]2-8-11 N Pollard 9/1: 40: 10th: Rear, modest late gains.   ½ **68**
3348 **MARY GRAY** 8 [8]2-8-11 J Fanning 25/1: 50: 11th: Led, hdd 2f out, sn wknd.   shd **67**
3035 **SHARABY** 22 [5]2-8-11 L Dettori 9/2: 30: 12th: Mid-div wide, hung & no extra ins fnl 2f: rider   ¾ **65**
reported mount was unsuited by grnd: btr 3035 (best).
     CASUAL GLANCE [1]2-8-11 Martin Dwyer 20/1: 0: 13th: Bhd, nvr a factor on debut.   5 **55**
13 Ran   Time 1m 29.18 (4.68)   Owned: Mr J L C Pearce   Trained: Newmarket

3555 5.00 De Boer European Breeders Fund Classified Stakes 3yo+ 0-95 (B)
£12296 £4664 £2332   7f rnd   Firm 12   -06 Slow   Inside

3113 **GOLDEN SAHARA** 19 [12] Saeed bin Suroor 3-8-9 t (95) L Dettori 8/1: 122-031: Cl-up, trav well & ev   **102**
ch dist, rdn out to lead cl-home: eff at 6/7f on firm & fast, prob handles gd/soft: acts with a t-strap: only
lightly rcd & is open to more improvement: see 3113.
3061* **MATERIAL WITNESS** 21 [10] W R Muir 7-9-6 (99) Martin Dwyer 5/1: 0201112: Tried to make all,   ½ **105**
caught cl-home: well bckd: in-form 7yo who lost little in defeat on bid for 4-timer: likes Goodwood, see 3061.
2915 **BOSTON LODGE** 26 [9] G A Butler 4-9-2 VIS (95) J Murtagh 8/1: 3240003: Slow away, hdwy when short   nk **100+**
of room dist, switchd & again sn short of room, styd on well, not btn far: blnks swapped for visor: prob unlucky &
worth keeping in mind for in-form stable: see 2206 & 790.

GOODWOOD   THURSDAY 29.07.04   Righthand, Sharpish, Undulating Track

3253 **MOONLIGHT MAN 13** [3] R Hannon 3-9-0 (100) R L Moore 14/1: 3-220024: Bhd, prog & ev ch bef 1f   ½   104
out, sn edged right & onepcd: bckd: rider received 1 day careless riding ban: btr 3253.
3077 **WIZARD OF NOZ 20** [7]4-9-5 (98) K Fallon 8/1: 40-26055: Mid-div, prog when short of room bef 2f   1½   99
out, no impress ins fnl 1f: see 3186 & 2228.
2278 **QUIET STORM 52** [5]4-8-13 (93) J F Egan 25/1: 324-0036: In tch, ev ch 2f out, no extra dist: abs.   ¾   91
3277 **SEWNSO CHARACTER 12** [4]3-8-9 BL (94) D Sweeney 16/1: 5-403447: Cl-up, wkng when no room dist.   hd   93
3441 **DIGITAL 5** [8]7-9-2 (90) S Hitchcott 10/1: 0522208: Al in rear: qck reapp: btr 3117 & 2684.   ½   92
3061 **MAGHANIM 21** [2]4-9-5 (98) R Hills 9/1: 0/0-53209: Held up, nvr a factor: twice below 2558.   ½   94
3441 **VICIOUS KNIGHT 5** [6]6-9-2 (95) A Nicholls 16/1: 15-00000: 10th: Al bhd: qck reapp.   3½   84
3059+**KEHAAR 21** [1]3-8-9 (93) E Ahern 7/2 FAV: 110: 11th: Held up wide, hung under press halfway, sn   ¾   82
btn: v well bckd on h'cap bow: lkd unhappy on today's trk & is worth another chance: btr 3059.
3061 **MAKFOOL 21** [11]3-8-11 (97) T E Durcan 14/1: 4021000: 12th: Cl-up 5f, sn wknd: btr 2212.   nk   83
12 Ran   Time 1m 25.81 (1.31)   Owned: Godolphin   Trained: Newmarket

---

3556   5.35 Valdoe Rated Stakes Handicap 3yo 0-95 (C)   [102]
£9613 £3647 £1823   **1m6f**   **Firm 12**   **-02 Slow**   Inside

2660 **LOCHBUIE 7** [7] G Wragg 3-9-2 (90) J F Egan 7/2 CO FAV: 40-41131: Mid-div, prog to lead dist, sn   99
edged right under press, rdn out to victory on: bckd: eff at 12f, apprec step up to 14f: acts on firm & gd grnd: v
progressive 3yo who can win again at this trip: see 1581 & 1174.
3015* **YOSHKA 22** [3] M Johnston 3-8-13 (87) R Ffrench 7/2 CO FAV: 1-3112: In tch, styd on to lead 3f   ¾   94
out, hdd dist, kept on but not quite pace of wnr: well bckd: fine eff on hat-trick bid: see 3015 (2m).
3200* **TUNGSTEN STRIKE 15** [10] Mrs A J Perrett 3-8-7 (81) Martin Dwyer 7/2 CO FAV: 400-0113: Prom,   1¾   86
outpcd over 2f out, kept on ins fnl 1f, no ch with front 2: well bckd on hat-trick bid: acts on firm & gd grnd:
apprec return to 2m: 10lb higher than recent win in 3200.
3274 **ANOUSA 12** [9] P Howling 3-9-7 (95) K Fallon 8/1: 0003104: Rear, hdwy 2f out, onepcd ins fnl 1f.   2½   98
3475 **TWOFAN 4** [4]3-8-6 (80) J Fanning 12/1: 221645: Cl-up, wknd fnl 2f: qck reapp: btr 3475.   3   80
3359 **MAN AT ARMS 7** [1]3-8-4 (3oh) (75) R L Moore 16/1: 4140046: Slow away, nvr nrr than mid-div.   nk   77
2668* **LEG SPINNER 36** [2]3-8-4 (1ow) (78) K Darley 8/1: 3317: Mid-div 12f, sn wknd: op 16/1: disapp,   nk   76
better expected over this trip: btr 2668 (mdn).
2919 **RED BIRR 26** [8]3-8-8 (82) L Dettori 16/1: 43-04108: Led, hdd 3f out, wknd: btr 2663 (10f).   11   70
3216 **WAZIRI 14** [6]3-8-4 (1oh) (77) K McEvoy 14/1: 464-109: Keen prom 11f, wknd: btr 2225.   7   59
9 Ran   Time 3m 0.78(1.98)   Owned: Mollers Racing   Trained: Newmarket

---

MUSSELBURGH   THURSDAY 29.07.04   Righthand, Sharp Track

Official Going GOOD/FIRM (FIRM IN PLACES)

3557   6.20 Famous Grouse Handicap Stakes Amateur Riders 4yo+ 35-55 (F)   [37]
£3374 £1038 £519   **2m**   **Good/Firm 29**   **-51 Slow**   Stands side

2850 **REGAL FANTASY 29** [3] P A Blockley 4-9-9 (32) Miss Faye Bramley(5) 10/1: 50/00-001: Chsd ldrs,   40
prog to lead ins fnl 1f, rdn out: tchd 16/1: imprvd for step up to 2m: acts on fast grnd & a sharp trk: first win.
3325 **SHERWOOD FOREST 9** [5] Miss L A Perratt 4-10-5 vis (42) Miss S Brotherton 10/1: 0-036052: Mid-div,   ¾   47
prog 4f out, styd on well ins fnl 1f, post came too sn: eff at 1m/11f, imprvd for step up to 2m: acts on fast & gd.
2964 **MR FORTYWINKS 24** [8] B Ellison 10-10-8 (45) Miss L Ellison(3) 11/2: 06-05063: Led till 11f out,   ½   49
styd prom & led again 4f out, hdd ins fnl 1f, no extra: op 4/1: recent plcd over hdles (nov, rtd 108h, stays around
2m1.5f on gd/soft): won this race 12 mths ago off a 6lb higher mark: btr 1551.
3398 **SARN 6** [2] M Mullineaux 5-10-4 (41) Miss M Mullineaux(7) 9/2 J FAV: 0320404: Held up, prog bef 2f   nk   44
out, nrst fin: qck reapp: prob stays 2m: see 2226 & 1406.
3190* **PETERS IMP 15** [10]9-11-0 (51) Mr D Grewer 12/1: 60/000-15: Rear, prog halfway, onepcd dist.   2½   51
2807 **WELSH DREAM 31** [1]7-10-9 (46) Mr C Storey 12/1: 14016/-66: Chsd ldrs 13f, o extra: see 2807.   3½   42
3325 **REPULSE BAY 9** [4]6-10-12 (49) Ms C Williams 15/2: 3050007: Mid-div, prog 5f out, fdd fnl 3f.   7   38
1819 **DOUBLE BLADE 72** [11]9-10-3 (40) Mrs N Wilson(3) 9/2 J FAV: 60404-68: Prom, led 11f out, hdd 4f   3½   25
out, wknd: op 11/2: recent wnr over fences (beginners chase, rtd 105c): see 1819.
2929 **SAN DIMAS 741** [12]7-9-12 vis (35) Miss J Riding(5) 14/1: 600/04/0/-9: gr g Distant View -   2   18
Chrystophard (Lyphear) Handy 11f, wknd: long jumps abs, h'cap hdle wnr on 1 of only 2 03/04 starts (rtd 100h,
stays 2m6.5f on firm or gd/soft, eff in visor): nvr hdle wnr in 02/03 (rtd 90h): modest Flat form previously.
2988 **OUTWARD 23** [7]4-10-8 (45) Miss R Bastiman(5) 40/1: 54-00000: 10th: Keen bhd, nvr a factor.   dist   0
3145 **WATERLINE SPIRIT 18** [9]4-10-3 (40) Miss A Bevan(7) 33/1: 00/000-00: 11th: b g Piccolo - Gina of   dist   0
Hithermoor (Reprimand) Chsd ldrs 10f, fdd: mod form in '03 (rtd 34, clmr): has tried visor: with P Evans.
11 Ran   Time 3m 35.3 (12.8)   Owned: Mr M J Wiley   Trained: Southwell

---

3558   6.50 Greengauge Home Turf Claiming Stakes 3yo+ (F)
£3513 £1081 £541   **1m rnd**   **Good/Firm 29**   **+01 Fast**   Outside

3426 **BAILIEBOROUGH 5** [6] D Nicholls 5-9-11 vis (70) Alex Greaves 4/1: 1301651: Mid-div, prog 3f out,   71
styd on to lead dist, rdn out: qck reapp: eff at 7/9f on firm & gd/soft: likes claim grade: see 2811.
3426 **KILLALA 5** [10] I Semple 4-9-4 (62) R Winston 5/2 FAV: 36-35522: Held up, hdwy halfway, styd on   1   60
ins fnl 1f, not pace of wnr: qck reapp: eff at 6f/1m: has shown enough to find similar: see 3426.
2947 **TOJONESKI 26** [2] I W McInnes 5-9-5 p (46) A Culhane 9/1: 2334203: Led after 5f, hdd dist, no extra.   1½   58$
2370 **ALAFZAR 48** [8] P D Evans 6-9-9-1 (58) S Donohoe(7) 9/1: 3130404: Handy 6f, sn no extra: 7 wk abs.   1½   59
3305 **SARRAAF 10** [4]8-9-9 (69) P Mulrennan(5) 7/2: 5333505: Rear, prog 3f out, no impress fnl 1f: op 5/2.   2½   54
3526 **SCRAMBLE 1** [7]6-9-2 t p (50) G Parkin 25/1: 3464-6006: Led 5f, sn wknd: unplcd yesterday: btr 1635.   7   33
622] **SOCIETY TIMES 1253** [1]11-9-7 T (16) J McAuley 150/1: 00/4500//-7: b g Imp Society - Mauna Loa   ¾   36$
(Hawaii) Nvr nrr than mid-div: reapp: missed '03 & '02: modest form back in '01 (rtd 32a, seller, A Bailey): eff
at 1m & handles fast grnd: with D A Nolan.
3325 **LUCKY LARGO 9** [9]4-9-3 bl (55) D McGaffin 25/1: 4026008: Chsd ldrs 5f, sn wknd: btr 2813.   1   30
2811 **ENVIRONMENTALIST 31** [3]5-9-2 t (40) C Haddon(7) 100/1: 06-00009: Al bhd.   6   17

1075

2991 **SHARABAD 23** [5]6-9-7 V Halliday 100/1: 5000: 10th: Handy 5f, fdd: btr 1894.   *16*   0
3324 **WARES HOME 9** [11]3-8-13 P (55) Darren Williams 12/1: 3433230: 11th: Handy, wkng/hung left 2f out.   ¾   0
11 Ran   Time 1m 39.76 (2.26)   Owned: Middleham Park Racing XVIII   Trained: Thirsk

---

3559   **7.20 Daily Record Maiden Auction Stakes 2yo   (E)**
£3380 £1040 £520   **7f30y rnd**   **Good/Firm 29**   **Inapplicable**   Outside

3189 **COLEORTON DANE 15** [2] K A Ryan 2-8-6   N Callan 13/8 FAV: 6321: Made all, clr after halfway, drvn   78
out cl-home to hold on: well bckd: eff at 7f on firm & fast grnd: see 3189 & 2776.
3239 **HEYBROOK BOY 13** [4] M Johnston 2-8-10 S Chin 7/2: 042: Handy, outpcd 3f out, rallied ins fnl   ¾   79
1f, not pace of wnr: eff at 6f, apprec step up to 7f: acts on fast & gd: improving with racing & can find similar.
2810 **CAVA BIEN 31** [6] J G Given 2-8-4   P Hanagan 3/1: 033: In tch, outpcd after 5f, rallied ins fnl   shd   72
1f, just held for 2nd: bckd from 6/1: imprvd effort after being gelded: see 2810.
3311 **BLACKCOMB MOUNTAIN 10** [5] M F Harris 2-7-13   J Mackay 9/1: 534: Cl-up, hung badly left under   ½   66
press dist, not recover: op 7/1: eff at 7f on fast grnd: closer but for hanging badly: see 3053.
3394 **KUMALA OCEAN 6** [8]2-7-13   J Bramhill 16/1: 25: Bhd, prog 2f out, styd on ins fnl 1f: qck reapp.   1   64
2505 **ISITLOVEYOURAFTER 42** [3]2-8-1   T Hamilton 100/1: 056: Handy, hung left halfway, wknd.   7   52
3239 **LIGHTENING FIRE 13** [7]2-8-6   D Kinsella 25/1: 07: b g Woodborough - Glowlamp (Glow) Dwelt, al   3½   50
in rear: Apr foal, cost £7,800: half-brother to wnrs at 7/12f: dam 9f wnr: sire Group wnr as a juv.
     FLY ME TO DUNOON [1]2-8-5 Darren Williams 25/1: 8: b f Rossini - Toledana (Sure Blade) Al bhd   10   29
on debut: Mar foal, cost £18,000: half-sister to a couple of wnrs at sprint dists: with K R Burke.
8 Ran   Time 1m 31.02 ()   Owned: Coleorton Moor Racing   Trained: Hambleton

---

3560   **7.50 Scottish Equitable/Jockey Association Nursery Handicap Stakes 2yo   (D)**   **[87]**
£8141 £2505 £1253   **7f30y rnd**   **Good/Firm 29**   **Inapplicable**   Outside

3351* **JANE JUBILEE 8** [1] M Johnston 2-9-11 (7ex) (84) S Chin 8/15 FAV: 352211: In tch, sltly outpcd   97+
after halfway, styd on to lead dist, pushed out, val bt more: eff at 6f, suited by recent step up to 7f, 1m will
suit: acts on fast grnd: in gd form & easily defied 7lb pen: can land hat-trick: see 3351.
3351 **BRACE OF DOVES 8** [3] T D Barron 2-8-10 (69) P Makin(5) 8/1: 052332: Led, hdd & edged left dist,   2   73
styd on, not pace easy wnr: eff at 6/7f: again fin bhd today's wnr in 3351.
2516 **WINDY PROSPECT 42** [2] P A Blockley 2-9-7 (80) N Callan 7/1: 352103: In tch over 5f, sn no extra.   6   74
3212 **PRINCELY VALE 14** [5] W G M Turner 2-9-1 p (74) C Haddon(7) 14/1: 0411134: Nvr nrr than mid-div.   nk   67
3393* **DICTION 6** [4]2-8-8 (7ex) (67) Darren Williams 16/1: 05115: Bhd, nvr a factor: qck reapp: btr 3393.   6   48
3259* **PREMIER TIMES 12** [6]2-8-0 (59) Dale Gibson 8/1: 516: Cl-up 5f, fdd: has been gelded.   3½   33
6 Ran   Time 1m 29.25 ()   Owned: Mrs Sheila Ramsden   Trained: Middleham

---

3561   **8.20 Rossleigh Land Rover Handicap For The Rossleigh Land Rover Trophy 3yo+ 0-70 (E)**   **[70]**
£6968 £2144 £1072   **5f str**   **Good/Firm 29**   **-02 Slow**   Stands side

3241 **CATCH THE CAT 13** [7] J S Wainwright 5-9-13 vis (69) G Parkin 8/1: 1650001: Handy, gd prog to lead   77
ins fnl 1f, drvn out: stays 6f, suited by sharp or stiff 5f on firm, soft & any trk, loves Beverley or Musselburgh:
eff with visor or blnks: fine eff to defy top-weight: see 2084.
3180 **VALIANT ROMEO 16** [9] R Bastiman 4-8-11 (53) P Mulrennan(5) 10/1: 5224052: Trkd ldrs, prog & ev ch   ½   58
ins fnl 1f, just held by wnr: only just denied & is h'capped to find similar: see 1555.
3403 **MORITAT 6** [11] P D Evans 4-8-11 (53) N Callan 12/1: 0206-063: Bhd, prog halfway, styd on ins fnl   1   55
1f: gd run from poor high draw: see 3403.
3527 **ALFIE LEE 1** [12] D A Nolan 7-8-1 t p (43) C Haddon(7) 33/1: 000400-74: Al handy, onepcd fnl 1f.   1¾   40
3427 **PIRLIE HILL 5** [10]4-8-9 (51) D Kinsella 16/1: 6044065: Dwelt, prog 2f out, kept on fnl 1f: qck reapp.   nk   47
2961 **HES A ROCKET 25** [4]3-9-0 bl (60) Darren Williams 14/1: 1136006: Handy till dist, no extra: btr 1605.   shd   55
3463 **RECTANGLE 4** [14]4-9-11 (67) Alex Greaves 12/1: 0000207: In tch 4f, no extra: qck reapp: btr 3244.   hd   61
3228 **PETERS CHOICE 13** [2]3-9-6 bl (66) R Winston 7/1 FAV: 0050028: Led, hdd dist, wknd: btr 3228.   nk   59
3018 **CHAMPAGNE CRACKER 22** [3]3-9-5 (65) T Hamilton(3) 33/1: 2-031509: In tch over 3f, wknd: btr 2227.   hd   57
3193 **SEA FERN 15** [6]3-8-1 (47) P Hanagan 50/1: 000-5000: 10th: Al in rear: btr 1392.   1½   34
3427 **STRAWBERRY PATCH 5** [5]5-8-13 p (55) S Chin 10/1: 600-0050: 11th: Bhd when sn short of room, nvr a   ½   40
factor: qck reapp: btr 3427.
3353 **Queen Of Night 8** [16]4-9-4 (60) A Culhane 16/1:0   3228 **Feu Duty 13** [15]3-9-5 (65) D McGaffin 50/1:0
2968 **Mutayam 24** [8]4-8-1 t(43) J McAuley 66/1:0   3417 **Star Applause 6** [13]4-7-12 (40) J Mackay 100/1:0
15 Ran   Time 59.08s (1.58)   Owned: Mr T W Heseltine   Trained: Malton

---

3562   **8.50 Bridgewell Securities Handicap Stakes 3yo+ 0-80 (D)**   **[83]**
£6773 £2084 £1042   **7f30y rnd**   **Good/Firm 29**   **Inapplicable**   Outside

3310 **ST SAVARIN 10** [4] J R Best 3-9-4 (73) M Savage(5) 4/1: 3100331: Led, hdd 5f out, led again 3f   78
out, rdn out to hold on ins fnl 1f: suited by around 7f, has tried 1m: acts on fast, soft grnd & loves polytrack:
has been in gd form & this was a deserved success: see 3310 & 3179.
3428 **KIRKBYS TREASURE 5** [3] A Berry 6-9-12 (74) F Lynch 7/2: 1301202: Held up, prog when no room sev   ¾   77+
times ins fnl 2f, fin well fnl 1f, poss came too sn: qck reapp: another gd eff here at Musselburgh & poss unlucky.
3328 **REGENTS SECRET 9** [10] J S Goldie 4-8-13 (61) P Mulrennan(5) 10/1: 4002403: Mid-div, prog 3f out,   2   60
styd on fnl 1f: promising but on long losing run: btr 2552.
     MISTER MARMADUKE 87 [1] I Semple 3-9-11 (80) D McGaffin 33/1: 11000-04: b g Marju - Lalique   ½   78
(Lahib) Rear, prog halfway, onepcd fnl 1f: long abs & Brit bow, ex-Irish, won twice in '03 (5f, firm & gd/soft).
3433 **DARK DAY BLUES 5** [7]3-8-12 (67) Darren Williams 12/1: 0001065: Keen handy over 5f, sn no extra.   hd   64
2990 **BLYTHE SPIRIT 23** [8]5-9-4 (66) P Hanagan 3/1 FAV: 45-50006: In tch, prog 3f out, no extra dist.   shd   62
3353 **RISK FREE 8** [9]7-8-11 vis (59) R Winston 14/1: 0535-067: Led 5f out till 3f out, wknd: see 3353.   nk   54
1897 **PROCREATE 26** [2]4-7-12 (4oh) (42) J McAuley 33/1: 500-0008: Prog 3f out, wkng when no room dist.   6   29
3229 **SILVER SEEKER 13** [6]4-8-6 (54) T Hamilton(3) 14/1: 5002069: Al bhd: btr 2102.   1   35

MUSSELBURGH THURSDAY 29.07.04 Righthand, Sharp Track

2086 **WHIPPASNAPPER 61** [5]4-9-5 (67) C Haddon(7) 7/1: 1032200: 10th: Dwelt, sn mid-div, wknd fnl 2f: abs. ¾ **46**
10 Ran Time 1m 28.96() Owned: Mr D S Nevison Trained: Maidstone

GOODWOOD FRIDAY 30.07.04 Righthand, Sharpish, Undulating Track

Official Going GOOD/FIRM.

3563 2.05 Listed Glorious Stakes 4yo+ (A)
£17400 £6600 £3300 **1m4f** **Firm 19** **-02 Slow** Outside

2948+**ALKAASED 27** [9] L M Cumani 4-8-12 (105) J Fortune 11/4 FAV: 2122-211: Chsd ldrs, imprvd to lead 2f out, jnd ent fnl 1f, pulled out more cl home, drvn out: well bckd: eff at 12/14f on gd & firm: handles a sharp/undul & gall trk: v smart, has a decent turn of foot & showed admirable battling qualities: Gr 3 shld now suit. **117**
2762* **FIRST CHARTER 34** [8] Sir Michael Stoute 5-9-1 (109) K Fallon 3/1: 1120-012: Chsd ldrs, prog to chall strongly ent fnl 1f, just held cl home: well bckd & clr of rem: fine run conceding wnr 3lbs: v smart colt. *nk* **118**
2898 **ALKAADHEM 28** [2] M P Tregoning 4-9-1 (108) R Hills 9/1: 1-541043: Held up, hdwy to chase ldrs when short of room 2f out, switched & kept on for 3rd, no ch with front 2: appeared to stay this longer 12f trip. *6* **109**
3030 **PERSIAN MAJESTY 23** [4] P W Harris 4-8-12 (113) J Murtagh 7/2: 1/1-63354: Held up, slightly short of room & switched 2f out, no impress fnl 1f: nicely bckd tho' op 11/4: below recent best, handled this trk well enough in 1843, see 2579. *1½* **104**
2898 **COMPTON BOLTER 28** [6]7-9-1 (107) E Ahern 12/1: 0325065: Prom, ev ch 4f out till wknd ins fnl 1f: tchd 16/1: won this race in '01 (h'cap): see 2898. *hd* **107**
2556 **PERSIAN LIGHTNING 42** [3]5-8-12 (107) S Drowne 14/1: 00-44146: Held up, nvr nr ldrs: 6 wk abs. *1¼* **102**
2914 **TIZZY MAY 27** [7]4-8-12 (100) Dane O'Neill 66/1: 0250407: Al rear: highly tried, flattered 2762. *3½* **97**
5012} **MILLSTREET 269** [5]5-8-12 t (110) L Dettori 12/1: 1/46240-8: ch g Polish Precedent - Mill Path (Mill Reef) Led till 2f out, wknd & eased on reapp: '02 stks rnr-up, also tried a t-strap: mdn & List wnr in '02 (J Oxx): eff at 10/12f on gd & softer grnd, handles fast: likes to force the pace: has been gelded. *1¾* **95**
2 Aug'03 Wind 11.6g/f 109-(110) C: 2 Sep'02 Leop 10gd 108- : 2 Aug'02 Leop 12gd 108- :
3233+**EASTERN BREEZE 14** [1]6-8-12 e (105) Paul Eddery 20/1: 120501P: Mid-div, when broke down 3f out, sn p,u,: sadly destroyed & a great loss. **0**
9 Ran Time 2m 34.40 (2.60) Owned: Mr M R Charlton Trained: Newmarket

3564 2.40 Gr3 Oak Tree Stakes Fillies 3yo+ (A)
£29000 £11000 £5500 **7f rnd** **Firm 19** **-03 Slow** Inside

3268 **PHANTOM WIND 13** [7] J H M Gosden 3-8-6 (98) S Drowne 16/1: 01-651: Trkd ldrs, short of room 2f out, rdn & qcknd to lead cl home: apprec this step up to 7f, acts on fast & firm grnd: handles a gall or sharp/undul trk: showed a decent turn of foot here & smart now: see 3268. **111**
2306 **NYRAMBA 54** [11] J H M Gosden 3-8-6 (107) J Fortune 13/2: 110-2552: Chsd ldrs, rdn to lead ins fnl 1f, not pace to repel wng stablemate cl home: bckd from 8/1, 8 wk abs: apprec this drop in grade & return to 7f. ½ **106**
2487 **CHIC 44** [10] Sir Michael Stoute 4-8-13 (97) K Fallon 10/3 FAV: 3621-603: Held up, short of room 2f out, fin well but no ch with front 2: hvly bckd from 9/2, 6 wk abs: not at home on this undul trk: has shown enough to win a Gr 3: see 2487 (1m). *1¼* **105**
2487 **GONFILIA 44** [12] Saeed bin Suroor 4-9-2 t (103) L Dettori 5/1: 0121104: Led till ins fnl 1f, no extra: op 15/2, 6 wk abs: rnr-up in this race last year & not disgraced under top-weight today: see 2211 (1m). *1* **106**
3075 **GOLDEN NUN 21** [6]4-9-2 bl (101) K Darley 25/1: 2313105: Keen & chsd ldrs, ev ch 2f out, onepcd fnl 1f: jt top-weight & ran as well as cld be expected at these weights: see 2457. *2* **102**
2918* **SILK FAN 27** [5]3-8-6 (95) D Holland 5/1: 2211-16: Mid-div wide, not pace to chall: well bckd. *nk* **98**
2457 **ENCHANTED 48** [1]5-8-13 (94) J Murtagh 40/1: 63-11007: Held up, no room at any stage: 7 wk abs: up in grade, no luck & must be given another chance, poss in List: see 1925. *1¼* **95+**
3365* **LUCKY PIPIT 8** [4]3-8-6 (102) M Hills 16/1: 103-5218: Chsd ldrs, btn fnl 1f: op 12/1. ¾ **93**
2736* **GREY PEARL 35** [3]5-8-13 (86) M Fenton 66/1: 6460419: Front rank, ev ch till wknd dist. ½ **92**
1932 **SAINT ETIENNE 69** [9]3-8-6 (90) Martin Dwyer 25/1: 150: 10th: Al rear: 10 wk abs: highly tried. *1* **90**
3268 **DOWAGER 13** [8]3-8-6 (100) Dane O'Neill 14/1: 61-54630: 11th: Al rear: btr 3268 (List, bt today's wnr). ½ **89**
2574+**LUCKY SPIN 41** [2]3-8-6 (104) R L Moore 11/2: 21110: 12th: Rear, eff 3f out, sn btn: well bckd tho' drifted from 7/2, 6 wk abs: something clearly amiss: most prog prev, see 2574 (List, crse rec time). *2* **85**
12 Ran Time 1m 26.10 (1.60) Owned: Mr K Abdulla Trained: Manton

3565 3.15 William Hill Mile Heritage Handicap 3yo+ (B) **[107]**
£58000 £22000 £11000 **1m rnd** **Firm 19** **+11 Fast** Inside

2154 **ANCIENT WORLD 58** [20] Saeed bin Suroor 4-9-10 (103) L Dettori 9/2 FAV: 4411-221: In tch, prog to lead ent fnl 1f, styd on strongly, rdn out: hvly bckd under top-weight, 8 wk abs & has been gelded, fast time: eff arnd 1m on firm & soft grnd: handles a gall or sharp/undul trk: excellent run under a big weight: v smart performance & List/Group company will now suit: see 2154 & 1649. **114**
3506 **IMPELLER 3** [19] W R Muir 5-8-8 (87) S Drowne 10/1: 0260522: Mid-div trav well, slightly short of room dist, kept on fnl 1f but carried head high: nicely bckd: qck reapp after again fin plcd in a big h'cap here 3 days ago: has plenty of ability, but is not an easy ride: see 3506. *1¼* **93**
2915 **TUNING FORK 27** [2] J Akehurst 4-8-10 (89) D Holland 80/1: 0-000003: Broke well from low draw & led till ent fnl 1f, no extra: fine run from this rank outsider from a poor draw: right back to form with t-strap left off: eff at 1m/10f, see 1843 (12f here). *2* **91**
3441 **EL COTO 6** [15] B A McMahon 4-9-7 (100) S Sanders 33/1: 5000404: Chsd ldrs, kept on under press fnl 1f: fine run with blnks left off: see 3061 (7f). *hd* **102**
3265 **DEFINITE GUEST 13** [4]6-8-2 (1ow) (80) J F Egan 66/1: 65-30005: Rear, styd on well on inside fnl 2f despite no room, nrst fin: poor low draw: right back to form & an eye-catching run: keep in mind, see 2207. ¾ **81+**
3265 **AUDIENCE 13** [14]4-8-11 p (90) J Quinn 14/1: 0000246: Mid-div, kept on v well fnl 1f despite not much room: another consistent run & overdue a win: see 3265 & 3001. *nk* **89**
3441 **UHOOMAGOO 6** [12]6-8-13 bl (92) N Callan 10/1: 0110037: Mid-div, prog wide 2f out, no impress ins fnl 1f: loves to come late off a strong pace: see 3441 & 2207. ¾ **89**

3029 **MYSTICAL GIRL 23** [9]3-8-7 (94) R Ffrench 14/1: 1213068: Trk ldr, ev ch till wknd fnl 1f: mod   ½   90
draw & used a lot of energy to get a decent early position: reportedly slipped on the bend: see 2250.
3124 **PENTECOST 20** [13]5-9-5 (98) Martin Dwyer 10/1: 0-060149: Held up, no room at any stage, fin   shd   94+
fast: nicely bckd: eye-catching run & must be given another chance: see 3124 & 2915.
2915 **UNSHAKABLE 27** [21]5-9-1 (94) F Norton 7/1: 00-00130: 10th: Mid-div, eff when hmpd 1.5f out, no   ½   89
ch after: well bckd: no luck, forgive this: see 2915 & 1351.
3077 **PUTRA KUANTAN 21** [17]4-9-7 (100) P Robinson 9/1: 0-631060: 11th: Chsd ldrs, wkng when hmpd ins   ½   94
fnl 1f: btr 2096.
3061 **AMANDUS 22** [16]4-9-2 (95) T P Queally 14/1: 4-002400: 12th: Held up, no room fnl 2f, forgive this.   1   87
3512 **OMAHA CITY 3** [10]10-7-12 (3oh) (74) D Kinsella 66/1: 0021000: 13th: Chsd ldrs, wknd fnl 1f.   ¾   67
2662* **FLOWERDRUM 37** [11]4-8-8 (87) E Ahern 16/1: 01-01410: 14th: Nvr nrr than mid-div.   nk   76
3443 **SAWWAAH 6** [22]7-8-1 (80) A Nicholls 14/1: 3400030: 15th: Mid-div, hmpd dist & no ch after: 2   65
nicely bckd, qck reapp: forgive this: see 3443.
3460* **WING COMMANDER 5** [7]5-9-3 (5ex) (96) P Hanagan 20/1: 4300010: 16th: Nvr nr ldrs: poor draw.   2   77
2489 **CONVENT CAR 44** [18]4-8-12 (91) R Havlin 100/1: 6-000000: 17th: Nvr a factor: 6 wk abs.   1   70
3265 Battle Chant 13 [6]4-9-9 (102) K Fallon 12/1:0   2915 Finished Article 27 [1]7-8-10 (89) Dane O'Neill 33/1:0
3443 Takes Tutu 6 [5]5-7-12 (3oh)bl(74) J F McDonald(3) 100/1:2265 Serieux 13 [8]5-8-11 (90) K Darley 50/1:0
21 Ran   Time 1m 38.10 (0.70)   Owned: Godolphin   Trained: Newmarket

---

3566   3.50 Gr2 Richmond Stakes Colts & Geldings 2yo (A)
£40600 £15400 £7700   6f str   Firm 19   -27 Slow   Stands Side

3046* **MONTGOMERYS ARCH 22** [5] P W Chapple Hyam 2-8-11   J Fortune 13/2: 11: Led till dist, rallied   109
gamely to regain lead on line: nicely bckd: eff at 6/7f, shld stay 1m: acts on firm & gd/soft grnd: fast
improving & clearly smart juv: remains one to follow, see 3046.
3028 **MYSTICAL LAND 23** [4] J H M Gosden 2-8-11   L Dettori 11/4: 21232: Prom, went on dist, worn down   nk   107
on line: hvly bckd: another smart run, deserves a List/Gr 3: see 3028 & 2516.
3407* **SILVER WRAITH 7** [7] N A Callaghan 2-8-11   J Murtagh 9/1: 4211313: Held up, kept on under press   2   101
fnl 1f, no ch with front 2: tchd 14/1: unsuited by this drop back to 6f, crying out for a return to 7f+.
3031* **STETCHWORTH PRINCE 23** [6] D R Loder 2-8-11   T P Queally 15/2: 14: Chsd ldrs, rdn dist, sn btn: 1½   97
more expected after useful debut in 3031.
3081 **AMAZIN 21** [8]2-8-11   K Fallon 5/1: 2125: Chsd ldrs wide, not pace to chall: bckd from 8/1:   2   91
better expected on this step up in grade: see 3081 (stks).
2516* **BLUE DAKOTA 43** [1]2-9-0   E Ahern 9/4 FAV: 11116: Keen in rear, prog to chall dist, sn wknd &   1¾   89
eased: well bckd tho' op 2/1, 6 wk abs: did not settle & prob failed to stay 6f: see 2516 (bt today's 2nd).
3266 **ALPAGA LE JOMAGE 13** [2]2-8-11   J F Egan 80/1: 4505147: V keen in rear, nvr dngrs: too keen.   3   77
3267 **OBE GOLD 13** [3]2-8-11 ViS T E Durcan 33/1: 31424U: Stumbled & u.r. after 1f: visor.   0
8 Ran   Time 1m 12.81 (2.81)   Owned: Franconson Partners   Trained: Newmarket

---

3567   4.25 Turf Club Rated Stakes Handicap 3yo 0-90 (C)   [97]
£9495 £3601 £1801   5f str   Firm 19   -08 Slow   Stands Side

3123 **JIMMY RYAN 20** [1] T D McCarthy 3-9-5 (88) T Quinn 12/1: 14-00121: Chsd ldrs stands side, qcknd   100
to lead ins fnl 1f, rdn out: stays 6f, ideally suited by 5f: acts on gd & firm grnd: handles a gall or sharp/undul
trk: clearly in top form, see 3123 & 2734.
3356 **TREASURE CAY 8** [18] P W D'Arcy 3-8-10 e t (79) K Darley 20/1: 3531032: Prom centre, led dist till   1½   84
ins fnl 1f, not pace to repel wnr: in fine form & deserves similar: see 3356.
2880 **HANDSOME CROSS 29** [3] H Morrison 3-8-11 (80) Dane O'Neill 25/1: 32-55603: Chsd ldrs stands side,   1¾   80
kept on under press fnl 1f: back to form on return to 5f: see 1525.
3193 **ICENASLICE 16** [5] J J Quinn 3-8-4 (7oh) (66) R Ffrench 66/1: 6-014104: Chsd ldrs, ev ch ent fnl   hd   72
1f, sn no extra: fine run from this outsider, acts on firm & gd/soft grnd: see 2731.
2950 **SKYHARBOR 27** [6]3-8-6 (75) J Fanning 25/1: 100-0505: Chsd ldrs stands side, onepcd fnl 1f: 1½   70
better run than 4th h'capped on last season's form: see 2591.
3356 + **ROYAL CHALLENGE 8** [21]3-8-7 (3ex) (76) K Fallon 2/1 FAV: 0-2116: Dwelt, hdwy centre halfway, nrst   ½   70
fin: hvly bckd: prob lost chance at the start today: rcd prom in 3356 & 2944.
3273 **RYDAL 13** [9]3-9-1 bl (84) L Dettori 20/1: 0406247: Rear stands side, fin well: longer priced   hd   78
stablemate of 6th: return to 6f will suit judged on this: see 3273.
2734 **INCISE 35** [19]3-9-0 (83) J Fortune 20/1: 1-600448: Chsd ldrs centre, onepcd fnl 1f.   hd   77
2268 **FIDDLE ME BLUE 53** [22]3-8-4 (1oh) (72) J Quinn 20/1: 31-5009: Prom & rcd alone far side, not pace   nk   66
of ldrs stands side: 8 wk abs, stablemate of 3rd: see 2268.
3466 **GREEN MANALISHI 5** [20]3-9-7 (90) T E Durcan 13/2: 0315500: 10th: Prom centre, onepcd fnl 1f: nk   82
bckd from 10/1, top-weight, qck reapp: see 3080.
3356 **DOLCE PICCATA 8** [15]3-8-8 bl (77) J F McDonald(3) 66/1: 5450000: 11th: Hmpd start, late prog   hd   69
centre, nvr a factor: lost all ch at the start.
3356 **BUY ON THE RED 8** [16]3-9-1 (84) R Miles(3) 10/1: 2211020: 12th: Held up centre, nvr dngrs.   nk   75
3356 **DIVINE SPIRIT 8** [10]3-9-2 p (85) J F Egan 12/1: 3610360: 13th: Held up stands side, late prog.   hd   76
3135 **LUALUA 19** [8]3-8-6 (75) P Hanagan 33/1: 4230430: 14th: Slow away, al rear stands side.   nk   65
3269 **SPANISH ACE 13** [12]3-9-4 vis (87) Martin Dwyer 9/1: 0000550: 15th: Led till halfway centre, wknd: 1¼   73
well bckd from 14/1: see 3269.
3135 **SILVER PRELUDE 19** [11]3-9-1 (84) P Robinson 25/1: 0003100: 16th: Chsd ldrs 3.5f centre.   shd   70
3427 **IMPERIAL ECHO 6** [4]3-8-9 vis (78) N Callan 11/1: 0040220: 17th: Al rear stands side: tchd 14/1.   nk   63
1822 Sessay 73 [17]3-8-4 (4oh)(69) A Nicholls 66/1:0   3543 Imperium 1 [14]3-8-4 (2oh)(71) F Norton 33/1:0
3228 Hello Roberto 14 [7]3-8-4 (1oh)(72) E Ahern 50/1:0   2407 Harry Up 48 [2]3-9-4 (87) M Fenton 33/1:0
21 Ran   Time 58.05 (1.35)   Owned: Mr James Ryan   Trained: Godstone

GOODWOOD FRIDAY 30.07.04 Righthand, Sharpish, Undulating Track

3568

5.00 European Breeders Fund Trundle Maiden Stakes Colts & Geldings 2yo (D)
£10693 £3290 £1645 **7f rnd** **Firm 19** **-32 Slow** Inside

2876 **JONQUIL 29** [11] J H M Gosden 2-8-11 J Fortune 7/2: 41: Made most, styd on strongly fnl 1f, rdn out: well bckd: eff at 7f, will stay 1m: acts on fast & firm grnd & on a sharp/undul or gall trk: clearly benefitted from recent debut & this was a useful effort: see 2876. **96**

LOOKS COULD KILL [4] G A Butler 2-8-11 K Fallon 11/2: 2: b c Red Ransom - Mingling Glances (Woodman) Mid-div, prog to chase wnr fnl 1f, nvr quite getting there: bckd from 10/1 on debut: Feb 1st foal, 40,000gns 2yo: dam a smart 1m/10f performer, sire a decent juv in the US: eff over a sharp/undul 7f on firm grnd: sure to learn from this & win races. *1½* **92**

SILENT JO [3] Saeed bin Suroor 2-8-11 L Dettori 9/2: 3: b c Sunday Silence - Jo Knows (The Minstrel) Slowly away, short of room & switched 2f out, styd on & nrst fin on debut: op 3/1, clr of rem: Feb foal, dam a smart mid-dist/stayer: sire a top-class performer in the US: eff at 7f on firm grnd: sure to learn from this encouraging run & be plcd to win races. *hd* **92+**

ZAMBOOZLE [5] D R C Elsworth 2-8-11 Dane O'Neill 50/1: 4: ch c Halling - Blue Sirocco (Bluebird) Dwelt, prog wide 2f out, nvr nr ldrs on debut: 35,000gns Feb foal: dam lightly rcd, but from a gd family: sire a top-class 10f performer: some encouragement here, will find easier races. *6* **80**

2766 **SILVERLEAF 34** [8]2-8-11 T E Durcan 14/1: 65: Chsd ldrs till wknd dist: ran green: btr 2766 (debut). *3½* **73**

KING MARJU [2]2-8-11 A McCarthy 12/1: 6: b c Marju - Katoushka (Hamas) Keen & dsptd early lead, wknd fnl 1f on debut: op 8/1: Apr foal, cost 34,000gns: dam unrcd, sire top-class over 1m/12f: sure to learn from this & improve, esp if settling better. *1* **71**

MY RASCAL [6]2-8-11 R L Moore 50/1: 7: Pushed in rear, nvr dngrs on debut. *shd* **71**

ELECTION SEEKER [12]2-8-11 A Quinn(5) 50/1: 8: Sn outpcd, nvr dngrs on debut. *½* **70**

2897 **GROUND RULES 28** [9]2-8-11 P Robinson 11/4 FAV: 29: Hmpd start, recovered to chase ldrs, wknd dist: well bckd & tchd 4/1: showed more on gd/soft grnd in 2897 (debut). *1½* **67**

ART ELEGANT [10]2-8-11 Martin Dwyer 14/1: 0: 10th: Chsd ldrs 5f, wknd on debut: tchd 50/1. *4* **59**

3302 **HIGHEST RETURN 11** [1]2-8-11 J Fanning 16/1: 40: 11th: Chsd ldrs, wknd 2f out. *5* **49**

PRIMED UP [7]2-8-11 E Ahern 50/1: 0: 12th: Slow away, al bhnd on debut. *13* **24**

12 Ran Time 1m 28.07 (3.57) Owned: Sheikh Mohammed Trained: Manton

3569

5.35 Stewards' Sprint Stakes Handicap 3yo+ (B) **[89]**
£13108 £4972 £2486 **6f str** **Firm 19** **-06 Slow** Stands Side

3537 **MERLINS DANCER 2** [5] D Nicholls 4-9-5 (80) A Nicholls 10/1: 5100041: Made all stands rail, clr fnl 1f, drvn out for a clr-cut win: nicely bckd & qck reapp: eff at 5f, apprec this return to 6f (all wins at this trip): acts on firm & gd/soft: suited by forcing tactics recently: in fine form, see 3537 & 2007. **89**

3518 **HIGH RIDGE 2** [4] J M Bradley 5-8-7 p (68) F Norton 9/1: 1234122: Rear stands side, fin v strongly into 2nd, not rch wnr: well bckd from 14/1: qck reapp: in fine form & apprec return to waiting tactics: see 3518. *1¼* **72**

3304 **DAME DE NOCHE 11** [2] J G Given 4-9-10 (85) N Callan 16/1: 0300053: Prom stands side, kept on fnl 1f despite flashing tail, caught for 2nd cl home: clearly likes Goodwood, won a 7f h'cap at this meeting last year. *½* **88**

2831 **ALBASHOOSH 31** [26] D Nicholls 6-8-9 (70) T E Durcan 12/1: 6561034: Dwelt, rear far side, prog to lead that group dist, kept on well but no ch with stands side: op 8/1: 1st home on far side & stablemate of wnr. *1¼* **69+**

3350 **ROMANY NIGHTS 9** [11]4-9-3 bl (78) D Sweeney 40/1: 2460205: Trkd ldrs stands side, kept on under press fnl 1f: see 3146. *½* **76**

3136 **HARD TO CATCH 19** [1]6-9-5 bl (80) M Savage(5) 40/1: 0113306: Rear stands side, styd on late. *¾* **75**

3463+**BALLYBUNION 5** [25]5-7-12 (6oh) (53) P Hanagan 16/1: 0000517: Mid-div far side, prog dist, no ch with stands side: gd run from out of the h'cap & on the wrong side: qck reapp & s/mate of 1st & 4th: see 3463. *1½* **50**

3436 **PAYS DAMOUR 6** [13]7-8-3 T (64) P Doe 66/1: 0305038: Chsd ldrs wide stands side, onepcd fnl 1f: tried a t-strap: s/mate of 1st & 4th: see 3436. *1½* **51**

3269 **IDLE POWER 13** [21]6-9-2 p (77) Martin Dwyer 14/1: 1102309: Dwelt, chsd ldrs far side, onepcd dist. *hd* **64**

3537 **ONLINE INVESTOR 2** [3]5-8-3 (64) E Ahern 12/1: 5500000: 10th: Rear stands side, prog when short of room dist, nvr nrr: qck reapp & s/mate of 1st & 4th: see 3537 (5f here). *shd* **51**

3341 **CURRENCY 9** [15]7-9-1 BL (76) J F Egan 33/1: 0406300: 11th: Chsd ldrs stands side, wknd fnl 1f: blnks. *½* **62**

3461* **UNDETERRED 5** [19]8-8-13 (3ex) (74) K Darley 13/2: 0044410: 12th: Nvr a factor far side: well bckd: won this race from a 1lb lower mark last term: see 3461. *shd* **60**

3220 **ATTORNEY 15** [8]6-7-12 (13oh)vis (46) D Kinsella 66/1: 5000600: 13th: Nvr btr than mid-div stands side. *½* **44**

3241 **PARKSIDE PURSUIT 14** [24]6-9-0 (75) R L Moore 25/1: 0413100: 14th: Al bhnd far side: btr 2838. *¾* **57**

3537 **TIME TO REMEMBER 2** [6]6-7-12 (2oh) (57) R Ffrench 10/1: 0600020: 15th: Speed till halfway stands side: tchd 16/1, qck reapp: s/mate & bt today's wnr over 5f here in 3537. *hd* **41**

3466 **PAX 5** [7]7-9-8 (83) Alex Greaves 33/1: 0100000: 16th: Slow away, no ch when short of room dist. *shd* **65**

3434 **LORD OF THE EAST 6** [23]5-8-13 (74) J Fanning 16/1: 3232100: 17th: Led till dist far side, wknd. *1¼* **52**

3241 **OBE ONE 14** [12]4-8-7 (68) P Mathers(5) 20/1: 2306040: 18th: Mid-div stands side, nvr dngrs. *hd* **46**

3269 **DEVON FLAME 13** [18]5-9-0 (75) J F McDonald(3) 33/1: 2122400: 19th: Front rank 5f far side: btr 3069. *½* **52**

3466 **PLATEAU 5** [20]5-9-9 (84) J Fortune 16/1: 00-60200: 20th: Rear far side, nvr dngrs: see 2253. *nk* **60**

2396 **LONG WEEKEND 48** [10]6-7-12 (16oh) (43) Joanna Badger 100/1: 6060000: 21th: Al bhnd stands side. *½* **34**

3434 **LOYAL TYCOON 6** [17]6-9-7 (3ex) (91) L Treadwell(5) 6/1 FAV: 0010550: 22th: Prom till dist far side, wknd & eased: well bckd: s/mate of 1st & 4th & much better expected, reportedly ran flat: see 3434. *shd* **57**

3518 **Prince Of Blues 2** [16]6-7-12 bl(59) S Righton 66/1:0 3352 **Sir Don 9** [14]5-8-5 vis(66) L Keniry(2) 66/1:0

2957 **Landing Strip 26** [9]4-8-11 (72) Dane O'Neill 66/1:0 3341 **Turibius 9** [22]5-9-3 (78) A Quinn(5) 33/1:0

26 Ran Time 1m 11.47(1.47) Owned: Chalfont Foodhalls Ltd Trained: Thirsk

THIRSK FRIDAY 30.07.04 Lefthand, Flat, Oval Track

Official Going GOOD/FIRM (FIRM places).

3570 2.30 Costa Claiming Stakes 2yo (E)
£3673 £1130 £565 **7f rnd** **Good/Firm 39** **-41 Slow** Inside

3349 **MAUREENS LOUGH 9** [9] T D Barron 2-8-1 N Mackay(3) 7/4 FAV: 3615441: Cl-up & led 3f out, in command dist, rdn out: bckd: clmd for M Chapman for 5,000: eff at 7f on firm & fast grnd, easy or gall trks: enjoy sell/claim grade: see 2294. **56**
3047 **COUNTRYWIDE SUN 22** [8] N P Littmoden 2-8-13 P T G McLaughlin 7/1: 0002: b g Benny The Dip - Sundae Girl (Green Dancer) Led till 3f out, sn outpcd by wnr, kept on ins last: first time cheek pieces, op 12/1: stay 7f in claim grade, breeding suggests 1m+ will suit: acts on fast grnd: see 3047. *2½* **62**
3412 **DANCING SHIRL 7** [3] C W Fairhurst 2-8-6 G Faulkner 8/1: 63: Chsd ldrs, styd on onepace for press fnl 3f: eff at 7f, get further: handles fast grnd: see 3412. *nk* **54**
2927 **LANAS TURN 27** [7] T D Easterby 2-8-5 W Supple 16/1: 05004: b f Mister Baileys - Lana Turrel (Trempolino) Mid-div, outpcd 3f out, kept on for press fnl 1f: imprvd eff on drop to claim grade: cheaply bght Apr foal, half-sister to a 7f 3yo scorer: dam a wnr over fences abroad: eff at 7f on fast in claim grade. *nk* **52**
3393 **GOLDHILL PRINCE 7** [5]2-8-11 p C Haddon(7) 11/4: 1111365: Chsd ldrs, no extra fnl 2f. *½* **57**
3172 **FAITHFUL FLASH 17** [4]2-8-6 BL B Reilly(3) 16/1: 6046: Held up, hmpd after 2f, late prog: blnks. *nk* **51**
3259 **SINGHALONGTASVEER 13** [10]2-8-7 J Bramhill 20/1: 0537: Rear, mod prog/short of room ins last. *½* **51**
3351 **ITSA MONKEY 9** [2]2-8-7 P K Ghunowa(7) 25/1: 06208: Dwelt, bhd, nvr a factor: cheek pieces: see 3093. *5* **42**
3349 **TEWITFIELD LASS 9** [1]2-8-4 D Fentiman(7) 20/1: 059: Mid-div, struggling from halfway. *5* **30**
GUNNERBERGKAMP [11]2-8-11 A Culhane 20/1: 0: 10th: Slow away & al rear. *¾* **36**
3349 **SPECIALISE 9** [6]2-8-2 Dale Gibson 25/1: 0P: Slow away, hung right & ran v wide on bend after 4f, sn t.o. & p.u., dismounted. **0**
11 Ran Time 1m 28.48 (5.58) Owned: Oghill House Stud Trained: Thirsk

3571 3.00 Skelton Castle Handicap Stakes 3yo+ 0-70 (E) [69]
£3858 £1187 £594 **7f rnd** **Good/Firm 39** **-10 Slow** Inside

3485 **HEADLAND 4** [7] D W Chapman 6-8-10 bl e (51) A Culhane 8/1: 0306221: Held up, prog wide 3f out & led ins last, pushed out to hold on: qck reapp: eff at 6/7f on both AWs, fast & hvy, prob any trk: see 227. **59**
2990 **BOLLIN EDWARD 24** [6] T D Easterby 5-9-8 vis (63) D Allan 4/1 JT FAV: 0-653202: Mid-div, styd on for press fnl 2f, not pace of wnr: nicely bckd, op 11/2: see 2752, 2466 & 2059. *¾* **68**
3016 **SAROS 23** [10] B Smart 3-8-9 (57) F Lynch 12/1: 1160203: Rear, rdn, styd on wide, not rch wnr. *nk* **62**
3210 **ROMAN MAZE 15** [13] W M Brisbourne 4-9-5 (60) S W Kelly 8/1: 4-050004: Mid-div, eff wide & led over 1f out, hdd ins last & no extra: gd eff from awkward high draw: see 2027 & 71. *1¼* **62**
3223 **FLASHING BLADE 15** [9]4-9-11 t (66) G Gibbons 12/1: 0001065: Trkd ldrs, onepace for press fnl 2f. *¾* **67**
2890 **JUBILEE STREET 28** [2]5-9-1 (56) G Hind 8/1: 0431006: Mid-div, onepace & held when short of room over 1f out: see 2080. *hd* **56**
1824 **ZAP ATTACK 73** [4]4-9-11 (66) M Lawson(5) 25/1: 10200-07: b g Zafonic - Rappa Tap Tap (Tap On Wood) Mid-div, rdn & no impress when short of room 2f out: 10 wk abs: mdn h'cap scorer '03 (M Channon): mdn plcd in '02 (rtd 75): eff btwn 6f/1m, tried 10f: handles firm & gd grnd, likes a gall trk. *1½* **63**
2 Aug'03 Ripo 6g/f 69-71 D: 1 Jul'03 Chep 6.1gd 72-68 E:
2935 **FLYING EDGE 27** [14]4-9-0 (55) W Supple 16/1: 5065008: Chsd ldrs, btn dist: see 2445 & 585. *½* **51**
3352 **TOPPLING 9** [11]6-8-12 p (53) C Catlin 33/1: 0004009: Keen & led early, no impress/ hmpd 2f out. *1* **47**
3490 **JEDEYDD 4** [12]7-8-12 BL t (53) L Enstone(3) 12/1: 4064000: 10th: Dwelt, held up, short of room 2f out, sn btn: qck reapp in blnks: btr 3490, 2967. *nk* **46**
3203* **THORNABY GREEN 15** [5]3-9-2 (64) P Makin(5) 4/1 JT FAV: 600-4410: 11th: Dsptd lead till over 1f out, wknd qckly: nicely bckd: btr 3203 (6f). *1¾* **54**
3378 **COTTINGHAM 8** [3]3-9-1 (63) K Dalgleish 25/1: 40-14660: 12th: Led/dsptd lead till 2f out, sn btn. *5* **44**
4761} **IRON TEMPTRESS 288** [8]3-9-3 (65) P Mulrennan(5) 66/1: 352000-0: 13th: ch f Piccolo - River Divine (Irish River) Held up, strugggling from halfway & hung badly right: reapp: auct mdn scorer in '03, subs h'cap rnr-up: winning form at 5f, stays gall 7f: acts on firm & gd grnd, stiff/gall trks. *15* **20**
2 Sep'03 Redc 7fm 70-74 E: 2 May'03 Donc 5gd 72- E: 1 Apr'03 Beve 5fm 74- E:
13 Ran Time 1m 26.33 (3.43) Owned: Mr Harold D White Trained: York

3572 3.35 Deepdale Solutions Nspcc Maiden Stakes 3yo+ (D)
£5616 £1728 £864 **1m rnd** **Good/Firm 39** **-25 Slow** Inside

2987 **TRIPLE JUMP 25** [4] T D Easterby 3-8-13 W Supple 8/13 FAV: 4-21: Chsd ldrs, shkn up & hdwy to lead 2f out, rdn out: hvly bckd, confirmed reapp promise: eff at 1m, 10f shld suit: acts on fast & gd: see 2987. **76**
2953 **RIVER NUREY 26** [10] B W Hills 3-8-13 (70) A Culhane 2/1: 052-3252: Mid-div, styd on for press fnl 2f, al held by wnr: stays an easy 1m well: see 2575 & 2148. *1* **73$**
3853} **THE NUMBER 340** [9] I Semple 3-8-13 K Dalgleish 25/1: 56-3: gr g Silver Wizard - Elite Number (Elmaamul) Trkd ldrs, hung left under press & not pace front pair dist: reapp: unplcd '03 (lightly rcd, mdns, rtd 75): eff at 1m, mid-dists could suit: handles fast grnd & an easy trk. *2½* **68**
1027} **SMIRFYS DANCE HALL 476** [12] W M Brisbourne 4-9-2 T G McLaughlin 100/1: 06-4: b f Halling - Bigger Dances (Moscow Ballet) Rear, styd on for press fnl 3f, nvr threaten ldrs: reapp: unplcd '03 (rtd 58, mdn): prob stays an easy 1m, tried 12f, rtn to mid-dists could suit: handles fast grnd: now qual for h'caps. *1½* **60**
2987 **DEE EN AY 25** [8]3-8-13 A Mullen(7) 100/1: 005: Led/dsptd lead 6f, fdd. *2½* **60**
2885 **JAVA DANCER 29** [7]3-8-13 D Allan 33/1: 06: Rear, only mod late prog. *6* **49**
4929} **ST JUDE 276** [3]4-9-7 J Bramhill 100/1: 00-7: Trkd ldrs till over 2f out: reapp, new yard. *¾* **48**
3195 **COCO POINT BREEZE 16** [11]3-8-8 S Chin 66/1: 08: Rear, nvr landed a blow. *1¼* **40**
1768 **JIDIYA 76** [2]5-9-7 C Catlin 33/1: 52-09: Dwelt & al rear, abs. *nk* **44**
3038 **TRINITY FAIR 23** [5]3-8-8 Dean McKeown 50/1: 000: 10th: Led till over 3f out, wknd qckly. *½* **38**
3480 **BALLET RUSE 4** [1]3-8-8 J Mackay 33/1: 000-00: 11th: Dwelt & al rear, qck reapp. *5* **29**
11 Ran Time 1m 40.52 (5.12) Owned: Mr and Mrs J D Cotton Trained: Malton

3573 **4.10 Crayke Handicap Stakes Fillies 3yo 0-70 (E)** **[74]**
£3751 £1154 £577 **1m4f** **Good/Firm 39** **-04 Slow** Inside

2960 **RICHTEE 26** [10] R A Fahey 3-9-7 (67) T Hamilton(3) 11/2: 060-1251: Chsd ldrs, qcknd to lead 2f out, rdn & held on well ins last: eff at 10/12f, could get further: acts on firm & gd/soft grnd, gall/easy trks: progressive profile, keep on side: see 2960, 2565 & 2299. **76**
3334 **VELVET WATERS 9** [1] R F Johnson Houghton 3-8-13 (59) S Carson 13/2: 0-364122: Mid-div, drvn & styd on fnl 2f, not able to reach wnr: remains on the upgrade: see 3334 & 2978. *¾* **66**
3373* **DONASTRELA 8** [3] A M Balding 3-9-3 (6ex)vis (63) N Chalmers(5) 11/2: 6001413: Held up, eff wide 2f out, styd on for press: stays 12f: in gd heart: see 3373. *hd* **69**
3052 **ON CLOUD NINE 22** [11] M L W Bell 3-9-4 (64) Hayley Turner(5) 25/1: 26004: Mid-div, styd on wide for press fnl 3f: stays an easy 12f: acts on fast & soft grnd: see 977. *1¼* **68**
3354* **LET IT BE 9** [2]3-8-0 (46) C Catlin 9/4 FAV: 2505115: Mid-div, briefly short of room over 1f out, kept on for press, not pace to chall: see 3354. *shd* **50**
3084 **PRELUDE 21** [13]3-9-0 (60) S W Kelly 66/1: 50066: Trkd ldrs, onepace fnl 2f: prob styd 12f. *shd* **63**
3459 **ROYAL DISTANT 5** [6]3-9-5 (65) Dale Gibson 20/1: 0000027: Bhd, hdwy over 2f out, no prog dist. *1¼* **66**
2478 **SILVER RHYTHM 44** [16]3-8-5 (1ow) (50) Dean McKeown 33/1: 0-3508: Chsd ldrs till dist: abs. *¾* **51**
2974 **ZURI 25** [4]3-9-5 (65) N Mackay(3) 12/1: 6409: Mid-div, no impress fnl 2f: longer trip, h'cap bow. *1¼* **63**
3354 **PRAIRIE SUN 9** [8]3-8-9 p (55) G Hind 20/1: 5100060: 10th: Rear, hung left, nvr threaten ldrs. *1¼* **51**
3377 **EBORACUM 8** [5]3-9-3 (63) D Allan 12/1: 20-00220: 11th: Rear, eff 3f out, no impress: btr 3377 (g/s). *1¼* **57**
1680 **PLAUSABELLE 79** [12]3-8-6 (52) W Supple 25/1: 006-0200: 12th: Al rear: abs: btr 1425 (1m, sft). *3½* **41**
3121 **POWER NAP 20** [7]3-8-1 t (47) Kim Tinkler 100/1: 00-600: 13th: Al bhd: longer trip. *2* **33**
3255 **LAND OF NOD 14** [14]3-9-2 BL (62) P Mulrennan(5) 16/1: 00-400: 14th: Keen & led/dsptd lead 10f, wknd qckly: blnks: btr 1089 (1m, soft). *3* **44**
3085 **LUCKY ARTHUR 21** [9]3-9-0 (60) J Mackay 14/1: 0503230: 15th: Al bhd: btr 3085 & 2978. *2* **39**
3312 **ADEES DANCER 11** [15]3-8-9 (55) F Lynch 66/1: 4-00500: 16th: Dwelt, hdwy wide to lead after 2f, ran wide on bend & hdd over 3f out, sn btn/eased: see 2893. *23* **4**
16 Ran Time 2m 36.69 (6.89) Owned: Terence Elsey and Richard Mustill Trained: Malton

3574 **4.45 Peter Bell Memorial Stakes Handicap 3yo+ 0-80 (D)** **[79]**
£5590 £1720 £860 **6f str** **Good/Firm 39** **+05 Fast** Stands Side

3375 **HARTSHEAD 8** [6] G A Swinbank 5-9-7 (72) Dean McKeown 100/30 FAV: 2061141: Held up, hdwy halfway & led ins last, rdn out: bckd, op 4/1: best time of day: stays 1m, suited by 6f on firm & gd grnd: progressive. **82**
3375 **SMIRFYS SYSTEMS 8** [12] W M Brisbourne 5-9-7 (72) T G McLaughlin 7/1: 2-005002: Handy & led over 1f out till ins last, not pace of wnr: op 9/1: won this in '03 off a 4lb lower mark: see 1598. *¾* **78**
3403 **LOCH INCH 7** [10] J M Bradley 7-8-1 bl (52) C Catlin 9/1: 0040423: Chsd ldrs, no extra dist: see 1867. *½* **57**
3136 **INTER VISION 19** [7] A Dickman 4-10-0 (79) P Mulrennan(5) 13/2: 4-005004: Mid-div, styd on onepace: op 9/2: top-weight: see 1767. *shd* **84**
3352 **NEMO FUGAT 9** [4]5-8-7 vis (58) J Carroll 7/1: 0056025: Dwelt, kept on late, not able to chall. *shd* **62**
3210 **BRANTWOOD 15** [1]4-8-8 t (59) G Gibbons 20/1: 0432306: Switched from high draw, led till dist. *1½* **58**
3463 **LAUREL DAWN 5** [2]6-8-10 (61) D Allan 20/1: 1525067: Chsd ldrs till dist: prefer a stiff 5f. *¾* **58**
3416 **MITSUKI 7** [11]5-8-12 (63) W Supple 9/2: 0400-058: Held up, rdn 2f out, no impress: btr 3416. *shd* **60**
2620 **CLIMATE 39** [3]5-9-12 bl (77) G Parkin 14/1: 4021639: Bhd, mod late prog: new yard, needs 7f+. *hd* **73**
3417 **MR SPLIFFY 7** [5]5-7-12 (3oh) (46) J Bramhill 50/1: 0000000: 10th: Held up, nvr dngrs: see 413. *nk* **44**
3352 **DRURY LANE 9** [8]4-8-2 bl (53) Hayley Turner(5) 14/1: 0400400: 11th: Strug halfway: btr 3289 (gd). *1½* **43**
11 Ran Time 1m 11.57 (2.07) Owned: Mr B Valentine Trained: Richmond

3575 **5.20 Teletext Hands And Heels Apprentice Maiden Handicap Stakes 3yo+ 0-70 (E)** **[63]**
£3809 £1172 £586 **6f str** **Good/Firm 39** **-17 Slow** Stands Side

2214 **OEUF A LA NEIGE 56** [19] G C H Chung 4-9-12 (61) Dean Williams 10/1: 530-5061: Chsd ldrs stands side, short of room 2f out, styd on under hand riding to lead well ins last: 8 wk abs: eff btwn 6f/1m on fast & gd. **68**
3262 **PRIDE OF KINLOCH 13** [15] J Hetherton 4-9-6 (55) M Halford 10/1: 0300032: Chsd ldrs stands side & led over 1f out till well ins last: see 3262 & 385. *½* **59**
3417 **AMANDAS LAD 7** [14] M C Chapman 4-9-6 (55) Lucy Russell(3) 12/1: 3545633: Chsd ldrs stands side, led over 2f out till over 1f out, onepace: see 2216, 487. *1¾* **54**
3231 **TROJAN FLIGHT 14** [4] Mrs J R Ramsden 3-9-6 (60) A Hamblett(3) 18/1: 4546064: Chsd ldrs far side & led that group over 1f out, not pace of ldrs stands side ins last: first home from far side group: eff around 6/7f on fast & gd/soft grnd: see 2166, 1628 & 1216. *1¼* **55+**
4046} **M FOR MAGIC 330** [2]5-8-6 (41) K Pierrepont(3) 33/1: 005045-5: ch g First Trump - Celestine (Skyliner) Led/dsptd lead far side 5f, no extra: reapp: mdn h'cap plcd in '03 (rtd 48, tried cheek pieces): unplcd '02 (blnks, J Spearing): eff over a gall 6f, tried 11f: handles fast grnd. *1* **33**
3193 **SIR LOIN 16** [6]3-9-3 (57) K Ghunowa(3) 10/1: 00-00526: Rider lost iron leaving stalls, chsd ldr far side till dist: btr 3193 (5f). *½* **47**
3417 **CELLINO 7** [8]3-8-5 (45) K Jackson(3) 66/1: 050-0407: Chsd ldrs far side, onepace fnl 2f: see 2219. *½* **33**
3129 **ORANGINO 20** [12]6-8-8 (43) R Kennemore(5) 10/1: 00-02028: Stands side, chsd ldrs 4f: btr 3129. *½* **29**
3262 **FLEET ANCHOR 13** [1]3-9-3 (57) C J Davies(3) 20/1: 50-009: Rcd far side, nvr pace to chall. *nk* **42**
3332 **AVERAMI 9** [7]3-8-10 vis (50) R J Killoran(3) 16/1: 4-050060: 10th: Held up far side, mod prog. *shd* **35**
3092 **MEGABOND 21** [5]3-9-3 (57) M Stainton(3) 20/1: 230-5040: 11th: Bhd far side, mod prog: btr 3092. *nk* **41**
3413 **GASPARINI 7** [20]3-9-4 (58) A Mullen 9/1: 0043030: 12th: Chsd ldrs stands side 4f: btr 3413 (7f). *1½* **37**
3262 **UHURU PEAK 13** [11]3-9-1 (55) M Howard 10/1: 0500320: 13th: Stands side, chsd ldrs, hung left & no impress fnl 2f: btr 3262. *hd* **33**
2125 **BELLS BOYS 59** [16]5-8-2 p (37) Donna Caldwell(3) 16/1: 0403300: 14th: Led stands side till over 2f out, sn btn & eased: 8 wk abs: btr 1989. *1½* **10**
3347 **HARRISONS FLYER 9** [10]3-9-11 bl (65) B O'Neill(3) 8/1 FAV: 4-02020: 15th: Dwelt & bhd stands side. *1¼* **34**
3228 **DARK CHAMPION 14** [9]4-9-8 p (57) J D O'Reilly 25/1: 3004500: 16th: Chsd ldrs far side 4f, btr 2527. *1½* **21**
682 **Aggi Mac 162** [13]3-8-4 (44) Suzanne France 50/1:0
1465 **Sweet Talking Girl 91** [3]4-7-12 T P(33) Hazel Boyd(3) 66/1:0
2683 **Caribbean Blue 36** [18]3-8-5 (45) Jemma Marshall(3) 14/1:0

THIRSK FRIDAY 30.07.04 Lefthand, Flat, Oval Track

3262 **Pure Imagination 13** [17]3-9-8 (62) H Poulton 11/1:0
20 Ran Time 1m12.84(3.34) Owned: Mr G C H Chung Trained: Newmarket

NOTTINGHAM FRIDAY 30.07.04 Lefthand, Galloping Track

Official Going GOOD/FIRM (GOOD places). All Times Slow.

3576 6.20 European Breeders Fund Maiden Stakes Fillies 2yo (D)
£5655 £1740 £870 **5f13y str** **Good/Firm** **Inapplicable** Stands side

2245 **ALL FOR LAURA 55** [1] D R Loder 2-8-11 T P Queally 3/1: 41: Prom, led 2f out, pushed clr fnl 1f,
val 4L+: 8 wk abs: eff at 6f, imprvd for drop back to 5f: acts on fast grnd: acts on a gall trk & goes well
fresh: showed plenty of speed today & can rate higher: see 2245. **92+**
    RASSEEM [2] Saeed bin Suroor 2-8-11 K McEvoy 8/1: 2: b f Fasliyev - Yorba Linda (Night Shift) 3 **80**
Led, hdd 2f out, kept on, most of wnr: debut: Feb first foal, cost 140,000gns: dam successful at 5/7f: sire
decent performer at sprint dists: eff at 5f, 6f shld suit: acts on fast grnd: encouraging effort.
    REGINA [4] Sir Michael Stoute 2-8-11 B Doyle 9/2: 3: b f Green Desert - Dazzle (Gone West) shd **79**
Dwelt, sn handy, onepcd ins fnl 1f: debut: Mar foal, half-sister to wnrs at 6/7f: dam Gr wnr at 6f/1m: sire
high-class performer at 6f/1m: eff at 6f on fast grnd: shld impr for today's experience.
    NEVERLETME GO [5] G Wragg 2-8-11 S Drowne 8/11 FAV: 4: b f Green Desert - Cassandra Go (Indian ½ **78**
Ridge) Handy 3f, sn outpcd, rallied late: debut: Mar first foal, dam decent sprint performer: sire high-class
performer at 6f/1m: eff at 5f, bred to apprec further: acts on fast grnd: ran green.
4 Ran Time 1m 3.80 (5.3) Owned: Lord Lloyd-Webber Trained: Newmarket

3577 6.50 96 Trent Fm Jo & Twiggy's Classified Stakes 3yo+ 0-65 (E)
£3721 £1145 £573 **5f13y str** **Good/Firm** **Inapplicable** Stands side

3307 **FOLEY MILLENNIUM 11** [9] M Quinn 6-9-2 (66) N Pollard 9/2 CO FAV: 1111021: Made all, rdn out ins **74**
fnl 2f to hold on: stay 6f, apprec return to 5f: acts on firm & hvy grnd: in-form pace setter: see 3307 & 2951.
3371* **CATCH THE WIND 8** [2] I A Wood 3-9-5 p (70) S Sanders 9/2 CO FAV: 0-055612: In tch, stdy on to 1½ **75**
chase wnr ins fnl 1f, al held: not disgraced but showed more in 3371 (first time cheek pieces).
3503 **BOAVISTA 3** [3] P D Evans 4-8-12 (62) S Hitchcott(3) 17/2: 0022033: Dwelt, mid-div, onepcd fnl 1f. 1¾ **59**
3485* **TALLY 4** [6] M J Polglase 4-9-8 (66) R Thomas(5) 7/1: 4430014: Rear, prog halfway, nrst fin: qck nk **67**
reapp: showed more in 3485 (6f, fibresand).
3165 **DUNN DEAL 18** [5]4-9-1 (62) B Swarbrick(5) 11/1: 2050665: Chsd ldrs 3f, sn outpcd, mod late gains. ½ **60**
3479 **KALLISTAS PRIDE 4** [7]4-8-12 (61) I Mongan 25/1: 0-020106: Handy halfway, sn extra: qck reapp. hd **56**
3350* **JUSTALORD 9** [4]6-9-9 bl (67) J Edmunds 8/1: 1230617: Prom 3f, sn wknd: btr 3350. ¾ **65**
3241 **TWICE UPON A TIME 14** [12]5-8-12 (65) A Culhane 9/2 CO FAV: 4000408: Nvr nrr than mid-div. 2 **48**
2268 **SHRINK 53** [10]3-8-8 (65) J Mackay 14/1: 2-214409: Dwelt, nvr a factor: 8 wk abs: btr 2048. 2½ **41**
3380 **KURINGAI 8** [1]3-8-11 (65) A Daly 66/1: 4300000: 10th: Chsd ldrs 3f, wknd: btr 1002 & 268. 3 **35**
3279 **PRIME RECREATION 8** [8]5-8-6 (66) Lisa Jones(3) 11/1: 0030040: 11th: Prom 3f, fdd: see 3279. ½ **35**
3371 **MELODY KING 8** [11]3-8-13 bl (67) F P Ferris(3) 33/1: 254365U: Short of room & u.r. start: btr 3036. **0**
12 Ran Time 1m 1.86 (3.36) Owned: Mrs S G Davies Trained: Wantage

3578 7.20 Campbell's Homepride Sauces Handicap Stakes 3yo 0-90 (C)
£10803 £3324 £1662 **1m1f213y** **Good/Firm** **Inapplicable** Inside **[87]**

3195* **NORDWIND 16** [6] P W Harris 3-9-2 (75) I Mongan 5/2: 3411: Chsd ldrs, prog & ev ch dist, rdn out **83**
to lead cl-home: eff at 1m, apprec step up to 10f: acts on fast, gd/soft & polytrack: unexposed in h'cap grade.
2994 **NIGHTSPOT 24** [5] R Charlton 3-9-7 (80) S Drowne 4/1: 5515-632: Al cl-up, stdy on to lead 2f out, hd **85**
hdd under press cl-home: lost little in defeat under top-weight: see 2994 & 1664.
3471* **DOCTORED 5** [1] P D Evans 3-9-4 (6ex)bl (77) S Donohoe(7) 7/1: 1011113: Handy, outpcd after nk **81**
halfway, rallied bef 1f out, just held in 3-way photo: qck reapp: has been in great form & this was an imprvd eff
in defeat: see 3471, 3201 & 3144.
3039 **SPRING JIM 23** [3] J R Fanshawe 3-9-6 (79) K McEvoy 15/8 FAV: 450-4124: Held up, prog halfway, ev 1 **81**
ch dist, sn onepcd: eff at 7/10f: just btr 3039.
3334 **ILE FACILE 9** [2]3-8-13 t (72) G Gibbons 14/1: 0204145: Led, hdd 2f out, fdd: btr 3192 (12f). 9 **61**
2660 **ZAFFEU 37** [4]3-8-11 (70) S Sanders 9/1: 6245106: Slow away, al in rear: btr 2413. 28 **24**
6 Ran Time 2m 10.87 (8.57) Owned: Mrs P W Harris Trained: Berkhamsted

3579 7.50 Konica East Direct Handicap Stakes 3yo+ 0-75 (E)
£3819 £1175 £588 **1m54y rnd** **Good/Firm** **Inapplicable** Centre **[75]**

3423 **SUMMER SHADES 6** [3] W M Brisbourne 6-9-6 (67) B Swarbrick(5) 11/1: 2443561: In tch, short of room **74**
2f out, prog & ev ch dist, drvn out to lead cl-home: qck reapp: eff at 1m/9f on firm, soft & fibresand: gd
confidence boost: see 2767 & 2108.
3242 **NEWCORP LAD 14** [9] Mrs G S Rees 4-8-12 (59) A Culhane 15/2: 4000442: In tch, prog to lead 2f ½ **64**
out, hdd under press cl-home: gd run in defeat & can find similar off this mark: see 3242 & 1397.
2958 **HILLTIME 26** [5] J J Quinn 4-8-4 (51) W Supple 14/1: 0/0-00003: Cl-up, led after 5f, hdd 2f out, 2½ **51**
no extra dist: eff at 1m on fast grnd: signs of encouragement & has drpd down the weights: see 1638.
3423 **NEARLY A FOOL 6** [7] G G Margarson 6-9-10 vis (71) N Pollard 3/1 FAV: 0210134: Held up, prog 3f 1¾ **67**
out, hung left & onepace dist: qck reapp: see 3423 & 1049.
4873) **NEW WISH 280** [2]4-9-5 (66) Dale Gibson 100/30: 000000-5: b g Ali Royal - False Spring (Petorius) ½ **61**
Keen in tch over 6f, sn no extra: reapp: plcd once in '03 (h'cap, rtd 89): med auct mdn wnr in '02: eff at 7f,
stays 1m: acts on firm & gd grnd: acts on any trk & has gone well fresh: shld impr on today & is well h'capped.
2 Aug'02 York 7g/f 91-89 C: 1 Jul'02 Epso 7gd 87- E: 2 May'02 York 6fm 91- D:
3185 **ARRY DASH 16** [6]4-10-0 (75) S Hitchcott(3) 13/2: 0030606: Slow away, nvr nrr than mid-div: btr 2313. ¾ **68**

1082

NOTTINGHAM   FRIDAY 30.07.04   Lefthand, Galloping Track

3187 **POLISH SPIRIT 16** [8]9-9-4 (65) S Drowne 12/1: 6015///5-07: b g Emarati - Gentle Star (Comedy   3   52
Star) Bhd, nvr a factor: 5th of 11 on sole '03 start (rtd 62, class stks): mdn chase wnr in 02/03 (rtd 95c, stays
2m5.5f on firm & gd, P J Hobbs): 5 times wnr on Flat in '00 (rtd 87, stks & 4 h'caps): eff at 1m/10f on gd & hvy
hvy grnd: acts on any trk & goes well fresh.
3045 **TATWEER 22** [1]4-8-6 vis (53) Darren Williams 50/1: 0-510008: Al bhd: btr 1682 (5f, soft).   3   34
3039 **BLUE MARINER 23** [4]4-9-9 (70) I Mongan 10/1: 0-032209: Led 5f, wknd: btr 2694.   1½   48
3524 **ZAFARSHAH 2** [10]5-8-13 vis (60) F P Ferris(3) 5/1: 2030040: 10th: Handy halfway, wknd: qck reapp.   7   25
10 Ran   Time 1m 45.65 (6.25)   Owned: Mr K Bennett   Trained: Nesscliffe

---

3580   8.20 Letheby & Christopher Handicap Stakes 3yo 35-55 (F)   [65]
£3332 £952 £476   **2m9y**   **Good/Firm**   **Inapplicable**   Inside

3312 **STRANGELY BROWN 11** [3] S C Williams 3-9-4 (55) S Sanders 13/8 FAV: 0030021: In tch, prog to lead   67+
2f out, pushed clr, eased cl-home, val 12L+: eff at 10f, imprvd for recent step up to 2m: acts on fast & hvy grnd:
unexposed performer who can follow up under a pen: see 3312.
3312 **SPRING BREEZE 11** [10] M Dods 3-9-4 BL (55) S W Kelly 7/1: 30-60232: Led, hdd 2f out, sn no extra: 9   57
first time blnks: prob stays 2m: again fin bhd today's wnr in 3312, see 2123.
3499 **FRAMBO 3** [11] J G Portman 3-8-3 bl (40) N Mackay(3) 20/1: 5064443: Handy, no extra fnl 2f.   5   35
3312 **MORNING HAWK 11** [14] J S Moore 3-8-5 BL (42) R Thomas(5) 33/1: 0-045604: Held up, prog 5f out, no   ½   38
impress fnl 2f: first time blnks: see 893.
3383* **BIENHEUREUX 8** [8]3-8-13 (5ex) (50) M Fenton 4/1: 0000215: Rear, nvr nrr than mid-div: 3   43
disappointing on step up to 2m: btr 3383 (12f).
3019 **TWILIGHT YEARS 23** [9]3-8-8 (45) W Supple 16/1: 0046: Cl-up over 12f, wknd: btr 3019 (14f).   ½   37
3367 **GENUINELY 8** [13]3-8-2 vis (39) J Mackay 9/1: 00-00637: Nvr nrr than mid-div: btr 3367.   3   28
3312 **ROMEOS DAY 11** [5]3-8-13 VIS (50) S Hitchcott(3) 20/1: 0243008: Handy 12f, wknd: first time visor.   1   38
2905 **CUNNING PURSUIT 28** [16]3-8-9 (46) A Culhane 14/1: 0656209: Cl-up 12f, fdd: btr 2346.   14   22
2996 **MISTER COMPLETELY 24** [14]3-8-9 (46) I Mongan 18/1: 0000160: 10th: Al in rear.   3   19
3026 **ILLEANA 23** [6]3-9-4 (55) P Makin(5) 9/1: 4001030: 11th: Bhd, nvr a factor: btr 3026 & 2163 (12f).   8   20
3383 **JANGO MALFOY 8** [15]3-9-1 t (52) A Daly 50/1: 50-00000: 12th: Mid-div, wknd 5f out.   6   11
3091 **SNOW CHANCE 21** [12]3-7-12 (1oh) (34) B Swarbrick(5) 66/1: 0040-000: 13th: Bhd, nvr a factor.   6   0
3294 **GREAT GIDDING 1** [2]3-9-4 BL (55) S Drowne 33/1: 030050: 14th: Cl-up 1m, fdd.   1¼   7
14 Ran   Time 3m 35.83 (11.63)   Owned: J T and K Worsley   Trained: Newmarket

---

3581   8.50 Citylife Magazine Median Auction Maiden Stakes 3yo (F)
£3304 £944 £472   **1m54y rnd**   **Good/Firm**   **Inapplicable**   Outside

3197 **CASHBAR 16** [8] J R Fanshawe 3-8-9 K McEvoy 4/5 FAV: 21: Cl-up, styd on to lead bef 2f out,   79+
pushed clr, eased cl-home, val 5L+: eff at 1m, will relish further: acts on fast grnd & polytrack: v sharp or gall
trk: can progress: see 3197 (debut).
1152 **MARSH ORCHID 108** [3] W Jarvis 3-9-0 S Drowne 4/1: 52: Handy, prog to chase wnr bef 1f out, al   3   76
held: long abs: eff at 7f/1m on fast & gd/soft grnd: drew clr of the 3rd & can be plcd to find similar: see 1152.
PLAY BOUZOUKI [4] L M Cumani 3-8-9 N Mackay(3) 5/1: 3: b f Halling - Balalaika (Sadler's Wells)   4   63
Slow away, prog halfway, nrst fin: debut: half-sister to useful 1m/10f List performer Alkaadhem: dam useful
around mid-dists: shld impr for today's experience & will apprec further.
1904 **MY MICHELLE 70** [1] B Palling 3-8-9 (68) A Culhane 16/1: 553-004: Rear, prog when short of room   1   61
2f out, sn switched, late gains: 10 wk abs.
2250 **OH GOLLY GOSH 55** [6]3-9-0 VIS (71) S Sanders 5/1: 2204205: Led till 2f out, wknd: visor.   nk   65
3197 **PORT SODRICK 16** [2]3-9-0 A Daly 33/1: 66: Slow away, modest late gains: see 3197.   nk   64
ZOOMIEZANDO [7]3-9-0 P Makin(5) 100/1: 7: b g Forzando - Zarah (Rudimentary) Handy over 5f, sn   3½   57
hung left & fdd: debut: with Mrs Lucinda Featherstone.
3208 **THROUGH THE SLIPS 15** [9]3-8-9 M Fenton 20/1: 08: Handy 6f, fdd: see 3208.   5   42
2656 **FIFTH COLUMN 38** [5]3-9-0 W Supple 25/1: 0-009: Mid-div 5f, fdd.   6   36
9 Ran   Time 1m 46.83(7.43)   Owned: Barford Bloodstock   Trained: Newmarket

---

NEWMARKET   FRIDAY 30.07.04   Righthand, Stiff, Galloping Track

Official Going GOOD/FIRM.

3582   6.05 Turftours Com Median Auction Maiden Stakes 2yo (E)
£3517 £1082 £541   **7f str**   **Good/Firm 30**   **-11 Slow**   Stands Side

3280 **FONGTASTIC 13** [17] B J Meehan 2-9-0 D Holland 9/2: 31: Made all stands side, rdn & styd on   91
strongly ins last: confirmed debut promise: eff at 6f, imprvd for step up to 7f: acts on fast grnd & a stiff/gall
trk: looks useful, clearly progressing: see 3280.
SPEAR [1] D R Loder 2-9-0 A Beech(3) 14/1: 2: b c Almutawakel - Les Hurlants (Barathea) Held   2   85+
up far side, hung right but styd on from over 1f out, not reach wnr stands side: 70,000gns Jan foal, half-brother to
a 7f/1m juv wnr, dam a 12f wnr in France: eff at 7f, sure to relish 1m+: acts on fast grnd & a stiff/gall trk:
most promising intro, still green, expect improvement.
3005 **FRITH 24** [3] B W Hills 2-9-0 M Hills 10/11 FAV: 23: Led far side, rdn & not pace of wnr from   nk   84
dist: well bckd: acts on firm & fast grnd, 1m shld suit: see 3005.
HOUSE MARTIN [16] A M Balding 2-8-9 R Mullen 25/1: 4: b f Spectrum - Guignol (Anita's Prince)   ¾   76
Dwelt, went up stands side, short of room over 2f out & switched, kept on late, no threat: Mar first foal, dam a 5f
Irish 3yo wnr: stays 7f, shaped as if 1m+ will suit: handles fast grnd: encouraging start.
3234 **TRAIANOS 14** [8]2-9-0 N De Souza(5) 25/1: 565: b c Mt Livermore - Shiitake (Green Dancer) Chsd   1½   77
ldr far side, onepace over 1f out: $95,000 May foal, half-brother to a high-class Gr 1 wnr, dam a 3yo US wnr: eff
at 7f, 1m shld suit: handles fast grnd.
KRISTINOR [14]2-9-0 J Murtagh 11/2: 6: Held up stands side, switched & hung left over 1f out,   ½   76
hung right ins last, kept on: green, op 9/2, likely improver.
FANTASY RIDE [10]2-9-0 R Price 66/1: 7: Chsd ldrs stands side, no impress distance.   1¼   73

3361 **DANEHILL WILLY 8** [6]2-9-0 P Dobbs 12/1: 28: Held up far side, kept on late, nrst fin: see 3361 (5f).	1	71
AKRAAN [15]2-8-9 R Hills 16/1: 9: Trkd ldrs stands side, btn over 1f out.	2½	61
MINK MITTEN [5]2-8-9 T S Whitworth 50/1: 0: 10th: Dwelt far side, nvr a threat: t-strap.	1¾	57
3239 **HOWS THAT 14** [11]2-8-9 G Carter 66/1: 00: 11th: Chsd ldrs stands side till halfway.	shd	57
2696 **TOMBOLA 36** [12]2-9-0 T Quinn 16/1: 40: 12th: Held up stands side, no impress fnl 2f: btr 2696.	nk	61
2927 **ROYAL ABIGAIL 27** [4]2-8-9 W Ryan 66/1: 00: 13th: Far side, chsd ldrs 4f.	2	52
PATAU [9]2-9-0 D Corby(3) 33/1: 0: 14th: Chsd ldrs stands side till over 2f out.	6	45
2714 **BREGAGLIA 35** [7]2-8-9 M Henry 66/1: 00: 15th: Chsd ldrs far side 4f.	9	22
ASSURED [13]2-8-9 Paul Eddery 50/1: 0: 16th: Stands side, dwelt at rear.	nk	21

16 Ran   Time 1m 26.83 (2.93)   Owned: Mr Stephen Dartnell   Trained: Upper Lambourn

---

3583 6.35 Turftours Com Go Racing In Paris Handicap Stakes 3yo+ 0-80 (D)   **[80]**
£5460 £1680 £840   **1m str**   Good/Firm 30   **-29 Slow**   Stands Side

2931 **HABSHAN 27** [9] N A Graham 4-9-1 (67) D Holland 7/2 JT FAV: 52-04351: Trkd ldr, short of room over 1f out, rdn to lead cl-home: bckd: eff around 1m on fast & gd/soft grnd: see 1891.		72
3310 **QUALITAIR WINGS 11** [6] J Hetherton 5-9-6 (72) D McGaffin 10/1: 3000202: Dwelt & held up, keen, hdwy over 2f out & rdn/led dist, hdd cl-home: see 1474.	nk	75
3465 **AFRICAN SAHARA 5** [7] Miss D Mountain 5-9-12 t (78) G Carter 7/2 JT FAV: 0060343: Held up, short of room over 1f out, drvn & kept on, not pace of wnr: qck reapp: see 3465 & 3225.	1	79
3225 **TOPTON 15** [8] P Howling 10-9-11 bl (77) J Murtagh 15/2: 0462654: Trkd ldrs, short of room when stumbled badly dist, onepace ins last: see 714.	½	77
3001 **TIBER TIGER 24** [5]4-9-12 bl (78) J P Guillambert(3) 13/2: 4102005: Held up & keen, outpcd 2f out, no impress ins last: btr 2600 & 1891.	3½	71
3257* **BOUNDLESS PROSPECT 14** [3]5-9-11 (77) M Hills 4/1: 0002316: Chsd ldr, rdn & onepace when badly hmpd dist, no ch after: op 3/1: btr 3257 (7f).	nk	69
2591 **GARDEN SOCIETY 41** [1]7-9-4 (70) W Ryan 25/1: 00/U06/-07: Chsd ldrs, hmpd when outpcd over 1f out: 6 wk abs: see 2591.	¾	60
2907 **KABEER 28** [4]6-9-4 (70) R Mullen 20/1: 4308: Dictated pace, qcknd from halfway, hung left & hdd dist, sn btn: h'cap bow: btr 2575, 2148.	hd	60

8 Ran   Time 1m 41.99 (4.79)   Owned: Alan & Jill Smith   Trained: Newmarket

---

3584 7.05 Breeders Cup In Texas With Turftours Handicap Stakes 3yo+ 0-90 (C)   **[89]**
£9549 £2938 £1469   **6f str**   Good/Firm 30   **+09 Fast**   Stands Side

3485 **JONNY EBENEEZER 4** [6] D Flood 5-8-10 (7ex)bl (71) L Dettori 13/8 FAV: 0221141: Keen in tch, short of room over 1f out, burst through gap ins last to lead nr fin, cosily: bckd, gd time, qck reapp: eff btwn 5/7f, stays stiff 1m: acts on firm, soft & fibresand: loves Newmarket, best held up & goes v well for L Dettori: prob more to come: see 3408.		83+
3279 **BEAUVRAI 13** [10] V Smith 4-8-11 p (72) M Tebbutt 20/1: 0053002: Held up when short of room over 1f out, switched & rdn to chal ins last, not pace of wnr nr line: well h'capped: now eff in cheek pieces: acts on firm, fast & both AWs: could be winning similar sn: see 2591, 1914 & 567.	1¼	78
3424 **SNOW BUNTING 6** [3] Jedd O'Keeffe 6-7-12 (1oh) (58) Leanne Kershaw(7) 6/1: 3020533: Chsd ldrs, rdn to lead ins last, sn hdd & not pace of wnr: qck reapp: see 3424, 2160 &1020.	hd	64
3409 **BOLEYN CASTLE 7** [4] P S McEntee 7-10-0 (89) L Fletcher(3) 50/1: 000-0004: Led, hdd ins last & no extra: cheek pieces omitted: see 2068.	2	88
2768 **FEARBY CROSS 34** [8]8-8-3 (64) R Mullen 9/1: 6045005: Held up, eff over 1f out, not pace to chal: won this race in '03 off a 1lb higher mark: see 698.	shd	63
4630] **DESERT LORD 650** [5]4-9-9 (84) J P Murtagh 6/1: 32210/-6: b c Green Desert - Red Carnival (Mr Prospector) Held up, outpcd 2f out, kept on late under kind ride, nvr a threat: reapp/long abs: missed '03: mdn scorer '02: stays 7f, winning form at 6f: acts on firm & gd grnd, gall/undul or sharp/turning trk: expect improv on this at 7f+. 1 Sep'02 Chep 6g/f 94- D: 2 Aug'02 Ches 7fm 86- D: 2 Aug'02 Donc 7gd 84- D:	½	82+
3408 **JUSTE POUR LAMOUR 7** [2]4-8-9 (70) D Holland 16/1: 0400047: Chsd ldrs, rdn & outpcd fnl 2f.	hd	68
3223 **STARBECK 15** [7]6-9-8 (83) P McCabe 20/1: 5400548: Slow away, held up, rdn & no impress fnl 1f.	nk	80
3543* **TONY THE TAP 1** [9]3-9-0 (80) D Fox(5) 7/2: 12225219: Trkd ldrs, short of room over 1f out, sn no extra: wnr last night: see 3543.	½	70
3002 **CORPS DE BALLET 24** [1]3-9-8 (88) T Quinn 16/1: 431-0100: 10th: Chsd ldr, ch over 1f out, no extra when bmpd ins last: btr 2155.	1	75

10 Ran   Time 1m 12.26 (1.26)   Owned: Mrs Ruth M Serrell   Trained: Hungerford

---

3585 7.35 Turftours Com For Sporting Hospitality Conditions Stakes 2yo (C)
£7273 £2759 £1379   **7f str**   Good/Firm 30   **+02 Fast**   Stands Side

2578 **BRECON BEACON 41** [2] P F I Cole 2-9-1 J P Murtagh 5/2 JT FAV: 1121: Made all, hung left under press bef 1f out, rdn out: nicely bckd after 6 wk abs: eff at 5/6f, imprvd for recent step up to 7f: acts on firm & soft grnd: goes well fresh: useful performer who is progressing with racing: see 2578 & 1937.		105
2695* **PERFECTPERFORMANCE 36** [8] Saeed bin Suroor 2-9-1 L Dettori 5/2 JT FAV: 12: Handy, kept on ins fnl 1f, not pace of wnr: nicely bckd: acts on fast & gd grnd: imprvd eff in defeat & shaped as tho' 1m will suit.	¾	102
3214* **IN THE FAN 15** [1] J L Dunlop 2-8-11 T Quinn 8/1: 213: Al cl-up, kept on ins fnl 1f, not pace front 2: gd eff in decent looking contest: see 3214 & 2594.	1¼	95
3120* **VISIONIST 20** [4] J A Osborne 2-8-11 D Holland 6/1: 14: Cl-up, ev ch 1f out, sn no extra: stays 7f, might just apprec drop back to 6f: acts on fast & gd grnd: see 3120 (debut).	nk	94
2792 **BUNNY RABBIT 32** [6]2-8-11 M Hills 40/1: 35: Bhd, outpcd 2f out, rallied ins fnl wk: eff at 7f, shaped as tho' 1m will suit: see 2792.	¾	90
2578 **PERFECT CHOICE 41** [3]2-9-1 W Ryan 33/1: 0106: Cl-up till dist, no extra: 6 wk abs: see 2348 (6f).	1¼	91
DIKTATORIAL [9]2-8-9 R Mullen 10/1: 7: b r c Diktat - Reason To Dance (Damister) Al bhd: debut: Feb foal, cost 45,000gns: half-brother to wnrs at 9/10f: dam successful at sprint dists: sire group wnr at sprint dists: with A M Balding.	1¼	81
3111* **LIAKOURA 20** [5]2-9-1 K Darley 11/4: 18: Al in rear: btr 3111 (debut, gd/soft).	¾	85

8 Ran   Time 1m 25.89 (1.99)   Owned: Elite Racing Club   Trained: Whatcombe

3586

8.05 Turftours Com Go Racing In Barbados E B F Maiden Stakes 2yo (D)
£4745 £1460 £730   **6f str   Good/Firm 30   -48 Slow**   Stands Side

SUN KISSED [2] Saeed bin Suroor 2-9-0 L Dettori 3/1: 1: ch c Sunday Silence - Flying Kiss **93**
(Sadler's Wells) Handy, styd on to lead cl-home, rdn out: debut: Mar foal: sire high-class performer abroad: eff
at 6f, will apprec further: acts on fast grnd & a stiff/gall trk: goes well fresh: potentially useful.

2766 **DANIEL THOMAS** 34 [3] Mrs A J Perrett 2-9-0 K Darley 5/6 FAV: 22: Al cl-up, styd on to lead 1f   *nk*   **90**
out, hdd cl-home: well bckd: eff at 6f, return to 7f will suit: another gd run in defeat & can lose mdn tag.

2473 **MY PRINCESS** 44 [1] N A Callaghan 2-8-9 D Fox(5) 16/1: 353: Led, hdd 1f out, kept on, not btn   *1*   **82**
far: 6 wk abs: ran with credit & now quals for h'caps: see 2263.

HAUNTING MEMORIES [4] M A Jarvis 2-9-0 P Robinson 8/1: 4: b c Barathea - King of All (King of   *¾*   **84**
Clubs) Mid-div, prog when short of room ins fnl 1f, sn no impress: op 5/1 on debut: Feb first foal, cost
30,000gns: dam won abroad, sire Gr 1 wnr at 1m: eff at 6f, will apprec further: acts on fast grnd.

WALKONTHEWILDSIDE [5]2-9-0 T P Queally 11/2: 5: b c Giant's Causeway - Wannabe Grand   *7*   **64**
(Danehill) Al in rear: debut: cost 160,000gns: half-brother to smart sprinter Bachelor of Arts: dam high-class
at 1m/9f: sire top-class 1m/10f performer: with D R Loder.

5 Ran   Time 1m 15.70 (4.70)   Owned: Godolphin   Trained: Newmarket

3587

8.35 Turftours Com Prix De L'arc De Triomphe Handicap Stakes 3yo+ 0-80 (D)   **[80]**
£5421 £1668 £834   **1m4f   Good/Firm 30   -51 Slow**   Centre

3040 **STOLEN HOURS** 22 [3] J Akehurst 4-8-11 (63) J Quinn 11/4: 0002231: In tch, gd prog to lead 3f   **70**
out, rdn out ins fnl 1f to hold on: op 7/2: eff at 12/14f on firm & fast, has disapp on gd/soft: acts on a
stiff/gall or sharp trk: made gd use of drop down weights to record first win: see 2869 & 2651.

3243 **GIFT VOUCHER** 14 [5] Sir Michael Stoute 3-9-2 T (80) K Fallon 2/1 FAV: 0302: Led, hdd 3f out,   *1½*   **84**
outpcd bef 1f out, rallied late, & held by wnr: nicely bckd: first time t-strap: stays a slowly run 12f on fast
grnd: only lightly rcd & is open to more improvement in h'caps: see 2862.

2735 **PIRI PIRI** 35 [1] P J McBride 4-9-1 (67) S Whitworth 7/2: 60-62303: Rear, prog to chase wnr 3f   *nk*   **70**
out, onepcd ins fnl 1f: op 9/2: see 2318.

2754 **DISTANT COUSIN** 34 [4] M A Buckley 7-8-6 vis (58) R Mullen 9/1: 6-053004: Cl-up 10f, sn no extra.   *2*   **58**

4954) **JASMICK** 273 [2]6-9-0 (76) L Fletcher(3) 10/3: 050260-5: Cl f Definite Article - Glass Minnow   *7*   **66**
(Alzao) Cl-up 10f, sn wknd: op 5/2: reapp: rnr-up once in '03 (h'cap): h'cap wnr in '02: eff at 12f, suited by
around 14f, poss stays 2m: acts on firm & gd/soft grnd: is best produced late: with H Morrison.

2 Oct'03 Good 12fm 75-73 C: 1 Jul'02 Kemp 14.4g/s 85-78 C: 2 Sep'01 York 11.8g/f 79-77 D: 1 Aug'01 Sali 12g/f 77-72 D:
5 Ran   Time 2m 38.03(9.83)   Owned: Mr A D Spence   Trained: Epsom

Official Going GOOD/FIRM

3588

6.20 Real Radio Apprentices Handicap Stakes Round 3 3yo+ 0-70 (E)   **[64]**
£4079 £1255 £628   **1m4f17y   Good/Firm 26   +00 Fast**   Stands side

3139 **EASIBET DOT NET** 20 [5] I Semple 4-9-10 p (60) W Hogg 7/2: 0230531: Made all, clr 2f out, readily: **69**
top-weight: eff at 9/12f on fast, gd/soft & fibresand, v sharp or stiff/undul trks: gd weight carrier: see 6.

3530* **COSMIC CASE** 3 [4] J S Goldie 9-9-1 (6ex) (51) K Pierrepoint(5) 5/2 FAV: 5230312: Mid-div, hdwy 4f   *6*   **49**
out, sn outpaced, kept on fnl 1f but no ch with wnr: qck reapp: shade btr 3530.

3426 **DONNAS DOUBLE** 7 [2] D Eddy 9-9-2 p (52) J D O'Reilly 9/2: 55-56343: Rear, hdwy 4f out, hung left   *2*   **47**
over 2f out, wknd fnl 1f: qck reapp: jock rec 3 day whip ban: see 3426.

3226 **SPREE VISION** 15 [3] P Monteith 8-9-1 (51) H Fellows(7) 7/2: 0/-604224: Nvr btr than mid-div.   *3½*   **41**

3134 **HOWARDS DREAM** 21 [1]6-7-12 (9oh)t (25) Donna Caldwell(5) 12/1: 4060005: Prom, wknd 4f out.   *dist*   **0**

5010) **BRIDGE PAL** 269 [6]4-9-6 (56) A Reilly(3) 10/1: 234200-6: ch f First Trump - White Domino (Sharpen   *10*   **0**
Up) Rcd in 2nd, wknd 4f out, t.o.: reapp: rnr up 3 of 10 '03 starts (h'caps, mdn h'cap, W Jarvis): unplcd sole
'02 start (mdn, rtd 58a): eff at 1m/10f, prob just stays 12f, acts on fast, gd & fibresand: now with P Monteith.

2 Jul'03 Muss 12gd 60-57 F: 2 Apr'03 Sout 10g/f 56-55 F: 2 Feb'03 Sout 8af 55a-55 F:
6 Ran   Time 2m 34.94 (3.14)   Owned: WWWEASIBET DOT NET   Trained: Carluke

3589

6.50 Ian Sorbie Memorial Novice Auction Stakes 2yo (E)
£4128 £1270 £635   **6f5y   Good/Firm 26   -33 Slow**   Stands side

3227 **HANSOMELLE** 15 [5] B Mactaggart 2-8-2 Dale Gibson 14/1: 41: Cl up, hdwy to lead ins fnl 1f, kept   **76**
on, rdn out: eff at 5f, imprvd for step up to 6f: acts on fast grnd, stiff/undul trks: imprvd from debut.

3202 **INVERTIEL** 16 [1] I Semple 2-8-13 G Hind 8/1: 42: Dwelt, sn cl up, not clr run over 2f out till   *½*   **83**
over 1f out, kept on: eff at 6f on fast: shade unlucky, win similar: see 3202.

2888* **MELALCHRIST** 29 [3] J J Quinn 2-9-5 (94) P Hanagan 4/6 FAV: 12213: Prom, led over 1f out till ins   *¾*   **87**
fnl 1f, no extra: top-weight: stays 6f but shade more expected after 2888.

3303 **SPEED DIAL HARRY** 12 [4] K R Burke 2-8-13 (83) Darren Williams 3/1: 3132104: Prom, wknd ins fnl 1f.   *3½*   **70**

3227 **KRISTIKHAB** 15 [2]2-8-11 (65) F Lynch 25/1: 5420005: Led till not much room over 1f out, no extra.   *8*   **44**

5 Ran   Time 1m 13.39 (3.59)   Owned: Corsby Racing   Trained: Hawick

3590   7.20 Robert Wiseman Dairies The One Nursery Handicap Stakes 2yo (D)   [91]
£5187 £1596 £798   **6f5y**   Good/Firm 26   -23 Slow   Stands side

3178 **BORDERLESCOTT 18** [5] R Bastiman 2-7-12 (1oh) (61) P Hanagan 11/2: 6031: Cl up, hdwy to lead 1f   75
out, rdn & styd on: h'cap bow: stays 6f on fast grnd & a stiff/undul trk: imprvd for a step up in trip.
3560 **WINDY PROSPECT 2** [4] P A Blockley 2-9-2 (80) Dean McKeown 6/1: 3521032: Prom, ev ch 1f out, kept   ½   90
on: qck reapp, clr of rem: acts on fast, gd & both AWs: back to form of 2051.
3202* **PROPELLOR 16** [2] A Dickman 2-9-7 (85) P Makin(5) 1/1 FAV: 313: Dwelt, sn handy, not much room 3f   3   86
out, led 2f out till 1f out, no extra: shade btr 3202 (mdn, made all).
3308* **BAYMIST 12** [3] M W Easterby 2-7-13 (63) Dale Gibson 5/1: 5614: Trkd ldrs, btn 2f out: btr 3308 (5f).   5   49
3224 **OCHIL HILLS DANCER 16** [1]2-8-2 (66) B Swarbrick(5) 12/1: 05045: Led to 2f out, no extra: see 2056.   5   37
3351 **REGAL LUSTRE 10** [6]2-7-12 (5oh) (57) D Fentiman(7) 20/1: 35266: Cl up, wknd over 1f out.   3½   22
6 Ran   Time 1m 12.74 (2.94)   Owned: Border Rail & Plant Limited   Trained: Wetherby

3591   7.50 European Breeders Fund Handicap Stakes Fillies 3yo+ 0-85 (D)   [81]
£6793 £2090 £1045   **5f4y**   Good/Firm 26   -09 Slow   Stands side

3135 **BARON RHODES 20** [6] J S Wainwright 3-9-9 (76) D McGaffin 9/1: 2313051: Trkd ldrs, hdwy to lead   85
ins fnl 1f, kept on well for press: suited by 5f on fast & soft, stiff/undul or sharp trks: imprvd for a drop into
fillies' grade: back to form of 2387.
3353* **ROXANNE MILL 10** [7] P A Blockley 6-9-10 p (73) F Lynch 5/1: 3235612: Led till ins fnl 1f, no   1   77
extra: new stable (prev with J Bradley): imprvd in defeat up in class: see 3353 (clmr).
3193 **SCOTTISH EXILE 17** [5] K R Burke 3-9-4 vis (71) Darren Williams 12/1: 1002103: Mid-div, kept on   hd   74
ins fnl 1f: back to form of 2784.
3416 **ROMAN MISTRESS 8** [4] T D Easterby 4-8-13 (62) D Allan 13/2: 4630504: Trkd ldrs, onepaced fnl 1f.   ½   63
3106 **DISPOL KATIE 21** [3]3-10-0 (81) P Makin(5) 2/1 FAV: 022-0635: Cl up, no impress over 1f out, kept   dht   82
on again ins fnl 1f: see 3106.
2614 **ROBWILLCALL 40** [1]4-8-1 (50) Dale Gibson 16/1: 00-05155: Prom, hung right over 2f out, one paced   ¾   49
over 1f out: 6 wk abs: 'hung right' throughout: see 2476.
3527* **BETTYS PRIDE 3** [8]5-8-7 (7ex) (56) P Hanagan 13/2: 4066017: Mid-div, btn 2f out: qck reapp: nk   54
reportedly not handle coming down hill: see 3527.
3416 **AMELIA 2** [2]6-8-10 (59) B Swarbrick(5) 6/1: 1325338: Al bhd: broke a blood vessel.   19   0
8 Ran   Time 59.85s (1.75)   Owned: Mr I Barran & Mr P Rhodes   Trained: Malton

3592   8.20 Variety Club Of Scotland Maiden Stakes 3yo (D)   [91]
£6182 £1902 £951   **1m1f36y**   Good/Firm 26   -29 Slow   Stands side

3236 **NOTABLE GUEST 15** [1] Sir Michael Stoute 3-9-0 (87) F Lynch 1/10 FAV: 22-531: Prom, hdwy to lead   84
halfway, pushed clr, cmftbly: eff at 7/10f on fast, stiff/undul trk: win more races: see 1259.
3328 **ARGENT 11** [7] Miss L A Perratt 3-9-0 p (48) Darren Williams 33/1: P020002: Trkd ldrs, ev ch 2f   5   66
out, hung right, not pace of wnr: acts on fast & soft: treat rating with caution: see 1630.
3079 **REEM TWO 22** [6] D McCain 3-8-9 L Enstone(3) 12/1: 63: Cl up, one paced 2f out: clr of rem: see 3079.   1½   58
3246 **DALKEYS LASS 15** [5] Mrs L B Normile 3-8-9 V Halliday 50/1: 04: gr f Wolfhound - Dalkey Sound   11   36
(Crash Course) Nvr btr than mid-div: Feb foal: NH bred, dam a smart chaser: imprvd from debut.
1527 **DANETTIE 89** [4]3-8-9 B Swarbrick(5) 50/1: 05: b f Danzero - Petite Heritiere (Last Tycoon)   shd   35
Prom, wknd over 3f out: long abs: Feb foal: dam unplcd at 2 & 3: with W Brisbourne.
2106 **AFTER LENT 61** [2]3-9-0 Dean McKeown 16/1: 06: b g Desert Style - Yashville (Top Ville) Rear,   ½   39
nvr nr ldrs: 9 wk abs: Apr foal, cost £12,000: half brother to a useful 7f wnr: dam unraced: with P Blockley.
3177 **RAYBERS MAGIC 18** [8]3-8-9 G Hind 50/1: 0007: Led to halfway, no extra over 3f out.   6   22
   BETFRED 0 [3]3-9-0 Dale Gibson 33/1: 8: Nvr a factor on debut.   24   0
8 Ran   Time 1m 59.05 (4.95)   Owned: Mr K Abdulla   Trained: Newmarket

3593   8.50 Handicap Stakes A Qualifier For The Totepool Handicap Series Final 3yo+ 0-75 (E)   [74]
£4908 £1510 £755   **1m1f36y**   Good/Firm 26   +08 Fast   Stands side

3325 **WAHOO SAM 11** [1] T D Barron 4-9-7 (67) P Makin(5) 5/1: 0031101: Made all, kept on well for press   75
fnl 1f: prev eff at 6/7f, suited by 1m/9f on fm, gd/soft & fibresand, any trk, loves Hamilton & dominating.
3328 **ANTHEMION 11** [10] Mrs J C McGregor 7-9-0 (60) D McGaffin 5/1: 0053132: Rcd in 2nd, outpaced over   1   64
2f out, kept on fnl 1f: continues in gd form: see 3250.
2828 **JORDANS ELECT 32** [9] I Semple 4-9-13 (73) G Hind 8/1: 1014043: Trkd ldrs, one paced fnl 1f: ½   76
top-weight: goes well here: likes Hamilton: back to form of 2179.
3250 **KRISTIANSAND 15** [8] P Monteith 4-9-4 (64) L Enstone(3) 33/1: 0505-064: Rear, hdwy & not much room   hd   66
over 1f out, kept on fnl 1f: see 3132.
3250 **ENCOUNTER 15** [5]8-8-1 (2ow) (45) D Allan 6/1: 3560025: Rear, mod late gains.   ¾   47
3242 **BASINET 15** [3]6-8-7 p (53) P Hanagan 7/1: 6-000406: Rear, not clr run 3f out, rdn/not much room   1½   50
over 1f out, not recover: much closer with clr run: see 2120.
3305 **CHERISHED NUMBER 12** [7]5-9-12 vis (72) Darren Williams 11/4 FAV: 6330447: Handy, wknd over 2f out. 7   55
3242 **ZAWRAK 15** [2]5-9-2 vis (62) W Hogg(7) 9/1: 3010528: Al bhd: btr 3242.   nk   44
3324 **FRANCIS FLUTE 11** [6]6-8-4 (1ow) (49) P Mulrennan 16/1: 0-024009: Cl up, wknd 4f out.   7   18
9 Ran   Time 1m 55.79(1.69)   Owned: Mr C A Washbourn   Trained: Thirsk

Official Going Good/Firm ALL TIMES SLOW EXCEPT 2.10

3594

1.00 Little Chef E B F Maiden Stakes 2yo (D)
£4992 £1536 £768   7f str   Good/Firm   Slow   Stands Side

LE CORVEE 0 [11] A King 2-9-0   J D Smith 66/1: 1: Trkd ldrs stands side & led over 1f out,   **98+**
pushed clr, readily: 27,000gns 2yo, Mar foal: half-brother to a 12f wnr: dam useful at 12f/2m: eff at 7f, shld
relish 1m+: acts on fast & goes well fresh: impressive start, looks useful, win more races.
3111 **MISTER GENEPI** 21 [9] W R Muir 2-9-0   Martin Dwyer 9/2: 52: Trkd ldrs, chall over 1f out, sn   3   **88**
outpcd by wnr: bckd, op 7/1: eff at 7f, handles fast & gd/soft: shld find a race: see 3111.
2766 **EQDAAM** 35 [2] J H M Gosden 2-9-0   R Hills 2/1 FAV: 33: Trkd ldrs & ch over 2f out, onepace.   1¼   **85**
SINGHALESE 0 [10] J A Osborne 2-8-9   S W Kelly 14/1: 4: Went left start, led till over 1f out,   nk   **79**
onepace: clr rem: £60,000 Mar foal, half-sister to a 6f/1m wnr Masterpoint, dam 5f wnr: eff at 7f on fast grnd:
ran well for a long way: entitled to progress.
MOBARHEN 0 [4]2-9-0   N Mackay(3) 10/1: 5: Sn pushed along chasing ldrs, kept on late, nvr threat.   5   **75**
3111 **DESERT COMMANDER** 21 [5]2-9-0   J Carroll 11/4: 46: Trkd ldrs, chall 3 out, rdn & no extra over 1f   ¾   **74**
out: well bckd: ahd of today's rnr-up in 3111 (g/s).
COEUR COURAGEUX 0 [3]2-9-0   J Murtagh 8/1: 7: V upset in stalls, slow away & bhd, switched wide   6   **63**
& hdwy halfway, no impress & position accepted fnl 2f: op 6/1: v green & unruly but showed ability.
FANTORINI 0 [8]2-9-0   R Havlin 25/1: 8: Cl-up, fdd fnl 2f.   hd   **62**
ROBINZAL 0 [6]2-9-0   D Allan 66/1: 9: Al towards rear, no ch fnl 3f.   shd   **62**
3078 **ZORIPP** 22 [1]2-9-0   M Fenton 66/1: 60: 10th: Went left start, struggling halfway.   shd   **61**
10 Ran   Time 1m 28.34 (5.14)   Owned: Mr David Mason   Trained: Barbury Castle

---

3595

1.35 Trade Union Unison Your Friend At Work Maiden Stakes 3yo+ (D)
£5559 £1710 £855   7f str   Good/Firm   Slow   Stands Side

1518 **LITERATIM** 89 [6] L M Cumani 4-9-7   N Mackay(3) 3/1: 41: Trkd ldr, went on halfway till hdd &   **84**
outpcd over 2f out, switched & rdn/rallied to lead cl-home: op 7/2: 12 wk abs: eff at 7f, 1m will suit: handles
gd/soft, imprvd on fast grnd today: likes a gall trk & goes well fresh: see 1518.
3237 **KAURI FOREST** 15 [1] J R Fanshawe 3-9-0 T J Murtagh 4/9 FAV: 322: Trkd ldr & smooth prog to lead   ½   **82**
over 2f out, edged right, rdn & carr head high when hdd well ins last: nicely bckd at odds on: clr of rem: wore a
t-strap today: has ability but not straightforward: see 3237 & 1136.
2756 **ZAZOUS** 35 [4] A King 3-9-0   (70) V Slattery 10/1: 03-63: Held up in tch, no impress on front pair   10   **65**
fnl 2f: longer 7f trip: see 2756.
3365 **LOTTIE** 9 [3] Miss V Haigh 3-8-9   S Chin 66/1: 054: Led till halfway, sn btn.   7   **46**
3365 **TREGENNA** 9 [5]3-8-9   M Henry 66/1: 45: Struggling halfway, al bhd: btr 3365.   15   **16**
OLLIJAY 0 [2]3-9-0   Martin Dwyer 14/1: 6: Slow away & bhd on debut, op 40/1.   5   **11**
6 Ran   Time 1m 27.74 (4.54)   Owned: Aston House Stud   Trained: Newmarket

---

3596

2.10 Unison Trade Union Positively Public Conditions Stakes 3yo+ (C)
£8632 £3274 £1637   6f str   Good/Firm   Fair   Stands Side

3268 **MAC LOVE** 14 [7] J Akehurst 3-8-9   (103) G Carter 5/1: 5422661: Rear, switched & strong run for   **108**
press to lead cl-home: op 4/1: eff at 5/6f on firm & gd grnd, poss handles soft: tough & v useful sprinter.
3075 **LOCHRIDGE** 22 [6] A M Balding 5-8-12   (102) Martin Dwyer 5/4 FAV: 30-20032: Led, drvn & hdd well   nk   **105**
ins last: well bckd: ran to useful best: see 3075, 2068.
1480 **MILK IT MICK** 91 [1] J A Osborne 3-9-3   (108) S W Kelly 5/2: 511-2503: Trkd ldrs, kept on for   2   **109**
press, not pace to chall ins last: 3 month abs: not disgraced conceding weight, return to 7f will suit.
2186 **TEDBURROW** 58 [3] E J Alston 12-9-0   (88) J Murtagh 12/1: 0605-534: Held up, eff over 2f out, not   3   **92**
able to chall: abs: see 1626.
2486 **TASHKIL** 45 [4]3-8-9   (103) R Hills 13/2: 4110-05: b g Royal Applause - Surprise Visitor (Be My   2½   **84**
Guest) Chsd ldr, rdn & btn over 1f out: been gelded, abs: mdn & nov stks wnr '03 (lightly rcd): both wins at 7f on
fast grnd, stiff/gall trks. 1 Sep'03 Sand 7.1g/f 99-(84) D: 1 Aug'03 Donc 7g/f 82- D:
3416 **SAFRANINE** 8 [2]7-8-9   (61) Ann Stokell 125/1: 0060006: In tch till outpcd from halfway: highly tried.   7   **59**
3375 **TELEPATHIC** 9 [5]4-9-0   (57) P Bradley 100/1: 0565407: Prom till halfway, sn struggling: see 1218.   2   **58**
3375 **JALOUHAR** 9 [8]4-9-0   (46) T Woodley 200/1: 0200608: Chsd ldrs, rdn & strugg halfway.   2½   **48**
8 Ran   Time 1m 13.01 (2.21)   Owned: Mr Vimal Khosla   Trained: Epsom

---

3597

2.40 Just Trays Handicap Stakes Fillies 3yo 0-85 (D)
£5606 £1725 £862   1m rnd   Good/Firm   Slow   Outside   **[91]**

2344* **PERLE DOR** 51 [6] W J Haggas 3-8-11   (74) A Culhane 5/2 FAV: 450-111: Trkd ldrs, switched & rdn to   **86+**
lead ins last, going away, val further: nicely bckd, 7 wk abs: eff at 7f/1m on fast grnd: goes well fresh: most
progressive & shld be kept on side, win again.
3378 **CHARNOCK BATES ONE** 9 [4] T D Easterby 3-8-7   (70) D Allan 3/1: 4-460122: Held up, hdwy & led over   1¾   **75**
1f out, edged left & hdd ins last, no ch with wnr: rest well covered & remains in fine form: acts on fm & gd/soft.
3273 **KEEPERS LODGE** 14 [5] B A McMahon 3-8-7   (70) G Gibbons 9/1: 4-400103: Held up, eff to chall 2f   2½   **70**
out, sn onepace: op 14/1: imprvd eff on rtn to 1m: acts on fast & gd grnd: see 2904.
2742* **KEYAKI** 35 [7] C F Wall 3-9-3   (80) J Murtagh 11/4: 66114: Trkd ldrs, led over 2f out, hdd over 1f   1   **78**
out & sn btn: op 2/1: btr 2742 & 2342 (7f).
3419 **MAGICAL MIMI** 7 [3]3-8-4   (67) Leanne Kershaw(7) 20/1: 0004505: Held up, eff wide 4f out, btn 3f out.   10   **48**
2877 **HAVE FAITH** 30 [2]3-9-7   (84) M Hills 9/2: 6210-366: Led, hdd over 2f out, sn btn: op 6/1: btr 2877.   ½   **64**
6 Ran   Time 1m 42.16 (6.06)   Owned: The Perle d'Or Partnership   Trained: Newmarket

DONCASTER SATURDAY 31.07.04 Lefthand, Flat, Galloping Track

3598
3.15 Weatherbys Bank Summer Cup Handicap 3yo+ 0-85 (D) [85]
£22835 £7026 £3513 **1m2f60y Good/Firm V Slow** Inside

3139 **OPENING CEREMONY 20** [9] R A Fahey 5-9-1 (72) T Hamilton(3) 11/1: 6242151: Trkd ldrs, led over 2f **78**
out, held on gamely for press ins last, all out: slow time: op 9/1: eff at 9/10.5f on fast & gd/soft grnd, any
trk: prev best delivered late & showed admirable resolution today: see 3099.
3501 **TEDSDALE MAC 4** [1] N Bycroft 5-8-0 (57) N Mackay(3) 7/1 CO FAV: 4252322: Trkd ldrs, briefly *shd* **62**
outpcd over 2f out, drvn & styd on strongly cl-home, just held: most consistent: stays 10.3f.
3358 **GREAT SCOTT 9** [13] M Johnston 3-8-13 (80) S Chin 25/1: 005-0053: Al handy & ch fnl 2f, drvn & *hd* **84**
kept on, just held: stays a slowly run 10.3f: see 2679.
3074 **GO TECH 22** [4] T D Easterby 4-9-2 (73) G Gibbons 14/1: 0624604: Mid-div, switched wide & styd on *hd* **76**
well for press cl-home, just held: stays slowly run 10.3f: see 2483.
3506 **KRUGERRAND 4** [2]5-9-13 (84) G Carter 12/1: 0013605: Rear, styd on well from over 1f out, nrst *nk* **86**
fin: qck reapp: stays a slowly run 10.3f: see 2404 (9f).
2890 **LES ARCS 29** [7]4-9-6 (77) A Culhane 7/1 CO FAV: 0-002136: Mid-div, outpcd over 2f out, kept on late. ¾ **78**
3216* **RONDELET 16** [10]3-9-0 (81) Martin Dwyer 8/1: 2023217: Trkd ldrs, drvn & onepace fnl 2f: see 3216. *nk* **81**
3099 **WAR OWL 21** [15]7-9-2 (73) J Murtagh 7/1 CO FAV: 1350108: Dwelt from start & bhd, keeping on when *shd* **73**
short of room dist, nvr able to chall: would have preferred a stronger pace: see 2265.
3236 **ALEKHINE 15** [11]3-9-1 e (82) R Hills 7/1: 6-230069: Held up, eff fnl 2f, kept on: eye-shield. ¾ **81**
3546 **COMPTON DRAGON 2** [3]5-9-3 vis (74) M Hills 25/1: 2252060: 10th: Dwelt, keeping on when short of *nk* **72**
room cl-home: qck reapp: fin 10th but only btn around 3L in a muddling event: see 2943, 2284 & 1519.
3184 **SWIFT ALCHEMIST 17** [6]4-8-0 (1ow) (56) A Daly 50/1: 0-003000: 11th: Al rear: btr 1537 (7f). 3½ **50**
2903 **INTRICATE WEB 29** [14]8-9-12 (83) D Allan 14/1: 1330100: 12th: Held up, eff wide, no impress fnl 2f. *nk* **75**
3430 **PAWAN 7** [5]4-9-1 (72) Ann Stokell 66/1: 6301050: 13th: Mid-div, struggling fnl 3f: btr 2962 (9f, g/s). 5 **57**
3430 **MBOSI 7** [12]3-9-3 (84) J Fanning 11/1: 15-33020: 14th: Led & allowed to dictate stdy pace, hdd 1 **68**
over 2f out & sn btn: btr 3430.
2233 **SOLO FLIGHT 56** [8]7-10-0 (85) L Fletcher(3) 8/1: 0206-260: 15th: Chsd ldrs wide, btn over 2f out: abs. 17 **45**
15 Ran Time 2m 14.99 (8.59) Owned: Mr H Hurst Trained: Malton

3599
3.50 Union In Front Is Unison Handicap Stakes 3yo 0-70 (E) [77]
£4321 £1330 £665 **5f str Good/Firm Slow** Stands Side

703 **BELLA BOY ZEE 159** [11] P A Blockley 3-8-8 (57) G Gibbons 14/1: 000-3251: Trkd ldr & led over 1f **61**
out, drvn & held on all out: op 12/1, 5 month abs: eff at 5.6f on firm, gd & fibresand, goes well fresh: see 485.
3193 **SHORT CHORUS 17** [5] J Balding 3-8-3 p (52) D Allan 7/1: 0401242: Al handy, drvn & styd on well *shd* **55**
ins last, just denied: in gd form: see 1605.
3215 **PICCLEYES 16** [10] R Hannon 3-8-11 bl (60) M Hills 8/1: 0001003: Held up, switched & styd on from *hd* **62**
over 1f out, nrst fin: op 10/1: acts on fast, gd/soft & fibresand: see 2586.
2728 **KAMENKA 36** [3] R A Fahey 3-9-7 (70) T Hamilton(3) 12/1: 63044-44: Trkd ldrs, chall over 1f out, onepace. ½ **70**
2950 **PICCOLO PRINCE 28** [6]3-9-4 (67) J Murtagh 9/1: 1202005: Mid-div, short of room over 1f out, ½ **65**
switched & kept on late, no threat: closer with a clr run: see 2011, 1344 & 1050.
3193* **NANNA 17** [4]3-9-6 (69) A Culhane 9/4 FAV: 2162116: Trkd ldrs, no extra ins last: well bckd, op 7/2. ¾ **65**
2944 **HAMAASY 28** [9]3-8-12 (61) J Fanning 25/1: 0600-507: Chsd ldrs, btn ins last: see 2485. *nk* **56**
3193 **OBE BOLD 17** [12]3-8-10 (59) P Bradley 6/1: 0150438: Held up, no impress dist: btr 3193. 1 **51**
3135 **FITZWARREN 20** [7]3-9-5 vis (68) Martin Dwyer 11/1: 402-0309: Dwelt, rear, only mod prog: btr 2961 (g/s) 2½ **52**
3213 **SMART STARPRINCESS 16** [8]3-8-8 bl (57) N Mackay 14/1: 1235000: 10th: Led till over 1f out, fdd. ½ **39**
3193 **FIRST ECLIPSE 17** [2]3-8-3 (2ow) (50) J Edmunds 28/1: 54600-00: 11th: Chsd ldrs till halfway: see 3193. 1¼ **30**
2808 **ONLY IF I LAUGH 33** [1]3-8-11 bl (60) G Parkin 10/1: 0230530: 12th: Al bhd: see 2493. 1½ **33**
12 Ran Time 1m 02.00(3.8) Owned: Transbuild Trained: Southwell

LINGFIELD Polytrack SATURDAY 31.07.04 Lefthand, V Sharp Track

Official Going Turf - Good/Firm, AW - Standard

3600
6.05 European Breeders Fund Maiden Stakes 2yo (D)
£4212 £1296 £648 **5f aw rnd Standard Inapplicable** Outside

SUMORA 0 [9] G A Butler 2-8-9 J Fortune 5/1: 1: b f Danehill - Rain Flower (Indian Ridge) Made **97a+**
all, pushed clr ins fnl 1f, val 4L+: debut: Feb first foal, cost 75,000gns: dam unrcd: sire decent performer at
6f/1m: eff at 5f, will apprec further in time: acts on polytrack & a v sharp trk: goes well fresh: promising.
3247 **COUNTDOWN 15** [4] Sir Mark Prescott 2-9-0 S Sanders 9/4: 32: Slow away, prog halfway, kept on 2 **90a**
ins fnl 1f, no ch with wnr: tchd 11/4: eff at 5f, will relish further: acts on firm grnd & polytrack: has shown
enough in both starts to date to find similar: see 3247 (debut).
3120 **BAHAMIAN MAGIC 21** [2] D R Loder 2-9-0 T P Queally 11/2: 43: Cl-up 4f, no extra ins fnl 1f: clr *nk* **89a**
rem: tchd 7/1: eff at 5f on polytrack: impr on debut, won a race: see 3120.
3280 **SIGN WRITER 14** [7] J Noseda 2-9-0 E Ahern 5/4 FAV: 624: Handy wide over 3f, wknd: disapp back 7 **70a**
at 5f on AW bow: btr 3280 (5f, fast).
2970 **GLOBAL BANKER 26** [3]2-9-0 T O Urbina 50/1: 05: b c Desert Prince - Luisa Demon (Baratthea) Chsd 5 **55a**
ldrs over 3f, fdd: first time t-strap: Feb first foal, dam successful at sprint dists: sire Gr 1 wnr at 1m.
GENERAL HAIGH 0 [5]2-9-0 M Savage(5) 33/1: 6: b g Mujahid - Stygian (Irish River) Al in rear: ½ **54a**
Mar foal, cost 20,000gns: half-brother to wnrs at 7/12f: dam wnr over sprint dists: sire Gr 1 7f wnr as a juv.
3020 **DANCING MOONLIGHT 24** [6]2-8-9 P C Haddon(7) 66/1: 6007: Bhd, nvr a factor: cheek pieces. 2½ **42a**
3160 **A QUI LE TOUR 19** [8]2-9-0 C Catlin 66/1: 08: Al in rear. 9 **22a**
8 Ran Time 1m 0.54 (2.74) Owned: Sangster Family Trained: Blewbury

Official Going Turf - Good/Firm, AW - Standard

3601
6.35 Derek Burridge Racing & Golf Trophies Median Auction Maiden Stakes 2yo   (F)
£3786 £1165 £583   7f140y rnd   Good/Firm 40   -26 Slow   Centre

3035 **TRIPLE ZERO** 24 [9] A P Jarvis 2-8-9 S Sanders 25/1: 001: b f Raise A Grand - Locorotondo   72
(Broken Hearted) Cl-up, led 2f out, rdn out to hold on: Feb foal, cost 36,000gns: half-sister successful at 7f:
dam won numerous times at mid-dists: sire group winning juv at 7f: eff at 7.6f, further will suit: acts on fast
grnd & a sharp/undul trk: improving with racing.

3329 **KEYNES** 10 [7] J H M Gosden 2-9-0 VIS J Fortune 14/1: 302: Led, hdd 2f out, rallied & ev ch from   ½   75
dist, just held by wnr: eff at 7.6f on fast grnd: imprvd eff with fitting of first time visor: see 2802.

3005 **YOUNG MICK** 25 [2] G G Margarson 2-9-0 A McCarthy 20/1: 03: br g King's Theatre - Just Warning   1½   72
(Warning) Cl-up over 4f, sn outpcd, rallied in fnl 1f: Feb first foal, dam unplcd: sire Gr 1 wnr at 12f: eff at
7.6f, 1m+ will suit: acts on fast grnd: encouraging display & can rate higher.

2522 **JAZRAWY** 44 [3] L M Cumani 2-9-0 D Holland 11/4: 44: Handy over 4f, sn outpcd, rallied late: 6   ¾   70
wk abs: eff at 7.6f, looks in need of further: acts on fast grnd: see 2522.

   SIR MONTY 0 [5]2-9-0 R L Moore 9/1: 5: ch c Cat's Career - Lady of Meadowlane (Pancho Jay)   ¾   68
Mid-div when hung right after halfway, kept on fnl 1f, nrst fin: op 16/1 on debut: Apr foal, cost 27,000gns:
half-brother to sprint wnrs in US: dam won numerous times abroad: sire useful at sprint dists: eff at 7.6f, shaped
as tho' further will suit: ran green today & is sure to impr with experience.

3329 **BEAUCHAMP TWIST** 10 [4]2-8-9 BL C Catlin 33/1: 0006: Held up, prog bef 1f out, nrst fin: blnks.   ½   62
2695 **FLAG POINT** 37 [15]2-9-0 T Quinn 9/4 FAV: 37: Chsd ldrs 4f, sn onepcd: disapp run & rider   1   65
reported mount ran too free to post: btr expected after promising 3rd in 2695 (debut).

3163 **DANGER ZONE** 19 [14]2-9-0 E Ahern 6/1: 08: Cl-up till dist, wknd: op 14/1.   ½   64
3285 **BLUE SPECTRUM** 14 [10]2-9-0 J D Smith 66/1: 09: Al in rear: see 3285.   2½   59
   CORDIER 0 [1]2-9-0 T P Queally 7/1: 0: 10th: Mid-div 5f, wknd: op 11/2 on debut.   1½   56
Pearls A Singer 0 [13]2-8-9 R Mullen 14/1:0   **Speedie Rossini** 0 [12]2-9-0 O Urbina 25/1:0
3234 **Rhoslan** 15 [8]2-9-0 R Havlin 33/1:0   **Hursley** 0 [16]2-8-9 Dane O'Neill 25/1:0
14 Ran   Time 1m 32.84 (5.04)   Owned: Quadrillian Partnership   Trained: Twyford

3602
7.05 Play A Round At Lingfield Club Handicap Stakes 3yo+ 35-55 (F)   [65]
£3122 £892 £446   6f str   Good/Firm 40   +02 Fast   Centre

3024 **UNITED SPIRIT** 24 [3] M A Magnusson 3-9-4 BL (55) E Ahern 8/1: 504-0631: Mid-div, prog halfway,   66
styd on to lead fnl 1f, rdn out: eff at 7f, apprec drop back to 6f: acts on fast & gd grnd: cheek pieces left
off, imprvd for fitting of first time blnks: see 3024 & 126.

3184 **COLD CLIMATE** 17 [7] Bob Jones 9-9-8 (54) J F Egan 6/1: 21-04052: Mid-div, prog & ev ch ins fnl   1¾   59
1f, al held by wnr: continues to run well: see 3184 & 144.

3289 **ENJOY THE BUZZ** 14 [15] J M Bradley 5-9-4 (50) C Catlin 5/1: 0102103: Bhd, outpcd halfway,   nk   54
rallied fnl 1f, nrst fin: return to fighting best will suit on this evidence: see 3050.

3403 **JAZZY MILLENNIUM** 8 [13] B R Millman 7-9-7 bl (53) D Holland 7/2 FAV: 0363304: Held up, prog when   ½   56+
short of room bef 1f out, switched & styd on ins fnl 1f, nrst fin: at least clr 2nd with a clr run: on a winning
mark & is worth keeping in mind for similar: see 3176 & 2957.

2633 **PRETTY KOOL** 40 [11]4-9-3 (49) O Urbina 10/1: 0/00-05: b f Inchinor - Carrie Kool (Prince Sabo)   ¾   50
Mid-div 3f, sn outpcd, rallied late: unplcd in both '03 starts (rtd 50, mdn): eff at 6f on fast grnd.

3289 **JAGGED** 14 [2]4-9-9 bl (50) T P Queally 5/1: 0-000236: Chsd ldrs, styd on to lead bef 1f out, hdd   nk   55
ins fnl 1f, no extra: btr 3289 & 2720.

3372 **LAKE VERDI** 9 [14]5-9-6 t (52) Dane O'Neill 16/1: 06-04307: Bhd, prog when hung right 2f out, nrst fin.   shd   51
3210 **ASTRAC** 16 [4]13-9-3 (49) S Drowne 14/1: 5002408: Bhd, prog bef 1f out, nrst fin: btr 2370.   shd   47
3403 **INDIAN BAZAAR** 8 [10]8-9-5 (51) R Miles(3) 20/1: 0020609: Handy over 4f, wknd: btr 2743.   1   46
3485 **ST IVIAN** 5 [12]4-9-9 vis (55) C Haddon(7) 33/1: 0000000: 10th: In tch when no room 2f out, sn btn.   1½   46
3232 **PIROUETTES** 15 [1]4-9-3 BL (49) D Corby(3) 66/1: 4340-000: 11th: Al in rear: first time blnks.   nk   39
2981 **TAPPIT** 26 [5]5-9-3 (49) M Savage(5) 33/1: 0030500: 12th: Cl-up till dist, wknd: btr 2412.   nk   38
3446 **NEBRASKA CITY** 7 [6]3-9-3 (54) S Whitworth 50/1: 0-060460: 13th: Al in rear: qck reapp.   5   28
2396 **MAYZIN** 49 [16]4-9-3 p (49) T Quinn 10/1: 1400000: 14th: Rcd stands side, cl-up over 4f, under   3   14
press when hmpd dist, not recover: 7 wk abs: btr 897 (polytrack).

3220 **BOANERGES** 16 [8]7-9-5 BL (51) R L Moore 14/1: 4005000: 15th: Handy 4f, fdd.   ½   15
2906 **PERFECT HINDSIGHT** 29 [9]3-9-4 BL (55) J Fortune 25/1: 005-0000: 16th: Led, hdd bef 1f out, fdd.   1½   15
16 Ran   Time 1m 11.08 (2.28)   Owned: East Wind Racing Ltd   Trained: Upper Lambourn

3603
7.35 Pleasure House Play After Racing Maiden Stakes 3yo+   (D)
£3533 £1087 £544   6f str   Good/Firm 40   -05 Slow   Centre

3218 **MR HULLABALOU** 16 [1] R Ingram 3-9-0 (61) E Ahern 10/1: 4500001: Cl-up, led bef 1f out, rdn out: 75
eff at 6f on fast & gd/soft grnd: see 1497.

   KOOL ACCLAIM 0 [6] S C Williams 3-8-9 O Urbina 12/1: 2: b f Royal Applause - Carrie Kool   1½   65
(Prince Sabo) Held up, prog 3f out, styd on to chase wnr ins fnl 1f, al held: op 8/1 on debut: dam successful at
5f: sire gr 1 wnr at 6f: eff at 6f on fast grnd: encouraging debut eff & can impr for today's experience.

2428 **BOLD BUNNY** 48 [4] S C Williams 3-8-9 Dane O'Neill 7/1: 33: Led, hdd bef 1f out, sn hung left &   2½   58
no extra: 7 wk abs: stablemate of 2nd: see 2428 (debut).

3469 **SYLVA ROYAL** 122 [8] C E Brittain 3-8-9 S Sanders 3/1: 44: Handy till dist, no extra: long abs.   1¼   54
3048 **PARADISE BREEZE** 23 [7]3-8-9 Lisa Jones(3) 25/1: 0-005: b f Perugino - Paradise Forum (Prince   2½   47
Sabo) Cl-up 4f, sn wknd: unplcd sole '03 start (mdn, rtd 53).

2870† **THOMAS LAWRENCE** 384 [2]3-9-0 (93) D Holland 10/11 FAV: 432-6: ch g Horse Chestnut - Olatha   1   49
(Miswaki) Cl-up 4f, sn wknd: bckd at odds-on: reapp: plcd on 2 of 3 '03 starts (mdns): eff at 5/7f, handles firm
& fast grnd: has been gelded since last term: with P F I Cole. 2 Jul'03 Hayd 6g/f 90- D:

2423 **COURT CHANCELLOR** 48 [3]3-9-0 BL (43) R L Moore 33/1: 000-007: Chsd ldrs over 3f, sn wknd: abs.   ½   48
3452 **INESCAPABLE** 7 [10]3-9-0 S Drowne 20/1: 08: Handy over 3f, sn fdd.   6   32

2700　JUST DASHING 37 [9]5-9-5　Natalia Gemelova(7) 66/1: 09: Al bhd.　½　31
3286　MANTEL MINI 14 [5]5-9-0 VIS (30) B Reilly(3) 66/1: 0600: 10th: Al in rear: first time visor.　½　25
10 Ran　Time 1m 11.54 (2.74)　Owned: Hullbran Bros　Trained: Epsom

3604	8.05 Sharp Minds Betfair Handicap Stakes 3yo 0-75 (E)				[82]
	£4459　£1372　£686	7f str	Good/Firm 40	+04 Fast　Centre	

3346　BLAEBERRY 10 [5] P L Gilligan 3-8-6 bl (60) J F Egan 13/2: 0554151: Mid-div, prog to lead dist,　　67
sn hung badly left, rdn out to hold on: fast time: suited by 7f, prob stays 1m: acts on fast & gd grnd: eff with
blnks & likes Lingfield: see 3024 & 1823.
3218　HEAD BOY 16 [6] S Dow 3-8-1 (55) Lisa Jones(3) 5/1: 0056542: Cl-up, styd on to lead 2f out, hdd　hd　60
dist, rallied fnl 1f, just denied: see 3218 & 1054.
3298　BAHAMA REEF 12 [7] B Gubby 3-8-1 (55) C Catlin 14/1: 0052033: Al handy, onepcd from dist: see 398.　2　56
3237　GLENCALVIE 15 [2] J Noseda 3-8-5 (59) E Ahern 7/2 FAV: 0504: Chsd ldrs, onepcd fnl 1f: tchd　hd　59
9/2: eff at 7f on fast grnd: see 2987.
3413*　WYCHBURY 8 [8]3-9-7 (75) D Corby(3) 5/1: 2-522015: Led, hdd 2f out, no extra fnl 1f: see 3413 (mdn).　1¼　73
3416　SHIFTY NIGHT 8 [11]3-7-12 (5oh) (47) A McCarthy 20/1: 0-004106: Chsd ldrs over 5f, sn no extra.　1¼　48
3283　MOLINIA 14 [1]3-8-1 (55) J Quinn 13/2: 0-0P4047: Cl-up over 4f, sn no extra: btr 3283.　2　47
3138　ACUZIO 20 [4]3-8-7 (61) T E Durcan 25/1: 660408: Chsd ldrs 4f, sn wknd: btr 2506.　nk　52
2953　REGAL FLIGHT 27 [10]3-7-12 (2oh) (50) R Thomas(1) 33/1: 505-6069: Keen bhd, nvr nrr than mid-div.　2½　38
4236*　MODEL FIGURE 320 [9]3-9-3 (71) D Holland 13/2: 401-0: 10th: b f Distant View - Sylph (Alleged)　nk　56
Chsd ldrs till halfway, sn wknd: tchd 8/1 on reapp: fills mdn wnr on last of only 3 '03 starts: eff at 6f, bred to
apprec 7f+: acts on firm & fast grnd, gall trk: with B W Hills. 1 Sep'03 Redc 6fm 72- D:
3331　LA LANDONNE 10 [13]3-8-12 (66) S W Kelly 12/1: 51-43660: 11th: Cl-up over 5f, fdd: btr 2624.　7　37
3283　Carlburg 14 [12]3-8-10 (64) J P Guillambert(3) 25/1:0
2645　Must Be So 39 [3]3-7-12 (20oh)t(32) C Haddon(7) 66/1:0
13 Ran　Time 1m 22.96 (2.56)　Owned: Lady Bland　Trained: Newmarket

Official Going Turf - Good/Firm, AW - Standard

3605	8.35 Come Back Next Saturday Handicap Stakes Fillies 3yo+ 35-55 (F)				[52]
	£2968　£848　£424	1m2f aw	Standard	Inapplicable　Inside	

3477　PIQUET 5 [6] J J Bridger 6-9-8 (46) T P Queally 14/1: 0006301: Cl-up, rdn out to lead cl-home:　　55a
qck reapp: suited by 1m/10f on firm & fast, likes polytrack/Lingfield, handles hvy & any trk: see 3025 & 538.
2741　SEMELLE DE VENT 35 [12] J H M Gosden 3-9-4 VIS (52) J Fortune 8/1: 56-33002: Held up wide, prog　½　59a
4f out, styd on to lead bef 1f out, hdd cl-home: eff at 10/12f: gd run in first time visor & can find similar: see 1165.
3487　MISS GLORY BE 5 [11] E R Oertel 6-9-11 p (49) D Holland 5/2 FAV: 06-03523: Mid-div, prog bef 1f　nk　55a
out, styd on, not btn far in 3rd: clr rem: qck reapp: likes W'hampton: see 3487 & 564.
386]　FLAMING SPIRT 564 [1] J S Moore 5-9-12 (50) Derek Nolan(7) 14/1: 60000/0-4: b f Blushing Flame -　5　49a
Fair Test (Fair Season)　Handy 1m, sn onepcd: reapp: unplcd sole '03 start (rtd 19a, h'cap): u.r. & p.u. in 2
02/03 hdles starts: med auct mdn & h'cap wnr in '02: eff at 1m/9f, prob stays 11f: acts on gd, gd/soft & fibresand:
has gone well fresh: sharper for this after a long layoff.
2 May'02 Hami 9.1gd 71-71 E: 1 Mar'02 Kemp 9gd 76-66 D: 1 Dec'01 Sout 8af 71a- F: 2 Nov'01 Sout 7af 69a- D:
3383　MRS BROWN 9 [2]3-9-7 (55) S Sanders 7/1: 35605: Handy, led briefly bef 2f out, wknd dist.　½　53a
2589　CUMBRIAN PRINCESS 42 [9]7-9-7 (45) R Thomas(5) 10/1: 0113636: Nvr nrr than mid-div: 6 wk abs.　2½　39a
3052　MADAME MARIE 23 [13]4-9-11 (49) Lisa Jones(3) 12/1: 0020607: Nvr nrr than mid-div: btr 2857.　1　41a
3492+　ELLOVAMUL 5 [7]4-10-1 (6ex) (53) M Savage(5) 8/1: 5-404018: Mid-div, no impress fnl 2f: qck reapp.　¾　43a
3295　HILARIOUS 12 [14]4-9-6 P (44) Lucy Russell(7) 25/1: 0-545649: Bhd, nvr a factor.　hd　33a
2910　RYANS BLISS 29 [10]4-9-6 (44) R Miles(3) 16/1: 2532000: 10th: Cl-up wide 1m, wknd: btr 1712.　2　30a
3492　ESTIMATE 5 [8]4-9-7 vis (45) S Whitworth 11/2: 0100220: 11th: Al in rear: qck reapp: btr 3492 & 2993.　3　27a
917　ARTZOLA 129 [4]4-9-12 (50) E Ahern 33/1: 050-00: 12th: Led, hdd bef 2f out, fdd: long abs.　4　26a
3505　HOLLY ROSE 4 [3]5-9-12 (50) J F Egan 7/1: 4044200: 13th: Cl-up 7f, fdd: tchd 10/1: btr 3052.　18　4a
3288　FIGURA 14 [5]6-10-0 (52) S W Kelly 16/1: 5000050: 14th: Al bhd: btr 3288.　7　0a
14 Ran　Time 2m 10.37(7.57)　Owned: Mr J J Bridger　Trained: Liphook

Official Going Firm ALL TIMES SLOW

3606	2.05 European Breeders Fund Thomas Lord Maiden Stakes 2yo (D)				
	£6214　£1912　£956	5f str	Firm	Slow　Stands Side	

2774　TURNAROUND 35 [6] Mrs J R Ramsden 2-9-0　I Mongan 4/7 FAV: 321: Trkd ldr trav well & led over 1f　　82+
out, readily asserted, val 3L+: hvly bckd at odds-on, op 10/11: eff at 5f/6f on firm & gd/soft grnd, easy or
stiff/gall trk: found this straightforward, potentially useful: see 2774 & 2241.
　　CARNIVORE 0 [3] T D Barron 2-9-0　Darren Williams 11/2: 2: ch c Zafonic - Ermine (Cadeaux　2½　72
Genereux)　Dwelt & held up, hdwy 2f out & chsd wnr ins last, al held: 58,000gns May foal, half-brother to a dual 6f
juv wnr, dam a 1m 3yo scorer: eff at 5f, shaped as if 6f shld suit: acts on firm grnd & an easy trk: encouraging.
2902　PETERS DELITE 29 [7] R A Fahey 2-9-0　P Hanagan 16/1: 03: b c Makbul - Steadfast Elite　½　70
(Glenstal)　Chsd ldrs, rdn & kept on from over 1f out, no ch with wnr: left debut bhd: 31,000gns Mar foal, brother
to 5/6f juv wnrs, dam a 5/6f juv wnr: eff at 5f on firm grnd.
3374　CHILALI 9 [4] A Berry 2-8-9 (60) Dale Gibson 14/1: 0330364: Led till over 1f out, fdd.　2　59
3411　ALGORITHM 8 [2]2-8-9　P M Quinn 20/1: 065: Held up, eff halfway, no prog dist: see 3258.　2　53
1752　KERNY 77 [1]2-9-0　G Hind 66/1: 06: b c Rossini - Queen of Sweden (Solid Illusion)　Chsd ldrs　3　49

till over 1f out, 11 wk abs: turf bow: 21,000gns 2yo, Mar first foal: dam plcd abroad as a 3yo.

2889 **WAYWARD SHOT** 29 [5]2-9-0 T Lucas 12/1: 57: Dwelt & al bhd: btr 2889.		nk	48
HALLA SAN 0 [8]2-9-0 L Goncalves 25/1: 8: b c Halling - St Radegund (Green Desert) Dwelt & al bhd: longer priced stablemate of wnr: 37,000gns Mar foal, half-brother to a 1m juv wnr, dam a 7f 3yo scorer.		1½	43
FEEL THE NEED 0 [9]2-9-0 P Mulrennan(5) 33/1: 9: Dwelt & sn bhd, t.o. on debut.		29	0
2360 **MELANDRE** 50 [10]2-8-9 (64) M Lawson(5) 6/1: 6045W: Ref to enter stalls, withdrawn: 7 wk abs.			0

10 Ran   Time 58.68 (1.68)   Owned: Mr J Musgrave   Trained: Thirsk

---

3607   **2.35 Hertel Nursery Handicap Stakes 2yo   (C)**   **[90]**
£9705   £2986   £1493   **5f**   **Firm**   **Slow**   Stands Side

3432 **WISE WAGER** 7 [1] R A Fahey 2-8-4 (66) P Hanagan 7/1: 23331: Led after 1f & crossed to stands rail fnl 2f, rdn & styd on well ins last: first win: suited by 5f on firm, gd & fibresand, prob any trk: likes to race with/force the pace, given a fine ride today: see 3432, 1652.			77
3432 **KATIE BOO** 7 [9] A Berry 2-9-2 (78) G Hind 6/1: 3213522: Dwelt, sn chsd ldrs, briefly short of room 2f out, rdn & styd on, al held by wnr: fin and of today's wnr latest: see 3432, 2711 & 2442.		1¼	84
3343* **BRAG** 10 [8] R Charlton 2-9-4 (80) D Sweeney 15/8 FAV: 24013: Chsd ldrs when short of room 2f out, kept on well cl-home, nrst fin: acts on firm & fast grnd: needs 6f now in similar: see 3343.		1¼	82
3115* **KEY SECRET** 21 [3] M L W Bell 2-9-5 (81) Hayley Turner(5) 5/1: 1114: Held up towards centre, styd on for press but nvr able to land a blow: unbeaten run ended but not disgraced from awkward low draw.		hd	82
2883 **AFRICAN BREEZE** 30 [6]2-9-5 (81) Dean McKeown 14/1: 04145: Dwelt, rear, eff to press ldrs from dist, hung left & no extra ins last: see 2883 & 2547.		shd	82
3227* **PRO TEMPORE** 15 [5]2-8-8 (70) I Mongan 14/1: 416: Chsd ldrs till dist: btr 3227.		1	68
3374 **FORZEEN** 9 [4]2-9-7 (83) M Fenton 4/1: 3423147: Held up, rdn & nvr able to chall: btr 3374, 3284.		½	79
3374 **OUR LOUIS** 9 [10]2-7-12 (6oh) (54) P M Quinn 66/1: 0541508: Led 1f & styd handy, hung left & btn dist.		3½	45
3271 **TOWN HOUSE** 14 [7]2-8-11 (73) Dale Gibson 20/1: 5021009: Cl-up, wknd qckly from halfway: btr1987.		7	39
3239 **NOODLES** 15 [2]2-8-11 (73) J Carroll 33/1: 0200: 10th: Slow away & sn struggling rear on h'cap bow.		4	29

10 Ran   Time 58.81 (1.81)   Owned: P Timmins & J Rhodes   Trained: Malton

---

3608   **3.10 Ekos Consulting Handicap Stakes 3yo+ 0-95   (C)**   **[94]**
£9588   £2950   £1475   **1m**   **Firm**   **V Slow**   Inside

3137 **EFIDIUM** 20 [3] N Bycroft 6-8-2 (68) P Hanagan 9/1: 3153541: Held up, hdwy to lead ins last, rdn out: suited by 7f/1m on firm, gd/soft & fibresand: v tough & genuine: continues to prog: see 2057.			75
3428 **RAPHAEL** 7 [8] T D Easterby 5-9-0 (80) A Mullen(7) 5/2 FAV: 3040222: Handy & led over 2f out till ins last, no extra: well bckd: continues to run well: see 3428, 3223 & 1474 (7f).		1	84
3210 **ALCHEMIST MASTER** 16 [6] R M Whitaker 5-8-6 p (72) Dean McKeown 9/1: 2211463: Trkd ldrs, styd on for press, not pace of wnr: 9lb higher than last win, likes Pontefract: see 2986.		1	74
3423 **ADOBE** 7 [2] W M Brisbourne 9-8-0 (66) B Swarbrick(5) 9/1: 3442004: Rear, kept on wide, nvr able to land blow: slipping to handy mark, likes Bath: see 3142, 2010.		hd	67
3423* **HARRY POTTER** 7 [4]5-9-0 vis (80) Darren Williams 7/2: 0603115: Held up when short of room halfway, onepace for press fnl 2f: see 3423.		½	80
3428 **SEA STORM** 7 [1]6-8-13 p (77) L Enstone(3) 8/1: 0100656: Chsd ldrs, no extra over 1f out: btr 3428.		1	77
3388 **ONLYTIME WILL TELL** 8 [5]6-9-11 (91) J Carroll 9/2: 0-005427: Led till over 2f out, fdd dist.		3½	82
3119 **MONTMARTRE** 21 [7]4-9-12 (92) P Mulrennan(5) 16/1: 23110-08: Cl up over 5f, wknd.		9	67

8 Ran   Time 1m 39.56 (4.16)   Owned: Hambleton Racing Partnership   Trained: Malton

---

3609   **3.45 Whitby Selling Handicap Stakes Ladies Race 3yo+ 35-55   (F)**   **[40]**
£4241   £1305   £653   **6f**   **Firm**   **V Slow**   Stands Side

3191 **ZIETZIG** 17 [13] D Nicholls 7-10-0 (40) Miss Kelly Harrison(3) 7/1: 0000561: Trkd ldrs stands side & led ins last, rdn clr: no bid: suited by 6/7f on firm & fast grnd, handles gd/soft: see 1635.			51
3527 **DANAKIM** 3 [19] J R Weymes 7-9-13 (39) Ms C Williams 13/2 FAV: 0000042: Led stands side, hdd ins last, sn held by wnr: qck reapp: can win similar: see 1988.		2½	41
2958 **FRIMLEYS MATTERRY** 27 [18] R E Barr 4-10-10 (50) Miss V Barr(7) 33/1: 0666503: Chsd ldrs stands side, drvn & styd on, no threat to wnr: acts on firm, fast & both AWs: see 2125.		¾	50
3229 **REDOUBTABLE** 15 [4] D W Chapman 13-10-13 (53) Miss H Cuthbert(5) 11/1: 0021604: Held up far side, hdwy & led that group over 1f out, al held by ldrs stands side ins last: finnise from unfav'd far side group.		nk	52+
3159 **ACE MA VAHRA** 19 [2]6-10-0 bl (40) Miss S Brotherton 14/1: 0306335: Sn prom far side & chall 2f out, onepace dist: acts on firm, fast & fibresand: see 2398, 677.		shd	39
3436 **AFRICAN SPUR** 7 [17]4-10-7 vis (47) Miss D Allman(5) 10/1: 5000046: Hndy stands side, no extra dist.		3½	35
3104 **GRAND VIEW** 21 [16]8-9-10 p (36) Miss Dawn Rankin(5) 33/1: 2100007: Nvr nrr than mid div stands side.		½	22
3180 **TORRENT** 18 [14]9-11-0 bl (54) Miss Lynsey Hanna 7/1: 0001208: Mid-div stands side, rdn & no impress over 1f out: btr 2702 & 2524 (5f).		nk	39
3289 **SABANA** 14 [5]6-10-7 p (47) Miss E J Jones 8/1: 0000169: Trkd ldrs far side & led that group 2f out, sn fdd: op 12/1: btr 3104.		½	30
3102 **ZAMYATINA** 21 [7]5-9-13 (39) Miss A Elsey 20/1: 0000500: 10th: Mid-div far side, no impress fnl 2f.		¾	20
3353 **BEYOND CALCULATION** 10 [12]10-10-11 bl (51) Mrs S Bosley 10/1: 0404450: 11th: Prom stands side 5f.		1	29
2615 **THE GAMBLER** 40 [8]4-10-8 p (48) Miss L Ellison(3) 25/1: 0020000: 12th: Mid-div far side, hdwy & led group 2f out, sn btn: 6 wk abs: btr 1553.		1¼	22
3191 **OLD BAILEY** 17 [3]4-10-3 p (43) Mrs N Wilson(3) 10/1: 1000550: 13th: Far side, nvr on terms: btr 3191.		¾	15
2951 **BLUES PRINCESS** 28 [9]4-10-4 bl (44) Miss V Tunnicliffe(5) 20/1: 000-0000: 14th: Led far side 4f, fdd.		3½	5
3575 **BELLS BOYS** 1 [10]5-9-11 p (37) Miss Charmaine O'Neill 16/1: 04033000: 15th: Mid-div stands side, btn 2f out, unplcd yesterday.		6	0
3478} **DISTANT KING** 358 [1]11-10-3 (43) Miss J Coward(2) 33/1: 000/650-0: 16th: Chsd ldr far side 4f, fdd.		4	0
1975 **WILHEHECKASLIKE** 17 [15]3-9-8 bl (35) Miss W Gibson(7) 66/1: 00-00060: 17th: Al bhd stands side.		hd	0
3324 **BLADES EDGE** 11 [20]3-10-0 VIS (45) Dr H McCarthy(7) 25/1: 3000000: 18th: V slow away & al t.o.		14	0

18 Ran   Time 1m 12.56 (3.06)   Owned: Mrs C L Swiers   Trained: Thirsk

THIRSK

SATURDAY 31.07.04   Lefthand, Flat, Oval Track

3610

4.20 Skipton Castle Maiden Stakes Fillies 3yo+   (D)
£5590 £1720 £860   7f   Firm   V Slow   Inside

3346 **MOON LEGEND 10** [8] W Jarvis 3-9-0 (66) Hayley Turner(5) 4/1: 06-0301: Held up, hdwy from halfway,   **71**
rdn & hung left over 1f out but styd on for press to narrowly assert cl-home: well bckd: eff at 7f, 1m+ shld suit:
acts on firm grnd, easy trk: see 2864 (h'cap).
   FASCINATION STREET 23 [7] M A Jarvis 3-9-0 (69) M Henry 8/1: 6-6502: b f Mujadil - Loon   nk **70**
(Kaldoun) Sn handy & narrow lead from 2f out, hdd well ins last, just held: op 5/1: clr rem: ex-French, unplcd
prev at up to 1m: eff over an easy 7f on firm ground.
2885 **ELTIHAAB 30** [2] Saeed bin Suroor 3-9-0 J Carroll 5/4 FAV: 03: Led aftr 1f till 2f out, btn   5 **60**
dist: hvly bckd, op 13/8: well btn debut prev: handles firm grnd, definitely one of stable's lesser lights.
4536} **MAGARI 304** [5] J G Given 3-9-0 M Fenton 6/1: 3-4: b f Royal Applause - Thatcher's Era (Never So   5 **50**
Bold) Handy, ch over 2f out, sn fdd: reapp: promise sole '03 start (rtd 62+, mdn): half-sister plcd at 7f, dam
styd up to 12f: eff over a stiff 7f on gd grnd.
2181 **PAY TIME 58** [6]5-9-7 (34) P Mulrennan(5) 100/1: 000-6005: Held up, rdn & no prog fnl 2f, 2 mth abs.   1½ **47**
   FIZZY POP 0 [10]5-9-7 L Enstone(3) 50/1: 6: Rear & bhd halfway, nvr a factor, 5 mth jumps abs.   3 **41**
2945 **ESTOILLE 28** [4]3-9-0 t Andrew Webb(7) 66/1: 0007: Trkd ldrs, rdn & btn 2f out, longer trip.   nk **40**
2849 **MISS CHANCELOT 31** [3]3-9-0 R Lappin 66/1: 08: Keen & led 1f, prom till 3f out, t.o..   11 **22**
365 **ELUSIVE KITTY 203** [1]3-9-0 T Mr J Mongan 7/2: 5255-6R: Ref to race: op 3/1, t-strap, abs.   **0**
9 Ran   Time 1m 2733 (4.43)   Owned: Mr Eugene Lismonde   Trained: Newmarket

---

3611

4.55 Richmond Castle Handicap Stakes 4yo+ 0-75 (E)   **[73]**
£4115 £1266 £633   2m   Firm   Slow   Inside

2685 **BEST PORT 37** [9] J Parkes 8-9-3 (62) M Lawson(5) 9/2: 4-010161: Held up, hdwy 3f out & rdn to   **67**
chall over 1f out, gamely prevailed on line in a thrilling fin, all out: suited by 14f/2m: acts on soft, loves
firm/fast grnd: v tough & genuine: see 2105.
2963 **MOST DEFINITELY 27** [7] T D Easterby 4-9-1 (60) A Mullen(7) 10/1: 222-2062: Held up, hdwy when   hd **65**
briefly short of room over 2f out, rdn to chall ins last & narrow lead cl-home, just hdd line: on soft: see 2444.
3387 **MOONSHINE BEACH 8** [3] P W Hiatt 6-9-4 (63) L Fletcher(3) 7/1: 54P1103: Handy & led over 3f out,   hd **67**
ev ch ins last, just hdd cl-home: rider received 1 day whip ban: acts on firm, gd & polytrack.
3105 **SONOMA 21** [4] M L W Bell 4-9-3 (62) Hayley Turner(5) 4/1 FAV: 0600144: Chsd ldrs, rdn & ch over   2 **64**
1f out, no extra ins last: acts on firm & fast grnd: see 2632.
3181 **GREENWICH MEANTIME 18** [10]4-9-13 (72) L Goncalves 16/1: 3003005: Trkd ldr & keen early, rdn & no   4 **69**
extra over 1f out: op 12/1: btr 2444 (14f).
2163 **BLACKTHORN 59** [8]5-8-12 (57) I Mongan 11/2: 02-403366: Dwelt & held up, drvn & btn 2f out: abs.   8 **49**
2444 **FREEDOM NOW 47** [1]6-9-9 (68) M Fenton 20/1: 60-00607: Led till 3f out, sn btn: 6 wk jumps abs.   8 **54**
3181 **CELTIC BLAZE 18** [2]5-8-11 t p (56) P Mulrennan(5) 10/1: 13060-38: Held up, drvn & btn 3f out: btr 3181.   22 **24**
2276 **ACADEMY 54** [6]9-8-12 (57) J Carroll 11/1: 0240-209: Rear & lost tch halfway, t.o.: abs: btr 1870.   1 **24**
3249 **PADDY MUL 15** [5]7-8-3 t (48) J Bramhill 11/2: 533144P: Mid-div, btn 2f out, eased & p.u. lame ins fnl 1f.   **0**
10 Ran   Time 3m 26.96(4.16)   Owned: Mr M Wormald   Trained: Malton

---

NEWMARKET

SATURDAY 31.07.04   Righthand, Stiff, Galloping Track

Official Going GOOD/FIRM.

3612

1.45 Helen Rollason Cancer Care Centre Appeal Handicap Stakes 3yo 0-80 (D)   **[84]**
£6838 £2104 £1052   7f str   Good/Firm 21   +21 Fast   Far Side

3421 **ATTUNE 7** [5] B J Meehan 3-9-7 BL (77) J F McDonald(3) 14/1: 4-401001: Trkd ldrs, led 2f out, rdn   **87**
clr: top-weight: eff at 7f/1m on gd & fast: likes a gall trk & woken up by blnks today: see 1770.
2427 **GRANSTON 48** [4] J D Bethell 3-9-5 (75) T Quinn 7/2 JT FAV: 1-316602: Nvr far away, kept on fnl   3 **78**
1f but no ch with wnr: op 5/1, 7 wk abs: bck to form, runs well fresh: see 1176.
3346 **SCARLETT ROSE 10** [1] Dr J D Scargill 3-8-9 (65) C Lowther 9/2: 360-6033: Nvr far away, sltly   shd **67**
short of room dist, kept on: stays a gall 1m: see 3346.
3378 **BRIGHT SUN 9** [3] N Tinkler 3-9-2 (72) Kim Tinkler 4/1: 0043034: Slowly away, styd on late, nvr   ¾ **73**
dngrs: ran in snatches today: see 3378.
3219 **GELLER 16** [2]3-8-9 (65) P Dobbs 10/1: 04-54005: Chsd ldrs, short of room 2f out, sn btn.   5 **56**
3283 **SPIN KING 14** [6]3-9-4 VIS (74) J Mackay 7/2 JT FAV: 0403406: Led till 2f out, wknd: nicely bckd: 2½ **60**
too keen today in first time visor: see 1496 (1m here).
3346 **LA PUCE 10** [7]3-8-6 T (62) Rachel Costello(7) 20/1: 0114607: Dwelt, nvr nr ldrs: tried a t-strap.   nk **47**
2950 **MIND ALERT 28** [8]3-8-11 (67) W Supple 8/1: 006-0208: Held up, nvr a factor: twice 2609.   nk **51**
8 Ran   Time 1m 23.84 (u0.06)   Owned: Wyck Hall Stud   Trained: Upper Lambourn

---

3613

2.20 Listed Fantasy Island Themed Family Resort Attraction E B F Stubbs Stakes 4yo+   (A)
£19040 £7040 £3520   1m str   Good/Firm 21   -09 Slow   Far Side

884 **PAWN BROKER 133** [1] D R C Elsworth 7-8-12 (105) W Supple 9/1: 66025-01: ch g Selkirk - Dime Bag   **109**
(High Line) Held up, hdwy dist, fin strongly to lead cl-home, won going away: long abs: '03 stks wnr, also rnr-up
in a Gr 3: eff at 1m, stays 10f well, has tried further: acts on firm & hvy grnd, any trk: has tried blnks, seems
btr without: runs well fresh: smart, only twice raced in '04.
2 Oct'03 Newm 9g/f 111-(105) A: 1 Mar'03 Asco 10g/f 109-(102) C: 2 Apr'01 Kemp 10hvy 117- A:
2915 **MINE 28** [5] J D Bethell 6-8-12 vis (108) T Quinn 6/4 FAV: 6-231152: Trkd ldr, went on ent fnl 1f   1 **106**
& kicked for home, not pace to repel wnr cl-home: well bckd: prefers big fields/fast run h'caps: see 2915 & 2489.
2252 **SUBLIMITY 56** [2] Sir Michael Stoute 4-9-2 t (110) S Drowne 7/2: 44-10403: Led till ent fnl 1f, no   1¼ **107**
extra: 8 wk abs: change of tactics & back to form: see 1862 & 1349.

3199* **ALWAYS ESTEEMED** 17 [3] G Wragg 4-8-12 (95) F Norton 6/1: 0-200414: Chsd ldrs, onepcd fnl 1f: hd   **103$**
imprvd run in this btr grade: see 3199 (AW).
2757   **TARJMAN** 35 [4]4-8-12 (111) T P Queally 7/2: 11234-05: Chsd ldrs, rdn & btn fnl 1f: yet to   1   **101**
recapture last season's progressive form, see 2757.
5 Ran   Time 1m 39.61 (2.41)   Owned: Mr Raymond Tooth   Trained: Whitsbury

---

3614   2.50 Siemens Smart Home Technology Nursery Handicap Stakes 2yo (B)   [100]
£13754 £4232 £2116   **6f str**   **Good/Firm 21**   **-05 Slow**   Far Side

3122* **TRANSACTION** 21 [5] J M P Eustace 2-8-13 (85) S Drowne 10/1: 3211: Held up, imprvd 1.5f out, led   **93**
ins fnl 1f, held on v gamely: eff at 6f on gd, fast grnd & polytrack: likes a gall trk: v tough & progressive.
3521   **PIDDIES PRIDE** 3 [10] P S McEntee 2-7-12 (70) F P Ferris(3) 12/1: 6641132: Led till halfway,   hd   **76**
regained lead 2f out till ins fnl 1f, rallied & only just btn: qck reapp: fine run, v tough performer.
2513   **SPACE SHUTTLE** 44 [4] T D Easterby 2-8-13 bl (85) W Supple 15/2: 32133: Keen in rear, fin well,   1¼   **87**
short of room cl-home: 6 wk abs: worth a try over 7f judged on this: see 2236 (first time blnks).
3418* **ENCANTO** 7 [1] J S Moore 2-8-11 (83) Derek Nolan(7) 10/1: 0622214: Held up, styd on under press   ½   **84**
fnl 1f, nvr nrr: worth a try at 7f: see 3418 (fill mdn).
3467   **SACRED NUTS** 6 [8]2-9-7 (93) J Mackay 3/1 FAV: 51135: Chsd ldrs, onepcd fnl 1f: well bckd, top-weight.   1¼   **90**
3406   **RED CHAIRMAN** 8 [6]2-8-10 (82) T P Queally 4/1: 0546: Prom, led halfway till 2f out, wknd fnl 1f: 1   **76**
bckd from 11/2: showed plenty of pace, see 3406.
3127   **NORCROFT** 21 [11]2-8-8 (80) J F McDonald(3) 40/1: 216007: Dwelt, hdwy 1.5f out, nvr dngrs: shd   **74**
3488   **HIGH CHART** 5 [2]2-8-10 (82) A McCarthy 33/1: 144038: Chsd ldrs 5f, sn btn.   1¾   **71**
2989* **PROSPECT COURT** 25 [3]2-8-11 (83) T Quinn 8/1: 03019: Speed 4f, wknd: btr 2989.   5   **57**
3212   **SAFENDONSEABISCUIT** 16 [1]2-8-6 BL (78) F Norton 14/1: 533420: 10th: Chsd ldrs 4f, wknd: blnks.   ¾   **49**
3290   **GENNIE BOND** 12 [9]2-8-7 (79) P Dobbs 7/1: 4320: 11th: Chsd ldrs, btn 2f out: btr 3290.   nk   **49**
11 Ran   Time 1m 12.56 (1.56)   Owned: Mr George Darling   Trained: Newmarket

---

3615   3.25 Lawshall Handicap Stakes 3yo+ 0-90 (C)   [88]
£13624 £4192 £2096   **1m2f**   **Good/Firm 21**   **-14 Slow**   Centre

3336   **BARRY ISLAND** 10 [10] D R C Elsworth 5-8-13 (73) J Mackay 14/1: 0030641: Chsd ldrs, imprvd to   **81**
lead dist, styd on strongly, drvn out, suited by 10f, stays 12f: acts on fast & firm, likes polytrack/Lingfield.
3325   **JEEPSTAR** 11 [7] T D Easterby 4-8-11 (71) W Supple 9/2: 53-00622: Led till dist, rallied fnl 1f &   ½   **77**
not btn far: op 11/2: another solid run, see 3325.
3070   **SILVALINE** 22 [4] T Keddy 5-9-6 (80) C Haddon(7) 14/1: 0601103: Chsd ldr, ev ch till no extra   1½   **83**
cl-home: back to form, see 2896 (gd/soft).
3421   **HELLO ITS ME** 7 [1] H J Collingridge 3-9-2 (86) M Tebbutt 16/1: 31-20254: Nvr far away, onepcd   ½   **88**
ins fnl 1f: reportedly hung right: see 2903 (1m).
2560   **TRUENO** 42 [5]5-9-10 (84) T P Queally 16/1: 524-1205: Keen in rear, styd on, nvr dngrs: 6 wk   ½   **84**
abs, top-weight: rcd too keenly today, see 2197 (gd grnd).
3256   **KENS DREAM** 15 [6]5-9-8 (82) P McCabe 7/1: 5/-034146: Hld up, hdwy/short of room dist, no impress.   hd   **83**
3295* **KARAOKE** 12 [9]4-8-8 (68) F Norton 12/1: 2000317: Held up, nvr a factor: btr 3295.   2   **66**
3358   **STRETTON** 9 [2]9-9-3 (83) T Quinn 8/1: 6003448: Held up, nvr nr ldrs.   1   **74**
3358   **ADAIKALI** 9 [3]3-9-3 (87) S Drowne 2/1 FAV: 0-02129: Keen in rear, prog 2f out, btn fnl 1f: well   2   **80**
bckd: reportedly fin distressed, much btr 3358 & 2277.
3430   **OLIVIA ROSE** 7 [8]5-9-9 (83) P Dobbs 12/1: 2314130: 10th: Chsd ldrs, btn 1.5f out: btr 3260 (g/s).   3   **71**
10 Ran   Time 2m 05.44 (3.54)   Owned: Mr Matthew Green   Trained: Whitsbury

---

3616   4.00 Hotel Felix Cambridge E B F Maiden Stakes Fillies 2yo (D)
£4813 £1481 £741   **7f str**   **Good/Firm 21**   **-36 Slow**   Far Side

3234   **ROAD RAGE** 15 [2] E A L Dunlop 2-8-11   T Quinn 8/11 FAV: 31: Chsd ldr, went on 2f out, styd on   **83**
well despite drifting right, rdn out: well bckd at odds on: confirmed recent debut promise, eff over a gall 7f,
shld stay 1m+ gvn time: acts on fast grnd: see 3234 (C/D).
     ELIZABETHAN AGE   [4] D R Loder 2-8-11   T P Queally 9/2: 2: b f King's Best - Dolydille (Dolphin   shd   **82**
Street) Chsd ldrs, ev ch fnl 1f, just btn in a thrilling fin on debut: drifted from 11/4: 85,000gns Mar first
foal: dam a mid-dist wnr, sire a high-class miler: eff over a stiff/gall 7f on fast grnd: sure to learn from this.
     CRYSTALLINE 15 [3] D R Loder 2-8-11   A Beech(3) 8/1: 3: b f Green Desert - Crown of Light (Mtoto)   1¼   **79+**
Held up, styd on fnl 1f, nrst fin on debut: tchd 12/1 & longer priced stablemate of rnr-up: Apr foal, half-sister
to mid-dist wnr Balkan Knight: dam a high-class mid-dist performer, sire a top-class sprinter/miler: eff over a
gall 7f on fast grnd, relish 1m+: v pleasing, improve.
     MOKARABA [1] J L Dunlop 2-8-11   S W Kelly 16/1: 4: ch f Unfuwain - Muhaba (Mr Prospector)   shd   **78**
Slowly away, recovered to chase ldrs, styd on fnl 1f on debut: op 12/1: Feb foal, dam styd mid-dists: sire a
top-class mid-dist performer: mid-dist bred for next term & sure to improve on this gvn time.
     THAKAFAAT [6]2-8-11   W Supple 7/1: 5: b f Unfuwain - Frappe (Inchinor) Slowly away, styd on   shd   **78**
well fnl 1f, nrst fin on debut: 160,000gns Feb foal: dam a 6f 2yo scorer, sire a top-class mid-dists performer.
     TOHAMA [3]2-8-11   S Drowne 16/1: 6: Prom, hmpd after 2f & lost pl, styd on late on debut.   shd   **78**
2876   **GARANCE** 30 [7]2-8-11   P Dobbs 16/1: 07: Led till 2f out, no extra.   1   **76**
7 Ran   Time 1m 27.93 (4.03)   Owned: Cliveden Stud   Trained: Newmarket

---

3617   4.35 Helen Rollason Live Well Experience Classified Stakes 3yo+ 0-90 (C)
£9471 £2914 £1457   **1m4f**   **Good/Firm 21**   **-09 Slow**   Centre

3278   **TAWNY WAY** 14 [4] W Jarvis 4-9-1 (86) T Quinn 14/1: 0-512601: Led till 3f out, regained lead   **93**
dist, held on gamely cl-home, all out: eff at 9/12f on gd & fast grnd, poss soft: handles a sharpish or stiff trk:
likes to run-up with/force the pace, v game today: see 1381.
2737* **WAIT FOR THE WILL** 36 [6] G L Moore 8-9-4 bl (90) A Quinn(5) 7/2 FAV: 6-000112: Chsd ldrs, went on   hd   **95**
2f out till collared dist, rallied gamely & only just btn: well bckd: in gd form but hit front too sn.
2582   **HIGHLAND GAMES** 42 [1] J G Given 4-9-4 (87) W Supple 9/2: 0-202453: Chsd ldrs, imprvd to lead 3f   1   **93**

out till 2f out, not qckn ins fnl 1f: nicely bckd, 6 wk abs: turn shld not be far away, see 2582.

3444 LODGER 7 [2] J Noseda 4-9-5 (91) S W Kelly 8/1: 3214-064: Prom, outpcd 3f out, rallied fnl 1f.	¾	90
1172 MILLVILLE 108 [3]4-9-4 (85) M Tebbutt 9/2: 101105: Held up, nvr nr ldrs: long abs: see 877 (AW).	3	86
3256* GOLD RING 15 [7]4-9-5 (91) S Carson 5/1: 2365316: Front rank, ev ch till wknd 1.5f out:	¾	85

reportedly unsuited by this fast grnd tho' won well enough on a fast surface in 3256.

3444 ARGONAUT 7 [5]4-9-4 (89) S Drowne 9/2: 31-637: Held up, nvr nrs ldrs: see 3444.	½	83
1344} HALLAND 454 [8]6-9-4 (82) Steven Harrison(7) 28/1: 0212//00-8: ch g Halling - Northshiel	nk	82

(Northfields) Held up, some hdwy 2f out, sn btn & fin last on comeback: 3 month jumps abs, rnr-up in a mdn hdle on debut (rtd 112h, eff at 2m1f on fast grnd): modest on both '03 Flat starts: missed prev term, '01 h'cap wnr for G Wragg, also 2L 2nd in Cambridgeshire: eff at 7/10f on firm, soft & any trk: now with N Littmoden.
2 Oct'01 Newm 9g/f 85-93 B: 1 Aug'01 Newb 10fm 94-87 C: 2 Jul'01 Newm 8g/f 89-81 C:
8 Ran Time 2m 31.83 (3.63) Owned: Rams Racing Club Trained: Newmarket

---

3618 5.10 Poslingford Handicap Stakes 3yo 0-70 (E) **[74]**
£3549 £1092 £546 1m4f Good/Firm 21 -19 Slow Centre

5016} WORCESTER LODGE 268 [15] R Charlton 3-9-2 (62) S Drowne 8/1: 040-1: Prom, led ins fnl 1f, hands		71+

& heels, going away: op 11/2 on reapp: lightly rcd in '03, mdn 4th at best (rtd 61), since been gelded: relished step up to 12f on fast grnd, 14f will suit: runs well fresh: unexposed, plenty more to come, win more races.

3367* INCHPAST 9 [3] M H Tompkins 3-9-2 bl (62) A Quinn(3) 9/2 FAV: 50-00412: Chsd ldrs, short of room	2	65

1.5f out, kept on cl-home but not reach wnr: gd run in this tougher grade, see 3367.

3108 JOLIZERO 21 [7] P W Chapple Hyam 3-8-11 (57) Derek Nolan(7) 6/1: 000-403: Chsd ldrs, went on 2f	shd	60

out till collared ins fnl 1f, no extra: bckd from 10/1: eff over a gall 12f on fast grnd: can find similar, see 3108.

3385 SCARRABUS 9 [9] B G Powell 3-9-5 (65) G Baker 25/1: 60-40634: Held up, hdwy to chall 2f out, not	1	66

qckn ins fnl 1f: stays a gall 12f on fast grnd: see 1140.

3419 CHARA 7 [13]3-9-5 (65) J F McDonald(3) 16/1: 5-310555: Held up, prog when short of room 3f out,	1¼	63

nrst fin: did not get the run of today's race: see 3419.

3108 TRILEMMA 21 [10]3-9-2 (62) J Mackay 20/1: 0006-006: Held up, styd on late, nvr dngrs: prob stays 12f.	¾	58
3192 SIEGFRIEDS NIGHT 17 [17]3-9-2 (62) A Beech(3) 9/1: 3355307: Chsd ldrs, onepcd fnl 1.5f.	nk	57
2960 SHARADI 7 [4]3-9-0 (60) M Tebbutt 10/1: 0456-008: Front rank, ev ch till hmpd dist, wknd &	½	54

eased: lost any ch when hmpd: worth another ch, see 2960.

2660 PANGLOSS 38 [14]3-9-7 BL (67) P Dobbs 14/1: 300-3059: Keen in rear, nvr a factor: blnks.	6	52
3334* ELLINA 10 [8]3-9-7 (67) R Price 10/1: 0464010: 10th: Slowly away, nvr a factor on hat-trick bid.	½	51
3201 POLAR DANCER 17 [1]3-8-13 (59) W Supple 7/1: 063-030: 11th: Rear & hmpd halfway, nvr a factor.	7	33
3454 NICK THE SILVER 7 [16]3-8-11 (57) S Carson 33/1: 0-060r00: 12th: Keen & chsd ldrs, btn 2f out.	hd	31
3161 ITS BLUE CHIP 19 [2]3-9-5 (65) Paul Eddery 14/1: 1464100: 13th: Slow away, al rear: op 20/1.	½	38
1514 DEVIOUS AYERS 7 [12]3-9-3 (63) S W Kelly 11/1: 3-400: 14th: Led till 3f out, wknd: abs, longer trip.	nk	35
2386 GREEK STAR 49 [11]3-8-2 (48) F Norton 22/1: 0-400: 15th: Held up, al bhnd: 7 wk abs.	1½	18

3312 Savannah River 12 [5]3-7-13 t(45) D Kinsella 14/1:0 3383 Vrisaki 9 [6]3-8-0 (46) F P Ferris(3) 28/1:0
17 Ran Time 2m 33.03(4.83) Owned: Lady Rothschild Trained: Beckhampton

---

Official Going GOOD/FIRM.

3619 2.00 Gr3 Vodafone Stakes Registered As The Lillie Langtry Stakesfillies 3yo+ (A)
£29000 £11000 £5500 1m6f Firm 11 +01 Fast Inside

3458* ASTROCHARM 6 [7] M H Tompkins 5-9-6 (83) N Callan 12/1: 1051211: Held up, hdwy & short of room		106

over 3f out, hdwy 2f out, led ins last, drvn out: qck reapp: v eff at 12f, relished first start at 14f: acts on firm & gd, any trk: thriving & most progressive this term, much imprvd here & unexposed over staying trips.

2946* PONGEE 28 [5] L M Cumani 4-9-11 (107) J Fortune 11/8 FAV: 110-3112: In tch, hdwy to lead 3f out,	¾	109

hdd 2f out, sn led again till ins last, no pace of wnr cl-home: hvly bckd, clr of rem: prob ran close to best & styd first attempt at 14f: on the upgrade: see 2946.

2946 SUMMITVILLE 28 [2] J G Given 4-9-6 (104) L Dettori 3/1: 302-3263: Held up, gd hdwy over 3f out,	4	98

led briefly 2f out, wknd tamely fnl 1f: nicely bckd: longer trip but lacking smart form of last term: see 1684.

3278 FÉAT 14 [6] J H M Gosden 3-8-6 (90) K McEvoy 21/1: 31664: Trkd ldr, lost place after 6f, hdwy	2	95

to lead briefly over 3f out, sn wknd: reportedly slipped on top bend, joc received a 2-day careless riding ban: up in class & trip: see 2124 (mdn).

3405* DARING AIM 8 [4]3-8-6 K Fallon 10/1: 4-515: Reluctant to enter stalls, in tch, hdwy to chall 3f	3	86

out, sn no extra & flashed tail: moody eff but not disgraced on this step up in trip & class: see 2405 (mdn).

3278 PORTRAIT OF A LADY 14 [3]3-8-6 (93) W Ryan 9/2: 3131136: Led till over 3f out, wknd qckly, t.o.:	dist	0

much btr expected after 3278 (12f, List), 2923.

2761 BALLERINA SUPREMA 35 [1]4-9-6 (85) D Holland 33/1: 31/-57: Keen cl-up, wknd over 3f out, t.o.	dist	0

7 Ran Time 3m 0.27 (1.47) Owned: Mystic Meg Limited Trained: Newmarket

---

3620 2.30 Listed Vodafone Thoroughbred Stakes 3yo (A)
£20300 £7700 £3850 1m rnd Firm 11 +06 Fast Inside

3253+ FONGS THONG 15 [9] B J Meehan 3-8-12 (108) J Fortune 6/4 FAV: 321-11: Made all, clr over 1f out,		112+

styd on strongly, rdn out, readily: hvly bckd: eff over 7f/1m on firm & fast grnd, prob any trk: best up with/forcing the pace: smart & in grand heart, looks one to follow for Gr class wnr: see 3253.

2521* MANDOBI 44 [6] A C Stewart 3-8-12 (102) L Dettori 5/2: 120-4212: In tch, hdwy & short of room	2	105

over 2f out, switched over 1f out, kept on to chase wnr ins last, no impress: 6 wk abs: acts on firm & gd grnd, any trk: ran right up to useful form of 2521 (val h'cap).

3061 KINGS POINT 23 [8] R Hannon 3-8-12 (98) Dane O'Neill 33/1: 0530403: Handy, hdwy to chase wnr	shd	105

over 1f out, kept on: ran to useful best: see 2421, 1040.

3059 RESPLENDENT ONE 23 [5] T G Mills 3-8-12 (97) R Miles 33/1: 01-6044: Keen with wnr, wknd over 1f	3	98

out: see 3059 (h'cap), 2069.
2558 **JACK SULLIVAN 43** [2]3-8-12 BL t (98) E Ahern 25/1: 15-24405: Keen held up, eff & short of room over 2f out till over 1f out, onepace: tried blnks: see 2558, 989. *1* **96**
3306 **KELUCIA 12** [1]3-8-7 (97) R Ffrench 25/1: 5056666: Slow away, held up, eff 2f out, sn no impress. *shd* **91**
2915 **THYOLO 28** [3]3-8-12 (99) R Smith 9/1: 11-20307: Held up, btn 2f out: btr 2521 (h'cap), 1496. *3½* **89**
2486 **AUDITORIUM 45** [7]3-8-12 (109) K Fallon 5/1: 1123-408: Handy, wknd over 1f out: abs, see 1932. *4* **81**
3441 **BAHIANO 7** [4]3-8-12 (105) D Holland 20/1: 3600409: Nvr trav well & al bhd, t.o.: surely something amiss: twice below 2486, see 885. *dist* **0**
9 Ran Time 1m 37.81 (0.41) Owned: Mr Joe L Allbritton Trained: Upper Lambourn

3621

3.05 Gr1 Vodafone Nassau Stakes Fillies 3yo+ (A)
£116000 £44000 £22000 **1m1f192y** **Firm 11** **-04 Slow** Inside

3004 **FAVOURABLE TERMS 25** [2] Sir Michael Stoute 4-9-2 (112) K Fallon 11/2: 1215-161: In tch, hdwy 2f out, styd on well to lead dist, just held on for press: eff at 1m/10f on firm & gd/soft, any trk: v smart & still on the upgrade, right back to form: genuine, see 2487. **118**
2898 **SILENCE IS GOLDEN 29** [1] B J Meehan 5-9-2 (101) J Fortune 12/1: 25-12022: Held up, hdwy 2f out, styd on strongly ins last, just failed: career best run in the highest grade & shld be winning in at least List class with a repeat of this: thriving whilst in foal, see 2898, 1111. *shd* **117**
2816* **CHORIST 35** [4] W J Haggas 5-9-2 (112) D Holland 6/4 FAV: 1013-113: Cl-up, led 3f out till over 1f out, pressed wnr but just held for press ins last: clr of rem & another smart run: Gr 1 wnr in 2816 (made all). *nk* **116**
2491 **ZOSIMA 45** [3] Saeed bin Suroor 3-8-6 t (107) L Dettori 2/1: 12115-34: In tch, rdn over 2f out, sn btn: 6 wk abs & btr expected after promising Brit debut in 2491 (1m). *7* **105**
1997 **ECHOES IN ETERNITY 70** [6]4-9-2 t (107) K McEvoy 9/1: 3011-445: Led till 3f out: nicely bckd, abs. *1¼* **103**
2460 **MENHOUBAH 48** [5]3-8-6 p (106) S Sanders 20/1: 2302106: Cl-up, wknd over 1f out: abs, btr 1999. *¾* **101**
6 Ran Time 2m 05.7 (1.5) Owned: Maktoum Al Maktoum Trained: Newmarket

3622

3.35 Vodafone Stewards' Cup Heritage Handicap 3yo+ (B) **[108]**
£58000 £22000 £11000 **6f str** **Firm 11** **-02 Slow** Stands Side

3466 **PIVOTAL POINT 6** [1] P J Makin 4-8-11 (3ex) (91) S Sanders 7/1 CO FAV: 52-00121: Slow away, sn cl-up, hdwy trav well to lead over 1f out, rdn out, readily: hvly bckd, qck reapp: eff at 5/6f on firm & gd grnd, any trk: v useful, lightly rcd & progressive, prob more to come in List/Gr class: see 3123. **105**
3424* **FANTASY BELIEVER 7** [24] J J Quinn 6-8-9 (5ex) (89) D Holland 10/1: 0041012: Dwelt, held up far side, strong hdwy when short of room over 1f out, 'flew' ins last, led that group cl-home, no ch with stands side wnr: eye-catching run & poss unlucky, poised to win again: see 3424. *1¼* **97+**
2878 **HIGH REACH 30** [28] T G Mills 4-8-11 (91) K Fallon 7/1 CO FAV: 44-36303: Led far side group, clr dist, kept on till hdd cl-home: well bckd: fine eff & running well in these big field/top h'cap sprints: see 2581. *nk* **98**
3434 **TWO STEP KID 7** [6] J Noseda 3-8-10 (95) E Ahern 9/1: 1-641344: Cl-up stands side, eff over 1f out, kept on: ran to useful best: see 3434. *½* **100**
3434 **SIMIANNA 7** [10]5-8-13 p (93) P Mathers(5) 40/1: 0200465: Bhd stands side, late gains, nrst fin: 6th in this race last term: see 2457. *hd* **97**
2727 **HALMAHERA 14** [29]9-9-4 (98) N Callan 40/1: 4660506: Cl-up far side, eff to chase ldr over 1f out, kept on: been running well in big field/val sprints for many yrs: see 1227. *nk* **101**
3073* **ARTIE 22** [9]5-8-6 (3ex) (86) B Doyle 50/1: 0210017: With ldr stands side, onepace over 1f out: gd run, likes easier grnd as in 3073 (5f). *shd* **88**
2253 **RACCOON 56** [2]4-8-10 vis (90) K Darley 20/1: 11-41108: Led stands side group till dist, no extra. *½* **90**
3555 **MATERIAL WITNESS 2** [4]7-9-0 (5ex) (94) L Dettori 14/1: 2011129: Handy stands side, some late gains: qck reapp, best at 7f as in 3555. *hd* **93**
3248 **CD EUROPE 15** [30]6-8-9 p (89) W Ryan 66/1: 1-000060: 10th: Held up rear far side, eff & hmpd 2f out, switched left & styd on strongly fnl 1f, nrst fin: eye-catching eff, much closer with a clr run: see 2581. *nk* **87+**
3466 **PROUD BOAST 6** [27]6-8-9 (89) K McEvoy 25/1: 0002300: 11th: Handy far side, hung & wknd dist. *nk* **86**
3279 **TEXAS GOLD 14** [25]6-8-9 (89) R Mullen 14/1: 3-240660: 12th: Held up far side, eff & short of room over 2f out, onepace: see 3279. *shd* **85**
2727+ **CARIBBEAN CORAL 36** [8]5-9-9 (103) R Winston 16/1: 12-02110: 13th: Dwelt, held up stands side, some late gains, nvr dngrs: btr expected after 2727 (5f). *shd* **98**
3441 **ROYAL STORM 7** [26]5-9-5 (99) J Fortune 16/1: 6-014600: 14th: With ldr far side till over 1f out, wknd: nicely bckd: see 2581, 1490. *1* **91**
3466 **SMOKIN BEAU 6** [5]7-9-2 (96) T G McLaughlin 40/1: 2000400: 15th: In tch stands side, wknd 2f out. *¾* **86**
3434+ **MUTAWAQED 7** [14]6-8-10 (5ex)t (90) R L Moore 10/1: 0-042010: 16th: Held up, hdwy & short of room over 2f out, some late gains: btr expected after 3434. *hd* **79**
3466 **PIC UP STICKS 6** [11]5-9-2 (96) T E Durcan 7/1 CO FAV: 3163600: 17th: Held up stands side, brief eff 2f out, sn wknd: hvly bckd: much btr expected after promising eff in 3466. *1¼* **81**
3466 **CORRIDOR CREEPER 6** [22]7-9-1 p (95) C Catlin 50/1: 2602360: 18th: With ldrs far side till dist. *¾* **78**
3116 **NATIVE TITLE 21** [23]6-8-7 (87) N Pollard 25/1: 4010030: 19th: Al bhd far side: see 3116, 2256. *hd* **69**
2758 **MARSAD 35** [13]10-8-8 (88) P Doe 100/1: 3-030200: 20th: In tch stands side, wknd dist: see 2357. *1½* **66**
3466 **WHITBARROW 6** [15]5-9-2 p (96) Dane O'Neill 66/1: 0000000: 21th: In tch, wknd over 2f out. *¾* **72**
2949 **CIRCUIT DANCER 28** [12]4-9-2 (96) R Ffrench 100/1: 3401050: 22th: In tch 4f stands side. *½* **70**
3466 **BLACKHEATH 6** [7]8-8-7 (5ex) (87) L Keniry(3) 28/1: 2641450: 23th: In tch stands side, wknd 2f out. *3½* **51**
2949 **DAZZLING BAY 28** [18]4-9-8 (102) J F Egan 20/1: 6-603520: 24th: Led to start, reluctant to enter stalls, in tch, wknd & hmpd over 1f out: mullish effort, much btr 2949. *nk* **65**
3061 **COCONUT PENANG 23** [17]4-9-2 BL (96) S Whitworth 20/1: 50-00200: 25th: In tch far side, btn when hmpd over 1f out: tried blnks: twice below 2581. *5* **44**
3253 **STORMONT 15** [20]4-9-10 vis (104) J Quinn 66/1: 4000000: 26th: Al bhd far side: lost action. *12* **16**
3466 **FUNFAIR WANE 6** [21]5-8-13 (93) Alex Greaves 50/1: 00-00400: 27th: In tch far side, wknd & eased 2f out: reportedly lost action: see 2532. *1½* **1**
2068 **PERUVIAN CHIEF 63** [19]7-9-1 vis (95) J P Guillambert(3) 100/1: 002000U: U.r. start: see 1207. **0**
28 Ran Time 1m 10.78 (0.78) Owned: Mr R A Bernard Trained: Marlborough

3623   4.10 Vodafone Racegoers Club Nursery Stakes Handicap 2yo (C)   [97]
£10823 £3330 £1665   6f str   Firm 11   -28 Slow   Stands Side

2241 **EASY FEELING 56** [7] R Hannon 2-8-8 (77) R L Moore 13/2: 3341: Handy, hdwy to lead just ins last,   87
rdn clr: 8 wk abs: apprec return to 6f & acts on firm & fast grnd, prob any trk: clearly runs well fresh: useful
eff, likely to reappear qckly under a pen: see 1920.
3374* **BIBURY FLYER 9** [3] M R Channon 2-8-13 (82) S Hitchcott(3) 100/30 FAV: 3522612: Held up, hdwy &   2½   85
short of room over 2f out, switched over 1f out, rdn & kept on ins last, no ch with ready wnr: well bckd: gd run &
clearly stays 6f: caught an improver: see 3374.
2263 **COME GOOD 54** [2] R Hannon 2-8-1 (70) R Smith 14/1: 5263: With ldrs, outpcd halfway, rallied &   nk   72
short of room over 1f out, kept on ins last: 8 wk abs: stays 6f on firm: shown enough to win a race: see 1900.
3284 **TALCEN GWYN 14** [4] M F Harris 2-8-10 (79) J F Egan 14/1: 41404: Set pace, rdn & hdd just ins   nk   80
last, no extra: prob stays 6f on firm & fast grnd: see 2430.
3445* **GIFTED GAMBLE 7** [8]2-8-13 bl (82) N Callan 6/1: 3332215: With ldr, no extra over 1f out: longer   1   80
trip & not disgraced: see 3445.
3115 **EMPIRES GHODHA 21** [5]2-9-5 (88) J Fortune 11/2: 2315346: Held up, eff well over 1f out, onepace.   ½   84
3303 **RANCHO CUCAMONGA 12** [9]2-8-5 (74) K Darley 15/2: 00107: Went right start, in tch, wknd qckly   10   40
over 1f out: thrice below 2251.
2697 **GORTUMBLO 37** [6]2-9-7 (90) S Sanders 8/1: 1308: Held up, wknd qckly dist: bckd, btr 2251.   1   53
3115 **BLUE MARBLE 21** [1]2-8-6 (75) K Fallon 7/1: 460109: Handy, wkng when short of room over 1f out: 6   20
twice below 2926 (5f, auct mdn).
9 Ran   Time 1m 12.35 (2.35)   Owned: Speedlith Group   Trained: Marlborough

3624   4.45 Vodafone Nursery Stakes Handicap 2yo (C)   [97]
£10969 £3375 £1688   7f rnd   Firm 11   -45 Slow   Inside

3290 **KEEP BACCKINHIT 12** [7] G L Moore 2-8-6 (75) Lisa Jones(3) 20/1: 3031: In tch, hdwy & short of   83
room over 2f out, styd on to lead ins last, drvn to hold on: imprvd for step up to 7f & acts on firm grnd &
sharp/undul trks: genuine, see 2733.
3053 **JUSTAQUESTION 23** [4] I A Wood 2-8-13 (82) K Fallon 7/1: 011032: Held up, short of room over 2f   shd 89+
out, switched & kept on ins last, just held for press: useful & lkd unlucky (this tricky trk only one that K Fallon
fails to excel at): acts on firm & soft: win again, see 1669.
2584* **LADY CHEF 42** [8] B R Millman 2-8-5 (74) T E Durcan 8/1: 0513: In tch, hdwy to lead over 1f out,   1   78
kept on till collared well ins last: 6 wk abs: acts on firm & fast grnd: going the right way: see 2584 (mdn auct).
2845* **AL GARHOUD BRIDGE 31** [6] M R Channon 2-9-7 (90) S Hitchcott(3) 7/4 FAV: 5014: Held up, hdwy 2f   2½   90
out, wknd fnl 1f: well bckd, joc received a 1-day careless riding ban: useful: see 2845 (auct mdn).
3266 **EXIT SMILING 14** [5]2-8-5 (74) R Ffrench 6/1: 2305: Chsd ldr till 2f out, wknd: btr 1744 (6f, gd).   5   64
3284 **ELISHA 14** [9]2-8-0 (69) D Fox(5) 12/1: 451066: Led till over 1f out, wknd: see 2020 (5f, gd).   nk   58
2870* **EMERALD PENANG 30** [3]2-8-9 (78) S Whitworth 4/1: 5417: In tch, hung right & wknd 2f out: best 2870.   ½   66
3031 **TREMPJANE 24** [1]2-8-11 (80) Dane O'Neill 33/1: 1558: Al bhd: see 2373.   1½   65
3386 **MISS MALONE 8** [2]2-8-11 (80) R L Moore 16/1: 00249: In tch, wknd 2f out: btr 3386 (6f), 3183.   ¾   63
9 Ran   Time 1m 28.43 (3.93)   Owned: Pleasure Palace Racing   Trained: Brighton

3625   5.20 Vodafone Apprentice Stakes Handicap 3yo+ 0-80 (D)   [89]
£10693 £3290 £1645   1m1f   Firm 11   -50 Slow   Inside

3512 **RINGSIDER 4** [5] G A Butler 3-9-2 (77) Lisa Jones 4/1 FAV: 01-0021: Held up, hdwy 2f out, styd on   87
to lead ins last, rdn clr: bckd: qck reapp & apprec step up to 9f: acts on firm & fast grnd: see 2250.
3256 **OCEAN OF STORMS 12** [12] Christian Wroe 9-9-10 t (76) S Hitchcott 33/1: 2100452: Slow away, sn in   1¾   82
tch, hdwy to lead briefly ins last, sn outpcd by wnr: gd run: acts on firm & soft: see 2207.
2967* **ARTISTIC STYLE 26** [2] B Ellison 4-8-11 (63) T Eaves 10/1: 3-060013: Held up, hdwy & hung over 1f   1½   66
out, kept on ins last: nicely bckd: acts on firm & soft: stays 9f: encouraging run stepped up from sell grade.
3083 **VOICE MAIL 22** [4] A M Balding 5-9-12 (78) T Block(7) 14/1: 1302034: Keen, cl-up trav well, led   nk   80
over 1f out, hdd & wknd ins last: see 3083.
3225* **PARNASSIAN 16** [8]4-9-5 (71) R Thomas(3) 5/1: 1305115: In tch, eff well over 1f out, sn wknd: 2½   68
well bckd: prob prefers easier grnd as in 3225.
1598 **HAIL THE CHIEF 85** [13]7-9-7 (73) N Chalmers(3) 12/1: 0-140306: Led till dist, wknd: 12 wk abs.   1   68
880 **DONT CALL ME DEREK 134** [10]3-8-1 (62) D Fox(3) 9/1: 04-5607: b g Sri Pekan - Cultural Role (Night   shd   56
Shift) Held up last, detached, wide bend over 3f out, some late gains, no dngr: long abs: big step up in trip &
shid stay 9f: prob handles polytrack.
3185 **SAY WHAT YOU SEE 17** [6]4-9-5 vis (71) H Gemberlu(7) 7/1: 5422048: In tch, wknd qckly dist: bckd.   1½   62
2920 **BAKER OF OZ 28** [1]3-8-11 (72) P Gallagher(5) 16/1: 0-264109: Al bhd: twice below 2264.   1¼   60
2540 **MAD CAREW 43** [7]5-9-8 bl e (74) H Poulton(5) 12/1: 0405540: 10th: Al bhd: abs: see 1849, 674.   ½   61
3034 **WIND CHIME 24** [3]7-9-0 (66) L Keniry 7/1: 0-020130: 11th: In tch, wknd 2f out: see 3034, 2600.   nk   52
3099 **LOW CLOUD 21** [11]4-9-10 (76) L Treadwell(5) 20/1: 3514540: 12th: Slow away, keen, handy 7f, wknd.   ¾   60
12 Ran   Time 1m 56.02(5.52)   Owned: Mr S A O'Donoghue & Mr M V Deegan   Trained: Blewbury

Official Going Good/Firm

3626   **2.00 Rock Capital Group E B F Maiden Stakes Fillies 2yo (D)**
£6188 £1904 £952   **6f8y str**   **Firm 11**   **-13 Slow**   Stands side

3252   **SWAN NEBULA 16** [11] Saeed bin Suroor 2-8-9 t   L Dettori   3/1: 351: Cl-up, ev ch dist, styd on to   **86**
lead ins fnl 1f, drvn out: apprec drop back to 6f: acts on firm & gd grnd: eff with a t-strap & acts on a gall trk.
2061   **COUNTY CLARE 64** [2] A M Balding 2-8-9   R Mullen   12/1: 02: ch f Barathea - Input (Primo Dominie)   *1*   **82+**
In tch, ev ch halfway, sn outpcd, rallied well ins fnl 1f, post came too sn: Feb foal, cost 39,000gns: sire Gr 1
wnr at 1m: eff at 6f, crying out for 7f+: acts on firm grnd: left debut eff bhd with promising run.
2151   **ENCOURAGEMENT 60** [1] R Hannon 2-8-9   R L Moore   20/1: 03: b f Royal Applause - Gentle Persuasion   *shd*   **79**
(Bustino) Led, hdd under press ins fnl 1f, no extra: 9 wk abs: Mar foal, sister to smart performers at 6f/1m: dam
smart sprint performer at 2: sire Gr 1 wnr at 6f: eff at 6f, shld get further: acts on firm grnd: improved on
debut eff (reportedly lost action) & can be plcd to find similar.
     NAZAAHA 0 [8] J L Dunlop 2-8-9   R Hills   11/1: 4: gr f Elnadim - Taatof (Lahib) Slow away, prog   *1¾*   **76**
after 4f, styd on ins fnl 1f: op 8/1 on debut: Feb first foal, dam unrcd: sire Gr 1 wnr at 6f: eff at 6f, shaped
as tho' 7f+ will suit: acts on firm grnd: impr for today's experience & rate higher.
3386   **DANCE FLOWER 9** [12]2-8-9   C Catlin   9/4 FAV: 235: Handy, kept on ins fnl 1f, nvr getting to ldrs: *1*   **73**
failed to build on promising 3rd in 3386.
     PIPERS ASH 0 [7]2-8-9   S Drowne   4/1: 6: b f Royal Academy - Merida (Warning) Slow away, sn mid   *nk*   **72**
div, prog 2f out, onepace fnl 1f: op 5/1 on debut: Apr foal, half-sister to a 6f wnr: dam successful miler.
3141   **MISS PATRICIA 21** [15]2-8-9   E Ahern   25/1: 07: Slow away, sn mid-div, no impress dist: see 3141.   *3½*   **62**
3342   **IFIT 11** [10]2-8-9   J Murtagh   33/1: 08: Rear, nvr nrr than mid-div.   *1*   **59**
     MANORSHIELD MINX 0 [9]2-8-9   J Fortune   25/1: 9: Rear, modest late gains.   *nk*   **58**
3021   **THE KEEP 25** [4]2-8-9   P Dobbs   14/1: 00: 10th: Handy over 4f, wknd.   *1½*   **54**
2492   **Sukuma 46** [6]2-8-9   N Chalmers(5) 66/1:0   **Doitforreel 0** [3]2-8-9   T P Queally 100/1:0
3103   **Mina Alsalaam 22** [13]2-8-9   S Whitworth   66/1:0   3071   **Tamora 23** [16]2-8-9   P Doe   11/1:0
14 Ran   Time 1m 13.04 (1.44)   Owned: Godolphin   Trained: Newmarket

---

3627   **2.30 Rsa Security & Bacyp Nursery Handicap Stakes 2yo (D)**   **[91]**
£5824 £1792 £896   **7f str**   **Firm 11**   **-04 Slow**   Stands side

3330   **KING OF BLUES 11** [4] M A Magnusson 2-8-8 t (71)   E Ahern   10/1: 0041: In tch, styd on to lead 1f   **80**
out, drvn out: eff at 7f, 1m will suit: acts on firm grnd & a gall trk: eff in a t- strap: imprvd effort on h'cap bow.
2970   **MUSICO 27** [2] B R Millman 2-8-9 (72)   G Baker   8/1: 4642: Chsd ldrs, prog to chase wnr bef 1f out,   *½*   **79**
styd on, not btn far: eff at 6f, imprvd for step up to 7f: acts on firm grnd: gd run in defeat on h'cap bow.
2287   **CALY DANCER 54** [12] D R C Elsworth 2-8-13 (76)   S Sanders   6/1: 05333: Slow away, rcd free & led   *nk*   **82**
after 2f, hdd 1f out, kept on, just held by front 2: 8 wk abs: eff at 5/6f, ran to form on step up to 7f: see 2287.
3266   **ALTA PETENS 15** [8] M L W Bell 2-9-1 (78)   J Mackay   6/1: 41004: Keen in tch, short of room bef 1f   *1½*   **81**
out, onepcd ins fnl 1f: eff at 5/6f, now stays 7f: acts on firm & hvy grnd: btr 1728.
2263   **FORTNUM 55** [10]2-8-2 (65)   R L Moore   18/1: 5305: In tch, ev ch fnl 1f, sn no extra: 8 wk abs: btr 1614.   *1*   **64**
2618   **HES A STAR 41** [3]2-7-13 (62)   R Smith   10/1: 0406: Rear, prog 3f out, no impress fnl 1f: 6 wk abs.   *nk*   **62**
3212   **SIMPLIFY 17** [5]2-9-0 bl (77)   T P Queally   10/1: 453257: Handy over 5f, sn no extra: btr 3022.   *2½*   **72**
3297   **HES A DIAMOND 13** [9]2-9-0 (77)   J Fortune   9/2 FAV: 5138: Led 2f, styd cl-up till wknd bef 1f out.   *2*   **68**
3302   **SHUJUNE AL HAWAA 13** [11]2-8-7 (70)   C Catlin   12/1: 5639: Chsd ldrs over 4f, sn wknd: btr 3302.   *5*   **51**
3368   **TRACKATTACK 10** [7]2-8-12 (75)   L Dettori   7/1: 3500: 10th: Rear, al bhd: has been gelded.   *2½*   **51**
2938   **THREE PENNIES 29** [1]2-8-11 (74)   S Drowne   16/1: 0130: 11th: Al bhd, nvr a factor: btr 2938 & 2652.   *12*   **28**
11 Ran   Time 1m 25.35 (1.05)   Owned: East Wind Racing Ltd   Trained: Upper Lambourn

---

3628   **3.05 Stones The Printers Handicap Stakes 3yo+ 0-95 (C)**   **[91]**
£9841 £3028 £1514   **5f34y str**   **Firm 11**   **+14 Fast**   Stands side

3537   **SALVIATI 4** [7] J M Bradley 7-9-0 p (77)   R L Moore   9/2 FAV: 0000451: Slow away, prog 2f out, styd   **86**
on to lead well ins fnl 1f, rdn out: qck reapp, fast time: eff at 5f, stays 6f: acts on firm & gd/soft grnd: eff
with/without cheek pieces: well h'capped 7yo & shld follow up: see 3537 & 2082.
3279   **CAPE ROYAL 15** [15] Mrs J R Ramsden 4-9-11 (88) J Murtagh   6/1: 0602032: Slow away, prog halfway,   *1*   **92**
styd on to lead 1f out, hdd well ins fnl 1f, not pace of wnr: op 8/1: remains in gd form: see 3279 & 2747.
3466   **WHISTLER 7** [10] J M Bradley 7-10-0 p (91) R Hills   20/1: 3101403: Mid-div, prog when short of room   *¾*   **93**
bef 1f out, kept on ins fnl 1f, nrst fin: qck reapp: stablemate of wnr: ran with credit under top-weight: see 2894.
3466   **MALAPROPISM 7** [3] M R Channon 4-9-5 (82) B O'Neill(7) 25/1: 6000604: Held up, prog after 3f, styd   *nk*   **83**
on ins fnl 1f: qck reapp: encouraging eff & has slipped back to a winning mark: see 1845.
3341   **KATHOLOGY 11** [8]7-9-2 (79)   T Quinn   12/1: 0-060035: Cl-up, no extra ins fnl 1f: just btr 3341.   *nk*   **79**
3257   **NIVERNAIS 16** [11]5-8-8 (71) Dane O'Neill   12/1: 0000606: Sn in tch, hdd bef 1f out, no extra.   *½*   **70**
3388   **THE LORD 9** [2]4-9-7 (84) C Haddon(7) 16/1: 06000-37: Handy, ev ch dist, sn no extra: see 3388.   *shd*   **82**
3466   **CONNECT 7** [4]7-9-10 bl (87)   P Doe   11/2: 2404148: Slow away, prog when short of room dist, sn   *shd*   **84**
onepcd: op 4/1: qck reapp: btr 3466 & 3279.
3123   **DANCING MYSTERY 22** [13]10-9-5 (82) S Carson   16/1: 0001459: Handy over 3f, no extra: btr 2420.   *shd*   **78**
3279   **FURTHER OUTLOOK 15** [1]10-9-7 (84) J Fortune   10/1: 0423000: 10th: Rcd alone centre, al cl-up,   *½*   **79**
prog & ev ch when switched to stands side group dist, sn wknd: btr 2698.
3537   **SIR EDWIN LANDSEER 4** [9]4-8-12 (75) R Thomas(5) 20/1: 00-00000: 11th: Reared up in stalls, rear,   *2*   **64**
prog when short of room dist, not recover: see 3269.
3269   **DANEHILL STROLLER 15** [5]4-9-6 p (83) S Sanders   7/1: 43-00040: 12th: Handy over 3f, wknd: op 9/1.   *nk*   **71**
3466   **LITTLE EDWARD 7** [14]6-9-13 (90) L Keniry(3) 25/1: 5005000: 13th: Led, hdd bef 1f out, wknd: qk reapp.   *2*   **72**
3341   **DOMIRATI 11** [6]4-9-5 (82) S Drowne   13/2: 4-042020: 14th: Handy, no extra when short of room   *7*   **43**
dist, sn eased: btr 3341 & 2698.
14 Ran   Time 1m 0.15 (u 0.15)   Owned: Mr J M Bradley   Trained: Chepstow

NEWBURY SUNDAY 01.08.04 Lefthand, Flat, Galloping Track

3629 **3.40 Listed European Breeders Fund Chalice Stakes Fillies 3yo+ (A)**
£17400 £6600 £3300 **1m4f5y** **Firm 11** **+03 Fast** Outside

2946 **SAHOOL 29** [2] M P Tregoning 3-8-4 (107) R Hills 4/6 FAV: 61-22221: In tch, styd on to lead dist, drvn to hold on: well bckd: eff at 1m/10f, suited by 12f: acts on firm & soft grnd: has been in consistent form & this was a deserved success: see 2946 & 2517. **101**
3474 **POLAR JEM 7** [1] G G Margarson 4-9-1 (92) A McCarthy 12/1: 1111632: Led, hdd bef 1f out, rallied & ev ch ins fnl 1f, just held by wnr: qck reapp: imprvd eff on step up in grade: most tough, see 3474. *nk* **100**
3278 **SELEBELA 15** [5] L M Cumani 3-8-4 (95) T P Queally 5/1: 0111223: Handy over 1m, sn outpcd, rallied fnl 1f, nvr getting to front 2: clr rem: op 7/2: worth a try at 14f now: btr 3278. *1¾* **97**
3335* **LIGHT OF MORN 11** [4] R Guest 3-8-5 (1ow) S Sanders 14/1: 2314: Rear, prog 4f out, onepcd bef 1f out: not disgraced on step up in grade, wants h'caps: see 3335. *3* **94**
2972+**LIGHT WIND 27** [6]3-8-4 (86) R L Moore 11/1: 5115: Slow away, prog after halfway, wknd bef 1f out. *3* **89**
2366* **MOCCA 51** [10]3-8-4 (87) E Ahern 25/1: 152-4516: Rear, nvr a factor: 7 wk abs: see 2366 (h'cap). *2* **86**
3216 **TIDAL 17** [3]5-9-1 (84) J Fortune 40/1: 6110347: Cl-up 9f, sn wknd: btr 3089. *3½* **81**
1719* **WELL KNOWN 80** [8]3-8-4 (92) S Drowne 10/1: 2-18: Keen bhd, nvr a factor: 11 wk abs: btr 1719 (mdn). *6* **72**
3089 **DOCTRINE 23** [9]3-8-4 (93) R Havlin 33/1: 116-4059: Keen handy over 1m, fdd: btr 3089. *9* **59**
9 Ran Time 2m 30.29 (0.99) Owned: Mr Hamdan Al Maktoum Trained: Lambourn

3630 **4.15 John Nike Leisuresport Handicap Stakes Fillies 3yo 0-85 (D)** **[92]**
£7248 £2230 £1115 **1m2f6y** **Firm 11** **-26 Slow** Outside

2860 **PORTMANTEAU 32** [4] Sir Michael Stoute 3-9-7 (85) J Murtagh 8/1: 0-0101: Keen handy, styd on to lead bef 2f out, rdn out, val bit more: suited by around 10f, 12f shld suit: acts on firm & fast grnd: lightly rcd performer who left disapp recent eff bhd with authoritative success: see 1835. **93+**
3391 **FOXILLA 9** [1] D R C Elsworth 3-7-12 (4oh) (58) Hayley Turner(5) 8/1: 0031432: Chsd ldrs over 6f, sn outpcd, rallied bef 1f out, kept on but not pace of wnr: op 11/1: acts on firm or gd grnd: continues in gd form. *1¾* **66**
3291* **DU PRE 13** [2] Mrs A J Perrett 3-8-10 (74) S Drowne 9/2: 30-0213: Trkd ldrs, kept on fnl 2f, nvr getting to front 2: eff at 1m, stays 10f: see 2391 (8.4f). *1* **76**
2991* **APSARA 26** [11] H R A Cecil 3-9-2 vis (80) W Ryan 3/1 FAV: 214: Reluctant to start & lost around 15L, sn mid-div, switched wide & prog bef 1f out, styd on well, nrst fin: fine run in circumstances & is worth bearing in mind for similar if learning to behave: see 2991. *hd* **81**
3240 **LADY BLADE 16** [7]3-7-12 (5oh) (57) C Haddon(7) 40/1: 360-0405: Bhd, prog after 6f, no impress fnl 1f. *1* **61**
3255 **TREE TOPS 16** [10]3-8-8 (72) J Fortune 11/2: 52336: Cl-up, led after 6f, hdd bef 2f out, sn wknd. *1¼* **69**
3255 **POWERFUL PARRISH 16** [9]3-8-10 T (74) T Quinn 20/1: 25-02407: Rear, prog 4f out, wknd 2f out. *5* **64**
3186 **PERSIAN GENIE 18** [8]3-7-13 (63) R Thomas(5) 16/1: 0-0008: Bhd, nvr a factor. *1* **51**
3223 **LIVE WIRE LUCY 17** [5]3-9-7 (85) R Mullen 50/1: 55-03009: Led 6f, sn wknd: btr 2421. *1¼* **71**
3128 **SAFFRON FOX 22** [6]3-9-1 (79) R L Moore 9/2: 20-40420: 10th: Bhd, nvr a factor: btr 3128 (1m). *12* **49**
10 Ran Time 2m 6.58 (3.78) Owned: Maktoum Al Maktoum Trained: Newmarket

3631 **4.45 Sfi Maiden Stakes 3yo (D)**
£6006 £1848 £924 **1m1f** **Firm 11** **-37 Slow** Outside

TAHTHEEB 0 [2] M P Tregoning 3-8-9 R Hills 9/2: 1: b f Muhtarram - Mihnah (Lahib) Slow away, ran green, switched wide when hung left 2f out, styd on well despite hanging left to lead well ins fnl 1f, pushed out, val 3L+: debut: eff at 9f, further will suit: acts on firm grnd & a gall trk: goes well fresh: defied greenness to win with a bit in hand & looks sure to impr for today. **78+**
3007 **OGILVY 26** [13] J H M Gosden 3-9-0 J Fortune 8/1: 002: Cl-up, styd on to lead dist, hdd well ins fnl 1f, not pace of wnr: eff at 9f on firm grnd: imprvd eff on only 3rd start & now quals for h'caps. *1¼* **78**
2248 **RED SAIL 57** [1] J R Fanshawe 3-8-9 J Murtagh 15/8 FAV: 33: Slow away, prog 3f out, kept on fnl 1f, no ch with front 2: 8 wk abs: eff at 1m/10f on firm & fast grnd: closer but for poor start & can find a race. *1¾* **70**
1130 **COPPICE 111** [8] L M Cumani 3-9-0 T P Queally 14/1: 64: Handy, prog 2f out, onepcd ins fnl 1f: long abs: eff at 9f on firm grnd: left debut eff behind. *hd* **74**
3385 **TOPKAT 10** [6]3-9-0 L Keniry(3) 7/1: 025: Chsd ldr 6f, sn outpcd, rallied ins fnl 1f: needs further. *nk* **73**
2974 **GAY ROMANCE 27** [3]3-8-9 W Ryan 40/1: 006: Led, hdd halfway, wknd dist: see 2974. *1¾* **63**
3186 **CHARMED BY FIRE 18** [12]3-9-0 R L Moore 25/1: 07: Handy, led halfway, hdd dist, wknd: see 3186. *1¼* **68**
2419 **TIPSY LADY 49** [10]3-8-9 Dane O'Neill 33/1: 0008: Nvr nrr than mid-div: 7 wk abs. *¾* **62**
SUNSHINE ON ME 0 [4]3-8-9 R Mullen 50/1: 9: Rear, modest late gains. *nk* **61**
2131 **BONSAI 61** [5]3-8-9 E Ahern 33/1: 0-000: 10th: Rear, prog after 3f, wknd fnl 3f. *4* **55**
BIG HURRY 0 [14]3-8-9 S Drowne 12/1: 0: 11th: b f Red Ransom - Call Me Fleet (Afleet) Chsd ldrs over 6f, wknd: op 9/1 on debut: with R Charlton. *nk* **54**
3282 **MUJAWER 15** [7]3-9-0 P Dobbs 10/1: 50: 12th: Handy, wknd 3f out: btr 3237. *2½* **55**
2056} **Sweep The Board 417** [11]3-9-0 S Sanders 33/1:0 3237 **Danze Romance 16** [9]3-8-9 T Quinn 16/1:0
14 Ran Time 1m 53.38(4.38) Owned: Mr Hamdan Al Maktoum Trained: Lambourn

CHESTER SUNDAY 01.08.04 Lefthand, Very Tight Track

Official Going GOOD/FIRM

3632 2.20 Warwick International Nursery Stakes A Handicap 2yo (D) [92]
   £4841 £1490 £745 **6f18y rnd** Firm 05 -20 Slow Outside

3348* **GOLDEN LEGACY 11** [10] R A Fahey 2-9-7 (85) P Hanagan 8/1: 2011: Slow away, hdwy bef halfway, sn **98+**
not clr run trav well, switched right & led over 1f out, rdn clr, v readily: eff at 6f on firm & fast, sharp or gall
trks: v useful run under top-weight & a high draw, keep on side: see 3348 (mdn).
3374 **IM AIMEE 10** [7] P D Evans 2-8-12 (76) F P Ferris(3) 8/1: 0402222: Handy, kept on over 1f out: consistent. 3½ **79**
3272 **MYTTONS BELL 15** [9] A Bailey 2-8-6 (70) D Allan 16/1: 2303: Rear, hdwy 2f out, kept on. 1 **70**
3115 **MISSPERON 22** [3] K A Ryan 2-8-13 (77) N Callan 100/30 FAV: 53134: Cl-up, not clr run over 1f nk **76**
out, sn lost pl, onepace: btr 2603 (fills mdn).
3323* **MADAME TOPFLIGHT 12** [1]2-9-2 (80) N Mackay(3) 7/2: 0215: Led till over 1f out, no extra ins fnl 1f. 1 **76**
3258 **ELSIE WAGG 15** [5]2-8-7 (71) K Darley 10/1: 3456: Bhd, nvr nr ldrs: see 2020. ½ **65**
3271* **MAKE US FLUSH 15** [4]2-8-9 (73) F Norton 7/1: 4040117: Outpcd in tch, staying on when not clr run ½ **65**
ins fnl 1f, no dngr, eased: op 10/1: btr 3271.
3432 **NOVA TOR 8** [8]2-9-2 (80) I Mongan 16/1: 1041548: Chsd ldrs, not clr run over 2f out, no impress 2½ **64**
over 1f out, eased when btn ins fnl 1f: btr 3082 (here, better draw).
3081 **TIVISKI 23** [2]2-8-13 (77) M Hills 8/1: 3410459: Cl-up, wknd over 1f out: see 1573. 8 **37**
9 Ran Time 1m 14.62 (1.52) Owned: Mr P N Devlin Trained: Malton

---

3633 2.50 Cheshire County Council Foster Care E B F Maiden Stakes 2yo (D)
   £4841 £1490 £745 **7f2y rnd** Firm 05 -46 Slow Inside

3272 **LOVE AND LAUGHTER 15** [2] T D Easterby 2-8-9 D Allan 2/1 FAV: 61: b f Theatrical - Hoh Dear (Sri **74**
Pekan) Trkd ldrs, hdwy to lead ins fnl 1f, kept on for press: Mar first foal: dam useful over 5/6f: sire wnr of
Breeders Cup Turf: relished this step up to 7f, acts on firm & a sharp trk: imprvd from debut: open to improvement.
3272 **WIZARDMICKTEE 15** [4] A Bailey 2-9-0 J Fanning 14/1: 02: b c Monashee Mountain - Epsilon 2 **73**
(Environment Friend) Led till ins fnl 1f, no extra: Mar first foal, cost 8,000gns: stays 7f on firm: shld find a mdn.
  OXFORD STREET PETE 0 [8] A Bailey 2-9-0 V Slattery 20/1: 3: b g Rossini - Thabeh (Shareef 1½ **70+**
Dancer) Slow away in rear, hdwy 4f out, not clr run & ran green over 1f out, kept on again ins fnl 1f on debut:
cost 10,000gns, Apr foal: half-brother to a useful 7f/1m wnr: eff at 7f on firm, friendly trk: pleasing start.
3368 **WATCHMYEYES 10** [12] N P Littmoden 2-9-0 J P Guillambert(3) 4/1: 64: Cl-up, ev ch over 1f out, onepcd. nk **69**
3097 **SWALLOW FALLS 22** [3]2-8-9 L Enstone(3) 16/1: 05: Cl-up, onepcd fnl 1f. nk **63**
2051 **ZANTERO 65** [11]2-9-0 T Hamilton(3) 10/1: 46: In tch, hdwy over 1f out, sn ran green, onepcd fnl 1f. 1¼ **65**
  KRISTALCHEN 0 [10]2-8-9 M Fenton 7/1: 7: Slow away, modest late gains: op 5/1, debut. 1¼ **57**
3081 **DEN PERRY 23** [5]2-9-0 P Mathers(5) 33/1: 60008: Mid-div, wknd over 1f out. 5 **52**
2802 **LORD CHALFONT 34** [1]2-9-0 P D Holland 16/1: 00009: Al bhd: tried cheek pieces. 11 **30**
  LAUROLLIE 0 [7]2-8-9 Lucy Russell(7) 40/1: 0: 10th: Slow away, nvr a factor on debut. 3 **19**
  BENNY THE BUS 0 [9]2-9-0 A Culhane 7/1: 0: 11th: Nvr a factor on debut: op 10/1. 2 **20**
11 Ran Time 1m 28.58 (3.58) Owned: Gold Star Partners Trained: Malton

---

3634 3.25 Halliwell Jones Bmw - Mile Handicap 3yo+ 0-90 (C) [88]
   £9724 £2992 £1496 **7f122y rnd** Firm 05 -02 Slow Inside

1812 **NASHAAB 75** [1] P D Evans 7-10-0 (88) F P Ferris(3) 5/1 J FAV: 0000231: Dwelt, rear, hdwy wide 2f **94**
out, led 1f out, hdd well ins fnl 1f, rallied to regain lead fnl stride: long abs: eff at 7f/1m on hvy & fibresand,
likes firm/fast & Chester: runs well fresh: game & tough, see 1598.
3571 **ROMAN MAZE 2** [8] W M Brisbourne 4-8-0 (60) F Norton 10/1: 4-0500042: Rear, not clr run over 2f shd **66**
out, switched right over 1f out, styd on to lead well ins fnl 1f, hdd fnl stride: long abs on 14/1, qck reapp: acts on firm,
fast & both AWs: fine run: see 71.
3428* **TRUE NIGHT 8** [13] D Nicholls 7-9-9 (83) D Holland 5/1 J FAV: 3303113: Mid-div, not much room & nk **88**
hmpd 2f out, ev ch ins fnl 1f, held cl-home: clr of rem: continues in gd form: see 3248.
3490 **ICED DIAMOND 6** [12] W M Brisbourne 5-7-12 (6oh)T (52) D Fentiman(7) 33/1: 0000044: In tch, hdwy 3½ **55**
when hmpd over 1f out, onepcd fnl 1f: qck reapp: tried a t-strap: stiff task at weights: see 558.
3017 **NO GROUSE 25** [11]4-8-8 p (68) P Hanagan 25/1: 3000005: In tch, not much room & hmpd just over 2f 1¼ **62**
out, onepcd fnl 1f: rider reported mount had hung RHd thr'out: see 632.
2871 **WATERSIDE 31** [10]5-9-8 (82) I Mongan 10/1: 0311246: Cl-up, led over 3f out to 1f out, no extra. nk **75**
3310* **ZANJEER 13** [4]4-8-10 (70) T Hamilton(3) 11/2: 0-016317: Handy, not much room 2f out, sn lost pl, btn. 3½ **56**
3461 **H HARRISON 7** [14]4-9-7 (81) R Ffrench 16/1: 4100358: Mid-div, hdwy over 2f out, no impress fnl 1f. nk **66**
3378 **FOOLISH GROOM 10** [2]3-8-1 1 p (68) Dale Gibson 14/1: 3456359: Rear, nvr nr ldrs. 1 **51**
3155 **MERDIFF 20** [7]5-7-13 (59) B Swarbrick(5) 11/2: 0002120: 10th: Cl-up, wknd over 1f out. 2 **38**
2389 **FLYING EXPRESS 50** [5]4-9-11 (85) M Hills 11/2: 4-602030: 11th: Led till over 3f out, sn no extra. 5 **54**
2712 **SUGAR CUBE TREAT 38** [9]8-7-12 (27oh) (31) S Righton 100/1: 0050060: 12th: Al bhd: see 2279. 12 **3**
12 Ran Time 1m 32.96 (0.56) Owned: Mr M W Lawrence Trained: Abergavenny

---

3635 4.00 Betting Exchange Curzon Park Rated Stakes Handicap 4yo+ 0-105 (B) [95]
   £13695 £4497 £2248 **2m2f147y** Firm 05 Inapplicable Outside

3475* **HIGH ACTION 7** [2] Ian Williams 4-9-4 (3ex)t (85) D Holland 5/4: 06-00011: Made all, rdn over 1f **89**
out, kept on well to hold on ins fnl 1f: landed double, qck reapp: eff at 15f/2m2.5f, acts on firm & fast, prob any
trk: tough, thriving, Ebor H'cap bound.
3125 **THEWHIRLINGDERVISH 22** [1] T D Easterby 6-9-2 (83) K Darley 1/1 FAV: 3403132: Rcd in 2nd, lost ¾ **84**
place when not much room 3f out, hdwy & ev ch ins fnl 1f, onepcd cl-home: remains in gd form: see 2607.
1828 **COUP DE CHANCE 75** [3] P A Blockley 4-9-3 bl (84) Dean McKeown 7/1: 0411-053: Held up, hdwy into 1 **84**
2nd 3f out, ev ch 2f out, flashed tail & lost place ins fnl 1f, no ch with first 2: eff at 11/12f, stays 2m2.5f.
3 Ran Time 4m 18.3 () Owned: Mr C N Barnes Trained: Alvechurch

CHESTER SUNDAY 01.08.04 Lefthand, Very Tight Track

3636 4.35 Listed Cheshire Life Queensferry Stakes 3yo+ (A)
£17850 £6600 £3300 6f18y rnd Firm 05 +06 Fast Outside

1918 **RUM SHOT 71** [2] H Candy 3-8-10 (100) D Sweeney 4/1: 611-401: Trkd ldrs, hdwy to lead well ins fnl 1f, kept on well, rdn out: abs: eff at 6f on firm & gd, sharp trks: runs well fresh: lightly rcd, career best.		106
3434 **TALBOT AVENUE 8** [1] M Mullineaux 6-9-0 (92) D Holland 5/2 J FAV: 5502202: Cl-up, led over 1f out till well ins fnl 1f, no extra: nicely bckd, top-weight: useful run: see 2894 & 1917.	½	102
3466 **NIGHTS CROSS 7** [3] M R Channon 3-8-10 (105) K Darley 5/2 J FAV: 4300003: Trkd ldrs, onepcd fnl 1f: op 7/4, qck reapp: see 1732.	1½	97
3075 **GOLDEVA 23** [5] R Hollinshead 5-8-13 t (100) A Culhane 5/1: 20-15054: Rear, asked for eff over 1f out, not pace of ldrs: best 952.	nk	95
3409 **VITA SPERICOLATA 9** [4]7-8-9 (81) R Ffrench 5/1: 3500055: Led till over 1f out, no extra: twice prev wnr of this race: see 1626.	2	85

5 Ran Time 1m 13.04 (u0.06) Owned: Mr H R Mould Trained: Wantage

3637 5.05 Aldford Glass & Hope House Handicap Stakes 3yo+ 0-90 (C)
£9490 £2920 £1460 1m4f66y Firm 05 -06 Slow Inside

[84]

3207 **SUALDA 17** [8] R A Fahey 5-9-0 (70) P Hanagan 5/1: 0-521231: Rear, hdwy over 1f out, led ins fnl 1f, drvn out: eff at 1m, suited by 10/12f, stays 13f: acts on firm & gd, sharp/turning, v tight or gall trks: continues in gd form: see 2892.		79
3261 **ALERON 15** [2] J J Quinn 6-9-1 p (71) D Holland 9/2: 1204352: Mid-div, hdwy over 2f out, led 1f out, hdd ins fnl 1f & hung in bhd wnr: handles firm, hvy & fibresand: gd run: see 1681.	½	77
3325+ **LENNEL 12** [5] A Bailey 6-8-12 b (68) M Fenton 11/2: 0406413: Rear, asked for eff over 2f out, styd on ins fnl 1f & nrst fin: suited by 10/11f, stays 12.5f: acts on firm & gd/soft: see 3325.	1½	72
3477 **GALLANT BOY 6** [1] P D Evans 5-8-10 vis t (66) F P Ferris(3) 9/2: 0640544: Rear, hdwy over 1f out, kept on ins fnl 1f: qck reapp: see 549.	¾	69
3083 **BEN HUR 23** [7]5-9-5 (75) S W Kelly 7/1: 0211545: Led to 1f out, no extra: btr 2745.	½	77
3437 **SPORTING GESTURE 8** [4]7-9-7 (77) P Mulrennan(3) 4/1 FAV: 0544436: Rcd in 2nd till over 1f out, wknd.	½	78
3256 **FINANCIAL FUTURE 16** [6]4-9-5 (75) J Fanning 8/1: 10-00007: Cl-up, wknd over 1f out: see 3256.	5	75
2901 **NOPEKAN 30** [3]4-9-10 (80) P Makin(5) 20/1: 06-56008: Nvr a factor: see 2582.	10	65

8 Ran Time 2m 37.78(1.38) Owned: Mr J H Tattersall Trained: Malton

WINDSOR MONDAY 02.08.04 Sharp, Fig 8 Track

Official Going GOOD/FIRM.

3638 6.05 Series Handicap Stakes For Gentleman Amateur Riders 3yo+ 0-75 (E)
£3513 £1081 £541 1m3f135y Firm 10 +01 Fast Inside

[46]

3538* **CRISTOFORO 4** [12] B J Curley 7-11-6 (66) Mr D Queally(7) 5/4 FAV: 1/-101111: Slow away, sn handy, gd hdwy to lead over 1f out, pushed clr, easily, val 8L+, hvly bckd, qck reapp: landed 4-timer: suited by 10/13f on firm, soft & both AWs, likes easy trks, esp Epsom: in grand heart & skillfully plcd, even more to come: see 3538.		82+
3481 **STOLEN SONG 7** [14] M J Ryan 4-10-8 (54) Mr S Walker 11/2: 1600632: Handy, hdwy to lead 2f out till over 1f out, cmftbly outpcd by wnr: another gd run, rtn to 14f+ shld suit: see 3481, 491.	3	59
2423 **REDI 50** [4] L M Cumani 3-10-10 (67) Mr G Arizkorreta 14/1: 054-0463: In tch, eff over 3f out, onepace: 7 wk abs: styd longer 11.6f trip & acts on firm & fast grnd: see 1042.	¾	71
4590} **PRECIOUS MYSTERY 303** [3] A King 4-10-11 (57) Mr G Tumelty(7) 20/1: 0/62016-4: ch f Titus Livius - Ascoli (Skyliner) In tch, rdn 4f out, some late gains, nvr dngrs on reapp: hdles rnr 3 months ago, earlier juv nov fill wnr (rtd 111h, 2m, hvy): '03 Flat mdn h'cap wnr for J Nicol: eff at 1m, prob stays 11.6f on firm & gd: has run well fresh & tried cheek pieces. 1 Sep'03 Yarm 8.0gd 55-51 F: 2 May'03 Newc 8.0g/f 53-49 F:	½	60
2912* **SKYLARKER 31** [8]6-12-0 (74) Mr L Jefford 11/1: 0004415: In tch, hdwy to lead 3f out till 2f out, onepcd.	hd	76
3398 **SOMAYDA 10** [11]9-9-10 (2oh) Mr J Doyle(7) 66/1: 0-000306: Led 5f out till over 3f out, wknd.	1½	41
3481+ **PONT NEUF 7** [6]4-11-5 (5ex)t (65) Mr L Newnes(3) 11/2: 0425117: Slow away, no threat: btr 3481.	1¼	62
3175 **BHUTAN 20** [10]9-10-0 (46) Mr J J Best(3) 14/1: 5130-028: Dwelt, held up, plenty to do over 3f out, wknd 2f out: btr 3175.	10	28
3276 **SADDLERS QUEST 16** [13]7-11-0 (60) Mr E Dehdashti(3) 50/1: 10650-09: b g Saddlers' Hall - Seren Quest (Rainbow Quest) Chsd leading pair till 4f out, wknd: 4th in a sell h'cap hdle 3 months ago (rtd 86h, 2m4.5f, gd): won reapp on the Flat in '03 (clmr, with C Morlock): eff arnd 10/11.5f on fast & soft: has run well fresh. 1 Jun'03 Wind 11.6g/f 57- F:	hd	41
3404 **PASO DOBLE 10** [9]6-10-9 (55) Mr J Millman(7) 33/1: 0542000: 10th: Held up, nvr a factor: see 2725.	2	33
3450 **BETTERWARE BOY 9** [2]4-11-12 (72) Mr J Morgan(5) 33/1: 545-00: 11th: In tch, wknd 2f out: see 3450.	1¾	47
3404 **DRAMATIC QUEST 10** [5]7-11-10 p (70) Mr Michael Murphy(2) 20/1: 0/0224-00: 12th: Al bhd: see 3404.	2	42

3538 Jalons Star 4 [1]6-10-11 (57) Mr M Walford(5) 50/1:0 4698} Dr Cool 647 [7]7-11-9 (69) Mr S Gascoyne(7) 33/1:0
14 Ran Time 2m 28.33 (1.03) Owned: Mr P Byrne Trained: Newmarket

3639 6.35 European Breeders Fund Maiden Stakes Fillies 2yo (D)
£5447 £1676 £838 6f rnd Firm 10 -63 Slow Inside

3290 **APPLE OF MY EYE 14** [16] J R Jenkins 2-8-11 W Ryan 14/1: 041: In tch, hdwy & short of room 2f out but sn led, pushed out, more in hand: showed more speed today & eff over an easy 6f on firm grnd: poss more to come in nxt: see 3290.		78
AMICA [8] G L Moore 2-8-11 R L Moore 50/1: 2: b f Averti - Friend For Life (Lahib) Dwelt, ran green & well bhd, hdwy 2f out, styd on ins last, no threat to wnr: Mar foal, cost 7,000gns: eff at 6f, 7f sure to suit: acts on firm grnd: ran v green & with plenty of promise, shld certainly improve & win a race.	1	74+

FLYING DANCER [13] A King 2-8-11 J D Smith 8/1: 3: b f Danzero - Alzianah (Alzao) Sn rdn bhd, eff 2f out, kept on, nrst fin on debut: Mar foal, cost 58,000gns: sister to a 6f juv wnr: dam useful sprinter h'capper: eff at 6f, shapes likes 7f will suit: acts on firm grnd: will learn plenty for this & improve. ¾ **72**
3418 **CASTEROSSA 9** [7] D Haydn Jones 2-8-11 Paul Eddery 16/1: 644: Cl-up, led over 1f out, sn hdd & no extra ins last: see 3418. *1½* **68**
3386 **CAONA 10** [14]2-8-11 E Ahern 7/1: 05: b f Miswaki - Hawzah (Green Desert) Cl-up, eff to chall over 1f out, sn no extra: Mar foal, cost 170,000gns: led to apprec 6/7f as a juv: drifter from 7/2. *1¼* **64**
3258 **NIGHT OUT 16** [12]2-8-11 D Holland 33/1: 06: In tch, wknd over 1f out. *½* **62**
ZONIC [1]2-8-11 B Doyle 14/1: 7: V slow away & left start, late gains despite short of room. *shd* **61**
RED FINESSE [5]2-8-11 P Robinson 2/1 FAV: 8: In tch, wknd dist on debut: well bckd. *nk* **60**
2970 **BLAZING VIEW 28** [3]2-8-11 W Supple 4/1: 59: In tch, wknd 2f out. *1½* **56**
GRAMADA [4]2-8-11 S Drowne 25/1: 0: 10th: Al bhd on debut. *3½* **46**
1717 **VERITABLE 81** [2]2-8-11 J F Egan 12/1: 40: 11th: Led till dist, wknd qckly: abs, btr 1717 (5f). *½* **44**
LIGHTED WAY [15]2-8-11 N Chalmers(5) 25/1: 0: 12th: Dwelt, sn handy, wknd over 2f out. *1* **41**
NIGHT CLUB QUEEN [10]2-8-11 T Quinn 20/1: 0: 13th: Al bhd. *3* **32**
13 Ran Time 1m 14.69 (4.39) Owned: Mr R B Hill Trained: Royston

3640

7.05 Sponsor A Race At Windsor Handicap Stakes 3yo+ 0-70 (E) **[69]**
£3494 £1075 £538 **5f10y rnd** **Firm 10** **-23 Slow** Inside

2396 **DAVIDS MARK 51** [11] J R Jenkins 4-8-9 (50) L Dettori 11/2: 0-034441: Made all, styd on gamely when prsd ins last, drvn out: 7 wk abs: eff at 5f, stays 6f on firm, gd & polytrack, likes sharp trks: eff with/without visor or cheek pieces: goes well fresh: back to form with forcing tactics & well h'capped: see 897. **58**
3537* **DOUBLE M 5** [6] Mrs L Richards 7-9-10 (7ex)vis (65) R Thomas(5) 9/2: 2136612: Held up, hdwy to chall just ins last, just held for press: well bckd: in fine form: see 3537. *shd* **72**
3574 **LOCH INCH 3** [16] J M Bradley 7-8-11 bl (52) R L Moore 7/2 FAV: 0404233: Held up, hdwy & short of room 2f out, kept on to chall ins last, just held, not btn far: qck reapp: see 3574. *nk* **58**
3403 **YORKIES BOY 10** [13] N E Berry 9-8-7 p (48) M Halford(7) 20/1: 5400004: Held up, hdwy & short of room over 2f out till over 1f out, kept on ins last, nrst fin: pleasing eff & a shade unlucky: see 1914. *1½* **50**
3165 **PULSE 21** [8]6-9-5 p (60) D Holland 14/1: 6453005: Handy trav well, eff & edged left dist, no extra. *nk* **61**
2957 **HARBOUR HOUSE 29** [4]5-8-5 (46) A Daly 16/1: 6313026: Slow away & bhd, eff & short of room 2f out, no dngr: see 1544 (banded). *2½* **40**
3537 **BLESSED PLACE 5** [12]4-8-10 (51) T Quinn 9/1: 3541507: In tch, eff dist, sn wknd: best 3165. *hd* **44**
3332 **ERRACHT 12** [7]6-9-6 (61) G Baker 20/1: 1600058: In tch, eff over 1f out, sn wknd: see 1371. *¾* **52**
3479 **BALLINGER EXPRESS 7** [2]4-9-7 bl (62) Martin Dwyer 14/1: 5320029: In tch, wknd 2f out: btr 3479 (6f). *1½* **49**
3537 **INTELLIBET ONE 5** [14]4-8-13 (54) N Callan 11/1: 0340000: 10th: In tch, eff well over 1f out, sn short of room but wknd: see 2951, 2599. *shd* **40**
3403 **AVIT 10** [15]4-7-12 (1oh) (38) A McCarthy 10/1: 0601450: 11th: Handy, wknd dist: op 16/1. *shd* **25**
1371 **TRIPTI 99** [9]4-8-8 (49) J F McDonald(3) 33/1: 0200000: 12th: Bhd, nvr a factor: 3 month abs. *¾* **33**
3332* **TENDER 12** [5]4-8-11 p (52) S Drowne 16/1: 5000410: 13th: In tch, wknd 2f out: btr 3332 (polytrk). *½* **34**
3403 **FLAPDOODLE 10** [3]6-8-7 (48) T P Queally 20/1: 050-5000: 14th: In tch, wknd qckly 2f out: see 2585. *½* **28**
3371 **MIRASOL PRINCESS 11** [1]3-9-11 (69) Dane O'Neill 20/1: 0466640: 15th: In tch, wknd over 1f out. *2½* **42**
2803 **CATCHTHEBATCH 35** [10]8-8-6 (47) S Carson 33/1: 0-430000: 16th: Chsd wnr 4f, wknd: see 619. *2* **14**
16 Ran Time 1m 0.67 (1.67) Owned: Miss C Roylance Trained: Royston

3641

7.35 Slough Estates Handicap Stakes 3yo+ 0-85 (D) **[81]**
£5493 £1690 £845 **1m67y rnd** **Firm 10** **+00 Fast** Inside

3184 **FEN GYPSY 19** [6] P D Evans 6-8-12 (65) N Callan 13/2: 2451241: Nvr far away, went on dist, held on well, drvn out: eff at 7f/1m, has tried 12f: acts on firm, gd/soft grnd & prob polytrack: handles a sharp or gall trk: mainly consistent sort who has broken blood vessels but seems over that now: see 3034. **72**
3524 **NAUTICAL 5** [4] A W Carroll 6-7-13 (1ow)(1oh) (50) C Catlin 20/1: 0464302: Dwelt, keen in rear, hdwy to chall fnl 1f, just btn: qk reapp & 1lb o/w may have proved v costly: acts on gd, fm & polytrack. *nk* **58**
3364 **RAFFERTY 11** [1] C E Brittain 5-10-0 (81) D Holland 7/2: 5000-053: Held up, drvn & styd on strongly fnl 1f, just btn in a 3-way photo: gd run under big weight: see 3001. *hd* **84**
3187 **JOHANNIAN 19** [7] J M Bradley 6-9-4 (71) R L Moore 12/1: 0350204: Front rank, led 2f out till dist, not qckn ins fnl 1f: op 9/1, clr of rem: see 2931. *1¼* **71**
3477+ **A ONE 7** [8]5-10-4 (6ex) (85) F P Ferris(3) 9/4 FAV: 1110115: Led till 2f out, sn lost pl, rallied late: hvly bckd under top-weight: did not appear suited by this drop back to 1m, most prog over 10f in 3477 (here). *3* **81**
3472 **MACLEAN 8** [5]3-9-3 vis (77) L Dettori 7/2: 2-213656: Trkd ldr, ev ch till wknd fnl 1f: bckd. *½* **72**
3408 **BARRANTES 10** [2]7-9-12 (79) N Chalmers(5) 25/1: 36000-07: Chsd ldrs, wknd 2f out: see 3408. *½* **73**
3465 **JOOLS 8** [3]6-9-9 (76) T Quinn 11/1: 044650U: Held up, slipped & u.r. halfway: unfortunate incident. **0**
8 Ran Time 1m 43.85 (0.85) Owned: Mr P D Evans Trained: Abergavenny

3642

8.05 Book Your Discounted Tickets On-Line Maiden Stakes 3yo (D)
£4290 £1320 £660 **1m2f7y** **Firm 10** **-01 Slow** Inside

4337} **POISE 318** [6] Sir Michael Stoute 3-8-9 L Dettori 1/3 FAV: 2-1: b f Rainbow Quest - Crepe Ginger (Sadler's Wells) Keen & prom, went on 1.5f out, pushed clr, cmftbly: well bkcd at odds on: rnr-up in a fill stks event on sole juv start: half-sister to a mid-dist wnr, cost 340,000gns: apprec this step up to 10f, 12f will suit: acts on fm & fast, sharp or gall trk: runs well fresh: simple task, will rate higher. **87**
2 Sep'03 Newb 7g/f 87- B:
3186 **MICHABO 19** [9] D R C Elsworth 3-9-0 (78) Dane O'Neill 10/1: 0-43262: Tried to make all, collared over 1f out, kept on but no ch with wnr: acts on gd & firm grnd: caught a tartar here, see 2700. *5* **80**
1965 **LAABBIJ 70** [4] M P Tregoning 3-9-0 BL (75) Martin Dwyer 8/1: 0-6053: Dwelt, chsd ldrs, onepcd fnl 1.5f in first time blnks: see 1965. *3* **74**
PLEASANT [8] L G Cottrell 3-8-9 J F Egan 33/1: 4: b f Topanoora - Devon Peasant (Deploy) Well bhd, styd on late, nvr dngrs on debut: ran v green: dam wng hdler. *2½* **64**
1130 **CELEBRE CITATION 112** [3]3-9-0 T O Urbina 16/1: 05: ch c Peintre Celebre - Kotama (Shahrastani) Chsd ldrs, btn 2f out: long abs & tried a t-strap: mid-dist bred, with J Fanshawe. *2* **65**
3480 **CEYLON ROUND 7** [7]3-8-9 D Corby(3) 33/1: 006: Front rank 1m, sn wknd: see 2953. *nk* **59**

WINDSOR **MONDAY 02.08.04 Sharp, Fig 8 Track**

STAGE SECRET [2]3-9-0 S Drowne 25/1: 7: ch c Zilzal - Tuxford Hideaway (Cawston's Clown) Keen in mid-div, rdn & btn 2f out on debut: unrcd for Mrs A Perrett & cost current connections 27,000gns: related to useful performers Desert Deer & Branston Abby (sprinter): now with Miss E Lavelle. *1¼* **62**

ONE OF DISTINCTION [1]3-8-9 W Supple 16/1: 8: Held up, al bhd on debut. *17* **23**

ITS MY SON [5]3-9-0 A Daly 33/1: 9: Al well bhd, t.o. in last on racecourse bow. *19* **0**

9 Ran Time 2m 07.13 (1.13) Owned: Cheveley Park Stud Trained: Newmarket

3643 **8.35 Come Racing This Sunday Handicap Stakes 3yo+ 0-70 (E)** **[70]**
£3650 £1123 £562 **6f rnd** **Firm 10** **-41 Slow** Inside

3364 **MICHELLE MA BELLE 11** [6] S Kirk 4-10-0 bl (70) J F Egan 25/1: 0220001: Mid-div, prog wide halfway, led dist, styd on strongly, rdn out: nicely bckd at long odds, top-weight: eff at 6/7f on firm, soft grnd & polytrack: handles any trk, carries weight well: wears blnks now & well h'capped, could follow up: see 799. **77**

3401 **FULL SPATE 10** [18] J M Bradley 9-9-10 (66) R L Moore 8/1: 6320002: Trkd ldrs, styd on strongly fnl 1f despite drifting left, not pace of wnr: usually runs well here at Windsor, see 2626 & 2451 (C/D). *1* **70**

3289 **JAGGED 2** [14] J R Jenkins 4-8-13 vis (55) L Dettori 11/2: 0002363: Trkd ldrs, kept on under press fnl 1f: qck reapp & swapped blnks for visor: sound run, but remains a mdn: see 3289. *nk* **58**

3569 **HIGH RIDGE 3** [13] J M Bradley 5-9-13 p (69) Dane O'Neill 9/4 FAV: 2341224: Held up, switched wide halfway, fin strongly but too late: qck reapp & shorter priced s/mate of rnr-up: continues in fine form, see 3568. *nk* **71**

2258 **B A HIGHFLYER 57** [5]4-9-2 (58) C Catlin 25/1: 6-050005: Held up, prog wide 2f out, nrst fin: 8 wk abs & modest low draw: encouraging run, spot on next time: see 1025. *hd* **59**

3289* **ADANTINO 16** [16]5-9-1 bl (57) T P Queally 11/2: 1336316: Trkd ldrs, ev ch dist, onepcd ins fnl 1f. *½* **56**

2396 **MAYZIN 2** [15]4-8-7 p (49) E Ahern 20/1: 4000007: Front rank, onepcd fnl 1f: qck reapp. *¾* **46**

3341 **AINTNECESSARILYSO 12** [12]6-8-13 (55) M Halford(7) 10/1: 6115368: Rear, styd on late, nvr dngrs. *nk* **51**

3490 **WARLINGHAM 7** [10]6-9-0 (56) S Drowne 25/1: 0505009: Nvr btr than mid-div: see 1731. *¾* **50**

3177 **PINK SUPREME 20** [3]3-8-6 (1ow) (51) N Callan 50/1: 0000060: 10th: Nvr btr than mid-div: mod draw. *nk* **45**

3401* **THREEZEDZZ 10** [4]6-9-5 t (61) S Donohoe(7) 16/1: 00/-00010: 11th: Front rank, wknd dist: poor draw. *½* **52**

3045 **FIREWORK 25** [19]6-9-6 p (62) T Quinn 8/1: 0650100: 12th: Led till dist, wknd: twice below 2715. *1¼* **49**

3109 **FORMALISE 23** [11]4-9-1 (57) R Thomas(5) 20/1: 0-005050: 13th: Swerved start, nvr btr than mid-div. *shd* **44**

2806 **SEMPER PARATUS 35** [2]5-8-12 bl (54) M Tebbutt 33/1: 4002030: 14th: Al well bhd from mod draw. *¾* **39**

123 **NATHAN DETROIT 247** [17]4-9-0 (56) D Sweeney 33/1: 0000-0: 15th: b c Entrepreneur - Mainly Sunset (Red Sunset) Al outpcd after long abs: mod AW form prev, incl in blnks: cost 16,000gns & related to sprint wnrs. *½* **39**

3333* **WOODBURY 12** [9]5-9-6 (62) G Baker 20/1: 260-0410: 16th: Chsd ldrs, wknd 2f out: btr 3333 (AW). *1½* **41**

2396 **NIGHT CAP 51** [7]5-8-1 (43) R Miles 12/1: 6002030: 17th: Front rank, wkng when hmpd dist: 7 wk abs. *nk* **21**

17 Ran Time 1m 13.35(3.05) Owned: Bill Allan & Mrs Michelle Cousins Trained: Upper Lambourn

RIPON **MONDAY 02.08.04 Righthand, Sharpish Track**

Official Going Good/Firm All Times Slow

3644 **2.15 Bbc Radio York Sandie Dunleavy E B F Novice Stakes 2yo (D)**
£5387 £1658 £829 **6f str** **Good/Firm** **V Slow** Stands Side

3266 **IMPERIAL SOUND 16** [2] T D Barron 2-9-5 (93) S Sanders 2/9 FAV: 1201: Sn led & made all, easily pulled clr over 1f out, val 9L+: well bckd at odds on: eff at 5f/easy 6f on fast & gd grnd: likes to race with/force the pace: useful, can rate higher: see 3266. **97+**

2959 **WOLF HAMMER 29** [3] J Howard Johnson 2-8-12 P Mulrennan(3) 25/1: 02: Went right start, sn trkd ldr, rdn & no impress over 1f out: gelded, op 16/1: caught a useful sort: see 2959 (7f). *5* **70**

3483 **UNLIMITED 7** [1] Mrs A Duffield 2-9-0 (77) J Quinn 20/1: 212503: Chsd wnr early, no impress halfway. *3½* **61**

ROCKPILER 0 [4] J Howard Johnson 2-8-8 R Winston 11/2: 4: b g Halling - Emma Peel (Emarati) Went right start, sn struggling & bhd, eased down fnl 2f: op 4/1, stablemate of rnr-up: Feb first foal, E300,000 purchase: dam a 6f juv wnr & a multiple winning 3yo sprinter. *dist* **0**

4 Ran Time 1m 15.35 (5.35) Owned: Mr J Stephenson Trained: Thirsk

3645 **2.45 Bbc Radio York Colin Hazelden Selling Handicap Stakes 3yo 35-55 (F)** **[65]**
£3251 £929 £464 **5f str** **Good/Firm** **V Slow** Stands Side

3371 **REHIA 11** [8] J W Hills 3-9-1 (52) M Hills 7/2 FAV: 4035031: Chsd ldr, led over 1f out, rdn & just held on: no bid: eff at 5f on fast, gd & polytrack, stiff or sharp trk: apprec rtn to sell grade: see 548. **57**

3180 **BURKEES GRAW 20** [3] Mrs S Lamyman 3-8-8 (45) R Winston 13/2: 0000202: Chsd ldrs, drvn & styd on well cl-home, just failed: snld find a sell h'cap: see 2219, 619. *nk* **49**

3024 **BARRAS 26** [4] Miss Gay Kelleway 3-9-1 vis (52) M Fenton 4/1: 0354003: Led till over 1f out, no extra. *1½* **51**

2849 **DESIGNER CITY 33** [1] A Berry 3-8-2 (39) F Norton 14/1: 0-000004: Held up, rdn & mod prog, no threat. *3½* **27**

3396 **BANK GAMES 10** [2]3-8-11 (48) P Mulrennan(3) 6/1: 0065: Rdn mid-div, nvr pace to land blow: h'cap bow. *1* **33**

3262 **SCOOBY DOOBY DO 16** [6]3-9-4 P (55) V Halliday 10/1: 60-5606: Mid-div, outpcd from halfway: btr 2728. *3* **32**

2808 **VAUDEVIRE 35** [7]3-8-2 bl (39) J Fanning 13/2: 6030447: Cl-up, btn over 1f out: op 8/1: btr 2808. *1½* **11**

3547 **GEMINI GIRL 4** [5]3-7-13 VIS (36) N Mackay(3) 7/1: 0000008: Sn struggling in rear: first time visor. *1¼* **4**

3226 **RUSTY BOY 17** [9]3-8-1 (38) D Fentiman(7) 50/1: 60-009: Prom towards centre, struggling from halfway. *6* **0**

9 Ran Time 1m 02.11 (4.31) Owned: Mr G and Mrs L Woodward Trained: Lambourn

3646 **3.15 Armstrong Memorial Rated Stakes Handicap 3yo+ 0-95 (C)** **[103]**
£10499 £3982 £1991 **6f str** **Good/Firm** **Slow** Stands Side

2770 **BYGONE DAYS 37** [1] W J Haggas 3-8-9 (84) D Holland 2/1 FAV: 02-13451: Made all stands rail, just held on for press cl-home, all out: nicely bckd: stay 7f well, suited by 6f on fast & soft grnd, stiff/gall or easy trks: loves to force the pace: useful & genuine gelding: see 946. **93**

3574 **INTER VISION 3** [2] A Dickman 4-8-8 (79) R Winston 9/2: 0050042: Chsd ldrs, styd on well for *shd* **87**

RIPON   MONDAY 02.08.04   Righthand, Sharpish Track

press cl-home, just failed: qk reapp, clr rem: likes this trk, on a fair mark, likes Ripon: see 1767.

3569 **ROMANY NIGHTS 3** [4] J W Unett 4-8-10 bl (81) S Hitchcott(3) 6/1: 4602053: Rdn chasing ldrs, kept   3½   78
on onepace, nvr threat: qck reapp: see 3146, 2286 & 2187.

3434 **BO MCGINTY 9** [9] R A Fahey 3-8-11 (86) P Hanagan 8/1: 1-012004: Rdn towards rear, little hdwy.   5   69

2950 **BONNE DE FLEUR 30** [6]3-9-1 (90) D McGaffin 33/1: 232-1005: Mid-div, rdn & no impress fnl 2f.   1¼   69

3434 **INDIAN SPARK 9** [8]10-8-12 (83) N Mackay(3) 16/1: 4600006: Rdn towards rear, nvr factor: see 1703.   shd   62

2950 **TIMES REVIEW 30** [7]3-8-8 (83) K Darley 33/1: 0-251007: Al rear, outpcd: btr 2137.   ½   60

2816} **IMPRESSIVE FLIGHT 388** [10]5-9-7 (92) P Makin(5) 16/1: 310/536-8: b f Flying Spur - Certain   nk   68
Impression (Forli) Dwelt, al rear: reapp: lightly rcd '03 (cond stks plcd, rtd 82): nov stks & h'cap wnr '02
(List rnr-up): eff at 5/6f on fast & gd/soft grnd, stiff/gall trks: can go well fresh.
1 Aug'02 Newm 6gd 96-88 B: 2 Jun'02 York 6g/s 90-83 B: 1 Apr'02 Thir 6fm 83- E:

3569 **DAME DE NOCHE 3** [3]4-9-0 (85) I Mongan 9/2: 3000539: Cl-up, btn 2f out: poss too soon after 3569.   2½   53
9 Ran   Time 1m 13.49 (3.49)   Owned: Mr J Hanson   Trained: Newmarket

3647   3.45 Tommy Shedden Challenge Trophy Handicap Stakes 3yo 0-85 (D)   [89]
£6825 £2100 £1050   1m2f   **Good/Firm**   **Slow**   Inside

3378* **DOUBLE VODKA 11** [5] Mrs J R Ramsden 3-8-3 (64) P Hanagan 9/4 FAV: 0624011: Held up & al trav   77+
well, shkn up to lead well ins last under hand riding, cosily, val 2L+: eff at 1m/10f, stays 11f: acts on fast &
gd/soft grnd: best held up: appeals as the type to progress, keep on side: see 3378, 2960.

3377* **RIO DE JUMEIRAH 11** [6] C E Brittain 3-9-7 (82) D Holland 13/2: 5-360512: Trkd ldr, rdn/chall &   ½   90
narrow lead over 1f out, edged left & hdd well ins last: op 4/1: another gd run: see 3377.

3309* **FUTOO 14** [4] G M Moore 3-8-5 (66) B Swarbrick(5) 5/1: 6513013: Led, hdd over 1f out, onepace.   2½   70

3358 **GREAT SCOTT 2** [3] M Johnston 3-9-5 (80) S Chin 3/1: 05-00534: Trkd ldrs, rdn & btn 2f out: bckd.   5   77

2627* **GAME DAME 42** [1]3-9-3 (78) M Hills 9/2: 33-415: Trkd ldrs, btn 2f out: op 7/2, abs: btr 2627 (1m mdn).   1¾   73

3413 **ROSIE MAC 10** [2]3-8-0 (2ow) (59) F Norton 14/1: 63466: Rear, no impress fnl 3f: flattered 3121 (7f).   3½   51
6 Ran   Time 2m 07.93 (4.63)   Owned: Mrs Alison Iles   Trained: Thirsk

3648   4.15 Black Sheep Brewery Maiden Stakes 3yo+ (D)
£4462 £1373 £686   1m2f   **Good/Firm**   **V Slow**   Inside

3789} **PAYOLA 346** [3] C E Brittain 3-8-7   S Sanders 13/2: 0-1: b f Red Ransom - Bevel (Mr Prospector)   70
Chsd ldrs, hdwy towards centre 3f out & led over 1f out, drvn out: unplcd sole '03 starts (rtd 72, fill mdn):
half-sister to a 1m wnr & a mid-dist scorer: apprec step up to 10f, may get further: acts on fast grnd & a sharpish
trk: goes well fresh: entitled to progress.

3572 **JIDIYA 3** [1] S Gollings 5-9-7   I Mongan 20/1: 52-002: b g Lahib - Yaqatha (Sadler's Wells) Sn   ½   73
handy, drvn to chall over 1f out, not pace of wnr nr fin: mod hdles form 03/04 (rtd 91h, unplcd, nov): mod form on
the level prev: eff around a sharpish 10f on fast grnd: improved run.

3292 **NEWS SKY 14** [2] B W Hills 3-8-12 (80) M Hills 1/6 FAV: 0223: Led till over 1f out, rdn & btn ins last.   4   67

3246 **ROUGE ET NOIR 17** [6] Mrs M Reveley 6-9-7 Neil Brown(7) 28/1: 004: Held up in tch, wknd 3f out.   12   49

1978 **BLUE NUN 8** [4]3-8-7 (47) J Quinn 100/1: 5005: Chsd ldrs, rdn & btn over 3f out: 10 wk abs.   5   37

3230 **ALETHEA GEE 17** [5]6-9-2 T Eaves(3) 100/1: 0-006: Rear & struggling from 4f out: longer trip, modest.   dist   0
6 Ran   Time 2m 10.23 (6.93)   Owned: Sheikh Marwan Al Maktoum   Trained: Newmarket

3649   4.45 Children's Day Handicap Stakes 3yo+ 0-70 (E)   [77]
£3747 £1153 £576   1m4f60y   **Good/Firm**   **V Slow**   Inside

3207 **HEARTHSTEAD DREAM 18** [8] J D Bethell 3-9-5 bl (68) J Fanning 5/1: 3215121: Chsd ldrs, smooth prog   74
to lead over 2f out, rdn & al holding rivals ins last: eff at 1m, suited by 12f on firm & soft: in fine form.

2960 **HERNANDOS BOY 29** [10] Mrs M Reveley 3-8-6 (55) T Eaves(3) 11/1: 00-50002: Chsd ldrs, short of   1   59
room over 1f out, rdn & no room again dist, kept on late: eff around 12f, shld get further: improved on fast.

3345 **TIGER FROG 12** [4] J Mackie 5-9-10 bl (62) Derek Nolan(7) 3/1 FAV: 0020/-153: Chsd ldrs, eff & chsd   hd   65
wnr over 1f out, no extra ins last: see 3345 & 3207.

3502* **SHOTLEY DANCER 6** [9] N Bycroft 5-8-2 (6ex) (40) F Norton 4/1: 0435314: Rear, hdwy towards centre   1¼   41
3f out, styd on for press, not able to chall: qck reapp: just btr 3502.

3207 **ARCHIRONDEL 18** [7]6-9-6 (58) P Mulrennan(3) 13/2: 2102155: Rear, styd on for press, not pace of   hd   58
wnr: nicely bckd: well clr of rem: see 2813.

2992 **ALL BLEEVABLE 27** [5]7-8-7 (45) J Quinn 14/1: 00///-66: Chsd ldrs, btn when short of room 2f out.   9   32

2653 **TURFTANZER 41** [6]5-7-12 (6oh)t (30) Kim Tinkler 28/1: 0000457: Led till over 2f out, fdd: 6 wk abs.   ¾   22

3502 **DALRIATH 6** [2]5-8-1 (39) Dean Williams(7) 16/1: 5035208: Al bhd: btr 3354.   7   15

3502 **ZAN LO 6** [1]4-8-13 (51) M Fenton 33/1: 0060009: Chsd ldr, drvn when hung right 3f out, qck reapp.   2½   23

2912 **TRUSTED MOLE 31** [3]6-9-6 (58) B Swarbrick(5) 5/1: 5162100: 10th: Mid-div, wknd over 3f out: btr 2782.   5   23
10 Ran   Time 2m 41.6(8.1)   Owned: Mr S A B Dinsmore   Trained: Middleham

CARLISLE   MONDAY 02.08.04   Righthand, Stiff Track, Uphill Finish

Official Going Firm (Good/Firm Places)

3650   6.20 Red Mills Irish Horsefeeds Lady Amateur Riders' Handicap Stakes 3yo+ 0-70 (E)   [47]
£3786 £1165 £583   7f200y rnd   **Good/Firm 26**   **-23 Slow**   Inside

3501 **GIFTED FLAME 6** [6] T D Barron 5-11-0 (61) Miss E J Jones 5/1 CO FAV: 0040031: Slow away, gd prog   72
to lead ins fnl 1f, rdn out: quick reapp: eff at 7/8.4f on firm & gd, prob not hvy: likes Carlisle: well h'capped.

3229 **PEPPER ROAD 17** [5] R Bastiman 5-10-6 (53) Miss R Bastiman(5) 5/1 CO FAV: 60-00122: Cl-up, styd on   1¾   59
to lead 2f out, hdd ins fnl 1f, not pace wnr: another gd run here at Carlisle: see 3229 & 2447.

3529 **JOEY PERHAPS 5** [15] J R Best 3-10-1 (55) Miss K Manser(5) 8/1: 0006323: Mid div, prog 3f out,   1¼   57
kept on fnl 1f, no ch with front two: qck reapp: mdn, see 3529 & 3309.

2688 **KELSEAS KOLBY** 39 [2] P A Blockley 4-10-8 vis (55) Miss Faye Bramley(5) 20/1: 0014344: Chsd ldrs,   ½   58
onepcd dist: likes Leicester & sell h'caps: see 2688 & 2431.

3949/ **FIROZI** 339 [8]5-10-2 (49) Miss V Tunnicliffe(5) 14/1: 450223-5: b f Forzando - Lambast (Relkino)   1   50
Mid-div, prog 2f out, onepcd fnl 1f: plcd on 2 of 3 03/04 hdle starts (rtd 90h, nov hdle): plcd 3 times in '03
(h'caps & sell): sell h'cap & clmg wnr in '02: eff at 7f/10f on fast & gd grnd: has gone well fresh: tried blnks,
eff with cheek pieces: with R A Fahey. 2 Aug'03 Carl 7.9m 48-49 E: 2 Aug'03 Newc 10.1g/f 44-(49) G:
2 Sep'02 Thir 8gd 57- E: 2 Aug'02 Beve 7.4g/f 43- E: 1 Aug'02 Carl 6.8g/f 55- F: 1 Jul'02 Thir 8g/f 60-55 F:

3363 **KAMAS WHEEL** 11 [3]5-8-13 (32) Miss Kelly Harrison(3) 33/1: 0D60-006: Handy over 6f, sn onepcd.   shd   32
2794 **NIGHT MARKET** 35 [12]6-10-5 (52) Mrs N Wilson(3) 9/1: 600-0107: In tch, no extra bef 1f out: btr 2572.   shd   51
3505 **RAINSTORM** 6 [4]9-9-7 (40) Mrs S Owen(3) 5/1 CO FAV: 6000028: Slow away, prog & ev ch bef 1f out,   nk   38
sn wknd: quick reapp: won this race 12 months ago off a 4lb higher mark: btr 3505.

3363* **OH SO ROSIE** 11 [16]4-10-8 p (55) Mrs S Moore(3) 13/2: 3250019: Slow away, nvr nrr than mid-div.   1½   50
2988 **MUTARED** 27 [1]6-9-9 p (42) Mrs Emma Littmoden(3) 33/1: 00-00000: 10th: No impress in mid-div.   nk   36
2988 **DARK CUT** 27 [9]4-9-4 (37) Miss Dawn Rankin(5) 33/1: 0000000: 11th: Al bhd: see 2708.   1   29
3426 **NOBLE PURSUIT** 9 [13]7-10-3 (50) Miss V Barr(7) 16/1: 0024030: 12th: Al in rear: btr 3426.   2   38
2544 **THWAAB** 45 [14]12-9-5 vis (38) Miss Victoria Casey(7) 50/1: 20600/-00: 13th: b g Dominion - Velvet   ½   25
Habit (Habitat) Al bhd: 6 wk abs: rnr-up once in '02 (class stks, rtd $65 & 49): h'cap wnr on fnl '01 start: eff
by 7f/1m, acts on gd/soft, loves firm or fast: eff with/without visor or blnks: with F Watson.
2 Aug'02 Carl 6.8m 65- E: 1 Sep'01 Sali 8g/f 55-48 E:

2315 **HEBENUS** 54 [10]5-9-12 (45) Miss H Cuthbert(5) 25/1: 5250-200: 14th: Cl-up 6f, fdd: 8 wk abs.   1   30
2811 **THE SPOOK** 35 [7]4-9-6 (39) Mrs S Bosley 40/1: 05300-00: 15th: Al in rear: see 2811.   nk   23
2688 **MAGIC MAMMAS TOO** 39 [11]4-10-1 (48) Ms C Williams 20/1: 2534050: 16th: Led 6f, fdd: see 334.   1¼   30
16 Ran   Time 1m 41.69 (3.99)   Owned: Mr Raymond Miquel   Trained: Thirsk

---

3651   6.50 Beadle And Hill Claiming Stakes 3yo (F)
£3164 £904 £452   **6f192y rnd**   **Good/Firm 26**   **-20 Slow**   Inside

3414 **CHUBBES** 10 [8] M D Hammond 3-8-4 bl (48) Hayley Turner(5) 13/2: 0-004401: Mid-div, prog 2f out,   48
drvn out to lead cl-home: eff at 7f/1m on fast, gd grnd & polytrack: eff with blnks: see 2932 &n 2704.

3298 **LOVE OF LIFE** 14 [2] Julian Poulton 3-8-3 (38) Lisa Jones(3) 16/1: 00602: Slow away, prog after   nk   45
5f, ev ch fnl 1f, just held by wnr: eff at 7f on fast grnd: best eff to date: see 2854.

3541 **LA CALERA** 4 [7] M F Harris 3-8-3 vis (65) A Nicholls 12/1: 0-310053: Led 4f, rallied to lead just   ¾   43
ins fnl 1f, hdd & no extra cl-home: quick reapp: claimed for 8,000: eff at 7f/7.5f on fast grnd: see 3541.

3262 **FIREBIRD RISING** 16 [1] T D Barron 3-8-5 (58) N Mackay(3) 3/1 FAV: 3-503604: Handy, styd on to   ½   44
lead 3f out, hdd fnl 1f, no extra: bckd: eff at 7f on fast grnd: see 2042.

3092 **GARNOCK VENTURE** 24 [4]3-8-10 bl (52) S Sanders 15/2: 0010055: Prom, ev ch halfway, wknd bef 1f out.5   39
3392 **MULTIPLE CHOICE** 10 [12]3-8-11 e t (64) J P Guillambert(3) 7/2: 0000246: Cl-up over 4f, wknd: btr 3091.   1½   37
3515 **DELUSION** 5 [3]3-8-2 (53) D Allan 10/1: 40-63007: Nvr nrr than mid-div: quick reapp.   1½   25
3153 **COMPASSION** 21 [13]3-7-13 p (46) P Hanagan 13/2: 0445368: Chsd ldrs 5f, sn wknd: btr 2969.   2½   17
3262 **BEAVER DIVA** 16 [10]3-7-13 (40) D Fentiman(7) 10/1: 4002209: Keen rear, nvr a factor: btr 2808 & 2541.   3½   10
3414 **MR MOON** 10 [6]3-8-3 BL (29) P Mathers(5) 20/1: 6600060: 10th: Al bhd: 1st time blnks.   hd   13
     BLACKPOOL JACK 0 [11]3-8-4 T Hamilton(2) 33/1: 0: 11th: Slow away, al bhd on debut.   8   0
11 Ran   Time 1m 27.17 (3.27)   Owned: Garden Shed Racing 1   Trained: Middleham

---

3652   7.20 Lloyd Bmw Maiden Auction Stakes 2yo (E)
£3478 £1070 £535   **5f rnd**   **Good/Firm 26**   **+ 02 Fast**   Inside

3355 **MONASHEE ROSE** 11 [4] J S Moore 2-8-2 N Mackay(3) 10/1: 01: Prom, styd on to lead dist, pushed   80+
out, val 3L+: bckd from 20/1: fast juv time: eff at 5f, shld get 6f: acts on fast grnd & a stiff trk: left debut eff
bhd with easy success & can rate higher: see 3355.

3525 **BOND BABE** 5 [5] B Smart 2-8-4 F Norton 7/1: 42: Slow away, prog halfway, ev ch 1f out, kept on   2   73
but not pace wnr: quick reapp: op 5/1: eff at 5f on fast grnd: see 3525 (debut).

3178 **BREAKING SHADOW** 20 [6] R A Fahey 2-8-9 P Hanagan 2/5 FAV: 23: Led, hdd dist, no extra: well   1¾   73
bckd at odds-on: disapp eff & reportedly hated today's fast grnd: showed more in 3178 (gd/soft).

3227 **SHATIN LEADER** 17 [3] Miss L A Perratt 2-8-2 R Ffrench 14/1: P634: Cl-up over 3f, hung right &, no extra.1   63
1401 **CREE** 97 [1]2-8-8 BL S Sanders 4/1: 005: b c Indian Ridge - Nightitude (Night Shift) Bhd, nvr a   2   63
factor: long abs & 1st time blnks: Mar foal, cost 10,000 gns: half brother to smart 1m performer abroad: dam
smart sprinter as a juv: sire decent performer at sprint dists: W R Muir.

     HITS ONLY CASH 0 [2]2-8-10 Dean McKeown 12/1: 6: b c Inchinor - Persian Blue (Persian Bold)   5   51
Slow away, wknd ins fnl 2f: debut: Feb foal, half brother $f wnr at 2: dam mid-dist plcd.
6 Ran   Time 1m 0.72 (1.22)   Owned: The Fairway Connection   Trained: Hungerford

---

3653   7.50 Coors Brewers Handicap Stakes 3yo 0-80 (D)
£5772 £1776 £888   **1m3f206y**   **Good/Firm 26**   **+17 Fast**   Outside   [83]

3261 **BAILEYS DANCER** 16 [1] M Johnston 3-9-6 (75) J Fanning 9/2: 0400201: Cl-up, styd on to lead 2f   82+
out, went clr under hand riding, eased cl-home, val 3L+: fast time: eff at 1m/10f, now stays 12f: acts on fast &
gd grnd: unexposed around this trk: see 2735.

3240* **CHARLOTTE VALE** 17 [4] M D Hammond 3-9-4 (73) M Fenton 3/1: 6521312: Mid-div, prog & ev ch bef 1f 1½   76
out, kept on, al held by wnr: proving consistent: see 3240.

4726/ **AURELIA** 294 [2] Sir Mark Prescott 3-9-7 (76) S Sanders 11/10 FAV: 6314-3: b f Rainbow Quest -   ½   78
Fern (Shirley Heights) Bhd, gd prog 2f out, onepcd ins fnl 1f: reapp: mdn wnr on 1 of 4 '03 starts: eff at
1m/10f, back to form on step up to 12f: acts on firm & fast grnd: unexposed in h'cap grade for shrewd trainer.
1 Sep'03 Bath 10.2fm 75- D:

3192 **EGO TRIP** 19 [5] M W Easterby 3-7-13 (54) Dale Gibson 10/1: 00-01304: Keen rear, nvr able to chall.   3½   51
3359 **GARSTON STAR** 11 [3]3-8-2 (57) F Norton 6/1: 6-312205: Led, sn clr, hdd 2f out, wknd: rcd too freely.   1   52
5 Ran   Time 2m 31.97 (1.17)   Owned: G R Bailey Ltd (Baileys Horse Feeds)   Trained: Middleham

CARLISLE   MONDAY 02.08.04   Righthand, Stiff Track, Uphill Finish

3654   8.20 Bank Of Scotland Classified Stakes 3yo+ 0-60 (F)
£3150 £900 £450   6f192y rnd   Good/Firm 26   -13 Slow   Inside

3447 **BEST DESERT 9** [7] J R Best 3-8-13 (63) N Pollard 11/1: 2-420051: Held up, prog 2f out, rdn out   **68**
to lead cl-home: first win: eff at 7f on fast grnd: acts on sharp or stiff trks: see 1982.
3574 **NEMO FUGAT 3** [4] D Nicholls 5-9-2 vis (60) A Nicholls 7/2: 0560252: Cl-up, styd on to lead dist,   shd   **63**
hdd cl-home: quick reapp: eff at 5/6f, now stays 7f: gd run in defeat & deserves to find similar: see 3352.
      MUSICAL TOP 71 [8] H Morrison 4-8-13 (60) L Fletcher(3) 16/1: 50-003: ch f Mt Livermore - Brief   1   **58**
Escapade (Brief Truce) Led, hdd dist, kept on, not btn in 3rd: 10 wk abs: Brit bow, ex-Irish, unplcd in all 4
starts to date: eff at 7f on fast grnd: encouraging start to Brit career & may do better.
3352* **NORTHERN GAMES 12** [1] K A Ryan 5-9-2 bl (59) G Parkin 7/1: 204-0014: Bhd, nvr nrr than mi-div.   6   **49**
3575* **OEUF A LA NEIGE 3** [6]4-9-3 (61) Dean Williams(7) 100/30: 30-50615: Handy 5f, sn wknd: btr   nk   **49**
expected after win in 3575 (6f, appr mdn h'cap).
3229 **WALTZING WIZARD 17** [2]5-9-2 (51) P Mathers(5) 16/1: 4063406: Al bhd: btr 2848.   nk   **47**
3571 **SAROS 3** [5]3-8-10 (57) D McGaffin 9/1: 1602037: In tch 5f, fdd: quick reapp: btr 3571.   6   **35**
3198 **PURE FOLLY 19** [3]3-8-7 (57) S Sanders 3/1 FAV: 4-3448: Al in rear: disapp on turf bow: btr 3198.   6   **20**
8 Ran   Time 1m 26.64 (2.74)   Owned: Mr Paul Hudson   Trained: Maidstone

3655   8.50 Lloyd Mini Handicap Stakes 3yo 35-55 (F)   **[64]**
£3234 £924 £462   5f193y rnd   Good/Firm 26   -08 Slow   Inside

3024 **DELLAGIO 26** [2] C A Dwyer 3-9-0 (50) F Norton 11/4: 0004001: In tch, styd on trav well to lead   **59**
bef 1f out, rdn out to hold on: eff at 5/6f, has tried further: acts on fast grnd & a stiff or gall trk: gd
confidence boost & has slipped down the weights: see 1942.
3213 **BOWLING ALONG 18** [12] M E Sowersby 3-9-4 (54) T Hamilton(3) 5/2 FAV: 5000432: Mid-div, prog to   ½   **61**
chase wnr ins fnl 1f, kept on, just held: clr rem: continues to run well: see 3213 & 1465.
2125 **ROYAL NITE OWL 62** [6] J O'Reilly 3-8-4 (40) D Allan 8/1: 00-00443: Prom, ev ch bef 1f out, sn no extra. 3   **38**
2961 **FROM THE NORTH 29** [5] A Dickman 3-9-2 vis (52) A Beech(3) 12/1: P0-0504: Handy over 3f, sn outpcd,   1¾   **45**
rallied late: shapes as though further will suit: btr 2075 (1st time visor).
3194 **ROYAL AWAKENING 19** [1]3-9-1 (51) T Eaves(3) 20/1: 30-0045: Bhd, prog halfway, styd on fnl 1f.   hd   **43**
3463 **GAME FLORA 8** [10]3-9-4 (54) P Mulrennan(3) 14/1: 0-140506: Led till halfway, wknd bef 1f out.   ½   **45**
3426 **LEOPARD CREEK 9** [4]3-9-0 (50) S Sanders 5/1: 2020007: Nvr nrr than mid-div: btr 2326.   nk   **40**
3527 **LOUIS PRIMA 5** [9]3-8-2 (38) R Ffrench 33/1: 00000-08: Prom, led halfway, hdd bef 1f out, wknd.   ½   **27**
3191 **AGUILERA 19** [11]3-8-4 (40) V Halliday 33/1: 0-000409: Al bhd: btr 3133.   1¾   **25**
1447 **TIZ WIZ 95** [7]3-8-7 (43) J Bramhill 9/1: 060-020: 10th: Al in rear: long abs: btr 1447 (gd/soft).   7   **10**
3156 **Lavish Times 21** [8]3-8-7 (43) P Mathers(5) 14/1:0   3203 **Yorkes Folly 18** [3]3-9-0 (50) G Faulkner 33/1:0
12 Ran   Time 1m 12.79(2.09)   Owned: Mrs J Parvizi   Trained: Newmarket

GALWAY   WEDNESDAY 28.07.04   Righthand, Turning Track, Stiff Finish

Official Going Good/Firm (Firm Places)

3656   3.00 HP Software H'cap 40-70 3yo ()   **[67]**
£6189 £1456 £642   7f rnd   Good/Firm

2619 **GENERAL FEELING 37** [12] S Kirk 3-9-12 (65) P B Beggy(7) 10/1: 3-33041: Held up, swtchd wide &   **78+**
strong run to lead ins last, sn clr, readily: 1st win for this raider from England: eff at 5/6f, imprvd for the step
up to 7f: acts on firm & soft ground: see 1575.
      PREMIER PROSPECT 11 [17] W P Browne 3-9-3 (56) R P Cleary(7) 7/1: 4-046562: Led till ins last.   3½   **60**
      NOK TWICE 18 [2] J C Hayden 3-9-9 (62) D P McDonogh 14/1: 4-005253: In tch, onepace.   shd   **66**
18 Ran   Time 1m 28.60 ()   Owned: The So Long Partnership   Trained: Upper Lambourn

CHANTILLY   THURSDAY 29.07.04   Righthand, Galloping Track

Official Going Good

3657   2.35 Gr 3 Prix Daphnis 3yo ()
£25704 £10282 £6426   1m1f rnd   Good

2825 **CACIQUE 32** [1] A Fabre 3-8-9 Gary Stevens 30/100 FAV: -11221: Made all, readily pulled clr over   **118+**
1f out, eased close home, readily: eff at 7f, now suited by 9/10f on gd & gd/sft ground: eff forcing the pace: v
smart display, more Gr success awaits: see 3657 (Gr 1).
2307 **ERSHAAD 53** [3] J E Hammond 3-8-9 C Soumillon 39/10: 364-1432: b c Kingmambo - Insight (Sadler's 1½   **110**
Wells) Mid-div, efft to chse ldr over 1f out, sn no impress.
      HIGH FLASH [5] P Bary 3-8-9 T Thulliez 84/10: 1-23123: Rear, kept on late, nvr threat.   1½   **107**
6 Ran   Time 1m 54.90()   Owned: K Abdulla   Trained: France

DEAUVILLE SUNDAY 01.08.04 Righthand, Galloping Track

Official Going Good

3658 2.15 Gr 3 Prix de Cabourg 2yo ()
£25704 £10282 £7711   6f str   Good

    LAYMAN [2] A Fabre 2-8-11 Gary Stevens 34/10: 11: ch c Sunday Silence - Laiyl (Nureyev) Made   **116+**
all & rdn clr dist, readily: ealrier made a winning debut at Deauville: eff at 6/7f, 1m will suit: acts on gd:
impressive success, held in high regard & can win in Gr1/Gr 2 company sn.
3169* **INHABITANT 21** [3] Mme C Head Maarek 2-8-11 O Doleuze 7/2: 112: Rear, hdwy halfway, styd on for   5   **102**
press, no threat to wnr: see 3169 (7f, Listed).
3008 **SALUT THOMAS 34** [6] R Collet 2-8-11 bl C Soumillon 61/10: 2131353: Keen, rear, styd on late.   1   **99**
7 Ran   Time ()   Owned: Sheikh Mohammed   Trained: France

3659 3.20 Gr 1 Prix d'Astarte Fillies & Mares 3yo+ ()
£80479 £32197 £16099   1m str   Good

2487 **MARBYE 46** [5] B Grizzetti 4-9-0 M Demuro 118/10: 13-14151: b f Marju - Hambye (Distant   **116**
Relative) Held up, hdwy wide 2f out, led ins last, drvn out: 6 wk abs: suited by 1m/9f: acts on firm & gd/sft,
with/without t-strap: smart, see 2487 (Gr 2). 1 Oct'03 San 12gd 105- :
3011 **MAJESTIC DESERT 29** [1] M R Channon 3-8-7 (111) T E Durcan 52/10: 2-107222: Chsd ldrs, swtchd &   ½   **114**
drvn/styd on ins last, not rch wnr: smart & consistent filly, dual Gr 1 rnr up this term: fine run, can win a Gr 2/3.
2470 **NEBRASKA TORNADO 47** [3] A Fabre 4-9-0 Gary Stevens 11/10 FAV: 1161-543: Led/dsptd lead till   ¾   **113**
over 1f out, not pace of front pair: rated higher 2470.
3004 **MONTURANI 26** [6] G Wragg 5-9-0 (104) O Peslier 122/10: 422-36244: Sn handy, kept on onepace.   snk **113**
8 Ran   Time ()   Owned: Teruya Yoshida   Trained: Italy

COPENHAGEN   SUNDAY 01.08.04

Official Going Good

3660 3.10 Gr 3 Scandinavian Open Championship 3yo+ ()
£28500 £9502 £4751   1m4f   Good

2898+ **CROCODILE DUNDEE 30** [8] Jamie Poulton 3-8-5 (105) J F Egan 36/10: 5-0632211: Chsd ldrs, hdwy to   **112**
chall 2f out, drvn & led close home, all out: eff at 10/12f on firm, gd/sft & polytrk: tough, & smart colt: see 2898.
2916 **MAKTUB 29** [4] M A Jarvis 5-9-6 (110) G Mosse 26/10 FAV: 200-06202: Trkd ldr, narrow led over 2f   shd **115**
out, just hdd close home: back to smart best dropped in grade & on gd grnd: see 1705.
    MITY DANCER [2] D K Richardson 4-8-11 L Hammer Hansen 37/1: 3: Chsd ldrs, rdn & styd on fnl 2f.   1   **104**
11 Ran   Time 2m 26.80 ()   Owned: R W Huggins   Trained: Telscombe

3661 1.53 Tuborg Classic 3-ars Mile 3yo ()
£1703 £851 £426   1m   Good

4737} **SOAP WATCHER** [7] L Reuterskiold 3-8-7 (60) M Santos : 04001: b g Revoque - Princess of Zurich   **73**
(Law Society) Narrowly prevailed in a tight fin.
2660 **TIGER TIGER 39** [3] Jamie Poulton 3-9-6 (84) J F Egan 7/10 FAV: 13120042: Trkd ldrs, led dist,   shd **85**
just hdd nr line: see 2250, 1500.
    THAI EXPRESS [6] B Olsen 3-8-5 Cathrine Weilby : 3: Not beaten far in a tight fin.   1   **68**
6 Ran   Time 1m 36.40 ()   Owned: Stall Lodder & Reuterskiold Hb   Trained: Sweden

MUNICH   SUNDAY 01.08.04   Lefthand, Galloping Track

Official Going Good

3662 3.40 Gr 1 Grosser Dallmayr-Preis Bayerisches Zuchtrennen 3yo+ ()
£64085 £25352 £12676   1m2f   Good

    INTENDANT [7] Frau A Bertram 3-8-9 J Palik 153/10: -13401: b c Lando - Incenza (Local Suitor)   **118**
Held up, rdn to lead well ins last, styd on strongly: eff at 10f on gd: improved run.
2916 **POWERSCOURT 29** [3] A P O'Brien 4-9-6 J P Spencer 3/5 FAV: 113-1252: Led till well ins last, not   1½ **117**
pace of wnr: smart run with forcing tactics: see 2916, 2004.
2916 **IMPERIAL DANCER 29** [5] M R Channon 6-9-6 (117) S Hitchcott 20/1: 10-36003: Held up, styd on for   1   **116**
press over 1f out, not pace to chall: ran to smart best: see 1230, 59.
3306 **SCOTTS VIEW 13** [8] M Johnston 5-9-6 (115) S Chin 87/10: 31330554: Handy, efft to chse wnr over   1¼ **113**
1f out, no extra ins last: see 2141, 1139.
8 Ran   Time ()   Owned: F Leve   Trained: Germany

COLOGNE SUNDAY 01.08.04

Official Going Good

3663 **2.40 Listed Globetrotter Trophy 3yo+** ()
£9155 £2817 £1408 **1m3f** **Good**

1556 **FOREIGN AFFAIRS 91** Sir M Prescott 6-9-6 (102) J Quinn 47/10: 46-40428131: Trkd ldr, rdn to 113
chall ins last & led nr fin: abs: eff btwn 10f/2m on firm, soft & fibresand: smart, back to best: see 987.
1859* **EPALO 77** A Schutz 5-9-6 T Hellier 30/100 FAV: 11222-112: Led till hdd well ins last, just nse 112
held: abs: btr expected after 1859 (Gr 1).
    ABSOLUT POWER A Wohler 3-8-9 E Pedroza : 3 : ch c Acatenango - All Our Dreams (Caerleon) 9 98
7 Ran   Time 2m 15.39 ()   Owned: Charles C Walker - Osborne House   Trained: Newmarket

3664 **3.55 Gr 3 Globetrotter Meile 3yo+** ()
£22535 £7042 £3251 **1m** **Good**

    PEPPERSTORM [6] J Ostmann 3-8-7 A Boschert 41/10: 1: br c Big Shuffle - Pasca (Lagunas) 112
Mid-div, hdwy 4f out & led over 1f out, styd on strongly: '03 Listed wnr: suited by 1m on gd & soft.
    EAGLE RISE [7] A Schutz 4-9-2 T Hellier 52/10: 2: Held up, styd on wide fnl 2f, nrst fin. nk 113
2915 **TAHREEB 29** [14] M P Tregoning 3-8-9 (108) Martin Dwyer 21/10 FAV: 44-421143: Trkd ldrs, chall ¾ 112
over 1f out, not pace of wnr well ins last: clr rem: ran to smart best: see 2637 (Gr 3).
14 Ran   Time 1m 34.20()   Owned: Gestut Hony-Hof   Trained: Germany

CATTERICK TUESDAY 03.08.04 Lefthand, Undulating, V Tight Track

Official Going GOOD/FIRM (FIRM places).

3665 **2.30 'redcar' Maiden Stakes 2yo** **(D)**
£4238 £1304 £652 **7f rnd** **Good/Firm 37** **-25 Slow** Inside

3329 **FOLLOWING FLOW 13** [6] W Jarvis 2-9-0 P Hanagan 5/1: 031: Handy, styd on to lead ins fnl 1f, 86
drvn out: op 8/1: eff at 7f, 1m will suit: acts on fast grnd & polytrack: improving with every start.
2750 **TCHERINA 38** [2] T D Easterby 2-8-9 D Allan 100/1: 002: Slow away, prog 3f out, kept on to grab 1½ 78
2nd well ins fnl 1f, no ch with wnr: imprvd for easier step up to 7f, shaped as tho' further will suit: acts on fast grnd:
encouraging eff & now quals for h'caps, win a race: see 2522.
3272 **MOZAFIN 17** [4] M R Channon 2-9-0 (88) T E Durcan 2/1 JT FAV: 6243: Prom, ev ch dist, onepcd ins shd 82
fnl 1f, just lost 2nd: well bckd: eff at 6f, now stays 7f: btr 2424.
    JAAMID [3] M Johnston 2-9-0 J Fanning 2/1 JT FAV: 4: b c Desert Prince - Strictly Cool nk 81
(Bering) Led, hdd ins fnl 1f, no extra: well bckd tho' tchd 5/4 on debut: Feb foal, cost 60,000gns: half-brother
to wnrs at 1m/10f, also to decent hdle performer: dam 2yo wnr abroad: sire Gr 1 wnr at 1m: eff at 7f, bred to
apprec further: acts on fast grnd: clearly held in some regard & will improve.
    VARENKA [5]2-8-9 S Sanders 9/2: 5: b f Fasliyev - Castara Beach (Danehill) Missed break, 1¼ 74
cl-up after 2f, short of room dist, sn no extra: tchd 15/2 on debut: Feb foal, cost 52,000gns: dam unplcd: sire
decent performer at sprint dists: learn from this: with Sir Mark Prescott.
    FASYLITATOR [8]2-9-0 S W Kelly 12/1: 6: b c Fasliyev - Obsessed (Storm Bird) Chsd ldrs over 3 73
5f, wknd: op 8/1 on debut: Apr foal, cost 36,000gns: half-brother successful at 7f: dam wnr at 6f.
    SI SI SI [7]2-8-9 N Callan 25/1: 7: Missed break & al bhd: debut. 8 52
7 Ran   Time 1m 27.36 (4.36)   Owned: Sales Race 2001 Syndicate   Trained: Newmarket

3666 **3.00 'doncaster' Selling Stakes 3-5yo** **(G)**
£2863 £818 £409 **1m7f177y** **Good/Firm 37** **-40 Slow** Inside

3312 **TELL THE TREES 15** [1] R M Beckett 3-8-2 (48) J Mackay 6/4 FAV: 000-0551: Cl-up, styd on to lead 62+
2f out, pushed clr, eased cl-home, val 7L+: bckd: sold for 12,600gns: apprec recent step up to 2m: acts on fast
grnd & an undul/tight trk: enjoyed drop to sell grade & can follow up: see 2664.
3395 **BOLD BLADE 11** [4] M J Polglase 3-8-13 (60) L Fletcher(3) 5/1: 5001002: Led, hdd 2f out, not pace 4 62
easy wnr: eff at 1m/12f, seemed to stay on first try at 2m: acts on fast grnd, likes fibresand: btr 2050 (12f clmr).
2924 **HOUSE OF BLUES 31** [7] J A Osborne 3-8-7 (57) S W Kelly 9/2: 000-0053: Keen rear, outpcd after 1½ 55
12f, rallied 2f out, nvr getting to front 2: tchd 6/1: first try at 2m: see 2203.
3400 **DESERT QUILL 11** [2] W M Brisbourne 4-9-3 (47) B Swarbrick(5) 4/1: 30-25004: Handy 12f, sn wknd. 7 43
1074 **ABUELOS 119** [6]5-9-8 (43) P Hanagan 12/1: 00-34005: Nvr nrr than mid-div: long abs & new stable. ½ 47
3327 **MIKASA 14** [8]4-9-8 BL (25) S Sanders 12/1: 0050006: Keen mid-div, prog after 12f, fdd bef 1f out. 10 38
2319 **SMEORACH 55** [5]3-8-2 R Ffrench 40/1: 007: In tch 12f, fdd: 8 wk abs: see 2319. 16 19
    GREEN CONVERSION [9]3-8-7 P Makin(5) 33/1: P: ch g Desert King - Blue Bangor (Thatching) Al in 0
rear, adrift when p.u. & dismounted 2f out: debut: with G Fierro.
8 Ran   Time 3m 33.25 (12.45)   Owned: Major R P Thorman   Trained: Lambourn

3667 **3.30 Eat Sleep At The Nag's Head Pickhill Handicap Stakes 3yo+ 35-55 (F)** [62]
£4472 £1376 £688 **5f rnd** **Good/Firm 37** **+09 Fast** Inside

3463 **BLUE MAEVE 9** [1] J Hetherton 4-9-3 (51) S Righton 11/2 FAV: 0042421: Led 4f out, rdn clr ins fnl 66
1f, readily: fast time: suited by around 5f: acts on fast & gd/soft: made gd use of plum draw in stall 1: shld follow
up under a pen: see 3463 & 2775.
3574 **MR SPLIFFY 4** [2] M C Chapman 5-8-9 (43) J P Guillambert(3) 10/1: 0000002: Led, hdd 4f out, styd 4 46
prom & ev ch dist, no extra ins fnl 1f: qck reapp: best eff for a while & has slipped down the h'cap: see 413.

CATTERICK   TUESDAY 03.08.04   Lefthand, Undulating, V Tight Track

3417 **MYSTERY PIPS** 11 [6] N Tinkler 4-8-9 vis (43) Kim Tinkler 14/1: 0040043: Handy, styd on fnl 1f,	nk	45
just held for 2nd: gd eff & is on a winning mark: see 2326.		
3353 **LOUGHLORIEN** 13 [16] R A Fahey 5-9-4 vis (50) P Hanagan 13/2: 0000334: Bhd, prog wide halfway,	shd	51+
styd on fnl 1f under hands & heels: gd run from poor high draw & is on a winning mark: just btr 3353 & 3191.		
2756 **DANE RHAPSODY** 38 [5]3-8-7 (44) S Hitchcott 25/1: 0505: Al in tch, onepace fnl 1f: see 2152.	½	44
3527 **JOYCES CHOICE** 6 [3]5-8-11 p (45) M Lawson(5) 15/2: 5400026: Bhd, prog 2f out, no impress fnl 1f.	¾	43
3609 **TORRENT** 3 [11]9-9-6 bl (54) P Makin(5) 14/1: 0012007: Handy till dist, onepcd: qck reapp: btr 2702.	nk	51
3350 **MAROMITO** 13 [15]7-9-7 (55) R Ffrench 10/1: 3110038: Handy, onepcd ins fnl 1f: btr 3350.	½	51
3575 **AMANDAS LAD** 4 [17]4-9-5 (53) S W Kelly 9/1: 5456339: Chsd ldrs over 3f, no extra: qck reapp.	1	46
3332 **PETANA** 13 [10]4-9-1 p (49) Lisa Jones(3) 20/1: 5040100: 10th: Mid-div, nvr able to chall: btr 2614.	1¾	37
3417 **ROSIES RESULT** 11 [14]4-9-2 (50) J Fanning 12/1: 0-000100: 11th: Mid-div, no impress fnl 2f: btr 3220.	¾	36
3230 **GOOD TIME BOBBY** 18 [7]7-9-3 (51) J D O'Reilly(7) 33/1: 3040: 12th: Nvr nrr than mid-div: btr 3230.	½	36
3220 **RUM DESTINY** 19 [9]5-8-8 bl (42) G Parkin 25/1: 00-00000: 13th: b g Mujadil - Ruby River (Red God)	hd	26
Al in rear: h'cap wnr in '03: unplcd in '02 (rtd 70, h'cap, A Berry): suited by 5f on fast & gd grnd: acts on		
any trk, likes to race with/force the pace: tried blnks, t-strap & cheek pieces, eff with visor.		
1 Jul'03 Catt 5g/f 59-52 E: 1 Aug'01 Good 5gd 94-89 C: 1 Jul'01 Beve 5g/f 86- D: 1 May'01 Muss 5gd 84- F:		
2846 **COUNT COUGAR** 34 [4]4-9-6 (54) Dale Gibson 25/1: 10-30060: 14th: Handy 3f, sn wknd: btr 2846.	nk	37
2280 **CLEVELAND JACK** 57 [12]4-8-10 vis (44) R Winston 25/1: 2262100: 15th: Bhd, nvr a factor: 8 wk abs.	3½	17
2803 **VALAZAR** 36 [13]5-8-12 (46) S Sanders 9/1: 0232340: 16th: Al bhd: btr 2702 & 1988.	1¼	15
4872} **SOLAR PRINCE** 284 [8]3-9-4 (55) R Lappin 50/1: 040000-0: 17th: b g Desert Prince - Quiche	2	18
(Formidable) Rear, nvr a factor on reapp: unplcd all 3 '03 Brit starts (rtd 59, nov auct stks, J C Fox).		
17 Ran Time 58.72 (1.42) Owned: Mr R G Fell Trained: Malton		

3668	4.00 'wetherby Steeplechases' Claiming Stakes 3yo+ (F)		
	£3474 £1069 £535 1m3f214y **Good/Firm 37** -16 Slow Inside		

3226 **PLATINUM CHARMER** 18 [13] K R Burke 4-9-7 p (55) L Enstone(3) 9/2: 2403251: Bhd & sn rdn, styd on		56
strongly to lead cl-home, rdn out: suited by arnd 12f on firm, soft & fibresand: eff with cheek pieces: likes		
claim/sell grade: see 2868 & 1819.		
3216 **ETON** 19 [14] D Nicholls 8-9-12 (73) Alex Greaves 4/5 FAV: 0512352: Led after 3f, clr trav well	½	59
dist with rider looking rnd, drvn & caught cl home: bckd at odds-on, top-weight: poss caught slightly napping.		
3557 **PETERS IMP** 5 [4] A Berry 9-9-7 (51) P Mathers(5) 12/1: 0/000-153: Held up, prog 3f out, nrst fin.	2½	50
3420 **THINK QUICK** 10 [9] R Hollinshead 4-8-11 (32) Stephanie Hollinshead(5) 22/1: 3006204: Rear, kept	nk	39
on fnl 1f, just held for 3rd: see 3154.		
3486 **CEZZARO** 8 [7]6-9-0 (36) Lisa Jones(3) 25/1: 0220005: Led 3f, styd cl-up, no extra bef 1f out.	½	41$
3190 **BALALAIKA TUNE** 20 [5]5-8-10 t (34) J Bramhill 14/1: 0460326: Nvr nrr than mid-div: see 3190.	2½	33$
3526 **CANLIS** 6 [3]5-9-0 (47) P Hanagan 16/1: 00-02007: Chsd ldrs & short of room after 1m, short of	2	34
room again 2f out, sn btn: qck reapp: btr 2442.		
4319} **DABUS** 320 [10]9-9-0 (28) J P Guillambert(3) 33/1: 006060-8: b g Kris - Licorne (Sadler's Wells)	nk	33$
Cl-up 10f, sn fdd: jumps fit, earlier plcd (rtd 95h, sell hdle, stays 2m1f on fast): sell h'cap hdle wnr in 03/04		
(rtd 93h): plcd on Flat in '03 (rtd 33, clmr): with M C Chapman.		
3206 **STEPASTRAY** 19 [8]7-9-7 (41) T Eaves 25/1: 0-500059: Handy 9f, sn wknd: btr 1821.	2½	36
2850 **NORMA SPEAKMAN** 34 [12]4-8-14 (40) A Mullen(7) 100/1: 220/-0600: 10th: Al bhd: see 2217.	½	25
3324 **Sandy Bay** 14 [6]5-9-3 (35) S Sanders 40/1:0 **Miss De Bois** [2]7-8-9 S W Kelly 20/1:0		
3085 **Grady** 25 [1]5-9-0 (30) B Swarbrick(5) 66/1:0 3190 **Marton Mere** 20 [11]8-9-0 (32) R Winston 50/1:0		
14 Ran Time 2m 37.59 (6.39) Owned: Spigot Lodge Partnership Trained: Leyburn		

3669	4.30 Catterickbridge Co Uk Handicap Stakes 3yo+ 0-70 (E)		[69]
	£4251 £1308 £654 1m5f175y **Good/Firm 37** -09 Slow Inside		

3354 **CHEVIN** 13 [5] R A Fahey 5-8-0 (41) P Hanagan 5/1: 5450-501: Held up, prog 3f out, styd on to		49
lead dist, rdn clr: eff at 11/14f on firm & fast grnd: apprec drop down h'cap: see 2813.		
3105 **MAJESTIC VISION** 24 [4] P W Harris 3-8-13 (67) N Callan 7/1: 34-062: Led, hdd dist, kept on, not	2½	71
pace of wnr: another gd run & can find similar: see 3105.		
3249 **RED FOREST** 18 [2] J Mackie 5-9-6 t (61) Derek Nolan(7) 4/1 FAV: 1150333: Chsd ldrs when short of	1½	64
room after 10f, kept on fnl 2f, not rch ldrs: suited by 12f, now stays 14f: see 3249 & 2998.		
2908 **THEATRE TINKA** 32 [8] R Hollinshead 5-9-2 p (57) S Sanders 11/2: 2405204: Cl-up 12f, no extra.	½	59
3505 **LAZZAZ** 7 [9]6-8-6 (47) Joanna Badger 15/2: 6434265: Prom, no extra dist: qck reapp: btr 3398.	2	47
3573 **PRAIRIE SUN** 4 [1]3-7-12 (52) J Mackay 20/1: 1000606: Handy when short of room 4f out, sn onepcd.	hd	51
3222 **PRINCE HOLING** 19 [7]4-9-10 t (65) R Winston 16/1: 22-50007: Rear, prog 5f out, no impress fnl 2f.	¾	63
3158 **NEXT FLIGHT** 28 [6]5-8-7 (48) P Mulrennan(3) 15/2: 4323468: Slow away, nvr a factor: btr 2685.	5	41
3502 **LADY STRATAGEM** 7 [3]5-8-1 (42) R Ffrench 16/1: 000/-0039: Chsd ldrs over 9f, sn fdd: qck reapp.	13	24
3140 **PERESTROIKA** 23 [10]6-8-11 (52) T Eaves(3) 9/1: 0/-004040: 10th: Chsd ldrs 1m, sn fdd: jumps fit.	9	26
10 Ran Time 3m 1.84 (6.44) Owned: Mr D M Beresford Trained: Malton		

3670	5.00 Saffie Joseph & Sons Handicap Stakes 3yo+ 35-55 (F)		[59]
	£4719 £1452 £726 7f rnd **Good/Firm 37** -18 Slow Inside		

3571 **JUBILEE STREET** 4 [9] Mrs A Duffield 5-9-10 (55) G Hind 11/1: 4310061: Chsd ldrs, styd on to lead		63
ins fnl 1f, rdn out to hold on: qck reapp: suited by 7f, poss stays 9f: acts on fast & gd/soft grnd: see 2080.		
3401 **BABY BARRY** 16 [6] Mrs G S Rees 7-9-1 (46) S Sanders 10/1: 0-000302: Mid-div, prog & ev ch dist,	shd	52
duelled with wnr ins fnl 1f, just held: on long losing run but has slipped to fair mark: see 3102.		
3242 **GOLDEN SPECTRUM** 18 [14] D Nicholls 5-9-10 VIS (55) Alex Greaves 40/1: 00-35003: Mid-div, prog	nk	60
dist, kept on & just btn in a cl fin: fine run in 1st time visor from high draw: h'capped to find a race.		
3547* **JOSHUAS GOLD** 5 [16] D Carroll 3-9-6 (6ex)VIS (57) D Tudhope(7) 12/1: 3600014: Handy wide, led 2f	1	60
out, sn rdn & briefly hung right, hdd ins fnl 1f, no extra: qck reapp & first time visor: gd effort racing so wide		
& is one to keep on side: ran to form of 3547 under a 6lb penalty.		
3427 **LINDENS LADY** 10 [15]4-9-8 (53) R Winston 66/1: 6056505: Held up, prog 2f out, nrst fin: eff at	2	52
5/6f, now stays 7f: gd eff from poor high draw: see 2280.		

CATTERICK   TUESDAY 03.08.04   Lefthand, Undulating, V Tight Track

3401   **OASES 11** [17]5-9-9 vis (54) T Hamilton(3) 14/1: 6000356: Dwelt, prog halfway, no impress fnl 1f.   ¾   51
3490   **SMITH N ALLAN OILS 8** [13]5-9-9 p (54) S W Kelly 7/1: 0522467: Nvr nrr than mid-div: btr 3017.   1   49
2730* **MISS WIZZ 39** [18]4-9-0 p (45) Rory Moore(7) 25/1: 1644518: Rear, nvr nrr than mid-div: btr 2730 (6f).   shd   39
3526   **LONER 6** [8]6-9-5 p (50) P Hanagan 3/1 FAV: 2500-029: Mid-div, prog 3f out, onepcd ins fnl 1f,   1¾   40
broke a blood vessel: well bckd: btr 3526.
2944   **BOWLEGS BILLY 31** [4]4-9-0 (45) J Edmunds 50/1: 5000-000: 10th: Handy over 5f, wknd: see 2657.   1   33
3609   **REDOUBTABLE 3** [2]13-9-8 (53) P Makin(5) 12/1: 0216040: 11th: Mid-div, no impress fnl 2f: qck reapp.   ¾   39
3569   **TIME TO REMEMBER 4** [7]6-9-10 (55) A Nicholls 11/1: 6000200: 12th: Led 5f, sn wknd: qck reapp.   shd   40
3545   **MR BOUNTIFUL 5** [3]6-9-3 BL t (48) Lisa Jones(3) 9/1: 0400640: 13th: Slow away, mod late gains.   1   31
2942‡ **STAR OVATION 383** [1]7-9-9 (54) R Lappin 50/1: 56/6064-0: 14th: ch g Fourstars Allstar - Standing   ⅓   36
Ovation (Godswalk): Prom 5f, fdd: reapp: unplcd in 4 '03 starts (rtd 58$, class stks, Mrs A M Naughton): rnr-up on
reapp in '02 (mdn, rtd 76$): eff at 1m on gd grnd: with Miss R Bowden. 2 Jul'02 Warw 8.1gd 76- D:
3352   **MASSEY 13** [5]8-9-7 (52) J Fanning 14/1: 0-101000: 15th: Chsd ldrs 4f, wknd: btr 3526.   5   24
2199   **PARKER 61** [10]7-9-10 bl (55) S Hitchcott(3) 25/1: 6060500: 16th: Handy over 4f, wknd.   1   25
2986   **BLUNHAM 29** [12]4-9-2 (47) J P Guillambert(3) 10/1: 4500620: 17th: Led early, styd prom, fdd dist.   nk   16
3191   **ONLY ONE LEGEND 20** [11]6-9-3 bl (48) N Callan 20/1: 0315000: 18th: Rear, nvr a factor: btr 2337.   2½   12
18 Ran   Time 1m 26.85(3.85)   Owned: Mr D W Holdsworth & Mr J A McMahon   Trained: Leyburn

BRIGHTON   TUESDAY 03.08.04   Lefthand, V Sharp, Undulating Track

Official Going FIRM

3671   2.15 Racing's Big Day Out For The Nspcc Median Auction Maiden Stakes 2yo   (E)
£3367 £1036 £518   **5f213y rnd**   **Firm 14**   **-16 Slow**   Inside

3355   **CUSOON 12** [6] G L Moore 2-9-0   R L Moore 11/8 FAV: 31: Mid-div on inner, hdwy to lead over 2f   84
out, drvn clr: well bckd: relished step up to 6f, acts on firm & fast, sharp/undul trk: see 3355.
3296   **MULBERRY LAD 15** [3] W R Muir 2-9-0 BL (68) Martin Dwyer 8/1: 5242: Bmpd start, dsptd lead, left   6   67
bhnd by wnr fnl 1f: tried blnks: see 2976.
2839   **CONNOTATION 34** [5] P W D'Arcy 2-8-9   D Holland 13/8: 223: Rear, eff halfway, high head carriage,   1   59
hung left & flashed tail over 1f out, no impress: well bckd: see 2839.
3284   **MAJESTICAL 17** [1] W R Muir 2-9-0 (58) S Drowne 25/1: 34004: With ldr till led over 3f out, hdd   1¾   59
over 2f out, wknd: stablemate of 2nd: see 1041.
3110   **WORTH A GRAND 24** [2]2-9-0   P Doe 10/1: 055: Led over 2f, wknd 2f out: see 3110.   4   47
3368   **MAKES PERFECT 12** [4]2-8-9   J F Egan 12/1: 06: b f Orpen - Practice (Diesis) Rear, nvr nr ldrs,   shd   41
returned lame: Feb foal, cost 7,000gns: half-sister to 4 US wnrs, dam a 2yo wnr: sire a Gr 1 6f 2yo wnr.
6 Ran   Time 1m 9.62 (1.82)   Owned: The Winning Hand   Trained: Brighton

3672   2.45 Tote Supports The Nspcc Handicap Stakes Fillies 3yo+ 0-70 (E)   [64]
£5499 £1692 £846   **6f209y rnd**   **Firm 14**   **-14 Slow**   Inside

3159   **ICECAP 22** [6] W G M Turner 4-8-13 (49) C Haddon(7) 12/1: 65002-01: Keen & cl-up, led over 2f out   56
& sn clr, held on: gamble from 20/1: eff at 7/10f on firm & both AWs, likes a sharp trk, acts on an undul one: gd
start for new yard (prev with Miss E Lavelle): see 267.
3479   **I WISH 8** [7] M Madgwick 6-9-7 (57) G Baker 6/1: 4155302: Keen in rear, hdwy over 1f out, fin   1½   59
well to snatch 2nd on post: tchd 8/1: handles firm, soft & polytrack: back to form of 1806.
3541   **LADY MO 5** [3] G G Margarson 3-9-10 (66) A McCarthy 7/2: 3061223: In tch, switched right & hdwy   shd   67
over 2f out, kept on: qck reapp, jt top-weight: remains in fine form, consistent: see 3215.
3364   **ZIET DALSACE 12** [2] A W Carroll 4-9-10 (60) R L Moore 9/4 FAV: 0020104: In tch, hdwy into 2nd 2f   nk   60
out, onepcd ins fnl 1f: well bckd, jt top-weight: back to form of 3176 (C/D).
3363   **CHERTSEY 12** [9]3-9-3 (59) E Ahern 14/1: 33505: Chsd ldrs, no impress fnl 1f.   1½   56
3548   **BLONDE EN BLONDE 5** [4]4-9-2 bl (52) D Holland 9/2: 3003056: Bhd, hdwy 2f out, not pace to chall.   1   47
1549   **STAGECOACH RUBY 91** [10]3-7-12 (1oh) (39) Hayley Turner(5) 14/1: 0054337: Prom, hung right over 2f   1¾   31
out, sn wknd: long abs: see see 1549.
2375   **AVERLLINE 53** [5]3-9-9 (65) N Chalmers(5) 20/1: 2210-008: Dwelt, sn in tch, wknd 2f out: 8 wk abs.   2½   51
1268   **TICTACTOE 105** [11]3-8-12 (54) C Catlin 14/1: 5361-669: Chsd ldrs wide, wknd 2f out: long abs.   1¾   37
2439   **MOSCOW MARY 50** [8]3-8-8 (50) S Whitworth 33/1: 240-0000: 10th: Led till over 2f out, wknd.   10   13
10 Ran   Time 1m 21.82 (2.02)   Owned: Mrs Anna L Sanders   Trained: Sherborne

3673   3.15 Daily Mail Supports The Nspcc Brighton Dash Handicap 3yo+ 0-80 (D)   [80]
£6663 £2050 £1025   **5f59y rnd**   **Firm 14**   **-07 Slow**   Inside

3341   **TABOOR 13** [6] J W Payne 6-8-1 h blt (53) Martin Dwyer 14/1: 5020601: Rear, hdwy over 1f out,   59
strong fin to lead cl home: eff over 5/6f on firm, gd/soft & both AWs, prob acts on any trk, likes a sharp/undul
one: wears a hd, blnks & t-strap: back to form: see 748.
3341   **JAYANJAY 13** [3] Miss B Sanders 5-10-0 (80) D Holland 7/2 FAV: 4343152: Bhd, hdwy 2f out, not clr   nk   85
run dist, switched right & fin well, only just btn: top-weight: poss a shade unlucky.
3372* **BYO 12** [8] M Quinn 6-9-3 (69) R L Moore 12/1: 0660013: Chsd ldrs, hdwy to lead 1f out, hdd & no   ¾   72
extra nr fin: likes fast grnd, acts on firm, hvy & polytrack: continues in gd form, see 3372 (clmr).
3537   **REDWOOD STAR 6** [7] P L Gilligan 4-8-4 (2ow)e (54) J F Egan 11/2: 0-400304: Chsd ldrs, ev ch ins   1   56
fnl 1f, sn onepcd: qck reapp: acts on firm, fast & polytrack: see 1867.
3424   **GONENDUNNETT 10** [5]5-8-8 vis (60) Dane O'Neill 6/1: 6103105: Made most to 1f out, no extra.   1¾   56
3463   **PORT ST CHARLES 9** [1]7-8-6 BL (58) R Thomas(5) 7/1: 3000406: Dwelt, hdwy into mid-div over 1f out,   nk   53
sn wknd: op 10/1, tried blnks: see 2189.
3537   **ROSES OF SPRING 6** [9]6-9-12 p (78) A Quinn(5) 11/2: 0300007: Dwelt, sn in tch, wknd 1f out.   1¾   69
3537   **STAGNITE 6** [4]4-8-7 p (59) N Chalmers(5) 9/2: 0-062108: Prom, wknd 1f out: qck reapp.   ½   48
2981   **TAMARELLA 29** [2]4-7-12 (3oh)bl (47) A McCarthy 25/1: 5000059: Prom, wknd halfway: see 767.   9   12
9 Ran   Time 1m 1.2 (1.2)   Owned: Mr T W Morley   Trained: Newmarket

1109

3674   3.45 Totesport Com Brighton Challenge Cup Handicap 3yo+ 0-80 (D)   [78]
£13650 £4200 £2100   1m3f196y   Firm 14   +12 Fast   Outside

3519* **DESERT ISLAND DISC 6** [3] J J Bridger 7-9-8 (72) J F McDonald(3) 9/1: 3061511: In tch, hdwy over   78
1f out, rdn to lead ins fnl 1f, just held on: fast time, op 7/1, qck reapp: eff arnd 12f on firm, hvy & handles
polytrack, acts on any trk, likes Kempton & Brighton: tough & in fine form: see 1381.

3637 **LENNEL 2** [13] A Bailey 6-9-4 bl (68) M Fenton 10/1: 4064132: Dwelt, rear 2f out, fin v strongly   shd   73
wide fnl 1f, just failed: qck reapp: remains in fine form: see 3637.

3481 **ABSINTHER 8** [4] M R Bosley 7-8-0 (50) Hayley Turner(5) 10/1: 00-02143: Dwelt bhd, switched wide   2½   51
3f out, kept on well fnl 1f & nrst fin: tchd 16/1: need a step up in trip? see 2836 (C/D).

3299* **BLAZE OF COLOUR 15** [8] Sir Michael Stoute 3-9-2 vis (77) B Doyle 4/1 FAV: 0-342314: Keen & led,   nk   77
clr 2f out, wknd fnl 1f & caught cl home: nicely bckd, clr of rem: poss went off too fast, see 3299.

3615 **KARAOKE 3** [2]4-9-4 (68) J F Egan 16/1: 0003105: In tch, hdwy into 2nd 2f out, hung left over 1f   3   63
out, wknd fnl 1f: qck reapp: see 3295.

3037 **MOSTARSIL 27** [12]6-9-4 p (68) R L Moore 7/1: 6341606: Chsd ldrs, onepcd 2f out.   1¼   61

3345* **PARTY PLOY 13** [1]6-9-6 (70) Darren Williams 7/1: 1101217: Cl-up, wknd over 1f out.   ¾   62

3208 **ANTIGIOTTO 19** [11]3-9-3 (78) D Holland 10/1: 0004228: Nvr btr than mid-div: rider reported his   ½   69
mount ran in snatches: see 3208.

3287 **DISPOL EVITA 17** [5]5-7-12 (48) A McCarthy 33/1: 0-042049: Bhd, nvr nr ldrs.   2½   35

3519 **MOST SAUCY 6** [10]8-8-4 (54) P Doe 10/1: 4504330: 10th: Rcd in 2nd to 5f out, btn over 1f out.   1¼   39

3261 **NORTHSIDE LODGE 17** [14]6-9-11 (75) Martin Dwyer 5/1: 0352000: 11th: Al bhd: op 7/1, top-weight.   3   55

1375 **ORINOCOVSKY 99** [9]5-8-9 (59) E Ahern 66/1: 2320130: 12th: Mid-div, wknd over 3f out: long abs: 3   34
reportedly failed to hanlde this trk & found grnd too fast: btr 1323 (AW seller).

1916 **HONOR ROUGE 73** [6]5-9-6 (70) V Slattery 16/1: 16000-60: 13th: Mid-div, wknd 5f out, eased: abs.   29   0

3450 **PAY THE SILVER 10** [7]6-9-0 p (64) I Mongan 2/1: 020330P: In tch, lost place over 4f out,
t.o./p.u. nr fin: rider reported his mount to be unsuited by this firm grnd: see 1530.

14 Ran Time 2m 28.5 (0.3) Owned: Mr W Wood   Trained: Liphook

---

3675   4.15 Video Meeting Company Supports The Nspcc Maiden Stakes 3yo+ (D)
£4017 £1236 £618   1m1f209y   Firm 14   -23 Slow   Outside

3255 **THIRTEEN TRICKS 18** [2] Mrs A J Perrett 3-8-5 (74) R L Moore 1/10 FAV: 034-0341: Prom, hdwy to   72
lead over 2f out, pushed clr ins fnl 1f, eased nr fin, val 8L+: eff at 9/10f on firm, gd/soft & polytrack, acts on a
v sharp/undul trk: simple task to open gd confidence boost: see 2680.

2352 **SO DETERMINED 54** [6] G A Butler 3-8-10 E Ahern 11/1: 00-02: b g Soviet Star - Memory Green   5   62
(Green Forest) Mid-div, hdwy into 2nd & ev ch 2f out, sn left bhnd by easy wnr: 8 wk abs: mdn unplcd both '03
starts (rtd 62a): has tried a t-strap.

2910 **DASH FOR GLORY 32** [1] J S King 5-9-5 (29) Hayley Turner(5) 33/1: 00-00003: Prom, outpcd halfway,   12   44$
wkng when hung left 2f out: see 1204.

2751 **WEST END WONDER 38** [5] M J Wallace 5-9-5 D Corby(3) 33/1: 04: b g Idris - Miss Plum (Ardross)   5   36
Led till over 2f out, wknd: twice rcd 5yo, seems modest.

4 Ran Time 2m 1.54 (3.74) Owned: Cheveley Park Stud   Trained: Pulborough

---

3676   4.45 Classic Fm Supports The Nspcc Classified Stakes 3yo+ 0-60 (F)
£4105 £1263 £632   7f214y rnd   Firm 14   -06 Slow   Inside

3448 **MISTER CLINTON 10** [3] D K Ivory 7-9-3 (59) D Holland 5/2 FAV: 3401201: Rear, hdwy over 2f out,   66
not clr run/switched right over 1f out, rdn & kept on well ins fnl 1f to lead fnl stride: eff btwn 6f/1m, stays 10f
well: acts on firm & gd, sharp trks, loves Brighton: back to form at favourite trk: see 761.

3448 **LONDONER 10** [4] S Dow 6-9-3 (60) R L Moore 11/2: 2105352: Chsd ldrs, hdwy to lead ins fnl 1f,   shd   66
hard rdn/hdd fnl stride: rider reported his mount hung left: likes Brighton: see 2334.

2857 **LIBERTY ROYAL 34** [1] P J Makin 5-9-7 p (64) D Sweeney 5/1: 0-606303: Chsd ldrs, hdwy to chall   1¾   66
over 1f out, onepcd ins fnl 1f: see 2220.

2958 **PRIME OFFER 30** [7] J Jay 8-9-8 (65) C Haddon(7) 6/1: 2412154: Sn led, hdd ins fnl 1f, no extra.   1½   64

3184 **FLORIAN 20** [8]6-9-3 (59) R Miles(3) 14/1: 133-0006: Keen in rear, hdwy over 1f out, sn onepcd.   2   55

3477 **OUR DESTINY 8** [9]6-9-3 (58) I Mongan 13/2: 1041056: Bhd, eff over 2f out, not pace of ldrs.   2½   50

3176 **POPPYLINE 21** [5]4-9-0 BL (51) S Drowne 16/1: 0U36307: Chsd ldrs, wknd 2f out, btn fnl 1f: blnks.   3½   40

3516 **BURLINGTON PLACE 6** [2]3-8-10 (60) J F Egan 13/2: 246-0028: With ldr, lost action over 2f out, sn   30   0
fdd: qck reapp: rider reported his mount failed to handle the trk & hung right: btr 3516.

8 Ran Time 1m 33.64 (1.64) Owned: Mr J B Waterfall   Trained: Radlett

---

3677   5.15 Piggybankkids Apprentice Maiden Handicap 3yo+ 35-55 (F)   [57]
£2975 £850 £425   6f209y rnd   Firm 14   -30 Slow   Inside

1711 **BRANDYWINE BAY 82** [5] A P Jones 4-8-9 p (38) T Block(5) 11/2: 3504-041: Bhd, hdwy 2f out, rdn over   41
1f out, styd on fnl 1f to lead fnl strides: long abs, op 8/1: eff btwn 6f/1m on firm, fast & fibresand, acts on
a gall or sharp/undul trk: runs well fresh: gd run out of banded grade: see 1073.

3219 **GROWLER 19** [9] J L Dunlop 3-9-6 VIS (55) W Hogg 7/2 FAV: 000-0302: Cl-up, led & swerved left over   hd   57
2f out, hit rail over 1f out, kept on with jock looking round, hdd fnl strides: joc 1 day careless riding ban: well
bckd: acts on firm & fast: back to form in visor: v modest ride, see 2434.

3372 **CAPTAIN CLOUDY 12** [7] M Madgwick 4-9-10 (53) R Lucey Butler 8/1: 0-566003: Mid-div, kept on ins   ½   54
fnl 1f: op 10/1, top-weight: eff at 5/7f on firm & gd/soft: see 607.

2834 **JOHNNY ALLJAYS 35** [2] J S Moore 3-8-1 (3oh)p (36) Laura Reynolds(7) 10/1: 0000044: Cl-up, not much   2½   32
room ins fnl 1f, sn onepcd: hdles fit (p.u., juv nov): gd eff here from 3lb out of the h'cap: see 1947.

3145 **BENJAMIN 23** [6]6-8-6 bl 11 (33) Dean Williams 11/2: 2250005: Led till hmpd over 2f out, sn no extra.   2   27

3380 **JASMINE PEARL 12** [11]3-8-11 (46) M Halford 6/1: 0402566: In tch, kept on from over 1f out, nrst fin.   shd   37

3301 **BLAISE WOOD 15** [8]3-8-12 bl (47) J Jones(5) 9/1: 6-060207: Keen in rear, eff 3f out, not pace of ldrs.   3   32

3197 **BUNKHOUSE 20** [4]4-9-4 P (47) B O'Neill(5) 20/1: 00008: ch g Wolfhound - Maid Welcome (Mummy's Pet)   2   28

BRIGHTON TUESDAY 03.08.04 Lefthand, V Sharp, Undulating Track

Dwelt, nvr a factor: mdn unplcd all earlier starts (with Miss E Lavelle): now with W Turner: tried cheek pieces.
3301 **COSTA DEL SOL 15** [10]3-8-2 (2oh)bl (37) Lucy Russell(5) 25/1: 0040069: ch g General Monash -   1¼   15
L'harmonie (Bering) Cl-up, wknd over 2f out: rnr-up twice in '03 (sellers, 1 for D Ivory): stays 6f on firm &
fast: has tried a visor, wears blnks: likes sellers. 2 Oct'03 Brig 5.3g/f 58-(55) G: 2 Jul'03 Brig 6.0fm 60- G:
3609 **BLADES EDGE 3** [3]3-8-10 (45) Natalie Hassall(7) 16/1: 0000000: 10th: Al bhd: qck reapp: see 673.   3   17
8   **GUARD 267** [1]4-8-8 t (37) Steven Harrison 14/1: 0/00000-0: 11th: b g Night Shift - Gaijin   shd   8
(Caerleon) Mid-div, wknd over 2f out on reapp: mdn & h'cap unplcd in '03 (rtd 62a): unplcd sole '02 start (mdn,
rtd 48a): wears a t-strap.
2716 **MRS BOZ 39** [13]4-8-4 (4oh) (29) K Jackson(5) 33/1: 060-400: 12th: ln tch, wknd 3f out.   ½   3
12 Ran   Time 1m 22.88(3.08)   Owned: Mrs K T Pilkington   Trained: Upper Lambourn

PONTEFRACT WEDNESDAY 04.08.04 Lefthand, Undulating Track, Stiff Uphill Finish

Official Going GOOD/FIRM (GOOD IN PLACES)

3678	2.20 Handicap Stakes For Gentleman Amateur Riders 3yo+ 0-80 (E)	[51]
	£4732 £1456 £728 **1m2f6y** **Good 58** -47 Slow Inside	

3222 **NIGHT SIGHT 20** [5] Mrs S Lamyman 7-11-2 (67) Mr J Morgan(5) 11/2: 4-023441: Mid-div, hdwy/trav   73
well over 1f out, led ins fnl 1f, kept on well nr fin: outstd by 10/12f on firm, gd/soft & fibresand, acts on any
trk, loves Doncaster: back to form on drop in trip: well h'capped on old form: see 2041.
3444 **BUCKS 11** [1] D K Ivory 7-12-0 (79) Mr Michael Murphy(5) 8/1: 2112502: Bhd, hdwy & ev ch ins fnl   ½   84
1f, no impress on wnr cl-home: top weight: eff over 10f/2m: fair run, return to further shld suit: see 2244.
3336 **MOVIE KING 14** [3] S Gollings 5-10-11 (62) Mr T Woodside(7) 14/1: 0020063: Led till ins fnl 1f, sn   2½   63
no extra: jock rec 3 day whip ban: see 1599.
3505* **OSCAR PEPPER 8** [2] T D Barron 7-11-4 (5ex)vis (69) Mr S Walker 4/1: 3452414: Trkd ldrs, no   3   65
impress over 1f out: see 3505.
3514* **REALISM 7** [6]4-12-0 (5ex) (79) Mr L Newnes(3) 11/8 FAV: 1211015: Rcd in 2nd, hdwy to chall 2f out,   3½   70
no impress ins fnl 1f: quick reapp: reportedly unsuited by the rain softened grnd: btr 3514 (fast).
3313 **DERWENT 16** [4]5-11-2 bl (67) Mr J J Best(3) 6/1: 3-000466: Keen in rear, hdwy over 2f out, no   2   55
impress over 1f out: see 2794.
6 Ran   Time 2m 18.68 (10.58)   Owned: Mr David Fravigar-Mr Alan Mann   Trained: Louth

3679	2.50 Dem Window Solutions Kbe Handicap Stakes 3yo 0-70 (E)	[76]
	£4300 £1323 £662 **1m4y** **Good 58** -24 Slow Inside	

3138* **SILVERHAY 24** [4] T D Barron 3-9-6 (68) N Callan 9/4 FAV: 23-42411: Prom, hdwy to lead over 3f   75
out, hung right & rider lost whip over 1f out, kept on ins fnl 1f: landed double: suited by 1m, stays 11f: acts on
fast, likes gd, soft & gall trks: improving, see 3138.
3455 **DAGOLA 11** [9] C G Cox 3-9-2 (64) P Robinson 4/1: 0-100342: Mid-div, switched to far rail after   ½   69
2f, ev ch over 1f out, not clr run just ins fnl 1f, kept on: clr of rem: in gd form: see 2971.
3455 **HANA DEE 11** [10] M R Channon 3-8-8 (56) S Hitchcott(3) 14/1: 0600453: Dwelt bhd, hdwy over 2f   3½   54
out, hung right over 1f out, wknd ins fnl 1f: see 3153.
1879 **MR MIDASMAN 76** [6] R Hollinshead 3-8-12 (60) D Sweeney 40/1: 1-600004: Rear, hdwy 2f out, kept   1¾   54
on fnl 1f but nvr going pace to reach ldrs: long abs: see 923.
3562 **DARK DAY BLUES 6** [1]3-9-4 (66) A Culhane 7/1: 0010655: ln tch, hdwy over 2f out, onepcd over 1f out.   1¾   56
3243 **SIERRA 19** [11]3-9-3 (65) R Hills 16/1: 0-566: Dwelt in rear, some mod late gains: see 2793.   1¾   51
3453 **QUEENSTOWN 11** [7]3-9-7 bl (69) D Holland 8/1: 122-0357: Led till over 3f out, sn no extra.   1½   52
2155 **ORPENBERRY 63** [2]3-9-0 (62) M Fenton 40/1: 3100-008: Chsd ldrs, no impress over 1f out: 9 wk   nk   44
abs: now with E Alston: see 2155.
3177 **ACCA LARENTIA 22** [5]3-8-2 (50) D Fox(5) 33/1: 62-00309: Mid-div, wknd 3f out.   9   14
3373 **MY HOPE 13** [3]3-9-1 (63) S Drowne 6/1: 0-000030: 10th: Bhd, nvr nr ldrs: see 2634.   2½   22
3309 **IMPULSIVE BID 16** [8]3-8-12 (60) P Hanagan 20/1: 4020500: 11th: Mid-div, wknd 2f out, t.o.   17   0
3499 **NAFFERTON HEIGHTS 8** [12]3-7-12 (4oh) (42) R Ffrench 25/1: 0500060: 12th: Handy, no impress 3f out.   1   0
12 Ran   Time 1m 48.37 (6.57)   Owned: D C Rutter P J Huntbach   Trained: Thirsk

3680	3.20 Chaplins Club Handicap Stakes 3yo+ 0-75 (E)	[75]
	£6906 £2125 £1063 **5f** **Good 58** +04 Fast Inside	

3482 **ON THE TRAIL 9** [13] D W Chapman 7-7-13 (46) A Nicholls 20/1: 2134331: Trkd ldrs, rdn to lead   55
well ins fnl 1f, kept on: stays 7f, best up with/forcing the pace around 5/6f on gd & both AWs, any trk.
3461 **NEVER WITHOUT ME 10** [7] J F Coupland 4-9-0 (61) D Holland 6/1: 3411242: Handy, ev ch well ins   nk   69
fnl 1f, no impress cl-home: loves fibresand, acts on fast & gd: remains in gd form: see 3213 & 3220.
3427 **KINGS COLLEGE BOY 11** [14] R A Fahey 4-8-13 bl (60) P Hanagan 6/1: 3230303: Trkd ldrs, bmpd over   nk   67
2f out, slt lead over 1f, no extra ins fnl 1f: op 8/1: see 2320.
2232 **CONSENSUS 60** [1] M Brittain 5-10-0 (75) P Robinson 11/1: 4003004: Led far rail, hdd & no extra   1   77
well ins fnl 1f: op 8/1, 9 wk abs: see 921.
3561 **QUEEN OF NIGHT 6** [15]4-8-13 (60) J Carroll 25/1: R011205: Dwelt, hdwy/bmpd over 2f out, kept on.   2½   56
2846 **VIGOROUS 35** [12]4-9-6 (67) A Mullen(7) 33/1: 40-05006: Dwelt, mod late gains: now with M Todhunter.   1¼   59
3537 **PLAYTIME BLUE 7** [10]4-8-13 (60) G Baker 15/2: 6053307: Prom, wknd over 1f out: op 10/1, qk reapp.   1   49
3561* **CATCH THE CAT 6** [6]5-10-1 (7ex)vis (76) G Parkin 12/1: 6500018: ln tch, hdwy into 2nd halfway,   1¼   61
fdd over 1f out: quick reapp, top weight: btr 3561 (fast grnd).
3241 **KARMINSKEY PARK 9** [9]5-9-3 (64) J Fanning 12/1: 3210009: Bhd, nvr a factor: op 16/1.   hd   48
3609 **DANAKIM 4** [16]7-7-12 (6oh) (39) D Fentiman(7) 33/1: 0000420: 10th: Cl-up, wknd over 1f out: qk reapp.   1¼   25
3503 **PERCY DOUGLAS 3** [2]4-9-12 (5oh)t (40) D Fox(5) 22/1: 0600050: 11th: Al bhd: stiff task at weights.   1   22
3241* **MIDNIGHT PARKES 19** [8]5-9-11 p (72) M Henry 8/1: 0350310: 12th: Handy, wknd 2f out: op 6/1.   ¾   47
3352 **COMPTON PLUME 14** [5]4-9-6 (67) V Halliday 20/1: 3D32100: 13th: Mid-div, wknd 2f out.   nk   41
3527 **SOAKED 7** [4]11-9-2 bl (63) A Culhane 10/1: 1215230: 14th: Handy, no impress over 1f out: qk reapp.   3½   26
3561 **VALIANT ROMEO 6** [3]4-8-6 (53) R Ffrench 11/2 FAV: 2240520: 15th: ln tch, rear & btn halfway.   2   10

15 Ran Time 1m 4.01 (2.71) Owned: Mr J M Chapman Trained: York

---

3681 3.50 Tony Sykes Sound Handicap Stakes 3yo+ 0-85 (D) [84]
£9303 £3529 £1764 1m4f8y Good 58 -15 Slow Inside

2899 **FLOTTA 33** [3] M R Channon 5-9-10 (80) S Hitchcott(3) 100/30: 5044301: Bhd, hdwy to lead 2f out, **86**
all out to hold on nr fin: suited by 12/14f on fm, gd & polytrack, prob any trk.
3345 **MEXICAN PETE 14** [5] P W Hiatt 4-9-8 (78) A Culhane 100/30: 0204432: Bhd, hdwy to dispute lead 2f ½ **82**
out, ev ch fnl 1f, no impress nr fin: remains in gd form, v consistent & shld find a race sn: clr of rem: see
1599.
3125 **SAHEM 25** [4] D Eddy 7-9-10 (80) P Hanagan 3/1 FAV: 0401203: Led 3f out, hdd/no extra 2f out. 3½ **79**
3437 **RAJAM 11** [1] D Nicholls 6-9-8 vis (78) Alex Greaves 7/2: 3065224: Handy, hdwy to chall over 2f 5 **69**
out, no impress over 1f out: see 3217 (fast grnd), 1796.
1828 **HIP HOP HARRY 78** [6]4-9-10 (80) W Ryan 15/2: 0212005: Rear, nvr nr ldrs: long abs. 11 **54**
3276 **THE ROUNDSILLS 18** [2]10-7-12 (19oh) (35) S Righton 100/1: 40//////-06: Led to 3f out, sn no 9 **14**
extra.
6 Ran Time 2m 42.93 (8.83) Owned: Mr W G R Wightman Trained: West Ilsley

---

3682 4.20 Birdsall Farms Maiden Stakes 2yo (D)
£5603 £1724 £862 6f Good 58 -30 Slow Inside

3122 **REQQA 25** [13] M Johnston 2-9-0 R Hills 6/5 FAV: 61: b c Royal Applause - Kangra Valley (Indian **98+**
Ridge) Trkd ldrs, hdwy to lead over 1f out, rdn clr readily: hvly bckd: Feb foal, cost 160,000 gns: half
brother to smart juv/sprinter Airwave: dam a 5f 2yo wnr: stays 6f, will get further: acts on gd grnd: v promising,
potentially v useful & can win better races.
3406 **YAJBILL 12** [12] M R Channon 2-9-0 A Culhane 11/4: 232: Led 1f, remained prom, ev ch 2f out, 5 **80**
styd on ins fnl 1f to go 2nd but no ch with wnr: shld find a race: see 3406.
3239 **ALONG THE NILE 19** [5] Mrs J R Ramsden 2-9-0 L Goncalves 28/1: 03: b g Desert Prince - Golden ¾ **78**
Fortune (Forzando) Dwelt bhd, hdwy over 2f out, chsd wnr just ent fnl 1f, sn no impress: Feb foal, cost 40,000 gns:
half brother to a 10f wnr: dam dual 6/7f wnr: improved from debut.
STREET BALLAD 0 [6] Mrs J R Ramsden 2-8-9 P Hanagan 25/1: 4: b f Fasliyev - Nancy Maloney 3 **64**
(Persian Bold) Slow away in rear, hdwy 2f out, styd on ins fnl 1f but not pace to chall on debut: Mar foal, cost
22,000 gns: sire top class 5/6f performer at 2.
2689 **IMPERIAL DYNASTY 41** [14]2-9-0 S Hitchcott(3) 33/1: 05: Led after 1f till over 1f out, no extra. 1¼ **65**
920 **YORKSHIRE LAD 132** [11]2-9-0 D Tudhope(7) 25/1: 06: Nvr btr than mid-div: long abs. 2½ **57**
2281 **CUTLASS GAUDY 57** [3]2-9-0 Stephanie Hollinshead(5) 33/1: 47: Cl-up, chsd wnr over 1f out, sn wknd. 1¾ **52**
3376 **TYBALT 13** [10]2-9-0 D Holland 8/1: 258: Mid-div, no impress 2f out: tchd 10/1. shd **51**
3473 **BESPOKE 9** [8]2-9-0 S Archer(7) 40/1: 569: Al bhd: see 3323. 4 **39**
ROCK HAVEN 0 [2]2-9-0 N Callan 40/1: 0: 10th: Al bhd on debut. 1½ **34**
2228 **PEVENSEY 61** [4]2-9-0 S Drowne 10/1: 60: 11th: Nvr a factor: tchd 12/1, 9 wk abs. 6 **16**
2424 **QUEUE UP 52** [9]2-9-0 M Fenton 16/1: 30: 12th: Mid-div, wknd over 2f out: 8 wk abs. shd **15**
COME TO DADDY 0 [7]2-9-0 D Kinsella 100/1: 0: 13th: Nvr a factor on debut. 8 **0**
13 Ran Time 1m 19.38 (5.28) Owned: Mr Hamdan Al Maktoum Trained: Middleham

---

3683 4.50 Matty Bown Memorial Maiden Stakes 3yo+ (D)
£5395 £1660 £830 1m4y Good 58 -66 Slow Inside

3237 **CLIPPERDOWN 19** [1] P W Harris 3-9-0 N Callan 5/2: 301: Trkd ldrs, hdwy to lead ins fnl 1f, kept **83**
on well for press: stays 1m, shld relish further: acts on gd: open to improvement.
2974 **ZATHONIA 30** [6] R Charlton 3-8-9 S Drowne 5/2: 232: Rcd in 2nd till led over 1f out, hdd ins 1¼ **73**
fnl 1f & no extra: handles firm & gd: see 2633.
3237 **ROYAL LUSTRE 19** [3] J H M Gosden 3-9-0 R Hills 11/8 FAV: 03: b c Deputy Minister - Snow Bride 2 **74**
(Blushing Groom) Led till over 1f out, no extra: well bckd: half brother to v smart Lammtarra & 2 other wnrs over
8/10f: dam smart mid-dist rnr: bred to apprec further.
PERRYWINKLE BOY 0 [2] M D Hammond 3-9-0 A Culhane 33/1: 4: b c Piccolo - Flower Arrangement 9 **56**
(Lomond) Bhd, nvr nr ldrs on debut: cost 11,500 gns: half brother to smart Italian 5/7f 2yo: dam unrcd.
3413 **DIUM MAC 12** [5]3-9-0 (70) P Hanagan 9/1: 24-05: Dwelt in rear, lost tch 3f out, t.o.: see 3413. dist **0**
5 Ran Time 1m 51.75 (9.95) Owned: Mrs G Godfrey & Mrs A Horner Trained: Berkhamsted

---

3684 5.20 August Classified Stakes 3yo 0-70 (E)
£4085 £1257 £629 6f Good 58 -04 Slow Inside

1417 **OUT AFTER DARK 98** [7] C G Cox 3-9-5 (75) P Robinson 5/2 FAV: 042-51: Made virtually all, kept on **80**
well for press ins fnl 1f to hold on nr fin: long abs: eff at 6f on fast & gd/soft, acts on a stiff/undul trk: joc
2 day careless riding ban: runs well fresh: imprvd for forcing tactics to gain 1st win here: see 1417.
3203 **FLYING BANTAM 20** [6] R A Fahey 3-9-0 (68) P Hanagan 13/2: 3-222402: Bhd, hdwy over 1f out, chsd nk **73**
wnr ent fnl 1f, kept on nr fin: op 10/1, clr of rem: back to form: see 1639.
3599 **FITZWARREN 4** [9] N Bycroft 3-9-0 (68) N Callan 12/1: 02-03003: With ldr, no extra fnl 1f: quick 5 **60**
reapp: joc 2 day careless riding ban: see 2961.
2884 **KEY OF GOLD 34** [5] D Carroll 3-9-0 (70) R Hills 12/1: 0120-004: Trkd ldrs, onepcd 1f out: see 2723. ¾ **58**
3379 **MARYSIENKA 13** [1]3-9-0 (73) K Pierrepont(7) 16/1: 20264-05: Trkd ldrs, wknd 1f out: see 3379. 3 **49**
3485 **EXTRA COVER 9** [4]3-9-5 bl (75) D Sweeney 4/1: 2223166: Rear, nvr a factor. 1¼ **50**
3543 **ASK THE CLERK 6** [8]3-9-1 (71) M Tebbutt 11/4: 3464337: Mid-div, hdwy & hmpd over 1f out, not 5 **31**
recover, eased in rear ins fnl 1f: well bckd, quick reapp: see 3543.
3485 **COMMANDER BOND 9** [2]3-9-1 (71) J Carroll 20/1: 4-001008: Slow away in rear, nvr a factor. 5 **16**
8 Ran Time 1m 17.84(3.74) Owned: The Night Owls Trained: Hungerford

KEMPTON WEDNESDAY 04.08.04 Righthand, Flat, Fair Track

Official Going Good/Firm (Good places)

3685 **6.00 Commitments Live Tonight Apprentice Handicap Stakes 3yo+ 0-75 (E)** **[73]**
£4124 £1269 £635 **1m rnd** **Good/Firm 33** **-18 Slow** Inside

3538 **BURGUNDY 6** [2] P Mitchell 7-9-0 bl (59) T P Queally 9/2: 3611121: Dwelt, held up, hdwy over 2f out, styd on to lead cl-home, rdn out: qck reapp: claim & sell wnr earlier: eff over 1m/10f on firm, soft & both AWs, likes Lingfield: in fine heart at present: see 3288, 145. **64**
3524 **THE GAIKWAR 7** [6] N E Berry 5-9-2 bl (61) M Savage 7/1: U000432: Slow away, sn in tch, hdwy to lead over 1f out, rdn & hdd cl-home: gd run: see 3401. ¾ **64**
3455* **MOSCOW TIMES 11** [5] D R C Elsworth 3-9-6 (72) Natalia Gemelova(3) 8/1: 00-65013: Slow away, held up, hdwy to chall just ins last, no extra cl-home: in gd heart, see 3455. ½ **74**
3641* **FEN GYPSY 2** [1] P D Evans 6-9-12 (6ex) (71) S Donohoe(3) 11/2: 4512414: In tch, eff 2f out, onepace. ¾ **71**
3490 **BALERNO 9** [4]5-9-0 (59) D Corby 7/2 FAV: 0402125: Held up, eff over 1f out, onepace: see 3184. ½ **58**
3524 **FLEETWOOD BAY 7** [11]4-3-8 t (67) N Chalmers 8/1: 0636026: Led over 2f out till over 1f out, wknd. ¾ **64**
2857 **GRAN CLICQUOT 35** [7]9-8-3 (48) C Haddon(3) 12/1: 0201027: In tch, eff over 1f out, sn no extra. 1½ **42**
3107 **LIZARAZU 25** [8]5-9-13 (72) R Miles 20/1: 62252-08: Held up, eff 2f out, wknd dist: see 2107. 1¾ **63**
3039 **CATCH THE FOX 28** [10]4-7-12 (1oh) (42) Lucy Russell(5) 33/1: 0200409: In tch, wknd over 1f out. 3 **28**
3215 **ESPADA 20** [9]8-8-7 bl (52) R Keogh(5) 20/1: 4150460: 10th: Led till 2f out, wknd: btr 2397 (7f). 5 **27**
3194* **LISTEN TO REASON 21** [3]3-8-13 (65) B Reilly 14/1: 50-10: 11th: In tch, wknd 2f out: btr 3194 (7f). 1¾ **36**
11 Ran Time 1m 40.9 (4.1) Owned: Mrs S Sheldon Trained: Epsom

3686 **6.30 O'callaghan Hotels Nursery Handicap Stakes 2yo (E)** **[91]**
£4163 £1281 £641 **6f str** **Good/Firm 33** **-14 Slow** Centre

3297 **TREAT ME WILD 16** [4] R Hannon 2-8-5 (68) R Smith 14/1: 1651: Cl-up, eff well over 1f out, styd on to lead cl-home, drvn: eff over 5/6f on fast & gd/soft grnd: genuine, see 1097. **76**
3521* **THE CROOKED RING 7** [3] P D Evans 2-9-10 (6ex) (87) S Donohoe(7) 6/5 FAV: 2134112: In tch, gd hdwy to lead 2f out, rdn & hdd ins last: hvly bckd: useful, most progressive & tough: top-weight, see 3521. shd **95**
3266 **EDGE FUND 18** [7] B R Millman 2-9-2 (79) K McEvoy 6/1: 3332303: With wnr, led halfway till 2f out, onepace: cheek pieces discarded: consistent: see 2367, 1256. 1½ **82**
3355 **PENNESTAMP 13** [5] Mrs P N Dutfield 2-8-5 (68) R Havlin 9/1: 06644: Keen, led to halfway, hung & wknd over 1f out: see 3355 (5f). 2 **65**
1567 **KING AFTER 91** [6]2-9-7 (84) M Savage(5) 10/1: 1665: With ldrs, wknd over 2f out: 3 month abs: much btr 1567 (5f, gd), 931 (polytrack). 8 **57**
3290 **EPITOMISE 16** [1]2-8-6 (69) Martin Dwyer 14/1: 6406: Held up, wknd well over 1f out: see 2847. 5 **27**
3361 **CHAIRMAN RICK 13** [2]2-8-3 VIS (66) T P Queally 4/1: 0647: Nvr trav well, al bhd, t.o.: not take to vis. ¾ **22**
7 Ran Time 1m 13.94 (2.84) Owned: The Old Downton Partnership Trained: Marlborough

3687 **7.00 Relay Technical Transport Maiden Stakes 3yo+ (D)**
£5369 £1652 £826 **5f str** **Good/Firm 33** **-10 Slow** Centre

197 **ELVINA 233** [9] A G Newcombe 3-8-9 L Dettori 9/1: 4-1: Rcd alone far rail, cl-up, led dist, drvn out: long abs: dam 5/6f scorer: eff at 5f on fast grnd: goes well fresh: gd enterprising ride. **61**
2649 **MILLINSKY 43** [7] R Guest 3-8-9 D Holland 8/11 FAV: 632: Held up, hdwy & short of room over 1f out, styd on to lead main group ins last, just held by far side wnr: 6 wk abs: see 2649, 2237. hd **61**
2645 **RYANS QUEST 43** [3] T D McCarthy 5-8-12 (39) R Miles(3) 20/1: 405-0003: Handy, led main group halfway till just ins last, no extra: 6 wk abs: eff at 5f on fast grnd: btr run, see 2645. 2½ **54**
3036 **SCARLETT BREEZE 28** [6] J W Hills 3-8-9 (46) M Hills 15/2: 5-000504: With ldrs, wknd over 1f out. ¾ **52**
HEAVENS WALK 0 [1]3-9-0 S Sanders 11/4: 5: ch c Compton Place - Ghost Dancing (Lion Cavern) Cl-up, wknd dist: bckd on debut: speedily bred: with P Makin. ¾ **55**
3413 **LORD WISHINGWELL 12** [4]3-9-0 vis (37) C Catlin 25/1: 0-033046: In tch, wknd 2f out: see 2125. 6 **37**
3165 **DIAPHANOUS 23** [8]6-8-12 bl (35) S Carson 33/1: 4-000007: Keen, led main group till halfway, wknd. 3 **23**
449 **IMPERIAL WIZARD 196** [5]3-9-0 A Daly 50/1: 08: Al bhd. 1 **25**
4870} **ANGEL MAID 285** [2]3-8-9 R Havlin 33/1: 000-9: Al bhd. 6 **2**
9 Ran Time 1m 0.46 (2.16) Owned: Patel Thomas Eagle & Capel Trained: Barnstaple

3688 **7.30 Mcgee Group Handicap Stakes 3yo+ 0-85 (D)** **[85]**
£8229 £2532 £1266 **1m6f92y** **Good/Firm 33** **+04 Fast** Inside

2899 **MR ED 33** [3] P Bowen 6-9-3 p (74) L Dettori 3/1 FAV: 6000-221: Rear, hdwy over 3f out, switched & rdn/led over 1f out, idled ins last, drvn out to hold on: nicely bckd: gd time: suited by 14f & stays 2m: acts on fast, gd/soft & any trk: genuine & tough: see 2391. **83**
3270 **MASKED 18** [11] J W Hills 3-8-5 (75) K McEvoy 9/1: 0041522: Mid-div, hdwy to chase ldrs over 2f out, sn outpcd by wnr but kept on well cl-home: styd longer 14f trip well, remains on the upgrade, can win again. ¾ **82**
3387 **FLAMENCO BRIDE 12** [6] D R C Elsworth 4-8-10 (67) J F Egan 16/1: 4500-003: Held up, hdwy halfway & led over 2f out till over 1f out, not pace of wnr: clr of rem: drpd in trip, best effort this term, win a h'cap. ¾ **72**
3519 **HEAD TO KERRY 7** [8] D J S ffrench Davis 4-7-12 t (55) J F McDonald(3) 7/1: 0353424: Keen in mid-div, chall 2f out, sn no extra: btr 3519 (12f). 6 **52**
3359 **BUKIT FRASER 13** [10]3-8-9 (79) S Sanders 11/2: 4-140005: Trkd ldrs, ch 2f out, fdd: op 7/1: yet to convince at 14f: rtn to 11/12f could suit: see 1140 (mdn, 11f). ½ **75**
2582 **OCEAN AVENUE 46** [7]5-9-12 (83) D Holland 4/1: 2431-106: Led & clr halfway, hdd over 2f out & fdd: nicely bckd, op 11/2: 6 wk abs: much btr 1916. 8 **67**
3587 **JASMICK 5** [9]6-9-5 (76) L Fletcher(3) 11/1: 50260-57: Held up, no impress over 2f out: qck reapp. 3 **56**
3519 **SUDDEN FLIGHT 7** [5]7-8-13 (70) R Havlin 16/1: 0431658: Rear, eff 4f out, sn btn: not enjoy fast grnd. 7 **40**
2391 **CANTRIP 53** [2]4-7-12 (4oh) (51) Lisa Jones 20/1: 0000139: Chsd ldrs, wknd 4f out: abs: btr 2391. 1 **23**
3057 **DARN GOOD 27** [12]3-8-1 bl (71) Martin Dwyer 10/1: 0601120: 10th: Chsd ldrs, lost pl 5f out, bhd. 1½ **37**
3114 **WESTERN 25** [1]4-9-3 (74) Dane O'Neill 50/1: 41-20000: 11th: Dwelt, al rear, bhd 3f out. 2½ **36**

KEMPTON   WEDNESDAY 04.08.04   Righthand, Flat, Fair Track

FAIT LE JOJO 1440 [4]7-10-0 (85) J Murtagh 14/1: 411351///-0: 12th: b g Pistolet Bleu - Pretty *dist* 0
Davis (Trempolino) Chsd ldr, wknd qckly from halfway, t.o. & eased: reportedly fin sore: v long Flat abs, 10 wk
jumps abs (unplcd, h'cap hdle): won 3 nov chases in 03/04 (rtd 132c, 2m, fast & soft grnd): last rcd on the level
'00, landed 3 h'caps: prev eff at 14/15f on fast grnd.
12 Ran   Time 3m 06.93 (4.13)   Owned: Mr Gwilym J Morris   Trained: Haverfordwest

3689   8.00 Byrne Group Classified Stakes 3yo+ 0-85 (C)
£11128 £3424 £1712   **1m rnd**   **Good/Firm 33**   **+04 Fast**   Inside

3006 **DAWN SURPRISE 29** [9] Saeed bin Suroor 3-8-11 t (89) L Dettori 11/4 FAV: 3-2151: Trkd ldr & narrow   **96**
lead 2f out, drvn & asserted ins last: well bckd: gd time: eff at 7f, suited by 1m/10f on firm & fast grnd,
stiff/gall or easy trk: lightly rcd & progressive filly: see 3006 & 2419.
3523* **WELCOME STRANGER 7** [8] J M P Eustace 4-9-9 (81) L Fletcher(3) 5/1: 0021212: Dwelt, sn trkd ldrs,   1½ **97**
rdn to chase wnr ins last, al held: nicely bckd: useful & progressive: see 3523, 2853.
3364* **WILL HE WISH 13** [4] S Gollings 8-9-7 bl (89) J F Egan 11/1: 0000013: Trkd ldrs, eff to chase wnr   ½ **94**
over 1f out, no extra ins last: confirmed rtn to form of latest: just best at 7f: see 3364 (7f).
3512 **HIGHLAND REEL 8** [7] D R C Elsworth 7-9-3 (85) Dane O'Neill 9/1: 1004033: Mid-div, kept on onepace.   1¾ **86**
3535* **DIAMOND LODGE 7** [6]3-9-1 (87) S W Kelly 3/1: 4121115: Trkd ldrs & ch 2f out, rdn & fdd ins last.   nk **90**
2753 **DUBROVSKY 39** [2]4-9-3 T (84) J Murtagh 5/1: 1/030-406: Held up, drvn & no impress dist: bckd.   2 **81**
3199 **SHARPLAW VENTURE 21** [3]4-9-3 (88) D Holland 25/1: 5230-307: Led racing freely, hdd 2f out & sn   shd **80**
btn: reportedly hanging left thr'out: see 2710.
3565 **SERIEUX 5** [1]5-9-6 (88) S Sanders 9/1: 0002008: Rear, no prog 3f out: qck reapp: btr 1231.   3½ **76**
2915 **OUR TEDDY 32** [5]4-9-3 bl (85) Martin Dwyer 20/1: 0054409: Rear, rdn & btn over 2f out: btr 2604.   6 **61**
9 Ran   Time 3m 39.15 (2.35)   Owned: Godolphin   Trained: Newmarket

3690   8.30 Mcardle Group Handicap Stakes 3yo 0-75 (E)
£4212 £1296 £648   **1m2f**   **Good/Firm 33**   **+00 Fast**   Centre
[82]

3384 **LITTLE EYE 13** [10] J R Best 3-8-8 vis (62) L Dettori 7/2 FAV: 3064021: Mid-div, prog 2f out, styd   **72**
on to lead ins fnl 1f, drvn out: bckd: eff at 7f, suited by 10f on frm, gd & both AW's: eff with visor: first win.
2919 **AMERICAN DUKE 32** [1] B J Meehan 3-8-10 (64) Paul Eddery 14/1: 4400-002: Bhd, hdwy for 3f out,   ½ **73**
chsd wnr ins fnl 1f, just denied: eff at 7f, now stays 10f: rider reported saddle had slipped & this was a gd eff.
3391* **IFFY 12** [14] P D Cundell 3-8-9 (63) C Catlin 5/1: 50-40413: Led, rcd along ins rail till   1½ **69**
switched to join main group turning in, hdd ins fnl 1f, no extra: did little wrong, raised 5lb since 3391.
3219* **DESERT REIGN 20** [8] A P Jarvis 3-9-3 (71) T P Queally 6/1: 000-514: Mid-div, prog when short of   1½ **74**
room bef 2f out, kept on fnl 1f, nrst fin: tchd 8/1: eff at 8.5f, now stays 10f: acts on fast & gd grnd.
2452 **LA PROFESSORESSA 51** [4]3-8-5 (59) R Havlin 25/1: 005-6005: Clp-up, ev ch dist, sn wknd: 7 wk abs.   1¼ **59**
3410 **BRIGHT FIRE 12** [12]3-7-12 (2oh) (50) Lisa Jones 14/1: 06-546: Mid-div, prog 3f out, onepcd fnl 1f.   nk **51**
3243 **SHARAAB 19** [6]3-9-2 t (70) D Holland 20/1: 0-605207: Cl-up 1m, wknd: ran without declared t-strap.   1½ **66**
2452 **ANDURIL 51** [15]3-8-10 (64) J F Egan 25/1: 6036408: Reared start, hdwy after halfway, fdd fnl 1f.   shd **60**
4665} **CIRCASSIAN 299** [3]3-8-7 (61) S Sanders 7/1: 0000-9: b g Groom Dancer - Daraliya (Kahyasi) Handy   1½ **54**
over 7f, sn wknd: reapp: unplcd in 4 '03 starts (rtd 61, med auct mdn): bred to apprec mid-dist: has been gelded.
3578 **DOCTORED 5** [7]3-8-7 (61) S Donohoe(7) 9/2: 0111130: 10th: Mid-div over 1m, wknd: qck   ½ **69**
reapp & 6lb pen: has been busy of late: btr 3471 & 3201.
2893 **SPRING DAISY 33** [11]3-8-10 (64) J Murtagh 25/1: 00-400: 11th: Handy over 7f, sn wknd: btr 2536.   1 **54**
2994 **CARTRONAGEERAGHLAD 29** [9]3-9-7 (75) Dane O'Neill 8/1: 0244540: 12th: Bhd, nvr a factor: btr 2994.   ½ **64**
3334 **Papeete 14** [7]3-8-2 (56) S Carson 33/1:0   3222 **Midshipman Easy 20** [5]3-9-2 e(70) S W Kelly 25/1:0
14 Ran   Time 2m 05.65(3.35)   Owned: Mr & Mrs R Dawbarn   Trained: Maidstone

---

BRIGHTON   WEDNESDAY 04.08.04   Lefthand, V Sharp, Undulating Track

Official Going Firm

3691   2.40 Chaplin's Bar At Burgess Hill Maiden Auction Stakes 2yo (E)
£3422 £1053 £526   **6f209y rnd**   **Firm 20**   **-12 Slow**   Inside

3586 **MY PRINCESS 5** [8] N A Callaghan 2-8-7 L Dettori 2/1: 3531: Cl-up, styd on for press to lead 1f   **80+**
out, pushed clr ins fnl 1f, val 4L+: bckd on quick reapp: eff at 6f, apprec step up to 7f: acts on firm & fast
grnd, stiff/gall or sharp/undul trk: see 3586 & 2263.
3342 **CHANTACO 14** [6] A M Balding 2-8-9 Martin Dwyer 15/8 FAV: 52: Led, hdd under press 1f out, sn   2½ **74**
outpcd by easy wnr: clr rem: acts on firm & fast grnd: imprvd on debut eff & can find a weak mdn.
3183 **AZUREE 21** [3] R Hannon 2-8-9 bl (77) P Dobbs 7/1: 263043: Cl-up over 5f, no extra: lngr trip.   2½ **69**
2618 **BUSACO 44** [7] J L Dunlop 2-8-9 I Mongan 16/1: 04: b c Mister Baileys - War Shanty (Warrshan)   ¾ **67**
Chsd ldrs 5f, sn onepcd: 6 wk abs: Apr foal, cost 10,000 gns: half brother plcd at 1m: dam unplcd.
BOLD COUNSEL 0 [5]2-8-8 S Sanders 7/1: 5: b c Titus Livius - Daisy Dobson (Gorytus) Dwelt, nvr   nk **65**
nrr than mid-div: debut: Apr foal, half brother to a Listed wnr abroad: sire decent performer at sprint dists.
SWEENEY TODD 0 [2]2-8-9 R Havlin 40/1: 6: ch g Raise A Grand - Optional (Prince Sabo) Rear,   5 **56**
nvr a factor on debut: Apr 1st foal, cost 9,000 gns: dam successful at 6f: sire decent 7f performer at 2.
WANDERING ACT 0 [4]2-8-11 T P Queally 7/1: 7: b c Brave Act - Cwm Deri (Alzao) Mid-div till   1¼ **56**
halfway, wknd: bckd from 16/1 on debut: May foal, cost 20,000 gns: half brother successful at 7f: dam unrcd.
7 Ran   Time 1m 22.04 (2.24)   Owned: Mr T Mohan   Trained: Newmarket

3692 3.10 Seaview At East Preston Selling Handicap Stakes 3yo+ 35-55 (G) [50]
£3322 £1022 £511   1m3f196y   Firm 20   -22 Slow   Outside

3049 **MR WHIZZ** 27 [7] A P Jones 7-8-12 p (34) Derek Nolan(7) 10/1: 4322051: Dwelt, prog halfway, styd on   44
for press to lead dist, rdn clr: bought in for 4,200 gns: recently fell over fences (beginner chase): eff at 1m,
now stays 12f, has tried further: acts on firm, hvy grnd & fibresand: prev eff in blnks & eye-shield, apprec
today's refitting of cheek pieces: see 3049 & 1643.
3294 **BLUE SAVANNA** 16 [4] J G Portman 4-9-4 bl (40) N Mackay(3) 8/1: 1056442: Cl-up, led after 7f, hdd   3   45
dist, no extra: rnr: see 3294 & 916.
3420* **BANNINGHAM BLAZE** 11 [3] A W Carroll 4-10-0 vis (50) I Mongan 11/4 FAV: 2365313: Rear, prog 3f   3   50
out, no impress bef 1f out: well bckd: btr 3420 (14f).
3486* **ROLEX FREE** 9 [1] D Flood 6-10-4 (6ex)vis (54) L Dettori 7/2: 0600314: Led 7f, sn no extra: tchd   1   52
9/2: disapp under 6lb pen on return to turf: btr 3486 (fibresand).
2589 **BLUE STREAK** 46 [2]7-9-12 bl (48) Dane O'Neill 10/1: 65220-05: ch g Bluebird - Fleet Amour   7   36
(Afleet) Handy, wknd 4f out: recently hdles unplcd (rtd 72h, sell): clmg hdle wnr in 03/04 (rtd 108h, stays 2m on
fast or hvy, eff with eye-shield: rnr-up twice here at Brighton in '03 (sell h'cap & clmr): clmg wnr in '02: eff
at 1m/12f on firm, fast & polytrack: best without blnks, eff in pieces & a t-strap.
2 Aug'03 Brig 11.9fm 57-(40) F: 2 Aug'03 Brig 11.9fm 49-40 G: 1 Aug'02 Brig 10g/f 48- E: 2 Dec'01 Ling 10ap 53a- D:
3383 **REGAL PERFORMER** 13 [6]3-9-5 (52) J F Egan 7/2: 0223456: Bhd, nvr a factor: op 5/1: btr 2576.   10   26
3292 **GLIDING BY** 16 [8]3-9-5 (52) S Sanders 16/1: 00-007: ch f Halling - Waft (Topsider) Mid-div till   18   0
halfway, sn fdd: unplcd sole '03 start (rtd 44a): with P R Charnings.
3420 **CRACOW** 11 [5]7-9-9 p (45) Martin Dwyer 8/1: 00-/20458: Cl-up, fdd 4f out: 'not handle fast grnd'.   20   0
8 Ran Time 2m 33.24 (5.04)   Owned: The Milk Sheiks   Trained: Upper Lambourn

3693 3.40 Ebony Room Brighton Sprint Handicap Stakes 3yo 0-80 (D) [87]
£6656 £2048 £1024   5f213y rnd   Firm 20   -06 Slow   Inside

2778 **WHOS WINNING** 38 [5] B G Powell 3-8-7 (66) S Sanders 13/2: 6-006021: In tch, styd on to lead 2f   74
out, drvn out ins fnl 1f to hold on: op 8/1, new stable: blnks left off: eff at 5/6f on firm & fast grnd, likes a
sharp/undul trk: imprvd eff on 1st start for new yard: see 2778 (C A Dwyer).
3543 **PERUVIAN STYLE** 6 [7] N P Littmoden 3-8-11 (70) T P Queally 7/1: 0500652: Mid-div, prog when   shd   76
short of room bef 2f out, swtchd & styd on well ins fnl 1f, post came too sn: qck reapp: reportedly lost a full
plate & this was a fine eff in circumstances, on a wng mark & can find similar: see 3543.
3416 **ESTIHLAL** 12 [3] E A L Dunlop 3-9-0 (73) W Supple 1/1 FAV: 4124143: Held up, prog halfway, ev ch   ½   78
ins fnl 1f, just held in 3-way photo: well bckd: continues to run well: 9lb higher than last win: see 3416.
2841 **ACE CLUB** 35 [4] W J Haggas 3-8-8 (67) L Dettori 4/1: 21-5004: Handy, short of room bef 1f out: 2½   65
sn switched & no impress ins fnl 1f: another below par run, btr 1570 (reapp, gd/soft).
3298 **BARABELLA** 16 [2]3-7-12 (2oh) (55) J F McDonald(3) 16/1: 5045045: Bhd, prog when short of room   2   49
halfway, switched when short of room again & styd on, no impress: shade closer with clr passage: btr 1404.
958 **EMARADIA** 128 [1]3-7-12 (3oh) (54) Lisa Jones 20/1: 2012266: Led, hdd 5f out, wknd fnl 2f: long abs.   3½   39
3293 **CHANCE FOR ROMANCE** 16 [6]3-9-7 VIS (80) Martin Dwyer 8/1: 050-2657: Led 5f out, hdd 2f out, sn   5   48
fdd: rcd too keenly in 1st time visor on h'cap bow: btr 2137 (reapp).
7 Ran Time 1m 9.37 (1.57)   Owned: Mrs Rachel A Powell   Trained: Winchester

3694 4.10 John Smith's Brighton Mile Challenge Trophy Rated Stakes Handicap 3yo+ 0-80 (D) [92]
£18966 £7194 £3597   7f214y rnd   Firm 20   +05 Fast   Inside

3363 **AESCULUS** 13 [10] L M Cumani 3-8-4 (1oh) (68) N Mackay(3) 12/1: 0530321: Chsd ldrs, styd on to lead   75
cl-home, pushed out: fast time: eff at 6f, suited by 1m: acts on fm, gd grnd & polytrack: impvg.
2172 **FLINT RIVER** 63 [7] H Morrison 6-9-0 (71) L Fletcher(3) 16/1: 0124002: Cl-up, styd on to lead   nk   75
dist, sn hung left & hdd, just held: 9 wk abs: loves Brighton & W'hampton: see 1598.
3565 **TAKES TUTU** 5 [2] K R Burke 5-9-5 bl (76) S Whitworth 33/1: 5502003: Held up, prog to lead ins fnl   ½   79
1f, hdd cl-home: quick reapp: gd run in defeat & is on wng mark: see 3210 & 2672.
3538 **KATIYPOUR** 6 [14] Miss B Sanders 7-9-4 (75) Lisa Jones 25/1: 2014034: Keen bhd, prog wide 3f out,   ½   77
styd on well, not btn far in 4th: quick reapp: likes sharp/undul trks & this was a decent eff: see 3538 & 1691.
3546 + **MASAFI** 6 [11]3-9-1 (3ex) (79) S Sanders 4/5 FAV: 1111115: Cl-up, ev ch 2f out, no extra ins fnl   ¾   79
1f: well bckd on quick reapp under 3lb pen: below form on bid for 8-timer & rider reported grnd was too firm.
3641 **JOOLS** 2 [12]6-9-5 (76) W Supple 25/1: 44650U6: Mid-div, prog 2f out, onepcd fnl 1f: qck reapp.   2   72
3199 **DANCE ON THE TOP** 21 [13]6-9-8 t (79) Martin Dwyer 25/1: 0-110657: Cl-up, led 2f out, hdd dist, no   hd   74
extra: saves best form for polytrack: btr 547.
3625 **VOICE MAIL** 4 [3]5-9-7 (78) T Block(7) 20/1: 3020438: Nvr nrr than mid-div: quick reapp: see 3083.   ½   72
3453* **HOH BLEU DEE** 11 [5]3-8-11 (75) J F Egan 16/1: 6-060219: Handy till halfway, sn outpcd, rallying   2   65
when short of room dist: btr 3453 (clmr).
3336 **FACTUAL LAD** 14 [4]6-9-1 (72) S W Kelly 33/1: 10-00100: 10th: Nvr nrr than mid-div: btr 2260.   nk   61
3423 **ARAGONS BOY** 11 [6]4-8-12 (69) Dane O'Neill 33/1: 4-001040: 11th: Led 6f, wknd: btr 3423.   6   46
3676 **LONDONER** 1 [15]6-8-5 (2oh) (60) C Catlin 20/1: 21053520: 12th: Handy 6f, sn hung left & fdd.   hd   38
3524* **TODLEA** 7 [8]4-9-5 (3ex) (76) L Dettori 9/2: 3622310: 13th: AI in rear: tchd 11/2: 'not enjoy fm'.   shd   51
2903 **BORREGO** 33 [1]4-9-5 (76) S Carson 50/1: 12-20600: 14th: Handy, fdd 2f out: btr 2389.   3½   44
3465 **A WOMAN IN LOVE** 10 [9]5-9-8 (79) T P Queally 15/2: 1111400: 15th: Keen bhd, nvr a factor: v   1¾   43
disapp run & surely something amiss: btr 3068,2587 & 2432.
15 Ran Time 1m 33.21 (1.21)   Owned: Duke of Devonshire   Trained: Newmarket

BRIGHTON WEDNESDAY 04.08.04 Lefthand, V Sharp, Undulating Track

3695 4.40 Coral Greyhound Stadia Handicap Stakes 3yo+ 0-70 (E) [68]
£5408 £1664 £832 **1m1f209y** **Firm 20** **-11 Slow** Outside

3250 **KIRKHAM ABBEY 19** [8] M A Jarvis 4-9-9 (63) S Sanders 7/2: 1-032651: Hld up, prog wide after halfway, drvn to lead cl home: eff at 8.5f/12f on fm & fibresand: vis discarded & likes Brighton. **73**
3392 **FORTUNE POINT 12** [3] A W Carroll 6-9-2 vis (56) W Supple 14/1: 2004062: Led, hdd under press ins fnl 1f, no extra: clr rem: back to form with re-introduction of visor: h'capped to find similar: see 912 & 718. 1½ **61**
3232 **FANTASY CRUSADER 19** [9] J A Gilbert 5-8-8 p (48) Dane O'Neill 11/1: 3032003: Handy, short of room 2f out, sn no extra: op 14/1: btr 2589. 7 **45**
3401 **OVER TO YOU BERT 12** [5] R J Hodges 5-8-4 (44) J F McDonald(3) 7/1: 0033104: Cl-up 1m, sn no extra: unproven beyond 1m: btr 3142 (1m h'cap). nk **40**
1712 **HUSKY 83** [7]6-8-5 p (45) A Daly 20/1: 00-51305: Slow away, nvr nrr than mid-div: recent hdles unplcd (rtd 82h, h'cap): btr 1412 & 1182. shd **40**
3676 **OUR DESTINY 1** [2]6-9-4 (58) I Mongan 8/1: 10410566: Handy over 7f, wknd: unplcd here yesterday. 1 **51**
2866 **KERNEL DOWERY 34** [6]4-9-10 e (64) Martin Dwyer 7/2: 0021107: Cl-up, fdd 2f out: another below par eff: fin ahead of today's wnr in 2433 (C/D). 2½ **53**
60 **SECOND OF MAY 259** [4]4-9-11 (65) J F Egan 10/1: 621542-8: Mid-div till halfway, grad wknd. ¾ **52**
3300 **FORGE LANE 16** [1]3-8-6 BL (55) S Whitworth 100/30 FAV: 0000429: Slow away, nvr travelling in blnks. shd **41**
9 Ran Time 2m 0.92 (3.12) Owned: Mr P D Savill Trained: Newmarket

3696 5.10 Club And Institute Union Classified Stakes 3yo+ 0-70 (E)
£3328 £1024 £512 **6f209y rnd** **Firm 20** **-15 Slow** Inside

3364 **SAMUEL CHARLES 13** [6] W M Brisbourne 6-9-3 (70) S W Kelly 9/2: 2334201: Made all, pushed clr fnl 1f: op 7/2: eff at 7f/8.5f on firm, gd/soft & both AWs: likes to force the pace: see 2920. **78+**
3443 **BRAVE DANE 11** [1] A W Carroll 6-9-7 (74) W Supple 7/2: 5612002: Held up, prog when short of room dist, sn switched wide & styd on, nvr getting to wnr: tchd 5/1: eff at 7f, crying out for return to 1m+: btr 1613. 2½ **75**
3433 **CARRY ON DOC 11** [2] J W Hills 3-9-2 (75) S Whitworth 9/4 FAV: 55-36153: Al handy, onepace fnl 1f: bckd from 7/2: will apprec return to 1m: btr 2953. ½ **76**
2954 **FRANKSALOT 31** [4] Miss B Sanders 4-9-3 (69) S Sanders 5/2: 22-01454: Keen cl-up, no extra ins fnl 1f: below form of win here in 2644 (h'cap). ½ **70**
2661 **OUR GAMBLE 42** [3]3-8-8 (70) Dane O'Neill 12/1: 10-60005: Al in rear: 6 wks abs. 2½ **62**
3672 **ZIET DALSACE 1** [5]4-9-0 (60) A Daly 8/1: 00201046: Prom, rcd keenly, wkng when short of room 2f out. 5 **52**
6 Ran Time 1m 22.29(2.49) Owned: Mr J F Thomas Trained: Nesscliffe

NEWCASTLE WEDNESDAY 04.08.04 Lefthand, Galloping, Stiff Track

Official Going Good/Soft (Good Places)

3697 2.30 Jazzy Geoff Ainsley Supports Nspcc Maiden Stakes 3yo+ (D)
£3435 £1057 £529 **1m1f9y rnd** **Good/Soft 64** **-09 Slow**

3263 **LITTLE BOB 18** [9] J D Bethell 3-8-13 (75) T E Durcan 11/10 FAV: 0-442301: Held up, smooth hdwy over 3f out & led over 2f out, edged right, drvn out: well bckd: eff at 9/10f on fast & gd/soft. **75**
2843 **ST BARCHAN 35** [1] W Jarvis 3-8-13 K Darley 11/4: 42: Dwelt, keen trkg ldrs, briefly short of room over 2f out, kept on, high head carraige: clr rem: op 11/8: eff at 9/10f on fast & gd/soft: see 2843. ½ **73**
3462 **KYBER 10** [8] R F Fisher 3-8-13 R Winston 10/1: 543: Trkd ldrs, onepace. 6 **61**
3263 **RIGONZA 18** [6] T D Easterby 3-8-13 (62) D Allan 5/1: 6-005034: In tch, outpcd 3f out, no impress. nk **60**
2947 **THE LOOSE SCREW 32** [2]6-9-7 p (35) B Swarbrick(5) 33/1: 0-000005: Led till over 2f out, fdd, needs sells. 4 **52$**
2987 **HIGH CLASS PET 30** [7]4-9-2 G Faulkner 100/1: 06: In tch, till over 2f out, sn bhd: no form. 12 **23**
2901 **RED MOUNTAIN 33** [4]3-8-13 L Enstone(3) 33/1: 0-07: Chsd ldrs, btn 3f out: see 2901. ½ **27**
3648 **BLUE NUN 2** [3]3-8-8 (47) G Gibbons 33/1: 50058: Chsd ldrs, no ch over 2f out: quick reapp: btr 3648. 7 **8**
1726} **DISTINCTLYTHEBEST 436** [5]4-9-7 T P Makin(5) 100/1: 0-9: b c Distinctly North - Euphyllia (Superpower) Bhd & no ch halfway: reapp in t-strap: unplcd & mod form sole '03 start (rtd 20, auct mdn). 4 **5**
9 Ran Time 1m 58.63 (6.53) Owned: Mr Robert Gibbons Trained: Middleham

3698 3.00 Mowden Park Estates Supports Nspcc Nursery Handicap Stakes 2yo (E) [92]
£3819 £1175 £588 **7f str** **Good/Soft 64** **-07 Slow**

2652 **LADY MISHA 43** [9] Jedd O'Keeffe 2-7-12 (62) J Mackay 16/1: 55031: Chsd ldrs, hdwy to lead dist, drvn out: 6 wk abs, 1st win on h'cap bow: eff at 7/7.5f on gd & gd/soft grnd, likes a stiff trk: lightly rcd, prog. **70**
3221 **SIR ANTHONY 20** [6] B Smart 2-9-7 (85) D McGaffin 5/1: 132: Rear, hdwy over 2f out, kept on for press, not pace of wnr: h'cap bow: styd longer 7f trip well: useful & improving: see 3221 & 2689. 1 **90**
3560 **BRACE OF DOVES 6** [3] T D Barron 2-8-5 (69) K Darley 11/4 FAV: 0523323: Trkd ldrs travelling well, led over 2f out till dist, not pace of front pair: fair run: see 3560, 2989 & 2682. 1½ **71**
3429 **SPINNAKERS GIRL 11** [12] J R Weymes 2-8-6 (70) R Winston 14/1: 0324: Mid-div, styd on onepace fnl 2f: acts on fast & gd/soft grnd: see 3429 (C/D). ½ **71**
3271 **MITCHELLAND 18** [11]2-8-10 (74) T Eaves(3) 12/1: 4106635: Dwelt, rear, short of room over 2f out, kept on late, nvr reach ldrs: op 9/1: longer 7f trip looks likely to suit, handles gd & hvy grnd, stiff/gall trks. 1¾ **72**
3189 **SOCIETY MUSIC 21** [10]2-9-2 (80) L Enstone(3) 10/1: 13136: Keen & held up, onepace fnl 2f: see 3189. ½ **77**
3393 **LORD JOHN 12** [8]2-8-0 (64) Dale Gibson 16/1: 040407: Chsd ldrs, rdn & no impress fnl 1f: see 3212. 2 **57**
2424 **SKIPPIT JOHN 52** [15]2-8-8 (72) Dean McKeown 25/1: 2668: Keen & handy, no impress over 1f out. nk **64**
3351 **TWICE NIGHTLY 14** [5]2-8-5 (69) T Hamilton(3) 10/1: 33659: Rear, rdn & only mod prog: btr 1780 (6f). hd **60**
3407 **HERES THE PLAN 12** [14]2-9-2 (80) P McCabe 6/1: 1060: 10th: Led till over 2f out, btn dist: bckd. hd **70**
2584 **MASTER JOSEPH 46** [1]2-8-0 (64) P M Quinn 16/1: 4000: 11th: Held up, no room over 2f out, no impress. ¾ **53**
2989 **Myttons Dream 29** [2]2-7-12 (2oh)(60) J Bramhill 20/1:0

3349⁰ Oredale 14 [13]2-8-4 (68) G Gibbons 12/1:0

13 Ran   Time 1m 29.06 (4.96)   Owned: Allen Kelly & Moore   Trained: Leyburn

---

3699   3.30 Lloyds Tsb Supports Nspcc Median Auction Maiden Stakes 2yo   (F)
£3052 £872 £436   6f str   Good/Soft 64   -02 Slow

3202   **SPY KING** 20 [13] M Johnston 2-9-0   K Darley 9/2: 21: Chsd ldrs far side & led dist, rdn out: 92
confirmed debut promise: eff at 6f on fast & gd/soft grnd, stiff/gall trks: looks potentially v useful: see 3202.
3148   **STRETFORD END** 23 [17] B Smart 2-9-0   D McGaffin 4/1: F2: b c Zieten - Creese (Diesis) Led & sn   ½   89+
in command stands side group, styd on well for press ins last, just held by wnr far side: cost 41,000 gns: May
foal: half brother to a 7f wnr: eff at 6f, 7f+ suit: acts on gd/soft: promising, win on.
3266   **TAGULA SUNRISE** 18 [12] R A Fahey 2-8-9 (85) T Hamilton(3) 3/1 FAV: 22203: Led far side after 2f   1   81
till dist, kept on onepace: op 5/2: stays a stiff 6f: acts on firm & gd/soft grnd: btr 2789 & 2165 (5f, fast).
3484   **GAME LAD** 9 [16] T D Easterby 2-9-0   D Allan 25/1: 34: Chsd ldrs stands side, rdn & kept on late: 1¼   82
styd longer 6f trip on turf bow: handles fibresand & gd/soft grnd: going the right way: see 3484.
2077   **PROFITS REALITY** 67 [2]2-9-0   Dean McKeown 10/1: 055: Chsd ldrs far side, onepace.   2   76
3451   **SUNSET STRIP** 11 [11]2-9-0 (78) T E Durcan 9/2: 2236: Led far side 2f, wknd 2f out: bckd, btr 3451.   2   70
2902   **UNION JACK JACKSON** 33 [15]2-9-0   J Bramhill 66/1: 407: Chsd ldrs stands side, no impress fnl 2f.   nk   67
         RIVER LIFFEY 0 [18]2-9-0   R Mullen 20/1: 8: b c Forzando - Rion River (Taufan) Dwelt, rdn & bhd   2   63
stands side, sn no impress: Apr foal, 15,000 gns purchase: half brother to juv wnrs at 6f/1m: dam 10f scorer.
2584   **FANTASY DEFENDER** 46 [10]2-9-0   G Faulkner 100/1: 00009: b g Fayruz - Mrs Lucky (Royal Match)   1¾   58
Held up far side, no impress from halfway: 6 wk abs: prev: cheaply bought Apr foal, half brother to multiple
Flat/hdles wnr Once More For Luck, dam a 6f 3yo scorer.
3517   **SUCCESSION** 7 [1]2-8-9   J Mackay 40/1: 00: 10th: Bhd far side, mod prog.   nk   52
         BALGARTH 0 [14]2-9-0   P Makin(5) 20/1: 0: 11th: Mid-div, far side, no impress fnl 2f.   shd   57
3376   **SHEKAN STAR** 13 [5]2-8-9   Dale Gibson 100/1: 00: 12th: Al rear far side.   1¼   48
3120   **AS HANDSOME DOES** 25 [6]2-9-0 t Kim Tinkler 66/1: 200: 13th: Pushed along & bhd far side, no dngr.   3   44
3376   **PLENTY CRIED WOLF** 13 [3]2-9-0   P Mulrennan(3) 66/1: 00: 14th: Mid-div far side, btn 2f out.   3   35
3178   **DETROIT DANCER** 22 [4]2-9-0   G Gibbons 100/1: 050: 15th: Chsd ldrs far side till over 2f out.   4   24
         AZAHARA 0 [8]2-8-9   L Enstone(3) 66/1: 0: 16th: Sn bhd far side.   10   0
         KASHTANKA 0 [7]2-9-0   R Winston 50/1: 0: 17th: Al rear far side.   ½   0
         PERRYWINKLE 0 [9]2-8-9   T Eaves 100/1: 0: 18th: Slow away & sn t.o. far side.   dist 0
18 Ran   Time 1m 15.28 (3.98)   Owned: Mr P D Savill   Trained: Middleham

---

3700   4.00 Yuill Homes Supports Nspcc Handicap Stakes 3yo+ 0-75   (E)   [71]
£4056 £1248 £624   7f str   Good/Soft 64   +02 Fast

3328   **PARISIAN PLAYBOY** 15 [9] Jedd O'Keeffe 4-8-2 (45) Leanne Kershaw(7) 9/2 JT FAV: 0000121: Rear, gd   54
hdwy over 1f out, led ins last, pushed out, more in hand: suited by 7f/1m, on gd & soft: improving, win again.
3426   **STORMVILLE** 11 [11] M Brittain 7-8-7 (50) M Lawson(3) 25/1: 500/0-002: Mid-div, rdn & styd on for   ½   57
press fnl 2f, not reach wnr: likes Newcastle & easy grnd: well h'capped: see 3426.
2655   **BOND PLAYBOY** 43 [18] B Smart 4-9-3 (60) D McGaffin 33/1: 6000003: Led & rdn clr over 1f out, hdd   1   65
ins last & no extra: gd run with enterprising tactics: abs: well h'capped, stays stiff 7f, spot on back at 6f.
3426   **TANCRED ARMS** 11 [8] D W Barker 8-7-12 (6oh)vis (35) Donna Caldwell(7) 100/1: 60-04004: Chsd ldrs,   1   44
kept on onepace: see 1448.
2986   **NOBLE PENNY** 30 [16]5-8-3 (46) A Elliott(7) 12/1: 0620465: Rdn & bhd, nrst fin: cheek pieces   ½   48
omitted, apprec a drop to 7f: acts on fast & gd/soft grnd: mdn: see 2080, 1661.
3117   **INCHDURA** 25 [7]6-9-10 (67) Kim Tinkler 9/1: 0000-006: Rdn & bhd halfway, nrst fin: well   hd   68
h'capped, looks to be coming to hand: handles gd/soft, prefers a faster surface: see 2684.
3102   **MALLARD** 25 [13]6-9-3 (60) K Darley 9/2 JT FAV: 1-302607: Held up, eff over 2f out, no impress dist.   2   57
3426   **MOUNT PEKAN** 11 [10]4-7-12 (41) J Mackay 33/1: 3060508: Rdn & bhd halfway, only mod prog.   1¼   35
3310   **CARLTON** 16 [17]10-9-1 (58) R Thomas(5) 9/1: 2220059: Trkd ldrs, btn dist: prefer sell/clmg grade.   ½   51
1661   **STELLITE** 86 [14]4-8-4 (47) T Hamilton(2) 13/2: 050-0100: 10th: Cl-up, btn over 1f out: abs: btr 1448. 1   38
2996   **TANCRED MISS** 29 [12]5-7-13 (42) J McAuley 25/1: 000-1030: 11th: Mid-div, no impress fnl 2f.   hd   32
1366   **THE WIZARD MUL** 102 [15]4-9-3 (60) J Bramhill 6/1: 0104-000: 12th: Cl-up early, btn 2f out: abs.   2   46
3426⁰ **MEHMAAS** 11 [4]8-8-13 vis (56) T Eaves(3) 12/1: 0040010: 13th: Prom 3f, sn struggling: btr 3426 (C/D).   nk   41
4052⁰ **PIPER** 335 [5]4-7-12 (5oh) (36) B Swarbrick(5) 66/1: 0/00000-0: 14th: ch g Atraf - Lady H (Never So   1½   23
Bold) Chsd ldrs, btn 2f out: reapp: unplcd '03 (rtd 45, h'cap, disapp in cheek pieces): unplcd '02 (rtd 43, mdn).
3229   **LIBRE** 19 [2]4-9-2 bl t (59) Dean McKeown 16/1: 0001000: 15th: Held up, rdn & btn out: btr 2655.   ¾   40
3529   Four Kings 7 [3]3-9-0 (63) P Mathers(5) 33/1:0   3378 Hevesham 13 [1]3-9-8 (71) L Enstone(3) 20/1:0
17 Ran   Time 1m 28.42 (4.32)   Owned: Playboy Partnership   Trained: Leyburn

---

3701   4.30 Tbi Wealth Management Supports Nspcc Handicap Stakes 3yo+ 0-75   (E)   [75]
£3790 £1166 £583   2m1f9y   Good/Soft 64   -29 Slow

2807⁰ **TONI ALCALA** 37 [4] R F Fisher 5-9-12 (73) P Mulrennan(3) 13/2: 3524511: Mid-div, rdn & hdwy over   77
2f out, led over 1f out, held on all out, gamely: eff at 12f, suited by 13f/2m1f on firm, gd/soft & fibresand, any
trk: most tough & genuine: see 2807.
3531   **RIYADH** 7 [5] M Johnston 6-9-5 (66) K Darley 7/2 FAV: 0300202: Held up, pushed along 4f out, rdn   hd   69
& hdwy to chall dist, drvn, just held: clr rem: in gd form but tricky ride now: see 3387, 1637.
2176   **FANTASTICO** 62 [9] Mrs K Walton 4-8-13 p (60) R Winston 10/1: 1430-403: Handy & led over 2f out   4   59
till over 1f out, no extra ins last: jumps flt, recent mares mdn hdle wnr (2m4f, rtd 96h, gd & gd/soft, 1st time
cheek pieces): stays a stiff 2m on the Level: gd run with cheek pieces applied: see 1923.
3249   **COLORADO FALLS** 19 [3] P Monteith 6-10-0 (75) L Enstone(3) 13/2: 06/-15404: Held up, late prog &   3   71
nrst fin, nvr a threat: longer trip: see 1506 (13f).
3359   **SHONGWENI** 13 [7]3-8-3 (65) R Mullen 15/2: 43305: Handy, rdn & short of room over 2f out, sn   ½   60
outpcd: longer trip: blnks omitted: btr 2788 & 2393 (mdns, 12f).
3158   **SIMPLE IDEALS** 23 [2]10-7-12 (10oh) (35) Kim Tinkler 10/1: 040-5406: Rear, only mod prog for press.   1½   39
3275   **ALLEZ MOUSSON** 18 [8]6-7-12 bl (45) J Bramhill 16/1: 030-0007: Held up, rdn & btn over 2f out.   ½   38
3275   **CALOMERIA** 18 [12]3-8-0 bl (62) J Mackay 10/1: 0004038: Handy & ev ch over 2f out, sn wknd: btr 3275.   ½   54

NEWCASTLE   WEDNESDAY 04.08.04   Lefthand, Galloping, Stiff Track

3240 **LEBENSTANZ 19** [11]4-9-4 (65) Dale Gibson 11/2: 66669: Keen & led till over 2f out, wknd qckly: 7 51
longer trip, needs to learn more restraint.
3309 **RIVER LINE 16** [10]3-7-12 (13oh) (47) B Swarbrick(5) 33/1: 000-4000: 10th; Chsd ldrs, btn 2f out. 7 40
10 Ran   Time 3m 40.33 (14.83)   Owned: Mr Alan Willoughby   Trained: Ulverston

---

3702   5.00 J & G Archibald Supports Nspcc Champagne Apprentice Classified Stakes 3yo+ 0-60 (G)
£2624 £750 £375   1m2f32y   Good/Soft 64   -14 Slow

3309 **PAY ATTENTION 16** [1] T D Easterby 3-8-5 (60) D Allan 4/1 JT FAV: 0-402021: Trkd ldrs & led dist, 66
rdn & styd on strongly: eff at 7f/1m, now stays a stiff 10f well, could get further: acts on firm, appears suited by
gd or hvy grnd: 1st career win, shld act as a confidence booster: see 1147.
1681 **MELODIAN 84** [8] M Brittain 9-9-5 bl (62) M Lawson(5) 5/1: 5451232: Handy & led halfway till over 2½ 66
1f out, not pace of wnr: 12 wk abs, gd run: see 1254.
3177* **FAIRLIE 22** [9] Mrs M Reveley 3-8-5 (59) T Eaves 12/1: 46-50013: Held up, rdn & styd on fnl 2f, 1 60
nrst fin: stays 10f: new yard: remains in gd heart after 3177 (7.5f, clmr).
3419* **ROCK LOBSTER 11** [7] J G Given 3-8-12 (64) P Makin(3) 4/1 JT FAV: 0563614: Trkd ldrs travelling ½ 66
well 3f out, sn short of room, onepace when in the clr dist: acts on fast, gd/soft & fibresand: see 3419.
3231 **PEARL OF YORK 19** [6]3-8-8 (63) L Enstone 9/2: 0025135: Trkd ldrs & rdn/led over 1f out, sn hdd & ½ 61
no impress on wnr: handles firm & gd/soft grnd: just btr 2969 (h'cap, 9f).
3309 **ORION EXPRESS 16** [4]3-8-8 (60) P Mulrennan(3) 12/1: 0046466: Held up, eff 2f out, no impress. 2½ 57
3119] **BEAMISH PRINCE 377** [5]5-9-3 (59) B Swarbrick(3) 16/1: 030033-7: ch g Bijou d'Inde - Unconditional ½ 56
Love (Polish Patriot). Keen & handy, rdn & btn 2f out: Flat reapp, 5 month jumps abs (unplcd, rtd 94h, nov): h'cap
plcd in '03 for M Johnston (rtd 59): '02 mdn wnr on debut: eff at 1m/9f on firm & gd grnd, stiff/undul trks: can
go well fresh: eff in blnks, wng form without. 1 May'02 Hami 9.1gd 71- D:
3413 **PURE VINTAGE 14** [2]3-8-8 (58) P Hamilton 6/1: 0608: Mid-div, rdn & btn 3f out, longer trip. 27 20
1590 **NORTH LANDING 90** [3]4-9-3 (40) A Reilly(7) 66/1: 20000-09: Led till halfway, sn struggling: jumps abs. 3 16
9 Ran   Time 2m 14.32(7.82)   Owned: Ryedale Partners No 6   Trained: Malton

---

YARMOUTH   WEDNESDAY 04.08.04   Lefthand, Flat, Fair Track

Official Going GOOD/FIRM (FIRM places).

3703   5.45 31st Running Of The Botton Brothers Handicap Stakes Ladies Race 3yo+ 0-75 (F)   [58]
£2905 £830 £415   1m6f17y   Good/Firm 34   -23 Slow   Inside

3387 **ASTYANAX 12** [1] Sir Mark Prescott 4-11-0 (72) Ms C Williams 4/1: 241-0501: Led early, regained 78
lead 6f out, styd on strongly, rdn out: top-weight: won this race from a 4lb lower mark last term: eff at 12/14f,
stays 2m well: acts on fast, gd/soft & fibresand, seems to handle any trk: see 3181.
3618 **SIEGFRIEDS NIGHT 4** [4] M C Chapman 3-9-5 (62) Miss S Brotherton 9/1: 3553002: Held up, prog to 1 65
chase wnr fnl 1f, nvr going to get there: clr of rem, qck reapp: eff around 10/12f, stays 14f: see 1785.
3531 **BOBSLEIGH 7** [2] Mrs A J Perrett 5-10-13 (71) Miss L J Harwood(3) 9/4 FAV: 40-60463: Chsd ldrs, 5 68
outpcd halfway, rallied late but no ch with front 2: back to usual C/D on a handy mark & btr expected: see 296.
3505 **EIGHT 8** [8] M R Channon 8-9-3 (47) Ms T Dzieciolowska(4) 40/1: 3200-004: Mid-div, hdwy to chase ¾ 43
wnr 4f out, btn dist: back up in trip: see 3398.
3147 **MAKARIM 24** [9]8-8-11 p (41) Mrs S Bosley 14/1: 0350405: Held up, late prog: see 2908 (2m). 2 34
3505 **THEATRE LADY 8** [5]6-9-5 (49) Miss E Folkes(3) 8/1: 6015106: Held up, nvr a factor: btr 3398. 1 40
3275 **EUIPPE 18** [3]3-9-12 (69) Miss E J Jones 7/2: 56-05147: Held up, nvr nr ldrs: btr 2905. 9 45
3531 **REDSPIN 7** [7]4-10-7 (65) Mrs S Moore(3) 16/1: 0444008: Chsd ldrs 12f, sn wknd. 6 32
2526 **MISCHIEF 48** [3]8-8-10 (4oh) (36) Miss Joey Ellis(5) 33/1: 60001-0P: ch g Generous - Knight's 0
Baroness (Rainbow Quest). Slowly away, recovered & led after 2f till 6f out, wknd qckly & p.u. 2f out: 7 wk abs &
something clrly amiss: '03 amat h'cap wnr: won that same race in '02: suited by 12/15f on firm & hvy, poss
fibresand: likes Carlisle: with K Bell. 1 Aug'03 Carl 14.1fm 37-33 E: 2 Aug'02 Carl 14.1fm 38-36 E:
2 Aug'01 Brig 10fm 32-30 F: 2 Jul'01 Folk 15.4g/f 37-35 E: 2 Dec'00 Ling 16ap 39a-43 E:
9 Ran   Time 3m 05.83 (8.03)   Owned: Lady Katharine Watts   Trained: Newmarket

---

3704   6.15 Constitution Motors Hyundai Claiming Stakes 3yo+ (F)
£2933 £838 £419   1m2f21y   Good/Firm 34   -41 Slow   Inside

3395 **ARMS ACROSSTHESEA 12** [2] J Balding 5-9-5 (57) J Edmunds 7/1: 2114001: Nvr far away, styd on 62
strongly to lead on line: slow time: eff at 9/12f on fd, gd/soft & f/sand: back to form, won 2054 (AW h'cap).
2231] **MORAHIB 413** [1] W J Musson 6-9-11 (88) G Carter 11/4 JT FAV: 5/514/15-2: ch c Nashwan - Irish shd 67
Valley (Irish River) Tried to make all, hdd on line: op 7/4, reapp: won first of 2 '03 starts (val h'cap) when
trained by M Tregoning, 5th in Royal Hunt Cup on sole other outing: '02 mdn wnr: eff at 7/10f on gd & fast grnd,
any trk: runs v well fresh: apprec drop to claim grade, capable of much btr for new connections.
1 May'03 Good 8g/f 88-83 C: 1 Jun'02 Beve 7.4gd 82- D:
3404 **PRIVATE SEAL 12** [5] Julian Poulton 9-9-1 t (43) M Halford(7) 14/1: 0003263: Held up, prog 2f out, ½ 56$
styd on well & only just btn in a close fin: see 3288 (AW).
3362 **BIG BAD BURT 13** [4] G C H Chung 3-8-10 (59) Dean Williams(7) 8/1: 0346004: Dwelt, sn recovered & 1 58
chsd ldrs, not qckn ins fnl 1f.
3144 **IVORY COAST 24** [6]3-8-7 (59) J Quinn 9/2: 4120005: Front rank, ev ch till onepcd ins fnl 1f. 1 53
3362* **SENOR EDUARDO 13** [3]7-9-5 (54) N Pollard 11/4 JT FAV: 5-003516: Chsd ldrs, onepcd fnl 1f. 1½ 53
3538 **KINGSTON TOWN 6** [7]4-9-6 bl (63) J P Guillambert(3) 10/1: 1-004067: Held up, nvr nr ldrs: qck reapp. 1¾ 51
7 Ran   Time 2m 11.72 (7.52)   Owned: Mr J Carter   Trained: Doncaster

3705 **6.45 Banham Poultry Handicap Stakes 3yo+ 0-80 (D)** **[77]**
£5720 £1760 £880 **6f3y str** **Good/Firm 34** **+03 Fast** Stands Side

3424 **MR MALARKEY 11** [8] Mrs C A Dunnett 4-10-0 bl T (77) Hayley Turner(5) 4/1: 4633061: Made all stands side, styd on well despite drifting left, rdn out: op 11/2, best time of day, top-weight & first time t-strap: deserved first win of this season: eff at 6f on firm & gd/soft grnd: likes to force the pace & best in blnks, apprec t-strap today: gd weight carrier: see 1354. **86**
3518* **MISTRAL SKY 7** [5] Mrs Stef Liddiard 5-9-7 (6ex)vis (70) F Norton 11/2: 3354012: Chsd ldrs centre, led that group dist, carr left fnl 1f but not pace to reach wnr: gd run under pen, see 3518. *1¼* **73**
3436* **TANCRED TIMES 11** [4] C F Wall 9-8-12 (61) J Quinn 7/1: 0331413: Led till dist centre, kept on well: fine first start for new connections, prev with D Barker: see 3436. *hd* **64**
3213 **ASBO 20** [9] Dr J D Scargill 4-8-11 (60) M Halford(7) 14/1: 00/00-54: Prom stands side, chsd wnr fnl 1f, sn no impress: op 11/1: see 3213. *1¼* **59**
3569 **CURRENCY 5** [2]7-9-13 p (76) C J Davies(7) 9/1: 4063005: Bhd centre, nrst fin: qck reapp: see 3033. *2* **69**
3424 **YOMALO 11** [1]4-9-1 (64) E Ahern 11/4 FAV: 0056256: Bhd centre, some hdwy 2f out, btn fnl 1f: bckd. *1¼* **53**
3403 **CORANGLAIS 12** [10]4-9-0 p (63) F P Ferris(3) 15/2: 0004107: Chsd wnr 4f stands side: btr 3143. *1¼* **48**
3184 **NIGHT WOLF 21** [3]4-8-13 (62) B O'Neill(7) 33/1: 0030008: Al rear stands side. *¾* **44**
3396 **STARGEM 12** [6]3-9-6 (73) R Price 11/1: 02-229: Keen & prom centre, wknd 2f out: btr 3396 (AW). *2* **49**
9 Ran Time 1m 12.30 (1.90) Owned: Mr T S Child Trained: Norwich

3706 **7.15 'enjoy A Night At The Ocean Rooms' Selling Handicap Stakes 3-4yo 35-55 (G)** **[55]**
£2653 £758 £379 **1m3y str** **Good/Firm 34** **-30 Slow** Stands Side

2149 **TAIYO 63** [6] J W Payne 4-9-1 (42) E Ahern 14/1: 4400P01: Chsd ldrs centre, left in lead over 2f out, rdn out fnl 1f: bght in for 7,600gns, 9 wk abs: eff at 6f/1m, prob stays a sharp 9.4f: acts on fast & fibresand, fair trk: made most of this drop into sell grade: see 561. **49**
3414* **ZONNEBEKE 12** [4] K R Burke 3-9-0 vis (48) T G McLaughlin 3/1 FAV: 3003412: Rear centre, hdwy to chase wnr over 1f out, not her pace ins fnl 1f: clmd for 6,000: remains in gd form: see 3414. *2* **50**
3300 **ANISETTE 16** [2] Julian Poulton 3-8-7 (41) M Halford(7) 6/1: 0640063: Handy centre, styd on fnl 1f: stays 1m, acts on fast & fibresand: see 126 (debut). *½* **42**
2981 **DANIFAH 30** [1] P D Evans 3-8-8 (42) F P Ferris(3) 9/1: 0004004: Chsd ldrs centre, onepcd fnl 1f. *2* **39**
3524 **ESPERANCE 7** [12]4-9-3 (44) G Carter 4/1: 0-005505: Slow away stands side, modest late gains. *½* **40**
3420 **LILIAN 11** [13]4-8-11 BL (38) Rachel Costello(7) 25/1: 6560006: Chsd ldrs stands side, no impress over 1f out: first time blnks: see 3025. *nk* **33**
3182 **LENWADE 22** [5]3-8-1 (4oh) (35) A McCarthy 20/1: 0-003007: Rear centre, nvr nr to chall. *1½* **27**
3087 **LEITRIM ROCK 26** [10]4-9-1 (42) F Norton 4/1: 00-00468: Slow away centre, nvr a factor: op 13/2. *2½* **29**
2854 **ROVING VIXEN 35** [11]3-8-6 bl (40) Hayley Turner(5) 12/1: 4033409: Led centre, hung right over 3f out, hdd over 2f out, wknd: see 2667. *15* **0**
3344 **KILMINCHY LADY 14** [9]3-8-6 (40) N Pollard 50/1: 006-500: 10th: Mid-div centre, btn halfway. *2½* **0**
3449 **NEWTOWN CHIEF 11** [7]3-8-9 BL (43) J P Guillambert(3) 66/1: 600-0000: 11th: Chsd ldrs centre, wknd over 2f out: first time blnks: see 3383. *1* **0**
11 Ran Time 1m 40.28 (5.18) Owned: Mrs J Morley Trained: Newmarket

3707 **7.45 Custom Kitchens Novice Stakes 2yo (D)**
£3335 £1026 £513 **7f3y str** **Good/Firm 34** **-53 Slow** Stands Side

3532 **WILKO 7** [2] J Noseda 2-9-5 (100) E Ahern 1/6 FAV: 3013321: Led early, regained lead dist, pushed out: qck reapp, top-weight: stays 7f, shld get 1m: acts on firm, fast & poss hvy: likes Yarmouth: confidence boosting win, can rate higher once rtnd to stronger company: see 3532. **103+**
3280 **SHRINE MOUNTAIN 18** [3] C E Brittain 2-8-12 J P Guillambert(3) 33/1: 02: b c Distorted Humor - Fancy Ruler (Half a Year) Led after 1f, hdd over 1f out, kept on: Mar foal: half-brother to 7f 2yo wnr Sohaib: sire a smart 7/8f rnr on dirt in the US: stays 7f on fast: imprvd here from debut. *½* **92**
LINNGARI [1] Sir Michael Stoute 2-8-8 G Carter 13/2: 3: ch c Indian Ridge - Lidakiya (Kahyasi) Chsd ldrs, onepaced fnl 1f on debut: Apr 1st foal: dam won thrice over 10/12f at 3, sire a high-class sprinter: prob stays 7f on fast: gd start, entitled to improve next time & will be plcd to win a race. *2½* **83**
3412 **ZABEEL PALACE 12** [4] D R Loder 2-8-12 N Pollard 20/1: 054: Keen in rear, nvr a factor: see 3126. *1¾* **83**
4 Ran Time 1m 28.70 (6.10) Owned: Mrs Susan Roy Trained: Newmarket

3708 **8.15 Bet365 08000 322365 Handicap Stakes 3yo+ 0-75 (E)** **[75]**
£3751 £1154 £577 **7f3y str** **Good/Firm 34** **-03 Slow** Stands Side

3643 **THREEZEDZZ 2** [1] P D Evans 6-9-0 t (61) F P Ferris(3) 9/2: 0/-000101: Made all, pushed clr ins fnl 1f, eased cl-home, val 7L+: acts on 7/2 on quick reapp: eff at 5/6f, now suited by 7f: acts on firm & gd grnd: improve for recent fitting of t-strap: likes to force the pace & enjoyed uncontested lead tonight: see 3401. **71+**
1142 **HAND CHIME 114** [4] W J Haggas 7-9-11 (72) Danielle Deverson(7) 8/1: 3-005002: Rear, prog 3f out, ev ch bef 1f out, not pace easy wnr: long abs: btr 262 (polytrack). *5* **70**
2955] **HAMMER OF THE GODS 746** [3] Julian Poulton 4-8-1 t (48) M Halford(7) 50/1: 0500/-3: ch g Tagula - Bhama (Habitat) Cl-up, wknd dist: reapp: missed '03: unplcd in 4 '02 starts (W Turner, rtd 60): tried a t-strap. *2½* **41**
3443 **LYGETON LAD 11** [2] Miss Gay Kelleway 6-9-7 t (68) M Fenton 5/2: 5100004: Handy over 5f, sn wknd: op 3/1: saves best form for the all weather: btr 1043 (polytrack). *½* **60**
3364 **BOBS BUZZ 13** [5]4-9-7 (68) T G McLaughlin 5/4 FAV: 110-0535: Keen rear, nvr a factor: well bckd. *2* **56**
3185 **INVADER 21** [6]8-10-0 t (75) J P Guillambert(3) 10/1: 6000106: Al rear: twice below 2840 (1m, aw). *8* **47**
6 Ran Time 1m 25.20(2.60) Owned: Mr Steve Evans Trained: Abergavenny

Official Going Good/Firm (Firm Places)

3709 2.30 European Breeders Fund Maiden Stakes 2yo (D)
£4749 £1461 £731   **6f str**   **Good/Firm 36**   -23 Slow   Stands Side

GHURRA 0 [2] E A L Dunlop 2-8-9   R Hills 12/1: 1: b f War Chant - Futuh (Diesis) Handy & led 2f   84
out, narrowly hdd over 1f out, shaken up & rallied well to lead on line: Mar foal, half sister to a top class 6f juv
Hayil: dam a 6f juv wnr: eff at 6f, shld stay 7f: acts on fast grnd & goes well fresh: shows plenty of speed.

MUNADDAM 0 [3] Saeed bin Suroor 2-9-0   L Dettori 4/9 FAV: 2: ch c Aljabr - Etizaaz (Diesis)   hd   88
Dwelt, sn handy & led over 1f out, rdn & hdd line: hvly bckd at odds-on: Apr foal, dam 7f/1m wnr: eff at 6f, 7f
sure to suit: acts on fast: promising start, shld find a race sn.

2870 **WISE DENNIS** 35 [5] A P Jarvis 2-9-0   E Stack 50/1: 003: Chsd ldrs, outpcd over 1f out, rdn &   hd   87
styd on well cl-home, just failed: significant improvement on prev effs: Apr foal, dam a multiple 5/6f wnr: eff at
6f, shaped as if 7f will suit: acts on fast grnd & an easy trk: interesting for nurs.

WINDERMERE ISLAND 0 [6] M L W Bell 2-8-9   R Mullen 20/1: 4: b f Cadeaux Genereux - Corndavon   2   76
(Sheikh Albadou) Held up, outpcd halfway, mod late prog, nvr threat: op 16/1: Feb foal, half sister to smart 6f
juv wnr Nevisian Lad: dam 6f scorer.

SANTA FE 0 [7]2-9-0   K Fallon 5/1: 5: Dwelt, sn trkd ldrs, rdn & outpcd over 1f out.   nk   80
LOVE THIRTY 0 [1]2-8-9   C Catlin 40/1: 6: Outpcd early, nvr pace to threaten.   hd   74
ROYAL WEDDING 0 [4]2-9-0   T P Queally 9/1: 7: Led 4f, no extra when hmpd ins last, only btn around 5L.1¾   74
7 Ran   Time 1m 13.91 (3.51)   Owned Mr Hamdan Al Maktoum   Trained Newmarket

3710 3.00 Bennetts Electrical Toshiba Claiming Stakes 3yo+ (F)
£2877 £822 £411   **6f str**   **Good/Firm 36**   +02 Fast   Stands Side

2477 **FORT MCHENRY** 50 [5] N A Callaghan 4-9-5 p (70) L Dettori 15/8: 1100-001: Made all, rdn & held on   62
well ins last: well bckd: 7 wk sble: eff btwn 5/7f on fast & gd/soft: enjoys forcing tactics & apprec reapp of
cheek pieces: goes well fresh & enjoyed this drop to clmg grade: see 2477.

3602 **LAKE VERDI** 5 [6] B Hanbury 5-8-9 t (52) R Hills 8/1: 6-043002: Sn cl-up, rdn & styd on, al just   nk   51
held: quick reapp: claimed by J T Billson for 6,000: see 3050, 2016 & 1806.

3558 **WARES HOME** 7 [4] K R Burke 3-8-7 (50) S Bushby(6) 16/1: 4332303: Trkd ldrs, hung left under press   1¼   49
& no extra fnl 100yds: clr rem: gd run: see 1975.

2023 **BLUE KNIGHT** 71 [3] A P Jarvis 5-9-4 (73) K Fallon 6/5 FAV: 2406204: Rdn rear early, no impress   5   43
on front trio over 1f out: well bckd: claimed by P Howling for 15,000: twice below 1914.

3705 **NIGHT WOLF** 1 [1]4-9-1 (62) C Catlin 14/1: 00300005: Rear, hdwy halfway, no prog: unplcd yesterday.   1   37
2925 **PARDON MOI** 33 [2]3-8-6 (47) Hayley Turner(5) 20/1: 4104006: Dwelt, sn rear, nvr land a blow: btr 1985.   5   19
6 Ran   Time 1m 12.46 (2.06)   Owned Mr M Tabor   Trained Newmarket

3711 3.30 Nspcc Handicap Stakes Fillies 3yo 0-75 (E)   [79]
£3868 £1190 £595   **7f str**   **Good/Firm 36**   -02 Slow   Stands Side

3339 **GLEBE GARDEN** 15 [10] M L W Bell 3-9-5 (70) L Dettori 4/1: 0-556001: Made most stands side, rdn &   76
styd on well: op 10/3: eff at 6/7f, prob stays 1m: handles soft, likes fast & gd: enjoyed switch to forcing tactics.

3380 **MUGEBA** 14 [5] Miss Gay Kelleway 3-8-9 t (60) I Mongan 3/1 FAV: 02-55122: In tch centre, rdn to   1   63
chall from over 1f out, not pace of wnr nr fin: well bckd: in gd form: see 330 & 2852 (C/D sell).

3479 **ZWADI** 10 [4] H Candy 3-9-6 (71) C Catlin 8/1: 24-40503: Al handy towards centre, rdn & led that   hd   73
group over 1f out, onepace ins last: eff at 6/7f, stays 1m: acts fast & prob fibresand: see 2072.

3291 **FLAME QUEEN** 17 [1] Miss K B Boutflower 3-9-1 (66) G Hind 14/1: 002-0004: Led centre group 5f, no   1¾   65
extra dist: prob stays an easy 7f: acts on firm & fast grnd: see 2590.

3024 **BEAUTIFUL NOISE** 29 [11]3-8-1 (52) J Mackay 5/1: 06-06555: Chsd ldrs stands side, no impress dist.   1¼   48
1841 **FABULOSO** 78 [9]3-7-12 (8oh) (41) D Fox(5) 33/1: 00000-56: b f Dr Fong - Shafir (Shaadi) Rear   ¾   44
stands side, mod late prog, no threat: abs: unplcd '03 (rtd 53 & 59a, S Keightley).

2925 **ANNIE MILLER** 33 [6]3-9-0 (65) K Fallon 5/1: 5305-07: Chsd wnr stands side, hung left & no impress.   ¾   59
3291 **HOLD UP** 17 [8]3-8-6 (57) B Reilly(3) 14/1: 0-00008: Chsd ldrs stands side, no impress fnl 2f: see 3007.   ½   50
3128 **FRAGRANT STAR** 26 [7]3-9-7 (72) R Hills 12/1: 05-00009: Stands side & struggling fnl 2f: btr 2592.   5   56
3492 **CARLA MOON** 10 [3]3-8-9 (60) R Mullen 5/1: 600-00000: 10th: b f Desert Prince - Khambani (Royal   2½   39
Academy) Held up centre, no impress fnl 2f: dropped in trip: unplcd '03 (rtd 72, debut): breathing probs prev.

2619 **SHEBAAN** 45 [2]3-7-12 (4oh) (45) Hayley Turner(5) 50/1: 050-0000: 11th: Prom in centre, wknd 2f out.   9   12
11 Ran   Time 1m 25.25 (2.65)   Owned Mr Christopher Wright & Mr WHCarson   Trained Newmarket

3712 4.00 Great Yarmouth Glass Selling Handicap Stakes 3yo 35-55 (G)   [65]
£2590 £740 £370   **1m str**   **Good/Firm 36**   -22 Slow   Stands Side

3344 **CITY GENERAL** 15 [11] J S Moore 3-8-12 p (49) S Chin 4/1: 3502051: Trkd ldrs, rdn & led dist, rdn   57
out: bckd: bt for 3,600 gns: eff at 7f/1m on fm, gd/soft & fibresand in cheek pieces: likes Yarmouth.

3344* **KINGS ROCK** 15 [8] K A Ryan 3-9-4 bl (55) K Fallon 5/4 FAV: 0063012: Al prom, rdn to chall over 1f   1½   59
out, not pace of wnr ins last: hvly bckd: ahead of today's wnr in 3344.

3515 **PERERIN** 8 [1] I A Wood 3-9-3 bl (46) T P Queally 17/2: 0-010003: Dwelt, sn trkd ldrs, rdn & led   shd   48
over 1f out, sn hdd & edged right, kept on: clr rem: quick reapp: stays an easy 1m with/without blnks.

3706 **LENWADE** 1 [4] G G Margarson 3-7-12 (35) D Fox(5) 16/1: 0-0030004: Dwelt & bhd, mod prog for more.   4   31
2667 **DIVERTED** 43 [12]3-7-13 (36) Nicol Polli(7) 40/1: 000005: b f Averti - Whittle Rock (Rock City)   hd   31
Chsd ldrs, hung left & no impress over 1f out: 6 wk abs: unplcd & mod form prev.

3363 **TARDIS** 14 [5]3-8-12 (49) R Mullen 9/1: 24-00006: Handy & led over 5f out, hung right & hdd over 1f out.   1½   41
3091 **BROTHER CADFAEL** 27 [6]3-7-13 (36) Hayley Turner(5) 25/1: 2666007: Chsd ldrs 5f: btr 1081.   3½   21
2852 **DAVIDS GIRL** 3 [13]3-8-1 (38) J Mackay 9/1: 5-566508: Pushed along rear, no impress thr'out.   6   11
1051 **STONOR LADY** 122 [9]3-8-9 (46) C Catlin 12/1: 6-000109: Held up, rdn & btn 2f out: abs: btr 865.   1¼   16
3087 **VARIETY CLUB** 27 [2]3-9-1 BL (52) R Hills 20/1: 000-000: 10th: Led till over 5f out, sn struggling, blnks.   14   0
10 Ran   Time 1m 39.71 (4.61)   Owned Mr A D Crook   Trained Hungerford

3713   4.30 Eventguard Maiden Auction Stakes 2yo   (E)
£3406 £1048 £524   1m str   Good/Firm 36   -08 Slow   Stands Side

3234 **BARADORE 20** [4] M G Quinlan 2-8-7   T P Queally 5/2: 21: Made all in centre, edged right & styd   88
on well for press ins last: well bckd: improved for step up to 1m, further shld suit: acts on fast: looks useful,
win more races: see 3234.
3252 **SILVER HIGHLIGHT 20** [2] A M Balding 2-8-7   R Mullen 10/1: 02: gr f Silver Charm - Rare   1½   84
Opportunity (Danzig Connection) Held up in centre, rdn & styd on well fnl 2f, not able to reach wnr: left debut
bhd: $50,000 Feb foal, half sister to a US juv wnr: apprec step up to 1m, mid-dists will suit on this evidence:
acts on fast grnd & an easy trk: win sn.
3003 **ARABIAN DANCER 30** [9] M R Channon 2-8-2   (88) C Catlin 10/11 FAV: 2653: Trkd ldrs stands side,   1¼   76
led that group over 2f out, onepace dist: clr rem: well bckd: styd longer 1m trip but btr 3003 & 2119 (6f).
3539 **ZOLASH 7** [1] J S Moore 2-8-8   S Chin 25/1: 50604: Chsd ldrs centre, no impress over 2f out: 12   61
longer trip, apprec h'cap company: see 1987.
3160 **CHAMPAGNE ROSSINI 24** [3]2-8-7   G Hind 66/1: 05: b g Rossini - Alpencrocus (Waajib) Dwelt,   ¾   57
centre, in tch 5f: 5,000 gns 2yo, Apr foal, half brother to a prolofic sprint wnr abroad: dam unplcd on sole start.
3431 **MILL BY THE STREAM 12** [6]2-8-9   E Stack 80/1: 0006: b c Lujain - Lonesome (Night Shift) Led   2½   56
stands side group 5f, sn btn: longer trip: 14,000 gns Mar foal, half brother to a 7f wnr.
       HALLOWED DREAM 0 [7]2-8-4   R Hills 12/1: 7: Slow away, stands side & nvr a factor.   3   45
3120 **SPENCE APPEAL 26** [5]2-8-11   K Fallon 14/1: 08: Chsd ldrs stands side till 2f out.   1¾   49
       CARIBBEAN DIAMOND 0 [10]2-8-2   P Doe 66/1: 9: Rear stands side, rdn & btn 2f out.   3½   33
2939 **AMANDERICA 33** [8]2-8-2   T D Fox(5) 100/1: 0000: 10th: Stands side, sn struggling: t-strap.   7   21
10 Ran   Time 1m 38.62 (3.52)   Owned: Mr L Cashman   Trained: Newmarket

3714   5.00 Bbc Radio Norfolk Maiden Handicap Stakes 3yo+ 35-55 (F)   [54]
£3038 £868 £434   1m3f101y   Good/Firm 36   -13 Slow   Inside

3383 **SCIENCE ACADEMY 14** [4] P F I Cole 3-10-0   (54) K Fallon 3/1: 00-05621: Handy & led over 1f out,   63
edged left & rdn clr ins last: eff at 11.5f/12f on fast & gd grnd, sharp/undul or easy trks: see 3383, 1648.
3362 **TATA NAKA 14** [8] Mrs C A Dunnett 4-9-13   (43) Hayley Turner(5) 12/1: 0050022: Held up, styd on for   3½   46
press fnl 2f, no impress on easy wnr: stays 11.5f: acts on fast & gd grnd: confirmed improvement of 3362.
3383 **SCOTT 14** [6] J Jay 3-9-10   (50) C Haddon(7) 50/1: 00603: gr g Polar Falcon - Circled (Cozzene)   nk   52
Held up & keen, styd on for press fnl 2f, no threat to wnr: eff over an easy 11.5f on fast grnd, mod form prev.
2978 **ROYAL STARLET 31** [14] Mrs A J Perrett 3-9-9   (49) I Mongan 20/1: 000-004: Led/dsptd lead till   1   50
over went over 2f out, hdd over 1f out & no extra: eff at 11.5f on fast grnd: see 2978.
3312 **HABITUAL 17** [7]3-9-10   (50) J Mackay 5/2 FAV: 00-0045: Chsd ldrs, dhvr over 1f out: nicely bckd.   3½   46
3367 **VANILLA MOON 14** [1]4-10-0 vis (44) S Chin 8/1: 5243646: Led 1f & al cl-up, btn dist: btr 3367.   nk   39
3383 **A MONK SWIMMING 14** [9]3-8-9   (35) G Carter 9/2: 060-437: Held up, eff 3f out, btn dist: btr 3383.   2½   26
2475 **KALAMANSI 50** [12]3-9-10   (50) D Fox(5) 40/1: 60008: Held up, no impress fnl 2f, 7 wk abs.   ¾   40
3449 **MACCHIATO GB 12** [2]3-9-9   (49) R Hills 50/1: 02-05009: Led after 2f till over 2f out, sn btn: btr 2842.   ¾   38
3128} **INSPECTOR BLUE 377** [3]6-9-5   (35) P Doe 66/1: 000-000-0: 10th: ch g Royal Academy - Blue Siren   1½   22
(Bluebird) In tch, btn 2f out: reapp: likely rcd & unplcd '03 (rtd 66, Miss J Feilden, mdn): unplcd in '02.
4963} **ITS A MYSTERY 279** [13]5-9-9 T (39) G Hind 50/1: 0000-0: 11th: b f Idris - Blue Infanta (Chief   3½   21
Singer) Kept in tch, btn 3f out: t-strap on reapp: unplcd '03 (rtd 44, no sand form, R Phillips).
3300 **ALLODARLIN 17** [5]3-9-10   (50) R Mullen 40/1: 50060-00: 12th: Chsd ldrs, btn 2f out.   ½   31
1922 **MAD MAURICE 75** [10]3-9-5 p (45) T P Queally 12/1: 0-0000: 13th: Held up, no ch fnl 3f: op 13/2, abs.   6   17
3618 **VRISAKI 5** [11]3-9-6   (46) O Urbina 14/1: 0363000: 14th: Slow away & held up, btn 2f out: quick reapp.   nk   17
14 Ran   Time 2m 28.39(5.59)   Owned: Sir Martyn Arbib   Trained: Whatcombe

BRIGHTON   THURSDAY 05.08.04   Lefthand, V Sharp, Undulating Track

Official Going FIRM

3715   5.55 Pleasure Palace Racing Lady Riders Series Claiming Stakes 3yo+   (F)
£3341 £1028 £514   1m3f196y   Good/Firm 37   -13 Slow   Outside

3398 **FINAL DIVIDEND 13** [5] J M P Eustace 8-9-13   (44) Miss Joanna Rees(3) 7/2: 43-05651: Trkd ldr till   55
led well over 1f out, pushed out fnl 1f, val 1L: suited by 12f, prob stays 2m: acts on firm, soft & polytrack:
likes Brighton & Lingfield: made most of this drop into clmg grade: see 107.
3692 **BANNINGHAM BLAZE 1** [1] A W Carroll 4-9-10   (50) Mrs S Bosley 100/30: 23653132: Bhd, hdwy over 2f   nk   50
out, pushed along & styd on well ins fnl 1f, nrst fin: op 9/4, 3rd here yesterday: wants 14f.
3486 **SALUT SAINT CLOUD 10** [6] G L Moore 3-9-6   (53) Miss Hayley Moore(5) 13/8 FAV: 6051333: Bhd,   2½   53
switched right & hdwy over 2f out, kept on but not pace of first 2: op 5/2: see 3486 & 2836.
3049 **JOELY GREEN 28** [3] N P Littmoden 7-9-11   (39) Mrs Emma Littmoden(3) 12/1: 0200004: In tch, onepce.   ½   46$
3051 **FIDDLES MUSIC 28** [4]3-9-1   (43) Ms D Goad(5) 25/1: 0-014565: Led till well over 1f out, no extra.   4   41
3398 **DUKES VIEW 13** [7]3-9-4   (58) Miss L J Harwood(3) 11/2: 6-005506: Chsd ldrs, no impress over 1f out.   ¾   43
2972 **LITTLE FOX 31** [2]9-10-1 (5ow) (45) Miss Donna Handley 25/1: 04500/-67: Al bhd: see 2972.   12   25
7 Ran   Time 2m 34.31 (6.11)   Owned: Mr Charles Curtis   Trained: Newmarket

3716   6.25 Chapel Down English Wine Median Auction Maiden Stakes Fillies 2yo   (E)
£3383 £1041 £520   6f209y rnd   Good/Firm 37   -10 Slow   Inside

       FAVOURITA 0 [3] C E Brittain 2-8-9   J P Guillambert(3) 16/1: 1: b f Diktat - Forthwith (Midyan)   76+
Slow away, rear, hdwy over 2f out, rdn ins fnl 1f, styd on to lead nr fin on debut: Mar foal: half sister to wnrs
over 7f/staying trips: dam 6f/10f scorer: eff at 7f, will stay further: acts on fast grnd: runs well fresh.
3483 **CHUTNEY MARY 10** [7] J G Portman 2-8-9   (72) A Beech(3) 9/2: 062252: Rcd in 2nd, hdwy to lead well   ½   73

ins fnl 1f, hdd cl-home: acts on fast, gd & fibresand: v consistent, shown enough to find similar: see 2652.
3381 **FANTAISISTE 14** [5] Sir Mark Prescott 2-8-9 S Carson 11/4 FAV: 03: b f Nashwan - Fantastic Belle (Night Shift) Led, hdd well ins fnl 1f, no extra: well bckd: Jan 1st foal: dam 6f wnr: eff at 7f, 1m+ shld suit. ¾ **71**
3163 **GRANDMAS GIRL 24** [1] R Guest 2-8-9 R Brisland 20/1: 04: b f Desert Style - Sakura Queen (Woodman) Keen & cl-up, onepcd fnl 1f: Mar foal: half sister to a 7f 2yo wnr: dam plcd over 8/10f at 3. ½ **70**
3381 **BONGOALI 14** [10]2-8-9 S Hitchcott(3) 100/30: 45: Rear on inner, hdwy over 2f out, kept on. 1¼ **67**
3407 **MADAM CAVERSFIELD 13** [8]2-8-9 (71) P Gallagher(7) 100/30: 503446: Bhd, hdwy over 3f out, onepcd. *shd* **66**
3381 **GEORGINA 14** [9]2-8-9 M Henry 16/1: 007: Trkd ldrs, no impress over 1f out. 3½ **59**
2257 **BLUE LINE 60** [6]2-8-9 G Baker 16/1: 058: Keen in tch, no impress over 1f out: 9 wk abs. 9 **41**
8 Ran Time 1m 23.14 (3.34) Owned: Wyck Hall Stud Trained: Newmarket

3717

6.55 Karma Brighton Marina Selling Handicap Stakes 3yo+ 35-55 (G) **[57]**
£2923 £835 £418 **5f213y rnd** **Good/Firm 37** **+03 Fast** Inside

3298 **RILEYS DREAM 17** [8] B J Llewellyn 5-9-0 p (43) D Corby(3) 11/2: 0010051: Rear, hdwy over 2f out, hard drvn to lead just ins fnl 1f: no bid: eff btwn 5/7f on fast & gd/soft, any trk, esp Brighton: runs well in cheek pieces: genuine, see 1284. **50**
3298 **CARGO 17** [4] B A Pearce 5-9-3 t p (46) S Sanders 5/2 FAV: 2320022: Rcd in 2nd till led 2f out, hdd just ins fnl 1f, no extra: clr of rem: see 544. 1¼ **49**
2801 **BANDBOX 38** [5] M Salaman 9-8-3 P (32) M Henry 8/1: 600-0503: Trkd ldrs, short of room 2f out, kept on ins fnl 1f: 1st time cheek pieces: shade closer to first 2 with a clr run: see 2501. 3 **26**
3298 **RATHMULLAN 17** [1] E A Wheeler 5-8-7 bl (36) S Carson 20/1: 1350004: Bhd, hdwy over 1f out, sn onepcd: reportedly lost a shoe: see 1710. *nk* **29**
3604 **MUST BE SO 5** [7]3-7-13 (3oh)t (32) Lucy Russell(7) 25/1: 0604005: Trkd ldrs, no impress fnl 1f. 1¼ **21**
3332 **LUCKY VALENTINE 15** [3]4-9-8 bl (51) S Hitchcott(3) 3/1: 00-24336: Mid-div, no impress fnl 1f: btr 3332. *nk* **39**
3672 **STAGECOACH RUBY 2** [2]3-8-6 (39) J Quinn 3/1: 0543307: Led to 2f out, no extra: quick reapp. 8 **3**
7 Ran Time 1m 9.86 (2.06) Owned: Mr Greg Robinson and Mr A N Jay Trained: Bargoed

3718

7.25 Venture Lifestyle Photography Handicap Stakes 3yo 0-70 (E) **[72]**
£3994 £1229 £614 **7f214y rnd** **Good/Firm 37** **+04 Fast** Inside

3656* **GENERAL FEELING 8** [6] S Kirk 3-9-13 (6ex) (71) J F Egan 6/4 FAV: 3-330411: Mid-div, hdwy over 3f out, hung left & led 1f out, drvn out fnl 1f: landed double: bckd, tchd 5/2, top weight: eff at 5/7f, now stays 1m well: acts on firm & soft: in fine form at present, gd weight carrying eff here: see 1575. **79**
3448* **MISS MADAME 12** [4] R Guest 3-9-7 (65) S Sanders 11/4: 60-33612: Rcd in 2nd, ev ch 1f out, onepcd nr fin: stays 1m: remains in gd form: see 3448. 1¼ **69**
3541 **INSTINCT 7** [5] R Hannon 3-9-1 (59) P Gallagher(7) 11/2: 0300033: Bhd, hdwy over 2f out, hung left over 1f out, kept on ins fnl 1f: op 10/1, quick reapp: eff at 6f/1m: see 3541. 1½ **60**
3291 **FILLIEMOU 17** [7] A W Carroll 3-8-12 (56) G Baker 5/1: 0-000524: Sn led, hdd 1f out, no extra. 1 **55**
3175 **EVEN EASIER 23** [1]3-8-8 bl (52) R Brisland 12/1: 0644505: Mid-div, no impress fnl 1f: see 2292. 1¾ **47**
3283 **FAITH HEALER 19** [2]3-8-11 bl (55) J Quinn 15/2: 0046106: Trkd ldrs, lost place 2f out, eased/btn fnl 1f. 12 **26**
6 Ran Time 1m 34.64 (2.64) Owned: The So Long Partnership Trained: Upper Lambourn

3719

7.55 Gleeson Classic Homes Apartments Palmeira Grande Handicap Stakes Fillies 3yo+ 0-70 (E) **[79]**
£4056 £1248 £624 **1m1f209y** **Good/Firm 37** **-05 Slow** Outside

3334 **OPTIMAL 15** [1] Sir Mark Prescott 3-8-10 BL (61) S Sanders 7/2: 400-061: Rcd in 2nd, hdwy & narrow lead over 2f out, drvn out ins fnl 1f: stays 10f on fast, sharp/undul trks: first win, sharpened up by blnks. **69**
3492 **SUNSET MIRAGE 10** [5] E A L Dunlop 3-9-3 vis (68) J F Egan 5/2: 6106042: Mid-div, kept on ins fnl 1f to take 2nd: tchd 9/2: remains in gd form: see 1953. ¾ **73**
3492 **NASSIRIA 10** [3] C E Brittain 3-9-0 P (65) J P Guillambert(3) 20/1: 660003: Led till over 2f out, still ev ch ent fnl 1f, no extra & lost 2nd ins fnl 1f: clr of rem: stays 10f on fast in cheek pieces: see 1495. ¾ **68**
3373 **SIENNA SUNSET 14** [6] W M Brisbourne 5-8-13 (55) G Baker 2/1 FAV: 00-06624: Keen in tch, hdwy over 3f out, no impress over 1f out: reportedly unsuited by this trk & grnd: see 3373. 7 **47**
3094 **MAGIC VERSE 27** [2]3-8-1 (52) J Quinn 10/1: 004445: Trkd ldrs, no impress over 1f out: see 2805. 1¾ **41**
39 **MAID FOR LIFE 264** [8]4-9-0 (56) D Corby(3) 13/2: 0464-6: b f Entrepreneur - Arandora Star (Sagace) Slow away in rear, hdwy 4f out, switched to inner over 2f out, sn wknd: reapp: 4th 2 of 4 '03 starts (mdns, rtd 58): eff at 1m on fast: with M Wallace. 5 **37**
1066 **JAHIA 121** [4]5-10-0 (70) R Lucey Butler(7) 33/1: 110/6-07: br f Jahafil - Lana (Tristrams Heritage) Al bhd: recent mod hlde rnr (with R Guest, tried a t-strap): 6th of 6 sole Flat '03 start in native NZ. 7 **40**
3605* **PIQUET 5** [7]6-8-7 (7ex) (49) Darren Williams 8/1: 0063018: Trkd ldrs, outpcd 4f out, wknd & eased, t.o.: quick reapp: reportedly not travel downhill on this grnd: btr 3605 (AW). 28 **0**
8 Ran Time 2m 2.02 (4.22) Owned: Lady O'Reilly Trained: Newmarket

3720

8.25 Curious Grape English Wine Classified Stakes 3yo+ 0-70 (E)
£3994 £1229 £614 **5f59y rnd** **Good/Firm 37** **+07 Fast** Inside

3503 **TRICK CYCLIST 9** [3] A M Balding 3-9-2 (72) S Sanders 2/1: 2406021: Made all, rdn out fnl 1f: nicely bckd: eff at 5/6f on fast, gd/soft & polytrack, acts on a gall or sharp/undul trk: gd run, see 3503. **77**
3567 **IMPERIUM 6** [1] Mrs Stef Liddiard 3-9-1 (71) J F Egan 9/2: 3000602: Rcd in 2nd, no impress on wnr ins fnl 1f: quick reapp: gd run, back to form at fav trk: see 1942 (C/D). 1½ **69**
3584 **BEAUVRAI 6** [5] V Smith 4-9-5 p (72) M Tebbutt 7/4 FAV: 0530023: Bmpd start, keen in tch, no impress fnl 1f, broke a blood vessel: quick reapp, top weight: see 3584. 5 **55**
3591 **SCOTTISH EXILE 5** [7] K R Burke 3-8-12 vis (71) Darren Williams 7/2: 0021034: Trkd ldrs, no impress over 1f out: quick reapp: btr 2784. *nk* **50**
3143 **RUN ON 25** [6]6-9-3 (46) S Righton 25/1: 6-000055: Al bhd: see 1788. 1¼ **48**
5 Ran Time 1m 1.67(1.67) Owned: Park House Partnership Trained: Kingsclere

Official Going Good/Firm (Firm Places)

3721
5.40 Louis's Triumph Median Auction Maiden Stakes 2yo (F)
£3521 £1006 £503 **7f str** **Good/Firm 38** **-17 Slow** Stands side

3122 **QUERIDO 26** [9] Saeed bin Suroor 2-9-0 L Dettori 1/3 FAV: 41: Made all far side rail, clr after 92+
halfway, pushed out fnl 1f, val 7L+: bckd at long odds-on: eff at 6f, apprec step up to 7f, further will suit:
acts on fast grnd & a sharp/undul trk: won in fine style, useful, will rate higher.
MANSIYA 0 [5] C E Brittain 2-8-9 K McEvoy 16/1: 2: ch f Vettori - Bay Shade (Sharpen Up) Al 4 71
handy, chsd wnr dist, al held ins fnl 1f: debut: May foal, cost 9,000 gns: half sister to a couple of 7f wnrs at
2: dam successful at 7f: sire Gr1 wnr at 1m: eff at 7f, shld get 1m: acts on fast: gd start bhd a useful sort..
HAATMEY 0 [1] M R Channon 2-9-0 T E Durcan 14/1: 3: b c Josr Algarhoud - Raneen Alwatar nk 75+
(Sadler's Wells) Cl-up over 4f, sn outpcd, rallied late, just held for 2nd: debut: Feb foal, half brother
successful at 1m: dam 12f wnr: sire useful performer at 1m: eff at 7f on fast, win sn at 1m.
2952 **LORD NORMACOTE 32** [3] C A Dwyer 2-9-0 R Havlin 66/1: 004: Cl-up 4f, sn outpcd, mod late gains. 3 69
KNIGHTSBRIDGE HILL 0 [4]2-9-0 J D Smith 20/1: 5: b c Raise A Grand - Desert Gem (Green Desert) ¾ 67
Bhd, nvr nrr than mid-div: op 10/1 on debut: Mar foal, half brother to numerous wnrs: dam plcd at 6f.
3046 **MERRYMADCAP 28** [6]2-9-0 D Sweeney 25/1: 0566: Al bhd: see 2263. nk 66
3046 **JAMAARON 28** [2]2-9-0 P Dobbs 7/1: 37: Chsd ldrs 5f, sn wknd: op 5/1: disapp run but 7 52
reportedly injured himself after leaving stalls: btr 3046 (debut, gd/soft).
RAFFISH 0 [7]2-9-0 L Fletcher(3) 40/1: 8: Chsd ldrs 4f, sn wknd: debut. ¾ 50
3601 **SPEEDIE ROSSINI 5** [8]2-9-0 V Halliday 66/1: 09: Cl-up 5f, fdd. ¾ 48
9 Ran Time 1m 28.09 (3.89) Owned: Godolphin Trained: Newmarket

3722
6.10 Chapel Down Maiden Stakes 2yo (D)
£4173 £1284 £642 **6f str** **Good/Firm 38** **-04 Slow** Stands side

3451 **MARCHING SONG 12** [1] R Hannon 2-9-0 (85) P Dobbs 11/10 FAV: 532421: Made all, clr halfway, eased 85+
fnl 1f, val 8L+: well bckd: eff at 5/7f on fast & gd: enjoyed forcing tactics & a confidence boost.
2976 **AVERTING 31** [2] R F Johnson Houghton 2-9-0 D Sweeney 25/1: 52: Prom 4f, sn outpcd, rallied 6 67
late, nvr getting to easy wnr: eff at 6f, shaped as tho' further will suit: acts on fast grnd: see 2976 (debut).
3438 **SAN DENG 12** [4] W R Muir 2-9-0 K McEvoy 50/1: 03: gr c Averti - Miss Mirror (Magic Mirror) ¾ 65
Chsd ldrs till over halfway, sn outpcd, rallied late: Apr foal, cost 25,000 gns: half brother to wnrs at 6/10f: dam
successful at 6f: sire decent performer at spring dists: looks in need of further.
3103 **ROYAL PARDON 26** [6] M L W Bell 2-8-9 M Fenton 3/1: 004: Rear, outpcd halfway, mod late gains. ¾ 58
1826 **INSIGNIA 79** [7]2-9-0 R Havlin 3/1: 55: Cl-up 4f, sn wknd: 11 wk abs: see 1826 (debut). ½ 62
2970 **LAMA ALBARQ 31** [3]2-9-0 L Dettori 100/30: 06: ch c Nureyev - Nuts In May (A P Indy) Rear, nvr 2½ 55
a factor: Mar 1st foal, cost £420,000: dam plcd over sprint dists: sire find performer at 1m: with Saeed Bin Suroor
3163 **VALIOS 24** [5]2-9-0 T E Durcan 20/1: 07: b c Royal Applause - Swing And Brave (Arctic Tern) 1 52
Prom, rcd keenly, wknd fnl 2f: Mar foal, dam wnr abroad: sire Gr1 wnr at 6f: with L M Cumani.
7 Ran Time 1m 13.57 (2.57) Owned: The Queen Trained: Marlborough

3723
6.40 Curious Grape Nursery Handicap Stakes 2yo (D) [84]
£5590 £1720 £860 **7f str** **Good/Firm 38** **-37 Slow** Stands side

3393 **LISA MONA LISA 13** [3] V Smith 2-9-0 (70) T E Durcan 5/1: 141041: Made all, rdn out ins fnl 1f to 75
hold on: eff at 5f, now suited by 7f: acts on fast & gd/soft: game, loves to dominate.
3171* **ROWAN LODGE 23** [2] M H Tompkins 2-9-7 (77) L Dettori 6/4 FAV: 0312: Keen cl-up, ev ch ins fnl shd 82
1f, just held: bckd: eff at 6/7f: lost little in defeat under top weight & task was not helped after bolting to start.
3342 **HALLUCINATE 15** [1] R Hannon 2-8-13 (69) P Dobbs 7/2: 0423: Handy, kept on ins fnl 1f, not btn ½ 73
far: gd run on h'cap bow: see 3342.
3467 **IM SPARTACUS 11** [5] I A Wood 2-8-12 (68) M Fenton 3/1: 1650654: In tch 5f, sn outpcd, rallied late. ½ 71
2670 **MEGELL 43** [4]2-8-12 (68) P McCabe 14/1: 6205: Hld up, gd prog 2f out, wknd fnl 1f: abs: lngr trip. 1 69
3296 **ARTADI 17** [6]2-8-1 e (57) A McCarthy 25/1: 0356: Keen rear, nvr a factor: btr 1574. 13 35
6 Ran Time 1m 29.47 (5.27) Owned: Mr Stephen Dartnell Trained: Newmarket

3724
7.10 Barretts Of Ashford Land Rover Handicap Stakes 3yo 0-70 (E) [72]
£3504 £1078 £539 **7f str** **Good/Firm 38** **-08 Slow** Stands side

3401 **IPHIGENIA 13** [7] P W Hiatt 3-9-7 (65) Lisa Jones 3/1: 5024531: Cl-up, led after 4f, pushed clr 79+
bef 1f out, val 7L+: eff at 5f, now suited by 7f, has tried further: acts on firm, gd grnd & fibresand: easily
defied top weight to record 1st win, fine confidence boost: see 3401 & 2716.
3197 **TRIFTI 22** [3] C A Cyzer 3-9-0 (58) K McEvoy 20/1: 400042: In tch, eff when short of room bef 2f 5 59
out, sn outpcd, rallied fnl 1f, al held by wnr: see 3197 & 2841.
2842 **PRINCESS GALADRIEL 24** [4] N Pollard 4/1: 2132063: Held up, prog when short 2 56
of room bef 1f out, kept on fnl 1f, nvr getting to front 2: shade closer with clr passage: btr 2344 & 1730.
3490 **YASHIN 10** [5] M H Tompkins 3-9-2 (60) L Dettori 11/4 FAV: 0-003204: Cl-up 4f, sn outpcd, briefly nk 56
rallied bef 1f out, wknd: btr 3218 (gd).
3346 **BEAUTY OF DREAMS 15** [8]3-9-7 (65) T E Durcan 20/1: 150-0005: Chsd ldrs over 4f, sn no extra. 1 59
3410 **BERTOCELLI 13** [1]3-9-5 (63) A McCarthy 8/1: 0034006: Al bhd: btr 2272. shd 56
3625 **DONT CALL ME DEREK 5** [2]3-9-4 (62) V Halliday 11/2: 04-56007: Slow away, sn mid div, no impress 2f. nk 54
3612 **LA PUCE 5** [6]3-9-4 (62) M Fenton 16/1: 1146008: Led, rcd keenly, hdd 3f out, styd cl-up till 1¼ 52
dist, fdd: quick reapp: btr 809 & 645 (fibresand).
8 Ran Time 1m 27.42 (3.22) Owned: Mr Clive Roberts Trained: Banbury

3725　　7.40 Seaholme Marquees Median Auction Maiden Stakes 3-4yo　(E)
　　　　£3348　£1030　£515　　**5f str**　　**Good/Firm 38**　　**+11 Fast**　Stands side

2152　**DANCE TO THE BLUES 64** [2] B De Haan 3-8-9　P Dobbs　9/4 FAV: 031: Prom, led bef 1f out, pushed　　　　**60+**
out, val 3L+: well bckd: fast time: 9 wk abs: eff at 5f, 6f shld suit: acts on fast grnd & a sharp/undul trk:
goes well fresh: only lightly rcd: see 2152.
3347　**LAKESIDE GUY 15** [3] P S McEntee 3-9-0　(56) L Dettori 3/1: 0403562: Led, hdd bef 1f out, not pace wnr.　1¾　57
2732　**SACCHARINE 41** [5] M J Polglase 3-8-9　K Ghunowa(7) 50/1: 00-03: Bhd, outpcd halfway, rallied fnl 1f.　3　43
3452　**BLACK SABBETH 12** [6] P J Makin 3-9-0　(69) D Sweeney 7/2: 00064: Chsd ldrs over 2f, sn outpcd,　1　45
mod late gains: tchd 9/2: showed more in 2907.
3347　**VITTORIOSO 15** [4]3-9-0 bl [51] M Fenton 11/1: 5332005: Cl-up 3f, sn wknd: btr 742.　1½　41
3332　**LADY JUSTICE 15** [7]4-8-12　(50) Lisa Jones 3/1: 50-04006: Rcd along far rail, nvr a factor: btr 2152.　hd　35
6 Ran　Time 59.79 (1.39)　Owned: Mrs D Vaughan　Trained: Lambourn

3726　　8.10 Wine For Home Handicap Stakes 3yo+ 35-55　(F)　　　　　　　　　　　　　　　　　**[55]**
　　　　£3122　£892　£446　　**1m1f149y**　　**Good/Firm 38**　　**-28 Slow**　Outside

3232　**ROYAL RACER 20** [14] J R Best 6-9-7 BL　(48) N Pollard 9/1: 0-136001: Led 3f, styd cl-up & led　　　**54**
again 2f out, rdn out to hold on cl-home: eff around 9f/sharp 10f on fast, soft & polytrack: likes Folkestone &
front rng tactics: tried visor, back to form with fitting of 1st time blnks: see 1273 & 1083.
2780　**SERRAVAL 754** [10] G B Balding 6-10-0　(55) R Havlin 2/1: 000000/-2: ch f Sanglamore - Saone　nk　59
(Bering) Hld up, prog bef 1f out, styd on well fnl 1f, post came too sn: rnr-up once over hdles in 02/03 (rtd 84h,
mdn hdle, stays 2m on gd, B S Rothwell): fills h'cap wnr in '02: eff at 9.7f/10f on fast & gd: tried visor: fine
eff under top-weight on first start for G Balding after long lay off, well h'capped. 1 Apr'02 Beve 10g/f 72-67 E:
3404　**FOREST TUNE 13** [11] B Hanbury 6-9-7 bl　(48) L Dettori 4/1 JT FAV: 6006453: Prom, led 5f out, hdd　1¾　49
2f out, kept on same pace:　not disgraced & is on a winning mark: btr 3238.
3238　**PRAIRIE LAW 20** [8] Ian Williams 4-9-1　(42) Lisa Jones 8/1: 52-10064: Mid-div, outpcd 3f out,　nk　42
rallied despite hanging left ins fnl 1f, nrst fin: op 13/2: eff at 9.7f/11.5f: see 3238.
3176　**SILISTRA 23** [13]5-8-13 p (40) Natalia Gemelova(7) 66/1: 00-00005: Chsd ldrs, no extra bef 1f out.　½　39
3232　**NO CHANCE TO DANCE 20** [9]4-9-6 t (47) T E Durcan 12/1: 0-004366: Rear, nvr nrr than mid-div: btr 2832.1¼　44
3238　**URSA MAJOR 20** [5]10-9-4　(45) K McEvoy 20/1: 00/-00607: Nvr nrr than mid-div: see 2146.　½　41
4370　**GIUST IN TEMP 14** [12]5-8-13　(40) M Fenton 25/1: 4206048: Cl-up over 6f, sn wknd: see 390.　2　34
3398　**BURNT COPPER 13** [15]4-9-11 VIS (52) M Savage(5) 6/1: 50-01009: Slow away, prog halfway, wknd 2f out. hd　45
2910　**TINTAWN GOLD 34** [2]4-9-7　(48) D Sweeney 4/1 JT FAV: 00-00420: 10th: Prom over 7f, wknd: btr 2910.　½　40
3524　**MY MAITE 8** [3]5-9-5 t p (46) N Day 5/1: 0160450: 11th: Al bhd: tchd 8/1: btr 3187.　1　36
3362　**Kyle Of Lochalsh 14** [7]4-9-5 (46) A McCarthy 20/1:0　2844　**Night Driver 36** [1]5-9-4 P(45) P Dobbs 25/1:0
13 Ran　Time 2m 4.42(6.42)　Owned: Mr & Mrs R Dawbarn　Trained: Maidstone

Official Going GOOD/FIRM.

3727　　2.20 Coca-Cola Handicap Stakes 3yo+ 35-55　(F)　　　　　　　　　　　　　　　　　**[53]**
　　　　£3136　£896　£448　　**1m4f23y**　　**Good 53**　　**-16 Slow**　Inside

2875　**ROYAL AXMINSTER 35** [5] Mrs P N Dutfield 9-9-1　(40) Amy Baker(7) 20/1: 5-0520U1: Made all, sn clr,　　**48**
held on well fnl 1f, rdn out: clrly none the worse for recent mishap: eff around 12f on fast, firm grnd & both AWs:
loves to front run & goes well for an inexperienced rider: see 2875 & 1287.
3056*　**DANEBANK 28** [17] J Mackie 4-9-12 P (51) Derek Nolan(7) 6/1: 600-0512: Nvr far away, ev ch fnl 1f,　hd　58
just btn in a tight fin: tried in cheek pieces & remains in fine form: see 3056.
3354　**MOLLYS SECRET 15** [19] C G Cox 6-9-5 p (44) J F Egan 9/1: 1000303: Mid-div, hdwy to chall fnl 1f,　nk　50
just btn in a close fin: gd run, see 2844 & 424.
3056　**BOJANGLES 28** [13] R Brotherton 5-9-10　(49) D Holland 9/2 FAV: 3034534: Prom, lost place halfway,　1¾　52
rallied 1.5f, nrst fin: again bhd today's rnr up in 3056.
3295　**LATIN QUEEN 17** [16]4-9-6　(45) F P Ferris(3) 20/1: 000-5055: Chsd wnr, ev ch till no extra　hd　47
cl-home: prob stays a gall/undul 12f on fast grnd: see 2422.
3200　**MARREL 22** [2]6-9-3　(42) Joanna Badger 15/2: 03/333-56: Slowly away, hdwy from rear 2f out, nrst　1½　41
fin: won a h'cap hdle at N Abbot 18 days ago (rtd 125h, eff at 2m/2m4f on gd & fast): see 3200.
3049　**JAVA DAWN 28** [1]4-9-1　(40) A Quinn(5) 25/1: 00-00367: Slowly away, styd on late, nrst fin.　½　38
3420　**LUNAR LORD 12** [18]8-9-11　(50) J Bramhill 10/1: 0004228: Held up, imprvd 3f out, btn fnl 1f: btr 3420.　nk　47
3057　**CHANFRON 28** [11]3-9-5　(55) Paul Eddery 11/1: 360-0559: Prom 10f, wknd: see 2134.　¾　50
3400　**FRIXOS 13** [12]4-9-11 bl (50) V Slattery 33/1: 60P0-660: 10th: Nvr btr than mid-div.　1　43
3454　**GREYFIELD 12** [14]8-9-6　(45) R Miles(3) 8/1: 0/-50600: 11th: Slowly away, nvr a factor.　¾　36
3049　**TOM BELL 28** [7]4-9-10 vis (49) N Chalmers(5) 10/1: 2044240: 12th: Slowly away, prog when slipped　nk　39
ent str, no ch after: lost all ch when slipped & this shld be forgiven: much btr 2937 (2m+).
3493　**LORD LAHAR 10** [6]5-9-1　(40) R Lappin 33/1: 0/00-6000: 13th: Held up, nvr nr ldrs.　1　28
3377†　**STAFFORD KING 728** [8]7-9-1　(40) D Kinsella 50/1: 060/020/-0: 14th: b c Nicolotte - Opening Day　hd　27
(Day Is Done) Al bhd on reapp: rnr-up sev times in nov/nov h'cap hdles in 02/03 (rtd 100h, eff at 2m/2m4f on firm &
gd/soft): missed '03 on the Flat, prev term rnr-up in a mdn h'cap: eff at 13f, stays 2m2f: acts on fast & hvy.
2 Jul'02 Chep 18g/s 41-40 E:
3276　**MR DIP 19** [10]4-9-9　(48) N Pollard 14/1: 6005260: 15th: Nvr nr ldrs: btr 3085.　1　33
3147　**Royal Trigger 25** [15]4-10-0 bl [53] A Daly 16/1:0
1580　**Rainsborough Hill 91** [9]3-8-12 (48) J F McDonald(3) 40/1:0
3579　**Tatweer 6** [4]4-10-0 vis(53) S Whitworth 33/1:0　　717†　**Hobart Junction 883** [3]9-8-12 (37) T Block(7) 50/1:0
19 Ran　Time 2m 39.44 (8.34)　Owned: Axminster Carpets Ltd　Trained: Seaton

3728 2.50 Guinness Median Auction Maiden Stakes 2yo (E)
£3523 £1084 £542 **5f16y str** **Good 53** **-24 Slow** Stands Side

3160 **LUCKY EMERALD** 24 [4] B Palling 2-8-9 F P Ferris(3) 12/1: 201: Nvr far away, styd on well despite 72
drifting left fnl 1f to lead cl-home, rdn out: eff over a gall/undul 5f, shld stay 6f: acts on gd grnd: see 2926.
3476 **OUR FUGITIVE** 10 [6] A W Carroll 2-9-0 N Pollard 7/1: 4032: Tried to make all, swerved ins fnl ½ 76
1f & caught cl-home: sound front rng eff, acts on gd & firm grnd: has enough to win similar, see 3476.
3160 **DANCING ROSE** 24 [11] C G Cox 2-8-9 R Smith 5/2: 23: Chsd ldrs, kept on under press fnl 1f, not shd 71
quite get there: well bckd: 6f looks sure to suit now: see 3160.
3355 **AGENT KENSINGTON** 14 [12] R Hannon 2-8-9 (67) D Holland 6/4 FAV: 225324: Chsd ldrs, kept on nk 70
under press fnl 1f, nvr nrr: well bckd from 2/1: consistent, but struggling to get her head in front: see 3355.
3361 **IL PRANZO** 14 [7]2-9-0 (72) J F Egan 12/1: 0635: Front rank, onepcd fnl 1f: see 3361. 1 72
TANNING [5]2-8-9 J F McDonald(3) 16/1: 6: b f Atraf - Gerundive (Twilight Agenda) Outpcd, nrst 2 61
fin on debut: Jan 1st foal, cost 2,200 gns: dam unrcd, sire a high-class sprinter: with H Morrison.
3157 **BLAKESHALL HOPE** 24 [8]2-9-0 Joanna Badger 33/1: 307: Chsd ldrs, wknd fnl 1f: see 2629 (debut). ¾ 63
SARTAENA [2]2-8-9 N Chalmers(5) 33/1: 8: b f Imperial Ballet - Joza (Marju) Speed till 1.5f 5 43
out alone on far side: Apr foal, cost 9,500 gns: half sister to 6f juv wnr Sweetest Revenge: dam 5f juv wnr.
STAR DUSTER [9]2-8-9 Paul Eddery 25/1: 9: gr f Paris House - To The Stars (Zieten) Slowly 1¾ 38
away, nvr a factor on race-course bow: 9,500 gns May 1st foal: sire a smart juv: with B Millman.
2287 **SECRET DIVA** 58 [3]2-8-9 D Kinsella 66/1: 000: 10th: Al outpcd after 8 wk abs. 1½ 34
Will The Till [1]2-9-0 S Whitworth 33/1:0 3368 **Theflyingscottie** 14 [10]2-9-0 V Slattery 66/1:0
12 Ran Time 1m 00.69 (3.89) Owned: Mr T Clarke Trained: Cowbridge

3729 3.20 Letheby & Christopher Nursery Handicap Stakes 2yo (E) [83]
£4173 £1284 £642 **6f16y str** **Good 53** **-19 Slow** Stands Side

2976 **DOVE COTTAGE** 31 [5] W S Kittow 2-8-5 (60) D Kinsella 14/1: 6531: Nvr far away, went on after 69
halfway, held on well despite drifting left, rdn out: apprec this step up to 6f & h'cap company: acts on gd & fast.
2911* **GODSEND** 34 [1] R Hannon 2-9-5 (74) D Holland 8/1 FAV: 212: Nvr far away, ev ch fnl 1f, not qckn ¾ 79
cl-home: well bckd: stays 6f: acts on gd & fast grnd: see 2911.
3212 **GAVIOLI** 21 [7] J M Bradley 2-8-10 t (65) S Whitworth 33/1: 5042003: Nvr far away, kept on under press. 1 67
3399 **GEISHA LADY** 13 [2] R M Beckett 2-9-7 (76) N Chalmers(5) 8/1: 6324: Rear, styd on late, nrst fin. 1 75
3517* **GOOD WEE GIRL** 8 [6]2-9-5 (7ex) (74) J F Egan 4/1: 00215: Prom till wknd ins fnl 1f: btr 3517. ¾ 70
3376 **WATERLINE LOVER** 14 [8]2-8-4 (59) F P Ferris(3) 12/1: 600406: Led till after halfway, wknd fnl 1f. shd 55
3491 **GENERAL NUISANCE** 10 [3]2-8-5 p (60) J F McDonald(3) 20/1: 4543237: Nvr nr ldrs: see 3491 & 3172. 2 50
3172 **GLASSON LODGE** 23 [4]2-8-0 (55) Joanna Badger 20/1: 6342268: Prom till halfway: btr 2977 (5f). nk 44
8 Ran Time 1m 13.13 (4.33) Owned: Mr Reg Gifford Trained: Cullompton

3730 3.50 Coors Brewers Selling Stakes 3yo+ (G)
£2653 £758 £379 **1m2f36y** **Good 53** **-03 Slow** Inside

3087 **GO GREEN** 27 [4] P D Evans 3-8-5 t (46) F P Ferris(3) 7/2: 0005021: Held up, prog 2f out, led dist, 56
held on well, drvn out: bought in for 6,800 gns: eff over a gall/undul 10f on firm & gd/soft: wears a t-strap.
3477 **COSI FAN TUTTE** 10 [8] M C Pipe 6-9-5 vis t (63) D Holland 7/4 FAV: 10/-23002: Prom, led 2f out hd 60
till dist, rallied well & only just btn: well bckd, clr of rem: apprec this drop to sell grade & shld find similar.
3211 **RELATIVE HERO** 21 [7] Miss S J Wilton 4-9-5 VIS (51) A Quinn(5) 8/1: 650-0023: Keen & prom, wknd 5 52
fnl 1f: too keen in 1st time visor: see 3211.
3294* **AMBERSONG** 17 [1] A W Carroll 6-9-10 (51) Derek Nolan(7) 10/3: 6433014: Slowly away, imprvd to 7 47
chase ldrs 3f out, sn btn: top weight: see 3294.
3344 **TAMARINA** 15 [9]3-8-5 bl (38) J F McDonald(3) 100/1: 4-000005: Keen & prom, led halfway till 2f out. 1 35
3104 **MY COUNTRY CLUB** 26 [6]7-9-5 (43) G Bartley(7) 40/1: 42-66006: Chsd ldrs till halfway, sn no ch. 1¾ 37
3294 **MISS WOODPIGEON** 17 [11]8-9-0 (40) V Slattery 100/1: 000-37: Chsd ldrs, btn 2f out: see 3294. nk 31
3344 **RUMOUR MILL** 15 [10]3-8-10 bl (40) R Miles(3) 25/1: 5000008: Nvr nr ldrs. 2½ 32
2436 **MANIKATO** 52 [5]10-9-5 (26) Kirby Harris(7) 25/1: 60-00009: Al bhd, 7 wk abs. ¾ 31$
3300 **KERRISTINA** 17 [3]3-8-5 (30) S Whitworth 50/1: 000000: 10th: Al rear. 5 18
3829] **ARTISTS RETREAT** 707 [2]5-9-0 (37) J Bramhill 50/1: 0/00000/-0: 11th: ch f Halling - Jumairah dist 0
Sunset (Be My Guest) Led till halfway, wknd qckly, t.o. in dist: missed '03: little form prev term for D Ffrench
Davis: mdn 4th in '01 (rtd 67): eff at 6f on fast grnd: now with B Leavy.
11 Ran Time 2m 09.74 (5.64) Owned: Mr P D Evans Trained: Abergavenny

3731 4.20 Food Partners Handicap Stakes Fillies 3yo+ 0-70 (E) [62]
£3965 £1220 £610 **1m14y str** **Good 53** **-00 Slow** Stands Side

3535 **TUSCARORA** 8 [4] A W Carroll 5-9-8 (56) R Miles(3) 15/8 FAV: 5261051: Rear, gd hdwy wide to lead 64
2f out, just held on: prev eff at 6f, now suited by 1m on firm, gd & polytrack, prob any trk: made most of this
drop in grade: continues in gd form: see 1465.
3363 **NAUGHTY GIRL** 14 [7] P D Evans 4-8-10 vis t (44) F P Ferris(3) 12/1: 0054402: Rear, hdwy over 2f shd 51
out, kept on ins fnl 1f: clr of rem: prev eff at 5/6f, now stays 1m: gd run, back to form: see 551.
3201 **TROIS ETOILES** 22 [2] J W Hills 3-9-2 (57) Derek Nolan(7) 4/1: 00-50553: Cl-up, led 3f out to 2f 3½ 57
out, no extra fnl 1f: see 2922.
3706 **DANIFAH** 1 [9] P D Evans 3-8-1 (42) Joanna Badger 16/1: 00040044: Led early, rem cl-up, not clr 3 36
run over 2f out, sn switched left, no impress dist: rcd yesterday (4th): shd closer with clr run.
3298 **IVY MOON** 17 [6]4-8-9 (43) S Whitworth 11/1: 0353405: Keen in rear, switched left 1f out, nvr a 3 31
factor: see 398.
3024 **YOUNG LOVE** 98 [8]3-8-11 VIS (52) J F McDonald(3) 12/1: 00-06406: Keen & cl-up, ev ch over 2f out, 1½ 37
no impress over 1f out: tchd 16/1: 1st time visor: see 2624.
3240 **TOCCATA ARIA** 20 [3]6-9-5 (53) D Holland 4/1: 006-1107: Sn led, hdd 3f out, no extra. hd 38

CHEPSTOW THURSDAY 05.08.04 Lefthand, Undulating, Galloping Track

3401 **ANNIJAZ 13** [1]7-9-3 (51) D Kinsella 9/1: 0460008: Rear, hdwy & ev ch 2f out, wknd. 2½ **31**

8 Ran Time 1m 36.15 (4.25) Owned: Pursuit Media Trained: Alcester

3732 **4.50 Merbury Catering Maiden Stakes 3yo+ (D)**
£3474 £1069 £535 **7f16y str** **Good 53** **+05 Fast** Stands Side

3480 **VIOLET PARK 10** [4] B J Meehan 3-8-8 J F McDonald(3) 9/4: 2231: With ldr till led 2f out, rdn over 1f out, kept up to work fnl 1f: fair time: eff at 7f/1m on fast & gd/soft, acts on a gall/undul trk: deserved win: can improve further: see 3048. **75**

3188 **TAAQAAH 22** [7] M P Tregoning 3-8-13 (80) A Daly 11/8 FAV: 62-2202: Dwelt & keen, hdwy over 3f out, chsd wnr ins fnl 1f, not her pace: bckd from 7/4: see 2463. 7 **65**

3292 **PRIMESHADE PROMISE 17** [1] D Burchell 3-8-8 J Bramhill 100/1: 003: ch f Opening Verse - Bonnie Lassie (Efisio) Led to 2f out, sn no extra: dam 1m wnr: best run thus far, now quals for h'caps. ½ **59**

3331 **NIKIFOROS 15** [3] J W Hills 3-8-13 (65) S Whitworth 20/1: 06044: b c Inchinor - Putout (Dowsing) Bhd, hdwy over 2f out, chsd wnr briefly 1f out, sn wknd: cost 75,000 gns: dam 5f wnr. ½ **63**

4870} **HOMEWARD 286** [2]3-8-8 D Kinsella 33/1: 0-5: ch f Kris - Home Truth (Known Fact) Prom, wknd over 2f out: mdn unplcd sole '03 start (rtd 33, with G Butler): now with A Balding. 1½ **55**

3379 **LIGNE DEAU 14** [5]3-8-13 (59) F P Ferris(3) 12/1: 00-05366: Mid-div, wknd over 2f out. 4 **52**

3282 **CAZENOVE 19** [8]3-8-13 Paul Eddery 20/1: 0467: Cl-up, wknd over 2f out. ¾ **50**

IRISH PLAYWRIGHT [6]4-9-5 V Slattery 50/1: 8: Slow away, nvr nr ldrs on debut: top weight. ¾ **48**

3595 **ZAZOUS 5** [10]3-8-13 (70) D Holland 9/2: 03-639: Nvr a factor: quick reapp. *hd* **48**

3048 **HOMEBRED STAR 28** [9]3-8-13 N Chalmers(5) 40/1: 000: 10th: Al bhd. 7 **34**

10 Ran Time 1m 23.18 (3.38) Owned: Mrs J Cash Trained: Upper Lambourn

3733 **5.20 Letheby & Christopher Stakes Handicap Ladies Race 3yo+ 0-70 (E)** **[52]**
£3858 £1187 £594 **1m14y str** **Good 53** **-02 Slow** Stands Side

3087 **LORD CHAMBERLAIN 27** [9] J M Bradley 11-9-12 bl (50) Miss Kelly Harrison(3) 12/1: 4030201: Held up, prog 3f out, styd on to lead 1f out, rdn out: eff at 7/8.5f on firm, hvy & f/sand: acts on any trk & eff with blnks. **55**

3142 **ADALAR 25** [14] P D Evans 4-10-6 (58) Miss A Bevan(7) 8/1: 6000402: Led, hdd under press 1f out, kept on but not pace wnr: tchd 11/1: gd run in defeat & can find similar off this mark: see 2866. 1½ **59**

3333 **CORMORANT WHARF 15** [13] T E Powell 4-11-0 (66) Miss J Powell(7) 11/1: 0500643: Slow away, prog 2f out, styd on ins fnl 1f, nrst fin: tchd 16/1: eff at 6/7f, now stays 1m: gd run with headgear left off. 1 **65**

2799 **SMOOTHLY DOES IT 38** [10] Mrs A J Bowlby 3-10-5 (64) Ms T Dzieciolowska(7) 10/1: 0-020604: Mid-div, prog & ev ch dist, sn no extra: btr 1647 (soft). *nk* **62**

3650 **RAINSTORM 3** [12]9-9-2 (40) Mrs S Owen(3) 6/1: 0000205: Cl-up, ev ch 1f out, sn no extra: qk reapp. 1¾ **34**

3398 **CRITICAL STAGE 13** [7]5-10-11 (63) Miss S Brotherton 10/1: 35-31306: Cl-up 6f, wknd: btr 595. ½ **56**

3512 **PAS DE SURPRISE 9** [1]6-10-0 (52) Miss E Folkes(3) 12/1: 5445407: Rear, nvr nrr than mid-div: btr 3328. 1½ **42**

3090 **DAYDREAM DANCER 27** [6]3-9-4 bl (49) Miss N Forde(5) 14/1: 0-500038: Nvr nrr than mid-div: btr 3090. ¾ **37**

3338 **LEAPING BRAVE 15** [11]3-10-11 (70) Miss E J Jones 10/1: 0-424009: Cl-up 6f, wknd: btr 2116 (C/D). 1½ **55**

3257 **CHANDELIER 20** [5]4-9-13 (51) Ms C Williams 5/1 FAV: 0320160: 10th: V slow away, al rear: below par run, reportedly lost blindfold in stalls & then shied at blind as stalls opened: worth another ch: btr 3087. 3 **30**

3109 **ARK ADMIRAL 26** [8]5-10-9 (61) Miss C Tizzard(3) 33/1: 0000-000: 11th: Mid-div 5f, sn wknd: jumps fit. 1 **38**

3650 **OH SO ROSIE 3** [2]4-10-3 p (55) Mrs S Moore(3) 6/1: 2500100: 12th: Rear, prog halfway, wknd fnl 2f. *nk* **31**

2589 **MAGIC WARRIOR 47** [4]4-10-0 (52) Miss Sarah Jane Durman(5) 33/1: 05-34600: 13th: Cl-up 6f, fdd. ¾ **26**

3515 **LYRICAL GIRL 8** [3]3-10-0 (59) Miss Joey Ellis(5) 20/1: 31-15060: 14th: Nvr a factor. 1 **31**

14 Ran Time 1m 36.32(4.42) Owned: Mr W C Harries Trained: Chepstow

HAYDOCK THURSDAY 05.08.04 Lefthand, Flat, Galloping Track

Official Going Good (Good/Soft places)

3734 **2.10 Gatehouse Handicap Stakes 3yo+ 0-80 (D)** **[85]**
£5746 £1768 £884 **1m3f200y** **Good 42** **+10 Fast** Outside

2238 **DALLOOL 61** [2] M A Jarvis 3-9-9 (80) P Robinson 3/1 FAV: 51441: Made all, kept on over 1f out, hands & heels, cosily: bckd, abs, gd time: v eff at 12f, shld stay further: likes to force the pace & acts on gd & gd/soft grnd, enjoys Haydock: runs well fresh: useful, lightly rcd & improving, win again. **90**

3052 **MAXILLA 28** [7] L M Cumani 4-9-9 (69) N Mackay(3) 10/1: 41-40562: Hel d up, gd hdwy over 2f out, styd on for press ins last, al just held by wnr: improved for step up to 12f, 14f suit: find a h'cap. ½ **76**

3222* **DICKIE DEADEYE 21** [1] G B Balding 7-9-9 (69) R Thomas(5) 7/2: 5223113: Handy, eff to chase wnr over 2f out, onepace fnl 1f: nicely bckd: tough & improving, likes easy grnd: see 3222. 2½ **71**

2984 **DR CERULLO 31** [12] C Tinkler 3-9-3 (74) E Ahern 14/1: 01-33024: In tch, sltly outpcd over 2f out, kept on over 1f out: worth a try over 14f now: see 2984, 238. 3 **72**

3140 **SMART JOHN 25** [4]4-9-10 (70) B Swarbrick(5) 5/1: 4142135: Chsd ldrs, wknd over 1f out: back at 12f & shade more expected: see 2900. *hd* **67**

3481 **SMOOTHIE 10** [11]6-9-3 (63) S Drowne 50/1: 66104-06: Bhd, some late gains: see 6. 2½ **56**

2785 **IRISH BLADE 39** [9]3-9-4 (75) Dane O'Neill 12/1: 0-4307: Chsd wnr, wknd 2f out: see 1501, 1259. 1 **67**

3437 **MERRYMAKER 12** [6]4-9-7 (67) S W Kelly 11/1: 4P12108: Slow away, in tch, eff 2f out, sn wknd. 6 **50**

3162 **TRANSCENDANTALE 24** [5]6-7-12 (2oh) (42) D Fentiman(7) 33/1: 0040459: In tch, wknd over 3f out. 5 **20**

3325 **TEMPLET 16** [3]4-9-4 (64) R Winston 25/1: 2345300: 10th: Held up, rdn & wknd 2f out: see 3149. 1 **38**

3514 **YOUNG ROONEY 8** [10]4-9-9 (69) W Supple 25/1: 04324-40: 11th: Handy, wknd 3f out: too keen. 3 **38**

2930 **TRULLITTI 33** [8]3-9-2 (73) K Darley 16/1: 65-35P: In tch, wknd halfway, t.o./p.u. lame 3f out. **0**

12 Ran Time 2m 31.63 (3.83) Owned: Sheikh Ahmed Al Maktoum Trained: Newmarket

3735 2.40 Haydock Park Annual Badgeholders Club Maiden Auction Stakes Div 1 2yo (E)
£3601 £1108 £554 **6f str** **Good 42** **-27 Slow** Centre

3272 **THROW THE DICE** 19 [2] K A Ryan 2-8-9 N Callan 11/4 FAV: 21: Handy, gd hdwy to lead over 1f out, **83**
rdn clr ins last, cosily: bckd tho' op 2/1: eff at 6f on gd & soft grnd, gall trks: just the type for a nurs.
3239 **PERSIAN CARPET** 20 [7] I A Wood 2-8-2 (70) F Norton 7/1: 0422: Prom, eff over 1f out, kept on but **1½ 67**
not pace of wnr: shown enough to win a modest race: see 2239, 2776.
2911 **PHLAUNT** 34 [14] R F Johnson Houghton 2-8-2 Martin Dwyer 14/1: 403: In tch, eff well over 1f **shd 66**
out, onepace: eff at 6f on fast & gd/soft: see 2537.
2774 **MIDDLE EASTERN** 40 [10] P A Blockley 2-8-7 Dean McKeown 25/1: 54: In tch, eff to chall over 1f **1 68**
out, onepace: sharper for debut & eff at 6f on gd grnd: see 2774.
1981 **TURKS WOOD** 72 [9]2-8-7 P Robinson 3/1: 45: In tch, eff dist, sn onepace: 10 wk abs: see 1981. **nk 67**
CHICKEN SOUP [1]2-8-11 S W Kelly 5/1: 6: br c Dansili - Radiancy (Mujtahid) In tch, no **nk 70**
impress over 1f out: Mar foal, cost 8,000gns: half-brother to a 2m scorer: dam styd 7f: sharper for this.
3212 **ENGLISH FELLOW** 21 [6]2-8-7 (76) G Gibbons 10/1: 34407: Led till dist, wknd: btr 2297, 1950. **2½ 59**
3376 **ADMITTANCE** 14 [5]2-8-4 L Goncalves 50/1: 08: Nvr a factor: see 3376. **½ 54**
CRIMSON BOW [12]2-8-4 W Supple 40/1: 9: ch f Night Shift - Carma (Konigsstuhl) Al bhd on **shd 53**
debut: Feb first foal, cost 20,000gns: dam useful over mid-dists.
3478 **SONNTAG BLUE** 10 [4]2-8-11 E Ahern 50/1: 00: 10th: b g Bluebird - Laura Margaret (Persian Bold) **nk 59**
Al bhd: Mar foal, cost 28,000gns: dam wnr abroad: bred to apprec 7f+ in time.
GRANDOS [11]2-8-11 R Winston 12/1: 0: 11th: Al bhd on debut. **1 56**
BELLA PLUNKETT [3]2-8-2 B Swarbrick(5) 80/1: 0: 12th: Slow away & al bhd on debut. **4 35**
2845 **HARRYS SIMMIE** 36 [13]2-8-2 Dale Gibson 100/1: 00: 13th: Dwelt, nvr a factor. **5 20**
PHANTOM SONG [8]2-8-9 D Tudhope(7) 100/1: 0: 14th: In tch, wknd over 2f out on debut. **1½ 23**
14 Ran Time 1m 15.47 (4.17) Owned: Pendle Inn Partnership Trained: Hambleton

3736 3.10 Haydock Park Annual Badgeholders Club Maiden Auction Stakes Div 2 2yo (E)
£3588 £1104 £552 **6f str** **Good 42** **-13 Slow** Centre

3163 **LOOK AT THE STARS** 24 [4] C G Cox 2-8-9 K Darley 16/1: 01: Handy, hdwy to lead over 1f out, styd **86**
on, drvn out: imprvd from debut & eff over a gall 6f on gd grnd: shld be more to come: see 3163.
3258 **MOLLY MARIE** 19 [10] T D Easterby 2-8-6 (78) D Allan 11/2: 2462: Chsd ldrs, eff over 1f out, kept **1 78**
on ins last, not pace of wnr: eff at 6f on gd grnd, 7f looks sure to suit: shown enough to win a race, see 2132.
3280 **DIAMONDS AND DUST** 19 [9] M H Tompkins 2-8-7 P Robinson 2/1 FAV: 43: Handy, eff & short of room **1 77**
over 1f out, switched left & kept on ins last, kept on: well bckd: looks sure to relish a step up to 7f: see 3280.
3425 **BEE STINGER** 12 [5] I A Wood 2-8-7 (76) F Norton 4/1: 03224: With ldr, eff dist, onepace: consistent. **1 74**
2310 **FLYING RIDGE** 57 [7]2-8-4 Martin Dwyer 25/1: 05: ch f Indian Ridge - Jarrayan (Machiavellian) **½ 69**
Led till over 1f out, sn flashed tail & no extra: Apr foal, cost 22,000gns: half-brother to a 1m wnr: dam plcd
over 6f: eff at 6f on gd grnd.
SECRET CAVERN [3]2-8-9 E Ahern 16/1: 6: b c Lion Cavern - River Dyna (Dynaformer) In tch, **½ 72**
kept on late: Apr first foal, cost £4,000: bred to apprec 7f in time & shld be sharper for this.
3632 **MYTTONS BELL** 4 [12]2-8-2 (70) J Fanning 12/2: 23037: Keen in tch, no extra dist: see 3632, **½ 63**
3381 **ISSY BLUE** 14 [2]2-8-5 (1ow) S W Kelly 25/1: 08: b f Inchinor - Mountain Bluebird (Clever Trick) **3½ 56**
Sn rdn & no extra: Feb foal, cost 18,000gns: half-sister to a 7f juv wnr, dam 1m scorer.
TURN ON THE STYLE [11]2-8-7 W Supple 20/1: 9: Nvr a factor on debut. **2 52**
3348 **CHOREOGRAPHIC** 15 [1]2-8-11 T Hamilton(3) 14/1: 030: 10th: Al bhd: btr 3348. **shd 56**
GLOBE TREKKER [6]2-8-4 R Ffrench 66/1: 0: 11th: Slow away & al bhd. **6 31**
MS THREE [8]2-8-2 B Swarbrick(5) 100/1: 0: 12th: Al bhd. **2½ 22**
MISTER MINTY [13]2-9-0 D Tudhope(7) 33/1: 0: 13th: Held up, al bhd. **7 13**
13 Ran Time 1m 14.59 (3.29) Owned: SBarrow A Parsons P Stevenson Trained: Hungerford

3737 3.40 Joan And Richie Thomas Golden Wedding Anniversary Handicap Stakes 3yo 0-70 (E) [74]
£3913 £1204 £602 **6f str** **Good 42** **-24 Slow** Centre

3356 **MORGAN LEWIS** 14 [17] G B Balding 3-9-3 (63) R Thomas(5) 2/1 FAV: 400-01: Bhd stands side, hdwy 2f **72**
out, hung left over 1f out but styd on to lead cl-home, drvn out, going away: bckd: apprec step up to 6f & confirmed
promise of debut run in 3356: acts on gd & fast: lightly rcd, rate higher.
2387 **AFTER THE SHOW** 54 [13] J R Jenkins 3-9-6 (66) Martin Dwyer 20/1: 51-60602: Cl-up, led over 2f **½ 73**
out, clr over 1f out, rdn & hdd cl-home: 8 wk abs: back to best: see 1166.
3575 **TROJAN FLIGHT** 6 [1] Mrs J R Ramsden 3-9-0 (60) R Winston 14/1: 5460643: Held up far side, hdwy **shd 66**
to chall dist, kept on, not btn far: qck reapp: many from this stable race in similar fashion: see 3575.
3203 **CALCULAITE** 21 [7] Mrs G S Rees 3-8-1 (47) J Fanning 7/1: 000-0664: Cl-up, led after 2f till **1¾ 48**
over 2f out, no impress: eff on gd grnd: see 3018.
3571 **THORNABY GREEN** 6 [19]3-9-4 (64) P Makin(5) 11/1: 00-44105: In tch, eff over 1f out, onepace. **nk 64**
3230* **FLASH RAM** 20 [20]3-9-7 bl (67) E Ahern 12/1: 6422616: Chsd ldrs, wknd 2f out: btr 3203 (7f, mdn). **1¼ 63**
3380 **ARFINNIT** 14 [14]3-8-12 vis (58) A Culhane 12/1: 6164007: In tch, onepace dist: see 2541 (clmr). **nk 53**
3153* **MUSIOTAL** 24 [11]3-8-9 (55) N Mackay(3) 12/1: 0550218: In tch, wknd over 1f out: btr 3153 (7f). **1 47**
2384 **DANTES DEVINE** 55 [19]3-8-1 (47) Dale Gibson 66/1: 0650409: Switched to race alone stands side, **nk 38**
in tch, modest late gains: 8 wk abs: see 2205.
3203 **TURKISH DELIGHT** 21 [12]3-8-13 (59) J Edmunds 14/1: 0-560030: 10th: Bhd, nvr a factor: btr 3203. **¾ 48**
2945 **INTAVAC BOY** 33 [3]3-9-0 (60) Dean McKeown 25/1: 6640: 11th: Dwelt, al bhd far side: see 2945. **1½ 45**
3203 **SMART DANNY** 21 [10]3-7-12 (44) R Ffrench 25/1: 5500050: 12th: Slow away & al bhd. **½ 27**
2985 **SHAMROCK TEA** 31 [9]3-8-13 (59) T Hamilton(3) 6/1: 00-05140: 13th: Slow away, sn in tch, wknd 2f **1¾ 37**
out: reportedly struck into & lost action: see 2985, 2683.
1457 **OL LUCY BROON** 97 [15]3-8-8 (54) T Eaves(3) 100/1: 62600-00: 14th: Al bhd: 3 month abs: see 1457. **3½ 22**
815 **WEAKEST LINK** 150 [5]3-8-12 (58) W Supple 25/1: 0-23300: 15th: Al bhd: see 636. **½ 24**
3095 **LA FONTEYNE** 27 [2]3-8-2 (48) J McAuley 50/1: 0-502050: 16th: Al bhd: see 2493. **8 0**
2784 **ORCHESTRATION** 39 [6]3-8-13 BL (59) A Nicholls 33/1: 26-44000: 17th: Led 2f, wknd 2f out: blnks. **3½ 0**
2398 **DISCO DIVA** 54 [4]3-8-11 (57) N Callan 33/1: 52-00000: 18th: Al bhd: 8 wk abs: see 933. **7 0**
18 Ran Time 1m 15.26 (3.96) Owned: Mrs G Smith Trained: Andover

3738   4.10 Diane Murphy 40th Birthday Handicap Stakes 3yo 0-90 (C)   [95]
£10205 £3140 £1570   **1m30y rnd**   **Good 42**   **+ 08 Fast**   Inside

3433 **MRS MOH 12** [3] T D Easterby 3-8-13 (80) D Allan 12/1: 2-005131: Trkd ldrs, rdn & led over 1f   90
out, held on well for press: eff at 7f/1m on fast, gd/soft & fibresand: tough & genuine: see 2749, 2427.
3421 **INCHLOSS 12** [2] B A McMahon 3-8-12 (79) J Fanning 9/1: 2006122: Trkd ldrs, short of room &   ¾   87
switched over 1f out, styd on for press, not reach wnr: remains on the up-grade: see 3421, 3107.
1206 **BORDER MUSIC 111** [7] A M Balding 3-8-10 (77) Martin Dwyer 16/1: 361-003: Held up, styd on for   1¼   82
press fnl 2f, not pace to chall: 4 month abs, fair run: acts on fast, gd & fibresand: see 879.
3273 **ISKANDER 19** [13] K A Ryan 3-8-6 bl (73) J Carroll 33/1: 6000064: Held up, short of room &   nk   77$
switched over 1f out, kept on for press ins last: closer with a clr passage: stays a gall 1m: now well h'capped &
shld be kept in mind for similar: see 1665.
3339 **KIBRYAA 15** [1]3-8-13 p (80) P Robinson 11/4 FAV: 21-62245: Trkd ldrs, short of room over 1f out   nk   83+
till ins last, kept on: luckless run, closer with a clr passage: nicely bckd, op 7/2: see 3339, 3179.
2904 **BAFFLE 34** [9]3-8-7 (74) K Darley 33/1: 026-1506: Led till dist, no extra: see 1108 (C/D mdn).   ½   76
4921} **FAMILIAR AFFAIR 282** [11]3-9-1 (82) D McGaffin 25/1: 14-7: b g Intikhab - Familiar (Diesis) Keen   2½   79
& prom, onepace for press when hmpd ins last: reapp: lightly rcd '03, debut wnr (auct mdn, subs nov stks 4th, rtd
84): eff at 7f, 1m shld suit: acts on fast grnd & goes well fresh. 1 Sep'03 Thir 7g/f 73- E:
2283 **WEET A HEAD 58** [6]3-8-10 (77) A Culhane 16/1: 3563468: Rear, mod prog for press: 2 month abs.   3½   67
2885* **BALAVISTA 35** [5]3-9-3 (84) S Drowne 7/2: 19: Mid-div, eff over 2f out, sn no prog: nicely bckd   3½   67
on h'cap bow tho' op 5/2: btr 2885 (C/D mdn).
3250 **ACE COMING 20** [12]3-8-2 bl (69) P Fessey 50/1: 0311000: 10th: Keen & trkd ldrs, btn 2f out: btr 1603.   3½   45
1825 **KEY PARTNERS 79** [8]3-9-1 (82) Dean McKeown 25/1: 52-10200: 11th: Al towards rear: 12 wk abs.   2   54
2519 **GOLDEN GRACE 49** [4]3-9-7 (88) W Supple 13/2: 31-04400: 12th: Trkd ldrs, lost pl 4f out: bckd, abs.   3½   53
12 Ran   Time 1m 43.22 (2.72)   Owned: Salifix   Trained: Malton

3739   4.40 Swan With Two Necks Maiden Claiming Stakes 3yo (F)
£3010 £860 £430   **1m30y rnd**   **Good 42**   **-04 Slow**   Inside

3448 **ONE UPMANSHIP 12** [4] J G Portman 3-8-10 (64) N Callan 11/2: 0063261: Trkd ldrs trav well, rdn to   64
lead well ins last: first win, bckd tho' op 9/2: eff at 7f/1m on fast & gd grnd, best without cheek pieces/blnks &
eye-shield: apprec drop to claim grade: see 3194, 2778 & 2369.
3410 **CAYMAN CALYPSO 13** [3] M A Jarvis 3-8-10 (62) P Robinson 4/1 FAV: 006062: Led, drvn & hdd well   nk   63
ins last: nicely bckd: imprvd eff on drop to claim: eff at 1m, tried 10f: acts on gd grnd & a gall trk.
3344 **TREASON TRIAL 15** [2] N Tinkler 3-8-7 (57) K Darley 5/1: 40-0643: Held up, kept on onepace: see 3344.   3   54
1876 **SOVIET SCEPTRE 77** [6] Miss D Mountain 3-9-0 T (70) A Culhane 7/1: 56-304: Held up, hdwy wide 2f   nk   60
out, no prog deal: 11 wk abs, t-strap: prev ran with G Butler: prob stays 1m in claim grade, 7f may prove ideal.
3515 **MISS PROCURER 8** [8]3-8-5 t (64) S Drowne 13/2: 65-5045: Dwelt, late prog, nvr factor: btr 3515.   2½   46
3572 **DEE EN AY 6** [9]3-8-12 D Allan 20/1: 0056: Held up, hdwy 3f out, no prog fnl 2f, qck reapp.   2½   48
3481 **FRANGIPANI 10** [1]3-8-9 (65) J Fanning 5/1: 334-3007: Chsd ldrs, rdn halfway, btn 2f out: btr 2261.   5   35
3481 **VENEZIANA 10** [10]3-8-7 (63) E Ahern 12/1: 030-08: ch f Vettori - Fairy Story (Persian Bold)   2½   28
Mid-div, no impress fnl 3f: lightly rcd in '03 (plcd, rtd 68a, mdn, turn unplcd, rtd 59): eff at 7f on polytrack.
4495} **BIG TOM 92** [5]3-9-0 (62) D Tudhope(7) 10/1: 504-5009: ch c Cadeaux Genereux - Zilayah (Zilzal)   5   25
Chsd ldr, btn 3f out: 3 month abs, unplcd in Ireland earlier this term: auct mdn rnr up '03: eff over a stiff/gall
6f on fast & gd grnd. 2 Jul'03 Carl 5.9gd 74- E:
3462 **BANANA GROVE 11** [7]3-9-0 P Mathers(5) 20/1: 30P: Rear & saddle slipped halfway, sn p.u.   0
10 Ran   Time 1m 44.17 (3.67)   Owned: Mr M J Vandenberghe   Trained: Compton

3740   5.10 Lccc Development Association 10th Anniversary Maiden Stakes 3yo+ (D)
£5746 £1768 £884   **1m2f120y**   **Good 42**   **-02 Slow**   Outside

3405 **ARTICULATION 13** [8] H R A Cecil 3-9-0 W Ryan 15/8 FAV: 421: Handy & led over 2f out, duelled &   89$
narrowly hdd by rnr-up over 1f out, styd on for press to lead again cl-home, gamely: well bckd: eff at 10.5f.12f on
firm & gd grnd: showed battling qualities, lightly rcd colt, entitled to progress: see 3405, 3007.
3237 **COUNTRYWIDE LUCK 20** [11] N P Littmoden 3-9-0 J Fanning 9/2: 62: Trkd ldrs, rdn & narrow lead   hd   88
over 1f out, just hdd cl-home: well bckd, op 6/1: left debut bhd over this longer 10.5f trip,
acts on gd grnd & a gall trk: find similar, see 3237.
2793 **CHANTELOUP 38** [5] J R Fanshawe 3-8-10 (1ow) (89) J Murtagh 9/2: 2443: Mid-div, kept on onepace,   6   74
no threat to front pair: nicely bckd: shld apprec h'cap company: acts on gd & soft grnd, disapp latest on fast.
3007 **MIKAO 30** [1] M H Tompkins 3-9-0 (80) P Robinson 7/2: 5324: Led 3f out till 2f out, fdd.   3½   72
3243 **BARANOOK 20** [9]3-9-0 E Ahern 66/1: 005: Mid-div, not able to chall fnl 3f.   3   67
715 **ROLLSWOOD 163** [6]4-9-10 K Darley 40/1: 56: Held up, rdn & btn 3f out, 5 month abs, turf bow.   1¼   65
 MITH HILL [4]3-9-0 W Supple 25/1: 7: b c Daylami - Delirious Moment (Kris) Pushed along   4   59
early, chsd ldrs, short of room over 3f out, sn no impress on debut, mid-dists shld suit.
 DREAM ALIVE [10]3-9-0 T N Callan 100/1: 8: Held up, rdn & btn 3f out, t-strap on debut.   3½   54
3237 **HOOPS AND BLADES 20** [13]3-9-0 T G McLaughlin 100/1: 00009: Dwelt & al rear, longer trip.   4   48
3186 **CUGINA NICOLA 22** [7]3-8-9 S Drowne 66/1: 00: 10th: Sn struggling rear.   1   41
3211 **BENS REVENGE 21** [3]4-9-10 L Treadwell(5) 100/1: 60: 11th: Keen, mid-div, btn 2f out: mod form.   12   28
2523 **JORDANS SPARK 49** [2]3-9-0 R Winston 66/1: 500: 12th: Led till over 3f out, sn btn: 7 wk abs.   9   12
12 Ran   Time 2m 14.7 (4.7)   Owned: Mr K Abdulla   Trained: Newmarket

3741   5.45 St Helens Handicap Stakes 3yo+ 0-75 (E)   [72]
£3705 £1140 £570   **1m2f120y**   **Good 42**   **-11 Slow**   Outside

3702 **MELODIAN 1** [1] M Brittain 9-9-4 bl (62) M Lawson(5) 13/2: 54512321: Cl-up, styd on to lead 3f out,   70
hdd dist, rallied to lead well ins fnl 1f, rdn out: fin 2nd only yesterday at Newcastle: eff at 7f, suited around
10/10.5f on firm, loves gd & hvy grnd: game & tough: see 3702 & 1633.
2483 **TROUBLE MOUNTAIN 50** [7] M W Easterby 7-9-10 (68) R Winston 10/1: 3524402: Bhd, prog 3f out, kept   1¼   73

HAYDOCK   THURSDAY 05.08.04   Lefthand, Flat, Galloping Track

on fnl 1f, not pace wnr: 7 wk abs: blnks left off: gd eff in defeat under top-weight: see 2284 & 1821.

3674 **LENNEL 2** [14] A Bailey 6-9-10 bl (68) P Makin(5) 4/1: 0641323: Mid-div, prog 4f out, styd on fnl 1f, just held for 2nd: op 11/4 on qck reapp: landed this prize 12 months ago off 9lb lower mark: in gd form. hd 72

2528 **MA YAHAB 49** [8] L M Cumani 3-9-4 (72) N Mackay(3) 8/1: 020-3304: Mid-div, prog to lead bef 1f out, hdd ins fnl 1f, no extra: 7 wk abs: back to form on drop back in trip: see 2162 & 1834. hd 75

3276 **BAND 19** [11]4-8-11 (55) Dane O'Neill 12/1: 0000405: Rear, prog 4f out, ev ch dist, sn no extra. 1¾ 55

3134 **SCURRA 26** [10]5-8-11 (55) P Mulrennan(3) 14/1: 6031246: Handy 1m, sn no extra: btr 2726 & 2545. 1½ 52

3238 **SINJAREE 20** [2]6-7-12 (2oh) (40) D Fentiman(7) 40/1: 0510607: Nvr nrr than mid-div: btr 821 (bndd). ¾ 38

3419 **MAMBINA 12** [5]3-8-8 (62) A Culhane 20/1: 0445048: Handy, ev ch 2f out, no extra dist: clr rem. nk 57

199 **PETROLERO 234** [4]5-8-0 (44) R Ffrench 66/1: 000040-9: gr g Perfect Parade - Louise (Farnesio) 11 21
Keen mid-div over 6f, sn wknd: reapp & new stable: unplcd in '03 (rtd 49a, Mrs S Liddiard): tried t-strap.

2987 **PHONE TAPPING 31** [6]3-8-2 (1ow) (55) P Robinson 7/2 FAV: 0660: 10th: Chsd ldrs over 7f, sn wknd: nk 32
bckd from 6/1: disapp eff & was found to be blowing after the race by vet: see 2987.

3108 **SANTA CATERINA 26** [12]3-9-3 (71) K Darley 6/1: 000-4520: 11th: Led, hdd 3f out, wknd: btr 3108. 7 35

3067 **FIT TO FLY 27** [9]3-9-2 (70) N Callan 33/1: 5156050: 12th: Mid-div over 6f, wknd: new stable. 10 0

3138 **Belshazzar 25** [3]3-9-0 (68) J Edmunds 33/1:0   2203 **Our Little Rosie 62** [13]3-8-6 (60) F Norton 40/1:0
14 Ran   Time 2m 15.6(5.6)   Owned: Mr Mel Brittain   Trained: Warthill

---

LINGFIELD   Polytrack   FRIDAY 06.08.04   Lefthand, Sharp, Undulating Track

Official Going Firm (Good/Firm Places)

3742

2.10 Lingfield Golf Club Maiden Stakes 3yo+   (D)
£3591 £1105 £553   **1m6f   Firm   Inapplicable**   Outside

3335 **MAGICAL QUEST 16** [6] Mrs A J Perrett 4-9-11   J Murtagh 6/1: 01: Led after 3f & rdn clr over 2f 88
out, decisively: left debut bhd: apprec step up to 14f, stoutely bred & shld get 2m+: acts on fm grnd & a sharp & a sharp/undul trk: gd weight carrier who learned plenty from intro, could prove useful, win again.

4737} **RED DAMSON 297** [5] Sir Mark Prescott 3-8-12 (80) S Sanders 8/11 FAV: 040222-2: b g Croco Rouge - 6 82
Damascene (Scenic) Led/dsptd lead 3f, remained handy, rdn over 4f out, onepace: hvly bckd at odds on, showed temperament in preliminaries on this reapp: thrice h'cap rnr-up '03, AW unplcd (rtd 17a, mdn): prev eff at 1m, styd this longer 14f trip & 2m could suit: acts on fast & gd/soft, prob handles firm.
2 Oct'03 Ayr 8g/s 81-77 D: 2 Aug'03 Ripo 8g/f 77-73 D: 2 Aug'03 Newc 8.0g/f 77-73 B:

3405 **GARNETT 14** [9] A King 3-8-12   D Holland 3/1: 433: Sn handy wide, chsd wnr 5f out, rdn & no 6 73
impress over 2f out: clr of rem: op 7/2, has been gelded: longer trip.

3233 **MY TRUE LOVE 21** [1] R J Baker 5-9-11   S Drowne 10/1: 504: Dwelt, rear, no ch over 5f out. 9 60$

3398 **BLACK SWAN 14** [3]4-9-11 (33) J Quinn 66/1: 0/50-05: Rear & no ch with ldrs halfway, only mod prog. 2 57

3335 **DUAL PURPOSE 16** [2]9-9-11 L Vickers 25/1: 06: Chsd ldrs till halfway, no ch fnl 3f: see 3335. 5 50

4458} **ICEY RUN 315** [8]4-9-11 S Righton 100/1: 000-7: b g Runnett - Polar Storm (Law Society) Chsd 1¼ 48
ldrs, struggling fnl 5f: reapp: unplcd at up to 12f in '03 (rtd 32 & 0a).

1940 **LYSANDERS QUEST 75** [10]6-9-11 (37) N Day 50/1: 50000-08: Mid-div, lost tch from 6f out, abs. 10 33

3335 **WHISPERING VALLEY 16** [4]4-9-6 Dane O'Neill 33/1: 0-09: Chsd ldrs, struggling fnl 5f: longer trip. 1,5 26

3288 **RUSSIAN ICON 20** [7]3-8-7 S Whitworth 100/1: 00-00: 10th: Dwelt, sn bhd & t.o. halfway: longer trip. dist 23
10 Ran   Time 3m 06.62 (10.12)   Owned: Mr K Abdulla   Trained: Pulborough

3743

2.40 Arthur Goddard Memorial Novice Stakes 2yo   (D)
£3474 £1069 £535   **5f aw rnd   Going 48   +07 Fast**   Outside

3355* **PITCH UP 15** [6] T G Mills 2-9-2 (81) K Fallon 9/2: 03611: Made all, rdn clr over 2f out, 100a+
readily: nicely bckd, best time on AW today: eff at 5f on fast grnd & polytrack, stiff or sharp/turning trk: loves to force the pace: pacey, progressive & useful, win more races.

3160* **SUNDANCE 25** [5] H J Collingridge 2-9-2 J Quinn 11/8 FAV: 12: Sn cl-up, kept on but not pace of 1½ 93a
wnr: hvly bckd: acts on gd grnd & polytrack: looks ready for 6f: see 3160.

3266 **CANTON 20** [8] R Hannon 2-9-2 (95) Dane O'Neill 5/2: 614453: Dwelt, sn chsd ldrs, onepace for 1 90a
press from over 1f out: consistent: see 3266.

3369 **WESTBROOK BLUE 15** [9] W G M Turner 2-9-0 (81) C Haddon(7) 20/1: 3134: Trkd ldrs, no impress fnl 2f. 4 76a

3284 **RUSSIAN ROCKET 20** [3]2-9-2 (80) Hayley Turner(5) 10/1: 052125: Handy, no impress fnl 2f. hd 77a

3476 **NINJA STORM 11** [2]2-8-12 E Ahern 14/1: 456: V slow away, rear & wide, short of room over 1f 1½ 68a+
out, no impress under kind ride: expect improvement, prob in h'cap company: see 3476 & 3160.

3451 **DIAMOND HOMBRE 13** [7]2-8-12 N Rollins 33/1: 467: Rdn mid-div, outpcd thr'out: btr 3451 (6f). hd 67a

3103 **MISTY PRINCESS 27** [1]2-8-7 M Tebbutt 100/1: 0560008: Mid-div, sn struggling: needs sellers. ¾ 60a

1424 **TARTATARTUFATA 100** [10]2-8-7 S Whitworth 100/1: 049: In tch wide, sn struggling: 3 month abs. 1¼ 56a

CHANTELLES DREAM 0 [4]2-8-4 P Doe 100/1: 0: 10th: ch f Compton Place - Polar Peak (Polar 13 14a
Falcon) Slow away & sn well bhd, t.o.: Apr first foal, 3,500gns purchase: dam a modest mdn.
10 Ran   Time 59.87 (2.07)   Owned: Mr B G Chamley   Trained: Epsom

3744

3.10 Totetrifecta Rated Stakes Handicap 3yo 0-80   (D)   [86]
£7202 £2216 £1108   **6f aw rnd   Going 48   -06 Slow**   Inside

2259 **FINDERS KEEPERS 61** [6] E A L Dunlop 3-9-0 (72) E Ahern 10/1: 2310001: Held up, keen, hung right 82a
but qcknd to lead ins last: 2 month abs: eff at 6/7f on fast, gd/soft & polytrack, likes a sharp trk: headstrong & needs strong handling but clearly has ability: see 1119, 1008 & 875.

3188 **THE JOBBER 23** [5] M Blanshard 3-9-6 (78) K Fallon 6/1: 021-4062: Trkd ldrs, rdn to lead ins ¾ 85a
last, sn hdd & not pace of wnr: op 8/1: acts on fast, gd/soft & polytrack: could find similar sn: see 2677.

3331 **SWEETEST REVENGE 16** [3] M D I Usher 3-9-0 (72) A Daly 8/1: 54-06033: Led/dsptd lead till ins 1½ 74a
last, no extra: stays 7f, 6f poss suites best: fair run: see 135.

3543 **EMTILAAK 8** [10] B Hanbury 3-9-4 (76) R Hills 9/2 JT FAV: 2310044: Held up in tch wide, kept on ½ 76a
for press, not able to chall: far from ideal passage, not disgraced: see 3543, 2042.

3218 **HERE TO ME** 22 [1]3-9-0 (72) Dane O'Neill 9/2 JT FAV: 3442135: Led/dsptd lead 4f, drvn & onepace: *shd* **72a**
acts on firm, gd/soft & polytrack: consistent: see 3218.
3331 **RAGGED JACK** 16 [2]3-8-12 (70) S W Kelly 11/1: U4-23156: Mid-div, drvn & not pace to threaten. ½ **68a**
1186 **TORONTO HEIGHTS** 113 [9]3-9-7 (79) Thomas Yeung(5) 8/1: 6-211007: Held up wide, eff 2f out, no 1¼ **73a**
impress: abs: awkward passage: btr 673.
3380 **SMOKIN JOE** 15 [11]3-8-7 (3oh)vis (62) N Pollard 25/1: 4050008: Rear, eff wide, no prog over 1f out. 2 **53a**
3331 **FOOLS ENTIRE** 16 [4]3-8-7 (2oh) (63) J Quinn 25/1: 3600009: Led/dsptd lead 4f, btn dist: btr 545 & 25. nk **52a**
3567 **HELLO ROBERTO** 7 [8]3-9-0 (72) L Fletcher(3) 12/1: 5301000: 10th: Mid-div, lost pl from halfway. 1 **56a**
3198 **CUT AND DRIED** 23 [7]3-8-7 (65) Martin Dwyer 7/1: 0546450: 11th: Keen, rear, no prog 2f out: btr 3198. 1¼ **45a**
11 Ran   Time 1m 13.61 (3.21)   Owned: Maktoum Al Maktoum   Trained: Newmarket

3745	**3.40 Golf And Gamble Selling Stakes Fillies 2yo** (G)				

£2940 £840 £420   **6f aw rnd**   **Going 48**   **-66 Slow** Inside

3491 **SAPPHIRE PRINCESS** 11 [5] I A Wood 2-8-11 (51) P Doe 16/1: 45561: Sn trkd ldrs, led over 1f out, **57a**
drvn out: no bid: v slow time: first win on AW bow: eff at 6f, acts on polytrack & prob handles fast grnd.
3342 **YELDHAM LADY** 16 [4] J Pearce 2-8-11 J Quinn 9/4 FAV: 002: b f Mujahid - Future Options (Lomond) 2 **50a**
Rear when stumbled & sltly hmpd after 1f, sn bhd, hdwy for press from halfway, not reach wnr: bckd, op 3/1: eff
4,000gns 2yo, Apr foal: half-sister to a 6f wnr, dam styd 1m: eff at 6f on polytrack, wants 7f.
2921 **CONCERT TIME** 34 [7] C R Dore 2-8-11 (46) R Thomas(5) 12/1: 036533: Keen, led/dsptd lead till over ½ **48a**
1f out, no extra: eff around 5/6f on fast grnd & polytrack in sell grade: clr of rem: see 2921 & 1831.
3209 **TURTLE MAGIC** 22 [9] W G M Turner 2-8-11 P (54) A Quinn(5) 5/1: 3664034: Led/dsptd lead till over 5 **34a**
1f out, wknd, cheek pieces: see 3209.
2721 **PETITE NOIRE** 42 [6]2-8-11 t E Ahern 20/1: 065: Wide & hmpd after 1f, nvr able to chall: 6 wk abs. 2 **28a**
3393 **QUEENS GLORY** 14 [8]2-8-11 VIS (66) D Holland 100/30: 2655006: Badly hmpd after 1f, sn in tch, eff ¾ **26a**
wide racing keenly from halfway, wknd qckly dist: tried visor: much btr 3212 & 3022.
2145 **ALICE KING** 65 [1]2-8-11 (50) C Haddon(7) 10/1: 440257: Sn outpcd & no ch halfway: op 8/1, abs. 9 **1a**
3209* **MARCELA ZABALA** 22 [2]2-9-2 (55) M Fenton 9/2: 018: Led/dsptd lead till over 2f out, rdn & losing 9 **0a**
pl when badly hmpd sn after, eased: breathing prob reported: btr 3209 (fast).
8 Ran   Time 1m 17.24 (6.84)   Owned: Sporting Occasions   Trained: Upper Lambourn

3746	**4.10 Chris Wotton Cup Handicap Stakes Fillies 3yo+ 35-55** (F)				[65]

£3003 £858 £429   **7f aw rnd**   **Going 48**   **-31 Slow** Inside

3602* **UNITED SPIRIT** 6 [14] M A Magnusson 3-9-10 (6ex)bl (61) E Ahern 5/1: 04-06311: Chsd ldrs wide, **70a**
styd on for press to lead well ins last: op 7/2, qck reapp: eff at 6/7f on fast, gd & polytrack: imprvd last twice
for twice for blnks & defied awkward wide passage today, could complete hat-trick: see 3602, 3024 & 126.
3286 **DIXIE DANCING** 20 [12] C A Cyzer 5-9-10 (55) Martin Dwyer 13/2: 030-5042: Sn handy/wide, led over nk **63a**
2f out & clr over 1f out, drvn & hdd cl-home: loves to force the pace but prob just undone by awkward draw.
3602 **PRETTY KOOL** 6 [11] S C Williams 4-9-4 (49) K McEvoy 11/2: 0/00-053: Mid-div, styd on onepace for 2½ **52a**
press: also bhd today's wnr latest: acts on fast & polytrack, stays a sharp 7f: see 3602.
3528 **TOKEWANNA** 9 [6] W M Brisbourne 4-9-2 t (47) S W Kelly 20/1: 40-00304: Keen in mid-div, only mod nk **49a**
prog for press, no threat: imprvd eff with t-strap reapplied: handles firm, gd/soft & polytrack: see 3079 & 2204.
3363 **RANNY** 15 [3]4-9-6 (51) R Miles(3) 4/1 FAV: 2206445: Dwelt, rear, hdwy wide over 2f out, no hd **52a**
impress for press fnl 1f: see 3363, 799 & 669.
3287 **WANNA SHOUT** 20 [10]6-9-9 (54) Lisa Jones 11/2: 2050636: Trkd ldrs, outpcd fnl 2f: btr 3287 (10f). 2 **51a**
3605 **ARTZOLA** 6 [7]4-9-5 (50) D Holland 16/1: 050-007: Rear, only mod prog for press, no threat: qck reapp. 2½ **42a**
2928 **BELLS BEACH** 34 [13]6-9-8 (53) S Drowne 16/1: 0441508: Held up wide, btn over 1f out: abs 2016 (6f). ½ **44a**
2347 **EMMERVALE** 57 [8]5-9-0 vis (45) J Murtagh 8/1: 100-5009: Led till over 2f out, sn btn: abs: btr 1730. 3 **30a**
3090 **DREAM OF DUBAI** 28 [5]3-9-4 (55) J F Egan 20/1: 05-00000: 10th: Mid-div, outpcd over 2f out, no 1 **38a**
impress when short of room dist: see 2617.
3334 **TEAM TACTICS** 11 [1]3-9-4 (55) A Daly 50/1: 0005-00: 11th: Dwelt, rear, no impress: see 3334. 1¼ **35a**
3177 **SOUL PROVIDER** 24 [4]3-9-1 BL (52) P Doe 25/1: 3240500: 12th: Rear, eff wide, btn 2f out: blnks. 4 **24a**
1778 **GUARDIAN SPIRIT** 83 [2]5-9-0 (45) J P Guillambert(3) 66/1: 6500/0-00: 13th: Hmpd early & rear. 3 **11a**
3371 **BAHAMA BELLE** 15 [9]3-9-1 bl (52) Dane O'Neill 33/1: 00-04000: 14th: Chsd ldrs wide 5f, sn btn. 1 **16a**
14 Ran   Time 1m 28.36 (5.56)   Owned: East Wind Racing Ltd   Trained: Upper Lambourn

3747	**4.40 Celebrate Your Wedding At Lingfield Racecourse Handicap Stakes 3yo+ 0-75** (E)				[85]

£4238 £1304 £652   **1m3f106y**   **Firm**   **Inapplicable** Outside

3192 **LA PETITE CHINOISE** 23 [6] R Guest 3-8-13 (70) J Murtagh 7/1: 6042251: Trkd ldr & led 3f out, sn **79**
strongly prsd but asserted for press ins last: first win: suited by 9/11f on firm & gd/soft grnd, sharp/undul or
stiff trk: best without blnks: see 2842, 2478 & 2025.
2866 **CARROWDORE** 36 [7] G A Huffer 4-9-9 (70) I Mongan 9/4 FAV: 0-243422: Trkd ldrs & chsd wnr over 2f 1¾ **75**
out, ch over 1f out, no extra ins last: bckd, tho' op 13/8: prev with C Allen: 1 win in 27.
3453 **ATAHUELPA** 13 [8] A King 4-9-12 (73) E Ahern 7/1: 10-00033: Held up, eff to chase front pair over 1¾ **75**
2f out, al held: prob stays a sharp 11.5f: see 888.
2869 **PERSIAN KING** 36 [4] J A B Old 7-9-0 (61) S Drowne 11/2: 0000634: Rear, rdn over 3f out, only mod 3 **59**
prog.
2930 **THE VIOLIN PLAYER** 34 [3]3-9-1 (72) J P Guillambert(3) 20/1: 13-00005: Chsd ldrs till lost pl over 2 **67**
3f out: new yard: btr 2247 (1m).
3334 **MUSTANG ALI** 16 [2]3-8-9 (66) D Holland 5/2: 0355356: Rear, lost tch over 4f out: nicely bckd, 2 **58**
op 4/1: jock reported mount lost action down the hill: btr 3334 & 2978.
2596 **SOVEREIGN DREAMER** 48 [1]4-9-12 (73) N De Souza(5) 12/1: 10-06007: Led till 3f out, sn btn: abs. nk **64**
3419 **BROOKLANDS LODGE** 13 [5]3-8-3 (60) S Righton 33/1: 450-6008: Keen in rear, no ch from halfway. 27 **13**
8 Ran   Time 2m 28.55 (5.15)   Owned: Mr N Elsass   Trained: Newmarket

LINGFIELD Polytrack FRIDAY 06.08.04 Lefthand, Sharp, Undulating Track

3748	5.10 Come Racing At Lingfield Handicap Stakes 3yo+ 35-55 (F)		[54]
	£3185 £910 £455 **1m2f** **Firm** **Inapplicable** Inside		

3695 **FANTASY CRUSADER 2** [4] J A Gilbert 5-9-8 p (48) Dane O'Neill 9/2 JT FAV: 0320031: Chsd ldrs, rdn **58**
to lead ins last, drvn out: nicely bckd: won this race last term off a 1lb lower mark: eff at 7f, suited by 10f on
firm, fast & polytrack, sharp/undul trks: eff in cheek pieces, tried a t-strap: in gd form.

3370* **DIDOE 15** [2] P W Hiatt 5-9-7 (47) P Doe 11/2: 30-00012: Led till ins last, no extra: confirmed 2 **53**
improvement of latest: see 3370 (seller).

3524 **MY MAITE 9** [13] R Ingram 5-9-6 t p (46) N Day 13/2: 0160453: Held up, styd on for press, nrst shd **52**
fin: acts on firm, gd & polytrack: see 1992.

3695 **HUSKY 2** [14] R M H Cowell 6-9-5 p (45) A Daly 9/1: 0-513054: Rear, hung right & lkd reluctant shd **50**
from over 2f out but kept on late, nrst fin: qck reapp: acts on firm, fast & polytrack: see 1182 (banded).

3605 **RYANS BLISS 6** [11]4-9-1 (41) J P Guillambert(3) 20/1: 5320005: Held up, eff wide 3f out, not able 1¾ **44**
to chall.

3505 **DEEKAZZ 10** [1]5-8-9 vis (35) E Ahern 25/1: 0406-006: Trkd ldrs, no extra over 1f out: see 3354. shd **38**

3477 **PACIFIC OCEAN 1** [6]5-9-13 t (53) S Drowne 9/2 JT FAV: 3604367: Trkd ldrs, trav well 3f out, 2½ **52**
found little fnl 2f: btr 2910.

3519 **ESCALADE 9** [7]7-9-7 vis (47) S W Kelly 13/2: 4343568: Mid-div, rdn & btn 2f out: bckd: btr 5 **39**
2892.

2628 **ZULETA 46** [10]3-9-5 (54) D Sweeney 33/1: 00044-09: Mid-div, struggling fnl 2f, 6 wk abs: see 5 **39**
2628.

2835 **MISS SHANGRI LA 38** [5]3-9-0 (49) D Holland 11/1: 0060: 10th: b f Rainbow Quest - Miss Rinjani 1½ **32**
(Shirley Heights) Handy, drvn halfway & sn struggling: h'cap bow: unplcd prev.

2954 **ESTRELLA LEVANTE 33** [3]4-9-8 (48) S Whitworth 33/1: 5306000: 11th: Trkd ldrs, btn 3f out: see 6 **22**
651.

11 Ran Time 2m 09.77(5.57) Owned: The Fantasy Fellowship Trained: Bury St Edmunds

NEWMARKET FRIDAY 06.08.04 Righthand, Stiff, Galloping Track

Official Going Good/Firm

3749	5.55 Stuart And Dave's Handicap Stakes 3yo+ 0-95 (C)		[93]
	£9568 £2944 £1472 **1m2f** **Good/Firm 31** **+ 05 Fast** Centre		

3439 **POLYGONAL 13** [3] Mrs J R Ramsden 4-9-6 (85) G Mosse 6/1: 0-136051: Handy, hdwy to lead over 1f **98**
out, styd on strongly, rdn clr: v eff at 10f, poss stays 12f: acts on fast & soft grnd: apprec sltly more positive
tactics today & the faster pace, clrly useful & can shld win again: see 2404.

2534* **ELMUSTANSER 49** [5] Saeed bin Suroor 3-9-7 t (95) L Dettori 5/2: 212: Set pace, hung left & hdd 6 **98**
over 1f out, not pace of wnr ins last: 7 wk abs: useful eff stepped up to h'cap company & prob more to come.

3439 **COURAGEOUS DUKE 13** [4] J Noseda 5-10-0 (93) K Fallon 5/4 FAV: 60-35023: Chsd ldr, eff over 1f 1 **94**
out, wknd ins last: likes Newmarket, acts on fast grnd: see 3439 & 2489.

2238 **FIRST CENTURION 62** [6] J W Hills 3-8-9 (83) M Hills 12/1: 6-1004: In tch, wknd over 1f out: 1 **82**
poss stays 10f on fast grnd, acts on hvy & h'cap polytrack: see 1511.

3216 **LILLI MARLANE 22** [2]4-8-7 (72) W Ryan 16/1: 6001005: Hld up, wknd over 1f out: up in class, see 2719. 3 **66**

3185 **LIQUID FORM 23** [1]4-9-1 (80) T E Durcan 10/1: 013-0006: Held up, btn well over 1f out: see 2185. 3 **69**

6 Ran Time 2m 04.46 (2.56) Owned: Mr R C Thompson Trained: Thirsk

3750	6.25 Mineral Star Selling Stakes 2yo (E)		
	£4085 £1257 £629 **7f str** **Good/Firm 31** **-41 Slow** Far Side		

3407 **DONT TELL TRIGGER 14** [11] J S Moore 2-8-11 (65) J D Smith 5/1: 061001: Made all stands side, **73**
kept on for press ins last: bght in for 9,500gns: relished rtn to sell grade & stays 7f on fast & gd grnd, gall trk.

3407 **LAKESDALE 14** [1] Mrs C A Dunnett 2-8-6 (60) Hayley Turner(5) 25/1: 0220402: In tch far side, hdwy 1¾ **64**
to lead that group till ins last, kept on, not pace of stands side wnr: encouraging run, best kept to this grade.

3393 **AMPHITHEATRE 14** [5] R F Johnson Houghton 2-8-11 (66) K Fallon 11/2: 503033: Chsd ldr far side, ¾ **67**
led that group over 2f out till ins last, no extra: stays 7f: see 3393.

3393 **ORPEN ANNIE 14** [3] Miss J Feilden 2-8-6 (65) B Reilly(3) 20/1: 03604: In tch far side, onepace nk **61**
over 1f out: prob stays 7f in sell grade: see 2603.

2882 **LADRUCA 36** [10]2-8-6 R Smith 25/1: 005: b f Dracula - Promissory (Caerleon) Held up far side, hd **60**
some late gains: Apr foal, half-sister to a 1m wnr: eff at 7f on fast grnd in sell grade.

2939* **PON MY SOUL 34** [12]2-9-2 P Dobbs 6/1: 16: Chsd wnr stands side, wknd over 1f out: btr 2939 (soft). ¾ **68**

3393 **HAROLDINI 14** [4]2-8-11 (70) R Havlin 4/1 FAV: 042627: Led far side till over 1f out, wknd: bght hd **62**
for 10,000: btr 3393 (6f, nurs h'cap, firesand).

3491 **JAY 11** [2]2-8-6 bl (52) T P Queally 12/1: 002028: Dwelt, sn rdn in tch, btn over 1f out: btr 3491. 1½ **54**

3570* **MAUREENS LOUGH 7** [6]2-8-11 (57) L Dettori 5/1: 6154419: Keen, handy, wknd over 1f out: now with 7 **45**
J Hetherton, btr 2570.

3601 **BLUE SPECTRUM 6** [7]2-8-11 Derek Nolan(7) 66/1: 000: 10th: Slow away, nvr a factor far side. 2 **41**

3488 **Ariane Star 11** [9]2-8-6 M Hills 11/1:0 3491 **Tip Toes 11** [8]2-8-6 (45) T E Durcan 33/1:0

12 Ran Time 1m 28.96 (5.06) Owned: Bigwigs Bloodstock Racing Club V Trained: Hungerford

3751
6.55 Bernard Lloyd/Hole In The Wall Handicap Stakes 3yo+ 0-80 (D)   [79]
£5616 £1728 £864   **6f str**   Good/Firm 31   -17 Slow   Far Side

3408 **SEMENOVSKII 14** [8] P W D'Arcy 4-9-4 (69) D Holland 6/1: 600-3601: Switched to race stands side,   75
made virtually all, kept on well for press, drvn out: suited by 6f on firm or gd, acts on gd/soft & polytrack, any
trk: right back to form with forcing tactics & has slipped to a v handy mark: see 516.
3602 **COLD CLIMATE 6** [11] Bob Jones 9-8-3 (54) J Quinn 11/2: 1-040522: Switched to race stands side,   nk   59
chsd wnr, eff over 1f out, styd on, just held: deserves similar: see 3602, 3184.
3569 **HARD TO CATCH 7** [1] D K Ivory 6-9-12 bl (77) M Savage(5) 9/1: 1133063: Dwelt, held up far side,   1¼   78
hdwy to lead that group over 1f out, styd on: fine run, reserves v best for Brighton: see 2598, 2269.
3584 **SNOW BUNTING 7** [12] Jedd O'Keeffe 6-8-11 (62) M Fenton 4/1 FAV: 0205334: Switched to race stands   nk   62
side, held up, hdwy over 1f out, nrst fin: consistent: see 3424, 2160.
3408 **PRINCE CYRANO 14** [10]5-9-6 (71) R Mullen 7/1: 0006035: Dwelt, switched race stands side, held   shd   70
up, eff to chall over 1f out, onepace: see 3408, 1481.
3333 **SALON PRIVE 16** [7]4-8-9 (60) L Dettori 7/1: 232-0026: Switched to race stands side, handy, hung   4   47
left & wknd over 1f out: btr 3333 (polytrack), 23.
3584 **JUSTE POUR LAMOUR 7** [4]4-9-5 (70) J F Egan 11/1: 4000407: With ldr far side, wknd fnl 1f: see 2090.   hd   56
2855 **MULTAHAB 37** [13]5-7-13 t (50) F P Ferris(3) 20/1: 4240008: In tch stands side, wknd over 1f out.   2   30
3408 **MIMIC 14** [2]4-8-12 (63) R Mills(7) 20/1: 140-0009: b f Royal Applause - Stripanoora (Ahonoora)   ½   41
In tch far side, wknd over 1f out: '03 dual h'cap & a class stks scorer: all 3 wins at 6f on firm or fast, acts on
polytrack: loves to dominate on an easy trk: tough & progressive last term. 1 Aug'03 Folk 6g/f 72-(63) E:
1 Aug'03 Yarm 6.0g/f 72-63 E: 2 Jul'03 Ling 6gd 63-61 E: 2 Jul'03 Kemp 5g/f 64-61 E: 1 Jun'03 Ling 6g/f 64-54 F:
3640 **YORKIES BOY 4** [6]9-7-12 (1oh)p (48) R Thomas(2) 14/1: 4000040: 10th: In tch far side, wknd 2f out.   ½   25
2871 **Silver Chime 36** [3]4-9-3 (68) Martin Dwyer 14/1:0   3341 **Strathclyde 16** [5]5-9-10 (75) C Catlin 25/1:0
12 Ran   Time 1m 13.9 (2.9)   Owned: Mr Peter Beaton-Brown   Trained: Newmarket

3752
7.25 Mykal Industries Maiden Stakes 2yo (D)
£4843 £1490 £745   **7f str**   Good/Firm 31   -17 Slow   Far Side

3337 **WINDSOR KNOT 16** [13] J H M Gosden 2-9-0   J Murtagh 4/5 FAV: 41: Made all, kept on well over 1f   94+
out, readily: eff at 7f, 1m sure to suit: acts on fast grnd & a gall trk: enjoyed forcing tactics & more to come.
     MONSOON RAIN 0 [15] Saeed bin Suroor 2-9-0   L Dettori 4/1: 2: b c Old Trieste - Smokey Mirage   2   87
(Holy Bull)   In tch, eff over 2f out, kept on ins last, not pace of wnr: Jan foal, cost $550,000: eff at 7f, 1m
sure to suit: acts on fast grnd: learn plenty from this & shld be winning sn.
2424 **GOLDEN FURY 54** [11] J L Dunlop 2-9-0   G Mosse 11/1: 43: Keen in tch, eff over 1f out, kept on: ¾   85
imprvd for debut & stays 7f on fast grnd: can win a minor trk mdn shortly, see 2424.
     GIVEN A CHOICE 0 [10] J G Given 2-9-0   I Mongan 16/1: 4: b c Trans Island - Miss Audimar (Mr   ¾   81+
Leader)   Held up, hdwy & short of room over 1f out, styd on strongly ins last, hands-and-heels: Mar foal, cost
E65,000: half-brother to high-class effort over 1m & caught the eye here, keep in mind.
     WOTCHALIKE 0 [5]2-9-0   N Pollard 66/1: 5: ch c Spectrum - Juno Madonna (Sadler's Wells)   Chsd   ¾   81
wnr, onepace over 1f out on debut: Feb foal, cost 13,000gns: half-brother to a 2m1f scorer: bred to relish
mid-dist next term & showed plenty of promise here.
     DUBAI VENTURE 0 [9]2-9-0   K Fallon 8/1: 6: ch c Rainbow Quest - Bombazine (Generous)   Sn rdn   hd   80
bhd, late gains, nvr dngrs: Apr foal, cost 200,000gns: full brother to a 12/15f scorer: dam 10f wnr: shaped with
plenty of promise here, will learn plenty from this & the type to win races over mid-dists later on.
3234 **THE COIRES 21** [1]2-9-0   Dane O'Neill 50/1: 07: In tch, wknd over 1f out.   1   78
     EBTIKAAR 0 [8]2-9-0   R Hills 14/1: 8: Slow away & nvr a factor on debut.   nk   77
     DESERT CLASSIC 0 [12]2-8-9   E Ahern 33/1: 9: Handy, wknd over 1f out.   3½   65
     WINGMAN 0 [2]2-9-0   M Hills 20/1: 0: 10th: Slow away & hmpd start, wknd over 1f out.   1½   67
2388 **South Othe Border 55** [6]2-9-0 R Miles(3) 50/1:0   3488 **Sherbourne 11** [3]2-8-9 Paul Eddery 66/1:0
   King Zafeen 0 [14]2-9-0 T E Durcan 33/1:0   2236 **Mr Kalandi 62** [4]2-9-0 D Holland 25/1:0
14 Ran   Time 1m 27.25 (3.35)   Owned: Sheikh Mohammed   Trained: Manton

3753
7.55 Firestone Products Nursery Handicap Stakes 2yo (D)   [87]
£4755 £1463 £732   **7f str**   Good/Firm 31   -28 Slow   Far Side

3342 **MIGHTY EMPIRE 16** [5] M H Tompkins 2-8-7 (66) L Dettori 9/4 FAV: 0041: Keen, handy, hdwy to lead   77
ins last, rdn clr, readily: first win: suited by a gall 7f on fast grnd, further shld suit: going the right way & a
gd confidence boost, more to come: see 2077.
3407 **ALRIGHT MY SON 14** [7] R Hannon 2-9-3 (76) Dane O'Neill 5/2: 02452: Set pace, hung left over 1f   3½   78
out, hdd & not pace of wnr ins last: more positive tactics & again shaped well: shld find a race: see 3407.
3297 **NORDHOCK 18** [4] N A Callaghan 2-8-1 (60) D Fox(5) 16/1: 6163: Sn rdn, handy, outpcd over 2f out,   ½   61
rallied ins last: stays 7f & well worth a try over 1m on this form: see 2865 (seller).
3103 **BURTON ASH 27** [6] J G Given 2-9-1 (74) M Fenton 12/1: 0434: With ldr, eff over 1f out, sn no   1   73
extra: not disgraced: poss stay 7f: see 3103.
3330 **FLYING PASS 16** [1]2-9-2 (75) D Holland 11/2: 030225: Handy, wknd fnl 1f: btr 3330.   1¼   71
3290 **GUINEA A MINUTE 18** [3]2-8-8 (67) R Mullen 7/1: 0366: Handy, wknd over 1f out: see 3041 (6f, gd/soft).   ¾   61
3412 **NOORAIN 14** [2]2-9-7 (80) T E Durcan 7/1: 3427: Keen with ldrs, hmpd & wknd over 2f out: btr 3412.   18   38
7 Ran   Time 1m 28.05 (4.15)   Owned: The Mighty Empire Partnership   Trained: Newmarket

NEWMARKET FRIDAY 06.08.04 Righthand, Stiff, Galloping Track

3754 **8.25 Bexhill Conditions Stakes 3yo+ (C)**
£8398 £3186 £1593 **1m2f** **Good/Firm 31** **+12 Fast** Centre

3464 **CORRIOLANUS 12** [5] P Mitchell 4-8-13 (94) D Holland 20/1: 0006061: Held up, hdwy over 1f out, styd on to lead ins last, rdn out: suited by 10f on fast, soft or polytrack: imprvd today & a useful effort: see 693. **103**
3264 **ELSHADI 20** [1] M P Tregoning 3-8-7 bl (104) Martin Dwyer 6/1: 114-0262: Set gd pace, rdn & hdd ins last, no extra: apprec drop in class & rtn to forcing tactics: useful: see 2554, 2254. *1¾* **102**
3233 **CARINI 21** [4] H Candy 3-7-13 (94) C Catlin 20/1: 11-363: In tch, eff & short of room over 1f out, kept on: running well but hard to place: see 1844. *¾* **93**
3043 **IMTIYAZ 29** [3] Saeed bin Suroor 5-9-2 t (108) L Dettori 4/6 FAV: 0631-224: Held up, eff well over 1f out, wknd tamely: smart form prev with forcing tactics & an odd switch here: shld do btr: see 3043, 2022. *¾* **99**
3563 **TIZZY MAY 7** [2]4-8-13 (100) Dane O'Neill 5/1: 2504005: Hld up, eff 2f out, wknd fnl 1f: busy: see 1478. *1½* **93**
4955} **ISLAND SOUND 280** [6]7-8-13 (102) K Fallon 7/1: 610246-6: b g Turtle Island - Ballet (Sharrood) Chsd ldr, wknd well over 1f out on reapp: '03 stks wnr: former nov chase wnr (2m1f, gd/soft, rtd 115c): eff at 1m/10f on firm & soft, handles hvy: likes to dominate & has tried a visor & cheek pieces. *dist* **0**
2 Aug'03 Epso 10.1g/f 112-(98) C: 1 Jul'03 Epso 10.1g/f 110-(99) C:
6 Ran Time 2m 03.79(1.89) Owned: Mr Richard J Cohen Trained: Epsom

HAYDOCK FRIDAY 06.08.04 Lefthand, Flat, Galloping Track

Official Going Good

3755 **6.10 Rectangle Group E B F Maiden Stakes 2yo (D)**
£4901 £1508 £754 **5f str** **Good 46** **-18 Slow** Centre

3600 **COUNTDOWN 6** [5] Sir Mark Prescott 2-9-0 S Sanders 4/9 FAV: 321: Al cl-up, styd on to lead 2f out, drvn out: quick reapp: eff at 5f, further will suit: acts on firm, gd grnd & polytrack: progressing well. **87**
ONE GREAT IDEA 0 [4] T D Barron 2-9-0 N Callan 4/1: 2: b g Night Shift - Scenaria (Scenic) Chsd ldrs, styd on to chase wnr fnl 1f, al held: clr rem on debut: Mar foal, half brother 7f Listed wnr: dam unrcd: sire speedily bred: eff at 5f, further will suit: acts on gd: clr rem, gd run in defeat & can rate higher. *1½* **79**
3431 **KOOL OVATION 13** [6] A Dickman 2-9-0 A Beech(3) 66/1: 03: b c Royal Applause - Carrie Kool (Prince Sabo) Led 3f, sn no extra: Apr foal, cost 3,000 gns: half brother to wnrs at sprint dists: dam 5f wnr. *4* **67**
1212 **LUCY PARKES 112** [7] E J Alston 2-8-9 M Henry 28/1: 04: Handy 3f, sn outpcd, rallied late: long abs. *1¾* **57**
1805 **DIKTATIT 81** [11]2-8-9 S Hitchcott(3) 11/1: 05: b f Diktat - Mystique Smile (Music Boy) Held up, nvr nrr than mid-div: long abs: Jan foal, cost 23,000 gns: half sister successful at 1m: dam wnr at 5f. *nk* **56**
3178 **MARLENES GIRL 24** [10]2-8-9 P Mathers(5) 100/1: 06: Nvr nrr than mid-div. *shd* **55**
3652 **HITS ONLY CASH 4** [3]2-9-0 Dean McKeown 33/1: 67: Al in rear: quick reapp. *½* **59**
3227 **SLATE GREY 21** [9]2-9-0 Darren Williams 66/1: 0008: Rear, mod late gains. *shd* **58**
3411 **PRINCEABLE LADY 14** [1]2-8-9 D Allan 22/1: 0009: Al bhd. *2* **47**
3633 **BENNY THE BUS 5** [8]2-9-0 A Culhane 66/1: 00: 10th: Cl-up 3f, fdd: quick reapp. *1¾* **47**
10 Ran Time 1m 2.02 (3.22) Owned: Cheveley Park Stud Trained: Newmarket

3756 **6.40 Countrywide Freight Nursery Handicap Stakes 2yo (E)** **[88]**
£3614 £1112 £556 **5f str** **Good 46** **-21 Slow** Centre

3590 **BAYMIST 6** [3] M W Easterby 2-8-3 (63) R Ffrench 25/1: 56141: Dwelt, rear, rdn & hdwy 2f out & led ins last, drvn out: apprec return to 5f, tried 6f: acts on gd grnd & a stiff/gall trk: see 3308. **70**
3632 **MAKE US FLUSH 5** [11] A Berry 2-8-13 (73) F Norton 11/1: 0401102: Held up in tch, rdn & styd on well from over 1f out, not pace of wnr nr fin: likes this trk, return to form: eff at 5/6f: see 3271. *1* **75**
3343 **ALSU 16** [4] A M Balding 2-8-11 (71) S Sanders 8/1: 310633: Mid-div, hdwy to lead over 1f out, hdd ins last, not pace of wnr: acts on fast & gd grnd: eff at 5/6f: see 3343 & 1744 (6f). *shd* **72**
2360* **DISTINCTLY GAME 56** [7] K A Ryan 2-9-7 (81) N Callan 13/8 FAV: 22214: Chsd ldrs travelling well, onepace for press ins last: see 2360. *¾* **80**
3431 **CAMPEON 13** [1]2-9-0 (74) K Darley 10/1: 5052435: Led till over 1f out, no extra: btr 3431 (6f). *1½* **69**
2744 **HANDSOME LADY 41** [6]2-9-3 VIS (77) P Hanagan 11/1: 16056: Cl-up, rdn & no extra ins last: tried vis. *½* **71**
3374 **RYEDANE 15** [2]2-8-5 (65) D Allan 7/1: 030537: Dwelt, rear, kept on late, nvr pace to chall: needs a return to 6f: see 3374, 2100. *1* **56**
3212 **CHILLY CRACKER 22** [9]2-8-11 (71) Dale Gibson 66/1: 26108: Chsd ldrs till over 1f out: btr 2498 (AW). *3* **53**
2165 **FLOSSYTOO 65** [5]2-9-0 (74) J D O'Reilly(7) 33/1: 01009: Dwelt, chsd ldrs, btn over 1f out: abs: btr 1343. *1¼* **52**
3271 **APOLOGIES 20** [8]2-9-2 (76) G Gibbons 16/1: 014060: 10th: In tch, outpcd from halfway: btr 1517. *1¾* **49**
3445 **SAUCEPOT 13** [10]2-8-5 (65) S Carson 16/1: 0620: 11th: Mid-div, struggling from halfway: btr 3445. *1* **35**
3343 **STRAFFAN 16** [12]2-8-0 (60) A Nicholls 11/1: 2541220: 12th: Dwelt, held up in tch, no impress halfway. *1¾* **25**
12 Ran Time 1m 2.16 (3.36) Owned: Mrs M E Curtis Trained: Sheriff Hutton

3757 **7.10 Premier Wealth Management Ltd Claiming Stakes 3yo+ (F)**
£3031 £866 £433 **6f str** **Good 46** **-23 Slow** Centre

3571 **JEDEYDD 7** [6] M Dods 7-9-1 bl t (53) R Winston 14/1: 0640001: Rear, hdwy from halfway, switched & rdn to lead well ins last: eff at 7f/1m, well suited tonight by 6f in clmg grade: now suited by blnks & a t-strap: best with waiting tactics, quirky & gvn a fine ride here: see 2057. **58**
3569 **PAYS DAMOUR 7** [8] D Nicholls 7-8-11 t (60) Alex Greaves 2/1 FAV: 3050302: Trkd ldrs, rdn to chall ins last, not pace of wnr nr fin: see 2337 & 1522. *¾* **50**
2999 **WHITE LEDGER 31** [13] R A Fahey 5-8-9 vis (50) P Hanagan 12/1: 0000-003: Led till well ins last, wknd. *shd* **47**
3547 **POLAR GALAXY 8** [14] C W Fairhurst 3-8-6 (45) G Faulkner 33/1: 400-0504: Chsd ldrs, onepace dist. *2½* **41**
3527 **AMERICAN COUSIN 9** [7]9-8-7 (55) A Nicholls 5/1: 2500665: Rear, kept on for press, no prog fnl 50yds. *hd* **37**
3104 **KING NICHOLAS 27** [9]5-8-13 t p (53) M Lawson(5) 11/2: 0104106: Mid-div, outpcd over 2f out. *1½* **39**

3545 **WILD TIDE** 8 [11]5-8-2 R Ffrench 100/1: 007: Chsd ldrs till halfway: mod form. 3 19
3482 **MALLIA** 11 [2]11-8-7 (44) P Makin(5) 6/1: 4163248: Held up in tch, no impress fnl 2f: btr 3000 (AW). 5 9
3417 **MATRIARCHAL** 14 [10]4-8-2 (30) Kim Tinkler 100/1: 00-05009: Dwelt, al rear: btr 2480. 1½ 0
2947 **BUTHAINA** 34 [3]4-9-0 (45) T Eaves(5) 50/1: 0000000: 10th: Mid-div, struggling fnl 2f: see 1660. nk 11
3426 **COUNTRYWIDE GIRL** 13 [1]5-8-6 (35) P Mathers(5) 25/1: 2153400: 11th: Chsd ldrs, btn 2f out: btr 2801. 1½ 0
2702 **Cloudless** 43 [4]4-8-8 (43) S Hitchcott(3) 20/1:0 3634 **Sugar Cube Treat** 5 [12]8-8-6 (31) P Varley(7) 33/1:U
13 Ran Time 1m 15.46 (4.16) Owned: Mr Neil Harrison Trained: Darlington

3758 **7.40 Mtb Group Classified Stakes 3yo+ 0-85 (C)**
£9237 £2842 £1421 **6f str** **Good 46** **+05 Fast** Centre

3434 **RIVER FALCON** 13 [2] J S Goldie 4-9-3 (84) N Mackay(3) 12/1: 0100301: Trkd ldr far side & led 92
overall 3f out, drvn & held on gamely, all out in a fast time: eff at 5/6f on firm or soft grnd, prefers gd or
softer: loves a gall trk: useful sprinter: see 1683.
3550 **COMPTONS ELEVEN** 8 [5] M R Channon 3-9-0 (86) S Hitchcott(3) 3/1 FAV: 0052122: Al handy in centre hd 92
& led that group halfway, edged left under press & kept on well, just failed: remains in fine form: see 3550.
3248 **PIETER BRUEGHEL** 21 [10] D Nicholls 5-9-4 (86) R Winston 9/1: 0400133: Led centre group till 1 89
halfway, onepace: see 3116.
3293 **KINGS CAPRICE** 18 [11] G B Balding 3-8-13 (85) S Carson 12/1: 0341044: Held up centre, styd on nk 87
for press, nrst line: has been gldd: see 3293, 2918 & 1756.
3434 **ELLENS ACADEMY** 13 [3]9-9-4 (86) W Supple 6/1: 2442235: Held up, kept on late, not land a blow. ½ 87
3424 **PINCHBECK** 13 [4]5-9-5 p (87) P Robinson 7/2: 0410146: Chsd ldrs centre, no impress over 1f out. 7 68
3461 **HITS ONLY MONEY** 12 [9]4-9-8 (90) Dean McKeown 25/1: 0-000007: Sn rdn in centre, no impress. nk 70
3596 **TELEPATHIC** 6 [6]4-9-3 (55) P Mathers(5) 200/1: 5654008: Held up, no ch fnl 2f: quick reapp. 1½ 61S
2438 **SOPHRANO** 53 [12]4-9-3 (60) G Faulkner 150/1: 0620-539: Chsd ldrs centre till halfway: abs: btr 2438. 4 49
1933 **PARTNERS IN JAZZ** 76 [7]3-9-2 (88) N Callan 7/2: 2221-50: 10th: Unruly stalls, dwelt, sn handy, nk 51
rdn & btn 2f out: 11 wk abs: got v warm & upset in preliminaries: much btr 1933.
3596 **JALOUHAR** 6 [1]4-9-3 (46) T Woodley 200/1: 2006000: 11th: Led far side till halfway, sn strugg: qk reapp. ½ 47
11 Ran Time 1m 13.81 (2.51) Owned: F Brady E Bruce & S Bruce Trained: Glasgow

3759 **8.10 Sproston Anniversary Handicap Stakes 3yo+ 0-70 (E)** [67]
£3848 £1184 £592 **1m30y rnd** **Good 46** **+09 Fast** Outside

2832 **DOUBLE RANSOM** 38 [3] Mrs L Stubbs 5-9-8 bl (61) P Hanagan 7/1: 1421621: Trkd ldrs, styd on for 70
press to lead well ins last: gd time: eff at 1m/10f on gd & polytrack: see 1504, 1278.
1661 **EXPLODE** 88 [7] Miss L C Siddall 7-8-10 (49) S Sanders 33/1: 0000-402: Al handy & led over 4f out ½ 56
till well ins last: eff around 1m on gd grnd: see 1536.
3562 **REGENTS SECRET** 8 [6] J S Goldie 4-9-6 (59) N Mackay(3) 12/1: 0024033: Held up, switched & styd on 1½ 63
for press ins last, not reach front pair: see 3562, 2552 & 1092.
3579 **NEWCORP LAD** 7 [5] Mrs G S Rees 4-9-6 (59) A Culhane 9/2 FAV: 0004424: Chsd ldrs, rdn to chall hd 62
ins last, no extra nr fin: likes Hamilton: see 3579.
3325 **APACHE POINT** 17 [8]7-9-1 (54) Kim Tinkler 15/2: 5455235: Chsd ldrs, onepace for press: btr 3325. 1¾ 53
3232 **QUICKS THE WORD** 21 [10]4-9-2 (55) K Darley 6/1: 4000226: Mid-div, styd on onepace: btr 3232. shd 53
463 **MOUNT HILLABY** 197 [17]4-9-6 (59) P Mulrennan(3) 16/1: 6000-107: Held up, rdn & mod prog: abs. 1¼ 55
2755 **ROUTE SIXTY SIX** 41 [2]8-8-8 (47) Dale Gibson 25/1: 00-06208: Rear, rdn & switched dist, nrst fin. hd 42
3593 **ENCOUNTER** 6 [4]8-8-6 (45) D Allan 12/1: 5600259: Held up, short of room repeatedly from over 2f nk 39+
out, kept on late: luckless run, prob much closer with clr run: see 3250 & 1388.
2891 **MAUREEN ANN** 35 [9]4-8-12 (51) J Bramhill 50/1: 0000-000: 10th: Keen in mid-div, no impress fnl 2f. 1 43
2931 **VERMILION CREEK** 34 [14]5-8-12 (51) Stephanie Hollinshead(5) 25/1: 6662060: 11th: Rear, mod hdwy 3½ 36
wide, nvr factor: btr 1348.
3401 **MEELUP** 14 [15]4-9-3 p (56) V Slattery 66/1: 0022000: 12th: Led 1f, prom till 2f out: btr 1748 (7f). shd 40
3360 **SILENT STORM** 15 [16]4-10-0 (67) N Chalmers(5) 16/1: 5/-330: 13th: Led after 1f till over 4f out, nk 50
btn 2f out: h'cap bow: btr 3360 & 2722.
3700* **PARISIAN PLAYBOY** 2 [13]4-8-12 (6ex) (51) Leanne Kershaw(7) 6/1: 0001210: 14th: Al rear: quick 1¾ 30
reapp under a pen: much btr 3700 (gd/soft, 7f).
2947 **RYMERS RASCAL** 34 [18]12-8-10 (49) W Supple 16/1: 2-320020: 15th: Mid-div wide, btn 2f out. nk 27
3490 **Kew The Music** 11 [1]4-9-6 (59) S Hitchcott(3) 33/1:0 3487 **Qobtaan** 11 [12]5-9-0 (53) G Baker 100/1:0
17 Ran Time 1m 43.50 (3.0) Owned: Tyme Partnership Trained: Malton

3760 **8.40 North West Racing Club Silver Jubilee Handicap Stakes 3yo+ 0-85 (D)** [84]
£5649 £1738 £869 **1m6f** **Good 46** **+02 Fast** Outside

3140+ **MAGIC COMBINATION** 26 [6] L Lungo 11-9-9 (79) P Mulrennan(3) 9/2: 0/-252211: Held up, bhd with 87+
plenty to do over 4f out, hdwy to lead ins last, rdn clr: eff at 10f/2m2f on fast & soft grnd: in rude health at
present depsite age: likes Haydock & wng run may continue: see 3140, 2963 & 2607.
3340 **TILLA** 16 [3] H Morrison 4-8-10 (66) S Sanders 2/1 FAV: 131-5602: Held up, smooth hdwy wide & led 2 69
over 1f out, sn rdn & hdd ins last, no extra: gd run: see 3340, 2607 & 2192.
3404 **YANKEEDOODLEDANDY** 14 [7] P C Haslam 3-8-8 (77) Rory Moore(7) 9/2: 1212323: Trkd ldrs, rdn & led 1¼ 79
over 2f out till over 1f out, not pace of front pair: cheek pieces omitted: consistent: see 1000 & 796.
PILGRIMS PROGRESS 405 [2] D W Thompson 4-9-3 (73) R Winston 50/1: 000130-4: b g Entrepreneur - hd 74
Rose Bonbon (High Top) Held up in tch, kept on onepace for press: 3 month jumps abs (p.u., nov hdle): ex-Irish,
'03 h'cap scorer: eff at 9f, wng form at 12f & stays 14f: likes soft & hvy grnd, handles gd.
3475 **WEET FOR ME** 12 [5]8-9-4 (74) N Callan 22/1: 33//-00265: Led till over 2f out, drvn & onepace: see 3101. ¾ 74
3125 **DR SHARP** 27 [1]4-9-10 (80) Dale Gibson 7/2: 4-012106: Trkd ldrs, lost place & outpcd over 3f ½ 79
out, kept on for press: btr 2887 (C/D).
2595 **LEOPARD SPOT** 762 [10]6-7-12 (4oh) (50) P Fessey 50/1: 25/02/40/-7: b g Sadler's Wells - 9 45
Savoureuse Lady (Caerleon) Slow away & rear, no ch over 2f out: long abs: unplcd on the Level '02 (lightly rcd, rtd
61, clmr, J J O'Neill): 02/03 nov h'cap hdle rnr-up (2m4f, soft): eff around 12f on gd & gd/soft: tried blnks.
3359 **SALAMBA** 15 [8]3-8-1 (70) P Robinson 12/1: 53-508: Handy, rdn & btn 3f out: see 1462. nk 60

HAYDOCK   FRIDAY 06.08.04   Lefthand, Flat, Galloping Track

3549   **PRIZE RING 8** [9]5-7-12 (2oh) (52) B Swarbrick(5) 12/1: 410-6269: Mid-div, struggling fnl 3f: btr 3140.   7   37
9 Ran   Time 3m 4.21(6.21)   Owned: SW Transport (Swindon) Ltd & R J Gilbert   Trained: Carrutherstown

AYR   SATURDAY 07.08.04   Lefthand, Galloping Track

Official Going Good/Firm (Good Places)

3761   6.05 Advertisingworks European Breeders Fund Maiden Stakes 2yo   (D)
£5460 £1680 £840   **6f str**   **Good/Firm 33**   **-28 Slow**   Far side

3386   **EPIPHANY 15** [1] E A L Dunlop 2-8-9 S Sanders 4/11 FAV: 21: Led, hdd dist, rallied to regain   78
lead ins fnl 1f, drvn out: eff at 6f, further will suit: acts on fast grnd & a gall trk: game & useful, open to
more improvement: see 3386 (debut).
      MINTLAW 0 [4] I Semple 2-8-9 R Winston 33/1: 2: b f Mujahid - Rynavey (Rousillon) Slow away,   shd   76
prog halfway, styd on to lead dist, hdd ins fnl 1f, just held by wnr on debut: Feb foal, half-sister to a number of
sprint wnrs at 2: dam unplcd: sire Gr 1 wnr at 7f: eff at 6f, 7f will suit: acts on fast grnd: win sn.
      BRANSTON LILY 0 [6] G A Swinbank 2-8-9 P Hanagan 12/1: 3: ch f Cadeaux Genereux - Indefinite   3   67
Article (Indian Ridge) Handy till dist, sn onepcd: debut: Apr foal, cost 25,000 gns: half-sister won numerous
times at sprint dists: dam unrcd: sire fine sprint performer: eff at 6f on fast grnd: can rate higher.
      EMERALD BAY 0 [7] M Johnston 2-9-0   J Fanning 7/2: 4: b c King's Best - Belle Etoile (Lead On   shd   71
Time) Chsd ldr over 4f, sn no extra: debut: Jan foal, half-brother 10f wnr: dam won abroad: Sire Gr 1 wnr at 1m:
eff at 6f, further will suit: acts on fast grnd: sharper for today.
3302   **GEOJIMALI 19** [5]2-9-0   J Currie(7) 66/1: 665: Al in rear: see 3148 (reapp).   8   50
3525   **QUICK GRAND 10** [3]2-8-9 R Ffrench 100/1: 666: Rear, nvr a factor.   3½   35
2682   **THE TERMINATOR 44** [2]2-9-0 P P Bradley 100/1: 0007: Cl up 4f, fdd: 6 wk abs, has been gelded.   6   24
7 Ran   Time 1m 13.01 (3.71)   Owned: Cliveden Stud   Trained: Newmarket

3762   6.35 Totesport Com Classified Stakes 3yo+ 0-80 (D)
£5337 £1642 £821   **1m2f**   **Good/Firm 33**   **+10 Fast**   Inside

2809   **BESSEMER 40** [4] I Semple 3-8-9 (81) R Winston 4/1: 310-5361: Cl up, led trav well ins fnl 1f,   86+
pushed out, val 3L+: fast time: 6 wk abs & new stable: eff at 6f/1m, impvd for step up to 10f: acts on fast & gd
grnd: likes Ayr: unexposed around this trip: see 2533 & 1460 (M Johnston).
3474   **BARKING MAD 13** [1] M L W Bell 6-9-7 (84) S Sanders 7/4 FAV: 6432162: Led, hdd under press ins   1¼   84
fnl 1f, not pace easy wnr: clr rem: back to form after disappointing in 3474, gd effort conceding weight all-round.
3598   **MBOSI 7** [2] M Johnston 3-8-12 (84) J Fanning 15/8: 5-330203: Cl up over 7f, fdd: qck reapp: 14   64
another below par effort: btr 3430 (gd) & 3042.
2602* **ON EVERY STREET 48** [3] R Bastiman 3-8-8 vis (77) R Ffrench 11/2: 5-4314: Prom 7f, fdd: 7 wk abs   14   40
& new stable: btr 2602 (mdn, firm), H R Cecil).
4 Ran   Time 2m 6.75 (2.35)   Owned: Mr Clarke Boon   Trained: Carluke

3763   7.05 Dm Hall Handicap Stakes 3yo+ 0-70 (E)
£5512 £1696 £848   **6f str**   **Good/Firm 33**   **-09 Slow**   Far side   [70]

3461   **MARSHALLSPARK 13** [5] R A Fahey 5-9-9 (65) P Hanagan 4/1: 0005101: Up front, styd on to lead bef   75
1f out, rdn out: eff at 6/7f, acts on fibresand & gd/soft, suited by firm & fast grnd: see 3213 & 1749.
3561   **STRAWBERRY PATCH 9** [6] Miss L A Perratt 5-8-10 p (52) S Sanders 6/1: 00-00502: Bhd, prog 2f out,   1½   57
styd on fnl 1f, not pace wnr: encouraging effort & is h'capped to win: likes Musselburgh: see 2542 (reapp)
3569   **ALBASHOOSH 8** [1] D Nicholls 6-9-13 (69) Alex Greaves 7/4 FAV: 5610343: Mid div, prog when short   1   71
of room bef 1f out, sn onepcd: continues in gd form: see 3569 & 2280.
3561   **STAR APPLAUSE 9** [7] J S Goldie 4-7-12 (5oh) (35) N Mackay(3) 33/1: 0060004: Chsd ldrs, no extra   ¾   40
fnl 1f: eff at 5/6f: acts on fast & fibresand: see 3514.
3528   **COLLEGE MAID 10** [8]7-9-3 vis (59) J Currie(7) 9/1: 3566665: Chsd ldr till dist, wknd: btr 2542.   1¼   55
3548   **PHARAOH HATSHEPSUT 9** [4]6-7-12 (14oh)bl (29) P Fessey 66/1: 0006006: Handy 4f, wknd dist.   1   33
3228   **TUSCAN FLYER 22** [2]6-9-5 bl (61) R Ffrench 9/2: 0304047: Led, hdd bef 1f out, wknd: btr 3228.   1½   50
3680   **DANAKIM 3** [3]7-7-12 (40) D Fentiman(7) 10/1: 0004208: In tch 4f, wknd: qck reapp: btr 3609.   1¾   24
8 Ran   Time 1m 11.87 (2.57)   Owned: Mr J J Staunton   Trained: Malton

3764   7.35 John Conroy Batchelor Claiming Stakes 3yo+ (E)
£3559 £1095 £548   **7f50y rnd**   **Good/Firm 33**   **-27 Slow**   Inside

3558* **BAILIEBOROUGH 9** [6] D Nicholls 5-9-9 vis (68) Alex Greaves 7/4 FAV: 3016511: Mid div, prog to   70
lead 2f out, rdn out to hold on: eff at 7/9f on firm & gd/soft grnd: in form 5yo who enjoys claiming grade.
3558   **SARRAAF 9** [8] J S Goldie 8-9-6 (65) N Mackay(3) 9/4: 3335052: Mid div, styd on to chase wnr ins   ½   65
fnl 1f, just held: clr rem: back to form today: see 2568.
3651   **COMPASSION 5** [9] Miss L A Perratt 3-8-2 p (46) R Ffrench 20/1: 4453603: Handy over 5f, sn onepcd.   7   39
2910   **PURI 36** [4] J G Given 5-9-4 VIS (50) J Fanning 25/1: 0-400P4: Cl up, wknd bef 1f out: 1st time visor.   1   47
3528   **ZAHUNDA 10** [2]5-8-8 (40) S Sanders 4/1: 3640245: Led 5f, fdd: btr 3324.   nk   36
3545   **VIJAY 9** [5]5-8-13 (45) R Winston 6/1: 0060026: Prom 5f, fdd: btr 3545 (5.9f).   2   37
3324   **NEEDWOOD BUCOLIC 18** [1]6-8-13 BL (33) D Fentiman(7) 100/1: 0000007: Al in rear: blnks, see 2369.   5   27
3324   **LIONS DOMANE 18** [3]7-9-1 (44) P Hanagan 33/1: P000008: Cl up, fdd 2f out: see 528.   3   23
3650   **THE SPOOK 5** [7]4-8-13 (39) P Mulrennan(3) 50/1: 5300-009: Slow away, nvr a factor: qck reapp.   dist   0
9 Ran   Time 1m 31.16 (4.36)   Owned: Middleham Park Racing XVIII   Trained: Thirsk

1135

3765
8.05 Totequadpot Handicap Stakes 3yo 0-70 (E)   [77]
£3575 £1100 £550   1m2f192y   Good/Firm 33   -03 Slow   Inside

3261 **RUTTERS REBEL 21** [3] G A Swinbank 3-9-7 (70) P Mulrennan(3) 15/2: 0402401: Chsd ldrs, styd on to   74
lead ins fnl 1f, rdn out: eff around 11/12f on fast & gd, disapp on gd/soft: see 2984.
3449* **QUARRYMOUNT 14** [1] Sir Mark Prescott 3-9-0 (63) S Sanders 11/8 FAV: 000-0212: Led, hdd under   ½   67
press ins fnl 1f, not pace wnr: eff at 8.5f, imprvd for recent step up to 10/11f: acts on fast & gd & polytrack.
3573* **RICHTEE 8** [2] R A Fahey 3-9-7 (70) P Hanagan 7/4: 60-12513: Prom, rcd keenly, ev ch dist, onepcd   ½   73
well ins fnl 1f: another gd run: see 3573.
3207 **SAAMEQ 23** [5] I Semple 3-8-0 (49) P Fessey 10/1: 0-600344: Rear, prog 2f out, onepcd ins fnl 1f.   ½   51
3529 **CHARLIE TANGO 10** [7]3-9-5 (68) R Winston 9/1: 0413435: Al cl up, no extra fnl 1f: btr 3529 (9f).   1¼   66
3573 **PRELUDE 8** [4]3-8-11 (60) J Fanning 16/1: 500666: Nvr nrr than mid div.   ¾   58
2515 **COLUMBIAN EMERALD 51** [6]3-8-3 (52) R Ffrench 50/1: 0457: Prom 1m, sn fdd: 7 wk abs.   17   27
7 Ran   Time 2m 20.01 (4.01)   Owned: Mrs Michele Rutter   Trained: Richmond

---

3766
8.35 Kidzplay Handicap Stakes 3yo+ 0-70 (E)   [64]
£3645 £1122 £561   1m1f20y   Good/Firm 33   -37 Slow   Inside

4381} **ROYAL INDULGENCE 320** [10] W M Brisbourne 4-8-7 (43) J Fanning 33/1: 660500-1: b g Royal Applause   50+
- Silent Indulgence (Woodman) Bhd, hdwy 3f out, styd on to lead ins fnl 1f, pushed out, val 3L+: reapp & new
stable: unplcd in '03 (rtd 50, clmr, M Dods): plcd in '02 (mdn, rtd 74 & 89$, M R Channon): eff at 6/7f, imprvd
for step up to 9f: acts on firm & gd, gall trk: goes well fresh: app switch to new stable, unexposed at this trip.
2179 **SKIDDAW JONES 65** [8] Miss L A Perratt 4-8-11 (47) R Ffrench 9/1: 00-05062: Cl up, styd on to   1¾   47
lead dist, hdd ins fnl 1f, no extra: encouraging run: see 2030.
3501 **CRYFIELD 11** [4] N Tinkler 7-9-10 (60) Kim Tinkler 6/1: 4001643: In tch, outpcd 2f out, rallied fnl 1f.   nk   59
3650* **GIFTED FLAME 5** [9] T D Barron 5-10-4 (6ex) (68) S Sanders 3/1 FAV: 0400314: Bhd, prog 3f out, ev   ½   66
ch 1f out, sn no extra: not disgraced under 6lb pen: btr 3650 (1m, Carlisle).
3328 **MARKET AVENUE 18** [1]5-9-8 (58) P Hanagan 4/1: 06-60505: Mid div, nvr able to challenge: btr 3132.   ¾   54
3328 **WOOD DALLING 18** [5]6-9-6 (56) R Winston 4/1: 5-006166: Led, hdd 6f out, ev ch 2f out, wknd fnl 1f.   5   45
3325 **FOREST AIR 18** [7]4-8-10 p (46) P Bradley 11/1: 1005267: Led 6f out, hdd dist, wknd.   ¾   33
2706 **COLLOSEUM 44** [11]3-8-10 (54) D McGaffin 33/1: 56-04008: Al prom: btr 1896.   shd   47
3246 **HOWARDS ROCKET 22** [3]3-8-3 (47) N Mackay(3) 10/1: 0069: Chsd ldrs 6f, sn wknd.   1   31
3558 **SOCIETY TIMES 9** [12]11-7-12 (10oh)t (24) D Fentiman(7) 100/1: 0/4500//-00: 10th: Al in rear: see 3558.   1   16
4559} **Zandeed 662** [2]6-9-10 (60) P Mulrennan(3) 25/1:0
3558 **Environmentalist 9** [6]5-7-12 (40oh)bl t(30) P Fessey 100/1:0
12 Ran   Time 1m 56.68(6.38)   Owned: Mr P G Evans   Trained: Nesscliffe

---

Official Going Good/Firm

3767
2.00 Come Racing Tomorrow Handicap Stakes 3yo+ 35-55 (F)   [61]
£4121 £1268 £634   6f str   Good/Firm 33   -26 Slow   Centre

3609 **FRIMLEYS MATTERRY 7** [4] R E Barr 4-9-2 (49) T Eaves(3) 20/1: 6665031: Mid-div, hdwy 2f out, drvn   56
& styd on to lead well ins last: eff at 6/7f both AWs: first win today: see 2125.
3372 **DIAMOND RING 16** [11] Mrs J Candlish 5-8-12 (45) G Hind 22/1: 5030362: Rear, switched & styd on   ½   49
for press, not pace of wnr cl-home: see 2412, 1336.
2967 **ROYAL WINDMILL 33** [15] M D Hammond 5-8-12 (45) P Mulrennan(3) 14/1: 0520663: Mid-div, hdwy over   shd   49
1f out, styd on well cl-home: eff at 6f/1m: see 1146.
3220 **LEVELLED 23** [10] D W Chapman 10-8-8 (41) Dean McKeown 25/1: 1065064: Led, drvn & hdd ins last.   nk   44
3228 **XANADU 22** [19]8-9-4 p (51) J Mackay 12/1: 0620065: Chsd ldrs stands side, kept on onepace for press.   1   51
3575 **PRIDE OF KINLOCH 8** [12]4-9-11 (58) W Ryan 10/1: 3000326: Slow away & bhd, hdwy from 2f out, not   nk   57
pace of ldrs cl-home: prob closer with a level break, could find a race after 3575 & 3262.
3667 **LOUGHLORIEN 4** [2]5-9-3 (50) T Hamilton(3) 11/2 FAV: 0003347: Mid-div, trav well 2f out, sn wknd.   hd   48
3352 **MICKLEDOR 17** [9]4-9-7 p (54) D Tudhope(7) 14/1: 0301108: Bhd, switched & only mod prog: btr 3129.   ¾   50
1897 **JOSHUAS BOY 78** [6]4-8-9 p (42) J Carroll 18/1: 600/0-309: Chsd ldrs till outpcd over 1f out: gelded.   hd   37
3609* **ZIETZIG 7** [7]7-9-0 (47) P J Benson(7) 15/2: 0005610: 10th: Handy, fbd over 1f out: btr 3609.   nk   41
3670 **MISS WIZZ 4** [17]4-8-12 p (45) Rory Moore(7) 12/1: 6445100: 11th: Chsd ldrs, no impress over 1f out.   ½   37
3670 **GOLDEN SPECTRUM 4** [3]5-9-8 vis (55) Alex Greaves 6/1: 0-350030: 12th: Trkd ldrs, btn 2f out.   shd   47
3667 **CLEVELAND WAY 4** [16]4-8-11 vis (44) D Nolan(3) 33/1: 2621000: 13th: Chsd ldrs, struggling fnl 2f.   1¾   31
3655 **BOWLING ALONG 5** [20]3-9-3 (54) D McGaffin 6/1: 0004320: 14th: Dwelt, bhd, only mod prog: qk reapp.   hd   40
3667 **Good Time Bobby 4** [8]7-9-4 (51) J D O'Reilly(7) 40/1:0
3609 **African Spur 3** [14]4-8-12 vis(46) Danielle McCreery(7) 25/1:0
859 **Lakelands Lady 144** [18]4-9-7 (54) J Edmunds 22/1:0   3487 **Warren Place 12** [5]4-8-7 (40) L Enstone(1) 100/1:0
3680 **Percy Douglas 3** [1]4-8-12 t(45) Ann Stokell 16/1:0
2326 **New Day Dawning 59** [13]3-8-10 (47) R Fitzpatrick 100/1:0
20 Ran   Time 1m 12.43 (3.53)   Owned: Mrs R E Barr   Trained: Middlesbrough

3768 **2.35 Tetley's Imperial Ale Rated Stakes Handicap 3yo+ 0-85 (D)** **[90]**
£18298 £5630 £2815 **1m str** **Good/Firm 33** **+01 Fast** Inside

3583 **AFRICAN SAHARA 8** [2] Miss D Mountain 5-9-2 t (78) O Urbina 7/1: 0603431: Held up, hdwy & rdn/led over 1f out, drvn & held on gamely, all out: eff at 1m/10f on firm, soft & both AWs: tough & genuine: see 800, 625. **83**
3608* **EFIDIUM 7** [3] N Bycroft 6-8-9 (71) Dean McKeown 14/1: 1535412: Held up, rdn to chall over 1f out, drvn & just held: op 12/1: in fine form: see 3608, 2057. *hd* **75**
3501 **TEDSTALE 11** [9] T D Easterby 6-9-2 bl (78) W Ryan 16/1: 5036453: Trkd ldrs, short of room 2f out, switched & styd on well ins last, nrst fin: on a fair mark for similar: see 1877. *1¼* **79**
3501 **ATLANTIC QUEST 11** [12] G A Harker 5-9-1 p (77) J Carroll 25/1: 0150B04: Rear, styd on from 2f out, hung left & not able to chall nr fin: imprvd eff with cheekpieces reapplied: see 1970. *½* **77**
3583 **TIBER TIGER 8** [5]4-9-0 bl (76) T G McLaughlin 25/1: 1020055: Held up, styd on for press, nrst fin. *nk* **75**
3283 **MOUNT VETTORE 21** [7]3-8-0 (5oh) (69) J Mackay 20/1: 0000066: Bhd, switched & mod prog for press, nrst fin: acts on fast, gd & fibresand: stays a gall 1m, best at 6/7f: see 955 & 481. *1* **66**
3553 **WOODY VALENTINE 9** [6]3-8-13 (82) S Chin 10/1: 1661207: Chsd ldrs, drvn & onepace fnl 2f: see 2874. *½* **78**
3583 **QUALITAIR WINGS 8** [10]5-8-10 (72) D McGaffin 20/1: 0002028: Held up, rdn & mod prog, no threat. *nk* **67**
3326* **OBRIGADO 18** [8]4-9-6 VIS (82) T P Queally 12/1: 16-02019: Keen & led after 1f till over 1f out, wknd. *1½* **74**
3565 **DEFINITE GUEST 8** [1]6-9-5 (81) T Hamilton(3) 11/2: 5-300050: 10th: Trkd ldrs 3f out, btn when short of room over 1f out: btr expected after 3565. *1½* **70**
3152* **TONY TIE 26** [4]8-9-8 (84) P Mulrennan(3) 14/1: 5021610: 11th: Trkd ldrs, fading when hmpd over 1f out. *shd* **73**
3634 **TRUE NIGHT 6** [13]7-9-7 (83) T Eaves(3) 4/1 FAV: 3031130: 12th: Mid-div, rdn & no impress dist: qk reapp. *1½* **69**
3443 **DISTANT COUNTRY 14** [16]5-8-9 p (71) L Goncalves 15/2: 6025250: 13th: Rear, smooth hdwy over 2f out, no prog dist & postion accepted: best at 7f: see 2425 & 2160. *1½* **54**
3598 **PAWAN 7** [15]4-8-8 (70) Ann Stokell 50/1: 3010500: 14th: Chsd ldrs 6f: see 2962 (g/s). *¾* **52**
2799 **BELTANE 40** [11]6-8-5 (25oh) (42) C Haddon(7) 200/1: 0012000: 15th: Led 1f, struggling halfway: abs. *12* **29**
3608 **RAPHAEL 7** [14]5-9-4 (80) A Mullen(7) 8/1: 0402220: 16th: Strugg halfway, sadly cut tendon & destroyed. *7* **30**
16 Ran Time 1m 37.33 (2.53) Owned: Miss Debbie Mountain Trained: Newmarket

3769 **3.05 Redcarracing Co Uk Selling Stakes 2yo (G)**
£3017 £862 £431 **6f str** **Good/Firm 33** **-37 Slow** Centre

3411 **THE PEN 15** [4] P C Haslam 2-8-6 G Faulkner 5/1: 01: ch f Lake Coniston - Come To The Point (Pursuit of Love) Dwelt, mid-div, styd on for press to lead well ins last: op 7/2: bght in for 9,000gns: Apr first foal, dam unrcd: eff at 6f, 7f shld suit in similar: acts on fast grnd & a gall trk: apprec drop to sell grade. **61**
3394 **PARIS TAPIS 15** [16] K A Ryan 2-8-6 J Carroll 6/1: 042: Trkd ldr & led over 1f out, drvn & hdd well ins last: eff at 6f: acts on fast grnd: suited by sell grade. *½* **58**
2939 **FRISBY RIDGE 35** [2] T D Easterby 2-8-6 bl (43) A Mullen(7) 9/1: 5055403: Led, rdn & edged right 2f out, hdd over 1f out & not pace of front pair: eff at 6f on fast grnd in sell grade: eff in blnks: see 1303. *1¾* **53**
3418 **CADOGEN SQUARE 14** [3] D W Chapman 2-8-6 Dean McKeown 33/1: 0004: Chsd ldrs, ch 2f out, no extra ins last: career best to date: eff at 6f on fast grnd & sell grade: see 3221. *½* **51**
3259 **MISS GOOD TIME 21** [9]2-8-6 BL J Bramhill 8/1: 060665: Dwelt, bhd, kept on despite hanging badly left from over 1f out, nrst fin: first time blnks: lkd a tricky ride. *1½* **46**
3504 **BLISSPHILLY 11** [8]2-8-6 T Hamilton(3) 14/1: 06: b f Primo Dominie - Majalis (Mujadil) Dwelt, bhd, mod late prog: 15,500gns Mar foal, dam plcd juv, subs 5f 3yo wnr. *2½* **38**
3560 **PREMIER TIMES 9** [17]2-9-3 (59) P Mulrennan(3) 5/1: 5167: Bhd, only mod prog: btr 3259 (g/s). *¾* **47**
2682 **KEYALZAO 44** [5]2-8-6 L Enstone 25/1: 08: Chsd ldrs till over 1f out: 6 wk abs. *nk* **35**
3457 **APETITE 13** [10]2-8-11 Suzanne France(7) 33/1: 09: Dwelt, bhd, mod prog. *¾* **38**
3429 **FOR NOWT 14** [14]2-8-11 W Ryan 7/1: 6000: 10th: Held up, eff when edged left 2f out, sn struggling. *1¼* **34**
3570 **GUNNERBERGKAMP 8** [7]2-8-11 P M Quinn 33/1: 00: 11th: Sn bhd. *3* **25**
3259 **DANEHILL FAIRY 21** [6]2-8-6 bl (47) G Hind 9/2 FAV: 0633320: 12th: Chsd ldrs, btn 2f out: btr 3259. *1¾* **15**
3014 **HUNIPOT 31** [13]2-8-8 (2ow) D McGaffin 50/1: 000060: 13th: Al bhd. *6* **1**
3504 **Peaceful Frontier 11** [12]2-8-6 R Fitzpatrick 33/1:0 3259 **Timmy 21** [1]2-8-11 bl T Eaves(3) 66/1:0
15 Ran Time 1m 13.08 (4.18) Owned: Middleham Park Racing XXVIII Trained: Middleham

3770 **3.40 European Breeders Fund Maiden Stakes Fillies 2yo (D)**
£4342 £1336 £668 **7f str** **Good/Firm 33** **-22 Slow** Centre

3252 **DUBAI SURPRISE 22** [6] D R Loder 2-8-11 T P Queally 10/11 FAV: 31: Trkd ldrs, smooth prog halfway & led over 1f out, rdn, going away: hvly bckd: eff at 7f, 1m will suit: acts on fast: more to come. **82**
ALDENTE 0 [4] Sir Mark Prescott 2-8-11 J Mackay 8/1: 2: gr f Green Desert - Alruccaba (Crystal Palace) Trkd ldrs, drvn & ch over 1f out, not pace of wnr ins last: nicely bckd, op 16/1: Apr foal, half-sister to a 6f/7f juv wnr, also wnrs at up to 14f: dam a 6f juv wnr: eff at 7f, 1m+ sure to suit: acts on fast & a gall trk: promising start, shld be winning soon. *1¼* **76+**
3381 **RESISTANCE HEROINE 16** [3] E A L Dunlop 2-8-11 O Urbina 25/1: 003: b f Dr Fong - Odette (Pursuit of Love) Chsd ldrs, rdn & kept on from over 1f out: left prev bhd: 125,000gns Mar foal, half-sister to v useful performer Silcas Gift, a wnr btwn 5f/7f: dam a 5/6f 3yo scorer: stays a gall 7f on fast: going right way. *¾* **75**
3202 **PATXARAN 23** [1] P C Haslam 2-8-11 G Faulkner 66/1: 054: Chsd ldrs, no extra over 1f out: see 3202. *3* **69**
3520 **AUTUMN MELODY 10** [7]2-8-11 t J Carroll 9/1: 565: Led, hdd over 1f out & wknd: see 3520 & 3035. *1* **67**
3071 **AFRICAN GIFT 29** [2]2-8-11 S Chin 16/1: 306: Cl-up, hung badly left under press over 1f out, fdd. *1¼* **64**
LOVE ME TENDER 0 [5]2-8-11 W Ryan 5/2: 7: b f Green Desert - Easy To Love (Diesis) Rear, eff over 2f out, no impress: op 6/4: Jan first foal, dam an 11f scorer & sister to Oaks wnr Love Divine. *6* **53**
7 Ran Time 1m 25.64 (3.84) Owned: Dr Ali Ridha Trained: Newmarket

3771   4.15 Mary Reveley Racing Club Claiming Stakes 3yo+ (E)
£3348 £1030 £515   1m6f19y   Good/Firm 33   -36 Slow   Inside

3190 **RIGHTY HO** 24 [4] W H Tinning 10-9-2 (43) Kristin Stubbs(7) 4/1: 0-133061: Trkd ldrs, prog to lead   50
3f out, rdn & al holding rival ins last: eff btwn 10f/2m on firm & soft: enjoys banded/claim company: see 1449.
2892 **LIFE IS BEAUTIFUL** 36 [3] W H Tinning 5-9-5 (53) T Eaves(3) 1/1 FAV: 0-615162: Led till 3f out,   1   51
kept on for press, not pace of stablemate: well bckd: stays 14f in claim grade: loves Beverley: see 2653 & 1945.
2905 **CRACKLEANDO** 36 [1] N P Littmoden 3-9-1 (60) Steven Harrison(7) 5/2: 0-303103: Chsd ldr, drvn &   1¼   58
onepace fnl 3f: acts on fast, poss prefer more give: clr of rem: see 1612.
3405 **FFIZZAMO GO** 15 [6] R M Beckett 3-8-5 bl J Mackay 10/1: 64: Dwelt, prog to go handy after 6f, rdn   11   32
& btn over 2f out: longer trip, little improvement: see 3405.
3142 **STEPPENWOLF** 27 [5]3-8-7 (37) C Haddon(3) 25/1: 0000005: Keen & chsd ldrs, lost tch from 5f out.   13   14
3609 **WILHEHECKASLIKE** 7 [7]3-8-3 (30) J Bramhill 33/1: 0-000606: Al bhd, much longer trip.   dist   0
6 Ran   Time 3m 07.42 (9.62)   Owned: Mr W H Tinning   Trained: York

3772   4.50 Go Racing In Yorkshire Maiden Handicap Stakes 3yo+ 0-75 (E)   [76]
£4745 £1460 £730   1m2f   Good/Firm 33   -01 Slow   Inside

3415 **HAVETOAVIT** 15 [4] J D Bethell 3-8-10 (58) T P Queally 5/1: 5324041: Made all, readily pulled clr   68+
fnl 3f, unchall: eff at 10/12f on fast, gd/soft & fibresand: likes to front run: see 2164, 1785.
3529 **MUNAAWESH** 10 [7] D W Chapman 3-8-8 bl (56) Dean McKeown 8/1: 0042042: Held up, rdn & styd on fnl 6   57
3f, nvr a threat to wnr: see 2969 & 1050.
3516 **STANLEY CRANE** 10 [10] B Hanbury 3-8-9 t (57) G Hind 7/1: 5-054543: Hld up, eff 3f out, no impress.   6   49
3573 **EBORACUM** 8 [8] T D Easterby 3-9-1 BL (63) A Mullen(7) 10/1: 0-002204: Trkd ldrs, rdn & no impress   2½   51
fnl 2f: blnks: btr 3377 & 2904 (gd & gd/soft).
4706] **RHETORICAL** 299 [9]3-8-9 (57) J Mackay 5/1: 0600-5: b g Unfuwain - Miswaki Belle (Miswaki) Rdn   1   44
rear, only mod prog: bckd tho' op 10/3: reapp: unplcd at up to 7f in '03 (rtd 56a & 52, mdns).
3299 **BUBBLING FUN** 19 [6]3-9-4 (66) W Ryan 7/4 FAV: 4043326: Chsd wnr, rdn & btn over 2f out: well bckd.   nk   52
3144 **ZARNEETA** 27 [2]3-8-2 (50) C Haddon(3) 100/1: 5000-007: Rdn & bhd, nvr a factor: see 2742.   4   30
3309 **CHISEL** 19 [5]3-8-7 (55) S Chin 14/1: 006008: Chsd ldrs, struggling over 3f out: btr 2325 (7.5f).   9   23
3573 **POWER NAP** 8 [11]3-7-12 (6oh)VIS t (40) Joanna Badger 66/1: 00-6009: Chsd ldrs wide, rdn & btn 3f out.   hd   13
3260 **FANLING LADY** 21 [1]3-9-10 (72) J Carroll 9/1: 3032-000: 10th: Rear, strugg 3f out, eased: see 3260.   5   32
10 Ran   Time 2m 05.72(3.42)   Owned: Mr John E Lund   Trained: Middleham

Official Going GOOD (GOOD/SOFT IN PLACES)

3773   1.40 Prince's Trust Shergar Cup Distaff Rated Stakes Handicapfillies 3yo+ 0-100 (B)   [103]
£22550 £7893 £3608   6f   Good 40   Inapplicable   Inside

3551 **TYCHY** 9 [7] S C Williams 5-9-3 (92) G Mosse 11/4 FAV: 0-530051: Handy, hdwy into 2nd over 2f   99
out, led ins fnl 1f, styd on well, rdn out: hvly bckd: enjoyed return to 6f, stays 7f on fm & gd & any trk: useful.
3235 **FRUIT OF GLORY** 22 [10] J R Jenkins 5-9-5 (94) L Dettori 11/2: 3042142: Trkd ldrs, hdwy 2f out,   1   96
kept on fnl 1f to go 2nd nr fin: well bckd: useful & consistent: see 3106.
2240 **CAVERAL** 63 [8] R Hannon 3-9-2 (95) W C Marwing 20/1: 31-00103: Keen in rear, hdwy halfway, styd   nk   96
on ins fnl 1f to go 3rd nr post: 9 wk abs: useful, back to form: see 1957.
2468 **SPEED COP** 53 [5] A M Balding 4-9-6 (95) J Murtagh 12/1: 10-23004: Led till ins fnl 1f, wknd: 8   hd   95
wk abs: stays 6f, v pacey & return to 5f will suit: on a fair mark: see 883.
3235 **FANNYS FANCY** 22 [1]4-8-13 (88) K Darley 5/1: 43-00035: Handy, kept on fnl 1f but not pace of ldrs.   hd   87
3622 **PROUD BOAST** 7 [9]6-9-1 (90) K Fallon 8/1: 0023006: Slow away, hdwy 2f out, kept on, not pace to chall. ½   87
3466 **FOREVER PHOENIX** 13 [3]4-9-3 (92) D Holland 9/2: 12R0237: Bhd, hdwy after 3f, sn btn: ominous   3½   78
drifter from 5/2: much btr expected after 3466 & 3304.
      MRS ST GEORGE 15 3-8-6 (3oh) (85) D Vargiu 16/1: 4201128: Bhd, hdwy over 2f out, sn extra.   ½   69
3641 **BARRANTES** 5 7-8-9 (3oh) (81) M J Kinane 40/1: 6000-009: Pressed ldr, no impress over 2f out: qk reapp. 7   47
3304 **BALI ROYAL** 5 [6]6-9-9 (98) D M Oliver 33/1: 4-640000: 10th: Keen in tch, no impress over 2f out.   2½   53
10 Ran   Time 1m 14.83 ()   Owned: Mr P Ellinas   Trained: Newmarket

3774   2.10 Porthault Shergar Cup Juvenile Auction Race 2yo (B)
£22550 £7893 £3608   7f   Good 40   Inapplicable   Inside

3624 **JUSTAQUESTION** 7 [5] I A Wood 2-8-10 (82) L Dettori 10/1: 0110321: Rear, gd hdwy wide 2f out, led   94+
nr fin, drvn out: qck reapp: stays 7f well: acts on firm & soft, any trk: v useful & progressive, showed a neat
turn of foot here: see 1669.
3254 **BEAVER PATROL** 22 [8] R F Johnson Houghton 2-9-6 (95) M J Kinane 14/1: 1321062: In tch, hdwy 2f   hd   104
out, chall well ins fnl 1f, just held: improved run at 7f: v useful effort conceding weight, win sn: see 2071.
3189* **LAMH EILE** 24 [7] T D Barron 2-8-7 D Vargiu 11/2: 113: Cl-up, hdwy into 2nd over 2f out, chall   nk   89
over 1f out, led ins fnl 1f, hdd nr fin: useful & lightly raced: see 3189.
3532 **DESTINATE** 10 [4] R Hannon 2-9-1 (95) D Holland 9/2: 01044: Trkd ldrs, lost place 3f out, styd on   ½   97
ins fnl 1f but not pace to reach ldrs: handles firm & gd: remains in gd form: see 3532.
2989 **SPIRIT OF FRANCE** 32 [10]2-9-2 (95) J P Spencer 4/1 FAV: 22125: Led till ins fnl 1f, wknd: lngr trip.   1   96
3337* **EMBOSSED** 17 [9]2-9-1 Y Take 5/1: 616: Slow away, hdwy 2f out, staying on when not clr run nr   ½   94
fin: more to come: see 3337.
3267 **KANDIDATE** 21 [6]2-8-12 G Mosse 10/1: 037: Bhd, nvr nr ldrs: wants mdn company.   5   81
3467 **GROUP CAPTAIN** 13 [2]2-8-12 (80) J Murtagh 12/1: 54228: In tch, no impress 2f out: tchd 16/1.   3½   74
3254 **STREET CRED** 22 [3]2-9-1 D M Oliver 33/1: 109: Rcd in 2nd till over 2f out, sn wknd.   1¼   74

3511 **MCELDOWNEY 11** [1]2-8-12 (77) K Darley 20/1: 322230: 10th: Trkd ldrs, fdd 2f out: btr 3511.   7   0
10 Ran   Time 1m 28.4 ()   Owned: Mr Christopher Shankland   Trained: Upper Lambourn

---

3775   2.45 Murphy's Fastflow Shergar Cup Mile Rated Stakes Handicap 4yo+ 0-100 (B)   [107]
         £22550 £7893 £3608   **1m**   **Good 40**   **+06 Fast**   Inside

3565 **PENTECOST 8** [6] A M Balding 5-9-7 (100) K Fallon 9/2 FAV: 0601401: Bhd, hdwy over 2f out, led   110+
ins fnl 1f, cmftbly: suited by stiff 1m, prob stays 9f: acts on firm & gd/soft, any trk, loves Ascot (won this race
last yr) v smart & has a turn of foot, thriving at present & can win in List/ Gr 3 class: see 3565, see 2915.
3441 **VORTEX 14** [5] Miss Gay Kelleway 5-9-10 e t (103) Y Take 6/1: 0130242: Trkd ldrs, hdwy to lead   1¼   107
over 1f out, hdd ins fnl 1f, no extra: top-weight: tough & v consistent: remains in fine form: see 1697.
3565 **WING COMMANDER 8** [7] R A Fahey 5-9-0 (3ex) (93) D Vargiu 9/1: 3000103: Trkd ldrs, hdwy over 1f   1   95
out, onepcd fnl 1f: op 12/1: gd run, back to form after 3565, see 3460.
2915 **COLISAY 35** [4] E Vaughan 5-9-7 VIS (100) J P Spencer 10/1: 4210-364: Rear, hdwy 2f out, kept on   1   100
ins fnl 1f but not pace to reach ldrs: gd run in a visor: see 1962.
3565 **UNSHAKABLE 8** [8]5-9-1 (94) L Dettori 11/2: 0-001305: In tch, hdwy & slt short of room over 1f   1¼   91
out, sn onepcd: twice below 2915.
3441 **GREENSLADES 14** [2]5-9-3 (96) G Mosse 8/1: 4420306: Rcd in 2nd till led just ins fnl 2f, hdd & no   1¼   90
extra over 6/7f: op 12/1: best over 6/7f: see 3061.
3441 **ST ANDREWS 14** [9]4-9-2 (95) W C Marwing 11/2: 14/-26257: In tch, hdwy & not clr run 1f out, sn wknd.   hd   88
3265 **CAMP COMMANDER 21** [3]5-9-1 t (94) D Holland 8/1: 4-045008: Bhd, nvr nr ldrs: see 2915 & 1624.   2   83
3460 **CALCUTTA 13** [10]8-9-4 (97) K Darley 20/1: 0002039: Bhd, nvr a factor.   1¼   83
3199 **SELECTIVE 24** [1]5-9-0 (93) J Murtagh 16/1: 30-40040: 10th: Led till just ins fnl 2f, no extra: 15   49
prev best with waiting tactics: see 3199.
10 Ran   Time 1m 41.24 (2.74)   Owned: J C J R and S R Hitchins   Trained: Kingsclere

---

3776   3.20 Sodexho Shergar Cup Stayers Rated Stakes Handicap 4yo+ 0-100 (B)   [107]
         £22550 £7893 £3608   **2m45y**   **Good 40**   **-02 Slow**   Inside

3510 **DOROTHYS FRIEND 11** [6] R Charlton 4-8-9 (88) M J Kinane 11/4 FAV: 11-01101: Rear, hdwy wide 2f   99
out, rdn to lead ins fnl 1f, going away: well bckd: relished return to 2m, acts on firm & gd, any trk, likes Ascot:
right back to form & remains on the upgrade at staying trips: win again, see 3125.
3552 **DOUBLE OBSESSION 9** [4] M Johnston 4-9-2 vis (95) D M Oliver 3/1: 0001542: Trkd ldrs, hdwy to lead   1   102
over 1f out, hdd & onepcd ins fnl 1f: well bckd: another fine run here at Ascot: see 3125, 2471.
3617 **HIGHLAND GAMES 7** [8] J G Given 4-8-8 (87) Y Take 10/1: 2024533: Trkd ldrs till lost place 7f   2   91
out, styd on wide for press from over 1f out but not pace of first 2: qck reapp: prev eff over 12f, stayed this 2m
well: unexposed at this trip.
2914 **GOLD MEDALLIST 35** [3] D R C Elsworth 4-9-7 (100) W C Marwing 25/1: 1603-604: Rcd in 2nd, hdwy to   1¾   103
lead over 3f out, hdd & no extra over 1f out: top-weight: fair run: see 2914.
2471 **PENNY PICTURES 53** [2]5-8-8 (87) K Fallon 9/2: 12234/-35: Dwelt & keen in rear, hdwy 6f out,   1¾   88
chall 2f out, sn onepcd: tchd 13/2, 8 wk abs: see 2471.
3510 **ALMAH 11** [7]6-8-11 (90) K Darley 25/1: 4630-006: Bhd, hdwy 3f out, sn onepcd: see 3125.   1½   89
3510 **MORSON BOY 11** [10]4-8-13 (92) D Holland 7/1: 51-00007: Led & sn clr, hdd over 3f out, no extra   hd   90
over 1f out: saddle reportedly slipped: see 3119.
3531 **ALBANOV 10** [9]4-9-2 (95) J P Spencer 14/1: 34522-08: Rear, nvr nr ldrs: see 3531.   6   87
3510 **SANTANDO 11** [1]4-8-11 vis (90) G Mosse 7/1: 3050049: Mid-div, hdwy just bef halfway, lost place   1½   80
over 4f out, wknd 2f out: rider reported his mount got tired: btr 3510 (14f).
1853] **NOSTRADAMUS 797** [5]5-9-0 (93) D Vargiu 40/1: 1460/-0: 10th: b c Gone West - Madam North (Halo)   16   67
Dwelt, mid-div, wknd 4f out, t.o.: reapp: hdles unplcd in 03/04 (rtd 79h, fell once): missed '03: won 1 of 4 '02
starts (mdn, 1m, fast, A O'Brien): stays 1m on fast: now with K Burke.
10 Ran   Time 3m 32.82 (6.82)   Owned: Mountgrange Stud   Trained: Beckhampton

---

3777   3.50 Carvill Shergar Cup Challenge Rated Stakes Handicap 4yo+ 0-100 (B)   [107]
         £22550 £7893 £3608   **1m4f**   **Good 40**   **-04 Slow**   Inside

3118 **DESERT QUEST 28** [1] A M Balding 4-8-13 bl (92) J P Spencer 14/1: 61-02401: Hld up last, hdwy on   99
rails over 1f out, styd on strongly to lead fnl strides, going away: eff around 10/12f on fm & soft, sharp or a
stiff/gall trk: best hld up, has a turn of foot: see 1746.
3464 **COUNSELS OPINION 13** [3] C F Wall 7-9-7 (100) W C Marwing 12/1: 0-340042: Dwelt in rear, hdwy   nk   105
wide over 2f out, styd on strongly fnl strides: jt top-weight: useful, likes Ascot: see 1111.
3439 **SWIFT TANGO 14** [2] E A L Dunlop 4-9-7 (100) D M Oliver 12/1: 4123643: In tch, hdwy 2f out, chall   nk   104
1f out, no impress & held nr fin: jt top-weight: remains in gd form & imprvd for this return to 12f: see 1759.
3185 **HAWRIDGE PRINCE 24** [8] L G Cottrell 4-9-2 (95) J Murtagh 7/1: 312-1124: In tch, hdwy over 2f   ½   98
out, not clr run over 1f out, kept on ins fnl 1f: stays 12f: remains in gd form: see 2694.
3118 **STARRY LODGE 28** [9]4-9-3 (96) L Dettori 6/4 FAV: 4121-135: Trkd ldrs, hdwy to lead briefly over   ¾   98
1f out, no extra ins fnl 1f: hvly bckd: shade more expected: see 2255.
3510 **HAMBLEDEN 11** [6]7-9-5 (98) K Fallon 5/1: 2-604406: Led till over 1f out, no extra: see 1585.   nk   99
3278 **DESERT ROYALTY 21** [4]4-8-13 (92) D Holland 22/1: 2124407: Trkd ldrs, chall 2f out, no impress fnl 1f.   ¾   92
3506 **SIR GEORGE TURNER 11** [5]5-9-2 (95) M J Kinane 10/1: 0000008: Bhd, hdwy 2f out, sn hung, no dngr.   1¾   92
3444 **MUHAREB 14** [10]5-9-1 (94) Y Take 20/1: 03004-59: Cl-up, fdd fnl 1f: see 3444.   10   76
1478 **AKASH 98** [7]4-8-12 (91) G Mosse 14/1: 220-1200: 10th: Trkd ldr, wkng when hmpd well over 1f out, wknd.10   58
10 Ran   Time 2m 34.32 (5.32)   Owned: Ballygallon Stud Ltd   Trained: Kingsclere

ASCOT   SATURDAY 07.08.04   Righthand, Stiff, Galloping Track

3778   4.20 Dubai Duty Free Shergar Cup Sprint Rated Stakes Handicap 3yo 0-100 (B)   [104]
£22550 £7893 £3608   6f   Good 40   Inapplicable Inside

3106 **PARADISE ISLE 28** [4] C F Wall 3-9-1 (91) W C Marwing 14/1: 211-0421: Made all, clr over 1f out, **109**
cmftbly: stays 5f, relished this return to 6f: likes firm & fast, acts on gd, poss handles gd/soft: prob acts on
any trk: enjoyed switch to forcing tactics, win again: see 2593.
3002* **ALDERNEY RACE 32** [5] R Charlton 3-9-7 (97) K Darley 3/1 J FAV: 4-521412: In tch, not clr run 2f   3   **105**
out, hdwy over 1f out, chsd wnr well ins fnl 1f, not her pace: well bckd under jt top-weight: remains in fine form.
3388+ **KHABFAIR 15** [9] Mrs A J Perrett 3-9-4 (3ex) (94) D Vargiu 7/2: 312-413: Trkd ldrs, hdwy 2f out,   ½   **100**
chsd wnr 1f out till well ins fnl 1f, onepace: shade btr 3388 (straight C/D, fast).
3098 **GLARAMARA 28** [8] A Bailey 3-9-7 (97) K Fallon 14/1: 2030044: Bhd, hdwy wide over 2f out, kept on   1½   **98**
but not pace of ldrs: jt top-weight: see 1583, 1150.
3379* **COMMANDO SCOTT 16** [1]3-9-0 (3ex) (90) M J Kinane 11/1: 2226115: Cl-up, hdwy into 2nd over 2f out,   nk   **90**
lost place & wknd qckly 1f out: btr 3379 (gd/soft).
3269 **DOITNOW 21** [10]3-8-13 (89) L Dettori 3/1 J FAV: 1226: Slow away in rear, hdwy over 2f out, no   ½   **87**
impress over 1f out: hvly bckd from 9/2: see 2950.
3388 **NEROS RETURN 15** [3]3-9-3 (93) Y Take 25/1: 6060057: In tch, no impress fnl 1f: see 1113.   1¾   **86**
3002 **HIGH VOLTAGE 32** [7]3-9-4 (94) D M Oliver 20/1: 0-136008: Rcd in 2nd till over 2f out, sn no impress.   ½   **85**
3235 **VALJARV 22** [2]3-9-2 VIS (92) J Murtagh 7/1: 0004429: Dwelt start, al bhd: tried a visor.   2   **77**
3466 **DANZIG RIVER 13** [6]3-9-3 (93) J P Spencer 25/1: 5-200000: 10th: Bhd, nvr a factor: joc reported   4   **66**
mount hung left throughout: see 1154.
10 Ran   Time 1m 14 47()   Owned: The Equema Partnership   Trained: Newmarket

NEWMARKET   SATURDAY 07.08.04   Righthand, Stiff, Galloping Track

Official Going GOOD/FIRM (FIRM places).

3779   1.45 Champions Health Club Handicap Stakes 3yo+ 0-90 (C)   [104]
£13676 £4208 £2104   2m24y   Good/Firm 20   -33 Slow   Stands Side

3359 **COVENTINA 16** [11] J L Dunlop 3-8-10 (86) R L Moore 8/1: 0-002331: Chsd ldrs, imprvd to lead   **97**
dist, styd on strongly, drvn out: deserved win & apprec this step up to 2m: acts on fast & firm grnd, handles a
sharp or stiff/gall trk: unexposed at this trip & can progress: see 3359 & 923.
3556 **TUNGSTEN STRIKE 9** [2] Mrs A J Perrett 3-8-7 (83) Martin Dwyer 2/1 FAV: 00-01132: Tried to make   1¼   **91**
all, collared dist, kept on but not pace of wnr: well bckd, clr of rem: apprec this return to 2m, see 3556.
3340 **COALITION 17** [6] H Candy 5-9-6 (81) Dane O'Neill 7/1: 162/-0223: Held up, imprvd 2f out, kept on   3   **86**
but not pace to chall: another consistent run, subs not getting any respite from the h'capper: clrly stays 2m.
3637* **SUALDA 6** [8] R A Fahey 5-9-0 (5ex) (75) G Parkin 16/1: 5212314: Held up, imprvd 3f out, onepcd   ½   **79**
fnl 1f: longer 2m trip & prob stays: quick reapp & 5lb pen for 3637 (12f, sharp trk).
3387 **RED SCORPION 15** [7]5-8-3 (64) B Swarbrick(5) 33/1: 5023065: Chsd ldrs, onepcd fnl 1f.   hd   **67**
3635 **THEWHIRLINGDERVISH 6** [10]6-9-8 (83) J Quinn 9/1: 4031326: Handy, onepcd fnl 1.5f: qck reapp.   hd   **85**
3475 **DOVEDON HERO 13** [12]4-8-11 bl (72) M Hills 20/1: 2046027: Held up, nvr nr ldrs: btr 3475.   5   **69**
2085* **JACK DAWSON 70** [4]7-9-1 (76) T E Durcan 9/1: 43540-18: Chsd ldrs, wknd & eased fnl 1f: 4th in a   ½   **72**
h'cap hdle (rtd 134h) since 2085 (14f).
3125 **RANDOM QUEST 28** [1]6-9-11 (86) S Whitworth 8/1: 50-00029: Keen in rear, btn 2f out: btr 3125.   20   **62**
3454* **THE VARLET 14** [3]4-8-9 p (70) S Hitchcott(3) 33/1: 05-03610: 10th: Keen in rear, nvr a factor.   ½   **45**
3510 **MAMCAZMA 11** [5]6-10-0 (89) M Tebbutt 16/1: 02-00400: 11th: Keen & prom, wknd 3f out: btr 3119 (14f). 3   **61**
11 Ran   Time 3m 31.10 (8.60)   Owned: Capt J Macdonald-Buchanan   Trained: Arundel

3780   2.15 Team Events Handicap Stakes Fillies 3yo+ 0-85 (D)   [87]
£6760 £2080 £1040   1m str   Good/Firm 20   -08 Slow   Stands Side

3072 **GOLDEN ISLAND 29** [1] J W Hills 3-9-10 (83) M Hills 11/2 CO FAV: 0-32151: Nvr far away, went on   **90**
dist, styd on strongly despite drifting right, drvn out: well bckd: eff at 1m/10f on fast & gd/soft grnd: handles
a stiff/gall or sharp/turning trk: lightly rcd & op to further improvement, see 2748 (mdn).
3579* **SUMMER SHADES 8** [6] W M Brisbourne 6-9-4 (70) B Swarbrick(5) 11/2 CO FAV: 4435612: Held up,   nk   **75**
switched & gd hdwy 1.5f out, fin well & only just btn: continues in fine form, see 3579.
3346 **ELA PAPAROUNA 17** [9] H Candy 3-8-13 (72) Dane O'Neill 11/2 CO FAV: 3-306323: Led till 2f out,   1¼   **74**
not qckn ins fnl 1f: clr of rem: styd this longer 1m trip: see 3346.
3223* **SCOTLAND THE BRAVE 23** [8] J D Bethell 4-9-4 p (70) Martin Dwyer 6/1: 0350414: Front rank, led 2f   3   **66**
out till dist, no extra: op 8/1: seems ideally suited by 7f: see 3223 (1st time cheek pieces).
4953} **RUSSIAN RUBY 281** [5]3-9-11 (84) J F Egan 16/1: 045116-5: b f Vettori - Pink Sovietstaia (Soviet   1½   **77**
Star) Keen & prom, wknd fnl 1f: won a fillis mdn & 2 h'caps in '03: eff at 6/7f on fast & firm: handles a
stiff/gall or sharp trk, best with waiting tactics: rcd too keenly on reapp today, sharper next time back at 7f.
1 Oct'03 Brig 7.0fm 82-79 E: 1 Oct'03 Newm 6g/f 80-73 C: 1 Jul'03 Nott 6.1fm 75- D: 2 May'03 Newm 6g/f 88- D:
3490 **SISTER SOPHIA 12** [7]4-8-10 (62) R Mullen 14/1: 060-0036: Slow away, styd on late, nvr dngrs.   nk   **54**
3456 **IN THE PINK 14** [4]4-9-6 (72) S Hitchcott(3) 11/2 CO FAV: 0012027: Rear, nvr nr ldrs: btr 3456 (7f).   1¾   **60**
3291 **HOT LIPS PAGE 19** [3]3-9-1 (74) R L Moore 13/2: 005-5148: Prom till wknd dist: btr 2624.   5   **52**
3456 **KINDLELIGHT DEBUT 14** [2]4-9-8 (74) N Callan 8/1: 100-0039: Keen & prom, wknd qckly 2f out.   28   **12**
9 Ran   Time 1m 39.46 (2.26)   Owned: Mr D M Kerr and Mr N Brunskill   Trained: Lambourn

3781 2.50 Gr3 Swynford Paddocks Hotel Sweet Solera Stakes Fillies 2yo (A)
£23200 £8800 £4400 **7f str** **Good/Firm 20** **-02 Slow** Stands Side

3357 **MAIDS CAUSEWAY 16** [10] B W Hills 2-8-8 (98) S Drowne 5/1: 2121: Trkd ldrs, qcknd to lead dist, 105
styd on strongly, rdn out: eff over a stiff/gall 7f, 1m looks sure to suit: acts on fast & gd/soft grnd, stiff/gall
or fair trk: fast imprvg & now useful filly: deserves her ch in the Fillies Mile, see 3357 & 2676.

2763* **SLIP DANCE 20** [2] E Tyrrell 2-8-11 J F Egan 10/1: 314162: Held up, prog 1.5f, fin well into 2nd 1¼ 103
but not reach wnr: Irish chall, stays a stiff/gall 7f well: v useful filly, see 2763 (6f here).

2553 **PARK ROMANCE 50** [9] B J Meehan 2-8-8 (90) R L Moore 10/1: 2153: Held up & outpcd, strong run 2f ½ 98
out till 1f out, onepcd: abs: has a gd turn of foot & can find a race in listed grade, poss over 1m: see 2553.

3520 **ARBELLA 10** [6] P W Harris 2-8-8 Martin Dwyer 9/1: 244: Chsd ldrs, ev ch till onepcd fnl 1f: op nk 97
16/1: must surely be plcd to find at least a mdn: see 3520 & 3035.

3254 **INDIANNIE STAR 22** [3]2-8-8 (87) S Hitchcott 50/1: 1605135: Chsd ldr, led 2f out till dist, no 1¾ 93
extra: rider reportedly gvn a 1 day ban for not keeping str early on: longer 7f trip, see 3086 (5f, gd/soft).

3252* **WINDSCREAMER 22** [7]2-8-8 M Hills 3/1 FAV: 16: Held up, hdwy 2f out, no impress fnl 1f: not hd 92
disgraced in grade tho' rtd higher 3252 (debut).

2763 **ROYAL ALCHEMIST 42** [1]2-8-8 A Daly 14/1: 127: Slowly away, styd on late, nvr dngrs: 6 wk abs: hd 91
closer to today's rnr-up in 2763 (6f here).

3440 **VALENTIN 14** [5]2-8-8 Dane O'Neill 5/1: 128: Keen & prom, wknd fnl 1f: rcd much too keenly over 3 85
this longer 7f trip: btr 3440 & 3071.

3412* **STRAWBERRY DALE 15** [11]2-8-8 T E Durcan 9/1: 119: Keen in rear, short of room 1.5f out, nvr shd 85
dngrs: up in grade, rcd too keenly & did not get the run of today's race: see 3412.

3003 **EXTREME BEAUTY 32** [8]2-8-8 (93) J Quinn 10/1: 61000: 10th: Chsd ldrs, wknd 1.5f out. nk 84

3614 **PIDDIES PRIDE 7** [4]2-8-8 (70) F P Ferris 66/1: 6411320: 11th: Led till 2f out, wknd: rider 6 72
reportedly given a 1 day ban for not keeping str: see 3614 (nurs h'cap).

11 Ran Time 1m 25.50 (1.60) Owned: Lady Richard Wellesley Trained: Lambourn

---

3782 3.25 Totesport Silver Salver Stakes Handicap 3yo+ 0-105 (B) [103]
£19500 £6000 £3000 **7f str** **Good/Firm 20** **+06 Fast** Stands Side

3584 **DESERT LORD 8** [19] Sir Michael Stoute 4-8-7 (82) Martin Dwyer 6/1 FAV: 32210/-61: Chsd ldrs 87+
stands side, short of room 2f out, styd on v strongly to lead on line, rdn out: well bckd, gd time: eff at 6/7f on
gd & firm grnd: handles a stiff/gall or sharp/turning trk: benefited from recent reapp, has been given plenty of
time to come to himself: open to more improvement & can win again, see 3584 (6f, here).

3622 **ROYAL STORM 7** [18] Mrs A J Perrett 5-9-8 (97) S Drowne 13/2: 0146002: Chsd ldrs stands side, led shd 101
well ins fnl 1f, caught on line: bckd from 9/1: right back to form, clrly loves Newmarket: see 1490 (6f here).

3375 **ARMAGNAC 16** [6] M A Buckley 6-8-4 (79) A Daly 14/1: 6002323: Held up stands side, hdwy to chall nk 82
ins fnl 1f, just btn in a close fin: deserves success, prob back at ideal 6f: see 3375 & 3269.

3512 **WHAT A DANCER 11** [13] G A Swinbank 7-7-13 (74) J F McDonald(3) 11/1: 0440654: Trkd ldrs stands ½ 76
side, led dist till ins fnl 1f, no extra: fine run, btn around 1L: see 887 (AW).

3555 **WIZARD OF NOZ 9** [9]4-9-6 VIS (95) S W Kelly 14/1: 0-260555: Chsd ldrs stands side, ev ch fnl 1f, ¾ 95
drifted left & no extra cl-home: tried a visor: see 3555.

4478} **FOLIO 315** [17]4-8-12 (87) R Mullen 50/1: 030000-6: b g Perugino - Bayleaf (Efisio) In tch shd 87+
stands side, short of room ins fnl 1f, styd on well, nrst fin: reapp: stks plcd at best in '03 (rtd 93): auct mdn &
2 stks wnr in '02 (Gr3 plcd, R Johnson Houghton): eff at 5/6f, stays 7f: acts on firm, soft & prob any trk:
eye-catching run, v well h'capped for W Musson & is one to keep on side: see 3584 (6f, here).
1 Jul'02 Bath 5g/f 96- D: 1 Jul'02 Wind 5g/f 94- E: 2 Jun'02 Nott 5gd 83- F: 2 May'02 Wind 5g/f 87- B:

3117* **LOOK HERES CAROL 28** [15]4-9-2 (91) G Carter 14/1: 4-336317: Chsd ldrs stands side, kept on fnl 1f. nk 90

3447* **MOLCON 14** [11]3-8-3 (84) J F Egan 16/1: 5344018: Mid-div, stands side, no pace to chall: see 3447. nk 82

2777 **KOOL 14** [2]5-9-0 (89) R L Moore 12/1: 0553549: Trkd ldr far side, led that group dist, kept on ½ 86+
but no ch with stands side: 6 wk abs: first home on far side: see 2777.

3441 **CAPRICHO 14** [10]7-9-13 (102) J Quinn 14/1: 140-0400: 10th: Held up stands side, nvr nr ldrs. shd 99

3584 **STARBECK 8** [16]6-8-6 (81) N Callan 25/1: 4005400: 11th: Rear stands side, nvr a factor. ½ 77

3441 **MARSHMAN 14** [14]5-8-11 (86) M Hills 14/1: 4-030000: 12th: Bhd stands side, nvr nr ldrs. hd 81

3073 **WATCHING 29** [20]7-8-5 (80) G Parkin 25/1: 2550000: 13th: Held up stands side, nvr dangerous: hd 74
new stable, prev with D Nicholls: see 1683 (5f).

3117 **KAREEB 28** [7]7-7-12 (73) C Catlin 9/1: 6004060: 14th: Chsd ldrs stands side, btn fnl 1f. 1 65

3441 **MASTER ROBBIE 6** [1]5-9-0 VIS (89) S Hitchcott(3) 14/1: 1600000: 15th: Held up far side, nvr hd 80
dangerous: tried visor & on the wrong side: see 2090 (C/D).

3634 **WATERSIDE 6** [8]5-8-7 (82) S Whitworth 25/1: 3112460: 16th: Led 5f stands side, wknd: qck reapp. 1½ 70

3077 **MYSTERINCH 29** [3]4-9-1 (90) I Mongan 3/1: 3002000: 17th: Led fnl dist far side, wknd. ½ 77

3061 **ATAVUS 30** [5]7-8-13 (88) A McCarthy 25/1: 4-060500: 18th: Chsd ldrs, led briefly dist, wknd. nk 74

3443* **HEY PRESTO 14** [4]4-7-12 (73) Lisa Jones 12/1: 0005610: 19th: Chsd ldrs far side, btn 2f out. 2 55

3441 **TAHIRAH 14** [12]4-8-10 (85) T E Durcan 14/1: 110-0000: 20th: Chsd ldrs stands side, wknd 2f out. 28 17

20 Ran Time 1m 24.88 (0.98) Owned: Cheveley Park Stud Trained: Newmarket

---

3783 4.00 Andromeda Maiden Stakes 3yo+ (D)
£5629 £1732 £866 **1m4f** **Good/Firm 20** **+04 Fast** Stands Side

3243 **MANDATUM 22** [9] L M Cumani 3-8-10 Martin Dwyer 9/4 FAV: 221: Front rank, led halfway, held on 82
gamely fnl 1f, all out: well bckd, gd time: deserved win & apprec this return to 12f: acts on gd & fast, handles a
sharpish or stiff/gall trk: half brother to decent stayer Boreaf & can improve further as he steps up in trip.

3114 **TURNSTILE 28** [10] R Hannon 3-8-10 (72) R L Moore 9/2: 4-42032: Nvr far away, chall fnl 1f & just ½ 79
btn in a tight fin: op 11/2: can find a race: see 3114.

102 **DAY ONE 255** [6] G Wragg 3-8-10 J F Egan 14/1: 0-3: ch c Daylami - Myself (Nashwan) Held up, 1¾ 77+
styd on nicely fnl 2f on reapp: unplcd on sole juv start (AW mdn): stays a stiff/gall 12f on fast grnd: not given
a hard time & superbly bred: sure to improve.

3236 **GANYMEDE 22** [4] M L W Bell 3-8-10 (77) R Mullen 6/1: 2322204: Chsd ldrs, onepcd fnl 1f: clr rem. 1½ 75

2992 **JAYER GILLES 32** [1]4-9-7 Dane O'Neill 7/2: 225: Chsd ldrs, wknd 3f out: op 11/4: btr 2992 & 2623. 13 55

2596 **SIMONS SEAT 49** [12]5-9-7 (62) M Hills 20/1: 5030-666: Slowly away, al bhd: 7 wk abs: new 17 25

stable, prev with C Drew: see 2596 (14f here).

3281 **LAHOB 21** [11]4-9-7 (58) S W Kelly 66/1: 2326-067: Led till halfway, hmpd 3f out & wknd qckly. *¾* **24**

2867 **WODHILL HOPE 37** [8]4-9-2 M Tebbutt 100/1: 438: Slowly away, al bhd: see 2867. *5* **11**

3335 **CEMGRAFT 17** [7]3-8-6 (1ow) S Drowne 11/1: 59: Sn bhd, nvr dangerous: see 3335. *8* **0**

2386 **JACOBIN 56** [2]3-8-10 S Whitworth 66/1: 00: 10th: b c Tamayaz - Simply Follow Me (Green Dancer) *¾* **3**
Prom, wknd 4f out: 8 wk abs: no form yet: with P J McBride.

RIVIERA RED [5]4-9-7 A McCarthy 66/1: 0: 11th: b g Rainbow Quest - Banquise (Last Tycoon) *dist* **0**
Slowly away, al well bhd, t.o. on debut: dam won over 2m: unrcd prev for J Dunlop, now with L Montague Hall.

GRAND MUSIC [3]4-9-7 I Mongan 50/1: 0: 12th: b c Grand Lodge - Abury (Law Society) Slowly *dist* **0**
away, al t.o. on debut: 70,000 gns purchase: dam a smart mid-dist performer: with J Sheehan.

12 Ran Time 2m 30.22 (2.02) Owned: Aston House Stud Trained: Newmarket

3784

4.30 Long Melford Maiden Stakes 3yo (D)
£5434 £1672 £836 **6f str** **Good/Firm 20** **-12 Slow** Stands Side

3452 **CONJUROR 14** [8] A M Balding 3-9-0 R J Killoran(7) 16/1: U1: b c Efisio - Princess Athena **86**
(Ahonoora) Trkd ldrs, qcknd to lead ins fnl 1f, won going away: clrly none the worse for unfortunate debut: eff over a stiff/gall 6f on fast grnd: showed a decent turn of foot.

2486 **IMTALKINGGIBBERISH 52** [3] J R Jenkins 3-9-0 (85) Martin Dwyer 3/1: 0502: b g Pursuit of Love - *1¼* **79**
Royal Orchid (Shalford) Tried ot make all, not pace to repel wnr cl-home: well bkcd, 7 wk abs: confirmed imprvd form of 2486 & shld find a mdn, poss back at 7f: acts on fast grnd & on a stiff/gall trk: runs well fresh.

3522 **FAREWELL GIFT 10** [2] R Hannon 3-9-0 (81) R L Moore 6/4 FAV: 3232333: Chsd ldrs, ev ch fnl 1f, *shd* **79**
not qckn cl-home: well bckd: yet another consistent eff but proving difficult to win with: see 3522.

2692 **TROPICAL STORM 44** [1] J Noseda 3-9-0 (70) S W Kelly 8/1: 24-304: Front rank, onepcd fnl 1f: abs. *1¾* **73**

2586 **RACHELS VERDICT 49** [5]3-8-9 Dane O'Neill 7/2: 45: Keen & prom, onepcd fnl 1f: 7 wk abs: more *nk* **66**
expected after encouraging debut in 2586, but prob rcd too keenly.

3282 **TIDES 21** [4]3-8-9 R Mullen 50/1: 06: b f Bahamian Bounty - Petriece (Mummy's Pet) Chsd ldrs, *7* **46**
btn dist: mod form to date: sprint bred, with W Musson.

2722 **CLASSIC EXPRESSION 43** [7]3-8-9 G Carter 33/1: 67: Al outpcd: 6 wk abs. *3* **37**

BIRD KEY [6]3-8-9 J F Egan 14/1: 8: Slowly away, al bhd & fin last on debut. *3* **28**

8 Ran Time 1m 12.99 (1.99) Owned: Kennet Valley Thorougbreds I Trained: Kingsclere

3785

5.00 Newmarketracecourses Co Uk Handicap Stakes 3yo+ 0-70 (E) **[70]**
£4154 £1278 £639 **1m2f** **Good/Firm 20** **-38 Slow** Stands Side

1693 **WELLINGTON HALL 87** [10] P W Chapple Hyam 6-9-6 (62) A McCarthy 11/4 FAV: 0500-101: Chsd ldrs, **69**
went on 2f out, held on well fnl 1f despite drifting right, drvn out: op 7/4, 3 month abs: apprec this return to a more gall trk: eff at 10/11f on fast & hvy grnd: runs well fresh, see 1693 & 1135.

3587 **PIRI PIRI 8** [2] P J McBride 4-9-11 (67) S Whitworth 11/2: 0-623032: Slowly away, hed from rear *shd* **72**
1.5f out, ev ch fnl 1f & just btn in a thrilling fin: op 7/1: fine run conceding wnr 5lbs, see 3587.

3367 **JACKIE KIELY 16** [3] P S McEntee 3-9-0 t (65) F P Ferris(3) 10/1: 1011003: Slowly away, hdwy to *1½* **68**
chall ent fnl 1f, no extra when short of room cl-home: see 3238.

3276 **IFTIKHAR 21** [7] W M Brisbourne 5-8-10 (52) S W Kelly 20/1: 224-0004: Slowly away, styd on late, *hd* **54**
nrst fin: back to form, prob on a fair mark now: see 1884.

3512 **REBATE 11** [5]4-9-2 t (58) J F Egan 8/1: 3363505: Keen in rear, nrst fin: op 11/1: btr 2979. *shd* **60**

3238 **GALEY RIVER 22** [13]5-7-12 (2oh) (38) Dean Williams(6) 25/1: 3504506: Chsd ldr, short of room & *½* **41**
lost place 2f out, rallied fnl 1f: did not get the run of today's race: sole win came in banded company in 1072.

3201 **RAJAYOGA 24** [12]3-8-8 (59) M Hills 10/1: 440-0047: Keen in rear, late hdwy: op 16/1: see 3201. *2* **57**

3238 **WELCOME SIGNAL 22** [9]4-9-9 p (65) Dane O'Neill 11/2: 035-0558: Chsd ldr, led 3f out till 2f out, wknd. *5* **55**

DARAB 307 [11]4-9-9 (65) Martin Dwyer 20/1: 113300-9: ch g Alywar - Damara (Pyjama Hunt) Dwelt, *3* **50**
recovered & prom till halfway, no ch after: unplcd in a recent juv nov hdle: won 3 times in native Poland (5/10f): acts on gd & fast grnd: with R Cowell.

3530 **DAIMAJIN 10** [8]5-8-0 (42) J McAuley 25/1: 0000060: 10th: Prom, ev ch till wknd 1.5f out. *2½* **23**

3437 **MARITIME BLUES 14** [4]4-9-6 (62) R Mullen 11/1: 0106300: 11th: Led till 3f out, wknd. *1¼* **41**

3471 **HAYDN 13** [6]3-8-13 (64) I Mongan 20/1: 5005060: 12th: Keen in rear, btn 2f out: new stable. *dist* **0**

12 Ran Time 2m 07.75(5.85) Owned: Allan Darke & Tom Matthews Trained: Newmarket

LINGFIELD **Polytrack** **SATURDAY 07.08.04 Lefthand, V Sharp Track**

Official Going Standard

3786

5.50 Lingfield-Racecourse Co Uk Maiden Stakes 2yo (D)
£3897 £1199 £600 **1m aw rnd** **Standard** **Inapplicable** Outside

3329 **RUSSIAN CONSORT 17** [6] A King 2-9-0 J D Smith 5/2 FAV: 21: Keen early, chsd ldrs, hdwy to lead **88a**
2f out, rdn clr: nicely bckd, op 11/4: confirmed debut promise: eff at 7f, apprec step up to 1m & shld get further: acts on polytrack: clearly going the right way: see 3329.

3285 **ZALAAL 21** [8] Saeed bin Suroor 2-9-0 R L Moore 3/1: 62: Chsd ldrs, rdn & styd on, not pace of *2½* **82a**
wnr: styd longer 1m trip, handles gd grnd & polytrack: can find a race: see 3285.

ELRAFA MUJAHID 0 [2] Julian Poulton 2-8-9 A Daly 50/1: 3: b f Mujahid - Fancier Bit (Lion *2½* **72a**
Cavern) Led till 2f out, kept on: cheaply bought Mar foal, dam unrcd, half sister to a 14f wnr: eff at 1m, stay further: acts on polytrack, promising start.

3330 **SAADIGG 17** [3] M A Jarvis 2-9-0 N Callan 4/1: 34: Chsd ldrs, rdn & no extra over 1f out: op 7/2. *2½* **72a**

3470 **ELTIZAAM 13** [4]2-9-0 N Pollard 5/1: 65: Trkd ldrs, rdn & no extra over 1f out: see 3470. *nk* **71a**

JUST DO IT 0 [12]2-9-0 T E Durcan 16/1: 6: b c Timber Country - Poised (Rahy) Slow away, held *4* **63a**
up wide, no impress fnl 2f: Jan 1st foal, dam plcd at 9f as a 3yo: sire high-class US performer around 1m/10f.

3500 **TERMINATE 11** [10]2-9-0 J Quinn 7/1: 07: Keen, trkd ldrs wide travelling well, wknd qckly fnl *5* **53a**
2f: again suffered awkward passage, likely capable of much btr: see 3500.

LOITOKITOK 0 [5]2-9-0 C Catlin 50/1: 8: b g Piccolo - Bonita Bee (King of Spain) V slow away & *7* **39a**

al bhd: Mar foal, half brother to multiple wnr h'capper Lady McNair, this 1m trip shld suit in time.
KRASIVIS BOY 0 [7]2-9-0 Lisa Jones 33/1: 9: Al bhd. *shd* **39a**
3517 **LITTLE WALTHAM 10** [9]2-8-9 D Sweeney 100/1: 00: 10th: Sn rear & struggling, nvr factor. *24* **0a**
LOUISE PARIS 0 [1]2-8-9 S Righton 100/1: 0: 11th: Pulled hard & cl-up till 3f out. *17* **0a**
11 Ran Time 1m 41.58 (5.38) Owned: Four Mile Racing Trained: Barbury Castle

3787 **6.20 Whips & Tees Median Auction Maiden Stakes 3-4yo (F)**
£2982 £852 £426 **1m2f aw rnd** **Standard** **Inapplicable** Inside

3992} **EXTERIOR 341** [9] Mrs A J Perrett 3-8-12 R L Moore 11/10 FAV: 3-1: ch c Distant View - Alvernia (Alydar) Trkd ldrs wide, prog & led 2f out, rdn well clr, easily: reapp/AW bow, nicely bckd: auct mdn plcd sole '03 start (rtd 75): apprec step up to 10f, 12f+ could suit: acts on fast grnd & polytrack, sharp/undul trk: goes well fresh: clearcut success, interesting for h'caps. **87a+**
3208 **DISPARITY 23** [5] J R Fanshawe 3-8-7 t T E Durcan 7/1: 042: Trkd ldr, outpcd when hmpd over 2f out, narrowly prevailed for remote 2nd: prob handles polytrack & fast , low grade h'caps shld now suit. *12* **64a**
3105 **BROUGH SUPREME 28** [6] H Morrison 3-8-12 (65) S Drowne 3/1: 0-54603: Led till 2f out, sn no ch with easy wnr: dropped in trip: handles polytrack: see 1384. *hd* **68a**
3581 **PORT SODRICK 8** [8] M D I Usher 3-8-12 A Daly 10/1: 664: Rear, prob 4f out, no impress fnl 2f. *2* **65a**
2741 **SHALATI PRINCESS 42** [4]3-8-7 (41) L Keniry(3) 16/1: 6040305: Mid-div, lost tch over 2f out: abs. *9* **47a$**
3090} **DINGLEY LASS 381** [3]4-9-2 J Quinn 33/1: 00-6: ch f Fleetwood - Riverine (Risk Me) Sn rdn & al bhd: reapp: unplcd '03 (lightly rcd, rtd 67 & 26a, mdns): with H Morrison. *2* **44a**
3195 **THE NIBBLER 24** [7]3-8-12 G Baker 16/1: 467: Rear, eff 4f out, sn bhd: longer trip: btr 2854 (1m). *1* **48a**
3405 **BLUE TRACK 15** [1]3-8-12 N Callan 50/1: 008: Trkd ldrs, wknd qckly 4f out, lame: AW bow. *dist* **0a**
8 Ran Time 2m 09.59 (6.79) Owned: Mr K Abdulla Trained: Pulborough

LINGFIELD Polytrack SATURDAY 07.08.04 Lefthand, Sharp, Undulating Track

Official Going Good/Firm

3788 **6.50 Lingfield Golf Club Handicap Stakes 3yo+ 35-55 (F)** **[58]**
£3185 £910 £455 **7f140y str** **Firm** **Inapplicable** Centre

3548 **CUT RIDGE 9** [5] J S Wainwright 5-9-2 (46) D Holland 11/2: 0000321: Al prom centre, led over 1f out, rdn & in command ins last: op 10/1: eff btwn 5/7.5f on firm & gd/soft grnd: see 2993. **56**
3288 **ENNA 21** [15] Mrs Stef Liddiard 5-9-1 (45) S Drowne 16/1: 6004042: Held up, styd on for press ins last, nvr threatened wnr: acts on firm & soft grnd: see 1284. *2½* **48**
3604 **BAHAMA REEF 7** [6] B Gubby 3-9-4 (55) C Catlin 20/1: 0520333: Chsd ldrs, styd on onepace, no threat: stays 7.5f: see 2016. *nk* **57**
3733* **LORD CHAMBERLAIN 2** [13] J M Bradley 11-9-12 (6ex)bl (56) C J Davies(7) 10/1: 0302014: Rdn towards rear, kept on late, nvr a threat: ran to form of win in 3733. *½* **57**
3541* **SCARROTTOO 9** [16]6-9-11 (55) R L Moore 4/1 FAV: 5140315: Rear, mod late prog: btr 3541 (clmr). *½* **55**
3443 **MOBO BACO 14** [9]7-9-10 (54) V Slattery 14/1: 0001506: Slow away, mid-div, no impress dist: btr 2909. *shd* **54**
3456 **SHIRLEY OAKS 14** [11]6-9-6 (50) N Chalmers(5) 14/1: 3120067: Held up, only mod prog: btr 2397. *shd* **49**
3604 **HEAD BOY 7** [1]3-9-8 (59) Lisa Jones 6/1: 0565428: Mid-div, eff over 2f out, sn btn: btr 3604. *nk* **57**
3558 **TOJONESKI 9** [7]5-9-2 p (46) J F McDonald(3) 5/1: 3342039: Led/dsptd lead till over 1f out: see 2440. *¾* **42**
3643 **MAYZIN 5** [3]4-9-3 (47) D Sweeney 16/1: 0000000: 10th: Held up, eff 3f out, no prog: qck reapp. *1¼* **40**
2644 **KINSMAN 46** [12]7-9-7 bl (51) J P Guillambert(3) 16/1: 1546000: 11th: Slow away & al bhd, 6 wk abs. *3* **38**
3449 **Whiplash 14** [8]3-9-2 (53) L Keniry(3) 33/1:0 3257 **Wood Fern 22** [14]4-9-8 (52) T E Durcan 20/1:0
3571 **Toppling 8** [2]6-9-6 p(50) N Callan 16/1:0
1938 **Easily Averted 76** [10]3-9-2 (53) R Lucey Butler(4) 33/1:0
15 Ran Time 30.24 (2.44) Owned: Mrs Chris Harrington Trained: Malton

3789 **7.20 Play Golf And Come Racing Classified Stakes 3yo+ 0-65 (F)**
£3601 £1108 £554 **6f str** **Firm** **Inapplicable** Centre

3346 **MISS JUDGEMENT 17** [6] W R Muir 3-8-9 (62) R Miles(3) 10/1: 3213001: Mid-div, rdn & qcknd to lead over 1f out, edged right under press, held on well: suited by 6f, tried 7f: acts on firm & fast grnd: see 2630. **67**
3705 **MISTRAL SKY 3** [4] Mrs Stef Liddiard 5-9-9 vis (72) S Drowne 15/8 FAV: 3540122: Reared start, sn trkd ldrs, rdn & styd on well ins last, not reach wnr: op 5/2, quick reapp: remains in gd heart: see 3705 & 3518. *¾* **77**
3479 **STOKESIES WISH 12** [1] J L Spearing 4-8-13 (62) Lisa Jones 8/1: 2054063: Handy & rdn to chall when carried right over 1f out, no extra nr fin: see 2535 & 1127. *¾* **65**
3577* **FOLEY MILLENNIUM 8** [5] M Quinn 6-9-10 (73) N Pollard 5/2: 1110214: Led till over 1f out, wknd: nicely bckd, tho' op 13/8: stays 6f, best at 5f: btr 3577 (5f). *2½* **68**
3446 **FAIR COMPTON 14** [8]3-8-9 (60) R L Moore 14/1: 4-465455: Rear, nvr pace to threaten: flattered 3446. *1¼* **53**
2598 **SWEET PICKLE 48** [2]3-8-13 (69) D Holland 4/1: 3010-246: Cl-up, wknd 2f out: op 5/1, abs: btr 2598. *shd* **57**
3744 **CUT AND DRIED 1** [7]3-8-12 (65) L Keniry(3) 25/1: 05464507: Chsd ldrs, btn 2f out: btr 3198. *6* **40**
7 Ran Time 1m 09.45 (0.65) Owned: Double D Partnership Trained: Lambourn

3790 **7.50 Furlongs And Fairways Handicap Stakes 3yo+ 35-55 (F)** **[60]**
£3206 £916 £458 **6f str** **Firm** **Inapplicable** Centre

3602 **JAZZY MILLENNIUM 7** [2] B R Millman 7-9-7 vis (53) D Holland 7/2 JT FAV: 3633041: Mid-div, hdwy over 1f out, drvn ot lead cl-home, all out: suited by 6/7f on firm, soft & polytrack, sharp/undul trk: see 2262. **59**
3602 **ENJOY THE BUZZ 7** [13] J M Bradley 5-9-4 (50) R L Moore 7/2 JT FAV: 1021032: Held up, drvn & styd on from over 1f out, just failed: acts on firm, gd/soft & fibresand: see 3050. *nk* **55**
3463 **LE MERIDIEN 13** [10] J S Wainwright 6-9-5 (51) N Pollard 10/1: 0065103: Handy, led 2f out, rdn & *shd* **56**

LINGFIELD Polytrack SATURDAY 07.08.04 Lefthand, Sharp, Undulating Track

hdd cl-home: appreciated return to 6f & remains on fair mark: see 3416.

3643 **NIGHT CAP 5** [8] T D McCarthy 5-8-11 (43) J P Guillambert(3) 9/1: 0020304: Mid-div, switched & styd on for press, not able to chall: quick reapp, op 12/1: see 328.	1	45
3561 **MORITAT 9** [7]4-9-8 (54) N Callan 11/2: 206-0635: Mid-div, onepcd for press fnl 2f: see 3561 (5f).	nk	55
3640 **HARBOUR HOUSE 5** [1]5-9-0 (46) A Daly 10/1: 3130266: Mid-div, not pace to chall fnl 2f: qck reapp.	1	44
3301* **MY GIRL PEARL 19** [11]4-9-2 (48) R Miles(3) 8/1: 4206417: Led till 2f out, no extra: btr 3301.	hd	45
3301 **BOLD WOLF 19** [4]3-8-8 (44) S Whitworth 33/1: 4440008: Mid-div, rdn & no impress fnl 3f.	2½	33
3023 **CEDRIC COVERWELL 31** [14]4-8-9 BL (41) J Quinn 33/1: 0000059: Dwelt, chsd ldrs till 1f out: blnks.	3½	19
3301 **CHATSHOW 19** [3]3-9-3 T (53) A McCarthy 25/1: 0040500: 10th: Slow away & at rear: t-strap: btr 3091.	nk	30
3543 **BLACK OVAL 9** [6]3-8-13 VIS (49) Lisa Jones 25/1: 3005000: 11th: Chsd ldrs till halfway: tried a visor.	½	24
3447 **Knight Onthe Tiles 14** [5]3-9-5 bl(55) G Baker 25/1:0 3403 **Old Harry 15** [9]4-8-10 t(42) C Catlin 33/1:0		
3347 **Night Worker 17** [12]3-9-0 (50) T E Durcan 16/1:0 3602 **Tappit 7** [15]5-9-0 (46) M Savage(5) 33/1:0		

15 Ran Time 1m 09.85 (1.05) Owned: Millennium Millionaires Partnership Trained: Cullompton

LINGFIELD Polytrack SATURDAY 07.08.04 Lefthand, V Sharp Track

Official Going Standard

3791	8.20 Lingfield Racecourse Handicap Stakes 3yo+ 0-85 (D)		[85]
	£5736 £1765 £883 **7f aw rnd** **Standard** **Inapplicable** Inside		

3001 **HARRISON POINT 32** [5] P W Chapple Hyam 4-9-12 (83) A McCarthy 3/1 FAV: 0-112201: Chsd ldrs, prog to chall dist, sn led, drvn out: nicely bckd, op 4/1: eff at 7f/1m on firm, fast & polytrack, loves Lingfield.		92a
3708 **BOBS BUZZ 3** [11] S C Williams 4-8-11 (68) A Daly 10/1: 10-05352: Dwelt, rear, hdwy wide over 2f out & kept on for press, not pace of wnr: quick reapp: gd AW bow, acts on firm, gd/soft & polytrack: see 2855.	1¼	73a
2223 **LAST APPOINTMENT 64** [14] J M P Eustace 4-9-7 (78) D Holland 7/1: 4210-503: Led after 1f, bmpd when strongly prsd over 1f out, sn hdd & no extra: op 10/1: abs: acts on firm, fast & polytrack: see 1817.	½	82a
3558 **ALAFZAR 9** [3] P D Evans 6-8-5 vis t (62) N Callan 20/1: 1304044: Mid-div, trav well, onepcd fnl 2f.	¾	65a
3216 **KENTUCKY KING 23** [12]4-9-10 (81) R Miles(3) 20/1: 0300035: Rear, mod late prog, prefer 1m.	¾	83a
3426 **TRE COLLINE 14** [2]5-9-8 (79) G Baker 14/1: 5146106: Mid-div, not pace to chall: btr 3286 (clmr, 1m).	nk	80a
3672 **BLONDE EN BLONDE 4** [9]4-8-11 bl (68) J P Guillambert(3) 14/1: 0030567: Mid-div, no impress dist.	½	68a
3286 **VARZANO 21** [13]4-9-3 (74) L Keniry(3) 16/1: 25160-28: Chsd ldr, btn over 1f out: new yard.	hd	73a
3257 **GALLERY BREEZE 22** [8]5-8-13 (70) V Slattery 20/1: 1120-109: Mid-div, rdn & strugg fnl 2f: btr 2755.	2	65a
3562* **ST SAVARIN 9** [7]3-8-10 (79) N Pollard 5/1: 1003310: 10th: Led 1f, btn over 1f out: new mark.	nk	70a
3088 **CHEESE N BISCUITS 29** [10]4-9-9 p (80) R L Moore 7/1: 0020000: 11th: Al bhd: btr 1616.	3½	67a
3441 **TARANAKI 14** [4]6-9-4 (75) S Whitworth 9/2: 4015000: 12th: Mid-div, rdn & hmpd 2f out, no ch after.	6	52a
3142 **HAVE SOME FUN 27** [6]4-8-2 (59) J Quinn 40/1: 6-32000: 13th: Mid-div, struggling fnl 3f: btr 476 (10f).	hd	35a

13 Ran Time 1m 27.38(4.58) Owned: Sangster Family M O'Donovan F Cook Trained: Newmarket

HAYDOCK SATURDAY 07.08.04 Lefthand, Flat, Galloping Track

Official Going Good

3792	1.55 Coral Co Uk Handicap Stakes 3yo+ 0-100 (C)		[98]
	£17862 £5496 £2748 **5f str** **Firm 09** +00 Fast Centre		

3622 **SMOKIN BEAU 7** [17] N P Littmoden 7-9-9 (93) J Fanning 25/1: 0004001: Made most stands side, styd on well fnl 1f, rdn out: eff over 5/6f on any grnd/trk, likes Goodwood: best up with/forcing the pace: right back to form & v well h'capped now: see 1137.		102
3537 **DEVISE 10** [8] M S Saunders 5-8-9 (79) R Miles(3) 11/1: 0155402: With ldr stands side, styd on over 1f out, not btn far: bckd from 16/1: fine run: see 2698, 1914.	½	86
3622 **CORRIDOR CREEPER 7** [2] J M Bradley 7-9-10 p (94) F Norton 25/1: 6023603: Chsd ldrs far side, kept on over 1f out: a fine run: see 2894, 1594.	¾	99
3628 **WHISTLER 6** [1] J M Bradley 7-9-6 p (90) R Hills 12/1: 1014034: Held up far side, hdwy & short of room 2f out, switched & styd on over 1f out, nrst fin: won this race last term off a 12lb lower mark & another useful effort: v tough: see 2628, 2894.	½	93
3241 **ZARZU 22** [6]5-8-9 (77) R Thomas(5) 25/1: 3000165: Bhd stands side, styd on late, nrst fin: encouraging, all 5 wins on sharper trks: see 2968.	nk	81
3150 **MAKTAVISH 26** [10]5-8-11 (81) P Hanagan 20/1: 1300046: With ldr stands side, onepcd over 1f out.	shd	83
3622 **RACCOON 7** [20]4-9-6 vis (90) S Sanders 100/30 FAV: 1-411007: Chsd ldr stands side, some late gains: hvly bckd, qck reapp: best form earlier when forcing the pace: see 2082, 1917.	shd	91
3628 **DANCING MYSTERY 6** [14]10-8-12 (82) S Carson 50/1: 0014508: Held up stands side, some late gains.	1	80
3628 **MALAPROPISM 6** [6]4-8-11 (81) A Culhane 16/1: 0006049: Led far side group till dist, no extra.	½	77
2894 **MATTY TUN 36** [11]5-9-3 (87) W Supple 20/1: 5500050: 10th: Slow away, in tch 3f stands side, wknd.	1	80
3628 **CONNECT 6** [18]7-9-10 bl (94) P Robinson 20/1: 4041400: 11th: Bhd stands side, nvr a factor.	½	85
3622 **BLACKHEATH 7** [13]8-9-4 (88) L Treadwell(5) 25/1: 6414500: 12th: Nvr a factor stands side: see 3466.	shd	78
3427* **AWAKE 14** [4]7-9-1 (85) A Nicholls 12/1: 0162010: 13th: In tch far side, wknd dist: btr 3427.	nk	74
3002 **LOCAL POET 32** [9]3-8-13 t (86) G Gibbons 25/1: 1505000: 14th: Handy stands side, wknd dist.	1	72
3279 **HENRY HALL 21** [19]8-9-9 (93) Kim Tinkler 33/1: 0030505: 15th: Al bhd stands side: see 2359.	¾	77
3622 **ARTIE 7** [3]5-9-3 (87) R Winston 10/1: 2100100: 16th: Led early far side, wknd appr fnl 1f: likes easier grnd: see 2622, 3073 (gd/soft).	hd	70
3628 **CAPE ROYAL 6** [7]4-9-4 (88) J Fortune 9/1: 6020320: 17th: Keen held up, nvr a factor: btr 3628.	hd	70
3628+ **SALVIATI 6** [15]7-8-13 (6exp) (83) E Ahern 15/2: 0004510: 18th: Dwelt, bhd stands side, short of room over 1f out, sn btn: much btr 3628.	nk	64
3150* **PTARMIGAN RIDGE 26** [5]8-9-2 (86) M Fenton 20/1: 1006510: 19th: Bhd far side, hmpd over 1f out, no impress: btr 3150.	2	61
3466 **PICCLED 13** [12]6-8-13 (83) D Allan 33/1: 001050R: Ref to race.		0

20 Ran Time 59.24 (0.44) Owned: Turf 2000 Limited Trained: Newmarket

3793 2.30 Gr3 Petros Rose Of Lancaster Stakes 3yo+ (A)
£37700 £14300 £7150 1m2f120y Firm 09 +05 Fast Outside

3439* **MISTER MONET 14** [6] M Johnston 3-8-7 (106) J Fanning 1/1 FAV: 31-2111: Led early, led again over 3f out, rdn clr appr fnl 1f, shade cmftbly: stays 10.5f well on firm & gd, likes gall trks: lightly rcd, fast improving & this was a high-class eff, shld be followed for Gr 1/2 success shortly: see 3439. **121**
3264* **MUQBIL 21** [4] J L Dunlop 4-9-3 (114) R Hills 5/2: 234-0112: Handy, eff to chase wnr over 2f out, hung left & onepace over 1f out: clr rem: smart, ran close to best bhd a high-class rival: see 3264 (List). 1½ **115**
3533 **CHECKIT 10** [2] M R Channon 4-9-3 (112) A Culhane 13/2: 3403403: Held up, eff 2f out, onepace. 5 **108**
1350 **FRANKLINS GARDENS 105** [5] M H Tompkins 4-9-3 (108) P Robinson 14/1: 21/110-44: Held up, modest late gains: over 3 mth abs: wants 12f: see 1350. 1¾ **105**
2470 **LATEEN SAILS 53** [3]4-9-3 t (110) K McEvoy 12/1: 0141-005: Sn led, hdd 3f out, wknd: 7 wk abs. 1 **103**
2916 **CHANCELLOR 35** [1]6-9-7 (110) J Fortune 40/1: 4-010006: In tch, wknd 2f out: likes easier grnd. ¾ **105**
6 Ran Time 2m 10.4 (0.4) Owned: Syndicate 2002 Trained: Middleham

3794 3.00 Totesport Stakes Heritage Handicap 3yo+ 0-105 (B) **[105]**
£43500 £16500 £8250 1m2f120y Firm 09 -06 Slow Outside

3430* **DUNASKIN 14** [2] D Eddy 4-8-6 (83) D Kinsella 50/1: 0056311: Made all, rdn clr 3f out, kept on ins last, rdn out: stays a sharp 12f, best dominating at 1m/10.5f on firm or gd/soft, any trk: tough & genuine, given a fine enterprising ride here: see 3430, 1668. **94**
3506* **COAT OF HONOUR 11** [11] Sir Mark Prescott 4-9-6 (97) S Sanders 5/1: 1132-012: Prom, eff 2f out, chall dist, not pace of wnr: useful & improving: acts on firm & gd/soft: shld continue to give a gd account. 1 **106**
2896 **SHAHZAN HOUSE 36** [14] M A Jarvis 5-9-5 p (96) P Robinson 14/1: 10-32333: In tch, eff 2f out, kept on, not pace of wnr: tough & consistent: handles firm & hvy: see 1296. nk **104**
3553 **MUTAFANEN 9** [12] E A L Dunlop 3-9-2 VIS (103) W Supple 14/1: 1333044: Held up, eff over 2f out, kept on ins last, no threat: gd run in first time visor: see 3553, 2520. 1½ **106**
3474* **KING OF DREAMS 13** [4]3-8-7 (94) R Ffrench 9/2 FAV: 42-1015: In tch, hdwy 3f out, kept on same pace over 1f out: hvly bckd: useful & improving: handles firm & gd, 12f shld suit: see 3474. 1¼ **96**
3506 **BONECRUSHER 11** [3]5-10-1 vis (106) A Beech(3) 9/1: 5205536: Held up, rdn over 3f out, onepace. 1¼ **105**
3464 **MUTASALLIL 13** [8]4-9-9 t (100) R Hills 9/1: 3-1127: In tch, eff 2f out, onepace: shade btr 3464. nk **98**
3506 **WINDY BRITAIN 11** [18]5-8-11 (88) J Fortune 10/1: 31-04268: Slow away, held up, eff over 2f out, short of room over 1f out, kept on same pace: showed more 3506, see 179. ½ **85**
2681 **SKI JUMP 45** [13]4-8-8 VIS (85) P Hanagan 33/1: 1601-169: Bhd, outpcd over 2f out, some late gains: 6 wk abs, tried visor: now with R Fahey & may do btr: see 2197. ¾ **80**
3615 **SILVALINE 7** [17]5-8-3 (80) P Doe 33/1: 6011030: 10th: Held up, eff 2f out, no impress: see 2896. 2 **71**
3265 **JAMES CAIRD 21** [16]4-8-9 (86) M Henry 25/1: 2-622200: 11th: In tch, wknd over 1f out. ½ **76**
3460 **CRIPSEY BROOK 13** [19]6-8-8 (85) Kim Tinkler 33/1: 6002560: 12th: Nvr a factor: see 2753, 2560. nk **74**
3185 **OFARABY 24** [15]4-8-13 (90) K McEvoy 25/1: 3164250: 13th: Keen in tch, short of room over 2f out, no impress: see 2184. ½ **78**
3506 **TELEMACHUS 11** [6]4-8-6 bl (83) M Fenton 50/1: 1000000: 14th: Chsd ldrs, wknd 2f out: see 3506. ½ **70**
3598 **INTRICATE WEB 7** [1]8-8-4 (81) F Norton 33/1: 3301000: 15th: Held up, btn 2f out: best 2560. ½ **67**
3460 **FLIGHTY FELLOW 13** [9]4-9-3 bl (94) D Allan 33/1: 6106240: 16th: Keen in tch, wknd over 2f out. 1¾ **76**
3430 **SCOTTISH RIVER 14** [5]5-8-5 (82) Hayley Turner(5) 50/1: 4661240: 17th: Dwelt, keen held up, btn 2f out. shd **64**
3118 **IONIAN SPRING 28** [10]9-9-4 (95) R Smith 20/1: 30-10100: 18th: Slow away & bhd, nvr a factor. hd **76**
3439 **FINE PALETTE 14** [20]4-8-11 (88) Paul Eddery 16/1: 2-115530: 19th: Handy, wknd 2f out: btr 3439. 4 **61**
3460 **PENRITH 13** [7]3-8-1 (88) J Fanning 10/1: 1-130350: 20th: In tch, wknd 2f out: something amiss? 4 **53**
20 Ran Time 2m 11.58 (1.58) Owned: Mrs I Battla Trained: Newcastle Upon Tyne

3795 3.35 Sodexho European Breeders Fund Novice Stakes Fillies 2yo (D)
£5018 £1544 £772 6f str Firm 09 -39 Slow Centre

3003 **SATIN KISS 32** [2] Saeed bin Suroor 2-9-2 (90) K McEvoy 2/1 FAV: 101: Made all, rdn clr fnl 1f: well bckd: v eff at 6f, shld stay further: acts on firm & fast grnd, gall trks: best up with/forcing the pace: back to useful best with ease in class: see 2399. **95**
3251 **INDIENA 22** [1] B J Meehan 2-8-9 J Fortune 3/1: 452: Keen, handy, eff to chase wnr over 1f out, kept on but not her pace: acts on firm & fast grnd: can win a minor trk mdn: see 3064. 1¼ **81**
RASHIDA [5] J Noseda 2-8-5 E Ahern 4/1: 3: b f King's Best - Nimble Lady (Fairy King) Dwelt, held up, some late gains, nvr a factor on debut, hands & heels: Jan first foal, cost E150,000: eff at 6f on firm grnd, 7f sure to suit: plenty more to come, educational intro. 1¼ **73**
2553 **SAPPHIRE DREAM 50** [4] A Bailey 2-9-2 (84) R Winston 7/1: 221604: Handy, wknd dist: 7 wk abs. nk **83**
3141* **BRIDGE TTHE STARS 27** [6]2-8-11 S Carson 5/1: 15: Held up, btn dist: up in class after 3141 (gd). ¾ **76**
5 Ran Time 1m 14.2 (2.9) Owned: Godolphin Trained: Newmarket

3796 4.10 Alan's 60th Birthday Handicap Stakes 4yo+ 0-70 (E) **[70]**
£3809 £1172 £586 6f str Firm 09 -10 Slow Centre

3643 **FULL SPATE 5** [16] J M Bradley 9-9-10 (66) F Norton 7/1: 3200021: Held up, al trav best, styd on well to lead ins last, rdn out: stays 1m, suited by 6f on firm & fast grnd, handles hvy & any trk, likes Windsor: on a winning mark, tough & clearly in fine heart, could win again: see 1103. **72**
3137 **FONTHILL ROAD 27** [8] R A Fahey 4-10-0 (70) J Fortune 100/30 FAV: 612-6132: Held up, hdwy well over 1f out, styd on ins last, not pace of wnr: fine run under top-weight & continues on the upgrade: acts on firm, likes gd/soft, soft & fibresand: win again: see 2831, 2477. ½ **76**
2884 **SMIRFYS PARTY 37** [19] D Nicholls 6-8-6 vis (48) A Nicholls 25/1: 106-0003: Handy, hdwy to lead over 2f out till ins last, no extra: back to form & h'capped to win similar shortly: see 2884. 1 **51**
3571 **FLYING EDGE 8** [12] E J Alston 4-8-11 (53) W Supple 14/1: 0650004: In tch, eff well over 1f out, styd on ins last: much more encouraging & h'capped to win over 7f shortly: see 2445, 585. ¾ **54+**

HAYDOCK SATURDAY 07.08.04 Lefthand, Flat, Galloping Track

3180 **SMIRFYS NIGHT 25** [15]5-8-8 (50) P Doe 33/1: 005/-0005: Led till over 1f out, onepace: see 2279. *hd* **50**
3424 **WILLIAMS WELL 14** [9]10-9-1 bl (57) Dale Gibson 16/1: 0-000506: Chsd ldrs, onepace over 1f out. *1½* **53**
3424 **FRIAR TUCK 14** [13]9-8-9 (51) A Beech(3) 25/1: 4000407: Bhd, late gains, nvr dngrs: see 1508. *nk* **46**
3574 **DRURY LANE 8** [18]4-8-9 bl (51) E Ahern 12/1: 4004008: Held up, eff dist, onepace: see 3289. *nk* **45**
3436 **HAULAGE MAN 14** [3]6-9-4 p (60) P Robinson 7/1: 40-02029: In tch, wknd dist: btr 3436 (clmr). *nk* **53**
3643 **AINTNECESSARILYSO 5** [17]6-8-13 (55) M Halford(7) 10/1: 1153600: 10th: Bhd, nvr a factor: see 2752. *nk* **47**
3146 **INDIAN MAIDEN 27** [7]4-9-10 (66) P Makin(5) 33/1: 600-0400: 11th: Held up, nvr a factor: see 2760. *¾* **56**
3427 **VIEWFORTH 14** [20]6-9-8 bl (64) V Halliday 9/1: 0430000: 12th: In tch, wknd 2f out: see 3150. *1¾* **49**
3561 **PIRLIE HILL 9** [6]4-8-7 (49) Hayley Turner(5) 25/1: 0440650: 13th: Bhd, wknd dist: see 2968. *shd* **33**
3402 **ELIDORE 15** [10]4-9-13 VIS (69) A Culhane 40/1: 3000-050: 14th: Handy, wknd 2f out: see 3402. *hd* **52**
3000 **LUCIUS VERRUS 32** [2]4-8-7 vis (49) Darren Williams 40/1: 0520560: 15th: Held up, btn over 2f out. *1* **29**
2080 **INDIAN SHORES 70** [11]5-8-6 (48) M Henry 40/1: 0600000: 16th: b f Forzando - Cottonwood (Teenoso) *½* **26**
Al bhd: 10 wk abs: '03 auct mdn fills wnr on reapp: eff at 5/6f on firm & gd, any trk: has run well fresh: with B Smart last term: has regressed. 1 May'03 Catt 6.0fm 65-(52) E:
3109 **CALUSA LADY 28** [4]4-8-11 (53) S Carson 16/1: 005-5020: 17th: In tch, wknd 3f out: see 3109 (g/s). *hd* **30**
3574 **BRANTWOOD 8** [14]4-9-2 t (58) G Gibbons 16/1: 4323060: 18th: Handy, wknd over 2f out: see 2884. *½* **33**
3427 **TRINITY 14** [1]8-8-6 (48) D Allan 25/1: 040-0000: 19th: In tch, wknd 2f out: see 1393. *¾* **21**
3417 **BLUEBERRY RHYME 15** [5]5-9-0 vis (56) M Fenton 40/1: 1015000: 20th: In tch, wknd over 2f out. *hd* **28**
20 Ran Time 1m 12.46 (1.16) Owned: Mr E A Hayward Trained: Chepstow

3797

4.40 Lester Piggott Rated Stakes Handicap 3yo+ 0-90 (C) **[95]**
£10180 £3132 £1566 **1m30y rnd** **Firm 09** **+01 Fast** Inside

3310 **YOUNG MR GRACE 19** [3] T D Easterby 4-8-11 (78) D Allan 9/2: 4251621: Handy, hdwy to lead over 2f out, kept on, drvn out: eff over 7f/1m now on firm or soft grnd: likes gall trks: genuine, imprvd this term. **85**
3565 **SAWWAAH 8** [9] D Nicholls 7-9-0 (81) A Nicholls 5/1: 4000302: Chsd ldrs, eff & hung left over 1f out, kept on ins last: gd run: see 3443, 1820 (7f). *1* **85**
1616 **IMPERSONATOR 92** [6] J L Dunlop 4-8-9 (76) P Doe 11/1: 0040-043: Handy, hdwy to lead over 3f out till over 2f out, kept on same pace: 3 mth abs: acts on firm & hvy: encouraging run: see 1616. *shd* **80**
3205+**LANGFORD 23** [4] M H Tompkins 4-9-5 (86) P Robinson 3/1 FAV: 6-210014: Keen in tch, hdwy trav well 2f out, onepcd over 1f out: well bckd: prob ran to winning form of 3205. *shd* **89**
3460 **TOUGH LOVE 13** [5]5-9-3 (84) W Supple 15/2: 0-000005: Held up, eff over 1f out, onepace: slipped down the weights & this was more encouraging: see 1151. *3* **81**
3216 **ACOMB 23** [2]4-8-10 (77) E Ahern 11/2: 6011006: Keen in tch, wknd 2f out: best 2129. *2½* **69**
2809 **NAMROUD 40** [7]5-8-13 (80) J Fortune 9/1: 0-060007: Held up, btn 2f out: 6 wk abs: see 2558, 1035. *2* **68**
1598 **SOLLER BAY 92** [8]7-8-8 (75) Darren Williams 12/1: 0466-208: Led till 3f out, wknd: 3 mth abs. *6* **51**
8 Ran Time 1m 41.21(0.71) Owned: Mr Norman Jackson Trained: Malton

WINDSOR SUNDAY 08.08.04 Sharp, Figure 8 Track

Official Going GOOD/FIRM.

3798

2.30 Dine In The Castle Restaurant Today Maiden Auction Stakes Div 1 2yo (E)
£3484 £1072 £536 **1m67y rnd** **Firm 14** **-19 Slow** Inside

3285 **BLAISE HOLLOW 22** [6] R Charlton 2-9-0 S Drowne 11/4 FAV: 051: Cl-up, styd on to lead dist, v comftbly, val 5L+: eff at 7f, imprvd for step up to 1m: acts on firm & gd: improving with racing, see 3285. **88+**
LITHOS [5] J A Osborne 2-9-0 L Dettori 7/1: 2: ch c Inchinor - Leisure (Fast Topaze) Chsd ldrs till hmpd bend after 3f & lost place, styd on to chase wnr fnl 1f, al held: debut: Mar foal, cost E27,000: dam successful abroad: sire decent performer around 7f: eff at 1m, shaped as tho' further will suit: acts on firm grnd: closer but for incident on bend & can impr for today's experience. *3* **78**
3489 **FADAEL 13** [8] P W D'Arcy 2-8-9 J Fortune 4/1: 063: b f In The Wings - Gift Box (Jareer) Led, hdd bef 1f out, wknd: Feb foal, cost 20,000gns: half-sister 7f wnr as a juv: dam unplcd: sire fine performer at mid-dists: now quals for h'caps. *4* **65**
3489 **GIBRALTAR BAY 13** [9] G G Margarson 2-8-6 A McCarthy 25/1: 04: b f Cape Cross - Secrets of Honour (Belmez) Missed break, sn in tch, onepcd fnl 2f: May foal, half-sister to wnrs at 1m/9f: dam unrcd: sire Gr 1 wnr at 1m: showed signs of encouragement. *1½* **59**
MAKTU [11]2-8-7 R L Moore 13/2: 5: Dwelt, nvr nrr than mid-div on debut: sharper for today. *½* **59**
2776 **HAWRIDGE KING 42** [2]2-8-7 S Carson 4/1: 356: Keen handy, hung badly left bend after 3f, no extra fnl 2f: clr rem, 6 wk abs: may do better in h'caps: btr 1964 (debut). *½* **58**
CROSS MY SHADOW [3]2-8-11 T Dane O'Neill 33/1: 7: Cl-up over 5f, sn fdd: debut. *13* **37**
3342 **DAVIDS SYMPHONY 18** [7]2-9-0 R Smith 16/1: 008: Prom over 5f, sn wknd. *1½* **37**
3633 **LORD CHALFONT 7** [10]2-8-7 bl K Ghunowa(7) 100/1: 000009: Rear, prog in mid-div when badly hmpd bend after 3f, no ch after: qck reapp. *7* **17**
3536 **CORNICHE DANCER 11** [4]2-8-9 L Harman(6) 16/1: 000: 10th: Dwelt, handy when hmpd after 3f, sn btn. *3* **13**
3342 **SEA MAP 18** [1]2-8-11 R Mullen 25/1: 00U: Veered left & u.r. at start: btr 3342. **0**
11 Ran Time 1m 45.81 (2.81) Owned: Mr D J Deer Trained: Beckhampton

3799

3.00 Attheraces Com Handicap Stakes Fillies 3yo 0-75 (E) **[79]**
£3601 £1108 £554 **1m67y rnd** **Firm 14** **-01 Slow** Inside

3540 **KRYSSA 10** [1] G L Moore 3-9-7 (72) R L Moore 4/1: 3513131: Held up, prog halfway, styd on to lead ins fnl 1f, rdn out to hold on: eff at 5f, now suited by 6f/1m on firm, gd/ soft & polytrack: remains in gd form & did well to defy top-weight: see 3090. **76**
3291 **DEIGN TO DANCE 20** [5] J G Portman 3-8-9 (60) L Dettori 7/2 FAV: 0051032: Mid-div, hdwy 2f out, ev ch ins fnl 1f, just held by wnr: tchd 9/2: gd run in defeat: see 3291 & 3090. *nk* **62**
3610 **ELUSIVE KITTY 8** [12] G A Butler 3-9-4 t (69) S Righton 20/1: 5255-6R3: b f Elusive Quality - Al Fahda (Be My Chief) Missed break, hdwy 3f out, kept on fnl 1f, not btn far: rider received 1 day whip ban: rnr-up on 1 of only 2 '03 starts (med auct mdn): eff around 1m on firm grnd & fibresand: eff with a t-strap: not *1½* **69**

straight-forward but has ability. 2 Oct'03 Ling 8ap 73a- E:

3718	**FILLIEMOU 3** [6] A W Carroll 3-8-5 (56) F P Ferris(3) 10/1: 0005244: Al cl-up, no extra fnl 1f: qck reapp: fin ahead of today's 2nd in 3291.	¾	54
3452	**ANNA PANNA 15** [11]3-9-6 (71) Dane O'Neill 8/1: 3-6255: In tch, prog bef 1f out, sn no extra: h'cap bow: first try at 1m: btr 2906 (6f).	½	68
2904	**NIGHT FROLIC 37** [8]3-8-12 (63) P Robinson 13/2: 00-13066: Led till ins fnl 1f: btr 1953.	nk	59
1761	**FARRIERS CHARM 85** [2]3-8-12 (63) J Fortune 14/1: 644-107: Sn well bhd, prog after 5f, staying on when bmpd dist, sn short of room, styd on cl-home: 12 wk abs: shade closer without interference: see 1376.	shd	58
3419	**PELLA 15** [9]3-8-12 (63) J Quinn 4/1: 6253238: Handy over 6f, no extra dist: btr 3419 & 3187.	shd	57
3175	**SONDERBORG 26** [4]3-8-1 bl (52) Lisa Jones 25/1: 0026009: Al bhd: btr 2218.	5	36
3090	**GENTLE RAINDROP 30** [3]3-8-11 (62) R Mullen 25/1: 05000: 10th: Handy over 6f, wknd: btr 1929.	hd	45
2661	**LA VIE EST BELLE 46** [7]3-9-3 (68) G Baker 20/1: 20-60400: 11th: Keen cl-up 5f, sn fdd: 7 wk abs.	2	47

11 Ran   Time 1m 44.30 (1.30)   Owned: Mr D J Deer   Trained: Brighton

---

3800   **3.30 Ian Hutchinson Memorial Conditions Stakes 2yo** (D)
£7027 £2162 £1081   **6f str**   **Firm 14**   **-18 Slow**   Inside

2194*	**CAESAR BEWARE 66** [2] H Candy 2-8-10 Dane O'Neill 11/10 FAV: 11: In tch, prog to lead dist, pushed clr, impressive, val 8L+: well bckd, 9 wk abs: eff at 6f on gd & firm, further will suit: acts on a sharp or stiff/gall trk: goes well fresh: lightly rcd, showed an impress turn of foot: smart & can make presence felt in List/Gr company: see 2194.		112+
3254	**AL QUDRA 23** [1] B J Meehan 2-8-12 (90) J Fortune 33/1: 51052: Bhd, prog wide 2f out, kept on cl-home to take 2nd, no ch with v easy wnr: acts on firm grnd & fibresand: caught a tartar.	6	96
3272*	**JOSH 22** [5] M A Jarvis 2-8-12 P Robinson 7/2: 13: Handy, styd on to chase wnr dist, no extra & just held for 2nd cl-home: op 5/2: shade below debut win in 3272 (soft).	nk	95
2783*	**AASTRAL MAGIC 42** [7] R Hannon 2-8-5 (87) R L Moore 9/1: 114: Led 3f, sn onepcd: 6 wk abs: disapp on hat-trick bid: btr 2783 (nov auct stk) & 1911 (mdn).	1½	84
3303	**DOCTOR HILARY 20** [3]2-8-10 (93) R Mullen 8/1: 412325: Cl-up, led halfway, hdd bef 1f out, fdd.	¾	87
3438*	**NIGHTFALL 15** [6]2-8-12 t L Dettori 4/1: 16: In tch 4f, sn wknd: failed to build on 3438 (debut).	2	83

6 Ran   Time 1m 12.24 (1.94)   Owned: Mill House Partnership   Trained: Wantage

---

3801   **4.00 Windsor-Racecourse Co Uk Rated Stakes Handicap 3yo 0-85** (D)   [92]
£6976 £2146 £1073   **1m2f7y**   **Firm 14**   **+08 Fast**   Inside

3474	**CREDIT 14** [5] R Hannon 3-9-6 (84) R L Moore 4/1: 3310041: Cl-up, styd on to lead dist, drvn out, gamely: fast time: eff at 1m, now stays 10f: acts on firm & gd/soft grnd: unexposed at this trip: see 1763.		94
3630*	**PORTMANTEAU 7** [6] Sir Michael Stoute 3-9-10 (3ex) (88) L Dettori 3/1: 0-01012: Chsd ldrs, styd on to chase wnr ins fnl 1f, al held: well bckd under a 3lb pen on qck reapp: ran to form of win in 3630.	1½	95
2919	**BREATHING SUN 36** [2] W J Musson 3-8-12 t (76) R Mullen 11/1: 011-0003: Slow away, prog 4f out, no impress fnl 1f: eff at 1m, now stays 10f: acts on firm & rain softened grnd: encouraging: see 2919.	¾	81
3246*	**ARRGATT 23** [4] M A Jarvis 3-9-5 (83) P Robinson 13/2: 0-32214: Led, rcd keenly, hdd dist, no extra: eff at 1m/11f: not disgraced in better co: see 3246 & 2549.	1¾	85
3292*	**MOTORWAY 20** [1]3-9-5 (83) J Fortune 11/4 FAV: 615: Handy 1m, no extra: h'cap bow: see 3292.	3	81
3471	**MAGIC AMIGO 14** [3]3-8-11 (75) N Pollard 16/1: 0230436: Mid-div, wknd 2f out: btr 3471.	½	72
3690	**AMERICAN DUKE 4** [7]3-8-4 (4oh) (64) Paul Eddery 8/1: 400-0027: Bhd, rcd keenly, nvr a factor.	3½	60

7 Ran   Time 2m 06.69 (0.69)   Owned: Highclere Thoroughbred Racing XV   Trained: Marlborough

---

3802   **4.30 Book Your Discounted Tickets On-Line Maiden Stakes Fillies 3yo+** (D)
£4251 £1308 £654   **1m2f7y**   **Firm 14**   **+05 Fast**   Inside

977	**BOOT N TOOT 131** [4] C A Cyzer 3-8-12 L Dettori 12/1: 01: b f Mtoto - Raspberry Sauce (Niniski) Handy, styd on for press to lead cl-home: long abs, gd time: dam a smart 10f performer: eff at 10f, 12f will suit: acts on firm grnd & goes well fresh: left debut eff well bhd & can progress.		78
1959	**UIG 76** [1] H S Howe 4-8-12 (77) Dane O'Neill 8/1: 0032: Led, rcd keenly, hdd under press cl-home: 11 wk abs: acts on firm & fast grnd: see 1959.	nk	77
3186	**PLUMMET 25** [8] J H M Gosden 3-8-12 J Fortune 8/15 FAV: 423: Cl-up, ev ch dist, kept on, just held in 3-way photo: well bckd at odds-on: acts on firm & gd grnd: continues to run well: see 3186 & 1959.	nk	76
2788	**SAMARIA 42** [3] C F Wall 3-8-12 R Mullen 33/1: 04: Held up, prog 4f out, styd on ins fnl 1f, not btn far: 6 wk abs: eff at 10f, worth another try over further: acts on firm grnd: see 2788.	shd	75
3186	**SAFIRAH 25** [10]3-8-12 P Robinson 7/1: 355: Rear, prog 4f out, onepcd fnl 1f: quals for h'caps.	1½	72
	ISMAHAAN [5]5-9-7 R L Moore 16/1: 6: ch f Unfuwain - River Divine (Irish River) Nvr nrr than mid-div: Flat debut: long jumps abs, unplcd in 3 bmpr starts to date (M J Wallace).	3	67
3477	**EFRHINA 13** [11]4-9-7 (63) S Drowne 12/1: 002-07: Handy 1m, no extra, eased fnl 1f: see 3477.	¾	65
	PATTERSON [9]3-8-12 G Baker 33/1: 8: Al adrift: debut.	22	35
2368	**PEARNICKITY 58** [6]3-8-12 P Doe 50/1: 009: Dwelt, al adrift: 8 wk abs.	6	27
2788	**LOOKOUTHEREICOME 42** [2]3-8-12 J Quinn 20/1: 0000: 10th: Missed break, sn handy, fdd 3f out.	½	26
2052	**CLOUD CATCHER 72** [7]3-8-12 S Righton 100/1: 0-000: 11th: Al adrift: 10 wk abs.	1½	23

11 Ran   Time 2m 6.91 (0.91)   Owned: Mrs Charles Cyzer   Trained: Horsham

---

3803   **5.00 National Hunt Racing Returns To Windsor Maiden Auction Stakes Div 2 2yo** (E)
£3474 £1069 £535   **1m67y rnd**   **Firm 14**   **-18 Slow**   Inside

2863	**GLORIOUS STEP 38** [7] J H M Gosden 2-8-9 L Dettori 1/1 FAV: 31: Made all, rcd green, pushed out ins fnl 1f to assert: well bckd: eff at 7f, apprec step up to 1m: acts on firm grnd: defied greenness to win well & there shld be more to come: see 2863 (debut).		87+
2959	**LITTLE MISS GRACIE 35** [9] P Burgoyne 2-8-6 L Keniry(3) 9/2: 332: Dwelt, sn cl-up, kept on ins fnl 1f, not pace of wnr: eff at 7f/1m on firm & gd/soft grnd: continues to do little wrong & quals for h'caps.	1½	80
3489	**CALL ME MAX 13** [8] E A L Dunlop 2-9-0 J Fortune 4/1: 43: Cl-up, no extra ins fnl 1f: eff at	¾	86

7f, imprvd for step up to 1m: acts on firm & gd grnd: lightly rcd performer who can lose mdn tag: see 3489.
1987 **FAIR ALONG 75** [4] W Jarvis 2-8-7 P Robinson 16/1: 0004: b g Alkalde - Fairy Tango (Acatenango) Keen mid-div, outpcd 2f out, rallied late: 11 wk abs: Mar foal, cost E10,000: dam wnr abroad: sire decent performer at 1m/11f in Germany: poss stays 1m on firm grnd; has been gelded. 1¾ **74**
3376 **BRIANNSTA 17** [1]2-8-11 Dane O'Neill 9/1: 65: Held up, prog halfway, kept on fnl 1f under hands & heels: left debut eff bhd on step up to 1m with encouraging run: see 3376. nk **79**
TRANQUILIZER [2]2-8-2 T J Quinn 25/1: 6: b f Dr Fong - Tranquillity (Night Shift) Slow away, nvr nrr than mid-div: t-strap fitted on debut: Feb foal, cost 4,000gns: half-sister to wnrs at 5/7f at 2: dam 1m wnr: sire fine performer at 1m/10f: with D J Coakley. 5 **63**
ARCH FOLLY [10]2-8-7 R Mullen 50/1: 7: b g Silver Patriarch - Folly Fox (Alhijaz) Al in rear: debut: Apr first foal, dam unrcd: sire Gr 1 wnr at 12/14f: with J G Portman. ½ **67**
3489 **BE BOP ALOHA 13** [3]2-8-2 P (58) P Doe 40/1: 063508: Mid-div over 6f, wknd. ¾ **60**
3163 **LOOKING GREAT 27** [6]2-9-0 S Carson 20/1: 009: Handy 6f, fdd. 3½ **67**
3110 **PIPS PEARL 29** [11]2-8-2 A McCarthy 50/1: 0000: 10th: Mid-div 5f, wknd. 9 **42**
10 Ran Time 1m 45.68 (2.68) Owned: Mr Saif Ali Trained: Manton

3804

5.30 Come Racing Again Tomorrow Night Handicap Stakes 3yo 0-75 (E) **[82]**
£3838 £1181 £591 **5f10y str** **Firm 14** **-13 Slow** Inside

3640 **MIRASOL PRINCESS 6** [11] D K Ivory 3-9-1 (69) Dane O'Neill 8/1: 4666401: Missed break, sn bhd, hdwy halfway, styd on to lead ins fnl 1f, rdn out: qck reapp: stays a sharp 6f, all wins at 5f: acts on firm or fast grnd: gd confidence boost & is h'capped to follow up: see 3371 & 3198. **76**
3372 **JINKSONTHEHOUSE 17** [1] M D I Usher 3-8-2 (56) Hayley Turner(5) 16/1: 1040142: Handy, ev ch dist, kept on, not pace of wnr: gd run back in h'cap grade: see 2808. 1½ **58**
3479* **WUNDERBRA 13** [3] M L W Bell 3-8-6 t (60) J Mackay 4/1: 34513: Cl-up, styd on to lead bef 1f out, hdd ins fnl 1f, no extra: op 3/1: eff at 5/6f: 5lb higher than recent win in 3479 (first time t-strap). nk **61**
4250} **KING EGBERT 327** [4] A W Carroll 3-8-6 (60) P Doe 40/1: 3000-4: b c Fasliyev - Exocet (Deposit Ticket) Dwelt, prog halfway, onepcd fnl 1f: reapp: plcd on first '03 start (rtd 67, mdn, J Dunlop): eff at 5f, bred to apprec further: acts on firm grnd: has tried blnks: signs of encouragement on h'cap bow. 1 **58**
3356 **BORZOI MAESTRO 17** [2]3-9-7 p (75) L Dettori 6/1: 3104305: Led, hdd bef 1f out, no extra dist. nk **72**
3599 **PICCLEYES 8** [7]3-8-7 bl (61) R L Moore 6/1: 0010036: Stumbled badly after leaving stalls, kept on fnl 1f, nrst fin: op 8/1: lost all ch at start: showed more in 3599. 1 **55**
3693 **PERUVIAN STYLE 4** [10]3-9-1 (69) J Fortune 5/2 FAV: 5006527: Handy till dist, wknd: bckd on qck reapp: showed more in 3693 (6f). 1 **60**
3023 **BLUE MOON HITMAN 32** [9]3-8-6 (60) F P Ferris(3) 12/1: 36-30338: Handy 3f, wknd: btr 3023 & 2784. 2 **45**
3561 **HES A ROCKET 10** [8]3-8-4 bl (58) N Chalmers(4) 15/2: 1360069: Al adrift: btr 1605 & 1547. 2 **37**
9 Ran Time 1m 0.35(1.35) Owned: Mr Anthony W Parsons Trained: Radlett

REDCAR SUNDAY 08.08.04 Lefthand, Flat, Galloping Track

Official Going FIRM (GOOD/FIRM IN PLACES)

3805

2.40 Tfm Roadshow Is Here Today Median Auction Maiden Stakes 3-4yo (E)
£3624 £1115 £558 **1m1f** **Good/Firm 33** **-24 Slow** Inside

3739 **BANANA GROVE 3** [5] A Berry 3-8-12 P Mathers(5) 33/1: 30P1: Mid-div, hdwy over 3f out, led 2f out, kept on well for press ins fnl 1f: qck reapp: stays 9f on fast, gall trk: unfortunate in 3739, see 3204. **72**
3581 **MARSH ORCHID 9** [7] W Jarvis 3-8-12 P Hanagan 1/2 FAV: 522: Mid-div, hung left over 4f out, hdwy to chase wnr dist, not his pace: bckd, clr of rem: stays 9f: find similar: see 3581. ¾ **69**
3581 **OH GOLLY GOSH 9** [1] N P Littmoden 3-8-12 p (69) T G McLaughlin 5/1: 2042053: Chsd ldrs, led 4f out till hung right & hdd 2f out, fdd over 1f out: see 1907. 3½ **62**
3413 **BORODINSKY 16** [6] R E Barr 3-8-12 (44) T Eaves(3) 10/1: 0-504024: Chsd ldrs, onepcd 5f out, kept on again fnl 2f: need further? see 3413. 3½ **55**
2428 **WONDER WOLF 56** [2]3-8-7 G Parkin 25/1: 0-05: b f Wolfhound - Wrangbrook (Shirley Heights) Slow away, bhd, modest late gains: 8 wk abs: mdn unplcd sole '03 start (rtd 36): with R Fahey. 4 **42**
2692 **ALPHA JULIET 45** [3]3-8-7 R Ffrench 8/1: 66: Prom, wknd over 3f out: 6 wk abs: see 2692. 2½ **37**
3581 **ZOOMIEZANDO 9** [4]3-8-12 P Makin(5) 66/1: 07: Chsd ldrs till over 3f out, sn wknd: see 3581. 9 **24**
3697 **DISTINCTLYTHEBEST 4** [8]4-9-6 P Mulrennan(3) 80/1: 0-08: Led till 4f out, sn no extra: qck reapp. 5 **14**
8 Ran Time 1m 54.0 (5.2) Owned: Mr Alan Berry Trained: Cockerham

3806

3.10 Funfair Is Here Today Classified Stakes 3yo+ 0-65 (E)
£3663 £1127 £564 **1m str** **Good/Firm 33** **-08 Slow** Centre

2475* **SHARP NEEDLE 53** [5] J Noseda 3-8-13 (70) E Ahern 13/8 FAV: 02511: Trkd ldrs, hdwy to lead well ins fnl 1f, cmftbly: 8 wk abs, well bckd: eff at 1m/9f, further shld suit: acts on fast & gd, prob any trk: runs well fresh: in fine form, remains on the upgrade: see 2475. **76**
3604* **BLAEBERRY 8** [4] P L Gilligan 3-8-8 bl (65) A Nicholls 11/2: 5541512: Dsptd lead till led & hung left over 2f out, hdd ins fnl 1f, no extra: suited by 7f, stays 1m: return to 7f prob suit: see 3604 (7f). ¾ **67**
3678 **OSCAR PEPPER 4** [11] T D Barron 7-9-6 vis (67) Alex Greaves 3/1: 4524143: Bhd, hdwy 3f out, hung left over 1f out, kept on ins fnl 1f: qck reapp, clr of rem: back to form of 3505. nk **71**
3571 **ZAP ATTACK 9** [3] J Parkes 4-9-4 (64) R Ffrench 9/1: 0200-004: Trkd ldrs, no impress over 1f out. 7 **55**
3768 **BELTANE 1** [1]6-9-4 (42) C Haddon(7) 33/1: 00120005: Nvr btr than mid-div: unplcd yesterday. ¾ **53**
3546 **GALA SUNDAY 10** [7]4-9-7 BL (68) Dale Gibson 7/1: 0000606: Led till 2f out, no extra: blnks. ¾ **54**
1745 **ATTACCA 86** [6]3-9-2 (70) D Allan 25/1: 021-6007: Rear, hdwy over 2f out, sn wknd: long abs. 1½ **53**
3650 **THWAAB 6** [2]12-9-4 vis (38) P Mulrennan(3) 100/1: 0600/-008: Chsd ldrs, wknd 2f out: qck reapp. 4 **40**
3263 **CHICAGO BOND 22** [9]3-8-8 (60) D McGaffin 28/1: 360-0069: Trkd ldrs, wknd over 2f out: see 2693. 8 **21**
9 Ran Time 1m 38.12 (3.32) Owned: Mr Arashan Ali Trained: Newmarket

REDCAR SUNDAY 08.08.04 Lefthand, Flat, Galloping Track

3807 **3.40 Toteexacta Nursery Stakes Handicap 2yo (C)** **[93]**
£10481 £3225 £1613 **6f str** **Good/Firm 33** **-10 Slow** Centre

3431 **CLARET AND AMBER 15** [1] R A Fahey 2-8-6 (71) P Hanagan 9/2: 3551: Bhd, hdwy over 2f out, not clr run dist, sn switched & styd on well to lead nr fin: h'cap bow: stays 6f on fast & gd: see 2889. **86**
3590 **WINDY PROSPECT 8** [8] P A Blockley 2-9-5 (84) M Fenton 13/2: 5210322: Trkd ldrs, hdwy to lead ins fnl 1f, sn hdd & no extra: remains in gd form: see 3590. *1¼* **93**
3614 **SPACE SHUTTLE 8** [5] T D Easterby 2-9-7 (86) D Allan 9/2: 321333: Trkd ldrs, onepcd over 2f out, kept on again fnl 1f: top-weight: looks to be crying out for a step up to 7f: remains in gd form: see 2236. *1* **92**
3504 **HILLSIDE HEATHER 12** [4] A Berry 2-8-4 (69) F Norton 12/1: 432024: Led till ins fnl 1f, no extra. *1¼* **71**
2845 **TARAS TREASURE 39** [2]2-8-8 (73) P Mulrennan(3) 12/1: 26435: Dwelt, sn handy, no impress dist. *2½* **67**
3348 **RASA SAYANG 18** [10]2-8-3 (68) N Mackay(3) 9/2: 0226: Trkd ldrs, no extra over 1f out, fin lame. *½* **60**
3115 **LADY DAN 29** [3]2-8-5 (70) Dale Gibson 10/1: 432067: Dsptd lead, lost place over 1f out, btn. *1* **59**
3525* **JERRYS GIRL 11** [6]2-8-7 (72) R Ffrench 25/1: 36418: Nvr a factor. *3* **52**
3623 **BIBURY FLYER 8** [9]2-9-5 (84) E Ahern 4/1 FAV: 5226129: Trkd ldrs, hung left/wknd over 1f out. *¾* **62**
9 Ran Time 1m 11.48 (2.58) Owned: The Matthewman Partnership Trained: Malton

3808 **4.10 Family Funday Handicap Stakes 3yo 0-85 (D)** **[87]**
£7027 £2162 £1081 **6f str** **Good/Firm 33** **+03 Fast** Centre

3599 **OBE BOLD 8** [5] A Berry 3-8-0 (2ow)(1oh) (59) F Norton 12/1: 1504301: Rear, hdwy to lead dist, kept on well for press: eff at 5/6f on firm, fast & f/sand: likes Redcar: see 2493. **69**
2656 **NISTAKI 47** [3] T D Easterby 3-8-8 (70) D Allan 13/8 FAV: 4642: Dwelt in rear, stumbled over 3f out, hdwy 2f out, kept on ins fnl 1f but not pace of wnr: well bckd, 7 wk abs: eff at 6f, stays 7f: acts on fast & gd/soft: gd run, win similar: see 3427. *¾* **75**
3567 **IMPERIAL ECHO 9** [7] T D Barron 3-9-4 vis (80) P Makin(5) 5/1: 0402203: Handy, one paced fnl 1f. *1¼* **81**
3188 **CELTIC THUNDER 25** [8] T J Etherington 3-9-7 (83) D McGaffin 7/1: 0502044: Led till hung left & hdd over 1f out, no extra, eased nr fin: top-weight: reportedly lost action: see 2677. *½* **82**
3379 **ABELARD 17** [1]3-8-0 (62) P Hanagan 7/2: 333-6505: Chsd ldrs wide, no impress 2f out: see 2227. *1¾* **56**
3684 **FITZWARREN 4** [6]3-8-5 (67) E Ahern 12/1: 2-030036: Chsd ldrs, no impress dist: qck reapp. *1* **58**
3655 **ROYAL AWAKENING 6** [2]3-7-12 (9oh) (51) D Fentiman(7) 40/1: 30-00457: Chsd ldrs, outpcd/btn 2f out. *1* **48**
3599* **BELLA BOY ZEE 8** [4]3-7-12 (60) Dale Gibson 10/1: 00-32518: Mid-div, wknd over 1f out, eased. *3½* **37**
8 Ran Time 1m 10.71 (1.81) Owned: Mr Alan Berry Trained: Cockerham

3809 **4.40 National Festival Circus Is Here Handicap Stakes 3yo+ 0-80 (D)** **[80]**
£7261 £2234 £1117 **7f str** **Good/Firm 33** **+08 Fast** Centre

3257 **YORKSHIRE BLUE 23** [15] J S Goldie 5-8-5 (57) N Mackay(3) 7/2 FAV: 0011051: Rear, hdwy over 2f out, led ins fnl 1f, styd on well for press despite saddle slipping: op 13/2, gd time: eff at 6f, suited by 7/7.5f: acts on fast, gd & fibresand: likes a gall trk, esp Redcar: gd eff: see 2235. **64**
3501* **SPLODGER MAC 12** [10] N Bycroft 5-8-1 (53) F Norton 25/1: 306-0012: Made most till ins fnl 1f, kept on nr fin: stays 7/8.5f: return to further shld suit: remains in gd form: see 3501 (8.5f). *¾* **56**
3768 **DISTANT COUNTRY 1** [14] Mrs J R Ramsden 5-9-5 p (71) M Fenton 7/1: 60252503: Slow away, hdwy over 2f out, not clr run dist, sn switched & kept on ins fnl 1f: unplcd yesterday: see 998. *hd* **73**
3608 **SEA STORM 8** [12] D R MacLeod 6-9-12 p (78) R Ffrench 20/1: 1006564: Prom, kept on fnl 1f: see 2087. *½* **79**
3768 **TIBER TIGER 1** [11]4-9-10 (76) T G McLaughlin 10/1: 10200555: Rear, hdwy over 2f out, kept on fnl 1f: 5th yesterday: see 1891. *½* **76**
3782 **WHAT A DANCER 1** [5]7-9-8 (74) P Mulrennan(3) 11/2: 04406546: Mid-div, hung left dist, onepcd. *½* **73**
3571 **BOLLIN EDWARD 9** [2]5-8-13 vis (65) D Allan 9/1: 6532027: Rear, hdwy 3f out, onepcd/hmpd fnl 1f. *½* **63**
3375 **BANJO BAY 17** [3]6-9-4 (70) Alex Greaves 25/1: 0300608: Chsd ldrs, onepcd when bmpd ent fnl 1f. *¾* **66**
3579 **NEW WISH 9** [9]4-8-12 (64) Dale Gibson 12/1: 00000-59: Nvr btr than mid-div: op 8/1: see 3579. *1* **58**
3646 **INTER VISION 6** [4]4-9-13 (79) T Eaves(3) 8/1: 0500420: 10th: Dwelt, sn handy, onepcd 1f out: qck reapp. *hd* **72**
3700 **MEHMAAS 4** [1]8-8-4 vis (56) P Mathers(5) 50/1: 0400100: 11th: Rcd alone far side, no impress nr side fnl 2f: qck reapp: joc 1 day ban for not riding to draw: see 3426. *½* **48**
3461 **LEGAL SET 14** [7]8-8-11 t (63) D Fox(5) 20/1: 0240020: 12th: Chsd ldrs, wknd qckly over 1f out. *1½* **52**
3395 **DOWNLAND 16** [13]8-9-3 (69) Kim Tinkler 20/1: 1651130: 13th: Nvr a factor. *nk* **57**
3634 **NO GROUSE 7** [16]4-9-2 p (68) P Hanagan 12/1: 0000050: 14th: Rear stands side, hdwy over 2f out, not pace to chall: qck reapp: see 632. *nk* **55**
3579 **Hilltime 9** [17]4-7-12 (50) P Fessey 28/1:0 3443 **Magic Amour 15** [6]6-8-3 (55) E Ahern 20/1:0
16 Ran Time 1m 23.56 (1.76) Owned: Mr John Mc C Hodge Trained: Glasgow

3810 **5.10 Redcar Cricket Club Stakes Handicap 3yo+ 0-75 (E)** **[73]**
£3643 £1121 £561 **2m4y** **Good/Firm 33** **+04 Fast** Inside

2963 **SPITTING IMAGE 35** [4] Mrs M Reveley 4-9-0 (59) T Eaves(3) 5/2 FAV: 0241231: Rcd in 2nd, hdwy to lead over 4f out, hdd over 2f out, kept on gamely to lead again ins fnl 1f, just held on: eff at 12/14f, stays 2m: acts on firm & soft, prob any trk, likes Redcar: v consistent, continues in fine form: game here: see 2298. **64**
3454 **CLARADOTNET 15** [5] M R Channon 4-9-3 (62) E Ahern 100/30: 0063032: Trkd ldrs, kept on for press ins fnl 1f, just held cl-home: prev eff at 11.7f, now stays 2m: gd run: see 3454. *nk* **65**
3475 **SKYES FOLLY 14** [1] J G Given 4-9-13 BL (72) M Fenton 4/1: 15-00033: Trkd ldrs till led over 2f out, hdd just ins fnl 1f, no extra: tried blnks: see 3475. *1* **74**
3668 **PETERS IMP 5** [2] A Berry 9-8-3 (48) P Mathers(5) 6/1: 000-1534: Rear, hdwy 4f out, no impress 1f out: tchd 8/1, qck reapp: stays 12f/2m: shade btr 3190 (12f, clmr). *4* **46**
3701* **TONI ALCALA 4** [7]5-10-6 (6ex) (79) P Mulrennan(3) 7/2: 5245115: Rear, hdwy 4f out, wknd over 1f out: top-weight, qck reapp: too sn after race 3701? *nk* **76**
3771 **STEPPENWOLF 1** [3]3-7-12 (21oh) (37) C Haddon(4) 66/1: 00000056: Led till over 4f out, no extra, t.o.: 5th yesterday: v stiff task at these weights: see 696. *dist* **15**

REDCAR SUNDAY 08.08.04 Lefthand, Flat, Galloping Track

6 Ran Time 3m 29.58(4.78) Owned: The Mary Reveley Racing Club Trained: Saltburn

LEICESTER SUNDAY 08.08.04 Righthand, Stiff, Galloping Track

Official Going Good/Firm

3811 2.20 E B F John Virgo Maiden Stakes 2yo (D)
£5798 £1784 £892 7f9y str **Firm 19** +00 Fast Stands side

3390 **CAPABLE GUEST** 16 [16] M R Channon 2-9-0 (100) J Fanning 5/4 FAV: 33321: Handy, led bef 3f out, **97+**
pushed out fnl 1f, val 3L+, op 9/4: eff at 6/7f on firm & gd/soft grnd: rarely runs a bad race & this was a
deserved victory: useful, gd confidence boost.
3280 **PIANOFORTE** 22 [2] D R Loder 2-9-0 T P Queally 14/1: 62: b c Grand Slam - Far Too Loud (No 1½ 92
Louder) Cl-up, kept on ins fnl 1f, not pace wnr: Feb foal, cost $190,000: dam wnr abroad: sire decent performer
at sprint dist/9f as a juv: eff at 7f, 1m shld suit: acts on firm grnd: improved & will find similar.
  BANCHIERI 0 [18] Saeed bin Suroor 2-9-0 K McEvoy 11/2: 3: b c Dubai Millennium - Belle Et nk 91
Deluree (The Minstrel) Cl-up, kept on ins fnl 1f, just held for 2nd: clr rem on debut: Feb foal, half brother to
Gr sprint wnr Dazzle, also half brother to a couple of 7f wnrs at 2: dam successful abroad: sire high-class
performer at 1m/10f: eff at 7f, further will suit: acts on firm grnd: sure to prog for today's experience.
3586 **WALKONTHEWILDSIDE** 9 [7] D R Loder 2-9-0 A Beech(3) 25/1: 54: Bhd, prog 3f out, no impress fnl 3 82
1f: stable-mate of rnr-up: improved for step up to 7f: acts on firm grnd: see 3586.
  HUMOUROUS 0 [9]2-9-0 T K Darley 11/1: 5: b c Darshaan - Amusing Time (Sadler's Wells) Handy 1½ 78
till dist, no extra: debut: Feb foal, half brother successful at 1m: dam smart 10f performer: sire Gr1 wnr at
12f: will need further in time: wore a t-strap.
3342 **PENNY ISLAND** 18 [17]2-9-0 J D Smith 16/1: 06: Nvr nrr than mid-div: see 3342. 1 75
  MOSTASHAAR 0 [10]2-9-0 R Hills 13/2: 7: b c Intikhab - Nasanice (Nashwan) Bhd, prog bef 1f nk 74
out, nrst fin: op 5/1 on debut: Feb foal, half brother to 7f/1m wnrs at 2: dam successful at 9f.
2629 **BADDAM** 48 [8]2-9-0 I Mongan 40/1: 48: Nvr nrr than mid-div: 7 wk abs: see 2629. ¾ 72
3500 **CHINESE PUZZLE** 12 [12]2-9-0 t W Ryan 16/1: 669: Cl-up, wknd fnl 2f. 1¾ 67
3234 **WUJOOD** 23 [6]2-9-0 W Supple 25/1: 00: 10th: Al in rear. 5 52
3163 **ARC OF LIGHT** 27 [4]2-9-0 M Hills 25/1: 500: 11th: Keen cl-up 4f, sn wknd. 1 49
  MOTHECOMBE DREAM 0 [3]2-9-0 J F McDonald(3) 33/1: 0: 12th: Cl-up till short of room 3f out, fdd. ¾ 47
  IMPERIOLI 0 [11]2-9-0 Dean McKeown 66/1: 0: 13th: Missed break, al in rear on debut. 2 41
3483 **DISHDASHA** 13 [15]2-9-0 R Thomas(5) 200/1: 00300: 14th: Cl-up, led after 3f, hdd bef 3f out, wknd. nk 40
  MYTORI 0 [14]2-8-9 S Whitworth 125/1: 0: 15th: Al bhd. 5 22
  PRESKANI 0 [1]2-9-0 R Fitzpatrick 125/1: 0: 16th: Led 3f, fdd. 12 0
16 Ran Time 1m 23.36 (1.36) Owned: Mr John Guest Trained: West Ilsley

3812 2.50 Leicester Tigers Selling Stakes 3-4yo (G)
£2968 £848 £424 7f9y str **Firm 19** -15 Slow Stands side

3515 **SHINKO FEMME** 11 [11] N Tinkler 3-8-10 (53) W Ryan 12/1: 0051001: Rear, prog 3f out, styd on to 53
lead ins fnl 1f, drvn out to hold on: op 9/1: no bid: stays 7f on fm & fast: enjoyed drop to sell.
3650 **KELSEAS KOLBY** 6 [12] P A Blockley 4-9-7 vis (55) Dean McKeown 7/2: 0143442: Mid-div, eff when shd 56+
short of room dist, styd on ins fnl 1f, post came too sn: qck reapp: clmd for 6,000: acts on firm & gd/soft grnd:
another gd run here at Leicester & prob wnr with clr passage: see 3650 & 1827.
3426 **FINGER OF FATE** 15 [7] M J Polglase 4-9-2 bl (42) G Gibbons 20/1: 4600303: Led, hdd under press 1 49
ins fnl 1f, no extra: see 3156.
3558 **KILLALA** 10 [10] R N Bevis 4-9-2 (58) K Darley 2/1 FAV: 6-355224: Cl-up, onepcd: new stable. shd 48
3262 **RUE DE PARIS** 22 [4]4-9-2 (40) T Hamilton(3) 33/1: 00000-05: Handy, ev ch 2f out, wknd fnl 1f. 2½ 43
3515 **CHIQITITA** 11 [9]3-8-5 (47) B Swarbrick(5) 33/1: 0000006: Cl-up over 4f, sn no extra: see 3094. ¾ 36
3515 **SWORN TO SECRECY** 11 [3]3-8-5 (54) J F McDonald(3) 11/1: 0006007: Handy 4f, sn no extra: op 8/1. 1¼ 34
3363 **WODHILL BE** 17 [14]4-8-11 (40) M Tebbutt 20/1: 5003008: Al bhd: btr 1827. 2 30
2615 **LUKE AFTER ME** 48 [1]4-9-2 (52) K McEvoy 5/2: 2043009: Bhd when short of room after 4f, sn btn. 6 24
2346 **PRINCESS ISMENE** 59 [8]3-8-10 bl (45) I Mongan 12/1: 340546R: Refused to race: 8 wk abs. 0
10 Ran Time 1m 24.43 (2.43) Owned: The Penniless Partnership Trained: Malton

3813 3.20 Coalville Glass & Glazing Handicap Stakes 3yo+ 0-85 (D) [80]
£6988 £2150 £1075 1m9y rnd **Firm 19** +04 Fast Inside

3185 **GIOCOSO** 25 [10] B Palling 4-9-10 (76) K Darley 11/1: 060-6001: Made all, clr after 2f out, eased 83
cl-home, val 3L+: op 16/1: fast time: eff at 1m/9f, has tried further: acts on firm & gd/soft grnd: made gd use of
drop down h'cap back at 1m & an uncontested lead: see 2860.
3490* **CONCER ETO** 13 [12] S C Williams 5-9-7 p (73) W Supple 7/2 FAV: 0023412: Rear, prog 3f out, kept 1½ 76
on ins fnl 1f, not pace wnr: op 9/2: gd run in defeat: in gd form: see 3490.
3512 **EPHESUS** 12 [14] Miss Gay Kelleway 4-9-12 vis (78) I Mongan 10/1: 4220003: Cl-up, chsd wnr dist, 1½ 78
sn no extra: back to foot form: see 2540.
3625 **PARNASSIAN** 8 [6] G B Balding 4-9-5 (71) R Thomas(5) 6/1: 3051154: Rear, prog 3f out, hung right 2½ 66
with no impress fnl 1f: op 9/2: prefers easier grnd: see 3225 (gd/soft).
3593 **CHERISHED NUMBER** 8 [8]5-9-4 (70) T Hamilton(3) 10/1: 3304405: Cl-up, no extra dist: see 2317. shd 64
3117 **MR VELOCITY** 29 [9]4-9-6 (72) T P Queally 4/1: 30-32106: Cl-up over 6f, no extra: btr 2564 (7f). nk 65
3583 **TOPTON** 9 [4]10-9-10 bl (70) R Hills 9/1: 4626547: Nvr nrr than mid-div: op 7/1: see 714. ½ 68
3608 **ADOBE** 8 [2]9-8-13 (65) B Swarbrick(5) 10/1: 4420048: Al bhd: saves best form for Bath: btr 3142. ½ 56
3276 **SHERIFFS DEPUTY** 22 [7]4-9-0 (66) S Whitworth 20/1: 42-00309: Handy 6f, sn wknd: btr 3142. ¾ 55
3501 **PRINCE OF GOLD** 12 [3]4-8-12 bl (64) J Fanning 20/1: 0100000: 10th: Al in rear: 1st time blnks. 2½ 48
3685 Lizarazu 4 [5]5-9-6 (72) R Miles(3) 20/1:0 3358 San Antonio 17 [1]4-9-7 (73) W Ryan 33/1:0
12 Ran Time 1m 39.44 (1.24) Owned: Mr W Devine & Mr P Morgan Trained: Cowbridge

LEICESTER   SUNDAY 08.08.04   Righthand, Stiff, Galloping Track

3814
3.50 Leicester City Football Club Rated Stakes Handicap 3yo 0-100 (B)   [104]
£12414 £4709 £2354   **7f9y str**   **Firm 19**   **+03 Fast**   Stands side

3263* **MY PARIS 22** [6] K A Ryan 3-8-4 (3oh) (80) J Fanning 10/1: 2252211: Made all, went on 2f out,   92+
eased cl-home, val bit more: eff at 7f/10f on firm & gd/soft: enjoyed forcing tactics: see 3263.
3555 **MOONLIGHT MAN 10** [1] R Hannon 3-9-7 (100) P Dobbs 8/1: 2200242: Al cl-up, styd on fnl 1f, not   1   104
pace wnr: continues to run well & did little wrong under top weight: see 3555 & 3253.
2403* **ROYAL PRINCE 57** [7] J R Fanshawe 3-8-10 (89) O Urbina 4/5 FAV: 34-4113: Keen in tch, onepcd   2½   88
dist: well bckd after 8 wk abs: btr expected after impress win in 2403 (C/D).
3338 **GO BANANAS 18** [4] B J Meehan 3-8-7 (86) J F McDonald(3) 16/1: 13516-64: Keen cl-up, no extra fnl 1f.   nk   84
3277 **APPALACHIAN TRAIL 22** [3]3-8-10 VIS (89) I Mongan 9/2: 2041665: Nvr nrr than mid-div: 1st time visor.   ½   86
3433 **RISING SHADOW 15** [5]3-8-5 (84) W Supple 12/1: 135-6246: Al rear: btr 3273.   3½   74
756 **FIREBELLY 162** [2]3-9-2 (95) K Darley 25/1: 1311-57: Handy 5f, fdd: long abs: btr 756.   10   67
7 Ran   Time 1m 23.31 (1.13)   Owned: J and A Spensley   Trained: Hambleton

3815
4.20 Stuart Pearce Handicap Stakes 3yo+ 0-85 (D)   [80]
£6949 £2138 £1069   **1m1f218y**   **Firm 19**   **-32 Slow**   Inside

3260 **ROTUMA 22** [1] M Dods 5-9-7 bl (73) D Tudhope(7) 6/1: 3161251: Cl-up, led 2f out, hdd briefly dist,   78
drvn out to hold on: stays 11f, 10f specialist on firm & hvy: suited by blnks: tough & proghressive.
3685* **BURGUNDY 4** [4] P Mitchell 7-8-11 bl (63) T P Queally 5/2 FAV: 6111212: Rear, prog 4f out, styd on   hd   67
to lead briefly dist, kept on, just denied: well bckd: quick reapp: remains in fine form: see 3685 & 3288.
3404* **JACARANDA 16** [8] Mrs A L M King 4-9-5 (71) J Fanning 4/1: 5002413: Handy, kept on ins fnl 1f,   2   72
not pace front 2: clr rem: fair run: see 3404 (amat h'cap).
3187 **GIUNCHIGLIO 25** [6] W M Brisbourne 5-8-12 (64) K McEvoy 6/1: 3103604: Cl-up 1m, sn wknd: op 8/1.   5   58
3598* **OPENING CEREMONY 8** [2]5-9-9 (75) T Hamilton(3) 3/1: 2421515: Rear, prog 4f out, wknd fnl 2f: too   1   67
sn after 3598?
1756} **THEATRE TIME 439** [5]4-9-13 (79) P Dobbs 11/1: 522/10-6: b g Theatrical - Kyka (Blushing John)   2½   67
Led, hdd 2f out, wknd: reapp: mdn wnr in 1 of only 2 '03 starts (B W Hills): mdn rnr-up twice in '02: eff at
7/10f on firm & gd grnd: acts on a gall trk & has gone well fresh: has been gelded: with Ian Williams.
1 May'03 Redc 10g/f 85-(85) D: 2 Sep'02 Hayd 7.1fm 86- D: 2 Sep'02 Epso 8.5gd 84- D:
6 Ran   Time 2m 7.67 (5.17)   Owned: Denton Hall Racing Ltd   Trained: Darlington

3816
4.50 PETER EBDON CLASS STKS 3yo+ 0-75 (D)
£5415 £1666 £833   **1m3f183y**   **Firm 19**   **-06 Slow**   Inside

3556 **LEG SPINNER 10** [4] M R Channon 3-8-8 (77) K Darley 7/2: 33101: Cl-up, led 2f out, drvn out to   84
hold on despite edging left fnl 1f: op 5/1: eff around 12f, tried further: acts on fm & fast: game & imprvg.
1399 **ALBAVILLA 103** [2] P W Harris 4-9-0 (75) I Mongan 5/1: 3/556-32: Rear, prog 3f out, ev ch ins fnl   shd   77
1f, just held: long abs: acts on firm, poss handles soft: shld win a race: see 1399.
3477 **LEIGHTON 13** [8] R M Stronge 4-9-3 (74) T P Queally 20/1: 0540203: Handy, short of room bef 1f   1¾   76
out, sn ev ch, onepcd when hmpd cl-home: eff at 7.4/10f, now stays 12f: see 3206 & 2030.
3471 **HATCH A PLAN 14** [3] R M Beckett 3-8-6 (74) K McEvoy 7/2: 0U01224: Rear, eff 2f out, onepace fnl 1f.   shd   75
4873} **SEEYAAJ 289** [1] R Hannon 3-9-1: 01300-5: b g Darshaan - Subya (Night Shift) Led, hdd 2f   ½   79
out, sn onepcd: hdles fit, earlier h'cap wnr (rtd 112h at best, stays 2m on gd & gd/soft grnd): mdn wnr in '03 (A C
Stewart): eff at 10f, further will suit: acts on firm & fast grnd: goes well fresh: with Jonjo O'Neill.
1 Jul'03 Pont 10.0g/f 86- D:
3681 **MEXICAN PETE 4** [7]4-9-6 (78) J Fanning 2/1 FAV: 2044326: Mid-div, no impress when hmpd ins fnl   nk   76
1f: on 3/1 on quick reapp: btr 3681 & 3345.
1005 **TAFFRAIL 130** [1]6-9-8 (80) Derek Nolan(7) 20/1: 00505-57: b g Slip Anchor - Tizona (Pharly)   23   43
Handy, fdd 2f out: 11 wk hdle abs, earlier plcd (h'cap, rtd 94h, stays 2m3.5f on fast): unplcd on Flat in '03 (J L
Dunlop, rtd 93, Listed): stks wnr in '02: 5 time h'cap wnr in '01: suited by 2m/2m2f on firm & gd/soft grnd:
tried cheek pieces: shadow of former self. 1 Sep'02 Pont 17.9fm 95- C: 1 Aug'01 Beve 16.1gd 95-83 D:
1 Jul'01 Asco 16.2g/f 84-71 D: 1 Jul'01 Beve 16.1fm 79-67 E: 1 Jun'01 Yarm 14g/f 67-59 E:
1 May'01 Nott 14g/s 59-47 E:
7 Ran   Time 2m 31.34(3.04)   Owned: Mr P D Savill   Trained: West Ilsley

LINGFIELD Polytrack MONDAY 09.08.04   Lefthand, V Sharp Track

Official Going Standard

3817
2.00 Lingfield-Racecourse Co Uk E B F Median Auction Maiden Stakes Div 1 2yo (F)
£3556 £1094 £547   **6f aw rnd**   **Going 52**   **+01 Fast**   Inside

3329 **CUPIDS GLORY 19** [4] Sir Mark Prescott 2-9-0 S Sanders 4/5 FAV: 61: Pushed along trkg ldrs, qknd   98a+
to lead ins last, rdn clr, readily: well bckd, op 5/4: gd juv time: eff at 7f, apprec drop to 6f: acts on
polytrack & a sharp/turning trk: showed a useful turn of foot, win more races: see 3329.
3418 **SCROOBY BABY 16** [7] J A Osborne 2-8-9 D Holland 8/1: 202: Led/dsptd lead, outpcd by wnr from   3   83a
dist: AW bow: eff at 6f on gd & polytrack: caught a decent sort: see 3141.
3296 **DANES CASTLE 21** [6] B J Meehan 2-9-0 (75) J Fortune 5/1: 3223: Led till ins last, not pace of   1½   83a
wnr: acts on both AWs, firm & fast grnd: consistent: see 3296, 3157 & 2970.
3103 **ICING 30** [2] W J Haggas 2-8-9 K Fallon 5/1: 64: br f Polar Falcon - Dance Steppe (Rambo Dancer)   3   69a
Mid-div, nvr pace to chall: AW bow: 54,000gns Feb foal, half-sister to an Italian/US List wnr.
3103 **ROSAPENNA 30** [5]2-8-9 G Baker 25/1: 505: b f Spectrum - Blaine (Lyphard's Wish) Trkd ldrs   ½   67a
wide, no extra over 1f out: AW bow: £40,000 Jan foal, half-sister to a 1m wnr: prob handles polytrack, will stay
further: awkward passage today, likely improver.

1151

PENANG SAPPHIRE 0 [1]2-9-0 T P Queally 8/1: 6: Trkd ldrs, rdn & no extra over 1f out, op 10/1. *1* **69a**
2109 **BOGAZ 70** [11]2-9-0 Martin Dwyer 12/1: 207: Led/dsptd lead wide, fdd over 1f out under a kind ride: 10 wk abs: awkward passage, not knocked about & can leave this bhd in h'caps: btr 1614 (5f). *nk* **68a**
DUROOB 0 [10]2-9-0 R Hills 10/1: 8: Dwelt, rear, hung right & some late gains under kind ride: bit reportedly slipped, do btr. *3* **59a+**
3735 **SONNTAG BLUE 4** [9]2-9-0 V Slattery 25/1: 009: Outpcd rear, nvr a factor, qck reapp. *6* **41a**
TIME TRAVELLER 0 [8]2-9-0 M Halford(7) 50/1: 0: 10th: Dwelt, sn bhd & flashed tail vigorously, t.o. *22* **0a**
10 Ran Time 1m 13.47 (3.07) Owned: Hesmonds Stud Trained: Newmarket

3818

2.30 Lingfield-Racecourse Co Uk E B F Median Auction Maiden Stakes Div 2 2yo (F)
£3549 £1092 £546 **6f aw rnd** **Going 52** **-07 Slow** Inside

3183 **WEDDING PARTY 26** [8] Mrs A J Perrett 2-8-9 K Fallon 11/10 FAV: 31: Dwelt, sn cl-up, wide on bend 2f out but led dist, rdn clr, readily: op 4/6: AW bow, confirmed debut promise: eff at 6f, 7f+ will suit: acts on gd grnd & polytrack, sharp/undul or easy trk: type to prog with racing, shld prove useful: see 3183. **79a+**
MUTANABI 0 [9] Saeed bin Suroor 2-9-0 L Dettori 7/4: 2: b c Wild Rush - Freudenau (Meadowlake) Led after 1f & sn pulled clr with wnr, hdd dist & no impress ins last: May foal, dam unrcd, related to a high-class US filly: sire top-class 7/9f dirt performer: eff at 6f on polytrack: encouraging start, rate higher. *4* **72a**
3337 **GUYANA 19** [10] S Kirk 2-9-0 J F Egan 20/1: 003: b c Lend A Hand - Romora (Sillery) Dwelt, pushed along chasing front pair halfway, kept on, al held: AW bow: Mar foal, 34,000gns purchase: half-brother to useful 5/6f juv wnr Clifden, dam unrcd: imprvd for drop to 6f on polytrack & a sharp/turning trk. *¾* **70a**
BOB BAILEYS 0 [5] P R Chamings 2-9-0 J Quinn 33/1: 4: b g Mister Baileys - Bob's Princess (Bob's Return) Rear, rdn & kept on wide fnl 1f, nrst fin: cheaply bght Mar foal, dam a 7f juv wnr: eff at 6f on polytrack, 7f likely to suit: can improve. *2½* **62a**
DANESCOURT 0 [4]2-9-0 Martin Dwyer 14/1: 5: Led 1f, no impress on front pair fnl 2f. *½* **60a**
BROOKLIME 0 [3]2-9-0 D Holland 7/1: 6: Dwelt, rear & taken wide, mod hdwy under kind ride. *hd* **59a**
1805 **ASPEN RIDGE 84** [6]2-8-9 S Drowne 10/1: 007: Pushed along mid-div, sn outpcd, 12 wk abs. *1* **51a**
KILLENA BOY 0 [1]2-9-0 J Fortune 16/1: 8: V slow away & rear, nvr a factor. *7* **35a**
2882 **WINTER MIST 39** [7]2-8-9 J P Guillambert(3) 50/1: 09: Sn struggling & bhd halfway. *6* **12a**
AUTUMN DAZE 0 [2]2-8-9 M Henry 100/1: 0: 10th: Chsd ldrs till halfway, wknd qckly. *1½* **8a**
10 Ran Time 1m 13.96 (3.56) Owned: Cheveley Park Stud Trained: Pulborough

3819

3.00 Come Evening Racing On 21st August Selling Stakes 3yo+ (G)
£2569 £734 £367 **1m4f aw** **Going 52** **-03 Slow** Inside

3692 **ROLEX FREE 5** [4] D Flood 6-9-12 vis (57) L Dettori 3/1 JT FAV: 6003141: Led after 2f, rdn from 3f out, al holding rival for press ins last: bght in for 7,200gns: qck reapp: suited by both AWs at 12f, tried 2m: gd weight-carrier, suited by forcing tactics & L Dettori: see 3486. **67a**
3730 **COSI FAN TUTTE 4** [1] M C Pipe 6-9-7 vis t (63) K Fallon 3/1 JT FAV: 0/-230022: Mid-div, hdwy to chase wnr over 2f out, drvn & no extra ins last: acts on fast, soft & polytrack: see 3730. *4* **55a**
3025 **ONE ALONE 33** [12] Jean Rene Auvray 3-8-5 BL (39) Martin Dwyer 14/1: 0-000043: V slow away, bhd, kept on late for press, no threat to front pair: first time blnks, modest improvement: see 2755. *4* **44a**
3492 **BOOGIE MAGIC 14** [6] G A Huffer 4-9-2 P (57) I Mongan 11/1: 00-02304: Trkd wnr trav well 4f out, wknd fnl 2f: chkpcs, drop to 10f in similar could suit: new yard: see 3164 & 2867. *2* **41a**
2267 **ANOTHER CON 63** [10]3-8-10 (60) R Mullen 11/2: 4500205: Mid-div, outpcd 4f out, nvr land blow. *3* **42a**
3692 **BLUE SAVANNA 5** [9]4-9-12 bl (50) D Holland 11/2: 0564426: Held up wide, hdwy halfway, btn 3f out. *18* **22a**
1238 **GOLDEN DUAL 114** [5]4-9-7 bl (56) C Haddon(7) 10/1: 0002007: Slow away & rdn, mod prog, new yard. *1* **16a**
2134 **EL MAGNIFICO 69** [11]3-8-10 BL (42) S Sanders 25/1: 06-60008: Mid-div, btn 4f out: blnks, jumps fit. *8* **5a**
3362 **BUCKENHAM STONE 18** [8]5-9-2 (30) R Price 66/1: 0-000009: Chsd wnr after 5f, btn over 3f out. *1¾* **0a**
3726 **NIGHT DRIVER 4** [3]5-9-7 bl e (62) J Fortune 16/1: 0-000000: 10th: Led 2f, struggling from halfway. *1¾* **1a**
2292 **HARRY CAME HOME 62** [7]3-8-10 (30) A McCarthy 50/1: 000000: 11th: Sn rear & t.o. from 4f out: abs. *5* **0a**
3025 **REGULATED 33** [2]3-9-1 (63) Dane O'Neill 11/1: 5516050: 12th: Dwelt, al bhd & no ch 4f out. *nk* **0a**
12 Ran Time 2m 35.80 (6.6) Owned: Mrs Ruth M Serrell Trained: Hungerford

3820

3.30 Lingfield Leisure Club Nursery Handicap Stakes 2yo (E) **[90]**
£3858 £1187 £594 **7f aw rnd** **Going 52** **-25 Slow** Inside

3330* **HYPNOTIC 19** [3] Sir Mark Prescott 2-9-12 (88) S Sanders 5/6 FAV: 411: Led/dsptd lead, asserted from 2f out, rdn out: eff at 7f on polytrack, will get further: v useful & imrpoving, win again. **98a**
3521 **LATERAL THINKER 12** [8] J A Osborne 2-8-7 (69) L Dettori 7/1: 2341052: Mid-div, styd on for press, nvr threat to wnr: styd longer 7f trip: acts on fast, gd/soft & polytrack: win again: see 3521, 3022. *2½* **71a**
3297 **GRYSKIRK 21** [12] P W D'Arcy 2-8-2 (64) A McCarthy 10/1: 4630003: Chsd ldrs, eff to chase wnr over 1f out, no impress ins last: stays an easy 7f, return to 6f could suit: gelded: handles fast & polytrack. *nk* **65a**
3559 **BLACKCOMB MOUNTAIN 11** [5] M F Harris 2-8-8 (70) D Holland 25/1: 5344: b f Royal Anthem - Ski Racer (Ski Chief) Led/dsptd lead racing wide, rdn & no extra fnl 1f: h'cap/AW bow: acts on fast grnd & polytrack: lkd much more straightforward today & caught the eye suffering a v wide passage, keep in mind for similar. *½* **70a+**
3126 **SKY CRUSADER 30** [1]2-9-8 (84) S Drowne 11/4: 165: Led/dsptd lead till over 1f out: bckd, AW bow. *2* **80a**
1934 **OUR CHOICE 79** [10]2-8-3 (65) T P Queally 20/1: 0406: Pushed along rear, eff wide & mod prog: abs. *½* **60a**
3349 **DARTANIAN 19** [2]2-7-12 (2oh) (58) F P Ferris(3) 33/1: 05637: Rear, rdn & little hdwy: see 3349. *¾* **54a**
3183 **BINT IL SULTAN 26** [11]2-8-4 (3ow) (63) J F Egan 20/1: 3008: Sn pushed along rear, only mod prog. *3* **54a**
3342 **LOUISE RAYNER 19** [9]2-7-12 (2oh) (58) J Mackay 16/1: 5409: Rear & drvn halfway, little hdwy: btr 2652. *2½* **43a**
2263 **PERIANTH 63** [6]2-8-3 (65) Martin Dwyer 20/1: 4000: 10th: Led/dsptd lead racing v wide, fdd under a kind ride fnl 2f: 2 mth abs, longer trip & AW bow: not knocked about, likely prove better than this in time. *5* **39a**
3172 **BELLALOU 27** [7]2-7-12 (5oh) (55) D Fox(5) 25/1: 0030: 11th: Sn struggling rear: btr 3172. *1½* **31a**
3221 **ELGIN MARBLES 25** [4]2-9-8 (84) Dane O'Neill 12/1: 160: 12th: Led/dsptd lead, wknd qckly 2f out. *5* **46a**
12 Ran Time 1m 28.22 (5.42) Owned: Cheveley Park Stud Trained: Newmarket

---

3821 4.00 Sponsor A Race At Lingfield Handicap Stakes 3yo+ 0-75 (E) [75]
£3907 £1202 £601 **7f aw rnd** **Going 52** +07 Fast Inside

3696 **FRANKSALOT** 5 [9] Miss B Sanders 4-9-8 (69) S Sanders 12/1: 2-014541: Mid-div, rdn & hdwy to lead **79a**
ins last, styd on strongly to assert: op 10/1, best time of day: qck reapp: eff at 6f/1m, 7f ideal: acts on firm,
gd/soft & polytrack, loves a sharp/undul trk: see 2644.
3490 **ARTISTRY** 14 [10] B J Meehan 4-9-0 (61) Dane O'Neill 16/1: 0-150052: Trkd ldrs, rdn & styd on fnl 3 **64a**
2f, not pace of wnr: likes this trk: see 1024 (C/D).
2801* **ALI BRUCE** 42 [5] G L Moore 4-9-3 (64) I Mongan 11/2: 5213: Cl-up & led 3f out, rdn & hdd ins hd **66a**
last, no extra: op 7/1, 6 wk abs: acts on both AWs & gd grnd: gd run for new yard: see 2801 (clmr).
3634 **MERDIFF** 8 [13] W M Brisbourne 5-9-2 (63) D Holland 10/1: 0021204: Held up in tch wide, kept on 2 **61a**
onepace, no threat: awkward passage, prob impr on this: acts on fast & both AWs: see 3102.
3583 **KABEER** 10 [11]6-9-5 (66) R Mullen 33/1: 43005: Rear, rdn & mod prog, nvr a threat: see 2575, 2148. 1¾ **61a**
3443 **ARCTIC DESERT** 16 [14]4-10-0 vis (75) Martin Dwyer 11/2: 0000006: Switched from start & settled nk **69a**
rear, eff wide 2f out, onepace dist: well h'capped: see 3088.
3708* **THREEZEDZZ** 5 [2]6-9-6 (6ex)t [9] F P Ferris(3) 5/1 JT FAV: 0001017: Led till 3f out, sn btn: qck reapp. ½ **60a**
3579 **NEARLY A FOOL** 10 [3]6-9-5 vis (66) N Pollard 5/1 JT FAV: 2101348: Sn pushed along chasing ldrs, 2 **55a**
no impress fnl 2f: btr 3423 & 1049.
3487* **ARRAN** 14 [7]4-8-11 (58) G Carter 7/1: 0-030219: Mid-div, short of room 2f out, sn btn: btr 3487 (f/sand). 1¾ **44a**
3759 **SILENT STORM** 3 [8]4-9-6 VIS (67) K Fallon 14/1: 5/-3300: 10th: Mid-div, btn 2f out: vis, qck reapp. 1¼ **50a**
3562 **Whippasnapper** 11 [12]4-9-8 (69) M Savage(5) 12/1:0   3710* **Fort Mchenry** 4 [4]4-10-1 (6ex)p(76) L Dettori 12/1:0
3142 **Have Some Fun** 2 [6]4-8-12 BL(59) J Quinn 33/1:0   3286 **Fulvio** 23 [1]4-8-9 (56) P Doe 16/1:0
14 Ran Time 1m 25.93 (3.13) Owned: Peter Crate Jane Byers Roger Knight Trained: Epsom

---

3822 4.30 Play Golf And Come Racing Handicap Stakes 4yo+ 35-55 (F) [63]
£2954 £844 £422 **2m aw** **Going 52** -08 Slow Inside

2868 **TOMMY CARSON** 39 [5] Jamie Poulton 9-8-3 (38) P Doe 10/1: 0/26/5-301: Al prom, pushed along from **43a**
halfway, drvn & led over 1f out, held on all out: recent h'cap chase wnr (2m6.5f): thorough stayer at 2m, get
further: acts on firm, hvy & both AWs.
3454 **DIAMOND ORCHID** 16 [8] P D Evans 4-8-10 vis (45) T E Durcan 4/1: 2215102: Mid-div, smooth hdwy nk **49a**
from 4f out & chsd wnr ins last, just failed: stays a sharp 2m: see 2856 (14f).
3549 **VANDENBERGHE** 11 [3] J A Osborne 5-9-2 (51) R Keogh(7) 9/1: 4356333: Mid-div, eff to chase ldrs 1 **54a**
when hmpd 2f out & short of room over 1f out, kept on well ins last: would have gone v close without interference:
stays an easy 2m: acts on firm, gd & both AWs: see 1657.
3158* **MAGIC RED** 28 [6] M J Ryan 4-9-4 (53) I Mongan 9/4 FAV: 0000-114: Led 4f & remained handy, led ¾ **55a**
again over 4f out till over 1f out, no extra nr line: acts on both AWs & fast grnd: stays an easy 2m: see 3158.
3450 **HEART SPRINGS** 16 [12]4-8-7 (42) A Daly 16/1: 00-00045: Dwelt & bhd, hdwy 3f out, no impress ins 3½ **41a**
last: poss stays an easy 2m: see 2868.
2739 **MANDOOB** 44 [9]7-9-6 t (55) N Pollard 13/2: 0020446: Rear, rdn & hdwy over 4f out, no prog fnl 2f, abs. 4 **50a**
3516] **SAORSIE** 725 [7]6-8-5 (40) D Fox(5) 25/1: 004020/-7: b g Emperor Jones - Exclusive Lottery 15 **23a**
(Presidium) Chsd ldrs, short of room over 3f out, sn btn: 5 mth jumps abs, dual 03/04 h'cap hdle scorer (rtd 106h
at best, 2m/2m1f on fast & gd/soft grnd): missed '03 on the level: h'cap rnr-up '02, AW unplcd (rtd 52a): stays a
stiff 14f, acts on fast grnd. 2 Jul'02 Sali 14g/f 47-45 E: 1 Jun'01 Sali 8gd 61-57 E:
3400 **INDIAN CHASE** 17 [11]7-8-6 (1ow) (40) D Sweeney 14/1: 2600048: Al rear & no ch fnl 4f. 3½ **21a**
3240 **RIBBONS AND BOWS** 24 [1]4-9-0 (49) S Whitworth 25/1: 0-060409: Mid-div, struggling from 4f out. 3 **32a**
3493 **POLANSKI MILL** 14 [10]5-9-1 T P (50) S Carson 5/1: 00-P0000: 10th: Led after 4f till over 4f out, 5 **22a**
sn bhd: t-strap & cheek pieces, no improvement.
3715 **LITTLE FOX** 4 [2]9-9-0 (49) A Beech(3) 50/1: 4500/-600: 11th: Dwelt, sn struggling & t.o. 2f out: qk reapp. 14 **10a**
3688 **CANTRIP** 5 [13]4-9-2 (51) S Sanders 8/1: 0001300: 12th: Cl-up, wknd qckly from 5f out: qck 2½ **10a**
reapp, reportedly nvr trav after halfway: btr 2274.
3493 **ROYALE PEARL** 14 [4]4-8-5 (40) G Carter 7/1: 0414550: 13th: Mid-div, btn 5f out, t.o.: 10 **0a**
reportedly ran lethargically: btr 1990.
13 Ran Time 3m 29.6 (9.6) Owned: Mr J Logan Trained: Lewes

3823 5.00 Lingfield Golf Club Apprentice Handicap Stakes 3yo+ 35-55 (F) [62]
£3024 £864 £432 **1m2f aw** **Going 52** -15 Slow Inside

2706 **MUSIC MIX** 46 [6] E A L Dunlop 3-9-7 (55) H Poulton 7/1: 466-001: Rear, hdwy over 3f out & led **67a+**
over 1f out, rdn clr, readily: first win: 6 wk abs: eyeshield omitted: eff at 10f, 12f+ may suit: acts on
polytrack & sharp trk: win again if repeating this:.
3288 **ZELOSO** 23 [13] M F Harris 6-9-3 vis (42) R Keogh(5) 16/1: 46/000/-62: Rear, rdn & hdwy over 2f 5 **46a**
out, kept on, no ch with wnr: acts on fast, gd/soft & polytrack: see 3288.
3605 **MISS GLORY BE** 9 [1] E R Oertel 6-9-13 p (52) Charlotte Kerton(7) 7/1: 6-035233: Mid-div, hdwy over nk **55a**
2f out, no extra fnl 1f: well h'capped: see 564.
3238 **GALEY RIVER** 2 [2] J J Sheehan 5-9-2 p (41) B O'Neill(5) 3/1: 5045064: Mid-div, hmpd & lost place 3 **40a**
3f out, kept on from over 1f out, nvr a threat: closer with clr passage, op 9/2: qck reapp: chkpcs reapplied.
3401 **SCARPIA** 17 [11]4-9-1 (40) K Jackson(5) 33/1: 0000-005: V slow away & bhd, mod late prog. 1 **38a**
3650 **JOEY PERHAPS** 7 [8]3-9-7 (55) Dean Williams 11/4 FAV: 0063236: Keen trkg ldr, led going well 3f hd **52a**
out, sn found little & wknd/hdd over 1f out: op 4/1: return to 1m & waiting tactics could suit: see 3650 & 3529.
3719 **PIQUET** 4 [5]6-9-11 (50) Lucy Russell(5) 8/1: 0630107: Mid-div, eff 3f out, no impress dist: qck reapp. 3½ **42a**
3605 **MRS BROWN** 9 [7]3-9-7 (55) S Archer(7) 8/1: 356058: Short of room early, held up, eff wide, btn dist. 1¼ **45a**
3602 **PIROUETTES** 9 [14]4-9-6 T (55) Jemma Marshall(5) 33/1: 340-0009: Led till 3f out, sn btn, tried t-strap. ½ **34a**
3187 **INDIAN BLAZE** 26 [3]10-9-11 (50) M Halford 7/2: 2036060: 10th: Mid-div, struggling fnl 2f: btr 3187. 1 **38a**
3677 **BLAISE WOOD** 6 [4]3-8-13 (47) J Jones(5) 12/1: 0602000: 11th: Rear & rdn/bhd fnl 3f: qck reapp. 8 **24a**
3395 **Midmaar** 17 [9]3-9-7 (55) Laura Pike(5) 33/1:0   3677 **Guard** 6 [10]4-9-2 t(41) Steven Harrison 25/1:0
13 Ran Time 2m 09.52(6.72) Owned: Mr Khalifa Sultan Trained: Newmarket

WINDSOR MONDAY 09.08.04 Sharp, Fig 8 Track

Official Going Good/Soft (Good places)

3824

5.45 Guinness Maiden Stakes 2yo (D)
£5343 £1644 £822 **6f rnd** **Good 44** **-06 Slow** Inside

3511 **ONE PUTRA 13** [5] M A Jarvis 2-9-0 P Robinson 100/30: 51: Made virtually all, styd on over 1f out, rdn out: imprvd from debut & eff at 6f on gd & a sharp trk: sure to relish 7f: useful, type to win more races. **94+**
REBUTTAL [8] B J Meehan 2-9-0 J Fortune 8/1: 2: b c Mr Greeley - Reboot (Rubiano) Slow away, sn in tch, eff over 1f out, kept on to chase wnr ins last, no impress: Mar foal, cost $400,000: dam sprint wnr in US: eff at 6f on gd grnd: learn plenty from this v pleasing start, looks sure to impr & win races. *1½* **89+**
3438 **MOTH BALL 16** [9] J A Osborne 2-9-0 D Holland 9/2: 23: With wnr, eff over 1f out, onepace under hands-&-heels: acts on fast & gd grnd: useful, must win a minor trk mdn: see 3438. *1¼* **85+**
SUDDEN DISMISSAL [14] G A Butler 2-9-0 T P Queally 33/1: 4: b c Inchinor - Suddenly (Puissance) In tch, eff well over 1f out, sn onepace on debut: Apr foal, cost E26,000: half-brother to a 1m wnr: dam 7f juv scorer: will apprec 7f in time: pleasing start, shld rate higher & win similar. *½* **83**
3478 **ENFORCER 14** [18]2-9-0 S Drowne 10/1: 45: Chsd ldrs, eff dist, onepace: shld find easier mdns. *2* **77**
2348 **GO MO 60** [1]2-9-0 J F Egan 66/1: 06: b c Night Shift - Quiche (Formidable) In tch, outpcd over 2f out, some late gains: May foal, cost E26,000: half-brother to sprint wnr, dam 6f scorer: speedily bred. *2* **71**
3438 **PRINCE SAMOS 16** [17]2-9-0 K Fallon 3/1 FAV: 47: In tch, wknd appr fnl 1f: btr 3438. *½* **69**
BOLODENKA [12]2-9-0 R Mullen 33/1: 8: In tch, some late gains, nvr dngrs on debut. *½* **67**
3478 **LADY LONDRA 14** [4]2-8-9 M Howard(5) 66/1: 09: In tch, wknd 2f out. *½* **60**
ONE GOOD THING [11]2-9-0 L Dettori 13/2: 0: 10th: In tch, rdn halfway, no impress. *1¼* **61**
3342 **SOUTHERN TIDE 19** [16]2-9-0 M Fenton 66/1: 00: 11th: Nvr a factor. *1¼* **57**
COME ON JONNY [13]2-9-0 N Chalmers(5) 50/1: 0: 12th: Slow away, nvr a factor. *¾* **55**
Ruby Murray [2]2-8-9 J Quinn 50/1:0 — **Kirkhammerton** [3]2-9-0 V Slattery 66/1:0
3361 **Dralion 18** [10]2-9-0 L Fletcher(3) 50/1:0 — 3342 **Reference 19** [6]2-9-0 P Dobbs 66/1:0
My Gacho [15]2-9-0 R Havlin 33/1:0 — 3476 **Eden Star 14** [7]2-8-9 Dane O'Neill 66/1:0
18 Ran Time 1m 13.31 (3.01) Owned: HRH Sultan Ahmad Shah Trained: Newmarket

3825

6.15 Nicholas Cunningham Memorial Auction Nursery Handicap Stakes Fillies 2yo (E) **[90]**
£4264 £1312 £656 **6f rnd** **Good 44** **-24 Slow** Inside

3245 **TEQUILA SHEILA 24** [7] K R Burke 2-9-2 (78) K Fallon 7/1: 0161: Held up, gd hdwy over 1f out, styd on to lead ins last, rdn out: back to best on gd grnd & v eff over a stiff or sharp 6f, shld get 7f: improving. **87**
3411 **CONSIDER THIS 17** [6] W M Brisbourne 2-9-3 (79) S Sanders 9/1: 2532: With ldrs, hdwy to lead over 1f out, hdd ins last, not pace of wnr: shown enough to win a race: see 3411, 2603. *1* **83**
3212 **IVANA ILLYICH 25** [8] S Kirk 2-8-8 (70) J F Egan 16/1: 50403: Held up, hdwy & short of room over 1f out, switched right & kept on ins last, nrst fin: shade unlucky & an encouraging run: see 2061. *shd* **73**
2697 **ALVARINHO LADY 46** [2] D Haydn Jones 2-8-12 (74) Paul Eddery 10/1: 1544: With ldrs, eff over 1f out, no extra ins last: 7 wk abs: see 2697, 1422. *1¼* **73**
3614 **ENCANTO 9** [3]2-9-7 (83) Derek Nolan(7) 7/1: 6222145: Bhd, eff to chall dist, no extra ins last. *¾* **80**
3614 **HIGH CHART 9** [9]2-9-0 T (76) A McCarthy 16/1: 1440306: In tch, wknd 2f out: see 1669, 1380. *3* **64**
2449 **DEBS BROUGHTON 56** [4]2-7-12 (4oh) (56) Lisa Jones 25/1: 0027: In tch, hung left 2f out, sn wknd. *¾* **46**
3504* **WITHERING LADY 13** [5]2-9-4 (80) R Havlin 8/1: 3462018: Keen in tch, wknd over 2f out: reportedly not handle grnd: see 3504 (mdn auct, fast). *¾* **64**
3536 **MADHAVI 12** [11]2-8-13 (75) P Dobbs 4/1 FAV: 0359: Al bhd: well back: btr 3251. *3½* **49**
3488 **EVANESCE 14** [12]2-8-12 (74) C Catlin 14/1: 2120040: 10th: With ldrs, wknd 2f out: btr 2442 (5f, fm). *½* **46**
3521 **ISLAND SWING 12** [1]2-9-6 (82) L Dettori 5/1: 01140: 11th: Led till dist, wknd & eased: best 2358. *¾* **52**
3284 **BAILEYS APPLAUSE 23** [10]2-8-2 bl (64) Hayley Turner(5) 20/1: 53600: 12th: Al bhd, saddle slipped over 2f out, t.o.: see 1652. *dist* **0**
12 Ran Time 1m 14.38 (4.08) Owned: Mr Lee Westwood Trained: Leyburn

3826

6.45 Talksport 1089/1053am 'porky' Parry Classified Stakes 3yo+ 0-80 (D)
£5493 £1690 £845 **1m67y rnd** **Good 44** **+07 Fast** Inside

3469+**TARFAH 15** [2] G A Butler 3-8-9 (82) S Sanders 11/4: 11: Cl-up, hdwy to lead over 1f out, sn pushed clr, easily: hvly bckd: eff at 8/3f, 10f sure to suit: acts on gd grnd & a stiff or sharp trk: looks useful, plenty more to come & one to keep on your side: see 3469. **97+**
3216 **KENTUCKY KING 2** [6] P W Hiatt 4-9-3 (80) L Dettori 9/2: 3000352: In tch, eff over 2f out, kept on ins last, not pace of wnr: gd run, shade further will suit now: see 3216, 1057. *5* **85**
2224+**CUT SHORT 66** [4] J H M Gosden 3-8-7 (80) J Fortune 9/4 FAV: 513: Led, rdn & hdd over 1f out, sn wknd: nicely bckd: 10 wk abs: mdn fills wnr in 2224. *1½* **79**
3641 **RAFFERTY 7** [5] C E Brittain 5-9-4 (81) D Holland 7/2: 000-0534: In tch, wknd qckly 2f out: btr 3641. *3* **77**
2313 **LINNING WINE 61** [3]8-9-4 (81) S Carson 16/1: 0240645: In tch, hung left & not go on over 2f out: 2 mth abs: tricky ride now: see 2313, 1877. *1* **75**
625 **JEWEL OF INDIA 177** [7]5-9-3 (80) S Drowne 33/1: 1/350-006: Al bhd: long abs: see 547. *4* **66**
3694 **JOOLS 5** [1]6-9-3 (75) Dane O'Neill 10/1: 4650U67: Al bhd: qck reapp: see 1057. *14* **38**
7 Ran Time 1m 46.1 (3.1) Owned: Mr Abdulla Al Khalifa Trained: Blewbury

3827 **7.15 Totequadpot Handicap Stakes 3yo+ 0-100 (C)** **[98]**
£12505 £4743 £2372 **6f rnd** **Good 44** **+07 Fast** Inside

3584+**JONNY EBENEEZER 10** [12] D Flood 5-8-9 bl (79) L Dettori 3/1 FAV: 2211411: In tch far side, qcknd to lead ins fnl 1f, pushed clr: bckd: suited by 5/7f, stays 1m on fm, soft & f/sand: best hld up, loves Newmarket: goes esp well for L Dettori: thriving this term & still on a handy mark, win again: see 3584. **94**
3673 **JAYANJAY 6** [5] Miss B Sanders 5-8-10 (80) S Sanders 7/1: 3431522: Chsd ldrs far side, styd on well into 2nd cl-home, no ch with wnr: qck reapp, op 9/1: met an in-form rival, see 3673. *1½* **86**
3268 **CRIMSON SILK 23** [6] D Haydn Jones 4-9-8 BL (92) Paul Eddery 16/1: 0000303: Front rank far side, led 2f out till ins fnl 1f, bmpd rail & caught for 2nd cl-home: apprec drop back to h'cap company & blnks. *2* **92**
3293 **PRESTO SHINKO 21** [13] R Hannon 3-8-9 (83) K Fallon 11/2: 1632134: In tch far side, kept on under press fnl 1f: nicely bckd: btr 2375. *½* **81**
3628 **LITTLE EDWARD 8** [1]6-9-4 (88) L Keniry(3) 25/1: 0050005: Slowly away far side, recovered to chase ldrs, onepcd fnl 1f: best conceding weight to inferior rivals in small fields: see 1845. *shd* **85**
3628 **FURTHER OUTLOOK 8** [7]10-9-0 (84) D Holland 25/1: 4230006: Led till 2f out far side, no extra. *1¼* **77**
3061 **ZILCH 32** [11]6-10-0 (98) R Mullen 12/1: 2140107: Rear far side, styd on late, nrst fin: see 2758. *hd* **90**
3622 **MARSAD 9** [3]10-9-2 (86) P Doe 14/1: 0302008: Rear far side, styd on late, nvr dangerous. *nk* **77**
3584 **BOLEYN CASTLE 10** [2]7-9-3 (87) L Fletcher(3) 25/1: 00-00049: Front rank till halfway far side. *3½* **68**
3577 **TALLY 10** [8]4-7-12 (1oh) (67) J Mackay 20/1: 4300140: 10th: Slowly away far side, nvr nr ldrs. *2½* **42**
3479 **MISS GEORGE 14** [10]6-8-11 (81) Dane O'Neill 12/1: 3060030: 11th: Slowly away & al outpcd far side: reportedly lost a shoe: see 3479. *¾* **53**
3269 **CAUSTIC WIT 23** [18]6-9-1 p (85) R Miles(3) 6/1: 1112200: 12th: Made all stands side, no ch with fav'd far side: on the wrong side, forget this: see 2758. *4* **45**
3643* **MICHELLE MA BELLE 7** [16]4-8-6 (6ex)bl (76) J F Egan 10/1: 2200010: 13th: Chsd ldrs stands side, no ch with far side from halfway: forgive this: much btr 3643. *¾* **34**
3165 **WILLHECONQUERTOO 28** [17]4-7-13 t (69) B Swarbrick(5) 16/1: 0035100: 14th: Chsd ldrs stands side, no ch when hmpd entering fnl 1f: on the wrong side: twice below 2975. *½* **25**
3372 **COMPTON BANKER 18** [14]7-7-12 (1oh) (67) F P Ferris(3) 33/1: 0652030: 15th: Al outpcd far side: new stable, prev with G Butler: see 3372. *shd* **24**
3434 **MINE BEHIND 16** [15]4-8-13 (83) M Savage(5) 20/1: 2000100: 16th: Chsd ldrs stands side, no ch halfway. *8* **15**
16 Ran Time 1m 12.52 (2.22) Owned: Mrs Ruth M Serrell Trained: Hungerford

3828 **7.45 Reading Evening Post Maiden Stakes 3yo+ (D)**
£4251 £1308 £654 **1m67y rnd** **Good 44** **-11 Slow** Inside

3480 **SEA NYMPH 14** [8] Sir Michael Stoute 3-8-9 K Fallon 4/7 FAV: 521: Chsd ldrs, imprvd to lead 1.5f out, rdn out, shade cosily: hvly bckd: deserved win, eff over a sharpish 1m on gd & firm grnd: open to improvement in h'caps, shld apprec further: see 3480 (C/D). **76**
NEWNHAM [6] L M Cumani 3-9-0 N Mackay(3) 14/1: 2: ch g Theatrical - Brief Escapade (Brief Truce) Rear, styd on well into 2nd ins fnl 1f, no ch with wnr: debut: eff over a sharp 1m, bred to apprec mid-dists: acts on gd grnd, runs well fresh: sure to learn from this & can find a race. *1¾* **74**
3469 **PAINTBOX 15** [7] Mrs A J Perrett 3-8-9 S Sanders 10/1: 63: Pushed in rear, styd on late, nvr dngrs: pleasing run, eff over an easy 1m on gd grnd, will stay further judged on this: see 3469. *2½* **64**
3592 **DANETTIE 9** [11] W M Brisbourne 3-8-9 B Swarbrick(5) 66/1: 054: Chsd ldrs, ev ch halfway, wknd fnl 1f. *1½* **61**
2394 **SECOND WARNING 58** [12]3-9-0 (60) L Dettori 20/1: 000-505: Chsd ldrs, held when bmpd 1.5f out: abs. *2½* **61**
3631 **SWEEP THE BOARD 8** [14]3-9-0 T P Queally 66/1: 0-06: b c Fasliyev - Fun Board (Saumarez) Led till 1.5f out, wknd: unplcd sole '03 start: lightly rcd & modest form to date for A Jarvis. *hd* **60**
2700 **LASSER LIGHT 46** [5]4-9-7 S Righton 50/1: 0-07: b g Inchinor - Light Ray (Rainbow Quest) Chsd ldrs, outpcd 2f out: 7 wk abs: no form yet. *1¼* **57**
3610 **MAGARI 9** [2]3-8-9 M Fenton 25/1: 3-48: Nvr nr ldrs. *nk* **51**
RUSSIAN APPLAUSE [1]4-9-7 J Quinn 33/1: 9: Chsd ldrs 6f, wknd on debut. *1¼* **53**
3477 **EL CHAPARRAL 14** [13]4-9-7 (68) Dane O'Neill 9/2: 6002020: 10th: Slowly away, v keen & hdwy to chall halfway, btn 2f out: op 6/1: capable of btr, rcd much too keenly here: see 3477 (10f). *nk* **52**
3480 **MEDICA BOBA 14** [10]3-8-9 S Drowne 50/1: 0000: 11th: Al rear. *2* **43**
RABBIT [9]3-8-9 V Slattery 50/1: 0: 12th: Slowly away, al bhd on debut. *3½* **36**
2987 **SPES BONA 35** [3]3-9-0 D Holland 20/1: 040: 13th: Al well bhd, fin last: see 2987. *14* **13**
13 Ran Time 1m 47.61 (4.61) Owned: Ballymacoll Stud Trained: Newmarket

3829 **8.15 Come Racing On Saturday Evening 28th August Handicap Stakes 3yo+ 0-70 (E)** **[70]**
£3533 £1087 £544 **1m3f135y** **Good 44** **-20 Slow** Inside

3481 **BAKIRI 14** [12] Andrew Reid 6-8-13 (55) J F Egan 20/1: 2324001: Chsd ldrs, imprvd to lead dist, styd on gamely but v sadly collapsed & died sn after finish. **62**
3638 **PONT NEUF 7** [11] P D Evans 4-9-9 (65) S Donohoe(7) 5/1: 4251102: Mid-div, imprvd 2f out, fin strongly but just failed: op 13/2: see 3481 (C/D). *¾* **70**
3674 **ABSINTHER 6** [8] M R Bosley 7-8-7 (49) Hayley Turner(5) 13/2: 0-021433: Slowly away, gd prog to lead 2f out, collared dist, not qckn cl-home: sound run, see 2836. *1½* **51**
3605 **FLAMING SPIRT 9** [13] J S Moore 5-8-8 (50) Derek Nolan(6) 33/1: 0000/0-44: Chsd ldrs, onepace. *nk* **52**
3392 **SAHAAT 17** [4]6-10-0 (70) L Fletcher(3) 33/1: 0005025: Led briefly early on, remained prom, onepcd. *1½* **70**
3638 **STOLEN SONG 7** [2]4-8-13 (55) S Whitworth 11/1: 6006326: Front rank, ev ch till onepcd fnl 1.5f. *¾* **54**
3598 **SWIFT ALCHEMIST 9** [9]4-8-13 P (55) G Baker 50/1: 0030007: Held up, styd on late: cheek pieces. *shd* **54**
3217 **MAN THE GATE 25** [14]5-9-3 (59) S Sanders 6/1: 0362158: Held up, keeping on/short of room dist. *nk* **58**
3404 **KALOU 17** [17]6-8-6 (48) T P Queally 11/4 FAV: 503-3039: Chsd ldrs, onepcd when stumbled dist, no ch after: hvly bckd: promising in 3404. *¾* **46**
3454 **SIR ALFRED 16** [1]5-8-13 (55) T E Durcan 20/1: 0630-040: 10th: Rear, hdwy to chall 3f out, sn btn. *nk* **52**
3295 **MALAK AL MOULOUK 21** [3]4-9-11 (67) D Holland 6/1: 425-420: 11th: Trkd ldrs, led briefly 3f out, wknd. *1* **62**
3114 **PRIVATE BENJAMIN 30** [7]4-8-4 (46) P Doe 25/1: 3010500: 12th: Hdwy to chase ldrs 2f out, sn btn. *1¾* **38**
4246] **DESERT AIR 686** [15]5-9-13 (69) J Fortune 20/1: 103230/-0: 13th: ch g Desert King - Greek Air (Ela Mana Mou) Sn led, hdd 3f out, wknd: 02/03 nov hdle wnr (first time visor, rtd 119h, eff at 2m on gd/soft & soft): '02 claim wnr for P Cole, also h'cap plcd & tried blnks: eff at 10/12f on gd & firm grnd: handles a *½* **60**

stiff/gall or sharpish trk. 2 Sep'02 Brig 11.8fm 67-68 E: 1 Jul'02 Newm 10g/f 70- D: 2 Aug'01 Leic 7gd 77- D:
3313 **INTERNATIONALGUEST 21** [6]5-10-0 P (70) N Pollard 14/1: 2005550: 14th: Mid-div, wknd dist.   1½   59
2180 **Saspys Lad 67** [10]7-9-4 (60) B Swarbrick(5) 33/1:0   3477 **Victory Venture 14** [5]4-9-9 (65) C Catlin 66/1:0
16 Ran   Time 2m 34.8(7.5)   Owned: Mr A S Reid   Trained: Mill Hill London

---

Official Going GOOD/SOFT - SOFT after 8.00. Rain Throughout Evening.

3830	**6.00 Sinnington Selling Handicap Stakes 3yo+ 35-55** (F)					**[57]**
	£3248 £928 £464	**1m rnd**	**Good/Soft**	**Inapplicable**	Inside	

3242 **DARA MAC 24** [6] N Bycroft 5-9-10 (53) Suzanne France(7) 6/1 CO FAV: 2631001: Held up, prog wide   64+
3f out, styd on to lead dist, pushed clr: no bid: eff at 7f/1m on fast & gd/soft: enjoys sell grade: see 2688.
3324 **ZARIN 20** [3] D W Chapman 6-9-6 (49) A Culhane 10/1: 0300062: Led, hdd dist, not pace easy wnr.   5   50
2850 **MILLKOM ELEGANCE 40** [16] K A Ryan 5-9-2 bl (45) N Callan 14/1: 5/0501-03: Chsd ldrs, ev ch dist,   1¼   44
no extra: recent p.u. over hdles: see 2850.
3159 **DONEGAL SHORE 28** [14] Mrs J Candlish 5-9-0 vis t (43) K McEvoy 16/1: 2430604: Rear, prog wide 3f   ¾   40
out, kept on fnl 1f: btr 1379 (fibresand).
3668 **CANLIS 6** [10]5-9-2 (45) P Hanagan 20/1: 0-020005: Bhd, prog 3f out, kept on fnl 1f: qck reappr.   1   40
3759 **RYMERS RASCAL 3** [5]12-9-6 (49) W Supple 6/1 CO FAV: 3200206: Bhd, nvr nrr than mid-div: qck   ½   43
reappr: won this race 2 yrs ago off a 2lb higher mark: btr 2947.
3426 **SUMMER SPECIAL 16** [8]4-8-13 p (42) L Enstone(3) 33/1: 5033007: Handy over 6f, sn wknd: btr 2544.   nk   35
3487 **SUPER DOMINION 14** [2]7-9-4 p (47) Stephanie Hollinshead(5) 33/1: 1401008: Prom 6f, wknd: btr 2725.   1¼   38
3650 **NOBLE PURSUIT 7** [15]7-9-7 (50) T Eaves(3) 16/1: 0240309: Al mid-div: qck reappr: btr 3426.   hd   40
2891 **ALPINE HIDEAWAY 38** [12]11-9-2 p (45) D Allan 20/1: 6140-060: 10th: Prom 6f, fdd: recently plcd   ½   34
over hdles (rtd 84h, sell h'cap): see 2891.
3406} **EASTERN SCARLET 90** [13]4-8-12 (41) F Norton(3) 6/1 CO FAV: 3555-050: 11th: b g Woodborough -   3   24
Cuddles (Taufan) Al bhd: earlier unplcd over hdles (mdn): mod Flat form in Ireland this yr: plcd once in '03 when
trained in Britain (rtd 50, sell, Mrs L Stubbs): auct mdn wnr in '02 (K A Ryan): prev eff at 5f, prob stays 9.7f:
acts on firm & fast grnd: eff on a sharp trk, tried blnks & cheek pieces: with V Smith.
2 Aug'02 Muss 5fm 73-72 D: 1 Jul'02 Muss 5g/f 75- E:
3548 **SPRING DANCER 11** [7]3-8-13 t (49) P Mulrennan(3) 12/1: 0005360: 12th: Handy 5f, wknd: btr 2205.   shd   31
3526 **SHAMWARI FIRE 12** [9]4-9-5 (48) R Ffrench 15/2: 6003300: 13th: In tch, fdd 2f out: btr 3242.   shd   29
3609 Ace Ma Vahra 9 [1]6-8-11 (40) J Bramhill 12/1:0   2335 Thumamah 60 [4]5-9-0 t(43) Darren Williams 50/1:0
3670 Blunham 6 [11]4-9-4 (47) R Winston 16/1:0
456   Magenta Rising 200 [18]4-9-11 (54) Rory Moore(7) 33/1:0
17 Ran   Time 1m 44.52 (9.12)   Owned: Mr N Bycroft   Trained: Malton

3831	**6.30 Beatrice Stephenson Maiden Auction Stakes 2yo** (E)				
	£3751 £1154 £577	**7f rnd**	**Good/Soft**	**Inapplicable**	Inside

3412 **THUNDERWING 17** [9] K R Burke 2-8-10 Darren Williams 6/1: 31: Chsd ldrs, styd on to lead dist,   86+
went clr, readily: op 9/2: eff at 7f, further will suit: acts on fast & gd/soft grnd: won with authority & has a
good future: see 3412 (debut).
      KINGS ACCOUNT [10] M Johnston 2-8-10 J Fanning 12/1: 2: ch c King of Kings - Fighting Countess   2½   78
(Ringside) Bhd, prog halfway, styd on fnl 1f, not pace easy wnr: op 8/1 on debut: May foal, cost 9,000gns:
half-brother to wnrs abroad: dam won numerous times abroad: sire Gr 1 wnr at 1m: eff at 7f, further will suit:
acts on gd/soft grnd: promising debut & can progress.
3594 **ROBINZAL 9** [13] T D Easterby 2-8-10 K Darley 33/1: 03: b g Zilzal - Sulitelma (The Minstrel)   ¾   76
Led till dist, no extra: Apr foal, half-brother 1m wnr as a juv: dam successful at 5f: sire Gr 1 wnr at 1m: eff
at 7f, 1m will suit: acts on gd/soft grnd: left debut effort bhd with encouraging effort.
3239 **COMICAL ERRORS 24** [8] P C Haslam 2-8-10 Rory Moore(7) 66/1: 04: b g Distorted Humor -   1½   73
Fallibility (Tom Rolfe) Rear, prog 3f out, nrst fin: Feb foal, half-brother to numerous wnrs abroad: dam unplcd:
sire decent performer around 1m abroad: eff at 7f, looks in need of further: acts on gd/soft grnd.
3239 **GOOD INVESTMENT 24** [2]2-8-10 G Faulkner 9/2: 35: Prom, ev ch dist, no extra: tchd 11/2.   ¾   71
3376 **ABLE CHARLIE 18** [14]2-8-10 R Winston 9/4 FAV: 26: Handy & keenly, wide bend turning for home,   ¾   69
sn ev ch, wknd dist: well bckd: btr expected after promising debut in 3376.
3500 **MISS ROSIE 13** [4]2-8-8 D Allan 5/1: 447: Cl-up 5f, wknd: op 7/1: btr 3500 (fast).   hd   66
      ANDY MAL [3]2-8-2 P Hanagan 25/1: 8: Nvr nrr than mid-div on debut: with R A Fahey.   9   44
3544 **HANNAHS TRIBE 11** [6]2-8-2 F Norton 50/1: 09: Bhd, nvr a factor.   2   40
3568 **MY RASCAL 10** [5]2-8-10 N Callan 7/1: 00: 10th: Cl-up fnl, fdd.   1   46
      Liability [7]2-8-2 Kim Tinkler 100/1:0   3429 Summer Silks 16 [11]2-8-2 T Hamilton(3) 18/1:0
      Smiling Starduster [1]2-8-7 D Tudhope(7) 66/1:0   Continental Flyer [12]2-8-5 V Halliday 66/1:R
14 Ran   Time 1m 32.44 (9.54)   Owned: Market Avenue Racing Club Ltd   Trained: Leyburn

3832	**7.00 E B F Calverts Carpets Median Auction Maiden Stakes 2yo** (E)				
	£4193 £1290 £645	**5f str**	**Good/Soft**	**Inapplicable**	Stands side

3082 **COLEORTON DANCER 31** [7] K A Ryan 2-9-0 (65) N Callan 16/1: 044401: Prom, styd on to lead dist,   86+
pushed clr: eff arnd 5f on firm & gd/soft: has been gelded & an imprvd run: see 2573.
2927 **OCEANICO DOT COM 37** [8] F Norton 40/1: 002: br f Hernando - Karen Blixen (Kris)   4   70
Prom, ev ch 2f out, no extra fnl 1f: Feb first foal, cost £10,000: dam unrcd: sire decent performer at mid-dists:
eff at 5f, further will suit in time: acts on gd/soft grnd.
3445 **NE OUBLIE 16** [2] J Mackie 2-9-0 Dale Gibson 25/1: 643: Handy wide over 3f, sn no extra: btr 3445.   2   69

3266 **CHISELLED** 23 [12] K R Burke 2-9-0 (85) Darren Williams 4/9 FAV: 42204: Led till dist, no extra: hd 68
well bckd at odds-on: disapp on today's rain softened grnd but handled such conditions in 1458, btr 1826.
3525 **ONE OF EACH** 12 [10]2-8-9 D Tudhope(7) 40/1: 55: Handy till dist, no extra: see 3525. ½ 62
   COCONUT MOON [4]2-8-9 P Hanagan 20/1: 6: b f Bahamian Bounty - Lunar Ridge (Indian Ridge) ¾ 60
Slow away, nvr nrr than mid-div: debut: Feb foal, cost 4,500gns: sire Gr winning sprinter as a juv.
3504 **JASMINE HILL** 13 [13]2-8-9 R Winston 66/1: 067: Rear, modest late gains. 5 47
3491 **HERENCIA** 14 [3]2-9-0 Dean McKeown 100/1: 008: Al bhd. ¾ 50
3525 **FOLGA** 12 [11]2-8-9 W Supple 20/1: 39: Bhd, nvr a factor: btr 3525 (fast). hd 44
3376 **DESERT BUZZ** 18 [1]2-9-0 M Tebbutt 80/1: 060500: 10th: Chsd ldrs 3f, wknd. hd 48
2795 **LIWAS LAKE** 42 [6]2-8-9 K McEvoy 11/2: 300: 11th: Handy 3f, sn fdd: 6 wk abs: btr 2097 (fast). 2 38
3504 **STAR OF KILDARE** 13 [9]2-8-9 Kim Tinkler 100/1: 0000: 12th: Mid-div 3f, fdd. 3 30
12 Ran Time 1m 2.03 (5.03) Owned: Coleorton Moor Racing Trained: Hambleton

---

3833 7.30 Weatherbys Printing Services Handicap Stakes 3yo 0-80 (D) [87]
   £5538 £1704 £852 5f str Good/Soft Inapplicable Stands side

3347* **TRUE MAGIC** 19 [13] J D Bethell 3-8-10 (69) J Fanning 7/1: 6-562211: Handy, ev ch bef 1f out, 76
styd on to lead ins fnl 1f, rdn out: op 5/1: eff at 5/6f on fast & gd/soft grnd: remains in gd form: see 3347.
3737 **TROJAN FLIGHT** 4 [7] Mrs J R Ramsden 3-8-0 (59) F Norton 6/1 FAV: 4606432: In tch, prog when hd 65+
short of room dist, switched & staying on when saddle slipped ins fnl 1f, just failed: qck reapp: eff at 5/7f: most
unfortunate, must be given another chance: see 3737 & 3575.
3591* **BARON RHODES** 9 [12] J S Wainwright 3-9-7 (80) T Eaves(3) 7/1: 3130513: Prom, led 2f out, hdd ins 1 83
fnl 1f, no extra: 4lb higher than recent win in 3591 (fills h'cap).
3599 **KAMENKA** 9 [14] R A Fahey 3-8-11 (70) P Hanagan 12/1: 3044-444: Chsd ldrs, prog dist, not rch 1¾ 68
ldrs: acts on fast & gd/soft grnd: see 2728.
3527 **WENDYS GIRL** 12 [9]3-8-3 bl (62) R Ffrench(3) 28/1: 0101655: Bhd, prog fnl 1f, nrst fin: acts on ½ 59
firm, gd/soft & fibresand: btr 3018 (6f).
2566 **BAYLAW STAR** 51 [10]3-8-10 p (69) N Callan 33/1: 6304006: Led 3f, no extra fnl 1f: 7 wk abs: btr 1387. hd 65
3599 **NANNA** 9 [15]3-8-10 (69) A Culhane 7/1: 1621167: Prom, no extra dist: op 11/2: btr 3193. hd 64
3575 **SIR LOIN** 9 [8]3-7-12 (57) Kim Tinkler 16/1: 0-005268: Prom over 3f, no extra: btr 3193 (fast). ½ 51
3684 **MARYSIENKA** 5 [17]3-9-0 (73) J Edmunds 40/1: 0264-059: In tch over 3f, wknd: qck reapp. ½ 66
3356 **JADAN** 18 [11]3-9-2 (75) W Supple 15/2: 0366150: 10th: Al bhd: btr 3518. ¾ 66
2734 **TIZZYS LAW** 45 [2]3-8-5 (64) J Bramhill 14/1: 0-164500: 11th: Handy 3f, wknd: 6 wk abs. 1 52
3433 **ELLIOTS CHOICE** 16 [16]3-8-4 (63) K McEvoy 16/1: 0436000: 12th: Bhd, prog when short of room hd 50
halfway, again short of room dist, sn eased: this is best forgiven: btr 2985.
3567 **LUALUA** 10 [5]3-9-0 VIS (73) Darren Williams 8/1: 2304300: 13th: Slow away, prog when badly short 2½ 53
of room bef 1f out, not recover: first time visor: btr 3135.
3808 **Bella Boy Zee** 1 [6]3-8-1 (60) D Fentiman(7) 14/1:0   3599 **Hamaasy** 9 [4]3-8-1 (60) A Nicholls 25/1:0
15 Ran Time 1m 1.62 (4.62) Owned: Mr T R Lock Trained: Middleham

---

3834 8.00 Black Sheep Brewery Stakes Handicap 4yo+ 35-55 (F) [60]
   £3484 £1072 £536 2m Soft Inapplicable Inside

3493 **SUPER FELLOW** 14 [8] C N Kellett 10-8-4 (36) J Bramhill 7/1: ///00///-31: Held up, prog 3f out, 45+
rdn out to lead ins fnl 1f, eased cl home: op 9/1: eff arnd 2m, further will suit: acts on gd & soft grnd:
lightly rcd & unexposed in h'cap grade: see 3493.
3397* **MERCURIOUS** 17 [5] J Mackie 4-8-9 (41) Dale Gibson 7/1: 4154212: Handy, prog to lead bef 1f out, 1¾ 47
wandered under press, hdd ins fnl 1f, no extra: op 4/1: acts on soft grnd & both AWs: just btr 3397.
3493 **OOPS** 14 [11] J F Coupland 5-8-12 (44) W Supple 7/2 FAV: 42-01623: Prom, led bef 2f out, hdd bef nk 49
1f out, sn onepcd: tchd 5/1: see 3493 & 2941.
3397 **DOCTOR JOHN** 17 [13] Andrew Turnell 7-8-11 p (43) C Catlin 10/1: 1622024: Rear, prog 4f out, ev ch 1½ 47
dist, sn no extra: see 3397 (fibresand).
3557* **REGAL FANTASY** 11 [2]4-8-4 (36) Dean McKeown 6/1: 0/00-0015: Mid-div, prog halfway, wknd dist. 3½ 37
3502 **ILOVETURTLE** 13 [1]4-9-0 (46) R Winston 9/2: 0-035U66: Handy 12f, wknd: tchd 7/1: jumps fit. 7 40
3701 **SIMPLE IDEALS** 5 [3]10-8-3 (35) Kim Tinkler 8/1: 40-54067: Bhd, prog fnl 1f, nrst fnl 2f: qck reapp. 3½ 26
3530 **SOVEREIGN STATE** 12 [6]7-9-4 p (50) F Norton 8/1: 00/-14528: Al rear: first try at 2m: btr 3530. 3½ 38
3486 **BANNERS FLYING** 14 [10]4-9-4 (50) A Culhane 33/1: 0040409: Led till 2f out, fdd: see 3154. 10 29
7 **GOLDEN FIELDS** 273 [12]4-8-12 (44) N Callan 50/1: 010020-0: 10th: b f Definite Article - dist 0
Quickstep Queen (Pampabird) Bhd, prog 6f out, hung badly right on bend 4f out, sn eased to walk: recently ref to
race over hdles: sell wnr in '03 (A P Jarvis): unplcd in '02 (rtd 65, mdn): eff at 10/11f, has tried further: acts
on fast grnd & a sharp/turning or gall trk: eff with a visor, has tried blnks.
2 Oct'03 Yarm 14.1sft 49-(45) G: 1 Jul'03 Warw 10.9g/f 48-(47) G:
10 Ran Time 3m 41.72 (24.32) Trained: Mr A M Egan Trained: Burton-On-Trent

---

3835 8.30 Ure Handicap Stakes 3yo 0-75 (E) [81]
   £3682 £1133 £567 1m rnd Soft Inapplicable Inside

3516* **SHES OUR LASS** 12 [9] D Carroll 3-9-7 (74) K McEvoy 7/2: 0131111: Rear, prog wide halfway, styd 79+
on to lead bef 1f out, pushed out, val 3L+: op 5/2: eff at 7f/1m on firm, soft & fibresand: v progressive 3yo who
easily landed 5th win of campaign: see 3516 & 2506.
3571 **COTTINGHAM** 10 [5] M C Chapman 3-8-6 (59) Stephanie Hollinshead(5) 16/1: 0-146602: Handy, prog to 1½ 58
lead 2f out, hdd dist, kept on, not pace easy wnr: acts on firm, soft grnd & fibresand: see 355.
3413 **DANCER KING** 17 [8] T P Tate 3-7-12 (51) R Ffrench 10/1: 5003: Mid-div, prog 3f out, styd on fnl ¾ 47
1f: h'cap bow: eff at 1m, shaped as tho' further will suit: acts on soft grnd: see 2692.
3501 **WRENLANE** 13 [6] R A Fahey 3-8-10 (63) P Hanagan 7/2: 30-26504: Keen cl-up, no extra dist: op 2 56
5/1: rcd far too keenly today: btr 2042.
3379 **COMPTON MUSIC** 18 [10]3-8-2 p (55) J Bramhill 20/1: 0605605: Hld up, prog 3f out, hung left & onepcd: ½ 47
3575 **UHURU PEAK** 10 [7]3-8-2 (55) Dale Gibson 7/1: 5003206: Chsd ldrs, no extra fnl 2f: btr 3262 (6f). 1¾ 43
3516 **LOUISIADE** 12 [1]3-8-9 (62) D Allan 11/4 FAV: 0300337: Led 6f, sn wknd: well bckd: prob hd 49
unsuited by today's soft grnd: btr 3516 (fast) & 3410 (firm).

THIRSK MONDAY 09.08.04 Lefthand, Flat, Oval Track

3007 **BOLD PHOENIX 34** [4]3-9-6 (73) K Darley 11/1: 0068: Mid-div, prog to chase ldr 5f out, wknd 2f out. **3 54**
3419 **CHEVERAK FOREST 16** [2]3-8-9 (62) Kim Tinkler 20/1: 3150-009: ch g Shinko Forest - Meranie Girl **7 30**
(Mujadil) Bhd, nvr a factor: sell, sell h'cap & claim wnr in '03 (M R Channon): suited by 6f on fast & gd/soft
grnd: acts on a stiff/gall or sharp trk: likes Newcastle: has tried a visor: with Don Enrico Incisa.
1 Oct'03 Newc 6fm 67-62 G: 1 Aug'03 Ripo 6g/f 66-(66) F: 1 May'03 Newc 6g/s 70- F:
9 Ran Time 1m 50.0(14.6) Owned: We-Know Partnership Trained: Warthilll

DEAUVILLE TUESDAY 03.08.04 Righthand, Galloping Track

Official Going Good/Soft

3836 2.20 Gr 3 Prix de Psyche 3yo Fillies ()
£25704 £10282 £7711 **1m2f Good/Soft**

QUILANGA [11] A Wohler 3-8-12 Gary Stevens 117/10: 1111: b f Lomitas - Quebrada (Devil's Bag) **112**
Sn handy & led over 1f out, styd on strongly: German trained filly who remains unbeaten from 4 career starts: May '04
wnr of a Listed contest at San Siro: suited by 10f on good/soft & soft ground: likes a gall trk: smart filly.
3089 **KINNAIRD 25** [12] P C Haslam 3-8-12 (110) K Darley 58/10: 111-4522: Handy, chance over 1f out, **1 110**
kept on, not pace of wnr ins last: tough & smart: see 3089, 2005.
2814 **CLOON 40** [10] N Clement 3-8-12 bl C P Lemaire 13/10: 1-452133: Held up, styd on for press, nrst fin. **½ 109**
2491 **BAY TREE 48** [6]3-8-12 (99) T P Queally 65/1: 107-6308: Rear, little hdwy: abs: see 1666, 1169. **6 99**
12 Ran Time () Owned: Stiftung Gestut Fahrhof Trained: Germany

DEAUVILLE SATURDAY 07.08.04 Righthand, Galloping Track

Official Going Good/Soft

3837 3.30 Gr 2 Prix de Pomone 3yo+ Fillies & Mares ()
£42148 £16268 £7764 **1m4f110y Good/Soft**

3013* **LUNE DOR 34** [5] R Gibson 3-8-11 T Jarnet 46/10: 2-3111: Held up, hdwy to chse ldr 2f out, rdn & **114**
styd on to lead well in last: eff at 12f on gd/sft & soft ground: smart & progressive filly: see 3013.
2946 **HIDDEN HOPE 35** [8] G Wragg 3-8-6 (106) D Bonilla 206/10: 00-21542: Trkd ldr, led over 2f out, no **½ 107**
extra when hdd well ins last: ran to best, shld win in List/Gr 3 comp: see 2946, 2517 & 1568 (Listed).
SWEET STREAM [9] J E Hammond 4-9-4 T Gillet 53/1: 03311-03: b f Shantou - Snug Dinner (Jareer) **nk 107**
Rear, styd on late for press, not pace of wnr.
2517 **RAVE REVIEWS 51** [13]3-8-6 (105) O Doleuze 39/1: 61-3109: Trkd ldrs, btn over 1f out, abs: btr 1733 (gd). **14 86**
3278+**BENEVENTA 21** [2]4-9-4 (110) T Thulliez 15/2: 40-112010: 10th: Led till over 2f out, wknd qckly: btr 3278. **¾ 86**
12 Ran Time () Owned: Mme P de Moussac Trained: France

DEAUVILLE SUNDAY 08.08.04 Righthand, Galloping Track

Official Going Good/Soft

3838 2.50 Gr 1 Prix Maurice de Gheest 3yo+ ()
£80479 £32197 £16099 **6f110y str Good/Soft**

3062 **SOMNUS 31** [2] T D Easterby 4-9-2 (117) Gary Stevens 146/10: 210-0251: Trkd ldr stands side, **120**
joined main group from halfway, led 3f out, drvn & held on most gamely, all out: 6f specialist, acts on fast/firm,
loves gd/sft ground: high class sprinter when encountering these conditions: spot on for Haydock.
1480 **WHIPPER 99** [10] R Collet 3-8-12 C Soumillon 33/10 FAV: 1141-152: Held up, prog 2f out, styd on **nk 121**
well ins last, just held: 3 mth abs: apprec return to sprinting & loves an easy surface: high-class, see 1480.
2306 **DOLMA 63** [4] N Clement 3-8-8 C P Lemaire 188/10: 2212313: b f Marchand de Sabie - Young Manila **nk 116**
(Manil) Led stands side group & left racing alone from halfway, styd on gamely for press: recent wnr of a 7f Listed
fillies event here at Deauville: earlier landed a 6f Listed event at Chantilly: eff btwn 6f/1m on gd & hvy ground.
2 Apr'04 Mais 7sft 105- A:
3062 **ASHDOWN EXPRESS 31** [6] C F Wall 5-9-2 (111) S Sanders 21/1: 10-302024: Held up, styd on for **hd 117**
press fnl 2f, not pace of wnr: remains in fine form after career best in 3062.
3167* **THE TRADER 29** [15]6-9-2 bl (113) D Sweeney 69/10: 26-13015: Rear, swtchd & hdwy 2f out, jinked **1 114**
left dist, styd on strongly, nrst fin: see 3167 (Listed).
3564 **GOLDEN NUN 9** [8]4-8-13 bl (101) R Winston 93/1: 23131057: Rear, late hdwy, nrst fin: wants Gr 3/List. **2¾ 103**
3062 **MONSIEUR BOND 31** [19]4-9-2 (117) F Lynch 55/1: 5-511069: Cl up, onepace bef dist: btr 1667 (Gr 2). **½ 104**
3062+**FRIZZANTE 31** [18]5-8-13 (111) J P Murtagh 43/10: 11-21310: 10th: Rear, nvr able to land a blow: **nk 100**
much btr expected after Gr 1 win in 3062.
2469 **BRUNEL 54** [12]3-8-12 (115) D Holland 27/1: 2215-1150: 11th: Led after 1f till 3f out, prom till over 1f out. **hd 104**
2769* **ROYAL MILLENNIUM 43** [11]6-9-2 (110) T E Durcan 34/1: 221425-10: 12th: Mid-div, rdn & hung right **nk 101**
over 1f out, fdd: 6 wk abs: btr 2769.
18 Ran Time () Owned: Legard Sidebottom & Sykes Trained: Great Habton

HOPPEGARTEN   SUNDAY 08.08.04

Official Going Good

3839 **3.35 Gr 3 Grosser Preis von Berlin 3yo+ ()**
£22535 £9155 £4577   **6f110y**   **Good**

FELICITY GER [1] P Rau 3-8-7 A Boschert 57/10: 1: ch f Inchinor - Felina (Acatenango) Held up, styd on strongly from 2f out to lead well ins last: eff at 6/7f on gd & soft.   **111**
KEY TO PLEASURE [3] M Hofer 4-9-5 J P Carvaiho 43/10: 2: Always handy & led 2f out, hdd ins last. ¾ **114**
GOLD TYPE [6] K Woodburn 5-9-5 A Helfenbein 23/1: 3: Held up, styd on well from over 1f out. 2½ **106**
3508 **NAAHY 12** [11]4-9-5 (106) S Hitchcott 58/10: 01-110446: Dsptd lead till 2f out, btn dist: btr 3508, 3320. 2 **100**
11 Ran   Time 1m 16.80()   Owned: Gestut Ittlingen   Trained: Germany

CURRAGH   SUNDAY 08.08.04   Righthand, Galloping Track

Official Going Good/Firm

3840 **2.45 Gr 2 Royal Whip Stakes 3yo+   ()**
£52260 £16549 £7839   **1m2f**   **Good/Firm**

3496 **SOLSKJAER 15** [4] A P O'Brien 4-9-6 J P Spencer 9/4: 0-1221: b c Danehill - Lyndonville (Top   **113**
Ville) Made all & dictated pace, held on all out under a well judged ride: op 4/1: eff at 7f/1m, imprvd last twice at 10f: likes fast ground & a gall trk: v smart colt: see 3496, 2820.
2 Jul'04 Leop 10g/f 108- : 2 Jun'04 Curr 8g/f 104- :
3322* **TROPICAL LADY 21** [5] J S Bolger 4-9-3 M J Kinane 11/8 FAV: 06-111112: Trkd ldrs, short of room hd **109**
2f out, swtchd & chall ins last, just held: stays 10f: tough, genuine & smart: see 3322, 3011.
3496 **MEDICINAL 15** [7] D K Weld 3-8-11 bl P J Smullen 7/1: 1-43143: Trkd ldr, kept on well for press nk **111**
fnl 1f, just held close home in a v tight fin: v useful: see 3496, 2456.
6 Ran   Time 2m 02.90 ()   Owned: Mrs A M O'Brien   Trained: Ballydoyle

3841 **3.45 Gr 1 Phoenix Fillies 2yo ()**
£118992 £38592 £18492   **6f**   **Good/Firm**

2490* **DAMSON 53** [1] D Wachman 2-8-11 K Fallon 8/11 FAV: 1111: b f Entrepreneur - Tadkiyra (Darshaan)   **117+**
Trkd ldrs, niggled hlafway, swtchd & qcknd to lead dist, rdn out: abs: eff at 5/6f, 7f will suit: acts on fast & gd/sft: v smart filly with a fine turn of foot, more Gr success beckons: see 2490, 2328.
1 Jun'04 Asco 5g/f 116-0 A: 1 Jun'04 Naas 6g/f 104- :
3319* **ORATORIO 21** [2] A P O'Brien 2-9-0 J A Heffernan 15/2: 1012: Cl up, briefly outpcd over 1f out, ¾ **117**
kept on ins last, not pace of wnr: smart effort, win again in Gr company, at 7f: see 3319 (Gr 3).
2819 **RUSSIAN BLUE 42** [4] A P O'Brien 2-9-0 J P Spencer 9/4: 11123: Led till dist, no extra when ½ **115**
edged right nr line: abs: smart run, relish a return to List/Gr 3: see 2819, 1994.
6 Ran   Time 1m 13.20 ()   Owned: Mrs John Magnier   Trained: Carrrick On Shore

3842 **4.15 Gr 3 Phoenix Sprint Stakes 3yo+   ()**
£32662 £9548 £4523   **6f**   **Good/Firm**

3318 **ONE COOL CAT 22** [7] A P O'Brien 3-9-8 J P Spencer 3/1 FAV: 41111-051: Held up trav well, qcknd   **120+**
to lead ins last & readily asserted, cmftbly: op 5/2: relished drop to 6f, stays 7f: acts on fast & gd today: to high class best at correct trip under a big weight: held in high regard regard by powerful stable & shld be followed in the top sprints from now on.
3268 **THE KIDDYKID 22** [6] P D Evans 4-9-7 (110) P J Smullen 8/1: 5-3014682: Always handy, rdn to lead 1 **110**
dist, hdd ins last & no chance with wnr: caught a tartar today & can win again in similar company: see 1996 (Gr 3).
3636 **NIGHTS CROSS 7** [2] M R Channon 3-9-0 BL (105) A Culhane 10/1: 43000033: Held up, hdwy from over ¾ **105**
1f out, not pace to chall: see 1732, 1106.
3622 **SIMIANNA 8** [5]5-9-1 p (93) P Shanahan 20/1: 02004657: Chsd ldrs, no extra dist: see 1162. 3 **93**
10 Ran   Time 1m 12.70 ()   Owned: Mrs John Magnier   Trained: Ballydoyle

3843 **5.15 Gr 2 Debutante Stakes 2yo ()**
£56615 £16549 £7839   **7f rnd**   **Good/Firm**

3314* **SILK AND SCARLET 25** [4] A P O'Brien 2-8-11 J P Spencer 13/8 FAV: 211: Rear, hdwy over 1f out &   **110+**
led ins last, readily asserted & eased close home, val 2L+: continues to progress after recent Listed success: eff at 6/7f, stays gd/sft ground: smart & progressive filly who should be kept on side.
LUAS LINE [1] D Wachman 2-8-11 K Fallon 3/1: 012: b f Danehill - Streetcar (In The Wings) ½ **103**
Trkd ldrs, rdn & led over 1f out, hdd ins last & no chance with easy wnr: rest well covered: recent easy wnr of a Cork mdn: eff at 6f, styd this longer 7f trip well: acts on firm & fast ground, gall trks: stepped up in grade & posted an encouraging effort, a likely type for Listed/Gr 3 success.
CHELSEA ROSE [7] C Collins 2-8-11 P Shanahan 7/2: 13: Led/dsptd lead till over 1f out, kept on. 2 **97**
8 Ran   Time 1m 25.40()   Owned: Mrs John Magnier   Trained: Ballydoyle

Official Going GOOD/FIRM.

3844   2.15 Saltwellsigns Co Uk Claiming Stakes 3yo+   (E)
£4115 £1266 £633   5f161y rnd   Good/Firm 22   -02 Slow   Inside

3466 **ATLANTIC VIKING** 16 [13] D Nicholls 9-9-5 (91) R Winston 1/1 FAV: 0-004001: Mid-div wide, prog **76**
halfway, styd on to lead dist, pushed out, val 2L+: suited by 5/6f, stays 7f: acts on firm & gd/soft
grnd: gd confidence boost on drop to claim grade: see 2359 & 2253.
3737 **ARFINNIT** 5 [14] M R Channon 3-8-6 vis (58) S Hitchcott(2) 20/1: 1640002: Slow away, prog 2f out, 1 **62**
kept on, not pace of wnr: back to form after a couple of disapp recent effs: see 2541.
3720* **TRICK CYCLIST** 5 [6] A M Balding 3-9-0 (72) Martin Dwyer 3/1: 4060213: Cl-up, styd on to lead 2f hd **69**
out, hdd dist, sn onepcd: qck reapp: remains in gd form: btr 3720 (class stks).
3673 **BYO** 7 [4] M Quinn 6-8-10 (69) F Norton 15/2: 6600134: Cl-up, no extra ins fnl 1f, not btn far: shd **60**
op 13/2 on qck reapp: likes Bath: btr 3673 & 3372.
2102 **CAYMAN BREEZE** 71 [8]4-8-8 (57) R L Moore 20/1: 0-054105: Bhd, prog wide dist, nrst fin: 10 wk ½ **57**
abs: return to 7f will suit: btr 708 (7f).
3436 **MILLFIELDS DREAMS** 17 [2]5-8-9 (57) B Swarbrick(5) 40/1: 4-100006: Chsd ldrs, no extra dist: btr 2372. 1¾ **53**
3289 **MAN CRAZY** 24 [11]3-7-12 bl (54) J Mackay 28/1: 6000407: Led, hdd 2f out, sn no extra: btr 3109. hd **45**
3577 **MELODY KING** 11 [7]3-8-3 bl (65) F P Ferris(3) 16/1: 54365U8: Cl-up till halfway, wknd: btr 3036. 3½ **40**
3482 **CONFUZED** 15 [9]4-8-7 bl e (40) G Hannon 66/1: 0000409: Prom 3f, fdd: btr 3301. 2 **34**
3396 **COCO REEF** 18 [12]3-7-12 (47) D Kinsella 66/1: 330-6050: 10th: Al bhd: btr 3396. ½ **28**
2928 **RIDICULE** 38 [10]5-8-7 bl t (44) S Drowne 66/1: 0000000: 11th: Nvr nrr than mid-div: see 1788. ½ **32**
      Java Gold [3]3-8-4 C Haddon(7) 100/1:0   3372 **Bennanabaa** 19 [1]5-9-0 t(46) B O'Neill(7) 80/1:0
13 Ran Time 1m 10.52 (1.42)   Owned: Mr David Faulkner   Trained: Thirsk

---

3845   2.45 Saltwell Signs Handicap Stakes 3yo 0-75 (E)   [82]
£3565 £1097 £549   1m3f144y   Good/Firm 22   -03 Slow   Inside

3573 **VELVET WATERS** 11 [2] R F Johnson Houghton 3-8-7 (61) S Carson 5/1: 3641221: Cl-up, styd on to **73**
lead 2f out, sn rdn clr: eff around 11/12f, prob stays 14f: acts on fast & gd grnd, likes Bath: see 3573.
3255 **PRINCIPESSA** 25 [6] B Palling 3-9-0 (68) J Fortune 10/1: 0002202: Led, hdd 2f out, kept on, not 3½ **73**
pace of wnr: eff arnd 1m/10f, now stays 11.6f: acts on fast & gd/soft: unexposed arnd this trip, see 2893.
3573 **DONASTRELA** 11 [11] A M Balding 3-8-9 vis (63) N Chalmers(5) 4/1: 0014133: Held up, styd on well nk **67**
fnl 1.5f, just held for 2nd: continues to run well, another gd eff here at Bath: see 3573 & 3373.
3300 **OKTIS MORILIOUS** 22 [8] A W Carroll 3-8-0 (54) C Haddon(7) 20/1: 2625104: Chsd ldrs 1m, no extra. 2½ **54**
3201 **AUTUMN FLYER** 27 [12]3-8-3 (57) R L Moore 33/1: 000-0005: Nvr nrr than mid-div: see 2452. 1½ **54**
3313 **MESSE DE MINUIT** 22 [10]3-9-7 (75) S Drowne 12/1: 31-036: Bhd, modest late gains: btr 3313. 2½ **68**
3334 **DESERT IMAGE** 20 [9]3-9-2 (70) D Corby(3) 14/1: 0332407: Bhd, prog halfway, wknd 3f out: btr 2413. nk **62**
3359 **BIENVENUE** 19 [5]3-9-5 (73) Martin Dwyer 3/1 FAV: 35-41268: Al bhd: op 9/4: much better 2½ **61**
expected & something amiss?: see 3161 & 2788.
3384 **MOMMKIN** 19 [1]3-9-0 VIS (68) T E Durcan 20/1: 25-55549: Handy 9f, wknd: 1st time visor. ½ **55**
3516 **KOMOTO** 13 [4]3-8-13 (57) T P Queally 14/1: 100: 10th: Bhd, nvr a factor: btr 3197 (1m, polytrk). 2 **51**
3578 **Zaffeu** 11 [3]3-9-1 (69) J P Guillambert(3) 20/1:0   3471 **Bailaora** 16 [7]3-9-1 bl(69) K Fallon 14/1:0
12 Ran Time 2m 27.94 (2.94)   Owned: Mr R Crutchley   Trained: Didcot

---

3846   3.15 Miss Hucklebridge Handicap Stakes 3yo 0-70 (E)   [77]
£4498 £1384 £692   1m5y rnd   Good/Firm 22   +05 Fast   Inside

3218 **RAYSOOT** 26 [12] E F Vaughan 3-8-7 T (56) K Fallon 9/2: 00-02501: Made all, rdn clr fnl 1f, **69+**
decisively: fast time: eff arnd 1m on fast & f/sand: imprvd for fitting of t-strap & switch to forcing tactics:
first wnr for trainer E Vaughan: see 2634 & 2205.
3219 **JARVO** 26 [2] N P Littmoden 3-8-11 (60) J P Guillambert(3) 50/1: 0-254002: Al cl-up, kept on fnl 2½ **66**
1f, al held by wnr: eff at 7f/1m, poss stays 10f: back to form with t-strap left off: can find similar.
3455 **MASTER MAHOGANY** 17 [5] R J Hodges 3-8-11 (60) S Drowne 14/1: 0654603: Chsd ldrs, kept on fnl 1f, 1½ **63**
no ch with front 2: eff at 1m, return to 10f will suit: acts on fast & gd grnd: see 2706.
3679 **DAGOLA** 6 [11] C G Cox 3-9-1 (64) J Fortune 13/8 FAV: 1003424: Mid-div, prog 3f out, onepcd bef nk **66**
1f out: well bckd on qck reapp: nvr able to get competitive & this was disapp: btr 3679 & 2971.
3515* **STEVEDORE** 13 [4]3-9-7 (70) G Baker 8/1: 4-000415: Chsd ldrs, no extra dist: btr 3515 (7f). nk **71**
3731 **DANIFAH** 5 [9]3-7-12 (5oh) F P Ferris(3) 16/1: 0400446: Keen cl-up over 6f, wknd: qck reapp. ½ **47**
3298 **BINNION BAY** 22 [6]3-8-10 (59) R L Moore 12/1: 00-00067: Nvr nrr than mid-div: see 2173. 8 **44**
2410 **MY SUNSHINE** 59 [7]3-8-13 (62) M Hills 11/1: 00-008: Nvr nrr than mid-div: 8 wk abs. ½ **46**
3679 **HANA DEE** 6 [8]3-8-7 (58)3 S Hitchcott(2) 10/1: 6004539: Slow away, al rear: qck reapp: btr 3679. nk **39**
2527 **AMBER FOX** 54 [10]3-7-12 (47) Joanna Badger 66/1: 004-5650: 10th: Bhd, nvr a factor: 8 wk abs. 1 **28**
696   **ROWAN PURSUIT** 171 [1]3-9-1 bl (64) T Quinn 10/1: 31-13500: 11th: Mid-div 5f, wknd: long abs. ¾ **43**
2495 **COUNT DRACULA** 55 [3]3-9-1 (64) Martin Dwyer 33/1: 020-1060: 12th: Rear, nvr a factor: new yard. 5 **33**
12 Ran Time 1m 39.72 (1.42)   Owned: Sheikh Ahmed Al Maktoum   Trained: Newmarket

---

3847   3.45 Tipto Two-Year-Old Selling Stakes 2yo (G)
£2548 £728 £364   5f11y rnd   Good/Firm 22   -21 Slow   Far side

      ARBORS LITTLE GIRL [7] B R Millman 2-8-6 S Drowne 8/1: 1: b f Paris House - Arbor Ealis (Woods **72**
of Windsor) Sn outpcd, prog 2f out, styd on under hands & heels to lead line: gamble from 25/1, debut, bght in for
4,400gns: Feb first foal: dam 5f wnr, also over hdles: sire speedy performer: eff at 5f, 6f will suit: acts on
fast grnd & goes well fresh: took a while to get the hang of things & shld improve.
3671 **MAJESTICAL** 7 [9] W R Muir 2-8-11 (58) Martin Dwyer 11/2: 340042: Al cl-up, styd on to lead ins shd **75$**
fnl 1f, hdd on line: op 9/2 on qck reapp: eff at 5f on fast grnd: apprec drop to sell grade: see 3671.

BATH   TUESDAY 10.08.04   Lefthand, Turning Track With Stiff Uphill Finish

3160 **RUBY MUJA 29** [1] R Hannon 2-8-6 R L Moore 11/2: 003: b f Mujahid - Ruby Julie (Clantime) Led   2½   63
4f out, hdd under press ins fnl 1f, no extra: clr rem: Feb foal, cost 5,000gns: dam unrcd: sire 7f Group wnr at
2: eff at 5f, further shld suit: acts on fast grnd.

3728 **BLAKESHALL HOPE 5** [10] P D Evans 2-8-11 VIS R Winston 5/1: 3004: Bhd, modest late gains: qck   4   56
reapp & first time visor: showed more in 2629 (debut).

3745* **SAPPHIRE PRINCESS 4** [6]2-8-11 (50) B Swarbrick(5) 9/1: 455615: Nvr nrr than mid-div: qck reapp.   hd   55

2977 **ZACHY BOY 36** [8]2-8-11 bl (58) Derek Nolan(7) 16/1: 0066546: Chsd ldrs 3f, sn wknd: btr 2977.   shd   54

3755 **DIKTATIT 4** [5]2-8-6 S Hitchcott(2) 9/2 FAV: 057: Chsd ldrs 3f, sn wknd: qck reapp: btr 3755 (mdn).   1½   45

3343 **LEONALTO 20** [3]2-8-11 bl (59) J Fortune 5/1: 053658: Led, hdd 4f out, wknd fnl 2f: btr 1367.   7   32

  TINKERS FIRST [4]2-8-6 C Haddon(7) 20/1: 9: b f First Trump - Tinker Osmaston (Dunbeath) Al in   5   14
rear: debut: Jan first foal, dam wnr at sprint dists: sire Gr 1 wnr at 6f: with W G M Turner.
9 Ran Time 1m 02.45 (2.15) Owned: Dr Ian R Shenkin Trained: Cullompton

---

3848   4.15 Wick Maiden Auction Stakes Fillies 2yo (E)
     £3585 £1103 £552   5f161y rnd   Good/Firm 22   -11 Slow   Inside

2618 **ROSIELLA 50** [7] M Blanshard 2-8-4 F Norton 10/1: 051: Chsd ldrs, styd on for press to lead   73
cl-home: tchd 14/1, 7 wk abs: eff at 5.8f, further will suit: acts on fast grnd & a goes well fresh: improving.

3728 **AGENT KENSINGTON 5** [6] R Hannon 2-8-3 (67) R L Moore 9/4: 2253242: Chsd ldrs, prog to chase wnr   nk   70
ins fnl 1f, sn ev ch, just held: well bckd on qck reapp: another gd run in defeat: see 3355 & 2927.

2927 **SHOSOLOSA 38** [4] B J Meehan 2-8-6 (72) J F McDonald(3) 13/8 FAV: 0223: Led bef 4f out, hdd under   ¾   71
press well ins fnl 1f, no extra: well bckd: acts on fast & gd grnd: fin just in front of today's 2nd in 2927.

3183 **MABELLA 27** [1] B R Millman 2-8-7 S Drowne 14/1: 0504: Sn bhd, styd on fnl 1f, nrst fin: see 2795.   3½   62

3251 **CABIN FEVER 25** [11]2-8-4 R Smith 20/1: 05: b f Averti - Julietta Mia (Woodman) Chsd ldrs till   1   56
dist, wknd: Feb foal, half-sister to a 5f wnr: dam a 7f wnr, sire decent sprinter: with J C Fox.

  PURPLE DOOR [3]2-8-4 Martin Dwyer 33/1: 6: b f Daggers Drawn - Carreamia (Weldnaas) Slow   ¾   54
away, nvr nrr than mid-div: Feb foal, cost 4,800gns: half-sister plcd at 5/8f: dam plcd around 1m: sire
decent performer at 2: with R M Beckett.

3399 **BARNBROOK EMPIRE 18** [9]2-8-4 (72) T P Queally 10/1: 0537: Cl-up 4f, wknd: btr 3399 (gd).   3   45

  FERRARA FLAME [8]2-8-5 D Corby(3) 50/1: 8: Al in rear: debut.   3½   36

2415 **FEMINIST 59** [5]2-8-13 (74) T E Durcan 20/1: 5309: Led, hdd bef 4f out, wknd halfway: 8 wk abs.   3½   34

1084 **RIBBONS OF GOLD 125** [10]2-8-8 S W Kelly 12/1: 60: 10th: Chsd ldrs till 3f out, wknd: long abs.   2   23

  MISS SUDBROOK [2]2-8-4 Paul Eddery 40/1: 0: 11th: Al bhd on debut.   ¾   17
11 Ran Time 1m 11.03 (1.93) Owned: Mrs R Wellman B McAllister D Hampson Trained: Upper Lambourn

---

3849   4.45 Hospitality At Bath Handicap Stakes Fillies 3yo+ 0-75 (E)   [70]
     £3546 £1091 £546   5f11y rnd   Good/Firm 22   -03 Slow   Far side

3567 **FIDDLE ME BLUE 11** [2] H Morrison 3-10-0 (70) S Drowne 7/2: 31-50001: Handy, styd on to lead 1f   77
out, pushed out, val 3L+: op 9/2: eff at 5/6f on fast & gd/soft grnd: fine win under top-weight, only lightly rcd
& can rate higher: see 3567 & 1229.

3640 **AVIT 8** [10] P L Gilligan 4-7-13 (38) A McCarthy 12/1: 6014502: Mid-div wide, prog 2f out, kept   1½   38
on ins fnl 1f, no ch with wnr: gd eff in defeat & can find similar: see 2331.

3537 **LADY PROTECTOR 13** [8] J Balding 5-9-4 (57) Dale Gibson 5/2 FAV: 0011333: Bhd, prog halfway, styd   ½   56
on ins fnl 1f, not rch wnr: op 4/1: continues in gd form: see 3537 & 2062.

3804 **JINKSONTHEHOUSE 2** [12] M D I Usher 3-9-0 (56) Hayley Turner(5) 13/2: 0401424: Chsd ldrs, styd on   ½   54
to lead bef 1f out, sn edged left & hdd dist, no extra: qck reapp: just btr 3804.

3479 **HAGLEY PARK 15** [8]5-8-6 (45) J F McDonald(3) 20/1: 3100005: Handy till dist, no extra: btr 1562 (bndd).   1   40

3577 **BOAVISTA 11** [6]4-9-8 (61) S Donohoe(7) 5/1: 0220336: Missed break, prog after 3f, onepcd fnl 1f.   hd   55

3640 **TENDER 8** [4]4-8-13 p (52) F Norton 10/1: 0004107: Nvr nrr than mid-div: btr 3332 (polytrack).   hd   45

3693 **EMARADIA 6** [9]3-8-12 (54) R L Moore 20/1: 0122668: Al bhd: qck reapp: btr 835 (fibresand).   1   44

3372 **INNCLASSIC 19** [5]3-9-7 bl (63) V Slattery 33/1: 0031209: Cl-up, led 3f out, hdd bef 1f out, wknd.   2½   46

3640 **BALLINGER EXPRESS 8** [11]4-9-11 bl (64) Martin Dwyer 8/1: 3200200: 10th: Led, hdd 3f out, wknd.   ½   46

1788 **ROYAL SUPREMACY 85** [7]3-8-5 T (47) C Catlin 33/1: 30U3-000: 11th: ch f Desert Prince - Saucy Maid   6   13
(Sure Blade) Cl-up till halfway, wknd: long abs & t-strap: plcd on fnl '03 start (h'cap, rtd 72 best, C G Cox):
eff at 5f, 6f shld suit: acts on fast grnd: with J M Bradley.
11 Ran Time 1m 1.59 (1.29) Owned: Mr David Dobson Trained: East Ilsley

---

BEVERLEY   WEDNESDAY 11.08.04   Righthand, Galloping Track, Stiff Finish

Official Going Good/Soft

3850   2.10 Wats On Claiming Stakes 3yo+ (E)
     £3572 £1099 £550   1m100y rnd   Good/Soft 68   -12 Slow   Inside

3830 **ALPINE HIDEAWAY 2** [8] J S Wainwright 11-9-2 p (45) D Allan 12/1: 140-0601: Chsd ldrs, led ins   51
last, duelled with rnr-up, just prevailed, all out: qck reapp: wnr of this race twice prev: suited by 7f/1m on firm,
gd/soft & fibresand: likes Beverley & claim grade: see 2891.

3739 **CAYMAN CALYPSO 6** [13] M A Jarvis 3-9-5 (62) N Callan 4/1 JT FAV: 0080622: Trkd ldrs, rdn & led   hd   60
over 1f out, hdd ins last, rallied, just held: acts on gd & gd/soft grnd: see 3739.

2313 **GEM BIEN 63** [10] D W Chapman 6-9-8 (76) A Culhane 4/1 JT FAV: 1640-003: Rear, styd on for press,   1½   53
not reach front pair: new yard, 2 mth abs: see 2313.

73] **ASH BOLD 1365** [11] B Ellison 7-8-10 (28) T Eaves(3) 100/1: 00/000///-4: ch g Persian Bold -   hd   40
Pasadena Lady (Captain James) Handy, rdn & no extra ins last: new yard, long abs: mod form back in 00/01 over
hdles (nov seller, p.u.): mod form on the level prev in '00: eff around 8.5f in claim grade on gd/soft.

3727 **LORD LAHAR 6** [14]5-9-6 (37) C Catlin 40/1: 00-60005: Chsd ldrs, onepace for press dist: qck   ¾   49
reapp: eff around 1m on gd/soft grnd: stays 8.5f in claim grade: see 1894.

3428 **MOBANE FLYER 18** [4]4-9-12 (63) P Hanagan 5/1: 0050-006: Mid-div, styd on late for press, nrst   nk   54
fin: op 8/1: stays 8.5f in claim grade: handles firm & gd/soft: awkward low draw today: see 3117.

4265] **DEE PEE TEE CEE 687** [12]10-9-12 (46) T Lucas 20/1: 040500/-7: b g Tidaro - Silver Glimpse *2* **50**
(Petingo) Led till over 1f out, fdd under press: long abs: missed '03: unplcd '02 (rtd 56, h'cap): back in '99 landed 4 h'caps: suited by 10f, stays 12f: acts on fast & hvy, prefers cut: handles any trk.
2967 **ERUPT 37** [7]11-9-0 (40) T Hamilton(3) 25/1: 60-50308: Dwelt & bhd, mod prog, nvr a factor. *1¾* **35**
3182 **FLYING SPUD 29** [16]3-8-13 (50) Dean McKeown 9/2: 5100029: Chsd ldrs, lost place from over 3f out. *½* **40**
3726 **GIUST IN TEMP 6** [9]5-8-12 (40) Darren Williams 20/1: 2060400: 10th: Chsd ldrs till over 1f out. *shd* **32**
3668 **STEPASTRAY 8** [1]7-9-4 vis (41) G Parkin 33/1: 5000500: 11th: Dwelt/bhd, mod prog from low draw. *nk* **37**
3548 **EFIMAC 13** [2]4-9-3 (38) A Reilly(7) 33/1: 0004000: 12th: Al rear from poor low draw. *1¼* **33**
3650 **DARK CUT 9** [15]4-9-6 (37) R Keogh(7) 50/1: 0000000: 13th: Mid-div, btn 3f out. *1½* **33**
857 **MOON ROYALE 148** [6]6-8-11 (34) Hayley Turner(5) 66/1: 500-0000: 14th: Mid-div wide, btn 2f out, abs. *hd* **23**
1083} **MAZRAM 483** [3]5-8-13 Natalia Gemelova(7) 100/1: 0-0: 15th: Sn bhd from poor draw, long abs. *2* **21**
3547 **GALLAS 13** [5]3-8-9 vis (49) R Ffrench 9/1: 0002000: 16th: Al bhd, poor low draw: btr 3177. *nk* **23**
16 Ran Time 1m 50.63 (6.83) Owned: Mr Peter Easterby Trained: Malton

3851

2.40 European Breeders Fund Journal Maiden Stakes 2yo (D)
£5577 £1716 £858 **7f100y rnd** **Good/Soft 68** **-10 Slow** Inside

3665 **VARENKA 8** [12] Sir Mark Prescott 2-8-9 S Sanders 3/1: 51: Made all from fav'ble high draw, **96+**
pulled clr over 1f out under hand riding, cmftbly: well bckd: eff at 7.5f, 1m+ will suit: acts on fast, enjoyed gd/soft grnd today with forcing tactics: clearly learnt plenty from intro, looks useful, win again.
BRAHMINY KITE 0 [2] M Johnston 2-9-0 R Ffrench 12/1: 2: b c Silver Hawk - Cope's Light *5* **89**
(Copelan) Mid-div, sn pushed along, kept on well from over 1f out, nvr threat to wnr: op 14/1: $300,000 purchase, Apr foal: half-brother to a multiple US juv wnr, dam a multiple US wnr: eff at 7.5f, shaped as if 1m+ will suit: handles gd/soft grnd: promising intro, shld learn plenty & find a race.
2959 **GONE FISHING 38** [8] M A Jarvis 2-8-9 N Callan 5/2 FAV: 023: Chsd ldr, hung right under press & *1* **82**
no prog dist: clr of rem: see 2959.
3234 **ETAAR 26** [10] N A Graham 2-9-0 W Supple 5/1: 44: Trkd ldrs, stumbled after 2f & lost several *6* **76**
lengths, rdn & btn 2f out: op 7/2: much btr 3234 (debut, fast).
RED RIOT 0 [9]2-9-0 K Darley 5/1: 5: b c Red Ransom - Musical Treat (Royal Academy) Rear, *1¼* **73**
shaken up & kept on fnl 2f, nvr a threat: op 8/1: Jan first foal, E120,000: dam a 7f plcd juv & subs useful at 7/10f as a 3yo: stay further & know more next time.
3311 **NOWADAY 23** [6]2-9-0 E Ahern 50/1: 066: Rear, mod late prog, no threat: see 3311. *1* **71**
3520 **BALLETOMAINE 14** [1]2-8-9 M Hills 8/1: 07: b f Sadler's Wells - Ivy (Sir Ivor) Cl-up, rdn & btn *shd* **66**
2f out: op 12/1: Apr foal, sister to smart 10/12f performers, dam plcd as a juv: strong mid-dist pedigree.
JUST WAZ 0 [3]2-9-0 P Hanagan 25/1: 8: Dwelt & al rear. *½* **70**
VIABLE 0 [11]2-9-0 A Culhane 50/1: 9: Slow away & sn bhd. *8* **56**
3500 **EBORARRY 15** [7]2-9-0 D Allan 50/1: 400: 10th: Bhd halfway. *½* **55**
1780 **METOLICA 87** [4]2-8-9 R Fitzpatrick 100/1: 000: 11th: Sn struggling rear, abs. *8* **36**
11 Ran Time 1m 36.67 (5.87) Owned: Lady Roborough Trained: Newmarket

3852

3.10 Toteplacepot Handicap Stakes 3yo+ 0-80 (D) **[80]**
£8418 £2590 £1295 **5f str** **Good/Soft 68** **+23 Fast** Inside

3833 **TROJAN FLIGHT 2** [17] Mrs J R Ramsden 3-8-7 (59) F Norton 3/1 FAV: 6064321: Sltly hmpd start & **71+**
bhd, switched & hdwy from halfway, rdn & hdwy to lead ins last, going away: qck reapp, hvly bckd: fast time: stays 7f, suited by 5/6f on fast & soft grnd: best without cheek pieces: deserved first success, win again.
550 **HOUT BAY 188** [11] R A Fahey 7-8-7 (56) P Hanagan 20/1: 500-1362: Mid-div, rdn & hdwy to lead *1½* **62**
dist, hung right & hdd ins last, no ch with wnr: gd run from moderate draw: 6 mth abs: see 415.
3375 **PADDYWACK 20** [13] D W Chapman 7-9-10 bl (73) A Culhane 7/1: 0110363: Mid-div, styd on for press, *1* **76**
not pace of wnr: tough gelding, likes this trk: see 2942 (C/D).
3463 **TANTRIC 17** [20] J O'Reilly 5-8-9 (58) S Sanders 6/1: 0300334: Chsd ldrs, switched when short of *1* **58**
room over 1f out, kept on: gd run from fav'ble high draw, needs further: see 3463.
3667+**BLUE MAEVE 8** [8]4-8-12 (7ex) (61) S Righton 12/1: 0424215: Chsd ldrs, onepace: gd run under pen *1¼* **57**
from moderate draw: prob more to come after 3667 (made most, fast).
3680 **CONSENSUS 7** [15]5-9-12 (75) K Darley 12/1: 0030046: Led till dist, wknd: btr 3680. *¾* **69**
3427 **BEYOND THE CLOUDS 18** [4]8-9-13 (76) G Parkin 20/1: 0020037: Rear, late gains, nrst fin: poor draw. *1* **67**
3463 **FAIRGAME MAN 17** [1]6-7-12 (1oh)p (46) P M Quinn 33/1: 2051008: Mid-div stands side, no impress. *¾* **36**
3375 **SOBA JONES 20** [19]7-9-9 (72) J Edmunds 13/2: 5654259: Chsd ldrs far side, no impress over 1f out. *½* **59**
3341 **SEVEN NO TRUMPS 21** [6]7-9-13 p (76) C J Davies(7) 20/1: 0400200: 10th: Bhd, mod late prog. *½* **61**
3150 **MUSICAL FAIR 30** [18]4-9-13 (76) E Ahern 16/1: 0215600: 11th: Mid-div, btn over 1f out: btr 2266 (fast). *1* **58**
3673 **PORT ST CHARLES 8** [9]7-8-7 bl (56) Hayley Turner(5) 25/1: 0004060: 12th: Mid-div, nvr land a blow. *½* **36**
2846 **CHICO GUAPO 42** [16]4-9-9 (72) W Supple 20/1: 0500000: 13th: Cl-up till over 1f out, 6 wk abs. *shd* **52**
3574 **LAUREL DAWN 12** [2]6-8-11 (60) R Ffrench 33/1: 5250600: 14th: Switched right from start & al bhd. *¾* **38**
3833 **ELLIOTS CHOICE 2** [10]3-8-11 (63) D Tudhope(7) 33/1: 4360000: 15th: Chsd ldrs, btn over 1f out. *¾* **39**
3503 **MISS CEYLON 15** [12]4-7-12 (8oh)bl (39) J McAuley 100/1: 00-00000: 16th: Sn struggling, nvr factor. *1* **20**
3503+**DISTANT TIMES 15** [3]3-9-10 (76) D Allan 20/1: 1300510: 17th: Rcd stands side, in tch till halfway. *5* **35**
3591 **DISPOL KATIE 11** [14]3-10-0 (80) N Callan 9/1: 22-06350: 18th: Chsd ldrs, hmpd over 1f out & *6* **23**
saddle slipped, eased right down: op 12/1: this best forgiven after 3591 & 3106.
18 Ran Time 1m 03.57 (2.27) Owned: Mr Timothy O'Gram Trained: Thirsk

3853

3.40 Charles Elsey Memorial Challenge Trophy Handicap 3yo+ 0-75 (E) **[72]**
£4134 £1272 £636 **2m35y** **Good/Soft 68** **-16 Slow** Inside

3611 **MOONSHINE BEACH 11** [1] P W Hiatt 6-9-7 (65) Darren Williams 5/1: 4P11031: Led 6f, remained trkg **75**
ldr, drvn to chall over 1f out & prevailed for press well ins last: eff at 2m/2m2f on fast, gd/soft & polytrack, prob any trk: thorough stayer: progressive profile: see 3147 & 3057.
3649 **SHOTLEY DANCER 9** [2] N Bycroft 5-8-0 (2ow) (42) F Norton 8/1: 4353142: Trkd ldr, rushed up to *1* **52**
lead after 6f, drvn & strongly pressed over 1f out, no extra when hdd well ins last: now stays 2m: see 3502.
3181 **VICARS DESTINY 29** [6] Mrs S Lamyman 6-9-5 (63) Andrew Webb(7) 5/1: 2000643: Held up, kept on for *3½* **68**
press but nvr threatened front pair: see 3181 & 1069.
2960 **WING COLLAR 38** [3] T D Easterby 3-8-7 (66) W Supple 11/4: 0-033204: Keen trkg ldrs, rdn & no *1¾* **69**

impress fnl 2f: nicely bckd: btr 2322 (12f).
3181* **CLARINCH CLAYMORE 29** [7]8-10-0 (72) T Eaves(3) 5/2 FAV: 6-205315: Held up, rdn & eff from over 2f   ¾   74
out, sn no impress: btr 3181 (C/D).
3611   **GREENWICH MEANTIME 11** [4]4-9-12 (70) L Goncalves 9/1: 0030056: Held up, eff 3f out, btn 2f out.   3   63
6 Ran   Time 3m 43.79 (13.49)   Owned: Mr Ken Read   Trained: Banbury

3854   4.10 East Riding Mail Handicap Stakes 3yo 0-70 (E)   [75]
£3731 £1148 £574   **1m2f**   **Good/Soft 68**   -20 Slow   Inside

162   **CAN CAN FLYER 247** [6] M Johnston 3-8-12 (59) R Ffrench 14/1: 006-1: ch c In The Wings - Can Can   69
Lady (Anshan) Chsd ldrs, rdn over 2f out, styd on for press to lead well ins last: first win on h'cap bow, 8 mth
abs: unplcd sole turf start in '03 (rtd 65, mdn, subs disapp on AW, rtd 39a, mdn): apprec step up to 10f, shaped as
if 12f+ will suit: acts on gd/soft grnd: goes well fresh: prog over further & with more racing.
3309   **SUPER KING 23** [8] N Bycroft 3-8-12 (59) E Ahern 9/1: 2-000052: Mid-div, rdn & hdwy to chall over   ½   67
1f out, narrow lead dist till well ins last, no extra: stays 10f: acts on firm & gd/soft grnd: see 2997.
3084   **MAGIC STING 33** [2] M L W Bell 3-9-7 (68) Hayley Turner(5) 9/2: 5611033: Keen & handy, led halfway   2   73
till over 1f out, no extra fnl 100y: see 2180.
3647   **FUTOO 9** [12] G M Moore 3-9-5 (66) B Swarbrick(5) 5/2 FAV: 5130134: Led till halfway, remained   hd   70
handy, drvn & onepace from dist: just btr 3309 (C/D, gd).
3263   **ASTON LAD 25** [7]3-8-3 (50) F Norton 9/1: 46625: Bhd, switched & kept on for press ins last, nrst   nk   53
fin: h'cap bow: stays 10f, has tried 14f & a return to 12f+ in similar could suit: acts on gd/soft: btr 3263 (mdn).
3505   **COME WHAT JULY 15** [1]3-8-8 bl (55) R Fitzpatrick 12/1: 0351036: Bhd, hdwy wide 3f out, no extra dist.   1½   56
3299   **ARMENTIERES 23** [10]3-8-8 bl (55) G Hind 33/1: 3530-607: b f Robellino - Perfect Poppy (Shareef   1½   54
Dancer) Chsd ldrs, no impress over 1f out: seller wnr in '03: eff at 7f/8.5f, yet to convince over further: acts
on fast, gd/soft & fibresand: eff in blnks, tried cheek pieces latest. 1 Oct'03 Nott 8.2g/s 57-(54) G:
3547   **MIDNIGHT PRINCE 13** [9]3-8-2 (49) Dale Gibson 11/1: 0006-658: Struggling rear halfway & nvr factor.   13   20
3309   **MISS ELOISE 23** [4]3-9-0 BL (61) W Supple 12/1: 2601009: Mid-div, rdn & btn 2f out: poor run in blnks.   2   29
2530   **SAIDA LENASERA 54** [3]3-9-3 (64) A Nicholls 20/1: 140-0660: 10th: Chsd ldrs 7f, sn bhd, 8 wk abs.   2   29
3108   **ABBEYGATE 32** [5]3-9-3 (64) N Callan 16/1: 006-00: 11th: Al bhd.   13   11
3354   **DANEFONIQUE 21** [11]3-8-3 (50) D Allan 10/1: 2256040: 12th: Chsd ldrs till 3f out, sn bhd: btr 3354 (fast). 12   0
12 Ran   Time 2m 11.11 (8.81)   Owned: Mr A W Robinson   Trained: Middleham

3855   4.40 Hull Daily Mail Maiden Stakes 3yo (D)
£4079 £1255 £628   **1m2f**   **Good/Soft 68**   -35 Slow   Inside

3740   **MITH HILL 6** [3] E A L Dunlop 3-9-0   E Ahern 5/2: 01: Held up & bhd halfway, styd on stdly for   72
press to lead well ins last: slow time: gd run 4/1: imprvd from intro: eff at 10f, shaped as if 12f may suit: acts on
gd/soft grnd: going the right way: see 3740.
3741   **MAMBINA 6** [2] M R Channon 3-8-9 (62) C Catlin 4/1: 4450402: Led, drvn & hdd well ins last: qck reapp. 2   63
2886   **PREMIER ROUGE 41** [1] E F Vaughan 3-9-0 N Callan 18 FAV: 443: Trckd ldr, rdn & chall 2f out, no   4   62
extra from dist: 6 wk abs: not see out this longer 10f trip: btr 2886 & 2325 (7.5f/1m).
3292   **ASPIRED 23** [4] J R Fanshawe 3-8-9 R Ffrench 4/1: 0P: Chsd ldr, hung badly left on home turn   0
over 2f out, sn p.u. & dismounted: op 3/1.
4 Ran   Time 2m 12.59 (10.29)   Owned: Mr Mohammed Jaber   Trained: Newmarket

3856   5.10 Downey's Diary Classified Stakes 3yo+ 0-60 (F)
£3339 £954 £477   **1m4f16y**   **Good/Soft 68**   -34 Slow   Inside

3618   **INCHPAST 11** [8] M H Tompkins 3-8-10 bl (64) N Callan 6/1: 0-004121: Trckd ldrs, drvn & led ins   70
last, gamely: acts on fast & gd/soft: suited by 11.5f/12f: shows a fine attitude, progressive profile: see 3618.
3618   **JOLIZERO 11** [1] P W Chapple Hyam 3-8-6 (59) Thomas Yeung(5) 9/1: 000-4032: Led, hung left under   ½   63
press 2f out, hdd ins last, just held cl-home: op 7/1: gd run with forcing tactics from awkward low draw: acts on
fast & gd/soft grnd: can be plcd to win sn: see 3618 & 3108.
3573   **ON CLOUD NINE 12** [10] M L W Bell 3-8-7 (64) Hayley Turner(5) 7/1: 260043: Held up, hdwy from 3f   1¼   63
out, rdn & not pace of wnr ins last: see 3573 & 977.
3702* **PAY ATTENTION 7** [4] T D Easterby 3-8-3 (60) D Allan 13/8 FAV: 4020214: Held up, hdwy wide to   nk   58
chall over 2f out, sn sltly hmpd, no extra ins last: well clr of rem: nicely bckd tho' op 11/8: styd longer 12f trip.
3299   **OUR EMMY LOU 23** [7]3-8-5 (62) E Ahern 13/2: 066-245: Held up, eff wide 3f out, btn 2f out: op 9/2.   9   49
3730   **RELATIVE HERO 6** [6]4-9-3 vis (51) A Quinn(5) 40/1: 50-00236: Chsd ldrs, drvn & btn 2f out: qck reapp. 5   44
3618   **ITS BLUE CHIP 11** [5]3-8-10 (64) J Carroll 14/1: 4641007: Dwelt & al bhd: btr 2804 (AW).   ½   47
4319} **BRAVE KNIGHT 328** [9]7-9-3 (32) F Norton 66/1: 00/0066-8: b g Presidium - Agnes Jane (Sweet   ½   42
Monday) Struggling halfway: lightly rcd & unplcd '03 (rtd 40, subs tried blnks & eye-shield, clmr): nov h'cap chase
rnr-up 03/04 (rtd 68a, modest form): h'cap plcd '02 on the level, rtd 41: eff around 1m/10f on fast & gd/soft.
3270   **SAXE COBURG 25** [11]7-9-3 (56) B Swarbrick(5) 7/1: 3035349: Chsd ldrs, btn 3f out: btr 3037.   2½   38
3310   **PEARL PRIDE 23** [2]3-8-6 (63) R Ffrench 20/1: 420-0000: 10th: Chsd ldr, btn 3f out, longer trip.   23   7
3502   **EDDIES JEWEL 15** [3]4-9-3 (39) T Hamilton 40/1: 00-25450: 11th: Mid-div, struggling from 3f out.   3   3
11 Ran   Time 2m 43.55(12.25)   Owned: Marcoe Racing Welwyn   Trained: Newmarket

Official Going GOOD/FIRM (GOOD places).

3857   5.40 Platinum Security Median Auction Maiden Stakes 2yo (E)
£4085 £1257 £629   5f6y str   Good/Firm 40   -08 Slow   Far Side

3626 **PIPERS ASH 10** [6] R Charlton 2-8-9 J Fortune 5/6 FAV: 61: Made all, drew clr over 1f out, v   **89**
easily: hvly bckd: much imprvd from debut with forcing tactics & eff at 5f on fast grnd & a stiff trk, 6f looks
sure to suit: looks v useful, plenty more to come, win more races: see 3626.
        KILLINGTON [3] G A Butler 2-9-0 S W Kelly 12/1: 2: ch c Kris - Miss Pickpocket (Petorius)   7   75
Reared stalls, dwelt, keen in tch, eff to chase wnr 2f out, no extra ins last on debut: Feb foal, half-brother to
wnrs over 5/6f: dam 5f juv scorer: eff over a stiff 5f on fast grnd: pleasing start, shld be sharper for this.
3438 **EDGE OF BLUE 18** [5] R Hannon 2-9-0 P Dobbs 6/1: 63: b c Bold Edge - Blue Goddess (Blues   ¾   73
Traveller) Chsd wnr till 2f out, onepace: Apr first foal, dam multiple 6f juv scorer: speedily bred & has shown
enough to win a minor trk mdn: eff at 5f on fast.
3488 **FARTHING 16** [4] G C Bravery 2-8-9 L Dettori 9/4: 24: Cl-up, no extra over 1f out: drifted from   shd   67
11/8 & did not prog from promising debut in 3488 (gd, fills mdn).
2839 **KINGSGATE BAY 42** [1]2-9-0 N Pollard 25/1: 055: Held up, eff 2f out, no impress fnl 1f: abs.   1   69
        BOLD MAGGIE [2]2-8-9 S Whitworth 25/1: 6: ch f Bold Edge - Vera's First (Exodal) Slow away &   3   55
al bhd on debut: Feb foal: half-sister to a 6f wnr: dam 7f juv scorer.
6 Ran   Time 1m 01.99 (2.39)   Owned: Mr K Abdulla   Trained: Beckhampton

3858   6.10 London Stock Exchange Maiden Stakes Fillies 3yo+ (D)
£5512 £1696 £848   1m14y rnd   Good/Firm 40   -22 Slow   Inside

2974 **LIBERTY FLAG 37** [4] J H M Gosden 3-8-11 J Fortune 8/11 FAV: 21: Handy, rdn over 3f out, styd on   73
over 1f out to lead ins last, rdn out: eff over a stiff or sharp 1m on firm & fast grnd: going the right way.
3480 **ALENUSHKA 16** [1] H Candy 3-8-11 (65) Dane O'Neill 3/1: 0642: Cl-up, led over 1f out, rdn & hdd   ¾   70
ins last, not pace of wnr: acts on a stiff or sharp trk, fast & firm grnd: ran to form of 3480.
        BATIK [8] L M Cumani 3-8-11 A Hamblett(7) 20/1: 3: gr f Peintre Celebre - Dali's Grey (Linamix)   nk   69
Slow away, gd hdwy 2f out, kept on well, hands & heels: dam 11f scorer: looks sure to relish a step up to 10f:
acts on fast grnd: learn plenty from this & one to keep on side over further with a more experienced jockey.
3469 **MERWAHA 17** [5] M P Tregoning 3-8-11 BL T E Durcan 5/1: 434: Slow away, keen held up, eff to   1½   66
chall over 1f out, wknd tamely: tried in first time blnks & poss temperament probs: see 3469, 2224.
3631 **TIPSY LADY 10** [7]3-8-11 N Pollard 20/1: 00005: b f Intikhab - Creme de Menthe (Green Desert)   1½   63
Led till over 1f out, no extra: bred to stay 1m+.
3446 **WITCHES BROOM 18** [6]3-8-11 L Dettori 11/2: 036: Handy, wknd over 1f out: btr 3446 (7f, gd).   8   47
3572 **COCO POINT BREEZE 12** [3]3-8-11 M Fenton 100/1: 007: b f Great Dane - Flying Colours (Fairy   5   37
King) Nvr a factor: breathing prob reported earlier.
        GENTLE WARNING [2]4-9-4 D Fentiman(7) 100/1: 8: Al bhd.   6   25
8 Ran   Time 1m 43.95 (4.95)   Owned: Mr W S Farish   Trained: Manton

3859   6.40 London Stock Exchange Conditions Stakes 2yo (C)
£7886 £2798 £1399   7f16y rnd   Good/Firm 40   -42 Slow   Inside

3390* **KAMAKIRI 19** [3] R Hannon 2-9-2 R L Moore 6/4 JT FAV: 011: Trkd ldr, hdwy to lead 2f out, styd   103
on well, pushed out: v eff over a stiff 7f on fast, 1m will suit: useful & progressive, more races can be won.
3489* **ACTIVE ASSET 16** [2] M R Channon 2-8-11 (85) T E Durcan 12/1: 212: Set pace till 2f out, kept on   2½   91
same pace: proving consistent: caught a useful sort, see 3489.
3520* **HACHITA 14** [4] H R A Cecil 2-8-11 W Ryan 7/2: 13: Keen held up, no extra over 1f out: up in   2½   86
class after mdn fills win in 3520.
3267 **BLUES AND ROYALS 25** [1] Saeed bin Suroor 2-9-2 L Dettori 6/4 JT FAV: 124: Slow away, held up,   8   75
wknd well over 1f out: something amiss? v useful eff earlier in 3267 & 2408.
4 Ran   Time 1m 32.15 (5.75)   Owned: Mr Michael Pescod   Trained: Marlborough

3860   7.15 London Stock Exchange Handicap Stakes 3yo 0-90 (C)   [97]
£10608 £3264 £1632   7f16y rnd   Good/Firm 40   +20 Fast   Inside

3550 **TAKE A BOW 13** [5] P R Chamings 3-9-7 (90) J Quinn 3/1 FAV: 02-1141: Mid-div, hdwy & qcknd to   104+
lead over 1f out, rdn clr, readily in a v fast time: hvly bckd: eff at 7f/1m on firm & gd/soft grnd, stiff or
sharp/undul trks: most progressive & has a turn of foot, win again.
3550 **FREE TRIP 13** [2] J H M Gosden 3-9-5 (88) J Fortune 4/1: 6025552: Held up, styd on for press fnl   3   93
2f, no ch with wnr: also bhd today's wnr in 3550, see 1983 & 955.
3283 **LORIEN HILL 25** [10] B W Hills 3-8-4 (73) Martin Dwyer 20/1: 6510203: Trkd ldrs & ch over 1f out,   nk   77
onepace: back to form after disapp in 3283, see 2742.
3179 **DR THONG 29** [12] P F I Cole 3-9-0 (83) P Dobbs 13/2: 4124104: Led, edged left & hdd dist, wknd.   1¼   84
3338 **FLIP FLOP AND FLY 21** [9]3-9-2 (85) L Dettori 4/1: 0010625: Rear, late prog: bckd: try 1m?   shd   85
2126 **JATH 71** [3]3-8-13 (82) N Pollard 50/1: 1-0606: Held up, hdwy 2f out, onepace when sltly hmpd dist.   1   80
3421 **BURLEY FLAME 18** [11]3-8-11 (80) M Fenton 20/1: 3103167: Held up, eff 2f out, little prog: btr 3179.   ½   77
3550 **BETTALATETHANNEVER 13** [1]3-9-1 (84) Dane O'Neill 12/1: 4002608: Mid-div wide, hdwy to press ldrs   shd   80
over 1f out, sn hung right & wknd: op 16/1: suffered an awkward wide passage & ran well for a long way.
3338 **CAMBERWELL 21** [8]3-9-2 (85) R Miles(3) 25/1: 1509: Bhd, hung badly right & little hdwy: btr 2291.   3½   74
3518 **GO YELLOW 14** [4]3-8-0 (69) D Fentiman(7) 25/1: 5246140: 10th: Chsd ldrs, btn 2f out: btr 3366.   shd   57
3048* **CORKY 34** [6]3-8-9 (78) R L Moore 8/1: 4310: 11th: Trkd ldrs, btn when hmpd over 1f out,   6   54
fdd/eased: btr 3048 (mdn, g/s).
3006 **FIRST CANDLELIGHT 36** [7]3-8-9 (78) I Mongan 40/1: 21-0000: 12th: Keen & led/dsptd lead till over   7   40
2f out, sn lost place & bhd.
12 Ran   Time 1m 27.8 (1.4)   Owned: Mrs J E L Wright   Trained: Basingstoke

SANDOWN WEDNESDAY 11.08.04 Righthand, Galloping Track, Stiff Finish

3861 7.45 Sharp Minds Betfair Handicap Stakes 3yo+ 0-80 (D) [93]
£5486 £1688 £844 2m78y Good/Firm 40 -21 Slow Inside

3580* **STRANGELY BROWN 12** [10] S C Williams 3-8-0 (65) Martin Dwyer 2/1 FAV: 0300211: Chsd ldr, hdwy to lead over 1f out, rdn & in command ins last: hvly bckd: eff at 2m on fast & hvy: unexposed stayer, win more races. **77**
3450* **BELLE ROUGE 18** [5] C A Horgan 6-9-1 (65) L Dettori 11/2: 2/-221212: Led, hdd over 1f out, not pace of wnr: acts on both AWs, fast & hvy grnd: v tough & prog: see 3450 & 768. *2½* **72**
3105 **RACE THE ACE 32** [1] J L Dunlop 3-8-5 (70) T Quinn 11/2: 45233: Rear, rapid hdwy over 5f out, styd on onepace fnl 2f: stays a stiff 2m: see 3105 & 2608. *1¼* **76**
3334 **POPES HILL 21** [3] L M Cumani 3-8-7 (72) D Holland 12/1: 0-44634: Mid-div, kept on onepace for press: prob styd longer 2m trip: acts on fast & gd grnd: see 3334, 2623 & 1885. *1¼* **75**
3340* **TOP TREES 21** [4]6-8-3 (53) N Mackay(3) 10/1: 010-0615: Mid-div, onepace for press fnl 2f: see 3340. *1* **56**
3688 **DARN GOOD 7** [2]3-8-6 bl (71) R L Moore 16/1: 6011206: Mid-div, lost place 3f out, no impress. *¾* **71**
3400* **TEORBAN 19** [6]5-8-8 (58) S Whitworth 20/1: 1010-617: Rear, only mod prog for press: reportedly lost both front shoes: see 3400. *hd* **59**
3454 **SAN HERNANDO 18** [11]4-9-6 (70) Dane O'Neill 9/1: 0040428: Bhd, hung right & mod prog. *1¼* **69**
3688 **JASMICK 7** [14]6-9-10 (74) J Fortune 16/1: 0260-509: Chsd ldrs, btn 2f out: see 3587. *2½* **70**
3340 **HENRY ISLAND 21** [9]11-8-10 (60) T E Durcan 33/1: 43-50400: 10th: Chsd ldrs till 2f out: btr 3057. *3½* **52**
3340 **LILLEBROR 21** [13]6-8-7 (57) S W Kelly 9/1: 000-0030: 11th: Mid-div, btn 2f out: op 13/2: btr 3340. *2* **47**
2879 **SONG OF THE SEA 41** [7]3-7-12 (1oh)t (62) J F McDonald(3) 25/1: 0-0040: 12th: Keen, rear, btn 2f out. *5* **48**
12 Ran Time 3m 39.75 (9.95) Owned: J T and K Worsley Trained: Newmarket

3862 8.15 Sharp Minds Betfair Rated Stakes Handicap 3yo 0-80 (D) [87]
£6212 £2356 £1178 1m2f7y Good/Firm 40 -14 Slow Inside

3072 **HASAIYDA 33** [2] Sir Michael Stoute 3-9-2 (75) J Fortune 9/4 FAV: 141: Handy, prog & ev ch 2f out, styd on to lead ins fnl 1f, rdn out: well bckd: eff at 9/10f, further shld suit: acts on fast & gd grnd: unexposed & improving: see 3072, 2013. **83**
3578* **NORDWIND 12** [10] P W Harris 3-9-4 (77) I Mongan 5/2: 34112: In tch, prog & ev ch bef 1f out, sn hung left & right, not pace of wnr: well bckd on hat-trick bid: did not impress with attitude under press. *1* **82**
3385* **FUEL CELL 20** [6] R Hannon 3-8-11 BL (70) R L Moore 14/1: 0033013: Cl-up, led 3f out, hdd under press ins fnl 1f, no extra: eff at 1m/10f: gd eff in first time blnks: see 3385. *¾* **73**
3339* **MR JACK DANIELLS 21** [1] W R Muir 3-9-2 (75) Martin Dwyer 7/2: 3630414: Held up, prog trav well 3f out, onepcd fnl 1f: prob stays 10f, return to 1m will suit: btr 3339. *1½* **75**
3453 **LOVE TRIANGLE 18** [7]3-9-2 (75) L Keniry(3) 25/1: 0-300045: Held up, prog 3f out, onepcd dist. *1½* **72**
3690 **DOCTORED 7** [3]3-9-4 bl (77) L Dettori 8/1: 1111306: Nvr nrr than mid-div: qck reapp: btr 3578 & 3471. *5* **66**
3785 **JACKIE KIELY 4** [9]3-8-6 t (65) S W Kelly 12/1: 0110037: Bhd, nvr a factor: qck reapp: btr 3785. *3* **49**
3292 **HAT TRICK MAN 23** [4]3-8-13 (72) Dane O'Neill 16/1: 00-68: Keen rear, wknd fnl 2f: btr 3292. *5* **48**
3523 **ARKHOLME 14** [8]3-9-7 (80) P Doe 12/1: 1-402129: Led till 3f out, wknd: disapp on step up to 10f. *7* **44**
9 Ran Time 2m 09.5(5.4) Owned: HH Aga Khan Trained: Newmarket

SALISBURY WEDNESDAY 11.08.04 Righthand, Galloping Track, Stiff Finish

Official Going Good/Firm (Good Places)

3863 2.30 Carmen Wines E B F Maiden Stakes 2yo (D)
£5902 £1816 £908 6f str Good/Firm 27 -26 Slow Far side

3478 **CAPE QUEST 16** [11] R Hannon 2-9-0 R L Moore 7/2: 031: Grabbed far rail & made all, drvn out fnl 1f: op 9/2: eff at 6f, further will suit: acts on firm & fast grnd: improving with racing, see 3478. **88**
NOTA BENE 0 [6] D R C Elsworth 2-9-0 L Keniry(3) 8/1: 2: b c Zafonic - Dodo (Alzao) Rear, prog halfway, styd on well ins fnl 1f, nrst fin: debut: Apr foal, cost 14,000gns: half-brother to smart 7f performer Tarjman: dam successful at 6f: sire Gr 1 wnr at 1m: eff at 6f, 7f/1m will suit: acts on fast grnd: showed signs of greenness but ran with some promise: impr on today & can find similar. *¾* **86+**
SOUND THE DRUM 0 [3] J H M Gosden 2-9-0 J Fortune 7/1: 3: b c Stravinsky - Uhavethebeat (Unbridled) Missed break, sn handy, chsd ldr bef 1f out, no extra ins fnl 1f: op 5/1 on debut: Mar foal, cost $200,000: dam unrcd: sire Gr 1 wnr at 6f: eff at 6f on fast grnd: encouraging start & can improve. *1½* **82**
TIGGERS TOUCH 0 [1] B R Millman 2-8-9 J Fanning 20/1: 4: b f Fraam - Beacon Silver (Belmez) Cl-up til halfway, wknd bef 1f out: clr rem: debut: Mar foal, dam plcd around mid-dists on Flat, also successful over hdles: sire useful performer around 1m: impr on today & will apprec further. *3* **68**
2970 **RUSKY DUSKY 37** [5]2-9-0 (79) P Dobbs 7/2: 0325: Rcd free in tch 4f, sn wknd: tchd 5/1: stablemate of wnr: needs to settle better: showed more in 2970 & 2666. *6* **57**
DESERT MOONBEAM 0 [2]2-8-9 R Havlin 50/1: 6: Nvr nrr than mid-div: debut. *1¼* **48**
2858 **AFRICAN STORM 42** [9]2-9-0 (81) L Dettori 5/2 FAV: 5227: Keen handy 4f, sn fdd, eased ins fnl 1f: bckd: rider reported mount rcd too freely on step up to 6f: btr 2858 & 2738 (5f). *1* **50**
PUSSY CAT 0 [7]2-8-9 Dane O'Neill 50/1: 8: Rear, nvr a factor: debut. *nk* **44**
2490 **MAKE IT HAPPEN NOW 56** [10]2-8-9 (50) A Daly 66/1: 0409: Handy over 3f, wknd: 8 wk abs. *2½* **37**
GRANITA 0 [4]2-8-9 D Sweeney 16/1: 0: 10th: Chsd ldrs till halfway, wknd. *nk* **36**
2472 **IAM FOREVERBLOWING 57** [8]2-8-9 (45) B O'Neill(7) 100/1: 545000: 11th: Handy 3f, sn hung left & fdd. *6* **20**
11 Ran Time 1m 15.28 (3.18) Owned: Mr Malih L Al Basti Trained: Marlborough

3864
3.00 Bembridge Claiming Stakes 2yo   (E)
£3562 £1096 £548   **6f212y str**   **Good/Firm 27**   **-41 Slow**   Far side

3750 **LADRUCA** 5 [2] R Hannon 2-8-2   R Smith 7/2: 0051: Handy, styd on to lead trav well bef 1f out, **61**
pushed clr, val bit more: clmd for 5,000: eff at 7f, 1m will suit: acts on fast grnd & a stiff/gall trk: see 3750.
3368 **SLITE** 20 [9] J A Osborne 2-8-5 (1ow) S W Kelly 20/1: 02: gr f Mind Games - Sapphire Mill **5** **52**
(Petong) Handy, led halfway, hdd bef 1f out, sn outpcd by easy wnr: clmd for 6,000: Feb first foal, cost 3,200
gns: dam unplcd: sire Group winning sprinter: eff at 7f on fast grnd: only lightly rcd & can rate higher.
3349 **LARAS GIRL** 21 [4] I A Wood 2-8-2 (40) P Doe 20/1: 04003: Handy, kept on fnl 1f, just held for **shd** **48**
2nd: eff at 7f on fast grnd: see 2640.
3713 **ZOLASH** 6 [8] J S Moore 2-9-1   Martin Dwyer 3/1 FAV: 506044: Held up, prog bef 1f out, nrst fin. **¾** **59**
1538 **LISTEN TO ME** 99 [1]2-8-7   R Havlin 20/1: 505: Led, hdd halfway, no extra bef 1f out: long abs. **nk** **50**
3491 **AHAZ** 16 [12]2-8-7 P (55) M Fenton 10/1: 060546: Chsd ldrs 5f, wknd: cheek pieces: btr 3491. **3½** **43**
3728 **SECRET DIVA** 6 [11]2-8-2   J F McDonald(3) 33/1: 0007: Handy over 3f, sn onepcd: qck reapp. **2** **34**
3691 **SWEENEY TODD** 7 [13]2-9-3   R L Moore 7/1: 68: Nvr nrr than mid-div: qck reapp: see 3691. **1¾** **45**
3394 **MUESTRA** 19 [5]2-8-2 (54) R Miles(2) 6/1: 0000539: No impress in mid-div: op 8/1: btr 3394 (AW). **nk** **29**
3394 **CHIN DANCER** 19 [6]2-8-0 bl t R Thomas(3) 33/1: 0060: 10th: Handy 5f, fdd: see 3394. **½** **26**
2449 **JOE NINETY** 58 [10]2-8-9 (47) J D Smith 14/1: 5600300: 11th: Bhd, nvr a factor: 8 wk abs. **½** **34**
2714 **Ardasnails** 47 [3]2-8-9 L Keniry(3) 100/1:0   **Jules Lee** 0 [7]2-9-3 C Haddon(7) 20/1:0
13 Ran   Time 1m 30.32 (4.82)   Owned: Mr R Hannon   Trained: Marlborough

3865
3.30 Listed Weatherbys Stonehenge Stakes 2yo   (A)
£20100 £6600 £3300   **1m str**   **Good/Firm 27**   **-28 Slow**   Far side

3585 **PERFECTPERFORMANCE** 12 [2] Saeed bin Suroor 2-8-11   L Dettori 4/5 FAV: 121: Held up in tch, prog **112**
halfway, styd on to lead bef 1f out, pushed clr, val 5L+: well bckd: eff at 7f, apprec step up to 1m: acts on fast
& gd grnd: likes Salisbury: v useful & showed a gd turn of foot, win in Gr class: see 3585 & 2695.
3267* **GRAND MARQUE** 25 [1] R Hannon 2-8-11 (100) J Fortune 13/8: 5112: Cl-up, led halfway, hdd bef 1f **3** **103**
out, sn no extra: op 11/8: eff at 7f/1m: far from disgraced against progressive rival: see 3267 & 2876.
3285* **MINNESOTA** 25 [3] H Candy 2-8-11 (83) Dane O'Neill 13/2: 213: Led till halfway, no extra bef 2f **5** **93**
out: tchd 8/1: stepped up in class after recent win in 3285 (mdn, 7f).
3 Ran   Time 1m 43.53 (4.43)   Owned: Godolphin   Trained: Newmarket

3866
4.00 Listed European Breeders Fund Upavon Stakes Fillies 3yo+   (A)
£26100 £9900 £4950   **1m1f198y**   **Good/Firm 27**   **+19 Fast**   Inside

2946 **NEW MORNING** 39 [6] M A Jarvis 3-8-5 (104) P Robinson 6/4 FAV: 4-21451: Made all, went 2 out clr **108**
bef 2f out, pushed out, al holding rivals: v well bckd: fast time: stays 12f, apprec drop back to 10f: acts on
fast or gd/soft grnd: authoritative success & has to be feared in Gr 3 grade: see 2517 & 1961.
3631* **TAHTHEEB** 10 [8] M P Tregoning 3-8-5   R Hills 13/2: 12: Rear, prog 3f out, styd on to chase wnr **1¾** **105+**
ins fnl 1f, al held: tchd 8/1: eff at 9f, appr for step up to 10f: acts on firm & fast grnd: fine eff on only
2nd ever start, 12f looks sure to suit & can win a Listed/Gr 3 sn: see 3631.
3389 **SNOW GOOSE** 19 [9] J L Dunlop 3-8-5 (103) J Fanning 7/2: 12-04233: Handy, chsd ldr after 6f, **2½** **101**
onepcd bef 1f out: clr rem: eff at 1m, ran to form on step up to 10f: see 3389 & 2917.
2761 **MANGO MISCHIEF** 46 [10] J L Dunlop 3-8-5 (92) R L Moore 16/1: 10-124: Held up, prog bef 2f out, **3½** **96**
no impress fnl 1f: needs h'caps: see 2761 (fills h'cap).
   BAYBERRY 304 [7]4-9-0   W Ryan 40/1: 430410-5: ch f Bering - Baya (Nureyev) In tch 1m, no extra: **2½** **92**
long abs & Brit bow: ex-French, wnr in '03 (9.5f, gd): with H R A Cecil.
3089 **INCHENI** 33 [3]3-8-9 (100) T E Durcan 11/1: 1-203146: In tch over 7f, wknd: twice below win of 2351. **3** **92**
   LA HERMANA 24 [2]3-8-5   Andreas Suborics 12/1: 15-55447: ch f Hernando - La Candela (Alzao) Nvr **6** **79**
nrr than mid-div: German raider, earlier plcd 4th in Gr 1 contest in native country (11f, gd): wnr in '03 (1m, soft).
2211 **TOP ROMANCE** 68 [4]3-8-5 (100) Martin Dwyer 8/1: 11-048: Chsd ldrs 7f, wknd: abs: btr 2211. **3** **75**
3629 **WELL KNOWN** 10 [5]3-8-6 (1ow) (92) Dane O'Neill 25/1: 2-109: Keen cl-up, fdd 3f out: btr 1719. **8** **65**
3448 **CUDDLES** 18 [1]5-9-0 (57) L Keniry 200/1: 5045300: 10th: Rear, nvr a factor: v stiff task: btr 3144. **6** **56**
10 Ran   Time 2m 5.39 (0.89)   Owned: Mr N R A Springer   Trained: Newmarket

3867
4.30 Violet Applin Challenge Cup Handicap Stakes 3yo+ 0-70   (E)   **[70]**
£3829 £1178 £589   **1m1f198y**   **Good/Firm 27**   **-17 Slow**   Inside

3336 **BLUEGRASS BOY** 21 [3] G B Balding 4-9-3 (59) R Thomas(5) 8/1: 0-300031: Held up, prog wide 3f out, **66**
drvn out to lead cl-home: eff around 10f on firm, gd/soft & polytrack: first win: see 3336 & 1098.
3512 **COMPTON DRAKE** 15 [13] G A Butler 5-9-10 (66) Andreas Suborics 9/2: 02111-02: Handy, prog & ev ch **½** **73**
bef 2f out, styd on to lead 1f out, hdd cl-home: op 7/1: back to form: see 249.
3802 **EFRHINA** 3 [12] Mrs Stef Liddiard 4-9-7 (63) R Havlin 20/1: 002-003: In tch, outpcd after 7f, **1½** **67**
rallied fnl 1f: qck reapp: acts on firm & fast grnd: see 3477.
3404 **KYLKENNY** 19 [6] H Morrison 9-10-0 t (70) R L Moore 4/1: 0653444: Held up, prog after halfway, **½** **73**
styd on to lead bef 2f out, hdd 1f out, no extra: bckd: top-weight: btr 2735 & 856.
3535 **PETROSA** 14 [10]4-10-0 (70) L Keniry(3) 7/2 FAV: 40323-45: Held up, prog 3f out, keeping on when **½** **72**
short of room ins fnl 1f, sn no impress: see 3535.
3579 **POLISH SPIRIT** 12 [9]9-9-4 (60) J Fanning 14/1: 015///5-006: Handy, ev ch bef 2f out, sn no extra. **nk** **61**
3573 **ZURI** 12 [1]3-8-12 (63) J Murtagh 17/2: 64007: Chsd ldrs 1m, wknd: see 2534. **6** **55**
3232 **MAMORE GAP** 26 [7]6-9-12 (60) P Gallagher(7) 8/1: 50-00058: Al bhd: btr 3232. **4** **54**
3455 **RUMBLING BRIDGE** 18 [8]3-8-8 (59) P Doe 25/1: 546-09: Al in rear: see 3455. **hd** **44**
3492 **DRY WIT** 16 [5]3-8-6 (57) Martin Dwyer 33/1: 260-0600: 10th: Cl-up, fdd 3f out, sn hdd & wknd. **3½** **37**
3053} **MARK YOUR WAY** 387 [14]4-8-13 (55) N Chalmers(5) 50/1: 600-0: 11th: b g Spectrum - Titania's Way **3½** **34**
(Fairy King) Bhd, nvr a factor: reapp: unplcd all 3 '03 starts (rtd 63, mdn): has been gelded.
1650 **DUSTY CARPET** 93 [4]6-9-4 (60) Joanna Badger 33/1: 0//-000000: 12th: Bhd, nvr a factor: long abs. **3½** **34**

SALISBURY WEDNESDAY 11.08.04 Righthand, Galloping Track, Stiff Finish

3748 **PACIFIC OCEAN 5** [2]5-8-10 P (52) A Daly 16/1: 6043600: 13th: Handy, ev ch 3f out, sn fdd: qck reapp. 1½ 23
RICHMOND LODGE 348 [11]4-9-0 (56) G Baker 33/1: 000310-0: 14th: br g Sesaro - Richmond Lillie 23 0
(Fairbairn) Led, hdd bef 2f out, fdd: ex-Irish, h'cap wnr at Tramore in '03: eff around 11/12f on fm & gd.
14 Ran Time 2m 8.90 (4.4) Owned: Supreme Team Trained: Andover

3868

5.00 Goldring Security Services Handicap Stakes Fillies 3yo+ 0-80 (D) **[88]**
£7384 £2272 £1136 **1m4f** **Good/Firm 27** **-04 Slow** Stands side

2867* **ASALEEB 41** [11] E F Vaughan 3-9-6 (80) R Hills 4/1: 32-211: In tch, styd on to lead trav well 3f out, rdn out ins fnl 1f to just hold on: 6 wk abs: eff at 10/11.5f, imprvd for step up to 12f: acts on firm & fast grnd: goes well fresh: unexposed & game: see 2867 & 2349. **87**
3345 **AONINCH 21** [7] Mrs P N Dutfield 4-8-11 (60) J Fanning 12/1: 5060262: Held up, prog 4f out, ev ch ins fnl 1f, just held: op 7/1: back to form on return to Salisbury: see 3114 & 801. *nk* **65**
3514 **ROYAL BATHWICK 14** [12] B R Millman 4-9-10 (73) G Baker 16/1: 40106-33: Held up, prog 4f out, ev ch dist, kept on fnl 1f, onepace front 2: clr rem: eff at 1m/12f: likes Warwick: see 3514. *¾* **76**
3217 **KEEP ON MOVIN 27** [5] T G Mills 3-8-13 (73) G Carter 16/1: 31-50204: Mid-div, prog 2f out, onepcd fnl 1f. *6* **67**
3481 **ANYHOW 16** [4]7-9-2 (65) D Nolan(3) 10/1: 5321055: Chsd ldrs 10f, wknd: btr 2651. *2½* **55**
3335 **WOMAN IN WHITE 21** [8]3-8-13 (73) R Havlin 16/1: 02636: Handy over 9f, wknd: btr 3335. *1½* **61**
3270 **ENCHANTED OCEAN 25** [9]5-8-4 (53) R Thomas(5) 33/1: 40//-0007: Nvr nrr than mid-div: see 2293. *5* **34**
2960 **PRENUP 38** [6]3-9-2 (76) J Murtagh 7/4 FAV: 0-411228: Keen cl-up, led 5f out, hdd 3f out, sn wknd: well bckd: rcd too keenly: much btr 2960 & 2530. *2½* **53**
3674 **DISPOL EVITA 8** [1]5-7-13 (48) J F McDonald(3) 25/1: 0420409: Rear, nvr a factor: btr 3287. *5* **18**
3340 **GAELIC ROULETTE 21** [2]4-9-7 (70) R L Moore 11/2: 1650-300: 10th: Handy 1m, sn wknd: btr 2923. *1½* **37**
1521 **OPERA BABE 100** [10]3-8-12 (72) S Carson 66/1: 4005-00: 11th: Bhd, nvr a factor. *12* **23**
3415 **KRISTALS DREAM 19** [3]3-9-2 T (76) T Quinn 20/1: 1-350250: 12th: Led, hdd 5f out, sn fdd: btr 2796. *dist* **2**
12 Ran Time 2m 36.14(3.74) Owned: Mr Hamdan Al Maktoum Trained: Newmarket

YARMOUTH WEDNESDAY 11.08.04 Lefthand, Fair, Flat Track

Official Going GOOD/FIRM (GOOD places).

3869

2.20 European Breeders Fund Maiden Stakes 2yo (D)
£4716 £1451 £726 **6f3y str** **Good 54** **-48 Slow** Stands Side

3594 **DESERT COMMANDER 11** [6] Saeed bin Suroor 2-9-0 T T P Queally 17/2: 461: Nvr far away, went on dist, styd on strongly, pushed out: apprec drop back to 6f, 7f will suit: acts on gd & gd/soft grnd, apprec first time t-strap today: see 3111. **89**
3120 **WAVERTREE WARRIOR 32** [7] N P Littmoden 2-9-0 J P Guillambert(3) 16/1: 032: Held up, outpcd, styd on strongly into 2nd cl-home, not reach wnr: sound run, shld find similar, poss over 7f: see 3120. *1½* **81**
2472 **JUANTORENA 57** [3] M L W Bell 2-9-0 (95) D Holland 4/11 FAV: 2243: Led till dist, caught for 2nd cl-home: hvly bckd, 8 wk abs: much better expected after 2472 & 2158. *1½* **77**
KINGS KAMA [5] Sir Michael Stoute 2-9-0 F Lynch 15/2: 4: b c Giant's Causeway - Maid For The Hills (Indian Ridge) Rdn in rear, nvr dngrs on debut: May foal, cost 350,000gns: half-brother to wnrsa over 7f/10f: dam a useful 6f juv wnr: likely to apprec 7f+. *½* **76**
3735 **TURKS WOOD 6** [2]2-9-0 M Henry 25/1: 455: Prom till halfway, sn no extra: see 1981 (debut). *shd* **74**
3280 **FIGHTING TOM CAT 25** [1]2-9-0 t R Mullen 20/1: 06: ch c Storm Cat - Elizabeth Bay (Mr Prospector) *2* **70**
Slowly away, nvr nr ldrs: longer priced stablemate of wnr: May foal, half-brother to a couple of 6f juv wnrs: dam a 6f 2yo scorer, sire a top-class juv in the US: with Saeed Bin Suroor & surely capable of better.
THREE BOARS [4]2-9-0 M Tebbutt 100/1: 7: ch c Most Welcome - Precious Poppy (Polish Precedent) *14* **30**
Slowly away, al well bhd, eased & fin last on debut: May first foal: dam styd mid-dists.
7 Ran Time 1m 16.52 (6.12) Owned: Godolphin Trained: Newmarket

3870

2.50 Parklands Leisure Holiday Caravans Handicap Stakes Fillies 3yo 0-70 (E) **[74]**
£3838 £1181 £591 **6f3y str** **Good 54** **-43 Slow** Stands Side

3273 **RISE 25** [12] Andrew Reid 3-9-4 bl (64) J F Egan 4/1: 6001201: Made all stands side, held on well fnl 1f, drvn out: eff at 5/6f on gd, fast grnd & both AWs: suited by blnks & handles a flat or stiff/gall trk. **74**
3479 **DARLA 16** [2] J W Payne 3-9-7 (67) T P Queally 15/2: 2306-052: Held up, smooth hdwy to chall dist, kept on but not pace of wnr cl-home: not disgraced under top-weight, has shown enough to win similar. *1½* **71**
3577 **SHRINK 12** [14] M L W Bell 3-9-2 T (62) R Mullen 16/1: 2144003: Chsd ldrs, onepcd fnl 1f: tried t-strap. *2½* **59**
2268 **URBAN ROSE 65** [1] R M H Cowell 3-9-3 t (63) M Henry 25/1: 44-00304: Mid-div, prog to chall 2f out, wknd cl-home: 9 wk abs: new stable, prev with J Unett: see 2118. *1½* **56**
3711 **BEAUTIFUL NOISE 6** [3]3-8-6 BL (52) J Quinn 9/1: 6-065555: Slowly away, no impress fnl 1f. *½* **44**
3672 **CHERTSEY 8** [7]3-8-13 (59) J P Guillambert(3) 11/1: 335056: Prom, wknd fnl 1f. *hd* **51**
3711 **MUGEBA 6** [9]3-9-0 BL t (60) D Holland 3/1 FAV: 2-551227: Cl-up till wknd fnl 1f: qck reapp & well bckd in first time blnks: reportedly hung & this was well below 3711 & 3380. *nk* **51**
3203 **INDRANI 27** [5]3-7-12 (2oh) (42) M Halford(5) 33/1: 4020508: Keen & prom, btn dist. *hd* **35**
3710 **PARDON MOI 6** [10]3-8-1 (47) D Kinsella 33/1: 1040069: Nvr nr ldrs: qck reapp. *1½* **34**
3604 **SHIFTY NIGHT 11** [8]3-8-1 (47) Dean Williams(7) 11/1: 0041060: 10th: Mid-div, btn 1.5f out: btr 3092. *nk* **33**
3331 **WAVERTREE GIRL 21** [13]3-9-7 bl (67) T G McLaughlin 20/1: 0504300: 11th: Slowly away, al bhd. *½* **52**
2925 **PARTY PRINCESS 39** [4]3-9-2 (62) J Mackay 12/1: 0014000: 12th: Prom 4f, wknd & eased. *11* **17**
2805 **Mitzi Caspar 44** [6]3-8-6 (52) A McCarthy 33/1:0 3737 **Turkish Delight 6** [11]3-8-13 (59) Lisa Jones 12/1:0
14 Ran Time 1m 16.24 (5.84) Owned: Mr A S Reid Trained: Mill Hill London

YARMOUTH WEDNESDAY 11.08.04 Lefthand, Fair, Flat Track

3871
3.20 Bet365 08000 322365 Selling Stakes 2yo (G)
£2520 £720 £360 6f3y str Good 54 -83 Slow Stands Side

3750 **JAY 5** [2] N A Callaghan 2-8-7 bl (53) D Holland 2/1 FAV: 0020201: V slowly away & lost 10L+, styd
on strongly fnl 1f to lead cl-home: no bid, slow time, qck reapp: first success: eff at 6/7f on gd & fast grnd:
clearly has ability but her share of temperament & wears blnks: see 3491 & 2640. **62**

3382 **HIS MAJESTY 20** [5] N P Littmoden 2-8-12 Steven Harrison(7) 14/1: 032: Chsd ldrs, went on
entering fnl 1f, caught cl-home: clr of rem: eff at 6f on gd grnd: see 3382. ¾ **63**

3729 **GENERAL NUISANCE 6** [3] J S Moore 2-8-12 bl (59) Derek Nolan(7) 4/1: 5432303: Led till entering fnl 1f. 3 **54**

3729 **GLASSON LODGE 6** [4] P D Evans 2-8-7 vis (55) F P Ferris(3) 4/1: 3422604: Chsd ldrs, btn over 1f shd **49**
out: reportedly fin lame, qck reapp.

3504 **RUSSIAN SERVANA 15** [1]2-8-7 (52) J Quinn 9/4: 0255: Chsd ldr, wknd dist: see 2921 (5f). 6 **31**
5 Ran Time 1m 18.62 (8.22) Owned: Mr G C Hartigan Trained: Newmarket

3872
3.50 Bennetts Electrical Toshiba Handicap Stakes 3yo+ 0-80 (D) [86]
£5512 £1696 £848 7f3y str Good 54 -47 Slow Stands Side

3718 **MISS MADAME 6** [3] R Guest 3-8-7 (65) T P Queally 3/1 JT FAV: 0-336121: Led till 2f out, rallied
to regain lead cl-home, rdn clr: eff at 5.7/7f, stays 1m: acts on gd, fast grnd & fibresand: in fine form. **73**

2532 **WARDEN WARREN 54** [2] Mrs C A Dunnett 6-9-7 p (73) T G McLaughlin 17/2: 0041002: Prom, led 2f out 1¼ **77**
till caught cl-home: 8 wk abs: won this race from a 4lb lower mark last term: v tough, see 2122.

1079 **AMMENAYR 126** [4] T G Mills 4-9-12 (78) D Holland 7/2: 50-00353: Chsd ldrs, onepcd fnl 1f: 2 **78**
top-weight, long abs: op 5/1 & sharper next time, see 1020.

3456* **AND TOTO TOO 18** [1] P D Evans 4-9-3 vis (69) F P Ferris(3) 3/1 JT FAV: 2044214: Dwelt, kept on 1¼ **66**
under press, not pace to chall: nicely bckd: btr 3456.

3408 **ANTONIO CANOVA 19** [5]8-9-10 (76) J F Egan 8/1: 0-001005: Held up, eff 2f out, sn no impress. 2 **69**

3708 **LYGETON LAD 7** [7]6-9-2 t (68) R Mullen 11/2: 1000046: Led stands duo, no ch with centre group fnl 1.5f. nk **60**

2148 **KING OF MUSIC 70** [6]3-8-10 (68) J Mackay 33/1: 350-07: ch g Jade Hunter - Hail Roberta (Roberto) 5 **50**
Chsd stands side ldr, eased fnl 1f: op 14/1, 10 wk abs: lightly rcd in '03, mdn plcd on debut (rtd 79): cost
$7,000 & half-brother to several wnrs in the US: eff at 7f on fast grnd: with G Prodromou.
7 Ran Time 1m 29.70 (7.10) Owned: Cosmic Greyhound Racing Partnership III Trained: Newmarket

3873
4.20 Munchies Cafe Maiden Stakes Fillies 3yo (D)
£3380 £1040 £520 6f3y str Good 54 -29 Slow Stands Side

3603 **KOOL ACCLAIM 11** [8] S C Williams 3-8-11 O Urbina 8/1: 21: In tch, hdwy to lead ins fnl 1f, drvn
out: tchd 14/1: stays 6f, shld get further: acts on fast & gd, flat/fair trk: built on encouraging debut, rate **74**
higher with further experience: see 3603 (debut).

1935 **ANTIGUA BAY 81** [6] J A R Toller 3-8-11 Lisa Jones 9/1: 002: b f Turtle Island - Vilanika (Top ¾ **71**
Ville) Bhd, outpcd halfway, styd on well ins fnl 1f despite edging left to go 2nd cl-home: op 6/1, 12 wk abs: cost
24,000gns: dam a 7/8f wnr: half-sister to useful 12f runner Largesse: stays 6f on gd, apprec a return to 7f/1m.

3366 **LAKE CHARLOTTE 20** [7] D R Loder 3-8-11 T P Queally 4/5 FAV: 323: Led till ins fnl 1f, no extra hd **70**
& lost 2nd cl-home: nicely bckd, clr of rem: stays 6f, return to 7f prob suit: find a small race: see 3121.

3610 **ELTIHAAB 11** [3] Saeed bin Suroor 3-8-11 T D Holland 3/1: 034: Slow away, nvr btr than mid-div: t-strap. 6 **52**

1688 **NOBLE DESERT 91** [5]3-8-11 J Mackay 40/1: 0-05: b f Green Desert - Sporades (Vaguely Noble) 5 **37**
Prom, wknd 2f out: long abs: unplcd sole '03 start (mdn, rtd 41a): with R Guest.

3603 **SYLVA ROYAL 11** [1]3-8-11 J P Guillambert(3) 20/1: 446: Rcd in 2nd, wknd qckly 2f out: see 1008. hd **37**

3448 **PICK A BERRY 18** [4]3-8-11 (55) J F Egan 20/1: 0-00607: In tch, wknd over 2f out: trainer 6 **19**
reported filly to be unsuited by this grnd: see 2906.

3784 **TIDES 4** [2]3-8-11 R Mullen 100/1: 068: Keen bhd, nvr a factor, eased fnl 1f: qck reapp: see 3784. 3 **10**
8 Ran Time 1m 15.38 (4.98) Owned: Carol Shekells & Associates Trained: Newmarket

3874
4.50 Vauxhall Holiday Park Claiming Stakes 3yo (F)
£2898 £828 £414 1m2f21y Good 54 -11 Slow Inside

3739 **TREASON TRIAL 6** [3] N Tinkler 3-8-9 (57) O Urbina 11/4 FAV: 40-06431: Prom, hdwy to lead over 1f **56**
out, rdn out ins fnl 1f: clmd for 7,000: bckd, qck reapp: eff at 1m/10f on fast & gd, flat/fair trk: see 3219.

3415 **AUROVILLE 19** [5] M L W Bell 3-9-1 (57) R Mullen 9/2: 4050062: Trkd ldrs, hdwy into 2nd 1f out, 2 **56**
btn when edged left ins fnl 1f: stays 10f on gd, prob handles fast & soft: see 1163.

3344 **TSHUKUDU 21** [8] M Blanshard 3-8-0 (38) D Kinsella 40/1: 00-00003: Keen & led, hdd 3f out, 3½ **36**
remained prom, no extra over 1f out: see 3344.

3515 **SOVIET SPIRIT 14** [4] C A Dwyer 3-8-10 (55) B Reilly(3) 16/1: 5053504: In tch, btn fnl 2f. 2½ **42**

3712 **LENWADE 6** [10]3-8-2 (35) A McCarthy 20/1: 0300045: Cl-up, wknd 2f out: qck reapp. ½ **33**

3300 **RUSSALKA 23** [7]3-8-8 (51) M Halford(7) 7/1: 0502606: Slow away & keen, nvr nr ldrs. nk **38**

3362 **MYSTIC MOON 20** [9]3-8-12 (48) J F Egan 16/1: 6040047: Pressed ldr till slt lead 2f out, hdd over 3 **37**
1f out, no extra, eased when btn ins fnl 1f: see 1280.

3455 **STARMIX 18** [2]3-9-11 (65) D Holland 9/2: 004008: Al bhd: top-weight: see 1815. 2 **47**

3704 **IVORY COAST 7** [11]3-9-0 (59) T P Queally 4/1: 1200059: Keen in rear, nvr a factor: op 7/1, qck 1¼ **34**
reapp: joc reported mount hung right: see 1953.

3712 **DIVERTED 6** [1]3-8-0 (36) J Mackay 40/1: 0000050: 10th: In tch, no impress over 3f out: qck 1¼ **18**
reapp: rider reported mount to be unsuited by this grnd: see 3712.
10 Ran Time 2m 10.77 (6.57) Owned: Elite Racing Club Trained: Malton

YARMOUTH WEDNESDAY 11.08.04 Lefthand, Fair, Flat Track

3875 5.20 Long Bar Classified Stakes 3yo+ 0-60 (F)
£3031 £866 £433   1m2f21y   Good 54   +10 Fast   Inside

1326* **BARTON SANDS** 110 [9] J Jay 7-9-3 (60) O Urbina 14/1: 60100-11: Held up, prog to lead dist, **71**
pushed clr, cmftbly: long abs: eff at 1m/11f on firm & gd/soft grnd: eff with visor or t-strap, left off today:
imprvd eff on first start for new yard (prev with M Pipe): see 1326 (sell).
2590 **PATRIXTOO** 53 [2] M H Tompkins 3-8-8 (57) M Henry 33/1: 00-0502: gr c Linamix - Maradadi **5 61**
(Shadeed) Rear, under press when hmpd 2f out, switched wide & styd on well fnl 1f, no ch with easy wnr: 8 wk abs:
unplcd both '03 starts (rtd 70, mdns): eff at 10f, shaped as tho' further will suit: acts on gd grnd.
3108 **GENERAL FLUMPA** 32 [5] C F Wall 3-8-12 (64) R Mullen 8/1: 6335263: Mid-div, outpcd after 6f, *shd* **65**
rallied fnl 1f, just held for 2nd: just btr 2780.
3490 **KIND EMPEROR** 16 [4] P L Gilligan 7-9-5 (62) A Mackay 10/1: 15150-04: Led, hdd bef 1f out, sn ½ **62**
edged right & no extra: op 7/1: won this race 12 mths ago: see 3490.
3201 **GOLDEN DRIFT** 28 [3]3-8-5 (60) J F Egan 9/2: 0-05025: Mid-div, short of room bef 2f out till just 3½ **52+**
ins fnl 1f, switched & styd on, ch had gone: op 7/2: no luck in running & worth another ch: btr 3201.
3704* **ARMS ACROSSTHESEA** 7 [6]5-9-9 (57) T P Queally 11/1: 1140016: Cl-up over 1m, sn wknd: qck reapp. *nk* **60**
3492 **CARRIACOU** 16 [8]3-8-9 (64) Derek Nolan(7) 7/2: 6450537: Nvr nrr than mid-div: btr 3492. 1½ **53**
3419 **SCRIPTORIUM** 18 [10]3-8-10 (62) D Holland 11/4 FAV: 0-602428: Handy over 7f, sn wknd: well bckd: ½ **53**
rider reported mount had hung left in straight: better expected after 3419 & 2120.
2530 **KING OF KNIGHT** 54 [7]3-8-10 (62) M Halford(7) 20/1: 00-45009: Al bhd: 8 wk abs: btr 1427. *shd* **53**
3492 **ABSOLUTELY SOAKED** 16 [11]3-8-5 (57) Lisa Jones 20/1: 30-56000: 10th: Keen in tch 1m: btr 1427. 1 **46**
2038 **DREAMS FORGOTTEN** 75 [1]4-9-0 (57) A McCarthy 14/1: 0/3200-40: 11th: Cl-up 7f, wknd & eased. 11 **31**
11 Ran   Time 2m 08.64(4.44)   Owned: Mr I N Chinn   Trained: Newmarket

HAMILTON WEDNESDAY 11.08.04 Righthand, Undulating Track, Stiff Uphill Finish

---

Official Going SOFT

3876 5.55 Lanarkshire Extra Claiming Stakes 3yo+ (E)
£4209 £1295 £648   1m1f36y   Good/Soft 71   -15 Slow   Inside

2854* **THE PRINCE** 42 [2] Ian Williams 10-9-4 (84) S Sanders 1/3 FAV: 21031-11: Trkd ldrs, hdwy to lead **71**
ins fnl 1f, pushed out: well bckd, abs: eff at 7.5/9f on firm, gd/soft & both AWs, acts on any trk: runs well fresh:
in gd form of late in clmg grade: see 2854.
3734 **TEMPLET** 6 [4] J Semple 4-10-0 bl (64) R Winston 10/1: 3453002: Rcd in 2nd till led over 3f out, 3½ **69**
hdd ins fnl 1f, no extra: quick reapp, clr of rem, top weight: much better run: see 1038.
2723 **WINGS OF MORNING** 47 [3] P A Blockley 3-8-6 VIS (65) J Bramhill 6/1: 1563003: Led till over 3f 6 **43**
out, no extra: 7 wks abs, tried a visor: see 1163.
3668 **SANDY BAY** 8 [5] A R Dicken 5-8-11 (35) P Fessey 80/1: 00-00004: Dwelt, sn cl-up, no impress 3f out. ½ **39**
2901 **CHARLIE GEORGE** 40 [1]3-9-0 P Mulrennan(3) 14/1: 065: ch g Idris - Faithful Beauty (Last Tycoon) 8 **34**
Keen in mid-div, no impress 4f out: 6 wk abs: mdn clmr & clmr unplcd prev: dam unrcd: with P Monteith.
5 Ran   Time 2m 1.85 (7.75)   Owned: Mr Patrick Kelly   Trained: Alvechurch

3877 6.25 Tnt International Novice Stakes A Qualifier For The Hamilton Park 2-Y-O Series Final 2yo (D)
£5532 £1702 £851   6f5y str   Good/Soft 71   -02 Slow   Far side

3699* **SPY KING** 7 [2] M Johnston 2-9-0 K Darley 4/6 FAV: 211: Made all, rdn & styd on well fnl 1f: **96**
well bckd, quick reapp: eff at 6f, 7f will suit: acts on fast & gd/soft, likes a stiff trk: useful, going the right
way & shld win more races: see 3699.
2570* **BUDDY BROWN** 53 [1] J Howard Johnson 2-9-5 R Winston 9/1: 12: Dwelt & outpcd in rear, pushed 1¾ **92**
along 1f out, hdwy over 1f out, styd on well ins fnl 1f to go 2nd cl home: 8 wk abs: improved again from debut &
crying out for a return to 7f, win again: see 2570.
3566 **OBE GOLD** 12 [5] M R Channon 2-9-5 (97) A Culhane 7/2: 31424U3: With wnr, onepcd: see 2823. *nk* **93**
3699 **PROFITS REALITY** 7 [4] P A Blockley 2-8-12 Dean McKeown 20/1: 0554: Chsd ldrs, outpcd 2f out, *shd* **85**
kept on fnl 1f but not pace to reach ldrs: quick reapp: stays 6f, 7f looks sure to suit: acts on gd/soft: see 2077.
3698 **MITCHELLAND** 7 [3]2-9-0 (74) S Sanders 8/1: 1066355: Trkd ldrs, no impress 2f out: quick reapp. 10 **57**
5 Ran   Time 1m 14.19 (4.39)   Owned: Mr P D Savill   Trained: Middleham

3878 6.55 Azure E B F Maiden Stakes 2yo (D)
£6890 £2120 £1060   1m65y rnd   Good/Soft 71   -03 Slow   Far side

3568 **LOOKS COULD KILL** 12 [5] G A Butler 2-9-0 S Sanders 8/11 FAV: 21: Mid-div, hdwy & ev ch over 1f **91**
out, rdn to lead ins fnl 1f, styd on well: nicely bckd tho' op 1/2: relished this step up to 8.5f, acts on firm &
gd/soft, undul/stiff trk: useful, shld get further & more races to be won: see 3568 (debut).
2938 **LOVE PALACE** 39 [2] M Johnston 2-9-0 K Darley 7/2: 22: Led, hdd ins fnl 1f & no extra: well clr 1½ **85**
of rem, bckd: stays 7.5/8.5f on gd/soft & soft: win similar: see 2938 (debut).
3078 **JACKADANDY** 33 [4] J Howard Johnson 2-9-0 R Winston 14/1: 43: Cl-up, onepcd 2f out: op 9/1. 8 **69**
HAIBAN 0 [1] G A Butler 2-9-0 P Hanagan 16/1: 4: b c Barathea - Aquarela (Shirley Heights) *shd* **68**
Mid-div, hdwy over 1f out, not pace to chall on debut: Mar foal: dam unplcd sole start, sire a smart miler: fair
start, entitled to learn from this & be sharper next time.
3500 **BALL BOY** 15 [3]2-9-0 (75) A Culhane 7/1: 0525: Handy, outpcd & btn over 2f out. 3 **32**
2109 **BALTHASAR** 72 [6]2-9-0 Dean McKeown 100/1: 06: b c Lujain - Anatase (Danehill) Chsd ldrs, no 3½ **25**
impress over 2f out: long abs: Jan first foal, cost 25,000: sire smart 2yo sprinter, dam unrcd: with P Blockley.
6 Ran   Time 1m 50.1 (6.3)   Owned: It's A Breeze   Trained: Blewbury

3879   7.30 Captain J C Stewart Rated Stakes Handicap 3yo+ 0-90 (C)   [91]
£12168   £4616   £2308   1m1f36y   Good/Soft 71   +07 Fast   Inside

3074   **DANELOR** 33 [2] R A Fahey 6-9-3 (80) P Hanagan 11/2: 4500501: Prsd ldr, led ins fnl 1f, kept on: 88
gd time: wng form at 7f, prob best btwn 1m/10f on firm & gd/soft, prob any trk: rdn more prom here: see 836.
3593 + **WAHOO SAM** 11 [6] T D Barron 4-8-7 (70) P Makin(5) 4/1: 0311012: Led till ins fnl 1f, no extra: see 3593.   1¾   74
3139   **ALLIED VICTORY** 31 [7] E J Alston 4-8-10 (73) Dean McKeown 14/1: 4-100203: Handy, onepcd fnl 2f.   6   65
3598   **WAR OWL** 11 [5] Ian Williams 7-8-10 (73) S Sanders 100/30 FAV: 3501004: Rear, hdwy 3f out, wknd.   5   55
3435   **GREY CLOUDS** 18 [1]4-9-2 (79) R Winston 9/2: 0123225: Nvr btr than mid-div.   1¼   58
3768   **TONY TIE** 4 [4]8-9-7 (84) P Mulrennan(3) 11/2: 0216106: Nvr a factor: quick reapp.   ½   62
2745   **HIAWATHA** 46 [3]5-8-9 (72) K Darley 10/1: 3001057: Keen & prom, wknd 3f out: op 14/1, 7 wk abs.   28   0
7 Ran   Time 1m 59.92 (5.82)   Owned: Mr Mark A Leatham   Trained: Malton

3880   8.00 Da Luciano Classified Stakes 3yo+ 0-75 (D)
£5343   £1644   £822   6f5y str   Good/Soft 71   -05 Slow   Far side

3350   **DIZZY IN THE HEAD** 21 [8] Paul Johnson 5-9-2 bl (77) P Hanagan 7/2: 1210001: Made all, drvn out   83
ins fnl 1f: eff at 5/6f on firm & soft, poss hvy, prob any trk: won for forcing tactics: see 1662.
1251   **ABBAJABBA** 114 [7] C W Fairhurst 8-9-3 (78) J Bramhill 7/2: 06-00002: Chsd ldrs, outpcd 2f out,   5   67
kept on again fnl 1f but no ch with wnr: well bckd, long abs, top weight: see 834.
3758   **SOPHRANO** 5 [1] P A Blockley 4-9-0 (60) Dean McKeown 20/1: 620-5303: Handy centre, onepcd 2f out.   nk   63
3809   **LEGAL SET** 3 [5] Miss A Stokell 8-9-0 t (63) P Makin(5) 9/2: 2400204: Prom, no impress 2f out: qk reapp.   ½   61
3758   **TELEPATHIC** 5 [2]4-9-0 (55) P Mathers(5) 50/1: 6540005: Cl-up, outpcd & btn 2f out: quick reapp.   1¾   56
3767   **PERCY DOUGLAS** 4 [6]4-9-0 t (45) Suzanne France(7) 66/1: 0005006: Nvr a factor: qck reapp: see 275.   ¾   54
3424   **ULYSEES** 18 [3]5-9-0 (73) R Winston 13/8 FAV: 0310507: Nvr a factor: nicely bckd from 9/4.   ¾   52
3430   **AXFORD LORD** 18 [4]4-9-0 (55) P Mulrennan(3) 100/1: 00204/-68: Al bhd: see 3430.   4   40
8 Ran   Time 1m 14.4 (4.6)   Owned: P and Mrs D M Johnson   Trained: Stanley

3881   8.30 Sytner Ferrari Owners Track Day Handicap Stakes 3yo 0-85 (D)   [91]
£6871   £2114   £1057   1m4f17y   Good/Soft 71   -35 Slow   Far side

3765   **RICHTEE** 4 [3] R A Fahey 3-8-7 (70) P Hanagan 5/2: 0-125131: Trkd ldrs, hdwy to lead ins fnl 1f,   72
drvn out: quick reapp: eff at 10/12f, could get further: acts on firm & gd/soft, gall/easy or stiff/undul trks:
tough, v consistent & enjoying a gd season: see 3573.
2972   **OBAY** 37 [2] E A L Dunlop 3-9-7 (84) S Sanders 15/8 FAV: 0-414232: Prsd ldr, hdwy to chall ins   hd   85
fnl 1f, kept on but just held nr fin: well bckd under top weight: gd eff, conceded wnr 14lbs: see 1213 (mdn).
3653   **CHARLOTTE VALE** 9 [4] M D Hammond 3-8-10 (73) A Culhane 2/1: 5213123: Trkd ldrs, no impress   1¼   72
fnl 1f: consistent, another gd run: win another fills h'cap: see 3240.
3666   **BOLD BLADE** 8 [1] M J Polglase 3-7-12 (1oh) (60) P Mathers(1) 7/1: 0010024: Led ins fnl 1f, no   hd   59$
extra: op 10/1: likes fibresand, acts on fast & gd/soft: fair run: see 3666.
4 Ran   Time 2m 44.6(12.8)   Owned: Terence Elsey and Richard Mustill   Trained: Malton

Official Going Good/Soft

3882   2.00 Downs Maiden Auction Stakes Div 1 2yo (E)
£3601   £1108   £554   6f212y str   Good 48   -03 Slow   Centre

3418   **SHARP AS A TACK** 19 [14] B J Meehan 2-8-9   J Fortune 5/1: 021: Rcd far side group, made all, drvn   85
out to assert ins fnl 1f despite flashing tail: eff at 6f, imprvd for step up to 7f: acts on fast & gd: improving.
3330   **MYSTERY LOT** 22 [8] A King 2-8-2   D Kinsella 12/1: 62: b f Revoque - Mystery Bid (Auction Ring)   1½   74
Cl-up stands side, ev ch bef 1f out, kept on but not pace of wnr far side: Mar foal, cost 9,500gns: half-sister to
wnrs at 5/7f: dam plcd at 6f/1m: eff at 7f, further will suit: acts on gd: encouraging.
        FOXHAVEN 0 [9] P R Chamings 2-9-0   Martin Dwyer 50/1: 3: ch c Unfuwain - Dancing Mirage   1½   83
(Machiavellian) Chsd ldrs far side, styd on to chase wnr ins fnl 1f, onepace: debut: Feb first foal, cost
40,000gns: dam successful at 7f: sire top-class performer at mid-dists: eff at 7f, bred to apprec further: acts on
gd grnd: encouraging eff & can impr with experience.
3399   **POLAR DAWN** 20 [12] R J Millman 2-8-2   A McCarthy 7/1: 264: Cl-up far side, no extra fnl 1f: see 2287.   nk   70
3601   **DANGER ZONE** 12 [3]2-8-7   S Drowne 20/1: 005: b c Danzero - Red Tulle (A P Indy) Handy stands   2   71
side over 5f, sn onepcd: Apr foal, half-brother mid-dist plcd: dam plcd at 10f: apprec 1m +.
3267   **JUST A TRY** 26 [7]2-9-0   P Dobbs 12/1: 06: Chsd ldrs stands side over 5f, sn wknd: see 3267.   4   70
3431   **SWIFT OSCAR** 19 [6]2-8-7   D Holland 4/1 FAV: 67: Handy stands side over 5f, sn btn: btr 3431 (debut).   1   61
        BORACAY DREAM 0 [11]2-8-9   J Quinn 10/1: 8: Al bhd stands side on debut.   3   57
3285   **DAHLIYEV** 26 [4]2-9-0   J Murtagh 11/2: 039: Led stands side group, hdd bef 1f out, fdd: op 9/2.   1¼   60
        EVA SONEVA SO FAST 0 [13]2-8-9   Dane O'Neill 25/1: 0: 10th: Al bhd far side.   1¼   53
3736   **ISSY BLUE** 7 [2]2-8-4   J F Egan 33/1: 000: 11th: Chsd ldrs stands side over halfway, wknd.   1½   45
3489   **PRIDE OF LONDON** 17 [1]2-8-2   P Doe 33/1: 000: 12th: Handy stands side 4f, fdd.   1   41
3399   **Mickey Pearce** 20 [16]2-8-7   D Fox(5) 100/1:0   **Whitland** 0 [15]2-8-7 T N Pollard 20/1:0
        Backstreet Lad 0 [5]2-8-11   G Baker 50/1:0   **Volitio** 0 [10]2-8-9 L Dettori 14/1:0
16 Ran   Time 1m 29.09 (3.59)   Owned: Mr P Minikes   Trained: Upper Lambourn

3883   2.30 Downs Maiden Auction Stakes Div 2 2yo   (E)
£3588 £1104 £552   **6f212y str**   **Good 48**   **-10 Slow**   Centre

JOINT ASPIRATION 0 [5] M R Channon 2-8-9   T E Durcan   6/1: 1: ch f Pivotal - Welcome Home (Most   **86+**
Welcome) Bhd stands side, prog halfway, styd on to lead ins fnl 1f, pushed out fnl 1f, going away: debut: May
foal, cost 36,000gns: dam successful at 12f: sire decent performer at sprint dists: eff at 7f, 1m + shld suit: acts
on gd grnd & a stiff/gall trk: goes well fresh: won with authority & looks to have a bright future.
3342 **SCARLET INVADER 22** [7] J L Dunlop 2-8-11   J P Murtagh   9/2: 402: Led, rcd stands side, hdd under   3   **79**
press ins fnl 1f, no extra: eff at 7f on gd grnd: gd eff in defeat & now quals for h'caps: see 2703.
GITCHE MANITO 0 [4] A King 2-8-11   J D Smith   16/1: 3: b c Namid - Chasing Rainbows (Rainbow   2   **75**
Quest) Cl-up stands side, wknd dist: debut: Mar foal, cost 17,000gns: half-sister wnr at 1m: dam unrcd: sire
fine performer at 6f: eff at 7f, 1m shld suit: acts on gd grnd: learn from this.
1401 **SEASONS ESTATES 107** [11] B R Millman 2-8-4   A McCarthy   20/1: 404: Handy stands side over 5f, wknd.3½   **61**
SILSONG 0 [12]2-8-2   R Smith   66/1: 5: ch f Stephen Got Even - Silver Trainor (Silver Hawk) Chsd   ½   **58**
ldrs stands side over halfway, sn no extra: debut: Feb foal, cost 9,000gns: half-sister to numerous wnrs: dam wnr
abroad: sire decent performer around 10f: with B R Millman.
3601 **SIR MONTY 12** [16]2-8-11   S Drowne   100/30 FAV: 56: Led far side group, kept on ins fnl 2f to go   1¼   **65**
clr of sole far side rival, nvr getting to stands side group: prob disadvantage racing on far side, see 3601.
CAPTAIN JOHNNO 0 [2]2-8-9   L Dettori   5/1: 7: b c Tagula - Thornby Park (Unfuwain) Keen in tch   hd   **62**
stands side, wknd bef 1f out: debut: Feb first foal, cost 20,000gns: dam successful at 14f.
3381 **FLAUNTING IT 21** [9]2-8-9   D Holland   6/1: 58: Chsd ldrs till halfway stands side, wknd.   4   **54**
NIP NIP 0 [13]2-8-2   D Fox(5)   66/1: 9: Chsd ldrs stands side 4f, wknd on debut.   nk   **46**
MONAD 0 [3]2-8-2   Amy Baker(7)   50/1: 0: 10th: Al in rear on debut.   10   **28**
THORNY MANDATE 0 [14]2-8-9   S Carson   12/1: 0: 11th: Chsd sole far side rival over 5f, sn wknd.   8   **19**
11 Ran   Time 1m 29.60 (4.1)   Owned: Ridgeway Downs Racing   Trained: West Ilsley

3884   3.05 Sovereign Windows & Conservatories Maiden Stakes 3yo   (D)
£5805 £1786 £893   **6f212y str**   **Good 48**   **-05 Slow**   Centre

4164} **CAPE VINCENT 337** [6] J H M Gosden 3-9-0   J Fortune   4/6 FAV: 03-1: b c Cape Cross - Samhat Mtoto   **91+**
(Mtoto) Handy, styd on for press to lead bef 1f out, pushed clr to lead fnl 1f, readily: well bckd on reapp: 3rd of 17
on last of only 2 '03 starts (rtd 90, mdn): eff at 7f, return to 1m + will suit: acts on gd grnd & a stiff/gall trk:
goes well fresh: only lightly rcd , useful & can rate higher.
2947} **PATTERDALE 392** [9] W J Haggas 3-9-0 (86)   L Dettori   9/1: 5200-2: b g Octagonal - Baize (Efisio)   4   **79**
Chsd ldrs, prog to chase wnr ins fnl 1f, al held: reapp: rnr-up on 1 of 4 '03 starts (med auct mdn, M Johnston):
eff at 6/7f on firm & gd grnd: encouraging display after such a long layoff. 2 Jun'03 Redc 6fm 84- E:
4758} **MRS SHILLING 301** [4] J R Fanshawe 3-8-9   O Urbina   15/2: 6-3: b f Dr Fong - Papaha (Green Desert)   2   **70**
Handy, onepcd 1f out: uplcd on sole '03 start (rtd 65, mdn): can be seen to btr effect over mid-dists.
3121 **NOORA 33** [10] M P Tregoning 3-8-9 (75) W Supple   5/1: 0-0024: Cl-up, led 2f out, hdd bef 1f out, wknd.   shd   **69**
3291 **SNOW JOKE 24** [7]3-8-9 (49) N Pollard   100/1: 0400005: Sn led, hdd 2f out, wknd: modest form to date.   3   **63$**
ENCORA BAY 0 [2]3-8-9   J Quinn   50/1: 6: Bhd, nvr nrr than mid-div: debut.   ¾   **61**
MISTER MUJA 0 [11]3-9-0 T I Mongan   33/1: 7: Bhd, nvr a factor.   ½   **65**
3209} **MINDSET 381** [1]3-8-9   D Holland   10/1: 23-8: b f Vettori - Eden (Polish Precedent) Handy 5f,   ½   **59**
fdd: reapp: plcd on both '03 starts (rtd 76, med auct mdn): eff at 7f on fast. 2 Jul'03 Folk 7g/f 76- F:
SUPERFLING 0 [5]3-9-0   P Dobbs   33/1: 9: Al in rear on debut.   5   **54**
KAJUL 0 [8]3-8-9   T Quinn   66/1: 0: 10th: Missed break, nvr a factor on debut.   1½   **46**
DINE N DASH 0 [3]3-9-0   L Keniry   66/1: 0: 11th: Al in rear: debut.   9   **35**
11 Ran   Time 1m 29.24 (3.74)   Owned: Sheikh Mohammed   Trained: Manton

3885   3.40 Stella Artois Handicap Stakes Fillies 3yo+ 0-85   (D)
£7124 £2192 £1096   **1m str**   **Good 48**   **-25 Slow**   Far side   **[87]**

2385 **ZWEIBRUCKEN 61** [6] S Kirk 3-9-7 (80) J F Egan   8/1: 2120-001: Cl-up, prog to lead bef 1f out, rdn   **87**
out to assert: op 6/1: 9 wk abs: now stays 1m: acts on fast & gd/soft grnd: acts on a stiff/gall or
sharp/undul trk: goes well fresh: see 2385.
3480* **NOUVEAU RICHE 17** [3] H Morrison 3-9-4 (77) S Drowne   7/4: 2312: Led, hdd under press bef 1f out,   1½   **81**
kept on but al held by wnr: well bckd: gd eff in defeat on h'cap bow: see 3480 & 2419.
3277 **ENFORD PRINCESS 26** [1] R Hannon 3-9-12 (85) J Fortune   8/1: 1100-403: Handy, eff 2f out, onepcd   2½   **84**
fnl 1f: eff at 6f, prob stays 1m: see 1498.
3162 **RED SAHARA 31** [5] W J Haggas 3-9-7 (80) L Dettori   5/4 FAV: 01-16624: Bhd, prog wide halfway,   2   **75**
wknd bef 1f out: disapp eff after fine 2nd in 3162 (3lb lower mark).
1110 **BETTY STOGS 124** [4]3-9-11 (84) L Keniry(3)   20/1: 0610-05: b f Perugino - Marabela (Shernazar)   1   **77**
Handy when short of room halfway, wknd fnl 2f: long abs: fills mdn wnr in '03 (N A Gaselee): eff at 7f, shld be
suited by further: acts on fast grnd & a stiff/gall trk: with D R C Elsworth.
1 Oct'03 Leic 7.0g/f 82- D:
5 Ran   Time 1m 44.98 (5.88)   Owned: Mr Eddie Tynan   Trained: Upper Lambourn

3886   4.15 Gr3 Totesport Sovereign Stakes Colts & Geldings 3yo+   (A)
£34800 £13200 £6600   **1m str**   **Good 48**   **+17 Fast**   Far side

3533 **NORSE DANCER 15** [12] D R C Elsworth 4-9-0 (115) T Quinn   3/1: 0-430441: Bhd, prog under press 3f   **117**
out, styd on to chall ins fnl 1f, drvn out to lead on line: bckd, blnks left off: fast time: stays 12f, suited by 1m
on fm & gd/soft: v smart & relished drop in class (has been running well in Gr 1's): resolution not in doubt here & a
gd confidence boost, see 3533.
4198*}**LUCKY STORY 335** [9] M Johnston 3-8-7 (118) D Holland   9/2: 41111-2: b c Kris S - Spring Flight   shd   **116+**
(Miswaki) Chsd ldrs, styd on to lead 1f out, sn edged left, hdd under press on line: op 3/1 on reapp: leading juv
performer last term winning 4 of 5 starts (mdn, stks & 2 Gr 2s): eff at 7f, suited by step up to 1m: acts on fast,
gd/soft & any trk: runs well fresh: excellent eff on first run against older rivals, one to follow.

SALISBURY THURSDAY 12.08.04 Righthand, Galloping Track, Stiff Finish

1 Sep'03 Donc 7gd 118-(100) A: 1 Jul'03 Good 7gd 112- A: 1 Jun'03 Pont 6g/s 104- C: 1 Jun'03 Ayr 6g/f 88- D:
3533 **HURRICANE ALAN 15** [2] R Hannon 4-9-5 (114) P Dobbs 25/1: 3150303: Handy, prog bef 1f out, kept on, nvr getting to front 2: fine run conceding weight to front 2: see 3124 & 1349. *2* **117**
3533 **PASSING GLANCE 15** [7] A M Balding 5-9-5 (118) Martin Dwyer 12/1: 2160-104: Led, hdd 1f out, onepcd when short of room ins fnl 1f: won this race 12 mths ago & ran with credit conceding 5lb to wnr: btr 2252. *shd* **116**
3124+**SHOT TO FAME 33** [11]5-9-3 (111) J Murtagh 12/1: 5011215: Handy, prog & ev ch bef 1f out, sn no extra. *1* **112**
3441 **AUTUMN GLORY 19** [1]4-9-0 (102) S Drowne 16/1: 40-11006: Handy over 6f, sn onepcd: see 1686. *¾* **107**
3316 **AFRICAN DREAM 29** [3]3-8-10 (112) J Quinn 16/1: 1111047: In tch over 6f, sn no extra: prob unsuited by drop back to 1m: btr 1595 (10f). *1* **108**
3565+**ANCIENT WORLD 13** [8]4-9-0 (110) L Dettori 5/2 FAV: 411-2218: Held up, prog wide halfway, no impress fnl 2f: well bckd: much better expected after 3565 (val h'cap, firm). *¾* **103**
3775* **PENTECOST 5** [4]5-9-0 (100) L Keniry 16/1: 6014019: Mid-div over 6f, sn wknd: qck reapp: btr 3775. *nk* **102**
3320 **TOUT SEUL 25** [6]4-9-0 (107) S Carson 33/1: 05-10060: 10th: Chsd ldrs 5f, sn wknd: proving disappointing: yet to recapture form of reapp win in 1356. *6* **91**
3613 **SUBLIMITY 12** [10]4-9-0 t (108) J Fortune 40/1: 4-104030: 11th: Slow away, nvr a factor: btr 3613. *hd* **90**
3265 **LAGO DORTA 26** [5]4-9-0 (100) Dane O'Neill 50/1: 6400660: 12th: Bhd, nvr a factor: btr 2489 (h'cap). *3½* **83**
12 Ran Time 1m 41.63 (2.53) Owned: Mr J C Smith Trained: Whitsbury

3887

4.50 Matthew Clark Handicap Stakes 3yo+ 0-70 (E) **[83]**
£3868 £1190 £595 **1m6f15y** **Good 48** **-15 Slow** No Stalls

3454 **ZALDA 19** [6] R Charlton 3-8-6 VIS (61) S Drowne 11/1: 06-16501: Cl-up, led 3f out, hdd under press well ins fnl 1f, rallied to lead on line: eff at 12f, now stays 14f: acts on fast & gd, stiff/gall trk: not straightforward but imprvd for fitting of first time visor: see 2905 & 2164. **70**
3760 **TILLA 6** [10] H Morrison 4-9-10 (66) J Murtagh 5/2 FAV: 31-56022: Held up, prog to chase wnr bef 1f out, styd on to lead well ins fnl 1f, hdd under press on line: clr rem: well bckd on qck reapp: continues to run well & deserves to get head in front: see 3760. *shd* **74**
1112 **TYPHOON TILLY 124** [9] C R Egerton 7-9-13 (69) L Dettori 7/2: 6436403: Slow away, prog 4f out, no impress bef 1f out: long abs & top-weight: btr 478 (polytrack). *7* **70**
3450 **COMPTON ECLAIRE 19** [1] G A Butler 4-9-5 vis (61) J Fortune 5/1: 4612424: Rear, prog when hung right 3f out, edged left & onepace dist: see 3450. *1¾* **60**
2912 **JAVELIN 41** [7]8-8-7 P (49) T E Durcan 20/1: 0/4045-65: Handy, outpcd over 3f out, rallied late. *1* **47**
2685 **RED SUN 49** [4]7-9-4 t (60) W Supple 9/1: 44-12606: Led, hdd 3f out, wknd: 7 wk abs. *6* **52**
1082 **RESONANCE 127** [5]3-8-9 (64) V Slattery 7/1: 043-2037: Chsd ldrs, fdd 3f out: long abs: btr 1082. *4* **52**
3147 **GIKO 32** [11]10-7-12 (3oh) (37) M Henry 25/1: 6062308: Handy 12f, wknd: btr 2912 (12f). *1¾* **26**
3333] **KWAHERI 1095** [3]6-8-3 (45) N Pollard 66/1: 40/0500//-9: b f Efisio - Fleeting Affair (Hotfoot) Chsd ldrs, fdd 4f out: recently unplcd over hdles: last seen on level back in '01 when unplcd in 4 starts (rtd 49). *20* **15**
3256 **VIN DU PAYS 27** [2]4-8-8 (50) I Mongan 33/1: 5116-000: 10th: Handy 10f, sn wknd: btr 1087. *1* **19**
10 Ran Time 3m 6.83 (8.83) Owned: Mr D J Deer Trained: Beckhampton

3888

5.20 Axminster Carpets Apprentice Handicap Stakes 3yo+ 0-80 (E) **[77]**
£3627 £1116 £558 **6f str** **Good 48** **-13 Slow** Far side

3751 **MIMIC 6** [12] R Guest 4-9-0 (63) R Mills(10) 14/1: 40-00001: Rcd far side, sn led far side pair, styd on to lead overall 1f out, rdn out: qck reapp: eff at 5f, suited by 6f on firm & gd, acts on polytrack: loves to dominate: on a winning mark: see 3751. **70**
3705 **CURRENCY 8** [5] J M Bradley 7-9-11 (74) C J Davies(8) 8/1: 0630052: Chsd ldrs stands side, led stands side group bef 1f out, styd on, not pace of wnr far side: gd run in defeat & is h'capped to find similar. *¾* **79**
3628 **NIVERNAIS 11** [6] H Candy 5-9-8 (71) C Cavanagh(8) 3/1 FAV: 0006063: Led stands side group till dist, no extra: op 9/2: not disgraced & is on a winning mark: see 2023. *2½* **69**
3643 **B A HIGHFLYER 10** [9] M R Channon 4-8-9 (58) B O'Neill(8) 11/2: 0500054: Chsd ldrs centre, hung right & onepcd bef 1f out: showed more in 3643. *2½* **49**
3443 **GAELIC PRINCESS 19** [4]4-10-0 (77) L Treadwell(3) 7/1: 0600005: Mid-div stands side, kept on fnl 1f. *2½* **61**
3790 **TAPPIT 5** [15]5-7-12 (1oh) (46) K Jackson(5) 33/1: 3050006: Cl-up far side till dist, wknd: qck reapp. *1* **28**
3708 **HAND CHIME 8** [3]7-9-9 (72) Danielle Deverson(10) 5/1: 0050027: Rear stands side, nvr nrr than mid-div: showed more in 3708 (7f, fast). *hd* **52**
3844 **BENNANABAA 2** [8]5-7-12 (1oh)t (46) Donna Caldwell(5) 50/1: 0000508: Handy stands side over 4f. *1½* **23**
3333 **TORQUEMADA 22** [10]3-8-6 (59) Dean Williams(5) 10/1: 3000309: Handy stands side, wknd bef 1f out. *1½* **31**
3602 **INDIAN BAZAAR 12** [1]8-8-0 p (49) M Halford(5) 33/1: 0206000: 10th: In tch stands side 3f, wknd. *1* **18**
3821 **FULVIO 3** [13]4-8-4 vis (53) Liam Jones(5) 33/1: 0-000500: 11th: Al bhd stands side: qck reapp. *hd* **21**
5025} **Fly More 279** [14]7-9-13 (76) N Chalmers 20/1:0 3602 **Nebraska City 12** [7]3-7-13 vis(52) A Medeiros 50/1:0
2861 **Golden Bounty 43** [11]5-9-5 (68) W Burton(10) 16/1:0 3453 **Awarding 19** [2]4-9-0 BL t(63) Lucy Russell(8) 25/1:0
15 Ran Time 1m 15.80(3.7) Owned: Mr C J Mills Trained: Newmarket

SANDOWN THURSDAY 12.08.04 Righthand, Galloping Track, Stiff Finish

Official Going Good/Soft

3889

2.20 Sharp Minds Betfair Handicap Stakes 3yo 0-85 (D) **[91]**
£6841 £2105 £1053 **5f6y str** **Good/Soft 68** **-03 Slow** Far Side

3567 **RYDAL 13** [8] G A Butler 3-9-6 VIS (83) S W Kelly 9/2: 4062401: Handy, hdwy over 1f out, squeezed out & styd on to lead last stride, drvn out: jock rec 2 day careless riding ban: has won at 1m, clearly has pace for 5f: acts on fast & polytrack, enjoys gd/soft: prev wore blnks, rcd more sweetly today in first time visor: gd confidence boost, useful. **88**
3577 **CATCH THE WIND 13** [6] I A Wood 3-9-3 p (80) S Sanders 9/1: 0556122: Made most, kept on till rdn & collared last stride: in-form sprinter: see 3371. *shd* **84**

3567 **DIVINE SPIRIT 13** [7] M Dods 3-9-7 (84) R Winston 7/2: 6103603: Held up, hdwy & short of room over 1f out, kept on ins last, not pace of front pair: see 3356, 2566. *1½* **84**

3599 **SHORT CHORUS 12** [5] J Balding 3-7-12 (7oh)p (54) J Bramhill 12/1: 4012424: Held up, eff well over 1f out, some late gains, nvr dngrs: gd run from 7oh: see 3599, 1605. *¾* **59**

2195* **IVORY LACE 70** [1]3-9-0 (77) D Sweeney 14/1: 1311415: Held up, eff dist, no impress: 10 wk abs. *2* **70**

3567 **TREASURE CAY 13** [4]3-9-5 e t (82) K Fallon 2/1 FAV: 5310326: Keen, in tch, rdn & wknd over 1f out: below best twice recently on gd/soft, best 2675 (gd grnd). *2½* **70**

3567 **DOLCE PICCATA 13** [3]3-8-11 bl (74) J F McDonald(3) 12/1: 4500007: With ldr, wknd over 1f out. *½* **61**

3379 **KABREET 21** [2]3-8-11 VIS (74) E Ahern 12/1: 1-310008: In tch, wknd 2f out: reportedly unsuited by easy grnd: tried a visor: see 494 (6f, polytrack). *7* **47**

8 Ran Time 1m 03.15 (3.55) Owned: Mr & Mrs G Middlebrook Trained: Blewbury

3890

2.50 E B F Mansell Plc & Ruddle Wilkinson Architects Maiden Stakes 2yo (D)
£5512 £1696 £848 **1m14y rnd** **Good/Soft 68** **-41 Slow** Inside

3337 **VELVET HEIGHTS 22** [2] J L Dunlop 2-9-0 G Carter 33/1: 001: b c Barathea - Height of Fantasy (Shirley Heights) Prom, rcd centre in straight, hdwy over 1f out, led ins last, rdn out, going away: Mar foal, dam 2m wnr: relished step up to 1m, mid-dists+ will suit next term: acts on gd/soft & a stiff trk: well rdn. **86**

3470 **KHARISH 18** [1] J Noseda 2-9-0 E Ahern 11/4 FAV: 432: Cl-up, led 3f out till ins last, no extra: nicely bckd: stays 1m & acts on fast & gd/soft: can find similar: see 3470. *2* **82**

3337 **KINGSHOLM 22** [8] A M Balding 2-9-0 K Fallon 100/30: 63: ch c Selkirk - Putuna (Generous) Chsd ldr to halfway, rallied fnl 1f: Feb foal, dam 10f wnr: stays 1m on gd/soft, type to prog in time over further. *1¾* **78**

3267 **WILLIAM TELL 26** [3] M R Channon 2-9-0 S Hitchcott(3) 50/1: 64: Held up, some late gains, nrst fin: stays 1m on gd/soft: minor trk mdns will suit: see 3267. *1* **76**

MAJESTIC MOVEMENT [4]2-9-0 R Havlin 25/1: 5: ch c Diesis - Zarara (Manila) Cl-up, wknd fnl 1f on debut: Apr first foal: bred to apprec mid-dists next term. *nk* **75**

FIGAROS QUEST [9]2-9-0 J Fanning 16/1: 6: Bhd, modest late gains on debut. *2½* **70**

2696 **CHAPTER 49** [10]2-9-0 R L Moore 11/2: 227: In tch, no extra well over 1f out: btr 2696 (gd). *shd* **70**

3285 **ASAATEEL 26** [7]2-9-0 M Hills 16/1: 08: Al bhd. *shd* **70**

3285 **CREATIVE CHARACTER 26** [11]2-9-0 N De Souza(5) 16/1: 49: Led to 3f out, wknd: see 3285. *7* **56**

1760 **ART LEGEND 89** [6]2-9-0 S Sanders 33/1: 400: 10th: Keen held up, hung & btn 2f out: 3 mth abs. *5* **46**

3470 **DAHMAN 18** [12]2-9-0 K McEvoy 7/2: 40: 11th: In tch, wknd qckly over 2f out: reportedly lost action in grnd: well bckd: see 3470 (7f, fast). *dist* **0**

11 Ran Time 1m 47.74 (8.74) Owned: Windflower Overseas Holdings Inc Trained: Arundel

3891

3.25 Rectangle Group Handicap Stakes 3yo+ 0-90 (C) **[90]**
£10634 £3272 £1636 **7f16y rnd** **Good/Soft 68** **+12 Fast** Inside

3001 **PRESUMPTIVE 37** [2] R Charlton 4-9-1 (77) K Fallon 2/1 FAV: 0/3-5301: Held up, plenty to do over 2f out, styd on strongly appr fnl 1f to lead ins last, drvn out: hvly bckd: eff at 7f/1m on gd, imprvd here on gd/soft grnd: acts on a stiff trk: imprvd here with Champ joc up & as mkt indicated he would: see 2662. **84**

3443 **SPIRITS AWAKENING 19** [6] J Akehurst 5-7-12 (2oh) (58) J Mackay 13/2: 2-063242: Chsd clr ldr, hdwy to lead over 1f out, hdd & not pace of wnr ins last: consistent: see 2350, 1849. *1* **64$**

2662 **NORTON 50** [3] T G Mills 7-10-0 (90) R Miles(3) 13/2: 0504003: Chsd ldrs, eff over 1f out, onepace: 7 wk abs: see 2662, 2489. *1* **92**

3465 **LIFTED WAY 18** [7] P R Chamings 5-9-2 (78) J Fanning 7/1: 0110654: Sn clr ldr, rdn & hdd over 1f out, no extra: went off too fast: see 1613 (polytrack), 1352 (1m). *¾* **76**

3441 **BINANTI 19** [1]4-9-9 (85) E Ahern 12/1: 0-066005: Rcd wide rear, nvr a factor: visor discarded. *1½* **82**

3689 **WILL HE WISH 8** [9]8-9-13 bl (89) S W Kelly 8/1: 0000136: In tch, wknd dist: see 3689. *shd* **85**

3265 **BLUE TROJAN 26** [5]4-9-10 (86) J D Walsh(7) 10/1: 4004207: In tch, wknd dist: see 3088. *1* **80**

3257 **POINT OF DISPUTE 27** [4]9-9-6 vis (82) S Sanders 7/1: 6302-528: Dwelt, nvr a factor: btr 3257, 2880. *2½* **71**

8 Ran Time 1m 30.33 (3.93) Owned: Ecurie Pharos Trained: Beckhampton

3892

4.00 Sharp Minds Betfair Classified Stakes 3yo+ 0-75 (D)
£6841 £2105 £1053 **1m1f** **Good/Soft 68** **+00 Fast** Inside

3260 **STRIDER 26** [8] Sir Michael Stoute 3-8-10 (76) K Fallon 7/1: 00-2441: Chsd ldrs, styd on under press to lead cl-home, drvn out: fair time, first success: eff at 9/10f on fast, gd/soft grnd & fibresand. **80**

3523 **RYANS FUTURE 15** [2] J Akehurst 4-9-3 (74) S Hitchcott(3) 25/1: 15-50052: Dwelt, hdwy from rear 2f out, fin well & only just failed: acts on firm, gd/soft & polytrack: seems best with waiting tactics, see 174. *nk* **78**

3339 **STRAW BEAR 22** [9] Sir Mark Prescott 3-8-11 (77) S Sanders 1/1 FAV: 5231-23: Trkd ldrs, ch 1f out, styd on well cl-home: hvly bckd: eff at 1m/9f, shld stay further: acts on fast, gd/soft & f/sand: see 3339. *shd* **80**

2521 **CELLO 56** [6] R Hannon 3-8-12 T (78) R L Moore 5/1: 5-216004: Mid-div, prog to lead 2f out & clr ent fnl 1f, collared cl-home: bckd from 10/1, 8 wk abs & first time t-strap: lkd wnr ent fnl 1f, 1m ideal? *¾* **79**

3694 **KATIYPOUR 8** [5]7-9-3 (75) Lisa Jones 12/1: 0140345: Held up, styd on cl-home but nvr figured. *½* **75**

3637 **BEN HUR 11** [10]5-9-3 (75) S W Kelly 25/1: 2115456: Prom, led halfway till 2f out, no extra fnl 1f. *1* **73**

3542 **MALIBU 14** [3]3-8-12 (78) E Ahern 33/1: 4650157: Nvr featured: reportedly unsuited by easy grnd. *5* **68**

4111*}**ELECTRIQUE 340** [7]4-9-8 (80) L Fletcher(3) 40/1: 4/33221-8: b g Elmaamul - Majmu (Al Nasr) Chsd ldrs, btn 2f out on reapp: booked for 2nd when fell on hdles bow in Feb '04 (rtd 107h?, eff at 2m on gd): won fnl '03 start (mdn): eff at 1m/10f on fast & firm, handles a stiff/gall trk: suited by forcing tactics: with J Osborne. *2½* **66**
1 Sep'03 York 10.4g/f 82-(75) D: 2 Aug'03 Newm 8fm 75-(75) D: 2 Aug'03 Sand 10.0g/f 78-(73) D:

3469 **ARCTIC SILK 18** [1]3-8-8 t (77) K McEvoy 7/1: 0329: Led till halfway, wknd qckly & eased, t.o.: amiss? *17* **32**

9 Ran Time 1m 57.34 (6.14) Owned: Cheveley Park Stud Trained: Newmarket

SANDOWN THURSDAY 12.08.04 Righthand, Galloping Track, Stiff Finish

3893	**4.35 Davert Banks Handicap Stakes 3yo 0-80 (D)**					[87]
	£7004 £2155 £1078	**1m6f**	Good/Soft 68	-11 Slow	Centre	

3359 **LEVITATOR** 21 [1] Sir Michael Stoute 3-8-9 (68) K Fallon 7/2: 0-02201: Held up, prog to chase ldr   76
2f out, went on dist, held on gamely, all out: tchd 9/2, first success: eff at 14f on fast & gd/soft: game.
3618 **SHARADI** 12 [6] V Smith 3-8-0 (59) Joanna Badger 20/1: 456-0002: Prom, led 5f out till dist,   shd 67
rallied gamely & just btn in a thrilling fin: imprvd form on this step up to 14f, acts on gd/soft grnd: see 3618.
3454 **WINSLOW BOY** 19 [3] C F Wall 3-8-1 (60) Lisa Jones 5/1: 0461263: Dwelt, styd on late into 3rd.   5 61
2746 **FIRE DRAGON** 47 [9] Jonjo O'Neill 3-9-7 P (80) F M Berry 7/1: 000-4154: Prom, led halfway till 5f   2 78
out, ev ch till wknd fnl 1f: tried cheek pieces: won a nov hdle (rtd 103h, eff at 2m1f on fast grnd) since 2746.
3192 **VICARIO** 29 [8]3-8-4 (63) J Mackay 12/1: 5133265: Chsd ldrs, btn over 3f out.   5 55
3359 **CONSIDINE** 21 [5]3-8-13 (72) K McEvoy 5/2 FAV: 0121026: Led till halfway, wknd 2f out: well   1¼ 62
bckd: again below form on rain softened grnd, btr 3359 & 2345.
3422 **SEEKING A WAY** 19 [7]3-8-11 (70) R Havlin 16/1: 21-237: Trkd ldrs, bhd 3f out: btr 3422 & 2668.   3 56
3161 **ABSOLUTELYTHEBEST** 31 [10]3-9-7 (80) E Ahern 10/1: 1226458: Led early, remained prom till styd   6 58
far side straight & sn well bhd: reportedly unsuited by this soft grnd: much btr 3161 & 2418.
3618 **CHARA** 12 [2]3-8-5 (64) J F McDonald(3) 10/1: 3105559: Held up, al bhd, t.o. in last.   16 16
9 Ran   Time 3m 06.09 (11.09)   Owned: Mr K Abdulla   Trained: Newmarket

3894	**5.10 Elmbridge Maiden Stakes 3yo (D)**				
	£5395 £1660 £830	**1m2f7y**	Good/Soft 68	-27 Slow	Inside

3642 **MICHABO** 10 [5] D R C Elsworth 3-9-0 (78) S Sanders 7/4: 0-432621: Made all, kept on gamely fnl   80
1f & rdn clr cl-home: hvly bckd from 11/4: deserved win, eff at 10f on firm & gd/soft: see 3642.
3038 **WAIT FOR SPRING** 36 [4] J H M Gosden 3-8-9 K Fallon 4/5 FAV: 52: Prom, chall fnl 1f, flashed   1½ 72
tail & no extra cl-home: well bckd: acts on fast & gd/soft: did not look as resolute as today's wnr, see 3038.
3469 **NIOBES WAY** 18 [2] P R Chamings 3-8-9 E Ahern 10/1: 043: Chsd ldrs, kept on under press fnl 1f: 1¾ 69
eff at 10f on gd/soft grnd: see 3038.
3292 **KILINDINI** 24 [1] Miss E C Lavelle 3-9-0 R Havlin 40/1: 6U54: Keen in rear, nvr nr to chall.   1½ 69
3631 **CHARMED BY FIRE** 11 [3]3-9-0 J Fanning 12/1: 005: b c Silver Charm - Mama Dean (Woodman) Slowly hd 70
away, recovered to trk ldrs, ev ch till fdd fnl 1f: mid-dist bred.
5 Ran   Time 2m 13.57(9.47)   Owned: Mrs Michael Meredith   Trained: Whitsbury

CHEPSTOW THURSDAY 12.08.04 Lefthand, Undulating, Galloping Track

Official Going GOOD (GOOD/SOFT IN PLACES)

3895	**5.45 Argus County Of Monmouthshire Family Day Apprentice Handicap Stakes 3yo+ 35-55 (G)**					[51]
	£2709 £774 £387	**1m2f36y**	Good/Soft 84	-50 Slow	Inside	

3276 **GOT TO BE CASH** 26 [11] W M Brisbourne 5-9-13 (50) B Swarbrick 100/30 FAV: 1053001: Rear, hdwy to   56
lead over 2f out, rdn out ins fnl 1f: top weight: eff at 1m/12.5f on firm, likes soft grnd, prob acts on any trk.
1384} **BLACK LEGEND** 464 [6] R Lee 5-9-5 t (42) S Donohoe(3) 15/2: 04002/0-2: b g Marju - Lamping   2½ 42
(Warning) Rear, hdwy over 2f out, kept on ins fnl 1f but not pace to reach wnr: op 12/1, well clr of rem: hdles fit
(sell unplcd, rtd 46h): well btn sole '03 start (h'cap, rtd 31): rnr-up 1 of 6 earlier starts in native Ireland
(10f h'cap, soft): stays 10f on gd/soft: wears a t-strap, tried blnks over timed.
1801 **TOMSK** 87 [7] Miss K M George 4-8-12 (35) W Hogg(5) 25/1: 0/04-63: Slow away in rear, hdwy over 3f   7 24
out, no impress ins fnl 1f: long abs: new stable (prev with A Berry): see 1801.
3087 **ZALKANI** 34 [12] B G Powell 4-9-10 (47) A Hindley(5) 16/1: 0005004: Slow away in rear, hdwy over   1 34
3f out, styg on when not clr run & switched right ins fnl 1f, not pace to chall: prob 3rd with a clr run: see 430.
2355} **STREET GAMES** 416 [5]5-8-12 (35) Jemma Marshall(5) 50/1: 000-00-5: b g Mind Games - Pusey Street   hd 21
(Native Bazaar) Slow away in rear, hdwy wide over 3f out, sn ev ch, no impress ins fnl 1f: reapp: unplcd both '03
starts (mdns, rtd 56, with J Gallagher): has tried a t-strap: now with D Bridgwater.
3605 **HILARIOUS** 12 [2]4-9-6 p (43) H Poulton(5) 7/1: 5456406: Cl-up, ev ch over 2f out, no impress fnl 1f.   1½ 27
3541 **NEWCORR** 14 [15]5-8-9 p (32) D Fox 12/1: 0632407: Slow away, nvr btr than mid-div.   3½ 11
3373 **MARGARETS WISH** 21 [14]4-9-3 bl (40) Stephanie Hollinshead(3) 14/1: 1000068: Mid-div, hdwy to lead   hd 18
over 5f out, hdd over 2f out, no extra: see 1333.
3727 **STAFFORD KING** 7 [14]7-9-3 (40) Steven Harrison(5) 20/1: 60/020/-09: Al bhd: quick reapp: see 3727.   8 6
2739 **COOLFORE JADE** 47 [13]4-9-4 (41) M Savage 11/1: 0006300: 10th: Mid-div, no impress over 2f out.   1¼ 5
891 **NASSAU STREET** 143 [10]4-9-0 (37) T Block(5) 12/1: 040-300: 11th: Cl-up, wknd 3f out, t.o.: long abs.   23 0
2722 **SILVER ISLAND** 48 [9]3-8-13 (45) Derek Nolan(3) 14/1: 00-000: 12th: ch g Silver Patriarch - Island   shd 0
Maid (Forzando) Rear, t.o.: 7 wk abs: mdn unplcd both '03 starts (rtd 47, with G Butler): seems mod.
2969 **SAUCY** 38 [3]3-9-0 bl (46) Thomas Yeung(3) 13/2: 6605350: 13th: Keen & led till over 5f out, no   20 0
extra 3f out, eased fnl 2f, t.o.: see 2664.
3677 **BUNKHOUSE** 9 [4]4-9-10 VIS (47) A Quinn 33/1: 000000: 14th: Chsd ldr till over 5f out, t.o.: visor.   1¾ 0
14 Ran   Time 2m 17.52 (13.42)   Owned: Mrs B Penton   Trained: Nesscliffe

3896	**6.15 Jack Brown Bookmakers Median Auction Maiden Stakes Fillies 2yo (F)**				
	£2933 £838 £419	**5f16y str**	Good/Soft 84	-59 Slow	Stands siders

2965 **TRIM IMAGE** 38 [6] W Jarvis 2-8-11 R Lappin 7/2: 23331: With ldr till led 3f out, rdn out ins   76
fnl 1f: eff at 5f on fast & gd/soft grnd, acts on a gall/undul trk: built on recent plcd effs: see 2547.
3639 **AMICA** 10 [2] G L Moore 2-8-11 D Holland 5/2: 22: Slow away, hdwy over 2f out, kept on ins fnl   nk 75
1f but just failed: clr of rem: eff at 5/6f, return to later will suit: acts on firm & gd/soft: win a race.
3536 **STARLIGHT RIVER** 15 [3] W R Muir 2-8-11 D Kinsella 20/2: 003: Handy, hdwy into 2nd over 2f out,   3 66
no impress fnl 1f: qual for h'caps: see 3536.

3368 **TASHYRA 21** [5] A M Balding 2-8-11   Martin Dwyer 7/4 FAV: 44: In tch, outpcd just bef halfway,   ¾   **64**
hdwy over 1f out, sn onepcd: op 11/4: see 3368.
3368 **TASKS MUPPET 21** [8]2-8-11   P Doe 10/1: 55: In tch, hdwy 3f out, no impress over 1f out: see 3368.   ½   **62**
EDGED IN GOLD 0 [4]2-8-11   D Sweeney 16/1: 6: ch f Bold Edge - Piccante (Wolfhound) Rear, hdwy   5   **47**
when not much room 2f out, sn btn on debut: op 10/1: Mar foal: dam uncrd, sire high-class older sprinter.
3728 **SARTAENA 7** [7]2-8-11   F P Ferris(3) 25/1: 07: Led 2f, no extra well over 1f out: quick reapp.   1½   **42**
3284 **MS POLLY GARTER 26** [1]2-8-11 [52] J F Egan 40/1: 40608: Chsd ldrs, no impress 1f out: see 1538.   ¾   **40**
8 Ran   Time 1m 3.95 (7.15)   Owned: Ms I Bristow   Trained: Newmarket

---

3897   6.45 Weatherbys Bank Nursery Handicap Stakes 2yo (E)   **[89]**
£4488 £1381 £691   **6f16y str**   **Good/Soft 84**   **-60 Slow**   Stands side

3478* **PERSIAN ROCK 17** [3] J A Osborne 2-9-7   (82) D Holland 15/8 FAV: 211: Made all, rdn out ins fnl   **91**
1f: landed a double: top weight: eff at 5/6f on gd/soft, sharp or an undul/gall trk: gd weight carrier:
lightly rcd, imprvg & more races to be won: see 3478.
3623 **COME GOOD 12** [1] R Hannon 2-8-9   (70) R L Moore 3/1: 52632: Rcd prom, ev ch 2f out, kept on ins   ½   **76**
fnl 1f: stays 6f on firm & gd/soft: acts on gd & gd/soft grnd: would have gone close with a clr run: see 1646.
3627 **MUSICO 11** [2] B R Millman 2-8-11   (72) S Drowne 9/4: 46423: Slow away, hdwy well over 1f out,   1   **75**
styng on when not clr run well ins fnl 1f: op 3/1: acts on firm & gd/soft grnd: would have gone close with a clr
run, rtn to 7f will suit: see 3627.
3407 **TIME FOR YOU 20** [6] P J McBride 2-8-8   (69) A Daly 12/1: 04104: Rear, mod late gains: op 9/1.   1¾   **67**
3729 **GAVIOLI 7** [4]2-8-4 t (65) J F Egan 7/1: 0420035: Trkd ldrs, no impress 2f out: tchd 12/1, qk reapp.   3½   **52**
3745 **QUEENS GLORY 6** [5]2-8-5   (66) Martin Dwyer 33/1: 6550066: Keen & prom, no impress over 1f out.   5   **38**
6 Ran   Time 1m 17.46 (8.66)   Owned: Waney Racing Group Inc & Karmaa Racing   Trained: Upper Lambourn

---

3898   7.15 Jack Brown Bookmakers Handicap Stakes 3yo+ 0-80 (D)   **[80]**
£6929 £2132 £1066   **1m14y str**   **Good/Soft 84**   **-06 Slow**   Stands side

3821 **THREEZEDZZ 3** [5] P D Evans 6-9-1 (6ex)t (67) F P Ferris(3) 7/1: 0010101: Made all, pushed clr ins   **83**
fnl 1f, readily: qck reapp: prev eff at 5/6f, now suited by 7f/1m: acts on firm & gd/soft, any trk, likes Chepstow:
right back to form on return to turf, loves forcing the pace & can win more h'caps: see 2199.
3524 **COOL TEMPER 15** [1] P F I Cole 8-8-10   (62) S Sanders 11/1: 6-530002: Handy, hdwy 3f out, on onepcd   7   **66**
halfway, wknd fnl 1f: see 1485.
3685 **THE GAIKWAR 8** [6] N E Berry 5-8-9 bl (61) R Miles(3) 9/2: 0004323: Slow away, hdwy 3f out, on onepcd.   2   **61**
3813* **GIOCOSO 4** [11] B Palling 4-10-2 (6ex) (82) D Holland 9/4 FAV: 60-60014: Dsptd lead 3f, onepcd fnl 2f.   ¾   **80**
3813 **TOPTON 4** [4]10-9-10 bl (76) S W Kelly 16/1: 6265405: Slow away, mod late gains: quick reapp.   ¾   **72**
3641 **JOHANNIAN 10** [10]6-9-5   (71) S Drowne 8/1: 3502046: Nvr a factor: see 2931.   2½   **62**
2374 **OAKLEY RAMBO 62** [7]5-9-10   (76) R L Moore 11/1: 0620607: Cl-up, wknd 2f out: 9 wk abs.   1¾   **63**
3733 **CHANDELIER 7** [8]4-7-13   (51) A McCarthy 12/1: 3201608: Slow away, hdwy 3f out, no impress 1f out.   2½   **33**
3443 **GEMS BOND 19** [9]4-9-11   (77) Derek Nolan(7) 33/1: 0-000009: b g Magic Ring - Jucinda (Midyan)   4   **51**
Rear, hdwy 2f out, sn no impress: won 2 of 10 '03 starts (h'caps, with R Hannon): won 1st 2 '02 starts (novs): eff
at 5/6f, stays a stiff 1m well: acts on firm & gd, likes a gall trk, handles a turning one: gd weight carrier, has
run well fresh: can force the pace: well h'capped.
1 Sep'03 Asco 8g/f 82-80 D: 1 Jul'03 Newm 8g/f 80-75 E: 2 Jul'03 Newb 7g/f 80-75 D: 2 Jul'03 Chep 8.1gd 76-73 E:
1 Aug'02 Bath 5.7fm 90-56 E: 1 Jul'02 Newb 6fm 91- D:
3479 **UNDER MY SPELL 17** [12]3-9-1   (74) J Fortune 25/1: 2510000: 10th: Rear, t.o..   27   **0**
2986 **PREMIER DREAM 38** [3]3-8-10   (69) D Sweeney 20/1: 6631040: 11th: Rear, hdwy 3f out, t.o.: new yard.   dist   **0**
3372} **RUSSIAN COMRADE 374** [2]8-9-1   (67) V Slattery 40/1: 000/010-P: b g Polish Patriot - Tikarna   **0**
(Targowice) Reluctant to race, p.u. sn after start: reapp: hdles unplcd in 03/04 (novs, rtd 59h): h'cap unplcd
sole '03 start (rtd 0), now suited by 1m2f+: acts on fast & soft: with J Tuck.
12 Ran   Time 1m 39.1 (7.2)   Owned: Mr Steve Evans   Trained: Abergavenny

---

3899   7.45 Bet Direct On 0800 211222 Median Auction Maiden Stakes 3-4yo (F)
£2905 £830 £415   **1m4f23y**   **Good/Soft 84**   **-34 Slow**   Inside

3638 **REDI 10** [5] L M Cumani 3-8-10   (67) D Holland 5/6 FAV: 54-04631: Led early, rem in 2nd, drvn into   **73**
lead again cl-home: stays 12f on firm & gd/soft, acts on a gall/undul trk: gd confidence booster: see 1042.
3642 **LAABBIJ 10** [1] M P Tregoning 3-8-10 bl (75) Martin Dwyer 7/4: 0-60552: Sn led, hdd cl-home: well   nk   **73**
clr of rem: stays 12f on gd/soft: shown enough to win similar: see 1965.
3208 **BAYOU PRINCESS 28** [4] B De Haan 3-8-5   (62) A McCarthy 50/1: 0053: ch f Bluegrass Prince -   11   **51**
Josifina (Master Willie) Rear, hdwy 5f out, no impress fnl 3f: dam won 3 hdles & plcd over fences.
LYES GREEN 0 [3] R M Beckett 3-8-10   S Sanders 11/1: 4: ch c Bien Bien - Dissolve (Sharrood)   6   **47**
Cl-up, lost place over 5f out, btn on debut: dam mdn on the Flat at 2, later mod wnr over hdles: learn from this.
3740 **BENS REVENGE 7** [2]4-9-7   V Slattery 100/1: 605: Al bhd: top weight, quick reapp: see 3740.   12   **29**
2014 **UNINTENTIONAL 78** [7]3-8-10 VIS (52) F P Ferris(3) 50/1: 52-6060P: Rear, hdwy over 5f out, no   **0**
impress over 2f out, p.u. ins fnl 1f: long abs: 1st time visor: see 238.
2879 **CHAPELCO 42** [6]3-8-10   J Fortune 16/1: 60P: b g Robellino - Lady Kris (Kris) Cl-up, lost place   **0**
bef halfway, t.o./p.u. ins fnl 1f: 6 wk abs: cost 11,000 gns: dam won & plcd at 9/12f at 3: with J Dunlop.
7 Ran   Time 2m 45.26 (14.16)   Owned: Equibreed SRL   Trained: Newmarket

---

3900   8.15 Monmouthshire Show Thursday 26th August Handicap Stakes 3yo 35-55 (F)   **[65]**
£3360 £960 £480   **7f16y str**   **Good/Soft 84**   **+ 05 Fast**   Stands side

3846 **DANIFAH 2** [2] P D Evans 3-8-5   (42) F P Ferris(3) 6/1: 4004461: Made all, rdn clr over 1f out,   **60**
kept on: quick reapp: prev eff at 5f, stays 7f on firm & gd/soft, likes Chepstow, handles a sharp/turning trk:
made most of this drop in grade, v well h'capped, win again: see 2118.
3575 **FLEET ANCHOR 13** [3] J M Bradley 3-9-3   (54) J F Egan 15/8 FAV: 50-0002: Cl-up, hdwy into 2nd over 3f   8   **58**
out, lost place over 2f out till went 2nd again ins fnl 1f, no ch with wnr: see 2906.
3291 **PAPPY 24** [12] A W Carroll 3-8-11   (48) P Doe 14/1: 3500-403: Keen & cl-up, hdwy into 2nd 2f out,   2   **48**

wknd ins fnl 1f: see 3291.
3480 **GRAND RAPIDE 17** [6] J L Spearing 3-9-0 (51) S Drowne 20/1: 6004: Rear, hdwy over 2f out, onepcd   1   49
ins fnl 1f: clr of rem: h'cap bow: see 3480.
3480 **TARTIRUGA 17** [13]3-8-8 (45) D Kinsella 12/1: 00-00005: b g Turtle Island - Palio Flyer (Slip   5   33
Anchor) Chsd ldrs, no impress fnl 2f: mdn unplcd both '03 starts (rtd 30a): with L Cottrell.
3788 **WHIPLASH 5** [1]3-9-2 BL (53) Thomas Yeung(5) 33/1: 0106006: Rcd in 2nd, no impress 2f out: blnks.   4   33
3194 **COMIC TALES 29** [4]3-8-12 BL (49) A McCarthy 33/1: 0-667: Slow away, hdwy over 2f out, no impress   1   27
over 1f out: 1st time blnks: see 3194.
      PRIMATECH 24 [18]3-8-11 (48) D Holland 6/1: 000008: b f Priolo - Ida Lupino (Statoblest) Rear,   1½   23
nvr nr ldrs: mdn & h'cap unplcd all earlier '04 starts in native Ireland: with M Cunningham.
3667 **DANE RHAPSODY 9** [19]3-8-8 (1ow) (44) S Sanders 6/1: 05059: Keen in tch, nvr a factor: see 2152.   shd   19
3790 **NIGHT WORKER 5** [11]3-8-13 (50) R L Moore 10/1: 0006500: 10th: Rear, nvr nr ldrs: quick reapp.   ¾   22
1183 **WEBBINGTON LASS 119** [9]3-8-3 VIS (40) A Daly 40/1: 0000- 0: 11th: Cl-up, no impress over 2f out: ¾   10
long abs: 1st time visor: see 1183.
794   **MAID THE CUT 162** [7]3-9-0 (51) V Slattery 33/1: 00-400: 12th: Al bhd: long abs: see 794.   hd   20
3346 **HI DARL 22** [15]3-8-13 (50) B Swarbrick(5) 20/1: 641-000: 13th: Rear, nvr a factor: see 2904.   hd   18
3712* **CITY GENERAL 7** [17]3-9-4 (6ex)p (55) Derek Nolan(7) 4/1 FAV: 5020510: 14th: Rcd stands rail, not   4   15
pace to chall over 1f out: quick reapp: btr 3712 (sell h'cap).
1497 **BOLD TRUMP 102** [16]3-9-4 (55) Martin Dwyer 16/1: 0- 400: 15th: In tch, btn 3f out: long abs.   2   11
2291 **COLLADA 65** [10]3-9-2 (53) J Fortune 0/1: 0060: 16th: b f Desert Prince - Bright Spells   7   0
(Alleged) Cl-up, lost place bef halfway, eased when btn ins fnl 1f: 9 wk abs: dam a 12f wnr in France.
3455 **Intitnice 19** [20]3-8-3 (40) Joanna Badger 40/1:0   3094 **Lola Lola 34** [14]3-8-6 (43) Dane O'Neill 20/1:0
18 Ran   Time 1m 25.39(5.59)   Owned: Mr E A R Morgans   Trained: Abergavenny

Official Going Heavy

3901	6.00 Kealshore Claiming Stakes 2yo (F)		
	£3052 £872 £436 5f str Good/Soft 86 -32 Slow Centre		

3308 **HOPELESSLY DEVOTED 24** [4] P C Haslam 2-8-4 Rory Moore(7) 16/1: 061: Handy when hung right & lost   60
place halfway, rallied for press to lead ins last, styd on well: bckd at long odds: eff at 5f & improved on gd/soft.
3769 **PARIS TAPIS 5** [5] K A Ryan 2-8-6 (1ow) N Callan 3/1 FAV: 0422: Al handy & led 2f out, rdn & hdd   ¾   59
ins last, no extra: well bckd: eff at 5/6f on fast & gd/soft grnd: could find similar in claim/sell grade: see 3769.
3308 **ROKO 24** [7] M W Easterby 2-8-10 (59) T Lucas 5/1: 000433: Chsd ldrs, hung left under press,   2   58
onepace from dist: op 6/1: handles gd & gd/soft grnd: see 3308, 3178.
3769 **DANEHILL FAIRY 5** [2] Mrs A Duffield 2-8-1 vis (47) N Mackay(3) 11/2: 6333204: Chsd ldrs, onepace.   1   47
      WEET N MEASURES 0 [9]2-9-1 A Culhane 16/1: 5: b c Weet A Minute - Weet Ees Girl (Common   ½   59
Grounds) Dwelt, bmpd start & bhd, late gains, nrst fin: op 10/1: May foal, half-brother to a 7f wnr: dam 5f scorer.
3308 **VON WESSEX 24** [3]2-8-10 T (63) C Haddon(7) 8/1: 1633146: Led till 2f out, hung right/btn dist: t-strap.   1½   50
      BEAUMONT GIRL 0 [1]2-8-7 p Dean McKeown 15/2: 7: ch f Trans Island - Persian Danser (Persian   1¼   42
Bold) Went left start & sn bhd, hung left & nvr a threat: bckd: Mar foal, cheaply bght: dam a 9f wnr.
3589 **KRISTIKHAB 12** [6]2-8-10 P (62) F Norton 8/1: 4200058: Slow away & bhd, btn/eased dist, chkpcs.   1¼   44
3097 **CARMANIA 33** [10]2-8-11 T Hamilton(3) 14/1: 059: Chsd ldrs, btn when no room over 1f out, op 10/1.   6   31
3330 **GALLEGO 22** [8]2-8-4 VIS S Righton 100/1: 000: 10th: Went right start, chsd ldrs till halfway, visor.   2½   17
10 Ran   Time 1m 04.7 (5.9)   Owned: Mr T E Pocock   Trained: Middleham

3902	6.30 Commhoist Co Uk Nursery Handicap Stakes 2yo (E)			[87]
	£3582 £1102 £551 6f str Good/Soft 86 -11 Slow Centre			

3756 **MAKE US FLUSH 6** [3] A Berry 2-9-0 (73) F Norton 3/1: 4011021: Held up, hdwy halfway & led over   77
1f out, rdn & held on well: bckd tho' op 2/1: eff at 5/6f on gd & soft grnd, Haydock specialist: see 3271 & 2882.
2989 **MONSIEUR MIRASOL 37** [7] K A Ryan 2-9-4 (77) N Callan 2/1 FAV: 335102: Held up, styd on well for   nk   80
press from dist, just held: gelded, apprec return to easy grnd: see 2682 (soft).
3632 **IM AIMEE 11** [2] P D Evans 2-9-3 (76) A Culhane 100/30: 4022223: Led 1f & remained handy, ev ch   nk   78
ins last, no extra cl-home: most tough & consistent, deserves similar: 3632, 3371 & 3271.
3351 **PARIS BELL 22** [1] T D Easterby 2-8-5 (64) D Allan 10/1: 35004: Held up in tch, kept on late, not   ¾   64
able to chall: imprvd eff, appears suited by gd/soft & soft grnd: see 1143.
3560 **PRINCELY VALE 14** [4]2-8-13 p (72) C Haddon(7) 14/1: 4111345: Led after 1f, hung right/hdd over 1f out.   1   69
2995 **MING VASE 37** [8]2-8-5 (64) G Gibbons 8/1: 6256: Chsd ldrs, onepace for press dist: op 10/1, h'cap bow.1   58
6 Ran   Time 1m 17.11 (5.81)   Owned: The Bath Tub Boys   Trained: Cockerham

3903	7.00 Commhoist Logistics Handicap Stakes 3yo+ 0-90 (C)			[87]
	£9854 £3032 £1516 6f str Good/Soft 86 +16 Fast Centre			

      SAHARA PRINCE 16 [4] Michael Cunningham 4-9-1 (74) K Darley 10/1: 2052321: b c Desert King -   86
Chehana (Posse) Chsd ldr & led dist, drvn out: op 8/1: Irish raider, dual h'cap rnr-up this term: eff at 6/7f on
firm & gd/soft grnd, sharp/turning or gd trks: first win, confidence booster.
3796 **FONTHILL ROAD 5** [8] R A Fahey 4-8-11 (70) P Hanagan 8/11 FAV: 12-61322: Chsd ldrs, rdn to press   nk   81
wnr ins last, struck by rival's whip, just held: qck reapp: clr of rem & another gd run: see 3796, 2831.
3569 **PRINCE OF BLUES 13** [1] M Mullineaux 6-8-0 bl (59) S Righton 25/1: 577303: Led till dist, no impress.   4   60
3088 **MARKER 34** [6] G B Balding 4-9-3 (76) R Thomas(5) 9/2: 0404004: Held up, eff over 2f out, no impress.   1   75
3428 **BALAKIREF 19** [2]5-8-9 (68) R Winston 13/2: 2U10005: Dwelt & rear, rdn & nvr able to chall: btr 2568.   nk   66
3628 **THE LORD 11** [5]4-9-11 (84) C Haddon(7) 12/1: 6000-306: Keen & chsd ldrs, btn over 1f out: btr 3388.   5   70
6 Ran   Time 1m 15.47 (4.17)   Owned: Mr Herb M Stanley   Trained: Ireland

---

3904 7.30 Commhoist Lifting Solutions Handicap Stakes 3yo+ 0-80 (D) [79]
£5688 £1750 £875 1m2f120y Good/Soft 86 -47 Slow Outside

3741 **TROUBLE MOUNTAIN** 7 [4] M W Easterby 7-9-3 (68) R Winston 7/2: 5244021: Held up, hdwy over 2f **75**
out, qcknd to lead ins last, rdn & sn asserted: v slow time: eff at 10/12f on fm, soft & fibresand, any trk: see 196.
2998 **ALPINE SPECIAL** 37 [1] P C Haslam 3-8-6 (67) Rory Moore(7) 11/2: 210-6042: Keen & trkd ldrs, rdn 1¼ **71**
to lead dist, hdd ins last, not pace of wnr: op 13/2: stays a slowly run 10.5f: acts on firm, gd/soft & fibresand.
3001 **DEVANT** 37 [5] M A Jarvis 4-9-13 (78) P Robinson 3/1: 5-040203: Held up, rdn & kept on fnl 2f, 1 **81**
nrst fin: well bckd: stays a slowly run 10.5f, gave the impress a stronger run race would have suited: see 2753.
3276 **PURE MISCHIEF** 26 [2] C R Dore 5-9-7 (72) R Thomas(5) 9/4 FAV: 1151324: Led early, remained handy, 1¼ **73**
ch ins last, no extra fnl 100y: nicely bckd tho' op 7/4: just btr 3276 & 2499.
3232 **SLALOM** 27 [3]4-9-7 p (72) M Fenton 7/1: 3-100505: Led & dictated pace, qcknd 4f out, edged right 2½ **70**
& hdd over 1f out, sn btn: uncontested lead but to no avail: btr 3107 & 939.
5 Ran Time 2m 24.07 (14.07) Owned: Mrs Jean Turpin Trained: Sheriff Hutton

---

3905 8.00 Commhoist Lifting Contractors Maiden Stakes 3yo+ (D)
£5655 £1740 £870 1m30y rnd Good/Soft 86 -09 Slow Inside

3230 **APERITIF** 27 [1] W J Haggas 3-9-0 (77) P Hanagan 4/6 FAV: 63-04331: Chsd front pair & rcd v keen **79+**
early, shaken up & hdwy to lead over 1f out, sn fnl clr & eased cl-home, val 8L: acts on fast, gd/soft & polytrack,
poss firm: suited by a gall 1m: see 3059, 2365 & 1707.
3572 **RIVER NUREY** 13 [6] B W Hills 3-9-0 (70) K Darley 7/4: 52-32522: Led till over 2f out, no ch with 7 **68**
wnr bef dist: see 3572, 2148 (firm & fast).
3413 **CLASSIC LEASE** 20 [3] R Hollinshead 3-9-0 A Culhane 33/1: 053: Held up, rdn & styd on fnl 2f. nk **67**
3462 **MOUNT COTTAGE** 18 [2] J G Given 3-8-9 M Fenton 11/1: 64: Pushed along rear & green early, hung 2 **58**
left over 2f out, mod late prog: well held debut prev.
3292 **START OF AUTHORITY** 24 [4]3-9-0 N Callan 33/1: 05: Keen & trkd ldr, led over 2f out till over 1f hd **62**
out, wknd qckly ins last: drop to 7f could suit.
4535} **WHITKIRK STAR** 316 [5]3-9-0 J McAuley 100/1: 0-6: Slow away & bhd, no ch 3f out, t.o., reapp. dist **0**
6 Ran Time 1m 48.12 (7.62) Owned: Stretton Manor Stud Trained: Newmarket

---

3906 8.30 Commhoist Super Skyrig Handicap Stakes 3yo 0-70 (E) [75]
£3669 £1129 £565 1m30y rnd Good/Soft 86 +04 Fast Inside

3547 **BOPPYS PRINCESS** 14 [3] R A Fahey 3-7-12 (45) P Hanagan 5/2 FAV: 0000-121: Mid-div, hdwy wide **59+**
from 3f out & led over 1f out, rdn clr: eff around 1m/8.5f on fm & gd/soft: improving.
3724 **DONT CALL ME DEREK** 7 [1] S C Williams 3-9-0 (61) D Allan 8/1: 4-560002: Keen, trkd front pair, 2½ **68**
styd on for press, not pace of wnr but clr rem: again attracted some mkt support: handles firm, gd/soft & polytrack:
seems suited by this 1m trip: lightly rcd type who could find a race: see 3625.
3132 **RARE COINCIDENCE** 33 [12] R F Fisher 3-9-4 p (65) D Nolan(3) 25/1: 0444003: Handy, no impress. 5 **63**
3690 **ANDURIL** 8 [5] J M P Eustace 3-9-3 (64) F Norton 13/2: 0364004: Dwelt, mid-div, nvr pace to threaten. 2½ **58**
3604 **ACUZIO** 12 [8]3-8-11 (58) R Winston(5) 25/1: 6604005: Led till over 1f out, wknd: btr 2506 (7f). 2 **49**
3257 **SABRINA BROWN** 27 [11]3-9-3 (64) R Thomas(5) 3/1: 006-2206: Held up, eff 2f out, wknd. 2 **52**
3138 **ALMOND WILLOW** 32 [2]3-9-5 (66) K Darley 6/1: 0361-027: Flashed tail, held up, nvr land a blow. nk **53**
4808} **MISS LADYBIRD** 297 [6]3-9-2 (63) M Fenton 25/1: 21336-8: b f Labeeb - Bird Dance (Storm Bird) 1 **48**
Mid-div, struggling fnl 3f on reapp: '03 auct mdn scorer, subs nov auct plcd (ntg 61a): acts on firm
& gd/soft grnd, sharp/turning or easy trks. 1 Aug'03 Warw 7.1fm 71- E: 2 Aug'03 Thir 7g/s 68- E:
2506 **MR LEWIN** 56 [10]3-8-10 (57) Darren Williams 25/1: 005-09: Held up, rdn & btn 2f out: 8 wk abs. ½ **41**
2656 **STEPHANO** 51 [4]3-9-1 (62) A Culhane 9/1: 50-050: 10th: Mid-div, lost place qckly from 4f out: abs. 1 **44**
10 Ran Time 1m 47.02(6.52) Owned: Mrs S Bond Trained: Malton

Official Going Good (Good/Soft Places) HEAVY RAIN

3907 1.50 Kentish Express I've Won A Competition Maiden Auction Stakes 2yo (F)
£2926 £836 £418 5f str Good Inapplicable Stands Side

3266 **GRAND PLACE** 27 [1] R Hannon 2-8-11 (73) Dane O'Neill 5/6 FAV: 0401: Trkd ldr & led over 1f out, **73**
rdn clr, rdly: well bckd: eff at 5f on fast & gd grnd, sharp/undul or easy trks: see 2858.
3652 **CREE** 11 [6] W R Muir 2-8-9 bl S Sanders 10/1: 0052: Led till over 1f out, sn no ch with wnr but 4 **61**
kept on: eff in blnks: eff at 5f on gd grnd, sharp/undul trk: shows speed, sell/clmg grade shld suit: see 3652.
3445 **DOCKLANDS GRACE** 20 [4] N P Littmoden 2-8-4 J Mackay 5/1: 553: Rdn & chsd ldrs, no impress dist. 1½ **51**
3600 **GENERAL HAIGH** 13 [3] J R Best 2-8-13 N Pollard 14/1: 64: Chsd ldrs, nvr land blow. 2 **54**
3380} **CAYENNE** 0 [7]2-8-8 Martin Dwyer 9/2: 5: ch f Efisio - Carola Rouge (Arazi) Slow away & well 3 **40**
bhd, mod late prog: 18,000 auct mdn scorer, subs nov auct plcd: sire tough & smart at 6f/1m.
3743 **CHANTELLES DREAM** 7 [2]2-8-2 P Doe 40/1: 06: Reluctant to race & sn well bhd: see 3743. 8 **12**
2983 **ALESHANEE** 39 [5]2-8-6 N Callan 20/1: 07: b f Bold Edge - Nesyred (Paris House) Cl-up 2f, wknd 10 **0**
qckly from halfway: Apr 1st foal, 15,000 gns purchase: dam a 6f 3yo wnr.
7 Ran Time 1m 0.12 (1.72) Owned: Mrs J K Powell Trained: Marlborough

3908

2.20 European Breeders Fund Maiden Stakes Div 1 Fillies 2yo (D)
£5174 £1592 £796 **7f str** **Good** **Inapplicable** Stands Side

RATUKIDUL [4] Sir Michael Stoute 2-8-11 D Holland 10/1: 1: b f Danehill - Whakilyric (Miswaki) **76**
Dwelt & held up, switched & hdwy wide over 2f out, rdn/styd on to lead line: op 8/1: Jan foal, half sister to high-class mid-dist performers Johann Quatz & Hernando: dam a smart juv abroad: eff at 7f, sure to apprec 1m: acts on gd grnd & a sharp/undul trk: goes well fresh: shld progress.
3386 **GHASIBA 21** [7] C E Brittain 2-8-11 S Sanders 4/1: 62: Chsd ldrs, rdn to lead well ins last, hdd line: op 13/2 & imprvd from debut: styd longer 7f trip well, acts on gd grnd: see 3386. *shd* **75**
3005 **NORTHERN SECRET 38** [3] A M Balding 2-8-11 Martin Dwyer 8/1: 03: b f Sinndar - Northern Goddess (Night Shift) Cl-up, ev ch fnl 2f, rdn & no extra well ins last: imprvd from debut: 20,000 gns Feb foal, half sister to a 2yo French scorer: dam a useful 5/6f performer: stays a sharp 7f, acts on gd grnd: going the right way. *1½* **72**
3554 **ELLENS PRINCESS 15** [1] R Hannon 2-8-11 P Dobbs 6/1: 54: Trkd ldrs travelling well, rdn to chall dist, no extra well ins last: handles firm & gd grnd: see 3554. *nk* **69**
2603 **ENTERTAINING 54** [9]2-8-11 Dane O'Neill 5/1: 65: b f Halling - Quaver (The Minstrel) Led, rdn & strongly prsd fnl 2f, hdd well ins last & no extra: imprvd from debut: Feb foal, half sister to 6f/1m juv wnrs: dam a 7f 3yo performer: eff over a sharp/undul 7f on gd grnd. *½* **70**
3035 **BIG HOO HAH 37** [8]2-8-11 D Sweeney 100/1: 06: Mid-div, lost place halfway, kept on late, not reach ldrs: apprec 1m & can improve. *1¼* **67**
3381 **SWEET LORRAINE 22** [6]2-8-11 R Miles(3) 7/2 FAV: 27: Rear, hdwy 3f out, not able to chall: bckd. *1* **65**
3381 **SABBIOSA 22** [10]2-8-11 N Callan 33/1: 008: Chsd ldrs, outpcd over 2f out. *¾* **64**
3381 **KRUMPET 22** [12]2-8-11 A McCarthy 16/1: 09: Dwelt, rear, nvr threatened ldrs. *2* **60**
3601 **HURSLEY 13** [5]2-8-11 V Slattery 100/1: 00: 10th: Mid-div, & sn pushed along, no impress fnl 2f. *nk* **59**
3520 **GREAT OPINIONS 16** [11]2-8-11 BL (75) R Havlin 9/1: 0200: 11th: Rear, no ch fnl 3f, blnks, op 7/1. *hd* **58**
LEGEND OF DANCE [2]2-8-11 T E Durcan 33/1: 0: 12th: Slow away, sn pushed along & bhd, some late hdwy, no impress but only btn around 8L. *hd* **57**
12 Ran Time 1m 27.63 (3.43) Owned: Niarchos Family Trained: Newmarket

3909

2.50 European Breeders Fund Maiden Stakes Div 2 Fillies 2yo (D)
£5161 £1588 £794 **7f str** **Good** **Inapplicable** Stands Side

3554 **KALMINI 15** [6] M R Channon 2-8-11 T E Durcan 9/2: 021: Pushed along mid-div, rdn & hdwy from halfway & led ins last, rdn out: confirmed recent improvement: eff at 7f on firm & gd grnd, sharp/undul trks: appears to need strong handling but the type to prog with racing at 1m+: see 3554. **77**
3381 **VELVETEEN RABBIT 22** [3] Saeed bin Suroor 2-8-11 K McEvoy 5/1: 032: Trkd ldrs & ev ch 2f out, narrow lead over 1f out till ins last, no extra: see 3381 (C/D). *¾* **75**
HASHIMA [4] C E Brittain 2-8-11 J P Guillambert(3) 16/1: 3: b f Kingmambo - Fairy Heights (Fairy King) Pushed along rear, styd on well from over 1f out, not able to reach wnr: $90,000 May foal, half sister to a 1m 3yo scorer, dam a 7f/1m high-class 2yo wnr: eff at 7f, get 1m: acts on gd grnd, promising. *½* **76**
3418 **MITRAILLETTE 20** [7] Sir Michael Stoute 2-8-11 D Holland 4/1: 654: Led till halfway, outpcd over 1f out: longer 7f trip: see 3418. *2* **72**
3451 **KOLYMA 20** [11]2-8-11 N Callan 66/1: 05: Chsd ldrs, onepace for press fnl 2f: left debut bhd: eff over a sharp 7f on gd grnd: see 3451. *1¼* **69**
MARCHETTA [10]2-8-11 N Pollard 20/1: 6: b f Mujadil - My Lewicia (Taufan) Mid-div, shaken up & not able to chall over 1f out: Mar foal, related to a plcd 10f 3yo, dam a 1m 3yo scorer: stay further. *nk* **68**
3582 **AKRAAN 14** [12]2-8-11 W Ryan 16/1: 07: Trkd ldrs trav well, outpcd fnl 2f, kind ride. *shd* **68+**
3554 **MIDCAP 15** [5]2-8-11 M Hills 6/1: 068: Cl-up & led halfway, hdd & flashed tail dist, sn btn. *1¼* **65**
2056 **TOMOBEL 77** [1]2-8-11 P Doe 50/1: 09: Slow away, hdwy halfway, no prog fnl 2f, abs, longer trip. *hd* **64**
3489 **MUSICAL DAY 18** [2]2-8-11 P Dobbs 14/1: 000: 10th: Al rear & sn pushed along, btn 2f out. *5* **55**
3616 **CRYSTALLINE 13** [8]2-8-11 S Sanders 7/2 FAV: 30: 11th: Mid-div, rdn & btn 2f out: bckd: jockey reported filly was nvr travelling: btr 3616 (debut, fast). *4* **47**
THE CHEQUERED LADY [9]2-8-11 R Miles(3) 66/1: 0: 12th: Slow away & al bhd. *¾* **46**
12 Ran Time 1m 28.10 (3.9) Owned: Sheikh Ahmed Al Maktoum Trained: West Ilsley

3910

3.25 Kmfm Classified Stakes 3yo+ 0-65 (E)
£3361 £1034 £517 **6f str** **Good/Soft** **Inapplicable** Stands Side

3244 **SEWMUCH CHARACTER 28** [7] M Blanshard 5-9-2 (62) D Sweeney 5/1: 4064201: Made all, qcknd clr 2f out, rdn to hold on cl-home: eff at 6/7f, tried 1m: acts on fast & gd/soft, any trk: enjoys forcing tactics today. **72**
3784 **TROPICAL STORM 6** [4] J Noseda 3-9-3 (70) S W Kelly 8/1: 24-3042: Chsd wnr, outpcd 2f out, kept on well for press cl-home, just held: quick reapp: eff at 6f, needs a return to 7f: see 1912 (7f, mdn). *nk* **76**
2174 **DANDOUCE 72** [3] P W Chapple Hyam 3-8-11 (67) Thomas Yeung(5) 7/2: 23-63403: Trkd ldrs, outpcd over 2f out, kept on late, not able to chall: eff at 6f, 7f poss ideal: acts on fast, gd/soft & polytrack: see 1956. *1¼* **66**
3054 **WHISTFUL 36** [5] C F Wall 3-8-12 (68) S Sanders 6/1: 2-303504: Rear, rdn & hdwy 2f out, nvr pace to chall: handles fast & gd/soft grnd: see 1239. *1¼* **63**
3705 **CORANGLAIS 9** [1]4-9-2 p (63) N Callan 8/1: 0041005: Chsd ldrs, no impress dist: btr 3143 (5f). *5* **50**
3796* **FULL SPATE 6** [6]9-9-9 (66) D Holland 2/1 FAV: 2000216: Dwelt, trkd ldrs, rdn & btn over 1f out: nicely bckd, quick reapp: acts on easy ground, prefers a fast surface: btr 3796 (firm). *1¼* **53**
3654 **OEUF A LA NEIGE 11** [8]4-9-3 (66) Dean Williams(7) 14/1: 0-506157: V free to post & sn struggling, t.o.: prob lost race bef start & this best forgiven: btr 3575 (mdn h'cap). *9* **24**
7 Ran Time 1m 13.26 (2.26) Owned: Aykroyd and Sons Ltd Trained: Upper Lambourn

3911   4.00 White's Transport 50 Year Anniversary Handicap Stakes Fillies 3yo+ 35-55 (F)   [57]
£3017 £862 £431   6f str   Good/Soft   Inapplicable   Stands Side

3746 **PRETTY KOOL 7** [2] S C Williams 4-9-5 (48) S Sanders 11/4 FAV: 0/00-0531: Led stands side pair & 　53
al prom, styd on for press to assert cl-home: eff at 6/7f on fast, gd/soft & polytrack: lightly rcd & can prog.
3788* **CUT RIDGE 6** [6] J S Wainwright 5-9-9 (6ex) (52) D Holland 7/2: 0003212: Led/dsptd lead far side, 　½ 54
edged left under press over 1f out, not pace of wnr nr line: nicely bckd & rest well covered, quick reapp.
3790 **MY GIRL PEARL 6** [3] M S Saunders 4-9-5 (48) V Slattery 8/1: 2064103: Prom far side, not pace 　1¾ 45
front pair from dist: back to form: acts on firm, gd/soft & fibresand: see 3301.
3643 **PINK SUPREME 11** [1] I A Wood 3-9-4 (51) P Doe 16/1: 0000604: Trkd wnr stands side, no extra 　nk 47
dist: handles gd & gd/soft grnd, stays a sharp 6f: see 2268.
3677* **BRANDYWINE BAY 10** [5]4-8-9 p (38) Hayley Turner(5) 8/1: 504-0415: Rdn & outpcd far side, kept on 　nk 33
late, no threat: op 10/1: eff at 6f, needs a return to 7f: handles firm, gd/soft & fibresand: see 3677 (7f).
3676 **POPPYLINE 10** [12]4-9-8 bl (51) K McEvoy 14/1: U363006: Trkd ldrs far side, outpcd fnl 2f: btr 2954. 　2 40
2925 **INDIAN LILY 41** [8]3-9-3 T (50) G Baker 10/1: 506007: Dwelt & held up far side, nvr land blow: t-strap. 　1¾ 34
3176 **KOMENA 31** [4]6-8-11 (40) N Callan 16/1: 0000508: Rear far side, only mod prog: btr 2928. 　¾ 22
3870 **INDRANI 2** [11]3-8-9 (42) N Pollard 14/1: 0205009: Led/dsptd lead far side till dist: needs 5f. 　shd 24
3289 **AKIRAMENAI 27** [7]4-9-5 BL (48) S W Kelly 25/1: 0406000: 10th: Sn rdn far side & al towards rear: 　1 27
blnks, no improvement: see 1659 (mdn).
3575 **AVERAMI 14** [13]3-9-0 (47) Martin Dwyer 14/1: 0500600: 11th: Mid-div far side, btn 2f out: 　2 21
reportedly unsuited by the grnd: btr 260 & 176 (AW mdns).
3575 **SWEET TALKING GIRL 14** [10]4-8-2 (1oh)t p (30) A McCarthy 66/1: 650-0000: 12th: Dwelt, sn chsd 　21 0
ldrs far side till halfway.
12 Ran   Time 1m 13.58 (2.58)   Owned: Carol Shekells & Associates   Trained: Newmarket

3912   4.30 European Breeders Fund Classified Stakes 3yo 0-90 (C)
£8195 £3109 £1554   1m1f149y   Good/Soft   Inapplicable   Outside

3550 **INVASIAN 15** [7] H R A Cecil 3-8-13 (86) W Ryan 14/1: 0-12001: Made all, travelling best over 2f 　102
out & shaken up & al holding rivals after: eff by 1m/9.7f on fast & likes gd/soft grnd: handles a gall or
sharp/undul trk: enjoys forcing tactics & was given a well judged ride today: see 3553 & 2231.
3421* **SECRETARY GENERAL 20** [6] P F I Cole 3-9-0 (91) S Sanders 5/1: 0205012: Mid-div, styd on for 　2½ 97
press, nvr threatened wnr: styd this sharp 9.7f, best prev arnd 7f/1m: see 3421 (1m, h'cap).
3465* **PRINCE OF THEBES 19** [4] A M Balding 3-8-13 (90) Martin Dwyer 5/1: 031-13: U.r. bef start, pulled 　3 91
hard early, sn trkd front pair, chsd wnr 2f out, no extra dist: handles fast or gd/soft grnd, return to 1m shld
suit: appears headstrong but has ability: see 3465.
3555 **SEWNSO CHARACTER 15** [5] M Blanshard 3-9-1 (92) D Sweeney 8/1: 4034404: Rear, late prog, no 　nk 92
threat: blnks omitted: see 2406, 1583.
3472 **MOMTIC 19** [2]3-8-13 (86) D Holland 6/1: 3044125: Trkd ldrs, no impress fnl 2f: reportedly 　1¼ 87
unsuited by the ground: btr 3472, 3039.
3553 **DANCING LYRA 15** [3]3-8-13 t (89) M Hills 3/1 FAV: 6112406: Rear, no impress fnl 2f: btr 2250. 　6 77
2785 **RINJANI 47** [1]3-8-13 t (90) K McEvoy 12/1: 41-07: Keen & trkd wnr, wknd qckly 2f out: abs: btr 2785. 　7 65
3553 **GAVROCHE 15** [8]3-8-13 (89) J P Guillambert(3) 11/2: 5114108: Rear, hdwy 4f out, wknd qckly 2f 　23 25
out, t.o.: much btr 3084.
8 Ran   Time 2m 05.21 (7.21)   Owned: Dr K Sanderson   Trained: Newmarket

3913   5.00 Eastwell Manor Handicap Stakes 3yo 35-55 (F)   [63]
£3010 £860 £430   1m4f   Good/Soft   Inapplicable   Outside

3714* **SCIENCE ACADEMY 8** [9] P F I Cole 3-9-11 (6ex) (60) N De Souza(5) 7/2: 0-056211: Mid-div, smooth 　68+
hdwy 3f out & led 2f out, rdn & sn in command: eff at 11/12f on fast & gd/soft grnd, sharp/undul or easy trks:
decisive scorer last twice, keep on side: see 3714.
2504 **TOP ACHIEVER 57** [6] Mrs L Stubbs 3-9-6 (55) S W Kelly 50/1: 5-00062: Mid-div, eff to chase wnr 　2 59
over 1f out, no impress in last: styd this sharp 12f well: blnks omitted: handles gd/soft: see 2504.
3383 **VENETIAN ROMANCE 22** [8] A P Jones 3-8-2 (37) Hayley Turner(5) 33/1: 5000003: Held up, kept on 　2 38
late for press, no threat: prob stays a sharp 12f on gd/soft grnd: see 1222.
3823* **MUSIC MIX 4** [14] E A L Dunlop 3-9-6 (55) W Ryan 13/8 FAV: 466-0014: Rear, hdwy 3f out, rdn & no 　¾ 55
extra over 1f out: hvly bckd, quick reapp: well clr of rem: stays a sharp 12f: acts on gd & polytrack: btr 3823.
3714 **ROYAL STARLET 8** [11]3-9-0 (49) P Dobbs 12/1: 000-0045: Chsd ldr till 3f out, sn hit rail & wknd, eased. 　10 38
3748 **ZULETA 7** [3]3-9-5 (54) A Putland(7) 33/1: 0044-006: Slow away & bhd, mod late prog: see 2628. 　3 39
3385 **SAYRIANNA 22** [1]3-9-0 (49) P Doe 33/1: 00: 0047: Keen & led, ran wide on bend after 2f, sn pulled 　7 26
clr but hdd & wknd 2f out: h'cap bow & longer trip.
3580 **ROMEOS DAY 14** [5]3-8-10 (45) Martin Dwyer 9/1: 2430008: Slow away & bhd, nvr factor, t.o. 　21 0
3449 **COBALT BLUE 20** [7]3-9-3 bl (52) D Holland 7/1: 0-061559: Sn rear, no ch fnl 3f, t.o.: btr 2613 (g/f). 　4 0
3499 **ONIZ TIPTOES 17** [4]3-8-5 (1ow)vis (39) N Callan 14/1: 00-06420: 10th: Keen, chsd ldr, wknd qckly 　17 0
3f out, t.o.: btr 3499.
3618 **POLAR DANCER 13** [12]3-9-6 (55) Dane O'Neill 9/1: 063-0300: 11th: Keen & trkd ldrs, wknd 3f out. 　5 0
3385 **PRESTON HALL 22** [2]3-9-0 (49) N Pollard 50/1: 00650: 12th: Keen & trkd ldrs, ran wide on bend 　23 0
after 2f & wknd qckly 4f out, t.o.: jockey reported a breathing prob, longer trip.
12 Ran   Time 2m 43.23 (11.73)   Owned: Sir Martyn Arbib   Trained: Whatcombe

3914   5.35 Kent Messenger Group Apprentice Handicap Stakes 3yo 0-75 (F)   [82]
£4108 £1264 £632   1m1f149y   Good/Soft   Inapplicable   Outside

2199 **NOUNOU 71** [1] D J Daly 3-8-6 (60) M Halford(3) 7/1: 05001: Chsd ldr, led over 1f out, rdn out: 　67
10 wk abs, 1st win: eff at 9.7f, 10f+ may yet suit: acts on gd grnd & a sharp/undul trk: unplcd prev.
3801 **MAGIC AMIGO 5** [4] J R Jenkins 3-9-7 (75) J Jeffrey(7) 3/1: 2304362: Led & sn clr, hdd over 1f 　1¼ 78
out, kept on: quick reapp: see 2283, 1580 (C/D).

FOLKESTONE   FRIDAY 13.08.04   Righthand, Sharpish, Undulating Track

3719   **SUNSET MIRAGE 8** [3] E A L Dunlop 3-9-2 (2ow)vis (68) L Treadwell 9/4 FAV: 1060423: Rear, smooth   1½   70
hdwy 3f out, ev ch 2f out but found less than looked likely: btr 3719 & 3492 (fast & gd).
3455   **TURTLE PATRIARCH 20** [2] Mrs A J Perrett 3-8-4 (58) Thomas Yeung 5/1: 60-0004: Chsd ldr, outpcd   ¾   57
over 2f out, kept on ins last, not able to chall: 10f+ in similar shld suit: see 3219.
3384   **KEEPERS KNIGHT 22** [5]3-8-8 (62) R J Killoran(5) 100/30: 3500035: Held up, eff 3f out, sn btn.   5   53
5 Ran   Time 2m 09.25(11.25)   Owned: Miss Anita Farrell   Trained: Newmarket

NEWBURY   FRIDAY 13.08.04   Lefthand, Flat, Galloping Track

Official Going GOOD/SOFT.

3915	**1.40** Stanjamesuk Com E B F Maiden Stakes Div 1 Fillies 2yo (D)

£5642 £1736 £868   **6f8y str**   **Good 57**   -06 Slow   Centre

SHANGHAI LILY [6] Sir Michael Stoute 2-8-11 K Fallon 3/1 FAV: 1: b f King's Best - Marlene D   101+
(Selkirk) Trkd ldrs, qcknd to lead 2f out, sn clr, impressive on debut: well bckd: Mar foal, cost E300,000: half
sister to a 7f juv wnr: dam won over 9f, sire a high-class miler: eff at 6f on gd grnd, 7f will suit: runs well
fresh: most impressive start, List/Group company now beckons.
     RUBY WINE [11] J M P Eustace 2-8-11 R Thomas(5) 12/1: 2: b f Kayf Tara - Cribella (Robellino)   4   85+
Held up, short of room over 2f out, kept on strongly fnl 1f under hands-&-heels, no ch with impress wnr: op 16/1,
debut: Apr 1st foal: dam a mid-dist wnr, sire won Ascot Gold Cup: eff at 6f, bred to stay much further: highly
encouraging debut behind a potentially smart rival: one to keep in mind.
     GOLD QUEEN [8] M R Channon 2-8-11 C Catlin 12/1: 3: b f Grand Lodge - Silver Colours (Silver   2   79
Hawk) Led till 2f out, no extra under a kind ride: 120,000gns Feb 1st foal: dam a 1m juv scorer, sire a top-class
1m/10f performer: eff at 6f on gd grnd: ran well for a long way & sure to learn plenty from this.
     PARK APPROACH [1] J Noseda 2-8-11 E Ahern 13/2: 4: gr f Indian Ridge - Abyat (Shadeed) Keen &   nk   78
trkd ldrs, onepcd fnl 1f: op 4/1, debut: 140,000gns Feb foal: half sister to a 10f wnr: dam unrcd but from a gd
family, sire a high-class sprinter: sure to learn from this & 7f shld suit.
     SCENT [7]2-8-11 J Quinn 16/1: 5: b f Groom Dancer - Sweet Pea (Persian Bold) Dwelt, hdwy when   2   72
short of room 1.5f out, nvr nr to chall on debut: May foal: dam a dual 1m wnr, sire a high-class 10f performer:
shld apprec 7f+ given time & will learn plenty from this.
     PONENTE [5]2-8-11 S Drowne 33/1: 6: Dwelt, rear, nvr nr ldrs on debut.   nk   71
     THIS IS MY SONG [9]2-8-11 J Murtagh 15/2: 7: Chsd ldrs, onepcd 2f on debut.   nk   70
     ROMANOVA [4]2-8-11 T P Queally 5/1: 8: Held up, nvr nr ldrs on debut.   1½   66
3639   **NIGHT CLUB QUEEN 11** [10]2-8-11 J F Egan 20/1: 09: Prom, short of room when wkng 2f out.   7   46
     ALULA [3]2-8-11 R L Moore 5/1: 0: 10th: Chsd ldrs till halfway on racecourse bow: op 9/1.   nk   45
     TANZANITE [2]2-8-11 G Carter 50/1: 0: 11th: Chsd ldrs 4.5f, wknd on debut.   3½   35
11 Ran   Time 1m 51.41 (3.81)   Owned: Cheveley Park Stud   Trained: Newmarket

3916	**2.10** Aja Ladies Invitation Fegentri Stakes Handicap 3yo+ 35-55 (F)

£3624 £1115 £558   **1m2f6y**   **Good 57**   -30 Slow   Outside

3727   **BOJANGLES 8** [2] R Brotherton 5-10-8 (49) Miss B de Granvilliers 9/2 FAV: 0345341: Nvr far away,   57
went on 3f out, kept on strongly under hands-&-heels: well bckd: eff at 1m/10f on firm, soft & f/sand, prob handles
hvy: can force the pace or come from bhnd: runs well for an amat: see 1334.
3829   **FLAMING SPIRT 4** [3] J S Moore 5-10-9 (50) Miss P Flierman 6/1: 000/0-442: Held up, hdwy to chase   2½   53
wnr 2f out & sn ev ch, no impress ins fnl 1f: op 9/2, qck reapp: see 3829 & 3605.
3726   **PRAIRIE LAW 8** [7] Ian Williams 4-10-1 (42) Miss A Elsey 6/1: 2-100643: Held up, styd on fnl 2f,   ½   44
nvr nrr: op 9/2, clr of rem: set plenty to do, see 3726 & 3238.
3605   **ESTIMATE 13** [6] John A Harris 4-10-12 vis (53) Miss S Brotherton 8/1: 1002204: Hdwy from rear 2f   6   46
out, btn fnl 1f.
3823   **GALEY RIVER 4** [12]5-9-11 (38) Miss E Johansson 8/1: 0450645: Prom till lost place 4f out,   3   26
rallied late: qck reapp.
2664   **LARAD 51** [8]3-9-12 bl (48) Mrs M Morris 16/1: 4610606: Held up, nvr nr ldrs: 7 wk abs.   3   31
3695   **OVER TO YOU BERT 9** [5]5-10-3 (44) Miss E J Jones 7/1: 0331047: Prom, wknd 2f out: btr 3142.   5   19
421   **COTE SOLEIL 211** [4]7-10-12 (53) Miss S Jischa 20/1: 0/6600-08: ch g Inchinor - Sunshine Coast   4   22
(Posse) Chsd ldrs 1m: mod form in '03: '02 dual h'cap scorer for M Bell: suited by 1m/9f, stays 10f: acts
on firm & hvy, poss handles fibresand: eff with/without blnks: loves a sharp trk, esp Musselburgh: with C Egerton.
1 Jul/02 Epso 8.5g/s 56-55 D: 2 Jul/'02 Yarm 8g/f 56-52 D: 1 Jun/'02 Muss 9gd 53-49 E: 1 Jul/'01 Muss 9g/f 65- E:
3727   **LATIN QUEEN 8** [9]4-10-4 (45) Miss E Folkes 9/1: 00-50559: Led till 3f out, wknd.   3   9
3685   **CATCH THE FOX 9** [11]4-10-1 (42) Mrs S Moore 25/1: 2004000: 10th: Front rank till halfway, wknd.   3   1
3367   **PANCAKE ROLE 22** [10]4-9-8 (5oh) (30) Miss D Lopez 50/1: 0/50-6000: 11th: Al rear: see 2782.   5   0
2448   **RAHEEL 60** [10]4-11-0 t (55) Miss N Volz 14/1: 6143000: 12th: V slowly away, al t.o.: 9 wk abs.   dist   0
12 Ran   Time 2m 11.52 (8.72)   Owned: Mr Alan Solomon   Trained: Pershore

3917	**2.40** Stanjamesuk Com E B F Maiden Stakes Div 2 Fillies 2yo (D)

£5616 £1728 £864   **6f8y str**   **Good 57**   -23 Slow   Centre

SALAMANCA [6] S Kirk 2-8-11 J F Egan 15/2: 1: ch f Pivotal - Salanka (Persian Heights) Held   88
up, prog 2f out, qcknd to lead well ins fnl 1f, won going away: op 11/2, debut: Feb foal, cost 35,000gns: half
sister to mid-dist wnr Kalapoi: dam a 10f wnr, sire a high-class sprinter: eff at 6f on gd grnd, runs well fresh:
showed a decent turn of foot & shld progress from here.
     HALLE BOP [2] Saeed bin Suroor 2-8-11 L Dettori 6/4 FAV: 2: b f Dubai Millennium - Napoleon's   ¾   84
Sister (Alzao) Mid-div, prog to lead briefly ins fnl 1f, not pace to reple wnr cl home: well bckd tho' op 5/4: Apr
foal, half sister to a 1m juv wnr: dam a 10f scorer, sire a top-class 1m/10f performer: eff at 6f on gd grnd, 7f+
will suit: plenty to like about this encouraging debut & will win similar.
3251   **MODRAJ 28** [8] J L Dunlop 2-8-11 W Supple 10/1: 03: b f Machiavellian - Saleela (Nureyev) Chsd   1¼   80
ldrs, prog to lead dist till ins fnl 1f, no extra: Apr foal, dam a mid-dist wnr: sire a top-class miler: eff at 6f
on gd grnd: much imprvd from debut & shld win similar.

1180

3626 **MISS PATRICIA 12** [9] J G Portman 2-8-11 T P Queally 40/1: 004: Rear, styd on fnl 1f under hands-&-heels, nvr dngrs: see 3141. 1 77
BLUEBERRY TART [5]2-8-11 S Drowne 9/1: 5: b f Bluebird - Tart (Warning) Chsd ldrs, kept on fnl 1f, not pace to chall on debut: op 7/1: Feb foal, cost 16,000gns: half sister to a mid-dist wnr abroad: dam a mid-dist wnr, sire a top-class sprinter: with B Meehan & sharper next time. ¾ 74
MISSIE BAILEYS [7]2-8-11 L Keniry(3) 33/1: 6: Very slowly away, styd on late on debut. 1 71
BAILEY GATE [3]2-8-11 J Fortune 14/1: 7: Dsptd lead, went on 2f out till dist, wknd on debut. shd 71
MONTECITO [4]2-8-11 R L Moore 20/1: 8: Deptd lead till 2f out, wknd on debut. shd 71
DESERT IMP [10]2-8-11 K Fallon 4/1: 9: Dwelt, switched far side, prog to lead 1.5f out till dist, wknd & eased: gamble from 8/1: with B Hills & much better clearly expected. 2½ 64
3639 **CAONA 11** [1]2-8-11 E Ahern 10/1: 050: 10th: Mid-div, btn dist: see 3639. nk 63
10 Ran Time 1m 16.43 (4.83) Owned: Wood Street Syndicate Trained: Upper Lambourn

3918

3.15 Stanjamesuk Com Handicap Stakes 3yo+ 0-90 (C) **[102]**
£9997 £3076 £1538 **1m5f61y** **Good 57** **-22 Slow** Outside

3468 **SOULACROIX 19** [5] Mrs A J Perrett 3-8-11 (85) J Murtagh 11/2: 3221-21: Rear, prog 2f out, led ins fnl 1f, styd on strongly, rdn out: op 9/2: stays 13f well, acts on firm & gd/soft grnd: lightly rcd & prog young stayer: see 3468 (12f, reapp). 95
3236 **LOST SOLDIER THREE 28** [3] L M Cumani 3-8-13 (87) K Fallon 9/2: 61542: Held up, prog when short of room 2f out & dist, fin well but wnr had got first run: op 3/1: styd this longer 13f trip well: did not get the run of today's race, see 3236 & 2196 (10f). ¾ 94
2960 **MEADAAF 40** [1] E F Vaughan 3-8-6 (80) S Drowne 12/1: 45-12363: Trkd ldrs, short of room dist, onepcd ins fnl 1f: 6 wk abs: stays 13f: see 2960. 1¾ 85
3534 **STAGE RIGHT 16** [7] D R C Elsworth 3-8-11 (85) L Keniry(3) 11/4 FAV: 46154: Chsd ldrs, outpcd fnl 2.5f: nicely bckd: shld stay 14f+: see 3534. 3½ 85
3510 **BENDARSHAAN 17** [4]4-10-0 (90) J Fanning 7/1: 0411205: Trkd ldr, led 2f out till ins fnl 1f, no extra. 1½ 88
2759 **SHREDDED 48** [2]4-9-3 T (79) J Fortune 10/1: 54-02106: Led till 2f out, no extra: 7 wk abs, tried a t-strap: btr 2192 (14f). ½ 76
3444 **GROOMS AFFECTION 20** [6]4-9-7 (83) L Dettori 11/2: 0/01-1607: Held up, nvr dngrs: tchd 7/1. 3½ 75
4600} **GONDOLIN 314** [8]4-9-8 (84) T P Queally 16/1: 120345-8: b g Marju - Galletina (Persian Heights) Keen in rear, nvr a factor: bckd at long odds, reapp: '03 mdn wnr, subs h'cap plcd: eff at 10f on fast & soft grnd: handles a sharp or gall trk: has tried a t-strap: with G Butler & better expected. 1 74
2 May'03 Hayd 10.5sft 82-80 C: 1 May'03 Wind 10.0g/s 84-(77) E:
8 Ran Time 2m 55.65 (10.55) Owned: Mr G C Stevens Trained: Pulborough

3919

3.50 Listed Stan James Stakes Registered As The Washington Singer Stakes 2yo (A)
£14875 £5500 £2750 **7f str** **Good 57** **-02 Slow** Centre

3406 **KINGS QUAY 21** [5] R Hannon 2-8-11 (91) R L Moore 3/1: 1021: Prom, went on 2f out, held on strongly fnl 1f, rdn out: well bckd from 5/1: apprec this step up to 7f, acts on gd & firm grnd: likes a gall trk: v useful juv, see 3406 & 2188. 104
3707* **WILKO 9** [1] J Noseda 2-8-11 (100) E Ahern 15/8: 0133212: Nvr far away, went after wnr dist, kept on well & not btn far: bckd from 5/2: v tough, continues in fine form: see 3707. ½ 103
3517 **SUBYAN DREAMS 16** [4] P W Chapple Hyam 2-8-7 (1ow) J Fortune 33/1: 533: Chsd ldrs, kept on under press fnl 1f, not pace of front 2: acts on gd & fast grnd: apprec this step up to 7f, looks nailed on to find a mdn. 1 95
3585* **BRECON BEACON 14** [3] P F I Cole 2-9-0 (100) J Murtagh 11/8 FAV: 11214: Led till 2f out, wknd ins fnl 1f & dismounted after line: top-weight, nicely bckd tho' drifted from 10/11: something clearly amiss, see 3585. 2½ 99
ROCAMADOUR [2]2-8-8 C Catlin 33/1: 5: b c Celtic Swing - Watch Me (Green Desert) Chsd ldrs, outpcd halfway, no ch after on debut: Feb foal, half-brother to a 5f juv wnr: dam a sprint wnr, sire a high-class mid-dist performer: with M Channon & highly tried on debut. ¾ 91
5 Ran Time 1m 28.46 (4.16) Owned: Mr J R May Trained: Marlborough

3920

4.20 Stanjamescasino Co Uk Handicap Stakes 3yo 0-80 (D) **[87]**
£5538 £1704 £852 **6f8y str** **Good 57** **+08 Fast** Centre

3447 **APEX 20** [14] E A L Dunlop 3-9-7 (80) K Fallon 3/1: 0-150321: Rear, prog 2f out, qcknd to lead ins fnl 1f, cmftbly: well bckd from 5/1, top-weight & gd time: stays 1m, prob suited by 6/7f: acts on fast, likes gd & soft grnd: gd weight-carrier who can run well fresh: showed a decent turn of foot today, see 3447 & 1526. 92
3744 **THE JOBBER 7** [13] M Blanshard 3-9-5 (78) F Norton 10/1: 21-40622: Held up, gd hdwy to lead entering fnl 1f, not pace to repel wnr ins fnl 1f: fine run, turn shld not be far away: see 3744. 2 82
3737* **MORGAN LEWIS 8** [16] G B Balding 3-8-10 (6ex) (69) R Thomas(5) 2/1 FAV: 400-013: Rear, styd on well fnl 1f, nrst fin: well bckd: see 3737. ½ 72
3452 **BEE MINOR 20** [8] R Hannon 3-8-12 (71) E Ahern 20/1: 0-020024: Rear, prog to chase ldrs 2f out, onepcd fnl 1f: see 3452. 1¾ 69
3684 **ASK THE CLERK 9** [6]3-8-12 (71) M Tebbutt 9/1: 4643305: Chsd ldrs, onepcd fnl 1f. nk 68
3213 **CHICKADO 29** [12]3-8-1 (60) D Fox(5) 33/1: 613-3606: Front rank, led briefly dist, no extra fnl 1f. 1½ 53
3379 **INSTANT RECALL 22** [11]3-9-7 bl (80) J Fortune 6/1: 5451247: Led till dist, no extra: jt top-weight: see 3188 & 2841 (AW). hd 72
2118 **BEEJAY 74** [7]3-9-1 (74) S Drowne 33/1: 31-1008: Chsd ldrs, wkng when hmpd dist: 10 wk abs. ½ 65
3542 **HILITES 15** [2]3-9-3 (76) Derek Nolan(7) 25/1: 0063049: Slow away, chsd ldrs, btn fnl 1f. nk 66
3401 **CYFRWYS 21** [5]3-8-3 (62) D Kinsella 14/1: 24-02260: 10th: Front rank, wknd fnl 1f: see 3095 (AW). ½ 51
3452* **KOSTAR 20** [4]3-9-4 (77) R Smith 14/1: 410: 11th: Chsd ldrs 4.5f, wknd: see 3452. ¾ 63
3804 **BORZOI MAESTRO 5** [15]3-9-2 (75) L Keniry(3) 20/1: 1043050: 12th: Chsd ldrs, ev ch till wknd dist. 2½ 54
3109 **SAINTLY PLACE 34** [1]3-8-1 (60) C Catlin 66/1: 060-00: 13th: Chsd ldrs 4f, sn btn: see 3109. shd 39
3480 **FISBY 18** [3]3-8-6 (65) J F Egan 20/1: 0-550: 14th: Chsd ldrs, btn 2f out. 1¾ 39
15 **SCARLET EMPRESS 275** [10]3-9-3 (76) R L Moore 50/1: 060140-0: 15th: b f Second Empire - Daltak (Night Shift) Front rank 4f, wknd into last: reapp: '03 AW nursery h'cap wnr (second time blnks): eff at 6f on firm, fast & polytrack, likes a sharp/turning trk: with R Hannon, blnks not worn today. ½ 49
1 Oct'03 Ling 6ap 79a-67 D:
15 Ran Time 1m 14.52 (2.92) Owned: Patrick Milmo and Stuart Tilling Trained: Newmarket

---

3921   4.50 Hamlyn Milne Mar-Key Marquees Maiden Stakes Fillies 3yo+ (D)
£5798 £1784 £892   **7f str**   **Good 57**   **-23 Slow**   Centre - Hand Timed

3648} **ENRAPTURE** 363 [4] Mrs A J Perrett 3-8-11 K Fallon 6/5 FAV: 5-1: b f Lear Fan - Cheviot Hills   **78**
(Gulch) Trkd ldrs, prog to lead 2f out, clr entering fnl 1f, held on drvn out: well bckd, reapp: 5th on sole juv
start (fills mdn): dam a mid-dist wnr: eff over a gall 7f on gd grnd, runs well fresh: can go on from here.
  WOODLAND GLADE [8] R Hannon 3-8-11 J Fortune 10/1: 2: b f Mark of Esteem - Incendio (Siberian   ½   **76**
Express) Chsd ldrs, kept on well fnl 1f, only just btn on debut: half-sister to smart 6/7f performer Barons Pit:
eff over a gall 7f on gd grnd: highly encouraging first run, must win similar.
2659 **TETCOTT** 51 [6] M P Tregoning 3-8-11 W Supple 10/3: 53: Chsd ldrs, onepcd fnl 1f: nicely bckd,   2½   **71**
7 wk abs: some improvement here, see 2659.
  FUTURE DEAL [7] C A Horgan 3-8-11 S Carson 33/1: 4: b f First Trump - Katyushka (Soviet Star)   ¾   **69**
Chsd ldrs, ev ch 2f out, no extra fnl 1f: dam is a top-class sprinter: eff at 7f on gd: sure to learn from this.
3048 **DEUXIEME** 36 [9]3-8-11 S Drowne 7/2: 335: Slowly away & keen, styd on late, nvr dngrs: tchd   1¾   **65**
9/1: btr 2352 (debut).
3446 **HIGHLAND LASS** 20 [5]3-8-11 N Chalmers(5) 50/1: 006: Chsd ldrs, led halfway till 2f out, wknd.   2   **61**
3038 **UNDER MY SKIN** 37 [10]3-8-11 t G Carter 25/1: 07: Led till halfway, sn wknd.   4   **53**
3237 **BONNETTS** 28 [3]3-8-11 C Catlin 33/1: 008: Slowly away, nvr a factor, flashed tail.   1   **51**
3282 **ALJAFLIYAH** 27 [2]3-8-11 A Hamblett(7) 33/1: U009: Slowly away, al bhd.   ¾   **49**
3452 **MISS MONZA** 20 [1]3-8-11 F Norton 33/1: 00: 10th: Chsd ldrs till halfway, sn btn & fin last.   6   **37**
10 Ran   Time 1m 19.10 (4.80)   Owned: Cheveley Park Stud   Trained: Pulborough

---

3922   5.25 Tom Mitchell 'half Century' Birthday Celebration Handicap Stakes 3yo+ 0-75 (E)   [72]
£4128 £1270 £635   **1m1f**   **Good 57**   **-42 Slow**   Outside

3232 **DIDNT TELL MY WIFE** 28 [9] C F Wall 5-9-5 (63) K Fallon 15/8 FAV: 1-660431: Chsd ldrs, squeezed   **68**
through to lead dist, styd on strongly fnl 1f, readily: well bckd: eff at 7/9f on firm, soft grnd & both AWs:
seems to handle any trk: see 3232 & 12 (AW).
3579 **ARRY DASH** 14 [2] M R Channon 4-10-0 (72) S Hitchcott(3) 3/1: 0306062: Chsd ldrs, ev ch 2f out,   1¼   **74**
not pace of wnr fnl 1f: top-weight: back to form here, well h'capped now: see 2313 & 758.
3556 **WAZIRI** 15 [11] H Morrison 3-9-9 (75) L Fletcher(3) 7/1: 464-1003: Rear, prog wide to chase ldrs   3½   **72**
dist, no impress fnl 1f: best 2225.
3398 **WIZARD OF EDGE** 21 [1] R J Hodges 4-9-9 (67) F Norton 20/1: 25/3-604: Rdn in rear, styd on late,   3½   **59**
nvr dngrs: see 3398.
2857 **PHRED** 44 [3]4-9-2 (60) S Carson 10/1: 6542005: Chsd ldrs, led 2f out till dist, wknd: 6 wk abs.   1   **50**
3605 **CUMBRIAN PRINCESS** 13 [10]7-8-1 (45) D Kinsella 16/1: 1136366: Prog to chase ldrs halfway, btn 2f out.1¼   **33**
2947 **HOWS THINGS** 41 [6]4-9-2 (60) R Havlin 20/1: 1223-607: Front rank, led 3f out till 2f out, wknd.   2   **45**
3391 **DESERT HAWK** 21 [5]3-9-2 (68) J Fortune 5/1: 005408: Chsd ldrs 7f, wknd: see 3039.   7   **43**
3719 **JAHIA** 8 [8]5-9-12 (70) R Lucey Butler(7) 50/1: 110/6-009: Led till 3f out, wknd: see 3719.   3   **40**
9 Ran   Time 1m 57.92(8.92)   Owned: Mr G D Newton   Trained: Newmarket

---

Official Going GOOD/SOFT

3923   5.45 Learndirect Classified Stakes 3yo 0-70 (E)
£4241 £1305 £653   **1m str**   **Good 43**   **+14 Fast**   Stands side

3612 **BRIGHT SUN** 13 [2] N Tinkler 3-9-2 (72) Kim Tinkler 4/1 J FAV: 0430341: Dwelt stands side, sn   **76**
cl-up, hdwy to lead 3f out, hung left dist, rdn out: fast time, bckd from 6/1: eff at 6f/1m on firm & gd/soft grnd,
acts on a stiff, undul or gall trk: gd run following recent plcd effs, see 2155.
3219 **ADORATA** 29 [5] J Jay 3-8-11 (67) O Urbina 16/1: 3202302: Mid-div stands side, hdwy & ev ch over   ½   **69**
1f out, kept on ins fnl 1f: clr of rem: eff at 6f/1m on firm & gd: gd run: see 2295.
3282* **SURREPTITIOUS** 27 [8] D R Loder 3-8-11 (68) T P Queally 4/1 J FAV: 13: Handy stands side, hung   3½   **62**
left 1f out & sn onepcd: shade btr 3282 (mdn, 7f, fast).
3384 **TANNOOR** 22 [1] M A Jarvis 3-9-5 P (75) P Robinson 8/1: 3-315064: Rcd alone far side, no impress   nk   **69**
stands side fnl 1f: 1st time cheek pieces: gd run in circumstances.
3282 **DREAM EASY** 27 [3]3-9-0 (70) R Price 16/1: 0545: With ldrs stands side, onepcd dist: see 3282.   1¼   **61**
1846 **HALABALOO** 86 [4]3-9-2 (75) J F Egan 5/1: 3-5036: Rear stands side, nvr a factor: long abs.   3   **57**
3625 **BAKER OF OZ** 13 [9]3-9-2 (72) R L Moore 8/1: 2641007: With ldr stands side, led over 3f out, sn   1   **55**
hdd, no extra fnl 1f: op 11/1: thrice below 2264.
3524 **PENDING** 16 [10]3-9-0 (70) J Murtagh 6/1: 05-3068: Chsd ldrs stands side, no impress over 1f out.   3   **47**
2748 **SHAABAN** 48 [7]3-9-0 (69) B Reilly(3) 33/1: 00059: Chsd ldrs stands side, wknd over 2f out: 7 wk   9   **29**
abs: now with Miss J Feilden: see 2748.
1369 **NEGWA** 110 [6]3-8-11 (70) T E Durcan 16/1: 433-500: 10th: Dwelt stands side, nvr a factor: abs.   10   **6**
2650 **MUTASSEM** 52 [12]3-9-0 (69) M Henry 50/1: 6-0000: 11th: b c Fasliyev - Fee Eria (Always Fair)   3½   **2**
Led stands side over 4f, no extra: 7 wk abs: mdn unplcd sole '03 start (rtd 70, E Dunlop): now with T Keddy.
11 Ran   Time 1m 39.59 (2.39)   Owned: Leeds Plywood and Doors Ltd   Trained: Malton

---

3924   6.15 Vibe Fm Handicap Stakes 3yo+ 0-80 (D)   [79]
£5538 £1704 £852   **6f str**   **Good 43**   **+11 Fast**   Stands side

3789 **MISTRAL SKY** 6 [5] Mrs Stef Liddiard 5-9-7 vis (72) J F Egan 4/1: 5401221: Keen & dsptd lead till   **80**
led over 1f out, drvn out ins fnl 1f: fast time, qck reapp: eff at 6/7f, stays 1m: acts on firm, gd & polytrack:
handles any trk, likes Leicester & Lingfield: in fine heart at present, v consistent & tough: see 3518.
3763 **ALBASHOOSH** 6 [4] D Nicholls 6-9-4 (69) Alex Greaves 4/1: 6103432: Keen & sn led, hdd over 1f   nk   **74**

---

out, kept on ins fnl 1f: quick reapp, well clr of rem: remains in gd form, win similar on this evidence: see 2280.
2023 **BEN LOMAND 79** [1] B W Duke 4-9-6 c (71) A Daly 25/1: 2000-003: ch g Inchinor - Benjarong (Sharpo)   9   **51**
Chsd ldrs, no impress 1f out: long abs: '03 h'cap & class stks wnr: rnr-up 1 of 2 '02 starts (mdn): suited by 6f
on firm & gd, rep suited by an easy surface: handles a sharp/undul or gall trk: wears an eye-cover.
2 Jul'03 Kemp 6g/f 79-(79) D: 1 Jun'03 Wind 6gd 80-75 D: 1 May'03 Brig 6.0fm 79-(70) E: 2 Nov'02 Newm 6gd 83- D:
3584 **FEARBY CROSS 14** [7] W J Musson 8-8-11 (62) R Mullen 4/1: 0450054: Rear, nvr nr ldrs: see 698.   hd   **41**
3424 **A TEEN 20** [8]6-8-3 (54) T P Queally 20/1: 0060005: Handy, wknd over 1f out: see 740.   ½   **31**
3710 **LAKE VERDI 8** [6]5-8-7-13 t (50) J Mackay 8/1: 0430026: Handy, wknd dist: now with Miss G Kelleway.   1¼   **23**
3720 **SCOTTISH EXILE 8** [2]3-9-2 vis (71) Darren Williams 16/1: 0210347: Rear, nvr nr ldrs.   ¾   **42**
2767 + **ST AUSTELL 401** [3]4-9-8 (73) Lisa Jones 14/1: 5/32021-6: b g Compton Place - Paris Joelle (Fairy   3½   **33**
King) Dwelt, sn cl-up, no impress over 1f out on reapp: top weight: won fnl '03 start (mdn): last of 5 sole '02
start (mdn, rtd 55): eff at 5f, has tried further: acts on firm & gd, sharp/undul trk: with J Toller.
1 Jul'03 Ling 5gd 67-(74) F: 2 Jun'03 Folk 5fm 74-(78) D: 2 Jun'03 Nott 5.1g/f 76- E:
3751 **COLD CLIMATE 7** [9]9-8-4 (55) J Quinn 7/2 FAV: 0405229: Mid-div, nvr a factor: op 5/1, qck reapp.   ½   **13**
9 Ran   Time 1m 12.96 (1.96)   Owned: Shefford Valley Stud   Trained: Hungerford

---

3925   6.45 Learndirect Maiden Stakes 2yo   (D)
£4804   £1478   £739   1m str   **Good 43**   -07 Slow   Stands side

MOTIVATOR [10] M L W Bell 2-9-0   K Fallon 3/1: 1: b c Montjeu - Out West (Gone West) Mid-div,   **100+**
hdwy to lead dist, sn clr, easily on debut, val 10L+: well bckd: Feb foal, cost 75,000gns: dam useful 1m scorer,
sire top-class mid-dist performer: stays 1m on gd, will relish further: runs well fresh: potentially smart,
deserves a step up in grade: keep on your side.
SUNDAY SYMPHONY [4] Saeed bin Suroor 2-9-0   K McEvoy 9/2: 2: br c Sunday Silence - Darrery   6   **85**
(Darshaan) Chsd ldrs, not pace to go with wnr over 1f out on debut: Mar foal, cost 250,000 gns: half brother juv
wnrs over 7f & 1m: dam dual 10/12f wnr, sire a smart US 3yo: prob stays 1m on gd: met a useful type here, shown
enough to win a mdn & entitled to improve for this.
3500 **TUMBLEWEED GALORE 17** [7] B J Meehan 2-9-0 (73) J F McDonald(3) 10/1: 0333: Dsptd lead till led 5f   ¾   **83**
out, hdd over 1f out, no extra: clr of rem: see 3500.
ROSECLIFF [6] A M Balding 2-9-0   J P Murtagh 16/1: 4: b c Montjeu - Dance Clear (Marju) Slow   4   **75**
away in rear, hdwy over 2f out, not pace to chall on debut: May foal, cost 150,000 gns: dam a 6f 2yo wnr, later a
7f scorer at 3: sire top class mid-dist performer: learn from this.
3470 **REBEL REBEL 19** [3]2-9-0   O Urbina 50/1: 005: Handy, wknd over 1f out.   1½   **72**
TAMATAVE [11]2-9-0 T K Darley 10/1: 6: Cl-up, hdwy into 2nd 3f out, wknd 2f out: tried a t-strap.   4   **64**
34 **MUTAMAASEK 19** [9]2-9-0   W Supple 5/2 FAV: 57: Nvr btr than mid-div: well bckd.   1¾   **60**
NOTABILITY [1]2-9-0   P Robinson 9/1: 8: Rear, nvr nr ldrs on debut.   hd   **59**
GARHOUD [8]2-9-0   E Ahern 20/1: 9: Slow away, hdwy 2f out, sn wknd on debut.   1¼   **56**
LEGALLY FAST [2]2-9-0   S Drowne 33/1: 0: 10th: Led till over 5f out, wknd on debut.   5   **46**
2766 **BIBI HELEN 48** [5]2-8-9   R Mullen 66/1: 600: 11th: Reared & slow away start, nvr dngrs.   nk   **40**
11 Ran   Time 1m 41.21 (4.01)   Owned: The Royal Ascot Racing Club   Trained: Newmarket

---

3926   7.15 Joe Jennings Bookmakers Handicap Stakes 3yo+ 0-90   (C)
£9666   £2974   £1487   1m4f   **Good 43**   -09 Slow   Centre   **[90]**

3617* **TAWNY WAY 13** [3] W Jarvis 4-9-11 (87) S Drowne 14/1: 5126011: Handy, hdwy to lead over 1f out,   **93**
drvn out fnl 1f: top-weight: eff at 9/12f on fast & gd, poss soft, sharpish or stiff/gall trks: gd weight carrier:
continues in excellent form & likes Newmarket: see 3617 (C/D).
2592 **FLING 55** [2] J R Fanshawe 3-8-9 (1ow) (81) J Murtagh 3/1: 1522: Rear, kept on for press ins fnl   1¾   **85**
1f but not pace to reach wnr: 8 wk abs: stays 12f: see 2592.
3587* **STOLEN HOURS 14** [9] J Akehurst 4-8-3 (65) J Quinn 14/1: 0022313: Rear, hdwy to lead over 2f out,   nk   **67**
sn hdd, still ev ch over 1f out, sn onepcd: acts on firm & gd, has disapp on gd/soft: gd run tho' shade btr 3587.
3734 **SMART JOHN 8** [5] W M Brisbourne 4-8-8 (70) K Fallon 8/1: 1421354: Mid-div, outpcd over 2f out,   1¼   **70**
kept on ins fnl 1f: see 2900.
2785 **RESERVOIR 47** [6]3-8-7 (80) D Holland 20/1: 043-2105: Rcd in 2nd, lost place after 5f & remained   1   **78**
handy, hdwy to lead 2f out, hdd over 1f out, no extra: 7 wk abs: btr 2222 (mdn).
3437 **DANAKIL 20** [8]9-9-1 (77) R L Moore 20/1: 2412246: Rear, hdwy over 1f out, no impress ins fnl 1f.   7   **64**
3510 **ANTICIPATING 17** [7]4-9-9 (85) K Darley 12/1: 0-040207: Dwelt, sn cl-up, rcd in 2nd over 5f out,   14   **51**
ev ch over 2f out, wknd over 1f out: see 877.
3734 + **DALLOOL 8** [1]3-8-12 (5ex) (85) P Robinson 11/8 FAV: 514418: Led over 9f, wknd.   nk   **50**
3653 + **BAILEYS DANCER 11** [4]3-8-7 (5ex) (80) J Fanning 16/1: 4002019: Cl-up, hdwy into 2nd 7f out till   16   **21**
over 5f out, wknd over 2f out: much btr 3653.
9 Ran   Time 2m 34.51 (6.31)   Owned: Rams Racing Club   Trained: Newmarket

---

3927   7.45 Vibe Fm Median Auction Maiden Stakes 2yo   (E)
£4339   £1335   £668   7f str   **Good 43**   -09 Slow   Stands side

3470 **FU MANCHU 19** [14] D R Loder 2-9-0   T P Queally 12/1: 01: b c Desert Style - Robsart (Robellino)   **87**
Mid-div, hdwy to lead well ins fnl 1f, drvn out: Feb foal, cost 75,000 gns: dam a dual 7/10f 3yo wnr: sire a
high-class 2yo, later best over 7f: stays 7f, 1m shld suit: acts on gd grnd & a stiff/gall trk: imprvd from debut.
3594 **MISTER GENEPI 13** [20] W R Muir 2-9-0   S Drowne 4/1: 522: Rear, hdwy over 3f out, led over 1f   ½   **84**
out, hdd well ins fnl 1f, no extra: consistent, must find a mdn: see 3594.
3047 **FAIRMILE 36** [13] P W Harris 2-9-0   J Murtagh 11/2: 33: Rear, hdwy over 1f out, kept on: op 8/1:   1   **82**
handles gd & gd/soft: gd run & can find similar on this showing: see 3047 (debut).
3272 **CHIEF SCOUT 27** [4] B J Meehan 2-9-0   K Fallon 5/1: 04: br c Tomba - Princess Zara (Reprimand)   ½   **81**
Made most over 5f, no extra ins fnl 1f: Mar foal: dam unrcd, sire useful 6f wnr, later high-class over 6/7f: stays
7f on gd: imprvd here from debut & has shown enough to win a mdn.
PATRONAGE [10]2-9-0   R Mullen 20/1: 5: b c Royal Applause - Passionate Pursuit (Pursuit of   hd   **80**
Love) Dwelt, hdwy over 3f out, ev ch over 1f out, no impress ins fnl 1f on debut: Feb 1st foal, cost 160,000 gns:
dam a 10f 3yo scorer, sire top class 2yo/sprinter: stays 7f on gd: gd start.
3122 **COUP DETAT 34** [18]2-9-0   K Darley 11/4 FAV: 426: Rear, hdwy over 1f out, kept on ins fnl 1f: nk   **79**
clr of rem: stays 7f: shade btr expected after 3122 (6f).

NEWMARKET FRIDAY 13.08.04 Righthand, Stiff, Galloping Track

PRESS EXPRESS [17]2-9-0 T E Durcan 50/1: 7: Nvr a factor on debut. *5* **69**
ATLANTIC STORY [6]2-9-0 K McEvoy 10/1: 8: Chsd ldrs, ev ch over 1f out, wknd on debut. *nk* **68**
SCARP [8]2-9-0 E Ahern 33/1: 9: Nvr btr than mid-div on debut. *1* **66**
3699 **SUCCESSION 9** [11]2-8-9 S Sanders 25/1: 000: 10th: Handy, hung left & no impress 2f out. *1* **59**
3234 **GURRUN 28** [3]2-9-0 O Urbina 66/1: 000: 11th: Handy, wknd over 1f out. *½* **63**
TIAMO [2]2-9-0 D Holland 33/1: 0: 12th: Slow away, nvr dangerous on debut. *1¾* **59**
STANCOMB WILLS [1]2-9-0 F P Ferris(3) 40/1: 0: 13th: Slow away, nvr a factor on debut. *shd* **58**
3568 **ELECTION SEEKER 14** [15]2-9-0 A Quinn(5) 66/1: 00: 14th: Mid-div, not much room 2f out, wknd. *3½* **51**
STAKHANOV [16]2-9-0 S W Kelly 50/1: 0: 15th: Slow away, al bhd on debut. *nk* **50**
3337 **SENDEED 23** [7]2-9-0 t W Supple 20/1: 00: 16th: Slow away, sn handy, no impress over 2f out. *1¾* **47**
ARCHIE WRIGHT [9]2-9-0 R L Moore 33/1: 0: 17th: Cl-up, wknd over 2f out on debut. *1* **45**
CAYUSE [12]2-8-9 R Price 100/1: 0: 18th: Slow away, nvr a factor on debut. *15* **10**
18 Ran Time 1m 27.59 (3.69) Owned: Egerton House Racing Trained: Newmarket

3928

8.15 Newmarket Nights Rated Stakes Handicapfillies 3yo+ 0-95 (C) **[95]**
£8589 £3258 £1629 **7f str** **Good 43** **-35 Slow** Stands side

3732* **VIOLET PARK 8** [7] B J Meehan 3-8-3 (3ex)(1oh) (70) J F McDonald(3) 9/4 J FAV: 22311: Trkd ldrs & keen, ev ch dist, hung left, led on line: well bckd: eff at 7f/1m on fast & gd/soft, acts on a gall/undul or stiff trk: tough, continues in fine form: see 3732. **77**
3006 **CUSCO 38** [3] R Hannon 3-9-7 (88) R L Moore 12/1: 5-260202: Led, wandered over 1f out, hdd post: top weight: back to form, fine eff: see 2736. *shd* **93**
3006 **SOLAR POWER 38** [1] J R Fanshawe 3-9-3 (84) J Murtagh 9/4 J FAV: 1-24443: Rcd in 2nd & keen, onepcd ins fnl 1f: well bckd, tchd 3/1: see 1930. *2½* **84**
3782 **STARBECK 6** [5] P Howling 6-9-6 (81) N Callan 10/1: 0054004: Mid-div, no impress ins fnl 1f. *¾* **79**
3791 **CHEESE N BISCUITS 6** [6]4-8-9 p (70) K Fallon 8/1: 0200005: Chsd ldrs, rdn/hmpd dist, sn onepcd. *nk* **67**
3235 **CHANTERELLE 28** [8]3-9-5 (86) K Darley 7/1: 441-66: Keen in rear, nvr nr ldrs: see 3235. *2½* **78**
3528* **GO BETWEEN 16** [4]3-9-4 (85) S Sanders 13/2: 0-206617: Keen in rear, nvr a factor. *9* **59**
1741 **ZERLINA 91** [2]3-8-13 (80) C Catlin 33/1: 201-008: Keen in rear, nvr dngrs: abs, new yard. *2½* **49**
8 Ran Time 1m 29.36(5.46) Owned: Mrs J Cash Trained: Upper Lambourn

CATTERICK FRIDAY 13.08.04 Lefthand, Undulating, Very Tight Track

Official Going SOFT (HEAVY IN PLACES)

3929

6.00 I R M Amateur Riders' Handicap Stakes 3yo+ 0-75 (F) **[50]**
£2996 £856 £428 **1m3f214y** **Soft 92** **-31 Slow** Outside

2724 **ROMIL STAR 49** [4] K R Burke 7-10-0 vis (50) Miss Kelly Burke(7) 16/1: 4113521: Stumbled start & bhd, stdy hdwy fnl 2f & led fnl strides: joc's first ride under Rules: 7 wk abs: eff at 12/14.7f on gd, hvy & fibresand: goes well fresh: see 2381. **56**
3471 **FORT CHURCHILL 19** [12] M H Tompkins 3-10-10 BL (71) Mr S Warren(7) 20/1: 00-5342: Chsd ldrs & led well over 1f out till hdd fnl strides: first time blnks, gd run: eff at 11.5f/12f on firm & soft grnd: see 2147. *½* **75**
3829 **PONT NEUF 4** [3] P D Evans 4-11-1 t (65) Miss Kelly Harrison(3) 9/2 FAV: 2511023: Rear, hdwy wide over 2f out, not pace of wnr cl-home: qck reapp: t-strap reapplied: acts on firm & soft grnd: see 3829 & 3481. *hd* **68**
3505 **LATE ARRIVAL 17** [14] M D Hammond 7-9-4 (40) Miss W Gibson(7) 33/1: 0002604: Held up, hdwy halfway, ch ins last, no extra cl-home: stays a sharp 12f: acts on firm, soft & fibresand: see 1954. *½* **42**
3140 **BRAMANTINO 33** [6]4-10-3 bl (53) Miss V Tunnicliffe(5) 10/1: 1025055: Held up, late prog, nrst fin. *1½* **53**
3715* **FINAL DIVIDEND 8** [15]8-9-13 (5ex) (49) Miss Joanna Rees(3) 14/1: 3-056516: Chsd ldrs, onepace fnl 3f. *5* **41**
3668* **PLATINUM CHARMER 10** [8]4-10-10 (5ex)p (60) Mr S Dobson(3) 8/1: 4032517: Mid-div, no impress dist. *nk* **51**
3140 **BUSHIDO 33** [7]5-10-6 (56) Miss Faye Bramley(5) 15/2: 0/3500/-68: Held up, late prog: jmps rnr. *½* **46**
3703 **EIGHT 9** [16]8-9-9 (45) Ms T Dzieciolowska(7) 20/1: 200-0049: Mid-div, no impress fnl 3f: btr 3703. *1* **33**
3096 **DASH OF MAGIC 55** [11]6-9-4 (40) Mrs S Bosley 14/1: 1063150: 10th: Slow away, mid-div, eff wide to lead 3f out, hdd 2f out & wknd: abs: btr 2340 (gd). *shd* **27**
3505 **SHALBEBLUE 17** [17]7-9-6 bl (42) Miss L Ellison(3) 20/1: 25-00000: 11th: Handy, led halfway till 3f out. *7* **18**
810* **MR MISCHIEF 161** [10]4-11-6 (70) Miss A Armitage(5) 9/1: 211-3010: 12th: Led till halfway, btn over 3f out: abs: btr 810 (AW). *hd* **45**
3419 **IMPERIAL ROYALE 20** [9]3-9-8 p (55) Mr D Weekes 66/1: 2-506000: 13th: Mid-div, btn 3f out: btr 2930. *1* **28**
3377 **APPETINA 22** [5]3-10-1 (62) Ms C Williams 25/1: 03-55440: 14th: Mid-div, eff 4f out, btn 2f out. *nk* **34**
2912 **CHAPTER HOUSE 42** [18]5-11-4 (68) Mr O Greenall(7) 50/1: 060/0-600: 15th: Chsd ldrs till 3f out: 6 wk abs: see 2725 (1m). *¾* **39**
3217 **ISAAF 29** [2]5-11-5 (69) Mrs Marie King(5) 13/2: 0244160: 16th: Mid-div, no ch fnl 3f: btr 3105 (gd). *6* **31**
3700 **FOUR KINGS 9** [13]3-9-13 t (60) Miss J Riding(5) 50/1: 0330600: 17th: Bhd halfway & t.o.: btr 2474. *dist* **0**
17 Ran Time 2m 46.03 (14.83) Owned: Mrs Elaine M Burke Trained: Leyburn

3930

6.30 Enter Tonight's Racecard Competition Selling Stakes 2yo (G)
£2632 £752 £376 **7f rnd** **Soft 92** **-33 Slow** Inside

3820 **DARTANIAN 4** [7] P D Evans 2-8-11 (58) R Winston 5/1: 056301: Handy & led over 2f out, rdn & styd on strongly ins last: bght in for 4,400gns: first win: qck reapp: eff at 7f on fast & soft grnd, sharp/turning trk: appreciates sell grade: see 3349 & 2597. **63**
3544 **TOLDO 15** [6] A Berry 2-8-11 (45) F Lynch 33/1: 000402: Rear, eff to chase wnr dist, al held: blnks omitted, imprvd eff: styd this sharp 7f & enjoyed soft grnd in sell grade: see 2933. *3½* **55**
3750 **LAKESDALE 7** [10] Mrs C A Dunnett 2-8-6 (60) N Mackay(3) 9/4 FAV: 2204023: Trkd ldrs, kept on onepace for press fnl 2f: clmd by Miss D Mountain for 6,000: see 1517. *½* **49**
3349 **NORTHERN REVOQUE 23** [13] A Berry 2-8-6 P Mathers(5) 66/1: 5005004: Chsd ldrs, hung left, onepce. *3* **43**
3209 **LANE MARSHAL 29** [1]2-8-11 bl T Eaves(3) 66/1: 6500065: Led till 2f out, sn outpcd: btr 2167. *¾* **46**
3750 **TIP TOES 7** [3]2-8-6 (49) T O'Brien(7) 20/1: 0604506: Mid-div, nvr able to chall: btr 3491 & 3259. *3* **35**
2077 **BELTON 76** [9]2-8-11 G Gibbons 7/1: 007: b c Lujain - Efficacious (Efisio) Dwelt, rear, only *1¾* **36**

mod prog, abs: longer trip: cheaply bght Mar foal, dam plcd at mid-dists as a 3yo.

3769 **PREMIER TIMES 6** [4]2-8-11 (59) A Culhane 9/2: 51608: Drvn mid-div, no prog fnl 2f: qck reapp. *1¾* **32**

3393 **DANES ROCK 21** [8]2-8-11 bl (65) G Faulkner 10/1: 406209: Handy when hung right on bend 4f out, btn 2f out: btr 2183 (6f). *1* **30**

2294 **HIGHBURY LASS 66** [2]2-8-6 Rory Moore(7) 33/1: 060: 10th: ch f Entrepreneur - Princess Victoria (Deploy) Slow away & al towards rear, 2 mth abs: Mar first foal, 8,500gns purchase: dam a 5f sell juv wnr. *3* **19**

3570 **TEWITFIELD LASS 14** [11]2-8-6 D Fentiman(7) 66/1: 0500: 11th: Mid-div, no prog fnl 3f. *3* **13**

3014 **CASH TIME 37** [5]2-8-6 (44) R Fitzpatrick 25/1: 6040: 12th: Dwelt, chsd ldrs till 2f out: btr 3014. *½* **12**

3769 **FOR NOWT 6** [15]2-8-11 D Allan 20/1: 60000: 13th: Sn drvn mid-div, btn 2f out: qck reapp. *5* **7**

3769 **GUNNERBERGKAMP 6** [14]2-8-11 P M Quinn 100/1: 000: 14th: Slow away & al bhd, qck reapp. *1¼* **4**

3349 **MISS TRENDSETTER 23** [12]2-8-6 P J Carroll 40/1: 000: 15th: Mid-div, struggling from halfway. *nk* **0**

15 Ran Time 1m 31.78 (8.78) Owned: Mr Garry Gardiner Trained: Abergavenny

3931

7.00 R M C Materials Nursery Handicap Stakes 2yo (D) **[84]**
£4823 £1484 £742 **6f rnd** **Soft 92** **-39 Slow** Inside

3723 **ROWAN LODGE 8** [4] M H Tompkins 2-9-7 (77) N Mackay(3) 3/1: 03121: Mid-div, rdn & hdwy to lead well ins last: nicely bckd, stays a sharp 7f well, both wins at 6f: acts on fast & soft grnd: progressive type. **85**

3544 **FAVOURING 15** [2] R A Fahey 2-8-8 (64) P Hanagan 11/4: 4002: Held up, hdwy halfway & chall ins last, sn not pace of wnr but rallied well cl-home, just held: hvly bckd, op 5/1: h'cap debut, much imprvd eff: eff over a sharp 6f & enjoys soft grnd: likely type for similar: see 1091. *nk* **68**

3245 **ANGELOFTHENORTH 28** [7] J D Bethell 2-8-12 (68) A Culhane 8/1: 34333: Led till hdd ins last & no extra: eff at 5/6f, handles fast & soft grnd: best effs to date both at Catterick: see 2847 & 2442. *2* **68**

3698 **LORD JOHN 9** [9] M W Easterby 2-8-6 (62) Dale Gibson 20/1: 0404004: Chsd ldrs, no extra dist. *2* **56**

3877 **MITCHELLAND 2** [6]2-9-4 VIS (74) T Eaves(3) 12/1: 0663555: Handy & ch over 1f out, wknd, visor. *1¼* **64**

2522 **STRATHTAY 57** [8]2-8-13 (69) Dean McKeown 10/1: 3056: Dwelt, chsd ldrs till over 1f out: abs, h'cap bow: btr 1974 (5f, fast). *1¼* **55**

3214 **SECRET PACT 29** [1]2-9-5 (75) R Ffrench 5/2 FAV: 4237: Trkd ldrs, sn lost place & struggling rear halfway, mod late prog: well bckd tho' op 2/1: h'cap bow: crying out for a return to 7f+ on this evidence. *1* **58**

2921 **JUSTENJOY YOURSELF 41** [3]2-7-12 (12oh) (42) Natalia Gemelova(7) 66/1: 60648: Dwelt, nvr on terms. *½* **35**

3698 **SKIPPIT JOHN 9** [5]2-9-2 (72) G Gibbons 25/1: 26609: Chsd ldrs till 2f out. *1¾* **48**

9 Ran Time 1m 18.19 (7.89) Owned: The Rowan Stud and Clique Partnership Trained: Newmarket

3932

7.30 Simon Bailes Peugeot Claiming Stakes 3yo+ (F)
£3031 £866 £433 **5f rnd** **Soft 92** **+05 Fast** Inside

3757 **WHITE LEDGER 7** [16] R A Fahey 5-8-11 vis (50) P Hanagan 9/2: 000-0031: Mid-div, hdwy when hit by rival's whip ins last, styd on for press to lead nr line: nicely bckd, op 6/1: eff at 6f, all wins at 5f: acts on fast, soft & both AWs: trainer/jockey combo in superb form: see 2999. **57**

3804 **HES A ROCKET 5** [13] K R Burke 3-8-13 P (58) G Faulkner 20/1: 3600602: Handy, narrow lead ins last, just hdd cl-home: qck reapp & tried cheek pieces: prob handles fast & f/sand, likes gd/soft & soft. *1* **57**

3680 **SOAKED 9** [8] D W Chapman 11-8-10 bl (62) A Culhane 11/2: 2152303: Led till ins last, kept on. *nk* **50**

4608} **OUTEAST 314** [15] G A Harker 4-8-3 (44) R Ffrench 50/1: 000000-4: b f Mujadil - Stifen (Burslem) Chsd ldrs, rdn & no extra well ins last: reapp, clmd for 4,000: unplcd in '03 (tried cheek pieces, h'cap): lightly rcd '02, auct mdn scorer for M Johnston: wng form at 5f: acts on firm & soft, gall or sharp trk. *nk* **42**
1 May'02 Redc 5fm 78- E: 2 Apr'02 Ripo 5g/f 68- D:

3403 **SO SOBER 21** [4]6-8-8 (37) R Winston 50/1: 0430005: Mid-div & hmpd early, styd on late for press, not able to chall: see 1544, 312. *hd* **46$**

2619 **SHIELALIGH 53** [14]3-8-8 p (70) M Fenton 10/1: 3-003066: Dwelt, mid-div, not pace to chall: see 1901. *1½* **44**

3757 **AMERICAN COUSIN 7** [9]9-8-10 (52) A Nicholls 12/1: 5006657: Dwelt, late prog, no dngr. *1¾* **38**

3545 **CAYMAN MISCHIEF 15** [5]4-8-3 (27) J Bramhill 100/1: 00-0068: Towards rear, only mod prog. *1¾* **26**

3591 **ROXANNE MILL 13** [11]6-9-0 p (74) F Lynch 7/4 FAV: 2356129: Led/dsptd lead, wknd qckly from dist. *hd* **36**

3763 **PHARAOH HATSHEPSUT 6** [12]6-8-5 bl (26) P Fessey 100/1: 0060060: 10th: Dwelt, al rear: qck reapp. *½* **25**

3482 **BOND SHAKIRA 18** [10]3-8-3 (47) D Allan 50/1: 0400450: 11th: Chsd ldrs, btn dist: btr 3482 (AW). *1* **23**

3655 **AGUILERA 11** [7]3-8-6 (3ow) (40) V Halliday 100/1: 0004000: 12th: Al towards rear & outpcd. *1¾* **21**

1765 **CASH 90** [1]6-9-5 p (59) N Mackay(3) 28/1: 5000100: 13th: Mid-div, sn outpcd: abs: btr 1555. *shd* **30**

3482 **HIGH ESTEEM 18** [3]8-8-8 BL (47) P Makin(5) 100/1: 000-4000: 14th: Chsd ldrs till 2f out: blnks. *nk* **18**

3000 **ALASTAIR SMELLIE 38** [2]8-8-10 vis (45) D Fentiman(7) 33/1: 2210000: 15th: Dwelt & al outpcd rear. *hd* **19**

2731 **BLUE POWER 49** [6]3-8-13 (60) P Mulrennan(3) 8/1: 3531020: 16th: Sn strug rear: abs: btr 2380. *1¼* **21**

16 Ran Time 1m 1.66 (4.36) Owned: Castlemead Developments Limited Trained: Malton

3933

8.00 Tennants Antique And Fine Art Auctioneers Handicap Stakes 3yo+ 0-70 (E) **[68]**
£3708 £1141 £571 **7f rnd** **Soft 92** **-05 Slow** Inside

2755 **PERTEMPS MAGUS 48** [4] R A Fahey 4-9-3 (57) P Hanagan 4/1 FAV: 50000-31: Mid-div, hdwy halfway, led ins last & rdn clr, decisively: nicely bckd, op 6/1: 7 wk abs: eff at 5f, now suited by 7f: acts on gd & soft grnd: goes well fresh: see 2755. **68+**

3724* **IPHIGENIA 8** [3] P W Hiatt 3-9-11 (6ex) (71) P Makin(5) 9/1: 0245312: Led till hdd ins last, no ch with wnr but kept on: another gd run: acts on soft but btr 3724 (fast, easily). *3* **73**

3000 **BOISDALE 38** [10] S L Keightley 6-8-9 (49) D Fentiman(7) 20/1: 1650103: Chsd ldrs, kept on onepace. *1½* **48**

3155 **ROMAN EMPIRE 32** [5] K A Ryan 4-8-11 bl (51) G Parkin 10/1: 0413354: Mid-div, rdn & styd on onepace fnl 2f: acts on both AWs & soft grnd: see 2502, 1750. *nk* **49**

3571* **HEADLAND 14** [6]6-9-1 bl e (55) A Culhane 10/1: 3062215: Chsd ldrs, no prog dist: see 3571, 227. *1½* **50**

3324* **ZHITOMIR 24** [13]6-8-12 (52) P Mulrennan(3) 9/1: 00-16616: Dwelt, mid-div, kept on: see 3324. *½* **46**

3651 **FIREBIRD RISING 11** [1]3-8-12 (58) N Mackay(3) 16/1: 5036047: Mid-div, kept on late: see 3651. *3* **46**

3670 **BABY BARRY 10** [17]7-8-6 (46) Dale Gibson 12/1: 0003028: Held up, short of room 2f out, late prog. *shd* **33**

1661 **THUNDERCLAP 95** [2]5-9-1 (55) T Hamilton(3) 25/1: 0-120009: Chsd ldrs till dist: 3 mth abs. *½* **41**

3670 **OASES 10** [8]5-9-0 vis (54) F Lynch 11/2: 0003560: 10th: Slow away, only mod prog: btr 3670. *nk* **39**

2768 **PHAROAHS GOLD 48** [14]6-8-11 (51) T Eaves(3) 33/1: 1000400: 11th: Dwelt & al rear: 7 wk abs. *1½* **33**

3417 **BELLA BEGUINE 21** [11]5-8-7 bl (47) M Fenton 14/1: 0204450: 12th: Mid-div, btn 2f out: btr 3180. *1½* **26**

3562 **RISK FREE 15** [16]7-9-2 vis (56) R Winston 16/1: 535-0600: 13th: Mid-div, no ch fnl 2f: see 3102. *hd* **34**

CATTERICK   FRIDAY 13.08.04   Lefthand, Undulating, Very Tight Track

3767 **GOLDEN SPECTRUM 6** [15]5-9-1 vis (55) J Carroll 16/1: 3500300: 14th: Al bhd, qck reapp: btr 3670.   2½   28
3654 **NEMO FUGAT 11** [9]5-9-6 vis (60) A Nicholls 10/1: 5602520: 15th: Keen in mid-div, bmpd 4f out & sn   1¾   30
struggling: much btr 3654 & 3352 (fast).
15 Ran   Time 1m 29.8 (6.8)   Owned: The Spinal Injuries Association   Trained: Malton

---

3934   8.30 Charity Night Maiden Stakes 3yo+   (D)
£3435 £1057 £529   1m3f214y   Soft 92   -35 Slow   Outside

3161 **GIRONDE 8** [5] Sir Michael Stoute 3-8-13 VIS (88) F Lynch 1/8 FAV: 5-43031: Held up, smooth hdwy   93
& led over 3f out, easily pulled clr, any amount in hand: bckd at long odds on in first time visor: eff at 12f on
gd & soft grnd: found this a straightforward task, shld act as a confidence boost: see 3161, 1148.
3697 **RIGONZA 9** [3] T D Easterby 3-8-13 (62) D Allan 16/1: 0050342: Held up, hdwy to chall for 2nd   15   62
over 2f out, nvr any ch with wnr: see 3697 & 3263 (9f).
3697 **KYBER 9** [1] R F Fisher 3-8-13   R Winston 14/1: 5433: Handy, drpd rear halfway, eff to chall for   1¾   59
2nd over 2f out, no ch with wnr.
2987 **TRANSKEI 39** [4] Mrs L Stubbs 3-8-8   R Ffrench 50/1: 04: Cl-up & pulled hard early, no ch fnl 3f.   dist   4
WIZARDS PRINCESS [2]4-9-5   P Mathers(5) 66/1: 5: b f Wizard King - Chalice (Governor General)   13   0
Led till over 3f out, wknd qckly, t.o. on Flat debut: 3 mth jumps abs (no form, bmpr).
5 Ran   Time 2m 46.46(15.26)   Owned: The Celle Syndicate Incorporated   Trained: Newmarket

---

RIPON   SATURDAY 14.08.04   Righthand, Sharpish Track

Official Going SOFT.

3935   2.10 Ripon Horn Blower Conditions Stakes 2yo   (C)
£7308 £2772 £1386   6f str   Good/Soft 83   -05 Slow   Stands Side

3221 **DARIO GEE GEE 30** [7] K A Ryan 2-9-0 (95) N Callan 9/4 FAV: 122021: Trkd ldrs, ev ch ent fnl 1f,   97
forged ahd cl home: well bckd: v eff at 5/6f on fast & soft grnd: handles a sharpish or gall trk: likes to run up
with the pace: useful juv, see 3221 & 924 (debut).
3544 **RAINBOW RISING 16** [3] J Howard Johnson 2-8-11   R Winston 7/1: 42: Tried to make all, collared cl   ½   93
home: clr of rem: eff at 6f, handles firm, much imprvd on soft: must find a mdn, see 3544 (debut).
3357 **SHIVAREE 23** [6] M R Channon 2-8-11 (92) J Fanning 11/4: 31403: Nvr far away, no extra fnl 1f: 5   83
handles soft, best run came on firm in 3003 (Gr 2).
3590 **PROPELLOR 14** [2] A Dickman 2-9-2 (85) A Beech(3) 11/2: 3134: Trkd ldrs, btn dist: op 8/1.   2   83
3224* **WORD PERFECT 30** [4]2-9-2 (93) Dale Gibson 5/1: 3115: Dwelt, nvr nr ldrs: longer 6f trip: see 3224.   5   72
3239* **EL REY ROYALE 29** [5]2-9-0   N Mackay(3) 16/1: 16: Dwelt, chsd ldrs till wknd after halfway: btr 3239 (gd).   5   59
3633 **DEN PERRY 13** [1]2-8-11   F Norton 200/1: 600007: Al rear, t.o.: v highly tried.   9   36
7 Ran   Time 1m 15.30 (5.30)   Owned: Crewe And Nantwich Racing Club   Trained: Hambleton

---

3936   2.45 Donal & Bernadette Mcwilliams Memorial Maiden Stakes 3yo+   (D)
£4741 £1459 £729   5f str   Good/Soft 83   -27 Slow   Stands Side

3396 **TROODOS JET 22** [3] A Berry 3-9-0 (64) F Norton 2/1: 464-4441: Made all, styd on strongly fnl 1f,   62
drvn out: nicely bckd: eff at 5/6f on fast, soft grnd & f/sand: eff forcing the pace: beat little today, see 3396.
3852 **ELLIOTS CHOICE 3** [2] D Carroll 3-9-0 VIS (63) D Nolan(3) 7/2: 3600002: Trkd ldrs, slightly short   ¾   59
of room clsd, kept on & not btn far: tchd 6/1, qck reapp & first time visor, well clr rem: see 2945.
ARIESANNE [4] R A Fahey 3-8-9   G Parkin 8/1: 3: ch f Primo Dominie - Living Legend (Archway)   8   38
Slow away & bhnd, styd on late, nvr dngrs: half sister to a wng hdler.
1876 **RAETIHI 86** [5] A Senior 3-8-9   N Callan 33/1: 04: b f Wizard King - Foreno (Formidable)   Prom,   1¼   35
wknd fnl 1f: 12 wk abs: no form yet.
4 Ran   Time 1m 03.30 (5.50)   Owned: Mr Anthony White   Trained: Cockerham

---

3937   3.15 William Hill Great St Wilfrid Stakes Heritage Handicap 3yo+ 0-105   (B)   [102]
£29000 £11000 £5500   6f str   Good/Soft 83   +22 Fast   Stands Side

3792* **SMOKIN BEAU 7** [11] N P Littmoden 7-9-10 (98) J Fanning 16/1: 0040011: Made all far side, clr fnl   112
1f, easily: fast time: eff over 5/6f on any grnd/trk, likes Goodwood: best up with/forcing the pace: v well
h'capped & right back to smart best: win more races: see 3792.
3758 **PIETER BRUEGHEL 8** [5] D Nicholls 5-8-12 (86) W Ryan 16/1: 4001332: Made all stands side, no ch   5   89
with impress wnr far side: excellent run on the wrong side (5 of 1st 6 on far side): acts on firm & soft grnd.
3375 **HICCUPS 23** [12] D Nicholls 4-8-5 (79) P M Quinn 40/1: 0310633: Prom far side, kept on well but   1¼   79
no ch with impress wnr: longer priced stablemate of 2nd & fine run for new stable (prev with Mrs J Ramsden): cheek
pieces omitted today: see 3375 & 2074.
3434 **MACHINIST 21** [20] D Nicholls 4-9-0 (83) A Nicholls 6/1: 0-000124: Held up far side, fin well but   nk   82
too late: bckd from 9/1 & shorter priced s/mate of 2nd & 3rd: acts on fast, soft & polytrack: in fine form.
3461 **CD FLYER 20** [21]7-8-13 (87) P Mulrennan(3) 12/1: 0410435: Chsd ldrs far side, left bhnd fnl 1f.   ½   85
2076 **HIDDEN DRAGON 77** [19]5-9-8 (96) G Faulkner 20/1: 00-22006: Prom far side, onepcd when short of   1   91
room fnl 1f: 11 wk abs: won this race from today's mark last year: fair run in the circumstances, see 1043.
3792 **ARTIE 7** [6]5-8-12 (86) R Winston 12/1: 1001007: Chsd ldr thro'out stands side: on the wrong side.   hd   80
3880 **ABBAJABBA 3** [13]8-8-4 (78) J Bramhill 25/1: 6-000028: Mid-div far side, nvr dngrs: qck reapp.   2½   66
3622 **HALMAHERA 14** [4]9-9-11 (99) N Callan 14/1: 6605069: Chsd ldrs stands side, nvr dngrs: poor draw.   nk   86
3622 **CD EUROPE 14** [10]6-8-13 p (87) J Carroll 22/1: 0000600: 10th: Prom far side, wknd fnl 1f: 1   71
eye-cathcing run in 3622 (Stewards Cup).
3116 **BOND BOY 35** [16]7-9-2 (90) D McGaffin 14/1: 4060300: 11th: Nvr btr than mid-div far side.   shd   74
3646 **IMPRESSIVE FLIGHT 12** [9]5-9-2 (90) P Makin(5) 50/1: 10/536-00: 12th: Slow away, al rear far side.   ½   73
3758 **PARTNERS IN JAZZ 8** [1]3-8-8 (86) N Mackay(3) 12/1: 2221-500: 13th: Prom stands side, wknd dist.   shd   69

3622 **DAZZLING BAY 14** [18]4-9-13 bl (101) D Allan 28/1: 6035200: 14th: Dwelt far side, nvr in it.   1½   80
3428 **SIERRA VISTA 21** [3]4-8-6 (80) T Eaves(3) 25/1: 0051600: 15th: Chsd ldrs 4f stands side.   1   56
3248 **TOM TUN 29** [14]9-9-9 bl (97) T Hamilton(3) 14/1: 0-020420: 16th: Slow away, al bhnd far side: op 10/1.   1   70
3827* **JONNY EBENEEZER 5** [17]5-8-9 (4ex)bl (83) S W Kelly 5/2 FAV: 2114110: 17th: Chsd ldrs far side,   hd   56
btn 1.5f out: hvly bckd: prev in great form, but this was softer grnd than has been racing on recently: see 3827.
5037} **Resplendent Cee 280** [7]5-9-12 (100) M Fenton 28/1:0 3045 **Kingscross 37** [8]6-8-3 (77) F Norton 20/1:0
19 Ran   Time 1m 13.65 (3.65)   Owned: Turf 2000 Limited   Trained: Newmarket

---

3938   3.50 European Breeders Fund Handicap Stakes Fillies 3yo+ 0-80 (D)   [79]
£10179 £3132 £1566   1m2f   Good/Soft 83   -21 Slow   Inside

3719 **SIENNA SUNSET 9** [6] W M Brisbourne 5-8-4 (55) B Swarbrick(5) 12/1: 0-066241: Waited with, prog 2f   61
out, styd on well to lead cl home, rdn out: eff at 10f on firm & soft: likes a sharp trk: made most of fav mark for
new year: see 3373 & 1348.
3597 **CHARNOCK BATES ONE 14** [1] T D Easterby 3-8-10 (70) R Winston 9/2: 4601222: Chsd ldrs, short of   nk   74
room 2f out, ev ch ins fnl 1f, only just btn: nicely bckd: styd this longer 10f trip well & remains in fine form.
3287 **HENESEYS LEG 28** [4] John Berry 4-9-12 (77) K Darley 13/2: 45-11153: Prom, led 2f out till ins   1¼   79
fnl 1f, no extra cl home: another fine run under top-weight: see 2674.
3435 **RANI TWO 21** [7] W M Brisbourne 5-9-3 (68) P Makin(5) 12/1: 0-006544: Led till 2f out, no extra   1½   68
fnl 1f: stablemate of wnr: see 2284.
2800 **MISS PEBBLES 47** [3]4-9-9 vis (74) M Fenton 4/1: 4005125: Trkd ldrs, onepcd fnl 1.5f: 7 wk abs &   hd   73
new stable (prev with B Johnson): see 2800 & 2761.
3759 **ROUTE SIXTY SIX 8** [5]8-7-12 (4oh) (45) Dale Gibson 16/1: 0-062006: Chsd ldrs, no impress fnl 2f.   2   45
3630 **SAFFRON FOX 13** [8]3-9-5 (79) N Callan 5/2: 0-404207: Trkd ldrs, onepcd when hmpd ins fnl 1f,   8   63
eased: may well have battled for minor placings: see 3128.
3702 **FAIRLIE 10** [2]3-7-13 (59) N Mackay(3) 7/2 FAV: 6-500138: Held up, nvr a factor: op 9/2.   5   35
8 Ran   Time 2m 13.69 (10.39)   Owned: Mr Ray Bailey   Trained: Nesscliffe

---

3939   4.25 Ripon-Races Co Uk Maiden Auction Stakes 2yo (E)
£5023 £1546 £773   6f str   Good/Soft 83   -23 Slow   Stands Side

3457 **ZOMERLUST 20** [14] J J Quinn 2-8-7 R Winston 6/1: 31: Prom far side, styd on strongly to lead cl   76
home, rdn out: eff over a sharpish 6f: improved for being gelded & soft grnd: see 3457 (debut).
3633 **WIZARDMICKTEE 13** [12] A Bailey 2-8-7 M Fenton 8/1: 022: Tried to make all far side, collared cl   hd   74
home: op 6/1, well clr rem: eff at 6/7f on firm & soft grnd: see 3633 (f, frm).
      BOLD HAZE [10] Miss S E Hall 2-8-7 Leanne Kershaw(7) 66/1: 3: ch g Bold Edge - Melody Park   5   63
(Music Boy) Dwelt far side, sn chsd ldrs, left bhnd by front 2 fnl 1f: Apr foal, cost 9,000gns: half brother to sev
wnrs, incl sprinter Creche: dam a juv wnr, sire a top-class sprinter: bred to be speedy, eff at 6f on soft grnd.
      BOO [11] K R Burke 2-8-11 Darren Williams 12/1: 4: b c Namaqualand - Violet (Mukaddamah) Trkd   nk   66
ldrs far side, onepcd fnl on debut: 24,000gns Mar 1st foal: dam a wng miler, sire a useful 1m performer.
3682 **YORKSHIRE LAD 10** [6]2-8-7 S W Kelly 12/1: 065: b c Second Empire - Villaminta (Grand Lodge)   1½   59
Prom stands side, led that group cl home, no ch with far side: first home on the wrong side: £10,000 Apr foal: sire
a high-class miler: prob eff at 6f on gd/soft grnd: gd effort in the circumstances.
3682 **ALONG THE NILE 10** [8]2-9-0 A Beech(3) 9/2 JT FAV: 036: Chsd ldrs stands side, kept on under   ½   65
press, no ch with far side: nicely bckd: see 3682.
3582 **HOWS THAT 15** [9]2-8-7 N Mackay(3) 16/1: 007: ch f Vettori - Royalty (Fairy King) Held up stands   2   48
side, styd on late: op 12/1: cheaply bght Mar 1st foal: dam unrcd, sire a high-class miler in France.
      MARK YOUR CARD [16]2-8-2 D Allan 14/1: 8: Dwelt, nvr dngrs far side on debut.   1   45
3429 **TILLINGBORN DANCER 21** [17]2-8-9 J Fanning 33/1: 00009: Slow away, nvr in it far side.   shd   52
3699 **SHEKAN STAR 1** [7]2-8-4 Dale Gibson 33/1: 000: 10th: Nvr dngrs stands side.   nk   46
3735 **ADMITTANCE 9** [19]2-8-4 L Goncalves 16/1: 000: 11th: Mid-div when short of room dist far side, no dngr. shd   46
3412 **GENERAL MAX 22** [5]2-8-11 G Faulkner 33/1: 300: 12th: Led till ins fnl 1f stands side, wknd.   1½   50
3120 **ARTIC FOX 35** [3]2-8-9 K Darley 9/2 JT FAV: 500: 13th: Chsd ldrs 4f stands side: op 7/1.   3   41
2039 **MIDNIGHT IN MOSCOW 78** [18]2-8-11 Rory Moore(7) 16/1: 60: 14th: Keen & prom 4f far side: gelded.   nk   42
      Street Dancer [13]2-8-9 F Norton 20/1:0   3607 **Noodles 14** [1]2-9-0 BL(69) T Eaves(3) 20/1:0
3425 **Negas 21** [2]2-8-9 P Mulrennan(3) 66/1:0   **Judge Damuss** [15]2-8-11 J Carroll 33/1:0
18 Ran   Time 1m 16.35 (6.35)   Owned: Mr P J Carr   Trained: Malton

---

3940   4.55 Ripon Cathedral Handicap Stakes 3yo 0-90 (C)   [86]
£10593 £3478 £1739   1m4f60y   Good/Soft 83   -18 Slow   Inside

2919* **HEZAAM 42** [1] J L Dunlop 3-9-7 (79) K Darley 1/1 FAV: 01-05011: Waited with, styd on well for   86
press to lead cl home: well bckd, 6 wk abs, top-weight: eff at 7f, clrly stays 10/12f well: acts on fast & soft,
handles a sharpish or gall trk: runs well fresh: unexposed at this trip: see 2919.
3760 **YANKEEDOODLEDANDY 8** [2] P C Haslam 3-9-5 (77) Rory Moore(7) 3/1: 2123232: Tried to make all, worn ½   82
down cl home: op 5/2: another consistent run, see 3760 (14f).
3649* **HEARTHSTEAD DREAM 12** [3] J D Bethell 3-8-13 bl (71) J Fanning 9/4: 2151213: Trkd ldr, ev ch till   3   71
no extra ins fnl 1f, short of room cl home: see 3649.
3 Ran   Time 2m 45.82(12.32)   Owned: Mr Hamdan Al Maktoum   Trained: Arundel

Official Going Good/Soft

3941 2.05 Ngk Spark Plugs Rated Stakes Handicap 3yo 0-105 (B) **[108]**
£17400 £6600 £3300 6f str Good/Firm 30 -07 Slow Far Side

3778 **ALDERNEY RACE** 7 [6] R Charlton 3-9-5 (99) S Drowne 4/1: 5214121: Trkd ldrs, rdn & led ins last, **108**
held on well for press: suited by a stiff 6f on firm & gd/soft grnd: v progressive & useful: see 3778 & 3002.

3550 **MAHMOOM** 16 [4] M R Channon 3-8-12 (92) T E Durcan 11/1: 0601262: Chsd ldrs, rdn over 1f out, nk **100**
styd on well ins last, just held: continues on an upward curve, win again: see 3002 & 2764 (C/D).

3842 **NIGHTS CROSS** 6 [13] M R Channon 3-9-5 VIS (99) S Hitchcott(3) 17/2: 0000333: Chsd ldrs, styd on ½ **105**
for press, not pace of wnr: first time visor: running well: see 3842, 1732 & 1106.

3338 **BENTLEYS BALL** 24 [11] R Hannon 3-8-8 (88) R L Moore 12/1: 32-60034: Led/dsptd lead, went on over ½ **92**
2f out, edged left & hdd ins last, no extra: see 2521.

2950* **FLIPANDO** 42 [10]3-8-6 (86) P Hanagan 5/1: 10-42215: Led 3f, edged right & onepace bef dist: abs. nk **89**

3778 **KHABFAIR** 7 [3]3-9-1 (95) P Robinson 6/1: 312-4136: Chsd ldrs, short of room 2f out till dist, nk **97**
onepace & not able to qckn ins last: no room at a crucial stage & can prob improve on this: see 3778, 3388.

3002 **TRAYTONIC** 39 [8]3-9-7 (101) J Murtagh 7/2 FAV: 0-501307: Held up, rdn & not pace to chall fnl 2f. shd **103**

2212 **BOTANICAL** 71 [1]3-9-3 t (97) S Sanders 20/1: 1204-508: Held up, nvr able to chall: abs: see 1732. 1 **96**

3778 **VALJARV** 7 [2]3-8-12 (92) J P Guillambert(3) 18/1: 0044209: Dwelt, pushed along rear, nvr a factor. nk **90**

3199 **HATCH** 31 [9]3-8-8 T (88) R Mullen 66/1: 3130400: 10th: Dwelt & held up, nvr pace to threaten: t-strap. 2½ **78**

3279 **SPLIFF** 28 [5]3-8-11 (91) D Sweeney 14/1: 21-10000: 11th: Slow away & held up, al bhd: blnks omitted. 2 **75**

11 Ran Time 1m 13.20 (2.2) Owned: Britton House Stud Ltd Trained: Beckhampton

---

3942 2.35 Sportingodds Com Grey Horse Handicap Stakes 3yo+ 0-80 (D) **[77]**
£10101 £3108 £1554 6f str Good/Firm 30 -00 Slow Far Side

3137 **MIDDLETON GREY** 34 [5] A G Newcombe 6-9-1 bl (64) J Murtagh 4/1: 3203521: Held up, rdn & hdwy over **74**
1f out, led ins last, rdn clr: eff at 6f on turf, best at 7/8.5f on sand: acts on fast, gd/soft & loves fibresand:
well h'capped on turf & this drop to 6f suited well, can win again: see 255.

3562 **KIRKBYS TREASURE** 16 [2] A Berry 6-9-13 (76) T E Durcan 6/1: 3012022: Pushed along rear, styd on 2 **79**
from over 1f out, nvr threatened wnr: eff over a stiff 6f, 7f ideal: loves Musselburgh: see 2809.

3751 **YORKIES BOY** 8 [10] N E Berry 9-7-12 (10h)p (46) J F McDonald(3) 12/1: 0000403: Held up, styd on nk **49**
for press, nvr threatened wnr: now seems suited by chkpcs: see 1914.

3104 **NICHOLAS NICKELBY** 35 [1] M J Polglase 4-8-5 p (54) R L Moore 33/1: 6200434: Chsd ldrs, no extra nk **55**
from dist: see 3104, 1966.

3121 **MECCAS MATE** 35 [4]3-8-2 (55) P Hanagan 50/1: 0-565: Dwelt, chsd ldrs & led 2f out, hdd ins last nk **55**
& no extra: h'cap bow: eff at 6f on fast grnd, unplcd prev: see 2944.

3279 **SIR DESMOND** 28 [7]6-10-0 p (77) S Sanders 9/4 FAV: 4-300356: Trkd ldrs, keeping on onepace when 1 **74**
short of room ins last, shade closer with clr run: topweight: btr 3279 & 3123 (5f).

3641 **NAUTICAL** 8 [8]6-8-3 (52) W Supple 14/1: 4643027: Slow away, held up, hdwy when switched & short hd **48+**
of room ins last, nvr able to chall: closer with clr run: rtn to 7f + shld suit: see 3641, 2589.

3852 **LAUREL DAWN** 3 [12]6-8-11 (60) Natalia Gemelova(7) 25/1: 2506008: Chsd ldrs, btn dist: prefer 5f. nk **55**

3751 **SILVER CHIME** 8 [11]4-9-4 (67) P Robinson 22/1: 4156609: Led/dsptd lead till over 2f out, btn dist. ½ **60**

3443 **FIVEOCLOCK EXPRESS** 21 [3]4-9-13 p (76) I Mongan 16/1: 2005200: 10th: Held up, no impress fnl 2f. 1¾ **64**

3068 **TE QUIERO GB** 36 [6]6-9-5 t (68) Rachel Costello(7) 25/1: 2000000: 11th: Chsd ldrs till 2f out: btr 141 (AW). 1¼ **52**

3350 **SILVER MASCOT** 24 [9]5-8-8 (57) R Ffrench 4/1: 0012000: 12th: Keen & led, hung right/hdd over 2f out. 6 **25**

12 Ran Time 1m 12.82 (1.82) Owned: Mr Andy Beard Trained: Barnstaple

---

3943 3.10 Bedford Lodge Hotel Nursery Handicap Stakes 2yo (C) **[97]**
£8210 £2526 £1263 5f str Good/Firm 30 +15 Fast Far Side

3632 **NOVA TOR** 13 [1] N P Littmoden 2-8-10 (79) I Mongan 33/1: 0415401: Chsd ldrs, drvn to lead ins **88**
last, styd on strongly to win in a fast time: all wins at 5f, tried 6f: acts on fast, gd/soft & fibresand,
sharp/turning or stiff trks: useful, v tough & progressive filly: see 3082.

3607* **WISE WAGER** 14 [6] R A Fahey 2-8-4 (73) P Hanagan 7/1: 233312: Dwelt, sn led, edged right from 1¼ **79**
halfway, hdd ins last & not pace of wnr: rest well covered & can win again after 3607.

3743 **CANTON** 8 [12] R Hannon 2-9-7 (90) R L Moore 12/1: 6144533: Held up, briefly short of room over 2 **90**
1f out, styd on well ins last, no threat: consistent type, can win again: see 3743, 3266 & 1041.

3607 **KEY SECRET** 14 [7] M L W Bell 2-8-12 (81) J Murtagh 11/1: 11144: Trkd ldrs, rdn & onepace dist. ¾ **79**

3743* **PITCH UP** 8 [2]2-9-7 (90) S Sanders 4/1 JT FAV: 036115: Chsd ldrs till lost pl bef halfway, mod ¾ **86**
rally from over 1f out, nvr threat: hvly bckd tho' op 3/1: btr 3743 (made all, polytrack).

3825 **BAILEYS APPLAUSE** 5 [5]2-7-12 (3oh)bl (64) Hayley Turner(5) 66/1: 536006: Hld up, eff 2f out, onepace. nk **62**

3457* **WITCHRY** 20 [4]2-9-2 (85) P Robinson 4/1 JT FAV: 4317: Dwelt, held up, short of room over 1f out, 1 **77**
no impres ins last: btr 3457 (mdn).

3623 **EMPIRES GHODHA** 14 [5]2-9-4 bl (87) J F McDonald(3) 14/1: 3153468: Held up, eff 2f out, no impress. shd **79**

3607 **BRAG** 14 [9]2-8-12 (81) S Drowne 5/1: 240139: Chsd ldrs, btn dist: btr 3607 & 3343. 3 **64**

3071 **LADY ANN SUMMERS** 36 [14]2-8-7 BL (76) W Supple 16/1: 0340: 10th: Dwelt & al rear in first time blnks. nk **58**

3082 **DETONATE** 36 [15]2-8-6 (75) C Haddon(3) 25/1: 640630: 11th: Chsd ldrs, btn over 1f out: btr 3082. 1 **54**

2100 **MONASHEE PRINCE** 75 [11]2-9-2 (85) N Pollard 20/1: 215340: 12th: Prom, struggling fnl 2f: 11 wk abs. ¾ **62**

3691 **AZUREE** 10 [8]2-8-2 bl (71) R Smith 33/1: 2630430: 13th: Dwelt & sn struggling rear: btr 3691 & 3183. 10 **22**

13 Ran Time 59.23 (0.73) Owned: Mr Nigel Shields Trained: Newmarket

---

3944   **3.40 Hoofbeats Tours Maiden Stakes Fillies 2yo (D)**
£5707 £1756 £878   **7f str**   **Good/Firm 30**   **-14 Slow**   Far Side

3252 **CASSYDORA** 29 [1] J L Dunlop 2-8-11 S Sanders 7/2 JT FAV: 61: b f Darshaan - Claxon (Caerleon)   **97+**
Led after 1f, qcknd clr fnl 2f, v readily: well bckd: Feb first foal, dam smart at 1m/10f: eff at 7f, 1m sure to
suit: acts on fast & a stiff trk: much imprvd from intro, v useful, keep on side.

      PLAYFUL ACT 0 [13] J H M Gosden 2-8-11 R Havlin 7/1: 2: b f Sadler's Wells - Magnificient Style   2½ **87+**
(Silver Hawk) Dwelt, held up, styd on fnl 2f, nvr threat to wnr: Apr foal, half-sister wnrs over 1m/10f: dam smart
over 10f: eff at 7f, 1m+ sure to suit: acts on fast grnd: promising start, will improve & win races.

3626 **COUNTY CLARE** 13 [7] A M Balding 2-8-11 R Mullen 7/2 JT FAV: 023: Led 1f & chsd wnr 2f out, rdn   2½ **82**
& no impress over 1f out: longer 7f trip will suit: acts on firm & fast grnd: see 3626.

      BAHJA 0 [15] J H M Gosden 2-8-11 W Supple 7/1: 4: ch f Seeking The Gold - Valentine Waltz (Be   nk **81**
My Guest) Dwelt & held up, switched & kept on fnl 2f, no threat: op 6/1: 500,000gns Mar foal, dam a high-class
7f/1m performer: sire top-class on dirt in US: handles fast grnd, stays 1m & will improve.

      DONYANA 0 [8]2-8-11 P Robinson 10/1: 5: b f Mark of Esteem - Albarsha (Mtoto) Chsd ldrs, no   1¼ **78**
impress dist: Feb first foal, dam plcd at 12f as a 3yo: stay further & can improve.

2863 **LUNAR SKY** 44 [12]2-8-11 R L Moore 14/1: 06: Dwelt & held up, hung left & nvr threaten ldrs: abs.   1 **76**
3520 **ALPINE GOLD** 17 [10]2-8-11 I Mongan 25/1: 07: Held up, nvr on terms with ldrs: op 33/1.   3 **70**
      ALLIED CAUSE 0 [5]2-8-11 S Drowne 7/1: 8: Held up, eff over 2f out, sn no impress: bckd.   ½ **69**
3473 **LOLA SAPOLA** 20 [11]2-8-11 A Mackay 50/1: 09: Held up, eff 2f out, no impress on ldrs.   ½ **68**
      MOONMAIDEN 0 [4]2-8-11 T E Durcan 10/1: 0: 10th: Slow away & pushed along rear early, late prog.   shd **68**
      JENNA STANNIS 0 [3]2-8-11 D Sweeney 66/1: 0: 11th: Trkd ldrs, btn when hmpd over 2f out.   ½ **67**
3381 **ROMANTIC GIFT** 23 [2]2-8-11 M Tebbutt 25/1: 0000: 12th: Chsd ldrs, no impress fnl 2f.   nk **66**
3280 **NEVER AWAY** 28 [14]2-8-11 J P Guillambert(3) 25/1: 000: 13th: Held up, eff when hung left 2f out, sn btn.   1½ **63$**
3582 **BREGAGLIA** 15 [9]2-8-11 O Urbina 100/1: 000: 14th: Chsd ldrs, no ch fnl 3f.   16 **63**
14 Ran Time 1m 27.0 (3.1) Owned: Hesmonds Stud Trained: Arundel

---

3945   **4.15 National Horseracing Museum Classified Stakes 3yo+ 0-80 (D)**
£5486 £1688 £844   **1m2f rnd**   **Good/Firm 30**   **-22 Slow**   Centre

3128 **BOULE DOR** 35 [5] R Ingram 3-9-0 (85) N Day 6/1: 0-414201: Held up, smooth hdwy over 2f out &led   **92**
over 1f out, rdn out: op 5/1: eff at 9/10f on fast & gd/soft grnd, stiff or sharp/undul trks: lightly rcd, useful
& on the upgrade: see 2919, 2353 & 2024.

3598 **SOLO FLIGHT** 14 [7] H Morrison 7-9-9 (85) R L Moore 11/1: 206-2602: Held up, styd on for press,   2 **88**
not able to chall: retains ability but on a long losing run: see 1890.

3128 **MARBUSH** 35 [4] M A Jarvis 3-8-12 T (83) P Robinson 6/1: 32153: Held up, rdn & chall over 1f out,   nk **85**
sn edged left & no extra: first time t-strap, gd grn: stays a stiff 10f, rtn to 1m/9f could suit: see 2081 (mdn).

3108* **CELLARMASTER** 35 [1] E F Vaughan 3-8-9 (79) S Sanders 11/4 FAV: 352-314: Prom & briefly led 2f   1½ **80**
out, sn outpcd by wnr: nicely bckd, op 7/2: just btr 3108 (h'cap).

3615 **TRUENO** 14 [3]5-9-6 (82) S Drowne 9/2: 24-12055: Held up & pulled hard, eff 2f out, onepace: btr 2197.   1 **81**
3762 **BARKING MAD** 7 [8]6-9-8 (84) I Mongan 13/2: 4321626: Led & sn clr, hdd 2f out, wknd: bckd: btr 3762.   4 **77**
3689 **DUBROVSKY** 10 [2]4-9-6 (82) J Murtagh 7/2: 030-4067: Held up, eff over 3f out, btn dist: bckd.   6 **66**
4879) **ADJWAR** 294 [6]6-9-7 (83) P Hanagan 22/1: 440610-8: b g Ashkalani - Adjriyna (Top Ville) Chsd   10 **53**
ldr 4f, well bhd fnl 2f: reapp: dual clmr wnr in '03 for H Morrison, AW h'cap unplcd (rtd 72a): class stks & h'cap
wnr in '02: eff at 10/12f on fast & gd/soft, poss hvy: eff in cheek pieces, best form without: handles any trk.
1 Oct'03 York 10.4g/f 83-(83) D: 1 Jul'03 Donc 12g/f 85-(85) D: 2 May'03 Wind 11.6g/f 84-82 D:
2 Apr'03 Epso 12.0g/f 82-80 D: 1 Aug'02 Epso 12g/f 80-74 D: 2 Aug'02 Brig 11.8g/f 77-74 D:
2 Jul'02 Kemp 10g/f 77-75 C: 1 Jul'02 Brig 12g/s 76- E: 2 Jun'01 Sali 12g/f 84-75 D:
8 Ran Time 2m 07.11 (5.21) Owned: Friends and Family Trained: Epsom

---

3946   **4.45 National Stud Conditions Stakes 3yo+ (B)**
£12287 £4543 £2272   **1m4f**   **Good/Firm 30**   **-20 Slow**   Centre

1483 **ORANGE TOUCH** 105 [5] Mrs A J Perrett 4-9-1 (101) J Murtagh 7/1: 51/54-61: Trkd ldr, rdn & led   **115**
over 1f out, rdn cl, cmftblyr: 3 month abs: lightly rcd '03 (unplcd, rtd 100, Gr 3): juv mdn scorer '02: relished
step up to 12f, further will suit: acts on fast & gd: goes well fresh: lightly rcd 4yo & v useful, more to come.

3507 **REMAADD** 18 [3] M P Tregoning 3-8-7 (107) S Sanders 4/7 FAV: 132: Led, rdn & hdd over 1f out, sn   6 **108**
no impress on wnr: clr of other pair but btr expected after 3507 (Gr 3).

3264 **MUSANID** 28 [2] Sir Michael Stoute 4-9-1 (107) W Supple 9/4: 33/1-3633: Chsd ldr 5f out, rdn &   12 **88**
btn over 1f out, eased: btr 3264 & 1483 (10f).

3083 **PHOENIX NIGHTS** 36 [1] A Berry 4-9-1 (52) P Mathers 66/1: 0-050064: Held up, rdn & no ch fnl 4f.   dist **0**
4 Ran Time 2m 34.18 (5.98) Owned: Cheveley Park Stud Trained: Pulborough

---

3947   **5.15 Rutland Arms Hotel Rated Stakes Handicap 3yo 0-85 (D)**
£5026 £1906 £953   **1m str**   **Good/Firm 30**   **-06 Slow**   Far Side   **[88]**

3339 **KING OF DIAMONDS** 24 [8] J R Best 3-8-10 (70) W Supple 16/1: 262001: Edged right start, held up,   **78**
hdwy/hung left & led 2f out, rdn clr: eff at 6f, now suited by a stiff 1m: acts on fast, gd & polytrack, stiff/gall
or sharp/undul trk: lightly rcd, win again: see 1044 & 898.

3522 **DUMNONI** 17 [6] Julian Poulton 3-9-6 (80) I Mongan 6/1: 3041322: Held up, rdn & kept on fnl 2f,   3 **83**
no threat to wnr: stays a stiff 1m: proving consistent: see 3522, 2590 (7f).

3339 **SONG OF VALA** 24 [5] R Charlton 3-9-1 (75) S Drowne 5/1: 42-05063: Chsd ldrs, rdn & onepace fnl   1¼ **75**
2f: op 4/1: t-strap omitted: handles fast & soft grnd: see 2113.

3523 **SWEET INDULGENCE** 17 [7] Dr J D Scargill 3-9-7 (81) M Tebbutt 14/1: 13-00534: Chsd ldrs, hmpd 2f   1 **79**
out, onepace dist: see 1930.

3654* **BEST DESERT** 12 [4]3-8-7 (1oh) (66) N Pollard 16/1: 4200515: Chsd ldrs, no extra fnl 1f: btr 3654 (7f).   shd **65**
3542* **HABANERO** 16 [1]3-9-5 (79) R L Moore 11/2: 5313316: Led/dsptd lead till 2f out, sn btn: op 13/2.   1¼ **74**
3738 **KIBRYAA** 9 [3]3-9-6 p (80) P Robinson 3/1 JT FAV: 1-622457: Led early, btn over 1f out: btr 3738.   2 **71**

3581* **CASHBAR 15** [2]3-9-3 (77) J Murtagh 3/1 JT FAV: 218: Chsd ldrs, no impress fnl 2f: op 5/2: btr 3581. 2 64
8 Ran Time 1m 40.11(2.92) Owned: Mr D Newland Trained: Maidstone

GOODWOOD SATURDAY 14.08.04 Righthand, Sharpish, Undulating Track

Official Going Good

3948 5.20 Bbci Apprentice Handicap Stakes 3yo+ 0-75 (E) [85]
£3406 £1048 £524 **1m3f** **Good 40** **-57 Slow** Outside

3653 **GARSTON STAR 12** [8] J S Moore 3-7-12 (55) Laura Reynolds(7) 12/1: 3122051: Led & sn clr, hdd over 66+
2f out, led again over 1f out & pulled clr, readily: op 8/1: eff at 11/12f on firm & gd/soft grnd, loves Goodwood &
sharp/undul trks: likes to force the pace & went well for an appr rider tonight: see 3040, 2019.

3481 **TRAVELLERS TALE 19** [2] P G Murphy 5-8-8 (55) Derek Nolan(3) 16/1: 6006062: Chsd clr ldr & sn well 7 57
clr of rem, led over 2f out till over 1f out, no impress from dist: on a fair mark: see 249.

3726 **SERRAVAL 9** [6] G B Balding 6-8-12 (59) R Thomas 11/2: 00000/-23: Rear, hdwy over 3f out, kept 1¾ 59
on, nvr threatened front pair: see 3726.

3401 **GOLD GUEST 22** [9] P D Evans 5-9-4 (65) S Donohoe(3) 5/1: 441-1004: Dwelt, rear, switched & kept shd 65
on late, no threat: jock rec a 9-day careless riding ban: see 339.

3829 **PRIVATE BENJAMIN 5** [4]4-7-13 (46) Liam Jones(5) 16/1: 0105005: Keen & held up, eff wide, onepace. 1¼ 44

3785 **REBATE 7** [10]4-8-11 t (58) P Gallagher(3) 7/1: 3635056: V slow away & bhd, only mod prog. 1 55

3387 **ONCE 22** [3]4-9-10 BL (71) R Keogh(5) 25/1: 300-3007: Keen & bhd, eff over 4f out, sn btn, blnks. 2 65

3829 **MAN THE GATE 5** [7]5-8-12 (59) N Chalmers 7/2 FAV: 3621508: Bhd, no impress when badly hmpd over 1 52
2f out, no ch after: op 9/2, qck reapp: btr 3040.

3477 **ICARUS DREAM 19** [5]3-8-11 P (68) H Muya(3) 50/1: 4620209: Keen & held up, no ch fnl 3f: chkpcs. 8 49

3085 **SHOLAY 36** [1]5-7-12 (45) Thomas Yeung(3) 25/1: 0-000040: 10th: Keen & held up, btn/hmpd 2f out. 4 20

3443 **TREETOPS HOTEL 21** [11]5-8-11 p (58) Dean Williams(5) 4/1: 0002420: 11th: Dwelt & held up, eff 4f 2 30
out, sn btn: bckd: best at 7f/1m: much btr 3443 (7f) & 2440.

11 Ran Time 2m 28.61 (10.71) Owned: East Garston Racing Trained: Hungerford

3949 5.50 Bbc Southern Counties Radio Stakes Handicap 3yo+ 0-90 (C) [84]
£10192 £3136 £1568 **1m1f192y** **Good 40** **-02 Slow** Inside

3358* **SKY QUEST GB 23** [8] P W Harris 6-10-0 t p (84) D Holland 6/1: 26P21-11: Rear, smooth hdwy from 2f 93
out & led ins last, rdn clr: stays 12f, suited by 10f on fm, gd/soft & polytrack: v progressive, loves a fast pace &
can win again: see 3358.

3534 **PRIME POWERED 17** [4] G L Moore 3-9-6 (85) A Quinn(5) 7/1: 021-5502: Trkd ldrs, hdwy to chall 2f 2 89
out, sn not pace of wnr: stays 10f: see 1192.

3185 **DREAM MAGIC 31** [1] M J Ryan 6-9-3 (73) M Henry 22/1: 4-405003: Led/dsptd lead till ins last, shd 77
kept on onepace for press: well h'capped & signs of a revival under forcing tactics tonight: see 1235.

3550 **PARKVIEW LOVE 16** [6] M Johnston 3-9-11 (90) S Chin 25/1: 3000004: Led/dsptd lead early, onepace: 2 91
poss stays 10f: well h'capped: see 1167.

3553 **WATAMU 16** [7]3-9-6 vis (85) G Carter 2/1 FAV: 0012635: Dwelt, held up, hdwy wide over 3f out & nk 85
chall going well over 2f out, rdn & no impress from dist: see 3553, 2021 & 1865.

3535 **WEE DINNS 17** [10]3-9-6 (85) J F Egan 3/1: 0522126: Trkd ldrs, smooth hdwy to lead over 2f out, 1½ 83
hdd dist & no extra: btr 3535 (here) & 3255.

3625 **OCEAN OF STORMS 14** [5]9-9-9 t (79) R Thomas(5) 16/1: 1004527: V slow away & rear, only mod prog. 2½ 73

3265 **GIG HARBOR 28** [3]5-9-9 (79) K McEvoy 33/1: 1560408: Held up in tch, eff over 2f out, no impress. 1 72

3506 **PRAIRIE WOLF 18** [9]8-9-7 (77) Derek Nolan(7) 8/1: 0005109: Cl-up, hung right & fdd fnl 2f: btr 3313. 2 67

3256 **SILVER CITY 29** [2]4-9-11 (81) E Ahern 22/1: 2610-200: 10th: Sn cl-up, btn 3f out: much btr 2874. 1¾ 69

10 Ran Time 2m 08.35 (4.15) Owned: Colourful Band Trained: Berkhamsted

3950 6.20 Bbc South Today Stakes Handicap 3yo 0-80 (D) [85]
£5499 £1692 £846 **1m rnd** **Good 40** **+11 Fast** Inside

2922 **FLYING ADORED 42** [6] J L Dunlop 3-8-12 (69) K Fallon 6/1: 040-301: Rear, hdwy over 2f out & led 79
ins last, rdn out, shade cosily: gd time, abs: eff at 6/7f, now stays sharp 1m well: acts on fast & gd/soft:
lightly rcd & open to further improvement with stable returning to form: see 1270.

3738 **BORDER MUSIC 9** [9] A M Balding 3-9-6 (77) T Block(7) 9/2: 361-0032: Rear, switched wide & hdwy to 1½ 82
chall dist, not pace of wnr: op 3/1: gd run, worth a try at 10f now: see 3738, 879.

2729 **MASTER THEO 50** [8] H J Collingridge 3-9-3 (74) D Holland 14/1: 35-03303: Trkd ldrs, rdn & led nk 78
over 1f out, hdd ins last, kept on: 7 wk abs: another gd run: see 2325 & 2106.

3292 **ZANGEAL 26** [2] C F Wall 3-9-5 (76) R Hills 4/1 FAV: 43444: Chsd ldrs, chall over 1f out, onepace. 1¾ 77

2474 **ON THE WATERFRONT 59** [4]3-8-9 (66) E Ahern 9/2: 5420425: Cl-up & led after 3f till over 1f out, wknd. 2 63

3471 **BELISCO 20** [3]3-9-1 T (72) K McEvoy 16/1: 50-006: Trkd ldrs, outpcd fnl 2f: t-strap: btr 3471. 1¼ 66

3550 **LORD LINKS 16** [5]3-9-7 (78) J F Egan 11/2: 40-40007: Held up, hmpd over 2f out, sn no impress, 2½ 67
prob closer with a clr run: see 1847.

3724 **BERTOCELLI 9** [1]3-8-3 (60) A McCarthy 12/1: 0340068: Led 3f, btn 2f out: btr 2634 & 2272. 6 37

3724 **TRIFTI 9** [7]3-8-1 (58) J Mackay 10/1: 4000429: Rear, eff wide 3f out, sn btn: btr 3724 (7f). 3 29

9 Ran Time 1m 39.68 (2.28) Owned: Mrs Mark Burrell Trained: Arundel

GOODWOOD   SATURDAY 14.08.04   Righthand, Sharpish, Undulating Track

---

3951   6.55 European Breeders Fund Chichester City Median Auction Maiden Stakes 2yo (E)
£4105 £1263 £632   **6f str**   **Good 40**   **-08 Slow**   Stands Side

3824 **MOTH BALL 5** [1] J A Osborne 2-9-0 D Holland 3/1: 231: Made all, dictating pace early, drvn &   87
held on well ins last: op 9/4, qck reapp: eff at 6f on fast & gd grnd, sharp/undul or stiff trks: reportedly prone
to bad behaviour but clearly useful & can win more races: see 3824 & 3438.

3682 **YAJBILL 10** [3] M R Channon 2-9-0 (82) T E Durcan 100/30: 2322: Chsd ldr, rdn to chall ins last,   ¾   83
no extra cl-home: op 9/2: acts on firm & gd grnd: shld find a race: see 3682, 3406.

3368 **GOODWOOD SPIRIT 23** [6] J L Dunlop 2-9-0 K Fallon 2/1 FAV: 223: Rear, outpcd over 2f out till   ½   81
drvn & styd on strongly ins last, closing fin: crying out for 7f+, can be plcd to win soon: see 3368, 2859.

STORM SILK 0 [2] Saeed bin Suroor 2-9-0 K McEvoy 6/1: 4: b c Stormin Fever - Carpenter's Lace   ½   79
(Woodman) Dwelt & held up, eff to press ldrs over 1f out, sn no extra: op 4/1: $100,000 Feb foal, half-brother to
a US List 4yo wnr, dam unplcd juv: sire high-class dirt performer: eff at 6f, get further: handles fast grnd.

CORDAGE 0 [5]2-9-0 T P Queally 25/1: 5: ch c Dr Fong - Flagship (Rainbow Quest) Held up in   2½   71
tch, not pace to chall fnl 2f: weak in the mkt: Apr foal, dam a 10f 3yo scorer: likely improver over further.

3111 **TRANSGRESS 35** [7]2-9-0 Dane O'Neill 8/1: 306: Trkd ldrs, no impress fnl 2f: btr 2876.   5   56
3722 **AVERTING 9** [9]2-9-0 S Carson 28/1: 527: Handy, btn over 1f out: btr 3722.   ¾   54

PENKENNA PRINCESS 0 [4]2-8-9 S Sanders 14/1: 8: b f Pivotal - Tiriana (Common Grounds) Dwelt,   ½   47
in tch till outpcd fnl 2f: May foal, half-sister to a dual 1m wnr: dam plcd abroad.

BYRON BAY 0 [8]2-9-0 N Chalmers(5) 66/1: 9: Dwelt, sn pushed along rear, no ch fnl 2f.   3½   41
9 Ran   Time 1m 12.88 (2.88)   Owned: Mountgrange Stud   Trained: Upper Lambourn

---

3952   7.30 Jilly Cooper Obe Stakes Handicapfillies 3yo+ 0-85 (D)   [81]
£6825 £2100 £1050   **6f str**   **Good 40**   **-07 Slow**   Stands Side

3269 **CANTERLOUPE 28** [3] P J Makin 6-9-4 (71) S Sanders 5/1: 16-00001: Hung right throughout, rear,   80
hdwy for press from over 1f out & drvn to lead cl-home: eff at 5f, suited by a sharp 6f on fm, gd/soft & fibresand.

3479 **MADDIES A JEM 19** [10] J R Jenkins 4-9-6 (73) T E Durcan 9/1: 1135642: Trkd ldrs, drvn to lead   ¾   78
ins last, hdd cl-home: op 11/1: gd run: likes sharp/undul trks: see 1269.

3746 **DIXIE DANCING 8** [5] C A Cyzer 5-8-2 (55) J Mackay 10/1: 30-50423: Dwelt, held up, smooth hdwy &   1¼   57
rdn/led over 1f out, hdd ins last & not pace of front pair: encouraging turf return: eff btwn 6f/sharp 1m: see 1024.

3643 **WOODBURY 12** [6] Mrs H Sweeting 5-8-7 (60) N Chalmers(5) 25/1: 60-04104: Led till 2f out, onepace.   2   56
3693 **ESTIHLAL 10** [8]3-9-2 (73) R Hills 3/1 FAV: 1241435: Trkd ldrs, eff over 1f out, no extra: btr 3693 & 2925.   hd   68
3537 **MADRASEE 17** [4]6-9-0 (67) D Holland 12/1: 5050006: Trkd ldrs, no room over 1f out, kept on, no   2   56
threat: shade closer with a clr run: well h'capped filly, this was more encouraging, loves Brighton: see 329.

3512 **MYTHICAL CHARM 18** [1]5-7-12 (2oh)t (49) D Fox(5) 25/1: 0003507: Dwelt, sn outpcd, mod late prog.   ½   38
2880 **CRAIC SA CEILI 44** [13]4-8-10 (63) R Miles(3) 10/1: 50-00048: Prom, briefly led 2f out, sn outpcd: op 6/1.   ½   48
3870 **URBAN ROSE 3** [9]3-8-6 t (63) M Henry 25/1: 4-003049: Cl-up 4f, wknd qckly: btr 3870.   6   32
3693 **CHANCE FOR ROMANCE 10** [7]3-9-8 (79) S Chin 33/1: 50-2600: 10th: Cl-up, lost place from halfway.   3½   37
3673 **ROSES OF SPRING 11** [12]6-9-10 p (77) E Ahern 12/1: 3000600: 11th: In tch till halfway, sn bhd.   shd   35
3380 **BELLA TUTRICE 23** [11]3-8-12 (69) K Fallon 15/2: 0340300: 12th: Cl-up, on btn & eased.   ¾   25
3448 **CONCUBINE 21** [2]5-8-5 BL (58) Hayley Turner(5) 12/1: 3024000: 13th: Chsd ldrs, struggling fnl 2f: blnks.   ¾   12
13 Ran   Time 1m 12.81 (2.81)   Owned: R A Ballin & The Billinomas   Trained: Marlborough

---

3953   8.00 Racing Uk Live On 425 Median Auction Maiden Stakes 3-4yo (E)
£4115 £1266 £633   **7f rnd**   **Good 40**   **-09 Slow**   Inside

2907 **MAJORS CAST 43** [5] J Noseda 3-8-12 E Ahern 1/1 FAV: 31: Trkd ldrs, led over 2f out & sn pulled   83
well clr, readily: well bckd to confirm debut promise: 6 wk abs: eff at 7f, shld get 1m: acts on fast grnd,
sharp/undul trks: goes well fresh: open to further improvement: see 2907.

1270 **RANGOON 116** [6] Mrs A J Perrett 3-8-12 (78) K Fallon 2/1: 3-2252: Led till over 2f out, sn hung   2½   77
badly left, kept on late but had lost all ch with wnr: worrying hanging tendency displayed but also shows ability &
was given a v kind ride tonight, no surprise to see improvement upon this if steering can be corrected: see 1270.

3446 **TEXT 21** [2] Mrs Stef Liddiard 3-8-12 (65) J F Egan 6/1: 6320-023: Rear, kept on fnl 2f but no   1¾   74$
threat to front pair: op 8/1: flattered 3446.

3603 **INESCAPABLE 14** [3] W R Muir 3-8-12 S Sanders 25/1: 004: Keen, held up in tch, no impress fnl 2f.   6   63
2659 **KHAFAYIF 52** [4]3-8-7 (63) R Hills 14/1: 0305: Trkd ldr, btn over 1f out: btr 2169.   5   49
5 Ran   Time 1m 27.93(3.43)   Owned: Mrs Susan Roy   Trained: Newmarket

---

NEWBURY   SATURDAY 14.08.04   Lefthand, Flat, Galloping Track

Official Going Good (Good/Soft back straight)

3954   1.00 Stan James 08000 383384 Rated Stakes Handicap 3yo+ 0-95 (C)   [102]
£9275 £3518 £1759   **7f str**   **Good/Firm 20**   **+08 Fast**   Centre

3797 **SAWWAAH 7** [14] D Nicholls 7-8-7 (81) P Doe 16/1: 0003021: Mid-div, prog when short of room dist,   88
styd on well for press to lead cl-home: val bit more: qck reapp, fast time: eff at 7/10.3f, suited by 7f: acts on
firm or hvy grnd: gd confidence boost: see 3797 & 3443.

3782 **KOOL 7** [7] P F I Cole 5-9-1 (89) D Holland 5/1 JT FAV: 5535402: Held up, prog 2f out, styd on   ½   93
well ins fnl 1f, just held by wnr: qck reapp: gd eff in defeat & is h'capped to find similar: see 3782 & 1126.

3791 **TARANAKI 7** [15] P D Cundell 6-8-12 (86) L Keniry(3) 20/1: 0150003: Handy, styd on to lead 1f out,   hd   89
hdd cl-home: qck reapp: back to form after a couple of recent disapp displays: 4lb higher than last win in 1817.

3068 **CRAIOVA 36** [9] B W Hills 5-8-7 (4oh) (77) K May(7) 11/1: 0000004: Keen mid-div, prog 3f out, ev ch   hd   83
dist, kept on, not btn far in 4th: encouraging eff from out of h'cap & is on a winning mark: see 2172.

2679 **JAY GEES CHOICE 52** [2]4-8-9 (83) C Catlin 33/1: 0030405: Cl-up, led briefly over 1f out, sn   dht   85

1191

onepcd: 7 wk abs: encouraging performance & is on a fair mark: see 2076.

3775	**GREENSLADES 7** [13]5-9-7 (95) K Fallon 5/1 JT FAV: 4203066: Handy, ev ch dist, sn onepcd: qck reapp. 1			95
3782	**ARMAGNAC 7** [4]6-8-7 (1oh) (80) A Daly 17/2: 0023237: Missed break, sn mid div, kept on well fnl	hd		80

1f, nrst fin: qck reapp: prob lost ch at start: btr 3782 & 3375.

3555	**DIGITAL 16** [8]7-9-2 (90) A Culhane 9/1: 5222008: Held up, styd on fnl 1f: btr 3117 & 2684.	hd		88
1686	**JAZZ MESSENGER 94** [16]4-9-7 (95) R Hughes 8/1: 1006-609: Held up, rider still motionless 2f out,	shd		92+

styd on well fnl 1f under a kind ride: well bckd after long abs: given plenty to do over this shorter 7f trip, will
appreciate return to 1m+: keep in mind, see 1351.

3782	**MARSHMAN 7** [3]5-8-10 (84) M Hills 17/2: 0300000: 10th: Nvr nrr than mid-div: qck reapp: btr 1151.	¾		79
3583	**BOUNDLESS PROSPECT 15** [12]5-8-7 (4oh) Derek Nolan(7) 16/1: 0023160: 11th: Dwelt, al bhd.	nk		75
3565	**TUNING FORK 15** [11]4-9-1 (89) J Quinn 10/1: 0000030: 12th: Led, hdd over 1f out, wknd: op 7/1.	3		77
3537	Willhewiz 17 [6]4-8-7 (4oh)(77) T P Queally 50/1:0		3782	**Master Robbie 7** [1]5-9-0 (88) K McEvoy 25/1:0
2389	King Carnival 63 [10]3-8-7 (87) Dane O'Neill 40/1:0		3550	**Fancy Foxtrot 16** [5]3-8-7 BL(87) J Fortune 12/1:0

16 Ran   Time 1m 25.20 (0.90)   Owned: Fayzad Thoroughbred Limited   Trained: Thirsk

---

3955   1.40 Stan James Supporting Wessex Heartbeat E B F Maiden Stakes Div 1 2yo   (D)
£6422 £1976 £988   **7f str**   **Good/Firm 20**   -20 Slow   Centre

	ETLAALA [6] B W Hills 2-9-0 R Hills 5/2 FAV: 1: ch c Selkirk - Portelet (Night Shift) Made			94+

all, rdn cl fnl 1f, readily on debut: Feb foal, cost 160,000gns: half-brothers to wnrs at 6f/1m: dam won numerous
times at 5f, sire decent performer at 1m: eff at 7f, further will suit: acts on fast grnd & a gall trk: goes well
fresh: won with authority & has a bright future.

	COUNT KRISTO [11] C G Cox 2-9-0 Dane O'Neill 25/1: 2: br c Dr Fong - Aryadne (Rainbow Quest)	2½		86+

Slow away, prog 2f out, styd on nicely fnl 1f under hands-&-heels on debut: Feb first foal, dam unrcd: sire decent
performer at 1m/10f: eff at 7f on fast, will apprec further: pleasing eff on debut behind a potentially decent rival.

	AMEEQ [10] M P Tregoning 2-9-0 R Hughes 15/2: 3: b c Silver Hawk - Haniya (Caerleon) Mid-div,	1¼		84

prog 3f out, chsd wnr ins fnl 1f, no extra cl-home: op 13/2 on debut: May foal, half-brothers to wnrs at 7/10f:
dam successful at 12f: sire decent performer at 1m: eff at 7f, bred to apprec further: acts on fast grnd.

3511	**OCEAN GIFT 18** [9] D R C Elsworth 2-9-0 J F Egan 7/2: 64: Handy, prog bef 2f out, onepcd fnl 1f.	1¾		80
	WINGSPEED [4]2-9-0 D Holland 9/1: 5: b c Bluebird - Aneeda (Rainbow Quest) Handy over 5f, sn	nk		79

onepcd: op 13/2 on debut: Feb foal, cost 28,000gns: half-brothers to wnrs at 7f/1m: dam appreciate sire decent
performer at sprint dists: with Mrs A J Perrett.

3511	**SUPERSTITIOUS 18** [2]2-9-0 G Gibbons 66/1: 006: Nvr nrr than mid-div: see 3122.	3		73
3513	**STORM FURY 17** [1]2-9-0 J Quinn 14/1: 037: Cl-up till dist, wknd: btr 3513 (6f).	3½		66
	FRONT STAGE [7]2-9-0 K Fallon 5/1: 8: Al in rear: debut.	1¼		64
	PRINCE VETTORI [3]2-9-0 E Ahern 33/1: 9: Missed break, nvr a factor on debut.	shd		63
	BOLD DIKTATOR [8]2-9-0 Martin Dwyer 50/1: 0: 10th: Handy 5f, fdd.	¾		61

10 Ran   Time 1m 27.14 (2.84)   Owned: Mr Hamdan Al Maktoum   Trained: Lambourn

---

3956   2.15 Listed Stanjamesuk Com St Hugh's Stakes Fillies 2yo   (A)
£14500 £5500 £2750   **5f34y str**   **Good/Firm 20**   +02 Fast   Centre

3600*	**SUMORA 14** [11] G A Butler 2-8-8 J Fortune 6/1: 11: Held up, prog to lead dist, sn edged left,			105+

qcknd clr, readily: op 9/2, gd time: eff at 5f, 6f will suit: acts on fast grnd & polytrack, gall or v sharp trk:
v smart run & looks a juv of the highest order: one to follow: see 3600.

2983*	**CASTELLETTO 40** [4] B A McMahon 2-8-8 (85) G Gibbons 50/1: 320212: Handy, prog & ev ch dist, kept	1½		99

on, not pace wnr: 6 wk abs: fine run stepped up in grade bhnd a v smart rival: see 2983 (mdn auct).

3440	**RIGHT ANSWER 21** [12] A P Jarvis 2-8-8 (98) K Fallon 5/1: 412253: In tch, ev ch bef 1f out,	¾		97

onepcd ins fnl 1f: tchd 13/2: gd eff on rtn to 5f: see 3115 (h'cap).

2858*	**NOTJUSTAPRETTYFACE 45** [5] H Morrison 2-8-8 R Hughes 7/1: 14: Chsd ldrs, ev ch 1f out, sn no	shd		96

extra: 6 wk abs: creditable eff on only 2nd start & can rate higher: see 2858 (debut, mdn).

3576*	**ALL FOR LAURA 15** [6]2-8-8 T P Queally 10/1: 415: In tch, outpcd after 3f, rallied ins fnl 1f:	½		95

op 20/1: rtn to 6f looks sure to suit on this evidence: see 3576 (mdn).

3509	**ROODEYE 18** [10]2-8-8 (94) Martin Dwyer 7/1: 2156: Bhd, styd on fnl 1f: btr 3509 & 2795.	2		89
3081	**OH DARA 36** [9]2-8-8 (90) Dean McKeown 50/1: 137: Led early 2f out, wknd: btr 3081.	1¾		83
3361*	**RUBYANNE 23** [3]2-8-8 D Holland 7/1: 618: Rdn in rear, nvr a factor: bckd: btr 3361 (mdn).	shd		82
3509	**MARY READ 18** [7]2-8-13 (100) F Lynch 8/1: 313129: Led early & again 2f out, hdd dist, wknd.	nk		86
3440	**SATIN FINISH 21** [2]2-8-8 (98) A Culhane 12/1: 4140: 10th: Al in rear: btr 3258 (mdn, gd/soft).	5		66
3130	**SWEET ROYALE 35** [8]2-8-8 (84) K McEvoy 100/1: 2150: 11th: Cl-up 3f, wknd: btr 2505 (mdn).	8		44
1709*	**DANCE AWAY 93** [1]2-8-8 J Mackay 9/2 FAV: 10-20: 12th: Chsd ldrs 3f, fdd: bckd after long abs: v	4		32

disapp eff & surely something amiss: btr 1709 (mdn, gd/soft).

12 Ran   Time 1m 1.23 (0.93)   Owned: Sangster Family   Trained: Blewbury

---

3957   2.50 Gr3 Stan James Online Hungerford Stakes 3yo+   (A)
£29000 £11000 £5500   **7f str**   **Good/Firm 20**   +24 Fast   Centre

3564	**CHIC 15** [7] Sir Michael Stoute 4-8-11 (101) K Fallon 9/2: 621-6031: Handy, led dist, rdn clr			115

despite edging left fnl 1f: well bckd, fast time: stays an easy 1m on gd & firm: has not had rub of
green recently, much imprvd with more positive tactics today: v smart, see 3564.

3508	**SUGGESTIVE 18** [11] W J Haggas 6-9-0 bl (111) M Hills 8/1: 5214022: Held up, styd on well fnl 1f,	1¾		113

not rch wnr: continues to run well: see 3508 & 3124.

3636*	**RUM SHOT 13** [6] H Candy 3-8-8 (100) Dane O'Neill 20/1: 611-4013: Handy, led 2f out till dist, no	¾		111

extra: eff at 6f, career best run on step up to 7f: can win a Group 3: see 3636.

3124	**BABODANA 35** [13] M H Tompkins 4-9-0 (108) D Holland 9/2: 0-163554: Mid-div, prog 2f out, onepcd	¾		109

ins fnl 1f: ran to form of 3rd in 1486, see 951.

3508	**SO WILL I 18** [8]3-8-8 (108) R Hills 12/1: 1-310405: Mid-div, prog 3f out, onepcd fnl 1f: see 1372.	1¾		105
2949*	**QUITO 42** [5]7-9-0 bl (108) A Culhane 14/1: 6106516: Mid-div, prog 2f out, onepcd fnl 1f: 6 wk	hd		104

abs: shade below win of 2949 (6f, stks).

1167	**CARRIZO CREEK 122** [10]3-8-8 (109) J Fortune 20/1: 31115-07: b c Charnwood Forest - Violet Spring	¾		102

(Exactly Sharp) Keen cl-up till dist, wknd: long abs: prog juv in '03, mdn, stks & Gr 2 wnr: eff arnd 6f on firm & gd/soft: loves gall or sharp/undul trk: with B J Meehan.
1 Jul'03 Good 6gd 107- A: 1 Jun'03 Curr 6.3g/s 99- : 1 May'03 Brig 6.0fm 94- E:

3320	**MILLENNIUM FORCE 27** [12]6-9-0 (108) C Catlin 25/1: 0042338: Rear, prog dist, nrst fin: btr 3320.		¾	100
3441	**POLAR WAY 21** [9]5-9-0 (114) R Hughes 7/2 FAV: 201-0329: Mid-div, prog 2f out, sn edged left & onepcd: op 11/4: much more expected after val h'cap win in 3441.		1½	97
2820	**DUCK ROW 48** [3]9-9-0 (106) Lisa Jones 25/1: 440-2050: 10th: Handy over 5f, wknd: 7 wk abs.		½	96
2470	**JUST JAMES 60** [4]5-9-5 (113) E Ahern 16/1: 5201-000: 11th: b g Spectrum - Fairy Flight (Fairy King) Chsd ldrs 5f, sn wknd: 9 wk abs: Gr 2 wnr on fnl '03 start (also rnr-up twice): prog in '02, won a val h'cap & Gr 3 Jersey: eff at 6f, suited by 7f: acts on firm & fast, handles soft: goes well fresh: likes to come late: v smart performer at best but yet to find form this term.		1	99
	1 Oct'03 Newm 7g/f 116-(115) A: 2 Jun'03 Newm 7fm 115-(115) A: 2 May'03 York 6.0fm 115-(108) A: 1 Jun'02 Asco 7g/f 111- A: 1 May'02 Newm 6fm 88-80 C: 1 Nov'01 Donc 6sft 80- D:			
3062	**COUNTRY REEL 37** [1]4-9-0 vis t (110) K McEvoy 12/1: 05-04400: 12th: Led 5f, wknd: first try at 7f.		3½	87
3098	**MAKHLAB 35** [2]4-9-0 bl (108) Martin Dwyer 16/1: 1-554220: 13th: Chsd ldrs 5f, fdd: btr 3098 (List).		¾	85

13 Ran   Time 1m 23.99 (u 0.31)   Owned: Cheveley Park Stud   Trained: Newmarket

---

3958   3.25 Gr2 Stan James Geoffrey Freer Stakes 3yo+   (A)
£62000 £22000 £11000   1m5f61y   Good/Firm 20   -22 Slow   Outside

4633}	**MUBTAKER 314** [4] M P Tregoning 7-9-3 (130) R Hills 30/100 FAV: 21/1112-1: ch c Silver Hawk - Gazayil (Irish River) Cl-up, led on bit over 2f out, pushed clr, easily: well bckd, reapp: v prog in '03, won List, Gr 3 & Gr 2 (this race), also less than 1L 2nd in Gr 1 Arc: won this race again in '02: eff at 10/13f on firm & hvy: goes well fresh: high-class 7yo, fine comeback & Gr 1 success beckons.			123+
	2 Oct'03 Long 12sft 132- A: 1 Sep'03 Kemp 12g/f 126-(118) A: 1 Aug'03 Newb 13.3fm 122-(117) A: 1 Jul'03 Newb 10.0fm 117- A: 1 Aug'02 Newb 13.2fm 121- A: 2 Jul'02 Newm 12g/s 119- A: 1 Oct'01 Newm 12g/f 119- A: 2 Sept'01 Newb 11fm 118- A: 1 Jun'01 Newm 12fm 119- A:			
2817	**DUBAI SUCCESS 49** [3] B W Hills 4-9-3 (112) M Hills 9/2: D3-14022: Led till over 2f out, kept on but no ch with wnr: 7 wk abs: gd eff bhnd high-class rival: see 2817 & 1230.		2½	114
3563	**COMPTON BOLTER 15** [2] G A Butler 7-9-3 (107) R Hughes 16/1: 3250653: Held up, prog 4f out, onepcd fnl 1.5f: needs to rtn to List/Gr3 grade: see 1862 & 1596.		1¾	111
3030	**THE GREAT GATSBY 38** [1] J H M Gosden 4-9-3 BL (112) J Fortune 16/1: 4/225-304: Cl-up, wknd dist in first time blnks: twice below 3rd in 2636 (reapp).		5	104

4 Ran   Time 2m 50.69 (5.59)   Owned: Mr Hamdan Al Maktoum   Trained: Lambourn

---

3959   4.00 Stan James Supporting Wessex Heartbeat E B F Maiden Stakes Div 2 2yo   (D)
£6396 £1968 £984   7f str   Good/Firm 20   -30 Slow   Centre

3438	**HALLHOO 21** [2] M R Channon 2-9-0 A Culhane 2/1: 31: Made all, edged right under press dist, rdn out: well bckd: eff at 6f, apprec step up to 7f: acts on fast grnd & a gall trk: gd eff to defy greeness & can progress: see 3438 (debut).			88
	TITIAN TIME [9] J H M Gosden 2-8-9 J Fortune 7/1: 2: b f Red Ransom - Timely (Kings Lake) Rear, prog to chase ldrs & hmpd ins fnl 1f, kept on, just held: Feb foal, half-sister to Group wnr at 5f: dam wnr at 1m: eff at 7f, shapes as further will suit: acts on fast grnd: shld find similar.		½	81
	MAYADEEN [8] M P Tregoning 2-9-0 Martin Dwyer 12/1: 3: b c King's Best - Inaaq (Lammtarra) Rear, prog 2f out, styd on well fnl 1f: op 20/1 on debut: Jan first foal, dam successful at 10f: sire Gr 1 wnr at 1m: eff at 7f, bred to apprec further: acts on fast grnd: pleasing eff & op to improvement.		½	85
	BERTROSE [6] J L Dunlop 2-9-0 E Ahern 25/1: 4: ch c Machiavellian - Tularosa (In The Wings) Rear, styd on well fnl 1f, nrst fin: debut: Mar foal, half-brother to wnrs at 1m/11f: dam successful abroad, sire high-class miler: eff at 7f on fast grnd, further will suit: encouraging start.		hd	84
	SPANISH RIDGE [7]2-9-0 P Doe 33/1: 5: Slow away, prog bef 1f out, nrst fin: debut: eff at 7f, 1m+ will suit: acts on fast grnd: can improve.		1½	81
3337	**SWELL LAD 24** [1]2-9-0 T P Queally 33/1: 006: Chsd ldrs over 5f, no extra: see 2578.		2½	76
	SAREM [3]2-9-0 R Hills 15/8 FAV: 7: b c Kingmambo - Storm Beauty (Storm Cat) Cl-up, ev ch dist, wknd: well bckd: Jan foal, cost $600,000: half-brother successful abroad: dam List wnr abroad, sire high-class miler: with M P Tregoning & will learn from this.		2½	71
	RAPID FLOW [4]2-9-0 R Hughes 12/1: 8: Handy over 5f, wknd: debut.		3½	64
2695	**GOLDEN DYNASTY 51** [5]2-9-0 P Dobbs 25/1: 09: Keen handy, wknd 2f out: 7 wk abs.		shd	63
3511	**WEMBURY POINT 18** [11]2-9-0 Dane O'Neill 33/1: 00: 10th: Handy 5f, sn fdd.		2	59
	DECORATION [10]2-9-0 K Fallon 12/1: 0: 11th: Mid-div 5f, fdd on debut.		3	53

11 Ran   Time 1m 27.85 (3.55)   Owned: Sheikh Ahmed Al Maktoum   Trained: West Ilsley

---

3960   4.35 Andrew Strode-Gibbons Supporting Wessex Heartbeat Handicap Stakes 3yo+ 0-85 (D)   [83]
£6474 £1992 £996   5f34y str   Good/Firm 20   -07 Slow   Centre

3763	**STRAWBERRY PATCH 7** [11] Miss L A Perratt 5-7-12 p (53) J Mackay 10/1: 0-005021: Handy, prog under press dist, styd on well to lead cl-home: op 16/1, qck reapp: eff at 5/6f on firm & fast grnd: eff with cheek pieces: gd confidence boost for this well h'capped 5yo who had been on a long losing run: see 3763.			61
3033	**BRAVE BURT 38** [4] D Nicholls 7-9-11 (80) K Fallon 6/1: 013-0002: Led, hung right ins fnl 1f, hdd cl-home: op 9/2: right back to form & is on a winning mark: see 2253.		nk	86
944	**ROMAN QUINTET 140** [3] D W P Arbuthnot 4-8-5 (60) E Ahern 33/1: 402-0003: Cl-up, hung right under press ins fnl 1f, just held when short of room cl-home: long abs: gd run in defeat & is on fair mark.		1½	62
3852	**SEVEN NO TRUMPS 3** [6] J M Bradley 7-9-7 p (76) D Holland 10/1: 4002004: Al handy, onepcd fnl 1f.		½	77
3827	**FURTHER OUTLOOK 5** [9]10-10-0 (83) Dane O'Neill 20/1: 2300065: Rear, prog 2f out, styd on ins fnl 1f: qck reap, top-weight: far from disgraced: see 2698 & 2266.		nk	83
3792	**MALAPROPISM 7** [13]4-9-12 (81) A Culhane 8/1: 0060406: Keen bhd, prog 2f out, nrst fin: qck reapp.		hd	80
3628	**SIR EDWIN LANDSEER 13** [12]4-9-10 (80) G Hind 16/1: 0-000007: Rear, prog 2f out, nrst fin: see 3269.		½	67
3792	**DANCING MYSTERY 7** [10]10-9-11 (80) S Carson 12/1: 0145008: Nvr nrr than mid-div: qck reapp.		¾	76
3640	**DOUBLE M 12** [8]7-8-11 vis (66) R Hughes 4/1 FAV: 1366129: Nvr nrr than mid-div: op 5/1: btr 3640.		nk	61
3792	**SALVIATI 7** [1]7-10-0 p (83) C J Davies(7) 9/1: 0045100: 10th: Al rear: qck reapp: btr 3628.		nk	77
3203	**SWEET CANDO 30** [5]3-8-4 p (62) Martin Dwyer 33/1: 6020500: 11th: Handy, wknd dist: see 2731.		¾	54

NEWBURY **SATURDAY 14.08.04 Lefthand, Flat, Galloping Track**

3792 **ZARZU 7** [7]5-9-9 (78) J Fortune 9/2: 0001650: 12th: Cl-up, fdd dist: qck reapp: disappointing. *1* **67**
3903 **THE LORD 2** [2]4-9-13 P (82) A Daly 14/1: 000-3060: 13th: Handy 3f, wknd: qck reapp & pieces. *2* **65**
13 Ran Time 1m 1.65 (1.35) Owned: Mrs Lucille Bone Trained: Ayr

3961 **5.05 Stan James Teletext P630 Handicap Stakes 3yo 0-85 (D)** **[92]**
£6611 £2034 £1017 **1m2f6y** **Good/Firm 20** **-32 Slow** Outside

3578 **NIGHTSPOT 15** [3] R Charlton 3-9-3 (81) Martin Dwyer 13/2: 515-6321: Made all, held on gamely co home: prev eff at 6f, now suited by 10f: acts on fast, handles soft grnd: lightly rcd performer who is op to more improvement: see 3578 & 2994. **85**
3468 **MAZUNA 20** [13] C E Brittain 3-8-4 (68) P Doe 12/1: 406-1232: Chsd ldrs, fin v strongly. post came too soon: op 8/1: continues to run well & can find similar back at 12f: see 3468 & 3255. *nk* **72**
3801+**CREDIT 6** [12] R Hannon 3-9-11 (5ex) (89) R Hughes 7/1: 3100413: Handy, prog when short of room 2f out & again dist, styd on well ins fnl 1f, just held in 3-way photo: op 5/1 on qck reapp: shade unlucky: see 3801. *nk* **92**
3237* **HERMITAGE COURT 29** [8] B J Meehan 3-9-6 (84) J Fortune 4/1 FAV: 14: Cl-up, ev ch bef 2f out, styd on, not btn far in 4th: op 6/1: eff at 1m, improved for step up to 10f: fine eff on only 2nd ever start. *½* **86**
3358 **WHITSBURY CROSS 23** [6]3-9-2 (80) L Keniry(3) 8/1: 5510435: Chsd ldrs, prog bef 1f out, nrst fin. *nk* **81**
3462 **KILLMOREY 20** [1]3-7-12 (62) J Mackay 14/1: 0026: Rear, kept on fnl 1f: eff at 1m/10f. *¾* **61**
3453 **TOP SPEC 21** [7]3-8-12 (76) P Dobbs 25/1: 1-005027: Dwelt, prog 3f out, nrst fin: btr 3453. *¾* **73**
3236 **WINNERS DELIGHT 29** [10]3-9-1 (79) K Fallon 11/2: 0055308: Held up, prog when no room dist, sn btn. *¾* **74**
2917 **DONNA VITA 42** [2]3-9-7 (85) J Quinn 40/1: 10-409: Nvr nrr than mid-div: 6 wk abs: btr 1619. *½* **79**
2732 **HAWKIT 50** [9]3-9-0 (78) D Tudhope(7) 16/1: 2101200: 10th: Bhd, prog 4f out, wknd fnl 2f: 7 wk abs. *1½* **70**
3734 **IRISH BLADE 9** [14]3-8-6 (70) Dane O'Neill 14/1: 0-43000: 11th: Handy 1m, sn wknd. *½* **61**
3522 **CONVINCE 17** [4]3-8-13 (77) A Daly 40/1: 0005650: 12th: Al in rear: see 1665. *½* **67**
3862 **MR JACK DANIELLS 3** [15]3-8-11 (75) R Miles(3) 6/1: 6304140: 13th: Handy 1m, wknd: too sn? *3* **61**
2680 **GRETNA 52** [5]3-8-13 BL (77) T P Queally 33/1: 6-10000: 14th: Handy 7f, fdd: 7 wk abs & blnks. *2½* **59**
14 Ran Time 2m 8.07(5.27) Owned: Mr D J Deer Trained: Beckhampton

BATH **SUNDAY 15.08.04 Lefthand, Turning Track with Uphill Finish**

Official Going GOOD/FIRM.

3962 **2.30 Ferndale Band Club Maiden Auction Stakes 2yo (F)**
£3350 £957 £479 **5f11y rnd** **Good/Firm 20** **-24 Slow** Far Side

3445 **DISPOL IN MIND 22** [11] I A Wood 2-8-2 P Doe 7/1: 231: Slow away, held up, hdwy 2f out, styd on to lead appr fnl 1f, rdn out: deserved win: eff at 5f on fast & gd grnd: see 3445, 3014. **69**
3728 **TANNING 10** [8] H Morrison 2-8-2 J F McDonald(3) 8/1: 62: Handy, eff over 1f out, kept on to go 2nd ins last: imprvd for debut & eff at 5f on gd: shld find a modest race, prob at 6f: see 3728. *¾* **66**
3756 **SAUCEPOT 9** [7] M D I Usher 2-8-2 (63) Hayley Turner(5) 9/1: 06203: Handy, hdwy to lead over 1f out, sn hdd & onepace: back to form of 3445. *shd* **66**
2976 **DANZILI BAY 41** [2] R M Beckett 2-8-13 N Chalmers(5) 16/1: 44: Chsd ldrs, eff & carr left appr fnl 1f, no extra ins last: joc rec a 2 day careless riding ban: 6 wk abs: btr eff conceding weight all round. *¾* **75**
2287 **ATSOS 68** [4]2-8-11 R L Moore 14/1: 6605: b g Imperial Ballet - Victim of Love (Damister) Sn outpcd, styd on well over 1f out, nrst fin: 10 wk abs: been gelded: May foal, cost E30,000: half-brother to a 5f juv wnr, dam 7f/1m scorer: crying out for a step up to 6f. *1¾* **68**
3745 **TURTLE MAGIC 9** [5]2-8-2 p (53) C Haddon(7) 20/1: 6640346: Handy, wknd fnl 1f: exposed: see 3745. *2* **53**
LITTLE WARNING [12]2-8-2 F Norton 9/1: 7: b f Piccolo - Iltimas (Dayjur) In tch, nvr a factor on debut: Apr foal, cost 8,000gns: half-sister to wnrs over 5/6f, dam 5/6f scorer: bred for speed. *nk* **52**
3513 **BEAU MARCHE 18** [3]2-8-7 D Sweeney 33/1: 58: Al bhd: see 3513. *nk* **56**
3686 **EDGE FUND 11** [6]2-8-13 (79) S Drowne 2/1 FAV: 3323039: In tch, hdwy to lead briefly 2f out, wkng when hmpd appr fnl 1f: btr 3686 (6f). *nk* **61**
3639 **NIGHT OUT 13** [1]2-8-6 D Holland 4/1: 060: 10th: b f Night Shift - My Lucky Day (Darshaan) Led till 2f out, wknd: Mar first foal, cost E35,000: bred to apprec 7f/1m in time. *1* **51**
SILVER CREEK [9]2-8-7 C Catlin 40/1: 0: 11th: Slow away & al bhd. *8* **28**
11 Ran Time 1m 02.52 (2.22) Owned: Thomas & Susan Blane Trained: Upper Lambourn

3963 **3.00 Totesport Com Mile Handicap Stakes Fillies 3yo+ 0-75 (E)** **[75]**
£5239 £1612 £806 **1m5y rnd** **Good/Firm 20** **+01 Fast** Inside

3748 **DIDOE 9** [7] P W Hiatt 5-8-0 (47) Joanna Badger 12/1: 0-000121: Led early, led again over 2f out, sn rdn clr: winning form over 1m/10f on firm & fast grnd, prob handles any trk, likes Bath: in form & improving. **53**
3423 **BRAZILIAN TERRACE 22** [8] M L W Bell 4-10-0 (75) Hayley Turner(5) 4/1 FAV: 0113022: Chsd ldrs, eff to over 1f out, kept on ins last, not pace of wnr: tough: see 3423, 2414. *1¾* **77**
3724 **BEAUTY OF DREAMS 10** [15] M R Channon 3-8-7 (61) C Catlin 25/1: 50-00053: Chsd ldrs wide, eff over 1f out, kept on, not pace of wnr: stays 1m, shapes likes even further will suit: see 2904. *1* **61**
3079 **HIRAYNA 37** [9] W M Brisbourne 5-8-3 (50) B Swarbrick(5) 20/1: 3044: In tch, outpcd over 2f out, rallied fnl 1f: stays 1m on fast grnd: see 2549. *hd* **49**
3746 **TOKEWANNA 9** [3]4-8-3 t (50) D Kinsella 25/1: 0-003045: Keen in tch, onepace dist: prob stays 1m. *nk* **48**
3174 **ISLAND RAPTURE 33** [11]4-9-10 (71) D Holland 13/2: 0040326: Cl-up, wknd fnl 1f: see 3174, 1891. *¾* **67**
3346 **HASAYIS 25** [5]3-9-0 (68) W Supple 15/2: 00-1047: Bhd, late gains, no dngr: see 1086 (mdn, sft). *½* **63**
3540 **MARNIE 17** [2]7-8-1 (48) N Mackay(3) 8/1: 0225558: Held up, btn 2f out: see 2032 (clmr), 845. *2* **39**
3788 **ENNA 8** [14]5-7-13 (1ow) (45) F Norton 7/1: 0040429: Slow away & al bhd: btr 3788, 1284. *¾* **35**
2993 **LARK IN THE PARK 40** [4]4-7-12 (5oh) (40) D Fentiman(7) 25/1: 06-00050: 10th: Al bhd: see 2604. *1* **32**
3540 **KINDNESS 17** [6]4-8-3 (50) R Thomas(5) 11/1: 0022020: 11th: Chsd ldr, wknd 2f out: btr 3540. *½* **36**
3731 **NAUGHTY GIRL 10** [13]4-7-13 vis t (46) F P Ferris(3) 7/1: 0544020: 12th: Slow away & al bhd: see 3731. *2* **28**
3672* **ICECAP 12** [10]4-8-6 (53) C Haddon(7) 12/1: 5002-010: 13th: Led after 1f till 2f out, wknd: btr 3672. *1* **33**
3731 **ANNIJAZ 10** [12]7-8-1 (48) R L Moore 16/1: 4600000: 14th: Al bhd: see 1540. *1½* **25**
14 Ran Time 1m 39.8 (1.5) Owned: Mrs Marion Wickham Trained: Banbury

---

3964   3.30 Bathwick Tyres Lady Riders' Derby Rated Stakes Handicap 3yo+ 0-90 (C)   **[77]**
£16250 £5000 £2500   **1m3f144y**   **Good/Firm 20**   **-05 Slow**   Inside

3345 **TENDER FALCON 25** [15] R J Hodges 4-9-8 (71) Miss C Hannaford 20/1: 14-51021: Held up, gd hdwy to   **83**
lead over 1f out, sn pushed clr: eff over 10/12f on firm & fast, handles gd/soft & likes stiff trks: tough &
genuine, well rdn off what is often a fast pace in these contests: see 2707, 2099.
3678 **BUCKS 11** [2] D K Ivory 7-10-2 (79) Miss L J Harwood(3) 6/1: 1125022: Slow away, sn in tch, eff 2f   5   **83**
out, not pace of wnr: another gd run: see 3678, 3444.
3694 **VOICE MAIL 11** [12] A M Balding 5-10-0 (77) Miss M Sowerby(5) 12/1: 0203403: Held up, eff 2f out,   3   **77**
kept on same pace: tough & consistent: loves Bath: see 3083, 2665.
3637 **GALLANT BOY 14** [6] P D Evans 5-9-4 (2oh)vis t (65) Miss E Folkes(3) 16/1: 6405444: In tch, hmpd &   1¼   **65**
lost pl 4f out, onepace over 2f out: on long losing run: see 549.
3066 **SANGIOVESE 38** [3]5-9-13 (76) Mrs S Bosley 13/2: 5231105: In tch trav well, hdwy to lead over 3f   shd   **74**
out till over 1f out, wknd: not disgraced: see 2681, 2354.
3815 **JACARANDA 7** [11]4-9-8 (71) Miss N Carberry 10/1: 0024136: In tch, no extra 2f out: best 3404 (10f).   5   **61**
2233 **BARMAN 71** [14]5-10-3 t (80) Ms C Williams 8/1: 42251-07: Trkd ldr, wknd over 1f out: see 2233.   ½   **69**
3681 **RAJAM 11** [13]6-10-0 vis (77) Miss Kelly Harrison(3) 12/1: 0652248: In tch 10f, wknd: see 3217, 1796.   3   **62**
3217* **FLYING SPIRIT 31** [10]5-9-13 (76) Miss E J Jones 11/2: 102-1119: In tch, wknd 2f out: best on   nk   **60**
sharp/undul trks as in 3217.
3641 **A ONE 13** [7]5-10-6 (83) Miss S Brotherton 16/1: 1101150: 10th: Led till 3f out, wknd: lngr trip.   2   **64**
2708 **LATALOMNE 52** [4]10-9-13 (76) Mrs N Wilson(3) 20/1: 500///0-140: 11th: Nvr a factor: unplcd h'cap   nk   **56**
chase rnr since 2708, 2525.
3360 **MINORITY REPORT 24** [5]4-10-1 (78) Mrs S Cumani(3) 4/1 FAV: 3020: 12th: Al bhd: btr 3360 (1m, mdn).   nk   **57**
3635 **COUP DE CHANCE 14** [9]4-10-7 bl (84) Miss Faye Bramley(5) 20/1: 411-0530: 13th: In tch, wknd 2f out.   2   **60**
3773 **Barrantes 8** [8]7-9-11 (74) Ms D Goad(5) 66/1:0   3826 **Kentucky King 6** [1]4-10-3 (80) Mrs Marie King(5) 25/1:R
15 Ran   Time 2m 27.97 (2.97)   Owned: Mr P E Axon   Trained: Somerton

---

3965   4.00 Listed European Breeders Fund Dick Hern Stakes Fillies 3yo+ (A)
£17400 £6600 £3300   **1m5y rnd**   **Good/Firm 20**   **+07 Fast**   Inside

3389 **BRINDISI 23** [6] B W Hills 3-8-7 (95) M Hills 7/1: 3414461: Held up outer, hdwy 2f out, styd on   **102**
well to lead ins last, rdn out: suited by 1m on firm & fast, handles gd/soft: likes gall trks: useful, imprvd run.
3389 **MOON DAZZLE 23** [2] W J Haggas 3-8-7 (104) D Holland 15/8 FAV: 14552: Slow away, held up, hdwy &   1½   **98**
short of room 2f out, switched dist, styd on strongly, too late: shade closer & well worth a try over 10f.
1863 **ZIETORY 87** [8] P F I Cole 4-9-0 (99) D Sweeney 20/1: 1242-503: Hld up, eff to go 2nd over 1f   shd   **98**
out, onepace: joc rec a 1 day careless riding ban: abs: ran to v best: acts on fast, likes gd/soft.
2917 **ITHACA 43** [9] H R A Cecil 3-8-7 (100) W Ryan 7/2: 20-36534: Led till just ins last, no extra: 6   nk   **97**
wk abs & ran close to form of 2917 with switch to forcing tactics: see 1150.
3565 **FLOWERDRUM 16** [5]4-9-0 (86) S W Kelly 8/2: 1-014105: Chsd ldrs, wknd when hmpd just ins last.   1   **95$**
3535 **WHY DUBAI 18** [4]3-8-7 (89) R L Moore 14/1: 0102-066: In tch, wknd over 1f out: see 3535.   1½   **92**
3872 **AND TOTO TOO 4** [11]4-9-0 bl (91) F Ferris 25/1: 0442147: Slow away & bhd, nvr a factor: qck   ½   **91$**
reapp, poss flattered by rating & will appr rtn to h'caps as in 3872, 3456 (7f).
3782 **TAHIRAH 8** [10]4-9-0 (85) S Drowne 28/1: 10-00008: In tch, eff 2f out, sn wknd: see 2289.   1   **89$**
3780* **GOLDEN ISLAND 8** [7]3-8-7 (83) S Whitworth 8/1: 0-321519: Slow away, in tch, wknd over 1f out.   1¾   **85**
3389 **KUNDA 23** [1]3-8-7 (94) F Norton 20/1: 2-623000: 10th: Al bhd: see 2574, 2211.   ½   **84**
3322 **CALDY DANCER 28** [3]3-8-7 (105) C Catlin 20/1: 00525-00: 11th: Keen, slow away, lost action after 3f.   nk   **83**
3089 **COTE QUEST 37** [12]4-9-0 (92) W Supple 20/1: 0044360: 12th: Chsd ldr, wknd qckly over 1f out.   2½   **78**
12 Ran   Time 1m 39.33 (1.03)   Owned: Mr M H Dixon   Trained: Lambourn

---

3966   4.30 John Smiths Extra Smooth Handicap Stakes 3yo+ 0-75 (E)   **[73]**
£4342 £1336 £668   **5f161y rnd**   **Good/Firm 20**   **+00 Fast**   Far Side

3888 **CURRENCY 3** [17] J M Bradley 7-9-13 (72) C J Davies(7) 11/2: 6300521: Held up, hdwy 2f out, led   **81**
appr fnl 1f, drvn out: eff over 5/6f on gd, likes firm, fast & polytrack, prob any trk: v tough, on a fair mark &
right back to form: tried cheek pieces & blnks this term: see 407.
3569 **DEVON FLAME 16** [8] R J Hodges 5-10-0 (73) S Drowne 7/1: 1224002: In tch, eff to chase wnr over   nk   **79**
1f out, kept on ins last, just held: right back to form under top-weight & likes Bath: see 2861, 2266.
3569 **BALLYBUNION 16** [1] D Nicholls 5-8-9 (54) A Nicholls 4/1 FAV: 0005103: Handy, eff dist, onepace.   2   **56**
2846 **YORKIE 46** [18] P A Blockley 5-8-11 (56) F P Ferris(3) 20/1: 0002204: Bhd, late gains, nvr dngrs: abs.   ½   **56**
3640 **PULSE 13** [14]6-8-13 p (58) F Norton 10/1: 4530055: In tch, some late gains, nvr dngrs: see 2743.   shd   **57**
3640 **BLESSED PLACE 13** [5]4-8-5 t (50) S Righton 33/1: 5415006: In tch, wknd dist: best 3165.   1   **46**
3744 **SWEETEST REVENGE 9** [11]3-9-4 P (67) J D Smith 16/1: 4-060337: Nvr a factor: tried cheekpieces.   nk   **62**
3643 **ADANTINO 13** [13]5-8-12 bl (57) S W Kelly 14/1: 3363168: In tch, eff dist, wknd: best 3289.   shd   **51**
3643 **FORMALISE 13** [12]4-8-10 (55) R Thomas(5) 28/1: 0050509: Trkd ldr, led 2f out till dist, wknd.   ¾   **47**
3680 **PLAYTIME BLUE 11** [7]4-9-0 (59) G Baker 20/1: 0533000: 10th: Handy, wknd 2f out: see 3228, 3165.   3½   **41**
3888 **INDIAN BAZAAR 3** [9]6-8-4 bl (49) J F McDonald(3) 40/1: 2060000: 11th: Led till 2f out, wknd.   2   **25**
3705 **CORANGLAIS 11** [3]4-9-2 p (61) R L Moore 40/1: 0041000: 12th: Slow away & al bhd: best 3143.   ½   **35**
3643 **NATHAN DETROIT 13** [2]4-8-6 P (51) D Sweeney 40/1: 0000-00: 13th: Slow away & al bhd: see 3643.   13   **0**
3888 **B A HIGHFLYER 3** [10]4-8-13 (58) C Catlin 7/1: 500054B: Bhd, b.d. over 2f out, sadly destroyed.   **0**
3640 **LOCH INCH 13** [19]7-8-7 bl (52) D Holland 6/1: 404233P: Bhd, sadly broke leg & p.u. 2f out, died.   **0**
15 Ran   Time 1m 10.23 (1.13)   Owned: Mr Robert Bailey   Trained: Chepstow

BATH   SUNDAY 15.08.04   Lefthand, Turning Track with Uphill Finish

---

3967   5.00 Jackie Coles Surprise 40th Birthday Celebrations Maiden Stakes 3yo   (D)
£3741 £1151 £576   1m3f144y   Good/Firm 20   -40 Slow   Inside

3335 **IDEALISTIC 25** [6] L M Cumani 3-8-9 (82) D Holland 8/13 FAV: 02221: Made all, styd on over 1f   77
out, cmftbly: bckd: stays 12f on fast & gd: enjoyed forcing tactics & a gd confidence boost.
3243 **TURN N BURN 30** [4] C A Cyzer 3-9-0 (78) R L Moore 5/2: 53-032: Keen in tch, eff to chase wnr   2½   75
over 3f out, no impress ins last: stays 11.5f on fast, gd & polytrack: shown enough to win a race: see 3243.
3422 **SOVIETTA 22** [1] R M Beckett 3-8-9 N Mackay(3) 8/1: 43: Slow away, cl-up, chall dist, sn no extra.   1   68
2368 **NINA FONTENAIL 65** [2] B R Millman 3-8-9 (40) F Norton 50/1: 06-00054: Slow away, keen bhd, btn   3   63
2f out: 2 month abs, prev with N Hawke: btr run: see 2368.
3480 **ANNA GAYLE 20** [5]3-8-9 S Drowne 25/1: 005: ch f Dr Fong - Urban Dancer (Generous) In tch, wknd   9   49$
over 2f out: bred to apprec mid-dist.
         MONTGOMERY [7]3-9-0 R Thomas(5) 25/1: 6: b g In Command - Lightening Reef (Bon Sang) Slow away1½   51
& al bhd: mid-dist bred.
3802 **CLOUD CATCHER 7** [3]3-8-9 S Righton 50/1: 0-0007: Keen in tch, wknd over 2f out: poor form.   30   6
7 Ran   Time 2m 32.01(7.01)   Owned: Fittocks Stud   Trained: Newmarket

---

PONTEFRACT   SUNDAY 15.08.04   Lefthand, Undulating Track, Stiff Uphill Finish

---

Official Going GOOD/SOFT.

3968   2.10 European Breeders Fund Sunday Plate Maiden Stakes 2yo   (D)
£8921 £2745 £1373   5f rnd   Good/Soft 61   -25 Slow   Inside

3457 **GRAZE ON 21** [7] J J Quinn 2-9-0 R Winston 7/1: 21: Trkd ldrs, imprvd to lead dist, styd on   82
strongly, drvn out: been gelded since last run: eff at 5f on gd & gd/soft, 6f shld suit: going the right way.
2158 **SENTIERO ROSSO 74** [11] B Ellison 2-9-0 J Fortune 11/1: 42: Chsd ldrs, ev ch ent fnl 1f, not   1   78
pace of wnr cl-home: op 8/1, 10 wk abs: eff at 5f on gd/soft: clearly runs well fresh: shld find a small race.
2970 **JE SUIS BELLE 41** [17] B W Hills 2-8-9 R Hills 11/2: 03: ch f Efisio - Blossom (Warning) Chsd   2½   66
ldrs wide, kept on under press fnl 1f but not pace of front 2: tchd 7/1, 6 wk abs: Mar first foal, dam unrcd: sire
a smart 6f/1m performer: eff at 5f on gd/soft, 6f will suit: promising run racing wide, shld pick up a small race.
2670 **ALEXIA ROSE 53** [8] A Berry 2-8-9 J Bramhill 100/1: 604: b f Mujadil - Meursault (Salt Dome)   2   60
Led till 2f out, no extra: 8 wk abs: £16,000 Mar foal: sire a speedy juv: first sign of form on this gd/soft.
         LESLINGTAYLOR [3]2-9-0 G Hind 50/1: 5: b g Orpen - Rite of Spring (Niniski) Chsd ldrs, wknd   1   62
fnl 1f: debut, longer priced stablemate of wnr: £8,000 Apr foal: brother to sprint wnr Artistic Belle: dam a
mid-dist wnr, sire a high-class juv sprinter: with J J Quinn.
2241 **HANSEATIC LEAGUE 71** [1]2-9-0 J Fanning 8/11 FAV: 226: Front rank, led briefly 2f out, wknd fnl   nk   61
1f: hvly bckd, 10 wk abs: clr front choice & most disapp, not handle this gd/soft grnd? much btr 2241 (gd).
3457 **HARRYS HOUSE 21** [18]2-9-0 P Hanagan 16/1: 47: Outpcd & rcd wide, styd on late, nvr dngrs: 1½   57
longer priced stablemate of wnr: see 3457 (C/D).
         ENTAILMENT [13]2-9-0 L Goncalves 40/1: 8: Rear, styd on late, nrst fin on debut.   nk   56
3272 **MICKLEDO 29** [4]2-9-0 M Fenton 100/1: 09: Nvr btr than mid-div.   1¼   52
3769 **APETITE 8** [5]2-9-0 A Reilly(7) 150/1: 000: 10th: Slowly away, nvr nr ldrs.   ½   51
3755 **LUCY PARKES 9** [2]2-8-9 M Henry 40/1: 040: 11th: Chsd ldrs 3.5f, sn wknd: see 3755.   ½   45
3606 **WAYWARD SHOT 15** [14]2-9-0 T Lucas 50/1: 500: 12th: Chsd ldrs 3.5f, wknd: best 2889 (debut).   ½   49
3606 **HALLA SAN 15** [9]2-9-0 A Beech(3) 66/1: 00: 13th: Al outpcd.   1½   45
3120 **PAULA JO 36** [10]2-8-9 G Parkin 37/1: 6000: 14th: Nvr btr than mid-div.   ½   39
3735 **Phantom Song 10** [15]2-9-0 E Ahern 100/1:0   3755 **Marlenes Girl 9** [16]2-8-9 P Mathers(5) 50/1:0
         Dolly Peel [6]2-8-9 Dean McKeown 40/1:0   3513 **Allizam 18** [12]2-9-0 G Carter 80/1:0
18 Ran   Time 1m 05.60 (4.30)   Owned: Mr J R Rowbottom   Trained: Malton

---

3969   2.40 Racecard Competition Handicap Stakes 3yo+ 0-100 (C)   [92]
£9373 £3555 £1778   1m4f8y   Good/Soft 61   -00 Slow   Inside

3615 **JEEPSTAR 15** [8] T D Easterby 4-8-10 (74) M Fenton 10/1: 3-006221: Made all, held on gamely fnl   81
1f, drvn out: winning form at 10/12f, acts on firm & gd/soft grnd: likes to run up with/force the pace: genuine.
         PRETTY STAR 106 [9] M Johnston 4-9-10 (88) J Fanning 25/1: 11660-02: b c Lando - Pretty   ¾   93
Ballerina (Sadler's Wells): Trkd wnr throughout, ev ch fnl 1f, just btn in a close fin: long abs, jt top-weight:
ex-German, won 3 times in native country in '03 (incl List): eff at 11/12f on gd & gd/soft grnd: has worn blnks,
not today: clearly runs well fresh & the type to win races.
3681 **SAHEM 11** [4] D Eddy 7-9-0 (78) P Hanagan 8/1: 4012033: Trkd ldrs, kept on under press fnl 1f: gd run.   1   81
3474 **DOUBLE ASPECT 21** [1] Sir Michael Stoute 3-8-11 (86) K Fallon 6/5 FAV: 4154: Chsd ldrs, switched   nk   88
wide dist, onepace: well bckd: prob styd this longer 12f trip: acts on fast & gd/soft: see 2700.
3119 **RANVILLE 36** [5]6-9-8 (86) M Henry 16/1: 2024/-005: Trkd ldrs, onepace fnl 1f: clr of rem: see 2759.   1   86
3861 **JASMICK 4** [3]6-8-8 (72) T P Queally 12/1: 260-5006: Held up, prog to chase ldrs 3f out, wkng   6   63
when short of room: qck reapp: see 3587.
3076 **UROWELLS 37** [2]4-9-10 (88) J Fortune 16/1: 6/41-007: Held up, nvr nr ldrs under jt top-weight.   1   77
3637 **ALERON 14** [6]6-8-8 p (72) E Ahern 7/1: 2043528: Chsd ldrs, wknd 2f out.   9   46
2567* **TRANCE 57** [7]4-9-9 (87) P Makin(5) 11/2: 01-04119: Chsd ldrs wide, btn 2f out: abs, btr 2567. dist 16
9 Ran   Time 2m 41.49 (7.39)   Owned: Miss E Jeeps and Partners   Trained: Malton

---

3970   3.10 Sportingoptions Co Uk Exchange Betting Handicap Stakes 3yo+ 0-65 (E)   [65]
£5772 £1776 £888   **2m1f22y**   Good/Soft 61   -47 Slow   Inside

3834* **SUPER FELLOW 6** [4] C N Kellett 10-8-5 (6ex) (42) J Bramhill 13/2: //00///-311: Held up, prog 3f   47
out, styd on strongly to lead cl-home, won going away: op 11/2: eff around 2m/2m1f on gd & soft grnd: lightly rcd
for a 10yo, progressing well over staying dists: see 3834.
3771 **CRACKLEANDO 8** [13] N P Littmoden 3-8-6 (58) J P Guillambert(3) 20/1: 3031032: Sn led, hdd dist,   1¼ 60
rallied to regain lead ins fnl 1f, not pace to repel wnr cl-home: styd this longer 2m1f trip on fav'd easy grnd.
3853 **VICARS DESTINY 4** [18] Mrs S Lamyman 6-9-12 (63) J Fortune 7/1: 0006433: Held up, prog to chase   ½ 66
ldrs 2f out, kept on under press: qck reappr, jt top-weight: consistent, see 3853.
3049 **HIGH DRAMA 38** [1] P Bowen 7-8-3 (40) T P Queally 7/1: 6/520-124: Led early, remained prom,   hd 42
2905 **HABITUAL DANCER 44** [17]3-8-6 (58) P Hanagan 25/1: 0-612305: Keen & led early, remained prom,   ¾ 59
onepcd fnl 1.5f: 6 wk abs: longer 2m1f trip & appears to stay: see 2827 & 1051 (10f).
3275 **PENNY STALL 29** [15]3-8-11 (63) K Fallon 7/4 FAV: 044-0426: Chsd ldrs, imprvd to lead dist,   hd 63
collared ins fnl 1f, wknd: hvly bckd from 5/2: rcd too keenly & subs failed to get home: stays 2m, see 3275.
2992 **MOLEHILL 40** [5]3-8-7 (59) M Fenton 16/1: 0547: Nvr far away, wknd 2f out: 6 wk abs, h'cap bow: 8 49
much longer 2m1f trip & prob failed to stay: see 2992.
3760 **LEOPARD SPOT 9** [7]6-8-11 (48) P Fessey 15/1: 5/02/40/-08: Held up, nvr nr ldrs: see 3760.   1½ 36
3701 **ALLEZ MOUSSON 11** [14]6-8-4 (41) D Allan 14/1: 30-00009: Rear, nvr nr ldrs.   ¾ 28
2964 **GREEN N GOLD 41** [2]4-9-2 (53) A Culhane 20/1: 1040000: 10th: Held up, nvr a factor: 6 wk abs.   nk 39
3692* **MR WHIZZ 11** [12]7-8-3 p (40) R Ffrench 20/1: 3220510: 11th: Chsd ldrs, ev ch 4f out, wknd fnl 2f.   3½ 22
3701 **FANTASTICO 11** [9]4-9-8 p (59) R Winston 11/1: 430-4030: 12th: Nvr btr than mid-div: btr 3701.   2½ 38
3139 **VALDESCO 35** [3]6-9-13 bl (64) P Mathers(5) 20/1: 1120/-000: 13th: Chsd ldrs, wknd 4f out: see 2673.   shd 43
3450 **Domenico 22** [6]6-9-12 (63) E Ahern 33/1:0   2664 **Purr 53** [11]3-7-12 (1oh)(49) M Henry 66/1:0
3460} **Special Branch 373** [16]4-8-11 (48) J Fanning 33/1:0 2533} **Jawwala 412** [10]5-9-8 (59) F Lynch 66/1:R
17 Ran   Time 3m 58.82 (18.52)   Owned: Mr A M Egan   Trained: Burton-On-Trent

---

3971   3.40 Listed Slatch Farm Stud Flying Stakes Fillies 3yo+ (A)
£29000 £11000 £5500   **6f rnd**   Good/Soft 61   +10 Fast   Inside

3636 **GOLDEVA 14** [8] R Hollinshead 5-9-4 (97) A Culhane 20/1: 0-150541: Held up, prog 2f out, qcknd to   106
lead well ins fnl 1f, pushed clr: gd time: suited by 6f on firm & hvy: handles any trk, runs well fresh: has tried
a t-strap: apprec this fast pace & a career best/improved run: see 952 (reapp).
3773 **FRUIT OF GLORY 8** [4] J R Jenkins 5-9-0 (94) F Lynch 10/1: 0421422: Chsd ldrs, imprvd to lead   2½ 99
dist, not pace to repel wnr cl-home: op 14/1, well clr rem: ran to best: tough & useful: see 3773.
3842 **SIMIANNA 7** [6] A Berry 5-9-0 p (94) R Winston 20/1: 0046503: Rear, prog when short of room after   4 89
halfway, nrst fin: did not get the run of today's race, see 2457.
3596 **LOCHRIDGE 15** [14] A M Balding 5-9-0 (101) T P Queally 7/2: 0-200324: Sn switched left & front   ½ 88
rank, led halfway till dist, no extra: often given a 5-day careless stating ban: see 3596.
3564 **NYRAMBA 16** [1]3-8-10 (107) J Fortune 5/2 JT FAV: 10-25525: Nvr btr than mid-div: needs further.   2 83
3636 **VITA SPERICOLATA 14** [9]7-9-0 (81) G Parkin 66/1: 5000556: Led till halfway, wknd fnl 1f.   2 78
3564 **DOWAGER 16** [13]3-8-10 (100) Dane O'Neill 25/1: 1-546307: Outpcd, nvr nr ldrs: btr 3268 (g/f).   1¾ 73
3773* **TYCHY 8** [7]5-9-0 (97) K Fallon 5/2 JT FAV: 5300518: Sn hmpd & lost place, hdwy wide 2f out, sn   1 70
no impress: well bckd from 7/1, disapp on this gd/soft grnd, beat today's 2nd in 3773 (gd).
3571 **FLASHING BLADE 16** [10]4-9-0 t (64) G Carter 100/1: 0010659: Al rear: v highly tried.   8 50
3790 **LE MERIDIEN 8** [12]6-9-0 p (51) R Ffrench 40/1: 0651030: 10th: Chsd ldrs 4f, wknd: highly tried.   3 43
3389 **NATALIYA 23** [5]3-8-10 (105) J Fanning 10/1: 13-30040: 11th: Chsd ldrs 4f, sn btn: op 7/1: btr 3389.   5 31
2305 **MILLYBAA 70** [2]4-9-0 (97) E Ahern 12/1: 020-2400: 12th: Chsd ldrs, wkng when hmpd 2f out, eased: abs.½ 30
12 Ran   Time 1m 17.20 (3.10)   Owned: Mr M Pyle & Mrs T Pyle   Trained: Upper Longdon

---

3972   4.10 Wakefield Unison Quality Services For Quality People Handicap Stakes 3yo 0-90 (C)   [94]
£9535 £3617 £1808   **1m4y rnd**   Good/Soft 61   +03 Fast   Inside

3647* **DOUBLE VODKA 13** [5] Mrs J R Ramsden 3-8-1 (67) P Hanagan 3/1: 6240111: Chsd ldrs, squeezed   77+
through to lead ins fnl 1f, rdn clr, readily: well bckd, gd time & completed hat-trick: eff at 1m/11f on fast &
gd/soft: suited by waiting tactics: most progressive gelding & winning run prob not at an end: see 3647.
3472 **ALSHAWAMEQ 21** [6] J L Dunlop 3-9-6 (86) R Hills 6/1: 5-310532: Sn rdn in rear, switched wide &   2½ 90
prog 2f out, kept on but not reach wnr: acts on fast & gd/soft grnd: in gd form: see 3472 & 2247.
3462* **CHOIR LEADER 21** [3] W J Haggas 3-9-5 (85) K Fallon 11/8 FAV: 013: Trkds ldrs, onepcd fnl 1f: ¾ 87
well bckd: not disgraced on h'cap bow: acts on gd & gd/soft grnd: see 3462 (C/D).
3679* **SILVERHAY 11** [4] T D Barron 3-8-7 (73) J Fortune 10/1: 3-424114: Prom, led 2f out till ins fnl   3 69
1f, no extra: op 7/1 on hat-trick bid: btr 3679.
3378 **HONEST INJUN 24** [9]3-8-8 (74) A Culhane 14/1: 1440545: Held up, prog 2f out, nvr dngrs: see 3378.   1 68
3107 **RILEY BOYS 36** [7]3-9-1 (81) M Fenton 10/1: 2122226: Chsd ldrs, wknd fnl 1f.   1 73
3339 **MISSION MAN 25** [2]3-8-13 (79) Dane O'Neill 20/1: 2140457: Led briefly 2f out, wknd fnl 1f.   ½ 70
2660 **RAREFIED 53** [11]3-9-0 (80) R Winston 33/1: 62-01008: Al bhd: 8 wk abs & new stabl (prev with R   15 46
Charlton): drop back in trip, see 1382 (12f).
3439 **FORTHRIGHT 22** [10]3-9-7 p (87) T P Queally 25/1: 0456009: Chsd ldrs, btn 2f out: top-weight.   3½ 47
3738 **FAMILIAR AFFAIR 10** [1]3-9-0 (80) F Lynch 25/1: 14-00: 10th: Led till over 2f out, wknd & eased: 3 34
saddle reportedly slipped: see 3738.
10 Ran   Time 1m 46.48 (4.68)   Owned: Mrs Alison Iles   Trained: Thirsk

---

3973   **4.40 Kids Come Free Maiden Stakes 3yo+   (D)**
£8921 £2745 £1373   **1m4y rnd**   **Good/Soft 61**   **-15 Slow**   Inside

3007 **STREAM OF GOLD 40** [5] Sir Michael Stoute 3-8-12   K Fallon 4/5 FAV: 51: Trkd ldrs, smooth hdwy to **84+**
lead 1f out, sn clr, easily: well bckd, 6 wk abs: full brother to top-class Spectrum: eff at 1m/10f on fm & gd/soft:
runs well fresh: clear cut win, plenty more to come.
4302½ **BABOOSH 333** [3] J R Fanshawe 3-8-7   R Ffrench 4/1: 2-2: b f Marju - Slipper (Suave Dancer) Led   3   70
till entering fnl 1f, kept on but no ch with wnr: reapp: rnr-up on sole juv start (fills mdn): eff at 1m on fast &
gd/soft grnd, 10f+ shld suit: prob met an above average rival & can find a small race. 2 Sep'03 Beve 7.5g/f 76- D:
   MEDALLA [12] M Brittain 4-9-5   T Williams 100/1: 3: gr c Medaaly - Sharp Cracker (Hamas)   ¾   73
Mid-div, prog 2f out, not pace to chall on debut: dam a 7f wnr: eff at 1m on gd/soft grnd: encouraging start.
3546 **FOSSGATE 17** [2] J D Bethell 3-8-12 VIS (70) J Fanning 8/1: 5-203644: Chsd ldrs 6f, wknd: tried a vis.   3½   68
2991 **CAPITOLE 40** [6]3-8-12   P McCabe 33/1: 045: Trkd ldrs, btn over 2f out: 6 wk abs.   5   60
3346 **TRUE 25** [10]3-8-7   (63) Andrew Webb(7) 12/1: 0203406: Chsd ldrs, not pace to chall: see 3016.   1   53
3230 **SONEARSOFAR 30** [11]4-9-5   M Lawson(5) 100/1: 067: Nvr a factor: see 3230.   9   43
3683 **PERRYWINKLE BOY 11** [9]3-8-12   A Culhane 33/1: 48: Al bhd: has been gelded: see 3683.   15   18
   THISTLE [7]3-8-12   J Fortune 9/1: 9: ch c Selkirk - Ardisia (Affirmed) Chsd ldrs, wknd 3f out   ½   17
on debut: related to mid-dist wnrs: with J Gosden & shld be capable of btr.
   SINAMAY [14]3-8-7   R Winston 50/1: 0: 10th: Al bhd on racecourse bow.   8   0
2124 **DONT TELL SIMON 75** [4]3-8-12   G Parkin 100/1: 000: 11th: Al outpcd, t.o.: recent jumps runner.   26   0
   City Lass [8]4-9-0 P Mulrennan(3) 100/1:0   **Rhum** [1]4-9-5 P Hanagan 25/1:P
13 Ran   Time 1m 47.88 (6.08)   Owned: Ballymacoll Stud   Trained: Newmarket

---

3974   **5.10 Go Racing In Yorkshire Handicap Stakes 3yo+ 35-55 (F)**   **[62]**
£4397 £1353   £677   **5f rnd**   **Good/Soft 61**   **-14 Slow**   Inside

3680* **ON THE TRAIL 11** [3] D W Chapman 7-9-0   (48) A Culhane 7/2: 1343311: Made all, clr dist, held on   54
drvn out: bckd from 11/2: stays 7f, best up with/forcing the pace around 5/6f: acts on gd, gd/soft & both AWs, any
trk, clearly likes Pontefract: in fine form, see 3680 & 1443.
3640* **DAVIDS MARK 13** [18] J R Jenkins 4-9-4   (52) K Fallon 10/3 FAV: 0344412: Held up, prog wide 2f   ½   57
out, fin well & only just btn: well bckd: in fine form, acts on firm, gd/soft & polytrack: see 3640.
3191 **MISTER MAL 32** [14] B Ellison 8-9-5   (53) R Miles(3) 16/1: 3-061003: Held up, hdwy wide 2f out,   1½   54
nrst fin: often likes to force the pace, see 1277.
3796 **SMIRFYS NIGHT 8** [16] D Nicholls 5-9-1   (49) J Fanning 8/1: 05/-00054: Held up, hdwy wide 2f out,   hd   50
nvr nrr: return to 6f will suit, see 3796.
3796 **SMIRFYS PRIDE 8** [9]6-9-1 vis (49) P M Quinn 9/1: 06-00035: Chsd ldrs, onepcd fnl 1f: s/mate of 4th.   1¾   45
3667 **ROSIES RESULT 12** [7]4-9-2   (50) Jemma Marshall(7) 20/1: 0001006: Chsd ldrs, onepcd fnl 1.5f.   ½   45
1824 **FENWICKS PRIDE 89** [5]6-9-7   (55) P Hanagan 7/1: 000/0-307: Rear, hdwy when short of room dist,   ½   49+
nrst fin: 3 mth abs: encouraging run from this well h'capped sort, stable in terrific form: keep in mind.
3852 **FAIRGAME MAN 4** [1]6-8-12 p (46) G Parkin 10/1: 0510008: Chsd ldrs, onepcd fnl 1.5f: qck reapp.   shd   40
3767 **LAKELANDS LADY 8** [15]4-9-1   (49) J Edmunds 40/1: 00-00009: Chsd ldrs wide, btn 2f out: see 859.   nk   42
3591 **ROBWILLCALL 15** [12]4-9-1   (49) P Mathers(5) 16/1: 0-051550: 10th: Chsd ldrs, onepcd fnl 2f.   1¼   38
3417 **BELLA BEGUINE 23** [4]5-8-13 bl (47) M Fenton 10/1: 0204450: 11th: Nvr btr than mid-div.   nk   35
3463 **ARCTIC BURST 21** [17]4-9-1 vis (49) Darren Williams 66/1: 0000000: 12th: Slowly away, nvr nr ldrs.   hd   37
3880 **TELEPATHIC 4** [11]4-9-7   (55) P Bradley 20/1: 5400050: 13th: Nvr btr than mid-div: qck reapp.   1¾   38
3575 **DARK CHAMPION 16** [2]4-9-6 (55) R Winston 33/1: 0045000: 14th: Rear, no room 1.5f out, nvr dngrs.   1¼   33
4269} **Petite Mac 334** [8]4-9-5 (53) A Reilly(7) 50/1:0
3767   **Good Time Bobby 8** [10]7-8-12 (46) P McCabe 50/1:0
3262 **Palvic Moon 29** [6]3-9-4 BL(55) R Fitzpatrick 66/1:0   2512 **Whinhill House 59** [13]4-9-0 (48) F Lynch 66/1:0
18 Ran   Time 1m 05.06(3.76)   Owned: Mr J M Chapman   Trained: York

---

Official Going GOOD (GOOD/FIRM places).

3975   **5.40 European Breeders Fund Maiden Stakes 2yo   (D)**
£5239 £1612   £806   **6f rnd**   **Good/Firm 28**   **-17 Slow**   Inside

3196 **SANT JORDI 33** [12] B J Meehan 2-9-0   J Fortune 3/1 CO FAV: 31: Made virtually all, styd on well   87
when hard pressed ins last, drvn out: eff over a sharp 6f on fast grnd: enjoyed switch to forcing tactics & a
game/useful effort here: see 3196.
   SOMETHING [17] T G Mills 2-9-0   G Carter 3/1 CO FAV: 2: b c Trans Island - Persian Polly   hd   86
(Persian Bold) Handy, hdwy to chall dist, kept on for press just ins last, just held on debut: Mar foal, cost
E100,000: half-brother to numerous wnrs incl a top-class sprinter: eff over a sharp 6f, shld stay further: acts on
fast grnd: excellent start, clr of rem & will be winning shortly.
3665 **FASYLITATOR 13** [1] J A Osborne 2-9-0   D Holland 12/1: 63: Rcd far side & led that small group,   3   75
not pace of stands side ins last: eff at 6f on fast grnd: encouraging: shld find similar: see 3665.
3818 **BROOKLIME 7** [2] J A Osborne 2-9-0   S W Kelly 50/1: 64: b c Namid - Wildflower (Namaqualand)   1   74
With ldr far side, no extra ins last: Jan first foal, cost E50,000: dam 7f juv scorer: improved from debut.
3478 **COOL PANIC 21** [7]2-9-0   J Murtagh 3/1 CO FAV: 025: Chsd wnr, wknd fnl 1f: nicely bckd, btr 3478.   ½   72
   SQUAW DANCE [11]2-8-9   M Hills 12/1: 6: ch f Indian Ridge - Likely Story (Night Shift) Bhd,   6   49
some late gains, nvr dngrs on debut: Feb foal, cost 68,000gns: half-sister to wnrs over 7f/2m: dam 6f scorer.
   BENEDICT [3]2-9-0   R Winston 12/1: 7: b c Benny The Dip - Abbey Strand (Shadeed) Slow away &   3½   44
bhd, some late gains, nvr dngrs on debut: Apr foal: half-brother to a useful 1m wnr: dam 1m scorer: sure to
relish 7f/1m+ in time & will learn plenty from this.
3818 **KILLENA BOY 7** [5]2-9-0   Martin Dwyer 20/1: 08: In tch far side, wknd over 1f out.   1¾   39

3163 **YOUNG BOLDRIC 35** [8]2-9-0 L Keniry(3) 66/1: 09: In tch, wknd 2f out. *nk* **38**
PEREZ [4]2-9-0 R Hughes 12/1: 0: 10th: Slow away & nvr a factor on debut. *nk* **37**
RED MARTEENEY [13]2-9-0 Dane O'Neill 25/1: 0: 11th: Slow away & al bhd on debut. *nk* **36**
1614 **HEART OF ETERNITY 101** [6]2-8-9 V Venkaya 50/1: 040: 12th: In tch, wknd 2f out. *3* **22**
2450 **LIGHTHORNE LAD 63** [14]2-9-0 J Jeffrey(7) 66/1: 000: 13th: In tch, wknd over 2f out. *2½* **20**
2970 **Worth Abbey 42** [9]2-9-0 P Dobbs 40/1:0 2970 **Cavaradossi 42** [16]2-9-0 J F McDonald(3) 50/1:0
Touch Of Spice [15]2-9-0 T E Durcan 50/1:0 3476 **Just Bonnie 21** [10]2-9-0 A Nicholls 50/1:0
17 Ran Time 1n 13.0 (2.7) Owned: Mr J S Threadwell Trained: Upper Lambourn

3976

6.10 Fireworks Extravaganza Saturday 6th November Handicap Stakes 3yo 0-85 (D) **[90]**
£5509 £1695 £848 **5f10y rnd** **Good/Firm 28** **+06 Fast** Inside

3804 **WUNDERBRA 8** [3] M L W Bell 3-7-12 t (60) Hayley Turner(5) 11/2: 345131: Handy, hdwy to lead over 1f out, styd on well ins last, drvn out: eff over 5/6f on fm & fast, likes Windsor: prog & genuine. **67**
3567 **SKYHARBOR 17** [10] A M Balding 3-8-11 (73) Martin Dwyer 4/1 FAV: 00-05052: In tch, outpcd halfway, strong run over 1f out, kept on ins last, just held: imprvd for switch to new stable (prev with D Nicholls) & looks poised to strike, prob over 6f: well h'capped: see 2591. *hd* **79**
3833 **MARYSIENKA 7** [1] J Balding 3-8-6 (68) J Edmunds 20/1: 264-0503: Held up, hdwy when short of room over 1f out, switched right & kept on ins last, no impress on front 2: encouraging eff tho' remains a mdn: see 3379. *1¼* **68**
3188 **SNOW WOLF 33** [2] J M Bradley 3-9-3 (79) R L Moore 12/1: 3-012004: With ldr, wknd ins last: gd run. *nk* **80**
3567 **INCISE 17** [5]3-9-5 (81) J Fortune 6/1: 6004405: Held up, hdwy & short of room over 1f out, switched right & kept on ins last, no threat: see 1400. *1* **79**
3920 **BORZOI MAESTRO 3** [7]3-8-13 (75) L Keniry(3) 16/1: 0430506: In tch, eff dist, no extra ins last. *1¼* **69**
3804 **KING EGBERT 8** [9]3-7-12 (60) T Dean(7) 10/1: 3000-47: Chsd ldrs, wkng when hmpd & switched ins last. *1* **51**
3737 **AFTER THE SHOW 11** [8]3-8-7 (69) T E Durcan 11/2: 1-606028: Slt lead till over 2f out, wkng when hmpd ins last: btr 3737, 1166. *nk* **59**
3567 **SILVER PRELUDE 17** [4]3-9-7 (83) D Holland 9/2: 0031009: With ldrs, led 2f out till dist, wknd. *2* **67**
9 Ran Time 1m 0.14 (1.14) Owned: Fitzroy Thoroughbreds Trained: Newmarket

3977

6.40 Finspreads Premier Claiming Stakes 3yo+ (D)
£5671 £1745 £873 **6f rnd** **Good/Firm 28** **-09 Slow** Inside

3608 **ONLYTIME WILL TELL 16** [8] D Nicholls 6-9-5 (91) R Winston 9/4 FAV: 0054201: Slow away, bhd, gd hdwy over 2f out & led over 1f out, shkn up ins last, cmfbly: well bckd: stays 1m, suited by 6f on firm, hvy & fibresand, any trk: relished drop into claim grade but is still useful & capable of winning decent races: see 888. **92**
3569 **LOYAL TYCOON 17** [9] D Nicholls 6-9-3 (87) A Nicholls 7/2: 0105502: In tch, short of room 2f out, hdwy to chase wnr ins last, kept on, al held: clr of rem, s/mate of wnr, clmd for 26,000. *½* **87**
1720 **ROCKET 95** [5] R Hannon 3-8-4 (57) R Smith 25/1: 04303: Bhd, hdwy over 2f out, styd on to take 3rd ins last, no dngr: 3 month abs, clmd for 6,000: acts on fast & soft: lightly rcd, see 1539. *3* **68**
3844* **ATLANTIC VIKING 6** [7] D Nicholls 9-9-2 (91) J Murtagh 11/4: 0040014: In tch, wknd fnl 1f: qck reapp. *1¼* **73**
3827 **WILLHECONQUERTOO 7** [4]4-9-3 t (69) J F Egan 8/1: 0351005: Set pace till dist, wknd: best 2975. *1¼* **70**
3301 **DEXILEOS 28** [2]5-8-9 t (40) S Hitchcott(3) 66/1: 0000036: Bhd, nvr a factor: see 3301, 1273. *1* **59$**
1021 **APPOLONIOUS 136** [3]3-8-6 Dane O'Neill 33/1: 007: b c Case Law - Supreme Thought (Emarati) Slow away & al bhd: long abs. *5* **44**
3804 **PICCLEYES 8** [10]3-8-6 bl (61) R L Moore 9/1: 0100368: In tch, wknd over 2f out: see 3599, 2586. *1½* **40**
1642 **PACKIN EM IN 98** [1]6-8-7 bl (45) V Venkaya 50/1: 3201009: Slow away, al bhd: best 969 (AW, 7f). *15* **0**
3640 **CATCHTHEBATCH 14** [6]8-8-7 bl (39) S Carson 66/1: 4300000: 10th: Cl-up, wknd qckly over 2f out. *5* **0**
10 Ran Time 1m 12.51 (2.21) Owned: Mr J Hair & Mr D Faulkner Trained: Thirsk

3978

7.10 Royal Windsor Rated Stakes Handicapfillies 3yo+ 0-90 (C) **[94]**
£8482 £3217 £1609 **1m67y rnd** **Good/Firm 28** **-10 Slow** Inside

3471 **MUNAAWASHAT 22** [4] K R Burke 3-8-5 (71) F Norton 7/1: 61-31201: Chsd ldrs, ev ch ent fnl 1f, forged ahd cl-home, drvn to hold on gamely: eff at 7f/1m, has tried 10f: acts on fast & gd/soft, stiff/undul or sharpish trk: likes to run-up with/force the pace: tough & progressive: see 2828. **77**
2620 **ULTIMATA 56** [2] J R Fanshawe 4-9-6 (80) O Urbina 3/1 JT FAV: 1-022: Chsd ldrs, ev ch 2f out, led dist till ins fnl 1f, rallied gamely & just btn in a thrilling fin: well bckd tho' op 2/1, 8 wk abs: acts on fast & gd/soft grnd: in fine form, deserves to go one btr: see 2620 (C/D). *shd* **85**
3446* **DESERT CRISTAL 23** [5] J R Boyle 3-8-12 (78) Martin Dwyer 4/1: 25-26313: Sn led, rcd wide, collared 2f out, rallied well & just btn in a close fin: well bckd: acts on fast & hvy grnd: lost more grnd when veering right than was eventually btn & prob unlucky: see 3446. *½* **82**
3365 **SURF THE NET 25** [6] R Hannon 3-9-7 (87) R Hughes 10/1: 16-30034: Led early, remained prom till regained led 2f out till collared dist, no extra: prob stays a sharp 1m: see 3365 & 2136. *1¾* **87**
3780 **SUMMER SHADES 9** [3]6-8-12 (72) B Swarbrick(5) 3/1 JT FAV: 4356125: Chsd ldrs, onepcd fnl 1.5f. *¾* **70**
3042 **MADAMOISELLE JONES 39** [1]4-8-7 (67) S Drowne 5/1: 0451646: Held up, hdwy to chall 2f out, sn wknd. *2½* **60**
6 Ran Time 1m 46.19 (3.19) Owned: Mr John A Duffy Trained: Leyburn

3979

7.40 Vccp/O2 Maiden Stakes 3yo (D)
£4199 £1292 £646 **1m67y rnd** **Good/Firm 28** **+00 Fast** Inside

1136 **DAY TO REMEMBER 126** [8] E F Vaughan 3-9-0 (80) D Holland 6/4 FAV: 43-51: Mid-div, gd hdwy to lead 2f out, sn clr, easily: well bckd, fair time, long abs: improved at 1m on gd, 10f sure to suit: more to come. **94**
SIMONDA [10] Mrs A J Perrett 3-8-9 R L Moore 13/2: 2: ch f Singspiel - Jetbeeah (Lomond) Held up, hdwy to chase wnr fnl 1f, kept on but no ch: debut, ran v green & clr of rem: half-sister to 6f wnr Dazilyn Lady & 10f scorer Miss Grace: dam a 1m wnr, sire high-class at mid-dists: eff over an easy 1m on fast: improve. *3½* **79**
3740 **DREAM ALIVE 11** [6] M Blanshard 3-9-0 t F Norton 16/1: 03: b c Unfuwain - Petite Sonnerie (Persian Bold) Chsd ldrs, onepcd fnl 2f: prob eff over an easy 1m on fast grnd: wears a t-strap. *5* **74**

WINDSOR   MONDAY 16.08.04   Sharp, Fig 8 Track

2767 **HUNTERS VALLEY 51** [7] R Hannon 3-8-9 (66) P Dobbs 9/1: 23-02404: Chsd ldr, wknd 1.5f out: abs. **2 65**
3631 **DANZE ROMANCE 15** [2]3-8-9 S Drowne 14/1: 005: b f Danzero - By Arrangement (Bold Arrangement) **2 61**
Rear, nvr nr ldrs on h'cap qual run: with J Dunlop & modest form to date.
2907 **MOORS MYTH 45** [4]3-9-0 (76) R Hughes 5/2: 0-3656: Led till 2f out, wknd: well bckd, 6 wk abs: **1 64**
btr expected, prob went off too fast: see 2907.
1763 **COUNT BORIS 93** [1]3-9-0 S Carson 33/1: 07: Rear, nvr a factor: 3 month abs. **shd 63**
3217} **DIEQUEST 385** [5]3-9-0 J F Egan 20/1: 0-8: Mid-div, btn 2f out on reapp. **1¼ 60**
3243 **EXPLICIT 31** [9]3-9-0 Martin Dwyer 25/1: 009: Chsd ldrs, btn 3f out & fin last. **10 40**
9 Ran   Time 1m 46.38 (2.38)   Owned: Racing For Gold   Trained: Newmarket

3980   8.10 Sandra Coltman Surprise 60th Birthday Classified Stakes 3yo+ 0-70 (E)
£3474 £1069 £535   **1m2f7y**   Good/Firm 28   +01 Fast   Inside

3828 **EL CHAPARRAL 7** [6] D K Ivory 4-9-1 (68) Dane O'Neill 14/1: 0020201: Held up, hdwy to chase ldrs **74**
when carr left 2f out, went on ent fnl 1f, held on, drvn out: fair time: settled btr today & gained first success:
suited by 10f on fast & firm grnd, likes Windsor: has tried cheek pieces, btr without: see 3477 (C/D).
3949 **DREAM MAGIC 2** [9] M J Ryan 6-9-4 (73) Martin Dwyer 4/1: 4050032: Chsd ldrs, imprvd to lead 2f **nk 77**
out, collared ent fnl 1f, kept on & only just btn: qck reapp, clr of rem: in fine form, see 3949.
3187 **RIDGE BOY 23** [2] R Hannon 3-8-7 (70) P Dobbs 12/1: 560103: Chsd ldrs, ev ch 2f out, sn onepcd: **3½ 68**
prob stays 10f: see 2971 (1m, here).
3734 **DICKIE DEADEYE 11** [7] G B Balding 7-9-1 (70) R Thomas(5) 11/4 FAV: 2231134: Chsd ldrs, ev ch 2f **4 62**
out, sn wknd: well bckd: btr 3222 (12f).
4426} **SERBELLONI 327** [8]4-9-1 (70) D Holland 16/1: 6/4660-5: b g Spectrum - Rose Vibert (Caerleon) **2 59**
Held up, some hdwy, nvr dngrs on reapp: unplcd in '03 (rtd 74): prob stays 10f & handles fast.
3744 **RAGGED JACK 10** [5]3-8-7 (70) S W Kelly 25/1: 4-231566: Held up, nvr nr ldrs: see 3133 (5f). **1½ 57**
3696 **BRAVE DANE 3** [10]6-9-5 (74) J Fortune 5/1: 6120027: Slowly away, nvr nr ldrs: btr 3696. **¾ 60**
3625 **HAIL THE CHIEF 16** [3]7-9-4 (73) R Smith 12/1: 1403068: Chsd ldrs 1m, sn wknd. **1¾ 56**
3791 **ZARIANO 9** [4]4-9-3 (72) L Keniry(3) 20/1: 5160-209: Made most till 3f out, wknd: btr 3286 (AW). **nk 54**
3630 **DU PRE 15** [1]3-8-8 (74) S Drowne 7/2: 30-02130: 10th: Led early, remained prom till regained **1 51**
lead 3f out till 2f out, sn wknd & eased: bckd from 5/1: btr clrly expected, see 3603 & 3291.
10 Ran   Time 2m 08.74(2.74)   Owned: Mr K T Ivory   Trained: Radlett

BRIGHTON   MONDAY 16.08.04   Lefthand, V Sharp, Undulating Track

Official Going GOOD/FIRM

3981   2.30 E B F /Totepool Median Auction Maiden Stakes 2yo (F)
£2947 £842 £421   **5f213y rnd**   Good/Firm 38   -26 Slow   Inside

3329 **ASIAN TIGER 26** [7] R Hannon 2-9-0 (83) R L Moore 15/8 FAV: 2253501: Mid-div, hdwy over 2f out, **81**
pushed out ins fnl 1f, led nr fin: bckd: stays 6f on fast & soft, any trk: gd confidence boost.
3473 **MANEKI NEKO 22** [1] M H Tompkins 2-9-0 F P Ferris(3) 9/2: 42: Handy, hdwy to lead ins fnl 1f, hdd **nk 79**
& just held: stays 6f on fast: joc 2 day careless riding ban: ran to form of 3473 (debut).
3411 **MOLLY DANCER 24** [2] M R Channon 2-8-9 T E Durcan 14/1: 003: b f Emarati - Perfect Partner (Be **1½ 69**
My Chief) Keen in 2nd, slt lead 2f out till ins fnl 1f, no extra: Jan first foal: dam unrcd: stays 6f on fast.
3817 **SCROOBY BABY 7** [8] J A Osborne 2-8-9 S W Kelly 4/1: 2024: Led to 2f out, sn no extra. **½ 67**
3473 **EASY MOVER 22** [3]2-8-9 J Mackay 25/1: 55: Dwelt, hdwy on inner when hmpd ins fnl 2f, switched **shd 66**
wide ins fnl 1f, staying on at fin: closer with a clr run, prob 3rd: see 3473.
3478 **POLLITO 21** [4]2-9-0 J Fortune 3/1: 56: b g Rossini - Bezee (Belmez) Cl-up, hmpd after 1f, hung **2 65**
left & no impress ins fnl 2f, btn when not much room 1f out: Mar foal, cost 25,000gns: half-brother to a 10f wnr.
2618 **PICOT DE SAY 56** [5]2-9-0 J F Egan 14/1: 07: b g Largesse - Facsimile (Superlative) Keen in **3½ 54**
mid-div, outpcd 2f out, no impress: op 25/1, 8 wk abs: Mar foal: dam plcd over 5/8f.
     VINO VENUS 0 [6]2-8-9 D Sweeney 66/1: 8: Keen in rear, nvr a factor on debut. **½ 47**
3343 **MISSED TURN 26** [9]2-8-9 (49) R Thomas(5) 50/1: 54469: Keen in rear, wide, nvr nr ldrs. **3½ 36**
9 Ran   Time 1m 11.66 (3.86)   Owned: The Waney Racing Group Inc   Trained: Marlborough

3982   3.00 Jimmy Heal Memorial Handicap Stakes 3yo 35-55 (F)
£2919 £834 £417   **1m1f209y**   Good/Firm 38   -20 Slow   Outside   **[63]**

3733 **DAYDREAM DANCER 11** [9] C G Cox 3-8-12 bl (47) R Smith 10/1: 5000301: Mid-div, hdwy over 2f out, **54**
rdn out ins fnl 1f, led fnl strides: first win: eff at 10f on fast, acts on a v sharp/undul trk.
3874 **LENWADE 5** [10] G G Margarson 3-8-0 (2oh) (33) D Fox(5) 33/1: 3000452: Cl-up, hdwy to lead well ins **hd 41**
fnl 1f, hdd fnl strides: qck reapp: eff at 10f on fast: gd run from 2lb out of the h'cap, not btn far: see 1454.
3913 **COBALT BLUE 3** [11] W J Haggas 3-9-3 VIS (52) J F Egan 10/1: 0615503: Led till well ins fnl 1f, no **1¼ 56**
extra: qck reapp: eff at 1m/10f: back to form of 2613 in first time visor.
3730* **GO GREEN 11** [6] P D Evans 3-9-5 t (54) S Donohoe(7) 3/1 FAV: 0050214: In tch, outpcd 4f out, kept **3 53**
on again fnl 2f: well bckd: up in class after 3730 (sell h'cap).
3900 **CITY GENERAL 4** [2]3-9-3 p (52) S Chin 10/1: 0205105: Keen & rcd in 2nd, wknd over 1f out: qck reapp. **nk 50**
3300 **WALTZING BEAU 28** [7]3-8-11 (46) G Baker 8/1: 0000236: Slow away in rear, late gains: clr of rem. **¾ 43**
3605 **SEMELLE DE VENT 16** [1]3-9-6 vis (55) J Fortune 4/1: 6-330027: Mid-div, no impress over 1f out. **11 35**
3695 **FORGE LANE 12** [3]3-9-6 bl (55) R L Moore 12/1: 0004208: Bhd, nvr a factor: jt top-weight. **1 33**
3913 **ROYAL STARLET 3** [4]3-8-13 VIS (48) P Dobbs 6/1: 00-00459: Cl-up, wknd 6f out: qck reapp: visor. **3 21**
2692 **MARY CARLETON 53** [12]3-8-5 (40) M Henry 12/1: 0600: 10th: ch f Halling - Anne Bonny (Ajdal) **6 4**
Slow away, nvr a factor: prev: abs h'cap bow, mdn unplcd prev: dam won over 8/10f: with R Cowell.
3300 **DON ARGENTO 28** [8]3-8-6 (1ow) (40) T E Durcan 33/1: 000U300: 11th: Slow away in rear, not clr run **2 2**
over 2f out, sn btn: rider reported mount to be unsuited by this trk: see 3175.
11 Ran   Time 2m 3.61 (5.81)   Owned: The Grey Lady Partnership   Trained: Hungerford

3983 **3.30 Fenton Timber Claiming Stakes 4yo+ (F)**
£2884 £824 £412 **1m3f196y** **Good/Firm 38** **+05 Fast** Outside

3038} **ARABIAN MOON 394** [2] R Brotherton 8-9-5 (71) D Nolan(3) 4/1: 04/0060-1: ch g Barathea - Excellent Alibi (Exceller) Rcd in 2nd till lead over 3f out, pushed clr ins fnl 1f: hdles fit (claim wnr, rtd 110h, stays 2m/3m on firm, gd & any trk, tried visor & cheek pieces, M Pipe): h'cap & cond stks unplcd in '03 (rtd 90, S Dow): rnr-up first '02 start (h'cap): eff at 10/12f, stays 2m: acts on firm, gd & polytrack, any trk. **67**
2 Feb'02 Ling 12ap 87a-81 C: 2 Jun'01 Newb 13.2g/f 83-84 D:
3715 **BANNINGHAM BLAZE 11** [4] A W Carroll 4-8-10 vis (48) R Thomas(5) 2/1: 6531322: Rear, hdwy over 2f out, no impress on wnr fnl 1f: see 3715. *5* **52**
4239} **ALAARED 336** [1] M R Channon 4-9-5 c (83) T E Durcan 7/4 FAV: 642214-3: b g King of Kings - Celtic Loot (Irish River) Bhd, hdwy over 2f out, sn onepcd: well bckd, long hdles abs (mdn 4th, rtd 90h, eye cover, B Gandolfo): won 1 of 6 '03 starts (mdn, J Dunlop): eff at 10f, suited by 12f, 14f+ could suit: acts on firm & gd, easy or stiff/gall trks: can force the pace. *7* **50**
1 Aug'03 Newm 12fm 83-(83) D: 2 Jul'03 Kemp 12g/f 76-(83) D: 2 Jun'03 Sali 9.9fm 84- D:
2623 **SHANNONS DREAM 56** [3] P W Hiatt 8-7-12 (18) J Mackay 50/1: 000/00//-04: Chsd lds, outpcd 4f out. *1¾* **26$**
2273 **GABOR 70** [5]5-8-13 bl (50) R L Moore 4/1: 4500-005: b g Danzig Connection - Kiomi (Niniski) Led till over 3f out, no extra 2f out: recent beg chase 6th (rtd 55, stays 2m on firm & gd, any trk, eff with/ without blnks/eye-shield): won a h'cap in '03: won a clmr & a class stks in '02: eff over 1m/12f on firm & gd/soft, stiff/gall or sharp/undul trks: wore blnks here, has run well in an eye-shield. *2* **38**
1 Aug'03 Brig 9.9fm 65-61 F: 2 Aug'03 Brig 9.9fm 61-(61) F: 1 Jul'02 Sali 12g/f 78- D: 1 Jun'02 Nott 9.9gd 78- E:
2 May'02 Ayr 9g/s 70- E: 2 Sep'01 Bath 8fm 77-74 C:
5 Ran Time 2m 32.22 (4.02) Owned: Mr Roy Brotherton Trained: Pershore

3984 **4.00 Weatherbys Insurance Handicap Stakes 3yo+ 0-75 (E)** **[71]**
£3747 £1153 £576 **5f59y rnd** **Good/Firm 38** **-06 Slow** RACE VOID

3403 **ONE WAY TICKET 24** [1] J M Bradley 4-9-12 p (69) R L Moore 7/1: 3100041: Stall opened late, sn led & made virtually all, drvn out ins fnl 1f: top-weight: eff over 5/7f & acts on firm, gd/soft & prob any trk: likes to force the pace, gd weight carrier: race subs declared void following stalls failure: see 2626. **73**
3673 **REDWOOD STAR 13** [13] P L Gilligan 4-8-11 e (54) D Sweeney 11/1: 4003042: In tch, hdwy 2f out, chsd wnr ins fnl 1f, kept on: race declared void following stalls failure: see 3673. *nk* **57**
3966 **YORKIE 1** [7] P A Blockley 5-8-13 (56) P Makin(5) 9/2 FAV: 00022043: Stall opened late, bhd, hdwy over 1f out, kept on: 4th yesterday, well bckd: race declared void following stalls failure: see 2044. *½* **57**
3759 **KEW THE MUSIC 10** [12] M R Channon 4-8-9 VIS (52) T O'Brien(7) 20/1: 0-000004: Mid-div, hung left 2f out, styd on fnl 1f: first time visor: see 976. *¾* **51**
3341 **FLARAN 26** [11]4-9-2 (59) K McEvoy 16/1: 01504-05: b g Emarati - Fragrance (Mtoto) Rcd in 2nd, onepcd 1f out: won 1 of 6 '03 starts (h'cap): mdn unplcd in '02 (rtd 64): eff at 6f on fast, acts on a gall trk: likes to run-up with/force the pace. 1 Aug'03 Hayd 6g/f 64-57 E: *1¼* **54**
3812 **FINGER OF FATE 8** [8]4-7-13 bl (42) D Fox(5) 16/1: 6003036: Stall opened late, fin well. *nk* **36**
3720 **IMPERIUM 11** [6]3-9-9 (68) J F Egan 5/1: 0006027: Rear, hung left 2f out, switched wide over 1f out, kept on but not pace to chall: see 3720. *½* **60**
3673* **TABOOR 13** [4]6-8-13 h bl t (56) S Hitchcott(3) 8/1: 0206018: Chsd ldrs, no impress over 1f out. *nk* **47**
3751 **MULTAHAB 10** [2]5-8-2 t (45) B Swarbrick(5) 16/1: 2400009: Stall opened late, rear, not clr run over 2f out till over 1f out, kept on fnl 1f: closer with a clr run: see 802 & 435. *shd* **35**
3640 **ERRACHT 14** [5]6-9-3 (60) G Baker 14/1: 6000500: 10th: Cl-up, wknd over 2f out: see 1371. *¾* **48**
3673 **GONENDUNNETT 13** [3]5-9-2 vis (59) S Chin 8/1: 1031050: 11th: Stall opened late, al bhd. *4* **35**
3602 **BOANERGES 16** [9]7-8-5 (48) F P Ferris(3) 16/1: 0050000: 12th: Stall opened late, nvr a factor. *nk* **23**
3371 **MALUTI 25** [10]3-8-9 (54) J Mackay 7/1: 0631420: 13th: Stall opened late & slow away, hdwy wide 3f out, wknd 2f out: btr 3371. *3* **20**
13 Ran Time 1m 2.42 (2.42) Owned: Saracen Racing Trained: Chepstow

3985 **4.30 Elvisthepokerplayer Com Median Auction Maiden Stakes 3-4yo (E)**
£3367 £1036 £518 **5f213y rnd** **Good/Firm 38** **+02 Fast** Inside

3884 **PATTERDALE 4** [7] W J Haggas 3-9-0 (86) R L Moore 4/7 FAV: 5200-21: Trkd ldrs, hdwy to lead 2f out, hung left over 1f out, pushed out fnl 1f: qck reapp: eff at 6/7f on firm & gd, acts on a v sharp/undul trk: sharper for & built on recent reapp: see 3884. **79**
3176 **CAFE AMERICANO 34** [3] D W P Arbuthnot 4-9-3 e (42) D Sweeney 33/1: 000-0502: Bhd, hdwy wide 3f out, chsd wnr ins fnl 1f, not his pace: stays 6f, rtn to 7f prob suit: see 2630. *1¾* **71$**
3610 **FASCINATION STREET 16** [1] M A Jarvis 3-8-9 (65) M Henry 7/2: 6-65023: Prsd ldr, onepcd dist. *1¼* **62**
3165 **MONTANA 35** [4] J L Spearing 4-9-3 (60) K McEvoy 10/1: 23000-04: Led to 2f out, no extra: op 7/1. *½* **65$**
3911 **POPPYLINE 3** [5]4-8-12 bl (48) S Chin 9/1: 3630065: Bhd, hdwy 2f out, wknd dist: qck reapp. *¾* **57$**
3725 **SACCHARINE 11** [6]3-8-9 (44) K Ghunowa(7) 20/1: 00-036: Handy, wknd over 2f out. *7* **36**
2493 **PHILLY DEE 61** [2]3-8-9 bl (42) R Thomas(5) 66/1: 0000007: Handy, no impress 2f out: 9 wk abs. *9* **9**
7 Ran Time 1m 10.01 (2.21) Owned: Mr & Mrs G Middlebrook Trained: Newmarket

3986 **5.00 Chapel Down English Wine Apprentice Handicap Stakes 3yo+ 0-70 (F)** **[70]**
£2954 £844 £422 **7f214y rnd** **Good/Firm 38** **-02 Slow** Inside

3751 **JUSTE POUR LAMOUR 10** [6] P L Gilligan 4-9-11 (67) D Fox 7/1: 0004001: In tch, hdwy over 1f out, rdn to lead well ins fnl 1f: stays 7f/1m on firm & fast, v sharp/undul or a gall trk: rdn with more restaint today. **76**
3733 **ADALAR 11** [9] P D Evans 4-9-2 (58) S Donohoe(3) 5/1 CO FAV: 0004022: Led, joined 2f out, hdd & no extra well ins fnl 1f: consistent, find similar: see 2866. *1½* **62**
2170 **LUCEFER 75** [4] G C H Chung 6-8-2 (44) Dean Williams(5) 5/1 CO FAV: 0034403: Rear, hdwy wide 3f out, chall 2f out till ins fnl 1f, no impress: long abs: won this race last year from a 1lb lower mark: see 1579. *¾* **46**
3676 **LIBERTY ROYAL 13** [12] P J Makin 5-9-6 p (62) A Quinn 5/1 CO FAV: 6063034: Bhd, hdwy over 2f out, onepcd fnl 1f: see 2220. *nk* **63**

BRIGHTON **MONDAY 16.08.04 Lefthand, V Sharp, Undulating Track**

3813 **ADOBE 8** [5]9-9-9 (65) B Swarbrick 13/2: 4200405: Bhd, hmpd over 3f out, hdwy & briefly not clr run well over 1f out, kept on well ins fnl 1f: shade closer with a clr run: well h'capped: see 2010. *2* **62**

3746 **RANNY 10** [11]4-8-4 (46) Stephanie Hollinshead(3) 5/1 CO FAV: 2064456: In tch, hung left 2f out, onepcd. *½* **42**

3726 **SILISTRA 11** [10]5-7-12 (1oh)p (39) Natalia Gemelova(3) 25/1: 0-000057: Handy, no impress 2f out. *hd* **35**

3733 **SMOOTHLY DOES IT 11** [8]3-9-1 (63) R Thomas 10/1: 0206048: Rear, modest late gains. *1½* **55**

3717 **CARGO 11** [3]5-8-5 t (47) P Makin 10/1: 3200229: Chsd ldrs, hmpd 5f out, no impress over 1f out. *1* **37**

3677 **JOHNNY ALLJAYS 13** [13]3-7-12 (12oh)p (34) Laura Reynolds(7) 25/1: 0000440: 10th: Handy, btn when carr left over 1f out: see 3677. *3* **30**

3714 **ALLODARLIN 11** [1]3-7-12 (1oh) (45) N De Souza 20/1: 0060-000: 11th: Cl-up, fdd 4f out: see 3300. *1* **28**

3677 **CAPTAIN CLOUDY 13** [7]4-8-11 (53) M Savage 12/1: 5660030: 12th: Keen in 2nd, wknd over 2f out. *hd* **34**

12 Ran Time 1m 35.21(3.21) Owned: Mr Ian Marks Trained: Newmarket

NOTTINGHAM **MONDAY 16.08.04 Lefthand, Galloping Track**

Official Going GOOD (GOOD/SOFT places).

3987

2.15 Racing Uk Nursery Handicap Stakes 2yo (E) **[91]**
£3916 £1205 £603 **5f13y str** **Good 43** **-01 Slow** Stands Side

3832* **COLEORTON DANCER 7** [9] K A Ryan 2-8-8 (6ex) (71) A Mullen(7) 5/4 FAV: 0444011: Chsd ldrs, hdwy/carried left over 1f out, qcknd to lead ins last & rdn clr, rdly: hvly bckd under a 6lb pen, op 7/4: eff at 5f on firm & gd/soft grnd, easy or gall trk: much imprvd for recent gldg & drop to min trip, can complete a hat-trick. **88+**

3536 **ON THE WATERLINE 19** [10] P D Evans 2-8-12 (75) S Drowne 14/1: 23042: Trkd ldrs, switched over 1f out & kept on, no ch with wnr ins last: see 3536, 1573 & 1237. *3½* **80**

3817 **DANES CASTLE 7** [8] B J Meehan 2-8-12 BL (75) L Dettori 10/1: 32233: Led till dist, kept on for press: gd run in 1st time blnks: h'cap bow: acts on firm, gd & both AWs: shld find a race: see 3817, 3296. *½* **78**

3369 **BOLD MINSTREL 25** [2] M Quinn 2-9-7 (84) F Norton 14/1: 032124: Handy, rdn & briefly led dist, sn hdd & outpcd: acts on firm & gd grnd: see 3369 & 3097. *shd* **86**

3623 **RANCHO CUCAMONGA 16** [7]2-8-7 (70) K Darley 11/1: 001005: Dwelt, pushed along rear, not pace to chall: btr 2927 (6f). *1¼* **69**

3607 **PRO TEMPORE 16** [11]2-8-4 (67) P Hanagan 11/1: 4166: Dwelt & rear, hdwy when no room & forced to switch over 1f out, kept on late: no luck here, keep in mind, poss over 6f: see 3607 & 3227. *hd* **65+**

3296* **LOUPHOLE 28** [3]2-9-5 (82) S Sanders 7/1: 3417: Cl-up, wknd over 1f out: h'cap bow: btr 3296. *1* **77**

3743 **TARTATARTUFATA 10** [1]2-7-12 (1oh) (60) Joanna Badger 50/1: 0408: Went left start & rcd alone, in tch till over 1f out: btr 1424 (soft). *¾* **54**

3606 **CHILALI 16** [4]2-7-12 (1oh) (60) Dale Gibson 50/1: 3303649: Chsd ldrs, btn when no room dist. *2* **48**

2490 **TARA TARA 61** [5]2-9-3 (80) R Winston 6/1: 1000: 10th: Mid-div, rdn/hmpd dist, sn bhd: abs. *2½* **59**

3041 **MAURO 39** [6]2-8-2 (65) J Quinn 25/1: 42460: 11th: Dwelt & al outpcd rear: btr 1805 & 1466. *1¾* **39**

11 Ran Time 1m 0.71 (2.21) Owned: Coleorton Moor Racing Trained: Hambleton

3988

2.45 Wright Brothers Maiden Auction Stakes 2yo (E)
£3916 £1205 £603 **5f13y str** **Good 43** **-21 Slow** Stands Side

2889 **EXPONENTIAL 45** [10] S C Williams 2-8-11 bl e D Allan 8/1: 01: b g Namid - Exponent (Exbourne) Al handy, led dist, rdn out: 6 wk abs, gamble from 100/1: 27,000gns 2yo, Apr foal: dam unrcd, related to 1m/10f juv wnrs: eff at 5f on fast grnd & a gall trk, shld stay further: eff in eye-shield & blnks: much imprvd from debut & landed a big gamble for shrewd stable. **81**

3728 **STAR DUSTER 11** [11] B R Millman 2-8-2 S Righton 66/1: 02: Chsd ldrs, switched & kept on ins last, not pace of wnr: imprvd from intro: eff at 5f on gd grnd: see 3728. *1* **69**

3652 **BREAKING SHADOW 14** [7] R A Fahey 2-8-9 P Hanagan 3/1 FAV: 233: Chsd ldrs, outpcd over 2f out, kept on for press ins last: gelded, nicely bckd: shld apprec h'caps: see 3652 & 3178. *shd* **76**

2933 **DISPOL ISLE 44** [8] T D Barron 2-8-2 J Fanning 5/1: 444: Badly bmpd start, hdwy to chase ldrs halfway, no extra ins last: 6 wk abs: can imporve on this & h'caps shld suit: see 2933 & 2360. *½* **67**

3431 **WIGWAM WILLIE 23** [15]2-8-11 K Darley 7/2: 45: Pushed along rear, styd on well ins last, nrst fin: gelded, unsuited by drop to min trip: handles fast & gd grnd: looks sure to improve back over 6f+. *1¾* **71+**

2360 **BEN CASEY 66** [2]2-8-9 F Lynch 50/1: 06: b c Whittingham - Hot Ice (Petardia) Rcd towards centre, chsd ldrs, no impress from dist: 2 month abs: 9,200 gns Feb 1st foal, dam a 5f juv wnr. *¾* **67**

INGLETON [6]2-8-9 G Gibbons 18/1: 7: b c Komaite - Dash Cascade (Absalom) Pushed along towards rear, kept on late, no threat: 10,000 gns Feb foal, half brother to 2 juv wnrs at 6f/1m, dam unrcd. *nk* **66**

3626 **DOITFORREEL 15** [1]2-8-2 F Norton 16/1: 08: Rcd far side early, switched & jnd main group halfway, kept on late, nrst fin: imprvd from intro & likely to apprec return to 6f+. *½* **57**

3431 **BLUSHING RUSSIAN 23** [12]2-8-7 G Faulkner 7/1: 09: Handy, led over 2f out till dist, sn btn. *1½* **57**

2625 **WIZZSKILAD 56** [14]2-8-7 (61) R Havlin 33/1: 0463040: 10th: Mid-div, no impress fnl 2f. *nk* **56**

3606 **KERNY 16** [5]2-8-11 G Hind 66/1: 060: 11th: Bhd, only mod late prog. *1¼* **56**

1466 **SAHARA MIST 108** [3]2-8-2 VIS Joanna Badger 100/1: 0650: 12th: Rcd far side early, switched halfway & al bhd: visor, abs. *4* **35**

3544 **LOVELORN 18** [9]2-8-7 T Lucas 20/1: 300: 13th: Chsd ldrs, struggling fnl 2f: btr 2336. *½* **38**

3517 **HEARTSONFIRE 19** [13]2-8-2 A McCarthy 8/1: 33040: 14th: Led, rdn halfway & sn hdd, sn bhd. *¾* **31**

SEASON TICKET [4]2-8-2 J Quinn 16/1: 0: 15th: Rcd on far side & al bhd. *¾* **29**

15 Ran Time 1m 01.72 (3.22) Owned: The Exponential Partnership Trained: Newmarket

3989

3.15 Weatherbys Bank Conditions Stakes 3yo+ (C)
£8694 £3298 £1649 **5f13y str** **Good 43** **+18 Fast** Stands Side

3062 **CONTINENT 39** [7] D Nicholls 7-8-11 (108) D Holland 11/4 FAV: 0600-301: Trkd ldrs, smooth hdwy to lead ins last, rdn clr: gd time. nicely bckd, op 7/2: suited by 5/6f, stays 7f: acts on firm, likes gd & soft: right back to form today, former Gr 1 wnr: see 2949. **111+**

3551 **BISHOPS COURT 18** [8] Mrs J R Ramsden 10-8-11 (105) L Dettori 7/2: 2033002: Trkd ldrs, rdn & narrow lead over 1f out, hdd & not pace of wnr ins last: op 11/4: see 2638 & 1207. *2* **105**

3773 **FOREVER PHOENIX 9** [4] R M H Cowell 4-8-6 (93) K Darley 3/1: 2R02303: Reared badly start, sn chsd   *1*   **97**
ldrs, kept on for press but not land a blow: lost ch at the start: see 3466, 3304 & 1615.
3551 **DRAGON FLYER 18** [5] M Quinn 5-8-6 (95) F Norton 9/2: 0034304: Led, edged left over 1f out, sn   *1*   **94**
hdd & no extra: op 6/1: see 3409, 3304.
3427 **STRENSALL 23** [3]7-8-11 (76) P Hanagan 66/1: 0340505: Cl-up, btn over 1f out: needs h'caps.   *3*   **90$**
3466 **FIRST ORDER 22** [1]3-8-9 (101) S Sanders 9/2: 2113-206: Cl-up, rdn & btn dist, eased: btr 3279.   *5*   **75**
3880 **PERCY DOUGLAS 5** [2]4-8-11 t (40) Ann Stokell 200/1: 0050067: Chsd ldrs, btn halfway: outclassed.   *3*   **66$**
7 Ran   Time 59.77 (1.27)   Owned: Lucayan Stud   Trained: Thirsk

---

3990   3.45 Nottinghamshire County Cricket Club Handicap Stakes 3yo 0-80 (D)   **[87]**
£5785 £1780 £890   **1m2f**   **Good 43**   **-34 Slow**   Inside

3231 **DANCE TO MY TUNE 31** [6] M W Easterby 3-8-1 (60) Dale Gibson 15/2: 06-01041: Held up in tch, rdn   **66**
& hdwy to lead ins last, drvn out: slow time: eff at 1m/slowly run 10f: acts on fast & soft grnd, stiff/gall trks.
3255 **IN DEEP 31** [4] Mrs P N Dutfield 3-8-5 (2ow) (62) R Havlin 14/1: 62-00602: Handy & led 3f out, hdd   *¾*   **68**
2f out, ch ins last, no extra nr fin: acts on fast & gd grnd, stays a gall 10f, tried further: see 2250.
3377 **SERRAMANNA 25** [5] H R A Cecil 3-9-0 (73) J Quinn 12/1: 62-653: Rear, switched wide & styd on for   *¾*   **76**
press, nrst fin: imprvd from h'cap bow: acts on fast & gd grnd, stays a gall 10f: could find similar: see 3377.
3161 **SPECTESTED 35** [3] A W Carroll 3-7-12 (11oh)p (46) M Halford(7) 33/1: 0-002504: Rear, prog when no   *shd*   **60**
room over 2f out & switched, kept on onepace for press: eff around 10/12f, handles fibresand & gd grnd.
3540* **DAMI 18** [11]3-9-4 p (77) D Holland 9/2: 5522115: Trkd ldrs, short of room & lost place over 4f   *nk*   **79**
out, switched & kept on onepace ins last: see 3540 & 2837.
3702 **ROCK LOBSTER 12** [2]3-8-5 (64) M Fenton 4/1 JT FAV: 5636146: Held up, hdwy 3f out, ch over 1f   *hd*   **65**
out, sn onepace for press: see 3702 & 3419.
3765 **CHARLIE TANGO 9** [9]3-8-8 (67) K Darley 4/1 JT FAV: 4134357: Held up, hdwy wide to lead 2f out,   *1¾*   **66**
hdd dist, wknd: op 11/2.
3862 **DOCTORED 5** [7]3-9-4 bl (77) S Drowne 8/1: 1113068: Trkd ldrs, short of room over 1f out, drvn &   *½*   **75**
no impress dist: btr 3578, 3471.
3630 **LIVE WIRE LUCY 15** [1]3-9-7 (80) P Hanagan 50/1: 5-030009: Led till 3f out, sn btn: btr 3630.   *13*   **61**
2853 **MOUNTCHARGE 47** [10]3-9-1 (74) S Sanders 15/2: 613-0050: 10th: Cl-up, btn 3f out: abs, new yard.   *3½*   **50**
10 Ran   Time 2m 10.04 (7.74)   Owned: R S Cockerill (Farms) Ltd   Trained: Sheriff Hutton

---

3991   4.15 European Breeders Fund Colwick Park Novice Stakes 2yo (D)
£4908 £1510 £755   **1m54y rnd**   **Good 43**   **-21 Slow**   Centre

2959* **NORTHERN SPLENDOUR 43** [1] Saeed bin Suroor 2-9-4 L Dettori 7/2: 311: Made all, qcknd 3f out,   **103**
rdn & in command ins last: eff at 7f, improve for step up to 1m with forcing tactics applied: acts on fast &
gd/soft grnd, gall trks: lightly rcd & prog colt, useful display: see 2959.
3585 **IN THE FAN 17** [2] J L Dunlop 2-9-2 (93) S Sanders 13/8 FAV: 2132: Trkd ldr, drvn & kept on, held   *2*   **96**
from dist: stays 1m: win again after 3585 & 3214.
3594* **LE CORVEE 16** [6] A King 2-9-4 J D Smith 2/1: 13: Trkd ldrs, styd on for press fnl 2f, al held: *1¾*   **95**
nicely bckd & clr of rem: stayd longer 1m trip: acts on soft grnd, see 3594 (7f).
2178 **HILL FAIRY 74** [7] T P Tate 2-8-7 J Fanning 33/1: 64: Went right start & held up, kept on late,   *7*   **72**
no threat to front trio: longer 1m trip & further will suit: see 2178.
3798* **BLAISE HOLLOW 8** [5]2-9-2 S Drowne 15/2: 0515: Chsd wnr, rdn & btn 2f out: op 6/1: btr 3798.   *1¾*   **78**
3811 **MYTORI 8** [3]2-8-7 Darren Williams 150/1: 06: ch f Vettori - Markievicz (Doyoun) Sn bhd & nvr a   *22*   **29**
factor: cheaply bought Apr foal, half sister to a 6f juv wnr, dam a 6f 3yo scorer.
ASHARON [4]2-8-12 J P Guillambert(3) 33/1: 7: b c Efisio - Arriving (Most Welcome) Dwelt, al   *¾*   **33**
bhd: Jan foal, 25,000 gns purchase: half brother to wnrs at 7f/1m, dam a multiple 10f 3yo scorer.
7 Ran   Time 1m 44.70 (5.3)   Owned: Godolphin   Trained: Newmarket

---

3992   4.45 Schools Out For Summer Apprentice Handicap Stakes 4yo+ 0-75 (E)   **[74]**
£3835 £1180 £590   **1m2f**   **Good 43**   **-16 Slow**   Inside

3625 **ARTISTIC STYLE 16** [1] B Ellison 4-9-3 (63) M Lawson 3/1 FAV: 0600131: Held up, hdwy halfway &   **75**
chsd ldr 2f out, rdn & led dist, hands & heels nr fin: eff at 1m/10f on firm & soft grnd, sharp or gall trks: prog
of late, keep on side: see 3625 & 2967.
2998 **MCQUEEN 41** [13] Mrs H Dalton 4-8-4 (50) A Mullen(3) 9/1: 0600602: Led & rdn clr 3f out, hdd dist   *1¼*   **59**
but kept on & well clr rem: abs: acts on fast, gd & both AWs: well h'capped on turf, win similar if repeating.
3501 **FIRST DYNASTY 20** [4] Miss S J Wilton 4-10-0 (74) H Poulton(3) 14/1: 023-1063: Mid-div, styd on   *6*   **74**
onepace fnl 2f, no ch with front pair: see 1340 (9f mdn, AW).
3895* **GOT TO BE CASH 4** [8] W M Brisbourne 5-8-10 (6ex) (56) P Mathers 11/2: 0530014: Held up, mod hdwy   *5*   **49**
fnl 3f, no threat: quick reapp under a pen, op 4/1: btr 3895 (gd/soft).
2998 **DANCE WORLD 41** [5]4-9-10 (70) L Treadwell 9/1: 4-103005: Mid-div, no impress fnl 3f, 6 wk abs.   *3*   **59**
3904 **PURE MISCHIEF 4** [2]5-9-12 (72) Rory Moore 7/2: 1513246: Held up, only mod prog: quick reapp.   *½*   **60**
3637 **NOPEKAN 15** [10]4-9-13 P (73) P Gallagher 16/1: 6-560007: Chsd ldr, btn 3f out, tried cheekpieces.   *9*   **50**
3492 **LEGALITY 21** [11]4-8-4 (50) M Halford(3) 16/1: 0006-068: Mid-div when hung right halfway & v wide   *2½*   **23**
on bend over 3f out, sn btn.
3678 **DERWENT 12** [7]5-9-4 bl (64) S Shaw(7) 14/1: 0004669: Al bhd: btr 2794.   *shd*   **37**
3325 **LUXOR 27** [6]7-8-2 (4ow)(1oh) (43) D J Cavanagh 20/1: 00-00000: 10th: Cl-up, wknd qckly fnl 3f.   *3½*   **16**
3295 **CURRAGH GOLD 28** [3]4-8-4 (50) Amy Baker(5) 33/1: 61300-00: 11th: Al bhd: see 3295.   *½*   **17**
842 **HUMDINGER 155** [9]4-7-12 (4oh) (40) Donna Caldwell(5) 50/1: 060-0000: 12th: Sn strug rear: abs.   *10*   **0**
1593 **MARENGO 102** [12]10-7-12 (19oh) (25) M Nem(7) 80/1: 6006400: 13th: Dwelt & al rear, new yard.   *3½*   **0**
13 Ran   Time 2m 08.2(5.9)   Owned: Mr & Mrs D A Gamble   Trained: Malton

YARMOUTH   MONDAY 16.08.04   Lefthand, Fair, Flat Track

Official Going Good/Firm (Good Places)

3993

5.25 Betfred 'the Bonus King' E B F Maiden Stakes 2yo (D)
£3682 £1133 £567   **5f43y str**   **Good 56**   **-27 Slow**   Stands side

3576 **REGINA 17** [4] Sir Michael Stoute 2-8-9 K Fallon 11/10 FAV: 31: Cl-up, styd on ins fnl 1f, pushed out, val 3L+: well bckd: eff at 5f on gd, 6f sure to suit: much improved, win more races. **92**

3411 **HONEY RYDER 24** [2] D R Loder 2-8-9 T P Queally 7/4: 22: Led, hdd under press ins fnl 1f, not pace wnr: clr rem: eff at 5f, rtn to 6f will suit: acts on fast & gd grnd: still ran green & can find similar, see 3411. *1¼* **82**

EMERALD LODGE 0 [3] J Noseda 2-9-0 E Ahern 16/1: 3: b c Grand Lodge - Emerald Peace (Green Desert) Handy over 3f, sn no extra: op 10/1 on debut: Feb first foal: dam 5f juv wnr. *7* **67**

2310 **STEPHANIES MIND 68** [5] G A Huffer 2-8-9 (78) R Mullen 7/2: 0344: Bhd, rcd keenly, nvr a factor: op 5/1, 10 wk abs: v disapp: btr 2310 (6f) & 2061. *1¾* **57**

WILLIAM JAMES 0 [1]2-9-0 A Culhane 80/1: 5: b g Mujahid - Pain Perdu (Waajib) Handy 3f, wknd: debut: Mar foal, half-brother to a 7f juv wnr: dam successful at 10f: sire Gr 1 wnr at 7f: with M J Wallace. *1½* **58**

5 Ran   Time 1m 4.25 (4.15)   Owned: Cheveley Park Stud   Trained: Newmarket

3994

5.55 Betfred Com In-Running Claiming Stakes 2yo (F)
£2926 £836 £418   **6f3y str**   **Good 56**   **-44 Slow**   Stands side

3723 **MEGELL 11** [6] M G Quinlan 2-8-7 (67) T P Queally 100/30: 62051: Keen cl-up, styd on to lead 1f out, drvn out to hold on: eff at 6f, tried further: acts on fast & gd grnd: apprec drop to claim grade. **65**

3756 **CAMPEON 10** [1] M J Wallace 2-9-2 (74) K Fallon 7/4 FAV: 0524352: Led, hdd under press 1f out, kept on, not pace wnr: bckd: continues to run well: see 3431 & 2952. *¾* **71**

3570 **GOLDHILL PRINCE 17** [5] W G M Turner 2-8-10 p (65) C Haddon(7) 9/1: 1113653: Cl-up, ev ch 1f out, kept on, just held for 2nd: op 13/2: likes sellers/claimers: see 2330 & 2177. *shd* **64**

3491* **TIPSY LILLIE 21** [4] Julian Poulton 2-8-8 (59) A Culhane 5/1: 0001414: In tch, onepcd fnl 1f. *¾* **60**

3699 **FANTASY DEFENDER 12** [2]2-8-11 E Ahern 12/1: 000005: Bhd, outpcd halfway, rallied late: op 9/1. *hd* **62**

3178 **ALZARMA 34** [3]2-8-12 (63) D Tudhope(7) 11/2: 0306: Prom, ev ch dist, sn no extra: btr 2882. *½* **62**

3847 **SAPPHIRE PRINCESS 6** [7]2-8-3 (54) P Doe 20/1: 4556157: Al in rear: qck reapp: btr 3745 (AW). *5* **38**

7 Ran   Time 1m 16.40 (6.0)   Owned: Mrs J Quinlan   Trained: Newmarket

3995

6.25 Betfred Com Now On-Line Handicap Stakes 3yo 0-75 (E)   **[80]**
£3877 £1193 £597   **7f3y str**   **Good 56**   **+04 Fast**   Stands side

3604 **GLENCALVIE 16** [4] J Noseda 3-8-7 VIS (59) E Ahern 11/2 JT FAV: 05041: In tch, styd on to lead bef 3f out, pushed clr fnl 1f, eased cl-home, val 6L+: eff at 7f on fast & gd grnd: much imprvd for visor & shld make a qk follow-up under a pen: see 3604. **73**

3363 **MORAG 25** [3] I A Wood 3-8-9 (61) S Sanders 6/1: 4000662: Chsd ldrs, prog to chase wnr bef 1f out, al held: cheek pieces left off: acts on firm & gd grnd: see 1359. *4* **62**

3604 **MOLINIA 16** [9] R M Beckett 3-8-1 T (53) N Mackay(3) 11/2 JT FAV: 0P40403: Missed break, prog 2f out, no impress fnl 1f: op 8/1: first time t-strap: btr 3283 (fast). *1½* **53**

3036 **ALCHERA 40** [12] R F Johnson Houghton 3-8-10 (62) R Mullen 14/1: 0064404: Rear stands side duo, prog despite hanging left bef 1f out, nvr getting to principals: 6 wk abs: been gelded, better run: see 2195. *½* **61**

3448 **VIOLET AVENUE 23** [11]3-8-5 (57) J Bramhill 20/1: 04-06405: Held up, prog 3f out, no impress fnl 1f. *1½* **53**

3739 **SOVIET SCEPTRE 11** [2]3-9-2 t (68) A Culhane 12/1: 56-3046: Nvr nrr than mid-div: see 3739 & 1464. *¾* **62**

2784 **GET TO THE POINT 50** [7]3-8-8 bl (60) B Reilly(3) 16/1: 2500057: Handy till dist, wknd: 7 wk abs. *½* **53**

3685 **LISTEN TO REASON 12** [6]3-8-13 (65) M Fenton 14/1: 50-108: In tch 4f, sn no extra: btr 3194. *2½* **53**

3870 **SHIFTY NIGHT 5** [8]3-7-12 (3oh) (47) Lisa Jones 18/1: 0410609: Chsd ldrs, wknd 2f out: qck reapp. *1¾* **34**

3378 **TYZACK 25** [10]3-8-8 (60) Dean McKeown 40/1: 240-5000: 10th: Nvr nrr than mid-div: btr 1088. *1¼* **42**

3679 **QUEENSTOWN 12** [1]3-8-12 bl (64) D Corby(3) 11/1: 22-03500: 11th: With majority of field in centre till bef 3f out, sn no extra: btr 3286. *½* **45**

3391 **ALI DEO 24** [14]3-9-7 (73) T P Queally 7/1: 00-13060: 12th: Switched to centre group, al rear: gelded. *6* **42**

3732 **CAZENOVE 11** [5]3-8-10 P (62) K Fallon 9/1: 04600: 13th: Cl-up 4f, sn wknd, veered fnl 1f: cheekpieces. *12* **9**

3655* **DELLAGIO 14** [13]3-8-4 (56) J Quinn 7/1: 0040010: 14th: Led stands side group, fdd fnl 3f: trainer reported mount was unsuited by ground: btr 3655 (fast, 6f). *1* **1**

14 Ran   Time 1m 26.30 (3.7)   Owned: Mrs Susan Roy   Trained: Newmarket

3996

6.55 Betfred Com Early Prices From 9 A M Handicap Stakes 3yo+ 35-55 (F)   **[59]**
£3423 £978 £489   **1m3y str**   **Good 56**   **-12 Slow**   Stands side

3741 **BAND 11** [12] B A McMahon 4-9-9 (54) S Sanders 5/1 JT FAV: 0004051: Mid-div, outpcd 3f out, rallied fnl 1f, styd on for press cl-home: eff at 7f/1m: acts on fast, likes gd & soft: first win: see 1883. **62**

3812 **KELSEAS KOLBY 8** [11] P Butler 4-9-10 vis (55) R Lucey Butler(7) 12/1: 1434422: In tch, prog & ev ch dist, led ins fnl 1f, sn edged right, hdd on line: new stable: continues in gd form & deserves to go one btr. *shd* **61**

3748* **FANTASY CRUSADER 10** [10] J A Gilbert 5-9-7 p (52) J Quinn 11/1: 3200313: Keen in tch, ev ch 1f out, kept on, not pace front 2: creditable eff in defeat: rtn to 10f will suit: see 3748. *¾* **56**

3733 **OH SO ROSIE 11** [20] J S Moore 4-9-10 p (55) Derek Nolan(7) 12/1: 5001004: Held up, prog 2f out, kept on ins fnl 1f: see 3363. *hd* **58**

3706* **TAIYO 12** [7]4-9-1 (46) E Ahern 20/1: 400P015: Cl-up, led dist, hdd well ins fnl 1f, no extra: sell h'cap wnr. *nk* **48**

3526 **EXPECTED BONUS 19** [17]5-8-13 (44) W Ryan 6/1: 00-04006: Bhd, prog 2f out, onepcd fnl 1f. *1½* **43**

3812 **WODHILL BE 8** [16]4-8-9 (40) M Tebbutt 66/1: 0030007: Held up, prog 2f out, no impress well ins fnl 1f. *½* **38**

2384 **PEARTREE HOUSE 66** [9]10-8-9 (40) A Culhane 40/1: 0666008: Prom over 6f, no extra: 9 wk abs. *1¾* **34**

2615* **SENNEN COVE 56** [15]5-8-13 t (44) R Ffrench 12/1: 6366119: Rear, prog to lead 2f out, hdd dist, wknd. *2½* **33**

3706 **ZONNEBEKE 12** [19]3-8-11 (48) B Reilly(3) 12/1: 0034120: 10th: Nvr nrr than mid-div: btr 3706 & 3414. *nk* **36**

2365 **GREEN FALCON 66** [1]3-9-4 T (55) R Mullen 20/1: 0330000: 11th: Rear, modest gains: 9 wk abs & t-strap. *2* **39**

893 **MIDNIGHT MAMBO 147** [3]4-8-9 (40) R Mills(7) 33/1: 05-5500: 12th: Handy 6f, wknd: long abs. *¾* **22**

3785 **DAIMAJIN 9** [13]5-8-8 p (39) A Beech(2) 40/1: 0000600: 13th: Al in rear: btr 3530. *½* **20**

YARMOUTH   MONDAY 16.08.04   Lefthand, Fair, Flat Track

3788 **SCARROTTOO 9** [14]6-9-10 (55) T P Queally 5/1 JT FAV: 1403150: 14th: Handy 6f, wknd: btr 3541 (7f). *½* **35**
3034 **PAGAN STORM 40** [18]4-9-10 t (55) Kristin Stubbs(7) 14/1: 5000300: 15th: Al in rear: 6 wk abs. *nk* **34**
3670 **BOWLEGS BILLY 13** [2]4-8-11 p (42) Dean McKeown 33/1: 000-0000: 16th: Keen mid-div, no impress. *hd* **20**
3024 **DIAL SQUARE 40** [8]3-9-1 (52) K Fallon 10/1: 2311100: 17th: Al in rear: 6 wk abs: 'lost action'. *2½* **25**
3764 **PURI 9** [4]5-9-3 bl (48) M Fenton 50/1: 0-400P40: 18th: Led 6f, fdd: btr 3764. *1½* **18**
3650 **Mutared 14** [6]6-8-8 p(39) Lisa Jones 20/1:0   3401 **Vertedanz 24** [5]4-8-13 (44) N Mackay(3) 66/1:0
20 Ran   Time 1m 40.60 (5.5)   Owned: Mr D J Allen   Trained: Tamworth

3997

7.25 Betfred 'we Pay Double Result' Maiden Stakes 3yo+ (D)
£3426 £1054 £527   **1m3f101y**   **Good 56**   **+07 Fast**   Inside

3587 **GIFT VOUCHER 17** [8] Sir Michael Stoute 3-9-0 t (80) K Fallon 1/2 FAV: 03021: Led after 2f, sn over 10L clr, started to idle bef 1f out, rdn out to hold on: well bckd: eff at 12f on fast & gd grnd: eff with a t-strap: only lightly rcd & can rate higher: see 3587. **83**
3802 **SAMARIA 8** [6] C F Wall 3-8-9 R Mullen 8/1: 042: Held up, prog halfway, styd on to chase ldr 2f out, kept on fnl 1f, just held: eff at 10/11.4f on firm & gd grnd: only lightly rcd & now quals for h'caps: see 3802. *1½* **75**
3335 **ENHANCER 26** [1] Mrs L C Jewell 6-9-9 J Quinn 33/1: 003: b g Zafonic - Ypha (Lyphard) In tch, prog 2f out, onepcd ins fnl 1f: unplcd sole bmpr start in 03/04: eff at 11.4f, further shld suit: acts on gd grnd. *1½* **74**
3340 **ONWARD TO GLORY 26** [7] J L Dunlop 4-9-9 (68) E Ahern 22/1: 5/60-004: Nvr nrr than mid-div. *6* **68**
3437 **TIMBER ICE 23** [4]4-9-4 (72) W Ryan 8/1: 0/43-05: Cl-up over 7f, sn rdn & no extra: see 3437. *shd* **62**
MENELAUS 0 [10]3-9-0 T P Queally 8/1: 6: b c Machiavellian - Mezzogiorno (Unfuwain) Nvr nrr than mid-div: debut: with D R Loder. *9* **54**
3675 **WEST END WONDER 13** [3]5-9-9 D Corby(3) 100/1: 047: Al bhd: see 3675. *5* **47**
2719] **REPENT AT LEISURE 767** [2]4-9-9 A Culhane 50/1: 40/-8: b g Bishop of Cashel - Sutosky (Great Nephew) Led, hdd after 2f, fdd 4f out: missed '03: unplcd both '02 starts (rtd 46, med auct mdn, W G M Turner). *1¾* **44**
HANAZAKARI 0 [9]3-9-0 S Sanders 12/1: 9: b c Danzero - Russian Rose (Soviet Lad) Al well adrift: debut. *1¼* **42**
35**TRINITY FAIR 17** [5]3-8-9 M Fenton 80/1: 0000: 10th: Al well adrift. *½* **36**
10 Ran   Time 2m 28.49 (5.69)   Owned: Ballymacoll Stud   Trained: Newmarket

3998

7.55 Betfred In Shops On Phone And On-Line Maiden Handicap Stakes 3yo+ 0-70 (E)   **[77]**
£3907 £1202 £601   **1m6f17y**   **Good 56**   **-29 Slow**   Stands side

3454 **MASTERMAN READY 23** [2] P W Harris 3-9-1 (64) E Ahern 7/1: 6-00601: Keen cl-up, styd on for press to lead cl-home: tchd 9/1: eff at 14f on gd grnd: unexposed around staying dists: see 2700. **68**
3772 **MUNAAWESH 9** [8] D W Chapman 3-8-6 bl (55) A Culhane 10/1: 0420422: Rear, prog wide 2f out, ev ch ins fnl 1f, just denied by wnr: prev eff at 9/11f, now stays 14f: shld find similar: see 3772. *hd* **58**
3208 **WELKINOS BOY 32** [6] J Mackie 3-8-13 (62) Dale Gibson 33/1: 0563: Keen cl-up, led 2f out, hdd under press cl-home: apprec step up to 14f: acts on gd grnd: see 2992. *hd* **64**
3292 **ROSSALL POINT 28** [5] J L Dunlop 3-8-13 (62) K Fallon 3/1: 4504: Bhd, prog 4f out, ev ch ins fnl 1f, not btn far in 4th: bckd: eff at 14f on gd grnd: see 2788. *1* **63**
2980 **SUNDAY CITY 42** [11]3-9-6 (69) T P Queally 9/1: 3355: Rear, prog 4f out, no impress fnl 1f: op 14/1. *½* **69**
3437 **LAWRENCE OF ARABIA 23** [4]4-9-7 (58) S Sanders 11/8 FAV: 004/-066: Mid-div, onepcd bef 1f out: bckd. *1¼* **57**
3340 **LARKING ABOUT 26** [1]4-9-1 BL (52) R Mullen 16/1: 20-00067: Nvr nrr than mid-div: 1st time blnks. *shd* **50**
3701 **LEBENSTANZ 12** [7]4-9-10 (61) N Mackay(3) 14/1: 666608: Al in rear: btr 3240. *3* **56**
3580 **MORNING HAWK 17** [9]3-7-12 (9oh)bl (38) J Quinn 33/1: 0456049: Cl-up, led 3f out, hdd 2f out, wknd. *2½* **40**
3783 **LAHOB 9** [10]4-9-4 (55) M Fenton 33/1: 326-0600: 10th: Led, hdd 3f out, sn wknd & eased: see 2530. *10* **40**
3783 **WODHILL HOPE 9** [3]4-8-11 (48) M Tebbutt 66/1: 4300: 11th: Al well adrift: btr 2867. *2* **31**
11 Ran   Time 3m 9.78(11.98)   Owned: The Mastermen   Trained: Berkhamsted

YORK   TUESDAY 17.08.04   Lefthand, Flat, Galloping Track

Official Going Good

3999

1.20 Ladbroke Knavesmire Stakes Handicap 3yo+ 0-95 (C)   **[93]**
£15925 £4900 £2450   **1m3f198y**   **Good 44**   **-07 Slow**   Inside

3779 **SUALDA 10** [19] R A Fahey 5-8-9 (74) S Sanders 33/1: 2123141: Swtchd start & rear, swtchd & hdwy wide 4f out, styd on for press to lead well ins last, all out: suited by 12f, stays 13f on fm & gd: tough, in form & progressive, stable in fine form: see 3637. **81**
3444 **COURT OF APPEAL 24** [3] B Ellison 7-9-8 t (87) T Eaves(3) 16/1: 4-113202: Trkd ldrs trav well & led 3f out, rdn & joined from over 1f out, hdd well ins last: nicely bckd: back to form after disapp latest: see 1599. *nk* **94**
3531 **KRISTENSEN 20** [1] D Eddy 5-8-12 p (77) J F McDonald(3) 25/1: 0625003: Trkd ldrs, outpcd over 3f out, styd on well for press fnl 1f, no threat: good run, 12f a minimum trip for this tough gelding nowadays. *3* **80**
3617 **MILLVILLE 17** [17] M A Jarvis 4-9-6 (85) P Robinson 16/1: 1011054: Held up, smooth hdwy wide over 3f out, rdn & onepace over 1f out: nicely bckd: shld win on turf: see 877 (AW). *nk* **87**
3029 **TORINMOOR 41** [4]3-9-2 (91) M J Kinane 12/1: 316-5335: Held up, gd hdwy wide 3f out, hung left under press over 1f out & no extra: bckd: abs: just stays 12f on fm & gd: see 3029. *¾* **92**
3794 **SKI JUMP 10** [8]4-9-4 vis (83) P Hanagan 25/1: 601-1606: Mid-div, late gains, nrst fin: shorter priced stablemate of wnr: prob stays 12f: see 2197. *1¼* **82**
1759 **LAGGAN BAY 94** [10]4-8-10 (75) L Keniry(3) 50/1: 5212-067: Bhd, late gains for press, nrst fin: abs. *1¾* **72**
3256 **GENGHIS 32** [2]5-9-2 (81) J Fortune 16/1: 24/3-2528: Handy & led 7f out till 3f out, fdd: see 3256. *1* **77**
3119 **PRINS WILLEM 38** [7]5-9-10 (89) J Murtagh 10/1: 10-23459: Mid-div, eff over 3f out, no impress fnl 2f. *1¼* **83**
3118 **JABAAR 38** [16]6-9-6 (85) J P Spencer 14/1: 0356250: 10th: Rear when hmpd bef halfway, late gains for press, nvr a threat: btr 2745 (10f). *4* **73**
3066 **CRATHORNE 40** [22]4-8-12 p (77) L Dettori 20/1: 30-43400: 11th: Held up, little hdwy: 6 wk abs. *1¾* **63**
2948 **TURBO 45** [18]5-10-0 p (93) S Drowne 28/1: 21-00400: 12th: Held up, no impress fnl 3f: abs: btr 1759. *3* **75**
WET LIPS 484 [12]6-8-11 bl t (76) Rory Moore(5) 50/1: 5000/00-0: 13th: ch g Grand Lodge - Kissing *nk* **57**

(Somalia) Stumbled start, sn handy, btn over 3f out: jumps fit (recent val h'cap hdle rnr-up, rtd 123h, 2m, blnks & t-strap), 03/04 h'cap hdle wnr (rtd 114h, firm & soft): ex-Australian Flat wnr at 7.5f/1m on fast & gd.

3345 **BEST BE GOING 27** [6]4-8-11 (76) E Ahern 20/1: 51-00540: 14th: Mid-div, eff over 4f out, btn 2f out.   *nk*   **56**

3969 **PRETTY STAR 2** [15]4-9-9 (88) J Fanning 16/1: 1660-020: 15th: Chsd ldrs, rdn halfway, sn strugg.   ½   **67**

3598 **LES ARCS 17** [14]4-8-12 (77) K Fallon 16/1: 0021360: 16th: Al bhd: btr 2828 (1m).   *hd*   **55**

3534 **ETMAAM 20** [9]3-9-5 (94) R Hills 15/2 FAV: 5121300: 17th: Al rear: bckd, has a problem?   6   **63**

1704 **BAGAN 96** [13]5-9-9 (88) T Gillet 11/1: 015-4440: 18th: Chsd ldrs, drvn & btn 3f out: won this in '03.   5   **50**

2771 **SPECTROMETER 52** [11]7-9-1 (80) D Holland 25/1: 1030-000: 19th: ch g Rainbow Quest - Selection Board (Welsh Pageant) Slow away, hmpd after 6f & al bhd: jumps fit (rnr-up, rtd 118c, nov chase): '03 class stks wnr on the level, val h'cap plcd (rtd 88): won this race back in '02: eff at 12/13f on fast, gd/soft & any trk, enjoys a gall one. 1 Aug'03 Hami 13.0gd 84-(77) D: 1 Aug'02 York 11.8gd 78-75 C: 3½   **37**

3794 **KING OF DREAMS 10** [21]3-9-5 (94) S Chin 12/1: 42-1015F: Handy when broke leg & fell over 6f out, died.   **0**

3637 **SPORTING GESTURE 16** [20]7-8-10 (75) T Lucas 33/1: 544436U: Rear, badly hmpd & u.r. over 6f out.   **0**

21 Ran   Time 2m 32.89 (6.09)   Owned: Mr J H Tattersall   Trained: Malton

---

4000	1.50 Gr2 Weatherbys Insurance Lonsdale Cup 3yo+ (A)
	£58000 £22000 £11000 1m7f198y Good 44 +06 Fast Inside

3563 **FIRST CHARTER 18** [1] Sir Michael Stoute 5-9-1 (112) K Fallon 7/1: 120-0121: Held up, hdwy 3f out, rdn/hung left dist, led ins last, drvn out: gd time: big drifter: eff at 12/14f, imprvd on step up to 2m: acts on fm & rain softened grnd: genuine, v smart & progressive.   **117**

2583 **DANCING BAY 59** [5] N J Henderson 7-9-1 (104) W Ryan 25/1: 10/31/-122: Held up, smooth hdwy over *nk* **116** 3f out, rdn & narrow lead over 1f out, hdd but kept on ins last, just held: jumps fit (unplcd, val h'cap): much imprvd up in class, win an easy grnd List/Gr 3 sn: see 2583.

1705+**MILLENARY 96** [10] J L Dunlop 7-9-4 bl (118) M J Kinane 11/8 FAV: 1042-313: Held up, smooth hdwy 3 **116** going best 3f out, rdn & no extra from dist: abs, hvly bckd: stays 2m but prob best at 14f: smart run conceding weight, win more Gr races: btr 1705 (14f).

2771 **SWING WING 52** [8] P F I Cole 5-9-1 (110) J Fortune 7/1: 33-50124: Handy & led over 3f out, drvn 2½ **111** & hdd over 1f out, not pace of winner: nicely bckd: 8 wk abs: smart, List/Gr 3 company ideal: see 2771 & 1998.

3552 **ROMANY PRINCE 19** [7]5-9-1 (109) R Hughes 16/1: 30-33255: Rear, hdwy 4f out, rdn & no impress 1½ **109** over 1f out: needs List/Gr 3: see 2914 (List).

2914 **CORRIB ECLIPSE 45** [6]5-9-1 (104) J F Egan 50/1: 166: Rear, late gains for press, no impress. 1¾ **107**

3552 **ROYAL REBEL 19** [4]8-9-1 vis (110) J Murtagh 14/1: 1/-504427: Chsd ldrs, ran in snatches & sn rdn 1½ **105** along, no impress fnl 3f: btr 3552.

1993 **BAILAMOS 16** [1]4-9-1 S Sanders 14/1: 0-532148: b c Lomitas - Bandeira (Law Society) Trkd ldrs, 1¾ **103** hdwy over 3f out, rdn & no impress fnl 2f: German raider, List wnr earlier this term: suited by 2m/2m1f on gd & soft grnd. 2 May'04 Bade 16gd 106- :

3552 **SILVER GILT 19** [3]4-9-1 (109) L Dettori 12/1: 34-33169: Led till over 3f out, sn btn: bckd: btr 2914 (List). 6 **97**

3507 **DUKE OF VENICE 21** [9]3-8-1 t (114) K McEvoy 13/2: 10-12150: 10th: Cl-up, rdn & btn 3f out: bckd. 5 **92**

10 Ran   Time 3m 25.94 (6.14)   Owned: Mr Saeed Suhail   Trained: Malton

---

4001	2.25 Gr2 Daily Telegraph Great Voltigeur Stakes Colts & Geldings 3yo (A)
	£78300 £29700 £14850 1m3f198y Good 44 -43 Slow Inside

2822 **RULE OF LAW 51** [2] Saeed bin Suroor 3-8-9 t (118) L Dettori 11/8 FAV: 113-2241: Dictated pace &   **121** qcknd tempo from 4f out, rdn & drew clr from over 1f out, styd on strongly: hvly bckd: slow time: padd pick, abs: eff at 10/12f, sure to get 14f on this evidence: acts on firm & gd/soft grnd: enjoyed forcing tactics today & will take all the beating in the St Leger: see 2822, 2254.

2822 **LET THE LION ROAR 51** [1] J L Dunlop 3-8-9 vis (118) M J Kinane 11/4: 12-13352: Trkd ldrs, eff to 2½ **116** chase wnr fnl 2f, rdn & no impress from dist: well bckd, 7 wk abs: 4th successive occasion finishing one place bhd this wnr: shld apprec 14f & finish close bhd this wnr again in St Leger.

3507 **GO FOR GOLD 21** [8] A P O'Brien 3-8-9 J P Spencer 7/1: 1-323: Held up, eff 3f out, kept on 1½ **114** onepace: bckd: relish drop into List/Gr 3: see 3507, 1706.

3534 **ALWAYS FIRST 20** [4] Sir Michael Stoute 3-8-9 (95) K Fallon 8/1: 1-0234: Trkd ldrs, chsd wnr from 1¼ **112** halfway, rdn & no impress fnl 2f: up in class & a smart run, will apprec drop to List/Gr 3: see 3534.

3274 **PUKKA 31** [5]3-8-9 (105) D Holland 8/1: 431-1025: Rear, eff over 3f out, no impress on ldrs: see 3274. 2½ **108**

3534 **RED LANCER 20** [6]3-8-9 (105) M Fenton 33/1: 1360606: Held up, eff to chase ldrs 3f out, btn 2f out. 2½ **104**

   RIO DE JANEIRO 25 [7]3-8-9 VIS J Murtagh 40/1: 0217: b c Sadler's Wells - Alleged Devotion 12 **88** (Alleged) Mid-div, rdn & struggling fnl 4f: Irish raider, first time visor: recent mdn wnr: winning form at 10f, 12f shld suit: acts on firm & gd grnd.

7 Ran   Time 2m 37.10 (10.3)   Owned: Godolphin   Trained: Newmarket

---

4002	3.00 Gr1 Juddmonte International Stakes 3yo+ (A)
	£266800 £101200 £50600 1m2f88y Good 44 +01 Fast Inside

3442 **SULAMANI 24** [9] Saeed bin Suroor 5-9-5 t (124) L Dettori 3/1: 115-4231: Held up, hdwy 3f out,   **126** styd on well to lead well ins last, drvn to assert: gd time: well bckd: eff at 10f, prob best at 12f: acts on firm, likes gd & soft grnd: top-class & game eff here, leading Arc candidate: see 2488.

3886+**NORSE DANCER 5** [1] D R C Elsworth 4-9-5 (116) J F Egan 16/1: 4304412: Trkd ldrs, led 2f out, ¾ **123** styd on well, drvn & hdd well ins last: qk reapp: up in class & confidence high now, this was a career best effort: win more Gr races: see 3886.

2825+**BAGO 51** [6] J E Pease 3-8-11 T Gillet 13/8 FAV: 1111-113: Trkd ldrs, rdn 4f out, styd on for ¾ **122** press fnl 2f, not pace of front two: hvly bckd French raider, clr rem: lost unbtn record against older horses but ran to top-class best: likes easy grnd: see 2825.

3657* **CACIQUE 19** [10] A Fabre 3-8-11 Gary Stevens 10/1: 112214: Held up, rdn 4f out, edged left & no 5 **115** impress from over 1f out: nicely bckd: needs Gr 3 as in 3657.

3563 **MILLSTREET 18** [4]5-9-5 t (110) K McEvoy 100/1: 46240-05: Led & pulled clr bef halfway, hdd 2f out ¾ **114** & no extra: set the required strong gallop for stablemate to prevail.

3306+**KALAMAN 29** [2]4-9-5 (116) K Fallon 6/1: 02-21316: Chsd ldrs, hdwy 3f out, rdn & no extra fnl 2f: ½ **113** hvly bckd: poss ideally suited by faster ground: btr 3306 (Gr 2).

3662 **IMPERIAL DANCER 16** [8]6-9-5 (114) T E Durcan 33/1: 0-360037: Rear, rdn & only mod prog fnl 3f, ½ **112**

nvr a dngr: btr 3662 (German Gr 1).

3840* **SOLSKJAER 9** [5]4-9-5 J Murtagh 33/1: 0-12218: Chsd ldr, hung left & btn over 2f out: btr 3840 (Gr 2). 6 **104**
3442 **TYCOON 24** [7]3-8-11 J P Spencer 7/1: 3215-369: Dwelt & rear, drvn & btn over 3f out, eased: *dist* **0**
much btr 3442 & 2822 (fast).
9 Ran Time 2m 11.82 (4.52) Owned: Godolphin Trained: Newmarket

---

4003 **3.35 Listed National Stud Never Say Die Club Acomb Stakes 2yo (A)**
£16250 £5000 £2500 **7f rnd** **Good 44** **-10 Slow** Inside

3078* **ELLIOTS WORLD 39** [5] M Johnston 2-8-13 J Fanning 5/2: 11: Trkd ldrs & led 2f out, sn edged left **106**
under press, drvn to hold on: hvly bckd, remains unbeaten: eff at 7f, shld get 1m: acts on gd & gd/soft grnd, likes
York: v useful juv with bags of scope, game eff & can win in Gr class.
3470* **OUDE 23** [1] Saeed bin Suroor 2-8-13 L Dettori 9/4 FAV: 12: Rcd keenly early, held up in tch, nk **105**
hdwy when briefly short of room over 2f out, edged left & styd on well for press from over 1f out, just denied: hvly
bckd tho' op 7/4: imprvd in defeat, acts on fast & gd grnd: 1m shld suit, keep on side for similar: see 3470 (mdn).
3470 **SHANNON SPRINGS 23** [2] B W Hills 2-8-10 M Hills 7/1: 23: Held up, rdn to chase ldr over 1f out, ½ **101**
no extra well ins last: just bhd today's rnr-up on debut: acts on fast & gd grnd: clearly useful, win races.
3811* **CAPABLE GUEST 9** [7] M R Channon 2-8-13 (100) T E Durcan 7/2: 333214: Dwelt, in tch, styd on 2 **100**
onepace for press fnl 2f: well bckd, op 11/2: see 3811.
3560* **JANE JUBILEE 19** [3]2-8-5 (95) S Chin 12/1: 3522115: Led/dsptd lead, rdn & no extra over 1f out: 1½ **89**
not beaten far & handles good but btr 3560 (h'cap, fast).
3329* **RAZA CAB 27** [6]2-8-10 (90) K Fallon 11/1: 316: Trkd ldrs, rdn & outpcd when short of room over shd **94**
2f out, no impress after: up in class: prev with C Allen: see 3329 (AW mdn).
3707 **SHRINE MOUNTAIN 13** [4]2-8-10 S Sanders 50/1: 027: Led till 2f out, btn when hmpd over 1f out: 1½ **91**
highly tried after 3707.
7 Ran Time 1m 25.06 (3.76) Owned: Atlantic Racing Limited Trained: Middleham

---

4004 **4.10 Irwin Mitchell Solicitors Stakes Nursery Handicap 2yo (C)** [101]
£11798 £3630 £1815 **6f str** **Good 44** **-03 Slow** Centre

3807 **SPACE SHUTTLE 9** [9] T D Easterby 2-8-13 (86) K Fallon 13/2: 3213331: Held up, hdwy halfway & **105+**
drvn to lead cl-home: nicely bckd: eff at 5f, both wins at 6f, 7f must surely suit on this evidence: acts on fast
& gd/soft grnd, with/without blnks: useful performance & on the upgrade, poss more to come over further: see 3807.
3756 **DISTINCTLY GAME 11** [15] K A Ryan 2-8-7 (80) N Callan 10/1: 222142: Trkd ldrs, led over 1f out, ½ **96**
drvn & hdd cl-home: imprvd for return to 6f, progressive profile: see 3756 & 2360.
3686 **THE CROOKED RING 13** [13] P D Evans 2-9-4 (91) S Donohoe(7) 16/1: 1341123: Held up, switched & 1 **104**
hdwy to chall over 1f out, no extra well ins last: well clr of rem: useful most progressive, keep on side.
3781 **PIDDIES PRIDE 10** [8] P S McEntee 2-8-1 (74) F P Ferris(3) 25/1: 4113204: Chsd ldrs, no impress on 5 **73**
front trio dist: see 3614, 3521 & 3382 (seller).
2578 **BOLTON HALL 59** [14]2-9-0 (87) P Hanagan 7/1: 165: Bhd halfway, late gains, no impress: bckd: 2 1¾ **81**
mth abs & h'cap bow: btr 2167 (cond stks, debut, 5f).
3614* **TRANSACTION 17** [12]2-9-3 (90) S Drowne 6/1: 32116: Mid-div, no impress over 1f out: bckd: btr 3614. ½ **82**
3691* **MY PRINCESS 13** [6]2-8-5 (78) E Ahern 16/1: 35317: Sltly hmpd start, chsd ldrs, btn dist: btr 3691 (fm). nk **69**
3544* **TOBYS DREAM 19** [1]2-8-9 (82) J Fanning 20/1: 018: Led till over 1f out, fdd: btr 3544 (fm). 2 **67**
3473* **LUBECK 23** [7]2-8-11 (84) T P Queally 13/2: 519: Dwelt, chsd ldrs till over 1f out: well bckd: btr 3473 (fast). ½ **67**
3589 **MELALCHRIST 17** [2]2-9-7 (94) D Holland 16/1: 122130: 10th: Rear, no impress fnl 2f: bckd, btr 3589. ¾ **75**
3432 **SELKIRK STORM 24** [5]2-8-8 (81) Dale Gibson 33/1: 12500: 11th: Hmpd start, in tch, wknd 2f out. nk **61**
2689 **RICH ALBI 54** [3]2-8-0 BL (73) F Norton 33/1: 6040: 12th: Drvn mid-div, no ch over 2f out: eased, blnks. 6 **37**
3606* **TURNAROUND 17** [4]2-8-8 (81) I Mongan 3/1 FAV: 3210: 13th: Swerved right start, chsd ldrs, hung 2½ **37**
left & wknd qckly over 1f out, eased: hvly bckd on h'cap bow: much btr 3606.
13 Ran Time 1m 12.23 (2.83) Owned: Jennifer Pallister & Jonathan Gill Trained: Malton

---

4005 **4.45 Patrington Haven Leisure Park Handicap Stakes 3yo+ 0-100 (C)** [98]
£11895 £3660 £1830 **6f str** **Good 44** **+16 Fast** Centre

3903 **FONTHILL ROAD 5** [8] R A Fahey 4-8-3 (73) P Hanagan 11/2: 2-613221: Towards rear, rdn & hdwy from **84**
halfway, drvn to lead line, all out in a fast time: qck reapp: eff at 5f, suited by 6/7f on fast, likes gd, soft &
fibresand, stiff/gall trks: v progressive & game, stable in cracking form: see 3903.
3782 **WATCHING 10** [7] R A Fahey 7-8-8 (78) T Eaves(3) 16/1: 5500002: Mid-div, hdwy over 2f out & led shd **88**
well ins last, hdd line: completed a fine stable one-two: only 2nd run for talented handler, enjoys gd or softer
grnd: h'capped to win sn: see 998.
3937 **TOM TUN 3** [10] J Balding 9-9-13 bl (97) T Lucas 20/1: 0204203: Al prom & led dist till well ins 1 **104**
last: qk reapp: tough & useful h'capper: loves easy grnd: see 3248 & 1703 (C/D).
3443 **CLOUD DANCER 24** [9] K A Ryan 5-8-6 (76) N Callan 16/1: 2213504: Chsd ldrs, outpcd halfway, kept 2 **77**
on for press ins last: acts on firm, on both AWs: see 2409 (C/D).
3408 **GOLDEN DIXIE 25** [6]5-8-12 (82) Martin Dwyer 12/1: 000-0255: Prom, hung right & drvn/led over 1f nk **82**
out, sn hdd & no extra nr fin: see 3136.
3424 **FAIR SHAKE 24** [14]4-7-12 vis (68) D Kinsella 12/1: 0035026: Outpcd early & bhd halfway, drvn & nk **67**
styd on well fnl 2f: ideally suited by a stiffer trk & prob more testing grnd: see 3424 & 1393.
3584 **TONY THE TAP 18** [18]3-8-10 (83) L Dettori 9/1: 2252107: Swerved left start & bhd, styd on tho' 1¾ **78**
wandered from over 1f out, no impress: progressive profile but now may benefit from headgear: see 3543.
3646 **INDIAN SPARK 15** [11]10-8-8 (78) T E Durcan 10/1: 6000068: Outpcd & bhd, prog//short of room over nk **72**
dist, nrst fin, kind ride: well h'capped 10yo who is one to note in the coming months on testing grnd.
3910 **FULL SPATE 4** [17]9-8-1 (71) F Norton 25/1: 0002169: Hmpd start, rear, styd on late under hand shd **65**
riding: qck reapp: not knocked about & can impr on this after what was a messy start today: see 998.
3622 **FANTASY BELIEVER 17** [3]6-9-11 (95) D Holland 5/1 FAV: 0410120: 10th: Chsd ldrs, ch dist, no shd **88**
extra ins last: hvly bckd but btr 3622, 3424.
3827 **TALLY 8** [15]4-7-12 (1oh) (67) J Quinn 33/1: 3001400: 11th: Towards rear, only mod prog: see 3485. 1 **58**
3434 **MISTER SWEETS 24** [5]5-8-2 (72) F P Ferris(3) 50/1: 0-601500: 12th: Outpcd rear, mod prog: btr 2768. nk **61**
3080 **MR WOLF 39** [4]3-8-1 (74) J Fanning 66/1: 1166000: 13th: Led till over 1f out, sn btn. nk **62**
3937 **ARTIE 3** [19]5-9-2 (86) J Fortune 10/1: 0010000: 14th: Swerved left start, chsd ldrs till over 1f nk **73**

YORK   TUESDAY 17.08.04   Lefthand, Flat, Galloping Track

out: well bckd: qck reapp, prefer 5f.

3751* **SEMENOVSKII 11** [1]4-8-3 VIS (73) T P Queally 20/1: 00-36010: 15th: Chsd ldrs, wknd halfway, vis.   1¼   56

952   **LAW BREAKER 143** [13]6-9-5 (89) B Reilly(3) 28/1: 21-55200: 16th: Chsd ldrs, hung right &   ¾   70
struggling from halfway: abs: btr 921 (Doncaster).

3960   **BRAVE BURT 3** [16]7-8-10 (80) K Fallon 9/1: 13-00020: 17th: Cl-up, wknd & eased down ins last: ¾   59
op 7/1: best at 5f: see 3960 (5f).

3248   **JOHNSTONS DIAMOND 32** [12]6-9-3 (87) S Sanders 20/1: 4620000: 18th: Prom till over 1f out, wknd.   hd   65

2684   **CHAPPEL CRESENT 54** [2]4-9-10 (94) A Nicholls 33/1: 5251500: 19th: Sn bhd & no ch 2f out, eased.   15   32

19 Ran   Time 1m 11.06(1.66)   Owned: Mrs Una Towell   Trained: Malton

HAMILTON   TUESDAY 17.08.04   Righthand, Undulating Track, Stiff Uphill Finish

Official Going GOOD/SOFT

4006   2.05 Knockhill Racing Circuit Median Auction Maiden Stakes 2yo   (E)
£4323 £1330 £665   6f5y str   Good/Soft   Inapp   Far side

3544   **MERCHANT 19** [4] M L W Bell 2-9-0 (78) R Mullen 13/8: 5321: Handy, hdwy to lead over 1f out, rdn   87
clr ins fnl 1f, shade cmftbly, val 6L: tchd 2/1: eff at 6f, 7f will suit: acts on firm & gd/soft, stiff/undul
trk: improving: see 3046.

    LORD MAYFAIR 0 [11] T D Barron 2-9-0 R Winston 6/1: 2: b c Silic - Spring Wedding (Prized) Led   3½   76
till over 1f out, kept on but not pace of wnr on debut: op 10/1: Apr 1st foal, cost $17,000: dam unrcd, sire
useful 1m 2yo scorer, later top-class turf miler: prob stays 6f on gd/soft: gd start, improve.

3877   **PROFITS REALITY 6** [3] P A Blockley 2-9-0 Dean McKeown 6/4 FAV: 05543: Cl-up, outpcd 2f out,   2½   68
rallied over 1f out, onepcd fnl 1f: well bckd, qck reapp, clr of rem: try 7f? see 3877.

3517   **LAKE WAKATIPU 20** [9] M Mullineaux 2-8-9 S Righton 25/1: 04: b f Lake Coniston - Lady Broker   4   51
(Petorius) In tch, outpcd, hdwy over 1f out, not pace to chall: Feb foal: half-sister to a 6f/1m wnr: dam 7f wnr.

3504   **RAINBOW IRIS 21** [7]2-8-9 F Lynch 14/1: 45: Chsd ldrs, outpcd 3f out, sn btn: see 3504.   ½   49

2882   **KERRYS BLADE 47** [10]2-9-0 G Faulkner 25/1: 056: Mid-div, outpcd halfway, btn: 7 wk abs: see 2882.   nk   53

3878   **BALTHASAR 6** [6]2-9-0 M Lawson(5) 80/1: 067: Handy, lost place over 1f out, btn: qck reapp.   nk   52

    LADY VEE 0 [8]2-8-9 T Hamilton(3) 66/1: 8: b f Rossini - Dama de Noche (Rusticaro) Rear, nvr a   2½   39
factor on debut: May foal, cost E1,600: half-sister to 3 dual 1m wnrs, dam unrcd, sire high-class 2yo sprinter.

    PERCHERON 0 [1]2-9-0 J Bramhill 40/1: 9: Bhd, nvr a factor on debut.   5   29

    OWED 0 [2]2-9-0 T W Supple 20/1: 0: 10th: Mid-div, green over 2f out, wknd on debut: t-strap.   7   8

3755   **BENNY THE BUS 11** [5]2-9-0 A Culhane 66/1: 000: 11th: Bhd, nvr nr ldrs.   21   0

11 Ran   Time 1m 12.85 (3.05)   Owned: HESheikh Rashid Bin Mohammed   Trained: Newmarket

4007   2.40 Horsepower Seiling Stakes 3yo+   (E)
£3608 £1110 £555   1m65y rnd   Good/Soft   Inapp   Inside

2008   **LORD OF METHLEY 83** [5] R M Whitaker 5-9-3 bl (46) V Halliday 10/1: 036-0001: gr g Zilzal -   49
Paradise Waters (Celestial Storm) Handy, hdwy over 3f out, wandered 2f out, ran on ins fnl 1f: no bid: long abs:
won a seller & a sell h'cap in '03: 4th at best in '02 (h'cap, rtd 62): eff at 1m/10f on firm & gd/soft, any trk:
eff in blnks/visor, tried cheek pieces: runs well fresh: goes well in sell grade.
1 Aug'03 Thir 8g/s 51-45 F: 1 Apr'03 Ripo 10gd 53-(58) F:

3727   **TATWEER 12** [7] D Shaw 4-9-8 vis (48) Darren Williams 14/1: 1000002: Rear, hdwy over 2f out, kept   shd   53
on ins fnl 1f but just held nr fin: eff btwn 5f/1m: likes easy grnd: see 1682.

3880   **SOPHRANO 6** [11] P A Blockley 4-9-3 (56) Dean McKeown 3/1 FAV: 20-53033: Made most till over 1f   2½   43
out, sn no extra: qck reapp, clr of rem: see 2438.

3850   **ERUPT 6** [3] R E Barr 11-9-3 (40) G Parkin 20/1: 0-503004: Rear, kept on from 2f out, nrst fin.   5   33

3809   **MEHMAAS 9** [6]8-9-3 vis (56) D Allan 11/2: 4001005: Bhd, hdwy 2f out, not pace to chall.   2   29

3788   **WOOD FERN 10** [9]4-9-3 (48) C Catlin 11/1: 0500006: Trkd ldrs, hdwy to dspt lead over 3f out,   1¾   25
lost place over 1f out, wknd: much btr 263 (mdn).

3700   **MOUNT PEKAN 13** [12]4-9-3 (39) W Supple 9/1: 0605007: Handy, no impress over 2f out: see 1748.   1½   22

3499   **BONJOUR BOND 21** [10]3-8-11 vis (44) D McGaffin 10/1: 0303058: Midfield, hung right over 3f out, wknd.   ½   21

3757   **WILD TIDE 11** [4]5-8-12 R Ffrench 66/1: 0009: In tch, hmpd over 4f out, sn wknd: see 3757.   3½   9

3666   **ABUELOS 14** [8]5-9-3 (43) S Williams 33/1: 0-340050: 10th: Slow away, nvr a factor.   nk   13

3764   **COMPASSION 10** [1]3-8-6 p (43) R Winston 8/1: 453603F: Dsptd lead, broke leg/fell over 4f out, sadly died.   0

2545   **MERLINS PROFIT 60** [2]4-9-3 (43) L Enstone(3) 7/1: 03-5420U: In tch, hmpd & u.r. over 4f out.   0

12 Ran   Time 1m 51.28 (7.48)   Owned: Mr R M Whitaker   Trained: Scarcroft

4008   3.15 Totepool Series Final Stakes Handicap 3yo+   (C)   [73]
£10160 £3126 £1563   1m1f36y   Good/Soft   Inapp   Inside

3137   **CRESKELD 37** [17] B Smart 5-9-5 (64) F Lynch 25/1: 3000001: Prom, hdwy to lead 2f out, all out to   70
hold on nr fin: eff at 7.4f/9f on fast, soft & polytrack, loves fibresand: acts on any trk: tough & genuine.

3505   **YENALED 21** [10] K A Ryan 7-9-10 (69) A Culhane 10/1: 5112242: Hld up, hdwy & not clr run over 2f   shd   75
out till over 1f out, rdn nr fin, just failed: wld have won with a clr run/stronger ride: tough & consistent.

3813   **CHERISHED NUMBER 9** [8] I Semple 5-9-11 (70) R Winston 12/1: 3044053: In tch, hdwy but not much   1   74
room over 2f out, sn switched left & hdwy over 1f out, nvr nrr: see 2317.

3588   **DONNAS DOUBLE 17** [5] D Eddy 9-8-5 VIS (50) D Allan 16/1: 5-563434: Bhd, hdwy over 3f out, onepcd   ¾   52
fnl 1f: first time visor: fair run, see 2832.

3759   **APACHE POINT 11** [7]7-8-9 (54) Kim Tinkler 8/1: 4552355: Mid-div, hdwy 2f out, onepcd ins fnl 1f.   ½   55

3759+   **DOUBLE RANSOM 11** [15]5-9-6 bl (65) C Catlin 11/2: 4216216: In tch, hdwy 2f out, onepcd.   hd   65

3726   **NO CHANCE TO DANCE 1** [9]4-8-0 t (45) M Halford(7) 8/1: 0043667: Cl-up, onepcd 2f out.   4   37

3759   **ENCOUNTER 11** [4]8-8-0 (45) B Swarbrick(5) 16/1: 6002508: Rear, hdwy over 3f out, wknd over 1f out.   shd   36

3764   **SARRAAF 10** [6]4-9-2 (54) V Halliday 25/1: 3350529: Nvr btr than mid-div.   2½   50

3593   **KRISTIANSAND 17** [13]4-9-5 (64) P Mulrennan(3) 16/1: 505-0640: 10th: In tch, hdwy 3f out, wknd 2f out.   ½   49

3879   **WAHOO SAM 6** [14]4-9-11 (70) P Makin(5) 9/2 FAV: 3110120: 11th: Led to 2f out, wknd: amiss?   3½   48

3759 **REGENTS SECRET 11** [6]4-9-0 (59) W Supple 12/1: 0240330: 12th: Bhd, nvr a factor: op 16/1.   ½   36
3134 **MILLENNIUM HALL 38** [11]5-9-3 (62) L Enstone(3) 25/1: 3110660: 13th: Trkd ldrs, no impress 2f out.   2½   34
3558 **Lucky Largo 19** [12]4-8-7 bl(52) R Ffrench 33/1:0   3593 **Anthemion 17** [3]7-9-1 (60) D McGaffin 25/1:0
3738 **Ace Coming 12** [2]3-9-0 bl(66) P Fessey 33/1:0
3933 **Pharoahs Gold 4** [9]6-8-6 vis(5l) Darren Williams 33/1:0
17 Ran   Time 2m 01.05 (6.95)   Owned: Creskeld Racing   Trained: Thirsk

---

4009   **3.50 Bill Mcharg Handicap Stakes 3yo+ 0-70 (E)**   [68]
£4485 £1380 £690   **6f5y str**   **Good/Soft**   **Inapp**   Far side

3700 **BOND PLAYBOY 13** [16] B Smart 4-9-6 (60) F Lynch 9/2 CO FAV: 0000031: Handy far side, hdwy to   70
lead ins fnl 1f, rdn out: nicely bckd: all 3 wins at 6f, stays 7f on fast, likes soft & fibresand: acts on any trk:
well h'capped: see 45.
2749 **MISARO 52** [7] P A Blockley 3-9-13 (70) Dean McKeown 20/1: 351-0562: Switched to far side & made   1   75
most till ins fnl 1f, styd on: 7 wk abs, top-weight: fine eff, improving of late & shld be winning sn: see 1627.
3228 **MY BAYARD 32** [5] J O'Reilly 5-9-5 (59) D Allan 14/1: 0104303: Handy stands side, switched to far   1¾   59
side over 3f out, ev ch over 1f out, onepcd: eff at 6f/1m, stays 11f: acts on gd & gd/soft, loves fibresand.
3737 **THORNABY GREEN 12** [3] T D Barron 3-9-7 (64) P Makin(5) 16/1: 0-441054: Handy stands side, led   2   58
group 2f out, kept on fnl 1f but no pace to reach far side group: gd run: see 3203.
3737 **CALCULAITE 12** [1]3-8-3 (46) W Supple 25/1: 00-06645: Prom stands side, hdwy 2f out, wknd 1f out.   nk   39
3767* **FRIMLEYS MATTERLY 10** [4]4-8-13 (53) P Mulrennan(3) 25/1: 6650316: Led stands side to 2f out.   2   40
3562 **SILVER SEEKER 19** [10]4-8-11 (51) C Catlin 50/1: 0020607: Rcd far side, outpcd, late chances.   ¾   36
3700 **THE WIZARD MUL 13** [14]4-9-3 (57) J Bramhill 16/1: 104-0008: Mid-div far side, no impress 2f out.   nk   41
3700 **CARLTON 13** [9]10-9-2 (56) B Swarbrick(5) 11/1: 2200509: Mid-div far side, outpcd 2f out.   nk   39
3933 **ROMAN EMPIRE 4** [8]4-8-11 bl (51) G Parkin 9/2 CO FAV: 4133540: 10th: Mid-div far side, hung right   nk   33
over 1f out, sn wknd: qck reappr: see 3933.
3670 **REDOUBTABLE 14** [15]13-8-11 (51) A Culhane 14/1: 2160400: 11th: Bhd far side, nvr a factor.   nk   32
3757 **MALLIA 11** [2]11-8-2 (42) P Fessey 20/1: 1632400: 12th: Cl-up stands side, hung right over 2f out, wknd.   2   17
3974 **FENWICKS PRIDE 2** [13]6-9-1 (55) T Hamilton(3) 9/2 CO FAV: 00/0-3000: 13th: Mid-div far side till   4   18
over 2f out, btn: qck reappr: btr expected after 3974.
2730 **FORMERIC 53** [12]8-7-13 (39) R Ffrench 50/1: 0-003000: 14th: Nvr a factor far side: 8 wk abs.   ¾   0
3575 **ORANGINO 18** [11]6-8-3 (43) R Kennemore(5) 20/1: 0-020200: 15th: Handy far side, lost place 3f out.   2½   0
3796 **PIRLIE HILL 10** [6]4-8-7 (47) R Winston 16/1: 4406500: 16th: Dwelt, switched to far side after   13   0
1f, hdwy 3f out, hung right over 1f out, wknd & eased fnl 1f: much btr 2181 (mdn h'cap, 5f).
16 Ran   Time 1m 13.62 (3.82)   Owned: Mr R C Bond   Trained: Thirsk

---

4010   **4.25 Parks Of Hamilton Classified Stakes 3yo+ 0-60 (F)**
£3066 £876 £438   **5f4y str**   **Good/Soft**   **Inapp**   Far side

3262* **RED MONARCH 31** [9] P A Blockley 3-9-7 (61) F Lynch 7/1: 0006211: Prom, hdwy to lead ent fnl 1f,   66
rdn out nr fin: tchd 10/1: eff at 5/6f, tried 1m: acts on fast & gd/soft, sharpish or stiff/undul trks: in fine
form & still improving: see 3262.
3569 **ONLINE INVESTOR 18** [4] D Nicholls 5-9-10 (62) R Winston 8/1: 5000002: Slow away, rear, not clr   ½   64
run & switched left over 1f out, fin fast: poss a shade unlucky: see 1523.
3852 **TANTRIC 6** [8] J O'Reilly 5-9-8 (58) D Allan 11/1: 3003343: Trkd ldrs, hdwy 2f out, kept on: qck   1   59
reappr: return to further will suit: see 3463.
3350 **SHARP HAT 27** [1] D W Chapman 10-9-11 (63) A Culhane 12/1: 0003024: Trkd ldrs, kept on fnl 1f.   shd   61
3427 **AAHGOWANGOWAN 24** [7]5-9-7 t (62) R Ffrench 2/1 FAV: 0521505: Led till entering fnl 1f, no extra.   nk   56
2951 **MYND 45** [5]4-9-10 (62) Dean McKeown 8/1: 1006406: Trkd ldrs, onepcd fnl 1f: 6 wk abs.   dht   59
3932 **HES A ROCKET 4** [6]3-9-6 p (58) B Swarbrick(5) 14/1: 6006027: Cl-up, onepcd fnl 1f: qck reapp.   shd   56
3680 **KARMINSKEY PARK 13** [2]5-9-7 (62) D McGaffin 9/1: 2100008: Mid-div, hdwy 2f out, wknd fnl 1f.   1   52
3680 **KINGS COLLEGE BOY 11** [3]4-9-9 bl (61) T Hamilton(3) 5/1: 2303039: Switched far rail & cl-up 3f.   1   51
3757 **PAYS DAMOUR 11** [10]7-9-8 t (57) P Makin(5) 8/1: 0503020: 10th: Nvr a factor: with Miss L Perratt.   13   11
10 Ran   Time 1m 01.84 (3.74)   Owned: Bigwigs Bloodstock III   Trained: Cockerham

---

4011   **5.00 Friends Of Scottish Racing Rating Related Maiden Stakes 3yo 0-70 (E)**
£3786 £1165 £583   **1m3f16y**   **Soft**   **Slow**   Stands side

3108 **LATE OPPOSITION 38** [1] E A L Dunlop 3-9-0 vis (68) W Supple 5/4 FAV: 2220031: Keen, led after 3f,   75
trav beat over 2f out, rdn & flashed tail ins fnl 1f: nicely bckd: eff around 11f, acts on gd & soft grnd,
stiff/undul trk: made most of this return to mdn grade: see 1260.
3855 **MAMBINA 6** [5] M R Channon 3-8-11 (60) C Catlin 100/30: 4504022: Keen & prom, hung right over 2f   5   62
out, wknd fnl 1f: qck reappr: see 3419.
3246 **HOLLYWOOD CRITIC 32** [3] P Monteith 3-9-0 (47) L Enstone(3) 7/1: 0053: Mid-div, hdwy over 3f out,   1¾   62$
sn onepcd: op 12/1: offic rtd 47, treat this with caution: see 3246.
3159 **KNIGHT OF HEARTS 36** [2] P A Blockley 3-9-0 (42) Dean McKeown 66/1: 55004: gr g Idris - Heart To   ½   61$
Heart (Double Schwartz) Mid-div, wknd 2f out: offic rtd 42, treat rating with caution.
3328 **AWESOME LOVE 28** [4]3-9-0 (70) R Ffrench 3/1: 3222605: Prom, wknd over 2f out.   9   46
3740 **JORDANS SPARK 12** [6]3-9-0 (49) P Fessey 25/1: 5006: Mid-div, wknd 3f out: see 1390.   12   28
6 Ran   Time 2m 31.64 (12.84)   Owned: Mr Saeed Maktoum Al Maktoum   Trained: Newmarket

---

4012   **5.30 Teletext Hands And Heels Apprentice Handicap 3yo+ 0-70 (E)**   [77]
£3868 £1190 £595   **1m4f17y**   **Soft**   **Fair**   Stands side

3414 **FARAWAY ECHO 25** [4] James Moffatt 3-7-12 (3oh) (47) M Halford 25/1: 0-063051: Mid-div, hdwy to   55
lead ins fnl 1f, pushed out: prev eff at 1m, relished this step up to 12f: acts on soft & a stiff/undul trk: gd
run from 3lb out of the h'cap & on first start for new yard (prev with M Bell): see 1740.
3904 **ALPINE SPECIAL 5** [1] P C Haslam 3-9-1 (67) G Bartley(7) 7/2: 10-60422: Handy & keen, led over 2f   1   69

HAMILTON TUESDAY 17.08.04 Righthand, Undulating Track, Stiff Uphill Finish

out till ins fnl 1f, no extra: qck reapp, clr of rem: stays 10.5/12f on firm, soft & fibresand: see 2277.

3588* **EASIBET DOT NET 17** [2] I Semple 4-9-11 p (67) W Hogg 2/1 FAV: 2305313: Led till 2f out, no extra.		17	43
3151 **KIDZPLAY 36** [5] J S Goldie 8-9-13 (69) H Poulton 100/30: 3421534: Rcd in 2nd, wknd over 3f out.		8	33
3588 **SPREE VISION 17** [3]8-8-7 vis (49) A Mullen 11/4: 6042245: Cl-up, wknd 3f out.		11	0

5 Ran Time 2m 43.35(11.55) Owned: Mr Alf Chadwick Trained: Cartmel

ARLINGTON SATURDAY 14.08.04 Lefthand, Flat, Oval Track, Short Run-In

Official Going Firm

4013 9.37 Grade 1 Beverley D Stakes (Fillies & Mares) 3YO+ (A)
£251397 £83799 £41899 **1m1f110y Firm**

2487 **CRIMSON PALACE 59** [9] Saeed Bin Suroor 5-8-11 (110) L Dettori 99/10: /4-14161: Prom wide, styd **118**
on to lead 1f out, rdn out: 8 wk abs: eff at 9/10.5f on firm & soft: goes well fresh: back to form after disapp
at R Ascot (unsuited by str trk): v smart, hds for Breeders Cup: see 2487.
4570*]**RISKAVERSE** [1] Patrick J Kelly 5-8-11 P Day 84/10: 561-4522: b f Dynaformer - The Bink ½ **115**
(Seeking The Gold) Mid div, kept on well fnl 1f, only just btn: eff at 9.5f on firm grnd: smart.
1 Oct'02 Keen 9gd 115- :
2210 **NECKLACE 71** [5] A P O'Brien 3-8-5 J P Spencer 254/10: 110-0643: Mid-div wide, eff 2f out, styd hd **116**
on well, post came too sn: 10 wk abs: has tried 12f, imprvd for drop back to 9.5f: acts on firm & fast grnd: has
shown enough to find a Gr 2/3 fillies contest: see 2210 & 2005.
11 Ran Time 1m 56.58 () Owned: Godolphin Trained: Newmarket

4014 10.35 Grade 1 Arllington Million 3YO+ (A)
£335196 £111732 £55866 **1m2f Firm**

3715*]**KICKEN KRIS** [4] M Matz 4-9-0 K Desormeaux 97/10: 12-36911: b c Kris S - Kicken Grass (Jade 1½ **119**
Hunter) Mid div, prog on rail when badly hmpd ins fnl 1f, kept on for 2nd, awarded race after stewards inquiry.
1 Aug'03 Arli 10gd 116- A:
3264 **MAGISTRETTI 28** [12] N A Callaghan 4-9-0 bl (121) E Prado 24/1: 022-6442: Bhd, prog 2f out, styd 1 **116**
on fnl 1f for 3rd, subs plcd 2nd: back to form on fav firm grnd: now stays in US.
3663 **EPALO 13** [7] A Schutz 5-9-0 A Starke 41/10 FAV: 222-1123: Chsd ldrs, led over 1f out, hdd & ½ **114**
hmpd 1f out, no extra, fin 4th, plcd 3rd: looked btn before being hmpd: acts on firm, gd & AW surface: see 3663.
3662 **POWERSCOURT 13** [10] A P O'Brien 4-9-0 vis J P Spencer 46/10: 13-12524: Rear, prog wide 3f out, **122**
styd on to lead 1f out, hung badly left, rdn out: fin 1st, subs demoted to 4th: likes firm & fast, acts on gd &
soft: wnr on merit, but an amateurish ride: high-class, can win another Group 1: see 3662.
3264 **VESPONE 28** [2]4-9-0 vis (118) L Dettori 19/2: 0-222020: 12th: Led till 2f out, sn fdd: 9½ **99**
disappointing run & prob unsuited by firm grnd: btr 3264 (fast) & 1858 (gd/soft).
13 Ran Time 2m 0.80 () Owned: Brushwood Stables Trained: Usa

4015 11.53 Grade 1 Secretariat Stakes 3YO (A)
£134078 £44693 £22346 **1m2f Firm**

KITTENS JOY 31 [1] Dale Romans 3-8-11 J D Bailey 9/10 FAV: 1-111211: ch c El Padro - Kittens **122**
First (Lear Fan) Bhd, prog to lead dist, sn edgd left, pushed out: won 6 of 7 starts to date: eff at 9/10f on firm
& gd/soft: won in good style & a probable for Breeders Cup Turf.
GREEK SUN [3] R J Frankel 3-8-9 E Prado 29/10: 11-12: Mid div, styd on fnl 1f, no ch with wnr. 3¼ **114**
2822 **MOSCOW BALLET 48** [6] A P O'Brien 3-8-7 J P Spencer 74/10: 25-66103: In tch, ev ch bef 1f out, 1¼ **110**
no extra cl home: 7 wk abs: appreciated return to 10f: see 2822 & btr 2520 (List).
2520 **SIMPLE EXCHANGE 21** [7] D K Weld 3-8-11 P J Smullen 79/10: 1251-414: In tch, ev ch bef 1f out, 1 **112**
sn no extra: recent wnr of Grade 2 American Derby here over 9.5f (firm): see 2520.
3316 **HAZYVIEW 31** [4]3-8-7 (110) L Dettori 9/1: 11121036: Cl up, wknd dist: btr 3316 (Gr 2, sft). 4¾ **102**
7 Ran Time 1m 59.65() Owned: Kenneth L & Sarah K Ramsey Trained: Usa

DEAUVILLE SATURDAY 14.08.04 Righthand, Galloping Track

Official Going Heavy

4016 3.20 Group 3 Prix Gontaut-Biron Le Royal Palm Hotel 4YO+ (A)
£25704 £10282 £7711 **1m2f Heavy Inapplicable**

3168 **SPECIAL KALDOUN 34** [6] D Smaga 5-8-11 D Boeuf 56/10: 100-0031: b c Alzao - Special Lady () **118**
Bhd, prog to lead ins fnl 1f, rdn out: Gr 3 & Gr 2 wnr in '03 (also 2L 2nd in Gr 1): Gr 3 wnr in '02: eff at 1m,
now stays 10f: acts on gd & hvy grnd: likes Deauville: high-class, win more Gr races.
1 Oct'03 Long 8sft 122- A: 1 Jul'03 Deau 8g/s 117- A: 1 Nov'02 Sain 8hvy 115- :
DEMON DANCER [2] Y de Nicolay 7-8-11 C Soumillon 31/10: /-331122: Mid div, prog wide 2f out, 1 **116**
kept on fnl 1f, nrst fin.
5012] **MAMOOL 284** [4] Saeed Bin Suroor 5-8-9 (115) C-P Lemaire 27/10: 153110-3: b c In The Wings - 1 **112**
Genovefa (Woodman) Led, hdd turning for home, regained lead bef 1f out, hdd ins fnl 1f, no extra: reapp: in fine
form last year winning 2 Gr 1's & a Gr 2 bef fracturing leg in Melbourne Cup: Gr 3 wnr in '02: eff at 12f/2m on
firm & hvy, goes well fresh, gd eff after long injury lay off, high class mid dist/stayer performer.
1 Sep'03 Colo 12sft 119- A: 1 Sep'03 Bade 12gd 119- A: 1 May'03 York 13.9fm 118-0 A: 1 Jun'02 Asco 16.2g/f 108- A:
1 Sep'01 Good 8gd 99- D: 2 Aug'01 Newb 7g/f 98- A: 2 Aug'01 Newm 7g/s 98- C:
7 Ran Time 2m 13.20 () Owned: Ecurie Chalhoub Trained: France

DEAUVILLE   SUNDAY 15.08.04   Righthand, Galloping Track

Official Going Soft

4017	**2.55 Group 1 Prix Jacques Le Marois 3YO+ (A)**
	£221317 £88542 £44271 **1m str Soft Inapplicable**

3838 **WHIPPER 7** [5] Robert Collet 3-8-11   C Soumillon 49/10: 141-1521: b c Miesque's Son - Myth To   **123**
Reality (Sadler's Wells) Mid div, styd on for press to lead 1f out, drvn out: qk reapp: eff between 6f/1m, handles
fm, suited by gd/soft & soft grnd: high class & versatile, at the top of his form & can win more top races:
see 3838. 2 Aug'04 Deau 6.5g/s 120- : 1 Apr'04 Mais 7sft 116- A: 1 Aug'03 Deau 6fsft 114- A:
2470 **SIX PERFECTIONS 61** [3] P Bary 4-9-1   T Thulliez 32/10: 2211-262: Mid div, prog 2f out, styd on   1   **117**
to chase wnr well ins fnl 1f, al held: 9 wk abs: won this contest 12 months ago: high class filly who returned to
form after finding grnd too fast at R Ascot in 2470, long term target is Breeders Cup Mile (won race 12 months ago).
2458* **MY RISK 63** [10] J-M Beguigne 5-9-4   O Peslier 127/10: 121-1513: Chsd ldrs, prog to lead bef 1f   1½   **117**
out, sn hdd & onepcd: 9 wk abs: smart run up in class, win again in Gr 2/3: see 2458.
3659 **MAJESTIC DESERT 14** [6] M R Channon 3-8-8 (111) T E Durcan 16/1: -1002224: Chsd ldrs, sytd on to   1½   **111**
lead bef 1f out, hdd 1f out, no extra: smart filly who was shade below best on today's easy grnd: btr 3659 (gd).
3124 **SALSELON 36** [7]5-9-4 (118) J P Murtagh 92/10: 10-02305: Bhd, hdwy halfway, no impress bef 1f   ½   **113**
out: twice below 2nd in 2470 (fast, Gr 1 Lockinge).
3508 **KHELEYF 19** [4]3-8-11 (112) L Dettori 123/10: 210-1036: Nvr nrr than mid div: btr 3508 (7f, fast).   3   **107**
3004 **BAQAH 40** [2]3-8-8   D Bonilla 99/10: 3121137: Chsd ldrs, no extra 2f out: 6 wk abs: btr 3004 (firm).   2½   **99**
3712} **FOMALHAUT** [8]5-9-4   C-P Lemaire 32/10: 240-3448: Led, hdd bef 1f out, fdd.   1   **100**
3508* **BYRON 19** [9]3-8-11 (111) K McEvoy 123/10: 331-3019: Mid div, wknd bef 1f out: btr 3508 (7f, Gr 2, fast).   2   **96**
3004 **ATTRACTION 40** [1]3-8-8 (119) K Darley 7/5 FAV: 11-11120: 10th: Prom, under press halfway, fdd 2f   10   **75**
out: 6 wk abs: disappointing effort & looked to be unsuited by today's soft grnd: high class filly who has been
busy this term: showed much more in 3004 (firm) & 2555 (fast).
10 Ran   Time 1m 38.40()   Owned: R C Strauss   Trained: France

COLOGNE   SUNDAY 15.08.04

Official Going Good

4018	**3.05 Group 1 Rheinland-Pokal der Stadssparkasse Koln 3YO+ (A)**
	£66901 £24648 £11972 **1m4f Good**

3497* **ALBANOVA 21** [7] Sir Mark Prescott 5-9-2 (111) T Hellier 57/10: /1026-11: Chsd ldrs, short of   **112**
room 2f out, styd on to lead well ins fnl 1f, rdn out: eff at 10/12f, has tried 2m: acts on gd & hvy grnd: v smart
5yo who remains in fine form & well plcd to land this val prize: see 3497 (reapp).
3442 **HIGH ACCOLADE 22** [6] M P Tregoning 4-9-6 vis (116) Martin Dwyer 28/10: 12-42302: Tried to make   ¾   **113**
all, not pace to repel wnr cl home: smart & consistent performer who rarely runs a bad race: see 3030.
3010 **MALINAS 42** [8] P Schiergen 3-8-8   A Suborics 9/10 FAV: 312123: b c Lomitas - Majoritat   3   **108**
(Koniosstuhl) Cl up, ev ch 2f out, sn no extra: eff at 12f on gd & hvy: smart colt.
2 Jul'04 Hamb 12hvy 109- :
7 Ran   Time ()   Owned: Miss K Rausing   Trained: Newmarket

LEOPARDSTOWN   SUNDAY 15.08.04   Lefthand, Galloping Track

Official Going Good/Firm

4019	**3.15 Listed Ballyroan Stakes 3YO+ (A)**
	£21808 £6398 £3048 **1m4f Good/Firm**

3663* **FOREIGN AFFAIRS 14** [7] Sir Mark Prescott 6-9-10 (102) J Quinn 7/1: 5-134511: Made all, held on   **111**
gamely drvn out: eff at 10f/2m on firm & soft: smart performer, suited by List company.
2138 **VINNIE ROE 81** [1] D K Weld 6-10-0 bl P J Smullen 1/1 FAV: /1154-22: Mid div, prog 2f out, styd   nk   **113**
on well fnl 1f, just denied: 11 wk abs: toip-weight: dual prev wnr of this race: will appr return to 14f in Irish
St Leger (won prev 3 season's): see 2138.
2817* **MKUZI 50** [2] John M Oxx 5-9-12   M J Kinane 9/2: -6605113: Mid div, bmpd dist, kept on fnl 1f,   ¾   **109**
nrst fin: op 7/2, 7 wk abs: continues in gd form & will enjoy return to further: btr 2817 (14f).
7 Ran   Time 2m 34.30 ()   Owned: Charles C Walker - Osborne House   Trained: Newmarket

4020	**4.15 Group 3 Desmond Stakes 3YO+ (A)**
	£30485 £8645 £4221 **1m rnd Good/Firm**

ACE 22 [4] A P O'Brien 3-8-13   J P Spencer 5/4 FAV: 111: b c Danehill - Tea House (Sassafras)   **118**
Cl-up, led 3f out, styd on strongly, easily: unbtn after wins at Naas (mdn) & here at Leopardstown (stks): eff at 1m
on fast & gd grnd: v smart & improving, deserves his chance in Gr 1/2 company now.
2455 **HAMAIRI 67** [1] John M Oxx 3-8-13   M J Kinane 7/1: 2122: Rear, prog wide 3f out, styd on for 2nd,   2   **111**
al held by easy wnr: eff at 7f, appreciated step up to 1m: can find similar: see 2455 & 1299.
2820* **GRAND PASSION 49** [3] G Wragg 4-9-6 (103) J F Egan 5/1: 4213: In tch, eff 2f out, no extra ins   1½   **108**
fnl 1f: 7 wk abs: see 2820 (List).
3496* **LATINO MAGIC 22** [2] R J Osborne 4-9-9   R M Burke 10/1: 5164: Led till 3f out, sn no extra.   2½   **106**
3840 **TROPICAL LADY 7** [5]4-9-6 P Shanahan 7/4: 1125: Mid div, onepcd over 2f out, eased when btn   hd   **102**
dist: qck reapp: v disappointing run: btr 3840 (10f) & 3322 (9f).
5 Ran   Time 1m 37.30()   Owned: Ballydoyle   Trained: Ballydoyle

YORK WEDNESDAY 18.08.04 Lefthand, Flat, Galloping Track

Official Going SOFT.

4021 **1.20 Motability Supported By Royal & Sunalliance Rated Stakes Handicap 3yo+ 0-105 (B)** **[109]**
£13305 £5047 £2523 **1m2f88y** **Good/Soft 77** **+07 Fast** Inside

3794* **DUNASKIN 11** [8] D Eddy 4-8-7 (1oh) (88) K Darley 8/1: 0563111: Made all, rdn clr 2f out, styd on strongly, unchall: stays a sharp 12f, best dominating at 1m/10.5f on firm or gd/soft, any trk: tough & genuine, useful now & thriving, rare ability to qckn from the front at present: see 3794. **102**
3474 **ZERO TOLERANCE 24** [10] T D Barron 4-8-8 (90) D Holland 9/2 JT FAV: 4-140002: Held up, hdwy to chase wnr well over 1f out, kept on but not his pace: back to useful best on fav soft grnd, win this autumn. *7* **94**
3794 **SHAHZAN HOUSE 11** [1] M A Jarvis 5-9-1 p (97) P Robinson 9/2 JT FAV: 0-323333: Cl-up, eff 2f out, onepace: tough & consistent: see 3794, 1296. *1¾* **98**
3118 **BLUE SPINNAKER 39** [2] M W Easterby 5-9-6 (102) P Mulrennan(3) 9/1: 4-014104: Held up, rdn & sltly outpcd over 3f out, eff over 2f out, no danger: back to useful form, clr of rem: see 2101. *¾* **102**
3794 **IONIAN SPRING 11** [6]9-8-11 (93) R Smith 12/1: 0-101005: In tch, gd hdwy 3f out, wknd 2f out. *4* **87**
3553 **GOLD HISTORY 20** [5]3-8-7 (97) J Fanning 25/1: 2135006: Chsd ldrs, wknd 2f out: best 1189 (g/f). *3* **87**
3775 **WING COMMANDER 11** [4]5-8-13 (95) P Hanagan 8/1: 0001037: In tch, wknd over 2f out: well bckd. *hd* **84**
3506 **BLYTHE KNIGHT 22** [12]4-9-7 (103) L Dettori 8/1: 1463008: Held up, btn 2f out: see 2556, 1478. *nk* **92**
3119 **BOURGEOIS 39** [3]7-9-2 (98) W Supple 11/1: 0-231009: Chsd wnr, wknd over 3f out: out of sorts. *14* **69**
2903 **BISHOPRIC 47** [11]4-8-12 (94) Dane O'Neill 16/1: 41-0100: 10th: Chsd ldrs, wknd 3f out: 7 wk abs. *21* **35**
3435 **RAINBOW QUEEN 25** [9]4-8-10 (92) K Fallon 10/1: 10/-30: 11th: In tch, wknd well over 3f out, virtually p.u.: 2 handlers in padd: something amiss? see 3435. *dist* **0**
11 Ran Time 2m 14.62 (7.32) Owned: Mrs I Battla Trained: Newcastle Upon Tyne

4022 **1.50 Gr2 Scottish Equitable Gimcrack Stakes Colts & Geldings 2yo (A)**
£75000 £28750 £14375 **6f str** **Good/Soft 77** **-05 Slow** Centre

3028 **TONY JAMES 42** [2] C E Brittain 2-8-11 (100) S Sanders 16/1: 1451: Handy, hdwy to lead appr fnl 1f, styd on well, hard drvn: 6 wk abs: v eff at 6f & acts on fast grnd, enjoyed this gd/soft: acts on gall trks: goes well fresh: v useful & genuine: see 2039. **110**
3247* **ANDRONIKOS 33** [4] P F I Cole 2-8-11 K Fallon 10/1: 12: Handy, eff well over 1f out, kept on for press: scope: eff at 6f, 7f looks sure to suit: acts on firm & gd/soft: v useful juv, looks plenty more to come. *1¼* **106**
3221* **ABRAXAS ANTELOPE 34** [3] J Howard Johnson 2-8-11 R Winston 100/30 FAV: 113: Set pace, rdn & hdd over 1f out, onepcd: well bckd, doing well physically: useful, will enjoy a drop into Listed/Gr3 class: see 3221. *½* **104**
3614 **SACRED NUTS 18** [6] M L W Bell 2-8-11 (93) R Mullen 40/1: 511354: Chsd ldrs, onepcd over 1f out: tough, useful & consistent: handles fast & gd/soft: see 3127. *¾* **102**
3163* **GALEOTA 37** [1]2-8-11 (85) R Hughes 20/1: 415: Cl-up, onepcd over 1f out: scope: not disgraced but a big step up in class: acts on fast & gd/soft: clr of rem, drop in class will suit: see 3163. *shd* **102**
3566 **STETCHWORTH PRINCE 19** [10]2-8-11 T P Queally 16/1: 146: Chsd ldrs, wknd 2f out: see 3031 (fast). *6* **90**
3319 **TURNKEY 31** [7]2-8-11 (100) T E Durcan 7/2: 21547: In tch, wknd 2f out: well bckd: see 2467. *1¼* **87**
3406* **CRIMSON SUN 26** [5]2-8-11 (97) K McEvoy 8/1: 2118: In tch 6f, wknd: scope: btr 3406 (made all). *1¼* **84**
3178* **BIG HASSLE 36** [8]2-8-11 (89) W Supple 22/1: 5219: Nvr a factor: btr 3178 (5f, mdn auct). *10* **0**
3509 **ROYAL ISLAND 22** [11]2-8-11 (100) J Fanning 20/1: 112000: 10th: Al bhd: best 2251 (List, fm). *13* **0**
3028 **COUNCIL MEMBER 42** [9]2-8-11 (100) L Dettori 4/1: 1220: 11th: Sn bhd, t.o./eased over 2f out: well bckd tho' op 11/4, 6 wk abs: something amiss on this easier grnd? much btr 3028 (fast grnd), 2467. *22* **0**
11 Ran Time 1m 14.3 (4.9) Owned: Mr A J Richards Trained: Newmarket

4023 **2.25 Totesport Ebor Heritage Handicap 3yo+ (B)** **[109]**
£130000 £40000 £20000 **1m5f197y** **Good/Soft 77** **-14 Slow** Inside

3510* **MEPHISTO 22** [3] L M Cumani 5-9-4 (7ex) (99) D Holland 6/1: 6-051111: Held up, hdwy 3f out, styd on strongly despite hanging left ins last, sn led, drvn & hdd cl-home but rallied to get up on line, gamely: well bckd: stays 14f well on fast & gd/soft grnd, any trk: most prog, useful & genuine gldg with a turn of foot: looks well up to Listed/Gr class, see 3510. **110**
3617 **GOLD RING 18** [15] G B Balding 4-8-10 (91) S Carson 12/1: 3653162: Cl-up, led 4f out, edged right appr fnl 1f but kept on, hdd ins last but rallied to lead cl-home, collared again on line: stays 14f: right back to useful best & likes easy grnd: see 3256, 3076. *shd* **100**
3507 **MIKADO 22** [13] A P O'Brien 3-8-13 (106) J P Spencer 9/1: 211-443: Held up, hdwy over 3f out, sn rdn, kept on nicely appr fnl 1f, nrst fin: excellent run under a big weight for a 3yo: acts on fast & gd/soft: looks sure to relish a step up to 2m & must be of interest at that trip: see 3507. *2½* **113**
2771 **DEFINING 53** [1] J R Fanshawe 5-9-0 (95) J Murtagh 16/1: 203-0304: Chsd ldrs, eff 2f out, kept on: 7 wk abs: another useful eff: see 2771, 2246. *nk* **101**
3510 **SELF DEFENSE 22** [18]7-9-5 (100) P Robinson 10/1: 450/-0655: In tch, eff 3f out, onepcd: useful. *¾* **105**
3119 **STAR MEMBER 39** [22]5-9-2 (97) K Fallon 7/1: 0-514126: Keen, prom, rdn over 2f out, no extra: hvly bckd: not disgraced but btr expected: rdn much closer to the pace today & may to btr: see 3119, 2355. *3½* **98**
3506 **FANTASTIC LOVE 22** [6]4-9-7 t (102) L Dettori 16/1: 22121-07: Chsd ldrs, eff to chase ldr over 3f out, wknd 2f out: may do btr back around 12f on faster grnd: see 3506. *hd* **103**
3510 **JAGGER 22** [7]4-9-2 (97) S Sanders 11/2 FAV: 6D11-038: In tch, eff over 3f out, wknd 2f out: real eye-catcher on faster grnd in 3510 & well worth another try on a sounder surface: see 2771. *1¼* **97**
3119 **COLLIER HILL 39** [16]6-9-8 (103) Dean McKeown 14/1: 03-01439: Held up, eff 2f out, sn no extra. *4* **99**
3776* **DOROTHYS FRIEND 11** [19]4-9-0 (7ex) (95) S Drowne 14/1: 1-011010: 10th: In tch, outpcd over 4f out, mod late gains: needs 2m & poss prefers a sounder surface as in 3776: prog earlier. *1* **90**
3125 **PAGAN DANCE 39** [11]5-8-13 p (94) M J Kinane 25/1: 3422600: 11th: In tch, wknd 2f out: see 3125. *¾* **88**
3776 **SANTANDO 11** [2]4-8-9 vis (90) J P Guillambert(3) 28/1: 0500400: 12th: Nvr a factor: boiled over. *1¼* **83**
2948 **CROW WOOD 46** [8]5-9-0 (95) A Culhane 33/1: 5-033520: 13th: In tch, wknd over 2f out: 7 wk abs. *2½* **86**
2948 **TRUST RULE 46** [20]4-8-10 (91) M Hills 25/1: 2-065000: 14th: Al bhd: 7 wk abs: see 2255. *8* **74**
1843 **SALSALINO 91** [14]4-9-8 (103) J D Smith 33/1: 243-6000: 15th: Al bhd: 3 mnth abs & gelded: plcd sev times in '03, incl when 3rd in this race: '02 mdn wnr: eff over 12/14f on firm & gd grnd, any trk. *½* **85**
3027 **TOP SEED 42** [21]3-8-12 (105) T E Durcan 25/1: 4-240320: 16th: In tch, wknd 2f out: 6 wk abs. *8* **79**
3119 **ROYAL CAVALIER 39** [4]7-9-2 (97) W Supple 40/1: 6-014500: 17th: Led till 3f out, wknd: see 950. *2½* **69**

YORK   WEDNESDAY 18.08.04   Lefthand, Flat, Galloping Track

2948 **GRAMPIAN 46** [12]5-9-7 (102) K Darley 22/1: 25/-26230: 18th: Al bhd: see 2948, 2234.   9   65
2771 **RAYSHAN 53** [17]4-8-9 (90) R Winston 50/1: 356-0000: 19th: In tch, wknd 3f out: 7 wk abs: see 2771.   8   45
19 Ran   Time 3m 06.1 (12.7)   Owned: Mrs Angie Silver   Trained: Newmarket

4024   3.00 Gr1 Aston Upthorpe Yorkshire Oaks Fillies 3yo+   (A)
£145000 £55000 £27500   1m3f198y   Good/Soft 77   -16 Slow   Inside

2517 **QUIFF 62** [3] Sir Michael Stoute 3-8-8 (105) K Fallon 7/2: 5-131: Held up, gd prog to lead 3f   120
out, pushed well clr fnl 1f, easily: hvly bckd tho' op 9/4, 9 wk abs: lightly rcd & prog into a high-class filly,
acts on fast, clrly relished this gd/soft grnd: runs v well fresh: eff at 12f 14f looks sure to suit & must run a
big race in the St Leger, esp on easy grnd: see 2517 & 1718.
3619 **PONGEE 18** [8] L M Cumani 4-9-4 (107) J Fortune 10/1: 10-31122: Chsd ldrs, outpcd ent str,   11   109
rallied to take 2nd but no ch with easy wnr: v useful run, will apprec a return to 14f judged on this: see 3619.
3321 **HAZARISTA 31** [9] John M Oxx 3-8-8   M J Kinane 9/2: 0-41133: Held up, prog to chase wnr 2f out,   1½   107
sn no impress & caught for 2nd cl-home: nicely bckd Irish challenger: struggled to last home on grnd prob softer
than ideal: rtd higher 3321 & 1857 (fast grnd).
3321 **PUNCTILIOUS 31** [10] Saeed bin Suroor 3-8-8 t (110) L Dettori 6/4 FAV: 13-13124: Led till halfway,   9   97
remained prom till wknd 2f out, eased: hvly bckd from 9/4: has shown form on soft grnd & something clrly amiss
today: prev v smart, see 3321 & 2517.
3629* **SAHOOL 17** [7]3-8-8 (107) R Hills 7/1: 1-222215: Trkd ldrs, rdn & wknd 2f out: prev most   8   89
consistent on gd & firm grnd this summer, did win on soft as a juv: capable of much btr, see 3629 (List).
3321 **DANELISSIMA 31** [1]3-8-8 VIS W Supple 33/1: 4412366: Trkd ldr, styd against far rail & led   4   85
halfway till 3f out, wknd qckly & eased: rcd keenly in 1st time visor & rider seemed to take wrong option.
2555 **ROYAL TIGRESS 31** [2]3-8-8 VIS J P Spencer 33/1: 3100507: Held up, t.o. fnl 3f: Irish   21   64
challenger, tried a visor: much longer trip & clrly something amiss: see 1330.
3621 **MENHOUBAH 18** [4]3-8-8 p (106) S Sanders 33/1: 3021068: Chsd ldrs 1m, wknd & t.o.: btr 1999.   5   59
8 Ran   Time 2m 38.03 (11.23)   Owned: Mr K Abdulla   Trained: Newmarket

4025   3.35 Listed Costcutter Roses Stakes Colts & Geldings 2yo   (A)
£16250 £5000 £2500   5f str   Good/Soft 77   -29 Slow   Centre

3509 **DANCE NIGHT 22** [2] B A McMahon 2-9-0 (94) G Gibbons 7/1: 2116061: Nvr far away, went on dist,   103
styd on strongly, rdn out: right back to form & clrly relishes gd & gd/soft grnd, handles fast: eff at 5f, shld
stay 6f: tough & v useful juv, see 3509 & 1567.
3028 **MOSCOW MUSIC 42** [3] M G Quinlan 2-8-11 (100) R L Moore 9/2: 21262: Outpcd rear, fin strongly   1½   96
into 2nd, no ch with wnr: 6 wk abs: acts on fast & gd/soft grnd, will relish a return to 6f judged on this.
3509 **BIGALOS BANDIT 22** [6] J J Quinn 2-8-11 (99) R Winston 7/1: 124043: led till dist, no extra: hd   95
beat today's wnr on faster grnd in 3509.
3509 **BECKERMET 22** [7] R F Fisher 2-9-0 (100) R Ffrench 5/4 FAV: 1121104: Trkd ldrs, onepcd fnl 1f: 1½   94
hvly bckd: showed v decent form when fav drawn, tackled tougher company today: see 3509 & 3081.
3266 **BOND CITY 32** [4]2-8-11 (95) F Lynch 4/1: 01335: Held up, nvr nr ldrs: nicely bckd & padd pick: 3   84
prob unsuited by this gd/soft grnd: see 3266 (fast).
5 Ran   Time 1m 02.13 (5.33)   Owned: Mr J C Fretwell   Trained: Tamworth

4026   4.10 Newitts Com Convivial Maiden Stakes 2yo   (D)
£10774 £3315 £1658   6f str   Good/Soft 77   -11 Slow   Centre

3586 **HAUNTING MEMORIES 19** [10] M A Jarvis 2-9-0 P Robinson 5/2: 41: Led till collared dist, rallied   99
gamely to regain lead cl-home: hvly bckd: clrly benefitted from recent debut: eff at 6f on fast, relishes gd/soft
grnd: op to further improvement & potentially v useful, see 3586 (debut).
3511 **RAJWA 22** [6] Saeed bin Suroor 2-9-0 t L Dettori 6/4 FAV: 22: Front rank, went on dist, collared   ½   97
cl-home: hvly bckd tho' drifted from 1/1, clr of rem: eff at 6f on fast & gd/soft: must find similar, poss over 7f.
      MY PUTRA [9] P F I Cole 2-9-0 J Fanning 8/1: 3: b c Silver Hawk - Petite Triomphe (Wild Again)   5   86
Chsd ldrs, onepcd fnl 2f on debut: btr for race: Jan 1st foal, cost $170,000: dam a sprinter in the US, sire a
high-class miler: eff at 6f on gd/soft, looks sure to benefit from 7f+: scopey sort, sure to learn from this.
      WORLD REPORT [3] R Hannon 2-9-0 R L Moore 10/1: 4: b c Spinning World - Miss Woodchuck   2   82
(Woodman) Hmpd start, hdwy from rear dist, nrst fin on debut: op from 16/1, btr for race: E70,000 Mar foal: half
brother to a sprinter in the US: dam a useful miler, sire a top class miler: scopey colt, sure to learn from this.
      BURNLEY AL [4]2-9-0 P Hanagan 11/1: 5: ch g Desert King - Bold Meadows (Persian Bold) Hmpd   4   74
start, outpcd till styd on late on debut: btr for race, bckd from 20/1: 6,000 gns Apr foal: half brother to sev
juv wnrs, around 5/9f: dam a juv scorer, sire a top class mid-dist performer: with R Fahey.
3148 **TARTAN SPECIAL 37** [5]2-9-0 Darren Williams 33/1: 46: Hmpd start, chsd ldrs 4f, sn btn.   shd   73
3425 **JEUNE LOUP 25** [1]2-9-0 Rory Moore(5) 33/1: 047: Held up, nvr nr ldrs.   1   71
3709 **ROYAL WEDDING 13** [8]2-9-0 T P Queally 11/1: 08: b c King's Best - Liaison (Blushing Groom)   ¾   69
Trkd ldrs 4f, sn wknd: 140,000 gns Mar foal: half brother to mid-dist wnr Lagudin: dam a wnr in France.
3939 **MIDNIGHT IN MOSCOW 4** [2]2-9-0 G Faulkner 50/1: 609: Chsd ldrs wide, btn 2f out: qck reapp, swtg. 16   37
9 Ran   Time 1m 14.67 (5.27)   Owned: Mr Lawrence Wosskow   Trained: Newmarket

4027   4.45 Eventmasters Falmouth Handicap Stakes 3yo 0-100   (C)
£11018 £3390 £1695   5f str   Good/Soft 77   +21 Fast   Centre   [106]

3080 **ENCHANTMENT 40** [5] J M Bradley 3-9-0 (92) R L Moore 14/1: 5211241: Broke well & made all, clr   103+
fnl 1f, cmftbly: 6 wk abs & fast time: v eff over 5/6f on firm & gd/soft grnd: handles any trk, likes a gall one:
best up with/forcing the pace: useful sprinter who shld make the step-up into Listed class: see 2390 & 2121.
3852 **DISPOL KATIE 7** [2] T D Barron 3-8-2 (80) Martin Dwyer 25/1: 2-063502: Nvr far away, left bhd by   3½   83
wnr fnl 1f: back to form after saddle slipped last time: acts on firm & gd/soft: met a most prog rival here.
3646* **BYGONE DAYS 16** [8] W J Haggas 3-8-11 (89) M Hills 7/2 FAV: 2-134513: Chsd ldrs, onepcd fnl 1f: 1   92
well bckd: prob unsuited by this drop back to 5f: see 3646 (6f, fast grnd).
3808 **IMPERIAL ECHO 10** [7] T D Barron 3-8-2 (80) P Fessey 20/1: 4022034: Rear, fin strongly, nvr nrr.   2   79

1213

YORK WEDNESDAY 18.08.04 Lefthand, Flat, Galloping Track

3937 **PARTNERS IN JAZZ** 4 [13]3-8-8 (86) P Makin(5) 10/1: 221-5005: Chsd ldrs stands side, onepcd fnl 1f. | 1 | 83
3852 **DISTANT TIMES** 7 [1]3-7-12 (76) P Hanagan 11/1: 3005106: Chsd ldrs, onepcd fnl 2f: btr 3503. | ½ | 72
3646 **BONNE DE FLEUR** 16 [9]3-8-7 (85) F Lynch 25/1: 32-10057: Chsd ldrs 3.5f, onepcd. | 2 | 77
3941 **NIGHTS CROSS** 4 [6]3-9-7 vis (99) S Hitchcott(3) 13/2: 0003338: Slowly away, mod late hdwy: op | 1 | 89
5/1, top weight & quick reapp: showed more over 6f in 3941 & 3842 (fast grnd).
3567 **ICENASLICE** 19 [12]3-7-13 (1ow)(6oh) (70) Rory Moore 12/1: 0141049: Handy stands side, wknd 2f out. | ½ | 66
3304 **BLUE CRUSH** 30 [14]3-8-12 (90) Darren Williams 33/1: 12-00000: 10th: Chsd ldrs, outpcd fnl 2f. | ½ | 78
3273 **FOUR AMIGOS** 32 [11]3-8-2 (80) J Fanning 14/1: 1063000: 11th: Rcd far side, nvr dangerous. | 2 | 64
3304 **NEEDLES AND PINS** 30 [3]3-8-12 (90) K Fallon 4/1: 25-40500: 12th: Al outpcd: bckd, btr 3304. | ½ | 73
3833 **Baron Rhodes** 9 [15]3-8-2 (80) R Ffrench 12/1:0   3241 **Sir Ernest** 33 [10]3-7-12 (76) D Kinsella 33/1:0
14 Ran   Time 59.61(2.81)   Owned: Ms A M Williams   Trained: Chepstow

---

KEMPTON WEDNESDAY 18.08.04 Righthand, Flat, Fair Track

Official Going Soft (Good/Soft Places), Rain through evening

4028 5.25 Evening Standard Maiden Stakes 2yo (D)
£4960 £1526 £763   **6f str**   **Soft**   **Inapplicable**   Far side

3824 **REBUTTAL** 9 [4] B J Meehan 2-9-0 J Fortune 5/6 FAV: 21: Made all, rdn out to hold on ins fnl 1f | | 99
despite hanging left: well bckd: eff at 6f on gd & soft: useful & improving.
1053 **TREMAR** 135 [3] T G Mills 2-9-0 G Carter 20/1: 432: Al cl-up, ev ch & edged left ins fnl 1f, | nk | 97
just denied: long abs: eff at 5f, improved for step up to 6f: acts on gd/soft & soft: can find similar.
3586 **DANIEL THOMAS** 19 [8] Mrs A J Perrett 2-9-0 K Darley 2/1: 223: Chsd ldrs, onepace from dist: op | 1¾ | 92
5/2: acts on fast & soft grnd: remains in gd form & return to 7f shld suit: see 3586 & 2766.
BAHIA BREEZE 0 [5] R Guest 2-8-9 S Drowne 66/1: 4: b f Mister Baileys - Ring of Love (Magic | ¾ | 85
Ring) In tch 4f, sn outpcd, rallied late: debut: Mar foal, cost 5,000 gns: dam 5f wnr: sire Gr1 wnr at 1m: eff
at 6f, will apprec further: acts on soft grnd: improve for today's experience.
3824 **PRINCE SAMOS** 9 [6]2-9-0 R Hughes 20/1: 405: Held up, nvr nrr than mid-div: twice below 3438 (fast). | 3 | 81
MISS TRIAL 0 [2]2-8-9 M Henry 50/1: 6: b f Zafonic - Perfect Alibi (Law Society) Keen handy | 2½ | 69
4f, sn wknd: debut: May foal, cost 20,000 gns: half sister to a smart 6f juv wnr: dam unrcd.
AVIATION 0 [7]2-9-0 Dane O'Neill 25/1: 7: b c Averti - Roufontaine (Rousillon) Al in rear on | hd | 73
debut: Apr foal, half brother plcd at 10f: dam mid-dist/bmpr wnr.
3476 **MIDDLE EARTH** 23 [1]2-9-0 L Keniry(3) 8/1: 28: Handy 4f, fdd: showed more in 3476 (debut, firm). | 1¾ | 68
8 Ran   Time 1m 16.61 (5.51)   Owned: Mr P Minikes   Trained: Upper Lambourn

4029 5.55 Retail Trust Maiden Stakes 3yo (D)
£5486 £1688 £844   **6f str**   **Soft**   **Inapplicable**   Far side

3784 **FAREWELL GIFT** 11 [10] R Hannon 3-9-0 VIS (80) R Hughes 11/4 FAV: 2323331: In tch, styd on to lead | | 82
dist, rdn out: well bckd: eff at 6/7f on fast & soft: consistent, sharper for 1st time visor.
3283 **DR SYNN** 32 [1] J Akehurst 3-9-0 (66) M Tebbutt 7/1: 0636502: Sn outpcd, hdwy 2f out, kept on fnl | 1¼ | 77$
1f, nvr getting to wnr: bckd from 14/1: improvd eff on return to soft grnd: see 1722 (h'cap).
3603 **THOMAS LAWRENCE** 18 [12] P F I Cole 3-9-0 (88) J Quinn 14/1: 432-63: In tch, prog when short of | nk | 76
room 2f out till dist, styd on to chase wnr ins fnl 1f, just held for 2nd: op 10/1: handles firm & soft grnd: lkd a
shade unlucky & is worth bearing in mind for similar: see 3603 (reappn).
1607 **VICTORIANA** 103 [9] H J Collingridge 3-8-9 K Darley 20/1: 64: Dspt lead, led outright 2f out, | 2½ | 64
hdd dist, no extra: long abs: eff at 6f on soft grnd: see 1607.
2291 **ILTRAVITORE** 71 [11]3-9-0 J F Egan 50/1: 005: Handy over 4f, no extra: 10 wk abs: see 2291. | 1¼ | 65$
3282 **POLAR SUN** 32 [4]3-9-0 O Urbina 5/1: 636: In tch wide, hdwy 2f out, wknd bef 1f out: op 3/1: | 2½ | 58
disapp on drop back in trip & switch to soft grnd: qual for h'caps: showed more in 3282 (7f, fast).
3603 **BOLD BUNNY** 18 [5]3-8-9 G Carter 11/1: 337: Nvr nrr than mid-div: btr 3603 & 2428 (fast). | 1¼ | 49
3687 **HEAVENS WALK** 14 [7]3-9-0 D Sweeney 12/1: 58: Dsptd lead 4f, sn fdd: btr 3687. | 9 | 36
PEARL FARM 0 [2]3-8-9 J Fortune 25/1: 9: Al bhd on debut. | 1½ | 27
3687 **IMPERIAL WIZARD** 14 [8]3-9-0 A Daly 100/1: 000: 10th: Cl-up over 3f, fdd. | shd | 31
3784 **IMTALKINGGIBBERISH** 11 [6]3-9-0 (81) E Ahern 100/30: 05020: 11th: Handy 4f, fdd: well bckd: | 6 | 18
disapp on today's soft grnd: btr 3784 (fast).
696 **SHANNKARAS QUEST** 179 [3]3-9-0 J Bramhill 66/1: 000: 12th: Sn bhd, adrift & eased ins fnl 1f. | dist | 0
12 Ran   Time 1m 17.72 (6.62)   Owned: Lady Whent and Friends   Trained: Marlborough

4030 6.25 Betfred Com 'the Bonus King' Handicap Stakes 3yo+ 0-85 (D)   [87]
£7134 £2195 £1098   **7f rnd**   **Soft**   **Inapplicable**   Inside

3758 **KINGS CAPRICE** 12 [7] G B Balding 3-9-12 (85) S Carson 7/1: 3410441: Cl-up, styd on to lead dist, | | 91
rdn out to hold on: eff at 6/7f on firm & fast, improvd today for switch to soft grnd: acts on a gall or sharp trk:
fine eff to defy top weight: appreciated recent gelding operation: see 3758.
3257 **AZREME** 33 [1] D K Ivory 4-9-2 (70) Dane O'Neill 7/1: 0454302: Chsd ldrs, prog & ev ch ins fnl | ½ | 73
1f, just held: likes soft: gd run in defeat & can find similar: see 3068 & 1537.
3257 **BI POLAR** 33 [13] D R C Elsworth 4-9-6 (74) L Keniry(3) 8/1: 0-002203: Handy, outpcd after 5f, | 1½ | 74
rallied fnl 1f: acts on firm & soft grnd: see 3034 & 2272.
3685 **FEN GYPSY** 14 [5] P D Evans 6-9-2 (70) S Donohoe(7) 6/1 FAV: 5124144: Led, hdd dist, no extra. | ¾ | 68
2880 **BLUE PATRICK** 48 [14]4-9-6 (74) L Fletcher(3) 16/1: 0002065: Chsd ldrs over 5f, no extra: 7 wk abs. | 3 | 66
3782 **KAREEB** 11 [11]7-9-3 (71) G Carter 14/1: 0040606: Held up, nvr nrr than mid-div: prefers faster grnd. | 1 | 61
3782 **MOLCON** 11 [6]3-9-11 (84) J F Egan 7/1: 3440107: Nvr nrr than mid-div: twice below 3447. | 1 | 72
3898 **OAKLEY RAMBO** 6 [4]5-9-8 (76) P Dobbs 25/1: 6206000: Bhd, mod late gains, quick reapp: btr 1624. | 2 | 60
3924 **BEN LOMAND** 5 [16]4-9-3 c (71) A Daly 25/1: 000-0039: Al bhd: quick reapp: see 3924. | shd | 54
3257 **OH BOY** 33 [10]4-9-3 (71) R Hughes 16/1: 0511000: 10th: Handy over 4f, fdd: btr 2647 (1m, firm). | 7 | 42
3685 **BALERNO** 14 [2]5-8-8 (62) N Day 13/2: 4021250: 11th: Al bhd: btr 3490 & 3184 (gd). | 1¼ | 31

3257 **JUST FLY 33** [1]4-9-7 (75) J Quinn 14/1: 2030000: 12th: Missed break, al bhd, eased dist: btr 1817.   *12*   **24**
3782 **HEY PRESTO 11** [9]4-9-5 (73) K Darley 9/1: 0056100: 13th: Bhd, nvr a factor: btr 3443 (fast).   *3½*   **15**
13 Ran   Time 1m 31.18 (7.08)   Owned: Miss B Swire   Trained: Andover

4031	**6.55 La Senza Lingerie Classified Stakes 3yo+ 0-80 (D)**
	£6841 £2105 £1053 **5f str** **Soft** **Inapplicable** Far side

3960 **FURTHER OUTLOOK 4** [11] D K Ivory 10-9-3 (83) M Howard(7) 6/1: 3000651: Made all, pushed out ins   **91**
fnl 1f, val 4L+: quick reapp: eff at 5/6f, stays 1m: acts on firm & polytrack, likes soft & hvy grnd & Kempton.
3960 **DANCING MYSTERY 4** [12] E A Wheeler 10-9-0 bl (80) S Carson 10/1: 1450002: Keen mid-div, prog to   *2½*   **80**
chase wnr bef 1f out, al held ins fnl 1f: op 7/1, quick reapp: v tough: see 2779 & 2420.
3827 **MISS GEORGE 9** [5] D K Ivory 6-8-12 (81) Dane O'Neill 8/1: 0600303: Missed break, prog halfway,   *2*   **72**
kept on fnl 1f, not getting to front 2: handles soft, return to faster grnd will suit: btr 3479 & 1383.
3567 **SPANISH ACE 19** [8] A M Balding 3-9-3 vis (85) J Fortune 4/1: 0005504: Cl-up till dist, wknd: *1*   **76**
bckd: best form has come on faster grnd: btr 3269 & 2212.
3827 **JAYANJAY 9** [6]5-9-2 (82) J Quinn 3/1 FAV: 4315225: Handy 3f, sn no extra: bckd: disapp effort.   *2½*   **66**
3827 **LITTLE EDWARD 9** [7]6-9-3 (83) L Keniry(3) 8/1: 0500056: Keen mid-div, 3f, wknd: btr 1845.   *3*   **58**
3705* **MR MALARKEY 14** [2]4-9-2 bl t (82) Hayley Turner(5) 11/2: 6330617: Al in rear: btr 3705 (fast).   *7*   **39**
3960 **ZARZU 4** [1]5-9-0 (78) R Thomas(5) 9/1: 0016508: Handy over 3f, fdd: quick reapp: btr 2968 (gd/soft).   *2½*   **30**
8 Ran   Time 1m 1.36 (3.06)   Owned: Mr K T Ivory   Trained: Radlett

4032	**7.25 Collingwood Team Services Handicap Stakes Fillies 3yo 0-75 (E)**	**[78]**
	£4319 £1329 £665 **1m1f** **Soft** **Inapplicable** Inside	

3799 **FARRIERS CHARM 10** [3] D J Coakley 3-8-13 (63) J Fortune 5/1: 644-1001: Chsd ldrs wide, styd on   **67**
for press to lead ins fnl 1f, drvn out: bckd: eff at 7f, apprec step up to 9f: acts on fibresand & soft grnd.
3449 **QUEEN LUCIA 25** [5] J G Given 3-8-3 (53) J Bramhill 14/1: 4445402: Cl-up, led 2f out, hdd ins fnl   *hd*   **56**
1f, rallied cl-home, just denied: eff at 1m/9f on gd & soft grnd: game performer who can find similar: see 1178.
3690 **LA PROFESSORESSA 14** [12] Mrs P N Dutfield 3-8-8 (58) R Havlin 5/1: 05-60053: In tch, prog 2f   *1¾*   **58**
out, onepcd ins fnl 1f: eff at 1m/9f on fast & soft grnd: see 3690 & 2031.
3875 **CARRIACOU 7** [8] P W D'Arcy 3-9-0 (64) L Keniry(3) 6/1: 4505304: Held up, prog wide 3f out, onepcd   *½*   **63**
fnl 1f: quick reapp: acts on gd, soft grnd & fibresand: much btr 3492.
3799 **DEIGN TO DANCE 10** [13]3-8-10 (60) E Ahern 4/1 FAV: 0510325: In tch, prog 2f out, no extra fnl   *1*   **57**
1f: bckd: btr 3799 & 3291 (1m, firm).
3799 **SONDERBORG 10** [10]3-8-2 bl (52) Hayley Turner(5) 33/1: 0260006: Bhd, prog wide 3f out, onepcd.   *1½*   **46**
3346 **BLUE DAZE 28** [11]3-8-11 (61) R Hughes 8/1: 0055507: Mid-div, 6f, sn onepcd: btr 2385.   *3*   **51**
2153 **ABINGTON ANGEL 77** [7]3-9-6 H BL (70) J F McDonald(3) 25/1: 2660-008: ch f Machiavellian - Band   *¾*   **58**
(Northern Dancer) Held up, nvr a factor: 11 wk abs & 1st time blnks & hood: plcd on 2 of 4 '03 starts (rtd 80,
fills mdn): eff at 6/7f, bred to apprec further: acts on firm & fast grnd: has tried a t-strap.
2 Jul'03 Newb 7g/f 83- D:
3630 **LADY BLADE 17** [2]3-8-9 BL (59) Lisa Jones 11/1: 60-04059: Al in rear: 1st time blnks.   *½*   **46**
3711 **FABULOSO 13** [6]3-7-12 (7oh) 4/1 J Quinn 9/1: 0000-560: 10th: Led 7f, fdd & eased: op 16/1: btr 1841.   *11*   **20**
3373 **Kalimenta 27** [9]3-9-1 (65) A Daly 14/1:0   1896 **Grande Terre 89** [4]3-8-10 (60) K Darley 20/1:0
12 Ran   Time 2m 0.33 (10.33)   Owned: Mr Alf Hall   Trained: West Ilsley

4033	**7.55 Williamhill Co Uk Handicap Stakes 3yo+ 0-70 (E)**	**[70]**
	£4271 £1314 £657 **1m4f** **Soft** **Inapplicable** Inside	

3398 **SILVER PROPHET 26** [2] M R Bosley 5-9-9 (65) Hayley Turner(5) 20/1: 0555001: Mid-div, hdwy 3f out,   **71**
rdn out to lead cl-home: eff at 10/12f, poss stays 14f: acts on fast & soft: back to form with no cheekpieces.
3948 **TRAVELLERS TALE 4** [7] P G Murphy 5-8-13 (55) Derek Nolan(7) 16/1: 0060622: In tch, al travelling   *hd*   **59**
well, styd on to lead ins fnl 1f, hdd under press cl-home: quick reapp: acts on fast & soft, poss handles
fibresand: continues to run well & is h'capped to find similar: see 3948.
3688 **SUDDEN FLIGHT 14** [5] P D Evans 7-9-11 (67) S J Donohoe(7) 12/1: 4316503: Bhd, prog 3f out, styd   *nk*   **70+**
on well ins fnl 1f, just btn in tight photo under kind ride: won with slightly stronger handling, see- 3101 (2m).
3856 **SAXE COBURG 7** [18] G A Ham 7-9-0 (56) J F McDonald(3) 25/1: 0353404: Held up, hdwy 3f out, styd   *nk*   **58**
on well ins fnl 1f, nvr btn far: quick reapp: see 3037 & 2156.
3688 **HEAD TO KERRY 14** [12]4-8-12 (54) E Ahern 9/2: 3534245: Prom, styd on to lead 2f out, hdd ins fnl   *½*   **55**
1f, no extra: acts on firm, soft & fibresand: just btr 3519 (fast).
3868 **AONINCH 7** [16]4-9-0 (60) R Hughes 6/1: 0602626: Held up, prog 4f out, staying on when short of   *½*   **60**
room dist, sn onepcd: quick reapp: btr 3868 & 3114.
3829 **SWIFT ALCHEMIST 9** [3]4-8-13 p (5) G Baker 33/1: 0300007: Cl-up, led 3f out, hdd 2f out, no extra.   *1¼*   **53**
3530 **ELLWAY HEIGHTS 21** [20]7-8-11 (53) J Fortune 10/1: 0-222538: Rear, hdwy 2f out, onepcd fnl 1f.   *nk*   **50**
3276* **MOUNT BENGER 32** [13]4-9-8 p (64) K Darley 7/1: 00-60419: Mid-div, hdwy 2f out, wknd fnl 1f: btr 3276.   *1¼*   **59**
3867 **EFRHINA 7** [11]4-9-7 (63) R Havlin 16/1: 002-0030: 10th: Cl-up over 10f, wknd: quick reapp: btr 3867.   *2½*   **54**
3630 **PERSIAN GENIE 17** [8]3-8-10 (62) S Carson 20/1: 0-00000: 11th: Al in rear: see 3186.   *2*   **50**
3688 **WESTERN 14** [10]4-10-0 (70) Dane O'Neill 5/1: 1-200000: 12th: Al in rear: top weight.   *6*   **50**
3618* **WORCESTER LODGE 18** [1]3-9-2 (68) S Drowne 7/2 FAV: 040-10: 13th: In tch over 1m, wknd: v disapp   *1¾*   **45**
on today's soft grnd: see 3618 (fast).
      FUTURE TO FUTURE 266 [15]4-8-12 (54) A Daly 50/1: F060-0: 14th: gr g Linamix - Finir En Beaute   *6*   **23**
(Groom Dancer) Al in rear: reapp & Brit bow: ex-French, mod form to date in 4 previous starts.
3638 **DR COOL 16** [14]7-9-10 (66) G Carter 25/1: 24510/-00: 15th: bl g Ezzoud - Vayavaig (Damister) Al   *2½*   **31**
in rear: missed '03: won 2 h'caps in '02 (also plcd numerous times): won 3 h'caps in '01: eff at 12/14f, prob
stays stiff 2m: acts on fast & hvy grnd, any trk: tried blnks/visor, prob btr without: with J Akehurst.
1 Oct'02 York 13.8g/f 69-69 D: 2 Aug'02 Sand 14g/s 72-70 C: 2 Jun'02 Sand 14g/s 72-69 D:
1 Jun'02 Sand 14gd 72-66 D: 2 May'02 Sali 12g/f 70-64 D: 2 Apr'02 Epso g/f 71-64 C:
1 Sep'01 Goog 12g/f 66-60 E: 1 Sep'01 Epso 12g/f 63-55 E:
3039 **MUST BE MAGIC 42** [17]7-9-0 vis (56) R Miles(3) 20/1: 4500000: 16th: Led, hdd 3f out, fdd: 6 wk abs.   *3*   **17**
3222 **SECRET JEWEL 34** [19]4-9-13 (69) J Quinn 25/1: 0/0-6050: 17th: Al adrift, eased 2f out: btr 3222.   *8*   **19**
17 Ran   Time 2m 46.08(16.08)   Owned: Mrs Jean M O'Connor   Trained: Wantage

Official Going Good/Soft (Good Places)

4034 5.40 Racing Uk Median Auction Maiden Stakes 3yo (F)
£3192 £912 £456 1m2f Good/Soft Inapplicable Inside

LOOK AGAIN 0 [5] Mrs A J Perrett 3-9-0 S Sanders 15/2: 1: ch g Zilzal - Last Look (Rainbow 87+
Quest) Dwelt & held up, hdwy & led over 2f out, edged left & styd on strongly to pull clr under hand riding: related
to a pair of mid-dist wnrs: eff at 10f, further will suit: acts on gd/soft grnd & a gall trk: goes well fresh: fine
start, looks potentially useful & likely to progress.
3186 **DUNDRY 35** [2] G L Moore 3-9-0 (78) I Mongan 9/2: 0-332: Chsd ldrs, rdn & kept on, no threat to 4 79
wnr: op 10/3: acts on gd & gd/soft grnd: see 3186 & 2700.
3007 **FLAMBOYANT LAD 43** [9] B W Hills 3-9-0 (80) R Hills 6/4 FAV: 2-333: Chsd ldr & led 7f out till nk 78
over 2f out, sn no extra: well bckd, op 7/4: 6 wk abs: clr of rem: just btr 3007 & 930.
2843 **PORT N STARBOARD 49** [6] C A Cyzer 3-9-0 N Callan 50/1: 454: Chsd ldrs, no impress fnl 3f: abs. 8 67
3581 **MY MICHELLE 19** [1]3-8-9 (64) A Culhane 20/1: 553-0045: Chsd ldrs, no impress over 2f out. 2 59
3828 **SECOND WARNING 9** [4]3-9-0 (60) J Murtagh 20/1: 000-5056: Cl-up, btn over 3f out, longer trip. 2½ 60
KIPSIGIS 0 [7]3-9-0 M Fenton 25/1: 7: b g Octagonal - Kisumu (Damister) Slow away & bhd, no ch 1¾ 58
fnl 3f on debut: half brother to a top class 10f performer.
NEW YORK CITY 0 [3]3-9-0 A Hamblett(7) 33/1: 8: Slow away & sn well bhd on debut. 18 33
3237 **ONE SO MARVELLOUS 33** [8]3-8-9 D Holland 5/2: 09: Led 3f, struggling halfway & eased: lost action. dist 0
9 Ran Time 2m 10.22 (7.92) Owned: Mr J H Richmond-Watson Trained: Pulborough

4035 6.10 Bbag Baden-Badener Yearling Sales Maiden Stakes Fillies 2yo (D)
£5083 £1564 £782 1m54y rnd Good/Soft Inapplicable Centre

2863 **NIGHT OF JOY 48** [10] M A Jarvis 2-8-11 N Callan 15/2: 441: Chsd ldrs & led over 2f out, drvn & 86
styd on well: op 6/1, abs: eff at 7f, improve for step up to 1m, further shld suit: acts on fm & fast, enjoyed
gd/soft tonight: handles a gall or easy trk: progressive, open to improvement in h'caps: see 2863.
DASH TO THE TOP 0 [16] L M Cumani 2-8-11 D Holland 14/1: 2: b f Montjeu - Millennium Dash 1 83+
(Nashwan) Dwelt & bhd, ran green & detached 3f out, 'flew home' fnl 2f, eye-catching: Feb 1st foal: dam 10f scorer:
eff at 1m, crying out for further: acts on gd/soft: penny dropped late on & made up an amazing amount of grnd, most
promising, keep on side.
3594 **SINGHALESE 18** [5] J A Osborne 2-8-11 S W Kelly 11/2 JT FAV: 43: Held up, switched & kept on shd 81
from over 1f out, not able to chall wnr: styd longer 1m trip well: acts on fast & gd/soft grnd: see 3594.
3616 **MOKARABA 18** [4] J L Dunlop 2-8-11 R Hills 6/1: 44: Handy, outpcd over 3f out, styd on late, not 1 81
pace of wnr: styd longer 1m trip, looks sure to relish mid-dists: acts on fast & gd/soft grnd: see 3616.
3601 **PEARLS A SINGER 18** [2]2-8-11 R Mullen 50/1: 05: ch f Spectrum - Cultured Pearl (Lammtarra) 2½ 74
Chsd ldrs, no impress fnl 1f: left debut bhd: Feb 1st foal, dam mdn: improved for debut.
3103 **AUTHENTICATE 39** [18]2-8-11 G Gibbons 11/2 JT FAV: 46: Held up, hdwy 4f out, rdn & no impress ¾ 75
bef dist: op 9/1: bred to apprec this longer 1m trip: handles gd & gd/soft grnd: see 3103 (6f).
3786 **ELRAFA MUJAHID 11** [8]2-8-11 I Mongan 20/1: 37: Chsd ldrs, edged left & fdd over 1f out: see 3786. hd 74
CREME DE LA CREME 0 [3]2-8-11 T P Queally 14/1: 8: b f Montjeu - Pride of Place (Caerleon) 2 70
Chsd ldrs, no impress over 2f: Feb foal, dam a 7f plcd juv: sire high-class mid-dist performer.
3633 **KRISTALCHEN 17** [11]2-8-11 A Culhane 28/1: 09: Mid-div, lost place after 3f, mod late prog. 1½ 67
TWYLA THARP 0 [14]2-8-11 T Durcan 7/1: 0: 10th: Dwelt & bhd, kept on late, nrst fin. ½ 66
SIDESHOW 0 [7]2-8-11 S Sanders 12/1: 0: 11th: Held up, rdn/hung left & btn 2f out. nk 65
3252 **USHINDI 33** [13]2-8-11 J Mackay 40/1: 00: 12th: Led 5f, btn over 1f out. 2½ 60
BAYREUTH 0 [17]2-8-11 M Fenton 40/1: 0: 13th: Sn towards rear & nvr factor. 5 51
KATANA 0 [9]2-8-11 J Murtagh 15/2: 0: 14th: Dwelt & al bhd. ¾ 50
3798 **Gibraltar Bay 10** [6]2-8-11 A McCarthy 66/1:0 **Line Ahead 0** [12]2-8-11 R Winston 12/1:0
3330 **Welsh Galaxy 28** [15]2-8-11 R Price 100/1:0 **Magdelaine 0** [1]2-8-11 C Catlin 66/1:0
18 Ran Time 1m 46.6 (7.2) Owned: Mr Saif Ali Trained: Newmarket

4036 6.40 Midlands Racing Handicap Stakes 3yo+ 0-80 (D) [86]
£7800 £2400 £1200 1m54y rnd Good/Soft Inapplicable Centre

3455 **BALEARIC STAR 25** [14] B R Millman 3-8-8 (66) R Winston 25/1: 6010061: Chsd ldr, led over 1f out, 78
rdn out: suited by 1m on firm & gd/soft grnd, sharp or gall trks: see 1956, 1007.
3759 **MOUNT HILLABY 12** [7] M W Easterby 4-8-5 (57) Dale Gibson 11/2: 000-1002: Trkd ldrs, styd on for 1½ 65
press, not able to reach wnr: back to form: see 378.
3898* **THREEZEDZZ 6** [11] P D Evans 6-9-10 (6ex)t (76) F P Ferris(3) 5/1 FAV: 0101013: Led 6f, no extra 1 82
for press fnl 1f: quick reapp under a pen, remains in gd heart: see 3898.
3964 **KENTUCKY KING 3** [4] P W Hiatt 4-10-0 (80) A Culhane 20/1: 00352R4: Dwelt & held up, switched & 1 84
styd on for press, not able to chall: quick reapp, left latest bhd: see 3216, 1057 &n 800.
3821 **ARRAN 9** [3]4-8-1 (53) Joanna Badger 2/1: 0302105: Dwelt & held up, short of room over 2f out, hd 56
kept on onepace: acts on fast & gd/soft grnd, loves fibresand: see 3487 (AW).
3809 **SPLODGER MAC 10** [13]5-8-1 (53) F Norton 11/1: 06-00126: Chsd ldrs, rdn & btn dist: new yard: btr 3809 & 3501. 2½ 51
3583* **HABSHAN 19** [12]4-9-3 (69) D Holland 11/2: 2-043517: Chsd ldrs, rdn & btn dist: new yard: btr 3583. ¾ 66
3829 **SAHAAT 9** [17]6-9-4 (70) J Murtagh 20/1: 0050258: Chsd ldrs till over 1f out: btr 3392 (fibresand). 1¾ 64
3768 **TEDSTALE 11** [8]6-9-12 bl (78) T E Durcan 14/1: 0364539: Slow away & bhd, mod prog: btr 3768 (fast). shd 72
3428 **OUT FOR A STROLL 25** [2]5-9-7 (73) R L Moore 7/1: 110-0000: 10th: In tch, rdn & btn over 1f out. shd 64
3505 **UNO MENTE 22** [9]5-7-13 VIS (52) Kim Tinkler 50/1: 0630000: 11th: Dwelt, rear, little hdwy in visor. 1¼ 44
2284 **SKIBEREEN 71** [5]4-9-1 (67) Natalia Gemelova(7) 33/1: 4503500: 12th: Handy, btn 2f out: btr 1775. 1 55
3042* **NIMELLO 41** [10]8-9-12 (78) L Dettori 11/2: 1-001010: 13th: Held up, eff over 2f out, sn btn: op 2½ 61
4/1: abs: longer 1m trip: acts on gd/soft grnd (gd ride, made alt).
3741 **SINJAREE 13** [6]6-7-12 (11oh) (39) D Fentiman 66/1: 5106000: 14th: Dwelt & held up, rdn & btn 2f out. nk 32
1021 **SEWMORE CHARACTER 138** [1]4-9-2 (68) N Callan 33/1: 61-46250: 15th: Mid-div, found little over 2f out. 1 48
3208 **WARNINGCAMP 34** [16]3-9-8 (80) S Sanders 14/1: 4630: 16th: Held up, rdn & btn 2f out: h'cap bow. 4 53

NOTTINGHAM WEDNESDAY 18.08.04 Lefthand, Galloping Track

16 Ran   Time 1m 44.42 (5.04)   Owned: Mr G W Dormer   Trained: Cullompton

4037   7.10 Simon Is Roughley 40 Today Handicap Stakes 3yo 35-55 (F)   [63]
£3556 £1016 £508   1m2f   Good/Soft   Inapplicable   Inside

3048 **ARGENTUM 41** [1] Lady Herries 3-9-3 (52) S Sanders 7/1: 00-051: Slow away & rear, hdwy over 3f   62
out & led over 1f out, drvn out, eased fnl strides: abs & h'cap bow: unplcd prev at up to 1m: apprec step up to
10f, 12f may suit: acts on gd/soft grnd & a gall trk: lightly rcd & open to further improvement: see 3048.
3690 **BRIGHT FIRE 14** [4] W J Musson 3-9-1 (50) R Mullen 8/1: 06-5462: Held up, rdn to chall over 1f   1½ 56
out, kept on, not pace of wnr: eff around 10f, handles fast & gd/soft grnd: shld find a race: see 3690, 750.
3982 **GO GREEN 2** [9] P D Evans 3-9-5 t (54) F P Ferris(3) 8/1: 0502143: Dwelt & held up, rdn & hdwy over   hd 59
3f out, chall over 1f out, no extra ins last: clr of rem: remains on an upward curve: see 3982 & 3730.
3913 **MUSIC MIX 5** [7] E A L Dunlop 3-9-6 (55) L Dettori 15/8 FAV: 66-00144: Held up, hdwy when hmpd   6 52
over 3f out, kept on late, no threat to front trio: shade closer when a clr run: bckd: btr 3913.
3383 **THE KING OF ROCK 27** [10]3-9-5 (51) J Murtagh 15/2: 5402465: Held up, eff over 3f out, sn edged   nk 50
left & no impress bef dist: see 2503.
3854 **ARMENTIERES 7** [8]3-9-6 bl (55) G Hind 33/1: 530-6006: Held up, prog 3f out, btn dist: btr 164 (AW).   1 50
3401 **COTTON EASTER 26** [3]3-9-2 (51) Paul Eddery 33/1: 006007: Slow away & bhd, late prog, nrst fin.   2 43
3874 **MYSTIC MOON 7** [2]3-8-13 (48) T E Durcan 50/1: 0400408: Chsd ldrs, fdd fnl 2f: btr 3362.   2½ 36
2982* **BISCAR TWO 44** [13]3-9-3 bl (52) V Halliday 10/1: 6222019: Slow away, held up, only mod prog: abs.   hd 39
3772 **STANLEY CRANE 11** [6]3-9-6 t (55) D Holland 10/1: 0545430: 10th: Led & around 4L clr halfway, hdd   12 27
over 2f out, fdd: btr 3772 (held up, fast).
3845 **OKTIS MORILIOUS 8** [14]3-9-5 (54) A Culhane 14/1: 6251040: 11th: Chsd ldrs, btn 2f out: btr 3055.   2 23
3835 **COMPTON MICKY 9** [11]3-9-6 p (55) K Pierrepont(7) 66/1: 6056050: 12th: Keen & prom, btn 3f out.   1½ 22
3874 **RUSSALKA 7** [12]3-9-5 (51) N Callan 25/1: 5026060: 13th: Chsd ldrs, rdn/edged right & hmpd   10 6
over 3f out, sn btn: 1st time visor, no improvement.
3288 **STYLISH SUNRISE 32** [16]3-9-4 t (53) P Doe 28/1: 0435030: 14th: Chsd ldrs, btn 3f out: btr 3288 (AW).   11 0
3422 **BREAKING THE RULE 25** [5]3-9-1 (50) R L Moore 40/1: 0650: 15th: Chsd ldrs till 3f out: h'cap bow.   nk 0
15 Ran   Time 2m 10.67 (8.37)   Owned: Lady Herries and Friends   Trained: Littlehampton

4038   7.40 Ed Lee 21st Birthday Celebration Handicap Stakes Fillies 3yo+ 0-75 (E)   [72]
£3770 £1160 £580   5f str   Good   Inapplicable   Stands Side

3591 **ROMAN MISTRESS 18** [2] T D Easterby 4-9-3 bl (61) D Allan 8/1: 6305041: Made all, rdn & in command   69+
dist, eased cl-home, val 2L+: eff at 5/6f, stays sharp 7f: acts on fast & gd/soft: improved for dominating in blnks.
3537 **CERULEAN ROSE 21** [8] A W Carroll 5-9-10 (68) R L Moore 4/1: 4020302: Rear, styd on late.   1¼ 68
3849 **TENDER 8** [4] Mrs Stef Liddiard 4-8-4 p (48) F Norton 12/1: 0041003: Dwelt & bhd, late gains: see 3332.   nk 47
3767 **DIAMOND RING 11** [10] Mrs J Candlish 5-8-5 (2ow) (47) G Hind 16/1: 0303624: Chsd wnr, wknd fnl 1f.   1½ 43
3888* **MIMIC 6** [7]4-9-0 (58) R Mills(7) 7/2 JT FAV: 0-000015: Held up, eff 2f out, no prog no dist: btr 3888 (6f).   ½ 50
3680 **QUEEN OF NIGHT 14** [6]4-8-12 (56) A Culhane 9/1: 0112056: Prom, fdd fnl 2f: btr 3680 & 3353.   3½ 37
2326 **WHITE O MORN 70** [9]5-7-12 p (42) D Fox(5) 33/1: 1020407: Slow away, nvr a factor: abs: btr 1948.   shd 23
3849 **LADY PROTECTOR 8** [11]5-8-13 (57) D Holland 7/2 JT FAV: 0113338: Chsd ldrs, outpcd when short of   ½ 36
room over 1f out, no impress.
3180 **LYDIAS LOOK 36** [3]7-8-4 (48) Kristin Stubbs(7) 33/1: 5451609: Dwelt & sn outpcd: btr 2326.   1¼ 23
3220 **RED LEICESTER 34** [5]4-8-3 vis (47) P Hanagan 14/1: 5160500: 10th: Chsd ldrs, btn 2f out: btr 3054.   2 16
3849 **JINKSONTHEHOUSE 8** [1]3-8-10 (56) S Sanders 12/1: 4014240: 11th: Prom, rdn & btn 2f out.   3 17
11 Ran   Time 1m 10.45 (1.95)   Owned: Mr W H Ponsonby   Trained: Malton

4039   8.10 Watch Racing Uk On Sky 425 Classified Stakes 3yo+ 0-70 (E)
£3640 £1120 £560   5f str   Good   Inapplicable   Stands Side

3952 **MADDIES A JEM 4** [6] J R Jenkins 4-9-0 (73) L Dettori 13/8 FAV: 1356421: Missed break & held up   77
rear, smooth hdwy over 1f out & switched to lead cl-home, cosily: quick reapp: eff at 5/6f: acts on firm & fast,
loves gd or softer, sharp/undul or gall trk: tough filly, type to prog & win again.
3789 **FOLEY MILLENNIUM 11** [5] M Quinn 3-9-3 (73) S Sanders 7/1: 1102142: Chsd ldr, led over 1f out   ½ 76
till well ins last: apprec drop back to minimum trip, tough & shld win again: see 3577 (C/D).
3852 **PADDYWACK 7** [3] D W Chapman 7-9-3 bl (73) A Culhane 3/1: 1103633: Chsd ldrs, briefly short of   1 73
room cl-home, styd on onepace for press: see 2942.
3684 **FLYING BANTAM 14** [2] R A Fahey 3-8-12 (70) P Hanagan 8/1: 2224024: Chsd ldrs, sn pushed along,   ¾ 68
onepace when short of room ins last: see 3684, 1639.
3852 **SOBA JONES 7** [4]7-9-2 (72) K Pierrepont(7) 9/1: 6542505: Chsd ldrs, no extra over 1f out: btr 3241.   ¾ 68
2698 **OK PAL 55** [8]4-9-5 bl (75) D Holland 8/1: U300606: Outpcd, switched left & no impress on ldrs: abs.   2 65
3751 **STRATHCLYDE 12** [7]5-9-0 (69) C Catlin 33/1: 000-0007: Led 3f, wknd qckly: val h'cap wnr '03 (J   ¾ 58
Cullinan): AW mdn & turf h'cap scorer '02: eff at 6f, loves a stiff 5f: acts on fm, gd/soft & polytrack, prob any trk.
3680 **CATCH THE CAT 14** [1]5-9-4 vis (74) G Parkin 16/1: 5000108: Sn struggling rear: btr 3561 (fast).   2 56
8 Ran   Time 1m 0.25(1.75)   Owned: Mrs Wendy Jenkins   Trained: Royston

SOUTHWELL Fibresand THURSDAY 19.08.04 Lefthand, Sharp, Oval Track

Official Going Standard

4040 **2.00 At The Races From 9 A M Nursery Handicap Stakes 2yo (E)** **[90]**
£3858 £1187 £594 **7f aw rnd** **Going 54** **-24 Slow** Inside

3807 **WINDY PROSPECT 11** [9] P A Blockley 2-9-8 (84) I Mongan 3/1 FAV: 2103221: Led/dsptd lead, went on over 2f out, drvn out: nicely bckd, op 7/2: eff at 6/7f on fast, gd & both AWs: useful & improving. **95a**
3560 **DICTION 21** [10] K R Burke 2-8-5 (67) L Enstone 8/1: 051152: Dwelt & held up, eff to press wnr 2f out, no extra ins last: loves fibresand, remains on an upward curve: see 3393. *1¼* **74a**
3483* **CAITLIN 24** [7] B Smart 2-8-8 (2ow) (68) F Lynch 5/1: 62413: Dwelt, sn mid-div, hung left but kept on for press fnl 2f, al held: ran to form of 3483 (C/D). *½* **76a**
3570 **COUNTRYWIDE SUN 20** [8] N P Littmoden 2-7-13 p (61) J Bramhill 14/1: 00024: Led till over 2f out, no extra: AW bow: handles fast grnd & fibresand: confirmed improvement of 3570 (clmr). *1¾* **64a**
3753 **GUINEA A MINUTE 13** [5]2-8-1 (63) J Mackay 14/1: 03665: Rear, hung left but styd on from over 1f out, no threat to ldrs: AW bow: prob handles fibresand: see 3041. *1* **64a**
3699 **UNION JACK JACKSON 15** [12]2-8-9 (71) G Baker 20/1: 4006: Mid-div, eff over 2f out, hung left & no impress bef dist: h'cap bow: see 2569. *1¼* **69a**
3227 **LORNA DUNE 34** [1]2-8-0 (62) D Kinsella 16/1: 36067: Chsd ldrs, no extra dist: longer trip, op 10/1. *½* **59a**
3698 **SPINNAKERS GIRL 15** [4]2-8-8 (70) P Makin(5) 16/1: 03248: Chsd ldrs, btn over 2f out: AW bow. *2½* **62a**
3351 **DANS HEIR 29** [3]2-7-12 (2oh)p (58) D Fentiman(7) 9/1: 02029: Al towards rear, nvr a factor: btr 3351. *2½* **47a**
3820 **GRYSKIRK 10** [13]2-8-2 e (64) T P Queally 6/1: 6300030: 10th: Dwelt, prom till over 1f out: btr 3820. *hd* **50a**
3750 **AMPHITHEATRE 13** [11]2-8-2 (64) S Carson 10/1: 5030330: 11th: Trkd ldrs wide, btn 2f out: btr 3750. *4* **43a**
3570 **Itsa Monkey 20** [2]2-7-12 (11oh)(49) K Ghunowa 50/1:0
3484 **Serene Pearl 24** [6]2-7-12 (3oh)t(57) Lisa Jones 40/1:0
13 Ran Time 1m 32.03 (5.43) Owned: bellhouseracingcom Trained: Cockerham

4041 **2.35 Midlands Racing - 9 Great Venues Selling Stakes 3yo+ (G)**
£2618 £748 £374 **6f aw rnd** **Going 54** **-23 Slow** Inside

1319 **SIRAJ 118** [3] Mrs J Candlish 5-9-2 (62) G Hind 13/2: 10025-01: Led/dsptd lead & went on over 1f out, held on all out: abs, prev with N Graham: sold to P McEntee for 9,000gns: eff at 5/6f on fast, soft & both AWs, with/without blnks: goes well fresh in sell grade: see 121. **63a**
3852 **PORT ST CHARLES 8** [7] C R Dore 7-9-2 (60) R Thomas(5) 3/1 FAV: 0040602: In tch, styd on well for press cl-home, just failed: blnks omitted, clmd for 6,000: back to form on fibresand: see 113. *hd* **62a**
3849 **EMARADIA 9** [9] A W Carroll 3-8-13 (60) L Enstone(3) 11/2: 1226603: In tch, outpcd halfway, late gains. *1½* **57a**
3876 **WINGS OF MORNING 8** [2] P A Blockley 3-9-4 vis (65) I Mongan 5/1: 5630034: Led/dsptd lead till over 1f out, no extra ins last: claimed for £6,000: btr 2723, 1163 & 488 (7f). *shd* **62a**
3344 **GO FREE 29** [5]3-8-13 (54) P Makin(5) 33/1: 00-2505: Chsd ldrs, not pace to chall: see 2339 (7f). *½* **55a**
3191 **INDIAN MUSIC 36** [6]7-9-7 (45) F Lynch 12/1: 2462006: Held up when hmpd halfway, nvr land a blow. *hd* **59a$**
3746 **BELLS BEACH 13** [8]6-9-2 (51) T P Queally 12/1: 4415007: In tch wide, nvr able to chall: flattered 2361. *1* **51a**
3757 **KING NICHOLAS 13** [1]5-9-7 t p (57) M Lawson(5) 7/1: 1041068: Slow away, sn in tch, hmpd halfway & nvr a factor: see 1606. *nk* **55a**
3545* **FIZZY LIZZY 21** [10]4-9-2 P (33) W Hogg(7) 16/1: 00-00019: Slow away & al bhd: chkpcs, new yard. *6* **34a**
3757 **POLAR GALAXY 13** [4]3-8-8 P (41) V Halliday 12/1: 00-05040: 10th: Slow away, in tch till over 2f out: cheek pieces: btr 3757. *3* **21a**
2559 **CASEYS HOUSE 61** [11]4-8-11 T Eaves(3) 50/1: 0000: 11th: Dwelt & al bhd, abs/AW bow, no form. *13* **0a**
11 Ran Time 1m 17.92 (4.62) Owned: Racing For You Limited Trained: Leek

4042 **3.10 At The Races Dedicated Racing Channel Maiden Stakes 3yo (D)**
£3361 £1034 £517 **1m aw rnd** **Going 54** **-05 Slow** Inside

3923 **ADORATA 6** [2] J Jay 3-8-9 (63) M Tebbutt 6/4 FAV: 2023021: Chsd ldrs, rdn to chall fnl 2f & duelled with rnr-up, prevailed line, all out: bckd: qck reapp: eff at 6/7f, suited by 1m: acts on firm, gd & fibresand, sharp or stiff/gall trk: see 3923, 2295. **67a**
3048 **NATIVE TURK 42** [5] J A R Toller 3-9-0 T P Queally 20/1: 0-002: b c Miswaki - Churn Dat Butter (Unbridled) Chsd ldr & led over 4f out, joined over 2f out, sn duelled with wnr, just denied on line: clr of rem: 6 wk abs, AW bow: blnks omitted: unplcd sole '03 start (rtd 73, mdn): imprvd for switch to fibresand, stays 1m. *shd* **71a**
3292 **NOBLE MIND 31** [7] P G Murphy 3-9-0 (68) D Kinsella 7/2: 2003: Chsd ldrs, btn over 1f out: op 3/1: drop to 6/7f may suit but btr 2622 (debut). *10* **56a**
2493 **BEAMSLEY BEACON 64** [1] Ian Emmerson 3-9-0 (47) V Halliday 66/1: 0040644: Led 3f, btn 2f out: abs. *3½* **50a**
3396 **RAGAZZI 27** [4]3-9-0 (65) P Makin(5) 10/1: 00035: Held up, no impress fnl 2f: btr 3396 (6f). *3½* **44a**
3572 **JAVA DANCER 20** [9]3-9-0 P M Quinn 25/1: 066: Dwelt, in tch till over 3f out: AW bow. *½* **43a**
3784 **CLASSIC EXPRESSION 12** [10]3-8-9 G Carter 20/1: 607: Wide & held up, bhd halfway: apprec h'caps. *1½* **35a**
TARKEEZ 55 [8]3-9-0 (70) F Lynch 9/2: 3-300308: b c Lear Fan - Mt Morna (Mt Livermore) Chsd ldrs till lost place bef halfway, no ch after: ex-Irish mdn, h'cap plcd earlier in '04: stays a gall 10f on fast. *2* **36a**
BONUS POINTS 0 [6]3-9-0 D Corby(3) 14/1: 9: Slow away & held up, no ch fnl 3f on debut: op 12/1. *3* **30a**
73**ALMANAC 175** [3]3-9-0 G Hind 66/1: 0-000: 10th: Sn struggling rear, 6 mth abs. *9* **14a**
10 Ran Time 1m 44.15 (4.75) Owned: Fremel and Friends Trained: Newmarket

4043 **3.45 Sky 415 Ntl 908 Telewest 534 Handicap Stakes 3yo+ 35-55 (F)** **[61]**
£3010 £860 £430 **5f aw str** **Going 54** **+15 Fast** Stands Side

3643 **JAGGED 17** [8] J R Jenkins 4-9-8 vis (55) T P Queally 5/1 FAV: 0023631: Trkd ldr, led ins last, drvn out: op 7/2: first win on 23rd start: eff btwn 5f/sharp 7f on fm, gd/soft & both AWs, likes a sharp trk: eff in blnks/visor: see 3643, 2720 & 1533. **64a**
3417 **KENNINGTON 27** [6] Mrs C A Dunnett 4-9-4 vis (51) Lisa Jones 11/2: 0200402: Chsd ldrs, styd on for press, not pace of wnr: visor reapplied, gd run: see 3220, 2347 & 416. *¾* **57a**
3353 **THE LEATHER WEDGE 29** [3] A Berry 5-8-12 p (45) P Bradley 20/1: 0525503: Led, hdd ins last & no extra: cheek pieces reapplied, gd run with forcing tactics: see 187 (C/D). *1¼* **47a**
3104 **BACK IN SPIRIT 40** [12] B A McMahon 4-8-5 t (38) G Carter 13/2: 0-000024: Towards rear, kept on *2½* **32a**

late, not reach front trio: bckd, op 8/1, 6 wk abs: see 3104 & 1799.
3655 **LEOPARD CREEK 17** [1]3-8-12 (47) I Mongan 12/1: 0200005: Rdn chasing ldrs halfway, onepace: acts on firm, gd/soft & fibresand: see 2326 & 1951. ½ **39a**
3932 **SO SOBER 6** [11]6-8-7 (40) F Lynch 8/1: 4300056: Chsd ldrs, no impress from dist: qck reapp. *nk* **31a**
3301 **SAVERNAKE BRAVE 31** [4]3-8-12 (47) G Baker 20/1: 5204007: Slow away & outpcd, mod gains. *nk* **37a**
3830 **DONEGAL SHORE 10** [9]5-8-10 vis t (43) G Hind 16/1: 4306048: Slow away & outpcd, nvr on terms. ¾ **31a**
3333 **THE BARONESS 29** [10]4-9-8 (55) D Corby(3) 25/1: 20545-09: Chsd ldrs, no extra dist, eased nr fin. *hd* **42a**
3220 **SCARY NIGHT 35** [15]4-9-4 p (51) J Edmunds 8/1: 0060200: 10th: Chsd ldrs, no impress over 1f out. 1½ **33a**
3687 **SCARLETT BREEZE 15** [5]3-8-11 (46) M Tebbutt 25/1: 0005040: 11th: Slow away & al towards rear. ½ **26a**
3180 **JOHN OGROATS 37** [2]6-9-4 BL e (51) P Makin(5) 14/1: 0000000: 12th: Sn struggling towards rear. ½ **29a**
3687 **DIAPHANOUS 15** [7]6-8-4 bl (37) Liam Jones(7) 50/1: 0000000: 13th: Slow away & outpcd, hung right. ½ **13a**
3767 **LEVELLED 12** [16]10-8-9 (42) J Mackay 12/1: 0650640: 14th: Slow away, sn handy till over 1f out. *1* **15a**
3569 **ATTORNEY 20** [14]6-9-3 vis (50) Derek Nolan(7) 14/1: 0006000: 15th: Slow away & sn struggling rear. *5* **9a**
15 Ran Time 59.23 (1.93) Owned: The Jagged Partnership Trained: Royston

4044

4.20 Arena Leisure Handicap Stakes 3yo 0-75 (E) **[81]**
£4264 £1312 £656 **1m aw rnd** **Going 54** **-09 Slow** Inside

3906 **DONT CALL ME DEREK 7** [10] S C Williams 3-8-5 (58) G Carter 9/4 FAV: 5600021: Chsd ldrs, led over 1f out, hung left under press but styd on strongly & eased cl-home: hvly bckd, op 3/1: first win: eff around 1m: acts on firm, gd/soft & both AWs: progressive of late, can win again: see 3906, 3625. **70a**
3529 **MISSION AFFIRMED 22** [9] T P Tate 3-8-12 (65) J Edmunds 8/1: 5104052: Slow away, mid-div halfway, styd on for press fnl 2f, nvr threatened wnr: enjoys this surface: see 2495 & 1198 (C/D). *3* **69a**
3392* **BOOK MATCHED 27** [1] B Smart 3-9-4 (71) F Lynch 15/2: 1406013: Led/dsptd lead, went on 3f out till over 1f out, no extra: confirmed improvement of latest, likes to race with/force the pace: see 3392 (C/D clmr). ¾ **74a**
3651 **MULTIPLE CHOICE 17** [8] N P Littmoden 3-8-11 e t (64) J P Guillambert(3) 16/1: 0002464: Led/dsptd lead 5f, no extra: stays 1m, interesting for 6/7f at Southwell in similar: see 3091, 1011. 1¾ **64a**
3515 **BLUE JAVA 22** [4]3-8-6 (59) T P Queally 7/2: 40-00025: Chsd ldrs till outpcd halfway, some late gains. *nk* **58a**
3679 **MR MIDASMAN 15** [6]3-8-4 (57) J Mackay 12/1: 6000046: Chsd ldrs till outpcd halfway, no impress. *1* **54a**
3854 **COME WHAT JULY 8** [11]3-9-3 vis (70) Lisa Jones 14/1: 3510367: Bhd, mod prog, nrst fin: see 3505. 1¼ **64a**
3741 **FIT TO FLY 14** [2]3-8-13 (66) G Hind 14/1: 1560508: Bhd, little prog: btr 3067, 2723 & 869. 1¾ **57a**
3177 **TURF PRINCESS 37** [5]3-8-4 (57) D Fentiman(7) 33/1: 2453049: Chsd ldrs, btn 2f out: btr 3177 & 1678. 1¼ **45a**
3571 **IRON TEMPTRESS 20** [3]3-8-7 (60) B Swarbrick(5) 33/1: 52000-00: 10th: Al struggling rear: see 3571. *5* **39a**
3138 **DISPOL VELETA 39** [7]3-9-7 (74) P Makin(5) 9/2: 3001000: 11th: Chsd ldrs wide till halfway, sn struggling. *2* **49a**
11 Ran Time 1m 44.4 (5) Owned: J Lloyd and E Warder Trained: Newmarket

4045

4.50 Come Racing Tomorrow Apprentice Handicap Stakes 3yo+ 35-55 (G) **[66]**
£2996 £856 £428 **1m6f aw** **Going 54** **-13 Slow** Inside

3715 **SALUT SAINT CLOUD 14** [12] G L Moore 3-9-1 p (53) A Quinn 7/2: 0513331: Slow away & held up, hdwy 5f out & led 2f out, styd on strongly to assert under hand riding ins last: eff btwn 10/14f on firm, gd & fibresand. **63a**
3822 **MAGIC RED 10** [11] M J Ryan 4-9-13 (53) M Halford(5) 2/1 FAV: 000-1142: Sn handy, outpcd halfway, styd on for press fnl 2f, not pace of wnr: apprec return to fibresand: remains in fine form: see 3822 & 3158. 2½ **58a**
3240 **STAFF NURSE 34** [14] Don Enrico Incisa 4-8-8 (2oh) (32) Janice Webster(7) 20/1: 3-004053: Held up, hdwy from halfway, kept on onepace for press: see 1840. 1¾ **37a**
3895 **BLACK LEGEND 7** [13] R Lee 5-9-2 t (42) B Swarbrick 8/1: 4002/0-24: Dwelt & held up, prog to lead over 3f out, hdd 2f out & wknd: clr of rem: prob handles fibresand & gd/soft: just btr 3895 (10f). *5* **38a**
3834 **MERCURIOUS 10** [3]4-9-11 (51) Derek Nolan(5) 7/2: 1542125: Chsd ldrs, lost tch fnl 3f. *14* **31a**
2479 **SALFORD ROCKET 64** [6]4-8-8 (4oh) (30) Laura Pike(5) 50/1: 0-00606: Held up, only mod prog: abs. 1¼ **12a**
2381 **THE LAST MOHICAN 69** [9]5-8-9 (35) Kristin Stubbs(5) 20/1: 0321007: Led 10f, sn struggling, abs. *1* **12a**
3714 **MACCHIATO GB 14** [15]3-8-6 (2oh)BL (44) Liam Jones(5) 33/1: 2-050008: Chsd ldrs, lost tch fnl 2f: blnks. 1¾ **19a**
1252 **THATS RACING 122** [1]4-8-8 (1oh) (33) K Ghunowa(5) 12/1: 000-2609: Held up & struggling fnl 4f: abs. *12* **0a**
2105 **TIOGA GOLD 80** [5]5-8-8 (4oh) (30) A Reilly(5) 50/1: 4400-500: 10th: Held up, no ch 4f out: abs. *9* **0a**
1087 **Munfarid 134** [10]4-10-0 t(54) M Lawson(3) 28/1:0
3668 **Think Quick 16** [4]4-8-9 (35) Stephanie Hollinshead(3) 14/1:0
2124 **Pointed 79** [7]3-8-7 (1oh)(45) P Makin 50/1:0
3549 **Sninfia 21** [8]4-9-6 (46) W Hogg(5) 25/1:0
3549 **Caper 21** [2]4-9-1 (41) H Fellows(7) 50/1:0
3312 **Pattern Man 31** [16]3-8-12 (50) D Fentiman(5) 50/1:0
16 Ran Time 3m 09.13(9.33) Owned: Mr A Grinter Trained: Brighton

CHESTER THURSDAY 19.08.04 Lefthand, Very Tight Track

Official Going GOOD (GOOD/SOFT places).

4046

2.20 Surrenda-Link Novice Stakes 2yo (D)
£5499 £1692 £846 **7f122y rnd** **Good/Firm 25** **-23 Slow** Inside

3539 **MASTMAN 21** [5] B J Meehan 2-8-12 t (80) J F McDonald(3) 8/1: 2541: Nvr far away, went on halfway, held on gamely cl-home, all out: deserved first win & apprec this step up to 7.5f: acts on fast & firm grnd, wears a t-strap: useful, game eff here: see 3539. **91**
3425* **SKIDROW 26** [4] M L W Bell 2-9-0 (88) M Fenton 7/2: 012: Trkd ldrs, fin strongly & just btn in a thrilling fin: confirmed recent improvement, acts on gd & fast grnd: eff at 7/7.5f, 1m will suit: see 3425. *shd* **92**
3532 **STAGBURY HILL 22** [3] J W Hills 2-9-5 R Hills 11/8 FAV: 163: Keen in rear, sltly short of room dist, kept on fnl 1f but not reach front 2: well bckd, clr of rem: far from disgraced under top-weight: see 3532. 1¼ **94**
3500 **MIRAGE PRINCE 23** [2] W M Brisbourne 2-8-12 S W Kelly 25/1: 60654: Led till halfway, ev ch till no extra fnl 1f: highly tried, will find easier races: see 3500. *4* **77**
3005 **LESCAPADE 44** [6]2-8-12 N Callan 9/4: 35: Stumbled start, keen & sn trkd ldrs, btn fnl 1f: bckd from 3/1, 6 wk abs: rcd too keenly & must be given another ch after encouraging debut in 3005. ¾ **75**

5 Ran   Time 1m 36.07 (3.67)   Owned: Kennet Valley Thoroughbreds III   Trained: Upper Lambourn

---

4047   2.55 Bentley Motors 40th Service Conditions Stakes 3yo (B)
£12006 £4554 £2277   7f122y rnd   Good/Firm 25   + 17 Fast   Inside

3550* **PETER PAUL RUBENS 21** [4] P F I Cole 3-9-1 (105) P Hanagan 11/10 FAV: 0415111: Keen & made all,   109+
styd on strongly fnl 1f, rdn out: fast time: top-weight, bckd from 7/4: completed hat-trick: eff at 7/7.5f, has
tried 1m: acts on fast & firm grnd & on a stiff/gall or sharp trk: v progressive & smart, one to keep on side in
List/Gr 3 company: see 3550 (val h'cap).
3550 **JEDBURGH 21** [5] J L Dunlop 3-8-12 (96) N Callan 7/1: 1-033202: Chsd wnr throughout, kept on   1   100
under press fnl 1f, not quite get there: ran to useful best: again bhd today's wnr in 3550, see 3113.
3596 **MILK IT MICK 19** [1] J A Osborne 3-8-10 (107) S W Kelly 2/1: 11-25033: Chsd ldrs, not pace to   2½   96
chall: drifted from 11/8, reportedly broke a blood vessel: see 3596.
3778 **GLARAMARA 12** [2] A Bailey 3-8-12 (97) M Fenton 8/1: 0300444: Chsd ldrs, onepace fnl 1.5f.   hd   96
1481* **OMAN SEA 464** [3]3-8-7 R Hills 10/1: 21-5: b f Rahy - Ras Shaikh (Sheikh Albadou) Sn bhd & nvr   20   61
dngrs on reapp: won fnl of 2 juv starts (nov): eff at 5/6f on gd & firm grnd, handles a stiff/gall trk: nvr
figured over this longer trip. 1 May'03 York 6.0fm 89- D: 2 Apr'03 Newm 5gd 92- D:
5 Ran   Time 1m 33.01 (0.61)   Owned: Richard Green (Fine Paintings)   Trained: Whatcombe

---

4048   3.30 Bet@Bluesq Com Handicap Stakes 3yo 0-95 (C)   [99]
£13975 £4300 £2150   6f18y rnd   Good/Firm 25   + 04 Fast   Inside

3778 **HIGH VOLTAGE 12** [2] K R Burke 3-9-7 t (92) N Callan 9/2 FAV: 1360001: Made all, held on gamely   101
fnl 1f, all out: nicely bckd, gd time, jt top-weight: made most of fav'ble low draw, loves to force the pace over
5/6f on fast & gd/soft grnd: see 1360 (reapp).
3758 **COMPTONS ELEVEN 13** [8] M R Channon 3-9-5 (90) S Hitchcott(3) 5/1: 0521222: Nvr far away, ev ch   shd   98
fnl 1f, just btn in a thrilling fin: tough & consistent, another fine run from a modest middle draw: see 3758.
3562 **MISTER MARMADUKE 21** [4] J Semple 3-8-7 (78) T Hamilton(3) 10/1: 1000-043: Mid-div, styd on well   1   83
fnl 1f, nrst fin: looks sure to apprec a return to 7f judged on this: acts on fast grnd: see 3562.
3778 **DANZIG RIVER 12** [5] B W Hills 3-9-5 (90) R Hills 10/1: 2000004: Held up, styd on fnl 1f, nrst   ¾   92
fin: did not make best use of fav'ble low draw: see 1154 (reapp).
2734 **TRIBUTE 55** [1]3-8-4 (75) P Fessey 12/1: 61-00555: Chsd ldrs, onepace fnl 1f: abs, now with K Ryan.   1   74
3844 **MELODY KING 9** [3]3-7-12 (4oh)bl (65) Hayley Turner(5) 25/1: 4365U06: Slowly away, styd on late,   1½   64
nvr dngrs: slow start negated fav'ble low draw: usually front runs, see 3036.
3808* **OBE BOLD 11** [6]3-7-12 (7ex)(3oh) (66) C Haddon(7) 20/1: 5043017: Chsd ldrs, onepace fnl 1f: btr 3808.   ½   63
3778 **COMMANDO SCOTT 12** [7]3-9-7 (92) P Mathers(5) 13/2: 2261158: Chsd ldrs, btn fnl 1f: jt top-weight.   3½   76
3833 **JADAN 10** [12]3-8-4 (75) M Fenton 25/1: 3661509: Prom till wknd dist: poor high draw: see 3135.   3½   49
3814 **RISING SHADOW 11** [14]3-8-13 (84) P Hanagan 12/1: 35-62460: 10th: Slow away, al bhd: poor draw.   2½   51
3646 **TIMES REVIEW 17** [16]3-8-10 (81) D Allan 50/1: 2510000: 11th: Slowly away, al rear: worst draw.   6   30
3567 **BUY ON THE RED 20** [9]3-9-1 (86) R Miles(3) 14/1: 2110200: 12th: Al rear: btr 3188.   shd   35
3269 **MORSE 33** [11]3-9-2 (87) S W Kelly 16/1: 1200600: 13th: Sn bhd & nvr dngrs: poor draw.   1   33
3920 **THE JOBBER 6** [13]3-8-7 (78) F Norton 9/1: 1-406220: 14th: Chsd ldrs 4f, wknd: poor draw.   1¾   19
14 Ran   Time 1m 14.77 (1.27)   Owned: Mrs K Halsall   Trained: Leyburn

---

4049   4.05 Gerrard Wealth Management Nursery Handicap Stakes 2yo (D)   [90]
£6874 £2115 £1058   5f16y rnd   Good/Firm 25   -12 Slow   Inside

3987* **COLEERTON DANCER 3** [1] K A Ryan 2-8-9 (6ex) (71) A Mullen(7) 1/1 FAV: 4440111: Mid-div, hdwy 3f   87
out, led well ins fnl 1f, going away: well bckd, qck reapp: eff at 5f on firm & gd/soft, tight or gall trk: made
full use of gd low draw but v progressive & can win again: see 3987.
3943 **WISE WAGER 5** [3] R A Fahey 2-8-11 (73) P Hanagan 9/4: 2333122: Prom, hdwy & ev ch ins fnl 1f, no   2   79
extra c-home: well bckd, qck reapp: remains in gd form: see 3607.
3432 **WONDERFUL MIND 26** [2] T D Easterby 2-8-10 BL (72) D Allan 14/1: 0521563: Led after 1f, hdd well   nk   77
ins fnl 1f, no extra: handles fast & gd: gd eff here in first time blnks: see 2889.
3795 **SAPPHIRE DREAM 12** [5] A Bailey 2-9-7 (83) Hayley Turner(5) 20/1: 2216044: Bhd, hdwy 2f out, kept   2   82
on but not pace to chall: return to 6f will suit.
3807 **HILLSIDE HEATHER 11** [9]2-8-7 (69) F Norton 25/1: 4320245: In tch, outpcd, hdwy 2f out, onepcd   1   65
ins fnl 1f: not disgraced from poor high draw.
3743 **WESTBROOK BLUE 13** [6]2-9-4 (80) C Haddon(7) 25/1: 31346: Mid-div, sh rm dist, kept on.   shd   76
3902 **IM AIMEE 7** [10]2-9-1 (77) S Hitchcott(3) 14/1: 0222237: Led 1f, wknd 2f out: qck reapp, poor draw.   3   64
3343 **NEXT TIME 29** [7]2-7-12 (1oh) (59) J F McDonald(3) 40/1: 4500448: Cl-up, wknd 2f out: see 954.   4   35
3863 **IAM FOREVERBLOWING 8** [4]2-7-12 (15oh) (45) Donna Caldwell(6) 100/1: 5450009: Outpcd, no ch when   8   11
joc lost irons over 1f out: v stiff task: see 1499.
3931 **ANGELOFTHENORTH 6** [8]2-8-6 (68) N Mackay(3) 25/1: 343330: 10th: Mid-div, wknd 2f out: qck reapp.   ¾   16
10 Ran   Time 1m 01.67 (1.87)   Owned: Coleerton Moor Racing   Trained: Hambleton

---

4050   4.40 European Breeders Fund Combermere Conditions Stakes Fillies 2yo (B)
£10205 £3871 £1935   6f18y rnd   Good/Firm 25   -16 Slow   Inside

3607 **KATIE BOO 19** [5] A Berry 2-8-8 (81) F Norton 7/1: 2135221: Made all, rdn out: tchd 10/1: eff   89
at 5/6f on firm & gd, prob acts on any trk: well deserved win following recent plcd effs: see 2442.
3357 **VONDOVA 28** [1] R Hannon 2-8-11 (83) P Dobbs 11/2: 30102: Trkd ldrs, switched right dist, bmpd &   ¾   88
went 2nd ins fnl 1f, sn struck by wnr's whip, not btn far: tchd 7/1: shade unfortunate.
3632* **GOLDEN LEGACY 18** [7] R A Fahey 2-8-11 (96) P Hanagan 4/6 FAV: 20113: Trkd ldrs, hdwy into 2nd   nk   87
over 2f out, onepcd fnl 1f: well bckd: shade btr expected after 3632 (C/D).
3795 **INDIENA 12** [2] B J Meehan 2-8-8 (79) J F McDonald 9/1: 4524: Keen in tch, onepcd over 1f out.   2½   77
3736 **FLYING RIDGE 14** [6]2-8-8 R Hills 20/1: 055: Rear, rdn & flashed tail bhd, nvr dngrs.   ½   76
3825* **TEQUILA SHEILA 10** [4]2-8-11 (78) N Callan 8/1: 01616: Mid-div, wknd 2f out.   6   61
3735 **BELLA PLUNKETT 14** [3]2-8-8 S Hitchcott 66/1: 07: ch f Daggers Drawn - Amazona (Tirol) Pressed   5   43

1220

wnr, no impress 2f out: Feb foal, cost 1,500gns: dam unplcd at 3, sire high-class 2yo over 6/7f: with W Brisbourne.
7 Ran   Time 1m 15.59 (2.49)   Owned: The Early Doors Partnership   Trained: Cockerham

4051   5.10 Blue Square 0800 587 0200 Apprentice Handicap Stakes 3yo+ 0-75 (E)   [75]
              £6971 £2145 £1073   **7f2y rnd   Good/Firm 25   -09 Slow** Inside

3313 **HILLS OF GOLD 31** [15] M W Easterby 5-9-13 (74) P Mulrennan 10/1: 4103221: Chsd ldrs, prog 3f   **78**
out, styd on to lead ins fnl 1f, rdn out: eff at 7f/1m, now stays 10f: acts on firm & soft grnd: won this race 12
mths ago off a 13lb lower mark & clearly likes Chester: did v well to overcome poor high draw: see 3313 & 3074.
3821 **MERDIFF 10** [3] W M Brisbourne 5-8-12 (59) P Mathers(5) 9/2 JT FAV: 0212042: In tch, styd on to   *1*   **61**
lead dist, hdd ins fnl 1f, not pace of wnr: op 8/1: acts on fast, soft grnd & both AWs: see 3821 & 3102.
3731* **TUSCARORA 14** [12] A W Carroll 5-8-12 (59) R Miles 12/1: 2610513: Missed break, prog 2f out, styd   *hd*   **60**
on well ins fnl 1f, not btn far: done no favours by slow start: poor high draw & one to keep in mind for similar.
3821 **WHIPPASNAPPER 10** [1] J R Best 4-9-5 (66) M Savage(3) 10/1: 3220004: Sn short of room, chsd ldrs,   *1½*   **64**
onepcd fnl 1f: see 1910 & 1354.
1896* **SHOWTIME ANNIE 90** [9]3-8-11 (63) N Mackay 16/1: 0-610415: Mid-div, prog 2f out, nrst fin: long   *1*   **59**
abs: return to a mile will suit: btr 1896.
3433* **NEON BLUE 26** [4]3-9-6 (72) Hayley Turner(3) 5/1: 1033316: Rear, styd on fnl 1f, nrst fin.   *2½*   **63**
3634 **ICED DIAMOND 18** [13]5-8-5 (52) J F McDonald 12/1: 0000447: Nvr nrr than mid-div: poor draw.   *hd*   **42**
3548 **SHAROURA 21** [5]8-9-5 (66) T Hamilton 6/1: 1034248: Cl-up 5f, sn wknd: btr 3416 (6f).   *¾*   **54**
3830* **DARA MAC 10** [14]5-8-12 (6ex) (59) Suzanne France(5) 14/1: 6310019: Missed break, prog wide 2f out,   *nk*   **46**
sn onepcd: poor high draw: btr 3830 (1m, gd/soft).
3813 **CONCER ETO 11** [6]5-9-12 p (73) L Fletcher 9/2 JT FAV: 0234120: 10th: Sh of room after 1f, nvr dngrs.   *½*   **59**
3643 **SEMPER PARATUS 17** [11]5-8-5 bl (52) C Haddon(5) 16/1: 0020300: 11th: Nvr nrr than mid-div: btr 2806.   *1¼*   **35**
3548 **PERFECT LOVE 21** [10]4-10-0 (75) D Allan 33/1: 12000-00: 12th: b f Pursuit of Love - Free Spirit   *shd*   **58**
(Caerleon) Led till dist, fdd: top-weight: mdn wnr on 1 of 3 '03 starts (G A Butler): eff at 6/7f on polytrack:
with E Alston. 2 Feb'03 Ling 7ap 81a- D: 1 Jan'03 Ling 6ap 76a- D:
3933 **Risk Free 6** [8]7-8-9 vis(56) S Hitchcott 33/1:0   3710 **Night Wolf 14** [16]4-8-10 (57) B O'Neill(7) 50/1:0
4317} **Miss Mytton 336** [2]3-9-1 (67) Natalie Hassall(7) 33/1:0 3684 **Key Of Gold 15** [7]3-8-13 (65) D Tudhope(5) 16/1:0
16 Ran   Time 1m 27.40(2.40)   Owned: Mr G Hart Mr D Scott & Mr G Sparkes   Trained: Sheriff Hutton

Official Going Good/Soft (Soft Places)

4052   5.40 Racecourse Garage Honda Median Auction Maiden Stakes 2yo (F)
              £3283 £938 £469   **6f16y str   Soft 110   -09 Slow**   Stands side

3975 **BROOKLIME 3** [6] J A Osborne 2-9-0 R Winston 9/2: 641: Cl-up far side, styd on to lead 1f out,   **83**
rdn out: op 9/2 on qck reapp: eff at 6f, 7f will suit: acts on fast, imprvd today for switch to soft grnd: acts
on a gall/undul trk: improving with racing: see 3975.
3431 **VIKING SPIRIT 26** [12] P W Harris 2-9-0 M Coumbe(7) 4/1: 022: Bhd stands side, prog halfway, kept   *1*   **80**
on well ins fnl 1f, just held by far side wnr: eff at 6f, looks in need of 7f: acts on fast & soft grnd: win a race.
3817 **DUROOB 10** [1] E A L Dunlop 2-9-0 J Fortune 9/2: 03: b c Bahhare - Amanily (Dayjur) Handy far   *hd*   **79**
side, styd on ins fnl 1f, just held for 2nd: bckd from 10/1: Jan foal, half-brother to wnrs at 6/7f: dam useful
performer as a juv: sire useful performer at 1m/10f: eff at 6f, further will suit: acts on soft grnd: promising run.
3633 **WATCHMYEYES 18** [9] N P Littmoden 2-9-0 J Bramhill 14/1: 644: ch g Royal Dome - Shadow Smile   *hd*   **79**
(Slip Anchor) Bhd stands side, prog 2f out, kept on well ins fnl 1f: Feb foal, half-brother eff at 7f, also reached
the frame over hdles: dam plcd at 10f: eff at 6f, 7f will suit: acts on soft grnd: now quals for h'caps.
3713 **ARABIAN DANCER 14** [2]2-8-9 (88) C Catlin 100/30 FAV: 26535: Rcd far side, led 5f, no extra: *shd*   **72**
op 9/4: rated much higher on fast grnd over further earlier: see 3713 (1m, fast).
3639 **LIGHTED WAY 17** [13]2-8-9 L Keniry(3) 50/1: 06: b f Kris - Natchez Trace (Commanche Run) Rcd   *1¾*   **67**
stands side, led that group till ins fnl 1f, no extra: Apr foal, cost 15,000gns: half-sister successful at 5f.
       BATHWICK FINESSE 0 [17]2-8-9 S Righton 25/1: 7: Rear, nvr nrr than mid-div: debut.   *¾*   **65**
3041 **ASTEEM 42** [5]2-9-0 S Carson 50/1: 058: Bhd far side, nvr nrr than mid-div: 6 wk abs: btr 3041.   *5*   **57**
       OVER TIPSY 0 [4]2-9-0 R Smith 33/1: 9: Handy far side 4f, wknd.   *3*   **48**
3818 **ASPEN RIDGE 10** [15]2-8-9 F P Ferris(3) 12/1: 0000: 10th: Al bhd stands side.   *¾*   **41**
       LYRIC DANCES 0 [7]2-8-9 N Day 33/1: 0: 11th: Al in rear stands side.   *1¼*   **37**
3330 **Inchcape Rock 29** [11]2-9-0 A Daly 100/1:0   3722 **San Deng 14** [14]2-9-0 S Chin 25/1:0
1123 **Blade Runner 129** [16]2-8-9 Paul Eddery 25/1:0   **Hillabilla 0** [8]2-8-9 D Sweeney 40/1:0
3817 **Penang Sapphire 10** [18]2-9-0 Joanna Badger 16/1:0 3473 **Mambazo 25** [3]2-9-0 O Urbina 14/1:0
17 Ran   Time 1m 15.95 (7.15)   Owned: Mr & Mrs I H Bendelow   Trained: Upper Lambourn

4053   6.10 Skybet Press Red To Bet Now Selling Handicap Stakes 3yo 35-55 (G)   [57]
              £2541 £726 £363   **1m4f23y   Soft 110   -15 Slow**   Inside

3547 **TRYSTING GROVE 21** [7] K A Ryan 3-8-11 (40) R Winston 5/1: 000501: Rear, prog halfway, styd on to   **49**
lead bef 1f out, sn pushed clr, eased nr line, val 9L: tchd 7/1, sold for 8,000gns: left prev modest form bhd on
step up to 12f: acts on soft grnd & a gall/undul trk: see 3177.
3913 **ZULETA 6** [2] M Blanshard 3-9-6 (49) D Sweeney 12/1: 044-0062: Handy, prog to chase wnr bef 1f   *6*   **50**
out, al held: op 8/1 on qck reapp: stays 12f on soft in sellers: see 2628.
3580 **FRAMBO 20** [1] J G Portman 3-8-7 bl t (36) F P Ferris(3) 9/2: 0644433: Missed break, prog halfway,   *1¾*   **34**
no impress fnl 2f: tchd 7/2: see 658.
3294 **KELTIC RAINBOW 31** [4] D Haydn Jones 3-9-2 (45) R Thomas(5) 12/1: 33-46004: Led 10f, fdd: btr 43.   *9*   **30**

3312	**INTRODUCTION 31** [3]3-8-6 (35) P Doe 7/2: 000-0005: Sn cl-up, fdd 3f out: see 845.	7	10
3692	**REGAL PERFORMER 15** [6]3-9-6 BL (49) J Fortune 3/1 FAV: 2234566: Missed break, al well adrift: disapp in first time blnks: btr 2642 (fast) & 2576 (firm).	16	4
3400	**BUCHANAN STREET 27** [5]3-9-1 (44) D Kinsella 11/2: 6-066257: Prom 6f, fdd: btr 2982 (10f, gd).	19	0
	7 Ran Time 2m 46.15 (15.05) Owned: Mrs B Hayes & Mrs J Ryan Trained: Hambleton		

4054 6.40 Skybet Watch And Bet Press Red Maiden Handicap Stakes 3yo 0-70 (E) **[73]**
£4615 £1420 £710 **6f16y str** **Soft 110** +13 Fast Stands side

3906	**SABRINA BROWN 7** [13] G B Balding 3-9-4 T (63) R Thomas(5) 5/1: 06-22061: Rcd stands side, made all, went clr 2f out, pushed out, val 4L+: tchd 13/2: fast time: qck reapp: stays 1m, imprvd eff today back at 6f: acts on gd & soft grnd: apprec fitting of first time t-strap: see 3090 & 2661.	75
3718	**INSTINCT 14** [9] R Hannon 3-8-11 (56) R Smith 5/1: 3000332: Missed break far side, styd on to chase wnr ins fnl 1f, al held: tchd 13/2: continues to run well: see 3718 (1m) & 3541 (7f).	2 60
3456	**INDIANA BLUES 26** [6] A M Balding 3-9-7 (66) L Keniry(3) 14/1: 0-400353: Chsd ldrs far side, onepcd ins fnl 1f: acts on fast & soft grnd: see 2953 & 1846.	1½ 66
3575	**PURE IMAGINATION 20** [2] J M Bradley 3-9-3 (62) S Carson 12/1: 630604: Cl-up far side 5f, no extra.	½ 61
3900	**FLEET ANCHOR 7** [15]3-8-9 (54) O Urbina 9/2 FAV: 50-00025: Cl-up stands side till dist, no extra.	1¼ 49
3401	**DANISH MONARCH 27** [10]3-9-1 (60) D Sweeney 25/1: 4-003006: Led far side group till dist, wknd.	½ 54
3732	**NIKIFOROS 14** [12]3-9-5 T (64) N Day 16/1: 060447: Cl-up stands side over 4f, wknd: 1st time t-strap.	1 55
3396	**FESTIVE CHIMES 27** [4]3-8-10 (55) R Winston 14/1: 0308: Cl-up far side over 4f, wknd: btr 3194 (fast).	½ 45
2756	**INDIAN EDGE 54** [16]3-9-3 (62) F P Ferris(3) 10/1: 6-052009: Nvr nrr than mid-div: 8 wk abs: btr 1607.	3 43
3575	**CELLINO 20** [17]3-7-12 (2oh) J McAuley 25/1: 50-04000: 10th: Nvr nrr than mid-div: btr 2219.	shd 23
3732	**LIGNE DEAU 14** [14]3-8-12 VIS (57) R Price 12/1: 0-053660: 11th: Rear, mod late gains, 1st time visor.	2 31
3693	**BARABELLA 15** [5]3-8-9 P (54) R Havlin 16/1: 0450450: 12th: Cl-up far side 4f, fdd: btr 3298 (7f).	½ 27
3804	**BLUE MOON HITMAN 11** [1]3-9-1 (60) D Nolan(3) 20/1: 6-303300: 13th: Al in rear far side: btr 3023 (5f).	1 30
3900	**WEBBINGTON LASS 7** [18]3-7-12 (3oh)vis (40) D Fox(5) 100/1: 0000-000: 14th: Al in rear.	nk 12
3920	**SAINTLY PLACE 6** [19]3-9-1 (60) C Catlin 33/1: 060-000: 15th: Rear, nvr a factor.	¾ 27
4153}	**CHAIN OF HOPE 344** [3]3-9-0 (59) P Doe 14/1: 006-0: 16th: ch g Shinko Forest - Fleeting Smile (Bluebird) Bhd, nvr a factor: on reapp: unplcd all 3 '03 starts (rtd 58, mdn): has been gelded.	shd 25
1078	**POWER TO BURN 134** [8]3-8-7 vis (52) D Kinsella 33/1: 600-3500: 17th: Cl-up far side 3f, fdd.	3½ 8
2906	**Eight Ellington 48** [11]3-8-13 (58) J Fortune 16/1:0	
139	**Katz Pyjamas 260** [7]3-8-2 (47) Joanna Badger 50/1:0	
	19 Ran Time 1m 14.66 (5.86) Owned: Miss B Swire Trained: Andover	

4055 7.10 Racecourse Garage Mitsubishi Maiden Stakes 3yo+ (D)
£3484 £1072 £536 **7f16y str** **Soft 110** -09 Slow Stands side

3237	**GENTLEMANS DEAL 34** [3] E A L Dunlop 3-9-0 J Fortune 1/3 FAV: 41: Chsd ldrs, prog trav well to lead 2f out, sn clr, pushed out, val 7L+: eff at 7f, return to 1m will suit: acts on fast & soft grnd, stiff/gall or undul trks: only lightly rcd & can impr: see 3237 (debut).	80
3985	**CAFE AMERICANO 3** [7] D W P Arbuthnot 4-9-5 e (42) D Sweeney 4/1: 00-05022: Rear, prog 3f out, styd on to chase wnr ins fnl 1f, al well held: qck reapp: see 3985 & 2630.	5 68
2339	**ARIANS LAD 70** [5] B Palling 3-9-0 F P Ferris(3) 20/1: 0003: b g Prince Sabo - Arian Da (Superlative) Led, rcd keenly till 2f out, sn no extraL 10 wk abs: modest form to date.	1½ 65
3742	**DUAL PURPOSE 13** [9] C Roberts 9-9-5 D Kinsella 25/1: 064: Cl-up 5f, fdd: quals for h'caps.	3½ 58
1518	**MACS ELAN 108** [2]4-9-5 J McAuley 66/1: 0-05: Nvr nrr than mid-div: long abs.	4 50
3595	**OLLIJAY 19** [6]3-9-0 R Winston 33/1: 66: Al in rear: see 3595 (debut).	19 18
3565}	**VELVET JONES 1092** [4]11-9-5 Joanna Badger 100/1: /0/0000//-7: gr g Sharrood - Cradle of Love (Roberto) Bhd, nvr a factor: v long abs: earlier p.u. in pts company: modest form when last seen on Flat in '01 (rtd 22, seller): with G F H Charles-Jones.	shd 17
2372	**ZAMBEZI RIVER 69** [8]5-9-5 (45) O Urbina 40/1: 000608: Handy 4f, sn fdd: 10 wk abs: see 1963.	13 0
	8 Ran Time 1m 28.19 (8.39) Owned: Khalifa Sultan And Mohammed Jaber Trained: Newmarket	

4056 7.40 Skybet - Red Button In Vision Betting Maiden Stakes Handicap 3yo+ 0-70 (E) **[65]**
£4183 £1287 £644 **2m2f** **Soft 110** -21 Slow Stands side

3822	**INDIAN CHASE 10** [13] Dr J R J Naylor 7-8-3 (40) R Thomas(5) 20/1: 6000401: Rear, prog 5f out, kept on for press to lead ins fnl 1f, pushed out, val bit more: eff at 2m/2m2f on soft grnd & polytrack: eff with/without visor: enjoyed testing trks: see 3400 & 1291.	49
3822	**HEART SPRINGS 10** [3] Dr J R J Naylor 4-8-3 (40) A Daly 12/1: 0-000452: Mid-div, prog after halfway, styd on to lead 1f out, sn hdd, outstyd by wnr: stablemate of wnr: eff at 2m/2m2f on soft grnd & polytrack.	¾ 46
3446	**ASSOON 26** [11] G L Moore 5-9-7 P (58) J Fortune 9/1 JT FAV: 23-03: Cl-up, led 2f out, hdd 1f out, no extra: first time cheek pieces: eff at 2m2f on soft grnd: see 3446.	1½ 63
3450	**BAKHTYAR 26** [2] R Charlton 3-8-2 bl (55) R Smith 11/2: 05-00454: Cl-up, no extra dist: btr 2621.	¾ 59
3335	**LORD NELLSSON 29** [9]8-9-8 (59) L Keniry 20/1: 4005: Held up, prog 6f out, onepcd fnl 2f: see 2668.	½ 60
2707	**HOH NELSON 56** [4]3-8-12 (65) R Havlin 20/1: 000-3006: Chsd ldrs, fdd 2f out: 8 wk abs: btr 1177.	6 62
3701	**CALOMERIA 15** [8]3-8-4 bl (57) S Carson 7/1: 0040307: Prom, led after 10f, hdd 4f out, sn wknd.	½ 53
3742	**BLACK SWAN 13** [12]4-8-3 (40) B Reilly(3) 33/1: 0/50-058: Cl-up, led 4f out, hdd 2f out, fdd.	11 27
3294	**DEVOTE 31** [7]6-8-2 (39) F P Ferris(3) 16/1: 506//-069: Mid-div, nvr a factor: btr 3294.	4 22
3895	**STAFFORD KING 7** [6]7-7-13 (36) D Kinsella 20/1: 0/020/-000: 10th: Missed break, al in rear: qck reapp.	1½ 18
2781	**FU FIGHTER 53** [1]3-9-3 (70) S W Kelly 5/1 JT FAV: 54-05430: 11th: Led 10f, fdd fnl half mile: 8 wk abs.	2½ 50
3740	**HOOPS AND BLADES 14** [15]3-7-12 (2oh)t (49) J Bramhill 25/1: 00000: 12th: Rear, nvr a factor: see 3237.	29 7
3861	**SONG OF THE SEA 8** [5]3-8-9 (62) N Day 33/1: 0-00400: 13th: Rear, nvr a factor.	20 0
3240	**OLYMPIAS 34** [14]3-8-3 (52) C Catlin 12/1: 500640: 14th: Mid-div, prog after 1m, fdd 4f out, sn eased.	2 0
3502	**SADLERS PRIDE 23** [10]4-10-0 (65) D Sweeney 10/1: 30-22400: 15th: Al adrift, eased ins fnl 2f.	dist 0
	15 Ran Time 4m 15.39 (23.5) Owned: The Indian Chase Partnership Trained: Shrewton	

4057 8.10 Skybet Press Red To Bet Now Handicap Stakes 3yo+ 0-70 (E) [70]
£4615 £1420 £710 1m14y str Soft 110 +05 Fast Stands side

3867 **COMPTON DRAKE 8** [4] G A Butler 5-9-10 (66) J Fortune 3/1 JT FAV: 2111-021: Held up, prog 75
halfway, styd on to lead ins fnl 1f, drvn out: eff at 1m/10f, stays 14f: acts on fast, soft grnd & both AWs: see 3867.
3796 **ELIDORE 12** [1] B Palling 4-9-8 (64) F P Ferris(3) 25/1: 000-0502: In tch far side, switched to nk 71+
stands side group halfway, styd on to lead dist, hdd ins fnl 1f, just denied: eff at 6/7f, now stays 1m: acts on
fast & soft, handles hvy grnd: back to form with visor left off: prob wnr but for switching sides & can win similar.
4036 **THREEZEDZZ 1** [8] P D Evans 6-10-6 (6ex)t (76) S Donohoe(7) 3/1 JT FAV: 01010133: Cl-up, led after 3½ 76
5f, hdd dist, no extra: remains in gd form after 3rd plcd eff yesterday in 4036.
3593 **BASINET 19** [15] J J Quinn 6-8-11 p (53) R Winston 7/1: 0004064: Chsd ldrs, onepcd fnl 1f: see 2120. ¾ 51
3481 **PETITE COLLEEN 24** [14]3-8-12 (60) D Kinsella 33/1: 5-040605: Rear, prog 2f out, nrst fin: btr 3161. 4 50
3963 **ENNA 4** [2]5-8-3 (45) S Carson 9/2: 0404206: Cl-up far side 6f, sn no extra: qck reapp: btr 3788. ½ 34
3650 **KAMAS WHEEL 17** [6]5-7-12 (9oh) (31) Natalia Gemelova(7) 50/1: D60-0067: Mid-div, no impress fnl 2f. 1½ 26
4930} **SEVEN SHIRT 296** [3]3-8-12 (60) D Fox(5) 50/1: 05400-8: b g Great Dane - Bride's Answer (Anshan) ¾ 44
In tch far side, sn no extra: reapp: unplcd in '03 (rtd 71, M R Channon): with E G Bevan.
3298 **ANOTHER DEAL 31** [10]5-9-4 (60) R Havlin 66/1: 03040-09: Al bhd: see 3298. 1½ 41
3090 **JUST ONE LOOK 41** [7]3-8-10 (58) D Sweeney 16/1: 0000060: 10th: Chsd ldrs 6f, fdd: 6 wk abs. 3½ 32
3788 **LORD CHAMBERLAIN 12** [9]11-8-13 bl (55) S W Kelly : v eff at 1m/10f (sprint bred) but shld stay 7f: btr 3788 & 3733. 2½ 24
CADORO 1385 [13]11-8-13 (55) R Thomas(5) 20/1: 302040///-0: 12th: ch g Cadeaux Genereux - Palace 5 15
Street (Secreto) Chsd ldrs over 6f, bmpd bef 1f out, sn wknd & eased: off trk since '00 when plcd 3 times (h'caps,
rtd 66): h'cap scorer in '99 (rtd 71): eff at 7f/1m on fast & gd, relishes gd/soft & hvy: has run well fresh.
3516 **MISTER TRICKSTER 22** [5]3-8-13 (61) Lisa Jones 14/1: 6001000: 13th: Led 5f, fdd: btr 2199. 2½ 16
2146 **Stars At Midnight 78** [11]4-8-6 (48) C Catlin 50/1:0
2288 **Frederick James 72** [12]10-7-12 (9oh)(31) J McAuley 100/1:0
15 Ran Time 1m 40.35(8.45) Owned: Mr Erik Penser Trained: Blewbury

---

Official Going SOFT.

4058 2.10 Listed E B F Galtres Stakes Fillies 3yo+ (A)
£22100 £6800 £3400 1m3f198y Good/Soft 70 -21 Slow Inside

10} **TARAKALA 17** [6] John M Oxx 3-8-8 bl M J Kinane 7/2: 0113321: ch f Dr Fong - Tarakana 103
(Shahrastani) Held up, gd hdwy to lead 2f out, rdn clr: nicely bckd: earlier won at Cork & Gowran Park: stays 12f
well on fast & soft grnd, wears blnks now: useful, imprvd today. 2 Nov'03 Leop 9gd 100-:
3629 **SELEBELA 18** [2] L M Cumani 3-8-8 (95) L Dettori 100/30 FAV: 1112232: Cl-up, led over 3f out till 4 98
2f out, not pace of wnr: proving v consistent & useful: acts on firm & soft: see 2422.
3777 **DESERT ROYALTY 12** [4] E A L Dunlop 4-9-4 (90) K Fallon 7/1: 1244003: Held up, hdwy 2f out, kept nk 97
on fnl 1f, no threat to wnr: back to form since 3076, 1721 (rtd h'cap).
3278 **GOSLAR 33** [1] H Candy 3-8-8 (90) Dane O'Neill 9/1: 3144: In tch, lost place over 3f out, kept on 1½ 95
fnl 2f: clr of rem: acts on fast & gd/soft: lightly rcd, shaped like step up to 14f will suit: see 2368.
3019* **SILVER SASH 43** [10]3-8-8 (79) R Mullen 16/1: 6315: Hmpd start, keen in tch, wknd over 2f out: 6 88$
wk abs: up in class after 3019 (auct mdn).
3648* **PAYOLA 17** [8]3-8-8 (66) S Sanders 25/1: 0-16: In tch, wknd over 3f out: up in class after mdn 5 81
win on fast grnd in 3648 (10f).
3422* **CASTAGNA 26** [7]3-8-8 (87) W Ryan 11/1: 0-417: In tch, wknd over 3f out: up in class after mdn 5 74
win on fast grnd & over 10f in 3422.
3322 **KISSES FOR ME 17** [3]3-8-8 J P Spencer 7/2: 1-500338: In tch, wknd over 2f out: hvly bckd: not 5 67
far bhd this wnr in Ireland last time on fast grnd: see 3322.
3802 **UIG 11** [9]3-8-8 (77) S Drowne 80/1: 00329: Keen, sn clr ldr, hdd 3f out, wknd: too head strong. 3 63
9 Ran Time 2m 37.68 (10.88) Owned: HH Aga Khan Trained: Ireland

---

4059 2.45 Gr2 Jaguar Lowther Stakes Fillies 2yo (A)
£51000 £19550 £9775 6f str Good/Soft 70 -38 Slow Centre

3440* **SOAR 26** [8] J R Fanshawe 2-9-0 (100) J Murtagh 2/1 FAV: 1211: Held up, gd hdwy & switched left 115+
over 1f out, sn qcknd to lead, v rdly, hands & heels: hvly bckd: v eff at 6f (sprint bred) but shld stay 7f: acts
on fast & gd/soft: high-class filly with a turn of foot, still imprvg & one to follow in Gr1 class: see 3440.
3003 **SALSA BRAVA 44** [4] N P Littmoden 2-8-11 (100) K Fallon 9/4: 1322: Handy, eff for press to lead 1½ 105
2f out, sn hdd & not pace of wnr but kept on: well bckd: 6 wk abs: prob caught a top class sort & acts on firm &
gd/soft: win a Gr3/Listed: see 3003.
2815 **SPIRIT OF CHESTER 55** [2] Mrs P N Dutfield 2-8-11 R Havlin 16/1: 4203: Sn led, rdn & hdd 2f out, 1½ 101
onepace, reportedly broke a blood vessel: scope, 8 wk abs: back to form after 2815: acts on fast & gd/soft.
3956 **NOTJUSTAPRETTYFACE 5** [5] H Morrison 2-8-11 S Drowne 8/1: 144: Cl-up, eff to chall 2f out, sn no 1 99
extra: fair run: see 2956, 2858.
3956 **CASTELLETTO 5** [10]2-8-11 (85) G Gibbons 10/1: 3202125: Cl-up, chall 2f out, held in 4th & short 3½ 92
of room dist: lengthy, looked superb: see 3956, 2983.
2763 **UMNIYA 54** [3]2-8-11 (91) A Culhane 14/1: 2133456: Rdn & al bhd: small, 8 wk abs: highly tried. 1¾ 88
3908 **GHASIBA 6** [9]2-8-11 S Sanders 20/1: 627: In tch, wknd 2f out: wants mdns: see 3908. nk 87$
3440 **KISSING LIGHTS 26** [6]2-8-11 (100) D Holland 14/1: 51638: Handy, wknd 2f out: btr 3440 (g/f). 7 73
8 Ran Time 1m 15.9 (6.5) Owned: Cheveley Park Stud Trained: Newmarket

---

4060	**3.20 Gr1 Victor Chandler Nunthorpe Stakes 2yo + (A)**

£116000 £44000 £22000   **5f str**   **Good/Soft 70**   **+08 Fast** Centre

3551 **BAHAMIAN PIRATE** 21 [5] D Nicholls 9-9-11 (110) S Sanders 16/1: 0000161: Handy, hdwy over 2f out,   **119**
styd on well to lead ins last, drvn out: eff over 5/6f on firm & fibresand, loves gd/soft & hvy: 1st Gr1 success at
age of 9! v smart & another fine example of his trainer's talents: see 3409, 1004.

3551 **THE TATLING** 21 [11] J M Bradley 7-9-11 (115) R L Moore 13/2: 2341032: Handy travelling well,   nk **118**
hdwy over 1f out, styd on ins last, not quite reach wnr: ran right up to smart best in top company.

3842* **ONE COOL CAT** 11 [15] A P O'Brien 3-9-9 J P Spencer 3/1 FAV: 111-0513: Held up off pace,   1 **118+**
switched & strong run well over 1f out, styd on strongly ins last, nrst fin, too much to do: hvly bckd: top class
sprinter with a fine turn of foot, likely wnr if rdn closer to pace & error-prone jock failed to impress again: acts
on fast & gd/soft: see 3842.

3551 **AVONBRIDGE** 21 [9] R Charlton 4-9-11 BL (114) S Drowne 8/1: 43-21544: Dwelt, sn cl-up, chall over   hd **115**
1f out, rdn & no extra well ins last: bckd: another smart run tried in blnks: wants Gr2/3.

2913* **ORIENTOR** 47 [14]6-9-11 (115) K Fallon 9/2: 4505315: Hld up, hdwy & switched left 2f out, styd on   hd **114**
ins last, nrst fin: ran to smart best up in class & on fav soft grnd: relish a return to Gr2/3 class on similar grnd.

3304* **AIRWAVE** 31 [3]4-9-8 (110) D Holland 6/1: 60-66016: Cl-up, led after 2f till just ins last, no   ½ **109**
extra: ran to useful win of 3304 (Listed fills) but will prob prefer faster grnd.

3409 **BALMONT** 27 [7]3-9-9 (113) E Ahern 13/2: 1110-327: Handy, eff dist, onepcd: well bckd: see 3409.   ½ **111**

3636 **TALBOT AVENUE** 18 [12]6-9-11 (90) K McEvoy 100/1: 5022028: Cl-up, onepace over 1f out: clrly in   ½ **109**
fine heart & will relish a return to Listed class as in 3636 (firm).

3062 **MOSS VALE** 42 [10]3-9-9 (112) M Hills 14/1: 3-411109: Chsd ldrs, wknd over 1f out: 6 wk abs: ½ **107**
twice well below 2421 (Listed, firm).

3062 **FAYR JAG** 42 [2]5-9-11 (113) W Supple 25/1: 10U-0100: 10th: Cl-up, chall over 1f out, sn wknd &   2 **103**
eased: 6 wk abs: much prefers faster grnd but now twice well below 2580.

3551 **FIRE UP THE BAND** 21 [8]5-9-11 (99) A Nicholls 33/1: 0340100: 11th: Led 2f, cl-up wknd over   2 **99**
1f out: twice below 3100 (fast grnd).

2913 **NIGHT PROSPECTOR** 47 [6]4-9-11 (105) J Murtagh 66/1: 100-0100: 12th: Al bhd: 7 wk abs: much   14 **71**
below best on easy grnd: much btr 2206 (fast grnd, 5f).

12 Ran   Time 59.89 (3.09)   Owned: Lucayan Stud   Trained: Thirsk

---

4061	**3.55 Persimmon Homes Rated Stakes Handicap 3yo + 0-105 (B)**	**[109]**

£14789 £5610 £2805   **7f205y rnd**   **Good/Soft 70**   **+16 Fast** Inside

3565 **AUDIENCE** 20 [4] J Akehurst 4-8-11 p (92) D Holland 11/1: 0002461: In tch, hdwy 2f out, styd on   **103**
well ins last to lead cl-home, drvn out: fast time: rng well in big field h'caps earlier: suited by 1m now & acts
on fast & gd, clrly relished this gd/soft grnd: likes gall trks: wears cheek pieces: proving tough & useful.

3860+ **TAKE A BOW** 8 [12] P R Chamings 3-8-6 (3ex)(1oh) (93) J Quinn 100/30 FAV: 02-11412: Handy, eff to   ½ **102**
chall dist, kept on, not quite reach of wnr: hvly bckd: v tough & prog, useful: see 3860.

3077+ **ST PETERSBURG** 41 [3] M H Tompkins 4-9-2 (97) P Robinson 13/2: 5-210213: Keen in tch, gd hdwy to   nk **105**
lead just ins last, hdd & no extra cl-home: v useful & another fine run on fav easy grnd: see 3077, 1066.

3775 **UNSHAKABLE** 12 [7] Bob Jones 5-8-12 (93) K Fallon 15/2: 0013054: Chsd ldrs, eff 2f out, onepcd.   2 **97**

3555 **VICIOUS KNIGHT** 21 [10]6-8-9 (90) A Nicholls 66/1: 5-000005: Set pace, rdn & hdd just ins last,   hd **93**
no extra: encouraging run: acts on firm & gd/soft: see 2489.

3077 **BLUE SKY THINKING** 41 [9]5-8-11 (92) Darren Williams 33/1: 1560346: Held up, eff 2f out, no impress.   7 **84**

3118 **CONSONANT** 40 [2]7-8-9 (90) A Culhane 25/1: 0602307: In tch, kept well over 1f out: 6 wk abs.   3 **76**

3565 **EL COTO** 20 [14]4-9-5 (100) S Sanders 13/2: 0004048: Bhd, brief eff 2f out, no impress: likes fast.   2 **82**

2207 **DUMARAN** 76 [6]6-8-7 (92) R Mullen 16/1: 3-002359: Dwelt, bhd, nvr a factor: 11 wk abs.   1¼ **71**

3954 **JAZZ MESSENGER** 5 [11]4-9-0 (95) M J Kinane 8/1: 006-6000: 10th: Held up, rdn & btn over 2f out,   1½ **71**
boiled over bef start: much btr expected after 2954, see 1351.

2757 **EXCELSIUS** 54 [16]4-9-4 (99) R L Moore 16/1: 301-0300: 11th: In tch, btn over 2f out: 8 wk abs.   2 **71**

951 **DARK CHARM** 145 [5]5-8-10 (91) R Ffrench 17/1: 20400-30: 12th: Dwelt, al bhd: long abs: btr 951.   2½ **58**

3613 **ALWAYS ESTEEMED** 19 [8]4-9-5 (100) S Drowne 28/1: 2004140: 13th: In tch, wknd over 2f out.   1½ **64**

3059 **STATE DILEMMA** 42 [13]3-8-6 (1oh) (93) M Hills 50/1: 14-51000: 14th: Al bhd: see 1665 (7f).   2 **53**

3506 **ANANI** 23 [15]4-9-7 (102) L Dettori 16/1: 4206040: 15th: In tch, wknd over 2f out: see 884.   2 **58**

15 Ran   Time 1m 40.12 (4.32)   Owned: Canisbay Bloodstock   Trained: Epsom

---

4062	**4.30 Kone Plc Melrose Rated Stakes Handicap 3yo 0-100 (B)**	**[104]**

£12946 £4910 £2455   **1m5f197y**   **Good/Soft 70**   **-10 Slow** Inside

3918 **LOST SOLDIER THREE** 6 [2] L M Cumani 3-8-11 (87) K Fallon 3/1 FAV: 615421: Held up, stdy hdwy 4f   **104+**
out, led dist & rdn clr, decisively: hvly bckd, qck reapp: eff at 13f, relished step up to 14f & 2m sure to suit:
acts on fast &n gd/soft: v prog stayer, must be kept on side this autumn: see 3918 & 2196.

3359* **PEAK OF PERFECTION** 28 [3] M A Jarvis 3-8-9 (85) P Robinson 10/1: 5351112: Led/dsptd lead, went   3½ **94**
on overall 4f out, hdd dist & no ch with wnr but kept on well: nicely bckd: lost little in defeat.

3249* **ELUSIVE DREAM** 34 [12] Sir Mark Prescott 3-8-5 (81) S Sanders 7/1: 00-11113: Keen in mid-div,   1¼ **89**
hdwy to chall dist, sn not pace of wnr: well bckd, clr rem: high in grade & a fine run, see 3249.

3556* **LOCHBUIE** 21 [13] G Wragg 3-9-7 (97) J F Egan 7/1: 0-411314: Held up, hdwy 6f out, no prog over   5 **100**
1f out: just btr 3556 (firm).

3261+ **LETS ROLL** 33 [4]3-8-7 (83) Dean McKeown 9/2: 6223115: Held up, rdn & hdwy over 3f out, no   5 **81**
impress fnl 2f: well bckd: btr 3261 (12f).

2517 **MODESTA** 63 [5]3-8-12 (88) R Hughes 12/1: 41206: Chsd ldrs, some hdwy 4f out, no prog over 2f   3½ **82**
out: 2 month abs: return to 12f & poss faster grnd will suit: btr 2238 (gd).

3918* **SOULACROIX** 6 [8]3-8-12 (3ex) (88) J Murtagh 8/1: 3221-217: In tch, hung left & btn 3f out: quick   ½ **81**
reapp: ahead of today's wnr in 3918 (gd).

3240 **SAND AND STARS** 34 [6]3-8-6 (1ow) (81) D Holland 22/1: 0-352128: Led/dsptd lead till 4f out, btn   2½ **72**
2f out: nicely bckd, op 40/1: btr 3240 & 2984 (12f, gd).

3534 **ALWAYS WAINING** 22 [1]3-9-6 (96) J Fanning 12/1: 3153169: Chsd ldrs, btn 3f out: btr 3444 (12f).   5 **81**

3249 **SOUND OF FLEET** 34 [11]3-8-9 (85) R L Moore 33/1: 4615020: 10th: Keen in rear, no ch fnl 3f, eased.   22 **48**

3926 **RESERVOIR** 6 [10]3-8-4 (80) Martin Dwyer 33/1: 43-21050: 11th: Chsd ldrs, btn 3f out & sn eased.   2 **41**

2946 **SI SI AMIGA 47** [9]3-9-2 (92) M Hills 100/1: 1-44500: 12th: Trkd ldrs, lost place halfway, t.o.   *28* **25**
3534 **LE TISS 22** [7]3-8-13 (89) T E Durcan 25/1: 4021400: 13th: Keen & chsd ldrs 10f, wknd.   *dist* **0**
13 Ran   Time 3m 04.67 (11.27)   Owned: Sheikh Mohammed Obaid Al Maktoum   Trained: Newmarket

---

4063 **5.00 Listed Len Mccormick City Of York Stakes 3yo+   (A)**
£19500 £6000 £3000   **6f217y rnd**   **Good/Soft 70**   **+01 Fast**   Inside

2684 + **POLAR BEAR 56** [7] W J Haggas 4-9-0 (103) A Culhane 2/1 FAV: 3/11-3011: Mid-div, rdn to chall   **111**
over 1f out, rdn & led line, all out: jockey given 1 day whip ban: hvly bckd, 8 wk abs: eff at 7f/1m on firm &
fibresand, relishes gd/soft: smart colt, progressing rapidly on easy ground: see 2684.
3009 **WELSH EMPEROR 47** [11] T P Tate 5-9-0 bl (107) D Holland 10/1: 26-14652: Wide & led after 1f, rdn   *shd* **109**
& hdd line: 7 wk abs: loves easy grnd & given an excellent front rng ride: see 1227.
3508 **VANDERLIN 23** [6] A M Balding 5-9-0 (109) Martin Dwyer 14/1: 3353103: Mid-div, styd on for press   *1½* **106**
fnl 2f, not pace of front pair: won this race in '03: acts on gd/soft, poss prefers a faster surface: see 3098 (g/f).
3622 **MATERIAL WITNESS 19** [4] W R Muir 7-9-0 (100) S Sanders 20/1: 0111204: Led 1f & remained handy,   *1* **104**
onepcd bef dist: up in grade & a gd run: see 3061 (val h'cap).
3782 **LOOK HERES CAROL 12** [3]4-8-9 (91) G Gibbons 28/1: 3363105: Chsd ldrs, no extra dist: see 3117.   *3* **94**
3957 **BABODANA 5** [5]4-9-5 (108) P Robinson 11/2: 1635546: Chsd ldrs, outpcd when hmpd ins last, no   *nk* **103**
extra: nicely bckd, quick reapp: likes to race with/force the pace & poss best at 1m: see 951 (1m).
3613 **MINE 19** [9]6-9-0 vis (108) L Dettori 3/1: 2311527: Rear, eff over 2f out, no impress on ldrs: *2½* **94**
well bckd, padd pick: btr 3613 & 2489 (1m, fast).
2455 **ROCKETS N ROLLERS 71** [12]4-9-5 (104) Dane O'Neill 25/1: 2314548: Chsd ldrs, lost place 4f out.   *5* **91**
3223 **PLAY THAT TUNE 35** [1]4-8-9 (90) W Ryan 25/1: 3-054339: Mid-div, drvn & strugg fnl 3f: new yard.   *2* **78**
3061 **HERETIC 42** [8]6-9-0 VIS (103) J Murtagh 12/1: 000-1400: 10th: Rear, btn 2f out: abs, visor.   *2½* **79**
3782 **CAPRICHO 12** [2]7-9-0 (100) J Quinn 16/1: 40-04000: 11th: Mid-div, struggling fnl 2f: see 2140.   *2* **75**
11 Ran   Time 1m 26.17 (4.87)   Owned: Mr B Haggas   Trained: Newmarket

---

4064 **5.30 Malton Nursery Handicap Stakes 2yo   (C)**   **[97]**
£11944 £3675 £1838   **6f217y rnd**   **Good/Soft 70**   **-16 Slow**   Inside

4006 + **MERCHANT 2** [2] M L W Bell 2-9-1 (6ex) (84) R Mullen 7/2 FAV: 53211: Held up, prog when short of   **101 +**
room & hit on head by whip 2f out, led dist, sn powered clr, easily: well bckd, qck reapp: eff at 6f, relished step
up to 7f: acts on firm, enjoys gd/soft: prog, can follow up under a pen: see 4006.
3729* **DOVE COTTAGE 14** [9] W S Kittow 2-7-12 (2oh) (65) A McCarthy 16/1: 65312: Cl-up, outpcd by easy   *7* **72**
wnr ins fnl 2f: eff at 6f, now prob stays 7f: acts on fast & gd/soft grnd: see 3729.
3047* **SPACED 42** [4] R Hannon 2-8-12 (81) R L Moore 13/2: 0613: Mid-div, prog 2f out, onepcd fnl 1f.   *hd* **85**
3723 **HALLUCINATE 14** [8] R Hannon 2-8-2 (71) Martin Dwyer 11/1: 04234: Handy over 5f, no extra: *½* **74**
proving consistent: see 3723 & 3342.
3407 **SEA HUNTER 27** [3]2-9-4 (87) T E Durcan 11/2: 014235: Nvr nrr than mid-div: well bckd: btr 3407 (fm).   *3½* **84**
3698 **SIR ANTHONY 15** [5]2-9-7 (90) D McGaffin 9/1: 1326: Missed break, prog halfway, fdd bef 1f out.   *nk* **86**
3736 **MOLLY MARIE 14** [11]2-8-8 (77) W Supple 12/1: 32-24627: Handy over 5f, sn wknd: op 8/1: rider   *nk* **72**
received a 2 day careless riding ban: btr 3736 (6f).
2883 **ROCKBURST 49** [7]2-8-9 (78) A Nicholls 16/1: 52138: Led, hdd dist, fdd: 7 wk abs: btr 2883 & 2178.   *8* **59**
3820 **BLACKCOMB MOUNTAIN 10** [6]2-8-1 (70) J F Egan 33/1: 53449: Handy 5f, fdd: see 3820.   *¾* **49**
3483 **SNOOKERED AGAIN 24** [12]2-7-13 (68) Dale Gibson 14/1: 51030: 10th: Handy wide 5f, fdd: btr 3483.   *1½* **44**
3302 **TOM FOREST 31** [1]2-8-13 (82) E Ahern 25/1: 62250: 11th: Rear, nvr a factor: btr 2522 & 2792.   *½* **57**
3467 **ARIODANTE 25** [10]2-8-11 (80) S Sanders 11/1: 3140: 12th: Bhd, prog halfway, fdd 2f out: btr 3021.   *3* **50**
12 Ran   Time 1m 27.3(6)   Owned: HESheikh Rashid Bin Mohammed   Trained: Newmarket

---

Official Going Rnd Crse - GOOD/SOFT (SOFT places); Str Crse - SOFT.

4065 **2.00 Betfred 'the Bonus King' Nursery Handicap Stakes 2yo   (D)**   **[88]**
£6841 £2105 £1053   **5f6y str**   **Soft**   **Slow**   Far Side

3755* **COUNTDOWN 14** [2] Sir Mark Prescott 2-9-7 (81) S Sanders 2/1 FAV: 3211: Chsd ldrs wide, imprvd to   **92**
lead dist, styd on strongly, rdn out: well bckd: eff at 5f on firm, soft & polytrack: gd weight carrier: useful.
3509 **KWAME 24** [3] Miss E C Lavelle 2-9-1 (75) S Drowne 16/1: 21202: Chsd ldrs, styd on under press   *1½* **80**
fnl 1f, not rch wnr: apprec this drop back in grade & return to easy grnd, acts on fast & soft: see 3509.
3943 + **NOVA TOR 6** [7] N P Littmoden 2-9-1 (6ex) (85) J Mongan 7/2: 4154013: Dsptd lead, led 2f out till   *nk* **89**
dist, no extra under top-weight: nicely bckd: acts on fast, soft & fibresand.
3931 **FAVOURING 7** [1] R A Fahey 2-8-4 (64) A McCarthy 11/4: 40024: Held up, mod late prog, nvr nrr: *1¾* **64**
bckd from 5/1: return to 6f will suit for in-form yard: see 3931 (6f).
3863 **RUSKY DUSKY 9** [5]2-9-5 (79) P Dobbs 25/1: 03255: Led early, chsd ldrs till halfway: better over   *1¾* **75**
6f on firm grnd in 2970 & prob worth another chance.
3756 **ALSU 14** [4]2-8-12 (72) Martin Dwyer 10/1: 3106336: Chsd ldrs, btn dist: see 3756 (gd).   *¾* **65**
3743 **NINJA STORM 14** [6]2-9-1 (75) R L Moore 7/1: 4567: Led after 1f till 2f out, wknd dist.   *1* **65**
7 Ran   Time 1m 05.21 (5.61)   Owned: Cheveley Park Stud   Trained: Newmarket

---

4066 **2.30 Combi Uk Conditions Stakes 2yo   (C)**
£8402 £2759 £1379   **1m14y rnd**   **Good/Soft 67**   **-27 Slow**   Inside

3851 **BRAHMINY KITE 9** [1] M Johnston 2-8-12 D Holland 2/1: 21: Trkd ldr, v green, chall 2f out & led   **103 +**
dist, drifted right but pushed out, readily: well bckd: stays a stiff 1m, will get further given time: acts on
gd/soft: v green today, open to plenty of further improvement & a potentially v smart colt: see 3851 (debut).
3774 **DESTINATE 13** [3] R Hannon 2-9-1 (100) P Dobbs 8/13 FAV: 010442: Led till dist, kept on but not   *2* **100**

pace of wnr cl home: clr of rem, hvly bckd, top-weight: prob stays 1m on gd/soft, acts on firm: useful juv.
2492* **SIMPLY ST LUCIA** 65 [2] J R Weymes 2-8-7   S Sanders 10/1: 13: Chsd ldrs, rdn & left bhnd by front   6   80$
2 fnl 1.5f: op 7/1, 9 wk abs: far from disgraced bhnd 2 well above average rivals: see 2492 (7f, AW).
3 Ran   Time 1m 46.54 (7.54)   Owned: Mr Abdulla BuHaleeba   Trained: Middleham

---

4067   3.05 Combi Uk Handicap Stakes 3yo+ 0-90 (C)   [90]
£12934 £4906   £2453   **1m14y rnd**   **Good/Soft 67**   **+ 02 Fast**   Inside

3891 **NORTON** 8 [4] T G Mills 7-10-0 (90) J Fortune 6/1: 5040031: Made all, 2L clr ent fnl 1f, styd on   99
strongly & won rdn out under top-weight: bckd from 8/1: overdue win: poss stays 12f, suited by 7.5f/1m on firm &
soft, any trk: has run well fresh: tried a visor, better without: well h'capped & best when able to dominate.
3595* **LITERATIM** 20 [2] L M Cumani 4-9-8 (84) D Holland 9/1: 412: Chsd ldrs, kept on well for press fnl   ¾   90+
1f, not rch wnr: drifted from 11/2: fine h'cap bow at olny 3rd start: acts on fast & gd/soft grnd, stays a gall 1m
well: open to more improvement, win a h'cap sn: see 3595 (mdn).
3813 **PARNASSIAN** 12 [9] G B Balding 4-8-9 (71) R Thomas(5) 5/1 CO FAV: 0511543: Mid-div, prog to chase   1½   74
ldrs 2f out, no impress fnl 1f: gd run on prob fav easy grnd: see 3225.
3768* **AFRICAN SAHARA** 13 [1] Miss D Mountain 5-9-6 † (82) O Urbina 6/1: 6034314: Held up, prog 2f out,   nk   84
rdn & kept on but not pace to chall: won this race from a 5lbs lower mark last year: see 3768.
3826 **LINNING WINE** 11 [8]8-9-5 (81) S Carson 33/1: 2406455: Held up, styd on late, nvr dngrs: see 3826.   1½   80
3891 **SPIRITS AWAKENING** 8 [3]5-7-12 (2oh) (58) J Mackay 5/1 CO FAV: 0632426: Trkd ldrs & v keen, wknd   1½   56
fnl 1f: too keen, see 3891.
3074 **RETIREMENT** 42 [5]5-9-4 (80) P Robinson 10/1: 12-13007: Mid-div, not pace to chall: op 14/1, 6 wk abs. hd   76
4778} **PAGAN PRINCE** 308 [10]7-8-11 (73) Lisa Jones 25/1: 002110-8: br g Primo Dominie - Mory Kante   nk   68
(Icecapade) Mid-div, nvr nr ldrs on reapp: dual h'cap wnr in '03: '02 turf & AW h'cap wnr: eff btwn 1m & 10f on
fast, gd/soft & f/sand: handles any trk, runs well fresh: sharper next time.
1 Oct'03 York 8.9g/f 33-67 D: 1 Sep'03 Asco 8g/f 69-61 B: 2 Sep'03 Epso 8.5gd 63-60 D: 1 Oct'02 Sout 8af 76a-67 E:
1 Jul'02 Beve 8.4g/s 67-63 D: 2 Jun'02 Carl 8g/f 67-60 D: 2 Jun'02 Leic 8gd 65-60 F: 1 Aug'01 Sand 8gd 62-57 E:
3565 **FINISHED ARTICLE** 21 [7]7-9-11 (87) Dane O'Neill 11/1: 0530009: Mid-div, eff & btn 2f out.   1¼   79
3891 **LIFTED WAY** 8 [6]5-9-2 (78) S Drowne 5/1 CO FAV: 1106540: 10th: Chsd ldrs, rdn & wknd 1.5f out.   ¾   68
10 Ran   Time 1m 44.27 (5.27)   Owned: Mr T G Mills   Trained: Epsom

---

4068   3.35 Combi Uk Premier Claiming Stakes 3yo (D)
£6711 £2065   £1033   **1m2f7y**   **Good/Soft 67**   **-32 Slow**   Inside

3961 **TOP SPEC** 6 [3] R Hannon 3-8-7 (76) R L Moore 6/4 FAV: 0050201: Chsd ldrs, prog to lead dist, rdn   80
well clr: well bckd, qck reapp: eff at 1m/10f on firm & gd/soft: likes a stiff/gall trk & suited by claim grade.
3453 **RABITATIT** 27 [4] J G M O'Shea 3-7-13 (62) Natalia Gemelova(7) 10/1: 4025562: V keen & led after   6   62
1f till collared dist, no extra: op 15/2, clr of rem: eff at 1m/10f on firm & gd/soft: too keen today, see 2475.
3874* **TREASON TRIAL** 9 [2] Mrs Stef Liddiard 3-8-6 (2ow) (57) S Drowne 7/2: 0-064313: Held up, nvr nr   5   59
ldrs: op 9/2: prob not handle this easy grnd: new stable, prev with N Tinkler: see 3874 (gd).
3236 **ANOTHER CHOICE** 35 [1] N P Littmoden 3-9-0 † (73) E Ahern 7/4: 3110004: Led 1f, remained prom till   1   65
rcd v wide rnd bend & lost many lengths, prog to chall for 2nd over 2f out, sn btn: nicely bckd op 6/4: went
searching for best grnd but gave away many lengths in the process: see 1403.
4 Ran   Time 2m 14.03 (9.93)   Owned: The Hill Top Partnership   Trained: Marlborough

---

4069   4.10 European Breeders Fund Combi Uk Maiden Stakes 2yo (D)
£7264 £2235   £1118   **7f16y rnd**   **Good/Soft 67**   **-02 Slow**   Inside

3585 **DIKTATORIAL** 21 [4] A M Balding 2-9-0   Martin Dwyer 7/1: 01: Made all, veered sharply left 2.5f   98+
out, clr ent fnl 1f, pushed out, cmftbly: clearly benefitted from recent debut: eff at 7f & relishes gd/soft grnd:
handles a gall trk & likes forcing tactics: open to more improvement & potentially useful: see 3585.
3337 **SURWAKI** 30 [9] C G Cox 2-9-0   P Robinson 13/2: 32: Chsd ldrs, kept on under press fnl 1f, just   5   88
shaded 2nd, no ch with wnr: op 5/1: acts on fast & gd/soft grnd: win a mdn: see 3337.
      GLEN IDA [7] M L W Bell 2-9-0   R Mullen 8/1: 3: ch c Selkirk - Yanka (Blushing John) Hld up,   shd   88
rdn to improve 2f out, kept on well for press, just pipped for 2nd: op 13/2, clr rem: 62,000gns Mar foal:
half brother to a wnr in the US: dam a wnr in the US, sire a top-class miler: eff at 7f on gd/soft, 1m will suit.
      TORRENS [6] M Johnston 2-9-0   D Holland 10/1: 4: b c Royal Anthem - Azure Lake (Lac Ouimet)   4   81
Mid-div, kept on steadily fnl 1f under hands & heels on debut: £100,000 Jan 1st foal: dam a wnr in the States, sire
a top-class mid-dist performer: plenty to like about this encouraging start, 1m shld suit & plenty more to come.
3568 **SILVERLEAF** 21 [1] J Mongan 25/1: 655: Chsd ldrs, ev ch 1.5f out, sn left bhnd: see 3568 (fm).   2   75
3234 **PENALTY KICK** 35 [1]2-9-0   O Urbina 33/1: 06: b c Montjeu - Dafrah (Danzig) Held up, styd on   1   75
under hands & heels: 50,000gns Apr foal: half brother to sev wnrs, incl 10f scorer Bold Demand: dam a 1m wnr, sire
a top-class mid-dist performer: not given a hard time & will improve over further.
      SPEIGHTSTOWN [12]2-9-0   E Ahern 3/1: 7: gr c Grand Lodge - Farfala (Linamix) Mid-div, rdn 3f   ½   74
out, not pace to chall on debut: well bckd from 6/1: Jan 1st foal: dam a mid-dist wnr in France, sire a top-class
mid-dist performer: with P Cole & shld do much better over further in time.
      NIGHT GUEST [13]2-9-0   Dane O'Neill 20/1: 8: Chsd ldrs, wknd 1.5f out on debut.   ½   73
      ONEIRO WAY [5]2-9-0   D Sweeney 33/1: 9: Held up, rdn & nvr nr ldrs on debut.   2   69
3752 **SOUTH OTHE BORDER** 14 [8]2-9-0   G Carter 33/1: 000: 10th: Held up, nvr in it on h'cap qual run.   3½   63
      SOVEREIGN SPIRIT [14]2-9-0   S Drowne 20/1: 0: 11th: Nvr better than mid-div under a kind ride.   1½   60
      WILTSHIRE [10]2-9-0   R Lappin 33/1: 0: 12th: Rdn in rear, nvr dngrs on debut.   nk   59
      STRIKE GOLD [2]2-9-0   P Dobbs 20/1: 0: 13th: Mid-div wide, btn 2f out on debut.   1¼   56
      RED ADMIRAL [11]2-9-0   L Dettori 11/4 FAV: 0: 14th: b c Red Ransom - Ausherra (Diesis) Trkd   6   46
ldrs, wknd qckly over 2f out, eased on debut: well bckd from 4/1: Feb foal, half brother to numerous wnrs, incl
smart stayer/hdler Yorkshire: dam a decent mid-dist performer: with Saeed bin Suroor & something clearly amiss.
14 Ran   Time 1m 31.24 (4.84)   Owned: Tweenhills Thurloe   Trained: Kingsclere

SANDOWN   FRIDAY 20.08.04   Righthand, Galloping Track, Stiff Finish

---

4070   4.45 Betfred 430 Branches Nationwide Handicap Stakes 3yo+ 0-75 (E)   [75]
£5642 £1736 £868   **5f6y str**   **Soft**   **Fair**   Far Side

3932* **WHITE LEDGER** 7 [5] R A Fahey 5-8-7 (6ex)vis (54) P Dobbs 7/4 FAV: 00-00311: Mid-div, switched   61
wide 1.5f out, rdn & strong run to lead cl home: hvly bckd: qck reapp: stays 6f, all wins at 5f: acts on fast,
soft & both AW's: in fine form & defied this step up in grade: well h'capped, see 3932 (claim).

3751 **PRINCE CYRANO** 14 [9] W J Musson 5-9-10 (71) R Mullen 7/2: 0060352: Chsd ldrs far rail, short of   nk   77
room 1.5f out, fin well but not as well as wnr: tchd 9/2, top-weight: acts on firm & gd/soft, handles soft grnd:
well h'capped & deserves to go one better: see 3408 & 1481.

3788 **MAYZIN** 13 [12] R M Flower 4-7-13 (46) A McCarthy 14/1: 0000003: Led till halfway, rallied &   ½   51
regained lead ins fnl 1f, no extra cl home: back to form with return to more forcing tactics: eff at 5f, will
apprec a return to 6/7f: acts on gd/soft & polytrack, handles fast grnd: well h'capped on turf: see 897 (AW).

3966 **PULSE** 5 [7] J M Bradley 6-8-11 p (58) P Fitzsimons 13/2: 5300554: Chsd ldrs, went on halfway till   nk   62
ins fnl 1f, no extra: qck reapp: see 2743 (gd/fm).

3537 **ELA FIGURA** 23 [8]4-7-13 p (46) Natalia Gemelova(7) 20/1: 3650005: Prom, onepcd fnl 1f.   1½   47

3924 **A TEEN** 7 [10]6-8-7 (50) R Kristin Stubbs(7) 14/1: 0600056: Mid-div, kept on under a quiet ride: ½   54
signs of a return to form under an inexperienced rider: see 740 (AW, K Fallon).

2502 **FREE WHEELIN** 64 [6]4-9-2 (63) M Tebbutt 9/1: 00-03007: Dwelt, styd on late, nvr dngrs: tchd   1½   60
12/1, 9 wk abs: return to 6f will suit: sharper next time: see 1345.

3380 **CREWES MISS ISLE** 29 [4]3-8-11 (60) L Keniry(3) 25/1: 1500058: Rdn rear, late prog.   nk   56

3984 **MULTAHAB** 14 [2]5-7-12 t (45) Liam Jones(2) 14/1: 2400009: Mid-div, onepcd when bmpd ent fnl 1f.   ¾   38

3984 **BOANERGES** 20 [1]7-8-1 (48) R Thomas(5) 25/1: 0050000: 10th: Prom, ev ch halfway, wknd dist.   1½   38

3577 **KALLISTAS PRIDE** 21 [3]4-8-13 VIS (60) I Mongan 16/1: 0201060: 11th: Dwelt, chsd ldrs, wknd fnl   ¾   47
1f: visor: reportedly clipped heels coming out of stalls.

11 Ran   Time 1m 05.21(5.61)   Owned: Castlemead Developments Limited   Trained: Malton

---

CHESTER   FRIDAY 20.08.04   Lefthand, Very Sharp Track

Official Going Soft

4071   2.10 Blue Square 0800 587 0200 Rated Stakes Handicap 3yo 0-90 (C)   [96]
£12482 £4734 £2367   **1m2f75y**   **Soft 130**   **-08 Slow**   Outside

3641 **MACLEAN** 18 [9] Sir Michael Stoute 3-8-8 P (76) K Fallon 10/1: 2136561: Made all, styd on fnl 2f,   83
drvn out: has lkd a tricky ride prev but right back to best with switch to forcing tactics over 10f in cheek pieces
& likes gd/soft & soft, acts on fast: tried visor: see 1462.

3826* **TARFAH** 11 [4] G A Butler 3-9-3 (3ex) (85) M J Kinane 4/5 FAV: 112: Keen, chsd wnr, eff to chall   2½   90
over 1f out, onepace: hvly bckd: lightly rcd & useful, first defeat but not disgraced: acts on gd & soft: stays 10f.

3572* **TRIPLE JUMP** 21 [10] T D Easterby 3-8-7 (75) W Supple 16/1: 4-213: Held up, eff over 1f out, kept   shd   80
on ins last, no threat: stays 10f & acts on fast & soft: may do btr with more positive tactics: see 3572.

3762+ **BESSEMER** 13 [8] I Semple 3-9-2 (84) F Lynch 20/1: 10-53614: Handy, eff to chall well over 1f   hd   88
out, sn hung left & onepcd: acts on gd & soft: prob ran to winning form of 3762 (class stks).

3597 **KEEPERS LODGE** 20 [6]3-8-4 (2oh) (70) J Quinn 33/1: 4001035: Held up, keen, eff 2f out, some late   1   74
gains, nvr dngrs: stays a sharp 10f on fast & soft: see 3597, 2904.

3236 **SWAGGER STICK** 35 [1]3-9-7 (89) S W Kelly 9/1: 4-116006: Held up, rdn over 2f out, no impress.   1¾   88

3647 **GREAT SCOTT** 18 [5]3-9-0 (82) S Chin 20/1: 5-005347: Held up, btn 2f out: see 2679 (7f).   2   78

3474 **ANNA PALLIDA** 26 [7]3-9-0 (82) N Callan 7/1: 0223128: In tch, wknd over 3f out, t.o.: not enjoy   21   48
soft grnd?: much btr 3474, 3038 (fast grnd, mdn fills).

3472* **TABLEAU** 26 [3]3-9-4 (86) R Hughes 10/1: 5-3119: In tch, wknd qckly over 2f out, eased: prob not   19   22
handle soft grnd, much btr on fast over 1m in 3472.

3553 **SENESCHAL** 22 [11]3-8-12 (80) C Catlin 50/1: 21-0000: 10th: Al bhd: see 3553, 1206.   shd   16

10 Ran   Time 2m 22.72 (14.22)   Owned: The Queen   Trained: Newmarket

---

4072   2.45 Shell Chemicals Premier Claiming Stakes 2yo (D)
£4901 £1508 £754   **7f2y rnd**   **Soft 130**   **-20 Slow**   Inside

3729 **GOOD WEE GIRL** 15 [4] S Kirk 2-8-2 (1ow) (74) J F Egan 100/30 FAV: 002151: Handy, hdwy to lead   74
dist, edged left but styd on, drvn out: nicely bckd, claimed for 15,000: eff over 6/7f on fast & soft grnd, stiff or
sharp trk: enjoyed drop in class & a game effort: see 3517, 3171.

3699 **RIVER LIFFEY** 16 [11] M L W Bell 2-9-0 M Fenton 8/1: 02: Dwelt, bhd, hdwy wide over 2f out, styd   shd   85
on to chall ins last, just held: imprvd from debut & apprec drop in class: stays a sharp 7f on soft & comes out
with plenty of credit from a poor draw & having to concede grnd: win similar, see 3699.

3483 **INDIBRAUN** 25 [2] P C Haslam 2-8-10 (77) G Faulkner 11/2: 514403: Set pace, rdd & hdd dist, no   2   76
extra ins last: well clr of rem: btr run from gd draw & stays 7f on fast & soft: see 1874.

3429* **ARABIAN ANA** 27 [6] B Smart 2-8-12 (83) F Lynch 4/1: 614: Held up, eff 2f out, sn onepace: drpd   5   72
in class & btr expected after 3429 (gd, mdn auct), poss not handle soft.

3686 **KING AFTER** 16 [7]2-9-2 (80) K Fallon 7/1: 16655: Chsd ldr, wknd dist: op 7/2: longer trip,   2   73
much btr over 5f earlier, see 1567, 931 (5f, polytrack).

3483 **DUSTY DANE** 25 [5]2-8-8 (71) A Daly 14/1: 565306: In tch, wknd 2f out: best 2952 (mdn auct, gd grnd).   3   60

3930 **NORTHERN REVOQUE** 7 [8]2-7-13 P J Quinn 50/1: 0050047: In tch, wknd 2f out: cheekpieces.   ½   50

3882 **MICKEY PEARCE** 8 [9]2-8-6 F Norton 40/1: 0008: b c Rossini - Lucky Coin (Hadeer) Al bhd: Jan   2   54
foal, cost 10,000gns: dam 11f scorer.

2802 **MISS CUISINA** 53 [1]2-7-13 P M Quinn 66/1: 009: b f Vettori - Rewardia (Petardia) Al bhd: 7 wk   hd   46
abs: Apr foal, cost 6,200gns: half-sister to wnrs over 5/6f: dam styd 7f as a juv.

3394 **POLESWORTH** 28 [3]2-7-13 M Halford(7) 25/1: 50: 10th: b f Wizard King - Nicholas Mistress   1¼   43
(Beveled) Dwelt, in tch, wknd 2f out: Mar foal: dam 6f scorer: speedily bred.

3627 **SHUJUNE AL HAWAA** 19 [10]2-8-3 (68) C Catlin 9/1: 56300: 11th: In tch, wknd over 2f out: btr 3302 (fast).   6   37

11 Ran   Time 1m 35.5 (10.5)   Owned: E Power & M Kavanagh   Trained: Upper Lambourn

---

4073   3.15 Chester Chronicle Rated Stakes Handicap 3yo+ 0-100 (B)   [98]
£12232 £4640 £2320   7f2y rnd   Soft 130   +08 Fast   Inside

3428 **KING HARSON** 27 [3] J D Bethell 5-8-7 (5oh)vis (77) K McEvoy 11/1: 0200601: Made all, styd on 87
well, rdn clr fnl 1f: 7f specialist who acts on firm & hvy grnd, any trk: loves to front run: right back to best.

3954 **DIGITAL** 6 [5] M R Channon 7-9-1 (90) C Catlin 4/1: 2220002: Held up, hdwy & short of room well   3   90
over 1f out, kept on ins last, no ch with wnr: likes easy grnd: tough: see 3117, 2684.

3954 **MARSHMAN** 6 [4] M H Tompkins 5-8-9 (84) K Fallon 2/1 FAV: 3000003: Chsd ldrs, onepace fnl 2f: ¾   83
well bckd: back on a fair mark: see 1151.

3622 **CIRCUIT DANCER** 20 [8] A Berry 4-9-5 (94) F Lynch 16/1: 4010504: Cl-up, no extra fnl 1f: just   ¾   92
caught out over longer trip, apprec rtn to 6f as in 2357 (fast).

3634* **NASHAAB** 19 [7]7-9-1 (90) N Callan 9/2: 0002315: Dwelt, bhd, some late gains, no threat: won   1½   85
here in 3634 (firm) & much prefers a fast surface.

3305 **STOIC LEADER** 32 [1]4-8-7 (1oh) (81) F Norton 11/1: 4265256: In tch, wknd over 1f out: btr 3152.   nk   77

3596 **TASHKIL** 20 [9]3-9-4 T (98) W Supple 10/1: 4110-057: Slow away, nvr a factor: see 3596 (fast).   nk   91

4165} **HUMID CLIMATE** 345 [6]4-8-7 (82) T Hamilton(3) 16/1: 0-/130-8: ch g Desert King - Pontoon (Zafonic)   dist   0
Al bhd: rnr-up in 2 hdles last winter (2m, rtd 117h, gd & fast): won first of 3 Flat starts for Mrs A Perratt
(mdn): eff at 10.5f on gd grnd: has gone well fresh. 1 May'03 Ling 10.3gd 85- D:
8 Ran   Time 1m 33.58 (8.58)   Owned: Mr C J Burley   Trained: Middleham

---

4074   3.50 Linpac Group Nursery Handicap Stakes 2yo (C)   [87]
£8444 £2598 £1299   7f2y rnd   Soft 130   -26 Slow   Inside

3807* **CLARET AND AMBER** 12 [4] R A Fahey 2-9-4 (6ex) (77) T Hamilton(3) 11/4 FAV: 35511: Dwelt, sn handy,   93
hdwy to lead over 2f out, pushed clr over 1f out: well bckd: clrly stays 7f well & acts on fast, relished this soft
grnd: acts on a gall or sharp trk: thriving at present, shld land quick-fire hat-trick: see 3807.

3665* **FOLLOWING FLOW** 17 [9] W Jarvis 2-9-7 (80) K Fallon 9/2: 0312: Held up, hdwy to go 2nd over 1f   6   86
out, not pace of wnr appr fnl 1f: well clr of rem & progressing well: acts on fast & polytrack, handles soft.

3053 **YOUNG THOMAS** 43 [7] M L W Bell 2-8-13 (72) M Fenton 9/1: 0443: Bhd, modest late gains, nvr a   5   70
factor: 6 wk abs: likes softer grnd: see 2810.

3266 **EARL OF LINKS** 34 [2] R Hannon 2-9-1 (74) R Hughes 9/2: 31604: Led 1f, led again 3f out till over   4   66
2f out, wknd: best 1531 (mdn, 5f).

3351 **NO COMMISSION** 30 [8]2-9-2 (75) J F Egan 14/1: 5402105: Held up, btn 2f out: twice below 3245 (fm).   1   66

3539 **WASALAT** 22 [3]2-9-6 (79) C Catlin 12/1: 423206: In tch, wknd over 3f out: btr 3297 (fast grnd), 2522.   ½   69

3723* **LISA MONA LISA** 15 [5]2-9-1 (74) J Quinn 17/2: 1410417: In tch, wknd 2f out: best 3723 (fast grnd).   21   34

3930* **DARTANIAN** 7 [1]2-8-6 (6ex) (2ow) (63) N Callan 9/2: 0563018: Led after 1f till 3f out, wknd: btr 3930.   ¾   24

3351 **CANARY DANCER** 30 [6]2-8-4 (63) M Halford(7) 25/1: 04209: In tch, wknd 2f out: twice below 2275 (fast).   shd   22
9 Ran   Time 1m 35.95 (10.95)   Owned: The Matthewman Partnership   Trained: Malton

---

4075   4.25 David Mclean Maiden Stakes Fillies 3yo (D)
£5330 £1640 £820   1m4f66y   Soft 130   -43 Slow   Inside

1892 **DAZE** 91 [5] Sir Michael Stoute 3-8-11 K Fallon 1/1 FAV: 31: Slow away, bhd, gd hdwy to lead   75
over 1f out, sn rdn clr, cmftbly: hvly bckd after 3 month abs: clrly stays 12.3f well, further will suit: acts on
soft grnd & a sharp trk: more to come in h'caps: see 1892.

3592 **REEM TWO** 20 [1] D McCain 3-8-11 W Supple 20/1: 632: Held up, hdwy over 2f out, kept on to take   8   66
2nd ins last, no ch with wnr: imprvd on firm, soft grnd & prob stays 12.3f: looks the type to apprec 14f+ in h'caps.

3105 **STOCKING ISLAND** 41 [4] B Hanbury 3-8-11 (71) K McEvoy 7/2: 023003: Handy, hdwy to lead over 2f   hd   66
out till over 1f out, wknd: not disgraced on much softer grnd: see 1885.

3845 **PRINCIPESSA** 10 [2] N Palling 3-8-11 (68) N Callan 5/2: 0022024: Handy, led over 5f out till over   4   60
2f out: nicely bckd: not enjoy v soft grnd?: btr 3845 (fast).

3828 **DANETTIE** 11 [6]3-8-11 S W Kelly 20/1: 0545: Led till over 5f out, wknd & t.o.: see 3592.   dist   0
5 Ran   Time 2m 57.68 (21.28)   Owned: Duke of Devonshire   Trained: Newmarket

---

4076   5.00 Handicap Stakes For Gentleman Amateur Riders 3yo+ 0-80 (E)   [51]
£3494 £1075 £538   1m4f66y   Soft 130   -67 Slow   Inside

3815 **GIUNCHIGLIO** 12 [4] W M Brisbourne 5-10-13 (64) Mr C Davies(5) 6/1: 1036041: Slow away, sn chsd   71
ldrs, hdwy to lead over 1f out, rdn clr: eff at 10f, styd this 12f well: winning form on fast & soft grnd, handles
polytrack: right back to best: see 1913, 1027.

2892 **CYBER SANTA** 49 [6] J Hetherton 6-9-10 (2oh) (45) Mr L Newnes(3) 16/1: 2430/-602: Set pace till   2½   50
over 1f out, no extra: 7 wk abs: imprvd eff & acts on fast, soft & polytrack: see 2244.

3741 **LENNEL** 15 [8] A Bailey 6-11-6 bl (71) Mr S Walker 5/2 FAV: 6413233: Chsd ldrs, rdn & sltly outpcd   1¾   71
over 2f out, kept on ins last, no threat: well bckd: in fine heart: acts on firm & soft: see 3637, 3325.

3481 **MILK AND SULTANA** 25 [5] G A Ham 4-10-2 (53) Mr E Dehdashti(3) 7/1: 6002024: In tch, eff to go 2nd   ¾   52
over 3f out, onepcd over 1f out: acts on firm, soft & fibresand: see 3481, 3145.

3964 **BUCKS** 5 [3]7-12-0 (79) Mr Michael Murphy(5) 11/4: 1250225: Held up, eff well over 1f out,   hd   77
onepace: nicely bckd: acts on firm, soft & polytrack: see 2244.

4544} **REVELINO** 676 [1]5-11-10 (75) Mr A Swinswood(7) 16/1: 3/40210/-6: With ldr, wknd 3f out: fit from   6   65
hdlg, plcd in a h'cap earlier (rtd 78h, 2m, fast, tried cheek pieces): last rcd on the Flat back in '02, won a h'cap
for E Dunlop: suited by 10f on fast or soft & acts on any trk.

3704 **BIG BAD BURT** 16 [7]3-9-12 (59) Mr S Warren(7) 14/1: 3460047: Al bhd: see 1778 (1m, gd/soft), 735.   10   34

3638 **SADDLERS QUEST** 18 [9]7-10-4 P (55) Mr S Dobson(3) 14/1: 0650-008: Al bhd: tried cheek pieces.   hd   30

2147 **GRAND WIZARD** 79 [2]4-11-0 (65) Mr J J Best(3) 10/1: 001-4009: Handy, wknd over 4f out, t.o.: abs.   dist   0
9 Ran   Time 3m 0.64(24.24)   Owned: Mr Nev Jones   Trained: Nesscliffe

Official Going Good/Soft

4077

5.35 Axminster Carpets Apprentice Handicap Stakes 3yo+ 0-70 (E)   [70]
£3835 £1180 £590   **1m str**   **Good/Soft 69**   **-45 Slow**   Far side

2647 **CRAIL 59** [9] C F Wall 4-10-0 (70) Lisa Jones 4/1: 010-3041: In tch, led 2f out, drvn out to hold   75
on: 8 wk abs: eff around 1m on firm & soft grnd: acts on a stiff/gall trk & goes well fresh: lightly rcd
performer who did well to defy top-weight, open to more improvement: see 2647 & 1423.
3996 **OH SO ROSIE 4** [3] J S Moore 4-8-13 p (55) Derek Nolan(8) 7/1: 0010042: Held up, prog 3f out, ev ch   ¾ 57
well ins fnl 1f, just held: qck reapp: gd eff in defeat: see 3996 & 3363.
3922* **DIDNT TELL MY WIFE 7** [2] C F Wall 5-9-13 (6ex) (69) S O'Hara(10) 7/2 FAV: 6604313: Bhd, prog   2½ 66
halfway, styd on to chase wnr bef 1f out, sn no extra: qk reapp: stablemate of wnr: in gd form.
3176 **LOCH LAIRD 38** [6] M Madgwick 9-8-6 (48) C Haddon(3) 16/1: 1050054: Chsd ldrs 5f, sn outpcd,   ½ 44
rallied late: btr 846 (7f, polytrack).
2170 **DASH FOR COVER 79** [5]4-9-3 (59) P Gallagher(8) 14/1: 0005605: Handy till dist, no extra: 11 wk abs.   1¾ 51
3898 **THE GAIKWAR 8** [8]5-9-6 bl (62) M Savage(6) 13/2: 0043236: In tch over 6f, no extra: btr 3898 & 3685.   1 52
3685 **FLEETWOOD BAY 16** [12]4-9-10 t (66) B Reilly 11/2: 6360267: Grabbed stands rail & led, hdd 2f out, wknd.1¼ 54
3176 **DUE TO ME 38** [4]4-8-2 p (44) J Jones(10) 12/1: 1463408: Bhd when no room 7f out, nvr nrr than mid-div.   nk 31
3512 **TERRAQUIN 24** [10]4-9-9 (65) A Beech 12/1: 0550009: Cl-up, ev ch 2f out, sn wknd: btr 2679.   7 39
3922 **CUMBRIAN PRINCESS 7** [11]7-8-3 (45) A Putland(7) 25/1: 1363660: 10th: In tch, ev ch bef 2f out, wknd.   ½ 18
3819 **HARRY CAME HOME 11** [7]3-7-12 (16oh)BL (30) Victoria Hill(2) 100/1: 0000000: 11th: Bhd, nvr a factor.   9 2
1402 **BREEZER 115** [1]4-8-10 (52) Frances Harper(10) 20/1: 0/5500-00: 12th: Rear, nvr a factor.   ¾ 0
12 Ran   Time 1m 48.27 (-45 Slow)   Owned: The Crail Partnership   Trained: Newmarket

---

4078

6.05 E B F Maiden Stakes 2yo (D)
£6078 £1870 £935   **1m str**   **Good/Soft 69**   **-35 Slow**   Far side

3390 **BAYEUX DE MOI 28** [6] Mrs A J Perrett 2-9-0 J Murtagh 13/8 FAV: 41: In tch stands side, styd on   82
to lead overall 1f out, rdn clr, val bit more: apprec step up to 1m, further will suit in time: acts on gd/soft
grnd & a stiff/gall trk: enjoyed today's test of stamina & is clearly going the right way: see 3390.
3786 **JUST DO IT 13** [11] M R Channon 2-9-0 T E Durcan 40/1: 62: In tch far side, led stands side   3 73
group bef 1f out, kept on fnl 1f, not pace of wnr stands side: eff at 1m on gd/soft grnd: left debut eff bhd with
encouraging display & can find similar: see 3786.
2897 **ALMANSHOOD 49** [1] J H M Gosden 2-9-0 R Hills 11/2: 53: b c Bahri - Lahan (Unfuwain) Handy   nk 73
stands side, kept on fnl 1f, just held for 2nd: 7 wk abs: Jan first foal, dam Gr 1 wnr at 1m: sire decent
performer at 1m: eff at 1m, further shld suit in time: acts on gd/soft grnd: showed promise under kind ride.
MY PORTFOLIO 0 [14] R Charlton 2-9-0 S Drowne 16/1: 4: b g Montjeu - Elaine's Honor (Chief's   ¾ 71
Crown) Rear far side, prog 3f out, nrst fin: Mar foal, cost 50,000gns: half-brother to a decent miler abroad: sire multiple Gr 1 wnr at 12f: eff at 1m, mid-dists will suit next term: gd start.
3594 **MOBARHEN 20** [8]2-9-0 D Holland 11/2: 55: b c Red Ransom - Fit For A Queen (Fit To Fight) In   1 69
tch stands side, led stands side group 2f out, hdd 1f out, no extra: Feb foal, cost $325,000: half-brother to decent
mid-dist performer abroad: dam decent miler abroad: sire well related: with Sir M Stoute.
3721 **KNIGHTSBRIDGE HILL 15** [12]2-9-0 D Kinsella 33/1: 56: Led far side group, hdd bef 1f out, no extra.   hd 68
3568 **ZAMBOOZLE 21** [13]2-9-0 S Carson 11/2: 47: Handy far side till dist, wknd: showed more in 3568 (firm).   1½ 65
3267 **VOIR DIRE 34** [2]2-9-0 R Havlin 50/1: 008: Nvr nrr than mid-div stands side: now quals for h'caps.   2 61
3554 **CASUAL GLANCE 22** [7]2-8-9 Martin Dwyer 20/1: 09: Missed break stands side, prog halfway, wknd dist.   hd 55
2714 **SARAH BROWN 56** [10]2-8-9 P P Doe 100/1: 000: 10th: Nvr a factor far side: cheek pieces.   2½ 50
2388 **MOSHKIL 59** [5]2-9-0 W Ryan 33/1: 00: 11th: Al in rear stands side: 10 wk abs.   5 46
3337 **SHAHAMA 30** [3]2-9-0 Paul Eddery 50/1: 00: 12th: Al bhd.   nk 45
3285 **RAGGED GLORY 34** [9]2-9-0 (77) R L Moore 9/1: 4620: 13th: Handy far side, swtchd stands side 3f   nk 44
out, wknd fnl 2f: btr 3285 (7f).
3390 **RIVER BISCUIT 28** [4]2-9-0 J Fortune 20/1: 050: 14th: Led stands side group 6f, fdd: btr 3390.   8 30
14 Ran   Time 1m 47.46 (8.36)   Owned: Lady Clague   Trained: Pulborough

---

4079

6.35 Gamebookers Com Nursery Handicap Stakes 2yo (E)   [91]
£3757 £1156 £578   **6f str**   **Good/Soft 69**   **-22 Slow**   Far side

3627 **CALY DANCER 19** [9] D R C Elsworth 2-9-0 (77) J Fortune 6/1 CO FAV: 053331: Held up, prog when   88
short of room 2f out, styd on to lead ins fnl 1f, drvn out: eff at 5/7f on firm & gd/soft: improving.
3521 **RIDDER 23** [10] D J Coakley 2-8-13 (76) E Ahern 7/1: 45022: Mid-div, prog to lead bef 1f out, hdd   1 83
ins fnl 1f, not pace of wnr: clr rem: acts on fast & gd/soft grnd: improving performer who can find similar.
3627 **FORTNUM 19** [13] R Hannon 2-8-0 (63) R Smith 10/1: 53053: Handy, onepace.   5 58
3686* **TREAT ME WILD 16** [3] R Hannon 2-8-10 (73) R L Moore 6/1 CO FAV: 16514: Rear, prog 2f out, no   shd 67
impress fnl 1f: btr 3686 (fast).
3716 **CHUTNEY MARY 15** [8]2-8-8 (71) Dane O'Neill 14/1: 0622525: Led, hdd bef 1f out, wknd: btr 3716 (fast).   nk 64
3753 **FLYING PASS 14** [2]2-8-11 VIS (74) D Holland 6/1 CO FAV: 0302256: Rcd stands side, sn switched to   hd 66
far side group, ev ch bef 1f out, wknd: first time visor: btr 3330 & 2870 (7f).
3807 **BIBURY FLYER 12** [4]2-9-7 (84) T E Durcan 6/1 CO FAV: 2261207: Stands side, sn joined far side   ¾ 74
group, prog when short of room bef 1f out, not recover: btr 3623 (firm) & 3374 (fast).
3520 **MULBERRY WINE 23** [1]2-9-0 (77) D Sweeney 16/1: 6458: Nvr a factor: btr 3047.   10 42
3330 **SASTRE 30** [6]2-8-2 (65) J F McDonald(3) 33/1: 0409: Cl-up over 4f, fading when short of room dist.   shd 29
3639* **APPLE OF MY EYE 18** [12]2-9-2 (79) W Ryan 9/1: 0410: 10th: Handy 4f, fdd: btr 3639 (firm).   3½ 34
3513 **Avertigo 23** [5]2-8-11 (74) S Drowne 14/1:0   3774 **Street Cred 13** [11]2-9-6 (83) Martin Dwyer 14/1:0
12 Ran   Time 1m 17.57 (5.47)   Owned: The Caledonian Racing Society   Trained: Whitsbury

SALISBURY FRIDAY 20.08.04 Righthand, Galloping Track, Stiff Finish

4080

7.05 Wilton Graphics Handicap Stakes 3yo 0-85 (D) [92]
£7488 £2304 £1152   1m4f   Good/Soft 69   +21 Fast   Inside

3631 **TOPKAT** 19 [1] D R C Elsworth 3-8-6 (70) Dane O'Neill 11/1: 0251: Keen bhd, prog 4f out, styd on   82
to lead bef 1f out, rdn out: fast time: eff at 9.5f, imprvd for step up to 12f: acts on gd & gd/soft grnd:
unexposed in h'cap grade & can rate higher: see 3385.
3690 **CIRCASSIAN** 16 [9] Sir Mark Prescott 3-7-12 (1oh) (61) J Mackay 7/2: 0000-02: In tch 1m, sn   ¾   72
outpcd, rallied bef 1f out, just held by wnr: apprec step up to 12f: acts on gd/soft grnd: lightly rcd performer
for v shrewd operation, can go one btr: see 3690.
3845* **VELVET WATERS** 10 [4] R F Johnson Houghton 3-8-3 (6ex) (67) S Carson 13/2: 6412213: In tch, styd   1¾   74
on to lead 2f out, hdd bef 1f out, no extra: acts on fast & gd/soft grnd: not disgraced under pen: just btr 3845.
3618 **PANGLOSS** 20 [11] G L Moore 3-8-1 p (65) R L Moore 16/1: 00-30504: Rear, prog 4f out, kept on fnl 1f.   2½   66
2919 **PAGAN MAGIC** 48 [8]3-8-12 (76) Lisa Jones 12/1: 05-30105: Mid-div, prog 2f out, no impress fnl 1f.   ½   78
3918 **STAGE RIGHT** 7 [3]3-9-7 (85) Martin Dwyer 5/2 FAV: 461546: Led 3f, styd cl-up & led again 3f out,   1¼   85
hdd 2f out, sn wknd: qck reapp: btr 3534 (firm).
3161 **INCURSION** 39 [5]3-9-5 (83) E Ahern 16/1: 63-10307: Sn in tch, wknd 2f out: btr 2631 (10f, fast).   3½   78
3783 **TURNSTILE** 13 [7]3-8-13 (77) R Hughes 8/1: 4-420328: Nvr nrr than mid-div: btr 3783 (fast).   4   66
3029 **QUARTINO** 48 [10]3-9-7 (85) J Fortune 20/1: 521-09: Led 9f out, hdd 3f out, wknd: 6 wk abs: see 3029.   5   67
3816 **HATCH A PLAN** 12 [2]3-8-10 (74) D Holland 10/1: U012240: 10th: Handy over 1m, wknd: btr 3471 (10f).   5   49
2923 **KARAMEA** 48 [6]3-9-2 (80) J Murtagh 16/1: 03-3150: 11th: Rear, prog halfway, fdd 3f out.   18   30
11 Ran   Time 2m 38.26 (5.86)   Owned: Mr R Standring   Trained: Whitsbury

4081

7.35 Sovereign Windows & Conservatories Maiden Stakes Fillies 3yo+ (D)
£5571 £1714 £857   6f str   Good/Soft 69   -34 Slow   Far side

3784 **RACHELS VERDICT** 13 [9] J R Fanshawe 3-8-11 J Murtagh 11/2: 451: Held up, prog halfway, hung   72
right under press from dist, styd on well to lead cl-home: eff at 6f, 7f will suit: acts on gd/soft & fast grnd:
still ran green but is improving with ev start: see 2586.
3711 **ZWADI** 15 [6] H Candy 3-8-11 (72) Dane O'Neill 9/2: 4-405032: Cl-up, hdd bef 2f out, kept on   hd   70
well, hdd cl-home: acts on firm & gd/soft grnd: see 3711.
3921 **MISS MONZA** 7 [3] B R Millman 3-8-11 T E Durcan 33/1: 003: Handy, eff 2f out, just held by front   1¾   65
2 fnl 1f: qck reapp: eff at 6f on gd/soft grnd: now quals for h'caps.
3921 **TETCOTT** 7 [1] M P Tregoning 3-8-11 D Holland 7/4 FAV: 534: Chsd ldrs, kept on fnl 1f, just held   shd   64
for 3rd: qck reapp: btr 3921 (7f, gd).
2352 **ALL QUIET** 71 [11]3-8-11 (75) R Hughes 4/1: 00-32355: Led, hdd bef 2f out, wknd dist: 10 wk abs.   1½   60
    MAGIC SPIN 0 [7]4-9-0 S Carson 14/1: 6: b f Magic Ring - Moon Spin (Night Shift) Nvr nrr than   nk   59
mid-div on debut: with R F Johnson Houghton.
3799 **GENTLE RAINDROP** 12 [4]3-8-11 BL (62) J Fortune 20/1: 050007: Rear, modest late gains: blnks.   nk   58
    SABANDER BAY 0 [5]3-8-11 R Havlin 8/1: 8: b f Lear Fan - Sambac (Mr Prospector) Missed break,   2½   51
nvr a factor: debut: with J H M Gosden.
511} **SOCIETY PET** 567 [8]5-9-0 (40) Derek Nolan(7) 100/1: 00000/0-9: Handy 4f, wknd.   5   38
    FIERY ANGEL 0 [10]3-8-11 L Keniry(3) 20/1: 0: 10th: Keen in tch till halfway, fdd.   10   13
10 Ran   Time 1m 18.32 (6.22)   Owned: Mr M Fisch   Trained: Newmarket

4082

8.05 European Breeders' Fund Classified Stakes 3yo+ 0-80 (D)
£8210 £2526 £1263   6f212y str   Good/Soft 69   -01 Slow   Far side

3293* **EISTEDDFOD** 32 [6] P F I Cole 3-9-2 (84) N De Souza(5) 7/4 FAV: 13311: In tch, short of room 2f   94
out, styd on to lead, rdn out to hold on: eff btwn 6/7f on firm & soft grnd: acts on a sharp or stiff/gall
trk: tough & useful performer who goes well for today's pilot: see 3293.
3210 **ST PANCRAS** 36 [7] N A Callaghan 4-9-3 (80) D Holland 7/2: 0201532: Missed break, prog wide 3f   hd   88
out, ev ch ins fnl 1f, just held: clr rem: remains in gd form: acts on firm & gd/soft grnd: see 3210 & 2665.
3782 **WATERSIDE** 13 [5] G L Moore 5-9-3 (80) R L Moore 11/2: 1124603: Led, hdd dist, no extra: see 2871.   4   80
3523 **VIENNAS BOY** 23 [1] R Hannon 3-9-0 (82) Dane O'Neill 11/2: 6052544: In tch, ev ch bef 1f out, wknd.   nk   81
2787 **STAR PUPIL** 54 [4]3-8-12 (79) Martin Dwyer 9/1: 2-420055: Mid-div, wknd dist: 8 wk abs: btr 1498.   1¾   75
3872 **AMMENAYR** 9 [3]4-9-3 VIS (78) J Fortune 14/1: 0-003536: Missed break, al in rear: first time visor.   2½   70
3402 **GOODENOUGH MOVER** 28 [2]8-9-5 (82) S Drowne 9/2: 2211527: Cl-up till halfway, wknd fnl 2f: 2½   67
disapp eff & surely something amiss: btr 3402 & 2880.
7 Ran   Time 1m 30.45 (4.95)   Owned: Elite Racing Club   Trained: Whatcombe

AYR FRIDAY 20.08.04 Lefthand, Galloping Track

Official Going SOFT (HEAVY IN PLACES ON BOTTOM BEND)

4083

2.20 Renault Trafic Median Auction Maiden Stakes 2yo (E)
£3700 £1138 £569   7f50y   Heavy 137   -53 Slow   Inside

3500 **FENRIR** 24 [5] J R Weymes 2-9-0 G Hind 100/1: 01: Mid-div, hdwy 3f out, led ins fnl 1f, rdn out: 85
shock 100/1! & stays 7f, much improved on hvy grnd: see 3500.
3831 **KINGS ACCOUNT** 11 [6] M Johnston 2-9-0 J Fanning 11/4: 22: Led till ins fnl 1f, kept on nr fin: nk   83
clr rem: handles gd/soft & hvy: shown enough to win a race: see 3831.
3582 **SPEAR** 21 [3] D R Loder 2-9-0 T P Queally 13/8 FAV: 23: Chsd ldrs, outpcd over 2f out, rallied   7   69
over 1f out, not pace to chall: nicely bckd: not enjoy hvy? much btr 3582 (debut, fast).
3721 **HAATMEY** 15 [1] M R Channon 2-9-0 A Culhane 8/1: 34: Mid-div hdwy after 3f, hdwy & not clr run   ¾   67
over 1f out, kept on ins fnl 1f: shade closer with a clr run: btr 3721 (debut, fast).
3272 **SYDNEYROUGHDIAMOND** 34 [7]2-9-0 L Enstone(3) 150/1: 05: b g Whittingham - November Song   1   65

(Scorpio) Prsd ldr, outpcd & btn 2f out: Mar foal: half brother stayed 12f: with M Mullineaux.
3425 **COCONUT SQUEAK 27** [4]2-8-9 Dean McKeown 14/1: 36: Cl-up, onepcd over 2f out.   ½   59
    WHITE STAR MAGIC 0 [10]2-9-0 B Swarbrick(5) 100/1: 7: ch c Bluegrass Prince - Bless (Beveled)   ¾   62
Bhd, nvr a factor on debut: cost 1,400gns, Apr first foal: dam a 12f 4yo scorer.
    THORNTOUN PICCOLO 0 [11]2-8-9 P Hanagan 66/1: 8: ch f Groom Dancer - Massorah (Habitat) Slow   2   53
away, hdwy on inner over 2f out,sn wknd: Jan foal, cost 9,000gns: half-sister to wnrs over 6/7f.
3831 **GOOD INVESTMENT 11** [8]2-9-0 G Bartley(7) 16/1: 359: Cl-up, outpcd & btn over 2f out.   ½   57
3682 **IMPERIAL DYNASTY 16** [2]2-9-0 P Makin(5) 25/1: 050: 10th: Bhd, nvr a factor.   4   49
3189 **HARBOUR LEGEND 37** [9]2-8-9 BL N Mackay(3) 100/1: 060: 11th: Al bhd in first time blnks.   10   24
3589 **INVERTIEL 20** [12]2-9-0 R Winston 13/2: 420: 12th: Handy to 2f out, fdd, eased, t.o.   30   0
12 Ran Time 1m 40.16 (13.36) Owned: Mr E G Moorey Trained: Middleham

---

4084   2.55 Arnold Clark Renault Handicap Stakes 3yo+ 0-75 (E)   [75]
         £3653 £1124 £562   **1m2f**   **Heavy 137**   +10 Fast   Inside

3785 **MARITIME BLUES 13** [4] J G Given 4-8-13 (60) A Culhane 6/1: 1063001: Handy, outpcd 2f out,   65
rallied/hdwy to lead ins fnl 1f, drvn out: fast time: eff at 1m/12f on firm, hvy & fibresand: back to form: see 1164.
460 **LOADED GUN 211** [1] W M Brisbourne 4-8-5 (52) B Swarbrick(5) 16/1: 205/00-02: ch g Highest Honor -   nk   55
Woodwardia (El Gran Senor) Mid-div, hdwy over 1f out, ev ch ins fnl 1f, held nr fin: long abs: h'cap unplcd both
'03 starts (rtd 54a, J Feilden): missed '02: eff at 10f on hvy: gd run on first start for new yard.
3734 **YOUNG ROONEY 15** [3] M Mullineaux 4-9-7 (68) T P Queally 8/1: 4324-403: Led till ins fnl 1f, no   1¼   69
extra: clr of rem: eff around 1m/10f on fast, hvy & fibresand: gd eff, back to form drop back to 10f: see 3514.
3598 **COMPTON DRAGON 20** [2] D Nicholls 5-9-13 vis (74) A Nicholls 7/2 FAV: 2520604: Rear, some late gains. 3   70
3741 **SCURRA 15** [5]5-8-7 (54) T Eaves(3) 4/1: 0312465: Cl-up to 2f out, kept on ins fnl 1f, not pace to chall.   2½   46
3766 **SKIDDAW JONES 13** [8]4-8-0 (47) P Hanagan 13/2: 0-050626: Bhd, nvr a factor: op 9/2.   ¾   38
3557 **REPULSE BAY 22** [6]6-7-13 (46) N Mackay(3) 5/1: 0500007: Nvr nr ldrs: op 7/1: see 1793.   nk   36
4008 **LUCKY LARGO 3** [7]4-8-5 bl (52) J Fanning 9/1: 2600008: Rcd in 2nd, no impress over 1f out: qck reapp. 3   37
8 Ran Time 2m 17.16 (12.76) Owned: Downlands Racing Trained: Gainsborough

---

4085   3.25 Parks Renault Handicap Stakes 3yo 0-80 (D)   [81]
         £5481 £1686 £843   **1m**   **Heavy 137**   -49 Slow   Inside

3906* **BOPPYS PRINCESS 8** [4] R A Fahey 3-7-12 (6ex) (51) P Hanagan 4/6 FAV: 000-1211: Led after 2f till   60
over 2f out, rallied to lead again ins fnl 1f, drvn out: landed a double: nicely bckd: eff around 1m/8.5f on firm
& hvy: v game eff here, tough & continues to improve: lightly rcd, win over dist: remains in gd form: see 3906.
3835* **SHES OUR LASS 11** [1] D Carroll 3-9-13 (6ex) (80) D Tudhope(7) 5/2: 1311112: Chsd ldrs, kept on ins   ¾   85
fnl 1f to go 2nd cl-home: top-weight: acts on firm, hvy & fibresand: gd eff on bid for 5-timer: see 3835.
3572 **THE NUMBER 21** [2] I Semple 3-8-12 (65) R Winston 20/1: 56-33: Keen, led 2f, remained in 2nd, led   shd   69
again over 2f out till ins fnl 1f, no extra nr fin & lost 2nd cl-home: handles fast & hvy: gd run bhd 2 improvers.
3737 **MUSIOTAL 15** [5] J S Goldie 3-8-2 (55) N Mackay(3) 11/1: 5502104: Cl-up, not pace of ldrs fnl 1f.   1¾   55
2049* **MISKINA 84** [3]3-8-5 T (58) B Swarbrick(5) 20/1: 24-03015: Mid-div, hdwy 2f out, sn no impress: t-strap.   15   28
5 Ran Time 1m 51.5 (14.9) Owned: Mrs S Bond Trained: Malton

4086   4.00 Renault Master Classified Stakes 3yo+ 0-70 (E)
         £3517 £1082 £541   **1m**   **Heavy 137**   -10 Slow   Inside

3546 **MILLAGROS 22** [1] I Semple 4-9-0 P (70) P Hanagan 6/1: 0446331: Cl-up, hdwy to lead appr fnl 1f,   76
drvn out ins fnl 1f: eff over 1m/10f on firm & hvy grnd, sharp, gall or stiff trks: enjoyed cheek pieces.
3780 **SCOTLAND THE BRAVE 13** [5] J D Bethell 4-9-0 p (70) T P Queally 7/2: 3504142: Prom, led briefly   1¾   70
appr fnl 1f, kept on ins fnl 1f but not pace of wnr: acts on fast & hvy grnd: remains in gd form: see 3223.
3922 **ARRY DASH 7** [2] M R Channon 4-9-5 (72) A Culhane 5/2 FAV: 3060623: Mid-div, hdwy over 1f out,   ½   74
kept on but not pace to chall: well bckd, qck reapp: handles fast, hvy & both AWs: fair run, rtn to further may suit.
3797 **SOLLER BAY 13** [3] K R Burke 7-9-6 (73) L Enstone(3) 4/1: 466-2004: Led till over 1f out, no extra.   2½   70
3634 **ZANJEER 19** [4]4-9-3 (70) M Lawson(5) 4/1: 0163105: Keen & handy, hdwy & ch over 1f out, sn outpcd.   7   53
5 Ran Time 1m 48.4 (11.8) Owned: Mr James A Cringan Trained: Carluke

---

4087   4.35 17th September Is Ladies Day Handicap Stakes 3yo+ 0-80 (D)   [78]
         £5554 £1709 £854   **6f**   **Heavy 137**   +06 Fast   Far side

3903 **BALAKIREF 8** [4] M Dods 5-9-4 (68) R Winston 5/2 J FAV: U100051: Cl-up, trav best over 1f out,   80
hdwy to lead ins fnl 1f, pushed out, val 4L: bckd: eff at 6/7f on fast & fibresand, likes gd, hvy & Ayr.
3424 **HIGHLAND WARRIOR 27** [8] J S Goldie 5-9-7 (71) N Mackay(3) 5/2 J FAV: 0466302: Keen in mid-div,   1½   75
hdwy over 1f out, kept on fnl 1f, no extra: handles firm & hvy: back to form at fav'd Ayr.
3763 **COLLEGE MAID 13** [3] J S Goldie 7-8-7 vis (57) P Hanagan 5/1: 5666653: Led till ins fnl 1f, no   nk   60
extra: back to winning form of 2508.
3880 **ULYSEES 9** [9] I Semple 5-9-9 P (73) T Eaves(3) 7/1: 3105004: Mid-div, hdwy over 2f out, kept on   1½   71
but not pace to chall: first time cheek pieces: see 2542.
3880 **LEGAL SET 9** [2]8-8-13 t (63) Ann Stokell 14/1: 4002045: Prom, ev ch over 1f out, onepcd: op 10/1.   1   58
3561 **CHAMPAGNE CRACKER 22** [5]3-8-11 (64) A Culhane 16/1: 0315006: Trkd ldrs, no impress 2f out.   11   26
4010 **PAYS DAMOUR 3** [1]7-8-7 (57) J Fanning 8/1: 5030207: Prom, lost pl 2f out, btn: tchd 11/1, qck reapp.   8   0
7 Ran Time 1m 17.16 (7.86) Owned: Septimus Racing Group Trained: Darlington

AYR **FRIDAY 20.08.04 Lefthand, Galloping Track**

4088 **5.10 Stewarts Turf Handicap Stakes 3yo+ 0-70 (E)** **[69]**
£3715 £1143 £572 **7f50y** **Heavy 137** **-06 Slow** Inside

3229 **LOCOMBE HILL 35** [13] N Wilson 8-9-4 (59) D Tudhope(7) 12/1: 0504401: Keen in mid-div, hdwy over **68**
1f out, led ins fnl 1f, kept on: tchd 20/1: eff at 6f, best at 7f/1m: acts on firm, hvy & fibresand, any trk: gd
run on first start for new yard (prev with D Nicholls): back to form & is well h'capped: see 417.
3759 **QUICKS THE WORD 14** [11] C W Thornton 4-8-13 (54) Dean McKeown 10/1: 0002262: Prom, led over 2f *1* **59**
out, hdd ins fnl 1f, no extra: gd run, remains in decent form & can find similar: see 2967 & 1532.
3766 **ZANDEED 13** [16] Miss L A Perratt 6-9-2 (57) J Fanning 33/1: 10/600/-03: b g Inchinor - Persian *1½* **59**
Song (Persian Bold) Bhd, hdwy over 2f out, kept on fnl 1f but not pace of ldrs: missed '03: unplcd in '02 (h'cap,
clmrs, rtd 35, with J Goldie): eff at 7f/10.5f on fast & hvy, gall/undul trk: prev eff visored: fair return.
1 Jul'01 Donc 10.2gd 82- E: 1 Jul'01 Chep 10.1g/f 72-66 D: 1 Jun'01 Nott 10gd 63- F: 1 Jun'01 Hayd 8.1gd 68-60 E:
3933 **ZHITOMIR 7** [12] M Dods 6-8-11 (52) L Enstone(3) 12/1: 0-166164: Mid-div, hdwy 3f out, kept on but *1¾* **50**
not pace to chall: qck reapp: shade btr 3324 (sell).
3155 **SANDORRA 39** [6]6-8-5 (46) T Williams 33/1: 0016005: Prom, ev ch over 2f out, no impress over 1f out. *1½* **41**
3933* **PERTEMPS MAGUS 7** [7]4-9-8 (6ex) (63) P Hanagan 1/1 FAV: 0000-316: Cl-up, ev ch 2f out, outpcd & *1* **56**
btn over 1f out: well bckd from 6/4, qck reapp: btr expected after 3933.
3700 **STELLITE 16** [10]4-8-5 (46) N Mackay(3) 9/1: 50-01007: Bhd, hdwy 2f out, onepcd fnl 1f: clr of rem. *2* **35**
3485 **IRUSAN 25** [9]4-9-3 (58) A Culhane 33/1: 6004658: Rear, outpcd, modest late gains: see 2722. *7* **33**
3700 **STORMVILLE 16** [5]7-8-13 (54) M Lawson(5) 9/1: 00/0-0029: Prom, wknd 2f out: op 7/1. *½* **28**
3766 **WOOD DALLING 13** [14]6-9-1 (56) R Winston 9/1: 0061660: 10th: Al bhd: op 12/1. *2* **26**
3766 **HOWARDS ROCKET 13** [2]3-7-13 (45) P Fessey 33/1: 00600: 11th: ch g Opening Verse - Houston *3* **9**
Heiress (Houston) Rear, hdwy over 2f out, wknd over 1f out: dam won in Italy: with J Goldie.
3670 **MASSEY 17** [1]8-8-9 (50) P Makin(5) 25/1: 1010000: 12th: Led till over 2f out, no extra. *½* **13**
3416 **CAPETOWN GIRL 28** [4]3-8-11 (57) A Nicholls 25/1: 1000000: 13th: Rear, nvr a factor. *1¾* **16**
3764 **ZAHUNDA 13** [15]5-7-12 (1oh) (38) B Swarbrick(4) 33/1: 6402450: 14th: Cl-up wide, hung left just *5* **0**
over 2f out, wknd: see 3324.
3880 **AXFORD LORD 9** [8]4-9-0 (55) J Carroll 150/1: 0204/-600: 15th: Slow away, al bhd: see 3430. *12* **0**
15 Ran Time 1m 36.85(10.05) Owned: Mr Ian W Glenton Trained: York

SOUTHWELL **Fibresand FRIDAY 20.08.04 Lefthand, Sharp, Oval Track**

Official Going STANDARD

4089 **5.20 At The Races On Ntl Ireland Median Auction Maiden Stakes 2yo (E)**
£3868 £1190 £595 **5f aw str** **Going 25** **-23 Slow** Stands side

2926 **KOMAC 48** [1] B A McMahon 2-9-0 (69) S Sanders 2/1 FAV: 62461: Chsd ldrs far side, styd on to **75a**
lead dist, rdn out: 7 wk abs & AW bow: eff at 5f, 6f+ will suit: acts on firm grnd & fibresand: goes well fresh.
3987 **TARTATARTUFATA 4** [3] D Shaw 2-8-9 (60) Joanna Badger 14/1: 04002: Prom, led 2f out, hdd dist, *¾* **66a**
kept on, not pace wnr: qck reapp: eff at 5f, further shld suit: acts on fibresand: see 1424.
SECOND REEF 0 [6] R A Fahey 2-9-0 G Parkin 14/1: 3: b c Second Empire - Vax Lady (Millfontaine) *1½* **66a**
Cl-up, ev ch bef 1f out, sn no extra: debut: clr rem: Apr foal, cost 5,000gns: half-brother successful at 5f:
dam 5f wnr: sire Gr 1 wnr at 1m: eff at 5f, 6f+ will suit: acts on fibresand: improve for today's experience.
3633 **ZANTERO 19** [5] R P Elliott 2-9-0 P Mulrennan(3) 10/1: 464: Mid-div far side, prog dist, nrst fin. *5* **51a**
3418 **EUKLEIA 27** [7]2-8-9 D Allan 6/1: 605: Led 3f, no extra: btr 2689. *shd* **45a**
3525 **DUCAL DIVA 23** [11]2-8-9 D Fentiman(7) 7/1: 026: Prom stands side over 3f, no extra: AW bow. *hd* **44a**
2297 **JESSICAS STYLE 73** [9]2-8-9 J Bramhill 33/1: 07: Chsd ldrs 3f, sn outpcd, rallied late: 10 wk abs. *hd* **43a**
DESPERATION 0 [13]2-9-0 Darren Williams 22/1: 8: b g Desert Style - Mauras Pride (Cadeaux *1¼* **44a**
Genereux) Missed break, nvr nrr than mid-div: debut: Mar foal, cost 1,000gns: half-brother successful at 10f.
RUSSIAN RIO 0 [15]2-9-0 Rory Moore(5) 4/1: 9: b g Imperial Ballet - L'harmonie (Bering) Handy *¾* **42a**
stands side 3f, sn wknd: debut: Mar foal, half-brother 5f wnr abroad: dam plcd at best.
3484 **ALL A DREAM 25** [12]2-8-9 D Corby(3) 25/1: 60: 10th: Al rear stands side. *2½* **29a**
3832 **ONE OF EACH 11** [14]2-8-9 Dale Gibson 16/1: 550: 11th: Cl-up stands side 3f, fdd. *¾* **27a**
3811 **Preskani 12** [2]2-9-0 R Fitzpatrick 66/1:0
3863 **Make It Happen Now 9** [4]2-8-9 (50) B O'Neill(7) 50/1:0
Mochaccino 0 [8]2-8-9 Hayley Turner(5) 28/1:0 **Imperatrice 0** [16]2-8-9 M Henry 20/1:0
15 Ran Time 1m 0.21 (2.41) Owned: Mrs J McMahon Trained: Tamworth

4090 **5.50 St Bernard Of Clairvaux's Selling Stakes 3yo+ (G)**
£2611 £746 £373 **1m aw rnd** **Going 25** **-22 Slow** Inside

3830 **ZARIN 11** [8] D W Chapman 6-9-4 (55) S Sanders 7/4 FAV: 3000621: Made all, rdn out ins fnl 1f, al **67a**
holding rivals: no bid: eff at 7f/1m on firm, hvy & both AWs: see 3830 & 744.
3704 **KINGSTON TOWN 16** [3] N P Littmoden 4-9-4 p (63) J P Guillambert(3) 4/1: 0040602: Cl-up, prog & ev *1½* **62a**
ch dist, kept on but not pace wnr: clr rem: can find similar: see 530 & 96.
3609 **OLD BAILEY 20** [11] T D Barron 4-9-9 vis (58) P Mulrennan(3) 11/1: 0005503: Mid-div, prog halfway, *6* **55a**
wknd bef 1f out: see 3129 & 2204.
3487 **BULAWAYO 25** [9] Andrew Reid 7-9-9 bl (51) D Corby(3) 9/2: 6421044: Cl-up, wknd dist: btr 2996. *1¾* **51a**
3830 **SUPER DOMINION 11** [4]7-9-9 p (46) Stephanie Hollinshead(5) 20/1: 4010005: Chsd ldrs over 6f, wknd. *1¼* **48a**
3482 **WILSON BLUEBOTTLE 25** [6]5-9-9 bl (48) Dale Gibson 7/2: 2000066: Chsd ldrs 4f, sn outpcd, rallied late. *1* **46a**
3575 **AGGI MAC 21** [7]3-8-7 e (40) Suzanne France(5) 33/1: 3005-507: Al bhd: new stable, btr 682. *¾* **34a**
3206 **JAMESTOWN 36** [1]7-9-4 (38) L Fletcher(3) 16/1: 0004048: Rear, nvr a factor: btr 3206. *6* **27a**
3992 **MARENGO 4** [2]10-9-4 (20) K Ghunowa(7) 66/1: 0064009: Missed break, sn mid-div, fdd 2f out: qk reapp. *1¼* **24a**
3392 **KUSTOM KIT FOR HER 28** [10]4-8-13 t (42) J Bramhill 33/1: 3224000: 10th: Missed break, nvr a factor. *8* **3a**
1181 **MISS CELERITY 127** [5]4-8-13 (30) Joanna Badger 66/1: 0040000: 11th: Handy over 5f, fdd, long abs. *6* **0a**
11 Ran Time 1m 43.23 (3.83) Owned: Mr J M Chapman Trained: York

4091 **6.20 John Salvin Retirement Handicap Stakes 3yo+ 0-70 (E)** **[67]**
£3432 £1056 £528 **6f aw str** **Going 25** **+01 Fast** Inside

3974 **MISTER MAL 5** [4] B Ellison 8-9-2 (55) P Mulrennan(3) 5/1: 0610031: Made all, edged right ins home str, drvn out to hold on: qck reapp: eff at 5/7f on firm, likes gd, hvy grnd & fibresand: in-form: see 3974. **65a**
3821 **SILENT STORM 11** [2] H J Cyzer 4-9-11 (64) J-P Guillambert(3) 12/1: 5/-33002: In tch, prog & ev ch dist, kept on, just held by wnr: lightly rcd performer who ran well with visor left off: can go one btr: see 3360. ½ **70a**
3744 **FOOLS ENTIRE 14** [1] J A Gilbert 3-9-0 e (56) G Baker 14/1: 6000003: Mid-div, prog halfway, no impress fnl 1f: btr 545. 1¾ **57a**
3995 **SHIFTY NIGHT 4** [7] Mrs C A Dunnett 3-8-7 P (49) Hayley Turner(5) 10/1: 4106004: Chsd ldrs, no extra fnl 1f: qck reapp in cheek pieces: btr 3092. 1¼ **46a**
3933 **HEADLAND 7** [12]6-9-2 bl e (55) S Sanders 11/4 FAV: 0622155: Bhd, prog wide halfway, nrst fin: qck reapp: appreciate return to 7f: btr 3571 (7f). ½ **50a**
4005 **TALLY 3** [10]4-9-11 (64) L Fletcher(3) 3/1: 0014006: Cl-up over 4f, no extra: qck reapp: btr 3485. nk **58a**
3812 **RUE DE PARIS 12** [8]4-8-1 (40) Dale Gibson 33/1: 0000-057: Prom over 4f, wknd: btr 3812. ½ **32a**
2716 **SET ALIGHT 56** [13]3-8-11 (53) Joanna Badger 20/1: 0438: Missed break, nvr a factor: 8 wk abs. 2 **39a**
3518 **CHEROKEE NATION 23** [9]3-10-0 e (70) D Allan 10/1: 2110359: Nvr nrr than mid-div. nk **55a**
2999 **SENOR BOND 45** [6]3-9-4 (60) D McGaffin 12/1: 0-630600: 10th: Bhd, nvr a factor. shd **44a**
2985 **XPRES DIGITAL 46** [5]3-9-13 t (69) J Bramhill 12/1: 0-040300: 11th: Bhd, nvr a factor: btr 2053. 3½ **42a**
2544 **PLATTOCRAT 63** [3]4-7-12 (2oh) (35) D Fentiman(7) 66/1: 5000: 12th: Bhd, nvr a factor: 9 wk abs. 3 **1a**
3446 **LADY FRANPALM 27** [11]4-8-8 (47) Darren Williams 25/1: 440-0000: 13th: Handy wide 3f, fdd. 14 **0a**
13 Ran Time 1m 14.79 (1.49) Owned: Mrs Andrea M Mallinson Trained: Malton

4092 **6.50 Kevin Voce - 25 Years At Southwell Handicap Stakes 3yo 35-55 (F)** **[63]**
£2989 £854 £427 **1m4f aw** **Going 25** **-03 Slow** Inside

3714 **SCOTT 15** [1] J Jay 3-9-1 (50) G Baker 12/1: 006031: Mid-div, prog 5f out, styd on to lead 2f out, pushed out fnl 1f, val 4L+: eff at 11.5f/12f on fast grnd & fibresand: imprvd eff today on switch to AW. **64a+**
2595 **RAWALPINDI 62** [2] J A R Toller 3-9-3 (52) Dale Gibson 25/1: 0-0002: In tch, prog & ev ch bef 1f out, not pace wnr: clr rem: 9 wk abs: h'cap bow: imprvd for step up to 12f: acts on fibresand: find similar. 2 **58a**
3192 **HOLLY WALK 37** [6] M Dods 3-9-1 p (50) Darren Williams 8/1: 5543203: Led 10f, fdd: btr 2804. 17 **30a**
4045 **SALUT SAINT CLOUD 1** [4] G L Moore 3-9-4 p (53) S Sanders 8/13 FAV: 05133314: Chsd ldrs, nvr trav, wknd 3f out: too sn after wng yesterday in 4045 (fast). 9 **19a**
2299 **MIDDLEHAM ROSE 73** [3]3-8-0 (2oh) (33) D Fentiman(7) 25/1: 00-66205: Prom 1m, fdd: jumps fit. 7 **0a**
3948* **GARSTON STAR 6** [8]3-9-6 (55) Laura Reynolds(7) 100/30: 1220516: In tch over 1m, wknd: btr 3948 (gd). ½ **9a**
3573 **SILVER RHYTHM 21** [7]3-9-0 (49) V Halliday 33/1: 0-35007: In tch over 1m, fdd: btr 1604. 1 **0a**
2503 **PEPE 64** [5]3-9-5 p (54) J Bramhill 25/1: 6301408: Bhd, nvr a factor: 9 wk abs. 10 **0a**
8 Ran Time 2m 37.66 (3.36) Owned: Mr Keith Wills Trained: Newmarket

4093 **7.20 At The Races Dedicated Racing Channel Classified Stakes 3yo+ 0-70 (E)**
£3361 £1034 £517 **7f aw rnd** **Going 25** **+07 Fast** Inside

1828 **KHANJAR 94** [4] K R Burke 4-9-1 (70) Darren Williams 10/1: 4/22-2401: ch g Kris S - Alyssum (Storm Cat) Cl-up, styd on to lead dist, hdd & under press when ins fnl 1f, rallied to get up on line: long abs: new stable: eff at 7/9f on fast grnd & fibresand: eff with visor, imprvd eff with it being left off here: goes well fresh: tough & game performer: see 1095 (D R Loder). **76a**
2 Apr'04 Muss 9g/f 78-(82) D: 2 May'03 Chep 8.1g/s 74-(90) D: 2 Sep'02 Leic 7g/f 90- D:
3809 **DOWNLAND 12** [8] N Tinkler 8-9-1 (69) Kim Tinkler 3/1: 6511302: Mid-div, prog to lead bef 1f out, hdd dist, rallied well to lead well ins fnl 1f, hdd on line: clr rem: apprec rtn to Southwell: see 3395 & 3155. shd **75a**
2551* **KINGSMAITE 63** [5] S R Bowring 3-9-1 bl (75) J Bramhill 2/1 FAV: 2-040513: Prom, ev ch bef 1f out, sn no extra: 9 wk abs: btr 2551 (6f). 4 **72a**
3395 **AIR MAIL 28** [2] Mrs N Macauley 7-9-1 (64) R Fitzpatrick 33/1: 0046064: Handy 5f, sn no extra. 2 **63a**
3210 **THE BONUS KING 36** [7]4-9-5 (74) G Baker 9/1: 0024005: Sn bhd, prog 3f out, no impress fnl 1f. 1¼ **64a**
4005 **MISTER SWEETS 3** [1]5-9-3 (72) D Nolan(3) 5/2: 6015006: Led, hdd 5f out, styd prom & ev ch bef 1f out, sn wknd: qck reapp: disapp on rtn to AW: btr 2768 (fast). 1¼ **59a**
3684 **COMMANDER BOND 16** [3]3-8-10 (70) D McGaffin 20/1: 0010007: Led 5f out, hdd 2f out, fdd. 5 **47a**
3850 **GEM BIEN 9** [6]6-9-4 (73) S Sanders 12/1: 640-0038: Prom till halfway, fdd: btr 3850 (gd/soft). 24 **2a**
8 Ran Time 1m 27.9 (1.3) Owned: Spigot Lodge Partnership Trained: Leyburn

4094 **7.50 Midlands Racing - 9 Great Venues Handicap Stakes 3yo 0-70 (E)** **[76]**
£3426 £1054 £527 **5f aw str** **Going 25** **-08 Slow** Stands side

3976* **WUNDERBRA 4** [6] M L W Bell 3-8-13 (6ex)t (61) Hayley Turner(5) 7/4 FAV: 3451311: In tch, prog halfway, styd on to lead ins fnl 1f, rdn out: qck reapp: eff at 5/6f on firm, fast grnd & fibresand: progressive. **69a**
3932 **BLUE POWER 7** [1] K R Burke 3-9-3 (65) Darren Williams 9/4: 5310202: In tch far side, prog to lead bef 1f out, hdd well ins fnl 1f, no extra: qck reapp: apprec rtn to fibresand & can find similar: see 2731. 1 **68a**
3833 **WENDYS GIRL 11** [13] R P Elliott 3-9-0 bl (62) P Mulrennan(3) 14/1: 1016553: Led, hdd dist, sn no extra. 1 **62a**
3744 **HELLO ROBERTO 14** [3] M J Polglase 3-9-7 (69) K Ghunowa(7) 14/1: 3010004: In tch far side, short of room halfway, switched & kept on fnl 1f: btr 3080 (fast). ½ **54a**
DUTCH KEY CARD 19 [12]3-9-1 (63) R Fitzpatrick 25/1: 0505005: b g Key of Luck - Fanny Blankers (Persian Heights) Sn outpcd, prog 2f out, nrst fin: Brit & AW bow: modest form prev in native Ireland. ¾ **46a**
3610 **ESTOILLE 20** [5]3-7-13 (1ow)(16oh)t (30) J Bramhill 100/1: 00006: Prom centre over 3f, wknd. nk **29a**
3654 **PURE FOLLY 18** [2]3-8-9 (57) S Sanders 7/2: 4-34407: Cl-up far side over 3f, no extra: btr 3198. 1½ **34a**
3347 **WESTBOROUGH 30** [4]3-8-0 (48) Kim Tinkler 16/1: 2505208: Handy over 3f, no extra: btr 3133. ½ **23a**
901 **PARK AVE PRINCESS 150** [8]3-9-0 (62) L Fletcher(3) 9/1: 0-225329: Al bhd: long abs: btr 901 (7f). ¾ **35a**
3645 **BURKEES GRAW 18** [11]3-7-12 (14oh) (32) D Fentiman(7) 25/1: 0002020: 10th: In tch 3f. 1¾ **14a**
3739 **BIG TOM 15** [10]3-8-11 (59) Dale Gibson 25/1: 04-50000: 11th: Al in rear: btr 3739. 12 **0a**
11 Ran Time 59.48(1.68) Owned: Fitzroy Thoroughbreds Trained: Newmarket

SANDOWN   SATURDAY 21.08.04   Righthand, Galloping Track, Stiff Finish

Official Going SOFT.

4095 1.40 Listed Variety Club Atalanta Stakes Fillies 3yo+ (A)
£17850 £6600 £3300 **1m14y rnd** **Good/Soft 86** -21 Slow Inside

3965 **ZIETORY 6** [2] P F I Cole 4-9-0 (99) L Dettori 4/1: 242-5031: Cl-up, hdwy to lead over 1f out,
edged left ins last but kept on well, drvn out: acts at 7f/1m, poss stays 12f: acts on fast & polytrack, loves
gd/soft & a sharp or gall trk: useful & genuine, not over-raced this term: see 1491. **99**

3866 **BAYBERRY 10** [3] H R A Cecil 4-9-0 (90) W Ryan 8/1: 30410-52: Handy, hdwy over 1f out, hdwy to nk **98**
chall ins last, just held: eff over 1m/9.5f on gd & gd/soft: useful filly, more to come: see 3866.

3365 **THREE SECRETS 30** [1] P W Chapple Hyam 3-8-8 (85) R Hughes 10/1: 20-0123: Set steady pace till ½ **97**
over 1f out, rallying when hmpd just ins last, kept on: up in class, stays 1m on fast & gd/soft: wld have gone v
close & 10f will suit: see 3365 & 2907.

3564 **SILK FAN 22** [5] P W Harris 3-8-8 (95) D Holland 5/4 FAV: 2211-164: Held up, hdwy 2f out, onepcd ¾ **95**
over 1f out: hvly bckd: stays 1m & prob ran to best: clrly even more expected aftr 3564 & 2918 (h'cap).

2211 **IMPERIALISTIC 78** [4]3-8-8 p (94) Darren Williams 7/2: 23-41105: In tch, eff over 2f out, sn no 3 **90**
extra: 11 wk abs: btr run: see 1305 (h'cap), 1105.
5 Ran Time 1m 47.57 (8.57) Owned: The Fairy Story Partnership Trained: Whatcombe

4096 2.15 Gr3 Iveco Daily Solario Stakes 2yo (A)
£26100 £9900 £4950 **7f16y rnd** **Good/Soft 86** +04 Fast Inside

3752* **WINDSOR KNOT 15** [2] J H M Gosden 2-8-11 L Dettori 9/2: 411: Made virtually all, styd on **111+**
strongly over 1f out, rdn clr: gd time: suited by 7f, 1m looks sure to suit: loves to dominate & acts on fast grnd,
clrly relished this gd/soft & a gall trk: potentially v smart, plenty more to come & can win more Gr races.

3774 **EMBOSSED 14** [4] R Hannon 2-8-11 (98) R L Moore 5/1: 6162: Handy, eff over 1f out, kept on to 2½ **106**
chase wnr ins last, not his pace: acts on fast & gd/soft: going the right way & will enjoy a drop into List class.

3126 **PROPINQUITY 42** [8] P W Harris 2-8-11 D Holland 12/1: 133: Held up, hdwy 2f out, onepcd over 1f nk **105**
out: acts on gd & gd/soft: would enjoy a drop into List class: see 3126, 2696.

3060 **PIVOTAL FLAME 44** [7] B A McMahon 2-8-11 R Hughes 8/1: 154: Held up, hdwy to chase wnr over 1f 2½ **101**
out, wknd ins last: 6 wk abs: consistent: see 3060, 1687.

3566 **SILVER WRAITH 22** [3]2-8-11 (100) T P Queally 9/1: 2113135: In tch, eff over 2f out, wknd over 1f 2 **97**
out: tough & consistent, poss prefers faster grnd as in 3407 (nurs h'cap, firm).

3532 **FOX 24** [5]2-8-11 (100) K Fallon 11/2: 21436: In tch, wknd dist: btr 3532 (g/f). 1¼ **95**

3110* **JOHNNY JUMPUP 42** [1]2-8-11 E Ahern 5/1: 117: In tch, eff over 2f out, sn no extra: 6 wk abs: hd **94**
shade btr expected stepped up in trip after gd/soft auct win in 3110.

2792* **LEOS LUCKY STAR 54** [6]2-8-11 R Hills 5/2 FAV: 118: In tch, wknd qckly dist: hvly bckd, 7 wk 2 **90**
abs: clrly much btr expected but this was his first start on easy grnd, lkd potentially smart on faster grnd earlier.
8 Ran Time 1m 32.12 (5.72) Owned: Sheikh Mohammed Trained: Manton

4097 2.50 William Hill Handicap Stakes 3yo+ 0-90 (C) [87]
£12644 £4796 £2398 **1m2f7y** **Good/Soft 86** -12 Slow Inside

3794 **TELEMACHUS 14** [12] J G Given 4-9-7 bl (80) M Fenton 16/1: 0000001: In tch, hdwy to lead dist, **89**
styd on well for press ins last: eff at 1m, suited by 10.5f on firm, soft or fibresand, prob any trk: wears blnks
now: has slipped to a v handy mark after some modest runs, stable rtng to form?: see 1519.

3794 **SILVALINE 14** [6] T Keddy 5-9-7 (80) J Murtagh 10/1: 0110302: Trkd ldr, led over 2f out till 1½ **86**
dist, kept on, not pace of wnr: won this race last term off a 9lb lower mark & another fine effort: likes Sandown.

3980 **DREAM MAGIC 5** [4] M J Ryan 6-9-2 (75) D Holland 15/2: 0500323: Handy, eff 2f out, onepace: gd run. 1¾ **78**

3186* **DEEP PURPLE 38** [10] M P Tregoning 3-9-4 (85) A Daly 12/1: 14: Held up last, styd on v well ins ½ **87+**
last, eye-catching: acts on gd & gd/soft: shaped with plenty of promise here, will relish 12f & will win soon: see 3186.

2363 **FAAYEJ 71** [2]4-9-10 (83) R Hills 11/2: 521-145: Held up, hdwy & hung right 2f out, kept on ½ **84**
ins last, nvr a threat: 10 wk abs & an encouraging run: see 2363, 2099.

3674+ **DESERT ISLAND DISC 18** [5]7-9-2 (75) T P Queally 9/1: 0615116: Led till over 2f out, wknd fnl 1f: nk **75**
carried head awkwardly, but v tough but last 8 wins have been at 12f: see 3674.

3892 **RYANS FUTURE 9** [11]4-9-2 (75) S Hitchcott(3) 8/1: 5-500527: In tch, eff 2f out, no extra: btr 3892. ¾ **74**

2759 **GOLANO 56** [8]4-9-7 (80) R Hughes 20/1: 3110-208: In tch 1m, wknd: now with P Webber, 8 wk abs. 3½ **74**

3216 **TRAVELLING BAND 37** [13]6-9-2 (75) L Keniry(3) 14/1: 024-0069: Bhd, btn 2f out: see 2903. 4 **64**

3029 **SILENT HAWK 45** [1]3-9-6 t (87) L Dettori 8/1: 2-41040: 10th: Chsd ldrs, hung right & wknd over 1f ¾ **75**
out: reportedly not handle grnd, 6 wk abs: best 1892 (mdn, gd).

3481 **SIR HAYDN 26** [14]4-8-5 bl (64) R L Moore 28/1: 0605300: 11th: Al bhd: btr 3295 (firm), 1006. nk **51**

3801 **BREATHING SUN 13** [7]3-8-8 t (75) R Mullen 9/1: 11-00030: 12th: Al bhd: reportedly distressed. 3½ **57**

3938 **MISS PEBBLES 7** [3]4-9-1 vis (74) N Pollard 14/1: 0051250: 13th: Al bhd: see 3938, 1927. 4 **51**

3615* **BARRY ISLAND 21** [9]5-9-4 (77) K Fallon 7/1: 0306410: 14th: Al bhd: reportedly lost action. 6 **46**
14 Ran Time 2m 13.9 (9.86) Owned: The Travellers Trained: Gainsborough

4098 3.25 Michael Shanly Rated Stakes Handicap 3yo+ 0-100 (B) [107]
£15314 £5809 £2904 **5f6y str** **Good/Soft 86** +04 Fast Far Side

3937+ **SMOKIN BEAU 7** [1] N P Littmoden 7-10-1 (108) K Fallon 2/1 FAV: 0400111: Handy, hdwy over 1f out, **112**
styd on well for press to lead cl-home, drvn & game: hvly bckd: v smart run under a big weight: eff over 5/6f on
any grnd or trk, likes Goodwood: best up with/forcing the pace: thriving now & right back to best after a spell in
the doldrums: see 3937.

3622 **MUTAWAQED 21** [5] M A Magnusson 6-8-10 t (89) R L Moore 7/2: 0420102: Slow away, sn in tch, gd hd **92**
hdwy over 1f out, slt lead cl-home, collared last stride: tough & useful sprinter who acts on fast & gd/soft grnd:
eff at 5f, poss just best at 6f: deserves another race, see 3434.

3792 **DEVISE 14** [7] M S Saunders 5-8-7 (4oh) (82) R Miles(3) 11/2: 1554023: With ldr, led 2f out, edged shd **88**
left ins last but styd on till collared cl-home, just btn: v useful eff from 4oh: in-form sprinter: see 3792, 1914.

1234

SANDOWN SATURDAY 21.08.04 Righthand, Galloping Track, Stiff Finish

3827 **CAUSTIC WIT 12** [2] M S Saunders 6-8-7 (1oh)p (85) D Holland 11/2: 1122004: Held up, eff & hung left dist, kept on ins last, not with ldrs: back to form: most prog & tough earlier: see 2758 & 2451. ¾ **86**
3971 **FRUIT OF GLORY 6** [3]5-9-2 (95) L Dettori 9/2: 4214225: With ldr, onepcd dist: shade btr 3971. ¾ **93**
3773 **SPEED COP 14** [4]4-9-2 (95) T Block(7) 11/1: 0-230046: Slt lead 3f, wknd fnl 1f: btr 3773 (gd). 1 **90**
6 Ran Time 1m 0.3.7 (4.1) Owned: Turf 2000 Limited Trained: Newmarket

4099

4.00 Currencies Direct Handicap Stakes 3yo 0-85 (D) **[92]**
£6874 £2115 £1058 **5f6y str** **Good/Soft 86** **+04 Fast** Far Side

3684* **OUT AFTER DARK 17** [5] C G Cox 3-8-12 (76) L Dettori 9/2: 042-511: Made virtually all, styd on strongly fnl 1f, shade cmftbly: eff over 5/6f on fast & gd/soft, stiff trks: lightly rcd, thriving from the front. **88**
3920 **MORGAN LEWIS 8** [2] G B Balding 3-8-4 (68) S Carson 3/1: 400-0132: Handy, hdwy to go 2nd over 2f out, hung right ins last but kept on, not pace of wnr: well bckd: eff over 5/6f on fast & gd/soft: consistent. 1¼ **75**
3976 **SKYHARBOR 5** [7] A M Balding 3-8-9 (73) D Holland 4/1: 0-050523: In tch, eff & edged right over 1f out, onepace: see 3976, 2591. 1 **78**
3889* **RYDAL 9** [3] G A Butler 3-9-9 vis (87) K Fallon 5/2 FAV: 0624014: In tch, no extra over 1f out: bckd: more expected after 3889. 2 **88**
3844 **TRICK CYCLIST 11** [1]3-8-9 (73) T Block(7) 14/1: 0602135: Held up, hdwy & short of room over 1f out, swtiched left & sn no impress: btr on fast grnd in 3720. ½ **73**
2985 **EXTREMELY RARE 47** [4]3-8-2 (66) J Quinn 25/1: 2010006: Nvr a factor: now with M Saunders, abs. 1 **64**
3543 **TREGARRON 23** [6]3-8-8 (72) R L Moore 7/1: 000-1427: Chsd wnr, wknd qckly dist: see 3543 (fm). 1¾ **66**
7 Ran Time 1m 03.7 (4.1) Owned: The Night Owls Trained: Hungerford

4100

4.35 Crown Personnel Nursery Handicap Stakes 2yo (D) **[89]**
£7280 £2240 £1120 **7f16y rnd** **Good/Soft 86** **-27 Slow** Inside

3723 **IM SPARTACUS 16** [2] I A Wood 2-8-8 (69) M Fenton 20/1: 6506541: In tch, hdwy over 1f out, styd on to lead ins last, rdn out: stays 7f on fast & gd/soft grnd, prob any trk: see 1367. **78**
3665 **MOZAFIN 18** [6] M R Channon 2-9-3 (78) L Dettori 9/2: 62432: Handy, hdwy to lead dist, hdd & no extra ins last: fine run: shown enough to win a race: stays 7f: acts on fast & gd/soft: see 3665, 2424. 1¼ **83**
3825 **IVANA ILLYICH 12** [4] S Kirk 2-8-12 (73) J F Egan 9/1: 504033: Held up, wide on bend 5f out, late gains, nvr dngrs: stays 7f on fast & gd/soft: see 3825, 2061. 1¾ **74**
3614 **NORCROFT 21** [7] N A Callaghan 2-9-2 BL (77) D Holland 12/1: 2160004: Led after 1f, clr 3f out, hung left over 1f out, sn hdd & wknd: tried blnks: best 1327. 1½ **75**
3624* **KEEP BACCKINHIT 21** [9]2-9-5 (80) R L Moore 10/1: 30315: In tch, wknd dist: btr 3624 (fm). 3 **72**
3431* **LITTLE DALHAM 28** [5]2-9-7 (82) K Fallon 13/8 FAV: 4216: In tch, wknd fnl 1f: hvly bckd: clrly btr expected & does handle gd/soft: see 3431. 1 **72**
3627* **KING OF BLUES 20** [3]2-9-0 t (75) E Ahern 9/2: 00417: Bhd, nvr a factor: bckd from 7/1: btr 3627 (fm). 9 **47**
3484 **HOMME DANGEREUX 26** [8]2-7-13 (60) J Quinn 14/1: 3058: In tch, wknd over 1f out: see 2382. 5 **22**
8 Ran Time 1m 34.7 (7.9) Owned: Mr John Purcell Trained: Upper Lambourn

4101

5.05 Capital Aviation Maiden Stakes Fillies 3yo (D)
£5486 £1688 £844 **1m14y rnd** **Good/Soft 86** **-20 Slow** Inside

4601} **PORTHCAWL 322** [5] Mrs A J Perrett 3-8-11 L Dettori 9/1: 0-1: b f Singspiel - Dodo (Alzao) Cl-up, hdwy to lead 2f out, pushed out ins last: well btn sole '03 start for M Bell: eff over a stiff 1m on gd/soft: goes well fresh: plenty to like about this, more to come. **78**
3799 **ANNA PANNA 13** [2] H Candy 3-8-11 (69) Dane O'Neill 9/1: 3-62552: Held up, hdwy 2f out, edged right ins last but kept on to go 2nd cl-home: stays 1m on fast & gd/soft, prob fibresand: worth a try in headgear. 1¼ **75**
3884 **NOORA 9** [6] M P Tregoning 3-8-11 (72) R Hills 9/2: 0-20243: Chsd ldrs, eff to chase wnr 2f out, not extra fnl 1f: well bckd: prob stays 1m on gd & gd/soft: consistent in defeat: see 3121, 1587. 1½ **72**
GO SUPERSONIC [9] Sir Michael Stoute 3-8-11 K Fallon 1/1 FAV: 4: b f Zafonic - Shirley Superstar (Shirley Heights) Cl-up, wkng when hmpd ins last: hvly bckd on debut: half-sister to an Oaks wnr. 2 **68**
3858 **TIPSY LADY 10** [3]3-8-11 (62) L Keniry(3) 16/1: 000055: Led till over 2f out, no extra: see 3858. 3½ **64**
3923 **HALABALOO 8** [1]3-8-11 BL (73) J F Egan 12/1: 3-50366: Keen in tch, wknd 2f out: tried blnks. 1¾ **60**
POETRY N PASSION [8]3-8-11 W Ryan 20/1: 7: b f Polish Precedent - Ghassanah (Pas de Seul) Slow away & al bhd on debut: bred to apprec 1m. 6 **50**
ABIGAIL ADAMS [10]3-8-11 D Holland 10/1: 8: Slow away & al bhd. ¾ **49**
8 Ran Time 1m 47.54(8.54) Owned: Usk Valley Stud Trained: Pulborough

CHESTER SATURDAY 21.08.04 Lefthand, Very Tight Track

Official Going SOFT.

4102

2.05 Blue Square 0800 587 0200 E B F Maiden Stakes 2yo (D)
£7280 £2240 £1120 **7f2y rnd** **Soft 112** **-10 Slow** Inside

3554 **CEIRIOG VALLEY 23** [2] B W Hills 2-8-9 M Hills 5/1: 01: b f In The Wings - Bodfari Quarry (Efisio) Chsd ldrs, short of room 2f out, prog to lead dist, pushed well clr fnl 1f, readily: clearly benefitted from recent debut: Feb foal, dam 9/12f wnr: sire a top-class mid-dist performer: eff over a sharp 7f, 1m+ shld suit: clrearly enjoys soft: potentially useful, win more races. **83+**
3878 **HAIBAN 10** [3] G A Butler 2-9-0 S W Kelly 8/1: 42: Chsd ldrs, went after wnr entering fnl 1f, not his pace: stays a sharp 7f on soft grnd: shld find a race: see 3878 (1m, debut). 8 **77**
3457 **ESKDALE 27** [15] R F Fisher 2-9-0 D Nolan(3) 66/1: 003: b g Perugino - Gilding The Lily (High Estate) Mid-div, styd on late, nvr dngrs on h'cap qual run: 11,000gns Mar foal: half-brother to a 10f wnr in Italy: sire a juv scorer: much imprvd over this longer 7f trip & on soft grnd: fine run from poor high draw. 2½ **73**
3411 **IGNITION 29** [9] W M Brisbourne 2-8-9 B Swarbrick(5) 33/1: 54: ch f Rock City - Fire Sprite ¾ **67**

(Mummy's Game) Mid-div, styd on late, nvr dngrs: Apr foal, cost 6,200gns: sister to mid-dist wnr TBM Can & half-sister sev wnrs, incl decent sprinter Always Alight: dam a dual 5f juv wnr, sire a high-class 2yo: imprvd run.
3735 **GRANDOS 16** [8]2-9-0 W Supple 25/1: 05: b c Cadeaux Genereux - No Reservations (Commanche Run) ½ 71
Chsd ldrs, btn fnl 1f: May foal, cost 37,000gns: half-brother to 6/7f wnr Hot Tin Roof: dam a 6f winning juv.
3544 **NASSEEM DUBAI 23** [16]2-9-0 P Mulrennan(3) 25/1: 06: Rear, keeping on when short of room dist. 1½ 69
2570 **MAKEPEACE 63** [12]2-9-0 A Culhane 20/1: 047: Rear, kept on late, nvr a factor: 9 wk abs, poor draw. 2½ 65
3511 **TOSHI 25** [1]2-9-0 S Chin 7/1: 08: Front rank, led halfway till dist, wknd qckly. ½ 64
3513 **LAYED BACK ROCKY 24** [14]2-9-0 S Righton 66/1: 69: Al bhd: poor draw. nk 63
3890 **MAJESTIC MOVEMENT 9** [10]2-9-0 K McEvoy 5/1: 50: 10th: Chsd ldrs 5f, wknd: modest draw. 2½ 59
EGYPTIAN LADY [11]2-8-9 T Hamilton(3) 66/1: 0: 11th: Slowly away, al bhd on racecourse bow. 6 44
2776 **ANSELLS LEGACY 55** [6]2-9-0 F Norton 50/1: 00: 12th: Slowly away, nvr a factor: 8 wk abs. 3 45
3633 **OXFORD STREET PETE 20** [7]2-9-0 R Winston 10/1: 30: 13th: Led till halfway, wknd qckly & eased. 10 30
3770 **ALDENTE 14** [4]2-8-9 S Sanders 5/2 FAV: 2P: Prog to chase ldrs when broke leg, sadly destroyed. 0
14 Ran Time 1m 33.6 (8.6) Owned: Mr R J McAlpine Trained: Lambourn

4103

2.40 Bet@Bluesq Com Handicap Stakes 3yo+ 0-100 (C) **[102]**
£14430 £4440 £2220 **7f122y rnd** **Soft 112** **+22 Fast** Inside

3277 **ZONUS 35** [14] B W Hills 3-9-2 BL (90) M Hills 8/1: 4230301: Held up, prog trav well when short of room 2f out, switched dist & sn led, pushed clr, readily: fast time, eff at 7/7.5f on fast & soft grnd: runs well fresh: impressive in first time blnks, follow-up with a repeat effort: see 2918. 100
3512* **PANGO 25** [10] H Morrison 5-9-3 (85) L Fletcher(3) 6/1: 0-221112: Chsd ldrs, imprvd to lead briefly dist, left bhd by wnr fnl 1f: lost little in defeat, acts on fast, soft grnd & both AWs: fine run from modest draw. 5 87
3809 **SEA STORM 13** [16] D R MacLeod 6-8-10 p (78) S Sanders 16/1: 0065643: Mid-div, kept on under press fnl 1f, not pace to chall: sound run from poor draw: acts on firm, soft grnd & polytrack: see 3809 & 2087. 2 76
3797 **NAMROUD 14** [8] R A Fahey 5-8-9 (77) P Hanagan 10/1: 0600004: Prom, led 2f out till dist, no extra: well h'capped now for in-form stable & worth keeping in mind back on preferred faster grnd: see 1035. 2 73+
3961 **HAWKIT 7** [11]3-8-4 T (78) Martin Dwyer 33/1: 1012005: Chsd ldrs, btn fnl 1f: t-strap, poor draw. 2 71
3942 **KIRKBYS TREASURE 7** [15]6-8-8 (76) F Lynch 12/1: 0120226: Held up, prog when short of room dist, nrst fin: not disgraced from poor high draw: see 3942 & 3562. 1 68
3512 **WINNING VENTURE 25** [1]7-8-13 (81) P Doe 11/2 FAV: 5-603207: Led till 2f out, wknd: nicely bckd. ½ 72
4047 **GLARAMARA 2** [5]3-9-9 (97) P Robinson 9/1: 3004448: Trkd ldrs trav well 6f, wknd. 1½ 86
3223 **STRONG HAND 37** [2]4-8-8 (76) P Mulrennan(3) 6/1: 110-6309: Trkd ldrs, wknd dist, sn eased: btr 1066. ¾ 64
3797 **TOUGH LOVE 14** [9]5-8-13 (81) D Allan 16/1: 0000050: 10th: Held up, nvr a factor: btr 3797 (fast). 1½ 67
3634 **H HARRISON 20** [3]4-8-11 (79) P Mathers(5) 14/1: 1003500: 11th: Slowly away, nvr a factor: see 3461. 5 58
3768 **TRUE NIGHT 14** [12]7-9-1 (83) R Winston 8/1: 0311300: 12th: Al rear: poor draw: btr 3634 & 3428 (gd). 1½ 60
3954+ **SAWWAAH 7** [17]7-9-2 (84) A Nicholls 18/1: 0030210: 13th: Al bhd, eased & t.o. fnl 1f: btr 3954 (fast). dist 0
13 Ran Time 1m 39.14 (6.74) Owned: Concord Racing Bonnycastle Grant Morton Trained: Lambourn

4104

3.15 Listed Blue Square Chester Rated Stakes Handicap 3yo+ 0-110 (A) **[114]**
£23200 £8800 £4400 **1m5f89y** **Soft 112** **-34 Slow** Inside

3777 **SWIFT TANGO 14** [3] E A L Dunlop 4-9-0 (100) P Hanagan 5/1: 1236431: Hld up, gd prog when short of room 1.5f out, switched wide & strong run to lead ins fnl 1f, rdn out: eff at 1m/12f, apprec this step up to 13f: acts on firm, soft grnd & polytrack: v tough & useful gelding who has been running well all season: see 3777. 107
4197} **MIDAS WAY 344** [4] P R Chamings 4-8-9 (95) S Sanders 8/1: 616320-2: ch g Halling - Arietta's Way (Darshaan) Tried to make all, not pace to repel wnr ins fnl 1f: reapp: trained by R Charlton to win at Salisbury (h'cap) in '03, has since been gelded: eff at 12/14f on firm & soft grnd: handles a sharp or gall trk: clearly runs well fresh & an excellent reapp. 1½ 100
2 Aug'03 York 13.9fm 97-93 B: 1 Jun'03 Sali 12fm 92-87 C: 1 Oct'02 Newb 8sft 88- D:
3777 **HAMBLEDEN 14** [7] M A Jarvis 7-8-10 (96) P Robinson 4/1 CO FAV: 6044063: Rdn in rear, styd on well fnl 1f, not quite get there: change of tactics, usually front runs: see 2948. ½ 100
3776 **ALBANOV 14** [9] M Johnston 4-8-9 (1oh) (94) S Chin 4/1 CO FAV: 4522-004: Chsd ldrs, ev ch entering fnl 1f, no extra cl-home: lightly rcd this term: see 3531 (tried blnks). nk 97
3777* **DESERT QUEST 14** [5]4-8-9 (1oh)bl (94) Martin Dwyer 4/1 CO FAV: 1-024015: Trkd ldrs, ev ch dist, wknd cl-home: btr 3777 (gd grnd). ½ 97
3233 **DELSARTE 36** [2]4-9-7 t (107) K McEvoy 4/1 CO FAV: 034-0256: Prom, ev ch till wknd fnl 1f: top-weight: unsuited by today's soft grnd, much btr on a fast surface: see 1757. ¾ 108
6 Ran Time 3m 09.33 (19.53) Owned: Mr Khalifa Sultan Trained: Newmarket

4105

3.50 Blue Square Pays Double Results Conditions Stakes Colts & Geldings 2yo (C)
£9118 £3458 £1729 **6f18y rnd** **Soft 112** **-01 Slow** Inside

3817* **CUPIDS GLORY 12** [2] Sir Mark Prescott 2-8-10 S Sanders 5/2: 611: Trkd ldrs, qcknd to lead ins fnl 1f, pushed clr, going away: well bckd, gd juv time: stays 7f, seems suited by 6f: acts on soft grnd & polytrack, likes a sharp trk: fast improving into a useful juv & deserves a step into List/Group company now: see 3817. 103
3532 **DAHTEER 24** [5] M R Channon 2-8-13 (90) A Culhane 9/1: 411602: Front rank, led briefly dist, left bhd by wnr ins fnl 1f: acts on fast & soft grnd: return to 7f shld suit, see 2367. 3½ 95
3824* **ONE PUTRA 12** [6] M A Jarvis 2-8-13 P Robinson 4/6 FAV: 513: Trkd ldrs, led dist till ins fnl 1f, no extra: hvly bckd: not disgraced but btr on gd grnd in 3824. ½ 93
3939 **WIZARDMICKTEE 7** [3] A Bailey 2-8-10 R Winston 12/1: 0224: Led till dist, wknd: will find easier races. 11 68
3935 **DEN PERRY 7** [1]2-8-10 P P Mathers(5) 40/1: 6000005: Al outpcd: tried cheek pieces: outclassed. 20 28
5 Ran Time 1m 19.89 (6.79) Owned: Hesmonds Stud Trained: Newmarket

CHESTER   SATURDAY 21.08.04   Lefthand, Very Tight Track

4106   4.25 Blue Square Games Handicap Stakes 3yo+ 0-85 (D)   [85]
£7020 £2160 £1080   1m7f195y   Soft 112   -25 Slow   Inside

3760 **DR SHARP** 15 [5] T P Tate 4-9-8 (79) R Winston 9/2: 0121061: Chsd ldrs, imprvd to lead 3f out,   87
styd on strongly, rdn out: eff at 14f/2m on gd & soft: acts on a gall or sharp trk: back to form, thorough stayer.
3359 **MASTER WELLS** 30 [10] J D Bethell 3-8-4 (75) P Hanagan 10/1: 1002002: Held up, hdwy 3f out, styd   1¼ 81
on fnl 1f & nrst fin: apprec return to fav'd soft grnd & clearly likes Chester: see 2746 (12f here).
3531 **ALMIZAN** 24 [13] M R Channon 4-9-11 vis (82) A Culhane 8/1: 4-004043: Held up, hdwy 3f out, nrst   hd 88
fin: thorough stayer, acts on firm & soft grnd: see 3531 (2m5f, first time visor).
3181 **CONTACT DANCER** 39 [14] M Johnston 5-9-13 (84) S Chin 10/1: 012/56-64: Rear, styd on under press   ½ 89
fnl 2f, nrst fin: top-weight, well clr rem: gd run: see 3181.
3810 **TONI ALCALA** 13 [15]5-9-6 (77) P Mulrennan(3) 14/1: 2451155: Held up, nvr nr ldrs: btr 3701.   15 67
2963* **LUCKY JUDGE** 48 [6]7-9-2 (73) K McEvoy 3/1 FAV: 4015116: Nvr nr to chall: nicely bckd, 7 wk abs.   1¾ 61
3531 **TERESA** 24 [7]4-9-2 (73) P Robinson 8/1: 3-266007: Front rank, wknd 2f out: reportedly hung right.   1¾ 59
3703* **ASTYANAX** 17 [4]4-9-5 (76) S Sanders 8/1: 41-05018: Nvr nrr than mid-div: op 6/1: btr 3703 (g/f).   12 50
3964 **RAJAM** 6 [12]6-9-6 (77) A Nicholls 25/1: 6522409: Nvr nr ldrs: qck reapp: longer trip, see 3437 (12f).   8 43
3918 **GONDOLIN** 8 [9]4-9-11 VIS (82) S W Kelly 25/1: 20345-00: 10th: Led till 3f out, wknd qckly &   30 18
eased: too keen in first time visor & not stay this longer 2m trip: see 3918.
3819* **ROLEX FREE** 12 [2]6-7-12 (4oh)vis (51) D Fentiman(7) 14/1: 0031410: 11th: Front rank till after   20 0
halfway, sn wknd & eased: see 3819 (12f, AW).
3549 **BRAVELY DOES IT** 23 [11]4-8-1 (2ow) (56) Martin Dwyer 25/1: 00620: 12th: Trkd ldrs till halfway,   dist 0
sn wknd & t.o. in last: btr 3549 (14f, firm grnd).
12 Ran   Time 3m 44.7 (22)   Owned: The Ivy Syndicate   Trained: Tadcaster

4107   4.55 Blue Square Casino Handicap Stakes 3yo+ 0-85 (D)   [83]
£6890 £2120 £1060   5f16y rnd   Soft 112   -10 Slow   Inside

4010 **KINGS COLLEGE BOY** 4 [10] R A Fahey 4-8-6 bl (61) Dale Gibson 16/1: 3030301: Held up, gd hdwy ent   71
str, strong run to lead ins fnl 1f, rdn out: qck reapp & fine run from mod high draw: deserved win, plcd many times
this season: eff at 5/6f on firm & soft: handles a gall or tight trk & suited by blnks: see 3680.
3279 **ENDLESS SUMMER** 35 [1] A W Carroll 7-9-4 (73) P Doe 10/1: 5504602: Held up, short of room   1½ 79
halfway, switched wide entering straight, fin well but not reach wnr: slow start negated advantage of low draw:
well h'capped now, but technically a mdn after disqualification of early career wins: see 2779 & 921.
3903 **PRINCE OF BLUES** 9 [8] M Mullineaux 6-8-2 bl (57) A McCarthy 14/1: 5003033: Chsd ldrs, onepcd fnl 1f.   3½ 56
3852 **HOUT BAY** 10 [5] R A Fahey 7-8-1 (56) P Hanagan 4/1: 00-13624: Chsd ldrs, onepcd fnl 1f: see 3852.   hd 54
3989 **STRENSALL** 5 [3]7-9-7 (76) T Eaves(3) 11/1: 3405055: Chsd ldrs, onepcd fnl 1f: qck reapp.   hd 73
3960 **THE LORD** 7 [4]4-9-12 (81) L Treadwell(5) 8/1: 00-30606: Led early, remained prom & regained lead   1½ 75
halfway, hdd ins fnl 1f & no extra: gd low draw: prob best on fast grnd: see 3388.
3106 **FRASCATI** 42 [2]4-9-8 (77) P Mathers(5) 7/2 FAV: 3011207: Held up, nvr dngrs: gamble from 6/1, abs.   4 63
3942 **LAUREL DAWN** 7 [12]6-8-3 (58) Natalia Gemelova(7) 28/1: 5060008: Chsd ldrs, btn sn after halfway.   nk 43
3503 **THE FISIO** 25 [7]4-9-5 vis (74) Martin Dwyer 14/1: 4102009: Prom, wkng when short of room halfway.   3 53
3463 **IZMAIL** 27 [13]5-9-1 (70) F P Ferris(3) 8/1: 0000100: 10th: Prom wide, wknd dist: new stable   6 37
(prev with D Nicholls): poor high draw: twice below 3228 (fast grnd).
4005 **BRAVE BURT** 4 [6]7-10-0 (83) S Sanders 4/1: 3-000200: 11th: Led till after halfway, wknd: qck   13 24
reapp & top-weight: 'nvr trav': twice below 3960 (fast grnd).
3852 **BLUE MAEVE** 10 [11]4-8-6 (61) S Righton 14/1: 4242150: 12th: Chsd ldrs 3f, wknd: btr 3667.   ½ 1
12 Ran   Time 1m 05.94(6.14)   Owned: The Dandy Dons Partnership   Trained: Malton

LINGFIELD   Polytrack   SATURDAY 21.08.04   Lefthand, Sharp, Undulating Track

Official Going GOOD/SOFT.

4108   5.20 Kgn Pillinger Maiden Auction Stakes 2yo (E)
£3806 £1171 £586   6f str   Good   Inapplicable   Stands Side

3824 **SUDDEN DISMISSAL** 12 [16] G A Butler 2-8-11 J Murtagh 11/8 FAV: 41: With ldr, hdwy to lead over   93
1f out, rdn clr over 1f out, cmftbly: bckd: eff over a sharp 6f, 7f sure to suit: acts on gd: progressive.
3824 **ENFORCER** 12 [17] W R Muir 2-8-9 S Drowne 9/2: 452: In tch, eff to chase wnr over 1f out, kept   2½ 83
on same pace: similar dist bhd this wk next time & eff at 6f on gd grnd: shld find a race: see 3478.
PINAFORE [11] H Morrison 2-8-2 D Kinsella 25/1: 3: ch f Fleetwood - Shi Shi (Alnasr Alwasheek)   2½ 69
In tch, eff 2f out, some late gains, nrst fin: Jan first foal: eff at 6f on gd grnd: encouraging start.
3907 **GENERAL HAIGH** 8 [20] J R Best 2-8-11 N Pollard 20/1: 644: Made most till over 1f out, no extra: 1 75
btr run at 6f on gd grnd: now quals for nurs h'caps: see 3600.
3020 **BAMZOOKI** 45 [12]2-8-4 O Urbina 8/1: 45: In tch trav well, onepcd dist: 6 wk abs: btr 3020.   1 65
3451 **LUCIFEROUS** 28 [15]2-8-4 R Miles(3) 16/1: 56: Veered right start, in tch, wknd dist: see 3451.   hd 64
3848 **CABIN FEVER** 11 [18]2-8-2 R Thomas(5) 25/1: 057: In tch, wknd & hmpd 2f out: see 3848.   2½ 55
3988 **SEASON TICKET** 5 [14]2-8-2 M Henry 10/1: 08: b f Kornado - Second Game (Second Set) Bhd, nvr a   ½ 53
factor: Apr foal, cost £7,500.
3376 **METHODICAL** 30 [7]2-8-3 (1ow) R Mullen 8/1: 49: In tch, wknd over 1f out: op 14/1: see 3376.   1 51
3544 **CROCODILE KISS** 23 [2]2-8-9 T P Queally 12/1: 550: 10th: Sn bhd, nvr a factor: see 3183.   2 51

Summer Charm [6]2-8-2 Hayley Turner(5) 66/1:0   3399 **Before The Dawn** 29 [10]2-8-2 C Catlin 33/1:0
3962 **Beau Marche** 6 [4]2-8-7 (1ow) I Mongan 66/1:0   **Slip Catch** [19]2-8-2 Lisa Jones 50/1:0
Bobs Flyer [13]2-8-4 J Mackay 20/1:0   **Amigra** [1]2-8-2 J F McDonald(3) 33/1:0
Sergeant Small [9]2-8-9 G Carter 66/1:0   3907 **Aleshanee** 8 [8]2-8-6 D Sweeney 66/1:0

18 Ran   Time 1m 11.82 (3.02)   Owned: The Schtum Partnership   Trained: Blewbury

---

4109   **5.50 Dreams Of Eastwell Manor Handicap Stakes Fillies 3yo+ 0-70 (E)**   **[69]**
£3582 £1102 £551   **6f str**   **Good**   **Inapplicable** Stands Side

3789 **FAIR COMPTON 14** [6] R Hannon 3-9-2 (57) R L Moore 10/1: 4654551: With ldr, narrow lead just ins   **64**
last, styd on wk out: eff at 6f on fast & gd grnd: confidence boosting first win today: see 1690.
3672 **I WISH 18** [2] M Madgwick 6-9-5 (57) G Baker 9/2: 1553022: Held up, hdwy over 1f out, styd on ins   hd **62**
last, just held for press: in gd form: see 3672, 1806.
3789 **STOKESIES WISH 14** [8] J L Spearing 4-9-8 (60) Hayley Turner(5) 7/2: 0540633: Keen, made most,   hd **65**
kept on till collared ins last, just held: encouraging run but 1 win in 28: see 2535, 1127.
4976} **RIQUEWIHR 294** [10] D R Loder 4-9-8 (60) T P Queally 7/1: 10-4: ch f Compton Place - Juvenilia   shd **64**
(Masterclass) In tch, eff well over 1f out, kept on ins last, just held in a close fin: prev with J Toller, reapp:
won a mdn in '03: eff at 6f on fast & gd grnd: has gone well fresh: encouraging return, lightly rcd.
1 Sep'03 Yarm 6.0g/f 56- D:
3911 **CUT RIDGE 8** [9]5-9-3 (55) E Ahern 13/8 FAV: 0032125: In tch, eff dist, sn onepace: clr rem, bckd.   1¾ **54**
3799 **LA VIE EST BELLE 13** [5]3-9-10 (65) G Baker 12/1: 0-604006: Keen with ldrs, wknd 2f out: see 1570.   5 **49**
3543 **ALIZAR 23** [7]3-9-2 (57) Lisa Jones 25/1: 6010007: Held up, btn 2f out: best 2435.   1¾ **36**
3456 **BAYONET 28** [3]8-8-2 (40) J F McDonald(3) 40/1: 00000-08: In tch, wknd 2f out: see 3456.   3 **10**
4041 **BELLS BEACH 2** [1]6-8-7 (45) R Mullen 12/1: 4150009: Al bhd.   2 **9**
3672 **AVERRLLINE 18** [4]3-9-5 T (60) D Kinsella 20/1: 210-0000: 10th: Slow away & al bhd: tried a t-strap.   5 **9**
10 Ran   Time 1m 11.23 (2.53)   Owned: Jubert Family   Trained: Marlborough

---

4110   **6.20 Kmfm: West Kent's Winning Music Station Handicap Stakes 3yo 0-80 (D)**   **[84]**
£5681 £1748 £874   **7f str**   **Good**   **Inapplicable** Stands Side

3846 **STEVEDORE 11** [2] B R Millman 3-8-13 (69) G Baker 20/1: 0004151: With ldr, hdwy to lead dist,   **77**
styd on well ins last, rdn out: suited by 7f now, stays a sharp 1m: acts on firm & gd grnd & fibresand, any trk.
2692* **POLAR MAGIC 58** [3] J R Fanshawe 3-9-0 (70) J Murtagh 1/1 FAV: 12: Keen in tch, eff to chase wnr   hd **77**
over 1f out, chall ins last, just held: abs, bckd: acts on soft & gd: going the right way, win a h'cap: see 2692.
3860 **CORKY 10** [9] R Hannon 3-9-7 (77) R L Moore 8/1: 43103: In tch, eff well over 1f out, onepcd fnl   1¾ **80**
1f: op 6/1: back to best on an easier surface: see 3048 (mdn).
3746* **UNITED SPIRIT 15** [5] M A Magnusson 3-8-9 bl (65) E Ahern 7/1: 4-063114: Keen, set pace till over   1¼ **65**
1f out, no extra: btr 3746 (polytrack).
3179 **SWEET REPLY 39** [8]3-9-3 (73) T P Queally 25/1: 4-051005: In tch, wknd over 1f out: best 2259.   1¼ **70**
3724 **PRINCESS GALADRIEL 16** [1]3-8-2 (58) D Kinsella 16/1: 1320636: Held up, eff & hung left 2f out, wknd.   ¾ **53**
3860 **LORIEN HILL 10** [4]3-9-3 (73) D Holland 4/1: 5102037: Nvr a factor: btr 3860 (fast grnd), 2169.   ½ **67**
4029 **DR SYNN 3** [6]3-8-10 (66) M Tebbutt 8/1: 6365028: Al bhd: btr 4029.   3½ **53**
3923 **MUTASSEM 8** [7]3-8-9 (65) M Henry 100/1: 6-00009: Keen in tch, wknd 2f out: see 3923.   8 **36**
9 Ran   Time 1m 24.0 (3.6)   Owned: Mrs S Clifford   Trained: Cullompton

---

Official Going STANDARD.

4111   **6.50 Mercedes-Benz Direct Maiden Stakes 3yo+ (D)**
£3640 £1120 £560   **1m4f aw**   **Going 44**   **+06 Fast** Inside

3742 **RED DAMSON 15** [12] Sir Mark Prescott 3-8-12 (80) J Mackay 7/2: 40222-21: Led early, remained   **84a**
prom, regained lead 4f out, rdn clr fnl 1f: op 2f: long overdue win: eff at 12/14f, shld stay 2m: acts
on fast, gd/soft & polytrack, prob handles firm: see 3742.
2793 **DALISAY 54** [7] Sir Michael Stoute 3-8-7 (74) K Fallon 5/2 FAV: 0-332: Trkd ldrs, went after wnr   2½ **75a**
3f out, no impress fnl 1f: op 11/8, 8 wk abs: eff at 10/12f on fast grnd & polytrack: see 2793.
2980 **MOUFTARI 47** [13] B W Hills 3-8-12 (80) D Holland 3/1: 0-54523: Sn led, hdd 4f out, onepcd after: 3½ **75a**
bckd from 5/1, 7 wk abs: eff at 10/12f on fast grnd & polytrack: see 2980.
       ALPH [6] R Ingram 7-9-8   R Havlin 100/1: 4: b g Alflora - Royal Birthday (St Paddy) Mid-div,   nk **74a**
kept on under press fnl 1f, nvr nrr on Flat debut: clr of rem: 7th in a nov hdle on hdles bow 3 months ago (rtd
96h): half-brother to smart hdler Royal Derby: eff at 12f on polytrack.
3631 **SUNSHINE ON ME 20** [10]3-8-7 R Mullen 20/1: 05: ch f Kris - Degannwy (Caerleon) Dwelt, well   7 **59a**
bhd, some late hdwy, nvr dngrs: mid-dist bred: with C Wall.
3740 **ROLLSWOOD 16** [8]4-9-8 p G Carter 25/1: 566: Keen & prom, wknd 2f out.   nk **63a**
3480 **CONSTRUCTOR 26** [1]3-8-12   D Sweeney 50/1: 07: b g So Factual - Love And Kisses (Salse) Trkd   shd **63a**
ldrs, btn 2f out: lightly rcd & only modest form: see C Cyzer.
3605 **MADAME MARIE 21** [9]4-9-3 (48) Lisa Jones 33/1: 0206006: Slowly away, nvr nr ldrs.   ¾ **56a$**
       SADLERS ROCK [5]6-9-8   R L Moore 7/1: 9: Slowly away, al towards rear on Flat debut.   1 **59a**
3854 **ABBEYGATE 10** [15]3-8-12 (64) M Henry 33/1: 006-000: 10th: Well bhd, nvr a factor.   hd **58a**
3675 **SO DETERMINED 18** [3]3-8-12 (60) E Ahern 10/1: 00-020: 11th: Nvr btn than mid-div: btr 3675 (turf).   3 **54a**
3802 **PATTERSON 13** [4]3-8-7 A Daly 66/1: 00: 12th: Chsd ldrs 1m, sn wknd.   10 **34a**
       CHARING CROSS [11]3-8-12 R Brisland 25/1: 0: 13th: Slowly away, al bhd on debut.   1 **37a**
3208 **PETERS PLOY 37** [2]4-9-8 J P Guillambert(3) 100/1: 000: 14th: Held up, al rear, t.o.: no form.   dist **0a**
3449 **STYLISH DANCER 28** [14]3-8-8 (1ow) (47) I Mongan 50/1: 05060: 15th: Al bhd, t.o. in last.   6 **0a**
15 Ran   Time 2m 33.78 (4.58)   Owned: W E Sturt-Osborne House V   Trained: Newmarket

LINGFIELD   Polytrack   SATURDAY 21.08.04   Lefthand, Sharp Track

4112   7.20 Mercedes-Benz Direct Claiming Stakes 3-4yo   (E)
£4225 £1300 £650   **1m2f aw**   **Going 44**   -07 Slow   Inside

3950 **BELISCO** 7 [1] Mrs A J Perrett 3-9-2 BL t (69) J Murtagh 7/1: 50-0061: Trkd ldrs, smooth hdwy to **70a**
lead dist, styd on well despite drifting left, rdn out: eff over a sharp 10f on polytrack: wears a t-strap,
sharpened up by blnks today: apprec drop in grade, see 3471.
3739* **ONE UPMANSHIP** 16 [4] J G Portman 3-9-2 (65) R L Moore 5/1: 0632612: Trkd ldrs, went after wnr   2   **66a**
fnl 1f, no impress cl-home: eff at 7/10f on gd, fast grnd & polytrack: continues in fine form, see 3739 (turf).
3419 **CANNI THINKAAR** 28 [6] P W Harris 3-8-6 (59) E Ahern 11/1: 6-600403: Prom, styd on under press   1¼   **53a**
fnl 1f, not pace of wnr: apprec this drop into claim grade, eff at 10f on gd grnd & polytrack: see 2345.
3404 **MARIA BONITA** 29 [11] R M Beckett 3-8-7 bl (63) D Holland 8/1: 03-40404: Held up, gd hdwy when   shd   **53a+**
short of room dist, nrst fin: apprec this drop in grade, did not get the run of today's race & poss a shade unlucky:
eff at 10f on fast grnd & polytrack: see 2979.
3706 **ESPERANCE** 17 [8]4-9-2 (48) S Hitchcott(3) 20/1: 0055055: Held up, some late hdwy, nvr dngrs.   ½   **53a**
3195 **FRENCH GIGOLO** 38 [10]4-9-4 (59) G Carter 20/1: 00/000-46: Prom, led 3f out till dist, wknd: see 3195.   3½   **50a**
2319 **PLATINUM PIRATE** 73 [5]3-9-6 vis (61) Darren Williams 7/1: 2136547: Nvr btr than mid-div: 10 wk abs.   ½   **59a**
3819 **ANOTHER CON** 12 [2]3-8-6 (1ow) (60) K Fallon 7/4 FAV: 5002058: Led till 3f out, wkng when hmpd   1½   **43a**
dist: well bckd from 3/1: see 2065.
3300 **BRETTON** 33 [12]3-9-6 (44) B Reilly(3) 33/1: 4430259: Al rear: see 3025.   nk   **56a$**
3480 **RICHIE BOY** 26 [9]3-9-6 (64) M Henry 14/1: 0-060: 10th: Dwelt, prog wide 2f out, sn btn: longer trip.   shd   **56a**
3895 **ZALKANI** 9 [3]4-9-2 (61) A Hindley(7) 25/1: 0050040: 11th: Held up, prog when hmpd over 1f out, no   nk   **43a**
ch after: lost al ch when hmpd & worth another chance: see 3895.
3748 **ESTRELLA LEVANTE** 15 [7]4-8-13 p (38) Lisa Jones 66/1: 3060000: 12th: Front rank, wknd 3f out.   6   **30a**
3874 **AUROVILLE** 10 [13]3-9-2 (57) R Mullen 8/1: 050062P: Mid-div, t.o./p.u. fnl 1f: reportedly lost action.   **0a**
13 Ran   Time 2m 07.89 (5.09)   Owned: Mr Michael H Watt   Trained: Pulborough

4113   7.50 Burden Group Handicap Stakes 3yo 35-55   (F)   [63]
£3066 £876 £438   **1m2f aw**   **Going 44**   -18 Slow   Inside

3580 **MISTER COMPLETELY** 22 [11] J R Best 3-9-0 (49) T P Queally 16/1: 0001601: Chsd ldrs, eff 2f out,   **55a**
styd on well to lead cl-home, drvn out: eff at 6f, suited by 1m/10f now, has tried 2m: acts on firm grnd &
polytrack, sharp/undul or stiff/turning trk: see 2667 (seller).
3967 **NINA FONTENAIL** 6 [10] B R Millman 3-8-5 (40) R Havlin 12/1: 6-000542: Held up, hdwy 2f out, fin   nk   **45a**
strongly but just btn: op 9/1: will apprec a rtn to 12f: acts on polytrack: see 3849 (12f mdn).
3292 **SIXTILSIX** 33 [3] W Jarvis 3-8-6 (1ow) (40) R Lappin 33/1: 0000-003: ch c Night Shift - Assafiyah   ¾   **44a**
(Kris) Trkd ldrs trav well, eff to lead briefly ins fnl 1f, no extra: modest imprvd form: modest for J Fox in '03,
also when trained in native Ireland: eff over a sharp 10f on polytrack.
3516 **MR BELVEDERE** 24 [6] A J Lidderdale 3-9-2 (51) E Ahern 10/1: 0003204: Mid-div, short of room 2f   ½   **53a**
out, kept on under press fnl 1f: op 16/1: stays an easy 10f on polytrack: see 2431 (1m seller, turf).
3449 **RUBAIYAT** 28 [13]3-9-4 (53) J F Egan 5/4 FAV: 6-004325: Held up, hdwy wide to lead 2f out, hdd dist.   ¾   **53a**
4032 **SONDERBORG** 3 [7]3-9-1 bl (50) Lisa Jones 10/1: 2600066: Held up & outpcd, styd on late, nvr dngrs.   1   **48a**
3715 **FIDDLES MUSIC** 16 [1]3-8-5 (40) C Catlin 14/1: 0145657: Prom, led 3f out till 2f out, wknd.   3   **33a**
3982 **FORGE LANE** 5 [12]3-9-3 bl (52) R L Moore 4/1: 0042008: Chsd ldrs, short of rm 2f out & no ch after.   7   **35a**
3300 **PRINCE VALENTINE** 33 [9]3-9-3 (52) M Tebbutt 20/1: 0354049: Trkd ldrs, wknd qckly dist.   nk   **34a**
2978 **ALMOST WELCOME** 47 [2]3-9-0 (49) I Mongan 25/1: 0035000: 10th: Al bhd: 7 wk abs.   1¾   **28a**
3874 **TSHUKUDU** 10 [8]3-8-1 (36) D Kinsella 20/1: 0-000030: 11th: Prom 6f, sn btn: btr 3874 (turf).   8   **3a**
3746 **DREAM OF DUBAI** 15 [4]3-9-1 P (50) K Fallon 7/1: 5-000000: 12th: Led till 3f out, wkng when hmpd 2f out. 2½   **13a**
12 Ran   Time 2m 08.98(6.18)   Owned: G G Racing   Trained: Maidstone

FOLKESTONE   SUNDAY 22.08.04   Righthand, Sharpish, Undulating Track

Official Going Good

4114   1.50 Garden Of England Maiden Auction Stakes Div 1 2yo   (E)
£3572 £1099 £550   **7f str**   **Good 41**   -09 Slow   Stands side

3520 **INNOCENT SPLENDOUR** 25 [12] E A L Dunlop 2-8-6 E Ahern 1/1 FAV: 21: In tch far side, styd on to   **83**
lead ins fnl 1f, pushed out, val 4L+: well bckd: eff at 7f, further shld suit: acts on fast, gd grnd & a
sharp/undul trk: won with something in hand & looks sure to progress: see 3520 (debut).
3803 **BRIANNSTA** 14 [16] M R Channon 2-8-9 S Hitchcott(3) 7/1: 652: Cl-up far side, led 3f out, hdd   2½   **78**
under press ins fnl 1f, no extra: eff at 7f, return to 1m will suit: gd run in defeat & now quals for h'caps: see 3803.
3399 **KAPAJE** 30 [10] P D Evans 2-8-2 Joanna Badger 25/1: 053: Prom far side, no extra ins fnl 1f: nk   **70**
eff at 6f, imprvd for step up to 7f: quals for h'caps: see 3399.
3489 **RINGAROOMA** 27 [8] M H Tompkins 2-8-8 P Robinson 12/1: 504: b f Erhaab - Tatouma (The Minstrel)   ½   **70**
Chsd ldrs far side till dist, sn onepcd: Mar foal, cost 10,000gns: half-sister successful at 7f: dam dual sprint
wnr at 2: sire Gr 1 wnr at 10f: quals for h'caps: see 3489: encouraging effort.
OASIS WAY 0 [13]2-8-4 R L Moore 33/1: 5: b f Wadood - Northern Moon (Ile de Bourbon) Missed   hd   **70**
break, bhd far side, prog bef 1f out, nrst fin: debut: Feb foal, cost 12,000gns: dam successful at 2: sire useful
performer as a juv: eff at 7f, further will suit: acts on gd grnd: pleasing eff after racing greenly.
STAR SIDE 0 [15]2-8-9 S Drowne 33/1: 6: b c Ashkalani - Rachel Pringle (Doulab) Nvr nrr than   4   **67**
mid-div far side: debut: Mar foal, half-brother to smart sprint/miler performer Cobourg Lodge: dam plcd at 5f.
3489 **DOUBLE KUDOS** 27 [14]2-9-0 I Mongan 7/2: 27: Prom far side over 5f, wknd: disapp eff: failed   ½   **71**
to build on promise shown in 3489 (debut).
MANGROVE CAY 0 [3]2-8-11 T P Queally 14/1: 8: Made all stands side group, no ch with far side   shd   **67**
group: debut: prob disadvantage by racing on unfav'd stands side & can rate higher.
3559 **KUMALA OCEAN** 24 [11]2-8-2 J Bramhill 33/1: 259: Led far side group 4f, sn wknd: see 3394.   1½   **55**
3601 **RHOSLAN** 22 [6]2-8-11 J D Smith 100/1: 000: 10th: Al in rear.   1   **62**
BONNABEE 0 [2]2-8-2 R Mullen 50/1: 0: 11th: Missed break, in tch stands side, outpcd halfway,   1½   **50**

1239

rallied late: debut: unseated rider bef start.
3962 **Silver Creek 7** [4]2-8-7 P Doe 100/1:0
3329 **Play Up Pompey 32** [7]2-8-7 J F McDonald(3) 100/1:0
     Luna Blu 0 [9]2-8-2 Hayley Turner(5) 100/1:0   3927 **Gurrun 9** [1]2-9-0 K Fallon 16/1:0
15 Ran   Time 1m 27.70 (3.5)   Owned: The Granite Partnership   Trained: Newmarket

---

4115   **2.20 Garden Of England Maiden Auction Stakes Div 2 2yo (E)**
         £3572 £1099 £550   **7f str**   **Good 41**   **-12 Slow**   Stands side

3329 **FONG SHUI 32** [10] P J Makin 2-8-9   D Sweeney 9/2: 401: In tch, styd on to lead bef 1f out, sn   **85**
clr, idled cl home, rdn out: op 7/1: eff at 7f on gd grnd: acts on a sharp/undul trk: improving.
3774 **GROUP CAPTAIN 15** [11] S Kirk 2-8-9 (88) R L Moore 11/4 FAV: 542202: Handy, short of room 2f out,   nk   **83**
sn outpcd, styd on well ins fnl 1f, nrst fin: gd run in defeat, shld find similar at a mile: see 3467.
     RED RIVER ROCK 0 [1] C Tinkler 2-8-9   S Hitchcott(3) 66/1: 3: b c Spectrum - Ann's Annie (Alzao)   ½   **87**
In tch, prog bef 1f out, kept on well, not btn far in 3rd: debut: Apr first foal, cost 24,000gns: dam successful
at 6f: sire Gr 1 wnr at 1m/10f: eff at 7f, further will suit: acts on gd grnd: impr for today's experience.
3736 **DIAMONDS AND DUST 17** [6] M H Tompkins 2-8-7   P Robinson 4/1: 434: Led, hdd over 1f out, styd on   hd   **79**
ins fnl 1f, not btn far: eff at 6f, ran to form on step up to 7f: now quals for h'caps: see 3736 & 3280.
3803 **CALL ME MAX 14** [8]2-8-7   E Ahern 8/1: 435: Prom when no room after 2f, held under press when no   1   **84**
room cl-home: just btr 3803 (1m).
     PRINCELYWALLYWOGAN 0 [15]2-8-7   T P Queally 25/1: 6: b c Princely Heir - Dublivia (Midyan)   Bhd,   2½   **72**
hdwy 2f out, nrst fin: debut: Mar foal, cost 2,500gns: half-brother successful at 7f: eff on gd grnd: imp plcd.
2995 **UNCLE BULGARIA 47** [14]2-8-9   L Keniry(3) 25/1: 37: Nvr nrr than mid-div: see 2995.   1   **70**
     WATER PISTOL 0 [13]2-9-0   S Drowne 12/1: 8: Nvr nrr than mid-div: op 9/1 on debut.   ¾   **75**
3601 **FLAG POINT 22** [16]2-8-11   K Fallon 66/1: 309: Handy ove 5f, sn no extra: 3/1: twice below 2695.   ¾   **70**
3939 **HOWS THAT 8** [5]2-8-2   R Mullen 66/1: 0000: 10th: Cl-up 5f, sn wknd: see 3582.   2½   **56**
3478 **Coombe Centenary 27** [3]2-8-2 P Doe 100/1:0   3633 **Laurollie 21** [12]2-8-2 A Daly 100/1:0
3882 **Volitio 10** [9]2-8-11 P Dobbs 66/1:0   3721 **Speedie Rossini 17** [4]2-8-9 J Bramhill 50/1:0
14 Ran   Time 1m 27.96 (3.76)   Owned: Camamile Hessert Scott Partnership   Trained: Marlborough

---

4116   **2.50 Come Racing In Kent Handicap Stakes 3yo 35-55 (F)**   **[65]**
         £3052 £872 £436   **6f str**   **Good 41**   **-01 Slow**   Stands side

3900* **DANIFAH 10** [14] P D Evans 3-9-5 (56) K Fallon 11/8 FAV: 0044611: Made all far side group, edged   **62**
left under press dist, edged right ins fnl 1f, pushed out, val bit more: eff at 5/7 on firm & gd/soft grnd: remains
well h'capped & shld land hat-trick: see 3900.
3058 **ROCKLEY BAY 45** [13] P J Makin 3-9-4 T (55) D Sweeney 25/1: 54-00002: In tch far side, styd on to   1¼   **53**
chase wnr dist, al held ins fnl 1f: 6 wk abs: eff at 6f on gd grnd: imprvd with fitting of t-strap, see 2619.
3480 **CRIMSON STAR 27** [11] C Tinkler 3-8-1 (38) D Kinsella 25/1: 00003: Al cl-up, no extra fnl 1f: 1¾   **33**
eff at 6f on gd grnd: see 1610.
4043 **SCARLETT BREEZE 3** [1] J W Hills 3-8-9 (46) Derek Nolan(4) 20/1: 0050404: Rcd alone stands side,   1   **38+**
al on terms with far side group, no extra from dist: qck reapp: eff at 6f on gd grnd: gd eff racing on unfav'd
stands side alone & is worth bearing in mind for similar: see 2649.
3094 **ESSEX STAR 44** [12]3-8-11 (48) B Reilly(3) 10/1: 000-0335: Prom, no extra dist: 6 wk abs: btr 3094.   nk   **39**
3155 **EMPEROR CAT 41** [9]3-8-8 (45) J Bramhill 28/1: 3000066: Bhd, prog halfway, onepcd fnl 1f: 6 wk abs.   hd   **35**
3687 **LORD WISHINGWELL 18** [10]3-8-0 (37) C Catlin 20/1: 0330467: Nvr nrr than mid-div: btr 3413.   1¾   **22**
3677 **COSTA DEL SOL 19** [2]3-7-12 (3oh) (32) J F McDonald(3) 50/1: 1040068: Nvr nrr than mid-div: btr 3301.   nk   **19**
3911 **PINK SUPREME 9** [6]3-8-12 (49) T P Queally 7/1: 0006049: Handy over 4f, wknd: btr 3911.   3   **24**
3870 **PARDON MOI 11** [8]3-8-6 (43) Hayley Turner(5) 12/1: 0400600: 10th: Al bhd: btr 2925.   ¾   **16**
3725 **LAKESIDE GUY 17** [4]3-9-4 (55) R L Moore 10/1: 4035620: 11th: Mid-div 4f, wknd: btr 3725 (5f, fast).   nk   **27**
3485 **TSARBUCK 27** [5]3-8-12 vis (49) E Ahern 6/1: 5252330: 12th: Chsd ldrs 4f, wknd: op 8/1: btr 3485 (AW).   shd   **20**
3677 **Jasmine Pearl 19** [3]3-8-7 (44) M Halford(7) 20/1:0   1985 **Joans Jewel 89** [7]3-8-11 (48) A McCarthy 33/1:0
14 Ran   Time 1m 53.55 (2.55)   Owned: Mr E A R Morgans   Trained: Abergavenny

---

4117   **3.20 Helen Santer 12th Birthday Classified Stakes 3yo+ 0-70 (E)**
         £4251 £1308 £654   **7f str**   **Good 41**   **+07 Fast**   Stands side

3821 **ARCTIC DESERT 13** [4] A M Balding 4-9-7 (72) K Fallon 4/1: 0000061: Mid-div, al trav well, styd   **77**
on to lead bef 1f out, sn pushed clr, eased cl-home, val 5L+: suited by around 7f on firm, gd, polytrack & prob
gd/soft: visor left off today, quals for h'caps: op 3/1: eff at 7f with easy success & is h'capped to win more races: see 3821.
3860 **GO YELLOW 11** [7] P D Evans 3-9-0 (67) N Callan 14/1: 2461402: Mid-div, prog to chase wnr 1f out,   2½   **66**
al held ins fnl 1f: see 3366 (mdn).
4077 **TERRAQUIN 2** [9] J J Bridger 4-9-5 (65) T P Queally 25/1: 05500003: Hld up, hdwy 3f out, styd on fnl 1f.   hd   **65**
3928 **CHEESE N BISCUITS 9** [2] G L Moore 4-9-2 p (68) R L Moore 7/1: 2000054: Bhd, hdwy 3f out, kept on.   shd   **61**
3821 **NEARLY A FOOL 13** [3]6-9-6 vis (71) A McCarthy 8/1: 1013405: Cl-up 5f, sn no extra: btr 3223 & 1049.   3½   **58**
3933 **IPHIGENIA 9** [5]3-9-0 (73) Lisa Jones 4/1: 2453126: Led, hdd bef 1f out, sn hung right & wknd: 2½   **52**
op 3/1: disappointing effort: btr 3933 & 3724.
4030 **AZREME 4** [6]4-9-5 (70) M Howard(7) 9/4 FAV: 4543027: Cl-up 5f, wknd: qk reapp: too sn after 4030? (soft).1   **50**
3518 **GENEROUS GESTURE 25** [8]3-8-11 (70) R Mullen 16/1: 6106568: Chsd ldrs 4f, sn wknd: btr 1441 (visor). 1   **45**
8 Ran   Time 1m 26.61 (2.41)   Owned: Holistic Racing Ltd   Trained: Kingsclere

FOLKESTONE SUNDAY 22.08.04 Righthand, Sharpish, Undulating Track

4118
3.50 Westenhanger Handicap Stakes Fillies 3yo+ 0-75 (E)
£4144 £1275 £638 5f str Good 41 +15 Fast Stands side [77]

3833 **TIZZYS LAW 13** [5] M A Buckley 3-8-11 (60) S Drowne 13/2: 1645001: Bhd stands side, hdwy to lead **68**
stands side group dist, kept on to lead overall cl-home: fast time: stays 6f, suited by 5f: acts on fast & soft grnd.
3932 **ROXANNE MILL 9** [6] P A Blockley 6-9-12 p (73) N Callan 11/2: 3561202: Cl-up far side, led 2f out, 1½ **75**
hdd well ins fnl 1f, no extra: gd run in defeat conceding weight all round: see 3591 & 3353.
3640 **FLAPDOODLE 20** [1] A W Carroll 6-7-12 (2oh)VIS (43) Lisa Jones(3) 7/1: 50-50003: Led stands side nk **46**
group, hdd dist, no extra: bckd from 12/1: back to form with first time visor fitted: see 2585.
3640 **TRIPTI 20** [7] J J Bridger 4-7-12 (1oh) (44) J F McDonald(3) 33/1: 2000004: In tch far side 3f, sn hd **45**
outpcd, rallied late: return to 6f will suit: btr 728 (polytrack, 6f).
4070 **KALLISTAS PRIDE 2** [2]4-8-13 VIS (60) K Fallon 11/2: 02010605: Bhd, sn switched to far side group, ½ **59**
prog 2f out, onepcd well ins fnl 1f: qck reapp & first time visor: see 4070 & btr 3109.
4038 **TENDER 4** [4]4-8-1 p (48) C Catlin 4/1 FAV: 0410036: In tch over 3f stands side, sn no extra: qck reapp. 1½ **43**
3416 **COLLEGE QUEEN 30** [8]6-9-2 bl (63) I Mongan 5/1: 6545207: Rcd far side, led 3f, sn no extra: btr 3050. ½ **57**
3725+ **DANCE TO THE BLUES 17** [3]3-8-8 (57) P Dobbs 9/2: 0318: Handy stands side 3f, wknd: btr 3725. ½ **50**
8 Ran Time 59.70 (1.30) Owned: North Cheshire Trading & Storage Ltd Trained: Stamford

4119
4.20 Nigel Collison Fuels Handicap Stakes 3yo+ 0-70 (E)
£4576 £1408 £704 1m4f Good 41 -15 Slow Outside [70]

3992 **DANCE WORLD 6** [9] Miss J Feilden 4-10-0 (70) B Reilly(3) 16/1: 1030051: Led, hdd 10f out, led **76**
again after 5f, hdd bef 1f out, rallied well cl-home to get up on line: qck reapp: eff at 12/14f on gd & fibresand:
apprec drop down weights: game 4yo: see 1516 & 1030.
3914 **TURTLE PATRIARCH 9** [13] Mrs A J Perrett 3-8-6 (58) R L Moore 8/1: 60-00042: Cl-up, styd on to hd **62**
lead bef 1f out, hdd ins fnl 1f, kept on, just denied: eff at 9f, imprvd for step up to 12f: acts on gd grnd.
3051 **WYOMING 45** [10] J A R Toller 3-8-4 (56) E Ahern 20/1: 00-30003: Cl-up, outpcd halfway, rallied 1½ **57**
bef 1f out, not btn far in 3rd: 6 wk abs: eff at 12f, shaped as tho' further will suit: acts on gd grnd: see 1617.
3964 **GALLANT BOY 7** [11] P D Evans 3-8-9 vis t (65) N Callan 15/2: 4054444: Bhd, outpcd halfway, ¾ **64**
rallied bef 1f out, nrst fin: qck reapp: see 3964 & 549.
3914* **NOUNOU 9** [12]3-8-11 (63) M Halford(7) 7/1: 050015: Held up, outpcd after 6f, rallied bef 1f out, 1 **60**
nrst fin: eff at 9.7f, stays 12f: see 3914.
3270 **MAKE MY HAY 36** [1]5-8-5 (47) T P Queally 10/1: 6125556: Rear, hdwy 3f out, kept on fnl 1f: btr 1960. ¾ **42**
3948 **MAN THE GATE 8** [4]5-9-0 (55) S Drowne 4/1 FAV: 6215007: Bhd, nvr nrr than mid-div: tchd 11/2.. 8 **39**
3648 **JIDIYA 20** [6]5-10-0 (70) I Mongan 8/1: 52-0028: Led 10f out, hdd 7f out, wknd 3f out: btr 3648 (10f). 4 **47**
3387 **BEST FLIGHT 30** [3]4-9-10 (66) K May(7) 17/2: 41-00409: Missed break, nvr a factor: btr 2973. 3 **39**
3887 **VIN DU PAYS 10** [14]4-8-3 (45) A McCarthy 33/1: 116-0000: 10th: Al bhd: btr 1087. 4 **12**
3692 **CRACOW 18** [7]7-8-0 p (42) Lisa Jones 33/1: 0/-204500: 11th: Cl-up, wknd 3f out: btr 3420. 2½ **5**
3477 **OUTSIDE INVESTOR 27** [5]4-10-0 (70) T Williams 25/1: 2232-000: 12th: In tch, fdd 3f out, sn eased. 10 **19**
3734 **SMOOTHIE 17** [2]6-9-2 (58) K Fallon 9/2: 6104-060: 13th: Bhd when ran wide after bend 10f out, 2½ **3**
hdwy 6f out, wknd bef 2f out: dismal effort, something amiss?: btr 6.
13 Ran Time 2m 30.30 (6.8) Owned: Stowstowquickquickstow Partnership Trained: Newmarket

4120
4.50 Family Fun Maiden Stakes 3yo+ (D)
£3897 £1199 £600 1m1f149y Good 41 -21 Slow Outside

1580 **PLAY THE MELODY 108** [4] C Tinkler 3-8-13 R Mullen 8/1: 31: Led after 1f, hdd bef 1f out, **76**
rallied to lead dist, rdn out to hold on: eff at 9/9.7f, further will suit: acts on gd grnd & a sharp/undul trk:
game performer who is only lightly rcd: see 1580.
4033 **EFRHINA 4** [7] Mrs Stef Liddiard 4-9-2 (64) R Havlin 8/1: 02-00302: In tch, prog & ev ch 2f out, nk **69**
styd on to lead bef 1f out, hdd dist, kept on, just held: clr rem: qck reapp: acts on firm & gd grnd: see 3867.
2066 **INNOCENT REBEL 85** [10] E A L Dunlop 3-8-13 E Ahern 10/1: 043: Mid-div, outpcd halfway, rallied 5 **66**
bef 1f out, no ch with front 2: 12 wk abs: shaped as tho' 10f+ will suit & now quals for h'caps: see 2066.
3845 **BAILAORA 12** [6] B W Duke 3-8-13 T (66) A Daly 16/1: 0630504: Led 1f, styd cl-up & ev ch 2f out, 1¼ **64**
sn no extra: first time t-strap: btr 2930.
3631 **COPPICE 21** [8]3-8-13 K Fallon 4/7 FAV: 645: Keen in tch, ev ch bef 2f out, sn no extra: bckd hd **63**
at odds-on: disapp eff: showed more in 3631 (firm).
3748 **RYANS BLISS 16** [5]4-9-2 (40) R Miles(3) 28/1: 3200056: Bhd, outpcd halfway, modest late gains. shd **57$**
SANDOKAN 0 [9]3-8-13 T P Queally 10/1: 7: Held up, modest late gains under hands & heels. 8 **51**
3970 **PURR 7** [1]3-8-13 (49) A Hamblett(7) 66/1: 0-06008: Al in rear: qck reapp. shd **50**
3742 **WHISPERING VALLEY 16** [11]4-9-2 R L Moore 33/1: 0-009: Bhd, nvr a factor. 1½ **42**
3858 **COCO POINT BREEZE 11** [3]3-8-8 I Mongan 50/1: 0000: 10th: In tch 7f, fdd. 10 **28**
3828 **RUSSIAN APPLAUSE 13** [2]4-9-7 S Drowne 33/1: 00: 11th: Cl-up when & hung badly left on bend 22 **5**
after 2f, fdd halfway: btr 3828 (debut).
11 Ran Time 2m 4.01(6.01) Owned: Doubleprint Trained: Compton

WINDSOR MONDAY 23.08.04 Sharp Fig 8 Track

Official Going Good/Soft

4121   5.25 Sharp Minds Winners Welcome Maiden Stakes 2yo (D)
£4966 £1528 £764   5f10y str   Good 40   -02 Slow   Inside

WOODCOTE [11] C G Cox 2-9-0 P Robinson 12/1: 1: b c Monashee Mountain - Tootle (Main Reef)   93
Cl-up stands side, styd on to lead dist, rdn clr: Apr foal, cost E11,000: half brother to juv wnrs over 6/7f: dam
scored in France: eff over a sharp 5f, 6f will suit: goes well fresh on gd grnd: useful start, shld rate more highly.
DIXIEANNA [12] B W Hills 2-8-9 M Hills 9/1: 2: ch f Night Shift - Dixielake (Lake Coniston)   1½   82
Overall ldr stands side, rdn & hdd dist, not pace of wnr on debut: Feb 1st foal, dam 1m scorer: eff at 5f, 6f sure
to suit: acts on gd grnd: fine start, must be wng similar shortly.
3915 **PARK APPROACH 10** [5] J Noseda 2-8-9 E Ahern 3/1: 43: Led far side group, hdd dist, kept on to   2½   76
retake lead on far side, not pace of stands side ldrs: eff at 5/6f: shld find a race, see 3915.
3869 **JUANTORENA 12** [3] M L W Bell 2-9-0 (92) R Mullen 6/4 FAV: 22434: Chsd ldr far side, led dist,   shd   80
hdd cl-home: bckd: try headgear? twice below 2472 (Listed), 2158.
THREE DEUCES [10]2-8-9 J Fortune 14/1: 5: gr f Two Punch - Too Fast To Catch (Nice Catch)   ½   73
Slow away stands side, sn in tch, onepace over 1f out on debut: Feb foal, cost $110,000: speedily bred.
2151 **LIMONIA 82** [9]2-8-9 D Sweeney 50/1: 5606: In tch stands side, hung left & onepace over 1f out: abs.   1½   70$
FOREST DELIGHT [8]2-8-9 J F Egan 25/1: 7: In tch stands side, no impress dist on debut.   1¼   66
ATTISHOE [2]2-8-9 S Drowne 16/1: 8: Nvr a factor far side on debut.   5   54
CESAR MANRIQUE [4]2-9-0 S Sanders 20/1: 9: In tch far side, wknd 2f out.   1½   56
3857 **EDGE OF BLUE 12** [14]2-9-0 R Hughes 11/1: 630: 10th: In tch stands side, wknd 2f out: btr 3857.   ¾   54
Sir Bluebird 0 [6]2-9-0 P Dobbs 33/1:0   **Tractor Boy** [7]2-9-0 D Holland 11/1:0
2921 **Jonny Foxs 51** [13]2-9-0 D Kinsella 100/1:0   **Aramat** [1]2-8-9 V Venkaya 66/1:0
14 Ran   Time 1m 01.13 (2.13)   Owned: Mr Dennis Shaw   Trained: Hungerford

4122   5.55 Sharp Minds Betfair Classified Stakes 3yo+ 0-80 (D)
£5525 £1700 £850   1m67y rnd   Good 40   +13 Fast   Inside

3598 **KRUGERRAND 23** [13] W J Musson 5-9-7 (85) G Carter 14/1: 0136051: Held up, gd hdwy over 1f out,   94
qcknd to lead ins last, going away, rdly: gd time: stays a slowly run 10f, suited by 1m/9f on firm or gd grnd, poss
handles gd/soft: useful, has a neat turn of foot off a strong pace: see 2404.
3512 **EVALUATOR 27** [11] T G Mills 3-8-13 (83) J Fortune 9/4 FAV: 0612202: Held up, hdwy to lead 1f   ½   90
out, hdd ins last, not pace of wnr: proving tough & consistent: see 2922, 2650.
3862 **ARKHOLME 12** [14] P Winkworth 3-8-10 bl (80) P Doe 20/1: 4021203: Chsd ldr, slt lead over 3f out   1½   84
till 1f out, no extra: back to best at 1m: see 3243, 3301 (clmr).
3210 **LEOBALLERO 39** [5] D J Daly 4-9-2 t (79) D Holland 20/1: 231-5354: Slow away, held up, plenty to   shd   83
do over 2f out, styd on well over 1f out, nrst fin: fair run: see 2532, 1891.
3898 **GIOCOSO 11** [2]4-9-5 (83) F P Ferris [3] 20/1: 0-600145: Led till 3f out, wknd fnl 1f: fair run: best 3813.   1¼   84
2250 **FREAK OCCURENCE 79** [7]3-8-11 (81) S Drowne 20/1: 0346306: In tch, wknd over 1f out: 11 wk abs.   3   77
3460 **LITTLE VENICE 28** [1]4-9-3 (84) R Hughes 16/1: 0531007: Keen in tch, wknd over 1f out: best 2767.   shd   76
3891 **BLUE TROJAN 11** [3]4-9-7 (85) J F Egan 10/1: 0042008: Bhd, eff over 2f out, wknd dist: see 3088.   1½   77
3465 **BEST BEFORE 29** [12]4-9-2 (80) E Ahern 8/1: 1333169: Al bhd: best 3232.   1   70
627 **BORDER EDGE 191** [8]6-9-7 vis (85) J F McDonald [3] 50/1: 2000-000: 10th: b g Beveled - Seymour Ann   1   73
(Krayyan) In tch, wknd over 2f out: '03 full time h'cap wnr & dual class stks scorer: eff at 7f/8.5f on fm, gd/soft
& both AWs, any trk: wears a visor, tried blnks: most tough & prog last term.
2 Oct'03 Brig 6.0fm 88-85 C: 1 Oct'03 Epso 7gd 85-(76) D: 1 Sep'03 Sali 8g/f 79-(74) D: 2 Aug'03 Leic 8.0gd 72-72 D:
2 Jul'03 Epso 8.5g/f 75-69 D: 2 Jun'03 Kemp 7fm 70-66 C: 1 Jun'03 Wind 8.3g/f 69-59 C: 1 May'03 Bath 8.0g/f 63-55 E:
1 Feb'03 Ling 7ap 62a-55 D: 1 Jan'03 Ling 7ap 59a-50 E: 2 May'02 Nott 10gd 58-48 F: 1 May'01 Warw 8.1gd 59-48 F:
1776* **SUPREME SALUTATION 100** [9]8-9-5 (83) M Howard(7) 16/1: 1101410: 11th: In tch, eff 2f out, sn   2   67
wknd: 3 month abs: btr 1776.
3689 **SERIEUX 19** [4]5-9-6 P (84) P Robinson 14/1: 0020000: 12th: In tch, wknd 2f out: tried cheekpieces.   2   64
3608 **HARRY POTTER 23** [10]5-9-2 vis (80) D Sweeney 10/1: 6031150: 13th: Nvr a factor: btr 3423.   2   56
3525] **LASANGA 378** [6]5-9-2 (80) S Sanders 14/1: 4/-32-0: 14th: res & Zamindar - Shall We Run (Hotfoot)   1¼   54
Bhd, nvr a factor: plcd in 2 mdns in '03: eff at 1m, prob stays an easy 10f on fast & polytrack.
2 Aug'03 Wind 8.3g/f 86- D:
14 Ran   Time 1m 45.29 (2.29)   Owned: The Square Table II   Trained: Newmarket

4123   6.25 Sharp Minds Betfair: Best Odds Nursery Handicap Stakes 2yo (E)   [88]
£3552 £1093 £547   5f10y str   Good 40   +01 Fast   Inside

3943 **KEY SECRET 9** [5] M L W Bell 2-9-6 (80) Hayley Turner(5) 4/1: 111441: Cl-up, led over 1f out, rdn   95
clr: gd juv time: v eff at 5f on firm, gd & fibresand, any trk: useful & v prog 2yo: see 3115.
4065* **COUNTDOWN 3** [4] Sir Mark Prescott 2-9-13 (6ex) (87) S Sanders 4/7 FAV: 32112: Sn rdn in tch, eff   5   91
to chase wnr fnl 1f, al held: well bckd: quick reapp & another useful eff: see 4065.
3686 **PENNESTAMP 19** [2] Mrs P N Dutfield 2-8-6 (66) R Havlin(5) 12/1: 066443: Cl-up, no extra fnl 1f: see 3355.½   68
3729 **WATERLINE LOVER 18** [3] P D Evans 2-7-12 (2oh) (56) J F McDonald(3) 20/1: 6004064: Rdn bhd, some   shd   60
late gains, nvr a factor: see 2221.
3907 **CREE 10** [7]2-7-13 bl (59) D Kinsella 11/1: 00525: Sn led, hung left & hdd dist, no extra: btr 3907.   nk   60
3086 **ROBMANTRA 45** [1]2-8-13 (73) F P Ferris(3) 16/1: 6536: Sn rdn & al bhd: see 3086, 2597.   9   56
6 Ran   Time 1m 0.95 (1.95)   Owned: Joy and Valentine Feerick   Trained: Newmarket

---

4124 **6.55 Sharp Minds Betfair: Back And Lay Premier Claiming Stakes 3yo+** (D)
£5655 £1740 £870 **1m2f7y** **Good 40** **-04 Slow** Inside

3945 **BARKING MAD** 9 [3] M L W Bell 6-9-9 (84) K Fallon 9/2: 3216261: Made all, clr fnl 1f, eased down, cmfbtly: op 5/2, val 3/4L: suited by 10f & gd & firm grnd, handles soft: handles any trk, loves a sharp one & forcing tactics: apprec this drop to clmg grade, sure 3083. 84

2939} **WHALEEF** 403 [1] B J Llewellyn 6-9-6 T P (82) F P Ferris(3) 20/1: 60/0512-2: br g Darshaan - Wilayif (Danzig) Prom, kept on well fnl 1f, but not rch wnr: jumps fit, mod h'cap hdle & nov h'cap chase form (P Webber): won 3 hdles in 03/04 (rtd 109h, eff arnd 2m1f on gd & fast): '03 clam wnr: eff at 1m/12f on gd, fast & polytrack: gd weight carrier: eff in t-strap & cheekpieces: fine reapp for new stable. 1½ 77
2 Jul'03 Hami 9.2g/f 80-(81) D: 1 Jul'03 Yarm 8.0g/f 80-(81) F: 2 Jan'02 Ling 12ap 98a-92 C: 1 Nov'01 Ling 12ap 100a- D: 1 Jun'01 Good 11g/f 97- D:

3892 **BEN HUR** 11 [7] W M Brisbourne 5-9-5 (74) E Ahern 8/1: 1154563: Chsd ldrs, kept on under press fnl 1f, not pace of wnr: clr of rem: drop to clmg grade, unable to lead today: again bhd today's wnr in 3083. 1½ 72
4036 **SAHAAT** 5 [10] M J Polglase 6-9-2 (69) D Holland 10/1: 0502504: Mid-div, imprvd to chase ldrs 2f out, sn no impress: quick reapp, op 16/1: see 3392 (1m, AW). 3 67
3867 **MAMORE GAP** 12 [5]6-9-3 (67) R Hughes 20/1: 0-000505: Rdn in rear, nvr nr ldrs. 6 59
903 **SCOTTYS FUTURE** 153 [6]6-9-8 (72) S Sanders 11/2: 0-010106: Held up, some prog, nvr dangerous: long abs & new stable (prev with D Loder): bckd from 7/1: see 738 (AW). 2½ 60
3391 **EPAMINONDAS** 31 [4]3-8-12 (65) J Fortune 20/1: 0002047: Chsd ldrs, btn 2f out: op 14/1. 7 48
3668 **MISS DE BOIS** 20 [8]7-8-9 Hayley Turner(5) 66/1: 08: ch f Elmaamul - Petite Melusine (Fairy King) Chsd ldrs 6f, wknd qckly & t.o.: lightly rcd 7yo, no form yet. 22 7
3668 **ETON** 20 [11]8-9-8 (69) A Nicholls 9/1: 5123529: Prom till halfway, wknd qckly: something clrly amiss. nk 20
3704 **MORAHIB** 19 [2]6-9-10 (80) G Carter 10/1: 514/15-20: 10th: Al well bhd, t.o.: btr 3704 (g/f). 20 0
4036 **KENTUCKY KING** 5 [9]4-9-8 (83) R Miles(3) 5/2 FAV: 0352R4R: Refused to race: well bckd fav, has now done this on 2 of last 3 starts & looks one to avoid. 0
11 Ran Time 2m 10.42 (4.42) Owned: Mr Christopher Wright Trained: Newmarket

---

4125 **7.25 Sharp Minds Betfair Maiden Stakes 3yo** (D)
£3523 £1084 £542 **1m2f7y** **Good 40** **-19 Slow** Inside

3292 **DAY OF RECKONING** 35 [4] Sir Michael Stoute 3-8-9 K Fallon 11/8 FAV: 31: Nvr far away, imprvd to lead ins fnl 1f, pushed clr despite flashing tail: well bckd: clrly benefitted from recent encouraging debut: eff at 10f, 12f+ will suit: handles firm, acts on gd grnd & on a sharp trk: going the right way, see 3292 (debut). 80
3642 **PLEASANT** 21 [1] L G Cottrell 3-8-9 I Mongan 25/1: 42: Trkd ldrs, imprvd to lead 3f out, not pace to repel wnr ins fnl 1f: imprvd run, eff over a sharp 10f on gd grnd: see 3642 (debut). 2 73
2602 **LINE DRAWING** 64 [9] B W Hills 3-9-0 (74) R Hughes 7/1: 2433: Trkd ldrs, onepcd fnl 1f: 9 wk abs. 1½ 76
3828 **NEWNHAM** 14 [2] L M Cumani 3-9-0 D Holland 11/4: 24: Prom, outpcd 3f out, rallied fnl 1f but not reach ldrs: nicely bckd & btr expected over this longer 10f trip after encouraging debut in 3828 (1m here). 4 70
  NEATH [6]3-8-9 S Drowne 14/1: 5: b f Rainbow Quest - Welsh Autumn (Tenby) Mid-div, outpcd 3f out, kept on cl-home on debut: bred from 25/1: sister to 1m wnr Rainwashed Gold: bred to apprec mid-dists. hd 64
5032} **DREAM VALLEY** 289 [8]3-8-9 M Hills 16/1: 00-06: b f Sadler's Wells - Vallee des Reves (Kingmambo) Rear, prog to chase ldrs 2f out, sn btn on reapp: unplcd on both juv starts: cost 110,000 gns & mid-dist bred. shd 64
3979 **COUNT BORIS** 7 [10]3-9-0 S Carson 50/1: 007: Rear, nvr troubled ldrs. 2½ 65
3979 **DIEQUEST** 7 [5]3-9-0 J F Egan 66/1: 0-08: ch c Diesis - Nuance (Rainbow Quest) Prog from rear to chase ldrs 3f out, sn btn: unplcd on sole juv start: with Jamie Poulton & no form yet. 3½ 60
3683 **ROYAL LUSTRE** 19 [7]3-9-0 J Fortune 12/1: 039: Led till 3f out, wknd: btr 3683 (1m). nk 60
  WINSLOW HOMER [11]3-9-0 R Havlin 33/1: 0: 10th: b c Peintre Celebre - Armorique (Top Ville) Slowly away, al bhd & t.o on debut: brother to a 10f wnr: with J Gosden & mid-dist bred. 24 24
3894 **CHARMED BY FIRE** 11 [3]3-9-0 T (68) S Sanders 14/1: 0050: 11th: Slowly away, al bhd, t.o. in last. 5 17
11 Ran Time 2m 11.91 (5.91) Owned: The Queen Trained: Newmarket

---

4126 **7.55 Sharp Minds Phone 0870 90 80 121 Handicap Stakes 3yo+ 0-75** (E)
£4901 £1508 £754 **6f str** **Good 40** **-16 Slow** Inside [75]

3888 **NIVERNAIS** 11 [16] H Candy 5-9-9 (70) Dane O'Neill 7/1: 0060631: Chsd ldrs, strong run to lead cl-home, rdn out: made most of fav mark & decent draw, 1st home on unfav side last time: eff at 5/6f, stays 7f: acts on firm & gd/soft grnd: see 2023. 79
3705 **TANCRED TIMES** 19 [20] C F Wall 9-9-0 (61) Hayley Turner(5) 7/1: 3314132: Led till halfway, again 2f out till caught cl-home: fine front rng eff, remains in great form: see 3436 (clmr). ½ 66
3184 **CHARLOTTEBUTTERFLY** 40 [15] T T Clement 4-8-6 (53) J F McDonald(3) 25/1: 53-04003: Mid-div, styd on strongly fnl 1f, nrst fin: 6 wk abs: lightly rcd & hinted at more to come today: acts on gd, firm & f/sand. 1½ 54
2282 **VAL DE MAAL** 76 [12] G C H Chung 4-9-8 (69) S Sanders 20/1: 40-30404: Chsd ldrs, onepcd fnl 1f: abs. ½ 68
3341 **POLAR IMPACT** 33 [18]5-10-0 (75) R L Moore 3/1 FAV: 1-105145: Rear, styd on strongly fnl 1f, nrst fin under top weight: gamble from 7/1: got going too late, see 2760. 1¼ 71
3790 **MORITAT** 16 [13]4-8-6 t (53) F P Ferris(3) 16/1: 06-06356: Front rank, led briefly halfway till 2f out, wknd. hd 48
3960 **DOUBLE M** 9 [5]7-9-5 vis (66) R Thomas(5) 33/1: 3661207: Chsd ldrs, onepcd fnl 1f: not disgraced from mod low draw: btr 3640 & 3537 (5f). ½ 59
3109 **EMERALD FIRE** 44 [19]5-9-2 (63) L Keniry(3) 14/1: 005-6008: Rear, styd on late, nvr dngrs: 6 wk abs. ¾ 54
3974 **SMIRFYS PARTY** 8 [6]6-8-2 vis (49) P Doe 10/1: 6-000359: Front rank, wknd fnl 1f: mod draw. 1 37
3921 **HIGHLAND LASS** 10 [8]3-8-8 (58) E Ahern 33/1: 0060: 10th: b f Nicolotte - Portvasco (Sharpo) Bmpd start, mod late prog on h'cap bow: lightly rcd & little form to date: prob worth another ch. hd 45
3984 **FLARAN** 33 [17]4-8-12 (59) R Hughes 25/1: 01504-00: 11th: Chsd ldrs, wkng when hmpd dist: see 3984. shd 46
3948 **TREETOPS HOTEL** 9 [3]5-8-11 T p (58) N Chalmers(5) 16/1: 0024200: 12th: Rear, nvr nr ldrs: t-strap. shd 45
4070 **FREE WHEELIN** 3 [14]4-9-2 (63) J Fortune 14/1: 0-030000: 13th: Held up, nvr dngrs: qck reapp. 2½ 44
3569 **SIR DON** 24 [2]5-9-2 vis (63) A Nicholls 20/1: 1035000: 14th: Nvr a factor: see 3017. 2 39
3872 **ANTONIO CANOVA** 12 [4]8-9-13 VIS (74) J F Egan 10/1: 0010050: 15th: Held up, nvr nr ldrs: visor. shd 49
3380+ **DAVE** 32 [9]3-8-13 (63) K Fallon 9/2: 0050-10: 16th: Front rank, wknd dist: bckd from 6/1: btr 3380. 5 24
3910* **SEWMUCH CHARACTER** 10 [10]5-9-8 (69) D Sweeney 14/1: 0642010: 17th: Chsd ldrs, wkng/hmpd dist. nk 29
17 Ran Time 1m 13.67(3.37) Owned: Mr M J M Tricks Trained: Wantage

---

SOUTHWELL Fibresand MONDAY 23.08.04 Lefthand, Sharp, Oval Track

Official Going SLOW

4127
5.10 National Plumbers Day Claiming Stakes 2yo (E)
£4115 £1266 £633 **6f aw rnd** **Going 80** **-43 Slow** Outside

3901 **ROKO 11** [11] M W Easterby 2-8-10 bl (59) T Lucas 10/1: 0004331: In tch, hdwy wide over 2f out, **59a**
drvn ins fnl 1f, led nr fin: clmd for 5,000: improved at 6f on gd, gd/soft & fibresand, acts on a sharp trk: first win.
2802 **HIAMOVI 56** [3] R M H Cowell 2-9-3 M Henry 20/1: 052: b c Monashee Mountain - Dunfern (Wolver ½ **63a**
Hollow) Led till hdd & no extra nr fin: 8 wk abs: Feb foal, cost E7,500: half-brother to a 7f 2yo wnr: dam wnr
over 7f at 3: sire high-class over 7f: eff at 6f on fibresand: shown enough to win a race.
3308 **FOLD WALK 35** [4] M W Easterby 2-8-7 (46) Dale Gibson 33/1: 04U053: In tch, hdwy over 2f out, ev nk **52a**
ch ins fnl 1f, onepace nr fin: eff at 6f on fibresand: see 1303.
3994 **CAMPEON 7** [1] M J Wallace 2-9-3 VIS (74) D Corby(3) 11/4 FAV: 5243524: Hmpd start, in tch, hdwy & 1½ **57a**
handy over 4f out, ev ch 2f out, onepcd ins fnl 1f: qck reapp: handles fast, gd & fibresand: visor: see 3431.
3901 **WEET N MEASURES 11** [5] 2-9-3 A Culhane 6/1: 55: Chsd ldrs, ev ch fnl 2f till onepcd ins fnl 1f. nk **56a**
3713 **CHAMPAGNE ROSSINI 18** [2] 2-9-7 L Vickers 40/1: 056: Chsd ldrs, onepcd over 1f out: see 3713. 1 **57a**
3931 **SKIPPIT JOHN 10** [12] 2-9-6 (65) Dean McKeown 16/1: 266007: Chsd ldrs, onepcd over 1f out. nk **55a**
3818 **DANESCOURT 14** [8] 2-9-3 C Catlin 100/30: 58: b c Danetime - Faye (Monsanto) Trkd ldrs, outpcd ½ **50a**
over 1f out, kept on again ins fnl 1f: cost 7,500gns, Apr foal: half-brother to wnrs at 5f & 1m.
3848 **FERRARA FLAME 13** [14] 2-8-12 L Fletcher(3) 33/1: 09: b f Titus Livius - Isolette (Wassl) In tch nk **44a**
till over 4f out, hdwy over 1f out, not pace to chall: Mar foal, cost E10,000: half-sister to a 10/12f wnr..
3901* **HOPELESSLY DEVOTED 11** [10] 2-8-9 (58) Rory Moore(5) 13/2: 0610: 10th: Handy, no impress over 1f 1½ **36a**
out: not enjoy fibresand? much btr 3901 (claim, gd/soft).
3930 **LANE MARSHAL 10** [13] 2-8-11 bl T Eaves(3) 40/1: 5000650: 11th: Chsd ldrs, hung left/wknd 1f out. 4 **26a**
3831 **SMILING STARDUSTER 14** [7] 2-8-13 D Tudhope(7) 40/1: 00: 12th: Nvr a factor. 1 **25a**
NIBBLES 0 [8] 2-9-7 T Hamilton(3) 33/1: 0: 13th: Rear, t.o. on debut. 25 **0a**
3769 **TIMMY 16** [9] 2-8-8 G Parkin 66/1: 0000500: 14th: Rear, hung right, fin well t.o. dist **0a**
14 Ran Time 1m 20.73 (7.43) Owned: Mr John Southway & Mr John Walsh Trained: Sheriff Hutton

4128
5.40 King Richard Iii Handicap Stakes 3yo+ 0-70 (E) [66]
£3341 £1028 £514 **1m4f aw** **Going 80** **-07 Slow** Inside

3154* **CROCOLAT 42** [6] Mrs Stef Liddiard 3-9-4 (56) F Norton 5/4 FAV: 0052411: Chsd ldrs, hdwy to lead **72a**
over 1f out, rdn clr ins fnl 1f, eased nr fin, val further: op 9/4, abs: landed double: eff around 12f on fast &
fibresand, likes Southwell: gd start for new yard (prev with N Callaghan): in fine form, win again: see 3154.
2724 **HEATHERS GIRL 59** [7] D Haydn Jones 5-9-10 (52) G Gibbons 8/1: 6242242: Trkd ldrs, hdwy to lead 8 **55a**
over 2f out till over 1f out, not pace of wnr: 8 wk abs: jt top-weight: see 1754 (claim).
4045 **STAFF NURSE 4** [4] Don Enrico Incisa 4-8-4 (32) Kim Tinkler 7/1: 0040533: Chsd ldrs, outpcd 5f 2 **32a**
out, kept on again over 1f out: qck reapp: clr of rem: does stay 14f & looks worth a step up in trip: see 1840.
3649 **DALRIATH 21** [5] M C Chapman 5-8-4 (32) Stephanie Hollinshead(5) 14/1: 0352004: Trkd ldrs, led 4 **26a**
over 3f out till over 2f out, sn hung left, no extra over 1f out: see 3354.
4012* **FARAWAY ECHO 6** [3] 3-8-9 (47) M Halford(7) 10/1: 0630515: Handy till outpcd 4f out, btn: qck reapp. 2½ **37a**
3856 **OUR EMMY LOU 12** [8] 3-9-9 BL (61) T P Queally 9/2: 066-2456: Led till over 3f out, no extra: blnks. 13 **31a**
3929 **DASH OF MAGIC 10** [1] 6-9-3 (45) M Tebbutt 7/1: 0631507: Slow away, al bhd: rep lost a front shoe. 6 **6a**
2781 **OPERA STAR 9** [2] 3-9-10 (62) A Culhane 14/1: 0-50368: Chsd ldrs, lost pl 7f out, sn btn: 8 wk 9 **9a**
abs, jt top-weight: joc reported a breathing problem: see 2668.
8 Ran Time 2m 44.82 (10.52) Owned: Mrs S Clifford Trained: Hungerford

4129
6.10 Festival Of Fire Selling Stakes Fillies 2yo (G)
£2541 £726 £363 **5f aw str** **Going 80** **-29 Slow** Outside

3901 **PARIS TAPIS 11** [7] K A Ryan 2-8-9 (58) P Fessey 1/1 FAV: 04221: Chsd ldrs, hdwy to lead over 1f **67a**
out, rdn out ins fnl 1f: bt in frm for 9,000gns: first win: eff at 5/6f on fast, gd/soft & fibresand: likes sellers.
3987 **CHILALI 7** [6] A Berry 2-8-9 (60) F Norton 9/4: 3036402: Trkd ldrs till led 2f out, sn hdd, no 2½ **57a**
extra: op 4/1, qck reapp: clr of rem: stays 5f on fibresand & fast: see 1458 (debut).
3944 **BREGAGLIA 9** [4] R M H Cowell 2-8-9 VIS M Henry 28/1: 0003: ch f Zaha - Strath Kitten (Scottish 5 **42a**
Reel) Outpcd in rear, hdwy 2f out, kept on ins fnl 1f: Mar foal: dam unplcd, sire a Gr 1 wnr at 2: tried a visor.
1968 **EMMAS VENTURE 91** [1] M W Easterby 2-8-9 (49) Dale Gibson 15/2: 526404: Led over 1f, remained shd **41a**
handy, no extra over 1f out, eased cl-home: long abs: joc reported mount moved badly thr'out & tired ins fnl 1f.
3723 **ARTADI 18** [9] 2-8-9 BL (50) C Catlin 14/1: 03565: Outpcd in rear, kept on over 1f out: blnks. shd **40a**
3736 **MS THREE 18** [5] 2-8-9 Joanna Badger 66/1: 06: b f Josr Algarhoud - Swing Along (Alhijaz) Dwelt, 5 **25a**
keen in tch, hdwy to lead over 3f out till over 2f out, sn no extra: May first foal, cost 4,000gns: dam a dual 7/9f wnr.
3832 **STAR OF KILDARE 14** [10] 2-8-9 Kim Tinkler 20/1: 00007: Slow away, nvr nr ldrs: see 3504. ½ **23a**
3517 **ISLE OF LIGHT 26** [8] 2-8-9 Lisa Jones 16/1: 08: b f Trans Island - Singled Out (Fairy King) 1¾ **18a**
Chsd ldrs, wknd over 1f out: Apr first foal, cost £2,000: dam unrcd, sire a high-class miler.
LA PROVIDENCE 0 [2] 2-8-9 BL e P M Quinn 40/1: 9: Slow away, green, al bhd on debut: tried blnks. 15 **0a**
30**ETERNAL SUNSHINE 45** [3] 2-8-9 BL (39) T Hamilton(3) 20/1: 00030: 10th: In tch, btn 2yf out: tried blnks. 1 **0a**
10 Ran Time 1m 3.27 (5.47) Owned: Calverts Carpets Trained: Hambleton

4130
6.40 St Rose Of Lima Handicap Stakes 3yo+ 35-55 (F) [60]
£3073 £878 £439 **6f aw rnd** **Going 80** **+04 Fast** Outside

4091 **HEADLAND 3** [3] D W Chapman 6-9-9 bl e (55) A Culhane 5/1: 6221551: In tch, hdwy 4f out, drvn into **63a**
lead nr fin: op 3/1, qck reapp: eff at 6/7f on both AWs, fast & hvy, prob any trk, likes Southwell: back to form.
4043+ **JAGGED 4** [4] J R Jenkins 4-10-1 (6ex)vis (61) L Dettori 2/1 FAV: 0236312: Led, hdd nr fin, no nk **67a**
extra: wel bckd, qck reapp, not btn far under top-weight: gd run, imprvd in defeat: see 4043.
3796 **LUCIUS VERRUS 16** [7] D Shaw 4-9-3 BL e (49) Darren Williams 14/1: 5205603: Rear, hdwy over 4f ½ **53a**
out, ev ch 1f out, sn onepcd: better run in blnks: see 1320.

1244

SOUTHWELL Fibresand   MONDAY 23.08.04   Lefthand, Sharp, Oval Track

3790	**BOLD WOLF 16** [16] J L Spearing 3-9-0 (49) G Hind 50/1: 4400004: Chsd ldrs, onepcd over 1f out.	1¼	49a
3830	**ACE MA VAHRA 14** [9]6-8-13 bl (45) J Bramhill 16/1: 0633505: Handy, outpcd over 2f out, kept on again fnl 1f: needs further: see 3609.	3½	34a
3482	**TRAVELLING TIMES 28** [11]5-9-1 vis (47) T Eaves(3) 11/2: 6004026: Chsd ldrs, outpcd over 2f out, kept on ins fnl 1f: tchd 9/1: btr 3482, 94.	1¼	32a
4009	**CALCULAITE 6** [6]3-8-11 (46) F Norton 10/1: 0-066457: Mid-div till over 3f out, some late gains.	1¼	27a
750	**OTYLIA 178** [5]4-9-1 (47) M Henry 33/1: 3544-548: Chsd ldrs, no impress over 1f out: long abs.	shd	27a
3873	**SYLVA ROYAL 12** [15]3-9-3 (52) J P Guillambert(3) 14/1: 4469: Rear, hung left 2f out, nvr nr ldrs.	¾	30a
3873	**NOBLE DESERT 12** [2]3-9-0 (49) T P Queally 14/1: 0-050: 10th: Chsd ldrs, wknd 2f out: see 3873.	2½	19a
2848	**EXTINGUISHER 54** [13]5-9-9 (55) M Fenton 25/1: 0000500: 11th: Al bhd: now with T FitzGerald.	1¾	20a
3655	**GAME FLORA 21** [8]3-9-0 (49) T Hamilton(3) 33/1: 1405060: 12th.	5	0a
3767	**MISS WIZZ 16** [12]4-8-11 p (43) Rory Moore(5) 12/1: 4451000: 13th: In tch till over 2f out, sn btn.	2	0a
2463	**KEY FACTOR 69** [14]3-9-6 (55) Dale Gibson 40/1: 4000: 14th: Al bhd: 10 wk abs: see 2104.	½	0a

14 Ran   Time 1m 17.89 (4.59)   Owned: Mr Harold D White   Trained: York

---

4131   **7.10 Gene Kelly Median Auction Maiden Stakes 3yo** (F)
£2919 £834 £417   **7f aw rnd**   **Going 80**   -01 Slow   Inside

3805	**OH GOLLY GOSH 15** [2] N P Littmoden 3-9-0 vis (66) T P Queally 9/2: 0420531: Prom, hdwy to lead over 4f out, came stands side 2f out, rdn out fnl 1f: eff over 7f/easy 8f on firm, soft & fibresand, sharp trk.		65a
2339	**ALIBA 74** [4] B Smart 3-9-0 (60) D McGaffin 25/1: 354-4002: ch g Ali Royal - Kiba (Tirol) Chsd ldrs, kept on ins fnl 1f, not btn far: abs, again unplcd in '03 (rtd 65): eff at 6/7f on gd & f/sand.	¾	62a
3581	**THROUGH THE SLIPS 24** [5] J G Given 3-8-9 M Fenton 33/1: 003: In tch, outpcd halfway, kept on again ins fnl 1f: step back up in trip shld suit: see 3208.	5	47a
	ROMAN LOVE 0 [6] J R Fanshawe 3-8-9 O Urbina 11/4: 4: ch f Perugino - Bordighera (Alysheba) Slow away, hdwy over 2f out, not pace to chall on debut: half-sister to smart mid-dist performer Grandera: dam a mid-dist wnr in France: will learn from this & do btr over further in time.	3½	40a
3870	**CHERTSEY 12** [3]3-8-9 (56) J P Guillambert(3) 11/2: 3350565: Chsd ldrs, no impress fnl 1f: op 8/1.	1	38a
3873	**ANTIGUA BAY 12** [1]3-8-9 (74) Lisa Jones 11/8 FAV: 0026: Chsd ldrs till 3f out, btn.	nk	37a
3985	**SACCHARINE 7** [7]3-8-9 (44) K Ghunowa(7) 40/1: 00-0367: Led till over 4f out, wknd 2f out.	6	25a
3979	**EXPLICIT 7** [8]3-9-0 C Catlin 50/1: 0008: ch c Definite Article - Queen Canute (Ahonoora) Sm outpcd, nvr a factor, qck reapp: dam lightly rcd mdn: with G Bravery.	16	0a
3177	**SKELTHWAITE 41** [9]3-9-0 (35) Darren Williams 100/1: 000-09: Dsptd lead till 4f out, sn btn: 6 wk abs: joc reportedly mount became tired in the later stages: see 3177.	13	0a

9 Ran   Time 1m 32.27 (5.67)   Owned: Mrs Gillian Curley   Trained: Newmarket

---

4132   **7.40 See You On 7th November Handicap Stakes 3yo+ 35-55** (F)   [59]
£3052 £872 £436   **1m aw rnd**   **Going 80**   +02 Fast   Inside

3487	**DUBONAI 28** [9] Andrew Turnell 4-9-5 (50) D Corby(3) 33/1: 0-003001: Chsd ldrs, led dist, drvn out: eff over 1m/12f on fast & f/sand & on a sharp trk: improved rdn closer to the pace today.		58a
2886	**GUSTAVO 53** [8] B W Hills 3-9-3 BL (54) Dean McKeown 20/1: 00002: b g Efisio - Washita (Valiyar) Chsd ldrs, ev ch 2f out, onepcd ins fnl 1f: 8 wk abs: stays 1m on f/sand: back to form in first time blnks.	½	59a
3867	**PACIFIC OCEAN 12** [2] Mrs Stef Liddiard 5-9-10 t (55) F Norton 7/1: 0436003: Rear, hdwy on outer 2f out, kept on well ins fnl 1f, not pace for 2: op 20/1: rtn to further suit: see 2910.	1½	57a
3766	**CRYFIELD 16** [4] N Tinkler 7-9-10 (55) Kim Tinkler 7/2 FAV: 0016434: Slow away, hdwy 4f out, onepcd.	1¼	54a
4007	**TATWEER 6** [1]4-9-3 BL e (48) Darren Williams 16/1: 0000025: Bhd, hdwy over 4f out, onepcd over 1f out: qck reapp: tried blnks: see 4007.	1½	44a
3242	**DUBAI DREAMS 38** [5]4-9-8 bl (53) B Swarbrick(5) 18/1: 4250006: Made most till dist, wknd.	2	45a
3823	**MISS GLORY BE 14** [14]6-9-7 p (52) S Hitchcott(3) 8/1: 0352337: Handy & wide, chall 3f out, wknd.	1	42a
1755	**SORBIESHARRY 100** [15]5-9-4 p (49) R Fitzpatrick 25/1: 5014058: Slow away, wide, some late gains.	1¾	35a
2805	**SUDRA 56** [16]7-9-8 bl (53) C Catlin 11/1: 4431439: In tch wide, sn outpcd, some late gains: 8 wk abs.	½	38a
3823	**MIDMAAR 14** [7]3-9-1 (52) M Tebbutt 100/1: 000-0000: 10th: In tch, wknd over 2f out: see 2998.	8	21a
3526	**ISLANDS FAREWELL 26** [11]4-9-6 (51) L Dettori 9/2: 00-00520: 11th: Handy & wide, wknd 2f out.	5	10a
3828	**MAGARI 14** [13]3-9-2 (53) M Fenton 12/1: 3-400: 12th: Al bhd: op 9/1: see 3610.	2½	7a
3486	**DISABUSE 28** [6]4-9-7 bl (52) Dale Gibson 6/1: 4454500: 13th: Al bhd: op 10/1: see 3105.	3	0a
3870	**MITZI CASPAR 12** [12]3-9-1 (52) R Price 66/1: 0321000: 14th: Rear, t.o.	18	0a
3366	**PRIVATE JESSICA 10** [10]3-9-4 (55) O Urbina 15/2: 0040: 15th: Dsptd lead till 3f out, wknd & t.o.	2½	0a

15 Ran   Time 1m 45.68(6.28)   Owned: Mr Geoff Jewson   Trained: Malton

---

HAMILTON   MONDAY 23.08.04   Righthand, Undulating Track, Stiff Uphill Finish

Official Going Good/Soft (Good Places)

4133   **2.15 Perfect Day Claiming Stakes 3yo+** (E)
£3494 £1075 £538   **1m1f36y**   **Good/Soft 66**   -14 Slow   Inside

4011	**JORDANS SPARK 6** [9] I Semple 3-8-10 P (49) R Winston 25/1: 50061: Chsd ldrs, styd on to lead ins fnl 1f, rdn out: qck reapp: eff around 9f on gd/soft grnd: acts on a stiff/undul trk: apprec fitting of cheek pieces & drop to claiming grade: see 1390.		57
3704	**SENOR EDUARDO 19** [5] S Gollings 7-9-3 (54) K Darley 11/4: 0035162: Mid-div, prog to lead bef 1f out, hdd ins fnl 1f, not pace wnr: qck rem: ran to form of win in 3362 (sell, 10f).	1¼	55
3764*	**BAILIEBOROUGH 16** [2] D Nicholls 3-9-13 vis (68) Alex Greaves 11/8 FAV: 0165113: In tch, led 2f out, hdd dist, no extra: well bckd under top-weight: last 5 wins have come on fast grnd: btr 3764 & 3558.	3½	60
4007	**MERLINS PROFIT 6** [6] M Dods 4-8-11 (43) P Hanagan 9/1: 3-5420U4: Bhd, prog 3f out, onepcd fnl 2f: tchd 20/1: qck reapp: btr 1946 (banded, fast).	2½	40
3772	**CHISEL 16** [8]3-8-3 (50) R Ffrench 11/2: 0060005: Handy 7f, wknd: op 7/2: btr 2325.	4	33
4007	**ABUELOS 6** [4]5-8-10 (43) T Williams 33/1: 3400506: Slow away, al in rear: qck reapp: see 652.	3½	28
3766	**SOCIETY TIMES 16** [7]11-8-11 t (24) D Fentiman(7) 25/1: 4500//-007: Led, hdd 2f out, wknd: see 3558.	shd	28$

1245

4558] **NEVER FORGET BOWIE 678** [1]8-8-10 (40) P Mathers(5) 20/1: 330404/-8: b g Superpower - Heldigvis 29 0
(Hot Grove) Cl-up 6f, fdd: missed '03: unplcd both 02/03 hdles starts (rtd 59h, mdn): plcd 3 times in '02 (rtd 47
at best, seller): eff at 1m/9f on fast or hvy grnd: with R Allan.
8 Ran Time 2m 1.30 (7.2) Owned: Ian Crawford & Brian Jordan Jnr Trained: Carluke

---

4134 **2.45 Royal Bank Of Scotland Maiden Stakes 2yo (D)**
£4804 £1478 £739 **5f4y str** **Good/Soft 66** **-02 Slow** Far side

CYCLICAL 0 [3] G A Butler 2-9-0 P Hanagan 5/6 FAV: 1: b c Pivotal - Entwine (Primo Dominie) 84
Dwelt, sn in tch, styd on to lead dist, sn edged left, pushed out, val bit more: well bckd: debut: Feb first
foal, dam dual 5f wnr as a juv: sire decent performer at sprint dists: eff at 5f, 6f shld suit: acts on gd/soft
grnd & goes well fresh: acts on a stiff/undul trk: improve for today's experience & rate higher.
3258 **HOWARDS PRINCESS 37** [4] J S Goldie 2-8-9 K Darley 9/4: 522: In tch, ev ch 1f out, kept on, not 1¼ 73
pace wnr: well bckd: another gd run & can find similar: see 3258.
3652 **BOND BABE 21** [1] B Smart 2-8-9 F Lynch 9/2: 423: Led, hdd dist, no extra: op 7/2: acts on 1½ 69
fast & gd/soft grnd: now qual for h'caps: see 3652.
2965 **NEE LEMON LEFT 49** [2] A Berry 2-8-9 (63) P Mathers(5) 25/1: 263064: Prom 3f, sn hung left & fdd. 12 39
4 Ran Time 1m 1.52 (3.42) Owned: Cheveley Park Stud Trained: Blewbury

---

4135 **3.15 Friends Of Scottish Racing Maiden Stakes 3yo+ (D)**
£5551 £1708 £854 **1m1f36y** **Good/Soft 66** **-09 Slow** Inside

3876 **TEMPLET 12** [9] I Semple 4-9-0 bl (60) R Winston 3/1: 4530021: In tch, prog & ev ch dist, rdn out 70
to lead on line: well bckd: eff at 9/12f on gd & hvy grnd: eff with/without blnks: gd confidence boost: see 3876.
3546 **JUST A FLUKE 25** [4] M Johnston 3-8-7 (74) R Ffrench 2/1 FAV: 4023052: Prom, led 2f out, hdd shd 68
under press on line: clr rem: well bckd: lost little in defeat & shld find a race: see 2687 & 2443.
3799 **ELUSIVE KITTY 15** [10] G A Butler 3-8-2 t (69) P Hanagan 4/1: 255-6R33: Chsd ldrs, onepcd & dist: 3½ 58
op 3/1: eff at 1m/9f on firm, gd/soft & fibresand: see 3799.
2164 **MOONSHAFT 82** [1] E A L Dunlop 3-8-7 (67) K Darley 9/1: 00404: Led, hdd 2f out, no extra: long abs. 4 57
2736} **FLIGHT COMMANDER 412** [a]4-9-0 D Allan 16/1: 55-5: b g In The Wings - Lucrezia (Machiavellian) ¾ 55
Chsd ldrs over 6f, no extra: reapp: unplcd on both '03 starts (rtd 65, mdn): has had leg problems.
SARENNE 0 [7]3-8-2 J Fanning 10/1: 6: b f Desert Sun - Fabulous Pet (Somethingfabulous) No dngr. 3 46
1121 **STRAVONIAN 134** [2]4-9-0 P P Mathers(5) 100/1: 07: Missed break, al in rear: long abs. 3 47
3610 **FIZZY POP 23** [8]5-8-9 D Fentiman(7) 66/1: 68: Rear, nvr a factor: see 3610. 26 7
3592 **DALKEYS LASS 23** [3]3-8-6 (4ow) V Halliday 100/1: 049: Handy 6f, sn fdd: btr 3592. nk 10
SWORDS AT DAWN 0 [5]3-8-5 (3ow) P Mulrennan 33/1: 0: 10th: ch f Daggers Drawn - Caraway dist 0
(Shadeed) Rear, nvr a factor: debut: with J Barclay.
10 Ran Time 2m 0.90 (6.8) Owned: J and J Hunter Trained: Carluke

---

4136 **3.45 Alex Salmond Pick A Winner Scottish Trophy Stakes Handicap 3yo+ 0-90 (C)** [86]
£10410 £3203 £1602 **1m65y rnd** **Good/Soft 66** **+10 Fast** Inside

3437 **NEVADA DESERT 30** [4] R M Whitaker 4-8-13 P (71) S Chin 10/1: 25-45201: Prom, styd on to lead ins 78
fnl 1f, rdn out: fast time: eff at 1m/11f on firm & gd/soft grnd: improved for cheek pieces: see 3260.
3794 **PENRITH 16** [8] M Johnston 3-9-5 J Fanning 11/1: 1303502: Cl-up, ev ch fnl 1f, just held ½ 91
by wnr: acts on fast, btr run on gd/soft & a return to 1m: see 3460.
3797* **YOUNG MR GRACE 16** [10] T D Easterby 4-9-8 (80) D Allan 8/1: 2516213: Led, hdd under press ins shd 84
fnl 1f, not btn far: another gd run: see 3797 (firm).
4051* **HILLS OF GOLD 4** [1] M W Easterby 5-9-2 (74) P Mulrennan(3) 13/2: 1032214: Bhd, prog 2f out, nrst shd 77
fin: qck reapp: btr 4051 (7f, Chester).
3892 **STRAW BEAR 11** [9]3-8-13 (77) J Mackay 4/1: 5231-235: Prom 7f, no extra: op 3/1: btr 3892 & 3339. 1½ 77
3768 **QUALITAIR WINGS 16** [6]5-9-0 (72) K Darley 20/1: 0020206: Mid-div, onepcd bef 1f out: btr 3583. 2½ 67
4008 **CHERISHED NUMBER 6** [3]5-8-11 (69) R Winston 7/2 FAV: 0440537: Rear, modest late gains: well nk 63
bckd on qck reapp: btr expected after 3rd here in 4008 (9f): likes Ayr.
3879* **DANELOR 12** [7]6-10-0 (86) P Hanagan 9/2: 5005018: Prom, rdn keenly, fdd dist: op 11/2: btr 3879 (9f). hd 79
3879 **TONY TIE 12** [2]8-9-12 (84) N Mackay(5) 22/1: 2161069: Chsd ldrs over halfway, sn no extra: btr 3152. 3½ 70
3625 **LOW CLOUD 23** [5]4-9-3 vis (75) Alex Greaves 33/1: 5145400: 10th: Missed break, al in rear: btr 3099. 5 51
10 Ran Time 1m 48.49 (4.69) Owned: Mr J Barry Pemberton Trained: Scarcroft

---

4137 **4.15 George Wimpey Handicap Stakes 3yo 0-75 (E)** [78]
£4209 £1295 £648 **1m1f36y** **Good/Soft 66** **-21 Slow** Inside

3772 **EBORACUM 16** [1] T D Easterby 3-8-12 bl (62) D Allan 100/30: 0022041: Prom, led bef 4f out, rdn 73
out fnl 1f: tchd 4/1: eff at 1m, suited by 9/10f on fast & gd/soft grnd: eff in blnks: see 3377.
3914 **SUNSET MIRAGE 10** [4] E A L Dunlop 3-9-4 BL (68) K Darley 5/2 JT FAV: 0604232: Mid-div, hdwy to 1½ 74
chase wnr 2f out, onepace: well bckd: ran to form with visor left off & first time blnks fitted.
3592 **ARGENT 23** [2] Miss L A Perratt 3-7-12 p (48) R Ffrench 5/1: 0200023: Handy 6f, sn outpcd, rallied late. 3½ 49
3805* **BANANA GROVE 15** [5] A Berry 3-9-7 (71) P Mathers(5) 14/1: 30P14: Missed break, sn in tch, no nk 71
extra 2f out: op 10/1: btr 3805 (fast).
3547 **KOODOO 25** [3]3-7-12 (5oh) (43) D Fentiman(7) 20/1: 0-060005: Led, hdd bef 4f out, wknd 3f out. 2½ 44
3618 **DEVIOUS AYERS 23** [6]3-8-11 (61) P Hanagan 5/2 JT FAV: 3-4006: Mid-div, hung right under press 6 48
after 6f, sn wknd: yet to convince on turf: btr 260 (polytrack).
6 Ran Time 2m 1.94 (7.84) Owned: Mr T D Easterby Trained: Malton

4138   4.45 Totepool Handicap Stakes 3yo+ 0-85 (D)   [82]
£8249 £2538 £1269   1m5f9y   Good/Soft 66   +00 Fast   Stands side

3969 **SAHEM 8** [6] C J Teague 7-9-10 (78) D Allan 7/1: 0120331: Mid-div, styd on for press to lead ins   **87**
fnl 1f, pushed out, val 3L+: op 5/1, new stable; eff at 10f, stays 14f well, tried further: acts on firm & gd/soft
grnd: likes a stiff/undul trk: imprvd eff to defy top-weight on first start for new yard: see 2444 (D Eddy).

3940 **YANKEEDOODLEDANDY 9** [5] P C Haslam 3-8-12 p (77) K Darley 7/2: 1232322: Led, hdd under press ins 1½   **82**
fnl 1f, no extra: clr rem: acts on firm, gd/soft & both AWs: continues to run well: see 3940 & 3404.

3701 **COLORADO FALLS 19** [7] P Monteith 6-9-5 (73) P Hanagan 3/1 FAV: 6/-154043: Cl-up, no extra from   3   **74**
dist: well bckd: see 3701 & btr 1506 (C/D).

2616 **MINIVET 63** [8] R Allan 9-7-12 (52) D Fentiman(6) 8/1: 0054-054: Handy, onepcd dist: op 6/1: new   hd   **52**
stable: recent wnr over hdles (clmr, rtd 116h, 2m6.5f on fast & soft): see 2616 (T D Easterby).

4012 **KIDZPLAY 6** [4]8-9-1 (69) N Mackay(3) 12/1: 4215345: Prom over 10f, no extra: qck reapp: see 3151.   1½   **66**

4008 **MILLENNIUM HALL 6** [2]5-8-8 (62) L Enstone(3) 12/1: 1106606: Mid-div, prog when no room 2f out, btn.   5   **52**

3970 **LEOPARD SPOT 8** [1]6-7-12 (40h)T P (48) R Ffrench 6/1: 02/40/-007: Slow away, nvr a factor: well   6   **34**
bckd: first time t-strap & cheek pieces: btr 3760.

3760 **PILGRIMS PROGRESS 17** [3]4-9-5 (73) R Winston 6/1: 00130-48: Cl-up over 10f, fdd: btr 3760.   1½   **52**
8 Ran   Time 2m 54.18(8.68)   Owned: Mr Robert Gray   Trained: Wingate

Official Going GOOD (GOOD/SOFT places); GOOD/SOFT Races 2-5; SOFT 6-7. Heavy Rain through Afternoon.

4139   2.00 European Breeders Fund Maiden Stakes 2yo (D)
£4774 £1469 £735   5f213y rnd   Good/Soft   Inapplicable   Inside

3951 **YAJBILL 10** [2] M R Channon 2-9-0 VIS (81) T E Durcan 5/1: 23221: Made all, held on gamely   **87**
cl-home: apprec first time visor & made best use of stands rail: overdue win, eff at 6f on firm & gd/soft grnd:
handles a stiff/gall or sharp/undul trk & suited by forcing tactics: see 3951 & 3120.

    OLIGARCH 10 [10] N A Callaghan 2-9-0   R Mullen 4/1: 2: b c Monashee Mountain - Courtier (Saddlers'   nk   **85+**
Hall) Held up, prog 2f out, fin strongly & only just failed: nicely bckd, clr of rem on debut: Feb foal, cost
E12,500: half-brother to 5/7f juv wnr Barbajuan: sire a high-class 7f performer: eff over a sharp/undul 6f on
gd/soft grnd: runs well fresh: fine debut, win similar sn.

    THE PHEASANT FLYER [6] B J Meehan 2-9-0   J F McDonald(3) 14/1: 3: ch g Prince Sabo - Don't Jump 2½   **79**
(Entitled) Prom, onepcd fnl 1f on debut: 6,000gns Mar foal: half-brother to 7f 2yo wnr Head Boy: dam a 1m wnr,
sire a high-class juv: eff at 6f on gd/soft grnd, 7f will suit: sharper next time.

3951 **CORDAGE 10** [1] G A Butler 2-9-0   E Ahern 10/1: 54: Sn outpcd, styd on strongly fnl 1f, nrst fin: hd   **78**
handles gd/soft grnd: crying out for 7f &/or a more gall trk: see 3951.

3103 **PEEPTOE 45** [12] R L Moore 11/4 FAV: 325: Chsd ldrs, onepcd fnl 1f: well bckd, 6 wk abs: 1¾   **70**
most disapp on this rain-softened grnd, much btr 3103 & 2658 (gd).

3975 **FASYLITATOR 8** [4]2-9-0 Dane O'Neill 9/2: 636: Prom 4.5f, wknd: tchd 11/2: btr 3975 (g/f).   3   **68**

3897 **COME GOOD 12** [9]2-9-0 (73) R Hughes 8/1: 526327: Chsd ldrs 4f, wknd: btr 3897.   1¼   **65**

3824 **KIRKHAMMERTON 15** [5]2-9-0   V Slattery 66/1: 08: ch c Grand Lodge - Nawara (Welsh Pageant)   7   **50**
Dwelt, nvr nr ldrs: 36,000gns Mar foal: half-brother to numerous wnrs, incl a decent wnr abroad.

3141 **DREAMERS LASS 44** [7]2-8-9 (60) S Drowne 50/1: 2069: Nvr nr ldrs: 6 wk abs: best 1786 (g/f).   3½   **37**

2625 **ANGELAS GIRL 64** [3]2-8-9   C Catlin 100/1: 000: 10th: Slowly away, al well bhd, t.o. in last: 9 wk abs.   20   **0**
10 Ran   Time 1m 12.57 (4.77)   Owned: Sheikh Ahmed Al Maktoum   Trained: West IIsley

4140   2.30 Manmatters Co Uk Handicap Stakes 3yo+ 0-75 (E)   [73]
£3387 £1042 £521   5f59y rnd   Good/Soft   Inapplicable   Inside

3463 **MOLOTOV 30** [12] I W McInnes 4-8-0 (45) Natalia Gemelova(7) 14/1: 00-10041: Made all, grabbed   **53**
stands side rail & styd on strongly fnl 1f, rdn out: eff at 5/6f, has tried 7f: acts on fast, gd/soft grnd &
fibresand: handles a stiff or sharp/undul trk & has reportedly broken blood vessels: see 3463 & 1948.

3984 **GONENDUNNETT 21** [8] Mrs C A Dunnett 5-9-0 vis (59) Dane O'Neill 10/1: 1031052: Prom, kept on   1½   **62**
under press fnl 1f, not pace of wnr: solid run, acts on firm, gd/soft & both AWs: see 2957 (C/D).

3984 **REDWOOD STAR 21** [10] P L Gilligan 4-8-9 e (54) D Fox(5) 12/1: 4003043: Chsd ldrs, outpcd halfway,   ½   **56**
rallied fnl 1f & not btn far: acts on fm, gd/soft & polytrack: likes Brighton: see 3984.

4010 **ONLINE INVESTOR 7** [6] N Tinkler 5-9-3 (62) T E Durcan 5/1: 0000024: Dwelt, sn mid-div, short of   nk   **63**
room after halfway, kept on but not pace to chall: see 4010.

3984* **ONE WAY TICKET 32** [9]4-9-10 p (69) R L Moore 7/2 FAV: 3100045: Chsd wnr till no extra fnl 1f: nk   **69**
bckd from 11/2, clr of rem: fine run under top-weight, landed C/D void race in 3984.

4070 **MULTAHAB 4** [1]5-8-0 t (45) B Swarbrick(5) 25/1: 4000006: Nvr btr than mid-div: qck reapp.   5   **33**

4070 **PULSE 4** [2]6-8-13 p (58) P Fitzsimons 7/1: 3005547: Al mid-div: qck reapp.   shd   **46**

3984 **YORKIE 9** [11]5-8-11 (56) Dean McKeown 13/2: 0022048: Chsd ldrs till wknd dist: btr 2846.   hd   **43**

4041 **EMARADIA 5** [3]3-8-0 (47) C Haddon(7) 20/1: 2266039: Chsd ldrs, btn 1.5f out: qck reapp.   2½   **28**

3809 **BANJO BAY 16** [5]6-9-9 (68) A Nicholls 6/1: 3006000: 10th: Slow away, nvr trbld ldrs: lost ch start.   6   **34**

3569 **LANDING STRIP 25** [4]4-9-7 (66) L Fletcher(3) 25/1: 0-005000: 11th: Al outpcd: see 2669.   5   **20**

3911 **SWEET TALKING GIRL 11** [7]4-7-12 (18oh)T p (25) F P Ferris(3) 100/1: 50-00000: 12th: Slowly away, al bhd 17   **0**
12 Ran   Time 1m 04.54 (4.54)   Owned: Ivy House Racing   Trained: Catwick

---

4141   3.00 Totesport Com Handicap Stakes 3yo+ 0-80 (D)   [74]
              £5525 £1700 £850   7f214y rnd   Good/Soft   Inapplicable   Inside

3986 **LUCEFER** 8 [7] G C H Chung 6-7-12 (6oh) (44) J F McDonald(3) 13/2: 0344031: Hld up, gd hdwy 2f out,   53
led in fnl 1f & sn 2L clr, put head in air & not go on, just prevailed: eff around 1m, stays a sharp 9.7f: acts on
fm, soft & polytrack: likes a sharp/undul trk, esp Brighton: gd eff from out of the h'cap but did his best to throw
this away, one to be cautious with: see 3986 & 1132.
3694 **FLINT RIVER** 20 [11] H Morrison 6-9-7 (73) L Fletcher(3) 11/2: 1240022: Trkd ldrs, went on 2f out   hd   75
till collared dist, rallied cl-home & only just failed: op 7/2: deserves to go one btr, see 3694.
3898 **JOHANNIAN** 12 [9] J M Bradley 6-9-3 (69) R L Moore   7/1: 5020463: Chsd ldrs, prog to lead dist   ¾   69
till collared ins fnl 1f, no extra: op 9/1: gd eff on grnd prob softer than ideal: see 2931 & 2087.
3364 **STAR SENSATION** 33 [2] P W Harris 4-9-12 (78) I Mongan 20/1: 0-656004: Dwelt, styd on well fnl 1f.   1   76
3986* **JUSTE POUR LAMOUR** 8 [4]4-9-1 (67) D Fox(5) 9/2 FAV: 0040015: Held up, hdwy 2f out, onepcd fnl 1f: ½   64
nicely bckd, clr of rem: btr 3986 (fast grnd).
3809 **TIBER TIGER** 16 [12]4-9-9 (75) T E Durcan   6/1: 2005556: Dwelt, nvr btr than mid-div: see 2600.   4   65
3694 **LONDONER** 20 [8]6-8-8 (60) P Doe 12/1: 0535207: Front rank, wknd 1.5f out: btr 3676 (firm grnd).   5   42
3963* **DIDOE** 9 [10]5-8-1 (6ex) (53) Joanna Badger 12/1: 0001218: Led till 2f out, wknd & eased: prev in   1½   32
fine form on fast grnd & worth another ch back on that surface: see 3963.
3791 **GALLERY BREEZE** 17 [3]5-9-3 (69) V Slattery 25/1: 120-1009: Chsd ldrs, wkng when short of room 2f out. 3½   42
3791 **ALAFZAR** 17 [5]6-8-5 bl t (57) F P Ferris(3) 12/1: 3040440: 10th: Keen & prom 5f, sn wknd.   1¼   28
3980* **EL CHAPARRAL** 8 [1]4-9-8 (6ex) (74) Dane O'Neill 11/1: 0202010: 11th: Slowly away, nvr a factor &   1½   43
fin last: almost certainly not at home on this easy grnd, all prev form on fast & firm: much btr 3980.
11 Ran   Time 1m 39.32 (7.32)   Owned: Mr Ian Pattle   Trained: Newmarket

---

4142   3.30 Ian Carnaby Selling Stakes 3yo (G)
              £2512 £718 £359   1m1f209y   Soft   Inapplicable   Outside

3874 **IVORY COAST** 13 [3] W R Muir 3-8-13 BL (57) S Drowne 3/1: 2000501: Chsd ldr, went on 3f out, rdn   54
well clr fnl 1f: bt in for 6,500gns: imprvd drpd to sell grade in blnks: eff at 10f on soft grnd & polytrack.
4113 **TSHUKUDU** 3 [5] M Blanshard 3-8-7 (36) D Kinsella 7/1: 0000302: Nvr far away, chsd wnr fnl 2f, no   5   40
impress: qck reappr: far from disgraced at today's weights, eff at 10f on soft grnd: see 3874.
3739 **MISS PROCURER** 19 [4] P F I Cole 3-8-7 (57) R L Moore 6/4 FAV: 65-50453: Waited wth, eff 3f out,   3   35
btn dist: hvly bckd: expected to do much btr but unproven on soft grnd: see 3515.
4076 **BIG BAD BURT** 4 [6] G C H Chung 3-8-12 (59) Dean Williams(7) 6/1: 4600404: Slowly away, nvr nr ldrs.   12   25
3730 **TAMARINA** 19 [7]3-8-7 bl (38) J F McDonald(3) 33/1: 0000005: Led till 3f out, sn wknd: see 240 (AW).   2   17
2849 **PRINCE RENESIS** 55 [2]3-8-12 S Righton 12/1: 0006: b g Mind Games - Stoneydale (Tickled Pink)   3   18
Al rear, t.o.: 8 wk abs: drpd to sell grade & much longer 10f trip: see 1539.
2812 **VENERDI TREDICI** 57 [1]3-8-7 (48) Dean McKeown 8/1: 0030-007: Chsd ldrs, wknd 3f out: 8 wk abs.   1   11
7 Ran   Time 2m 12.76 (14.96)   Owned: Mrs J M Muir   Trained: Lambourn

---

4143   4.00 Farm Fresh Supplies Handicap Stakes Fillies 3yo+ 0-70 (E)   [71]
              £3414 £1050 £525   1m3f196y   Soft   Inapplicable   Outside

3690 **PAPEETE** 20 [4] Miss B Sanders 3-8-9 (52) S Drowne 20/1: 00-44001: Trkd ldrs, outpcd 2f out, rdn   62
out to lead ins fnl 1f: prev eff at 7f: relished this step up to 12f: acts on fast & soft, prob any trk: see 2133.
3638 **PRECIOUS MYSTERY** 22 [2] A King 4-9-10 (57) E Ahern 6/1: 62016-42: With ldr till led over 2f out,   ½   65
hdd ins fnl 1f, styd on: clr of rem: eff at 1m, stays 12f: acts on firm & soft: gd run: see 3638.
3714 **TATA NAKA** 19 [7] Mrs C A Dunnett 4-8-10 (43) Lisa Jones 7/1: 0500223: Bhd, hdwy 3f out, hung   4   45
left over 1f out, no impress: see 3714.
3690 **SPRING ADIEU** 20 [6] Mrs A J Perrett 3-9-5 (62) R L Moore 16/1: 00-4004: Led till over 2f out,   2½   60
hung left & no extra 1f out: see 2893.
3948 **SERRAVAL** 10 [8]6-9-10 (57) R Thomas(5) 4/1: 0000/-235: Bhd, hdwy 2f out, sn no impress.   3   50
3913* **SCIENCE ACADEMY** 11 [5]3-9-10 (67) N De Souza(5) 1/1 FAV: 0562116: Cl-up, wknd over 2f out, btn   6   52
when hung left over 1f out: well bckd: not handle this soft grnd? much btr 3913 & 3714 (fast).
3605 **ELLOVAMUL** 24 [9]4-9-6 (53) P Makin(5) 20/1: 4040107: In tch, rear & btn 3f out: op 12/1.   5   31
3230 **SPOT IN TIME** 39 [10]4-9-8 (55) Natalia Gemelova(7) 25/1: 00008: In tch to 4f out, t.o.: with I McInnes.   dist   0
8 Ran   Time 2m 41.07 (12.87)   Owned: Mr Mark L Champion   Trained: Epsom

---

4144   4.30 Alexander Catering Classified Stakes 3yo+ 0-60 (F)
              £3052 £872 £436   6f209y rnd   Soft   Inapplicable   Inside

1956 **LANDUCCI** 92 [1] J W Hills 3-9-3 T (63) S Drowne 25/1: 00-2061: Rcd alone on inner, joined main   67
stands side group 3f out, led well over 1f out, drvn out ins fnl 1f, just held on: long abs: eff at 7f, prob stays
8.4f: acts on soft, prob fibresand: back to form in first time t-strap: see 1220.
3676 **PRIME OFFER** 21 [14] A Jay 8-9-9 (64) G Baker 8/1: 4121542: Mid-div, short of rm & switched left   shd   67
over 2f out, styd on well fnl 1f, kept on nr fin: acts on gd/soft & soft, loves firm/fast: in gd form.
3785 **WELCOME SIGNAL** 17 [16] J R Fanshawe 4-9-8 p (63) J D Smith 12/1: 35-05503: Dwelt & outpcd, hdwy   1¼   63+
when not clr run over 1f out, pushed through to chall ins fnl 1f, nrst fin: handles fast, soft & polytrack: closer
to first 2 with a clr run, poss wnr: keen in mind: see 2529.
3634 **ROMAN MAZE** 23 [4] W M Brisbourne 4-9-6 (61) R Hughes 6/1: 5000424: Chsd ldrs, no impress fnl 2f.   2   57
3573 **LAND OF NOD** 25 [18]3-8-11 VIS (60) E Ahern 14/1: 00-4005: In tch, kept on ins fnl 1f: tried visor.   1¼   50
3676* **MISTER CLINTON** 21 [3]7-9-7 (62) Dane O'Neill 10/1: 4012016: In tch, hdwy 4f out, no impress 2f   hd   54
out: best on faster grnd: see 3676.
3995 **MORAG** 8 [11]3-8-12 (61) P Doe 8/1: 0006627: Dwelt, bhd, hdwy 4f out, no impress over 1f out.   2½   46
2148 **ICE DRAGON** 83 [8]3-9-0 (63) P Robinson 14/1: 62-08: b f Polar Falcon - Qilin (Second Set)   ¾   46
Cl-up, wknd over 1f out: long abs: rnr-up last of 2 '03 starts (fills mdn): eff at 7f on polytrack: with M
Tompkins. 2 Sep'03 Ling 7ap 70a- D:
3788 **HEAD BOY** 17 [9]3-9-0 (59) R L Moore 16/1: 5654209: Handy till lost place after 2f, hdwy 2f out, wknd.   1½   44

BRIGHTON   TUESDAY 24.08.04   Lefthand, V Sharp, Undulating Track

4126 **DAVE 1** [15]3-9-3 (63) M Savage(5) 12/1: 0050-100: 10th: Rcd in 2nd, lost place 2f out, wknd: op 9/1. ½ 46
4109 **STOKESIES WISH 3** [5]4-9-2 (60) Lisa Jones 10/1: 5406330: 11th: Led alone in centre, hdd over 1f out. hd 39
3963 **BEAUTY OF DREAMS 9** [13]3-8-12 (61) S Hitchcott(3) 5/1 FAV: 0-000530: 12th: Nvr a factor. 1½ 38
3933 **Nemo Fugat 11** [17]5-9-7 vis(62) T E Durcan 20/1:0   4126 **Sir Don 1** [6]5-9-8 vis(63) A Nicholls 25/1:0
2723 **Nine Red 60** [7]3-8-11 (59) P Fitzsimons 33/1:0   3846 **Rowan Pursuit 14** [10]3-8-11 (60) C Catlin 20/1:0
16 Ran Time 1m 28.97 (9.17)   Owned: Mr R J Tufft   Trained: Lambourn

4145   5.00 Express Chef Amateur Riders Handicap Stakes 3yo+ 35-55 (F)   [34]
£3038 £868 £434   1m1f209y   Soft   Inapplicable Outside

3512 **LUCAYAN DANCER 28** [12] D Nicholls 4-11-7 (55) Miss Kelly Harrison(3) 14/1: 34-65501: In tch, hdwy 62
over 1f out, rdn out ins fnl 1f, led fnl strides: eff btwn 7/10.5f, tried further: acts on firm & soft, any trk,
likes Brighton: capitalised on fav'ble h'cap mark: see 1049.
4037 **GO GREEN 6** [16] P D Evans 3-10-12 t (54) Miss E Folkes(3) 12/1: 5021432: Handy, hdwy to lead 4f nk 60
out, hdd fnl strides: qck reapp: acts on firm & soft: gd run, continues in fine form & is consistent: see 3730.
3505 **EMPERORS WELL 28** [13] M W Easterby 5-11-7 bl (55) Miss S Brotherton 16/1: 04146-03: Cl-up, ev ch 2½ 57
over 1f out, sn onepcd: suited by forcing the pace at 1m/8.5f, now stays 10f: acts on fast & soft: fair run.
3704 **PRIVATE SEAL 20** [3] Julian Poulton 9-10-11 t (45) Mr A Chahal(7) 25/1: 0032634: Slow away in rear, ½ 46
kept on well from 2f out & nrst fin: see 3288.
3669 **LAZZAZ 21** [1]6-10-11 (45) Mrs Marie King(5) 7/1: 4342655: In tch, some late gains. nk 45
3727 **MOLLYS SECRET 19** [2]6-10-13 BL (47) Miss N Forde(5) 12/1: 0003036: Rear, hdwy 3f out, ev ch over 1¼ 45
1f out, sn no impress: clr of rem: tried blnks: see 2844.
3242 **HEALEY 39** [11]6-10-11 (45) Mr S Dobson(3) 25/1: 4032-007: Bhd, hdwy over 2f out, no impress over 3½ 38
1f out: now with I McInnes: see 2988.
3963 **HIRAYNA 9** [15]5-11-2 (50) Mr C Davies(5) 8/1: 30448: Handy, no impress over 1f out. 7 34
3895 **COOLFORE JADE 12** [9]4-10-7 (41) Mr Joshua Harris(7) 50/1: 0063009: In tch, rcd far side straight, 1 23
no impress over 1f out: on unfavored side: see 2381.
3715 **DUKES VIEW 19** [10]3-10-13 (55) Miss L J Harwood(3) 16/1: 0055060: 10th: Mid-div, rcd far side ½ 36
straight, no impress over 1f out: on unfavoured side: see 2837.
3373 **JESSINCA 33** [8]8-10-4 (38) Mr E Dehdashti(3) 10/1: 6032050: 11th: Chsd ldrs, no impress over 1f out. 8 7
3829 **ABSINTHER 15** [17]7-11-1 (49) Mrs S Bosley 5/1 FAV: 0214330: 12th: Bhd/slow away, mod late gains. 5 11
3651* **CHUBBES 22** [20]3-10-9 bl (51) Miss A Frieze(7) 20/1: 0044010: 13th: Mid-div wide, outpcd over 5f ¾ 12
out, sn btn: now with B Llewellyn: btr 3651 (clmr, fast).
4113* **MISTER COMPLETELY 3** [14]3-10-9 (6ex) (51) Miss K Manser(5) 9/1: 0016010: 14th: Cl-up, wknd 2f out. 1½ 10
3605 **HOLLY ROSE 24** [7]5-11-5 p (53) Ms C Williams 14/1: 0442000: 15th: No danger. 10 0
4113 **Prince Valentine 3** [4]3-10-10 P(52) Mr N Storey(7) 25/1:0
3916 **Flaming Spirt 11** [19]5-11-2 (50) Mrs S Moore(3) 7/1:0
3650 **Night Market 22** [5]6-11-3 P(51) Mrs N Wilson(3) 16/1:0
2431 **Margery Daw 71** [18]4-10-12 (46) Miss J C Duncan(5) 50/1:0
19 Ran Time 2m 14.18(13.38)   Owned: Lucayan Stud   Trained: Thirsk

YARMOUTH   TUESDAY 24.08.04   Lefthand, Flat, Fair Track

Official Going SOFT; HEAVY after race 3. Heavy Rain through Afternoon.

4146   2.15 Peter Higby Racecourse Photographer Selling Nursery Handicap Stakes 2yo (G)   [78]
£2576 £736 £368   6f3y str   Soft   Inapplicable Stands Side

3745 **MARCELA ZABALA 18** [8] J G Given 2-8-4 (54) J Fanning 10/1: 0101: Cl-up, hdwy to lead just ins 59
last, styd on, rdn out: bght in for 5,200gns: eff at 5/6f on fast or soft grnd, gall or fair trks: no signs of
breathing problems that were reported last time: see 3209.
3393 **CHICAGO NIGHTS 32** [4] P C Haslam 2-7-13 (49) D Fentiman(7) 15/2: 40052: Set pace, rdn & hdd ins hd 53
last, kept on, just held: eff at 6f & imprvd for forcing tactics on this soft grnd & drop to sell company: see 2921.
3931 **JUSTENJOY YOURSELF 11** [5] C A Dwyer 2-7-12 (60h) (42) Hayley Turner(5) 16/1: 606403: Held up, hdwy 2½ 47
2f out, kept on ins last, no threat to 1st 2: btr effort at 6f on soft grnd in sell h'cap company: see 2921.
3864 **JOE NINETY 13** [6] J S Moore 2-7-12 (1oh) (47) N Mackay(5) 12/1: 6003004: In tch, onepcd over 1f ½ 46
out: eff at 6f on soft: see 2449, 2294.
3570 **FAITHFUL FLASH 25** [3]2-8-1 (51) F Norton 8/1: 60465: Rdn bhd, late gains: tried blnks 3570. shd 48
3871 **HIS MAJESTY 13** [1]2-8-12 (62) Steven Harrison(7) 10/1: 0326: Chsd ldr, wknd fnl 1f: see 3871 (gd). 2 55
3745 **YELDHAM LADY 18** [7]2-8-0 (50) J Quinn 10/2 RV: 0027: Dwelt, nvr a factor: see 3745. 1¼ 40
3504 **EMERAUDE DU CAP 28** [10]2-8-1 (51) J Mackay 4/1: 0038: Nvr a factor: see 2927. 2 37
3871 **GENERAL NUISANCE 13** [9]2-8-5 p (55) S Chin 13/2: 4323039: In tch, wknd 2f out: op 9/1: btr 3491. ½ 40
9 Ran Time 1m 17.86 (7.46)   Owned: Zaha Racing Syndicate   Trained: Gainsborough

4147   2.45 Haven Caister Holiday Park Maiden Stakes 2yo (D)
£3829 £1178 £589   1m3y str   Soft   Inapplicable Inside

3582 **FANTASY RIDE 25** [5] J Pearce 2-9-0 J Quinn 16/1: 01: b c Bahhare - Grand Splendour (Shirley 96
Heights) Slow away, sn in tch, hdwy to lead over 1f out, rdn clr: Jan foal: half-brother to a 6/7f scorer: stays
1m well & much imprvd for this front 2: looks useful, win again under similar conditions.
      INCA WOOD 4 [4] M Johnston 2-8-9 J Fanning 11/1: 2: b f Timber Country - Lady Icarus (Rainbow 11 74
Quest) In tch stands side, eff over 1f out, not pace of wnr: Apr foal: op 8/1: poss eff at 1m on soft grnd: learn
plenty from this & shld rate more highly.
3470 **SAND REPEAL 30** [1] Miss J Feilden 2-9-0 B Reilly(3) 40/1: 03: b g Revoque - Columbian Sand 2 76
(Salmon Leap) Switched to race stands side, led that group 2f, cl-up, wknd over 1f out: Mar foal: half-brother to
wnrs over 7f/hdles: btr effort.
3811 **PIANOFORTE 16** [9] D R Loder 2-9-0 T P Queally 5/6 FAV: 624: Led stands side group after 2f till 1 74

over 1f out, wknd: hvly bckd: much btr expected after 3811 (firm, 7f) & poss not enjoy soft grnd.

| | | | | ½ | 70 |
3786 **TERMINATE 17** [6]2-9-0 S Sanders 25/1: 005: In tch stands side, wknd 2f out: quals for h'caps. ½ 70
3991 **ASHARON 8** [3]2-9-0 K Fallon 14/1: 06: Slow away, hdwy to lead centre group after 1f till dist. 10 56
3691 **WANDERING ACT 20** [2]2-9-0 J Fortune 66/1: 07: Handy centre, wknd over 2f out. 7 46
IRISH BALLAD [7]2-9-0 N Callan 20/1: 8: Slow away & al bhd stands side. dist 1
3786 **ZALAAL 17** [8]2-9-0 L Dettori 3/1: 629: Al bhd stands side: not enjoy soft? btr 3786 (polytrk). 16 0

9 Ran Time 1m 45.51 (10.41) Owned: Mr J P Hayes Trained: Newmarket

---

4148

3.15 Bbc Look East Classified Stakes 3yo 0-80 (D)
£6734 £2072 £1036 **7f13y str** **Soft** **Inapplicable** Stands Side

3860 **JATH 13** [4] Julian Poulton 3-8-9 (80) N Callan 5/1: 1-06061: Trkd ldr, hdwy to chall over 1f 83
out, styd on well ins last, led line, drvn out: eff at 7f/1m on fast & soft grnd: see 1931.
3978 **DESERT CRISTAL 8** [2] J R Boyle 3-8-9 (78) L Dettori 7/4 FAV: 5-263132: Led till over 1f out, shd 82
rallied to lead again ins last, drvn & collared on line: game run & deserves similar: see 3978, 3446.
3953* **MAJORS CAST 10** [3] J Noseda 3-9-3 (85) J Murtagh 15/8: 313: Handy, hdwy to lead over 1f out, sn ½ 89
hdd, rallied to lead again ins last, sn hdd & no extra: drifted from 6/5: acts on fast & soft: going the right way.
3597 **KEYAKI 24** [1] C F Wall 3-8-9 (80) S Sanders 7/2: 661144: In tch, hdwy to lead over 1f out, hdd & nk 80
no extra ins last but not btn far: acts on fast & soft: consistent: see 2742, 2343.

4 Ran Time 1m 31.46 (8.86) Owned: Meddler Bloodstock Trained: Newmarket

---

4149

3.45 Listed Saltwell Signs Virginia Rated Stakes Handicapfillies 3yo+ 0-110 (A)
£17400 £6600 £3300 **1m2f21y** **Soft** **Inapplicable** Inside [111]

3236 **POSTERITAS 39** [9] H R A Cecil 3-7-13 (8oh) (82) J Quinn 10/1: 32151: Mid-div, switched centre 4f 91
out, styd on to lead dist, rdn out: eff at 1m, imprvd for recent step up to 10f, further could suit: acts on firm &
soft grnd: lightly rcd 3yo who made gd use of feather weight in today's testing grnd: can rate higher: see 2793.
3435* **LA PERSIANA 31** [10] W Jarvis 3-8-13 (96) K Darley 9/1: 0-521152: Cl-up, ev ch dist, kept on fnl 1 104
1f, not pace of wnr: op 7/1: acts on firm & soft: v progressive, imprvd again in defeat: see 3435.
1619 **BOWSTRING 108** [11] J H M Gosden 3-8-13 (96) J Fortune 10/1: 0-1223: Led 3f, styd in tch & 1 101
switched centre to lead 3f out, sn hung left, hdd dist, no extra: long abs: continues to run well: see 1619.
2772* **ICE PALACE 59** [3] J R Fanshawe 4-9-7 (96) J Murtagh 15/8 FAV: 140-3214: Mid-div, eff 2f out, no 1 100
impress in fnl 1f: well bckd tho' op 5/2: 8 wk abs: not disgraced under top-weight on today's grnd: see 2772.
3565 **MYSTICAL GIRL 25** [5]3-8-9 (92) J Fanning 12/1: 2130605: Handy, prog & ev ch dist, no extra. 2 93
3949 **WEE DINNS 10** [12]3-8-2 (5oh) (85) F Norton 20/1: 5221266: Rear, prog 3f out, wknd dist: clr rem. 1 84
3794 **WINDY BRITAIN 17** [7]5-8-13 (88) D Holland 10/1: 1-042607: Nvr nrr than mid-div: btr 3072 (gd). 5 80
3754 **CARINI 18** [6]3-8-11 (94) D Sweeney 33/1: 11-3638: Led after 3f till 3f out, wknd: btr 3754 (g/f). 3½ 81
3978 **ULTIMATA 8** [8]4-8-7 (2oh) (80) O Urbina 14/1: 1-0229: Al bhd: btr 3978 (1m, fast). 1¼ 67
3965 **FLOWERDRUM 9** [1]4-8-11 (86) K Fallon 10/1: 0141050: 10th: In tch, wknd 3f out: btr 2662 (1m, gd). 13 53
2210 **CRYSTAL 81** [4]3-8-10 (93) L Dettori 11/2: 0-2150: 11th: Rear, nvr a factor: long abs: disapp 1¼ 58
on today's soft grnd: showed more in 1384 (mdn, gd).
3458 **QUDRAH 30** [2]4-8-7 (2oh) (80) S Sanders 66/1: 0054050: 12th: Dwelt, nvr a factor: see 1005. dist 0

12 Ran Time 2m 14.29 (10.09) Owned: Mr K Abdulla Trained: Newmarket

---

4150

4.15 Haven Seashore Holiday Park Claiming Stakes 3-4yo (E)
£4027 £1239 £620 **6f3y str** **Soft** **Inapplicable** Stands Side

3720 **BEAUVRAI 19** [5] V Smith 4-8-8 p (75) K Fallon 4/6 FAV: 5300231: Rider slow to remove blindfold & 53
missed break, prog halfway, styd on to lead ins fnl 1f, readily, val 3L+: bckd, clmd for 8,000: eff at 5/6f on firm,
soft grnd & both AWs: eff at cheek pieces: apprec drop to claim grade: see 3720 & 3584.
3911 **INDRANI 11** [3] John A Harris 3-7-12 p (38) Hayley Turner(5) 14/1: 2050002: Rcd centre, led, hdd 1½ 41
ins fnl 1f, not pace of wnr: ran well in defeat: see 2925 & 1641.
3708 **HAMMER OF THE GODS 20** [1] Julian Poulton 4-9-0 VIS t (45) N Callan 7/1: 0500/-33: Cl-up centre, 1¼ 47
ev ch dist, sn hung left & no extra: clr rem: first time visor: eff at 6f on soft grnd: gd eff under top-weight.
3936 **ELLIOTS CHOICE 10** [4] D Carroll 3-8-7 BL (60) S Sanders 3/1: 6000024: Cl-up stands side alone, 10 25
wknd dist: v disapp in first time blnks: yet to convince at this trip: showed more 3936 (1st time visor, 5f).
2431 **TRUSTED INSTINCT 71** [2]4-8-6 (57) B Reilly(3) 25/1: 0-000005: In tch centre 3f, sn hung right & fdd. 8 5

5 Ran Time 1m 17.95 (7.55) Owned: Mr R J Baines Trained: Newmarket

---

4151

4.45 Aylsham Bathroom & Kitchen Centre Handicap Stakes 3yo+ 0-70 (E)
£4085 £1257 £629 **2m** **Soft** **Inapplicable** Stands Side [70]

1064 **SENDINTANK 140** [5] S C Williams 4-9-6 (62) N Callan 2/1 FAV: 0-111131: Held up, smooth prog 4f 70+
out, led dist, pushed clr, val 8L+: gamble from 9/2: long abs: eff at 12f, imprvd for today's step up to 2m: acts
on fibresand, soft & hvy grnd: goes well fresh: v easy wnr for yard that rarely gets it wrong when money is down:
unexposed at this trip, see 1064.
3998 **LARKING ABOUT 8** [10] W J Musson 4-8-10 bl (52) K Fallon 11/1: 0-000602: Missed break, prog to 5 55
lead 4f out, hdd under press dist, not pace v easy wnr: op 7/1, clr rem: eff at 13f, now stays 2m: acts on soft
grnd & polytrack: has slipped down the weights, caught a tartar here, see 1899.
3049 **PEAK PARK 47** [1] J A R Toller 4-8-4 vis (46) T P Queally 25/1: 60-00203: Handy, styd on to lead 17 36
5f out, hdd 4f out, hung right & sn fdd: 7 wk abs: btr 2856 (fast).
3611 **SONOMA 24** [3] M L W Bell 4-9-6 (62) Hayley Turner(5) 10/1: 6001444: Rear, nvr nrr than mid-div. 5 47
3200 **MADIBA 41** [7]5-9-0 (56) J Fanning 20/1: 22000P5: Handy 9f, sn fdd: 6 wk abs. dist 0
3701 **RIYADH 20** [6]6-9-13 (69) K Darley 5/1: 3002026: Al bhd: btr 3701. 7 0
3493 **VANBRUGH 29** [2]4-7-12 (3oh)vis t (37) J McAuley 33/1: 0000007: Led, hdd 5f out, fdd: btr 336. 28 0
1163} **SEATTLE PRINCE 490** [4]6-8-9 (51) D Holland 20/1: 431/004-8: gr g Cozzene - Chicken Slew (Seattle 11 0
Slew) Handy 4f, sn wknd: reapp: plcd on last of only 3 '03 starts (h'cap, rtd 50): h'cap scorer in '02 (R
Hannon): dual h'cap wnr in '01: eff at 10/12f, stays 2m well: acts on firm, gd & prob any trk, likes Salisbury:
best without blnks/visor: with S Gollings.

YARMOUTH   TUESDAY 24.08.04   Lefthand, Flat, Fair Track

1 Oct'02 Brig 12gd 56- F: 1 Aug'01 Sali 12g/f 79-75 E: 2 Jul'01 Chep 10.1g/f 76-74 D: 1 Jun'01 Sali 9.9g/f 75-68 D:
3998 **LAWRENCE OF ARABIA 8** [9]4-9-2 (58) S Sanders 9/4: 004/-0669: Cl-up, fdd after 1m: well bckd: v   1½   0
disapp on today's soft grnd & step up to 2m: showed more in 3998 & 3437.
3783 **SIMONS SEAT 17** [8]5-9-4 (60) M Fenton 33/1: 030-6660: 10th: Bhd, al well adrift: btr 1003.   1¼   0
10 Ran   Time 3m 45.02(21.72)   Owned: Steve Jones and Phil McGovern   Trained: Newmarket

CURRAGH   SATURDAY 21.08.04   Righthand, Galloping Track

Official Going Good/Firm

4152	2.45 Listed Emerald Bloodstock Belgrave Stakes 3YO+ (A)

£23273 £6828 £3253   6f str   Good/Firm   Inapplicable

3495* **ULFAH 28** [10] Kevin Prendergast 3-9-0   D P McDonogh 7/1: 1-061151: Prom, led 3f out, drvn out to   109
hold on fnl 1f: eff at 6/6.5f on fast grnd: likes a gall trk & Curragh: game, useful & improving.
    DESERT FANTASY 13 [9] C Roche 5-9-6 tbl F M Berry 9/2 JT FAV: 011-0362: b g Desert King - Petite   hd   110
Fantasy (Mansooj) Missed break, hdwy 3f out, kept on ins fnl 1f, just held by wnr: won 3 times in '03 including
this race (also 2 h'caps): eff at 6/7f on fast & soft grnd: likes Curragh: eff with t-strap & blnks: smart.
2486 **GRAND REWARD 21** [7] A P O'Brien 3-9-0   J P Spencer 11/2: 5-2501U3: Bhd, prog bef 1f out, styd   1   104
on, nrst fin: earlier stks wnr at Naas (6f, fast): btr 1995 & 1559.
3441 **NEW SEEKER 28** [12]4-9-3 (103) R Smith 9/2 JT FAV: 11-24060: 10th: Cl up 4f, sn fdd: see 3441 & 2558. 1¾ 98
12 Ran   Time 1m 11.60 ()   Owned: Hamdan Al Maktoum   Trained: Ireland

4153	3.50 Tattersalls Ireland Sale Stakes 2YO ()

£95550 £37050 £22425   6f str   Good/Firm   Inapplicable

3774 **BEAVER PATROL 14** [15] R F Johnson Houghton 2-8-12 (95) M J Kinane 9/2: 13219621: Cl up, styd on   111
to lead 2f out, hdd bef 1f out, rallied to lead again ins fnl 1f, rdn out: eff at 6/7f on firm & gd/soft grnd: acts
on a gall or easy trk: useful & still improving: can hold his own in listed/Group 3 class: see 3774.
3319 **INDESATCHEL 34** [8] David Wachman 2-8-12   J P Spencer 6/4 FAV: 4132: Bhd, prog halfway, led bef   1   106
1f out, hdd ins fnl 1f, not pace wnr: gd run in defeat & will appreciate return to 7f: see 3319.
3585 **VISIONIST 22** [5] J A Osborne 2-8-12   P J Smullen 11/2: 143: Mid div, prog bef 1f out, nrst fin: 1   103
fine eff on only 3rd ever start & sure to apprec return to 7f: see 3585 & 3120.
3266 **CELTIC SPA 35** [3] Mrs P N Dutfield 2-8-7   N G McCullagh 16/1: 105304: Handy, onepcd bef 1f out: 3   89
poss stays 6f, return to 5f will suit: see 2786.
3623* **EASY FEELING 21** [7]2-8-7 (77) J A Heffernan 6/1: 33415: Led, hdd 2f out, no extra: btr 3623 (fm).   2   83
2902 **MALINSA BLUE 50** [14]2-8-8 (1ow) F M Berry 16/1: 6226: Bhd, nvr nrr than mid div: 7 wk abs.   nk   83
3750* **DONT TELL TRIGGER 15** [12]2-8-7 (65) J D Smith 25/1: 610018: Nvr nrr than mid div: up in class.   1   79$
3632 **TIVISKI 20** [4]2-8-7 (77) P Shanahan 20/1: 104509: Cl up 4f, wknd: btr 3081.   2   73
3736* **LOOK AT THE STARS 16** [11]2-8-12 R Smith 12/1: 010: 14th: Rear, nvr a factor: btr 3736 (mdn auct). 1¼ 74
16 Ran   Time 1m 12.80 ()   Owned: G C Stevens   Trained: Blewbury

4154	4.25 Group 2 Galileo EBF Futurity Stakes 2YO (A)

£52390 £16055 £7605   7f rnd   Good/Firm   Inapplicable

3841 **ORATORIO 13** [2] A P O'Brien 2-9-0   J P Spencer 5/4 FAV: 10121: Cl up, styd on to lead bef 2f   117+
out, sn clr, eased ins fnl 1f, val 4L+: eff at 7f, 1m will suit: acts on fast & gd grnd: likes a gall
trk: v smart juvenile, can rate higher & win in Gr 1 class: see 3841.
2819* **DEMOCRATIC DEFICIT 55** [1] J S Bolger 2-9-4   M J Kinane 7/2: 112: In tch, styd on to chase wnr 2f   2   112
out, styd on, not his pace: 8 wk abs: stays 7f: smart 2yo who ran well conceding weight all round.
3494* **ELUSIVE DOUBLE 28** [4] D K Weld 2-9-0   P J Smullen 13/2: 113: Held up, nvr nrr than mid div: not   1   106
disgraced up in grade: see 3494 (listed).
    CARNEGIE HALL 34 [3] A P O'Brien 2-9-0   J A Heffernan 6/1: 14: b c Danehill - Bolshaya (Cadeaux   nk   105
Genereux) In tch, eff 3f out, onepcd fnl 1f: recent mdn wnr here at the Curragh: eff at 7f on fast.
2897* **MELROSE AVENUE 50** [5]2-9-0 R Ffrench 9/2: 515: Led, always hung right, hdd bef 2f out, fdd: op   6   93
7/2, 7 wk abs: more expected after 2897 (gd/soft, mdn).
5 Ran   Time 1m 25.70()   Owned: Mrs John Magnier   Trained: Ireland

DEAUVILLE   SATURDAY 21.08.04   Righthand, Galloping Track

Official Going HEAVY.

4155	1.05 Listed Prix de la Vallee d'Auge 2YO (A)

£15845 £5546 £5546   5f   Heavy

    BEAUTIFIX [3] C Laffon-Parias 2-8-9   O Peslier 9/2: 1: b f Bering - Beautimix (Linamix)   95
Narrowly prevailed in a v tight fin: eff at 5f on hvy grnd: useful filly.
3376* **CAMMIES FUTURE 30** [7] P W Chapple-Hyam 2-8-11   O Doleuze : 312: Front rank, bmpd dist, ev ch fnl ½ 95
1f & just btn in a thrilling fin: eff at 5/6f, return to the latter will suit: acts on gd/soft & hvy: see 3376.
3632 **MADAME TOPFLIGHT 20** [5] Mrs G S Rees 2-8-8 (80) D Bohilla : 02152: Chsd ldrs, fin strongly &   dht   92
ddhtd for 2nd In a thrilling fin: eff at 5f, return to 6f will suit: acts on firm & hvy see 3632 & 3323.
3509 **SIENA GOLD 25** [4] B J Meehan 2-8-8   T E Durcan : 110184: Led till dist, sn bmpd, kept on well   shd   91
under press & btn under 1L: gd front running effort, acts on fast & hvy: see 3266.
2094 **PRINCE CHARMING 82** [2]2-8-11   J Fanning : 1186: Prom, imprvd to lead dist till ins fnl 1f, no extra. 1 91
9 Ran   Time 1m 02.80 ()   Owned: Wertheimer Et Frere   Trained: France

---

4156   1.35 Listed Criterium du Fonds European de L'Elevage 2YO   (A)
£42958 £17183 £12887   **1m rnd**   **Heavy**

3532 **BERKHAMSTED 24** [6] J A Osborne 2-8-11 Gary Stevens 7/2: 16251: Prom, led dist, held on a shade   **101**
cosily: eff at 7f/1m: acts on firm, clearly relishes gd/soft & hvy: well plcd for this val prize, see 3532 & 3126.
    GLAZED FROST [2] P Bary 2-8-8   T Thulliez : 2: gr f Verglas - Vol Sauvage (Always Fair)   hd   **94**
    DOCTOR DINO [1] R Gibson 2-8-11   T Jarnet : 3: ch c Muhtathir - Logica (Priolo)   1   **95**
7 Ran   Time 1m 52.30 ()   Owned: Richard Leslie   Trained: Upper Lambourn

---

4157   2.05 Group 3 Prix du Calvados - Haras du Logis (Fillies) 2YO   (A)
£25704 £10282 £7711   **7f str**   **Heavy**

2553 **COURS DE LA REINE 64** [5] P W Chapple-Hyam 2-8-9   C Soumillon 13/1: 301: Trkd ldr, went on 2f out   **103**
till hdd dist, rallied gamely to regain lead on line: 9 wk abs: much imprvd form on this hvy grnd: stays 7f well &
runs well fresh: useful, see 2310 (debut, mdn).
    ROYAL COPENHAGEN [4] R Gibson 2-8-9   T Jarnet 6/4 FAV: 112: b f Inchinor - Amnesia (Septieme   snk   **102**
Ciel) Chsd ldrs, chall strongly fnl 1f, just btn in a thrilling finish: well bckd: prev unbtn, stays 7f on hvy.
    GORELLA [8] J de Rouaille 2-8-9   E Legrix 68/10: 213: ch f Grape Tree Road - Exciting Times   snk   **101**
(Jeune Homme) Rear, hdwy to lead dist, caught dying strides: eff at 7f on hvy grnd: useful.
3803* **GLORIOUS STEP 13** [9]2-8-9   J Fortune 91/10: 318: Led till 2f out, wknd & eased: see 3803 (fm).   18   **71**
8 Ran   Time 1m 32.30 ()   Owned: Classic St Gatien Partnership   Trained: Newmarket

---

4158   2.35 Group 2 Prix Guillaume d'Ornano 3YO   (A)
£42146 £16268 £7764   **1m2f**   **Heavy**

3793* **MISTER MONET 14** [8] M Johnston 3-8-11 (106) J Fanning 9/5 FAV: 31-21111: Made all, pushed clr   **122**
fnl 1f, cmftbly: another impressive win, completed 4-timer today: suited by 10f on drm & hvy grnd: likes forcing
tactics on a gall trk: high-class, still unexposed & Gr 1 success surely awaits: see 3793.
3316 **DELFOS 38** [2] C Laffon-Parias 3-8-11   M Blancpain 26/10: -2111022: Chsd ldrs, went after wnr 2f   4   **114**
out, no impress fnl 1f: eff at 10f on hvy grnd: met a high-class rival: see 3316.
    ISLERO NOIR [1] Y de Nicolay 3-8-11   S Pasquier 132/10: 215-1623: b c Septieme Ciel - Mioura   1½   **112**
(Saumarez) Chsd ldrs, onepcd fnl 1.5f: eff at 10f on hvy grnd: smart.
    APEIRON [5] Mario Hofer 3-8-11   T Thulliez 89/10: 11-10034: b c Devil River Peek - Asuma   nk   **111**
(Surumu) Rear, styd on late nvr dngrs: German chall, eff at 10f on hvy grnd: smart.
3553 **GATWICK 23** [6]3-8-11 (104) T E Durcan 23/1: 13110605: Nvr btr than mid-div: see 1919.   3   **106**
3274 **LORD MAYOR 35** [4]3-8-11 (103) Gary Stevens 138/10: 31-31556: Trkd wnr, wknd 2f out: btr 2520.   5   **98**
9 Ran   Time 2m 14.40()   Owned: Syndicate 2002   Trained: Middleham Moor

---

DEAUVILLE   SUNDAY 22.08.04   **Righthand, Galloping Track**

Official Going Very Soft

4159   2.20 Group 1 Prix Morny Casinos Barriere (Colts & Fillies) 2YO   (A)
£100599 £40246 £20123   **6f str**   **Soft**   **Inapplicable**

3498* **DIVINE PROPORTIONS 28** [9] P Bary 2-8-11   C-P Lemaire 33/10: 1111: Chsd ldrs, styd on to lead ins   **120+**
fnl 1f, rdn out, val more: relished step up to 6f, 7f/1m sure to suit: acts on gd, imprvd on soft: high-class &
exciting filly who is unbeaten in 4 starts, win more Gr 1's & a strong 1000 Guineas candidate for '05.
3658* **LAYMAN 21** [8] A Fabre 2-9-0   Gary Stevens 7/10 FAV: 112: Led, hung right from dist, hdd ins fnl   1½   **117**
1f, not pace wnr: acts on gd & soft grnd: fine eff on step up to Group 1 grade, win more Gr races: see 3658.
3841 **RUSSIAN BLUE 14** [6] A P O'Brien 2-9-0   J P Spencer 78/10: 111233: Al prom, ev ch dist, no extra   1½   **113**
fnl 1f: acts on fast & soft grnd: not disgraced & drop to Gr 2 comp will suit: see 3841 & 1994.
3028* **CAPTAIN HURRICANE 46** [7] P W Chapple-Hyam 2-9-0   J Fortune 14/1: 2214: Bhd, prog wide halfway,   3   **104**
no impress bef 1f out: 6 wk abs: reportedly unsuited by testing grnd: btr 3028 (Gr 2, fast).
3566 **MYSTICAL LAND 23** [4]2-9-0   L Dettori 7/10 FAV: 212325: Chsd ldrs, wknd 2f out: btr 3566 (Gr 2, fm).   5   **91**
3509* **TOURNEDOS 26** [2]2-9-0   T E Durcan 31/1: 122017: Al bhd: btr 3509 (5f, fast, Gr 3).   4½   **79**
3511* **DOCTORS CAVE 26** [5]2-9-0   O Peslier 27/1: 000018: Mid div 4f, fdd: btr 3511 (mdn, fast).   2½   **72**
9 Ran   Time 1m 12.80 ()   Owned: Niarchos Family   Trained: France

---

4160   2.50 Group 2 Prix Jean Romanet (Fillies & Mares) 4YO+   (A)
£42148 £16268 £7764   **1m2f**   **Soft**   **Inapplicable**

4625} **WHORTLEBERRY 323** [5] F Rohaut 4-8-12 bl   T Gillet 104/10: 21-44161: ch f Starborough - Rotina   **118**
(Crystal Glitters) Prom, led bef 1f out, rdn out: Gr 3 & Gr 2 wnr in '03: eff at 10/12.5f on gd & hvy grnd: eff
with blnks: v smart. 2 Oct'03 Long 12.5sft 116- A: 1 Aug'03 Deau 102- :
3012 **PRIDE 49** [9] A de Royer-Dupre 4-8-12 (80) D Bonilla 38/10: 10-41352: Mid div, prog bef 1f out,   2   **114**
nrst fin: another gd run: apprec Gr 3 company: see 3012 & 2143.
3621 **CHORIST 22** [4] W J Haggas 5-9-2 (112) D Holland 6/4 FAV: 013-1133: Led, hdd 3f out, sn regained   nk   **117**
lead, hdd bef 1f out, no extra: ran to smart -best under top-weight: see 3621 & 2816 (Gr 1).
3659 **MONTURANI 21** [7]5-8-12 (104) T E Durcan 26/1: 2-362445: Cl up over 1m, no extra: btr 3004 (fm).   3½   **108**
2816 **SOLDERA 57** [8]4-8-12 (103) J P Murtagh 32/1: 4140-349: Cl up 1m, wknd: 8 wk abs.   3½   **103**
3089+ **FELICITY 44** [6]4-8-12 (94) J Fortune 163/10: 35-03410: 11th: Cl up, led 3f out, hdd bef 2f out,   **2**
wknd: 6 wk abs: btr 3089 (gd/soft, Gr 3).
2816 **HANAMI 57** [1]4-8-12 (110) L Dettori 22/1: 6100-360: 12th: Al bhd: 8 wk abs: btr 1997.   **2**

DEAUVILLE SUNDAY 22.08.04 Righthand, Galloping Track

13 Ran Time 2m 12.90 () Owned: J Beres Trained: France

4161 **3.20 Group 2 Prix Kergorlay 3YO+ (A)**
£42148 £16268 £7764 **1m7f Soft Inapplicable**

3776 **GOLD MEDALLIST 15** [9] D R C Elsworth 4-9-4 (100) R Hughes 321/10: 603-6041: Led bef 13f out, **113**
drvn out ins fnl 1f: suited by 15/16f on firm, improved on soft here: likes to force the pace: smart.

3497 **BRIAN BORU 28** [5] A P O'Brien 4-9-8 J P Spencer 4/1: 3-155552: Bhd, prog bef 1f out, styg on **1½ 115**
when short of room just ins fnl 1f, kept on, nvr getting to wnr: stays 15f: smart, better run.

4628} **CUT QUARTZ** [3] R Gibson 7-9-4 T Jarnet 86/10: 0-011143: b h Johann Quatz - Cutlass (Sure **nse 110**
Blade) In tch, styd on to chase wnr bef 1f out, no extra cl home: earlier won stks & listed race: won Gr 3 in '03:
won this race in '02 (also Gr1 3rd): eff at 10/15.5f on gd & soft grnd: acts on a stiff/gall trk: useful.
1 May'03 Long 15.5sft 114- A: 1 Aug'02 Deau 15g/s 112- :

3776 **DOUBLE OBSESSION 15** [2] M Johnston 4-9-4 vis (95) J F Egan 137/10: 00015424: Cl up, no extra bef **2 108**
1f out: not disgraced: loves Ascot: see 3776 (gd, h'cap).

3958 **THE GREAT GATSBY 8** [7]4-9-4 bl (112) L Dettori 54/10: 225-3048: Chsd ldrs, 13f, wknd: btr 2636. **14½ 95**
9 Ran Time 3m 20.90() Owned: J C Smith Trained: Whitsbury

FAIRYHOUSE SUNDAY 22.08.04 Righthand, Stiff, Undulating Track

Official Going GOOD/SOFT.

4162 **4.35 Listed Ballycullen Stakes 3YO+ (A)**
£21157 £6207 £2957 **1m6f Good/Soft**

2583 **HOLY ORDERS 23** [8] W P Mullins 7-9-7 bl (110) D J Condon 8/1: 6U0-4461: Held up, smooth hdwy to **113**
lead 2f out, sn clr, easily: eff at 12/14f, poss not quite stay 2m6f: handles firm, wng form on gd & soft grnd: gd
weight carrier who wears blnks: smart stayer who has proved v profitable for connections: see 2583.

4019 **MKUZI 7** [10] John M Oxx 5-9-12 M J Kinane 13/8 FAV: 66051132: Chsd ldrs, kept on under press **3½ 113**
fnl 2f, no ch with wnr: well bckd from 9/4, qck reapp: eff at 10/14f on firm & soft: see 4019 & 2817.

4227} **MAHARIB 57** [4] D K Weld 4-9-7 P Shanahan 10/1: 1145-203: b c Alhaarth - Diali (Dayjur) Waited **¾ 107**
with, styd on fnl 2f, nvr nrr: tchd 16/1, 8 wk abs: List & Gr 3 wnr in '03: eff at 10/14f on gd & soft grnd, likes
a gall trk: lightly rcd & running into form. 1 Jun'03 Curr 14gd 110- A: 1 Jun'03 Lime 12g/s 111- A:

4309} **ONE OFF 339** [7]4-9-7 (87) S Sanders 6/1: 111112-7: b g Barathea - On Call (Alleged) Led till 2f **9 98**
out, wknd on reapp: won 6 successive h'caps in '03: eff at 12f/2m on fast, gd grnd & fibresand: gd weight carrier
who handles any trk: tough & v prog last year: ran well for a long way on grnd prob too soft: sharper next time.
2 Sep'03 Yarm 16gd 88-87 C: 1 Aug'03 Sand 14g/f 93-82 D: 1 Aug'03 Newc 14.4g/f 85-72 E: 1 Jul'03 Folk 15.4g/f 74-66 E:
1 Jul'03 Hayd 14gd 69-60 E: 1 Jun'03 Wolv 12af 66-61 E: 1 Jun'03 Brig 11.9g/f 67-54 E:
11 Ran Time 3m 0.10() Owned: A McLuckie Trained: Ireland

BRIGHTON WEDNESDAY 25.08.04 Lefthand, V Sharp, Undulating Track

Official Going Heavy

4163 **2.10 Wellington Maiden Auction Stakes 2yo (E)**
£3429 £1055 £528 **6f209y rnd Soft 90 -11 Slow Inside**

3489 **DAISY BUCKET 30** [4] D M Simcock 2-8-2 C Catlin 9/4: 031: Keen mid-div, prog halfway, styd on to **72**
lead bef 1f out, pushed clr despited tail flashing, val bit more: eff at 7f on gd & soft: improving, see 3489.

2584 **GRAND WELCOME 67** [10] C Tinkler 2-8-9 BL S Drowne 5/1: 0002: b g Indian Lodge - Chocolate Box **3 72**
(Most Welcome) Led, hdd bef 1f out, not pace wnr: clr rem: Mar foal, cost 6,000 gns: dam successful at 13f: sire
Gr1 wnr at 1m: eff at 7f, further will suit: acts on soft grnd: imprvd eff with 1st time blnks.

3735 **PHLAUNT 20** [5] R F Johnson Houghton 2-8-2 (70) S Carson 5/4 FAV: 4033: Held up, rcd keenly, prog **5 56**
3f out, wknd bef 1f out: well bckd: prob unsuited by soft grnd on 1st try at 7f: btr 3735 (6f, gd).

3285 **PRALIN STAR 38** [8] H S Sweeting 2-8-11 G Baker 33/1: 04: ch c Daggers Drawn - Polaregina (Rex **1½ 62**
Magna) Mid-div, rcd alone down centre of trk after halfway, hung left & wknd bef 1f out: Apr foal, cost 10,000 gns:
half brother to numerous wnrs: dam unrcd: sire decent performer at sprint dists.

3798 **CROSS MY SHADOW 17** [7]2-8-13 t Dane O'Neill 10/1: 05: b c Cape Cross - Shadowglow (Shaadi) Keen **½ 63**
cl-up till halfway, sn outpcd, rallied 2f out, fdd dist: Apr foal, cost 20,000 Euros: half brother to listed 14f
wnr Holy Orders, also Grade 1 3m wnr over hdles: sire Group 1 wnr at 1m.

2802 **UGLY SISTER 58** [3]2-8-5 L Keniry(2) 25/1: 006: Keen cl-up 4f, sn outpcd, rallied 2f out, sn fdd. **2 49**
6 Ran Time 1m 26.90 (7.1) Owned: Old Suffolk Stud Trained: Newmarket

4164 **2.40 Dearle & Henderson Selling Stakes 3yo+ (G)**
£2584 £738 £369 **6f209y rnd Soft 90 -09 Slow Inside**

4007 **WOOD FERN 8** [6] M R Channon 4-9-1 vis (48) C Catlin 14/1: 5000061: Cl-up, styd on to lead **50**
cl-home, drvn out: no bid: eff at 7f/1m, has tried 12f: acts on firm, soft grnd & polytrack: apprec refitting of vis.

3717* **RILEYS DREAM 20** [3] B J Llewellyn 5-9-1 p (48) D Corby(3) 5/1: 0100512: Handy, styd on for press **nk 48**
to lead ins fnl 1f, hdd cl-home: acts on fast & soft grnd: another gd eff from 5lb h'cap: see 3717 (sell h'cap).

3844 **CONFUZED 15** [2] D Flood 4-9-1 e (40) S Hitchcott(3) 20/1: 0004003: Keen bhd, prog 3f out, ev ch **nk 47**
ins fnl 1f, just held in photo: eff at 7f: improved for step up to 7f: acts on soft grnd & polytrack: see 3301.

3731 **YOUNG LOVE 20** [8] Miss E C Lavelle 3-8-5 (49) Martin Dwyer 9/1: 0-064064: Chsd ldrs 4f, sn **hd 41**
outpcd, rallied bef 1f out, not btn far in 4th: visor left off: eff at 7f, return to 1m will suit: acts on fast & soft.

3515 **ELSINORA 28** [14]3-8-5 (42) D Kinsella 9/1: 0002635: Held up, prog halfway, no impress fnl 1f. **2½ 36**

1253

3676 **FLORIAN** 22 [9]6-9-1 (57) K Fallon 7/2: 33-00056: Led, sn clr, hdd ins fnl 1f, no extra: btr 2799 (fast).   nk   40
4057 **ENNA** 6 [16]5-8-10 (45) S Drowne 5/2 FAV: 4042067: Cl-up till halfway, no extra: qk reapp: btr 3788.   2½   30
3215 **SOCIAL CONTRACT** 41 [17]7-9-1 vis (44) T P Queally 8/1: 0000008: Al in rear: 6 wk abs: btr 783.   4   28
3888 **FULVIO** 13 [4]4-9-1 vis (49) P Doe 20/1: 0005009: Rear, nvr a factor: btr 3286.   3   22
9 Ran   Time 1m 26.75 (6.95)   Owned: Wooden Tops Partnership   Trained: West IIsley

---

4165   3.10 C Brewer And Sons Handicap Stakes Fillies 3yo 35-55 (F)   [63]
£3052 £872 £436   **7f214y rnd**   **Soft 90**   **-05 Slow**   IInside

4113 **FIDDLES MUSIC** 4 [2] Miss S West 3-8-5 (40) C Catlin 12/1: 1456501: Made all, drvn out ins fnl   48
1f: quick reapp: stays 10f, apprec drop back to 1m: acts on gd & soft grnd: see 1134.
4037 **ARMENTIÈRES** 7 [3] J L Spearing 3-9-4 bl (53) S Drowne 13/2: 30-60062: Handy, styd on to chase ldr   4   53
2f out, kept on but al held fnl 1f: quick reapp: acts on gd/soft, soft & fibresand: enjoyed return to 1m, see 164.
3651 **LA CALERA** 23 [12] G C H Chung 3-9-0 vis (49) O Urbina 5/1: 3100533: Mid-div, prog halfway, hdd   2½   44
when short of room 2f out & dist, no extra: op 4/1: new stable, see 3651 (M F Harris).
3719 **MAGIC VERSE** 20 [9] R Guest 3-9-0 (49) R L Moore 100/30 FAV: 0044454: Bhd, hmpd 4f out, mod gains.   2½   39
4053 **KELTIC RAINBOW** 6 [8]3-8-10 (45) F McDonald(3) 10/1: 3-460045: Chsd ldrs till halfway, sn no extra.   1½   32
3996 **ZONNEBEKE** 9 [6]3-8-13 (48) Dane O'Neill 7/1: 0341206: In tch, prog to lead bef 3f out, sn hdd,   5   26
wknd fnl 2f: op 5/1: twice below 3706 (fast).
3874 **SOVIET SPIRIT** 14 [10]3-9-4 (53) R Thomas(5) 10/1: 0535047: Al in rear: btr 3291.   13   9
4037 **MYSTIC MOON** 7 [15]3-8-10 (45) R Mullen 10/1: 4004008: Cl-up 5f, fdd: quick reapp.   5   0
3291 **GREAT BLASKET** 37 [4]3-9-3 (52) K Fallon 7/1: 30004-09: Bhd, short of room halfway, wknd fnl 2f.   13   0
9 Ran   Time 1m 39.61 (7.61)   Owned: Mr Michael Moriarty   Trained: Lewes

---

4166   3.40 Army Benevolent Fund Diamond Jubilee Handicap Stakes 3yo 0-70 (E)   [75]
£3819 £1175 £588   **1m3f196y**   **Soft 90**   **-31 Slow**   Outside

3765 **QUARRYMOUNT** 18 [5] Sir Mark Prescott 3-9-2 (63) J Mackay 10/11 FAV: 00-02121: Made all, went clr   76+
3f out, eased fnl 1f, val 10L+: well bckd: eff at 10/11f, apprec step up to 12f: acts on fast, gd & polytrack,
enjoyed today's soft grnd: acts on v sharp/undul trk: prog 3yo who can win more h'caps for shrewd stable.
3867 **RUMBLING BRIDGE** 14 [2] J L Dunlop 3-8-9 (56) P Doe 7/1: 546-002: Chsd ldrs, styd on to chase wnr   7   60
bef 1f out, sn hung left & no ch with easy wnr: clr rem: prob stays 12f on soft grnd: see 3455.
4068 **TREASON TRIAL** 5 [4] Mrs Stef Liddiard 3-8-10 (57) S Drowne 4/1: 0643133: Keen bhd, prog 6f out,   5   54
wknd 2f out: quick reapp: disapp on step up to 12f in today's soft grnd: showed more in 3874 (10f, gd).
3845 **KOMOTO** 15 [6] G A Butler 3-9-2 VIS (63) T P Queally 8/1: 1004: Prom, wkng when hung left ins fnl 1f.   nk   59
3091 **HINODE** 47 [3]3-9-2 (63) M Tebbutt 8/1: 0035: Prom 10f, fdd: 7 wk abs: op 13/2: btr 3091 (1m, aw).   3½   54
5 Ran   Time 2m 42.76 (14.56)   Owned: Lady Fairhaven   Trained: Newmarket

---

4167   4.10 Montpelier Re Handicap Stakes 3yo+ 0-70 (E)   [70]
£3507 £1079 £540   **1m1f209y**   **Soft 90**   **-12 Slow**   Outside

3232 **SECLUDED** 40 [5] E F Vaughan 4-9-8 BL (64) S Drowne 11/4: 355-5001: Held up, prog 5f out, styd on   71
to lead 1f out, eased cl home, val 6L+: abs: eff at 10f on fast, improved for soft & blnks.
2701 **MISS INKHA** 62 [10] R Guest 3-8-11 (61) Martin Dwyer 7/2: 00662: Handy, styd on to lead 2f out,   4   63
hdd 1f out, no extra: clr rem: 9 wk abs: eff at 1m, imprvd for step up to 10f: acts on gd & soft grnd: see 2701.
3923 **PENDING** 12 [9] J R Fanshawe 3-9-6 p (70) Dane O'Neill 7/2: 05-30603: Led 1m out, hdd 2f out, wknd.   5   65
3695 **KERNEL DOWERY** 21 [2] P W Harris 4-9-7 p (63) E Ahern 5/2 FAV: 0211004: Bhd, nvr able to chall: ¾   56
well bckd: not handle soft? btr 2433 (C/D, fast).
3867 **RICHMOND LODGE** 14 [6]4-8-12 (54) G Baker 12/1: 00310-05: Led till after 2f, hung left/wknd 1f out.   17   22
5 Ran   Time 2m 8.00 (10.2)   Owned: Racing For Gold   Trained: Newmarket

---

4168   4.40 Brighton Square Supports The Martlets Hospice Handicap Stakes 3yo+ 0-70 (E)   [69]
£3523 £1084 £542   **6f209y rnd**   **Soft 90**   **+09 Fast**   Inside

2927} **PLUM** 406 [9] E F Vaughan 4-9-12 (67) K Fallon 5/1: 443-1: br f Pivotal - Rose Chime (Tirol)   74
Bhd, prog 2f out, styd on under hands & heels to lead cl-home: bckd on reapp: plcd on last of only 3 '03 starts
(auct mdn, rtd 69 best, A C Stewart): eff at 7f, 1m+ will suit: handles firm & fast, enjoyed today's soft grnd:
acts on a v sharp/undul trk & goes well fresh: fine eff to defy long abs on h'cap bow.
3790* **JAZZY MILLENNIUM** 18 [11] B R Millman 7-9-1 vis (56) S Drowne 9/2 CO FAV: 6330412: In tch, styd on   hd   61
to lead 2f out, hdd under pres cl-home: another gd run here at Brighton: see 3790 & 3176.
4077 **LOCH LAIRD** 5 [2] M Madgwick 9-8-7 (48) C Haddon(7) 7/1: 0500543: Rear, prog & ev ch dist, sn   2   49
edged left & onepace: quick reapp: see 846.
3286 **ZINGING** 39 [10] J J Bridger 5-7-12 (3oh) (36) Hayley Turner(5) 25/1: 6556004: Held up, prog 3f   shd   39
out, ev ch 1f out, no extra: see 2216.
3790 **HARBOUR HOUSE** 18 [1]5-8-4 (45) A Daly 14/1: 1302665: Led 6f out, hdd halfway, styd cl-up & ev ch   2½   40
bef 1f out, no extra: btr 2957 (5f, gd).
3174 **TEMPER TANTRUM** 43 [15]6-9-2 p (57) N Pollard 7/1: 2040546: Bhd, outpcd halfway, sn short of room,   ½   51
rallied late: 9 wk abs: tchd 12/1: see 3144.
3788 **TOJONESKI** 18 [18]5-8-4 p (45) J F McDonald(3) 9/2 CO FAV: 3420307: Cl-up, led halfway till 2f out, wknd.½   38
3895 **HILARIOUS** 13 [13]4-8-12 BL (43) R Thomas(5) 25/1: 4564068: Chsd ldrs 4f, no extra: 1st time blnks.   3   30
3654 **MUSICAL TOP** 23 [12]4-9-4 (59) M Fenton 12/1: 50-0039: led, hdd 6f out, styd cl-up, wknd 2f out,   ¾   44
btn when sn hung left: btr 3654 (Brit bow, fast).
3888 **HAND CHIME** 13 [14]7-10-0 (69) T P Queally 9/2 CO FAV: 0500200: 10th: Handy, wknd 2f out: btr 3708.   1   52
10 Ran   Time 1m 25.52 (5.72)   Owned: Sir Robert Stewart   Trained: Newmarket

BRIGHTON   WEDNESDAY 25.08.04   Lefthand, V Sharp, Undulating Track

4169   5.10 Manmatters Co Uk Classified Stakes 3yo 0-60 (F)
£2940 £840 £420   5f59y str   Soft 90   +14 Fast   Inside

4094* **WUNDERBRA** 5 [6] M L W Bell 3-9-3 t (60) Hayley Turner(5) 9/4: 4513111: In tch, styd on to lead   **77**
dist, pushed clr, val 5L+: quick reapp: fast time: eff at 5/6f on firm, soft grnd & fibresand: eff in a t-strap:
most progressive, win again: see 4094 & 3976.

3693   **ACE CLUB** 21 [9] W J Haggas 3-9-4 (64) T P Queally 2/1 FAV: 21-50042: Trkd ldrs, styd on ins fnl   3½   67
1f, not pace easy wnr: well bckd: acts on fast & soft grnd: see 1570.

4094   **WENDYS GIRL** 5 [7] R P Elliott 3-8-12 bl (61) T Hamilton(3) 8/1: 0165533: Led, hdd dist, no extra: ¾   59
quick reapp: showed more in 4094 (fibresand).

3844   **ARFINNIT** 15 [3] M R Channon 3-9-0 vis (58) S Hitchcott(3) 5/1: 6400024: Nvr nrr than mid-div: btr 3844.   3   53

3143   **ARDKEEL LASS** 45 [2]3-8-11 (58) Paul Eddery 12/1: 06-00245: Chsd ldrs till halfway, wknd: 6 wk abs.   nk   49

1942   **CHEEKY CHI** 94 [11]3-8-11 (60) R L Moore 13/2: 1400006: Cl-up, fdd bef 1f out: tchd 10/1: long abs.   12   24

3788   **EASILY AVERTED** 18 [10]3-9-0 t (48) R Thomas(5) 33/1: 0000607: Missed break, nvr a factor: btr 492 (AW).6   14

7 Ran   Time 1m 4.04(4.04)   Owned: Fitzroy Thoroughbreds   Trained: Newmarket

---

MUSSELBURGH   THURSDAY 26.08.04   Righthand, Sharp Track

Official Going Good/Firm (Str Course - Gd Places). Rnd Course- Fm Places)

4170   2.30 Racing Uk Apprentice Handicap Stakes 3yo+ 0-70 (E)   [67]
£3393 £1044 £522   1m6f   Good/Firm 40   -26 Slow   Inside

3669   **RED FOREST** 23 [3] J Mackie 5-9-8 t (61) D Nolan 5/1 FAV: 1503331: In tch, styd on to lead 2f out,   **72**
pushed out, val bit more: suited by 12/14f on fast, gd grnd & fibresand: eff in a t-strap: consistent, see 3669.

3502   **TURN OF PHRASE** 30 [7] R A Fahey 5-9-1 VIS (54) T Hamilton 15/2: 5213-002: Rear, prog to chase wnr   1¾   62
2f out, styd on fnl 1f, al held: clr rem: eff at 12/13f, now stays 14f: imprvd eff with fitting of 1st time visor.

3703   **REDSPIN** 22 [8] J S Moore 4-9-7 (60) Derek Nolan(3) 20/1: 4440003: Bhd, prog 3f out, onepcd dist.   3   62

3649   **ZAN LO** 24 [1] B S Rothwell 4-8-5 (44) T Eaves 25/1: 0600004: Mid-div, eff 2f out, kept on fnl 1f.   1¾   46

3588   **COSMIC CASE** 26 [11]9-8-10 (49) N Mackay 8/1: 2303125: Nvr nrr than mid-div: op 11/2: btr 3588.   shd   50

3557   **SHERWOOD FOREST** 28 [2]4-8-5 vis (44) Leanne Kershaw(3) 14/1: 0360526: Prom over 12f, no extra.   nk   44

4138   **MILLENNIUM HALL** 3 [9]5-9-9 (62) P Mulrennan 11/1: 1066067: Nvr nrr than mid-div: qck reapp.   1   61

4084   **REPULSE BAY** 6 [6]6-8-7 (46) Lisa Jones 12/1: 5000008: Keen in tch 12f, no extra: qck reapp.   ¾   44

3881   **BOLD BLADE** 15 [10]3-8-9 (60) K Ghunowa(5) 16/1: 0100249: Saddle slipped sn after start, led till   2   56
2f out, wknd: worth another ch: showed more in 3666.

3810   **CLARADOTNET** 18 [5]4-9-10 (63) S Hitchcott 7/1: 0630320: 10th: Mid-div 12f, wknd: btr 3810.   ¾   58

3929* **ROMIL STAR** 13 [12]7-9-1 vis (54) S Bushby(7) 11/1: 1135210: 11th: Chsd ldrs 12f, wknd: btr 3929 (soft).   3   46

4012   **ALPINE SPECIAL** 9 [4]3-9-2 (67) G Bartley(7) 15/2: 0-604220: 12th: Rcd keenly, saddle slipped sn   dist 34
after start, cl-up over 11f, wknd & eased: ignore this: btr 4012 & 3904.

12 Ran   Time 3m 5.75 (9.25)   Owned: Mr P Riley   Trained: Church Broughton

4171   3.00 Dm Hall Selling Stakes 2yo (E)
£6903 £2124 £1062   7f30y rnd   Good/Firm 40   -35 Slow   Far side

3930   **TOLDO** 13 [7] A Berry 2-8-11 (53) F Lynch 33/1: 0004021: Stumbled after leaving stalls, prog 3f   **72**
out, no room bef 1f out, styd on despite hanging left to lead ins fnl 1f, rdn out: bght in for 7,000gns: imprvd for
recent step up to 7f: acts on fast or soft grnd: likes sell grade: see 3930.

4102   **ESKDALE** 5 [6] R F Fisher 2-8-11   D Nolan(3) 8/1: 0032: Handy, outpcd 2f out, rallied fnl 1f, nrst   ¾   69
fin: qck reapp: acts on fast & soft grnd: can find similar, prob at 1m: see 4102.

3864   **ZOLASH** 15 [4] J S Moore 2-8-11 (65) Derek Nolan(3) 14/1: 5060443: Mid-div, prog 2f out, kept on fnl 1f.   1¾   65

4072   **INDIBRAUN** 6 [3] P C Haslam 2-9-2 (77) G Faulkner 5/1: 5144034: Cl-up, led bef 3f out, hdd well   ¾   68
ins fnl 1f, no extra: bckd: qck reapp: shade disapp: showed more in 4072 (soft).

3736   **MYTTONS BELL** 21 [11]2-8-6 (69) D Allan 9/2 FAV: 230305: In tch over 5f, no extra: bckd: btr 3632.   1   56

3239   **ROYAL FLYNN** 41 [8]2-8-11 (70) P Makin(5) 20/1: 6406: Bhd, outpcd 2f out, rallying when short of   hd   60
room well ins fnl 1f: 6 wk abs: see 2511.

3698   **TWICE NIGHTLY** 22 [10]2-8-11 (66) J Fanning 6/1: 336507: Led over 3f, ev ch dist, wknd: op 9/1.   shd   59

3931   **STRATHTAY** 13 [1]2-8-6 P (66) K Darley 14/1: 30568: Nvr nrr than mid-div: cheek pieces.   ½   53

2959   **MR MAXIM** 53 [12]2-8-11   Dean McKeown 16/1: 0509: Chsd ldrs over 5f, wknd: 8 wk abs.   2   54

3848   **PURPLE DOOR** 16 [9]2-8-6   F Norton 8/1: 60: 10th: Mid-div 5f, sn wknd: btr 3848.   2½   44

3769   **BLISSPHILLY** 19 [14]2-8-6   P Hanagan 16/1: 060: 11th: Chsd ldrs 5f, fdd: btr 3769.   6   33

      BRONZE DANCER 0 [2]2-8-11   P Mulrennan(3) 33/1: 0: 12th: b g Entrepreneur - Scrimshaw (Selkirk)   shd   37
Al in rear: debut: Mar foal, half-brother successful at 1m: dam unrcd: sire Gr 1 wnr at 1m: with G A Swinbank.

4069   **WILTSHIRE** 6 [5]2-8-11   A Culhane 10/1: 00: 13th: br c Spectrum - Mary Magdalene (Night Shift)   7   25
Al in rear: qck reapp: Apr foal, cost 35,000 euros: half-sister 6f wnr: dam successful at 5f.

4129   **LA PROVIDENCE** 3 [13]2-8-6 bl e J Bramhill 100/1: 00: 14th: Keen rear, nvr a factor: qck reapp.   dist 0

14 Ran   Time 1m 30.18 (5.28)   Owned: Mr Anthony White   Trained: Cockerham

4172   3.30 Watch Live On Racing Uk Nursery Stakes A Handicap 2yo (D)   [95]
£6890 £2120 £1060   5f str   Good/Firm   Slow   Stands side

3652* **MONASHEE ROSE** 24 [7] J S Moore 2-8-5 (72) N Mackay(3) 9/2: 011: Slow away, prog halfway, styd on   **78**
to lead ins fnl 1f, rdn out: tchd 7/1: eff at 5f, shld get 6f: acts on fast grnd & a sharp or stiff trk: unexposed.

4049   **WONDERFUL MIND** 7 [4] T D Easterby 2-8-4 (71) D Allan 7/2: 5215632: Prom, led halfway, hdd ins   nk   74
fnl 1f, just held by wnr: qck reapp: gd eff with blnks left off: see 4049 & 2889.

3425   **LLAMADÁS** 33 [12] M Dods 2-7-12 (1oh)BL (64) P Fessey 25/1: 303403: Missed break, prog 2f out,   hd   68
styd on well ins fnl 1f, post came too sn: acts on fast & gd grnd: back to form with cheek pieces left off & first

time blnks fitted: worth another try at 6f on this evidence: see 2995.
3756 **HANDSOME LADY 20** [11] I Semple 2-8-7 (74) P Hanagan 12/1: 160564: In tch, kept on ins fnl 1f, *nk* **76**
not btn far in 4th: acts on fast & gd/soft grnd: visor left off: btr 1445.
3956 **OH DARA 12** [9]2-9-7 (88) Dean McKeown 7/1: 1305: Led, hdd halfway, no extra dist: fair run, see 3081. *2* **84**
3590 **OCHIL HILLS DANCER 26** [10]2-7-12 (3oh)T (62) D Fentiman(7) 50/1: 050456: Bhd, pog 2f out, nrst fin. *nk* **60**
3770 **AFRICAN GIFT 19** [8]2-8-1 (68) J Bramhill 25/1: 3067: Rear, prog bef 1f out, nrst fin: btr 2228 (6f). *nk* **62**
4105 **WIZARDMICKTEE 5** [6]2-8-10 (77) K Darley 14/1: 02248: Cl-up over 3f, no extra: qck reapp: btr 3939. *1¼* **67**
3488* **SMIDDY HILL 31** [3]2-9-1 (82) R Ffrench 11/4 FAV: 2414519: Cl-up 3f, sn hung right & no extra: *hd* **71**
made all to win 3488 (auct).
3832 **NE OUBLIE 17** [1]2-8-0 (67) Dale Gibson 10/1: 6430: 10th: Al in rear: btr 3832 (gd/soft). *2* **50**
3652 **SHATIN LEADER 24** [2]2-8-0 (2ow)(4oh) (61) F Norton 25/1: P6340: 11th: Chsd ldrs 3f, wknd: btr 3227. *3* **41**
4134 **NEE LEMON LEFT 3** [5]2-7-12 (2oh)BL (63) Lisa Jones 33/1: 2630640: 12th: Al in rear: 1st time blnks. *11* **9**
12 Ran Time 1m 0.97 (3.47) Owned: The Fairway Connection Trained: Hungerford

4173

4.00 Gebals Premier Claiming Stakes 3yo+ (D)
£5538 £1704 £852 **1m1f** **Good/Firm 40** **+09 Fast** Inside

4008 **YENALED 9** [2] K A Ryan 7-9-5 (69) Donna Caldwell(7) 3/1: 1122421: Rear, prog to lead 2f out, **74**
pushed out to assert, val 3L+: fast time: eff at 7f/9f, stays 10f well: acts on fm, soft & fibresand: see 4008.
4133 **BAILIEBOROUGH 3** [6] D Nicholls 5-9-5 vis (68) Alex Greaves 100/30: 1651132: Keen cl-up, ev ch bef *1¼* **68**
1f out, sn hung right & not pace of wnr: tchd 4/1 on qck reapp: back to best on return to fast grnd: see 4133.
4008 **SARRAAF 9** [3] J S Goldie 8-9-2 (64) N Mackay(3) 5/1: 3505203: Mid-div, prog when short of room 2f *hd* **64**
out till dist, kept on ins fnl 1f, nrst fin: clr rem: prob 2nd with clr run: see 3764 & btr 2568.
3946 **PHOENIX NIGHTS 12** [1] A Berry 4-9-2 (52) P Mathers(5) 25/1: 0500644: Nvr nrr than mid-div: see 423. *6* **53**
3694 **TAKES TUTU 22** [8]5-9-10 vis (76) Darren Williams 9/4 FAV: 5020035: Keen cl-up, ev ch bef 1f out, *1½* **58**
sn hung right & fdd: well bckd: v disapp on drop in grade: showed more in 3694 (1m) & 3210 (7f).
4920} **QUINTOTO 303** [7]4-9-10 (69) P Hanagan 14/1: 600000-6: b g Mtoto - Ballet (Sharrood) Led 7f, *1½* **55**
wknd: earlier p.u. over hdles (nov): h'cap wnr in '03 (T G Mills): showed mdn promise in '02 (rtd 85): eff at 10f
on fast grnd & a sharp trk: has gone well fresh: with R A Fahey.
1 Apr'03 Brig 9.9g/f 79-67 E:
1240 **MYANNABANANA 131** [4]3-8-7 vis (46) K Darley 25/1: 4405007: Prom 7f, fdd: long abs. *¾* **43**
4133 **SOCIETY TIMES 3** [9]11-8-10 t (24) D Fentiman(7) 100/1: 500//-0008: In tch 7f, fdd: qck reapp. *½* **38$**
8 Ran Time 1m 53.52 (2.82) Owned: The Fishermen Trained: Hambleton

4174

4.30 Quality Racing On Racing Uk Handicap Stakes 3yo+ 0-90 (C) **[90]**
£10277 £3162 £1581 **5f str** **Good/Firm** **Fair** Stands side

3577 **JUSTALORD 27** [11] J Balding 6-8-10 bl (72) J Edmunds 16/1: 2306101: Prom, led dist, pushed out, **83**
val 4L+: eff at 6f, all wins have come at 5f: acts on firm, gd & loves both AWs: likes sharp trks.
4107 **STRENSALL 5** [7] R E Barr 7-9-0 (76) P Mathers(5) 14/1: 4050552: Cl-up, styd on fnl 1f, not pace *2* **79**
of wnr: qck reapp: gd eff in defeat: just btr 2690.
3852 **MUSICAL FAIR 15** [3] J A Glover 4-8-13 (75) A Culhane 20/1: 2156003: Rear, prog 2f out, nrst fin. *¾* **77**
3569 **OBE ONE 27** [15] A Berry 4-8-4 (66) Dale Gibson 10/1: 3060404: Sn in rear, hdwy 2f out, styd on *hd* **67**
fnl 1f: gd run from poor high draw & is on winning mark: see 3241 & 2559.
4048 **MISTER MARMADUKE 7** [14]3-9-0 (78) D Allan 11/1: 000-0435: Rear, prob halfway, onepcd fnl 1f. *½* **78**
3577 **TWICE UPON A TIME 27** [10]5-8-1 (63) F Norton 33/1: 0004006: Nvr nrr than mid-div: btr 3106. *1¼* **59**
3646 **DAME DE NOCHE 24** [5]4-9-11 (87) Dean McKeown 10/1: 0005307: Cl-up over 3f, no extra: btr 3569 (6f). *hd* **82**
3833* **TRUE MAGIC 17** [12]3-8-10 (74) J Fanning 9/1: 5622118: Cl-up 4f, no extra: btr 3347. *shd* **68**
3937 **HICCUPS 12** [13]4-9-2 (78) Alex Greaves 11/2 FAV: 3106339: Nvr nrr than mid-div: well bckd: btr 3937. *hd* **71**
4027 **BLUE CRUSH 8** [4]3-9-12 (90) Darren Williams 50/1: 2-000000: 10th: Cl-up till dist, wknd. *1* **80**
3937 **IMPRESSIVE FLIGHT 12** [16]5-9-11 (87) K Darley 25/1: 0/536-000: 11th: In tch wide 3f, wknd: btr 3646. *¾* **75**
3792 **MAKTAVISH 19** [17]5-9-4 p (80) P Hanagan 13/2: 3000460: 12th: Rcd alone far side, nvr a factor. *shd* **67**
3852 **CHICO GUAPO 15** [6]4-8-7 p (69) P Mulrennan(3) 25/1: 5000000: 13th: Led, hdd dist, wknd. *nk* **55**
4039 **CATCH THE CAT 8** [9]5-8-12 vis (74) G Parkin 14/1: 0001000: 14th: Al in rear: btr 3561. *½* **59**
3852 **BEYOND THE CLOUDS 15** [2]8-8-13 (75) T Eaves(3) 10/1: 0200300: 15th: Chsd ldrs 3f, wknd. *¾* **58**
4118 **ROXANNE MILL 4** [1]6-8-11 p (73) F Lynch 8/1: 5612020: 16th: Cl-up 3f, fdd: disapp: btr 4118. *¾* **54**
16 Ran Time 59.16 (1.66) Owned: Mr T H Heckingbottom Trained: Doncaster

4175

5.00 Rectangle Group Handicap Stakes 3yo 0-70 (E) **[72]**
£4193 £1290 £645 **7f30y rnd** **Good/Firm 40** **-12 Slow** Far side

3654 **SAROS 24** [10] B Smart 3-9-0 (58) F Lynch 10/1: 6020301: Prom, styd on to lead 2f out, sn edged **65**
badly left, rdn out: eff at 7f/sharp 1m on fast grnd & fibresand: loves Southwell: see 3571 & 2812.
3670 **JOSHUAS GOLD 23** [11] D Carroll 3-8-11 vis (55) D Tudhope(7) 9/2 FAV: 6000142: Keen handy, prog bef *1¼* **59**
1f out, kept on, not pace of wnr: bckd: clr rem: 4lb higher than last win in 3547 (1m).
3737 **FLASH RAM 21** [6] T D Easterby 3-9-7 (65) D Allan 10/1: 4226163: Cl-up till dist, no extra: btr 3230. *3* **63**
3906 **RARE COINCIDENCE 14** [3] R F Fisher 3-9-7 p (65) D Nolan(3) 20/1: 4440034: Led 5f, sn no extra. *½* **62**
4085 **THE NUMBER 6** [7]3-9-7 (65) T Eaves(3) 6/1: 56-335: Chsd ldrs over 4f, sn onepcd: btr 4085 (1m). *½* **61**
3702 **PURE VINTAGE 22** [8]3-9-0 (58) P Hanagan 10/1: 06006: Nvr nrr than mid-div: see 1971. *nk* **53**
4009 **THORNABY GREEN 9** [5]3-9-6 (64) P Makin(5) 10/1: 4410547: Nvr nrr than mid-div: btr 4009. *nk* **58**
4051 **SHOWTIME ANNIE 7** [4]3-9-5 (63) N Mackay(3) 10/1: 6104158: Chsd ldrs 5f, no extra: qck reapp. *nk* **56**
3526* **SON OF THUNDER 29** [1]3-9-3 (61) L Enstone(3) 7/1: 6162019: Rear, modest late gains: btr 3526 (1m). *1¼* **52**
3767 **BOWLING ALONG 19** [2]3-9-0 (58) T Hamilton(3) 16/1: 0043200: 10th: Al in rear: btr 3655 (6f). *nk* **48**
3528 **Graceful Air 29** [9]3-8-11 VIS(55) K Darley 16/1:0
3995 **Listen To Reason 10** [14]3-9-7 (65) A Culhane 20/1:0
3679 **Dark Day Blues 22** [13]3-9-6 (64) Darren Williams 12/1:0
3016 **Mister Regent 50** [12]3-9-2 bl(60) G Parkin 50/1:0
14 Ran Time 1m 28.56(3.66) Owned: Pinnacle Desert Sun Partnership Trained: Thirsk

Official Going Standard

4176 2.20 Hays Montrose Novice Stakes 2yo (D)
£3562 £1096 £548 **7f aw rnd** **Going 32** **-06 Slow** Inside

3707 **LINNGARI 22** [5] Sir Michael Stoute 2-8-12 K Fallon 3/1: 31: Cl-up, led over 1f out, styd on **98a**
well fnl 1f, rdn out: much imprvd from debut & stays 7f well on polytrack: looks useful, plenty more to come, win
more races: see 3707.
4003 **RAZA CAB 9** [6] G A Huffer 2-9-2 (90) D Holland 5/2: 3162: Cl-up, eff to chall just ins last, ½ **98a**
kept on, al just held: proving consistent & useful: see 4003, 3329.
3820* **HYPNOTIC 17** [2] Sir Mark Prescott 2-9-6 (96) J Mackay 2/1 FAV: 4113: Set pace till over 1f out, 1¼ **99a**
onepace: well bckd: not disgraced conceding weight all round: useful & improving: see 3820 (nursery h'cap).
3585 **BUNNY RABBIT 27** [7] B J Meehan 2-8-12 M Hills 11/2: 354: In tch wide, onepace fnl 2f: stays 7f 2 **86a**
on fast & prob polytrack: win a mdn: see 2792.
     TAKHLEED [4]2-8-8 R Hills 16/1: 5: b c Stravinsky - Bold Threat (Bold Ruckus) Slow away, nvr 2½ **76a**
a factor on debut: Jan foal: dam juv scorer: speedily bred but this was a stiff intro, mdns will suit.
     ABERDEEN [3]2-8-8 J F Egan 50/1: 6: b c Xaar - Olivia Jane (Ela Mana Mou) In tch, short of 1 **74a**
room ove 2f out, no extra: debut: Mar foal, cost E30,000: half-brother to wnrs over 7f/12f: bred to need 1m+.
3438 **ANTONIO STRADIVARI 33** [1]2-8-12 Martin Dwyer 33/1: 07: b c Stravinsky - Dearest (Riverman) 2½ **73a**
Slow away, sn in tch, wknd over 2f out: Mar foal, cost E75,000, dam plcd over sprint trips: speedily bred.
     TURTLE BAY [8]2-8-3 E Stack 66/1: 8: Al bhd on debut. 5 **54a**
8 Ran Time 1m 25.5 (2.7) Owned: HH Aga Khan Trained: Newmarket

---

4177 2.50 Castlemaine Xxxx Nursery Handicap Stakes 2yo (E) **[97]**
£3601 £1108 £554 **7f aw rnd** **Going 32** **-03 Slow** Inside

4105* **CUPIDS GLORY 5** [5] Sir Mark Prescott 2-10-0 (7ex) (97) J Mackay 7/4 FAV: 6111: With ldr, led over **111a**
2f out, styd on well over 1f out, drvn out: hvly bckd, qck reapp: eff over 6/7f on soft grnd & polytrack, likes
sharp trks, esp Lingfield: fast improving, useful & can carry big weights, looks well up to List/Gr 3 class.
3065 **LANGSTON BOY 49** [7] M L W Bell 2-8-1 (70) J Quinn 20/1: 42302: Handy trav well, eff to chall 1½ **80a**
appr fnl 1f, not pace of wnr ins last: 7 wk abs: imprvd for gelding op & stays 7f on polytrack, handles soft:
shown enough to win a race: see 1631, 1353.
3709 **WISE DENNIS 21** [1] A P Jarvis 2-8-9 (78) E Stack 20/1: 0033: Slow away, hld up, hdwy trav well 1¼ **85a+**
over 2f out, sn short of room, styd on well over 1f out, nrst fin: stays 7f, 1m sure to suit: acts on fast grnd &
polytrack: promising, win sn: see 3709.
3818* **WEDDING PARTY 17** [4] Mrs A J Perrett 2-8-11 (80) K Fallon 15/8: 314: Led after 2f till over 2f 1¼ **84a**
out, no extra ins last: bckd tho' op 9/4: shld stay 7f & more expected after 3818 (auct mdn, 6f).
3798 **HAWRIDGE KING 18** [2]2-8-1 (70) D Kinsella 33/1: 3565: In tch, wknd over 1f out: see 3798, 1964. 1¾ **70a**
3820 **LATERAL THINKER 17** [6]2-8-2 (71) Martin Dwyer 11/1: 3410526: Led 2f, cl-up till wknd dist. 4 **63a**
3407 **CLINET 34** [11]2-8-0 (2ow)(2oh) (65) C Catlin 40/1: 0520507: Dwelt, sn bhd, wide bend 2f out, no dngr. nk **60a**
3897 **TIME FOR YOU 14** [8]2-7-12 (1oh) (66) F P Ferris(3) 21/1: 041048: In tch, wknd 1.5f out: best 3020. nk **57a**
3285 **DREEMON 40** [9]2-8-5 (74) J F Egan 33/1: 0309: Keen, al bhd: 6 wk abs: see 2870. nk **63a**
3795 **BRIDGE TTHE STARS 19** [3]2-8-7 (76) S Carson 33/1: 150: 10th: Slow away & nvr a factor: btr 3141 (6f). ½ **64a**
3800 **NIGHTFALL 18** [10]2-9-3 t (86) L Dettori 10/1: 160: 11th: Handy, wknd 2f out: best 3438 (debut, 6f, fast). 1½ **71a**
3981 **SCROOBY BABY 10** [12]2-8-6 (75) D Holland 20/1: 20240: 12th: Al bhd. nk **59a**
3671 **CONNOTATION 23** [14]2-8-0 (69) A McCarthy 16/1: 2230: 13th: In tch, wknd 2f out: btr 3671, 2839. 2 **49a**
3943 **LADY ANN SUMMERS 12** [13]2-8-4 P (73) J F McDonald(3) 20/1: 03400: 14th: In tch, wknd 2f out: nk **52a**
tried cheek pieces: see 3943, 2858 (5f, fast).
14 Ran Time 1m 25.28 (2.48) Owned: Hesmonds Stud Trained: Newmarket

---

4178 3.20 Castlemaine Xxxx Median Auction Maiden Stakes Div 1 2yo (E)
£3504 £1078 £539 **6f aw rnd** **Going 32** **-25 Slow** Inside

3536 **TOFFEE VODKA 29** [1] J W Hills 2-8-9 R Hills 3/1 FAV: 631: Made all, kept on over 1f out, drvn **75a**
out ins last: eff at 6f on gd & firm & polytrack, sharp trks: see 3536.
3798 **CORNICHE DANCER 18** [5] M R Channon 2-8-9 T E Durcan 66/1: 0002: Dwelt, sn bhd, hdwy over 1f hd **74a**
out, kept on ins last, just failed: much imprvd drpd back to 6f & on polytrack: win a race, 7f will suit.
3735 **CHICKEN SOUP 21** [9] J A Osborne 2-9-0 D Holland 9/2: 63: Held up trav well, eff to press wnr shd **78a**
dist, kept on for press, just btn: eff at 6f on polytrack, poss gd grnd: shown enough to win a race: see 3735.
3639 **FLYING DANCER 24** [7] A King 2-8-9 J D Smith 5/1: 34: Handy, eff over 1f out, kept on same pace nk **72a**
ins last, not btn far: acts on firm & polytrack: going the right way: see 3639.
     BEAUCHAMP TURBO [3]2-9-0 L Dettori 10/1: 5: ch g Pharly - Compton Astoria (Lion Cavern) Bhd, 2½ **70a**
eff dist, kept on ins last, no threat: debut: Mar first foal: eff at 6f, 7f sure to suit: handles polytrack.
3824 **GO MO 17** [4]2-9-0 J F Egan 6/1: 066: With ldrs, wknd fnl 1f: see 3824. 1 **67a**
     DEPRESSED [6]2-8-9 S Drowne 25/1: 0: ch f Most Welcome - Sure Care (Caerleon) Dwelt, sn in 3 **53a**
tch, wknd over 1f out: debut: Apr foal, cost 3,000gns: half-sister to wnrs over 5/7f: dam 12f scorer.
3722 **INSIGNIA 21** [11]2-9-0 J Fortune 25/1: 558: Bhd, outpcd 2f out: see 1826. 1 **55a**
3857 **KILLINGTON 15** [2]2-9-0 T S W Kelly 12/1: 29: Dwelt, keen cl-up, wknd well 2f out: gelded, tried t-strap. 3½ **45a**
     FOXY GWYNNE [10]2-8-9 Martin Dwyer 50/1: 0: 10th: b f Entrepreneur - Nahlin (Slip Anchor) ¾ **38a**
Slow away & al bhd: reportedly not handle kick-back on debut: Feb foal, cost 15,000gns: bred to need 7f+ in time.
3824 **EDEN STAR 17** [8]2-8-9 Dane O'Neill 66/1: 000: 11th: Handy, wknd over 2f out. hd **37a**
     STORM CHASE [12]2-9-0 K Fallon 6/1: 0: 12th: Al bhd. 5 **27a**
12 Ran Time 1m 13.84 (3.44) Owned: Mr G and Mrs L Woodward Trained: Lambourn

LINGFIELD Polytrack THURSDAY 26.08.04 Lefthand, V Sharp Track

4179 3.50 Castlemaine Xxxx Median Auction Maiden Stakes Div 2 2yo (E)
£3504 £1078 £539 **6f aw rnd** **Going 32** **-11 Slow** Inside

4028 **TREMAR 8** [1] T G Mills 2-9-0 G Carter 5/4 FAV: 4321: Made all, kept on over 1f out, cmftbly: stays 6f well, 7f shld suit: acts on soft & polytrack: can force the pace: useful, more to come in nurseries. **94a**
3716 **FANTAISISTE 21** [2] Sir Mark Prescott 2-8-9 J Mackay 12/1: 032: With wnr, onepace well over 1f out: eff over 6/7f on fast grnd & polytrack: shld be plcd to win a race, prob over further: see 3716. *2* **79a**
4028 **PRINCE SAMOS 8** [9] R Hannon 2-9-0 K Fallon 6/1: 4053: In tch, eff over 1f out, onepace: eff at 6f on fast grnd & polytrack: see 3438. *½* **82a**
2795 **BEAUTIFUL MOVER 59** [12] J W Hills 2-8-9 (76) R Hills 10/1: 2304: In tch, eff over 1f out, onepace: 2 mth abs: acts on firm, gd & polytrack: see 2297, 1887. *hd* **76a**
OPTIMUS [6]2-9-0 L Dettori 7/2: 5: ch c Elnadim - Ajfan (Woodman) In tch, outpcd over 2f out, some late gains: bckd from 7/1 on debut: May foal, cost E52,000: half-brother to wnrs over 6/10f: dam useful over 7f/1m: sure to relish further & will come on plenty for this. *2½* **74a**
3930 **LAKESDALE 13** [10]2-8-9 (59) O Urbina 25/1: 2040236: With ldr, wknd dist: with Miss D Mountain. *¾* **67a**
BEAUCHAMP TRUMP [7]2-9-0 S W Kelly 25/1: 7: b g Pharly - Beauchamp Kate (Petoski) Dwelt, nvr a factor on debut: Mar foal: half-brother to wnrs over 9/11f: bred to need 1m+ in time. *1½* **68a**
SECRET AFFAIR [4]2-9-0 J D Smith 12/1: 8: b c Piccolo - Secret Circle (Magic Ring) Nvr a factor on debut: Apr foal, cost 34,000gns: half-brother to a 7f wnr: speedily bred. *3½* **58a**
SAVOY CHAPEL [8]2-9-0 D Holland 20/1: 9: Dwelt, al bhd on debut. *1¼* **54a**
EDGE OF ITALY [11]2-8-9 C Catlin 50/1: 0: 10th: Dwelt, hung right & nvr a factor on debut. *nk* **48a**
2056 **GOGETTER GIRL 90** [5]2-8-9 (68) N Callan 25/1: 6240460: 11th: Keen in tch, wknd qckly 2f out: abs, reportedly hung right: see 1826. *1¼* **44a**
TAKEMETOYOURHEART [3]2-8-9 P Doe 40/1: 0: 12th: Dwelt, al bhd. *7* **23a**
12 Ran Time 1m 12.98 (2.58) Owned: Mr T Jacobs Trained: Epsom

4180 4.20 Lingfield-Racecourse Co Uk Handicap Stakes 3yo+ 0-85 (D) **[90]**
£6923 £2130 £1065 **7f aw rnd** **Going 32** **+10 Fast** Inside

3550 **DISTANT CONNECTION 28** [13] A P Jarvis 3-9-9 (85) K Fallon 4/1 FAV: 2153201: Prom, went on 2f out, clr fnl 1f, cmftbly: bckd from 6/1, gd time: stays 1m, suited by 7f: acts on gd, fast grnd & polytrack: handles a sharp or gall trk: likes to run up with the pace: v useful: see 3433 & 2525. **96a**
3768 **OBRIGADO 19** [8] W J Haggas 4-9-11 (82) S W Kelly 16/1: 6-020102: Led till 2f out, kept on but no ch with wnr: acts on gd, firm grnd & polytrack: met a progressive rival, see 3326 (turf). *2½* **85a**
2877 **DOCTORATE 56** [5] E A L Dunlop 3-9-7 (83) E Ahern 6/1: 4-01253: Trkd ldrs, kept on under press fnl 1f, just lost out in battle for 2nd: 8 wk abs: AW bow, acts on fast, gd/soft & polytrack: see 2166 & 1270. *hd* **85a**
3891 **POINT OF DISPUTE 14** [4] P J Makin 9-9-8 vis (79) J Fortune 12/1: 302-5204: Dwelt, hdwy from rear when short of room dist, nrst fin: encouraging: see 3257 & 2880. *1¾* **77a**
3891 **BINANTI 14** [3]4-9-12 vis (83) J Quinn 12/1: 0660055: Mid-div, kept on under press, not pace to chall. *¾* **79a**
4103 **H HARRISON 5** [6]4-9-8 (79) L Fletcher(3) 20/1: 0035006: Prom, wknd fnl 1f: qck reapp. *1¼* **73a**
3751 **HARD TO CATCH 20** [11]6-9-6 (77) M Savage(5) 20/1: 1330637: Slowly away, nvr nr ldrs: see 3751 (6f). *shd* **70a**
3791 **TRE COLLINE 19** [12]5-9-7 (78) R Mullen 9/1: 1461068: Nvr btr than mid-div: btr 3286. *nk* **70a**
3634 **FLYING EXPRESS 25** [2]4-9-12 (83) M Hills 14/1: 6020309: Nvr nr ldrs: btr 2389 (turf). *nk* **74a**
4031 **MISS GEORGE 8** [9]6-10-0 (85) Dane O'Neill 9/1: 6003030: 10th: Front rank, wknd 1.5f out: top-weight. *¾* **74a**
3700 **MALLARD 22** [14]6-9-6 (77) M Fenton 10/1: 3026000: 11th: Rear wide, nvr dngrs. *½* **65a**
4117 **CHEESE N BISCUITS 4** [1]4-9-7 p (78) R L Moore 11/1: 0000540: 12th: Slow away, al bhd: qck reapp. *3½* **59a**
3791 **LAST APPOINTMENT 19** [7]4-9-8 (79) D Holland 13/2: 210-5030: 13th: Prom, wkng when stumbled 2f out, eased: btr 3791. *½* **59a**
1925 **HIGH FINANCE 96** [10]4-9-6 (77) R Hills 33/1: 0455-560: 14th: Al bhd, fin last: 3 mth abs. *2* **53a**
14 Ran Time 1m 24.37 (1.57) Owned: Mrs Ann Jarvis Trained: Twyford

LINGFIELD Polytrack THURSDAY 26.08.04 Lefthand, Sharp, Undulating Track

Official Going Good (Good/Soft places)

4181 4.50 Castlemaine Xxxx Selling Stakes 3yo+ (G)
£2933 £838 £419 **1m3f106y** **Good/Soft** **Inapp** Outside

4909} **PERELANDRA 304** [6] M J Wallace 4-9-0 (75) K Fallon 9/4 JT FAV: 66610-1: ch f Cadeaux Genereux - Larentia (Salse) Trkd ldrs, went on 2f out, pushed well clr: gamble from 4/1, reapp & bght in for 17,000gns: trained by J Noseda to win a mdn in '03: eff at 12f on gd/soft & polytrack: likes a sharp trk, runs v well fresh: apprec this drop in grade, can rate higher. 1 Sep'03 Ling 12ap 74a-(76) D: **70+**
3875+ **BARTON SANDS 15** [2] J Jay 7-9-11 (69) D Holland 9/4 JT FAV: 0100-112: Held up, prog to chall 2f out, left bhd fnl 1f: op 11/8, clmd by A Reid for 6,000: prev in fine form, caught a tartar today: see 3875. *7* **69**
3730 **AMBERSONG 21** [3] A W Carroll 6-9-11 (51) J Fortune 7/1: 4330143: Slowly away, styd on late, no ch with ldrs: fine run at today's weights: see 3294 (firm). *2½* **66$**
4106 **ROLEX FREE 5** [5] D Flood 6-9-11 vis (51) E Ahern 4/1: 0314104: Led till 2f out, wknd: qck reapp. *5* **60**
3692 **BLUE STREAK 22** [7]7-9-5 bl (45) R L Moore 14/1: 5220-055: Prom till wknd 2f out: no easy grnd form. *¾* **53**
3486 **WHITE PARK BAY 31** [8]4-9-0 (54) M Halford(7) 12/1: 330-5206: Chsd ldrs 1m, sn btn: btr 3164. *9* **38**
2800 **ENVIRONMENT AUDIT 59** [1]5-9-5 vis (60) J Jeffrey(7) 20/1: 0-000007: Keen in rear, nvr dngrs: well btn in a nov hdle 2 wks ago (rtd 92h): see 1484 & 979. *3½* **39**
375 **SPLENDID TOUCH 227** [4]4-9-0 (35) R Mullen 50/1: 00000-08: b f Distinctly North - Soft Touch (Horst Herbert) Reared start, chsd ldrs & v keen, btn halfway, t.o.: reapp, reportedly has a breathing problem. *dist* **0**
8 Ran Time 2m 33.97 (10.57) Owned: Lucayan Stud Trained: Newmarket

LINGFIELD Polytrack THURSDAY 26.08.04 Lefthand, Sharp, Undulating Track

| **4182** | 5.20 Castlemaine Xxxx Handicap Stakes 3yo 0-75 (E) | | | | | | [81] |
| | £3611 £1111 £556 **1m2f** **Good/Soft** Inapp Inside | | | | | | |

3449 **WILLHEGO** 33 [3] J R Best 3-8-4 (57) Martin Dwyer 8/1: 00-00231: Made all, held on gamely fnl 1f, drvn out: eff at 10f on polytrack & gd/soft: likes to force the pace on a sharp/undul trk: see 2604 (AW here). **65**

3854 **MAGIC STING** 15 [1] M L W Bell 3-9-1 (68) Hayley Turner(5) 11/2: 6110332: Chsd ldrs, kept on well fnl 1f, not btn far: another consistent run: see 3084. ¾ **75**

3238 **PLANTERS PUNCH** 41 [13] R Hannon 3-9-0 (67) K Fallon 12/1: 0010003: Trkd wnr, ev ch till no extra cl-home: clr rem, abs: fine run, btn less than 1L: acts on gd & gd/soft grnd: see 2135. hd **73**

3875 **GENERAL FLUMPA** 15 [4] C F Wall 3-8-11 (64) R Mullen 8/1: 3352634: Held up, prog 3f out, no impress fnl 1f: acts on firm & soft: see 3875. 3 **66**

3862 **FUEL CELL** 15 [8]3-9-3 bl (70) R L Moore 5/1 FAV: 0330135: Held up, styd on late, nvr dngrs. 1¼ **70**

2203 **AMWELL BRAVE** 83 [5]3-8-3 (56) J F McDonald(3) 25/1: 5050006: Held up, nvr nr ldrs: abs, gelded. 2 **53**

4032 **CARRIACOU** 8 [6]3-8-10 (63) L Keniry(3) 10/1: 5053047: Slowly away, keen, nvr nr ldrs. 1½ **58**

3906 **ANDURIL** 14 [11]3-8-10 (63) J F Egan 16/1: 3640048: Slowly away, nvr btr than mid-div: see 3906 (1m). 1 **56**

3468 **UNCLE JOHN** 32 [2]3-8-7 (60) P Dobbs 14/1: 5-004249: Trkd ldrs, wknd 2f out: see 3173 (g/f). 3 **49**

3922 **WAZIRI** 13 [7]3-9-7 (74) S Drowne 8/1: 64-10030: 10th: Trkd ldrs 1m, sn wknd: btr 3922. 6 **54**

3675* **THIRTEEN TRICKS** 23 [12]3-9-7 (74) L Dettori 13/2: 34-03410: 11th: Mid-div, btn 2f out: top-weight: reportedly spread a plate: much btr 3675 (mdn, firm grnd). ¾ **53**

3772 **RHETORICAL** 19 [9]3-8-4 BL (57) J Mackay 12/1: 0600-50: 12th: Prom 7f, wknd: tchd 20/1, tried blnks. shd **36**

2835 **AL SHUUA** 58 [10]3-9-7 (74) D Holland 16/1: 36-2040: 13th: Al rear: 8 wk abs: btr 2835 (fm). 1¾ **50**

13 Ran Time 2m 12.78(8.58) Owned: G G Racing Trained: Maidstone

---

GOODWOOD FRIDAY 27.08.04 Righthand, Sharpish, Undulating Track

Official Going Str Crse - SOFT (HEAVY places); Rnd Crse - GOOD/SOFT.

| **4183** | 2.05 Coors Fine Light Beer Stakes Handicap 3yo+ 0-85 (D) | | | | | | [84] |
| | £7020 £2160 £1080 **1m4f** **Soft 110** -23 Slow Outside | | | | | | |

3437* **JACK OF TRUMPS** 34 [8] G Wragg 4-9-3 (73) F Norton 7/2: 1004111: Chsd ldrs, chall 2f out, led ins fnl 1f, all-out to hold on: bckd from 9/2: eff at 10f, suited by 12f: acts on fast, soft grnd & polytrack, any trk. **77**

3940* **HEZAAM** 3 [3] J L Dunlop 3-9-0 (80) W Supple 5/2 FAV: 1-050112: Mid-div, prog to chall when short of room cl-home, swtched wide dist, drvn & styd on well, only just failed: well bckd: improving. hd **84**

3894* **MICHABO** 15 [6] D R C Elsworth 3-8-11 (77) J F Egan 10/1: 4326213: Tried to make all, brought field along stands side, worn down cl home: clr of rem: eff at 10/12f on firm & soft grnd: gd run. ¾ **80**

3868 **ROYAL BATHWICK** 16 [7] B R Millman 4-9-5 (75) G Baker 12/1: 0106-334: Dwelt, hdwy to chase ldrs 3f out, left bhnd fnl 1.5f: first try on soft: btr 3868 (fast). 4 **72**

3904 **DEVANT** 15 [5]4-9-7 (77) J Murtagh 13/2: 0402035: Mid-div, nvr nr ldrs: lngr trip. 3 **70**

3961* **NIGHTSPOT** 13 [4]3-9-3 (83) S Drowne 5/1: 15-63216: Trkd ldr, wknd 3f out: ' unsuited by soft'. 10 **62**

3444 **GALLERY GOD** 34 [9]8-9-13 (83) L Smith(7) 16/1: 30-00007: Held up & v keen, prog to chase ldr after 3f, wknd over 3f out: top-weight: see 2255. hd **61**

3983* **ARABIAN MOON** 11 [1]8-9-6 (5ex) (76) D Nolan(3) 20/1: 4/0060-18: Hld up, nvr nr ldrs: unproven on soft. 9 **40**

2973 **LITTLETON TELCHAR** 19 [2]4-9-6 (76) M Henry 33/1: 51009: Chsd ldrs, wknd 3f out: btr 2453 (g/f). dist 5

9 Ran Time 2m 47.87 (16.07) Owned: Mollers Racing Trained: Newmarket

---

| **4184** | 2.40 Ladbrokes Com Handicap Stakes 3yo+ 0-95 (C) | | | | | | [92] |
| | £18966 £7194 £3597 **6f str** **Soft 110** +02 Fast Stands Side | | | | | | |

3903 **MARKER** 15 [7] G B Balding 4-8-9 (73) R Thomas(5) 8/1: 4040041: Chsd ldrs, went on dist, styd on strongly, rdn out: bckd from 14/1: stays 6f, suited by 6f: acts on firm & soft grnd: eff with/without a visor. **84**

3937 **KINGSCROSS** 13 [11] M Blanshard 6-8-11 (75) D Sweeney 16/1: 4210502: Held up, prog 2f out, ev ch fnl 1f, just btn: back to form on fav soft grnd: best held up for a late chall: see 1523. ½ **84**

4005 **WATCHING** 10 [3] R A Fahey 7-9-0 (78) P Hanagan 5/2 FAV: 5000023: Trkd ldrs & v keen, ev ch ent fnl 1f, no extra cl home: well bckd from 7/2: rider given 2 1-day careless riding bans: in gd form, see 4005. ¾ **85**

3942 **SIR DESMOND** 13 [6] R Guest 6-8-13 p (77) J Murtagh 11/1: 3003564: Rear, prog 2f out, nrst fin: best with waiting tactics & a gd run: likes easy grnd: see 3942 & 3123. ¾ **81**

3937 **MACHINIST** 13 [9]4-9-4 (82) Alex Greaves 6/1: 0001245: Mid-div, drvn & kept on fnl 1f. 1¼ **83**

3937 **CD FLYER** 13 [1]7-9-8 (86) S Hitchcott(3) 8/1: 4104356: Chsd ldrs, short of room & stumbled 1.5f out, no room after, fin well: nicely bckd: no luck at any stage, must be given another chance: see 3461. ½ **86**+

3952 **MADRASEE** 13 [2]6-8-1 (65) J F McDonald(3) 25/1: 0500067: Led till dist, no extra. 1¾ **62**

3952* **CANTERLOUPE** 13 [5]6-8-12 (76) D Holland 9/1: 6-000018: Held up, al rear: btr 3952 (gd). 2½ **67**

4126 **POLAR IMPACT** 4 [12]5-8-11 (75) R L Moore 7/1: 1051459: Chsd ldrs wide, wknd dist: qck reapp. 1¾ **62**

3937 **BOND BOY** 13 [8]7-9-10 (88) W Supple 12/1: 0603000: 10th: Mid-div, ch 1.5f out, sn btn: top-weight, reportedly lost a shoe: out of sorts: see 3116. shd **75**

3966 **DEVON FLAME** 12 [10]5-8-9 (73) S Drowne 16/1: 2240020: 11th: Mid-div wide till halfway: op 12/1. 3½ **52**

3827 **MICHELLE MA BELLE** 18 [4]4-8-11 bl (75) J F Egan 25/1: 2000100: 12th: Chsd ldrs, btn sn after halfway: reportedly nvr trav: btr 3643 (fm). 3½ **46**

12 Ran Time 1m 16.51 (6.51) Owned: Miss B Swire Trained: Andover

4185 3.15 Racing Post Rated Stakes Handicap 3yo 0-100 (C)   [97]
£10569 £3252 £1626   1m1f   Soft 110   -24 Slow   Inside

3787* **EXTERIOR** 20 [1] Mrs A J Perrett 3-9-0 (83) S Drowne 11/1: 3-11: Chsd ldrs, went on 3f out, push   **97**
clr fnl 1f, easily: mkt drifter: eff at 9/10f, 12f will suit: acts on fast & polytrack, clearly relished this soft
grnd: fast improving & potentially v useful: see 3787 (AW mdn).
3892 **CELLO** 15 [2] R Hannon 3-8-9 t (78) R L Moore 7/2: 2160042: Held up, prog to chase wnr 3f out,   6   **80**
left bhnd fnl 1f: bckd from 5/1: see 3892.
3553 **WARRAD** 29 [5] G A Butler 3-9-5 (88) P Hanagan 9/2: 1-4353: Chsd ldrs, onepace: op 3/1: see 3553.   ½   **89**
2250 **VANTAGE** 83 [4] N P Littmoden 3-8-9 P (78) D Holland 11/1: 2314504: Led till 3f out, grad wknd: 9   3   **74**
wk abs & tried cheek pieces: see 1308 (mdn).
3884* **CAPE VINCENT** 15 [3]3-9-7 (90) J Murtagh 1/1 FAV: 03-15: Trkd ldr & keen, wknd 3f out, eased &   15   **66**
t.o.: well bckd, reported fin lame: lkd a decent prospect in 3884 (mdn, gd).
5 Ran   Time 2m 02.64 (12.14)   Owned: Mr K Abdulla   Trained: Pulborough

4186 3.50 P P S Softwoods Classified Stakes 3yo+ 0-75 (D)
£5642 £1736 £868   7f rnd   Soft 110   -01 Slow   Inside

4082 **WATERSIDE** 7 [2] G L Moore 5-9-8 (80) R L Moore 7/2: 1246031: Chsd ldrs, prog to chall 2f out,   **85**
led dist & rdn well clr: eff at 6/7f on firm, soft & polytrk: handles any trk, likes to run up with or force the pace.
3569 **IDLE POWER** 28 [1] J R Boyle 6-9-6 p (78) J Murtagh 7/2: 1023002: Held up, styd on into 2nd, no ch   7   **75**
with wnr: grnd prob softer than ideal: see 2374 (C/D) & 2045.
3402 **SAVILES DELIGHT** 35 [3] R Brotherton 5-9-5 (77) D Nolan(3) 2/1 FAV: 1201143: Trkd ldr, led 2f out   4   **67**
till dist, no extra: well bckd: see 3137.
4091 **FOOLS ENTIRE** 7 [4] J A Gilbert 3-8-12 e (59) D Holland 20/1: 0000034: Keen rear, rdn halfway, no dngr.   3½   **60**
4073+ **KING HARSON** 7 [5]5-9-11 vis (77) W Supple 10/3: 2006015: Led till 2f out, wknd: btr 4073.   5   **60**
5 Ran   Time 1m 32.31 (7.81)   Owned: Mr Nigel Shields   Trained: Brighton

4187 4.25 Royal Sussex Regiment Nursery Handicap Stakes 2yo (D)   [90]
£4810 £1480 £740   5f str   Soft 110   -33 Slow   Stands Side

3296 **MISS CASSIA** 39 [5] R Hannon 2-8-8 (70) R L Moore 5/1: 32S31: Chsd ldrs, imprvd to lead 2f out,   **76**
held on gamely, all out: first win: eff at 5f on gd & fast, clearly revels in soft.
4123 **CREE** 4 [1] W R Muir 2-7-12 (10h) (59) P Hanagan 5/1: 005252: Chsd ldrs, outpcd halfway, fin well: ¾   **63**
qck reapp: acts on gd & soft grnd, 6f shld now suit: see 3907 (mdn auct).
4079 **BIBURY FLYER** 7 [3] M R Channon 2-9-7 (83) S Hitchcott(3) 4/1: 2612003: Dwelt & pushed in rear, gd   nk   **85**
prog 2f out, kept on: top-weight, op 3/1: return to 6f will suit: see 3623.
3284 **KEMPSEY** 41 [2] J J Bridger 2-8-5 P (67) A Daly 5/1: 06444: Mid-div wide, ev ch ent fnl 1f, no   1   **66**
extra: 6 wk abs, tried cheek pieces: see 3284 (gd).
3623 **TALCEN GWYN** 27 [6]2-9-3 (79) D Holland 7/2 FAV: 414045: Chsd ldrs, ev ch dist, no extra.   1¼   **76**
3863 **AFRICAN STORM** 16 [4]2-8-12 (74) J F Egan 4/1: 52206: Led till 2f out, wknd: much better on fast   6   **58**
grnd prev & reportedly lost action: see 2858 & 2738 (gd/fm).
6 Ran   Time 1m 03.87 (7.17)   Owned: Mr William Durkan   Trained: Marlborough

4188 5.00 August Median Auction Maiden Stakes 3-4yo (E)
£4076 £1254 £627   1m3f   Soft 110   Inapplicable   Outside - Heavy Rain

3734 **TRULLITTI** 22 [3] J L Dunlop 3-8-7 BL (73) W Supple 11/2: 65-35P1: In tch, imprvd to lead 2f out,   **82**
rdn clr: apprec 1st time blnkrs: eff at 10/11f on gd/soft & soft grnd: handles a sharp/undul trk: see 1365.
4034 **DUNDRY** 9 [5] G L Moore 3-8-12 P (77) R L Moore 11/8 FAV: 0-3322: Trkd ldr, chall 2f out, left   3½   **81**
bhnd fnl 1f: well bckd: fair run in cheek pieces: consistent, eff at 10/11f on gd & soft: see 4034.
4898} **LOMAPAMAR** 307 [1] Mrs A J Perrett 3-8-7 (78) P Hanagan 9/4: 030-3: b f Nashwan - Morina   nk   **75**
(Lyphard) Chsd ldrs, onepcd fnl 1.5f: op 7/4, reapp: plcd on mid of 3 juv starts (mdn, rtd 76+): 40,000gns half
sister to a smart stayer: eff at 1m on fast grnd, prob stays 11f & worth another chance back on better grnd.
4034 **PORT N STARBOARD** 9 [4] C A Cyzer 3-8-12 J F Egan 7/1: 4544: Led till 2f out, wknd & t.o.   16   **60**
3828 **LASSER LIGHT** 18 [2]4-9-7 S Righton 16/1: 0-005: Prom 1m, sn wknd, t.o.: see 3828.   2   **57**
5 Ran   Time 2m 38.26 (20.36)   Owned: Mrs Sonia Rogers   Trained: Arundel

4189 5.35 Bollinger Champagne Series Hcap For Gentleman Amateurs 3yo+ 35-55 (F)   [26]
£3591 £1105 £553   1m rnd   Soft 110   Inapplicable   Inside - Heavy Rain

3992 **MCQUEEN** 11 [14] Mrs H Dalton 4-11-10 (50) Mr S Walker 7/4 FAV: 6006021: Sn led, clr halfway, rdn   **63**
fnl 1f but al well in command: well bckd: made most of fav'ble turf h'cap mark: stays 12f, seems suited by 1m/10f:
acts on fast & gd, revels in soft grnd & on both AWs: likes a sharp/undul trk: see 3992 & 99.
3952 **MYTHICAL CHARM** 13 [2] J J Bridger 5-11-8 t (48) Mr D H Dunsdon 14/1: 0035002: Held up, prog wide   6   **52**
to chase wnr fnl 1f, no impress: acts on soft grnd & both AWs: met a well h'capped rival: see 427.
4132 **ISLANDS FAREWELL** 4 [1] D Nicholls 4-11-11 (51) Mr M Walford(5) 14/1: 0-002503: Held up, prog wide   3½   **50**
2f out, nvr nr ldrs: op 10/1, qck reapp: acts on firm & soft grnd: still a mdn, see 3246.
3916 **CATCH THE FOX** 14 [4] J J Bridger 4-11-0 (40) Mr J Morgan(3) 14/1: 0040004: Held up, btn 2f out.   5   **31**
3638 **SOMAYDA** 25 [12]9-10-13 p (39) Mr J Doyle(7) 15/2: 0003065: Led early, remained prom till wknd over   ½   **29**
2f out: trying a variety of trips: see 3109 (6f).
3706 **ANISETTE** 23 [13]3-10-9 (41) Mr A Chahal(7) 14/1: 6400636: V slowly away, nvr a factor: btr 3706 (g/f).   3   **26**
3916 **COTE SOLEIL** 14 [9]7-11-10 (50) Mr T Greenall 12/1: 6600-007: Trkd ldrs till btn 3f out: see 3916.   4   **28**
3225 **OPEN HANDED** 43 [10]4-11-9 t (49) Mr S Dobson(3) 4/1: 0105508: Nvr btr than mid-div: bckd from   1½   **25**
13/2, 6 wk abs: reportedly has a breathing problem: see 1160.
3788 **MOBO BACO** 20 [8]7-12-0 (54) Mr J J Best(3) 12/1: 0015069: Nvr btr than mid-div: top-weight.   ½   **29**

GOODWOOD FRIDAY 27.08.04 Righthand, Sharpish, Undulating Track

3730 **RUMOUR MILL 22** [5]3-10-8 (40) Mr Joshua Harris(6) 33/1: 0000000: 10th: Nvr a factor. ½ **14**
3051 **HIGH VIEW 50** [11]3-11-8 (54) Mr J Owen(3) 33/1: 000000: 11th: Prom, btn sn after halfway: 7 wk abs. 1 **26**
3718 **EVEN EASIER 22** [3]3-11-4 bl (50) Mr E Dehdashti(3) 12/1: 6445050: 12th: Slow away, nvr btr than mid-div. 10 **7**
483 **Chorus 214** [7]7-11-8 (48) Mr J Millman(7) 16/1:0
3541 **Mutabari 29** [6]10-10-8 (8oh)(26) Mr John Evans(7) 33/1:P
14 Ran Time 1m 49.37(11.97) Owned: Mr R Edwards and Mr W J Swinnerton Trained: Shifnal

NEWMARKET FRIDAY 27.08.04 Righthand, Stiff, Galloping Track

Official Going SOFT.

4190 1.15 Sandals E B F Maiden Stakes Div 1 Colts & Geldings 2yo (D)
£5512 £1696 £848 7f str Good 53 -31 Slow Stands Side

3927 **CHIEF SCOUT 14** [11] B J Meehan 2-8-11 K Fallon 4/1: 041: Made all, rdn out to assert ins fnl 1f: eff at 7f, 1m+ will suit: acts on gd grnd & a stiff/gall trk: improving with every start: see 3927. **88**
1133 **RED AFFLECK 137** [8] P W Chapple Hyam 2-8-11 A McCarthy 12/1: 32: In tch, prog & ev ch dist, sn edged left & not pace of wnr: long abs: eff at 5f, imprvd for step up to 7f & being gelded: lost little in defeat. ¾ **85**
3451 **PALATINATE 34** [2] H Candy 2-8-11 Dane O'Neill 5/1: 43: Handy, ev ch 1f out, sn no extra: tchd 7/1: ran to form of debut on this step up to 7f: acts on gd grnd: see 3451. 1½ **82**
TOP THE CHARTS [5] R Hannon 2-8-11 R Hughes 14/1: 4: b c Singspiel - On The Tide (Slip Anchor) Missed break, prog 2f out, hung right & no impress fnl 1f: debut: Apr foal, cost 80,000gns: half-brother to wnrs at 1m/10f: dam successful at 1m: sire Gr 1 wnr at mid-dists: eff at 7f on gd, further will suit. 1 **80**
WAR AT SEA [12]2-8-11 Martin Dwyer 7/1: 5: b c Bering - Naval Affair (Last Tycoon) Bhd, prog 1f out, nrst fin: debut: Feb first foal, dam successful at 7f: sire decent performer at 12f: impr for experience. 1½ **77**
BOXHALL [4]2-8-11 N Callan 33/1: 6: b c Grand Lodge - March Hare (Groom Dancer) Nvr nrr than mid-div on debut: Feb foal, half-brother won numerous times around 10f: sire Gr 1 wnr at 1m/10f. ¾ **75**
3927 **STANCOMB WILLS 14** [10]2-8-11 P Robinson 100/1: 07: In tch over 5f, wknd: see 3927. 1¾ **71**
USTAD [7]2-8-11 R Hills 20/1: 8: Missed break, nvr a factor on debut. 1½ **68**
2970 **JACK THE GIANT 53** [1]2-8-11 M Hills 3/1 FAV: 09: b c Giant's Causeway - State Crystal (High Estate) Cl-up, wknd bef 1f out: op 9/4: 8 wk abs: May foal, cost E80,000: half-brother to wnrs at 7/12f: dam 12f Gr 3 wnr: sire numerous Gr 1 wnr at 7f/10f: with B W Hills. shd **67**
ROSSBEIGH [3]2-8-11 J Fortune 8/1: 0: 10th: Handy 4f, wknd fnl 2f on debut. hd **66**
3883 **GITCHE MANITO 15** [9]2-8-11 J D Smith 16/1: 30: 11th: Handy 5f, fdd: showed more in 3883. 8 **52**
11 Ran Time 1m 29.82 (5.92) Owned: Mr J R Good Trained: Upper Lambourn

4191 1.45 Beaches Resorts E B F Maiden Stakes Div 1 Fillies 2yo (D)
£5499 £1692 £846 7f str Good 53 -31 Slow Stands Side

3616 **THAKAFAAT 27** [8] J L Dunlop 2-8-11 R Hills 9/2: 51: Handy, styd on for press to lead ins fnl 1f, sn hung left, rdn out: tchd 7/1: eff at 7f, further will suit: acts on gd grnd & a stiff/gall trk: see 3616. **84**
CELTIQUE [3] Sir Michael Stoute 2-8-11 K Fallon 5/1: 2: b f Celtic Swing - Heart's Harmony (Blushing Groom) In tch, styd on to lead dist, sn hung left & hdd ins fnl 1f, not pace of wnr: op 7/2 on debut: Apr foal, half-sister to wnrs at 6/7f: sire high-class mid-dist performer: eff at 7f, further looks sure to suit: acts on gd grnd: can imprve for today's experience & find similar. 1 **81**
4035 **SINGHALESE 9** [6] J A Osborne 2-8-11 L Dettori 3/1 FAV: 433: Mid-div, eff 2f out, onepcd ins fnl 1f: bckd: continues to run well & now quals for h'caps: see 4035 & 3594. 1¾ **77**
3917 **BLUEBERRY TART 14** [11] B J Meehan 2-8-11 J Fortune 9/2: 54: Led, hung left & hdd dist, no extra: imprvd sltly for step up to 7f: acts on gd grnd: see 3917. nk **76**
3770 **LOVE ME TENDER 20** [2]2-8-11 W Ryan 8/1: 05: Handy over 5f, no extra: see 3770. 2½ **71**
ZAYN ZEN [7]2-8-11 P Robinson 8/1: 6: ch f Singspiel - Roshani (Kris) Nvr nrr than mid-div on debut: Jan first foal, dam successful at 1m/10f: sire Gr 1 wnr at mid-dists: with M A Jarvis. nk **70**
HOH MY DARLING [10]2-8-11 R Mullen 20/1: 7: br f Dansili - Now And Forever (Kris) Missed break, cl-up after 2f, wknd fnl 2f: debut: Apr foal, half-sister successful at 7f: sire smart miler. 4 **62**
MAKE IT SNAPPY [1]2-8-11 Dane O'Neill 20/1: 8: Dwelt, nvr a factor on debut. ½ **61**
3713 **HALLOWED DREAM 22** [4]2-8-11 R Hughes 33/1: 09: Cl-up 5f, wknd. hd **60**
3752 **SHERBOURNE 21** [9]2-8-11 Paul Eddery 100/1: 00600: 10th: Keen cl-up 5f, fdd. 13 **35**
10 Ran Time 1m 29.80 (5.9) Owned: Mr Hamdan Al Maktoum Trained: Arundel

4192 2.15 Beaches Resorts E B F Maiden Stakes Div 2 Fillies 2yo (D)
£5499 £1692 £846 7f str Good 53 -30 Slow Stands Side

3944 **PLAYFUL ACT 13** [8] J H M Gosden 2-8-11 J Fortune 8/15 FAV: 21: Made all, pushed out ins fnl 1f to assert, val 4L+: bckd at odds-on: eff at 7f, 1m+ looks sure to suit: acts on fast & gd grnd: improving & won with with plenty in hand today: see 3944 (debut). **90**
NAIVETY [5] C E Brittain 2-8-11 R Hills 33/1: 2: ch f Machiavellian - Innocence (Unfuwain) Keen cl-up, styd on ins fnl 1f, al held by wnr: debut: May foal, cost 70,000gns: half-sister successful at 6f: sire high-class miler: eff at 7f, further looks sure to suit: acts on gd grnd: encouraging eff & can be seen to btr effect over further. 1¾ **81**
3915 **THIS IS MY SONG 14** [2] Mrs A J Perrett 2-8-11 L Dettori 16/1: 03: b f Polish Precedent - Narva (Nashwan) Cl-up, no extra ins fnl 1f: Mar foal, half-sister successful at 1m: dam unrcd: sire decent performer around 1m: eff at 7f, 1m looks sure to suit: acts on gd grnd. 1¼ **81**
BOWLED OUT [9] P J McBride 2-8-11 G Carter 100/1: 4: b f Dansili - Braissim (Dancing Brave) In tch over 4f, sn outpcd, modest late gains: debut: May foal, cost 2,000gns: half-sister successful abroad: dam unrcd: sire decent performer around 1m: sharper for this. 5 **71**
NAPAPIJRI [3]2-8-11 Dane O'Neill 33/1: 5: Dwelt, sev places, wknd fnl 1f on debut. 1 **69**
BRONWEN [6]2-8-11 E Ahern 20/1: 6: Al in rear on debut. 1¼ **67**
3554 **LOVE AFFAIR 29** [1]2-8-11 R Hughes 11/2: 27: Cl-up 5f, wknd: showed more in 3554 (firm). ½ **66**
RAZE [7]2-8-11 K Fallon 5/1: 8: Sn cl-up, fdd fnl 2f: op 3/1 on debut. hd **65**

3944 **LOLA SAPOLA 13** [4]2-8-11 A Mackay 66/1: 009: Al in rear. *2* **61**
9 Ran Time 1m 29.75 (5.85) Owned: Sangster Family Trained: Manton

4193

2.50 Coco Reef Resort And Golden Caribbean Nursery Handicap Stakes 2yo (C) **[85]**
£8522 £2622 £1311 **1m str** **Good 53** **-22 Slow** Stands Side

4064* **MERCHANT 8** [6] M L W Bell 2-9-13 (6ex) (84) Hayley Turner(5) 8/11 FAV: 532111: Keen rear, prog 3f out, styd on to lead dist, pushed clr, val 4L+: well bckd: eff at 6f, relished recent step up to 7f/1m: acts on firm, enjoys gd & gd/soft grnd: v progressive juv who easily defied pen: open to more improvement & now worth a try in List/Group company: see 4064 & 4006. **98**
3698 **MASTER JOSEPH 23** [11] M R Channon 2-8-3 (60) J Fanning 50/1: 40002: Cl-up, led 2f out, hdd dist, not pace easy wnr: apprec step up to 1m: acts on gd grnd: caught a tartar, see 1900. *2½* **65**
3394* **VALE DE LOBO 35** [13] A W Carroll 2-9-1 (72) N Callan 20/1: 513: In tch, eff bef 1f out, kept on fnl 1f: new stable, h'cap & turf bow: eff at 7f/1m on gd grnd & fibresand: see 3394 (Sir M Prescott, AW seller). *1¼* **75**
3753 **ALRIGHT MY SON 21** [4] R Hannon 2-9-6 (77) Dane O'Neill 14/1: 024524: Rear, prog 2f out, no impress ins fnl 1f: just btr 3753 (7f, fast). *shd* **79**
4004 **MY PRINCESS 10** [10]2-9-7 (78) E Ahern 16/1: 353105: Rear, prog bef 1f out, onepcd cl-home. *1¾* **76**
3925 **TUMBLEWEED GALORE 14** [8]2-9-7 (78) J Fortune 14/1: 03336: Missed break, nvr nrr than mid-div. *2* **72**
3820 **OUR CHOICE 18** [2]2-8-5 (62) J Bramhill 50/1: 04067: Led, hdd 2f out, no extra: btr 1386. *shd* **55**
4072* **GOOD WEE GIRL 7** [9]2-9-9 (6ex) (80) L Dettori 16/1: 0021518: Rear, prog 3f out, short of room bef 1f out, sn btn: qck reapp: showed more in 4072 (7f, soft). *3* **67**
3803 **FAIR ALONG 19** [1]2-9-1 (72) P Robinson 16/1: 00049: Rcd alone far side & cl-up 4f: btr 3803. *1¾* **55**
3624 **EMERALD PENANG 27** [12]2-9-6 (77) K Fallon 10/1: 54100: 10th: Al in rear: twice below 2870. *1¼* **58**
3381* **HIDDEN CHANCE 36** [7]2-9-1 (72) Martin Dwyer 20/1: 010: 11th: Missed break, nvr a factor. *¾* **51**
3539 **DISCOMANIA 29** [5]2-9-4 (75) R Hughes 9/1: 0460: 12th: Handy 6f, wknd: tchd 14/1 on h'cap bow. *1¼* **52**
3721 **LORD NORMACOTE 22** [3]2-8-11 (68) T E Durcan 66/1: 0040: 13th: Cl-up, fdd 2f out: btr 3721. *½* **44**
13 Ran Time 1m 43.26 (6.06) Owned: HESheikh Rashid Bin Mohammed Trained: Newmarket

4194

3.25 Sandals E B F Maiden Stakes Div 2 Colts & Geldings 2yo (D)
£5499 £1692 £846 **7f str** **Good 53** **-23 Slow** Stands Side

3752 **THE COIRES 21** [3] R Hannon 2-8-11 R Hughes 8/1: 001: b c Green Desert - Purple Heather (Rahy) Cl-up, styd on to lead 2f out, sn hung right, rdn out: Mar first foal, dam successful at 10f: sire decent performer at sprint dists/1m: eff at 7f, 1m+ will suit: imprvd today for slt ease in grnd: acts on a stiff/gall trk. **90**
DHAULAR DHAR [8] B W Hills 2-8-11 M Hills 12/1: 2: b c Indian Ridge - Pescara (Common Grounds) In tch, eff when short of room dist, kept on ins fnl 1f, unable to catch wnr: debut: May foal, sire top-class performer at sprint dists: eff at 7f on gd grnd: encouraging start to career. *1½* **87**
2408 **THE DUKE OF DIXIE 76** [4] P F I Cole 2-8-11 K Fallon 5/4 FAV: 33: Cl-up, ev ch bef 1f out, sn short of room & no extra: well bckd after 11 wk abs: eff at 6f, stays 7f & further shld suit: acts on fast, handles gd grnd: failed to prog from debut in 2408. *1½* **84**
MUTAJAMMEL [5] Sir Michael Stoute 2-8-11 R Hills 7/1: 4: b c Kingmambo - Irtifa (Lahib) Cl-up till halfway, sn outpcd, rallied ins fnl 1f: op 5/1: debut: May foal, cost 525,000gns: half-brother to numerous wnrs: dam successful at 6f: sire Gr 1 performer at 1m: eff at 7f, further will suit: showed signs of greenness. *nk* **83+**
3882 **EVA SONEVA SO FAST 15** [1]2-8-11 J Quinn 50/1: 05: Rear, prog 2f out, kept on ins fnl 1f: see 3882. *shd* **82**
3927 **PRESS EXPRESS 14** [2]2-8-11 T E Durcan 14/1: 06: Handy over 5f, no extra: see 3927. *hd* **79**
BILLY ONE PUNCH [12]2-8-11 A McCarthy 10/1: 7: b c Mark of Esteem - Polytess (Polish Patriot) Handy over 5f, wknd: op 7/1 on debut: Mar foal, half-brother to wnrs at 6/8f: dam plcd at mid-dists: sire multiple Gr 1 performer at 1m: with P W Chapple Hyam. *4* **73**
BATTLEDRESS [7]2-8-11 Martin Dwyer 20/1: 8: Missed break, nvr a factor: debut. *nk* **72**
3582 **DANEHILL WILLY 28** [9]2-8-11 R Mullen 10/1: 209: Cl-up over 4f, wknd. *1* **70**
COST ANALYSIS [10]2-8-11 P Robinson 14/1: 0: 10th: Led, hdd 2f out, wknd. *1¼* **68**
3927 **Scarp 14** [6]2-8-11 E Ahern 20/1:0 **Bahamian Spring** [11]2-8-11 J Fortune 14/1:0
12 Ran Time 1m 29.24 (5.34) Owned: The Queen Trained: Marlborough

4195

4.00 Half Moon Claiming Stakes 3yo (E)
£4163 £1281 £641 **7f str** **Good 53** **-04 Slow** Stands side

4082 **VIENNAS BOY 7** [14] R Hannon 3-9-7 (82) Dane O'Neill 4/1: 0525441: Rcd centre, prog halfway, styd on to lead dist, rdn out despite hanging left ins fnl 1f: well bckd on qck reapp: clmd for 20,000: eff at 5/7f, prob not stay 1m: acts on firm & gd/soft grnd: enjoyed drop to claim grade & this was a gd confidence boost. **78**
3972 **HONEST INJUN 12** [11] B W Hills 3-9-7 (74) M Hills 7/2 FAV: 4405452: Rear centre, prog to lead 2f out, hdd bef 1f out, kept on, not pace of wnr: bckd: apprec drop back to 1m on drop in grade: find similar. *1½* **74**
3846 **JARVO 17** [13] N P Littmoden 3-9-2 (62) K Fallon 15/2: 2540023: Missed break, prog centre to lead bef 3f out, hdd 2f out, no extra dist: clr rem: remains in gd form: see 3846. *2½* **64**
3694 **HOH BLEU DEE 23** [5] S Kirk 3-9-3 bl (75) J Fortune 6/1: 0602104: Bhd centre, prog 3f out, onepcd fnl 2f: twice below 3453 (1m, first time blnks). *3½* **58**
1617 **BLAKE HALL LAD 112** [7]3-8-11 B Reilly(3) 50/1: 005: Cl-up centre, wknd 2f out: long abs. *4* **44**
3712 **DAVIDS GIRL 22** [2]3-8-1 (38) J Mackay 50/1: 5665006: In tch centre 5f, sn wknd: btr 2704. *nk* **33**
3746 **SOUL PROVIDER 21** [10]3-8-4 P (44) J Fanning 40/1: 2405007: Rcd centre, led till bef 3f out, wknd dist. *½* **35**
3995 **SOVIET SCEPTRE 11** [12]3-8-12 t (68) O Urbina 14/1: 56-30468: Nvr nrr than mid-div centre: btr 1876. *2½* **38**
3487 **PETROLINA 32** [15]3-8-6 T (53) Martin Dwyer 50/1: 00409: Cl-up, fdd fnl 2f. *2* **28**
2344 **PLEASURE SEEKER 78** [1]3-8-4 (57) Ashleigh Horton(7) 40/1: 00-0000: 10th: Missed break, nvr a factor. *nk* **25**
3711 **SHEBAAN 22** [6]3-8-1 (42) A McCarthy 66/1: 50-00000: 11th: Handy centre over 4f, edged left & wknd. *1½* **19**
3980 **RAGGED JACK 11** [4]3-9-2 P (70) S W Kelly 14/1: 2315660: 12th: Handy 4f centre, sn wknd. *1¼* **32**
3612 **SPIN KING 27** [8]3-8-13 (72) R Mullen 9/2: 4034060: 13th: Rear, nvr a factor centre: btr 2922. *1½* **26**
3724 **YASHIN 22** [16]3-8-13 (59) N Callan 25/1: 0032040: 14th: Cl-up alone stands side 4f, fdd: btr 3724. *27* **0**
14 Ran Time 1m 27.95 (4.05) Owned: Mr M Sines Trained: Marlborough

	4.35 Breheny Handicap Stakes 3yo+ 0-95 (C)			[95]
4196	£9763 £3004 £1502 **1m6f175y** **Good 53** +**14 Fast** Stands side			

4151* **SENDINTANK** 3 [11] S C Williams 4-8-0 (5ex) (67) Martin Dwyer 7/4 FAV: 1111311: Held up, prog 3f   80
out, styd on to lead trav well dist, pushed clr despite hanging right, val 5L+: fast time: well bckd under pen on
qck reapp: eff at 12f, imprvd for recent step up to 15f/2m: acts on fibresand, gd & hvy grnd: looks ahd of the
h'capper at present & can land quick-fire hat-trick: see 4151.
3531 **PROMOTER** 30 [14] J Noseda 4-9-8 (89) E Ahern 18/1: 0020402: Rear, prog 3f out, kept on fnl 1f,   3½ 94
no ch with easy wnr: acts on firm & gd grnd: back to form after disapp last time out: see 3125 & 2471.
3249 **ACT OF THE PACE** 42 [4] M Johnston 4-8-11 (78) J Fanning 28/1: 5-41263: Led, hdd dist, no extra: 1 82
6 wk abs: eff around 12f, ran to form on step up to 15f: see 2882 & 2484.
3617 **ARGONAUT** 27 [2] Sir Michael Stoute 4-9-8 (89) K Fallon 16/1: 31-6304: Rear, prog 1m out, ev ch   ¾ 92
3f out, no extra bef 1f out: eff at 12f, prob stays 15f: see 3444.
3387 **HIGH POINT** 35 [1]6-8-10 (77) Dane O'Neill 33/1: 2333605: In tch, ev ch bef 2f out, no extra dist.   3 77
3887 **TILLA** 15 [8]4-8-3 (70) J Quinn 10/1: 1-560226: Rear, prog 4f out, wknd fnl 2f: showed more in 3887.   1 69
3999 **LAGGAN BAY** 10 [3]4-8-8 (75) B Reilly(3) 25/1: 212-0607: Mid-div, prog 5f out, wknd 2f out: btr 1759.   5 69
3969 **RANVILLE** 12 [6]6-9-5 (86) P Robinson 9/2: 024/-0058: Cl-up 12f, sn outpcd, modest late gains.   ½ 79
3531 **TEN CARAT** 30 [16]4-10-0 (95) R Hughes 12/1: 1110-309: Cl-up, fdd 3f out: btr 3032 (reapp).   1½ 87
3688 **BUKIT FRASER** 23 [13]3-7-12 (1oh)T (77) J Mackay 25/1: 1400050: 10th: Al in rear: 1st time t-strap.   5 65
3779 **MAMCAZMA** 20 [15]6-9-5 (86) M Tebbutt 28/1: 2-004000: 11th: Handy 12f, wknd: btr 3119.   1 72
3970 **DOMENICO** 12 [9]6-7-12 (2oh) (63) Hayley Turner(5) 100/1: 2-030600: 12th: Al in rear: stiff task.   3 48
3125 **THEATRE** 48 [5]5-8-13 (80) R Mullen 33/1: 0S22300: 13th: Bhd, prog 1m out, fdd fnl 4f: 7 wk abs.   1½ 62
3027 **BUMPTIOUS** 51 [7]3-8-10 bl (90) R Hills 33/1: 3314430: 14th: Mid-div over 12f, fdd: 7 wk abs.   3 69
1916 **CAPTAIN MILLER** 97 [10]8-8-5 T (72) W Ryan 15/2: 206/0//-220: 15th: Rear, prog 6f out, fdd 3f out: 17 38
long abs & first time t-strap: showed more in 1916 & 1689.
3918 **GROOMS AFFECTION** 14 [12]4-9-1 T (82) N Callan 16/1: 01-16000: 16th: Keen rear, fdd 3f out.   22 30
3556 **ANOUSA** 29 [17]3-8-13 (93) J Fortune 20/1: 0031040: 17th: Cl-up, fdd 4f out: btr 3027 (4 rnr List). shd 40
17 Ran Time 3m 11.35 (5.85) Owned: Steve Jones and Phil McGovern Trained: Newmarket

	5.05 Air Jamaica Handicap Stakes 3yo+ 0-85 (D)			[79]
4197	£6864 £2112 £1056 **5f str** **Good 53** +**11 Fast** Stands Side			

4107 **HOUT BAY** 6 [9] R A Fahey 7-8-5 (56) J Quinn 11/2: 0-136241: In tch, styd on to lead ins fnl 1f,   64
rdn out: qck reapp: fast time: best around 5f, prob stays 7f: acts on firm, gd/soft & both AWs: has
been running well & this was a deserved success: see 3852 & 451.
3984 **TABOOR** 24 [5] J W Payne 6-8-5 h bl t (56) Martin Dwyer 16/1: 0206012: Rear, prog bef 1f out, styd   ½ 61
on, post came too sn: continues in gd form & has apprec recent fitting of t-strap: see 3984 & 3673.
3960 **SWEET CANDO** 13 [8] Miss L A Perratt 3-8-5 p (58) T E Durcan 33/1: 0205003: Bhd, prog fnl 1f,   ¾ 61
nrst fin: gd run in defeat & is fairly weighted: just btr 2566.
4038 **CERULEAN ROSE** 9 [2] A W Carroll 5-9-3 (68) J Fortune 4/1 FAV: 0203024: Mid-div, prog & ev ch ins   ½ 70
fnl 1f, no extra: bckd: won this race last year off 63: showed more in 4038.
4005 **MR WOLF** 10 [7]3-9-7 (74) J Fanning 16/1: 1660005: Led, hdd ins fnl 1f, no extra: btr 1477 (6f). hd 75
3537 **POLISH EMPEROR** 30 [12]4-9-10 e (75) N Callan 7/1: 0310006: Sn cl-up, no extra from dist. nk 75
3960* **STRAWBERRY PATCH** 13 [10]5-8-7 p (58) J Mackay 7/1: 0050217: Handy over 4f, no extra: btr 3960. nk 57
4039 **FOLEY MILLENNIUM** 9 [4]6-9-8 (73) N Pollard 10/1: 1021428: Handy 4f, wknd: disapp run: btr 4039.   5 58
4070 **PRINCE CYRANO** 7 [6]5-9-6 (71) R Mullen 5/1: 0603529: Missed break, nvr a factor: qck reapp.   ¾ 54
4041* **SIRAJ 8** [11]5-9-3 (6ex) (68) Hayley Turner(5) 16/1: 0025-010: 10th: Handy 3f, wknd: new stable.   6 35
3924 **ST AUSTELL** 14 [3]4-9-5 (70) E Ahern 25/1: 32021-00: 11th: Handy 3f, sn hung left & wknd. hd 36
3577 **PRIME RECREATION** 28 [1]7-9-0 (65) Lisa Jones 16/1: 0300400: 12th: Missed break, handy 3f, wknd.   2½ 24
12 Ran Time 1m 0.60(2.1) Owned: Northumbria Leisure Ltd Trained: Malton

Official Going GOOD/SOFT (GOOD places).

	5.10 Cantor Odds Novice Auction Stakes 2yo (E)			
4198	£3682 £1133 £567 **5f161y rnd** **Good/Soft 70** -**25 Slow** Far Side			

3266 **HAPPY EVENT** 41 [3] B R Millman 2-8-13 (83) G Baker 10/1: 1001: Slow away, sn in mid-div, hdwy   87
over 1f out, kept on well ins fnl 1f to lead cl-home: 6 wk abs: eff at 5.5/6f, 7f shld suit: acts on fast &
gd/soft, sharp or a turning trk: back to form on drop in grade: see 2263 (debut).
3987 **BOLD MINSTREL** 11 [4] M Quinn 2-8-13 (84) C Catlin 4/1: 0321242: Led, no extra & hdd cl-home: 1 84
eff at 5/5.5f on firm & gd/soft: consistent, win another race: see 3097.
3848* **ROSIELLA** 17 [7] M Blanshard 2-8-8 (71) F Norton 5/1: 0513: Slow away, hdwy 2f out, no   2 73
impress fnl 1f: handles fast & gd/soft: remains in gd form, see 3848.
3671* **CUSOON** 24 [5] G L Moore 2-8-13 (83) I Mongan 2/1 FAV: 314: Mid-div, outpcd, kept on fnl 1f but   1¼ 74
not pace of ldrs: btr 3671 (firm).
3825 **WITHERING LADY** 18 [9]2-8-6 (77) R Havlin 7/1: 4620105: Mid-div, no impress 1f out: tchd 9/1.   1¼ 63
3800 **AASTRAL MAGIC** 19 [2]2-9-0 (87) P Dobbs 9/2: 1146: Rcd in 2nd, no impress over 2f out: top weight.   5 56
     IN THE SHADOWS [6]2-8-4 D Kinsella 40/1: 7: b f Lujain - Addicted To Love (Touching Wood)   1¾ 42
Rear, outpcd & nvr a factor on debut: Mar foal, cost 13,000 gns: half sister to 6f & 1m wnrs: dam 10/14f wnr.
3883 **NIP NIP** 15 [1]2-8-2 C Haddon(7) 66/1: 08: b f Royal Applause - Rustie Bliss (Kris) Slow away,   3½ 30
nvr a factor: Mar 1st foal: dam unrcd: sire smart 2yo/sprinter: with A Smith.
8 Ran Time 1m 14.43 (5.33) Owned: Mr Robin Lawson Trained: Cullompton

4199　5.40 Cantorodds Com Selling Stakes 3-4yo　(G)
　　　　£2548　£728　£364　　1m3f144y　　Good/Soft 70　　-18 Slow　　Inside

4037　**OKTIS MORILIOUS** 9 [8] A W Carroll 3-9-2　(53) L Dettori　7/2 FAV: 2510401: Bhd, hdwy over 4f out,　　　　　　**60**
led 1f out, rdn clr: no bid: eff at 10/11.5f on firm, gd/soft & polytrack, sharp or turning trks: back to form.

4053　**ZULETA** 8 [10] M Blanshard 3-8-6　(49) D Kinsella　4/1: 44-00622: Cl-up, led 3f out to 1f out, no　　　　　*6*　　**40**
extra: claimed for 6,000: clr of rem: rated higher 4053.

4077　**BREEZER** 7 [7] G B Balding 4-9-7　(52) R Havlin　12/1: 5500-003: Rear, mod late gains: quick reapp.　　　*5*　　**37**

3856　**RELATIVE HERO** 16 [2] Miss S J Wilton 4-9-7 vis (50) A Quinn(5)　4/1: 0-002364: Trkd ldrs, hdwy into　　　*5*　　**29**
2nd 3f out, no impress over 1f out.

3913　**ROMEOS DAY** 14 [1]3-8-11 vis (42) C Catlin　11/2: 4300005: Rcd in 2nd to 3f out, no impress over 1f out.　*7*　　**19**

3771　**FFIZZAMO GO** 20 [6]3-8-11 bl　F Norton　16/1: 646: Slow away in rear, nvr a factor: see 3405.　　　　　*½*　　**18**

3819　**REGULATED** 18 [9]3-9-2 BL (62) J P Guillambert(3)　16/1: 5160507: Led for 1f, rear 4f out, t.o.: blnks.　*dist*　**0**

3802　**PEARNICKITY** 19 [4]3-8-6　R Smith　33/1: 0008: b f Bob's Return - The Robe (Robellino)　Slow away,　*2*　　**0**
al rear, t.o.: dam a multiple sell hdle wnr: mod eff thus far.

4053　**INTRODUCTION** 8 [5]3-8-11 VIS (35) R Miles(3)　16/1: 00-00059: Mid-div, lost place after 3f, fin t.o.　*nk*　　**0**

4045　**SNINFIA** 8 [3]4-9-2 P (46) I Mongan　12/1: 0400000: 10th: Cl-up till led over 5f out, hdd 3f out,　　*2½*　**0**
sn fdd, t.o.: 1st time cheek pieces: see 1399.

10 Ran　Time 2m 35.14 (10.14)　Owned: Mr Dennis Deacon　Trained: Alcester

4200　6.10 Cantor Odds/E B F Maiden Stakes Fillies 2yo　(D)
　　　　£4163　£1281　£641　　5f11y rnd　　Good/Soft 70　　-18 Slow　　Far Side

3728　**DANCING ROSE** 22 [9] C G Cox 2-8-11　R Smith　6/1: 231: Trkd ldrs till led 2f out, drvn out ins　　　　**78**
fnl 1f: stays 5f on gd & gd/soft, acts on a turning trk: built on prev plcd effs, 6f shld now suit.

　　　　RUBIES [10] R F Johnson Houghton 2-8-11　S Carson　6/1: 2: ch f Inchinor - Fur Will Fly (Petong)　　*¾*　　**74**
Bhd, short of room over 2f out, styd on well for press ins fnl 1f, not pace of wnr on debut: op 8/1: Feb foal,
cost 6,000 gns: half sister to a 6f 2yo wnr: dam plcd over 6f at 3, sire smart 2yo, later high-class over 7f: eff
at 5f on gd/soft: v pleasing start, can learn from this & has shown enough to find similar.

　　　　WORLD MUSIC [8] Saeed bin Suroor 2-8-11　S Drowne　14/1: 3: b f Dixieland Band - Headline　　　　*1½*　**70**
(Machiavellian)　Slow away, hdwy over 2f out, styd on ins fnl 1f but not pace of 1st 2 on debut: Apr foal: half
sister to a US Gr1 wnr at 12f: stays 5f, 6f shld suit: acts on gd/soft.

　　　　MAY MORNING [7] B W Hills 2-8-11　K May(7)　14/1: 4: b f Danehill - Golden Digger (Mr Prospector)　*nk*　**69**
Bhd, late gains on debut: May foal: half sister to smart dual 7f 2yo scorer Naheef & a 6f 2yo scorer: dam unplcd,
sire a smart sprinter/miler: stays 5f on gd/soft: learn from this.

2373　**AUWITESWEETHEART** 77 [12]2-8-11 T F Norton　33/1: 55: Wide in tch, hdwy over 2f out, no impress　*1¼*　**65**
ins fnl 1f: long abs: tried a t-strap.

4052　**LIGHTED WAY** 8 [3]2-8-11　L Keniry(3)　25/1: 066: Led to 2f out, no extra over 1f out.　　　　　　*1¼*　**61**

3576　**RASSEEM** 28 [4]2-8-11　L Dettori　7/4 FAV: 27: Bhd, hdwy when short of room over 1f out, sn　　　*hd*　**60**
switched right, wknd: nicely bckd, tchd 5/2: shorter priced stable-mate of 3rd: btr 3576 (fast).

3993　**STEPHANIES MIND** 11 [6]2-8-11 P (78) Derek Nolan(7)　12/1: 03448: Mid-div, no impress 1f out.　　　*6*　　**45**

3896　**EDGED IN GOLD** 15 [2]2-8-11　D Sweeney　40/1: 69: Mid-div wide, wknd over 1f out.　　　　　　*nk*　**44**

3626　**ENCOURAGEMENT** 26 [1]2-8-11　P Dobbs　7/2: 030: 10th: Rcd in 2nd, no impress over 1f out.　　　*hd*　**43**

1866　**SOME NIGHT** 99 [11]2-8-11　R Havlin　20/1: 50: 11th: Mid-div, no impress 2f out: long abs.　　　　*4*　　**31**

11 Ran　Time no 04.74 (4.44)　Owned: The Eighteen Dreamers　Trained: Hungerford

4201　6.40 Cantorodds Com Classified Stakes 3yo+ 0-80　(D)
　　　　£5811　£1788　£894　　5f11y rnd　　Good/Soft 70　　+16 Fast　　Far Side

4031　**SPANISH ACE** 9 [10] A M Balding 3-9-5 H BL (85) S Drowne　11/1: 0055041: Bhd, prog 2f out, rdn out　　　**93**
to lead cl-home: visor left off, fast time: stays 6f, now suited by 5f: acts on firm & gd/soft: has tumbled down
the weights this term & apprec today's fitting of 1st time blnks & hood: see 4031 & 3269.

4098　**DEVISE** 6 [3] M S Saunders 5-9-4　(82) R Miles(3)　10/3: 5540232: Chsd ldrs, styd on to lead dist,　　*hd*　**90**
hdd under press cl-home: qck reapp: in form, deserves similar: see 4098 & 3792.

3567　**ROYAL CHALLENGE** 28 [11] G A Butler 3-9-0　(80) L Dettori　2/1 FAV: 0-21163: Sn bhd, prog bef 1f　　*2½*　**81**
out, nrst fin: bckd: gd run & is worth a try at 6f: see 3356.

3954　**WILLHEWIZ** 13 [9] R M Stronge 4-9-2　(77) J F McDonald(3)　25/1: 1100004: Cl-up, ev ch bef 1f out,　　*1*　　**78**
no extra: showed more in 2591 (6f, firm).

4031*　**FURTHER OUTLOOK** 9 [8]10-9-9　(81) M Howard(7)　10/1: 0006515: Led 1f, styd cl-up, wknd dist: fin　*¾*　**82**
ahead of today's wnr in 4031.

3960　**MALAPROPISM** 13 [6]4-9-2 (80) C Catlin　7/1: 0604066: Chsd ldrs 3f, no extra: btr 3628 (firm).　　　*shd*　**75**

3960　**SEVEN NO TRUMPS** 13 [5]7-9-2 p (75) F Norton　11/1: 0020047: Nvr nrr than mid-div: frustrating.　　*2½*　**69**

4259}　**LORD KINTYRE** 346 [1]9-9-5　(83) G Baker　25/1: 361030-8: b g Makbul - Highland Rowena (Royben)　　*2*　　**66**
Missed break, nvr a factor on reapp: h'cap wnr in '03: plcd at best in '02 (rtd 88, rtd h'cap): stks & Listed wnr
back in '00: stays 6f, prob best at 5f: handles firm, loves firm & gd grnd, any trk: eff with cheek pieces: likes
to force the pace & has gone well fresh: can break blood vessels. 1 Jun'03 Sali 5fm 84-82 D:

4031　**DANCING MYSTERY** 7 [7]10-9-2 bl (78) S Carson　10/1: 4500029: Led after 1f till dist.　　　　　　*1¾*　**57**

3960　**SALVIATI** 13 [4]7-9-4 p (82) P Fitzsimons　14/1: 0451000: 10th: Dwelt, nvr a factor: btr 3628.　　　　*3½*　**50**

2253　**PALAWAN** 83 [2]8-9-2　(74) R J Killoran(7)　25/1: 0600000: 11th: Bhd, nvr a factor: 12 wk abs.　　　*3*　　**39**

11 Ran　Time 03.00 (2.70)　Owned: The Farleigh Court Racing Partnership　Trained: Kingsclere

4202　7.10 Cantor Odds Handicap Stakes 3yo 35-55　(F)　　　　　　　　　　　　　　　　　**[65]**
　　　　£3416　£976　£488　　1m5y rnd　　Good/Soft 70　　-02 Slow　　Inside

3900　**GRAND RAPIDE** 15 [13] J L Spearing 3-8-11　(48) S Drowne　8/1: 60041: Mid-div, prog 3f out, rdn out　　**58**
to lead cl-home: eff at 1m, further shld suit: acts on gd/soft grnd: unexposed in h'caps: see 3900.

3526　**OTAGO** 30 [4] J R Best 3-9-2　(53) I Mongan　7/1: 3045042: Chsd ldrs, styd on for press to lead　　*nk*　**59**
dist, hdd cl-home: clr rem: eff at 6f/1m on firm & gd/soft grnd: find similar, see 2985.

BATH   FRIDAY 27.08.04   Lefthand, Turning Track with Uphill Finish

4032 **QUEEN LUCIA 9** [15] J G Given 3-9-2 (53) L Dettori 9/4 FAV: 4454023: Cl-up, no extra fnl 1f: showed more in 4032 (9f, soft). *5* **51**
3547 **FARNBOROUGH 29** [6] R J Price 3-8-13 (50) R Miles(3) 40/1: 5000004: Bhd, prog 3f out, onepcd fnl 1f. *2* **44**
3900 **MAID THE CUT 15** [12]3-8-8 (45) A Daly 50/1: 00-4005: Nvr nrr than mid-div: showed more in 1984. *½* **38**
3982 **CITY GENERAL 11** [10]3-9-1 p (52) Derek Nolan(7) 12/1: 2051056: Led till dist, no extra: btr 3712. *2½* **41**
3515 **FIZZY LADY 30** [1]3-9-4 t (55) M Savage(5) 25/1: 4410007: Nvr nrr than mid-div. *1* **42**
4165 **GREAT BLASKET 2** [8]3-9-1 (52) J P Guillambert(3) 33/1: 0004-008: Nvr nrr than mid-div: qck reapp. *½* **38**
3900 **NIGHT WORKER 15** [9]3-8-9 (46) P Dobbs 16/1: 0065009: No impress in mid-div: btr 3347. *hd* **32**
2344 **WELSH EMPRESS 78** [14]3-8-13 (50) S Carson 33/1: 603-0300: 10th: Cl-up wide 6f, fdd. *1¼* **34**
3982 **COBALT BLUE 11** [3]3-9-0 vis (51) D Sweeney 7/2: 6155030: 11th: Handy 5f, wknd: btr 3982 (10f, fast). *5* **25**
3846 **HANA DEE 17** [5]3-9-1 (52) C Catlin 10/1: 0045300: 12th: Cl-up 6f, fdd: btr 3679. *1¾* **23**
3900 **WHIPLASH 15** [16]3-8-11 bl (48) D Corby(3) 20/1: 1060060: 13th: Cl-up 6f, fdd. *3½* **13**
2667 **LADY PREDOMINANT 65** [11]3-8-8 (45) Frances Pickard(7) 66/1: 6010500: 14th: Dwelt, nvr a factor. *1¾* **7**
2019 **MR STROWGER 93** [7]3-8-8 (45) R Smith 16/1: 0000-630: 15th: Al well adrift: long abs. *24* **0**
15 Ran Time 1m 44.06 (5.76) Owned: Mr A J & Mrs L Brazier Trained: Kinnersley

4203
7.40 Cantorodds Com Handicap Stakes 3yo+ 0-70 (E) **[70]**
£4173 £1284 £642 **1m5f22y** **Good/Soft 70** **-14 Slow** Inside

3861 **BELLE ROUGE 16** [2] C A Horgan 6-9-10 (66) L Dettori 7/2 JT FAV: 2212121: Chsd ldrs, led dist trav well, pushed clr, val 4L+: eff btwn 12f/2m on fast, hvy grnd & both AWs: tough & prog performer who is a credit to connections: see 3861 & 3450. **76**
3887 **TYPHOON TILLY 15** [5] C R Egerton 7-9-12 (68) S Drowne 7/2 JT FAV: 4364032: Mid-div, prog bef 1f out, al held by wnr cl-home: encouraging eff & can find similar: see 3887 & 605. *2½* **73**
3727 **DANEBANK 22** [8] J Mackie 4-8-12 p (54) S Carson 7/1: 00-05123: Handy, prog to lead 3f out, hdd dist, no extra: eff around 12/12.5f, now stays 13f: acts on firm & gd/soft grnd: 7lb higher than last win in 3056. *hd* **58**
75 **SPRING PURSUIT 280** [13] E G Bevan 8-8-4 (46) R Miles(3) 14/1: 004/000-4: b g Rudimentary - Pursuit of Truth (Irish River) Chsd ldrs, eff 2f out, onepcd ins fnl 1f: earlier unplcd over hdles (rtd 103h, h'cap): nov h'cap hdle wnr in 03/04 (R Price, plcd numerous times, rtd 113h, stays 2m4.5f on gd & soft): unplcd both Flat starts in '03 (rtd 47, h'cap): best at 10/12f, stays 14f: acts on gd, loves soft & hvy: on fair mark. *½* **49**
2 Mar'02 Donc 12sft 66-64 E: 2 Oct'01 Brig 11.8sft 69-66 E: 1 Apr'01 Epso 12hvy 84-72 C:
3398 **HASHID 35** [7]4-9-6 (62) I Mongan 33/1: 3-630065: Cl-up, no extra bef 1f out: btr 2596. *nk* **64**
4033 **SAXE COBURG 9** [12]7-8-11 (53) J F McDonald(3) 7/1: 3534046: Nvr nrr than mid-div: btr 4033. *1½* **53**
3969 **JASMICK 12** [9]6-10-0 (70) L Fletcher(3) 14/1: 60-50067: Nvr nrr than mid-div: btr 3587. *¾* **69**
3861 **TOP TREES 16** [15]6-8-10 (52) F Norton 12/1: 10-06158: Al in rear: btr 3340. *3½* **46**
3887 **JAVELIN 15** [14]8-8-3 BL (45) C Haddon(7) 20/1: 4045-659: Bhd, nvr a factor: showed more in 2912. *½* **38**
3787 **DINGLEY LASS 20** [4]4-8-7 (1ow) (48) P Dobbs 33/1: 00-60: 10th: Led 1f, fdd 3f out. *1½* **40**
4033 **TRAVELLERS TALE 9** [11]5-8-10 (52) Derek Nolan(7) 5/1: 0606220: 11th: Led 5f out till 3f out, fdd. *1½* **41**
3868 **ENCHANTED OCEAN 16** [6]5-8-7 (49) R Thomas(5) 50/1: 40//-00000: 12th: Rear, nvr a factor. *5* **30**
3779 **The Varlet 20** [3]4-9-13 p(69) D Corby(3) 25/1:0   3727 **Royal Trigger 22** [10]4-8-7 bl t(49) C Catlin 50/1:0
14 Ran Time 2m 56.53(11.03) Owned: Mrs B Woodford Trained: Ogbourne Maizey

THIRSK   FRIDAY 27.08.04   Lefthand, Flat, Oval Track

Official Going GOOD/SOFT (SOFT IN PLACES)

4204
1.55 Farmers Inn - Helperby Maiden Auction Stakes Div 1 2yo (E)
£3653 £1124 £562 **7f rnd** **Good/Soft 82** **-31 Slow** Inside

DESERT MOVE 0 [9] M R Channon 2-8-9 A Culhane 9/2: 1: b f Desert King - Campestral (Alleged) Trkd ldrs, hdwy to lead over 2f out, rdn over 1f out, kept on well ins fnl 1f: op 7/1, debut: Apr foal, cost E50,000: half-sister to an 11f wnr: dam a 7f 2yo scorer, sire smart 2yo: stays 7f, 1m will suit: acts on gd/soft, flat trk: runs well fresh: fine start, entitled to come on for this & can win more races. **80**
4102 **NASSEEM DUBAI 6** [10] Mrs A Duffield 2-9-0 G Hind 8/1: 062: ch c Silver Hawk - Fleur de Nuit (Woodman) Mid-div, hdwy wide over 2f out, chall over 1f out, onepcd fnl 1f: op 12/1, qck reapp, clr of rem, top-weight: Mar foal, cost 35,000gns: half-brother to 2yo wnrs at 7f/1m: dam wnr of a US Gr 3, sire smart miler: stays 7f, 1m will suit: acts on gd/soft grnd: shld win a race. *1¼* **80**
3478 **RED RUDY 32** [3] R M Beckett 2-8-9 K McEvoy 4/1: 63: ch c Pivotal - Piroshka (Soviet Star) Trkd ldrs, onepcd over 1f out: Mar foal, cost 14,000gns: half-brother to a 2yo wnr: dam unrcd, sire smart sprinter. *3* **69**
2462 **TIT FOR TAT 73** [2] J G Given 2-8-6 M Fenton 14/1: 054: Prom, onepcd 2f out: long abs: new stable (prev with M Johnston): see 2462. *1½* **63**
3831 **COMICAL ERRORS 18** [5]2-8-9 G Faulkner 12/1: 045: Hmpd start, sn in tch, hdwy 2f out, nrst fin. *3½* **59**
3831 **ANDY MAL 18** [8]2-8-2 T Hamilton 20/1: 06: In tch, hdwy over 2f out, sn no impress. *shd* **51**
3908 **NORTHERN SECRET 14** [1]2-8-4 K Darley 9/4 FAV: 037: Led till over 2f out, sn no extra. *1½* **50**
SHANKLY BOND 0 [11]2-8-11 F Lynch 16/1: 8: Slow away in rear, hdwy over 2f out, not pace to chall. *¾* **55**
312 **LAST PIONEER 48** [13]2-8-7 J Edmunds 25/1: 09: Rear, modest late gains: 7 wk abs. *nk* **50**
3425 **MORNING MAJOR 34** [4]2-8-7 P Fessey 50/1: 000: 10th: In tch, wknd over 2f out. *1¼* **49**
3939 **ADMITTANCE 13** [14]2-8-4 L Goncalves 20/1: 0000: 11th: Al bhd. *nk* **45**
3425 **TRIGONY 34** [6]2-8-9 G Gibbons 66/1: 00: 12th: Al bhd. *nk* **49**
3939 **MARK YOUR CARD 13** [7]2-8-2 D Allan 25/1: 00: 13th: Cl-up, wknd over 2f out. *11* **31**
BRAVE TARA 0 [12]2-8-2 P M Quinn 33/1: 0: 14th: Al bhd on debut. *12* **19**
14 Ran Time 1m 30.81 (7.91) Owned: Mr Jaber Abdullah Trained: West Ilsley

4205 2.25 European Breeders Fund Maiden Stakes 2yo (D)
£7319 £2252 £1126 **6f str** **Good/Soft 82** **-09 Slow** Stands side

3968 **ENTAILMENT 12** [12] Mrs J R Ramsden 2-9-0 L Goncalves 33/1: 01: b g Kris - Entail (Riverman) **80**
Trkd ldrs stands side, hdwy to chall over 1f out, led ins fnl 1f, drvn out: Mar first foal, cost 30,000gns: dam 7/8f wnr: sire top-class miler: eff over 6f on gd/soft: rate higher.
4006 **RAINBOW IRIS 10** [6] B Smart 2-8-9 D McGaffin 33/1: 452: Led stands side, hdd ins fnl 1f, no extra: stays 6f on gd/soft grnd: see 3504 (debut). *nk* **73**
3824 **COME ON JONNY 18** [14] R M Beckett 2-9-0 M Fenton 33/1: 03: b c Desert King - Idle Fancy (Mujtahid) Mid-div stands side, hdwy over 1f out, kept on: May foal, cost 20,000gns: half-brother wnrs at 5/6f: dam 1m wnr: stays 6f, 7f shld suit: acts on gd/sof. *1¼* **74**
3699 **STRETFORD END 23** [5] B Smart 2-9-0 F Lynch 4/6 FAV: F24: Led far side group, ev ch over 1f out, no extra nr fin: nicely bckd: btr expected after 3699. *shd* **73**
3968 **HALLA SAN 12** [16]2-9-0 A Beech(3) 50/1: 005: Bhd stands side, switched left well over 1f out, hdwy fnl 1f, nrst fin: needs further: see 3606. *1* **70**
PREMIER FANTASY 0 [3]2-9-0 Darren Williams 11/2: 6: b c Pivotal - Hemaca (Distinctly North) *1¾* **65**
Trkd ldrs far side, hdwy to chall over 1f out, ev ch 1f out, no impress ins fnl 1f on debut: Feb first foal, cost 60,000gns: dam unrcd, sire a smart sprinter: learn from this.
ECOLOGICALLY RIGHT 0 [8]2-8-9 A Culhane 33/1: 7: Mid-div stands side, onepcd 2f out on debut. *nk* **59**
4102 **GRANDOS 6** [15]2-9-0 G Gibbons 20/1: 058: Chsd ldrs stands side, onepcd over 1f out: qck reapp. *1¼* **60**
3699 **GAME LAD 23** [7]2-9-0 D Allan 12/1: 349: Rear stands side, modest late gains. *hd* **59**
3665 **JAAMID 24** [1]2-9-0 K Darley 13/2: 40: 10th: Prom far side, wknd 2f out. *2½* **51**
3227 **TAHLAL 42** [13]2-9-0 G Hind 33/1: 50: 11th: Chsd ldrs stands side, wknd over 2f out: 6 wk abs. *1½* **46**
DAISY POOTER 0 [2]2-8-9 P Makin(5) 33/1: 0: 12th: Trkd ldrs far side, wknd over 1f out on debut. *1¾* **36**
1818 **FALCON GOER 101** [4]2-8-9 Joanna Badger 100/1: 00: 13th: Dwelt, switched to stands side sn after start, nvr a factor: long abs. *3½* **25**
CUT TO THE CHASE 0 [11]2-9-0 T Kim Tinkler 66/1: 0: 14th: Handy stands side, wknd 2f out: t-strap. *3* **21**
LOVE FROM RUSSIA 0 [10]2-9-0 R Ffrench 50/1: 0: 15th: Slow away, al bhd on stands side on debut. *nk* **20**
GRACEFUL FLIGHT 0 [9]2-8-9 R Fitzpatrick 80/1: 0: 16th: Al bhd stands side on debut. *3* **6**
16 Ran Time 1m 15.01 (5.51) Owned: Mr Nigel Munton Trained: Thirsk

4206 3.00 Helmsley Selling Stakes 2yo (F)
£3255 £930 £465 **7f rnd** **Good/Soft 82** **-54 Slow** Inside

3901 **BEAUMONT GIRL 15** [6] G A Swinbank 2-8-6 Dean McKeown 9/1: 01: Mid-div, hdwy over 2f out, led 1f out, drvn out ins fnl 1f: no bid: op 7/1: relished this step up to 7f, acts on gd/soft: see 3901. **61**
3968 **APETITE 12** [12] N Bycroft 2-8-11 A Reilly(7) 25/1: 0002: ch g Timeless Times - Petite Elite (Anfield) Bhd, hdwy 2f out, chall ins fnl 1f, no impress nr fin: Mar foal, cost 500gns: half-brother to a couple of 2yo wnrs: dam plcd over 7f at 4, sire a 2yo wnr: improved at 7f on gd/soft. *nk* **64**
3864 **LARAS GIRL 16** [3] I A Wood 2-8-6 (51) P Doe 9/1: 040033: Mid-div, hdwy over 2f out, onepcd fnl 1f: handles fast & gd/soft: see 3864. *2* **55**
3832 **HERENCIA 18** [13] P A Blockley 2-8-11 F Lynch 11/1: 0004: Mid-div wide, lost place 3f out, styd on again over 1f out, nrst fin: try 1m? see 3491. *2½* **55**
3750 **MAUREENS LOUGH 21** [5]2-8-12 (55) N Mackay(3) 4/1 FAV: 1544105: Trkd ldrs till led 2f out, hdd entering fnl 1f, no extra: see 3750. *2* **52**
3570 **LANAS TURN 28** [4]2-8-6 BL (52) D Allan 15/2: 050046: Dwelt, sn handy, ev ch well over 1f out, sn wknd. *1¼* **43**
4074 **CANARY DANCER 7** [1]2-8-6 (63) G Faulkner 6/1: 042007: Led to 2f out, no extra over 1f out: qck reapp. *hd* **42**
3832 **DESERT BUZZ 18** [10]2-8-11 K Darley 5/1: 0605008: Rear, hdwy 2f out, sn wknd: see 1987. *shd* **46**
3570 **SINGHALONGTASVEER 28** [14]2-8-11 (51) Darren Williams 12/1: 05309: Mid-div wide, wknd 3f out. *1½* **43**
3097 **XEIGHT EXPRESS 48** [2]2-8-6 R Ffrench 33/1: 0000: 10th: b f Ashkalani - Believing (Belmez) Rcd in 2nd, no impress over 1f out: 7 wk abs: Mar first foal, cost 5,500gns: dam a 5f 2yo wnr. *½* **37**
4127 **FOLD WALK 4** [11]2-8-6 (46) T Lucas 12/1: 04U0530: 11th: Chsd ldrs, wknd 2f out: op 15/2, qck reapp. *3½* **30**
3429 **MIST OPPORTUNITY 34** [8]2-8-11 G Bartley(7) 50/1: 0000: 12th: b g Danetime - Lady of The Mist (Digamist) Al bhd: 15,000gns Apr foal: dam unplcd at 2, sire smart sprinter: with P Haslam. *3* **29**
3189 **FILEY BUOY 44** [7]2-8-11 V Halliday 33/1: 000: 13th: In tch, rear & btn over 3f out: 6 wk abs. *6* **17**
LISEBERG 0 [9]2-8-11 B Swarbrick(5) 28/1: 0: 14th: Slow away, al bhd on debut. *24* **0**
14 Ran Time 1m 32.47 (9.57) Owned: Mr G Stephenson Trained: Richmond

4207 3.35 Farmers Inn - Helperby Maiden Auction Stakes Div 2 2yo (E)
£3653 £1124 £562 **7f rnd** **Good/Soft 82** **-39 Slow** Inside

3386 **SECRET HISTORY 35** [6] M Johnston 2-8-6 (76) K Darley 2/1 FAV: 2351: Prom, hdwy to lead 3f out, rdn over 1f out, kept on well ins fnl 1f: prev eff at 6f, stays 7f & 1m shld suit: acts on fast & gd/soft grnd, turning trk: most deserved success, win more races: see 2610 (debut). **82**
3831 **ROBINZAL 18** [8] T D Easterby 2-8-9 D Allan 6/1: 032: Prom, hdwy & ev ch 3f out, onepcd fnl 1f. *2½* **78**
3429 **ASKWITH 34** [3] J D Bethell 2-8-9 K McEvoy 3/1: 53: Chsd ldrs, styd on fnl 1f: op 13/2: stays 7f, 1m will suit: acts on gd/soft: find a race: see 3429. *1* **76**
3239 **TIDAL FURY 42** [5] J Jay 2-8-11 A Culhane 14/1: 04: b c Night Shift - Tidal Reach (Kris S) Chsd ldrs, onepcd over 1f out: 6 wk abs, top-weight: Mar foal, cost 28,000gns: half-brother to 2yo wnrs at 5f/1m: dam a 1m wnr at 2: much imprvd from debut, can find a race. *¾* **76**
MR MARUCCI 0 [9]2-8-9 T Eaves(3) 25/1: 5: b c Miner's Mark - Appealing Style (Valid Appeal) *2* **70**
Dwelt, hdwy over 3f out, onepcd over 1f out on debut: clr of rem: Mar foal, cost 15,000gns: dam unplcd, sire smart dirt runner: fair start, entitled to come on for this next time.
3699 **KASHTANKA 23** [14]2-8-7 M Fenton 66/1: 06: ch c Ashkalani - Spark (Flash of Steel) Chsd ldrs, onepcd 2f out: 2,500gns Apr foal: dam a wnr over 6f at 2, sire smart 2yo, later high-class miler: with J Quinn. *4* **60**
4083 **COCONUT SQUEAK 7** [2]2-8-2 Dale Gibson 13/2: 367: Led to 3f out, sn no extra: qck reapp. *nk* **54**
3851 **NOWADAY 16** [4]2-8-9 R Ffrench 18/1: 0668: Mid-div, wknd 3f out. *shd* **60**
4006 **PERCHERON 10** [11]2-8-9 Dean McKeown 40/1: 09: In tch, not much room after 2f, nvr nr ldrs. *¾* **58**
3376 **CALA FONS 36** [12]2-8-4 Kim Tinkler 66/1: 00: 10th: Al bhd. *1* **51**
JEFFSLOTTERY 0 [10]2-8-7 G Hind 33/1: 0: 11th: Al bhd on debut. *1¼* **51**

THIRSK   FRIDAY 27.08.04   Lefthand, Flat, Oval Track

3425 **ALLSTAR PRINCESS 34** [13]2-8-2 T Hamilton 25/1: 0000: 12th: In tch, rear & btn over 3f out. *shd* **45**
2492 **SATIN ROSE 72** [7]2-8-4 G Gibbons 12/1: 560: 13th: Slow away, al bhd: long abs. *3* **41**
3376 **GOLDEN SQUAW 36** [1]2-8-2 P M Quinn 25/1: 600: 14th: Slow away, nvr a factor. *hd* **38**
14 Ran   Time 1m 31.38 (8.48)   Owned: Mr J Shack   Trained: Middleham

4208   4.10 Bridlington Classified Stakes 3yo+ 0-90 (C)
£8567 £3249 £1625   **1m rnd**   **Good/Soft 82**   **-21 Slow**   Inside

3689* **DAWN SURPRISE 23** [5] Saeed bin Suroor 3-8-9 t (91) K McEvoy 2/1 FAV: 3-21511: Rcd in 2nd, hdwy to **100**
lead well over 2f out, pushed out ins fnl 1f: landed double: eff at 7f, suited by 1m/10f on firm & gd/soft, any
trk: progressive, can rate higher: see 3689.
4061 **BLUE SKY THINKING 8** [3] K R Burke 5-9-5 (92) Darren Williams 4/1: 5603462: Trkd lrds, hdwy over *1¼* **98**
2f out, wknd fnl 1f: clr of rem: won this race last yr: back to form: see 519.
4061 **VICIOUS KNIGHT 8** [1] D Nicholls 6-9-3 (90) A Nicholls 3/1: 0000053: Led, hdd well over 2f out, no extra. *5* **86**
3782 **MYSTERINCH 20** [4] Jedd O'Keeffe 4-9-3 (87) N Mackay(3) 10/1: 0020004: Chsd lrds, btn 2f out: op 17/2.*1¼* **83**
3782 **WIZARD OF NOZ 20** [7]4-9-8 vis (95) K Darley 4/1: 2605555: Chsd lrds, wknd over 2f out: top-weight. *nk* **87**
4173 **PHOENIX NIGHTS 1** [6]4-9-3 (52) P Mathers(5) 125/1: 05006446: Al bhd: ran yesterday: see 423. *24* **34**
6 Ran   Time 1m 43.7 (8.3)   Owned: Godolphin   Trained: Newmarket

4209   4.45 Wiske Handicap Stakes 3yo+ 0-85 (D)   [91]
£5616 £1728 £864   **2m**   **Good/Soft 82**   **-11 Slow**   Inside

4106 **MASTER WELLS 6** [5] J D Bethell 3-8-12 (75) K McEvoy 3/1 J FAV: 0020021: Mid-div, hdwy 4f out, **84**
led well over 1f out, drvn out fnl 1f: qck reapp: eff over 10/12f, clearly stays 2m well: acts on gd/soft & soft,
stiff/undul or a turning trk, likes Chester: open to further improvement.
3970 **VICARS DESTINY 12** [1] Mrs S Lamyman 6-8-12 (61) Andrew Webb(7) 7/1: 0064332: Bhd, hdwy 6f out, ev *½* **68**
ch 2f out, kept on ins fnl 1f: in gd form: see 1069 & 926.
3437 **TOMASINA 34** [6] K G Reveley 6-9-7 t (70) K Darley 16/1: 6-460103: Prom, hdwy to lead over 3f out *2½* **74**
till well over 1f out, sn no extra: see 3226.
3861 **POPES HILL 16** [4] L M Cumani 3-8-9 (72) N Mackay(3) 3/1 J FAV: 0-446344: Trkd lrds, onepcd 2f out. *2* **74**
4106 **LUCKY JUDGE 6** [3]7-9-10 (73) Dale Gibson 4/1: 0151165: Mid-div, wknd over 2f out: qck reapp. *2* **73**
3359 **HATHLEN 36** [2]3-8-13 (76) A Culhane 6/1: 6656156: Al bhd: btr 2376 (gd). *11* **65**
3853 **GREENWICH MEANTIME 16** [7]4-9-2 (65) L Goncalves 9/1: 0300567: Led till over 3f out, sn no extra. *10* **44**
7 Ran   Time 3m 37.7 (14.9)   Owned: Mr Jordan Ellison Lund   Trained: Middleham

4210   5.20 Greta Apprentice Stakes Handicap Fillies 3yo+ 0-70 (E)   [70]
£3624 £1115 £558   **5f str**   **Good/Soft 82**   **+20 Fast**   Stands side

3942 **MECCAS MATE 13** [2] D W Barker 3-8-13 (55) A Mullen(5) 6/1: 0-5651: Rear, hdwy 2f out, rdn over 1f **62**
out, pushed into lead nr fin: fast time: first win: op 5/2: gd run, back to form of 2944.
4010 **AAHGOWANGOWAN 10** [8] M Dods 5-9-8 t (62) W Hogg(5) 13/8 FAV: 5215052: Led, no extra & hdd nr fin: *shd* **67**
op 5/2: gd run, back to form of 2830.
4070 **ELA FIGURA 7** [3] A W Carroll 4-8-6 p (46) Natalia Gemelova(3) 8/1: 6500053: Prom, hdwy & ev ch fnl *½* **49**
1f, onepcd nr fin: qck reapp: handles fast & gd/soft: gd run: see 1371.
2791 **MARABAR 4** [4] D W Chapman 6-9-2 (56) Dean Williams(5) 10/1: 1226604: Mid-div, hdwy over 1f out, *nk* **58**
kept on: 9 wk abs: eff at 5f, stays 6/7f & a return to further will suit: back to form of 1804.
3932 **SHIELALIGH 14** [6]3-9-11 p (67) L Treadwell(3) 16/1: 0030665: Chsd lrds, onepcd fnl 1f. *¾* **67**
4038 **QUEEN OF NIGHT 9** [1]4-9-2 (56) P Mathers(3) 8/1: 1120566: Mid-div, onepcd fnl 1f: op 6/1. *2½* **48**
3974 **PETITE MAC 12** [5]4-8-13 (53) A Reilly(5) 25/1: 05100-07: b f Timeless Times - Petite Elite *2½* **37**
(Anfield) Al bhd: won 1 of 15 '03 starts (with h'cap): rnr-up 2 '02 starts (fills mdn, auct mdn): eff at 5/6f on
firm, soft & fibresand, prob any trk: best without cheek pieces: goes well in sell grade: with N Bycroft.
1 Aug'03 Ripo 5g/f 55-49 F: 2 Oct'02 Redc 6sft 65- D: 2 Aug'02 Carl 5g/f 64- E:
4094 **ESTOILLE 7** [9]3-7-12 (10oh)t (30) Leanne Kershaw(3) 20/1: 000068: Dwelt, sn handy, wknd over 1f *shd* **23**
out: qck reapp: stiff task at weights: see 2945.
3574 **MITSUKI 28** [7]5-9-7 (61) J Cavanagh(7) 6/1: 400-0509: Slow away, al bhd: see 3116. *1* **41**
9 Ran   Time 1m 0.13(3.13)   Owned: Mr David T J Metcalfe   Trained: Richmond

NEWCASTLE   FRIDAY 27.08.04   Lefthand, Galloping, Stiff Track

Official Going Heavy

4211   5.25 Cantorsport Co Uk Apprentice Handicap Stakes 3yo+ 35-55 (F)   [61]
£3171 £906 £453   **6f str**   **Heavy 143**   **-33 Slow**   Stands Side

4090 **OLD BAILEY 7** [2] T D Barron 4-8-8 vis (41) P Makin 9/2 FAV: 0055031: Prom far side, led over 2f **50**
out, kept on, rdn out: wng form over 5/7f: acts on fibresand, fast & hvy grnd, any trk, likes W'hampton: eff in
blnks or a visor: slipped to a handy mark: see 2204, 1277.
3575 **M FOR MAGIC 28** [6] C W Fairhurst 5-8-7 (40) K Pierrepont(5) 9/1: 05045-52: Prom far side, eff *1¼* **46**
over 1f out, kept on: acts on fast & hvy grnd: mdn after 20 but lightly rcd this term: see 3575.
3767 **MICKLEDOR 20** [8] M Dods 4-9-6 p (53) D Tudhope(3) 10/1: 3011003: Handy far side, outpcd 2f out, *1¼* **56**
rallied fnl 1f: acts on fast & hvy grnd: back to form of 3129.
4009 **REDOUBTABLE 10** [5] D W Chapman 13-9-4 (51) M Halford(5) 12/1: 1604004: Held up far side, eff over *shd* **53**
1f out, sn onepcd, jock eased down cl home & lost 3rd, banned for 10 days: best 2891 (sell h'cap, gd grnd).
4041 **INDIAN MUSIC 8** [4]7-8-9 (42) C Ely(7) 14/1: 4620065: Held up, eff & hmpd 3f out, some late gains. *½* **43**
3609 **THE GAMBLER 27** [9]4-8-12 p (45) Stephanie Hollinshead(3) 50/1: 0200006: Led far side till over 2f *hd* **45**
out, no extra: see 1553, 1393.
3710 **WARES HOME 22** [14]3-8-10 (46) S Bushby(7) 14/1: 3323037: Handy, led centre group halfway, hung *2* **42**

NEWCASTLE FRIDAY 27.08.04 Lefthand, Galloping, Stiff Track

left & no extra over 1f out: gd run on unfav side: see 3710 (clmr), 1975.

3888 **BENNANABAA** 15 [15]5-8-9 t (42) B O'Neill(5) 33/1: 0005008: Handy centre, onepcd over 1f out.	1	36
3485 **LORD ARTHUR** 32 [3]3-9-3 (53) T Block(5) 25/1: 00-0409: In tch, wknd 2f out: see 3095.	½	46
3974 **DARK CHAMPION** 12 [11]4-9-7 (54) H Poulton(5) 40/1: 0450000: 10th: Handy centre, wknd over 1f out.	1¼	44
2683 **SAM THE SORCERER** 64 [12]3-8-9 (45) M Lawson(3) 9/1: 00-01030: 11th: Sn bhd, nvr a factor: abs.	1¼	33
3487 **DESERT FURY** 32 [7]7-8-8 (41) B Swarbrick 6/1: 00-00650: 12th: Nvr a factor far side: btr 3487 (1m).	6	17
3974 **ROSIES RESULT** 12 [1]4-9-3 (50) Jemma Marshall(5) 10/1: 0010060: 13th: In tch 4f far side.	11	4
4044 **TURF PRINCESS** 8 [10]3-9-3 (53) D Fentiman(3) 12/1: 4530400: 14th: In tch, wknd 2f out: see 3177.	½	6
3984 **KEW THE MUSIC** 21 [13]4-9-5 VIS (52) T O'Brien(7) 16/1: 0-000000: 15th: Led centre, wknd 2f out.	6	0

15 Ran Time 1m 21.86 (10.56) Owned: Mr J Baggott Trained: Thirsk

4212 5.55 Cantorindex Co Uk Novice Auction Stakes 2yo (F)
£2933 £838 £419 1m3y str Heavy 143 -48 Slow Inside

3831* **THUNDERWING** 18 [1] K R Burke 2-9-1 Darren Williams 11/8: 311: Keen in tch, hdwy & short of room		98

2f out, switched & styd on to lead ins last, rdn out: eff at 7f, styd this 1m well: acts on fast, clrly goes well on gd/soft & hvy: useful & prog, more to come: see 3831, 3412.

4046 **SKIDROW** 8 [2] M L W Bell 2-8-13 (88) M Fenton 5/4 FAV: 0122: Handy, hdwy to lead over 2f out	2	92

till ins last, not pace of wnr: nicely bckd: stays 1m on fast & hvy grnd: ran to useful form of 4046 & 3425.

4066 **SIMPLY ST LUCIA** 7 [4] J R Weymes 2-8-6 G Hind 8/1: 133: Cl-up, chall 2f out, wknd: see 4066.	13	65
2236 **SAINT CLEMENTS** 83 [3] M Johnston 2-8-12 S Chin 12/1: 004: b c Lemon Drop Kid - Sophisticated	27	31

Lynn (Clever Trick) Led till over 2f out, wknd: abs: Mar foal, cost $34,000: dam useful wnr in US.
4 Ran Time 1m 52.28 (15.28) Owned: Market Avenue Racing Club Ltd Trained: Leyburn

4213 6.25 Cantorsport Co Uk Claiming Stakes 2yo (F)
£3003 £858 £429 1m rnd Heavy 143 -41 Slow Inside

4171* **TOLDO** 1 [4] A Berry 2-8-13 (53) F Lynch 100/30: 00040211: Dwelt, held up, gd hdwy over 2f out,		67

styd on to lead ins last, pushed out, cmftbly: claimed for 8,000: eff at 7f/1m on fast grnd & hvy, easy or gall trks: likes clmrs & sells: won at Musselburgh yesterday, clrly in grand heart: see 4171.

3716 **BONGOALI** 22 [1] M R Channon 2-9-2 D Allan 11/4 FAV: 452: b f Fraam - Stride Home (Absalom) In	1	68

tch, hdwy to lead over 1f out, hdd this ins last, not pace of wnr: clr of rem: Mar foal: full sister to a 6f/1m scorer: dam 5f wnr: stays 1m on gd & hvy: shld win similar.

3570 **DANCING SHIRL** 28 [2] C W Fairhurst 2-8-12 L Enstone(3) 11/1: 633: Handy, onepcd over 1f out:	3½	58

poss handles fast & hvy: see 3570 (7f).

3930 **DANES ROCK** 14 [8] P C Haslam 2-8-3 bl (59) D Fentiman(7) 9/1: 4062004: Keen, sn clr ldr, hung to	1½	47

stands side enr str, hdd over 2f out, no extra: claimed for 3,000: looks exposed: see 2183 (blnks).

EASTERN MANDARIN [9]2-9-7 M Fenton 16/1: 5: b g Tipsy Creek - Hotel Street (Alleged) Slow	1¼	63

away, nvr a factor: claimed for 12,000 on debut: Mar foal, half brother to wnrs over 7/12f.

2051 **DRAMATIC REVIEW** 91 [3]2-9-1 VIS T G Faulkner 10/1: 0506: Held up, hung left over 2f out, wknd:	1¼	55

3 month abs: gldd, visor, t-strap: see 1744.

3349 **TONIGHT** 37 [10]2-8-7 (60) B Swarbrick(5) 7/1: 34367: In tch, wknd 2f out: see 1906.	½	46
3930 **BELTON** 14 [7]2-9-7 Dean McKeown 20/1: 0008: In tch, wknd over 2f out: see 3930.	½	59
4083 **WHITE STAR MAGIC** 7 [6]2-9-3 G Hind 9/1: 09: Handy, led 2f out till 1f out, wknd: see 4083.	1¼	53
2563 **FRANSISCAN** 69 [5]2-8-13 vis G Bartley(7) 50/1: 0060: 10th: In tch, wknd 2f out: abs: see 2563.	1¾	46

10 Ran Time 1m 25.74 (14.75) Owned: Mr Anthony White Trained: Cockerham

4214 6.55 Cantorindex Co Uk Novice Stakes 2yo (D)
£3416 £1051 £526 5f str Heavy 143 -23 Slow Stands Side

3968 **SENTIERO ROSSO** 12 [3] B Ellison 2-8-12 T Eaves(3) 4/6 FAV: 421: Handy trav well, styd on to lead		78

ins last, pushed clr, cmftbly: eff at 5f on gd/soft & hvy, 6f will suit: going the right way, more to come in nurs.

3644 **WOLF HAMMER** 25 [1] J Howard Johnson 2-8-12 P Mulrennan(3) 6/1: 022: Led till just ins last, not	1¼	75

pace of wnr: prob acts on fast grnd & hvy: see 3644.

3606 **PETERS DELITE** 27 [2] R A Fahey 2-8-12 T Hamilton(3) 100/30: 033: In tch, no extra dist: see 3606.	1¾	71
PARCHMENT [4] J Howard Johnson 2-8-8 R Ffrench 9/1: 4: ch c Singspiel - Hannalou (Shareef	11	45

Dancer) In tch, wknd over 2f out on debut: Jan foal, cost 100,000 gns: dam stays 1m: bred to need 7f/1m+ in time.
4 Ran Time 1m 06.5 (8.3) Owned: Mr Graeme Redpath Trained: Malton

4215 7.25 Cantorsport Co Uk Handicap Stakes 3yo+ 0-70 (E)
£3689 £1135 £568 1m1f9y Heavy 143 +22 Fast Inside [70]

3992* **ARTISTIC STYLE** 11 [13] B Ellison 4-9-7 (63) T Eaves(3) 7/2 FAV: 6001311: In tch, hdwy 2f out,		72

styd on to lead ins last, rdn clr: fast time: eff over 1m/10f on firm & hvy, sharp or gall trks: imprvg, see 3992.

3392 **GENERAL GB** 35 [3] C R Dore 7-9-9 (65) M Fenton 12/1: 2000532: In tch, eff to chall over 1f out,	1¾	69

styd on to lead briefly ins last, kept on: gd run from new yard: see 1295, 856.

3850 **MOBANE FLYER** 16 [10] R A Fahey 4-9-4 (60) T Hamilton(3) 20/1: 050-0063: In tch, hdwy to lead over	1	64

2f out till ins last, no extra: acts on firm & hvy: see 3850, 3117.

3423 **TAGULA BLUE** 34 [7] J A Glover 4-9-11 (67) Dean McKeown 12/1: U0R3654: Slow away, sn in tch, eff	3	67

2f out, sn no impress: see 2901 (10f, clmr, gd), 2010.

4008 **APACHE POINT** 10 [15]7-8-12 (54) Kim Tinkler 6/1: 5523555: Chsd ldrs, no extra dist: btr 3325.	1½	52
3741* **MELODIAN** 22 [9]9-9-9 bl (65) M Lawson(5) 4/1: 5123216: Dwelt, bhd, nvr a factor: likes this grnd	3½	58

& usually races more prom: much btr 3741.

3526 **HOHS BACK** 30 [14]5-8-9 p (51) Stephanie Hollinshead(5) 25/1: 5000007: Hld up, nvr a factor: see 1214.	¾	43
3459 **THIRD EMPIRE** 33 [6]3-9-1 (64) P Fessey 16/1: 0-305248: Led till 2f out, wknd: btr 3231 (g/f).	9	42
4036 **MOUNT HILLABY** 9 [4]4-9-1 (57) Dale Gibson 5/1: 00-0029: Keen cl-up, wknd dist: see 4036.	hd	34
2162 **KINGS ENVOY** 86 [8]5-9-4 (60) D McGaffin 66/1: 0/0-43500: 10th: Handy, wknd 2f out: 3 month abs.	1½	35
3992 **GOT TO BE CASH** 11 [1]5-8-12 (54) B Swarbrick(5) 15/2: 5300140: 11th: In tch, wknd 2f out: best 3895.	2½	25
1602 **SHARDDA** 112 [12]4-9-7 (63) P Mulrennan(3) 50/1: 430-300: 12th: Held up, wknd 2f out: long abs.	12	16

NEWCASTLE FRIDAY 27.08.04 Lefthand, Galloping, Stiff Track

12 Ran Time 2m 03.06 (10.96) Owned: Mr & Mrs D A Gamble Trained: Malton

4216 7.55 Cantorindex Co Uk Maiden Stakes 3yo+ **(D)**
£3474 £1069 £535 **7f str** **Heavy 143** -25 Slow Inside

3910 **TROPICAL STORM** 14 [4] J Noseda 3-9-0 (73) K Darley 4/11 FAV: 24-30421: Cl-up, led over 2f out, **73**
kept on fnl 1f, rdn out: apprec return to 7f: acts on fast & hvy grnd: consistent: see 3910, 1912.
4462} **QUEENS ECHO** 336 [3] M Dods 3-8-9 L Enstone(3) 9/1: 5-2: b f Wizard King - Sunday News'n'echo hd **67$**
(Trempolino) Handy, eff over 1f out, kept on, just held: clr of rem: reapp: unplcd sole '03 start (rtd 64): eff
at 7f, bred to stay further: handles hvy grnd: encouraging return.
3737 **LA FONTEYNE** 22 [8] C B B Booth 3-8-9 (44) T Hamilton(3) 33/1: 5020503: Dwelt, in tch, eff over 1f 5 **58$**
out, sn onepcd: treat rating with caution, seemingly imprvd on this hvy grnd at 7f, handles fibresand: see 2493.
1636 **GREY FORTUNE** 111 [5] M Brittain 5-9-0 M Lawson(5) 28/1: 04: gr f Grey Desire - Mere Melody 3½ **52**
(Dunphy) In tch, eff to chall 2f out, sn no extra: mod form to date.
2117 **INK IN GOLD** 88 [2]3-9-0 P Bradley 16/1: 05: Dwelt, in tch, btn 2f out: abs: bred to apprec 7f/1m. ½ **56**
3462 **SPEED RACER** 33 [10]3-8-9 Kim Tinkler 14/1: 05-05036: Dsptd lead after 2f till over 2f out, wknd. 2 **48**
    SWINTON [9]3-9-0 T Williams 25/1: 7: Slow away & nvr a factor on debut: bred to apprec 7f/1m. shd **53**
3805 **BORODINSKY** 19 [7]3-9-0 (47) T Eaves(3) 12/1: 5040248: Led till 2f out, wknd: see 3805 (fast). ¾ **52**
3592 **AFTER LENT** 27 [6]3-9-0 Dean McKeown 28/1: 069: Held up, nvr a factor: see 3592. 11 **36**
3973 **PERRYWINKLE BOY** 12 [1]3-9-0 Darren Williams 50/1: 400: 10th: In tch, wknd 2f out: see 3973. 28 **0**
10 Ran Time 1m 35.87(11.77) Owned: Lucayan Stud Trained: Newmarket

WINDSOR SATURDAY 28.08.04 Sharp, Figure 8 Track

Official Going Good/Soft (Good Places)

4217 5.05 European Breeders Fund Novice Median Auction Stakes 2yo **(D)**
£5265 £1620 £810 **6f str** **Good/Soft** Inapplicable Inside rail

3290* **ANGEL SPRINTS** 40 [5] L G Cottrell 2-9-1 (86) A Daly 9/2: 33611: Made all, rdn out ins fnl 1f to **93**
assert: 6 wk abs: eff at 5f, imprvd for recent step up to 6f: acts on firm & gd/soft grnd: likes Windsor & goes
well further: progressing well: see 3290.
3110 **DEEDAY BAY** 49 [6] C F Wall 2-9-1 (87) G Baker 7/2: 142: Cl up, kept on bef 1f out, al held by 1¾ **87**
wnr: 7 wk abs: continues in gd form & now qual for h'caps: see 3110 & 2750.
3943 **CANTON** 14 [2] R Hannon 2-9-4 (89) K Fallon 4/1 FAV: 1445333: Mid div, al hanging right, no room 1½ **86**
halfway, no impress dist: clr rem: acts on firm, gd & polytrack, handles gd/soft: see 3943 (5f, fast).
    TEN CENTS 0 [4] C A Cyzer 2-8-3 P Doe 16/1: 4: b f Dansili - Daylight Dreams (Indian Ridge) 5 **57**
Missed break, nvr able to chall: debut: May foal, half-sister successful at 1m: dam 5f wnr at 2.
3682 **COME TO DADDY** 24 [1]2-8-12 R Havlin 66/1: 05: ch g Fayruz - Forgren (Thatching) Missed break, 3½ **57**
prog 3f out, hung left & fdd fnl 2f: Apr foal, dam unrcd: sire speedy bred: with F Jordan.
3863 **PUSSY CAT** 17 [3]2-8-7 J Fanning 33/1: 06: b f Josr Algarhoud - Swan Lake (Lyphard) Cl up 4f, 8 **31**
fdd: Mar first foal, dam modest: sire useful around 1m: with K O Cunningham- Brown.
6 Ran Time 1m 14.95 (4.65) Owned: Mrs Lucy Halloran Trained: Cullompton

4218 5.35 Rectangle Group Selling Stakes 2yo **(E)**
£3377 £1039 £520 **5f10y str** **Good/Soft** Inapplicable Inside rail

3847 **RUBY MUJA** 18 [2] R Hannon 2-8-6 (55) R Smith 11/2: 0031: Keen cl up, styd on to lead dist, **65**
pushed out, val 4L+: sold for 8,400 gns: eff at 5f, further shld suit: acts on fast, imprvd for gd/soft.
4127 **CAMPEON** 5 [6] M J Wallace 2-8-11 vis (71) K Fallon 1/1 FAV: 2435242: Keen bhd, prog 2f out, styd 2 **64**
on, not pace wnr: qck reapp: bought for 6,000: handles fast, gd/soft & fibresand: see 4127 & 3431.
3988 **WIZZSKILAD** 12 [4] Mrs P N Dutfield 2-8-11 (60) R Havlin 10/1: 4630403: Led, hdd dist, no extra. 1½ **60**
3962 **TURTLE MAGIC** 13 [3] W G M Turner 2-8-6 p (53) A Daly 10/1: 6430464: Keen bhd, no threat. 1¾ **49**
3864 **SLITE** 17 [7]2-8-6 E Ahern(3) 100/30: 025: Nvr nrr than mid div: btr 3864 (7f, fast, J A Osborne). 5 **36**
3901 **VON WESSEX** 16 [5]2-9-2 C Haddon(7) 12/1: 6331466: Keen cl up 4f, fdd: btr 2321. 3 **37**
2976 **OUR NIGEL** 54 [1]2-8-11 J Fanning 20/1: 007: Mid div 3f, wknd: 8 wk abs. ½ **31**
2977 **FIRE AT WILL** 54 [8]2-8-11 VIS P Doe 25/1: 008: Al well bhd: 8 wk abs & 1st time visor. ¾ **29**
8 Ran Time 1m 2.83 (3.83) Owned: Mr William J Kelly Trained: Marlborough

4219 6.05 Listed Stanjamesuk Com August Stakes 3yo+ **(A)**
£17400 £6600 £3300 **1m3f135y** **Good/Soft** Inapplicable Inside rail

3030 **NAHEEF** 52 [3] Saeed bin Suroor 5-9-2 vis t (109) K McEvoy 100/30: 125-3501: Al prom, led 2f out, **111**
rdn out to hold on: 7 wk abs: eff at 9/10f, now stays 12f: acts on firm, gd/soft & any trk: eff with t-strap &
visor: smart 5yo who enjoyed drop to listed grade: see 2004.
3777 **HAWRIDGE PRINCE** 21 [2] L G Cottrell 4-9-2 (95) K Fallon 9/4: 12-11242: Bhd, prog 2f out, styd on 1½ **108**
ins fnl 1f, al held by wnr: well bckd: acts on fast & gd/soft grnd: progressive 4yo who is unexposed at this trip.
3958 **COMPTON BOLTER** 14 [6] G A Butler 7-9-2 (109) J Fortune 15/8 FAV: 2506533: Led, hdd 2f out, no 1¼ **106**
extra ins fnl 1f: clr rem: shade better expected dropped in grade: see 2898.
4825} **OVAMBO** 658 [7] P J Makin 6-9-2 D Sweeney 12/1: 2/36243/-4: b g Namaqualand - Razana (Kahyasi) 6 **97**
Cl up 9f, wknd bef 1f out: reapp: missed '03: close 3rd of 6 at best in '02 (Gr 3, also twice plcd in listed): won
3 h'caps in '01: eff at 10/14f on firm & gd, handles soft: acts on any trk & has gone well fresh: tough & smart at
best, has been gelded. 2 Jun'02 Newm 12fm 111- A: 2 Aug'01 York 13.8g/f 103-95 B: 1 Aug'01 Good 12fm 97-90 C:
1 Jul'01 Sali 12g/f 92-80 D: 1 Jun'01 Wind 12g 82-76 D:
3754 **TIZZY MAY** 22 [5]4-9-2 (97) P Dobbs 12/1: 5040055: Cl up 9f, wknd: needs h'caps, see 1478. 6 **88**
3506 **FOODBROKER FOUNDER** 32 [1]4-9-2 (94) E Ahern 16/1: 00-06606: Chsd ldrs 7f, fdd: see 1862. 6 **79**
4111 **SADLERS ROCK** 7 [4]6-9-2 R Brisland 100/1: 07: Rear, nvr a factor: qck reapp. 7 **69**

WINDSOR SATURDAY 28.08.04 Sharp, Figure 8 Track

7 Ran Time 2m 33.27 (5.97) Owned: Godolphin Trained: Newmarket

4220 **6.35 Gr3 Stan James Winter Hill Stakes 3yo+ (A)**
£29000 £11000 £5500 **1m2f7y** **Good/Soft** **Inapplicable** Inside rail

3886 **ANCIENT WORLD 16** [1] Saeed bin Suroor 4-9-0 (110) K McEvoy 5/1: 11-22101: Mid div, prog trav well to lead 2f out, rdn out: eff at1m, enjoyed step up to 10f: acts on firm & soft grnd: back to smart best. **116**
3306 **GATEMAN 40** [3] M Johnston 7-9-4 (114) J Fanning 15/8 FAV: 2031222: Cl up, led 3f out, hdd 2f out, sn went clr with wnr, just held ins fnl 1f: clr rem: 6 wk abs: eff at 7/10f: smart & consistent: see 3306. *1½* **117**
3306 **FRUHLINGSSTURM 40** [6] M A Jarvis 4-9-8 (112) P Robinson 10/1: 151-5103: Cl up 1m, no extra: 6 wk abs: gd run conceding weight all round: see 3043. *4* **115**
3613* **PAWN BROKER 28** [5] D R C Elsworth 7-9-0 (109) K Fallon 11/2: 6025-014: Bhd, prog 4f out, wknd dist. *3½* **102**
2128 **NYSAEAN 88** [4]5-9-4 (114) R Hughes 5/2: 4521345: Bhd, nvr nrr than mid div: 12 wk abs: btr 2004. *2* **103**
3957 **DUCK ROW 14** [2]9-9-0 (104) E Ahern 20/1: 40-20506: Rear, prog 4f out, fdd fnl 2f: btr 2252. *nk* **98**
3964 **A ONE 13** [8]5-9-0 (83) D Sweeney 50/1: 1011507: Led 7f, fdd: stiff task: btr 3477 (C/D, h'cap). *5* **91**
3954 **TUNING FORK 14** [9]4-9-0 (89) M Tebbutt 50/1: 0000308: Al bhd, adrfift when eased bef 1f out. *dist* **61**
8 Ran Time 2m 8.97 (2.97) Owned: Godolphin Trained: Newmarket

4221 **7.05 Stanjamesuk Com Rated Stakes Handicap 3yo+ 0-85 (D)** **[90]**
£5494 £2084 £1042 **1m67y rnd** **Good/Soft** **Inapplicable** Inside rail

4067 **PAGAN PRINCE 8** [10] J A R Toller 7-8-10 (72) E Ahern 14/1: 02110-01: Held up, prog 2f out, led ins fnl 1f, rdn out: eff btwn 1m & 10f on fast, gd/soft & fibresand: win again on this evidence: see 4067 (reapp). **80**
4067 **AFRICAN SAHARA 8** [8] Miss D Mountain 5-9-6 t (82) O Urbina 5/1: 0343142: Mid div, prog 4f out, led ins fnl 1f, sn hdd & no extra: continues to run well: see 3768. *1¾* **85**
3797 **IMPERSONATOR 21** [6] J L Dunlop 4-9-0 (76) P Doe 6/1: 040-0433: Led, hdd 6f out, led again 2f out, hdd ins fnl 1f, no extra: another encouraging run & is on a winning mark: see 3797. *½* **78**
4122 **SUPREME SALUTATION 5** [13] D K Ivory 8-9-7 (83) M Howard(7) 25/1: 1014104: Sn mid div, eff 3f out, styd on fnl 1f: qck reapp: 5lb higher than win in 1776 (10f). *nk* **84**
3512 **FREELOADER 32** [1]4-9-2 (78) R L Moore 11/2: 0430145: Held up, prog 3f out, ev ch dist, no extra. *1* **77**
4117* **ARCTIC DESERT 6** [5]4-8-13 (3ex) (75) K Fallon 9/4 FAV: 0000616: Bhd, prog when no room bef 2f out, sn btn: qck reapp: btr 4117 (7f, gd). *½* **73**
3995 **ALCHERA 12** [2]3-8-1 (15oh) (60) C Haddon(7) 33/1: 0644047: Nvr nrr than mid div: stiff task. *2½* **60**
4122 **FREAK OCCURENCE 5** [3]3-8-13 vis (81) S Drowne 8/1: 3463068: Cl upover 6f, wknd: qk reapp: btr 2126. *1* **72**
4141 **EL CHAPARRAL 4** [11]4-8-11 (73) D Sweeney 12/1: 2020109: Al in rear: qck reapp: btr 3980 (10f, fast). *½* **63**
1377* **SUBMISSIVE 124** [4]3-8-7 (75) K May(7) 16/1: 010: 10th: Cl up 6f, fdd: long abs: btr 1377 (mdn, AW). *½* **64**
3978 **MADAMOISELLE JONES 12** [12]4-8-7 (3oh) (66) J F McDonald(3) 20/1: 4516460: 11th: Mid div 6f, wknd. *5* **48**
3813 **LIZARAZU 20** [7]5-8-7 (69) R Miles(3) 20/1: 252-0000: 12th: Bhd, nvr a factor. *3* **42**
3762 **MBOSI 21** [9]3-9-0 BL (82) J Fanning 16/1: 3302030: 13th: Led 6f out, hdd 2f out, fdd: 1st time blnks. *1½* **53**
13 Ran Time 1m 47.42 (4.42) Owned: Gap Partnership & Mrs J Toller Trained: Newmarket

4222 **7.35 Mark & Julie Lancaster Handicap Stakes Fillies 3yo+ 0-85 (D)** **[90]**
£5801 £1785 £893 **1m67y rnd** **Good/Soft** **Inapplicable** Inside rail

3978* **MUNAAWASHAT 12** [8] K R Burke 3-8-11 (73) J Fanning 10/1: 1-312011: Prom, led after 3f, styd on well for press fnl 1f: eff at 7f/1m, tried 10f: acts on fast & gd/soft: likes Windsor: likes to race with/force the pace: tough & progressive 3yo who can land hatrick: see 3978. **81**
3828* **SEA NYMPH 19** [4] Sir Michael Stoute 3-9-0 (76) K Fallon 15/8 FAV: 5212: Mid div, prog to chase wnr ins fnl 1f, al held: acts on firm & gd/soft grnd: gd run on h'cap bow & can rate higher: see 3828 (mdn). *2* **79**
4051 **TUSCARORA 9** [7] A W Carroll 5-8-5 (61) R Miles(3) 9/2: 6105133: Held up, prog wide 3f out, no impress fnl 1f: acts on firm, gd/soft & polytrack: see 4051 & 3731. *1½* **61**
4058 **UIG 9** [2] H S Howe 3-8-13 (75) P Doe 25/1: 003204: Led 3f, styd in tch, onepcd dist: eff at 1m, return to 10f will suit: acts on firm & fast, handles gd/soft: btr 3802. *½* **74**
4032* **FARRIERS CHARM 10** [10]3-8-4 (66) E Ahern 14/1: 44-10015: Chsd ldrs over 6f, sn onepcd: btr 4032. *nk* **64**
3287 **CZARINA WALTZ 42** [6]5-9-13 (83) R Mullen 20/1: 040-2066: Cl up, wknd fnl 1f: 6 wk abs: btr 2265. *1½* **79**
3866 **CUDDLES 17** [1]5-8-1 (57) J F McDonald(3) 16/1: 0453007: Bhd, nvr nrr than mid div: btr 3144. *nk* **52**
4101 **ANNA PANNA 7** [5]3-8-10 (72) Dane O'Neill 12/1: 3-625528: Missed break, prog halfway, no impress. *1½* **65**
3963 **BRAZILIAN TERRACE 13** [11]4-9-5 (75) S Drowne 8/1: 1130229: Mid div 6f, wknd: btr 3963 (fast). *14* **42**
3780 **HOT LIPS PAGE 21** [13]3-8-11 (73) R L Moore 25/1: 05-51400: 10th: Mid div 5f, grad wknd: btr 2624. *2½* **35**
3885 **RED SAHARA 16** [12]3-9-2 (78) P Robinson 6/1: 1-166240: 11th: Al in rear: btr 3162. (gd). *1¾* **36**
11 Ran Time 1m 48.24(5.24) Owned: Mr John A Duffy Trained: Leyburn

NEWMARKET SATURDAY 28.08.04 Righthand, Stiff, Galloping Track

Official Going GOOD/SOFT.

4223 **1.55 Mckeever St Lawrence E B F Maiden Stakes 2yo (D)**
£4891 £1505 £753 **6f str** **Good 50** **-02 Slow** Stands Side

ECHELON [4] Sir Michael Stoute 2-8-9 N Mackay(3) 7/1: 1: b f Danehill - Exclusive (Polar Falcon) Held up, gd hdwy over 1f out to lead ins last, hands-and-heels, cmftbly: Apr foal: half-sister to a top-class 1m wnr Chic: dam smart 7f/1m wnr: eff at 6f, 7f/1m sure to suit: goes well fresh on gd grnd & a gall trk: most promising, just the sort to develop into a top-class performer, keep on side. **105+**
NEWSROUND [8] M A Jarvis 2-9-0 P Robinson 6/1: 2: ch c Cadeaux Genereux - Ring The Relatives (Bering) Set pace, edged left over 1f out, hdd & not pace of wnr ins last but well clr of rem on debut: Feb first foal, cost 220,000gns: dam styd 10f: eff at 6f, 7f sure to suit: acts on gd grnd: useful start bhd a smart sort. *2* **100**
RIVER ROYALE [1] P W Chapple Hyam 2-9-0 A McCarthy 11/2: 3: b c Royal Applause - Trundley Wood *5* **87**

(Wassl) In tch, eff to chall over 1f out, no extra ins last: debut: Feb foal, cost 36,000gns: half-brother to a sprint wnr: dam 7f juv wnr: bred to apprec 6/7f: shld find easier mdns.

2408	**WISE OWL 77** [2] M Johnston 2-9-0 J Fanning 3/1 FAV: 24: With ldrs, wknd fnl 1f: well bckd, 11 wk abs: showed more on faster grnd in 2408.	nk	86
	BREATHING FIRE [3]2-9-0 R Mullen 33/1: 5: b c Pivotal - Pearl Venture (Salse) Slow away, held up, some late gains, no dngr on debut: Apr foal, cost 15,000gns: bred to apprec 7f/1m in time: gd start.	2	81
	VICTORY DESIGN [5]2-9-0 E Ahern 4/1: 6: In tch, wknd 2f out.	nk	80
	MUSAHIM [11]2-9-0 R Hills 17/2: 7: Held up, some late gains, hands-and-heels, improve.	shd	80
3959	**RAPID FLOW 14** [10]2-9-0 R Hughes 25/1: 08: In tch, wknd 2f out.	¾	78
4121	**SIR BLUEBIRD 5** [7]2-9-0 J F Egan 50/1: 09: In tch, wknd 2f out.	1	75$
	PACIFIC PIRATE [9]2-9-0 S W Kelly 50/1: 0: 10th: In tch, wknd 2f out on debut.	nk	74
	PADRAO [6]2-9-0 K Darley 20/1: 0: 11th: With ldrs, wknd over 2f out on debut.	¾	72
	SELIKA [13]2-9-0 N Callan 100/1: 0: 12th: Slow away & al bhd on debut.	7	54
3975	**PEREZ 12** [12]2-9-0 Paul Eddery 50/1: 00: 13th: Handy, hung left & wknd over 2f out.	hd	53

13 Ran   Time 1m 14.14 (3.14)   Owned: Cheveley Park Stud   Trained: Newmarket

---

4224   2.25 Siemens Smart Home Technology Nursery Handicap Stakes 2yo (B)   [97]
£14040 £4320 £2160   **6f str**   **Good 50**   **-08 Slow**   Stands Side

4049*	**COLEORTON DANCER 9** [3] K A Ryan 2-8-13 (82) N Callan 5/1: 4401111: Hld up centre, hdwy 2f out, styd on well to lead ins last, rdn out: eff at 5f, clrly stays 6f well on fm, gd/soft & on any trk: thriving, useful & tough.		91
3722*	**MARCHING SONG 23** [11] R Hannon 2-9-3 (86) R Hughes 8/1: 5324212: Slow away centre, held up, hdwy 2f out to lead dist, sn hdd & not pace of wnr but kept on: excellent run up in class: see 3722.	½	93
3877*	**SPY KING 17** [6] M Johnston 2-9-7 (90) K Darley 4/1 FAV: 2113: In tch centre, eff to chall over 1f out, kept on same pace ins last: continues to improve: useful, made all 3877 (nov stks).	2	92
3251	**ALEXANDER CAPETOWN 43** [8] B W Hills 2-8-2 (1ow) (70) R Mullen 14/1: 2564: In tch, hdwy to lead 4f out till dist, onepace: 6 wk abs: gd run & stays 6f: see 1709, 1524.	½	71
4065	**KWAME 8** [1]2-8-9 (78) T E Durcan 14/1: 212025: Slow away, held up centre, hdwy dist, onepace.	1¼	75
4004	**BOLTON HALL 11** [7]2-9-2 (85) P Hanagan 8/1: 1656: Handy, onepcd dist: see 4004, 2167 (5f).	shd	81
3698	**SOCIETY MUSIC 24** [9]2-8-9 (78) E Ahern 50/1: 131367: In tch centre, hung right & onepace dist.	nk	73
4072	**KING AFTER 8** [4]2-8-6 (75) C Haddon(7) 33/1: 166558: Sn rdn & nvr a factor centre, see 1567, 931 (5f).	1½	66
3931*	**ROWAN LODGE 15** [16]2-8-12 (81) P Robinson 14/1: 031219: Made most stands side, no extra 1f out.	nk	71
4052*	**BROOKLIME 9** [15]2-8-9 (78) S W Kelly 14/1: 6410: 10th: In tch stands side, hung left & btn fnl 1f.	nk	64
3987	**ON THE WATERLINE 12** [12]2-8-7 (76) N Chalmers(5) 12/1: 230420: 11th: In tch, wknd over 1f out.	1¾	56
3614	**PROSPECT COURT 28** [13]2-8-13 (82) K McEvoy 25/1: 030100: 12th: In tch stands side, wkng & hmpd ins last: twice below 2989.	2½	61
3943	**MONASHEE PRINCE 14** [14]2-8-12 (81) D Kinsella 33/1: 2153400: 13th: With ldrs, wknd 2f out: see 2100.	hd	59
3407	**WHATATODO 36** [2]2-8-3 (72) J Mackay 16/1: 030120: 14th: In tch, wknd 2f out: btr 3407, 3297.	½	48
3907*	**GRAND PLACE 15** [5]2-8-4 (73) J F Egan 14/1: 04010: 15th: Keen, handy centre, wknd over 1f out: reportedly lost action: btr 3907 (5f, mdn auct).	1¾	45
3544	**NAVAL FORCE 30** [10]2-8-10 t (79) M Fenton 14/1: 0430: 16th: Led centre 2f, wknd 2f out: see 3544.	1¼	47

16 Ran   Time 1m 14.46 (3.45)   Owned: Coleorton Moor Racing   Trained: Hambleton

---

4225   2.55 Chris Blackwell Memorial Handicap Stakes 3yo 0-90 (C)   [96]
£14170 £4360 £2180   **7f str**   **Good 50**   **+00 Fast**   Stands Side

3814*	**MY PARIS 20** [5] K A Ryan 3-9-5 (87) A Mullen(7) 13/2: 2522111: Slow away, sn handy, hdwy to lead over 1f out, hung left ins last, kept on, drvn out: eff over 7f/10f on firm & gd/soft: best up with/forcing the pace: genuine & improving, useful: see 3814.		98
1496	**ALFONSO 118** [2] B W Hills 3-8-5 (73) M Hills 8/1: 04-1002: Prom, eff & sltly short of room ins last, styd on cl-home, just held: shade unlucky & a fine run after a 4 month abs: imprvd for gelding op.	shd	81
3941	**FLIPANDO 14** [4] T D Barron 3-9-4 (86) K Darley 4/1 FAV: 0-422153: In tch, eff & hung right over 1f out, kept on: nicely bckd: another useful run: see 2950.	1¾	92
3472	**HAZEWIND 34** [12] P D Evans 3-7-12 (1oh)vis t (65) N Mackay(3) 12/1: 0251164: Led after 1f till over 1f out, kept on same pace: back to form: best 3283.	nk	71
3612	**GRANSTON 28** [6]3-8-7 (75) P Robinson 9/1: 3166025: Handy, eff to chall over 1f out, held when hmpd ins last: see 3612, 1176.	¾	78
3778	**DOITNOW 21** [8]3-9-7 (89) P Hanagan 8/1: 12266: Held up, eff dist, onepace: see 2950, 2485.	½	91
3860	**BURLEY FLAME 17** [9]3-8-11 (79) M Fenton 16/1: 1031607: Held up, eff dist, no impress: btr 3179.	shd	80
3923+	**BRIGHT SUN 15** [1]3-8-7 (75) Kim Tinkler 11/1: 4303418: In tch, no extra dist: btr 3923 (1m).	1¼	74
4071	**SENESCHAL 8** [7]3-8-7 (75) T E Durcan 9/1: 21-00009: Held up, nvr a factor: see 3553, 1206.	¾	72
3947*	**KING OF DIAMONDS 14** [10]3-8-9 (77) N Callan 6/1: 2620010: 10th: Keen held up, nvr a factor.	3½	68
3972	**MISSION MAN 13** [11]3-8-10 (78) R Hughes 11/1: 1404500: 11th: Led till 5f out, wknd dist.	2½	65
3002	**BIG BRADFORD 53** [3]3-9-6 vis (88) D Kinsella 20/1: 420-2000: 12th: Dwelt, held up, btn over 2f out: 7 wk abs: see 1933 (6f, fast grnd).	1¾	71

12 Ran   Time 1m 27.42 (3.52)   Owned: J and A Spensley   Trained: Hambleton

---

4226   3.30 Listed Sharp Minds Betfair Be Hopeful Stakes 3yo+ (A)
£17400 £6600 £3300   **6f str**   **Good 50**   **+00 Fast**   Stands Side

3069*	**PRINCE AARON 50** [6] C N Allen 4-9-0 (89) G Carter 3/1 FAV: 2131511: Held up, hdwy over 1f out, hung left ins last but styd on well to lead, drvn out: 7 wk abs: suited by 6/6.5f on firm, gd & polytrack, sharp & gall trks: goes well fresh: has thrived this term, useful now & still on the up-grade: see 3069.		100
3782	**ATAVUS 21** [3] G G Margarson 7-9-0 (85) J Mackay 16/1: 0605002: Chsd ldr, led dist, sn hdd but kept on, not btn far: best eff for some time back at 6f, best prev at 7f: likes Newmarket & on a handy mark now.	½	98
3379	**RED ROMEO 37** [1] G A Swinbank 3-8-11 (92) P Hanagan 6/1: 4411123: Handy, eff & hung left over 1f out, kept on, not btn far: useful & v progressive, fine effort: see 3188.	hd	97
3971	**MILLYBAA 13** [7] R Guest 4-8-9 (97) K Darley 9/1: 20-24004: Sn handy, eff over 1f out, no extra well ins last: gd run: see 1773.	¾	90
3622	**COCONUT PENANG 28** [2]4-9-0 (95) E Ahern 7/2: 0-002005: Handy, eff over 1f out, onepace: tried blnks 3622, prob ran to form of 2581.	hd	94

3551 **CELTIC MILL** 30 [8]6-9-4 (106) L Enstone 6/1: 4011006: Led till dist, no extra: best 1958.   *1* **95**
3564 **ENCHANTED** 29 [4]5-8-9 (94) J F Egan 13/2: 3-110007: Held up, btn dist: see 3564, 1925 (7f).   *hd* **85**
3971 **DOWAGER** 13 [5]3-8-6 (100) R Hughes 15/2: 5463008: Held up, wknd over 1f out: see 3268.   *2½* **80**
8 Ran   Time 1m 14.02 (3.02)   Owned: Black Star Racing   Trained: Newmarket

---

4227	**4.00 Dettori's Italian Ice Cream Challenge Rated Stakes Handicap 3yo+ 0-95 (C)**	**[105]**
	£15428 £5852 £2926 **1m2f** **Good 50** **+08 Fast** Stands Side	

4924*}**BORDER CASTLE** 305 [9] Sir Michael Stoute 3-8-4 (3oh) (81) N Mackay(3) 4/1: 441-1: b c Grand Lodge - Tempting Prospect (Shirley Heights) Held up, hdwy over 2f out, styd on to lead ins last, rdn clr: reapp: won last of 3 '02 starts (mdn): enjoyed step up to 10f, further could suit: acts on fast & gd/soft, gall trks: clrly runs well fresh: useful & progressive, plenty more to come. 1 Oct'03 Nott 8.2g/s 84- D: **93**
4021 **ZERO TOLERANCE** 10 [5] T D Barron 4-9-7 (90) M Fenton 9/2: 1400022: Keen, handy, eff to chase ldrs 4f out, led over 1f out till ins last, no extra: not pace of wnr: running well on easy grnd: see 4021, 2489.   *2* **98**
3794 **OFARABY** 21 [2] M A Jarvis 4-9-5 (88) P Robinson 9/1: 1642503: Held up, eff well over 1f out, kept on same pace: gd run: see 2185, 964.   *1¾* **93**
3999 **TORINMOOR** 11 [3] Mrs A J Perrett 3-8-13 (90) K Darley 100/30 FAV: 16-53354: Chsd ldr, led centre group 7f out till over 1f out, onepace: nicely bckd: consistent: see 3999 (12f).   *½* **94**
4136 **DANELOR** 5 [1]6-9-3 (86) P Hanagan 16/1: 0050105: Led stands side, hdd dist, sn wknd: qck reapp.   *2* **87**
4097 **SILVALINE** 7 [8]5-8-13 (82) T E Durcan 5/1: 1103026: Handy, hung left dist, no impress: btr 4097.   *½* **82**
3794 **CRIPSEY BROOK** 21 [6]6-9-1 (84) Kim Tinkler 22/1: 0025607: Keen, handy, wknd over 2f out.   *3½* **79**
4082 **ST PANCRAS** 8 [7]4-8-13 (82) N Callan 10/1: 2015328: Slow away, held up, btn 2f out: see 4082.   *5* **70**
3945 **SOLO FLIGHT** 14 [4]7-9-2 (85) R Hughes 16/1: 06-26029: Dwelt, nvr a factor: not enjoy easy grnd.   *1¼* **71**
9 Ran   Time 2m 06.11 (4.21)   Owned: The Queen   Trained: Newmarket

---

4228	**4.35 New Tigra Arrives At Marshall Ely Maiden Stakes 3yo+ (D)**	
	£5616 £1728 £864 **1m str** **Good 50** **+00 Fast** Stands Side	

  EYES ONLY [10] H R A Cecil 3-8-6 R Hughes 7/4 FAV: 1: b f Distant View - Yashmak (Danzig) Cl-up, hdwy to lead over 1f out, sn clr, hands & heels, readily: hvly bckd: styd 1m well, shld get further: goes well fresh on gd grnd: impressive start, plenty more to come.   **82+**
3973 **THISTLE** 13 [15] J H M Gosden 3-8-11 R Hills 25/1: 02: Led till over 1f out, not pace of wnr: improved from debut & eff at 1m on gd grnd: shld find a modest mdn: see 3973.   *6* **76**
4721} **HIGH RESERVE** 320 [4] J R Fanshawe 3-8-6 O Urbina 8/1: 35-3: b f Dr Fong - Hyabella (Shirley Heights) Held up, eff over 1f out, onepace: plcd in a mdn in 1 of 2 '03 starts: dam smart miler: eff at 1m, further looks sure to suit: acts on fast & gd grnd: can improve in h'caps, shld win a race.   *½* **70**
3581 **PLAY BOUZOUKI** 29 [16] L M Cumani 3-8-6 N Mackay(3) 5/1: 34: Handy, eff over 1f out, no impress: nicely bckd: stays 1m on gd grnd: see 3581.   *¾* **68**
1729 **RIVER OF BABYLON** 106 [5]3-8-6 (64) J Mackay 11/1: 50-265: Keen, handy, wknd dist: see 1129.   *shd* **68**
3446 **RESIDENTIAL** 35 [14]3-8-11 P Hanagan 9/1: 5-46: In tch, hung left & wknd over 1f out: see 3446.   *3* **68**
  HARRYCAT [17]3-8-11 G Carter 50/1: 7: b g Bahhare - Quiver Tree (Lion Cavern) Held up, some late gains, nvr dngrs on debut: bred to apprec 1m+.   *1* **66**
  RIVER OF DIAMONDS [8]3-8-11 J F Egan 50/1: 8: Nvr a factor.   *nk* **65**
5023} **NADIR** 295 [3]3-8-11 M Hills 11/1: 3-9: Al bhd on reapp.   *1¼* **63**
3921 **BONNETTS** 15 [13]3-8-6 M Fenton 66/1: 0000: 10th: Held up, hung left over 1f out, sn btn.   *1* **56**
2087} **CORBEL** 443 [9]4-8-12 (72) T E Durcan 40/1: 23/3-0: 11th: Hld up, wknd dist: with Miss G Kelleway.   *6* **46**
3642 **CELEBRE CITATION** 26 [6]3-8-11 t R Mullen 33/1: 050: 12th: In tch, wknd over 1f out.   *shd* **51**
3732 **HOMEWARD** 23 [11]3-8-6 D Kinsella 50/1: 0-50: 13th: Handy, wknd 2f out.   *½* **45**
3595 **TREGENNA** 28 [2]3-8-6 M Henry 66/1: 450: 14th: Handy, wknd over 2f out.   *hd* **44**
3921 **ALJAFLIYAH** 15 [12]3-8-6 A Hamblett(7) 50/1: U0000: 15th: Held up, wknd over 2f out.   *2½* **40**
3894 **WAIT FOR SPRING** 16 [1]3-8-6 K Darley 14/1: 520: 16th: Handy, wknd over 1f out, eased: btr 3894.   *1½* **37**
  ARCTIC COVE [7]3-8-11 N Callan 50/1: 0: 17th: Slow away & bhd: reportedly fin stiff.   *dist* **0**
17 Ran   Time 1m 41.21 (4.01)   Owned: Mr K Abdulla   Trained: Newmarket

---

4229	**5.10 Brettenham Handicap Stakes 3yo+ 0-85 (D)**	**[83]**
	£5811 £1788 £894 **6f str** **Good 50** **+01 Fast** Stands Side	

4005+**FONTHILL ROAD** 11 [4] R A Fahey 4-9-9 (78) P Hanagan 6/4 FAV: 6132211: Handy, keen, lost pl over 2f out but rallied well over 1f out to lead cl-home, drvn out: suited by 6/7f & handles fast, likes gd & soft & fibresand, gall trks: most progressive & game: see 4005.   **86**
744 **NISR** 898 [6] J W Payne 7-9-4 (73) J F Egan 33/1: 56/6530/2-: b g Grand Lodge - Tharwa (Last Tycoon) Handy, eff & edged left over 1f out, led ins last, collared cl-home, no extra: last rcd back in '02, plcd in a class stks (rtd 79a): '01 h'cap wnr: eff at 6/7f on firm, gd & polytrack: excellent rtn after such a long abs. 1 Jul'01 Folk 7g/f 80-77 D: *hd* **80**
4087* **BALAKIREF** 8 [11] M Dods 5-9-4 (73) N Callan 9/2: 1000513: Held up, eff over 1f out, kept on ins last, just held: fine run: see 4087 (Ayr).   *nk* **79**
3482* **BRANSTON TIGER** 33 [8] P D Evans 5-8-7 VIS (62) N Chalmers(5) 6/1: 0650014: In tch, eff over 1f out, kept on ins last, not btn far: fine run in a visor having been gelded & on first start for new trainer.   *nk* **67**
4005 **TONY THE TAP** 11 [2]3-9-10 (82) N Mackay(3) 9/1: 2521005: Led 3f out till ins last, not btn far.   *nk* **86**
3924 **FEARBY CROSS** 15 [1]8-8-6 (61) R Mullen 10/1: 4500546: In tch, eff dist, no impress: see 698.   *hd* **64**
3146 **WYATT EARP** 48 [10]3-9-4 (76) K Darley 20/1: 046-0107: Held up, eff dist, onepace: 7 wk abs.   *¾* **77**
1881 **STORMY NATURE** 99 [13]3-9-1 (73) M Fenton 25/1: 420-3008: Slow away & nvr a factor.   *3* **67**
3269 **NAJEEBON** 42 [7]5-9-9 (78) T E Durcan 10/1: 0363009: Dwelt, held up over 1f out: gelded.   *2* **67**
2272 **MANDARIN SPIRIT** 82 [3]4-9-0 (69) M Henry 33/1: 000-0550: 10th: Led till 3f out, wknd over 1f out.   *1½* **55**
4126 **ANTONIO CANOVA** 5 [9]8-9-5 (74) D Kinsella 14/1: 0100500: 11th: Al bhd: see 4126 (visor), 1743.   *shd* **59**
3744 **TORONTO HEIGHTS** 22 [5]3-9-3 (75) A McCarthy 20/1: 2110000: 12th: In tch, wknd 2f out: see 673.   *nk* **59**
12 Ran   Time 1m 13.95(2.95)   Owned: Mrs Una Towell   Trained: Malton

Official Going Rnd Crse - GOOD/SOFT; Str Crse - SOFT (HEAVY places).

4230   2.00 Listed Travelsphere Holidays March Stakes 3yo+   (A)
£17850   £6600   £3300   **1m6f**   **Good/Soft 82**   **+06 Fast**   Inside

3946* **ORANGE TOUCH 14** [3] Mrs A J Perrett 4-9-7 (112) J Murtagh 5/4 FAV: 51/54-611: Trkd Idr, led 3f   **118+**
out, sn well clr, v easily: hvly bckd, gd time: eff at 12/14f, shld stay further: acts on fast & gd/soft, handles
a sharp/undul or stiff/gall trk: runs well fresh: developing into a v smart stayer, must win in Gr class sn.
4104* **SWIFT TANGO 7** [5] E A L Dunlop 4-9-10 (100) J Fortune 5/2: 2364312: Waited with, went after wnr   11   **106**
3f out, sn no impress: sound run, but met a v smart rival: see 4104 (List h'cap).
4080   **STAGE RIGHT 8** [4] D R C Elsworth 3-8-7 (85) Martin Dwyer 7/1: 4615463: Trkd Idrs, rdn & btn 2f   4   **94$**
out: fine run at today's weights in this btr company: see 3864 (mdn).
3552   **SUPREMACY 30** [2] Sir Michael Stoute 5-9-10 (105) K Fallon 6/1: 021-0404: Led till 3f out, wknd: 1½   **97**
drifted from 9/2: no soft grnd form, best on fast & firm: see 3233.
3617   **WAIT FOR THE WILL 28** [1]8-9-7 bl (90) R L Moore 14/1: 0001125: Held up, al bhd: see 3617 & 2737.   3   **90**
5 Ran   Time 3m 09.47 (10.67)   Owned: Cheveley Park Stud   Trained: Pulborough

---

4231   2.30 Totepool Rated Stakes Handicap 3yo+ 0-105   (B)   [107]
£12841   £4871   £2435   **7f rnd**   **Good/Soft 82**   **-17 Slow**   Inside

4063   **MATERIAL WITNESS 9** [8] W R Muir 7-9-7 (100) Martin Dwyer 11/2: 1112041: Made all, clr fnl 1f,   **107**
drvn to hold on cl-home: top-weight: stays 1m, ideally suited by 7f: acts on firm, soft grnd & polytrack, handles
any trk, likes Goodwood: loves to dominate: v useful, career best effort.
4073   **DIGITAL 8** [1] M R Channon 7-8-9 (88) C Catlin 6/1: 2200022: Rear, drvn to improve 2f out, fin   ¾   **93**
fast but too late: another fine run, loves easy grnd, but is an infrequent wnr now: see 4073.
3954   **KOOL 14** [2] P F I Cole 5-8-11 (90) D Holland 7/2 JT FAV: 5354023: Chsd Idrs, onepcd fnl 1f: 2½   **91**
nicely bckd, clr of rem: on a decent mark & a fair run: see 3954 & 1146.
3775   **SELECTIVE 21** [5] E F Vaughan 5-8-12 (91) S Drowne 10/1: 0-400404: Chsd Idrs wide, btn fnl 1f: 6   **82**
tchd 14/1: best form on fast grnd: see 3911.
4030* **KINGS CAPRICE 10** [7]3-8-5 (2oh) (89) S Carson 7/2 JT FAV: 4104415: Trkd wnr 5f, grad wknd: well bckd. 2½   **76**
3954   **TARANAKI 14** [6]6-8-8 (87) L Keniry(3) 12/1: 1500036: Chsd Idrs, wknd qckly 1.5f out: see 3954.   ½   **73**
3775   **CAMP COMMANDER 21** [4]5-8-13 (92) J Fortune 12/1: 0450007: Chsd Idrs till halfway, eased   21   **48**
considerably, t.o.: reportedly hung right thr'out: unproven on soft grnd: see 1926.
3441   **GRIZEDALE 35** [3]5-9-0 t (93) K Fallon 11/2: 0020-508: Prom till wknd qckly 2f out, virtually   7   **39**
p.u.: lightly rcd this term, struggling to recapture form: see 3061.
8 Ran   Time 1m 31.45 (6.95)   Owned: Mr M J Caddy   Trained: Lambourn

---

4232   3.05 Gr2 Totesport Celebration Mile 3yo+   (A)
£58000   £22000   £11000   **1m rnd**   **Good/Soft 82**   **+10 Fast**   Inside

3957+ **CHIC 14** [5] Sir Michael Stoute 4-8-12 (101) K Fallon 4/1: 21-60311: Held up, outpcd halfway,   **120+**
strong run fnl 1f to lead cl-home, won going away: gd time: eff at 7f/1m on firm & gd/soft: fast improving filly
who is developing into a high-class performer, can win a Gr 1: see 3957.
3533   **NAYYIR 31** [2] G A Butler 6-9-1 (120) M J Kinane 5/4 FAV: 102-3022: Waited with, prog to lead   1¼   **120**
1.5f out & sn clr, collared cl-home: hvly bckd, gd time: usually runs well at Goodwood, poss in front too sn
today: high-class gelding, acts on firm, gd/soft & polytrack: see 3533 & 991.
3886   **HURRICANE ALAN 16** [3] R Hannon 4-9-4 (114) P Dobbs 11/2: 1503033: Mid-div, imprvd to chase Idr   5   **115**
dist, sn no impress: bckd from 8/1: not disgraced under jt top-weight: see 3886 & 1349.
3441+ **COURT MASTERPIECE 35** [4] E A L Dunlop 4-9-1 (110) J Fortune 8/1: 1-354214: Held up, prog to   nk   **111**
chall for 2nd dist, sn held: confirmed recent imprvd form, acts on fast, handles gd/soft grnd: see 3441.
3886   **PASSING GLANCE 16** [6]5-9-4 (118) Martin Dwyer 12/1: 160-1045: Dsptd lead & clr halfway, went on   5   **106**
3f out till collared 1.5f out, wknd: tchd 16/1: close rnr-up in this race last year, got into a battle for early
lead today & went off too fast: see 3886 & 2252.
3838   **BRUNEL 20** [7]3-8-12 (113) D Holland 12/1: 15-11506: Keen in rear, nvr nr Idrs: much too free.   2½   **102**
3839   **NAAHY 20** [1]4-9-1 (92) J Murtagh 25/1: 1104467: Dsptd lead & clr halfway, hdd 3f out, wknd &   25   **69**
eased: went off too fast in this soft grnd: best at 7f, see 2455.
7 Ran   Time 1m 43.22 (5.82)   Owned: Cheveley Park Stud   Trained: Newmarket

---

4233   3.40 Chapel Down English Wines Maiden Auction Stakes 2yo   (D)
£4969   £1529   £765   **1m rnd**   **Good/Soft 82**   **-44 Slow**   Inside

3721   **JAMAARON 23** [9] R Hannon 2-8-13   R L Moore 6/1: 301: Trkd Idrs, prog to lead 2f out, styd on   **83**
strongly fnl 1f, drvn out: clrly non the worse for unfortunate experience in 3721: apprec this sharp 1m, acts on
gd/soft grnd: can prog further, see 3046 (debut).
3786   **KRASIVIS BOY 21** [6] G L Moore 2-8-10 D Holland 33/1: 02: b c Swain - Krasivi (Nijinsky) Front   1¼   **77**
rank, ev ch ent fn 1f, not pace of wnr cl-home: much imprvd on turf bow: 15,000gns Apr foal: half-brother to a
couple of wnrs in the US: eff over an easy 1m on gd/soft: op to improvement.
3811   **PENNY ISLAND 20** [15] A King 2-8-12 J D Smith 6/1: 063: Keen in mid-div, kept on fnl 1f, nvr   ½   **78**
nrr: swtg: acts on fast & gd/soft grnd: now qual for h'caps, see 3342.
3883   **SIR MONTY 16** [2] Mrs A J Perrett 2-8-13 M J Kinane 11/2: 564: Mid-div, sltly short of room 2f   2   **76**
out & again dist, hands & heels: bckd: acts on fast & gd/soft, stays 1m: now quals for h'caps.
3399   **LORD OF DREAMS 36** [10]2-8-13 Martin Dwyer 33/1: 05: ch c Barathea - The Multiyorker (Digamist)   ¾   **74**
Rear, short of room 2f out, nrst fin: Feb foal, cost 27,000gns: half-brother to 6f juv wnr Siptitz Heights: dam a
7f wnr, sire a top-class miler: with D Arbuthnot.
3798   **LITHOS 20** [3]2-8-11 J Murtagh 9/2 FAV: 26: Led till 2f out, wknd: bckd: btr 3798 (debut, fm).   1¾   **69**
3908   **SABBIOSA 15** [5]2-8-7 Dane O'Neill 14/1: 0007: b f Desert Prince - Alla Marcia (Marju) Prom,   2½   **61**
wkng when short of room 2f out, no ch after: 22,000gns Mar first foal: dam a top-class miler, sire a top-class miler.
3520   **SPINNING COIN 31** [7]2-8-4 R Miles(3) 6/1: 0608: Rear, short of room halfway, nvr a factor: bckd.   1½   **56**

GOODWOOD SATURDAY 28.08.04 Righthand, Sharpish, Undulating Track

3927 **ELECTION SEEKER 15** [11]2-8-13 A Quinn(5) 25/1: 009: Nvr btr than mid-div.	1 63
4114 **PLAY UP POMPEY 6** [1]2-8-8 J F McDonald(3) 33/1: 00000: 10th: Drvn in rear, nvr nr ldrs: qck reapp.	1¾ 56
PROPRIOCEPTION [4]2-8-5 C Catlin 14/1: 0: 11th: Sn outpcd, nvr a factor on debut.	2 50

4035 **Katana 10** [8]2-8-6 (2ow) S Drowne 14/1:0   3803 **Looking Great 20** [13]2-8-11 S Carson 33/1:0
   Yankey 14/1:2-8-8 J Fortune 25/1:0   3803 **Tranquilizer 20** [12]2-8-3 t Hayley Turner(5) 14/1:U
15 Ran   Time 1m 47.54 (10.14)   Owned: Mr N A Woodcock   Trained: Marlborough

---

4234 4.15 E B F Progressive Maiden Stakes Fillies 2yo (D)
£4979 £1532 £766 **6f str** **Soft** **Inapplicable** Stands Side

ANNALS [5] H Candy 2-8-11 Dane O'Neill 7/2: 1: b f Lujain - Anna of Brunswick (Rainbow Quest)   **88+**
Chsd ldrs, imprvd to lead ent fnl 1f, styd on strongly, readily: op 9/4, debut: Feb foal, half-sister to a winning
miler in Germany & mid-dist scorer Goslar: dam a mid-dist scorer, sire a top-class juv sprinter: eff over a sharp
6f, 7f+ will suit: acts on soft grnd: runs well fresh: plenty more to come.
3968 **JE SUIS BELLE 13** [1] B W Hills 2-8-11 D Holland 11/10 FAV: 032: Trkd ldrs, short of room after   1½   81
halfway, kept on ins 2nd but no ch with wnr: hvly bckd: imprvd eff back at 6f on soft grnd: see 3968.
3071 **THEAS DANCE 50** [3] D R Loder 2-8-11 M J Kinane 6/1: 503: b f Danzig - Teggiano (Mujtahid) Led   1½   74
till ent fnl 1f, no extra: abs, clr of rem: Apr first foal, dam a top-class 1m juv wnr: eff at 6f on soft, handles fm.
3883 **FLAUNTING IT 16** [2] J A Osborne 2-8-11 S Drowne 14/1: 504: Dwelt, al rear: btr 3381 (gd).   6   63
ZEENA [4]2-8-11 Martin Dwyer 4/1: 5: b f Unfuwain - Forest Fire (Never So Bold) Front rank   hd   63
4f, grad wknd on debut: tchd 11/2: Mar first foal: dam a 1m wnr, sire a top-class mid-dist performer.
5 Ran   Time 1m 18.78 (8.78)   Owned: Major M G Wyatt   Trained: Wantage

---

4235 4.50 Horizon Maiden Stakes Handicap 3yo 0-70 (E)   [77]
£3874 £1192 £596 **2m** **Good/Soft 82** **-21 Slow** Inside

3861 **RACE THE ACE 17** [4] J L Dunlop 3-9-7 (70) J Murtagh 5/2 FAV: 452331: Keen & prom, went on over   80
1f out, rdn clr: hvly bckd: top-weight: deserved first win, suited by 2m now: acts on fast & gd/soft grnd:
handles a stiff/gall or sharp/undul trk: lightly rcd & improving young stayer, see 3861.
3893 **SHARADI 16** [2] V Smith 3-9-2 (65) Joanna Badger 11/2: 56-00022: Led after 4f & sn clr, hdd dist,   4   69
no extra: nicely bckd: styd this longer 2m trip: in gd form: see 3893.
3961 **IRISH BLADE 14** [10] H Candy 3-9-2 (68) Dane O'Neill 8/1: 0-430003: Keen in rear, prog to chase   1¼   70
ldrs 2f out, sn onepcd: prob stays an easy 2m: see 1501.
4056 **HOH NELSON 9** [9] H Morrison 3-8-13 (62) S Drowne 14/1: 00-30064: Rear, prog 2f out, nvr nrr: 2   62
prob stays 2m: see 1177.
4080 **PANGLOSS 8** [12]3-9-1 bl (64) R L Moore 5/1: 0-305045: Rear, nvr nr ldrs: longer 2m trip.   3   61
3899 **BAYOU PRINCESS 16** [7]3-8-9 (58) L Keniry(3) 50/1: 00536: Nvr btr than mid-div: longer 2m trip.   4   51
4119 **WYOMING 6** [11]3-8-7 (56) Martin Dwyer 7/1: 3-300037: Rear, prog to chase ldrs 2f out, wknd &   nk   48
eased: qck reapp & longer 2m trip: see 4119 (12f).
3970 **MOLEHILL 13** [1]3-8-7 (56) I Mongan 10/1: 05408: Prom 14f, wknd.   1   47
4056 **FU FIGHTER 9** [5]3-9-5 (68) D Holland 8/1: 4-054309: Led 4f, remained prom till wknd qckly 2f   10   49
out, eased: tchd 12/1: reportedly unsuited by this soft grnd: btr 2781 (firm grnd).
3948 **ICARUS DREAM 14** [6]3-9-2 (65) S Carson 50/1: 6202000: 10th: Prom 14f, sn wknd.   7   39
2130 **BLUE HILLS 88** [3]3-9-2 (65) R Miles(3) 33/1: 052-0500: 11th: Chsd ldrs 12f, wknd & t.o.: 12 wk   14   24
abs: prev trained by M Johnston, now with P Hiatt: reportedly unsuited by soft grnd: see 1507 (12f).
3982 **ROYAL STARLET 12** [8]3-7-12 (2oh) (45) C Catlin 20/1: 0-004500: 12th: Mid-div, wknd 4f out, t.o.   23   0
12 Ran   Time 3m 40.84 (16.54)   Owned: I H Stewart-Brown & M J Meacock   Trained: Arundel

---

4236 5.25 Stayin Alive Stakes Handicap 3yo 0-80 (D)   [85]
£5473 £1684 £842 **5f str** **Soft** **Inapplicable** Stands Side

4109 **LA VIE EST BELLE 7** [5] B R Millman 3-8-3 (60) Martin Dwyer 16/1: 6040061: Led till dist, rallied   67
gamely to regain lead cl-home: eff at 5/6.5f on firm & soft grnd: likes to run-up with/force the pace, any trk.
4169+**WUNDERBRA 3** [4] M L W Bell 3-9-2 (7ex)t (73) Hayley Turner(5) 11/8 FAV: 5131112: Keen & trkd ldrs,   ¾   77
smooth hdwy to lead dist, caught cl-home: hvly bckd: imprvd again in defeat & remains in tremendous form.
3984 **IMPERIUM 23** [3] Mrs Stef Liddiard 3-8-11 (68) D Holland 12/1: 0006023: Trkd ldr, onepcd fnl 1f: 1¼   68
love Brighton: see 3720 & 1942.
4027 **FOUR AMIGOS 10** [7] J G Given 3-9-7 (78) I Mongan 6/1: 0630004: Held up, styd on late, nvr dngrs.   1¾   73
4118+**TIZZYS LAW 6** [6]3-8-10 (7ex) (67) S Drowne 9/2: 6450015: Keen in rear, nvr nr ldrs: qck reapp.   hd   62
4169 **ARFINNIT 3** [2]3-8-11 vis (58) C Catlin 8/1: 4000246: Front rank, wknd halfway: qck reapp: btr 3488.   3½   44
3804* **MIRASOL PRINCESS 20** [1]3-9-2 (73) Dane O'Neill 9/1: 6664017: Reared & slowly away, al rear: op   1   56
12/1: blinkers taken off late & lost all ch start: forget this, see 3804 (fm).
7 Ran   Time 1m 03.18(6.48)   Owned: Mr Robin Lawson   Trained: Cullompton

---

BEVERLEY SATURDAY 28.08.04 Righthand, Oval Track with Stiff, Uphill Finish

Official Going Good/Soft

4237 2.05 Priory Park Volkswagen Maiden Stakes 3yo+ (D)
£3543 £1090 £545 **5f str** **Good/Soft 64** **-13 Slow** Inside

3873 **LAKE CHARLOTTE 17** [10] D R Loder 3-8-9 (70) N Pollard 13/8 FAV: 3231: Made all, kept on, shade   66
cmftbly: well bckd: eff at 6/7f, apprec drop to 5f: acts on gd & soft grnd, stiff/gall or easy trk.
3833 **SIR LOIN 19** [5] N Tinkler 3-9-0 (55) W Ryan 9/1: 0052602: Chsd wnr, kept on for press, al held ins last.   1   64
3194 **BRAIN WASHED 45** [11] T D Easterby 3-8-9 (70) R Winston 9/2: 04253: Dwelt, sn chsd front pair,   ½   57

switched & kept on, nvr able to chall: 6 wk abs: eff at 5f, rtn to 6f in similar could suit: see 2728.

3942 **NICHOLAS NICKELBY 14** [9] M J Polglase 4-9-2 (53) S Sanders 6/1: 2004344: Chsd ldrs, no impress over 1f out: handles fast, gd/soft & fibresand: see 3104 & 1966.	2½	55
4029 **VICTORIANA 10** [4]3-8-9 J Quinn 14/1: 645: Pushed along mid-div, not pace to chall.	½	48
4094 **WESTBOROUGH 8** [3]3-9-0 (54) A Culhane 20/1: 5052006: Held up, mod prog from halfway, no threat.	1½	49
3936 **ARIESANNE 14** [8]3-8-9 T Hamilton(3) 5/1: 37: Chsd ldrs till halfway: op 14/1: see 3936.	2½	37
3767 **WARREN PLACE 21** [6]4-9-2 (35) W Supple 66/1: 0000-008: Al towards rear: see 3487.	nk	41
3645 **DESIGNER CITY 26** [2]3-8-9 (35) F Norton 50/1: 0000049: Sn struggling rear: needs sellers.	6	21
4094 **BIG TOM 8** [7]3-9-0 (54) D Tudhope(7) 25/1: 4-500000: 10th: Al bhd & outpcd: see 3739 (1m).	2	21
HOME FRONT 0 [1]3-9-0 (0): 0: 11th: b g Intikhab - Felicita (Catrail) Sn struggling.	6	6

11 Ran   Time 1m 05.16 (3.86)   Owned: Sheikh Mohammed   Trained: Newmarket

---

4238   2.40 Listed Totepool Beverley Bullet Sprint Stakes 3yo+   (A)
£17400 £6600 £3300   5f str   Good/Soft 64   +10 Fast   Inside

3248 **CHOOKIE HEITON 43** [6] I Semple 6-8-12 (98) T Eaves 40/1: 10-45001: Chsd ldrs, switched to far rail & squeezed through gap to lead ins last, drvn out: 6 wk abs: eff over a stiff 5f/6f on firm & gd/soft grnd: goes well fresh: useful, back to useful best: see 952.		112
3971 **SIMIANNA 13** [3] A Berry 5-8-7 p (94) W Supple 16/1: 0465032: Rear, switched wide & styd on for press ins last, not reach wnr: tough & genuine mare, deserves a nice prize: see 3971, 2457 & 1162 (C/D).	1¼	102
3466* **BALTIC KING 34** [10] H Morrison 4-8-12 t (106) S Sanders 11/4 FAV: 100-6013: Short of room & drpd to rear early, hdwy when short of room again dist, kept on for press: closer with a clr passage: acts on firm, gd/soft & handles soft: useful & in form: see 3466.	shd	107
4027+ **ENCHANTMENT 10** [7] J M Bradley 3-8-5 (92) F Norton 3/1: 2112414: Led, rdn & hdd dist, no extra.	hd	101
3989 **BISHOPS COURT 12** [9]10-8-12 (103) A Culhane 13/2: 0330025: Trkd ldrs, edged left/no extra dist.	1¼	103
3989 **FOREVER PHOENIX 12** [2]4-8-7 (93) J Quinn 12/1: R023036: Chsd ldrs, hung dist & no extra fnl 1f.	1	96
3989+ **CONTINENT 12** [4]7-8-12 (108) A Nicholls 6/1: 600-3017: Mid-div, switched right early, short of room halfway, nvr land a blow: op 7/2: btr 3989.	2	96
4027 **BARON RHODES 10** [8]3-8-5 (80) D Allan 100/1: 3051308: Chsd ldrs, btn when hmpd over 1f out.	1¾	87
3971 **VITA SPERICOLATA 13** [11]7-8-7 vis (81) G Parkin 25/1: 0005569: Cl-up, btn/hmpd over 1f out.	1¼	84
3073 **ABSENT FRIENDS 50** [5]7-8-12 (89) J Edmunds 50/1: 0-060600: 10th: Cl-up, btn over 1f out: 7 wk abs.	nk	88
3622 **CARIBBEAN CORAL 28** [1]5-8-12 (102) R Winston 7/1: 2-021100: 11th: Sn struggling rear: bckd.	1½	84

11 Ran   Time 1m 00.99 (2.69)   Owned: Hamilton Park Members Syndicate   Trained: Carluke

---

4239   3.15 Totesport Stakes Heritage Handicap 3yo 0-105   (B)   [110]
£29000 £11000 £5500   1m1f207y   Good/Soft 64   +16 Fast   Inside

4158 **GATWICK 7** [10] M R Channon 3-9-6 (102) S Hitchcott(3) 7/1: 1106051: Held up, rdn/hdwy & switched over 1f out, styd on strongly for press to lead well ins last, fast time: eff at 1m/10f, tried 12f: acts on fast & gd/soft grnd, poss hvy, handles any trk: tough, smart & genuine colt: see 1919.		111
3912* **INVASIAN 15** [1] H R A Cecil 3-8-13 (95) W Ryan 11/2: 0-120012: Led, drvn & hdd well ins last, no extra: loves to dominate & confirmed improvement of 3912.	1	101
3615 **HELLO ITS ME 28** [9] H J Collingridge 3-8-3 (85) J Quinn 11/1: 1-202543: Chsd ldrs, styd on onepace for press fnl 2f: acts on fast & gd/soft grnd: see 2903 & 1192.	½	90
3738 **INCHLOSS 23** [11] B A McMahon 3-8-3 (3ow) (81) G Gibbons 7/1: 0061224: Trkd front pair, no extra for press dist: prob styd longer 10f trip: see 3421 & 3107 (1m).	1	86
4021 **GOLD HISTORY 10** [4]3-8-12 (94) R Ffrench 20/1: 1350065: Cl-up, ch over 2f out, edged right & no extra bef dist: btr 1189 (List).	1½	96
3912 **SEWNSO CHARACTER 15** [5]3-8-8 (90) S Sanders 8/1: 0344046: Held up, late prog, no threat.	¾	91
3947 **SWEET INDULGENCE 14** [7]3-7-13 (1ow)(1oh) (79) F Norton 25/1: 3-005347: Chsd ldrs, btn over 1f out.	1¼	80
3912 **GAVROCHE 15** [6]3-8-7 (89) J P Guillambert(3) 25/1: 1141008: Dwelt, bhd, mod late progr: btr 3084 (fast).	¾	87
3625* **RINGSIDER 28** [2]3-8-2 (84) Lisa Jones 8/1: 01-00219: Dwelt, rear, nvr factor: btr 3625 (firm).	nk	81
3794 **MUTAFANEN 21** [3]3-9-7 vis (103) W Supple 4/1 FAV: 3330440: 10th: Mid-div, btn 2f out: btr 3794.	1½	98
3066 **BURNING MOON 51** [8]3-8-4 (86) Dale Gibson 11/1: 50-5100: 11th: Mid-div, eff 2f out, sn btn, abs.	1¼	79

11 Ran   Time 2m 07.13 (4.83)   Owned: Mr W H Ponsonby   Trained: West Ilsley

---

4240   3.45 Will It Be A Winston Winner Handicap Stakes 3yo+ 0-75   (E)   [75]
£6019 £1852 £926   5f str   Good/Soft 64   -13 Slow   Inside

4197* **HOUT BAY 1** [13] R A Fahey 7-9-1 (6ex) (62) R Ffrench 9/2 FAV: 0-1362411: Chsd ldrs, switched & styd on for press to lead well ins last, held on all out: eff at 6f, suited by a stiff 5f: acts on firm, likes gd/soft, soft & both AWs, any trk: won at Newmarket yesterday: tough: see 415.		71
4091* **MISTER MAL 8** [14] B Ellison 8-8-7 (54) S Sanders 11/2: 6100312: Bhd & hmpd halfway, switched & styd on strongly ins last, just denied: in gd heart: see 4091.	shd	62
3463 **BRIGADIER MONTY 34** [7] Mrs S Lamyman 6-8-5 (52) J Quinn 33/1: 0025503: Rear, hdwy when short of room dist, switched & kept on well cl-home, nrst fin: see 2846 & 2214.	1¾	56
3974* **ON THE TRAIL 13** [15] D W Chapman 7-8-7 (54) A Culhane 7/1: 3433114: Chsd ldrs, led 2f out, hdd ins last & no extra: btr 3974 (made all).	¾	56
3796 **BRANTWOOD 21** [12]4-8-9 t (56) G Gibbons 16/1: 3230605: Trkd ldrs, hung right halfway, onepace when short of room over 1f out: see 2884, 2502 & 1774.	nk	57
4174 **BEYOND THE CLOUDS 2** [3]8-10-0 P (75) R Winston 20/1: 2003006: Handy, drvn & no extra bef dist.	nk	75
3680 **COMPTON PLUME 24** [10]4-9-4 (65) Dale Gibson 50/1: D321007: Rear, kept on late, nrst fin: btr 2849.	½	63
4107 **LAUREL DAWN 7** [18]6-8-9 (56) Natalia Gemelova(7) 7/1: 0600008: Mid-div, badly hmpd & lost pl early, kept on late, nrst fin: closer with a clr run: see 2657 (C/D).	¾	52
4107* **KINGS COLLEGE BOY 7** [16]4-9-7 bl (68) T Hamilton(3) 6/1: 0303019: Dwelt, bhd, nrst fin: qck reapp.	½	62
4038* **ROMAN MISTRESS 10** [6]4-9-6 bl (67) D Allan 16/1: 3050410: 10th: Chsd ldrs out til over 1f out, mod draw.	¾	59
3353 **TOMTHEVIC 38** [4]6-8-2 (49) F Norton 50/1: 0-000040: 11th: Prom, fdd under press fnl 2f: new yard.	½	39
4010 **MYND 11** [9]4-9-6 (63) Dean McKeown 16/1: 0064050: 12th: Mid-div, hmpd early & drpd rear, nvr factor.	1¼	48
3888 **FLY MORE 16** [8]7-9-13 (74) C J Davies(7) 40/1: 00000-00: 13th: ch g Lycius - Double River (Irish River) Al bhd, 6 wk abs: landed 3 h'caps in '03: h'cap wnr '02: best at 5f, stays 6f: acts on firm & gd/soft.	1¾	57

1 Aug'03 Newb 5.2g/f 81-76 C: 2 Jul'03 Warw 5.5g/f 75-75 D: 1 Jun'03 Newc 5gd 76-69 E: 2 Jun'03 Warw 6.1fm 74-(69) E:

2 Jun'03 Wind 5.0g/f 69-(68) E: 1 May'03 Good 5g/f 67-64 E: 1 Jul'02 Chep 5gd 72-66 E: 2 Jul'02 Bath 5.7g/f 71-68 D:
2 Oct'01 York 5g/s 76-74 D: 1 Jul'01 Wind 5g/f 78-69 E: 1 Jul'01 Folk 5g/f 66-63 E: 1 Jul'01 Bath 5gd 68-63 F:
4150 **ELLIOTS CHOICE 4** [11]3-8-11 bl (60) Lisa Jones 50/1: 0000240: 14th: Nvr a factor: qck reapp: btr 3936. *nk* **42**
3503 **TOMMY SMITH 32** [19]6-9-10 bl (71) T Eaves(3) 12/1: 0010000: 15th: Led till 2f out, fdd under press. *1¾* **49**
3852 **Consensus 17** [1]5-9-11 (72) T Williams 33/1:0 3350 **Chairman Bobby 38** [2]6-9-6 (67) F Lynch 33/1:0
3932 **Soaked 15** [5]11-9-0 bl(61) A Nicholls 25/1:0 1749 **Regal Song 106** [17]8-9-3 bl(64) D McGaffin 16/1:0
19 Ran Time 1m 05.14 (3.84) Owned: Northumbria Leisure Ltd Trained: Malton

4241

4.20 John Jenkins Memorial Handicap Stakes 3yo+ 0-70 (E) **[70]**
£4082 £1256 £628 **7f100y** **Good/Soft 64** **-02 Slow** Inside

3310 **RISKA KING 40** [11] R A Fahey 4-9-11 (67) T Hamilton(3) 7/1: 0043361: Chsd ldrs, smooth prog halfway & led over 1f out, rdn out: op 11/2, 6 wk abs: stays 1m, suited by 7/7.5f on fast & soft, handles hvy & polytrack, prob any trk: well h'capped, shld score again: see 318. **76**
3670* **JUBILEE STREET 25** [14] Mrs A Duffield 5-9-1 (57) G Hind 8/1: 3100612: Chsd ldrs, styd on for press, not pace of wnr: see 3670. *1½* **63**
3766 **GIFTED FLAME 21** [4] T D Barron 5-9-11 (67) P Makin(5) 7/1: 4003143: Held up, styd on for press late. *½* **71**
3933 **OASES 15** [5] D Shaw 5-8-10 P (52) Lisa Jones 16/1: 0035604: Rear, styd on wide for press, nrst fin: first time cheek pieces, visor omitted: see 3184, 976 & 940. *¾* **56**
4088* **LOCOMBE HILL 8** [8]8-9-8 (64) D Tudhope(7) 6/1 FAV: 5044015: Prom, no extra dist: see 4088. *nk* **67**
4041 **KING NICHOLAS 9** [13]5-8-10 t p (52) Rory Moore(5) 16/1: 0410606: Led/dsptd lead till over 1f out, fdd. *½* **54**
3443 **COLEMANSTOWN 35** [1]4-9-0 (56) T Eaves(3) 20/1: 0000007: Rear, kept on late, nrst fin: see 3872. *½* **57**
3973 **TRUE 13** [6]3-9-0 (61) R Winston 14/1: 2034068: Rear, eff 2f out, only mod prog, nrst fin: btr 3016. *½* **61**
3107 **MOTU 49** [2]3-9-6 (67) S Sanders 7/1: 0-000009: Rear, nvr a factor: 7 wk abs: see 1930, 1417. *5* **58**
4009 **CARLTON 11** [9]10-8-12 (54) R Ffrench 16/1: 2005000: 10th: Mid-div, eff 2f out, sn fdd under press. *¾* **44**
3017 **TAP 52** [10]7-9-2 p (58) D Fentiman(7) 9/1: 000-1150: 11th: Led till over 2f out, sn btn: abs: btr 1635. *2* **44**
2496 **YORKER 73** [12]6-9-4 (60) S Hitchcott(3) 16/1: 2000360: 12th: Chsd ldrs, btn over 1f out: abs: btr 2338. *1* **44**
3813 **PRINCE OF GOLD 20** [7]4-9-8 p (64) W Supple 10/1: 1000000: 13th: Mid-div wide, btn 2f out: btr 2324. *½* **47**
4036 **SEWMORE CHARACTER 10** [3]4-9-8 (64) F Norton 16/1: 1-462500: 14th: Al bhd: btr 697 (AW). *10* **32**
14 Ran Time 1m 35.72 (4.92) Owned: Market Avenue Racing Club Ltd Trained: Malton

4242

4.55 Ebf Bp Saltend Maiden Stakes Fillies 2yo (D)
£5623 £1730 £865 **7f100y** **Good/Soft 64** **-44 Slow** Inside

3915 **GOLD QUEEN 15** [12] M R Channon 2-8-11 A Culhane 4/1: 31: Trkd ldrs, styd on for press to lead line, all out: op 11/4: confirmed debut promise: eff at 6f, apprec step up to 7.5f, 1m+ shld suit: acts on gd & gd/soft grnd, stiff/gall trk: showed a willing attitude, type to progress with racing: see 3915. **80**
3909 **MUSICAL DAY 15** [11] B J Meehan 2-8-11 F Norton 33/1: 0002: ch f Singspiel - Dayville (Dayjur) Handy & led halfway, drvn & hdd line: Mar foal, 20,000gns purchase: half-sister to a 10/12f wnr: dam multiple 6f scorer: imprvd for forcing tactics & enjoyed gd/soft: stays 7.5f. *shd* **79**
INTRIGUED 0 [10] Sir Mark Prescott 2-8-11 S Sanders 10/11 FAV: 3: gr f Darshaan - Last Second (Alzao) Dwelt, settled mid-div, short of room 2f out till over 1f out, switched & kept on well cl-home, nrst fin, shade unlucky: bckd: Feb foal, sister to a 7f juv wnr: dam top-class over 10f: eff at 7.5f, 1m+ sure to suit: acts on gd/soft: well regarded filly, expect improvement. *½* **78+**
3411 **CALAMARI 36** [5] Mrs A Duffield 2-8-11 J Carroll 66/1: 04: ch f Desert King - Mrs Fisher (Salmon Leap) Held up, kept on late, nrst fin but not threaten front trio: Apr foal, sister to multiple 1m/10f wnr Masafi, dam a multiple 7f scorer: prob handles gd/soft grnd: imprvd from intro today. *5* **68**
3425 **SCORPIO SALLY 35** [6]2-8-11 P M Quinn 66/1: 0565: Led, hdd halfway & fdd. *½* **67**
MELODY QUE 0 [8]2-8-11 R Winston 12/1: 6: Chsd ldrs, no impress over 2f out, op 16/1. *½* **66**
3682 **STREET BALLAD 24** [2]2-8-11 J Quinn 18/1: 47: Rear, eff over 2f out, only mod prog, longer trip. *nk* **65**
3616 **TOHAMA 28** [1]2-8-11 W Ryan 14/1: 68: Rear, mod late prog. *shd* **65**
2863 **RIYMA 58** [4]2-8-11 F Lynch 14/1: 09: Chsd ldrs, btn 2f out, 2 month abs. *¾* **64**
CARIBBEAN DANCER 0 [7]2-8-11 R Ffrench 16/1: 0: 10th: Al towards rear. *3* **58**
3554 **SHARABY 30** [9]2-8-11 W Supple 7/1: 300: 11th: Mid-div, btn 2f out: btr 3035. *2* **54**
MOUNTAIN BREEZE 0 [3]2-8-11 Lisa Jones 66/1: 0: 12th: Dwelt, sn struggling. *30* **1**
12 Ran Time 1m 38.91 (8.11) Owned: Mr Jaber Abdullah Trained: West Ilsley

4243

5.30 Teletext Racing Hands And Heels Apprentice Maiden Handicap Stakes 3yo+ 35-55 (F) **[61]**
£3413 £975 £488 **1m1f207y** **Good/Soft 64** **-38 Slow** Inside

3419 **SNOWED UNDER 35** [1] J D Bethell 3-9-8 (55) J Cavanagh(6) 12/1: 0-555001: Handy & led over 1f out, styd on strongly under hand riding: eff around 10f on gd/soft grnd: see 2322. **60**
3854 **DANEFONIQUE 17** [16] D Carroll 3-9-3 (50) Neil Brown(3) 11/1: 2560402: Chsd ldrs, kept on to chase wnr dist, onepace: see 1836, 1240 & 1051. *2½* **50**
3573 **PLAUSABELLE 29** [15] T D Easterby 3-9-1 bl (48) W Hogg 8/1: 06-02003: Chsd ldrs, led over 2f out till over 1f out, no extra: handles gd/soft & soft grnd: prob stays 10f, rtn to 1m could suit: back to form with blnks reapp: see 1425. *1¼* **46**
2552 **MANDINKA 71** [8] J F Coupland 4-8-7 (32) S Yourston(3) 40/1: 00500-04: b g Distinctly North - Primo Panache (Primo Dominie) Dwelt, bhd, kept on late & wide, no threat: 10 wk abs: unplcd '03 (rtd 43, mdn): prob stays a stiff 10f on gd/soft grnd. *2½* **26**
3651 **MR MOON 26** [5]3-7-12 (10oh) (29) Donna Caldwell(3) 25/1: 6000605: Mid-div, kept on late, nvr a factor: prev with M Hammond, blnks omitted: see 1798. *4* **19**
3856 **EDDIES JEWEL 17** [3]4-8-12 (37) R Keogh(3) 6/1 FAV: 0-254506: Led till over 2f out, fdd: flattered 3310. *hd* **24**
3835 **DANCER KING 19** [4]3-9-4 (51) H Poulton 13/2: 50037: Mid-div, no impress fnl 2f: btr 3835 (1m). *3* **34**
4855} **AMALFI COAST 311** [6]5-9-10 (49) K Pierrepont(3) 50/1: 5440U-8: b g Emperor Jones - Legend's Daughter (Alleged) Chsd ldrs, fdd under press fnl 3f, reapp: unplcd '03 (lightly rcd, rtd 62, poss flattered, mdn). *1¼* **30**
3505 **AWWAL MARRA 32** [17]4-9-5 (44) Dean Williams 12/1: 2/-0309: Rear, mod late prog, nvr factor. *½* **24**
3505 **BENEKING 32** [9]4-9-12 (51) H Fellows(6) 10/1: 0306050: 10th: Rear, only mod late prog: btr 3505. *1¼* **29**
4536} **BOPPYS BABE 332** [10]3-7-12 (9oh) (30) K Jackson(3) 12/1: 00000-0: 11th: Al bhd, reapp & new yard. *2½* **5**

BEVERLEY SATURDAY 28.08.04 Righthand, Oval Track with Stiff, Uphill Finish

1947 **MONKEY OR ME 96** [14]3-8-0 (6oh) (33) M Halford 7/1: 0423340: 12th: Prom, fdd fnl 2f, 3 month abs. *nk* **6**
3973 **SONEARSOFAR 13** [11]4-9-5 (44) K Ghunowa(3) 25/1: 0600: 13th: Nvr a factor, h'cap bow & longer trip. *1¼* **15**
3499 **CAMPBELLS LAD 32** [13]3-8-6 (39) C Ely(6) 9/1: 5400530: 14th: Bhd/wide, no impress: btr 3499. *5* **3**
1518 **Lucky Piscean 117** [2]3-9-7 (54) Andrew Webb(3) 25/1:02812 **Grey Orchid 61** [18]3-8-7 (40) Liam Jones(3) 50/1:0
3354 **Quay Walloper 38** [12]3-7-12 (13oh)(26) T Dean(5) 40/1:0487 **Inmom 33** [7]3-9-7 (54) A Reilly(3) 14/1:0
18 Ran Time 2m 12.53(10.23) Owned: Mrs G Fane Trained: Middleham

REDCAR SATURDAY 28.08.04 Lefthand, Flat, Galloping Track

Official Going GOOD/SOFT.

4244 5.20 Ladies Evening Median Auction Maiden Stakes 2yo (F)
£3679 £1051 £526 **6f str** **Good 55** **-16 Slow** Inside

3148 **TSAROXY 47** [9] J Howard Johnson 2-9-0 P Mulrennan(3) 9/4 FAV: 331: Made all, clr dist, drvn out to hold on: 7 wk abs: eff at 6f on gd & gd/soft: acts on a gall trk & goes well fresh: see 3148 & 2774. **81**
3988 **WIGWAM WILLIE 12** [6] M J Wallace 2-9-0 D Corby(3) 5/2: 452: Al cl-up, kept on ins fnl 1f, just held by wnr: tchd 4/1: apprec return to 6f: quals for h'caps: see 3988 & 3431. *½* **79**
3968 **LESLINGTAYLOR 13** [2] J J Quinn 2-9-0 B Swarbrick(5) 5/1: 53: Cl-up, no extra from dist: clr rem: imprvd for step up to 6f: acts on gd grnd: see 3968. *1¾* **74**
3348 **MISTER BUZZ 38** [8] M D Hammond 2-9-0 (60) Darren Williams 25/1: 00044: Chsd ldrs 4f, no extra. *5* **61**
SWEET POTATO [4]2-8-9 P Fessey 25/1: 5: b f Monashee Mountain - Villafranca (In The Wings) Cl-up 4f, sn outpcd, modest gains: debut: Mar foal, cost 2,700gns: dam won a couple of times over mid-dists abroad: sire decent performer around 7f: with T D Barron. *shd* **55**
1780 **DANCING DEANO 104** [5]2-9-0 V Halliday 22/1: 06: b g Second Empire - Ultimate Beat (Go And Go) Dwelt, nvr nrr than mid-div: long abs: Mar foal, cost 8,000gns: sire Gr 1 wnr at 1m. *¾* **58**
ENBORNE AGAIN [7]2-9-0 G Faulkner 20/1: 7: ch c Fayruz - Sharp Ellie (Sharp Victor) Missed break, modest late gains: debut: May foal, cost E3,500: dam unrcd: sire 5/6f performer: with R A Fahey. *nk* **57**
BLADES BOY [3]2-9-0 G Parkin 14/1: 8: Al in rear: debut. *2½* **50**
4089 **JESSICAS STYLE 8** [1]2-8-9 J Bramhill 14/1: 009: Bhd, nvr a factor. *3½* **35**
INTERWOVEN [10]2-9-0 S Chin 7/1: 0: 10th: Missed break, nvr a factor on debut. *3* **31**
10 Ran Time 1m 13.21 (4.31) Owned: Andrea & Graham Wylie Trained: Crook

4245 5.50 Better Half Classified Stakes 3yo+ 0-60 (F)
£3436 £982 £491 **6f str** **Good 55** **+10 Fast** Inside

4009* **BOND PLAYBOY 11** [3] B Smart 4-9-7 (66) F Lynch 7/2: 0000311: Made all, drifted under press dist, rdn out to hold on: fast time: all wins at 6f, stays 7f: acts on fast, likes gd, soft grnd & fibresand: in-form 4yo, h'capped to land hat-trick: see 4009. **70**
3809 **BOLLIN EDWARD 20** [5] T D Easterby 5-9-5 vis (64) D Allan 5/1: 5320202: Bhd, prog 2f out, styd on well ins fnl 1f, post came too sn: another gd run in defeat & is h'capped to find a race: see 3571 & 2752. *shd* **66**
3796 **WILLIAMS WELL 21** [6] M W Easterby 10-9-1 bl (55) P Mulrennan(3) 12/1: 0005063: Held up, prog bef 1f out, nrst fin: encouraging eff & is on a fair mark: see 2884. *1¾* **57**
750 **JILLY WHY 183** [8] Ms Deborah J Evans 3-8-9 (60) A Nicholls 100/1: 6340-04: b f Mujadil - Ruwy (Soviet Star) Cl-up 5f, sn no extra: long abs: plcd on 1 of 4 '03 starts (rtd 67, mdn): eff at 6f on fast & gd grnd: lightly rcd & open to more improvement. *nk* **53**
4010 **KARMINSKEY PARK 11** [12]5-8-12 (60) Kristin Stubbs(7) 12/1: 1000005: Handy till dist, onepcd: btr 2712. *½* **52**
4009 **FRIMLEYS MATTERRY 11** [4]4-9-1 (53) P Mathers(5) 33/1: 6503166: Mid-div, no impress bef 1f out. *1* **52**
4087 **LEGAL SET 8** [7]8-9-1 t (60) Leanne Kershaw(7) 14/1: 0020457: Nvr nrr than mid-div: btr 3461 & 2713. *hd* **51**
3796 **VIEWFORTH 21** [9]6-9-3 VIS (62) V Halliday 7/1: 4300008: Rear, modest late gains: 1st time visor. *1¼* **49**
3989 **PERCY DOUGLAS 12** [2]4-9-1 t (40) M Stainton(7) 66/1: 0500609: Rear, nvr able to chall: see 275. *7* **28**
4010* **RED MONARCH 11** [1]3-9-1 (63) L Fletcher(3) 9/4 FAV: 0062110: 10th: Cl-up over 3f, wknd: v well bckd on hat-trick bid: disapp & might have come too sn after recent win in 4010. *2* **25**
4051 **Key Of Gold 9** [11]3-8-12 (60) Darren Williams 20/1:0 3936* **Troodos Jet 14** [10]3-9-2 (64) A Culhane 12/1:0
12 Ran Time 1m 11.65 (2.75) Owned: Mr R C Bond Trained: Thirsk

4246 6.20 Ladies Night Out Handicap Stakes 3yo+ 0-80 (D) [80]
£11242 £3459 £1730 **1m str** **Good 55** **+04 Fast** Centre

4088 **ZANDEED 8** [12] Miss L A Perratt 6-8-5 (57) P Fessey 14/1: 0/600/-031: Missed break, prog after 1f, kept on well to lead ins fnl 1f, rdn out: rider received a 5-day ban for excessive use of whip: eff at 7/10.5f on fast & hvy grnd: well h'capped & more prizes await: see 4088. **62**
3099 **CATS WHISKERS 49** [3] M W Easterby 5-9-13 (79) Dale Gibson 11/1: 00-03402: Prom, led 4f out, hdd well ins fnl 1f, not pace of wnr: 7 wk abs: fine eff under top-weight on return to 1m: h'capped to find similar. *¾* **82**
4136 **QUALITAIR WINGS 5** [6] J Hetherton 5-9-6 (72) D McGaffin 16/1: 0202063: Bhd, prog 2f out, ev ch well ins fnl 1f, not pace front 2: qck reapp: see 1474. *shd* **74**
4008* **CRESKELD 11** [4] B Smart 5-9-2 (68) F Lynch 4/1 JT FAV: 0000014: Cl-up, ev ch 1f out, sn no extra: bckd: 4lb higher than recent win in 4008 (9f). *¾* **68**
4090* **ZARIN 8** [2]6-8-1 (53) A Nicholls 6/1: 0006215: Cl-up, ev ch bef 1f out, sn no extra: well bckd, shade disappointing on return to turf: btr 4090 (AW). *1½* **50**
4051 **DARA MAC 9** [5]5-8-10 (62) Dean McKeown 16/1: 3100106: Held up, prog halfway, onepcd fnl 1f. *shd* **58**
3972 **RAREFIED 13** [7]3-9-4 (76) D Allan 33/1: 2-010007: Nvr nrr than mid-div: btr 1382 (11.5f). *1¼* **70**
4008 **PHAROAHS GOLD 11** [10]6-7-12 (1oh)vis (49) B Swarbrick(4) 50/1: 0040008: Bhd, nvr a factor. *2* **40**
3242 **FAIR SPIN 43** [8]4-8-10 (62) A Culhane 4/1 JT FAV: 000-0309: Al in rear: 6 wk abs: btr 2947. *nk* **51**
4036 **SPLODGER MAC 10** [11]5-8-3 (55) J Bramhill 10/1: 6-001260: 10th: Cl-up 6f, wknd: btr 3809 & 3501. *1* **42**
3759 **PARISIAN PLAYBOY 22** [9]4-7-12 (1oh) (49) Leanne Kershaw(7) 9/2: 0012100: 11th: Nvr in it. *3* **31**

4086 **SOLLER BAY 8** [1]7-9-6 (72) Darren Williams 14/1: 66-20040: 12th: Led 4f, sn wknd: btr 1059.   2   49
12 Ran   Time 1m 38.88 (4.08)   Owned: Miss L A Perratt   Trained: Ayr

---

4247	6.50 Fairer Sex Novice Median Auction Stakes 2yo (E)		
	£5070 £1560 £780 **7f str** **Good 55** **-05 Slow** Centre		

3975 **COOL PANIC 12** [6] M L W Bell 2-8-12 (78) R Winston 5/2: 0251: In tch, styd on to lead dist,   87
pushed out: well bckd: eff at 6f on gd & firm, imprvd for step up to 7f: won with a bit in hand.
4064 **SIR ANTHONY 9** [7] B Smart 2-9-4 (90) F Lynch 10/11 FAV: 13262: Bhd, prog 2f out, kept on ins fnl   2½   85
1f, no ch with wnr: well bckd under jt top-weight: acts on gd & gd/soft grnd: gd eff conceding wnr 6lb: see 3698.
      IL COLOSSEO [8] Mrs L Stubbs 2-8-12   D Allan 33/1: 3: b g Spectrum - Valley Lights (Dance of   shd   78
Life) Cl-up, led after 4f, hdd dist, onepcd when eased & lost 2nd cl home: rider received 10 day ban for not riding
out for best poss placing: debut: Feb foal, half-brother to wnrs at 6/12f: dam unplcd: sire Gr 1 wnr at 1m/10f:
eff at 7f, further will suit: acts on gd grnd: improve with experience.
2959 **PARIS HEIGHTS 55** [4] R M Whitaker 2-8-12   Dean McKeown 25/1: 064: Handy 4f, sn onepcd: 8 wk abs. 6   65
4083* **FENRIR 8** [2]2-9-4 (86) P Mulrennan 4/1: 015: Cl-up 5f, wknd: op 11/4: btr 4083 (hvy).   1¼   71
3500 **FORPETESAKE 32** [3]2-8-12   A Nicholls 50/1: 06606: Led 4f, sn wknd: btr 2939.   4   58
3699 **AZAHARA 24** [5]2-8-7   A Culhane 50/1: 07: b f Vettori - Branston Express (Bay Express) Bhd, nvr   4   46
a factor: Feb foal, half-sister to wnrs at 5/6f: dam unrcd, sire Gr 1 wnr at 1m: with K G Reveley.
      COOL SANDS [1]2-8-12 Darren Williams 20/1: 8: b c Trans Island - Shalerina (Shalford) Rear,   dist 21
fdd 1f out: debut: Apr foal, half-brother to wnrs at 5/7f: sire decent performer at 1m: with D Shaw.
8 Ran   Time 1m 26.05 (4.25)   Owned: D W & L Y Payne   Trained: Newmarket

---

4248	7.20 Don't Be Late Stakes Handicap 3yo+ 0-70 (E)		[67]
	£5343 £1644 £822 **1m2f** **Good 55** **-12 Slow** Inside		

4033 **SWIFT ALCHEMIST 10** [4] Mrs H Sweeting 4-8-13 p (52) Darren Williams 7/1: 3000001: Chsd ldrs, prog   58
& ev ch 1f out, rdn out to lead cl-home: eff at 7f/1m, now stays 10f: acts on fast, hvy grnd & polytrack: eff with
cheek pieces: apprec big drop down the weights: see 1537.
3990* **DANCE TO MY TUNE 12** [9] M W Easterby 3-9-1 (62) Dale Gibson 7/2: 6-610412: Keen rear, prog 3f   shd   67
out, styd on to lead dist, hdd under press cl-home: clr rem: well bckd: continues to run well: see 3990.
4033 **MOUNT BENGER 10** [7] R M Beckett 4-9-9 p (62) F Lynch 3/1 FAV: 0-604103: Held up, prog 3f out,   3½   62
onepcd fnl 1f: reportedly hung right throughout: showed more in 3276 (soft).
2163 **JAKE BLACK 87** [6] J J Quinn 4-9-5 (58) R Winston 9/2: 5315044: Prom, led 3f out, hdd dist, no   ¾   56
extra: long abs: 8lb higher than win in 1430 (soft).
4008 **ENCOUNTER 11** [2]8-8-6 (45) D Allan 9/1: 0025005: Rear, prog 3f out, onepcd dist: btr 3250.   1½   40
5010} **BEADY 297** [3]5-9-5 (58) D McGaffin 25/1: 142500-6: b g Eagle Eyed - Tales of Wisdom (Rousillon)   4   47
Chsd ldrs prog 7f, no extra: reapp: won 2 h'caps on the AW in early '03: plcd in '02 (rtd 62a & 71, mdns): eff around
12/14f on fibresand, prob handles gd & soft, stiff or sharp trks: with B Smart.
2 Feb'03 Sout 12af 61a- F: 1 Jan'03 Sout 12af 66a-58 G: 1 Jan'03 Sout 12af 65a-58 F:
4084+ **MARITIME BLUES 8** [5]4-9-10 (63) A Culhane 5/1: 0630017: Chsd ldrs 6f, wknd: top-weight.   1½   49
3850 **STEPASTRAY 17** [8]7-8-1 (40) P Mathers(3) 22/1: 0005008: Cl-up 1m, sn hung left & wknd: btr 1821.   1   24
4045 **THATS RACING 9** [1]4-7-12 (6oh) (31) S Righton 33/1: 00-26009: Led 7f, wknd: btr 906 (fibresand).   3½   16
9 Ran   Time 2m 9.01 (6.71)   Owned: The Kennet Connection   Trained: Marlborough

---

4249	7.50 Best Dressed Lady Handicap Stakes 3yo 35-55 (F)		[65]
	£3848 £1184 £592 **1m6f19y** **Good 55** **-24 Slow** Inside		

2905 **RESTART 57** [9] P C Haslam 3-9-4 (55) G Faulkner 16/1: 6030-001: Chsd ldrs, styd on to lead 2f   62
out, rdn out: 8 wk abs: eff at 7f, imprvd for recent step up to 14f: acts on gd grnd & fibresand: see 2905.
3573 **LET IT BE 29** [11] K G Reveley 3-9-0 (51) A Culhane 11/4: 5051152: Held up, prog 4f out, styd on   1¾   55
to chase wnr ins fnl 1f, al held: tchd 4/1: eff at 12f, apprec step up to 14f: can find similar: see 3354.
2893 **NODS STAR 57** [5] Miss J A Camacho 3-8-6 (1ow) (42) R Winston 25/1: 500003: Rear, prog 4f out, ev   nk   46
ch 2f out, styd on, just held for 2nd cl-home: clr rem: 8 wk abs: imprvd eff on step up to 14f: acts on gd grnd.
3618 **SAVANNAH RIVER 28** [12] C W Thornton 3-8-6 t (43) P Mulrennan(3) 14/1: 2543604: In tch, ev ch 2f   3½   43
out, sn no extra: see 3192 (12f, fast).
3580 **SPRING BREEZE 29** [2]3-9-1 bl (52) L Enstone(3) 9/4 FAV: 0-602325: Led 12f, no extra: well bckd: 1¾   50
showed more in 3580 (2m, fast).
3344 **DEFANA 38** [7]3-8-13 (50) D Tudhope(7) 20/1: 53-53306: Nvr nrr than mid-div: see 3055.   2½   46
3312 **BARTON FLOWER 40** [4]3-8-5 BL (45) Dale Gibson 50/1: 0-000007: Cl-up 12f, wknd: first time blnks.   hd   37
3854 **ASTON LAD 17** [3]3-8-13 (50) Darren Williams 11/2: 466258: Rear, mod late hdwy: btr 3263 (9f).   3   42
3192 **BAY SOLITAIRE 45** [14]3-8-8 (45) S Sanders 11/2: 000-609: Chsd ldrs, prog 7f out, wknd 2f out.   nk   36
3580 **TWILIGHT YEARS 29** [8]3-8-6 (43) D Allan 14/1: 00460: 10th: Bhd, nvr a factor: btr 3019.   3   31
3312 **OVER THE YEARS 40** [1]3-7-13 (1ow)BL (35) J Quinn 16/1: 00-5400: 11th: Handy 10f, sn wknd.   ½   23
3913 **VENETIAN ROMANCE 15** [10]3-8-0 (37) B Swarbrick(5) 12/1: 0000030: 12th: Mid-div over 10f, wknd.   3½   21
1961 **SES SELINE 96** [13]3-8-5 (2ow)P (40) Dean McKeown 50/1: 4500: 13th: Prom 10f, fdd: abs & pieces.   21   8
13 Ran   Time 3m 8.99(11.19)   Owned: Mr J Roundtree   Trained: Middleham

YARMOUTH SUNDAY 29.08.04 Lefthand, Flat, Fair Track

Official Going SOFT (HEAVY places)

4250
2.20 Great Yarmouth Racecourse Bookmakers/E B F Maiden Stakes 2yo (D)
£4833 £1487 £744   **6f3y str**   **Good/Soft 84**   **-29 Slow**   Stands side

3869 **FIGHTING TOM CAT** 18 [8] Saeed bin Suroor 2-9-0 t L Dettori 3/1: 061: Made most, kept on well for **84**
press ins fnl 1f & just held on: stays 6f, 7f shld suit: relished this gd/soft grnd, acts on a flat trk: imprvd
here with a switch to forcing tactics: prob more to come & can rate higher: see 3869.
3709 **LOVE THIRTY** 24 [2] M R Channon 2-8-9 T E Durcan 11/4: 62: b f Mister Baileys - Polished Up   *shd* **78**
(Polish Precedent) Chsd ldrs, ev ch when hung left dist, kept on ins fnl 1f: clr of rem: Mar first foal, cost
120,000gns: sire a high-class miler: stays 6f on gd/soft, 7f looks sure to suit: win similar.
3600 **SIGN WRITER** 29 [3] J Noseda 2-9-0 (83) E Ahern 15/8 FAV: 6243: Mid-div, onepcd fnl 1f.   *3½* **72**
2766 **RUDAKI** 64 [4] M G Quinlan 2-9-0 M Tebbutt 9/1: 04: ch g Opening Verse - Persian Fountain   *2½* **64**
(Persian Heights) Slow away & outpcd, modest late gains: op 15/2, 9 wk abs: Mar foal, cost 10,500gns:
half-brother to a dual 5f 2yo scorer: dam a 7f 2yo wnr, sire a smart miler.
MUDDY [1]2-9-0 J Quinn 11/1: 5: ch g Monashee Mountain - Schonbein (Persian Heights) Cl-up,   *1* **61**
wknd over 1f out on debut: Apr foal, cost 14,000gns: half-brother to sev 2yo wnrs: dam plcd at 2, sire high-class
7f wnr: with G Huffer & can learn from this.
3559 **FLY ME TO DUNOON** 31 [5]2-8-9 VIS Darren Williams 20/1: 06: b f Rossini - Toledana (Sure Blade)   *5* **41**
Dwelt, hdwy to dispute lead after 1f, wknd fnl 1f: tried a visor: no form yet.
GREAT GENERAL [7]2-9-0 M Fenton 40/1: 7: Outpcd, nvr a factor on debut.   *8* **22**
3786 **LITTLE WALTHAM** 22 [6]2-8-9 P Hanagan 100/1: 008: Chsd ldrs to 5f out, no impress 3f out, t.o.   *dist* **0**
8 Ran Time 1m 17.2 (6.8)

4251
2.55 Let's Talk Handicap Stakes Fillies 3yo+ 0-80 (D)   [81]
£6682 £2056 £1028   **7f3y str**   **Good/Soft 84**   **-13 Slow**   Stands side

4110 **PRINCESS GALADRIEL** 8 [6] J R Best 3-8-3 (56) W Supple 16/1: 3206361: Held up stands side, hdwy   **63**
2f out, led 1f out, kept on well for press: eff at 6f/1m, acts on fast & soft, sharp/undul trks, likes Yarmouth:
back to form on this drop into fillies grade: see 1576.
3711* **GLEBE GARDEN** 24 [9] M L W Bell 3-9-7 (74) L Dettori 9/2: 5560012: Led stands side, hdd 1f out,   *nk* **79**
bmpd ins fnl 1f, kept on: clr of rem: back to recent winning form of 3711.
4088 **PERTEMPS MAGUS** 9 [5] R A Fahey 4-9-2 (64) P Hanagan 9/4 FAV: 000-3163: Chsd ldrs stands side,   *4* **61**
hung left over 2f out, no impress fnl 1f: op 10/3: twice below 3933.
3780 **IN THE PINK** 22 [4] M R Channon 4-9-10 (72) T E Durcan 8/1: 0120204: Dwelt stands side, hdwy over   *1¼* **66**
1f out, no impress fnl 1f: op 12/1, top-weight: see 3456.
3672 **LADY MO** 26 [8]3-8-13 (66) A McCarthy 10/1: 0612235: Handy stands side, wknd 1f out.   *2* **56**
2974 **DOUBLE DAGGER LADY** 55 [3]3-8-9 (62) E Ahern 7/2: 6456: Led centre, no extra fnl 1f: 8 wk abs.   *½* **51**
3780 **SISTER SOPHIA** 22 [7]4-8-13 (61) M Fenton 10/1: 60-00367: Slow away stands side, nvr dngrs.   *7* **36**
4091 **SET ALIGHT** 9 [2]3-7-12 (1oh) (50) Lisa Jones 14/1: 04308: Handy stands side, hung left 2f out, wknd.   *½* **25**
946 **EMSAM BALLOU** 155 [10]3-8-13 (66) M Tebbutt 20/1: 3339: Cl-up stands side & keen, wknd 2f out: *2* **36**
long abs: now with V Smith: see 946.
3541 **BAD INTENTIONS** 31 [1]4-8-12 (60) O Urbina 50/1: 00-60060: 10th: Rcd in 2nd centre, wknd 2f out.   *5* **20**
10 Ran Time 1m 29.42 (6.82) Owned: Mrs Pam Akhurst Trained: Maidstone

4252
3.30 Lowestoft Journal Classified Stakes 3yo 0-60 (F)
£3530 £1086 £543   **1m3y str**   **Good/Soft 84**   **-17 Slow**   Stands side

3799 **PELLA** 21 [7] M Blanshard 3-8-10 (61) L Dettori 5/1: 2532301: Bhd, hdwy well over 1f out, led 1f   **69**
out, kept on well for press ins fnl 1f: eff at 1m/9f, stays 10f: handles fast & gd/soft, flat trk: rdn with more
restraint today: first win: see 2153.
3855 **PREMIER ROUGE** 18 [4] E F Vaughan 3-9-3 (65) P Robinson 8/1: 4432: Rear, hdwy over 2f out, hmpd   *1¼* **70**
when ev ch 1f out, an onepcd: stays 7.5f/1m: back to form on this drop back to 1m: find a race: see 2325 (debut).
4044* **DONT CALL ME DEREK** 10 [15] S C Williams 3-9-4 (66) S W Kelly 13/8 FAV: 6000213: Chsd ldrs, hdwy   *2* **68**
& ev ch 1f out, an not pace of first 2: nicely bckd: shade btr 4044 (AW).
3875 **KING OF KNIGHT** 18 [1] G Prodromou 3-8-12 (60) J Quinn 25/1: 0-450004: Slow away in rear, hdwy   *shd* **61**
over 1f out, kept on: see 2530.
4186 **FOOLS ENTIRE** 2 [6]3-8-12 e (58) B Reilly(3) 25/1: 00000345: Prom till led over 4f out, hdd over 1f   *2* **57**
out, no extra when hmpd ins fnl 1f: qck reapp: see 4186.
3872 **KING OF MUSIC** 15 [5]3-8-12 (60) O Urbina 40/1: 350-006: Dwelt, rear, hdwy over 2f out, onepcd   *1* **55**
over 1f out: clr of rem: see 3872.
3995 **VIOLET AVENUE** 13 [3]3-8-9 (55) M Fenton 22/1: 4-064057: Bhd, hdwy 2f out, no impress: see 2904.   *6* **40**
3711 **FLAME QUEEN** 24 [2]3-8-13 (64) Lisa Jones 20/1: 02-00048: Bhd, hdwy 4f out, no impress over 1f   *2* **40**
out: now with Mrs C Dunnett: see 3711.
3799 **NIGHT FROLIC** 21 [14]3-8-10 (61) M Hills 9/2: 0-130669: Cl-up, hmpd & lost pl 3f out, sn btn.   *4* **29**
3929 **APPETINA** 16 [12]3-8-9 (60) S Chin 25/1: 3-554400: 10th: Led over 3f, no extra well over 1f out.   *½* **27**
2243 **MY PENSION** 85 [9]3-9-3 (65) T E Durcan 16/1: 04300: 11th: Al bhd: long abs.   *¾* **33**
3947 **BEST DESERT** 15 [11]3-9-3 (65) N Pollard 16/1: 2005150: 12th: Handy, lost pl 3f out, no ch after.   *shd* **32**
3604 **La Landonne** 29 [13]3-8-12 ViS(63) M Howard(7) 25/1:0 3785 **Haydn** 22 [10]3-9-0 VIS(62) Derek Nolan(7) 33/1:0
14 Ran Time 1m 43.2 (8.1) Owned: The Pella Partnership Trained: Upper Lambourn

---

4253   **4.05 John Smith's Extra Smooth Handicap Stakes 3yo+ 0-80 (D)**   **[80]**
£6968 £2144 £1072   **5f43y str**   **Good/Soft 84**   **+06 Fast**   Stands side

4197   **PRIME RECREATION** 2 [9] P S Felgate 7-8-13 (65) Lisa Jones 22/1: 03004001: Made all, rdn out ins   **73**
fnl 1f: qck reapp: suited by 5f on fast, likes gd/soft, hvy & fibresand, acts on any trk: loves to race with/force
the pace: back to form here, slipped to a handy mark & could follow up: see 660.

3680   **NEVER WITHOUT ME** 25 [6] J F Coupland 4-8-10 (62) W Supple 13/2: 4112422: Chsd ldrs, ev ch just   1   **67**
over 1f out, onepcd ins fnl 1f: clr of rem: loves fibresand, acts on fast & gd/soft: most consistent: see 2720.

3680   **VALIANT ROMEO** 25 [1] R Bastiman 4-8-3 P (55) F P Ferris(3) 16/1: 2405203: In tch, hdwy over 2f   3   **51**
out, onepcd over 1f out: tried cheek pieces: see 3561.

4043   **KENNINGTON** 10 [2] Mrs C A Dunnett 4-7-13 vis (51) A McCarthy 12/1: 2004024: Chsd ldrs, onepcd fnl 1f.   1½   **42**

3933   **BOISDALE** 16 [10]6-7-12 (2oh) (48) J Quinn 8/1: 6501035: Bhd, modest late gains.   nk   **40**

4039*   **MADDIES A JEM** 11 [5]4-9-9 (75) L Dettori 2/1 FAV: 3564216: Bhd, nvr nr ldrs: nicely bckd.   shd   **64**

3763   **TUSCAN FLYER** 22 [8]6-8-8 bl (60) Darren Williams 28/1: 3040407: Cl-up, wknd fnl 1f.   1¼   **45**

4070*   **WHITE LEDGER** 9 [7]5-8-6 (58) P Hanagan 9/4: 0-003118: Bhd, hmpd 3f out, nvr a factor: much btr   1¼   **39**
expected after recent winning form: see 4070.

1683   **TRINCULO** 109 [3]7-10-0 p (80) M Savage(5) 11/1: 2500609: Handy, wknd dist: op 8/1, long abs.   ½   **59**
9 Ran   Time 1m 4.0 (3.9)   Owned: Mr Michael Heywood   Trained: Melton Mowbray

---

4254   **4.40 Great Yarmouth Mercury Classified Stakes 3yo+ 0-70 (E)**
£4557 £1402 £701   **1m2f21y**   **Good/Soft 84**   **+07 Fast**   Inside

4068   **ANOTHER CHOICE** 9 [9] N P Littmoden 3-8-12 t (73) T E Durcan 12/1: 1100041: Slow away, rcd far   **80**
side str, hdwy to lead over 1f out, kept on well for press: prev eff at 1m, now suited by 10f on firm & soft: acts
on a flat trk, likes a stiff fin: back to form: see 1306.

3815   **OPENING CEREMONY** 21 [2] R A Fahey 5-9-5 (75) P Hanagan 7/2 FAV: 4215152: Trkd ldrs & keen,   1½   **76**
remained far side ent str, led over 4f out, hdd over 1f out, sn no extra: clr of rem: back to form of 3598.

3519   **RECOUNT** 32 [6] J R Best 4-9-8 (75) M Savage(5) 12/1: 5002343: Rear, remained far side ent str,   5   **71**
hdwy over 2f out, not pace to chall: see 3477.

3674   **PARTY PLOY** 26 [7] K R Burke 6-9-3 (70) Darren Williams 4/1: 1012104: Rcd in 2nd, carr to stands   ¾   **65**
side ent str, led over 2f out, no impress fnl 1f: closer but for interference: see 3345.

3992   **PURE MISCHIEF** 13 [5]5-9-5 (72) M Fenton 13/2: 5132465: Rear, remained far side ent str, hdwy   ½   **66**
over 2f out, no impress over 1f out: see 3276.

3914   **MAGIC AMIGO** 16 [8]3-9-0 (75) L Dettori 9/2: 3043626: Cl-up, far side ent str, wknd fnl 1f.   nk   **68**

3875   **KIND EMPEROR** 18 [10]7-9-3 (62) A Mackay 12/1: 5150-047: Led, came stands side ent str, hdd over   ½   **62**
2f out, sn no extra: see 3490.

3829   **INTERNATIONALGUEST** 20 [3]5-9-3 bl (60) A McCarthy 11/1: 0055508: Rear far side, btn 2f out.   7   **51**

3805   **MARSH ORCHID** 21 [1]3-9-0 (75) M Tebbutt 6/1: 5229: Handy, left in lead far side well over 4f   22   **23**
out, sn hdd, wknd over 2f out: op 8/1.
9 Ran   Time 2m 11.94 (7.74)   Owned: Mr A A Goodman   Trained: Newmarket

---

4255   **5.15 Dfds Handicap Stakes 3yo+ 0-75 (E)**   **[82]**
£4605 £1417 £709   **1m6f17y**   **Good/Soft 84**   **-01 Slow**   Stands side

3405   **PATRIXPRIAL** 37 [2] M H Tompkins 3-9-2 (70) P Robinson 12/1: 0-551: Chsd ldrs till led over 1f   **78**
out, kept on well for press fnl 1f: op 9/1: relished this step up to 14f, 2m may suit: acts on gd/soft, flat
trks: first win, more staying races to be won: see 1597.

3493*   **ANNAKITA** 34 [10] W J Musson 4-7-12 (40) Lisa Jones 10/1: 0-000412: Bhd, hdwy over 3f out, onepcd   2½   **42**
ins fnl 1f: stays 14f, rtn to 2m shld suit: acts on gd & gd/soft: remains in gd form: see 3493 (2m).

3998*   **MASTERMAN READY** 13 [8] P W Harris 3-8-12 (66) M Fenton 7/1: 6-006013: Bhd, hdwy 2f out, onepcd   2½   **64**
fnl 1f: btr 3998 (gd grnd).

3893*   **LEVITATOR** 17 [1] Sir Michael Stoute 3-9-6 (74) L Dettori 6/4 FAV: 0-022014: Trkd ldrs, hdwy to   1   **70**
chall 3f out, no impress ins fnl 1f: shade btr 3893.

3856   **JOLIZERO** 18 [3]3-8-8 (62) A McCarthy 7/2: 00-40325: Led, hung right & bit slipped through mouth   ¾   **57**
after 6f, hdd over 1f out, sn no extra: forgive this.

3893   **WINSLOW BOY** 17 [7]3-8-5 (59) J Quinn 13/2: 4612636: Rear, hdwy & ev ch dist, sn wknd.   ¾   **53**

4151   **VANBRUGH** 5 [9]4-7-12 (3oh)vis t (37) J McAuley 40/1: 0000007: Dwelt, nvr a factor: qck reapp.   2½   **30**

3997   **REPENT AT LEISURE** 13 [5]4-8-6 (48) M Halford(7) 66/1: 40/-08: Rcd in 2nd & keen, no impress over   18   **11**
2f out: v stiff task at weights: see 3997.

4045   **SALFORD ROCKET** 10 [6]4-7-12 (11oh) (29) F P Ferris(3) 66/1: 0-006069: Cl up/keen, wknd 2f out.   shd   **2**

3281   **MUSKATSTURM** 43 [4]5-9-10 (66) S W Kelly 16/1: 000-0000: 10th: Cl-up, wknd over 3f out: op 8/1.   13   **7**
10 Ran   Time 3m 9.71(11.91)   Owned: Mr P H Betts   Trained: Newmarket

---

Official Going Good/Soft   All Times Slow

4256   **2.30 Johnson Wedding Anniversary Claiming Stakes 3yo (E)**
£3549 £1092 £546   **7f100y rnd**   **Soft**   **Inapplicable**   Inside

3712   **KINGS ROCK** 24 [13] K A Ryan 3-8-11 bl (55) N Callan 7/2 JT FAV: 0630121: Made all & rdn clr over   **61**
1f out, styd on strongly: clmd by J T Billson for £10,000: eff at 7.5f/1m on fast, soft & fibresand, prob any trk:
enjoys sell/claim grade & relished forcing tactics today: see 3344.

4130   **GAME FLORA** 6 [11] M E Sowersby 3-8-5 (51) T Eaves(1) 16/1: 4050602: Chsd ldrs, styd on to chase   4   **49**
wnr dist, al well held: qck reapp: prob stays 7.5f in claim grade: see 1426 (6f).

3812*   **SHINKO FEMME** 21 [12] N Tinkler 3-8-4 (53) D Allan 13/2: 0510013: Rear, kept on late for press,   2½   **44**

nrst fin, nvr a threat: handles firm & soft grnd: see 3812.

3547 **LORD BASKERVILLE 31** [5] W Storey 3-8-11 (53) J Bramhill 14/1: 0022404: Handy, chsd wnr over 2f | 1¼ | 49$
out, no impress bef dist: see 3203 (6f).

779* **TWO OF CLUBS 181** [10]3-8-8 p (68) G Faulkner 5/1: 454-3315: Mid-div, kept on late for press, op | 4 | 39
7/2, jumps fit: see 779 (AW).

4144 **BEAUTY OF DREAMS 5** [8]3-8-6 (60) A Culhane 7/2 JT FAV: 0005306: Dwelt & well bhd, late gains. | 1½ | 35

3933 **FIREBIRD RISING 16** [3]3-8-6 (53) D Mernagh 6/1: 0360407: Chsd ldrs wide till over 1f out, mod draw. | 4 | 28

4042 **BEAMSLEY BEACON 10** [14]3-8-9 (47) V Halliday 50/1: 0406448: Mid-div, nvr able to chall: btr 4042. | 2 | 28

3697 **BLUE NUN 25** [2]3-8-1 (40) J Mackay 50/1: 500509: Well bhd, only mod late prog. | 3 | 15

3655 **TIZ WIZ 27** [4]3-8-1 (41) Rory Moore(5) 33/1: 060-0200: 10th: Chsd ldrs wide, btn 2f out: btr 1447. | nk | 14

3645 **Bank Games 27** [1]3-8-6 (43) T Lucas 3/1:1:0   3651 **Garnock Venture 27** [7]3-8-12 bl(49) F Lynch 16/1:0
42 **Faites Vos Jeux 286** [6]3-8-2 (50) T Williams 50/1:0   3805 **Zoomiezando 21** [9]3-8-11 P Makin(5) 100/1:0
14 Ran   Time 1m 40.58 (9.78)   Owned: Miss Claire King and Mr Peter McBride   Trained: Hambleton

---

4257   3.05 E B F Joan Graves Birthday Celebration Median Auction Maiden Stakes 2yo (E)
£4485 £1380 £690   1m100y rnd   Soft   Inapplicable   Inside

3919 **ROCAMADOUR 16** [8] M R Channon 2-9-0 A Culhane 13/8 FAV: 51: Handy & led 3f out, drvn & styd on | | 89
strongly ins last: nicely bckd, confirmed debut promise: eff at 7f, styd this longer 8.5f trip well & will get
further: acts on gd & soft grnd, stiffish/gall trk: well regarded & useful, can prog with racing over further.

4072 **RIVER LIFFEY 9** [4] M L W Bell 2-9-0 R Mullen 15/8: 022: Trkd ldrs trav well halfway, eff to | 1 | 86
chall wn carried head high from dist, held well ins last: nicely bckd, op 11/4: styd longer 8.5f trip: shown
enough to find a race: see 4072 (clmr).

3665 **TCHERINA 26** [11] T D Easterby 2-8-9 (73) D Allan 10/1: 0023: Mid-div, styd on for press, not | 2 | 78$
able to chall: op 7/1, clr rem & confirmed latest improv: stays 8.5f, handles fast & soft grnd: can find a race.

3601 **YOUNG MICK 29** [10] G G Margarson 2-9-0 N Callan 11/1: 034: Prom, short of room & stumbled 2f | 5 | 75
out, rdn & no extra bef dist: this longer 8.5f trip shld suit, prob handles fast & soft grnd: see 3601.

3909 **AKRAAN 16** [6]2-8-9 R Hills 11/1: 005: ch f Erhaab - Nafhaat (Roberto) Sn handy wide, fdd over | 1¾ | 68
1f out: op 9/1: caught the eye prev: Mar foal, strong mid-dist pedigree, dam a 12f 3yo scorer: suffered an
awkward wide passage & likely prove better than this, also eyecatching latest & could be one to note in h'caps.

3927 **SUCCESSION 16** [12]2-8-9 J Mackay 14/1: 0006: Slow away & bhd, late gains, nrst fin: op 10/1: | 5 | 61+
mid-dist pedigree, likely impr on this in h'cap company over further: see 3517.

4040 **ITSA MONKEY 10** [2]2-9-0 BL (43) D Nolan(3) 100/1: 0620007: Led till 3f out, fdd: tried blnks. | 2½ | 62$

INDONESIA 0 [3]2-9-0 R Ffrench 12/1: 8: ch c Lomitas - Idraak (Kris) Slow away & sn well bhd, | 15 | 41
mod late prog, op 7/1: Apr foal, half-brother to 2yo wnrs at 6f/1m, dam unplcd: v green on intro but got the hang of
things late on, impr with experience over further.

3798 **LORD CHALFONT 21** [1]2-9-0 bl K Ghunowa(7) 100/1: 0000009: Chsd ldrs, hung badly left & wknd 2f out. 5 | | 34

3376 **FRENCH KISSES 38** [5]2-8-9 Dean McKeown 100/1: 000: 10th: Mid-div, struggling from halfway. | 4 | 23

2563 **LADY INDIANA 71** [7]2-8-9 P M Quinn 100/1: 0000: 11th: Dwelt & sn struggling, 10 wk abs, longer trip. | 5 | 16

TIME TO SUCCEED 0 [9]2-9-0 G Parkin 50/1: 0: 12th: b g Pennekamp - Ivory League (Last Tycoon) | 16 | 0
Dwelt & al bhd: Apr foal, 10,000gns purchase: half-brother to a 10f 3yo scorer, dam modest btwn 7f/2m1f.
12 Ran   Time 1m 55.5 (11.7)   Owned: Mr Salem Suhail   Trained: West Ilsley

---

4258   3.40 Britannia Rescue Nursery Handicap Stakes 2yo (C)
£10758 £3310 £1655   5f str   Soft   Inapplicable   Inside   [97]

3003 **NUFOOS 54** [4] M Johnston 2-9-2 (85) R Hills 11/4 FAV: 31001: Chsd ldrs, hdwy towards centre over | | 97+
1f out, sn led & rdn cir, decisively: nicely bckd, op 7/2: 8 wk abs: prev wn at 6f, much imprvd for return to a
stiff 5f: acts on fast, loved soft grnd today: smart performance, could make her mark in fills List company.

3968* **GRAZE ON 14** [3] J J Quinn 2-8-13 (82) R Winston 4/1: 212: Held up, rdn & styd on fnl 2f, no ch | 3 | 84
with wnr: h'cap bow: acts on gd & soft grnd, lightly rcd & progressive: see 3968, 3457.

3756 **APOLOGIES 23** [1] B A McMahon 2-8-2 BL (71) G Gibbons 22/1: 0140603: Mid-div, styd on for press, | shd | 73
not pace to chall: first time blnks, imprvd eff: suited by 5f & loves soft grnd: see 1107.

3902 **MONSIEUR MIRASOL 17** [5] K A Ryan 2-8-10 (79) N Callan 4/1: 3351024: Held up, styd on for press, | 2 | 76
nvr a threat: eff at 5f, return to 6f shld suit: see 2682 (6f).

3003 **MISS MEGGY 54** [2]2-9-7 (90) D Allan 6/1: 11065: Switched right from start & rear, kept on late, | 1 | 85
nvr land a blow: 8 wk abs: prob handles soft grnd but btr 2165 (List, fast).

3756* **BAYMIST 23** [7]2-7-12 (67) F Norton 7/1: 561416: Trkd ldrs, led halfway till over 1f out, sn fdd. | 2 | 57

4049 **HILLSIDE HEATHER 10** [6]2-7-12 P (67) F Norton 16/1: 3202457: Mid-div, fdd from halfway: chkpcs. | 5 | 45

4089 **TARTATARTUFATA 9** [9]2-7-12 (2oh) (65) Joanna Badger 16/1: 040028: Cl-up, hanging left throughout, | 6 | 30
struggling from halfway: op 12/1: btr 4089 (AW mdn).

3115 **SOWERBY 50** [8]2-7-12 (3oh) (64) D Mernagh 25/1: 06409: Prom till halfway, sn bhd, 7 wk abs: btr 2889. | 3½ | 21

3607 **OUR LOUIS 29** [10]2-7-12 (12oh) (54) P M Quinn 50/1: 5415000: 10th: Led bhd halfway, wknd qckly. | 1 | 19
10 Ran   Time 1m 07.15 (5.85)   Owned: Mr Hamdan Al Maktoum   Trained: Middleham

---

4259   4.15 Nigel Briggs 50th Birthday Handicap Stakes 3yo+ 0-75 (E)
£5086 £1565 £783   1m4f16y   Soft   Inapplicable   Inside   [74]

3929 **BRAMANTINO 16** [4] R A Fahey 4-8-6 bl (52) T Hamilton(3) 7/1: 0250551: Trkd ldrs, chall 2f out & | | 62
narrow lead dist, held on all out, gamely: suited by 11/12f, tried 14f: acts on firm, hvy & fibresand, prob any
trk: best in cheek pieces/blnks: see 1034 & 746.

3854* **CAN CAN FLYER 18** [1] M Johnston 3-8-7 (63) R Ffrench 4/1: 006-12: Held up in tch wide, eff to | shd | 72+
chall over 1f out, styd on well for press, just denied: nicely bckd tho' op 3/1: styd longer 12f trip well, shld
get further: acts on gd/soft & soft grnd: excellent eff despite suffering wide passage, keep on side: see 3854.

3734 **MERRYMAKER 24** [12] W M Brisbourne 4-9-5 (65) P Mathers(5) 20/1: P121003: Dwelt, rear, hdwy wide | hd | 73
over 2f out & chall dist, drvn & just held cl-home: clr of rem: back to form: acts on fast & soft grnd: see 3270.

3502 **EAST CAPE 33** [14] Don Enrico Incisa 7-7-12 (2oh) (42) Kim Tinkler 16/1: 0063524: Bhd, late prog, | 5 | 46
nrst fin, no threat to front trio: see 724 (AW).

3598 **TEDSDALE MAC 29** [9]5-8-13 (59) F Norton 9/2: 2523225: Held up, eff 2f out, nvr able to chall. | 1 | 60

4170* **RED FOREST** 3 [10]5-9-1 t (61) Dale Gibson 3/1 FAV: 5033316: Keen & trkd ldr, ev ch 3f out, sn   hd   61
wknd, qck reapp: disappointing effort: btr 4170 (fast).
3879 **ALLIED VICTORY** 18 [2]4-9-12 T (72) Dean McKeown 25/1: 1002037: Led, hdd 2f out, fdd.   1¾   70
4076 **CYBER SANTA** 9 [11]6-8-4 (1ow) (49) D Allan 14/1: 430/-6028: Trkd ldr, rdn & led 2f out, hdd dist & fdd.   ½   47
3741* **MELODIAN** 24 [6]9-9-5 bl (65) M Lawson(5) 15/2: 5123219: Trkd ldrs, short of room over 1f out, fdd.   hd   61
2526 **MICHAELS DREAM** 73 [13]5-7-12 (2oh) (42) S Righton 25/1: 6330400: 10th: Chsd ldrs, rdn & btn 2f out.   1½   38
4922} **COLWAY RITZ** 306 [3]10-9-1 (61) J Bramhill 50/1: 600422-0: 11th: Trkd ldrs trav well, fdd qckly   hd   54
fnl 2f: dual h'cap rnr-up '03: dual apr h'cap wnr '02, also landed a class stks: suited by 10/14f on fm, gd/soft
& any trk, likes York: eff with/without cheek pieces: ran well for a long way, sharper for this on faster grnd.
3222 **FIELD SPARK** 45 [5]4-8-12 p (58) R Winston 10/1: 1523020: 12th: Sn struggling rear: abs: btr 3222.   14   31
12 Ran   Time 2m 50.00 (18.7)   Owned: Mrs Kenyon A Rhodes Haulage P Timmins   Trained: Malton

---

4260   4.50 Jim And Mary Richardson Ruby Anniversary Handicap Stakes Fillies 3yo+ 0-75 (E)   [72]
       £4303   £1324   £662   1m1f207y   Soft   Inapplicable   Inside

3853 **SHOTLEY DANCER** 18 [6] N Bycroft 5-8-2 (46) F Norton 6/1: 3531421: Handy & led over 2f out, held   51
on well ins last: eff at 1m, now seems suited by 12f/2m on fast, soft & fibresand: likes Beverley: genuine, can
win again in modest company: see 3853 & 3502.
4071 **KEEPERS LODGE** 9 [10] B A McMahon 3-9-4 (70) G Gibbons 7/1: 0010352: Trkd ldrs, hdwy when short   nk   74+
of room over 1f out, forced to switch & kept on well cl-home, lkd unlucky: may have won this with clr run: eff at
1m/10f on gd & soft grnd: see 4071 & 2904.
3938* **SIENNA SUNSET** 15 [9] W M Brisbourne 5-9-0 (58) B Swarbrick(5) 11/2: 0662413: Held up, hdwy trav   2   60
well from halfway, drvn & no extra ins last: clr of rem: see 3938.
3325 **MEGANS MAGIC** 40 [1] W Storey 4-9-10 e (68) J Bramhill 5/1: 2003644: Dwelt, bhd, hdwy wide   6   64
halfway, no impress over 1f out: 6 wk abs: see 3325, 1307 (C/D).
3856 **PAY ATTENTION** 18 [7]3-8-11 (63) D Allan 4/1 JT FAV: 0202145: Chsd ldrs, wknd over 3f out.   8   51
3719 **MAID FOR LIFE** 24 [3]4-8-12 (56) R Winston 12/1: 0464-66: Chsd ldrs, btn 3f out: see 3719.   1¼   42
2706 **CHARMATIC** 26 [11]3-8-13 (65) Dean McKeown 4/1 JT FAV: 2215457: Led, btn 2f out: 2 mth abs.   hd   50
3916 **ESTIMATE** 16 [8]4-8-9 vis (53) N Callan 20/1: 0022048: Chsd ldrs, struggling halfway: btr 3916.   13   25
3812 **PRINCESS ISMENE** 21 [4]3-7-12 (5oh) S Righton 66/1: 40546R9: Al bhd: btr 2019.   2½   19
3730 **ARTISTS RETREAT** 24 [2]5-7-12 (5oh) J Mackay 66/1: 00000/-00: 10th: Sn strugg rear: see 3730.   24   0
10 Ran   Time 2m 16.49 (14.19)   Owned: Mr J A Swinburne   Trained: Malton

---

4261   5.25 Beverley Lions Maiden Stakes 3yo+   (D)
       £3829   £1178   £589   1m1f207y   Soft   Inapplicable   Inside

3422 **AUTUMN WEALTH** 36 [6] Mrs A J Perrett 3-8-8   A Culhane 1/1 FAV: 221: Chsd ldrs wide, hung badly   79
left on home turn behd over 3f out, hung behd to stands rail & led over 1f out, drvn out: hvly bckd, op 11/8: eff
at 10f on fast & soft grnd: won this despite v awkward passage, could prog in h'caps if steering can be corrected.
3848} **TRICKY VENTURE** 371 [7] P W Hiatt 4-9-7 (65) P Makin(5) 24/1: 540452-2: gr g Linamix - Ukraine   4   77$
Venture (Slip Anchor) Held up, hdwy over 3f out, chall over 1f out, not pace of wnr ins last: reapp: rnr-up on fnl
'03 start (this race, earlier AW unplcd, rtd 60a, mdn): stays a stiff 10f, handles fast & soft grnd, prob fibresand.
2 Aug'03 Beve 9.9g/f 74-(46) D:
3697 **ST BARCHAN** 25 [9] W Jarvis 3-8-13   D Nolan(3) 4/1: 423: Trkd ldrs, led 3f out, hung badly left   1½   75
under press 2f out, hdd over 1f out & no extra: now qual for h'caps: handles fast & soft grnd: see 3697 & 2843.
3979 **DREAM ALIVE** 13 [11] M Blanshard 3-8-13 t   N Callan 6/1: 034: Chsd ldrs, hdwy over 2f out, edged   1¼   74
left & no extra bef dist: well clr of rem: prob stays a stiff 10f: handles fast & soft grnd: see 3979 (1m).
3973 **MEDALLA** 24 [4]4-9-7   M Lawson(5) 6/1: 35: Chsd ldrs, sn strugg 2f out, longer trip.   13   61
3905 **MOUNT COTTAGE** 17 [13]3-8-8   J Bramhill 14/1: 646: Mid-div, eff over 3f out, sn struggling.   8   48
3572 **ST JUDE** 30 [12]4-9-7   D Allan 50/1: 00-07: b c Deploy - Little Nutmeg (Gabitat) Led till 3f   6   47
out, sn btn, longer trip: unplcd '03 for K Ryan (rtd 40, mdn).
2381 **SHAMELESS** 79 [10]7-9-7 t   R Keogh(7) 100/1: 08: Dwelt & al bhd, 6 wk jumps abs.   1¾   45
    PARISI PRINCESS 0 [8]3-8-8   P Mulrennan(3) 50/1: 9: Dwelt, sn struggling rear.   13   27
5024} **LADY LUCINDA** 296 [5]3-8-8   Dean McKeown 50/1: 0-0: 10th: Mid-div, rdn & btn halfway, reapp.   7   20
3858 **GENTLE WARNING** 18 [1]4-9-2   D Fentiman(7) 50/1: 00: 11th: Al bhd & eased 3f out, longer trip.   dist   0
11 Ran   Time 2m 16.04(13.74)   Owned: Mr D J Burke   Trained: Pulborough

---

GOODWOOD   SUNDAY 29.08.04   Righthand, Sharpish, Undulating Track

Official Going Rnd Course - Good/Soft, Str Course - Soft (Hvy Places)

4262   2.10 Britannia Rescue Median Auction Maiden Stakes 3-4yo (E)
       £5408   £1664   £832   6f str   Soft   Inapplicable   Stands side

3677 **GROWLER** 26 [5] J L Dunlop 3-9-0 vis (56) R Hughes 5/1: 00-03021: Cl-up, led trav well dist, rdn   74
out, val bit more: stays 7f on firm & fast, imprvd for drop back to 6f on soft grnd: apprec recent fitting of visor.
3705 **STARGEM** 25 [1] J Pearce 3-8-9 (66) K Fallon 7/2 FAV: 02-2202: Led, hdd dist, not pace of wnr: 2½   64
acts on firm, soft grnd & fibresand: see 3396 & 2756.
3705 **ASBO** 25 [6] Dr J D Scargill 4-8-12 (59) K Darley 4/1: 00/00-543: Mid-div, prog 2f out, onepcd   1¾   59
4029 **HEAVENS WALK** 11 [9] P J Makin 3-9-0   D Sweeney 12/1: 504: Held up, prog halfway, onepcd fnl 2f.   5   51
3953 **TEXT** 15 [3]3-9-0 (65) J F Egan 7/1: 320-0235: Prom, outpcd 3f out, mod gains when no room dist.   2½   44
3884 **DINE N DASH** 17 [8]3-9-0   L Keniry(3) 66/1: 06: Al in rear: see 3884.   3½   35
4055 **CAFE AMERICANO** 10 [4]4-9-3 e (48) J Fortune 8/1: 0-050227: Bhd, nvr a factor: got restless in stalls.   2½   28
3347 **SOKOKE** 39 [4]3-9-0   R L Moore 11/2: 238: Cl-up 4f, fdd: rider reported mount was unsuited by grnd.   13   0
1078 **SILVER REIGN** 144 [2]3-9-0   R Thomas(5) 25/1: 569: In tch when short of room 2f out, sn fdd: long abs.   4   0
9 Ran   Time 1m 16.56 (6.56)   Owned: Mr P D Player   Trained: Arundel

---

4263   **2.45 Seafrance Stakes Handicap Fillies 3yo 0-85 (D)**
£7036 £2165 £1083   **7f rnd**   **Soft 100**   **-00 Slow**   Inside   **[91]**

2886 + **NEW ORDER** 59 [2] B W Hills 3-8-8 (71) R Hughes 9/2: 311: Cl-up, styd on to lead bef 1f out trav   82
well, sn hung right, pushed out, val 3L+: eff at 7f, return to 1m+ will suit: acts on gd & soft, any trk: goes well
fresh: going the right way, win more: see 2886.
4054 + **SABRINA BROWN** 10 [4] G B Balding 3-8-8 t (71) R Thomas(5) 13/2: 6-220612: Led, hdd bef 1f out,   1¾   76
kept on but not pace of wnr: another gd eff after recent fitting of t-strap: ran to form of 4054.
3921* **ENRAPTURE** 16 [6] Mrs A J Perrett 3-9-2 (79) K Fallon 13/8 FAV: 5-13: Mid-div, prog 2f out, no   1¼   82
impress fnl 1f: v well bckd on h'cap bow: acts on gd & soft grnd: ran to form of mdn win in 3921.
3885 **ENFORD PRINCESS** 17 [5] R Hannon 3-9-7 (84) R L Moore 14/1: 100-4034: Held up, prog wide 3f out,   nk   84
no impress fnl 1f: not disgraced under top-weight: see 3885 & 3277.
3447 **SARISTAR** 36 [7]3-9-6 (83) J Fanning 10/1: 010-1005: Held up, hdwy 3f out, no impress fnl 1f: 1   83
more encouraging after twice below 1154 (6f).
3744 **HERE TO ME** 23 [3]3-8-9 (72) J Fortune 16/1: 4421356: Mid-div, no impress fnl 2f: btr 2906 (6f, fast).   ½   71
3612 **SCARLETT ROSE** 29 [8]3-8-2 (65) Martin Dwyer 11/1: 60-60337: In tch 5f, sn no extra, eased ins fnl 1f.   3½   57
3923 **SURREPTITIOUS** 16 [1]3-8-5 (68) K Darley 13/2: 138: Chsd ldrs 5f, fdd: well bckd: btr 3923 (gd).   6   48
8 Ran   Time 1m 31.51 (7.01)   Owned: Mr K Abdulla   Trained: Lambourn

---

4264   **3.20 Gr3 Citroen C5 Prestige Stakes Fillies 2yo (A)**
£23200 £8800 £4400   **7f rnd**   **Soft 100**   **-11 Slow**   Inside

3770* **DUBAI SURPRISE** 22 [10] D R Loder 2-8-9 (84) R L Moore 16/1: 311: Bhd, outpcd after 3f, prog when   104
short of room 2f out, styd on for press to lead cl-home: eff at 7f, 1m will suit: acts on fast, imprvd here on
soft: v useful & lighty raced, win more Gr races: see 3770.
   NANABANANA 19 [11] Mme C Head Maarek 2-8-9   K Darley 9/2: 42122: b f Anabaa - Tanabata (Shining   ½   101
Steel) Cl-up, led trav well 2f out, under press ins fnl 1f, hdd cl-home: clr rem: well bckd from 10/1: French
raider, Feb foal, dam plcd at 7f: sire Gr 1 wnr at 6f: earlier won in French provinces: eff at 7f: acts on soft: v
useful, win at least a List.
3539* **RED PEONY** 31 [9] Sir Mark Prescott 2-8-9   J Murtagh 3/1 JT FAV: 13: In tch, outpcd 3f out,   3   95
rallied ins fnl 1f, no ch with front 2: well bckd: acts on firm & soft grnd: useful eff stepped up in grade on
only 2nd ever start, sure to improve at 1m: see 3539 (mdn, debut).
3716* **FAVOURITA** 24 [1] C E Brittain 2-8-9   J P Guillambert 50/1: 14: Mid-div, short of room & lost   shd   94
place halfway, sn switched wide, styd on ins fnl 1f: on fast & soft: improved run & looks sure to relish 1m: see 3716.
3774* **JUSTAQUESTION** 22 [2]2-8-9 (93) P Doe 12/1: 1103215: Held up, hdwy 3f out, onepcd ins fnl 1f.   1   92
4059 **UMNIYA** 10 [6]2-8-9 VIS (91) C Catlin 50/1: 1334566: Bhd, prog when short of room bef 2f out &   ½   91
again 2f out, styd on ins fnl 1f, nvr getting to principals: first time visor: see 2553 (6f).
3843 **LUAS LINE** 21 [4]2-8-9   K Fallon 3/1 JT FAV: 0127: Bhd, prog after 3f, outpcd 3f out, briefly   2½   86
rallied bef 1f out, sn no impress: well bckd Irish raider, prob unsuited by today's soft grnd: showed more in 3843.
3781 **ROYAL ALCHEMIST** 22 [13]2-8-9 (94) A Daly 10/1: 1208: Bhd, nvr able to chall: btr 2763 (6f, fast).   2   82
3919 **SUBYAN DREAMS** 16 [7]2-8-9 (95) R Hughes 14/1: 5339: Led 5f, sn wknd: btr 3919 (gd).   3   76
4003 **JANE JUBILEE** 12 [12]2-8-9 (95) J Fanning 12/1: 5221150: 10th: Mid-div 5f, wknd: btr 3560 (fast, h'cap).   5   66
3554* **MISS LAUGEVAL** 31 [8]2-8-9 (82) Martin Dwyer 20/1: 410: 11th: Mid-div when short of room after   2   62
3f, wknd 2f out: btr 3554 (firm, mdn).
3882* **SHARP AS A TACK** 17 [5]2-8-9 (83) J Fortune 20/1: 0210: 12th: Handy over 4f, sn hung right & fdd.   9   46
12 Ran   Time 1m 32.30 (7.8)   Owned: Dr Ali Ridha   Trained: Newmarket

---

4265   **3.55 Motoring & Leisure Stakes Handicap 3yo 0-85 (D)**
£7134 £2195 £1098   **1m rnd**   **Soft 100**   **+04 Fast**   Inside   **[92]**

3950 + **FLYING ADORED** 15 [7] J L Dunlop 3-8-10 (74) K Fallon 5/2 FAV: 040-3011: Mid-div, hdwy halfway,   80
styd on to lead dist, rdn out: well bckd: eff at 6/7f, imprvd for recent step up to 1m: acts on fast & soft grnd:
likes Goodwood: progressing well & can land hat-trick on this evidence: see 3950.
3860 **DR THONG** 18 [8] P F I Cole 3-9-4 (82) K Darley 3/1: 1241042: Cl-up, led 4f out, hdd bef 1f out,   2   85
kept on, not pace of wnr: op 4/1: acts on firm & soft grnd: continues to run with credit: see 3860 & 2922.
3979* **DAY TO REMEMBER** 13 [2] E F Vaughan 3-9-7 (85) J Fortune 5/1: 43-513: In tch, prog 2f out, sn   1¾   84
outpcd, rallied well ins fnl 1f: clr rem: op 7/2: acts on gd & soft grnd: not disgraced under top-weight.
3718* **GENERAL FEELING** 24 [5] S Kirk 3-8-12 (76) J F Egan 13/2: 3304114: Held up, prog & ev ch 2f out,   5   66
sn wknd: disapp on that-trick bid: 5lb higher than last win in 3718 (fast).
4110* **STEVEDORE** 8 [1]3-8-9 (73) G Carter 8/1: 0041515: Led 4f, rcd stands side in home straight, sn   1   61
outpcd, rallied late: btr 4110 (gd).
2590 **LORD OF THE SEA** 71 [4]3-7-12 (1oh) (61) D Kinsella 28/1: 4000406: Prom 6f, sn wknd: abs, gelded.   3   44
3535 **TAMINOULA** 32 [3]3-9-2 (80) J Murtagh 7/1: 0311-07: Chsd ldrs, switched to stands rail in   11   43
straight, fdd 2f out: op 10/1: btr 3535.
4781↓ **LITTLE LONDON** 317 [6]3-9-1 (79) R L Moore 14/1: 0352-P: b g Bahhare - North Kildare (Northjet)   0
Missed break, lost tch halfway, sn p.u. & dismounted: clearly something amiss on reapp: plcd twice in '03 (mdns):
eff at 7f/1m on firm & gd grnd: with J L Dunlop. 2 Oct'03 Brig 8.0fm 78-(80) E:
8 Ran   Time 1m 45.09 (7.69)   Owned: Mrs Mark Burrell   Trained: Arundel

---

4266   **4.30 Trundle Premier Claiming Stakes 3yo+ (D)**
£5616 £1728 £864   **1m1f**   **Soft 100**   **-39 Slow**   Inside

3876* **THE PRINCE** 18 [5] Ian Williams 10-9-2 (84) C Catlin 9/2: 1031-111: Mid-div, prog to chase wnr   73
bef 1f out, styd on to lead trav well ins fnl 1f, rdn out: no bid: qck reapp: came 2nd just 2 days ago in claim race at
Deauville (AW): eff at 7.5/9f on firm, soft grnd & both AWs: enjoys claim grade: see 3876 & 2854.
4097 **TRAVELLING BAND** 8 [2] A M Balding 6-9-5 VIS (72) L Keniry(3) 10/1: 24-00602: In tch, styd on to   2   71
lead trav well 2f out, sn clr, under press & tiring when hdd well ins fnl 1f: eff at 1m/9f on fast & soft grnd:
apprec fitting of first time visor on drop to claim grade: see 2903.

GOODWOOD SUNDAY 29.08.04 Righthand, Sharpish, Undulating Track

4112 **ONE UPMANSHIP 8** [8] J G Portman 3-8-12 (65) R L Moore 14/1: 6326123: In tch, prog 2f out, onepcd   2½   **67**
ins fnl 1f: clr rem: just btr 4112 (polytrack) & 3739 (gd).
3689 **HIGHLAND REEL 25** [1] D R C Elsworth 7-9-7 (87) R Hughes 2/1 FAV: 0040344: Held up, prog 3f out,   6   **61**
no impress fnl 2f: reportedly unsuited by today's soft grnd: btr 3512 (h'cap).
4067 **LINNING WINE 9** [3]8-9-7 (80) S Carson 9/2: 4064555: Mid-div, wknd bef 1f out: disapp eff: all   1¼   **59**
wins have come on polytrack: btr 928 & 547.
3967 **MONTGOMERY 14** [9]3-8-7   N Chalmers(5) 50/1: 66: Al in rear: see 3967.   1   **50**
602 **KNOCKTOPHER ABBEY 200** [4]7-9-0 bl (60) S Hitchcott(3) 50/1: 34050/-07: ch g Pursuit of Love -   1½   **47**
Kukri (Kris) Sn adrift, modest late gains: modest hdles form in 03/04 (rtd 93h, nov hdle, also p.u. 3 times, B R
Millman, eff around 2m1f on fast & gd): mdn hdle wnr on last of 3 02/03 starts (rtd 107h, Miss V Williams): plcd on
Flat in '02 (h'caps, rtd 68): h'cap wnr in late '01: prev eff at 6/10f on firm, gd/soft & polytrack, handles soft.
1 Dec'01 Ling 10ap 72a-69 E: 2 Jul'01 Asco 8g/f 73-71 C: 2 Jun'01 Ling 7.6fm 71-68 E:
3690 **CARTRONAGEERAGHLAD 25** [6]3-9-5 bl (75) Martin Dwyer 10/1: 2445408: Led, hdd 2f out, fdd: btr 2994.1   **58**
4124 **BEN HUR 6** [10]5-9-5 (74) K Darley 5/1: 1545639: Cl-up 6f, sn fdd: qck reappp: disapp: btr 4124 (gd).   1½   **48**
9 Ran   Time 2m 3.01 (12.51)   Owned: Mr Patrick Kelly   Trained: Alvechurch

---

4267	5.05 Picnic Handicap Stakes 3yo+ 0-75 (E)					[75]
	£4310 £1326 £663	**1m16f**	**Soft 100**	**-05 Slow**	Inside	

2607 **STOOP TO CONQUER 70** [5] J L Dunlop 4-9-11 (72) J Murtagh 11/4 FAV: 56-00141: Led, hdd 10f out,   **80**
styd cl-up, sltly outpcd 2f out, rallied well ins fnl 1f to lead cl-home, rdn out: well bckd: 10 wk abs: eff at
14f/2m1f on fast & soft grnd: game tough 4yo who enjoyed today's stamina test: fine eff under top-weight, see 2276.
4203 **JASMICK 2** [2] H Morrison 6-9-6 (67) L Fletcher(3) 6/1: 60-500672: Chsd ldrs, styd on to lead 2f   nk   **75**
out, sn grabbed stands side rail, hdd under press cl-home: clr rem: qk reapp: acts on fm & soft: well h'capped.
3415 **MARKET LEADER 37** [3] Mrs A J Perrett 3-8-12 (71) R Hughes 7/2: 502-33: In tch, onepcd bef 1f   7   **72**
out: op 5/1: prob unsuited by soft grnd on first try at 14f: see 3415.
3387 **ESTABLISHMENT 37** [1] C A Cyzer 7-9-4 (65) D Sweeney 13/2: 0000004: Led 10f out, hdd 2f out, wknd.   ½   **65**
293 **HIGH HOPE 239** [4]6-9-10 (71) R L Moore 4/1: 00003-05: ch g Lomitas - Highness Lady (Cagliostro)   3½   **68**
Mid-div 12f, sn fdd: reapp: rnr-up once in early '03 (h'cap): unplcd both 02/03 hdles starts (rtd 109h, stays
around 2m on gd/soft): amat h'cap wnr in late '02: ex-French, wnr in native country back in '02: eff at 12/13f on
polytrack & soft: likes a sharp trk: been gelded. 2 Jan'03 Ling 12ap 83a-82 C: 1 Nov'02 Ling 12ap 81a-78 F:
3255 **GOODWOOD FINESSE 44** [7]3-9-2 (75) G Carter 7/1: 55-156: Held up, nvr a factor: op 5/1: 6 wk abs.   ½   **71**
4033 **DR COOL 11** [6]7-8-13 (60) P Doe 20/1: 4510/-007: Al bhd, fin well adrift: see 4033.   21   **38**
7 Ran   Time 3m 13.55 (14.75)   Owned: H Stewart-Brown & M J Meacock   Trained: Arundel

---

4268	5.40 Harvest Stakes Handicap 3yo+ 0-75 (E)					[75]
	£4358 £1341 £671	**1m1f192y**	**Soft 100**	**+03 Fast**	Inside	

3867 **POLISH SPIRIT 18** [10] B R Millman 9-8-13 (60) J Fortune 5/1: 15//5-0061: Mid-div, prog to lead   **65**
2f out, drvn out to hold on cl-home: op 7/1: eff at 1m/10f on gd & hvy grnd: showed battling qualities today.
4086 **ARRY DASH 9** [12] M R Channon 4-9-12 (73) S Hitchcott(3) 9/2: 0606232: Held up, prog trav well bef   hd   **77**
1f out, styd on well ins fnl 1f, post came too sn: continues to run well but finds it difficult to win: see 4086.
4143 **SERRAVAL 5** [2] G B Balding 6-8-10 (57) R Thomas(5) 8/1: 000/-2353: Rear, prog 3f out, ev ch 1f   nk   **60**
out, kept on, just held in photo: op 13/2 on qck reapp: acts on fast & soft grnd: encouraging effort.
4033 **HEAD TO KERRY 11** [1] D J S ffrench Davis 4-8-7 (54) K Fallon 9/4 FAV: 5342454: Mid-div, prog 4f   ½   **56**
out, ev ch dist, kept on, not btn far in 4th: well bckd: gd eff back at 10f: see 4033 & 3519.
2800 **COMPETITOR 62** [4]3-8-10 (65) G Carter 22/1: 10-2005: Bhd, sn adrift & t.o. after halfway, modest   6   **59**
late gains: 9 wk abs: looks in need of step up to 12f+: see 365.
3922 **DESERT HAWK 16** [9]3-8-13 (68) R L Moore 16/1: 0054006: Led 1m, sn wknd: btr 3039 (fast).   1½   **59**
3996 **GREEN FALCON 13** [8]3-7-12 (53) D Kinsella 28/1: 3300007: Rear, prog 4f out, fdd fnl 2f: btr 697 (AW).   ½   **43**
4120 **EFRHINA 7** [13]4-9-2 (63) R Havlin 9/1: 2-003028: Keen mid-div, ev ch 2f out, sn wknd: qck reapp.   1   **51**
4120 **PURR 7** [7]3-7-12 (80h) A Hamblett(5) 9/1: 0-060009: Cl-up 7f, sn fdd: qck reapp.   8   **30**
3173 **KIROV KING 47** [5]4-9-1 (62) A Hindley(7) 33/1: 0-000060: 10th: Prom, rcd alone far rail in   ½   **38**
straight, wknd bef 2f out: 7 wk abs: btr 2099.
3449 **AFRICAN STAR 36** [6]3-7-13 (1ow)(1oh)P C Catlin 12/1: 05-65640: 11th: Cl-up 7f, fdd.   16   **115**
1128 **ROZANEE 139** [3]4-8-13 (60) J Murtagh 16/1: 333-600: 12th: Mid-div 6f, sn fdd: long abs.   dist   **0**
12 Ran   Time 2m 13.99(9.79)   Owned: Mrs Izabel Palmer   Trained: Cullompton

---

WARWICK MONDAY 30.08.04 Lefthand, Sharp, Turning Track

Official Going Good/Soft (Gd Places) FAST TIMES SUGGEST RECONFIGURED TRACK

4269	2.00 Sandall House Maiden Auction Stakes Div 1 2yo (E)				
	£4004 £1232 £616	**7f26y rnd**	**Good**	**Inapplicable**	Inside

4114 **BRIANNSTA 8** [10] M R Channon 2-8-11   S Hitchcott(3) 9/2 JT FAV: 6521: Held up, rdn & hdwy 2f out,   **78**
styd on for press to lead well ins last: eff at 7f, rtn to 1m shld suit: acts on firm & gd grnd, sharp/undul &
turning trks: lightly rcd & progressive, interesting for h'caps: see 4114, 3803.
  MOON FOREST 0 [1] P W Chapple Hyam 2-8-11   A McCarthy 9/2 JT FAV: 2: br c Woodborough - Ma   nk   **78**
Bella Luna (Jalmood) Handy & led over 4f out till rdn & hdd well ins last: bckd: £12,000 May foal, half-brother
to a dual 5f juv wnr, dam a 7f 3yo scorer: eff over a sharp 7f on gd grnd: encouraging intro, can find a race.
4102 **IGNITION 9** [4] W M Brisbourne 2-8-4   B Swarbrick(5) 7/1: 543: Handy & chsd wnr over 2f out, edged   2½   **64**
left & no extra dist: op 9/1: stays 7f on gd grnd, nvr quals for h'caps: see 4102.
3521 **GRAND OPTION 33** [14] B W Duke 2-8-9 (71) A Daly 11/1: 2325004: Prom, no extra dist, longer trip.   3½   **64**
3909 **TOMOBEL 9** [8]2-8-2   M Henry 25/1: 005: b f Josr Algarhoud - Eileen's Lady (Mtoto) Dwelt, rear,   1   **55+**
kept on wide, nrst fin: cheaply bght Mar foal, plcd at 10f, mid-dist pedigree: caught the eye late on, expect
improvement at 1m+: with M H Tompkins.
2870 **TUVALU 60** [17]2-8-12   K Darley 8/1: 056: Held up, eff 3f out, no impress dist, abs: see 2870.   shd   **64**
3927 **ARCHIE WRIGHT 17** [15]2-8-9   O Urbina 20/1: 07: ch c Lake Coniston - Roisin Clover (Faustus)   1¼   **58**

Held up, eff 3f out, edged left & no impress dist: cheaply bght Mar first foal, dam a 12f wnr as a 3/5yo: shld stay further & can improve: with R Hannon.
3467 **LADY LUISA 36** [12]2-8-2 N Mackay(3) 11/1: 058: Dwelt, held up, mod prog, op 8/1. 1¾ **48**
4163 **CROSS MY SHADOW 5** [11]2-8-12 t K McEvoy 14/1: 059: Led 2f, btn 2f out: op 10/1, qck reapp. 1 **56**
3818 **BOB BAILEYS 21** [2]2-8-7 J Quinn 10/1: 40: 10th: Dwelt, sn in tch, no impress fnl 2f: op 12/1. shd **51**
3883 **MONAD 18** [16]2-8-8 (4ow) R Havlin 100/1: 00: 11th: Mid-div, btn 2f out. 1½ **49**
STOLEN 0 [9]2-8-9 S Drowne 66/1: 0: 12th: Dwelt & al rear. 1½ **47**
SAXON LIL 0 [13]2-8-2 Joanna Badger 33/1: 0: 13th: Slow away & al bhd. nk **39**
Dewin Coch 0 [5]2-8-7 S W Kelly 66/1:0
Flower Seeker 0 [6]2-8-7 E Ahern 16/1:0
3883 **Silsong 18** [3]2-8-6 S Righton 20/1:0
3798 **Davids Symphony 22** [7]2-8-13 Paul Eddery 50/1:0
17 Ran Time 1m 23.94 (1.54) Owned: Mr B Brooks Trained: West Ilsley

4270

2.30 Law Commission Conditions Stakes 3yo+ (C)
£9951 £3680 £1840 **7f26y rnd** **Good** **Inapplicable** Inside

3957 **POLAR WAY 16** [1] Mrs A J Perrett 5-9-0 (114) R Hughes 8/11 FAV: 01-03201: Trkd front pair, smooth hdwy & qcknd to lead over 1f out, rdn out: well bckd: eff at 6f, all wins at 7f: acts on firm & soft, any trk: back to form after disappointing last time (reportedly lost action), gd confidence boost: see 2581 (Gr 1). **112**
3253 **DESERT DESTINY 45** [4] Saeed bin Suroor 4-8-11 t (110) K McEvoy 5/2: 054-0252: Held up in tch, pushed along over 2f out, chsd wnr ins last, al held: 6 wk abs: see 2765, 2184. ½ **107**
3253 **PRINCE TUM TUM 45** [3] J L Dunlop 4-8-11 (97) K Darley 9/2: 11/1-0643: Chsd ldr, briefly led over 1f out, sn outpcd by wnr: clr rem: 6 wk abs: see 1686. 2 **103$**
3605} **ROMARIC 382** [2] J R Norton 3-8-6 (85) J Bramhill 50/1: 103-4: b g Red Ransom - Eternal Reve (Diesis) Held up, no impress fnl 2f: reapp: debut scorer '03 for D Loder (AW mdn, subs turf h'cap unplcd, rtd 85, 1st time visor): eff at 6/7.5f on fast & fibresand: eff in visor, can go well fresh & likes a sharp/turning trk. 5 **94$**
1 May'03 Wolv 6af 81a- D:
2037 **DANCING KING 94** [5]8-9-0 (48) Joanna Badger 150/1: 6262555: Led till over 1f out, fdd: abs. 1 **95$**
5 Ran Time 1m 22.73 (0.33) Owned: Mr K Abdulla Trained: Pulborough

4271

3.00 Sandall House Maiden Auction Stakes Div 2 2yo (E)
£4017 £1236 £618 **7f26y rnd** **Good** **Inapplicable** Inside

3882 **POLAR DAWN 18** [4] B R Millman 2-8-2 (70) S Righton 7/2 FAV: 2641: Held up in tch, switched & styd on for press to lead cl-home: eff at 6/7f on firm & gd grnd, stiff or sharp/turning trk: can progress. **75**
3729 **GEISHA LADY 25** [7] R M Beckett 2-8-2 (74) S Carson 5/1: 63242: Handy & led over 1f out till cl-home: styd longer 7f trip well: see 3729, 3399 & 3141. ½ **73**
3824 **MY GACHO 21** [9] Mrs P N Dutfield 2-8-11 R Havlin 40/1: 03: b c Shinko Forest - Floralia (Auction Ring) Led after 1f, hung left under press & hdd over 1f out, kept on: left debut bhd: cheaply bght Feb foal, half-brother to sev wnrs, incl a mulitple 6/7f 3yo scorer, dam a dual 7f/1m juv wnr: eff over a sharp 7f on gd grnd: encouraging effort & can find a race. hd **81**
3721 **RAFFISH 25** [6] J M P Eustace 2-8-12 (1ow) L Fletcher 40/1: 04: ch g Atraf - Valadon (High Line) Held up, rdn & kept on fnl 2f, not pace to chall: imprvd from intro: 10,000gns Feb foal, half-brother to sev wnrs, incl a multiple wnr at 7f/12f: dam a 3yo scorer: eff at 7f, shapes as if 1m+ will suit: handles gd grnd. nk **81**
3342 **HIGH DYKE 40** [13]2-8-9 G Gibbons 9/2: 0565: Mid-div, eff to press ldrs over 1f out, edged left & onepace dist: op 6/1, 6 wk abs: handles fast & gd grnd: see 3342. 1 **74**
3811 **BADDAM 22** [1]2-8-12 S Drowne 7/1: 406: Rear, kept on late, no threat: apprec 1m+: see 2629. 3 **73**
4050 **BELLA PLUNKETT 11** [16]2-8-2 B Swarbrick(5) 66/1: 007: Towards rear, late gains, nvr threat: may improve in h'caps, poss over further: see 4050. ½ **62**
4205 **TAHLAL 3** [2]2-8-11 G Hind 20/1: 508: Mid-div, prog/short of room over 1f out, sn onepcd. 1½ **65**
3626 **THE KEEP 29** [12]2-8-4 Paul Eddery 14/1: 009: ch f Shinko Forest - Poyle Amber (Sharrood) Handy, btn dist: cheaply bght Apr foal, half-brother to 2 6f wnrs, incl a juv scorer: dam plcd at 6f. shd **60**
3489 **CAPTAIN MARGARET 35** [14]2-8-7 t A McCarthy 8/1: 050: 10th: In tch, rdn & no impress over 1f out. shd **64**
TRAPPETO 0 [3]2-8-13 R Hughes 14/1: 0: 11th: Dwelt & al towards rear, op 10/1. 1½ **67**
4108 **SUMMER CHARM 9** [10]2-8-4 K McEvoy 20/1: 00: 12th: Rear, late prog under kind ride, can improve. ½ **57+**
4046 **MIRAGE PRINCE 11** [8]2-8-11 (73) S W Kelly 16/1: 606540: 13th: Led 1f, cl-up, btn 2f out. ¾ **63**
Indian Well 0 [17]2-8-9 O Urbina 20/1:0
4114 **Silver Creek 8** [15]2-8-7 J Bramhill 40/1:0
Overtop Way 0 [11]2-8-11 J Quinn 33/1:0
Poppyfields 0 [5]2-8-2 A Daly 40/1:0
17 Ran Time 1m 25.39 (2.79) Owned: Mr T E Pocock Trained: Cullompton

4272

3.35 Warwickracecourse Co Uk Handicap Stakes 3yo+ 0-70 (E) **[70]**
£4095 £1260 £630 **6f21y rnd** **Good** **Inapplicable** Inside

3809 **MAGIC AMOUR 22** [4] Ian Williams 6-8-11 VIS (53) K Darley 11/1: 2604001: Led early, sn trkd ldrs, rdn to lead ins last, drvn out: eff at 7f/1m, suited by drop to 6f: acts on firm & gd grnd, prob any trk: suited by application of visor today: see 2057. **61**
3654 **NORTHERN GAMES 28** [10] K A Ryan 5-9-3 bl (59) G Parkin 12/1: 04-00142: Led early, remained handy & led again over 1f out, hdd ins last, ev ch nr fin, just held: reportedly broke blood vessel: op 10/1: see 3352. ½ **65**
4229 **BRANSTON TIGER 2** [1] P D Evans 5-9-6 vis (62) S Hitchcott(3) 9/2 FAV: 6500143: Handy & led 4f out, drvn & hdd over 1f out, kept on: op 7/2: qck reapp: see 4229, 3482 (AW clmr). hd **67**
4054 **INDIANA BLUES 11** [8] A M Balding 3-9-6 (65) K McEvoy 13/2: 4003534: Held up, late gains, not threat front trio: remains a mdn: see 4054 & 2953. 1½ **65**
3790 **ENJOY THE BUZZ 23** [12]5-8-10 (52) S W Kelly 5/1: 0210325: Towards rear, late gains for press. ½ **50**
4126 **VAL DE MAAL 7** [13]4-9-13 (69) O Urbina 11/1: 0-304046: Trkd ldrs, no extra dist: see 1337. nk **66**
4041 **PORT ST CHARLES 11** [7]7-8-12 (54) E Ahern 7/1: 0406027: Chsd ldrs 5f, new yard. 1¾ **46**
4005 **FULL SPATE 13** [5]9-10-0 (70) C J Davies(7) 12/1: 0021608: Mid-div, no impress over 1f out: see 4005. nk **61**
4030 **BEN LOMAND 12** [11]4-9-9 c (65) A Daly 40/1: 00-00309: Bhd, little hdwy: btr 3924. ¾ **54**
4077 **FLEETWOOD BAY 10** [3]4-9-10 (66) R Hughes 13/2: 3602600: 10th: Chsd ldrs, btn dist: btr 3524 (1m). nk **54**

3232 **MACS TALISMAN 45** [6]4-8-10 (52) M Tebbutt 20/1: 0002300: 11th: Al bhd, 6 wk abs: btr 2967, 2801. 2 34
2951 **Full Pitch 58** [14]8-9-9 (65) L Fletcher(3) 20/1:0 203 **Romantic Drama 258** [9]3-9-2 (61) S Drowne 40/1:0
13 Ran Time 1m 10.78 (0.18) Owned: Mrs Maggie Bull Trained: Alvechurch

4273 4.10 Saltisford Nursery Handicap Stakes 2yo (E) [95]
£3978 £1224 £612 **6f21y rnd** **Good** **Inapplicable** Inside

3627 **SIMPLIFY 29** [2] D R Loder 2-8-6 bl (73) K Darley 12/1: 4532501: Dwelt, sn rdn towards rear, strong run for press fnl 1f, led well ins last for first success: eff at 6f, tried 7f, may yet suit: handles firm & gd grnd, stiff/gall or sharp/turning trks: eff in blnks: see 3022, 2597 & 1205. 80
3536 **UNREAL 33** [4] B W Hills 2-8-13 (80) R Hughes 3/1: 6262: Trkd ldrs trav well, rdn & led dist, hdd well ins last: h'cap bow: handles fast & gd grnd: see 3063. *1½* 81
3284 **TESARY 44** [11] E A L Dunlop 2-8-8 (75) E Ahern 7/1: 621433: Chsd ldrs wide, lost pl after 2f, styd on well for press wide fnl 1f, nrst fin: bckd: eff at 5/6f: suffered awkward wide passage, remains interesting for similar: see 3284, 2738. *hd* 75+
2467 **CATWALK CLERIC 76** [14] M J Wallace 2-9-7 (88) A Mullen(7) 10/1: 41204: Held up, kept on wide for press, not able to chall: back to form after lastest: stays a sharp 6f: see 2303 & 1571. *nk* 87
3644 **UNLIMITED 28** [3]2-8-5 (72) G Hind 33/1: 2125035: Led till dist, no extra: stays a sharp 6f, rtn to 5f could suit: see 1868, 1439. *¾* 69
3639 **CASTEROSSA 28** [5]2-8-5 (72) G Gibbons 25/1: 6446: In tch, edged right & no impress fnl 1f. *shd* 69
3951* **MOTH BALL 16** [6]2-9-2 (83) S W Kelly 7/4 FAV: 2317: Dwelt, sn trkd ldrs, rdn & btn dist: well bckd & better expected on h'cap bow: btr 3951. *1¼* 76
3825 **ISLAND SWING 21** [8]2-9-0 (81) S Drowne 33/1: 011408: Chsd ldrs, btn ins last: btr 3521, 2358. *shd* 74
3955 **STORM FURY 16** [7]2-8-3 (70) A McCarthy 25/1: 0309: Held up, eff over 2f out, btn dist, h'cap bow. *½* 61
3848 **MABELLA 20** [12]2-7-13 (66) S Righton 25/1: 05040: 10th: Dwelt & al towards rear: btr 3848. *shd* 57
2109 **DANTES DIAMOND 91** [10]2-8-12 (79) J Quinn 25/1: 22550: 11th: Al rear, abs: btr 1173. *1¾* 65
3614 **Safendonseabiscuit 30** [9]2-8-6 (73) K McEvoy 14/1:0 3825 **Alvarinho Lady 21** [1]2-8-7 (74) Paul Eddery 16/1:0
13 Ran Time 1m 11.53 (0.93) Owned: Jumeirah Racing Trained: Newmarket

4274 4.45 Hoys Co Uk Handicap Stakes 3yo+ 0-75 (E) [74]
£4046 £1245 £623 **1m4f134y** **Good** **Inapplicable** Inside

3926 **SMART JOHN 17** [7] W M Brisbourne 4-9-9 (69) B Swarbrick(5) 11/2: 4213541: Mid-div, hdwy over 3f out, rider drpd whip over 1f out, led ins last & narrowly prevailed under hand riding: eff at 10/12f, stays gall 14f well: acts on fast & gd/soft grnd, prob any trk, likes Haydock: tough & genuine, progressive profile: see 2900. 77
3519 **GREAT VIEW 33** [2] Mrs A L M King 5-9-4 vis (64) J Quinn 14/1: 2402302: Held up, hdwy & narrow lead ins last, just hdd line: bckd at long odds, op 25/1: find similar: see 2830 & 1373. *shd* 71
3785* **WELLINGTON HALL 23** [1] P W Chapple Hyam 6-9-5 (65) A McCarthy 3/1 FAV: 500-1013: Handy & led going well over 2f out, sn rdn & hdd ins last, held cl-home: stays 12.5f, rtn to 10/11f could suit: see 3785. *nk* 71
3734 **DR CERULLO 25** [6] C Tinkler 3-9-2 (73) S Hitchcott(3) 6/1: 1-330244: Rear, styd on for press fnl 2f, not able to reach front trio: see 3734, 2984 & 238. *1½* 77
4033* **SILVER PROPHET 12** [11]5-9-7 (67) Derek Nolan(7) 10/1: 5550015: Dwelt & bhd, late prog for press, no threat: showed more in 4033 (soft). *3* 67
3299 **KYTHIA 42** [8]3-9-1 (72) S Drowne 16/1: 15-43206: Mid-div, hdwy to chall over 1f out, sn outpcd. *¾* 71
3929 **FORT CHURCHILL 17** [4]3-9-1 bl (72) K Darley 9/1: 00-53427: Rear, eff 3f out, no impress dist: op 11/1. *1¼* 69
3929 **ISAAF 17** [13]5-9-8 (68) P Makin(5) 20/1: 2441608: Trkd ldrs, btn 2f out: btr 3105. *3½* 60
4119 **BEST FLIGHT 8** [12]4-9-6 (66) E Ahern 33/1: 1-004009: Chsd ldr, btn over 1f out: btr 2973 (10f, firm). *1¼* 56
4033 **AONINCH 12** [9]4-9-2 (62) R Havlin 11/1: 6026260: 10th: Held up, hdwy wide 3f out, onepcd fnl 2f. *1½* 50
3816 **LEIGHTON 22** [5]4-10-0 (74) R Hughes 20/1: 5402030: 11th: Held up, eff over 3f out, btn 2f out. *2½* 58
2998 **CAROUBIER 55** [10]4-9-9 (69) K McEvoy 33/1: 1000060: 12th: Al towards rear, 8 wk abs: btr 1059 (1m). *½* 52
4119* **DANCE WORLD 8** [3]4-10-0 (6ex) (74) B Reilly(3) 7/1: 0300510: 13th: Led till over 2f out, sn struggling: reportedly unsuited by the grnd: btr 4119. *9* 46
13 Ran Time 2m 43.64 (4.34) Owned: Mr & Mrs D J Smart Trained: Nesscliffe

4275 5.15 Raymond Tooth Racing Maiden Stakes 3yo+ (D)
£4290 £1320 £660 **7f26y rnd** **Good** **Inapplicable** Inside

4483} **VONADAISY 338** [5] W J Haggas 3-8-8 (70) S W Kelly 7/2: 60344-1: b f Averti - Vavona (Ballad Rock) Dwelt, sn trkd ldrs, rdn/led dist, eased final strides: op 9/2, reapp: mdn/h'cap plcd '03 (lightly rcd, rtd 70): eff btwn 6/7f, tried 1m, may yet suit: acts on fast & gd grnd, sharp/turning or gall trk: goes well fresh: lightly rcd, entitled to progress. 73
2510} **BLUEBOK 429** [8] D R Loder 3-8-13 K Darley 5/1: 5-2: Handy, rdn & led over 1f out, hdd dist & not pace of wnr: reapp: unplcd '03 (sole start, mdn, rdn 69): styd this longer 7f trip, 1m could suit: handles gd. *2* 73
3884 **ENCORA BAY 18** [16] P R Chamings 3-8-8 J Quinn 16/1: 63: b f Primo Dominie - Brave Revival (Dancing Brave) Handy, rdn to chall over 1f out, not pace of wnr ins last: 20,000gns purchase, half-sister to a 7f juv wnr, also a 6f juv scorer: dam a 1m 2/3yo wnr: eff around a sharp 7f on gd grnd. *nk* 67
4120 **RUSSIAN APPLAUSE 8** [11] P R Chamings 4-9-4 S Hitchcott(3) 50/1: 004: Rear, rdn & hung left dist but kept on: little form prev, imprvd for drop to sharp 7f on gd grnd. *nk* 71
4081 **MAGIC SPIN 10** [9]4-8-13 S Carson 10/1: 65: Dwelt & held up, hdwy/no room & switched over 1f out, hung left & no extra ins last: op 8/1, longer trip. *2* 62
3884 **MISTER MUJA 18** [10]3-8-13 t E Ahern 9/1: 06: Mid-div, eff 2f out, held dist, broke blood vessel. *nk* 66
2106 **ZALEBE 91** [12]3-8-8 A McCarthy 100/1: 07: Mid-div, eff to press ldrs 2f out, sn no extra, abs. *nk* 60
4952} **MANNYMAN 304** [6]3-8-8 M Tebbutt 33/1: 0-8: Prom, fdd dist, reapp. *nk* 59
4144 **NINE RED 6** [14]3-8-8 (59) P Fitzsimons 20/1: 0-000209: Dwelt, hung right on bend over 3f out, sn btn. *1¼* 56
4055 **OLLIJAY 11** [7]3-8-13 G Gibbons 100/1: 660: 10th: Dwelt & sn bhd, joc reported gelding outpcd. *2½* 56
3631 **MUJAWER 29** [13]3-8-13 BL A Daly 6/1: 500: 11th: Chsd ldrs, struggling fnl 2f, first time blnks. *3* 50
3396 **TANNE BLIXEN 38** [15]3-8-8 G Parkin 100/1: 00: 12th: Led, hdd over 1f out & sn struggling. *8* 31
MASTER RAT 0 [3]3-8-13 R Havlin 50/1: 0: 13th: Dwelt, sn well bhd, t.o: debut. *18* 3
13 **HELIBEL 292** [1]3-8-8 (72) S Drowne 11/4 FAV: 4424-W: U.r. & bolted bef start, withdrawn. 0

WARWICK   MONDAY 30.08.04   Lefthand, Sharp, Turning Track

14 Ran   Time 1m 25.57 (3.17)   Owned: BSmith/ADuke/JNetherthorpe/JGuthrie   Trained: Newmarket

4276	**5.45 Email Warwick@Rht Net Handicap Stakes** 3yo+ 0-70 (E) £4856 £1494 £747 **2m39y** **Good** **Inapplicable** Inside	**[70]**

3853* **MOONSHINE BEACH** 19 [11] P W Hiatt 6-9-13 (69) P Makin(5) 4/1 FAV: P110311: Chsd ldrs, rdn & 77
outpcd 3f out, styd on for press to lead nr line: eff at 2m/2m2f, shapes as a thorough stayer: acts on fast,
gd/soft & polytrack: tough, a credit to connections: see 3853.
3861 **HENRY ISLAND** 19 [2] Mrs A J Bowlby 11-9-1 (57) E Ahern 10/1: 3-504002: Held up, smooth hdwy to ½ 63
lead over 1f out, rdn & hdd nr fin: won this race last term off a 7lb higher mark, loves this trk: see 3057.
2856 **ASTROMANCER** 61 [12] M H Tompkins 4-8-7 (49) K Darley 16/1: 5003103: Held up, rdn & outpcd 3f nk 54
out, styd on for press ins last, not pace of wnr cl-home: 2 month abs: stays 2m well: see 2562 (14f).
2632 **SNOWS RIDE** 70 [4] W R Muir 9-9-4 (60) Paul Eddery 11/1: 0000064: Held up, styd on for press fnl nk 64
2f, not pace of wnr: 10 wk abs, imprvd turf effort: looks well h'capped on turf in comparison to AW form: see 140.
2632 **CALAMINTHA** 70 [13]4-9-8 (64) K McEvoy 9/2: 01-26135: Handy & led 4f out, hdd over 1f out & no extra: 1½ 67
3861 **DARN GOOD** 19 [7]3-8-12 bl (68) R Hughes 8/1: 0112066: Held up, rdn halfway, btn 3f out: btr 3057. 8 64
3861 **TEORBAN** 19 [5]5-9-1 (57) J Quinn 20/1: 010-6107: Rear, eff 2f out, sn no impress: btr 3400. 1 52
3549 **COURT ONE** 32 [15]6-8-4 (46) B Swarbrick(5) 25/1: 0011008: Bhd, hung left over 1f out, sn btn. nk 40
4170 **BOLD BLADE** 4 [10]3-8-4 (60) G Gibbons 33/1: 1002409: Led till 4f out, btn dist, eased: btr 3666. nk 53
2577 **CALIBAN** 72 [16]6-8-5 (47) R Fitzpatrick 14/1: 550-0030: 10th: Keen rear, no ch fnl 2f, abs: btr 2577. 7 33
2035 **SASHAY** 95 [1]6-8-3 (45) Stephanie Hollinshead(5) 22/1: 4-520360: 11th: Prom, lost pl from 6f out, wknd. 1½ 30
3998 **ROSSALL POINT** 14 [6]3-8-6 (62) S Drowne 8/1: 45040: 12th: Mid-div, hdwy 4f out, btn 3f out: btr 3998. 5 42
3502 **FLEETFOOT MAC** 34 [3]3-8-10 VIS (66) S Hitchcott(2) 14/1: 1003400: 13th: Led/dsptd lead, wknd 6f out. 14 35
4119 **VIN DU PAYS** 8 [9]4-8-3 (45) S Carson 33/1: 16-000000: 14th: Mid-div, struggling fnl 4f. 11 5
3307] **BUSINESS TRAVELLER** 395 [14]4-8-3 (45) R Miles(3) 8/1: 5/50540-0: 15th: ch g Titus Livius - 11 0
Dancing Venus (Pursuit of Love) Sn rdn & drpd rear bef halfway, t.o.: 5 month abs: juv nov h'cap scorer
03/04 (rtd 108h+, 2m3f, gd): Flat unplcd '03 (rtd 45, h'cap, G Swinbank).
3970 **JAWWALA** 15 [8]5-9-3 p (59) R Havlin 100/1: 250/00-R0: 16th: b f Green Dancer - Fetch N Carry 5 5
(Alleged) Mid-div, lost pl from halfway, t.o.: unplcd '03 (rtd 59, h'cap): '02 h'cap rnr-up for J Payne): stays
14f, handles gd/soft & hvy grnd, gall or easy trk: with J R Jenkins.
2 Aug'02 Redc 14g/s 72-67 E: 1 Oct'01 Yarm 8hvy 79- D:
16 Ran   Time 3m 33.63(6.13)   Owned: Mr Ken Read   Trained: Banbury

RIPON   MONDAY 30.08.04   Righthand, Sharpish Track

Official Going Good/Soft

4277	**2.20 Bank Holiday Is For Racing Selling Stakes** 2yo (F) £3270 £934 £467 **6f str** **Good 53** **-49 Slow** Inside	

4206 **APETITE** 3 [8] N Bycroft 2-8-11 C Catlin 5/1: 00021: Dwelt & towards rear, rdn & styd on from 66
over 1f out to lead well ins last: op 4/1: no bid: first win: eff at 6/7f on gd & gd/soft grnd: likes sell grade.
4115 **HOWS THAT** 8 [7] P J McBride 2-8-6 R Mullen 12/1: 00002: Rdn towards rear, hdwy to lead over 1f ½ 58
out, hdd ins last, no extra: clr of rem, clmd by K Burke for £6,000: eff at 6f on gd grnd in sell grade: see 3939.
2983 **OUTRAGEOUS FLIRT** 56 [4] A Dickman 2-8-6 R Winston 11/1: 0003: Held up, eff over 2f out, not 6 41
pace of front pair: 8 wk abs, moderate form to date: see 2213.
3348 **THORNBER COURT** 40 [1] A Berry 2-8-6 F Norton 7/1: 04: b f Desert Sun - Goldfinch (Zilzal) nk 40
Handy & led 2f out, hdd over 1f out & fdd: well bckd, op 10/1, 6 wk abs: Jan first foal, £10,500 purchase: dam
unplcd at 6f/1m: sire a smart 6f/1m performer.
4127 **LANE MARSHAL** 7 [9]2-8-11 bl T Eaves(3) 33/1: 0006505: Led/dsptd lead 4f, wknd: btr 3930. 3 37
4006 **BALTHASAR** 13 [3]2-8-11 Dean McKeown 2/1 FAV: 0606: Handy & dsptd lead till halfway, sn fdd. 2½ 30
2939 **SHUCHBAA** 58 [2]2-8-6 (40) N Callan 20/1: 3007: Mid-div, btn 2f out, 2 mth abs: see 1968. nk 24
3901 **DANEHILL FAIRY** 18 [5]2-8-6 bl (45) J Carroll 9/1: 3332048: Prom till halfway, sn btn: btr 3901. 8 3
2882 **ELLIEBOW** 60 [6]2-8-6 D Allan 9/1: 009: br f Pharly - Primo Donna Magna (Primo Dominie) Sn ¾ 1
struggling rear, 2 mth abs: cheaply bght Mar foal, dam unrcd, related to numerous wnrs.
9 Ran   Time 1m 16.09 (6.09)   Owned: Mr N Bycroft   Trained: Malton

4278	**2.50 Billy Nevett Memorial Handicap Stakes** 3yo 0-80 (D) £6201 £1908 £954 **6f str** **Good 53** **-24 Slow** Inside	**[87]**

4027 **IMPERIAL ECHO** 12 [20] T D Barron 3-9-7 (80) P Fessey 12/1: 0220341: Al handy far side & led 2f 88
out, held on well for press: eff at 5f, prob suited by 6/7f: acts on fast & gd/soft: best without visor: see 1460.
3852+ **TROJAN FLIGHT** 19 [19] Mrs J R Ramsden 3-8-15 (64) R Winston 6/4 FAV: 0643212: Held up far side, nk 71+
hdwy over 2f out, short of room repeatedly from over 1f out till well ins last, styd on well cl-home, lkd unlucky:
hvly bckd, op 9/4: remains one to keep on side: see 3852.
4099 **TREGARRON** 9 [18] R Hannon 3-8-12 (71) R Hills 12/1: 00-14203: Chsd ldrs far side, rdn to chall ½ 76
over 1f out, no extra ins last: clr of rem: acts on firm & gd grnd: see 3543, 2649.
4009 **MISARO** 13 [2] P A Blockley 3-9-0 (73) Dean McKeown 10/1: 51-05624: Stands side & led that group 3½ 67+
throughout, styd on for press ins last, no impress on front trio far side: first home from unfav'd stands side
group: acts on gd & gd/soft grnd: worth another look after 4009.
4240 **ELLIOTS CHOICE** 2 [12]3-8-1 bl (60) Danielle McCreery(7) 50/1: 0002405: Slow away & towards rear nk 53
far side, keeping on when short of room over 2f out, no threat to ldrs: qck reappr: mdn: see 3936, 2945 & 1229.
3567 **SESSAY** 31 [6]3-8-9 (68) A Nicholls 16/1: 20-43506: Stands side, in tch, no impress dist: btr 1570. ¾ 59
4039 **FLYING BANTAM** 12 [9]3-8-11 (70) R Ffrench 14/1: 2240247: Mid-div far side, no impress over 1f out. 1½ 56
3599 **PICCOLO PRINCE** 30 [1]3-8-8 (67) F Norton 20/1: 2020058: Chsd ldrs stands side, no impress fnl 1f. 2 47
3131 **BRIDGEWATER BOYS** 51 [14]3-9-7 bl (80) T Eaves(3) 14/1: 3112159: Two well: mod prog, abs. 1¼ 56
3463 **FOX COVERT** 36 [17]3-7-12 (2oh)vis (55) J McAuley 25/1: 2350400: 10th: Led far side 4f, fdd: btr 3203. nk 32
4027 **DISTANT TIMES** 12 [15]3-9-2 (75) D Allan 10/1: 0051060: 11th: Stumbled start, al bhd far side. 1¼ 46
HALLAHOISE HYDRO 94 [8]3-7-12 (57) P M Quinn 66/1: 60-10000: 12th: ch g Lake Coniston - Flo Bear 1 25

(Prince Rupert) Dwelt & al towards rear far side: 3 mth abs, Brit bow: ex-Irish: earlier in '04 landed a h'cap: winning form at 5f on gd/soft grnd: with B S Rothwell.
2439 **OPEN MIND 77** [3]3-7-12 (9oh) (48) Natalia Gemelova(7) 66/1: 40-43060: 13th: Mid-div stands side, no impress fnl 2f, abs: stiff task from out of h'cap: btr 1949. *1½* **20**
4048 **OBE BOLD 11** [13]3-8-9 (68) J Carroll 33/1: 0430100: 14th: Chsd ldrs far side 4f: btr 3808. *shd* **31**
3833 **BAYLAW STAR 21** [7]3-8-8 p (67) N Callan 20/1: 3040060: 15th: Cl-up stands side till over 1f out. *hd* **29**
3806 **ATTACCA 22** [16]3-8-6 (65) C Catlin 50/1: 21-60000: 16th: Chsd ldrs far side till 2f out. *nk* **26**
3833 **Kamenka 21** [5]3-8-10 (69) T Hamilton(3) 16/1:0
3645 **Scooby Dooby Do 28** [11]3-7-12 (7oh)p(50) Hayley Turner(3) 66/1:0
3870 **Party Princess 19** [4]3-8-1 (60) D Fentiman(7) 50/1:0
3273 **George The Best 44** [10]3-8-8 (3ow)(64) Darren Williams 40/1:0
20 Ran Time 1m 14.64 (4.64) Owned: Mr J Stephenson Trained: Thirsk

4279

3.25 Barry Pemberton 60th Birthday Ripon Rowels Stakes Handicap 3yo+ 0-100 (C) **[101]**
£12273 £4655 £2328 **1m rnd** **Good 53** **+10 Fast** Inside

3152 **ANOTHER BOTTLE 49** [13] T P Tate 3-8-10 (83) R Winston 8/1: 33-01131: Trkd ldrs, led 2f out, drvn & held on gamely, all out in a fast time: op 6/1, 7 wk abs: eff at 7f, suited by 1m/9f on fast & gd grnd, goes well fresh: progressive profile, keep on side: see 3152, 2877. **91**
3891 **WILL HE WISH 18** [12] S Gollings 8-9-8 bl (89) T Eaves(3) 33/1: 0001362: Mid-div, drvn to press ldr ins last, just held: stays an easy 1m well: see 3364 (7f). *nk* **96**
3460 **VICIOUS WARRIOR 36** [8] R M Whitaker 5-9-5 (86) Dean McKeown 13/2: 0530223: Al handy trav well, briefly outpcd 2f out, rallied to chall ins last, just held cl-home: well h'capped, can find a race: see 3460. *shd* **93**
3904* **TROUBLE MOUNTAIN 18** [4] M W Easterby 7-8-4 (71) R Ffrench 16/1: 2440214: Pushed along towards rear, switched wide & styd on for press, not pace to chall: eff at 1m, ideally suited by 10f: see 3904, 196. *½* **77**
4095 **IMPERIALISTIC 9** [1]3-9-6 (93) Darren Williams 12/1: 3-411055: Rear, staying on when no room over 2f out till ins last, styd on, hands & heels: much closer with clr passage: eye-catching, keep in mind on easy grnd. *½* **98+**
3546 **GOODBYE MR BOND 32** [7]4-8-4 (71) F Norton 6/1 FAV: 1111326: Held up, short of room over 1f out, kept on late, not able to chall: shade closer with clr run: see 2672. *hd* **75**
4071 **TABLEAU 10** [11]3-8-13 (86) M Hills 10/1: 5-31107: Cl-up, no extra dist: see 3472. *2* **86**
4136+ **NEVADA DESERT 7** [3]4-8-10 (6ex)p (77) S Chin 8/1: 5-452018: Mid-div, eff 2f out, btn dist: btr 4136. *1¼* **74**
4136 **YOUNG MR GRACE 7** [6]4-8-13 (80) D Allan 7/1: 5162139: Led till 2f out, fdd: btr 4136, 3797. *¾* **76**
3608 **ALCHEMIST MASTER 30** [9]5-8-5 p (72) Hayley Turner(3) 14/1: 2114630: 10th: Rear, eff 2f out, no dngr. *shd* **68**
4067 **RETIREMENT 10** [10]5-8-11 (78) N Callan 15/2: 2-130000: 11th: Mid-div, btn when hmpd ins last. *1¼* **71**
4103 **STRONG HAND 9** [5]4-8-7 (74) T Lucas 12/1: 10-63000: 12th: Chsd ldrs trav well over 2f out, sn wknd. *½* **66**
2915 **ACE OF HEARTS 58** [2]5-9-10 (91) R Mullen 14/1: 0211100: 13th: Bhd, eff over 2f out, sn fdd & eased. *8* **70**
13 Ran Time 1m 40.96 (3.46) Owned: Mr J Hanson Trained: Tadcaster

4280

4.00 Listed Ripon Champion Two Yrs Old Trophy 2004 2yo (A)
£15660 £5940 £2970 **6f str** **Good 53** **-24 Slow** Inside

4004* **SPACE SHUTTLE 13** [2] T D Easterby 2-8-11 (93) D Allan 12/1: 2133311: Trkd ldrs, qcknd to lead 2f out, drvn & held on well ins last: op 10/1: eff at 6f, 7f will suit: acts on fast & gd/soft grnd: v useful & progressive performer who deserves chance in Gr 3 company: see 4004. **105**
4022 **ABRAXAS ANTELOPE 12** [4] J Howard Johnson 2-8-11 (100) R Winston 5/4 FAV: 1132: Narrow lead till 2f out, briefly outpcd, rallied well, just held cl-home: hvly bckd: continues in gd form: see 4022. *½* **102**
4214* **SENTIERO ROSSO 3** [6] B Ellison 2-8-11 T Eaves 20/1: 4213: Held up in tch, styd on for press, not pace to chall wnr: qck reapp & up in grade, gd run: acts on gd & hvy grnd: win again after 4214. *nk* **101**
3682* **REQQA 26** [5] M Johnston 2-8-11 R Hills 5/2: 614: Trkd ldrs, outpcd 2f out, kept on cl-home under a kind ride, not pace to chall: well bckd: stronger gall/7f will suit: not knocked about, can impr on this. *½* **99**
3935* **DARIO GEE GEE 16** [1]2-8-11 (95) N Callan 11/2: 1220215: Went left start, held up, no impress fnl 1f. *3* **90**
3956 **SATIN FINISH 16** [3]2-8-6 (97) C Catlin 12/1: 41406: Cl-up, wknd qckly 2f out: btr 3258 (5f). *5* **72**
6 Ran Time 1m 14.63 (4.63) Owned: Jennifer Pallister & Jonathan Gill Trained: Malton

4281

4.35 Family Day Maiden Stakes 3yo+ (D)
£4095 £1260 £630 **1m4f60y** **Good 53** **-02 Slow** Inside

2862 **QUDRAAT 61** [5] E F Vaughan 3-8-13 R Hills 4/1: 501: Handy & led over 2f out, styd on for press to narrowly assert ins last: well bckd, op 13/2: 2 mth abs: eff at 12f, 14f+ may suit: acts on gd grnd: goes well fresh & handles a sharpish trk: lightly rcd & entitled to prog: see 2193. **81**
4125 **LINE DRAWING 7** [9] B W Hills 3-8-13 (74) M Hills 5/2 FAV: 24332: Led, qcknd tempo over 3f out, hdd over 2f out, kept on for press tho' held nr fin: nicely bckd: prob imprvd with forcing tactics, styd this longer 12f trip well: see 2602, 2386 & 1597. *¾* **79**
3990 **SERRAMANNA 14** [1] H R A Cecil 3-8-8 (73) W Ryan 9/2: 62-6533: Chsd ldrs, styd on for press, not pace to chall: clr rem: op 11/4: longer 12f trip may yet suit: see 3990 (h'cap). *1¾* **72**
3997 **SAMARIA 14** [3] C F Wall 3-8-8 (74) R Mullen 3/1: 0424: Mid-div when stumbled halfway, drvn & no impress on ldrs fnl 3f: clr of rem: btr 3997. *5* **65**
3802 **ISMAHAAN 22** [8]5-9-4 F Norton 12/1: 65: Chsd ldrs, no impress fnl 2f: see 3802. *12* **49**
3805 **ALPHA JULIET 22** [7]3-8-8 N Pollard 40/1: 666: Held up, hdwy 4f out, no prog fnl 3f, longer trip. *2* **46**
2383 **SWEET AT HEART 80** [6]3-8-8 Dean McKeown 100/1: 07: b f Catrail - Lost Shadow (First Trump) Al towards rear & nvr a factor, abs: E11,000 first foal: dam unrcd, related to a high-class mid-dist performer. *10* **35**
1964} **MITRASH 452** [2]4-9-9 A Nicholls 66/1: 6-8: b c Darshaan - L'Ideale (Alysheba) Al bhd, reapp: unplcd sole '03 start (rtd 69, mdn, B Hanbury): half-brother to a 1m/10f wnr. *7* **31**
4216 **INK IN GOLD 3** [11]3-8-13 N Callan 33/1: 059: Mid-div, no impress fnl 3f, qck reapp, longer trip. *1½* **29**
3230 **MINSTRELS DOUBLE 45** [4]3-8-13 T Eaves(3) 100/1: 50: 10th: Sn struggling rear, abs, longer trip. *3* **25**
3671} **PAGAN CEREMONY 379** [10]3-8-13 R Winston 11/1: 0-0: 11th: Prom, btn 4f out, reapp. *½* **24**
11 Ran Time 2m 40.11 (6.61) Owned: Mr Hamdan Al Maktoum Trained: Newmarket

---

4282   **5.05 Pateley Bridge Handicap Stakes 3yo 0-70 (E)**
£3864 £1189 £594   **1m2f**   **Good 53**   **-07 Slow**   Inside   [75]

3765 **PRELUDE 23** [11] W M Brisbourne 3-8-9 (56) D Allan 10/1: 5006661: Trkd ldrs, hdwy to duel with
rnr-up fnl 2f, carried head high but drvn to prevail line, all out: first win: eff at 10f, stays an easy 12f: acts
on fast & gd grnd: does not look entirely straightforward, benefitted from a v strong ride today: see 3573, 1587. 63
3854 **FUTOO 19** [9] G M Moore 3-9-5 (66) N Pollard 4/1 JT FAV: 1301342: Led, duelled with wnr fnl 2f,
just denied on line: rest well covered: see 3309.   hd   72
3499 **TANCRED IMP 34** [12] D W Barker 3-7-12 (5oh) (40) D Fentiman(7) 33/1: 3-053003: Mid-div, styd on
for press fnl 2f, not pace to reach front pair: stays 10f: see 1505.   4   45
1163 **QUICKSTYX 138** [8] M R Channon 3-9-7 (68) C Catlin 4/1 JT FAV: 1454: Dwelt & held up, hdwy 3f
out, no impress on front pair over 1f out: 4 mth abs: longer 10f trip may yet suit: see 1163, 1007.   ¾   67
3631 **GAY ROMANCE 29** [2]3-9-1 (62) M Hills 10/1: 0065: Handy, ch 2f out, wknd under press: h'cap bow.   1   60
3182 **BORIS THE SPIDER 48** [10]3-8-3 (50) Hayley Turner(5) 20/1: 2005546: Held up, no dngr.   ¾   47
3201 **LILLIANNA 47** [4]3-9-1 (62) W Ryan 10/1: 40307: Rear, only mod prog for press, abs: btr 2656 (1m).   3   55
4037 **MUSIC MIX 12** [5]3-9-3 (64) R Mullen 11/2: 6-001448: Mid-div, no impress fnl 2f: bckd: btr 3823 (AW).   nk   56
4173 **MYANNABANANA 4** [7]3-7-13 vis (46) R Ffrench 20/1: 4050009: Chsd ldrs, btn 2f out, qck reapp.   nk   37
4249 **SAVANNAH RIVER 2** [1]3-7-12 t (45) F Norton 11/1: 5436040: 10th: Sn struggling rear, t.o.: btr 4249.   19   10
2431 **SMART BOY PRINCE 77** [3]3-8-11 (58) G Edwards(7) 28/1: 1050300: 11th: Prom wide till halfway,
t.o., abs: new yard: btr 1193 (1m, AW).   6   15
3850 **CAYMAN CALYPSO 19** [6]3-9-3 (64) R Winston 8/1: 0606220: 12th: Mid-div, rdn & struggling fnl 3f,
eased: prev with M Jarvis: btr 3850 (1m).   1¾   19
12 Ran   Time 2m 09.33(6.03)   Owned: Mr A P Burgoyne   Trained: Nesscliffe

---

Official Going SOFT (HEAVY places).

4283   **2.15 Unison Family Day E B F Maiden Stakes 2yo (D)**
£4527 £1393 £697   **7f str**   **Soft 91**   **-29 Slow**   Stands Side

3851 **JUST WAZ 19** [7] R M Whitaker 2-9-0 F Lynch 25/1: 01: ch c Woodman - Just Tops (Topsider)
Dwelt, switched & gd hdwy 2f out, led ins fnl 1f, styd on strongly, rdn out: much imprvd for recent debut: Mar
$40,000 foal: eff over a stiff/gall 7f on soft: open to more improvement.   72
ALANI [4] Jedd O'Keeffe 2-8-9 M Fenton 33/1: 2: b f Benny The Dip - Toi Toi (In The Wings)
Front rank, ev ch fnl 1f, only just btn on debut: 7,500gns Mar foal: half-sister to a 9f juv wnr abroad: dam won
over 14f: eff over a stiff/gall 7f, bred to stay mid-dists next term: acts on gd grnd: fine start.   nk   66
ONYERGO [5] J R Weymes 2-9-0 P Mulrennan(3) 33/1: 3: b c Polish Precedent - Trick (Shirley
Heights) Chsd ldrs, kept on under press fnl 1f, just btn in a close fin on debut: Mar foal, cost 7,500gns:
half-brother to wnrs at 6f/12f: dam a mid-dist wnr: eff over a stiff/gall 7f on soft, will stay further: learn from this.   shd   71
3968 **HARRYS HOUSE 15** [8] J J Quinn 2-9-0 J Fanning 11/1: 404: Keen & tried to make all, collared ins
fnl 1f: fine run, btn under 1L: apprec this step up to 7f, acts on soft grnd: see 3968 & 3457.   ½   70
4089 **DESPERATION 10** [6]2-9-0 L Enstone(3) 16/1: 05: Dwelt, recovered to chase ldrs, short of room 2f
out, kept on & btn not far over 1L: apprec this step up to 7f & soft grnd: see 4089 (AW, debut).   ½   69
4171 **ESKDALE 4** [2]2-9-0 (73) P Hanagan 13/2: 00326: Trkd ldrs, onepcd fnl 1f: qck reapp: see 4171 (g/f).   shd   69
TETRA SING [3]2-8-9 G Faulkner 25/1: 7: Dwelt, chsd ldrs wide, btn fnl 1f on debut.   3½   58
4100 **MOZAFIN 9** [1]2-9-0 (81) S Sanders 4/11 FAV: 624328: Front rank, wknd fnl 1f: hvly bckd: had
the best form on offer, incl on easy grnd & something clearly amiss today: see 4100.   ¾   61
8 Ran   Time 1m 32.52 (8.42)   Owned: Mrs L Ziegler   Trained: Scarcroft

---

4284   **2.45 Unison Family Day Claiming Stakes 3yo+ (F)**
£2954 £844 £422   **1m3y str**   **Soft 91**   **-42 Slow**   Stands Side

3232 **EASTERN HOPE 45** [11] Mrs L Stubbs 5-9-11 (59) Kristin Stubbs(7) 10/1: 0300301: Dwelt, hdwy from
rear 2f out, led dist, held on well, rdn out: 6 wk abs: eff over 7f/1m on fast & soft grnd: eff with/without blnks:
runs well fresh & apprec this drop into claim grade: see 1823.   60
3850 **ASH BOLD 19** [13] R E Barr 7-8-11 (40) P Mulrennan(3) 9/1: 0/000///-42: Nvr far away, led briefly
dist, kept on well & not btn far: acts on gd/soft & soft grnd: apprec sell h'caps: see 3850.   nk   44
4007 **ERUPT 13** [8] R E Barr 11-8-11 (40) M Lawson(4) 14/1: 5030043: Held up, imprvd 2f out, ran on fnl
1f & nrst fin: sound run, btn under 1L: has ability when in the mood, best held up for a late chall: see 2497.   nk   43
3830 **SUMMER SPECIAL 21** [5] D W Barker 4-8-11 (45) L Enstone(3) 14/1: 0330004: Prom, ev ch till no
extra cl-home: only btn around 1L: yet to score, see 2544 (seller).   ¾   41
4090 **KINGSTON TOWN 10** [3]4-9-7 p (57) J P Guillambert(3) 13/2: 0406025: Held up, switched & hdwy 2f
out, nrst fin: op 11/2: see 4090 (AW).   hd   50
4008 **DONNAS DOUBLE 13** [4]9-9-3 p (50) P Hanagan 9/4 FAV: 5634346: Chsd ldrs, onepcd fnl 1f: well bckd
on drop to claim grade: first time visor in 4008.   shd   46
4007 **MEHMAAS 13** [12]8-9-1 vis (53) P Mathers(5) 11/1: 0010057: Led till dist, no extra.   2½   40
3830 **NOBLE PURSUIT 21** [1]7-9-1 (49) S Sanders 10/1: 2403008: Chsd ldrs, hmpd & lost place 2f out.   5   32
3700 **TANCRED MISS 26** [2]5-8-8 (40) T Williams 16/1: 00-10309: Chsd ldrs 6f, wknd.   8   11
3649 **TURFTANZER 28** [9]5-8-13 t (30) Janice Webster(7) 66/1: 0004500: 10th: Chsd ldrs, wknd 3f out.   1   14
4133 **CHISEL 7** [7]3-8-5 (50) J Fanning 10/1: 0600050: 11th: Al bhd: clmd for 3,000: see 4133.   ¾   10
3414 **DELTA LADY 38** [10]3-7-12 (40) D Mernagh 33/1: 0605000: 12th: Prom 6f, wknd & fin last.   14   0
12 Ran   Time 1m 47.65 (10.67)   Owned: Mr T C Chiang   Trained: Malton

4285 3.20 Chisholm Bookmakers Blaydon Race A Nursery Handicap 2yo (C) [94]
£10322 £3176 £1588   1m3y str   Soft 91   -34 Slow   Stands Side

4035* **NIGHT OF JOY 12** [6] M A Jarvis 2-9-0 (80) P Robinson 9/2: 4411: Keen & prom, went on 2f out, 5L   94
clr dist, eased down: eff over a stiff/gall 1m, shld stay further: acts on firm & soft grnd: handles a gall or easy
trk: most progressive filly, land qk hat-trick: see 4035.
3698* **LADY MISHA 26** [9] Jedd O'Keeffe 2-8-9 (69) P Hanagan 13/2: 550312: Chsd ldrs, short of room 2f   1¼   73+
out, kept on v well fnl 1f: well clr rem: gd run bhd a prog filly, eff at 7f/1m on gd & soft: see 3698.
4074 **YOUNG THOMAS 10** [2] M L W Bell 2-8-6 (72) M Fenton 10/1: 04433: Chsd ldrs, outpcd fnl 1.5f: 5   68
longer 1m trip: see 4074.
4072 **ARABIAN ANA 10** [7] B Smart 2-8-13 (79) F Lynch 16/1: 6144: Led till 2f out: btr 3429 (gd).   ½   74
3909* **KALMINI 17** [1]2-9-0 (80) S Sanders 7/2 JT FAV: 0215: Rdn in rear, modest late hdwy: bckd from   1   73
11/2: much btr prev on gd & faster grnd: see 3909.
3770 **PATXARAN 23** [3]2-8-4 (70) Rory Moore(5) 16/1: 0546: Chsd ldrs, btn dist: btr 3770 (7f, g/f).   shd   63
3890* **VELVET HEIGHTS 18** [8]2-9-7 (87) G Carter 7/2 JT FAV: 0017: Held up, prog 2f out, sn btn: nicely   1¾   77
bckd under top-weight: more expected for 3890.
3902 **MING VASE 18** [5]2-7-12 (2oh) Dale Gibson 16/1: 62568: Front rank 6f, wknd: see 2802 (AW).   1¾   51
3351 **SHARP N FROSTY 40** [4]2-7-12 (1oh) M Halford(7) 14/1: 4044U: Held up, u.r. after 2f: 6 wk abs.   0
9 Ran Time 1m 47.00 (10.00)   Owned: Mr Saif Ali   Trained: Newmarket

4286 3.55 Unison Family Day Median Auction Maiden Stakes 3-4yo (E)
£3647 £1122 £561   1m2f32y   Soft 91   -34 Slow   Inside

3459 **TYTHEKNOT 36** [3] Jedd O'Keeffe 3-8-13 (74) P Hanagan 11/10 FAV: 2-236431: Trkd ldrs, smooth prog   70
to lead dist, held on gamely cl-home, all out: hvly bckd: deserved win after several gd plcd efforts: eff at 1m,
stays a stiff/gall 10f well: acts on gd & soft grnd, likes to run up with/force the pace: see 3459 & 1108.
626 **ZAKFREE 198** [1] N P Littmoden 3-8-13 bl (66) J P Guillambert(3) 11/2: 04030-22: Dwelt, chsd ldrs,   shd   68
fin well but too late, just failed: long abs: clearly runs well fresh: see 626 (AW clmr).
3854 **SUPER KING 19** [6] N Bycroft 3-8-13 (61) P Robinson 5/2: 0005523: Prom, led briefly 2f out,   nk   67
rallied fnl 1f & just btn in a tight fin: nicely bckd, clr of rem: see 3854 (h'cap).
2886 **CRONKYVODDY 60** [2] Miss Gay Kelleway 3-8-13 t (58) S Sanders 7/1: 6064: Led till 2f out, wknd: 9   9   54
wk abs: only modest form: see 2148 (debut).
3973 **RHUM 15** [5]4-9-7 P Mulrennan(3) 20/1: P5: ch g Bahamian Bounty - Rynavey (Rousillon) Prom, wkng   2½   51
when short of room 3f out: with I Semple & no form yet.
2633 **SUPER BOSTON 70** [4]4-9-7 J Fanning 40/1: 06: b g Saddlers' Hall - Nasowas (Cardinal Flower)   5   44
Chsd ldrs 7f, sn wknd: 10 wk abs & new stable (prev with R Woodhouse): no Flat or bmpr form.
6 Ran Time 2m 19.06 (12.56)   Owned: Arthur Walker and Paul Chapman   Trained: Leyburn

4287 4.30 Chisholm Bookmakers Handicap Stakes 3yo+ 0-80 (D) [76]
£5343 £1644 £822   1m6f97y   Soft 91   No Standard Time   Flip Start

4196+ **SENDINTANK 3** [4] S C Williams 4-9-6 (6ex) (68) S Sanders 1/2 FAV: 1113111: Chsd ldrs, hdwy to   81
lead dist, styd on strongly, readily: well bckd at odds-on: qck reapp & has now won 7 of last 8 starts: eff at
12f, suited by 14f/2m on fibresand, gd & hvy grnd: highly progressive stayer who may make another qck reapp this
Thurs/Fri & will prove hard to beat: see 4196.
4011* **LATE OPPOSITION 13** [5] E A L Dunlop 3-8-8 vis (68) P Robinson 4/1: 2200312: Held up, prog to   1¼   75
chase wnr fnl 1f, flashed tail & kept on well: bckd from 13/2: eff at 11f, stays a gall 14f: met a most prog rival.
3998 **WELKINOS BOY 14** [6] J Mackie 3-8-3 (63) Dale Gibson 20/1: 05633: Prom, led 2f out till dist, no   3½   65
extra: op 14/1: only lightly rcd, acts on gd & soft grnd: see 3998.
4138 **COLORADO FALLS 7** [3] P Monteith 6-9-11 (73) P Hanagan 9/1: 1540434: Chsd ldrs, btn 2f out.   4   69
2963 **EBINZAYD 57** [2]8-9-11 (73) J Fanning 25/1: 45//0//-005: Led till 2f out, wknd: 8 wk abs: see 2444.   2½   66
4106 **TONI ALCALA 9** [1]5-9-13 (75) P Mulrennan(3) 14/1: 4511556: Chsd ldrs 12f, sn wknd: top-weight.   hd   67
6 Ran Time 3m 14.20 ()   Owned: Steve Jones and Phil McGovern   Trained: Newmarket

4288 5.00 North East Motor Show Handicap Stakes 3yo 0-75 (E) [81]
£3533 £1087 £544   1m4f93y   Soft 91   +29 Fast   Inside

3961 **KILLMOREY 16** [1] S C Williams 3-8-9 (62) G Carter 4/1: 00261: Chsd ldr, went on dist, styd on   75
strongly, rdn out: gamble from 6/1, fast time: first success: eff at 1m/10f, apprec this step up to 12f: acts on
gd & soft grnd: stable can do little wrong on the gambling front recently: see 3462.
4166* **QUARRYMOUNT 5** [4] Sir Mark Prescott 3-9-2 (6ex) (69) S Sanders 1/1 FAV: 0-021212: Led till dist,   2½   77
kept on but not pace of wnr: well bckd: qck reapp under a pen, well clr rem: see 4166.
2103 **MARINE CITY 91** [2] M A Jarvis 3-9-7 (74) P Robinson 7/1: 0-1663: Chsd ldr, outpcd halfway, no ch   7   72
with front 2 fnl 2f: top-weight: best 1272 (reapp).
3881* **RICHTEE 19** [3] R A Fahey 3-9-5 (72) P Hanagan 5/2: 1251314: Chsd ldrs, btn 2f out: btr 3881.   3   65
4 Ran Time 2m 45.60(7.70)   Owned: Wood Farm Stud (Waresley) Partnership   Trained: Newmarket

Official Going Good (Good/Soft places)

4289   2.10 European Breeders Fund Roger White Median Auction Maiden Stakes 2yo (D)
£5668 £1744 £872   **7f rnd**   **Good 51**   **-39 Slow**   Inside

3927 **ATLANTIC STORY 17** [6] Saeed bin Suroor 2-9-0 L Dettori 8/1: 01: b c Stormy Atlantic - Story   93
Book Girl (Siberian Express) Made all, clr over 1f out, pushed out to hold on: Apr foal: dam unrcd: much imprvd
from debut & eff over a sharp/undul 7f on gd grnd, pushed out sure to suit: relished switch to forcing tactics: useful.
3554 **RUMBALARA 32** [7] J H M Gosden 2-8-9 J Fortune 9/2: 02: b f Intikhab - Bint Zamayem (Rainbow   ½   86
Quest) Chsd wnr, eff for press over 1f out, flashed tail but kept on, al just held: Feb foal, cost 70,000gns:
half-sister to wnrs over 6f/1m: dam 10f scorer: eff over a sharp/undul 7f, 1m sure to suit: win similar.
3927 **MISTER GENEPI 17** [3] W R Muir 2-9-0 (86) Martin Dwyer 11/4 FAV: 5223: Keen held up, eff over 2f   2   87
out, kept on ins last, nvr a threat: well bckd: consistent, wants the minor trks: see 3927.
3981 **POLLITO 14** [11] B J Meehan 2-9-0 J F McDonald(3) 50/1: 564: Handy, came to nr side rail 3f out,   2½   82
onepace: see 3981.
3927 **PATRONAGE 17** [8]2-9-0 J Murtagh 4/1: 55: Dwelt & bmpd start, in tch, eff 2f out, onepace: see 3927.   nk   81
3786 **ELTIZAAM 23** [9]2-9-0 Dane O'Neill 33/1: 656: Dwelt & bmpd start, bhd, came to stands side 3f   nk   80
out, no impress: see 3470.
4178 **CHICKEN SOUP 4** [1]2-9-0 R L Moore 8/1: 637: Handy, wknd over 1f out: btr 4178 (polytrk, 6f).   3   74
3975 **BENEDICT 14** [4]2-9-0 K Fallon 9/2: 08: In tch, wknd over 2f out: see 3975.   3½   67
3626 **IFIT 29** [2]2-8-9 T Dean(7) 66/1: 009: b f Inchinor - Robin (Slip Anchor) Dwelt, hmpd after 1f,   shd   61
al bhd: Apr first foal, cost E50,000: bred to apprec 7f+.
4179 **BEAUCHAMP TRUMP 4** [5]2-9-0 Lisa Jones 50/1: 00: 10th: In tch, wknd over 2f out.   1¼   64
3993 **WILLIAM JAMES 14** [10]2-9-0 VIS P Doe 66/1: 50: 11th: In tch, wknd over 3f out: visor.   11   42
11 Ran   Time 1m 25.7 (5.6)   Owned: Godolphin   Trained: Newmarket

---

4290   2.40 Jra Golden Jubilee Conditions Stakes 3yo+ (B)
£12122 £4598 £2299   **1m2f18y**   **Good 51**   **-04 Slow**   Inside

3042} **SIGHTS ON GOLD 406** [2] Saeed bin Suroor 5-8-13 t (114) L Dettori 1/1 FAV: 12/2612-1: ch c Indian   107
Ridge - Summer Trysting (Alleged) Handy, hdwy to lead over 1f out, styd on ins last, pushed out: hvly bckd on
reapp: won 1 of 4 '03 starts (Gr 3): won twice in '02, incl in List: suited by 10f, stays 12f on fast & soft grnd,
any trk: wears a t-strap & runs well fresh: sweat at best, prob more in hand here & can rate more highly.
2 Jul'03 Ayr 10gd 114-(114) A: 1 May'03 Sand 10.0g/f 115-(111) A: 1 Sep'02 Leop 10gd 113- :
2 Aug'02 Curr 10sft 113- : 2 Apr'02 Leop 8g/f 103- :
3565 **BATTLE CHANT 31** [3] Mrs A J Perrett 4-8-13 (103) J Murtagh 11/2: 4030-302: Unruly bef race, held   ¾   104
up, hung over 1f out but styd on ins last, not btn far: stays 10f & close to best but looks a moody customer.
3754 **ISLAND SOUND 24** [4] D R C Elsworth 7-8-13 (98) J Fortune 14/1: 10246-63: Rdn to lead, hdd 4f   hd   103
out, sn outpcd, rallied ins last, not btn far: v encouraging & shaped like worth a try over 12f now: see 3754.
1478 **FAMOUS GROUSE 121** [6] R Charlton 4-8-13 (98) R Kingscote 33/1: 1/2020-04: b g Selkirk - Shoot   nk   101$
Clear (Bay Express) In tch, eff over 1f out, kept on ins last, not btn far: 4 mth abs: rnr-up on 2 of 4 '03 starts
(h'caps): won 2 nov stks in '02: stays 10f on fast & soft grnd, any trk: poss best fresh: useful, ran to best.
2 Aug'03 Good 9.9g/f 102-95 B: 2 May'03 Wind 10.0g/f 97-95 C: 1 Oct'02 Nott 8.2sft 97- D:
1 Aug'02 Nott 8.2gd 89- D: 2 Jul'02 Newb 7g/f 90- D:
2772 **CRYSTAL CURLING 65** [5]3-8-0 (99) Martin Dwyer 11/1: 21-33055: With ldr, led over 4f out till   shd   96
over 1f out, held when short of room ins last: 2 mth abs: see 1568.
3464 **ALPHECCA 36** [1]3-8-6 (1ow) (95) K Fallon 11/4: 0-136: Nvr a factor: bckd: see 3464, 2843.   4   96
6 Ran   Time 2m 09.3 (5.5)   Owned: Godolphin   Trained: Newmarket

---

4291   3.15 Toteexacta Sprint Stakes Handicap 3yo+ 0-105 (B)
£23200 £8800 £4400   **5f str**   **Good**   **Inapp**   Stands Side   **[103]**

3977 **ATLANTIC VIKING 14** [9] D Nicholls 9-8-13 (88) L Keniry(3) 10/1: 0400141: Handy, hdwy over 1f out,   93
sn led, kept on, rdn out: best at 5f, stays 7f: acts on firm & gd/soft: back to useful best despite advancing
years, loves Epsom (won this race in '02 off a 2lb lower mark): see 3844.
3622 **TEXAS GOLD 30** [7] W R Muir 6-8-12 (87) J D Smith 8/1: 2406602: Held up, plenty to do over 2f   ½   90
out, styd on ins last, nrst fin, not btn far: back to useful best, made up plenty of grnd: see 1845.
3569 **PLATEAU 31** [10] D Nicholls 5-8-7 (82) P Doe 7/1: 0-602003: Sn rdn in tch, eff stands rail over   nk   84
1f out, nrst fin: joc received a 3-day careless riding ban: ran a similar race here in 2253, h'capped to win.
3971 **TYCHY 15** [2] S C Williams 5-9-8 (92) J Murtagh 8/1: 3005104: Handy, trav well till rdn over 1f   ¾   97
out, onepace: useful run: see 3773 (6f, fills h'cap, stiff tk).
3792 **CORRIDOR CREEPER 23** [1]7-9-6 p (95) R L Moore 11/1: 0236035: Handy, eff over 1f out, onepace: hd   94
won this race off a 10lb lower mark, gd run here: see 2894, 1594.
4238 **BISHOPS COURT 2** [8]10-10-0 (103) L Dettori 5/1 FAV: 3300256: Held up, plenty to do over 1f out,   ½   100
styd on ins last, nrst fin: nicely bckd: top-weight: useful run: see 4238.
3792 **HENRY HALL 23** [4]8-9-2 (91) Kim Tinkler 25/1: 3030007: In tch, eff dist, onepace: see 2359.   nk   87
4031 **JAYANJAY 12** [3]5-8-7 (82) Lisa Jones 14/1: 3152258: Handy, wknd fnl 1f: btr 3827 (6f), 3673.   shd   78
4098 **SPEED COP 9** [6]4-9-5 VIS (94) Martin Dwyer 16/1: 2300469: With ldrs, wknd fnl 1f: joc received a   shd   89
2-day careless riding ban: see 3773.
3567 **GREEN MANALISHI 31** [5]3-8-12 (89) J Fortune 20/1: 3155000: 10th: In tch, hung left dist, wknd.   ½   82
4107 **BRAVE BURT 9** [12]7-8-7 (82) K Fallon 7/1: 0002000: 11th: Made most stands rail, hdd over 1f out,   1¼   71
sn wknd & hmpd cl-home: see 4107, 3960.
4201 **FURTHER OUTLOOK 3** [11]10-9-1 (90) Dane O'Neill 12/1: 0065150: 12th: With ldr, wknd over 1f out.   ¾   77
3622 **WHITBARROW 30** [14]5-9-3 bl (92) R Thomas(5) 12/1: 0000000: 13th: Slow away, bhd, no impress.   2½   72
4027 **SIR ERNEST 12** [13]3-7-12 (1oh)P (74) J F McDonald(3) 50/1: 2042000: 14th: Dwelt, bhd, hmpd over 3f   3   46
out: cheek pieces: see 2227.
14 Ran   Time 55.52 (1.22)   Owned: Mr David Faulkner   Trained: Thirsk

4292 **3.50 Burton & Smith Amateur Derby A Handicap For Gentleman Amateur Riders 3yo+ 0-90 (C) [55]**
£12180 £4620 £2310 **1m4f10y** **Good 51** **-20 Slow** Centre

3964* **TENDER FALCON 15** [8] R J Hodges 4-11-7 (76) Mr A E Lynch 9/2 FAV: 4-510211: Chsd ldrs, hdwy to lead over 2f out, kept on ins last, rdn out: nicely bckd: eff at 10/12f on firm & fast, handles gd/soft & any trk: tough & genuine, in fine form: see 3964. **84**
3964 **FLYING SPIRIT 15** [6] G L Moore 5-11-7 (76) Mr S Walker 5/1: 02-11102: Prom, hdwy to lead over 3f out till over 2f out, sn hung left but kept on, not pace of wnr: back to form on fav'd sharp/undul trk: see 3217. *1¼* **81**
4097 **DESERT ISLAND DISC 9** [5] J J Bridger 7-11-6 (75) Mr S Dobson 9/1: 6151163: In tch, eff 2f out, sn onepace: gd run: see 4097, 3674. *2½* **76**
3794 **SCOTTISH RIVER 23** [2] M D I Usher 5-11-12 (81) Mr L Newnes 14/1: 6612404: Slow away & bhd, eff 2f out, hung left & onepace fnl 2f: prob stays 12f: see 3044. *¾* **81**
3638 **SKYLARKER 28** [11]6-11-5 (74) Mr T Callejo 11/1: 0044155: Dsptd lead till 3f out, wknd dist. *hd* **73**
3681* **FLOTTA 26** [3]5-12-0 (83) Mr E Dehdashti 9/1: 0443016: Bhd, some late gains, no dngr: btr 3681. *1¼* **80**
4076 **LENNEL 10** [10]6-11-2 bl (71) Mr J J Best 9/1: 4132337: In tch, no impress 2f out: consistent prev. *hd* **67**
3926 **ANTICIPATING 17** [1]4-12-0 (83) Mr L Jefford 7/1: 0402008: Dsptd lead, wknd 2f out: see 877. *2½* **75**
4106 **RAJAM 9** [4]6-11-6 vis (75) Mr H Engblom 14/1: 5224009: Al bhd: see 3437. *6* **58**
2471 **WASTED TALENT 76** [9]4-11-7 vis (76) Mr Loek van der Ham 12/1: 531-1200: 10th: Dsptd lead, wknd over 2f out: 11 wk abs: see 2114, 1399. *1½* **57**
3926 **DANAKIL 17** [12]9-11-6 (75) Mr C Guimard 14/1: 4122460: 11th: Al bhd: see 2681, 1986. *3½* **51**
2874 **DISSIDENT 60** [7]6-12-0 vis (83) Mr O Sauer 16/1: 2145650: 12th: Al bhd: 2 mth abs: see 1516, 1484. *10* **44**
12 Ran Time 2m 43.36 (8.56) Owned: Mr P E Axon Trained: Somerton

4293 **4.25 Toteplacepot Handicap Stakes 3yo+ 0-90 (C) [84]**
£10426 £3208 £1604 **1m2f18y** **Good 51** **+11 Fast** Inside

1759 **WIGGY SMITH 107** [7] H Candy 5-9-10 (80) Dane O'Neill 14/1: 15/41-501: Handy, hdwy trav well over 3f out, led over 1f out, styd on, rdn to assert: gd time: eff over 10/11f, stays a slow run 12f on fast & soft, reportedly not firm: any trk: useful & imprvd run: see 1381. **89**
2759 **CAMROSE 65** [6] J L Dunlop 3-9-9 (87) J Fortune 6/1: 21-43252: Handy, hdwy to lead 2f out, hdd over 1f out, onepace: 2 mth abs: gd run, shld find a h'cap: see 2290, 1865. *1½* **93**
4097 **DREAM MAGIC 9** [1] M J Ryan 6-9-5 (75) Martin Dwyer 8/1: 5003233: Dwelt, held up, eff over 1f out, kept on ins last: consistent at present: see 3980, 3949. *hd* **80**
3598 **RONDELET 30** [9] R M Beckett 3-9-3 (81) J Murtagh 9/2: 0232104: Held up, eff & hung left over 1f out, kept on ins last, short of room cl-home: bckd from 7/1: prob ran to form of 3216. *1½* **83**
3815 **BURGUNDY 22** [4]7-8-8 bl (64) P Doe 7/1: 1112125: Slow away, held up, hdwy over 1f out, sn hung left & no extra: btr 3815, 3685. *shd* **66**
2919 **OVER THE RAINBOW 58** [10]3-9-4 (82) K May(7) 33/1: 30-10006: Handy, wknd over 1f out: 2 mth abs. *1* **81**
3892 **KATIYPOUR 18** [8]7-9-5 (75) Lisa Jones 14/1: 1403457: Nvr a factor: see 3694, 3538. *1* **73**
3949 **PRIME POWERED 16** [11]3-9-9 p (87) R L Moore 7/1: 21-55028: In tch, wknd 2f out: btr 3949, 1192. *¾* **83**
3694 **FACTUAL LAD 26** [5]6-9-1 (71) L Keniry(3) 50/1: 0-001009: In tch, outpcd 2f out, mod late gains. *nk* **66**
3938 **RANI TWO 16** [3]5-8-12 (68) N Chalmers(5) 20/1: 0065440: 10th: In tch, wknd 2f out: with W Muir. *¾* **61**
4071* **MACLEAN 10** [2]3-9-2 p (80) K Fallon 3/1 FAV: 1365610: 11th: Rdn to lead, hdd 2f out, sn rdn & wknd tamely: hvly bckd: showed much more enthusiasm in first time cheek pieces in 4071 (soft). *5* **65**
11 Ran Time 2m 09.76 (4.04) Owned: Mrs George Tricks Trained: Wantage

4294 **4.55 Chantilly Claiming Stakes 3yo+ (E)**
£4836 £1488 £744 **6f rnd** **Good 51** **+01 Fast** Outside

4150* **BEAUVRAI 6** [4] D Flood 4-9-6 BL (75) Martin Dwyer 100/30 JT FA: 3002311: Handy trav well, hdwy to lead over 1f out, sn pushed clr, cmftbly: well bckd for new stable: clmd for 12,000: eff at 5/6f on firm, soft & both AWs, likes sharp trks: wore cheek pieces to win last week, first time blnks here: enjoying clmrs: see 4150. **83**
2853 **HURRICANE FLOYD 61** [3] D Nicholls 6-9-12 (77) J Fortune 100/30 JT FA: 3-000042: Dwelt, held up rear, eff over 1f out, kept on ins last, no threat to wnr: clmd for 15000, prev with D Loder, abs: enjoyed drop in trip & class, shld win a clmr/seller: see 1512: *5* **76**
3541 **GAMESETNMATCH 32** [11] W G M Turner 3-8-3 p (57) R Thomas(5) 15/2: 065-6043: With ldr, eff over 1f out, sn outpcd: see 3541, 2873. *¾* **54**
3643 **FIREWORK 28** [6] J Akehurst 6-8-10 (59) K Fallon 4/1: 6501004: In tch, eff over 1f out, onepace. *½* **56**
4118 **TRIPTI 8** [1]4-8-3 (45) J F McDonald(3) 16/1: 0000045: In tch, no extra dist: see 4118, 728. *1¼* **45**
4164 **SOCIAL CONTRACT 5** [2]7-8-8 vis (45) Dane O'Neill 40/1: 0000006: Nvr a factor: see 783, 556. *½* **48**
3976 **BORZOI MAESTRO 14** [10]3-8-13 (72) L Keniry(3) 11/2: 4305067: Led till dist, wknd: best 2048. *nk* **55**
3609 **BEYOND CALCULATION 30** [5]10-8-6 bl (48) Lisa Jones 12/1: 4044508: Held up rear, nvr a factor. *3½* **35**
4070 **BOANERGES 10** [8]7-8-12 (45) R L Moore 20/1: 0500009: In tch, wknd 2f out: lost form: see 1886. *1¾* **36**
4054 **CHAIN OF HOPE 11** [9]3-8-11 (54) J Murtagh 33/1: 006-00: 10th: Al bhd: see 4054. *shd* **37**
4090 **MARENGO 10** [7]10-8-8 (30) P Doe 50/1: 0640000: 11th: Dwelt, al bhd: see 1430. *½* **29**
11 Ran Time 1m 10.8 (3) Owned: Mr Alan Smith (Edinburgh) Trained: Hungerford

4295 **5.30 Mark Tracey 40th Birthday Handicap Stakes 3yo+ 0-80 (D) [85]**
£10660 £3280 £1640 **1m114y rnd** **Good 51** **-08 Slow** Inside

3696 **CARRY ON DOC 26** [14] J W Hills 3-9-3 (74) R L Moore 16/1: 5-361531: Bhd, eff to lead appr fnl 1f, rdn clr: eff at 7f/8.5f on fast, gd & fibresand, likes sharp/undul trks: improving: see 2953, 1321. **82**
4057* **COMPTON DRAKE 11** [2] G A Butler 5-9-8 (72) J Fortune 7/2 FAV: 111-0212: In tch, eff to chall over 1f out, onepace: continues in fine heart: see 4057, 3867. *1¾* **78**
3813 **MR VELOCITY 22** [3] E F Vaughan 4-9-7 (71) J F McDonald(3) 6/1: 0-321063: In tch, eff & short of room 3f out & over 1f out, styd on well ins last: back to form of 2564 & stays 8.5f. *½* **76**
3862 **JACKIE KIELY 19** [5] P S McEntee 3-8-8 t (65) J Brennan(7) 33/1: 1100304: Held up rear, hdwy over 1f out, nrst fin: gd run: wants a return to 10f as in 3238. *1½* **67**

EPSOM   MONDAY 30.08.04   Lefthand, Very Sharp, Undulating Track

3821* **FRANKSALOT 21** [12]4-9-6 (70) J Murtagh 10/1: 0145415: In tch, eff over 2f out, sn onepace: prob nk **71**
just best at 7f as in 3821.
3331* **GRANDALEA 40** [6]3-9-7 (78) K Fallon 6/1: 236-5316: Handy, hdwy to lead dist, sn hdd & wknd. 1 **77**
4067 **PARNASSIAN 10** [1]4-9-6 (70) R Thomas(5) 11/2: 5115437: Held up, eff & short of room over 2f out, hd **68**
sn onepace: see 4067, 3225.
3980 **HAIL THE CHIEF 14** [9]7-9-6 (70) P Doe 20/1: 4030608: Sn led till hdd dist, wknd: see 360. ¾ **66**
3542 **GO SOLO 32** [8]3-9-5 (76) K May(7) 14/1: 63-033539: In tch, wknd over 1f out: see 2901. 1¼ **69**
3826 **JOOLS 21** [10]6-9-10 (74) Dane O'Neill 20/1: 650U600: 10th: In tch, eff dist, nvr a factor: best 1057. ¾ **65**
3963 **ISLAND RAPTURE 15** [11]4-9-7 (71) Lisa Jones 20/1: 0403260: 11th: Slow away, nvr a factor: see 3174. ½ **61**
4456*]**THE PLAYER 339** [7]5-9-8 (72) L Keniry(3) 11/1: 4/41-0: 12th: b g Octagonal - Patria (Mr ½ **61**
Prospector) Keen bhd, nvr a factor: '03 mdn wnr: stays 7f well on fibresand: goes well fresh on a sharp trk.
1 Sep'03 Sout 7af 73a- D:
4141 **TIBER TIGER 6** [13]4-9-11 bl (75) Steven Harrison(7) 16/1: 0055560: 13th: In tch, wknd over 2f out. ¾ **62**
3694 **DANCE ON THE TOP 26** [15]6-9-13 t (77) Martin Dwyer 25/1: 1106500: 14th: Handy, wknd qckly 2f out. 7 **50**
14 Ran   Time 1m 46.82(5.02)   Owned: Stuart Whitehouse & Abbott Racing Partne   Trained: Lambourn

CHEPSTOW   MONDAY 30.08.04   Lefthand, Undulating, Galloping Track

Official Going SOFT

4296   2.25 European Breeders Fund Maiden Stakes Fillies 2yo (D)
£3572 £1099 £550   1m14y   Good/Soft 85   -31 Slow   Stands side

3944 **ALPINE GOLD 16** [3] J L Dunlop 2-8-11 I Mongan 7/1: 001: b f Montjeu - Ski For Gold (Shirley   **80**
Heights) In tch, styd on to lead ins fnl 1f, pushed out, val 4L+: May foal, dam successful at 7f, also plcd up to
2m: sire won numerous Gr1s at 12f: eff at 1m, further will suit in time: acts on gd/soft grnd & an undul/gall trk:
apprec today's step up in trip & is progressing with experience.
3716 **MADAM CAVERSFIELD 25** [11] R Hannon 2-8-11 (71) R Smith 7/1: 5034462: Led 4f, led again 2 out, 2 **72**
hdd ins fnl 1f, not pace easy wnr: eff at 7f, ran to form on step up to 1m: acts on firm & gd/soft grnd: see 3407.
2714 **YOU FOUND ME 66** [9] C Tinkler 2-8-11 D Kinsella 20/1: 063: Mid-div, hung right after halfway, 1½ **69**
styd on fnl 1f, nrst fin: 9 wk abs: signs of encouragement on step up to 1m, acts on gd/soft grnd.
3908 **BIG HOO HAH 17** [5] C A Cyzer 2-8-11 D Sweeney 25/1: 064: Handy over 6f, sn onepcd: clr rem: 1 **67**
stays 1m & now quals for h'caps: see 3908.
3944 **MOONMAIDEN 16** [6]2-8-11 T E Durcan 4/1: 05: ch f Selkirk - Top Table (Shirley Heights) Chsd 7 **53**
ldrs 5f, sn no extra: Feb foal, cost 85,000 gns: half sister to wnrs at 6f/2m: dam plcd at mid-dists: sire decent
performer around 1m: with M R Channon.
FINE LADY [10]2-8-11 D Holland 7/2: 6: ch f Selkirk - Rua d'Oro (El Gran Senor) Cl-up, led ¾ **51**
halfway, hdd 2f out, sn wknd: debut: Jan foal, cost 24,000 gns: half sister to wnr at 7f: dam successful at
6f/1m: sire decent performer around 1m: with M Johnston.
3770 **RESISTANCE HEROINE 23** [8]2-8-11 (78) J F Egan 11/4 FAV: 0037: Handy over 5f, wknd: disapp on 6 **39**
step up to 1m tho' rider reported mount lost action: btr 3770 (7f, fast).
3616 **GARANCE 30** [1]2-8-11 P Dobbs 14/1: 008: Handy over 5f, wknd: see 3616. ½ **38**
3086 **DIZZY LIZZY 52** [7]2-8-11 J Mackay 25/1: 059: Missed break, nvr a factor: 7 wk abs. 20 **0**
4078 **SARAH BROWN 10** [2]2-8-11 p F P Ferris(3) 50/1: 0000: 10th: Cl-up over 3f, fdd: see 2714. dist **0**
SILVER DREAMER [4]2-8-11 A Beech(3) 33/1: 0: 11th: Al well adrift: hung left thr'out on debut. dist **0**
11 Ran   Time 1m 41.21 (9.31)   Owned: Windflower Overseas Holdings Inc   Trained: Arundel

4297   2.55 European Breeders Fund Maiden Stakes Colts & Geldings 2yo (D)
£3543 £1090 £545   1m14y str   Good/Soft 85   -40 Slow   Stands side

4069 **TORRENS 10** [5] M Johnston 2-8-11 D Holland 4/6 FAV: 41: Chsd ldrs, styd on to lead 2f out, drvn   **83**
out to hold on fnl 1f: bckd: apprec step up to 1m, further will suit: acts on gd/soft grnd & a gall/undul trk:
lightly rcd performer who showed battling qualities today: see 4069.
4052 **INCHCAPE ROCK 11** [6] L G Cottrell 2-8-11 D Kinsella 66/1: 0002: ch c Inchinor - Washm (Diesis) ½ **81**
Led 6f, styd cl-up ch ins fnl 1f, just held by wnr: Mar foal, cost 18,000 gns: dam unplcd: sire decent
performer around 7f: left prev mod form bhd on step up to 1m: acts on gd/soft grnd: can find similar.
3798 **MAKTU 22** [4] P F I Cole 2-8-11 N De Souza(5) 16/1: 53: ch c Bien Bien - Shalateeno (Teenoso) 1½ **78**
Rear, hung left under press & lkd held halfway, styd on fnl 1f, nrst fin: Mar foal, cost 4,000 gns: dam successful
at 10f: sire decent performer abroad: eff at 1m, looks in need of further: acts on gd/soft grnd.
3890 **ASAATEEL 18** [1] J L Dunlop 2-8-11 I Mongan 8/1: 004: br c Unfuwain - Alabaq (Riverman) Chsd 2½ **73**
ldrs, prog bef 1f out, no extra ins fnl 1f: Apr foal, dam a smart 10f performer: sire high-class mid-dist performer:
eff at 1m, further will suit: acts on gd/soft grnd.
4078 **JUST DO IT 10** [8]2-8-11 T E Durcan 7/2: 625: Handy over 5f, sn hung left & wknd: reportedly 5 **63**
unsuited by today's easy grnd: showed more in 4078.
3959 **GOLDEN DYNASTY 16** [7]2-8-11 P Dobbs 33/1: 006: Handy 6f, wknd: see 3959. 3 **57**
3053 **SCALE THE HEIGHTS 53** [3]2-8-11 J Mackay 16/1: 007: Rear, nvr a factor. 2 **53**
3721 **MERRYMADCAP 25** [2]2-8-11 J F Egan 20/1: 05668: Handy over 4f, sn wknd: btr 3046. 22 **9**
MOUNT ARAFAT [9]2-8-11 D Sweeney 40/1: 9: Bhd, nvr a factor on debut. 7 **0**
9 Ran   Time 1m 41.92 (10.02)   Owned: Sheikh Mohammed   Trained: Middleham

4298   3.30 Ethel Gold Memorial Sponsored By Pickwicks Nursery Stakes Handicap 2yo (D)   [89]
£4804 £1478 £739   5f16y str   Good/Soft 85   -41 Slow   Stands side

3728 **OUR FUGITIVE 25** [5] A W Carroll 2-9-0 (75) D Holland 11/4 FAV: 40321: Led, hdd well over 1f out,   **87**
regained lead ins fnl 1f, pushed out, val 3L+: eff around 5f on firm & gd/soft grnd: imprvg with every start &
unexposed in h'cap grade: see 3728 & 3476.
3902 **PRINCELY VALE 18** [1] W G M Turner 2-8-8 p (69) C Haddon(7) 9/1: 1113452: Handy, styd on to lead 1¾ **74**
well over 1f out, hdd ins fnl 1f, no extra: eff at 5/7f: see 3212 & 2833.
4187 **BIBURY FLYER 3** [3] M R Channon 2-9-7 (82) B O'Neill(7) 7/2: 6120033: Bhd, prog halfway, kept on 1¾ **82**

1293

ins fnl 1f, no ch with front 2: quick reapp: showed more in 4187 & 3623.
4049 **IM AIMEE 11** [2] P D Evans 2-9-1 (76) F P Ferris(3) 4/1: 2222304: Cl-up till halfway, sn no extra.   2   70
3981 **MOLLY DANCER 14** [4]2-8-10 (71) T E Durcan 7/1: 0035: Handy 3f, sn hung left & wknd: op 9/2.   4   53
4074 **EARL OF LINKS 10** [6]2-8-10 (71) P Dobbs 4/1: 316046: Rear, nvr a factor: btr 1531.   5   38
6 Ran   Time 1m 3.12 (6.32)   Owned: Mr Serafino Agodino   Trained: Alcester

---

4299   4.05 Racecourse Garage Honda Handicap Stakes 3yo+ 35-55 (F)   [57]
£3507 £1002 £501   1m2f36y   Good/Soft 85   -37 Slow   Inside

4189* **MCQUEEN 3** [5] Mrs H Dalton 4-10-1 (6ex) (58) J F Egan 11/4 FAV: 0060211: Made all, went clr 3f   68
out, eased cl-home, val 7L+: op 9/4 on qck reapp: stays 12f, seems suited by 1m/10f on fast & gd, likes gd/soft,
soft & both AWs: acts on a sharp/undul or gall trk: in-form 4yo who can land qck hat-trick.
3916* **BOJANGLES 17** [13] R Brotherton 5-9-10 (53) D Nolan(3) 7/2: 3453412: Handy, styd on to chase wnr   5   57
bef 1f out, al held: tchd 9/2: gd run in defeat: 4lb higher than recent win in 3916.
4037 **COTTON EASTER 12** [3] Mrs A J Bowlby 3-8-12 (49) T Block(7) 33/1: 0060003: Held up, prog wide 3f   2   50
out, nrst fin: showed signs of encouragement on step up in trip & shaped as tho' further will suit: see 2971.
3822 **RIBBONS AND BOWS 21** [9] C A Cyzer 4-9-8 (51) D Sweeney 33/1: 0604004: Prog 4f out, onepcd fnl 1f.   ¾   51
3056 **DENISE BEST 53** [15]6-9-7 p (50) I Mongan 25/1: 0/0501-05: In tch, ev ch 3f out, wknd bef 1f out.   5   42
4145 **GO GREEN 6** [10]3-9-3 t (54) F P Ferris(3) 4/1: 0214326: Chsd ldrs over 7f, no extra: quick reapp: 3   41
disapp eff: showed more in 4145 & 4037.
3850 **LORD LAHAR 19** [11]5-9-2 (45) T E Durcan 20/1: 0-600057: Nvr nrr than mid-div: see 3850.   shd   31
4112 **ZALKANI 9** [7]4-9-2 (45) A Hindley(7) 33/1: 0500408: Rear, prog wide halfway, wknd 2f out: btr 3895.   ½   30
4045 **BLACK LEGEND 11** [2]5-9-2 t (45) J Mackay 10/1: 002/0-249: Rear, prog 5f out, fdd 3f out: btr 3895.   3   25
3395 **MIDSHIPMAN 38** [16]6-9-12 vis t (55) D Holland 6/1: 0022240: 10th: Cl-up & ev ch 3f out, fdd fnl 2f.   5   27
4057 **ANOTHER DEAL 11** [4]5-9-12 (55) D Kinsella 14/1: 3040-000: 11th: Handy 7f, fdd: hung right.   5   19
1564 **Bevier 117** [8]10-8-11 (40) R Smith 25/1:0   3867 **Mark Your Way 19** [6]4-9-9 (52) C Haddon(7) 33/1:0
3996 **Midnight Mambo 14** [1]4-8-11 (40) P Dobbs 50/1:0   2199 **Blue Quiver 88** [14]4-9-11 (54) G Baker 25/1:0
15 Ran   Time 2m 16.39 (12.29)   Owned: Mr R Edwards and Mr W J Swinnerton   Trained: Shifnal

---

4300   4.40 Hayes Electrical Contractors Handicap Stakes 3yo+ 0-70 (E)   [76]
£4053 £1247 £624   1m14y str   Good/Soft 85   -02 Slow   Stands side

3986 **SMOOTHLY DOES IT 14** [12] Mrs A J Bowlby 3-9-0 (62) J F Egan 8/1: 2060401: Mid-div, prog over 3f   69
out, rdn out to lead well ins fnl 1f, styd on well: stays around 1m on fast & soft grnd: 1st win: see 3733 & 1647.
4141 **JOHANNIAN 6** [3] J M Bradley 6-9-13 (69) R Smith 11/2: 0204632: Held up, prog halfway, styd on to   1¾   72
chase wnr ins fnl 1f, al held: quick reapp: anthr gd eff & is v well h'capped: see 4141.
4030 **FEN GYPSY 12** [14] P D Evans 6-10-0 (70) D Nolan(3) 11/2: 1241443: Cl-up, led after 3f, hdd 1f   nk   72
out, no extra wknd ins fnl 1f: tchd 13/2: gd eff, 5lb higher than last win in 3641.
4057 **ELIDORE 11** [15] B Palling 4-9-13 (66) F P Ferris(3) 9/2 FAV: 00-05024: Led, hdd 5f out, styd in   3   66
tch, no extra dist: showed more in 4057.
4124 **MAMORE GAP 7** [4]6-9-11 (67) P Dobbs 25/1: 0005055: Rear, prog 2f out, nrst fin: quick reapp.   ½   63
3898 **CHANDELIER 18** [2]4-8-7 (49) T E Durcan 20/1: 2016006: Dwelt, prog 2f out, nrst fin: btr 3087.   nk   44
4910* **BATHWICK BRUCE 308** [1]6-9-9 (65) G Baker 16/1: 600004-7: b g College Chapel - Naivity (Auction   3½   55
Ring) Handy 5f, no extra fnl 2f: reapp: plcd twice in '03 (h'cap & class stks, rtd 74): prog in '02, won class
stks & 2 h'caps: eff at 7/10f on fast, soft grnd & polytrack: has gone well fresh.
1 Oct'02 Ling 8ap 79a-74 E: 1 Jul'02 Nott 8.2g/f 71- E: 1 Aug'01 Chep 7sft 75- D:
2 Jun'01 Sali 7g/f 80- D:
4141* **LUCEFER 6** [8]6-8-9 (6ex) (51) Dean Williams(7) 6/1: 3440318: Chsd ldrs, wknd dist: qck reapp.   1¼   39
4055 **DUAL PURPOSE 11** [7]9-9-3 (59) D Kinsella 14/1: 0649: Handy over 6f, no extra: btr 4055.   1   45
3922 **HOWS THINGS 17** [10]4-9-1 (57) A Beech(3) 25/1: 223-6000: 10th: Handy 5f, sn wknd: btr 700 (AW).   2½   39
3867 **DUSTY CARPET 19** [11]6-8-13 (55) I Mongan 25/1: 0000000: 11th: In tch over 5f, sn wknd: see 605.   3½   32
4112 **RICHIE BOY 9** [9]3-9-1 P (63) A Quinn(5) 25/1: 0-0600: 12th: Dwelt, sn mid-div, wknd 2f out.   1½   38
3898 **COOL TEMPER 18** [5]8-9-6 (62) D Holland 9/2 J FAV: 5300020: 13th: Rear, nvr a factor: well bckd: 6   28
disapp eff & rider reported mount was reluctant to race: btr 3898 (C/D).
4057 **Seven Shirt 11** [13]3-8-12 (60) J Mackay 50/1:0   1830 **Logger Rhythm 104** [6]4-9-0 (56) D Sweeney 50/1:0
15 Ran   Time 1m 38.88 (6.98)   Owned: Michael Bowlby Racing   Trained: Wantage

---

4301   5.10 Racecourse Garage Mitsubishi Classified Stakes 3yo+ 0-80 (D)   [76]
£5785 £1780 £890   7f16y str   Good/Soft 85   +01 Fast   Stands side

4057 **THREEZEDZZ 11** [4] P D Evans 6-9-2 t (78) F P Ferris(3) 9/2: 0101331: Made all, under press &   83
carried right ins fnl 1f, drvn out: op 3/1: prev eff at 5/6f, now suited by 7f/1m: acts on firm & gd/soft grnd, eff
in a t-strap & loves Chepstow: continues to progress: see 4057 & 3898.
4103 **WINNING VENTURE 9** [7] A W Carroll 7-9-3 (81) G Baker 13/2: 6032002: Keen rear, prog to chase wnr   nk   83
dist, ev ch when hung right ins fnl 1f, just held: clr rem: well h'capped, but on a long losing run.
4073 **MARSHMAN 10** [5] M H Tompkins 5-9-4 BL (82) D Holland 2/1 FAV: 0000033: Rear, prog 3f out, no   3½   77
impress fnl 1f: 1st time blnks: showed more in 4073.
4122 **GIOCOSO 7** [8] B Palling 4-9-4 (82) J F Egan 11/2: 6001454: Cl-up 5f, sn wknd: quick reapp: 5   67
showed more in 3813 (firm).
4082 **STAR PUPIL 10** [9]3-8-11 (76) D Sweeney 10/1: 4200555: Handy 5f, sn wknd: see 1621 & btr 1498.   1½   62
3954 **JAY GEES CHOICE 16** [3]4-9-5 (83) T E Durcan 9/2: 0304046: Al in rear: op 6/1: btr 3954 (fast).   10   45
4007 **SOPHRANO 13** [2]4-9-2 (55) P Bradley 50/1: 0-530337: Handy till halfway, wknd: btr 3880.   5   32
2715 **CRAFTY CALLING 66** [6]4-9-2 (80) N De Souza(5) 16/1: 54-00048: Cl-up over 3f, wknd: 9 wk abs.   1½   29
8 Ran   Time 1m 25.69 (5.89)   Owned: Mr Barry McCabe   Trained: Abergavenny

CHEPSTOW   MONDAY 30.08.04   Lefthand, Undulating, Galloping Track

4302   **5.40 County Of Monmouthshire Raceday Handicap Stakes 3yo 35-55 (F)**   [65]
£3241 £926 £463   **2m49y**   **Good/Soft 85**   -41 Slow   Inside

4092 **SALUT SAINT CLOUD 10** [2] G L Moore 3-9-2 p (53) A Quinn(5) 3/1 FAV: 1333141: Mid-div, led trav v   74
well 4f out, sn went clr, eased cl-home, val 20L+: eff at 10/14f, imprvd for step up to 2m: acts on firm, gd/soft &
fibresand: eff with cheek pieces: won v easily & is unexposed arnd this trip: more prizes await.
3990 **SPECTESTED 14** [4] A W Carroll 3-9-4 p (55) D Holland 7/1: 0025042: Rear, prog 4f out, styd on for   16   57
clr 2nd, no ch v easy wnr: 1st try at 2m: btr 3990.
3580 **GENUINELY 31** [7] W J Musson 3-8-6 (3ow)vis (40) T E Durcan 10/1: 0-006303: Rear, prog 6f out, no   8   37
impress on clr front 2 ins fnl 3f: btr 3367.
3998 **MORNING HAWK 6** [6] J S Moore 3-8-3 bl (40) J F Egan 12/1: 4560404: Led 12f, wknd: btr 3580 (fast).   4   30
3383 **RINNEEN 39** [3]3-8-9 vis (46) P Dobbs 9/2: 0-005345: Handy 9f, wknd over 1m: op 13/2: btr 3051 (12f).   1½   34
4053 **FRAMBO 11** [8]3-7-12 bl t (35) F P Ferris(3) 5/1: 6444336: In tch, chsd ldr after 1m, fdd 4f out.   ¾   22
3572 **BALLET RUSE 31** [5]3-8-11 (48) J Mackay 7/2: 000-007: ch f Rainbow Quest - El Opera (Sadler's   dist   0
Wells) Bhd, prog bef halfway, fdd over 5f out, t.o.: v disapp on step up in trip: mod form in '03 (rtd 53, mdn).
4011 **KNIGHT OF HEARTS 13** [1]3-8-9 (46) I Mongan 14/1: 550048: Handy over 1m, fdd: see 4011.   11   0
8 Ran   Time 3m 48.05(20.25)   Owned: Mr A Grinter   Trained: Brighton

RIPON   TUESDAY 31.08.04   Righthand, Sharp Track

Official Going GOOD/SOFT (SOFT places).

4303   **2.15 Black Sheep Brewery Maiden Auction Stakes 2yo (E)**
£4072 £1253 £626   **5f str**   **Good**   **Fair**   Stands side

3832 **OCEANICO DOT COM 22** [11] A Berry 2-8-5 (67) F Norton 11/4 JT FAV: 0021: Rcd far side, made all,   74
rdn clr dist, styd on well: bckd: eff at 5f on gd & gd/soft, shld stay further: much imprvd, see 3832.
2965 **BOND PUCCINI 57** [13] B Smart 2-8-10   D McGaffin 20/1: 02: Cl-up far side, onepcd fnl 1f: 8 wk   4   67
abs: eff at 5f, 6f + will suit: acts on gd grnd: encouraging eff conceding wnr 5lb: see 2965.
4134 **BOND BABE 8** [3] B Smart 2-8-9   F Lynch 9/2: 4233: Led stands side group, went clr of that group   1¼   63+
ins fnl 1f, al held by far side: shorter priced stablemate of 2nd: op 3/1: gd eff racing on unfav'd stands side.
4108 **BOBS FLYER 10** [7] J G Given 2-8-9   Dean McKeown 10/1: 04: br f Lujain - Gymcrak Flyer (Aragon)   2   57
Sn switched to far side & in tch, hung left & no extra fnl 1f: tchd 16/1: Jan first foal, cost 13,000gns: dam wnr
at 6f/1m: sire decent performer at sprint dists: signs of encouragement.
DISPOL CHARM [14]2-8-2 P Fessey 10/1: 5: br f Charnwood Forest - Phoenix Venture (Thatching)   1¾   45
In tch far side over 3f, no extra: debut: half-sister to a 7f wnr: dam also successful at 7f: sire decent Group
performer around 1m: with T D Barron.
DANETHORPE LADY [10]2-8-6 (1ow) Darren Williams 25/1: 6: b f Brave Act - Annie's Travels (Mac's   1¼   45
Imp) Sn switched far side, nvr nrr than mid-div: debut: Apr foal, cost 7,000gns: half-sister successful at 6f:
dam unrcd: sire group wnr at 7f, later decent performer in US: with D Shaw.
EL POTRO [4]2-8-7 S Sanders 11/4 JT FAV: 7: Bhd stands side, prog halfway, no impress fnl 1f.   2½   39
4089 **MOCHACCINO 11** [6]2-8-2 Hayley Turner(3) 16/1: 08: Cl-up stands side till dist, wknd: see 4089.   nk   33
3761 **THE TERMINATOR 24** [1]2-8-10 P Bradley 100/1: 00009: Handy stands side till halfway, sn wknd.   1   38$
2100 **KIMBERLEY HALL 92** [12]2-8-2 P Hanagan 20/1: 09: Al in rear far side.   ¾   28
2603 **AGREAT DAYOUTWITHU 72** [8]2-8-4 (2ow) R Fitzpatrick 100/1: 00: 11th: Handy stands side 3f, fdd.   2½   23
LIGHTNING PROSPECT [2]2-8-5 G Faulkner 10/1: 0: 12th: Al in rear stands side.   1   21
2336 **MINDFUL 82** [9]2-8-10 K Ghunowa(7) 50/1: 0600: 13th: Al bhd stands side: 8 wk abs.   2½   19
13 Ran   Time 1m 00.84 (3.04)   Owned: The Red and The Green   Trained: Cockerham

4304   **2.45 Green-Tech Classic Premier Claiming Stakes 3-4yo (D)**
£5429 £1670 £835   **1m rnd**   **Good**   **Fast**   Inside

3972 **FAMILIAR AFFAIR 16** [7] B Smart 3-8-9   (78) F Lynch 9/1: 14-001: Made all, went 2L clr halfway,   79
rdn out ins fnl 1f to hold on: clmd for 20,000, op 11/2: eff at 7f/1m on fast & gd grnd: lightly rcd performer who
appreciated gd ride from front on drop to claim grade: see 4921.
4093* **KHANJAR 11** [4] K R Burke 4-9-9   (73) Darren Williams 7/1: 22-24012: Bhd, prog 3f out, styd on to   1   81
chase wnr ins fnl 1f, al held: acts on fast, gd grnd & fibresand: see 4093.
3694 **TODLEA 27** [5] J A Osborne 4-9-3   (78) D Holland 7/4 FAV: 6223103: Keen bhd, eff when short of   nk   76
room 2f out, switched & styd on ins fnl 1f, nrst fin: well bckd: shade closer with clr run: btr 3524 (h'cap).
3973 **FOSSGATE 16** [3] J D Bethell 3-8-9 p (70) P Robinson 13/2: 2036444: Handy 4f, hung right & onepcd   5   64
4093 **COMMANDER BOND 11** [2]3-8-6   (68) J Fanning 25/1: 0100005: Bhd, prog after 2f, wknd fnl 2f: btr 2723.   6   49
3813 **EPHESUS 23** [1]4-9-3 vis (78) I Mongan 5/2: 2200036: Handy over 6f, wknd: see 2540.   ¾   52
4137 **BANANA GROVE 8** [6]3-8-11   (71) F Norton 20/1: 30P147: Al in rear: btr 3805 (med auct mdn).   ½   51
7 Ran   Time 1m 39.7 (2.27)   Owned: Pinnacle Intikhab Partnership   Trained: Thirsk

4305   **3.15 City Of Ripon Stakes Handicap 3yo+ 0-90 (C)**   [88]
£9396 £3564 £1782   **1m2f**   **Good**   **Fast**   Inside

3615 **STRETTON 31** [9] J D Bethell 6-9-1   (75) P Robinson 9/1: 0034401: Mid-div, prog dist, rdn out to   83
lead cl-home: eff at 1m, suited by 10f: acts on firm, gd & handles soft: best delivered late off a strong pace: on
a fair mark & could follow up: see 2896 & 2560.
2483 **LA SYLPHIDE GB 76** [2] G M Moore 7-9-4   (78) S W Kelly 12/1: 10-25602: Led, went clr bef 2f out,   shd   85
under press well ins fnl 1f, hdd cl-home: 11 wk abs: lost little in defeat & can find similar: see 1346.
3029 **GALVANISE 55** [7] B W Hills 3-9-3   (78) R Hughes 13/2: 0-6103: In tch, ev ch 2f out, onepcd fnl   1¾   89
1f: 8 wk abs: acts on fast & gd grnd: shade btr 2523 (fast, mdn).
4036 **TEDSTALE 13** [6] T D Easterby 6-9-4 bl (78) D Allan 33/1: 3645304: Rear, eff when short of room 2f   1½   79

out, kept on ins fnl 1f, no impress: btr 3768 & 1877.

4097* **TELEMACHUS** 10 [4]4-9-11 bl (85) M Fenton 7/1: 0000015: Keen bhd, prog 4f out, no impress dist.		shd	85
3276 **JIMMY BYRNE** 45 [12]4-9-4 (78) T Eaves(3) 14/1: 0561136: Handy, ev ch 3f out, no extra bef 1f out.		½	77
4246 **CATS WHISKERS** 3 [14]5-9-5 (79) Dale Gibson 11/1: 0-034027: In tch over 1m, no extra: qck reapp:		½	77

best form has come at 1m: btr 4246 (1m).

3999 **JABAAR** 14 [10]6-9-9 BL (83) P Mulrennan(3) 7/1: 3562508: Held up, nvr nrr than mid-div: blnks.		shd	80
3815* **ROTUMA** 23 [5]5-9-1 bl (75) D Tudhope(7) 20/1: 1612519: Rear, hmpd after 4f, prog 4f out, wknd dist.		2	69
4084 **COMPTON DRAGON** 11 [11]5-9-0 vis (74) S Sanders 20/1: 5206040: 10th: Missed break, nvr a factor.		2	65
3777 **AKASH** 24 [8]4-10-0 (88) J Fanning 11/1: 20-12000: 11th: Handy 1m, wknd: btr 1437.		5	72
2929ª **RASID** 59 [13]6-9-4 (78) D Holland 12/1: 1005310: 12th: In rear when hit rail after 4f, sn btn:		1½	59

8 wk abs: btr 2929 (gd/soft).

1668 **KENTUCKY BLUE** 112 [3]4-9-8 (82) R Winston 25/1: 0550-300: 13th: In rear when short of room after		10	49

4f, sn btn & eased: long abs: btr 1346.

3892* **STRIDER** 19 [1]3-8-10 VIS (78) K Fallon 9/2 FAV: 00-24410: 14th: In tch over 7f, sn wknd, eased		6	36

fnl 1f: well bckd in first time visor: v disapp: showed more in 3892 (gd/sft).
14 Ran   Time 2m 06.30 (3.0)   Trained: Middleham   Trained: Mr M J Dawson

---

4306   3.45 **Steve Nesbitt Challenge Trophy Nursery Handicap Stakes 2yo   (D)**   [97]
£4887 £1504 £752   6f str   Good   Slow   Stands side

3988 **BREAKING SHADOW** 15 [6] R A Fahey 2-8-3 (72) P Hanagan 4/1: 2331: In tch far side, short of room			83

over 1f out, styd on to lead ins fnl 1f, rdn out: h'cap bow: rider received 3 day whip ban: eff at 5f, imprvd for
step up to 6f: handles fast, acts on gd & gd/soft grnd: open to more improvement: see 3988 & 3652.

3939* **ZOMERLUST** 17 [2] J J Quinn 2-8-9 (78) R Winston 10/1: 312: Cl-up stands side, led that group		2½	80

after 4f, kept on, not pace of wnr far side: acts on gd & gd/soft grnd: imprvd eff in defeat on h'cap bow.

3559* **COLEORTON DANE** 33 [9] K A Ryan 2-8-9 (78) N Callan 7/1: 63213: Led far side group until fnl 1f,		nk	79

no extra: eff at 6f: return to 7f will suit: acts on firm & gd grnd: gd run on h'cap bow: see 3559.

3303 **GENEROUS OPTION** 43 [10] M Johnston 2-9-2 (85) J Fanning 3/1 FAV: 5134: In tch far side, eff when		nk	85

short of room dist, sn switched & kept on, just held for 3rd: well bckd: 6 wk abs: showed more in 3303 (fast).

4224 **BROOKLIME** 3 [8]2-8-9 (78) D Holland 9/1: 64105: In tch far side till dist, no extra: qck reapp.		½	77
2165 **ROSEIN** 90 [7]2-8-9 (78) S Sanders 11/1: 106: In tch far side over 4f, sn hung badly left &		¾	75

onepced: long abs: see 1752 (fibresand).

3902* **MAKE US FLUSH** 19 [1]2-8-7 (76) F Norton 10/1: 0110217: Nvr nrr than mid-div stands side: btr 3902.		2½	66
3935 **WORD PERFECT** 17 [5]2-9-7 (90) K Fallon 7/1: 31158: Al bhd far side: btr 3224 & 1173 (5f).		2½	73
3939 **ALONG THE NILE** 17 [4]2-8-6 (75) L Goncalves 20/1: 0369: In tch stands side over 3f, sn hung		½	57

right & no extra: h'cap bow: btr 3682.

3245 **MELVINO** 46 [3]2-8-7 vis (76) M Fenton 20/1: 40340: 10th: Led 4f stands side, wknd.		1¾	53

10 Ran   Time 1m 14.06 (4.06)   Owned: Mr G Morrill   Trained: Malton

---

4307   4.15 **Sapper Conditions Stakes 2yo   (C)**
£7252 £2751 £1375   5f str   Good   Fair   Stands side

3743 **SUNDANCE** 25 [3] H J Collingridge 2-8-12 J Quinn 9/4: 121: In tch, styd on to lead trav well			100

dist, rdn out: well bckd: eff at 5f on gd grnd & polytrack: likes a sharp trk: improving performer who deserves
step up to List/Group company: see 3743 & 3160.

4025 **BOND CITY** 13 [1] B Smart 2-8-12 (95) F Lynch 9/2: 013352: In tch, prog to chall ins fnl 1f, not		1	95

pace of wnr: op 7/2: back to form on return to sounder surface: see 3266.

4025 **BIGALOS BANDIT** 13 [2] J J Quinn 2-9-0 (99) R Winston 2/1 FAV: 1240433: In tch, ev ch dist, sn no		1¾	92

extra: bckd under top-weight: fin ahd of today's 2nd in 4025 (gd/soft).

3115 **WORLD AT MY FEET** 52 [8] N Bycroft 2-8-9 (85) F Norton 10/1: 21304: In tch, onepcd & sltly short		shd	86

of room ins fnl 1f: clr rem: 7 wk abs: btr 1764 (fast).

MALAIKA [7]2-8-2 Stephanie Hollinshead(5) 66/1: 5: b f Polar Prince - Gold Belt (Bellypha)		5	64

Missed break, prog halfway, fdd dist: debut: Apr foal, sister successful at 1m: half-sister wnr at 5/6f: dam plcd
at 6f: sire decent performer at 1m/10f: with R Hollinshead.

3509 **THEATRE OF DREAMS** 35 [5]2-8-12 (89) A Nicholls 9/1: 54106: Led till dist, wknd & eased: btr 2083.		1	71
2321 **STEAL THE THUNDER** 83 [6]2-8-10 P Mathers(5) 200/1: 055007: Missed break, al in rear.		6	52
4105 **DEN PERRY** 10 [4]2-8-10 C Ely(7) 200/1: 0000058: Missed break, nvr a factor: stiff task.		shd	51

8 Ran   Time 1m 0.10 (2.3)   Owned: Mr Richard Farquhar   Trained: Newmarket

---

4308   4.45 **Eat Sleep Drink At Nags Head Pickhill Handicap Stakes 3yo+ 0-75   (E)**   [79]
£3778 £1162 £581   2m   Good   Fast   Inside

3618 **TRILEMMA** 31 [1] Sir Mark Prescott 3-8-10 (61) S Sanders 9/2: 006-0061: Rear, prog after halfway,			68

styd on to lead ins fnl 1f, rdn out: left prev form bhd on first try at 2m: acts on gd grnd & a sharp trk:
unexposed at this trip & can win more prizes for shrewd trainer: see 3618.

3834 **OOPS** 22 [3] J F Coupland 5-8-8 (45) N Mackay(3) 3/1 FAV: 2-016232: In tch, styd on to lead 3f		¾	50

out, carried head high under press & hdd ins fnl 1f, no extra: bckd from 9/2, clr rem: continues in gd form.

3940 **HEARTHSTEAD DREAM** 17 [6] J D Bethell 3-9-6 (71) J Fanning 5/1: 1512133: Rear, prog 5f out, no		5	71

impress bef 1f out: btr 3649 (12f, fast).

3893 **VICARIO** 19 [7] M L W Bell 3-8-10 (61) J Mackay 11/1: 1332654: Nvr nrr than mid-div: btr 3051 (12f).		7	54
3834 **SIMPLE IDEALS** 22 [8]10-7-12 (35) Kim Tinkler 16/1: 0-540605: Rear, modest late gains: see 90.		nk	27
3810* **SPITTING IMAGE** 23 [4]4-9-10 (61) T Eaves(3) 5/1: 2412316: Led 1f, led again 9f out, hdd 3f out,		5	48

sn wknd: below par effort: btr 3810 (fast).

3611 **CELTIC BLAZE** 31 [9]5-9-3 t p (54) R Winston 12/1: 3060-307: Al in rear: btr 3181.		3	38
3970 **HABITUAL DANCER** 16 [2]3-8-7 (58) P Hanagan 13/2: 6123058: Led after 1f, hdd 9f out, fdd 3f out.		shd	41
3954} **SUBADAR MAJOR** 368 [5]7-7-13 (10w)(50h) (30) J Quinn 100/1: 30/0000-9: b g Komaite - Rather		dist	0

Gorgeous (Billion) In tch 12f, sn wknd & eased, t.o.: reapp: unplcd in all 4 '03 starts (h'caps, rtd 18): plcd
once in '02 (h'cap, rtd 29): mdn h'cap wnr in '01: eff at 13f on fast grnd: with Mrs G S Rees.
1 Jun'01 Ayr 13g/f 32-27 E:
9 Ran   Time 3m 28.10 (3.3)   Owned: Mrs Sonia Rogers   Trained: Newmarket

DEAUVILLE   TUESDAY 24.08.04   Righthand, Galloping Track

Official Going Very Soft

4309   **12.10 Gr 3 Prix de La Nonette 3yo Fillies** ()
£28274 £10282 £7711   **1m2f**   **Very Soft**

2460   **GREY LILAS 72** [8] A Fabre 3-9-0 Gary Stevens : 62-11231: Dictated pace, qcknd 3f out & in   **116+**
command dist, easily: 10 wk abs: earlier 3rd in the French Derby: suited by 10/11f on fast & v soft: goes well fresh:
likes to force the pace: v smart, cld land a valuable prize this autumn: see 2460.
        TRINITY JOY [1] R Gibson 3-9-0   T Jarnet : 2: b f Vettori - Triple Joy (Most Welcome) Held up,   5   **106**
rdn & kept on fnl 3f, no ch with wnr: prob eff at 10f on v soft grnd: useful.
        POLYFIRST [5] Mme C Head Maarek 3-9-0   O Peslier : 3: b f Poliglote - First Turn (Alleged)   ¾   **104**
4 Ran   Time 2m 29.80 ()   Owned: Gestut Ammerland   Trained: France

4310   **1.50 Gr 3 Prix Minerve 3yo Fillies** ()
£25704 £10282 £7711   **1m4f110y**   **Very Soft**

2304* **SILVERSKAYA** [7] J C Rouget 3-9-0 I Mendizabal 17/10 FAV: 111171: Held up, hmpd over 2f out,   **112**
styd on for press to lead ins last: reportedly in season when disapp last time: prev unbtn in 4 career starts: suited
by 12f on gd & v soft grnd: smart, entitled to progress this autumn: see 2304.
2304   **REVERIE SOLITAIRE** [3] C Laffon Parias 3-8-10   O Peslier 67/10: 41342: Trkd ldrs, led briefly dist.   1   **106**
4274} **ANABAA REPUBLIC** [8] F Doumen 3-8-10   E Legrix 16/1: 330-0223: Led 2f out till dist, no extra.   nk   **105**
9 Ran   Time 2m 55.90 ()   Owned: Earl Champ Gignoux   Trained: France

DEAUVILLE   SUNDAY 29.08.04   Righthand, Galloping Track

Official Going Heavy

4311   **2.15 Gr 3 Prix Quincey Fouquet's Barriere 3yo+** ()
£25704 £10282 £7711   **1m str**   **Heavy**

3886   **AUTUMN GLORY 17** [7] G Wragg 4-9-0 (102) S Drowne 411/10: 0-110061: Cl up, led over 1f out, drvn   **108**
& gamely prevailed, all out: suited by 1m, acts on fast, relishes gd/sft & hvy grnd: proving v progressive on an easy
surface & win again in Gr company this autumn: see 1686.
1496*]**KELTOS** [9] C Laffon Parias 6-9-0   M Blancpain 59/10: 011/1222: gr c Kendor - Loxandra (Last   snk   **107**
Tycoon) Trkd ldrs, hdwy & drvn to chall ins last, just held: recent List rnr-up at Vichy, earlier won at M-Laffitte
(stks): missed '03, went to stud but proved a failure: Gr2 wnr & also landed Gr1 Lockinge in '02: suited by 1m on
fast & hvy grnd: smart colt.
1 May'02 Newb 8g/f 124- A: 1 May'02 Sain 8gd 117- : 1 Nov'01 Sain 8hvy 113- : 1 Jun'01 Asco 8gd 116- A:
1851* **MISTER SACHA** [10] J C Rouget 3-9-1   J C Rouget 44/10: 11153: Trkd ldrs & chall dist, no extra.   ¾   **113**
11 Ran   Time 1m 43.20 ()   Owned: Mollers Racing   Trained: Newmarket

4312   **2.45 Gr 2 Grand Prix de Deauville Lucien 3yo+** ()
£52183 £20141 £9613   **1m4f110y**   **Heavy**

1852   **CHERRY MIX** [7] A Fabre 3-8-8 (2ow) T Gillet 5/1: 2-323211: Held up, hdwy to lead dist, sn   **123+**
asserted under hand riding: 2 mth abs: suited by 11/12.5f on gd/sft & hvy grnd: likes a gall trk: smart display,
confirmed mud lover who reportedly now has the Arc as his target in early Oct: see 1158.
1493   **MARTALINE** [5] A Fabre 5-9-3 Gary Stevens 33/10: 124-0512: Led till 2f out, no ch with wnr fnl 1f.   4   **116**
3542} **BAILADOR** [2] A Fabre 4-9-3 A Fabre 54/10: 5-110613: Rear, hdwy to lead 2f out till dist, no extra.   shd   **116**
4000   **SWING WING 12** [4] P F I Cole 5-9-3 (110) S Drowne 66/10: 3-501244: Trkd ldr, ch 2f out, fdd: btr 4000.   3   **112**
3793   **FRANKLINS GARDENS 22** [6]4-9-3 (108) D Boeuf 103/10: /110-447: Cl up till 2f out, wknd: see 1350.   11½   **99**
7 Ran   Time 2m 55.10 ()   Owned: Lagardere Family   Trained: France

4313   **3.20 Gr 3 Prix de Meautry Royal Barriere 3yo+** ()
£25704 £10282 £7711   **6f str**   **Heavy**

2458   **STAR VALLEY 77** [7] J C Rouget 4-9-0 I Mendizabal 74/10: 22-54331: b c Starborough - Valleyrose   **116**
(Royal Academy) Held up, swtchd & drvn to lead well ins last: 11 wk abs: 1m List wnr in '03: stays 1m, suited by
this drop to 6f: acts on gd & hvy grnd: goes well fresh: smart display & further Gr success awaits.
3167   **SWEDISH SHAVE** [6] R Gibson 4-9-0   T Jarnet 11/2: 6-220282: Handy & led just ins last, no extra   2   **110**
when hdd well in last: eff at 6f on hvy: v useful.
952   **STRIKING AMBITION 155** [2] R Charlton 4-9-0 (113) S Drowne 20/1: 1070-903: b c Makbul - Lady   2½   **105**
Roxanne (Cyrano de Bergerac) Led/dsptd lead, briefly led again dist, not pace of front pair: 5 mth abs, prev with G
Bravery: dual '03 List wnr, mdn & List wnr in '02: suited by 6f on fast & hvy: can go well fresh: likes a stiff/gall trk.
1 May'03 Newb 6.0g/f 116-111 A: 1 Apr'03 Asco 6gd 118-108 A: 1 Nov'02 Sain 6hvy 105- : 1 Aug'02 Nott 6g/f 89- E:
3957   **RUM SHOT 15** [8]3-8-11 (100) Dane O'Neill 89/10: 611-40136: Cl up, led 2f out till dist, wknd.   5   **95**
3842   **THE KIDDYKID 21** [9]4-9-5 (110) Gary Stevens 51/10: 5-30146827: Cl up 4f: btr 3842.   ½   **99**
4027   **NIGHTS CROSS 11** [10]3-8-11 vis (99) T Thulliez 20/1: 00033380: 10th: Cl up, wknd qckly over 1f out.   8¾   **77**
10 Ran   Time 1m 13.00()   Owned: A Caro   Trained: France

LINGFIELD **Polytrack** **WEDNESDAY 01.09.04** **Lefthand, V Sharp Track**

Official Going Standard

4314 **1.50 East Grinstead Maiden Stakes Div 1 3yo+ (D)**
£3790 £1166 £583 **1m4f aw** **Going 37** **+09 Fast** Inside

3335 **WEDDING CAKE 42** [1] Sir Michael Stoute 3-8-8 (73) N Mackay(3) 3/1 FAV: 0341: Chsd ldrs, rdn & hdwy to lead dist, styd on well for press: nicely bckd, AW bow, abs: gd time: eff at 10f, suited by this longer 12f trip, could get further: handles fast, gd & polytrack, sharp/turning trks: lightly rcd, entitled to progress: see 3335. **72a**
2740 **CHAMPAGNE SHADOW 67** [8] G L Moore 3-8-13 bl (69) J Fortune 7/1: 4020232: Mid-div, kept on for press, al held by wnr: 10 wk abs: ran to form: see 2740, 2393. 1½ **74a**
3719 **NASSIRIA 27** [7] C E Brittain 3-8-8 p (64) J P Guillambert(3) 16/1: 6600033: Trkd ldrs, wide on bend after 3f, rdn to chall over 1f out, no extra: clr rem: stays 12f on fast & polytrack, in cheekpieces. 2½ **65a**
3967 **TURN N BURN 17** [3] C A Cyzer 3-8-13 (78) Martin Dwyer 4/1: 53-0324: Led till dist, fdd: op 5/2: btr 3967. 5 **63a**
3997 **HANAZAKARI 16** [2]3-8-13 J Quinn 33/1: 05: Rear, lost tch over 2f out, AW bow. 20 **35a**
2879 **FOUR PENCE 62** [9]3-8-13 (68) S Sanders 7/2: 40-426: Slow away, sn handy till over 3f out: abs. 1 **34a**
4056 **SONG OF THE SEA 13** [6]3-8-8 (58) E Ahern 33/1: 0-004007: Prom till halfway, sn struggling. 1½ **27a**
4111 **PETERS PLOY 11** [4]4-9-8 M Henry 100/1: 0008: Chsd ldr, rdn & btn 4f out, t.o., modest form. dist **0a**
AETHELING 0 [5]3-8-8 R Hughes 10/1: 9: b f Swain - Etheldreda (Diesis) V slow away & sn bhd, t.o. 12 **0a**
41**ALPH 11** [10]7-9-8 N Day 7/1: 4W: Withdrawn, ref to enter stalls: see 4111. **0a**
10 Ran Time 2m 32.55 (3.35) Owned: Ballymacoll Stud Trained: Newmarket

4315 **2.20 East Grinstead Maiden Stakes Div 2 3yo+ (D)**
£3780 £1163 £582 **1m4f aw** **Going 37** **-03 Slow** Inside

4032 **ABINGTON ANGEL 14** [7] B J Meehan 3-8-8 h bl (67) J Fortune 10/1: 660-0001: Rear, smooth hdwy wide 3f out & led 2f out, rdn clr, easily, val 10L+: op 8/1: unplcd prev at up to 9f, significant improvement for step up to 12f, will stay further: acts on fm, fast & polytrack: eff in hood & blnks: unexposed at mid-dists: see 4032. **78a+**
3740 **MIKAO 27** [1] M H Tompkins 3-8-13 (80) D Holland 2/1 FAV: 53242: Trkd ldrs, rdn & kept on fnl 2f, no ch with easy wnr: bckd: longer 12f trips may yet suit: handles firm, fast & polytrack: see 3007. 8 **68a**
3618 **SCARRABUS 32** [8] B G Powell 3-8-13 (66) D Sweeney 5/1: 0-406343: Prom, short of room 2f out, onepace: handles fast & polytrack: see 3618 (h'cap). 1 **67a**
3405 **ZUMA 40** [3] R Hannon 3-8-13 P (73) R Hughes 5/1: 0305544: Mid-div, outpcd 3f out, kept on late, no threat: tried cheek pieces, 6 wk abs: see 3405, 3084 & 2386. nk **66a**
3742 **LYSANDERS QUEST 26** [6]6-9-8 (40) N Day 50/1: 0000-005: br g King's Theatre - Haramayda (Doyoun) Rear, eff wide over 2f out, no impress on wnr: unplcd '03 (rtd 45a & 48, h'caps, tried visor, L Montague Hall): dual h'cap rnr-up in '02, AW unplcd (rtd 47a, C/D h'cap): eff btwn 12/14f on fast, gd or polytrack, stiff or sharp trks. nk **65a$**
2 Sep'02 Sand 14g/f 49-49 D: 2 Sep'02 Epso 12gd 53-47 E:
4125 **DREAM VALLEY 9** [9]3-8-8 S Sanders 4/1: 00-66: Chsd ldr & ch 2f out, wknd qckly, longer trip, AW. 3½ **55a**
4111 **CHARING CROSS 11** [4]3-8-13 R Brisland 25/1: 07: Held up & al towards rear. 5 **53a**
MAD 0 [2]3-8-8 J F Egan 12/1: 8: br f Pursuit of Love - Emily Mou (Cadeaux Genereux) Dwelt, in tch, btn 3f out: debut, op 10/1: dam a 1m/10f scorer. nk **47a**
4111 **CONSTRUCTOR 11** [5]3-8-13 Martin Dwyer 14/1: 009: Keen, led till over 2f out, sn wknd. 3 **48a**
9 Ran Time 2m 34.01 (4.81) Owned: Mr F C T Wilson Trained: Upper Lambourn

LINGFIELD **Polytrack** **WEDNESDAY 01.09.04** **Lefthand, Sharp, Undulating Track**

Official Going Good/Firm

4316 **2.50 Crawley Selling Stakes 2yo (G)**
£2961 £846 £423 **6f str** **Good/Firm** **Inapplicable** Stands Side

4179 **LAKESDALE 6** [11] Miss D Mountain 2-8-6 (59) O Urbina 7/2: 0402361: Trkd ldrs, rdn to lead ins last, drvn out: nicely bckd, op 4/1: no bid: qck reapp, first win: eff at 6/7f on fast & soft grnd, stiff/gall or sharp/undul trk: apprec drop to sell grade: see 3930, 3750 & 2115. **60**
4108 **BEAU MARCHE 11** [9] I A Wood 2-8-11 I Mongan 20/1: 5002: Handy, rdn & kept on fnl 1f, not pace of wnr: eff at 6f on fast grnd in sell grade: see 3513. ½ **62**
4127 **DANESCOURT 9** [12] J A Osborne 2-8-11 D Holland 3/1 FAV: 503: Led till rdn & hdd ins last, kept on for press: nicely bckd, op 9/2: clmd for 6,000: turf bow: eff at 6f on fast in sell: clr rem. shd **62**
4129 **ARTADI 9** [18] P M Phelan 2-8-6 bl (50) C Catlin 20/1: 035654: Dwelt, in tch when short of room over 1f out, kept on late, not able to chall: prob handles fast & soft grnd: eff in blnks: see 1574. 2½ **49**
3803 **PIPS PEARL 24** [14]2-8-6 VIS T N Pollard 50/1: 00005: Dwelt, mid-div, kept on late, no threat: vis & t-strap. 1½ **44**
4089 **IMPERATRICE 12** [5]2-8-6 E Ahern 20/1: 06: b f Emperor Jones - Fine Honor (Highest Honor) Chsd ldrs, no impress over 1f out: Feb first foal, dam a dual 10f 3yo scorer abroad. 1½ **39**
4127 **FERRARA FLAME 9** [6]2-8-6 Martin Dwyer 14/1: 007: Dwelt, mid-div, nvr a factor. ¾ **37**
4108 **CABIN FEVER 11** [7]2-8-6 R Smith 11/2: 0508: Mid-div, no impress fnl 2f: see 3848. 1¾ **32**
3864 **SECRET DIVA 21** [15]2-8-6 J F McDonald(3) 50/1: 00009: ch f Dr Devious - Deerussa (Jareer) Chsd ldrs, struggling from halfway: 2,000 Feb foal, half-sister to a dual 5f wnr, also a hdles scorer: dam unrcd. nk **31**
2865 **TIGER HUNTER 62** [8]2-8-11 J Fortune 50/1: 00: 10th: Prom, btn over 1f out, abs. ½ **34**
4146 **JOE NINETY 8** [2]2-8-11 P (47) Derek Nolan(7) 25/1: 0030040: 11th: In tch till over 1f out: cheekpieces. ½ **32**
3627 **TRACKATTACK 31** [3]2-8-11 BL (70) S W Kelly 7/1: 35000: 12th: Mid-div, strugg fnl 2f in blnks. ¾ **30**
4129 **BREGAGLIA 9** [4]2-8-6 vis M Henry 20/1: 00030: 13th: Chsd ldrs till halfway: flattered 3944. ½ **23**
3864 **Listen To Me 21** [17]2-8-11 Paul Eddery 14/1:0
3864 **Ahaz 21** [1]2-8-11 bl(55) S Sanders 12/1:0
3847 **Tinkers First 22** [13]2-8-6 C Haddon(7) 50/1:0
3817 **Time Traveller 23** [10]2-8-11 BL Dane O'Neill 50/1:0
17 Ran Time 1m 11.9 (3.1) Owned: Mr A Cavanagh Trained: Newmarket

4317	3.25 Reigate Handicap Stakes 3yo 56-70 (E)	[77]

£3611 £1111 £556 **6f str** **Good/Firm** **Inapplicable** Stands Side

3333 **CHIMALI 42** [9] J Noseda 3-9-4 VIS (67) E Ahern 10/1: 4-1431: Handy & led over 1f out, rdn out: **77**
op 12/1: eff at 5/6f on fast, soft & polytrack, sharp/undul or stiff trk: goes well fresh & sharpened by vis.
3870* **RISE 21** [12] Andrew Reid 3-9-7 bl (70) J F Egan 10/1: 0012012: Mid-div, styd on for press fnl 2f: see 3870. 1½ **74**
4116* **DANIFAH 10** [5] P D Evans 3-8-13 (6ex) (62) F P Ferris(3) 12/1: 0446113: Led till over 1f out, onepace. ½ **64**
3920 **ASK THE CLERK 19** [17] V Smith 3-9-7 (70) Rory Moore(5) 12/1: 6433054: Mid-div, switched & short ½ **70**
of room/switched again over 1f out, kept on late: shade closer with a clr run, prob not trouble wnr: see 3543.
4110 **UNITED SPIRIT 11** [16]3-9-2 (65) J Fortune 5/1 FAV: 0631145: Reared start, bmpd & held up towards nk **64**
rear, kept on well fnl 1f, nrst fin: not helped by tardy start, prob worth another look: see 3746 (7f).
3870 **DARLA 21** [4]3-9-6 (69) J Murtagh 12/1: 306-0526: Switched right start, rear, kept on late, no danger. 1 **65**
2784 **INNSTYLE 66** [10]3-8-11 (60) S Hitchcott(3) 40/1: 3440-607: b f Daggers Drawn - Tarneem (Zilzal) ¾ **54**
Chsd ldrs, btn dist, 2 month abs: nurs h'cap rnr-up '03 (B Meehan, also mdn plcd): eff at 5f, prob best at 6f:
handles fast & gd grnd, sharp or gall trks: eff in blnks, poss best without. 2 Jul'03 Ling 6gd 74-74 E:
4054 **PURE IMAGINATION 13** [7]3-8-11 (60) R Thomas(5) 25/1: 6306048: In tch, btn dist: btr 4054 (soft). hd **53**
4054 **DANISH MONARCH 13** [18]3-8-8 (57) C Catlin 33/1: 0030069: Mid-div, no impress fnl 2f: btr 3332. ½ **48**
3332 **MINIMUM BID 42** [20]3-8-8 (57) S Sanders 8/1: 3-002020: 10th: Hung right throughout, mod late gains. hd **47**
4169 **ACE CLUB 7** [14]3-8-8 (57) D Holland 11/2: 1-500420: 11th: Rear, hdwy 2f out, no prog dist: btr 4169. ¾ **52**
4054 **NIKIFOROS 13** [13]3-8-12 (61) N Day 40/1: 0604400: 12th: Mid-div, btn over 1f out: btr 3331. 1 **46**
4110 **MUTASSEM 11** [2]3-8-9 (58) M Henry 66/1: 6-000000: 13th: In tch, short of room 2f out, sn struggling. shd **43**
3744 **SMOKIN JOE 26** [11]3-8-8 vis (57) N Pollard 20/1: 0500000: 14th: Chsd ldrs, btn 2f out: btr 3774 (AW). shd **44**
3870 **TURKISH DELIGHT 21** [19]3-8-8 P (57) J Edmunds 14/1: 6003000: 15th: Al towards rear: btr 3203. ½ **39**
3858 **WITCHES BROOM 21** [15]3-8-8 (57) Martin Dwyer 33/1: 0360: 16th: Al bhd, reportedly lost action. 1¼ **35**
3789* **MISS JUDGEMENT 25** [3]3-9-1 (64) R Miles(3) 9/1: 2130010: 17th: In tch, struggling fnl 2f: joc 4 **30**
reported he was nvr able to restrain filly from her low draw: btr 3789 (C/D).
3725 **BLACK SABBETH 27** [1]3-9-1 (64) D Sweeney 50/1: 000640: 18th: In tch, rdn & struggling from halfway. shd **30**
4109 **Alizar 11** [6]3-8-7 (1oh)(55) Lisa Jones 50/1:0   3789 **Sweet Pickle 25** [8]3-9-3 (66) Dane O'Neill 33/1:0
20 Ran   Time 1m 10.33 (1.53)   Owned: Mrs Susan Roy   Trained: Newmarket

Official Going Standard

4318	3.55 Horsham Handicap Stakes 3yo 71-85 (D)	[92]

£7155 £2202 £1101 **7f aw rnd** **Going 37** **+06 Fast** Inside

4148 **MAJORS CAST 8** [3] J Noseda 3-9-7 (85) E Ahern 8/1: 3131: Al handy trav well & led ins last under **95a**
hand riding: gd time: h'cap/AW bow: eff at 7f on fast & soft grnd, imprvd again here on polytrack: prog.
3550 **ECCENTRIC 34** [2] Andrew Reid 3-9-2 (80) J F Egan 8/1: 1042202: Led, hdd & hung right ins last, nk **89a**
rallied gamely, al just held: tough front running type who loves this trk: see 3331, 3198 & 933 (C/D).
4180+ **DISTANT CONNECTION 6** [5] A P Jarvis 3-9-13 (6ex) (91) D Holland 6/4 FAV: 1532013: Trkd front 2½ **95a**
pair, eff to chall over 1f out, no extra ins last: nicely bckd, useful: see 4180.
3928 **ZERLINA 19** [10] W J Musson 3-9-3 (81) C Catlin 66/1: 201-0004: Rear, late gains for press, no threat. shd **85a**
2767 **OUR JAFFA 67** [9]3-9-5 (83) J Murtagh 20/1: 42-41125: Mid-div, eff 2f out, no prog dist: abs: see 2767. 1½ **84a**
3972 **FORTHRIGHT 17** [6]3-9-7 p (85) J P Guillambert(3) 33/1: 4560006: Chsd ldrs, btn over 1f out: btr 325 (10f). ½ **85a**
3216 **WHITGIFT ROCK 48** [4]3-8-11 (75) J Quinn 12/1: 0003207: Chsd ldrs early, sn lost pl & nvr factor: abs. 5 **66a**
3447 **I WONT DANCE 39** [7]3-8-9 (73) R Hughes 20/1: 12-00048: Rear, nvr land a blow: btr 3447. hd **63a**
3814 **GO BANANAS 24** [1]3-9-6 (84) J Fortune 16/1: 3516-649: Mid-div, btn 2f out: btr 3338. 1¾ **71a**
1770 **DAVORIN 109** [8]3-9-5 VIS (83) S Sanders 12/1: 160: 10th: Slow away, sn rdn, al rear: abs, lkd 1½ **67a**
reluctant in first time visor: btr 1152 (g/s).
3791 **ST SAVARIN 25** [13]3-8-12 (76) N Pollard 20/1: 0033100: 11th: Mid-div, struggling from halfway. 3 **54a**
3744* **Finders Keepers 26** [14]3-9-1 (79) Dane O'Neill 16/1:0 3684 **Extra Cover 28** [12]3-8-8 (72) R Mullen 33/1:0
13 Ran   Time 1m 24.95 (2.15)   Owned: Mrs Susan Roy   Trained: Newmarket

4319	4.30 Andrew Macfarlane Handicap Stakes 3yo+ 46-55 (F)	[63]

£2946 £842 £421 **2m aw** **Going 37** **-14 Slow** Inside

3674 **MOST SAUCY 29** [8] A Wood 8-9-4 (53) J Murtagh 7/1: 5043301: Rear, hdwy from halfway, styd on **58a**
for press to lead well in last: eff at 10f/2m on firm, hvy & both AWs: loves Lingfield: see 1286.
4151 **PEAK PARK 8** [11] J A R Toller 4-8-11 vis (46) E Ahern 9/2: 0-002032: Handy & chsd ldr trav well ½ **49a**
from over 4f out, sltly hmpd over 1f out & briefly led ins last, nt pace wnr: acts on firm, fast & polytrack.
1960 **MONTOSARI 100** [2] P Mitchell 5-9-5 (54) D Holland 12/1: 1631203: Mid-div, hdwy wide to lead over nk **56a**
2f out, hdd ins last & no extra: 3 month abs: styd longer 2m trip well: see 1412, 1243.
3822 **VANDENBERGHE 23** [6] J A Osborne 5-9-4 (53) S W Kelly 7/2 FAV: 3563324: Mid-div, onepace fnl 2f. 3½ **52a**
4037 **STYLISH SUNRISE 14** [10]3-8-2 (9oh)VIS t (50) D Kinsella 33/1: 4350305: In tch, hmpd 2f out, onepace. 1 **48a**
3982 **WALTZING BEAU 16** [7]3-8-7 (4oh) (55) R Miles(3) 33/1: 0002366: Mid-div, led 7f out till over 2f nk **52a**
out, sn short of room but no extra: btr 3055 (11f).
3887 **COMPTON ECLAIRE 20** [4]4-9-6 bl (55) J Fortune 4/1: 6124247: Dwelt & rear, late gains, no threat. ½ **51a**
4111 **MADAME MARIE 11** [13]4-9-2 (51) Lisa Jones 33/1: 2060008: Keen & al bhd: longer trip. 8 **39a**
3493 **CIRCUS MAXIMUS 37** [1]7-9-4 p (53) S Sanders 11/2: 0-040239: Mid-div, sn rdn & struggling fnl 3f. 19 **26a**
3765 **COLUMBIAN EMERALD 25** [9]3-8-0 (11oh) (48) Martin Dwyer 33/1: 04500: 10th: Bhd, btn 4f out. 21 **4a**
3454 **ASH HAB 39** [12]6-9-6 P (55) Derek Nolan(7) 66/1: 13000//-00: 11th: Al rear: cheek pieces, new yard. 1¾ **9a**
3819† **FINNFOREST 375** [5]4-9-4 (53) J F Egan 20/1: 004025-0: 12th: ch g Eagle Eyed - Stockrose (Horage) 3 **4a**
Keen & led after 3f till 7f out, sn wknd: reapp: h'cap rnr up '03: auct mdn plcd '02 (rtd 66): eff at 1m/10f on
firm & fast ground: handles a sharp/undul or gall trk. 2 Aug'03 Brig 9.9fm 53-53 F:

LINGFIELD Polytrack WEDNESDAY 01.09.04 Lefthand, V Sharp Track

204 **QUEENSBERRY** 260 [14]5-9-2 BL (51) I Mongan 20/1: 020412-0: 13th: b g Up And At 'em - Princess   *dist* **0a**
Poquito (Hard Fought) Chsd ldrs, struggling fnl 3f: blnks, 5 month jumps abs: dual AW clmr wnr '03 for N Littmoden:
mdn placed '02 (rtd 66a): both wins at 8.5f, stays 12f: likes fibresand & a sharp trk: eff in vis/chkpcs, tried blnks.
2 Dec'03 Sout 11af 46a-(49) F: 1 Dec'03 Sout 8af 54a-49 F: 2 Oct'03 Wolv 12af 54a-(57) F: 2 Mar'03 Wolv 8.5af 63a-(65) G:
1 Feb'03 Wolv 8.5af 68a-(58) G: 1 Feb'03 Wolv 8.4af 61a- F: 2 Jan'03 Wolv 6af 58a- G:
4033 **FUTURE TO FUTURE** 14 [3]4-9-0 (49) C Catlin 50/1: F060-00: 14th: Led 3f, bhd from halfway, t.o.   3½ **0a**
14 Ran   Time 3m 28.11 (8.11)   Owned: Mrs A M Riney   Trained: Upper Lambourn

4320   5.00 Redhill Apprentice Classified Stakes 3yo+ 0-60 (E)
     £3474 £1069 £535   1m aw rnd   Going 37   -12 Slow   Outside

4141 **LONDONER** 8 [10] S Dow 6-9-3 (60) Lisa Jones 5/1: 5352001: Made all, pulled clr over 1f out, in   **69a+**
command dist, readily: eff at 7f/10f on firm, gd & polytrack: likes to force the pace on sharp trk: see 2334.
4044 **BLUE JAVA** 13 [12] H Morrison 3-8-12 (59) L Fletcher 6/1: 0-000252: Mid-div wide, styd on to   2½ **63a**
chase wnr, at held: eff at 7f/1m on gd grnd, prob handles both AWs: see 4044 & 3515.
3516 **KNICKYKNACKIENOO** 35 [4] A G Newcombe 3-8-12 (59) D Nolan 4/1 FAV: 0310253: Held up, short of   ½ **62a**
room 2f out, kept on for press, nrst fin: closer with a clr passage: acts on firm, soft & polytrk: see 3455 & 2701.
4126 **TREETOPS HOTEL** 9 [1] B R Johnson 5-9-3 VIS t (60) N Chalmers(3) 11/2: 0242004: Trkd ldrs, switched   nk **61a**
& kept on for press despite awkward head carriage, no threat: first time visor, op 8/1: btr 3443.
3996 **KELSEAS KOLBY** 16 [8]4-9-3 vis (57) R Thomas(3) 11/2: 4344225: Keen & prom, chsd wnr over 2f out   ¾ **60a**
till dist, no extra: just btr 3996 & 3812.
1618* **STATE OF BALANCE** 117 [6]6-9-0 (60) L Keniry 6/1: 040-0416: Rear, wide, only mod prog: btr 1618 (10f).2 **53a**
3916 **RAHEEL** 19 [7]4-9-3 t (60) S Hitchcott 10/1: 1430007: Mid-div, btn over 1f out: btr 757 (10f).   3½ **49a**
3846 **MY SUNSHINE** 22 [9]3-8-9 (59) A Medeiros(3) 33/1: 00-0008: b f Alzao - Sunlit Ride (Ahonoora)   1 **44a**
Mid-div wide, btn 2f out: unplcd '03 (rtd 68, mdn, debut).
4032 **LADY BLADE** 14 [11]3-8-9 bl (60) C Haddon(3) 20/1: 0-040509: Chsd ldrs, chsd wnr 4f out till over   ½ **43a**
2f out, sn wknd: btr 3630.
2485 **CHICA ROCA** 77 [5]3-8-9 t (60) J F McDonald 50/1: 50-00600: 10th: Keen in mid-div, struggling halfway.   1¼ **40a**
1791 **REIGN OF FIRE** 107 [3]3-8-9 (60) Derek Nolan(5) 12/1: 46-000: 11th: Mid-div, btn 3f out, abs, new yard.   6 **30a**
3604 **CARLBURG** 32 [2]3-8-12 (60) J P Guillambert 25/1: 200-0000: 12th: Chsd wnr, wknd qckly 2f out.   5 **24a**
12 Ran   Time 1m 40.12(3.92)   Owned: Mr P McCarthy   Trained: Epsom

YORK WEDNESDAY 01.09.04 Lefthand, Flat, Galloping Track

Official Going Good/Soft changing to Good after 2.40

4321   2.10 Patrington Haven Leisure Park Stakes Handicap 3yo 56-70 (E)   [76]
     £5660 £1742 £871   7f205y rnd   Good 40   -00 Slow   Inside

4137* **EBORACUM** 9 [1] T D Easterby 3-9-6 (6ex)(68) D Allan 9/1: 0220411: Chsd ldrs, styd on to lead   **81**
dist, rdn out, val bit more: eff at 1m/10f on fast & gd/soft: eff in blnks: improving, see 4137.
4044 **DISPOL VELETA** 13 [3] T D Barron 3-9-3 (65) N Callan 9/1: 0010002: Bhd, prog halfway, styd on to   2½ **70**
chase wnr ins fnl 1f, al held: back to form after a couple of disapp efforts: btr 2495 (fibresand).
3410 **CHIGORIN** 40 [8] J M P Eustace 3-9-3 (65) T E Durcan 10/1: 03-06003: Chsd ldrs, prog 3f out,   1 **68**
short of room dist, kept on fnl 1f, no extra: see 6 wk abs: encouraging eff & can find a race: see 2773.
3979 **HUNTERS VALLEY** 16 [16] R Hannon 3-9-4 (66) L Dettori 14/1: 3-024044: Led, hdd dist, no extra.   ½ **68**
3679 **SIERRA** 28 [5]3-9-0 (62) K McEvoy 25/1: 0-5665: Handy over 6f, no extra: see 2692.   1¾ **60**
3906 **ALMOND WILLOW** 20 [4]3-9-3 (65) T P Queally 10/1: 361-0206: Mid-div, prog bef 1f out, nrst fin.   hd **62**
3700 **HEVERSHAM** 28 [13]3-9-5 (67) M Tebbutt 40/1: 0425007: Nvr nrr than mid-div: btr 2854 (fast, clmr).   ½ **63**
3835 **WRENLANE** 23 [9]3-9-0 (62) P Hanagan 6/1 FAV: 0-265048: Mid-div when no room bef 1f out, sn onepcd.½ **57**
3990 **CHARLIE TANGO** 16 [15]3-9-4 (66) K Darley 12/1: 1343509: Nvr nrr than mid-div: btr 3529.   1 **59**
3647 **ROSIE MAC** 30 [17]3-8-9 (57) F Norton 40/1: 634660: 10th: Handy over 6f, no extra: see 2692.   nk **49**
3548 **MISTRESS TWISTER** 34 [19]3-9-6 (68) P Makin(7) 16/1: 0-33030: 11th: Missed break, nvr dngrs.   ½ **59**
4042* **ADORATA** 13 [20]3-9-7 (69) G Baker 16/1: 0230210: 12th: No impress in mid-div: showed more in 4042.   hd **47**
3702 **ORION EXPRESS** 28 [18]3-8-10 (58) P Mulrennan(3) 22/1: 0464660: 13th: Missed break, mod late gains.   nk **55**
3573 **ROYAL DISTANT** 33 [2]3-9-5 (67) T Lucas 7/1: 0000200: 14th: Mid-div, no impress bef 2f out: op 5/1.   ½ **44**
3835 **COTTINGHAM** 23 [14]3-8-12 (60) Stephanie Hollinshead(5) 16/1: 1466020: 15th: Prom, ev ch 2f out, wknd.2 **44**
3835 **CHEVERAK FOREST** 23 [7]3-8-12 (60) Kim Tinkler 100/1: 150-0000: 16th: Al in rear: see 3419.   ¾ **42**
4903} **Passion Fruit** 310 [6]3-8-9 (57) J Fanning 40/1:0
4094 **Park Ave Princess** 12 [10]3-9-0 (62) G Gibbons 33/1:0
4044 **Book Matched** 13 [12]3-9-0 (62) F Lynch 12/1:0   2055 **Named At Dinner** 96 [11]3-9-0 (62) J Carroll 100/1:0
20 Ran   Time 1m 39.03 (3.23)   Owned: Mr T D Easterby   Trained: Malton

4322   2.40 Basf Handicap Stakes 3yo+ 86-100 (C)   [107]
     £12783 £4849 £2424   6f str   Good 40   +06 Fast   Centre

4027 **PARTNERS IN JAZZ** 14 [11] T D Barron 3-8-5 (4oh) (84) W Supple 9/1: 21-50051: Led after 1f, rdn   **92**
out ins fnl 1f to just hold on: fast: eff at 5f/6f on fast, gd & rain-softened grnd: acts on a stiff, undul
or gall trk: still only lightly rcd & remains unexposed in h'cap grade: see 1933 (reapp).
3827 **MARSAD** 23 [10] J Akehurst 10-8-7 (1oh) (85) P Doe 11/2: 3020002: Mid-div, prog halfway, kept on   nk **90**
well ins fnl 1f, just denied: another gd eff here at York & is h'capped to find similar: see 2357 & 1703.
2684 **MYSTIC MAN** 69 [7] K A Ryan 6-8-9 (1ow) (87) N Callan 12/1: 0013043: Bhd, prog bef 1f out, styd on   nk **91**
well fnl 1f, ran't came too sn: eff ad eff, tk t: fine eff back in trip & can rtn to winning ways.
3977* **ONLYTIME WILL TELL** 16 [2] D Nicholls 6-8-12 (91) J Fanning 9/1: 0542014: Chsd ldrs, ev ch when   hd **93**
hung left dist, kept on ins fnl 1f, not btn far in 4th: remains in gd form & is on a fair mark: just btr 3977 (clmr).
4005 **TOM TUN** 15 [13]9-9-6 bl (99) T Lucas 12/1: 2042035: Handy, kept on ins fnl 1f, just held for 4th: gd run.   hd **100**
3758 **ELLENS ACADEMY** 26 [5]9-8-7 (86) F Norton 8/1: 4422356: Keen in tch, no extra ins fnl 1f: btr 3434.   1 **84**
4073 **CIRCUIT DANCER** 12 [9]4-9-0 (93) T E Durcan 20/1: 0105047: Led, hdd 5f out, styd in tch, no extra dist.   1½ **87**

1300

3941 **KHABFAIR 18** [8]3-9-0 (95) L Dettori 100/30 FAV: 12-41368: Bhd, prog halfway, bmpd dist, no ½ 88
impress & btn when hmpd & eased ins fnl 1f: well bckd: shade btr expected: btr 3941 & 3778.
927 **SMART HOSTESS 159** [1]5-9-0 (93) P Hanagan 25/1: 11011-09: gr f Most Welcome - She's Smart 2 80
(Absalom) In tch wide over 4f out, no extra: long abs: v progressive in '03 winning no less than 6 times (5 h'caps
& class stks): mdn wnr in light '02 campaign: eff at 6f, best form has come at 5f: acts on fast, soft grnd &
fibresand, handles firm: gd weight carr who has brkn blood vessels: with J J Quinn.
1 Oct'03 Donc 5g/f 93-86 B: 1 Oct'03 Pont 5g/f 96-83 D: 1 Oct'03 Redc 5g/f 80-(84) E: 1 Sep'03 Ripo 6g/f 85-70 E:
1 Feb'03 Sout 6af 82a-70 E: 1 Feb'03 Wolv 6af 75a-66 E: 2 Sep'02 Newc 6g/s 69-64 F: 1 Aug'02 Beve 5g/f 53- D:
3758 **PINCHBECK 26** [6]5-8-7 p (86) P Robinson 9/1: 4101460: 10th: Rear, nvr able to chall: btr 3424 & 3136. hd 72
3920 +**APEX 19** [3]3-8-8 (89) S Drowne 5/1: 1503210: 11th: Bhd, nvr able to get competitive: amiss: btr 3920. 2½ 68
4005 **Law Breaker 15** [4]6-8-8 (87) K Darley 20/1:0   1356 **Aleutian 130** [12]4-9-7 (100) T P Queally 33/1:0
13 Ran Time 1m 11.45 (2.05) Owned: Sporting Occasions Racing No 2 Trained: Thirsk

---

4323 **3.15 Gr3 Sportingoptions Co Uk Betting Exchange Strensall Stakes 3yo+ (A)**
£31000 £11000 £5500 **1m208y** **Good 40** **-26 Slow** Inside

2555 **RED BLOOM 75** [4] Sir Michael Stoute 3-8-8 (113) K Fallon 1/1 FAV: 311-431: Cl-up, rdn to lead 114
ins fnl 1f, styd on well, val bit more: well bckd after 11 wk abs: eff at 1m, imprvd for step up to 9f, 10f shld
suit: acts on firm & gd grnd: goes well fresh: gd confidence boost: smart, see 2555.
4017 **SALSELON 17** [3] L M Cumani 5-9-3 VIS (118) L Dettori 2/1: 0-023052: Hld up, prog trav well 2f ½ 115
out, onepace for press: well bckd: smart run in visor but poss keeping something for himself: see 4017.
4002 **IMPERIAL DANCER 15** [2] M R Channon 6-9-3 (110) T E Durcan 9/2: 3600303: Chsd ldrs 7f, sn outpcd, nk 114
rallied well ins fnl 1f, not btn far: smart performer: see 3662 & 1230.
4063 **BABODANA 13** [1] M H Tompkins 4-9-3 BL (107) P Robinson 12/1: 6355464: Led, hdd under press ins nk 113
fnl 1f, no extra: gd run stepped up in grade with first time blnks: wants Listed: see 4063 & 951.
4 Ran Time 1m 54.74 (5.94) Owned: Cheveley Park Stud Trained: Newmarket

---

4324 **3.45 Elite Homes Garrowby Handicap Stakes 3yo 86-100 (C)** [107]
£12482 £4734 £2367 **1m3f198y** **Good 40** **+ 02 Fast** Inside

3236 +**INTO THE DARK 47** [1] Saeed bin Suroor 3-9-7 vis t (100) L Dettori 1/1 FAV: 111: Made all, rcd 114+
trav well, went clr from dist, eased cl-home: val 5L+: well bckd after 7 wk abs: eff at 10f, improved for step up
to 12f: acts on fast & gd grnd: eff in t-strap & visor: progressive performer who easily defied top-weight with
impressive display: unbtn, keep on your side in Gr class: see 3236.
3912 **SECRETARY GENERAL 19** [6] P F I Cole 3-8-12 (91) N De Souza(5) 20/1: 2050122: Held up, prog 4f 2½ 96
out, styd on to chase wnr ins fnl 1f, al held: eff at 7f/1m, ran to form on step up to 12f: see 3912.
3961 **CREDIT 18** [2] R Hannon 3-8-11 (90) T P Queally 16/1: 1004133: Al cl-up, no extra bef 1f out: 1¾ 92
prob stays 12f, rtn to 10f will suit: just btr 3961 & 3801.
4062 **ALWAYS WAINING 13** [3] M Johnston 3-9-2 (95) J Fanning 16/1: 1531604: Prom over 10f, sn no extra. 1 95
3534 **LARKWING 35** [8]3-8-9 (88) F Norton 9/2: 4-23125: Chsd ldrs 10f, sn onepcd: btr 3534 (firm). nk 87
3999 **ETMAAM 15** [7]3-8-13 BL (92) R Hills 16/1: 1213006: Rear, wknd 2f out: blnks, again disapp. 3½ 86
2519 **KEELUNG 76** [5]3-8-9 (88) P Robinson 18/1: 2213207: Keen rear, prog 3f out, hung left & onepcd dist. hd 81
3059 **REHEARSAL 55** [9]3-9-2 (95) K Darley 16/1: 21568: Rear, nvr a factor: 8 wk abs: btr 1495 (1m, firm). 12 72
3534 **PROTECTIVE 35** [4]3-8-9 (88) W Supple 100/1: 401409: Missed break, al in rear: btr 2230. ½ 64
3534 **ODIHAM 35** [10]3-8-8 (87) S Drowne 6/1: 002-1040: 10th: Chsd ldrs till halfway, grad wknd: amiss? ¾ 61
10 Ran Time 2m 31.40 (4.6) Owned: Godolphin Trained: Newmarket

---

4325 **4.20 Champions Are Sold In Ireland Maiden Auction Stakes 2yo (E)**
£9542 £2936 £1468 **7f205y rnd** **Good 40** **+01 Fast** Inside

XTRA TORRENTIAL 0 [9] D M Simcock 2-8-10 N Callan 16/1: 1: b c Torrential - Offering (Majestic 91 +
Light) Missed break, prog halfway, staying on when hung left ins fnl 1f, pushed out to lead cl-home, val bit more:
debut: Feb foal, cost 14,000 gns: half-brother to sprint wnrs abroad: dam plcd at sprint dists, sire decent at
10f: eff at 1m, further will suit: acts on gd & goes well fresh: fine start, win more races.
3337 **WOODSLEY HOUSE 42** [14] Mrs P N Dutfield 2-8-7 R Havlin 11/8 FAV: 222: Led, kept on under press nk 86
ins fnl 1f, hdd cl-home: well bckd after 6 wk abs: eff at 7f/1m: win a mdn: see 3337 & 3111.
4064 **HALLUCINATE 13** [7] R Hannon 2-8-10 (70) L Dettori 2/1: 042343: Cl-up, ev ch ins fnl 1f, sn no 1¼ 87
extra: bckd: eff at 7f/1m on fast & gd: appears much improved, interesting back in h'caps.
3736 **GLOBE TREKKER 27** [4] James Moffatt 2-8-8 R Ffrench 66/1: 04: gr f Aljabr - Amazonia (Deputy 1¼ 83
Minister) In tch, kept on ins fnl 1f, well clr of rem: Apr foal, cost 15,000gns: half-sister to a couple of rnrs
plcd abroad: dam unrcd: sire high-class juv performer, subs decent miler: eff at 1m on gd grnd.
BOSCHICE 0 [2]2-8-5 K McEvoy 16/1: 5: b f Dansili - Secret Dance (Sadler's Wells) Bhd, nvr 8 66
nrr than mid-div: debut: Mar foal, half-sister to a couple of wnrs: dam unrcd: sire decent performer at 1m.
3831 **LIABILITY 23** [1]2-8-2 Joanna Badger 125/1: 06: Cl-up over halfway, sn no extra: see 3831. 2½ 58
3559 **CAVA BIEN 34** [3]2-8-7 (70) M Fenton 10/1: 0337: Nvr nrr than mid-div: showed more in 3559 (7f, fast). hd 62
2236 **SHINGLE STREET 88** [6]2-8-13 P Robinson 25/1: 008: Rear, modest late gains: long abs. 4 60
3939 **ARTIC FOX 18** [5]2-8-13 D Allan 25/1: 5009: Bhd, nvr a factor. 6 48
3429 **DIXIE QUEEN 39** [13]2-8-5 (65) P Hanagan 14/1: 50030: 10th: Rear, modest late gains. 2 36
2492 **LAUREN LOUISE 77** [12]2-8-2 t Kim Tinkler 125/1: 000: 11th: Al in rear. 3½ 26
4204 **Mark Your Card 5** [8]2-8-5 W Supple 33/1:0   4035 **Welsh Galaxy 14** [10]2-8-6 (1ow) R Price 125/1:0
13 Ran Time 1m 38.97 (3.17) Owned: The Wight Wons Trained: Newmarket

---

4326   4.50 E B F Prince Of Wales's Own Regiment Of Yorkshire Maiden Stakes 2yo   (D)
£5210 £1603 £802   **6f217y rnd**   **Good 40**   **-23 Slow**   Inside

SUBPOENA 0 [9] M A Jarvis 2-9-0 P Robinson 10/1: 1: b c Diktat - Trefoil (Kris) In tch, styd on to lead dist, pushed out, val 3L+: debut: May foal, half-brother to Three Graces who was successful at 7f/1m: dam 10f List wnr: sire decent performer at sprint dists: eff at 7f, 1m shld suit: acts on gd grnd & a gall trk: goes well fresh: much to like about this debut success & looks one to follow.		96+
3031 **PAPER TALK 56** [4] B W Hills 2-9-0 M Hills 15/8: 32: Led, hdd dist, kept on, not pace wnr: well bckd after 8 wk abs: eff at 6f, imprvd for step up to 7f: acts on firm & gd grnd: gd eff in defeat: see 3031.	2	91
3811 **BANCHIERI 24** [1] Saeed bin Suroor 2-9-0 L Dettori 7/4 FAV: 33: Chsd ldrs, prog & ev ch bef 1f out, sn no extra: well bckd: acts on firm & gd grnd: win a mdn: see 3811.	1½	88
3878 **LOVE PALACE 21** [2] M Johnston 2-9-0 J Fanning 5/1: 224: Cl-up over 5f, no extra: acts on gd & soft grnd: see 3878 & 2938.	½	87
3752 **WINGMAN 26** [5]2-9-0 R Hills 33/1: 05: Chsd ldrs over 5f, no extra: see 3752.	2½	82
GIDAM GIDAM 0 [7]2-9-0 T E Durcan 50/1: 6: b c King's Best - Flamands (Sadler's Wells) Missed bread, nvr a factor: debut: May foal, half-brother successful at 12/14f: dam wnr at 12/14f.	4	74
RAINBOW TREASURE 0 [8]2-8-9 K Fallon 33/1: 7: ch f Rainbow Quest - Gaily Royal (Royal Academy) Al in rear on debut: Mar foal, cost 65,000gns: half-sister plcd at 1m/10f: dam won a couple of time abroad.	2½	64
SUGITANI 0 [3]2-9-0 T K McEvoy 16/1: 8: b c Kingmambo - Lady Reiko (Sadler's Wells) Rear, nvr a factor on debut: Apr foal, half-brother successful abroad: dam wnr at 9f: sire Gr 1 wnr at 1m.	3	63

8 Ran   Time 1m 25.75 (4.45)   Owned: Sheikh Mohammed   Trained: Newmarket

---

4327   5.20 Bollinger Champagne Series Handicap For Gentlemen Amateur Riders 4yo+ 56-70 (D)   **[42]**
£5055 £1555 £778   **1m3f198y**   **Good 40**   **-28 Slow**   Inside

4259* **BRAMANTINO 3** [9] R A Fahey 4-11-2 (6ex)bl (58) Mr R Stephens(3) 5/1: 2505511: Rear, prog over 3f out, styd on to lead ins fnl 1f, rdn out: well bckd on qck reapp: suited by 11/12f, has tried 14f: acts on firm, hvy & fibresand: eff in cheek pieces or blnks: in form 4yo who can land hat-trick on this evidence: see 4259.		68
1777 **CALATAGAN 109** [11] J M Jefferson 5-11-7 (63) Mr M Seston(3) 11/1: 30/-31552: Prom, styd on to lead 2f out, hdd ins fnl 1f, kept on, just held: clr rem: long abs: imprvd eff in defeat & go one better: see 997.	½	71
4133 **SENOR EDUARDO 9** [8] S Gollings 7-11-0 (2oh) (54) Mr T Woodside(7) 33/1: 0351623: Rear, prog 5f out, no impress dist: longer trip: btr 4133 & 3362.	5	55
4084 **LOADED GUN 12** [6] W M Brisbourne 4-11-0 (2oh) (54) Mr C Davies(5) 8/1: 05/00-024: Mid-div, eff over 2f out, onepcd fnl 1f: just btr 4084 (10f, hvy).	½	56
3678* **NIGHT SIGHT 28** [5]7-11-13 (69) Mr J Morgan(3) 13/2: 0234415: Bhd, prog 4f out, ev ch bef 1f out, wknd.	1¾	66
4170 **ROMIL STAR 6** [4]7-11-0 (2oh)vis (54) Mr S Dobson(3) 20/1: 1352106: Chsd ldrs, ev ch 2f out, sn wknd.	2	50
1109 **MIDDLETHORPE 144** [13]7-11-9 bl (65) Mr T Greenall 10/1: 055-1567: Nvr nrr than mid-div: long abs.	nk	58
4056 **SADLERS PRIDE 13** [3]4-11-7 T (63) Mr Nicky Tinkler 33/1: 0-224008: Chsd ldrs till halfway, no extra.	2½	52
3980 **DICKIE DEADEYE 16** [2]7-12-0 (70) Mr J J Best(3) 4/1 FAV: 2311349: Prom, led 6f out, hdd 2f out, fdd: well supported: 13lb higher than last win in 3222.	hd	58
3638 **DRAMATIC QUEST 30** [1]7-12-0 p (70) Mr Michael Murphy(5) 33/1: 0224-000: 10th: In tch, wknd 2f out: long abs.	1¼	56
1777 **ARCHIE BABE 109** [10]8-11-10 (66) Mr S Walker 8/1: 00-01500: 11th: Rear, fdd 2f out: long abs.	14	32
2062} **KINGS SQUARE 448** [7]4-11-0 (16oh) (40) Mr O Greenall(7) 100/1: 0000-0: 12th: b g Bal Harbour - Prime Property (Tirol) Led 6f, sn wknd: modest hdles form in 03/04 (rtd 78h, juv nov hdle): unplcd all 4 '03 Flat starts (rtd 46, mdn): with M W Easterby.	3	18
4170 **SHERWOOD FOREST 6** [12]4-12-0 (11oh)vis (45) Mr E Whillans(7) 40/1: 3605260: 13th: Handy over 1m.	1	16
3867 **KYLKENNY 21** [14]9-12-0 (70) Mr J Rees 9/1: 6534440: 14th: Mid-div wide over 7f, sn fdd: btr 3867.	5	23

14 Ran   Time 2m 35.03(8.23)   Owned: Mrs Kenyon A Rhodes Haulage P Timmins   Trained: Malton

---

Official Going GOOD (GOOD/FIRM places). Pace Figs Inapplicable due to Reconfigured Track

---

4328   1.50 Whitsbury Manor Stud E B F Novice Stakes 2yo (D)
£7046 £2168 £1084   **1m str**   **Good**   **Inapplicable**   Far side

3585 **LIAKOURA 34** [4] Mrs A J Perrett 2-9-5 P J Murtagh 6/1: 101: Held up, prog despite hanging left dist, rdn out to lead cl-home: eff at 7f, imprvd for step up to 1m: acts on gd & gd/soft grnd: likes Salisbury: apprec fitting of cheek pieces & deserves step up to List/Group company: see 3585 & 3111.		101
3586* **SUN KISSED 34** [1] Saeed bin Suroor 2-9-5 L Dettori 7/4: 12: Rear, prog halfway, styd on to lead 2f out, hdd under press cl-home: bckd: eff at 6f, ran to form on step up to 1m: acts on fast & gd grnd: lightly rcd performer who ran well in defeat: see 3586 (debut).	1	97
3532 **SOLENT 36** [2] R Hannon 2-9-5 Dane O'Neill 16/1: 103: Cl-up over 6f, sn outpcd, rallied ins fnl 1f, just held for 2nd: eff at 7f/1m, looks in need of further: acts on gd & gd/soft grnd: see 2766 (debut).	hd	96
3752 **GOLDEN FURY 27** [3] J L Dunlop 2-8-12 K Fallon 5/1: 434: Led 6f, kept on ins fnl 1f, not btn far in 4th: eff at 7f, imprvd for step up to 1m: acts on gd grnd: can find a mdn: see 3752.	hd	88
4096 **PROPINQUITY 12** [5]2-9-5 (100) D Holland 13/8 FAV: 1335: Keen prom over 6f, sn no extra: well bckd: disapp eff on step up to 1m: showed more in 4096 (Gr 3, 7f, gd/soft).	¾	93

5 Ran   Time 1m 42.75 (3.65)   Owned: Mr Mark Tracey   Trained: Pulborough

---

4329   2.20 European Breeders Fund Quidhampton Maiden Stakes Div 1 Fillies 2yo (D)
£10725 £3300 £1650   6f212y str   Good   Inapplicable   Centre

3944 **DONYANA** 19 [14] M A Jarvis 2-8-11   P Robinson 4/1 JT FAV: 51: Made all, went clr ins fnl 1f, rdn   91
out: eff at 7f, bred to apprec further: acts on gd grnd & a stiff/gall trk: much to like about today's win, see 3944.

   MISS THE BOAT [13] J L Dunlop 2-8-11   Dane O'Neill 50/1: 2: b f Mtoto - Missed Again (High Top)   2   85
Cl-up, sltly outpcd 2f out, kept on ins fnl 1f, no ch with wnr: debut: Mar foal, half-sister to wnrs at 5/15f: dam
successful at 10f: sire Gr 1 wnr at mid-dists: eff at 7f, further looks sure to suit: acts on gd grnd: encouraging
eff & can impr with experience.

   NICE TUNE [2] C E Brittain 2-8-11   R Hills 40/1: 3: b f Diktat - Military Tune (Nashwan) Held   1   83
up, prog bef 1f out, nrst fin: debut: Nov foal, cost 23,000gns: half-sister to wnrs at 6f: sire unrcd: sire
decent performer at sprint dists: eff at 7f, will apprec further: acts on gd grnd: impr for today's experience.

   LOVE ALWAYS [3] Mrs A J Perrett 2-8-11   J Murtagh 33/1: 4: b f Piccolo - Lady Isabell (Rambo   hd   82
Dancer) Mid-div, prog 2f out, kept on ins fnl 1f: debut: Feb foal, half-sister successful at mid-dists: dam
unplcd: sire Gr 1 wnr at 6f: eff at 7f, shld get further: acts on gd grnd: promising start to career.

   CLASSICISM [5] 2-8-11   L Dettori 9/2: 5: b f A P Indy - Colour Chart (Mr Prospector) Cl-up, ev   2   78
ch bef 1f out, no extra when eased ins fnl 1f, returned lame: bckd: Apr foal, half-sister to decent juv performer
in US, also to 7f/10f Group wnr Equerry: dam successful at 1m/10f: sire fine performer abroad.

   ABIDE [4] 2-8-11   R L Moore 25/1: 6: Handy over 5f, sn onepcd: debut.   ½   77
2970 **MAGGIE TULLIVER** 59 [7] 2-8-11   D Holland 40/1: 07: Nvr nrr than mid-div: 8 wk abs.   1   75
3944 **JENNA STANNIS** 19 [16] 2-8-11   N Chalmers(5) 66/1: 08: Cl-up, no extra bef 1f out: see 3944.   nk   74
   RED DUCHESS [9] 2-8-11   K Fallon 9/2: 9: Bhd, nvr nrr than mid-div: debut.   nk   73
4035 **AUTHENTICATE** 15 [11] 2-8-11   G Gibbons 16/1: 460: 10th: Handy 5f, sn no extra: btr 3103.   shd   72
   INTENDED [12] 2-8-11   Martin Dwyer 50/1: 0: 11th: Chsd ldrs over 5f, wknd: debut.   shd   71
   ASK FOR RAIN [8] 2-8-11   M Hills 20/1: 0: 12th: Al in rear.   2½   66
3554 **SOMETHING EXCITING** 35 [10] 2-8-11   J F Egan 10/1: 400: 13th: Mid-div over 5f, wknd.   shd   65
3103 **MONTJEU BABY** 54 [6] 2-8-11   P Dobbs 10/1: 00: 14th: Bhd, nvr a factor.   6   53
2646 **CLASSIC GUEST** 72 [15] 2-8-11   T E Durcan 20/1: 460: 15th: Missed break, nvr a factor.   4   45
   TRICK OF LIGHT [1] 2-8-11   R Hughes 4/1 JT FAV: W: Withdrawn at start on debut.   0
16 Ran   Time 1m 28.72 (3.22)   Owned: Sheikh Ahmed Al Maktoum   Trained: Newmarket

---

4330   2.50 European Breeders Fund Quidhampton Maiden Stakes Div 2 Fillies 2yo (D)
£10693 £3290 £1645   6f212y str   Good   Inapplicable   Centre

3064 **ALMANSOORA** 56 [3] Saeed bin Suroor 2-8-11   L Dettori 4/1: 21: Mid-div, prog & ev ch dist, styd   90
on under hands & heels to get up on line: op 3/1, 8 wk abs: eff at 6/7f, further shld suit: acts on fast & gd
grnd: eff on a stiff/gall trk & goes well fresh: only lightly rcd & can progress: see 3064.

3616 **ELIZABETHAN AGE** 33 [8] D R Loder 2-8-11   T P Queally 14/1: 22: Cl-up, led 2f out, under press   shd   88
when chall ins fnl 1f, hdd on line: acts on fast & gd grnd: lost little in defeat & has shown enough to find similar.

3944 **BAHJA** 19 [5] J H M Gosden 2-8-11   R Hills 5/2 JT FAV: 43: Cl-up, ev ch bef 1f out, kept on well,   ½   87
not btn far in 3rd: well bckd: rider reported mount hung left throughout: eff at 7f, shld get 1m: acts on fast &
gd grnd: imprvd on debut eff & can find similar: see 3944.

   HIGHLAND DIVA [1] Sir Michael Stoute 2-8-11   K Fallon 20/1: 4: ch f Selkirk - Drama Class   3½   80+
(Caerleon) Bhd, sn in mid-div, kept on fnl 1f under kind ride on debut: Feb first foal, dam successful at 10f:
sire decent performer at 1m: eff at 7f, will apprec further: acts on gd grnd: promising eff & will rate higher.

   TAMALAIN [7] 2-8-11   J Murtagh 40/1: 5: b f Royal Academy - Woodland Orchid (Woodman) Bhd, prog   ¾   78
bef 1f out, nrst fin: debut: Mar foal, cost 200,000gns: half-sister successful at 6f: dam unplcd: sire Gr 1 wnr
at 6f/1m: with Mrs A J Perrett.

3252 **PROUD SCHOLAR** 48 [15] 2-8-11   R Hughes 5/2 JT FAV: 26: In tch over 5f, sn no extra: bckd after 7   shd   77
wk abs: failed to prog from debut eff in 3252 (fast).

   AMALIE [12] 2-8-11   T E Durcan 66/1: 7: b f Fasliyev - Princess Amalie (Rahy) Nvr nrr than   1   75
mid-div: debut: Apr foal, cost 12,000gns: half-sister to a couple of performers plcd at 10f: dam unplcd: sire
decent performer at sprint dists: with C E Brittain.

3917 **MONTECITO** 20 [10] 2-8-11   R L Moore 66/1: 08: In tch, no extra bef 1f out: see 3917.   ½   74
3863 **TIGGERS TOUCH** 22 [6] 2-8-11   S Drowne 33/1: 49: Nvr nrr than mid-div: showed more in 3863.   ½   73
3582 **HOUSE MARTIN** 34 [11] 2-8-11   Martin Dwyer 8/1: 40: 10th: Led 5f, grad wknd: btr 3582.   ½   72
   Brandexe [2] 2-8-11 M Hills 100/1:0   3915 **Scent 20** [9] 2-8-11 J Fortune 16/1:0
4217 **Pussy Cat 5** [4] 2-8-11 L Keniry(3) 150/1:0   3752 **Desert Classic 27** [13] 2-8-11 E Ahern 40/1:0
   Swift Dame [16] 2-8-11 Dane O'Neill 9/2:0   4052 **Hillabilla 14** [14] 2-8-11 D Sweeney 125/1:0
16 Ran   Time 1m 28.52 (3.02)   Owned: Godolphin   Trained: Newmarket

---

4331   3.20 E B F Lochsong Stakes Handicap Fillies 3yo+ 86-100 (C)
£15239 £5781 £2890   6f212y str   Good   Inapplicable   Centre   [104]

3612+ **ATTUNE** 33 [13] B J Meehan 3-8-7 (2oh) (83) J F McDonald(3) 9/1: 4010011: Made all, rdn clr ins fnl   96
1f: eff at 7f/1m on gd & fast grnd: likes a stiff/gall trk: eff with blnks, left off today: in form performer who
did well to win from out of h'cap, see 3612.

4063 **LOOK HERES CAROL** 14 [10] B A McMahon 4-9-3 (91) K Fallon 6/1: 3631052: Rcd cl-up, styd on ins   1¾   96
fnl 1f, not pace of wnr: proving consistent: 4lb higher than last win in 3117.

3965 **GOLDEN ISLAND** 18 [9] J W Hills 3-8-7 (85) R Hills 12/1: 3215103: Chsd ldrs, kept on ins fnl 1f,   ½   89
no ch with wnr: eff at 7f, return to 1m/10f will suit: just btr 3780 (1m).

4095 **SILK FAN** 12 [8] P W Harris 3-9-3 (95) D Holland 4/1: 211-1644: Handy, onepcd bef 1f out: nk   98
3lb higher than last win: see 2918 & 3564.

3773 **FANNYS FANCY** 26 [14] 4-9-0 (88) J Fortune 9/2: 3-000355: Keen cl-up till dist: first try at 7f.   1½   88
3565 **CONVENT GIRL** 34 [5] 4-9-0 (88) R Havlin 16/1: 0000006: Dwelt, rcd in rear, prog bef 1f out, nrst   hd   87+
fin: signs of encouragement & has slipped to a fair mark, worth keeping in mind back at 1m: see 2207 & 1686.

4263 **ENFORD PRINCESS** 4 [6] 3-8-7 (1oh) (84) Dane O'Neill 25/1: 00-40347: Nvr nrr than mid-div: qck reapp.   nk   83

3456 **MUSIC MAID 40** [7]6-8-11 (21oh) (64) D Kinsella 50/1: 15-01008: Keen bhd, nvr nrr than mid-div.   1¾   81$
3928 **CUSCO 20** [12]3-8-12 (90) R L Moore 14/1: 2602029: Cl-up, wknd bef 1f out: showed more in 3928.   ½   85
3773 **CAVERAL 26** [11]3-9-3 (95) R Hughes 10/1: 1-001030: 10th: Keen in tch 5f, wknd: btr 3773 & 1957.   1½   87
4095* **ZIETORY 12** [4]4-9-11 (99) L Dettori 6/1: 42-50310: 11th: Bhd, prog when short of room bef 1f   1½   88
out, sn btn: tchd 9/1: disapp back at 7f: showed more in 4095 (1m, gd/soft, List).
1919 **ASIA WINDS 103** [1]3-9-1 (93) M Hills 12/1: 1155-500: 12th: Rear, nvr a factor: long abs: btr 1919.   1   80
3928 Go Between 20 [2]3-8-7 (85) E Ahern 33/1:0   3885 **Betty Stogs 21** [3]3-8-7 (5oh)(80) Martin Dwyer 50/1:0
14 Ran   Time 1m 27.10 (1.6)   Owned: Wyck Hall Stud   Trained: Upper Lambourn

---

4332   3.50 Listed E B F /Irish Thoroughbred Marketing Dick Poole Stakes Fillies 2yo (A)
£18850 £7150 £3575   **6f str**   **Good**   **Inapplicable**   Far side

3536* **SUEZ 36** [3] M A Jarvis 2-8-9   P Robinson 8/11 FAV: 11: Made all, pushed clr fnl 1f, val 4L+:   111+
well bckd: eff at 6f, 7f shld suit: acts on firm & gd grnd: acts on a sharp/undul or stiff/gall trk: won today
with plenty in hand & an exciting prospect: now heads for Gr 1 Cheveley Park & will be hard to beat: see 3536.
4059 **CASTELLETTO 14** [2] B A McMahon 2-8-9 (99) G Gibbons 28/1: 2021252: Cl-up, kept on ins fnl 1f, no   2½   99
ch with v easy wnr: eff at 5f, best eff to date today over 6f: gd run in defeat & can find similar: see 4059.
3956 **ROODEYE 19** [5] R F Johnson Houghton 2-8-9 (94) Martin Dwyer 25/1: 21563: In tch over 4f, sn   1   96
onepcd: eff at 5f, imprvd for step up to 6f: see 3509 & 2795.
3795* **SATIN KISS 26** [1] Saeed bin Suroor 2-8-9 (88) L Dettori 12/1: 1014: Mid-div, prog halfway,   nk   95
onepcd bef 1f out: see 3795 (nov fills stks, gd/soft, made all).
3956 **ALL FOR LAURA 19** [9]2-8-9 (95) T P Queally 14/1: 4155: Mid-div, prog when hmpd bef 1f out,   nk   94
switched & kept on ins fnl 1f: clr rem: ran to form on return to 6f: see 3956 & 3576.
3993* **REGINA 17** [10]2-8-9 K Fallon 11/2: 316: Handy over 4f, no extra: disapp on step up to 6f.   3   85
3709* **GHURRA 28** [7]2-8-9 R Hills 14/1: 17: Nvr nrr than mid-div: see 3709 (mdn, debut).   ½   84
3781 **VALENTIN 26** [11]2-8-9 (100) R Hughes 12/1: 1208: Al bhd: twice below gd 3rd in 3440 (Gr 3).   hd   83
4050 **VONDOVA 14** [8]2-8-9 (84) Dane O'Neill 40/1: 301029: Keen bhd, nvr a factor: btr 4050 (stks).   2½   76
3251* **FREE LIFT 48** [4]2-8-9 S Drowne 10/1: 10: 10th: Cl-up 4f, fdd: 7 wk abs: btr 3251 (mdn).   3   67
3064 **SAFFA GARDEN 56** [6]2-8-9 D Holland 100/1: 000: 11th: Al in rear: 8 wk abs.   6   50
11 Ran   Time 1m 13.46 (1.36)   Owned: Sheikh Mohammed   Trained: Newmarket

---

4333   4.20 Ely Fund Managers Conditions Stakes 3yo+ (C)
£9251 £3509 £1755   **1m6f15y**   **Good**   **Inapplicable**   Flag start

3315* **BAROLO 50** [2] P W Harris 5-9-10 (106) D Holland 4/1: 14-01011: Cl-up, styd on for press to lead   113
dist, drvn out to hold on: bckd after 7 wk abs: eff at 10/12f, suited by 14f: acts on firm & gd grnd: acts on a
stiff/gall or sharp trk: goes well fresh: career best eff conceding weight all round: v game & deserves step up to
Gr 2/3: see 3315 & 1861.
4023 **GRAMPIAN 15** [3] J G Given 5-9-1 (102) K Fallon 7/1: 5/-262302: Handy, prog & ev ch ins fnl 1f,   nk   103
just held by wnr: eff at 10/12.3f, now stays 14f: back to form after disapp in 4023, see 2948.
1746 **FIGHT YOUR CORNER 111** [7] Saeed bin Suroor 5-9-1 t (107) L Dettori 4/1: 15/520-03: b c Muhtarram   1½   101
- Dame Ashfield (Grundy) Led & sn clr, hdd bef 1f out, kept on but not pace front 2: List rnr-up on first of only 2
'03 Brit starts, earlier 5th in a Dubai Gr 3: Gr 3 wnr in '02 (M Johnston, subs 5th in Gr 1 Epsom Derby, subs
injured): stays 13/14f, shld get further: acts on firm & gd/soft: eff with a t-strap. 2 May'03 Newb 13.3gd 111- A:
1 May'02 Ches 12.3fm 107- A: 1 Oct'01 Asco 8g/s 112- A: 1 Sep'01 Newb 8fm 102- B: 1 Aug'01 Newc 6g/s 73- F:
3233 **WESTMORELAND ROAD 48** [1] Mrs A J Perrett 4-9-1 (108) J Murtagh 5/4 FAV: 1310-224: Mid-div, prog   hd   100
trav well 2f out, kept on ins fnl 1f, no impress on principals: clr rem: 7 wk abs: eff at 11/12f, now stays a
slowly run 14f: sltly disapp run & prob prefers stronger pace: showed more in 3233 & 2762 (12f).
2914 **GULF 61** [6]5-9-1 T (105) R Hughes 13/2: 606-0355: Held up, nvr a factor: 9 wk abs & t-strap.   6   94
        TOILE [4]3-7-13 D Kinsella 200/1: 6: ch f Zafonic - Princess Sadie (Shavian) Rear, sn t.o.   dist 49
3114 **HERODOTUS 34** [5]6-9-1 t (55) Dane O'Neill 250/1: 050-0007: Sn bhd, eased after halfway, t.o.: 8   dist 4
wk abs: rider reported mount had a breathing problem: see 2759.
7 Ran   Time 3m 8.00 (10.0)   Owned: Mrs P W Harris   Trained: Berkhamsted

---

4334   4.50 Wiltshire Life Handicap Stakes 3yo+ 56-70 (E)
£3731 £1148 £574   **1m str**   **Good**   **Inapplicable**   Far side   [79]

3986 **LIBERTY ROYAL 17** [6] P J Makin 5-8-11 p (62) D Sweeney 8/1: 0630341: Held up, prog 3f out, styd   70
on for press to lead cl-home: op 12/1: eff at 1m, prob stays 10f: acts on gd & polytrack: handles firm: eff with
cheek pieces: apprec big drop in weights & shld be able to find similar: see 3676 & 2220.
3980 **RIDGE BOY 17** [1] R Hannon 3-9-0 (70) R L Moore 14/1: 5601032: Handy, styd on to lead 2f out, hdd   hd   76
under press cl-home: prob stays 10f, enjoyed return to 1m: acts on firm & gd grnd: unexposed in h'cap grade.
4036 **HABSHAN 15** [5] C F Wall 4-9-4 (69) D Holland 5/1: 0435103: Held up, prog wide 3f out, styd on   shd   74
well despite hanging badly right well ins fnl 1f, just held in 3 way photo: op 7/1: clr rem: prob wnr if keeping a
straight line ins fnl 1f: has the ability to find similar: see 3583.
4222 **TUSCARORA 5** [11] A W Carroll 5-8-10 (61) J Fortune 9/2 FAV: 1051334: Mid-div, prog 2f out,   3½   59
onepcd fnl 1f: qck reapp: showed more in 4222 & 3731.
4385* **YOUNG ALEX 346** [2]6-9-2 p (67) Martin Dwyer 11/1: 456343-5: ch g Midhish - Snipe Hunt (Stalker)   1½   63
Bhd, prog halfway, edged right & no impress dist: reapp: rnr-up once in '03 (h'cap, K R Burke): h'cap wnr in '02:
h'cap wnr in '01: eff at 7f, stays 1m: acts on firm, gd grnd & polytrack: tried cheek pieces: encouraging eff &
is well h'capped, can be plcd to gd effect by M C Pipe.
2 Jun'03 Chep 7.1g/f 74-72 D: 2 Oct'02 Sand 7g/f 75-70 D: 2 Sep'02 Muss 7.1g/f 72-70 D: 1 Sep'02 Sali 6.9fm 71-64 D:
2 Jan'02 Ling 6ap 92a- C: 2 Apr'01 Wind 8.3g/f 79- D: 2 Feb'01 Ling 6ap 83a-80 D: 1 Feb'01 Ling 7ap 80a-69 E:
4117 **TERRAQUIN 11** [4]4-8-12 p (63) T P Queally 20/1: 5000036: Nvr nrr than mid-div: btr 4117.   ½   58
4252* **PELLA 4** [3]3-8-11 (6ex) (65) L Dettori 11/2: 5323017: Nvr nrr than mid-div: qck reapp: btr 4252 (g/s).   2   58
3980 **ZARIANO 17** [14]4-9-4 (69) L Keniry(3) 33/1: 160-2008: Handy, wknd fnl 2f: btr 3286.   2   56
3922 **JAHIA 20** [15]5-8-12 (63) G Baker 100/1: 10/6-0009: Al in rear: see 3719.   2¾   45
3920 **FISBY 20** [9]3-8-8 (65) J F Egan 14/1: 0-5500: 10th: Handy, wknd bef 1f out.   shd   45
3829 **MALAK AL MOULOUK 24** [16]4-9-2 (67) J Tate 16/1: 425-4200: 11th: Al adrift: btr 3295.   nk   47
2650 **OFF BEAT 72** [7]3-8-9 (65) S Carson 66/1: 6300000: 12th: Handy till halfway, wknd: 10 wk abs.   1¼   43

SALISBURY   THURSDAY 02.09.04   Righthand, Galloping Track, Stiff Finish

4077 **DASH FOR COVER 13** [8]4-8-6 (57) P Dobbs 14/1: 0056050: 13th: Cl-up 6f, wknd.   *2* **31**
1849 **PRIORS DALE 106** [12]4-9-1 (66) Dane O'Neill 16/1: 20-26640: 14th: Mid-div when short of room   *3* **34**
after halfway, wknd: showed more in 1849.
4030 **OH BOY 15** [10]4-9-5 (70) R Hughes 16/1: 5110000: 15th: Cl-up, led 3f out, sn hdd & fdd.   *7* **24**
1136 **HALLINGS OVERTURE 143** [13]5-9-5 (70) R Hills 12/1: 500/-6020: 16th: Led, hdd 3f out, wknd.   *10* **6**
16 Ran   Time 1m 41.96 (2.86)   Owned: T W Wellard & Partners   Trained: Marlborough

4335   5.20 Axminster Carpets Apprentice Handicap Stakes 3yo+ 56-70 (E)   [76]
£5026 £1546 £773   **5f str   Good   Inapplicable** Far side

3667 **MAROMITO 30** [3] R Bastiman 7-8-7 (55) A Mullen(5) 12/1: 1100301: Cl-up, led 2f out, rdn out ins   **66**
fnl 1f: eff at 5f on firm, gd grnd & both AWs, handles soft: see 3350 & 1408.
3693* **WHOS WINNING 29** [15] B G Powell 3-9-4 (67) A Hindley(5) 9/1: 0060212: In tch, chsd wnr & hung   *2* **71**
left ins fnl 1f, al held: op 13/2, acts on firm & gd: see 3693 (6f, firm).
3687 **MILLINSKY 29** [11] R Guest 3-8-7 (56) R Mills(5) 11/4 FAV: 6323: Bhd, prog bef 1f out, nrst fin: *1* **57**
h'cap bow: app step up to 6f on this evidence: see 3687 & 2649.
3966 **FORMALISE 18** [8] G B Balding 4-8-7 (3oh)p (52) R Thomas 12/1: 0505004: Led stands side group,   *shd* **55**
kept on fnl 1f, no ch with far side: encouraging eff back at minimum trip & has slipped to a fair mark: see 3109.
4240 **TOMTHEVIC 5** [7]6-8-7 (6oh) (49) C Haddon(3) 20/1: 0000405: Mid-div when short of room after 2f,   *1* **52**
prog 2f out, no impress fnl 1f: qck reapp: btr 2585.
3673 **STAGNITE 30** [16]4-8-10 p (58) A Quinn 12/1: 0621006: Led, hdd 2f out, sn no extra: btr 3403.   *½* **54**
    CHANTELLE 41 [1]4-8-8 (56) J D Walsh(5) 33/1: 0100507: b f Lake Coniston - Kristabelle (Elbio)   *nk* **51**
Chsd ldrs stands side group, switched to far side after halfway, sn onepcd: 6 wk abs & Brit bow: ex-Irish, earlier
appr h'cap wnr at Navan (5f, gd/soft): with S Kirk.
3844 **BYO 23** [9]6-9-7 (69) K May(5) 10/1: 6001348: Handy, no extra dist: btr 3673 & 3372.   *nk* **63**
4126 **DOUBLE M 10** [2]7-9-4 vis (66) M Howard(5) 7/1: 6612009: Cl-up stands side, no extra dist: btr 3640.   *nk* **59**
4140 **PULSE 9** [6]6-8-10 p (58) Derek Nolan(5) 10/1: 0055400: 10th: Nvr nrr than mid-div.   *hd* **50**
4140 **ONE WAY TICKET 9** [13]4-9-7 p (69) C J Davies(5) 13/2: 1000450: 11th: Chsd ldrs, wknd dist: see 3984.   *2* **55**
4118 **Kallistas Pride 11** [12]4-8-11 vis(59) M Savage 12/1:0 4211   **Bennanabaa 6** [5]5-8-7 (10oh)BL t(45) B O'Neill(5) 66/1:0
4029 **Iltravitore 15** [10]3-9-2 (65) N Chalmers 25/1:0
3977 **Catchthebatch 17** [4]8-8-7 (15oh)bl(40) Liam Jones(5) 66/1:0
15 Ran   Time 1m 0.11(0.31)   Owned: Mrs C B Bastiman   Trained: Wetherby

REDCAR   THURSDAY 02.09.04   Lefthand, Flat, Galloping Track

Official Going GOOD/FIRM (FIRM places)

4336   2.10 Crab Maiden Stakes 3yo+ (D)
£3552 £1093 £547   **1m1f   Firm 18   -12 Slow** Inside

    FOCUS GROUP [1] H R A Cecil 3-9-0 W Ryan 9/2: 1: b c Kris S - Interim (Sadler's Wells) Rear,   **82**
hdwy over 3f out, led just ins fnl 1f, drvn out on debut: full brother to a 10f 3yo scorer in France: dam smart
mid-dist runner: eff at 9f, will stay further: acts on firm, runs well fresh & acts on a gall trk: gd start.
    NAMAT [4] M P Tregoning 3-8-9 W Supple 13/2: 2: b f Daylami - Masharik (Caerleon) Dwelt, hdwy   *1* **73**
to lead over 1f out till just ins fnl 1f, no extra on debut: dam a 3yo wnr at 10f: eff at 9f, will stay further:
acts on firm grnd: fair start, entitled to learn from this & impr next time.
2988! **DREAM SCENE 412** [7] J H M Gosden 3-8-9 S Sanders 7/2: 4-3: b f Sadler's Wells - Highest   *hd* **72**
Accolade (Shirley Heights) With ldr till led 3f out, hdd over 1f out, no extra on reapp: 4th sole '03 start (fills
mdn, rtd 76): eff at 7/9f on firm & fast grnd: poss ndd this following lengthy absence.
3741 **MA YAHAB 28** [5] L M Cumani 3-9-0 (72) N Mackay(3) 100/30 FAV: 20-33044: Rear, hdwy 3f out, onepcd   *1* **75**
when not much room ins fnl 1f: handles firm & gd/soft: see 1834.
1661 **BUSINESS MATTERS 10** [9]4-9-1 (45) B Swarbrick(5) 25/1: 00-00035: Chsd ldrs, onepcd over 1f out: *½* **69$**
clr of rem: now with Miss R Bowden: see 1661.
3079 **HEARTS DESIRE 55** [10]3-8-9 (70) A Culhane 7/1: 52-626: Led to 3f out, wknd dist: op 5/1.   *8* **53**
    LADY KARR [11]3-8-9 J Fanning 7/1: 7: Chsd ldrs, wknd over 2f out on debut: op 10/1.   *1¼* **50**
3934 **WIZARDS PRINCESS 20** [2]4-9-1 A McCarthy 150/1: 58: Slow away, nvr nr ldrs.   *12* **38**
2974 **ROSINGS 59** [8]3-8-9 M Fenton 33/1: 09: Chsd ldrs, hung left 4f out, sn wknd: 8 wk abs.   *5* **33**
9 Ran   Time 1m 51.58 (2.78)   Owned: Mr K Abdulla   Trained: Newmarket

4337   2.40 Cray Fish Nursery Handicap Stakes 2yo 0-75 (E)   [79]
£4329 £1332 £666   **7f str   Firm 18   -16 Slow** Centre

4040 **CAITLIN 14** [17] B Smart 2-9-5 (70) F Lynch 12/1: 624131: Made all, hung left 3f out, drvn &   **78**
flashed tail ins fnl 1f, just held on cl-home: joc 1 day careless riding ban: eff at 6f, now suited by 7f & shld
stay 1m+: acts on firm & fibresand: most tough, see 2336.
3769* **THE PEN 26** [16] P C Haslam 2-8-5 (56) G Faulkner 6/1: 012: Dwelt, sn handy, styd on v well ins   *hd* **62**
fnl 1f, only just btn: h'cap bow: eff at 6/7f, 1m will suit: acts on fast & firm, likes Redcar: see 3769.
3517 **CEREBUS 36** [20] N P Littmoden 2-9-0 (72) L Fletcher(3) 10/1: 6423: Chsd ldrs, kept on ins fnl 1f: *½* **77**
stays 7f: acts on firm & fast: gd run: see 3517 (mdn).
3005 **DRAX 58** [9] D R Loder 2-9-6 (71) K Darley 10/1: 3004: Prom, hdwy & ev ch over 1f out, onepcd ins   *hd* **75**
fnl 1f: op 7/1, 8 wk abs: h'cap bow & a pity: see 2462.
4193 **MASTER JOSEPH 6** [13]2-8-9 (60) A Culhane 5/1 FAV: 400025: Chsd ldrs, hdwy over 2f out, kept on   *1½* **61**
fnl 1f: qck reapp: return to 1m shld suit: acts on firm & gd: see 4193.
3606 **ALGORITHM 33** [15]2-8-7 (58) W Supple 50/1: 0656: Bhd, hdwy over 2f out, kept on: see 3258.   *hd* **58**
3699 **AS HANDSOME DOES 29** [5]2-9-0 t (65) W Ryan 25/1: 007: Slow away, hdwy over 2f out, kept on.   *1¼* **62**
4064 **SNOOKERED AGAIN 14** [19]2-8-13 (64) P Mulrennan(3) 20/1: 510308: Handy, onepcd 2f out.   *1½* **58**
3753 **BURTON ASH 27** [11]2-9-7 (72) M Fenton 20/1: 04349: Swerved & joc lost iron start, in tch, kept   *½* **65**
on fnl 2f but not pace of ldrs: see 3753.

3429 **ZANDO 40** [3]2-8-11 (62) D Fentiman(7) 66/1: 0060: 10th: b g Forzando - Rockin' Rosie (Song)   *nk*   **54**
Prom, no impress over 1f out: 6 wk abs: h'cap bow: cost 10,500gns: sire smart performer at up to 9f.
4083 **IMPERIAL DYNASTY 13** [8]2-8-12 (63) S Sanders 10/1: 0500: 11th: b c Devil's Bag - Leasears (Lear   *1¼*   **52**
Fan) Chsd ldrs, no impress over 1f out: cost $25,000: dam a French 3yo wnr, sire high-class US 2yo.
3682 **TYBALT 29** [4]2-9-1 (65) R Winston 10/1: 2500: 12th: In tch, nvr nrr.   *3½*   **48**
3994 **FANTASY DEFENDER 17** [2]2-8-9 (60) J Fanning 40/1: 0000050: 13th: Slow away, some late gains.   *3*   **36**
2959 **LOYALTY LODGE 60** [7]2-8-8 (59) J Fanning 40/1: 0600: 14th: Nvr nr ldrs: 9 wk abs: see 2522.   *1½*   **32**
3831 **SUMMER SILKS 24** [14]2-8-11 (62) P Hanagan 16/1: 0400: 15th: Handy, no impress when hmpd 3f out.   *½*   **34**
2911 **TOWN END TOM 62** [6]2-8-9 (60) C Catlin 14/1: 5660: 16th: In tch, wknd 2f out: op 10/1, 9 wk abs.   *¾*   **30**
3871* **Jay 22** [1]2-8-10 P(61) N Mackay(3) 20/1:0   2927 **Sweet Marguerite 61** [10]2-8-12 (63) D Allan 25/1:0
3864* **Ladruca 22** [12]2-8-9 (60) A McCarthy 14/1:0   2792 **Tantien 66** [18]2-9-0 (65) Dean McKeown 50/1:0
20 Ran   Time 1m 24.24 (2.44)   Owned: EKOS Pinnacle Partnership   Trained: Thirsk

---

4338   **3.10 Cockle Maiden Auction Stakes 2yo   (E)**
       £2975   £850   £425   **5f str**   **Firm 18**   **-14 Slow**   Centre

3962 **DANZILI BAY 18** [2] R M Beckett 2-8-13   S Sanders 9/1: 441: Prom, hdwy to lead well over 1f out,   **82**
drvn out ins fnl 1f: jt top-weight: eff at 5f on firm grnd, acts on a gall trk: gd weight-carrying eff: see 2976.
3699 **TAGULA SUNRISE 29** [1] R A Fahey 2-8-8 (82) P Hanagan 2/5 FAV: 222032: Dwelt in rear, hdwy over   *nk*   **76**
2f out, chsd wnr fnl 1f, hdd far: well bckd at odds-on: return to 6f will suit: see 3699.
3988 **BEN CASEY 17** [5] B Smart 2-8-7   R Winston 25/1: 063: Led till dist, no extra: stays 5f on firm.   *2½*   **67$**
1974 **HIGH PETERGATE 100** [7] M W Easterby 2-8-6   P Mulrennan(3) 14/1: 54: Handy, onepace fnl 1f: abs.   *1½*   **61**
3178 **TIGER BOND 51** [3]2-8-7   D Allan 33/1: 05: br c Diktat - Blackpool Belle (The Brianstan)   *1¾*   **57**
Mid-div, nvr nrr: 7 wk abs: Feb foal, cost 8,200gns: half-brother to smart winning sprinter Croft Pool: dam dual
5f 2yo wnr, later won over 6f: sire smart older sprinter: with B Smart.
     SHARP DIVERSION [11]2-8-6   M Fenton 28/1: 6: ch f Diesis - Jamie de Vil (Digression) Cl-up,   *1½*   **51**
fdd over 1f out on debut: Apr foal, cost $10,000: dam unplcd, sire a smart 2yo: learn from this.
4089 **DUCAL DIVA 13** [10]2-8-2 (66) J Quinn 25/1: 0267: Trkd ldrs & keen, wknd over 1f out.   *shd*   **46**
3832 **JASMINE HILL 24** [9]2-8-2   C Catlin 100/1: 0608: Handy to halfway, sn btn: see 2504.   *5*   **31**
3457 **TYRONE SAM 39** [8]2-8-13   N Callan 10/1: 09: b g Mind Games - Crystal Sand (Forzando) Slow away,   *3*   **33**
nvr a factor under jt top-weight: 34,000gns Apr foal: half-brother to smart 5/6f 2yo Cumbrian Venture: dam unrcd,
sire a smart 2yo/sprinter: with K Ryan.
     ISLE DREAM [4]2-8-3 (1ow) J Edmunds 100/1: 0: 10th: In tch, rear & btn over 2f out on debut.   *8*   **0**
10 Ran   Time 58.12s (1.62)   Owned: The Mid-Landers   Trained: Lambourn

---

4339   **3.40 Albert Clamp Memorial Handicap Stakes 3yo+ 56-70   (E)**   **[84]**
       £4329   £1332   £666   **6f str**   **Firm 18**   **+01 Fast**   Centre

4278 **TROJAN FLIGHT 3** [9] Mrs J R Ramsden 3-8-8 (64) R Winston 7/4 FAV: 6432121: In tch, still trav   **72**
well when not clr run over 1f out, rdn ins fnl 1f & flew to lead cl-home: qck reapp: suited by 5/6f, stays 7f: acts
on firm & soft, stiff/gall trks: showed a gd turn of foot here, tough & can win again: see 3852.
4005 **FAIR SHAKE 16** [7] D Eddy 4-8-13 vis (67) K Darley 10/1: 0350262: Bhd, hdwy over 2f out, styd on   *shd*   **73**
well ins fnl 1f to lead cl-home, hdd post: acts on firm & soft grnd: gd eff: see 1393.
3417+ **PLAYFUL DANE 41** [11] W S Cunningham 7-8-13 (67) D Fentiman(7) 10/1: 00-15013: Sn led, hung left   *nk*   **72**
for press ins fnl 1f, hdd cl-home: 6 wk abs: acts on firm & gd: remains in gd form, see 3417.
4174 **OBE ONE 7** [6] A Berry 4-8-12 (66) F Lynch 14/1: 0604044: In tch, kept on well fnl 1f: qck   *hd*   **70**
reapp: suited by 5f, stays 6f: in gd form at present & is well h'capped: see 1977.
4118 **COLLEGE QUEEN 11** [13]6-8-9 (63) W Supple 33/1: 5452005: Cl-up, hdwy into 2nd over 2f out, no   *1¼*   **63**
impress ins fnl 1f: see 3050 & 1873.
4197 **STRAWBERRY PATCH 6** [4]5-8-4 p (58) J Fanning 12/1: 0502106: Mid-div, styd on fnl 1f: qck reapp.   *nk*   **57**
3751 **SNOW BUNTING 27** [12]6-8-8 (62) M Fenton 10/1: 2053347: Bhd, hdwy over 1f out, kept on fnl 1f.   *shd*   **60**
4245 **LEGAL SET 5** [1]8-8-6 t (60) Leanne Kershaw(7) 33/1: 0204508: Cl-up, onepcd dist: qck reapp.   *¾*   **56**
3680 **MIDNIGHT PARKES 29** [2]5-9-2 p (70) M Henry 20/1: 3503109: Prom, onepcd 1f out.   *½*   **64**
4240 **CHAIRMAN BOBBY 5** [10]6-8-13 (67) L Enstone(3) 20/1: 2500000: 10th: Handy, onepcd over 2f out.   *shd*   **60**
3942 **SILVER CHIME 19** [3]4-8-11 (65) S Sanders 16/1: 1566000: 11th: Mid-div, onepcd 2f out.   *shd*   **57**
4051 **SHAROURA 14** [14]8-8-11 (65) P Hanagan 16/1: 0342400: 12th: Bhd, hdwy/not clr run 2f out, no impress.   *hd*   **56**
4087 **COLLEGE MAID 13** [15]7-8-3 vis (57) N Mackay(3) 20/1: 6666530: 13th: Rear, not clr run 2f out, sn btn.   *½*   **46**
3352 **RONNIE FROM DONNY 43** [19]4-8-7 (61) T Eaves(3) 28/1: 0555000: 14th: Al bhd: 6 wk abs: see 241.   *nk*   **49**
4107 **Blue Maeve 12** [8]4-8-6 (60) S Righton 12/1:0   4093 **Kingsmaite 13** [18]3-8-12 bl(68) J Bramhill 14/1:0
3808 **Fitzwarren 25** [20]3-8-7 vis(63) C Catlin 33/1:0   3561 **Feu Duty 35** [5]3-8-7 (63) R McAuley 100/1:0
18 Ran   Time 1m 9.94 (1.04)   Owned: Mr Timothy O'Gram   Trained: Thirsk

---

4340   **4.10 Clam Handicap Stakes 3yo+ 46-55   (F)**   **[64]**
       £2983   £852   £426   **1m6f19y**   **Firm 18**   **-34 Slow**   Inside

4170 **ZAN LO 7** [11] B S Rothwell 4-8-9 (1oh) (45) R Winston 18/1: 6000041: Rear, hdwy wide 6f out, drvn   **52**
ins fnl 1f, led nr fin: qck reapp: op 14/1: eff at 12/14f on firm & fast, acts on a gall trk: gd run, see 1681.
3834 **SOVEREIGN STATE 24** [4] D W Thompson 7-8-12 p (49) L Enstone(3) 12/1: 0/-1602000: Rear, hdwy to lead 1½   **52**
1f out, hdd & no extra nr fin: prev eff at 1m, now stays 12/14f: gd run: see 2850.
3648 **ROUGE ET NOIR 31** [2] K G Reveley 6-8-13 T (50) T Eaves(3) 7/1: 0043: b g Hernando - Bayrouge   *nk*   **52**
(Gorytus) Rear, hdwy 4f out, ev ch 1f out, onepcd ins fnl 1f: rnr-up 1 of 2 03/04 bmpr starts (M Reveley, 2m, gd):
stays 14f on firm grnd: tried t-strap here.
4657] **REGENCY RED 682** [12] W M Brisbourne 6-8-9 (1oh) (45) B Swarbrick(5) 25/1: 232100/-4: ch g Dolphin   *1*   **46**
Street - Future Romance (Distant Relative) Bhd, hdwy halfway, hung left but led over 2f out, hdd 1f out, sn no
extra: missed '03: won a sell in '02 (R Ford): eff at 12f/2m on firm & fast, prob any trk.
1 Aug'02 Catt 15.8g/f 44- G: 2 Jul'02 Nott 14g/f 36-35 G: 2 Jun'02 Brig 11.8g/f 30-33 E: 2 Jun'01 Nott 10g/f 37-35 G:
3367* **MUSLIN 42** [14]3-8-6 (54) O Urbina 7/1: 030025: Trkd ldrs, rdn/not clr run over 1f out, kept on   *½*   **53**

ins fnl 1f: 6 wk abs: shade closer with a clr run: eff around 11.5/14f on fm & gd: see 3367.

3230	**NARCISO 48** [5]4-8-12 (49) P Mulrennan(3) 50/1: 00006: ch g Acatenango - Notturna (Diu Star)		nk	47

Handy, styd on fnl 1f: 7 wk abs: h'cap bow, mdn unplcd prev: with M Easterby.

3669* **CHEVIN 30** [3]5-8-9 (46) P Hanagan 5/2 FAV: 450-5017: Trkd ldrs, chall 2f out, wknd 1f out. — 1 — 42

4249* **RESTART 5** [6]3-8-13 (6ex) (61) G Faulkner 8/1: 030-0018: In tch, onepcd 2f out: qck reapp. — ¾ — 56

3701 **RIVER LINE 29** [9]3-8-0 (1ow) (47) C Catlin 100/1: 00-40009: Led till 2f out, wknd 1f out. — 5 — 35

3771* **RIGHTY HO 26** [10]10-8-13 (50) Kristin Stubbs(7) 16/1: 1330610: 10th: Rcd in 2nd to 3f out, wknd. — 6 — 28

2790 **THEATRE BELLE 66** [15]3-8-2 (1ow) (49) D Allan 40/1: 0-000650: 11th: Handy, wknd over 4f out. — 7 — 17

3834 **BANNERS FLYING 24** [1]4-8-9 (1oh) (45) A Culhane 40/1: 0404000: 12th: In tch till 3f out, sn btn. — 8 — 1

4151 **LARKING ABOUT 9** [8]4-9-0 (51) K Darley 3/1: 0006020: 13th: Slow away in rear, t.o.: nicely — dist — 0
bckd: puzzling run & something clearly amiss: see 4151 (soft).

13 Ran   Time 3m 5.12 (7.32)   Owned: Mr D J Coles   Trained: Nawton

---

4341   4.40 Lobster Classified Stakes 3yo+ 0-75 (D)
£6988 £2150 £1075   **7f str   Firm 18   +10 Fast   Centre**

3574* **HARTSHEAD 34** [6] G A Swinbank 5-9-3 (75) Dean McKeown 4/1 FAV: 0611411: Rear, hdwy 2f out, drvn — — 82
ins fnl 1f & led cl-home: fast time: stays 1m, suited by 6/7f on firm & gd, likes Redcar: see 3574.

1825 **NIGHT AIR 107** [3] D R Loder 3-8-13 (74) K Darley 9/2: 152: Dwelt, sn in mid-div, hdwy 2f out, — nk — 80
led over 1f out, hdd cl-home: long abs: eff at 7f on firm & gd/soft: continues to prog: see 1473 (debut).

3433 **REIDIES CHOICE 40** [9] J G Given 3-8-13 (73) A Culhane 12/1: 0204203: Bhd, hdwy over 1f out, kept — 1½ — 77
on well ins fnl 1f to go 3rd cl home: 6 wk abs: back to form: see 1879.

3694 **BORREGO 29** [1] C E Brittain 4-9-3 BL (72) S Sanders 20/1: 2-206004: Trkd ldrs, hdwy to chall over — nk — 76
1f out, no impress fnl 1f: tried blnks: see 2235.

3937 **ABBAJABBA 19** [7]8-9-3 (74) J Fanning 14/1: 0000205: In tch, hdwy over 1f out, kept on. — hd — 75

3696* **SAMUEL CHARLES 29** [2]6-9-3 (75) B Swarbrick(5) 12/1: 3342016: Led till over 1f out, styd on. — shd — 74

4051 **NEON BLUE 14** [13]3-8-13 (72) S Chin 10/1: 0333167: In tch, no impress 2f out. — 2½ — 69

3950 **MASTER THEO 19** [4]3-8-13 (74) J Quinn 8/1: 5-033338: Chsd ldrs, wkng when hmpd ins fnl 1f. — ½ — 68

3768 **EFIDIUM 26** [12]6-9-3 (74) C Catlin 9/2: 5354129: Rear, hdwy over 2f out, sn wknd. — ½ — 67

3433 **VADEMECUM 40** [8]3-8-13 (73) F Lynch 12/1: 413-6000: 10th: Rear, hdwy when not clr run over 1f — nk — 66
out, sn no impress: 6 wk abs: see 1305.

3356 **SION HILL 42** [5]3-8-13 (75) P Hanagan 33/1: 202-000: 11th: Chsd ldrs, wknd qckly 2f out: 6 wk — 1¼ — 63
abs: new with J O'Reilly: see 3241.

2153 **MARINAITE 92** [14]3-8-10 (73) J Bramhill 20/1: 1522030: 12th: Prom, no impress 2f out: long abs. — ¾ — 58

4051 **PERFECT LOVE 14** [10]4-9-0 (70) D Allan 50/1: 2000-000: 13th: Bhd, hung right 3f out, fin t.o.. — 22 — 36

13 Ran   Time 1m 22.41 (0.61)   Owned: Mr B Valentine   Trained: Richmond

---

4342   5.10 Mussel Handicap Stakes 3yo 56-70 (E)   [77]
£4198 £1292 £646   **1m2f   Firm 18   -02 Slow   Inside**

3906 **STEPHANO 21** [12] B W Hills 3-8-10 (59) P Hanagan 25/1: 50-0501: Bhd, hdwy to lead 2f out, rdn — — 72
out: first win: relished step up to 10f: acts on firm grnd, gall trk: win again over this trip: see 2656.

3772* **HAVETOAVIT 26** [8] J D Bethell 3-9-2 (65) J Fanning 9/2: 3240412: Trkd ldrs till led 3f out, hdd — 2½ — 70
2f out, no extra: acts on firm, gd/soft & fibresand: continues in decent form & goes well at Redcar: see 3772.

3853 **WING COLLAR 22** [4] T D Easterby 3-9-2 (65) W Supple 11/1: 0332043: Bhd, hdwy 4f out, kept on: — nk — 69
acts on firm & soft: gd run: see 2322.

4248 **DANCE TO MY TUNE 5** [9] M W Easterby 3-8-13 (62) P Mulrennan(3) 6/1: 6104124: Rear, hdwy & not clr — ½ — 65
run over 2f out, pulled out to chall, styd on: qck reapp: shade closer with a clr passage.

2633 **BLUETONIA 73** [5]3-9-5 (68) Dean McKeown 50/1: 0-405: Bhd, hdwy 3f out, wandered & kept on. — nk — 70

4321 **COTTINGHAM 1** [15]3-8-11 (60) Stephanie Hollinshead(5) 33/1: 14660206: Rear, hdwy 3f out, styd on. — hd — 61

3950 **BERTOCELLI 19** [1]3-8-7 (56) A McCarthy 50/1: 3400607: Chsd ldrs, no impress over 1f out. — 2½ — 53

3391 **EDGEHILL 41** [7]3-9-1 (64) M Fenton 9/2: 00-428: Handy, no impress over 1f out: 6 wk abs. — ¾ — 60

3998 **MUNAAWESH 11** [11]3-8-7 bl (56) A Culhane 14/1: 4204229: Rear, hdwy 4f out, no impress 2f out. — 2 — 49

3391 **TURNER 41** [13]3-9-7 (70) B Swarbrick(5) 50/1: 60-63300: 10th: Bhd, nvr nr ldrs: 6 wk abs. — hd — 62

3875 **GOLDEN DRIFT 22** [3]3-8-11 (60) K Darley 9/1: 0-050250: 11th: Chsd ldrs, wknd/eased over 1f out. — 4 — 46

3410 **DAN DI CANIO 41** [6]3-9-0 t (63) N Callan 16/1: 50550: 12th: In tch, wknd 3f out: 6 wk abs: see 2106. — 7 — 38

4112* **BELISCO 12** [14]3-9-6 VIS t (69) B Reilly(3) 14/1: 50-00610: 13th: Chsd ldrs, hung left 3f out, sn — 7 — 33
wknd: tried a visor: new with C Dwyer: much btr 4112 (cirm, AW).

3719* **OPTIMAL 28** [2]3-9-1 bl (64) S Sanders 4/1 FAV: 400-0610: 14th: Led to 3f out, sn no extra & fdd, — dist — 0
eased over 1f out, t.o.: reportedly suffered nasal discharge: forgive this, see 3719.

14 Ran   Time 2m 4.37(2.07)   Owned: Mr Guy Reed   Trained: Lambourn

---

Official Going GOOD (GOOD/SOFT places).

4343   2.30 Sands Maiden Auction Stakes 2yo (E)
£3150 £900 £450   **5f rnd   Good/Firm 35   -05 Slow   Inside**

4050 **FLYING RIDGE 14** [3] A M Balding 2-8-6 R Mullen 5/1: 0551: Handy & led 2f out, flashed tail — — 80
under press but held on well ins last: eff over a stiff 5f/6f on fast & gd grnd: handles a sharp/turning or
stiff/gall trk: shows temperament but also ability & could make her mark in nurseries: see 4050 & 3736.

3832 **CHISELLED 24** [1] K R Burke 2-8-10 T (80) Darren Williams 3/1 FAV: 422042: Trkd ldrs, eff to chase — ¾ — 81
wnrs ins last, al just held: imprvd eff in first time t-strap, back on faster surface: see 3266, 1826 & 1458.

3807 **LADY DAN 25** [4] M W Easterby 2-8-3 (68) Dale Gibson 6/1: 4320603: Rdn towards rear, kept on — 1¾ — 69
late, not threaten front pair: see 2360.

3988 **DISPOL ISLE 17** [8] T D Barron 2-8-2 (65) P Fessey 4/1: 4444: Dwelt, towards rear, kept on late, — ¾ — 66
nvr a threat: see 3988, 2933 & 2360.

4089 **RUSSIAN RIO 13** [9]2-8-9 Rory Moore(5) 22/1: 05: Led till 2f out, no extra: turf bow, imprvd — hd — 72

from intro: handles fast grnd: see 4089.
4172 **LLAMADAS 7** [7]2-8-10 bl (64) S W Kelly 8/1: 3034036: Pushed rear, not pace to chall. ½ **69**
3457 **WAGGLEDANCE 39** [11]2-8-9 G Parkin 40/1: 5007: Cl-up, outpcd from halfway: see 2167. 1¾ **65**
4102 **EGYPTIAN LADY 12** [2]2-8-2 T Hamilton 80/1: 08: ch f Bold Edge - Calypso Lady (Priolo) Pushed along rear, no impress: cheaply bght Jan foal, half-sister to a plcd 6f juv, dam a 6f 2yo scorer. *nk* **57**
1632 **JOE JO STAR 117** [12]2-8-9 Hayley Turner(3) 20/1: 669: b c Piccolo - Zagreb Flyer (Old Vic) Chsd ldrs, no impress halfway: 4 mth abs: 14,000gns Feb foal: half-brother to a useful 6/7f juv wnr Venturi. 2½ **56**
3735 **MIDDLE EASTERN 28** [10]2-8-9 P Bradley 10/1: 540: 10th: Chsd ldrs, struggling halfway: btr 3735. *shd* **56**
GEORDIE DANCER [6]2-8-9 P Mathers(5) 20/1: 0: 11th: b c Dansili - Awtaar (Lyphard) Dwelt, sn outpcd: bckd at long odds: 15,000gns Feb foal, half-brother to a dual 12f 3/4yo scorer, dam plcd as a juv. *hd* **55**
FERN HOUSE [5]2-8-9 R Ffrench 25/1: 0: 12th: Dwelt & al rear on debut. ½ **53**
12 Ran Time 1m 01.5 (2.0) Owned: Mr E N Kronfeld Trained: Kingsclere

4344

3.00 Border Construction Nursery Handicap Stakes 2yo 0-75 (E) **[80]**
£5506 £1694 £847 **5f193y rnd** **Good/Firm 35** **-24 Slow** Inside

3857 **KINGSGATE BAY 22** [1] J R Best 2-9-0 (66) N Pollard 12/1: 0551: Sn cl-up from awkward low draw, led over 2f out, edged right under press & flashed tail but held on well: op 10/1: first win on h'cap bow: eff at 6f, shld get further: acts on fast grnd & a stiff trk: imprvd for racing up with/forcing the pace today, overcame awkward berth in fine style, worth following in similar. **80+**
3589* **HANSOMELLE 33** [9] B Mactaggart 2-9-6 (72) R Ffrench 12/1: 412: Mid-div, styd on to chase wnr fnl 1f, al held: h'cap bow: confirmed improvement of 3589. 1½ **80**
3987 **PRO TEMPORE 17** [3] Mrs J R Ramsden 2-8-13 (65) A Beech(3) 5/1 FAV: 41663: Rear, switched/hung right over 1f out, kept on, al held: styd longer 6f trip: caught the eye 3987, cld find similar. 1½ **66**
3722 **ROYAL PARDON 28** [6] M L W Bell 2-8-6 (58) R Mullen 8/1: 0044: Pushed along towards rear, kept on fnl 2f, no dngr: bckd on h'cap bow: eff over a stiff 6f, looks worth a try at 7f in similar: acts on fast grnd. ½ **59**
4127 **HOPELESSLY DEVOTED 10** [13]2-8-6 (58) Rory Moore(5) 25/1: 06105: Keen, trkd ldrs, no extra dist. 2½ **51**
4089 **ZANTERO 13** [7]2-8-13 (65) J Mackay 20/1: 4646: Pushed along towards rear, late hdwy, no threat: h'cap bow: 7f in similar shld suit: prob handles fast grnd: see 2051. ¾ **56**
3686 **CHAIRMAN RICK 29** [19]2-8-13 (65) Alex Greaves 25/1: 06407: Mid-div, nvr pace to chall: new yard. *hd* **55**
3736 **CHOREOGRAPHIC 28** [16]2-8-9 (61) T Hamilton(3) 6/1: 0308: Hmpd start, towards rear, only mod prog. 1¼ **47**
4074 **NO COMMISSION 13** [10]2-9-7 (73) D Nolan(3) 12/1: 4021059: Mid-div, no impress fnl 2f: btr 3245. *hd* **58**
3931 **LORD JOHN 20** [5]2-8-3 (55) Dale Gibson 10/1: 4040040: 10th: Rear, mod gains: btr 3212. *shd* **40**
2847 **KILMOVEE 64** [18]2-9-3 (69) Kim Tinkler 40/1: 50550: 11th: Led till 2f out, wknd: abs: btr 2847. 1¼ **50**
3756 **RYEDANE 27** [8]2-8-13 (65) S W Kelly 14/1: 0305300: 12th: Held up, no impress fnl 2f: btr 3374 (5f). *shd* **46**
4244 **MISTER BUZZ 5** [17]2-8-8 (60) Lisa Jones 16/1: 000440: 13th: Mid-div, no impress from halfway. 1¾ **36**
3239 **Zarova 48** [14]2-8-4 (56) T Lucas 25/1:0 3053 **Kaggamagic 56** [2]2-9-3 (69) Darren Williams 20/1:0
4206 **Maureens Lough 6** [12]2-8-3 (55) Hayley Turner(3) 25/1:0 4089 **Eukleia 13** [15]2-8-13 (65) P Fessey 20/1:0
2569 **Zendaro 75** [11]2-8-5 (57) S Hitchcott 14/1:0 3901 **Kristikhab 21** [4]2-8-4 (56) P Mathers(4) 20/1:0
19 Ran Time 1m 14.26 (3.56) Owned: Mr John Mayne Trained: Maidstone

4345

3.30 Willy Holme Handicap Stakes 3yo+ 46-55 (F) **[67]**
£3296 £942 £471 **6f192y rnd** **Good/Firm 35** **-28 Slow** Inside

3526 **MON SECRET 36** [4] B Smart 6-8-12 (51) D McGaffin 14/1: 4006061: Rear, rdn & hdwy halfway, led ins last, drvn out: 7f specialist, tried 1m: acts on fast, gd/soft & both AWs, sharp or stiff trk: see 193. **56**
4051 **ICED DIAMOND 14** [9] W M Brisbourne 5-8-11 t (50) S Hitchcott(3) 8/1: 0004402: Dwelt, held up, hdwy & switched over 1f out, rdn to chall ins last, carried head high & not pace of wnr cl-home: t-strap reapplied. *nk* **54**
4175 **JOSHUAS GOLD 7** [5] D Carroll 3-8-12 vis (55) D Tudhope(7) 13/2: 0001423: Sn cl-up & ev ch fnl 2f, rdn & no extra ins last: trav well in a race, tough & consistent, shld win more races: see 4175, 3547. ¾ **58**
3670 **LINDENS LADY 30** [6] J R Weymes 4-8-12 (51) A Beech(3) 16/1: 0565054: Rear, styd on wide for press, not pace of front trio: confirmed improvement of latest, well h'capped & looks to be coming to hand. 1¼ **51**
4215 **APACHE POINT 6** [10]7-9-1 (54) Kim Tinkler 8/1: 5235555: Rear, outpcd halfway, kept on, 1m+. *nk* **53**
4088 **WOOD DALLING 13** [15]6-9-2 (55) P Fessey 9/1: 0616606: Trkd ldrs, edged right & no extra dist. 1¾ **51**
4109 **CUT RIDGE 12** [13]5-9-2 (55) R Ffrench 8/1: 0321257: Keen, led/dsptd lead till ins last: btr 3911. *hd* **50**
4009 **THE WIZARD MUL 16** [11]4-9-1 (54) Hayley Turner(3) 50/1: 04-00008: Handy, fdd dist: see 1366. *hd* **48**
4132* **DUBONAI 10** [3]4-9-1 (6ex) (54) D Corby(3) 10/1: 0030019: Mid-div, no impress fnl 2f: op 14/1. *nk* **47**
4088 **ZHITOMIR 13** [12]6-8-11 (50) S W Kelly 6/1 FAV: 1661640: 10th: Mid-div, btn dist: btr 3324 (sell). *hd* **42**
3654 **WALTZING WIZARD 31** [1]5-8-12 (51) P Mathers(5) 16/1: 0634060: 11th: Al rear: btr 2935. *hd* **42**
3933 **GOLDEN SPECTRUM 20** [8]5-9-0 vis (53) Alex Greaves 14/1: 5003000: 12th: Rear, btn 2f out: btr 3670. 1¼ **41**
4088 **Stormville 13** [7]7-9-1 (54) M Lawson(5) 25/1:0 4009 **Fenwicks Pride 16** [2]6-9-0 (53) T Hamilton(3) 20/1:0
14 Ran Time 1m 28.29 (4.39) Owned: Pinnacle Monash Partnership Trained: Thirsk

4346

4.00 Carlisle Glass Handicap Stakes 3yo+ 56-70 (E) **[79]**
£5328 £1639 £820 **7f200y rnd** **Good/Firm 35** **-01 Slow** Inside

4202 **OTAGO 6** [16] J R Best 3-8-2 (53) R Ffrench 11/2: 0450421: Sn prom & led over 1f out, edged left, drvn & held on gamely: first win, qck reapp: imprvd of late at 1m, acts on firm & gd/soft grnd, sharp or stiff/turning trk: shows a willing attitude, could win again: see 4202, 3526. **61**
3492 **HULA BALLEW 38** [14] M Dods 4-8-13 p (59) S W Kelly 9/1: 5501552: Mid-div, hdwy when briefly short of room over 1f out, chall ins last, just held cl-home: see 2993. ½ **66**
3137 **ABLE MIND 53** [15] A C Whillans 4-8-11 (57) P Fessey 14/1: 233-0063: Mid-div, styd on for press despite hanging right, not pace of front pair: 8 wk abs: stays a stiff 1m: see 2726. 1½ **61**
4135* **TEMPLET 10** [5] I Semple 4-9-6 (6ex) (66) G Parkin 14/1: 5300214: Bhd early, rdn & styd on fnl 2f, nrst fin: eff at 1m, crying out for a return to 9f+ in similar: acts on fast & hvy: worth another look. ¾ **69+**
4241* **RISKA KING 5** [18]4-9-13 (6ex) (73) T Hamilton(3) 6/1: 0433615: Chsd ldrs, no extra dist: see 4241. *nk* **75**
4241 **GIFTED FLAME 5** [13]5-9-7 (67) P Makin(5) 5/1 FAV: 0031436: Rear, hdwy/short of room over 1f out, *shd* **69**

no extra ins last: qck reapp: see 3650 (C/D).

3996* **BAND 17** [12]4-8-11 (57) S Hitchcott(3) 11/2: 0040517: Held up, eff 2f out, no prog ins last.   nk   58
4246 **ZARIN 5** [4]6-8-7 (53) N Pollard 16/1: 0062158: Keen & led/dsptd lead, no extra dist: qck reapp.   hd   53
4132 **CRYFIELD 10** [8]7-9-0 (60) Kim Tinkler 14/1: 0164349: Held up, nvr able to chall: see 2890.   1   58
4175 **GRACEFUL AIR 7** [3]3-8-4 (55) Joanna Badger 50/1: 0544500: 10th: Mid-div, no impress fnl 2f.   nk   52
3850 **FLYING SPUD 22** [6]3-8-2 (5oh) (48) Lisa Jones 25/1: 1000200: 11th: Cl-up, btn 2f out: btr 3182 (g/s).   1½   47
3526 **TIME TO REGRET 36** [2]4-8-7 (1oh) (52) P Mathers(5) 25/1: 2401000: 12th: Led till dist, wknd.   ¾   46
4246 **PHAROAHS GOLD 5** [1]6-8-7 (4oh)P (49) Darren Williams 50/1: 0400000: 13th: Keen & held up, hung   1¾   43
right & btn 2f out, qck reapp: tried cheek pieces: btr 1388.
3759 **NEWCORP LAD 27** [7]4-8-11 VIS (59) J Mackay 10/1: 0044240: 14th: In tch, hung right & btn 2f out.   nk   48
4211 **LORD ARTHUR 6** [10]3-8-2 BL (53) Dale Gibson 50/1: 00-04000: 15th: Trkd ldrs, hung right & btn 2f   8   29
out, qck reapp: blnks: btr 3095 (6f, AW).
15 Ran   Time 1m 40.57 (2.87)   Owned: Mrs L M Askew   Trained: Maidstone

---

4347   4.30 Denton Holme Median Auction Maiden Stakes 3-4yo (E)
£3136 £896 £448   1m1f61y   Good/Firm 35   -00 Slow   Inside

3740 **COUNTRYWIDE LUCK 28** [8] N P Littmoden 3-8-12 J P Guillambert(3) 4/9 FAV: 621: Chsd ldrs, hdwy to   78
lead over 1f out, hung right, rdn out: hvly bckd at odds-on to confirm recent promise: eff at 9/10.5f on fast & gd
grnd, stiff/gall trks: lightly rcd gelding, could prog in h'cap company: see 3740.
4084 **YOUNG ROONEY 13** [14] M Mullineaux 4-9-4 (68) R Mullen 6/1: 324-4032: Rcd keen early, sn led &   2½   72
hung left throughout, edged towards stands side fnl 2f & hdd over 1f out, kept on: clr of rem: headstrong type but
not without ability, can find a race: see 4084 (h'cap).
3923 **DREAM EASY 20** [13] P L Gilligan 3-8-12 (70) R Price 11/1: 05453: Rear, late gains, no threat to   6   61
front pair: see 3282, 2595.
3547 **GRELE 35** [12] R Hollinshead 3-8-7 (45) P Makin(5) 50/1: 0-0564: Held up, kept on fnl 3f, no   ¾   55$
threat: apprec low grade h'caps: see 3079.
3182 **SCHINKEN OTTO 51** [9]3-8-12 (45) T Hamilton(3) 66/1: 060-0605: Slow away, mod prog, abs.   5   51
4135 **SARENNE 10** [4]3-8-7 R Ffrench 16/1: 66: b f Desert Sun - Fabulous Pet (Somethingfabulous) Held   ¾   45
up, no ch over 3f out, mod late prog: well bhd on debut: op 12/1: bred to apprec 1m+.
4075 **REEM TWO 13** [6]3-8-7 (55) J Mackay 16/1: 6327: Chsd ldrs, struggling fnl 2f: flattered 4075.   2½   40
2054 **ROYALTEA 97** [1]3-8-7 (47) Joanna Badger 66/1: 664008: Rear, hung right & btn 3f out: abs.   nk   39
4129} **BOBERING 360** [2]4-9-4 P Mathers(5) 100/1: 0-9: b g Bob's Return - Ring The Rafters (Batshoof)   15   17
Mid-div, struggling fnl 3f: reapp: no form sole '03 start (rtd 13).
3934 **TRANSKEI 20** [7]3-8-7 S W Kelly 100/1: 040: 10th: Held up, struggling fnl 3f: modest form.   6   2
4809} **WELL CONNECTED 318** [5]4-9-4 (45) D McGaffin 66/1: 006030-0: 11th: Handy, wknd fnl 3f, reapp.   2   3
4132} **STARBRIGHT 359** [11]3-8-12 T Lucas 80/1: 0-0: 12th: Keen & cl-up, struggling fnl 3f, reapp.   7   0
         Jonnyem [3]3-8-12 Dale Gibson 28/1:0   **La Mago** [10]4-8-13 D Mernagh 100/1:0
14 Ran   Time 1m 58.64 (3.24)   Owned: Countrywide Steel & Tubes Ltd   Trained: Newmarket

---

4348   5.00 Battle Holme Handicap Stakes 3yo+ 46-55 (F)
£3242 £926 £463   1m3f206y   Good/Firm 35   +08 Fast   Outside   [64]

4170 **TURN OF PHRASE 7** [17] R A Fahey 5-9-4 vis (54) T Hamilton(3) 15/8 FAV: 213-0021: Mid-div, hdwy 2f   63
out, rdn to chall ins last, led ins last, all out: gd time, well bckd, op 5/2: eff btwn 12/14f: acts on firm, gd &
polytrack, shapr or stiff trk: eff in blnks, suited by application of visor last twice: see 4170 & 3502.
4084 **SCURRA 13** [8] A C Whillans 5-9-3 (53) D Tudhope(7) 12/1: 3124652: Held up, hdwy to lead 2f out,   shd 61
drvn & strongly chall ins last, just hdd line: well clr of rem: eff at 9/12f: see 2726 & 2545.
3850 **DEE PEE TEE CEE 22** [12] M W Easterby 10-8-10 (46) T Lucas 16/1: 40500/-03: Led, hdd 2f out, no extra. 11   41
3771 **LIFE IS BEAUTIFUL 26** [4] W H Tinning 5-9-0 (50) Dale Gibson 7/1: 6151624: Mid-div, kept on fnl   1¼   43
3f, no threat to front pair: see 2653 (clmr, Beverley).
3549 **MR MIDAZ 35** [2]5-8-9 (45) R Ffrench 18/1: 4000/-555: Mid-div, no impress fnl 2f: see 3276.   2½   34
4243 **DANEFONIQUE 5** [1]3-8-5 (50) R Mullen 10/1: 5604026: Led/dpstd lead till 2f out: qck reapp.   ¾   38
3830 **CANLIS 24** [10]5-8-9 P (45) D Mernagh 12/1: 0200057: Keen, mid-div, btn 2f out: chkpcs: btr 2402.   nk   32
4327 **SHERWOOD FOREST 1** [15]4-8-9 vis (45) D Corby(3) 20/1: 36052608: Bhd, mod prog, unplcd yesterday.   nk   31
3275 **CANTEMERLE 47** [5]4-8-10 bl (46) S W Kelly 12/1: 0-200609: Held up, strugg halfway, nvr factor.   hd   31
3558 **SHARABAD 35** [16]6-8-9 (45) D McGaffin 100/1: 50000: 10th: Chsd ldrs, btn 2f out: see 1894.   ½   29
4045 **Caper 14** [9]4-8-9 (5oh) (40) J Mackay 66/1:0
3420 **Border Terrier 40** [13]6-8-9 (5oh)VIS(40) Hayley Turner(3) 12/1:0
4076 **Saddlers Quest 13** [7]7-9-0 (50) Darren Williams 28/1:0 3669   **Lady Stratagem 30** [14]5-8-9 (5oh) (40) G Parkin 40/1:0
1776} **Needwood Spirit 463** [11]9-8-9 (10oh)(35) P Mathers(5) 40/1:0
3970 **Special Branch 18** [6]4-8-9 (45) N Pollard 16/1:0
16 Ran   Time 2m 34.04(3.24)   Owned: Jacksons Transport (West Riding) Ltd   Trained: Malton

---

HAYDOCK   FRIDAY 03.09.04   Lefthand, Flat, Galloping Track

Official Going GOOD (GOOD/SOFT places).

4349   2.30 European Breeders Fund Maiden Stakes 2yo (D)
£4979 £1532 £766   5f str   Good/Firm 31   -16 Slow   Centre

4205 **PREMIER FANTASY 7** [9] T D Barron 2-9-0 P Hanagan 4/1: 61: Dwelt, sn handy, hdwy to lead ins   94+
last, styd on, hands & heels: much imprvd from debut & eff at 5f on fast: useful, win more races.
4121 **JUANTORENA 11** [6] M L W Bell 2-9-0 (92) R Mullen 13/8 FAV: 224342: Set pace, kept on & rdn over   1¼   88
1f out, hdd ins last, not pace of wnr: hvly bckd: clr of rem & a gd run from the front but remains a mdn after 6.
BEAUNE [10] W J Haggas 2-9-0 S W Kelly 11/1: 3: b c Desert Prince - Tipsy (Kris) Chsd ldrs,   3   78
eff over 1f out, kept on ins last, no threat to front pair: Feb 1st foal: dam 1m/12f wnr: eff at 5f, sure to

relish 6f+: acts on fast grnd: will improve plenty for this & be wng races over further shortly.
AYNSLEY [2] M A Jarvis 2-8-9 P Robinson 14/1: 4: ch f Tomba - Eggy (Risk Me) Rcd alone far side, handy, no extra over 1f out: Apr 1st foal, cost 6,500 gns: cheaply bred & will learn from this. *3* **63**
3993 **EMERALD LODGE 18** [8]2-9-0 D Holland 5/1: 35: Handy, wknd over 1f out: see 3993. *hd* **67**
1170 **CILLAS SMILE 142** [7]2-8-9 D Allan 50/1: 06: b f Lake Coniston - Tinkerbird (Music Boy) Slow away, in tch, wknd over 1f out: Mar foal: half sister to a 5f scorer: dam 5/6f wnr. *1* **59**
GUADIARO [4]2-9-0 K Darley 14/1: 7: Nvr a factor. *nk* **63**
CAVALARRA [11]2-9-0 A Culhane 12/1: 8: Slow away & went right start, nvr a factor. *3* **53**
DANZATRICE [5]2-8-9 Dean McKeown 66/1: 9: Slow away & al bhd. *7* **28**
2870 **COOL CRISTAL 64** [1]2-8-9 P Mulrennan(3) 66/1: 00: 10th: Slow away & al bhd. *5* **13**
RANDALLS TOUCH [3]2-9-0 D Mernagh 66/1: 0: 11th: Slow away & al bhd. *9* **0**
11 Ran Time 1m 01.18 (2.38) Owned: Mr J Browne Trained: Thirsk

4350

3.05 European Breeders Fund Classified Stakes 3yo+ 0-80 (D)
£9074 £2792 £1396 **6f str** **Good/Firm 31** **-08 Slow** Centre

3928 **SOLAR POWER 21** [8] J R Fanshawe 3-8-11 (83) J Murtagh 4/1: 1-244431: Went right start, chsd ldrs, hdwy & short of room 2f out, styd on to lead over 1f out, rdn out: stays a stiff 1m, relished this drop back to 6f: acts on fast & soft grnd, gall trk: consistent: see 1419, 131. **89**
4184 **KINGSCROSS 7** [5] M Blanshard 6-8-13 (75) D Sweeney 13/2: 2105022: Held up, hdwy over 1f out, styd on ins last, not pace of wnr: fine run, enjoys easier grnd: see 4184, 1523. *1* **85**
4099* **OUT AFTER DARK 13** [2] C G Cox 3-8-12 (81) P Robinson 2/1 FAV: 042-5113: Cl-up, eff to chall over 1f out, sn onepcd: hvly bckd: continues to go the right way: lightly rcd, made virtually all 4099. *nk* **85**
3326 **FLUR NA H ALBA 45** [10] I Semple 5-9-1 p (82) R Winston 25/1: 000-1034: Handy, hdwy to lead over 1f out, no extra ins last: 6 wk abs: last 2 wins have been over 7f at Ayr: see 1909. *1¾* **81**
3937 **SIERRA VISTA 20** [9]4-8-10 (79) L Enstone(3) 14/1: 0516005: Held up, hdwy short of room 2f out, switched & onepace ins fnl 1f: best 2770. *1¼* **72**
4098 **CAUSTIC WIT 13** [7]6-9-4 p (85) D Holland 11/2: 1220046: Handy, wknd fnl 1f: see 2758, 2451. *1¾* **75**
3569 **PAX 35** [1]7-8-13 (80) A Nicholls 16/1: 1000007: In tch, eff & short of room over 1f out, no extra: reportedly broke a blood vessel: best 2059. *½* **69**
3535 **TOTALLY YOURS 37** [11]3-8-13 (85) F Norton 20/1: 0-040508: Held up, eff over 1f out, no impress. *hd* **70**
4027 **BONNE DE FLEUR 16** [6]3-8-8 (80) F Lynch 12/1: 2-100509: Handy, led till over 1f out, no extra, lame. *2½* **58**
2137 **LITTLE RIDGE 94** [3]3-8-13 (82) L Fletcher(3) 50/1: 36011-00: 10th: Led till halfway, wknd over 2f out. *13* **33**
3784* **CONJUROR 27** [4]3-9-0 (83) R J Killoran(7) 14/1: U10: 11th: Al bhd, sadly fin lame: see 3784. *5* **19**
11 Ran Time 1m 13.65 (2.35) Owned: Deln Ltd Trained: Newmarket

4351

3.35 National Stud Never Say Die Club Median Auction Maiden Stakes 2yo (E)
£3611 £1111 £556 **1m30y rnd** **Good/Firm 31** **-06 Slow** Inside

3786 **SAADIGG 27** [1] M A Jarvis 2-9-0 P Robinson 8/1: 341: Made all, kept on over 1f out, rdn out: relished switch to turf & clrly stays a gall 1m well, shld get further: acts on fast grnd: enjoyed forcing tactics. **89**
4069 **GLEN IDA 14** [8] M L W Bell 2-9-0 R Mullen 6/5 FAV: 32: Slow away, held up, hdwy to chall over 1f out, no extra ins last: hvly bckd: stays 1m: acts on fast & gd/soft: shown enough to win a race: see 4069. *1½* **86**
4115 **CALL ME MAX 12** [6] E A L Dunlop 2-9-0 K Darley 10/1: 4353: Keen, prom, eff to chall over 1f out, no extra ins last: prob ran to form of 3803, see 3489. *1½* **83**
KAMES PARK [2] I Semple 2-9-0 R Winston 50/1: 4: b g Desert Sun - Persian Sally (Persian Bold) Slow away, keen, some late gains, nvr a factor: Apr foal, cost 3,500 gns: half brother to a 7f/10f scorer. *1½* **80**
4233 **LITHOS 6** [7]2-9-0 S W Kelly 14/1: 265: Handy, no extra over 1f out: see 3798. *½* **79**
3120 **COMMENDABLE COUP 55** [3]2-9-0 P Hanagan 22/1: 506: b c Commendable - Bird Dance (Storm Bird) Al bhd: 8 wk abs: Mar foal: half brother to a 7f juv wnr. *8* **64**
4207 **CALA FONS 7** [5]2-8-9 Kim Tinkler 100/1: 007: Keen in tch, wknd & hung right over 4f out. *8* **44**
GRIZEBECK [10]2-9-0 L Fletcher(3) 66/1: 8: b g Trans Island - Premier Amour (Salmon Leap) Slow away & nvr a factor on debut: Apr foal, cost 7,500 gns: half brother to wng milers: dam 11f scorer. *14* **24**
8 Ran Time 1m 43.46 (2.96) Owned: Sheikh Ahmed Al Maktoum Trained: Newmarket

4352

4.10 Kings Regiment Cup Handicap Stakes 3yo+ 71-85 (D) **[86]**
£7362 £2265 £1133 **1m30y rnd** **Good/Firm 31** **+19 Fast** Inside

4279 **GOODBYE MR BOND 4** [5] E J Alston 4-8-13 (71) F Norton 4/1 FAV: 1113261: Held up, hdwy over 2f out, styd on to lead ins last, rdn out: gd time: 5th win this term: v eff over 1m/9f on fast, soft grnd, handles fibresand & any trk: most tough & prog this term, fine advert for his talented trainer: see 2672. **81**
4221 **AFRICAN SAHARA 6** [2] Miss D Mountain 5-9-10 t (82) O Urbina 11/2: 3431422: In tch, eff & short of room over 1f out, switched & kept on ins last, not pace of wnr: in fine heart: see 4221, 3768. *1½* **88**
3961 **MR JACK DANIELLS 20** [6] W R Muir 3-8-12 (75) J Murtagh 10/1: 3041403: Led till halfway, led again over 1f out, hdd ins last, no extra: jockey received a 1 day whip ban: back to form of 3339. *¾* **79**
4073 **STOIC LEADER 14** [4] R F Fisher 4-9-8 (80) L Fletcher(3) 20/1: 2652564: In tch, eff over 1f out, onepace. *1¼* **82**
3443 **PLAY MASTER 41** [15]3-8-10 (73) Paul Eddery 50/1: 2010305: Bhd, some late gains, nvr dangerous. *¾* **73**
4136 **HILLS OF GOLD 11** [13]5-9-6 (78) P Mulrennan(3) 11/1: 0322146: Chsd ldrs, onepcd over 1f out. *hd* **77**
3905* **APERITIF 22** [11]3-9-0 (77) S W Kelly 9/1: 3-043317: Held up, short of room over 5f out, eff over 2f out, no danger: up in class after mdn win on gd/soft in 3905. *1½* **73**
2543 **LAURO 77** [10]4-9-2 (74) R Winston 10/1: 14-32448: In tch, eff over 1f out, no extra: 11 wk abs: see 2323. *hd* **69**
4180 **DOCTORATE 8** [8]3-9-6 (83) P Hanagan 14/1: 4-012539: In tch, wknd 2f out: btr 4180 (7f, polytrack). *¾* **76**
3152 **BRIEF GOODBYE 53** [12]4-9-9 (81) M Fenton 40/1: 3-140140: 10th: In tch, wknd over 1f out: 7 wk abs. *¾* **72**
3885* **ZWEIBRUCKEN 22** [3]3-9-7 (84) D Holland 14/1: 120-0010: 11th: Keen in tch, wknd 2f out: btr 3885. *hd* **74**
3697* **LITTLE BOB 30** [7]3-8-12 (75) P Robinson 16/1: 4423010: 12th: Slow away & al bhd: btr 3697 (mdn). *3½* **58**
3738 **BAFFLE 29** [9]3-8-10 (73) K Darley 22/1: 26-15060: 13th: Led halfway till over 1f out, wknd: btr 1108 (1m). *2* **52**
2835 **MISS MONICA 66** [14]3-8-6 (4oh) (69) W Ryan 11/1: 6430: 14th: Nvr a factor: 2 month abs: see 2835. *1¾* **44**
4048 **MORSE 15** [1]3-9-8 (85) D Sweeney 33/1: 2006000: 15th: In tch, wknd over 2f out: see 2841, btr 1771 (6f). *1¼* **58**
15 Ran Time 1m 41.5 (1) Owned: Mr Peter J Davies Trained: Preston

4353   4.40 Rectangle Group Handicap Stakes 3yo+ 71-85 (D)   [85]
£6997 £2153 £1076   1m3f200y   Good/Firm 31   -05 Slow   Outside

4287* **SENDINTANK** 4 [5] S C Williams 4-8-11 (6ex) (68) K Darley 4/5 FAV: 1131111: Hld up, hdwy to lead   **81**
trav well over 1f out, pushed clr, cmftbly, val further: hvly bckd: 8th win this term: eff at 12f, stays 2m well on
fast, hvy & fibresand, sharp or gall trks: proving most tough & prog, great credit to connections: see 4287.

4062 **RESERVOIR** 15 [6] W J Haggas 3-8-11 (77) A Culhane 10/1: 3-210502: Handy, eff to chall over 1f   2½   **82**
out, not pace of wnr ins last: encouraging run: mdn wnr in 2222.

3999 **GENGHIS** 17 [7] H Morrison 5-9-9 (80) L Fletcher(3) 5/1: 4/3-25203: Keen in tch, eff to chall over   1½   **83**
1f out, onepcd: bckd from 8/1: shown enough to win a race: see 2737.

4259 **ALLIED VICTORY** 5 [1] E J Alston 4-9-1 t (72) D Allan 25/1: 0020304: Led till over 1f out, no: stays 12f.   hd   **74**

3740 **CHANTELOUP** 29 [4]3-9-0 (80) J Murtagh 7/1: 24435: Held up, outpcd over 2f out, some late gains: hd   **82**
shapes like even further will suit, stays 12f: enjoyed easy grnd earlier: see 3740, 1304.

4097 **GOLANO** 13 [3]4-9-8 (79) D Holland 14/1: 110-2006: Handy, wknd over 2f out: see 4097, btr 2392.   3   **77**

3815 **THEATRE TIME** 26 [2]4-9-6 (77) P Robinson 28/1: 522/10-67: Slow away, al bhd: see 3815.   6   **66**

4080 **KARAMEA** 14 [8]3-8-11 (77) S W Kelly 25/1: 03-31508: Held up, btn over 2f out, eased: 'lost action'.   22   **36**

8 Ran   Time 2m 32.08 (4.28)   Owned: Steve Jones and Phil McGovern   Trained: Newmarket

4354   5.10 Three Sisters Handicap Stakes For Gentleman Amateur Riders 3yo+ 56-70 (E)   [38]
£3463 £1066 £533   1m2f120y   Good/Firm 31   -42 Slow   Outside

4076 **MILK AND SULTANA** 14 [1] G A Ham 4-11-0 (4oh) (52) Mr E Dehdashti(3) 7/2: 0020241: Hld up, hdwy   **62**
over 2f out, led over 1f out, kept on, rdn out: eff over 10/12f on fm, soft & fibresand, prob any trk: see 3145.

2890 **IBERUS** 63 [7] S Gollings 6-11-13 (69) Mr R Stephens(3) 5/2 FAV: 5-000542: Hld up, eff well over   2½   **70**
1f out, edged left but onepace ins last: well bckd, clr of rem after abs: styd 10.5f on fast & hvy.

4119 **JIDIYA** 12 [8] S Gollings 5-12-0 (70) Mr T Woodside(7) 13/2: 52-00203: Held up, onepace: btr 3648.   4   **66**

3398 **KING HALLING** 42 [4] R Ford 5-11-0 (1oh)BL (55) Mr L Newnes(3) 8/1: 400/-0604: Led till over 1f out, wknd.   nk   **51**

3056 **BOING BOING** 57 [3]4-11-0 (4oh) (52) Mr A Swinswood(7) 7/1: 5001-065: Slow away & al bhd.   7   **41**

4282 **SMART BOY PRINCE** 4 [5]3-10-8 (6oh) (58) Mr R C Morris(7) 20/1: 0503006: In tch, wknd over 1f out.   ¾   **41**

3929 **CHAPTER HOUSE** 21 [6]5-11-9 (65) Mr T Greenall 6/1: 60/0-6007: Al bhd: see 2725.   6   **38**

3992 **LUXOR** 18 [2]7-11-0 (11oh) (45) Mr S Walker 12/1: 0-000008: Chsd ldr, wknd over 2f out: see 1884.   26   **0**

8 Ran   Time 2m 17.49(7.49)   Owned: Mr D M Drury   Trained: Axbridge

Official Going Good (Good/Firm Places)

4355   1.35 Rukba Senate Consulting E B F Maiden Stakes Div 1 2yo (D)
£5161 £1588 £794   1m rnd   Good/Firm 20   -36 Slow   Inside

3890 **KHARISH** 22 [3] J Noseda 2-9-0 (83) E Ahern 9/4 FAV: 4321: Sn handy & rdn to chall 2f out, narrow   **91**
lead & dist to stay on for press to assert cl-home: hvly bckd: eff at 7f/1m on gd/fm & gd/soft: consistent.

3882 **FOXHAVEN** 22 [1] P R Chamings 2-9-0 Martin Dwyer 9/1: 32: Led, hdd narrowly dist, styd on well,   ¾   **89**
just held cl-home: confirmed promise of intro: stays 1m on fast & gd: win a race.

3955 **AMEEQ** 20 [9] M P Tregoning 2-9-0 R Hills 11/4: 33: Trkd ldrs, shaken up & kept on under hand   ½   **88**
riding ins last, not pace to chall: styd longer 1m trip well, relish further: shld be wng soon.

   LUIS MELENDEZ 0 [7] P F I Cole 2-9-0 R L Moore 25/1: 4: ch c Horse Chestnut - Egoli (Seeking   2   **84**
The Gold) Trkd ldrs, outpcd over 2f out, kept on well ins last: op 20/1: Mar foal: dam a 7f 3yo scorer: stays 1m
on fast, will apprec further: pleasing intro, can improve.

3959 **BERTROSE** 20 [12]2-9-0 S Sanders 9/1: 45: Keen & held up, outpcd over 2f out, kept on ins last.   1¾   **81**

   ESQUIRE 0 [13]2-9-0 L Dettori 4/1: 6: b c Dubai Millennium - Esperada (Equalize) Handy, ch   2½   **76**
over 1f out, edged left & fdd ins last: op 4/1: Mar foal, dam a champion juv filly abroad: sire 1m juv scorer &
subs top class 1m/10f performer: ran well for a long way & not knocked about, likely to progress.

4078 **MY PORTFOLIO** 14 [4]2-9-0 J Fortune 25/1: 47: Mid-div, nvr pace to chall ldrs: see 4078.   2   **72**

2213 **OUR KES** 91 [14]2-8-9 Dane O'Neill 100/1: 08: Dwelt, keen towards rear, no impress, abs, new yard.   1   **65**

   INDIAN PIPE DREAM 0 [10]2-9-0 J Fortune 25/1: 9: br c Indian Danehill - Build A Dream (Runaway   3½   **63**
Groom) Towards & no impress fnl 2f: 70,000 gns Apr foal, half brother to a 10f plcd juv abroad.

4115 **UNCLE BULGARIA** 12 [5]2-9-0 M Hills 50/1: 300: 10th: Al towards rear: btr 2995 (AW).   nk   **62**

3981 **PICOT DE SAY** 18 [2]2-9-0 J F McDonald(3) 50/1: 000: 11th: Rear, no impress.   5   **53**

4069 **NIGHT GUEST** 14 [8]2-9-0 R Hughes 33/1: 00: 12th: Mid-div, no impress fnl 3f.   ¾   **52**

   AMPELIO 0 [11]2-9-0 K Fallon 8/1: 0: 13th: Al rear & eased over 2f out, t.o.: op 11/2.   14   **26**

13 Ran   Time 1m 41.21 (4.41)   Owned: Mrs Susan Roy   Trained: Newmarket

4356   2.10 Rukba Senate Consulting E B F Maiden Stakes Div 2 2yo (D)
£5161 £1588 £794   1m rnd   Good/Firm 20   -26 Slow   Inside

3811 **HUMOUROUS** 26 [1] Saeed bin Suroor 2-9-0 t L Dettori 5/2 FAV: 51: Made all, strongly prsd ins   **92**
last, rdn & held on all out: well bckd: eff at 7f, improved for step up to 1m & will get further: acts on fast
grnd: eff in t-strap: showed battling qualities, type to prog with racing: see 3811.

   FORWARD MOVE 0 [9] R Hannon 2-9-0 R Hughes 20/1: 2: ch c Dr Fong - Kissing Gate (Easy Goer)   shd   **91**
Keen & handy, shaken up & chall ins last, just held: May foal, half brother to 2 plcd 3yos at 1m/12f: dam a 1m juv
wnr: eff over an easy 1m on fast grnd, will stay further: weak in mkt but a fine start.

3955 **FRONT STAGE** 20 [8] Sir Michael Stoute 2-9-0 K Fallon 9/1: 03: b c Grand Lodge - Dreams (Rainbow   1¾   **88**
Quest) Trkd ldrs, shaken up to chall 2f out, no extra from dist: left debut bhd: 65,000 gns Feb foal, half brother
to a useful 10f wnr, dam a 10f 3yo scorer: eff at 1m, will stay further: clr rem, win a race.

   NIGHT HOUR 0 [6] M P Tregoning 2-9-0 Martin Dwyer 6/1: 4: b c Entrepreneur - Witching Hour   4   **80+**

(Alzao) Towards rear, outpcd over 2f out, kept on eyecatchingly under hand riding, fnl 2f, nrst fin: Mar foal, half brother to a 9f 3yo scorer, dam a 6f juv wnr: will relish 9f+ & a sure-fire improver.
3568 **ART ELEGANT 35** [14]2-9-0 M Hills 14/1: 05: Held up, hdwy over 2f out, no impress over 1f out. *¾* **79**
3337 **OFF COLOUR 44** [5]2-9-0 S Sanders 6/1: 406: Dwelt, chsd ldrs wide, no impress fnl 2f. *4* **71**
4069 **SILVERLEAF 14** [7]2-9-0 S Hitchcott(3) 10/1: 6557: Handy, wknd qckly over 1f out, longer trip. *1¼* **68**
4069 **PENALTY KICK 14** [10]2-9-0 BL N Callan 10/1: 068: Pulled hard trkg ldrs, lost place from over 2f out: op 8/1, not settle in 1st time blnks: btr 4069. *1* **66**
3951 **BYRON BAY 20** [2]2-9-0 J F McDonald(3) 100/1: 09: Chsd ldrs, no impress over 2f out, longer trip. *6* **56**
3786 **LOITOKITOK 27** [3]2-9-0 Dane O'Neill 100/1: 00: 10th: Dwelt & al bhd, no ch 3f out. *6* **46**
3890 **FIGAROS QUEST 22** [4]2-9-0 R L Moore 8/1: 60: 11th: Sn pshd along/wide & twds rear, nvr dngr. *¾* **45**
SILVER SONG 0 [12]2-9-0 S Drowne 20/1: 0: 12th: Dwelt & al rear, left bhd 3f out. *hd* **44**
3329 **Eastwell Magic 44** [13]2-8-9 J Bramhill 66/1:0 **Brego 0** [11]2-9-0 J Fortune 25/1:0
14 Ran Time 1m 40.39 (3.59) Owned: Godolphin Trained: Newmarket

4357

2.40 Rukba Cantor Sport E B F Maiden Stakes Div 1 Fillies 2yo (D)
£5239 £1612 £806 **6f str** **Good/Firm 20** **+08 Fast** Stands Side

3917 **HALLE BOP 21** [4] Saeed bin Suroor 2-8-11 L Dettori 6/4 FAV: 21: Made all trav well stands rail, hands & heels, cosily: gd time: confirmed debut promise: eff at 6f on fast & gd grnd, gall or easy trk: looks useful, win again: see 3917. **91+**
HOLLY SPRINGS 0 [7] J H M Gosden 2-8-11 J Fortune 33/1: 2: b f Efisio - Anotheranniversary (Emarati) Trkd wnr, rdn to chall over 1f out, no ch with wnr ins last: 120,000 gns Feb foal, half sister to a plcd 6f performer, dam a dual 5f 2yo wnr: eff at 6f on fast grnd & an easy trk: most pleasing start. *1¼* **84**
3917 **DESERT IMP 21** [10] B W Hills 2-8-11 M Hills 6/1: 03: b f Green Desert - Devil's Imp (Cadeaux Genereux) Sn trkd ldrs, switched & hdwy to press ldrs dist, no ch with wnr: nicely bckd, op 11/1: Mar foal, dam 6/7f wnr: eff at 6f on fast grnd: much imprvd today, win a race. *¾* **82**
BIRIYANI 0 [6] P W Harris 2-8-11 E Ahern 20/1: 4: b f Danehill - Breyani (Commanche Run) Trkd ldrs, onepace under hands & heels: E180,000 Mar foal, half sister to a top class Irish 1m wnr: dam multiple scorer at 11f/2m: sure to relish 7f+ & improve plenty for this. *2* **76**
3576 **NEVERLETME GO 35** [12]2-8-11 S Drowne 5/2: 45: Cl-up, wknd from dist: btr 3576 (5f). *1¾* **71**
VERBIER 0 [9]2-8-11 N Callan 33/1: 6: Dwelt, mid-div, outpcd fnl 2f. *1½* **66**
3908 **ELLENS PRINCESS 21** [11]2-8-11 R L Moore 14/1: 547: Trkd ldrs, btn over 1f out, op 11/1: see 3908. *nk* **65**
DIAMOND KATIE 0 [15]2-8-11 R Hughes 50/1: 8: Mid-div, no impress under kind ride fnl 2f, imprve. *hd* **64**
38 **RUBY MURRAY 25** [3]2-8-11 K McEvoy 50/1: 09: Pushed along towards rear, only mod prog. *¾* **62**
3639 **VERITABLE 32** [1]2-8-11 A Daly 50/1: 400: 10th: Slow away & rear, tkn wide, little prog: reportedly hung right & subs found to be lame on left fore. *2½* **54**
3896 **TASHYRA 22** [13]2-8-11 Dane O'Neill 33/1: 440: 11th: Chsd ldrs, btn 2f out: see 3368. *¾* **52**
3357 **LADY PILOT 43** [14]2-8-11 S Sanders 8/1: 00: 12th: Prom, btn 2f out, 6 wk abs: btr 3357 (7f). *1* **49**
3639 **BLAZING VIEW 32** [2]2-8-11 K Fallon 25/1: 500: 13th: Al bhd & no ch halfway: bckd at long odds. *5* **34**
3915 **NIGHT CLUB QUEEN 21** [5]2-8-11 R Hills 66/1: 000: 14th: Dwelt & rear, nvr factor. *1½* **29**
DANAATT 0 [8]2-8-11 Martin Dwyer 33/1: 0: 15th: Sn struggling. *4* **17**
15 Ran Time 1m 11.76 (0.66) Owned: Godolphin Trained: Newmarket

4358

3.15 Rukba Cantor Sport E B F Maiden Stakes Div 2 Fillies 2yo (D)
£5239 £1612 £806 **6f str** **Good/Firm 20** **+06 Fast** Stands Side

3951 **PENKENNA PRINCESS 20** [3] R M Beckett 2-8-11 S Sanders 16/1: 01: Sn cl-up & rdn/narrow lead over 1f out, duelled with rnr-up & prevailed for press fnl 50yds, gd time: op 20/1, left debut bhd: eff at 6f, relished this fast grnd & an easy trk: significant improvement, could prove useful: see 3951. **91**
2399 **CODE ORANGE 83** [10] J H M Gosden 2-8-11 J Fortune 4/6 FAV: 22: Led/dsptd lead, hdd narrowly over 1f out, continued to chall, just held cl-home: hvly bckd at odds-on, 12 wk abs: win a race. *½* **88**
SHEBOYGAN 0 [4] J G Given 2-8-11 J Bramhill 25/1: 3: ch f Grand Lodge - White Satin (Fairy King) Chsd ldrs, kept on for press, not able to chall front pair: 34,000 gns Feb foal, dam a 7f juv wnr: eff at 6f, get further: acts on fast: v pleasing start, win sn. *¾* **86**
4217 **TEN CENTS 6** [1] C A Cyzer 2-8-11 I Mongan 33/1: 44: Rear, rdn & styd on well from over 1f out, nrst fin: qck reapp: eff at 6f, 7f+ shld suit, handles fast: penny dropped closing stages, clr rem & a likely imprvr. *2½* **78**
2437 **XEERAN 81** [2]2-8-11 N Callan 10/1: 555: Stumbled start, chsd ldrs, no impress fnl 2f: abs: see 2097. *5* **63**
LOYAL LOVE 0 [8]2-8-11 L Dettori 4/1: 6: b f Danzig - Always Loyal (Zilzal) Trkd ldrs, no impress over 1f out: op 10/3: May foal, half sister to a dual turf US wnr. *½* **61**
2646 **FOLLOW MY LEAD 73** [11]2-8-11 M Hills 33/1: 007: Rear, struggling halfway, mod late prog, abs. *hd* **60**
CUP OF LOVE 0 [6]2-8-11 Martin Dwyer 50/1: 8: ch f Behrens - Cup Of Kindness (Secretariat) Mid-div, no impress from halfway: half sister to 4 US sprint wnrs, dam unrcd. *nk* **59**
3917 **BAILEY GATE 21** [12]2-8-11 R Hughes 10/1: 09: Mid-div, no impress over 1f out, eased,. *½* **57**
DAISYS GIRL 0 [14]2-8-11 R Hills 25/1: 0: 10th: Sn prom, wknd over 1f out. *¾* **55**
3944 **NEVER AWAY 20** [5]2-8-11 E Ahern 50/1: 0000: 11th: Al struggling towards rear. *1* **52**
MUSIC TEACHER 0 [13]2-8-11 S Drowne 14/1: 0: 12th: Chsd ldrs, wknd qckly from halfway. *5* **38**
ALEYAH 0 [9]2-8-11 R L Moore 50/1: 0: 13th: Slow away & al bhd, t.o. *13* **0**
13 Ran Time 1m 11.89 (0.79) Owned: Mrs H M Chamberlain Trained: Lambourn

4359

3.45 Rukba Pafs E B F Conditions Stakes Fillies 2yo (C)
£7308 £2772 £1386 **7f rnd** **Good/Firm 20** **-21 Slow** Inside

3883* **JOINT ASPIRATION 22** [2] M R Channon 2-8-8 S Hitchcott(3) 3/1: 11: Pushed along chsg ldrs halfway, rdn & hdwy to lead over 1f out, styd on strongly: op 5/2: eff at 7f, 1m+ looks sure to suit: acts on fast & gd grnd, stiff/gall or easy trk: useful filly, more to come: see 3883. **96**
TAHRIR 0 [7] B W Hills 2-8-8 R Hills 20/1: 2: gr f Linamix - Miss Sacha (Last Tycoon) Dwelt, trkd ldrs, switched & qcknd to chall over 1f out, not pace of wnr ins last: op 16/1: May foal, 350,000 gns purchase: half sister to wnrs at 7f/9f: dam 5f wnr: eff at 7f on fast: useful start, must win soon. *1½* **90**
3959 **TITIAN TIME 20** [5] J H M Gosden 2-8-8 J Fortune 11/8 FAV: 23: Sn cl-up & led 2f out, hdd over 1f out & no extra: hvly bckd, rest well covered: win a minor trk mdn: see 3959. *1½* **87**

LIGHT OF DUBAI 0 [3] Saeed bin Suroor 2-8-8 L Dettori 7/2: 4: b f Gone West - A P Assay (A P Indy) Led till 2f out, wknd ins last under a kind ride: op 3/1: Feb foal, cost $1,600,000: dam a high-class US performer & sire top class 1m/9f performer on dirt.	3½	80

3909 **MARCHETTA 21** [6]2-8-8 R L Moore 33/1: 65: Held up in tch, outpcd over 2f out, kept on late, nvr landed blow: prob handles firm & gd grnd, 1m & return to mdn company shld suit: see 3909. **shd 80**

INSINUATION 0 [4]2-8-8 K Fallon 15/2: 6: b f Danehill - Hidden Meaning (Gulch) Dwelt, rear, in tch, shaken up & kept on fnl 2f, nvr threat: Apr foal, 260,000 gns purchase: dam unrcd, related to a high-class US performer: sire top class sprinter/miler: kind ride & a likely imprvr, mdn company shld suit. **¾ 79**

GRAND GIRL 0 [1]2-8-8 A Daly 100/1: 7: Dwelt, in tch, left bhd fnl 2f. **10 59**
7 Ran   Time 1m 26.92 (2.82)   Owned: Ridgeway Downs Racing   Trained: West Ilsley

---

4360 4.20 Rukba Ubs Laing And Cruickshank Handicap Stakes 3yo+ 71-85 (D)   [90]
£10250 £3888 £1944   **1m4f**   **Good/Firm 20**   **+05 Fast**   Inside

3688 **OCEAN AVENUE 30** [7] C A Horgan 5-9-6 (82) L Dettori 4/1: 431-1061: Made all, pulled clr over 2f out, eased down, val 3/4L: gd time: best when able to dominate at 12/14.5f on fm or gd. **90**

3674 **BLAZE OF COLOUR 31** [1] Sir Michael Stoute 3-8-6 (3oh)vis (77) K Fallon 7/2 FAV: 3423142: Rear, hdwy to chase wnr over 1f out, al held: bckd: see 3674 & 3299. **2 80**

3779 **DOVEDON HERO 27** [5] P J McBride 4-8-9 (1oh)bl (70) M Hills 8/1: 0460203: Rear, kept on fnl 2f despite hanging, nvr threat to wnr: slipped down the weights: see 3475 & 2391. **1 73**

3459* **MR TAMBOURINE MAN 40** [6] P F I Cole 3-8-13 (84) J Fortune 8/1: 6001314: Rear, rdn & hdwy over 2f out, no impress dist: prob stays an easy 12f: see 3459 (10f). **nk 85**

3816 **ALBAVILLA 26** [10]4-8-13 (75) I Mongan 10/1: 3/556-325: Chsd wnr, no extra over 1f out: see 3816. **¾ 75**

4377*)**REGAL SETTING 349** [2]3-8-6 (3oh) (77) S Sanders 6/1: 21-6: br g King's Theatre - Cartier Bijoux (Ahonoora) Rear, rdn halfway, no prog fnl 3f: op 4/1, reapp/h'cap bow: turf bow: AW mdn scorer on 2nd of just 2 '03 starts: eff at 1m/8.5f, mid-dist pedigree: acts on fibresand & a sharp trk. **4 71**
1 Sep'03 Wolv 8.5af 79a- D: 2 Sep'03 Sout 8af 72a- D:

3945 **TRUENO 20** [4]5-9-6 (82) S Drowne 12/1: 4-120557: Chsd wnr 6f out, btn 2f out: btr 3615 (10f). **1¾ 74**

4292 **DESERT ISLAND DISC 4** [8]7-8-13 (75) J F McDonald(3) 11/2: 1511638: Held up in tch, no impress fnl 2f. **hd 66**

4274 **LEIGHTON 4** [3]4-8-12 (74) Lisa Jones 25/1: 4020309: Keen & chsd wnr early, struggling from 4f out. **17 42**
9 Ran   Time 2m 31.67 (1.67)   Owned: Mrs Wendy Gillings   Trained: Ogbourne Maizey

---

4361 4.50 Rukba Morgan Stanley Handicap Stakes 3yo+ 56-70 (E)   [73]
£3507 £1079 £540   **2m**   **Good/Firm 20**   **-13 Slow**   Inside

4203 **TYPHOON TILLY 7** [11] C R Egerton 7-9-9 (68) S Drowne 6/1: 3640321: Mid-div, hdwy & chsd ldrs over 1f out, led ins last, rdn out: eff at 12f/2m on firm, gd/soft & polytrack, prob any trk: see 404. **75**

4203* **BELLE ROUGE 7** [8] C A Horgan 6-9-13 (6ex) (72) L Dettori 5/1 FAV: 2121212: Handy & led over 1f out, hdd ins last & not pace of wnr: op 4/1: remains in fine form: see 4203. **1¾ 78**

4128* **CROCOLAT 11** [3] Mrs Stef Liddiard 3-8-4 (6ex)(70h) (62) N Mackay(3) 6/1: 0524113: Rear, kept on wide for press, nrst fin: set plenty to do but clrly stays this longer 2m trip: win again. **hd 67**

4166 **TREASON TRIAL 9** [1] Mrs Stef Liddiard 3-7-13 (12oh) (57) Lisa Jones 25/1: 6431334: Keen in mid-div, styd on onepace for press fnl 2f: prob styd this longer 2m trip: see 4166, 3874. **1 61**

3669 **MAJESTIC VISION 31** [13]3-8-9 (2oh) (67) R L Moore 14/1: 34-0625: Trkd ldrs, no extra dist: longer 2m trip may yet suit: see 3669 (14f). **½ 70**

1753 **MACARONI GOLD 111** [17]4-8-13 (58) S Sanders 16/1: 4450336: Towards rear, kept on late, no threat. **¾ 60**

4151 **RIYADH 10** [4]6-9-9 (68) R Ffrench 11/1: 0020267: Trkd ldrs, no impress dist: btr 3701. **1 69**

3861 **SAN HERNANDO 23** [15]4-9-9 (68) Dane O'Neill 7/1: 0404208: Rear, short of room 3f out till 2f out, kept on late, closer with a clr run: op 9/1: see 3454. **shd 69**

3387 **BEECHY BANK 42** [14]6-9-4 (63) N Pollard 20/1: 1-005359: Led, hdd over 1f out, fdd. **4 60**

3531 **DANCE LIGHT 37** [16]5-8-13 (58) E Ahern 25/1: 0-005300: 10th: Trkd ldrs, btn 2f out: btr 2941. **½ 54**

4143* **PAPEETE 10** [3]3-8-0 (6ex)(11oh) (58) J F McDonald(3) 16/1: 0-440010: 11th: Held up, short of room 2f out till over 1f out, sn no ch: closer with a clr run: see 4143 (12f, soft). **1 53**

3779 **RED SCORPION 27** [10]5-9-4 (63) K Fallon 8/1: 0230650: 12th: Rear/wide, no ch fnl 2f. **1¾ 56**

3200 **Moon Emperor 51** [5]7-9-11 (70) N McEvoy 20/1:0   3340 **Rome 44** [9]5-9-5 (64) R Hughes 33/1:0
3400 **Simonovski 42** [2]3-8-2 (9oh)(60) R Miles 33/1:0   4203 **The Varlet 7** [6]4-9-10 t(69) Martin Dwyer 66/1:0
16 Ran   Time 3m 29.41 (5.21)   Owned: Mrs Evelyn Hankinson   Trained: Chaddleworth

---

4362 5.25 Rukba Mobility Bureau Apprentice Handicap Stakes 3yo+ 71-85 (D)   [97]
£7092 £2182 £1091   **1m rnd**   **Good/Firm 20**   **-06 Slow**   Inside

4122 **ARKHOLME 11** [15] P Winkworth 3-8-4 (80) M Savage(3) 10/1: 0212031: Mid-div, switched & hdwy 2f out, styd on for press to lead well ins last: eff around 1m on fast & gd grnd, stiff/gall or easy trk: suited by blnks. **87**

3950 **BORDER MUSIC 20** [5] A M Balding 3-8-9 (78) T Block(7) 9/2: 61-00322: Trkd ldrs & led travelling well over 2f out, hdd well ins last & al pace: acts on fast, gd & fibresand: see 3950, 3738 & 879. **1 82**

4148 **DESERT CRISTAL 10** [13] J R Boyle 3-8-9 (78) D Corby 10/1: 2631323: Trkd ldrs, drvn & kept on, not pace of wnr: acts on fast & hvy grnd: see 3978 & 3466. **½ 81**

4221* **PAGAN PRINCE 6** [6] J A R Toller 7-9-0 (6ex) (78) Lisa Jones 7/2 JT FAV: 2110-014: Dwelt, rear, hdwy wide from over 1f out, not able to chall: quick reapp: see 4221. **1 79**

3535 **HONORINE 37** [9]4-9-0 (78) A Beech 20/1: 1243-605: Dwelt & rear, kept on late, not able to chall. **1½ 76**

3708 **INVADER 30** [4]8-8-8 bl t (72) N Mackay 25/1: 0001066: Rear, hdwy 2f out, no prog dist: see 2840. **1½ 67**

3780 **KINDLELIGHT DEBUT 27** [3]4-8-10 (74) M Howard(5) 25/1: 00-00307: Rear, eff 2f out, not able to chall. **1¾ 66**

3954 **BOUNDLESS PROSPECT 20** [1]5-8-13 (77) Derek Nolan(5) 25/1: 0231608: Dwelt, rear, no prog fnl 2f. **1 67**

4122 **BORDER EDGE 11** [11]6-9-7 vis (85) J F McDonald 50/1: 000-0009: Reared start & v slow away, bhd. **1½ 72**

3738 **ISKANDER 29** [8]3-8-4 (3oh)bl (73) A Mullen(5) 7/2 JT FAV: 0000640: 10th: Handy & led over 2f out, hung left & sn hdd, sn btn: see 3738. **¾ 59**

3685 **MOSCOW TIMES 36** [14]3-8-3 (4oh) (72) Natalia Gemelova(5) 10/1: 0-650130: 11th: Al bhd. **hd 57**

4030 **BLUE PATRICK 16** [7]4-8-8 (72) S Hitchcott 10/1: 0020650: 12th: Led racing freely till over 2f out, wknd. **3 51**

3964 **BARRANTES 19** [2]7-8-10 (74) N Chalmers(3) 50/1: 00-00000: 13th: Cl-up, wknd fnl 2f. **hd 52**

KEMPTON   FRIDAY 03.09.04   Righthand, Flat, Fair Track

3860 **CAMBERWELL** 23 [12]3-9-0 (83) R Miles 25/1: 15000: 14th: Cl-up, struggling fnl 2f: btr 3113 (7f).   2   57
3550 **DESERT DREAMER** 36 [10]3-9-2 (85) K May(7) 6/1: 0-50600W: Bolted bef start, withdrawn.   0
15 Ran   Time 1m 38.82(2.02)   Owned: Mr I Russell   Trained: Godalming

CHEPSTOW   FRIDAY 03.09.04   Lefthand, Undulating, Galloping Track

Official Going GOOD

4363   2.20 Ron Ullah Maiden Auction Stakes 2yo (F)
£3474 £1069 £535   1m14y   Good/Soft 65   -14 Slow   Stands side

4052 **BATHWICK FINESSE** 15 [1] B R Millman 2-8-2 S Righton 12/1: 01: b f Namid - Lace Flower (Old Vic)   80
  Keen & made most, clr 3f out, rdn out nr fin: 12,000 gns Apr foal: dam wnr over 9/13f: eff at 1m, shld stay 9f:
  acts on gd/soft: much imprvd wiht forcing tactics.
4083 **KINGS ACCOUNT** 14 [10] M Johnston 2-8-9 J Fanning 6/4 FAV: 222: Cl-up, hdwy into 2nd over 4f   1½   82
  out, onepcd fnl 1f: nicely bckd: stays 1m: rnr-up yet again, now qual for h'caps: see 4083.
4115 **GROUP CAPTAIN** 12 [7] S Kirk 2-8-7 (88) J F Egan 7/4: 5422023: Cl-up, asked for eff 3f out,   nk   79
  onepcd over 1f out: tchd 5/2: stays 1m & acts on fast & gd/soft: see 2388.
4072 **DUSTY DANE** 14 [8] W G M Turner 2-8-7 (67) C Haddon(7) 50/1: 5653064: Rear, hdwy 4f out, onepcd.   1½   76
3890 **WILLIAM TELL** 22 [5]2-9-0 C Catlin 8/1: 645: Mid-div, outpcd 3f out, kept on again ins fnl 1f.   3   77
3803 **ARCH FOLLY** 26 [9]2-8-7 F P Ferris(3) 66/1: 06: Rear, mod late gains: see 3803.   shd   69
3882 **JUST A TRY** 22 [4]2-9-0 P Dobbs 20/1: 067: Bhd, hdwy over 2f out, no impress fnl 1f: see 3267.   3   70
3955 **PRINCE VETTORI** 20 [2]2-8-9 T P Queally 50/1: 08: b c Vettori - Bombalarina (Barathea) Bhd, nvr   3   59
  nr ldrs: Feb 1st foal, cost 20,000 gns: dam unrcd, sire wnr of French Guineas: with D Coakley.
4115 **WATER PISTOL** 12 [11]2-8-9 J Quinn 14/1: 09: b g Double Trigger - Water Flower (Environment   1¾   55
  Friend) Mid-div, no impress over 3f out: Feb 1st foal, cost 24,000 gns: dam wnr over 12f/hdles.
4115 **LAUROLLIE** 12 [3]2-8-2 R Thomas(5) 100/1: 000: 10th: Cl-up, wknd over 3f out.   ½   47
4269 **LADY LUISA** 4 [6]2-8-2 S Carson 25/1: 0500: 11th: Dwelt, nvr a factor: quick reappr.   6   35
11 Ran   Time 1m 38.28 (6.38)   Owned: Mrs S Clifford   Trained: Cullompton

4364   2.50 Russell Reynolds Claiming Stakes 3yo+ (F)
£2604 £744 £372   1m4f23y   Good/Soft 65   -01 Slow   Inside

3856 **ON CLOUD NINE** 23 [2] M L W Bell 3-8-4 (62) Hayley Turner(3) 9/4 FAV: 2600431: Rear, hdwy over 4f   63
  out, led well over 1f out till 1f out, drvn ins fnl 1f to lead again, kept on cl-home: claimed for 8,000: stays 12f
  on fast & soft grnd, acts on a gall/undul trk: made most of this drop in grade: game: see 977.
3983 **BANNINGHAM BLAZE** 18 [5] A W Carroll 4-9-3 vis (48) T P Queally 9/2: 5313222: Slow away in rear,   1   63
  hdwy over 4f out, led 1f out till ins fnl 1f, no extra: op 7/1: clr of rem: acts on firm, gd/soft & polytrack.
4181 **ROLEX FREE** 8 [6] D Flood 6-9-6 vis (51) J F Egan 8/1: 3141043: Led till well over 1f out, sn no extra.   4   60
3970 **MR WHIZZ** 13 [3] A P Jones 7-9-3 p (40) D Nolan(3) 14/1: 2205104: Bhd, hdwy & ev ch 2f out, no impress.nk   56$
4299 **BLACK LEGEND** 4 [3]5-9-0 (45) B Swarbrick(5) 9/1: 02/0-2405: Bhd, hdwy 3f out, no impress 1f out.   6   44
4124 **SAHAAT** 11 [7]6-9-4 (68) K Ghunowa(7) 5/1: 5025046: Rear, hdwy over 5f out, no impress over 2f   3½   43
  out: claimed for £8,000: see 3392.
3772 **ZARNEETA** 27 [12]3-8-4 (45) P Doe 100/1: 000-0007: Cl-up, hdwy into 2nd over 4f out, wknd 3f out.   5   30
3400 **OUR IMPERIAL BAY** 42 [11]5-9-4 vis (45) J P Guillambert(3) 20/1: 3036308: Rear, wknd 3f out.   4   29
4165 **KELTIC RAINBOW** 9 [1]3-7-12 (40) R Thomas(2) 40/1: 4600459: Chsd ldr, lost place over 4f out, no   1¾   15
  impress over 3f out: see 3294.
1975} **TWEED** 455 [9]7-9-2 (50) D Kinsella 20/1: 4/40002-0: 10th: ch g Barathea - In Perpetuity (Great   6   15
  Nephew) Nvr a factor on reapp: rnr-up fnl '03 start (clmr, B Ellison, earlier with J Best): won 4 h'caps & a clmr
  in '02: best at 2m, fibresand/Southwell specialist, handles soft: tried cheek pieces & blnks: now with C Roberts.
  2 Jun'03 Wolv 14.8af 67a-(68) F: 1 Feb'02 Sout 16af 85a-76 D: 1 Feb'02 Sout 16af 75a-62 E: 1 Jan'02 Sout 16af 68a-57 E:
  1 Jan'02 Wolv 16af 62a-54 D: 1 Jan'02 Sout 16af 55a- F:
3675 **DASH FOR GLORY** 31 [4]5-9-0 (30) V Slattery 100/1: 0-000030: 11th: Cl-up, fdd over 5f out: jumps fit.   1¾   10
3733 **LYRICAL GIRL** 29 [8]3-8-4 (54) F P Ferris(3) 16/1: 1-150600: 12th: Rear, hdwy over 4f out, no   4   3
  impress 3f out, fin last: jockey reported mount lost her action & was hanging.
12 Ran   Time 2m 39.06 (7.96)   Owned: Mrs Alison C Farrant   Trained: Newmarket

4365   3.25 Escape Design Handicap Stakes 3yo+ 56-70 (E)
£3675 £1131 £565   1m2f36y   Good/Soft 65   -01 Slow   Inside   [83]

4182 **MAGIC STING** 8 [2] M L W Bell 3-8-13 (68) Hayley Turner(3) 3/1: 1103321: Rear, hdwy to lead 2f   79
  out, drvn clr ins fnl 1f: eff at 10f/11f, 12f+ shld suit: acts on fast & soft, likes a stiff/undul or gall trk: consistent.
2452 **CORNISH GOLD** 81 [15] N J Henderson 3-8-7 (62) J Mackay 9/1: 0056-02: Rear, hdwy 5f out, led   3½   66
  over 2f out but sn hdd, no extra: long abs: see 2452.
4011 **MAMBINA** 17 [9] M R Channon 3-8-4 (3oh) (59) C Catlin 11/1: 5040223: Rear, hdwy 3f out, onepcd fnl 1f.   ½   62
  WILD POWER 805 [13] J G M O'Shea 6-8-7 (55) R Havlin 25/1: 020/230/-4: b g Turtle Island - White   ½   57
On Red (Konigsstuhl) Bhd, hdwy over 2f out, kept on: chase fit: plcd in a nov chase in 04/05 (rtd 89c, eff around
2m on firm & fast, sharp trk, I Williams): former German mdn wnr: eff at 10f on gd/soft.
3144 **BILLY BATHWICK** 54 [14]7-8-11 (59) F P Ferris(3) 10/1: 0033105: Rear, hdwy over 4f out, onepcd fnl 1f.   nk   60
4222 **CUDDLES** 6 [10]5-8-9 (57) J F Egan 12/1: 4530006: Slow away in rear, hdwy over 3f out, onepcd 2f out.   2½   54
3926 **STOLEN HOURS** 21 [6]4-9-3 (65) J Quinn 5/2 FAV: 0223137: Rear, hdwy & not clr run over 4f out, sn   ½   61
  switched right, not pace to chall: op 4/1: 'nvr travelling': needs faster grnd: see 3926.
3695 **OUR DESTINY** 30 [7]6-8-2 (56) R Thomas(5) 4/1: 4105668: Rear, hdwy over 2f out, not pace to chall.   1¾   49
3695 **FORTUNE POINT** 30 [5]6-8-11 vis (59) T P Queally 8/1: 0040629: Led till over 2f out, no extra over 1f out.   2½   48
2632 **STARRY MARY** 74 [16]6-8-7 (3oh) (52) B Swarbrick(5) 20/1: 06-22050: 10th: Al bhd: now with R Price.   1   42
4057 **PETITE COLLEEN** 15 [12]3-8-4 (3oh) (59) A McCarthy 25/1: 0406050: 11th: Cl-up, no impress 2f out.   4   40
4300 **DUAL PURPOSE** 4 [8]9-8-11 (59) D Kinsella 50/1: 06400: 12th: Cl-up, no impress 3f out: quick reappr.   nk   39
4032 **LA PROFESSORESSA** 16 [4]3-8-3 (4oh) (58) J Fanning 11/1: 5-600530: 13th: Cl-up, hdwy & ev ch over   6   29
  3f out, no impress over 2f out: see 4032.

CHEPSTOW FRIDAY 03.09.04 Lefthand, Undulating, Galloping Track

2931 **AMONG FRIENDS 62** [1]4-8-7 (1oh) (54) P Doe 50/1: 6-600000: 14th: Nvr a factor: 9 wk abs: see 1079. *3* **21**
4032 **KALIMENTA 16** [3]3-8-7 (62) S Chin 25/1: 4266000: 15th: Mid-div, no impress 4f out. *8* **16**
3336 **GLIMMER OF LIGHT 44** [11]4-9-7 BL (69) S Carson 25/1: 50-60000: 16th: Rcd in 2nd, lost place over 4f out, fdd over 3f out: 6 wk abs, top weight: tried blnks: see 2735. *shd* **22**
16 Ran Time 2m 10.7 (6.6) Owned: Mrs P T Fenwick Trained: Newmarket

4366

3.55 Make-A-Wish Classified Stakes 3yo+ 0-60 (F)
£3497 £1076 £538 **1m14y** **Good/Soft 65** **+06 Fast** Stands side

3579 **ZAFARSHAH 35** [10] P D Evans 5-9-2 (59) B Swarbrick(5) 12/1: 0300401: Rear, hdwy 4f out, drvn out ins fnl 1f, led nr fin: suited by 7f/1m on firm, soft & both AWs, any trk, likes Lingfield: back to form: see 366. **68**
226} **REDSWAN 625** [4] A E Jones 9-9-2 t (59) D Nolan(3) 14/1: 30/3300/-2: ch g Risk Me - Bocas Rose (Jalmood) Led, hung left over 1f out, hdd & no extra nr fin: op 33/1, reapp, clr of rem: missed '03: 3rd 2 of 4 '02 starts (clmr, class stks, rtd 71, A Carroll): eff at 7f/1m on firm, gd/soft & both AWs, handles soft, any trk, likes stiff/gall ones: suited by t-strap, eff with/without blnks: has broken blood vessels. *1¼* **63**
3542 **JOMUS 36** [1] L Montague Hall 3-8-11 (58) P Dobbs 33/1: 2000403: Rear, hdwy over 2f out, kept on. *3½* **56**
3540 **ARCHERFIELD 36** [14] J W Hills 3-8-8 t (60) T P Queally 7/1: 0023344: Rear, hdwy 4f out, onepcd fnl 1f. *1* **51**
3952 **CRAIC SA CEILI 20** [3]4-8-13 (60) J Fanning 7/1: 0-000405: Keen in tch, hdwy over 4f out, ev ch 2f out, no impress ins fnl 1f: see 1423. *hd* **50**
4144 **LAND OF NOD 10** [5]3-8-8 vis (60) S Chin 16/1: 00-40056: Cl-up, no impress fnl 1f: see 1089. *3½* **43**
3806 **BELTANE 26** [2]6-9-2 (46) R Smith 100/1: 1200057: Rear, hdwy over 2f out, not pace to chall. *½* **45**
4144 **HEAD BOY 10** [11]3-8-11 (59) P Doe 28/1: 6542008: Bhd, hdwy over 2f out, no impress fnl 1f. *hd* **44**
3986 **ADALAR 18** [12]4-9-2 (58) F P Ferris(3) 9/2 FAV: 0040229: Handy, no impress 2f out. *1* **42**
3846 **MASTER MAHOGANY 24** [19]3-8-11 (60) L Keniry(3) 9/1: 6546030: 10th: Cl-up stands side, no impress. *nk* **41**
4054 **INDIAN EDGE 15** [6]3-8-11 (58) D Kinsella 50/1: 0520000: 11th: Rear, switched left over 5f out, no impress *1* **39**
3155 **TEEHEE 53** [8]6-9-2 bl (58) J Quinn 14/1: 6002340: 12th: Cl-up, no impress over 2f out: 8 wk abs. *2* **35**
1647 **LORD GREYSTOKE 116** [7]3-8-11 (55) R Havlin 80/1: 0400-000: 13th: b c Petardia - Jungle Story (Alzao) In tch, rear & btn 4f out: long abs: 4th at best in '03 (mdn, rtd 61a, rtd 75 at best): with C Morlock. *5* **25**
4077 **HARRY CAME HOME 14** [9]3-8-11 bl (30) P Gallagher(7) 100/1: 0000000: 14th: b g Wizard King - Kirby's Princess (Indian King) Nvr a factor: mdn, sell & h'cap unplcd all earlier starts: with J Fox. *hd* **24**
3524 **SENIOR MINISTER 37** [13]6-9-2 (60) A Quinn(5) 50/1: 0100000: 15th: Cl-up, no impress over 2f out. *6* **12**
2701 **FIRST DAWN 71** [18]3-8-8 (60) C Catlin 25/1: 06-0000: 16th: Rear, nvr a factor: long abs. *1¾* **5**
3875 **DREAMS FORGOTTEN 23** [16]4-8-13 (57) A McCarthy 25/1: 3200-400: 17th: Bhd, nvr a factor. *8* **0**
3676 **BURLINGTON PLACE 31** [15]3-8-11 (60) J F Egan 16/1: 46-00200: 18th: Rear, no ch & eased over 2f out: jockey reported mount was changing legs for most of race. *10* **0**
3922 **PHRED 21** [17]4-9-2 (58) S Carson 6/1: 5420050: 19th: Slow away, rear, t.o.: 'breathing prob'. *17* **0**
19 Ran Time 1m 36.66 (4.76) Owned: Waterline Racing Club Trained: Abergavenny

4367

4.30 Betfred 'the Bonus King' Handicap Stakes 3yo+ 46-55 (F) **[62]**
£2747 £785 £392 **7f16y** **Good/Soft 65** **+05 Fast** Stands side

3942 **NAUTICAL 20** [11] A W Carroll 6-9-4 (52) P Dobbs 6/1: 6430201: Rear, hdwy to lead ins fnl 1f, drvn out: op 15/2: eff at 7/10f on firm, gd/soft & polytrack, gall/undul trk: see 2589. **61**
4057 **LORD CHAMBERLAIN 15** [10] J M Bradley 11-9-7 bl (55) C J Davies(7) 16/1: 0201402: Mid-div, hdwy to lead well over 1f out, hdd ins fnl 1f, no extra: op 25/1: gd run, back to form: see 2733. *1¼* **57**
4165 **ARMENTIERES 9** [14] J L Spearing 3-9-1 bl (53) Hayley Turner(3) 12/1: 0-600623: Chsd ldrs till over 3f out, rallied 2f out, kept on ins fnl 1f: return to further will suit: see 4165 (1m). *½* **56**
4189 **MOBO BACO 7** [2] R J Hodges 7-9-6 (54) L Keniry(3) 25/1: 0150604: Rear, hdwy 2f out, no impress fnl 1f. *1* **55**
4057 **JUST ONE LOOK 15** [5]3-9-3 (55) R Thomas(5) 40/1: 0000605: Rear, hdwy over 1f out, kept on ins fnl 1f. *hd* **55**
4057 **STARS AT MIDNIGHT 15** [6]4-8-12 (46) R Smith 66/1: 0100-006: b f Magic Ring - Boughtbyphone (Warning) Handy, wknd fnl 1f: won 1 of 6 '03 starts (h'cap, with I Wood): unplcd in '02 (mdns, nov, rtd 54, with J Naylor): eff over a sharp 1m on fast grnd: with J Bradley. 1 Jul'03 Wind 8.3g/f 49-46 E: *4* **38**
3911* **PRETTY KOOL 21** [12]4-9-5 (53) T P Queally 9/2: 00-05317: Cl-up, hdwy/ev ch 2f out, no impress 1f out. *shd* **44**
3759 **MEELUP 28** [9]4-9-6 p (54) V Slattery 33/1: 0220008: Led till well over 1f out, no extra. *hd* **44**
3184 **LOGISTICAL 51** [18]4-9-4 (52) J Fanning 16/1: 0-005009: Held up stands side, nvr a factor: 7 wk abs. *2* **38**
4168 **LOCH LAIRD 9** [8]9-8-13 P (47) G Baker 8/1: 5005430: 10th: Nvr a factor in 1st time cheek pieces. *nk* **32**
3788 **TOPPLING 27** [17]6-9-0 BL (48) P Fitzsimons 33/1: 0400000: 11th: Led stands side, no extra 2f out. *1¼* **30**
4202 **WELSH EMPRESS 7** [7]3-8-12 (50) J F Egan 33/1: 03-03000: 12th: Nvr a factor: quick reapp: jockey reported mount was unsuited by this grnd: see 1798. *3* **26**
4036 **ARRAN 16** [13]4-9-5 (53) J Quinn 4/1 FAV: 3021050: 13th: Rear, hdwy 2f out, no impress over 1f out. *shd* **28**
4202 **FIZZY LADY 7** [1]3-9-3 t (55) M Halford(7) 40/1: 4100000: 14th: Nvr a factor: quick reapp. *1¼* **27**
3963 **ICECAP 19** [15]4-9-5 (53) A Quinn(5) 16/1: 002-0100: 15th: Keen & cl-up, wknd over 2f out. *¾* **23**
3963 **ANNIJAZ 19** [3]7-8-12 P (46) F P Ferris(3) 16/1: 6000000: 16th: Cl-up, no impress 2f out: cheekpieces. *4* **8**
3884 **SNOW JOKE 22** [16]3-9-1 (53) R Havlin 33/1: 4000050: 17th: Slow away, sn cl-up on stands side, no impress 2f out: jockey reported mount did not come down the hill: see 3884. *nk* **14**
1147 **POKER 144** [19]3-9-3 (55) J P Guillambert(3) 25/1: 060-100: 18th: In tch stands side, rear & btn 3f out: long abs: now with Mrs J Candlish: btr 656 (mdn h'cap). *2½* **11**
3953 **INESCAPABLE 20** [20]3-9-1 (53) S Chin 33/1: 0040: 19th: b c Cape Town - Danyross (Danehill) In tch stands side, rear & btn 3f out: h'cap bow: mdn unplcd all earlier starts: with W Muir. *1¼* **6**
4164* **WOOD FERN 9** [4]4-9-6 (6ex)vis (54) C Catlin 16/1: 0000610: 20th: Cl-up, no impress 2f out. *5* **0**
20 Ran Time 1m 24.05 (4.25) Owned: Mr Gary J Roberts Trained: Alcester

4368

5.00 Rita Naylor Birthday Handicap Stakes 3yo+ 46-55 (F) **[65]**
£2670 £763 £381 **6f16y** **Good/Soft 65** **+05 Fast** Stands side

3942 **YORKIES BOY 20** [16] N E Berry 9-8-9 p (46) R Thomas(5) 10/1: 0004031: Rear, hdwy over 1f out, drvn ins fnl 1f & led cl-home: op 8/1: best up with/forcing the pace at 5/6f, stays 7f well: acts on firm & gd/soft, any trk: rdn with restraint today: tough 9yo, on a handy mark: see 1914. **55**
3751 **SALON PRIVE 28** [5] C A Cyzer 4-9-2 (53) J F Egan 12/1: 32-00262: Led, hdd & no extra cl-home: handles firm, gd/soft soft & polytrack: gd run: see 23. *¾* **58**
4126 **MORITAT 11** [19] P D Evans 4-9-2 t (53) F P Ferris(3) 8/1: 6-063563: Rear, hdwy over 2f out, kept *½* **56**

CHEPSTOW FRIDAY 03.09.04 Lefthand, Undulating, Galloping Track

on ins fnl 1f: stays 5/6f on fast & gd/soft, has disapp on firm: see 3403.
3986 **CAPTAIN CLOUDY 18** [8] M Madgwick 4-9-2 (53) L Keniry(3) 33/1: 6600304: Mid-div, hdwy over 1f out, *1* 53
kept on ins fnl 1f: see 3677.
4272 **ENJOY THE BUZZ 4** [1]5-9-1 (52) T P Queally 7/1: 2103255: Handy, onepcd ins fnl 1f: quick reapp. *nk* 51
3911 **MY GIRL PEARL 21** [10]4-8-10 (47) V Slattery 12/1: 0641036: Cl-up, no impress ins fnl 1f: see 3911. *nk* 45
4070 **A TEEN 14** [14]6-8-13 (50) D Kinsella 11/1: 6000567: Rear, no room 2f out till just ins fnl 1f, *hd* 47
styd on ins fnl 1f & nrst fin: much closer with a clr run, well handicapped & is one to keep in mind: see 740.
4211 **KEW THE MUSIC 7** [18]4-9-1 vis (52) C Catlin 33/1: 0000008: Rear, hdwy 1f out, kept on: quick *nk* 48
reapp: handles fast & gd/soft: see 976.
4038 **DIAMOND RING 16** [20]5-8-10 (47) B Reilly(3) 16/1: 3036249: Rear, hdwy over 1f out, no impress fnl 1f. *nk* 42
3844 **MILLFIELDS DREAMS 24** [9]5-9-4 (55) D Nolan(3) 20/1: 1000060: 10th: Cl-up, no impress ins fnl 1f. *shd* 49
2439 **YAMATO PINK 81** [6]3-8-13 (52) G Baker 14/1: 0-012530: 11th: Bhd, hdwy over 1f out, not pace to chall. *nk* 45
4051 **SEMPER PARATUS 15** [7]5-8-12 bl (49) M Tebbutt 25/1: 0203000: 12th: Rear, mod late gains. *shd* 41
4044 **MULTIPLE CHOICE 15** [11]3-9-2 e t (55) J P Guillambert(3) 14/1: 0024640: 13th: Rear, nvr a factor. *nk* 46
587 **MR PERTEMPS 207** [4]6-9-3 p (54) T Hamilton(3) 11/2 FAV: 00-31250: 14th: Cl-up, rcd in 2nd to 2f *hd* 44
out, no impress ins fnl 1f: op 10/1, long abs: now with J Quinn.
4054 **BARABELLA 15** [2]3-8-11 (50) S Carson 33/1: 4504500: 15th: Rear, hdwy far side over 1f out, no impress. *¾* 38
3604 **REGAL FLIGHT 34** [15]3-8-11 (50) R Smith 66/1: 05-60600: 16th: Handy, no impress over 2f out. *1* 35
4164 **RILEYS DREAM 9** [3]5-8-11 p (48) R Havlin 16/1: 1005120: 17th: Chsd ldrs, no impress 1f out. *2* 27
3900 **PAPPY 22** [13]3-8-7 (2oh) (46) P Doe 12/1: 500-4030: 18th: Bhd, hung left & not clr run 2f out, sn btn. *½* 23
4116 **ROCKLEY BAY 12** [12]3-9-2 t (55) J Mackay 14/1: 4-000020: 19th: In tch till over 3f out, sn btn. *2* 26
4189 **CHORUS 7** [17]7-8-11 (48) J Quinn 33/1: 406-0300: 20th: Chsd ldrs, no impress over 2f out: quick reapp. *3* 10
20 Ran   Time 1m 12.44(3.64)   Owned: Paul & Ann de Weck   Trained: Earlswood

FOLKESTONE SATURDAY 04.09.04 Righthand, Sharpish, Undulating Track

Official Going Good/Firm

4369 11.30 Barretts Of Ashford Maiden Auction Stakes 2yo (H)
£1372 £392 £196   6f str   Good/Firm 36   +17 Fast   Stands Side

4028 **BAHIA BREEZE 17** [5] R Guest 2-8-7 C Catlin 15/8 FAV: 41: Made all & rdn clr over 2f out, 91+
easily: well bckd, op 5/2: confirmed debut promise: eff at 6f, will get further: acts on soft ground, relished fast
ground today: eff forcing the pace: impressive success, looks useful & can win more races: see 4028.
4079 **AVERTIGO 15** [4] W R Muir 2-8-12 (74) R Miles 12/1: 53202: Cl up, readily outpcd by wnr over 2f *7* 74
out but kept on for press: caught a tartar: appre return to fast ground: could find a race: see 3513, 3171.
3962 **TANNING 20** [12] H Morrison 2-8-5 T P Queally 9/2: 623: Slow away, sn mid-div, styd on for *nk* 66
press, nrst fin: styd longer 6f trip, 7f will suit: nursery type: see 3962, 3728.
PINK BAY 0 [3] W S Kittow 2-8-7 L Keniry(3) 100/1: 4: b f Forzando - Singer On The Roof (Chief *2½* 60
Singer) Mid-div, outpcd 2f out, kept on fnl 1f, no threat: chepaly bought Apr foal, half sister to 2 wnrs
abroad, dam a 1m 3yo wnr: eff at 6f, apprec further: handles fast ground: some encouragement on intro.
3896 **TASKS MUPPET 23** [11]2-8-7 J F Mcdonald(3) 50/1: 555: Prom, no impress from over 2f out: see 3368. *3* 51
3735 **PERSIAN CARPET 30** [1]2-8-5 (70) I Mongan 3/1: 04226: Trkd ldrs, btn over 2f out: btr 3735, 3239 (gd). *1* 46
4146 **YELDHAM LADY 11** [13]2-8-6 (50) A McCarthy 25/1: 00207: Dwelt, pushed along rear, late gains. *nk* 46
LORD OF ADVENTURE 0 [6]2-8-12 P Doe 25/1: 8: b c Inzar - Highly Fashionable (Polish Precedent) *½* 50
Dwelt, twds rear, mod prog: cheaply bought Mar foal: half brother to 2 1m 3yo wnrs: dam a 7f juv wnr.
4108 **BEFORE THE DAWN 14** [14]2-8-4 F P Ferris(3) 25/1: 0009: Chsd ldrs till halfway, sn btn. *½* 40
3504 **SUNNY TIMES 39** [10]2-8-6 Hayley Turner(3) 25/1: 500: 10th: Always rear: btr 3021 (gd, debut). *1* 39
4218 **TURTLE MAGIC 7** [2]2-8-5 VIS (51) A Daly 66/1: 4034640: 11th: Chsd ldrs till wknd & hung right fnl 2f. *2* 32
4108 **AMIGRA 14** [9]2-8-4 D Kinsella 100/1: 00: 12th: Always bhd. *1¼* 27
3489 **LIAMELISS 40** [8]2-8-3 N Chalmers(3) 100/1: 6000: 13th: Sn bhd, abs. *nk* 25
3343 **COMINTRUE 45** [15]2-8-7 (56) S Carson 50/1: 000200: 14th: Keen & prom 2f, sn strugg, abs: btr 2321. *17* 0
2450 **DIAMOND JOSH 82** [7]2-8-11 R Havlin 5/1: 3W: Ref to enter stalls, withdrawn. 0
15 Ran   Time 1m 12.16 (1.16)   Owned: Mr F Nowell   Trained: Newmarket

4370 11.55 Lancaster Banded Stakes 3yo+ 0-45 (H)
£1540 £440 £220   6f str   Good/Firm 36   -04 Slow   Stands Side

4368* **YORKIES BOY 1** [7] N E Berry 9-9-7 p (46) M Savage(5) 11/2: 00040311: Stumbled start, pshd along 56
mid-div, styd on for press to lead close home: scored at Chepstow yesterday: eff btwn 5/7f, 6f ideal: acts on firm &
gd/sft: genuine 9yo, in great heart: see 4368.
4164 **ELSINORA 10** [15] H Morrison 3-8-12 bl (45) L Fletcher(3) 14/1: 0026352: Trkd ldrs, rdn to chall *½* 46
ins last, hung left & not pace of wnr close home: see 2932 (sell).
4140* **MOLOTOV 11** [14] I W McInnes 4-9-5 (50) Natalia Gemelova(7) 5/1 FAV: 0-100413: Dsptd lead, went on *nk* 50
after 2f, rdn & hdd close home: genuine front runner, win again in this type of company: see 4140.
3985 **POPPYLINE 19** [10] W R Muir 4-9-2 bl (47) J F McDonald(3) 16/1: 6300654: Slow away, rear, styd on *1½* 42
for press from halfway, unable to chall: eff at 6f/8.5f: see 2954, 2149 & 1849.
4070 **MAYZIN 15** [16]4-9-2 (47) T P Queally 6/1: 0000035: Dsptd lead 2f, no extra over 1f out: btr 4070 (sft, 5f). *1¼* 38
2435 **LITTLE FLUTE 82** [11]3-8-13 (46) P Doe 20/1: 0000166: Chsd ldrs, no impress dist: abs: see 1312. *1* 34
3672 **MOSCOW MARY 32** [12]3-8-12 (45) F P Ferris(3) 33/1: 0000900: Rear, mod gains for press: see 1218. *2½* 25
3977 **DEXILEOS 19** [3]5-9-0 t (45) C Catlin 25/1: 0000368: Rear, outpcd, mod prog: flattered 3977. *2½* 17
3986 **CARGO 19** [2]5-9-2 p (47) R Miles(3) 9/1: 2002209: Prom towards centre 4f: btr 3298. *3½* 8
3924 **LAKE VERDI 22** [4]5-9-1 t (46) I Mongan 9/2: 4300260: 10th: Dwelt & always twds rear: op 10/1: btr 3710. *nk* 6
1613 **SUPERCHIEF 120** [13]9-9-0 t (45) S Carson 14/1: 3552500: 11th: Mid-div, outpcd from halfway: op 20/1. *nk* 4
4165 **LA CALERA 10** [8]3-9-0 bl (47) O Urbina 10/1: 1005330: 12th: Rear till wknd over 4f out. *½* 4
3401 Lily Of The Guild 43 [1]5-9-5 (50) L Keniry(3) 12/1:0   3673 Tamarella 32 [9]4-9-1 (46) A McCarthy 25/1:0
4130 Otylia 12 [6]4-9-3 (48) M Henry 33/1:0   4116 Pink Supreme 13 [5]3-9-1 (48) D Nolan(3) 25/1:0
16 Ran   Time 1m 13.37 (2.37)   Owned: Paul & Ann de Weck   Trained: Earlswood

FOLKESTONE SATURDAY 04.09.04 Righthand, Sharpish, Undulating Track

4371 **12.25 Hurricane Apprentice Banded Stakes 3yo+ 0-40 (H)**
£1320 £377 £189 **7f str** **Good/Firm 36** **-20 Slow** Stands Side

4043 **SAVERNAKE BRAVE 16** [1] Mrs H Sweeting 3-8-12 (40) D Corby 22/1: 2040001: Trkd ldr stands side, drvn to lead that pair ins last & sn clr of far side group: 1st win: eff at 5f/sharp 7f: acts on firm, fast & fibresand. **47**
4116 **CRIMSON STAR 13** [2] C Tinkler 3-8-12 (40) L Fletcher 12/1: 000032: Led stands side pair & always prom, hdd & not pace of wnr ins last, clr of rem far side: eff at 6/7f on fast & gd grnd: see 4116, 1610. *¾* **45**
3895 **NASSAU STREET 23** [6] D J S ffrench Davis 4-9-2 (40) A Hindley(7) 33/1: 040-3003: Rear far side, styd on for press to lead that group well ins last, nrst fin & no impress on front pair stands side: handles fast ground & fibresand, prob apprec 1m in similar: see 668. *5* **35**
3176 **COPPINGTON FLYER 53** [14] B W Duke 4-9-2 T (40) R Miles 8/1: 0404004: Dsptd lead far side, onepace: abs: imprvd effort in t-strap: see 474 (AW). *hd* **34**
3717 **STAGECOACH RUBY 30** [13]3-8-12 (40) Jemma Marshall(7) 18/1: 5433005: Dstpd lead far side, onepace. *hd* **33**
3986 **SILISTRA 19** [15]5-9-2 p (40) Natalia Gemelova(5) 16/1: 0000506: Trkd ldrs far side, not pace to chall. *nk* **32**
4168 **ZINGING 10** [9]5-9-2 (40) Hayley Turner 7/1: 5560047: Mid-div far side, unable to land a blow: btr 4168. *¾* **31**
3301 **MR UPPITY 47** [10]5-9-2 e (40) M Halford(5) 4/1 FAV: 5365428: Chsd ldrs far side, no impress over 1f out. *¾* **30**
3911 **BRANDYWINE BAY 22** [7]4-9-2 p (40) T Block(7) 11/2: 04-04159: Twds rear far side, liltte hdwy: see 3677. *nk* **29**
3363 **BALMACARA 44** [4]5-9-2 (40) A Beech 16/1: 4-006050: 10th: Rear far side, mod prog: abs: btr 3363. *3* **23**
1839 **TINY TIM 108** [16]6-9-2 (40) R J Killoran(7) 13/2: 2215220: 11th: Trkd ldrs far side 5f, fdd: abs: see 1839. *hd* **22**
3996 **Vertedanz 19** [11]4-9-2 (40) N Chalmers(3) 50/1:0 2396 **Badou 84** [5]4-9-2 vis(40) J F McDonald 8/1:0
3911 **Komena 22** [8]6-9-2 (40) T P Queally 14/1:0
4091 **Rue De Paris 15** [12]4-9-2 P(40) Dean Williams(5) 16/1:0
15 Ran Time 1m 28.15 (3.95) Owned: Mr P Sweeting Trained: Marlborough

4372 **12.50 Carl Scarrott 40th Birthday Tri-Banded Stakes 3yo 0-45 (H)**
£1509 £431 £216 **1m1f149y** **Good/Firm 36** **-16 Slow** Inside

3580 **CUNNING PURSUIT 36** [10] M L W Bell 3-8-11 (45) T P Queally 11/4 FAV: 6562001: Mid-div inner trav well, hdwy to lead over 1f out, drvn out: op 11/2: 1st win: eff at 9.7f/11.5f, has tried 2m: acts on fast ground. **53**
3982 **LENWADE 19** [4] G G Margarson 3-8-1 (35) A McCarthy 5/1: 0004522: Mid-div, styd on for press fnl 2f. *1¾* **41**
4131 **SKELTHWAITE 12** [7] Miss D A McHale 3-8-1 (35) J McAuley 100/1: 000-003: Chsd ldr, no extra dist: eff arnd 9.7f in banded company: see 3177. *3½* **34**
2716 **PRINCESS BANKES 71** [14] Miss Gay Kelleway 3-8-11 (45) I Mongan 20/1: 5-060004: Chsd ldr, no extra bef dist: abs: see 2049. *1½* **41**
4189 **ANISETTE 8** [13]3-8-6 (40) A Daly 10/1: 4006365: Keen, mid-div, not pace to chall: see 3706. *½* **35**
4165* **FIDDLES MUSIC 10** [9]3-8-12 (46) C Catlin 4/1: 4565016: Led, hdd over 1f out, wknd: btr 4165 (sft). *½* **40**
4142 **TSHUKUDU 11** [5]3-8-1 (35) J F McDonald(3) 6/1: 0003027: Mid-div, wide on bend over 2f out, no hdwy. *nk* **28**
3812 **CHIQITITA 27** [8]3-8-11 (45) Derek Nolan(7) 25/1: 0000068: Dwelt, rear, little hdwy: see 1576. *2* **34**
3392 **JAOLINS 43** [6]3-8-6 (40) D Kinsella 12/1: 0000659: Slow away, rear, no prog fnl 2f: abs: btr 3392. *1½* **26**
3712 **BROTHER CADFAEL 30** [3]3-8-1 T (35) Hayley Turner(3) 25/1: 6660000: 10th: Mid-div, strugg fnl 2f: t-strap. *5* **12**
3967 **ANNA GAYLE 20** [11]3-8-11 (45) S Carson 12/1: 0050: 11th: Chsd ldrs, btn 2f out: btr 3967. *2½* **17**
4189 **Rumour Mill 8** [1]3-8-6 (40) F P Ferris(3) 33/1:0 4112 **Bretton 14** [12]3-8-6 p(40) B Reilly(3) 10/1:0
13 Ran Time 2m 03.05 (5.05) Owned: Mrs Maureen Buckley Trained: Newmarket

4373 **1.20 Hambridge Ruby Banded Stakes 4yo+ 0-45 (H)**
£1712 £489 £245 **1m1f149y** **Good/Firm 36** **-13 Slow** Inside

3830 **SHAMWARI FIRE 26** [13] I W McInnes 4-9-2 (47) J F McDonald(3) 14/1: 0033001: Mid-div, hdwy 2f out & swtchd/styd on for press to lead cl home: eff at 7f/9.7f on firm & gd/sft: enjoys banded company: see 1944. **49**
4299 **MIDNIGHT MAMBO 5** [9] R Guest 4-9-0 (40) R Mills(7) 66/1: 5-550002: Mid-div, led over 1f out, hdd close home: qck reapp: eff at 9.7f on fast grnd & polytrk: see 828. *½* **45**
3748 **MY MAITE 29** [14] R Ingram 5-9-1 t p (46) N Day 5/1: 6045033: Rear, styd on for press fnl 2f, nrst fin. *½* **45**
3766* **ROYAL INDULGENCE 28** [1] W M Brisbourne 4-9-3 (48) M Savage(5) 3/1 JT FAV: 60500-14: Slow away, rear, efft 2f out, no impress ins last: see 3766. *¾* **46**
3052 **HAVANTADOUBT 58** [5]4-9-5 T (50) G Baker 33/1: 000-0005: Rear, rdn & late prog, no threat: abs, t-strap. *3½* **41**
4132 **MISS GLORY BE 12** [15]6-9-0 p (45) D Corby(3) 17/2: 3523306: Cl up, outpcd over 1f out: btr 3823. *shd* **36**
4077 **DUE TO ME 15** [12]4-9-0 p (45) I Mongan 12/1: 4634007: Mid-div, no prog fnl 2f: btr 2334 (7f). *1¾* **33**
3685 **GRAN CLICQUOT 31** [2]9-9-3 (48) Derek Nolan(7) 14/1: 2010208: Trkd ldrs, efft wide over 2f out, sn btn. *¾* **35**
4145 **PRIVATE SEAL 11** [7]9-9-0 t (45) A Daly 20/1: 0326349: Rear, only mod prog: btr 3704. *¾* **31**
4145 **MARGERY DAW 11** [8]4-9-0 (45) F P Ferris(3) 50/1: 6300500: 10th: Cl up, wknd over 1f out: btr 2431. *nk* **30**
3401 **BALLARE 43** [3]5-9-0 P (45) D Kinsella 20/1: 6104000: 11th: Mid-div, btn 2f out: chkpcs: see 1073 (1m). *¾* **29**
1451 **LADY LIESEL 128** [4]4-9-0 (45) Hayley Turner(3) 50/1: 0300400: 12th: Keen, rear, no prog fnl 2f: abs. *½* **28**
3823 **PIQUET 26** [6]6-9-0 (45) T P Queally 33/1: 6301000: 13th: Trkd ldrs, short of room over 1f out, sn btn. *¾* **27**
3963 **KINDNESS 20** [10]4-9-5 (50) C Catlin 8/1: 0220200: 14th: Led , hung left & hdd over 1f out. *hd* **31**
3996 **EXPECTED BONUS 19** [11]5-9-0 (45) R Havlin 3/1 JT FAV: 0-040060: 15th: Mid-div, lost place 2f out. *½* **25**
15 Ran Time 2m 02.8 (4.8) Owned: Ivy House Racing Trained: Catwick

4374 **1.45 Spitfire Banded Stakes 3yo+ 0-45 (H)**
£1719 £491 £246 **1m4f** **Good/Firm 36** **-39 Slow** Outside

4315 **LYSANDERS QUEST 3** [3] R Ingram 6-9-7 (40) N Day 14/1: 000-0051: Chsd ldrs, drvn to lead close home: qck reapp: 1st win: eff btwn 12f/14f on fast, gd or polytrk: see 4315. **47**
3726 **TINTAWN GOLD 30** [16] S Woodman 4-9-9 P (47) C Catlin 8/1: 0-004202: Mid-div, smooth prog to lead over 1f out, rdn & found little, hdd close home: gd run in chkpcs but extreme waiting tactics may suit: see 2718. *hd* **48**
2222 **OPEN BOOK 92** [12] H Morrison 3-9-2 (49) L Fletcher(3) 33/1: 00003: b f Mark of Esteem - Sweetness Herself (Unfuwain) Keen, mid-div, hdwy to chall dist, no extra close home: abs: eff arnd a sharp 12f on fast ground. *½* **49**

FOLKESTONE   SATURDAY 04.09.04   Righthand, Sharpish, Undulating Track

4143 **TATA NAKA 11** [1] Mrs C A Dunnett 4-9-7 (45) Hayley Turner(3) 6/1: 5002234: Rear, late gains.	½	**44**
3822 **CANTRIP 26** [9]4-9-11 (49) S Carson 8/1: 0013005: Led after 2f till over 1f out, no extra: see 2391.	½	**47**
4145 **COOLFORE JADE 11** [17]4-9-7 (40) M Savage(5) 20/1: 0630006: Keen, mid-div, no room 3f out, onepace.	nk	**42**
4319 **VANDENBERGHE 3** [14]5-9-9 (47) R Keogh(7) 11/4 FAV: 5633347: Twds rear, swtchd wide, mod prog.	1¼	**42**
4145 **ABSINTHER 11** [4]7-9-11 (49) G Baker 3/1: 2143308: Dwelt, rear, only mod prog wide fnl 2f.	1	**43**
4045 **MACCHIATO GB 16** [5]3-8-12 bl (40) J Mackay 20/1: 0500009: Rear, rdn & btn 2f out.	2½	**35**
3887 **GIKO 23** [10]10-9-7 (35) R Miles(3) 21/1: 0623000: 10th: Chsd ldr 4f out, btn over 1f out.	1	**34**
4255 **REPENT AT LEISURE 6** [11]4-9-10 (48) R Havlin 66/1: 40/-000: 11th: Chsd ldrs halfway, btn 2f out.	shd	**37**
4168 **HILARIOUS 10** [15]4-9-7 bl (40) A Daly 33/1: 5640600: 12th: Keen & led 2f out, prom 10f.	1¾	**32**
3714 **MAD MAURICE 30** [7]3-8-12 BL (45) T P Queally 10/1: 0-00000: 13th: ch g Grand Lodge - Amarella	4	**26**

(Balleroy) Held up, btn 2f out, blnks: no form sole '03 start for J Noseda: tried in chkpcs prev this season.
4268 **Purr 6** [6]3-9-2 (49) J McAuley 50/1:0   1238 **Retail Therapy 140** [13]4-9-7 BL(45) M Henry 33/1:0
15 Ran   Time 2m 40.04(9.04)   Owned: Mrs E N Nield   Trained: Epsom

THIRSK   SATURDAY 04.09.04   Lefthand, Flat, Oval Track

Official Going Firm (Good/Firm Places) ALL TIMES SLOW

4375   1.50 Richmond Castle Maiden Auction Stakes Div 1 2yo (E)
£3504 £1078 £539   **7f rnd**   **Firm**   **V Slow** Inside

3691 **CHANTACO 31** [3] A M Balding 2-8-11 W Ryan 2/1: 521: Led, qcknd from halfway & in command over   **77+**
1f out, pushed out, readily: nicely bckd, op 10/3: eff at 7f, on fm & fast, 1m shld suit: likes to dominate:
interesting for nurseries: see 3691 & 3923.
3691 **BOLD COUNSEL 31** [2] B J Meehan 2-8-7 F Norton 9/1: 52: Trkd wnr, styd on for press, al held: 2½   **66**
op 10/1: stays an easy 7f, acts on firm grnd: see 3691.
3988 **BLUSHING RUSSIAN 19** [5] P C Haslam 2-8-7 G Faulkner 12/1: 003: b g Fasliyev - Ange Rouge   2½   **61**
(Priolo) Rear, rdn & styd on well from over 1f out, no threat to wnr: E11,000 Mar foal, half-brother to a 3yo wnr
abroad, dam a French 10f scorer: improves off this longer 7f trip, stay further: handles firm grnd.
ABSTRACT FOLLY 0 [8] J D Bethell 2-8-7 A Culhane 25/1: 4: b g Rossini - Cochiti (Kris) Rear,   1½   **58**
late gains, no threat: Apr first foal, dam unplcd as a juv & subs plcd at 12f as a 3yo & over hdles.
3907 **CAYENNE GER 22** [7]2-8-6 D Allan 20/1: 55: Keen in rear, switched wide & drvn, mod prog, longer trip.   nk   **56**
4207 **KASHTANKA 8** [9]2-8-7 J Fanning 40/1: 066: Chsd ldrs, no impress over 1f out: see 4207.   2½   **52**
3736 **SECRET CAVERN 30** [10]2-8-11 S W Kelly 7/4 FAV: 67: Trkd ldrs, btn over 1f out: see 3736.   ¾   **55**
4204 **ANDY MAL 8** [4]2-8-2 T Hamilton 20/1: 068: b f Mark of Esteem - Sunflower Seed (Mummy's Pet)   3½   **39**
Dwelt & al bhd: 7,500 Apr foal, half-sister to a 7f/1m 3yo scorer, dam plcd at up to 12f as a 3yo.
4207 **MR MARUCCI 8** [6]2-8-11 T Eaves(3) 6/1: 59: Keen & trkd ldrs, struggling over 1f out: btr 4207 (g/s).   1¼   **45**
LINZIS LAD 0 [1]2-8-7 N Callan 28/1: 0: 10th: Dwelt, chsd ldrs 5f.   2   **37**
2492 **LADY SUESANNE 80** [11]2-8-2 Dale Gibson 100/1: 000: 11th: Sn pushed along & al rear, 12 wk abs.   ¾   **31**
11 Ran   Time 1m 26.31 (3.4)   Owned: The Pink Hat Racing Partnership   Trained: Kingsclere

4376   2.25 European Breeders Fund Maiden Stakes 2yo (D)
£5707 £1756 £878   **1m rnd**   **Firm**   **Gd Juv Time** Inside

3925 **SUNDAY SYMPHONY 22** [9] Saeed bin Suroor 2-9-0 J Carroll 6/4 FAV: 21: Trkd ldrs, hung right &   **91+**
hdwy to lead over 1f out, readily pulled clr in a juv course record time: hvly bckd: relished step up to 1m & 10f+
should suit in time: acts on fm & gd: sure to rate higher & win more races: see 3925.
4078 **MOBARHEN 15** [10] Sir Michael Stoute 2-9-0 N Mackay(3) 7/1: 552: Led till over 1f out, no ch with   5   **78**
wnr but kept on: op 11/2: handles firm grnd, stays 1m, get further: see 4078.
3811 **CHINESE PUZZLE 27** [8] H R A Cecil 2-9-0 t W Ryan 10/1: 6603: Mid-div, styd on onepace, no   1¼   **75**
impress on wnr over 1f out: longer 1m trip shld suit: prob handles firm & gd/soft grnd: see 3500 & 3111.
3752 **KING ZAFEEN 29** [2] M R Channon 2-9-0 T A Culhane 25/1: 04: b c Lend A Hand - Groom Dancing   1   **73+**
(Groom Dancer) Dwelt & bhd, shaken up & styd on well fnl 2f, nrst fin: first time t-strap, left debut bhd:
50,000gns Feb first foal, dam a dual 2/3yo French wnr: not knocked about, likely improver in similar.
4204 **CHINESE PUZZLE DUBAI 8** [13]2-9-0 G Gibbons 5/1: 0625: Cl-up, wknd 2f out: bckd: btr 4204 (gd/soft).   ¾   **72**
1739 **TRUCKLE 113** [11]2-9-0 J Fanning 16/1: 06: b c Vettori - Proud Titania (Fairy King) Chsd ldrs,   2   **68**
no impress fnl 2f, op 20/1, abs: Mar foal, half-brother to a 12f 4yo scorer, dam a 7f 2/3yo wnr.
3890 **KINGSHOLM 23** [14]2-9-0 N Callan 4/1: 637: Trkd ldrs, hung left & btn over 1f out: bckd tho' op 7/2.   1½   **65**
4171 **BRONZE DANCER 9** [3]2-9-0 S W Kelly 100/1: 08: Chsd ldrs, no impress fnl 3f, longer trip.   ¾   **64**
BODDEN BAY 0 [7]2-9-0 F Norton 100/1: 9: Dwelt, nvr a factor.   6   **54**
4171 **WILTSHIRE 9** [5]2-9-0 T O'Brien(7) 100/1: 000: 10th: Dwelt & al towards rear.   1¼   **51**
Be Bop 0 [6]2-9-0 Kim Tinkler 40/1:0   3559 **Lightening Fire 37** [12]2-9-0 D Allan 100/1:0
3878 **Jackadandy 24** [4]2-9-0 P Mulrennan(3) 25/1:0   3644 **Rockpiler 33** [1]2-9-0 T Eaves(3) 50/1:0
14 Ran   Time 1m 37.97 (2.57)   Owned: Godolphin   Trained: Newmarket

4377   3.00 Totesport Hambleton Cup Handicap 3yo+ 71-85 (D)   [90]
£7073 £2176 £1088   **1m4f**   **Firm**   **Slow** Inside

4327 **NIGHT SIGHT 3** [16] Mrs S Lamyman 7-8-7 (69) R Thomas(5) 16/1: 2344151: Held up, smooth hdwy to   **74**
lead dist, rdn & held on all out cl-home: qck reapp: acts on fm, gd/soft & fibresand: see 1969.
3999 **SPORTING GESTURE 18** [4] M W Easterby 7-8-13 (75) P Mulrennan(3) 10/1: 44436U2: Chsd ldrs, outpcd   hd   **79**
over 3f out, switched & styd on well cl-home, just failed: see 1969.
4274* **SMART JOHN 5** [12] W M Brisbourne 4-8-10 (3ex) (72) B Swarbrick(5) 7/1: 2135413: Mid-div, switched   ¾   **75**
wide & kept on for press, not pace to chall: qck reapp: acts on firm & gd/soft: ran to form of 4274.
4254 **PARTY PLOY 6** [8] K R Burke 6-8-8 (70) L Enstone(3) 12/1: 0121044: Chsd ldrs & led over 1f out, sn   nk   **72**
hdd & no extra nr fin: qck reapp: see 3345.

3674 **NORTHSIDE LODGE 32** [11]6-8-8 (70) S W Kelly 12/1: 3520005: Chsd ldrs, styd on onepace fnl 2f.   nk   71
3868 **PRENUP 24** [5]3-8-5 (2oh) (76) N Mackay(3) 6/1: 4112206: Led till over 1f out, no extra: back to form.   ¾   76
3637 **FINANCIAL FUTURE 34** [2]4-8-8 BL (70) J Fanning 16/1: 0-000007: Chsd ldrs, kept on in 1st time blnks.   nk   67
3437 **STALLONE 42** [1]7-8-8 (70) T Hamilton(3) 12/1: 0343608: Dwelt & rear, only mod prog for press, amiss.   ¾   68
3816 **MEXICAN PETE 27** [14]4-9-3 (79) D Allan 25/1: 0443269: Rear, switched wide & mod prog, nvr a threat.   nk   76
4181* **PERELANDRA 9** [10]4-8-13 (75) A Mullen(7) 16/1: 66610-10: 10th: Rear, eff over 2f out, nvr able to chall.   1   70
3765* **RUTTERS REBEL 28** [13]3-8-1 (6oh) (72) F Norton 16/1: 4024010: 11th: Mid-div, no impress fnl 2f.   1   67
4227 **CRIPSEY BROOK 7** [6]6-9-6 (82) Kim Tinkler 16/1: 0256000: 12th: Bhd & pushed along, no impress.   nk   76
3999 **CRATHORNE 18** [3]4-8-13 p (75) A Culhane 11/1: 0-434000: 13th: Held up, no impress: btr 2465.   shd   69
1781 **PETRULA 111** [9]5-9-5 (81) N Callan 25/1: 4034-260: 14th: Mid-div, drvn/btn 2f out: abs: btr 1586.   1¼   73
3868* **ASALEEB 24** [17]3-9-0 (85) W Ryan 11/2 FAV: 32-2110: 15th: Sn handy, btn 2f out: amiss?   5   70
3938 **Heneseys Leg 21** [7]4-9-1 (77) Lisa Jones 33/1:0
3458 **Conquering Love 41** [15]6-9-7 (83) T Eaves(3) 100/1:P
17 Ran   Time 2m 33.61 (2.11)   Owned: Mr David Fravigar-Mr Alan Mann   Trained: Louth

---

4378   3.30 B D O Stoy Hayward Stakes Handicap Fillies 3yo+ 71-85 (D)   [84]
         £6937 £2134 £1067   1m rnd   Firm   Slow   Inside

2904 **POPPYS FOOTPRINT 64** [3] K A Ryan 3-9-5 (75) N Callan 20/1: 05340P1: Dwelt, held up in tch,   83
hdwy/short of room over 2f out, led over 1f out, drvn out: reportedly banged head in stalls when p.u. latest: eff
at 6f, now suited by 1m: acts on firm & gd grnd: right back to best: see 1707.
3971 **FLASHING BLADE 20** [2] B A McMahon 4-8-13 t (64) G Gibbons 16/1: 0106502: Trkd ldrs, edged right &   1   69
no extra fnl 1f: op 12/1: back to form on firm: see 2633.
4086* **MILLAGROS 15** [8] I Semple 4-9-9 p (74) T Eaves(3) 8/1: 4463313: Held up, styd on onepace for press.   1¼   76
3806* **SHARP NEEDLE 27** [1] J Noseda 3-9-3 (73) S W Kelly 7/2: 025114: Dwelt, hdwy when short of room   ½   74
over 2f out, kept on onepace ins last: not disgraced: btr 3806.
3597* **PERLE DOR 35** [6]3-9-10 (80) A Culhane 2/1 FAV: 450-1115: Chsd ldrs, no extra over 1f out: bckd.   2   77
3872* **MISS MADAME 24** [4]3-8-13 (69) N Mackay(3) 5/1: 3361216: Led after 1f till over 2f out, no extra: op 15/2.   hd   65
2993 **SHARP SECRET 60** [5]6-8-6 (57) Lisa Jones 12/1: 265-5107: Chsd ldrs, lost place halfway, no threat.   1¼   50
4222* **MUNAAWASHAT 7** [7]3-9-10 (80) J Fanning 9/2: 3120118: Led/dsptd lead till over 1f out: btr 4222 (g/s).   2   69
8 Ran   Time 1m 38.14 (2.74)   Owned: Kimian Barfly   Trained: Hambleton

---

4379   4.05 Taskmaster Selling Stakes 3yo+ (F)
         £3059 £874 £437   1m rnd   Firm   V Slow   Inside

3830 **RYMERS RASCAL 26** [13] E J Alston 12-9-0 (48) D Allan 8/1: 2002061: Held up, hdwy over 2f out &   52
styd on for press to lead cl-home: no bid: op 11/2: eff at 7/8.3f on firm, hvy & any trk, likes Redcar.
4246 **SPLODGER MAC 7** [3] N Bycroft 5-9-6 (53) A Reilly(7) 3/1 FAV: 0012602: Led, rdn & hdd cl-home: ½   56
well bckd, op 9/2: acts on firm & fast grnd: see 3809, 3501.
3850 **EFIMAC 24** [1] N Bycroft 4-8-9 (40) F Norton 28/1: 0040003: Rear, styd on for press, nrst fin: nk   44
stablemate of rnr-up: handles firm, gd/soft & fibresand: stays an easy 1m in sell grade: see 1522.
539   **DANCING TILLY 214** [2] R A Fahey 6-8-9 p (40) T Hamilton(3) 8/1: 06-42464: Mid-div, drvn & kept on   1   42
onepace: 7 mth abs: chkpcs reapplied: see 375 & 302.
4211 **THE GAMBLER 8** [12]4-9-0 p (45) D Fentiman(7) 16/1: 2000065: Dwelt, held up in tch, only mod prog.   3   41
4133 **ABUELOS 12** [1]5-9-0 (40) T Williams 100/1: 4005066: Chsd ldrs, btn dist: see 3666 (2m).   hd   40
3734 **TRANSCENDANTALE 30** [10]6-8-9 (40) R Thomas(5) 9/1: 0404507: Dwelt, in tch, no impress fnl 2f.   nk   34
4215 **HOHS BACK 8** [6]5-9-0 p (49) Lisa Jones 9/2: 0000008: Chsd ldrs 4f out, btn over 1f out.   shd   39
4348 **CANLIS 2** [15]5-9-0 p (45) L Enstone(3) 20/1: 2000509: Mid-div, nvr able to chall: see 3830.   nk   38
4007 **WILD TIDE 18** [9]5-8-9 (30) P Mathers(5) 100/1: 00000: 10th: Mid-div, switched wide & no impress.   1¾   30
4051 **NIGHT WOLF 16** [4]4-9-0 (52) A Culhane 15/2: 0000500: 11th: Held up, eff 3f out, sn btn: longer trip.   ½   34
3609 **ZAMYATINA 35** [8]5-8-9 (40) R Kennemore(5) 25/1: 0005000: 12th: Chsd ldrs, drvn & btn 2f out.   6   19
3685 **ESPADA 31** [11]8-9-6 bl (50) S W Kelly 50/1: 1504600: 13th: Chsd ldrs till over 2f out: likes to dominate.   1½   27
4256 **Blue Nun 6** [7]3-8-4 P(40) J Fanning 50/1:0   3190 **Natmsky 52** [5]5-9-0 (30) P Mulrennan(3) 100/1:0
15 Ran   Time 1m 38.88 (3.48)   Owned: Mr Brian Chambers   Trained: Preston

---

4380   4.35 Rjf Homes Maiden Stakes 3yo+ (D)
         £4115 £1266 £633   6f str   Firm   Slow   Stands Side

4245 **JILLY WHY 7** [6] Ms Deborah J Evans 3-8-7 (57) A Nicholls 8/1: 6340-041: Led & asserted from   71
halfway, in command dist, ran & heels, readily: op 13/2: eff at 6f on firm & gd grnd: enjoyed forcing tactics.
3575 **HARRISONS FLYER 36** [4] R A Fahey 3-8-12 (67) T Hamilton(3) 6/1: 4-020202: Cl-up, hung left & no   3½   63
impress over 1f out: handles firm & soft grnd: blnks omitted today: see 3347, 2944 & 2849.
3655 **YORKES FOLLY 33** [9] C W Fairhurst 3-8-7 VIS (45) Lisa Jones 50/1: 50-00003: Chsd ldrs, outpcd bef   3½   47
halfway, kept on late to snatch 3rd, nvr a dngr: first time visor: see 2936.
4081 **ZWADI 15** [2] H Candy 3-8-7 (72) D Sweeney 11/10 FAV: 4050324: Cl-up, rdn/btn over 1f out: hvly   1   44
bckd, op 6/4: btr 4081 (g/s).
3220 **ROAN RAIDER 51** [5]4-9-0 vis (57) K Ghunowa(7) 14/1: 3502025: Chsd ldrs, nvr pace to chall: abs.   1   46
4237 **ARIESANNE 7** [8]3-8-7 N Lawes(7) 20/1: 306: Sn outpcd, nvr on terms with ldrs, longer trip.   5   26
4029 **THOMAS LAWRENCE 17** [1]3-8-12 BL (80) J Fanning 100/30: 432-637: Sn rdn & struggling towards rear,   14   0
bhd 2f out: first time blnks, nicely bckd but no improvement: see 4029 & 3603.
2701} **CHANTILLY SUNSET 425** [10]3-8-7 J Bramhill 66/1: 0-8: b f General Monash - Alpine Sunset   11   0
(Auction Ring) Reared start & hmpd early, al bhd, reapp: no form sole '03 start (rtd 26, A Berry).
      DEJEEJE 0 [7]3-8-12 A Culhane 20/1: 9: Slow away & sn well bhd, t.o..   dist   0
9 Ran   Time 1m 11.46 (1.96)   Owned: Mr Paul Green (Oaklea)   Trained: Lydiate

---

4381   5.05 Richmond Castle Maiden Auction Stakes Div 2 2yo (E)
£3494 £1075 £538   **7f rnd   Firm   V Slow** Inside

3981 **EASY MOVER** 19 [9] R Guest 2-8-6   N Mackay(3) 5/1: 551: Mid-div, pushed along halfway, switched   **81**
wide & rdn/styd on strongly ins last to lead cl-home, going away: nicely bckd: apprec step up to 7f, looks sure to
relish 1m: acts on firm & fast grnd, sharp/undul or easy trks: lightly rcd & progressing, keep in mind for h'caps..
4153 **MALINSA BLUE** 14 [2] J A Glover 2-8-6 (77) F Norton 11/4: 62262: Trkd ldrs & led over 1f out till   ½   **80**
cl-home: nicely bckd: styd longer 7f trip well: acts on firm & gd grnd: shown enough to find a race: see 4153.
VANCOUVER GOLD 0 [3] K R Burke 2-8-2   Dale Gibson 25/1: 3: b f Monashee Mountain - Forest   hd   **75**
Berries (Thatching) Dwelt & held up, hdwy/switched to press ldrs ins last, no extra nr fin: op 33/1: Apr foal,
half-sister to wnrs at 5f/1m, dam unrcd: eff at 7f, 1m shld suit in time: handles firm: gd start.
3699 **PLENTY CRIED WOLF** 31 [10] R A Fahey 2-8-7   T Hamilton(3) 33/1: 004: b g Wolfhound - Plentitude   1½   **77**
(Ela Mana Mou) Handy & led 2f out, sn hdd & no extra ins last: Mar foal, dam unrcd, related to a prolific 11f/2m
scorer, also a hdles wnr: imprvd over this longer 7f trip, likely to stay much further in time: acts on fm.
4343 **EGYPTIAN LADY** 2 [1] 2-8-2   D Fentiman(7) 33/1: 005: Held up, hdwy when hung left 2f out, kept on   ½   **71**
onepace: well clr of rem, qck reapp: styd longer 7f trip, handles firm grnd: see 4343.
4207 **ROBINZAL** 8 [5] 2-8-11 (75) D Allan 9/2: 0326: Led till 2f out, sn btn: btr 4207 (g/s).   6   **70**
3774 **McELDOWNEY** 28 [6] 2-8-11 BL (82) J Fanning 9/4 FAV: 3222307: Chsd ldrs & drvn/hmpd 4f out, btn 2f   1¼   **67**
out & eased ins last: hvly bckd in first time blnks: btr 3511 & 3245.
SADIES STAR 0 [4] 2-8-2   P Fessey 14/1: 8: b f Indian Lodge - Nishiki (Brogan) Trkd ldrs, btn 2f   ½   **57**
out: 10,000gns 2yo purchase, Apr foal: half-sister to a 5/6f juv wnr, dam a 4yo hdles scorer.
2802 **HIDDEN JEWEL** 68 [8] 2-8-7 (48) G Gibbons 25/1: 0669: Sn outpcd & al bhd.   hd   **61$**
MISS BEAR 0 [11] 2-8-6   D McGaffin 14/1: 0: 10th: Swerved right start & al rear, op 16/1.   3   **54**
3939 **STREET DANCER** 21 [7] 2-8-11   N Callan 50/1: 00: 11th: Mid-div, struggling 3f out.   2½   **54**
11 Ran   Time 1m 26.61(3.71)   Owned: Wendals Herbs Ltd   Trained: Newmarket

---

Official Going Good

4382   1.35 Stanleybet Be Friendly Handicap Stakes 3yo+ 86-100 (C)   [99]
£21376 £8108 £4054   **5f str   Firm 13   -01 Slow** Inside

4238 **FOREVER PHOENIX** 7 [16] R M H Cowell 4-9-7 (92) A Quinn(5) 7/1: 0230361: Held up, hdwy over 2f out   **102**
& led dist, styd on strongly to assert, pushed out: suited by 5/6f on firm, gd/soft & both AWs: back to best.
4201 **DEVISE** 8 [13] M S Saunders 5-9-1 (86) D Holland 7/2 FAV: 5402322: Chsd ldrs & led halfway till   1¼   **91**
dist, not pace of wnr: well bckd, op 5/1: remains on the upgrade, can win again: see 3792, 1914.
3792 **PTARMIGAN RIDGE** 28 [12] Miss L A Perratt 8-9-1 (86) M Fenton 16/1: 0065103: Mid-div, edged left   ½   **89**
& styd on for press, not pace of wnr: gd run, likes this venue: acts on firm, loves gd & hvy, any trk: see 3150.
4184 **BOND BOY** 8 [6] B Smart 7-9-1 (86) F Lynch 20/1: 6030004: Towards rear, styd on for press from   ½   **87**
over 1f out, reportedly hung RHd & lost an off-fore shoe, gd run in the circumstances: prefer more give.
3646 **BO McGINTY** 33 [14] 3-8-12 (84) P Hanagan 10/1: 0120045: Mid-div, styd on for press, unable to   ½   **83**
chall: acts on firm & gd grnd: see 1745.
3622 **FUNFAIR WANE** 35 [1] 5-9-5 (90) A Nicholls 25/1: 0-004006: Prom halfway, styd on onepace: imprvd   hd   **88**
eff, looks to be coming to hand & on a fair mark: spot on at 6f, '02 wnr of the Ayr Gold Cup off a 10lb higher mark.
4291 **WHITBARROW** 5 [11] 5-9-7 bl (92) J F Egan 16/1: 0000007: Sn handy, no extra dist: qck reapp: see 1845.¾   **88**
4238 **ABSENT FRIENDS** 7 [8] 7-9-1 (86) J Edmunds 16/1: 0606008: Chsd ldrs, no impress dist: see 1626.   1½   **77**
4174 **MAKTAVISH** 9 [4] 5-8-10 (2oh)p (79) R Winston 12/1: 0004609: Led till halfway, prefer easy ground.   1½   **68**
4253 **TRINCULO** 6 [10] 7-8-10 (1oh)p (80) J P Guillambert(3) 33/1: 5006000: 10th: Chsd ldrs, no extra dist.   nk   **67**
3758* **RIVER FALCON** 29 [3] 4-9-5 (90) T E Durcan 9/1: 1003010: 11th: Mid-div, no impress over 1f out.   1½   **71**
3622 **PERUVIAN CHIEF** 35 [9] 7-9-10 vis (95) K Darley 33/1: 002000U0: 12th: Dwelt, nvr on terms with ldrs.   nk   **75**
3792 **BLACKHEATH** 28 [2] 8-9-2 (87) Alex Greaves 16/1: 4145000: 13th: Mid-div, no impress fnl 2f: btr 3248.   nk   **66**
4005 **JOHNSTONS DIAMOND** 18 [7] 6-8-13 BL (84) W Supple 20/1: 6200000: 14th: Rdn halfway, nvr factor.   1¼   **59**
3792 **WHISTLER** 28 [15] 7-9-5 p (90) M Hills 7/1: 0140340: 15th: Dwelt & al bhd: bckd: reportedly   2   **59**
stumbled leaving the stalls & hung RHd: btr 3628.
4107 **PRINCE OF BLUES** 14 [5] 6-8-10 (25oh)bl (56) S Righton 100/1: 0030330: 16th: Al struggling rear.   hd   **49**
16 Ran   Time 59.50 (0.7)   Owned: Mr J M Greetham   Trained: Newmarket

---

4383   2.05 Stanleybet Com Old Borough Cup Stakes Heritage Handicap 3yo+ 0-105 (B)   [109]
£52000 £16000 £8000   **1m6f   Firm 13   -04 Slow** Inside

4023 **DEFINING** 17 [1] J R Fanshawe 5-9-3 (98) J Murtagh 11/1: 03-03041: Chsd ldrs & al trav well,   **109+**
smooth prog to lead over 1f out, hung left but in command ins last, pushed out, val 2L+: eff at 12f, now seems
suited by 14f: acts on firm, gd/soft & both AWs, any trk: v useful performance: List/Gr 3 potential: see 2246.
3510 **SERGEANT CECIL** 39 [7] B R Millman 5-8-12 (93) S Drowne 10/1: 0-035122: Held up, rdn & hdwy to   ¾   **99**
chase wnr dist, kept on, al held: continues to run well: acts on firm, hvy: see 3510, 3070.
4353* **SENDINTANK** 1 [12] S C Williams 4-8-1 (5ex) (82) Martin Dwyer 7/1: 11311113: Held up, no room &   hd   **87+**
lost pl over 3f out, hdwy when forced to switch over 1f out, fin strongly, would have gone v close with a clr run:
wnr here yesterday: acts on firm, hvy & fibresand: has been v busy but remains ultra progressive, keep on side.
4062 **LOCHBUIE** 16 [3] G Wragg 3-8-5 (97) J F Egan 11/2 JT FAV: 4113144: Mid-div, styd on onepace for   shd   **102**
press fnl 2f: gd run in defeat: see 3556.
3999 **MILLVILLE** 18 [11] 4-8-4 (85) P Robinson 7/1: 0110545: Held up, short of room 2f out, styd on well   ½   **89+**
ins last: styd longer 14f trip well, acts on firm, gd & polytrack: remains progressive: see 3999 & 877.
4023 **CROW WOOD** 17 [6] 5-9-0 (95) K McEvoy 33/1: 0335206: Mid-div, short of room/lost pl 3f out, late   1   **98**
rally, no threat: apprec rtn to faster surface & this longer 14f trip may yet suit: see 2101, 1296.
3999 **SKI JUMP** 18 [9] 4-8-0 vis (81) P Hanagan 25/1: 01-16067: Mid-div, styd on onepace fnl 2f, no dngr.   nk   **83**
3635* **HIGH ACTION** 34 [15] 4-8-9 t (90) J P Spencer 12/1: 6-000118: Led over 2f out till bef 1f out, wknd.   ¾   **91**
3617 **LODGER** 35 [16] 4-8-8 (89) R Hughes 16/1: 214-0649: Held up, eff 3f out, no prog dist: btr 3617 (12f).   2   **87**

3076 **LOVES TRAVELLING 57** [4]4-8-9 (90) D Holland 11/2 JT FAV: 123-2120: 10th: Held up, prog/hmpd over 1f out, sn no extra: shade closer without interference: nicely bckd, longer trip & 8 wk abs: btr 3076 (12f, g/s). *nk* **87**
3969 **TRANCE 20** [10]4-8-6 (87) P Makin(5) 100/1: 1-041100: 11th: Held up, eff 3f out, no impress: btr 2567. *nk* **83**
4138* **SAHEM 12** [20]7-8-3 (84) W Supple 66/1: 1203310: 12th: Keen & trkd ldrs, btn 2f out: btr 4138. *3* **76**
3444 **ITS THE LIMIT 42** [19]5-8-11 (92) M J Kinane 12/1: 131/42-40: 13th: Reared start, bhd, little prog. *shd* **84**
4106* **DR SHARP 14** [8]4-8-1 (82) J Quinn 25/1: 1210610: 14th: Dwelt, mid-div, eff 3f out, sn btn: btr 4106. *2* **71**
2771 **JOROBADEN 70** [2]4-8-6 (87) R Mullen 66/1: 1610600: 15th: Mid-div, struggling fnl 2f, eased, abs. *½* **75**
4023 **TRUST RULE 17** [18]4-8-9 (90) M Hills 25/1: 0650000: 16th: Al towards rear: btr 1484. *nk* **77**
3776 **ALMAH 28** [14]6-8-6 (1ow) (86) R Winston 66/1: 630-0060: 17th: Dwelt, chsd ldrs till 3f out: btr 3776. *1* **72**
3918 **BENDARSHAAN 22** [17]4-8-8 (89) R Ffrench 66/1: 4112050: 18th: Mid-div, btn 3f out: btr 3458. *½* **73**
4104 **ALBANOV 14** [5]4-8-13 (94) K Darley 33/1: 522-0040: 19th: Keen & prom, hmpd when btn over 1f out. *1¼* **76**
4490] **PUSHKIN 232** [13]6-9-10 (105) S Chin 100/1: 00526-30: 20th: b c Caerleon - Palmeraie (Lear Fan) *2½* **83**
Led, hdd over 2f out, sn wknd: Brit bow, long abs: AW rnr-up in Middle East '03, ex French, List & Gr 2 in '02 (E Lellouche): eff at 14f/15.5f on gd & soft grnd: with M Johnston.
2 Oct'02 Long 20gd 116- : 1 Jul'02 Mais 14gd 113- :
20 Ran Time 3m 0.43 (2.43) Owned: Mrs V Shelton Trained: Newmarket

4384 **2.35 Gr1 Stanleybet Sprint Cup 3yo+ (A)**
£130500 £49500 £24750 **6f str** **Firm 13** **+08 Fast** Inside

3075* **TANTE ROSE 57** [14] R Charlton 4-8-11 (111) R Hughes 10/1: 3040-111: Towards rear, hdwy over 1f out, qknd to lead line: op 12/1: fast time: 8 wk: eff at 7f, now proving v smart at 6f: acts on firm & gd/soft, any trk: goes well fresh: game, still improving & has a fine turn of foort. **120**
3838* **SOMNUS 27** [5] T D Easterby 4-9-0 (118) M J Kinane 7/1: 10-02512: Al handy & rdn/led over 1f out, just hdd line: nicely bckd: high-class sprinter who lost nothing in defeat, won this race last term: acts on firm/fast but prob ideally suited by more give: see 3838, 1667. *shd* **121**
3062 **PATAVELLIAN 58** [4] R Charlton 6-9-0 bl (114) S Drowne 14/1: 5111-303: Dwelt, trkd ldrs, rdn to chall ins last, no extra nr line: 2 month abs, stablemate of wnr: rtn to 5f shld suit, poss with more give, spot on now for Prix L'Abbaye (wnr last term): see 1856. *¾* **119**
3838 **ROYAL MILLENNIUM 27** [8] M R Channon 6-9-0 (111) T E Durcan 50/1: 1425-104: Rear, prog/forced to switch over 1f out, kept on for press: fine run, spot on back at Gr 2/Gr 3 level: see 2769. *1½* **114**
3838 **MONSIEUR BOND 27** [19]4-9-0 BL (115) F Lynch 33/1: 5110605: Prom, ch over 1f out, onepace ins last: fine run in first time blnks on unsuitably fast grnd: high-class performer when granted give: see 1667. *hd* **113**
4060 **ONE COOL CAT 16** [7]3-8-12 J P Spencer 6/4 FAV: 11-05136: Mid-div, eff over 1f out, onepace: hvly bckd: inconsistent, promising 4060. *1* **110**
4060 **ORIENTOR 16** [16]6-9-0 (115) W Supple 25/1: 5053157: Mid-div, styd on onepace: gd run, ideally suited by more give: see 2913 (Gr 3, g/s). *½* **108**
4063 **WELSH EMPEROR 16** [17]5-9-0 bl (107) R Winston 66/1: 6-146528: Led till over 1f out, no extra. *hd* **107**
3838 **ASHDOWN EXPRESS 27** [13]5-9-0 (117) R Mullen 16/1: 3020249: Pushed along rear, mod late gains. *½* **105**
4472} **RATIO 35** [1]6-9-0 t P Robinson 18/1: 11010-10: 10th: ch g Pivotal - Owdbetts (High Estate) Held up, eff 2f out, no impress on ldrs: French raider, recent List wnr: landed val Woking h'cap & Gr 3 in '03: suited by 5/6f on firm & soft grnd, prob any trk: high-class sprinter at best. *hd* **104**
1 Sep'03 Newb 5.2fm 113- A: 1 Jun'03 Asco 6fm 109-99 B: 2 Aug'01 Deau 8sft 102- : 2 May'01 Yarm 7gd 88- C: 1 May'01 Sali 6gd 89- D:
4060 **AIRWAVE 16** [12]4-8-11 (110) K Darley 16/1: 0-660160: 11th: Trkd ldrs, btn dist: btr 3304 (List). *¾* **99**
4060+ **BAHAMIAN PIRATE 16** [9]9-9-0 (110) D Holland 40/1: 0001610: 12th: Rear, short of room over 1f out, little prog: needs more give: see 4060 (5f, g/s). *nk* **101**
3596* **MAC LOVE 35** [6]3-8-12 (104) J F Egan 100/1: 4226610: 13th: Chsd ldrs, btn 2f out: btr 3596 (cond). *1* **98**
3971 **LOCHRIDGE 20** [3]5-8-11 (101) Martin Dwyer 100/1: 2003240: 14th: Chsd ldrs, btn over 1f out: btr 3596. *nk* **94**
4291 **TYCHY 5** [10]5-8-11 (98) P Hanagan 200/1: 0051040: 15th: Chsd ldrs, btn over 1f out: qck reapp. *hd* **93**
4063 **CAPRICHO 16** [2]7-9-0 (100) J Quinn 150/1: 0-040000: 16th: Mid-div, outpcd from halfway: see 2140. *nk* **95**
3838 **FRIZZANTE 27** [18]5-8-11 (115) J Murtagh 13/2: 1-213100: 17th: Held up, sn pushed along & nvr factor: nicely bckd but reportedly btn in the early stages & nvr trav: much btr 3062 (Gr 1). *¾* **90**
3268 **CARTOGRAPHY 49** [11]3-8-12 t (106) K McEvoy 50/1: 310-3320: 18th: Trkd ldrs, btn 2f out, abs: reportedly lost action around halfway: btr 3268 & 2486. *nk* **92**
3838 **THE TRADER 27** [15]6-9-0 bl (114) D Sweeney 20/1: 6-130150: 19th: Al in rear: reportedly struck into. *1* **89**
19 Ran Time 1m 11.58 (0.28) Owned: Mr B E Nielsen Trained: Beckhampton

4385 **3.05 Stanleybet Mobile E B F Maiden Stakes 2yo (D)**
£5720 £1760 £880 **6f str** **Firm 13** **-42 Slow** Inside

ZOHAR 0 [12] B J Meehan 2-9-0 M J Kinane 14/1: 1: b c Aljabr - Dafnah (Housebuster) Towards rear, pushed along & hdwy from halfway, rdn & led dist, rdn out: $26,000 Feb foal, dam an unrcd half-sister to a useful 1m/10f performer: eff at 6f, looks sure to apprec 7f+: acts on firm grnd & a gall trk: goes well fresh: potentially useful & can rate higher. **94**
3709 **MUNADDAM 30** [9] Saeed bin Suroor 2-9-0 W Supple 4/1: 22: Dwelt & towards rear, rdn & styd on fnl 2f, not pace of wnr: nicely bckd tho' op 3/1: acts on firm & fast grnd: shld find a race: see 3709. *1¼* **88**
4028 **AVIATION 17** [6] R Hannon 2-9-0 R Hughes 50/1: 03: Rear, rdn & styd on well from over 1f out, nrst fin: left soft grnd debut bhd: eff at 6f, looks sure to apprec 7f+: acts on firm grnd: keep in mind for 7f+. *¾* **86$**
MUSEEB 0 [11] J L Dunlop 2-9-0 J Murtagh 9/2: 4: b c Danzig - Elle Seule (Exclusive Native) Dwelt & bhd, styd on well from over 1f out, nrst fin: bckd, May foal, half-brother to top-class 1m filly, dam a high-class 2/3yo: eff at 6f, 7f/1m shld suit: handles firm grnd: got the hang of thing late on, will improve. *nk* **85+**
3755 **ONE GREAT IDEA 29** [13]2-9-0 P Hanagan 7/1: 25: Chsd ldrs, hung left & no extra dist: styd longer 6f trip, handles firm & gd grnd: see 3755. *½* **83**
GROSVENOR SQUARE 0 [8]2-9-0 K McEvoy 7/2 FAV: 6: b c Dubai Millennium - Embassy (Cadeaux Genereux) Pushed along towards rear, kept on late, nvr able to chall: hvly bckd, op 9/2: Mar foal, dam a top-class juv at 6f & related to a high-class 10f performer: styd further, prob improve. *nk* **82**
3272 **SACRANUN 49** [3]2-9-0 D Holland 6/1: 237: Chsd ldrs, outpcd over 1f out: abs: see 3272. *1¼* **78**
4083 **SYDNEYROUGHDIAMOND 15** [1]2-9-0 R Mullen 200/1: 058: Cl-up, led over 1f out till dist, wknd: improved effort on this faster surface. *shd* **78**
4204 **SHANKLY BOND 8** [4]2-9-0 F Lynch 33/1: 09: Pushed along towards rear, only mod prog. *2½* **70**
4006 **OWED 18** [5]2-9-0 t T E Durcan 200/1: 00: 10th: Outpcd, nvr a factor. *6* **52**
2553 **TOUCH OF SILK 78** [2]2-8-9 (73) M Hills 7/1: 5200: 11th: Chsd ldrs till halfway, op 9/1. *nk* **46**

DISTINCTIVE MIND 0 [10]2-9-0 M Fenton 66/1: 0: 12th: Led till over 1f out, wknd qckly. *3* **42**
DE BULLIONS 0 [7]2-9-0 Martin Dwyer 66/1: 0: 13th: Sn outpcd & struggling. *5* **28**
4247 **COOL SANDS 7** [14]2-9-0 R Winston 200/1: 00: 14th: Dwelt, in tch to halfway, sn bhd. *25* **0**
14 Ran Time 1m 14.6 (3.3) Owned: E H Jones (Paints) Ltd Trained: Upper Lambourn

4386 **3.40 Listed Stanleybet Robert Sangster Superior Mile 3yo+ (A)**
£23200 £8800 £4400 **1m30y rnd** **Firm 13** **-03 Slow** Inside

1758 **WITH REASON 112** [5] Saeed bin Suroor 6-9-2 t (115) K McEvoy 11/2: 16121-01: Made all, styd on strongly ins last, drvn out: op 9/2: 4 month abs: eff at 7f/1m on firm, gd/soft & fibresand, any trk, likes Haydock: goes well fresh: likes to force the pace: smart performance: see 1758. **114**
4797} **TROUBADOUR 45** [9] A P O'Brien 3-8-11 J P Spencer 2/1 FAV: 135-12: b c Danehill - Taking Liberties (Royal Academy) Mid-div, rdn & styd on to chase wnr ins last, al held: hvly bckd Irish raider, 6 wk abs: earlier this term landed a cond event at Naas in easy fashion: mdn wnr in '03: eff at 1m: acts on firm & gd grnd, stiff or gall trks: up in grade & clrly smart. 1 Aug'03 Curr 6gd 109- : *1* **111**
4061+**AUDIENCE 16** [1] J Akehurst 4-9-2 p (98) J Quinn 14/1: 0024613: Keen, mid-div, styd on well for press fnl 2f, not pace of wnr: clr of rem: up-graded & a smart performance: acts on firm & gd/soft grnd: see 4061. *1¼* **108$**
4061 **EXCELSIUS 16** [7] J L Dunlop 4-9-2 BL (96) K Darley 66/1: 01-03004: Keen & held up, outpcd 3f out, drvn & some late prog, no dngr: blnks: poss suited by more give: see 108 (List, soft). *5* **99**
3886 **SHOT TO FAME 23** [2]5-9-7 (111) J Murtagh 4/1: 0112155: Trkd ldr, rdn & btn over 1f out. *1* **102**
4061 **ST PETERSBURG 16** [8]4-9-2 (101) D Holland 9/1: 2102136: Chsd wnr 5f out, btn over 1f out: op 12/1: btr 4061, 3077 (h'caps). *1¼* **94**
2458 **PUTRA PEKAN 83** [4]6-9-5 bl (110) P Robinson 11/2: 010-1107: Keen & held up, wide on bend 4f out, btn 2f out: abs: btr 1649 (led, soft). *6* **86**
3957 **MILLENNIUM FORCE 21** [6]6-9-2 (106) T E Durcan 16/1: 0423308: Held up, strugg fnl 2f, wants 7f & give. *3½* **76**
8 Ran Time 1m 41.8 (1.3) Owned: Godolphin Trained: Newmarket

4387 **4.15 Stanleybet 0808 100 1221 Nursery Handicap Stakes 2yo (B)** **[93]**
£15474 £5870 £2935 **1m30y rnd** **Firm 13** **-26 Slow** Inside

4064 **SPACED 16** [6] R Hannon 2-9-2 (81) R Hughes 20/1: 06131: Trkd ldrs, rdn to lead over 1f out, drvn ins last, held on all out: eff at 7f/1m on firm & gd/soft grnd: shows a find attitude, progessive: see 4064. **91**
3959* **HALLHOO 21** [1] M R Channon 2-9-2 (81) T E Durcan 7/2: 312: Mid-div, short of room 2f out, drvn & styd on well ins last, just failed: hvly bckd, op 9/2: styd longer 1m trip well on h'cap bow: acts on firm & fast grnd: progressing with racing: see 3959. *shd* **90**
4177 **WISE DENNIS 9** [4] A P Jarvis 2-9-0 (79) K McEvoy 11/1: 00333: Keen in mid-div, rdn & styd on well ins last, nrst fin: bckd: styd longer 1m trip well: acts on firm, fast & polytrack, sharp or gall trk: significantly imprvd last thrice, shld find a race: see 4177 & 3709. *¾* **87**
3878* **LOOKS COULD KILL 24** [2] G A Butler 2-9-7 (86) J Murtagh 5/2 FAV: 214: Held up, short of room 2f out, shkn up & hung left ins last but kept on under min pressure, nrst fin: hvly bckd on h'cap bow: closer with a clr passage, not knocked about & can improve from this: see 3878. *1½* **91+**
4100* **IM SPARTACUS 14** [9]2-8-10 (75) M Fenton 16/1: 5065415: Handy, rdn & hung left over 1f out, no extra: op 20/1: longer 1m trip may yet suit: acts on firm & gd/soft grnd: see 4100 (7f). *hd* **79**
4212 **SIMPLY ST LUCIA 8** [11]2-8-10 (75) R Winston 100/1: 1336: Led till over 1f out, fdd: see 4066 & 2492. *2½* **74**
3582 **TRAIANOS 36** [10]2-9-0 (79) N De Souza(5) 33/1: 5657: Keen & chsd ldrs, no impress over 1f out. *¾* **77**
3065 **ADORATION 58** [5]2-8-13 (78) R Ffrench 25/1: 32508: Held up, eff over 2f out, little hdwy, abs. *shd* **76**
4285* **NIGHT OF JOY 5** [3]2-9-8 (6ex) (87) P Robinson 7/2: 44119: Keen & mid-div, rdn & btn over 1f out: nicely bckd under a 6lb pen: joc reported the race came too sn after 4285 (soft). *2½* **80**
3869 **TURKS WOOD 24** [8]2-8-10 (75) D Holland 33/1: 4550: 10th: Mid-div, btn 2f out: h'cap bow, longer trip. *¾* **67**
4102* **CEIRIOG VALLEY 14** [7]2-9-6 (85) M Hills 7/1: 010: 11th: Pushed along towards rear halfway, sn btn: bckd: disappointing on h'cap bow: btr 4102 (7f, soft). *½* **76**
11 Ran Time 1m 43.74 (3.24) Owned: De La Warr Racing Trained: Marlborough

4388 **4.45 Stanley Casinos Handicap Stakes 3yo 56-70 (E)** **[77]**
£5543 £1706 £853 **1m2f120y** **Firm 13** **-20 Slow** Outside

4342* **STEPHANO 2** [10] B W Hills 3-8-13 (3ex) (62) M Hills 2/1 FAV: 50-05011: Mid-div, rdn & hdwy to lead over 1f out, edged left but styd on strongly for press: nicely bckd, qck reapp under a 3lb pen: imprvd at 10f/10.5f last twice, shld get further: likes firm grnd & a gall trk: hat-trick on the cards: see 4342, 2656. **71**
2799 **CAPTAIN MARRYAT 68** [4] P W Harris 3-8-10 (59) W Supple 6/1: 0-202232: Trkd ldrs, rdn & kept on fnl 2f, not pace of wnr: 10 wk abs: styd longer 10f trip well, deserves to find similar: see 2799, 2634 & 2423 (1m). *3* **64**
4044 **MR MIDASMAN 16** [2] R Hollinshead 3-8-7 (1oh) (55) J Quinn 25/1: 0000463: Held up, rdn & styd on fnl 2f, not threaten front pair: stays 10.5f, 12f could suit: handles firm & soft grnd: see 923. *1½* **59**
3875 **PATRIXTOO 24** [7] M H Tompkins 3-8-11 (60) P Robinson 10/1: 00-05024: Led till over 1f out, onepace: confirmed improvement on latest: handles firm & gd grnd: see 3875. *¾* **62**
3801 **AMERICAN DUKE 27** [13]3-9-3 (66) Paul Eddery 20/1: 00-00205: Mid-div, kept on onepace: see 3690. *1½* **66**
4119 **TURTLE PATRIARCH 13** [1]3-8-11 (60) S Drowne 10/1: 0-000426: Chsd ldrs, rdn & no extra fnl 1f, eased cl-home: btr 4119 (12f). *¾* **59**
3741 **SANTA CATERINA 30** [12]3-9-7 (70) K Darley 25/1: 00-45207: Keen & prom, wknd over 1f out: btr 3108. *2½* **65**
1978 **ESTEPONA 102** [9]3-9-2 (65) R Winston 33/1: 4008: Mid-div, drvn & no prog fnl 2f: h'cap bow, abs. *1* **59**
3679 **IMPULSIVE BID 31** [11]3-8-7 (56) P Hanagan 66/1: 0205009: Mid-div, rdn & no impress fnl 2f: btr 1678. *shd* **50**
3905 **CLASSIC LEASE 23** [8]3-8-12 (61) F Lynch 40/1: 0530: 10th: Rear, no impress fnl 3f, h'cap bow. *1* **54**
4167 **MISS INKHA 10** [14]3-8-12 (61) Martin Dwyer 40/1: 006620: 11th: Mid-div, rdn & btn 2f out: btr 4167. *1¾* **52**
3845 **ZAFFEU 25** [5]3-9-3 BL (66) T E Durcan 50/1: 4510600: 12th: Dwelt, rear, no impress fnl 2f, blnks. *1¾* **55**
3854 **MISS ELOISE 24** [17]3-8-9 (58) M Fenton 50/1: 6010000: 13th: Stumbled start & sn bhd. *2* **44**
2974* **HILLTOP RHAPSODY 61** [15]3-9-6 (69) J Murtagh 12/1: 0010: 14th: Chsd ldrs, btn 2f out: h'cap bow. *6* **46**
4260 **KEEPERS LODGE 6** [16]3-9-7 (70) D Holland 5/1: 0103520: 15th: Al towards rear, reportedly nvr trav & lost action in the home straight: much btr 4260 (soft). *7* **37**
3410 **Supamach 43** [6]3-9-2 (65) J F Egan 33/1:0 4342 **Turner 2** [3]3-9-7 VIS(70) R Hughes 33/1:0
17 Ran Time 2m 0.54(3.54) Owned: Mr Guy Reed Trained: Lambourn

Official Going Good/Firm (Good places)

4389　　2.10 Pentax 'perfect Image' Handicap Stakes 3yo 86-100 (C)　　　　　[102]
£12145　£4607　£2303　　**1m Jub**　　**Firm 05**　　-05 Slow　　Inside

4149　**MYSTICAL GIRL** 11 [5] M Johnston 3-9-3　(91) K Fallon　5/2 FAV: 1306051: Made all, styd on well　　　　101
over 1f out, rdn out: hvly bckd: right back to useful best with a rtn to forcing tactics & suited by 1m, stays 10f:
acts on firm & soft grnd, gall or easy trk: tough: see 2126, 1865.

3689　**DIAMOND LODGE** 31 [6] J Noseda 3-9-4　(92) E Ahern　7/2: 1211152: Handy, eff to chase wnr over 2f　　2　　97
out, kept on same pace fnl 1f: well bckd: another tough & useful run: progressive: see 3535.

4563*)**PEDRILLO** 338 [4] Sir Mark Prescott 3-8-13　(87) S Sanders　9/2: 321-3: b g Singspiel - Patria (Mr　　nk　　91
Prospector)　Slow away, held up, eff well over 1f out, kept on, no threat to wnr: reapp: won last of 3 '03 starts
(mdn): styd this fair 1m well, shld get further: acts on firm & gd grnd: lightly rcd, stable likely to extract more
improvement & shld be winning sn, poss over 10f.　1 Oct'03 Brig 7.0g/f 86- D:　2 Sep'03 Chep 6.1g/f 68- D:

4061　**STATE DILEMMA** 16 [10] B W Hills 3-9-3　(91) R Hills　20/1: 4-510004: Held up, hdwy over 2f out, onepcd.　nk　　94
3318　**JAZZ SCENE** 49 [7]3-9-7　(95) S Hitchcott(3) 8/1: 2-002245: Dwelt, held up, rdn & no impress over　½　　97
2f out, some late gains: 7 wk abs: fair run: see 2749, 2521.

3113　**SGT PEPPER** 56 [9]3-9-4　(92) R L Moore　25/1: 140-0046: In tch, onepcd fnl 2f: abs: likes Salisbury.　½　　91
3067　**TRANQUIL SKY** 57 [1]3-8-9　(83) L Keniry(3) 14/1: 0052047: In tch, wknd over 1f out:　8 wk abs: see 2040.　1¾　　80
3860　**FLIP FLOP AND FLY** 24 [2]3-8-11　(85) J Fortune　9/1: 0106258: Hld up, hung badly left into str, no impress2　　78
3978　**SURF THE NET** 19 [8]3-8-11 P　(85) Dane O'Neill　33/1: 6-300349: Handy, wknd 2f out: cheekpieces.　1¾　　76
3059　**QASIRAH** 58 [3]3-9-6 bl　(94) L Dettori　10/1: 0-053600: 10th: Handy, wknd qckly over 2f out:　8 wk abs.　6　　73
10 Ran　Time 1m 37.64 (0.84)　Owned: T T Bloodstocks　Trained: Middleham

---

4390　　2.40 Gr3 Pentax Sirenia Stakes 2yo (A)
£23200　£8800　£4400　　**6f str**　　**Firm 05**　　+09 Fast　　Stands Side

3065*　**SATCHEM** 58 [5] C E Brittain 2-8-11　(95) K Fallon　3/1: 2111: Handy, hdwy to lead over 1f out,　　　　115
styd on fnl 1f, drvn out: gd time, abs: eff over 6/7f on fm & fast, stiff or fair trks: runs well fresh: prev with
D Loder but this was an improved/smart run for new stable, win another Gr race: see 3065.

4022　**COUNCIL MEMBER** 17 [1] Saeed bin Suroor 2-8-11　(100) L Dettori　15/8 FAV: 12202: Set pace till　　1½　　110
over 1f out, kept on but not pace of wnr: well bckd: back to form on a sound surface & can find a List/Gr 3.

4153　**VISIONIST** 14 [2] J A Osborne 2-8-11　J Fortune　7/1: 1433: Chsd ldrs, eff over 1f out, onepace:　　1½　　105
well worth another try at 7f in List: see 4153.

4179*　**TREMAR** 9 [4] T G Mills 2-8-11　(90) G Carter　20/1: 43214: With ldrs, no extra over 1f out: gd　　nk　　104
run: acts on firm, soft & polytrack: wants stks/List: see 4179.

4022　**GALEOTA** 17 [7]2-8-11 P　(100) R L Moore　5/1: 4155: With ldrs, no extra over 1f out: needs ease in grade.　shd　　103
4046　**STAGBURY HILL** 16 [3]2-8-11　(100) R Hills　20/1: 1636: Dwelt, sn bhd, some late gains, no dngr:　　nk　　102
needs ease in grade & step up in trip: see 4046 (7f, nov stks), 3532.

4108*　**SUDDEN DISMISSAL** 14 [8]2-8-11　(87) S Sanders　12/1: 417: Al bhd: up in class after 4108 (mdn auct).　2　　96
3509　**SAFARI SUNSET** 39 [6]2-8-11　(99) P Doe　16/1: 13438: With ldrs, wknd over 2f out: btr 3509, 2472.　1¾　　91
8 Ran　Time 1m 10.87 (u0.24)　Owned: Sheikh Hamdan Bin Mohammed Al Maktoum　Trained: Newmarket

---

4391　　3.15 Gr3 Pentax Uk September Stakes 3yo+ (A)
£29750　£11000　£5500　　**1m4f**　　**Firm 05**　　-04 Slow　　Inside

4016　**MAMOOL** 21 [5] Saeed bin Suroor 5-9-3 t　(118) L Dettori　3/1: 53110-31: Trkd ldr, hdwy to lead over　　　　117
2f out, rdn out: eff over 12f/2m on firm & hvy, any trk: right back to v smart best after long injury
lay-off, game & more Group races to be won: see 4016.

3563*　**ALKAASED** 36 [1] L M Cumani 4-9-3　(113) J Fortune　6/4 FAV: 122-2112: Held up, hdwy to chall appr　½　　115
fnl 1f, kept on, al just held for press: proving tough, game & progressive: can find a Gr 3: see 3563.

3442　**BANDARI** 42 [4] M Johnston 5-9-8　(119) R Hills　15/8: 1110103: Set pace till over 2f out, onepace:　　1¼　　118
nicely bckd: 6 wk abs: rival to best conceding weight to smart rivals: see 3030 (Gr 2).

4023　**JAGGER** 17 [2] G A Butler 4-9-3　(101) E Ahern　11/1: D11-0304: Held up, eff over 2f out, sn no　　4　　107
impress: back to form on a sound surace but needs a drop into h'cap/List: see 3510, 2771.
4 Ran　Time 2m 31.13 (1.13)　Owned: Godolphin　Trained: Newmarket

---

4392　　3.50 Pentax 'digital Camera' Handicap Stakes 3yo+ 71-85 (D)　　　　[91]
£10236　£3883　£1941　　**1m2f**　　**Firm 05**　　-05 Slow　　Inside

3629　**TIDAL** 34 [1] A W Carroll 5-9-6　(83) L Dettori　14/1: 1103401: Handy, led 3f out, kept on for　　　　90
press ins last, just held on: eff over 10/12f & likes firm & gd grnd, handles soft: enjoys Chepstow: thrived this
term & enjoyed another fine positive L Dettori ride: see 2371.

4068*　**TOP SPEC** 15 [2] R Hannon 3-8-6 (1oh)　(76) R L Moore　20/1: 0502012: Held up, gd hdwy over 1f out,　nk　　82
kept on well ins last, just held: fine run up in class & shld win a h'cap shortly: see 4068 (clmr), 3453.

4268　**ARRY DASH** 6 [9] M R Channon 4-8-10　(73) S Hitchcott(3) 8/1: 6062323: Dwelt, bhd, eff well over 1f　1¼　　76
out, onepace: qck reapp: another gd plcd run: see 4268.

3066　**STREET LIFE** 58 [14] W J Musson 6-8-9　(72) G Carter　10/1: 3343544: Dwelt, held up, hdwy & short　½　　75
of room over 2f out, kept on well ins last, nrst fin: 2 month abs & an encouraging run: on a winning mark & likes
Windsor: acts on firm & gd, enjoys soft & hvy: see 391.

3230　**OUNINPOHJA** 50 [8]3-8-3 (1ow)(5oh)　(72) Dean McKeown　7/2 FAV: 4325: Held up, hdwy & badly over 2f　½　　75+
out, styd on well over 1f out, nrst fin: hvly bckd: 7 wk abs: would have gone close with clr run: acts on firm &
gd: one to keep in mind, lightly rcd: see 3230.

2101　**PAGAN SKY** 96 [15]5-9-7　(84) T P Queally　20/1: 6161-006: ch g Inchinor - Rosy Sunset (Red Sunset)　nk　　85
Chsd ldrs, no extra appr fnl 1f: 3 month abs: won 2 of 7 '03 starts (h'caps): suited by 10f & acts on fast &
gd/soft, any trk: has run well fresh.　1 Oct'03 Newb 10.0gd 86-80 B:　1 Sep'03 Pont 10.0g/f 83-78 C:
2 May'03 Good 8g/f 79-76 D:　2 Jul'02 Sand 8g/f 81- D:　1 Jun'02 Good 7g/f 75- D:　2 Jun'02 Good 8g/s 77- D:

3785*　**PIRI PIRI** 28 [11]4-8-7 (1oh)　(69) C Catlin　25/1: 6230327: Dwelt, bhd, some late gains, no dngr: see 3785.　½　　70

3749 **LIQUID FORM** 29 [4]4-8-12 (75) A McCarthy 33/1: 13-00068: Dwelt, bhd, hdwy over 1f out, sn no impress. 1½ 72
3514 **FORTUNES PRINCESS** 38 [17]3-8-7 (77) K Fallon 9/1: 22129: Chsd ldrs, onepcd over 1f out: btr 3514. shd 73
4182 **FUEL CELL** 9 [12]3-8-0 (7oh)bl (70) R Smith 25/1: 3301350: 10th: Handy, wknd well over 1f out: see 3862. ¾ 65
3391 **VAMP** 43 [10]3-8-7 (77) S Sanders 25/1: 023150: 11th: In tch, short of room over 2f out, no impress: abs. ½ 71
3964 **VOICE MAIL** 20 [6]5-9-0 (77) L Keniry(3) 25/1: 2034030: 12th: Nvr a factor: see 3964, 3083. 1½ 68
3070 **PENZANCE** 57 [20]3-8-10 (80) O Urbina 12/1: 13-64100: 13th: In tch, short of room over 2f out, sn shd 70
wknd: gelded after 2 month abs: twice below 2631.
3964 **SANGIOVESE** 20 [18]5-8-13 (76) L Fletcher(3) 8/1: 2311050: 14th: In tch, wknd over 2f out: see 2681. 1 64
4122 **LEOBALLERO** 12 [16]4-9-2 t (79) E Ahern 12/1: 31-53540: 15th: In tch, wknd well over 1f out: see 4122. shd 66
3999 **BEST BE GOING** 18 [7]4-8-12 (75) Dane O'Neill 12/1: 1-005400: 16th: In tch, wknd 2f out: see 3345. 5 55
4122 **LASANGA** 12 [13]5-9-0 (77) P Doe 66/1: 4/32-00: 17th: With ldr, wknd over 2f out: see 4122. 8 45
3892 **ELECTRIQUE** 23 [19]4-8-12 (75) I Mongan 33/1: 33221-00: 18th: Led after 3f till 3f out, wknd: see 3892. nk 42
2680 **SUNISA** 73 [3]3-8-12 (82) R Hills 33/1: 4-213020: 19th: Chsd ldrs, wknd over 3f out, sn eased & fin lame. dist 0
19 Ran   Time 2m 03.29 (0.99)   Owned: Mrs B Quinn   Trained: Alcester

---

4393   **4.25 Pentax 'light & Image' Conditions Stakes Colts & Geldings 2yo (C)**
          £7291 £2765 £1383   **7f rnd   Firm 05   -32 Slow   Inside**

3951 **STORM SILK** 21 [4] Saeed bin Suroor 2-8-10 L Dettori 2/1 JT FAV: 41: Made all, drew clr over 1f 104
out on bit, v easily, val 7L +, hvly bckd: much imprvd from debut & stays 7f well, 1m sure to suit: acts on firm &
fast grnd: enjoyed forcing tactics & looks potentially v smart, well up to winning in Group class: see 3951.
      PERUVIAN PRINCE 0 [6] J A R Toller 2-8-10 E Ahern 12/1: 2: b c Silver Hawk - Inca Dove (Mr 3½ 89
Prospector) With wnr, not his pace over 1f out: Apr foal, cost $45,000: eff at 7f on firm grnd: v pleasing start
bhd a smart sort, will win similar soon.
      RAIN STOPS PLAY 0 [8] M R Channon 2-8-10 S Hitchcott 20/1: 3: b c Desert Prince - Pinta 3 83
(Ahonoora) In tch, eff over 1f out, onepace: Mar foal, cost E110,000: half-brother to wnrs over 6f/1m: dam useful
5f juv scorer: learn plenty from this encouraging start.
      KERASHAN 0 [5] Sir Michael Stoute 2-8-10 K Fallon 6/1: 4: b c Sinndar - Kerataka (Doyoun) With nk 82
ldrs, lost pl over 2f out, onepce: May first foal: dam 1m wnr: bred to relish 1m in time & will learn from this.
4190 **GITCHE MANITO** 8 [1]2-8-10 J D Smith 33/1: 305: Chsd ldrs, wknd over 1f out: see 3883. 1 80
      MOLEM 0 [3]2-8-10 R Hills 12/1: 6: Held up, nvr a factor. 1¼ 77
      PILLARS OF WISDOM 0 [9]2-8-10 J Fortune 8/1: 7: Dwelt, held up, nvr a factor: bckd. 2 73
      PARTY BOSS 0 [2]2-8-10 S Sanders 25/1: 8: Slow away & al bhd. 9 55
8 Ran   Time 1m 26.7 (2.6)   Owned: Godolphin   Trained: Newmarket

---

4394   **4.55 Pentax 'perfect' Handicap Stakes 3yo+ 71-85 (D)**   [92]
          £7111 £2188 £1094   **6f str   Firm 05   +06 Fast   Stands Side**

2451 **THURLESTONE ROCK** 82 [2] B J Meehan 4-8-11 (75) C Catlin 25/1: 001-0501: With ldrs stands side, 80
hdwy to lead just ins last, rdn out: 11 wk abs: suited by 6f on firm & fast grnd, both AWs: likes sharp trks, esp
Kempton: runs well fresh: right back to best: see 2707.
4229 **NAJEEBON** 7 [3] M R Channon 5-8-12 (76) S Hitchcott(3) 8/1: 3630002: Sn bhd stands side, hdwy over nk 80+
1f out, styd on well ins last, just held: back to form after recent gelding op & poised to strike off a v handy mark.
4956} **AVERSHAM** 154 [7] R Charlton 4-9-7 (85) J Fortune 20/1: 230-0003: b c Averti - Vavona (Ballad hd 88+
Rock) Sn bhd stands side, hdwy over 1f out, styd on strongly ins last, just held: unplcd in Dubai last spring:
plcd for R Hannon in '03: auct mdn & nov stks wnr in '02: eff at 6/7f on firm & soft grnd, prob any trk: right
back to best for new stable who do expertly with sprinters, will be winning off this mark shortly.
2 Oct'03 Leic 7.0fm 93-(92) C: 2 Oct'02 Yarm 6sft 97- C: 1 Sep'02 Leic 7fm 80- D: 1 Jul'02 Bath 5.7g/f 82- F:
4031 **LITTLE EDWARD** 17 [1] B G Powell 6-9-4 (82) L Keniry(3) 16/1: 5000564: In tch stands side, eff ¾ 81
over 1f out, onepace: see 1845.
4126* **NIVERNAIS** 12 [12]5-8-11 (75) Dane O'Neill 10/1: 0606315: In tch stands side, eff to chall over hd 75
1f out, onepace: ran to form of 4126.
4031 **MR MALARKEY** 17 [11]4-9-4 bl (82) Hayley Turner(3) 20/1: 3306106: Made most stands side, rdn & hdd shd 80
ins last, no extra: gd run: see 3705.
3827 **MINE BEHIND** 26 [17]4-9-4 (82) L Dettori 8/1: 0001007: Chsd far side ldrs, led that group over 1f ½ 79
out, kept on, no ch with stands side group: nicely bckd: won race on wrong side & one to keep in mind: see 3146.
4005 **GOLDEN DIXIE** 18 [5]5-9-3 (81) K Fallon 8/1: 00-02558: In tch stands side, no extra over 1f out: see 3136. ½ 75
4229 **WYATT EARP** 7 [4]3-8-9 (75) E Ahern 16/1: 46-01009: Chsd ldrs, btn over 1f out: best 1734. ½ 67
3628 **DANEHILL STROLLER** 34 [20]4-9-4 p (82) S Sanders 6/1 FAV: 3-000400: 10th: In tch far side, some 1 71
late gains, no ch with stands side group.
3954 **ARMAGNAC** 21 [18]6-9-2 (80) G Carter 7/1: 0232300: 11th: Nvr a factor far side: see 3782, 3375. nk 68
4180 **HARD TO CATCH** 9 [6]6-8-13 bl (77) M Savage(5) 20/1: 3306300: 12th: Bhd stands side, btn over 1f out. nk 64
4186 **SAVILES DELIGHT** 8 [14]5-8-13 (77) D Nolan(3) 12/1: 2011430: 13th: Handy far side, wknd over 1f out. hd 63
1847 **TREASURE HOUSE** 108 [19]3-9-5 (85) G Baker 33/1: 10-00500: 14th: Al bhd far side: now with J Jay. ½ 69
4180 **MISS GEORGE** 9 [16]6-9-1 (77) M Howard(7) 14/1: 0030300: 15th: Al bhd: see 4031, 3479. 1 60
4005 **SEMENOVSKII** 18 [15]4-8-9 vis (73) R L Moore 16/1: 0-360100: 16th: Led far side till wknd over 1f out. nk 53
4201 **WILLHEWIZ** 8 [10]4-8-12 (76) J F McDonald(3) 20/1: 1000040: 17th: Handy stands side, wknd 2f out. ½ 54
3808 **CELTIC THUNDER** 27 [13]3-9-3 (83) R Hills 25/1: 5020440: 18th: In tch stands side, wknd 2f out. 1¼ 56
3210 **MIDNIGHT BALLARD** 51 [9]3-8-13 BL (79) M Carson 33/1: 6420100: 19th: With ldrs, wknd over 2f out: 8 28
7 wk abs, blnks: twice below 2716 (7f, auct mdn).
19 Ran   Time 1m 11.01 (u0.09)   Owned: Mr N Attenborough & Mrs L Mann   Trained: Upper Lambourn

---

4395   **5.25 Pentax 'optical Excellence' Handicap Stakes 3yo 71-85 (D)**   [89]
          £6861 £2111 £1056   **1m6f92y   Firm 05   -24 Slow   Inside**

3816* **LEG SPINNER** 27 [6] M R Channon 3-9-4 (79) L Dettori 13/2: 331011: Cl-up, led 2f out, kept on ins 87
last, rdn out: eff at 12f, enjoyed step up to 14.5f & acts on firm & fast grnd, prob any trk: game & progressive.
4111* **RED DAMSON** 14 [7] Sir Mark Prescott 3-9-10 (85) S Sanders 8/1: 0222-212: Led till 2f out, kept hd 92
on for press, just held: progressive & game: stays 14.5f on firm, gd/soft & polytrack: shld win again: see 4111.
4080 **VELVET WATERS** 15 [3] R F Johnson Houghton 3-8-10 (1oh) (70) S Carson 12/1: 4122133: Handy, eff 2 75
over 1f out, onepace: continues in gd heart: see 3845.

KEMPTON SATURDAY 04.09.04 Righthand, Flat, Fair Track

3893 **CONSIDINE** 23 [13] J M P Eustace 3-8-11 (72) J Fortune 12/1: 1210264: In tch, onepace fnl 2f: see 3359. 1¼ 74
3845 **DONASTRELA** 25 [2]3-8-10 (6oh)vis (65) N Chalmers(5) 33/1: 0141335: In tch, eff over 1f out, onepace. 1 70
4080 **TURNSTILE** 15 [5]3-9-0 (75) R L Moore 20/1: 4203206: In tch, lost pl over 3f out, some late gains. shd 75
4080+ **TOPKAT** 15 [8]3-9-2 (77) Dane O'Neill 5/1: 02517: Bhd, no impress over 2f out: best 4080 (12f, gd/soft). 1¾ 74
4058 **SILVER SASH** 16 [4]3-9-5 (80) K Fallon 6/1: 63158: Hld up, wknd over 2f out: btr 3019 (auct mdn). 1½ 75
3742 **GARNETT** 29 [1]3-9-0 (75) J D Smith 33/1: 4339: Nvr a factor: see 3742, 3405. hd 69
3556 **MAN AT ARMS** 37 [10]3-9-1 (76) S Hitchcott(3) 20/1: 1400460: 10th: Al bhd: see 2538. ½ 69
3688 **MASKED** 31 [11]3-9-4 (79) E Ahern 3/1 FAV: 0415220: 11th: In tch, wknd over 2f out: bckd: btr 3688. hd 72
4062 **SOUND OF FLEET** 16 [9]3-9-9 (84) T P Queally 12/1: 6150200: 12th: Al bhd. 2½ 73
3868 **KEEP ON MOVIN** 24 [12]3-8-10 (71) G Carter 25/1: 1-502040: 13th: In tch, wknd over 2f out: reportedly not enjoy grnd: see 2923 (12f), 1017 & 116. 11 44
13 Ran Time 3m 07.09(4.29) Owned: Mr P D Savill Trained: West Ilsley

YORK SUNDAY 05.09.04 Lefthand, Flat, Galloping Track

Official Going Good/Firm (Firm Places)

4396 2.05 Sarah Coggles Nursery Handicap Stakes 2yo 0-85 (D) [86]
£5870 £1806 £903 6f217y rnd Good/Firm 21 -26 Slow Inside

4115 **DIAMONDS AND DUST** 14 [17] M H Tompkins 2-9-5 (77) P Robinson 7/1: 4341: Handy wide, styd on to lead 2f out, rdn out: eff at 6f, now suited by 7f: acts on fast & gd grnd: improving with every start, see 4115. 84
4337 **ALGORITHM** 3 [16] T D Easterby 2-8-0 (58) R Ffrench 16/1: 06562: In tch wide, kept on ins fnl 1f, not pace of wnr: qck reapp: eff at 7f on firm & fast grnd: see 4337. 1½ 62
4205 **GAME LAD** 9 [3] T D Easterby 2-9-1 (73) D Allan 6/1: 3403: Dwelt, prog when short of room 2f out, short of room again 1f out, styd on ins fnl 1f, nrst fin: eff at 6/7f on fast, gd/soft grnd & fibresand: prob 2nd but for interference & can find similar: see 3699. nk 76
2959 **AIRE DE MOUGINS** 63 [11] P C Haslam 2-9-3 (75) G Faulkner 12/1: 0444: Chsd ldrs, edged left & onepcd ins fnl 1f: 9 wk abs: eff at 7f on fast grnd: gelded for h'cap bow: see 2959. shd 77
4224 **SOCIETY MUSIC** 8 [4]2-9-2 (74) S W Kelly 12/1: 1313605: Prom, edged right & no extra dist. nk 75
3407 **BALLYCROY GIRL** 44 [1]2-9-0 (72) E Ahern 14/1: 625106: Bhd, prog halfway, no impress fnl 1f. 3 67
4258 **MONSIEUR MIRASOL** 7 [5]2-9-7 (75) N Callan 10/1: 3510247: Handy over 5f, no extra: likes soft. ½ 73
4108 **ENFORCER** 15 [6]2-9-6 (78) S Drowne 5/1 FAV: 4528: Nvr nrr than mid-div: bckd, btr 4108 (6f). nk 71
4153 **TIVISKI** 15 [2]2-9-1 (73) M Fenton 33/1: 1045009: Nvr nrr than mid-div: btr 1573. 1¼ 64
4277* **APETITE** 6 [12]2-8-6 (5ex) (64) J Quinn 14/1: 000210: 10th: Sn short of room, al in rear. ½ 54
3478 **DARKO KARIM** 41 [13]2-9-6 VIS (78) T P Queally 14/1: 4000: 11th: Sn short of room, al bhd. 1¼ 66
4127* **ROKO** 13 [14]2-8-1 VIS (59) P Hanagan 20/1: 0043310: 12th: Handy over 5f, wknd: first time visor & new stable: btr 4127 (6f, fibresand, M W Easterby, claimer). ¾ 45
3939 **GENERAL MAX** 22 [7]2-8-6 (64) R Winston 33/1: 3000: 13th: Bhd, nvr a factor. 1¼ 48
4004 **SELKIRK STORM** 19 [9]2-9-5 (77) P Robinson 33/1: 125000: 14th: Led after 2f, hdd 2f out, wknd. 2½ 56
4344 **MAUREENS LOUGH** 3 [10]2-7-12 (3oh) (53) N Mackay(3) 50/1: 4410500: 15th: Led, hdd 6f out, wknd fnl 2f. 2 31
4074 **Dartanian** 16 [8]2-8-2 (60) F P Ferris(3) 20/1:0 3735 **English Fellow** 31 [15]2-8-12 (70) G Gibbons 33/1:0
17 Ran Time 1m 24.65 (3.35) Owned: Mrs S Ashby Trained: Newmarket

4397 2.35 Drs For Sony 'premier' Claiming Stakes 3yo+ (D)
£6370 £1960 £980 1m208y Good/Firm 21 -10 Slow Inside

3775 **CALCUTTA** 29 [10] B W Hills 8-9-5 (95) M Hills 11/4: 0020301: Mid-div, prog to lead trav well bef 1f out, rdn out, val bit more: well bckd: no claim: eff at 7f, best around 1m/9f: likes firm & fast, handles gd/soft: best without binks & likes a gait lift: apprec drop to claim grade: distil useful: see 3460. 93
4103 **TRUE NIGHT** 15 [8] D Nicholls 7-8-9 (83) E Ahern 5/1: 3113002: Led, hdd under press bef 1f out, kept on, no pace of wnr: op 7/2: stays 9f, return to 7f/1m will suit: see 3634 & 3428 (h'caps). 1½ 79
4122 **HARRY POTTER** 13 [4] K R Burke 5-8-12 vis (79) D Sweeney 12/1: 0311503: In tch, prog when short of room dist, switched & kept on fnl 1f, no ch with front 2: eff at 7f/9f: see 3423 & 3328. 1¼ 80
4136 **CHERISHED NUMBER** 13 [13] I Semple 5-8-9 p (70) R Winston 10/1: 4405304: Held up, prog 3 out, onepcd ins fnl 1f: see 4008. ¾ 75
4124 **SCOTTYS FUTURE** 13 [6]6-8-12 (72) T P Queally 22/1: 0101065: Keen in tch over 6f, sn outpcd, rallying when short of room ins fnl 1f: see 4124. 1½ 75
3762 **ON EVERY STREET** 29 [2]3-8-13 BL (77) R Ffrench 50/1: 5-43146: Prom, ev ch bef 1f out, sn wknd. nk 79
4021 **IONIAN SPRING** 18 [12]9-9-2 (91) P Robinson 9/4 FAV: 1010057: Held up, prog 3f out, wknd fnl 2f: well bckd: v disappointing on drop in grade: btr 2185 (h'cap). 2½ 74
4061 **DARK CHARM** 17 [11]5-9-10 (90) P Hanagan 7/1: 0400-308: Held up, nvr a factor: twice below 951. 6 73
8 Ran Time 1m 51.60 (2.8) Owned: The Hon Mrs J M Corbett & Mr C Wright Trained: Lambourn

4398 3.10 Smith Brothers Handicap Stakes 3yo+ 56-70 (E) [84]
£6198 £1907 £954 6f217y rnd Good/Firm 21 -02 Slow Inside

4225 **HAZEWIND** 8 [18] P D Evans 3-8-9 vis t (65) F P Ferris(3) 10/1: 2511641: In tch wide, styd on to lead fnl 1f, rdn out: eff at 1m/10f, now seems suited by 7f: acts on fast, gd grnd & polytrack: improving. 74
4144 **ROMAN MAZE** 12 [5] W M Brisbourne 4-8-9 (61) S W Kelly 10/1: 0004242: In tch when short of room bef 1f out, kept on ins fnl 1f, not pace of wnr: apprec return to faster surface & can go one btr: see 3634. 1 67
4241 **LOCOMBE HILL** 8 [7] N Wilson 8-8-12 (64) D Tudhope(7) 20/1: 0440153: Keen cl-up, led 2f out, hdd ins fnl 1f, no extra: running well: see 4088. shd 69
4030 **KAREEB** 18 [9] W J Musson 7-9-3 (69) G Carter 6/1: 0406064: Chsd ldrs, onepcd from dist: btr 3117. 1¾ 70
3809 **NO GROUSE** 28 [14]4-8-12 p (64) P Hanagan 16/1: 0000505: Mid-div, prog bef 1f out, nrst fin: see 3634. ½ 64
4093 **DOWNLAND** 16 [12]8-9-0 (66) Kim Tinkler 25/1: 5113026: Handy 6f, no extra: btr 4093 (fibresand). nk 65
4140 **BANJO BAY** 12 [4]6-8-13 (65) Alex Greaves 20/1: 0060007: In tch over 5f, no extra: see 2074. 1¼ 62
4278 **SESSAY** 6 [16]3-8-12 (68) A Nicholls 28/1: 0-435068: In tch, led halfway, hdd 2f out, no extra. ½ 64

1325

4131* **OH GOLLY GOSH 13** [11]3-8-10 vis (66) T E Durcan 28/1: 4205319: Missed break, nvr nrr than mid-div. 3½ **55**
3809+**YORKSHIRE BLUE 28** [1]5-8-9 (61) N Mackay(3) 7/2 FAV: 0110510: 10th: Rear, prog halfway, wknd dist: well bckd: showed more in 3809. ¾ **48**
4245 **BOLLIN EDWARD 8** [15]5-8-12 vis (64) D Allan 9/1: 3202020: 11th: Stumbled start, al in rear: btr 4245. ½ **50**
3809 **NEW WISH 28** [17]4-8-9 (61) T Lucas 16/1: 0000-500: 12th: Bhd, nvr a factor: jumps fit. ¾ **45**
3516 **PHLUKE 39** [10]3-8-12 (68) S Carson 33/1: 1204060: 13th: Handy over 5f, wknd. 2 **48**
3791 **BOBS BUZZ 29** [3]4-9-2 (68) R Mullen 15/2: 0-053520: 14th: Keen bhd, nvr a factor: btr 3791. ¾ **46**
4341 **PERFECT LOVE 3** [13]4-9-4 (70) E Ahern 50/1: 000-0000: 15th: Led till halfway, grad wknd: qck reapp. 1¼ **46**
3806 **Zap Attack 28** [19]4-8-10 (62) M Lawson(5) 33/1:0 3138 **Desert Leader 56** [8]3-8-11 (67) G Gibbons 16/1:0
17 Ran Time 1m 22.94 (1.64) Owned: Waterline Racing Club Trained: Abergavenny

4399

3.45 Monks Cross Shopping Park Handicap Stakes 3yo+ 56-70 (E) **[79]**
£6829 £2101 £1051 **7f205y rnd** **Good/Firm 21** **+15 Fast** Inside

4215 **MOUNT HILLABY 9** [6] M W Easterby 4-8-9 (60) P Mulrennan(3) 9/1: 0-100201: In tch, styd on to lead dist, drvn out to hold on: fast time; eff at 7f/1m, has tried 10f: acts on fast, gd/soft & fibresand: see 4036. **66**
4259 **TEDSDALE MAC 7** [15] N Bycroft 5-8-8 (59) F Norton 8/1 JT FAV: 5232252: Rear, prog 3f out, styd on to chase wnr ins fnl 1f, al held: qck reapp: continues to run well: see 3598. 1 **60**
4144 **NEMO FUGAT 12** [16] D Nicholls 5-8-9 vis (60) A Nicholls 25/1: 0252003: Al cl-up, ev ch ins fnl 1f, no extra: eff at 5/7f, now stays 1m: see 3654. ½ **62**
4173 **SARRAAF 10** [10] J S Goldie 8-8-13 (64) T E Durcan 20/1: 5052034: Chsd ldrs, kept on fnl 1f, nrst fin. ½ **65**
2529 **QUEEN CHARLOTTE 79** [7]5-8-13 (64) J Fanning 12/1: 10-20005: Cl-up, led 4f out, hdd bef 1f out, wknd. ¾ **63**
4008 **REGENTS SECRET 19** [1]4-8-8 (59) N Mackay(3) 12/1: 2403306: Bhd, prog when short of room just ins fnl 2f, nrst fin: longstanding mdn: see 3759. 1 **56**
4321 **HEVERSHAM 4** [4]3-8-11 (67) M Tebbutt 33/1: 4250007: Mid-div, prog under press when short of room just ins fnl 1f, sn no impress: qck reapp: btr 2854. ½ **63**
3505 **SANTIBURI LAD 40** [12]7-9-3 (68) T Hamilton(3) 16/1: 3211208: Led 4f, ev ch bef 1f out, wknd. ½ **63**
4173 **BAILIEBOROUGH 10** [11]5-9-3 vis (68) Alex Greaves 14/1: 6511329: Nvr nrr than mid-div: btr 4173. hd **62**
3986 **ADOBE 20** [5]9-8-13 (64) M Savage(4) 8/1 JT FAV: 2004050: 10th: Nvr nrr than mid-div: likes Bath. 1 **56**
3583 **GARDEN SOCIETY 37** [18]7-9-1 (66) G Carter 33/1: 0/U06/-000: 11th: Rear, nvr able to chall: see 2591. ½ **57**
3806 **OSCAR PEPPER 28** [13]7-9-2 vis (67) R Winston 9/1: 5241430: 12th: Bhd, modest late gains: btr 3806. 2 **54**
4215 **TAGULA BLUE 9** [8]4-9-2 t (67) Dean McKeown 12/1: 0R36540: 13th: Missed break, no dngr. 1¾ **50**
4246 **DARA MAC 8** [20]5-8-10 (61) Suzanne France(7) 40/1: 1001060: 14th: Al in rear: btr 3830. 1 **42**
4077 **DIDNT TELL MY WIFE 16** [17]5-9-2 (67) R Mullen 10/1: 6043130: 15th: Al in rear: btr 4077 & 3922. 1¼ **46**
3806 **GALA SUNDAY 28** [2]4-9-0 (65) Dale Gibson 20/1: 0006060: 16th: Mid-div over 5f, wknd: btr 3806. ¾ **42**
4036 **SKIBEREEN 18** [19]4-9-0 (65) R Ffrench 50/1: 5035000: 17th: Handy 4f, sn wknd: btr 1972. 3 **36**
4300 **FEN GYPSY 6** [14]6-9-5 (70) F P Ferris(3) 10/1: 2414430: 18th: Mid-div over 6f, wkng when eased ins fnl 1f, saddle slipped & fin lame: qck reapp: btr 4300. 2 **37**
4175 **FLASH RAM 10** [9]3-8-8 (64) D Allan 14/1: 2261630: 19th: Handy 5f, sn wknd & eased, returned lame. 6 **20**
19 Ran Time 1m 36.28 (0.48) Owned: The Woodford Group Limited Trained: Sheriff Hutton

4400

4.20 Layerthorpe Volkswagen Beetle Handicap Stakes 3yo+ 71-85 (D) **[90]**
£13183 £5001 £2500 **1m5f197y** **Good/Firm 21** **+02 Fast** Inside

3964 **BARMAN 21** [14] P F I Cole 5-9-4 t (80) J Fanning 25/1: 2251-001: In tch, styd on to lead 1f out, rdn out: eff at 12f, imprvd for step up to 14f: acts on firm, gd/soft & polytrack: eff with/without t-strap: left recent form bhd on step up in trip & is unexposed over staying dists: see 2233. **87**
3531 **VALANCE 39** [10] C R Egerton 4-9-3 (79) S Drowne 7/1: 3-351402: Trkd ldrs, styd on to lead 2f out, hdd 1f out, kept on, not pace of wnr: tchd 9/1: can find similar: see 3032. 1¾ **80**
3810 **SKYES FOLLY 28** [3] J G Given 4-8-10 bl (72) M Fenton 14/1: 5-000333: Mid-div, prog 4f out, onepcd. 1½ **74**
3734 **MAXILLA 31** [7] L M Cumani 4-8-12 (74) N Mackay(3) 6/1: 1-405624: Mid-div, prog 4f out, onepcd. shd **75**
4196 **TILLA 9** [2]4-8-9 (2oh) (69) J Quinn 10/1: 5602265: Held up, prog 4f out, kept on ins fnl 1f: btr 3887. 1½ **71**
3760 **WEET FOR ME 30** [6]8-8-10 (72) N Callan 33/1: 3//-002656: Led 6f, led again 3f out, hdd 2f out, wknd. ½ **71**
3510 **FOURTH DIMENSION 40** [8]5-9-5 (81) A Nicholls 10/1: 000-0407: Nvr nrr than mid-div: 8 wk abs. nk **79**
3969* **JEEPSTAR 21** [15]4-9-1 (77) G Gibbons 6/1: 0062218: Cl-up, led after 6f, hdd 3f out, wknd: btr 3969. 2½ **73**
3611* **BEST PORT 36** [17]8-8-9 (7oh) (64) M Lawson(5) 14/1: 0101619: Al in rear: btr 3611. 3 **64**
3999* **SUALDA 19** [4]5-9-2 (78) P Hanagan 3/1 FAV: 1231410: 10th: Keen mid-div, btn when eased ins fnl 2f: op 4/1: v disappointing back at 14f: btr 3999 (12f). 8 **64**
3760* **MAGIC COMBINATION 30** [13]11-9-9 (85) P Mulrennan(3) 9/1: 2522110: 11th: Al in rear: btr 3760 (gd). 2½ **69**
3964 **LATALOMNE 21** [1]10-9-0 (76) T Hamilton(3) 25/1: 00///0-1400: 12th: Rear, prog halfway, wknd bef 2f out, sn eased: poor effort on first try at 14f: btr 2526 13 **48**
12 Ran Time 2m 56.11 (2.71) Owned: Sir George Meyrick Trained: Whatcombe

4401

4.50 One Call Insurance Maiden Auction Stakes 2yo (E)
£10205 £3140 £1570 **6f str** **Good/Firm 21** **-09 Slow** Inside

4079 **RIDDER 16** [12] D J Coakley 2-8-13 (81) E Ahern 5/2 FAV: 450221: Mid-div, prog bef 1f out, rdn out to lead cl-home: well bckd: eff around 6f on fast & gd/soft, 7f shld suit: see 4079. **85**
SAMS SECRET 0 [14] J A Glover 2-8-5 F Norton 20/1: 2: b f Josr Algarhoud - Twilight Time (Aragon) Keen mid-div, prog to lead ins fnl 1f, hdd cl-home: debut: Apr foal, cost 13,000gns: half-sister to a couple of useful sprint wnrs: dam unrcd: sire useful performer around 1m: eff at 6f, further looks sure to suit: acts on fast grnd: sure to impr for today's experience & go one better. shd **75**
3445 **JOHN ROBIE 43** [5] G A Butler 2-8-13 S W Kelly 11/2: 63: Prom, led dist, hdd ins fnl 1f, no extra: op 4/1: 6 wk abs: imprvd eff on step up to 6f: acts on fast grnd: lost little in defeat: see 3445. ½ **82**
3988 **INGLETON 20** [11] B A McMahon 2-8-10 G Gibbons 20/1: 04: Cl-up, edged left & onepcd dist: eff at 6f on fast grnd: improved run: see 3988. 1¾ **74**
OCEANCOOKIE 0 [6]2-8-2 R Mullen 33/1: 5: b f Dashing Blade - Sankaty Light (Summer Squall) Bhd, prog 3f out, kept on ins fnl 1f: debut: Feb foal, cost 3,600gns: dam plcd at 7f: sire decent performer as a juv: eff at 6f, further looks sure to suit: acts on fast grnd: imprvd for today's experience. hd **65**
3939 **BOO 22** [3]2-8-13 J Fanning 10/1: 46: Cl-up, ev ch dist, sn no extra: see 3939. 1¼ **72**

YORK   SUNDAY 05.09.04   Lefthand, Flat, Galloping Track

COSMIC DESTINY 0 [9]2-8-5 S Drowne 4/1: 7: b f Soviet Star - Cruelle (Irish River) Led, hdd   *hd*   63
dist, no extra: well bckd on debut: Apr foal, cost 11,000gns: dam fine performer around 6f/1m.
RAPID RIVER 0 [10]2-8-2 R Ffrench 50/1: 8: In tch over 4f, no extra: debut.   ½   59
HAENERTSBURG 0 [17]2-8-2 J Bramhill 33/1: 9: Nvr nrr than mid-div on debut.   ½   58
4026 BURNLEY AL 18 [19]2-8-7 P Hanagan 6/1: 50: 10th: Bhd, nvr a factor.   4   51
NAVIGATION 0 [8]2-8-7 T E Durcan 50/1: 0: 11th: Missed break, nvr nrr than mid-div.   nk   50
4192 BOWLED OUT 9 [7]2-8-2 J Quinn 14/1: 40: 12th: Chsd ldrs over 4f, wknd: btr 4192.   ½   44
GUADALOUP 0 [16]2-8-5 K Darley 33/1: 0: 13th: Al in rear.   nk   46
BIRTHDAY STAR 0 [18]2-8-10 Lisa Jones 66/1: 0: 14th: Missed break, nvr a factor on debut.   ¾   49
Ginger Cookie 0 [15]2-8-2 D Allan 33/1:0   3939 Bold Haze 22 [2]2-8-10 P Robinson 16/1:0
4108 Season Ticket 15 [13]2-8-2 N Mackay(3) 50/1:0   Woodford Wonder 0 [1]2-8-3 (1ow) P Mulrennan 66/1:0
4257 Time To Succeed 7 [4]2-8-10 G Parkin 100/1:0   4108 Sergeant Small 15 [20]2-8-10 G Carter 100/1:0
20 Ran   Time 1m 11.20 (1.80)   Owned: Mr Chris van Hoorn   Trained: West Ilsley

4402

5.20 Evening Press Compact Apprentice Handicap Stakes 3yo+ 56-70 (E)   [75]
£4872 £1499 £750   1m2f88y   Good/Firm 21   -09 Slow   Inside

4248 JAKE BLACK 8 [11] J J Quinn 4-8-11 (58) D Tudhope(3) 8/1: 3150441: In tch, styd on to lead 2f   65
out, sn clr, eased cl-home, val 4L+: eff at 1m/10.4f on fast, soft grnd & fibresand: see 1541 & 1430.
4259 COLWAY RITZ 7 [12] W Storey 10-9-0 (61) Rory Moore(3) 10/1: 00422-02: Missed break, prog wide 3f   2   65
out, kept on to chase wnr ins fnl 1f, al held: qck reapp: won this race 2yrs ago off a mark of 45: see 4259.
4215 MOBANE FLYER 9 [14] R A Fahey 4-8-13 (60) P Makin 100/30 FAV: 50-00633: Held up, prog 5f out, no   1   62
impress dist: acts on firm & hvy grnd: just btr 4215 (hvy).
4124 ETON 13 [9] D Nicholls 8-9-7 (68) P J Benson(7) 8/1: 1235204: Led after 1f, hdd 2f out, no extra.   2½   66
3948 GOLD GUEST 22 [16]5-9-1 (62) S Donohoe(3) 7/1: 41-10045: Nvr nrr than mid-div: btr 3948.   1   58
2691 WESTCOURT DREAM 73 [1]4-8-7 (2oh) P Mathers(3) 7/1: 333-3106: Keen in tch, no extra bef 1f out.   ½   49
3785 IFTIKHAR 29 [4]5-8-7 (2oh) (52) B Swarbrick 8/1: 24-00047: Missed break, sn in tch, wknd fnl 2f.   1   47
4243 BENEKING 8 [13]4-8-7 (3oh) (51) Stephanie Hollinshead(3) 33/1: 3060508: Nvr nrr than mid-div.   1   45
3260 CHAMPAIN SANDS 50 [8]5-8-7 (1oh) (53) R Thomas 14/1: 3425009: Chsd ldrs over 7f, wknd: 7 wk abs.   2½   41
3929 IMPERIAL ROYALE 23 [15]3-8-0 (7oh)p (54) M Halford(5) 50/1: 5060000: 10th: Handy over 1m, wknd.   ½   40
2955 LITTLESTAR 63 [17]3-8-0 (7oh) (54) D Fentiman(3) 16/1: 0-000020: 11th: Al in rear: 9 wk abs: btr 2955.   7   30
3505 WUXI VENTURE 40 [18]9-9-1 (62) M Savage 20/1: 60-06000: 12th: Bhd, nvr a factor: jumps fit.   1   36
4340 NARCISO 5 [7]4-8-7 (5oh) (49) Dean Williams(5) 33/1: 000060: 13th: In tch 1m, sn hung left & wknd.   1   26
4173 QUINTOTO 10 [3]4-9-4 (65) Natalia Gemelova(3) 20/1: 00000-60: 14th: Led, swerved right, hdd & rcd   *dist*   7
wide after 1f, rcd wide again on bend turning for home, sn fdd & eased, t.o.: btr 4173.
14 Ran   Time 2m 10.48(3.18)   Owned: Mr G A Lucas   Trained: Malton

NEWCASTLE   MONDAY 06.09.04   Lefthand, Galloping, Stiff Track

Official Going Good

4403

2.30 European Breeders Fund Maiden Stakes 2yo (D3)
£4813 £1481 £741   6f str   Good/Firm 34   -04 Slow   Centre

POTENT HEIR 0 [1] Saeed bin Suroor 2-9-0 K McEvoy 2/1 FAV: 1: b c Forest Wildcat - Penniless   95+
Heiress (Pentelicus) Chsd ldrs, switched & briefly rdn to lead ins last, sn asserted, going away: hvly bckd:
$475,000 Feb foal, brother to a high-class US juv & subs sprint performer: dam a dual US sprint wnr: eff at 6f on
fast, 7f will suit: goes well fresh: looks useful, win more races.
CROSSPEACE 0 [3] M Johnston 2-9-0 R Ffrench 12/1: 2: b c Cape Cross - Announcing Peace   1   88
(Danehill) Led till ins last, rdn & not pace of wnr cl-home: 32,000gns 2yo, Apr first foal: dam unplcd: eff at 6f,
7f will suit: handles fast grnd: v encouraging intro with rest well covered, win sn.
4223 MUSAHIM 9 [4] B W Hills 2-9-0 R Hills 11/4: 03: b c Dixieland Band - Tabheej (Mujtahid)   2½   80
Led/dsptd lead, outpcd fnl 1f: nicely bckd tho' 7/4: Mar first foal, dam a useful 5/6f 2yo scorer: handles fast.
4205 COME ON JONNY 10 [10] R M Beckett 2-9-0 S Sanders 5/2: 034: Cl-up, no impress fnl 1f: nicely bckd.   2½   72
4176 ANTONIO STRADIVARI 11 [8]2-9-0 VIS N Callan 12/1: 005: Dwelt, sn chsd ldrs, outpcd fnl 2f: tried vis.   1¼   68
4213 WHITE STAR MAGIC 10 [9]2-9-0 P Hanagan 66/1: 006: Held up, nvr pace to threaten ldrs: see 4083.   nk   67
2689 PEE JAYS DREAM 74 [2]2-9-0 Dale Gibson 50/1: 607: ch g Vettori - Langtry Lady (Pas de Seul)   4   55
Outpcd, no impress halfway: dam: cheaply bght Apr foal, half-brother to a 6f juv wnr & also a multiple mid-dist
scorer Nowell House: dam wnr at 6f/9f.
4205 FALCON GOER 10 [11]2-8-9 Kim Tinkler 100/1: 008: Chsd ldrs till halfway.   1   47
4349 COOL CRISTAL 3 [5]2-8-9 P Mulrennan(3) 100/1: 009: Went badly left start & sn t.o.   *dist*   0
ROSS IS BOSS 0 [6]2-9-0 T Eaves(3) 100/1: 0: 10th: Started v slowly & al t.o.   7   0
10 Ran   Time 1m 13.56 (2.26)   Owned: Godolphin   Trained: Newmarket

4404

3.00 Kpmg Maiden Stakes 3yo+ (D3)
£3455 £1063 £532   5f str   Good/Firm 34   -15 Slow   Centre

3561 MUTAYAM 39 [2] D A Nolan 4-9-0 t (45) P Mathers(5) 66/1: 00-60601: Chsd ldrs, rdn to lead well ins   59
last: eff at 5f on fast, stiff/sharp trk: eff in a t-strap: improved run: see 2713.
999 SONG KOI 159 [8] J G Given 3-8-8 (60) M Fenton 12/1: 44-02: Led till well ins last, no extra   1   50
cl-home: 5 month abs: unplcd both '03 starts (rtd 67, mdn): dam a 5f scorer: eff over a stiff 5f on fast grnd.
4278 FOX COVERT 7 [1] D W Barker 3-8-13 vis (55) L Enstone(3) 5/1: 3504003: Al prom, onepace.   nk   54
3976 MARYSIENKA 21 [11] J Balding 3-8-8 (60) J Edmunds 7/2: 64-05034: Keen & handy, ev ch dist, no extra.   nk   48
982 ABOUSTAR 160 [10]4-9-0 (35) M Lawson(5) 50/1: 6/00-5055: Chsd ldrs, not able to chall: abs: see 771.   2   47
4317} JUNIPER BANKS 354 [5]3-8-13 (67) A Culhane 12/1: 060420-6: ch g Night Shift - Beryl (Bering)   1   44
Bhd, late prog, no dngr: reapp, has been gelded: nurs h'cap rnr-up '03: eff over a stiff 6f on fast grnd: eff in a

t-strap, not worn today: has tried cheek pieces prev. 2 Sep'03 Hami 6.0g/f 67-66 D:

4237	**WESTBOROUGH 9** [9]3-8-13 VIS (52) Kim Tinkler 12/1: 0520067: Towards rear, only mod prog in visor.	nk	43
3932	**AGUILERA 24** [12]3-8-8 (30) V Halliday 100/1: 0040008: Rdn & rear, mod prog, no threat: see 3133.	1¼	34
4237	**WARREN PLACE 9** [15]4-9-0 (35) S Sanders 20/1: 0000009: Led stands side trio till dist, no impress.	½	37
3936	**RAETIHI 23** [14]3-8-8 Dean McKeown 33/1: 040: 10th: Led stands side dist, no ch with far side.	1½	27
3655	**LOUIS PRIMA 35** [6]3-8-13 (35) R Ffrench 50/1: 0000-000: 11th: Mid-div far side, no impress fnl 2f.	1½	27
1766	**SELF BELIEF 114** [3]3-8-8 (67) N Callan 8/1: 4340-00: 12th: b f Easycall - Princess of Spain	1¾	17

(King of Spain) Chsd ldrs far side 4f: abs: auct mdn plcd '03 (lightly rcd, rtd 71, D Cantillon): eff over a
sharp 5f, tried 6f: acts on fast grnd.

	SECRET OF SECRETS 0 [13]3-8-13 J McAuley 33/1: 0: 13th: Al outpcd stands side.	13	0
3575	**HARRISONS FLYER 2** [4]3-8-13 VIS (67) P Hanagan 11/4 FAV: 020202U: U.r. start: qck reapp in vis.		0

14 Ran   Time 1m 0.67 (2.47)   Owned: Miss M McFadyen-Murray   Trained: Wishaw

---

4405   **3.30 Stephen Easten Handicap Stakes 3yo+ 56-70 (E3)**   [81]
£3743 £1152 £576   **2m19y**   **Good/Firm 34**   **-45 Slow**   Inside

4308*	**TRILEMMA 6** [6] Sir Mark Prescott 3-9-0 (6ex) (67) S Sanders 4/7 FAV: 06-00611: Held up in tch,		77

smooth prog & led over 1f out, qcknd clr under hand riding, eased fnl stides: qck reapp under a pen: suited last
twice by 2m, acts on fast & gd grnd, stiff or sharpish trk: more to come, win again: see 4308, 3618.

4151	**MADIBA 13** [2] P Howling 5-9-0 (54) M Fenton 25/1: 2000P52: Held up in tch, outpcd 2f out, kept	1¾	57

on late to take 2nd, no ch with wnr: see 1753, 1637, 690 & 306.

3549*	**LITTLE TOBIAS 39** [1] Andrew Turnell 5-9-1 (55) R Thomas(5) 5/1: 010-6013: Handy & led over 2f out	¾	53

till dist, no extra: gd run: see 3549 (14f).

4209	**GREENWICH MEANTIME 10** [7] Mrs J R Ramsden 4-9-6 (60) L Goncalves 9/1: 3005604: Held up in tch,	½	59

no run over 2f out till ins last, styd on: op 7/1: much closer with clr run: see 3611.

4308	**CELTIC BLAZE 6** [3]5-9-0 t p (54) A Culhane 25/1: 060-3005: Trkd ldrs, outpcd fnl 2f: see 3181.	½	52
3970	**FANTASTICO 22** [5]4-9-4 p (58) P Mulrennan(3) 14/1: 30-40306: Led till over 2f out, sn no impress.	2	54
	ARCHIAS 456 [4]5-9-11 (65) R Winston 14/1: 5115/0-7: b g Darshaan - Arionette (Lombard) Trkd	2½	59

ldrs, btn 2f out: 12 wk jumps abs, May '04 h'cap hdle scorer (R Guest, rtd 103h, h'cap hdle, 2m & gd/soft, tried
cheek pieces & t-strap): ex German, 32 wnr: winning Flat form at 11/12f on soft & hvy grnd.
7 Ran   Time 3m 38.19 (12.69)   Owned: Mrs Sonia Rogers   Trained: Newmarket

---

4406   **4.00 Bet365 Call 08000 322 365 Handicap Stakes 3yo+ 56-70 (E3)**   [77]
£3836 £1180 £590   **1m2f32y**   **Good/Firm 34**   **-14 Slow**   Inside

3766	**MARKET AVENUE 30** [5] R A Fahey 5-8-9 (58) R Winston 9/2 JT FAV: 6-605051: Keen & held up, smooth		64

hdwy to chase wnr 2f out, drvn to lead cl-home: bckd, op 11/2: eff at 9/11f on firm & gd, handles gd/soft, any trk.

4703]	**INCROYABLE 330** [1] Sir Mark Prescott 3-8-3 (4oh) (59) J Mackay 16/1: 0006-2: gr f Linamix -	½	63

Crodelle (Formidable) Trkd front pair & led trav well over 2f out, rdn & hdd well ins last: op 8/1, reapp/h'cap
bow: unplcd at up to 1m in '03 (rtd 55, mdn): imprvd for step up to 10f on fast, further shld suit: impressed with
the way she trav thr' the race & can find similar on this evidence.

3992	**DERWENT 21** [9] J D Bethell 5-8-13 VIS (62) S Sanders 12/1: 0046603: Held up, switched wide & kept	1¾	64

on for press, nvr reaching front pair: imprvd eff in first time visor: well h'capped, likes Pontefract: see 2794.

4246*	**ZANDEED 9** [13] Miss L A Perratt 6-8-10 (59) T Eaves(3) 8/1: 600/-0314: Held up, pushed along	hd	60

halfway, styd on for press fnl 2f, nrst fin: see 4246 (1m).

4248	**MARITIME BLUES 9** [7]4-9-0 (63) A Culhane 12/1: 6300105: Mid-div, outpcd over 2f out, kept on onepce.	shd	64
4133*	**JORDANS SPARK 14** [4]3-8-1 (6oh)p (57) P Fessey 16/1: 500616: Keen & trkd ldrs, not pace to chall.	1½	56
4135	**FLIGHT COMMANDER 14** [2]4-9-3 (66) D Allan 33/1: 55-57: Mid-div, nvr able to threaten: h'cap bow.	4	59
4282	**FUTOO 7** [3]3-8-10 (66) N Pollard 9/2 JT FAV: 3013428: Led /dsptd lead till over 2f out: bckd, btr 4282.	3½	54
4260	**MEGANS MAGIC 8** [8]4-9-5 BL e (68) J Bramhill 8/1: 0036449: Slow away & rear, little hdwy in blnks.	1¾	54
4259	**MELODIAN 8** [6]9-9-2 bl (65) M Lawson(5) 9/1: 2321600: 10th: Led /dsptd lead over 3f out, sn btn.	1¼	49
530	**BOND MILLENNIUM 216** [3]6-8-10 (59) F Lynch 12/1: 02455-00: 11th: Held up, eff/short of room over	1¼	41

2f out, no after: abs: much closer here with a clr passage: see 530.

3876	**Sandy Bay 26** [11]5-8-7 (26oh)(30) P Makin(4) 100/1:0 2673 **Gran Dana 75** [10]4-9-7 (70) R Ffrench 12/1:0

13 Ran   Time 2m 11.36 (4.86)   Owned: Market Avenue Racing Club Ltd   Trained: Malton

---

4407   **4.30 Saltwell Signs Maiden Stakes 3yo+   (D3)**
£3523 £1084 £542   **1m rnd**   **Good/Firm 34**   **-14 Slow**   Inside

1747	**BACKGAMMON 115** [5] D R Loder 3-8-12 S Sanders 5/4 FAV: 231: Chsd ldrs, drvn to lead ins last,		80

styd on strongly: hvly bckd, op 2/1: 4 month abs: eff at 1m/10f on fast & soft grnd, stiff/undul trks: goes well
fresh: showed a willing attitude, can progress in h'cap company: see 1428.

4228	**THISTLE 9** [7] J H M Gosden 3-8-12 K McEvoy 4/1: 022: Led, rdn & hdd ins last, kept on & clr of	¾	78

rem: op 7/2: acts on fast & gd grnd: likely type for similar this autumn: see 4228 & 3973.

4994]	**LAKE DIVA 307** [11] J G Given 3-8-7 M Fenton 40/1: 00-3: ch f Docksider - Cutpurse Moll (Green	7	59+

Desert) Rear, late gains for press, not threat to front pair: reapp/h'cap bow: unplcd both '03 starts (rtd 53a &
42, mdns, M Wallace): half-sister to wnrs at up to 7f, dam a 7f wnr: not knocked about.

3905	**RIVER NUREY 25** [2] B W Hills 3-8-12 (68) R Hills 11/2: 2-325224: Chsd ldrs, no impress on front pair.	1½	61
4216	**QUEENS ECHO 10** [8]3-8-7 L Enstone(1) 12/1: 5-25: Chsd ldrs, no impress fnl 2f: btr 4216 (7f, hvy).	1¼	53
4228	**NADIR 9** [12]3-8-12 R Winston 7/1: 3-06: b c Pivotal - Along The Stars (Midyan) Held up in tch,	1¼	55

hung left over 2f out & no impress: plcd on sole '03 start (mdn, rtd 80): eff at 7f on gd.

4261	**MEDALLA 8** [1]4-9-3 M Lawson(5) 14/1: 357: Towards rear, rdn & little hdwy, op 10/1.	shd	55
4216	**SWINTON 10** [6]3-8-12 T Williams 40/1: 08: Held up, rdn & no impress over 3f out.	10	39
3414	**SVENSON 45** [10]3-8-12 (30) P M Quinn 150/1: 0-00009: Chsd ldrs 7f, sn btn, jumps fit.	½	38
4623]	**FORREST GUMP 336** [4]4-9-3 bl T Eaves(3) 150/1: 00-0: 10th: Chsd ldrs till 3f out, reapp.	9	23
4215	**Shardda 10** [9]4-8-12 T(60) P Hanagan 33/1:0 **Silloth Spirit 0** [3]4-9-3 N Pollard 66/1:0

12 Ran   Time 1m 42.8 (3.8)   Owned: Jumeirah Racing   Trained: Newmarket

NEWCASTLE MONDAY 06.09.04 Lefthand, Galloping, Stiff Track

4408 **5.00 St James Security Handicap Stakes 3yo+ 46-55 (F4)** **[67]**
£3006 £859 £429 **6f str** **Good/Firm 34** **+05 Fast** Centre

4009 **ROMAN EMPIRE 20** [12] K A Ryan 4-8-10 (49) N Callan 9/1: 1335401: Sn handy far side & led 2f out, drvn & held on all out: best time of day: first turf success: blnks omitted: eff at 6/7f on both AWs, fast & soft grnd, sharp/turning or stiff trk: eff with/without blnks: see 1750. **56**
3966 **BALLYBUNION 22** [2] D Nicholls 5-9-1 (54) A Nicholls 13/2 FAV: 0051032: Mid-div far side, short of room over 2f out till dist, drvn & strong run cl-home, just failed: in gd heart: see 3966, 3463. *shd* **60**
4245 **WILLIAMS WELL 9** [5] M W Easterby 10-9-2 bl (55) P Mulrennan(3) 7/1: 0050633: Held up far side, styd on well for press, nrst fin: see 4245 & 2884. *nk* **60**
4256 **LORD BASKERVILLE 8** [4] W Storey 3-8-12 (53) M Lawson(5) 20/1: 0224044: Al prom far side & ch dist, not pace of front trio cl-home: see 1509. ½ **54**
4240 **ON THE TRAIL 9** [3]7-9-1 (54) A Culhane 9/1: 4331145: Prom far side, kept on onepace. 1½ **52**
4211 **MICKLEDOR 10** [13]4-9-0 p (53) D Tudhope(7) 16/1: 0110036: Mid-div far side, styd on onepace. 1½ **46**
3767 **XANADU 30** [14]8-8-11 p (50) R Ffrench 25/1: 6200657: Prom far side, no extra dist: btr 3767. 1¾ **38**
4245 **FRIMLEYS MATTERRY 9** [19]4-9-0 (53) T Eaves(3) 25/1: 5031668: Trkd ldrs stands side, led that group ins last, no ch with ldrs far side: first home from unfav'd stands side group: see 3767. *shd* **41+**
3757* **JEDEYDD 31** [1]7-9-2 bl t (55) R Winston 12/1: 6400019: Mid-div far side, nvr land a blow: btr 3575. ½ **41**
3575 **MEGABOND 38** [11]3-8-13 (54) F Lynch 20/1: 30-50400: 10th: Bhd far side, late prog under min press. *hd* **39**
3463 **FLYING TACKLE 43** [8]6-8-11 p (50) L Enstone(3) 33/1: 3210000: 11th: Mid-div far side, no impress: abs. *hd* **34**
2615 **THE OLD SOLDIER 77** [7]6-8-12 (51) A Beech(3) 10/1: 200-0020: 12th: Never on terms far side, abs. *shd* **35**
4211 **REDOUBTABLE 10** [15]13-8-11 (50) P Makin(5) 33/1: 6040040: 13th: Cl-up stands side & led that group over 1f out till ins last, sn btn. 1 **31**
4345 **THE WIZARD MUL 4** [16]4-9-1 BL (54) J Bramhill 50/1: 4-000000: 14th: Led stands side till over 1f out, sn struggling, qck reapp in blnks. ½ **33**
4009 **SILVER SEEKER 20** [9]4-8-9 (48) P Fessey 33/1: 0206000: 15th: Bhd far side, nvr factor. ½ **25**
2752 **QUANTICA 72** [20]5-9-2 (55) Kim Tinkler 14/1: 2-600000: 16th: Sn far side & no impress thr'out, abs. ½ **30**
4211 **TURF PRINCESS 10** [6]3-8-9 (50) D Fentiman(7) 50/1: 5304000: 17th: Chsd ldrs far side 4f. ¾ **23**
4368 **A TEEN 3** [18]6-8-11 (50) S Sanders 8/1: 0005600: 18th: Mid-div far side, hung left & btn over 1f out. 3 **14**
3796 **Drury Lane 30** [10]4-8-10 bl(49) N Pollard 25/1:0 3548 **Gaiety Girl 39** [17]3-8-12 (53) D Allan 100/1:0
20 Ran Time 1m 13.02(1.72) Owned: Yorkshire Racing Syndicates Trained: Hambleton

BATH MONDAY 06.09.04 Lefthand, Turning Track with Uphill Finish

Official Going FIRM

4409 **2.10 Mitie Engineering Maiden Auction Stakes Fillies 2yo (E4)**
£3108 £888 £444 **5f11y** **Good/Firm 21** **-06 Slow** Far side

4052 **ARABIAN DANCER 18** [5] M R Channon 2-8-2 (82) C Catlin 7/2 J FAV: 265351: Mid-div, hdwy over 1f out, led ins fnl 1f, pushed out: stays 1m, relished this drop back to 5f: acts on fast grnd: see 2119. **79**
3857 **FARTHING 26** [11] G C Bravery 2-8-5 S Whitworth 9/1: 242: Chsd ldrs, hdwy to lead over 1f out, hdd ins fnl 1f, no extra: op 14/1: handles fast & gd: shown enough to win similar: see 3488. 1½ **75**
3988 **DOITFORREEL 21** [8] I A Wood 2-8-2 F Norton 12/1: 003: b f Princely Heir - Chehana (Posse) Chsd ldrs, onepcd fnl 1f: op 10/1: May foal, cost E5,000: half sister to a couple of 2yo wnrs: eff at 5f on fast: best run thus far here, can find a race based on this. ½ **70**
4298 **IM AIMEE 7** [6] P D Evans 2-8-2 (76) F P Ferris(3) 5/1: 2223044: Sn led till over 1f out, onepace. ½ **68**
2437 **BORN FOR DANCING 84** [2]2-8-8 BL W Supple 7/1: 25: Rear, mod late gains: long abs: tried blnks. ¾ **72**
3962 **SAUCEPOT 22** [10]2-8-2 (63) Hayley Turner(3) 25/1: 062036: Prom, hdwy/ev ch 2f out, no impress fnl 1f. *hd* **65**
3962 **LITTLE WARNING 22** [3]2-8-2 N Mackay(3) 10/1: 07: Handy, no impress 2f out: see 3962. ½ **63**
4303 **BOBS FLYER 6** [9]2-8-5 T E Durcan 33/1: 048: Rear, hdwy 2f out, no pace to chall: quick reapp. ¾ **64**
3848 **AGENT KENSINGTON 27** [1]2-8-2 (69) R L Moore 7/2 J FAV: 2532429: Chsd ldrs, no impress 2f out. *nk* **60**
3988 **STAR DUSTER 21** [4]2-8-2 S Righton 6/1: 020: 10th: Slow away, nvr a factor. 1 **57**
4178 **EDEN STAR 11** [7]2-8-2 Martin Dwyer 100/1: 0000: 11th: b f Soviet Star - Gold Prospector (Spectrum) Slow away, nvr a factor: Mar 1st foal, cost 7,000 gns: dam plcd over 7f/1m at 2. 9 **30**
11 Ran Time 1m 1.67 (1.37) Owned: Mr Jaber Abdullah Trained: West Ilsley

4410 **2.40 Betfred Com In-Running Nursery Handicap Stakes 2yo 0-85 (D2)** **[84]**
£6019 £1852 £926 **1m5y** **Good/Firm 21** **-10 Slow** Inside

4177 **CLINET 11** [3] P M Phelan 2-8-7 (63) J F Egan 20/1: 5205001: Slow away in rear, hdwy 3f out, led just ins fnl 2f, drvn out ins fnl 1f: 1st win: prev eff at 5f, relished this step up to 1m: acts on fast & gd. **71**
3959 **SWELL LAD 23** [11] P F I Cole 2-9-0 BL (70) N De Souza(5) 12/1: 0062: Led after 1f, hdd just ins fnl 2f, sn no extra: op 7/1: stays 1m on fast: gd run in 1st time blnks: see 2578 (debut). 1½ **72**
3890 **CHAPTER 25** [1] R Hannon 2-9-7 (77) R L Moore 100/30 FAV: 2203: Handy, lost pl over 4f out, hdwy over 2f out, onepcd fnl 1f: stays 1m: back to form on fast: see 2696. ¾ **78**
4079 **FLYING PASS 17** [7] D J S ffrench Davis 2-9-2 (72) S Whitworth 14/1: 3022564: Rear, hdwy over 3f out, not pace to chall: stays 1m: gd run: see 3330. *shd* **72**
4213 **BONGOALI 10** [4]2-8-11 (67) C Catlin 7/1: 4525: Slow away in rear, hdwy over 2f out, onepcd fnl 1f. 1¼ **64**
4171 **ZOLASH 11** [6]2-8-6 (62) Martin Dwyer 10/1: 0604436: Handy, onepcd 2f out: op 12/1, clr of rem. 1¾ **55**
4153 **DONT TELL TRIGGER 16** [12]2-8-13 (69) Derek Nolan(7) 8/1: 6100107: Chsd ldrs, no impress 2f out. 3½ **55**
3624 **LADY CHEF 37** [2]2-9-6 (76) T E Durcan 4/1: 05138: Led 1f, no extra over 1f out: btr 3624 (7f). 4 **54**
4233 **SPINNING COIN 9** [9]2-8-11 (67) N Mackay(3) 8/1: 06009: Rear, mod late gains: tchd 10/1: see 3035. 2 **41**
4177 **DREEMON 11** [8]2-9-0 (70) F Norton 14/1: 03000: 10th: Chsd ldrs, no impress 2f out: rep hung left. 4 **36**
4089 **MAKE IT HAPPEN NOW 17** [5]2-7-12 (9oh) (45) S Righton 66/1: 040000: 11th: b f Octagonal - Whittle Woods Girl (Emarati) Keen & handy, no impress: Mar foal, cost 13,000 gns: half sister to 5/7f wnrs: dam 6f wnr. 1½ **17**
3141 **SIRCE 57** [10]2-7-12 (9oh) (45) F P Ferris(3) 66/1: 0600: 12th: Nvr a factor: 8 wk abs: see 2783. 4 **9**

12 Ran Time 1m 40.84 (2.54) Owned: Wood Hall Stud Limited Trained: Shenley

4411 **3.10 Betfred The Bonus King Selling Handicap Stakes 3-4yo 46-55 (G4)** **[57]**
£2624 £750 £375 **1m5y** **Good/Firm 21** **-04 Slow** Inside

3963 **NAUGHTY GIRL 22** [10] P D Evans 4-9-3 vis t (46) F P Ferris(3) 5/1: 5440201: Handy, trav best over 2f out, hdwy into 2nd 2f out, led over 1f out, drvn out ins fnl 1f: no bid: op 7/1: prev eff at 5/6f, now seems suited by 1m: acts on fast & gd/soft, stiff/undul, sharp or turning trks: made most of this drop in grade: see 551. **50**
4112 **ESPERANCE 16** [2] J Akehurst 4-9-2 (45) R L Moore 4/1 FAV: 0550552: Slow away in rear, hdwy over 2f out, chsd wnr ins fnl 1f, nrst fin: gd run, does stay further & a step up in trip will suit: see 2799. *shd* **48**
4164 **CONFUZED 12** [5] D Flood 4-9-2 e/s (45) J F Egan 9/1: 0040033: Keen & handy, poised to chall when hmpd 1f out, kept on ins fnl 1f: op 7/1: prev eff at 5f, imprvd last twice for step up to 7f/1m: acts on fast, soft & polytrack: closer but for interference: see 737. *1* **46**
4164 **YOUNG LOVE 12** [11] Miss E C Lavelle 3-8-11 (45) R Havlin 11/1: 0640644: In tch, hdwy 2f out, onepcd. *1½* **43**
4054 **SAINTLY PLACE 18** [9]3-9-2 (50) S Hitchcott(3) 33/1: 060-0005: Rcd in 2nd till led over 2f out, hdd over 1f out, sn no extra: see 3109. *1¼* **45**
3867 **DRY WIT 26** [13]3-9-5 (53) N Mackay(3) 16/1: 60-06006: Rear, some late gains: see 2249. *¾* **46**
4202 **CITY GENERAL 10** [14]3-9-2 p (50) Laura Reynolds(7) 12/1: 0510567: Chsd ldrs, no impress over 1f out. *hd* **42**
3712 **PERERIN 32** [4]3-8-12 bl (46) Hayley Turner(3) 12/1: 0100038: Mid-div, hdwy 3f out, fdd 2f out. *7* **24**
3344 **MAGICO 47** [7]3-9-2 bl (50) Martin Dwyer 11/1: 0-000329: Keen in tch, wknd 2f out: now with A Haynes. *2* **24**
4145 **CHUBBES 13** [8]3-9-3 bl (51) S Whitworth 7/1: 0440100: 10th: Rear, nvr a factor. *1* **23**
3731 **IVY MOON 32** [1]4-9-2 (45) D Corby(3) 20/1: 3534050: 11th: Mid-div, wknd 2f out: rep moved badly. *½* **16**
4372 **RUMOUR MILL 2** [6]3-8-6 (5oh)bl (40) C Catlin 66/1: 0000000: 12th: b c Entrepreneur - Pursuit of Truth (Irish River) Led till over 2f out, fdd: quick reapp: nurs & mdn unplcd in '03 (rtd 68a, part with Sir M Prescott): wears blnks, tried cheek pieces. *7* **0**
4054 **KATZ PYJAMAS 18** [3]3-8-11 (45) Joanna Badger 100/1: 00000-00: 13th: b f Fasliyev - Allepolina (Trempolino) Al bhd: sell, mdn, nurs & clmg unplcd in '03 (rtd 56, with Mrs A Duffield): tried blnks. *3½* **0**
4300 **CHANDELIER 7** [12]4-9-6 (49) T E Durcan 9/2: 016006R: Refused to race. **0**
14 Ran Time 1m 40.36 (2.06) Owned: Mrs S J Lawrence Trained: Abergavenny

4412 **3.40 Betfred Com Now Online Handicap Stakes 3yo+ 56-70 (E3)** **[76]**
£6107 £1879 £940 **5f161y** **Good/Firm 21** **+11 Fast** Inside

3952 **WOODBURY 23** [1] Mrs H Sweeting 5-8-10 (58) G Baker 10/1: 0-041041: Chsd ldrs, hdwy on inner to lead 1f out, rdn out: fast time: suited by 5.5/6f on firm, fast & polytrack, handles gd/soft: likes Bath. **66**
4130 **JAGGED 14** [17] J R Jenkins 4-8-10 vis (58) T E Durcan 13/2 FAV: 2363122: Prom, hdwy to chall 2f out, styd on ins fnl 1f but not pace of wnr: op 5/1: remains in fine form at present: see 4043. *hd* **64**
4317 **INNSTYLE 5** [2] J L Spearing 3-8-10 (60) S Hitchcott(3) 20/1: 440-6003: Chsd ldrs, no room over 1f out till just ins fnl 1f, styd on well ins fnl 1f, just failed: op 14/1, quick reapp: looked unlucky: see 4317. *hd* **65+**
3977 **WILLHECONQUERTOO 21** [6] Andrew Reid 4-9-7 t (69) J F Egan 11/1: 3510054: Sn led, hdd 1f out, no extra: gd run: ran to wng form of 2975. *1½* **69**
4335 **STAGNITE 4** [12]4-8-10 p (58) D Corby(3) 10/1: 6210065: Prom, outpcd & btn ins fnl 1f: op 14/1. *1* **55**
4335 **PULSE 4** [19]6-8-9 p (57) P Fitzsimons 9/1: 0554006: Cl-up, styd on fnl 1f but not pace to chall. *nk* **53**
3602 **ASTRAC 37** [10]13-8-7 (7oh) (48) Joanna Badger 16/1: 0024007: Rear, hdwy over 1f out, not pace to chall. *nk* **50**
3966 **CORANGLAIS 22** [8]4-8-11 bl (59) R L Moore 16/1: 4100508: Rear, hdwy 2f out, not pace of ldrs. *¾* **52**
3966 **INDIAN BAZAAR 22** [7]8-8-7 (10oh) (45) L Keniry(3) 33/1: 0600009: Chsd ldrs, no impress fnl 1f. *½* **46**
3995 **DELLAGIO 21** [9]3-8-6 (1oh) (56) C Catlin 14/1: 0400100: 10th: Nvr btr than mid-div. *½* **45**
4197 **ST AUSTELL 10** [3]4-9-3 (65) S Whitworth 20/1: 2021-000: 11th: Slow away in rear, hdwy over 2f out, no impress ins fnl 1f: see 3924. *shd* **53**
4169 **ARDKEEL LASS 12** [4]3-8-7 (57) R Havlin 25/1: 6-002450: 12th: Rear, some late gains. *¾* **43**
4317 **MISS JUDGEMENT 5** [15]3-9-0 (64) F Norton 9/1: 1300100: 13th: Rear, mod late gains: quick reapp. *nk* **49**
4107 **IZMAIL 16** [18]5-9-7 (69) S Donohoe(7) 20/1: 0001000: 14th: Rear, hdwy 2f out, not pace to chall. *shd* **53**
3827 **COMPTON BANKER 28** [11]7-9-1 bl (63) F P Ferris(3) 8/1: 6520300: 15th: Handy, wknd over 2f out. *1* **44**
4168 **MUSICAL TOP 12** [14]4-8-9 (57) Martin Dwyer 14/1: 50-00300: 16th: Handy, wknd 2f out. *½* **36**
2627 **NINAH 77** [5]3-8-8 (58) Hayley Turner(3) 66/1: 240-0000: 17th: b f First Trump - Alwal (Pharly) Prom, wknd over 2f out: long abs: rnr-up 3 of 12 '03 starts (mdns): stays 5f, 6f shld suit: acts on fast & fibresand. 2 Sep'03 Chep 7.1g/f 76-(70) F: 2 Sep'03 Chep 7.1gd 69-(66) D: 2 Apr'03 Sout 5af 64a- F: *¾* **35**
4164 **FLORIAN 12** [13]6-8-7 (55) R Miles(3) 11/1: 3-000560: 18th: Nvr a factor: see 2799. *¾* **30**
18 Ran Time 1m 9.7 (0.6) Owned: Mr P Sweeting Trained: Marlborough

4413 **4.10 Betfred We Pay Double Result Maiden Stakes 3yo (D3)**
£3595 £1106 £553 **5f161y** **Good/Firm 21** **-01 Slow** Inside

3403 **COMERAINCOMESHINE 45** [13] T G Mills 3-8-9 (62) G Carter 9/1: 3642001: Rear, wide, hdwy over 2f out, led 1f out, rdn out: 6 wk abs: eff at 5/5.5f on fast & polytrack, turning trk: imprvd for waiting tactics. **72**
3921 **DEUXIEME 24** [6] R Charlton 3-8-9 (72) D Sweeney 5/2: 3352: Slow away in rear, hdwy & hung left over 2f out, short of rm 1f out, kept on ins fnl 1f, nrst fin: eff over 5.5/7f: return to further will suit. *¾* **68**
4272 **INDIANA BLUES 7** [4] A M Balding 3-8-9 (65) Martin Dwyer 9/4 FAV: 0035343: With ldr, slight advantage over 3f out to 1f out, no extra ins fnl 1f: quick reapp: see 4054. *nk* **67**
3884 **SUPERFLING 25** [10] R Hannon 3-9-0 R L Moore 20/1: 04: ch g Superpower - Jobiska (Dunbeath) Rear, wide, hdwy over 1f out, not pace to chall: dam unplcd at 2 & 3: eff at 5.5f on fast: imprvd from debut. *1¾* **67**
3900 **DANE RHAPSODY 25** [2]3-8-9 (45) S Hitchcott(3) 20/1: 050505: Chsd ldrs, not much room over 1f out, sn onepcd: see 2152. *nk* **61$**
706 **KNEAD THE DOUGH 196** [1]3-9-0 J F Egan 8/1: 26: Slight led till over 3f out, no extra over 1f out. *1¾* **61**
4116 **SCARLETT BREEZE 15** [12]3-8-9 (45) M Tebbutt 20/1: 0504047: Mid-div, nvr nrr: see 4116. *hd* **55$**
4262 **SOKOKE 8** [8]3-9-0 N Mackay(3) 9/1: 2308: Chsd ldrs, no impress fnl 1f. *¾* **58**
4029 **IMPERIAL WIZARD 19** [9]3-9-0 S Chin 100/1: 0009: ch g Magic Ring - Paula's Joy (Danehill) Handy & wide, no impress over 1f out: mdn unplcd all earlier starts: with M Usher. *1¾* **53$**
3900 **BOLD TRUMP 25** [7]3-9-0 VIS (52) R Mullen 66/1: 0-4000: 10th: Prom, wknd over 2f out: tried visor. *4* **41**
4262 **DINE N DASH 8** [11]3-9-0 S Whitworth 66/1: 060: 11th: ch g Komaite - Instinction (Never So Bold) Slow away, nvr a factor: dam unrcd: with A Newcombe. *½* **39**

BATH
MONDAY 06.09.04 Lefthand, Turning Track with Uphill Finish

4081	**MISS MONZA 17** [3]3-8-9 (68) T E Durcan 14/1: 0030: 12th: Cl-up early, sn no impress: op 10/1.				2	28
49	**BERESFORD BOY 293** [5]3-9-0 C Catlin 50/1: 06-P: Slow away, bhd, p.u. over 1f out: lost action.					0

13 Ran   Time 1m 10.33 (1.23)   Owned: John Humphreys (Turf Accountants) Ltd   Trained: Epsom

---

4414   **4.40 Betfred In Shops On Phone And On-Line Maiden Stakes Fillies & Mares 3yo+ (D3)**
£3663 £1127 £564   **1m3f144y   Good/Firm 21   -15 Slow   Inside**

3979	**SIMONDA 21** [11] Mrs A J Perrett 3-8-10 R L Moore 5/4 FAV: 21: Bhd, hdwy over 3f out, led 2f out, pushed out ins fnl 1f: well bckd: eff over an easy 1m, relished this step up to 11.5f: acts on fast grnd, turning trk: imprvd from debut, more races to be won around this trip: see 3979 (debut).		80
3186	**TASHREEFAT 54** [9] E F Vaughan 3-8-10 W Supple 3/1: 342: Rcd in 2nd till led over 3f out, hdd 2f out, not pace to go with wnr: 8 wk abs: met a useful rival: see 2534.	8	65
1864	**RUGGTAH 109** [10] M R Channon 3-8-10 T E Durcan 33/1: 03: gr f Daylami - Raneen Alwatar (Sadler's Wells) Chsd ldrs, hmpd & lost place over 3f out, styd on again fnl 1f: long abs: dam a 12f wnr.	½	64
	LETS PRETEND 0 [2] B W Hills 3-8-10 R Mullen 8/1: 4: b f Rainbow Quest - Imaginary (Dancing Brave) Slow away, sn in mid-div, hdwy into 2nd 3f out, onepcd 2f out on debut: sister to smart older stayer Rainbow High: dam a lightly rcd 10f wnr at 3: fair start: acts on Flat debut & will improve.	shd	63
	EUROBOUND 66 [8]3-8-10 (74) C Catlin 7/1: 4455: b f Southern Halo - Eurostorm (Storm Bird) Cl-up, sn bhd, nvr a factor: op 10/1, 9 wk abs: Brit bow: mdn 4th 1 of 3 earlier '04 starts in Ireland (1m, firm, with J Oxx): stays 1m, further likely: acts on firm: with D Daly.	3½	58
3194	**STORMY DAY 407** [1]4-9-5 L P Keniry(3) 50/1: 60-6: Keen in mid-div, no impress over 2f out on reapp.	2	55
	MRS PHILIP 0 [7]5-9-5 V Slattery 33/1: 7: Al bhd on Flat debut: NH fit.	6	46
3630	**POWERFUL PARRISH 36** [3]3-8-10 (72) S Chin 14/1: 5-024008: Chsd ldrs, no impress 3f out: op 10/1.	1½	44
3967	**SOVIETTA 22** [4]3-8-10 Martin Dwyer 9/1: 439: Chsd ldrs, wknd 3f out: rep unsuited by grnd.	shd	43
	MOON SPINNER 0 [6]7-9-5 J F Egan 40/1: 0: 10th: Led till over 3f out, sn no extra on Flat debut.	7	32

10 Ran   Time 2m 29.17 (4.17)   Owned: Mr S P Tindall   Trained: Pulborough

---

4415   **5.10 Betfred Com Early Prices From 9 A M Maiden Handicap Stakes 3yo+ 56-70 (E3)**   **[74]**
£3673 £1130 £565   **1m5f22y   Good/Firm 21   -01 Slow   Inside**

2288	**POLAR TRYST 444** [1] Lady Herries 5-9-2 (62) N Mackay(3) 100/30 FAV: 454/022-1: ch f Polar Falcon - Lovers Tryst (Castle Keep) Stumbled leaving stalls, sn led, drvn out fnl 1f: reapp: rnr-up fnl 2 '03 starts (h'cap, mdn h'cap): lightly rcd in '02 (unplcd, h'cap, rtd 63): eff btwn 10/13f on firm & gd, turning trk: runs well fresh: seemingly much imprvd, win again in this form.		74

2 Jun'03 Ayr 13.1g/f 63-60 E: 2 Jun'03 Hami 13.0gd 63-60 F:

3998	**SUNDAY CITY 21** [12] D R Loder 3-8-13 (69) R L Moore 9/2: 33552: Chsd ldrs, hdwy into 2nd over 2f out, not pace to go with wnr: see 2608.	6	70
4056	**OLYMPIAS 18** [11] H Morrison 3-7-12 (12oh)BL (52) F P Ferris(3) 25/1: 5006403: Rear, hdwy over 3f out, hung left 2f out, kept on fnl 1f: tried blnks: stiff task at weights: see 2376.	½	54
4299	**LORD LAHAR 7** [9] M R Channon 5-8-8 (9oh) (45) T E Durcan 25/1: 6000504: Rear, mod late gains: stiff task at weights.	2½	49
4092	**RAWALPINDI 17** [4]3-8-0 (8oh) (56) F Norton 9/2: 0-00025: Bhd, mod late gains: stiff task at weights.	1	50
3893	**SEEKING A WAY 25** [5]3-8-12 (68) W Supple 7/1: 21-2306: Mid-div, hdwy into 2nd 10f out, lost place over 2f out & sn no impress.	nk	61
4143	**SPRING ADIEU 13** [2]3-8-4 (4oh)BL (60) Martin Dwyer 14/1: 00-40047: Rcd in 2nd till after 3f, no impress fnl 1f: tried blnks: see 2893.	½	52
4056	**LORD NELLSSON 18** [3]8-8-12 (58) Hayley Turner(3) 16/1: 40058: Chsd ldrs, no impress 3f out: see 4056.	1	48
3894	**KILINDINI 25** [10]3-8-12 (68) R Havlin 14/1: 6U549: Al bhd: see 3292.	13	38
3948	**ONCE 23** [8]4-9-8 bl (68) J F Egan 14/1: 00-30000: 10th: Mid-div, hdwy over 5f out, fdd 4f out.	17	12
1297	**EMBASSY SWEETS 138** [7]3-8-1 (7oh) (57) N de Souza(5) 11/1: 00-40: 11th: Nvr a factor: long abs.	12	0

11 Ran   Time 2m 48.47(2.97)   Owned: Lady Herries and Friends   Trained: Littlehampton

---

WARWICK
MONDAY 06.09.04 Lefthand, Sharp, Turning Track

Official Going Good/Firm

4416   **2.20 European Breeders Fund Maiden Stakes Colts & Geldings 2yo (D2)**
£6396 £1968 £984   **7f26y rnd   Good/Firm   Inapplicable   Inside**

3811	**WALKONTHEWILDSIDE 29** [1] D R Loder 2-8-11 VIS T P Queally 3/1: 541: Made all, went clr dist, pushed out, val 4L+: eff at 7f, further will suit: acts on fast grnd: improving, apprec visor.		87
	NOTNOWCATO 0 [6] Sir Michael Stoute 2-8-11 K Darley 28/1: 2: ch c Inchinor - Rambling Rose (Cadeaux Genereux) Al cl-up, styd on ins fnl 1f, al held by wnr: debut: Mar foal, half-brother plcd over 1m: dam successful at 1m, also Group decent performer around 7f: sire decent performer around 7f: eff at 7f, further will suit: acts on fast grnd: encouraging start & sure to progress with experience.	2	79
	CROIX ROUGE 0 [2] Mrs A J Perrett 2-8-11 R Hughes 16/1: 3: b c Chester House - Rougeur (Blushing Groom) Cl-up, kept on ins fnl 1f, just held for 2nd: debut: Mar foal, half-brother decent performer abroad at mid-dists: dam successful at 10/12f abroad: sire Gr 1 wnr at 10f in USA: eff at 7f, further will suit: acts on fast grnd: pleasing intro & can rate higher next time out.	hd	78
3869	**KINGS KAMA 26** [5] Sir Michael Stoute 2-8-11 K Fallon 7/4 FAV: 44: Held up, prog halfway, staying on when short of room 1f out, kept on ins fnl 1f under hands & heels: well bckd: eff at 7f, will apprec 1m+: acts on fast grnd: prob plcd with clr run & shld be capable of finding a mdn: see 3869.	1	76+
	RIVER ALHAARTH 0 [9]2-8-11 J Fortune 28/1: 5: b c Alhaarth - Sudden Interest (Highest Honor) Prom, no extra dist: debut: May foal, half-brothers to wnrs at 6/12f: dam success abroad.	¾	74
	COMPTON QUAY 0 [4]2-8-11 J D Smith 50/1: 6: Dwelt, prog 2f out, nrst fin on debut.	shd	73
3811	**WUJOOD 29** [11]2-8-11 I Mongan 40/1: 007: Bhd, nvr nrr than mid-div: quals for h'caps.	1	71
3438	**TAJ INDIA 44** [8]2-8-11 J Fanning 17/2: 58: Mid-div over 5f, no extra: tchd 10/1: 6 wk abs.	hd	70
3831	**MY RASCAL 28** [13]2-8-11 A McCarthy 66/1: 009: Rear, nvr a factor.	3	64

3470 **LITTLE INDY 43** [12]2-8-11 D Nolan(2) 150/1: 000: 10th: Mid-div 5f, sn wknd. ½ **63**
3959 **WEMBURY POINT 23** [14]2-8-11 Dane O'Neill 125/1: 000: 11th: Missed break, nvr a factor. 1 **61**
4179 **Savoy Chapel 11** [7]2-8-11 D Holland 25/1:0 3582 **Tombola 38** [10]2-8-11 S Drowne 16/1:0
13 Ran Time 1m 23.84 (1.44) Owned: Mr M Tabor Trained: Newmarket

4417

2.50 European Breeders Fund Maiden Stakes Div 1 Fillies 2yo (D2)
£5954 £1832 £916 **7f26y rnd** **Good/Firm** **Inapplicable** Inside

LITERATURE 0 [8] Saeed bin Suroor 2-8-11 L Dettori 7/2: 1: b f Notebook - Deputy's Mistress (Deputy Minister) Cl-up, led despite edg left fnl 1f, pushed out, val more: op 5/2 on debut: Mar foal, sister well related: dam unrcd: sire decent performer around 6f/1m: eff at 7f, shld stay further: acts on fast grnd & a sharp trk: fresh: much to like about this, rate higher. **81+**
LYSANDRA 0 [12] Sir Michael Stoute 2-8-11 K Fallon 5/2 FAV: 2: b f Danehill - Oriane (Nashwan) Sn upfront, edged left under press dist, kept on, no ch with easy wnr: debut: Mar foal, half-sister to wnrs at 7/8f: dam successful at 1m: sire fine performer at 6f/1m: eff at 7f, 1m will suit: acts on fast grnd: ran well enough for debut & looks sure to find similar. 1¾ **73**
4178 **FOXY GWYNNE 11** [4] A M Balding 2-8-11 Dane O'Neill 50/1: 03: Cl-up, ev ch dist, sn no extra: left debut bhd on step up to 7f, acts on fast grnd: encouraging display: see 4178 (debut). hd **72**
3915 **ROMANOVA 24** [1] D R Loder 2-8-11 T P Queally 11/2: 04: b f Grand Lodge - Millitrix (Doyoun) Led, hdd under press ins fnl 1f, no extra: tchd 9/2: Feb foal, cost 60,000gns: half-sister plcd at sprint dists: dam plcd at 7f: sire Gr 1 wnr at 1m/10f: eff at 7f, shld get further: acts on fast grnd. nk **71**
3716 **GRANDMAS GIRL 32** [11]2-8-11 K Darley 13/2: 045: Cl-up over 5f, sn hung left & no extra: see 3716. 1 **68$**
4108 **SLIP CATCH 16** [9]2-8-11 Lisa Jones 50/1: 06: Missed break, nvr nrr than mid-div: see 4108. 3½ **62**
OVERJOY WAY 0 [6]2-8-11 J Quinn 20/1: 7: Nvr nrr than mid-div on debut. 1¾ **58**
TARABUT 0 [7]2-8-11 J Fortune 20/1: 8: Missed break, modest at late gains: debut. ½ **57**
3915 **PONENTE 24** [3]2-8-11 M Hills 9/2: 69: Mid-div 5f, sn wknd: op 6/1. ¾ **55**
PIROETTA 0 [5]2-8-11 S Drowne 16/1: 0: 10th: Missed break, al in rear. 1½ **52**
4296 **Silver Dreamer 7** [10]2-8-11 P Doe 100/1:0 **Tiegs 0** [2]2-8-11 J F McDonald(3) 100/1:0
12 Ran Time 1m 23.43 (1.03) Owned: Godolphin Trained: Newmarket

4418

3.20 European Breeders Fund Maiden Stakes Div 2 Fillies 2yo (D2)
£5954 £1832 £916 **7f26y rnd** **Good/Firm** **Inapplicable** Inside

3252 **SADIE THOMPSON 52** [8] M R Channon 2-8-11 J Fanning 8/1: 01: b f King's Best - Femme Fatale (Fairy King) Cl-up, styd on to lead dist, rdn out to hold on: op 13/2: 7 wk abs: Feb first foal, cost 130,000gns: dam 6f wnr: eff at 7f, 1m+ will suit: acts on fast: goes well fresh. **79**
3520 **HEAT OF THE NIGHT 40** [4] J L Dunlop 2-8-11 L Dettori 4/1: 402: Missed break, prog 2f out, ev ch ins fnl 1f, just held by wnr: 6 wk abs: lost little in defeat & now quals for h'caps: see 3035. hd **77**
3909 **MIDCAP 24** [3] B W Hills 2-8-11 (73) M Hills 14/1: 0603: Held up, prog 2f out, kept on ins fnl 2f, no ch with front 2: eff at 7f on fast grnd: see 3554. 2½ **72**
4035 **USHINDI 19** [2] M L W Bell 2-8-11 J Fortune 33/1: 004: Led, hdd dist, sn no extra: eff at 7f on fast. nk **71**
ORLAR 0 [1]2-8-11 S W Kelly 33/1: 5: b f Green Desert - Soviet Maid (Soviet Star) Cl-up, no extra dist: debut: Apr foal, cost 100,000gns: half-sister to 7f wnr: dam unrcd. nk **70**
DALIYA 0 [9]2-8-11 BL K Fallon 9/2: 6: b f Giant's Causeway - Dalara (Doyoun) Missed break, sn cl-up, hung left & wknd dist: op 6/1 on debut: 1st blnks fitted: May foal, half-sister & half-brother to Group wnrs at 12/16f: dam mid-dists wnr: with Sir M Stoute. 2 **66**
3046 **LOTTIE DUNDASS 60** [5]2-8-11 D Holland 9/2: 527: Cl-up over 5f, sn hmpd & wknd: btr 3046. ¾ **64**
3795 **RASHIDA 30** [7]2-8-11 E Ahern 5/2 FAV: 38: Nvr nrr than mid-div: rider reported mount ran v green. 1¼ **62**
2970 **GYPSY ROYAL 63** [12]2-8-11 N Day 33/1: 09: Cl-up 5f, wknd: 9 wk abs. 5 **52**
4072 **POLESWORTH 17** [10]2-8-11 M Halford(7) 150/1: 500: 10th: Missed break, nvr a factor. 1 **50**
3818 **Winter Mist 28** [11]2-8-11 J P Guillambert(3) 100/1:0 **Ciendra Girl 0** [6]2-8-11 D Nolan(3) 100/1:0
12 Ran Time 1m 24.03 (1.63) Owned: Sheikh Mohammed Trained: West Ilsley

4419

3.50 Colombe Claiming Handicap Stakes 3yo+ 46-55 (F4) **[65]**
£2590 £740 £370 **1m2f188y** **Good/Firm** **Inapplicable** Inside

3145 **HEATHYARDS PRIDE 57** [6] R Hollinshead 4-8-12 (49) K Fallon 5/1: 4-10451: Mid-div, eff over 3f out, styd on to lead 1f out, edgd left for press, rdn out: 8 wk abs: eff at 1m/9f, now stays 11f: acts on firm, fast grnd & fibresand: apprec drop in grade: see 1954 & 299. **57**
3538 **ICANNSHIFT 39** [4] S Dow 4-9-2 (53) D Holland 9/2: 6303042: Led, hdd under press 1f out, kept on but no pace wnr: recently unplcd over hdles (rtd 61h, mdn): eff at 7f/10f, now stays 11f: gd run in defeat. ¾ **59**
4145 **MOLLYS SECRET 13** [9] C G Cox 6-8-10 bl (47) P Robinson 9/2: 0030363: Missed break, prog 4f out, no impress fnl 1f: op 7/2: just btr 3727. 3½ **48**
4164 **ENNA 12** [11] Mrs Stef Liddiard 5-8-8 (45) S Drowne 16/1: 0420604: Rear, prog bef 1f out, nrst fin. shd **45**
3367 **COMPTON AVIATOR 46** [12]8-8-12 t (49) L Dettori 7/2 FAV: 4-605065: Held up, prog wide 4f out, no impress dist: 6 wk abs: rider reported mount has breathing prob: see 1986. ¾ **47**
4181 **AMBERSONG 11** [5]6-9-0 (51) J Fortune 5/1: 3301436: Nvr nrr than mid-div: btr 4181 (gd/soft). ½ **48**
3834 **GOLDEN FIELDS 28** [8]4-8-8 bl (45) I Mongan 40/1: 10020-07: Cl-up 9f, sn wknd: jumps fit. 1½ **39**
4243 **MANDINKA 9** [1]4-8-7 (9oh) (35) S Yourston(7) 40/1: 0500-048: Missed break, nvr nrr than mid-div. 6 **29**
4282 **TANCRED IMP 7** [3]3-7-13 (12oh) (40) Lisa Jones 14/1: 0530039: Al in rear: qck reapp: btr 4282. 2 **26**
4299 **MARK YOUR WAY 7** [2]4-9-1 (52) J Quinn 50/1: 600-000: 10th: Cl-up over 1m, wknd: qck reapp. 2½ **30**
705 **EUROLINK ZANTE 196** [7]8-8-13 (50) E Ahern 33/1: 060-0600: 11th: Rear, prog 4f out, fdd fnl 2f. 3½ **23**
2649} **Mulsanne 430** [13]6-8-7 (14oh)(30) A Mackay 100/1:0
3486 **Legion Of Honour 42** [10]5-8-8 (45) J F McDonald(3) 66/1:0
13 Ran Time 2m 16.91 (0.71) Owned: Mr L A Morgan Trained: Upper Longdon

---

4420   **4.20 Prevention & Detection Holdings / Site Sentry Nursery Stakes Handicap 2yo 0-85 (D2)**   **[87]**
£6162 £1896 £948   **6f21y rnd**   **Good/Firm**   **Inapplicable**   Inside

4052 **VIKING SPIRIT** 18 [3] P W Harris 2-9-0 (73) D Holland 9/2: 0221: Led, hdd after 1f, styd cl-up &   86
led again 2f out, edged right from dist, pushed clr ins fnl 1f, val bit more: tchd 13/2: eff at 6f, 7f looks sure to
suit: acts on fast & soft grnd: progressive, shld make a qk follow-up: see 4052.
3476 **CUMMISKEY** 42 [12] J A Osborne 2-9-4 (77) S Drowne 2/1 FAV: 5342: Al cl-up, edged left under   3   80
press ins fnl 1f, no ch with easy wnr: bckd after 6 wk abs: eff at 5.8f/6f: gd run.
3729 **GODSEND** 32 [6] R Hannon 2-9-4 (77) Dane O'Neill 8/1: 2123: Rear, prog 2f out, kept on fnl 1f, no   1¾   75
ch with front 2: op 6/1: showed sltly more in 3729.
4224 **ALEXANDER CAPETOWN** 9 [9] B W Hills 2-8-11 (70) M Hills 6/1: 25644: Rear, prog 2f out, no impress.   nk   67
3411* **TOP FORM** 45 [8]2-9-7 (80) L Dettori 13/2: 0515: Led after, hdd 2f out, sn no extra: abs, btr 3411.   1½   73
3752 **MR KALANDI** 31 [7]2-8-4 (63) A McCarthy 33/1: 3006: Missed break, prog after 2f, wknd dist.   ½   55
3951 **AVERTING** 23 [2]2-8-6 (65) S Carson 50/1: 5207: Nvr nrr than mid-div: showed more in 3722.   ¾   55
2983 **MISS COTSWOLD LADY** 63 [13]2-9-0 (73) K Fallon 25/1: 54208: Nvr nrr than mid-div: 'unsuited by grnd'. 1   60
4214 **PETERS DELITE** 10 [4]2-8-10 (69) T Hamilton(3) 14/1: 0339: Al in rear: btr 4214 & 3606.   nk   55
3686 **EPITOMISE** 33 [10]2-8-6 T (65) J Quinn 100/1: 64060: 10th: Bhd, nvr a factor: first time t-strap.   hd   50
3355 **Mister Aziz** 46 [5]2-8-6 (65) J Tate 50/1:0   4004 **Piddies Pride** 20 [11]2-9-0 (73) T P Queally 16/1:0
3160 **Agilete** 56 [1]2-9-2 (75) A Daly 20/1:0   3728* **Lucky Emerald** 32 [14]2-8-13 (72) K Darley 25/1:0
14 Ran   Time 1m 10.65 (0.05)   Owned: The Masterminds   Trained: Berkhamsted

---

4421   **4.50 Ian Williams Racing Median Auction Maiden Stakes 3yo (F4)**
£3276 £936 £468   **1m22y rnd**   **Good/Firm**   **Inapplicable**   Inside

3953 **RANGOON** 23 [4] Mrs A J Perrett 3-9-0 (77) R Hughes 15/8 FAV: 3-22521: Cl-up, styd on to lead   73
dist despite edging left, rdn out: eff at 1m on fast & & soft: confidence boost.
3985 **FASCINATION STREET** 21 [3] M A Jarvis 3-8-9 (65) P Robinson 5/2: 6-650232: Led, hdd under press   ¾   66
dist, kept on, just held by wnr: eff at 6/7f, ran to form on rtn to 1m: see 3985 & 3610.
4113 **RUBAIYAT** 16 [5] G Wragg 3-9-0 (53) S Drowne 100/30: 0043253: Mid-div, eff when short of room bef   1¾   67
1f out, hung right & no impress fnl 1f: tchd 13/2: eff at 1m, acts prev on 10/12f: acts on fast & fibresand.
4034 **MY MICHELLE** 19 [2] B Palling 3-8-9 (62) K Darley 15/2: 53-00454: Rear, prog 2f out, styd on ins fnl 1f.   2   58
2243 **VELOCITAS** 93 [12]3-9-0 (54) D Holland 20/1: 0-40005: Nvr nrr than mid-div: long abs.   1¾   59
3900 **TARTIRUGA** 25 [1]3-9-0 (45) A Daly 40/1: 0-000056: Mid-div 6f, wknd: see 3900.   4   51
4125 **COUNT BORIS** 14 [7]3-9-0 S Carson 18/1: 0007: Missed break, nvr a factor.   3½   44
3802 **LOOKOUTHEREICOME** 29 [9]3-8-9 (45) J Quinn 100/1: 00008: Missed break, nvr a factor.   9   23
3905 **START OF AUTHORITY** 25 [10]3-9-0 I Mongan 33/1: 059: Keen cl-up 6f, fdd.   ¾   26
4042 **ALMANAC** 18 [8]3-9-0 (49) T Woodley 100/1: 0-0000: 10th: Rear, nvr a factor.   shd   25
10 Ran   Time 1m 38.44 (1.64)   Owned: Mr K Abdulla   Trained: Pulborough

---

4422   **5.20 Bott Founders Maiden Auction Stakes 2yo (F4)**
£3598 £1028 £514   **6f21y rnd**   **Good/Firm**   **Inapplicable**   Inside

4139 **THE PHEASANT FLYER** 13 [4] B J Meehan 2-8-11 J F McDonald(3) 7/4 FAV: 31: Made all, styd on well   86
for press ins fnl 1f despite edging to hold on: bckd: eff at 6f, further will suit: acts on fast & gd grnd: see 4139.
3568 **KING MARJU** 38 [7] P W Chapple Hyam 2-9-0 J Fortune 3/1: 62: Prom, ev ch ins fnl 1f, just held   shd   87
by wnr: imprvd for drop back to 6f: acts on gd grnd: shown enough to find similar: see 3568.
4028 **MISS TRIAL** 19 [10] M A Jarvis 2-8-6 P Robinson 3/1: 63: Cl-up, onepcd ins fnl 1f: eff at 6f on fast.   1¾   74
4271 **THE KEEP** 7 [6] R Hannon 2-8-4 R Smith 18/1: 0004: Mid-div over 4f, no extra bef 1f out: qck reapp.   7   53
4026 **TARTAN SPECIAL** 19 [11]2-8-11 Darren Williams 18/1: 465: Keen mid-div, prog halfway, wknd bef 1f out.½   59
3975 **RED MARTEENEY** 21 [13]2-8-11 Dane O'Neill 50/1: 06: Mid-div, wknd dist.   nk   58
ITALIAN TOUCH 0 [9]2-8-9 I Mongan 66/1: 7: b g Rossini - Attached (Forest Wind) Nvr nrr than   shd   55
mid-div on debut: Apr foal, dam unrcd: sire decent sprint performer at 2: with J A Glover.
4250 **MUDDY** 8 [3]2-8-9 J Quinn 20/1: 58: Nvr nrr than mid-div: showed more in 4250.   hd   54
MONICAS REVENGE 0 [2]2-8-4 T P Queally 66/1: 9: b f Josr Algarhoud - Unimpeachable   shd   48
(Namaqualand) Missed break, nvr a factor on debut: Feb first foal, cost 10,000gns: dam successful at 1m.
BLADE OF GOLD 0 [1]2-8-5 S W Kelly 22./1: 0: 10th: Missed break, nvr a factor on debut.   nk   48
4271 **Summer Charm** 7 [14]2-8-3 Lisa Jones 66/1:0   **Nodina** 0 [12]2-8-13 E Ahern 12/1:0
Vague Star 0 [8]2-8-13 N Day 40/1:0   **Rooks Bridge** 0 [5]2-8-8 A Daly 100/1:0
14 Ran   Time 1m 11.12 (0.52)   Owned: The Second Pheasant Inn Partnership   Trained: Upper Lambourn

---

4423   **5.50 Crown Farm Apprentice Handicap Stakes 3yo+ 46-55 (F4)**   **[61]**
£3170 £906 £453   **2m39y**   **Good/Firm**   **Inapplicable**   Inside

4145 **LAZZAZ** 13 [2] P W Hiatt 6-8-12 (1oh) (45) P Gallagher(3) 14/1: 3426551: Made all, rdn out ins fnl   54
1f to hold on: eff at 9/13f, apprec step up to 2m: acts on firm, gd/soft & fibresand: likes W'hampton.
3611 **ACADEMY** 37 [12] Andrew Turnell 9-9-7 (55) N Chalmers 20/1: 240-2002: Rear, prog 3f out, ev ch   ½   61
ins fnl 1f, just held by wnr: bckd to form after disapp on last 2 starts, see 1870.
4364 **BANNINGHAM BLAZE** 3 [4] A W Carroll 4-9-0 (48) M Halford(5) 10/1: 3132223: Held up, prog 2f out,   ½   53
kept on ins fnl 1f, not btn far: qck reapp: eff at 12/14f, now stays 2m: just btr 4364 & 3983.
4308 **OOPS** 6 [11] J F Coupland 5-8-12 (1oh) (45) Dean Williams(5) 7/2: 0162324: Rear, prog after   2   49
halfway, staying on when short of room dist, switched & sn no impress: qck reapp: just btr 4308 & 3834.
4299 **BOJANGLES** 7 [3]5-9-5 (53) M Savage 10/1: 4534125: Mid-div, eff bef 2f out, onepcd dist: lngr trip.   nk   55
4255 **VANBRUGH** 8 [13]4-8-12 (11oh)vis t (35) W Hogg(5) 66/1: 0000006: Al cl-up, edged left & no extra dist.   ½   47$
3493 **GALANDORA** 42 [6]4-9-2 (50) T Block(5) 16/1: 1203307: Nvr nrr than mid-div: 6 wk abs: btr 3147 & 3049.   ½   50

WARWICK   MONDAY 06.09.04   Lefthand, Sharp, Turning Track

4302* **SALUT SAINT CLOUD** 7 [8]3-8-12 (6ex)p (59) A Quinn 13/8 FAV: 3331418: Rear, prog halfway, no   ¾   58
impress fnl 2f: well bckd on qck reapp: showed more in 4302 (gd/soft).
3916 **PRAIRIE LAW** 24 [9]4-8-12 (1oh) (45) A Mullen(3) 8/1: 1006439: Mid-div over 12f, sn no impress.   4   41
3742 **MY TRUE LOVE** 31 [7]5-9-7 (55) C J Davies(5) 50/1: 5040: 10th: Mid-div, grad wknd fnl 3f.   nk   49
4276 **COURT ONE** 7 [10]6-8-12 (46) B Swarbrick 14/1: 0110000: 11th: Rear, prog 7f out, wknd 3f out.   hd   39
4203 **DINGLEY LASS** 10 [5]4-8-12 (1oh) (45) Derek Nolan(3) 50/1: 00-600: 12th: Cl-up 13f, wknd.   hd   38
4056 **BLACK SWAN** 18 [1]4-8-12 (11oh) (35) Steven Harrison(5) 100/1: 0/50-0500: 13th: Cl-up 13f, fdd.   6   33
4056 **HEART SPRINGS** 18 [15]4-8-12 (1oh) (45) C Haddon(3) 50/1: 0004520: 14th: V slow away, prog 6f out,   1   32
fdd bef 3f out: btr 4056 (soft).
14 Ran   Time 3m 34.90(7.4)   Owned: Mr Phil Kelly   Trained: Banbury

BADEN BADEN   TUESDAY 31.08.04   Lefthand, Sharpish, Turning Track

Official Going Soft

4424	3.25 Gr 2 Darley Oettingen Rennen 3yo+ ()		
	£35211 £14085 £7042 **1m rnd** **Soft**		

3664* **PEPPERSTORM** 30 U Ostmann 3-8-7 A Boschert 21/10: 11: br c Big Shuffle - Pasca (Lagunas) Rear,   115
smooth hdwy to lead dist, rdn & styd on strongly: suited by 1m on good & soft ground: v smart colt: see 3664 (Gr 3).
1 Aug'04 Colo 8gd 112- :
3793 **CHECKIT** 24 M R Channon 4-9-0 (112) A Culhane 32/10: 34034032: Handy & ev ch over 1f out, drvn &   2   111
not pace of wnr: see 1349.
3166 **ASSIUN** 51 P Schiergen 3-8-7 A Suborics 6/5 FAV: 1323: Led/dsptd lead till dist, no extra: 2½   106
handles soft ground tho' btr 3166 (gd).
7 Ran   Time 1m 41.77 ()   Owned: Gestut Hony-Hof   Trained: Germany

BADEN BADEN   WEDNESDAY 01.09.04   Lefthand, Sharpish, Turning Track

Official Going Soft

4425	1.35 Listed Kaba Badener Steher Cup 3yo+ ()		
	£13380 £5282 £2465 **1m6f** **Soft**		

    SOTERIO W Baltromei 4-9-3 I Ferguson : 1: b c Lavirco - So Rarely (Arctic Tern) Narrowly   102
prevailed to land this Listed contest.
    KASUS P Vovcenko 6-8-13 A Starke : 2: br g Second Set - Kettwig (Acatenango) Just denied at   hd   97
the end of this 14f trip.
4504} **NO REFUGE** 338 Sir Mark Prescott 4-9-0 (94) T Hellier : 31121323: ch c Hernando - Shamarra   2   96
(Zayyani) Dictated pace till over 1f out, not pace of front pair: reapp: most prog '03, landing 4 h'caps, incl a val
h'cap at Goodwood: suited by 12/13f, stayed 14f today: acts on fast, soft & both AW's: handles any trk: eff in
blnks: tough & useful. 2 Sep'03 Hami 13.0gd 100-94 B: 1 Jul'03 Good 12gd 96-86 C: 2 Jul'03 Ripo 12.3g/f 87-82 D:
1 Jul'03 Hami 12.1gd 86-77 E: 1 Jun'03 Ling 12ap 89-74 E: 1 Jun'03 Wolv 12af 77-61 E:
4 Ran   Time 3m 10.38 ()   Owned: Frau J Kumpernas   Trained: Germany

4426	3.26 Gr 2 Fahrhof Goldene Peitsche 3yo+ ()		
	£45775 £18310 £9155 **6f rnd** **Soft**		

    RAFFELBERGER M Hofer 3-8-13 A Suborics 162/10: 1: b g Auenadler - Royal Cat (Royal Academy)   116
Mid-div, pshd along & hdwy to chall over 1f out, led ins last, rdn out: List wnr at Maisons Laffitte earlier this
year: eff at 5/7f on gd & hvy ground: handles a sharp & gall trk: smart gelding.
3839 **KEY TO PLEASURE** 24 M Hofer 4-9-2 J P Carvalho 101/10: 22: Handy, styd on for press, not pace   ½   114
of wnr ins last.
3009* **LUCKY STRIKE** A Trybuhl 6-9-2 A de Vries 23/10 FAV: 40-21115313: Led, rdn & hdd ins last, wknd.   ¾   113
3838 **GOLDEN NUN** 24 4-8-12 bl (101) R Winston 96/10: 231310575: Mid-div, styd on onepace for press.   2½   104
4060 **FAYR JAG** 13 5-9-2 (113) A Culhane 3/1: 10U-01009: Pshd along rear, nvr on terms: needs faster.   4½   99
16 Ran   Time 1m 09.47 ()   Owned: Stall Jenny   Trained: Germany

BADEN BADEN   FRIDAY 03.09.04   Lefthand, Sharpish, Turning Track

Official Going Good

4427	3.27 Gr 2 Maurice Lacroix Trophy 2yo ()		
	£37324 £14085 £7746 **6f rnd** **Good**		

    DARING LOVE U Ostmann 2-8-9 A Boschert 11/10 FAV: 111: b f Big Shuffle - Daring Action   101
(Arazi) Held up, strong run for press fnl 1f to lead nr line, all out: unbeaten German trained filly whose previous
2 wins included a Listed contest at Cologne: eff at 6/7f, return to latter should suit: acts on good ground: useful.
    BEIRUT P Schiergen 2-8-7 A Starke 63/10: 2: br f Turtle Island - Bajonette (Lomond) Trkd   nk   97
ldrs, rdn to lead narrowly over 1f out, hdd close home: bhd this wnr prev.
4159 **TOURNEDOS** 12 M R Channon 2-9-2 T E Durcan 6/4: 1220173: Prom & chall over 1f out, no extra   ¾   105
close home: eff at 5/6f: see 3509 (Gr 3, 5f).
8 Ran   Time 1m 11.16 ()   Owned: Gestut Auenquelle   Trained: Germany

BADEN BADEN   SUNDAY 05.09.04   Lefthand, Sharpish, Turning Track

Official Going Soft

4428   3.40 Gr 1 Grosser Preis Von Baden 3yo+   ()
£352113 £98592 £52817   1m4f   **Soft**

3442 **WARRSAN 43** C E Brittain 6-9-6 (120) K McEvoy 78/10: 33-531291: Mid-div, hdwy wide 4f out & rdn   **122**
to lead ins last, edged left, held on gamely: eff at 10/14f, high class performer at 12f: acts on firm & soft ground,
any trk: v tough & genuine, superbly handled by trainer: see 2916, 2219.

EGERTON 35 P Rau 3-8-9 A Helfenbein 39/1: 4-520022: b c Groom Dancer - Enrica (Niniski)   nk   **119**
Mid-div, hdwy 2f out & drvn/styd on well ins last, just held: eff at
10/12f on gd & soft ground: high class effort from this big priced contender.

3010* **SHIROCCO 63** A Schutz 3-8-9 A Suborics 42/10: -21313: Mid-div, hdwy to lead over 1f out, hdd &   ¾   **118**
just held when slightly hmpd ins last: 2 mth abs: German Derby wnr, not btn far & reportedly could reoppose this wnr
in the Arc next month: see 3010.

3442 **GAMUT 43** 5-9-6 (117) K Fallon 47/10: 123-21145: Trkd ldr, briefly led over 2f out, no extra from   4   **116**
dist: 6 wk abs: btr 3442, 3012.

3958* **MUBTAKER 22** 7-9-6 (130) R Hills 9/10 FAV: 21/1112-17: Keen & led after 1f, briefly hdd over 2f   2   **114**
out, hdd over 1f out & fdd: connections reportedly felt colt disadvantaged by racing on slower ground towards the
inside of the track: btr 3958 (fast).

8 Ran   Time 2m 32.79()   Owned: Saeed Manana   Trained: Newmarket

CRAON   SATURDAY 04.09.04

Official Going Good/Soft

4429   2.20 Listed Darley Criterium de l'Ouest 2yo   ()
£15845 £6338 £4754   1m55y rnd   **Good/Soft**

4176 **HYPNOTIC 9** Sir Mark Prescott 2-9-2 (96) J B Eyquen 7/1: 41131: Mid-div outer, rdn & hdwy to   **102**
lead dist, drvn out: eff at 7f, imprvd over this longer 8.3f trip: acts on polytrk & gd/sft ground: useful &
progressive colt, superbly placed by trainer: see 4176, 3820.

RIVERBRIDE N Clement 2-8-13 S Pasquier : 2: br f Kingmambo - Anklet (Wild Again) Half length   ½   **97**
adrift in 2nd to this British raider.

LOUVAIN R Gibson 2-8-13 T Jarnet : 3: b f Sinndar - Flanders (Common Grounds) Beaten less   nk   **96**
than a length in 3rd.

11 Ran   Time 1m 36.50()   Owned: Chevely Park Stud   Trained: Newmarket

CAPANNELLE   SUNDAY 05.09.04   Righthand, Flat, Galloping Track

Official Going Good

4430   3.05 Listed Premio Repubbliche Marinare Tattersalls 2yo Fillies   ()
£24648 £10845 £5915   7f110y   **Good**

KYKUIT L Brogi 2-8-9 M Pasquale : 1: b f Green Desert - Cromac (Machiavellian) Decisive 2L   **103**
winner of this Listed contest.

3851* **VARENKA 25** Sir Mark Prescott 2-8-9 S Sanders : 512: Up in grade & a useful effort finishing 2L   2   **98**
2nd with the rest well covered: acts on gd & gd/sft: see 3851.

VEGAS QUEEN S Santella 2-8-9 A Corniani : 3: br f Celtic Swing - Dwingeloo (Dancing   3   **92**
Dissident) No impress on front pair in closing stages.

8 Ran   Time 1m 33.90()   Owned: Allevamento La Nuova Sbarra   Trained: Italy

CURRAGH   SUNDAY 05.09.04   Righthand, Galloping Track

Official Going Good/Firm

4431   2.45 Gr 3 Round Tower Stakes 2yo   ()
£34894 £10238 £4878   6f str   **Good/Firm**

CHEROKEE A P O'Brien 2-8-11 J P Spencer 5/2: 1: b f Storm Cat - Totemic (Vanlandingham)   **109+**
Rear, swtchd & rdn/strong run fnl 1f to lead line: well fancied to make this winning debut in Gr company: half sister
to a useful Gr 2 3yo US wnr: dam a US Gr 3 wnr: eff at 6f, 7f shld suit: acts on fast grnd & a gall trk: goes well
fresh: v useful start, improve & win more Gr races.

3494 **LOCK AND KEY 43** E Lynam 2-8-11 Catherine Gannon 10/1: 351122: Trkd ldrs, swtchd & hdwy to lead   shd   **108**
over 1f out, hdd line: tough & useful: see 3494 (7f).

4153 **INDESATCHEL 15** D Wachman 2-9-0 M J Kinane 2/1 FAV: 41323: Held up, short of room 2f out, kept   1½   **106**
on ins last, prob shade closer with a clr run: prob ran to form of 4153, 3319.

11 Ran   Time 1m 12.10 ()   Owned: Mrs John Magnier   Trained: Ballydoyle

CURRAGH   SUNDAY 05.09.04   Righthand, Galloping Track

4432
4.20 Gr 1 Moyglare Stud Stakes 2yo Fillies   ()
£112962 £38592 £18492   **7f rnd**   **Good/Firm**

3843 **CHELSEA ROSE 28** C Collins 2-8-11 P Shanahan 9/1: 131: ch f Desert King - Cinnamon Rose   109
(Trempolino) Trkd ldrs, rdn to lead over 2f out, held on most gamely ins last, drvn out: earlier this term landed a
Leopardstown mdn: eff at 7f, stay further: acts on fast ground & likes a gall trk: smart, genuine & improving.
2328 **PICTAVIA 90** J S Bolger 2-8-11 K J Manning 8/1: 7122: Mid-div, rdn & outpcd 2f out, styd on   ¾ 107
well for press ins last, not able to reach wnr: 3 mth abs: must win a Gr race at 1m sn: see 2328.
SAOIRE 21 Ms F M Crowley 2-8-11 P J Smullen 6/1: 213: ch f Pivotal - Polish Descent (Danehill)   ¾ 105
Held up, rdn & styd on strongly ins last, not able to chall: Leopardstown mdn wnr last month: eff at 7f, shld apprec
1m on this evidence: acts on fast & gd grnd: likes a stiff/gall trk: lightly rcd, useful & prog filly.
4264 **UMNIYA 7** M R Channon 2-8-11 BL (91) A Culhane 14/1: 13345664: Rear, drvn & styd on fnl 1f, not   hd 104
pace to chall: prob career best in 1st time blnks, vis omitted: stays a gall 7f well: see 2553, 2328.
BELLE ARTISTE 17 2-8-11 BL J A Heffernan 33/1: 5: b f Namid - Beltisaal (Belmez) Trkd ldrs,   shd 103
drvn to chall dist, no extra well ins last: 1st time blnks: earlier won a Tipperary auct mdn: winning form at 5f,
stays a gall 7f: acts on fast & gd ground, sharp or gall trk.
3781 **SLIP DANCE 29** 2-8-11 J F Egan 16/1: 3141626: Held up, hdwy over 2f out, no extra from dist.   ¾ 101
3843* **SILK AND SCARLET 28** 2-8-11 J P Spencer 11/8 FAV: 2117: Held up, efft wide but no prog bef dist.   shd 100
3003* **JEWEL IN THE SAND 61** 2-8-11 M J Kinane 5/2: 1110: 11th: Held up, efft 2f out, sn btn: 'nvr   2½ 95
trav': longer trip but much btr 3003.
12 Ran Time 1m 24.20 () Owned: Mrs A J Donnelly Trained: The Curragh

4433
5.25 Gr 3 Flying Five 3yo+   ()
£0 £0 £0   **5f str**   **Good/Firm**

3551+ **RINGMOOR DOWN 38** D W P Arbuthnot 5-9-1 (106) M J Kinane 5/2: 61342411: Held up, hdwy over 1f   111
out, chall ins last & just prevailed, all out: op 3/1: eff at 5/6f on firm & gd/sft.
3170 **BENBAUN 56** M J Wallace 3-9-0 bl (93) D Corby 11/2: 20-1012132: Trkd ldrs, rdn to lead over 2f   hd 110
out, strongly pressed ins last, hdd nr line: op 9/2: v tough & genuine: see 3170, 2390.
2818* **OSTERHASE 70** J E Mulhern 5-9-1 bl (94) F M Berry 13/8 FAV: -0611143: Led, hdd over 1f out,   nk 109
rallied well ins last: 4th in a Gr 3 since 2818.
8 Ran Time () Owned: Prof C D Green Trained: Upper Lambourn

LONGCHAMP   SUNDAY 05.09.04   Righthand, Stiff, Galloping Track

Official Going Good/Soft

4434
2.50 Gr 1 Prix du Moulin de Longchamp 3yo+   ()
£120718 £48296 £24147   **1m rnd**   **Good/Soft**

4309* **GREY LILAS 12** A Fabre 3-8-8 E Legrix 5/1: 62-112311: Trkd ldr, led over 2f out, rdn & held on   118
well ins last: eff at 1m/1f on fast & v soft: likes to race with/force the pace: tough, high class & improving.
3168 **DIAMOND GREEN FR 56** A Fabre 3-8-12 T Gillet 87/10: 111-32222: Rear, styd on from over 1f out,   1 119
not able to chall: 8 wk abs: tough & high-class: see 3168, 2469 & 1855.
3533 **ANTONIUS PIUS 39** A P O'Brien 3-8-12 J P Murtagh 194/10: 10-453053: Mid-div, hdwy to chall ins   nse 119
last, kept on, not pace to chall: back to high-class best: see 2469.
1432 **DENEBOLA** P Bary 3-8-8 C P Lemaire 349/10: 131-3274: Handy, efft to chse wnr over 1f out, no extra.   nk 114
4017* **WHIPPER 21** 3-8-12 C Soumillon 23/10 FAV: 41-15215: Rear, kept on late, no dngr: btr 4017.   ¾ 117
991* **PAOLINI** 7-9-2 E Pedroza 26/1: 302-1006: Held up, hdwy/hmpd halfway, kept on from over 1f out.   snk 115
3886 **LUCKY STORY 24** 3-8-12 (118) D Holland 96/10: 41111-27: Led till over 2f out, sn outpcd, kept on   nk 115
late, no dngr: not disgraced in top company: see 3886.
3533 **LE VIE DEI COLORI 39** 4-9-2 L Dettori 54/10: 21-11438: Trkd ldrs, keen early, kept on onepace: btr 3533. nse 114
11 Ran Time 1m 37.50 () Owned: Gestut Ammerland Trained: France

4435
4.10 Gr 3 Prix du Petit Couvert 3yo+   ()
£25704 £10282 £7711   **5f str**   **Good/Soft**

3622* **PIVOTAL POINT 36** P J Makin 4-8-12 (91) L Dettori 52/10: 52-001211: Handy, led over 1f out, drvn   115
out: eff at 5/6f on firm & gd grnd: v smart & progressive: keep on side: see 3622 (val h'cap).
4060 **THE TATLING 17** J M Bradley 7-9-4 (115) R L Moore 13/10 FAV: 23410322: Mid-div, hdwy to chse ldr   1 117
dist, kept on, al held: smart: see 4060, 3551.
2638* **CHINEUR 76** M Delzangles 3-8-11 E Legrix 79/10: 21-34613: Rear, kept on from over 1f out, no   2 105
threat to front pair: abs: btr 2638 (List).
9 Ran Time 56.50() Owned: R A Bernard Trained: Ogbourne Maisey

CATTERICK TUESDAY 07.09.04 Lefthand, Undulating, Very Tight Track

Official Going Good/Firm ALL TIMES SLOW

4436 **2.30 Beckside Maiden Auction Stakes 2yo (E4)**
£2947 £842 £421 **6f rnd** **Good/Firm** **Inapplicable** Inside

4178 **CORNICHE DANCER 12** [2] M R Channon 2-8-8 (75) A Culhane 5/1: 00021: Held up in tch, trkg ldrs trav well when short of room 2f out, rdn to lead ins last, all out: op 3/1: confirmed improvement of latest: eff at 6f on polytrack & fast grnd, sharp/turning trks: see 4178, 3536. **72**
4114 **RINGAROOMA 16** [3] M H Tompkins 2-8-4 (69) K Darley 6/4 FAV: 5042: Trkd ldrs, briefly short of room over 2f out, drvn to chall well ins last, just held: well bckd, op 2/1: eff at 6/7f on fast & gd grnd: see 4114. *shd* **68**
4242 **STREET BALLAD 10** [6] Mrs J R Ramsden 2-8-8 A Beech(3) 6/1: 403: Held up, rdn & kept on ins last, not pace of front pair: handles fast & gd grnd, stays a sharp 6f: shld apprec h'cap company: see 3682. *2* **66**
2110 **BEVERLEY BEAU 99** [1] Mrs L Stubbs 2-8-7 (60) Kristin Stubbs(7) 25/1: 5544: Handy & led over 2f out till hdd ins last & no extra: 3 mth abs: handles firm & fast grnd: see 2110 (clmr). *hd* **64**
4006 **LADY VEE 21** [7]2-8-2 D Mernagh 12/1: 05: Rdn chasing ldrs, ch over 1f out, sn no extra: bckd, see 4006. *1* **56**

HANNAHS DREAM 0 [4]2-8-6 R Ffrench 7/1: 6: b f King's Best - Meritxell (Thatching) Broke well but sn outpcd & drpd rear, kept on late for press, no threat: 14,000gns Apr foal, dam a French mid-dist wnr: looks sure to apprec 7f+ will know more next time, shld improve. *¾* **58+**
3736 **TURN ON THE STYLE 33** [8]2-8-7 S Chin 12/1: 07: ch g Pivotal - Elegant Rose (Noalto) Led till over 2f out, no extra under press: 5,000gns 2yo purchase, May foal: dam 6f scorer. *shd* **59**
2682 **FLAXBY 75** [10]2-8-9 R Mullen 33/1: 08: b g Mister Baileys - Harryana (Efisio) Dwelt, sn handy wide, rdn & btn 2f out, 11 wk abs: 9,000gns Apr first foal, dam a dual 5f 2yo scorer. *10* **34**
4244 **BLADES BOY 10** [9]2-8-7 N Callan 14/1: 09: Dwelt, prom till hmpd over 1f out, sn bhd, gelded. *3* **23**
KNOT IN WOOD 0 [5]2-8-9 G Parkin 33/1: 0: 10th: V slow away & t.o. throughout. *1¼* **21**
10 Ran Time 1m 14.15 (3.85) Owned: Mrs A M Jones Trained: West Ilsley

4437 **3.00 'sponsor A Race At Catterick' Nursery Handicap Stakes 2yo 0-75 (E3)** **[80]**
£3533 £1087 £544 **5f rnd** **Good/Firm** **Inapplicable** Inside

3606 **MELANDRE 88** [7] M Brittain 2-8-12 (64) T Williams 12/1: 60451: Sn cl-up & led 2f out, drvn out: 12 wk abs, first win on h'cap bow: imprvd over this sharp 5f on fast grnd with forcing tactics: temperament problems prev but appeared much calmer today & could progress: see 2360, 2056. **74**
4344 **LORD JOHN 5** [1] M W Easterby 2-8-1 BL (53) Dale Gibson 10/1: 0400402: Sn pushed along chasing ldrs, short of room halfway, switched & styd on well for press cl-home, not reach wnr: would have gone v close with a clr passage: imprvd in first time blnks: eff at 5/6f on fast grnd: see 3212. *½* **60**
4303* **OCEANICO DOT COM 7** [2] A Berry 2-9-7 (6ex) (73) F Norton 3/1 FAV: 00213: Sn handy, drvn & kept on, not pace to chall: hvly bckd under a 6lb pen on h'cap bow: handles fast & gd grnd: just btr 4303. *1¼* **76**
4198 **ROSIELLA 11** [10] M Blanshard 2-9-7 (73) N Callan 7/1: 05134: Pushed along towards rear, styd on for press, not able to chall: gd run from an awkward draw: found this sharp 5f against her on h'cap bow. *½* **74**
3987 **RANCHO CUCAMONGA 22** [8]2-9-2 (68) K Darley 6/1: 0010055: Mid-div & drvn, not able to chall. *½* **67**
4258 **APOLOGIES 9** [9]2-9-5 bl (71) G Gibbons 7/1: 1406036: Dwelt & towards rear, hdwy for press halfway when short of room, nvr a pace to chall: btr 4258 (soft). *½* **68**
4258 **OUR LOUIS 9** [3]2-8-2 (54) R Ffrench 25/1: 4150007: Gd speed to lead 3f, wknd qckly: needs sells. *1½* **46**
3769 **CADOGEN SQUARE 31** [4]2-7-12 (1oh) (49) P M Quinn 16/1: 00048: Sn handy, btn 2f out: see 3769. *2½* **34**
3896 **STARLIGHT RIVER 26** [6]2-8-12 (64) S Chin 16/1: 0039: Handy when hmpd & lost pl halfway, sn btn. *2½* **40**
3988 **KERNY 22** [11]2-7-13 (51) P Fessey 16/1: 0600: 10th: Mid-div & sn outpcd, nvr a factor: h'cap bow. *shd* **27**
4049 **NEXT TIME 19** [5]2-8-3 (55) R Mullen 20/1: 5004400: 11th: Mid-div & sn struggling, nvr land blow. *1¼* **27**
3825 **EVANESCE 29** [13]2-9-5 (71) A Culhane 12/1: 1200400: 12th: Al rear from poor high draw: btr 3488. *1¼* **39**
3901 **CARMANIA 26** [14]2-8-1 (53) D Mernagh 33/1: 0500: 13th: Sn struggling from poor high draw, h'cap bow. *nk* **20**
4172 **OCHIL HILLS DANCER 12** [12]2-8-9 t (61) D Fentiman(7) 20/1: 0504560: 14th: Sn outpcd, poor high draw. *hd* **27**
14 Ran Time 1m 0.24 (2.94) Owned: Mr Mel Brittain Trained: Warthill

4438 **3.30 Catterickbridge Co Uk Handicap Stakes 3yo+ 56-70 (E3)** **[70]**
£5511 £1696 £848 **7f rnd** **Good/Firm** **Inapplicable** Inside

4241 **JUBILEE STREET 10** [14] Mrs A Duffield 5-9-2 (58) A Beech(3) 11/2 JT FAV: 1006121: Mid-div, strong run for press fnl 1f to lead cl-home, going away: stays 9f, suited by 7f: acts on fast & gd/soft, any trk, likes Catterick: remains on an upward curve at present: see 4241 & 3670. **64**
4339 **LEGAL SET 5** [9] Miss A Stokell 8-9-2 t (58) L Fletcher(3) 16/1: 2045002: Sn handy wide, rdn to lead ins last, hdd nr line & no extra: qck reapp: veteran, in gd heart at present: see 2713 (6f). *½* **62**
4044 **MISSION AFFIRMED 19** [11] T P Tate 3-9-0 (60) R Winston 9/1: 1040523: Trkd ldrs halfway, styd on for press, not pace of wnr: eff at 7f, return to 1m shld suit: acts on fast grnd & fibresand: see 4044 & 1198 (AW). *½* **63**
4272 **NORTHERN GAMES 8** [6] K A Ryan 5-9-3 bl (59) G Parkin 11/2 JT FAV: 4-001424: Slow away, rear, briefly short of room dist, switched & strong run cl-home, nrst fin: gd late hdwy, likes this trk: see 4272. *¾* **60**
4229 **MANDARIN SPIRIT 10** [1]4-9-8 bl (64) R Mullen 10/1: 00-05505: Cl-up & led over 1f out, rdn & hdd ins last, no extra: imprvd eff from fav'ble low draw with blnks reapplied: see 2045. *nk* **64**
4342 **COTTINGHAM 5** [2]3-9-0 (60) S Chin 16/1: 6602066: Chsd ldrs, not pace to chall, qck reapp: see 3835. *nk* **57**
3694 **ARAGONS BOY 34** [8]4-9-11 (67) D Allan 11/1: 0010407: Sn pushed along mid-div, no impress dist: prev with H Candy & best form to date when dominating: see 2641. *2½* **61**
2295 **WASHBROOK 91** [10]3-8-12 (58) A Nicholls 18/1: 640-0038: Mid-div, no prog fnl 2f: abs: btr 2295. *¾* **51**
4175* **SAROS 12** [17]3-9-4 (64) F Lynch 9/1: 0203019: Dwelt & towards rear, eff wide, no prog dist. *½* **56**
4175 **DARK DAY BLUES 12** [16]3-9-2 (62) Darren Williams 25/1: 1065500: 10th: Towards rear, mod hdwy. *¾* **53**
4130* **HEADLAND 15** [7]6-9-2 bl e (58) A Culhane 7/1: 2215510: 11th: Dwelt & towards rear, nvr land a blow. *1¼* **46**
2985 **RENE BARBIER 64** [4]3-9-2 (62) F Norton 16/1: 0415600: 12th: Chsd ldrs early, sn lost place, some mod late hdwy when short of room dist: 2 mth abs: up in trip & visor omitted: see 2237 (5f mdn). *½* **49**
2655 **WEET WATCHERS 77** [3]4-9-6 (62) N Callan 16/1: 43051P0: 13th: Led/dsptd lead till over 1f out, wknd. *nk* **48**
3679 **ORPENBERRY 34** [18]3-8-11 (57) P M Quinn 66/1: 100-0000: 14th: Sn struggling rear: see 3679, 2155. *¾* **42**
4321 **NAMED AT DINNER 6** [12]3-9-2 (62) J Carroll 100/1: 24-00000: 15th: Al rear, qck reapp. *nk* **46**
2806 **KISS THE RAIN 71** [5]4-9-1 (57) G Gibbons 66/1: 0334-600: 16th: Led till over 4f out, sn btn, abs: see 3853 **35**

CATTERICK TUESDAY 07.09.04 Lefthand, Undulating, Very Tight Track

3392 **CROSS ASH 46** [15]4-9-4 (60) K Darley 28/1: 100-0000: 17th: Mid-div, struggling halfway, 6 wk abs. 2½ 33
3541 **MAJHOOL 40** [13]5-9-1 (57) R Ffrench 20/1: 0-045100: 18th: Chsd ldrs, no ch fnl 2f, abs: new yard. 2½ 25
18 Ran Time 1m 26.63 (3.63) Owned: Mr D W Holdsworth & Mr J A McMahon Trained: Leyburn

4439	4.00 Goracing Co Uk Handicap Stakes 3yo 56-70 (E3)			[71]
	£5265 £1620 £810 1m5f175y Good/Firm Inapplicable Inside			

3856* **INCHPAST 27** [1] M H Tompkins 3-9-10 bl (67) N Callan 3/1: 0041211: Trkd ldrs & al trav well, rdn 78
to lead 2f out, sn in command, rdn out: well bckd, op 7/2: eff at 11.5f/12f, imprvd for step up to 14f & 2m may
suit: acts on fast & gd/soft grnd: tough & progressive: see 3856, 3618.
4259 **CAN CAN FLYER 9** [6] M Johnston 3-9-6 (63) R Ffrench 10/11 FAV: 006-122: Cl-up & led over 2f out, 2 69
hdd 2f out & not pace of wnr, kept on for press: hvly bckd & styd this longer 14f trip: acts on fast & soft grnd.
3669 **PRAIRIE SUN 35** [5] Mrs A Duffield 3-8-10 (5oh) (48) A Beech(3) 16/1: 0006063: Trkd ldrs, rdn to 1¼ 57
chall over 2f out, sn outpcd by wnr: recent jumps runner (rnr-up, rtd 99h, juv nov, 2m, gd/soft)): stays 14f.
4342 **MUNAAWESH 5** [4] D W Chapman 3-8-13 bl (56) A Culhane 7/1: 2042204: Held up in tch, eff fnl 2f, no 1½ 58
extra from dist: qck reapp: see 3998 & 3772.
3703 **SIEGFRIEDS NIGHT 34** [7]3-9-8 (65) L Vickers 9/1: 5530025: Rdn twds rear 3f out, no impress: jumps fit. 6 58
4044 **IRON TEMPTRESS 19** [8]3-8-13 (56) D Allan 50/1: 2000-006: Drvn rear 4f out, nvr land blow: see 3571. 1½ 47
4276 **BOLD BLADE 8** [3]3-9-3 (60) L Fletcher(3) 28/1: 0024007: Led till over 2f out, sn btn: see 3881, 3666. ½ 50
3192 **JALOUSIE DREAM 55** [2]3-8-10 (8oh) (45) P M Quinn 100/1: 05308: Rear, drvn & outpcd fnl 4f, abs. 6 34
8 Ran Time 3m 02.35 (6.95) Owned: Marcoe Racing Welwyn Trained: Newmarket

4440	4.30 'entertain In Style At Catterick' Median Auction Maiden Stakes 3-4yo (F4)		
	£2919 £834 £417 7f rnd Good/Firm Inapplicable Inside		

4228 **RIVER OF BABYLON 10** [7] M L W Bell 3-8-9 (64) R Mullen 9/4: 50-2651: In tch, hdwy to lead over 70
1f out, rdn clr ins last, decisively: well bckd: poss stays a stiff 1m, suited by return to 7f on fast & gd grnd.
3195 **REVENIR 55** [1] E F Vaughan 3-9-0 (74) N Callan 4/7 FAV: 0222: Handy & led over 1f out, sn hdd & 4 66
outpcd by wnr ins last: rest well covered: hvly bckd at odds-on: eff at 7f, return to 1m could suit: handles
fast, gd & polytrack: see 3195 & 2886.
1982 **NEW YORK 105** [3] W J Haggas 3-8-9 t (65) A Culhane 11/1: 324-003: b f Danzero - Council Rock 3½ 54
(General Assembly) Held up, kept on for press fnl 2f, no threat to front pair: 3 mth abs: auct mdn rnr-up '03, AW
mdn plcd (rtd 72a): eff at 7f, tried 1m, may suit: handles fast grnd & polytrack, sharp/turning trks: worn a
t-strap last twice. 2 Nov'03 Muss 7.1g/f 69- E:
3808 **ROYAL AWAKENING 30** [4] R E Barr 3-9-0 (49) M Lawson(5) 33/1: 0-004504: Rear, only mod prog. 1¼ 56
2523 **GOVERNMENT 82** [8]3-9-0 A Beech(3) 33/1: 045: Handy & led after 2f till over 1f out, wknd qckly, 3 50
abs, drpd in trip: prev with J H M Gosden: see 2523.
3679 **ACCA LARENTIA 34** [5]3-8-9 (47) V Halliday 66/1: 2-003006: In tch, outpcd fnl 2f: btr 2693 (soft). 1 43
4091 **PLATTOCRAT 18** [2]4-9-4 (30) S Chin 150/1: 50007: Cl-up, struggling from halfway, needs sellers. 3 42
3805 **DISTINCTLYTHEBEST 30** [6]4-9-4 R Winston 200/1: 0-008: Dsptd lead early, struggling halfway: gelded. 9 26
8 Ran Time 1m 26.97 (3.97) Owned: Mr CWright & The Hon Mrs JMCorbett Trained: Newmarket

4441	5.00 'special Package Deal' Maiden Stakes 3yo (D3)		
	£3455 £1063 £532 1m3f214y Good/Firm Inapplicable Inside		

1365 **EXCLUSIVE DANIELLE 136** [6] B W Hills 3-8-9 A Culhane 8/1: 3-51: Made all, pressed from 2f out, 77
rdn & held on well ins last: op 6/1: 5 mth abs: plcd sole '03 start (fills mdn, promise, rtd 82+): imprvd for
this step up to a sharp 12f, may get further: acts on fast & gd, any trk: goes well fresh: genuine.
3261 **MAGNETIC POLE 52** [3] Sir Michael Stoute 3-9-0 (83) R Winston 4/9 FAV: 3-2302: Trkd wnr, rdn to ½ 80
chall 2f out, drvn & no extra well ins last: hvly bckd at odds-on, 7 wk abs: stays a sharp 12f: see 1783 & 1398.
3783 **GANYMEDE 31** [1] M L W Bell 3-9-0 (75) R Mullen 3/1: 3222043: Trkd ldrs, drvn & kept on fnl 2f, 1 79
al held: well clr of rem: bckd tho' op 5/2: stays a sharp 12f: see 2843, 2222 & 1019.
2515 **CHESTALL 82** [4] R Hollinshead 3-9-0 R Kennemore(7) 50/1: 44: Chsd ldrs, hung right on bend after 16 58
4f, lost tch fnl 3f, t.o.: gelded, abs: btr 2515.
4281 **SWEET AT HEART 8** [5]3-8-9 N Callan 80/1: 005: Held up in tch, drvn/hmpd 3f out, sn lost tch. 12 36
2081 **TAILI 101** [2]3-8-9 (30) J McAuley 150/1: 000-06: Slow away, sn rdn rear, no ch from halfway: abs. dist 0
6 Ran Time 2m 38.50(7.3) Owned: Mr John C Grant Trained: Lambourn

LINGFIELD Polytrack TUESDAY 07.09.04 Lefthand, V Sharp Track

Official Going Turf - Good/Firm, AW - Standard

4442	1.50 E B F Sis Sports Data Maiden Stakes Div 1 Fillies 2yo (D3)		
	£5200 £1600 £800 7f aw rnd Going 48 -14 Slow Inside		

PROMOTED DEPUTY 0 [6] Saeed bin Suroor 2-8-11 K McEvoy 8/15 FAV: 1: b f Deputy Minister - 75a
Shouldnt Say Never (Meadowlake) Slow away, prog after 1f, styd on to lead ins fnl 1f, pushed out, val 2L+: well
bckd on debut: Apr foal, half-sister to a couple of sprint wnrs abroad: dam successful in US: sire well related:
eff at 7f, further will suit: acts on polytrack & a v sharp trk: goes well fresh: impr with experience.
2245 **IMPROVISE 94** [10] C E Brittain 2-8-11 R Hills 100/30: 62: In tch, styd on to lead dist, hdd 1 72a
under press well ins fnl 1f, not pace of wnr: long abs: apprec step up to 7f, 1m shld suit: acts on polytrack:
encouraging eff & can be plcd to find a mdn: see 2245.
4089 **ALL A DREAM 8** [4] R Guest 2-8-11 E Ahern 22/1: 603: In tch, prog bef 1f out, styd on, no ch 2½ 67a
with front 2: apprec step up to 7f, acts on polytrack: now quals for h'caps: see 3484.
3381 **FRENCH SCHOOL 47** [8] D R Loder 2-8-11 S Sanders 4/1: 04: b f Desert Prince - Bint Shihama 1 65a
(Cadeaux Genereux) Led, hdd under press dist, no extra: 7 wk abs: Jan foal, half-sister to Cheese N Biscuits, 7f
h'cap wnr: dam successful at 7f: sire Gr 1 wnr at 1m: eff at 7f, shld get 1m: acts on polytrack.

LINGFIELD Polytrack TUESDAY 07.09.04 Lefthand, V Sharp Track

4330 **SWIFT DAME 5** [9]2-8-11 R L Moore 14/1: 05: b f Montjeu - Velvet Appeal (Petorius) Sn cl-up, ev ch bef 1f out, sn hung badly left & wknd: rider reported mount hung left in fnl 4 furlongs: qck reapp: Feb foal, half-sister to wnrs at 6/7f: dam successful at 1m: sire multiple Gr 1 wnr at mid-dists: with R Hannon. *2* **61a**

1084 **KINDLELIGHT DREAM 153** [7]2-8-11 Dane O'Neill 33/1: 06: Missed break, nvr nrr than mid-div. *¾* **59a**

3183 **ROCKYS GIRL 55** [2]2-8-11 M Henry 50/1: 07: Nvr nrr than mid-div: 8 wk abs. *2½* **54a**

JOYEAUX 0 [5]2-8-11 J Fortune 25/1: 8: Cl-up, wknd bef 2f out: debut. *shd* **53a**

4115 **COOMBE CENTENARY 16** [1]2-8-11 J Quinn 66/1: 0009: Al bhd: modest form to date. *1* **51a**

4316 **TINKERS FIRST 6** [3]2-8-11 P C Haddon(7) 100/1: 000: 10th: Rear, nvr a factor. *15* **23a**

10 Ran Time 1m 27.14 (4.34) Owned: Godolphin Trained: Newmarket

LINGFIELD Polytrack TUESDAY 07.09.04 Lefthand, Sharp, Undulating Track

Official Going Turf - Good/Firm, AW - Standard

4443

2.20 Sis/At The Races International Service E B F Median Auction Maiden Stakes 2yo (F4)
£3213 £918 £459 **6f str** **Good 45** **-04 Slow** Stands side

3342 **MISSED A BEAT 48** [9] M Blanshard 2-8-9 (62) D Sweeney 16/1: 0401: Mid-div, hdwy halfway, styd on to lead dist, rdn out to assert: 7 wk abs: 33/1: eff at 6f: acts on gd, handles firm grnd: goes well fresh & acts on a sharp/undul trk: left prev form bhd & can progress: see 2287. **78**

2424 **KANAD 86** [8] B Hanbury 2-9-0 t (77) R Hills 15/2: 3202: Mid-div, hdwy halfway, ev ch ins fnl 1f, not pace of wnr: 12 wk abs: gd eff after abs & can find a weak mdn: see 1987 & 1727. *1¼* **77**

GLAD BIG 0 [16] J A Osborne 2-9-0 M Fenton 33/1: 3: b c Big Shuffle - Glady Sum (Surumu) Missed break, hdwy halfway, kept on ins fnl 1f, just held for 2nd: debut: Feb foal, half-brother to a couple of wnrs abroad: dam unrcd: sire decent performer at sprint dists: eff at 6f, shld stay further: acts on gd grnd: promising eff & can leave this eff bhd with more experience. *shd* **76**

DALDINI 0 [3] J A Osborne 2-9-0 S W Kelly 16/1: 4: b c Josr Algarhoud - Arianna Aldini (Habitat) Bhd, hdwy over 2f out, no impress ins fnl 1f: debut: Apr foal, half-brother to 6f wnr: dam unrcd: sire useful performer around 1m: sharper for today & will apprec further. *2½* **69**

4178 **BEAUCHAMP TURBO 12** [15]2-9-0 J Murtagh 7/2 FAV: 55: Led 4f, sn no extra: bckd from 6/1: sltly below form on switch to turf: showed more in 4178 (debut, polytrack). *1¼* **65**

4171 **PURPLE DOOR 12** [13]2-8-9 J Mackay 33/1: 606: Missed break, prog bef 1f out, nrst fin: signs of encouragement & now quals for h'caps: see 3848. *nk* **59**

2341 **RIGHT TO ROAM 89** [14]2-9-0 BL E Ahern 10/1: 47: Keen cl-up, led 2f out, hdd dist, wknd: 1st blnks. *1¼* **60**

3752 **WOTCHALIKE 32** [4]2-9-0 N Pollard 5/1: 58: Sn struggling, nvr nrr than mid-div: btr 3752 (7f). *1½* **56**

PICKAPEPPA 0 [2]2-8-9 S Carson 33/1: 9: ch f Piccolo - Cajole (Barathea) Handy over 4f, wknd: debut: Jan first foal, dam plcd at 7f: sire Gr 1 wnr at sprint dists: with R F Johnson Houghton. *1* **48**

4052 **OVER TIPSY 19** [6]2-9-0 R L Moore 14/1: 00: 10th: Nvr nrr than mid-div. *¾* **51**

4121 **ATTISHOE 15** [12]2-8-9 S Drowne 12/1: 00: 11th: Handy, wknd bef 1f out. *hd* **45**

BEST GAME 0 [7]2-9-0 Joanna Badger 50/1: 0: 12th: Al in rear on debut. *shd* **49**

STORYVILLE 0 [11]2-9-0 S Sanders 5/1: 0: 13th: br c Lujain - Slow Jazz (Chief's Crown) Handy 4f, fdd: op 7/2 on debut: Mar foal, half-brother to wnrs at 6f/1m: dam smart performer at 1m. *¾* **47**

4052 **San Deng 19** [17]2-9-0 (63) K McEvoy 25/1:0 4052 **Penang Sapphire 19** [10]2-9-0 J Fortune 33/1:0

April Shannon 0 [5]2-8-9 Natalia Gemelova(7) 100/1:0 4108 **Aleshanee 17** [1]2-8-9 J Quinn 50/1:0

17 Ran Time 1m 11.76 (2.96) Owned: The First Timers Trained: Upper Lambourn

4444

2.50 Sis Producers Of At The Races Nursery Handicap Stakes 2yo 0-75 (E3) **[82]**
£3757 £1156 £578 **7f str** **Good 45** **-01 Slow** Stands side

3909 **MITRAILLETTE 25** [17] Sir Michael Stoute 2-9-5 (73) N Mackay(3) 7/1 FAV: 6541: Handy, styd on for press to lead dist, drvn out to hold on: eff at 6f, now suited by around 7f: acts on fast & gd grnd: acts on a sharp/undul trk: imprvd eff on h'cap bow & can rate higher: see 3909 & 3418. **84**

4052 **WATCHMYEYES 19** [11] N P Littmoden 2-9-5 (73) J P Guillambert(3) 12/1: 6442: Prom, ev ch dist, kept on ins fnl 1f, just held by wnr: eff at 6f, apprec return to 7f: acts on gd & soft grnd: gd run in defeat. *½* **81**

3883 **SEASONS ESTATES 26** [8] B R Millman 2-8-8 (62) S Drowne 25/1: 4043: Mid-div, hdwy halfway, kept on ins fnl 1f, no ch with front 2: eff at 7f on gd grnd: encouraging eff on h'cap bow: see 1401. *2* **66**

3925 **REBEL REBEL 25** [7] N A Callaghan 2-9-0 (68) O Urbina 10/1: 0054: b c Revoque - French Quarter (Ile de Bourbon) Missed break, hdwy halfway, staying on when short of room dist & again ins fnl 1f, nrst fin: Mar foal, half-brother successful at 7/12f: dam successful 3 times: sire Gr 1 wnr around 1m: eff at 7f, shld apprec return to further: acts on gd grnd: shade closer with clr passage. *½* **71**

4040 **GRYSKIRK 19** [15]2-8-10 (64) J Quinn 16/1: 3000305: Held up, prog 2f out, styd on ins fnl 1f. *½* **66**

2194 **SHAHEER 96** [18]2-9-5 (73) J Fortune 10/1: 6206: In tch over 4f, sn outpcd, rallied late: long abs, stays 7f. *nk* **74**

4100 **IVANA ILLYICH 17** [14]2-9-5 (73) Dane O'Neill 14/1: 5040337: Mid-div, prog when short of room bef 1f out & again ins fnl 1f, kept on late under kind ride: worth a try at a mile on this evidence & can impr: see 4100. *nk* **73+**

4193 **HIDDEN CHANCE 11** [16]2-9-2 (70) R L Moore 8/1: 0108: Chsd ldrs wide over 5f, sn onepcd. *hd* **69**

4193 **GOOD WEE GIRL 11** [6]2-9-3 (71) J Murtagh 14/1: 0215109: In tch, onepcd when hmpd bef 1f out. *¾* **68**

4139 **FASYLITATOR 14** [2]2-9-4 (72) S W Kelly 11/1: 6360: 10th: Led, hdd bef 1f out, wknd: btr 3975 (6f). *shd* **68**

4079 **CHUTNEY MARY 18** [5]2-9-2 (70) E Ahern 25/1: 6225250: 11th: Prom till dist, wknd: btr 3716. *¾* **64**

4079 **MULBERRY WINE 18** [9]2-9-4 (72) D Sweeney 50/1: 64500: 12th: Cl-up 5f, sn wknd: btr 3047. *1* **64**

3521 **ARTHUR WARDLE 41** [19]2-9-2 VIS (70) J Mackay 16/1: 25060: 13th: Bhd, nvr able to chall: 6 wk abs. *hd* **61**

3825 **HIGH CHART 29** [12]2-9-5 (73) A McCarthy 33/1: 4403060: 14th: Handy over 5f, sn wknd: btr 3488. *½* **63**

3882 **DANGER ZONE 26** [3]2-9-2 (70) S Sanders 14/1: 0050: 15th: Handy over 5f, wknd: btr 3882. *hd* **59**

3627 **HES A DIAMOND 37** [20]2-9-7 (75) G Carter 12/1: 51300: 16th: Held up, nvr a factor: btr 2952. *1* **62**

3520 **IMPERIAL MISS 41** [10]2-8-12 (66) A Daly 100/1: 060600: 17th: Mid-div over 4f, wknd. *2½* **48**

4102 **MAKEPEACE 17** [4]2-8-12 (66) S Hitchcott(3) 33/1: 0400: 18th: Bhd, nvr a factor: btr 2570. *1¾* **44**

3296 **THREE ACES 50** [1]2-8-11 BL (65) K McEvoy 50/1: 0560: 19th: Missed break, al bhd: first time blnks. *5* **33**

2188 **EXTRA MARK 96** [13]2-9-7 (75) N Pollard 10/1: 2240: 20th: Rear, nvr a factor: long abs: btr 1752. *2½* **38**

20 Ran Time 1m 23.65 (3.25) Owned: Miss K Rausing Trained: Newmarket

4445 3.20 Isis Display System Maiden Stakes 3yo+ (D3)
£4033 £1241 £621 7f str Good 45 +04 Fast Stands side

3029} **KODIAC** 416 [5] J L Dunlop 3-9-0 S Sanders 5/2 FAV: 3-1: b c Danehill - Rafha (Kris) Mid-div, 80
styd on to lead bef 1f out, pushed out to assert, val bit more: bckd on reapp: 3rd of 12 on sole '03 start (mdn,
rtd 83): eff at 6f, apprec step up to 7f, further will suit: acts on firm & gd grnd, sharp/undul trk & goes well
fresh: fine eff after long lay off due to injury, bright future ahead.

2092 **GREAT EXHIBITION** 100 [12] Saeed bin Suroor 3-9-0 t (80) K McEvoy 3/1: 32-0032: Cl-up, ev ch dist, 1¾ 75
kept on ins fnl 1f, not pace of wnr: tchd 4/1: long abs: acts on firm & gd grnd: can find a race: see 2092.

       SUBTLE BREEZE 0 [14] J H M Gosden 3-8-9 J Fortune 4/1: 3: ch f Storm Cat - Morning Devotion shd 69
(Affirmed) Prom, led 2f out, hdd dist, sn no extra: tchd 5/1 on debut: eff at 7f, will apprec further: acts on gd
grnd: much to like about debut eff & can rate higher with experience.

3884 **MRS SHILLING** 26 [1] J R Fanshawe 3-8-9 O Urbina 9/1: 6-34: Handy wide, ev ch bef 1f out, sn no extra. 2 65

4081 **ALL QUIET** 18 [4]3-8-9 (70) R L Moore 12/1: 0-323555: In tch, ev ch bef 1f out, sn no extra: see 2031. nk 64

4262 **TEXT** 9 [8]3-9-0 (65) S Drowne 14/1: 20-02356: Nvr nrr than mid-div: 'lost front shoe'. 1½ 66

4112 **ESTRELLA LEVANTE** 17 [16]4-9-4 bl (45) E Ahern 10/1: 0600007: ch g Abou Zouz - Star of Modena ½ 65$
(Waajib) Mid-div over 5f, sn onepcd: rider reported mount had hung left: modest form to date.

       POLISH ROSE 0 [13]3-8-9 R Hills 12/1: 8: ch f Polish Precedent - Messila Rose (Darshaan) In hd 59
tch, prog 2f out, wknd dist: debut: with E F Vaughan.

3977 **APPOLONIOUS** 22 [11]3-9-0 Dane O'Neill 66/1: 0009: Mid-div over 5f, sn wknd. 3½ 57$

4275 **ENCORA BAY** 8 [17]3-8-9 J Quinn 16/1: 630: 10th: Led 5f, wknd: showed more in 4275. 2½ 47

3788 **BAHAMA REEF** 31 [9]3-9-0 (55) L Keniry(3) 20/1: 5203330: 11th: Cl-up 4f, grad wknd: see 3788. 1½ 49

       Golden Bankes 0 [6]3-8-9 D Sweeney 33/1:0   **Charlie Masters** 0 [3]3-9-0 S W Kelly 66/1:0
       Dark Parade 226 [7]3-9-0 J Jones(7) 33/1:0   **Nelsons Luck** 0 [2]3-9-0 S Carson 100/1:0
15 Ran Time 1m 23.33 (2.93) Owned: Prince A A Faisal Trained: Arundel

---

Official Going Turf - Good/Firm, AW - Standard

4446 3.50 Ladbrokes Com Handicap Stakes 3yo+ 71-85 (D2) [90]
£6828 £2101 £1051 7f aw rnd Going 48 +10 Fast Inside

4186 **IDLE POWER** 11 [10] J R Boyle 6-8-13 p (75) E Ahern 8/1: 0230021: In tch, styd on trav well to 85a
lead dist, pushed clr fnl 1f, val 4L+: eff around 6/7f on firm, gd/soft & polytrack: eff in cheek pieces: has been
in gd form this term & won today with authority, more prizes await on this evidence: see 4186 & 3069.

3338 **WARDEN COMPLEX** 48 [9] J R Fanshawe 3-9-5 (85) J Murtagh 5/1 JT FAV: 3211052: Mid-div, sltly 2½ 87a
outpcd after 4f, staying on when headed, kept on cl-home, no ch with easy wnr: 7 wk abs: creditable eff.

4394 **MISS GEORGE** 3 [6] D K Ivory 6-9-7 (83) Dane O'Neill 14/1: 0303003: Missed break, hdwy 3f out, ½ 84a
kept on ins fnl 1f, just held for 2nd: qck reapp: see 4031 & 3479.

4180 **MALLARD** 12 [3] J G Given 4-9-0 (76) M Fenton 16/1: 0260004: In tch, no extra from dist: btr 2840. ½ 76a

4231 **TARANAKI** 10 [4]6-8-13 (75) L Keniry(3) 5/1 JT FAV: 5000365: Led 1f, styd cl-up, still trav well 1¾ 71a
over 1f out, sn rdn & no extra.

4225 **BIG BRADFORD** 10 [5]3-9-2 bl (82) D Kinsella 33/1: 20-00006: Keen cl-up, ev ch bef 1f out, sn no extra. shd 77a

4279 **ALCHEMIST MASTER** 8 [14]5-9-1 p (77) Dean McKeown 12/1: 1146307: Mid-div wide, outpcd 3f out, shd 71a
modest late gains: showed btr 3608 (1m).

2760 **ANOTHER GLIMPSE** 73 [7]6-9-2 t (78) S Sanders 12/1: 0023208: Held up wide, short of room bef 2f ¾ 70a
out, modest late gains: 10 wk abs: btr 2053 (6f, fibresand).

4180 **POINT OF DISPUTE** 12 [2]9-9-2 vis (78) D Sweeney 11/1: 02-52049: Keen rear, nvr able to chall. shd 69a

4180 **OBRIGADO** 12 [11]4-9-6 (82) S W Kelly 7/1: 0201020: 10th: Led 6f out, hdd dist, wknd: btr 4180. nk 72a

3920 **INSTANT RECALL** 25 [8]3-9-4 bl (84) J Fortune 15/2: 4512400: 11th: Nvr nrr than mid-div: btr 3379. 1 72a

4221 **FREAK OCCURENCE** 10 [12]3-9-0 vis (80) S Drowne 14/1: 4630600: 12th: Mid-div wide 5f, sn wknd: 5 58a
rider reported mount did not face the kickback: btr 2250.

4207} **Blackmail** 13 [13]6-9-2 bl(78) S Carson 50/1:0   4394 **Hard To Catch** 3 [1]6-8-13 bl(75) M Savage(3) 25/1:0
14 Ran Time 1m 25.50 (2.7) Owned: The Idle B'S Trained: Epsom

---

4447 4.20 E B F Sis Sports Data Maiden Stakes Div 2 Fillies 2yo (D3)
£5200 £1600 £800 7f aw rnd Going 48 -23 Slow Inside

3817 **ICING** 29 [5] W J Haggas 2-8-11 S W Kelly 10/1: 641: Cl-up, styd on to lead bef 1f out, rdn out: 80a
apprec step up to 7f, acts on polytrack & a v sharp trk: progressing with racing: see 3103.

       ONE TO WIN 0 [2] J Noseda 2-8-11 E Ahern 15/2: 2: b f Cape Cross - Safe Exit (Exit To Nowhere) ½ 78a
Chsd ldrs, prog to chase wnr ins fnl 1f, just held: debut: op 11/2: Feb first foal, dam successful abroad: sire Gr
1 wnr around 1m: eff at 7f, will apprec further: acts on polytrack: gd eff in defeat & can find a race.

3851 **GONE FISHING** 27 [9] M A Jarvis 2-8-11 (80) P Robinson 10/11 FAV: 0233: Led, hdd bef 1f out, sn 1½ 75a
rdn & no extra: well bckd: disapp on AW bow, handles polytrack, acts on gd/soft grnd: btr expected after 3851.

3841 **JALISSA** 0 [3] R Charlton 2-8-11 S Drowne 14/1: 4: b f Mister Baileys - Julia Domna (Dominion) ¾ 73a
Slow away, sn in tch, outpcd 2f out, rallied late: debut: May foal, half-sister successful at 7/12f: dam unplcd.

3917 **MISSIE BAILEYS** 25 [6]2-8-11 L Keniry(3) 8/1: 65: ch f Mister Baileys - Jilly Woo (Environment 1½ 70a
Friend) Handy over 5f, no extra: Apr foal, half-sister successful at mid-dists: dam plcd at 6f.

       SAND IRON 0 [4]2-8-11 J Fortune 66/1: 6: Sn bhd, hdwy halfway, no impress fnl 2f: debut. 1½ 67a

3639 **ZONIC** 36 [1]2-8-11 N Mackay(3) 9/2: 07: Cl-up 4f, wknd fnl 2f: disappointing on AW bow. nk 66a

3851 **BALLETOMAINE** 27 [7]2-8-11 K May(7) 20/1: 008: Al adrift. 8 50a
8 Ran Time 1m 27.81 (5.01) Owned: Cheveley Park Stud Trained: Newmarket

4448
4.50 Sislink Upod 'premier' Claiming Stakes 3-4yo (D3)
£5720 £1760 £880   **1m2f aw**   **Going 48**   -02 Slow   Inside

4112 **PLATINUM PIRATE 17** [14] K R Burke 3-8-5 vis (61) J Quinn 14/1: 1365401: Held up, prog wide 3f   **65a**
out, styd on to lead 1f out, rdn out: eff around 10f on gd, soft grnd & polytrack: now suited by a visor: see 1280.
4241 **SEWMORE CHARACTER 10** [7] M Blanshard 4-9-5 (66) D Sweeney 20/1: 4625002: Held up, prog 4f out, 1½ **69a+**
short of room 2f out till dist, styd on well ins fnl 1f, post came too sn: apprec today's drop in grade, would have
gone v close with clr passage: see 697 & 131.
3362 **RED SKELTON 47** [8] W J Haggas 3-8-3 (75) N Mackay(3) 16/1: 01-00003: Held up wide, prog after 3f,   1½ **58a**
onepcd dist: clmd for 6,000: eff at 7f, now stays 10f: acts on both AWs: see 1427.
3291 **SEA OF GOLD 50** [5] H J Cyzer 3-8-7 (70) K McEvoy 8/1: 06264: Bhd, hdwy 4f out, no impress ins   ½ **61a**
fnl 1f: 7 wk abs: showed more in 2835 (firm).
3948 **REBATE 24** [4]4-9-0 t (65) R L Moore 11/4 FAV: 6350565: Led, hdd under press 1f out, no extra: op 4/1. hd **60a**
4042 **BONUS POINTS 19** [6]3-8-7 L Keniry(3) 20/1: 06: Missed break, nvr nrr than mid-div: see 4042.   1¾ **56a**
4266 **ONE UPMANSHIP 9** [9]3-8-10 (65) E Ahern 5/1: 3261237: Prom over 1m, no extra: btr 4266 & 4112.   ¾ **57a**
4342 **BELISCO 5** [10]3-9-3 bl t (69) J Murtagh 8/1: 0-006108: Cl-up, ev ch bef 1f out, sn rdn & wknd: nk **63a**
rider reported mount hung badly left: qck reapp: showed more in 4112.
4221 **EL CHAPARRAL 10** [1]4-9-5 (72) Dane O'Neill 8/1: 0201009: Nvr nrr than mid-div: btr 3980.   2½ **54a**
4284 **KINGSTON TOWN 8** [4]4-8-12 p (62) J P Guillambert(3) 12/1: 4060250: 10th: Cl-up over 1m, wkng when 4 **41a**
short of room ins fnl 1f: btr 4090 (1m, fibresand).
3423 **WESTERN ROOTS 45** [11]3-8-9 (72) S Drowne 12/1: 0615500: 11th: Handy over 7f, wknd: 6 wk abs.   6 **37a**
4137 **DEVIOUS AYERS 15** [13]3-8-7 (62) S Sanders 16/1: 3-40060: 12th: Cl-up 1m, fdd: see 260.   ½ **34a**
2706 Lawaaheb 75 [12]3-8-12 (67) N Pollard 20/1:0   Golden Queen 0 [2]3-8-7 A Daly 66/1:0
14 Ran   Time 2m 7.85 (5.05)   Owned: Spigot Lodge Partnership   Trained: Leyburn

4449
5.20 Sis Vital Link Median Auction Maiden Stakes 3-4yo (F4)
£2891 £826 £413   **1m4f aw**   **Going 48**   +03 Fast   Inside

4188 **DUNDRY 11** [8] G L Moore 3-8-13 p (79) R L Moore 13/8 FAV: 0-33221: Sn cl-up, styd on to lead 2f   **84a**
out, sn went clr, eased cl-home, val 14L+: bckd: eff at 10/11f, imprvd for step up to 12f: acts on gd, soft grnd &
polytrack: apprec recent fitting of cheek pieces: see 4188.
1089 **ALEXEI 153** [2] J R Fanshawe 3-8-13 Dane O'Neill 33/1: 02: Chsd ldrs, kept on for press ins fnl 11 **68a**
2f, no ch with v easy wnr: long abs & AW bow: see 1089.
4395 **GARNETT 3** [3] A King 3-8-13 (75) E Ahern 3/1: 43303: Led, hdd 10f out, styd cl-up, no extra fnl 1 **66a**
2f: qck reapp: tchd 9/2: btr 3742 (14f, firm).
      MOANING MYRTLE 0 [7] J R Fanshawe 3-8-8   O Urbina 20/1: 4: br f Desert King - Grinning   nk **60a**
(Bellypha) In tch, trav well over 2f out, sn hung badly & no extra: debut: sharper for today.
4315 **SCARRABUS 6** [6]3-8-13 (66) T Quinn 9/1: 4063435: Led 10f out, hdd 2f out, fdd: op 7/1 on qck reapp. 5 **58a**
4113 **SONDERBORG 17** [4]3-8-8 bl e (49) Lisa Jones 20/1: 6000666: Prom 1m, sn wknd: see 4032.   1 **51a**
3787 **DISPARITY 31** [1]3-8-8 (65) J Murtagh 13/2: 0427: Chsd ldrs till halfway, fdd: v disapp on step up to 12f. 29 **11a**
      CZECH SUMMER 0 [11]3-8-13 D Sweeney 66/1: 8: Missed break, al well adrift on debut.   dist **0a**
4075 **STOCKING ISLAND 18** [5]3-8-8 (70) S Sanders 5/1: 023003P: P.u. after 2f, dismounted: btr 4075.   **0a**
9 Ran   Time 2m 34.60(5.4)   Owned: Mr D J Deer   Trained: Brighton

LEICESTER   TUESDAY 07.09.04   Righthand, Stiff, Galloping Track

Official Going GOOD/FIRM (GOOD IN PLACES)

4450
2.10 European Breeders Fund Filbert Maiden Stakes Fillies 2yo (D2)
£5681 £1748 £874   **1m9y**   **Good/Firm 32**   -15 Slow   Stands side

4035 **DASH TO THE TOP 20** [2] L M Cumani 2-8-11 D Holland 15/8: 21: Mid-div, hdwy halfway, led over 1f   **85+**
out, rdn out ins fnl 1f: bckd: stays 1m, will relish further: acts on fast & gd/soft, stiff/gall trk: imprvd from
debut & still ran a shade green, will progress again & win more races.
3046 **BAZELLE 61** [13] P W D'Arcy 2-8-11 J F Egan 33/1: 042: Cl-up, hdwy to chall ins fnl 1f, not pace   ½ **82**
of wnr: 9 wk abs, clr of rem: eff at 1m on fast: has imprvd with each start, win a race: see 3046.
4191 **CELTIQUE 11** [7] Sir Michael Stoute 2-8-11 K Fallon 5/4 FAV: 23: Sn led, hdd over 1f out, no   3 **76**
extra ins fnl 1f: nicely bckd: shade btr 4191 (debut, 7f on gd).
4191 **ZAYN ZEN 11** [1] M A Jarvis 2-8-11 M Hills 8/1: 64: Trkd ldrs, onepcd 2f out: tchd 12/1: see 4191.   shd **75**
      INTERIM PAYMENT 0 [5]2-8-11 R Hughes 20/1: 5: b f Red Ransom - Interim (Sadler's Wells) Prom,   nk **74**
chall over 1f out, sn onepcd, not given hard time on debut: op 14/1: half-sister to wnrs at 9/12f: dam useful over
8/10f: sire smart 2yo: with R Charlton & can learn from this.
      HIGHER LOVE 0 [12]2-8-11 Martin Dwyer 20/1: 6: b f Sadler's Wells - Dollar Bird (Kris)   3½ **67**
Mid-div, no impress over 1f out on debut: op 11/1: Feb first foal, cost E340,000: dam a 1m wnr at 2, sire smart at
8/12f: with M Bell & entitled to impr for this next time.
4035 **KRISTALCHEN 20** [3]2-8-11 J Fanning 66/1: 007: b f Singspiel - Crystal Flite (Darshaan) Al bhd: 1 **65**
Mar first foal: dam wnr over 12f, sire a smart 2yo & later at 10/12f: likely type for nurseries.
4191 **HALLOWED DREAM 11** [9]2-8-11 W Supple 100/1: 008: Keen & cl-up, no impress over 1f out.   ½ **64**
3915 **ALULA 25** [4]2-8-11 P Dobbs 50/1: 09: Nvr a factor.   2½ **59**
4289 **IFIT 8** [6]2-8-11 T E Durcan 66/1: 0000: 10th: Al bhd.   ¾ **57**
      RELEASED 0 [11]2-8-11 L Dettori 66/1: 0: 11th: Slow away, nvr a factor on debut.   ½ **56**
3909 **KOLYMA 25** [8]2-8-11 I Mongan 66/1: 050: 12th: Al bhd.   nk **55**
3908 **LEGEND OF DANCE 25** [10]2-8-11 J F McDonald(3) 66/1: 00: 13th: Nvr a factor.   shd **54**
13 Ran   Time 1m 42.0 (3.8)   Owned: Helena Springfield Ltd   Trained: Newmarket

---

4451	2.40 Ggbet Com Betting Exchange Selling Nursery Handicap Stakes 2yo 0-65 (G4)	[70]

£3038 £868 £434   7f9y   Good/Firm 32   -53 Slow   Stands side

4040 **AMPHITHEATRE** 19 [8] R F Johnson Houghton 2-9-6 (62) L Dettori 9/2 J FAV: 0303301: Mid-div, hdwy over 1f out, led ins fnl 1f, drvn out: bght in for 7,000gns: tchd 13/2: stays 7f on fast & fibresand, stiff/gall trks: made most of this drop in grade: see 1880. — **70**

4206 **HERENCIA** 11 [15] P A Blockley 2-8-10 P (52) I Mongan 12/1: 00042: Rear, hdwy over 2f out, kept on ins fnl 1f but no pace to reach wnr: stays 7f, 1m will suit: acts on fast grnd: tried cheek pieces: see 3491. — 1 — **56**

3825 **DEBS BROUGHTON** 29 [10] W J Musson 2-9-0 (56) R Hughes 11/1: 00003: Cl-up, hdwy to lead 2f out till ins fnl 1f, sn no extra, fin 3rd, disqual & plcd 4th: stays 7f: see 2449. — shd — **59**

4040 **LORNA DUNE** 19 [13] Mrs J R Ramsden 2-9-4 (60) K Fallon 9/2 J FAV: 360604: Mid-div, hdwy over 1f out, staying on when hmpd cl-home, fin 4th, promoted to 3rd: clmd for 6,000: stays 7f on fast & hvy: see 1677. — nk — **62**

4218 **SLITE** 10 [1]2-8-12 (54) Martin Dwyer 20/1: 0255: Dwelt in rear, hdwy when not clr run over 1f out, kept on ins fnl 1f: clmd for 6,000: gd run on return to 7f, 1m likely to suit: shade closer with a clr run. — ½ — **55**

4316 **ARTADI** 6 [19]2-8-8 bl (50) C Catlin 14/1: 0356546: Cl-up, onepcd fnl 1f: qck reapp. — hd — **50**

4040 **DANS HEIR** 19 [16]2-9-2 p (58) G Faulkner 16/1: 020207: Mid-div, onepcd fnl 1f. — shd — **57**

3750 **ORPEN ANNIE** 32 [2]2-9-3 (59) B Reilly(3) 14/1: 036048: Mid-div, hdwy & ev ch 2f out, no impress fnl 1f. — hd — **57**

4337 **JAY 5** [7]2-9-4 (60) D Holland 14/1: 2020109: Slow away in rear, hdwy over 2f out, onepcd fnl 1f. — 1¼ — **55**

4213 **TONIGHT** 11 [4]2-9-1 BL (57) B Swarbrick(5) 40/1: 343600: 10th: Bhd, hdwy 3f out, not pace to chall: blnks¾ — **50**

3308 **PROCRASTINATE** 50 [17]2-8-12 (54) J F Egan 14/1: 6530520: 11th: Cl-up, hdwy & ev ch over 2f out, no impress fnl 1f out: 7 wk abs: see 3308. — 2½ — **42**

3698 **MYTTONS DREAM** 34 [14]2-9-2 (58) A Mullen(7) 8/1: 6610400: 12th: In tch, nvr nrr: op 10/1. — ¾ — **44**

4146 **HIS MAJESTY** 14 [3]2-9-4 (60) Steven Harrison(7) 25/1: 03260: 13th: Prom, no impress 3f out. — ¾ — **44**

4146 **CHICAGO NIGHTS** 14 [5]2-8-10 P (52) Rory Moore(5) 12/1: 400520: 14th: Led to 2f out: cheekpieces. — shd — **35**

4191 **SHERBOURNE** 11 [6]2-8-5 (47) Paul Eddery 33/1: 006000: 15th: Rear, hdwy 3f out, wknd fnl 1f, eased. — nk — **29**

4193 **LORD NORMACOTE** 11 [9]2-9-7 (63) R Havlin 20/1: 00400: 16th: Nvr a factor. — ½ — **44**

4213 **BELTON** 11 [18]2-8-13 (55) S Righton 40/1: 00000: 17th: Slow away in rear, hdwy over 3f out, no impress. 2½ — **31**

3803 **BE BOP ALOHA** 30 [11]2-9-1 (57) L Enstone(3) 25/1: 0635000: 18th: In tch, hdwy over 3f out, not clr run over 2f out, sn no impress: see 2492. — 4 — **25**

3994 **SAPPHIRE PRINCESS** 22 [12]2-8-5 (47) P Doe 33/1: 5561500: 19th: Mid-div, not much room over 2f out, sn btn. — 1¾ — **11**

4163 **UGLY SISTER** 13 [20]2-8-10 (52) T E Durcan 33/1: 0060: 20th: gr f Aljabr - Cinderella Ball (Nureyev) Nvr a factor: Feb foal, cost 6,500gns: dam unrcd, sire unbeaten Gr 1 wnr at 2, later a smart miler. — 14 — **0**

20 Ran   Time 1m 27.99 (5.99)   Owned: Mr R F Johnson Houghton   Trained: Didcot

---

4452	3.10 Terry O'farrell Memorial Handicap Stakes 3yo+ 56-70 (E3)	[79]

£3843 £1182 £591   7f9y   Good/Firm 32   -27 Slow   Stands side

3888 **TORQUEMADA** 26 [15] W Jarvis 3-8-4 (3oh) (55) P Doe 33/1: 0003001: In tch, hdwy 2f out, led entering fnl 1f, pushed out: relished this step up to 7f, acts on fast & polytrack, stiff/gall trk: gd run from 3lb out of the h'cap: back to form & can win more races over this trip: see 898. — **65**

4144 **WELCOME SIGNAL** 14 [11] J R Fanshawe 4-9-2 p (63) L Dettori 4/1 FAV: 5-055032: Slow away in rear, hdwy over 1f out, styd on well ins fnl 1f, nrst fin: stays further & a step up in trip will suit: see 4144 & 2529. — ½ — **70**

3768 **MOUNT VETTORE** 31 [14] Mrs J R Ramsden 3-9-2 (67) K Fallon 4/1 J FAV: 0000663: Slow away, hdwy over 2f out, kept on: clr of rem: see 3768. — 2 — **70**

3198 **TICERO** 55 [6] C E Brittain 3-9-0 bl (65) T E Durcan 50/1: 04-00004: Bhd, hdwy when short of room over 2f out, kept on fnl 1f: 8 wk abs: need further? see 2403. — 3 — **62**

4398 **BOBS BUZZ** 2 [10]4-9-7 (68) D Holland 6/1: 0535205: Made most to 3f out, no extra fnl 1f: qck reapp. — ¾ — **63**

3562 **BLYTHE SPIRIT** 40 [8]5-9-3 p (64) T Hamilton(3) 8/1: 5-500066: Cl-up, hdwy to lead 3f out till entering fnl 1f, no extra: 6 wk abs: see 1977. — 1¼ — **56**

4144 **MORAG** 14 [16]3-8-9 (60) L Enstone(3) 25/1: 0066207: Handy, no impress over 1f out. — nk — **51**

1976 **RAHEED** 105 [12]3-8-11 (62) Hayley Turner(3) 100/1: 46-6008: b g Daggers Drawn - In Due Course (A P Indy) Handy, no impress well over 1f out: long abs: mdn unplcd both '03 starts (rtd 66, E Dunlop). — ½ — **52**

4175 **SHOWTIME ANNIE** 12 [19]3-8-10 (61) J Fanning 33/1: 1041509: Bhd, modest late gains. — 1 — **49**

3806 **BLAEBERRY** 30 [7]3-9-0 bl (65) J F Egan 12/1: 5415120: 10th: In tch, short of room over 2f out, sn btn. shd — **52**

2971 **CARTE NOIRE** 64 [20]3-8-6 (1oh) (57) J F McDonald(3) 100/1: 30-51000: 11th: Nvr btr than mid div. — 1¼ — **41**

4252 **FOOLS ENTIRE** 9 [17]3-8-7 e (58) B Reilly(3) 33/1: 0003450: 12th: Cl-up, no impress over 1f out. — hd — **41**

4345 **JOSHUAS GOLD** 5 [13]3-8-7 vis (58) W Supple 12/1: 0014230: 13th: Cl-up, wknd 2f out: qck reapp. — shd — **40**

4278 **ELLIOTS CHOICE** 8 [5]3-8-5 (2oh)bl (56) A Mullen(7) 20/1: 0024050: 14th: Al bhd. — hd — **37**

4263 **SCARLETT ROSE** 9 [1]3-8-13 (64) I Mongan 14/1: 0-603300: 15th: Cl-up, wknd 3f out. — ½ — **44**

4317 **DANIFAH** 6 [4]3-8-11 (62) F P Ferris(3) 10/1: 4461130: 16th: Pressed ldr, wknd over 3f out: qck reapp. — nk — **41**

2403 **FIVE GOLD 87** [2]3-8-11 (62) Martin Dwyer 50/1: 2410-000: 17th: Mid-div, no impress over 2f out. — nk — **40**

4256* **KINGS ROCK** 9 [9]3-8-10 (6ex)bl (61) R Hughes 14/1: 6301210: 18th: Nvr a factor: btr 4256 (soft). — ¾ — **37**

4366 **SENIOR MINISTER** 4 [18]6-8-13 (60) R Miles(3) 50/1: 1000000: 19th: Slow away, rcd alone far side, wknd over 2f out, eased: qck reapp: wrong side. — 25 — **0**

19 Ran   Time 1m 26.17 (4.17)   Owned: Canisbay Bloodstock   Trained: Newmarket

---

4453	3.40 Zurich Risk Services Maiden Stakes 3yo+ (D3)	

£4358 £1341 £671   1m1f218y   Good/Firm 32   +06 Fast   Inside

4034 **ONE SO MARVELLOUS** 20 [3] L M Cumani 3-8-9 D Holland 6/1: 001: ch f Nashwan - Someone Special (Habitat) Mid-div, hdwy over 2f out, chsd ldr over 1f out, drvn ins fnl 1f, led cl-home: sister to smart performer at 10f: dam smart: eff at 10f, will stay further: acts on fast grnd, stiff/gall trk: back to form. — **81**

4034 **FLAMBOYANT LAD** 20 [11] B W Hills 3-9-0 (79) M Hills 6/4 FAV: 2-3332: Rcd in 2nd till led over 2f out, hdd & no extra cl-home: nicely bckd, well clr of rem: plcd yet again, see 3007. — nk — **84**

4912} **KABIS BOOIE** 316 [9] H R A Cecil 3-9-0 Paul Eddery 10/1: 24-3: ch c Night Shift - Perfect Welcome (Taufan) Mid-div, hdwy over 1f out, no impress over 1f out: reapp: rnr-up 1st of 2 '03 starts (mdn): eff at 1m on firm, prob handles polytrack: poss ndd this. 2 Oct'03 Bath 8.0fm 80- D: — 12 — **66**

4252 **FLAME QUEEN** 9 [10] Mrs C A Dunnett 3-8-9 (64) Hayley Turner(3) 18/1: 2-000404: Led till over 2f out, no extra: op 25/1: see 3711. — ½ — **60**

1342

3997 **TIMBER ICE 22** [2]4-9-2 (65) W Ryan 5/1: 0/43-055: Cl-up, no impress over 1f out: see 3437. *5* **52**
3246 **BIJOU DAN 53** [7]3-9-0 T Eaves(3) 16/1: 46: In tch, not much room/lost place over 6f out, sn wknd. *hd* **56**
3292 **SURFACE TO AIR 50** [8]3-9-0 R Havlin 50/1: 0007: b g Samraan - Travelling Lady (Almoojid) Bhd, sn in tch, no impress over 3f out: 7 wk abs: dam unplcd in NH bmpr. *3* **51**
WYVERN 0 [5]3-9-0 R Hughes 11/2: 8: Handy, no impress over 2f out on debut. *2½* **47**
3740 **CUGINA NICOLA 33** [13]3-8-9 R Thomas(5) 50/1: 009: Al bhd. *16* **18**
4101 **ABIGAIL ADAMS 17** [4]3-8-9 Martin Dwyer 20/1: 00: 10th: In tch, no impress over 4f out. *7* **7**
UP THE AISLE 0 [1]7-9-7 L Enstone(3) 100/1: 0: 11th: Slow away, nvr a factor on debut. *13* **0**
4261 **LADY LUCINDA 9** [12]3-8-9 I Mongan 100/1: 0-00: 12th: Al bhd. *4* **0**
4261 **GENTLE WARNING 9** [6]4-9-2 BL S Righton 150/1: 000: 13th: Slow away & keen, nvr a factor: tried blnks. *23* **0**
13 Ran Time 2m 5.18 (2.68) Owned: Helena Springfield Ltd Trained: Newmarket

4454

4.10 Manmatters Co Uk Conditions Stakes 3yo+ (C2)
£6165 £2339 £1169 **5f2y** **Good/Firm 32** **+05 Fast** Stands side

3989 **DRAGON FLYER 22** [6] M Quinn 5-8-3 (1ow) (93) J F Egan 10/1: 0343041: Cl-up, hdwy 1f out, drvn & styd on well to lead nr fin: suited by 5f on firm, hvy & polytrack, any trk: 1st win this term, v useful. **101**
4060 **TALBOT AVENUE 19** [4] M Mullineaux 6-8-7 (99) K Fallon 11/4 FAV: 0220202: Cl-up, hdwy to lead halfway, hdd nr fin, kept on cl-home: clr of rem: fine eff conceding weight: deserves another race: see 2894. *nk* **104**
2359 **MAGIC GLADE 88** [8] R Brotherton 5-8-7 (86) D Nolan 66/1: 1213003: Cl-up, outpcd over 1f out, sn btn: long abs: new stable (prev with C Dore): back to form: see 2082. *3½* **93**
3937 **HIDDEN DRAGON 24** [12] P A Blockley 5-8-7 (94) Hayley Turner(3) 12/1: 0-220064: Mid-div, styd on fnl 1f: return to 6f will suit: see 887. *nk* **92**
4238 **CONTINENT 10** [2]7-9-4 (107) D Holland 3/1: 00-30105: Slow away in rear, hdwy 2f out, kept on: top weight: likes easier grnd & return to 6f may now suit: see 3989. *nk* **102**
3123 **FROMSONG 59** [10]6-8-7 (95) I Mongan 16/1: 4440066: Cl-up, no impress over 1f out: op 12/1, 8 wk abs. *2½* **83**
1421 **RUSSIAN VALOUR 132** [11]3-8-12 BL (108) J Fanning 14/1: 1211-067: Slow away, nvr a factor: op 10/1, long abs: tried blnks: imprvd here but has struggled this term to recapture smart 2yo form. *¾* **87**
4291 **SPEED COP 8** [3]4-8-2 vis (94) Martin Dwyer 4/1: 3004608: Cl-up, no impress over 1f out. *2* **70**
4382 **ABSENT FRIENDS 3** [1]7-8-7 (86) J Edmunds 20/1: 6060009: Led to halfway, no extra over 1f out. *1¼* **71**
3827 **BOLEYN CASTLE 29** [5]7-8-7 (86) F P Ferris(3) 40/1: 0-000400: 10th: Al bhd: see 2068. *1* **68**
EFISTORM 121 [9]3-9-3 (88) L Dettori 20/1: 211-1400: 11th: Mid-div, wknd over 2f out: long abs. *3½* **68**
659} **FOREST RAIL 565** [7]4-8-2 J F McDonald(3) 200/1: 3126/64-0: 12th: b f Catrail - Forest Heights (Slip Anchor) Al bhd on reapp: sell & h'cap unplcd both '03 starts (rtd 50a, with R Wilman): '02 W'hampton scorer (sell, with D Morris): wng form at 5f, acts on both AWs & likes a sharp/turning trk: enjoys sell grade & can force the pace: now with J Harris: has tried blnks. 2 Jul'02 Ling 5ap 69a-67 E: 1 Jul'02 Wolv 5af 69a- G: *2* **46**
12 Ran Time 59.68s (1.38) Owned: Marchwood Aggregates Trained: Wantage

4455

4.40 E B F Racecourse Video Services Maiden Stakes 2yo (D2)
£5811 £1788 £894 **7f9y** **Good/Firm 32** **-31 Slow** Stands side

3709 **SANTA FE 33** [3] Sir Michael Stoute 2-9-0 K Fallon 7/1: 51: b c Green Desert - Shimna (Mr Prospector) Mid-div, hdwy over 1f out, led ins fnl 1f, pushed out: Mar foal, cost 210,000 gns: dam plcd at 3, sire smart 2yo, later v smart sprinter/miler: stays 7f, 1m will suit: acts on fast grnd: useful, win again. **93**
3568 **SILENT JO 39** [4] Saeed bin Suroor 2-9-0 L Dettori 4/5 FAV: 32: Prom, hdwy to lead 1f out & sn hdd, kept on but not pace of wnr: nicely bckd: acts on firm & fast: win a mdn: see 3568. *hd* **91**
3781 **ARBELLA 31** [17] P W Harris 2-8-9 (98) D Holland 85/40: 2443: Mid-div, hdwy over 2f out, ev ch ins fnl 1f, onepcd nr fin: continues to perform with credit, shown enough to win a race: see 3781. *1¼* **83**
4046 **LESCAPADE 19** [7] A M Balding 2-9-0 Martin Dwyer 16/1: 354: Led to 3f out, not much room 1f out, no extra ins fnl 1f: see 4046. *2* **84**
ART ROYAL 0 [6]2-9-0 J Fanning 40/1: 5: b c Royal Academy - Chelsea Green (Key To The Mint) Cl-up, hdwy to lead over 2f out till 1f out, no extra on debut: 64,000 gns Apr foal: dam wnr in the US, sire top class sprinter/miler: with A Perrett & will learn from this. *1* **82**
4223 **PEREZ 10** [13]2-9-0 P Dobbs 100/1: 006: b c Mujadil - Kahla (Green Desert) Prom, hdwy to lead 3f out till over 2f out, still ev ch over 1f out, no extra ins fnl 1f: Mar foal, cost E36,000: dam unrcd. *1¼* **79**
3988 **HEARTSONFIRE 22** [8]2-8-9 Paul Eddery 150/1: 330407: Keen in rear, hdwy over 1f out, no dngr. *½* **73**
4179 **SECRET AFFAIR 12** [11]2-9-0 J D Smith 100/1: 08: In tch, nvr nrr. *½* **77**
WESTER LODGE 0 [1]2-9-0 J Tate 100/1: 9: Rear, some late gains on debut. *½* **76**
GINGIEFLY 0 [9]2-9-0 I Mongan 100/1: 0: 10th: Slow away, sn in tch, no impress over 1f out on debut. *6* **64**
33**BROAD TO HEAVEN 48** [5]2-9-0 W Ryan 33/1: 300: 11th: Dwelt & rear, hdwy over 2f out, sn btn: 7 wk abs. *2½* **59**
32**LIQUID LOVER 52** [15]2-9-0 R Smith 100/1: 0000: 12th: Mid-div, no impress over 2f out: 7 wk abs. *nk* **58**
RED APACHE 0 [14]2-9-0 J F Egan 100/1: 0: 13th: Rear, hdwy over 2f out, wknd over 1f out on debut. *1¼* **55**
OPTIMUM 0 [12]2-9-0 R Hughes 25/1: 0: 14th: Cl-up, no impress 2f out on debut. *shd* **54**
CITY TRADER 0 [10]2-9-0 T E Durcan 100/1: 0: 15th: Dwelt, nvr a factor on debut. *6* **42**
15 Ran Time 1m 26.47 (4.47) Owned: The Celle Syndicate Incorporated Trained: Newmarket

4456

5.10 Free Bets @ Gg Com Apprentice Handicap Stakes 3yo+ 56-70 (E3) **[77]**
£4257 £1310 £655 **1m1f218y** **Good/Firm 32** **+01 Fast** Inside

4119 **SMOOTHIE 16** [16] Ian Williams 6-8-9 p (58) L Enstone 22/1: 104-0601: Bhd, hdwy over 2f out, drvn ins fnl 1f, led post: best over 10/12f on fast, gd & fibresand, handles soft & any trk: right back to form. **61**
4293 **RANI TWO 8** [1] W R Muir 5-9-5 (68) N Chalmers 20/1: 0654402: Bhd, hdwy over 3f out, led well ins fnl 1f, hdd post: gd run: on a handy mark: see 2284. *shd* **71**
4327* **BRAMANTINO 6** [8] R A Fahey 4-8-9 (6ex)bl (58) T Hamilton 11/4 FAV: 5055113: Rear, hdwy to lead over 1f out, hdd well ins fnl 1f, no extra: quick reapp: not disgraced on bid for hat-trick, return to further will suit: eff at 10f & suited by 11/12f, tried 14f: see 4327 (12f). *½* **60**
3747 **CARROWDORE 32** [5] G A Huffer 4-9-7 p (70) D Tudhope(3) 7/1: 2434224: Cl-up, no room/pulled out to chall 1f out, sn short of room, kept on cl-home: closer with a clr run but is a tricky ride: see 3747. *nk* **71**
4167 **KERNEL DOWERY 13** [6]4-8-13 e (62) M Coumbe(5) 20/1: 2110045: Rcd in 2nd, hdwy & ev ch 2f out, no impress ins fnl 1f: clr of rem: back to form on fast grnd: see 2433. *1¼* **61**
4243* **SNOWED UNDER 10** [7]3-8-2 (5oh) (58) J Cavanagh(5) 25/1: 5550016: Trkd ldrs, no impress over 1f out. *3* **52**

LEICESTER   TUESDAY 07.09.04   Righthand, Stiff, Galloping Track

3867* **BLUEGRASS BOY 27** [10]4-9-0 (63) R Thomas 12/1: 3000317: Slow away/rear, hdwy 3f out, onepcd.   nk   56
4057 **BASINET 19** [3]6-8-7 (3oh) (53) P Mulrennan 12/1: 0040648: Slow away in rear, hdwy bef halfway, no   nk   48
impress over 1f out: hdles fit (nov h'cap wnr), rtd 110h): see 2120.
4402 **QUINTOTO 2** [14]4-9-2 (65) D Nolan 40/1: 0000-609: Led till over 1f out, no extra: quick reapp.   nk   56
4295 **JACKIE KIELY 8** [17]3-8-9 t (65) F P Ferris 15/2: 1003040: 10th: Rear, hdwy 1f out, not pace to chall.   1   54
4143 **ELLOVAMUL 14** [11]4-8-7 (5oh) (51) P Makin 66/1: 0401000: 11th: In tch, hdwy over 3f out, sn btn.   1¼   43
4260 **SIENNA SUNSET 9** [12]5-8-9 (58) B Swarbrick 12/1: 6624130: 12th: Rear, not clr run over 2f out, sn btn.   hd   44
4342 **BLUETORIA 5** [15]3-8-12 (68) J F McDonald 10/1: 0-4050: 13th: Keen in tch, hmpd & lost place 6f   nk   53
out, sn btn: op 16/1, quick reapp: see 1978.
3514 **ACTIVE ACCOUNT 41** [9]7-8-10 (59) A Mullen(3) 25/1: 5663000: 14th: Mid-div, wknd 4f out: 6 wk abs.   nk   43
4402 **ETON 2** [2]8-9-5 (68) P J Benson(7) 16/1: 2352040: 15th: Cl-up, short of room 3f out, sn btn.   2½   48
2881 **INFIDELITY 68** [13]3-8-1 (6oh) (57) Natalie Hassall(7) 50/1: 0606350: 16th: Nvr a factor: 10 wk abs.   5   29
3875 **ARMS ACROSSTHESEA 27** [4]5-8-11 (60) T Eaves 25/1: 1400160: 17th: Mid-div, no impress over 3f out.   6   23
4248* **SWIFT ALCHEMIST 10** [18]4-8-7 p (56) D Corby 12/1: 0000010: 18th: Al bhd.   7   8
3747 **BROOKLANDS LODGE 32** [16]3-8-0 (7oh) (56) Steve Harrison 100/1: 50-60000: 19th: Slow away, saddle   12   0
slipped halfway, btn: forgive this: see 3419.
19 Ran   Time 2m 5.66(3.16)   Owned: Miss S Howell   Trained: Alvechurch

DONCASTER   WEDNESDAY 08.09.04   Lefthand, Flat, Galloping Track

Official Going Good/Firm. Headwind may exaggerate fast times.

4457   1.15 European Breeders Fund Carrie Red Nursery Stakes Handicap Fillies 2yo (B1)   [97]
£26000 £8000 £4000   6f110y str   Firm -11   -13 Slow   Stands Side

3626* **SWAN NEBULA 38** [22] Saeed bin Suroor 2-8-13 t (82) L Dettori 5/1: 3511: Dwelt, sn trkd stands   92+
side trav well, led ins last, rdn & styd on strongly: hvly bckd: crse rec time: h'cap bow: eff at 6f/6.5f on firm
& gd grnd, looks sure to relish return to 7f+: acts on firm & gd grnd, gall trks: most scopey filly who posted a
useful display, can improve again, prob over further.
4050 **INDIENA 20** [15] B J Meehan 2-8-5 (74) C Catlin 16/1: 45242: Led stands side, hdd ins last, kept   1¾   81
on, not pace of wnr: gd run in h'cap bow: eff at 6f/6.5f: mdn but shld find a race sn on this evidence: see 3795.
4298 **BIBURY FLYER 9** [21] M R Channon 2-8-13 (82) T E Durcan 20/1: 1200333: Held up stands side trav   hd   88
well, styd on for press fnl 1f, not pace of wnr: imprvd eff over this longer 6.5f trip: can win again: see 3623.
3626 **DANCE FLOWER 38** [13] M R Channon 2-8-8 (77) A Culhane 12/1: 2354: Mid-div stands side, styd on   1   80
for press, not able to chall: bckd at long odds in the morning: h'cap bow: styd longer 6.5f trip, shapes as if 7f
will now suit: acts on firm & gd grnd: shld find a race: see 3386 & 3071.
3022 **ABERDOVEY 63** [17]2-8-8 (77) R Mullen 12/1: 5135: Sn pushed along towards rear stands side, styd   nk   79
on for press, nvr threatened: bckd, op 16/1, 2 month abs: handles firm & gd grnd, cying out for 7f in similar.
4258 **MISS MEGGY 10** [12]2-9-7 (90) M J Kinane 14/1: 110656: Sn handy stands side, outpcd by ldrs from   nk   91
over 1f out: longer trip, prob handles firm & gd: eff at 6f/6.5f on firm & gd grnd: see 4258 & 2165 (5f).
3825 **CONSIDER THIS 30** [14]2-8-13 (82) K Darley 25/1: 25327: Chsd ldrs stands side, rdn & not able to chall.   ¾   81
2783 **HIGHLAND CASCADE 73** [18]2-8-9 (78) J Tate 14/1: 1328: Chsd ldrs stands side, hung left & no   hd   76
extra dist: nicely bckd: abs: just btr 2341.
3781 **STRAWBERRY DALE 32** [4]2-9-7 (90) T Quinn 10/1: 1109: Chsd ldr far side & led that group over 4f   1¼   84
out, rdn & no ch with ldrs stands side from over 1f out: first home from far side group, prob worth another look.
4064 **MOLLY MARIE 20** [1]2-8-8 (77) P Robinson 22/1: 246200: 10th: Chsd ldrs far side, no impress fnl 2f.   1   68
3607 **AFRICAN BREEZE 39** [19]2-8-11 (80) Dean McKeown 25/1: 041450: 11th: Dwelt & held up stands side,   ½   69
only mod prog: see 2547 (5f).
4153 **EASY FEELING 18** [3]2-9-2 (85) R Hughes 20/1: 334150: 12th: Led far side 2f, no impress fnl 2f: btr 3623.   nk   73
3774 **LAMH EILE 32** [16]2-9-5 (88) N Mackay(3) 9/2 FAV: 1130: 13th: Chsd ldrs stands side, hung right &   ½   74
btn over 1f out: hvly bckd on h'cap bow: btr 3774 & 3189 (7f).
3624 **MISS MALONE 39** [5]2-8-6 (75) Dane O'Neill 50/1: 002400: 14th: Sn prom stands side & chsd ldr   1½   56
over 2f out, wknd from dist: btr 3183.
4059 **GHASIBA 20** [11]2-8-13 (82) J Mackay 20/1: 6200: 15th: Stands side, dwelt, al towards rear: h'cap bow.   ½   61
3614 **GENNIE BOND 39** [20]2-8-10 (79) R L Moore 20/1: 43200: 16th: Stands side, dwelt, nvr a factor: btr 3290.   1¼   54
4100 **KEEP BACCKINHIT 18** [6]2-8-11 (80) J Fortune 33/1: 303150: 17th: Held up far side, no impress.   hd   54
4079 **Apple Of My Eye 19** [5] W Ryan 40/1:0   4273 **Alvarinho Lady 9** [2]2-8-5 (74) Paul Eddery 66/1:0
4224 **On The Waterline 11** [9]2-8-7 (76) F P Ferris(3) 40/1:0   3115 **Dorn Dancer 60** [7]2-8-12 (81) D Holland 50/1:0
21 Ran   Time 1m 17.95 (.15)   Owned: Godolphin   Trained: Newmarket

4458   1.50 #200000 St Leger Yearling Stakes 2yo (B1)
£173400 £69360 £34680   6f str   Firm -11   -19 Slow   Stands Side

3800* **CAESAR BEWARE 31** [12] H Candy 2-8-11 Dane O'Neill 13/8 FAV: 111: Mid-div towards centre, rdn &   112+
hdwy 2f out, led well ins last, sn clr, readily in a course rec time: remains unbtn: eff at 6f, 7f will suit: acts
on firm & gd: only small but a v smart gelding with a fine turn of foot, most taking effort, keep on side in Gr class.
4004 **DISTINCTLY GAME 22** [17] K A Ryan 2-8-11 (81) N Callan 25/1: 2221422: Trkd ldrs & led over 2f out   2   104
to ins last, no ch with wnr fnl 100yds: acts on firm & gd grnd: continues to progress & can land a nice prize.
4025 **MOSCOW MUSIC 21** [19] M G Quinlan 2-8-11 (100) R Hughes 33/1: 212623: Held up, styd on for press   1½   99
fnl 2f, no ch with wnr: acts on firm & gd/soft grnd: consistent & useful: see 4025, 1614.
OMASHERIFF 38 [10] Bruce Hellier 2-9-2 bl T Hellier 33/1: 1124: ch c Shinko Forest - Lady of   1   101
Leisure (Diesis) Sn handy & ch over 1f out, rdn & no extra from dist: blinkered German raider, rnr-up a Gr 2 event
earlier this term, prev won twice, incl a List contest: eff at 5/6.5f on firm & soft grnd: clrly useful.
4074* **CLARET AND AMBER 19** [20]2-8-11 T Hamilton 22/1: 355115: Pushed along towards rear, styd on well   shd   96+
from over 1f out, not reach ldrs: handles firm & gd grnd: continues to progess & needs return to 7f+.
4155 **CAMMIES FUTURE 18** [21]2-8-11 M J Kinane 16/1: 3126: Led stands side till over 2f out, sn   nk   95
onepace: handles firm & hvy grnd: see 4155, 3376 (C/D mdn).
3800 **JOSH 31** [18]2-8-11 P Robinson 16/1: 137: Chsd ldrs, outpcd halfway, kept on fnl 1f, no threat: nk   94
op 20/1: looks in need of 7f+ now: see 3800, 3272.

4004 **TRANSACTION 22** [13]2-8-11 T E Durcan 66/1: 321168: Chsd ldrs, nvr able to chall: see 3614. | 2½ | 86
3935 **RAINBOW RISING 25** [4]2-8-11 R Winston 66/1: 429: Chsd ldrs far side & led that group nr line, | ½ | 84+
nvr any ch with principals stands side: first home from smaller unfav'd far side group, will surely find a mdn.
4139 **OLIGARCH 15** [9]2-8-11 L Dettori 22/1: 20: 10th: Switched right start & chsd ldrs stands side, | nk | 83
no impress when short of room over 1f out, kept on late: shld do better back in mdn company: see 4139 (mdn).
4025* **DANCE NIGHT 21** [3]2-9-2 (92) T Quinn 33/1: 1160610: 11th: Chsd ldrs far side, no impress fnl 2f. | nk | 87
3897* **PERSIAN ROCK 27** [14]2-8-11 D Holland 50/1: 2110: 12th: Swerved right start & bhd, mod late prog. | shd | 83
4217 **CANTON 11** [11]2-8-11 (87) R L Moore 50/1: 4453330: 13th: Rear, nvr a factor: btr 3743. | shd | 81
3432* **MIMI MOUSE 46** [2]2-8-6 (79) K Darley 25/1: 643110: 14th: Chsd ldrs far side, no impress fnl 2f: abs. | shd | 76
4307 **BIGALOS BANDIT 8** [6]2-8-11 (91) J Murtagh 66/1: 2404330: 15th: Led far side till well in last, | shd | 80
nvr ch with ldrs stands side: see 4307, 4025.
4159 **CAPTAIN HURRICANE 17** [15]2-9-4 J Fortune 4/1: 22140: 16th: Bmpd start & held up, no impress on | nk | 86
ldrs fnl 2f: well bckd: joc reportedly colt may have gone over the top for the season: btr 4159 & 3028.
3644* **IMPERIAL SOUND 37** [16]2-8-11 E Ahern 20/1: 12010: 17th: Mid-div, struggling halfway: btr 3644. | hd | 78
3122 **FOR LIFE 60** [5]2-8-11 M Hills 33/1: 30: 18th: Dwelt, far side & nvr a factor: abs: see 3122. | shd | 78
4280 **DARIO GEE GEE 9** [22]2-9-0 (95) J Carroll 33/1: 2202150: 19th: Sn outpcd & nvr a factor: btr 3935. | 1½ | 76
3956 **RIGHT ANSWER 28** [8]2-8-6 (95) K McEvoy 20/1: 4122530: 20th: Switched early & rcd stands side, | nk | 67
chsd ldrs 4f, sn btn: btr 3115.
3607 **FORZEEN 39** [7]2-8-11 (74) C Catlin 100/1: 4231400: 21th: In tch far side till halfway: see 3284 (5f). | 7 | 53
3254* **DON PELE 8** [1]2-9-2 (84) J F Egan 20/1: 02110: 22th: Chsd ldrs far side, hung left & btn 2f out, abs. | 5 | 45
22 Ran   Time 1m 09.64 (u1.16)   Owned: Mill House Partnership   Trained: Wantage

---

4459 2.25 Totesport Portland Heritage Handicap 3yo+ 0-110 (B1)   [102]
£32500 £10000 £5000   5f140y str   Firm -11   +09 Fast   Stands Side

3937 **HALMAHERA 25** [13] K A Ryan 9-9-10 (98) N Callan 11/1: 6050601: Held up stands side, switched & | | 107
strong run for press ins last, led line to win in a fast time: stays 7f, suited by 5/6f on firm & hvy, loves
Doncaster: 3rd successive victory in this v competitive h'cap, a superb performance by all concerned.
4291 **TEXAS GOLD 9** [1] W R Muir 6-8-13 (87) Martin Dwyer 16/1: 4066022: Chsd front pair far side & rdn | hd | 95
to lead that group over 1f out, drvn & hdd cl-home: useful sprinter, win a val h'cap: see 4291 & 106.
4382 **PTARMIGAN RIDGE 4** [8] Miss L A Perratt 8-8-12 (86) N Mackay(3) 33/1: 0651033: Chsd ldrs stands | nk | 93
side, styd on well for press ins last: has nvr been the most consistent but in grand heart.
4382 **WHISTLER 4** [12] J M Bradley 7-9-2 (90) R Hills 40/1: 1403404: Held up stands side, hung left | nk | 96
but kept on from over 1f out, not able to chall: qck reappp: see 2894.
4382 **WHITBARROW 4** [3]5-9-4 bl (92) J F Egan 40/1: 0000005: Led far side trio 4f: gd run, eff in blnks. | ½ | 96
4382* **FOREVER PHOENIX 4** [17]4-9-11 (7ex) (99) A Quinn(5) 8/1: 2303616: Held up stands side, short of | shd | 103+
room over 1f out, kept on well ins last, not reach btr: qck reappp under a pen: plcd with a clr passage.
4291 **CORRIDOR CREEPER 9** [19]7-9-7 p (95) R L Moore 14/1: 2360357: Led/dsptd lead stand side, led that | hd | 98
group over 1f out, no extra ins last.
3937 **JONNY EBENEEZER 25** [25]5-9-2 bl (90) L Dettori 12/1: 1141108: Held up stands side, kept on: needs 6f. | nk | 92
4098 **MUTAWAQED 18** [22]6-9-2 t (90) E Ahern 7/1: CO FAV: 4201029: Held up stands side, hmpd over 1f out, | nk | 91
kept on ins last: closer with a clr passage & rtn to 6f shld suit: see 4098 & 3434.
4382 **PERUVIAN CHIEF 4** [10]7-9-7 (95) R Mullen 66/1: 2000U00: 10th: Held up stands side, kept on ins last. | ¾ | 94
3002 **FUN TO RIDE 64** [5]3-9-2 (92) M Hills 28/1: 22-12000: 11th: Chsd ldrs stands side, btn over 1f out, abs. | nk | 90
4382 **FUNFAIR WANE 4** [4]5-9-2 (90) D Holland 20/1: 0040060: 12th: Chsd ldr far side, no impress dist. | nk | 87
3569* **MERLINS DANCER 40** [21]4-8-13 (87) A Nicholls 17/1: CO FAV: 1000410: 13th: Dsptd lead stands side | nk | 83
4f, sn btn: bckd, op 9/1: abs: see 3569.
1703 **POMFRET LAD 118** [20]6-9-8 (96) Alex Greaves 66/1: 052-0000: 14th: b g Cyrano de Bergerac - Lucky | shd | 92
Flinders (Free State) Mid-div stands side, nvr land a blow, 4 month abs: rtd h'cap scorer '03, subs class stks
rnr-up: rtd h'cap rnr-up '02: eff at 6f/7f on firm & fast grnd, stiff/gall trks: best without blnks: improve at 6f+.
2 Sep'03 Newm 7g/f 101-(100) B: 1 Aug'03 Newb 7frm 100-94 C: 2 Jul'02 Newb 6g/f 105-102 B:
3792 **CONNECT 32** [15]7-9-5 bl (93) P Robinson 25/1: 0414000: 15th: Held up stands side, nvr able to chall. | ½ | 87
3622 **PIC UP STICKS 39** [16]5-9-7 (95) T E Durcan 7/1: CO FAV: 1636000: 16th: Dwelt stands side, held | 1 | 86
up, nvr land a blow: well bckd: btr 3466.
4291* **ATLANTIC VIKING 9** [14]9-9-10 (10ex) (98) R Winston 40/1: 4001410: 17th: Dwelt, stands side, no dngr. | nk | 88
4201 *SPANISH ACE 12** [11]3-8-13 h bl (89) J Murtagh 25/1: 0550410: 18th: Held up stands side & al bhd. | ½ | 77
3792 **Raccoon 32** [6]4-9-1 vis(89) K Darley 14/1:0   4005 **Fantasy Believer 22** [9]6-9-6 (94) T Hamilton(3) 18/1:0
4048* **High Voltage 20** [7]3-9-6 t(96) Darren Williams 20/1:0 1771* **Lake Garda 116** [18]3-9-3 (93) T Quinn 40/1:0
22 Ran   Time 1m 05.64 (u1.16)   Owned: Mr J Duddy and Mrs G Quinn   Trained: Hambleton

---

4460 3.00 Gr2 National Stud Never Say Die Club Park Hill Stakes Fillies & Mares 3yo+ (A1)
£60000 £23000 £11500   1m6f132y   Firm -11   -30 Slow   Inside

3621 **ECHOES IN ETERNITY 39** [3] Saeed bin Suroor 4-9-3 t (106) L Dettori 5/1: 011-4451: Trkd ldrs & | | 107
hdwy trav well 3f out, led over 1f out, drvn out: bckd, padd pick: slowest time of the day: prev winning from at
1m/10f, now stays a gall 14.7f well, 2m could suit: acts on firm & fast: v useful filly, comes gd in autumn.
3961 **MAZUNA 25** [6] C E Brittain 3-8-5 (69) R L Moore 100/1: 06-12322: Keen in mid-div, styd on for | 1 | 104
press to take 2nd cl-home: nvr threatened to reach wnr: much imprvd over this longer 14.7f trip (btn off 68 last
time!): acts on firm & gd grnd: see 3961, 2842 (h'cap).
4149 **BOWSTRING 15** [5] J H M Gosden 3-8-6 (1ow) (97) J Fortune 10/1: 0-12233: Trkd ldr & led over 4f | ½ | 104
out, drvn/hung left & hdd over 1f out, no extra: bckd: styd longer 14.7f trip: acts on firm & hvy grnd: see 4149.
4058* **TARAKALA 20** [2] John M Oxx 3-8-5 bl M J Kinane 5/2 FAV: 1133214: Trkd ldrs, drvn & styd on, not | ½ | 102
able to chall: acts on firm & gd grnd: stronger gallop may well have suited: see 4058.
4062 **MODESTA 20** [4]3-8-5 (88) W Ryan 18/1: 412065: Rear, styd on for press fnl 2f, not able to land blow. | nk | 101
3629 **LIGHT OF MORN 38** [1]3-8-5 (92) K Darley 14/1: 23146: Slow away in rear, kept on wide, nvr a threat. | 1¾ | 99
3619* **ASTROCHARM 39** [7]5-9-3 (103) P Robinson 7/2: 0512117: Mid-div, outpcd 3f out, kept on, nvr able | hd | 98
to land blow: hvly bckd, op 9/2: another poss unsuited by stdy early pace: btr 3619.
1494 **OPERA COMIQUE 129** [9]3-8-5 t K McEvoy 18/1: 13-68: b f Singspiel - Grace Note (Top Ville) Led & | 8 | 87
qcknd from 5f out, hdd over 1f out, sn btn/eased: 4 month abs: mdn scorer for J Oxx in '03, subs Gr 3 plcd (rtd
101): eff at 7/9f on fast & gd grnd.
4058 **DESERT ROYALTY 20** [8]4-9-3 (92) J Murtagh 25/1: 2440039: Rear, eff wide, btn 2f out, eased. | hd | 86

4058 **SELEBELA 20** [10]3-8-5 (95) T E Durcan 11/2: 1122320: 10th: Keen tracking ldrs, rdn & hung right   7   76
over 2f out, sn struggling & eased: hvly bckd: much btr 4058 & 3629.
10 Ran   Time 3m 05.82 (2.82)   Owned: Godolphin   Trained: Newmarket

4461 3.35 Mckeever St Lawrence Conditions Stakes 2yo (C2)
£6432 £2378 £1189   **7f str**   **Firm -11**   **-03 Slow**   Stands Side

3234* **LIBRETTIST 54** [5] Saeed bin Suroor 2-9-1 L Dettori 1/1 FAV: 11: Made all, qcknd tempo over 1f   114+
out & in command ins last under hand ride, readily: hvly bckd, padd pick: 8 wk abs: remains unbtn: eff at 7f, 1m
wil suit: acts on firm & fast grnd, stiff/gall trks: eff forcing the pace: goes well fresh: potentially top-class,
shld be followed in Group company: see 3234.
4096 **EMBOSSED 18** [1] R Hannon 2-9-1 (100) R L Moore 100/30: 61622: Sn handy & eff to chase wnr over   1½ 106
2f out, kept on, al held: well bckd: acts on firm & gd/soft grnd: scopey colt, prob ran to form of 4096.
3280* **CAMACHO 53** [4] H R A Cecil 2-9-1 R Hughes 5/1: 13: Trkd ldrs, outpcd by front pair over 1f out,   3½   99
kept on: op 4/1, 8 wk abs: longer 7f trip, shapes as if 1m wil suit: prob handles firm & fast grnd: see 3280.
3991 **LE CORVEE 23** [3] A King 2-9-1 J D Smith 18/1: 134: Held up, rdn & no impress on front pair over 1f out. 2   95
3451* **MOTARASSED 46** [2]2-9-1 (88) R Hills 13/2: 315: Dwelt, sn chsd wnr, rdn & btn 2f out: abs: btr 3451 (6f). 12   74
5 Ran   Time 1m 22.61 (u0.59)   Owned: Godolphin   Trained: Newmarket

4462 4.10 Thwaites Smooth Beer E B F Maiden Stakes 2yo (D2)
£7066 £2174 £1087   **1m str**   **Firm -11**   **-21 Slow**   Stands Side

3752 **MONSOON RAIN 33** [3] Saeed bin Suroor 2-9-0 L Dettori 6/4: 21: Led till over 2f out, briefly   99+
outpcd by rnr-up, led ins last, hand riding: hvly bckd: scopey colt who imprvd for step up to 1m, get further:
acts on firm & fast grnd, stiff/gall trks: useful & set for more success: see 3752.
4003 **SHANNON SPRINGS 22** [8] B W Hills 2-9-0 M Hills 5/4 FAV: 232: Led/dsptd lead, went on trav best   ¾   97
over 2f out, rdn/hdd ins last & not pace of wnr nr fin: hvly bckd, op 7/4: styd longer 1m trip well: acts on firm &
gd grnd: must surely find a mdn nr: see 4003 & 3470.
      SANCHI 0 [4] J H M Gosden 2-9-0 K Darley 25/1: 3: b c Darshaan - Samara (Polish Patriot) Rear,   2   93+
shkn up & styd on well from over 1f out under hand riding, not threaten front pair: 36,000gns Apr foal, half-brother
to a useful 12f 3yo scorer, also a hdles wnr: dam a dual 1m 3yo wnr: eff at 1m, breeding suggests further sure to
suit: strong, scopey colt who ndd this, expect improvement, looks sure to win races.
      SPEAR THISTLE 0 [11] J H M Gosden 2-9-0 J Fortune 20/1: 4: ch c Selkirk - Ardisia (Affirmed)   nk   92
Swerved left start, held up in tch, hdwy from halfway & kept on ins last, nvr threat to front pair: stablemate of
3rd, op 16/1: Mar foal, half-brother to a v useful 12f+ performer, also a 13f wnr: dam a multiple 10f scorer: tall
& strong colt with a stoute pedigree, sure to relish 10f+ & win races.
2876 **NORTH SHORE 69** [2]2-9-0 R L Moore 14/1: 65: b c Soviet Star - Escape Path (Wolver Hollow)   1¾ 89$
Mid-div, eff 3f out, sn outpcd by ldrs, kept on: op 10 wk abs: 37,000gns Apr foal, half-brother to a wnr at 5/7f, dam
plcd over hdles: workmanlike colt who imprvd from intro & poss still needed this, enjoy a minor trk mdn.
4147 **ASHARON 15** [9]2-9-0 E Ahern 100/1: 066: Chsd ldrs, rdn & no impress over 1f out.   shd 89$
      SUBTLE AFFAIR 0 [7]2-8-9 J Murtagh 22/1: 7: Keen & trkd ldrs, btn over 1f out.   5   75
2766 **HIGH TREASON 74** [1]2-9-0 Dean McKeown 66/1: 08: Keen, in tch, no impress fnl 2f, 10 wk abs.   ½ 79$
      WHOOPSIE 0 [5]2-8-9 R Winston 66/1: 9: Dwelt & al rear, no ch fnl 2f.   11   56
      PERFORMING ART 0 [10]2-9-0 R Hughes 12/1: 0: 10th: Slow away, rdn/hung badly left over 3f out &   2½   56
sn struggling: op 8/1: strong colt but v backward in appearance, learn plenty from this experience.
4205 **LOVE FROM RUSSIA 12** [6]2-9-0 N Callan 200/1: 00: 11th: Chsd ldrs till 3f out, sn struggling.   3½   49
11 Ran   Time 1m 37.32 (0.82)   Owned: Godolphin   Trained: Newmarket

4463 4.45 Thoroughbred Breeders' Association Classified Stakes 3yo+ 0-85 (C2)
£14053 £4324 £2162   **1m2f60y**   **Firm -11**   **-22 Slow**   Inside

3072* **TARTOUCHE 61** [11] Lady Herries 3-8-12 (89) R L Moore 4/1 JT FAV: 111: Mid-div, pushed along over   96
4f out & rdn/styd on to lead well ins last: hvly bckd, op 7/1: 2 month abs, remains unbtn: eff at 10/10.3f, 12f
shld suit: acts on firm & gd/soft grnd, stiff/gall or easy trks: goes well fresh: useful & v progressive.
3629 **MOCCA 38** [3] D J Coakley 3-8-10 (87) J Fortune 20/1: 52-45162: Cl-up & led over 1f out, drvn &   ½   92
hdd well ins last, no extra: useful: acts on firm & gd grnd: see 2366.
3794 **JAMES CAIRD 32** [4] M H Tompkins 4-9-4 (84) P Robinson 12/1: 6222003: Held up, hdwy to chase ldrs   1¼   91
over 1f out, no extra from dist: ran to best: see 2860, 2101.
4034* **LOOK AGAIN 21** [9] Mrs A J Perrett 3-8-11 (85) J Murtagh 11/1: 14: Trkd ldrs & led over 3f out   1½   89
till over 1f out, no extra ins last: handles firm & gd/soft grnd: confirmed promise of 4034 (mdn debut).
3534 **FORT 42** [8]3-9-0 (88) J Fanning 14/1: 3-303205: Cl-up, led 4f out, sn hdd, kept on for press: 6 wk abs.   ¾   91
4149* **POSTERITAS 15** [5]3-8-11 (88) R Hughes 9/2: 321516: Held up, short of room after 4f, kept on   1¼   86
late, nvr land a blow: nicely bckd: just btr 4149 (soft).
4305 **GALVANISE 8** [6]3-8-11 T (85) M Hills 10/1: 0-61037: Rear, eff when short of room over 2f out, no impress. nk   85
4067 **LITERATIM 19** [7]4-9-5 (86) D Holland 7/1: 4128: Keen in rear, hung left under press & only mod prog.   nk   85
4071 **SWAGGER STICK 19** [12]3-9-0 (88) K Darley 14/1: 1160069: Chsd ldrs, no impress fnl 3f.   ¾   86
3553 **ODDSMAKER 41** [1]3-9-0 (88) Dean McKeown 50/1: 0153000: 10th: Keen in mid-div, kept on late, abs.   1   85
4097 **SILENT HAWK 18** [10]3-8-13 t (87) K McEvoy 33/1: 2-410400: 11th: Trkd ldrs, rdn & btn 3f out: btr 3029.   3   80
4239 **INCHLOSS 11** [13]3-8-11 (84) T Quinn 25/1: 0612240: 12th: Chsd ldrs, no impress fnl 2f: btr 3738.   5   71
3076 **DESTINATION DUBAI 61** [2]3-9-2 t (90) L Dettori 4/1 JT FAV: 22-13000: 13th: Led & hung right   12   61
thr'out, hdd 4f out & sn struggling: eased over 1f out: joc reported colt hung RHd thr'out: 2 month abs: btr 2021.
13 Ran   Time 2m 07.49 (1.09)   Owned: Lady Herries   Trained: Littlehampton

Official Going Good (Good/Firm Places)

4464 2.15 Pkf E B F Maiden Stakes 2yo (D3)
£5434 £1672 £836 1m114y rnd Good 41 -04 Slow Inside

4242 **INTRIGUED 11** [3] Sir Mark Prescott 2-8-9 S Sanders 4/11 FAV: 31: Rear, prog trav well to lead **91+**
2f out, sn hung left, pushed out ins fnl 1f, v easily, val 8L+: bckd at odds on: eff at 7.5f, apprec step to 8.5f,
relish further: acts on gd, gd/soft & a stiff or sharp/undul trk: left debut performance bhd with easy success:
sure to improve & win more prizes: see 4242.
4147 **INCA WOOD 15** [2] M Johnston 2-8-9 R Ffrench 5/1: 22: Led, hdd bef 6f out, led over 3f out, hdd 5 78
2f out, kept on, no ch with easy wnr fnl 1f: clr rem: acts on gd & soft grnd: see 4147.
3851 **RED RIOT 28** [4] D R Loder 2-9-0 T P Queally 7/1: 53: In tch over 6f, no extra: see 3851. 6 71
4269 **ARCHIE WRIGHT 9** [1] R Hannon 2-9-0 P Dobbs 33/1: 004: Led over 6f out, hdd bef 3f out, fdd. 18 36
4233 **YANKEY 11** [5]2-9-0 K Fallon 33/1: 05: b c Amfortas - Key (Midyan) Sn in rear & adrift: Mar dist 0
first foal, cost 3,500gns: dam successful at 8f: sire mid-dists performer: with C E Brittain.
5 Ran Time 1m 45.66 (3.86) Owned: Mr Faisal Salman Trained: Newmarket

---

4465 2.50 Mitie Generation Handicap Stakes 3yo 71-85 (D2) [85]
£9687 £2981 £1490 7f rnd Good 41 -05 Slow Inside

3804 **PERUVIAN STYLE 31** [2] N P Littmoden 3-8-13 (70) T P Queally 12/1: 0065201: Cl-up, styd on to 77
lead despite hanging left 1f out, drvn out to hold on: eff at 5/6f, ran to form on first try at 7f: acts on firm,
gd grnd & polytrack: likes a sharp/undul trk: on a winning mark & remains of interest: see 3693 & 914.
4317 **ASK THE CLERK 7** [6] V Smith 3-8-13 (70) Rory Moore(5) 13/2: 4330542: Missed break, plenty to do ½ 74
turning in, hdwy wide bef 1f out, kept on well ins fnl 1f, just held by wnr: tch 8/1: fine run.
4144* **LANDUCCI 15** [12] J W Hills 3-8-8 t (65) S Drowne 7/1: 00-20613: Held up in mid-div, hdwy bef 2f 1¼ 67
out, hung left & no impress dist: acts on gd, soft grnd & prob fibresand: remains in gd form: see 4144 (class stks).
3950 **LORD LINKS 25** [10] R Hannon 3-9-7 (78) P Dobbs 16/1: 0-400004: Bhd, prog wide bef 1f out, 'flew hd 79
home': not straightforward but caught the eye & well h'capped.
3421 **LITTLE JIMBOB 46** [1]3-9-4 (75) R Ffrench 11/2 FAV: 42-12435: Led, hdd & under press dist, no shd 75
extra: 6 wk abs: eff at 7f, will apprec rtn to further: btr 3421 & 2705.
4117 **IPHIGENIA 17** [7]3-9-1 (72) Lisa Jones 16/1: 4531266: Mid-div, hdwy 2f out, onepcd when no room dist. 1¼ 70
3985* **PATTERDALE 23** [4]3-9-5 (76) S W Kelly 17/2: 5200-217: Handy over 5f, sn onepcd: btr 3985 (6f, mdn). shd 73
3920 **HILITES 26** [8]3-9-3 P (74) S Whitworth 25/1: 0630408: Nvr nrr than mid-div: cheek pieces. ½ 70
691* **SAVIOURS SPIRIT 200** [5]3-9-3 (74) K Fallon 8/1: 053-2219: Keen in tch over 5f, no extra: long abs. ¾ 68
4251 **GLEBE GARDEN 10** [14]3-9-3 (74) S Sanders 7/1: 5600120: 10th: Handy wide over 4f, wknd: poor draw. 2½ 63
4318 **ST SAVARIN 7** [11]3-9-5 (76) N Pollard 25/1: 0331000: 11th: In tch 5f, wknd: qck reapp: btr 3562. ½ 64
3892 **MALIBU 27** [9]3-9-7 VIS (78) J Quinn 40/1: 6501500: 12th: Al in rear: first time visor. shd 65
4110 **SWEET REPLY 18** [13]3-9-0 (71) F Norton 25/1: 0510050: 13th: Rear, nvr a factor. ¾ 56
4225 **SENESCHAL 11** [3]3-8-13 (70) S Hitchcott(3) 10/1: 1-000000: 14th: Bhd, nvr a factor. hd 54
14 Ran Time 1m 23.34 (3.24) Owned: M C S D Racing Ltd Trained: Newmarket

---

4466 3.25 Sterling Construction Composites Companies E B F Median Auction Maiden Stakes 2yo (E3)
£5486 £1688 £844 6f rnd Good 41 -09 Slow Outside

3896 **AMICA 27** [5] G L Moore 2-8-9 I Mongan 5/2: 221: Cl-up, styd on to lead trav well just after 2f 82
out, rdn out, val bit more: bckd: eff at 5f, suited by 6f, acts on firm & gd/soft grnd: acts on a gall or
sharp/undul trk: progressing well & now quals for h'caps: see 3639.
  MARKET TREND 0 [8] M Johnston 2-8-9 R Ffrench 6/1: 2: b f Selkirk - Equity Princess (Warning) 1½ 76
Chsd ldrs wide, styd on to chase wnr ins fnl 1f, al held: debut: op 4/1: Jan foal, dam smart performer around 1m:
sire decent around 1m: eff at 6f, further will suit: acts on gd grnd: sure to improve for today & rate higher.
3476 **REGAL DREAM 44** [7] J W Hills 2-9-0 S Drowne 16/1: 03: Rear, hdwy halfway, kept on ins fnl 1f: hd 80
6 wk abs: left debut eff bhd on step up to 6f: acts on gd grnd: see 3476.
4139 **CORDAGE 15** [2] G A Butler 2-9-0 S Sanders 15/8 FAV: 544: Led, hdd just after 2f out, sn no 2 74
extra: bckd: acts on gd & gd/soft grnd: can be seen to better effect now qualified for h'caps: see 4139 & 3951.
4121 **EDGE OF BLUE 16** [4]2-9-0 (68) K Fallon 9/2: 6305: Cl-up, al hanging right, wknd fnl 2f: lkd 2½ 67
unsuited by today's trk: showed more in 3857 (5f).
  BRIANNIE 0 [6]2-8-9 T P Queally 25/1: 6: b f Xaar - Annieirwin (Perugino) Missed break, sn in nk 61
mid-div, wknd fnl 2f: debut: Feb first foal, cost 32,000: dam success at 8/9f: sire top-class juv performer at 7f.
2750 **NAN JAN 74** [3]2-8-9 N Day 25/1: 07: b f Komaite - Dam Certain (Damister) Missed break, nvr a 1 58
factor: 11 wk abs: Apr foal, half-sister successful at 9f: a muliple wnr around 7/9f: sire successful at 7f.
7 Ran Time 1m 10.84 (3.04) Owned: Mr D J Deer Trained: Brighton

---

4467 4.00 Withersnet Classified Stakes 3yo+ 0-90 (C1)
£15367 £5829 £2914 1m2f18y Good 41 +03 Fast Inside

3565 **IMPELLER 40** [5] W R Muir 5-9-4 (90) S Drowne 11/2 FAV: 2605221: Chsd ldrs, hdwy to lead 2f out, 97
drvn out to hold on ins fnl 1f: op 13/2: 6 wk abs: eff at 1m/10f on firm & gd grnd: gd confidence boost for
talented 5yo who has been in fine form without getting head in front: see 3565.
3866 **MANGO MISCHIEF 28** [8] J L Dunlop 3-8-10 (92) S Sanders 7/1: 10-1242: Bhd, hdwy 2f out when nk 94
repeatedly barged into eventual 3rd, chsd wnr fnl 1f, al just held: fine run in defeat; see 2761.
2489 **ZONERGEM 84** [7] Lady Herries 6-9-6 p (92) T P Queally 7/1: 603-0633: Mid-div, sn lost pl, hdwy 2f ½ 96
out when repeatedly barged into 2nd, kept on well ins fnl 1f, not btn far: 12 wk abs: quirky but talented 6yo who
canb find a race off this mark on this evidence: btr 2489 (Royal Hunt Cup).
3945* **BOULE DOR 25** [10] R Ingram 3-8-11 (89) N Day 8/1: 4142014: Held up, prog wide to chase wnr bef 1 92
1f out, no extra well ins last: clr rem: ran to form of win in 3945.
4021 **WING COMMANDER 21** [3]5-9-8 (94) R Ffrench 6/1: 0010305: In tch, eff bef 2f out, wknd dist: btr 3755. 5 89
4061 **JAZZ MESSENGER 20** [4]4-9-7 (93) S W Kelly 6/1: 06-60006: Mid-div over 1m, sn wknd: btr 3954. 3½ 83

3278	**NUZOOA 53** [6]3-8-10 BL (92) W Supple 8/1: 2-157: Led, hdd 2f out, wknd: 8 wk abs & 1st time blnks.	1½	76
4219	**FOODBROKER FOUNDER 11** [12]4-9-6 (92) N Pollard 33/1: 0-066068: Cl-up over 7f, fdd: btr 3506.	5	72
2406	**NUNKI 88** [1]3-8-11 (87) J Quinn 25/1: 3109: In tch over 7f, wknd: long abs: btr 1922.	9	57
1861	**COLD TURKEY 11** [9]4-9-4 (90) S Whitworth 7/1: 3241240: 10th: Held up, nvr a factor: long abs.	1¾	54
3777	**MUHAREB 32** [11]5-9-6 (92) J P Guillambert(3) 20/1: 3004-500: 11th: Handy over 6f, sn fdd: btr 3444.	15	34

11 Ran   Time 2m 7.67 (3.87)   Owned: D G Clarke & C L A Edginton   Trained: Lambourn

---

4468   4.35 Group Two Robowatch Handicap Stakes 3yo 71-85 (D2)   [90]
£9632 £2964 £1482   **1m4f10y**   **Good 41**   **-00 Slow**   Centre

3862	**NORDWIND 28** [4] P W Harris 3-9-3 (79) I Mongan 4/1: 341121: Made all, drvn out ins fnl 1f to hold-on: op 5/1: eff at 1m/10f, ran to form of step up to 12f: acts on fast, gd/soft & polytrack: has high head carriage but is proving consistent: see 3862 & 3578.		86
3458	**HORNER 45** [11] P F I Cole 3-9-5 (81) J Quinn 33/1: 0421032: Held up, hdwy wide over 2f out, styd on chase wnr ins fnl 1f, al held: gd run in defeat & can find similar: see 2411 (mdn).	¾	85
4062	**SAND AND STARS 20** [5] M H Tompkins 3-9-5 (81) M Henry 8/1: 3521203: In tch, styd on to chase wnr 2f out, no extra ins fnl 1f: back to form on rtn to 12f: see 3240 & 3984.	¾	83
4080	**PAGAN MAGIC 19** [7] J A R Toller 3-8-13 (75) Lisa Jones 11/1: 5-301054: Held up, hdwy 3f out, onepcd.	½	76
4058	**PAYOLA 20** [10]3-8-10 (72) S Sanders 14/1: 0-165: Nvr nrr than mid-div: see 4058 & 3648 (10f).	6	65
3845	**BIENVENUE 29** [3]3-8-11 (73) A Daly 20/1: 5-412606: Nvr nrr than mid-div: btr 3161.	3	62
3747	**THE VIOLIN PLAYER 33** [1]3-8-7 (1oh) (68) J P Guillambert(3) 50/1: 3-000057: Missed break, cl-up after 1f, wknd 2f out: btr 2247.	1	56
3862*	**HASAIYDA 28** [6]3-9-4 (80) K Fallon 6/4 FAV: 1418: Mid-div, under press when no room 2f out, sn no impress: v well bckd: reportedly struck into during race: first time at 12f: beat today's wnr in 3862 (10f).	6	59
4395	**MAN AT ARMS 4** [2]3-9-0 P (76) F Norton 16/1: 4004609: Missed break, nvr a factor: qck reapp.	7	45
3287	**CHERUBIM 53** [9]3-8-13 (75) T P Queally 20/1: 32-55120: 10th: Cl-up 9f, wknd: 8 wk abs: btr 3287.	¾	42
4183	**NIGHTSPOT 12** [8]3-9-7 (83) S Drowne 13/2: 5-632160: 11th: Cl-up 10f, fdd & sn eased: rider reported mount tired badly fnl 1f.	1¾	47

11 Ran   Time 2m 39.80 (5.0)   Owned: Mrs P W Harris   Trained: Berkhamsted

---

4469   5.10 Chanton Group Handicap Stakes 3yo+ 71-85 (D2)   [85]
£9792 £3013 £1506   **1m114y rnd**   **Good 41**   **+02 Fast**   Inside

4295	**MR VELOCITY 9** [12] E F Vaughan 4-9-0 (71) K Fallon 2/1 FAV: 3210631: Mid-div, hdwy 3f out, styd on to lead 1f out, rdn out: bckd: eff at 7f/8.5f on firm, gd/soft & polytrack: acts on a sharp/undul or stiff/gall trk.		81
4141	**JUSTE POUR LAMOUR 15** [9] P L Gilligan 4-9-1 (72) R Miles(3) 16/1: 0400152: Bhd, hdwy over 2f out, styd on well ins fnl 1f, post came too sn: acts on firm & gd grnd: remains fairly treated on old form.	½	79
4295	**FRANKSALOT 9** [10] Miss B Sanders 4-8-13 (70) S Sanders 10/1: 1454153: In tch, styd on to lead 2f out, hdd 1f out, no extra: another gd run on a sharp/undul trk: see 4295 & 3821.	¾	75
4225	**KING OF DIAMONDS 11** [4] J R Best 3-9-0 (77) W Supple 14/1: 6200104: Held up, hdwy despite hanging left 2f out, no impress ins fnl 1f: back to form on rtn to 1m: 7lb higher than win in 3947.	½	81
4141	**FLINT RIVER 15** [1]6-9-3 (74) L Fletcher(3) 7/1: 2400225: Sn no room & bhd, hdwy 3f out, onepcd dist.	1	76
3961	**HERMITAGE COURT 25** [7]3-9-7 (84) S W Kelly 6/1: 146: Keen cl-up, ev ch 2f out, sn no extra: shade btr expected on drop back to 1m: btr 3961 (10f).	1½	83
4173	**TAKES TUTU 13** [3]5-9-5 vis (76) I Mongan 12/1: 0200357: Held up, nvr nrr than mid-div: btr 3694.	2½	70
4362	**INVADER 5** [2]8-9-1 bl (72) J P Guillambert(3) 20/1: 0010668: Nvr nrr than mid-div: qck reapp.	¾	64
3947	**HABANERO 25** [6]3-9-2 (79) F Norton 14/1: 3133169: Led, hdd after 1f, led 3f out, hdd 2f out, wknd.	2½	66
4221	**MADAMOISELLE JONES 11** [13]4-8-9 (66) D Kinsella 40/1: 5164600: 10th: Led after 1f, hdd 3f out, wknd.	7	40
4295*	**CARRY ON DOC 9** [8]3-9-3 (6ex) (80) S Whitworth 8/1: 3615310: 11th: Held up wide, nvr a factor: btr expected after recent win 4295.	2½	49
4318	**WHITGIFT ROCK 7** [11]3-8-10 (73) J Quinn 33/1: 0032000: 12th: Cl-p over 5f, sn hung right & wknd.	1½	39
4221	**MBOSI 11** [5]3-9-1 bl (78) R Ffrench 33/1: 3020300: 13th: Keen cl-up till halfway, wknd: btr 3762.	6	32

13 Ran   Time 1m 45.13(3.33)   Owned: Mr A M Pickering   Trained: Newmarket

---

Official Going Good/Firm (Good Places)

4470   2.15 H & V News General E B F Median Auction Maiden Stakes 2yo (E3)
£5564 £1712 £856   **7f rnd**   **Good/Firm 22**   **-39 Slow**   Inside

3951	**GOODWOOD SPIRIT 26** [1] J L Dunlop 2-9-0 (79) R L Moore 8/11 FAV: 2231: Cl-up, styd on to lead after 4f, rdn out ins fnl 1f to hold-on: eff around 6f, apprec step up to 7f: acts on fast & gd, any trk consistent.		82
3955	**WINGSPEED 26** [3] Mrs A J Perrett 2-9-0 P Hanagan 5/2: 52: In tch, styd on to chase ldr well over 1f out, kept on well ins fnl 1f, just denied: clr rem: eff at 7f, 1m will suit on this evidence: acts on fast grnd: lost little in defeat & can find similar: see 3955 (debut).	shd	79
	CHASM 0 [6] M Johnston 2-9-0 S Chin 10/1: 3: b c Gulch - Subito (Darshaan): Cl-up till halfway, sn outpcd, rallied late, no ch with front 2: debut: Feb first foal, dam successful at 7f.	5	70
4289	**BEAUCHAMP TRUMP 10** [2] G A Butler 2-9-0 S W Kelly 33/1: 004: Handy over 5f, sn onepcd: see 4179.	shd	69
3951	**TRANSGRESS 26** [4]2-9-0 (69) Dane O'Neill 10/1: 3065: Led 4f, sn no extra: btr 2876.	nk	68
3955	**BOLD DIKTAT 26** [5]2-9-0 J Quinn 66/1: 06: b c Diktat - Madam Bold (Never So Bold): Rear, nvr a factor: Mar foal, half-brother to wnrs at 5/6f: dam unrcd: sire decent performer at sprint dists: with W R Muir.	6	56

6 Ran   Time 1m 24.42 (4.32)   Owned: Goodwood Racehorse Owners Group (Ten)   Trained: Arundel

4471   2.50 Vokera Nursery Handicap Stakes 2yo 0-85 (D2)   [90]
£8346 £2568 £1284   **6f rnd   Good/Firm 22   + 04 Fast   Inside**

4139* **YAJBILL 16** [2] M R Channon 2-9-7 vis (83) J Quinn 3/1 FAV: 232211: Made all, went clr dist, rdn   **99**
out, val bit more: bckd: eff at 6f on firm & gd/soft grnd: likes a sharp/undul trk: apprec recent fitting of
visor: vastly imprvd eff on h'cap bow & can follow up: see 4139 & 3951.
3624   **ELISHA 40** [11] D M Simcock 2-8-5 (67) M Fenton 20/1: 4510662: Cl-up, chsd wnr well over 1f out,   5   **71**
al held ins fnl 1f: 6 wk abs: eff at 5/6f on fast & gd grnd: see 2020 (auct mdn).
4224   **KWAME 12** [5] Miss E C Lavelle 2-9-2 VIS (78) S W Kelly 10/1: 2120253: In tch when hung badly   nk   **79**
right on bend after 1f, prog bef 1f out, just held for 2nd cl-home: ran to form with first time visor fitted: see 4065.
4198   **CUSOON 13** [14] G L Moore 2-9-7 (83) A Quinn(5) 12/1: 3144: Held up, prog bef 1f out, nrst fin: 2½   **78**
op 9/1: h'cap bow: btr 3671 (firm).
4198   **BOLD MINSTREL 13** [4]2-9-7 (83) P Hanagan 10/1: 3212425: Cl-up over 4f, wknd dist: btr 4198 (gd/soft). nk   **78**
4004   **TOBYS DREAM 23** [7]2-9-6 (82) S Chin 16/1: 0106: Rcd wide, nvr nrr than mid-div: btr 3544.   ½   **76**
3987   **LOUPHOLE 24** [10]2-9-6 (82) R Smith 25/1: 34107: Chsd ldrs wide, prog halfway, wknd dist.   ¾   **74**
4273* **SIMPLIFY 10** [8]2-9-3 (6ex)bl (79) R L Moore 6/1: 5325018: Rear, prog when short of room dist &   nk   **70**
again ins fnl 1f, sn eased: closer but for trouble in running: showed more in 4273.
4187   **TALCEN GWYN 13** [12]2-9-2 (78) A Daly 33/1: 4140459: Nvr nrr than mid-div.   hd   **68**
4273   **STORM FURY 10** [3]2-8-6 BL (68) A McCarthy 25/1: 03000: 10th: Chsd ldrs wide over 4f, wknd: 1st time blnks.   ½   **57**
4100   **NORCROFT 19** [13]2-8-13 bl (75) O Urbina 16/1: 1600040: 11th: Al in rear: btr 4100.   shd   **63**
4224   **KING AFTER 12** [9]2-8-9 (71) N Pollard 20/1: 1665500: 12th: Mid-div over 4f, sn wknd & eased.   nk   **58**
4273   **TESARY 10** [6]2-8-13 (75) Dane O'Neill 11/2: 6214330: 13th: Sn in rear, saddle slipped: best forgiven.   14   **31**
3817   **BOGAZ 31** [1]2-8-2 VIS (64) J Mackay 12/1: 2000: 14th: Rear, nvr a factor: first time visor: btr 1614.   3½   **10**
14 Ran   Time 1m 8.89 (1.09)   Owned: Sheikh Ahmed Al Maktoum   Trained: West Ilsley

4472   3.25 Listed Vaillant Fortune Stakes 3yo+   (A1)
£20300 £7700 £3850   **7f rnd   Good/Firm 22   + 05 Fast   Inside**

4384   **MAC LOVE 5** [5] J Akehurst 3-8-12 (104) G Carter 20/1: 2266101: Held up, prog wide bef 1f out,   110
pushed out to lead on line, val bit more: qck reappr: eff at 5/6f, imprvd eff on step up to 7f: acts on firm & gd,
poss handles soft: tough & useful performer who is unexposed at this trip: see 3596 & 2421.
4047+ **PETER PAUL RUBENS 21** [6] P F I Cole 3-8-12 (105) R L Moore 13/8 FAV: 4151112: Led 6f out, went   nk   **109**
clr halfway, hdd under press cl-home: bckd tho' op 11/8: lost little in defeat: ran to form of win in 4047 & 3550.
4063   **VANDERLIN 21** [8] A M Balding 5-9-2 (107) L Keniry 4/1: 3531033: Handy, prog wide 2f out, styd on   1½   **106**
well ins fnl 1f, nvr getting to front 2: op 5/1: continues to run with credit: see 4063 & 3098.
4270   **DESERT DESTINY 10** [2] Saeed bin Suroor 4-9-2 t (110) K McEvoy 11/2: 54-02524: Chsd ldrs, eff when   ½   **105**
short of room well over 1f out, sn switched & kept on ins fnl 1f: see 4270 (gd/soft).
3268   **IQTE SAAB 54** [4]3-8-12 (102) R Hills 10/1: 12-1605: Held up, prog wide 2f out, nrst fin: 6 wk   nk   **104**
abs: shade btr after disapp on last 2 starts, see 1150 (reapp).
4231* **MATERIAL WITNESS 12** [1]7-9-2 (105) J Quinn 8/1: 1120416: Led, hdd after 1f, styd cl-up, no extra   shd   **103**
dist: best when able to dominate & was unable to today: showed more in 4231 (made all, gd/soft).
3620   **KINGS POINT 40** [3]3-8-12 (100) Dane O'Neill 20/1: 5304037: Handy over 5f, no extra: 6 wk abs.   1¼   **101**
3782   **ROYAL STORM 33** [7]5-9-2 (99) P Hanagan 9/1: 1460028: In tch 5f, sn fdd: 'lost action'.   5   **91**
8 Ran   Time 1m 21.34 (1.24)   Owned: Mr Vimal Khosla   Trained: Epsom

4473   4.00 Fujitsu Handicap Stakes 3yo+ 71-85 (D2)   [92]
£9401 £3566 £1783   **1m2f18y   Good/Firm 22   -39 Slow   Inside**

3039   **RESONATE 64** [11] A G Newcombe 6-8-8 (72) Dane O'Neill 9/1: 2006-401: Mid-div, prog wide over 3f   82
out, styd on to lead dist, pushed clr, val 4L+: 9 wk abs: eff btwn 5/9f, imprvd for step up to 10f: acts on firm &
soft grnd: goes well fresh & acts on a stiff/gall or sharp/undul trk: unexposed around this trip: see 3039.
4392   **ARRY DASH 5** [4] M R Channon 4-8-9 (73) J Quinn 11/2: 0623232: Trkd ldrs, prog & ev ch dist, kept   2½   **76**
on ins fnl 1f, al held: continues to go well but proving difficult to win with: see 4392 & 4268.
1721   **MAYSTOCK 119** [6] G A Butler 4-8-8 (72) S W Kelly 25/1: 0-103003: Rear, prog wide 3f out, kept on   nk   **74**
fnl 1f, nrst fin: long abs: visor left off: acts on fast & polytrack, handles firm grnd: see 876 & 342.
4097   **RYANS FUTURE 19** [2] J Akehurst 4-8-11 (75) G Carter 10/1: 5005204: Missed break, prog bef 1f   2   **74**
out, late gains.
3768   **WOODY VALENTINE 33** [3]3-8-10 (81) S Chin 13/2: 6612005: In tch over 1m, no extra: btr 3205 (1m).   nk   **79**
3678   **REALISM 26** [10]4-9-5 (83) Darren Williams 16/1: 2110156: In tch, led well over 2f out, hdd dist, wknd.   2½   **77**
4293   **KATIYPOUR 10** [5]7-8-11 (75) Lisa Jones 11/1: 4034507: In tch when short of room 3f out, sn lost   hd   **68**
place, modest late gains: btr 3694.
4227   **DANELOR 12** [9]6-9-7 (85) P Hanagan 4/1 FAV: 0501058: Led after 3f, hdd well over 2f out, sn wknd.   1   **76**
4183   **GALLERY GOD 13** [12]8-9-2 (80) L Smith(7) 33/1: 0-000009: Rear, modest late gains: see 2255.   nk   **70**
4292   **SCOTTISH RIVER 10** [13]5-9-3 (81) Hayley Turner(3) 12/1: 6124040: 10th: Missed break, nvr a factor.   ½   **70**
3695* **KIRKHAM ABBEY 36** [8]4-8-7 (2oh) (69) R L Moore 11/2: 0326510: 11th: Mid-div 1m, wknd: btr 3695.   1½   **57**
3949   **SILVER CITY 26** [1]4-9-1 (79) K McEvoy 20/1: 610-2000: 12th: Led after 1f, hdd 7f out, wknd fnl 3f.   ½   **64**
3949   **PRAIRIE WOLF 26** [7]8-8-11 (75) M Fenton 5/1: 0051000: 13th: Led 1f, styd in tch, fdd bef 2f out.   5   **53**
13 Ran   Time 2m 9.92 (6.12)   Owned: Mr S Langridge   Trained: Barnstaple

4474   4.35 Denco Maiden Stakes 3yo (D3)
£5330 £1640 £820   **1m114y rnd   Good/Firm 22   -24 Slow   Inside**

3237   **TADAWUL 55** [3] E F Vaughan 3-8-9   R Hills 4/5 FAV: 01: b f Diesis - Barakat (Bustino) Made all,   70
edged right from dist, pushed out, val bit more: 8 wk abs: eff around 1m, further shld suit: acts on fast grnd & a
sharp/undul trk: goes well fresh: still showed signs of greenness & can rate higher.
3828   **PAINTBOX 31** [1] Mrs A J Perrett 3-8-9   R L Moore 9/4: 632: Chsd ldrs, prog & ev ch 2f out, kept   1½   **66**
on ins fnl 1f, not pace of wnr: tchd 5/2, clr rem: eff around 1m on fast & gd: see 3828 & 3469.
    SIAN THOMAS 0 [2] M P Tregoning 3-8-9   A Daly 20/1: 3: ch f Magic Ring - Midnight Break (Night   3   **60**

EPSOM
THURSDAY 09.09.04 Lefthand, V Sharp, Undulating Track

Shift) Held up, prog 2f out, kept on but no ch with front 2 fnl 1f: debut: bred to apprec further:

3447	**SACHIN** 47 [6] J R Boyle 3-9-0 (62) Dane O'Neill 20/1: 340-0604: Cl-up over 6f, no extra: 7 wk abs.	1½	62
4042	**NATIVE TURK** 21 [4]3-9-0 (69) K McEvoy 6/1: 0-0025: Handy 6f, sn wknd: op 8/1: btr 4042 (AW).	2½	57
4032	**FABULOSO** 22 [7]3-8-9 (45) J Quinn 33/1: 000-5606: Bhd, nvr a factor.	4	45
4300	**SEVEN SHIRT** 10 [5]3-9-0 (60) P Doe 50/1: 5400-007: Rear, carried hd high & no impress fnl 2f.	nk	49

7 Ran   Time 1m 45.71 (3.91)   Owned: Mr Hamdan Al Maktoum   Trained: Newmarket

4475
5.10 H & V 05 Exhibition Handicap Stakes 3yo+ 56-70 (E3)   **[77]**
£5684 £1749 £874   **7f rnd**   **Good/Firm 22**   **-11 Slow**   Inside

4438	**MANDARIN SPIRIT** 2 [1] G C H Chung 4-9-1 bl (64) O Urbina 5/1: 0-055051: Cl-up, led after 3f, rdn out ins fnl 1f to just hold on: eff at 7f/8.5f on fast, gd & fibresand: likes a sharp/undul trk: eff with blnks: on a winning mark & can follow up on this evidence: see 2045.		71
4168	**JAZZY MILLENNIUM** 15 [15] B R Millman 7-8-9 bl (58) G Baker 8/1: 3304122: Led, hdd 4f out, styd cl-up, styd on well ins fnl 1f, just denied: in-form performer who loves a sharp/undul trk: see 4168 & 3790.	shd	63
3996	**SCARROTTOO** 24 [9] S C Williams 6-8-7 (1oh) (55) R L Moore 9/2-FAV: 4031503: Held up, prog wide well over 2f out, styd on well ins fnl 1f, not btn far: another gd eff here at Epsom: see 3541 (clmr).	1	59
3924	**COLD CLIMATE** 27 [14] Bob Jones 9-8-8 (57) J Mackay 16/1: 4052204: Slow away, late gains.	hd	59
4251	**LADY MO** 11 [7]3-8-13 (66) A McCarthy 12/1: 6122355: Chsd ldrs, lost place halfway, rallied well fnl 1f.	hd	67
4030	**BALERNO** 22 [16]5-8-12 (61) N Day 12/1: 0212506: Chsd ldrs, onepcd bef 1f out: btr 3490.	2½	57
4367	**ICECAP** 6 [12]4-8-7 (3oh) (53) A Daly 66/1: 02-01007: In tch over 5f, sn wknd: qck reappr: btr 3672.	2	48
4144	**MISTER CLINTON** 16 [11]7-8-13 (62) Dane O'Neill 12/1: 0120168: Handy over 5f, sn wknd: btr 3676.	hd	53
3469	**LADY TAVERNER** 46 [10]3-8-4 (3oh) (57) P Hanagan 50/1: 0059: Missed break, nvr nrr than mid-div.	½	47
4317	**MINIMUM BID** 8 [3]3-8-4 (3oh) (57) J Quinn 14/1: 0020200: 10th: Rear, modest late gains: btr 3332 (5f).	½	46
4295	**HAIL THE CHIEF** 10 [6]7-9-7 (70) P Doe 12/1: 0306000: 11th: In tch 5f, sn wknd: btr 511.	hd	58
4317	**DANISH MONARCH** 8 [8]3-8-4 (3oh) (57) N Chalmers(5) 40/1: 0300600: 12th: Mid-div over 4f, sn wknd.	2	41
4051	**WHIPPASNAPPER** 21 [17]4-9-2 (65) N Pollard 14/1: 2200040: 13th: Handy over 4f, sn wknd: see 1910.	1½	48
4339	**SILVER CHIME** 7 [5]4-9-2 (65) M Fenton 25/1: 5660000: 14th: Al bhd: reportedly unsuited by trk.	¾	46
4272*	**MAGIC AMOUR** 10 [4]6-8-10 (6ex)vis (59) K McEvoy 13/2: 6040010: 15th: Handy till halfway, wknd, lame.	3	34

15 Ran   Time 1m 22.46(2.36)   Owned: Mr Peter Tsim   Trained: Newmarket

DONCASTER
THURSDAY 09.09.04 Lefthand, Flat, Galloping Track

Official Going Good/Firm FOLLOWING WIND POSS EXAGGERATING FAST TIMES

4476
1.15 Gr2 Betfair Com May Hill Stakes Fillies 2yo (A1)
£42000 £16100 £8050   **1m rnd**   **Firm -13**   **-04 Slow**   Outside

4192*	**PLAYFUL ACT** 13 [7] J H M Gosden 2-8-10 (90) J Fortune 8/1: 211: Trkd ldrs, qcknd & led over 1f out, drvn out: eff at 7f, imprvd for step up to 1m, get further: acts on firm & gd grnd, stiff/gall trks: lightly rcd, smart filly who has plenty of scope, win more Gr races: see 4192.		109
3357*	**QUEEN OF POLAND** 49 [8] D R Loder 2-8-10 T P Queally 11/4-FAV: 112: Chsd ldrs, drvn & styd on, not pace of wnr: well bckd, 7 wk abs: styd longer 1m trip well: improving, win a Gr race.	¾	107
3781*	**MAIDS CAUSEWAY** 33 [5] B W Hills 2-8-13 (100) M Hills 9/2: 21213: Held up in tch, rdn to press ldr over 1f out, no extra well ins last: clr rem: hvly bckd: stays 1m on firm & gd/soft: smart, see 3781.	shd	110
3944*	**CASSYDORA** 26 [2] J L Dunlop 2-8-10 T Quinn 15/2: 614: Led/dsptd lead till over 1f out: padd pick: longer 1m trip shld suit, would have preferred an uncontested lead: ahd of today's winner in 3944 (mdn).	5	97
4264	**FAVOURITA** 11 [4]2-8-10 J Murtagh 16/1: 145: Reluctant to go to start, sn pushed along rear, late gains for press, nvr landed blow: longer 1m trip: tricky ride.	hd	96
4264	**RED PEONY** 11 [3]2-8-10 S Sanders 7/2: 136: Led/dsptd lead, rdn/hung left & btn 2f out: nicely bckd: would have preferred an uncontested lead: see 4264 & 3539 (made all).	2	92
3781	**WINDSCREAMER** 33 [1]2-8-10 E Ahern 12/1: 167: Dwelt, chsd ldrs, btn 2f out: btr 3252.	5	82
3616*	**ROAD RAGE** 40 [6]2-8-10 L Dettori 16/1: 318: Unruly start, sn strugg btn over 1f out, eased, abs.	25	37

8 Ran   Time 1m 35.40 (u0.7)   Owned: Sangster Family   Trained: Manton

4477
1.50 Gr2 Gner Park Stakes 3yo+ (A1)
£60000 £23000 £11500   **7f str**   **Firm -13**   **+09 Fast**   Stands Side

3268*	**PASTORAL PURSUITS** 54 [7] H Morrison 3-8-10 (110) S Drowne 5/1: 2111-211: Dwelt, sn pushed along chasing ldrs, hdwy 2f out & styd on for press to lead ins last, in command nr line: fast time (crse rec): eff at 6/7f on firm & gd/soft: goes well fresh: lightly rcd, prog & smart, win more Gr races.		117
1758	**FIREBREAK** 117 [1] Saeed bin Suroor 5-9-4 t (115) L Dettori 5/2-FAV: 1005-142: Trkd ldr, rdn to chall 2f out, not pace of wnr ins last: hvly bckd, op 7/2: 4 mth abs: v smart run conceding weight.	1¼	116
4232	**COURT MASTERPIECE** 12 [3] E A L Dunlop 4-9-0 (110) K Fallon 13/2: 3542143: Chsd ldrs, kept on over 1f out, not pace of wnr ins last: hvly bckd, op 7/2: acts on firm & gd/soft: win again at Gr 3/List level: see 4232.	1½	109
4426	**GOLDEN NUN** 8 [4] T D Easterby 4-8-11 bl (104) R Winston 33/1: 3105054: Chsd ldrs, styd on for press late, nvr landed blow: see 2457 (6f, Gr 3).	1½	103
3620*	**FONGS THONG** 40 [8]3-8-10 (108) J Fortune 9/2: 321-115: Led/dsptd lead & went on overall over 2f out, hdd ins last & btn/eased cl-home: abs: ominous drifter from 11/4 & reportedly returned stiff: prog earlier.	½	105
3957	**SUGGESTIVE** 26 [5]6-9-0 bl (111) M Hills 9/1: 2140226: Chsd ldrs, carried hd high & no impress fnl 1f.	nk	104
4232	**NAAHY** 12 [2]4-9-0 (107) S Hitchcott 50/1: 1044607: Led/dsptd lead till over 2f out: needs List/Gr 3.	2½	99
3533	**TILLERMAN** 43 [6]8-9-0 (115) R Hughes 7/2: 0330-568: Held up, eff over 2f out, sn btn & eased: hvly bckd but ran as if something amiss: 6 wk abs: btr 3533 & 2470.	4	91

8 Ran   Time 1m 21.66 (u1.54)   Owned: The Pursuits Partnership   Trained: East Ilsley

DONCASTER THURSDAY 09.09.04 Lefthand, Flat, Galloping Track

4478 **2.25 Gr2 Gner Doncaster Cup 3yo+ (A1)**
£60000 £23000 £11500 **2m2f** **Firm -13** **-09 Slow** Inside

4000 **MILLENARY 23** [4] J L Dunlop 7-9-4 bl (117) T Quinn 7/1: 042-3131: Held up, smooth hdwy 4f out & **119**
rdn/narrow lead ins last, joined on line: nicely bckd: prev best at 12/14f, now stays a gall 2m2f well: acts on
firm & gd/soft, handles soft: seems best blnkd & extreme waiting tactics are poss ideal: v smart: see 4000, 1705.
4794} **KASTHARI 327** [8] J Howard Johnson 5-9-1 (112) J Murtagh 14/1: 220/303-1: gr g Vettori - Karliyka *dht* **115**
(Last Tycoon) Trkd ldr & al trav well, went on over 2f out, rdn & hdd ins last, rallied gamely to force ddht on
line: 4 mth jumps abs (dual nov hdle scorer 03/04, rtd 127h, 2m4f, gd/sft & hvy): Gr 2 plcd '03, (rtd 112, Sir M
Stoute): auct mdn wnr & subs val h'cap rnr-up '02: suited by 14f/2m2f on firm & soft, any trk: v smart styr.
2 Sep'02 Donc 14.6fm 101-96 B: 2 Aug'02 York 13.8g/f 102-92 B: 1 May'02 Wind 10sft 92- E:
4000 **DANCING BAY 23** [6] N J Henderson 7-9-1 (116) K Fallon 5/1: 0/31/-1223: Trkd ldrs, hdwy over 3f *3½* **111**
out, not pace of front pair fnl 2f: another fine eff, Gr 3/List level shld prove ideal & likes easier grnd.
4018 **HIGH ACCOLADE 25** [2] M P Tregoning 4-9-1 vis T (115) Martin Dwyer 5/1: 2-423024: Held up, hung *2* **109**
left under press over 3f out & nvr landed blow: op 7/2, tried a t-strap over this longer trip: btr 4018 (12f).
3552* **DARASIM 42** [7]6-9-4 vis (115) J Fanning 6/4 FAV: 30-61315: Led, hdd over 2f out & sn btn: hvly *3* **109**
bckd, 6 wk abs: better expected after 3552.
4000 **CORRIB ECLIPSE 23** [5]5-9-1 (106) J F Egan 18/1: 1666: Rear, only mod prog, nvr pace to threaten: *¾* **105**
thorough stayer, prob needs 2m4f+: see 2583 (2m6f).
4000 **ROMANY PRINCE 23** [1]5-9-1 (108) R Hughes 16/1: 0-332557: Rear, hdwy 9f out, rdn & struggling fnl 2f. *1¼* **104**
4000 **SILVER GILT 23** [3]4-9-1 (108) L Dettori 16/1: 4-331608: Chsd ldr, lost place qckly over 2f out, eased. *12* **94**
8 Ran Time 3m 51.86 (u0.64) Owned: Elliott Brothers Trained: Crook

---

4479 **3.00 Listed Jra Golden Jubilee Sceptre Stakes Fillies & Mares 3yo+ (A1)**
£19500 £6000 £3000 **7f str** **Firm -13** **-00 Slow** Stands Side

4331* **ATTUNE 7** [7] B J Meehan 3-8-6 (82) K Darley 12/1: 0100111: Trkd ldrs, rdn over 2f out, drvn & **104**
led well ins last, gamely: suited by 7f, stays 1m: acts on firm & gd grnd, stiff/gall trks: eff with/without
blnks: rapidly progressing filly of late, v useful display today, keeps on side: see 4331 & 3612.
3564 **GONFILIA 41** [2] Saeed bin Suroor 4-9-1 t (102) L Dettori 5/1: 1211042: Led small group towards *1* **106**
centre, drvn & narrow ldr overall over 1f out, rdn & hdd well ins last: nicely bckd, 6 wk abs: tough & useful.
3965 **ITHACA 25** [13] H R A Cecil 3-8-6 (100) R Hughes 7/1: 0-365343: Led/dsptd lead till over 1f out, *½* **100**
drvn & kept on: drpd in trip & enjoyed forcing tactics today: acts on firm & gd/soft grnd: see 2917 & 1150.
4226 **ENCHANTED 12** [8] N A Callaghan 5-8-10 (92) J Murtagh 33/1: 1100004: Trkd ldrs, styd on for *¾* **99**
press, not pace of wnr: imprvd eff: see 1925.
3971 **NYRAMBA 25** [5]3-8-6 (106) J Fortune 7/2 FAV: 0-255255: Trkd ldrs, styd on onepace for press: bckd. *hd* **98**
4331 **CAVERAL 7** [3]3-8-6 (95) E Ahern 66/1: 0010306: Dwelt, switched right to chase ldrs stands side, *½* **97**
kept on for press, not able to chall: stays a gall 7f: acts on firm & gd grnd: see 3773 & 1957.
4331 **LOOK HERES CAROL 7** [10]4-8-10 (91) K Fallon 10/1: 6310527: Held up, eff over 2f out, mod prog: *½* **96**
3965 **TAHIRAH 25** [11]4-8-10 (83) S Drowne 50/1: 0-000008: Rear, late gains, nvr a threat: see 2289. *½* **95**
   THE CATS WHISKERS 124 [4]4-8-10 P Robinson 28/1: 1021029: b f Tale Of The Cat - Good Faith *3* **89**
(Straight Strike) Chsd ldr far side, btn over 1f out: 4 mth abs: ex-NZ, dual wnr earlier in '04: winning form at
7f/1m on firm grnd, handles gd/soft: trav well for a long way, could prove sharper for this.
3965 **WHY DUBAI 25** [9]3-8-6 (89) Martin Dwyer 66/1: 102-0660: 10th: Dwelt & al towards rear: btr 3965. *nk* **88**
3621 **ZOSIMA 40** [1]3-8-6 t (107) T E Durcan 9/2: 2115-340: 11th: Trkd ldr towards centre, btn over 1f *shd* **88**
out: bckd tho' op 3/1, stablemate of rnr-up: 6 wk abs: btr 3621 & 2491.
4933} **POETICAL 19** [15]3-8-6 N G McCullagh 12/1: 222-310: 12th: ch f Croco Rouge - Abyat (Shadeed) *shd* **87**
Rear, eff when short of room 2f out, sn btn: Irish raider: recent mdn scorer: winning form at 1m: acts on fast &
gd grnd. 2 Oct'03 Curr 8g/s 100- :
3928 **STARBECK 27** [6]6-8-10 (79) N Callan 100/1: 0540040: 13th: Switched right from start, al rear: see 3928. *3* **81**
3564 **LUCKY PIPIT 41** [14]3-8-6 (100) M Hills 11/1: 03-52100: 14th: Bolted bef start, led till over 2f *dist* **0**
out, btn when hmpd over 1f out, eased right down: 6 wk abs: lost race in preliminaries: see 3365.
3971 **NATALIYA 25** [12]3-8-6 VIS (102) S Sanders 12/1: 3-30040P: Chsd ldrs, sadly broke leg over 1f out, dead. **0**
15 Ran Time 1m 22.26 (u0.94) Owned: Wyck Hall Stud Trained: Upper Lambourn

---

4480 **3.35 Ralph Raper Memorial Prince Of Wales Cup Nursery Handicap 2yo (B1)** **[101]**
£18200 £5600 £2800 **1m str** **Firm -13** **-14 Slow** Stands Side

4191 **SINGHALESE 13** [9] J A Osborne 2-8-6 (1ow) (79) S Drowne 20/1: 4331: Rear, switched over 1f out & **93**
rdn to lead well ins last, styd on strongly: first win on h'cap bow: eff at 7f, imprvd for return to 1m: acts on
fast & gd grnd, reportedly relished this firm surface: likes a stiff/gall trk: lightly rcd & useful filly: lightly
raced & scopey filly, entitled to prog again: see 4191 & 4035.
3753* **MIGHTY EMPIRE 34** [1] M H Tompkins 2-8-2 (76) P Robinson 8/1: 00412: Switched to race stands side *2* **83+**
early, mid-div & pulled hard early, smooth hdwy to lead dist, rdn & hdd ins last, nvr extra: styd longer 1m trip
well: acts on firm & fast grnd: fine run despite pulling hard early with no cover, remains one to keep on side.
4247 **SIR ANTHONY 12** [12] B Smart 2-8-13 (87) F Lynch 33/1: 132623: Rear, switched wide over 2f out & *1* **93**
styd on for press, not pace of wnr: styd longer 1m trip well: acts on firm & gd/soft: progressive profile, a gd
run despite far from ideal passage today, can win similar: see 4247, 3698 & 2689.
4355* **KHARISH 6** [3] J Noseda 2-9-0 (5ex) (88) E Ahern 6/1 JT FAV: 43214: Switched right & settled near, *1* **92**
styd on for press fnl 2f, not able to land blow: nicely bckd, qck reapp under pen, h'cap bow: acts on firm & gd/soft.
4193 **MY PRINCESS 13** [11]2-8-1 (75) M Henry 33/1: 3531055: Led/dsptd lead till dist, kept on for *hd* **78**
press: stays 1m with forcing tactics: see 3969.
4194* **THE COIRES 13** [5]2-8-13 (87) R Hughes 16/1: 0016: Switched right from start & sn cl-up, no extra *nk* **89**
dist: h'cap bow, shaped as if this longer 1m trip will suit: handles firm & gd grnd: see 4194 (7f).
4193 **ALRIGHT MY SON 13** [10]2-8-3 (77) J F Egan 20/1: 0245247: Trkd ldrs when no room from over 1f out *¾* **78+**
& pos accepted: bckd at long odds, op 33/1: much closer with a clr run.
4176 **BUNNY RABBIT 14** [14]2-8-13 (87) L Dettori 6/1 JT FAV: Trkd ldrs, poised to chall when no *hd* **87+**
room from over 1f out, pos accepted: nicely bckd on h'cap bow: luckless passage, lkd sure to be involved.
4176 **RAZA CAB 14** [2]2-9-7 (95) K Fallon 15/2: 31629: Switched start & sn prom, btn/eased ins last, op 13/2. *1½* **92**
4064 **SEA HUNTER 21** [15]2-8-13 (87) S Hitchcott(3) 14/1: 0142350: 10th: Chsd ldrs, not pace to chall fnl 2f. *¾* **83**

1351

4257 **TCHERINA 11** [7]2-7-13 (73) A Nicholls 25/1: 00230: 11th: Towards rear, only mod prog for press.   ¾   68
3451 **CELESTIAL ARC 47** [4]2-7-12 (72) F P Ferris(3) 50/1: 3000: 12th: Switched from start, mid-div, no impress. 1   65
3500* **BANKNOTE 44** [6]2-8-5 (79) Martin Dwyer 17/2: 4410: 13th: Restless stalls, al bhd.   6   60
4306 **COLEORTON DANE 9** [13]2-8-4 (78) J Fanning 20/1: 632130: 14th: Cl-up till lost place qckly 2f out.   5   49
4074 **FOLLOWING FLOW 20** [8]2-8-9 (83) K Darley 14/1: 03120: 15th: Bhd when hmpd over 2f out, sn btn.   14   29
4003 **SHRINE MOUNTAIN 23** [16]2-9-2 (90) S Sanders 33/1: 0200: 16th: Led till over 3f out, sn hmpd & btn.   3½   29
3877 **BUDDY BROWN 29** [17]2-9-1 (89) R Winston 9/1: 120: 17th: Bhd, hmpd when switched left over 2f   4   20
out, sn hung left & btn/eased: nicely bckd: btr 3877 (6f) & 2570 (g/s).
17 Ran   Time 1m 36.55 (u0.05)   Owned: Mr Paul J Dixon   Trained: Upper Lambourn

---

4481   **4.10 Listed Earth Mortgages Scarbrough Stakes 2yo+   (A1)**
£16250 £5000 £2500   **5f str   Firm -13   +05 Fast**   Stands Side

4226 **CELTIC MILL 12** [6] D W Barker 6-9-12 P (104) L Dettori 15/2: 0110061: Made all & rdn/held on well   109
ins last, v fast time (crse rec): eff at 5/7f, stays 1m: acts on firm, gd & fibresand, any trk: best dominating &
much imprvd for application of chkpieces today: win a Gr race in this form: see 1958.
4454 **TALBOT AVENUE 2** [7] M Mullineaux 6-9-9 (99) K Fallon 13/2: 2202022: Trkd ldrs trav well halfway,   ½   104
rdn to press wnr dist, al held ins last: qck reapp & another fine eff, deserves a race: see 4454, 2894.
4238 **CARIBBEAN CORAL 12** [8] J J Quinn 5-9-9 (101) R Winston 13/2: 0211003: Sn pushed along, styd on   1¼   100
for press from halfway, nvr landed blow: see 2727 (val h'cap).
4238 **ENCHANTMENT 12** [2] J M Bradley 3-9-3 (101) J Murtagh 9/2: 1124144: Cl-up, edged left & no extra   2½   87
bef dist: nicely bckd, op 11/2: twice below 4027 (g/s, made all).
4291 **BISHOPS COURT 10** [4]10-9-9 (102) S Sanders 15/2: 3002565: Towards rear, short of room 2f out but   nk   91
nvr a pace to land blow: see 3989, 2638 & 1207.
4238 **BALTIC KING 12** [3]4-9-9 t (106) J Fortune 6/4 FAV: 00-60136: Outpcd rear, eff from halfway, nvr   ¾   89
threatened: hvly bckd but nvr got competitive on this fast grnd: btr 4238 & 3466 (gd).
4089* **ENCHANTMENT 20** [1]2-8-3 (72) Martin Dwyer 100/1: 624617: Swerved left start, chsd ldrs, struggling fnl 2f.   5   78
4060 **NIGHT PROSPECTOR 21** [9]4-10-2 BL (102) P Robinson 33/1: 00-01008: Chsd ldrs, btn/eased dist: blnks.1¼   79
3551 **IF PARADISE 42** [5]3-9-11 (100) R Hughes 40/1: 5-106009: Al outpcd rear, hung left over 1f out, abs.   hd   74
9 Ran   Time 57.28 (u0.92)   Owned: Mr P Asquith   Trained: Richmond

---

4482   **4.45 Queen's Own Yorkshire Dragoons Ladies Day Stakes Handicap 3yo+ 71-85   (D2)**
£7561 £2326 £1163   **7f str   Firm -13   -13 Slow**   Stands Side   **[91]**

4341 **BORREGO 7** [10] C E Brittain 4-8-9 bl (72) S Hitchcott(3) 25/1: 2060041: Handy & led over 1f out,   77
drvn & held on well ins last: eff at 7f, stays 10f well: acts on firm & gd grnd: imprvd last twice in blnks: likes
to race with/force the pace: well ridden near the front of meaty messy race: see 2235.
4221 **ARCTIC DESERT 12** [16] A M Balding 4-9-0 (77) K Fallon 9/2 FAV: 0006162: Chsd ldrs, no run over   ¾   82+
1f out, drvn & styd on well, too late: well bckd, op 11/2: lkd unlucky, v well h'capped & must be kept on side.
4225 **GRANSTON 12** [14] J D Bethell 3-8-7 (74) T Quinn 12/1: 1660253: Chsd ldrs, hmpd over 1f out, drvn   shd   78
& kept on: see 3612 & 1176.
4103 **SAWWAAH 19** [19] D Nicholls 7-9-7 (84) A Nicholls 20/1: 0302104: Rear, switched wide for eff over   hd   87
1f out, pressed wnr ins last, nvr a threat fnl 50y: gd run: see 3954.
4005 **CLOUD DANCER 23** [22]5-8-12 (75) N Callan 6/1: 2135045: Rear, prog/no room over 1f out, kept on   1¼   75+
ins last, pressed wnr ins last, kept on: see 4005, 2791 & 2409.
4030 **BI POLAR 22** [11]4-8-10 (73) R Hughes 33/1: 0022036: Mid-div, switched & kept on onepace.   hd   72
1598 **QUEENS RHAPSODY 125** [17]4-9-5 (82) J Fanning 50/1: 2404007: Mid-div, hdwy/short of room over 1f   nk   80
out, kept on ins last, abs.
3809 **DISTANT COUNTRY 32** [12]5-8-9 p (72) S Sanders 10/1: 2525038: Rear, hdwy when no room over 1f out, ¾   69
kept on under kind ride cl-home, nvr a threat: another hard luck story in a messy race.
4122 **SERIEUX 17** [15]5-9-3 p (80) J Murtagh 14/1: 0200009: Held up, short of room over 1f out, kept on   ½   76+
under min press & much closer with a clr run: eff in chkpcs: see 1231 (1m).
4051 **CONCER ETO 21** [8]5-8-10 p (73) Martin Dwyer 12/1: 2341200: 10th: Mid-div, no room 2f out, nvr   nk   68
land blow: little room & can do better: see 3490.
4352 **STOIC LEADER 6** [3]4-9-3 (80) J F Egan 33/1: 6525640: 11th: Dwelt, sn trkd ldrs, ch over 1f out, no extra. shd   75
4362 **DESERT DREAMER 42** [6]3-9-4 (85) M Hills 6/1: 0-506000: 12th: Mid-div, ch over 1f out, fdd, abs.   ½   79
3791* **HARRISON POINT 33** [18]4-9-7 (84) J Fortune 6/1: 1122010: 13th: Mid-div when badly hmpd twice   1   76+
from 2f out, no ch after, forgive this: see 3791.
4301* **THREEZEDZZ 10** [2]6-9-7 (6ex)t (84) F P Ferris(3) 14/1: 1013310: 14th: Led/dsptd lead till over 1f out.   ½   75
4103 **TOUGH LOVE 19** [9]5-9-1 (78) T E Durcan 14/1: 0000500: 15th: Mid-div, no impress over 1f out.   shd   69
4362 **KINDLELIGHT DEBUT 6** [7]4-8-11 (74) P Robinson 66/1: 0-003000: 16th: Chsd ldrs, badly hmpd & lost   shd   64
place 2f out, qck reapp.
2427 **OVERDRAWN 88** [5]3-9-3 (84) E Ahern 33/1: 5-000000: 17th: Dwelt, al towards rear, 12 wk abs.   ½   73
4030 **HEY PRESTO 22** [21]4-8-9 (72) K Darley 20/1: 0561000: 18th: Sn struggling rear: btr 3443.   hd   60
4103 **SEA STORM 19** [1]6-9-1 p (78) T P Queally 33/1: 0656430: 19th: Chsd ldrs 5f, sn btn: btr 4103, 3809.   ½   65
3569 **LORD OF THE EAST 41** [13]5-9-1 (78) T Eaves(3) 50/1: 2321000: 20th: Led till 2f out, sn hung left/fdd.   3½   58
4341 **EFIDIUM 7** [4]6-8-11 (74) R Winston 40/1: 3541200: 21th: Al rear: btr 3608.   8   40
21 Ran   Time 1m 23.21 (0.01)   Owned: Monarch Thoroughbreds Racing   Trained: Newmarket

---

CHEPSTOW   THURSDAY 09.09.04   Lefthand, Undulating, Galloping Track

Official Going GOOD/FIRM

4483   2.00 'gravells Renault' E B F Maiden Stakes 2yo (D3)
£3621 £1114 £557   7f16y   Good 46   -13 Slow   Stands side

4194 **PRESS EXPRESS 13** [6] M R Channon 2-9-0 C Catlin 4/1: 061: ch c Entrepreneur - Nawaji   79
(Trempolino) Prom, hdwy fnl 1f, sn drvn along, led nr fin: Mar foal, cost E18,000: dam plcd over 12/13f: sire v
smart over 1m: eff at 7f, 1m will suit: acts on gd, gall/undul trk: confidence boost.
4296 **FINE LADY 10** [3] M Johnston 2-8-9 D Holland 6/1: 62: With ldr till led 4f out, hdd nr fin: nk 72
stays 7f on gd: much imprvd from debut, shld find similar: see 4296.
4069 **STRIKE GOLD 20** [1] S Kirk 2-9-0 W Supple 25/1: 03: b c Mujahid - Gracious Beauty (Nijinsky)   shd 76
Mid-div, hdwy & ev ch well ins fnl 1f, kept on: Mar foal, cost 22,000gns: half-brother to wnrs at 1m/12f: dam plcd
over 7/10f: sire v smart 2yo over 7f: stays 7f, 1m will suit: acts on gd grnd: much imprvd from debut.
4078 **KNIGHTSBRIDGE HILL 20** [12] A King 2-9-0 J D Smith 8/1: 564: Mid-div, hdwy over 1f out, kept on: shd 75
clr of rem: stays 7f, 1m shld suit: acts on gd grnd: see 3721.
4330 **BRANDEXE 7** [4]2-8-9 K May(7) 20/1: 05: b f Xaar - Tintara (Caerleon) In tch, wknd over 1f out: 5 60
qck reapp: May foal, cost E24,000: dam plcd at 1m, wnr over 13f: sire a smart 2yo: with B Hills.
4026 **WORLD REPORT 2** [13]2-9-0 P Dobbs 7/4 FAV: 46: Bhd, hdwy 2f out, onepcd fnl 1f: well bckd: ¾ 63
joc reported mount was nvr travelling: see 4026.
4069 **SOVEREIGN SPIRIT 20** [14]2-9-0 I Mongan 20/1: 07: Chsd ldrs, onepcd 2f out.   3 57
     PIRAN 0 [2]2-9-0 J F McDonald(3) 16/1: 8: Slow away, nvr a factor on debut.   nk 56
3890 **CREATIVE CHARACTER 28** [7]2-9-0 R Mullen 12/1: 409: Slow away, hung left over 2f out, hdwy over   shd 55
1f out, not pace to chall: see 3285.
4052 **ASTEEM 21** [9]2-9-0 (55) S Carson 33/1: 0500: 10th: Cl-up, no impress over 2f out.   1½ 52
     CRYSTAL MYSTIC 0 [11]2-9-0 BL R Miles(3) 50/1: 0: 11th: Slow away, hdwy over 4f out, no impress.   1¼ 49
4329 **MONTJEU BABY 7** [15]2-8-9 F Norton 33/1: 000: 12th: Al bhd: qck reapp.   nk 43
     BACK TO REALITY 0 [5]2-9-0 D Sweeney 33/1: 0: 13th: Nvr a factor on debut.   2 44
3863 **DESERT MOONBEAM 29** [10]2-8-9 R Havlin 33/1: 60: 14th: Cl-up, wknd bef halfway.   7 25
4123 **ROBMANTRA 17** [8]2-9-0 P (70) S Whitworth 50/1: 65360: 15th: Led 3f, no extra over 2f out: cheekpieces. 5   20
15 Ran Time 1m 23.95 (4.15) Owned: Mr Tareq Al-Mazeedi & Adnan Bahbahani Trained: West Ilsley

4484   2.35 Renault Kangoo Van Median Auction Maiden Stakes 2yo (E3)
£3669 £1129 £565   1m14y   Good 46   -04 Slow   Stands side

3520 **SHES MY OUTSIDER 43** [14] I A Wood 2-8-9 F Norton 9/4: 031: Keen & cl-up, led over 2f out,   84
pushed out ins fnl 1f: 6 wk abs: eff at 7f, imprvd for this step up to 1m: acts on fast & gd, gall/undul trk.
4035 **MOKARABA 22** [3] J L Dunlop 2-8-9 W Supple 7/4 FAV: 442: Mid-div, hdwy & ev ch over 2f out, sn   1¼ 79
onepcd: consistent, now quals for h'caps & has shown enough to win a race: see 4035.
     SOLARIAS QUEST 0 [7] A King 2-9-0 J D Smith 14/1: 3: b g Pursuit of Love - Persuasion   nk 83+
(Batshoof) Bhd, hdwy over 2f out, kept on under hands & heels ins fnl 1f on debut: op 20/1: Feb foal, cost
16,000gns: half-brother to 1m wnrs: dam a dual 10/12f wnr: v pleasing start, win sn.
     CLOONAVERY 0 [11] J A Osborne 2-9-0 V Slattery 20/1: 4: b c Xaar - Hero's Pride (Hero's Honor)   ½ 82
Dwelt in rear, hdwy over 2f out, kept on fnl 1f: op 33/1, debut: 28,000gns Apr foal: dam wnr over 10f: sire a
v smart 2yo: eff at 1m, shld stay further: fine start, improve.
4114 **OASIS WAY 18** [13]2-8-9 D Sweeney 13/2: 55: Slow away, sn cl-up, ev ch over 2f out, onepcd fnl 1f.   1¾ 73
3214 **YARDSTICK 56** [12]2-9-0 C Catlin 40/1: 06: ch c Inchinor - Fair Verona (Alleged) Rear, sn in   4 70
tch, onepcd 2f out: 8 wk abs: May foal, cost 12,500gns: dam unplcd, sire smart 2yo, later smart 7f runner.
     NOBBLER 0 [8]2-9-0 S Whitworth 25/1: 7: Slow away in rear, hdwy over 2f out, not pace to chall.   nk 69
4356 **BREGO 6** [9]2-9-0 R Havlin 40/1: 08: Led 3f, no extra over 1f out: qck reapp.   ¾ 67
3626 **MANORSHIELD MINX 39** [2]2-8-9 I Mongan 16/1: 09: Mid-div, hdwy over 2f out, no impress over 1f out. 1¼ 59
4325 **WELSH GALAXY 8** [5]2-8-9 R Price 100/1: 0000: 10th: Nvr nr ldrs, no impress over 1f out: wknd.   nk 58$
4115 **VOLITIO 18** [10]2-9-0 P Dobbs 66/1: 000: 11th: Dsptd lead till led 5f out, hdd over 2f out, no extra.   ½ 62
4269 **STOLEN 10** [4]2-9-0 R Mullen 40/1: 00: 12th: Mid-div, no impress when short of room over 1f out.   shd 61
4297 **SCALE THE HEIGHTS 10** [1]2-9-0 D Holland 12/1: 0000: 13th: Rear, t.o.: op 20/1.   14 33
     CHESTMINSTER GIRL 0 [6]2-8-9 G Hannon 100/1: 0: 14th: Bhd, t.o. on debut.   16 0
14 Ran Time 1m 35.9 (4.0) Owned: Lewis Caterers Trained: Upper Lambourn

4485   3.10 Renault Trafic Van Selling Stakes 3yo+ (G4)
£2765 £790 £395   1m14y   Good 46   +09 Fast   Stands side

4141 **ALAFZAR 16** [2] P D Evans 6-9-8 vis t (55) S Donohoe(7) 8/1: 0404401: Rear, hdwy over 3f out, led   62
2f out, pushed out ins fnl 1f: no bid: eff at 7f/1m on firm, gd & polytrack: enjoyed drop in class.
4367 **FIZZY LADY 6** [6] N E Berry 3-8-12 t (52) R Mullen 33/1: 1000002: Rear, hdwy over 2f out, rcd in   1 53
2nd fnl 1f, kept on: qck reapp: eff at 7f/1m & poss get further: back to winning form of 613.
4367 **MOBO BACO 6** [17] R J Hodges 7-9-8 (52) J F McDonald(3) 3/1 FAV: 1506043: Rear, hdwy & ev ch over   2 54
2f out, onepcd fnl 1f: op 9/1, qck reapp, clr of rem: see 2909.
4365 **OUR DESTINY 6** [8] A W Carroll 6-9-8 (56) D Holland 9/2: 1056604: Bhd, hdwy over 2f out, no impress.   3 48
4270 **DANCING KING 10** [18]8-9-8 (48) P Gallagher(7) 6/1: 2625555: Led to 2f out, sn no extra.   1¼ 45
3916 **OVER TO YOU BERT 27** [3]5-9-8 (45) M Savage(5) 12/1: 3310406: Chsd ldrs, no impress over 1f out.   nk 44
3996 **WODHILL BE 24** [9]4-8-12 (40) M Tebbutt 20/1: 0300007: Dwelt, hdwy over 1f out, onepcd fnl 1f.   1 32
4368 **MILLFIELDS DREAMS 6** [5]5-9-8 (55) I Mongan 10/1: 0000608: Cl-up, no impress fnl 1f: qck reapp.   1 40
3844 **CAYMAN BREEZE 30** [19]4-9-8 (57) C J Davies(7) 10/1: 0541059: Rcd in 2nd, no impress over 1f out.   3 34
2372 **LYRICAL LADY 90** [13]3-8-7 p (45) R Thomas(3) 33/1: 546-0000: 10th: Cl-up, wknd over 2f out: long abs.   2 20
4142 **TAMARINA 16** [10]3-8-7 bl (35) F Norton 50/1: 0000550: 11th: Cl-up, wknd bef halfway: see 240.   1 18
3727 **FRIXOS 35** [12]4-9-3 bl (47) V Slattery 50/1: 0P0-6600: 12th: Cl-up, no impress: p.u. over hdles.   4 15
4043 **DIAPHANOUS 21** [15]6-8-12 (35) Liam Jones(7) 100/1: 0000000: 13th: Keen in tch, no impress.   shd 9
     LYNS RESOLUTION 0 [16]4-9-3 R Price 66/1: 0: 14th: b g Awesome - Our Resolution (Caerleon)   2 10
Slow away, sn t.o., modest late gains: Flat debut, National Hunt fit: unplcd in 2 bmprs in 04/05: with D Burchell.
4411 **RUMOUR MILL 3** [1]3-8-12 (40) R Miles(3) 50/1: 0000000: 15th: Rcd alone far side, no impress well   ½ 9
over 1f out: qck reapp: see 4411.
     PICO ALTO 0 [7]3-8-7 D Sweeney 18/1: 0: 16th: b f Lugana Beach - Noble Canonire (Gunner B)   1½ 1
Dwelt, nvr a factor on debut: dam a wnr at 11f: with B Palling.

4124 **MISS DE BOIS** 17 [4]7-8-12   B Swarbrick(5) 66/1: 000: 17th: Dwelt, nvr a factor: see 4124.   ½   0
4260 **PRINCESS ISMENE** 11 [14]3-8-12 (45) S Righton 66/1: 0546R0R: Ref to race.   0
18 Ran   Time 1m 34.88 (2.98)   Owned: Waterline Racing Club   Trained: Abergavenny

---

4486 **3.45 Renault Master Van Maiden Stakes 3yo (D3)**
£3533 £1087 £544   **1m4f23y**   **Good 46**   **-01 Slow**   Inside

2751 **DUNE RAIDER** 75 [4] K A Ryan 3-9-0   F Norton 13/2: 001: b c Kingmambo - Glowing Honor (Seattle   78
Slew) Rear, hdwy 4f out, drvn ins fnl 1f, led cl-home: long abs: cost $120,000: dam smart US wnr: stays 12f,
further may suit: acts on gd grnd, gall/undul trk: runs well fresh: gd start here for new yard (prev Sir M Stoute).
4125 **NEWNHAM** 17 [5] L M Cumani 3-9-0   N Mackay(3) 6/5 FAV: 242: Led early, remained in 2nd, led again   hd   76
over 1f out, hdd cl-home: clr of rem: stays 12f: find a race: see 3828 (debut).
4267 **MARKET LEADER** 11 [3] Mrs A J Perrett 3-8-9 BL (71) W Supple 15/8: 502-333: Sn led, hdd over 1f   7   60
out, no extra fnl 1f: tried blnks: see 4267.
1871 **DANCING BEAR** 112 [2] Julian Poulton 3-9-0 (60) I Mongan 14/1: 0-4034: Rear, hdwy over 5f out, no   9   51
impress 3f out: op 9/1, long abs: see 1871.
4315 **DREAM VALLEY** 8 [1]3-8-9 H (60) D Holland 12/1: 00-665: Nvr a factor: op 8/1: tried a hood: see 4125.   1½   44
4111 **PATTERSON** 19 [6]3-8-9   S Whitworth 100/1: 006: br f Turtle Island - Richmond Lillie (Fairbairn)   30   0
Rear, t.o.: dam plcd over 7f: with M Madgwick.
6 Ran   Time 2m 36.74 (5.64)   Owned: Mr Tariq Al Nisf   Trained: Hambleton

---

4487 **4.20 Totesport Handicap Stakes 3yo 56-70 (E3)**   [77]
£3936 £1211 £606   **1m2f36y**   **Good 46**   **-09 Slow**   Inside

162 **NUTS FOR YOU** 276 [2] R Charlton 3-8-12 (61) D Sweeney 16/1: 002-1: b f Sri Pekan - Moon Festival   72
(Be My Guest) Cl-up, hdwy into 2nd after 2f, led 2f out, rdn out nr fin: reapp, op 12/1: rnr-up fnl '03 start
(mdn): eff at 1m/10f, acts on gd & fibresand, sharp or an undul/gall trk: runs well fresh: gd run on h'cap bow,
lightly rcd & open to further improvement. 2 Dec'03 Sout 8af 62a- F:
4388* **STEPHANO** 5 [10] B W Hills 3-9-2 (6ex) (65) D Holland 5/6 FAV: 0-050112: In tch, hdwy 4f out, chsd   ¾   72
wnr fnl 1f, kept on: qck reapp: likes firm, acts on gd: gd run on bid for hat-trick, continues in fine form: see 4388.
4388 **CAPTAIN MARRYAT** 5 [13] P W Harris 3-8-10 (59) W Supple 5/1: 2022323: In tch, hdwy & not clr run   2½   62
over 2f out, styd on ins fnl 1f: qck reapp: did not get run of race, closer to first two with a clr run: see 4388.
4282 **QUICKSTYX** 10 [4] M R Channon 3-9-5 (68) C Catlin 8/1: 14544: Keen in tch, hdwy 4f out, onepcd.   nk   69
3854 **SAIDA LENASERA** 29 [1]3-9-0 (63) N Mackay(3) 33/1: 40-06605: Rcd in 2nd for 2f, remained cl-up, ev   hd   64
ch 2f out, no impress ins fnl 1f: see 1708.
3747 **MUSTANG ALI** 34 [8]3-9-2 (65) F Norton 20/1: 3553566: Rear, hdwy 2f out, onepcd ins fnl 1f.   1½   64
4068 **RABITATIT** 20 [9]3-8-13 (62) B Swarbrick(5) 14/1: 0255627: Led to 2f out, no extra over 1f out.   2   58
4334 **OFF BEAT** 7 [11]3-9-2 (65) S Carson 33/1: 3000008: Rear, nvr nr ldrs: qck reapp.   1   59
4182 **UNCLE JOHN** 14 [15]3-8-9 (58) V Slattery 33/1: 0042409: In tch, no impress 2f out.   nk   51
1939 **TWELVE BAR BLUES** 109 [3]3-9-4 (67) R Havlin 28/1: 0050: 10th: Cl-up, wknd over 1f out: long abs.   nk   59
3828 **MEDICA BOBA** 31 [7]3-8-10 (59) P Dobbs 50/1: 00000: 11th: Al bhd: see 2419.   2½   47
4321 **SIERRA** 8 [6]3-8-13 (62) J P Guillambert(3) 25/1: 0-56650: 12th: Cl-up, wknd 2f out: see 2793.   4   44
4299 **GO GREEN** 10 [14]3-8-7 (1oh)t (55) R Mullen 11/1: 2143260: 13th: Slow away, rear, hdwy 6f out, wknd.   1¾   35
3898 **PREMIER DREAM** 28 [5]3-9-6 (69) S Whitworth 66/1: 6310400: 14th: Slow away, rear, t.o..   14   27
14 Ran   Time 2m 9.68 (5.58)   Owned: Mountgrange Stud   Trained: Beckhampton

---

4488 **4.55 Renault Vans Handicap Stakes 3yo+ 46-55 (F4)**   [69]
£3126 £893 £447   **7f16y**   **Good 46**   **+06 Fast**   Stands side

4368 **MY GIRL PEARL** 6 [19] M S Saunders 4-8-6 (47) N Mackay(3) 20/1: 6410361: With ldr till led over 2f   52
out, rdn out ins fnl 1f: qck reapp: eff at 6/7f on firm, gd/soft & fibresand, sharp, undul or a gall trk.
3650 **PEPPER ROAD** 38 [11] R Bastiman 5-8-12 (53) D Holland 9/2 FAV: 0-001222: In tch, slt short of   ¾   57
room & switched left over 2f out, hdwy over 1f out, kept on: consistent: rtn to further will suit: see 3229 & 2447.
3024 **ACCENDERE** 64 [15] R M Beckett 3-8-10 (55) R Mullen 20/1: 0050103: Bhd, hdwy over 1f out, kept   nk   58
on: 9 wk abs: acts on firm & gd: gd run, back to former form of 2292.
4367 **ARMENTIERES** 6 [18] J L Spearing 3-8-7 bl (52) J F McDonald(3) 10/1: 6006234: Cl-up, onepcd fnl 1f: nk   54
qck reapp: acts on gd, soft & fibresand: see 3854.
4168 **TEMPER TANTRUM** 15 [17]6-9-0 p (55) M Savage(5) 6/1: 0405465: Rear, hdwy 2f out, onepcd ins fnl 1f.   ½   56
4345 **ICED DIAMOND** 7 [1]5-8-9 t (50) C Catlin 7/1: 0044026: Rear, hdwy over 1f out, onepcd ins fnl 1f.   ¾   49
4368 **CAPTAIN CLOUDY** 6 [16]4-8-12 (53) S Whitworth 20/1: 6003047: Slow away, rear, hdwy over 2f out,   ¾   50
onepcd fnl 1f: qck reapp: see 3677.
4175 **MISTER REGENT** 14 [14]3-8-10 bl (55) F Norton 33/1: 300008: 12th: Cl-up, no impress ins fnl 1f.   ½   51
2768 **CAERPHILLY GAL** 75 [9]4-8-9 (50) D Corby(3) 20/1: 040-0009: Cl-up, wknd ins fnl 1f: long abs.   ¾   44
4379 **ESPADA** 5 [13]8-8-9 bl (50) V Slattery 28/1: 5046000: 10th: Led till over 2f out, no extra over 1f out. ¾   42
3996 **PAGAN STORM** 24 [12]4-8-13 (54) Kristin Stubbs(7) 20/1: 0003000: 11th: Slow away, hdwy over 1f   nk   45
out, no impress ins fnl 1f: see 2768.
4370* **YORKIES BOY** 5 [20]9-8-11 (6ex)p (52) R Thomas(3) 7/1: 0403110: 12th: Cl-up, no impress over 2f   1   41
out: qck reapp: been busy, could come too qckly after race 4370.
3548* **BINT ROYAL** 42 [10]6-9-0 (55) J-P Guillambert(3) 12/1: 5000210: 13th: Chsd ldrs, wknd from 3f out: hd   43
6 wk abs: joc one day whip ban: btr 3548 (fillies h'cap).
4367 **LOGISTICAL** 6 [6]4-8-11 (52) D Sweeney 25/1: 0050000: 14th: In tch, wknd 3f out: qck reapp: see 2063.   1½   37
2384 **EXTEMPORISE** 90 [8]4-8-11 (52) K Jackson(7) 50/1: 0351160: 15th: In tch, rear & btn 2f out: long abs.   nk   36
3670 **PARKER** 37 [7]7-8-10 T (51) R Miles(3) 20/1: 0605000: 16th: Handy, wknd over 1f out: tried a t-strap.   nk   34
4141 **DIDOE** 16 [4]5-8-10 (51) Joanna Badger 20/1: 0012100: 17th: Slow away, nvr a factor.   2   30
3799 **FILLIEMOU** 32 [5]3-8-9 (54) W Supple 20/1: 0052440: 18th: Chsd ldrs, no impress 2f out.   hd   32
3537 **SUPER SONG** 43 [3]4-8-10 t (51) I Mongan 14/1: 0000000: 19th: Rear, nvr a factor: 6 wk abs: see 1214.   5   19
1788 **ARABIAN KNIGHT** 115 [1]4-8-10 (51) R Havlin 100/1: 0000000: 20th: Al bhd: long abs: see 960.   6   7
20 Ran   Time 1m 22.66 (2.86)   Owned: Mr T A Godbert   Trained: Wells

CHEPSTOW THURSDAY 09.09.04 Lefthand, Undulating, Galloping Track

4489 5.25 Renault Clio Van Handicap Stakes 3yo+ 56-70 (E3) [74]
£3823 £1176 £588 5f16y Good 46 +06 Fast Stands side

3537 **INCH BY INCH** 43 [10] P J Makin 5-8-7 (2oh)bl (53) C Catlin 40/1: 300-0401: Cl-up, hdwy to lead 65
just over 1f out, drvn out ins fnl 1f: 6 wk abs: eff at 5f, suited by 6f: acts on gd & polytrack, any trk.
4140 **REDWOOD STAR** 16 [5] P L Gilligan 4-8-7 (1oh)e (54) D Sweeney 10/1: 0030432: Rear, hdwy over 1f ¾ 61
out, kept on well ins fnl 1f: consistent: see 4140.
4339 **COLLEGE QUEEN** 7 [12] S Gollings 6-8-13 (61) W Supple 14/1: 4520053: In tch, not clr run 2f out, ¾ 65
kept on ins fnl 1f: qck reapp: fraction closer with a clr run: see 3050 & 1873.
4335* **MAROMITO** 7 [6] R Bastiman 7-8-7 (55) D Holland 2/1 FAV: 1003014: With ldr till led over 2f out, ½ 57
hdd just over 1f out, no extra ins fnl 1f: qck reapp: not disgraced tho' a shade btr 4335.
4412 **CORANGLAIS** 3 [15]4-8-11 bl (59) F Norton 25/1: 1005005: Rear, hdwy over 2f out, fin well: qck reapp. 1½ 56
4412 **ARDKEEL LASS** 3 [4]3-8-8 (57) R Havlin 33/1: 0024506: Mid-div, hdwy over 1f out, sn onepcd: qck reapp.
1B'&a3150h-1R ½ 51
4144 **STOKESIES WISH** 16 [8]4-8-12 (60) J F McDonald(3) 12/1: 4063307: Led till over 2f out, no extra fnl 1f. nk 54
4412 **INDIAN BAZAAR** 3 [1]8-8-7 (10oh) (45) R Thomas(3) 33/1: 6000008: Mid-div till over 2f out, modest ½ 47
late gains: qck reapp: stiff task at weights: see 2743.
4412 **PULSE** 3 [7]6-8-9 p (57) P Fitzsimons 10/1: 5540069: In tch, hdwy 1f out, sn onepcd: qck reapp. ½ 47
3974 **DAVIDS MARK** 25 [16]4-8-8 (56) I Mongan 7/2: 3444120: 10th: Rear, hdwy 2f out, no impress ins fnl 1f. 1 43
4335 **TOMTHEVIC** 7 [13]6-8-7 (9oh) (46) B Swarbrick(5) 20/1: 0004050: 11th: In tch, onepcd fnl 1f: qck reapp. shd 41
4412 **IZMAIL** 3 [9]5-9-7 (69) S Donohoe(7) 14/1: 0010000: 12th: Dsptd lead, no impress 1f out: qck reapp. nk 54
3888 **TAPPIT** 28 [2]5-8-7 (10oh)bl (45) R Miles(3) 50/1: 0500060: 13th: Cl-up, wknd over 1f out: see 1963. 1 37
4368 **MORITAT** 6 [14]4-8-7 (4oh)t (51) R Mullen 8/1: 0635630: 14th: Rear, no dngr. ½ 35
4055 **ZAMBEZI RIVER** 21 [11]5-8-7 (15oh) (40) Joanna Badger 66/1: 0006000: 15th: Slow away, nvr a factor. 2½ 27
15 Ran Time 58.82s(2.02) Owned: Mrs Anna L Sanders Trained: Marlborough

DONCASTER FRIDAY 10.09.04 Lefthand, Flat, Galloping Track

Official Going Good/Firm (Firm Places)

4490 1.15 Dbs St Leger Yearling Stakes 2yo (B1)
£27000 £10800 £5400 6f str Firm 02 -17 Slow Stands Side

4338 **TAGULA SUNRISE** 8 [8] R A Fahey 2-8-6 (81) P Hanagan 8/1: 2220321: Pushed along chasing ldrs, rdn 79
2f out & drvn/styd on to lead cl-home, all out: first win: eff at 5/6f on firm & gd/soft: tough.
3521 **ROYAL ORISSA** 44 [17] D Haydn Jones 2-8-11 (78) L Dettori 14/1: 45302: Trkd ldrs, rdn to chall nk 83
ins last, just held fnl strides: gd run in t-strap: acts on firm & gd: mdn, looks sure to find a race, see 3163.
4271 **MY GACHO** 11 [18] Mrs P N Dutfield 2-8-11 R Havlin 33/1: 033: Chsd ldrs, drvn & narrow lead well shd 83
ins last, hdd cl-home: eff at at 6/7f on firm & gd grnd: can find a race: see 4271 (7f).
4224 **GRAND PLACE** 13 [3] R Hannon 2-8-11 (71) R L Moore 33/1: 040104: Held up, styd on well for press shd 82$
from over 1f out, nrst fin: eff at 5/6f on firm & gd grnd: improved, 7f shld suit: see 3907.
4200* **DANCING ROSE** 14 [20]2-8-6 (77) R Smith 9/1: 2315: Chsd ldrs, hmpd over 1f out, kept on ins last: ¾ 75+
lkd unlucky, would have gone close without interference: eff at 5/6f on firm & gd/soft grnd: see 4200.
4065 **RUSKY DUSKY** 21 [15]2-8-11 VIS (75) Dane O'Neill 33/1: 032556: Cl-up, wandered under press & nk 79
narrow lead over 1f out, hdd ins last & no extra: first time visor: see 2970.
4178* **TOFFEE VODKA** 15 [6]2-8-6 (77) R Hills 14/1: 6317: Rear, switched wide & mod prog, no threat. 2 68
4192 **LOVE AFFAIR** 14 [14]2-8-6 M Hills 25/1: 208: Rdn rear, switched wide & kept on late: needs 7f. 1 65
4457 **MOLLY MARIE** 2 [22]2-8-6 (77) T E Durcan 7/1 FAV: 2462009: Trkd ldrs, going well & poised to hd 64+
chall when badly hmpd over 1f out & not able to recover: qck reapp: unlucky, must surely have gone close.
4306* **BREAKING SHADOW** 10 [7]2-8-11 (72) K Darley 9/1: 23310: 10th: Chsd ldrs, no extra dist: see 4306. nk 68
4049 **SAPPHIRE DREAM** 28 [16]2-8-6 (80) R Winston 9/1: 2160440: 11th: Led, hdd/hmpd over 1f out & sn btn. nk 62
3632 **MISSPERON** 40 [2]2-8-6 (76) N Callan 20/1: 531340: 12th: Cl-up, btn dist: abs: btr 2603. 1 59
4233 **LORD OF DREAMS** 13 [11]2-8-11 K McEvoy 100/1: 050: 13th: Mid-div, nvr paced to chall: see 4233 (1m).nk 63
4205 **RAINBOW IRIS** 14 [9]2-8-6 (70) C Catlin 40/1: 4520: 14th: Rear, only mod prog: see 4205. ½ 54
4177 **SCROOBY BABY** 15 [10]2-8-6 (72) E Ahern 66/1: 202400: 15th: Mid-div, no impress fnl 2f: btr 3817 (AW). ½ 54
3897 **MUSICO** 29 [13]2-8-11 (74) S Drowne 15/2: 464230: 16th: Mid-div, hung right & no impress fnl 2f. 1½ 54
4178 **FLYING DANCER** 15 [4]2-8-6 J D Smith 50/1: 340: 17th: Mid-div, struggling from halfway: btr 4178. ½ 44
4306 **MELVINO** 10 [1]2-8-11 (76) D Mernagh 100/1: 403400: 18th: Mid-div, struggling fnl 2f: btr 3245. 1¾ 47
4244 **WIGWAM WILLIE** 13 [5]2-8-11 (75) K Fallon 11/1: 450: 19th: Al rear: op 14/1: see 4244 f 3988. 3 42
2144 Striking Endeavour 100 [12]2-8-11 (81) T Quinn 20/1:0 3955 **Superstitious** 27 [21]2-8-11 (70) W Ryan 50/1:0
21 Ran Time 1m 11.91 (1.11) Owned: Mr David M Knaggs & Mel Roberts Trained: Malton

4491 1.50 Totepool Mallard Stakes Handicap 3yo+ 96-110 (B1) [121]
£23200 £8800 £4400 1m6f132y Firm 02 -04 Slow Inside

4062* **LOST SOLDIER THREE** 22 [2] L M Cumani 3-8-4 (97) N Mackay(3) 5/2 FAV: 6154211: Trkd ldrs, al trav 105+
well, briefly short of room over 3f out, rdn & hdwy to lead dist, styd on strongly: hvly bckd: eff at 13/14.7f, 2m
looks sure to suit: acts on firm & gd/soft, loves a gall trk: v progressive, List/Gr 3 potential this autumn.
4383 **SERGEANT CECIL** 6 [5] B R Millman 5-8-12 (93) J Fortune 5/1: 0351222: Rear, hdwy when short of 1¼ 98
room 2f out, switched & kept on, not able to reach wnr: set too much to do, fine run: see 4383.
4023 **FANTASTIC LOVE** 23 [3] Saeed bin Suroor 4-9-6 t (101) L Dettori 9/1: 2121-003: Trkd ldrs, qcknd & hd 105
led over 2f out, hdd dist & no extra fnl 100yds: nicely bckd, op 10/1: acts on firm & gd grnd: stays 14.7f but
again shaped as if 12f would not go amiss: see 4023 & 3506.
4383 **TRUST RULE** 6 [13] B W Hills 4-8-10 (1oh)t T P (90) M Hills 33/1: 6500004: Held up, kept on late for 2½ 91
press, no threat to front trio: imprvd eff in t-strap & chkpcs: prob stays 14.7f: see 1484 (12f).
4383 **HIGH ACTION** 6 [10]4-8-10 (1oh)t (90) K Darley 20/1: 0001105: Held up, short of room over 2f out, 2½ 87
late prog, nvr a threat: qck reapp: see 3635 (2m2f).

1355

4023 **STAR MEMBER 23** [15]5-9-2 (97) K McEvoy 12/1: 5141266: Held up, mod prog for press, no threat. **1½ 91**
4104 **MIDAS WAY 20** [12]4-9-0 (95) E Ahern 20/1: 16320-27: Chsd ldr, btn over 1f out: btr 4104 (soft). **1½ 87**
1295 **HEISSE 142** [1]4-8-12 (93) R L Moore 50/1: 120-5008: Mid-div, short of room over 2f out when no **1½ 83**
impress on ldrs: 5 month abs, visor omitted: see 950.
4230 **SUPREMACY 13** [4]5-9-10 (105) K Fallon 20/1: 21-04049: Led till over 2f out, sn lost pl & struggling. **1 94**
4023 **SANTANDO 23** [9]4-8-10 (10h)vis (90) R Hills 25/1: 5004000: 10th: Mid-div, no impress over 2f out. **1 79**
3556 **YOSHKA 43** [14]3-7-13 (10h) (92) R Ffrench 4/1: 1-31120: 11th: Chsd ldrs, rdn 4f out, hung left & **shd 80**
btn from 2f out, fin lame: hvly bckd, 6 wk abs: see 3015.
4021 **Bourgeois 23** [7]7-9-1 (96) R Winston 50/1:0
3776 **Highland Games 34** [8]4-8-10 (1oh)(90) T Quinn 20/1:0
2771 **Zibeline 76** [6]7-8-10 (3oh)bl(88) Dane O'Neill 20/1:0   4023 **Salsalino 23** [11]4-9-5 (100) J D Smith 50/1:0
15 Ran   Time 3m 03.9 (0.9)   Owned: Sheikh Mohammed Obaid Al Maktoum   Trained: Newmarket

---

4492   **2.25 Gilbey Brothers Silver Microphone Conditions Guaranteed Sweepstakes 3-5yo   (B1)**
£11600 £4400 £2200   **1m2f60y**   **Firm 02**   **-03 Slow**   Inside

3496 **BIG BAD BOB 48** [3] J L Dunlop 4-9-2 (110) L Dettori 7/2: 110-3451: Led & qcknd clr after 2f, **114**
drvn & al holding rivals from dist: well bckd, 7 wk abs: best dominating at 10f, yet to convince at 12f: acts on
firm & gd/soft grnd: smart colt, fine ride: see 1862.
3118 **RED FORT 62** [4] M A Jarvis 4-9-2 (113) P Robinson 5/6 FAV: 40-13142: Held up, styd on for press **¾ 112**
to take 2nd well ins last, nvr reaching wnr: abs: acts on firm & gd/soft: smart, gave wnr too much rope.
4095 **BAYBERRY 20** [2] H R A Cecil 4-8-11 (93) W Ryan 16/1: 0410-523: Chsd wnr, styd on for press fnl **nk 106**
2f, just lost 2nd well ins last: styd longer 10.3f trip well: acts on firm & gd/soft: lightly rcd, useful & progressive.
3264 **KAIETEUR 55** [6] B J Meehan 5-9-8 (111) J Fortune 8/1: 230-6054: Chsd ldrs, eff to chase wnr over **6 108**
3f out, no impress fnl 2f: op 13/2, 8 wk abs: poss prefer more give: see 2128 (g/s).
2641} **ARTISTIC LAD 434** [5]4-9-2   K Fallon 7/1: 1/0-5: ch c Peintre Celebre - Maid For The Hills **9 91**
(Indian Ridge) Trkd ldrs, rdn & btn 3f out: long abs: unplcd sole '03 start (List, rtd 90): mdn wnr on sole '02
start: winning form at 7f on soft grnd, bred to apprec 1m/10f. 1 Oct'02 Leic 7sft 95- D:
1068 **LOVE YOU ALWAYS 157** [1]4-9-2 (92) B Reilly 100/1: 13/-06: ch g Woodman - Encorenous (Diesis) **½ 90$**
Rear, no ch fn 3f: 5 month abs: missed '03 (lightly rcd '02 for M Johnston, debut scorer, mdn, subs unplcd in cond
stks): winning form at 1m on fast grnd a stiff/undul trk: has gone well fresh. 1 Sep'02 Hami 8.2g/f 94- D:
6 Ran   Time 2m 06.89 (.49)   Owned: Windflower Overseas Holdings Inc   Trained: Arundel

---

4493   **3.00 Gr2 Sgb Champagne Stakes Colts & Geldings 2yo   (A1)**
£60000 £23000 £11500   **7f str**   **Firm 02**   **-00 Slow**   Stands Side

3955* **ETLAALA 27** [3] B W Hills 2-8-10   R Hills 6/1: 11: Dwelt & keen in rear early, no run 3f out & **117+**
till 1f out, qcknd to lead, readily/impressive: well bckd: eff at 7f, 1m sure to suit: acts on fm & fast: unbtn, v
smart & most eye-catching here, more to come & shld be followed in Gr 1 class: see 3955.
2467* **ICEMAN 87** [2] J H M Gosden 2-9-1 (100) K Fallon 5/2 JT FAV: 2112: Swerved right start, sn pushed **½ 117+**
along in tch, rdn & hdwy to lead ins last, hdd & not pace of wnr well ins last: rest well covered: hvly bckd &
imprvd in defeat under a pen: styd longer 7f trip, 1m shld suit: acts on firm & fast, handles soft: win more Gr races.
4003 **OUDE 24** [9] Saeed bin Suroor 2-8-10   L Dettori 5/2 JT FAV: 123: Keen trkg ldrs, led over 2f out **2½ 107**
till ins last, not pace of front pair: hvly bckd tho' op 2/1: acts on firm & gd: win a Listed.
3919 **WILKO 28** [5] J Noseda 2-8-10 (100) E Ahern 16/1: 1332124: Chsd ldrs, drvn & kept on fnl 2f, not **1¼ 104**
pace of front pair: tough & consistent type, a drop to List/Gr3 level shld suit: see 3919.
3865 **GRAND MARQUE 30** [7]2-8-10 (96) R L Moore 50/1: 51125: Chsd ldrs, outpcd halfway, kept on for **nk 103**
press ins last, nvr threat: rtn to 1m looks sure to suit: will apprec List/Gr 3: see 3865 & 3267.
4003* **ELLIOTS WORLD 24** [1]2-8-10   J Fanning 11/2: 116: Trkd ldrs & ch 2f out, fdd under press: well **1½ 100**
bckd: fastest ground encountered to date: btr 4003 (List, gd).
4289 **MISTER GENEPI 11** [10]2-8-10   (86) S Drowne 100/1: 52237: Held up, pushed along halfway, nvr threat. **nk 99**
3568* **JONQUIL 42** [12]2-8-10   J Fortune 11/1: 418: Chsd ldrs, rdn & btn 2f out: stablemate of rnr-up, abs. **2 95**
4069 **SURWAKI 11** [8]2-8-10   P Robinson 100/1: 329: Led, hung right & hdd over 3f out, sn struggling. **5 86**
4096 **LEOS LUCKY STAR 20** [6]2-8-10   K Darley 16/1: 1100: 10th: Led/dsptd lead till over 2f out, wknd qckly. **1½ 83**
10 Ran   Time 1m 23.33 (.12)   Owned: Mr Hamdan Al Maktoum   Trained: Lambourn

---

4494   **3.35 Listed Orderit-Online Com Troy Stakes 3yo+   (A1)**
£19500 £6000 £3000   **1m4f**   **Firm 02**   **+04 Fast**   Inside

3119* **DISTINCTION 62** [2] Sir Michael Stoute 5-9-6 (111) K Fallon 5/2 FAV: 015-0511: Trkd ldrs, **116**
rdn/edged left & hdwy to lead over 1f out: drvn out: best time of day: hvly bckd, op 11/4: 2 month abs: eff at
12/14f, stays 2m: acts on firm & gd/soft: progressive, just the type for Melbourne Cup.
4219 **COMPTON BOLTER 13** [6] G A Butler 7-9-1 (109) E Ahern 11/2: 5065332: Led, qcknd tempo from over **¾ 109**
3f out, hdd over 1f out, kept on for press: gd run with forcing tactics: see 82.
4230 **SWIFT TANGO 13** [3] A L Dunlop 4-9-6 (102) P Hanagan 10/1: 3643123: Rear, short of room over 2f **1½ 112**
out, drvn & kept on, not pace to chall: smart run, improving: see 4104.
4104 **DELSARTE 20** [1] Saeed bin Suroor 4-9-1 VIS t (106) L Dettori 5/1: 34-02564: Rear, eff 3f out, onepace. **nk 106**
3777 **STARRY LODGE 34** [7]4-9-1 (96) J Fortune 9/2: 121-1355: Chsd ldr, rdn & outpcd when short of room **3 102**
over 1f out, no impress after: hvly bckd: see 3118 & 2255 (h'caps).
4312 **FRANKLINS GARDENS 12** [5]4-9-1 (108) P Robinson 9/2: 110-4406: Chsd front pair, no impress over **½ 101**
1f out: nicely bckd: btr 1350 (reapp, g/s).
2004 **PRIVATE CHARTER 110** [4]4-9-1 (105) M Hills 20/1: 45-02067: Held up, eff when outpcd over 3f out, **5 94**
sn no impress & eased ins last: 4 month abs: btr 1483 (10f).
7 Ran   Time 2m 29.62 (u0.18)   Owned: Highclere Thoroughbred Racing Ltd   Trained: Newmarket

4495   **4.10 Centex Fairclough Homes Trophy A Conditions Guaranteed Sweepstakes 3yo   (C2)**
£8700   £3300   £1650   **1m rnd**   **Firm 02**   **+02 Fast**   Outside

2555 **SECRET CHARM 84** [9] B W Hills 3-8-6 (110) M Hills 11/2: 11-5501: Led/dsptd lead, went on after   **112**
2f, strongly pressed from dist, drvn & held on gamely: gd time: 12 wk abs: eff at 7f/1m, mid-dists may yet suit:
acts on firm & gd grnd: relished forcing tactics today & goes well fresh: game & smart, stable back to best.
4047 **MILK IT MICK 22** [2] J A Osborne 3-8-11 (107) K Fallon 9/2: 1-250332: Keen, pushed along & hdwy   ½   **115**
to chall over 1f out, drvn/edged right & no extra fnl 100yds: stays 1m but lkd likely wnr at the dist today: tough &
deserves a win this term: see 1040.
3487*}**MANSFIELD PARK 398** [3] Saeed bin Suroor 3-8-6 (100) K McEvoy 11/2: 21-3: b f Green Desert - Park   1   **108**
Appeal (Ahonoora) Dwelt, rdn & outpcd 3f out, switched & kept on ins last, no reach front pair: well bckd tho' op
4/1: reapp: lightly rcd '03, won 2nd of just 2 starts (fill mdn, rtd 105+): eff at 7f/1m, shapes as if mid-dists
could suit: acts on firm & fast grnd, gall trks: encouraging comeback, could improve.
1 Aug'03 Redc 7g/f 105- D: 2 Jul'03 Newm 7g/f 86- D:
1188 **FANTASTIC VIEW 148** [1] R Hannon 3-8-11 (113) R L Moore 6/1: 12112-54: Trkd ldrs, kept on for   hd   **112**
press, not pace to chall: 5 month abs: may improve on this when racing on or close to the pace: handles firm & gd.
4683*}**ORIENTAL WARRIOR 335** [4]3-8-11   R Hills 8/1: 11-5: b c Alhaarth - Oriental Fashion (Marju) Trkd   1¾   **109**
ldrs, no extra dist: reapp: lightly rcd '03 (unbtn both starts, landing a mdn & cond event): winning form at 6/7f,
styd this gall 1m: acts on firm & gd grnd, stiff/gall trks: goes well fresh.
1 Oct'03 Asco 7gd 99- C: 1 Sep'03 Newb 6.0g/f 96- D:
3814 **MOONLIGHT MAN 33** [5]3-8-11 (100) Dane O'Neill 14/1: 2002426: Led till 5f out, no impress over 1f   2   **105**
out: nicely bckd, op 16/1: see 3814 7 3253 (7f).
1701 **MISS CHILDREY 12** [7]3-8-6 t D M Grant 66/1: 4-530007: Rear, eff 3f out, sn btn, Irish raider.   8   **86**
1317* **THAJJA 140** [8]3-9-2 (98) L Dettori 11/4 FAV: 1-18: Rcd keenly in mid-div, restrained & drpd to   4   **89**
rear halfway, rdn & no impress fnl 2f: hvly bckd, 5 month abs: not settle in early stages but much btr 1317 (g/s).
4799} **TAROT CARD 328** [5]3-8-6 (100) P Hanagan 33/1: 150-9: b f Fasliyev - Well Beyond (Don't Forget   1¼   **76**
Me) Held up, hung right thr'out & no ch fnl 2f: reapp, stablemate of wnr: lightly rcd '03 (debut wnr, fill mdn,
subs not disgraced in Gr 1 company, rtd 102, 5th): winning form at 6f, prob stays a stiff 1m: acts on firm & gd
grnd: can go well fresh. 1 Jul'03 Good 6gd 91- D:
9 Ran   Time 1m 36.07 (u0.03)   Owned: Maktoum Al Maktoum   Trained: Lambourn

4496   **4.45 Wilfreda Beehive Handicap Guaranteed Sweepstakes 3yo+ 71-85 (D2)**   **[91]**
£6500   £2000   £1000   **5f str**   **Firm 02**   **-09 Slow**   Stands Side

4201 **MALAPROPISM 14** [17] M R Channon 4-9-1 (78) S Hitchcott(3) 13/2: 6040661: Trkd ldrs trav well,   **84**
briefly btwn of room over 1f out, led dist, edged left under press, held on all out: well bckd, op 7/1: best btwn
5/5.7f & stays 6f: acts on firm or soft, any trk: has slipped to attractive mark & come to hand of late: see 1845.
4240 **BEYOND THE CLOUDS 13** [10] J S Wainwright 8-8-10 p (73) R Winston 12/1: 0030062: Trkd ldrs, drv to   shd   **78**
chall when carr left ins last, just held: cllrly eff in cheek pieces: well h'capped for similar: loves Beverley.
4339 **MIDNIGHT PARKES 8** [3] E J Alston 5-8-7 (70) M Henry 33/1: 5031003: Led far side & drvn/styd on   ¾   **73+**
well, just held in front pair stands side nr fin: fine eff, decisive wnr of the smaller far side group: keep in mind.
3966* **CURRENCY 26** [19] J M Bradley 7-9-0 (77) R L Moore 6/1 FAV: 3005214: Rdn rear, hdwy when short of   hd   **79+**
room briefly dist, styd on strongly cl-home, nrst fin: would have gone v close without brief interference.
4031 **ZARZU 23** [2]5-9-0 (77) R Thomas(3) 16/1: 0165005: Rear, prog/short of room over 1f out, kept on.   hd   **78**
3763* **MARSHALLSPARK 34** [15]5-8-8 (71) P Hanagan 10/1: 0051016: Rear, styd on for press, not reach   shd   **72**
ldrs: eff at 5f, 6f ideal: see 3763 (6f).
3809 **INTER VISION 33** [7]4-9-5 (82) A Beech(3) 16/1: 5004207: Chsd ldrs, onepace dist.   ¾   **81**
4039 **PADDYWACK 23** [1]7-8-9 bl (72) J Fanning 16/1: 1036338: Dwelt, trkd ldrs far side, no impress fnl 1f.   ½   **69**
4027 **DISPOL KATIE 23** [6]3-9-3 (81) N Callan 11/1: 0635029: Cl-up far side, no extra dist: btr 4027.   nk   **77**
3792 **MATTY TUN 34** [22]5-9-6 (83) J Bramhill 4/1: 5000500: 10th: Rear, short of room dist, mod late prog.   nk   **78**
2747 **WANCHAI LAD 76** [2]3-9-7 (85) A Nicholls 33/1: 60-30500: 11th: Trkd ldrs far side, no extra dist, abs.   nk   **79**
4174 **MUSICAL FAIR 15** [13]4-8-12 (75) F Norton 10/1: 1560030: 12th: Trkd ldrs, onepace.   hd   **68**
4174 **TRUE MAGIC 15** [18]3-8-10 (74) K McEvoy 14/1: 6221100: 13th: Cl-up, no extra over 1f out: btr 3833.   hd   **66**
4201 **DANCING MYSTERY 14** [4]10-9-1 bl (78) G Baker 16/1: 5000200: 14th: Trkd ldrs far side, btn over 1f out.   hd   **69**
4099 **TRICK CYCLIST 20** [5]3-8-8 (72) S Drowne 25/1: 6021350: 15th: Held up in tch far side, btn 2f out.   nk   **62**
3792 **PICCLED 34** [16]6-9-6 (83) T E Durcan 25/1: 01050R0: 16th: Slow away & lost around 8L, nvr   1½   **69**
factor: has developed an aversion to starting & is best watched until able to kick the habit: see 3792, 3466.
3976 **SILVER PRELUDE 25** [11]3-9-4 (82) P Robinson 33/1: 0310000: 17th: Cl-up, btn over 1f out.   shd   **68**
4201 **PALAWAN 14** [14]8-8-7 (70) C Catlin 50/1: 6000000: 18th: Led stands side, btn dist: see 205.   shd   **55**
4601] **Calypso Dancer 22** [20]4-8-9 (72) K Darley 25/1:0   2400   **Fyodor 90** [12]3-9-1 (79) E Ahern 33/1:0
20 Ran   Time 58.74(0.54)   Owned: Mr Michael A Foy   Trained: West Ilsley

SANDOWN   FRIDAY 10.09.04   Righthand, Galloping Track, Stiff Finish

Official Going Good (Good Firm places)

   2.00 Marshall Arts E B F Maiden Stakes 2yo   (D2)
£5538   £1704   £852   **5f6y str**   **Good 40**   **-54 Slow**   Far Side

4273 **UNREAL 11** [6] B W Hills 2-8-9 (80) R Hughes 3/1 JT FAV: 62621: Handy, hdwy over 1f out, styd on   **81**
despite edging left ins last to lead fnl 100yds, rdn out: eff over 5/6f on fm & gd: confidence boost.
4121 **PARK APPROACH 18** [3] J Noseda 2-8-9   S W Kelly 4/1: 432: Keen, led over 3f out till ins last,   ½   **78**
not pace of wnr: consistent, shld find a minor trk event: see 3915.
3968 **ALEXIA ROSE 26** [4] A Berry 2-8-9 (61) W Supple 33/1: 6043: Dwelt, keen held up, hdwy over 1f   ¾   **76**
out, kept on ins last for press: imprvd run at 5f on gd grnd with more patient tactics: see 3968.
4200 **ENCOURAGEMENT 14** [5] R Hannon 2-8-9 (75) J Murtagh 11/1: 0304: Led till over 3f out, onepcd when   ½   **74**
short of room ins last: eff at 5/6f on firm & gd: see 3626.

4121 **CESAR MANRIQUE** 18 [8]2-9-0 A Culhane 40/1: 05: ch c Vettori - Norbella (Nordico) Keen held up,   *hd*   **78**
hdwy & short of room over 1f out, kept on ins last: Mar foal: half-brother to wnrs over 5f/1m: eff at 5f on gd grnd.
4200 **RUBIES** 14 [7]2-8-9 S Carson 100/30: 26: Keen, slow away, wkng when hmpd ins last: btr 4200.   *1½*   **69**
        SMALL STAKES 0 [9]2-9-0 S Sanders 3/1 JT FAV: 7: b c Pennekamp - Poker Chip (Bluebird) In tch,   *2*   **68**
eff 2f out, no impress on debut: Mar foal, cost 20,000gns: dam 5f juv wnr.
        WINDWOOD 0 [2]2-9-0 D Holland 20/1: 8: b c Piccolo - Presently (Cadeaux Genereux) Slow away &   *5*   **53**
al bhd: reportedly hung left: Apr foal, cost 60,000gns: half-brother to wnrs over 5/6f, dam 5f scorer.
        ELMS SCHOOLBOY 0 [1]2-9-0 J Tate 33/1: 9: Slow away, keen, handy, wknd 2f out.   *1*   **50**
9 Ran   Time 1m 04.36 (4.76)   Owned: Mr K Abdulla   Trained: Lambourn

---

4498   **2.35 Clear Channel Classified Stakes 3yo+ 0-80 (D2)**
        £6776 £2085 £1043 **5f6y str** **Good 40** **-14 Slow**   Far Side

4174 **DAME DE NOCHE** 15 [4] J G Given 4-9-3 (85) A Culhane 5/1: 0053001: In tch, hdwy over 1f out, styd   **89**
on to lead dist, rdn clr: clrly has the pace for a stiff 5f, stays 1m: acts on firm & gd grnd, prob any trk: prev
eff with forcing tactics: back to form & h'capped to win again: see 1115.
4201 **ROYAL CHALLENGE** 14 [5] G A Butler 3-9-0 (79) S Sanders 5/2 FAV: 0-211632: Cl-up, rdn dist, not   *1½*   **82**
pace of wnr: bckd: ran to best: see 4201, 3356.
3849* **FIDDLE ME BLUE** 31 [2] H Morrison 3-8-11 (77) J Murtagh 13/2: 1-500013: Held up, eff & hung over   *hd*   **78**
1f out, kept on: prob ran close to form of fill h'cap win in 3849.
3628 **DOMIRATI** 40 [3] R Charlton 4-9-3 (82) D Holland 4/1: 0420204: Held up, eff & short of room over   *hd*   **82**
1f out & ins last, kept on: 6 wk abs: shade closer with a clr run: see 3341, 2698.
3479 **BOHOLA FLYER** 46 [1]3-8-11 (78) R Hughes 20/1: 1145205: Held up, eff over 1f out, no impress: abs.   *1½*   **73**
4394 **LITTLE EDWARD** 6 [6]6-9-3 (82) L Keniry(3) 3/1: 0005646: Led till over 1f out, wknd: bckd, qck reapp.   *1¼*   **74**
6 Ran   Time 1m 02.3 (2.7)   Owned: The G-Guck Group   Trained: Gainsborough

---

4499   **3.10 Whatsonwembley Com Handicap Stakes 3yo 86-100 (C1)**   **[105]**
        £12151 £4609 £2305 **1m14y rnd** **Good 40** **+07 Fast**   Inside

3860 **FREE TRIP** 30 [2] J H M Gosden 3-8-12 (89) R Hughes 5/1: 0255521: Handy, hdwy trav well to lead   **99**
over 1f out, sn rdn clr: eff at 7f, apprec this step up to 1m: acts on fast & rain-softened grnd, prob any trk:
useful, unexposed at this trip: see 955.
4061 **TAKE A BOW** 22 [4] P R Chamings 3-9-7 (98) J Quinn 9/4 FAV: 2-114122: Handy, eff well over 1f   *1½*   **105**
out, kept on, not pace of wnr: useful & proving v tough: see 3860.
3814 **ROYAL PRINCE** 33 [1] J R Fanshawe 3-8-12 (89) J Mayaasa 5/1: 34-41133: Held up, plenty to do over   *hd*   **95+**
2f out, kept on over 1f out, nrst fin: set too much to do & stays 1m: winning earlier with more positive rides &
looks sure to go close next time: see 2403, 2148.
3973* **STREAM OF GOLD** 26 [5] Sir Michael Stoute 3-8-12 (89) S Sanders 11/2: 514: Held up, eff well over   *2*   **91**
1f out, sn no extra: up in class after mdn win on gd/soft in 3973.
2877 **BARATHEA DREAMS** 71 [3]3-8-7 (1oh) (83) J F Egan 20/1: 1413005: Set gd pace, hdd & wknd over 1f   *3½*   **79**
out: 10 wk abs: best 1315 (gd/soft).
2521 **MASTER MARVEL** 85 [7]3-8-12 (89) D Holland 9/2: 211006: Handy, wknd over 2f out: 3 month abs.   *1½*   **81**
4239 **SEWNSO CHARACTER** 13 [6]3-8-11 (88) D Sweeney 10/1: 3440467: Slow away, in tch, wknd over 2f out.   *½*   **79**
7 Ran   Time 1m 41.71 (2.71)   Owned: Mr K Abdulla   Trained: Manton

---

4500   **3.45 3a Handicap Stakes 3yo+ 71-85 (D2)**   **[89]**
        £8724 £2684 £1342 **7f16y rnd** **Good 40** **-02 Slow**   Inside

4394 **ARMAGNAC** 6 [6] M A Buckley 6-9-5 (80) A Culhane 8/1: 2323001: Held up, hdwy over 1f out, styd on   **86**
well for press to lead cl-home: deserved win after sev nr misses earlier: winning form over 6/7f on firm or soft
grnd, likes Haydock: tough, come from bhd h'capper: see 1138.
4776} **SATTAM** 329 [10] M P Tregoning 5-9-2 vis (77) R Hughes 12/1: 553210-2: b g Danehill - Mayaasa   *nk*   **82**
(Lyphard) Held up, hdwy & short of room 2f out, hung left over 1f out but kept on ins last, just held: reapp: '03
h'cap wnr: eff over 7f/1m on firm & fast grnd, stiff or sharp trks: eff in a visor, tried blnks: gelded since last
term & v encouraging rtn, tho' poss not totally straightforward.
1 Sep'03 Sali 7.0g/f 78-70 D: 2 Aug'03 Folk 7g/f 72-(69) E: 2 Apr'03 Epso 8.5g/f 71- D:
4180 **BINANTI** 15 [8] P R Chamings 4-9-5 (80) J Quinn 11/2 FAV: 6600553: In tch, hdwy to lead over 1f   *nk*   **84**
out, edged left & hdd ins last, not btn far: gd run, slipped down the weights: see 3441, 2777.
3512 **PINTLE** 45 [5] J L Spearing 4-8-13 (74) J Murtagh 7/1: 15-41164: Cl-up, led 2f out till over 1f out, onepace.   *1¼*   **75**
3898 **GEMS BOND** 29 [13]4-9-0 (75) Derek Nolan(7) 50/1: 0000005: In tch, eff over 1f out, onepace: see 3898.   *¾*   **74**
1847 **ANUVASTEEL** 114 [2]3-8-9 (74) J F Egan 12/1: 132-6006: Held up, hdwy & short of room over 1f out,   *shd*   **72**
kept on ins last, no dngr: 4 month abs & showed more here, poss more to come: see 177, 132 (polytrack).
4125*}**MAREN** 368 [4]3-9-4 T (83) W Supple 11/1: 31-7: b c Gulch - Fatina (Nashwan) In tch, hdwy over 1f   *nk*   **80**
out, sn btn & easd on reapp: won 2nd of 2 '03 starts (mdn): eff at 7f, shld stay 1m+: acts on firm & fast grnd,
sharp trks: tried a t-strap today. 1 Sep'03 Warw 7.1fm 85-D:
3360* **SERRE CHEVALIER** 50 [3]3-9-0 (79) D Holland 8/1: 218: Handy, eff & short of room over 1f out,   *¾*   **74**
onepace: 7 wk abs: up in class after win in 3360.
2370 **LOCKSTOCK** 91 [1]6-8-10 (71) R Miles(3) 33/1: 4-001009: Bhd, wide, nvr a factor: abs, best 1542.   *1¼*   **63**
3565 **OMAHA CITY** 42 [15]5-8-10 (71) L Keniry(3) 20/1: 0210000: 10th: Held up, staying on when hmpd   *hd*   **62**
dist, not recover: 6 wk abs: 10yo but still clrly retains ability & prob capable of another win at Goodwood.
4331 **MUSIC MAID** 8 [9]6-8-7 (4oh) (64) D Kinsella 20/1: 5-010000: 11th: Held up, eff over 1f out, no extra.   *shd*   **58**
4186* **WATERSIDE** 14 [7]5-9-7 (82) I Mongan 7/1: 2460310: 12th: Handy, wknd over 1f out: btr 4186 (7f, soft).   *2*   **68**
4071 **GREAT SCOTT** 21 [12]3-9-1 BL (80) S Chin 14/1: 0053400: 13th: Handy, wknd 2f out: blnks: see 2679.   *5*   **56**
4067 **LIFTED WAY** 21 [11]5-9-1 (76) S Sanders 10/1: 1065400: 14th: Led till 2f out, wknd: see 1613, 1352.   *nk*   **51**
4082 **GOODENOUGH MOVER** 21 [14]8-9-7 (82) Hayley Turner(3) 14/1: 2115200: 15th: Handy, wknd over 1f out.*1¾*   **53**
15 Ran   Time 1m 29.34 (2.94)   Owned: Mr C C Buckley   Trained: Stamford

4501

4.20 Mean Fiddler Maiden Stakes 3yo (D3)
£5564 £1712 £856   **1m2f7y**   **Good 40**   **-05 Slow**   Inside

2751 **MARAAKEB 76** [7] J H M Gosden 3-9-0 W Supple 3/1: 3-61: Made all, trav best over 2f out, sn   **84**
pushed clr, unchall, cmftlby, val more: well bckd after 11 wk abs: stays 10f on gd grnd, 12f looks sure to suit:
more to come in h'caps: enjoyed forcing tactics: see 2751.
3243 **BARATHEA BLUE 56** [4] P W Harris 3-9-0 S Carson 25/1: 52: Handy, outpcd by wnr over 2f out,   3   **74**
onepace over 1f out: 8 wk abs: stays 10f on gd grnd: see 3243.
4125 **NEATH 18** [1] Mrs A J Perrett 3-8-9 S Sanders 12/1: 53: Bhd, outpcd over 2f out, onepace over 1f   *shd*   **69**
out: clr of rem: prob stays 10f on gd: see 4125.
4034 **KIPSIGIS 23** [2] Lady Herries 3-9-0 J Quinn 66/1: 04: Nvr a factor: see 4034.   7   **62**
1148 **PARLIAMENT SQUARE 150** [8]3-9-0 T P Queally 2/1 FAV: 35: Handy, wknd over 1f out: long abs.   2½   **58**
4871} **TIZI OUZOU 322** [5]3-8-9 I Mongan 100/1: U0-6: ch f Desert Prince - Tresor (Pleasant Tap) Al   2½   **49**
bhd: modest to date.
      ARDERE 0 [3]3-8-9 R Hughes 12/1: 7: ch f El Prado - Flaming Torch (Rousillon) Handy, wknd 3f   6   **39**
out: saddle reportedly slipped: mid-dist bred.
      KATAYEB 0 [9]3-8-9 D Holland 10/1: 8: b f Machiavellian - Fair of The Furze (Ela Mana Mou)   13   **21**
Slow away & al bhd on debut: mid-dist bred.
3631 **RED SAIL 40** [6]3-8-9 J Murtagh 11/4: 339: In tch, wknd qckly over 2f out: hvly bckd: 6 wk   8   **9**
abs: much btr expected after 3631 but reportedly got upset in the stalls.
9 Ran Time 2m 08.6 (4.5) Owned: Mr Hamdan Al Maktoum Trained: Manton

4502

4.55 Dc Entertainment Handicap Stakes 3yo 71-85 (D2)   **[88]**
£8619 £2652 £1326   **1m2f7y**   **Good 40**   **-26 Slow**   Inside

4392 **TOP SPEC 8** [8] R Hannon 3-9-2 (76) R Hughes 7/2 FAV: 5020121: Slow away, keen, held up, hdwy to   **84**
lead over 1f out, kept on for press ins last: suited by 10f now on firm or gd/soft, likes a stiff trk, esp Sandown.
3578 **SPRING JIM 42** [7] J R Fanshawe 3-9-5 (79) J Murtagh 4/1: 50-41242: Dwelt, held up, hung over 2f   ¾   **85**
out, eff to chall dist, kept on, not btn far: 6 wk abs: stays 10f: see 2634.
4362 **BORDER MUSIC 7** [3] A M Balding 3-9-4 (78) T Block(7) 7/1: 1-003223: Held up, gd hdwy to chall   *shd*   **83**
over 1f out, sn onepace: stays 10f: in gd form: see 4362.
3257 **STAR OF LIGHT 56** [5] B J Meehan 3-9-3 (77) J F McDonald(3) 11/2: 0621-34: Keen held up, eff over   nk   **81**
1f out, kept on ins last, not btn far: clr rem: big step up in trip & stays 10f: shld win again: see 3257, 52.
4293 **RONDELET 11** [2]3-9-7 (81) S Sanders 11/2: 2321045: In tch, hdwy 2f out, sn onepace: see 4293.   4   **79**
3339 **SECRET FLAME 51** [4]3-9-2 (76) A Culhane 8/1: 5-33106: Keen in tch, no impress over 1f out: 7 wk abs.   1   **72**
3108 **JAKARMI 62** [10]3-9-2 (76) R Miles(3) 25/1: 2321107: Handy, wknd over 1f out: 2 month abs.   1¼   **70**
3604 **WYCHBURY 41** [9]3-8-13 (73) T P Queally 25/1: 5220158: Keen bhd, nvr a factor: best 3413 (7f, mdn).   nk   **66**
3802* **BOOT N TOOT 33** [6]3-9-2 (76) J F Egan 25/1: 019: Al bhd: drop in class after mdn fill win in 3802.   6   **59**
3674 **ANTIGIOTTO 38** [1]3-9-4 BL (78) D Holland 20/1: 0042200: 10th: Cl-up, led 3f out till over 1f out,   3   **56**
wknd qckly & hmpd in last: tried blnks: see 3208, 2663.
3630 **TREE TOPS 40** [11]3-8-12 (72) W Supple 16/1: 523360: 11th: Handy, wknd qckly over 2f out: btr 3255.   4   **44**
3990 **LIVE WIRE LUCY 25** [12]3-8-13 (73) S W Kelly 100/1: 0300000: 12th: Led 3f out, wknd: see 3630.   nk   **44**
12 Ran Time 2m 10.72(6.62) Owned: The Hill Top Partnership Trained: Marlborough

Official Going Good/Firm

4503

11.10 Cantor Fitzgerald Memorial Median Auction Maiden Stakes 2yo (H5)
£1554 £444 £222   **6f192y rnd**   **Firm 12**   **-66 Slow**   Inside

3931 **SECRET PACT 29** [3] M Johnston 2-9-0 (75) R Ffrench 3/1 FAV: 42301: Trkd ldrs, carried v wide on   **79+**
bend after 3f, pshd along 3f out, hdwy to lead over 1f out, rdn clr: slow time: eff at 6f/7f, 1m looks sure to suit:
acts on firm or soft ground, stiff or sharp/undul trk: overcame an awkward passage to win decisively, rate higher.
4114 **KUMALA OCEAN 20** [15] P A Blockley 2-8-9 (62) G Parkin 12/1: 2502: Mid-div, hdwy to chse ldrs   3   **67**
when hmpd over 1f out, kept on ins last, no threat to decisive wnr: handles firm grnd & fbsand: shld get 1m.
4283 **HARRYS HOUSE 12** [1] J J Quinn 2-9-0 (68) P Mulrennan(3) 9/2: 4043: Keen & handy, held by wnr when   hd   **71**
hmpd over 1f out, onepace: handles firm & soft grnd: see 4283.
4269 **IGNITION 12** [8] W M Brisbourne 2-8-9 (67) B Swarbrick(5) 7/2: 5434: Keen & led after 2f, hdd over   ½   **65**
1f out, no extra: handles firm & gd grnd: see 4102.
4206 **SINGHALONGTASVEER 15** [14]2-9-0 (49) J Bramhill 33/1: 053005: Cl up & ch over 1f out, sn edged   1   **68**
left & no extra: handles firm & gd/sft ground: offic rtd 49: see 3259 (sell).
4416 **WEMBURY POINT 5** [2]2-9-0 T Eaves(3) 11/1: 0006: gr c Monashee Mountain - Lady Celina (Crystal   1½   **65**
Palace) Mid-div, nvr pace to chall: qck reapp: Apr foal, cost 32,000 euros: dam a wnr abroad.
4381 **PLENTY CRIED WOLF 7** [7]2-9-0 (71) T Hamilton(3) 6/1: 0047: Chsd ldrs, rdn/hmpd over 1f out, no extra.   ¾   **64**
4376 **BODDEN BAY 7** [6]2-9-0 Dale Gibson 33/1: 08: b g Cayman Kai - Badger Bay (Salt Dome) Mid-div,   1½   **61**
btn 2f out: Apr foal, half brother to a 6f juv wnr: dam placed at up to 1m.
      CALFRAZ 0 [11]2-9-0 G Faulkner 33/1: 9: Outpcd, mod late hdwy.   ½   **60**
3570 **SPECIALISE 43** [10]2-8-9 T Williams 80/1: 0P0: 10th: Slow away & nvr a factor, 6 wk abs.   4   **47**
      DEMOLITION FRANK 0 [4]2-9-0 P M Quinn 33/1: 0: 11th: Dwelt, always struggling.   *shd*   **52**
4204 **BRAVE TARA 15** [12]2-8-9 A Nicholls 50/1: 00: 12th: Keen & led till ran wide on bend after 2f, sn strugg.   12   **23**
      CASALESE 0 [5]2-9-0 M Tebbutt 33/1: 0: 13th: Al outpcd & bhd.   ¾   **27**
4257 **ITSA MONKEY 13** [9]2-9-0 bl (49) D Nolan(3) 50/1: 6200000: 14th: Always strugg rear.   2½   **22**
14 Ran Time 1m 29.38 (5.48) Owned: Jumeirah Racing Trained: Middleham

4504

11.40 Cantor Sport Maiden Claiming Stakes 3yo+   (H5)
£1544 £441 £221   **6f192y rnd   Firm 12   -44 Slow**   Inside

4408 **MEGABOND** 5 [6] B Smart 3-8-12 P (54) D McGaffin 5/1: 0-504001: Made all & drvn clr over 2f out,   **65**
eased right down cl home, easily, val 7L+: qck reapp, clmd by C Dwyer: eff at 5/6f, much improved at 7f in banded
company: acts on firm, fast & fbsnd: suited by drop in grade, forcing tactics & 1st time chkpcs.
4237 **NICHOLAS NICKELBY** 14 [5] M J Polglase 4-9-2 p (53) L Fletcher(3) 4/1 FAV: 0043442: Chsd ldrs, rdn   4   **52**
& kept on, nvr chance with wnr: see 4237, 3942.
4256 **FIREBIRD RISING** 13 [14] T D Barron 3-8-7 (50) P Makin(5) 8/1: 3604003: Chsd wnr, rdn & no impress   1   **45**
fnl 2f, lost 3rd nr fin: see 3651, 2042.
4301 **SOPHRANO** 12 [1] P A Blockley 4-9-0 (55) P Bradley 10/1: 5303304: Mid-div, mod prog for press.   2½   **43**
4132 **MAGARI** 19 [3]3-8-7 (53) J Bramhill 25/1: 3-4005: Mid-div, drvn & btn over 2f out: see 3610.   nk   **39**
4054 **FESTIVE CHIMES** 23 [7]3-8-7 (52) P Mulrennan(3) 12/1: 03006: Held up, mod prog for press: btr 3194.   1¾   **36**
4438 **NAMED AT DINNER** 4 [9]3-8-12 (55) M Tebbutt 11/1: 4-000007: ch g Halling - Salanka (Persian   1¼   **38**
Heights) Mid-div, nvr any impress, qck reapp: dual mdn rnr up in '03 for B Meehan: eff at 6/7f on fast grnd,
sharp/undul or gall trk: has tried up to 10f (mid dist pedigree).
2 Oct'03 Brig 7.0g/f 76-(75) D: 2 Sep'03 Nott 6.1g/f 75- D:
3850 **MAZRAM** 31 [12]5-8-7 BL T Hamilton(3) 66/1: 0-08: b f Muhtarram - Royal Mazi (Kings Lake) Dwelt &   3   **23**
rdn early, mod late prog in blnks: mod form prev.
3522 **MEMORY MAN** 45 [13]3-8-12 (65) D Kinsella 11/2: 04309: Chsd ldrs early, sn lost place & strugg: abs.   4   **24**
3655 **FROM THE NORTH** 40 [10]3-8-7 vis (50) A Beech 8/1: P0-05040: 10th: Handy, btn 3f out, abs.   nk   **18**
4042 **RAGAZZI** 23 [8]3-8-10 (60) D Mernagh 20/1: 000350: 11th: Sn rdn & al rear: btr 3396 (AW).   11   **1**
2608 **DEANGATE** 83 [2]3-8-12 T R Fitzpatrick 100/1: P0: 12th: Sn bhd & nvr factor, t-strap, abs.   dist   **0**
3177 **MICKLEGATE** 60 [4]3-8-7 (58) B Swarbrick(5) 7/1: 443-440P: Bhd, lost action & p.u. 2f out.   **0**
13 Ran   Time 1m 27.88 (3.98)   Owned: The Bond Girls Partnership   Trained: Thirsk

4505

12.10 Cantor Index Banded Stakes 3yo+ 0-40 (H5)
£1537 £439 £220   **1m1f61y   Firm 12   -26 Slow**   Inside

4379 **DANCING TILLY** 7 [12] R A Fahey 6-9-4 p (40) T Hamilton(3) 7/2 FAV: 6-424641: Twds rear & sn pushed   **49**
along, hdwy from halfway & rdn to lead ins last, rdn out: 1st win: eff btwn 1m/11f on firm & fbsnd, stiff or sharp
trk: now suited by chkpcs: see 375.
4243 **CAMPBELLS LAD** 14 [11] A Berry 3-8-12 (40) P Mathers(5) 12/1: 4005302: Trkd ldrs trav well, smooth   3   **42**
prog to lead 2f out, hdd/went badly left under press ins last, kept on cl home: eff btwn 9f/12f in mod company,
handles firm & fast grnd: see 3499 (sell).
4133 **MERLINS PROFIT** 19 [16] M Dods 4-9-4 (40) L Enstone 6/1: 5420U43: Chsd ldrs, outpcd/short of room   1¾   **39**
over 2f out, kept on ins last: handles firm & fast gnrd: see 1819 (11f).
4243 **EDDIES JEWEL** 14 [5] J S Wainwright 4-9-4 (40) G Parkin 17/2: 2545064: Keen, cl up, no extra bef dist.   1   **37**
4379 **ABUELOS** 7 [8]5-9-4 (40) T Williams 20/1: 0050665: Chsd ldrs, no extra fnl 1f: see 3666.   hd   **36**
3744} **NEVER PROMISE** 350 [9]6-9-4 vis (40) A Medeiros(5) 40/1: 000/600-6: b f Cadeaux Genereux -   1½   **33**
Yazeanhaa (Zilzal) Held up, late prog for press: jmps fit (no form): unplcd '03 (rtd 36, h'cap): '02
h'cap wnr (J Neville): eff at 1m/10f on firm & gd grnd, any trk: handles any trk & likes to force the pace.
1 Jul'02 Wind 8.3gd 48-45 E: 2 Apr'02 Sout 10gd 59-58 F: 2 Jul'01 Folk 9.6g/f 60-59 E: 1 Jul'01 Chep 10.1gd 60-56 E:
4248 **STEPASTRAY** 14 [7]7-9-4 vis (40) D Tudhope(7) 12/1: 0050007: Mid-div wide no impress fnl 2f.   nk   **32**
331 **NIGHT MAIL** 249 [2]4-9-4 (40) T Lucas 22/1: 044U0-68: Wide/rear, only mod prog: abs: see 331.   5   **22**
4284 **ERUPT** 12 [6]11-9-4 (45) M Lawson(5) 7/1: 0300439: Sn rdn rear & btn fnl 4284 (stf).   1½   **19**
3102 **HORMUZ** 12 [15]8-9-4 (40) A Nicholls 10/1: 40-00040: 10th: Led till 2f out, wknd qckly: btr 3102.   5   **9**
3963 **LARK IN THE PARK** 27 [4]4-9-4 t (40) B Swarbrick(5) 11/1: 6-000500: 11th: Held up, nvr a threat: btr 2993.   2½   **4**
3996 **DAIMAJIN** 26 [1]5-9-4 (40) A Beech(3) 16/1: 0006000: 12th: Prom, btn 3f out: btr 3530.   ½   **3**
3102 **LARK IN THE PARK** — (see above)
4348 **LADY STRATAGEM** 9 [3]5-9-4 (40) G Faulkner 20/1: 0-003000: 13th: Chsd ldrs, strugg from 3f out.   3   **0**
4120 **COCO POINT BREEZE** 20 [10]3-8-12 BL (40) P Mulrennan(3) 50/1: 00000: 14th: Keen, handy, btn 2f out.   4   **0**
4299 **BEVIER** 12 [13]10-9-4 (40) L Fletcher(3) 8/1: 4204000: 15th: Hampd early & dropped rear, dng out.   3   **0**
15 Ran   Time 1m 57.97 (2.57)   Owned: The 'We Believe In Miracles' Partnership   Trained: Malton

4506

12.40 Cantorindex Co Uk Banded Stakes 4yo+ 0-45 (H5)
£1554 £444 £222   **7f200y rnd   Firm 12   -22 Slow**   Inside

3526 **PENWELL HILL** 45 [9] T D Barron 5-9-3 (50) P Makin(5) 13/2: 2060031: Made all, drvn & held on well   **54**
ins last: 6 wk abs: stays 11f, suited by rdn on firm, fast & fibresand: improved for forcing tactics.
3933 **BABY BARRY** 29 [13] Mrs G S Rees 7-9-0 (47) A Beech(3) 6/1: 0030202: Trkd ldrs, rdn & kept on fnl   ½   **49**
2f: stays 1m in banded company: see 2445.
4373* **SHAMWARI FIRE** 7 [15] I W McInnes 4-9-2 (49) L Fletcher(3) 9/2 FAV: 0330130: Mid-div, rdn/hung   ¾   **50**
left over 1f out, kept on for press: eff at 1m, prob 9f+ ideal: see 4373 (9.7f).
3963 **TOKEWANNA** 27 [12] W M Brisbourne 4-9-2 t (49) P Mathers(5) 9/1: 0030454: Held up, efft wide, no dngr.   ½   **49**
4379 **HOHS BACK** 7 [11]5-8-12 p (45) A Nicholls 12/1: 0000005: Held up, mod prog for press, no dngr.   1¾   **42**
4145 **NIGHT MARKET** 18 [14]6-9-3 (50) M Lawson(5) 12/1: 0-010006: Dwelt, rear, some prog, nvr threat.   3   **41**
3996 **SENNEN COVE** 26 [8]5-8-12 t (45) G Faulkner 25/1: 3661107: Trkd ldrs trav well 3f out, wknd over 1f out.   hd   **35**
4084 **LUCKY LARGO** 22 [2]4-9-1 bl (48) J P Guillambert(3) 33/1: 6000008: Trkd ldrs, btn 2f out: see 1160.   3½   **31**
2947 **GEMINI LADY** 70 [17]4-8-12 (45) M Tebbutt 33/1: 20-02009: Held up, rdn & little prog: abs: btr 1992.   1   **26**
3270} **MASTER NIMBUS** 408 [1]4-9-2 (49) P Mulrennan(3) 66/1: 000000-0: 10th: b g Cloudings - Miss Charlie   3½   **23**
(Pharly) Bhd & rdn, nvr a factor: reapp: unplcd '03 (rtd 54, h'cap): best effort at 5f on gd grnd.
4347 **WELL CONNECTED** 9 [3]4-8-12 (45) L Enstone 20/1: 06030-00: 11th: b g Among Men - Wire To Wire   ½   **18**
(Welsh Saint) Mid-div, btn 2f out: dual h'cap plcd '03 (rtd 52, incl C/D): eff at 1m on firm & gd/sft grnd.
2986 **Jessie** 68 [16]5-8-12 vis(45) Kim Tinkler 12/1:0
3974 **Good Time Bobby** 27 [6]7-8-12 (45) J D O'Reilly(6) 20/1:0
4084 **Skiddaw Jones** 22 [5]4-9-0 (47) D Mernagh 12/1:0
2316} **Touch Of Ebony** 408 [7]5-9-1 (48) A Medeiros(5) 12/1:0
3159 **Ash Laddie** 61 [4]4-8-12 BL(45) G Parkin 100/1:0
4150 **Trusted Instinct** 18 [10]4-9-3 P(50) Dale Gibson 66/1:0
17 Ran   Time 1m 40.38 (2.68)   Owned: Mrs Liz Jones   Trained: Thirsk

CARLISLE   SATURDAY 11.09.04   Righthand, Stiff Track, Uphill Finish

---

4507   **1.10 Cantorsport Co Uk Tri-Banded Stakes 3yo 0-45 (H5)**
£1505 £430 £215   **7f200y rnd**   **Firm 12**   **+16 Fast**   Inside

4130   **CALCULAITE** 19 [17] Mrs G S Rees 3-9-5   (45) A Beech(3) 6/1: 0664501: Dpstd lead, went on after 3f   **60+**
& rdn clr over 2f out, won easily in best time of day: 1st win: eff at 6f, apprec return to 1m & banded company: acts
on firm & gd grnd: suited by forcing tactics: can win again in modest company if able to repeat this: see 3018.
3547   **ROMAN THE PARK** 44 [5] T D Easterby 3-9-5   (45) P M Quinn 7/2 FAV: 2313432: Mid-div, hung left &   10   **46**
kept on for press to take 2nd, nvr any impress on wnr: 6 wk abs: see 3547, 2969 & 2613.
3414   **BARGAIN HUNT** 50 [9] W Storey 3-9-5   (45) J Bramhill 9/1: 0360043: Chsd ldrs 3f out, kept on, no threat.   ½   **45**
3900   **PRIMATECH** 30 [3] K A Morgan 3-9-5 P (45) P Fitzsimons 33/1: 0000004: Held up, rdn & mod prog, no   1   **43**
dngr: new yard: tried chkpcs: see 3900.
4372   **CHIQITITA** 7 [13]3-9-0   (40) L Fletcher(2) 20/1: 0000605: Mid-div, nvr a threat to wnr: see 3094.   ½   **37**
2982   **BALLIN ROUGE** 68 [15]3-8-9 t (35) P Mulrennan(3) 50/1: 00-006: Held up, drvn & nvr able to chall: abs.   1   **30**
1330* **COURANT DAIR** 141 [12]3-9-0 (40) Rory Moore(5) 5/1: 0-036517: Trkd ldrs 3f out, sn no impress: jmps fit.   hd   **34**
4090   **AGGI MAC** 22 [11]3-9-0   (40) Suzanne France(7) 20/1: 005-5008: Bhd, efft wide, little prog: see 682.   ¾   **33**
4284   **DELTA LADY** 12 [2]3-9-0   (40) J P Guillambert(3) 33/1: 6050009: Held up, hung right 2f out, no impress.   ½   **32**
4054   **CELLINO** 23 [4]3-9-0   (40) A Nicholls 12/1: 0-040000: 10th: Mid-div, btn 2f out, longer trip.   3½   **25**
4347   **GRELE** 9 [6]3-9-5   (45) L Enstone 11/2: 0-05640: 11th: Chsd ldrs 6f, sn btn: flattered 4347.   8   **16**
4130   **NOBLE DESERT** 19 [10]3-9-5   (45) B Reilly(3) 16/1: 0-0500: 12th: Chsd ldrs, btn 2f out: flattered 1688 (7f).   1   **14**
4407   **SVENSON** 5 [14]3-8-9   (30) P Bradley 66/1: 0-000000: 13th: Keen. dsptd lead 2f, strugg fnl 3f, qck reapp.   1   **2**
4116   **Lord Wishingwell** 20 [1]3-8-9 vis(35) G Parkin 12/1:0   4243   **Monkey Or Me** 14 [7]3-8-9 (35) R Fitzpatrick 14/1:0
15 Ran   Time 1m 40.09 (u0.29)   Owned: Maggie and Eric Hemming   Trained: Preston

---

4508   **1.40 Cantorsport Co Uk Banded Stakes 3yo+ 0-45 (H5)**
£1512 £432 £216   **5f rnd**   **Firm 12**   **-24 Slow**   Inside

3767   **LOUGHLORIEN** 35 [8] R E Barr 5-9-4   (49) D Tudhope(7) 5/1: 0033401: Mid-div, rdn & styd on to lead   **55**
well ins last: prev with R Fahey: eff at 6f, stiff 5f ideal: acts on firm & gd/sft: apprec drop in grade: see 1886.
4408   **FLYING TACKLE** 5 [10] M Dods 6-9-5 p (50) L Enstone 10/1: 2100002: Mid-div, rdn to chall ins last,   nk   **55**
just outpcd by wnr close home: qkc reapp: see 2981.
4370   **MOLOTOV** 7 [14] I W McInnes 4-9-5   (50) L Fletcher(5) 5/2 FAV: 1004133: Led over 2f out till ins last.   1   **52**
4412   **ASTRAC** 5 [4] Mrs A L M King 13-9-3   (48) P M Quinn 10/1: 0240004: Mid-div, kept on for press, no dngr.   ½   **48**
3974   **ROBWILLCALL** 27 [17]4-9-2 p (47) P Mathers(5) 8/1: 0515505: Led till over 2f out, no extra: btr 2614.   nk   **46**
436   **SUITCASE MURPHY** 236 [11]3-8-13   (45) A Beech(3) 33/1: 00004-06: b g Petardia - Noble Rocket   3   **35**
(Reprimand) Mid-div, no impress fnl 2f, long abs: unplcd '03 (rtd 53a & 52): unplcd '03 (rtd 53a & 49).
4088   **MASSEY** 22 [5]8-9-2 vis (47) D Mernagh 12/1: 0100007: Mid-div, drvn & btn 2f out: needs further.   ¾   **35**
3900   **HI DARL** 30 [13]3-8-13   (45) Rory Moore(5) 40/1: 641-0008: Bhd, mod prog: see 2904.   hd   **32**
4009   **PIRLIE HILL** 25 [12]4-9-2   (47) G Parkin 12/1: 4065009: Chsd ldrs, outpcd fnl 2f: btr 2181.   ¾   **32**
3667   **PETANA** 39 [16]4-9-4 p (49) Joanna Badger 20/1: 0401000: 10th: Bhd, only mod prog: btr 2614.   nk   **33**
4211   **ROSIES RESULT** 15 [7]4-9-3   (48) Jemma Marshall(7) 16/1: 0100600: 11th: Bhd, rdn & no impress.   shd   **32**
4043   **John Ogroats** 23 [15]6-9-2 (47) A Nicholls 12/1:0   4502}   **Las Ramblas** 348 [3]7-9-3 t p(48) P Bradley 50/1:0
3767   **Royal Windmill** 35 [2]5-9-2 (47) P Mulrennan(3) 10/1:0
3737   **Ol Lucy Broon** 37 [1]3-9-3 VIS(49) R Fitzpatrick 40/1:0
15 Ran   Time 1m 01.32(1.82)   Owned: Mr P Cartmell   Trained: Middlesbrough

---

CHESTER   SATURDAY 11.09.04   Lefthand, V Sharp Track

Official Going Good

4509   **1.55 Hallows Associates Nursery Handicap Stakes 2yo 0-95 (C2)**   **[99]**
£8141 £2505 £1253   **7f2y rnd**   **Good/Firm 24**   **-06 Slow**   Inside

3311   **COMIC STRIP** 54 [7] Sir Mark Prescott 2-9-3   (88) M Hills 11/4: 141: Held up, hdwy 3f out, styd on   **99+**
well to lead ins last, rdn, going away: well bckd after 7 wk abs: stays 7f well, further will suit: acts on
fibresand & fast grnd, sharp trk: runs well fresh: useful, more to come as he steps up in trip, win again.
4224   **ROWAN LODGE** 14 [1] M H Tompkins 2-8-9 (1ow) (79) N Callan 6/1: 0312102: Led early, led again over   1½   **85**
3f out till ins last, not pace of wnr: clr of rem & right back to form: see 3931, 3723.
4105   **DAHTEER** 21 [2] M R Channon 2-9-7   (92) C Catlin 9/4 FAV: 4116023: With ldr, led over 5f out till   5   **89**
over 3f out, wknd fnl 1f: btr 4105, 2367.
4177   **LANGSTON BOY** 16 [3] M L W Bell 2-8-2   (73) R Mullen 7/1: 423024: Cl-up, sltly short of room over   hd   **69**
1f out but sn wknd: btr on polytrack in 4177.
4224   **BOLTON HALL** 14 [5]2-8-12   (83) R Winston 9/2: 16565: Handy, outpcd over 2f out, some late gains.   1¼   **77**
2926   **TRANSVESTITE** 70 [6]2-8-4   (75) W Ryan 9/1: 5436: Al bhd: 10 wk abs: btr 2926 (5f), 2618.   5   **59**
3623   **GORTUMBLO** 42 [4]2-9-1   (86) D Corby(3) 20/1: 13007: Al bhd: been gelded, 6 wk abs: btr 2251 (6f).   8   **54**
7 Ran   Time 1m 27.11 (2.11)   Owned: Neil Greig - Osborne House   Trained: Newmarket

---

4510   **2.25 Listed Totesport Henry Gee Stakes Fillies & Mares 3yo+ (A1)**
£20300 £7700 £3850   **6f18y rnd**   **Good/Firm 24**   **+20 Fast**   Inside

4238   **SIMIANNA** 14 [1] A Berry 5-8-13 p (97) R Winston 9/2: 4650321: Cl-up, trav well & short of room   **102**
over 1f out, squeezed through & styd on to lead ins last, rdn out: deserved win after several plcd efforts: winning
form over 5/6f & acts on firm, hvy & polytrack, likes Chester: tough & useful, gd confidence boost: see 2457, 1162.
       BLUE DREAM 23 [4] T Hogan 4-8-13 P M Hills 14/1: 0-024342: b f Cadeaux Genereux - Hawait Al Barr   ½   **101**
(Green Desert) Chsd ldr, eff to chall over 1f out, kept on, not btn far: Irish raider, plcd there earlier: stks

---

1361

wnr in France in '03: eff over 5/6f on fast & gd grnd: clearly eff in cheek pieces: useful.
4098 **FRUIT OF GLORY 21** [3] J R Jenkins 5-8-13 (95) W Ryan 7/1: 2142253: Led, rdn & hdd just ins last, no extra: ran to best: see 3971, 3773. *1¼* **97**
2727} **PEARL GREY 431** [2] Saeed bin Suroor 3-8-11 T (108) J Carroll 4/1 FAV: 3112-4: gr f Gone West - Zelanda (Night Shift) In tch, eff & switched right over 1f out, kept on ins last: long abs: '03 mdn & List wnr for D Loder: eff over 5/6f on firm & fast grnd, prob any trk: wore a t-strap here: useful. *shd* **96**
2 Jul'03 Newm 6g/f 100- A: 1 Jun'03 Newm 6fm 101- A: 1 Jun'03 Nott 5.1g/f 97- D:
3971+**GOLDEVA 27** [5]5-9-2 (105) D Sweeney 11/2: 1505415: Held up, hdwy & short of room over 1f out, kept on ins last, no threat: shade btr 3971 (gd/soft). *1¼* **95**
3965 **AND TOTO TOO 27** [7]4-8-13 bl (75) D Nolan 33/1: 4421406: Slow away & bhd, some late gains, no threat: relish h'caps & 7f: see 3872, 3456. *3* **83**
3778* **PARADISE ISLE 35** [12]3-8-11 (100) R Mullen 6/1: 11-04217: Held up, hdwy wide over 2f out, wknd over 1f out: gave up too much grnd on this v sharp trk: btr 3778. *1* **80**
4317 **RISE 10** [11]3-8-11 bl (70) D Kinsella 66/1: 0120128: In tch, lost place & short of room over 1f out, held when hmpd ins last: needs h'caps: see 4317. *1¾* **75**
4384 **TYCHY 7** [8]5-8-13 (97) N Callan 11/2: 0510409: In tch, wknd over 1f out: poor draw: see 4291, 3773. *shd* **74**
4226 **DOWAGER 14** [6]3-8-11 BL (96) C Catlin 16/1: 4630000: 10th: Al bhd: tried blnks: btr 3268. *1½* **70**
3564 **GREY PEARL 43** [10]5-8-13 (86) Darren Williams 25/1: 4604100: 11th: Handy wide, wknd over 1f out: 6 wk abs, poor draw & gave up too much grnd: twice below 2736. *6* **52**
11 Ran Time 1m 13.33 (0.23) Owned: Mr T G & Mrs M E Holdcroft Trained: Cockerham

4511

3.00 Legat Owen E B F Maiden Stakes 2yo (D3)
£5086 £1565 £782 **7f2y rnd** **Good/Firm 24** **-14 Slow** Inside

4194 **DHAULAR DHAR 15** [1] B W Hills 2-9-0 M Hills 2/5 FAV: 21: Made all, pushed clr over 1f out, v cmftbly: well bckd: stays 7f well on fast & gd grnd, sharp or gall trk, 1m sure to suit: disposed of modest field in gd style, more to come: see 4194. **89**
4102 **LAYED BACK ROCKY 21** [6] M Mullineaux 2-9-0 C Catlin 33/1: 602: ch c Lake Coniston - Madam Taylor (Free State) Chsd wnr, not pace of wnr over fnl 2f: poss stays 7f on fast grnd. *11* **63**
4006 **LAKE WAKATIPU 25** [2] M Mullineaux 2-8-9 R Mullen 14/1: 043: Held up, brief eff over 2f out, onepace. *2½* **53**
4303 **THE TERMINATOR 11** [3] A Berry 2-9-0 (35) N Callan 40/1: 000004: b g Night Shift - Surmise (Alleged) Handy, wknd over 1f out. *1* **56**
POLAR PASSION 0 [5]2-8-9 D Sweeney 25/1: 5: b f Polar Prince - Priorite (Kenmare) Al bhd on debut: Apr foal: half-sister to a 7f wnr: dam 7f juv scorer. *nk* **50**
TAVALU 0 [4]2-9-0 J Carroll 4/1: 6: Al bhd. *shd* **54**
4102 **OXFORD STREET PETE 21** [7]2-9-0 A Daly 10/1: 307: Held up, wknd well over 1f out: best 3633. *5* **44**
7 Ran Time 1m 27.64 (2.64) Owned: Maktoum Al Maktoum Trained: Lambourn

4512

3.35 University Of Liverpool Handicap Stakes 3yo+ 56-70 (E3) **[73]**
£5236 £1611 £806 **1m7f195y** **Good/Firm 24** **-35 Slow** Inside

ROOFTOP PROTEST 27 [5] T Hogan 7-9-4 T (63) M Hills 4/1 FAV: 3311611: b g Thatching - Seattle Siren (Seattle Slew) Made all, pushed clr over 1f out, cmftbly: Irish raider, 3-time h'cap wnr there prev this term: stays 2m well, further will suit: acts on firm & gd grnd & clearly eff in a t-strap: v progressive, defy a pen. **77**
4235 **IRISH BLADE 14** [8] H Candy 3-8-10 (1oh) (68) D Sweeney 13/2: 4300032: Prom, eff over 1f out, kept on but not pace of wnr: stays 2m & caught a progressive type: shld certainly find a mdn h'cap: see 1501. *8* **72**
3887 **RED SUN 30** [9] J Mackie 7-8-11 t (56) Dale Gibson 6/1: 4-126063: Keen cl-up, eff over 2f out, sn onepace. *1¼* **59**
4274 **ISAAF 12** [15] P W Hiatt 5-9-7 (66) Darren Williams 25/1: 4416004: Chsd ldrs, onepace over 1f out. *½* **68**
3140 **NORTHERN NYMPH 62** [1]5-9-6 (65) Stephanie Hollinshead(5) 16/1: 5623405: In tch, no impress fnl 2f. *1* **66**
4033 **ELLWAY HEIGHTS 24** [2]7-8-11 (5oh) (51) R Mullen 14/1: 2225306: Held up, eff & short of room well over 1f out, sn btn: see 2964, 2813. *1* **55**
4183 **ARABIAN MOON 15** [16]8-9-11 (70) D Nolan(3) 25/1: 0060-107: Bhd, modest late gains: best 3983 (12f). *shd* **70**
4170 **REDSPIN 16** [4]4-9-1 (60) Derek Nolan(7) 10/1: 4400038: In tch, outpcd over 3f out, no impress: see 2471. *hd* **59**
4276 **TEORBAN 12** [6]5-8-11 (1oh) (55) W Ryan 16/1: 10-61009: Chsd wnr till over 5f out, wknd over 1f out, sn eased: best 3400 (clmr). *1¾* **53**
4276 **HENRY ISLAND 12** [11]11-8-13 (58) D Kinsella 15/2: 5040020: 10th: Nvr a factor: btr 4276. *nk* **54**
4340 **REGENCY RED 9** [7]6-8-11 (10oh) (46) B Swarbrick(5) 25/1: 32100/-40: 11th: Held up, no impress. *¾* **51**
3822 **DIAMOND ORCHID 33** [3]4-8-12 vis (57) Lisa Jones 8/1: 2151020: 12th: Slow away & al bhd: btr 3822. *hd* **51**
4119 **GALLANT BOY 20** [14]5-9-5 vis t (64) N Callan 9/1: 0544440: 13th: Slow away & al bhd: see 3964 (12f). *2* **56**
4276 **DARN GOOD 12** [10]3-8-9 (2oh)bl (67) J Carroll 16/1: 1120660: 14th: Nvr a factor: see 3057, 2908. *1¾* **57**
4308 **SUBADAR MAJOR 11** [12]7-8-11 (26oh) (30) Hayley Turner(3) 100/1: 0/0000-00: 15th: Handy, wknd 4f out. *dist* **0**
15 Ran Time 3m 32.1 (9.4) Owned: M G Byrne Trained: Ireland

4513

4.05 European Breeders Fund Conditions Stakes 2yo (C2)
£7735 £2745 £1372 **7f122y rnd** **Good/Firm 24** **-19 Slow** Inside

4096 **JOHNNY JUMPUP 21** [3] R M Beckett 2-9-0 (93) N Callan 5/2: 1101: In tch, hdwy to lead 1f out, styd on well, drvn clr: stays 7.5f well on fast & soft, stiff or sharp trks: useful, genuine & improving: see 3110. **102**
3859 **HACHITA 31** [1] H R A Cecil 2-8-9 (83) W Ryan 11/2: 132: Set pace till over 3f out, kept on to take 2nd ins last: stays 7.5f, 1m sure to suit: going the right way: see 3520. *2½* **91**
3060 **COUNTRY RAMBLER 65** [2] B W Hills 2-9-0 (98) M Hills 11/8 FAV: 0103: Led over 3f out till dist, wknd: nicely bckd, 2 mth abs: shade more expected after 2597 (7f, made all). *1¼* **94**
2851* **PERSONIFY 73** [4] Saeed bin Suroor 2-9-0 J Carroll 7/2: 14: Slow away, nvr a factor: abs: btr 2851 (6f). *3½* **87**
4 Ran Time 1m 35.62 (3.22) Owned: Mr & Mrs A Briars Trained: Lambourn

CHESTER **SATURDAY 11.09.04 Lefthand, V Sharp Track**

4514 **4.40 Rectangle Group Handicap Stakes 3yo+ 71-85 (D2)** **[85]**
£6770 £2083 £1042 **5f16y rnd** **Good/Firm 24** **-28 Slow** Inside

4380* **JILLY WHY 7** [6] Ms Deborah J Evans 3-8-10 (67) B Swarbrick(5) 10/1: 340-0411: Prom wide, gd hdwy to lead over 1f out, pushed clr: eff over 5/6f on firm & gd grnd: best up with/forcing the pace: eye-catching win conceding grnd by racing wide, clearly thriving & shld be followed: see 4380. **77+**
4240 **KINGS COLLEGE BOY 14** [4] R A Fahey 4-8-12 bl (68) Dale Gibson 5/1: 3030102: Handy, eff & short of room well over 1f out, kept on ins last, no threat to wnr: fine run & likes Chester: see 4107. *1¼* **71**
4294* **BEAUVRAI 12** [8] G C H Chung 4-9-7 bl (77) O Urbina 9/2 FAV: 0023113: In tch, eff well over 1f out, onepace: nicely bckd: prev with D Flood: gd run from modest draw & in fine heart: see 4294 (clmr, 6f). *3½* **70**
4107 **FRASCATI 21** [9] A Berry 4-9-6 (76) P Mathers(5) 9/1: 0112004: Sn bhd, short of room 2f out, kept on nicely up straight, racing wide: fine run conceding grnd from poor draw: see 2747. *¾* **67**
4489 **IZMAIL 2** [1]5-8-13 (69) N Callan 11/2: 0100005: Led till over 1f out, no extra: well drawn. *¾* **58**
4291 **SIR ERNEST 12** [5]3-9-0 (71) L Fletcher(3) 16/1: 0420006: Held up, eff well over 1f out, no extra: see 4291. *nk* **59**
4094 **HELLO ROBERTO 22** [12]3-9-0 (71) K Ghunowa(7) 20/1: 0100047: Slow away, in tch, onepace over 1f out. *shd* **58**
4174 **STRENSALL 16** [13]7-9-7 (77) C Catlin 20/1: 0505528: Held up, nvr a factor: btr 4174, 2690. *1* **61**
4144 **SIR DON 18** [7]5-8-10 (5oh)vis (61) J Bramhill 25/1: 3500009: Slow away, nvr a factor: best 2477. *¾* **48**
4382 **PRINCE OF BLUES 7** [2]6-8-10 (10oh)bl (56) L Enstone 14/1: 0303300: 10th: Handy, wknd well over 1f out. *hd* **47**
3561 **RECTANGLE 44** [10]4-8-10 (66) A Nicholls 12/1: 0002000: 11th: Handy, wknd over 1f out: 6 wk abs. *2½* **40**
4382 **JOHNSTONS DIAMOND 7** [16]6-9-10 (80) M Hills 11/1: 2000000: 12th: Al bhd: see 1977, 687. *nk* **53**
4174 **CHICO GUAPO 16** [3]4-8-11 bl (67) W Ryan 6/1: 0000000: 13th: Handy, wknd over 2f out: see 1476. *2½* **33**
13 Ran Time 1m 02.39 (2.59) Owned: Mr Paul Green (Oaklea) Trained: Lydiate

4515 **5.10 Astbury Wren Insurance Brokers Handicap Stakes 3yo+ 56-70 (E3)** **[77]**
£5689 £1750 £875 **1m2f75y** **Good/Firm 24** **-28 Slow** Outside

4354* **MILK AND SULTANA 8** [7] G A Ham 4-8-10 (59) A Daly 14/1: 0202411: Held up, hdwy over 2f out, styd on for press to lead cl-home, drvn out: eff over 10/12f on firm, soft & fibresand, prob any trk: improving. **67**
4347 **YOUNG ROONEY 9** [15] M Mullineaux 4-9-5 P (68) L Enstone 20/1: 24-40322: Led, rdn & hdd cl-home, just held: fine run, deserves a race: see 4347, 4084. *nk* **75**
4388 **MR MIDASMAN 7** [1] R Hollinshead 3-8-0 (55) Dale Gibson 8/1: 0004633: In tch, onepace. *1* **61**
4456 **INFIDELITY 4** [2] A Bailey 3-8-1 p (57) Hayley Turner(3) 25/1: 6063504: Slow away, hdwy & short of room 2f out, edged left ins last but kept on: qck reapp: see 2881, 2509. *½* **61**
4167* **SECLUDED 17** [4]4-9-5 bl (68) R Mullen 7/1: 55-50015: Slow away, hed up, eff 2f out, onepace: clr rem. *1¼* **70**
4076* **GIUNCHIGLIO 22** [6]5-9-7 (70) B Swarbrick(5) 20/1: 0360416: Held up, nvr a factor: btr 4076 (soft). *7* **62**
3845 **DESERT IMAGE 32** [5]3-8-12 (68) D Corby(3) 33/1: 3324007: Held up, eff over 2f out, sn no extra: btr 2413. *1¾* **57**
4299* **MCQUEEN 12** [11]4-9-3 (66) D Sweeney 9/2: 0602118: Handy, wknd 3f out: btr 4299 (soft). *1½* **53**
4268 **HEAD TO KERRY 13** [9]4-8-7 (1oh)P (55) W Ryan 7/1: 3424549: Held up, nvr a factor: btr 4268. *¾* **41**
4134} **INVESTMENT AFFAIR 368** [10]4-8-11 (60) J Carroll 50/1: 136000-0: 10th: b g Sesaro - Superb Investment (Hatim) Al bhd: now with D McCain: '03 dual h'cap wnr for M Johnston: suited by forcing tactics at 1m & acts on fast & gd/soft grnd, gall or sharp trks. *3* **41**
1 Jun'03 Muss 8g/f 71-57 E: 1 May'03 Ayr 8g/s 55-52 F:
4406* **MARKET AVENUE 5** [17]5-9-1 (6ex) (64) Darren Williams 8/1: 6050510: 11th: Slow away, sn in tch, saddle slipped over 3f out: ignore this: see 4406. *2* **42**
4402* **JAKE BLACK 6** [14]4-8-9 (58) D Tudhope(7) 3/1 FAV: 1504410: 12th: Handy, wknd over 2f out: bckd. *7* **26**
3335 **ARMATORE 52** [3]4-9-5 (68) A Nicholls 100/1: 44330-00: 13th: b g Gone West - Awesome Account (Lyphard) Chsd ldr, wknd over 2f out: prev plcd in the French provinces at around 10f on gd grnd. *3½* **31**
4342 **HAVETOAVIT 9** [16]3-8-9 (65) C Catlin 10/1: 2404120: 14th: In tch, wknd over 2f out: btr 4342, 3772. *8* **16**
4354 **LUXOR 8** [13]7-8-7 (11oh) (45) Lisa Jones 66/1: 0000000: 15th: Al bhd: see 1884. *½* **6**
3812 **KILLALA 34** [12]4-8-7 (1oh) (55) N Callan 33/1: 3552240: 16th: Slow away & al bhd: btr 3558 (clmr). *7* **0**
16 Ran Time 2m 13.83(5.33) Owned: Mr D M Drury Trained: Axbridge

MUSSELBURGH **SATURDAY 11.09.04 Righthand, Sharp Track**

Official Going Good (Good/Firm places)

4516 **1.50 Totesport Com Handicap Stakes 3yo 86-100 (C1)** **[101]**
£15103 £5729 £2864 **1m** **Good 58** **+12 Fast** Far Side

4225 **FLIPANDO 14** [6] T D Barron 3-8-13 (86) M Fenton 7/2: 4221531: In tch, styd on to lead 2f out, drvn out ins fnl 1f: tchd 9/2, fast time: eff at 6/7f, imprvd for step up to 1m: acts on fast & gd, prob soft. **94**
3738+**MRS MOH 37** [5] T D Easterby 3-8-11 (84) J Mackay 9/2: 0051312: Handy, ev ch well bef 1f out, styd on ins fnl 1f, just held by wnr: continues in gd form: 4lb higher than recent win in 3738. *½* **90**
4136 **PENRITH 19** [8] M Johnston 3-8-13 (86) R Ffrench 100/30 FAV: 3035023: Al cl-up, ev ch 1f out, sn no extra: tchd 4/1: just btr 4136 (gd/soft). *1¼* **89**
1317 **UNITED NATIONS 141** [3] D R Loder 3-9-7 VIS (94) T P Queally 7/1: 134: Chsd ldrs, eff over 2f out, onepcd dist: long abs & first time visor: h'cap bow: btr 1317 & 1166. *2* **93**
3949 **PARKVIEW LOVE 28** [2]3-9-1 (88) W Hogg(7) 11/1: 0000045: Held up, prog 3f out, kept on ins fnl 1f. *¾* **85**
1665 **REDWOOD ROCKS 123** [1]3-8-9 (82) F Lynch 16/1: 100-0106: Led 6f, no extra: long abs, btr 1460 (7f). *½* **78**
3620 **KELUCIA 42** [7]3-9-6 (93) Paul Eddery 12/1: 0566667: Missed break & nvr a factor: 6 wk abs, op 9/1. *8* **73**
4174 **MISTER MARMADUKE 16** [4]3-8-7 (1oh) (79) T Eaves(3) 8/1: 00-04358: In tch over 5f, sn wknd, eased. *16* **28**
8 Ran Time 1m 41.21 (3.71) Owned: Mrs J Hazell Trained: Thirsk

---

4517	2.20 John Smith's Extra Smooth Median Auction Maiden Stakes 2yo (E3)
	£4095 £1260 £630 5f Good 58 -29 Slow Stands Side

3832 **FOLGA 33** [6] J G Given 2-8-9   J Mackay 20/1: 301: Keen in tch, styd on to lead 1f out, rdn out: **75**
new stable: eff at 5f on fast, gd grnd & a sharp trk: imprvd for switch to J G Given yard, see 3525 (R P Elliott).
4409 **BOBS FLYER 5** [1] J G Given 2-8-9   R Ffrench 12/1: 0402: In tch, prog 2f out, kept on ins fnl 1f,   1   **71**
not pace wnr: shorter priced stablemate of wnr: qck reapp: eff at 5f on gd grnd: see 4303.
4207 **PERCHERON 15** [8] P A Blockley 2-9-0   G Gibbons 100/1: 003: ch g Perugino - Silvery Halo (Silver   1   **73**
Ghost) Prom, ev ch dist, sn no extra: Apr foal, half-brother successful abroad: dam plcd at 7f: sire well
related: eff at 5f, further shld suit: acts on gd grnd: imprvd eff today & now quals for h'caps.
4134 **HOWARDS PRINCESS 19** [2] J S Goldie 2-8-9 (73) T P Queally 5/2: 5224: In tch over 2f out, sn   ¾   **66**
outpcd, rallied dist: op 7/4: showed more in 4134 & 3258 (gd/soft).
3258 **PEDLAR OF DREAMS 56** [3]2-8-9   M Fenton 15/8 FAV: 35: In tch over 3f, sn no extra: well bckd, 8   1   **63**
wk abs: showed more in 3258 (debut, gd/soft).
4343 **LLAMADAS 9** [4]2-9-0 bl (67) T Eaves(3) 13/2: 0340366: Missed break, nvr a factor: btr 4172.   1   **64**
4303 **BOND PUCCINI 11** [7]2-9-0   F Lynch 9/2: 027: Led, sn switched to stands rail, hdd 1f out, wknd.   shd   **63**
4277 **THORNBER COURT 12** [5]2-8-9   Paul Eddery 33/1: 048: Missed break, nvr a factor: see 4277.   1¼   **54**
8 Ran   Time 1m 01.84 (4.34)   Owned: Mr Peter Onslow   Trained: Gainsborough

---

4518	2.50 Bliss Maiden Auction Stakes 2yo (E3)
	£4076 £1254 £627 7f30y Good 58 -14 Slow Far Side

4006 **PROFITS REALITY 25** [4] P A Blockley 2-8-11 (77) G Gibbons 7/2: 055431: Handy, prog to lead dist,   **86**
pushed clr, val 4L+: eff at 6f, imprvd for step up to 7f: acts on gd, gd/soft grnd & a sharp trk: see 4006.
4381 **MCELDOWNEY 7** [7] M Johnston 2-8-10 (77) R Ffrench 11/2: 2223002: Led, hdd dist, kept on, not   2¼   **78**
pace easy wnr: clr rem: qck reapp: back to form with blnks left off: see 3511 & 3245.
3798 **FADAEL 34** [2] P W D'Arcy 2-8-5 (72) M Fenton 11/2: 0633: Chsd ldrs over 5f, no extra: see 3798 (firm).   4   **65**
4114 **MANGROVE CAY 20** [5] D R Loder 2-8-10   T P Queally 6/5 FAV: 04: b c Danetime - Art Duo (Artaius)   ½   **69**
Prom, ev ch 2f out, grad wknd: well bckd: Apr foal, half-brothers to wnrs at 6/8f: dam unplcd.
4242 **SCORPIO SALLY 14** [6]2-8-3 (63) J Mackay 16/1: 05655: Rear, nvr a factor.   4   **54**
4102 **ANSELLS LEGACY 21** [1]2-8-10   F Lynch 25/1: 006: b c Charnwood Forest - Hanzala (Akarad) Missed   ½   **57**
break, al in rear: Apr foal, half-brother successful at 1m: dam List wnr abroad.
4127 **SMILING STARDUSTER 19** [3]2-8-7   T Eaves(3) 66/1: 007: b c Danehill Dancer - Evriza (Kahyasi)   12   **33**
Bhd, nvr able to chall: May foal, dam wnr at 14f, also a wnr over hdles: sire useful performer at sprint dists.
7 Ran   Time 1m 29.94 (5.04)   Owned: Phones Direct Partnership   Trained: Cockerham

---

4519	3.25 Kronenbourg Nursery Handicap Stakes 2yo 0-75 (E3)	[80]
	£6942 £2136 £1068 1m Good 58 -06 Slow Far Side	

4257 **SUCCESSION 13** [8] Sir Mark Prescott 2-8-11 (63) J Mackay 7/1: 00061: Handy, styd on to lead 2f   **74**
out, sn clr, rdn out: eff at 1m, further will suit: acts on gd grnd & a sharp trk: imprvd dramatically on h'cap bow
as most of his stablemates do: more prizes await on this evidence: see 4257.
4006 **KERRYS BLADE 25** [9] P C Haslam 2-8-11 (63) G Faulkner 16/1: 0562: Bhd, prog wide 3f out, kept on   2   **69**
ins fnl 1f, no ch with wnr: imprvd for step up to 7f on h'cap bow: acts on gd grnd: can find similar.
4213 **DANCING SHIRL 15** [6] C W Fairhurst 2-8-6 (58) Leanne Kershaw(7) 33/1: 6333: Held up, prog wide 3f   3½   **57**
out, kept on ins fnl 1f, no ch with front 2: h'cap bow: see 2413 & 3570.
3500 **LODGICIAN 46** [13] J J Quinn 2-9-4 (70) T Hamilton(3) 12/1: 4304: Dwelt, sn in mid-div, no impress fnl 1f.   1½   **66**
4171 **ROYAL FLYNN 16** [4]2-8-13 (65) T Eaves(3) 33/1: 64065: Nvr nrr than mid-div: see 4171.   2   **57**
4074 **LISA MONA LISA 22** [7]2-9-7 (73) M Lawson(5) 10/1: 4104106: Handy over 6f, no extra: btr 3723 (7f).   3   **59**
2721 **DIATONIC 78** [3]2-8-10 (62) M Fenton 33/1: 00027: Rear, moderate late gains: long abs & new stable.   nk   **47**
4344 **ZANTERO 9** [14]2-8-10 (62) G Gibbons 6/1: 46468: Trkd ldrs over 6f, sn hung right & wknd: tchd 10/1.   1¾   **43**
3376 **BRACE OF DOVES 38** [11]2-8-10 (62) Paul Eddery 7/1: 5009: ch g Zafonic - Seeker (Rainbow Quest) Al   ¾   **41**
in rear: 7 wk abs: Feb first foal, cost 20,000gns: dam successful at 12f: sire Gr 1 wnr at 1m: with P W D'Arcy.
3698 **DAVY CROCKETT 44** [5]2-9-3 (69) F Lynch 11/1: 00560: 11th: Led 6f, sn wknd: 6 wk abs & new stable.   2   **43**
3214 **SPEAGLE 58** [10]2-8-11 (63) T P Queally 20/1: 0560: 12th: Chsd ldrs 6f, wknd: 8 wk abs.   1½   **34**
3624 **EXIT SMILING 42** [2]2-9-6 (72) R Ffrench 9/1: 23050: 13th: In tch, wknd bef 2f out: 6 wk abs.   ½   **42**
3698 **UREDALE 38** [12]2-9-0 (66) M Tebbutt 25/1: 5065100: 14th: Bhd, nvr a factor: btr 3349.   3   **30**
14 Ran   Time 1m 42.6 (5.1)   Owned: Dr Catherine Wills   Trained: Newmarket

---

4520	3.55 Stephen Hay Associates Maiden Stakes 3yo (D3)
	£4066 £1251 £626 1m Good 58 -05 Slow Far Side

4135 **JUST A FLUKE 19** [5] M Johnston 3-9-0 (72) R Ffrench 5/4 FAV: 0230521: Mid-div, prog 2f out, styd   **68**
on to lead ins fnl 1f, drvn out to hold on: well bckd: eff at 1m/10f on firm & gd/soft grnd: deserved this.
4175 **THE NUMBER 16** [2] I Semple 3-9-0 (64) T Eaves(3) 9/1: 56-3352: Mid-div, prog halfway, styd on to   nk   **67**
lead dist, sn hung under press, hdd ins fnl 1f, kept on but just denied: tchd 11/1: see 4085.
4346 **GRACEFUL AIR 9** [4] J R Weymes 3-8-9 (52) T Hamilton(3) 25/1: 5445003: In tch, prog & ev ch dist, wknd. 3   **56**
222 **FIVE YEARS ON 267** [6] W J Haggas 3-9-0 (73) M Fenton 15/8: 024-4: Led, hdd after 2f, styd on to   shd   **60**
lead again 3f out, hdd dist, wknd: bckd after long abs: prob styd on first try at 1m: btr 76 (5f).
4228 **HARRYCAT 14** [1]3-9-0   J Mackay 11/2: 05: In tch, ev ch 2f out, sn wknd: see 4228.   2   **56**
3766 **COLLOSEUM 35** [3]3-9-0 (52) Kristin Stubbs(7) 100/1: 6-040006: Led after 2f, hdd 3f out, wknd.   10   **36**
6 Ran   Time 1m 42.59 (5.09)   Owned: Maktoum Al Maktoum   Trained: Middleham

MUSSELBURGH   SATURDAY 11.09.04   Righthand, Sharp Track

4521   4.30 Watch Live On Racing Uk Handicap Stakes 3yo+ 56-70 (E3)   **[68]**
£6812 £2096 £1048   **1m6f**   **Good 58**   **-01 Slow**   Inside

4138 **MINIVET 19** [3] R Allan 9-8-11 (51) P Mulrennan(3) 11/1: 054-0541: In tch, prog after halfway,   **64**
styd on to lead dist, drvn clr: op 9/1: eff at 9/12f, now stays 14f: acts on fast & soft grnd: see 4138.
4235 **SHARADI 14** [7] V Smith 3-9-1 (66) Joanna Badger 9/2: 6-000222: Led, hdd bef 1f out, sn no extra: 3 **74**
clr rem: op 7/2: has been gelded since last run: continues to run well: see 4235 & 3893.
3611 **MOST DEFINITELY 42** [8] T D Easterby 4-9-8 (62) M Fenton 5/1: 22-20623: Mid-div, prog halfway,   3 **66**
styd on to lead trav well bef 3f out, sn hdd & no extra: 6 wk abs: showed more in 3611 (2m, firm).
4348+**TURN OF PHRASE 9** [4] R A Fahey 5-9-6 vis (60) T Hamilton(3) 2/1 FAV: 13-00214: Rear, prog 5f out,   1¼ **63**
onepcd fnl 2f: bckd: 6lb higher than win in 4348 (12f).
3475 **THE RING 48** [5]4-9-11 VIS (65) T Eaves(3) 7/1: 2305055: Keen in tch, wknd bef 3f out: 7 wk abs &   5 **62**
visor.
4182 **RHETORICAL 16** [1]3-8-4 (7oh) (55) J Mackay 7/1: 0600-506: Cl-up 10f, sn fdd: op 9/1: see 3772.   6 **44**
4708) **CULCABOCK 334** [2]4-8-11 (1oh) (50) G Faulkner 40/1: 062560-7: b g Unfuwain - Evidently (Slip   3 **36**
Anchor) Bhd, nvr a factor: earlier unplcd over hdles (rtd 91h, h'cap): juv nov hdle in early 03/04 (rtd 107h at
best, stays 2m on gd grnd): unplcd in 3 '03 Flat starts (rtd 39, appr seller): ex Irish, mdn wnr at Bellewstown in
'02: eff at 1m/11f on fast & gd/soft grnd: with P Monteith.
4170 **COSMIC CASE 16** [9]9-8-11 (3oh) (48) T P Queally 10/1: 3031258: In tch till halfway, wknd: btr   9 **24**
3588.
3588 **BRIDGE PAL 42** [6]4-8-12 (52) R Ffrench 66/1: 34200-69: Handy, wknd over 1m out: 6 wk abs: see   11 **11**
3588.
9 Ran   Time 3m 04.83(8.33)   Owned: Mr R Allan   Trained: Cornhill-On-Tweed

---

GOODWOOD   SATURDAY 11.09.04   Rigthand, Sharpish, Undulating Track

Official Going Good/Firm

4522   2.00 European Breeders Fund Gg Racing Club Maiden Stakes 2yo (D2)
£5629 £1732 £866   **1m rnd**   **Good/Firm 39**   **-27 Slow**   Inside

EMILE ZOLA 0 [12] M P Tregoning 2-9-0 N De Souza(5) 12/1: 1: b c Singspiel - Ellie Ardensky   **87+**
(Slip Anchor) Trkd ldrs, pushed along when hdwy 2f out, switched & styd on under minimal press to lead cl-home: Jan
foal, half-brother to a useful 1m 3yo scorer, dam a 10f 3yo List wnr: eff at 1m, will relish 10f: acts on fast grnd
& a sharp/undul trk, goes well fresh: potentially useful, expect significant prog.
4194 **EVA SONEVA SO FAST 15** [14] J L Dunlop 2-9-0 J Quinn 7/2: 052: ch c In The Wings - Azyaa (Kris)   shd **84**
Dwelt, sn handy, rdn & narrow lead ins last, hdd line: nicely bckd: May foal: half brother to a 12f wnr: dam a 7f
wnr: eff at 1m, mid-dists shld suit in time: handles fast & gd, any trk: win a race soon.
ROYAL JET 0 [7] M R Channon 2-9-0 A Culhane 7/1: 3: b c Royal Applause - Red Bouquet (Reference   nk **83+**
Point) Dwelt, pushed along rear early, switched & shaken up from over 1f out, strong run cl-home, nrst line:
58,000gns May foal, superb mid-dist pedigree, dam a 12/13f 4yo scorer: eff at 1m, crying out for 10f+: acts on fast:
eyecatching, expect significant improvement for this & over further.
3925 **TAMATAVE 29** [9] Saeed bin Suroor 2-9-0 t W Supple 5/2 FAV: 64: b c Darshaan - Manuetti (Sadler's   hd **82**
Wells) Keen & trkd ldr, led 3f out, rdn & hdd ins last, no extra nr line: btn less than 1L, hvly bckd: left debut
bhd: Apr foal: half brother to a 12f/hdle wnr: dam styd 11f: eff at 1m, will get further: handles fast grnd.
LOCH QUEST 0 [4]2-9-0 J Fanning 16/1: 5: Al handy & ch 2f out, no extra well ins last but not btn far.   ¾ **81**
3927+**TAMO 29** [2]2-9-0 F P Ferris(3) 20/1: 06: Handy & ch 2f out, btn dist.   3 **75**
HONOUR HIGH 0 [5]2-9-0 I Mongan 12/1: 7: In tch, lost place & no impress fnl 3f.   6 **65**
2970 **IN DREAMS 68** [1]2-9-0 E Ahern 9/1: 008: Led till 3f out, sn rdn, abs.   1 **63**
RAISE A TUNE 0 [10]2-9-0 V Slattery 25/1: 9: Rear, drvn & nvr a factor.   nk **62**
GROUNDCOVER 0 [6]2-9-0 S Drowne 8/1: 0: 10th: Sn outpcd rear & no ch fnl 3f.   shd **62**
SOLE AGENT 0 [3]2-9-0 R Brisland 20/1: 0: 11th: Dwelt, rear, no ch fnl 3f.   2½ **57**
4163 **PRALIN STAR 17** [13]2-9-0 G Baker 50/1: 040: 12th: Held up, eff 3f out, wknd qckly 2f out.   4 **50**
12 Ran   Time 1m 42.69 (5.29)   Owned: Sheikh Mohammed   Trained: Lambourn

---

4523   2.35 Chichester Observer Handicap Stakes 3yo+ 86-100 (C1)   **[106]**
£12554 £4762 £2381   **7f rnd**   **Good/Firm 39**   **+14 Fast**   Inside

3441 **ETTRICK WATER 49** [12] L M Cumani 5-9-2 vis (94) N Mackay(3) 9/1: 13-51101: Trkd ldrs, led over 1f   **103+**
out, rdn out, decisively: 7 wk abs: fast time: suited to 7f/1m on firm & soft grnd: goes well fresh: likes to
dominate but imprvd again today with more restrained tactics: v tough & progressive, keep on side: see 2532.
3555 **BOSTON LODGE 44** [8] G A Butler 4-9-4 vis (96) E Ahern 12/1: 2400032: Mid-div, switched & styd on   1¾ **100**
well ins last, al held by wnr: confirmed improvement of latest: can win again: see 3555, 2206 & 790.
3555* **GOLDEN SAHARA 44** [11] Saeed bin Suroor 3-9-2 t (98) W Supple 8/1: 122-0313: Trkd ldrs, styd on   nk **101**
for press, not pace of wnr ins last: abs: useful, just abd of today's rnr-up in 3555 (C/D).
4103 **PANGO 21** [3] H Morrison 5-8-8 (86) S Drowne 8/1: 2211124: Mid-div, styd on for press, no threat   1¼ **86**
to wnr: tough & progressive: see 4103, 3512 (1m).
4047 **JEDBURGH 23** [1]3-9-3 (99) I Mongan 5/1 FAV: 0332025: Trkd ldrs & led over 2f out till over 1f out.   1 **97**
4231 **KOOL 14** [7]5-8-11 (89) N De Souza(5) 12/1: 3540236: Horse still wearing hood when stalls opened,   hd **86**
held up, late prog, not able to land blow: see 4231, 3954.
4073 **NASHAAB 22** [5]7-8-12 (90) F P Ferris(3) 33/1: 0023157: Pushed along rear, mod prog for press.   ½ **86**
3954 **MASTER ROBBIE 28** [9]5-8-8 (86) T O'Brien(7) 20/1: 0000008: Mid-div wide, not able to land a blow.   hd **81**
4472 **ROYAL STORM 2** [10]5-9-7 (99) J Crowley 4/1: 4600029: Chsd ldr, wknd from dist: btr 3782.   shd **94**
2777 **VINDICATION 76** [2]4-8-10 t (88) R Miles(3) 25/1: 10-06600: 10th: Rear, hung right & only mod prog.   ½ **82**
3777 **SIR GEORGE TURNER 35** [15]5-9-0 (92) J Fanning 33/1: 0000000: 11th: Chsd ldrs, short of room over   shd **86**
1f out & sn no impress: big drop in trip: see 3506, 2101.
4231 **DIGITAL 14** [14]7-8-12 (90) A Culhane 7/1: 2000220: 12th: Dwelt, keen in mid-div, btn 2f out: btr 4231.   nk **83**
3277 **BARBAJUAN 56** [1]3-8-10 bl (92) S Whitworth 50/1: 5000000: 13th: Rear, little prog, 8 wk abs.   1 **83**

GOODWOOD   SATURDAY 11.09.04   Rigthand, Sharpish, Undulating Track

3565 **UHOOMAGOO** 43 [4]6-9-2 bl (94) A Mullen(7) 11/1: 1100300: 14th: Sn pshd along rear: 'nvr trav'.   2½   80
4231 **GRIZEDALE** 14 [6]5-8-12 t (90) J Quinn 20/1: 020-5000: 15th: Rear, no ch fnl 2f: see 3061.   2½   71
3522* **PIZAZZ** 45 [16]3-8-10 bl (92) J F McDonald(3) 7/1: 5220310: 16th: Led & rcd too freely, hdd over 2f   2½   68
out & wknd qckly: 6 wk abs: dominated a much weaker field in first time blnks latest: see 3522.
16 Ran   Time 1m 26.25 (1.75)   Owned: Mrs E H Vestey   Trained: Newmarket

4524 3.05 Listed Stardom Stakes 2yo (A1)
£14500 £5500 £2750   1m rnd   Good/Firm 39   -09 Slow   Inside

3060 **HEARTHSTEAD WINGS** 65 [4] M Johnston 2-8-11 (99) J Fanning 100/30: 1461: Made all, strongly   105
pressed from 2f out, rdn & styd on strongly to assert ins last: nicely bckd, op 4/1: 2 mth abs: eff at 6/7f,
imprvd at 1m today: acts on fm & fast: v useful colt: see 2578.
4066 **DESTINATE** 22 [3] R Hannon 2-8-11 (100) E Ahern 9/2: 0104422: Trkd front pair, rdn & outpcd 2f   1¼   101
out, kept on to take 2nd cl-home, not able to reach wnr: tough & useful: see 4066.
4003 **CAPABLE GUEST** 25 [1] M R Channon 2-8-11 (100) A Culhane 2/1 FAV: 3332143: Cl-up, rdn & chall   shd   101
over 2f out, no extra ins last & lost 2nd line: well bckd: styd longer 1m trip: see 4003 & 3811 (7f).
4329 **NICE TUNE** 9 [2] C E Brittain 2-8-6 J Quinn 10/1: 34: Held up, rdn & kept on late, nvr able to   nk   95
chall: acts on fast & gd grnd: likely rcd & useful on this evidence, must win a mdn: see 4329.
3627 **ALTA PETENS** 41 [6]2-8-6 (77) S Drowne 20/1: 410045: Trkd ldrs, ch over 1f out, sn no extra: 1¼   92$
abs, prob styd longer trip: poss flattered: see 1728.
3357 **PARK LAW** 51 [5]2-8-6 (89) R Havlin 100/30: 2156: Rear, eff over 2f out, no prog: abs: longer trip.   3½   85
6 Ran   Time 1m 41.26 (3.86)   Owned: Hearthstead Homes Ltd   Trained: Middleham

4525 3.40 Mirror Image Stakes Handicap 3yo+ 86-100 (C1)   [110]
£13878 £4270 £2135   1m1f rnd   Good/Firm 39   -26 Slow   Inside

4239 **GOLD HISTORY** 14 [9] M Johnston 3-8-10 (92) J Fanning 10/1: 3500651: Trkd ldrs trav well, led   97
over 1f out, drvn out to hold on: both wins at 9f this term, stays 10f & has tried 12f: acts on fast & gd: useful.
3265 **KINGS COUNTY** 56 [2] L M Cumani 6-9-3 (93) N Mackay(3) 10/1: 2-303002: Mid-div, styd on well for   hd   97
press ins last, just held: 8 wk abs: eff at 7f/9f: useful: see 2860.
3506 **CHINKARA** 46 [7] B J Meehan 4-8-13 (89) J F McDonald(3) 7/1: 0-000403: Keen in mid-div, no room   nk   92+
over 2f out till over 1f out, kept on late for press: lkd unlucky, shld find similar: abs: see 2860.
4185* **EXTERIOR** 15 [10] Mrs A J Perrett 3-8-9 (91) S Drowne 7/4 FAV: 3-114: Trkd ldrs, onepace for   1   92
press over 1f out: bckd: acts on fast, soft & polytrack: lightly rcd, see 4185 (soft).
4122+ **KRUGERRAND** 19 [5]5-8-13 (89) E Ahern 8/1: 1360515: Trkd ldrs & ch over 1f out, no extra ins last.   1   88
3506 **ALRAFID** 46 [6]5-8-9 (85) I Mongan 12/1: 0562006: Held up, mod prog for press, no threat, abs: btr 2207. hd   83
4061 **CONSONANT** 23 [1]7-8-13 (89) S Righton 25/1: 6023007: Rear, only mod prog for press: btr 2903.   ½   86
5016* **VAUGHAN 310** [11]3-8-10 (92) A Culhane 14/1: 01-8: b c Machiavellian - Labibeh (Lyphard) Dwelt &   8   76
held up, no ch over 2f out: reapp/h'cap bow, stablemate of 4th: lightly rcd in '03, landed a mdn: winning form at
1m, dam a smart 12f wnr: acts on soft grnd & a gall trk. 1 Nov'03 Nott 8.2sft 97- D:
4220 **TUNING FORK** 14 [4]4-8-12 (88) J Quinn 14/1: 0003009: Led till over 1f out, wknd qckly, eased: 1½   69
reportedly hung right: btr 3565.
3555 **MAGHNIAM** 8 [8]4-9-7 (97) W Supple 8/1: 0-532000: 10th: Held up, eff over 2f out, no impress: abs.   nk   77
3797 **LANGFORD** 35 [3]4-8-10 (86) F P Ferris(3) 8/1: 2100140: 11th: Pulled hard & trkd ldr, wknd qckly   1½   63
over 1f out: not settle in the early stages, much btr 3205.
11 Ran   Time 1m 56.35 (5.85)   Owned: Mr Abdulla BuHaleeba   Trained: Middleham

4526 4.15 Listed Starlit Stakes 3yo+ (A1)
£17400 £6600 £3300   6f str   Good/Firm 39   +02 Fast   Stands Side

VAR 253 [2] C E Brittain 5-9-0 BL J Quinn 16/1: 14016-11: b c Forest Wildcat - Loma Preata   116
(Zilzal) Went right start, sn led & dictated pace, drvn & al holding rivals ins last: Brit bow, long abs: ex-US,
clmr wnr in '04, won 4 times in '03: suited by 5/6f on firm & gd, sharp/undul or turning trks: likes to force the
pace: suited by blnks & goes well fresh: smart & genuine, win again.
3495 **RUBY ROCKET** 49 [7] H Morrison 3-8-7 (105) S Drowne 14/1: 4-523232: Chsd wnr halfway, drvn &   1½   105
kept on, al held: hvly bckd, 7 wk abs: useful & consistet: see 3495, 3075 & 2769.
3957 **SO WILL I** 28 [1] M P Tregoning 3-9-2 (106) W Supple 7/2: 3104053: Mid-div, rdn & outpcd over 2f   ½   112
out, kept on ins last: bckd, op 5/1: improved run: see 1732 (List).
2468 **LYDGATE** 88 [6] Saeed bin Suroor 4-9-7 t (106) E Ahern 4/1: 2442104: Held up, eff from over 1f   1½   110
out, no extra dist: nicely bckd, 12 wk abs: see 2468.
3409 **COLONEL COTTON** 50 [3]5-9-0 (98) A Culhane 14/1: 5503065: Hmpd start, rear, little hdwy, abs.   1½   98
4226 **ATAVUS** 14 [5]7-9-0 (92) A McCarthy 9/1: 6050026: Chsd wnr, outpcd fnl 2f: op 11/1: btr 4226.   3   92
4226 **COCONUT PENANG** 14 [4]4-9-0 (93) S Whitworth 12/1: 002005P: Held up in tch, no impress when broke   0
down badly distance, sadly destroyed.
7 Ran   Time 1m 12.20 (2.2)   Owned: Mr Mohammed Rashid   Trained: Newmarket

4527 4.50 Racing Uk Live On 432 Stakes Handicap 3yo+ 71-85 (D2)   [88]
£6939 £2135 £1068   2m   Good/Firm 39   -07 Slow   Inside

3032 **LAND N STARS** 66 [3] Jamie Poulton 4-9-5 (79) R Miles(3) 15/2: 22-01541: Trkd ldrs, went on 2f   88
out, rdn to hold on ins last: 2 mth abs: suited by 2m, prob stays a stiff 2m4f: likes firm & fast: progressive.
3125 **ESCAYOLA** 63 [12] W J Haggas 4-9-11 vis (85) W Supple 7/1: 11-02002: Keen & held up, drvn & styd   hd   93
on well from over 1f out, just failed: 2 mth abs: encouraging, apprec a stronger pace.
3634} **CORTON** 393 [6] P F I Cole 5-9-6 (80) E Ahern 33/1: 020250-3: gr g Definite Article - Limpopo   1¼   84
(Green Desert) Trkd ldrs trav well, briefly led over 2f out, styd on onepace for press ins last: clr of rem on
reapp: dual h'cap rnr-up in '03: lightly rcd & unplcd in '02 (rtd 55, h'cap): eff around 12f, now stays 2m: acts
on fast & gd/soft grnd, any trk, likes a sharp/undul one: can force the pace: gd return.
2 Jul'03 Asco 12g/f 82-79 C: 2 May'03 Brig 11.9g/f 79-76 D: 1 Aug'01 Folk 7g/f 83- E:
4361 **RIYADH** 8 [11] M Johnston 6-8-11 (5oh) (66) J Fanning 11/1: 0202604: Dwelt & held up, smooth hdwy   5   72

1366

GOODWOOD SATURDAY 11.09.04 Rigthand, Sharpish, Undulating Track

to press ldrs over 2f out, sn short of room, onepace from dist: shade closer with a clr run: see 3701.

3997 **ENHANCER 26** [14]6-8-13 (73) J F McDonald(3) 33/1: 0035: Held up, eff to chase ldrs 4f out, no   *1*   **73**
impress fnl 2f: h'cap bow & longer trip: btr 3997 (11.5f).

4209 **POPES HILL 15** [5]3-7-12 (13oh)BL (71) N Mackay(3) 9/1: 4463446: Held up, eff wide form 4f out, no   *nk*   **70**
prog fnl 2f: blnks: btr 3861, 3334.

4196 **THEATRE 15** [1]5-9-3 (77) A McCarthy 16/1: S223007: Chsd ldrs, lost place from 3f out, kept on late.   *½*   **75**

3653 **AURELIA 40** [13]3-8-4 (7oh) (77) J Quinn 6/1: 6314-38: Dwelt & rear, hdwy 3f out, wknd bef dist, abs.   *1*   **74**

4267* **STOOP TO CONQUER 13** [7]4-9-3 (77) I Mongan 7/1: 6-001419: Led after 6f till 6f out, wknd.   *3½*   **71**

4106 **ALMIZAN 21** [9]4-9-8 vis (82) A Culhane 9/2 FAV: 0040430: 10th: Chsd ldrs, btn 3f out: much btr 4106.   *3*   **73**

3742* **MAGICAL QUEST 36** [8]4-9-11 (85) S Drowne 8/1: 010: 11th: Led for 6f, btn 3f out: btr 3742 (14f, mdn).   *1*   **75**

4267 **ESTABLISHMENT 13** [4]7-8-11 (8oh) (63) S Whitworth 33/1: 0000040: 12th: Held up, slipped badly on   *2*   **59**
bend after 4f, al rear: see 1484.

4276* **MOONSHINE BEACH 12** [10]6-8-11 (71) A Quinn(5) 8/1: 1103110: 13th: Led 6f out till over 2f out, sn   *2*   **57**
outpcd: btr expected after 4276 (weaker h'cap).

13 Ran   Time 3m 31.59 (7.29)   Owned: Mr Kenneth Wilkinson   Trained: Lewes

---

4528	**5.25 Plantation Stakes Handicap 3yo 56-70 (E3)**				**[77]**
	£3496 £1076 £538	**5f str**	**Good/Firm 39**	**-20 Slow** Stands Side	

4335 **WHOS WINNING 9** [1] B G Powell 3-9-6 (69) J Fanning 4/1 FAV: 0602121: Made all stands side trav   **79**
well, drvn out ins last: well bckd, op 6/1: eff at 5/6f on firm & gd grnd, likes a sharp/undul trk: progressive.

4237 **SIR LOIN 14** [16] N Tinkler 3-8-11 VIS (60) A Culhane 9/1: 0526022: Rcd virtually alone towards   *1*   **66**
centre, al prom & drvn to chall ins last, no extra cl-home: acts on fast & gd/soft grnd: gd run in a vis racing away
from main group: shown enough to find a race: see 4237, 2227.

3976 **KING EGBERT 26** [3] A W Carroll 3-8-7 (56) W Supple 25/1: 3000-403: Pushed along towards rear,   *hd*   **61**
short of room 2f out, styd on late for press, nrst fin: encouraging: see 3804.

3952 **URBAN ROSE 28** [13] R M H Cowell 3-8-11 t P (60) M Henry 25/1: 0030404: Held up, hdwy halfway, not   *¾*   **63**
pace of front pair, gd run in cheek pieces on return to 5f: eff in a t-strap: eff at 5/6f: see 2118.

4236 **TIZZYS LAW 14** [7]3-9-2 (65) J Quinn 11/1: 4500155: Went right start, bmpd, chsd ldrs, no impress.   *¾*   **66**

3889 **DOLCE PICCATA 30** [6]3-9-7 bl (70) J F McDonald(3) 14/1: 5000006: Cl-up, fdd fnl 1f.   *¾*   **69**

3984 **MALUTI 51** [8]3-8-7 (1oh) (55) N Mackay(3) 11/1: 0631027: Hmpd start & bhd, only mod prog: abs.   *½*   **53**

4236* **LA VIE EST BELLE 14** [10]3-9-1 (64) G Baker 13/2: 0400618: Prom, outpcd over 1f out: btr 4236 (soft).   *½*   **59**

4048 **MELODY KING 23** [15]3-8-12 vis (61) F P Ferris(3) 14/1: 365U069: Dwelt, chsd ldrs till outpcd from halfway. *nk*   **55**

3789 **CUT AND DRIED 35** [9]3-9-0 (63) S Whitworth 25/1: 4645000: 10th: Bmpd start, rear, little prog for press. *nk*   **56**

4278 **BAYLAW STAR 12** [2]3-9-1 BL (64) A Mullen(7) 14/1: 0400600: 11th: Prom 2f, btn over 1f out, blnks.   *2½*   **49**

3717 **MUST BE SO 37** [11]3-8-7 (26oh)T (30) C Haddon(7) 50/1: 6040050: 12th: Sn rdn & outpcd, nvr a factor. *nk*   **40**

3889 **SHORT CHORUS 30** [4]3-8-9 p (58) I Mongan 10/1: 0124240: 13th: Mid-div, struggling from halfway. *nk*   **40**

4236 **IMPERIUM 14** [12]3-9-4 (67) S Drowne 14/1: 0060230: 14th: Chsd ldrs, btn over 1f out: btr 4236 & 3984.   *½*   **48**

4144 **DAVE 18** [5]3-8-13 (62) N De Souza(5) 6/1: 050-1000: 15th: Cl-up till halfway, fdd under press: btr 3380. *hd*   **42**

2387 **SIMPSONS MOUNT 91** [14]3-9-3 (66) E Ahern 14/1: 3050150: 16th: Dwelt, chsd ldrs 3f, sn btn: abs.   *1¼*   **42**

16 Ran   Time 59.64(2.94)   Owned: Tony Head and Caroline Andrus   Trained: Winchester

---

DONCASTER SATURDAY 11.09.04 Lefthand, Flat, Galloping Track

Official Going Firm (Good/Firm Places)

4529	**1.35 Gner Conditions Stakes 2yo (C2)**				
	£6343 £2345 £1173	**6f str**	**Firm 11**	**-18 Slow** Stands Side	

4390 **GALEOTA 7** [1] R Hannon 2-9-1 (100) R L Moore 4/1: 41551: Led, qcknd from halfway, rdn & in   **112**
command ins last: op 5/1: eff at 6f on firm & gd/soft grnd, sharp or gall trks: likes to force the pace & best
without cheek pieces: smart colt: see 4022 & 3163.

4026 **RAJWA 24** [4] Saeed bin Suroor 2-8-11 t K McEvoy 6/4 FAV: 222: Cl-up, rdn & chall over 1f out,   *2*   **102**
hung right & no extra ins last: well bckd, padd pick: useful, but once again found less than lkd likely: see 4026.

3877 **OBE GOLD 31** [5] M R Channon 2-9-1 (89) R Fallon 8/1: 1424U33: Chsd ldrs, pushed along halfway,   *2½*   **98**
onepace: see 2823, 2251 & 1716.

4280 **REQQA 12** [2] M Johnston 2-9-1 R Hills 7/4: 6144: Trkd ldrs, wknd over 1f out: bckd: something amiss?   *13*   **63**

4 Ran   Time 1m 12.52 (1.72)   Owned: Mr J A Lazzari   Trained: Marlborough

---

4530	**2.05 Ladbrokes Com Stakes Handicap 3yo+ 96-110 (B1)**				**[112]**
	£17400 £6600 £3300	**1m2f60y**	**Firm 11**	**-17 Slow** Inside	

3775 **COLISAY 35** [4] E F Vaughan 5-9-1 (99) K Fallon 4/1: 210-3641: Trkd ldrs, led dist, rdn out: eff   **105**
around 1m/10f on firm & gd/soft: v useful gelding, reportedly a Cambridgeshire possible: see 1962.

3749 **COURAGEOUS DUKE 36** [2] J Noseda 5-8-9 (93) S Sanders 9/2: 0-350232: Trkd ldrs, rdn & ch dist,   *nk*   **98**
not pace of wnr ins last: well bckd: running well, likes Newmarket: see 3749 & 3439.

1584 **ROEHAMPTON 128** [1] Sir Michael Stoute 3-8-6 (1oh)VIS (97) Martin Dwyer 16/1: 01-653: Trkd ldr &   *1¼*   **98**
rcd keenly early, led over 2f out, hdd dist, onepace: padd pick, abs: 1st time visor, t-strap omitted: eff around
1m/10f on firm & soft grnd: imprvd eff, can find a race: see 1584 & 1189.

3794 **BONECRUSHER 35** [7] D R Loder 5-9-7 vis (99) R L Moore 4/1: 2055364: Dwelt, sn in tch, eff from   *¾*   **106**
over 1f out, onepace for press: nicely bckd: just btr 3506.

3439 **WEECANDOO 49** [6]6-8-7 (7oh) (84) G Carter 33/1: 3154-005: Chsd ldrs, onepace fnl 2f: 7 wk abs.   *¾*   **91**

4290 **FAMOUS GROUSE 12** [5]4-9-0 (98) D Holland 12/1: 2020-046: Led till over 2f out, sn btn: see 4290.   *1¼*   **96**

4208 **BLUE SKY THINKING 15** [8]5-8-8 (92) S W Kelly 7/1: 6034627: Chsd ldrs, hung left & btn over 1f out.   *2½*   **86**

3749* **POLYGONAL 36** [3]4-8-10 (94) J Fortune 3/1 FAV: 1360518: Held up, carr head high when eff over 2f   *1*   **87**
out, sn btn, fin lame: see 3749.

8 Ran   Time 2m 09.33 (2.93)   Owned: Mr M Hawkes   Trained: Newmarket

---

4531	2.40 Porcelanosa Stakes Handicap 3yo+ 96-110 (B1)				[115]

£17400 £6600 £3300 1m str Firm 11 -05 Slow Stands Side

4397* **CALCUTTA** 6 [12] B W Hills 8-8-11 (3ex) (98) R Hills 8/1: 0203011: Hdwy over 1f out & styd on for **105**
press to lead well ins last: qck reapp: won this race for the 3rd time: eff at 7f, best at 1m/9f on firm, fast &
handles gd/soft: loves Doncaster: best held up off a sound pace: v useful & in form 8yo.

3186} **FUNFAIR** 413 [8] Mrs A J Perrett 5-9-2 (103) R L Moore 14/1: 10/1020-2: b g Singspiel - Red nk **109**
Carnival (Mr Prospector) Trkd ldrs, rdn & led over 1f out, just hdd cl-home: just sharper for this on reapp:
lightly rcd '03, List h'cap scorer for Sir M Stoute, subs val h'cap rnr-up: mdn & val h'cap wnr in '02: suited by
1m/10f on firm & gd/soft, stiff or sharp trk, likes York: fine reapp for new yard & can win soon.
2 Jul'03 Sand 8.1g/f 105-100 B: 1 May'03 York 7.9fm 103-94 A: 1 Aug'02 York 8g/f 94-88 B: 1 Jun'02 Carl 9.2g/s 89- D:

4630} **DESERT STAR** 693 [5] Sir Michael Stoute 4-8-11 (98) K Fallon 8/1: 310/-3: Trkd ldrs, short of shd **104**
room over 2f out, rdn & chall ins last, just held: fine eff after v long abs: missed '03: lightly rcd '02, mdn
scorer: eff at 7f/1m on firm grnd, stiff/gall trks: excellent comeback, will sn be winning races.

3794 **FLIGHTY FELLOW** 35 [14] T D Easterby 4-8-7 (2oh)bl (92) G Carter 20/1: 1062404: Rear, rdn & hdwy shd **99**
to chall well ins last, just held cl-home: back to best, apprec rtn to 1m: acts on firm & soft grnd: see 3077, 1833.

4063 **MINE** 23 [2]6-9-7 vis (108) T Quinn 13/2: 3115205: Held up, hdwy over 1f out & chall ins last, nk **112**
hung right & no extra well ins last: most tough & still improving (top-weight here): see 2489.

4021 **BLUE SPINNAKER** 24 [15]5-9-1 (102) S W Kelly 6/1 FAV: 0141046: Rear & briefly outpcd over 2f out, 1 **104**
styd on for press, not able to chall: wants a return to 10f: see 2101 (10f).

3118 **LUNDYS LANE** 63 [7]4-8-7 (94) S Sanders 25/1: 00-40007: Dwelt, kept on, not land blow, abs. nk **95**

3689 **WELCOME STRANGER** 38 [3]4-8-7 (2oh) (92) D Holland 15/2: 0212128: Mid-div, chall dist, no extra. ¾ **94**

3886 **PENTECOST** 30 [6]5-9-5 (106) L Keniry(3) 8/1: 0140109: Rear, eff over 1f out, not pace to chall: see 3775. nk **105**

2234 **BAYEUX** 98 [9]3-8-8 t (100) K McEvoy 8/1: 102-5300: 10th: Cl-up & led 2f out, sn hdd & no extra: shd **99**
well bckd, 3 month abs: only btn around 3L in a v tight fin: see 1482.

4279 **WILL HE WISH** 12 [13]8-8-7 (5oh)bl (89) R Thomas(3) 14/1: 0013620: 11th: Cl-up & led over 3f till 2f out. 4 **85**

3027 **ISIDORE BONHEUR** 66 [11]3-8-6 (1oh) (98) Dane O'Neill 50/1: 14-44440: 12th: Chsd ldrs, no dngr. ½ **88**

4061 **ALWAYS ESTEEMED** 23 [4]4-8-11 (98) Martin Dwyer 16/1: 0041400: 13th: Chsd ldrs, pushed along 2½ **83**
halfway & sn lost pl: see 3199.

3460 **ROSKILDE** 48 [1]4-8-11 (98) J Fortune 33/1: 03002-00: 14th: Cl-up, wknd qckly over 1f out, 7 wk abs. 3 **77**

2406 **AQUALUNG** 91 [10]3-8-2 (7oh) (92) F Norton 33/1: 4-0100: 15th: Led till 3f out, wknd qckly: abs. 6 **63**
15 Ran Time 1m 37.74 (1.24) Owned: The Hon Mrs J M Corbett & Mr C Wright Trained: Lambourn

---

4532	3.15 Gr1 Betfair Com St Leger Stakes Colts 3yo (A1)			

£240000 £92000 £46000 1m6f132y Firm 11 -11 Slow Inside

4001* **RULE OF LAW** 25 [9] Saeed bin Suroor 3-9-0 t (120) K McEvoy 3/1 JT FAV: 13-22411: Dictated pace, **122**
qcknd from over 2f out, held on most gamely for press ins last under a superbly judged ride: eff at 10/12f, styd
longer 14.7f trip well, shld get 2m: acts on firm & gd/soft, loves to force the pace: top-class & most willing colt,
more Gr 1 success likely: see 4001, 2822 & 2254.

4024* **QUIFF** 24 [4] Sir Michael Stoute 3-8-11 (119) K Fallon 3/1 JT FAV: 5-1312: Trkd ldrs, short of hd **118**
room & switched for eff over 2f out, drvn & chall ins last, just held cl-home: styd longer 14.7f trip well, will get
2m: acts on firm & fast, poss gd/soft ideal: high-class, win a Gr 1: see 4024 (g/s).

4002 **TYCOON** 24 [6] A P O'Brien 3-9-0 T D Holland 6/1: 215-3603: Held up, trav well & jock 1½ **119+**
motionless till over 1f out, styd on well, too much to do: clearly stays 14.7f trip & acts on fm & gd/soft: enjoyed
t-strap: eye-catching, must surely go v close next time with a positive ride, keep on side.

3507* **MARAAHEL** 46 [5] Sir Michael Stoute 3-9-0 (112) R Hills 4/1: 414-2214: Trkd ldrs, eff to chall 2f 1 **118**
out, no extra from dist: 6 wk abs: styd longer 14.7f trip tho' joc reported a rtn to 12f may suit: acts on fm & soft.

4023 **MIKADO** 24 [7]3-9-0 J Fortune 25/1: 211-4435: Trkd wnr, drvn & styd on onepace: relish Gr 3/2. hd **117**

4726} **DARSALAM** 13 [10]3-9-0 S Chin 33/1: 2111116: Chsd ldrs, pushed along & outpcd over 3f out, kept 1½ **115**
on, nvr land a blow: Czech raider, multiple wnr in native land this term: unplcd mdn for M Johnston in '03 (rtd
25): suited by 10/14f on firm & gd grnd: only btn around 5L, smart effort.

4001 **GO FOR GOLD** 25 [1]3-9-0 S Sanders 12/1: 1-3237: Chsd ldrs, no impress fnl 3f: see 4001 & 3507. 3 **111**

4001 **LET THE LION ROAR** 25 [2]3-9-0 vis (118) T Quinn 9/2: 2-133528: Sweating & edgy in padd, not 6 **102**
settle rear early, eff from 3f out, sn hung right & btn: may have lost any ch in the preliminaries & early stages of
the race: longer trip & bhd this wnr sev time sthis year.

3274* **FRANK SONATA** 56 [8]3-9-0 (105) R L Moore 16/1: 0-613119: Rear, pushed along from halfway, nvr a nk **101**
factor: 8 wk abs, prob prefer more give & an ease in grade.
9 Ran Time 3m 06.29 (3.29) Owned: Godolphin Trained: Newmarket

---

4533	3.45 Gr2 Polypipe Flying Childers Stakes 2yo (A1)			

£42000 £16100 £8050 5f str Firm 11 -32 Slow Stands Side

3028 **CHATEAU ISTANA** 66 [7] N P Littmoden 2-8-12 T (98) S Sanders 11/1: 61101: Broke well & sn trkd **108**
ldrs, led over 1f out, drvn & styd on strongly: 2 month abs: all wins at 5f, tried 6f, shld suit: acts on firm &
fast grnd, stiff/gall trks: goes well fresh & imprvd for first time t-strap today: smart colt: see 2472 (List).

4427 **TOURNEDOS** 8 [3] M R Channon 2-9-1 (100) T Quinn 11/2: 2201032: Held up in tch, hdwy to press wnr 2 **105**
dist, sn outpcd but kept on: nicely bckd, op 8/1: acts on firm & gd grnd, eff at 5/6f: proving tough & durable,
rtn to List/Gr 3 company shld suit: see 4427 & 3509 (Gr 3).

4059 **KISSING LIGHTS** 23 [12] M L W Bell 2-8-9 (100) D Holland 20/1: 516303: Pushed along towards rear, ¾ **97**
prog when short of room over 3f out, not able to chall: looks worth another try at 6f: useful filly: see 3440.

3566 **AMAZIN** 43 [4] R Hannon 2-8-12 (97) R L Moore 16/1: 21254: Slow away & rear, rdn & kept on from 1 **97**
over 1f out, not land a blow: abs: eff at 5f, rtn to 6f shld suit: see 3081 & 2859.

4307 **BOND CITY** 11 [10]2-8-12 (95) D McGaffin 33/1: 0133525: Trkd ldrs, outpcd over 1f out: see 4307, 3266. 1¾ **92**

3956* **SUMORA** 28 [9]2-8-9 J Fortune 11/8 FAV: 116: Keen & led/dsptd lead till 3f out, no extra over 1f hd **88**
out: edgy & 2 handlers in the padd: hvly bckd tho' op 11/10: apprec more cover in the early stages as in 3956.

3943 **PITCH UP** 28 [11]2-8-12 BL (87) G Carter 33/1: 0361157: Chsd ldrs, outpcd over 1f out, blnks: see 3743. ½ **89**

2895 **BUNDITTEN** 71 [5]2-8-9 (96) F Norton 25/1: 13448: Chsd ldrs till over 1f out, abs: btr 2490, 2094. shd **86**

4390 **SAFARI SUNSET** 7 [6]2-8-12 (99) R Smith 33/1: 134309: Chsd ldrs, no impress over 1f out: btr 3509. nk **88**

3509 **SKYWARDS** 46 [2]2-8-12 T (100) K McEvoy 7/1: 51300: 10th: Cl-up, hung left & led 2f out, hdd over nk **87**

DONCASTER SATURDAY 11.09.04 Lefthand, Flat, Galloping Track

1f out & sn btn: abs, t-strap: much btr 2516 & 2089.
4025 **BECKERMET 24** [8]2-8-12 (100) K Fallon 11/2: 1211040: 11th: Cl-up, edged left & btn 1f out. *hd* **86**
11 Ran   Time 1m 0.36 (2.16)   Owned: Mr Ivan Allan   Trained: Newmarket

---

4534	4.20 Torne Valley Farm & Country Store Handicap Stakes 3yo+ 96-110 (B1)	[111]

£13796 £4245 £2122   **1m4f**   **Firm 11**   **+16 Fast**   Inside

3794 **MUTASALLIL 35** [9] Saeed bin Suroor 4-9-3 t (100) R Hills 9/2: 3-11201: Led & dictated pace, qcknd   **108**
from over 4f out, narrowly hdd dist but rallied gamely for press to lead again cl-home, all out: fast time: well
bckd: eff at 10f, imprvd for 12f today: acts on firm & gd grnd, loves to force the pace: v useful & progressive.
4023 **PAGAN DANCE 24** [8] Mrs A J Perrett 5-8-9 p (92) R L Moore 9/2: 4226002: In tch, smooth hdwy to   *shd* **98**
chall over 1f out & narrow lead dist, carr head high & hung left under press, just hdd cl-home: hvly bckd: useful
gelding who apprec rtn to 12f: plenty of ability but is ungenuine: clr of rem: see 2771.
3464* **WUNDERWOOD 48** [6] Lady Herries 5-9-7 (104) S Sanders 7/4 FAV: 4-001113: Trkd ldrs & chall over   5 **104**
2f out, btn over 1f out: hvly bckd: 7 wk abs: not disgraced: see 3464, 2582.
3999 **BAGAN 25** [1] H R A Cecil 5-8-7 (3oh) (87) K McEvoy 10/1: 15-44404: In tch, rdn & no impress fnl 2f.   2½ **86**
4239 **HELLO ITS ME 14** [5]3-7-12 (12oh) (87) R Thomas(2) 7/1: 2025435: Chsd ldrs, btn 2f out: btr 4239 (10f).   2 **83**
4056*]**TOTAL TURTLE 729** [3]5-9-6 (103) J Fortune 12/1: 312011/-6: b g Turtle Island - Chagrin d'Amour   2½ **92**
(Last Tycoon) Dwelt & rear, little prog: op 20/1, long abs: gelded: missed '03: prog '02, landing 3 h'caps: eff
at 10f, by 14.5f & 2m could suit: acts on firm, soft & fibresand: not knocked about after long break, could improve
over further. 1 Sep'02 Donc 14.6fm 101-91 B: 1 Aug'02 York 13.8g/f 97-86 B: 2 Jun'02 York 10.3g/s 93-83 B:
1 Jun'02 Good 9.8sft 85-77 D: 2 Apr'02 Sout 7gd 76-74 D: 1 Jul'01 Sout 6af 80a- F:
3999 **TURBO 25** [4]5-8-8 p (91) S Carson 12/1: 1-004007: Rear, eff wide, no impress fnl 3f: btr 1759.   3 **76**
4383 **ALBANOV 7** [2]4-8-10 (93) K Fallon 14/1: 22-00408: Chsd ldrs, lost pl qckly over 2f out, eased ins last.   1¾ **76**
8 Ran   Time 2m 29.15 (u0.65)   Owned: Godolphin   Trained: Newmarket

---

4535	4.55 Trilogy Nightclub Doncaster Nursery Handicap Stakes 2yo 0-85 (D2)	[91]

£7280 £2240 £1120   **7f str**   **Firm 11**   **-49 Slow**   Stands Side

4381 **MALINSA BLUE 7** [11] J A Glover 2-8-12 (75) F Norton 20/1: 622621: Held up trav well, smooth hdwy   **81**
over 1f out & qcknd to lead ins last, rdn out: first win on h'cap bow: eff at 6f, suited by 7f, 1m may suit: acts
on firm & gd grnd, stiff/gall or easy trks: imprvd today for more restrained tactics: see 4381, 2902 & 2236.
4004 **TURNAROUND 25** [4] Mrs J R Ramsden 2-9-1 (78) J Fortune 8/1: 32102: Rear, switched & smooth hdwy   ¾ **83**
2f out, rdn & kept on ins last, not able to reach wnr: set plenty to do but styd longer 7f trip well: shld win again.
4337 **CEREBUS 9** [10] N P Littmoden 2-8-10 (73) K Fallon 4/1: FAV: 64233: Chsd ldrs, ch over 1f out, no extra.   ¾ **77**
4306 **ZOMERLUST 11** [6] J J Quinn 2-9-3 (80) R Winston 5/1: 3124: Held up, styd on for press fnl 2f,   1½ **81**
not able to chall: styd longer 7f trip: acts on firm & gd/soft: see 4306 & 3939.
4064 **DOVE COTTAGE 23** [14]2-8-5 (68) R Thomas(3) 7/1: 653125: Cl-up & led over 3f out till dist, kept   ¾ **68**
on: handles firm & gd/soft: see 4064, 3729.
3311 **DRY ICE 54** [2]2-9-7 (84) Dane O'Neill 8/1: 5156: Trkd ldrs & led over 1f out till ins last, no extra: abs.   *hd* **83**
4207* **SECRET HISTORY 15** [15]2-8-12 (75) R Hills 10/1: 23517: Chsd ldrs, rdn & btn dist: btr 4207 (g/s).   5 **65**
3863* **CAPE QUEST 31** [9]2-9-6 (83) R L Moore 7/1: 0318: Cl-up, btn over 1f out: btr 3863.   1½ **70**
4079 **TREAT ME WILD 22** [12]2-8-10 (73) R Smith 25/1: 165149: Mid-div, drvn & btn 2f out: btr 3686 (6f).   2½ **65**
4306 **ALONG THE NILE 11** [1]2-8-7 (70) Martin Dwyer 20/1: 03600: 10th: V slow away & lkd reluctant to   *nk* **51**
race, mod late prog but lost all ch start: stablemate of rnr-up: much btr 3682.
2297 **Vision Victory 95** [8]2-7-12 (1oh)(60) D Fox(5) 66/1:0   3627 **Three Pennies 41** [5]2-8-9 (72) S W Kelly 50/1:0
2902 **Tiffin Deano 71** [7]2-7-13 (62) D Fentiman(7) 66/1:0
3633* **Love And Laughter 41** [13]2-8-12 (75) S Sanders 7/1:0
14 Ran   Time 1m 27.43(4.23)   Owned: Mrs Andrea M Mallinson   Trained: Worksop

---

GOODWOOD SUNDAY 12.09.04 Righthand, Sharpish, Undulating Track

Official Going Good/Firm

4536	2.00 Celer Et Audax Nursery Stakes Handicap 2yo 0-85 (D2)	[92]

£5655 £1740 £870   **6f str**   **Good/Firm 38**   **-33 Slow**   Stands side

4134* **CYCLICAL 20** [4] G A Butler 2-9-7 (85) L Dettori 3/1: 11: Held up, hdwy wide halfway, styd on to   **95 +**
lead 1f out, pushed out, val 3L+: eff at 5f, apprec step up to 6f: acts on fast or gd/soft grnd: eff on a
stiff/undul or sharp trk: v lightly rcd, open to improvement, win more races: see 4134.
4420 **CUMMISKEY 6** [7] J A Osborne 2-8-13 (77) S Drowne 7/4 FAV: 53422: In tch, styd on to lead well   1½ **81**
over 1f out, sn flashed tail & hdd 1f out, not pace wnr: op 9/4: qck reapp: continues in gd form: see 4420.
4187 **CREE 16** [9] W R Muir 2-7-12 (3oh) (59) Lisa Jones 10/1: 0052523: Cl-up, styd on to lead halfway,   1½ **62**
hdd over 1f out, no extra: eff at 5/6f on fast & soft grnd: just btr 4187 (5f).
4139 **PEEPTOE 19** [6] J L Dunlop 2-8-11 (70) T Quinn 11/2: 3254: Held up, prog wide halfway, no impress.   1¼ **71**
4420 **PIDDIES PRIDE 6** [3]2-8-9 (73) F P Ferris(3) 14/1: 1320405: Handy well over 4f, no extra: qck reapp.   2½ **62**
4187 **KEMPSEY 16** [8]2-8-1 p (65) J F McDonald(3) 16/1: 064446: Cl-up 4f, sn wknd & eased: btr 3284.   7 **34**
3632 **ELSIE WAGG 42** [1]2-8-7 (1ow) (70) K Fallon 10/1: 34567: Prom, wknd bef halfway: reported by vet   10 **15**
to have higher heart rate than normal: btr 2020.
3624 **TREMPJANE 43** [5]2-9-2 (80) R Hughes 33/1: 15508: Led till halfway, fdd: 6 wk abs: btr 2373.   5 **11**
8 Ran   Time 1m 14.30 (4.30)   Owned: Cheveley Park Stud   Trained: Blewbury

4537   2.35 Totepool Stakes Handicap 3yo+ 86-100 (C1)   [103]
£15300 £5804 £2902   6f str   Good/Firm 38   -05 Slow   Stands side

3959 **TEXAS GOLD** 4 [8] W R Muir 6-9-0 (89) S Drowne 7/2: 0660221: In tch, hdwy halfway, styd on to 101
lead dist, pushed out, val bit more: qck reapp: op 5/2: eff at 5f, stays sharp 6f: acts on firm, gd/soft &
polytrack, likes Lingfield & Goodwood: big ch under pen in Ayr Gold Cup if grnd is fast.

3937 **CD EUROPE** 29 [7] J J Quinn 6-8-10 p (85) R Winston 17/2: 0006002: Held up, prog when short of   1¾ 90
room bef 1f out, switched & kept on for 2nd ins fnl 1f, no ch with wnr: encouraging eff on first start for new yard,
on a winning mark & can be plcd to find similar: see 2581 (K A Ryan).

3959 **PERUVIAN CHIEF** 4 [13] N P Littmoden 7-9-3 (92) K Fallon 10/1: 000U003: In tch, prog bef 1f out,   shd 96
kept on ins fnl 1f, just held for 2nd: qck reapp: decent eff in defeat: see 1207.

3622 **TWO STEP KID** 43 [1] J Noseda 3-9-7 (98) E Ahern 5/2 FAV: 6413444: Chsd ldrs, eff when short of   hd 101
room dist & again ins fnl 1f, kept on cl-home, nrst fin: did not get run of race & plcd with clr run.

3941 **SPLIFF** 29 [11]3-8-12 (89) Dane O'Neill 20/1: 1-100005: Cl-up, styd on to lead 2f out, hdd dist,   shd 91
no extra cl-home: signs of encouragement today: see 1933 & btr 1498 (gd/soft).

4174 **IMPRESSIVE FLIGHT** 17 [4]5-8-8 (83) R L Moore 9/1: 536-0006: Bhd, outpcd after halfway, rallied late. ½ 84

4322 **MYSTIC MAN** 11 [6]6-8-12 (88) N Callan 5/1: 0130437: Bhd, eff when no room dist & again ins fnl   ½ 88
1f, sn onepcd: wants further: see 4322.

4382 **DEVISE** 8 [12]5-8-13 (88) R Miles(3) 9/1: 4023228: Held up, hdwy wide halfway, wknd dist: btr 4382. 2 82

3584 **CORPS DE BALLET** 44 [9]3-8-10 (87) T Quinn 33/1: 31-01009: Led 4f, wknd fnl 1f: 6 wk abs: btr 2155. hd 80
9 Ran   Time 1m 12.62 (2.62)   Owned: Mr C L A Edginton   Trained: Lambourn

4538   3.05 Gr3 Select Racing Uk On Sky 432 Stakes 3yo+ (A1)
£29000 £11000 £5500   1m1f192y   Good/Firm 38   +15 Fast   Inside

3563 **ALKAADHEM** 44 [8] M P Tregoning 4-9-0 BL (107) W Supple 11/2: 5410431: In tch, al trav well, styd 114
on to lead bef 1f out, pushed clr, val 4L+: op 8/1, fast time: eff at 1m, suited by 10f, prob stays 12f: acts on fm &
gd: goes well fresh & likes Goodwood: enjoyed first time blnks, win more Gr races with repeat.

4290 **BATTLE CHANT** 13 [6] Mrs A J Perrett 4-9-0 (102) R L Moore 7/2: 030-3022: Held up, prog 4f out,   2½ 108
sltly short of room dist, swtchd & kept on ins fnl 1f, no ch with easy wnr: another gd eff, wants List.

4323 **SALSELON** 11 [4] L M Cumani 5-9-0 bl (118) K Fallon 7/2: 0230523: Mid-div, prog to chase wnr bef   shd 107
1f out, no extra just lost 2nd cl-home: op 5/2: clr rem: stays 10f: blnks refitted & visor left off: lacking
resolution in finish: btr 4323 (9f) & 2470 (Gr 1, 1m).

3793 **MUQBIL** 36 [7] J L Dunlop 4-9-0 (114) R Hills 11/8 FAV: 34-01124: Al cl-up, ev ch 3f out, wknd   5 100
bef 1f out: well bckd: fin 2nd in this race 12 months ago: has been in gd form & this was disapp: btr 3793.

4014 **VESPONE** 29 [3]4-9-0 t (112) L Dettori 7/2: 2220205: Led, hdd bef 1f out, wknd: twice below 3264. 1¼ 98

4220 **PAWN BROKER** 15 [1]7-9-0 (109) Dane O'Neill 16/1: 025-0146: Held up, nvr a factor: btr 3613 (1m). ¾ 96

4097 **SIR HAYDN** 22 [2]4-9-0 (62) E Ahern 50/1: 6053007: Cl-up, wknd over 3f out: stiff task: btr 3295. 12 50
7 Ran   Time 2m 6.54 (2.34)   Owned: Mr Hamdan Al Maktoum   Trained: Lambourn

4539   3.40 Fegentri World Cup Of Nations Stakes Handicap Amateur Riders Trophy 3yo+ 56-70 (E3)   [45]
£6789 £2089 £1045   1m1f   Good/Firm 38   -66 Slow   Inside

3996 **FANTASY CRUSADER** 27 [2] J A Gilbert 5-10-7 (3oh)p (52) Mr C Fais 5/1 FAV: 2003131: Cl-up, styd on 62
to lead 2f out, rdn out to lead fnl 1f to hold on: eff at 7f, suited by 9/10f: acts on firm, fast grnd &
polytrack: likes a sharp/undul trk: eff with cheek pieces: rider won race for 3rd year in a row: see 3996.

3733 **CORMORANT WHARF** 38 [8] T E Powell 4-11-3 (65) Mr C Von Ballmoos 10/1: 5006432: In tch, prog to nk 71
chase wnr ins fnl 1f, styd on well, post came too sn: eff at 6f/1m, now stays 9f: see 3733.

4456 **JACKIE KIELY** 5 [11] P S McEntee 3-10-11 t (65) Miss Judith Patterson 10/1: 0030403: Bhd, still   1¾ 67
plenty to do 3f out, staying on for press bef 1f out, nrst fin: qck reapp: apprec rtn to 10f: see 4295 & btr 3785.

4181 **BARTON SANDS** 17 [4] Andrew Reid 7-11-7 t (69) Mr F Ollivaud 8/1: 100-1124: Bhd, hdwy wide 4f out, 1¼ 69
styd on to chase wnr dist, sn no extra: btr 4181 (11.5f) & 3875 (10f).

4367 **LORD CHAMBERLAIN** 9 [5]11-10-7 bl (55) Mr S Walker 7/1: 2014025: Missed break, nvr nrr than mid-div. nk 54

4419 **ICANNSHIFT** 6 [12]4-10-7 (2oh) Ms A Amy Herbert 6/1: 3030426: Led, clr halfway, hdd 2f out, no extra. 2 51

3625 **WIND CHIME** 43 [9]7-11-4 (66) Miss C Gatta 13/2: 0201307: Nvr nrr than mid-div: 6 wk abs: btr 3034. 3½ 57

4365 **BILLY BATHWICK** 9 [1]7-10-11 (59) Miss N Volz 12/1: 0331058: Cl-up 7f, sn wknd: btr 2866. ¾ 48

4366 **PHRED** 9 [7]4-10-7 t (55) Ms C Williams 8/1: 4200509: In tch over 6f, wknd: btr 2448. 2 41

4199 **REGULATED** 16 [6]3-10-3 (4oh) (57) Miss Melanie Sauer 50/1: 1605000: 10th: Bhd, nvr a factor. 3 38

4452 **MORAG** 5 [3]3-10-6 (1oh) (60) Mr C De Smet 12/1: 0662000: 11th: Cl-up, ev ch bef 1f out, fdd: qck reapp. 1 39

4112 **CANNI THINKAAR** 22 [10]3-10-5 (2oh)P (59) Miss Celine Monfort 25/1: 6004030: 12th: Mid-div 5f, wknd. 1 36
12 Ran   Time 1m 59.90 (9.40)   Owned: The Fantasy Fellowship   Trained: Bury St Edmunds

4540   4.15 Lesley Dolphin European Breeders Fund Maiden Stakes 2yo (D2)
£5538 £1704 £852   6f str   Good/Firm 38   -37 Slow   Stands side

3196 **WAZIR** 60 [5] J H M Gosden 2-9-0 L Dettori 4/11 FAV: 21: Led 4f, sn outpcd, rallied ins fnl 1f   84
to lead cl-home, val bit more: bckd at odds on: 9 wk abs: eff at 6f, further will suit on this evidence: acts on
fast grnd & polytrack: eff on a sharp/undul trk & goes well fresh: see 3196.

4176 **ABERDEEN** 17 [3] P Mitchell 2-9-0 R L Moore 11/1: 62: Held up, prog halfway, ev ch ins fnl 1f,   ½ 81
btn far: eff at 6f, further shld suit: acts on fast grnd: see 4176.

DR ZALO 0 [6] P J Makin 2-9-0 D Sweeney 14/1: 3: ch c Dr Fong - Azola (Alzao) In tch, led 2f   shd 80
out, still trav well 3f out, hdd under press cl-home: tchd 20/1 on debut: Mar foal, half-brother successful at 6/7f,
also plcd over 1m: dam successful at 1m: sire fine performer at mid-dists on 3rd: eff at 6f, further will suit in
time: acts on fast grnd: plenty to like about this debut eff & can progress.

2263 **ARCHIE GLENN** 97 [7] M S Saunders 2-9-0 P McCabe 25/1: 004: Bhd, hdwy halfway, kept on ins fnl   ½ 79
1f, not btn far in 4th: long abs: eff at 6f on fast grnd: now quals for h'caps: see 1955.

4385 **AVIATION** 8 [8]2-9-0 R Hughes 5/1: 035: Handy over 4f, sn wknd, eased ins fnl 1f: btr 4385 (firm). 3½ 69

3196 **CHEK OI** 60 [2]2-9-0 S Drowne 50/1: 0006: In tch, prog & ev ch bef 1f out, sn wknd: 9 wk abs. 4 58

SUNDAY 12.09.04 Righthand, Sharpish, Undulating Track

4139 **KIRKHAMMERTON 19** [4]2-9-0 V Slattery 25/1: 007: Rear, nvr a factor: see 4139.	8	36
2976 **DOMINER 69** [1]2-9-0 P (40) C Catlin 66/1: 6668: Cl-up 4f, sn wknd: 10 wk abs & cheek pieces.	nk	35

8 Ran Time 1m 14.50 (4.50) Owned: H R H Princess Haya of Jordan Trained: Manton

---

4541 **4.50 Adenstar Maiden Stakes 3yo (D2)**
£6955 £2140 £1070 **1m1f192y** **Good/Firm 38** **-33 Slow** Inside

4937} **CORSICAN NATIVE 319** [5] Mrs A J Perrett 3-9-0 R Hughes 15/8 FAV: 3-1: Made all, pushed clr bef 1f out despite wandering under press, eased cl-home, val bit more: well bckd on reapp: 3rd of 14 on sole '03 start (rtd 77, mdn): eff at 7f, apprec upto 10f: acts on fast & soft grnd: goes well fresh & acts on a sharp/undul trk: could not have won with more ease & can progress.		79
4125 **ROYAL LUSTRE 20** [6] J H M Gosden 3-9-0 (67) L Dettori 5/2: 0302: Al cl-up, easily outpcd by wnr fnl 2f.	9	65
3913 **POLAR DANCER 30** [2] Mrs A J Perrett 3-8-9 (53) S Drowne 13/2: 63-03003: Chsd ldrs, no extra bef 1f out.1¾		57
4305} **TYUP POMPEY 361** [8] D R C Elsworth 3-9-0 L Keniry(3) 8/1: 3-4: ch g Docksider - Cindy's Baby (Bairn) In tch over 7f, sn fdd: reapp: 3rd of 12 on sole '03 start (rtd 60, auct mdn, B Smart).	7	52
4266 **MONTGOMERY 14** [9]3-9-0 S Whitworth 14/1: 665: Missed break a al well adrift: see 3967.	10	37
MARIDAY 0 [1]3-9-0 Paul Eddery 5/1: 6: Chsd ldrs 6f, fdd: debut: with Lady Herries.	1½	34
2320} **KWAI BABY 449** [4]3-8-9 J F McDonald (3) 50/1: 000-7: gr f Charnwood Forest - Roses In The Snow (Be My Guest) Chsd ldrs, fdd 4f out: reapp: unplcd in all 3 '03 starts (rtd 41, fill stks): with J J Bridger.	12	13

7 Ran Time 2m 11.36 (7.16) Owned: Mr K Abdulla Trained: Pulborough

---

4542 **5.25 Seabeach Apprentice Stakes Handicap 3yo+ 56-70 (E3)** **[76]**
£3531 £1086 £543 **1m rnd** **Good/Firm 38** **-12 Slow** Inside

4300 **JOHANNIAN 13** [4] J M Bradley 6-9-7 (69) L Fletcher 12/1: 2046321: Held up, prog wide 2f out, rdn out to lead cl-home: eff at 1m/10.5f on firm & soft grnd: in form 6yo who remains fairly treated: see 4300 & 4141.		76
4189 **MYTHICAL CHARM 16** [13] J J Bridger 5-8-7 (7oh)t (48) J F McDonald 20/1: 0350022: Mid-div, prog to lead 2f out, hdd cl-home: acts on fast, soft grnd & both AWs: see 4189.	¾	59
4320 **KELSEAS KOLBY 11** [11] P Butler 4-8-9 (57) D Nolan 20/1: 3442253: Bhd, hdwy 3f out, styd on ins fnl 1f.	½	60
4293 **BURGUNDY 13** [17] P Mitchell 7-9-2 bl (64) T P Queally 11/2: 1121254: Held up, prog 3f out, nrst fin.	¾	65
4077 **OH SO ROSIE 23** [6]4-8-10 p (58) Derek Nolan(5) 14/1: 0100425: Held up, styd on to chase ldr well over 1f out, no extra ins fnl 1f: just btr 4077.	1	57
4320* **LONDONER 11** [16]6-8-12 (60) Lisa Jones 6/1: 3520016: Led 6f, hdd 2f out, no extra: btr 4320 (AW).	½	58
4221 **ALCHERA 15** [7]3-8-7 (60) C Haddon(5) 16/1: 6440407: Held up, eff when no room 2f out, mod late gains. ½		57
798 **TREVIAN 192** [3]3-9-0 (67) R Reilly 20/1: 6-016658: Handy over 6f, wknd: long abs: 'struck into'.	1	62
4067 **SPIRITS AWAKENING 23** [14]5-8-12 (60) S Hitchcott 7/2 FAV: 6324269: In tch over 6f, wknd: btr 3891.	1	53
3524 **LITTLE ENGLANDER 46** [5]4-8-10 (58) N Chalmers(3) 16/1: 5005100: 10th: Al bhd: twice below 2931.	4	43
4320 **KNICKYKNACKIENOO 11** [15]3-8-6 (1oh) (59) L Keniry 8/1: 3102530: 11th: Cl-up 6f, fdd: btr 4320.	2½	39
4265 **LORD OF THE SEA 14** [10]3-8-6 (1oh) (59) R Miles 20/1: 0004060: 12th: Bhd, nvr a factor: see 2378.	nk	38
4346* **OTAGO 0** [1]3-8-5 (2oh) (58) F P Ferris 8/1: 4504210: 13th: Led, hdd 6f out, wknd after halfway.	1¾	33
4195 **JARVO 16** [12]3-8-9 (62) J P Guillambert 12/1: 5400230: 14th: Cl-up over 4f, wknd: btr 4195 & 3846.	2½	32

14 Ran Time 1m 41.43(4.03) Owned: Ms A M Williams Trained: Chepstow

---

MONDAY 13.09.04 Lefthand, Turning Track with Uphill Finish

Official Going GOOD

4543 **2.30 Sharp Minds Betfair Median Auction Maiden Stakes 2yo (E3)**
£3614 £1112 £556 **5f161y** **Good 58** **-12 Slow** Far side

3600 **BAHAMIAN MAGIC 44** [8] D R Loder 2-9-0 T P Queally 7/2: 431: Rcd keen & cl-up, hdwy over 2f out, kept on well for press in fnl 1f to lead cl-home: 6 wk abs: eff at 5/5.5f, 6f will suit: acts on polytrack & gd.		83
4200 **LIGHTED WAY 17** [4] A M Balding 2-8-9 (64) L Keniry(3) 20/1: 0662: Keen & prom, hdwy to lead 2f out, hdd cl-home: stays 5.5f on gd: shld find a small race: see 4052.	½	75
INKA DANCER 0 [11] B Palling 2-8-9 F P Ferris(3) 66/1: 3: ch f Intikhab - Grannys Reluctance (Anita's Prince) Slow away, rear, hdwy over 1f out, nrst fin on debut: Mar 1st foal: dam plcd at 6f/1m: eff at 5.5f, 6f will suit: reportedly lost a shoe & this was a pleasing start, improve.	½	73+
3473 **DISGUISE 50** [3] B W Hills 2-9-0 M Hills 11/8 FAV: 524: Led to 2f out, no extra ins fnl 1f: well bckd from 7/4, 7 wk abs: btr 3473 (6f).	1	75
CHINALEA 0 [9]2-9-0 R Smith 5/1: 5: b c Danetime - Raise A Secret (Classic Secret) Slow away, sn handy, onepcd 2f out on debut: Apr foal, cost 26,000 gns: half brother to a 1m wnr.	½	73
4179 **EDGE OF ITALY 18** [6]2-8-9 S Whitworth 100/1: 06: ch f Bold Edge - Brera (Tate Gallery) Rear, hdwy over 1f out, kept on: Mar foal: dam unplcd over 5/7f: sire prog into a top class sprinter: with K Bell.	1¼	64
3728 **IL PRANZO 39** [2]2-9-0 (71) J F Egan 14/1: 06357: Chsd ldrs, onepcd 2f out.	1	66
4455 **PEREZ 6** [10]2-9-0 T Dobbs 14/1: 0068: In tch, wknd 2f out: op 20/1, quick reapp.	shd	65
LATIN EXPRESS 0 [5]2-9-0 Martin Dwyer 9/1: 9: Cl-up, no impress well over 1f out on debut: op 12/1.	9	38
ROSIE MUIR 0 [7]2-8-9 D Sweeney 100/1: 0: 10th: Slow away, nvr a factor on debut.	5	18
SATURDAYS CHILD 0 [1]2-8-9 R Miles(3) 100/1: 0: 11th: Slow away, t.o. on debut.	18	0

11 Ran Time 1m 12.97 (3.87) Owned: Lucayan Stud Trained: Newmarket

---

4544 **3.00 Sharp Minds Winners Welcome Maiden Stakes 2yo (D3)**
£3663 £1127 £564 **1m5y** **Good 58** **-05 Slow** Inside

4289 **RUMBALARA 14** [7] J H M Gosden 2-8-9 J Fortune 15/8: 021: Made virtually all, flashed tail ins fnl 1f, rdn out: relished this step up to 1m, further shld suit: open to improvement.		81
3713 **SILVER HIGHLIGHT 39** [4] A M Balding 2-8-9 Martin Dwyer 1/1 FAV: 022: Cl-up, kept on ins fnl 1f: handles fast & gd: rng well, shown enough last twice to find a race: see 3713.	nk	80

4194 **BATTLEDRESS** 17 [2] M P Tregoning 2-9-0 N De Souza(5) 7/1: 03: b c In The Wings - Chaturanga ¾ 83
(Night Shift) In tch, outpcd 2f out, kept on ins fnl 1f: Mar foal: dam unrcd, sire top class over 12f: stays 1m,
further will suit: gd run, rate higher & win.

    RIGHTFUL RULER 0 [3] B W Hills 2-9-0 M Hills 14/1: 4: b c Montjoy - Lady of The Realm (Prince hd 82+
Daniel) Rear, hdwy over 1f out, kept on on debut: Mar foal: half brother to an 11f wnr: sure to relish further & an
encouraging start.

2897 **SPILL A LITTLE** 73 [8]2-9-0 S Hitchcott 20/1: 65: b c Zafonic - Lypharitissima (Lightning) Keen hd 81
& dsptd lead, ev ch 2f out, onepcd nr fin: long abs, clr of rem: Mar foal: half brother to wnrs at 9/12f: eff over
1m on gd: gd run, imprvd from debut & has shown enough here to find a race.

4078 **MOSHKIL** 24 [6]2-9-0 S Drowne 25/1: 006: Cl-up, no impress over 1f out. 6 69
4218 **FIRE AT WILL** 16 [9]2-9-0 R L Moore 100/1: 0007: Nvr a factor. 19 31
4297 **MOUNT ARAFAT** 14 [11]2-9-0 A Daly 100/1: 08: Dwelt, nvr nr ldrs. 2 27
    LAMBRIGGAN LAD 0 [10]2-9-0 P Dobbs 100/1: 9: Mid-div, wknd 3f out on debut. shd 26
    EDITH BANKES 0 [1]2-8-9 C Haddon(7) 100/1: 0: 10th: Slow away, nvr a factor on debut. 2½ 16
4418 **CIENDRA GIRL** 7 [5]2-8-9 D Nolan 100/1: 00: 11th: Rear, t.o.: quick reapp. 24 10
11 Ran   Time 1m 43.4 (5.1)   Owned: Mr Peter Maher   Trained: Manton

---

4545   3.30 Sharp Minds Betfair: Best Odds Nursery Handicap Stakes 2yo 0-75 (E4)   [82]
    £3108 £888 £444   **5f161y**   Good 58   -06 Slow   Far side

3847* **ARBORS LITTLE GIRL** 34 [9] B R Millman 2-8-4 (58) A Daly 9/2 F FAV: 11: Rear, hdwy 2f out, hung 71
left 1f out, led ins fnl 1f, pushed out: landed double: eff at 5/5.5f, 6f will suit: acts on fast & gd, likes Bath:
still green, ore to come & can rate higher: see 3847 (debut, led).

4172* **MONASHEE ROSE** 18 [10] J S Moore 2-9-7 (75) N Mackay(3) 9/2 J FAV: 0112: Mid-div, hdwy to lead 1¾ 79
just over 2f out, hdd ins fnl 1f, no extra: stays 5.5f, shld get 6f: acts on fast & gd: remains in gd form: see 4172.

3820 **PERIANTH** 35 [11] B J Meehan 2-8-7 (61) K Fallon 9/1: 40003: Cl-up, bmpd & not much room 1f out, 1¼ 62
hmpd when ev ch ins fnl 1f, not recover: stays 5.5f on gd: poss rnr-up with clr run: see 1646 (debut).

3847 **MAJESTICAL** 34 [4] W R Muir 2-8-6 (60) S Drowne 8/1: 3400424: Led till just over 2f out, no extra 1 58
fnl 1f: reportedly hung right: see 3847.

4409 **IM AIMEE** 7 [6]2-9-5 (73) S Donohoe(7) 6/1: 2230445: In tch, hdwy over 1f out, not pace to chall. ¾ 69
3962 **ATSOS** 29 [12]2-9-0 (68) R L Moore 9/1: 66056: Dwelt, rear, hdwy over 1f out, kept on: see 3962. ½ 62
4269 **CROSS MY SHADOW** 14 [3]2-8-9 t (63) S Hitchcott 25/1: 0507: Cl-up, no impress over 1f out: 'hung right'. shd 56
3399 **MISTER BELL** 52 [8]2-8-6 (60) D Sweeney 50/1: 3608: Slow away, nvr a factor: 7 wk abs. 3 44
4409 **SAUCEPOT** 7 [2]2-8-9 (63) T Quinn 11/1: 0620369: Keen & cl-up, no impress over 1f out: qk reapp. 1¼ 43
4369 **TASKS MUPPET** 9 [5]2-8-7 (61) J F McDonald(3) 12/1: 5550: 10th: Handy, no impress over 1f out. 2 35
4357 **TASHYRA** 10 [1]2-8-10 (64) Martin Dwyer 10/1: 4400: 11th: Slow away, nvr nr ldrs: see 3368. ½ 36
4139 **DREAMERS LASS** 20 [7]2-8-2 (56) F P Ferris(3) 25/1: 20600: 12th: Cl-up, wknd over 1f out. nk 27
12 Ran   Time 1m 12.63 (3.53)   Owned: Dr Ian R Shenkin   Trained: Cullompton

---

4546   4.00 Sharp Minds Betfair: Back And Lay Handicap Stakes 3yo 56-70 (E3)   [74]
    £3702 £1139 £570   **1m5y**   Good 58   -04 Slow   Inside

4366 **MASTER MAHOGANY** 10 [9] R J Hodges 3-8-13 (59) S Drowne 11/1: 5460301: Cl-up, hdwy to lead well 67
over 2f out, drvn out ins fnl 1f: stays 1m/10f, tried 12f: acts on fast & gd: 1st win: see 2353.

4268 **DESERT HAWK** 15 [7] R Hannon 3-9-6 (66) R L Moore 16/1: 0540062: In tch, hdwy over 2f out, kept ½ 71
on: stays 1m/9f, 10f shld suit: acts on fast & gd: gd run: see 2378.

4054 **FLEET ANCHOR** 25 [14] J M Bradley 3-8-10 (4oh) (52) J F Egan 10/1: 0-000253: Rear, hdwy over 2f shd 60
out, kept on: stays 1m on gd: gd eff from 4lbs out of the h'cap: see 2906.

3973 **CAPITOLE** 29 [8] E F Vaughan 3-9-1 VIS (61) P McCabe 17/2: 0454: Rear, kept on late: stays 1m in a vis. nk 64
2971 **KINBRACE** 70 [12]3-8-13 (59) Martin Dwyer 11/2: 050-655: Rear, hdwy over 3f out, ev ch over 2f 1 60
out, onepcd ins fnl 1f: long abs: reportedly hung left: see 2098.

3731 **TROIS ETOILES** 39 [1]3-8-10 (1oh) (55) K Fallon 3/1 FAV: 0-505536: In tch, hdwy over 2f out, no 2½ 52
impress ins fnl 1f: well bckd from 5/1: btr expected: see 2922.

3995 **ALI DEO** 28 [10]3-9-10 P (70) T P Queally 14/1: 0-130607: Cl-up, no impress over 1f out: cheekpieces. 1¾ 62
4256 **BEAUTY OF DREAMS** 15 [4]3-8-11 (57) S Hitchcott 8/1: 0053068: Mid-div, wkng when hmpd over 2f out. 4 41
3867 **ZURI** 33 [5]3-9-2 (62) N Mackay(3) 12/1: 640009: Cl-up, no impress over 1f out, eased: see 2534. 1¼ 43
4603} **ROYAL ZEPHYR** 345 [3]3-9-4 (64) J Mackay 14/1: 360-0: 10th: b f Royal Academy - Cassation (Lear nk 44
Fan) In tch, wknd over 2f out: op 9/1, reapp: 3rd 1st of 3 '03 starts (mdn, rtd 68).

4320 **MY SUNSHINE** 12 [2]3-8-10 (2oh) (54) M Hills 33/1: 00-00000: 11th: Al bhd: see 4320. 3 30
4321 **CHARLIE TANGO** 12 [13]3-9-4 BL (64) T Quinn 8/1: 3435000: 12th: Keen, led over 6f out till well 12 14
over 2f out, fdd: reportedly ran too free early on: tried blnks.

4272 **ROMANTIC DRAMA** 14 [6]3-8-10 (1oh) (55) D Sweeney 66/1: 00460-00: 13th: b f Primo Dominie - dist 0
Antonia's Choice (Music Boy) Led over 1f, fdd 3f out, eased: 4th at best in '03 (fills mdn, rtd 67a, with B
Meehan): eff at 7f on polytrack: tried blnks.
13 Ran   Time 1m 43.28 (4.98)   Owned: Villagers Five   Trained: Somerton

---

4547   4.30 Sharp Minds Betfair Maiden Stakes Fillies 3yo (D3)
    £3536 £1088 £544   **1m2f46y**   Good 58   +10 Fast   Inside

3858 **BATIK** 33 [9] L M Cumani 3-8-11 N Mackay(3) 2/1: 31: Rear, plenty to do 2f out, hdwy well over 1f 78
out, drvn out ins fnl 1f, led cl-home: fast time: relished step up to 10f, further shld suit: acts on fast & gd,
turning trk: improved from debut: see 3858 (debut).

4222 **UIG** 16 [1] H S Howe 3-8-11 (74) J Fortune 13/2: 0032042: Led till hdd & no extra cl-home: acts 1 75
on firm & gd/soft: see 4222.

4075 **PRINCIPESSA** 24 [4] B Palling 3-8-11 (70) T Quinn 11/1: 0220243: Rcd in 2nd, hdwy & ev ch fnl 1f, nk 74
sn onepcd: well clr of rem: see 3845.

4101 **GO SUPERSONIC** 23 [6] Sir Michael Stoute 3-8-11 K Fallon 7/4 FAV: 44: Cl-up, no impress fnl 1f. 7 63
2378 **TENNYS GOLD** 94 [2]3-8-11 (70) M Hills 7/1: 02-435: Rear, hdwy over 6f out, no impress over 2f out. 5 55
1166 **KEY IN** 152 [5]3-8-11 S Drowne 40/1: 06: ch f Unfuwain - Fleet Key (Afleet) Nvr a factor: long 6 46
abs: cost 30,000 gns: mid-dist bred: with B Hills.

4364 **ZARNEETA** 10 [8]3-8-11 (40) R Smith 200/1: 00-00007: Al bhd: see 2742. 1 44

BATH MONDAY 13.09.04 Lefthand, Turning Track with Uphill Finish

4165 **MYSTIC MOON** 19 [3]3-8-11 (40) R L Moore 100/1: 0040008: Nvr a factor: see 1280.	½	43
2974 **GOLD RELIC** 70 [7]3-8-11 Martin Dwyer 33/1: 09: b f Kingmambo - Gold Bust (Nashwan) Nvr a factor: long abs: dam a wnr over 10f: with A Balding.	2½	39

9 Ran   Time 2m 10.8 (4.8)   Owned: Aston House Stud   Trained: Newmarket

4548   5.00 Sharp Minds Phone 0870 90 80 121 Handicap Stakes 3yo + 56-70 (E3)   [76]
£5884   £1810   £905   5f161y   Good 58   +01 Fast   Far side

3910 **OEUF A LA NEIGE** 31 [3] G C H Chung 4-9-2 (64) O Urbina 25/1: 5061501: Rear, hdwy over 1f out, drvn out ins fnl 1f, led nr fin: eff at 5.5f/1m on fast: back to form: see 2214.		75
3960 **ROMAN QUINTET** 30 [5] D W P Arbuthnot 4-8-12 (60) T Quinn 7/1: 02-00032: Cl-up, hdwy to lead ins fnl 1f, hdd nr fin: gd eff: acts on fast, gd & polytrack: see 231.	nk	69
4335 **DOUBLE M** 11 [4] Mrs J Richards 7-9-3 vis (65) A Daly 14/1: 6120003: Slow away, styd on late.	½	72
4412 **JAGGED** 7 [6] J R Jenkins 4-8-10 vis (58) K Fallon 2/1 FAV: 3631224: Led till ins fnl 1f, no extra.	nk	64
4489 **PULSE** 4 [13]6-8-8 p (56) P Fitzsimons 16/1: 5400605: Cl-up, ev ch when carried right well over 1f out, onepcd ins fnl 1f: quick reapp: see 1532.	nk	61
4126 **SEWMUCH CHARACTER** 21 [8]5-9-7 (69) D Sweeney 33/1: 6420106: Mid-div, onepcd fnl 1f.	½	72
4412+ **WOODBURY** 7 [12]5-9-2 (6ex) (64) G Baker 10/1: 0410417: Rear, hdwy over 2f out, hmpd on stands rail ins fnl 1f & no ch after: quick reapp: closer with a clr run, forgive this.	1	64+
4412 **INNSTYLE** 7 [2]3-8-7 (57) S Hitchcott 6/1: 40-60038: Rear, hdwy/not clr run over 2f out, onepcd fnl 1f.	½	55
4197 **TABOOR** 17 [1]6-8-11 h bl t (59) Martin Dwyer 8/1: 2060129: Al bhd.	2	51
4485 **CAYMAN BREEZE** 4 [7]4-8-9 (57) J F Egan 33/1: 5410500: 10th: Mid-div, no impress over 1f out.	nk	48
4412 **STAGNITE** 7 [11]4-8-9 p (57) N Chalmers(5) 14/1: 2100650: 11th: Cl-up, no impress 2f out: quick reapp.	2½	40
4335 **FORMALISE** 11 [9]4-8-7 (1oh) p (54) R Thomas(3) 8/1: 5050040: 12th: Cl-up, no impress 2f out.	1¼	34
4317 **PURE IMAGINATION** 12 [10]3-8-8 (58) R L Moore 25/1: 3060400: 13th: Dwelt in rear, hdwy over 3f out, no impress over 1f out: see 1912.	3	28

13 Ran   Time 1m 12.25(3.15)   Owned: Mr G C H Chung   Trained: Newmarket

MUSSELBURGH MONDAY 13.09.04 Righthand, Sharp Track

Official Going Good/Firm (Good Places)

4549   2.20 Sharp Minds Betfair Maiden Auction Stakes 2yo (E3)
£3387   £1042   £521   5f str   Good/Firm 29   -48 Slow   Stands Side

4436 **BLADES BOY** 6 [1] K A Ryan 2-8-8 (1ow) N Callan 16/1: 001: ch g Paris House - Banningham Blade (Sure Blade) Made all, hung right under press but held on all out cl-home: qk reapp: Mar foal, dam useful sprinter: eff at 5f on fast grnd: improved effort.		67
2989 **HYMN OF VICTORY** 69 [5] T J Etherington 2-8-7 (72) J Fanning 7/2: 05262: Rdn & outpcd early, strong run ins last, just failed: 10 wk abs: eff at 5f, needs a stiffer trk &/or further: handles gd/soft & fast grnd.	nk	64
4451 **PROCRASTINATE** 6 [4] R F Fisher 2-8-10 (54) R Winston 10/1: 5305203: Chsd ldrs, rdn & switched ins last, kept on for press, just held: qck reapp: handles fast & gd grnd: see 3308, 2177 & 1037.	shd	68
4517 **BOBS FLYER** 2 [7] J G Given 2-8-8 M Fenton 6/4 FAV: 04024: Chsd ldrs, onepace: qck reapp: btr 4517.	3½	55
OUR LITTLE SECRET 0 [2]2-8-2 F Norton 8/1: 5: ch f Rossini - Sports Post Lady (M Double M) Cl-up & ch 2f out, wknd bef dist: op 11/2: cheaply bght May foal, half-sister to a 5f juv wnr: dam multiple 5f wnr.	1	46
3323 **COMPTON CLASSIC** 55 [6]2-8-13 T Eaves(3) 50/1: 06: Al outpcd, 8 wk abs: see 3323.	3½	46
2056 **MISS JELLYBEAN** 108 [3]2-8-5 P Mulrennan(3) 5/1: 07: b f Namid - Elfin Queen (Fairy King) Cl-up & ch 2f out, fdd under press: bckd: Apr foal, 12,000gns 2yo: half-sister to a Greek wnr at up to 1m, dam a 5f plcd juv.	4	26

7 Ran   Time 1m 01.37 (3.87)   Owned: Crown Select   Trained: Hambleton

4550   2.50 Sharp Minds: Best Odds 'premier' Claiming Stakes 3yo + (D2)
£6916   £2128   £1064   1m1f rnd   Good/Firm 29   +12 Fast   Outside

4266* **THE PRINCE** 15 [7] Ian Williams 10-8-13 (79) C Catlin 4/1 JT FAV: 31-11211: Rear, smooth hdwy halfway trav well, qcknd to lead over 1f out & rdn clr, readily in a fast time: nicely bckd tho' op 11/4: eff at 7.5f/9f on firm, soft & both AWs: thriving in claimers: see 4266, 3876.		77+
4124* **BARKING MAD** 21 [3] M L W Bell 6-9-9 (85) M Fenton 4/1 JT FAV: 2162612: Led, drvn & hdd over 1f out, onepace: see 4124.	3	79
4304 **TODLEA** 13 [11] J A Osborne 4-9-7 (76) S W Kelly 8/1: 2231033: Trkd ldrs, onepace fnl 2f.	½	76
4397 **SCOTTYS FUTURE** 8 [8] D Nicholls 6-9-10 (72) J Fanning 25/1: 1010654: Towards rear, styd on late.	¾	78
4397 **DARK CHARM** 8 [10]5-9-8 (90) T Hamilton(3) 9/1: 400-3005: Trkd ldrs, onepace for press fnl 2f: see 951.	1	74
4399 **SARRAAF** 8 [1]8-8-11 (64) R Winston 14/1: 0520346: Held up, switched & no impress over 1f out.	shd	63
4173+ **YENALED** 18 [5]7-9-2 (72) Donna Caldwell(7) 9/2: 1224217: Slow away & bhd, eff wide, little prog: bckd.	3½	61
4305 **TEDSTALE** 13 [4]6-9-5 bl (77) W Supple 11/2: 6453048: Mid-div, rdn & no impress over 1f out: op 7/1.	½	63
4208 **PHOENIX NIGHTS** 17 [9]4-8-12 (52) P Mathers(5) 150/1: 0064469: In tch, no impress fnl 2f: see 423.	3½	49
3151 **AMBUSHED** 63 [6]8-8-9 (50) P Mulrennan(3) 150/1: 030-6400: 10th: Chsd ldrs, btn 2f out: jumps fit.	¾	45
1507 **LANGE BLEU** 134 [2]5-8-9 A Nicholls 200/1: 2/50-00: 11th: Prom till halfway, sn bhd: 5 month abs.	dist	0

11 Ran   Time 1m 52.26 (1.56)   Owned: Mr Patrick Kelly   Trained: Alvechurch

4551   3.20 Sharp Minds Betfair Bet In Running Nursery Handicap Stakes 2yo 0-95 (C1)   [96]
£13728   £4224   £2112   5f str   Good/Firm 29   -14 Slow   Stands Side

4437 **OCEANICO DOT COM** 6 [12] A Berry 2-7-13 (1ow)(3oh) (67) F Norton 12/1: 002131: Al handy, styd on for press to lead well ins last: qck reapp: eff at 5f on fast & gd, easy trks: likes to race with/force the pace.		77
4172 **SMIDDY HILL** 18 [8] R Bastiman 2-8-10 (82) A Mullen(7) 16/1: 4145102: Handy, led over 1f out, hdd well ins last: bckd to form after latest, loves to race with/force the pace: see 3488.	nk	87
4273 **MOTH BALL** 14 [3] J A Osborne 2-8-11 (83) S W Kelly 5/1 JT FAV: 23103: Hmpd start, sn chsd ldrs,	shd	88

switched & kept on for press, nrst fin: needs 6f &/or stiffer trk: see 3951.

4471 **TALCEN GWYN 4** [5] M F Harris 2-8-6 (78) A Nicholls 50/1: 1404504: Hmpd start & well bhd, styd on *1¼* **79**
strongly fnl 1f, nrst fin: qck reapp: closer without a slow start: keep in mind for similar: see 3623, 2430.

4258 **GRAZE ON 15** [10]2-8-12 (84) R Winston 10/1: 2125: Towards rear, switched & kept on for press fnl *shd* **85**
1f: handles fast & soft grnd: wants 6f/stiffer trk: see 4258, 3968.

4458 **IMPERIAL SOUND 5** [4]2-9-7 (93) P Fessey 7/1: 120106: Hmpd start, chsd ldrs, onepace. *nk* **93**

4049 **WISE WAGER 25** [7]2-8-5 (77) T Hamilton(3) 6/1: 3331227: Led/dsptd lead 3f, no extra dist: btr 4049. *nk* **76**

3266 **ANNATALIA 58** [2]2-8-9 (81) C Catlin 15/2: 46108: Hmpd start & towards rear, prog/no room over 1f *1½* **75**
out, nvr able to chall: abs: best forgiven: see 2976.

3623 **GIFTED GAMBLE 44** [13]2-8-8 (80) N Callan 25/1: 3322159: Chsd ldrs, btn over 1f out, abs: btr 3445. *shd* **74**

2490 **GLOVED HAND 89** [9]2-9-3 (89) M Fenton 10/1: 100: 10th: Mid-div, outpcd from halfway: 12 wk abs. *nk* **82**

4065 **NOVA TOR 24** [1]2-9-1 (87) I Mongan 5/1 JT FAV: 1540130: 11th: Chsd ldrs, btn over 1f out: btr 4065. *1* **77**

3896* **TRIM IMAGE 32** [11]2-8-2 (74) B Swarbrick(5) 50/1: 233310: 12th: Struggling halfway: btr 3896 (g/s). *5* **50**

4172 **WONDERFUL MIND 18** [6]2-8-2 bl (74) W Supple 10/1: 2156320: 13th: Chsd ldrs, btn halfway: amiss? *¾* **48**

13 Ran Time 59.66 (2.16) Owned: The Red and The Green Trained: Cockerham

4552

3.50 Sharp Minds Betfair Back And Lay Maiden Auction Stakes 2yo (E3)
£3414 £1050 £525 **1m rnd** **Good/Firm 29** **-25 Slow** Outside

4351 **LITHOS 10** [1] J A Osborne 2-8-13 (77) S W Kelly 100/30: 2651: Held up in tch, hdwy halfway, rdn **84**
to lead over 1f out, styd on strongly: nicely bckd: eff at 1m on firm & fast grnd, sharp or gall trk: useful eff.

3981 **MANEKI NEKO 28** [6] M H Tompkins 2-8-10 N Callan 10/11 FAV: 422: Trkd ldrs, rdn to lead over 2f *2* **76**
out, hdd over 1f out & no extra well ins last: hvly bckd & styd this longer 1m trip well: can find a race: see 3981.

4064 **BLACKCOMB MOUNTAIN 25** [2] M F Harris 2-8-2 (68) A Nicholls 8/1: 534403: Cl-up when carr badly *3* **62+**
wide on bend after 3f, sn bhd, rapid hdwy over 2f out to chase ldrs, no extra bef dist: would have gone close without severe interference: this longer 1m trip looks set to suit: handles fast, gd & polytrack.

4283 **ESKDALE 14** [4] R F Fisher 2-8-10 (67) P Mulrennan(3) 13/2: 003264: Chsd ldrs, rdn & btn 2f out: btr 4171. *3* **64**

4343 **GEORDIE DANCER 11** [7]2-8-13 P Mathers(5) 33/1: 05: Cl-up & left in lead on bend after 3f, hdd *3½* **60**
over 2f out, sn btn: see 4343.

4271 **BELLA PLUNKETT 14** [5]2-8-2 B Swarbrick(5) 20/1: 0006: Led/dsptd lead till ran v wide on bend *9* **34**
after 3f, sn drpd to rear: lkd difficult to stear today: see 4271 & 4050.

6 Ran Time 1m 41.84 (4.34) Owned: Mr J McGarry Trained: Upper Lambourn

4553

4.20 Sharp Minds Betfair Musselburgh Gold Cup A Handicap 3yo+ 71-85 (D2) **[88]**
£10109 £3110 £1555 **1m4f** **Good/Firm 29** **-09 Slow** Inside

4400 **JEEPSTAR 8** [8] T D Easterby 4-9-3 (77) M Fenton 4/1: 0622101: Made all, strongly pressed fnl 3f **84**
& went right under press over 1f out, held on most gamely: won this race in '03 off a 6lb lower mark: winning form at 10/12f: acts on firm & gd/soft: best when dominating: tough & genuine: see 3969, 2078.

4360 **MR TAMBOURINE MAN 10** [10] P F I Cole 3-9-1 (84) C Catlin 11/2: 0013142: Held up, rdn & hdwy to *¾* **89**
chall over 1f out, no extra nr fin: nicely bckd: stays 12f well: see 4360 & 3459.

4383 **SAHEM 9** [5] C J Teague 7-9-9 (83) W Supple 20/1: 2033103: Trkd ldrs, rdn to chall 2f out, onepace. *½* **87**

4012 **EASIBET DOT NET 27** [2] I Semple 4-8-9 (3oh)p (66) R Winston 20/1: 3053134: Held up, kept on for *hd* **72**
press fnl 2f, not able to land blow: back to form after disapp latest on soft grnd: see 3588.

4259 **MERRYMAKER 15** [1]4-8-10 (70) P Mathers(5) 12/1: 1210035: Dwelt, rear, kept on wide for press, no dngr. *hd* **72**

4377 **RUTTERS REBEL 9** [4]3-8-2 (7oh) (71) P Fessey 16/1: 0240106: Trkd ldrs, rdn & short of room when *½* **72**
switched ins last, onepace: only btn around 2L in a tight fin: see 3765.

4383 **SKI JUMP 9** [3]4-9-7 vis (81) T Hamilton(3) 6/1: 1-160607: In tch, eff 2f out, no extra bef dist: see 3999. *¾* **81**

3926 **BAILEYS DANCER 31** [6]3-8-12 (81) J Fanning 12/1: 0020108: Chsd wnr, btn 2f out: btr 3653. *3* **77**

4183* **JACK OF TRUMPS 17** [7]4-9-4 (78) F Norton 5/2 FAV: 0041119: In tch, chall over 2f out, fdd under *2* **71**
press over 1f out: well bckd: something amiss? btr 4183.

9 Ran Time 2m 35.21 (4.61) Owned: Miss E Jeeps and Partners Trained: Malton

4554

4.50 Sharp Minds Betfair Phone 0870 90 80 121 Classified Stakes 3yo+ 0-60 (F3)
£3523 £1084 £542 **1m rnd** **Good/Firm 29** **-02 Slow** Outside

4402 **MOBANE FLYER 8** [3] R A Fahey 4-9-3 (60) T Hamilton(3) 5/1: 0-006331: Trkd ldrs trav well, rdn & **66**
led over 1f out, sn duelled with rnr-up, prevailed all out: nicely bckd: stays 10f, apprec rtn to 1m: acts on firm & gd/soft grnd: prob handles any trk: travels well: see 3850 & 3117.

4406 **BOND MILLENNIUM 7** [1] B Smart 6-9-3 (59) F Norton 17/2: 2455-002: Held up, hdwy wide to chall *shd* **65**
over 1f out, drvn & just held: apprec drop to 1m & has come to hand, on a handy mark.

4346 **NEWCORP LAD 11** [6] Mrs G S Rees 4-9-3 (59) J Fanning 7/1: 0442403: Trkd ldrs, smooth prog to *1½* **62**
lead over 2f out, rdn & edged right over 1f out, sn hdd & not pace of front pair: visor omitted: likes Hamilton.

4438 **LEGAL SET 6** [10] Miss A Stokell 8-9-3 t (57) L Fletcher(3) 14/1: 0450024: Chsd ldrs, drvn & kept *hd* **61**
on: qck reapp: now stays an easy 1m well: continues in gd heart: see 2713.

4452 **JOSHUAS GOLD 6** [5]3-8-12 (57) D Tudhope(7) 20/1: 0142305: Bhd, styd on wide for press, nrst fin: *2* **57**
qck reapp: back to form with a change in tactics (normally prom): see 4345, 4175 & 3547.

1535 **COMMITMENT LECTURE 132** [7]4-9-0 t (57) S W Kelly 12/1: 200-5146: Mid-div, rdn & no impress fnl 2f. *nk* **53**

3702 **BEAMISH PRINCE 40** [9]5-9-3 (57) M Fenton 33/1: 30033-07: Rear, mod prog for press, abs: see 3702. *1½* **53**

4399 **NEMO FUGAT 8** [12]5-9-3 vis (60) A Nicholls 9/2 FAV: 2520038: Led till over 2f out, wknd: see 4399. *shd* **53**

4008 **ANTHEMION 27** [2]7-9-3 (60) D McGaffin 16/1: 5313209: Mid-div, eff wide, btn over 1f out: btr 3593. *shd* **52**

3835 **LOUISIADE 35** [4]3-8-12 (60) W Supple 10/1: 3003300: 10th: Chsd ldr, btn over 1f out: btr 3516 & 3410. *1¼* **49**

4399 **REGENTS SECRET 8** [13]4-9-3 (59) P Mulrennan(3) 10/1: 4033060: 11th: Mid-div, eff when edged right *shd* **49**
2f out, sn btn: op 14/1.

4406 **ZANDEED 7** [11]6-9-3 (59) P Fessey 12/1: 00/-03140: 12th: Al rear & nvr paced to chall: btr 4406. *nk* **48**

4345 **WOOD DALLING 11** [14]6-9-3 (54) R Winston 16/1: 6166060: 13th: Chsd ldrs, btn when no room 2f out. *14* **24**

13 Ran Time 1m 40.00 (2.5) Owned: Mr P N Devlin Trained: Malton

MUSSELBURGH MONDAY 13.09.04 Righthand, Sharp Track

4555
5.20 Sharp Minds Betfair Handicap Stakes 3yo+ 56-70 (E3) [77]
£3359 £1034 £517 **2m** **Good/Firm 29** **-20 Slow** Stands Side

4521 **SHARADI 2** [4] V Smith 3-9-3 (66) N Callan 2/1 FAV: 0002221: Trkd ldr, led over 2f out & rdn well **74**
clr, decisively: hvly bckd, op 5/2: qck reapp: deserved this after fin rnr-up last thrice: eff at 14f/2m on fast
& gd/soft grnd, prob any trk: shapes as a progressive stayer & imprvd today for stronger handling: see 4521.
4249 **SPRING BREEZE 16** [5] M Dods 3-8-3 (8oh)VIS (52) P Fessey 11/2: 6023252: Led till over 2f out, **6** **56**
kept on for press but no ch with wnr: clr of rem: first time visor: op 4/1: see 3580, 3312 & 2123.
4151 **SONOMA 20** [2] M L W Bell 4-9-11 (66) M Fenton 7/2: 0014443: Held up in tch, rdn 5f out, nvr any threat. **10** **56**
2685 **GARGOYLE GIRL 81** [1] J S Goldie 7-9-8 (58) W Supple 9/2: 0510604: Bhd & rdn 5f out, only mod **hd** **52**
prog: nicely bckd: jumps fit (recent h'cap hdle scorer): btr 1551 (C/D).
4361 **DANCE LIGHT 10** [6]5-9-6 (56) J Fanning 8/1: 0053005: Chsd ldrs, drvn & btn 3f out: btr 2941. **12** **40**
4170 **MILLENNIUM HALL 18** [3]5-9-9 (59) R Winston 8/1: 0660606: Struggling 5f out & al bhd: btr 2479. **19** **27**
6 Ran Time 3m 30.28(7.78) Owned: Mr R J Baines Trained: Newmarket

REDCAR MONDAY 13.09.04 Lefthand, Flat, Galloping Track

Official Going Firm (Good/Firm Places)

4556
2.10 Sharp Minds Winners Welcome Nursery Handicap Stakes 2yo 0-75 (E3) [82]
£4225 £1300 £650 **5f str** **Firm 14** **-11 Slow** Centre

4177 **CONNOTATION 18** [11] P W D'Arcy 2-8-12 VIS (66) L Dettori 8/1: 22301: Bhd, prog 2f out, pushed out **75**
to lead cl-home, val bit more: eff at 5f, tried further: acts on firm, fast grnd & polytrack: improved for vis.
3476* **CLOVE 49** [15] B W Hills 2-9-7 (75) R Hughes 2/1 FAV: 412: Led 4f out, edged left under press ins ½ **81**
fnl 1f, hdd cl-home: 7 wk abs: gd run on h'cap bow under top-weight: ran to form of win in 3476 (mdn).
4437 **LORD JOHN 6** [3] M W Easterby 2-7-13 bl (53) Dale Gibson 9/2: 4004023: Al prom, ev ch just ins ½ **58**
fnl 1f, sn onepcd: acts on firm & fast grnd: continues to run well: see 4437 & 3212.
4344 **HOPELESSLY DEVOTED 11** [7] F C Haslam 2-8-2 (56) Rory Moore(5) 14/1: 061054: Prom, ev ch dist, sn **2** **55**
no extra: paddock pick: btr 3901 (gd/soft, clmr).
4303 **BOND BABE 13** [8]2-9-0 (68) S Sanders 9/2: 42335: Led, hdd after 1f, styd prom, no extra bef 1f 1¼ **63**
out: op 6/1: below form of today's firm grnd: showed more in 4303 (gd) & 4134 (gd/soft).
4258 **HILLSIDE HEATHER 15** [12]2-8-10 p (64) Dean McKeown 7/1: 2024506: Nvr nrr than mid-div: op 9/1. ¾ **57**
4437 **OUR LOUIS 6** [13]2-8-0 (54) R Ffrench 25/1: 1500007: Cl-up over 3f, no extra: qck reapp. nk **46**
3902 **PARIS BELL 32** [1]2-8-10 (64) K Darley 12/1: 350048: Nvr nrr than mid-div: btr 3902. 1 **53**
4179 **GOGETTER GIRL 18** [5]2-8-12 P (66) T E Durcan 25/1: 2404609: Nvr nrr than mid-div: cheek pieces. hd **54**
4437 **CADOGEN SQUARE 6** [9]2-7-12 (3oh) P M Quinn 50/1: 000400: 10th: Missed break, nvr a factor. ½ **39**
4344 **Kilmovee 11** [10]2-8-13 (67) E Ahern 25/1:0   4437 **Carmania 6** [6]2-7-13 (53) D Fentiman(7) 40/1:0
3968 **Paula Jo 29** [14]2-7-12 (7oh)P(45) D Mernagh 50/1:0
3559 **Isitloveyourafter 46** [2]2-7-12 (2oh)(50) J Quinn 50/1:0
14 Ran Time 57.78 (1.28) Owned: Hyperion Bloodstock Trained: Newmarket

4557
2.40 Sharp Minds Betfair/European Breeders Fund Maiden Stakes Fillies 2yo (D3)
£3926 £1208 £604 **6f str** **Firm 14** **+06 Fast** Centre

4330 **AMALIE 11** [5] C E Brittain 2-8-11 S Sanders 7/2: 01: Missed break, prog & ev ch halfway, styd **93+**
on to lead clr, pushed clr, eased cl-home, val 5L+: op 5/1: imprvd eff on drop to 6f, further shld suit in time:
acts on firm grnd & a gall trk: displayed a gd turn of foot & has a bright future: see 4330.
4200 **MAY MORNING 17** [12] B W Hills 2-8-11 R Hughes 5/2 FAV: 42: Prom, styd on ins fnl 1f, not pace **3** **81**
easy wnr: bckd: eff at 5f, imprvd for step up to 6f: acts on firm & gd/soft grnd: shown enough to find a mdn.
4200 **RASSEEM 17** [4] Saeed bin Suroor 2-8-11 L Dettori 11/4: 203: Led, hdd dist, no extra: clr rem: ½ **80**
eff at 5f, prob stays 6f: acts on firm & fast grnd: just btr 3576 (debut, 5f).
3761 **BRANSTON LILY 37** [10] G A Swinbank 2-8-11 Dean McKeown 8/1: 34: Handy over 4f, no extra. **6** **64**
KINDLING 0 [3]2-8-11 R Ffrench 12/1: 5: br f Dr Fong - Isle of Flame (Shirley Heights) Rear, 1¼ **60**
prog bef 1f out, nrst fin: debut: May foal, half-sister to wnrs at 7/10f: dam unrcd.
NEPAL 0 [1]2-8-11 D Mernagh 16/1: 6: ch f Monashee Mountain - Zetonic (Zafonic) Nvr nrr than nk **59**
mid-div: debut: Feb first foal, cost 10,500: dam successful at 11f: sire descent performer around 7f.
MUSARDIERE 0 [7]2-8-11 L Goncalves 28/1: 7: b f Montjeu - Majestic Image (Niniski) In rear, ½ **58**
nvr nrr than mid-div on debut: Apr foal, cost 34,000gns: half-sister to wnrs at 12/16f: dam successful numerous
times around 14f/2m: sire mulitple Gr 1 wnr at 12f: just sharper for today.
3103 **MERCARI 65** [11]2-8-11 N Pollard 66/1: 008: Handy 4f, wknd: 9 wk abs. ½ **57**
SORCERESS 0 [6]2-8-11 T E Durcan 50/1: 9: Mid-div over 4f, wknd. **6** **41**
4205 **GRACEFUL FLIGHT 17** [8]2-8-11 R Fitzpatrick 100/1: 00: 10th: Mid-div 3f, sn fdd. 13 **8**
Factual Lady 0 [13]2-8-11 K Darley 16/1:0   **Sterling Supporter 0** [9]2-8-11 L Enstone 50/1:0
12 Ran Time 1m 9.39 (0.49) Owned: Mr Saeed Manana Trained: Newmarket

4558
3.10 Sharp Minds Betfair : Best Odds/European Breeders Fund Maiden Stakes 2yo (D3)
£3926 £1208 £604 **1m1f** **Firm 14** **-26 Slow** Inside

4083 **SPEAR 24** [4] D R Loder 2-9-0 S Sanders 7/2: 231: Made all, drvn out ins fnl 1f, op 2/1, padd **84**
pick: eff at 7f, apprec step up to 9f: acts on firm & fast, disapp on hvy last time out: see 4083.
4083 **HAATMEY 24** [6] M R Channon 2-9-0 T E Durcan 9/1: 342: In tch, prog & ev ch ins fnl 1f, just shd **82**
denied: op 8/1: eff at 7f, apprec step up to 9f: acts on firm & fast grnd: again just fin bhd today's wnr in 4083.
4376 **CHINESE PUZZLE 9** [11] H R A Cecil 2-9-0 t (71) R Hughes 11/4 FAV: 66033: Rear, prog 4f out, 2½ **78**

onepcd ins fnl 1f: tchd 4/1: eff at 1m, ran to form & stays 9f.
3944 **LUNAR SKY 30** [9] C E Brittain 2-8-9 J Quinn 5/1: 064: Rear, prog after halfway, no impress ins   nk   72
fnl 1f: prob stays 9f on firm grnd: see 2863.
     TIMBER SCORPION 0 [5]2-9-0 R Ffrench 9/1: 5: b c Timber Country - Aqraba (Polish Precedent)   3   73
Prom over 7f, sn wknd: debut: Mar first foal, dam successful at 1m: sire high-class performer around 7/9f abroad.
4204 **TRIGONY 17** [3]2-9-0 K Darley 100/1: 006: In tch till halfway, no extra.   2½   69
4114 **DOUBLE KUDOS 22** [8]2-9-0 L Dettori 11/2: 207: Handy 6f, sn wknd: btr 3489 (7f).   nk   68
4257 **INDONESIA 15** [10]2-9-0 Dean McKeown 33/1: 08: Al in rear: see 4257.   3   64
4376 **BE BOP 9** [7]2-9-0 Kim Tinkler 80/1: 09: Sn in mid-div, wknd 3f out: still lkd burly.   1¼   62
     CABOPINO LAD 0 [1]2-9-0 Joanna Badger 66/1: 0: 10th: b g Comic Strip - Roxanne (Woodman)   3   57
Missed break, nvr a factor on debut: May foal, cost 7,500gns: half-brother successful at sprint dist abroad: sire
decent miler in US: with Mrs L Stubbs.
10 Ran   Time 1m 52.44 (3.64)   Owned: Highclere Thoroughbred Racing XXIV   Trained: Newmarket

---

| **4559** | 3.40 Sharp Minds Betfair : Back & Lay Handicap Stakes 3yo+ 56-70 (E3) | | [86] |
| | £7553 £2324 £1162   **1m6f19y**   **Firm 14**   **-34 Slow**   Inside | | |

4439* **INCHPAST 6** [8] M H Tompkins 3-9-1 (6ex)bl (73) L Dettori 7/4 FAV: 0412111: In tch, styd on to   81
lead 3f out, rdn out to hold on: qck reapp: well bckd: eff at 11.5f/12f, apprec recent step up to 14f, 2m shld
suit: acts on firm & gd/soft grnd: tough & progressive performer: see 4521.
4521 **MOST DEFINITELY 2** [5] T D Easterby 4-9-1 (62) T E Durcan 6/1: 2-206232: Held up, prog bef 2f   ½   68
out, styd on to chase wnr ins fnl 1f, kept on, not btn far: op 8/1: qck reapp: continues in gd form: see 4521.
3587 **DISTANT COUSIN 45** [2] M A Buckley 7-8-9 vis (56) A Culhane 20/1: 0530043: Prom, ev ch trav best   1½   58
2f out, rdn & no extr from dist: 6 wk abs: signs of encouragement today & is on a winning mark: see 1980.
4400 **BEST PORT 8** [1] J Parkes 8-9-3 (64) M Lawson(5) 7/1: 1016104: Chsd ldrs, ev ch dist, sn no extra.   ¾   67
2156 **ETCHING 103** [6]4-8-13 (60) R Hughes 12/1: 210-1005: Held up, prog 3f out, no impress when hung   1   62
right dist: long abs: just ndd race: showed more in 1399.
4255 **MASTERMAN READY 15** [4]3-8-8 (1oh) (66) E Ahern 5/1: 0060136: Cl-up over 12f, no extra: btr 4255.   nk   67
4259 **EAST CAPE 15** [10]7-8-9 (11oh) (45) Kim Tinkler 25/1: 0635247: Al in rear: stiff task from out of h'cap.   3   54
4151 **LAWRENCE OF ARABIA 20** [7]4-8-11 (58) S Sanders 5/1: 04/-06608: Led, hdd 3f out, wknd: bckd: nk   55
starting to prove disappointing: see 4151 & btr 3437.
4267 **DR COOL 15** [9]7-8-9 (1oh) (55) J Quinn 50/1: 510/-0009: Held up, nvr a factor: see 4033.   dist 28
9 Ran   Time 3m 4.52 (6.72)   Owned: Marcoe Racing Welwyn   Trained: Newmarket

---

| **4560** | 4.10 Sharp Minds Betfair Selling Handicap Stakes 3-5yo 46-55 (G4) | | [67] |
| | £3515 £1082 £541   **1m2f**   **Firm 14**   **-17 Slow**   Inside | | |

4249 **DEFANA 16** [12] M Dods 3-8-9 (48) L Enstone 12/1: 3-533061: In tch, prog 2f out, rdn out to lead   55
cl-home: no bid: eff at 10f, poss stays 12f: acts on firm & gd grnd: first win: see 3055 & 2790.
4243 **PLAUSABELLE 16** [6] T D Easterby 3-8-9 bl (48) E Ahern 7/1: 6-020032: Prom, led 3f out, hdd under   ¾   53
press well ins fnl 1f, no extra: handles firm & soft grnd: shown enough to find similar: see 4243.
3182 **ATHOLLBROSE 62** [13] T D Easterby 3-8-10 bl (49) K Darley 7/1: 2454003: Cl-up, ev ch bef 1f out,   2½   50
sn no extra: tchd 12/1: 9 wk abs: acts on firm & soft grnd: btr 1306.
4411 **ESPERANCE 7** [10] J Akehurst 4-8-13 (45) S Sanders 5/1 FAV: 5505524: Mid-div, prog 3f out, no   ¾   44
impress dist: qck reapp: btr 4411 (1m).
4440 **ACCA LARENTIA 6** [16]3-8-8 (47) Hayley Turner(3) 16/1: 0030065: Mid-div, prog 4f out, onepcd.   2½   42
3486 **ANTONY EBENEEZER 49** [4]5-8-8 (40) J Bramhill 5/1: 0150026: Rear, prog 4f out, no impress fnl 2f: shd 34
earlier hdles plcd (rtd 92h, sell h'cap): btr 3486 (12f, fibresand).
4282 **MYANNABANANA 14** [5]3-8-6 (1oh)vis (45) J Quinn 12/1: 0500007: Handy 7f, sn no extra: btr 441.   2   36
4379 **CANLIS 9** [3]5-8-8 (40) R Ffrench 8/1: 0005008: Led 7f, wknd: btr 442.   1   29
4243 **MR MOON 16** [14]3-8-0 (16oh) (30) Lisa Jones 20/1: 0006059: Missed break, nvr a factor: stiff task.   3   24
4037 **RUSSALKA 26** [8]3-8-11 vis (50) A Culhane 12/1: 0260600: 10th: Al in rear: btr 3175.   5   28
4202 **Great Blasket 17** [2]3-8-9 (48) J P Guillambert(3) 16/1:0
3499 **Dame Nova 48** [1]3-8-1 (6oh)(40) Rory Moore(5) 20/1:0
3547 **Alpha Zeta 16** [15]3-8-1 (6oh)(40) Dale Gibson 50/1:0   4103] **Amaretto Express 373** [7]5-8-8 (40) G Parkin 50/1:0
14 Ran   Time 2m 5.43 (3.13)   Owned: Denton Hall Racing Ltd   Trained: Darlington

---

| **4561** | 4.40 Sharp Minds Phone 0870 90 80 121 Maiden Stakes 3yo+ (D3) | | |
| | £3497 £1076 £538   **7f str**   **Firm 14**   **+13 Fast**   Centre | | |

3979 **MOORS MYTH 28** [1] B W Hills 3-9-0 (73) R Hughes 7/2: 0-36561: Made all, clr 2f out, eased   70
cl-home, val bit more: op 5/2: eff at 7f, has tried 1m: acts on firm & gd/soft grnd: gd confidence boost.
4216 **BORODINSKY 17** [5] R E Barr 3-9-0 (47) M Lawson(5) 25/1: 0402402: Al prom, kept on but no ch with   7   59
easy wnr fnl 2f: clr rem: acts on firm & fast grnd: see 3413.
4216 **SPEED RACER 17** [3] Don Enrico Incisa 3-8-9 (49) Kim Tinkler 33/1: 5-050363: Cl-up over 3f, sn   3½   47
outpcd, modest late gains: btr 3462.
4211 **M FOR MAGIC 17** [8] C W Fairhurst 5-9-4 (45) K Pierrepont(7) 12/1: 5045-524: Nvr nrr than mid-div.   shd 51
     ESHAADEH 0 [4]3-8-9 T L Dettori 1/3 FAV: 5: b f Storm Cat - Sarayir (Mr Prospector) In tch 5f,   hd   45
sn flashed tail & wknd: bckd at long odds-on debut: padd pick: related to wnrs at 7/10f.
3900 **COMIC TALES 32** [9]3-9-0 bl (45) S Righton 100/1: 0-6606: Missed break, nvr a factor.   4   42
4380 **DEJEEJE 9** [6]3-9-0 A Culhane 100/1: 07: Sn adrift, eased fnl 1f: still lkd in need of race.   28   2
7 Ran   Time 1m 21.90 (0.10)   Owned: Mr K Abdulla   Trained: Lambourn

4562 5.10 Sharp Minds Betfair Apprentice Handicap Stakes 3yo+ 56-70 (E3) [82]
£3749 £1154 £577 6f str Firm 14 +09 Fast Centre

4175 **BOWLING ALONG 18** [2] M E Sowersby 3-8-3 (57) T Dean(7) 33/1: 0432001: Cl-up, prog 2f out, rdn out   65
to lead cl-home: eff at 5/7f on firm & gd/soft grnd: acts on a gall or sharp trk: see 3655 & 3213.

4408 **ON THE TRAIL 7** [1] D W Chapman 7-8-2 (54) Liam Jones(4) 9/1: 3311452: Handy, ev ch dist, kept on ¾ 58
ins fnl 1f, not pace wnr: qck reapp: acts on firm, gd/soft & both AWs: see 4240 & 3974.

3503 **WINTHORPE 48** [16] J J Quinn 4-9-2 (68) K Ghunowa(4) 9/1: 3205443: Mid-div, prog bef 1f out, nrst hd 71
fin: 7 wk abs: tchd 12/1: acts on firm, soft grnd & fibresand: slipped to a fair mark: see 3427 & 2942.

4278 **FLYING BANTAM 14** [14] R A Fahey 3-9-1 (69) N Lawes(7) 14/1: 2402404: Prom, led 3f out, hdd ins ¾ 70
fnl 1f, no extra: not disgraced: btr 3684.

4398 **BANJO BAY 8** [5]6-8-13 (65) P J Benson(7) 8/1: 0600005: Mid-div, prog when short of room dist, nk 65
switched & kept on: signs of encouragement here & v well h'capped on old form: see 4398 & 2704.

4339 **SNOW BUNTING 11** [9]6-8-9 (61) T Block(4) 9/2: 0533406: Nvr nrr than mid-div: btr 3584. 1½ 57

4514* **JILLY WHY 2** [13]3-9-5 (6ex) (73) R J Killoran(4) 5/1: 40-04117: Nvr nrr than mid-div: warm in ½ 68
padd on qck reapp: poss too sn after recent win in 4514.

3796 **HAULAGE MAN 37** [10]6-8-6 p (58) W Hogg 4/1 FAV: 0-020208: Slow away, nvr nrr than mid-div. nk 52

2053 **GLOBAL ACHIEVER 108** [3]3-8-6 (60) Dean Williams 33/1: 2100009: Prom 4f, wknd: long abs. 5 40

3984 **FINGER OF FATE 36** [8]4-8-2 (9oh)bl (45) M Nem(7) 33/1: 6003030: 10th: Led 3f, grad wknd: btr 3984. 1 31

4038 **MIMIC 26** [15]4-9-2 (68) R Mills(4) 12/1: 0000150: 11th: Al in rear: btr 3888. 1¼ 41

4321 **Park Ave Princess 12** [11]3-8-4 (58) J D O'Reilly 20/1:0
1198 **Simply The Guest 151** [4]5-8-7 t(59) Janice Webster(7) 66/1:0
4466} **Whittle Warrior 353** [6]4-8-13 (65) K Pierrepont(4) 66/1:0
3767 **Pride Of Kinloch 37** [7]4-8-5 (57) A Reilly(4) 16/1:0
15 Ran Time 1m 9.25(0.35) Owned: Keith Brown Properties (Hull) Ltd Trained: York

Official Going Good

4563 2.05 Gr 3 Prix d'Arenberg 2yo ()
£25704 £10282 £7711 5f110y str Good

TOUPIE F Rohaut 2-8-8 J B Eyquem 213/10: 115251: Trkd ldrs, chall over 1f out, rdn & held on 108
gamely ins last: eff at 5/6f on gd & hvy grnd, likes a gall trk: v useful filly.

CROSSOVER H A Pantall 2-8-8 T Jarnet 81/10: 522: Trkd ldrs, styd on well from over 1f out, just held. snk 107

365 **SALUT THOMAS** R Collet 2-8-11 bl C Soumillon 94/10: 3135363: Hled up, kept on from over 1f out, hd 109
nrst fin & only just held in a thrilling fin.

4123* **KEY SECRET 16** 2-8-8 (80) Hayley Turner 101/10: 1114416: Cl up, rdn & no extra dist: see 4123. 3½ 95

4155 **SIENA GOLD 18** 2-8-8 J F McDonald 22/1: 1101847: Led 1f, dsptd lead to halfway, sn lost place. 2 89

4123 **COUNTDOWN 16** 2-8-11 bl (87) T Thulliez 6/1: 321128: Dsptd lead till halfway, sn lost place. snk 91
9 Ran Time 1m 02.90() Owned: J Gispert Trained: France

Official Going Good

4564 1.50 Gr 3 Prix la Rochette 2yo ()
£25704 £10282 £7711 7f rnd Good

EARLY MARCH Mme C Head Maarek 2-8-11 O Peslier 38/10: 11: br c Dansili - Emplane (Irish 115
River) Led, in command ins last under hand riding; remains unbeaten, a winner on debut at Clairefontaine prev: eff
over a gall 7f on good ground: well regarded juv who should rate higher.

STOP MAKING SENSE A Fabre 2-8-11 C Soumillon 8/5 FAV: 3112: Dwelt, held up in tch, styd on late. 1½ 109

OSIDY X Nakkachdji 2-8-11 G Benoist 113/10: 1153: Rear, kept on fnl 2f, not able to land a blow. hd 108
6 Ran Time 1m 22.20 () Owned: K Abdulla Trained: France

4565 2.50 Gr 3 Prix de Lutece 3yo ()
£25704 £10282 £7711 1m7f Good

ETENDARD INDIEN A Fabre 3-8-9 C Soumiillon 62/10: -0151: b c Selkirk - Danseuse Indienne 113
(Danehill) Led after 1f & dictated pace, qcknd from 5f out, rdn & styd on well: 10f wnr at Maisons Laffitte earlier
this term: now suited by 15f & acts on gd, handles soft: lightly raced & progressive stayer.

2308 **REEFSCAPE 95** A Fabre 3-8-9 T Gillet 1/1 FAV: 25-31102: Early leader, soon trkd wnr, outpcd 3f 2 109
out, kept on ins last, not able to chall: 3 mth abs: styd longer 15f trip: see 2308.

DOUBLE GREEN F Head 3-8-6 O Peslier 3/1: 3334113: Held up, hdwy to chse ldr 3f out, no impress. 1½ 104
6 Ran Time 3m 29.00 () Owned: Baron E de Rothschild Trained: France

Official Going Soft

4566   **2.15 Gr 2 Prix Niel 3yo** ()
£44155 £17042 £8134   **1m4f**   **Soft**

3316* **VALIXIR** 60 A Fabre 3-9-2 E Legrix 36/10: 12-13311: Chsd ldrs, rdn & chall over 1f out, drvn to   121
lead close home: 2 mth abs: suited by 10/12f on fast & soft ground: likes a gall trk: goes well fresh: v smart colt
who heads now for the Arc in fine form: see 3316 (Gr 2).
2824* **PROSPECT PARK** 77 C Laffon Parias 3-9-2 O Peslier 7/2: 3-112212: Trkd ldrs & led over 2f out,   nse   120
joined over 1f out & just denied close home: abs: tough & high-class: see 2824 (Gr 3).
4002 **BAGO** 26 J E Pease 3-9-2 T Gillet 14/10 JT FAV: 1111-1133: Held up, eff 2f out, onepace: styd   1   119
this longer 12f trip but just btr 4002 & 2825 (10f).
2308 **LORD DU SUD** 98 J C Rouget 3-9-2 I Mendizabal 84/10: 1-11164: Held up, kept on fnl 2f, not pace   nk   117
of front pair: not beaten far & clr of remaining quartet: 3 mth abs: ahead of today's rnr up in 1852 (C/D).
8 Ran   Time 2m 29.40 ()   Owned: Lagardere Family   Trained: France

4567   **2.51 Gr 1 Prix Vermeille Fillies 3 & 4yo** ()
£100599 £40246 £20123   **1m4f**   **Soft**

3837 **SWEET STREAM** 36 J E Hammond 4-9-2 T Gillet 308/10: 3311-031: Mid-div, pushed along over 3f out   117
& hdwy over 2f out, rdn to lead ins last: Listed wnr in '03: suited by 12f, acts on gd/sft, loves soft & hvy: v smart.
3317 **ROYAL FANTASY** 36 H Steinmetz 4-9-2 E Botti 44/1: 1111-252: Mid-div, rdn to chall over 1f out, kept on. ½   115
4160 **PRIDE** 21 A de Royer Dupre 4-9-2 (80) D Bonilla 40/1: 0-413523: Rear, drvn & styd on late to   ½   114
take 3rd, not rch wnr: eff at 10/12f: see 1699 (Gr 3).
     VALLERA 21 U Ostmann 3-8-7 A Boschert 26/1: 2-330114: b f Monsun - Val d'Etoile (Big Shuffle)   snk   113
Mid-div, styd on for press fnl 2f, not rch ldrs: German trained filly, Gr 3 success at Hamburg & Bremen earlier this
term: eff at 11/12f on good & sft ground: not beaten far & evidently a smart filly.
     DIAMOND TANGO 19 3-8-7 O Peslier 87/10: 1545: Held up, late prog, not land a blow.   hd   112
4310* **SILVERSKAYA** 19 3-8-7 I Mendizabal 64/10: 1111016: Mid-div, kept on for press, nrst fin.   snk   111
3012 **VISORAMA** 36 4-9-2 E Legrix 87/1: 11-52307: Held up, late prog, nvr dangerous.   hd   110
2460* **LATICE** 91 3-8-7 C Soumillon 1/1 FAV: 11-118: Trkd ldrs, led over 2f out till well ins last: shd   110
lost her unbeaten record today: only btn arnd 2L & stayed longer 12f trip but btr 2460 (10.5f).
4160* **WHORTLEBERRY** 21 4-9-2 bl C P Lemaire 133/10: 1-441619: Mid-div, no impress fnl 2f: btr 4160.   2½   106
13 Ran   Time 2m 29.50 ()   Owned: Team Valor   Trained: France

4568   **3.20 Gr 2 Prix Foy 4yo+** ()
£44155 £17042 £8134   **1m4f**   **Soft**

3012 **POLICY MAKER** 70 E Lellouche 4-9-2 O Peslier 11/8 FAV: 110-5121: Made all, pushed along fnl 2f   119+
but always in command, readily: 10 wk abs: suited by 12f on good & soft ground: high class colt who won this
stylishly although today's jockey reportedly prefers Prospect Park for the Arc.
3012 **SHORT PAUSE** 70 A Fabre 5-9-2 T Gillet 4/1: 42-31342: Trkd ldr, rdn over 1f out, styd on but   2   115
nvr able to chall wnr: 10 wk abs: suited by 12f & stays 2459.
4220 **NYSAEAN** 15 R Hannon 5-9-2 (114) J Fortune 13/2: 45213453: Trkd ldr, kept on press, always held.   1½   113
3012 **POLISH SUMMER** 70 A Fabre 7-9-2 C Soumillon 2/1: 12-11504: Rear, nvr able to mount a chall: 10   ¾   112
wk abs: bhd this front pair when last seen & may be best on a faster surface: btr 990 (fast).
4 Ran   Time 2m 38.70 ()   Owned: Ecurie Wildenstein   Trained: France

4569   **4.35 Gr 3 Prix Gladiateur 4yo+** ()
£25704 £10282 £7711   **1m7f110y**   **Soft**

2518 **WESTERNER** 70 E Lellouche 5-9-6 O Peslier 17/10: 11-12201: Held up, hdwy over 2f out & chall   122
over 1f out, rdn & led dist, held on all out: 10 wk abs: suited by 15f+, stays stiff 2m4f well: acts on fast, loves
gd/sft & soft: high class performance under topweight, hard to beat once again in Prix Cadran next month.
4161 **CUT QUARTZ** 21 R Gibson 7-8-13 T Jarnet 81/10: -0111432: Held up in tch, hdwy over 1f out &   snk   114
strong run for press ins last, just failed: smart effort: see 4161 (Gr 2).
3317 **CLEAR THINKING** 21 A Fabre 4-8-13 C Soumillon 1/2 FAV: 15333303: Handy & chsd ldr halfway, hdwy 2½   111
to lead 2f out, no extra: also bhd this wnr in 2000.
4161* **GOLD MEDALLIST** 21 4-9-4 (100) J Fortune 37/10: 603-60415: Led till 2f out, no extra dist: see 4161. 2   114
8 Ran   Time 3m 26.60()   Owned: Ecurie Wildenstein   Trained: France

Official Going Firm

4570   **3.30 Gr 2 Bosphorus Cup 3yo+** ()
£83799 £33520 £16760   **1m4f**   **Firm**

2636* **SENEX** H Blume 4-9-6 W Mongil 33/4: 226-33511: German raider.   118
3660 **MAKTUB** 41 M A Jarvis 5-9-6 (110) T Jarnet 95/20: 200-062022: Trkd ldr, led over 1f out, hdd   ½   116
well ins last: 6 wk abs: acts on firm & hvy: another smart run: see 3660, 2636.
2141* **TOUCH OF LAND** 4-9-6 H A Pantall 4-9-6 C P Lemaire 95/20: 0311240313: No extra well in last.   1   115
11 Ran   Time 2m 26.47()   Owned: Stall Meerbusch   Trained: Germany

LEOPARDSTOWN   SATURDAY 11.09.04   Lefthand, Galloping Track

Official Going Good/Firm

4571   3.31 Gr 1 Irish Champion Stakes 3yo+   ()
£387930 £126630 £59630   1m2f   Good/Firm

2469* **AZAMOUR 88** John M Oxx 3-8-11   M J Kinane 8/1: 11-3211: b c Night Shift - Asmara (Lear Fan)   **124**
Rear, rdn & strong run for press from over 1f out to lead ins last: 12 wk abs: eff at 1m, relished this step up
to 10f, shld get 12f: acts on fast & gd/sft: goes well fresh: top-class & still improving, more Gr 1's to be won.
1 Jun'04 Asco 8g/f 123-0 A: 2 May'04 Curr 8g/f 118- : 1 Oct'03 Curr 8g/s 110- :
4002 **NORSE DANCER 25** D R C Elsworth 4-9-4 (116) J F Egan 20/1: 43044122: Trkd ldrs, rdn & hdwy to   ½   **122**
lead ins last, hdd cl home: most tough & more reliable of late: high class performer: see 4002, 3886.
4014 **POWERSCOURT 28** A P O'Brien 4-9-4 BL J P Spencer 11/1: 13-125243: Trkd ldr, led over 2f out, hdd   nk   **121**
ins last, no extra nr fin: vis omitted but another fine run with 1st time blnks: see 4014. 4014.
2822* **GREY SWALLOW 76** D K Weld 3-8-11   P J Smullen 9/2: -14314: Held up, kept on for press, not pace   ¾   **120**
to chall: 10 wk abs: gd run, next month's Arc is reportedly the main target this autumn: see 2822 (Irish Derby, 12f).
2916 **RAKTI 70** 5-9-4 (121) P Robinson 5/1: 0/1212-185: Held up, kept on for press, not able to land a   ½   **119**
blow: 10 wk abs: reportedly banged his head leaving the stalls, settled better today but btr 2488.
4323 **IMPERIAL DANCER 10** 6-9-4 (110) S Hitchcott 66/1: 36003036: Rear, rdn & no impress on ldrs: needs   2   **116**
Gr 2/ Gr3 company: see 4323, 3662 & 1230.
3442* **DOYEN 49** 4-9-4 (124) L Dettori 4/5 FAV: 1124-2117: Trkd ldrs, btn 2f out & eased down ins last: **0**
7 wk abs: connections puzzled by this well below par display: v impressive 3442 (King George).
4002 **MILLSTREET 25** 5-9-4 t (110) T E Durcan 100/1: 46240-058: Ked till over 2f out, sn btn & eased: **0**
pacemaker for stablemate Doyen: see 4002, 3563.
8 Ran   Time 2m 01.90 ()   Owned: H H Aga Khan   Trained: Currabeg

4572   4.10 Gr 1 Pegasus Matron Stakes Fillies & Mares 3yo+   ()
£113230 £33098 £15678   1m   Good/Firm

3533+ **SOVIET SONG 45** J R Fanshawe 4-9-2 (115) J P Murtagh 8/13 FAV: 5-2312111: Settled towards rear,   **122**
hdwy over 2f out & rdn to lead well ins last: 6 wk abs: 3 successive Gr 1 victories: suited by 1m on firm or soft
ground, any trk: most tough & high class, has a turn of foot & shld remain hard to beat: see 3533, 3004.
4017 **ATTRACTION 27** M Johnston 3-8-11 (119) K Darley 7/2: 11-111202: Tried to make all, drvn & hdd   ½   **120**
well ins last: clr rem: best 3yo miler but keeps finding Soviet Song too gd: back to form after flopping on soft.
3564* **PHANTOM WIND 43** J H M Gosden 3-8-11 (98) R Hughes 9/1: 01-6513: Trkd ldrs, kept on for press   5   **110**
but no chance with the front pair at the distance: abs: longr trip & needs an ease in grade: see 3564 (Gr 3, 7f).
3318* **RED FEATHER 56** E Lynam 3-8-11 t N G McCullagh 20/1: 20-21314: Chsd ldrs, rdn & btn over 1f out.   4½   **101**
4915} **YESTERDAY 322** 4-9-2   J P Spencer 7/1: 124223-5: b f Sadler's Wells - Jude (Darshaan) Chsd ldrs,   3½   **94**
rdn & btn 2f out: belated reappearance, reportedly nearly died earlier this year from colitis: Gr 1 Irish 1000
Guineas wnr in '03, subs Gr 1 rnr up on 3 occasions, incl Epsom Oaks: Gr 2 plcd '03 (rtd 106): eff btwn 1m & 12f on
firm & soft, any trk: formerly high class. 2 Oct'03 Long 10sft 117- A: 2 Sep'03 Long 12g/s 118- :
2 Jun'03 Epso 12.0g/f 115-0 A: 1 May'03 Curr 8sft 118- A: 2 Aug'02 Curr 7sft 100- :
6 Ran   Time 1m 36.80()   Owned: Ellite Racing Club   Trained: Newmarket

TABY   SUNDAY 12.09.04

Official Going Fast

4573   2.15 Listed Nickes Minneslopning 3yo+   ()
£11646 £5823 £2795   1m rnd   Fast

3775 **VORTEX 36** Miss Gay Kelleway 5-9-4 (103) N Cordrey 4/6 FAV: 01302421: Trkd ldr, led 2f out, all   **106a**
out to hold on close home, gamely: eff at 7f/8.5f on firm, gd & loves AW surface, any trk: v tough & useful.
       HOVMAN Ms C Erichsen 5-9-4 M Larsen : 2: Just denied close home by the British raider.   hd   **105a**
3123] **HANZANO** A Hyldmo 6-9-4 (95) K Andersen : 3440103: No extra close home.   2   **99a**
10 Ran   Time 1m 39.90 ()   Owned: Coriolis Partnership   Trained: Newmarket

TABY   SUNDAY 12.09.04

Official Going Good

4574   3.45 Gr 3 Stockholm Cup International 3yo+   ()
£31056 £15528 £7453   1m4f   Good

4023 **COLLIER HILL 25** G A Swinbank 6-9-4 (103) Dean McKeown 92/10: 03-014391: Rear, hdwy to chall   **108**
dist, drvn & led line, all out: eff at 7f/8.5f on firm, gd & loves AW surface, any trk: v tough & smart.
4019* **FOREIGN AFFAIRS 28** Sir Mark Prescott 6-9-4 (102) S Sanders 9/5: 5-1345112: Led, drvn & caught   shd   **107**
line: tough & smart: see 4019 (Listed).
1697 **MANDRAKE EL MAGO** F Castro 5-9-4 M Santos 7/10 FAV: 23: Mid-div, hdwy to chall 2f out, onepace.   2   **104**
9 Ran   Time 2m 27.80()   Owned: R H Hall & Ashley Young   Trained: Melsonby

SALISBURY TUESDAY 14.09.04 Righthand, Galloping Track, Stiff Finish

Official Going Soft (Good/Soft Places)

4575 **1.40 Racing Uk On Channel 432 Median Auction Maiden Stakes Div 1 2yo (E3)**
£3666 £1128 £564 **6f212y str** **Soft 114** **-04 Slow** Centre

BRECON 0 [8] D R C Elsworth 2-8-9 T Quinn 12/1: 1: ch f Unfuwain - Welsh Valley (Irish River) **80+**
Rear, prog halfway, kept on to lead cl-home, pushed out: debut: Feb first foal, dam plcd at 6f: sire decent mid-dist performer: eff at 7f, 1m sure to suit: acts on soft grnd & a stiff/gall trk: goes well fresh: showed signs of greenness & looks sure to impr with more experience.
2695 **HAWRIDGE STAR 82** [5] W S Kittow 2-9-0 W Supple 9/1: 62: b c Alzao - Serenity (Selkirk) Held up, prog 3f out, kept on to lead ins fnl 1f, hdd cl-home: op 12/1, 12 wk abs: Feb foal, half-brother successful at 1m: dam successful at 6f: eff at 7f, will apprec further: acts on soft: win sn. *nk* **83**
ASTRONOMICAL 0 [2] B W Hills 2-9-0 M Hills 15/2: 3: b c Mister Baileys - Charm The Stars (Roi Danzig) Rear, prog halfway, styd on to lead well over 1f out, hdd ins fnl 1f, not btn far in 3rd: debut: Apr foal, cost 14,000gns: half-brother to wnrs at 7f/12f: dam unplcd: sire Gr 1 wnr at 1m: eff at 7f, bred to apprec further: acts on soft grnd: gd start to career & looks sure to impr & find a race. *½* **82**
VILLARRICA 0 [4] Sir Michael Stoute 2-8-9 K Fallon 7/2 FAV: 4: ch f Selkirk - Melikah (Lammtarra) Missed break, prog in mid-div after 1f, prog ins fnl 1f, nrst fin: debut: Feb first foal, dam useful performer at mid-dists: eff at 7f, 1m+ will suit: acts on soft grnd: improve. *½* **76**
4242 **TOHAMA 17** [10]2-8-9 R L Moore 5/1: 605: In tch when short of room dist, sn onepcd: eff at 7f on soft. *1¼* **72**
4330 **TIGGERS TOUCH 12** [1]2-8-9 Dane O'Neill 7/1: 406: Led, hdd 5f out, led again 3f out, hdd well over 1f out, no extra: improving with racing & now quals for h'caps: see 3863. *½* **73**
4443 **BEST GAME 7** [6]2-9-0 J Fortune 50/1: 07: Chsd ldrs over 5f, wknd: qck reapp. *5* **68**
3882 **WHITLAND 33** [9]2-9-0 t R Havlin 100/1: 08: Missed break, nvr nrr than mid-div. *1* **66$**
3330 **SAMSON QUEST 55** [7]2-9-0 Martin Dwyer 6/1: 59: Led after 2f, hdd 3f out, sn wknd: 8 wk abs. *1¾* **62**
FINAL PROMISE 0 [15]2-9-0 S Carson 50/1: 0: 10th: Al in rear on debut. *2½* **57**
3478 **RUM CREEK 50** [3]2-9-0 P Dobbs 33/1: 000: 11th: In tch till halfway, wknd. *1¾* **53**
3126 **PATRONOFCONFUCIUS 66** [13]2-9-0 D Sweeney 66/1: 00: 12th: Handy over 5f, fdd. *10* **35**
3368 **GOLD MAJESTY 54** [12]2-8-9 S Hitchcott 50/1: 0000: 13th: In tch 4f, wknd. *1¼* **28**
MELS MOMENT 0 [11]2-9-0 S Drowne 10/1: 0: 14th: Mid-div, wknd 3f out: debut. *6* **22**
14 Ran Time 1m 33.78 (8.28) Owned: Mr K J Mercer & Mrs S Mercer Trained: Whitsbury

4576 **2.10 Racing Uk On Channel 432 Median Auction Maiden Stakes Div 2 2yo (E3)**
£3666 £1128 £564 **6f212y str** **Soft 114** **-24 Slow** Centre

4190 **PALATINATE 18** [4] H Candy 2-9-0 Dane O'Neill 9/4 FAV: 431: Keen bhd, prog 3f out, ev ch dist, rdn out to lead cl-home: bckd: eff at 6f, suited by 7f, further shld suit: acts on gd, soft grnd & stiff/gall trk. **86**
4443 **WOTCHALIKE 7** [12] D R C Elsworth 2-9-0 J Fortune 11/2: 502: Led till halfway, led again 2f out, hdd under press cl-home: op 7/1, qck reapp: eff at 7f, further will suit: acts on soft grnd: find similar. *nk* **84**
3473 **SALINJA 51** [5] Mrs A J Perrett 2-9-0 S Drowne 5/2: 33: In tch, ev ch bef 1f out, sn onepcd: bckd, 7 wk abs: eff at 6f, ran to form on step up to 7f: acts on fast & soft grnd: see 3473. *1½* **81**
4234 **ZEENA 17** [10] M P Tregoning 2-8-9 Martin Dwyer 7/1: 54: Held up, prog 3f out, nrst fin: 'hung left'. *3½* **69**
4356 **BYRON BAY 11** [1]2-9-0 J F McDonald(3) 100/1: 005: In tch, led halfway, hdd 2f out, no extra: imprvd eff today & now quals for h'caps: see 4356. *½* **73$**
4297 **MERRYMADCAP 15** [6]2-9-0 (63) T Quinn 33/1: 056606: Nvr nrr than mid-div: see 2263. *¾* **71**
4233 **ELECTION SEEKER 17** [11]2-9-0 R L Moore 20/1: 0007: b g Intikhab - Scottish Eyes (Green Dancer) In tch 4f, sn outpcd, rallied late: Feb foal, half-brother successful at 1m/9f: dam unrcd. *hd* **70$**
4269 **MONAD 15** [13]2-8-9 R Havlin 100/1: 008: Handy over 5f, no extra: now quals for h'caps. *1¼* **63**
3882 **BACKSTREET LAD 33** [3]2-9-0 G Baker 50/1: 09: b c Fraam - Forest Fantasy (Rambo Dancer) Missed break, nvr a factor: Mar foal, half-brother successful at 5f: dam wnr at 1m/9f: sire useful performer around 1m. *¾* **66**
4484 **MANORSHIELD MINX 5** [8]2-8-9 P Dobbs 20/1: 000: 10th: Handy 5f, wknd. *1* **59**
4359 **GRAND GIRL 11** [14]2-8-9 A Daly 100/1: 00: 11th: Missed break, nvr a factor. *hd* **58**
3883 **Thorny Mandate 33** [9]2-9-0 S Carson 50/1:0 **Mister Troubridge 0** [2]2-9-0 R Thomas(3) 16/1:0
13 Ran Time 1m 35.16 (9.66) Owned: Crichel Racing Trained: Wantage

4577 **2.40 Sydenhams Maiden Stakes 2yo (D2)**
£5844 £1798 £899 **6f str** **Soft 114** **-10 Slow** Centre

3163 **LOADERFUN 64** [2] H Candy 2-9-0 Dane O'Neill 2/1 FAV: 421: Made all, went clr ins fnl 2f, eased cl-home, val more: 9 wk abs: eff at 5f, suited by 6f: acts on firm & gd, imprvd today for soft grnd: acts on a sharp or stiff/gall trk: goes well fresh: won with authority, win more races. **100+**
ANCHOR DATE 0 [4] B W Hills 2-9-0 R Hughes 5/1: 2: b c Zafonic - Fame At Last (Quest For Fame) Missed break, bhd, plenty to do no room bef 1f out, kept on for clr 2nd ins fnl 1f under hands & heels: clr rem on debut: Apr first foal, dam successful at 7f: sire Gr 1 wnr at 1m: eff at 6f, 7f/1m will suit: acts on soft grnd: not given hard time today & a sure-fire improver. *5* **85+**
3280 **DESERT DEMON 59** [1] B W Hills 2-9-0 M Hills 11/4: 53: Keen in tch, no extra bef 1f out: 8 wk abs: ruined ch by failing to settle in today's soft grnd: showed more in 3280 (fast). *3½* **75**
2364 **DRUM DANCE 95** [5] R F Johnson Houghton 2-9-0 S Carson 4/1: 224: Handy over 4f, wknd dist: long abs: rcd far too keenly on first try at 6f: showed more in 2364 (5f, gd). *1* **72**
4200 **AUWITESWEETHEART 18** [9]2-8-9 S Drowne 12/1: 555: Cl-up over 4f, wknd: see 4200. *hd* **66**
1716 **WOOD SPIRIT 124** [7]2-8-9 R Havlin 16/1: 66: b f Woodborough - Windomen (Forest Wind) Missed break, nvr a factor: long abs: reportedly did not handle today's grnd: Apr first foal, cost E4,500: dam unrcd. *½* **65**
BELLE CHANSON 0 [3]2-8-9 D Sweeney 33/1: 7: b f Kingsinger - Tallulah Belle (Crowning Honors) Bhd, nvr a factor: debut: May first foal, dam successful at 6/11f: sire useful 1m performer: with J R Boyle. *¾* **63**
4233 **PLAY UP POMPEY 17** [8]2-9-0 (58) J F McDonald(3) 100/1: 000008: Chsd ldrs, wknd 2f out. *3* **59**
8 Ran Time 1m 19.54 (7.44) Owned: Paul & Linda Dixon Trained: Wantage

SALISBURY TUESDAY 14.09.04 Righthand, Galloping Track, Stiff Finish

4578

3.10 Herbert H Harrison 90th Birthday Maiden Stakes Fillies 3yo (D3)
£5727 £1762 £881 **1m str** **Soft 114** **-05 Slow** Far side

2342 **ZAMEYLA 96** [4] M A Jarvis 3-8-11 (74) P Robinson 100/30: 0221: Handy, switched far side after halfway, sn led, went clr ins fnl 1f, rdn out: long abs: eff at 7f, apprec step up to 1m: acts on firm & fast, imprvd today for switch to soft grnd: acts on a stiff/gall or fair trk, goes well fresh: clearly at home in the mud. **85**
3921 **WOODLAND GLADE 32** [11] R Hannon 3-8-11 J Fortune 11/4 FAV: 22: In tch, styd centre, kept on to chase wnr well over 1f out, al held: clr rem: eff at 7f, ran to form on step up to 1m: acts on gd & soft grnd: again shaped with promise & can find a race: see 3921. *5* **76**
3780 **ELA PAPAROUNA 38** [7] H Candy 3-8-11 (72) Dane O'Neill 100/30: 3063233: Cl-up, led halfway, hdd well over 2f out, wknd: bckd: shade below form in today's soft grnd: showed more 3780 & 3346 (fast). *4* **68**
1511 **DANDYGREY RUSSETT 134** [1] G L Moore 3-8-11 R L Moore 10/1: 044: Missed break, nvr nrr than mid-div: long abs: now quals for h'caps: see 1511. *4* **60**
4135 **ELUSIVE KITTY 22** [6]3-8-11 (68) K Fallon 13/2: 55-6R335: Missed break, sn mid-div, onepcd fnl 2f. *nk* **59**
3783 **CEMGRAFT 38** [5]3-8-11 S Drowne 33/1: 506: Al in rear: see 3335. *7* **48**
4899} **SHES A FOX 323** [3]3-8-11 P Dobbs 100/1: 0-7: b f Wizard King - Foxie Lady (Wolfhound) Bhd, nvr a factor on reapp: unplcd sole '03 start (rtd 22): with A W Carroll. *¾* **46**
4081 **SABANDER BAY 25** [9]3-8-11 R Havlin 20/1: 08: Missed break, sn in tch, wknd bef 2f out. *5* **37**
4388 **SUPAMACH 10** [12]3-8-11 (63) T Quinn 25/1: 344009: In tch 4f, sn wknd: 'lost action'. *24* **0**
4315 **MAD 13** [10]3-8-11 S Carson 66/1: 00: 10th: Sn led, hdd halfway, fdd. *1¼* **0**
10 Ran Time 1m 48.63 (9.53) Owned: Sheikh Ahmed Al Maktoum Trained: Newmarket

4579

3.40 Milford Hall Hotel Claiming Stakes 3yo (E3)
£3497 £1076 £538 **1m4f** **Soft 114** **+19 Fast** Stands side

4274 **FORT CHURCHILL 15** [9] M H Tompkins 3-9-5 bl (71) P Robinson 3/1: 0-534201: Made all, clr fnl 3f, eased ins fnl 1f, readily: fast time: clmd for £31,000: eff at 11.5f/12f on fm & soft grnd: eff with blnks: imprvd eff on drop to claim grade & enjoyed today's mud: see 3929. **86**
4033 **PERSIAN GENIE 27** [2] G B Balding 3-8-6 (60) R Havlin 12/1: 0-000002: In tch, prog to chase ldr well over 1f out, al well held: see 3186. *13* **57**
4487 **GO GREEN 5** [6] P D Evans 3-8-4 t (55) F P Ferris(3) 7/1: 1432603: Rear, prog halfway, no impress fnl 2f: qck reapp: showed more in 4145 (10f). *3* **53**
3051 **VARUNI 68** [5] J G Portman 3-8-7 (57) T Quinn 9/1: 1020054: Cl-up 10f, fdd: 10 wk abs: btr 1165. *1¾* **53**
1790 **SILKEN JOHN 120** [1]3-9-0 G Baker 50/1: 05: Nvr nrr than mid-div: long abs. *1¾* **57**
4235 **PANGLOSS 17** [3]3-9-2 bl (62) R L Moore 11/4 FAV: 3050456: Rear, hdwy 4f out, hung right & wknd bef 1f out: bckd: disapp run in today's soft grnd: btr 1260. *nk* **58**
2978 **SIGNORA PANETTIERA 71** [4]3-8-4 (40) S Hitchcott 25/1: 0-606007: Chsd ldrs over 6f, wknd: 10 wk abs. *1½* **44**
4195 **HOH BLEU DEE 18** [7]3-8-10 (73) J Fortune 4/1: 6021048: Bhd, prog 5f out, fdd bef 2f out: btr 3453. *nk* **49**
4315 **CHARING CROSS 13** [8]3-8-9 R Brisland 25/1: 009: Al in rear: see 4315. *3* **44**
4281 **PAGAN CEREMONY 15** [10]3-8-11 S Drowne 25/1: 0-00: 10th: Cl-up over 1m, fdd. *3* **42**
10 Ran Time 2m 43.86 (11.46) Owned: Mr P H Betts Trained: Newmarket

4580

4.10 Axminster Carpets Nursery Handicap Stakes 2yo 0-85 (D3) **[87]**
£5077 £1562 £781 **1m str** **Soft 114** **-23 Slow** Far side

4329 **SOMETHING EXCITING 12** [7] D R C Elsworth 2-8-12 (71) J Fortune 12/1: 4001: Held up, prog wide 2f out, pushed out to lead cl-home, val 3L+: apprec step up to 1m, acts on soft grnd & a stiff/gall trk: unexposed in h'cap grade & appreciated today's stamina test: see 3252 (debut). **83**
4363 **WILLIAM TELL 11** [5] M R Channon 2-9-3 (76) T Dean(7) 25/1: 6452: Held up, prog halfway, styd on to lead 2f out, hung left & hdd dist, no extra well ins fnl 1f: eff at 1m on soft grnd: gd eff on h'cap bow: see 3267. *1¾* **83**
4040 **GUINEA A MINUTE 26** [4] M L W Bell 2-8-2 (61) Hayley Turner(3) 11/1: 036653: In tch, ev ch well over 1f out, sn hung left, no extra cl home: eff at 7f, stays 1m: acts on soft grnd & fibresand. *nk* **67**
4363* **BATHWICK FINESSE 11** [8] B R Millman 2-9-6 (79) G Baker 12/1: 014: Chsd ldrs, styd on for press to lead dist, hdd well ins fnl 1f, no extra: acts on gd/soft & soft grnd: gd run on h'cap bow: ran to form of 4363. *nk* **84**
4177 **HAWRIDGE KING 19** [11]2-8-9 (68) W Supple 20/1: 35655: Handy over 6f, no extra: clr rem: btr 1964. *2½* **68**
3883 **SCARLET INVADER 33** [6]2-9-7 (80) T Quinn 7/1: 4026: Nvr nrr than mid-div: first try at 1m & is prob unsuited by today's grnd: showed more in 3883 (7f, gd). *8* **66**
4297* **TORRENS 15** [10]2-9-6 (79) K Fallon 13/8 FAV: 417: Chsd ldrs 6f, fdd: v well bckd on h'cap bow: reportedly nvr trav & is prob unsuited by today's soft grnd: showed more in 4297 (mdn, gd/soft). *hd* **64**
3682 **BESPOKE 41** [2]2-8-3 (62) J Mackay 10/1: 5608: Missed break, sn in tch, wknd bef 1f out: 6 wk abs. *1¾* **43**
4233 **SIR MONTY 17** [1]2-9-0 (73) S Drowne 13/2: 5649: Chsd ldrs over 5f, wknd: btr 4233 (gd/soft). *¾* **52**
4269* **BRIANNSTA 15** [12]2-9-7 (80) S Hitchcott 9/1: 65210: 10th: Led 7f out, hdd 2f out, fdd: btr 4269 (7f, gd). *1½* **57**
3671 **WORTH A GRAND 42** [3]2-8-7 (66) R Thomas(3) 20/1: 0550: 11th: Led, hdd after 1f, fdd halfway: abs. *8* **29**
3467 **BENEDICT BAY 51** [13]2-8-11 (70) S Carson 40/1: 6000: 12th: Al bhd: 7 wk abs. *3* **27**
12 Ran Time 1m 50.07 (10.97) Owned: Setsquare Recruitment Trained: Whitsbury

4581

4.40 Wadworth 6x Classified Stakes 3yo+ 0-70 (E3)
£5571 £1714 £857 **1m str** **Soft 114** **-07 Slow** Far side

4228 **HIGH RESERVE 17** [8] J R Fanshawe 3-8-10 (70) O Urbina 11/4: 35-31: Stumbled after leaving stalls, sn in tch, sltly short of room & switched bef 1f out, styd on to lead cl-home, val bit more: bckd: eff at 1m, will apprec further: acts on fast & soft grnd: acts on a stiff/gall trk: only lightly rcd & can rate higher. **75**
4374 **GIKO 10** [2] Jane Southcombe 10-9-4 (35) Hayley Turner(3) 100/1: 6230002: Led, hdd under press well ins fnl 1f, not pace of wnr: acts on firm, soft grnd & both AWs: gd eff back at 1m tho' prob shade flattered. *1* **74$**
4295 **PARNASSIAN 15** [1] G B Balding 4-9-4 (70) R Thomas(3) 7/4 FAV: 1154303: Chsd ldrs, styd on to chase ldr despite hanging right ins fnl 1f, sn no extra: bckd: fair run: see 4067. *1¾* **70**
838 **LAKOTA BRAVE 185** [4] Mrs Stef Liddiard 10-9-4 (70) S Drowne 16/1: 2400064: In tch, styd on to chase ldr halfway, no extra fnl 1f: long abs: acts on fast & both AW's, prob soft grnd: see 360 & 5. *¾* **68**

SALISBURY TUESDAY 14.09.04 Righthand, Galloping Track, Stiff Finish

4362 **BLUE PATRICK 11** [3]4-9-4 (70) L Fletcher(3) 8/1: 0206505: Missed break, nvr nrr than mid-div. *2* **64**
4398* **HAZEWIND 9** [5]3-9-5 vis t (65) F P Ferris(3) 7/2: 5116416: Cl-up, wknd dist: not handle soft? *shd* **69**
4334 **OH BOY 12** [6]4-9-4 (67) Dane O'Neill 12/1: 1100007: Al in rear: btr 2647 (firm). *5* **55**
7 Ran Time 1m 48.78 (9.68) Owned: Helena Springfield Ltd Trained: Newmarket

4582 **5.10 Salisburyracecourse Co Uk Handicap Stakes 3yo+ 56-70 (E3)** **[80]**
£3843 £1182 £591 **6f212y str** **Soft 114** **-23 Slow** Centre

4229 **FEARBY CROSS 17** [7] W J Musson 8-8-9 bl (61) K Fallon 7/2 FAV: 5005461: Hld up, prog wide 3f out, styd on to lead well ins fnl 1f, drvn out: eff at 6/7f on fm, soft & polytrack, prob hvy: loves Newmarket. **71**
4334 **YOUNG ALEX 12** [4] M C Pipe 6-8-13 VIS (65) P Makin(5) 8/1: 56343-52: Held up, prog 3f out, styd on to lead ins fnl 1f, sn hdd & no extra: acts on firm, soft grnd & polytrack: gd run in first time vis. *1* **71**
4110 **DR SYNN 24** [3] J Akehurst 3-8-10 (66) S Hitchcott 11/1: 3650203: In tch, led 2f out, hdd ins fnl 1f, no extra: enjoyed return to soft surface: see 4029 & 1722. *1¾* **68**
1393 **MAJIK 141** [2] D J S ffrench Davis 5-8-7 (59) Liam Jones(7) 14/1: 0340404: In tch, ev ch 2f out, no extra fnl 1f: long abs: btr 419 (fibresand). *2½* **56**
4126 **EMERALD FIRE 22** [9]5-8-8 (60) L Keniry(3) 12/1: 05-60005: Chsd ldrs over 5f, no extra: see 3109. *2* **53**
1080 **RUSSIAN SYMPHONY 160** [10]3-8-13 BL (69) S Drowne 40/1: 05-06: ch c Stravinsky - Backwoods Teacher (Woodman) Rear, nvr nrr than mid-div: long abs & first time blnks: unplcd both '03 starts (rtd 71, mdn). *1¼* **60**
4032 **BLUE DAZE 27** [15]3-8-3 (59) R L Moore 16/1: 0555007: Nvr nrr than mid-div: btr 2385. *nk* **49**
1103 **SUNDRIED TOMATO 159** [5]5-9-4 (70) L Fletcher(3) 14/1: 6460608: Led 5f, wknd: long abs. *¾* **58**
4141 **GALLERY BREEZE 21** [11]5-9-1 P (67) V Slattery 40/1: 20-10009: Nvr nrr than mid-div: cheekpieces. *shd* **54**
4272 **BEN LOMAND 15** [8]4-8-8 c (60) A Daly 25/1: 0-003000: 10th: Handy over 5f, wknd: btr 3924 (6f, gd). *hd* **46**
4180 **CHEESE N BISCUITS 19** [16]4-8-13 p (65) J Fortune 11/1: 0005400: 11th: Al in rear: btr 1616 (gd/soft). *¾* **49**
4452 **KINGS ROCK 7** [1]3-8-4 bl (60) Hayley Turner(3) 16/1: 3012100: 12th: Sn in tch, wknd bef 1f out. *1¼* **42**
1136* **POULE DE LUXE 155** [13]3-8-13 (69) T Quinn 4/1: 04-10: 13th: Handy 5f, fdd: long abs: btr 1136 (gd). *1¾* **47**
4334 **TERRAQUIN 12** [12]4-8-9 VIS (61) J F McDonald(3) 9/1: 0000360: 14th: Handy when short of room bef 2f out, wknd: first time visor: btr 4117. *1* **37**
4101 **Tipsy Lady 24** [6]3-8-6 (62) Dane O'Neill 12/1:0 4228 **Corbel 17** [14]4-8-13 (65) J P Guillambert(3) 40/1:0
16 Ran Time 1m 35.15(9.65) Owned: Mrs Rita Brown Trained: Newmarket

YARMOUTH TUESDAY 14.09.04 Lefthand, Flat, Fair Track

Official Going GOOD/FIRM (GOOD IN PLACES)

4583 **2.20 Jack Leader Challenge Trophy Nursery Handicap Stakes Fillies 2yo 0-85 (D2)** **[88]**
£5772 £1776 £888 **7f3y** **Good/Soft 68** **-15 Slow** Stands side

4519* **SUCCESSION 3** [7] Sir Mark Prescott 2-8-9 (6ex) (69) S Sanders 9/4 FAV: 000611: Made all, drvn out/flashed tail ins fnl 1f: landed double: nicely bckd, quick reapp: eff at 7f/1m, further will suit: acts on gd & gd/soft, sharp or flat trks: tough & in fine form, type to win again: see 4519. **80**
4457 **BIBURY FLYER 6** [6] M R Channon 2-9-7 (81) T E Durcan 11/2: 2003332: Rear, hdwy over 2f out, kept on fnl 1f: op 7/1, quick reapp, not btn far under joint top weight: stays 7f: most consistent: see 3374. *½* **89**
3917 **MISS PATRICIA 32** [14] J G Portman 2-9-0 (74) N Callan 20/1: 0043: Bhd, hdwy into 2nd over 2f out, ev ch over 1f out, onepcd ins fnl 1f: stays 7f on gd/soft: fair run: see 3141. *1½* **79**
4224 **WHATATODO 17** [1] M L W Bell 2-8-12 (72) J Quinn 20/1: 0301204: Chsd ldrs, onepcd ins fnl 1f. *1½* **74**
3943 **AZUREE 31** [5]2-8-7 bl (67) J F Egan 50/1: 6304305: Trkd ldrs, onepcd 1f out: clr of rem. *1* **67**
4234 **FLAUNTING IT 17** [16]2-8-3 (63) C Catlin 33/1: 5046: Cl-up, no impress over 1f out: see 3381. *7* **49**
3909 **VELVETEEN RABBIT 32** [12]2-9-0 (74) L Dettori 9/2: 0327: Rear, nvr nr ldrs: btr 3909 (gd). *hd* **59**
4177 **LATERAL THINKER 19** [3]2-8-10 (70) K McEvoy 16/1: 4105268: Rcd in 2nd till over 2f out, no impress. *½* **54**
4234 **THEAS DANCE 17** [4]2-8-5 (65) T P Queally 10/1: 5039: Slow away, hdwy 2f out, no impress 1f out. *nk* **48**
4316* **LAKESDALE 13** [8]2-7-12 (58) A McCarthy 20/1: 4023610: 10th: Handy, wknd 2f out: btr 4316 (sell). *1* **39**
4358 **NEVER AWAY 11** [10]2-7-13 (59) D Kinsella 66/1: 00000: 11th: b f Royal Applause - Waypoint (Cadeaux Genereux) Dwelt in rear, nvr a factor: May foal: half sister to a smart 2yo sprinter: dam wnr at 6/7f. *¾* **38**
1353 **GREZIE 143** [15]2-8-0 (60) R Ffrench 28/1: 4430: 12th: Bhd, nvr nr ldrs: long abs. *10* **19**
4337 **TANTIEN 12** [11]2-8-0 (60) Lisa Jones 66/1: 540500: 13th: Chsd ldrs, wknd over 2f out: see 1677. *3½* **12**
3221 **KRYNICA 61** [13]2-9-7 (81) E Ahern 10/1: 140: 14th: Mid-div, btn when short of room over 1f out: 9 wk abs, jt top weight: 'saddle slipped': btr 3221, 2610. *7* **19**
14 Ran Time 1m 28.45 (5.85) Owned: Dr Catherine Wills Trained: Newmarket

4584 **2.50 Trett Consulting Claiming Stakes 3yo (F4)**
£3024 £864 £432 **1m3f101y** **Good/Soft 68** **-09 Slow** Inside

4128 **OUR EMMY LOU 22** [1] Sir Mark Prescott 3-8-5 (1ow) (60) S Sanders 7/2: 66-24561: Rear, hdwy over 4f out, led over 1f out, pushed clr ins fnl 1f, val 9/10L: stays 11.5/12f, further may suit: handles fast, acts on gd/soft: made most of this drop into clmg grade & apprec removal of blnks: see 3192. **68**
4235 **FU FIGHTER 17** [7] J A Osborne 3-8-11 (68) L Dettori 11/4 FAV: 0543002: Rcd alone after 1f, led 8f out till over 2f out, sn no extra, kept on again nr fin: clmd for 9,000: back in trip. *7* **62**
4112 **MARIA BONITA 24** [4] R M Beckett 3-8-2 bl (63) J Quinn 4/1: 3-404043: Mid-div, hdwy to lead over 2f out, hdd over 1f out, no extra fnl 1f: clmd for 7,000: see 4112. *2* **50**
4166 **HINODE 20** [6] J A R Toller 3-8-13 (60) T P Queally 16/1: 00354: Rear, some late gains. *hd* **60**
4112 **AUROVILLE 24** [10]3-8-11 (57) R Mullen 14/1: 50062P5: Led over 3f, rem handy, no extra over 1f out. *½* **57**
4145 **DUKES VIEW 21** [2]3-8-13 (53) E Ahern 14/1: 0550606: Handy, wknd over 2f out. *8* **47**
4282 **LILLIANNA 15** [5]3-8-6 (60) W Ryan 11/2: 403007: Chsd ldrs, no impress over 1f out. *3* **35**
4235 **ROYAL STARLET 17** [8]3-8-8 (45) I Mongan 33/1: 0045008: Mid-div, no impress 2f out: see 3714. *1¼* **35**
4388 **ZAFFEU 10** [9]3-9-9 bl (65) T E Durcan 16/1: 5106009: Slow away in rear, nvr a factor. *2½* **46**
4456 **BROOKLANDS LODGE 7** [3]3-8-4 P (56) P Doe 33/1: 0-600000: 10th: Handy, wknd over 3f out: quick reapp: tried cheek pieces: 'coughed after race': see 2529. *22* **0**

4372 **SKELTHWAITE 10** [11]3-9-9 (35) W Hogg(7) 100/1: 000-0030: 11th: Chsd ldrs, wknd over 3f out. *1½* **11**
11 Ran Time 2m 31.7 (8.9) Owned: Lady Roborough Trained: Newmarket

4585

3.20 Toteplacepot Sprint Handicap Stakes 3yo+ 71-85 (D2) **[97]**
£9331 £3539 £1770 **5f43y** **Good/Soft 68** **-13 Slow** Stands side

4394 **MINE BEHIND 10** [1] J R Best 4-8-13 (82) L Dettori 4/1 FAV: 0010001: Rear, hdwy over 2f out, led ins fnl 1f, pushed out: eff over 5/7f, does stay 1m: acts on firm, gd/soft & polytrack, sharp, gall or turning trks: confirmed improvement of race 4394, relished this return to the minimum trip: see 3146. **92**

4229 **TONY THE TAP 17** [4] N A Callaghan 3-8-12 (82) T P Queally 9/1: 5210052: In tch, outpcd over 2f out, kept on ins fnl 1f but not pace to reach wnr: acts on firm, gd/soft & polytrack: in gd form, wants 6f. *1½* **86**

4496 **MUSICAL FAIR 4** [8] J A Glover 4-8-6 (75) F Norton 12/1: 5600303: Rear, hdwy over 2f out, kept on fnl 1f: quick reapp: acts on firm & gd/soft: 'hung left': see 1973. *½* **77**

4454 **ABSENT FRIENDS 7** [9] J Balding 7-9-0 (83) K McEvoy 16/1: 0600004: Prom, ev ch over 1f out, onepcd. *nk* **84**
4197 **FOLEY MILLENNIUM 18** [11]6-8-5 (74) N Pollard 20/1: 0214205: Led till ins fnl 1f, no extra. *¾* **73**
4498 **FIDDLE ME BLUE 4** [5]3-8-7 VIS (77) J Quinn 8/1: 5000136: Dwelt, no factor: 'nvr trav' in vis. *¾* **74**
4496* **MALAPROPISM 4** [15]4-8-12 (3ex) (81) B O'Neill(7) 11/2: 0406617: Mid-div, no extra over 1f out. *½* **76**
4253* **PRIME RECREATION 16** [10]7-8-2 (71) Lisa Jones 20/1: 0040018: Handy, wknd over 2f out. *1½* **61**
4201 **SALVIATI 18** [6]7-8-11 (80) P Fitzsimons 20/1: 4510009: Slow away, nvr a factor. *5* **55**
4197 **POLISH EMPEROR 18** [2]4-8-6 (1ow)e (74) N Callan 6/1: 3100060: 10th: Handy, wknd 2f out. *½* **48**
4140 **GONENDUNNETT 21** [3]5-8-0 (9oh)vis (60) A McCarthy 40/1: 0310520: 11th: Chsd ldrs, no impress. *nk* **41**
4394 **MR MALARKEY 10** [7]4-8-13 bl (82) C Catlin 14/1: 3061060: 12th: Chsd ldrs, wknd 2f out. *½* **52**
12 Ran Time 1m 4.16 (4.06) Owned: M Folan R Lees R Crampton Trained: Maidstone

4586

3.50 Thomas Prior Maiden Stakes 3yo+ (D3)
£4095 £1260 £630 **6f3y** **Good/Soft 68** **-21 Slow** Stands side

4054 **INSTINCT 26** [1] R Hannon 3-8-12 (58) L Dettori 2/1 FAV: 0003321: Mid-div, trav best 2f out, sn made hdwy into 2nd, hard rdn ins fnl 1f to lead post: eff at 6f/1m on firm & soft, flat trk: overdue win. **64**

4262 **STARGEM 16** [2] J Pearce 3-8-7 (64) J Quinn 5/2: 02-22022: Led & keen, hdd post: see 4262. *shd* **58**

4131 **ANTIGUA BAY 22** [7] J A R Toller 3-8-7 (70) Lisa Jones 9/4: 00263: Rcd in 2nd over 4f out till over 1f out, sn onepcd: clr of rem: handles gd & gd/soft: see 3873. *2½* **50**

4452 **RAHEED 7** [6] Mrs C A Dunnett 3-8-12 VIS (62) A McCarthy 14/1: 46-60004: Handy, wknd over 1f out: quick reapp: tried a visor: see 4452. *6* **37**

NOPLEAZINU 0 [5]4-8-9 Joanna Badger 40/1: 5: ch f Sure Blade - Vado Via (Ardross) Slow away, hung left 3f out, nvr a factor on debut: with Mrs N Macauley & entitled to learn from this. *21* **0**

TERENURE GIRL 0 [4]3-8-7 N Callan 16/1: 6: br f Averti - Royal Fontaine (Royal Academy) Slow away, hdwy over 3f out, sn no impress on debut: with P Felgate. *8* **0**

6 Ran Time 1m 15.78 (5.38) Owned: Mr Jim Horgan Trained: Marlborough

4587

4.20 Racing Welfare Selling Stakes 3yo (G4)
£2723 £778 £389 **7f3y** **Good/Soft 68** **-24 Slow** Stands side

4275 **ZALEBE 15** [1] J Pearce 3-8-7 J Quinn 20/1: 001: b f Bahamian Bounty - Alo Ez (Alzao) Rear, hdwy/hung left over 2f out, led ins fnl 1f, drvn out: no bid: dam a smart sprinter at 3: eff at 7f, poss stay further: acts on gd/soft, flat trk: enjoyed drop in class. **53**

4411 **SAINTLY PLACE 8** [7] M R Channon 3-8-12 (50) T E Durcan 10/1: 60-00052: Chsd ldrs till led over 2f out, hdd ins fnl 1f, kept on: clmd for 6,000: clr of rem: stays 7f on gd/soft: see 3109. *nk* **56$**

4195 **YASHIN 18** [8] M H Tompkins 3-8-12 (57) L Dettori 7/2 FAV: 0320403: Led till over 5f out, remained handy, outpcd over 2f out, kept on again fnl 1f: need further? *3* **50**

4370 **ELSINORA 10** [18] H Morrison 3-8-7 bl (45) D Kinsella 8/1: 0263524: Cl-up, onepcd fnl 1f: op 6/1. *nk* **44**

848 **BULBERRY HILL 184** [12]3-8-12 T P Queally 12/1: 055: b g Makbul - Hurtleberry (Tirol) Mid-div, onepcd over 1f out: tchd 25/1, long abs: dam a wnr btwn 6f/1m: with M Quinlan. *2* **45**

4195 **DAVIDS GIRL 18** [2]3-8-7 (40) B Reilly(3) 40/1: 6650066: Chsd ldrs, no impress fnl 1f: see 1416. *1¼* **37**

4275 **MANNYMAN 15** [13]3-8-7 G Carter 25/1: 0-07: b f Dr Devious - Lithe Spirit (Dancing Dissident) Trkd ldrs & keen, no impress fnl 1f: well btn sole '03 start (mdn, rtd 11). *1¼* **34**

4256 **SHINKO FEMME 16** [6]3-8-12 (51) W Ryan 9/2: 5100138: Rear, hdwy over 1f out, not pace to chall. *hd* **38**
3182 **KILLOCH PLACE 63** [5]3-8-12 vis (40) F Norton 20/1: 0003409: Dwelt in rear, nvr a factor: 9 wk abs. *5* **28**
3712 **TARDIS 40** [10]3-8-7 (45) R Mullen 20/1: 4-000060: 10th: Cl-up, wknd over 1f out: 6 wk abs. *2* **19**
4041 **WINGS OF MORNING 26** [17]3-9-3 (63) D Nolan(3) 12/1: 6300340: 11th: Nvr a factor: now with D Carroll. *5* **19**
4132 **MITZI CASPAR 22** [11]3-8-12 BL (45) J F Egan 40/1: 3210000: 12th: Bhd, nvr a factor in 1st time blnks. *nk* **13**
4150 **INDRANI 21** [16]3-8-7 (40) Natalia Gemelova(7) 25/1: 0500020: 13th: Led over 5f out till over 2f out, no extra over 1f out: btr 4150. *1* **6**
3995 **MOLINIA 29** [14]3-8-7 t (51) S Sanders 4/1: P404030: 14th: Slow away, nvr a factor: 'breathing prob'. *2½* **1**
4380 **CHANTILLY SUNSET 10** [3]3-8-7 J Edmunds 66/1: 0-00: 15th: Handy, wknd 3f out. *dist* **0**
15 Ran Time 1m 29.1 (6.5) Owned: Mr T H Rossiter Trained: Newmarket

4588

4.50 Elm Contracts Conditions Stakes 3yo+ (C2)
£9048 £3432 £1716 **6f3y** **Good/Soft 68** **-01 Slow** Stands side

4510 **DOWAGER 3** [4] R Hannon 3-8-1 (96) F Norton 12/1: 6300001: Cl-up centre, hdwy to lead over 1f out, rdn out ins fnl 1f: quick reapp: stays 7f well, prob best suited by 6f: acts on firm & gd/soft, prob handles soft: acts on a stiff or easy trk: blnks removed & an improved run. **100**

3957 **COUNTRY REEL 31** [5] Saeed bin Suroor 4-8-8 vis t (110) L Dettori 1/1 FAV: 5-044002: Held up centre, hdwy over 2f out, rcd in 2nd over 1f out, kept on: nicely bckd: shade btr expected on this drop in grade. *¾* **101**

4526 **COLONEL COTTON 3** [8] N A Callaghan 5-8-8 vis (98) W Ryan 6/1: 5030653: Held up centre, hdwy over 2f out, onepcd fnl 1f: quick reapp: fair run: see 1159. *1¼* **97**

4459 **WHITBARROW 6** [2] J M Bradley 5-8-8 bl (90) J F Egan 7/2: 0000054: Led centre, hung left thr'out, hdd over 1f out, no extra: quick reapp, clr of rem: see 1845. *2* **91**

YARMOUTH TUESDAY 14.09.04 Lefthand, Flat, Fair Track

FLUSHING MEADOWS 366 [7]3-8-6 T K McEvoy 7/1: 1315-5: b c Grand Slam - Sheepish Grin (Our Native) Held up centre, no impress over 1f out: Brit bow: long abs: won 2 of 4 '03 starts in native USA (5/6f, 3rd in a Gr2 & unplcd in a Gr1): stays 5/6f: tried a t-strap here. *3½* **80**
4454 **BOLEYN CASTLE 7** [9]7-8-8 BL (86) T P Queally 33/1: 0004006: Rcd alone stands side & prom 4f, sn btn. *2* **74**
4454 **RUSSIAN VALOUR 7** [6]3-8-13 bl (108) S Sanders 20/1: 211-0607: Dwelt centre, sn cl-up, no impress. *3½* **70**
4454 **FOREST RAIL 7** [3]4-8-3 Lisa Jones 200/1: 126/64-08: Chsd ldr centre, no impress 3f out: quick reapp. *17* **7**
8 Ran Time 1m 14.57 (4.17) Owned: Plantation Stud Trained: Marlborough

4589

5.20 Bennetts Electrical Toshiba Handicap Stakes 3yo+ 56-70 (E3) **[85]**
£6037 £1858 £929 **1m3f101y** **Good/Soft 68** **+08 Fast** Inside

4080 **CIRCASSIAN 25** [5] Sir Mark Prescott 3-8-10 (67) S Sanders 2/1 FAV: 0000-021: Cl-up, hdwy into 2nd over 3f out, eff to lead over 1f out, pushed clr ins fnl 1f: nicely bckd: eff at 11.5/12f on gd/soft, further will suit: confirmed recent improvement & is unexposed at mid-dists: win again: see 3690. **81+**
4254 **KIND EMPEROR 16** [11] P L Gilligan 7-8-13 (62) A Mackay 33/1: 150-0402: Led till over 1f out, no extra. *4* **65**
4456 **CARROWDORE 7** [7] G A Huffer 4-9-7 p (70) I Mongan 6/1: 4342243: Rear, hdwy 2f out, not pace to chall. *1¼* **71**
4274 **GREAT VIEW 15** [2] Mrs A L M King 5-9-4 vis (67) L Dettori 13/2: 4023024: Rear, hdwy 3f out, wknd fnl 1f. *2½* **64**
4274 **WELLINGTON HALL 15** [15]6-9-4 (67) A McCarthy 9/2: 00-10135: Mid-div, onepcd 2f out. *1¼* **62**
2735 **BLAZING THE TRAIL 81** [3]4-9-1 (64) E Ahern 25/1: 1323066: Rear, hdwy over 3f out, no impress fnl 1f. *2½* **55**
2707 **PERFECT PUNCH 82** [10]5-9-3 (66) R Mullen 33/1: 540-2007: Chsd ldrs, wknd over 2f out: long abs. *hd* **56**
4259 **FIELD SPARK 16** [12]4-8-9 p (58) F Norton 20/1: 5230208: Bhd, hdwy over 1f out, not pace to chall. *1¾* **45**
4392 **PIRI PIRI 10** [1]4-9-6 (69) S Whitworth 8/1: 2303209: Slow away, rear, hdwy 1f out, not pace to chall. *hd* **55**
3514 **ZEIS 48** [9]4-9-4 t (67) J F Egan 40/1: 0001100: 10th: Slow away in rear, some late gains. *shd* **52**
3139 **MI ODDS 65** [8]8-8-13 (62) Joanna Badger 66/1: 1500000: 11th: Handy, wknd 3f out: 9 wk abs. *12* **29**
4539 **BILLY BATHWICK 2** [6]7-8-10 (59) C Catlin 33/1: 3310500: 12th: Handy, wknd over 2f out: quick reapp. *nk* **25**
3618 **ELLINA 45** [13]3-8-8 (65) J Quinn 25/1: 4640100: 13th: Al bhd: 6 wk abs. *1¼* **29**
4261 **DREAM ALIVE 16** [14]3-8-13 t (70) N Callan 33/1: 0340: 14th: Cl-up, no impress 2f out. *2* **31**
4167 **PENDING 20** [4]3-8-12 p (69) K McEvoy 20/1: 5-306030: 15th: Al bhd. *1* **28**
3593 **ZAWRAK 45** [16]5-8-12 (61) R Ffrench 40/1: 0105200: 16th: In tch, no impress 4f out: 6 wk abs. *8* **8**
16 Ran Time 2m 29.79(6.99) Owned: Lady Katharine Watts Trained: Newmarket

THIRSK TUESDAY 14.09.04 Lefthand, Flat, Oval Track

Official Going Good/Firm

4590

2.30 Penyghent Median Auction Maiden Stakes 2yo (E4)
£3273 £935 £468 **6f str** **Good/Firm 39** **-18 Slow** Stands Side

3807 **TARAS TREASURE 37** [6] J J Quinn 2-8-9 (71) R Winston 5/2 JT FAV: 264351: Trkd ldrs, briefly short of room 2f out, drvn to lead well ins last: nicely bckd: eff at 6f/sharp 7f on fast grnd. **74**
MONKEY MADGE 0 [8] B Smart 2-8-9 F Lynch 7/1: 2: br f Cape Cross - Runelia (Runnett) Handy & led over 2f out till well ins last: nicely bckd, op 12/1: 8,500gns Feb foal, half-sister to juv wnrs at 5/7f, dam unplcd: eff over an easy 6f on fast grnd, shld get further & can progress. *1* **70**
3376 **ORPEN WIDE 54** [2] M C Chapman 2-9-0 D Fox(5) 100/1: 03: b c Orpen - Melba (Namaqualand) Handy & ch dist, rdn & no extra ins last: left debut bhd, 8 wk abs: cheaply bght Mar first foal, dam a lightly rcd mdn: sire a Gr 1 US 6f juv wnr: eff at 6f on fast grnd. *1¼* **71**
4385 **OWED 10** [13] Mrs G S Rees 2-9-0 Dale Gibson 33/1: 004: b c Lujain - Nightingale (Night Shift) Dwelt & towards rear, kept on for press from halfway, no threat to front trio: imprvd eff, t-strap omitted: Feb foal. *3* **65**
2682 **SOUND AND VISION 82** [5]2-9-0 BL (66) S W Kelly 7/1: 56565: Led/dsptd lead till over 2f out, no extra: op 11/1, blnks: 12 wk abs, has been gelded: see 2511. *1½* **60**
1950 **MOSSMANN GORGE 113** [4]2-9-0 Dean McKeown 20/1: 06: Rdn chasing ldrs halfway, no prog when short of room distance, 4 mth abs, has been gelded. *1¼* **56**
3831 **ABLE CHARLIE 36** [12]2-9-0 A Culhane 5/2 JT FAV: 267: Reared start & v slow away, lost all ch, some late prog: well bckd tho' op 2/1: excuses last twice: h'caps shld suit: see 3376. *2* **50**
4381 **STREET DANCER 10** [7]2-9-0 M Fenton 100/1: 008: Cl-up, hmpd halfway, no prog fnl 2f. *shd* **50**
KOMREYEV STAR 0 [11]2-9-0 P Hanagan 8/1: 9: Al outpcd towards rear. *nk* **49**
2926 **INDEPENDENT SPIRIT 73** [1]2-9-0 T Hamilton(3) 66/1: 00: 10th: Sn struggling towards rear, abs. *3* **40**
4325 **MARK YOUR CARD 13** [10]2-8-9 K Darley 22/1: 0000: 11th: Dwelt, mid-div, btn 2f out. *2* **29**
AVIZANDUM 0 [9]2-9-0 J Fanning 50/1: 0: 12th: Al bhd & t.o.. *11* **5**
4303 **KIMBERLEY HALL 14** [3]2-8-9 G Gibbons 40/1: 000: 13th: Bolted bef start, slow away & hung left, sn t.o. *dist* **0**
13 Ran Time 1m 12.84 (3.34) Owned: Tara Leisure Trained: Malton

4591

3.00 Brough Castle Maiden Stakes 2yo (D3)
£4342 £1336 £668 **7f rnd** **Good/Firm 39** **-04 Slow** Inside

3539 **HADRIAN 47** [3] M Johnston 2-9-0 J Fanning 9/4 FAV: 621: Made all, drvn to hold on cl-home, all out: hvly bckd, abs: eff up with/forcing the pace at 7f: acts on firm & fast: goes well fresh. **89**
4283 **MOZAFIN 15** [10] M R Channon 2-9-0 VIS (79) A Culhane 7/1: 6243202: Trkd ldrs, rdn to chase wnr over 2f out, kept on for press, just failed: back to form on a faster surface with visor applied: can find a race. *nk* **88**
DAVID JUNIOR 0 [5] B J Meehan 2-9-0 R Hills 5/2: 3: ch c Pleasant Tap - Paradise River (Irish River) Mid-div, onepace: well bckd newcomer: Apr foal, dam plcd in US as a 4yo, related to a top-class 1m/12f performer: eff at 7f, shaped as if 1m+ will suit: handles fast grnd: clr of rem. *1¼* **85**
4205 **HALLA SAN 18** [7] Mrs J R Ramsden 2-9-0 L Goncalves 25/1: 0054: Bhd, switched wide & late gains, no threat: longer 7f trip & further will suit: prob handles fast grnd: once again fin eyecatchingly. *7* **73+**
4006 **LORD MAYFAIR 28** [12]2-9-0 R Winston 4/1: 25: Prom, rdn & btn 2f out: nicely bckd, gelded. *shd* **73**
4385 **SHANKLY BOND 10** [13]2-9-0 F Lynch 50/1: 006: b c Danehill Dancer - Fanellan (Try My Best) Mid-div, eff 3f out, no prog over 1f out: Apr foal, 28,000gns purchase: half-brother to a hdles wnr: dam 6f scorer. *hd* **72**
4376 **BRONZE DANCER 10** [6]2-9-0 Dean McKeown 100/1: 007: Keen & twds rear, nvr land a blow. *¾* **71**
4026 **ROYAL WEDDING 27** [1]2-9-0 K Darley 9/1: 008: Trkd ldrs, fdd under press fnl 2f: see 4026. *1½* **68**

3769 **KEYALZAO 38** [8]2-8-9 L Enstone 150/1: 009: b f Alzao - Key Partner (Law Society) Al towards rear: 12,500gns Apr foal, half-sister to a 5f 2yo scorer, also a 7f 3yo wnr: dam a wnr at 9/12f & over hdles. *9* **47**
SOOYOU SIR 0 [2]2-9-0 G Gibbons 80/1: 0: 10th: Mid-div, sn rdn & nvr a factor. *1½* **49**
LILLAS FOREST 0 [11]2-9-0 G Faulkner 100/1: 0: 11th: Dwelt & al towards rear. *3½* **42**
4244 **DANCING DEANO 17** [4]2-9-0 P Hanagan 33/1: 060: 12th: Al bhd, op 50/1. *5* **33**
12 Ran Time 1m 25.88 (2.98) Owned: Highclere Thoroughbred Racing XXIII Trained: Middleham

4592

3.30 Racing Uk On Channel 432 Handicap Stakes 3yo+ 56-70 (E3) **[79]**
£4555 £1402 £701 **1m rnd** **Good/Firm 39** **+04 Fast** Inside

3423 **HUXLEY 52** [1] M G Quinlan 5-9-5 t (70) G Faulkner 12/1: 0000401: Sn mid-div trav well, led over 1f out & readily asserted, val 3L+: 7 wk abs: suited by 7f/1m on fast & soft grnd, now eff in a t-strap & goes well fresh: win again on this evidence: see 3232, 1423. **83+**
4399 **HEVERSHAM 9** [7] J Hetherton 3-8-9 (65) Dean McKeown 16/1: 2500002: Chsd ldrs, chall 2f out, not pace of wnr over 1f out: gd run: see 2854 & 623. *2* **68**
4346 **HULA BALLEW 12** [6] M Dods 4-8-11 p (62) S W Kelly 7/1: 5015523: Chsd ldrs over 2f out, kept on. *½* **64**
4399 **DARA MAC 9** [2] N Bycroft 5-8-10 (61) Suzanne France(7) 16/1: 0010604: Mid-div, eff to chall over 1f out, sn no extra: see 3830 (C/D sell h'cap). *¾* **62**
4406 **MEGANS MAGIC 8** [8]4-9-2 bl e (67) J Bramhill 14/1: 0364405: Slow away & bhd, kept on late for press but lost winning ch start: interesting for similar when getting a level break: see 4260, 3325 & 1307 (10f). *¾* **67**
4399 **QUEEN CHARLOTTE 9** [5]5-8-13 (64) J Fanning 6/1 FAV: 0-200056: Handy & led halfway till over 1f out. *shd* **64**
4399 **ADOBE 9** [10]9-8-13 (64) A Culhane 11/1: 0040507: Mid-div, nvr pace to land a blow: see 2010. *hd* **63**
4346 **GIFTED FLAME 12** [9]5-9-2 (67) R Winston 13/2: 0314368: Dwelt & towards rear, no prog. *1½* **63**
3700 **INCHDURA 41** [16]6-9-1 (66) Kim Tinkler 14/1: 000-0069: Mid-div, eff wide, little hdwy, abs: see 3700. *¾* **61**
3670 **TIME TO REMEMBER 42** [11]6-8-6 (57) P Hanagan 7/1: 0002000: 10th: Held up & keen, mod prog: abs, new yard: prob best at 6/7f: see 3537, 1910. *1¾* **49**
3546 **WESSEX 47** [4]4-9-3 (68) T Eaves(3) 33/1: 0600500: 11th: Trkd ldrs, wknd 2f out: abs: btr 3328, 1970. *½* **59**
3512 **ATLANTIC ACE 49** [12]7-8-12 (63) F Lynch 8/1: 0060000: 12th: Held up, eff 3f out, no prog: abs. *1¾* **51**
3678 **MOVIE KING 41** [14]5-8-9 (60) Dale Gibson 16/1: 0200630: 13th: Led till halfway, abs, best dominating. *½* **47**
1465 **GRANDMA LILY 137** [18]6-8-10 (61) D Tudhope(7) 33/1: 0000030: 14th: Al rear & t.o., long abs, sprinter. *11* **30**
3597 **Magical Mimi 45** [13]3-8-8 (64) Darren Williams 33/1:0 3690 **Sharaab 41** [17]3-8-12 t(68) R Hills 16/1:0
16 Ran Time 1m 38.16 (2.76) Owned: Mr Liam Mulryan Trained: Newmarket

4593

4.00 Rogan's Seat Maiden Stakes 3yo (D3)
£4186 £1288 £644 **1m rnd** **Good/Firm 39** **-02 Slow** Inside

IKTIBAS 0 [5] Saeed bin Suroor 3-9-0 T R Hills 8/15 FAV: 1: b c Sadler's Wells - Bint Shadayid (Nashwan) Led & readily pulled clr fnl 3f, any amount in hand on debut: hvly bckd at odds-on: eff forcing the pace over an easy 1m, 10f wil suit: acts on fast grnd & goes well fresh: eff in a t-strap: untested, rate higher. **86+**
4241 **TRUE 17** [4] Mrs S Lamyman 3-8-9 (58) R Winston 4/1: 0340602: Mid-div, hdwy halfway, kept on for press, nvr any ch with wnr: see 3016 & 2215. *9* **62**
2443 **THE RIP 92** [2] T D Easterby 3-9-0 (70) K Darley 18/1: 004-03: ch g Definite Article - Polgwynne (Forzando) Chsd wnr halfway, drvn & sn no impress: 3 mth abs: lightly rcd '03, mdn unplcd (rtd 73): dam a 7f wnr: eff around a sharp 7f: prob handles firm & fast grnd. *4* **59**
4347 **JONNYEM 12** [1] G A Swinbank 3-9-0 Dean McKeown 40/1: 04: Held up, only mod prog for press. *¾* **58**
3581 **FIFTH COLUMN 46** [7]3-9-0 (60) L Enstone 66/1: 0-0005: b g Allied Forces - Miff (Beau Genius) Rdn & btn 2f out: abs: unplcd sole '03 start (J Fanshawe, rtd 45). *1½* **55**
3787 **THE NIBBLER 38** [6]3-9-0 (52) M Henry 20/1: 4606: Al bhd: btr 2854. *9* **37**
1978 **UNPRECEDENTED 112** [9]3-9-0 vis (50) J Fanning 33/1: 00-00407: Chsd wnr, strugg halfway, abs. *6* **25**
2772} **ATTACK MINDED 432** [3]3-9-0 T Williams 200/1: 0-8: Dwelt & al bhd, reapp. *½* **24**
2295 **TOP LINE DANCER 98** [8]3-9-0 T (65) A Culhane 11/1: 54-4009: Al bhd, 3 mth abs, t-strap, new yard. *5* **14**
9 Ran Time 1m 38.64 (3.24) Owned: Godolphin Trained: Newmarket

4594

4.30 Buckden Pike Handicap Stakes 3yo+ 46-55 (F4) **[71]**
£3210 £917 £459 **1m4f** **Good/Firm 39** **-04 Slow** Inside

3653 **EGO TRIP 43** [11] M W Easterby 3-8-9 BL (52) Dale Gibson 12/1: 0-013041: Trkd ldrs, rdn to lead over 2f out, drvn out: op 16/1, 6 wk abs: eff at 1m/10f, now stays an easy 12f well: acts on firm & gd grnd: imprvd today for first time blnks: see 2299 & 1872. **60**
4365 **WILD POWER 11** [5] J G M O'Shea 6-9-7 (55) B Swarbrick(5) 11/1: 20/230/-42: Mid-div trav well, smooth prog 2f out, rdn & not pace of wnr ins last: eff at 10/12f on fast & soft grnd, return to 10f could suit: travels stylishly in a race, poss not entirely straightforward but appeals at the type to win similar: see 4365. *1* **61**
3669 **THEATRE TINKA 42** [9] R Hollinshead 5-9-7 p (55) F Lynch 7/1: 4052043: Rear, short of room when hdwy 2f out, styd on well ins last, nrst fin: 6 wk abs: gd late work, worth another try at 14f+: see 2601, 679 & 191. *1¾* **59**
1396 **BROUGHTON KNOWS 141** [10] Miss Gay Kelleway 7-9-4 bl (52) K Darley 14/1: 1112464: In tch wide, hdwy to chall over 2f out, no extra ins last: recently took part in a charity race at Fontwell, 5 mth Rules abs: prev with W J Musson: acts on fast grnd & fibresand: caught the eye suffering an awkward passage, keep in mind. *nk* **55+**
4439 **MUNAAWESH 7** [14]3-8-11 bl (54) A Culhane 11/1: 0422045: Dwelt & hmpd early, hdwy & chall 2f out, no extra for press from dist: see 3998, 3772. *1* **56**
4340 **MUSLIN 12** [17]3-8-11 (54) S W Kelly 15/2: 0300256: Mid-div wide, ch over 1f out, no extra. *hd* **55**
3649 **ALL BLEEVABLE 43** [13]7-8-12 (6oh) (40) J Bramhill 50/1: 00///-667: Mid-div, eff 2f out, no extra, abs. *1½* **45**
4340 **SOVEREIGN STATE 12** [16]7-9-2 p (50) L Enstone 14/1: 1452028: Mid-div, eff over 2f out, sn no extra. *2* **46**
4340 **CHEVIN 12** [8]5-8-12 (46) P Hanagan 13/2: 50-50109: Held up, rdn 3f out, little prog: btr 3669. *1¼* **40**
4249 **LET IT BE 17** [12]3-8-8 (51) Neil Brown(7) 5/1 FAV: 0511520: 10th: Chsd ldrs wide 9f. *¾* **44**
4243 **AMALFI COAST 17** [4]5-9-0 (48) G Faulkner 100/1: 5440U-00: 11th: Led over 3f out till over 2f out. *½* **40**
4032 **GRANDE TERRE 27** [2]3-8-12 (55) M Fenton 66/1: 00-P0000: 12th: Mid-div, btn 2f out: see 1896 (1m). *4* **41**
4423 **PRAIRIE LAW 8** [7]4-8-12 (1oh) (45) A Nicholls 14/1: 0064300: 13th: Al bhd: btr 3916. *½* **31**
4402 **WESTCOURT DREAM 9** [6]4-9-4 (52) P Mulrennan(3) 16/1: 33-31060: 14th: Chsd ldrs, btn 3f out. *3½* **32**
2850 **FAIRY MONARCH 76** [18]5-9-1 p (49) R Fitzpatrick 25/1: 000-2020: 15th: Mid-div, btn 3f out, abs. *shd* **29**
4243 **AWWAL MARRA 17** [3]4-8-12 (1oh) (45) Dean McKeown 50/1: 2/-03000: 16th: Chsd ldrs, btn 3f out. *6* **17**

THIRSK TUESDAY 14.09.04 Lefthand, Flat, Oval Track

3996 **DIAL SQUARE 29** [15]3-8-9 (52) J Fanning 40/1: 3111000: 17th: Al bhd: btr 1454 (AW, banded). *5* **16**
3327 **WOODWIND DOWN 56** [1]7-9-0 (48) R Winston 25/1: 50/20//-100: 18th: Led till over 3f out, wknd qckly & eased: abs: btr 2966. *2½* **8**
1871} **MISTER MERLIN 471** [19]3-8-3 (45) D Tudhope(1) 100/1: 350-0: 19th: ch g Titus Livius - Official Secret (Polish Patriot) Al rear, h'cap bow, long abs: gelded: unplcd in '03 at up to 6f (mdns, rtd 51). **0**
19 Ran Time 2m 34.95 (5.15) Owned: Mr K Hodgson & Mrs J Hodgson Trained: Sheriff Hutton

4595 **5.00 Scarborough Castle Handicap Stakes 3yo 46-55 (F4)** **[67]**
£3086 £882 £441 **6f str** **Good/Firm 39** **-02 Slow** Stands Side

4404 **FOX COVERT 8** [1] D W Barker 3-9-0 vis (53) L Enstone 7/1: 5040031: Made all far side, drvn out: eff at 5/6f, stays 7f: acts on firm & gd grnd, prob not gd/soft or softer: handles any trk & suited by a visor. **62**
4404 **WESTBOROUGH 8** [2] N Tinkler 3-8-13 T (52) Kim Tinkler 20/1: 5200602: Sn chsd wnr far side, kept on, al held: imprvd eff in first time t-strap: eff at 5/6f: see 1682. *1½* **55**
4508 **SUITCASE MURPHY 3** [19] Ms Deborah J Evans 3-8-7 (45) B Swarbrick(5) 12/1: 0004-063: Trkd ldrs stands side, rdn to lead that group well ins last, not pace of front pair far side: qck reapp: eff at 6f on fast. *½* **47**
4368 **YAMATO PINK 11** [17] Mrs H Sweeting 3-8-12 (51) S W Kelly 6/1 JT FAV: 0125304: Led/dsptd lead stands side, ch ins last, no extra: see 1985, 1453 (banded). *¾* **50**
4380 **YORKES FOLLY 10** [5]3-8-7 vis (45) R Winston 20/1: 0-000035: Chsd ldrs far side, kept on for press. *nk* **44**
3561 **SEA FERN 47** [12]3-8-7 (45) P Fessey 16/1: 00-50006: Chsd ldrs stand side, rdn & no extra dist, abs. *hd* **43**
4504 **FROM THE NORTH 3** [7]3-8-11 P (50) A Beech(3) 33/1: 0-050407: Mid-div far side, not pace to chall. *1* **44**
3835 **UHURU PEAK 36** [18]3-9-0 BL (53) P Mulrennan(3) 6/1 JT FAV: 0032068: Rdn start, dsptd lead stands side 4f, fdd under press in first time blnks: op 9/1: btr 3262 (g/s). *shd* **47**
4116 **TSARBUCK 23** [14]3-8-8 (47) G Faulkner 10/1: 2523309: Chsd ldrs stands side, not land a blow. *¾* **39**
3725 **VITTORIOSO 40** [11]3-8-7 (45) Darren Williams 20/1: 3320050: 10th: Towards rear stands side, switched right & only mod prog, nrst fin, abs. *nk* **37**
3133 **RED HOT RUBY 66** [3]3-8-7 (46) P Hanagan 15/2: 0330: 11th: Chsd ldrs far side, nvr land a blow: abs. *¾* **35**
4347 **SCHINKEN OTTO 12** [10]3-8-7 (45) T Eaves(3) 33/1: 60-06050: 12th: Towards rear stands side, not able to chall: flattered 4347 (9f). *hd* **34**
4317 **TURKISH DELIGHT 13** [13]3-9-2 (55) A Culhane 12/1: 0030000: 13th: Cl-up stands side, btn 2f out. *2½* **35**
4252 **APPETINA 16** [6]3-9-2 BL (55) K Darley 12/1: 5544000: 14th: Hmpd start & al outpcd stands side: blnks. *3½* **24**
4256 **FAITES VOS JEUX 16** [8]3-8-7 (45) Dale Gibson 33/1: 64430-00: 15th: Chsd wnr far side 4f. *1* **12**
4278 **OPEN MIND 15** [15]3-8-9 (48) Dean McKeown 20/1: 0-430600: 16th: Led/dsptd lead stands side 3f. *½* **12**
3595 **LOTTIE 45** [16]3-8-7 (45) J Fanning 40/1: 0540: 17th: Al bhd stands side, abs/h'cap bow. *5* **0**
4278 **HALLAHOISE HYDRO 15** [20]3-9-0 (53) M Fenton 18/1: 0-100000: 18th: Dwelt & al bhd stands side. *5* **0**
4237 **BIG TOM 17** [4]3-8-10 (49) D Tudhope(7) 33/1: 5000000: 19th: Chsd ldrs far side till halfway, sn struggling. *7* **0**
19 Ran Time 1m 11.95(2.45) Owned: Mr D W Barker Trained: Richmond

BEVERLEY WEDNESDAY 15.09.04 Righthand, Oval Track with Stiff, Uphill Finish

Official Going Good/Firm

4596 **1.50 Brecks Saab Maiden Stakes Div 1 2yo (D3)**
£4209 £1295 £648 **5f str** **Good/Firm 25** **-15 Slow** Inside

2505 **SPACE MAKER 90** [11] M L W Bell 2-9-0 R Mullen 100/30: 401: Made all & rdn clr over 1f out, easily: op 5/2, 3 month abs: reportedly fin lame when disapp latest: eff at 5f/6f on fast & gd grnd: can force the pace & goes well fresh: handles a sharp or stiff trk: useful display, can win again: see 2263. **85+**
4343 **WAGGLEDANCE 13** [3] J S Wainwright 2-9-0 P (56) T Eaves(3) 20/1: 50002: Chsd ldrs, eff to chase wnr over 1f out, kept on but nvr any impress: fair run in first time cheek pieces: h'caps shld suit: see 2167. *6* **66**
4338 **BEN CASEY 13** [1] B Smart 2-9-0 (66) F Lynch 5/1: 0633: Chsd ldrs, drvn & kept on onepace, nvr threat: poor low draw: handles firm & fast grnd, shld apprec h'caps: see 4338 & 3988. *nk* **65**
4303 **DANETHORPE LADY 15** [2] D Shaw 2-8-9 Darren Williams 50/1: 64: In tch, mod prog. *6* **44**
4343 **RUSSIAN RIO 13** [10]2-9-0 G Faulkner 3/1 FAV: 055: Cl-up, rdn & btn over 1f out: btr 4343. *nk* **48**
BOPPYS DREAM 0 [4]2-8-9 P Hanagan 7/1: 6: ch f Clan of Roses - Laurel Queen (Viking) Bhd, mod late hdwy: op 9/1: cheaply bght May foal, half-sister to a 1m wnr: dam mulitple 7f juv wnr. *2½* **35**
LUGANA POINT 0 [8]2-9-0 F Norton 33/1: 7: b c Lugana Beach - Raisa Point (Raised Socially) Bhd, modest late prog: Apr foal, dam plcd at 5f, sire a smart sprint performer. *shd* **40**
2789 **HAMBURG SPRINGER 79** [9]2-9-1 L Fletcher 100/1: 058: Dwelt & al towards rear, nvr factor, abs. *1* **38**
HOLIDAY COCKTAIL 0 [5]2-9-0 P M Quinn 20/1: 9: b g Mister Baileys - Bermuda Lily (Dunbeath) V slow away & al bhd: Apr foal, half-brother to sev wnrs, incl 5/6f juv scorers: dam a 5f 2yo wnr. *1¾* **32**
3968 **LUCY PARKES 31** [6]2-8-9 (51) M Henry 10/1: 0400: 10th: Chsd ldrs towards centre, sn bhd. *shd* **27**
PRIMARILY 0 [7]2-9-0 R Winston 12/1: 0: 11th: Dwelt, al bhd. *1½* **27**
AMAZING GRACE MARY 0 [12]2-8-9 J Bramhill 16/1: 0: 12th: In tch, hung badly left halfway, wknd. *6* **5**
12 Ran Time 1m 03.30 (2.0) Owned: HESheikh Rashid Bin Mohammed Trained: Newmarket

4597 **2.20 Racing Uk On Channel 432 Selling Nursery Handicap Stakes 2yo 0-65 (F4)** **[65]**
£3147 £899 £450 **7f100y rnd** **Good/Firm 25** **-26 Slow** Inside

4451 **BELTON 8** [15] Ronald Thompson 2-9-4 (55) K McEvoy 20/1: 000001: Mid-div, styd on wide for press to lead well ins last: bght in for 4,000gns: first win: eff at 7.5f, tried 1m, shld suit: acts on fast in sell grade. **62**
4396 **MAUREENS LOUGH 10** [7] J Hetherton 2-8-13 (50) R Winston 7/1: 4105002: Chsd ldrs & led over 1f out, drvn & hdd well ins last: eff at 7/7.5f: see 3570 (clmr). *nk* **55**
4277 **OUTRAGEOUS FLIRT 16** [11] A Dickman 2-8-8 (45) P Hanagan 9/1: 00033: Trkd ldrs, switched to chall ins last, just held cl-home: styd longer 7.5f trip on h'cap bow: handles fast & gd grnd: see 4277. *hd* **50**
4171 **MR MAXIM 20** [10] R M Whitaker 2-9-6 (57) Dean McKeown 12/1: 05004: Chsd ldrs, kept on onepace. *1½* **59**
4213 **FRANSISCAN 19** [5]2-8-8 P (45) G Faulkner 33/1: 00605: Mid-div, mod late prog, no threat: chkpcs. *1½* **44**
3769 **MISS GOOD TIME 39** [16]2-8-8 bl (45) J Bramhill 8/1: 0606656: Mid-div, eff over 2f out, not able to chall. *½* **43**
4556 **CADOGEN SQUARE 2** [12]2-8-12 (49) J Fanning 12/1: 0004007: Led till over 4f out, no extra dist. *½* **46**

4206 **DESERT BUZZ 19** [4]2-9-5 P (56) M Tebbutt 14/1: 6050008: Cl-up & led over 4f out till over 1f out, chkpcs. ¾   52
4206 **LANAS TURN 19** [14]2-9-1 bl (52) G Gibbons 10/1: 0500469: Unruly start, mid-div, no prog fnl 2f: btr 3570. 1½   45
4204 **ADMITTANCE 19** [13]2-9-7 (58) A Culhane 9/2 FAV: 00000: 10th: Mid-div, no prog over 2f out: op 6/1.   3½   44
4503 **Itsa Monkey 4** [8]2-8-12 bl(49) R Mullen 20/1:0   2939 **Riverweld 74** [3]2-9-6 (57) N Pollard 12/1:0
4206 **Fold Walk 19** [6]2-8-9 (46) Dale Gibson 25/1:0   4451 **Be Bop Aloha 8** [2]2-9-6 (57) N Callan 28/1:0
4146 **Justenjoy Yourself 22** [1]2-8-9 (46) F Norton 12/1:0   3348 **Zanderido 56** [9]2-8-13 (50) P Mulrennan(3) 16/1:0
16 Ran   Time 1m 34.61 (3.81)   Owned: Mr J M Phillips   Trained: Doncaster

---

4598	2.50 Mac And Leni Memorial Handicap Stakes 3yo+ 46-55 (F4)				[67]
	£3685 £1134 £567	1m100y rnd	Good/Firm 25	+07 Fast Inside	

4145 **EMPERORS WELL 22** [5] M W Easterby 5-9-2 bl (55) T Lucas 20/1: 4146-031: Made all, awkward low   65
draw, rdn clr over 1f out, decisively: eff at 1m/8.5f, stays a sharp 10f well: loves to front run on fast & soft.
4346 **TIME TO REGRET 13** [17] J S Wainwright 4-8-11 (50) T Eaves(3) 22/1: 4010002: Chsd ldrs, styd on   2   55
for press, no threat to wnr: see 3242.
4345 **GOLDEN SPECTRUM 13** [15] D Nicholls 5-8-12 (51) P J Benson(7) 20/1: 0030003: Trkd ldrs, kept on   nk   55
for press, not threat to wnr ins last: now stays 8.5f: see 3670 & 1508.
4379 **SPLODGER MAC 11** [16] N Bycroft 5-9-0 (53) F Norton 9/2: 0126024: Chsd wnr, drvn & no extra dist.   ¾   56
4085* **BOPPYS PRINCESS 26** [12]3-8-11 (55) P Hanagan 3/1 FAV: 00-12115: Held up, eff 2f out, onepace.   1   56
4402 **CHAMPAIN SANDS 10** [13]5-9-0 (53) B Swarbrick(5) 25/1: 4250006: Handy, short room 1f out, kept on.   nk   53
3501 **SEDGE 50** [9]4-9-1 (54) R Fitzpatrick 50/1: 10007: Held up, eff over 2f out, not able to chall, 7 wk abs.   ¾   53
4456 **BASINET 8** [3]6-9-0 p (53) R Winston 14/1: 0406408: Dwelt, short of room over 1f out, mod prog.   nk   51
4345 **APACHE POINT 13** [10]7-9-0 (53) Kim Tinkler 8/1: 2355559: Chsd ldrs wide, fdd under press fnl 2f.   3   45
4488 **DIDOE 6** [14]5-8-12 (51) Joanna Badger 16/1: 0121000: 10th: Keen, chsd ldrs, btn 2f out, qck reapp.   1½   40
4345* **MON SECRET 13** [8]6-9-2 (55) F Lynch 14/1: 0060610: 11th: Al towards rear: btr 4345 (7f).   ½   43
3733 **PAS DE SURPRISE 41** [7]6-8-11 (50) S Donohoe(7) 6/1: 4454000: 12th: Mid-div, eff wide, btn 2f out, abs.   1   36
4418} **AQRIBAA 358** [11]6-8-13 (52) P Mulrennan(3) 33/1: 0/01000-0: 13th: b g Pennekamp - Karayb (Last   1   36
Tycoon) Dwelt at bkd: reapp: '03 C/D amat riders h'cap wnr, mod form subs: unplcd '02 (rtd 43): eff at 8.5f on
fast grnd. 1 Aug'03 Beve 8.5g/f 54-50 E:
3737 **Weakest Link 41** [4]3-8-11 (55) N Callan 25/1:0   4327 **Senor Eduardo 14** [2]7-9-1 (54) K McEvoy 16/1:0
15 Ran   Time 1m 45.36 (1.56)   Owned: Mr M W Easterby   Trained: Sheriff Hutton

---

4599	3.25 Brecks Saab Maiden Stakes Div 2 2yo (D3)			
	£4209 £1295 £648	5f str	Good/Firm 25	-18 Slow Inside

4349 **JUANTORENA 12** [6] M L W Bell 2-9-0 (83) R Mullen 10/11 FAV: 2243421: Chsd ldr, hung right under   85
press over 1f out, chall ins last, prevailed all out: well bckd: eff at 5/6f on fast & gd grnd, prob any trk.
4385 **ONE GREAT IDEA 11** [7] T D Barron 2-9-0 P Hanagan 7/2: 252: Led, edged right early, kept on for   shd   84
press, just hdd line: op 11/4: shown enough to find a race: see 4385 & 3755.
       GOLDEN ASHA 0 [1] N A Callaghan 2-8-9 F Norton 25/1: 3: ch f Danehill Dancer - Snugfit Annie   1¼   75+
(Midyan) Slow away & bhd, styd on from halfway, nrst fin: Feb foal, half-sister to useful 5/7f wnr Enchanted, dam
plcd at 6f: eff over a stiff 5f, apprec 6f+ on this evidence: handles fast grnd: caught the eye, improve.
4436 **BEVERLEY BEAU 8** [5] Mrs L Stubbs 2-9-0 (60) Kristin Stubbs(7) 22/1: 55444: Chsd ldrs, not able to   1¼   76$
chall fnl 1f but clr of rem: shld apprec h'caps: see 4436, 2110.
4129 **MS THREE 23** [8]2-8-9 Joanna Badger 100/1: 065: Hmpd early, chsd ldrs 3f: see 4129.   7   50
4298 **MOLLY DANCER 16** [9]2-8-9 (67) C Catlin 10/1: 00356: Chsd ldrs till over 1f out: btr 3981.   2   44
4178 **STORM CHASE 20** [10]2-9-0 K McEvoy 11/2: 07: b c Awad - Night Duja (Dayjur) Hmpd early on, nvr   shd   49
a factor: turf bow: Apr foal, cost £45,000: dam a US sprint wnr.
4385 **DISTINCTIVE MIND 11** [11]2-9-0 G Gibbons 22/1: 08: b g Mind Games - Primum Tempus (Primo   nk   48
Dominie) Hmpd early, chsd ldrs, struggling fnl 2f: Feb foal, half-brother to 3 5f juv wnrs: dam unplcd.
       GRANDMA RYTA 0 [4]2-8-9 T Lucas 50/1: 9: Dwelt, chsd ldrs till halfway.   1½   38
       SPRING TIME GIRL 0 [12]2-8-9 T Eaves(3) 33/1: 0: 10th: Slow away & al outpcd rear.   nk   37
       PRETTY WOMAN 0 [2]2-8-9 N Pollard 33/1: 0: 11th: V slow away & sn bhd.   3½   29
11 Ran   Time 1m 03.46 (2.16)   Owned: HESheikh Rashid Bin Mohammed   Trained: Newmarket

---

4600	3.55 European Breeders Fund Maiden Stakes Fillies 2yo (D3)			
	£5805 £1786 £893	7f100y rnd	Good/Firm 25	-47 Slow Inside

4357 **VERBIER 12** [7] N A Callaghan 2-8-11 F Norton 9/2: 61: b f Fusaichi Pegasus - Oh Nellie (Tilt   79
The Stars) Trkd ldr, rdn to lead over 1f out, styd on well for press: Jan foal, half-sister to a 7f juv wnr, dam a
high-class miler: apprec step up to 7.5f, 1m could suit: acts on fast grnd: shld progress again.
4436 **HANNAHS DREAM 8** [8] M Johnston 2-8-11 J Fanning 9/1: 62: Led, hdd over 1f out, kept on for   1   76
press: op 15/2: imprvd from intro over this longer 7.5f trip, acts on fast grnd: see 4436.
       SHARAIJI BLOSSOM 0 [12] Saeed bin Suroor 2-8-11 K McEvoy 100/30: 3: b f Saint Ballado - Lilac   ¾   75
Garden (Roberto) Held up, eff when edged right 2f out, nrst fin: May foal, half-sister to wnrs abroad: dam a
multiple US sprint wnr: stays 7.5f, 1m+ will suit: handles fast: improve.
3418 **SHAMROCK BAY 53** [4] J G Given 2-8-11 J Bramhill 25/1: 04: b f Celtic Swing - Kabayil (Dancing   nk   74
Brave) Chsd ldrs, no extra under press over 1f out: 8 wk abs: Apr foal, half-sister to useful stayer Dancing Bay,
also a 7f juv wnr: dam a 10f 3yo scorer & subs prolific hdles wnr: likely to apprec 1m+: handles fast grnd.
4035 **PEARLS A SINGER 28** [3]2-8-11 R Mullen 9/1: 055: Chsd ldrs wide, onepcd dist: btr 4035.   ½   71
4205 **ECOLOGICALLY RIGHT 19** [10]2-8-11 A Culhane 10/1: 06: Trkd ldrs, edged right over 1f out, no extra.   nk   72
4192 **NAIVETY 19** [2]2-8-11 J P Guillambert(3) 15/8 FAV: 27: Rear, eff over 2f out, sn btn: nicely bckd.   1   70
3626 **TAMORA 45** [9]2-8-11 N Callan 16/1: 608: Chsd ldrs, btn over 1f out, abs, longer trip.   hd   69
4283 **TETRA SING 16** [1]2-8-11 G Faulkner 50/1: 09: Al bhd.   nk   68
9 Ran   Time 1m 36.19 (5.39)   Owned: Mrs Doreen Tabor   Trained: Newmarket

4601 4.30 Katie And Paul Wedding Celebration Handicap Stakes 3yo 56-70 (E3) [77]
£5636 £1734 £867 1m4f16y Good/Firm 25 -31 Slow Inside

4342 **WING COLLAR 13** [1] T D Easterby 3-9-2 (65) G Gibbons 7/1: 3320431: Chsd ldrs, led over 1f out, 75
drvn out: first win: eff at 10/12f, poss stays 2m: acts on fast & soft grnd: see 2322, 1663 & 1174.
4037* **ARGENTUM 28** [5] Lady Herries 3-8-7 (56) A Culhane 9/4 FAV: 00-0512: Mid-div wide, drvn/styd on 1¾ 63
for press fnl 2f, not pace of wnr: nicely bckd: styd longer 12f trip: acts on fast & gd/soft grnd: see 4037.
4342 **GOLDEN DRIFT 13** [3] G Wragg 3-8-10 (59) R Ffrench 16/1: 0502503: Chsd ldrs, drvn & kept on 2 61
onepace: stays 12f: acts on fast & gd grnd: see 3201.
4308 **HEARTHSTEAD DREAM 15** [12] J D Bethell 3-9-7 (70) K McEvoy 6/1: 5121334: Held up, late gains. ½ 73
4282* **PRELUDE 16** [7]3-8-12 (61) B Swarbrick(5) 12/1: 0066615: Held up, eff when hung right over 1f out, wknd. hd 63
4487 **QUICKSTYX 6** [10]3-9-5 (68) C Catlin 9/1: 145446: Rear, eff from 3f out, onepace: see 4282, 1163. 1¾ 68
4321 **ROYAL DISTANT 14** [6]3-9-2 (65) Dale Gibson 16/1: 0002007: Rear, hdwy over 2f out, no prog bef dist. 1 64
4388 **PATRIXTOO 11** [11]3-8-11 (60) N Callan 11/2: 0-050248: Keen, led till over 1f out, wknd: btr 3875 (10f). 2½ 55
4274 **KYTHIA 16** [4]3-9-7 (70) L Fletcher(3) 12/1: 5-432069: Cl up, lost pl over 1f out, eased: btr 2956. 7 55
4439 **IRON TEMPTRESS 8** [14]3-8-7 BL (56) N Pollard 50/1: 000-0060: 10th: Keen rear, strugg fnl 2f: blnks. 9 30
3828 **SWEEP THE BOARD 37** [9]3-8-13 (62) R Winston 40/1: 0-060: 11th: Chsd ldrs, struggling fnl 2f. 1¾ 34
3893 **CHARA 34** [8]3-8-13 (62) R Mullen 16/1: 1055500: 12th: Mid-div wide, no ch fnl 3f. 1 33
12 Ran Time 2m 37.97 (6.67) Owned: Mr and Mrs J D Cotton Trained: Malton

4602 5.00 Thank You To The Stalls Handlers Maiden Auction Stakes 2yo (E3)
£3621 £1114 £557 7f100y rnd Good/Firm 25 +04 Fast Inside

4363 **KINGS ACCOUNT 12** [10] M Johnston 2-8-9 (82) J Fanning 1/1 FAV: 2221: Made all, pulled clr over 83
1f out, hand riding: hvly bckd: gd time: eff at 7f/1m on fast & gd/soft grnd, gall or easy trk: enjoyed forcing
tactics today: displays a willing attitude & the type to progress with racing: see 4363, 4083.
4190 **STANCOMB WILLS 19** [11] M H Tompkins 2-8-9 N Callan 10/1: 002: b c Trans Island - First Nadia 2½ 77
(Auction Ring) Chsd wnr, edged left under press over 1f out, kept on but al held: rest well covered: £12,000 Feb
foal, half-brother to multiple wnrs abroad: stays 7.5f, 1m could suit: handles fast grnd.
ZAGREUS 0 [8] M W Easterby 2-8-13 P Mulrennan(3) 50/1: 3: gr g Fasliyev - Zephyrine (Highest 3½ 74
Honor) Chsd ldrs, kept on onepace, nvr a threat: 30,000gns Apr foal, dam unrcd half-sister to top-class Mutaman:
sire a high-class 5/6f juv: handles fast grnd.
3975 **KILLENA BOY 30** [7] W Jarvis 2-8-9 M Tebbutt 33/1: 004: b g Imperial Ballet - Habaza (Shernazar) 1 68
Chsd ldrs, rdn & no extra fnl 2f: longer trip: 9,500gns Mar foal, dam unplcd: sire 1m wnr.
PAPARAAZI 0 [9]2-8-7 P Hanagan 16/1: 5: Swerved badly left start & lost arnd 10L, in tch wide 1¾ 63+
halfway, kept on fnl 2f, nvr threat: green on intro & lost chance start, impressed in recovery.
4207 **SATIN ROSE 19** [4]2-8-4 (54) G Gibbons 33/1: 5606: Al bhd. ½ 59
4204 **RED RUDY 19** [3]2-8-9 K McEvoy 3/1: 637: Al towards rear: see 4204. shd 64
4207 **ASKWITH 19** [6]2-8-9 C Catlin 7/1: 538: Chsd wnr, rdn & btn 2f out: see 4207 (g/s). 6 54
4207 **GOLDEN SQUAW 19** [5]2-8-2 BL (47) P M Quinn 66/1: 6009: Al bhd in first time blnks. 11 28
4464 **YANKEY 7** [2]2-8-7 J P Guillambert(3) 66/1: 050: 10th: Mid-div, rdn & struggling from halfway: mod form. 10 15
10 Ran Time 1m 32.37 (1.57) Owned: Brian Yeardley Continental Ltd Trained: Middleham

4603 5.35 Subscribe To Racing Uk On 08700 860432 Handicap Stakes 3yo+ 56-70 (E3) [76]
£4092 £1259 £630 5f str Good/Firm 25 -10 Slow Inside

4240 **COMPTON PLUME 18** [3] W H Tinning 4-9-0 (62) Dale Gibson 33/1: 3210001: Mid-div, styd on for 68
press to lead well ins last: eff at 5f/6f on fm & gd: fine run from poor draw.
3667 **TORRENT 43** [13] D W Chapman 9-8-7 (2oh)bl (53) J Fanning 25/1: 0120002: Chsd ldrs, styd on for ¾ 58
press, not pace of wnr cl-home: see 2524.
2951 **MALAHIDE EXPRESS 74** [16] E J Alston 4-8-9 (57) J D O'Reilly(7) 9/1: 5541003: Led till well ins nk 59
last, no extra: 10 wk abs: see 2320.
4140 **ONLINE INVESTOR 22** [17] D Nicholls 5-9-0 (62) Alex Greaves 13/2: 0000244: Dwelt, hdwy for press ½ 62
halfway, edged right, onepace cl-home: see 1765, 1523.
4339 **OBE ONE 13** [2]4-9-5 (67) F Lynch 14/1: 6040445: Bhd, no room over 1f out styd on well for press ½ 65
ins last, nrst fin: gd run from poor draw & is well h'capped, but on long losing run: see 2359, 1977.
3591 **BETTYS PRIDE 46** [15]5-8-7 (3oh) (52) P Mulrennan(3) 14/1: 0660106: Reared start & bhd, kept on late. hd 52
4174 **TWICE UPON A TIME 20** [12]5-8-13 (61) F Norton 12/1: 0040067: In tch, onepace. nk 57
4091 **TALLY 26** [7]4-9-3 (65) L Fletcher(3) 25/1: 0140068: Bhd, eff wide, mod prog: moderate draw. nk 60
4240 **SOAKED 18** [18]11-8-11 bl (59) A Culhane 13/2: 5230309: Mid-div, nvr able to chall: best dominating. ½ 52
4240 **BRIGADIER MONTY 18** [20]6-8-7 (2oh) (53) C Catlin 4/1 FAV: 0255030: 10th: Mid-div when short of ½ 46
room over 1f out, nvr able to chall: btr 4240.
4253 **TUSCAN FLYER 17** [9]6-8-10 bl (58) R Ffrench 20/1: 0404000: 11th: Mid-div, nvr able to chall: btr 3228. 1 46
4404 **HARRISONS FLYER 9** [10]3-9-3 (66) T Eaves(3) 20/1: 20202U0: 12th: Swerved left start & bhd, nvr factor. nk 53
4496 **MIDNIGHT PARKES 5** [8]5-9-7 (69) M Henry 11/1: 0310030: 13th: Stumbled start, short of room shd 56
over 1f out, no dngr: qck reapp: btr 4496.
4240 **TOMMY SMITH 18** [14]6-9-6 bl (68) R Winston 9/1: 0100000: 14th: Chsd ldrs, rdn & btn dist. 3½ 44
3808 **ABELARD 38** [4]3-8-11 (60) P Hanagan 25/1: 33-65050: 15th: Al bhd: btr 3808. hd 35
4010 **Hes A Rocket 29** [19]3-8-6 bl(55) Darren Williams 9/1:0
3667 **Count Cougar 43** [11]4-8-7 (2oh)(53) J McAuley 100/1:0
17 Ran Time 1m 03.06(1.76) Owned: Mr W H Tinning Trained: York

Official Going Good

4604

2.30 Queen Elizabeth's Foundation Charity Day Handicap Stakes 3yo 71-85 (D2)   **[90]**
£8303 £2555 £1277   **5f6y str**   **Good 44**   +01 Fast Far side

4382 **BO MCGINTY 11** [11] R A Fahey 3-9-7 (83) G Parkin 6/1: 1200451: Trkd ldrs, kept on to lead cl   89
home, rdn out: eff at 5/6f on firm & gd grnd: acts on a stiff/undul, sharp or gall trk, fine eff under top-weight.
4350 **OUT AFTER DARK 12** [3] C G Cox 3-9-5 (81) R Smith 5/1 JT FAV: 42-51132: Mid-div, prog bef 1f out,   shd 85
kept on cl-home, post came too soon: continues to run well & likes Sandown: see 4350 & 4099.
4236 **MIRASOL PRINCESS 18** [12] D K Ivory 3-8-11 (73) Dane O'Neill 16/1: 6640103: Held up, hdwy wide   nk 76
halfway, kept on well ins fnl 1f, not btn far: acts on firm or gd grnd: on fair mark & can find similar, see 4236.
4099 **SKYHARBOR 25** [6] A M Balding 3-9-0 VIS (76) Martin Dwyer 10/1: 0505234: Dsptd lead till lead   ½ 77
overall just ins fnl 1f, hdd cl-home: ran up to form in first time vis: see 4099 & 3976.
4394 **CELTIC THUNDER 11** [13]3-9-6 (82) R Havlin 16/1: 0204405: In tch, kept on fnl 1f, not btn far.   nk 82
3920 **BEEJAY 33** [9]3-8-11 (73) N De Souza(5) 25/1: 31-10006: Handy over 4f, sn onepcd: btr 1239 (6f).   nk 72
3036 + **RED SOVEREIGN 70** [4]3-8-13 (75) S Sanders 14/1: 366-0017: Mid-div wide till dist, onepcd: 10 wk abs.   hd 73
3567 **HANDSOME CROSS 47** [15]3-9-4 (80) J Fortune 5/1 JT FAV: 2-556038: Dsptd lead over 4f, no extra.   hd 73
4236 **FOUR AMIGOS 18** [1]3-9-0 (76) T Quinn 14/1: 6300049: Bhd, prog when no room dist, kept on fnl 1f.   hd 72
4496 **SILVER PRELUDE 5** [10]3-9-6 (82) S Drowne 20/1: 3100000: 10th: Nvr nrr than mid-div: qck reapp.   ½ 76
4404 **MARYSIENKA 9** [5]3-8-7 P (68) J Edmunds 33/1: 4-050340: 11th: Mid-div, prog halfway, no extra fnl 1f.   ½ 67
3873* **KOOL ACCLAIM 35** [7]3-9-0 (76) O Urbina 10/1: 210: 12th: Al in rear: btr 3873 (6f).   ½ 67
3889 **IVORY LACE 34** [8]3-9-1 (77) D Sweeney 25/1: 3114150: 13th: Held up, prog 2f out, staying on when   hd 67
short of room ins fnl 1f, sn no extra: btr 2195.
3976 **SNOW WOLF 30** [2]3-9-3 (79) M Fenton 25/1: 0120040: 14th: Handy wide over 3f out, hung right & wknd. 2½ 62
4278 **TREGARRON 16** [14]3-8-11 (73) R L Moore 6/1: 0-142030: 15th: Al in rear: disapp run: btr 4278 & 3543. 5 42
15 Ran Time 1m 1.75 (2.15) Owned: Paddy McGinty & Bo Turnbull Trained: Malton

---

4605

3.05 Queen Elizabeth's Foundation 'premier' Claiming Stakes 3yo+ (D3)
£5590 £1720 £860   **5f6y str**   **Good 44**   +01 Fast Far side

4039 **OK PAL 28** [11] T G Mills 4-9-7 (72) J Fortune 13/2: 3006061: Hugged far rail & made all, rdn out   84
fnl 1f: eff at 5/6f on gd, gd/soft grnd & fibresand: likes to force the pace: back to form with blnks left off.
3989 **FIRST ORDER 30** [5] Sir Mark Prescott 3-9-6 (100) S Sanders 11/8 FAV: 113-2062: Handy, styd on to   1¾ 77
chase wnr dist, kept on but al held ins fnl 1f: clmd for £20,000: acts on firm & gd, handles gd/soft: formerly v
useful sprinter: btr 3279 (h'cap).
4291 **FURTHER OUTLOOK 16** [1] D K Ivory 10-9-2 (87) Dane O'Neill 5/1: 0651503: Held up, prog halfway,   ¾ 70
hung right & no impress fnl 1f: btr 4031 (soft).
3844 **MAN CRAZY 26** [12] R M Beckett 3-8-0 bl (50) J Mackay 25/1: 0004004: Handy till dist, no extra.   ½ 52
4294 **BORZOI MAESTRO 16** [2]3-8-8 p (69) R Miles(3) 25/1: 3050605: Keen in tch till dist, no extra: see 2048.   1½ 58
4118 **TENDER 24** [7]4-8-6 p (48) S Drowne 20/1: 4100366: Nvr nrr than mid-div: see 4038.   ½ 54
4514 **HELLO ROBERTO 4** [9]3-8-7 (71) Martin Dwyer 10/1: 1000407: Nvr nrr than mid-div: qck reapp.   ½ 55
3696 **OUR GAMBLE 42** [10]3-8-3 (1ow) (65) R L Moore 16/1: 0-600058: Mid-div, no impress fnl 2f: 6 wk abs.   hd 50
3790 **BLACK OVAL 39** [4]3-8-3 (2ow) (45) P Doe 100/1: 0050009: Al bhd.   1½ 48
4394 **WILLHEWIZ 11** [8]4-9-7 vis (73) L Keniry(3) 13/2: 0000400: 10th: Cl-up over 3f, wknd: btr 4201.   ½ 62
4317 **Alizar 14** [3]3-8-0 (53) R Smith 66/1:0   4275 **Master Rat 16** [6]3-9-1 R Havlin 100/1:0
12 Ran Time 1m 1.77 (2.17) Owned: Sherwoods Transport Ltd Trained: Epsom

---

4606

3.35 Halewood International Futures Novice Stakes 2yo (D2)
£10192 £3136 £1568   **7f16y rnd**   **Good 44**   -30 Slow Inside

4176* **LINNGARI 20** [2] Sir Michael Stoute 2-9-4 (93) R L Moore 8/15 FAV: 311: Al cl-up, styd on to lead   100+
2f out, sn pushed clr, eased cl-home, val 5L+: bckd at odds on: eff at 7f, relish further: acts on fast, gd &
polytrack: fast improving & looks smart, win Gr races: see 4176.
4381* **EASY MOVER 11** [3] R Guest 2-8-11 (76) S Sanders 6/1: 5512: Handy, styd on to chase wnr from   3½ 77
dist, al held ins fnl 1f: acts on firm & gd grnd: gd eff in defeat: ran to form of 4381 (aust mdn).
3865 **MINNESOTA 35** [5] H Candy 2-9-4 (85) Dane O'Neill 4/1: 2133: Led 5f, no extra: see 3865 (List).   2½ 81
4285 **KALMINI 16** [4] M R Channon 2-8-13 (76) S Hitchcott 12/1: 02154: Mid-div over 4f, grad wknd: op 7/1.   hd 75
4 Ran Time 1m 31.64 (5.24) Owned: HH Aga Khan Trained: Newmarket

---

4607

4.10 Man Group Handicap Stakes Fillies 3yo 71-85 (D2)   **[87]**
£8334 £2564 £1282   **1m14y rnd**   **Good 44**   +06 Fast Inside

4101* **PORTHCAWL 25** [3] Mrs A J Perrett 3-9-2 (75) S Sanders 8/1: 0-11: In tch, styd on to lead dist,   82
rdn out: h'cap bow: fast time: eff at 1m, further shld suit: acts on gd & gd/soft: acts on stiff/gall trk, likes
Sandown: only lightly rcd & is open to more improvement in h'cap grade: see 4101.
4318 **ZERLINA 14** [7] W J Musson 3-9-2 (75) P Doe 16/1: 01-00042: Held up, prog wide 3f out, ev ch   1¼ 79
dist, kept on ins fnl 1f, not pace wnr: eff at 7f/1m on fast, gd grnd & polytrack: find similar on this evidence.
3885 **NOUVEAU RICHE 34** [1] H Morrison 3-9-4 (77) S Drowne 12/1: 23123: Cl-up, led 2f out, hdd dist,   shd 80
not pace front 2: continues to run well: see 3885 7 3480.
4331 **ENFORD PRINCESS 13** [4] R Hannon 3-9-9 (82) R L Moore 10/1: 0-403404: Held up, eff when short of   ¾ 83
room 2f out, prog wide ins fnl 1f, nrst fin: op 16/1: eff at 6f, now stays 1m: see 1498.
4265* **FLYING ADORED 17** [5]3-9-7 (80) T Quinn 6/1: 40-30115: Held up, prog wide 3f out, no impress ins   hd 80
fnl 1f: shade btr expected on h'cap bid: 6lb higher than last win in 4265.
4265 **TAMINOULA 17** [6]3-9-4 (77) Dane O'Neill 20/1: 0311-006: Held up, prog when short of room 2f out,   1¼ 75
switched & sn no impress: btr 3535.
4318 **OUR JAFFA 14** [14]3-9-10 (83) M Fenton 11/1: 411257: Handy over 6f, sn short of room & no extra.   nk 80
2767 **MRS PANKHURST 81** [12]3-8-12 (71) R Hills 33/1: 10-50568: Keen mid-div, under press when badly   nk 67

SANDOWN WEDNESDAY 15.09.04 Righthand, Galloping Track, Stiff Finish

hmpd dist, not recover: 10 wk abs: see 923.
4362 **DESERT CRISTAL 12** [10]3-9-5 (78) V Venkaya 12/1: 6313239: Keen in tch, badly hmpd & nrly lost footing dist, wknd: op 9/1: btr 4362 & 4148. 1¼ 72
2153 **CITRINE SPIRIT 105** [9]3-9-1 (74) J Fortune 11/1: 0-61300: 10th: Al in rear: long abs: btr 1610. 2 64
3799* **KRYSSA 38** [11]3-9-2 (75) I Mongan 7/1: 5131310: 11th: Mid-div when hmpd dist, not recover: btr 3799. 3½ 58
3542 **PICKLE 48** [13]3-9-7 (80) Martin Dwyer 11/2 FAV: 3611120: 12th: Led 6f out, hdd 2f out, wkng when hmpd dist: 7 wk abs: btr 3542 & 3410 (firm). ¾ 61
4222 **SEA NYMPH 18** [2]3-9-5 (78) J Mackay 13/2: 52120: 13th: Led, hdd 6f out, styd cl-up, fdd bef 1f out: disapp run & reportedly lost action: btr 4222 & 3828. 13 37
13 Ran Time 1m 42.04 (3.04) Owned: Usk Valley Stud Trained: Pulborough

4608 4.40 Queen Elizabeth's Foundation E B F Maiden Stakes 2yo (D2)
£6874 £2115 £1058 **1m14y rnd** **Good 44** **-07 Slow** Inside

4194 **MUTAJAMMEL 19** [4] Sir Michael Stoute 2-9-0 R Hills 13/8 FAV: 41: Handy, prog wide to lead dist, pushed out, val bit more: eff at 7f, apprec step up to 1m: acts on gd grnd & a stiff/gall trk: only lightly rcd & still showed signs of greeness, can rate higher: see 4194 (debut). 91
4328 **GOLDEN FURY 13** [1] J L Dunlop 2-9-0 (87) S Sanders 11/4: 4342: Mid-div, hdwy & ev ch dist, sn carr left & not pace wnr: continues to run well & deserves to find similar: see 4328 & 3752. ¾ 88
4355 **LUIS MELENDEZ 12** [7] P F I Cole 2-9-0 R L Moore 2/1: 43: Chsd ldrs, prog bef 1f out, kept on but not pace front 2: tchd 4/1: acts on fast & gd grnd: again showed signs of encouragement: see 4355. 2 84
3594 **FANTORINI 46** [6] J H M Gosden 2-9-0 J Fortune 20/1: 04: b c Theatrical - Beyrouth (Alleged) Led, hdd dist, no extra: 6 wk abs: Feb foal, half-brother to sprint h'cap wnr Golden Dixie: dam successful abroad: sire top-class performer at 12f: eff at 1m, will apprec further: can rate higher. 1¼ 82
CAVE OF THE GIANT 0 [8]2-9-0 T Quinn 33/1: 5: b c Giant's Causeway - Maroussie (Saumarez) Missed break, bhd, hdwy ins fnl 1f, nrst fin: debut: Apr foal, cost 25,000gns: half-brother to wnrs at 7/9f: dam fine performer around 10f abroad: sire multiple Group 1 wnr at 7/10f: ran green but showed ability. 1¾ 78
3285 **SNOW TEMPEST 60** [3]2-9-0 R Miles(3) 50/1: 0006: Al bhd: 9 wk abs. 5 68
4190 **USTAD 19** [2]2-9-0 P Doe 16/1: 07: br c Giant's Causeway - Winsa (Riverman) Al in rear: Feb foal, half brother to wnrs at 7/12f: dam successful at mid dists: sire multiple Gr 1 wnr at 7/10f: with J L Dunlop. nk 67
4376 **WILTSHIRE 11** [5]2-9-0 L Harman(7) 100/1: 0008: Cl-up over 6f, fdd: stiff task. 6 56
8 Ran Time 1m 43.14 (4.14) Owned: Mr Hamdan Al Maktoum Trained: Newmarket

4609 5.15 Queen Elizabeth's Foundation Handicap Stakes 3yo+ 71-85 (D2) [97]
£8533 £2626 £1313 **1m2f7y** **Good 44** **-01 Slow** Inside

DIEGO CAO 109 [8] G L Moore 3-8-9 (78) R L Moore 50/1: 2161: b g Cape Cross - Lady Moranbon (Trempolino) In tch, prog bef 1f out, rdn out to lead well ins fnl 1f: long abs on Brit bow, ex French, earlier won 1 of 3 starts in provinces (9.5f, gd/soft): eff around 10f on gd & gd/soft grnd: acts on stiff/gall trk & goes well fresh: lightly rcd performer & made gd start to Brit career, can progress. 89
3598 **GO TECH 46** [9] T D Easterby 4-8-12 (74) T Quinn 12/1: 6246042: Hld up, prog wide 3f out, ev ch 1f out, kept on, just held by wnr: 6 wk abs: gd run but on long losing run: see 3598. ½ 82
4293 **DREAM MAGIC 16** [4] M J Ryan 6-9-1 (77) Martin Dwyer 7/1: 0032333: Led, hdd under press well ins fnl 1f, no extra: continues in gd form: see 4293 & 3980. ¾ 83
4221 **FREELOADER 18** [11] J W Hills 4-9-2 (78) R Hills 7/1: 4301454: Held up, hdwy wide 3f out, no impress. 1¾ 81
4473 **ARRY DASH 6** [12]4-8-13 (75) S Hitchcott 11/2: 6232325: Mid-div, hdwy 2f out, onepcd ins fnl 1f. nk 77
4254* **ANOTHER CHOICE 17** [3]3-8-9 t (78) Dane O'Neill 16/1: 1000416: Nvr nrr than mid-div: btr 4254. 1¼ 78
4221 **IMPERSONATOR 18** [10]4-9-0 (76) P Doe 10/1: 40-04337: Cl-up, ev ch well over 1f out, sn wknd. nk 75
3256 **UNSUITED 61** [5]5-8-7 (1oh) (68) Natalia Gemelova(7) 14/1: 6411138: Bhd, gd prog over 1f out, nrst fin. ½ 67
4254 **RECOUNT 17** [13]4-8-13 (75) I Mongan 25/1: 0023439: In tch over 1m, no extra when short of room dist. ¾ 71
3964 **JACARANDA 31** [1]4-8-9 (71) S Drowne 20/1: 0241360: 10th: Al in rear: btr 3815 & 3404 (firm). ¾ 65
4080 **HATCH A PLAN 26** [15]3-8-3 (72) J Mackay 25/1: 0122400: 11th: Mid-div over 1m, sn no impress. 1 64
4468 **HASAIYDA 7** [14]3-8-11 (80) J Fortune 3/1 FAV: 14100: 12th: Held up, nvr able to chall: qck reapp: again disapp: twice below 3862 (fast). nk 71
4268 **COMPETITOR 17** [7]3-8-0 (65) D Kinsella 33/1: 10-20050: 13th: In tch over 7f, wknd: btr 365 (AW). ¾ 58
3879 **WAR OWL 35** [16]7-8-11 (73) S Sanders 12/1: 5010040: 14th: Bhd, nvr a factor: showed more in 3879. 1½ 59
4221 **Supreme Salutation 18** [6]8-9-7 (83) M Howard(7) 14/1:0
4318*} **Lord Eurolink 363** [2]10-8-10 (72) F P Ferris(3) 25/1:0
16 Ran Time 2m 8.67(4.57) Owned: Vetlab Supplies Ltd Trained: Brighton

YARMOUTH WEDNESDAY 15.09.04 Lefthand, Flat, Fair Track

Official Going GOOD (GOOD/SOFT IN PLACES IN STRAIGHT)

4610 2.10 European Breeders Fund Maiden Stakes Fillies 2yo (D3)
£5216 £1605 £803 **6f3y** **Good 41** **-14 Slow** Stands side

DIVINELY DECADENT 0 [1] P W Chapple Hyam 2-8-11 K Fallon 7/1: 1: br f Turtle Island - Divine Prospect (Namaqualand) Dwelt in rear, hdwy over 2f out, led ins fnl 1f, rdn out on debut: Feb 1st foal, cost E27,000: dam 7f, stayed 10f: sire smart 2yo/miler: eff at 6f, will stay further: acts on gd, flat trk: runs well fresh: gd start to racing, potentially useful & can win more races. 88+
2902 **PEPPERMINT TEA 75** [14] M L W Bell 2-8-11 P Robinson 40/1: 002: b f Intikhab - Karayb (Last Tycoon) Made most over 4f, not pace of wnr: long abs: May foal, cost E38,000: half sister to a 10f wnr: dam & sire both wnrs over 6f at 2, sire later a smart miler: eff at 6f, will stay further: acts on gd: win similar. 2 79
4357 **DESERT IMP 12** [12] B W Hills 2-8-11 M Hills 13/8 FAV: 033: Chsd ldrs till led over 1f out, hdd ins fnl 1f, no extra: nicely bckd: acts on fast & gd: shade btr 4357. shd 78
4358 **TEN CENTS 12** [3] C A Cyzer 2-8-11 D Holland 8/1: 444: Chsd ldrs, onepcd fnl 1f: op 12/1: see 4358. 2½ 70
FASHION HOUSE 0 [5]2-8-11 L Dettori 5/1: 5: b f Quiet American - Polish Style (Danzig) Handy, onepcd over 1f out on debut: op 11/4: Apr foal: half sister to wnrs at 7f/1m: dam 6f 2yo wnr. ¾ 68

4357 **LADY PILOT 12** [4]2-8-11 J Murtagh 11/1: 006: Dsptd lead, hung left over 1f out, sn no impress. *1¾* **63**
4178 **DEPRESSED 20** [11]2-8-11 J F Egan 50/1: 07: Chsd ldrs, hung left over 1f out, sn btn. *½* **61**
2399 **QAWAAFIL 95** [10]2-8-11 W Supple 25/1: 58: Rear, some late gains: long abs. *nk* **60**
MAGIC FLO 0 [2]2-8-11 S Whitworth 66/1: 9: In tch, nvr nrr on debut. *1½* **56**
PESQUERA 0 [6]2-8-11 K Darley 20/1: 0: 10th: Hmpd start, in tch, hdwy 2f out, no impress 1f out. *1* **53**
NEFERURA 0 [16]2-8-11 S W Kelly 40/1: 0: 11th: Nvr a factor on debut. *3* **44**
4375 **LADY SUESANNE 11** [17]2-8-11 W Ryan 150/1: 0000: 12th: In tch, wknd 3f out. *¾* **42**
FRAMBROISE 0 [8]2-8-11 VIS T P Queally 16/1: 0: 13th: Hmpd start, sn cl-up, no impress 1f out: visor. *4* **30**
LADY LAKOTA 0 [7]2-8-11 J F McDonald(3) 50/1: 0: 14th: Hmpd start, in tch, wknd 3f out on debut. *½* **28**
LASTING IMAGE 0 [9]2-8-11 A McCarthy 50/1: 0: 15th: Slow away, nvr a factor on debut. *1½* **24**
FOUR PLEASURE 0 [13]2-8-11 T E Durcan 50/1: 0: 16th: Slow away, al bhd on debut. *shd* **23**
3582 **ASSURED 47** [15]2-8-11 J Quinn 66/1: 00: 17th: Slow away, nvr a factor: 7 wk abs. *2* **17**
17 Ran Time 1m 13.7 (3.3) Owned: Mrs Sue Catt Trained: Newmarket

4611

2.40 European Breeders Fund/Norton Peskett Legal Services Maiden Stakes 2yo (D3)
£5255 £1617 £809 **7f3y** **Good 41** **-12 Slow** Stands side

3234 **HOME AFFAIRS 61** [4] Sir Michael Stoute 2-9-0 K Fallon 8/13 FAV: 51: b c Dansili - Orford Ness (Selkirk) Slow away, rear far side, hdwy over 3f out, led over 2f out, rdn out ins fnl 1f: nicely bckd, 9 wk abs: Mar foal: half brother to a smart 9/10f rnr: dam wnr over 1m, sire prog into a smart miler: eff at 7f, 1m looks sure to suit: acts on gd, flat trk: runs well fresh: looks potentially smart, more races to be won. **92+**
3925 **NOTABILITY 33** [7] M A Jarvis 2-9-0 P Robinson 25/1: 02: b c King's Best - Noble Rose (Caerleon) *3* **84** Led stands side, onepcd fnl 1f: May foal: half brother to a 6f wnr: dam wnr over 7f at 2, later useful at 11/14f: sire a smart miler: eff at 7f on gd, 1m will suit: imprvd from debut, 'wrong side' winner & can find similar.
ALQAAHIR 0 [9] Saeed bin Suroor 2-9-0 L Dettori 9/2: 3: b c Swain - Crafty Example (Crafty *nk* **83** Prospector) Slow away, rear far side, hdwy to chase wnr over 1f out, not his pace on debut: tchd 7/1: Apr foal: half brother to a 6f/1m wnr: stays 7f on gd: pleasing start, rate higher.
BURGUNDIAN 0 [8] J Noseda 2-9-0 T E Durcan 25/1: 4: Chsd ldr stands side, ev ch over 1f out, onepcd. *¾* **81**
39**ALLIED CAUSE 32** [6]2-8-9 N Mackay(3) 10/1: 05: Chsd ldrs far side, no impress ins fnl 1f: op 7/1. *2* **72**
TREBLE SEVEN 0 [12]2-8-9 M Hills 20/1: 6: Chsd ldrs stands side, ev ch 2f out, no impress fnl 1f. *1¾* **68**
PHI 0 [5]2-9-0 K Darley 33/1: 7: Made most towards far side over 4f, no extra fnl 1f on debut. *¾* **71**
ESKIMOS NEST 0 [11]2-8-9 S W Kelly 100/1: 8: Dwelt, switched towards far side & sn cl-up, no impress. *shd* **65**
4223 **SELIKA 18** [14]2-9-0 W Ryan 150/1: 09: In tch stands side, no impress over 1f out. *¾* **68**
4190 **BOXHALL 19** [1]2-9-0 J Murtagh 12/1: 60: 10th: Rear far side, no impress over 1f out. *hd* **67**
4422 **MUDDY 9** [13]2-9-0 W Supple 66/1: 500: 11th: Handy stands side, no impress over 1f out. *shd* **66**
4052 **MAMBAZO 27** [2]2-9-0 J F Egan 100/1: 000: 12th: Rcd in 2nd far side till over 2f out, no impress 1f out. *9* **48**
MISSY CINOFAZ 0 [10]2-8-9 T P Queally 100/1: 0: 13th: In tch stands side, btn 3f out on debut. *1¾* **39**
MONT SAINT MICHEL 0 [3]2-9-0 D Holland 25/1: 0: 14th: In tch far side, lost action over 5f out. *shd* **43**
14 Ran Time 1m 26.36 (3.76) Owned: Mr K Abdulla Trained: Newmarket

4612

3.15 Danny Wright Selling Stakes 3-4yo (G4)
£2632 £752 £376 **1m2f21y** **Good 41** **-37 Slow** Inside

4372 **LENWADE 11** [5] G G Margarson 3-8-5 (40) A McCarthy 11/1: 0045221: Chsd ldrs, hdwy to lead over 1f out, pushed out ins fnl 1f: bought in for 10,400 gns: eff at 10f on fast & gd, flat trk: 1st win: see 1454. **50**
4399 **SKIBEREEN 10** [4] I W McInnes 4-9-3 (65) D Holland 5/1: 0350002: Cl-up, kept on ins fnl 1f: *nk* **53** claimed for 6,000: clr of rem: imprvd for this drop into sell grade: see 1006.
4448 **GOLDEN QUEEN 8** [3] M D I Usher 3-8-5 Ashleigh Horton(7) 100/1: 03: b f Unfuwain - Queen Linear *3* **43** (Polish Navy) Cl-up, hdwy into 2nd over 4f out, led over 2f out till over 1f out, no extra ins fnl 1f: cost 55,000 gns: dam a US sprint wnr: prob stays 10f on gd: much imprvd for recent debut.
4199 **ROMEOS DAY 19** [2] M R Channon 3-8-10 vis (40) T E Durcan 16/1: 3000054: Led till over 2f out, no extra. *nk* **47**
3787 **PORT SODRICK 39** [1]3-8-10 (62) Hayley Turner(3) 7/1: 6645: Rcd in 2nd, lost place over 6f out, *1½* **45** rdn/not much room over 1f out, onepcd ins fnl 1f: see 3197.
4506 **SHAMWARI FIRE 4** [8]4-9-8 (49) J F McDonald(3) 7/1: 3300136: Rear, hdwy over 3f out, onepcd 1f out. *nk* **49**
4165 **SOVIET SPIRIT 21** [6]3-8-5 (51) D Fox(5) 16/1: 5350407: Mid-div, onepcd over 1f out. *1¾* **36**
4199* **OKTIS MORILIOUS 19** [9]3-9-1 (55) L Dettori 9/4 FAV: 5104018: Dwelt, nvr a factor: claimed for 6,000. *nk* **45**
4195 **SOVIET SCEPTRE 19** [10]3-8-10 (62) K Fallon 5/1: 6-304609: Keen in rear, hung right & no impress. *9* **26**
3449 **FOX HOLLOW 53** [7]3-8-10 (35) J Quinn 66/1: 6230000: 10th: Al bhd: 8 wk abs. *3* **21**
10 Ran Time 2m 12.01 (7.81) Owned: The Lenwade Partnership Trained: Newmarket

4613

3.45 Totejackpot Stakes Handicap For The Golden Jubilee Trophy 3yo+ 71-85 (D2) **[66]**
£10561 £3250 £1625 **1m2f21y** **Good 41** **-07 Slow** Inside

4374 **TATA NAKA 11** [7] Mrs C A Dunnett 4-8-7 (21oh) (45) Hayley Turner(3) 100/1: 0022341: Mid-div, hdwy to lead 2f out, drvn out ins fnl 1f: stays 11.5f on fast & gd, massive improvement back at 10f. **71**
3522 **RIVER TREAT 49** [2] G Wragg 3-8-12 (78) J F Egan 16/1: 4-165042: Rear, hdwy over 2f out, kept on: *1* **80** 7 wk abs: prev eff at 6/7f, stayed first start at 10f: gd run: see 1125.
3961 **WINNERS DELIGHT 32** [13] A P Jarvis 3-8-13 (79) K Darley 6/1: 0553003: Mid-div, keen, hdwy over *nk* **80** 1f out, kept on: tchd 8/1: see 2919.
4392 **VAMP 11** [5] R M Beckett 3-8-9 (75) J Quinn 20/1: 0231504: Rear, no run over 2f out till over 1f *1½* **74+** out, styd on ins fnl 1f: acts on firm & gd: much closer with a clr run, one to keep in mind for sim: see 2980.
4392 **LIQUID FORM 11** [3]4-9-0 (73) K Fallon 9/2 J FAV: 3-000605: Rear, not clr run over 2f out, styd *hd* **71** on fnl 1f: shade closer with a clr run: see 2185.
4185 **VANTAGE 19** [1]3-8-11 bl (77) T E Durcan 20/1: 3145046: Rear, some late gains. *1½* **73**
4305* **STRETTON 15** [12]6-9-7 (80) L Dettori 9/2 J FAV: 0344017: Chsd ldrs, not much room & lost *½* **75** position well over 1f out, no ch after: closer with a clr run: see 4305.
3377 **TREW CLASS 55** [4]3-8-11 (77) P Robinson 8/1: 001138: Chsd ldrs, no impress fnl 1f: 8 wk abs. *hd* **71**
2185 **BALTIC BLAZER 104** [14]4-9-2 (75) D Holland 9/1: 21-59: Rcd in 2nd, no impress ins fnl 1f: op 14/1. *hd* **68**
3879 **GREY CLOUDS 35** [8]4-9-6 (79) W Supple 13/2: 1232250: 10th: Rear, btn when hmpd over 2f out. *5* **64**
LADYS VIEW 31 [15]3-9-4 (84) J Murtagh 20/1: 41-300: 11th: Slow away, sn handy, no impress. *nk* **68**
4453 **FLAME QUEEN 8** [9]3-8-0 (62) Lisa Jones 66/1: 0004040: 12th: Keen & sn led to 2f out, no extra fnl 1f. *2½* **46**

3961 **DONNA VITA 32** [11]3-9-3 (83) T P Queally 20/1: 10-4000: 13th: Rear, nvr nr ldrs: see 1619. *14* **42**
13 Ran Time 2m 9.02 (4.82) Owned: Mr Andy Middleton Trained: Norwich

4614

4.20 Listed John Musker Stakes Fillies & Mares 3yo+ (A1)
£17400 £6600 £3300 **1m2f21y** **Good 41** **+10 Fast** Inside

3629 **POLAR JEM 45** [5] G G Margarson 4-8-13 (98) A McCarthy 5/2: 1116321: Made virtually all, drvn out to hold on ins fnl 1f: fast time: nicely bckd, 6 wk abs: loves to dominate over 9/10f on firm or gd, easy or stiff trks: 5th win this term, most tough, progressive & useful: see 2592. **104**
3089 **SHAMARA 68** [4] C F Wall 4-8-13 (90) J Murtagh 18/1: 10-22402: Mid-div, hdwy into 2nd over 1f out, kept on: abs: useful, improved run: see 1781. *½* **102**
4149 **LA PERSIANA 22** [11] W Jarvis 3-8-6 (100) K Darley 15/8 FAV: 5211123: Trkd ldrs & keen, onepcd ins fnl 1f: nicely bckd: continues to run well: see 4149. *2* **99**
4331 **SILK FAN 13** [9] P W Harris 3-8-6 (95) D Holland 11/2: 11-16444: Slow away in rear, hdwy over 2f out, wknd fnl 1f: clr of rem: see 2918 & 3564. *1¼* **97**
3990 **DAMI 30** [3]3-8-6 p (77) T P Queally 40/1: 5221155: Cl-up, outpcd & btn from 2f out: stiff task. *4* **91$**
4502 **BOOT N TOOT 5** [6]3-8-6 (76) J F Egan 100/1: 0106: Rear, nvr a factor: poss flattered. *nk* **90$**
4530 **WEECANDOO 4** [12]6-8-13 (84) G Carter 33/1: 154-0057: Al bhd: quick reapp. *nk* **89$**
4149 **CRYSTAL 22** [7]3-8-6 (93) M Hills 8/1: 0-21508: Rcd in 2nd, lost place & wknd 2f out: op 12/1. *1* **87**
3615 **OLIVIA ROSE 46** [8]5-8-13 (83) J Quinn 33/1: 3141309: Rear, nvr a factor: 7 wk abs. *2½* **83**
4392* **TIDAL 11** [10]5-8-13 (88) L Dettori 10/1: 1034010: 10th: Cl-up, wknd 2f out: 'not suited by grnd'. *2* **80**
4021 **RAINBOW QUEEN 28** [1]4-8-13 (88) K Fallon 20/1: 10/-300: 11th: Trkd ldrs, no impress 2f out: 'stumbled twice 2f out'. *20* **50**
11 Ran Time 2m 7.36 (3.16) Owned: Norcroft Park Stud Trained: Newmarket

4615

4.50 Sea-Deer Levy Board Handicap Stakes 3yo+ 71-85 (D2) **[89]**
£7685 £2915 £1458 **1m3y** **Good 41** **-12 Slow** Stands side

4122 **LITTLE VENICE 23** [2] C F Wall 4-9-7 (82) K Darley 20/1: 5310001: With ldr till led 1f out, drvn out: eff at 7f/1m on firm & gd, handles soft: acts on any trk, likes Newmarket: best up with/forcing the pace. **92**
4542* **JOHANNIAN 3** [9] J M Bradley 6-8-8 (69) N Mackay(3) 3/1 FAV: 0463212: Rear, hdwy over 1f out, kept on to go 2nd post: quick reapp: remains in gd form: see 4542. *¾* **76**
4222 **BRAZILIAN TERRACE 18** [13] M L W Bell 4-9-0 (75) Hayley Turner(3) 16/1: 1302203: Chsd ldrs, kept on fnl 1f: gd run, back to form of 2414. *shd* **81**
4482 **CONCER ETO 6** [5] S C Williams 5-8-12 p (73) L Dettori 5/1: 3412004: Trkd ldrs, kept on fnl 1f. *shd* **78**
4180 **H HARRISON 20** [8]4-9-4 (79) L Vickers 25/1: 0350065: Led, hung left & hdd 1f out, sn no extra: suited by a sharp 7f, now stays 1m: back to form of 2282. *¾* **82**
2672 **SALINOR 84** [12]4-9-5 (80) K Fallon 7/2: 323-1106: Rear, eff 4f out, short of room ins fnl 1f, pulled out & kept on: long abs: shade closer with a clr run: gd eff, back to form of 1915. *shd* **82**
3826 **RAFFERTY 37** [4]5-9-6 bl (81) D Holland 8/1: 00-05347: Trkd ldrs, onepcd ins fnl 1f: see 3001. *¾* **81**
4222 **RED SAHARA 18** [6]3-8-11 (77) S W Kelly 25/1: 1662408: Chsd ldrs, onepcd ins fnl 1f. *nk* **76**
4141 **STAR SENSATION 22** [10]4-9-2 (77) M Coumbe(7) 20/1: 6560049: Slow away, nvr a factor: see 1231. *1¼* **73**
4295 **TIBER TIGER 16** [11]4-8-11 bl (72) T E Durcan 16/1: 0555600: 10th: Slow away in rear, nvr a factor. *hd* **67**
4469 **KING OF DIAMONDS 7** [14]3-8-11 (77) W Supple 8/1: 2001040: 11th: Rear, nvr a factor: quick reapp. *3½* **65**
11 Ran Time 1m 39.35 (4.25) Owned: Hintlesham SPD Partners Trained: Newmarket

4616

5.25 Teletext 'hands And Heels' Apprentice Handicap Stakes 3yo+ 46-55 (F4) **[65]**
£3037 £868 £434 **7f3y** **Good 41** **-05 Slow** Stands side

3232 **HALCYON MAGIC 61** [6] M Wigham 6-8-9 bl (46) Laura Pike(5) 14/1: 0020601: Chsd ldrs, hdwy to lead ins fnl 1f, kept on: 9 wk abs: eff at 6f/1m on fast & gd/soft, handles firm: acts on any trk, loves Yarmouth: runs well fresh: won this race 2 years ago off a 10lb higher mark: gd start for new yard (prev with J Feilden). **52**
2999 **FEAST OF ROMANCE 71** [7] G A Huffer 7-8-9 (1oh)bl (45) T Block(5) 40/1: 0306402: Led till ins fnl 1f, kept on: long abs: new stable (prev with C Allen): gd eff: see 2347. *¾* **49**
4345 **LINDENS LADY 13** [1] J R Weymes 4-8-13 (50) T Dean(7) 12/1: 5650543: Chsd ldrs, onepcd fnl 1f. *1¾* **49**
4488* **MY GIRL PEARL 6** [5] M S Saunders 4-9-1 (6ex) (52) W Hogg 13/2: 4103614: Handy, hdwy & ev ch over 1f out, sn onepcd: quick reapp: remains in decent form: see 4488. *½* **50**
4300 **LUCEFER 16** [4]6-9-1 (52) Jemma Marshall(5) 8/1: 4403105: Rear, hdwy over 2f out, onepcd fnl 1f. *1* **48**
3996 **TAIYO 30** [9]4-8-9 (46) R J Killoran(5) 12/1: 00P0156: Chsd ldrs, onepcd fnl 1f. *shd* **41**
846 **BLAKESEVEN 185** [13]4-8-11 (48) A Rutter(5) 20/1: 0-322307: Chsd ldrs, onepcd over 1f out: long abs. *¾* **41**
4488 **TEMPER TANTRUM 6** [11]6-9-4 p (55) H Poulton 9/2: 4054658: Slow away in rear, mod late gains. *nk* **47**
4539 **LORD CHAMBERLAIN 3** [16]11-9-4 bl (55) C J Davies(3) 10/1: 0140259: Slow away in rear, mod late gains. *shd* **46**
3911 **INDIAN LILY 33** [15]3-8-6 (47) S O'Hara(3) 50/1: 5060000: 10th: Nvr a factor: see 2439. *2½* **33**
4150 **HAMMER OF THE GODS 22** [10]4-8-9 (1oh)t (45) A Hindley(5) 25/1: 0500/-330: 11th: Chsd ldrs, no impress over 1f out: lost a front shoe. *½* **31**
4165 **ZONNEBEKE 21** [3]3-8-5 (46) B O'Neill(5) 25/1: 3412060: 12th: Slow away, hdwy 3f out, no impress. *¾* **29**
4367 **WOOD FERN 12** [8]4-8-12 (49) T O'Brien(7) 33/1: 0006100: 13th: In tch, btn over 1f out. *1* **30**
3759 **MAUREEN ANN 40** [14]4-8-11 (48) K Pierrepont(5) 20/1: 000-0000: 14th: Nvr a factor: 6 wk abs. *½* **28**
4126 **CHARLOTTEBUTTERFLY 23** [2]4-9-2 (53) K Jackson(5) 12/1: 3-040030: 15th: Handy, wknd over 2f out. *½* **32**
4475 **SCARROTTOO 6** [12]6-9-4 (55) Dean Williams 7/2 FAV: 0315030: 16th: Cl-up, lost place 2f out, sn eased, saddle slipped: quick reapp. *17* **0**
16 Ran Time 1m 25.85(3.25) Owned: The Magic Partnership Trained: Newmarket

Official Going Good/Soft HEAVY RAIN THROUGH THE AFTERNOON

4617

2.10 Audi A4 Maiden Auction Stakes 2yo (E3)
£3458 £1064 £532 **6f str** **Good/Soft** **Inapplicable**

4401 **INGLETON 11** [18] B A McMahon 2-8-7 G Gibbons 5/1: 041: Made all, rdn & just held on cl-home: eff at 6f on fast & gd/soft grnd, gall trks: improved for forcing tactics: see 4401, 3988. **88**
REAL QUALITY 0 [3] I Semple 2-8-11 Dean McKeown 66/1: 2: br g Elusive Quality - Pleasant Prize (Pleasant Colony) Dwelt & towards rear, hdwy 2f out & styd on well under kind hand ride ins last, just failed: May foal, half-brother to several US wnrs, dam unrcd: eff at 6f, 7f will suit: acts on gd/soft & a gall trk: promising. *hd* **91+**
3883 **CAPTAIN JOHNNO 35** [13] D R Loder 2-8-9 BL K Darley 16/1: 03: Cl-up, rdn & no extra from dist: blnks, has been gelded, imprvd eff: eff at 6f on gd/soft grnd, get further: see 3883. *2½* **82**
4269 **MOON FOREST 17** [6] P W Chapple Hyam 2-8-7 A Culhane 1/1 FAV: 24: Chsd ldrs, kept on fnl 2f, not able to land a blow: btr 4269 (7f, gd, debut). *2* **75**
3755 **HITS ONLY CASH 41** [16]2-8-9 N Callan 33/1: 605: Chsd ldrs, rdn & no extra over 1f out: 6 wk abs. *2½* **70**
4549 **COMPTON CLASSIC 3** [14]2-8-9 N Mackay(3) 100/1: 066: Keen & held up, mod late prog, nvr a threat. *2* **65**
4401 **HAENERTSBURG 11** [11]2-8-2 P Mathers(3) 50/1: 07: b f Victory Note - Olivia's Pride (Digamist) Chsd ldrs, no impress fnl 2f: Apr foal, cheaply bght: sister to a 6f juv wnr: dam unrcd. *5* **46**
4337 **SWEET MARGUERITE 14** [17]2-8-2 (60) C Catlin 33/1: 544608: Cl-up, btn over 1f out. *¾* **44**
BLACKNYELLO BONNET 0 [15]2-8-4 J Fanning 20/1: 9: Dwelt, sn chsd ldrs, btn 2f out. *1¾* **42**
4338 **HIGH PETERGATE 14** [10]2-8-6 T Lucas 33/1: 540: 10th: Chsd ldrs, struggling halfway: btr 4338 (fm). *¾* **42**
ORPENDONNA 0 [1]2-8-4 P Fessey 14/1: 0: 11th: Al towards rear, nvr a factor. *¾* **38**
3755 **SLATE GREY 41** [7]2-8-7 VIS (57) Darren Williams 100/1: 00000: 12th: Held up, not land blow, vis, abs. *2½* **34**
STANLEY ARTHUR 0 [2]2-8-9 A Nicholls 66/1: 0: 13th: Sn rdn & bhd, only mod prog. *3½* **27**
4244 **ENBORNE AGAIN 19** [9]2-8-7 P Hanagan 25/1: 00: 14th: Bhd, no ch over 2f out. *½* **23**
4171 **MYTTONS BELL 21** [12]2-8-2 (65) Hayley Turner(3) 10/1: 2303050: 15th: Cl-up when saddle slipped early, struggling halfway. *3* **11**
MOUNT KELLET 0 [4]2-8-9 D Holland 25/1: 0: 16th: Dwelt & al bhd. *3½* **9**
Sonic Anthem 0 [5]2-9-0 Alex Greaves 50/1:0 4172 **Shatin Leader 21** [8]2-8-2 (59) Dale Gibson 50/1:0
18 Ran Time 1m 14.41 (5.11) Owned: Mr J C Fretwell Trained: Tamworth

4618

2.40 All New Audi A6 Handicap Stakes 3yo+ 56-70 (E3) **[73]**
£7202 £2216 £1108 **5f str** **Good/Soft** **Inapplicable**

3796 **BLUEBERRY RHYME 40** [27] P A Blockley 5-8-7 (2oh)vis (52) N Callan 50/1: 0150001: Cl-up/dsptd lead stands side, led that group over 1f out, rdn & held on well cl-home: 6 wk abs: suited by 5f on fast, gd/soft & both AWs: likes to race with/force the pace & goes well fresh: see 960 & 742. **62**
4339 **STRAWBERRY PATCH 14** [26] Miss L A Perratt 5-8-10 p (57) P Fessey 20/1: 5021062: Chsd ldrs stands side, kept on well ins last, not reach wnr: acts on firm & gd/soft grnd: see 3960. *½* **62**
4240* **HOUT BAY 19** [22] R A Fahey 7-9-6 (67) P Hanagan 13/2: 3624113: Mid-div stands side, styd on well for press, nrst fin: remains in gd form: see 4240. *1¾* **69**
4514 **KINGS COLLEGE BOY 5** [1] R A Fahey 4-9-7 bl (68) Dale Gibson 14/1: 0301024: Trkd ldrs far side, drvn & led that group ins last, just held by stands side cl-home: qck reapp & still in fine form, stablemate of 3rd. *hd* **69**
4010 **SHARP HAT 30** [5]10-9-2 (63) A Culhane 25/1: 0030245: Led/dsptd lead far side, no extra well ins last. *shd* **64**
4398 **SESSAY 11** [16]3-9-3 (65) P M Quinn 33/1: 4350606: Rdn towards rear stands side, kept on, nrst fin. *hd* **65**
4240 **MISTER MAL 19** [3]8-8-11 (58) J Fanning 10/1: 1003127: Dwelt, chsd ldrs far side, no extra ins last. *nk* **57**
4240 **BRANTWOOD 19** [12]4-8-8 t (55) G Gibbons 16/1: 2306058: Mid-div stands side, some hdwy for press. *1¾* **51**
4339* **TROJAN FLIGHT 14** [19]3-9-5 (67) R Winston 3/1 FAV: 4321219: Held up stands side, eff halfway, nvr able to chall: btr 4339 (6f, fm). *1* **61**
4197 **SWEET CANDO 20** [20]3-8-11 p (59) D Holland 14/1: 2050030: 10th: Held up stands side, nvr dngr. *½* **51**
4210 **AAHGOWANGOWAN 20** [23]5-9-2 t (63) S W Kelly 16/1: 2150520: 11th: Led stands side till over 1f out. *hd* **54**
4094 **BLUE POWER 27** [2]3-8-12 (60) Darren Williams 50/1: 3102020: 12th: Chsd ldrs far side, btn over 1f out. *hd* **50**
4408 **BALLYBUNION 10** [24]5-8-7 (54) A Nicholls 9/1: 0510320: 13th: Bhd stands side, mod hdwy: btr 4408. *hd* **43**
3667 **MYSTERY PIPS 44** [21]4-8-7 (9oh)vis (45) Kim Tinkler 100/1: 0400430: 14th: Chsd ldrs stands side, btn over 1f out, abs: see 3667. *nk* **42**
4508 **ROBWILLCALL 5** [6]4-8-7 (7oh) (47) P Bradley 100/1: 5155050: 15th: Chsd ldrs far side 4f, qck reapp. *½* **40**
4408 **WILLIAMS WELL 10** [14]10-8-8 bl (55) K Darley 20/1: 0506330: 16th: Mid-div stands side, nvr land blow. *shd* **41**
4339 **COLLEGE MAID 14** [7]7-8-10 vis (57) N Mackay(3) 33/1: 6665300: 17th: Bhd far side, sn rdn & nvr factor. *hd* **42**
4514 **RECTANGLE 5** [15]4-9-5 (66) Alex Greaves 50/1: 0020000: 18th: Chsd ldrs stands side, btn 2f out. *¾* **49**
4508 **LAS RAMBLAS 5** [25]7-8-7 (1ow)(6oh)t p (48) D Nolan 100/1: 00640-00: 19th: b g Thatching - Raise A Warning (Warning) Al bhd stands side, nvr a factor, qck reapp: plcd '03 (rtd 48, h'cap): unplcd '02 (rtd 62, h'cap): eff at 6f on firm, gd/soft & fibresand, any trk: eff with/without visor, now wears a t-strap. *¾* **35**
2 May'01 Nott 6g/s 69-66 G: 2 Mar'01 Wolv 6af 67a- E:
4240 **REGAL SONG 19** [4]8-8-13 bl (60) D McGaffin 100/1: 5-000000: 20th: Al bhd far side & nvr a factor. *1* **38**
4404* **Mutayam 10** [10]4-8-7 (3ex)(6oh)t(48) P Mathers(2) 66/1:0
4240 **Roman Mistress 19** [17]4-9-5 bl(66) T Lucas 33/1:0
3482 **Spy Master 52** [18]6-8-7 (19oh)t p(35) Hayley Turner(3) 100/1:0
4245 **Viewforth 19** [9]6-8-12 bl(59) C Catlin 14/1:0
4087 **Champagne Cracker 27** [8]3-9-0 (62) J Carroll 100/1:0 3942 **Silver Mascot 33** [11]5-8-10 (57) T Eaves(3) 66/1:0
26 Ran Time 1m 0.19 (3.59) Owned: Mr Nigel Shields Trained: Cockerham

4619

3.10 Audi Tt Chase European Breeders Fund Novice Stakes 2yo (D2)
£5408 £1664 £832 **1m rnd** **Good/Soft** **Inapplicable**

4212* **THUNDERWING 20** [5] K R Burke 2-9-4 (91) Darren Williams 7/4 JT FAV: 3111: Trkd front pair, prog & led over 2f out, rdn out, decisively: suited by 1m, shld get further: acts on fast, relishes gd/soft & hvy grnd, stiff/gall or easy trk: tough, useful & progressive: see 4212, 3831. **100**
4257* **ROCAMADOUR 18** [3] M R Channon 2-9-2 (88) A Culhane 9/4: 512: Trkd ldr, ch over 2f out, onepace. *2½* **92**
4247 **FENRIR 19** [4] J R Weymes 2-9-2 (83) R Winston 25/1: 0153: Held up in tch, eff to chase ldr 2f out, no impress ins last: fair run, stays 1m: likes gd/soft & hvy grnd: see 4083 (7f, hvy). *1½* **87**
4154 **MELROSE AVENUE 26** [1] M Johnston 2-9-5 J Fanning 7/4 JT FAV: 5154: Sn led but hung right throughout, hdd over 2f out & sn btn: continued tendency to hang right: see 4154 & 2897. *½* **91**
4 Ran Time 1m 44.63 (8.03) Owned: Market Avenue Racing Club Ltd Trained: Leyburn

4620

3.40 New Ayr Audi 'premier' Claiming Stakes 3yo+ (D2)
£7033 £2164 £1082 **1m1f20y** **Good/Soft** **Inapplicable**

4550+**THE PRINCE 3** [7] Ian Williams 10-9-2 (79) C Catlin 7/4 FAV: 1-112111: Rear, pushed along over 3f out, styd on for press to lead well ins last, gamely: qck reapp, completed a hat-trick: eff at 7.5f/9f on firm, soft & both AWs: most tough & genuine 10yo loves claim grade: see 4550, 4266. **75**
4284 **DONNAS DOUBLE 17** [17] D Eddy 9-8-10 p (49) K Darley 25/1: 6343462: Chsd ldrs, rdn to chall over 1f out, not pace of wnr well ins last: much btr run, shld find a claim: see 2832. *1¼* **63**
4397 **CHERISHED NUMBER 11** [2] I Semple 5-9-10 p (70) R Winston 10/1: 4053043: Mid-div, styd on for press, not pace of wnr: see 2317. *1* **75**
4550 **YENALED 3** [8] K A Ryan 7-9-5 (72) N Callan 10/1: 2242104: Held up, kept on late for press, no dngr. *hd* **69**
4305 **CATS WHISKERS 16** [10]5-9-10 (79) Dale Gibson 7/1: 0340205: Handy & led over 2f out till ins last. *½* **73**
4012 **SPREE VISION 30** [3]8-8-10 vis (47) P Hanagan 66/1: 0422456: Mid-div, hdwy over 2f out, no extra dist. *2* **55**
695 **YORK CLIFF 208** [14]6-9-2 (76) P Mathers(5) 14/1: 00-05457: Rear, mod late prog, nvr a threat: 7 mth abs. *½* **60**
4550 **SCOTTYS FUTURE 3** [9]6-9-10 (72) J Fanning 12/1: 0106548: Held up, eff 2f out, btn dist: qck reapp. *hd* **67**
4550 **SARRAAF 3** [12]8-9-2 (64) A Culhane 20/1: 5203469: Mid-div, no impress fnl 1f: 7f/1m poss best. *4* **52**
4598 **PAS DE SURPRISE 1** [5]6-8-10 (50) D Nolan(2) 50/1: 44540000: 10th: Handy, btn 2f out: unplcd yesterday. *½* **45**
4246 **SOLLER BAY 19** [4]7-9-5 (69) Darren Williams 25/1: 6-200400: 11th: Led till over 2f out, sn btn: btr 4086. *2* **50**
4266 **TRAVELLING BAND 18** [11]6-9-8 vis (72) D Holland 6/1: 4-006020: 12th: Held up, rdn & no impress. *1½* **50**
4377 **CRATHORNE 12** [15]4-9-10 p (71) N Mackay(3) 16/1: 4340000: 13th: Held up, no impress fnl 3f: see 1668. *shd* **52**
4266 **Ben Hur 18** [13]5-9-2 (72) S W Kelly 20/1:0
4336 **Business Matters 14** [6]4-9-5 Hayley Turner(3) 100/1:0
4088 **Axford Lord 27** [1]4-8-12 vis(45) T Eaves(3) 100/1:0 **Lexicon 0** [16]4-9-5 J Carroll 150/1:0
17 Ran Time 2m 0.63 (No Std Time) Owned: Mr Patrick Kelly Trained: Alvechurch

4621

4.10 Audi A8 Classic Handicap Stakes 3yo 71-85 (D2) **[87]**
£6851 £2108 £1054 **1m rnd** **Soft** **Inapplicable**

4321* **EBORACUM 15** [10] T D Easterby 3-9-2 bl (75) K Darley 7/1: 2204111: Handy & led over 2f out, drvn out: completed hat-trick: eff at 1m/10f in blnks: acts on fast & soft, loves a gall trk: most game & progressive. **83**
4452 **SHOWTIME ANNIE 9** [4] A Bailey 3-8-7 (5oh) (61) R Winston 25/1: 0415002: Trkd ldrs, rdn & styd on well ins last, not pace to chall wnr: eff at 7f, apprec return to 1m: acts on fast, soft or fibresand: see 1896 (C/D). *1* **71**
3972 **SILVERHAY 32** [5] T D Barron 3-8-13 (72) J Fanning 11/2: 4241143: Led till over 2f out, kept on for press. *1½* **74**
4225 **ALFONSO 19** [8] B W Hills 3-9-4 (77) D Holland 6/4 FAV: 04-10024: Held up, styd on for press fnl 2f, not able to reach front trio: stays 1m, handles soft grnd but btr 4225 (gd, 7f). *¾* **78**
4286* **TYTHEKNOT 17** [7]3-9-1 P (74) P Hanagan 25/1: 2364315: Held up, eff 3f out, onepace: cheekpieces. *¾* **74**
4225 **BRIGHT SUN 19** [6]3-9-0 (73) Kim Tinkler 10/1: 3034106: Pulled hard chasing ldrs, btn over 1f out. *1¼* **70**
4085 **SHES OUR LASS 27** [11]3-9-7 (80) D Tudhope(7) 9/1: 3111127: Mid-div, eff over 2f out, sn btn: btr 4085. *3* **71**
4341 **NEON BLUE 14** [2]3-8-13 (72) Hayley Turner(3) 25/1: 3331608: Trkd ldrs, rdn & btn 2f out: btr 3433 (7f). *6* **53**
2525 **WEST HIGHLAND WAY 91** [3]3-9-5 (78) T Eaves(3) 25/1: 2502-159: Keen in mid-div, btn over 2f out: 2 mth abs: btr 1907 (mdn, 7f, firm). *1¾* **56**
4378* **POPPYS FOOTPRINT 12** [1]3-9-6 (79) N Callan 12/1: 5340P10: 10th: Held up, rdn & btn 2f out: btr 4378. *2* **53**
966 **GLENCAIRN STAR 171** [9]3-8-7 (2oh) (64) N Mackay(3) 33/1: 05-00: 11th: b c Selkirk - Bianca Nera (Salse) Bhd & no ch from halfway: h'cap bow, 6 mth abs: unplcd in '03 (lightly rcd, rtd 71, mdn). *dist* **0**
11 Ran Time 1m 45.36 (8.76) Owned: Mrs K Arton Trained: Malton

4622

4.40 Allroad Challenge Handicap Stakes 3yo+ 56-70 (E3) **[77]**
£7056 £2171 £1086 **7f50y rnd** **Soft** **Inapplicable**

4398 **LOCOMBE HILL 11** [2] N Wilson 8-9-1 (64) D Tudhope(7) 7/1: 4401531: Keen & sn led, narrowly hdd ins last but rallied gamely to prevail line, all out: eff at 6f, best at 7f/1m on firm, hvy & fibresand, any trk, likes Ayr: eff forcing the pace: see 4088 & 417. **73**
4438 **NORTHERN GAMES 9** [9] K A Ryan 5-8-12 bl (61) N Callan 14/1: 0014242: Keen in mid-div, smooth prog to chall ins last, narrow lead, just hdd line: acts on fast, soft & fibresand: in fine form but remains a tricky ride for whom extreme waiting tactics prob suit: see 4438, 4272 & 3352. *shd* **69**
4339 **SHAROURA 14** [11] R A Fahey 8-9-1 (64) T Eaves(3) 25/1: 3424003: Trkd ldrs, onepace. *2½* **68**
4398 **BOLLIN EDWARD 11** [6] T D Easterby 5-9-1 vis (64) A Culhane 16/1: 2020204: Trkd ldrs, styd on onepace for press: handles soft, prob prefer firm & gd: see 2466, 2059. *5* **60**
4398 **DOWNLAND 11** [7]8-9-3 (66) Kim Tinkler 12/1: 1130265: Mid-div, drvn & onepace fnl 2f: btr 4093 (AW). *½* **61**
4251 **PERTEMPS MAGUS 18** [4]4-9-0 P (63) P Hanagan 7/1: 00-31636: Mid-div, no impress over 1f out. *2* **55**
4554 **ANTHEMION 3** [1]7-8-11 (60) D McGaffin 50/1: 3132007: Chsd ldrs, outpcd fnl 2f, qck reapp: btr 3593. *2* **49**
4272 **BRANSTON TIGER 17** [17]5-9-1 vis (64) D Holland 10/1: 5001438: Towards rear, rdn & mod prog. *¾* **52**
4086 **SCOTLAND THE BRAVE 27** [16]4-9-7 (70) C Catlin 14/1: 5041429: Mid-div, btn 2f out: btr 4086 & 3223. *½* **57**
4175 **RARE COINCIDENCE 21** [13]3-8-11 T (63) D Nolan(3) 33/1: 4400340: 10th: Rear, eff 2f out, sn btn: t-strap. *½* **49**

3244 **BUNDY 62** [8]8-9-0 (63) R Winston 25/1: 2320440: 11th: Held up, no impress fnl 2f, abs: btr 3129. *3* **44**
4398 **ROMAN MAZE 11** [3]4-8-12 (61) S W Kelly 10/1: 0042420: 12th: Al towards rear & nvr a factor: btr 4398. *6* **33**
4398 **YORKSHIRE BLUE 11** [14]5-8-12 (61) N Mackay(3) 14/1: 1105100: 13th: Held up, rdn & btn halfway. *3½* **28**
4339 **FAIR SHAKE 14** [5]4-9-6 vis (69) K Darley 13/2 FAV: 3502620: 14th: Bhd, no impress: btr 4339 (6f). *3½* **31**
4051 **Merdiff 28** [10]5-8-12 (61) P Mathers(5) 14/1:0 4514 **Sir Don 5** [18]5-8-12 (61) A Nicholls 33/1:0
4398 **Desert Leader 11** [15]3-9-1 (67) G Gibbons 50/1:0
1196* **Constable Burton 154** [12]3-8-13 (65) J Fanning 33/1:0
18 Ran Time 1m 33.76 (6.96) Owned: Mr Ian W Glenton Trained: York

4623

5.10 Audi A3 Guaranteed Sweepstakes Handicap For The Kilkerran Cup 3yo+ 56-70 (E3) **[77]**
£3250 £1000 £500 **1m2f192y Soft Inapplicable**

4215+**ARTISTIC STYLE 20** [11] B Ellison 4-9-5 (68) T Eaves(3) 100/30 FAV: 0013111: Mid-div, hdwy & led over 1f out, sn asserted, eased cl home, val 4L: eff at 1m/11f on fm & hvy: v progressive, win again. **80+**
4342 **DANCE TO MY TUNE 14** [16] M W Easterby 3-8-9 (65) Dale Gibson 14/1: 1041242: Mid-div, smooth hdwy to chase wnr over 1f out, kept on but held ins last: rest well covered: styd longer 11f trip: see 3990. *2½* **72**
1776 **CHAMPION LION 124** [3] M R Channon 5-9-4 (67) C Catlin 11/1: 0050633: Rear, smooth hdwy 3f out, no impress on front pair ins last: well clr of rem: 4 mth abs: acts on fast & soft, poss hvy: see 1295. *2* **70**
4145* **LUCAYAN DANCER 23** [12] D Nicholls 4-8-8 (57) J Fanning 8/1: 4-655014: Mid-div, smooth prog to chall over 1f out, no extra bef dist: see 4145. *6* **56**
4554 **ZANDEED 3** [8]6-8-10 (59) P Fessey 20/1: 0/-031405: Rear, late gains for press, no threat: qck reapp. *½* **57**
4138 **KIDZPLAY 24** [6]8-9-2 P (65) N Mackay(3) 12/1: 2153456: Led till over 2f out: chkpcs: see 2507. *½* **62**
4327 **LOADED GUN 15** [2]4-8-7 (2oh) (54) P Mathers(5) 20/1: 5/00-0247: Trkd ldrs, no extra fnl 2f: see 4084. *2* **51**
4406 **MARITIME BLUES 10** [14]4-9-0 (63) Dean McKeown 16/1: 3001058: Held up, nvr land a blow: see 4084. *5* **53**
4255 **JOLIZERO 18** [9]3-8-6 (62) A Culhane 8/1: 0-403259: Chsd ldrs, btn 2f out: bckd: btr 3856, 3618. *nk* **51**
4248 **MOUNT BENGER 19** [7]4-8-13 p (62) R Winston 14/1: 6041030: 10th: Held up, efft 3f out, no impress. *hd* **50**
4506 **LUCKY LARGO 5** [4]4-8-7 (8oh)bl (48) Leanne Kershaw(7) 100/1: 0000000: 11th: Keen, mid-div, btn 2f out. *3* **41**
1777 **THE FAIRY FLAG 124** [18]6-8-8 p (57) Hayley Turner(3) 25/1: 3436-400: 12th: Handy & led over 2f out till over 1f out, wknd qckly, abs. *3* **39**
4515 **GIUNCHIGLIO 5** [17]5-9-7 (70) S W Kelly 33/1: 3604160: 13th: Rear, little hdwy for press: btr 4076 (12f). *5* **47**
3667} **TARAWAN 396** [10]8-9-7 vis (70) D Holland 33/1: 040360-0: 14th: ch g Nashwan - Soluce (Junius) Rdn & bhd over 4f out, nvr a factor, reapp: landed 3 h'caps in '03, incl AW h'cap, amat riders & appr events: dual h'cap rnr-up in '03 (amat & appr h'caps): suited by 1m/10f, tried 12f+: acts on firm, hvy & polytrack, any trk: suited by a visor & a gd weight-carrier. 1 Mar'03 Leic 10.0g/f 74-65 D: 1 Mar'03 Donc 10.3g/s 68-60 E: 1 Mar'03 Ling 10ap 61a-52 E: 2 Feb'03 Ling 10ap 56a-52 F: 2 Jun'02 Hayd 10.5sft 65-63 G: 2 May'02 Pont 10gd 64-63 E: 2 Sep'01 Pont 10fm 68-67 E: 2 Jun'01 Good 9g/f 72-73 E: 1 Jun'01 Bath 10.2fm 75-67 F: *12* **35**
4215 **KINGS ENVOY 20** [13]5-8-10 (59) D McGaffin 100/1: 0-435000: 15th: Held up, rdn & btn 3f out. *9* **15**
3249 **NAKWA 62** [15]6-9-2 (65) N Callan 20/1: 2126000: 16th: Led/dsptd lead 9f, sn btn, 2 mth abs. *3* **18**
4170 **REPULSE BAY 21** [5]6-8-7 (11oh) (45) K Darley 33/1: 0000000: 17th: Sn well bhd & t.o.. *13* **0**
4327 **CALATAGAN 15** [1]5-9-6 (69) P Hanagan 7/1: 0/-315520: 18th: Pulled hard & cl-up, wknd 3f out, eased. *4* **5**
18 Ran Time 2m 29.46(13.46) Owned: Mr & Mrs D A Gamble Trained: Malton

PONTEFRACT THURSDAY 16.09.04 Lefthand, Undulating Track, Stiff Uphill Finish

Official Going Firm

4624

2.20 Betfair Com Apprentice Series Round 4 Handicap Stakes 3yo+ 46-55 (F4) **[61]**
£3605 £1109 £555 **1m2f6y Good/Firm 26 -18 Slow** Inside

780 **TIME MARCHES ON 199** [14] K G Reveley 6-8-7 T (40) Neil Brown(5) 20/1: 36/20-401: b g Timeless Times - Tees Gazette Girl (Kalaglow) Held up, prog wide 4f out, styd on to lead 1f out, pushed clr: long abs: unplcd sole 03/04 hdles start (rtd 55h, h'cap): rnr-up on 1 of only 2 '03 Flat starts (sell h'cap): sell h'cap wnr in '01: stays 12f, best around 10/11f: acts on fast & gd/soft, handles fibresand, goes well fresh & eff in t-strap. 2 Apr'03 Ripo 12.3g/f 39-38 F: 2 Jul'02 Pont 10g/s 41-39 F: 1 Jun'01 Nott 10g/f 31-26 G: **51**
4189 **ISLANDS FAREWELL 20** [3] D Nicholls 4-9-2 (49) P J Benson(7) 8/1: 0025032: Chsd ldrs, kept on ins fnl 1f 2nd, no ch with wnr: eff around 1m, ran to form on first try at 10f: see 4189 & 3246. *5* **51**
281 **FIRST EAGLE 258** [6] A L Forbes 5-8-7 vis (40) H Fellows(7) 22/1: 0/0032-03: b g Hector Protector - Merlin's Fancy (Caerleon) Mid-div, prog to chase wnr bef 1f out, kept on, just held for 2nd cl-home: long abs: plcd twice in '03 (rtd 57a, mdn, Mrs N Macauley): eff at 1m/10f on fast grnd & fibresand: eff with visor, tried pieces. 2 Nov'03 Wolv 9.4af 53a-(44) D: 2 Feb'02 Wolv 7af 62a- D: 2 Feb'02 Wolv 7af 61a-55 E: *nk* **41**
4373 **ROYAL INDULGENCE 12** [13] W M Brisbourne 4-9-1 (48) D Fentiman 9/2: 0500-144: Missed break, prog wide 3f out, hung left & no impress fnl 1f: btr 3766. *¾* **47**
4284 **TURFTANZER 17** [4]5-8-7 (10oh)t (30) Janice Webster(7) 50/1: 0045005: Handy over 1m: btr 2548. *3½* **34**
3370 **LUCKY ARCHER 56** [12]11-8-12 (45) C Haddon 20/1: 00-00006: Held up, prog bef 3f out, staying on when hmpd dist, not recover: shade closer but for interference: see 2135. *nk* **38**
4132 **DUBAI DREAMS 24** [7]4-8-12 T (45) R J Killoran(5) 9/1: 2500067: In tch, prog 4f out, wknd fnl 2f: t-strap. *2½* **34**
3995 **TYZACK 31** [9]3-9-2 (55) K Pierrepont(5) 16/1: 40-50008: Led after 1f, hdd dist, fdd: btr 1088. *3½* **39**
3929 **LATE ARRIVAL 34** [1]7-8-7 (40) A Mullen 4/1 FAV: 0026049: Al in rear: bckd: btr 3929. *½* **23**
4340 **BANNERS FLYING 14** [2]4-8-12 (45) K Ghunowa(3) 33/1: 4040000: 10th: Bhd, nvr a factor: see 3486. *21* **2**
4113 **SIXTILSIX 26** [5]3-8-6 (45) Dean Williams 16/1: 000-0030: 11th: Led 1f, styd handy, fdd fnl 2f. *4* **0**
4320 **REIGN OF FIRE 15** [8]3-9-0 (53) K May(3) 18/1: 46-0000: 12th: Al in rear: op 16/1. *16* **0**
2333 **WAKE UP HENRY 98** [10]3-9-2 VIS (55) R Kingscote(7) 6/1: 006-0340: 13th: Keen in tch over 7f, wknd. *1¾* **0**
3868 **DISPOL EVITA 36** [11]5-8-12 (45) H Poulton 9/1: 420400U: Held up, rcd wide on bend, slipped up & u.r. after 4f: see 3287. **0**
14 Ran Time 2m 12.50 (4.4) Owned: Mrs M B Thwaites Trained: Saltburn

4625 **2.50 Reg Vardy Rotherham Renault Median Auction Maiden Stakes 2yo (E3)**
£4124 £1269 £635 **5f rnd** **Good/Firm 26** **-21 Slow** Inside

SEAMUS SHINDIG 0 [5] H Candy 2-9-0 Dane O'Neill 3/1: 1: b g Aragon - Sheesha (Shadeed) Led early, styd cl-up, styd on to lead 1f out, rdn out, val bit more: debut: tchd 4/1: Apr foal, cost 2,800gns: half-brother to wnrs at 6/7f: dam unrcd: sire fine performer around 1m: eff at 5f, sure to apprec further: acts on fast grnd & a stiff/undul trk: goes well fresh: sure to impr for this & has a bright future. **90+**
4497 **ALEXIA ROSE 6** [1] A Berry 2-8-9 (63) W Supple 12/1: 60432: Bhd, prog halfway, ev ch just ins fnl 1f, kept on but not pace of wnr: qck reapp: op 9/1: acts on fast & gd grnd: another gd run: see 4497. *¾* **81**
4401 **SAMS SECRET 11** [2] J A Glover 2-8-9 F Norton 4/5 FAV: 23: Sn led, hdd 1f out, no extra: eff at 5/6f: ran to form of debut in 4401. *1¾* **76**
4497 **CESAR MANRIQUE 6** [4] B W Hills 2-9-0 M Hills 6/1: 054: Keen in tch 3f, sn outpcd, rallied late: op 9/2 on qck reapp: needs further: see 4497. *¾* **79**
4349 **AYNSLEY 13** [6]2-8-9 M Henry 12/1: 45: In tch over 3f, sn wknd, eased ins fnl 1f: see 4349. *8* **52**
5 Ran Time 1m 3.68 (2.38) Owned: Mr Henry Candy Trained: Wantage

4626 **3.20 John And Diane's 50th Birthday Bash Selling Handicap Stakes 3yo+ 46-55 (F4)** **[64]**
£3605 £1109 £555 **1m4y rnd** **Good/Firm 26** **-20 Slow** Inside

3759 **VERMILION CREEK 41** [15] R Hollinshead 5-8-13 p (49) K Fallon 6/1 FAV: 6620601: Held up, prog wide 2f out, rdn out to lead cl-home: no bid: 6 wk abs: eff btwn 1m/12f on fast, gd/soft & fibresand: goes well fresh: apprec re-fitting of cheek pieces: enjoys coming late off a strong pace: see 1348. **56**
4379* **RYMERS RASCAL 12** [8] E J Alston 12-8-12 (48) W Supple 8/1: 0020612: Mid-div, prog 3f out, styd on to lead 1f out, hdd cl-home: continues to run well: ran to form of win in 4379. *nk* **53**
4248 **ENCOUNTER 19** [3] J Hetherton 8-8-9 (45) D Fentiman(7) 7/1: 0250053: Mid-div, prog when short of room over 2f out & bef 1f out, kept on, no ch with front 2: has ability & is on a fair mark. *1½* **47**
4090 **SUPER DOMINION 27** [4] R Hollinshead 7-8-11 p (47) Dane O'Neill 20/1: 0100054: Held up, prog wide 3f out, no impress ins fnl 1f: stablemate of wnr: see 2725. *hd* **48**
4485 **DANCING KING 7** [1]8-8-12 (48) P Makin(5) 9/1: 6255555: Led 7f, no extra: qck reapp: btr 1535. *2½* **44**
4507 **DELTA LADY 5** [7]3-8-0 (40) M Henry 50/1: 0500006: Rear, nvr nrr than mid-div: qck reapp: see 1591. *2* **32**
3850* **ALPINE HIDEAWAY 36** [19]11-8-13 p (49) G Parkin 16/1: 40-06017: Handy over 6f, wknd: recent rnr-up over hdles (rtd 97h, h'cap): showed more in 3850 (gd/soft). *1¼* **39**
3700 **TANCRED ARMS 43** [11]8-8-4 vis (40) Donna Caldwell(7) 25/1: 0-040048: Missed break, no dngr. *¾* **28**
3805 **WONDER WOLF 39** [18]3-8-8 (48) R Ffrench 12/1: 0-059: In tch over 6f, wknd: see 3805. *1¼* **34**
4411* **NAUGHTY GIRL 10** [5]4-9-2 (6ex)vis t (52) F P Ferris(3) 9/1: 4402010: 10th: Handy over 6f, wknd. *¾* **36**
3830 **MILLKOM ELEGANCE 38** [12]5-8-9 bl (45) A Mullen(7) 7/1: 0501-030: 11th: Mid-div, prog halfway, wknd fnl 2f: recently unplcd over hdles (rtd 60h, h'cap): btr 3830. *1¼* **27**
3262 **DISPOL VERITY 61** [2]4-8-5 (1ow) (40) S Hitchcott 33/1: 00/-00000: 12th: Chsd ldrs 6f, wknd: 9 wk abs. *shd* **22**
4284 **SUMMER SPECIAL 17** [17]4-8-9 (45) L Enstone 20/1: 3300040: 13th: In tch 6f, wknd: btr 4284. *¾* **24**
4130 **Ace Ma Vahra 24** [10]6-8-4 (40) J Bramhill 16/1:0
4379 **Transcendantale 12** [14]6-8-4 (40) R Thomas(3) 16/1:0
3996 **Peartree House 31** [13]10-8-4 (40) N Pollard 20/1:0 2891 **Delightful Gift 76** [16]4-8-9 (45) T Williams 50/1:0
17 Ran Time 1m 45.55 (3.75) Owned: Mr M Johnson Trained: Upper Longdon

4627 **3.50 Dixon Renault Stakes Handicap Fillies & Mares 3yo+ 71-85 (D2)** **[92]**
£6796 £2091 £1046 **6f rnd** **Good/Firm 26** **-07 Slow** Inside

4263 **SARISTAR 18** [2] P F I Cole 3-9-4 (82) K Fallon 5/1: 10-10051: Ld, hdd after 1f, styd on to lead again 2f out, sn clr, eased cl home, val 4L+: tried 7f, apprec drop back to 6f: acts on fast, gd/soft & fibresand: still only lightly rcd & is open to more improvement: see 1154. **88**
4253 **MADDIES A JEM 18** [1] J R Jenkins 4-8-13 (75) W Ryan 8/1: 5642162: Held up, prog bef 1f out, kept on for 2nd, no ch with wnr: another gd eff, can find similar poss on easier surface: see 4039 & 3952. *2½* **74**
3428 **FAVOUR 54** [3] Mrs J R Ramsden 4-8-7 (2oh) (67) J F Egan 7/1: 3-206003: Rear, prog when short of room bef 1f out, switched & kept on, just held for 2nd: 8 wk abs: gd run from out of h'cap: just btr 1878. *½* **67**
4278 **OBE BOLD 17** [6] A Berry 3-8-5 (67) F Norton 25/1: 4301004: Handy over 4f, no extra: just btr 3808. *1¼* **64**
4537 **IMPRESSIVE FLIGHT 4** [8]5-9-7 (83) W Supple 7/2 FAV: 36-00065: Bhd, prog when short of room bef 1f out, switched & kept on under kind ride: qck reapp: btr 3646 (reapp). *¾* **76**
4237* **LAKE CHARLOTTE 19** [7]3-8-6 T (70) N Pollard 13/2: 32316: Keen rear, prog halfway, fdd dist: first time t-strap: drop back to 5f will suit: showed more in 4237 (5f mdn, gd/soft). *2* **57**
2990* **COMPLICATION 72** [9]4-8-8 bl (70) Lisa Jones 4/1: 0624217: Sn bhd, nvr a factor: 10 wk abs: btr 2990. *½* **56**
4240 **CONSENSUS 19** [5]5-8-9 (71) T Williams 8/1: 3004608: Rcd keenly & led after 1f, hdd 2f out, sn hung left & wknd: showed more in 3852 & 3680 (5f). *8* **35**
3920 **SCARLET EMPRESS 34** [4]3-8-7 (71) Dane O'Neill 33/1: 60140-09: Handy over 4f, wknd: see 3920. *1* **32**
9 Ran Time 1m 16.41 (2.0) Owned: Mr R A Instone Trained: Whatcombe

4628 **4.20 Phil Bull Trophy Conditions Stakes 3yo+ (C2)**
£8978 £3406 £1703 **2m1f216y** **Good/Firm 26** **-02 Slow** Inside

4478 **CORRIB ECLIPSE 7** [4] Jamie Poulton 5-9-10 (106) J F Egan 6/4 FAV: 16661: Cl-up, led 5f out, under press well over 1f out, styd on strongly: bckd: qck reapp: eff at 2m2f/2m6f on firm & fast grnd: out & out stayer who apprec slt drop in grade: see 4478 & 2583. **106**
4383 **PUSHKIN 12** [2] M Johnston 6-9-2 (100) K Fallon 3/1: 0526-302: Rear, prog 4f out, styd on to chase ldr well over 1f out, kept on ins fnl 1f, not pace of wnr: clr rem: tchd 4/1: eff at 14f/15.5f, now stays 2m2f: acts on fast & soft grnd: see 4383. *1¾* **96**
4209 **VICARS DESTINY 20** [5] Mrs S Lamyman 6-8-11 (64) Dane O'Neill 16/1: 0643323: Held up, eff 6f out, no impress fnl 3f: stiff task at weights: see 4209 & 1069 (h'caps). *15* **75$**
4162 **ONE OFF 25** [6] Sir Mark Prescott 4-9-2 (90) J Mackay 2/1: 11112-04: In tch, ev ch over 4f out, *10* **70**

PONTEFRACT   THURSDAY 16.09.04   Lefthand, Undulating Track, Stiff Uphill Finish

sn wknd: v disapp: btr 4162 (reapp).
1753   **JAMAICAN FLIGHT 124** [1]11-9-2 (45) R Thomas(3) 25/1: 3444455: Led, hdd 5f out, sn wknd: long abs.   *21*   **48**
5 Ran   Time 3m 57.07 (5.07)   Owned: Mr M Ioannou   Trained: Lewes

---

4629   4.50 Harratts Renault Classified Stakes 3yo+ 0-80 (D2)
£6939 £2135 £1068   **1m4y rnd**   **Good/Firm 26**   **+04 Fast**   Inside

4301   **JAY GEES CHOICE 17** [8] M R Channon 4-9-2 (82) S Hitchcott 11/2: 3040461: Dictated slow pace, hdd   **89**
2f out, rallied to lead again 1f out, rdn out to hold on: op 7/1: eff at 7f/1m on firm & soft grnd: apprec gd
tactical ride today in slow run race: gd confidence boost & is well h'capped: see 3954 & 2076.
3112   **NAMROC 68** [3] E F Vaughan 3-9-1 (85) K Fallon 11/8 FAV: 142: Handy, outpcd after 5f, rallied ins   ½   **89**
fnl 1f, not btn far: 10 wk abs: well bckd: gd run on only 3rd ever start: further will suit, see 3112 & 2595.
4071   **ANNA PALLIDA 27** [7] P W Harris 3-8-9 (82) Dane O'Neill 7/2: 2231203: Cl-up, styd on to lead 2f   ½   **82**
out, hdd under press 1f out, sn no extra: eff at 1m, return to 10f will suit: apprec return to fast surface: see 3474.
4482   **STOIC LEADER 7** [2] R F Fisher 4-9-0 (78) J F Egan 7/1: 5256404: Bhd, prog bef 1f out, nvr dngrs.   3½   **76**
3794   **INTRICATE WEB 40** [4]8-9-0 (80) W Supple 9/1: 3010005: Handy 6f, no extra: 6 wk abs: btr 2560 (10f).   3½   **69**
3999   **LES ARCS 30** [6]4-9-0 (76) F Norton 12/1: 0213606: Keen in tch 6f, fdd: recent hdles unplcd.   10   **51**
4073   **HUMID CLIMATE 27** [1]4-9-0 (78) G Parkin 50/1: 0/130-07: Reluctant start, al adrift: see 4073.   12   **29**
7 Ran   Time 1m 43.62 (1.82)   Owned: Mr John Guest   Trained: West IIsley

---

4630   5.20 Lady Balk Maiden Stakes 3yo+ (D3)
£5629 £1732 £866   **1m2f6y**   **Good/Firm 26**   **+02 Fast**   Inside

4453   **FLAMBOYANT LAD 9** [2] B W Hills 3-9-0 (79) M Hills 8/11 FAV: 2-33321: Cl-up, led 2f out, sn   **89**
pushed clr, eased cl-home, val 12L+: eff around 10f on firm & gd/soft grnd: gd confidence boost: see 4453 & 4034.
4441   **MAGNETIC POLE 9** [4] Sir Michael Stoute 3-9-0 BL (83) K Fallon 6/4: 3-23022: Led, hdd under press   10   **75**
2f out, no extra: clr rem: btr 4441 (12f).
4354   **JIDIYA 13** [5] S Gollings 5-9-6 (68) J F Egan 14/1: 2-002033: Chsd ldrs, no extra over 4f out.   6   **66**
4407   **SILLOTH SPIRIT 10** [1] Mrs A M Naughton 4-9-6 N Pollard 125/1: 04: Missed break, nvr a factor.   *dist* **31**
4453   **UP THE AISLE 9** [3]7-9-6 L Enstone 100/1: 05: Handy over 6f, fdd.   10   **17**
5 Ran   Time 2m 10.55(2.45)   Owned: Maktoum Al Maktoum   Trained: Lambourn

---

YARMOUTH   THURSDAY 16.09.04   Lefthand, Flat, Fair Track

Official Going GOOD (GOOD/SOFT IN PLACES)

4631   2.30 European Breeders Fund Maiden Stakes 2yo (D3)
£5099 £1569 £785   **1m3y**   **Good/Soft 63**   **-04 Slow**   Stands side

4069   **RED ADMIRAL 27** [10] Saeed bin Suroor 2-9-0 L Dettori 6/1: 01: Rcd in 2nd, hdwy to lead over 3f   **92**
out, pushed out ins fnl 1f: relished this step up to 1m, will stay further: acts on gd/soft, flat trk: much imprvd
from debut, more to come & can win btr races: see 4069 (debut).
3126   **CLASP 68** [4] M L W Bell 2-9-0 R Mullen 13/2: 02: Rear, hdwy over 3f out, onepcd fnl 1f: 10 wk   2   **86**
abs: eff at 1m on gd/soft: shown enough both starts to find a race: see 3126 (debut).
4458   **OLIGARCH 8** [8] N A Callaghan 2-9-0 J Murtagh 5/6 FAV: 203: Cl-up, hdwy into 2nd 3f out, onepcd   nk   **85**
ins fnl 1f: nicely bckd: stays 1m: see 4139.
CLUELESS 0 [1] W J Haggas 2-9-0 T P Queally 25/1: 4: b c Royal Applause - Pure (Slip Anchor)   nk   **84+**
Rear, hdwy & hung right over 1f out, styd on well ins fnl 1f on debut: clr of rem: Feb foal, cost 26,000gns: dam
unrcd: eff at 1m on gd/soft: pleasing start, will come on for this & can find similar.
FORCE NINE 0 [6]2-9-0 K Ahern 16/1: 5: br c Stormin Fever - Screener (Major Impact) Dwelt in   6   **72**
rear, hdwy 4f out, no impress over 1f out on debut: Mar foal, cost $38,000: half-brother to a 2yo sprint wnr in the
US: dam a mid-dist wnr, sire smart at 7f/1m: with J Noseda & potential to do btr on this.
4326   **GIDAM GIDAM 15** [9]2-9-0 R L Moore 25/1: 66: Cl-up, no impress 2f out: see 4326.   2   **68**
RIVER CARD 0 [3]2-8-9 P Robinson 33/1: 7: ch f Zaha - Light Hand (Star Appeal) Al bhd on   ½   **62**
debut: Feb foal: half-sister to a dual 5/6f 2yo wnr: dam wnr over 10f, sire smart over 9f at 2: with M Tompkins.
KAHIRA 0 [7]2-8-9 S Sanders 20/1: 8: Al bhd on debut.   1   **60**
4376   **KING ZAFEEN 12** [2]2-9-0 t T E Durcan 9/1: 049: Slow away, rear, hdwy 3f out, no impress 1f out.   nk   **64**
3489   **PROPHETS CALLING 52** [11]2-9-0 J McAuley 150/1: 00: 10th: Led over 4f, no extra 2f out: 7 wk abs.   7   **50**
10 Ran   Time 1m 40.46 (5.36)   Owned: Godolphin   Trained: Newmarket

---

4632   3.00 Racing Welfare Selling Nursery Handicap Stakes 2yo 0-65 (G4)   **[71]**
£2618 £748 £374   **1m3y**   **Good/Soft 63**   **-34 Slow**   Stands side

4451   **LORNA DUNE 9** [14] J G M O'Shea 2-9-3 (60) D Sweeney 10/1: 3606031: Cl-up stands side, hdwy to   **67**
lead over 1f out, pushed out ins fnl 1f: bght in for 6,800gns: first win: stays 7f, relished this step up to 1m:
acts on fast & hvy, stiff or flat trk: gd start for new yard (prev with J Ramsden): win again at this trip: see 1677.
4451   **ORPEN ANNIE 9** [16] Miss J Feilden 2-9-2 (59) B Reilly(3) 16/1: 0360402: Held up stands side, hdwy   1½   **61**
over 2f out, hung left & ev ch over 1f out, onepcd ins fnl 1f: stays 1m & handles fast & gd/soft: gd eff: see 2603.
4369   **YELDHAM LADY 12** [15] J Pearce 2-8-7 P (50) J Quinn 12/1: 002003: Rear stands side, hdwy over 2f   ½   **51**
out, onepcd ins fnl 1f: clr of rem: stays 1m, handles polytrack & gd/soft: see 3745.
3930   **TIP TOES 34** [10] M R Channon 2-8-2 (45) T Dean(7) 40/1: 6045064: Chsd ldrs stands side, hdwy to   3   **40**
lead group over 5f out, hdd over 1f out, sn no extra: see 3259.
4451   **DEBS BROUGHTON 9** [4]2-8-13 (56) R Mullen 8/1: 002045: Rear far side, hdwy over 2f out, led group   2   **47**
ins fnl 1f, kept on but no ch with stands side: won race on wrong side, gd run.
4451   **ARTADI 9** [7]2-8-7 bl (50) T P Queally 12/1: 3565466: Chsd ldrs far side, hdwy to lead group 2f   1¾   **38**
out till ins fnl 1f, no extra: see 4316.
4451   **LORD NORMACOTE 9** [13]2-9-6 BL (63) J P Guillambert(3) 33/1: 004007: Handy stands side, hung left &   3   **45**

1397

no impress over 1f out: tried blnks: see 2952.
4451 **TONIGHT 9** [11]2-9-0 (57) B Swarbrick(5) 25/1: 3436008: Led stands side till over 5f out, no extra 2f out. *3* **33**
4410 **ZOLASH 10** [9]2-9-5 (62) Derek Nolan(7) 8/1: 6044369: Cl-up far side, wknd over 1f out. *1¾* **35**
4213 **DRAMATIC REVIEW 20** [8]2-9-7 P (64) G Faulkner 20/1: 05060: 10th: Chsd ldrs far side, hdwy to lead group 3f out to 2f out, sn no extra: tried cheek pieces: see 1744. *1¾* **34**
4206 **LARAS GIRL 20** [12]2-8-8 (51) P Doe 16/1: 0400330: 11th: Cl-up stands side, wknd over 2f out. *1¾* **18**
4127 **CHAMPAGNE ROSSINI 24** [2]2-9-3 (60) R L Moore 20/1: 0560: 12th: Led far side 5f, no extra over 1f out. *1¾* **24**
4583 **LAKESDALE 2** [5]2-9-1 (58) O Urbina 8/1: 0236100: 13th: Chsd ldrs far side, wknd over 2f out. *1½* **19**
4451 **SHERBOURNE 9** [3]2-8-4 (47) Paul Eddery 33/1: 0060000: 14th: In tch far side, rear & btn 3f out. *shd* **7**
4206* **BEAUMONT GIRL 20** [6]2-8-12 (55) L Dettori 15/8 FAV: 010: 15th: Held up far side, hdwy over 3f out, no impress over 1f out: nicely bckd from 5/2: 'swallowed tongue': forgive this: see 4206. *1* **13**
4257 **LORD CHALFONT 18** [1]2-7-12 (11oh)bl (30) M Nem(7) 150/1: 0000000: 16th: Handy far side, no impress. *24* **0**
16 Ran Time 1m 42.9 (7.8) Owned: Mr Gary Roberts Trained: Westbury On Severn

4633

3.30 John Slapp Bookmakers Norwich Novice Stakes 2yo (D2)
£6747 £2076 £1038 **6f3y** **Good/Soft 63** **-12 Slow** Stands side

4458 **JOSH 8** [4] M A Jarvis 2-9-5 P Robinson 100/30: 1301: Slow away, sn handy, hdwy to lead over 1f out, sn edged right, drvn out ins fnl 1f: joc 3 day careless riding ban: stays 6f, shld apprec further: acts on gd/soft & soft, gall or flat trks: gd run, clearly useful with give in the grnd: see 3272. **99**
3513+**ARMY OF ANGELS 50** [1] Saeed bin Suroor 2-9-5 t L Dettori 10/11 FAV: 212: Rcd in 2nd, hdwy to chall over 2f out, hmpd 1f out, sn pulled out to chall, kept on cl-home: 7 wk abs: acts on firm & gd/soft: poss wnr here with clr run, remains on the upgrade & can return to winning form sn: see 3513. *nk* **98**
4273 **ISLAND SWING 17** [3] J L Spearing 2-8-13 (78) S Drowne 50/1: 0114003: Mid-div, hdwy over 1f out, kept on: acts on fast & gd/soft: gd run, back to form of 2358. *1½* **87$**
4332 **ROODEYE 14** [2] R F Johnson Houghton 2-8-11 (96) J Murtagh 9/4: 215634: Led over 4f, pushed along when hmpd 1f out, kept on: acts on firm & gd/soft: shade closer but for interferance, prob 3rd: see 4332. *shd* **84**
4 Ran Time 1m 14.9 (4.5) Owned: Mr T G & Mrs M E Holdcroft Trained: Newmarket

4634

4.00 R M Levitt 'another Year In Practice' Handicap Stakes 3yo+ 71-85 (D2) **[89]**
£9225 £3499 £1750 **2m** **Good/Soft 63** **+12 Fast** Inside

4196 **HIGH POINT 20** [7] G P Enright 6-9-0 (75) J Murtagh 13/2: 3336051: Cl-up, hdwy 2f out, drvn out ins fnl 1f, led nr fin: fast time: eff over 12f/2m on firm, gd/soft & loves polytrack: tough 6yo: see 83. **85**
4106 **ASTYANAX 26** [12] Sir Mark Prescott 4-9-1 (76) S Sanders 9/1: 1-050102: Handy, hdwy to lead over 3f out, hdd nr fin: tchd 12/1: gd eff, only just caught: back to winning form of 3703 (Yarmouth). *½* **84**
4527* **LAND N STARS 5** [3] Jamie Poulton 4-9-10 (6ex) (85) P Doe 7/1: 2-015413: Chsd ldrs till over 4f out, not clr run 3f out, hdwy over 1f out, kept on: qck reapp: acts on fm & gd/soft: continues on the upgrade, shade unlucky: see 4527. *1* **92**
4288 **MARINE CITY 17** [10] M A Jarvis 3-7-13 P (72) D Fox(5) 10/1: 0-16634: In tch, lost place 6f out, kept on late: stays 12f/2m, may want further judged on this: acts on gd/soft & soft: fair run in cheek pieces. *1* **78**
3475 **KING FLYER 53** [8]8-9-0 (75) B Reilly(3) 14/1: 3020005: Bhd, hdwy over 2f out, onepace fnl 1f: 8 wk abs. *1½* **79**
4361* **TYPHOON TILLY 13** [11]7-8-12 (73) S Drowne 4/1 FAV: 6403216: Rear, hdwy after 1m, rcd in 2nd over 2f out, onepcd fnl 1f: op 6/1: continues in gd form: see 4361. *shd* **76**
4209 **HATHLEN 20** [6]3-8-2 (75) J Quinn 20/1: 6561567: Rear, hdwy after 1m, lost place over 5f out, kept on again over 1f out, not dangerous: see 2376. *1½* **76**
4255* **PATRIXPRIAL 18** [5]3-8-5 (78) P Robinson 6/1: 0-5518: In tch, onepcd 2f out. *½* **78**
3779 **THEWHIRLINGDERVISH 40** [4]6-9-7 (82) T E Durcan 8/1: 0313269: Handy, no impress 1f out: 6 wk abs. *2* **80**
3617 **HALLAND 47** [2]6-9-7 (82) J P Guillambert(3) 50/1: 212//00-00: 10th: Rear, hdwy over 3f out, no impress 2f out: 7 wk abs: see 3617. *¾* **79**
3015 **TUDOR BELL 71** [1]3-8-10 (83) D Sweeney 16/1: 1162130: 11th: Led 2f, rem handy, no extra 2f out. *12* **68**
4468 **CHERUBIM 8** [13]3-8-2 (75) T P Queally 33/1: 2-551200: 12th: Led after 2f till over 3f out, no extra. *1¾* **58**
4865} **KING EIDER 328** [9]5-9-10 (85) R L Moore 14/1: 22/5603-0: 13th: b g Mtoto - Hen Harrier (Polar Falcon) Rear, hdwy 3f out, sn wknd: won 1 of 6 hdles starts in 03/04 (mdn, rtd 125h at best, eff at 2m on fast & gd/soft, N Henderson): 3rd 1 of 4 '03 starts on the level (h'cap, rtd 90, J Dunlop): wnr of 3 of 9 '02 starts (h'caps): eff at 12f, suited by 14f/2m on firm & soft, any trk: now with B Ellison: sharper for this. *6* **62**
2 Oct'02 Newb 16sft 87-87 C: 2 Sep'02 Redc 14g/f 88-85 C: 1 Sep'02 Sand 14gd 84-80 D: 1 Aug'02 Brig 11.8g/f 80-75 D:
2 Jul'02 Sali 12g/s 75-73 D: 1 May'02 Warw 12.6fm 75-70 D: 2 Apr'02 Brig 10fm 70-69 E:
13 Ran Time 3m 31.51 (8.21) Owned: The Aedean Partnership Trained: Lewes

4635

4.30 Lottie And Albert Botton Memorial Nursery Handicap Stakes 2yo 0-75 (E3) **[82]**
£4043 £1244 £622 **1m3y** **Good/Soft 63** **-08 Slow** Stands side

4444 **REBEL REBEL 9** [8] N A Callaghan 2-9-0 (68) L Dettori 2/1 FAV: 00541: Held up centre, hdwy over 2f out, led over 1f out, pushed clr ins fnl 1f: first win: nicely bckd: eff at 7f, relished return to 1m: acts on gd & gd/soft, flat trk: gd eff, confidence boosted & looks capable of following up based on this eff: see 4444. **85**
4269 **TOMOBEL 17** [7] M H Tompkins 2-8-6 (60) P Robinson 20/1: 0052: Rcd in 2nd centre, onepcd fnl 1f. *3½* **66**
4376 **MOBARHEN 12** [1] Sir Michael Stoute 2-9-5 (73) R Hills 9/2: 5523: Held up far side, hdwy over 3f out, led group over 2f out, kept on but no ch with centre group: clr of rem: won race on wrong side: keep in mind. *nk* **78**
4040 **UNION JACK JACKSON 28** [9] J G Given 2-8-11 (65) M Fenton 50/1: 40064: Led centre over 6f, no extra. *3* **64**
4355 **UNCLE BULGARIA 13** [11]2-8-11 (65) S Whitworth 33/1: 3005: Chsd ldrs stands side, wknd 2f out. *1½* **61**
4519 **KERRYS BLADE 5** [20]2-8-9 (63) G Faulkner 7/1: 05626: Chsd ldrs stands side, hdwy to lead group/hung left over 2f out, sn hdd & no extra: qck reapp: see 4519. *6* **47**
4296 **BIG HOO HAH 17** [6]2-8-13 (67) K McEvoy 40/1: 0647: Rear centre, modest late gains: see 3908. *½* **50**
3750 **PON MY SOUL 41** [13]2-8-11 (65) T P Queally 33/1: 168: Held up stands side, nvr a factor: 6 wk abs. *1½* **45**
4285 **SHARP N FROSTY 17** [16]2-8-9 (63) B Swarbrick(5) 66/1: 4044U9: Nvr a factor stands side: see 1237. *3* **37**
4444 **GRYSKIRK 9** [14]2-8-10 (64) J Quinn 16/1: 0003050: 10th: In tch stands side, hdwy 3f out, no impress. *2* **34**
4444 **GOOD WEE GIRL 9** [19]2-9-3 (71) J Murtagh 20/1: 2151000: 11th: Led stands side over 5f, sn no extra. *4* **33**
4271 **CAPTAIN MARGARET 17** [18]2-9-0 P (68) R L Moore 33/1: 0500: 12th: b f Royal Applause - Go For Red (Thatching) Al bhd stands side: 13,000gns Apr foal: half-brother to a 1m/12f wnr: dam unrcd. *1¾* **26**
4257 **YOUNG MICK 18** [4]2-9-5 (73) A McCarthy 33/1: 0340: 13th: Rcd in 2nd far side, hdwy to lead well *1* **29**

YARMOUTH THURSDAY 16.09.04 Lefthand, Flat, Fair Track

over 2f out, sn hdd & no extra: see 4257.
4147 **TERMINATE 23** [12]2-8-13 (67) S Sanders 9/2: 0050: 14th: In tch stands side, hdwy 3f out, no impress. *2½* **18**
4444 **HES A DIAMOND 9** [5]2-9-7 (75) G Carter 50/1: 513000: 15th: Cl-up centre, wknd over 2f out. *1* **24**
2584 **SILVER VISAGE 89** [17]2-8-9 BL (63) B Reilly(3) 50/1: 5550: 16th: b g Lujain - About Face (Midyan) *¾* **10**
Bhd stands side, saddle slipped: long abs: Mar foal, cost 800gns: half-brother to a 7f wnr: dam unrcd.
4410 **BONGOALI 10** [3]2-8-13 (67) T Dean(7) 33/1: 45250: 17th: Chsd ldrs far side, wknd over 3f out. *3* **8**
4040 **COUNTRYWIDE SUN 28** [2]2-8-7 p (61) J P Guillambert(3) 40/1: 000240: 18th: Led far side over 5f. *hd* **0**
4204 **TIT FOR TAT 20** [10]2-8-7 (61) S Drowne 50/1: 0540: 19th: Slow away in centre, sn cl-up, wknd 3f out. *8* **0**
4356 **SILVERLEAF 13** [15]2-9-4 (72) T E Durcan 40/1: 65500: 20th: Al bhd stands side: see 3568. *2* **0**
20 Ran Time 1m 40.85 (5.75) Owned: Six Star Racing Trained: Newmarket

4636 **5.00 Bbc Look East Handicap Stakes 3yo+ 46-55 (F4)** **[69]**
£3370 £963 £481 **6f3y** **Good/Soft 63** **-03 Slow** Stands side

4368 **KEW THE MUSIC 13** [9] M R Channon 4-8-8 vis (49) T E Durcan 20/1: 0000001: Dwelt & outpcd, hdwy to **59**
lead 1f out, drvn out ins fnl 1f: eff btwn 5/6f on fast & gd/soft, acts on a gall or flat trk: back to form, well h'capped.
4317 **MUTASSEM 15** [14] T Keddy 3-8-9 (52) P Doe 50/1: 0000002: Rear, hdwy over 1f out, ev ch ins fnl *nk* **61**
1f, kept on: clr of rem: stays 6f on gd/soft: gd eff, rdn with more restraint today: see 3923.
4240 **LAUREL DAWN 19** [6] I W McInnes 6-9-0 (55) W Hogg(7) 14/1: 6000003: Chsd ldrs, onepcd 1f out. *3½* **53**
4508 **MOLOTOV 5** [18] I W McInnes 4-8-9 (50) Natalia Gemelova(7) 15/2: 0041334: Led 5f, no extra ins fnl 1f. *3* **39**
4253 **KENNINGTON 18** [16]4-8-9 (50) Joanna Badger 12/1: 0040245: Chsd ldrs, no impress fnl 1f. *½* **37**
4408 **QUANTICA 10** [7]5-9-0 (55) M Fenton 8/1: 6000006: In tch, hung left & no impress over 1f out. *shd* **41**
4562 **ON THE TRAIL 3** [2]7-8-13 (54) S Sanders 6/1: 3114527: Chsd ldrs, hung right & no impress over 1f out. *1½* **36**
4412 **FLORIAN 10** [10]6-9-0 (55) G Carter 28/1: 0005608: Handy, no impress over 1f out: see 2799. *shd* **36**
4368 **ENJOY THE BUZZ 13** [4]5-8-10 (51) R L Moore 10/1: 1032559: Rear, hdwy 2f out, no impress 1f out. *shd* **31**
4488 **YORKIES BOY 7** [5]9-8-12 p (53) R Miles(3) 12/1: 4031100: 10th: In tch, no impress 2f out: qck reapp. *1¾* **28**
4368 **SALON PRIVE 13** [15]4-9-0 (55) L Dettori 7/2 FAV: 2-002620: 11th: Dsptd lead over 3f, no extra 1f out. *1¾* **25**
1982 **STAR FERN 114** [8]3-8-9 (52) E Ahern 50/1: 4-550000: 12th: Dwelt in rear, nvr a factor: long abs. *½* **20**
4367 **PRETTY KOOL 13** [11]4-8-11 (52) K McEvoy 9/1: 0-053100: 13th: Handy, wknd 2f out. *shd* **19**
3176 **DOCTOR DENNIS 65** [12]7-8-10 vis (51) A McCarthy 25/1: 1601060: 14th: Cl-up, wknd 2f out: 9 wk abs. *1½* **13**
1750 **BAYTOWN FLYER 124** [1]4-8-10 (51) T P Queally 33/1: 1211200: 15th: Nvr a factor: long abs. *nk* **12**
4489 **TOMTHEVIC 7** [20]6-8-10 (51) P Fitzsimons 25/1: 0040500: 16th: Chsd ldrs, wknd over 1f out: qck reapp. *½* **10**
3643 **WARLINGHAM 45** [17]6-8-13 (54) R Mullen 20/1: 5050000: 17th: Chsd ldrs, wknd over 2f out: 6 wk abs. *2½* **5**
3985 **MONTANA 31** [19]4-9-0 (55) S Drowne 22/1: 3000-040: 18th: Cl-up, wknd 2f out: see 3165. *5* **0**
3024 **FORZENUFF 71** [3]3-8-8 (51) D Sweeney 50/1: 0600000: 19th: In tch, wknd 2f out: long abs: see 217. *2* **0**
19 Ran Time 1m 14.4(4.0) Owned: Miss Bridget Coyle Trained: West Ilsley

NEWBURY FRIDAY 17.09.04 Lefthand, Flat, Galloping Track

Official Going Good/Firm (Good places). Rain Throughout Afternoon.

4637 **1.20 E B F Dubai Tennis Championships Maiden Stakes 2yo (D2)**
£6646 £2045 £1023 **6f8y str** **Good/Firm** **Inapp** Centre

4223 **NEWSROUND 20** [9] M A Jarvis 2-9-0 P Robinson 2/5 FAV: 21: Made all, pushed clr over 1f out, v **101+**
cmftbly: well bckd at odds-on: eff at 6f, 7f/1m sure to suit: acts on fast & gd grnd, gall trks: useful, plenty
more to come in stronger company, win more races.
ORANMORE CASTLE 0 [5] B W Hills 2-9-0 M Hills 10/1: 2: b c Giant's Causeway - Twice The Ease *2½* **89+**
(Green Desert) Keen held up, eff over 1f out, kept on hands & heels, not pace of wnr on debut: Jan first foal, cost
E150,000: v pleasing start & eff at 6f, 7f sure to suit: acts on fast grnd: clr of rem, learn plenty from this, win sn.
4329 **ASK FOR RAIN 15** [11] B W Hills 2-8-9 D Holland 33/1: 03: gr f Green Desert - Requesting *5* **70**
(Rainbow Quest) Held up, eff & edged left 2f out, onepace: Apr foal: bred to relish 1m in time & needs minor trks.
AWAASER 0 [8] M P Tregoning 2-8-9 R Hills 6/1: 4: ch f Diesis - Forest Storm (Woodman) Cl-up, *¾* **68**
wknd over 1f out on debut: Feb foal, cost E300,000: bred to want 1m+ in time.
4108 **METHODICAL 27** [2]2-8-9 R Mullen 50/1: 405: Bhd, modest late gains, no threat: see 3376. *½* **66**
4223 **SIR BLUEBIRD 20** [10]2-9-0 R Hughes 66/1: 006: Chsd ldr to 3f out, wknd. *1¾* **66**
PAGAN QUEST 0 [4]2-9-0 Lisa Jones 16/1: 7: Slow away, nvr a factor. *½* **64**
3975 **WORTH ABBEY 32** [6]2-9-0 Dane O'Neill 66/1: 0008: Cl-up, wknd over 2f out. *1½* **59**
SPEEDY SPIRIT 0 [7]2-8-9 S Whitworth 100/1: 9: Slow away & al bhd. *5* **39**
JUBILEE COIN 0 [1]2-8-9 R Thomas(3) 66/1: 0: 10th: In tch, wknd over 2f out. *4* **27**
10 Ran Time 1m 13.42 (1.82) Owned: Sheikh Mohammed Trained: Newmarket

4638 **1.50 Listed Dubai Duty Free Cup 3yo+ (A1)**
£17400 £6600 £3300 **7f str** **Good/Firm** **Inapp** Centre

4523 **ROYAL STORM 6** [12] Mrs A J Perrett 5-9-0 (99) D Holland 16/1: 6002001: Led stands side group **109**
after 2f, kept on for press & led overall over 1f out, styd on well: loves to dominate & stays 1m, suited by 6/7f on
firm, gd or polytrack, any trk, likes Newmarket: v useful & genuine, career best run: see 3782, 1490.
1486 **MESHAHEER 139** [4] Saeed bin Suroor 5-9-0 t (105) R Hills 12/1: 6/0241-02: Held up far side, hdwy *½* **107**
& short of room over 2f out, kept on over 1f out, held by wnr ins last: over 4 mth abs: right back to useful best,
likes Newbury: shld find another nice prize: see 1486.
3564 **LUCKY SPIN 49** [6] R Hannon 3-8-6 (102) R L Moore 10/1: 211103: In tch far side, hdwy to lead *½* **98**
that group over 2f out till over 1f out, onepace: 7 wk abs: back to form, enjoys fills contest: see 2574, 2136.
2069 **AZAROLE 111** [3] J R Fanshawe 3-8-11 (106) J Murtagh 12/1: 1144-544: Handy far side, eff over 1f *½* **105**
out, kept on same pace: has had a wind op since 2069 (3 mths ago): useful & consistent: see 2069.
3421 **OASIS STAR 55** [11]3-8-6 (89) T Quinn 33/1: 1151205: Handy stands side, onepcd over 1f out: 8 wk *½* **99**
abs: ran to best up in class: see 3006 (fills h'cap).
4477 **SUGGESTIVE 8** [8]6-9-0 bl (111) M Hills 9/2 FAV: 1402266: Held up far side, eff over 1f out, no *1* **102**
impress: needs everything to fall right: see 4477, 3957.

4472 **MATERIAL WITNESS 8** [5]7-9-0 (105) Martin Dwyer 16/1: 1204167: Led far side group till over 2f   1½   99
out, no extra: likes to dominate: see 4231 (rtd h'cap).
4472 **KINGS POINT 8** [14]3-8-11 (103) R Hughes 33/1: 3040308: In tch stands side, wknd over 1f out: see 3620.1½   96
4866} **SABBEEH 329** [1]3-8-11 T (110) L Dettori 5/1: 1016-9: b c Red Ransom - Capistrano Day (Diesis)   ½   95
Led stands side group 2f, handy, wknd over 1f out: '03 mdn & stks wnr for M Jarvis: eff at 6/7f & enjoys gd & soft
grnd, sharp or gall trks: has run well fresh: tried a t-strap here.
1 Sep'03 Donc 7gd 112- C: 1 May'03 Ripo 6sft 98- D:
4103+ **ZONUS 27** [1]3-8-11 bl (100) K Fallon 6/1: 2303010: 10th: Held up far side, wknd over 1f out: btr   ½   94
expected after 4103 (h'cap, first time blnks).
3886 **LAGO DORTA 36** [9]4-9-0 (99) P Robinson 16/1: 4006600: 11th: Slow away, sn in tch, wknd 2f out.   nk   93
3620 **BAHIANO 48** [7]3-8-11 (104) T E Durcan 33/1: 6004000: 12th: In tch far side, wknd 2f out: see 2486.   2   89
4523 **PIZAZZ 6** [10]3-8-11 bl (92) J Fortune 50/1: 2203100: 13th: In tch stands side, wknd 2f out: shd   88
twice well below 3522 (made all, first time blnks).
4313 **RUM SHOT 19** [2]3-8-11 (108) Dane O'Neill 15/2: 1-401360: 14th: Slow away & nvr a factor: 'lost action'.   2½   83
14 Ran   Time 1m 24.64 (0.24)   Owned: The Cloran Family   Trained: Pulborough

---

4639   2.20 Gr3 Dubai Duty Free Arc Trial 3yo+   (A1)
£29000 £11000 £5500   1m3f5y   Good/Firm   Inapp   Outside

4290* **SIGHTS ON GOLD 18** [3] Saeed bin Suroor 5-9-2 t (114) L Dettori 3/1 FAV: 2/2612-11: Held up, gd   115
hdwy to lead well over 1f out, sn rdn clr, held on ins last: suited by 10/12f on fast & soft grnd, any trk: smart,
fresh for further success this autumn: see 4290.
4571 **IMPERIAL DANCER 6** [7] M R Channon 6-9-2 (110) T E Durcan 7/2: 0030362: Held up, eff over 2f out,   1   112
kept on ins last, al just held: tough & smart, enjoys easier grnd: see 2571.
4494 **COMPTON BOLTER 7** [4] G A Butler 7-9-2 (109) D Holland 11/1: 0653323: In tch, eff over 2f out,   1   110
kept on same pace: another smart run: see 4494, 82.
2308 **DAY FLIGHT 103** [8] J H M Gosden 3-8-9 (114) R Hughes 7/2: 1144: Held up, eff & short of room   ½   109
over 2f out, kept on over 1f out, nvr dngrs: long abs: handles fast grnd, smart effs earlier on easier grnd:
likely more to come: see 2308 (Gr 1), 1706.
3274 **ALBINUS 62** [1]3-8-9 bl (104) Martin Dwyer 14/1: 3-021135: Chsd ldr, led over 2f out, sn hung   1½   106
badly right & hdd over 1f out, no extra: 2 mth abs & ran to form of 3274 (soft), see 2660.
4568 **NYSAEAN 5** [5]5-9-5 (112) R L Moore 20/1: 2134536: Held up, hdwy qckly over 2f out, dismounted.   6   97
4333 **WESTMORELAND ROAD 15** [2]4-9-2 (106) J Murtagh 12/1: 310-2247: Slow away, sn rdn to lead, hdd   8   78
over 2f out, wknd qckly: something amiss? much btr 4333.
4001 **ALWAYS FIRST 31** [6]3-8-9 (110) K Fallon 5/1: 1-02348: In tch, wknd when hmpd over 2f out, eased: dist   0
something amiss? btr 4001.
8 Ran   Time 2m 18.07 (2.27)   Owned: Godolphin   Trained: Newmarket

---

4640   2.55 Haynes Hanson And Clark Conditions Stakes Colts & Geldings 2yo   (B1)
£10874 £4021 £2010   1m str   Good/Firm   Inapp   Centre

4193* **MERCHANT 21** [4] M L W Bell 2-8-10 (99) R Mullen 4/5 FAV: 5321111: Handy, hdwy to lead over 1f   92
out, hung right & kept on well, pushed out: hvly bckd: stays 1m well & acts on firm & gd/soft, likes gall trks:
useful & tough, has thrived this term: see 4193.
NOBLE DUTY 0 [5] Saeed bin Suroor 2-8-10 L Dettori 5/2: 2: b c Dubai Millennium - Nijinsky's   2½   86+
Lover (Nijinsky) Held up, hdwy to chase wnr over 1f out, kept on same pace: debut: Feb foal: dam won in US:
stays 1m, further will suit next term: acts on fast grnd: useful debut, will appreciate a hard time, win races.
4046* **MASTMAN 29** [3] B J Meehan 2-9-1 t (85) J Fortune 14/1: 25413: Trkd wnr, eff over 2f out, onepace: ¾   89
gd run up in class & stays 1m: see 4046.
PITTSBURGH 0 [1] A M Balding 2-8-10 K Fallon 11/1: 4: ch c Nashwan - Oatey (Master Willie) In   ¾   80
tch, rdn & sltly outpcd over 2f out, some late gains: debut: Mar foal, cost 24,000gns: half-brother to a 1m wnr:
dam 5f scorer: stays 1m, shld get further next term: pleasing start, can find a mdn.
4176 **TAKHLEED 22** [2]2-8-10 R Hills 7/1: 55: Led till over 1f out, wknd: see 4176.   3   76
5 Ran   Time 1m 40.25 (3.45)   Owned: HESheikh Rashid Bin Mohammed   Trained: Newmarket

---

4641   3.30 Dubai Duty Free Full Of Surprises E B F Conditions Stakes Fillies 2yo   (B1)
£10652 £4040 £2020   7f str   Good/Firm   Inapp   Centre

3915* **SHANGHAI LILY 35** [5] Sir Michael Stoute 2-8-13 K Fallon 4/7 FAV: 11: In tch, gd hdwy to lead   104+
over 1f out, pushed clr, v cmftbly: hvly bckd: stays 7f well, 1m sure to suit: acts on fast & gd grnd:
potentially v smart & looks one to follow when stepped up to Gr class: see 3915.
4264 **SHARP AS A TACK 19** [2] B J Meehan 2-8-8 BL (83) J Fortune 14/1: 02102: Set pace till over 1f out,   2½   89
sn flashed tail & not pace of wnr: ran to best in first time blnks & stays 1m: see 3882 (mdn auct).
4359 **TAHRIR 14** [3] B W Hills 2-8-8 R Hills 11/4: 23: Cl-up, no extra over 1f out: will apprec mdn company.   ¾   87
4234* **ANNALS 20** [6] H Candy 2-8-13 Dane O'Neill 15/2: 14: Handy, wknd well over 1f out: up in class & trips.   6   80
4 Ran   Time 1m 26.09 (1.79)   Owned: Cheveley Park Stud   Trained: Newmarket

---

4642   4.05 Dubai Duty Free Foundation Stakes Handicap 3yo+ 71-85   (D2)
£7914 £2435 £1218   7f str   Good/Firm   Inapp   Centre   [92]

3443 **CHATEAU NICOL 55** [18] B G Powell 5-9-3 (81) T Quinn 20/1: 4156601: In tch, hdwy 2f out, styd on   87
ins last to lead last strides: 8 wk abs: best at 7f, stays 1m on fast, hvy & fibresand, any trk, likes sharp ones.
4122 **BLUE TROJAN 25** [4] S Kirk 4-9-5 (83) J Daly(7) 16/1: 0420002: Set pace, hung left & clr 2f out,   shd   88
in command till joc started persistently looking around fnl 1f & eased closing strides: hdd line: joc received
28-day ban: v modest ride from his inexperienced pilot & shld have won this: see 3088, 1883.
1971* **MUTAMARED 116** [21] M P Tregoning 4-9-4 (82) R Hills 5/1: 226-13: In tch, eff over 1f out, kept   shd   86
on ins last, not btn far: a fine run after 4 mth abs: looks sure to relish 1m now & will be winning shortly.
4482 **SERIEUX 8** [23] Mrs A J Perrett 5-9-2 p (80) J Murtagh 7/1: 2000004: Held up, eff over 1f out,   ½   82
kept on ins last, not btn far: again showed promise & is well h'capped: see 4482.

NEWBURY **FRIDAY 17.09.04 Lefthand, Flat, Galloping Track**

4251 **IN THE PINK 19** [17]4-8-7 (1oh) (70) S Hitchcott 25/1: 1202045: Slow away, held up, hdwy over 1f out, styd on well, nrst fin: encouraging, see 3456. *nk* **72**
4469 **JUSTE POUR LAMOUR 9** [14]4-8-8 (72) D Fox(5) 12/1: 4001526: In tch, eff over 1f out, onepace. *¾* **72**
4500* **ARMAGNAC 7** [20]6-9-7 (6ex) (85) Dane O'Neill 16/1: 3230017: Held up, some late gains, nrst fin. *shd* **84**
4301 **WINNING VENTURE 18** [6]7-9-3 P (81) D Holland 16/1: 0320028: In tch, onepace fnl 2f: cheekpieces. *1¾* **76**
4482 **ARCTIC DESERT 8** [13]4-8-13 (77) K Fallon 100/30 FAV: 0061629: In tch, eff well over 1f out, wknd. *nk* **71**
4500 **OMAHA CITY 7** [8]10-8-7 (1oh) (70) L Keniry(3) 40/1: 2100000: 10th: In tch, wknd 2f out: likes Goodwood. *hd* **64**
4398 **KAREEB 12** [24]7-8-7 (2oh) (69) R Mullen 12/1: 4060640: 11th: Held up, some late gains: see 4398. *nk* **63**
3954 **CRAIOVA 34** [19]5-9-2 (80) K May(7) 12/1: 0000040: 12th: In tch, wknd over 2f out: see 3954. *½* **71**
4030 **JUST FLY 30** [5]4-8-8 (72) S Whitworth 40/1: 0300000: 13th: Nvr a factor. *nk* **62**
4110 **CORKY 27** [26]3-8-10 (77) R L Moore 16/1: 431030: 14th: Al bhd. *2* **63**
4082 **Ammenayr 28** [2]4-8-11 (75) G Carter 50/1:0
4362 **Border Edge 14** [3]6-9-4 vis(82) A Beech(3) 66/1:0
4318 **Go Bananas 16** [25]3-9-1 (82) J Fortune 33/1:0
4394 **Danehill Stroller 13** [12]4-9-2 p(80) Martin Dwyer 33/1:0
4498 **Little Edward 7** [9]6-9-4 (82) R Hughes 50/1:0
3443 **Quantum Leap 55** [16]7-8-8 vis(72) Lisa Jones 50/1:0
4482 **Kindlelight Debut 8** [15]4-8-8 (72) P Robinson 33/1:0
232 **Caledonian 272** [22]3-9-1 (82) N Pollard 66/1:0
4180 **Flying Express 22** [1]4-9-4 (82) M Hills 33/1:0
4048 **Tribute 29** [10]3-8-6 (73) T E Durcan 33/1:0
24 Ran Time 1m 25.23 (0.93) Owned: Basingstoke Commercials Trained: Winchester

4643

4.40 Dubai Grand Prix Handicap Stakes 3yo+ 71-85 (D2) **[92]**
£7221 £2222 £1111 **1m3f5y** **Good/Firm** **Inapp** Outside

4227 **SOLO FLIGHT 20** [6] H Morrison 7-9-7 (85) R L Moore 25/1: 6-260201: Slow away, held up, hdwy 2f out, strong run to lead cl-home, rdn out: winning form over 10/12f & handles soft, enjoys firm & fast, any trk: best coming late off a strong pace & a fine ride from his v progressive joc: tough, see 1890. **91**
4428*]**TIP THE DIP 359** [11] J H M Gosden 4-9-6 (84) J Fortune 10/1: 2131-2: ch c Benny The Dip - Senora Tippy (El Gran Senor) Prom, hdwy to lead over 1f out, kept on ins last, collared cl-home on reapp: won 2 of 4 '03 starts (auct mdn & class stks): eff over 10/12f on fast grnd & any trk: runs well fresh: yet to run a poor race, excellent return & shld be winning soon. *nk* **89**
1 Sep'03 Good 12g/f 84-(80) D: 1 Aug'03 Nott 10.0g/f 84- F: 2 Aug'03 Wind 8.3g/f 71- D:
3945 **CELLARMASTER 34** [7] E F Vaughan 3-8-8 (79) K Fallon 7/1: 352-3143: In tch, eff over 1f out, kept on ins last, not btn far: ran to best: see 3108. *½* **83**
4295 **COMPTON DRAKE 18** [5] G A Butler 5-8-8 (72) L Dettori 4/1: 11-02124: Keen in tch, eff over 1f out, onepace: continues in fine heart: see 4295, 4057. *hd* **75**
4292 **FLOTTA 18** [12]5-9-4 (82) S Hitchcott 20/1: 4430165: Held up, eff over 1f out, onepace: see 3681. *½* **82**
4097 **DEEP PURPLE 27** [3]3-9-0 (85) Martin Dwyer 3/1 FAV: 146: Slow away, sn in tch, eff over 1f out, kept on, nvr dngrs: shade more expected after 4097 (gd/soft). *2* **84**
4075* **DAZE 28** [15]3-8-5 (1ow) (75) R Hills 10/1: 317: In tch, wknd over 1f out: btr 4075 (soft, 12f). *1* **73**
3867 **PETROSA 37** [13]4-8-7 (1oh) (70) T Quinn 16/1: 0323-458: Slow away, keen, in tch, nvr a factor: see 3535. *½* **67**
3816 **SEEYAAJ 40** [14]4-9-1 (79) W Ryan 40/1: 01300-59: Slow away & nvr a factor: recent 4th in a h'cap hdle. *nk* **75**
1689 **NAWOW 128** [9]4-8-10 (74) D Holland 10/1: 26-03560: 10th: Held up, eff over 2f out, sn wknd: see 1003. *nk* **70**
4305 **RASID 17** [2]6-9-0 (78) Dane O'Neill 25/1: 0053100: 11th: Slow away, nvr a factor: best 2929 (10f, gd/soft) *hd* **73**
4292 **ANTICIPATING 18** [16]4-9-3 (81) R Mullen 25/1: 4020000: 12th: Slow away, nvr a factor: see 877. *½* **75**
3255 **CAUSE CELEBRE 63** [4]3-8-7 (78) M Hills 25/1: 24-10160: 13th: Led till over 1f out, wknd: 2 mth abs. *shd* **72**
4392 **PENZANCE 13** [1]3-8-9 (80) J Murtagh 10/1: 3-641000: 14th: In tch, wknd over 2f out: see 2631. *1¾* **72**
1352 **SIR LAUGHALOT 146** [8]4-8-7 (1oh) (70) T E Durcan 33/1: 2032320: 15th: In tch, wknd 2f out: btr 1352. *½* **62**
15 Ran Time 2m 22.27(6.47) Owned: Lady Hardy Trained: East Ilsley

NOTTINGHAM **FRIDAY 17.09.04 Lefthand, Galloping Track**

Official Going GOOD/SOFT

4644

2.10 Sarrego Memorial E B F Maiden Stakes 2yo (D2)
£6338 £1950 £975 **6f15y** **Good/Soft 60** **-27 Slow** Far side

THE ABBESS 0 [7] H Candy 2-8-9 D Sweeney 10/1: 1: gr f Bishop of Cashel - Nisha (Nishapour) Mid-div, asked for eff over 2f out, led well ins fnl 1f, pushed out on debut: Apr foal: half-sister to a couple of 1m wnrs: dam unplcd, sire a smart 2yo, later smart over 7f/1m: eff at 6f, 7f looks sure to suit: acts on gd/soft, gall trk: runs well fresh: fine start to racing, entitled to come on for this & win more races. **87+**
3863 **SOUND THE DRUM 37** [14] J H M Gosden 2-9-0 K McEvoy 7/4 FAV: 32: Rcd in 2nd, hdwy to lead over 3f out, hdd well ins fnl 1f, no extra: handles fast & gd/soft: find similar: see 3863. *1½* **85**
THREE DEGREES 0 [5] R M Beckett 2-8-9 N Chalmers(5) 50/1: 3: gr f Singspiel - Miss University (Beau Genius) Slow away, outpcd, hdwy/hung left over 1f out, styd on well ins fnl 1f on debut: clr of rem: Feb foal, cost 20,000gns: dam unpcld, sire a smart 2yo & later top-class over 10/12f: eff at 6f & further looks sure to suit: acts on gd/soft: pleasing debut, will learn from this & win over further. *1½* **75+**
3851 **ETAAR 37** [11] E A L Dunlop 2-9-0 W Supple 4/1: 444: b c Zafonic - Hawayah (Shareef Dancer) Slow away in rear, hdwy over 2f out, onepcd fnl 1f: Mar foal, cost 36,000gns: half-brother to wnrs over 7f/1m: dam a 7f wnr at 2, sire top-class 2yo/miler: new stable here (prev with N Graham): by drop back in trip here. *3* **71**
4349 **CAVALARRA 14** [10]2-9-0 E Ahern 20/1: 05: Chsd ldrs, no impress ins fnl 1f. *2½* **63**
4349 **BEAUNE 14** [3]2-9-0 S W Kelly 9/4: 36: Chsd ldrs, no impress ins fnl 1f. *1¾* **59**
LEIGHTON BUZZARD 0 [1]2-9-0 R Havlin 20/1: 7: Slow away & outpcd, modest late gains on debut. *nk* **58**
EFORETTA 0 [6]2-8-9 M Tebbutt 66/1: 8: Slow away in rear, nvr a factor on debut. *2* **47**
4422 **ITALIAN TOUCH 11** [16]2-9-0 I Mongan 40/1: 09: Slow away, al bhd. *½* **50**
3817 **SONNTAG BLUE 39** [4]2-9-0 T P Queally 66/1: 0000: 10th: Al bhd. *¾* **48**
3682 **QUEUE UP 44** [8]2-9-0 M Fenton 25/1: 300: 11th: Led till over 3f out, no extra 1f out: 6 wk abs. *1¾* **44**
TEMPLE BELLE XPRES 0 [12]2-8-9 J Bramhill 66/1: 0: 12th: Cl-up, wknd over 2f out on debut. *½* **37**
4089 **PRESKANI 28** [2]2-9-0 R Fitzpatrick 100/1: 000: 13th: Cl-up, lost place after 1f, no impress 3f out. *5* **27**

4540 **KIRKHAMMERTON 5** [15]2-9-0 V Slattery 100/1: 0000: 14th: Slow away, nvr a factor: qck reapp.   2   21
3975 **JUST BONNIE 32** [13]2-9-0 (35) P Fitzsimons 100/1: 6000: 15th: Slow away, hdwy 4f out, wknd 3f   2½   13
out.
15 Ran   Time 1m 16.01 (5.21)   Owned: Girsonfield Ltd   Trained: Wantage

---

4645   2.45 Ziminski Golden Wedding Celebration Nursery Handicap Stakes 2yo 0-75 (E3)   [82]
£4404 £1355 £678   6f15y   Good/Soft 60   -33 Slow   Far side

4420* **VIKING SPIRIT 11** [11] P W Harris 2-9-11 (6ex) (79) I Mongan 2/1 FAV: 02213: Chsd ldrs stands   94
side, hdwy to lead group & overall ldr well over 1f out, rdn out ins fnl 1f: landed double under top-weight: eff at
6f, 7f looks sure to suit: acts on fast & soft: see 4420.
4471 **TESARY 8** [4] E A L Dunlop 2-9-7 (75) E Ahern 11/1: 2143302: Trkd ldrs far side, hdwy to lead   2½   80+
over 2f out, kept on, not pace of winner on wrong side: acts on fast & gd/soft: see 4273.
4437 **APOLOGIES 10** [10] B A McMahon 2-9-4 bl (72) N Chalmers(5) 16/1: 4060363: Chsd ldrs far side, onepcd. 1¼   73
4490 **GRAND PLACE 7** [1] R Hannon 2-9-3 (71) P Dobbs 5/1: 0401044: Rear, hdwy 2f out, wknd fnl 1f.   1½   67
4545* **ARBORS LITTLE GIRL 4** [14]2-8-10 (6ex) A Daly 13/2: 115: Mid-div stands side, eff over 2f   ½   58
out, outpcd over 1f out: qck reapp: too sn after 4545?
4437 **ROSIELLA 10** [5]2-9-5 (73) D Sweeney 16/1: 051346: Slow away far side, sn cl-up, onepcd fnl 1f.   1   64
3212 **GAUDALPIN 64** [8]2-8-11 (65) A McCarthy 66/1: 340407: Chsd ldrs far side, wknd over 1f out: 9 wk abs. nk   55
4171 **TWICE NIGHTLY 22** [3]2-8-9 (63) K McEvoy 25/1: 3365008: Cl-up far side, wknd over 1f out.   1¼   49
4123 **PENNESTAMP 25** [6]2-8-11 (65) R Havlin 25/1: 0664439: Led far side over 3f, no extra 1f out: 'hung right'. shd 50
4146* **MARCELA ZABALA 24** [2]2-8-4 (58) N Mackay(3) 25/1: 01010: 10th: Rear far side, modest late gains.   shd   42
4556 **GOGETTER GIRL 4** [12]2-8-12 p (66) M Fenton 80/1: 4046000: 11th: Slow away stands side, no dngr.   nk   49
4171 **INDIBRAUN 22** [9]2-9-4 P (72) Rory Moore(5) 25/1: 1440340: 12th: Handy far side, wknd 1f out.   3   46
3484 **SISTER GEE 53** [16]2-8-7 (61) W Supple 50/1: 4320: 13th: Prom stands side, hdwy to lead halfway,   hd   34
hdd 2f out, no extra over 1f out: 8 wk abs.
3994* **MEGELL 32** [17]2-8-11 (65) T P Queally 33/1: 620510: 14th: Made most stands side to halfway, no extra. 1½   33
3266 **PEOPLETON BROOK 62** [15]2-8-13 (67) S W Kelly 50/1: 5600: 15th: Mid-div, keen, no impress.   shd   34
4343 **JOE JO STAR 15** [20]2-8-3 (57) P Bradley 33/1: 6600: 16th: Slow away stands side, no dngr.   nk   23
3750 **HAROLDINI 42** [7]2-8-11 (65) J Edmunds 28/1: 0426200: 17th: Chsd ldrs far side, no impress.   1¼   27
4437 **RANCHO CUCAMONGA 10** [13]2-9-0 (68) S Sanders 12/1: 0100550: 18th: Handy, wknd 1f out.   5   33
4420 **AVERTING 11** [19]2-8-11 BL (65) S Carson 40/1: 52000: 19th: Dsptd lead stands side, lost place   1½   7
halfway, no extra over 2f out: blnks: see 3722.
19 Ran   Time 1m 15.93 (5.53)   Owned: The Masterminds   Trained: Berkhamsted

---

4646   3.15 Ibetx Com Sports Betting Exchange Handicap Stakes Fillies & Mares 3yo+ 56-70 (E3)   [75]
£4150 £1277 £639   6f15y   Good/Soft 60   -16 Slow   Far side

4489 **STOKESIES WISH 8** [17] J L Spearing 4-8-13 (60) B Swarbrick(5) 16/1: 0633001: Rear stands side,   71
hdwy 3f out, drvn out to lead ins fnl 1f: eff at 5/6f on firm & gd/soft, likes a sharp/undul trk, esp Goodwood.
3705 **YOMALO 44** [19] R Guest 4-9-3 (64) C Catlin 14/1: 0562562: Rear stands side, hdwy 2f out, kept on   ¾   71
ins fnl 1f: 6 wk abs: acts on fast, gd/soft & fibresand: see 2034.
4109 **RIQUEWIHR 27** [9] D R Loder 4-8-13 (60) T P Queally 8/1: 10-43: Mid-div far side, hdwy 2f out,   ½   65
led over 1f out, styd on: lightly rcd, try 7f now? acts on fast & gd/soft: see 4109.
4528 **LA VIE EST BELLE 6** [5] B R Millman 3-9-1 (64) A McCarthy 20/1: 4006104: Led far side group, hdd   1   66
over 1f out, no extra ins fnl 1f: qck reapp: back to form: see 4236.
4262 **ASBO 19** [20]4-8-11 (58) D Corby(3) 16/1: 0/00-5435: Rear stands side, hdwy 2f out, styd on well   hd   59
ins fnl 1f: acts on fast & gd/soft: see 3213.
4548 **WOODBURY 4** [15]5-9-3 (6ex) (64) G Baker 14/1: 4104106: Mid-div stands side, styd on ins fnl 1f.   1   62
1908* **CEFIRA 118** [8]3-9-4 (67) M Henry 14/1: 0-3017: Rear far side, hdwy over 1f out, kept on: long abs.   nk   64
4126 **TANCRED TIMES 25** [13]9-9-3 (64) S Sanders 13/2 J FAV: 3141328: Sn led stands side, hdd over 2f   ¾   59
out, led again over 1f out, hdd & no extra ins fnl 1f.
4117 **GENEROUS GESTURE 26** [14]3-9-3 (66) W Supple 33/1: 1065609: Handy stands side, wknd 2f out.   shd   60
4475 **SILVER CHIME 8** [10]4-9-2 BL (63) M Fenton 66/1: 6600000: 10th: Chsd ldrs far side, no impress 2f out. hd   56
4229 **STORMY NATURE 20** [7]3-9-7 (70) P Dobbs 16/1: 20-30000: 11th: Prom far side, no impress over 1f out. nk   62
2268 **GOJO 102** [4]3-9-5 (68) D Sweeney 33/1: 60-42000: 12th: Handy far side, wknd far out: long abs.   1½   55
3849 **BALLINGER EXPRESS 38** [16]4-9-1 bl (62) N Chalmers(5) 33/1: 2002000: 13th: Mid-div stands side, wknd. 1¼   45
4317 **UNITED SPIRIT 16** [3]3-9-1 bl (64) E Ahern 13/2 J FAV: 6311450: 14th: Nvr a factor far side.   ½   45
4489 **COLLEGE QUEEN 8** [6]6-9-0 (61) S Carson 10/1: 5200530: 15th: Handy far side, wknd 2f out.   ½   40
4317 **DARLA 16** [11]3-9-6 (69) K McEvoy 8/1: 06-05260: 16th: Cl-up stands side, hdwy to lead over 2f   1   45
out, hdd & no extra over 1f out: see 3870.
4278 **PARTY PRINCESS 18** [1]3-8-9 (58) I Mongan 16/1: 1400000: 17th: Handy far side, wknd 2f out.   shd   33
4412 **MISS JUDGEMENT 11** [18]3-9-1 (64) R Miles(3) 14/1: 3001000: 18th: Handy stands side, wknd 2f out.   nk   38
2999 **DIAMOND SHANNON 73** [2]3-8-9 (58) Joanna Badger 33/1: 0051200: 19th: Slow away, nvr a factor.   1¼   28
2395J **WALL STREET RUNNER 34** [12]3-8-13 (62) Natalia Gemelova(7) 50/1: 1106520: 20th: Bhd, saddle   5   17
slipped, no ch: now with C Dwyer: forgive this.
20 Ran   Time 1m 15.31 (4.51)   Owned: Mr Byron J Stokes   Trained: Kinnersley

---

4647   3.50 Stora Enso/Reel Paper Company Handicap Stakes 3yo+ 71-85 (D2)   [99]
£12034 £3703 £1851   1m6f15y   Good/Soft 60   +15 Fast   Inside

4360 **REGAL SETTING 14** [3] Sir Mark Prescott 3-8-6 (77) S Sanders 7/1: 21-61: Trkd ldrs, hdwy 4f out,   90
drvn out to lead ins fnl 1f: op 5/1: fast time: eff at 1m/8.5f, relished this step up to 14f: acts on gd/soft &
fibresand, sharp or gall trk: unexposed, type to win more races.
3688* **MR ED 44** [6] P Bowen 6-9-5 p (80) K McEvoy 7/2 FAV: 000-2212: Rear, hdwy wide 3f out, styd on ins 1¼   88
fnl 1f, onepcd cl-home: hdles fit (val h'cap wnr, rtd 150h): gd run, in excellent form this term: see 3688.
4353 **GENGHIS 14** [13] H Morrison 5-9-5 (80) L Fletcher(3) 14/1: 3-252033: Led till hdd & no extra ins   1¼   86
fnl 1f: stays 12/14f: acts on firm & gd/soft: most consistent: see 2737.
4400 **SKYES FOLLY 12** [4] J G Given 4-8-11 bl (72) M Fenton 11/1: 0003334: Bhd, hdwy 3f out, kept on: 1½   76
handles firm, gd/soft & poss polytrack: see 3475.
4377 **SPORTING GESTURE 13** [5]7-9-1 (76) T P Queally 14/1: 4436U25: Mid-div, outpcd over 5f out, hdwy   2½   76

3f out, onepcd over 1f out: see 4377.
4076 **BUCKS 28** [15]7-9-4 (79) M Howard(7) 14/1: 2502256: In tch, hdwy after 7f, onepcd fnl 1f: clr of rem. 1½ 77
4383 **TRANCE 13** [10]4-9-11 (86) P Makin(5) 20/1: 0411007: Rear, hdwy over 3f out, wknd 2f out. 3½ 79
4281 **SERRAMANNA 18** [9]3-8-1 (72) Paul Eddery 16/1: 62-65338: In tch, nvr nrr. ¾ 64
3899* **REDI 36** [1]3-8-0 (71) N Mackay(3) 5/1: 4-046319: Chsd ldrs, hdwy 3f out, wknd over 1f out: op 8/1. nk 62
4196 **MAMCAZMA 21** [11]6-9-10 (85) M Tebbutt 25/1: 0040000: 10th: In tch, hdwy halfway, wknd 2f out. 4 70
3688 **FAIT LE JOJO 44** [16]7-9-10 (85) E Ahern 40/1: 11351///-00: 11th: Chsd ldrs, wknd over 1f out. 1¼ 68
4553 **SKI JUMP 4** [12]4-9-6 vis (81) T Hamilton(3) 12/1: 1606000: 12th: Trkd ldrs, wknd over 2f out: qck reapp. shd 63
3881 **OBAY 37** [2]3-9-0 (85) W Supple 14/1: 4142320: 13th: Al bhd: op 20/1. 27 26
4400 **WEET FOR ME 12** [18]8-8-11 (72) D Sweeney 33/1: 0026560: 14th: Rcd in 2nd, wknd over 3f out. 1½ 11
4395 **SOUND OF FLEET 13** [7]3-8-11 (82) P Dobbs 28/1: 1502000: 15th: Nvr a factor. ¾ 20
4149 **QUDRAH 24** [17]4-9-3 (78) R Ffrench 100/1: 0540500: 16th: Slow away, nvr a factor: see 1005. 23 0
4106 **TERESA 27** [8]4-8-10 (71) I Mongan 16/1: 2660000: 17th: In tch, rear 3f out, fin t.o.: 'hung RH'd'. dist 0
17 Ran Time 3m 4.47 (6.17) Owned: W E Sturt - Osborne House Trained: Newmarket

4648

4.25 European Breeders Fund Trent Maiden Stakes 2yo (D2)
£6315 £1943 £972 **1m54y** **Good/Soft 60** **-57 Slow** Centre

3063 **CATCH A STAR 71** [7] N A Callaghan 2-8-9 (80) N Mackay(3) 9/1: 35031: Dwelt, rear, hdwy over 2f out, switched wide fnl 1f, drvn out ins fnl 1f, led post: op 7/1, long abs: relished this step up to 1m, further likely to suit: acts on gd/soft, gall trk: runs well fresh: win more races: see 1887. 83
4326 **BANCHIERI 16** [6] Saeed bin Suroor 2-9-0 K McEvoy 85/40: 332: Bhd, hdwy over 3f out, ev ch ins fnl 1f, kept on: stays 1m on fm & gd/soft: consistent, sure to win a race: see 4326 & 3811. nk 86
4069 **SPEIGHTSTOWN 28** [3] P F I Cole 2-9-0 S Sanders 8/1: 03: Led after 1f, hdd post: stays 1m, further will suit in time: acts on gd/soft: imprvd for recent debut, shown enough to win a race: see 4069. hd 85
3925 **MUTAMAASEK 35** [9] J L Dunlop 2-9-0 W Supple 20/1: 504: Trkd ldrs, ev ch ins fnl 1f, kept on: op 14/1: stays 1m, relish further in time: acts on gd/soft: win similar: see 3470. shd 84
4296 **MOONMAIDEN 18** [4]2-8-9 C Catlin 33/1: 055: Cl-up, hdwy into 2nd over 2f out, ev ch over 1f out, onepcd nr fin: stays 1m on gd/soft: see 4296. ¾ 77
FEN GAME 0 [10]2-9-0 R Havlin 40/1: 6: b c Montjeu - Hatton Gardens (Auction Ring) Handy, not clr run well over 1f out, onepcd fnl 1f on debut: Feb foal, cost 50,000gns: half-brother to wnrs at 2: dam smart 2yo, sire v smart mid-dist performer: with J Gosden. 2 78
3752 **GIVEN A CHOICE 42** [1]2-9-0 I Mongan 5/4 FAV: 47: Mid-div & keen, onepcd fnl 1f: nicely bckd, 6 wk abs: reportedly unsuited by grnd & slow early pace: see 3752. ¾ 76
4269 **SILSONG 18** [2]2-8-9 R Smith 150/1: 508: Led 1f, no extra 2f out: see 3883. 1½ 68
4115 **RED RIVER ROCK 26** [8]2-9-0 E Ahern 14/1: 39: Nvr a factor. 2 69
4147 **IRISH BALLAD 24** [11]2-9-0 M Fenton 50/1: 00: 10th: b c Singspiel - Auenlust (Surumu) Nvr a factor: 35,000gns Apr foal: half-brother to a 7f 2yo wnr: dam a wnr in Germany. 8 53
MISS DEFYING 0 [5]2-8-9 R Miles(3) 125/1: 0: 11th: b f Shambo - Dugy (Risk Me) Slow away, nvr a factor on debut: Apr first foal: dam unrcd, sire smart 12/14f runner: with R Curtis. dist 0
11 Ran Time 1m 48.68 (9.28) Owned: Mr M Tabor Trained: Newmarket

4649

5.00 Hblb City Life Magazine Maiden Stakes 3yo (D3)
£4966 £1528 £764 **1m54y** **Good/Soft 60** **-38 Slow** Centre

2991 **CANTARNA 73** [12] J Mackie 3-8-9 (73) R Ffrench 9/2: 555-2351: Prom, hdwy to lead over 3f out, drvn out ins fnl 1f: op 10/1, long abs: eff at 1m, further may suit: acts on fast & gd/soft, gall trk: runs well fresh. 74
3366 **MENEEF 57** [5] M P Tregoning 3-9-0 W Supple 7/2: 4-32: Led till over 3f out, not much room entering fnl 1f, kept on nr fin: 8 wk abs: stays 1m, further will suit: handles fm & gd/soft: see 3366. ½ 76
4120 **COPPICE 26** [4] L M Cumani 3-9-0 (74) N Mackay(3) 11/2: 6453: Cl-up, onepcd nr fin: stays 1m/9f: acts on firm & gd/soft: see 4120. 1 74
ALL BLUE 0 [6] Saeed bin Suroor 3-9-0 T K McEvoy 8/1: 4: b g Green Desert - Talented (Bustino) Mid-div, hdwy 3f out, onepcd fnl 1f on debut: dam smart over 10/12f: poss stays 1m, further will suit in time: prob acts on gd/soft: tried a t-strap: learn from this. 1¼ 71
3870 **BEAUTIFUL NOISE 37** [16]3-8-9 bl (49) M Tebbutt 33/1: 0655555: Mid-div, hdwy 3f out, kept on. 1¼ 63$
MISS POLARIS 0 [13]3-8-9 M Fenton 25/1: 6: b f Polar Falcon - Sarabah (Ela Mana Mou) Rear, hdwy 2f out, styd on ins fnl 1f on debut: cost 30,000gns: dam wnr over 10f. ¾ 61
4445 **SUBTLE BREEZE 10** [2]3-8-9 R Havlin 11/4 FAV: 37: Chsd ldrs, wknd fnl 1f. 1¾ 58
CIRRIOUS 0 [11]3-8-9 D Sweeney 100/1: 8: gr f Cloudings - Westfield Mist (Scallywag) Bhd, hdwy 3f out, hung left 2f out, sn wknd on debut: dam wnr of a National Hunt bmpr: with B Palling. ½ 57
BOBBY CHARLES 0 [10]3-9-0 T P Queally 80/1: 9: Slow away, modest late gains on debut. ¾ 60
PORTMEIRION 0 [3]3-8-9 S Sanders 12/1: 0: 10th: Mid-div, wknd over 1f out on debut: op 9/2. 1 53
2953 **EIJAAZ 75** [7]3-9-0 (67) P Dobbs 66/1: 0040: 11th: Al bhd: long abs: now with G Bravery. 1 56
4474 **SIAN THOMAS 8** [8]3-8-9 A Daly 20/1: 30: 12th: In tch, outpcd & btn over 2f out. ¾ 49
DESIREE 0 [9]3-8-9 Frances Pickard(7) 150/1: 0: 13th: Slow away, nvr a factor on debut. 2½ 44
1136 **ROYAL FLIGHT 158** [1]3-9-0 E Ahern 28/1: 5-00: 14th: Handy, wknd over 2f out: long abs. nk 48
3422 **KIKIS GIRLS 55** [14]3-8-9 J Brennan(7) 150/1: 00: 15th: Slow away, nvr a factor: now with M Wigham. 24 0
15 Ran Time 1m 47.23 (7.83) Owned: Gwen K DotCom Trained: Church Broughton

4650

5.30 Ibetx Com - The Punter's Choice Madame Jones Classified Stakes 3yo+ 0-60 (E3)
£4111 £1265 £633 **1m1f213y** **Good/Soft 60** **-42 Slow** Inside

4406 **INCROYABLE 11** [4] Sir Mark Prescott 3-8-9 (59) S Sanders 4/5 FAV: 0006-21: Trkd ldrs, hdwy into 2nd over 2f out, drvn out ins fnl 1f, led nr line: stays 10f well, further shld suit: acts on fast & gd/soft, gall trk: lightly rcd, can impr further: game: see 4406. 65
4365 **MAMBINA 14** [6] M R Channon 3-8-9 (59) C Catlin 8/1: 0402232: Led, hdd & no extra nr line: clr of rem: most consistent: see 3419 & 1648. nk 64
4321 **WRENLANE 16** [15] R A Fahey 3-8-12 (60) T Hamilton(3) 16/1: 2650403: Dwelt, sn in mid-div, hdwy & handy over 2f out, sn onepcd. 5 59
4515* **MILK AND SULTANA 6** [12] G A Ham 4-9-7 (59) A Daly 15/2: 2024114: Bhd, hdwy 3f out, onepace. ½ 61
4366 **JOMUS 14** [5]3-8-12 (58) R Miles(3) 28/1: 0004035: Slow away, hdwy over 3f out, styd on well ins 5 50

NOTTINGHAM FRIDAY 17.09.04 Lefthand, Galloping Track

fnl 1f: 'unsuited by this grnd': see 4366.
4438 **COTTINGHAM 10** [11]3-8-12 (59) B Reilly(3) 28/1: 6020666: Bhd, hdwy 3f out, styd on well ins fnl 1f. ½ **49**
4456 **SIENNA SUNSET 10** [13]5-9-1 (58) B Swarbrick(5) 14/1: 6241307: Al bhd. *2* **43**
4515 **JAKE BLACK 6** [8]4-9-4 (58) D Tudhope(7) 9/1: 5044108: Cl-up, wknd over 1f out: qck reapp. ½ **45**
2804 **ROYAL APPROACH 81** [9]3-8-9 (60) D Sweeney 80/1: 60-509: Al bhd: long abs: see 2804. *1½* **40**
1648 **AIRGUSTA 130** [2]3-8-12 (59) S Carson 80/1: 000-0000: 10th: Cl-up, wknd 3f out: now with C Morlock. ½ **42**
4346 **CRYFIELD 15** [10]7-9-4 (59) Kim Tinkler 25/1: 1643400: 11th: Al bhd. ½ **41**
2617 **SAHARAN SONG 88** [3]3-8-9 (59) E Ahern 25/1: 4-0000: 12th: Chsd ldrs, wknd over 3f out: long abs. *23* **3**
4456 **ARMS ACROSSTHESEA 10** [7]5-9-4 (60) J Edmunds 50/1: 4001600: 13th: Mid-div, wknd 3f out. *3* **1**
13 Ran Time 2m 12.44(10.14) Owned: Lady O'Reilly Trained: Newmarket

AYR FRIDAY 17.09.04 Lefthand, Galloping Track

Official Going Soft

4651

2.05 Listed Aon Consulting Harry Rosebery Stakes 2yo (A1)
£17400 £6600 £3300 **5f str** **Good/Soft 87** **+02 Fast** Stands side

4155 **PRINCE CHARMING 27** [12] J H M Gosden 2-8-11 (98) J Fanning 6/1: 11061: In tch, styd on to lead dist trav well, pushed out, val 2L+: bckd: eff at 5f on gd/soft & soft grnd: acts on a stiff/gall trk: showed imprvd form today & more List/Group prizes await on this evidence: see 1422 & 1114. **107**
3956 **MARY READ 34** [3] B Smart 2-8-9 (100) F Lynch 10/1: 3131202: Led, hdd dist, kept on, not pace easy wnr: back to form after disapp last time in 3956, see 3509 & 2786. *1* **100**
4458 **DANCE NIGHT 9** [4] B A McMahon 2-9-2 (100) G Gibbons 6/1: 1606103: Cl-up, no extra from dist: op 8/1: appreciated return to 5f with give & ran well under top-weight: see 4025. *2* **101**
2472 **NEXT TIME AROUND 94** [10] Mrs L Stubbs 2-8-11 (97) R Winston 20/1: 13504: Cl-up, no extra ins fnl 1f. ¾ **94**
4533 **BECKERMET 6** [11]2-9-0 (100) J F Egan 20/1: 2110405: Cl-up over 3f, no extra: qck reapp: see 4025. *1½* **93**
4307* **SUNDANCE 17** [1]2-8-11 (98) J Quinn 5/1 JT FAV: 1216: Chsd ldrs wide over 3f, onepcd: op 4/1: first try on easy grnd: showed more in 4307 (stks, gd). ½ **89**
4563 **KEY SECRET 9** [9]2-8-6 (93) Hayley Turner 10/1: 1144167: Nvr nrr than mid-div: twice below 4123 (h'cap). *1¾* **80**
4458 **MIMI MOUSE 9** [8]2-8-6 (88) K Darley 25/1: 6431108: Al in rear: btr 3432 (fast, h'cap). *2* **74**
4280 **SENTIERO ROSSO 18** [7]2-8-11 (96) T Eaves 6/1: 42139: Al in rear: btr 4280 (6f). *2* **73**
4059 **NOTJUSTAPRETTYFACE 29** [2]2-8-6 (100) S Drowne 5/1 JT FAV: 1440: 10th: Al bhd: btr 4059 (Gr 2, 6f). *2* **62**
4172 **Handsome Lady 22** [5]2-8-6 (75) P Hanagan 50/1:0
4307 **Theatre Of Dreams 17** [6]2-8-11 (86) A Nicholls 66/1:0
12 Ran Time 1m 00.85 (4.25) Owned: Sheikh Mohammed Trained: Manton

4652

2.35 Totesport Ayr Silver Cup Handicap 3yo+ (B1) **[93]**
£18050 £6846 £3423 **6f str** **Good/Soft 87** **+11 Fast** Stands side

4082* **EISTEDDFOD 28** [22] P F I Cole 3-9-8 (87) N De Souza(5) 8/1: 133111: In tch stands side, styd on to lead ins fnl 1f, rdn out: bckd: fast time: eff btwn 6/7f on firm & soft grnd acts on a sharp or stiff/gall trk: progressive 3yo who is still unexposed in h'cap grade: can win more races: see 4082 & 3293. **100**
4537 **CD EUROPE 5** [14] J J Quinn 6-9-8 p (85) R Winston 14/1: 0060022: Held up stands side, prog after halfway, kept on ins fnl 1f, not pace of wnr: qck reapp: gd run: well h'capped. ¾ **93**
4514 **JOHNSTONS DIAMOND 6** [28] E J Alston 6-9-7 (84) J Quinn 33/1: 0000003: Prom stands side, led that group after 4f, hdd ins fnl 1f, not btn far in 3rd: qck reapp: back to form on gd/soft. *hd* **91**
4229 **BALAKIREF 20** [26] M Dods 5-8-10 (73) S Drowne 9/1: 0005134: Cl-up stands side when short of room after halfway, styd on ins fnl 1f, not btn far in 4th: bckd from 14/1: remains in gd form: see 4229 & 4087. *hd* **79**
4482 **QUEENS RHAPSODY 8** [24]4-9-5 (82) J Fanning 20/1: 4040005: Cl-up stands side, no extra fnl 1f. *2* **82**
4229* **FONTHILL ROAD 20** [6]4-9-4 (3ex) (81) P Hanagan 10/1: 1322116: Mid-div far side, prog halfway, styd on to lead far side group ins fnl 1f, no ch with stands side group: won race on unfav'd far side: see 4229. *1* **78+**
4184 **MACHINIST 21** [11]4-9-5 (82) Alex Greaves 16/1: 0012457: Led far side group till ins fnl 1f, no extra: gd race on unfav'd far side: btr 3434. *1½* **75**
4350 **SIERRA VISTA 14** [13]4-9-2 (79) L Enstone 50/1: 5160058: Handy stands side over 4f, no extra. ¾ **70**
3136 **MILLION PERCENT 68** [25]5-9-0 (77) Darren Williams 18/1: 0622669: In tch stands side over 4f, no extra. *2* **62**
3622 **NATIVE TITLE 48** [3]6-9-9 (86) A Nicholls 22/1: 0100300: 10th: Chsd ldrs far side, no extra bef 1f out: 7 wk abs: won this race 12 mths ago off a 9lb lower mark: btr 3116 (gd) & 2256 (firm). *hd* **70**
4603 **OBE ONE 2** [9]4-8-3 (66) P Mathers(5) 33/1: 0404450: 11th: Bhd far side, nvr nrr than mid-div. *nk* **49**
4537 **MYSTIC MAN 5** [27]6-9-10 (87) N Callan 7/1 FAV: 1304300: 12th: Cl-up stands side when short of room 2f out, sn btn: well bckd: qck reapp: shade btr expected: showed more in 4322 & 2684. *hd* **69**
2189 **ZOOM ZOOM 106** [16]4-8-12 (75) J P Guillambert(3) 25/1: 31/-1050: 13th: Nvr nrr than mid-div. ½ **56**
4465 **HILITES 9** [17]3-8-9 p (74) Derek Nolan(7) 100/1: 6304000: 14th: Al in rear stands side: btr 3545. ½ **54**
4048 **RISING SHADOW 29** [12]3-9-3 (82) K Darley 66/1: 5-624600: 15th: Cl-up far side 4f, wknd: btr 3433. ½ **61**
3937 **PIETER BRUEGHEL 34** [20]5-9-9 (86) P Doe 12/1: 0013320: 16th: Led stands side group 4f, wknd. ½ **64**
4103 **KIRKBYS TREASURE 27** [4]6-8-12 (75) F Lynch 40/1: 1202260: 17th: Nvr nrr than mid-div far side. *nk* **52**
4184 **CD FLYER 21** [1]7-9-9 (86) T Eaves(3) 25/1: 1043560: 18th: In tch far side, wknd bef 1f out. *1* **60**
4245+* **Bond Playboy 20** [19]4-8-3 (66) G Gibbons 16/1:0 4184 **Sir Desmond 21** [5]6-9-0 p(77) J Mackay 33/1:0
4322 **Ellens Academy 16** [2]9-9-9 (86) F Norton 33/1:0
2747 **Skip Of Colour 83** [21]4-8-8 (71) Dean McKeown 33/1:0
4005 **Indian Spark 31** [23]10-8-12 (75) J F Egan 20/1:0 4394 **Golden Dixie 13** [8]5-9-4 (81) A Culhane 25/1:0
4582 **Cheese N Biscuits 3** [18]4-8-5 p(68) Hayley Turner(3) 50/1:0
4382 **Blackheath 13** [10]8-9-10 (87) P J Benson(7) 66/1:0
26 Ran Time 1m 13.90 (4.6) Owned: Elite Racing Club Trained: Whatcombe

4653
3.05 James Barr European Breeders Fund Maiden Stakes 2yo (D2)
£5512 £1696 £848   **7f50y rnd**   **Good/Soft 87**   **-50 Slow**   Inside

4466 **MARKET TREND 9** [13] M Johnston 2-8-9 J Fanning 15/8 FAV: 21: Cl-up, led under press well over **85**
1f out, styd on well: well bckd: eff at 6f, apprec step up to 7f, further will suit: acts on gd & gd/soft grnd:
eff on a sharp/undul or gall trk: only lightly rcd & can progress: see 4466.

4457 **CONSIDER THIS 9** [3] W M Brisbourne 2-8-9 (82) K Darley 100/30: 253202: Led 5f, rallied to chase   1¼   **81**
wnr ins fnl 1f, al held: bckd: clr rem: eff at 6f, ran to form on step up to 7f: acts on fast & gd/soft grnd.

4376 **NASSEEM DUBAI 13** [9] Mrs A Duffield 2-9-0 (76) J Quinn 13/2: 06253: Keen in tch, led 2f out, sn   3   **80**
hdd, no extra: bckd: apprec return to 7f: see 4204.

4483 **BRANDEXE 8** [11] B W Hills 2-8-9 A Culhane 11/1: 054: Missed break, prog ins fnl 2f, nrst fin: 2   **71**
now quals for h'caps & will be of interest at a mile: see 4483.

4083 **THORNTOUN PICCOLO 28** [6]2-8-9 P Hanagan 33/1: 05: Bhd, prog 3f out, no impress fnl 1f: see 4083. hd   **70**

4326 **RAINBOW TREASURE 16** [1]2-8-9 T Eaves(3) 33/1: 06: Chsd ldrs 5f, wknd: see 4326.   3½   **63**

BESTBYFAR 0 [2]2-9-0 N Callan 16/1: 7: b c King's Best - Pippas Song (Reference Point) Handy   2½   **63**
over 4f, wknd: debut: Apr foal, cost 50,000gns: half-brother to wnrs at 5/8f: dam mid-dist wnr.

MAYS DREAM 0 [10]2-8-9 A Nicholls 25/1: 8: b f Josr Algarhoud - Amber Mill (Doulab) Missed   11   **37**
break, al bhd on debut: Apr foal, cost 27,000gns: half-sister to sprint wnr Golden Nun: dam sprinter.

PLUNGINGTON TAVERN 0 [5]2-9-0 Dean McKeown 66/1: 9: Missed break, nvr a factor on debut.   4   **34**

DEGREE OF HONOR 0 [12]2-8-9 R Winston 25/1: 0: 10th: In tch over 4f, sn wknd & eased: debut.   9   **13**

VICTOR BUCKWELL 0 [7]2-9-0 J F Egan 8/1: 0: 11th: Missed break, nvr a factor on debut.   ½   **17**

11 Ran   Time 1m 36.73 (9.93)   Owned: Maktoum Al Maktoum   Trained: Middleham

4654
3.40 Hbg Properties Handicap Stakes 3yo+ 71-85 (D2)   [88]
£6976 £2146 £1073   **5f str**   **Good/Soft 87**   **+05 Fast**   Stands side

4618 **HOUT BAY 1** [5] R A Fahey 7-8-7 (3oh) (67) P Hanagan 8/1: 36241131: Held up, prog halfway, styd on **78**
to led ins fnl 1f, rdn out: fin 3rd in similar event here yesterday: eff at 6f, suited by a stiff 5f: acts on
firm, likes gd/soft, soft & both AWs: tough & in-form 7yo who is thriving at present: see 4618 & 4240.

4197 **MR WOLF 21** [6] D W Barker 3-8-9 (73) L Enstone 20/1: 6600052: Cl-up, styd on to lead ins fnl 1f,   1¼   **76**
sn hdd & no extra: apprec return to easy surface & can find similar: see 1477 & 1392.

4496 **PICCLED 7** [15] E J Alston 6-9-6 (83) S Drowne 28/1: 1050R03: Bhd, prog halfway, onepace.   hd   **85**

4496 **PADDYWACK 7** [1] D W Chapman 7-8-9 bl (72) A Culhane 16/1: 0363304: Bhd, prog 2f out, kept on ins shd   **73**
fnl 1f, not btn far: qck reapp: just btr 4039 & 3852.

4382 **TRINCULO 13** [4]7-8-12 bl e (75) J P Guillambert(3) 33/1: 0060005: Rcd alone far rail, kept on ins   1½   **72**
fnl 1f, not pace stands side group: gd run in circumstances & is on a gd mark: see 927.

4087 **HIGHLAND WARRIOR 28** [2]5-8-8 (71) J F Egan 14/1: 4663026: Missed break, prog when short of room nk   **67**
bef 1f out, switched & kept on cl-home: shade closer with a clr run, apprec return to 6f: btr 4087 & 3307.

4005 **ARTIE 31** [10]5-9-7 (84) R Winston 7/1: 0100007: Handy till dist, onepcd: btr 3073.   ½   **79**

4350 **PAX 14** [9]7-9-2 (79) A Nicholls 33/1: 0000008: Nvr nrr than mid-div: btr 2059 (fast).   ½   **73**

4291 **PLATEAU 18** [16]5-9-6 (83) Alex Greaves 6/1 FAV: 6020039: Cl-up when hung left after halfway, sn btn. hd   **76**

4291 **BRAVE BURT 18** [14]7-9-3 (80) J Fanning 10/1: 0020000: 10th: Led stands side grp over 4f, no extra. ½   **72**

4496 **DISPOL KATIE 7** [12]9-9-3 (81) N Callan 11/1: 6350200: 11th: Chsd ldrs over 3f, wknd: btr 4027.   ½   **72**

4618 **KINGS COLLEGE BOY 1** [3]4-8-7 (2oh)bl (68) Dale Gibson 14/1: 03010240: 12th: Al in rear: too sn? nk   **60**

4278 **MISARO 8** [8]3-8-9 (73) Dean McKeown 14/1: 1-056240: 13th: Chsd ldrs wide 3f, sn hung left & wknd. 2½   **56**

4382 **MAKTAVISH 13** [11]5-9-1 p (78) T Eaves(3) 13/2: 0046000: 14th: Prom 3f, wknd: bckd: btr 1594.   ¾   **59**

4496 **WANCHAI LAD 7** [13]3-9-7 (85) K Darley 11/1: 0-305000: 15th: Mid-div 3f, wknd: qck reapp.   8   **44**

15 Ran   Time 1m 0.70 (4.1)   Owned: Northumbria Leisure Ltd   Trained: Malton

4655
4.15 Knight Frank Nursery Handicap Stakes 2yo 0-85 (D2)   [92]
£7046 £2168 £1084   **6f str**   **Good/Soft 87**   **-21 Slow**   Stands side

4234 **JE SUIS BELLE 20** [6] B W Hills 2-8-5 (69) A Culhane 7/2: 0321: In tch, prog when sltly short of   **75**
room ins fnl 1f, rdn out to lead cl-home: bckd tho' op 5/2: eff at 5f, suited by 6f & further shld suit: acts on
gd/soft & soft grnd: unexposed in h'cap grade & can progress: see 4234 & 3968.

4490 **MISSPERON 7** [8] K A Ryan 2-8-12 p (76) N Callan 10/1: 5313402: Prom, styd on to lead ins fnl 1f,   shd   **80**
hdd cl-home: qck reapp: back to form at fast & gd/soft grnd: back to form with fitting of cheek pieces: see 3115 & 2603.

4343 **DISPOL ISLE 15** [5] T D Barron 2-8-1 (65) P Fessey 8/1: 44443: Cl-up, ev ch ins fnl 1f, kept on,   nk   **68**
not btn far in 3rd: eff at 5f, apprec step up to 6f on h'cap bow: acts on fast & gd/soft grnd: see 4343 & 3988.

4306 **GENEROUS OPTION 17** [10] M Johnston 2-9-6 (84) J Fanning 100/30 FAV: 51344: Led, hdd ins fnl 1f,   ¾   **85**
no extra: tchd 4/1: acts on fast & gd/soft: see 4306 & 3303.

4306 **WORD PERFECT 17** [7]2-9-7 (85) Dale Gibson 20/1: 311505: Bhd, eff when short of room halfway,   hd   **85**
kept on ins fnl 1f: top-weight: eff at 5f, now stays 6f: see 3224.

4457 **DORN DANCER 9** [9]2-9-3 (81) L Enstone 33/1: 015006: Cl-up 5f, no extra: clr rem: btr 2281.   nk   **80**

4065 **FAVOURING 28** [2]2-8-0 (64) P Hanagan 7/2: 400247: Bhd, nvr a factor: well bckd: btr 4065.   4   **51**

4457 **AFRICAN BREEZE 9** [1]2-9-3 (80) Hayley Turner(3) 12/1: 0414508: Al bhd: btr 2883.   4   **55**

4343 **MIDDLE EASTERN 15** [11]2-8-4 (68) Dean McKeown 20/1: 5409: Cl-up till dist, fdd.   4   **31**

4273 **UNLIMITED 6** [4]2-8-5 (69) J Quinn 16/1: 1250350: 10th: Cl-up 3f, sn hung left & fdd.   6   **16**

10 Ran   Time 1m 15.79 (6.49)   Owned: Mr Guy Reed   Trained: Lambourn

4656
4.50 Westsound Handicap Stakes 3yo+ 71-85 (D2)   [96]
£7056 £2171 £1086   **1m2f**   **Good/Soft 87**   **-10 Slow**   Inside

4136 **STRAW BEAR 25** [4] Sir Mark Prescott 3-8-9 (77) J Mackay 13/2 FAV: 231-2351: Chsd ldrs, under   **89**
press when short of room & took place after 6f, rallied bef 1f out, rdn out to lead cl-home: bckd: eff at 1m/9f,
imprvd for step up to 10f, 12f will suit: acts on fast, gd/soft grnd & fibresand: prog again & win more races.

4279 **TROUBLE MOUNTAIN 18** [11] M W Easterby 7-8-9 (71) J F Egan 7/1: 4402142: Bhd, prog 3f out, styd   ½   **78**
on to lead dist, hdd under press cl-home: clr rem: tchd 10/1: rider received 1 day whip ban: see 4279.

4352 **APERITIF** 14 [19] W J Haggas 3-8-9 (77) J Quinn 12/1: 0433103: In tch, styd on to lead 2f out,   *5*   **80**
hdd dist, no extra: prob stays 10f, return to 1m will suit: see 3905 (1m mdn).

4254 **OPENING CEREMONY** 19 [5] R A Fahey 5-8-13 (75) P Hanagan 9/1: 2151524: Mid-div, prog 3f out, no   *1¾*   **75**
impress fnl 1f: shade btr 4254.

4292 **LENNEL** 18 [13]6-8-9 bl (71) Hayley Turner(3) 16/1: 1323305: Rear, prog 4f out, no impress fnl 2f.   *1*   **69**

4279 **STRONG HAND** 18 [9]4-8-10 (72) Dale Gibson 16/1: 0-630006: Nvr nrr than mid-div: btr 1066 (1m).   *¾*   **68**

4352 **LITTLE BOB** 14 [16]3-8-5 (73) J Fanning 40/1: 4230107: Nvr nrr than mid-div: btr 3697.   *2*   **66**

4246 **QUALITAIR WINGS** 20 [1]5-8-10 (72) D McGaffin 20/1: 2020638: Rear, prog 4f out, ev ch 2f out, wknd.   *1*   **63**

4305 **ROTUMA** 17 [7]5-8-13 bl (75) L Enstone 16/1: 6125109: Chsd ldrs 7f, wknd: showed more in 3815 (firm).   *3½*   **61**

4239 **BURNING MOON** 20 [20]3-9-3 VIS (85) K Darley 20/1: 50-51000: 10th: Chsd ldrs 7f, wknd: 1st time visor.   *2½*   **67**

3969 **UROWELLS** 33 [6]4-9-7 VIS (83) S Drowne 20/1: 6/41-0000: 11th: Led, hdd after 2f, styd cl-up, wknd dist.   *hd*   **64**

4612} **NECKAR VALLEY** 347 [12]5-9-1 (77) G Parkin 50/1: 205530-0: 12th: b g Desert King - Solar   *6*   **50**
Attraction (Salt Dome) Rear, modest late gains: reapp: h'cap wnr in '03: ex Irish, h'cap wnr in '02: eff at
9/12f on fast & gd/soft grnd: with R A Fahey.
2 Jul'03 Hami 9.2g/f 80-(74) E: 1 Jul'03 Hami 11.1g/f 77-68 E:

4305 **JIMMY BYRNE** 17 [3]4-9-2 (78) T Eaves(3) 12/1: 5611360: 13th: Nvr nrr than mid-div: btr 3276 & 3139.   *1*   **49**

4551} **LEWIS ISLAND** 704 [2]5-9-4 (80) J Carroll 33/1: 216630/-0: 14th: b g Turtle Island - Phyllode   *¾*   **49**
(Pharly) Al in rear: h'cap hdle wnr in 03/04 (rtd 127h, stays 2m4f on firm & hvy, N A Twiston Davies): h'cap wnr
on Flat in '02 (T G Mills): eff at 9f, suited by 12f: acts on fast & soft grnd: prob handles any trk.
1 Jun'02 Kemp 12sft 89-80 D: 2 May'02 Good 11g/f 82-78 D: 2 Sep'01 Kemp 8g/f 79- D: 2 Sep'01 Hayd 8.1g/s 77- E:

4295 **GO SOLO** 18 [8]3-8-7 (75) A Culhane 25/1: 0335300: 15th: Handy 7f, fdd.   *6*   **36**

4377 **PETRULA** 13 [10]5-9-4 bl (80) N Callan 16/1: 034-2600: 16th: Prom, ev ch 4f out, sn wknd.   *2*   **38**

4136 **LOW CLOUD** 25 [15]4-8-11 (73) F Norton 66/1: 1454000: 17th: Missed break, nvr a factor.   *5*   **24**

4279 **NEVADA DESERT** 18 [18]4-8-11 p (73) Dean McKeown 16/1: 4520100: 18th: Prom, led 4f out, hdd 2f out.   *hd*   **23**

4071 **BESSEMER** 28 [17]3-9-2 (84) R Winston 7/1: 0-536140: 19th: Mid-div 6f, fdd: something amiss?   *dist*   **0**

3879 **HIAWATHA** 37 [14]5-8-10 (72) G Gibbons 50/1: 0010500: 20th: Led 1f out, hdd 4f out, sn fdd.   *25*   **0**

20 Ran   Time 2m 14.12 (9.72)   Owned: Mr Chris Jenkins   Trained: Newmarket

---

4657	5.20 Strachans Motor Handicap For The Eglinton & Winton Challenge Cup 3yo+ 71-85 (D2)	[94]
	£6830 £2102 £1051 **2m1f105y** **Good/Soft 87** **-44 Slow** Inside	

3861* **STRANGELY BROWN** 37 [8] S C Williams 3-8-5 (71) P Hanagan 13/8 FAV: 3002111: Keen rear, prog 3f   **75**
out, stdy on to lead fnl 1f, rdn out: v well bckd: suited by around 2m/2m1.5f on fast & hvy grnd: unexposed
around this trip & may not be at end of winning run: see 3861 & 3580.

4287 **LATE OPPOSITION** 18 [3] E A L Dunlop 3-8-4 vis (70) F Norton 6/1: 2003122: Cl-up, led 2f out, hdd   *1¼*   **72**
ins fnl 1f, sn flashed tail for press, not pace of wnr: eff at 11/14f, tan to form on step up to 2m1.5f: see 4287.

3233 **HISTORIC PLACE** 63 [2] G B Balding 4-9-12 (80) S Drowne 9/1: 2403: Cl-up, no extra ins fnl 1f: 9   *1*   **81**
wk abs: h'cap bow: eff at 12f, apprec step up to 2m1.5f: see 2230.

4209* **MASTER WELLS** 21 [6] J D Bethell 3-8-13 (79) A Culhane 7/2: 0200214: Mid-div, prog when short of   *shd*   **79**
room bef 2f out, again short of room ins fnl 1f, late prog when short of room cl-home: bckd: prob stays 2m1.5f:
did not get run of race & is worth keeping in mind for similar: see 4209.

4287 **EBINZAYD** 18 [5]8-9-3 (71) J Fanning 25/1: 5//0//-0055: Led, hdd 2f out, no extra: see 2444.   *2½*   **69**

4504} **ALAM** 354 [1]5-9-6 (74) L Enstone 66/1: 5/0346/0-6: b g Silver Hawk - Ghashtah (Nijinsky) Cl-up,   *6*   **66**
wknd bef 1f out: plcd twice over hdles in 03/04 (rtd 117h at best, stays 2m on gd/soft & hvy): won 2 juv
nov hdles in 02/03 (rtd 112h): modest Flat form in 4 '02 starts (rtd 71, class stks): with P Monteith.

4287 **TONI ALCALA** 18 [4]5-9-4 (72) D Nolan(5) 25/1: 5115567: Mid-div, nvr a factor: btr 3810.   *1¾*   **62**

3999 **KRISTENSAN** 31 [7]5-9-9 p (77) K Darley 11/2: 6250038: Al in rear: btr 3999 (12f).   *shd*   **66**

8 Ran   Time 4m 5.91(23.61)   Owned: J T and K Worsley   Trained: Newmarket

---

Official Going Standard

4658	11.30 Welney Maiden Auction Stakes 2yo (H5)	
	£1491 £426 £213 **7f aw rnd** **Going 46** **+00 Fast** Inside	

4035 **ELRAFA MUJAHID** 31 [8] Julian Poulton 2-8-4 Lisa Jones 4/1 CO FAV: 301: In tch, prog bef 1f out,   **69a**
rdn out to lead cl home: tchd 11/2: eff at 7f/1m, turned well: acts on polytrack: see 3786.

4108 **PINAFORE** 28 [10] H Morrison 2-8-3 T P Queally 4/1 CO FAV: 32: Led, hdd under press cl home: op   *nk*   **66a**
3/1: AW bow: eff at 6f, imprvd for step up to 7f: acts on gd grnd & polytrack: gd eff in defeat: see 4108 (debut).

4444 **DANGER ZONE** 11 [4] Mrs A J Perrett 2-8-12 (66) P Dobbs 12/1: 00503: In tch trav well, kept on   *1¾*   **71a**
fnl 1f, not pace front 2: AW bow: eff at 7f, bred to apprec further: acts on polytrack: see 3882.

   BIRD OVER 0 [3] R M Beckett 2-8-3 J Mackay 40/1: 4: b f Bold Edge - High Bird (Polar Falcon)   *hd*   **61a**
Bhd, hdwy 3f out, kept on fnl 1f, nrst fin: debut: May first foal, cost 900 gns: dam decent sprint
performer: eff at 7f, shapes as though further will suit: acts on polytrack: signs of encouragement.

4401 **OCEANCOOKIE** 13 [6]2-8-6 R Mullen 4/1 CO FAV: 55: Rear, prog 3f out, no impress dist: AW bow: *1*   **62a**
eff at 6f, ran to form on step up to 7f: acts on fast grnd & polytrack: see 4401.

4375 **BOLD COUNSEL** 14 [13]2-8-12 BL J Fortune 4/1 CO FAV: 526: Cl up over 5f, no extra: 1st time blnks.   *1½*   **65a**

4114 **BONNABEE** 27 [9]2-8-5 D Kinsella 25/1: 07: b f Benny The Dip - Samhat Mtoto (Mtoto) Bhd wide,   *5*   **48a**
prog when no room 2f out, swtchd & kept on late: Feb foal, cost 2,400 gns: half sister plcd at a mile: dam
successful abroad: sire Gr 1 wnr at 12f: closer with clr run & will enjoy further.

4163 **PHLAUNT** 24 [5]2-8-3 (68) S Carson 9/1: 40338: Bhd, nvr nrr than mid div: btr 4163 (soft).   *4*   **38a**

3975 **TOUCH OF SPICE** 33 [12]2-8-9 R Havlin 66/1: 09: Nvr nrr than mid div.   *4*   **36a**

4271 **SILVER CREEK** 19 [11]2-8-9 D Fox(5) 33/1: 0000: 10th: Cl up 5f, wknd.   *3*   **30a**

4422 **Summer Charm** 12 [7]2-8-9 (2ow) M Tebbutt 40/1:0   **Sperrin Valley 0** [1]2-8-5 R Miles(3) 66/1:0

4422 **Rooks Bridge** 12 [2]2-8-8 A Daly 66/1:0

4442 **Kindlelight Dream** 11 [14]2-8-8 (1ow) M Howard 33/1:R

14 Ran   Time 1m 26.04 (3.24)   Owned: Mr Giovanni Favarulo & Mr Manan Khawaja   Trained: Newmarket

LINGFIELD Polytrack SATURDAY 18.09.04 Lefthand, V Sharp Track

4659 **11.55 Titchwell Banded Stakes 3yo+ 0-40 (H5)**
£1491 £426 £213 **1m aw rnd** **Going 46** **-11 Slow** Outside

905 **LEVANTINE 179** [3] Miss J Feilden 7-9-0 (40) Kirsty Milczarek(7) 12/1: 633-3561: In tch trav well, prog when no room 2f out & again dist, found room & styd on well to lead cl home, pushed out, val 2L+: long abs & new stable: eff at 7f/1m on fast, soft & both AW's: tried pieces, blnks & visor, imprvd without them today, goes well fresh: gd start for current trainer & can win again in this grade. **49a**
4371 **CRIMSON STAR 14** [4] C Tinkler 3-8-10 (40) D Kinsella 5/1: 0000322: Handy, led 2f out, hdd cl home: op 4/1: eff at 6/7f, now stays 1m: acts on fast, gd & polytrack: can find similar: see 4371. *½* **43a**
4419 **ENNA 12** [2] Mrs Stef Liddiard 5-9-0 (40) R Havlin 9/2: 4206043: Mid div, hdwy bef 1f out, kept on, not pace front 2: clr rem: acts on firm, soft & polytrack: worth another try over further on this evidence. *2½* **38a**
3288 **RAGASAH 63** [5] E R Oertel 6-9-0 (40) Lisa Jones 33/1: 0060/0-04: Led 5f, sn no extra: 9 wk abs. *2½* **33a**
4299 **DENISE BEST 19** [12]6-9-0 p (40) D Nolan(3) 5/1: 0501-055: Missed break, nvr nrr nrr than mid div. *nk* **32a**
4211 **DESERT FURY 22** [11]7-9-0 (40) T P Queally 11/4 FAV: 0-006506: Slow away, prog 2f out, mod late gains: bckd: better expected on drop in grade for polytrack bow: btr 3487. *1¼* **30a**
4189 **CATCH THE FOX 22** [8]4-9-0 (40) A Daly 11/1: 0400047: Al bhd: btr 4189. *½* **29a**
4445 **ESTRELLA LEVANTE 11** [6]4-9-0 bl (40) S Carson 16/1: 6000008: Cl up, led 3f out, hdd 2f out, wknd. *hd* **28a**
2840] **TAP DANCER 795** [10]6-9-0 (40) A Hindley(7) 33/1: 410060/-9: b g Sadler's Wells - Watch Out (Mr Prospector) Keen in tch 5f, fdd: mod form in 2 02/03 hdle starts (rtd 72h, nov): h'cap wnr in '02: ex Irish mdn: eff at 10f, tried further: acts on gd/soft grnd & a sharp/undul trk: 1 May'02 Brig 10g/s 46-42 F: *¾* **26a**
3717 **RATHMULLAN 44** [7]5-9-0 bl (40) Liam Jones(7) 16/1: 3500040: 10th: Handy 5f, sn hung badly & wknd. *2½* **21a**
4131 **Explicit 26** [1]3-8-10 (40) J Mackay 33/1:0 3286 **Singularity 63** [9]4-9-0 bl(40) B Reilly(3) 66/1:R
12 Ran Time 1m 40.82 (4.62) Owned: City Racing Club Trained: Newmarket

4660 **12.20 Amy & Jessica Rix Banded Stakes 3yo+ 0-45 (H5)**
£1701 £486 £243 **7f aw rnd** **Going 46** **+03 Fast** Inside

4130 **SYLVA ROYAL 26** [4] C E Brittain 3-9-1 (49) J P Guillambert(3) 12/1: 44601: Mid div, hdwy halfway, led ins fnl 1f, pushed out, val bit more: imprvd for step up to 7f, further will suit: acts on polytrack. **54a**
4373 **BALLARE 14** [5] Bob Jones 5-9-5 vis (50) T Williams 5/1: 1040002: Cl up, led 2f out, hdd ins fnl 1f. *1½* **50a**
4507+**CALCULAITE 7** [14] Mrs G S Rees 3-9-7 (55) Rory Moore(5) 3/1 FAV: 6645013: Prom, ev ch bef 1f out, no extra: qck reapp: acts on firm & gd, handles polytrack: btr 4507 (firm, 1m). *1¾* **51a**
3823 **PIROUETTES 40** [3] E R Oertel 4-9-0 (45) Lisa Jones 25/1: 40-00004: Bhd, hdwy halfway, no impress. *2* **37a**
3197 **LABELLED WITH LOVE 66** [2]4-9-3 T (48) V Venkaya 28/1: 0-25605: Keen handy over 5f, sn no extra. *3* **34a**
3911 **AVERAMI 36** [13]3-9-2 BL (50) R J Killoran(7) 28/1: 5006006: Nvr nrr than mid div: 1st time blnks. *nk* **35a**
4367 **LOCH LAIRD 15** [10]9-9-4 (49) C Haddon(7) 8/1: 0054307: Bhd, mod gains: op 13/2: btr 4168 (soft). *½* **33a**
4616 **TAIYO 3** [1]4-9-4 (49) R Havlin 10/1: 0P01568: Handy 5f, wknd: qck reapp. *nk* **32a**
4488 **LOGISTICAL 9** [7]4-9-2 (47) C Cavanagh(6) 16/1: 0500009: Missed break, nvr a factor. *½* **29a**
4130 **BOLD WOLF 26** [11]3-9-0 (48) D Corby(3) 7/1: 4000040: 10th: In tch, fdd 2f out: op 10/1: btr 4130. *½* **29a**
491} **SPINETAIL RUFOUS 598** [8]6-9-3 bl t (48) S Carson 7/1: 006/000-0: 11th: b g Prince of Birds - Miss Kinabalu (Shirley Heights) Led, trav best halfway, hdd 2f out, fdd: reapp & new stable: unplcd in '03 (rtd 49a, D W P Arbuthnot): rnr up in '02 (AW h'cap): mdn & h'cap wnr in '01: eff at 5/6f, prev eff on equitrack & fibresand: likes a sharp trk: eff with t-strap. 2 Oct'02 Sout 6af 63a-58 E: 2 Mar'01 Ling 5ap 73a-71 D: 1 Feb'01 Ling 5ap 74a-66 E: 1 Feb'01 Ling 5ap 62a- D: 2 Dec'00 Sout 6af 59a-55 E: *¾* **27a**
4195 **SOUL PROVIDER 22** [12]3-8-11 p (45) R Miles(3) 25/1: 4050000: 12th: Al in rear. *5* **14a**
365 **Spring Whisper 252** [9]3-9-1 BL(49) D Fox(5) 28/1:0 3849 **Hagley Park 39** [6]5-9-2 (47) D Nolan(3) 25/1:0
14 Ran Time 1m 25.87 (3.07) Owned: Eddy Grimstead Ltd Trained: Newmarket

4661 **12.50 Filey Maiden Claiming Stakes 3yo+ (H5)**
£1488 £425 £213 **1m2f aw** **Going 46** **+04 Fast** Inside

4120 **RYANS BLISS 27** [9] T D McCarthy 4-9-1 (45) R Miles(3) 4/1: 2000561: Cl up, led 3f out, clr bef 1f out, eased cl home, val 5L+: eff at 10f on poltrack, likes Lingfield: appreciated drop in grade: see 3748 & 970. **61a**
4299 **ZALKANI 19** [8] B G Powell 4-9-6 (57) A Hindley(7) 7/2 FAV: 5004002: Bhd, outpcd after 5f, rallied to chase wnr 2f out, kept on but always held: clr rem: see 430. *3* **59a**
1456 **LADY LAKSHMI 142** [7] M Madgwick 4-9-1 T (40) C Haddon(7) 8/1: 5030-323: Held up, outpcd after halfway, mod gains: op 9/2, new stable: 1st time t-strap: needs further: btr 1456 (13f, R Guest). *8* **42a**
4411 **YOUNG LOVE 12** [6] Miss E C Lavelle 3-8-9 (45) R Havlin 13/2: 6406444: Mid div 6f, outpcd, rallied late. *½* **41a**
4445 **DARK PARADE 11** [14]3-9-0 J Jones(7) 33/1: 505: An bhd, hdwy when no room 2f out, swtchd & nrst fin. *2* **43a**
3547 **RICKY MARTAN 51** [4]3-8-10 (45) D Nolan(3) 20/1: 0000606: In tch 6f, no extra. *1¼* **37a**
4379} **DAMASK DANCER 364** [12]5-9-4 P (45) P McCabe 33/1: 0/55000-7: Handy 6f, wknd. *shd* **38a**
4373 **MARGERY DAW 14** [3]4-9-1 (45) J Brennan(7) 10/1: 3005008: In tch 7f, sn wknd. *1¼* **33a**
4372 **ANNA GAYLE 14** [13]3-8-7 (40) S Carson 20/1: 00509: Bhd, nvr a factor. *nk* **30a**
4448 **BONUS POINTS 11** [1]3-9-0 BL D Corby(3) 4/1: 060: 10th: Led, clr halfway, hdd 3f out, fdd: blnks. *9* **24a**
3819} **Trigger Mead 392** [11]4-8-11 (50) D Kinsella 16/1:0 2907 **Jimmy Hay 78** [5]3-8-8 Victoria Hill(7) 66/1:0
3911 **Akiramenai 36** [2]4-9-1 (45) Kristin Stubbs(7) 25/1:0 2393 **Seagold 98** [10]3-8-5 bl(45) T Williams 66/1:0
14 Ran Time 2m 7.02 (4.22) Owned: Mr James Ryan Trained: Godstone

4662	1.15 Slimbridge Banded Stakes 3yo+ 0-35 (H5)
	£1281 £366 £183 1m2f aw Going 46 -23 Slow Inside

4371 **STAGECOACH RUBY 14** [12] G L Moore 3-8-10 (35) R Brisland 12/1: 4330051: Keen handy, prog to lead **40a**
well ins fnl 1f, pushed out, val 3L+: eff at 6/7f, appreciated step up to 10f: acts on firm, gd & polytrack.
   SAMMAGEFROMTENESSE 65 [5] A E Jones 7-9-2 p (35) T Williams 10/1: 2060-652: b g Petardia -   *1½* **36a**
Canoora (Ahonoora) In tch, led bef 2f out, hdd well ins fnl 1f, not pace wnr: ex Irldh, unplcd both Flat starts
this term: sell h'cap hdle wnr in 02/03 (rtd 80h, stays 2m1f on gd): Irish h'cap wnr on Flat in '00 (9f, gd/soft):
eff at 9/10f on gd/soft & polytrack.
3530 **SMARTER CHARTER 52** [9] Mrs L Stubbs 11-9-2 (35) Kristin Stubbs(7) 6/1: 5045643: Bhd, prog when no *1¾* **33a**
room bef 1f out, nrst fin: 7 wk abs; shade closer but for interference: see 1287.
   MAEVEEN 105 [8] V Smith 4-9-2 e (35) Rory Moore(5) 12/1: 000-004: Handy, eff 2f out, wknd fnl 1f.   *1¾* **30a**
3096 **KALANISHA 71** [11]4-9-2 bl (35) D Corby(3) 3/1 FAV: 00-0008: In tch 1m, no extra: abs & new stable.   *¾* **28a**
3895 **STREET GAMES 37** [6]5-9-2 (35) S Righton 7/1: 000/00-56: Keen bhd, hdwy 2f out, wknd ins fnl 1f.   *shd* **27a**
4055 **MACS ELAN 30** [10]4-9-2 (35) L Fletcher(3) 16/1: 0-057: Nvr nrr than mid div.   *¾* **25a**
1026 **PRINCE IVOR 169** [13]4-9-2 vis T (35) B Reilly(3) 66/1: 0000-008: In tch 5f, fdd: jumps fit & new yard.   *nk* **24a**
4373 **LADY LIESEL 14** [4]4-9-2 (35) J P Guillambert(3) 16/1: 3004009: Al in rear.   *2* **21a**
3895 **TOMSK 37** [1]4-9-2 (35) D Nolan(3) 6/1: 0/04-630: 10th: Missed break, nvr a factor: btr 3895 (gd/soft).   *8* **10a**
4372 **TSHUKUDU 14** [14]3-8-10 (35) S Carson 16/1: 0030200: 11th: Led, hdd 3f out, fdd: op 10/1: btr 4142.   *7* **0a**
4505 **DAIMAJIN 7** [3]5-9-2 VIS (35) Derek Nolan(7) 50/1: 0: 0060000: 12th: Keen & led after 3f, hdd bef 2f out.   *½* **0a**
4116 Costa Del Sol 27 [2]3-8-10 P(35) R Miles(3) 25/1:0   4584 Skelthwaite 4 [7]3-8-10 (35) J McAuley 28/1:U
14 Ran   Time 2m 9.77 (6.97)   Owned: Mr Richard Dean   Trained: Brighton

4663	1.45 Minsmere Banded Stakes 3yo+ 0-45 (H5)
	£1495 £427 £214 2m aw Going 46 -10 Slow Inside

3714 **HABITUAL 44** [7] Sir Mark Prescott 3-8-13 (49) J P Guillambert(3) 9/4 FAV: 00-00451: In tch, eff **57a**
3f out, led dist, pushed clr, val 5L+: op 5/4, 6 wk abs: enjoyed return to 2m, acts on polytrack & goes well fresh:
easy wnr dropped in grade & can follow up for shrewd trainer: see 3312.
4056* **INDIAN CHASE 30** [8] Dr J R J Naylor 7-9-7 (45) L Vickers 7/1: 0004012: Mid div, hdwy 4f out,   *3½* **47a**
kept on fnl 1f, no pace easy wnr: op 11/1: continues in gd form: see 4056 (mdn h'cap).
4704↑ **CODY 342** [4] G A Ham 5-9-7 t (45) T Williams 25/1: 300/040-3: ch g Zilzal - Ibtihaj (Raja Baba)   *2* **45a**
Cl up, no extra dist: recent hdles p.u: rnr up twice in 03/04 (both h'caps, stays 3m on gd & fast): unplcd in '03
(mdn, rtd 76): plcd in '02 (mdn 'hcap, rtd 50): eff at 12f, poss stays 2m: acts on gd/sft & polytrack.
3714 **VANILLA MOON 44** [2] J R Jenkins 4-9-7 vis (45) P McCabe 14/1: 2436464: Led, hdd adter 3f, led   *shd* **44a**
again 6f out, hdd dist, wknd: 6 wk abs: see 3367 (11.5f).
4423 **GALANDORA 12** [6]4-9-2 (50) Natalia Gemelova(7) 7/1: 2033005: Bhd, prog 3f out, no impress dist.   *1* **48a**
3742 **ICEY RUN 43** [11]4-9-7 (45) S Righton 33/1: 000-06: Nvr nrr than mid div: 6 wk abs.   *2* **41a**
4374 **OPEN BOOK 14** [1]3-8-13 (49) L Fletcher 11/2: 000037: Handy 9f, no extra 3f out: btr 4374 (fast).   *nk* **44a**
3481 **MAXIMINUS 54** [10]4-9-12 (50) R Lucey Butler(7) 12/1: 00-40608: Nvr nrr than mid div.   *2½* **43a**
4372 **BRETTON 14** [5]3-8-9 (45) Rory Moore(5) 25/1: 3025009: Rear, mod late gains.   *3* **35a**
3715 **JOELY GREEN 44** [3]7-9-7 p (45) Steven Harrison(7) 7/1: 2000040: 10th: Bhd, nvr nrr than mid div.   *3½* **32a**
4374 **CANTRIP 14** [14]4-9-11 (49) S Carson 12/1: 0130050: 11th: Cl up 12f, fdd.   *13* **25a**
3992 **CURRAGH GOLD 33** [13]4-9-9 (47) Amy Baker(7) 50/1: 1300-000: 12th: Handy 10f, fdd.   *nk* **22a**
   COLD ENCOUNTER 1471 [9]9-9-12 (50) D Corby(3) 50/1: /32/00///-0: 13th: held up, fdd 3f out.   *6* **19a**
4319 **ASH HAB 17** [12]6-9-7 bl (45) Derek Nolan(7) 50/1: 3000//-000: 14th: Led after 3f, hdd 6f out, fdd.   *dist* **0a**
14 Ran   Time 3m 29.0(9.0)   Owned: P J McSwiney - Osborne House   Trained: Newmarket

---

Official Going Good/Soft

4664	2.10 Gallions Maiden Stakes 2yo (D3)
	£4495 £1383 £692 7f26y rnd Good/Soft 61 -00 Slow Inside

4190 **RED AFFLECK 22** [1] P W Chapple Hyam 2-9-0 A McCarthy 4/6 FAV: 321: Made all, drvn out ins last: **85**
eff at 7f, acts on fast & gd/soft grnd, stiff/gall or sharp/turning trk: eff forcing the pace: see 4190 & 1133.
2498 **BELLY DANCER 8** [8] P F I Cole 2-9-0 N De Souza(5) 13/2: 642: Chsd ldrs, switched & rdn/styd on   *1¼* **76**
ins last, not able to reach wnr: op 9/2, 3 month abs: styd longer 7f trip well: handles firm, gd/soft & fibresand.
4359 **MARCHETTA 15** [9] P W Harris 2-8-9 S W Kelly 15/2: 653: Sn cl-up, rdn & no extra from dist: op   *1¾* **73**
11/2: handles fast & gd/soft grnd: see 4359 & 3909.
4273 **DANTES DIAMOND 19** [5] F Jordan 2-9-0 (75) G Baker 16/1: 225504: In tch, rdn & styd on well ins   *nk* **77**
last, not reach front trio: rest well covered: stays a sharp 7f, handles firm & gd/soft grnd: see 1001.
3280 **ROYAL MOUGINS 63** [7]2-9-0 S Whitworth 66/1: 05: br c Daylami - Miss Riviera Golf (Hernando)   *3* **71**
Rear, eff wide, late gains, nvr threat: Jan first foal, dam a useful 1m 3yo scorer: sire top-class at 1m/12f.
4466 **BRIANNIE 10** [13]2-8-9 D Sweeney 33/1: 66: Chsd ldrs, btn 2f out: see 4466 (6f).   *2* **62**
   MR MAYFAIR 0 [2]2-9-0 P Fitzsimons 50/1: 7: ch g Entrepreneur - French Gift (Cadeaux Genereux)   *1½* **64**
Dwelt, late gains, no impress fnl 2f: Jan foal, half-brother to several sprint wnrs: dam 6f scorer.
   BLUE TORPEDO 0 [12]2-9-0 J Crowley 33/1: 8: ch c Rahy - Societe Royale (Milford) Dwelt, rear,   *1½* **61**
mod late prog, no threat: Apr foal, half-brother to a useful 7f/1m scorer: dam unrcd.
   ESRAR 0 [6]2-9-0 O Urbina 10/1: 9: Dwelt, mid-div, no impress fnl 3f.   *1¼* **58**
4250 **GREAT GENERAL 20** [10]2-9-0 R Fitzpatrick 150/1: 00: 10th: Prom, btn 2f out.   *nk* **57**
   EMPANGENI 0 [4]2-9-0 I Mongan 40/1: 0: 11th: Sn struggling rear.   *1* **55**
3594 Zoripp 49 [11]2-9-0 S Chin 50/1:0   4416 Savoy Chapel 12 [3]2-9-0 V Slattery 100/1:0
13 Ran   Time 1m 26.75 (4.35)   Owned: Dr JWilson Tom McNaughton John Porter   Trained: Newmarket

4665   **2.40 Beechy Bank Classified Stakes 3yo+ 0-50 (G4)**
£3101 £886 £443   1m4f134y   Good/Soft 61   -20 Slow   Inside

4423* **LAZZAZ 12** [6] P W Hiatt 6-9-6 (50) P Gallagher(7) 9/2: 4265511: Chsd ldr, rdn & led over 2f out, **56**
drvn out: eff 9f/2m on firm, gd/soft & fibresand: tough & versatile: see 4423.

4423 **BANNINGHAM BLAZE 12** [2] A W Carroll 4-9-3 (50) M Halford(7) 4/1 JT FAV: 1322232: Rear, hdwy 4f ½ **52**
out, styd on for press, not pace to reach wnr: most consistent: see 4423 & 3420.

4566} **CROIX DE GUERRE 352** [7] P J Hobbs 4-9-6 bl (50) V Slattery 4/1 JT FAV: 015532-3: gr g Highest 1¼ **53**
Honor - Esclava (Nureyev) Held up, rdn & styd on well fnl 2f, not pace of wnr: bckd, op 6/1: jumps fit, dual nov
hdle scorer last summer (rtd 117h, rnr-up, h'cap, 2m1f/2m4f, firm & gd, blnks): h'cap wnr '03 on the level (Sir M
Prescott): eff at 10/12f on fast & gd/soft, with/without blnks.
2 Oct'03 Brig 9.9g/f 53-51 F: 1 Jul'03 Brig 9.9g/f 52-50 E:

3481 **TASNEEF 54** [1] T D McCarthy 5-9-6 bl (50) S Whitworth 13/2: 40-06604: Led till over 2f out, no extra: abs. 3 **49**
4203 **TOP TREES 22** [13]6-9-6 (50) I Mongan 13/2: 0-061505: Slow away & bhd, prog halfway, btn over 1f out. 2 **46**
3727 **LUNAR LORD 44** [11]8-9-6 (49) J Tate 8/1: 0042206: Bhd, hdwy 4f out, btn over 1f out: 6 wk abs. 3 **42**
3998 **LAHOB 33** [3]4-9-6 (50) S W Kelly 40/1: 26-06007: Chsd ldrs, btn 3f out: see 2530. 5 **35**
4276 **CALIBAN 19** [4]6-9-6 (46) R Fitzpatrick 14/1: 50-00308: Held up, rdn & struggling from halfway. 3½ **30**
2754 **FIGHT THE FEELING 84** [12]6-9-6 vis (45) O Urbina 14/1: 0506059: Held up, eff 4f out, btn 2f out: abs. 3½ **25**
3998 **WODHILL HOPE 33** [9]4-9-3 (45) A McCarthy 100/1: 43000: 10th: Mid-div, struggling fnl 4f: btr 2867. 3½ **17**
3383 **OCEAN ROCK 58** [5]3-8-11 (50) Paul Eddery 25/1: 0-00000: 11th: Al rear: abs: see 873, see 3383. 4 **14**
4366 Lord Greystoke 15 [8]3-8-11 (48) D Sweeney 80/1:0   4189 High View 22 [10]3-8-11 (49) G Baker 100/1:0
13 Ran   Time 2m 49.62 (10.32)   Owned: Mr Phil Kelly   Trained: Banbury

4666   **3.15 Electrolux Nursery Handicap Stakes 2yo 0-85 (D3)**   [88]
£4622 £1422 £711   7f26y rnd   Good/Soft 61   +05 Fast   Inside

4194 **DANEHILL WILLY 22** [1] N A Callaghan 2-8-11 (71) N De Souza(5) 4/1 JT FAV: 2001: Mid-div, rdn over **80**
1f out, styd on for press to lead well in last: op 5/1, gd time: first win on h'cap bow: at 5f, now stays a
sharp 7f well & 1m could suit: acts on gd & gd/soft grnd, sharp/turning or easy trk: entitled to progress again.

4306 **BROOKLIME 18** [3] J A Osborne 2-9-2 (76) S W Kelly 9/2: 641052: Led, drvn & hdd well in last: ¾ **83**
styd longer 7f trip well: enjoys gd/soft & soft grnd: see 4052 (6f, soft, mdn).

4289 **ELTIZAAM 19** [4] E A L Dunlop 2-9-2 (76) O Urbina 13/2: 6563: Held up, styd on for press fnl 2f, 3½ **78**
no threat to front pair: h'cap bow: prob handles fast, gd/soft & polytrack, stiff or sharp trk: see 4289, 3470.

4115* **FONG SHUI 27** [5] P J Makin 2-9-7 (81) D Sweeney 4/1 JT FAV: 4014: Held up, switched for effort ¾ **82**
over 1f out, not able to chall: op 7/2: h'cap bow: handles gd & gd/soft grnd: see 4115.

2666 **ABERDEEN PARK 87** [9]2-8-8 (68) Joanna Badger 28/1: 50045: Trkd ldrs, rdn & no extra dist: abs. nk **68**
4269 **GRAND OPTION 19** [10]2-8-9 bl (69) G Baker 16/1: 3250046: Rear, eff wide, no impress fnl 2f: btr 4269. 1 **68**
4271 **HIGH DYKE 19** [2]2-8-12 (72) S Whitworth 10/1: 05657: Handy, rdn & btn dist: see 4271. 1 **70**
4420 **MR KALANDI 12** [8]2-7-13 (59) A McCarthy 8/1: 30068: Mid-div, rdn & no impress fnl 2f: see 1874. ¾ **56**
4297 **ASAATEEL 19** [7]2-8-13 (73) I Mongan 8/1: 0049: Cl-up, rdn & btn over 1f out: h'cap bow: see 4297. 7 **60**
9 Ran   Time 1m 26.37 (3.97)   Owned: Mr T Mohan   Trained: Newmarket

4667   **3.50 Zachary White Claiming Stakes 3yo (E3)**
£3754 £1155 £578   7f26y rnd   Good/Soft 61   -02 Slow   Inside

4352 **MORSE 15** [6] J A Osborne 3-9-7 (83) S W Kelly 9/2: 0060001: Led/dsptd lead, went on after 3f, **80**
drvn out: eff at 6/7f, tried 1m: acts on fast, soft & polytrack: apprec drop to claim grade: see 1621.

1007 **PENEL 171** [1] B R Millman 3-8-8 (58) P Fitzsimons 28/1: 6540-602: Handy, rdn & styd on for press 1 **64**
ins last, not pace of wnr: 6 month abs: stays a sharp 7f: acts on gd/soft grnd: see 713.

4081 **TETCOTT 29** [2] M P Tregoning 3-8-1 (72) N De Souza(5) 2/1 FAV: 5343: Held up, rdn & styd on fnl shd **57**
2f, not able to reach wnr: handles gd & gd/soft grnd: see 3921 (mdn).

3995 **QUEENSTOWN 33** [10] B J Meehan 3-8-4 H bl (60) R Fitzpatrick 14/1: 2-035004: Cl-up & ch 2f out, no hd **59**
extra ins last: see 213 & 88.

4341 **REIDIES CHOICE 16** [4]3-9-7 (73) I Mongan 6/1: 2042035: Held up, eff wide, drvn & onepace: see 4341. 1¾ **73**
4366 **HEAD BOY 15** [9]3-8-6 (55) S Whitworth 12/1: 5420006: Rear, eff wide over 2f out, not able to chall. ¾ **57**
4413 **KNEAD THE DOUGH 12** [13]3-8-6 A McCarthy 16/1: 267: Chsd ldrs, btn 2f out: btr 706. 1¾ **54**
4317 **SWEET PICKLE 17** [14]3-8-11 (63) O Urbina 20/1: 10-24608: Held up, eff 2f out, no impress dist. nk **58**
3923 **BAKER OF OZ 36** [5]3-8-10 (72) Paul Eddery 7/1: 6410009: Al bhd: btr 2264. 9 **41**
4452 **FIVE GOLD 11** [7]3-8-11 (55) G Baker 16/1: 410-0000: 10th: Slow away & hung right thr'out, al rear. hd **41**
4304 **COMMANDER BOND 18** [8]3-8-6 (60) D Sweeney 20/1: 1000050: 11th: Led after 1f till over 4f out. 5 **27**
4485 Pico Alto 9 [3]3-7-13 Joanna Badger 100/1:0
3853} Pearl Island 390 [11]3-9-0 Frances Pickard(7) 50/1:0
13 Ran   Time 1m 26.80 (4.4)   Owned: Turf 2000 Limited   Trained: Upper Lambourn

4668   **4.25 Cers Handicap Stakes 3yo+ 56-70 (D3)**   [77]
£3887 £1196 £598   1m22y rnd   Good/Soft 61   -10 Slow   Inside

4399 **TAGULA BLUE 13** [4] A J Glover 4-9-1 t (64) J Crowley 12/1: R365401: Dwelt, rear, smooth hdwy from 75+
over 3f out & switched to lead ins last, pushed clr, readily: suited by 1m on fast, likes gd & gd/soft: eff in a
t-strap, tried blnks & visor: moody & a habitual slow starter but suited by a quiet ride today & is well h'capped.

4263 **HERE TO ME 20** [5] R Hannon 3-9-3 (70) P Gallagher(7) 10/1: 4213562: Cl-up, rdn & led over 1f out, 3 **74**
hdd ins last & no extra: op 8/1: see 2906.

4241 **MOTU 21** [17] J L Dunlop 3-8-11 BL (64) S W Kelly 20/1: 0000003: Held up, styd on for press fnl 1¾ **65**
2f, nvr threatened wnr: first time blnks, imprvd eff: handles fast & gd/soft grnd: see 1930, 1417.

3821 **ALI BRUCE 40** [3] G L Moore 4-9-1 (64) A Quinn(5) 5/1:˜52134: Led, rdn & hdd over 1f out, no ½ **64**
extra: 6 wk abs: stays 1m, 7f poss ideal: see 3821 & 2801.

4300 **ELIDORE 19** [6]4-9-5 (68) J P Guillambert(3) 10/1: 0-050245: Keen & cl-up, btn over 1f out: see 4057. shd **68**

4399 **DIDNT TELL MY WIFE 13** [1]5-9-4 (67) S Whitworth 13/2: 0431306: Rear, eff 3f out, no impress.   2½   62
4300 **BATHWICK BRUCE 19** [9]6-9-0 (63) G Baker 14/1: 00004-07: Prom till over 1f out: see 4300.   nk   57
1385 **ZONIC BOOM 145** [16]4-8-13 (62) O Urbina 4/1 FAV: 00-538: Held up, eff 2f out, only mod prog: abs.   2½   51
4334* **LIBERTY ROYAL 16** [13]5-9-2 p (65) D Sweeney 8/1: 6303419: Dwelt & held up, eff over 3f out, fdn   nk   53
when short of room over 1f out: btr 4334 (gd).
3835 **BOLD PHOENIX 40** [8]3-9-2 (69) J McAuley 50/1: 00600: 10th: Mid-div, rdn & btn over 1f out, 6 wk abs.   1¾   54
4592 **ADOBE 4** [15]9-8-13 (62) M Savage(5) 20/1: 0405000: 11th: Held up, struggling from halfway, nvr factor.   hd   46
2401 **ANNA WALHAAN 98** [7]5-9-7 (70) Dean Williams(7) 20/1: 05-00250: 12th: Rear, forced wide over 3f   7   42
out, sn no impress, jumps fit.
3990 **MOUNTCHARGE 33** [11]3-9-3 (70) I Mongan 22/1: 13-00500: 13th: Held up, brief eff 3f out, sn btn.   ¾   41
3631 **Bonsai 48** [10]3-8-12 T(65) A McCarthy 40/1:0   4456 **Quintoto 11** [12]4-9-0 (63) D Nolan(3) 20/1:0
3023} **Scalloway 427** [2]4-9-5 (68) V Slattery 33/1:0   4251 **Sister Sophia 20** [14]4-8-10 (59) Paul Eddery 25/1:0
17 Ran   Time 1m 42.53 (5.73)   Owned: Boston R S Ian Bennett   Trained: Worksop

4669	4.55 Edward Joseph Handicap Stakes 3yo+ 46-55 (F4)		[67]
	£3606 £1030 £515 **1m2f188y** **Good/Soft 61** **-10 Slow** Inside		

4423 **BOJANGLES 12** [10] R Brotherton 5-9-0 (53) D Nolan(3) 4/1 FAV: 5341251: Handy & led over 3f out,   61
rdn clr over 2f out, held on well for press ins last: op 7/1: eff at 1m/11f, stays a sharp 2m: acts on firm, soft
& fibresand, prob handles hvy & any trk: see 3916, 1334.
4132 **GUSTAVO 26** [5] B W Hills 3-8-8 bl (54) O Urbina 13/2: 000022: Handy & chsd wnr over 1f out, rdn &   1   59
no extra well ins last: confirmed improvement of latest: acts on fibresand & gd/soft: shld find a race.
3481 **DUCS DREAM 54** [11] D Morris 6-8-12 (51) Paul Eddery 16/1: 0100503: Prom, styd on onepace.   2   53
658 **KILLING ME SOFTLY 214** [16] J Gallagher 3-8-5 (51) R Fitzpatrick 33/1: 01-204: Handy, rdn & no   ½   52
extra over 1f out: 2 month jumps abs: stays a sharp 11f, rtn to 1m/10f could suit: handles fibresand & gd/soft.
4299 **RIBBONS AND BOWS 19** [7]4-8-12 (51) D Sweeney 14/1: 6040005: Held up, hdwy 3f out, no dngr.   1   50
5001} **MY LAST BEAN 319** [13]7-9-2 (55) R Fletcher(3) 16/1: 2/55436-6: gr g Soviet Lad - Meanz Beanz   4   48
(High Top) Chsd ldrs, btn 2f out: 5 month jumps abs: 03/04 nov hdle wnr (rtd 124h, 2m, fast): class stks plcd '03
on the level (rtd 56 & 60, h'cap): mdn & appr wnr '02: eff at 10/12f on gd & fibresand, with/without blnks.
2 Dec'02 Sout 12af 74a-65 E: 2 Jun'02 Brig 11.8g/s 58- E: 1 Mar'02 Sout 12af 75a-64 F: 1 Feb'02 Wolv 12af 67a- D:
2 Jan'02 Wolv 12af 58a-57 E:
3829 **KALOU 40** [17]6-8-8 (47) S W Kelly 9/2: 03-30307: Rear, hdwy 3f out, no prog over 1f out: jumps fit.   ½   39
4485 **OUR DESTINY 9** [8]6-9-0 (53) M Halford(7) 12/1: 0566048: Mid-div, eff 3f out, no impress: btr 4485 (1m).   2   42
4373 **HAVANTADOUBT 14** [14]4-8-9 t (48) G Baker 25/1: 00-00059: Held up, rdn & switched over 1f out, wknd.   2½   33
4215 **GOT TO BE CASH 22** [9]5-9-1 (54) M Savage(5) 14/1: 3001400: 10th: Held up, prog when short of room   2   36
over 3f out, sn btn: btr 3895.
4365 **CUDDLES 15** [19]5-9-1 BL (54) S Whitworth 16/1: 5300060: 11th: V slow away, held up, no impress: blnks. 1   34
4542} **MIGHTY PIP 353** [18]8-8-10 (49) Joanna Badger 33/1: 010200-0: 12th: b g Pips Pride - Hard To Stop   4   23
(Hard Fought) Rear, eff 3f out, no impress: reapp: clmr wnr in '03: aman h'cap & AW seller rnr-up in '02: eff at
1m/10f on firm, hvy & polytrack, likes Brighton. 2 Sep'03 Warw 10.9fm 50-48 F: 1 Aug'03 Brig 9.9fm 51-(36) F:
2 Jun'03 Brig 9.9g/f 43-(33) F: 2 Aug'02 Brig 9.9g/f 39-37 F: 2 Feb'02 Ling 8ap 46a- E:
4252 **VIOLET AVENUE 20** [15]3-8-7 BL (53) S Chin 28/1: 0640500: 13th: Mid-div, rdn & btn over 1f out: blnks.   2   24
1240* **BE WISE GIRL 154** [20]3-8-9 (55) I Mongan 17/2: 03-310: 14th: Rcd wide, led till over 3f out,   6   17
wknd qckly: joc reported filly blew up appr 3f out: see 1240.
4120 **Whispering Valley 27** [4]4-8-13 (2ow)(50) J Crowley 80/1:0
4033 **Must Be Magic 31** [12]7-9-0 vis(53) J P Guillambert(3) 25/1:0
4113 **Forge Lane 28** [1]3-8-7 p(53) A Quinn(2) 25/1:0   2589 **Fairland 91** [3]5-8-8 (47) P Fitzsimons 16/1:0
18 Ran   Time 2m 23.91 (7.71)   Owned: Mr Alan Solomon   Trained: Pershore

Official Going Firm (Good/Firm Places)

4670	1.55 European Breeders Fund Maiden Stakes 2yo (D3)		
	£4212 £1296 £648 **5f212y rnd** **Good/Firm 39** **-23 Slow** Inside		

4244 **LESLINGTAYLOR 21** [10] J J Quinn 2-9-0 G Parkin 7/2: 531: Held up wide, bit slipped through   79
mouth 3f out, styd on to lead 1f out, pushed clr, val 5L+: eff at 6f on fast & gd grnd: acts on a gall or v
tight/undul trk: improving with practice, likely to go well for h'caps: see 4244.
2882 **MAS O MENOS 79** [4] Ms Deborah J Evans 2-9-0 N Chalmers(5) 50/1: 2002: Prom, led 3f out, hdd 1f   3   68
out, sn no extra: 11 wk abs: eff at 5/6f on fast & soft grnd: back to form: see 1658 (debut).
       ON ACTION 0 [9] Mrs A Duffield 2-9-0 A Beech(3) 20/1: 3: b c Miswaki - Dancing Action   ¾   66
(Danzatore) Handy when short of room 2f out, sn switched & kept on, no ch with wnr: debut: Feb first foal, cost
36,000gns: dam successful at 1m: sire decent performer as a juv: improve for today.
       BALKAN LEADER 0 [3] Saeed bin Suroor 2-9-0 J Carroll 4/7 FAV: 4: b c Stravinsky - Baydon Belle   hd   65
(Al Nasr) Sn in tch, onepcd bef 1f out: debut: May foal, half-brother to a couple of decent
performers in US: dam unplcd, sire Gr 1 wnr at 6f: does not look one of stable's leading lights.
       MISSIN MARGOT 0 [1]2-8-9 B Swarbrick(5) 25/1: 5: b f Fraam - Abstone Queen (Presidium) Bhd,   3½   50
prog 3f out, wknd bef 1f out: debut: Feb foal, cost 10,000gns: dam successful at 6f: dam successful at 6/7f.
       KATIES BISCUIT 0 [8]2-8-9 N Pollard 40/1: 6: Missed break, nvr a factor on debut.   2   44
4462 **LOVE FROM RUSSIA 10** [7]2-9-0 Dale Gibson 66/1: 007: Led 3f, fdd: btr 4462.   ½   48
4303 **DISPOL CHARM 18** [6]2-8-9 P Fessey 12/1: 58: Handy 4f, fdd.   ¾   41
       EKATERINA 0 [2]2-8-9 J Bramhill 40/1: 9: Missed break, nvr a factor on debut.   8   20
9 Ran   Time 1m 14.02 (3.72)   Owned: Mr Derrick Bloy   Trained: Malton

CATTERICK   SATURDAY 18.09.04   Lefthand, Undulating, V Tight Track

4671   2.25 Scorton Selling Stakes 3yo (G4)
£2993 £855 £428   1m5f175y   Good/Firm 39   -15 Slow   Inside

4092 **PEPE** 29 [9] R Hollinshead 3-8-11 p (54) R Ffrench 9/1: 3014001: In tch, prog 4f out, ev ch over   57
1f out, drvn out to lead cl-home: no bid: op 14/1: eff at 12f, apprec step up to 14f: acts on fast grnd &
fibresand: eff with/without cheek pieces: enjoyed drop to sell grade: see 1444 & 1030.
4199 **ZULETA** 22 [7] J G M O'Shea 3-8-5 (45) B Swarbrick(5) 7/2 JT FAV: 4-006222: Mid-div, prog 6f out,   hd   50
styd on to lead 2f out, hdd under press cl-home: clr rem, new stable: eff at 12f, ran to form on step up to 14f:
acts on fast & soft grnd: can find similar: see 4199 & 4053 (M Blanshard).
4056 **CALOMERIA** 30 [11] R M Beckett 3-8-5 bl (54) N Chalmers(5) 7/2 JT FAV: 0403003: Led, hdd 2f out, wknd. 6   44
4579 **SIGNORA PANETTIERA** 4 [3] M R Channon 3-8-5 (40) J Carroll 8/1: 6060004: Bhd, nvr nrr than mid-div.   7   37
4007 **BONJOUR BOND** 32 [8]3-8-10 P (45) D McGaffin 12/1: 3030505: In tch over 10f, wknd: cheek pieces.   6   36
4439 **BOLD BLADE** 11 [4]3-9-2 (55) D Tudhope(7) 4/1: 0240006: Nvr nrr than mid-div: tchd 5/1: btr 3666.   ½   41
4261 **PARISI PRINCESS** 20 [1]3-8-5 J Edmunds 100/1: 07: Bhd, nvr a factor: see 4261.   1   29
4601 **IRON TEMPTRESS** 3 [6]3-8-5 (53) N Pollard 12/1: 00-00608: Handy 10f, fdd: qck reapp: see 3571.   11   19
4560 **MYANNABANANA** 5 [2]3-8-10 vis (45) A Beech(3) 16/1: 5000009: Prom 10f, fdd: qck reapp.   5   19
2790 **WEAVER SPELL** 82 [5]3-8-10 VIS (35) A Mullen(7) 100/1: 06-56400: 10th: Mid-div over 1m, grad wknd.   20   1
608 **AMAR** 219 [12]3-8-10 (35) G Parkin 33/1: 460-000: 11th: Rear, nvr a factor: long abs.   30   0
11 Ran Time 3m 2.96 (7.56) Owned: Mr J D Graham Trained: Upper Longdon

4672   3.00 Weatherbys Bank September Stakes Handicap 3yo+ 56-70 (E3)   [80]
£7190 £2212 £1106   1m3f214y   Good/Firm 39   -04 Slow   Inside

4589+ **CIRCASSIAN** 4 [13] Sir Mark Prescott 3-9-7 (6ex) (73) J Carroll 5/6 FAV: 000-0211: In tch, prog to   81
lead 2f out, drvn out fnl 1f to hold on: well bckd on qck reapp under 6lb pen: eff at 11.5f/12f, further will suit:
acts on gd/soft & fast grnd: rider reported mount was unsuited by grnd & trk: unexposed around mid dists.
4402 **COLWAY RITZ** 13 [5] W Storey 10-9-3 (61) J Bramhill 14/1: 0422-022: Held up, prog 4f out, ev ch   hd   66
ins fnl 1f, just held by wnr: continues in gd form: see 4402.
4405 **GREENWICH MEANTIME** 12 [4] Mrs J R Ramsden 4-9-2 (60) L Goncalves 8/1: 0056043: Mid-div, prog 3f 1   64
out, ev ch dist, kept on, no btn far in 3rd: encouraging eff & has slipped to a fair mark: btr 2444 (14f).
4395 **DONASTRELA** 14 [9] A M Balding 3-9-0 vis (66) N Chalmers 11/1: 1413354: In tch over 1m, sn   nk   69
outpcd, rallied ins fnl 1f: clr rem: 14f+ will suit on this evidence: see 3573 & 3373.
4327 **SADLERS PRIDE** 17 [10]4-9-2 (60) D Mernagh 50/1: 2240005: Cl-up over 10f, no extra: btr 1742(soft).   5   56
4377 **STALLONE** 14 [11]7-9-12 (70) D Tudhope(7) 16/1: 3436006: Mid-div, prog wide 4f out, onepcd dist.   hd   65
3649 **TRUSTED MOLE** 47 [14]6-8-12 (1oh) (55) B Swarbrick(5) 40/1: 1621007: In tch, prog halfway, wknd dist.   2   48
4448 **RED SKELTON** 11 [3]3-8-8 (60) P Makin(5) 28/1: 1-000038: Missed break, nvr nrr than mid-div.   3   47
3572 **SMIRFYS DANCE HALL** 50 [8]4-8-13 (57) N Pollard 50/1: 06-49: Mid-div, hung left & fdd bef 1f out.   nk   43
4399 **TEDSDALE MAC** 13 [1]5-9-2 (60) R Ffrench 7/1: 2322520: 10th: In tch 10f, fdd: btr 4399 (1m).   ½   45
3747 **SOVEREIGN DREAMER** 43 [7]4-9-12 t (70) Dale Gibson 25/1: 0-060000: 11th: Prom, led after 5f, hdd   2   52
2f out, fdd: 6 wk abs: rider reported mount had a breathing problem.
465 **SPITFIRE BOB** 239 [12]5-9-3 (61) A Mullen(7) 66/1: 02100-00: 12th: b g Mister Baileys - Gulf   2   40
Cyclone (Sheikh Albadou) Rear, nvr a factor: long abs: won 2 h'caps in '03 (T D Barron): mdn h'cap wnr in '02:
eff btwn 1m/10f on firm, fast & fibresand: has gone well fresh & likes W'hampton.
1 Aug'03 Pont 10.0fm 62-57 E: 2 Jul'03 Beve 9.9g/f 61-57 E: 2 Jun'03 Newc 10.1g/f 57-54 F:
1 Jan'03 Wolv 9.3af 71a-63 E: 2 Oct'02 Pont 8fm 62-58 D: 1 Sep'02 Wolv 8.4af 64a-58 F:
2 Jan'02 Wolv 7af 64a- D:
3373 **BOND MAY DAY** 58 [6]4-9-4 (62) D McGaffin 40/1: 0-004400: 13th: Missed break, nvr a factor.   12   25
4377 **FINANCIAL FUTURE** 14 [2]4-9-11 bl (69) W Hogg(7) 20/1: 0000000: 14th: Led, hdd after 5f, wknd 4f out.   15   11
14 Ran Time 2m 36.14 (5.2) Owned: Lady Katharine Watts Trained: Newmarket

4673   3.35 Constant Security Nursery Handicap Stakes 2yo 0-75 (E3)   [82]
£7573 £2330 £1165   7f rnd   Good/Firm 39   -08 Slow   Inside

4503* **SECRET PACT** 7 [3] M Johnston 2-9-7 (75) R Ffrench 9/2 FAV: 423011: Prom, led bef 3f out, rdn   84
out: qck reapp: well bckd: eff at 6f, suited by 7f, 1m shld suit: acts on firm or soft grnd: improving.
4337* **CAITLIN** 16 [5] B Smart 2-9-5 (73) D McGaffin 5/2: 6241312: Handy, prog to chase wnr well over 1f   ¾   77
out, sn hung left, not pace wnr: continues in gd form: acts on firm, fast grnd & fibresand: consistent.
4396 **ALGORITHM** 13 [1] T D Easterby 2-8-5 (59) J Bramhill 7/1: 065623: In tch, prog bef 1f out, kept on.   ¾   62
4535 **ALONG THE NILE** 7 [8] Mrs J R Ramsden 2-9-2 (70) L Goncalves 14/1: 036004: Mid-div, prog 3f out,   shd   72
kept on ins fnl 1f: eff at 6f, now stays 7f: acts on fast & gd/soft grnd: see 3682.
3968 **WAYWARD SHOT** 34 [17]2-8-4 (58) Dale Gibson 50/1: 5005: Mid-div, prog bef 2f out, staying on when   ½   59
short of room ins fnl 1f, nrst fin: h'cap bow: signs of promise on step up to 7f: see 2889.
4519 **ZANTERO** 7 [18]2-8-5 (59) D Fentiman(7) 16/1: 464606: Mid-div, prog wide 3f out, styd on ins fnl 1f.   1½   58
4519 **BRACE OF DOVES** 7 [11]2-9-2 (70) P Makin(5) 14/1: 2332307: Mid-div, prog halfway, staying on when   1   67
short of room well ins fnl 1f: qck reapp: just btr 3698 (gd/soft).
4503 **KUMALA OCEAN** 7 [10]2-8-10 (64) P Bradley 12/1: 25028: Prom, ev ch well over 1f out, wknd: qck reapp. ½   60
4344 **PRO TEMPORE** 16 [15]2-8-10 (64) A Beech(3) 7/1: 416639: Keen in tch 5f, wknd: btr 4344 (6f).   3   54
4503 **IGNITION** 7 [4]2-8-10 (64) B Swarbrick(5) 16/1: 54340: 10th: Nvr nrr than mid-div, qck reapp.   ½   54
4519 **LODGICIAN** 7 [9]2-9-0 (68) G Parkin 14/1: 43040: 11th: Missed break, nvr a factor: qck reapp.   nk   56
3811 **DISHDASHA** 41 [16]2-8-3 (3ow) (54) J Edmunds 80/1: 003000: 12th: Handy 5f, wknd: btr 2563 (gd/soft).   ½   44
4171 **STRATHTAY** 23 [6]2-8-6 (60) N Chalmers(5) 40/1: 305600: 13th: Missed break, nvr a factor.   2½   42
4297 **JUST DO IT** 19 [12]2-9-7 (75) J Carroll 16/1: 6250: 14th: Missed break, al in rear.   nk   56
4517 **LLAMADAS** 7 [13]2-8-13 bl (67) P Fessey 25/1: 3403660: 15th: Bhd, nvr able to chall.   ¾   46
4632 **BEAUMONT GIRL** 2 [7]2-8-1 (55) M Henry 14/1: 0100: 16th: Mid-div, short of room well 4f out, sn btn.   nk   33
4247 **PARIS HEIGHTS** 21 [2]2-9-0 (68) D Mernagh 33/1: 0640: 17th: Led, hdd bef 3f out, fdd.   1¼   44
3302 **KING HENRIK** 61 [14]2-8-7 (61) N Pollard 66/1: 4600: 18th: Bhd, nvr a factor.   5   28
18 Ran Time 1m 26.34 (3.34) Owned: Jumeirah Racing Trained: Middleham

CATTERICK SATURDAY 18.09.04 Lefthand, Undulating, V Tight Track

4674 4.05 John Gill Limited Chrysler Jeep Maiden Stakes 3yo (D3)
£3406 £1048 £524 **7f rnd** **Good/Firm 39** **-07 Slow** Inside

4421 **FASCINATION STREET 12** [10] M A Jarvis 3-8-9 (65) M Henry 7/2: 6502321: Handy, styd on for press to lead well ins fnl 1f, rdn out: eff at 6f/1m on firm & fast grnd: has been in gd form & this was deserved. **70**
4413 **INDIANA BLUES 12** [4] A M Balding 3-8-9 (63) N Chalmers(5) 7/2: 0353432: Led, clr ins fnl 2f, hdd well ins fnl 1f, no extra: op 9/2: another plcd effort: see 4413 & 4054. *1* **67**
4380 **ZWADI 14** [1] H Candy 3-8-9 (72) Dale Gibson 3/1 FAV: 0503243: Prom over 5f, no extra: see 4081. *1½* **64**
4075 **DANETTIE 29** [6] W M Brisbourne 3-8-9 (62) B Swarbrick(5) 25/1: 05454: Handy, onepace from dist: eff at 7f on fast grnd: see 3828. *nk* **62**
4256 **BEAMSLEY BEACON 20** [9]3-9-0 (45) N Pollard 100/1: 4064405: Cl-up, no extra dist: see 4042. *1¾* **64$**
3339 **STRAWBERRY FAIR 59** [3]3-8-9 t (70) J Carroll 5/1: 2-4006: Rear, modest late gains: 8 wk abs. *hd* **58**
3219 **ROSACARA 65** [2]3-8-9 t (68) R Ffrench 9/2: 504-2207: Handy 4f, wknd: 9 wk abs: twice below 2971. *4* **50**
4507 **AGGI MAC 7** [5]3-8-9 e (35) Suzanne France(7) 66/1: 05-50008: Missed break, nvr a factor. *4* **42**
4593 **JONNYEM 4** [8]3-9-0 P Fessey 33/1: 049: Mid-div 4f, fdd: qck reapp: btr 4593. *hd* **46**
9 Ran Time 1m 26.26 (3.26) Owned: Mr N R A Springer Trained: Newmarket

4675 4.40 Richmond Handicap Stakes 3yo+ 46-55 (F4) [70]
£3092 £883 £442 **1m7f177y** **Good/Firm 39** **+05 Fast** Inside

4555 **SPRING BREEZE 5** [11] M Dods 3-8-10 vis (52) D Tudhope(7) 11/2: 0232521: Made all, clr 3f out, pushed out, val 7L+: qck reapp: eff at 12f, suited by 14f/2m on fast & gd grnd: imprvd eff with blnks left off & visor refitted: more staying h'caps await on this evidence: see 3580 & 3312. **62**
3929 **BUSHIDO 36** [2] Mrs S J Smith 5-9-9 (53) M Lawson(5) 18/1: 3500/-602: Mid-div, prog 5f out, chsd wnr bef 1f out, al held: recently unplcd over hdles (rtd 114h, h'cap): eff at 2m on fast grnd: see 3140. *5* **56**
4405 **LITTLE TOBIAS 12** [18] Andrew Turnell 5-9-10 (54) D Mernagh 11/1: 10-60133: In tch, eff 4f out, onepace. *4* **53**
4423 **OOPS 12** [1] J F Coupland 5-9-4 (48) A Beech(3) 5/1 FAV: 1623243: In tch, prog 7f out, styd on to chase wnr 4f out, fdd bef 1f out: bckd: disapp run: showed more in 4308. *6* **41**
3970* **SUPER FELLOW 34** [10]10-9-2 (1oh) (45) J Bramhill 10/1: /00///-3115: Missed break, prog bef 2f out, kept on but no ch with principals: disapp on hat-trick bid: showed more in 3970 (gd/soft) & 3834 (soft). *5* **34**
4402 **NARCISO 13** [13]4-9-5 (49) Dale Gibson 10/1: 0000606: Nvr nrr than mid-div: see 4340. *hd* **36**
4340 **THEATRE BELLE 16** [4]3-8-5 (47) G Parkin 66/1: 0006507: Cl-up over 12f, wknd: see 2691. *3* **31**
3810 **PETERS IMP 41** [20]9-9-2 (1oh) (45) P Bradley 16/1: 00-15348: Nvr nrr than mid-div: jumps fit. *¾* **29**
4340 **ROUGE ET NOIR 16** [15]6-9-7 t (51) Neil Brown(7) 10/1: 00439: Missed break, nvr a factor: btr 4340 (14f). *½* **33**
4521 **RHETORICAL 7** [17]3-8-8 (50) P Fessey 9/1: 600-5060: 10th: Cl-up 12f, fdd: tchd 7/1 on qck reapp. *4* **28**
4260* **SHOTLEY DANCER 20** [16]5-9-5 (49) D McGaffin 16/1: 5314210: 11th: Chsd ldrs 12f, wknd: btr 4260. *3½* **24**
3834 **DOCTOR JOHN 40** [6]7-9-2 (1oh) (45) M Henry 33/1: 6220240: 12th: Al bhd: 6 wk abs: btr 3834 & 3397. *1¾* **19**
3240 **PAINT THE LILY 64** [14]3-8-12 (54) R Ffrench 100/1: 00400: 13th: Mid-div over 1m, wknd: 9 wk abs. *shd* **26**
4348 **CAPER 16** [7]4-9-2 (6oh) (40) J Edmunds 100/1: 060-0000: 14th: Mid-div 10f, fdd. *¾* **17**
4340* **ZAN LO 16** [5]4-9-6 (50) P Aspell(3) 16/1: 0000410: 15th: Bhd, nvr a factor: btr 4340 (14f). *1½* **20**
4348 **NEEDWOOD SPIRIT 16** [12]9-9-2 (11oh) (35) N Pollard 100/1: 2//0004-00: 16th: Rear, nvr a factor. *13* **5**
4415 **LORD LAHAR 12** [19]5-9-3 (47) J Carroll 25/1: 0005040: 17th: In tch, wknd 3f out, sn eased: btr 4415. *21* **0**
4512 **SUBADAR MAJOR 7** [9]7-9-2 (16oh) (30) P Makin(5) 100/1: 0000-000: 18th: Chsd ldrs over 12f, sn wknd. *dist* **0**
4423 **ACADEMY 12** [3]9-10-0 (58) N Chalmers(5) 8/1: 40-2002P: Bhd when p.u. 10f out, broke leg & sadly died. **0**
19 Ran Time 3m 26.25 (5.45) Owned: Sheridan Fabrications Ltd Trained: Darlington

4676 5.10 Catterickbridge Co Uk Handicap Stakes Fillies & Mares 3yo+ 46-55 (F4) [63]
£3044 £870 £435 **7f rnd** **Good/Firm 39** **-03 Slow** Inside

4488 **BINT ROYAL 9** [5] Miss V Haigh 6-9-6 (55) M Henry 8/1: 0002101: Made all, went clr after 2f out, drvn out to hold on: suited by 6/7f on firm, soft grnd & polytrack, loves fibresand: tough. **61**
1985 **DUBAIAN MIST 116** [1] A M Balding 3-9-0 (52) N Chalmers(5) 10/1: 05-052: In tch, prog well over 1f out, kept on ins fnl 1f, just held: long abs: eff at 6f, now stays 7f: only lightly rcd & is unexposed in h'caps. *hd* **56**
4506 **TOKEWANNA 7** [10] W M Brisbourne 4-8-12 t (47) B Swarbrick(5) 7/1: 0304543: Missed break, prog wide 2f out, kept on despite hanging left ins fnl 1f, not btn far: op 10/1 on qck reapp: see 3746 & 3079. *nk* **50**
4506 **GEMINI LADY 7** [2] Mrs G S Rees 4-8-11 (1oh)BL (45) J Carroll 25/1: 0-020004: Chsd ldrs, prog bef 1f out, kept on cl-home, just held for 3rd: back to form with fitting of blnks: eff at 7f, rtn to further will suit. *hd* **48**
4408 **MICKLEDOR 12** [9]4-9-3 p (52) D Tudhope(7) 7/1: 1100365: Mid-div, prog 2f out, kept on ins fnl 1f. *1* **52**
3830 **SPRING DANCER 40** [8]3-8-9 t (47) A Mullen(7) 10/1: 0053606: Missed break, prog over 2f out, nrst fin. *nk* **46**
4616 **MAUREEN ANN 3** [7]4-8-13 (48) D McGaffin 14/1: 00-00007: Bhd, prog 2f out, no impress ins fnl 1f. *1½* **45**
4616 **LINDENS LADY 3** [11]4-9-1 (50) A Beech(3) 5/1 FAV: 6505438: Held up, prog wide 3f out, no impress. *shd* **46**
4504 **FESTIVE CHIMES 7** [15]3-8-12 P (50) P Fessey 28/1: 030069: Prom over 5f, wkng/short of room dist. *1½* **43**
822 **KATY OHARA 194** [3]5-8-11 (1oh) (45) N Pollard 20/1: 000-0260: 10th: Missed break, nvr nrr than mid-div. *1½* **36**
4130 **MISS WIZZ 26** [16]4-8-11 (1oh)p (45) M Lawson(5) 25/1: 4510000: 11th: Handy 5f, wknd: btr 3670. *½* **35**
4321 **PASSION FRUIT 17** [17]3-9-3 (55) R Ffrench 50/1: 00630-00: 12th: b f Pursuit of Love - Reine de Thebes (Darshaan) Chsd ldrs, fdd dist: plcd once in '03 (h'cap, rtd 59): eff at 7f on fast grnd. *1½* **42**
4345 **CUT RIDGE 16** [13]5-9-5 (54) G Parkin 10/1: 3212500: 13th: Prom 5f, fdd: btr 3911 (6f, gd/soft). *½* **40**
4504 **FIREBIRD RISING 7** [14]3-8-9 (47) P Makin(5) 10/1: 6040030: 14th: Bhd, nvr a factor: qck reapp. *3½* **26**
3176 **Susiedil 67** [12]3-8-11 (49) Dale Gibson 16/1:0
4131 **Through The Slips 26** [6]3-8-13 (51) J Bramhill 20/1:0
16 Ran Time 1m 25.94(2.94) Owned: Miss V Haigh Trained: Bawtry

NEWBURY SATURDAY 18.09.04 Lefthand, Flat, Galloping Track

Official Going GOOD - GOOD/SOFT after race 3 - Heavy Rain.

4677 1.50 Dubai Duty Free Golf World Cup Maiden Stakes 2yo (D2)
£6240 £1920 £960 7f str Good/Firm 25 -06 Slow Centre

4355 **ESQUIRE 15** [3] Saeed bin Suroor 2-9-0 L Dettori 5/1: 61: Made all, clr ent fnl 1f, styd on strongly, readily: clearly benefitted from debut, eff over a gall 7f on fast: useful, win more races. **92+**
4385 **MUSEEB 14** [15] J L Dunlop 2-9-0 R Hills 3/1 FAV: 42: Prom, chsd wnr fnl 2f, kept on: well bckd: apprec this step up to 7f, acts on fast & firm: prob met an above average rival & can win similar. *1¾* **86**
ALFIE NOAKES [2] Mrs A J Perrett 2-9-0 P Robinson 25/1: 3: b c Groom Dancer - Crimson Rosella (Polar Falcon) Slowly away, imprvd halfway, nrst fin, hands & heels: 36,000gns Apr foal: brother to a 1m/10f wnr: dam stayed 12f: will relish a step up to 7f+ & bundles of promise here, one for the notebook. *1½* **83+**
4190 **TOP THE CHARTS 22** [8] R Hannon 2-9-0 R L Moore 9/2: 44: Prom, onepcd fnl 1f: bckd from 15/2: acts on gd & fast grnd, 1m will now suit: see 4190. *shd* **82**
SPARKWELL [1]2-9-0 R Hughes 8/1: 5: b c Dansili - West Devon (Gone West) Dwelt, recovered to chase ldrs, wknd fnl 1f, hands & heels: clr of rem: Mar foal, half-brother to 6f juv wnr Salcombe: dam unrcd, sire a high-class miler: ran well for a long way, with B Hills & sure to learn from this. *1¼* **79**
BARBARY COAST [13]2-9-0 Martin Dwyer 80/1: 6: b c Anabaa - Viking's Cove (Miswaki) Slowly away, styd on late, nvr dngrs on debut: E105,000 Apr foal: dam unrcd but from a high-class family. *5* **69**
IN THE LEAD [10]2-8-9 T Quinn 50/1: 7: b f Bahri - Air de Noblesse (Vaguely Noble) Chsd ldrs, outpcd halfway, styd on cl-home on debut: longer priced stablemate of rnr-up: $8,000 Mar foal: half-sister to a mid-dist wnr in France: sire a top-class miler: with J Dunlop & shld learn from this. *1¼* **61**
4393 **RAIN STOPS PLAY 14** [7]2-9-0 C Catlin 16/1: 38: Prom till wknd dist: btr 4393 (debut). *1½* **63**
4483 **PIRAN 9** [12]2-9-0 J Fortune 66/1: 09: Chsd ldrs 5f, wknd. *3* **57**
BULWARK [4]2-9-0 E Ahern 25/1: 0: 10th: Nvr btr than mid-div: debut, stablemate of 3rd. *½* **56**
KING GABRIEL [11]2-9-0 R Smith 100/1: 0: 11th: Nvr nr ldrs on racecourse bow. *¾* **54**
3955 **COUNT KRISTO 35** [9]2-9-0 Dane O'Neill 4/1: 20: 12th: Chsd ldrs till halfway, sn btn: well bckd: disapp run, much btr expected after 3955 - reportedly still weak. *¾* **52**
4443 **OVER TIPSY 11** [16]2-9-0 P Dobbs 100/1: 000: 13th: Chsd ldrs till halfway, wknd. *2½* **47**
PLANET [6]2-9-0 N Mackay(3) 22/1: 0: 14th: Slowly away, nvr a factor on debut. *1¾* **44**
Atacama Star [14]2-9-0 L Keniry(3) 50/1:0 **Chiracahua** [5]2-9-0 R Winston 66/1:0
16 Ran Time 1m 26.52 (2.22) Owned: Godolphin Trained: Newmarket

4678 2.20 Gr3 Dubai International Airport World Trophy 3yo+ (A1)
£29000 £11000 £5500 5f34y str Good/Firm 25 +18 Fast Centre

4435 **THE TATLING 13** [6] J M Bradley 7-9-4 (116) R L Moore 5/1: 4103221: Chsd ldrs, styd on strongly to force head in front cl-home: fast time: deserved win, earlier rnr-up in Gr 1 Nunthorpe: stays 6f, prob best over a stiff 5f & likes gd & firm, acts on soft & any trk: best without a t-strap: relishes a fast pace: high-class run under a pen, must go cl in the Abbaye (3rd last yr). **120**
4526* **VAR 7** [1] C E Brittain 5-8-13 bl R Hills 10/1: 4016-112: Rcd wide, led 1.5f out, caught dying strides: fine run on this return to 5f, stays 6f well: likes to force the pace & clearly smart, see 4526. *hd* **114**
4384 **AIRWAVE 14** [7] H Candy 4-8-10 (108) T Quinn 5/1: 6601603: Held up, short of room & switched wide halfway, styd on fnl 1f & nrst fin: nicely bckd: seems to get on best with D Holland: see 3304. *1¼* **107**
4537* **TEXAS GOLD 6** [10] W R Muir 6-8-13 (89) Martin Dwyer 16/1: 6602214: Rear, fin fast but too late: fine run in this much btr grade, recent h'cap wnr off a mark of 89: looks sure to apprec a return to 6f, thriving. *nk* **109**
4435* **PIVOTAL POINT 13** [5]4-9-2 (113) L Dettori 5/2 FAV: 0012115: Chsd ldrs, wknd fnl 1f: bckd, btr 4435. *1¼* **108**
3551 **MAJESTIC MISSILE 51** [4]3-8-12 (112) J Fortune 10/1: 1161-506: Rear, switched left dist, nrst fin: nicely bckd, 7 wk abs: has failed to prog from reapp in 2468. *½* **104**
4481 **TALBOT AVENUE 9** [3]6-8-13 (101) P Dobbs 33/1: 2020227: Chsd ldrs, wknd fnl 1f. *¾* **101**
4481* **CELTIC MILL 9** [8]6-8-13 p (107) L Enstone 16/1: 1100618: Led till dist, no extra: btr 4481. *shd* **100**
3622 **HIGH REACH 49** [11]4-8-13 (94) R Mullen 20/1: 4-363039: Chsd ldrs, onepcd when hmpd ins fnl 1f: 7 wk abs: wld have fin on the heels of the ldrs: see 3622 (6f). *½* **99**
3551 **BOOGIE STREET 51** [9]3-8-12 t (110) R Hughes 8/1: 3216420: 10th: Front rank, ev ch till wknd fnl 1f: 7 wk abs: disapp eff, btr 3551. *shd* **98**
4481 **CARIBBEAN CORAL 9** [2]5-8-13 (100) R Winston 14/1: 2110030: 11th: Al towards rear: btr 4481. *nk* **97**
11 Ran Time 1m 00.68 (0.38) Owned: Dab Hand Racing Trained: Chepstow

4679 2.50 Watership Down Stud Sales Race Fillies 2yo (B1)
£146150 £58460 £29230 6f110y str Good/Firm 25 No Standard Time Centre

3917* **SALAMANCA 36** [18] S Kirk 2-8-9 L Dettori 5/1 FAV: 11: Held up stands side, gd hdwy 2f out, fin strongly to lead on line in a thrilling fin: well bckd: unbeaten, eff at 6/6.5f on gd & fast grnd: likes a gall trk & has a fine turn of foot: well plcd to land this v val prize, clearly useful: see 3917. **96**
4409* **ARABIAN DANCER 12** [21] M R Channon 2-7-12 C Catlin 13/2: 2653512: Chsd ldrs stands side, led entering fnl 1f, caught on line: well bckd from 10/1, rider given a 2-day whip ban: eff at 5/6.5f, stays 1m. *shd* **84**
4432 **UMNIYA 13** [16] M R Channon 2-8-8 vis T Quinn 8/1: 3456643: Rear stands side, hdwy when switched entering fnl 1f, fin strongly & just btn in a v exciting fin: op 6/1: longer priced stablemate of rnr-up: tried blnks in 4432, back in a visor today: v consistent & useful, see 4432. *shd* **94**
4583 **BIBURY FLYER 4** [19] M R Channon 2-8-8 R Havlin 14/1: 0033324: Rear stands side, styd on strongly fnl 1f, nrst fin: qck reapp, stablemate of 2nd & 3rd: will apprec a return to 7f: see 4583. *1¼* **90**
4250 **LOVE THIRTY 20** [24]2-9-0 R Hills 33/1: 625: Chsd ldrs stands side, ev ch fnl 2f, no extra cl-home: mdn, stablemate of 2nd, 3rd & 4th: acts on fast & gd/soft grnd: must find at least a mdn, see 4250. *½* **95**
4524 **ALTA PETENS 7** [8]2-7-12 J Mackay 12/1: 4100456: Chsd ldrs far side, led that group entering fnl 1f, no ch with stands side: first home on far side over this shorter 6.5f trip, styd 1m in 4524 (List). *¾* **76+**
4357 **DIAMOND KATIE 15** [22]2-8-4 E Ahern 33/1: 07: b f Night Shift - Fayrooz (Gulch) Slowly away & rear stands side, fin well fnl 1f, nvr nrr: 16,000gns Mar foal: half-sister to mid-dist wnr Beryl: dam a 7f juv wnr, sire a decent miler: eff at 6.5f on fast grnd: fine run on only 2nd start, will find much easier races. *1¼* **78**
2763 **BALTIC DIP 84** [4]2-8-11 R Hughes 8/1: 148: Slowly away far side, styd on strongly fnl 1f, no ch *shd* **84+**

with stands side: bckd from 12/1, 12 wk abs: severely hmpd by slow start (lost around 6L) & on the wrong side: must be given another ch, see 2763 & 1866 (debut).
4264 **JUSTAQUESTION 20** [7]2-8-5 L Enstone 13/2: 1032159: Bhd far side, styd on fnl 1.5f, nvr nrr: *shd* **77**
nicely bckd: on the wrong side: much btr 3774.
3848 **SHOSOLOSA 39** [26]2-8-2 D Kinsella 66/1: 02230: 10th: Front rank stands side, ev ch till wknd fnl 1f. *nk* **73**
4357 **HOLLY SPRINGS 15** [2]2-9-0 J Fortune 12/1: 20: 11th: Led till ent fnl 1f far side, wknd: see 4357. *shd* **84**
4242 **MUSICAL DAY 21** [11]2-8-6 R Winston 40/1: 00020: 12th: Front rank 5f far side, wknd: btr 4242. *nk* **75**
3369* **LADY LE QUESNE 58** [27]2-8-7 Martin Dwyer 16/1: 62110: 13th: Led till dist, no extra: 8 wk abs. *nk* **75**
3993 **HONEY RYDER 33** [25]2-8-8 T P Queally 20/1: 220: 14th: Rear stands side, nvr nr ldrs: btr 3993. *½* **75**
3944 **COUNTY CLARE 35** [14]2-8-8 R Mullen 25/1: 0230: 15th: Front rank stands side, wknd dist. *hd* **74**
4484 **OASIS WAY 9** [20]2-8-2 Lisa Jones 100/1: 550: 16th: Rear stands side, nvr nr ldrs. *1* **65**
4187* **MISS CASSIA 22** [13]2-8-8 P Dobbs 66/1: 32S310: 17th: Rear far side, mod late gains: btr 4187. *hd* **70**
4329 **AUTHENTICATE 16** [5]2-8-6 C Haddon 100/1: 4600: 18th: Chsd ldrs 4f far side. *hd* **67**
4273 **Casterossa 19** [6]2-8-10 W Ryan 100/1:0
4420 **Top Form 12** [12]2-8-11 P Robinson 50/1:0
4369 **Persian Carpet 14** [15]2-7-12 N Mackay 100/1:0
4444 **High Chart 11** [17]2-8-2 D Fox 100/1:0
3825 **Madhavi 40** [9]2-8-6 BL Dane O'Neill 40/1:0
4457 **Gennie Bond 10** [23]2-8-8 R L Moore 40/1:0
4409 **Agent Kensington 12** [1]2-7-13 (1ow) R Smith 66/1:0
4436* **Corniche Dancer 11** [10]2-8-6 L Keniry 100/1:0
26 Ran Time 1m 20.09 () Owned: Wood Street Syndicate Trained: Upper Lambourn

4680 **3.25 Gr2 Dubai Duty Free Mill Reef Stakes 2yo (A1)**
£40600 £15400 £7700 **6f8y str** **Good/Firm 25** **-12 Slow** Centre

4529* **GALEOTA 7** [6] R Hannon 2-8-12 (100) R L Moore 7/1: 415511: Made all, styd on strongly fnl 1f, **114**
rdn out: op 5/1: eff at 6f on firm & gd/soft grnd, shld stay 7f: loves to force the pace, handles a sharp or gall trk: has tried cheek pieces, best without: developing into a v smart colt, see 4529.
4159 **MYSTICAL LAND 27** [5] J H M Gosden 2-8-12 VIS (100) L Dettori 10/3: 2123252: Chsd ldrs, went after *1* **110**
wnr fnl 1f, kept on but nvr going to get there: nicely bckd in first time visor: back to form on fav'd fast grnd.
4028* **REBUTTAL 31** [3] B J Meehan 2-8-12 J Fortune 8/1: 213: Held up, short of room & switched dist, *shd* **109**
fin strongly but too late: lightly rcd & unlucky not to be 2nd: acts on fast & soft grnd: useful, see 4028.
4059 **SALSA BRAVA 30** [1] N P Littmoden 2-8-9 (100) T P Queally 3/1 FAV: 13224: Rear, hdwy to chase *2½* **99**
ldrs halfway, left bhd fnl 1f: op 9/4: this is not her form, much btr 4059.
4264 **ROYAL ALCHEMIST 20** [7]2-8-9 (94) A Daly 50/1: 12005: Chsd ldrs, wknd fnl 1f: see 2763. *1¾* **94**
4105 **ONE PUTRA 28** [9]2-8-12 (91) P Robinson 6/1: 5136: Front rank, wknd fnl 1f: op 8/1: btr 3824. *¾* **94**
4022 **ANDRONIKOS 31** [2]2-8-12 T Quinn 4/1: 127: Chsd ldrs, wknd fnl 1f: btr 4022 . *¾* **91**
3955 **OCEAN GIFT 35** [4]2-8-12 Martin Dwyer 50/1: 648: Al towards rear: mdn, highly tried. *1¼* **87**
4159 **DOCTORS CAVE 27** [8]2-8-12 (89) R Hills 66/1: 0000109: Prom 4.5f, sn wknd: btr 3511. *1* **84**
9 Ran Time 1m 13.84 (2.24) Owned: Mr J A Lazzari Trained: Marlborough

4681 **4.00 John Smith's Stakes Heritage Handicap 3yo+ 0-105 (B1)** **[106]**
£58000 £22000 £11000 **1m2f6y** **Good** **Fair** Outside

3439 **SPURADICH 56** [7] L M Cumani 4-8-12 (90) N Mackay(3) 14/1: 110-0361: Mid-div, hdwy to lead over 1f **100**
out, hung left under press, drvn out: joc given 2-day careless riding ban: op 10/1, 8 wk abs: suited by 9/10f on fast & gd grnd, stiff/gall trks: useful colt: see 1833.
4305 **JABAAR 18** [12] M W Easterby 6-8-5 (83) T P Queally 18/1: 5625002: Trkd ldrs, rdn & outpcd *¾* **90+**
briefly 3f out, short of room 2f out, switched & styd on well for press, wnr had first run: joc given 3-day careless riding ban: hmpd at a crucial stage & poss unlucky: h'capped to win.
4531 **BLUE SPINNAKER 7** [14] M W Easterby 5-9-10 (102) R Winston 14/1: 1410463: Mid-div, hdwy 4f out, *¾* **107**
staying on for press when forced to switch ins last, not able to recover: closer without interference: op 10/1
4392 **PAGAN SKY 14** [1] J A R Toller 5-8-6 (84) Lisa Jones 20/1: 161-0064: Dwelt & bhd, styd on for *1* **87**
press fnl 2f, not able to reach ldrs: op 16/1: see 4392.
4239+ **GATWICK 21** [3]3-9-9 (5ex) (107) T Quinn 10/3 FAV: 1060515: Mid-div, short of room 2f out & again *hd* **110+**
over 1f out, styd on well for press, nrst fin: well bckd under a 5lb pen: no luck in running & wld have gone v close: remains interesting for the Cambridgeshire h'cap next month: see 4239.
4061 **DUMARAN 30** [11]6-8-12 (90) C Catlin 14/1: 0023506: Chsd ldrs, styd on onepace: btr 1704. *nk* **92**
4463 **SWAGGER STICK 10** [20]3-8-4 BL (88) D Kinsella 25/1: 1600607: Chsd ldrs, btn ins last: blnks. *1½* **88**
4305 **TELEMACHUS 18** [8]4-8-7 bl (85) J Mackay 20/1: 0000158: Led/dsptd lead till over 1f out, no extra. *½* **84**
3506 **SPANISH DON 53** [15]6-9-3 (95) L Keniry(3) 12/1: 0051159: Rear, late gains, nvr a threat: abs. *¾* **93**
4104 **DESERT QUEST 28** [13]4-9-2 bl (94) Martin Dwyer 25/1: 0240150: 10th: Dwelt, mod prog. *hd* **92**
4525 **LANGFORD 7** [5]4-8-8 (86) R Hills 66/1: 1001400: 11th: Rear, eff 3f out, no impress over 1f out: *shd* **84**
poss best dominating: btr 3205 (fast, 1m).
3949* **SKY QUEST GB 35** [9]6-8-13 t p (91) R L Moore 11/1: 6P21-110: 12th: Rear, nvr able to chall. *1½* **87**
4534 **TURBO 7** [2]5-8-13 p (91) S Carson 20/1: 0040000: 13th: Rear, only mod prog fnl 2f: see 1759. *1¼* **85**
4324 **KEELUNG 17** [6]3-8-4 (88) P Robinson 14/1: 2132000: 14th: Led after 1f till over 3f out, sn btn. *nk* **81**
3620 **THYOLO 49** [19]3-8-13 (97) R Smith 25/1: 1-203000: 15th: Nvr in it: 7 wk abs: btr 2521. *1¾* **88**
4219 **HAWRIDGE PRINCE 21** [17]4-9-3 (95) L Dettori 7/2: 2-112420: 16th: Chsd ldrs wide, wknd qckly 2f *3* **81**
out, eased: well bckd: awkward high draw, nvr trav & hung: btr 4219, 3189.
3777 **Counsels Opinion 42** [16]7-9-8 (100) R Mullen 14/1:0
4231 **Camp Commander 21** [18]5-9-0 t(92) R Hughes 33/1:0
18 Ran Time 2m 08.16 (5.36) Owned: Scuderia Rencati Srl Trained: Newmarket

NEWBURY SATURDAY 18.09.04 Lefthand, Flat, Galloping Track

4682
4.35 Scottish Courage Berkshire Brewery Silver Jubilee Conditions Stakes 3yo+ (B2)
£8949 £3309 £1654 **1m1f** **Good** **Slow** Outside

4531 **PENTECOST 7** [3] A M Balding 5-8-11 (106) Martin Dwyer 4/1: 1401001: Trkd ldrs, smooth prog & led 2f out, rdn out: nicely bckd: suited by 1m/9f on firm & gd/soft grnd, any trk: tough & smart: see 3775. **112**
4424 **CHECKIT 18** [4] M R Channon 4-8-11 (110) J Fortune 7/4 FAV: 3403622: Held up, hdwy to chase wnr ins last, drvn & kept on, al held: clr rem: hvly bckd: tough & genuine, deserves a race: see 4424, 1349. *¾* **109**
4290 **ISLAND SOUND 19** [1] D R C Elsworth 7-8-11 (99) T Quinn 5/1: 0246-633: Led & sn clr, hdd 2f out & sn btn: nicely bckd, op 8/1: see 4290 & 3754. *6* **100**
2252 **PARASOL 105** [2] D R Loder 5-8-11 vis (111) L Dettori 5/2: 262-2004: Trkd ldr trav well, chall 3f out, sn rdn & hung left, lkd reluctant over 1f out: well bckd: 3 mth abs, has been gelded: less than enthusiastic in the closing stages today, one to treat with caution at present: see 1505. *5* **92**
4389 **SGT PEPPER 14** [5]3-8-6 (89) R L Moore 16/1: 40-00465: Sn rdn & al bhd: see 4389, 3113 (1m). *nk* **91**
5 Ran Time 1m 55.71 (6.71) Owned: J C J R and S R Hitchins Trained: Kingsclere

4683
5.05 John Smith's Woolston Trades And Labour Club Handicap Stakes 3yo 71-85 (D2) **[91]**
£7587 £2334 £1167 **7f str** **Good** **Fair** Centre

4352 **DOCTORATE 15** [2] E A L Dunlop 3-9-4 (81) E Ahern 22/1: 0125301: Chsd ldrs trav well far side, led over 1f out, drvn out: suited by 7f, tried 1m, may yet suit: acts on fast, gd/soft & polytrack, prob any trk. **91**
4341 **NIGHT AIR 16** [16] D R Loder 3-8-13 (76) T P Queally 10/1: 1522: Rcd towards centre, eff to chall 2f out, hung left under press but kept on ins last: lightly rcd type with a progressive profile, can win again. *1½* **81**
2880 **PRIMO WAY 79** [15] B W Hills 3-9-5 (82) L Dettori 6/1 FAV: 5-136303: Rear centre, drvn & styd on fnl 2f, nrst fin: well bckd, op 9/1: 11 wk abs: back to form, shown enough to find a race. *hd* **86**
4301 **STAR PUPIL 19** [1] A M Balding 3-8-10 vis (73) Martin Dwyer 33/1: 2005554: Chsd ldrs far side, overall ldr 2f out, drvn & hdd over 1f out, no extra: see 1498, 1152. *½* **76**
4465 **SENESCHAL 10** [17]3-8-7 (67) T O'Brien(7) 40/1: 0000005: Bhd centre, kept on late, no threat: imprvd eff under an inexperienced rider, well h'capped & poss worth another look in similar: see 3553, 1206. *1¾* **70**
2575+**KALI 91** [22]3-8-13 (76) Dane O'Neill 12/1: 2-33216: Mid-div stands side, drvn & styd on fnl 3f, no ch with ldrs centre to far side: 3 mth abs: rcd from unfav'd group & worth another look in similar: see 2575. *nk* **75+**
4029* **FAREWELL GIFT 31** [21]3-9-3 vis (80) R Hughes 25/1: 3233317: Chsd ldrs stands side, kept on onepace. *¾* **77**
4465 **LORD LINKS 10** [27]3-9-1 (78) P Dobbs 33/1: 4000048: Chsd ldrs stands side, onepace for press. *shd* **75**
4148 **KEYAKI 25** [24]3-9-2 (79) R Mullen 25/1: 6611449: Stands side, dwelt, late prog: btr 4148. *1* **74**
4465 **SAVIOURS SPIRIT 10** [13]3-8-9 (72) R Miles(3) 33/1: 53-22100: 10th: Led centre 5f, hung right & wknd over 1f out: reportedly unsuited by the ground: btr 691 (6f, AW). *1* **65**
2716 **TRUMAN 85** [23]3-8-7 (70) Lisa Jones 50/1: 5-0350: 11th: Held up stands side, nvr land a blow: abs. *½* **62**
3928* **VIOLET PARK 36** [3]3-8-12 (75) J Fortune 15/2: 223110: 12th: Chsd ldrs far side, btn over 1f out. *nk* **66**
4265 **STEVEDORE 20** [8]3-8-10 (73) R Winston 20/1: 0415150: 13th: Led far side group 5f, wknd: btr 4110. *nk* **63**
4265 **GENERAL FEELING 20** [14]3-8-13 (76) J D Walsh(7) 40/1: 3041140: 14th: In tch 5f centre: 'made noise'. *¾* **64**
1177* **ASHWAAQ 156** [18]3-9-1 (78) R Hills 12/1: 4-10: 15th: Dwelt stands side, mod prog: abs. *½* **65**
4446 **FREAK OCCURENCE 11** [26]3-9-0 vis (77) R Havlin 25/1: 6306000: 16th: Chsd ldrs 5f far side. *1* **62**
3928 **CHANTERELLE 36** [19]3-9-7 (84) P Robinson 33/1: 441-660: 17th: In tch centre, btn when hmpd dist. *1½* **66**
4263 **ENRAPTURE 20** [10]3-9-2 (79) R L Moore 7/1: 5-130: 18th: In th 5f centre: btr 4263. *1¾* **57**
4389 **SURF THE NET 14** [7]3-9-5 VIS (82) R Smith 66/1: 3003400: 19th: Far side & nvr on terms: visor. *½* **59**
4465 **ASK THE CLERK 10** [20]3-8-9 (72) Rory Moore(5) 12/1: 3305420: 20th: Stands side, in tch 4f. *½* **48**
4275* **VONADAISY 19** [4]3-8-7 (70) T Quinn 14/1: 60344-10: 21th: Far side, dwelt, hung left & btn 2f out. *1¼* **43**
1141 **PICK OF THE CROP 159** [6]3-8-9 (72) W Ryan 50/1: 25-12000: 22th: Slow away & al bhd far side: abs. *1¼* **42**
2740 **PINE BAY 84** [11]3-8-7 (64) L Keniry(2) 100/1: 6000: 23th: Bhd in centre halfway, abs, new stable. *2½* **35**
3379 **SOLINIKI 58** [25]3-8-13 (76) S Carson 66/1: 1-000: 24th: Led stands side group 5f, sn btn: abs. *3* **35**
4352 **MR JACK DANIELLS 15** [9]3-8-12 BL (75) N Mackay(3) 10/1: 0414030: 25th: Chsd ldrs far side 4f. *nk* **33**
25 Ran Time 1m 27.72(3.42) Owned: Mr P G Goulandris Trained: Newmarket

AYR SATURDAY 18.09.04 Lefthand, Galloping Track

Official Going Soft (Heavy places)

4684
2.00 Gr3 Tsg Firth Of Clyde Stakes Fillies 2yo (A1)
£23200 £8800 £4400 **6f str** **Soft 118** **-16 Slow** Stands Side

4050 **GOLDEN LEGACY 30** [1] R A Fahey 2-8-8 (96) P Hanagan 7/1: 201131: Held up, hdwy & short of room over 1f out, styd on well to lead ins last, going away: bckd: v eff at 6f on any trk: winning form on firm or soft: useful & improving: see 3632. **104**
4332 **CASTELLETTO 16** [11] B A McMahon 2-8-8 (98) G Gibbons 13/2: 0212522: Led after 2f, kept on till collared ins last, not btn far despite edging left, fin 2nd, disqual & plcd 3rd: joc received a 3-day careless riding ban: stays 6f well on fast & soft, sharp or gall trks: proving tough, useful & consistent. *nk* **103**
4258* **NUFOOS 20** [10] M Johnston 2-8-8 (94) W Supple 15/8 FAV: 310013: Handy, eff to chall dist, onepcd when hmpd cl-home, fin 3rd, promoted to 2nd: hvly bckd: confirmed useful h'cap win of 4258, likes soft grnd. *¾* **101**
4457 **MISS MEGGY 10** [5] T D Easterby 2-8-11 VIS (88) K Darley 16/1: 1106564: With ldrs, onepace over 1f out: encouraging run in first time visor, return to h'caps will suit: see 4457. *2½* **99**
3956 **DANCE AWAY 35** [2]2-8-8 (97) D Holland 8/1: 2105: Held up, eff & switched over 1f out, onepace. *1¼* **93**
3357 **GOLDEN ANTHEM 58** [9]2-8-8 (90) J Quinn 16/1: 10366: In tch, wknd over 1f out: abs, wants h'caps. *½* **92**
4457* **SWAN NEBULA 10** [8]2-8-8 t (82) K McEvoy 5/1: 35117: Handy, wknd over 1f out: not handle soft? *8* **76**
4155 **MADAME TOPFLIGHT 28** [6]2-8-8 (93) A Culhane 14/1: 021528: In tch, wknd over 2f out: btr 4155 (5f). *14* **48**
4307 **WORLD AT MY FEET 18** [7]2-8-8 (87) F Norton 33/1: 213049: Cl-up, wknd over 2f out: see 4307, 1764. *3* **42**
9 Ran Time 1m 17.36 (8.06) Owned: Mr P N Devlin Trained: Malton

---

4685   2.35 Totepool Ayrshire Handicap Stakes 3yo+ 86-100 (C1)   [100]
£12267 £4653 £2327   **1m rnd**   **Soft 118**   **-32 Slow**   Inside

4279 **YOUNG MR GRACE** 19 [11] T D Easterby 4-8-8 (80) D Allan 8/1: 1621301: With ldr, led over 3f out,   **89**
kept on well, pushed out: bckd: eff over 7f/1m on fm & soft grnd, likes gall trks: tough & prog.
4389 **JAZZ SCENE** 14 [1] M R Channon 3-9-3 (93) A Culhane 4/1: 0022452: Cl-up, eff over 1f out, kept on   1¼ **99**
but not pace of wnr ins last: nicely bckd: acts on firm & soft grnd: see 2749, 2521.
4523 **SIR GEORGE TURNER** 7 [2] M Johnston 5-9-3 (89) J Fanning 9/1: 0000003: Handy, eff over 1f out,   1½ **93**
onepace: acts on firm & soft: see 3506, 2101.
3460 **EVEREST** 55 [3] B Ellison 7-8-13 (85) T Eaves(3) 7/2 FAV: 0001104: Held up, eff well over 1f out,   ½ **88**
kept on, no threat: nicely bckd after 8 wk abs: ran to best: see 3265.
4136 **TONY TIE** 26 [8]6-8-10 (82) D Holland 14/1: 1610605: Chsd ldrs, onepcd over 1f out: see 3152, 2543.   1½ **82**
4463 **ODDSMAKER** 10 [10]3-8-10 (86) Dean McKeown 9/1: 1530006: Keen in tch, eff well over 1f out, wknd   shd **85**
ins last: see 2753, 1707.
4467 **WING COMMANDER** 10 [7]5-9-7 (93) P Hanagan 6/1: 0103057: Held up, eff over 2f out, sn no extra.   1 **90**
4397 **HARRY POTTER** 13 [9]5-8-7 vis (79) Darren Williams 10/1: 3115038: In tch, eff well over 1f out, no extra.   3 **71**
4977} **DUKE OF MODENA** 322 [4]7-9-0 (86) R Thomas(3) 12/1: 320400-9: ch g Salse - Palace Street (Secreto)   5 **70**
In tch, wknd over 2f out on reapp: won 1 of 8 '03 starts (rtd h'cap): '02 class stks & rtd h'cap wnr: suited by
1m on any grnd, likes gd or soft: acts on any trk: useful at best.   2 May'03 Sand 8.1g/f 93-92 B:
1 Apr'03 Sand 8.1gd 96-85 C: 1 Apr'02 Sand 8g/s 98-94 C: 2 Apr'02 Wind 8.3g/f 96- C: 2 May'01 Sand 8gd 103-100 B:
4005 **CHAPPEL CRESENT** 32 [5]4-9-7 (93) A Nicholls 50/1: 2515000: 10th: Led till over 3f out, wknd.   3½ **71**
10 Ran   Time 1m 48.63 (12.03)   Owned: Mr Norman Jackson   Trained: Malton

---

4686   3.10 Totesport Ayr Gold Cup Heritage Handicap 3yo+ (B1)   [112]
£70000 £26552 £13276   **6f str**   **Soft 118**   **+04 Fast**   Stands Side

4459 **FUNFAIR WANE** 10 [8] D Nicholls 5-8-6 (90) P Doe 33/1: 0400601: Made all, sn clr, flashed tail   **103**
for press fnl 1f but styd on strongly: best at 6f, just stays 1m: acts on firm, clearly enjoyed this soft grnd:
loves to front run: won this race 2 seasons ago off a 10lb higher mark & clearly likes this trk: tough, well
h'capped & another typically expert training performance: see 2532.
4459 **FANTASY BELIEVER** 10 [16] J J Quinn 6-8-11 (95) T Hamilton(3) 14/1: 1012002: Chsd ldrs stands   2 **103**
side, eff well over 1f out, kept on ins last but not pace of wnr: right back to form: v tough sprinter: see 3622.
4454 **CONTINENT** 11 [18] D Nicholls 7-9-10 (108) D Holland 18/1: 0-301053: Held up stands side, hdwy &   2½ **111**
short of room over 2f out, switched & kept on fnl 1f, nvr a threat: smart run under a big weight: former Gr 1 wnr.
4459 **MUTAWAQED** 10 [20] M A Magnusson 4-8-6 t (90) K McEvoy 8/1: 2010204: Held up stands side,   nk **92**
eff over 1f out, kept on, no threat to wnr: keeps running well in big sprint h'caps: see 4098 (gd/soft), 3434.
3957 **QUITO** 35 [23]7-9-8 bl (99) A Culhane 11/1: 1065165: Dwelt, held up stands side, no room halfway   ½ **107+**
till ins last, styd on strongly: won this race last term off a 14lb lower mark: relishes a fast pace/big field &
must have gone close with any sort of run here: see 2949, 1703.
4322 **ONLYTIME WILL TELL** 17 [10]6-8-7 (91) J Fanning 33/1: 5420146: Handy stands side, onepace.   1½ **89**
4454 **HIDDEN DRAGON** 11 [6]5-8-10 (94) G Faulkner 33/1: 2200647: Handy centre, onepace over 1f out.   ½ **90**
3827 **ZILCH** 40 [24]6-8-13 (97) S Sanders 8/1 JT FAV: 1401008: In tch stands side, eff over 1f out, sn   ¾ **91**
no impress: nicely bckd: abs, likes soft grnd: see 2758.
4384 **CAPRICHO** 14 [4]7-9-1 (99) J Quinn 33/1: 0400009: Held up centre, eff over 1f out, no extra.   1 **91**
4322 **TOM TUN** 17 [27]9-9-1 bl (99) T Lucas 14/1: 0420350: 10th: In tch stands side, wknd over 1f out.   2 **87**
4459 **RACCOON** 10 [28]4-8-5 T (89) K Darley 20/1: 1100000: 11th: With ldrs stands side, wknd over 1f out.   2 **73**
4238+ **CHOOKIE HEITON** 21 [25]6-9-7 (7ex) (105) T Eaves(3) 16/1: 0-450010: 12th: In tch stands side, wknd   ½ **88**
over 1f out: much btr 4238 (List, 5f, gd/soft).
4322 **CIRCUIT DANCER** 17 [26]4-8-9 (93) F Lynch 33/1: 1050400: 13th: In tch, wknd 2f out: see 2357.   ½ **75**
4382 **BOND BOY** 14 [17]7-8-4 (88) G Gibbons 16/1: 0300004: 14th: Nvr a factor stands side: btr 4382.   hd **71**
3061 **CARDINAL VENTURE** 72 [22]6-8-9 (93) N Callan 11/1: 0001000: 15th: With ldrs stands side, wknd   ½ **73**
qckly 2f out: 10 wk abs: btr expected, see 2187.
4231 **KINGS CAPRICE** 21 [7]3-8-3 (89) R Thomas(3) 33/1: 1044150: 16th: In tch, wknd 2f out: see 4030.   1½ **66**
4103 **GLARAMARA** 28 [11]3-8-9 (95) Hayley Turner(3) 50/1: 0044400: 17th: In tch stands side, wknd dist.   shd **71**
4382 **RIVER FALCON** 14 [9]4-8-6 (90) W Supple 50/1: 0030100: 18th: Chsd wnr centre till over 1f out, wknd.   1 **64**
4459 **CONNECT** 10 [5]7-8-9 bl (93) F P Ferris(3) 100/1: 4140000: 19th: Held up centre, wknd over 1f out.   1¼ **64**
3002 **PHILHARMONIC** 74 [15]3-9-0 (100) P Hanagan 14/1: 2114-400: 20th: In tch, eff 2f out, sn hung left   3 **65**
& wknd: 10 wk abs, much btr on reapp in 2727.
4060 **FIRE UP THE BAND** 6 [13]5-9-1 vis (99) A Nicholls 20/1: 4010000: 21th: Handy stands side, hung   1¾ **60**
left & wknd 2f out: see 3100 (fast grnd).
4459 **POMFRET LAD** 10 [21]6-8-12 (96) Alex Greaves 66/1: 52-00000: 22th: Al bhd: see 4459.   ½ **56**
4459 **JONNY EBENEEZER** 10 [1]5-8-6 bl (90) F Norton 33/1: 1411000: 23th: Held up, wknd over 2f out.   1¾ **46**
4226* **PRINCE AARON** 21 [3]4-8-12 (7ex) (96) G Carter 12/1: 1315110: 24th: Held up centre, wknd over 2f   14 **24**
out: not handle soft? much btr 4226 (gd), 3069.
24 Ran   Time 1m 16.15 (6.85)   Owned: Mrs Jean Keegan & Mr D Nicholls   Trained: Thirsk

---

4687   3.45 Listed Weatherbys Bank Stakes Registered As The Doonside Cup 3yo+ (A1)   [116]
£17400 £6600 £3300   **1m2f192y**   **Soft 118**   **+11 Fast**   Inside

4324* **INTO THE DARK** 17 [6] Saeed bin Suroor 3-8-4 vis t (114) K McEvoy 5/4: 1111: Cl-up, led over 4f   **119+**
out, clr over 1f out, cmftbly: unbeaten: stays 12f well on fast & soft grnd, gall trks: eff in t-strap & visor: v
smart & fast improving, type to thrive in a Gr 1 class performer, keep on side: see 4324, 3236.
2822 **PERCUSSIONIST** 83 [1] J H M Gosden 3-8-11 (118) K Darley 1/1 FAV: 32-11402: Chsd ldrs, rdn over   5 **118**
3f out & sn outpcd, rallied over 1f out, no threat to wnr: hvly bckd: 3 mth abs: prob caught a high-class sort &
was conceding weight: v interesting in Group company over 14f: see 2254 (4th in Derby), 1622.
4530 **BONECRUSHER** 7 [3] D R Loder 5-8-11 vis (105) S Sanders 9/1: 0553643: Slow away, held up, hdwy to   ½ **110**
chase wnr over 3f out, flashed tail & wknd over 1f out: not disgraced but finding it hard to be plcd to advantage.
3588 **HOWARDS DREAM** 49 [5] D A Nolan 6-8-11 t (30) D Allan 500/1: 0600004: Al bhd, t.o.: abs, offic 30.   28 **70$**
4173 **SOCIETY TIMES** 23 [4]11-8-11 t (30) P Mathers 500/1: 00//-00005: Led till over 4f out, wknd, t.o.: 11yo.   14 **48**
3999 **COURT OF APPEAL** 32 [2]7-8-11 t (90) T Eaves 25/1: 1132026: In tch, wknd 3f out, t.o.: needs h'caps.   dist **0**

6 Ran Time 2m 27.85 (11.85) Owned: Godolphin Trained: Newmarket

4688

4.15 Totesport Com Nursery Handicap Stakes 2yo 0-95 (C1) **[102]**
£12319 £4673 £2336 **1m rnd** **Soft 118** **-49 Slow** Inside

4509* **COMIC STRIP 7** [10] Sir Mark Prescott 2-9-8 (96) S Sanders 100/30: 1411: Mid-div, smooth prog to lead over 2f out, pshd out: well bckd: eff at 7f, imprvd for step up to 1m, shld get further: acts on fast, soft & fibresand, sharp or gall trk: progressive: see 4509. **108**
4387 **HALLHOO 14** [1] M R Channon 2-8-11 (85) A Culhane 3/1 FAV: 3122: Chsd ldrs, rdn & outpcd over 2f out, styd on for press ins last, not reach wnr: hvly bckd: clr of rem: acts on firm & soft grnd: can find similar. *1* **95**
4387 **LOOKS COULD KILL 14** [6] G A Butler 2-8-12 (86) P Hanagan 100/30: 2143: Held up, hdwy to go handy 3f out, sn no impress on wnr: well bckd, also bhd today's wnr of latest: handles firm & soft grnd: see 4387. *3½* **90**
4273 **CATWALK CLERIC 19** [8] M J Wallace 2-8-12 (86) K Darley 20/1: 412044: Trkd ldrs, drvn & onepace over 2f out: this longer 1m trip looks likely to suit: acts on gd & soft grnd: see 2303. *2* **87**
4285 **YOUNG THOMAS 19** [3]2-7-12 (2oh) (70) J Quinn 20/1: 044335: Handy & ch 3f out, sn outpcd by ldrs. *1¼* **71**
3390 **TAKHMIN 57** [2]2-8-10 (84) W Supple 12/1: 0236: Led/dsptd lead till over 2f out, sn outpcd & short of room, no impress after: clr of rem: 8 wk abs, h'cap bow: longer 1m trip shld suit: btr 3390 & 2689. *1¼* **81**
4396 **BALLYCROY GIRL 13** [7]2-7-12 (1oh) (71) Hayley Turner(3) 25/1: 6251067: Mid-div, eff 3f out, sn btn. *8* **55**
4387 **TURKS WOOD 14** [11]2-7-12 BL (72) F P Ferris(3) 50/1: 45508: Dwelt, rear, eff 3f out, sn btn, blnks. *2* **52**
3467 **JOHN FORBES 55** [5]2-8-13 (87) T Eaves(3) 25/1: 01009: Held up, rdn 3f out, sn struggling, 8 wk abs. *4* **61**
4396 **APETITE 13** [4]2-8-0 (2ow)(12oh) (60) F Norton 66/1: 0002100: 10th: Slow away & al bhd: btr 4277 (6f). *1¼* **46**
2938* **GYPSY JOHNNY 77** [9]2-8-11 VIS (85) D Holland 8/1: 10: 11th: Dwelt & rear, hdwy & led after 2f till 3f out, sn wknd: abs, visor: btr 2938 (debut). *5* **49**
11 Ran Time 1n 50.02 (13.42) Owned: Neil Greig - Osborne House Trained: Newmarket

4689

4.50 Keyline Builders Merchants Handicap Stakes 3yo+ 71-85 (D2) **[92]**
£12616 £4785 £2393 **7f50y str** **Soft 118** **-85 Slow** Inside

4117 **AZREME 27** [14] D K Ivory 4-8-8 (72) A Culhane 14/1: 5430201: Held up, hdwy & led ins last, drvn out: eff at 7f, stays 1m: acts on both AWs & fast grnd, loves gd/soft & hvy, prob any trk: see 1537. **81**
4482 **SEA STORM 9** [7] D R MacLeod 6-8-12 (76) G Carter 25/1: 6564302: Rear, drvn & styd on well ins last, just held: see 4103, 3809 & 2087. *nk* **84**
4184 **WATCHING 22** [4] R A Fahey 7-9-4 (82) P Hanagan 9/2: 0000233: Held up, styd on for press fnl 2f, not pace of wnr: hvly bckd, op 7/1: now stays a gall 7f well: well h'capped & loves easy grnd: see 4184, 4005. *1* **88**
2684 **BANDOS 86** [1] I Semple 4-8-10 t (74) D Allan 66/1: 220-3004: Keen & led, remained alone on far rail in straight, hdd well ins last & no extra: 12 wk abs: acts on fast & soft grnd: see 2122. *1¼* **76**
4301 **MARSHMAN 19** [6]5-9-2 (80) F P Ferris(3) 10/1: 0000335: Held up, drvn & styd on fnl 2f, not reach ldrs: worth another try at 1m: see 4301, 4073. *nk* **83**
4352 **HILLS OF GOLD 15** [11]5-8-13 (77) D Holland 15/2: 3221466: Trkd ldrs, styd on onepace: clr of rem. *1* **78**
4087 **ULYSEES 29** [5]5-8-7 (71) W Supple 20/1: 1050047: Keen in mid-div, hung left & btn over 1f out. *7* **62**
4304 **KHANJAR 18** [9]4-9-0 (78) Darren Williams 20/1: 2-240128: Dwelt & held up, eff wide, no impress. *¾* **68**
4103 **NAMROUD 28** [2]5-8-11 (75) T Hamilton(3) 7/1: 6000049: Chsd ldrs, no impress fnl 2f: btr 4103. *¾* **64**
3574 **SMIRFYS SYSTEMS 50** [10]5-8-9 (73) N Callan 66/1: 0050020: 10th: Held up, prog/ch over 2f out, sn btn: abs: btr 3574. *1* **60**
4654 **WANCHAI LAD 1** [8]3-9-1 (82) P Doe 66/1: 0-30500000: 11th: Cl-up, btn 2f out, unplcd yesterday. *3½* **64**
4397 **TRUE NIGHT 13** [3]7-9-5 (83) Alex Greaves 20/1: 1130020: 12th: Chsd ldrs, btn over 2f out: btr 4397. *hd* **64**
4350 **FLUR NA H ALBA 15** [16]5-9-3 p (81) T Eaves(3) 33/1: 00-10340: 13th: Mid-div, strug fnl 2f: btr 3326. *8* **48**
4294 **HURRICANE FLOYD 19** [15]6-8-10 BL (74) S Sanders 14/1: 0000420: 14th: Mid-div wide, struggling fnl 2f, blnks: btr 4294 (6f clmr). *14* **19**
3924 **ALBASHOOSH 36** [17]6-8-7 (71) A Nicholls 10/1: 1034320: 15th: Cl-up, btn 2f out: btr 3924, 3763. *14* **0**
1225 **LADY MYTTON 154** [12]4-9-6 (84) J Fanning 100/1: 2351/4-50: 16th: Held up, no ch fnl 3f: abs. *1¾* **4**
3891+**PRESUMPTIVE 37** [13]4-9-4 BL (82) K Darley 4/1 FAV: 0/3-53010: 17th: Rear, struggling from halfway: tried blnks, poor run: btr 3891 (g/s). *16* **0**
4186 **KING HARSON 22** [18]5-9-7 vis (85) K McEvoy 25/1: 0060150: 18th: Mid-div, struggling 3f out: much btr 4073 (made all). *dist* **0**
18 Ran Time 1m 38.04 (14.24) Owned: Halcyon Partnership Trained: Radlett

4690

5.20 Glasgow Audi - The World's Largest Audi Centre Handicap Stakes 3yo+ 71-85 (D2) **[94]**
£8284 £2549 £1275 **1m5f13y** **Soft 118** **-54 Slow** Inside

4062 **ELUSIVE DREAM 30** [6] Sir Mark Prescott 3-9-1 (81) S Sanders 1/2 FAV: 0-111131: Chsd ldrs, hdwy & led over 2f out, edged right, rdn out: hvly bckd at odds-on: eff at 12/14f: acts on firm, soft & fibresand: most progressive: see 4062 & 3249. **94**
4062 **LETS ROLL 30** [9] C W Thornton 3-9-3 (83) Dean McKeown 11/2: 2231152: Held up, styd on for press fnl 2f, nvr a threat to wnr: op 4/1: bhd this wnr latest: acts on fast & soft grnd: see 4062 & 3261. *5* **88**
4097 **FAAYEJ 28** [3] Sir Michael Stoute 4-9-12 P (83) W Supple 7/1: 521-1453: Trkd ldrs, rdn & no impress over 1f out: cheekpieces: prob handles soft grnd & stays a gall 13f: see 4097, 2099 (10f). *2* **85**
4377 **PERELANDRA 14** [4] M J Wallace 4-9-1 (72) N Callan 66/1: 6610-104: Held up, smooth prog to chall over 2f out, sn rdn & no extra: clr of rem: ran well for a long way: acts on soft, gd/soft & polytrack: see 4181. *nk* **74**
4553 **MERRYMAKER 5** [1]4-8-13 (70) P Mathers(5) 25/1: 2100355: Chsd ldrs, no impress fnl 2f, qck reapp. *7* **65**
4656 **LENNEL 1** [7]6-8-12 bl (69) Hayley Turner(3) 16/1: 13233056: Held up, no impress fnl 3f, unplcd yesterday. *nk* **64**
3181 **NESSEN DORMA 67** [8]3-9-3 (83) D Holland 33/1: 2133007: Led till over 2f out, sn strug: 2 mth abs. *1½* **76**
4209 **TOMASINO 22** [5]6-8-13 t (70) K Darley 16/1: 4601038: Chsd ldrs, rdn & btn 3f out: btr 3226 (fast). *dist* **0**
8 Ran Time 3m 06.94(22.34) Owned: Cheveley Park Stud Trained: Newmarket

Official Going Soft (Good/Soft Places), Rain throughout afternoon

---

4691

2.25 Bellway Homes Maiden Stakes 2yo (D2)
£5863 £1804 £902 1m65y rnd Soft Inapplicable Inside

4326 **LOVE PALACE** 18 [5] M Johnston 2-9-0 (85) J Fanning 8/13 FAV: 2241: Made all, clr 3f out, pushed out, val 12L+: bckd at odds-on: eff at 7f, suited by 1m: acts on gd/soft & soft grnd: improving.		95
4351 **KAMES PARK** 16 [4] I Semple 2-9-0 R Winston 13/2: 42: Rear, prog to chase wnr 3f out, al held ins fnl 2f: clr rem: op 11/2: encouraging run: see 4351 (debut).	9	81
4102 **HAIBAN** 29 [2] G A Butler 2-9-0 P Hanagan 11/2: 423: Keen cl-up 6f, wknd: see 4102, 3878.	3½	74
4401 **BOO** 14 [1] K R Burke 2-9-0 Darren Williams 12/1: 464: Cl-up 6f, fdd: see 4401 & 3939.	4	66
4283 **ALANI** 20 [3]2-8-9 M Fenton 14/1: 25: Prom till halfway, sn edged right & fdd: btr 4283 (7f).	5	52
3811 **IMPERIOLI** 42 [6]2-9-0 G Gibbons 11/1: 06: b c Fraam - Jussoli (Don) Chsd ldrs 5f, fdd: 6 wk abs: Apr foal, half-brother successful at 7/8f: dam wnr at 7/10f: sire useful performer around 1m.	8	43
PETER ROUGHLEY 0 [7]2-9-0 P Bradley 100/1: 7: b g Inchie Lodge - Dahabiah (Soviet Star) Al in rear on debut: Jan first foal, dam unplcd: sire Gr 1 wnr at 1m: with A Berry.	¾	41
7 Ran Time 1m 51.47 (7.67) Owned: Mr M Doyle Trained: Middleham		

4692

2.55 Gala Casinos Merchant City 2-Y-O Final Handicap For The Lord Hamilton Trophy 2yo (B1) [97]
£12087 £4585 £2292 6f5y str Soft Inapplicable Far side

4040* **WINDY PROSPECT** 31 [15] P A Blockley 2-9-6 (89) M Fenton 9/2 FAV: 1032211: Made all, edged left under press ins fnl 1f, just held on: eff at 6/7f on fast, soft grnd & both AWs: likes to force the pace: improving.		102
4551 **GIFTED GAMBLE** 6 [5] K A Ryan 2-8-11 (80) R Winston 16/1: 3221502: Mid-div, prog wide halfway, styd on well ins fnl 1f, just denied: qck reapp: eff at 5f, now stays 6f: acts on firm & soft grnd: see 3445.	shd	91
4518* **PROFITS REALITY** 8 [11] P A Blockley 2-8-12 (81) G Gibbons 5/1: 0554313: Chsd ldrs, outpcd after 4f, rallied ins fnl 1f, just held when short of room cl-home: acts on gd & soft grnd: gd run in defeat, see 4518 (7f).	1	89
4344 **HANSOMELLE** 17 [6] B Mactaggart 2-8-6 (75) Dale Gibson 9/1: 4124: Mid-div, pog 2f out, onepcd.	2½	76
4518 **MCELDOWNEY** 8 [9]2-8-7 (76) J Fanning 7/1: 2230025: Cl-up over 4f, no extra: btr 4518 (7f, gd).	5	64
4490 **RAINBOW IRIS** 9 [3]2-8-1 (70) F P Ferris(3) 16/1: 45206: Prom over 4f, wkng when hmpd dist: btr 4205.	½	57
4050 **TEQUILA SHEILA** 31 [2]2-9-1 (84) Darren Williams 20/1: 016167: Nvr nrr than mid-div: btr 3825 (gd).	½	70
4344 **KRISTIKHAB** 17 [13]2-7-13 (1ow)(14oh) (53) P Fessey 66/1: 0005008: Dsptd lead 4f, wknd: stiff task.	1¾	49
4224 **MONASHEE PRINCE** 22 [7]2-8-9 (78) S Sanders 20/1: 1534009: Al in rear: btr 2100.	1¼	55
4083 **INVERTIEL** 30 [14]2-8-11 (80) P Hanagan 16/1: 4200: 10th: Mid-div 4f, fdd: btr 3589 (fast).	9	34
4437 **OCHIL HILLS DANCER** 12 [4]2-7-12 (8oh)t (59) D Fentiman(7) 66/1: 5045000: 11th: Al in rear: see 2056.	shd	20
4306 **MAKE US FLUSH** 19 [12]2-8-5 (74) F Norton 12/1: 1102100: 12th: Al bhd: btr 3902 (gd/soft).	1	24
4344 **No Commission** 17 [10]2-8-2 (71) R Ffrench 25/1:0 4444 **Extra Mark** 12 [8]2-8-3 (72) A Nicholls 16/1:0		
14 Ran Time 1m 13.91 (4.11) Owned: bellhouseracingcom Trained: Cockerham		

4693

3.30 Listed Betfair Com Flower Of Scotland Stakes Fillies & Mares 3yo+ (A1)
£20300 £7700 £3850 5f4y str Soft Inapplicable Far side

3235* **KIND** 65 [5] R Charlton 3-8-11 (89) R Hughes 8/1: 4-311111: In tch trav well, styd on to lead well ins fnl 1f, pushed out, op 11/2, 9 wk abs: eff at 6/7f, imprvd eff today for drop back to 5f: acts on firm & soft grnd: v progressive sprinter who can win more races in this grade: see 3235 & 2677.		103+
3551 **AUTUMN PEARL** 52 [10] M A Jarvis 3-8-11 (97) S Sanders 5/1: 1-123602: Led, hdd under press well ins fnl 1f, not pace of wnr: 7 wk abs: appreciated return to easy surface: see 2593 & 2206.	½	99
4514 **FRASCATI** 8 [2] A Berry 4-8-12 (76) F Lynch 100/1: 1120043: Cl-up, ev ch despite edging right dist, kept on, not pace front 2: acts on firm, soft grnd & fibresand: fine eff up in grade: see 2968 & 2747 (h'cap).	¾	97$
4481 **ENCHANTMENT** 10 [11] J M Bradley 3-8-11 (100) R L Moore 2/1 FAV: 1241444: Cl-up, no extra ins fnl 1f: acts on firm & soft grnd: see 4481 & btr 4027.	1¼	93
4510+ **SIMIANNA** 8 [7]5-9-2 p (97) R Winston 6/1: 6503215: Held up, prog 2f out, nrst fin: btr 4510 (6f, fast).	1½	93
4459 **FOREVER PHOENIX** 11 [1]4-8-12 (98) E Ahern 5/1: 3036166: Bhd, prog halfway, onepcd ins fnl 1f: op 7/2: below form on today's soft grnd: btr 4459 & 4382 (h'caps, firm).	1	86
4238 **BARON RHODES** 22 [8]3-8-11 (80) T Eaves 100/1: 0513007: Prom 4f, no extra: btr 3833.	¾	84
4479 **ENCHANTED** 10 [4]5-8-12 (92) A Culhane 20/1: 1000048: Al in rear: btr 4479 (7f, firm).	3	75
4322 **SMART HOSTESS** 18 [3]5-8-12 (91) P Hanagan 20/1: 1011-009: Mid-div, fdd dist: btr 4322.	½	74
2741) **SISTER MOONSHINE** 14 [6]3-8-11 BL Martin Dwyer 14/1: 0-315060: 10th: ch f Piccolo - Cootamundra (Double Bed) Cl-up, fdd dist: French raider, earlier stks wnr in native country (5f, gd/soft).	nk	73
4454* **DRAGON FLYER** 12 [9]5-8-12 (98) F Norton 5/1: 3430410: 11th: Al in rear: showed more in 4454 (fast).	2	67
11 Ran Time 1m 0.80 (2.7) Owned: Mr K Abdulla Trained: Beckhampton		

4694

4.05 Super Sunday 'premier' Claiming Stakes 3-4yo (D2)
£8249 £2538 £1269 1m1f36y Soft Inapplicable Inside

4352 **LAURO** 16 [2] Miss J A Camacho 4-8-6 (72) R Winston 2/1 JT FAV: 4-324401: Chsd ldrs, styd on to lead dist, pushed out, val 7L+: stays 1m/9f: acts on fast, soft grnd & fibresand.		75
4365* **MAGIC STING** 16 [5] M L W Bell 3-8-10 (75) J Mackay 2/1 JT FAV: 1033212: Keen cl-up, kept on fnl 1f, no ch with easy wnr: bckd, eff at 9f, return to further will suit: just btr 4365 (1m, gd).	5	76
4304* **FAMILIAR AFFAIR** 19 [8] T D Barron 3-8-11 (78) R L Moore 3/1: 14-0013: Keen prom, led 2f out, hdd dist, no extra: see 4304 (1m, gd).	¾	75
4487 **RABITATIT** 10 [4] J G M O'Shea 3-7-13 P (60) Natalia Gemelova(7) 12/1: 2556204: Led 7f, wknd: cheek pieces: twice below 4068 (10f).	3½	58
4362 **ISKANDER** 16 [1]3-8-8 bl (72) J Carroll 11/1: 0006405: Al in rear: btr 3738.	9	54
4304 **BANANA GROVE** 19 [3]3-8-8 (68) F Lynch 33/1: 30P1406: Mid-div over 5f, wknd: btr 3805 (fast).	22	26
4397 **ON EVERY STREET** 14 [7]3-9-4 bl (77) R Ffrench 33/1: 5-431467: Keen prom 6f, fdd.	1½	33
3548 **DEVINE LIGHT** 52 [9]4-8-4 p (50) P Hanagan 66/1: 01-00608: Mid-div over halfway, wknd: 7 wk abs.	hd	13

HAMILTON   SUNDAY 19.09.04   Righthand, Undulating Track, Stiff Uphill Finish

8 Ran   Time 2m 3.95 (9.85)   Owned: Shangri-La Racing Club   Trained: Malton

4695   4.40 Hamilton Park Classified Stakes 3yo+ 0-85 (C2)
£10166 £3128 £1564   **1m65y rnd**   **Soft**   **Inapplicable**   Inside

4389 **PEDRILLO** 15 [7] Sir Mark Prescott 3-8-12 (87) S Sanders 8/11 FAV: 321-31: In tch, prog trav well   102
to lead ins fnl 1f, pushed clr, val 7L+: bckd at odds-on: eff around 1m, further will suit: acts on firm & gd,
seemed to relish today's soft grnd: lightly rcd 3yo who is open to plenty more improvement, more races await.
4516 **MRS MOH** 8 [2] T D Easterby 3-8-8 (86) D Allan 3/1: 0513122: Prom, led bef 2f out, hdd ins fnl   5   88
1f, no extra: acts on fast, soft grnd & fibresand: continues to run well: see 4516 & 3738.
4071 **BESSEMER** 30 [4] I Semple 3-8-10 (84) R Winston 7/1: 0-536143: Keen prom, led 3f out, sn hdd, wknd.   3   84
4629 **STOIC LEADER** 3 [1] R F Fisher 4-9-0 (78) P Hanagan 10/1: 2564044: Mid-div 6f, wknd: qck reapp.   6   73
       KING SUMMERLAND 413 [3]7-9-0 (50) R Ffrench 150/1: 242160-5: b g Minshaanshu Amad - Alaskan   9   53
Princess (Prince Rupert) Led 5f, wknd: earlier jumps unplcd (rtd 71h, mdn hdle): ex-German, won numerous times in
Europe at at 6/10f: with B Mactaggart.
4550 **PHOENIX NIGHTS** 6 [6]4-9-0 (52) P Mathers(5) 150/1: 0644606: Mid-div, wknd bef 2f out: see 4173.   3½   52
6 Ran   Time 1m 51.77 (7.97)   Owned: Hesmonds Stud   Trained: Newmarket

4696   5.10 Scottish Racing Handicap Stakes 3yo 56-70 (E3)   [77]
£5135 £1580 £790   **6f5y str**   **Soft**   **Inapplicable**   Far side

4548 **PURE IMAGINATION** 6 [8] J M Bradley 3-8-9 (58) R L Moore 20/1: 0604001: Rear, styd on well to   64
lead dist, rdn clr despite edging right, val bit more: eff at 6f, has tried further: relished this soft grnd.
4175 **THORNABY GREEN** 24 [11] T D Barron 3-8-13 (62) P Makin(5) 11/2: 4105402: Prom, outpcd bef 1f out,   2½   63
rallied ins fnl 1f, no ch with wnr: op 7/1: acts on fast & soft grnd: see 4009 & 3203.
4210+**MECCAS MATE** 23 [16] D W Barker 3-8-8 (57) L Enstone 5/1: 0-56513: Keen in tch, led 2f out, hdd   1   55
dist, no extra: tchd 13/2: acts on fast & soft grnd: just btr 4210 (5f).
4618 **TROJAN FLIGHT** 3 [9] Mrs J R Ramsden 3-9-4 (67) R Winston 15/8 FAV: 3212104: Mid-div, prog & ev   1½   61
ch dist, sn no extra: well bckd on qck reapp: twice below win of 4339 (firm).
4278 **PICCOLO PRINCE** 20 [5]3-9-3 (66) E Ahern 14/1: 0200505: Rear, prog bef 1f out, nrst fin: see 3599.   1½   56
4528 **BAYLAW STAR** 8 [2]3-8-12 (61) D Mernagh 25/1: 4006006: Cl-up stands side, hung left into centre   1   48
after halfway, no extra bef 1f out: btr 1387.
4252 **BEST DESERT** 21 [6]3-9-1 (64) G Gibbons 14/1: 0051507: Nvr nrr than mid-div: btr 3654 (7f, fast).   5   38
4618 **SWEET CANDO** 3 [12]3-8-10 p (59) S Sanders 10/1: 0500308: Bhd, modest late gains: qck reapp.   hd   32
3612 **MIND ALERT** 50 [14]3-9-1 BL (64) D Allan 20/1: 06-02009: Led 4f, wknd: 7 wk abs & blnks.   1¼   33
4341 **VADEMECUM** 17 [15]3-9-7 (70) F Lynch 16/1: 13-60000: 10th: Cl-up, fdd dist: btr 1745.   6   24
4278 **KAMENKA** 20 [3]3-9-4 (67) P Hanagan 16/1: 44-44000: 11th: Mid-div far side 4f, wknd: btr 3833.   ¾   19
4627 **Obe Bold** 3 [13]3-9-4 t(67) F Norton 20/1:0   4245 **Troodos Jet** 22 [1]3-9-1 (64) F P Mathers(5) 50/1:0
3667 **Solar Prince** 25 [10]3-8-7 (48) F P Ferris(3) 100/1:0   4404 **Louis Prima** 13 [4]3-8-7 (30) R Ffrench 100/1:0
15 Ran   Time 1m 15.53(5.73)   Owned: Dab Hand Racing   Trained: Chepstow

LEICESTER   MONDAY 20.09.04   Righthand, Stiff, Galloping Track

Official Going Good/Soft

4697   2.00 Ibetx Com - The Punter's Choice Nursery Handicap Stakes Fillies 2yo 0-85 (D2)   [91]
£5759 £1772 £886   **6f str**   **Good 40**   **+01 Fast**   Stands Side

3440 **MAGICAL ROMANCE** 58 [8] B J Meehan 2-9-6 (83) R Winston 13/2: 4161: Made all, rdn clr over 1f out   98
& in command ins last, eased fnl strides: op 8/1: 2 month abs: h'cap bow: eff up with/forcing the pace at 6f on
fast, likes gd grnd: goes well fresh: likely to improve: see 3183.
2666 **ABERDEEN PARK** 2 [10] Mrs H Sweeting 2-8-5 (68) P Doe 25/1: 500452: Held up in tch, styd on for   3   74
press fnl 2f, not pace to chall: qck reapp: stays 2m6f on firm & gd grnd: see 2666.
4457 **HIGHLAND CASCADE** 12 [4] J M P Eustace 2-8-12 (75) J Tate 12/1: 13203: Chsd ldrs, kept on onepace   ½   79
chall: h'cap bow: eff at 6f, shapes as if 7f+ could suit: handles fast & gd grnd: see 2097.
4358 **XEERAN** 17 [12] M A Jarvis 2-7-13 (62) D Fox(5) 9/1: 5554: Held up, kept on late, not able to   ¾   64
chall: h'cap bow: eff at 6f, shapes as if 7f+ could suit: handles fast & gd grnd: see 2097.
4052 **ASPEN RIDGE** 32 [7]2-7-12 (4oh) (57) P Hanagan 40/1: 00005: ch f Namid - Longueville Lady (Hamas)   nk   62
Chsd ldrs, no extra fnl 1f: imprvd on gd grnd today, h'cap bow: £20,000 Mar first foal, dam a dual 3yo wnr abroad:
prob stays a stiff 6f & handles gd grnd.
4535 **CEREBUS** 9 [1]2-8-11 (74) R Mullen 5/1: 642336: Held up, eff from halfway, no prog dist.   nk   74
3761* **EPIPHANY** 44 [5]2-9-7 (84) K McEvoy 7/1: 217: Held up, sn pushed along, nvr on terms: btr 3761.   2   78
4420 **ALEXANDER CAPETOWN** 14 [11]2-8-6 (69) A Culhane 9/2 FAV: 256448: Keen early, trkd ldrs, btn dist.   hd   62
4471 **KWAME** 11 [6]2-9-1 vis (78) S Drowne 9/1: 1202539: Chsd ldrs till dist: btr 4471 & 4065.   ¾   69
4535 **THREE PENNIES** 9 [9]2-8-5 (1ow) (67) S W Kelly 40/1: 013000: 10th: Prom, struggling halfway: btr 2938. 4   47
4422 **THE KEEP** 14 [13]2-7-12 (3oh) (58) R Thomas 33/1: 00040: 11th: Prom till lost pl from halfway.   5   26
4357 **ELLENS PRINCESS** 17 [2]2-8-9 (72) P Dobbs 14/1: 5400: 12th: Chsd ldrs, struggling fnl 2f: bckd, op 20/12½   29
4436 **RINGAROOMA** 13 [3]2-8-6 (69) P Robinson 7/1: 50420: 13th: Prom, btn over 2f out: btr 4436.   2   20
13 Ran   Time 1m 12.06 (2.26)   Owned: Mr F C T Wilson   Trained: Upper Lambourn

4698   2.30 Golden Hand Selling Stakes 3yo   (G4)
£3073 £878 £439   **7f str**   **Good 40**   **-37 Slow**   Stands Side

4367 **INESCAPABLE 17** [7] W R Muir 3-8-11 (49) S Drowne 33/1: 00401: Trkd ldr, drvn to lead well ins   56
last: first win, bt in for 4,500gns: eff at 7f, 1m may yet suit: acts on gd: apprec drop to sell grade.
3875 **ABSOLUTELY SOAKED 40** [10] Dr J D Scargill 3-8-6 BL (54) K McEvoy 7/1: 0-560002: Led, rdn & hdd   1   48
well ins last: 6 wk abs: gd run with forcing tactics in first time blnks: acts on fast & gd grnd: see 1247.
3515 **RED ROCKY 54** [13] R Hollinshead 3-8-6 p (45) R Ffrench 8/1: 5020353: Chsd ldrs, styd on for   ½   47
press, not pace of press: 8 wk abs: acts on fast & gd grnd: see 2704 (C/D).
4528 **MELODY KING 9** [18] P D Evans 3-9-2 bl (58) R Winston 5/1 FAV: 65U0604: Mid-div, hdwy over 2f out,   shd   57
styd on onepace ins last: stays a stiff 7f in sell grade: see 1903.
4560 **RUSSALKA 7** [5]3-8-6 (50) M Halford(7) 20/1: 2606005: Pushed along towards rear, late gains, nrst fin.   hd   46
4582 **BLUE DAZE 6** [1]3-8-11 (59) P Dobbs 7/1: 5550006: Trkd ldrs, drvn & onepace fnl 2f: qck reapp.   ½   50
4595 **VITTORIOSO 6** [6]3-8-11 (45) B Reilly(3) 20/1: 3200507: Handy, outpcd over 2f out, kept on ins last.   ½   49$
4587 **BULBERRY HILL 6** [16]3-8-11 D R McCabe 16/1: 0558: Mid-div, no impress over 1f out, qck reapp.   3½   42
4370 **LA CALERA 16** [20]3-8-11 (45) O Urbina 10/1: 0053309: Prom, rdn & btn over 1f out: see 4165 & 3651.   1   40
4504 **NAMED AT DINNER 9** [17]3-8-11 BL (50) R Mullen 40/1: 0000000: 10th: Slow away, in tch till over 1f out.   hd   39
4088 **CAPETOWN GIRL 31** [19]3-8-11 (52) Darren Williams 20/1: 0000000: 11th: Dwelt, sn handy, btn 2f out.   ¾   38
4438 **ORPENBERRY 13** [3]3-8-11 (50) D Allan 20/1: 00-00000: 12th: Mid-div, rdn/btn 2f out: btr 4438 & 3679.   4   30
2834 **MAC THE KNIFE 83** [15]3-9-2 (50) A Culhane 20/1: 0-000000: 13th: Bhd, no impress, new yard, abs.   7   23
4595 **LOTTIE 6** [12]3-8-6 (45) P Doe 50/1: 05400: 14th: Sn struggling & nvr a factor, qck reapp: btr 3595.   5   4
4081J **MUNAAHEJ 380** [11]3-8-11 P Hanagan 11/2: 05-0: 15th: b c Soviet Star - Azyaa (Kris) Chsd ldrs   ¾   8
till over 2f out: op 9/1, reapp: lightly rcd, unplcd in '03 (rtd 63, mdn, B Hills): brother to wnrs at 7f/1m.
3772 **POWER NAP 44** [9]3-8-6 BL (40) G Carter 66/1: 00-60000: 16th: Swerved left start, al rear, abs.   4   0
4278 Scooby Dooby Do 21 [4]3-8-6 p(49) S W Kelly 33/1:0   **Nippy Nipper 0** [8]3-8-6 N Pollard 33/1:0
18 Ran   Time 1m 27.32 (5.32)   Owned: Mr M J Caddy   Trained: Lambourn

4699   3.05 E B F Kegworth Novice Stakes 2yo   (D2)
£5408 £1664 £832   **7f str**   **Good 40**   **-33 Slow**   Stands Side

4096 **PIVOTAL FLAME 30** [6] B A McMahon 2-9-5 (100) G Carter 7/4: 1541: Trkd ldr halfway, rdn & led   102
over 1f out, hung left under press, styd on well: eff at 6/7f on fast & gd/soft grnd, stiff/gall trks: useful.
4026* **HAUNTING MEMORIES 33** [1] M A Jarvis 2-9-5 R Robinson 8/13 FAV: 412: Led, hung right thr'out,   1   99
hdd & briefly outpcd over 1f out, rallying for press when hmpd ins last, not able to chall nr fin: clr of rem:
handles fast & gd/soft grnd: stays 7f: see 4026.
4590 **ORPEN WIDE 6** [3] M C Chapman 2-8-12 K McEvoy 50/1: 033: Chsd ldr, no impress on front pair fnl   5   83$
2f: qck reapp: longer 7f trip shld suit, can find a race when rtnd to mdn company: see 4590.
4198* **HAPPY EVENT 24** [5] B R Millman 2-9-4 (86) G Baker 16/1: 10014: Chsd ldrs, no impress fnl 3f: lngr trip.   5   80
        COURT RULER 0 [4]2-8-8 O Urbina 150/1: 5: b g Kayf Tara - Fairfields Cone (Celtic Cone) Dwelt   dist   0
& al outpcd rear: Feb foal, 9,000gns May foal, dam a multiple wnr over hdles: stoutly bred.
        SILVER COURT 0 [7]2-8-8 P Hanagan 100/1: 6: b c Silver Patriarch - Double Stake (Kokand)   1¾   0
Swerved right start & al outpcd in rear: 16,000gns May foal, dam a US stks wnr, sire 10f 2yo List scorer.
6 Ran   Time 1m 27.02 (5.02)   Owned: Mr R L Bedding   Trained: Tamworth

4700   3.40 Betting With Ibetx Com Handicap Stakes 3yo+ 71-85   (D2)
£7264 £2235 £1118   **5f str**   **Good 40**   **+14 Fast**   Stands Side   [92]

4107 **ENDLESS SUMMER 30** [12] A W Carroll 7-8-12 (76) P Doe 4/1 JT FAV: 5046021: Al prom, led over 1f   87
out, drvn out: bckd, op 6/1: gd time: eff at 5/6f on firm & soft grnd, any trk: has broken blood vessels, best
without t-strap: well h'capped & enjoyed racing whn/forcing the pace today: see 921.
4605* **OK PAL 5** [8] T G Mills 4-9-0 (6ex) (78) G Carter 8/1: 0060612: Led 3f, drvn & kept on, not pace   1   85
of wnr: nicely bckd & gd run under a 6lb pen: see 4605 (clmr).
4496 **DANCING MYSTERY 10** [7] E A Wheeler 10-8-13 bl (77) P Robinson 14/1: 0002003: Chsd ldrs, switched   nk   83
& kept on for press: tough & well h'capped 10yo: see 4031.
4585* **MINE BEHIND 6** [3] J R Best 4-9-0 (6ex) (88) K McEvoy 4/1 JT FAV: 0100014: Held up stands side,   1   91
late gains, nrst fin: qck reapp: just btr 4585.
4654 **PADDYWACK 3** [4]7-8-8 bl (72) A Culhane 5/1: 3633045: Held up, kept on for press fnl 2f, no threat.   shd   75
4253 **NEVER WITHOUT ME 22** [2]4-8-7 (6oh) (65) P Makin(5) 8/1: 1124226: Chsd ldrs, no extra from dist.   ¾   72
4496 **BEYOND THE CLOUDS 10** [1]8-8-12 p (76) R Winston 12/1: 0300627: Sn rdn, nvr pace to chall: btr 4496.   nk   76
4322 **LAW BREAKER 19** [15]6-9-7 (85) B Reilly(3) 20/1: 5520008: Prom, no extra fnl 1f: likes Doncaster.   ½   83
4184 **DEVON FLAME 24** [5]5-8-13 (77) S Drowne 16/1: 2400209: Chsd ldrs, no extra fnl 1f: btr 3966.   nk   74
3569 **TURIBIUS 52** [10]5-8-9 vis (73) S W Kelly 20/1: 3000000: 10th: Held up, nvr land a blow, abs: see 755.   4   59
3569 **PARKSIDE PURSUIT 52** [16]6-8-9 (73) P Fitzsimons 25/1: 4131000: 11th: Chsd ldrs till 2f out: btr 2838.   nk   57
4514 **PRINCE OF BLUES 9** [14]6-8-7 (15oh)p (56) Liam Jones(7) 66/1: 3033000: 12th: Prom 3f, sn wknd.   ½   53
4197 Prince Cyrano 24 [11]5-8-8 (72) R Mullen 14/1:0   4394 **Treasure House 16** [17]3-9-1 (80) G Baker 40/1:0
3131 Lets Get It On 72 [6]3-8-9 (74) Darren Williams 28/1:0 4107 The Fisio 30 [13]4-8-9 vis(72) T Eaves(3) 33/1:0
16 Ran   Time 59.6 (1.3)   Owned: Seasons Holidays   Trained: Alcester

4701   4.10 Henry Alken Claiming Stakes 3-4yo   (E3)
£4251 £1308 £654   **1m1f218y**   **Good 40**   **-38 Slow**   Inside

4448* **PLATINUM PIRATE 13** [7] K R Burke 3-8-7 vis (65) Rory Moore(5) 5/1: 3654011: Held up, prog & led   67
over 2f out, held on well for press ins last: suited by 10f on fast, soft & polytrack, any trk: enjoys claimers.
4579 **GO GREEN 6** [6] P D Evans 3-7-12 t (54) Natalia Gemelova(7) 8/1: 4326032: Dwelt, chsd ldrs, styd on   ½   56
for press, not able to reach wnr: qck reapp: apprec rtn to 10f: see 4145 & 3730 (seller).

LEICESTER   MONDAY 20.09.04   Righthand, Stiff, Galloping Track

4304 **EPHESUS 20** [10] Miss Gay Kelleway 4-9-3 vis (76) A Culhane 7/2 FAV: 2000363: Trkd ldrs, onepace.   2½   65
4261 **TRICKY VENTURE 22** [12] P W Hiatt 4-8-13 (73) P Makin(5) 5/1: 40452-24: Chsd ldrs, rdn/short of   ½   60
room dist, onepace ins last: flattered 4261 (mdn).
4625] **SELKIRK GRACE 703** [1]4-9-7 P Hanagan 7/1: 3/-5: b g Selkirk - Polina (Polish Precedent) Slow   ½   67
away & held up, kept on late, not able to land a blow: v long abs, missed '03: promise sole start in '02 (mdn, rtd
95): half-brother to a 6f juv wnr: eff at 1m/10f on fast & gd grnd, stiff/gall trks.
4076 **GRAND WIZARD 31** [8]4-8-9 (60) R Mullen 33/1: 01-40006: Held up, pushed along halfway, late gains.   nk   54
4448 **REBATE 13** [5]4-8-9 t (58) P Dobbs 6/1: 3505657: Keen & prom, no extra dist: btr 4448.   nk   53
4492 **LOVE YOU ALWAYS 10** [3]4-9-7 (92) B Reilly(3) 12/1: 13/-068: Chsd ldrs, hung right & btn 2f out.   5   58
4142* **IVORY COAST 27** [11]3-8-2 bl (57) P Doe 14/1: 0005019: Led 7f, sn btn: btr 4142 (soft).   6   36
       INDIANS LANDING 105 [4]3-9-1 R Winston 40/1: 0000: 10th: Held up, struggling fnl 3f, abs.   25   17
5019] **RUSTIC CHARM 319** [9]4-8-12 (67) A Nicholls 25/1: 3340-P: b f Charnwood Forest - Kabayil (Dancing   0
Brave) Held up, rdn & btn 3f out, t.o./p.u. ins last: Flat reapp, 3 months jumps abs, 04/05 dual nov seller wnr &
(rtd 103h, 2m/2m1.5f, fast & gd): plcd on the level '03 (C Cox, fill mdn, rtd 74): eff around 1m/10f on gd & gd/soft.
11 Ran   Time 2m 10.18 (7.68)   Owned: Spigot Lodge Partnership   Trained: Leyburn

---

4702   4.40 Highfields Classified Stakes 3yo+ 0-75 (D2)
            £7261 £2234 £1117   **1m rnd**   **Good 40**   **-15 Slow**   Inside

4578* **ZAMEYLA 6** [10] M A Jarvis 3-8-13 (74) P Robinson 11/4 FAV: 02211: Chsd ldrs, led 2f out, edged   84
left, rdn out, eased fnl strides: qck reapp: eff at 7f, imprvd at 1m last twice: acts on firm & soft: see 4578.
4195 **HONEST INJUN 24** [9] J G M O'Shea 3-8-10 (72) S W Kelly 9/1: 4054522: Held up, drvn & styd on,   1   77
not able to reach wnr: gd run for new yard: see 4195, 3378.
4341 **MASTER THEO 18** [6] H J Collingridge 3-8-10 (73) R Winston 25/1: 0333303: Trkd ldrs, chall 2f   ½   76
out, not pace of wnr but kept on: mdn, shown enough to find a race: see 3950, 2729.
4346 **RISKA KING 18** [7] R A Fahey 4-9-0 (72) P Hanagan 7/1: 4336154: Held up in tch, eff & onepace dist.   ½   75
4465 **ST SAVARIN 12** [5]3-8-10 (74) R Ffrench 33/1: 3310005: Held up, eff over 2f out, hung right & no   1   73
extra ins last: prefer 7f: see 3562.
4474* **TADAWUL 11** [1]3-8-7 (75) K McEvoy 4/1: 016: Held up, hmpd over 1f out, not pace to chall: bckd.   1¾   67
4093 **THE BONUS KING 31** [8]4-9-0 (75) G Baker 40/1: 0240057: Led 6f, btn ins last: see 688.   nk   69
3738 **WEET A HEAD 46** [4]3-8-10 (75) A Culhane 12/1: 5634608: Trkd ldrs, rdn & btn over 1f out, 6 wk abs.   ½   68
3942 **FIVEOCLOCK EXPRESS 37** [2]4-9-0 p (71) T Eaves(3) 16/1: 0052009: Hld up, hdwy 5f out, wknd 2f out.   ¾   67
4077* **CRAIL 31** [3]4-9-0 (75) S Drowne 7/2: 10-30410: 10th: Chsd ldrs, btn 2f out: much btr 4077 (g/s).   2   63
10 Ran   Time 1m 42.54(4.34)   Owned: Sheikh Ahmed Al Maktoum   Trained: Newmarket

---

CHEPSTOW   MONDAY 20.09.04   Lefthand, Undulating, Galloping Track

Official Going HEAVY

4703   2.20 Allprint Median Auction Maiden Stakes Div 1 2yo (F4)
            £3066 £876 £438   **7f16y str**   **Heavy 146**   **-01 Slow**   Stands side

       SONGERIE [1] Sir Mark Prescott 2-8-9 S Sanders 7/4 FAV: 1: b f Hernando - Summer Night   89+
(Nashwan) Rear, hdwy to lead 1.5f out, pushed out fnl 1f despite drifting right: nicely bckd: Mar 1st foal: dam a
6f wnr, sire top class at 12f: eff at 7f, will stay further: acts on hvy, gall/undul trk: runs well fresh: v
pleasing start, learn from this & rate higher in future.
3882 **MYSTERY LOT 39** [2] A King 2-8-9 J D Smith 5/2: 622: Mid-div, hdwy & ev ch well over 1f out, sn   5   77
carried right, not pace of wnr: clr of rem: handles gd & hvy: met a decent rival.
4330 **SCENT 18** [8] J L Dunlop 2-8-9 I Mongan 11/1: 503: Rear, hdwy 2f out, no impress fnl 1.5f.   5   67
4483 **CRYSTAL MYSTIC 11** [3] B Palling 2-9-0 bl F P Ferris(3) 40/1: 04: b c Anita's Prince - Out On Her   4   64
Own (Superlative) Led 1.5f out, wknd: half brother to a 6f juv wnr, sire smart sprinter.
       TURNOVER [5]2-8-9 D Corby(3) 25/1: 5: ch f Gold Away - Turn To Vodka (Polish Precedent) Slow   1¾   55+
away, kept on under hands & heels fnl 1f on debut: Feb 1st foal: dam smart, sire smart sprinter.
4416 **LITTLE INDY 14** [12]2-9-0 D Nolan(3) 100/1: 0006: Cl-up, wknd 1.5f out.   3   54
4483 **STRIKE GOLD 11** [6]2-9-0 T P Queally 7/2: 037: Rcd in 2nd till over 2f out, sn wknd.   ½   53
4422 **MONICAS REVENGE 14** [4]2-8-9 N Chalmers(5) 20/1: 08: Cl-up, wknd 2f out.   ¾   46
       PATRICIAN DEALER [7]2-9-0 V Slattery 33/1: 9: Slow away, nvr a factor on debut.   5   41
3975 **YOUNG BOLDRIC 35** [10]2-9-0 L Keniry(3) 66/1: 000: 10th: In tch, wknd after 3f.   6   29
       OAKLEY ABSOLUTE [9]2-9-0 Dane O'Neill 14/1: 0: 11th: Slow away, nvr a factor on debut: op 10/1.   5   19
11 Ran   Time 1m 30.15 (10.35)   Owned: Miss K Rausing   Trained: Newmarket

---

4704   2.55 Allprint Median Auction Maiden Stakes Div 2 2yo (F4)
            £3059 £874 £437   **7f16y str**   **Heavy 146**   **-05 Slow**   Stands side

3285 **KARLU 65** [7] J L Dunlop 2-9-0 I Mongan 2/1: 01: ch c Big Shuffle - Krim (Lagunas) Slow away,   81
hdwy over 2f out, led ins fnl 1f, rdn out: 9 wk abs: Feb foal, cost 32,000gns: half brother to a 2yo wnr: dam
unrcd, sire a top class sprinter: eff at 7f, shld stay further: acts on hvy, gall/undul trk: runs well fresh:
imprvd from debut & is open to further improvement.
       SPECTAIT [2] Sir Mark Prescott 2-9-0 S Sanders 8/1: 2: b g Spectrum - Shanghai Girl (Distant   ½   78+
Relative) Dwelt, hdwy when green halfway, styd on well under hands & heels fnl 1f to take 2nd on post debut: op 7/2:
Mar foal: dam a 5/6f wnr, sire smart performer at 8/10f: eff at 7f, 1m shld suit: acts on hvy: pleasing start,
learn from this & shld be winning shortly.
4052 **DUROOB 32** [11] E A L Dunlop 2-9-0 W Supple 7/4 FAV: 033: Mid-div, hdwy to lead 1f out, hdd ins   shd   77
fnl 1f, kept on: stays 7f on soft & hvy: shown enough last twice to find a race: see 4052.
3848 **MISS SUDBROOK 41** [10] D Haydn Jones 2-8-9 M Fenton 100/1: 04: ch f Daggers Drawn - Missed   2½   67
Opportunity (Exhibitioner) Mid-div, hdwy to lead well over 2f out, hdd 1f out, no extra: Apr foal, cost
E7,500: half sister to wnrs at 7f & 10f: dam a 7f 2yo scorer, sire smart 2yo at 6/7f: prob stays 7f on hvy.
       MAXAMILLION [8]2-9-0 T P Queally 8/1: 5: Slow away, hdwy & ev ch 1f out, sn edged left & btn.   ½   71
       VALIANT ACT [6]2-8-9 C Catlin 20/1: 6: Cl-up, no impress ins fnl 1f: op 33/1, debut.   3   60

1421

CHEPSTOW   MONDAY 20.09.04   Lefthand, Undulating, Galloping Track

4269 **DEWIN COCH 21** [5]2-9-0 B Swarbrick(5) 25/1: 07: Led early, ev ch dist, carried left & wknd fnl 1f.   ½   64
4576 **GRAND GIRL 6** [12]2-8-9 A Daly 40/1: 008: Nvr a factor: quick reapp.   3½   52
4269 **FLOWER SEEKER 21** [9]2-8-9 S Whitworth 66/1: 09: Slow away, nvr a factor.   11   30
3824 **SOUTHERN TIDE 42** [3]2-9-0 N Mackay(3) 25/1: 000: 10th: Led after 2f till over 2f out.   7   21
4484 **BREGO 11** [1]2-9-0 BL R Havlin 16/1: 000: 11th: Mid-div, wknd 3f out, t.o.: tried blnks.   21   0
11 Ran   Time 1m 30.42 (10.62)   Owned: Pat Eddery Racing (Rainbow Quest)   Trained: Arundel

4705   3.30 European Breeders Fund Maiden Stakes 2yo (D3)
£3572 £1099 £550   6f16y str   Heavy 146   -12 Slow   Stands side

4443 **DALDINI 13** [5] J A Osborne 2-9-0 T P Queally 3/1: 41: Mid-div, hdwy over 2f out, led over 1f   82
out, drvn out ins fnl 1f: op 6/1: eff at 6f, shld apprec further: acts on hvy, gall/undul trk: improved from
recent debut, came go on from here: see 4443.
4540 **ARCHIE GLENN 8** [2] M S Saunders 2-9-0 P McCabe 4/1: 0042: Keen, led 3f, rem prom, ev ch fnl 1f,   ½   79
kept on: clr of rem: acts on fast & hvy: shown enough last twice to win a race: see 4540.
2437 **INAGH 98** [8] M J Wallace 2-8-9 D Corby(3) 33/1: 63: b f Tipsy Creek - Compton Amber (Puissance)   3½   63
Cl-up, hdwy to lead 3f out, hdd over 1f out, no extra: long abs: Jan foal, cost 6,000 gns: dam plcd over 5/7f,
later plcd over timber: sire smart juv: some improvement from debut here.
3418 **RAPID ROMANCE 58** [6] E A L Dunlop 2-8-9 W Supple 11/1: 564: Mid-div, hdwy 2f out, onepcd fnl 1f.   nk   62
       DEVILS ISLAND [7]2-9-0 S Sanders 4/1: 5: b c Green Desert - Scandalette (Niniski) Rear, nvr a   6   49
factor on debut: Mar foal, cost 50,000 gns: half brother to smart miler Gateman: dam unrcd, sire a smart 2yo, later
top class sprinter/miler: not handle hvy?
3991 **MYTORI 35** [1]2-8-9 S Whitworth 100/1: 066: Cl-up, no impress over 2f out: see 3991.   9   17
       FLYING HIGHEST [4]2-8-9 Dane O'Neill 15/8 FAV: 7: b f Spectrum - Mainly Sunset (Red Sunset)   1   14
Mid-div, no impress over 2f out on debut: Mar foal, cost 36,000 gns: half sister to sev sprint wnrs: dam once rcd,
sire top class 8/10f rnr: more expected here, not handle this hvy grnd?
7 Ran   Time 1m 18.31 (9.51)   Owned: Mr Paul J Dixon   Trained: Upper Lambourn

4706   4.00 Allprint Nursery Handicap Stakes 2yo 0-75 (E3)   [79]
£4134 £1272 £636   5f16y str   Heavy 146   -06 Slow   Stands side

4536 **CREE 8** [6] W R Muir 2-8-8 (59) S Sanders 2/1 FAV: 0525231: Trkd ldrs, hdwy to lead ent fnl 1f,   68
soon veered right, drvn out: eff at 5/6f on fast & hvy, sharp/undul or gall trk: 1st win, relished these conds.
4543 **LIGHTED WAY 7** [11] A M Balding 2-8-12 (63) L Keniry(3) 5/2: 06222: Cl-up, hdwy to lead over 2f   2   66
out till ent fnl 1f, no extra: quick reapp: stays 5/5.5f on gd & hvy: gd eff: see 4052.
2450 **KNOCK BRIDGE 98** [10] P D Evans 2-9-0 (65) Joanna Badger 16/1: 4203: Slow away, hdwy over 1f out,   shd   67+
styd on well under hands & heels fnl 1f: long abs: 6f will suit based on this: acts on firm & hvy: see 2083.
4483 **ROBMANTRA 11** [2] B J Llewellyn 2-8-12 p (63) S Whitworth 33/1: 653604: Rear, styd on fnl 1f.   1¾   60
4457 **MISS MALONE 12** [7]2-9-6 (71) Dane O'Neill 4/1: 0024005: Led over 2f, no extra fnl 1f: op 13/2.   1¼   64
4580 **WORTH A GRAND 6** [5]2-9-1 (66) J F McDonald(3) 16/1: 05506: Handy till over 3f out, keeping on   ½   57
when not clr run ins fnl 1f: quick reapp, op 12/1: shade closer with a clr run: see 3110.
4121 **LIMONIA 28** [1]2-9-0 (65) C Catlin 11/1: 56067: Cl-up, no impress ins fnl 1f: see 1531.   hd   55
4396 **ROKO 15** [8]2-8-8 vis (59) W Supple 12/1: 0433108: In tch, btn 1f out: op 16/1.   ¾   47
2017 **LADY ERICA 117** [9]2-8-8 (59) L Enstone 20/1: 25439: Dsptd lead, wknd over 1f out: long abs.   2   14
9 Ran   Time 1m 4.41 (7.61)   Owned: Inflite Partners   Trained: Lambourn

4707   4.30 Arthur Llewellyn Jenkins Classified Stakes 3yo+ 0-50 (G4)
£3087 £882 £441   7f16y str   Heavy 146   -17 Slow   Stands side

4368 **SEMPER PARATUS 17** [17] V Smith 5-9-3 bl (47) M Tebbutt 4/1 FAV: 2030001: Rear, hdwy over 2f out,   55
rdn out/carried right ins fnl 1f, led cl-home: eff at 6f, suited by 7f on firm, hvy & f/sand, prob any trk: see 74.
4345 **ZHITOMIR 18** [15] M Dods 6-9-3 (48) L Enstone 5/1: 6616402: Rear, hdwy over 1f out, carried right   nk   53
ins fnl 1f, kept on: acts on firm & hvy: gd run: just btr 3324 (sell).
3846 **AMBER FOX 41** [5] P D Evans 3-8-11 (45) R Havlin 50/1: 04-56503: Rear, hdwy to lead over 2f out,   nk   49
edged right fnl 1f, hdd cl-home: 6 wk abs: eff at 7f on hvy: gd run: see 1908.
4616 **WOOD FERN 5** [13] M R Channon 4-9-3 (49) C Catlin 10/1: 0061004: Cl-up, hdwy & ev ch over 2f out,   2   48
onepcd 1f out: quick reapp: acts on firm, hvy & polytrack: shade below wng form of 4164 (sell).
4616* **HALCYON MAGIC 5** [19]6-9-3 bl (46) Laura Pike(7) 7/1: 0206015: Held up stands side, hdwy over 2f   shd   47
out, kept on ins fnl 1f: quick reapp: handles firm & hvy, acts on fast & gd/soft: fair run, see 4616.
4474 **SEVEN SHIRT 11** [10]3-9-0 (50) R Miles(3) 50/1: 400-0006: Dsptd lead & edged to far rail over   ½   46
3f out, hdd over 2f out, no extra: see 4057.
4202 **NIGHT WORKER 24** [18]3-9-0 (45) Dane O'Neill 25/1: 0650007: Bhd, hdwy over 2f out, onepace.   nk   45
4616 **MY GIRL PEARL 5** [16]4-9-0 (50) N Mackay(3) 9/2: 1036148: Cl-up till over 3f out, kept on fnl 1f.   1¼   39
4370 **DEXILEOS 16** [20]5-9-3 t (45) N Chalmers(5) 33/1: 0073609: Slow away stands side, hdwy 2f out, sn btn.   hd   41
4346 **PHAROAHS GOLD 18** [4]6-9-3 p (48) S Whitworth 14/1: 4000000: 10th: Rear, hdwy over 1f out, no dngr.   1   39
4368 **BARABELLA 17** [2]3-8-11 (47) V Slattery 25/1: 5045000: 11th: Rear, nvr a factor: see 1404.   6   24
3790 **CHATSHOW 44** [12]3-9-0 (50) I Mongan 10/1: 0405000: 12th: Cl-up, no impress over 1f out: op   2½   22
20/1, 6 wk abs: now with A Carroll: see 3091.
4488 **SUPER SONG 11** [14]4-9-3 VIS t (48) F P Ferris(3) 16/1: 0006000: 13th: Keen in tch, led over 5f out   nk   21
till over 3f out, no extra 2f out: tried a visor: see 1214.
4043 **BACK IN SPIRIT 32** [11]4-9-3 t (40) G Gibbons 33/1: 0000240: 14th: Led over 1f, no extra over 1f out.   10   1
4113 **DREAM OF DUBAI 30** [7]3-8-11 BL (48) Hayley Turner(3) 40/1: 0000000: 15th: Slow away, rear, t.o.: blnks.   16   0
4116 **EMPEROR CAT 29** [6]3-9-0 (45) P Bradley 40/1: 0000660: 16th: Handy, no impress over 2f out, t.o..   7   0
16 Ran   Time 1m 31.23 (11.43)   Owned: Exeter Stables Partnership   Trained: Newmarket

CHEPSTOW MONDAY 20.09.04 Lefthand, Undulating, Galloping Track

4708 **5.00 Country Land & Business Association Raceday 2nd Oct Hcap 3yo 46-55 (F4)** **[67]**
£3349 £957 £478 **1m2f36y** **Heavy 146** **-20 Slow** Inside

4299 **COTTON EASTER 21** [8] Mrs A J Bowlby 3-8-10 (49) R Thomas(3) 3/1 FAV: 0600031: Rear, hdwy over 3f out, led over 1f out, rdn out ins fnl 1f: eff at 10f on hvy, gall/undul trk: 1st win, confirmed recent improvement. **55**
4421 **TARTIRUGA 14** [5] L G Cottrell 3-8-7 (1oh) (45) A Daly 8/1: 0000562: Keen, led after 1f till over 6f out, led again 3f out, hdd over 1f out, no extra: clr of rem: stays 10f on hvy: see 3900. *1½* **48**
CHARLOTTINE 54 [1] M P Sunderland 3-9-1 P (54) S Sanders 7/1: 5053503: b f Spectrum - Lady Dulcinea (General) Mid-div, hdwy 4f out, no impress over 1f out: 8 wk abs: Brit bow: 3rd earlier in '04 in native Ireland (h'cap, 1m, firm): mdn & nurs unplcd in '02: tried cheek piece & blnks. *5* **48**
4485 **FIZZY LADY 11** [7] N E Berry 3-8-11 t (50) C Catlin 9/1: 0000024: Bhd, hdwy 3f out, onepcd over 1f out. *3* **39**
4202 **FARNBOROUGH 24** [12]3-8-9 (48) R Miles(3) 7/1: 0000045: Bhd, hdwy over 3f out, no impress fnl 1f. *1½* **35**
4195 **PLEASURE SEEKER 24** [4]3-8-13 (52) I Mongan 33/1: 00-00006: b f First Trump - Purse (Pursuit of Love) Rear, hdwy over 4f out, no impress over 1f out: mdn & auct unplcd in '03 (rtd 55). *1¼* **37**
4182 **AMWELL BRAVE 25** [3]3-9-2 (55) T P Queally 7/1: 0500067: Rear, hdwy over 5f out, no impress 2f out. *8* **28**
3906 **ACUZIO 39** [2]3-9-2 (55) B Swarbrick(5) 12/1: 6040058: Cl-up, no impress over 3f out. *7* **17**
4111 **STYLISH DANCER 30** [10]3-8-7 (1oh) (45) R Havlin 25/1: 050609: In tch, wknd 2f out: see 2222. *1¾* **5**
3899 **UNINTENTIONAL 39** [6]3-8-13 (52) D Nolan(3) 33/1: 2-6060P0: 10th: Led over 6f out till 3f out. *¾* **10**
4202 **MR STROWGER 24** [13]3-8-7 (1oh) (45) W Supple 25/1: 000-6300: 11th: Led 1f, rem cl-up, no extra 3f out. *nk* **3**
4487 **UNCLE JOHN 11** [9]3-9-2 (55) Dane O'Neill 5/1: 0424000: 12th: Cl-up, no impress over 3f out, t.o. *18* **0**
12 Ran Time 2m 20.74 (16.64) Owned: The Reg Partnership Trained: Wantage

4709 **5.30 Jump Season Begins Here Saturday 2nd October Handicap Stakes 3yo 56-70 (E3)** **[77]**
£3986 £1227 £613 **1m14y str** **Heavy 146** **+12 Fast** Stands side

4452 **DANIFAH 13** [8] P D Evans 3-9-0 (63) D Nolan(3) 12/1: 4611301: Made all, drvn out to hold on ins fnl 1f: fast time: eff at 5f/1m on firm & hvy, prob any trk, loves Chepstow: tough, loves to force the pace: see 2118. **72**
4300* **SMOOTHLY DOES IT 21** [13] Mrs A J Bowlby 3-9-3 (66) R Thomas(3) 2/1 FAV: 0604012: Rear, hdwy over 3f out, onepcd fnl 1f: clr of rem: acts on fast & hvy: gd run, continues in fine form: see 4300. *1¼* **71**
4252 **PREMIER ROUGE 22** [3] E F Vaughan 3-9-4 (67) S Sanders 7/2: 44323: Rear, hdwy 4f out, rcd in 2nd 2f out till onepcd ins fnl 1f: see 4252. *3* **66**
4252 **NIGHT FROLIC 22** [1] J W Hills 3-8-10 (59) T P Queally 12/1: 1306604: Mid-div, hdwy into 2nd 3f out to 2f out, no impress ins fnl 1f: see 1953. *¾* **56**
4546 **FLEET ANCHOR 7** [14]3-8-7 (4oh) (52) C Catlin 8/1: 0002535: Keen & cl-up, no impress over 1f out. *8* **37**
4054 **LIGNE DEAU 32** [9]3-8-7 (3oh) (53) F P Ferris(3) 25/1: 0536606: In tch, hdwy 3f out, no impress 1f out. *1* **35**
4182 **WAZIRI 25** [6]3-9-7 (70) L Fletcher(3) 12/1: 4-100307: Cl-up, no impress over 2f out. *2* **45**
3732 **PRIMESHADE PROMISE 46** [12]3-8-8 (57) R Price 33/1: 0038: Al bhd: btr 3732 (gd). *4* **24**
1534 **SUCHWOT 139** [11]3-8-9 (58) R Havlin 16/1: 600-0629: Slow away, nvr a factor: long abs. *10* **5**
4546 **DESERT HAWK 7** [7]3-9-3 (66) Dane O'Neill 10/1: 5400620: 10th: Al bhd: qck reapp. *nk* **12**
4281 **INK IN GOLD 21** [2]3-8-7 (1oh) (55) P Bradley 40/1: 0500: 11th: In tch, rear & btn 3f out: see 4216. *shd* **1**
2951 **GREEN RIDGE 79** [10]3-8-11 (60) Hayley Turner(3) 28/1: 06-24000: 12th: In tch, no impress over 2f out: long abs: now with Miss A Newton-Smith. *8* **0**
2840 **ATHBOY 82** [4]3-9-5 vis (68) D Corby(3) 20/1: 0-011000: 13th: Bhd, nvr nr ldrs: abs: btr 729 (polytrk). *6* **0**
13 Ran Time 1m 42.62(10.72) Owned: Mr E A R Morgans Trained: Abergavenny

KEMPTON MONDAY 20.09.04 Righthand, Flat, Fair Track

Official Going Good/Firm (Last race abandoned because of unsafe ground)

4710 **2.10 Norman Hill Memorial E B F Maiden Stakes Div 1 Fillies 2yo (D3)**
£5265 £1620 £810 **7f rnd** **Good/Firm 31** **-16 Slow** Inside

FEN SHUI 0 [7] Saeed bin Suroor 2-8-11 L Dettori 3/1 FAV: 1: b f Timber Country - Crystal Gazing (El Gran Senor) Prom, led 2f out, pushed clr, eased cl-home, val 8L+: tchd 4/1 on debut: Mar foal, half-sister to wnrs at sprint dists/10f: dam 7f Gr 3 wnr: sire high-class performer around 9f: eff at 7f, further will suit: acts on fast grnd & goes well fresh: impressive debut & has a v bright future. **97+**
4329 **ABIDE 18** [8] R Hannon 2-8-11 R Hughes 11/2: 62: ch f Pivotal - Ariadne (Kings Lake) Dsptd lead 5f, kept on but no ch with easy wnr, eased cl home: Mar foal, cost 30,000gns: half-sister successful abroad: dam successful in Germany: eff at 7f on fast grnd: caught a smart sort, win sn. *6* **80**
PHOEBE WOODSTOCK 0 [4] P W Harris 2-8-11 E Ahern 20/1: 3: ch f Grand Lodge - Why So Silent (Mill Reef) Mid-div, sltly outpcd 3f out, rallied ins fnl 1f, no ch with wnr: debut: Apr foal, half-sister to wnrs at 7/10f, incl Group wnr Leporello: dam unrcd: pleasing start, will improve. *1¼* **78+**
WITWATERSRAND 0 [10] B W Hills 2-8-11 M Hills 16/1: 4: b f Unfuwain - Valley of Gold (Shirley Heights) Held up, eff when short of room 2f out & again dist, switched & kept on cl-home: debut: Apr foal, half-sister to wnrs at 7f/2m: dam decent performer at mid-dists: sire decent mid-dist performer, showed signs of greeness & looks sure to improve for today's experience when tried over further. *1½* **75**
SHINY THING 0 [6]2-8-11 D Kinsella 33/1: 5: Nvr nrr than mid-div: debut. *½* **74**
3817 **ROSAPENNA 42** [9]2-8-11 (64) D Holland 33/1: 5056: Stumbled after start, bhd, prog when short of room bef 2f out, switched & kept on late: 6 wk abs. *¾* **72$**
BEST ABOUT 0 [12]2-8-11 T R L Moore 11/1: 7: Sn in tch, prog well over 1f out, wknd ins fnl 1f: t-strap. *nk* **71**
3063 **PAPALITY 74** [1]2-8-11 T Quinn 4/1: 58: Dsptd lead 5f, wknd: 11 wk abs: failed to build on 3063. *1* **69**
TI ADORA 0 [11]2-8-11 A McCarthy 12/1: 9: Prom 5f, fdd on debut. *1* **67**
ZAVILLE 0 [13]2-8-11 M Henry 25/1: 0: 10th: Prom 4f, wknd fnl 2f on debut. *½* **66**
ROYAL JELLY 0 [2]2-8-11 J Fortune 12/1: 0: 11th: Al in rear on debut. *nk* **65**
MISS TOLERANCE 0 [14]2-8-11 K Fallon 11/1: 0: 12th: Sn cl-up, fdd fnl 2f on debut. *nk* **64**
1911 **SMART DAWN 121** [15]2-8-11 S Hitchcott 66/1: 00: 13th: In tch, fdd bef 1f out. *¾* **62**
Pavilion 0 [3]2-8-11 F Norton 33/1:0 4442 **Rockys Girl 13** [5]2-8-11 K Darley 50/1:0

15 Ran   Time 1m 27.44 (3.34)   Owned: Godolphin   Trained: Newmarket

---

4711   2.45 Norman Hill Memorial E B F Maiden Stakes Div 2 Fillies 2yo (D3)
£5265 £1620 £810   **7f rnd**   **Good/Firm 31   -41 Slow**   Inside

3251 **QUICKFIRE** 66 [2] Sir Michael Stoute 2-8-11 K Fallon 8/13 FAV: 21: Keen prom, led 2f out, hung   92
badly ins fnl 1f towards stands rail, pushed out to hold on, val bit more: bckd at odds on: 9 wk abs: eff at 6f,
impr for step up to 7f, 1m will suit: acts on fast: goes well fresh: will improve again.
4329 **LOVE ALWAYS** 18 [3] Mrs A J Perrett 2-8-11 L Dettori 4/1: 42: Prom, styd on to chase wnr from   1¾   85
dist, kept on but al held: acts on fast or gd grnd: gd run in defeat & can sn go one better: see 4329.
     AUNT JULIA 0 [8] R Hannon 2-8-11 R Hughes 50/1: 3: b f In The Wings - Original (Caerleon)   1   83
Mid-div, hdwy over 2f out, kept on ins fnl 1f, hands & heels: debut: Feb first foal, cost 21,000gns: dam unrcd:
sire high-class performer at mid-dists: eff at 7f, looks sure to appr further: acts on fast grnd.
     SEVEN MAGICIANS 0 [10] Sir Michael Stoute 2-8-11 K Darley 25/1: 4: b f Silver Hawk - Mambo   ¾   81+
Jambo (Kingmambo) Held up, styd on strongly for hands & heels fnl 1f, nrst fin: Mar foal, half-sister to useful
mid-dist performer: dam successful at 12f: eff at 7f, will relish 1m+: acts on fast grnd: most promising start, type
to win plenty of races, one for the notebook.
4443 **PICKAPEPPA** 13 [4] 2-8-11 S Carson 66/1: 05: Cl-up, gd bef 3f out, hdd 2f out, sn no extra: see 4443.   ½   80
     CLARA BOW 0 [5] 2-8-11 M Hills 10/1: 6: b f Sadler's Wells - Brigid (Irish River) In tch wide   ¾   78
over 5f, no extra: debut: Mar foal, cost 750,000gns: sister to wnrs at 6/7f: dam successful at 1m.
     DANZARE 0 [11] 2-8-11 R Hills 16/1: 7: b f Dansili - Shot of Redemption (Shirley Heights)   3½   71
Missed break, nvr nrr than mid-div: debut: Feb foal, cost 11,000gns: half-sister to wnrs abroad: dam plcd abroad.
4447 **MISSIE BAILEYS** 13 [1] 2-8-11 J Fortune 33/1: 658: Nvr nrr than mid-div: quals for h'caps: see 4447.   hd   70
     SIGN OF LUCK 0 [14] 2-8-11 D Holland 20/1: 9: Cl-up 5f, wknd on debut.   hd   69
     FRANELA 0 [6] 2-8-11 R L Moore 33/1: 0: 10th: Keen bhd, nvr able to challenge.   2   65
     BALLET BALLON 0 [13] 2-8-11 M Henry 25/1: 0: 11th: In rear & ran green, nvr able to challenge.   3   59
4198 **IN THE SHADOWS** 24 [7] 2-8-11 T E Durcan 100/1: 00: 12th: Keen mid-div 5f, wknd.   3½   52
     ROMA VALLEY 0 [9] 2-8-11 E Ahern 66/1: 0: 13th: Mid-div 4f, grad wknd.   3½   45
3183 **MYSTERY MAID** 68 [12] 2-8-11 (45) A McCarthy 100/1: 06000: 14th: Rcd keenly, led, hdd bef 3f out, fdd.   4   37
14 Ran   Time 1m 29.18 (5.08)   Owned: Mr K Abdulla   Trained: Newmarket

---

4712   3.20 Dennis Hutchings E B F Maiden Stakes 2yo (D3)
£5304 £1632 £816   **1m rnd**   **Good/Firm 31   -30 Slow**   Inside

     AUSTRALIAN 0 [11] J H M Gosden 2-9-0 J Fortune 8/1: 1: b c Danzero - Auspicious (Shirley   88
Heights) In tch, styd on to lead 2f out, rdn out ins fnl 1f to hold on: debut: Feb foal, half-brother to 7f/1m wnr
Doctrine: dam smart performer around 10f: sire decent performer in Australia: eff at 1m, 10f+ will suit: acts on
fast grnd & goes well fresh: defied greenness to win here & looks sure to progress.
4393 **KERASHAN** 16 [6] Sir Michael Stoute 2-9-0 K Fallon 2/1: 42: Handy, sltly outpcd under press bef   nk   86
1f out, styd on well ins fnl 1f, nrst fin: bckd: apprec step up to 1m, further suit on this evidence: acts on
fast grnd: gd eff in defeat despite showing signs of greenness, can loose mdn tag sn: see 4393.
4455 **LESCAPADE** 13 [2] A M Balding 2-9-0 (85) D Holland 7/1: 3543: In tch, prog bef 1f out, styd on   nk   85
ins fnl 1f, not btn far in 3rd: eff at 7f, ran to form on step up to 1m: see 4455 & 3005.
     THE COMPOSER 0 [10] M Blanshard 2-9-0 F Norton 10/1: 4: b c Royal Applause - Superspring   nk   84+
(Superlative) Sn well bhd, ran green, hdwy over 1f out, 'flew home', nrst fin: debut: Mar foal, cost 26,000gns:
half-brother to wnr at 11f: dam unrcd: sire Gr 1 wnr at sprint dists: crying out for 10f & a v eye-catching run,
will improve bundles for this & win races.
     ASHKAL WAY 0 [12] 2-9-0 E Ahern 25/1: 5: ch c Ashkalani - Golden Way (Cadeaux Genereux) Prom,   shd   83
no extra under press well ins fnl 1f: debut: Jan first foal, dam 10f wnr: eff at 1m, 10f shld suit: acts on fast grnd.
     UNFURLED 0 [7] 2-9-0 T Quinn 14/1: 6: Bhd, prog 3f out, no impress fnl 1f: debut.   2   79
4297 **GOLDEN DYNASTY** 21 [1] 2-9-0 R Hughes 50/1: 0067: Al cl-up, no extra dist: see 3957.   1½   76
4356 **LOITOKITOK** 17 [4] 2-9-0 D Sweeney 66/1: 008: Keen handy 6f, sn wknd.   4   68
4355 **AMEEQ** 17 [9] 2-9-0 R Hills 1/1 FAV: 339: Led, hung left & hdd 2f out, wknd: bckd: 'hung left': btr 4355.   1   66
3811 **MOTHECOMBE DREAM** 43 [8] 2-9-0 K Darley 66/1: 00: 10th: Keen cl-up over 5f, fdd: 6 wk abs.   10   48
10 Ran   Time 1m 41.73 (4.93)   Owned: Sheikh Mohammed   Trained: Manton

---

4713   3.50 Renault Master Van Stakes Handicap 3yo 71-85 (D2)
£8420 £2591 £1295   **6f str**   **Good/Firm 31   +14 Fast**   Centre   [92]

4528* **WHOS WINNING** 9 [4] B G Powell 3-8-10 (74) T Quinn 9/1: 6021211: Made all stands side, al trav   86
well, pushed out ins fnl 1f, val 2L+: fast time: eff at 5/6f on firm & gd grnd: v progressive, see 4528.
4394 **WYATT EARP** 16 [1] J A R Toller 3-8-10 (74) K Darley 12/1: 6-010002: Held up stands side, hdwy to   1¼   81
chase wnr over 1f out, kept on ins fnl 1f, al held: back to best: see 1734.
4317* **CHIMALI** 19 [9] J Noseda 3-8-9 vis (73) E Ahern 13/2: 4-14313: Cl-up stands side, no extra from   3½   70
dist: 6lb higher than recent win in 4317 (first time visor).
3920 **KOSTAR** 38 [2] C G Cox 3-8-12 (76) R Smith 25/1: 4104: In tch stands side, prog 2f out, no extra fnl 1f.   ½   72
4048 **THE JOBBER** 32 [12] 3-9-0 (78) F Norton 16/1: 4062205: Cl-up far side, led that group after 4f,   1   71+
kept on ins fnl 1f, no ch with principals on stands side: gd eff on unfavoured far side.
4498 **BOHOLA FLYER** 10 [3] 3-9-0 (78) R Hughes 12/1: 1452056: In tch stands side, no extra bef 1f out.   ¾   69
4318 **EXTRA COVER** 19 [7] 3-8-7 bl (69) N De Souza(5) 33/1: 2316607: Missed break stands side, nvr nrr.   nk   61
4498 **ROYAL CHALLENGE** 10 [11] 3-9-1 (79) L Dettori 3/1 FAV: 2116328: Reared at start, bhd far side,   hd   68
hdwy bef 1f out, kept on, no ch with wnr far side ldr: v well bckd: not disgraced.
4350 **TOTALLY YOURS** 17 [8] 3-9-4 (82) Paul Eddery 33/1: 0405009: In tch stands side over 4f, wknd: btr 2136.   nk   70
4604 **TREGARRON** 5 [6] 3-8-9 (73) R L Moore 20/1: 1420300: 10th: Bhd stands side, nvr a factor: qck reapp.   ½   66
3188 **BATHWICK BILL** 68 [14] 3-9-3 (81) J Fortune 20/1: 0-062300: 11th: Bhd far side, nvr a factor: 10 wk abs.   hd   67
4482 **DESERT DREAMER** 11 [10] 3-9-4 (82) M Hills 7/1: 5060000: 12th: Cl-up far side till dist, wknd.   hd   67
4604 **SKYHARROR** 5 [5] 3-8-12 vis (76) D Holland 8/1: 5052340: 13th: In tch stands side 4f, wknd: qck reapp.   ½   60
4446 **BIG BRADFORD** 13 [16] 3-9-7 bl (85) D Kinsella 20/1: 0-200060: 14th: Led far side group 4f, fdd.   2   63
4091 **CHEROKEE NATION** 31 [13] 3-8-7 (70) K Fallon 12/1: 1103500: 15th: Bhd far side, nvr a factor.   2½   42
15 Ran   Time 1m 12.15 (1.05)   Owned: Tony Head and Caroline Andrus   Trained: Winchester

4714

4.20 Renault Trafic Van Handicap Stakes 3yo+ 71-85 (D2) [90]
£10278 £3163 £1581 1m rnd Good/Firm 31 +01 Fast Inside

4642 **BLUE TROJAN 3** [9] S Kirk 4-9-7 (83) D Holland 6/1 JT FAV: 4200021: Handy, styd on to lead well 94
over 1f out, sn hung left, rdn out: qck reapp: suited by around 7f/1m, stays sharp 10f: acts on firm, gd/soft &
fibresand: deserved compensation for 4642, in fine form.
4642 **JUST FLY 3** [7] S Kirk 4-8-10 (72) R L Moore 33/1: 3000002: Mid-div, hdwy 3f out, styd on to 1¼ 79
chase wnr when carr sltly left dist, kept on but al held ins fnl 1f: clr rem: eff at 6/7f, now stays 1m: slipped
back to a winning mark & can similar on this evidence: see 1817 & 518.
4500 **SATTAM 10** [1] M P Tregoning 5-9-3 vis (79) R Hills 8/1: 53210-23: Held up, hdwy over 2f out, kept 4 78
on ins fnl 1f, no ch with front 2: showed more on reapp in 4500.
4362* **ARKHOLME 17** [16] P Winkworth 3-9-3 bl (83) M Savage(5) 14/1: 2120314: Mid-div, hdwy over 1f out, hd 81
no impress well ins fnl 1f: showed more in 4362 (C/D).
4110 **LORIEN HILL 30** [6]3-8-7 (73) M Hills 25/1: 1020305: Bhd, hdwy wide 2f out, nrst fin: btr 3860. shd 70
4362 **PAGAN PRINCE 17** [8]7-9-2 (78) Lisa Jones 8/1: 110-0146: Mid-div wide, hdwy over 2f out, onepcd. shd 74
4265 **DR THONG 22** [15]3-9-3 (83) N De Souza(5) 9/1: 2410427: Keen cl-up, led 3f out, hdd well over 1f ¾ 77
out, wknd: showed more in 4265 (soft).
4482* **BORREGO 11** [10]4-8-13 bl (75) S Hitchcott 16/1: 0600418: Nvr nrr than mid-div: showed more in 4482. nk 68
4301 **GIOCOSO 21** [4]4-9-4 (80) K Darley 16/1: 0014549: Cl-up, ev ch 2f out, sn wknd: btr 4301. 1 71
4295 **DANCE ON THE TOP 21** [11]6-8-13 t (75) J Fortune 16/1: 1065000: 10th: Bhd, nvr nrr than mid-div. nk 65
4500 **MUSIC MAID 10** [14]6-8-7 (5oh) (64) A McCarthy 33/1: 0100000: 11th: Rear, nvr a factor: btr 2312. 1¾ 55
4469 **FRANKSALOT 12** [3]4-8-8 (70) T Quinn 16/1: 4541530: 12th: Mid-div wide over 6f, wknd: btr 4469. hd 55
4550 **TODLEA 7** [20]4-9-0 (76) L Dettori 6/1 JT FAV: 2310330: 13th: Cl-up, ev ch 2f out, sn lost action & eased. 3 55
4609 **SUPREME SALUTATION 5** [2]8-9-7 (83) M Howard(7) 33/1: 1410400: 14th: Handy 6f, wknd: qck reapp. shd 61
2620 **ILE MICHEL 91** [8]7-9-0 (76) D Sweeney 33/1: 0-004300: 15th: Al bhd: long abs: btr 2356. 1¼ 52
4378 **MISS MADAME 16** [19]3-8-3 (69) M Henry 25/1: 3612160: 16th: Led 5f, fdd: btr 3872. 14 20
4030 **MOLCON 33** [17]3-9-4 (84) W Ryan 20/1: 4401000: 17th: Al in rear: btr 3447. 17 5
4500 **MAREN 10** [12]3-9-2 t (82) K Fallon 13/2: 31-00: 18th: Bhd, no impress ins fnl 2f, eased ins fnl 1f. 1¾ 0
18 Ran Time 1m 39.25 (2.45) Owned: The Ex Katy Boys Trained: Upper Lambourn

4715

4.50 Renault Kangoo Van E B F Classified Stakes 3yo+ 0-90 (C1)
£12267 £4653 £2327 1m4f Good/Firm 31 -00 Slow Inside

4293 **CAMROSE 21** [1] J L Dunlop 3-8-9 (89) J Fortune 14/1: 1-432521: In tch, ev ch over 1f out, drvn 96
out to lead on line: eff at 10/11f, now stays 12f: acts on firm & gd/soft grnd: in fine form: see 4293.
3749 **ELMUSTANSER 45** [13] Saeed bin Suroor 3-9-0 t (95) L Dettori 4/1 FAV: 2122: Cl-up, led trav well shd 100
2f out, hdd under press on line: bckd: 6 wk abs: eff at 10f, ran to form on step up to 12f: see 3749 & 2534.
4324 **CREDIT 19** [10] R Hannon 3-8-9 (90) K Fallon 5/1: 0041333: Mid-div, prog 2f out, styd on ins fnl 2 92
1f, no ch with front 2: bckd: continues to run well: see 4324 & 3961.
4525 **VAUGHAN 9** [6] Mrs A J Perrett 3-8-9 (90) K Darley 16/1: 01-04: In tch, sltly outpcd over 2f out, hd 91
styd on ins fnl 1f: eff at 1m, against today's step up to 12f: acts on fast & soft grnd: still only lightly rcd.
3468 +**VINANDO 57** [4]3-8-13 t (94) M Hills 10/1: 5-1015: Cl-up, no extra from dist: 8 wk abs: btr 3468 (gd). nk 94
3029 **LUNAR EXIT 75** [5]3-8-11 (92) E Ahern 25/1: 315-606: Nvr nrr than mid-div: 11 wk abs: btr 2406. 4 86
4360* **OCEAN AVENUE 17** [12]5-9-3 (88) D Holland 17/2: 31-10617: Led 10f, sn wknd: showed more in 4360. hd 83
4324 **SECRETARY GENERAL 19** [11]3-8-13 (94) T Quinn 9/1: 0501228: Bhd, modest prog: bckd: btr 4324 (gd). 2 84
4219 **TIZZY MAY 23** [3]4-9-8 (95) T E Durcan 25/1: 0400559: Al in rear: see 1478. nk 84
4230 **WAIT FOR THE WILL 23** [9]8-9-3 bl (90) R L Moore 12/1: 0011250: 10th: Held up, nvr a factor: btr 3617. 2 76
4463 **POSTERITAS 12** [8]3-8-6 (88) R Hughes 10/1: 3215160: 11th: Held up when hmpd 4f out, sn wknd. 8 62
4228] **HASTY PRINCE 373** [14]6-9-3 (88) J Mackay 20/1: 01450/0-S: ch g Halling - Sister Sophie 0
(Effervescing) Bhd, slipped up on bend 4f out: long jumps abs, val h'cap & cond hdle wnr in 03/04 (rtd 165h, eff at
2m/2m4f on fast & hvy): unplcd sole '03 Flat start (rtd 84, h'cap): won 2 nov hdles in 02/03: h'cap wnr on Flat in
'02 (B Hanbury): eff at 10/12f on firm & gd/soft, stiff/gall trk: gd weight carrier.
1 Jul'02 Hayd 10.5g/f 92-86 C: 1 Jun'01 Donc 10.2g/f 85- D:
4324 **LARKWING 19** [2]3-8-9 (88) F Norton 5/1: 4-23125S: Bhd, slipped up on bend 4f out: btr 3534 & 1936. 0
13 Ran Time 2m 33.83(3.83) Owned: Mr Nicholas Cooper Trained: Arundel

Official Going GOOD/FIRM (FIRM places).

4716

2.10 Racing Uk On Channel 432 Selling Stakes 3yo+ (G4)
£3504 £1078 £539 1m4f16y Good/Firm 33 -49 Slow Inside

4512 **REGENCY RED 10** [6] W M Brisbourne 6-9-5 (46) B Swarbrick(5) 9/1: 2100/-401: Mid-div, prog 53
halfway, styd on to lead 2f out, sn clr, eased cl-home: op 14/1: eff at 12f/2m on firm & fast: likes sell grade.
4128 **STAFF NURSE 29** [11] Don Enrico Incisa 4-9-0 (35) Kim Tinkler 10/1: 0405332: Sn adrift, prog 4f 7 37
out, kept on fnl 1f, no ch with easy wnr: another plcd eff: see 4128 & 4045 (fibresand).
4340 **RIGHTY HO 19** [7] W H Tinning 10-9-10 (48) Kristin Stubbs(7) 8/1: 3306103: Mid-div, prog 5f out, 1 45
styd on to chase wnr dist, no extra ins fnl 1f: showed more in 3771 (14f).
4374 **COOLFORE JADE 17** [8] N E Berry 4-9-5 (40) M Savage(5) 10/1: 6300064: 10th: In tch, ev ch 2f out, no extra. 1½ 37
4364 **OUR IMPERIAL BAY 18** [2]5-9-10 p (40) A Daly 16/1: 0363005: Rear, nvr nrr than mid-div: btr 2724. hd 41
3370 **FORBEARING 61** [10]7-9-5 (62) D Sweeney 7/2: 1610-326: Chsd ldrs 10f, wknd: tchd 5/2, 9 wk abs & 1¾ 33
new stable, clmd for 6,000: disappointing on switch to J G M O'Shea yard: btr 3370 & 3211 (M C Pipe).
4512 **ELLWAY HEIGHTS 10** [3]7-9-5 (51) S W Kelly 13/8 FAV: 2253067: Led, hdd after 1f, led again 3f 6 24
out, hdd 2f out, fdd: bckd: disapp & reportedly bled from nose: showed more in 3530 & 2964.
4419 **GOLDEN FIELDS 15** [5]4-9-0 bl (45) M Fenton 25/1: 0020-008: Led after 1f, hdd 3f out, fdd. 6 10
4261 **SHAMELESS 23** [1]7-9-5 t R Keogh(7) 80/1: 009: Handy 1m, fdd: see 2381. 13 0
MODULOR 3459 [12]12-9-5 T Williams 40/1: 0////////-0: 10th: gr g Less Ice - Chaumontaise hd 0

(Armos) Bhd, adrift & nvr a factor: hdles fit, p.u. in 2 of 3 04/05 starts (rtd 84h at best, h'cap): 4th at best in 03/04 (h'cap hdle, earlier with M Pipe): well btn sole completed 02/03 start (Cheltenham Gold Cup, rtd 120c, eff at 2m/2m5f, prob stays 3m3f on firm & hvy, tried visor, t-strap & pieces).

3640} **BENVOLIO 403** [4]7-9-5 Natalia Gemelova(7) 66/1: 0///00-0: 11th: br g Cidrax - Miss Capulet   **¾**   **0**
(Commanche Run) In tch 1m, fdd: recently chase unplcd (amat h'cap): unplcd both '03 Flat starts.
11 Ran   Time 2m 41.20 (9.9)   Owned: Mrs J M Russell   Trained: Nesscliffe

---

4717   2.40 Children In Need Pantomime Horse Race Novice Stakes 2yo (D3)
£5512 £1696 £848   **5f rnd**   Good/Firm 33   -39 Slow   Inside

2490 **SHARPLAW STAR 97** [5] W J Haggas 2-9-0 M Hills 8/13 FAV: 131: Mid-div, prog halfway, led trav   **96**
well ins fnl 1f, pushed out, val 4L+: bckd at odds-on, long abs: eff over a stiff 5f, 6f shld suit: acts on fast & gd grnd: goes well fresh: won with a bit in hand & deserves return to List/Group grade.
3682 **CUTLASS GAUDY 48** [6] R Hollinshead 2-8-12 D Sweeney 100/1: 402: Rear, prog 2f out, kept on ins   2   **85**
fnl 1f, no ch with wnr: 7 wk abs: apprec return to 5f: acts on fast grnd: gd eff & must find a mdn.
3484* **SAFSOOF 57** [1] Saeed bin Suroor 2-9-5 (93) K McEvoy 11/4: 2013: Cl-up till halfway, kn outpcd,   nk   **91**
rallied ins fnl 1f, just held for 2nd: 8 wk abs: acts on fast, gd grnd & fibresand: not disgraced conceding weight all round & will apprec 6f: see 3484.
3303 **BOLD MARC 64** [4] K R Burke 2-9-4 (88) Darren Williams 16/1: 4121064: Handy till dist: 9 wk abs.   nk   **89**
4471 **BOLD MINSTREL 12** [2]2-9-2 (83) F Norton 20/1: 2124255: Led till ins fnl 1f: see 4198 (g/s).   nk   **86**
4551 **GLOVED HAND 8** [7]2-9-0 (89) A Culhane 9/1: 1006: Handy over 3f, wkng under press when short of   6   **68**
room bef 1f out, sn eased: op 15/2: again disapp, btr 2151 (debut).
6 Ran   Time 1m 04.91 (3.61)   Owned: Miss Tina Miller   Trained: Newmarket

---

4718   3.15 Violet And Eddie Smith Memorial Conditions Stakes 3yo+ (C2)
£8746 £3318 £1659   **5f rnd**   Good/Firm 33   -10 Slow   Inside

4481 **BALTIC KING 12** [5] H Morrison 4-8-9 t (104) S Drowne 7/4 FAV: 0-601361: Held up, prog & short of   **108**
room halfway, swtchd wide & styd on to lead ins fnl 1f, pushed clr, val 5L+: well bckd: stays 6f, suited by 5f: acts on firm & gd, poss handles soft grnd: eff in a t-strap: right back to form & List/Gr races await.
4481 **IF PARADISE 12** [6] R Hannon 3-8-8 (98) R Thomas(3) 14/1: 1060002: Cl-up, styd on to lead dist, sn   3½   **98**
hdd & not pace easy wnr: back to form with creditable eff: see 1106.
3937 **DAZZLING BAY 38** [9] T D Easterby 4-8-9 bl (99) D Allan 7/2: 0352003: Held up, prog wide 2f out,   hd   **97**
kept on ins fnl 1f, just held for 2nd: appreciate return to 6f: just btr 2949.
4588 **COLONEL COTTON 7** [12] N A Callaghan 5-8-9 vis (97) S W Kelly 7/2: 0306534: Bhd, prog when hmpd   nk   **96**
dist, switched & kept on ins fnl 1f: clr rem: qck reapp: see 4588 & 2913.
2758 **BONUS 87** [1]4-8-9 (98) M Hills 14/1: 15-60005: Chsd ldrs, wknd bef 1f out: poor low draw.   3½   **86**
stiff task from poor low draw: btr 1187.
4174 **BLUE CRUSH 26** [2]3-8-3 (85) P Hanagan 66/1: 0000006: In tch, wknd bef 1f out: poor low draw.   1¼   **77**
4585 **ABSENT FRIENDS 7** [10]7-8-9 (83) K McEvoy 6/1: 6000047: Led, hdd dist, wknd: qck reapp: btr 1917.   nk   **81**
4510 **GREY PEARL 10** [11]5-9-0 t P (86) M Fenton 25/1: 6041008: Handy 3f, wknd: first time pieces.   1½   **82**
4514 **STRENSALL 10** [8]7-8-9 (76) T Eaves(2) 40/1: 5055209: In tch over 3f, wknd: btr 4174.   1   **74**
4496 **BEYOND THE CLOUDS 11** [3]8-8-9 p (76) R Winston 20/1: 0300620: 10th: Sn cl-up, wknd 2f out.   5   **61**
10 Ran   Time 1m 03.49 (2.19)   Owned: Thurloe Thoroughbreds VIII   Trained: East Ilsley

---

4719   3.45 Paul And Lucy Woolfitt Happy Anniversary Handicap Stakes 3yo+ 56-70 (E3)   **[77]**
£5086 £1565 £783   **7f100y rnd**   Good/Firm 33   +04 Fast   Inside

4592 **GIFTED FLAME 7** [16] T D Barron 5-9-4 (67) P Makin(5) 5/1 FAV: 3143601: Chsd ldrs, prog 3f out,   **76**
styd on to lead bef 1f out, sn clr & idled, rdn out: qk reapp: eff at 7/8.4f on fm & gd, prob not hvy, likes Beverley.
4445 **MRS SHILLING 14** [15] J R Fanshawe 3-8-13 (65) R Winston 8/1: 6-342: In tch, prog when short of   1   **70**
room over 1f out, switched & kept on, nrst fin: eff at 7.4f, furthest off pace: acts on fast grnd: fine run.
4446 **ALCHEMIST MASTER 14** [4] R M Whitaker 5-9-7 (70) K McEvoy 11/1: 1463003: Held up, prog 2f out,   1   **73+**
staying on when short of room dist, kept on ins fnl 1f, nrst fin: fine run from poor low draw, shade unlucky.
4398 **NO GROUSE 16** [2] R A Fahey 4-9-0 p (63) P Hanagan 11/1: 0005054: Bhd, prog wide 2f out, kept on late.   shd   **65**
4241 **PRINCE OF GOLD 24** [6]4-8-13 p (62) D Sweeney 25/1: 0000005: In tch, staying on when short of room   hd   **63**
1f out, switched & kept on, nrst fin: showed more in 2324 (C/D).
4650 **CRYFIELD 4** [10]7-8-10 vis (59) Kim Tinkler 20/1: 6434006: Chsd ldrs, staying on when short of   1¼   **58**
room dist, switched & styd on ins fnl 1f: qck reapp: btr 2890.
4592 **DARA MAC 7** [14]5-8-10 (59) Suzanne France(7) 14/1: 0106047: Mid-div, prog when short of room over   ½   **57**
1f out, switched & hit in face with whip ins fnl 1f, no impress: qck reapp: not get run of race: btr 4592.
4438* **JUBILEE STREET 14** [9]5-8-13 (62) A Beech(3) 13/2: 0061218: Held up, prog wide 3f out, onepace.   nk   **59**
4554 **LEGAL SET 8** [8]8-8-11 t (60) D Tudhope(7) 16/1: 4500249: Handy over 5f, sn short of room & wknd dist.   5   **56**
4399+ **MOUNT HILLABY 16** [7]4-9-0 (63) T Lucas 13/2: 1002010: 10th: Led, edged wide on bend & hdd after   1½   **56**
2f, styd cl-up, wknd ins fnl 1f: showed more in 4399.
4117 **NEARLY A FOOL 30** [13]6-9-6 vis (69) N Pollard 20/1: 0134050: 11th: Prom, led after 2f, hdd over 1f out.   3   **56**
4399 **Gala Sunday 16** [3]4-8-11 (60) Dale Gibson 28/1:0
4589 **Zawrak 7** [12]5-8-12 vis(61) Natalia Gemelova(7) 14/1:0   4592 **Atlantic Ace 7** [11]7-9-0 p(63) D McGaffin 12/1:0
3215 **Captain Saif 68** [5]4-9-7 (70) T Hamilton(3) 16/1:0
15 Ran   Time 1m 32.98 (2.18)   Owned: Mr Raymond Miquel   Trained: Thirsk

---

4720   4.20 Brian Merrington Memorial Stakes Handicap 3yo+ 46-55 (F4)   **[68]**
£3681 £1133 £566   **1m1f207y**   Good/Firm 33   +10 Fast   Inside

4598* **EMPERORS WELL 6** [5] M W Easterby 5-9-7 (6ex)bl (61) T Lucas 15/2: 146-0311: Grabbed rail & made   **70**
all, clr bef 1f out, pushed out, val bit more: fast time: op 8/1 on qck reapp: eff at 1m/10f acts on fast & soft grnd, likes Beverley: eff with blnks & likes to force the pace: in-form 5yo who did well to defy 6lb pen: see 4598.
4348 **LIFE IS BEAUTIFUL 19** [15] W H Tinning 5-8-8 (48) R Winston 7/1: 1516242: Mid-div, prog 2f out,   ½   **53**

staying on when short of room bef 1f out, kept on ins fnl 1f, nrst fin: tchd 9/1: eff at 10f, return to 12f will suit.

4598 **SENOR EDUARDO 6** [14] S Gollings 7-9-0 (54) A Nicholls 25/1: 5162303: Handy, styd on ins fnl 1f, not btn far: qck reapp: back to form with creditable eff: see 4327 & 4133.		nk	58
4594 **WILD POWER 7** [13] J G M O'Shea 6-9-1 (55) D Sweeney 5/1 FAV: 0/230/-424: Chsd ldrs, eff over 1f out, no impress ins fnl 1f: qck reapp: just btr 4594 (12f).		1¼	57
4598 **TIME TO REGRET 6** [19]4-8-10 (50) T Eaves(3) 10/1: 0100025: Bhd, prog when short of room & switched over 1f out, styd on ins fnl 1f, nrst fin: qck reapp: eff at 7/9.3f, now stays 10f: see 4598 & 3242.		1	50
3726* **ROYAL RACER 47** [2]6-8-12 bl (52) N Pollard 16/1: 1360016: Handy over 1m, no extra: 7 wk abs.		½	51
4626 **ALPINE HIDEAWAY 5** [9]11-8-9 p (49) D Allan 33/1: 0-060107: Mid-div, prog over 2f out, no impress.		shd	47
4594 **FAIRY MONARCH 7** [16]5-8-9 p (49) R Fitzpatrick 20/1: 00-20208: Rear, nvr nrr than mid-div: qck reapp.		1	45
4612 **SHAMWARI FIRE 6** [18]4-8-9 (49) R Ffrench 12/1: 3001369: Nvr nrr than mid-div: qck reapp: btr 4373.		½	44
4456 **ELLOVAMUL 14** [12]4-8-11 (51) P Makin(5) 20/1: 4010000: 10th: Mid-div over 1m, sn onepcd: btr 3492.		nk	45
4145 **HIRAYNA 28** [10]5-8-8 (48) S W Kelly 14/1: 304400: 11th: Nvr nrr than mid-div: btr 3963.		nk	41
2788 **DANCE PARTY 86** [4]4-9-1 (55) Dale Gibson 22/1: 0040000: 12th: Bhd, modest gains: 12 wk abs.		1½	45
4202* **GRAND RAPIDE 25** [3]3-8-8 (54) S Drowne 40/1: 600410: 13th: Handy 1m, wknd.		½	43
4402 **BENEKING 5** [17]4-8-9 (49) A Culhane 14/1: 0605000: 14th: Bhd, prog 3f out, staying on when short of room dist, not recover: btr 2080.		¾	36
4598 **AQRIBAA 6** [11]6-8-12 (52) P Mulrennan(3) 40/1: 01000-00: 15th: Missed break, nvr a factor: qck reapp.		1¾	36
4620 **DONNAS DOUBLE 5** [6]9-8-9 p (49) K Darley 9/1: 3434620: 16th: Chsd ldrs, prog 3f out, fdd bef 1f out.		½	32
4594 **AMALFI COAST 7** [7]5-8-8 (48) D Tudhope(5) 100/1: 440U-000: 17th: Bhd, nvr a factor: qck reapp.		3	27
4970} **SHEER FOCUS 325** [1]6-8-8 P (48) Natalia Gemelova(7) 40/1: 604303-0: 18th: Prom, fdd 2f out: reapp.		8	16
4036 **UNO MENTE 34** [8]5-8-8 vis (48) Kim Tinkler 40/1: 6300000: 19th: Rear, nvr a factor.		nk	15

19 Ran   Time 2m 4.62 (2.32)   Owned: Mr M W Easterby   Trained: Sheriff Hutton

---

4721   4.50 Subscribe To Racing Uk On 08700 860432 Handicap Stakes 3yo 56-70 (E3)   [75]
£4355   £1340   £670   1m100y rnd   Good/Firm 33   -04 Slow   Inside

4334 **PELLA 19** [12] M Blanshard 3-9-2 (63) D Sweeney 9/1: 3230101: Mid-div, prog halfway, styd on for press to lead well ins fnl 1f, rdn out: acts on fast & gd/soft grnd: enjoys coming late.			68
4592 **HEVERSHAM 7** [17] J Hetherton 3-9-4 (65) M Tebbutt 5/1 FAV: 5000022: In tch, prog 2f out, styd on to lead disp, hdd under press cl-home: qck reapp: continues to run well & can find a race off this mark: see 4592.		nk	68
4251* **PRINCESS GALADRIEL 23** [16] J R Best 3-9-0 (61) K Darley 6/1: 2063613: Held up, prog 2f out, kept on ins fnl 1f, just held in 3-way photo: gd run: 5lb higher than recent win in 4251.		nk	63
4546 **CHARLIE TANGO 8** [6] N Tinkler 3-9-3 (64) R Winston 14/1: 4350004: Rear, prog 2f out, short of room over 1f out, sn switched & styd on: gd run from poor low draw: btr 2565.		¾	64
4339 **KINGSMAITE 19** [14]3-9-6 bl (67) J Bramhill 12/1: 4051305: Led, hdd dist, no extra: btr 4093 (7f, AW).		1¼	65
4260 **CHARMATIC 23** [5]3-9-4 (65) S Drowne 7/1: 2154506: Bhd, prog wide 2f out, styd on fnl 1f: poor draw.		¾	61
4554 **JOSHUAS GOLD 8** [10]3-8-10 vis (57) D Tudhope(7) 9/1: 1423057: Keen in tch, hung right & no extra dist.		nk	52
3419 **KALISHKA 59** [9]3-8-11 BL (58) A Nicholls 33/1: 00-65008: Bhd, prog halfway, kept on ins fnl 1f: blnks.		1¼	51
4438 **DARK DAY BLUES 14** [11]3-8-12 (59) Darren Williams 33/1: 0655009: Handy over 6f, wknd: btr 2295.		nk	51
4341 **SION HILL 19** [3]3-9-7 (68) J D O'Reilly(7) 66/1: 202-0000: 10th: Keen handy wide over 6f, wknd.		¾	58
4546 **CAPITOLE 8** [7]3-9-0 vis (61) K McEvoy 7/1: 04540: 11th: Al in rear: btr 4546.		¾	49
4282 **CAYMAN CALYPSO 22** [15]3-9-3 (64) P Hanagan 16/1: 6062200: 12th: Mid-div over 6f, wknd: btr 3850.		1¾	48
341 **FREDDIE FRECCLES 258** [13]3-9-4 (65) M Fenton 33/1: 10-60: 13th: In tch over 6f, wknd: long abs.		shd	48
4593 **TRUE 7** [2]3-8-11 (58) R Thomas(3) 14/1: 3406020: 14th: Bhd, nvr a factor.		1½	38
3828 **SPES BONA 43** [4]3-8-12 (59) A Culhane 14/1: 0400: 15th: Bhd, nvr a factor.		1¼	37
1030 **IT MUST BE SPEECH 172** [1]3-8-13 (60) R Fitzpatrick 40/1: 000-5250: 16th: Mid-div 5f, fdd: been gelded.		8	24
3177 **ALWAYS FLYING 70** [8]3-9-0 (61) P Mulrennan(3) 20/1: 2660200: 17th: Chsd ldrs wide over 5f, fdd.		5	16

17 Ran   Time 1m 46.95(3.15)   Owned: The Pella Partnership   Trained: Upper Lambourn

---

Official Going GOOD/FIRM. Strong tailwind made pace figs dubious.

4722   2.20 Robinsons Mercedes-Benz Median Auction Maiden Stakes 2yo (E3)
£4358   £1341   £671   1m str   Firm   Inapplicable   Centre

4356 **FORWARD MOVE 18** [7] R Hannon 2-9-0 R L Moore 2/1 FAV: 21: Cl-up, led halfway & rdn clr over 1f out, impressive: hvly bckd, confirmed debut promise: eff at 1m, 10f+ may suit: acts on firm & fast grnd, stiff/gall or easy trks: looks v useful & the type to make his mark in List/Gr company: see 4356.			101+
4026 **MY PUTRA 34** [4] P F l Cole 2-9-0 T Quinn 5/1: 32: Handy, kept on fnl 2f, no ch with wnr: styd longer 1m trip, handles firm & gd/soft grnd: showed enough to find a race: see 4026 (6f).		5	87
4289 **PATRONAGE 22** [9] M L W Bell 2-9-0 K Fallon 11/2: 553: Dwelt, sn trkd ldrs, shaken up & styd on fnl 1f, no threat to easy wnr: styd longer 1m trip, handles firm & gd grnd: h'caps may now suit.		shd	87
MAIDANNI [11] Saeed bin Suroor 2-9-0 L Dettori 5/1: 4: b c Private Terms - Carley's Birthday (Marfa) Chsd ldrs, no extra fnl dist: Mar foal, dam a multiple US scorer & sire a top-class 9f dirt performer: handles firm grnd: not knocked about, likely improver.		1½	82
2594 **ROBESON 94** [15]2-9-0 L Keniry(3) 100/1: 05: br g Primo Dominie - Montserrat (Aragon) Trkd ldrs, outpcd fnl 2f: Feb foal, half-brother to a dual 6f/7f juv wnr, dam a 5f juv wnr: imprvd from entries.		1¾	77
4522 **ROYAL JET 10** [18]2-9-0 D Holland 7/1: 36: Pushed mid-div, no impress fnl 2f: btr 4522.		nk	76
4194 **SCARP 25** [8]2-9-0 E Ahern 50/1: 007: b c Gulch - Rhetorical Lass (Capote) Chsd ldrs, no impress fnl 1f: Mar foal, half-bother to 6f juv wnr, also a 1m 3yo scorer: dam uncrd, related to a top-class mid-dist performer: breathing suggests mid-dists will suit.		3	67
ELOQUENT KNIGHT [1]2-9-0 S Sanders 33/1: 8: Dwelt, late gains, nvr a factor.		1¼	63
PENNY WEDDING [10]2-8-9 W Ryan 33/1: 9: Dwelt & towards rear, nvr a threat.		1¼	54
3869 **THREE BOARS 41** [2]2-9-0 J Fortune 66/1: 00: 10th: Al towards rear: 6 wk abs.		2½	51
ROYAL SAILOR [5]2-9-0 J Tate 50/1: 0: 11th: Mid-div, no impress fnl 2f.		nk	50
4115 **SPEEDIE ROSSINI 30** [6]2-9-0 BL A McCarthy 66/1: 0000: 12th: Led till halfway, sn fdd: blnks.		1¾	45
SWORDS [13]2-9-0 C Catlin 66/1: 0: 13th: Slow away & al outpcd rear.		nk	44
ROSS MOOR [14]2-9-0 P Robinson 66/1: 0: 14th: Dwelt, in tch till over 2f out.		4	32
Chief Dipper [17]2-9-0 T P Queally 66/1:0			

Polish Index [12]2-9-0 T E Durcan 100/1:0   **La Musique** [3]2-9-0 J Mackay 66/1:0
~~Fantastic Luck~~ [16]2-9-0 G Carter 40/1:0
18 Ran   Time 1m 35.70 (u0.8)   Owned: The Queen   Trained: Marlborough

---

4723
2.50 Robinsons Mercedes-Benz E B F Maiden Stakes Fillies 2yo   (D2)
£5538 £1704 £852   **1m str**   **Firm**   **Inapplicable**   Centre

4359 **TITIAN TIME 18** [11] J H M Gosden 2-8-11   J Fortune 11/4 JT FAV: 231: Made all, rdn & styd on strongly ins last: well bckd, confirmed prev promise: eff at 7f/1m on firm & fast grnd, stiff/gall or easy trks: could prove useful: see 4359 & 3959.   **91**

4450 **HALLOWED DREAM 14** [8] C E Brittain 2-8-11   T P Queally 66/1: 0002: b f Alhaarth - Salul (Soviet Star) Handy & keen, rdn & styd on ins last, not pace of wnr: imprvd over this longer 1m trip: Feb foal, half-sister to 7f/1m wnrs: eff at 1m on firm, 10f may suit: handles a stiff/gall trk: going the right way.   **1¼**   **87**

RUSSIAN REVOLUTION [12] Saeed bin Suroor 2-8-11   L Dettori 11/4 JT FAV: 3: b f Dubai Millennium - Russian Snows (Sadler's Wells) Al prom, rdn & onepace bef dist: t-strap on debut: half-sister to a useful 10f 3yo scorer, dam a smart 10/12f performer: eff at 1m, mid-dist pedigree: handles firm grnd & a stiff/gall trk: likely improver, particularly when tackling further.   **1¼**   **84**

4330 **TAMALAIN 19** [4] Mrs A J Perrett 2-8-11   R L Moore 7/1: 54: Chsd ldrs, kept on onepace ins last: styd longer 1m trip: prob handles firm & gd grnd: see 4330.   **½**   **83**

AYAM ZAMAN [6]2-8-11   P Robinson 33/1: 5: b f Montjeu - Kardashina (Darshaan) Held up & keen early, outpcd 3f out, styd on eye-catchingly ins last, nrst fin: 95,000gns Feb foal, half-sister to 3yo wnrs at 10/12f: dam a multiple mid-dist wnr: eff at 1m, looks sure to relish further: handles firm grnd: expect improvement & one to keep in mind.   **¾**   **82+**

4450 **BAZELLE 14** [9]2-8-11 (83) S Sanders 15/2: 0426: Chsd ldrs till dist: btr 4450.   **nk**   **81**
BASSERAH [10]2-8-11   R Hills 25/1: 7: Slow away, chsd ldrs, no extra fnl 1f: clr rem.   **nk**   **80**
DANCINGINTHECLOUDS [5]2-8-11   T Quinn 10/1: 8: Slow away, only mod prog.   **6**   **68**
4329 **RED DUCHESS 19** [7]2-8-11   K Fallon 8/1: 09: Held up, no impress from halfway.   **5**   **58**
SHADES OF GREEN [14]2-8-11   D Holland 33/1: 0: 10th: Prom, lost place after 2f, nvr a factor.   **½**   **57**
4355 **OUR KES 18** [13]2-8-11   J Mackay 100/1: 000: 11th: Held up & no ch fnl 3f.   **½**   **55**
4358 Cup Of Love 18 [1]2-8-11 E Ahern 66/1:0   Queen Tomyra [3]2-8-11 N Mackay(3) 16/1:0
Tale Of Dubai [15]2-8-11 C Catlin 33/1:0   Queens Dancer [2]2-8-11 T E Durcan 50/1:0
15 Ran   Time 1m 36.22 (u.28)   Owned: Lady Bamford & The Sangster Family   Trained: Manton

---

4724
3.25 Scottish Equitable E B F Maiden Stakes Colts & Geldings 2yo   (D2)
£5681 £1748 £874   **7f str**   **Firm**   **Inapplicable**   Centre

4385 **GROSVENOR SQUARE 17** [8] Saeed bin Suroor 2-8-11   L Dettori 2/1 FAV: 61: Made all & al trav well, shaken up & rdn clr from over 1f out: nicely bckd: imprvd from this step up to 7f, 1m+ shld suit in time: acts on firm grnd & a stiff/gall trk: clearly progressing & lkd useful today: see 4385.   **97+**

3511 **COUNCELLOR 56** [5] R Hannon 2-8-11 (81) R L Moore 5/1: 3442: Prom, outpcd by wnr from over 1f out: rest well covered: 8 wk abs: acts on firm & fast grnd: shown enough to find a race: see 3511, 2348.   **4**   **82**

4393 **PILLARS OF WISDOM 17** [1] J L Dunlop 2-8-11   J Fortune 14/1: 03: ch c Desert Prince - Eurolink Mischief (Be My Chief) Chsd ldrs, eff over 2f out, not pace to chall but kept on: op 20/1 & imprvd from intro: Apr foal, half-brother to several wnrs, incl 4 juv wnrs: dam a 12f 3yo scorer: eff at 7f, 1m+ likely to suit: handles firm grnd: encouraging, shld be winning in time.   **2½**   **77**

3959 **SPANISH RIDGE 38** [13] J L Dunlop 2-8-11   T Quinn 13/2: 54: Chsd ldrs, eff over 2f out, kept on but not able to chall: op 8/1, stablemate of 3rd: handles firm & fast grnd: see 3959.   **1¼**   **74**

REGISTRAR [12]2-8-11   S Sanders 14/1: 5: ch c Machiavellian - Confidante (Dayjur) Slow away, in tch till over 1f out: Apr foal, half-brother to a 7f 3yo scorer, dam a dual 7f 3yo wnr.   **3**   **68**

4194 **COST ANALYSIS 25** [2]2-8-11   P Robinson 9/1: 06: ch c Grand Lodge - Flower Girl (Pharly) Chsd ldrs, no extra fnl 2f: 100,000gns Feb foal, half-brother to a high-class 1m French 2yo performer.   **¾**   **66**

KINGS MAJESTY [9]2-8-11   K Fallon 6/1: 7: Chsd ldrs, no impress fnl 2f.   **5**   **57**
TRAFALGAR SQUARE [4]2-8-11   E Ahern 25/1: 8: Held up, btn & hung right over 1f out.   **½**   **56**
MINERAL STAR [11]2-8-11   N Callan 33/1: 9: Dwelt, held up & nvr a factor.   **1¾**   **52**
JOSTLE [10]2-8-11   T P Queally 25/1: 0: 10th: Slow away & al rear: lost ch start.   **¾**   **50**
GREEN PIRATE [6]2-8-11   D R McCabe 50/1: 0: 11th: Keen & prom, btn over 2f out.   **5**   **41**
LINDAS COLIN [3]2-8-11   D Holland 16/1: 0: 12th: Slow away & held up, no ch fnl 2f.   **¾**   **39**
SHATIN STAR [7]2-8-11   O Urbina 50/1: 0: 13th: Slow away & sn struggling rear.   **shd**   **39**
13 Ran   Time 1m 22.95 (u0.25)   Owned: Godolphin   Trained: Newmarket

---

4725
4.30 Uae Equestrian And Racing Federation Nursery Handicap Stakes 2yo 0-95   (C1)   **[101]**
£13884 £4272 £2136   **1m str**   **Firm**   **Inapplicable**   Centre

4480 **BUNNY RABBIT 12** [2] B J Meehan 2-9-0 (87) L Dettori 2/1 FAV: 35401: Chsd ldrs, rdn & led dist, duelled with rnr-up & narrowly hdd ins last, prevailed line, all out: hvly bckd: eff at 7f, suited by 1m & could get further: acts on firm, fast & polytrack, stiff/gall or sharp trk: lightly rcd, appeals as a type to progress.   **98**

4480 **ALRIGHT MY SON 12** [8] R Hannon 2-8-3 (76) R L Moore 5/1: 2452402: Led/dsptd lead, went on 3f out till over 1f out, rallied for press & narrow lead ins last, just hdd line: nicely bckd, op 6/1: closely matched with this wnr on prev form, can find comp: see 4480, 3753 & 1646.   **hd**   **86**

4100 **KING OF BLUES 31** [9] M A Magnusson 2-8-3 (1ow)f (75) E Ahern 25/1: 004103: Sn prom, rdn & kept on ins last, not pace of front pair: styd longer 1m trip: see 3627.   **2**   **82**

4329* **DONYANA 19** [13] M A Jarvis 2-8-13 (86) P Robinson 5/1: 514: Rcd alone & cl-up towards far side, not pace of front pair ins last: bckd tho' op 11/4: h'cap bow: styd longer 1m trip: handles firm & gd grnd.   **hd**   **91**

4233 **PENNY ISLAND 24** [7]2-8-1 (74) D Kinsella 20/1: 0635: Chsd ldrs, rdn & kept on onepace: h'cap bow: handles firm & gd/soft grnd: see 4233.   **2**   **75**

3774 **SPIRIT OF FRANCE 45** [5]2-9-7 (94) D Holland 10/1: 221256: Led 5f, no extra fnl 1f: abs.   **shd**   **95**
4480 **MIGHTY EMPIRE 12** [10]2-8-7 (80) N Callan 6/1: 004127: Held up, hdwy halfway, no prog bef dist.   **1¼**   **78**
4417 **GRANDMAS GIRL 15** [12]2-7-12 (1oh) (70) N Mackay(3) 20/1: 0458: Prom 2f, no impress after.   **nk**   **68**

NEWMARKET TUESDAY 21.09.04 Righthand, Stiff, Galloping Track

4410 **SWELL LAD 15** [1]2-7-13 (72) J F McDonald(3) 25/1: 00629: Chsd ldrs, btn over 1f out: btr 4410.	1½	66
3935 **SHIVAREE 38** [4]2-9-0 (87) T E Durcan 25/1: 314030: 10th: Chsd ldrs, no ch fnl 2f: btr 3935 (6f).	hd	80
4285 **VELVET HEIGHTS 22** [3]2-8-12 (85) G Carter 25/1: 00100: 11th: Dwelt & al rear: btr 3890 (g/s).	5	68
4471 **NORCROFT 12** [6]2-8-0 bl (73) F P Ferris(3) 40/1: 6000400: 12th: Prom, btn 3f out: btr 4100 (7f).	12	36
4462 **ASHARON 13** [11]2-8-7 (80) S Sanders 33/1: 0660: 13th: Dwelt, in tch till over 2f out, h'cap bow.	6	33

13 Ran   Time 1m 35.98 (u0.52)   Owned: Gold Group International Ltd   Trained: Upper Lambourn

4726 5.00 Louise Steel Median Auction Maiden Stakes 2yo (E3)
£4212 £1296 £648   6f str   Firm   Inapplicable   Centre

4422 **KING MARJU 15** [1] P W Chapple Hyam 2-9-0 J Fortune 10/11 FAV: 621: Al prom & led over 1f out, rdn out: hvly bckd, confirmed prev promise: suited by 6f last twice, has tried 7f: acts on firm & fast grnd, sharp/turning or stiff/gall trk: see 4422 & 3568.		92
4442 **IMPROVISE 14** [7] C E Brittain 2-8-9 S Sanders 8/1: 622: Al prom, rdn & kept on ins last, not pace of wnr: eff at 6/7f on firm grnd & polytrack: see 4442.	1¼	78
4497 **ENCOURAGEMENT 11** [13] R Hannon 2-8-9 (75) R L Moore 8/1: 03043: Led 4f, no extra ins last: eff at 5/6f on firm & gd grnd: clr of rem & h'caps may now suit: see 4497 & 3626.	hd	77
KENMORE [2] B W Hills 2-9-0 K Fallon 8/1: 4: b c Compton Place - Watheeqah (Topsider) Dwelt & held up, kept on late, nvr able to threaten: 38,000gns Mar foal, dam a 5f 3yo wnr: prob handles firm grnd: not given hard time on intro, likely improver.	3½	71
4443 **KANAD 14** [6]2-9-0 t (77) R Hills 12/1: 32025: Chsd ldrs, no impress bef dist: btr 4443 & 1987.	¾	69
4223 **PACIFIC PIRATE 24** [11]2-9-0 T P Queally 25/1: 06: b c Mujadil - Jay And A (Elbio) Chsd ldrs, btn over 1f out: Feb foal, half-brother to a plcd 6f 3yo performer: dam a useful Irish sprinter.	1	66
BORN FOR DIAMONDS [5]2-8-9 E Ahern 33/1: 7: b f Night Shift - Kirri (Lycius) Held up, late gains, no threat to ldrs: Mar first foal, cost E65,000: stay further & likely improver.	¾	59
SILVER BARK [3]2-8-9 L Dettori 12/1: 8: Mid-div, no impress over 1f out.	½	57
PAMIR [8]2-9-0 N Mackay(3) 25/1: 9: Dwelt, pushed along rear, nvr on terms.	1¼	58
HAWKES BAY [4]2-9-0 P Robinson 33/1: 0: 10th: Dwelt, outpcd, mod late prog, nrst fin.	½	56
PERFECT NATION [12]2-8-9 Lisa Jones 33/1: 0: 11th: Chsd ldrs, no impress over 2f out.	½	49
4329 **CLASSIC GUEST 19** [10]2-8-9 (60) T E Durcan 50/1: 4600: 12th: Chsd ldrs, btn 2f out: btr 2373.	2½	41
BRANSTON PENNY [9]2-8-9 D Holland 50/1: 0: 13th: Al outpcd & rear.	9	16

13 Ran   Time 1m 10.49 (u0.31)   Owned: Mr Bryan Fry   Trained: Newmarket

4727 5.30 Robinsons Mercedes-Benz Nursery Handicap Stakes 2yo 0-85 (D2)
£5577 £1716 £858   6f str   Firm   Inapplicable   Centre   [91]

4422* **THE PHEASANT FLYER 15** [5] B J Meehan 2-9-4 (81) J Fortune 3/1 FAV: 311: Led/dsptd lead throughout, asserted ins last, drvn out: op 10/3: h'cap bow: eff at 6f, handles gd/soft, likes firm & fast grnd, stiff/gall or sharp/turning trk: lightly rcd & progressive gelding: see 4422.		92
3820 **ELGIN MARBLES 43** [6] R Hannon 2-9-3 (80) R L Moore 16/1: 1602: Trkd wnr, outpcd halfway, rdn & chall over 1f out, no extra well ins last: op 20/1, 6 wk abs: back to form of debut: eff at 5/6f on firm & gd.	1¼	86
4358* **PENKENNA PRINCESS 18** [1] R M Beckett 2-9-7 (84) S Sanders 5/1: 013: Chsd ldrs, rdn & kept on, not pace of wnr: well bckd on h'cap bow: handles firm & fast grnd: see 4358.	shd	90
4457 **KEEP BACCKINHIT 13** [3] G L Moore 2-9-4 (78) A Quinn(5) 12/1: 3031504: Chsd ldrs, rdn & styd on for press, not able to chall: eff at 6f, return to 7f could suit: see 3624 (7f).	1	81
4396 **MONSIEUR MIRASOL 16** [8]2-8-12 (75) N Callan 7/1: 5102405: Mid-div, no impress dist: btr 3902.	1¾	73
4556* **CONNOTATION 8** [2]2-8-9 (6ex)vis (72) L Dettori 4/1: 223016: Held up, eff over 2f out, no prog dist: well bckd under a 6lb pen: btr 4556 (5f).	2½	62
4224 **PROSPECT COURT 24** [9]2-9-2 (79) T Quinn 16/1: 0301007: Trkd ldrs early, btn 2f out: btr 2989.	shd	69
3284 **FIRST RULE 66** [10]2-8-9 (72) E Ahern 20/1: 04408: Chsd ldrs, no impress fnl 2f, abs: btr 2738 (5f).	nk	61
4509 **ROWAN LODGE 10** [4]2-9-7 (84) P Robinson 7/2: 3121029: Prom, strug 2f out: nicely bckd.	2½	65
4484 **WELSH GALAXY 12** [7]2-7-12 (8oh) (53) D Fox(5) 50/1: 00000: 10th: Al outpcd & struggling rear.	4	31

10 Ran   Time 1m 10.52(u0.28)   Owned: The Second Pheasant Inn Partnership   Trained: Upper Lambourn

CHANTILLY MONDAY 13.09.04 Righthand, Galloping Track

Official Going Good

4728 1.20 Gr 3 Prix d'Aumale 2yo Fillies ()
£25704 £10282 £7711   1m rnd   Good

BIRTHSTONE [3] H A Pantall 2-8-9 C P Lemaire 7/10 JT FAV: 11: ch f Machiavellian - Baya (Nureyev) Handy, led over 1f out, readily asserted under hand riding: remains unbeaten after an earlier Deauville success: eff at 1m on good & v soft ground: likes a gall trk: smart filly, can rate higher at Gr2/Gr1 level.		113+
3498 **PORTRAYAL** [2] A Fabre 2-8-9 C Soumillon 7/10 JT FAV: 31342: Held up in tch, swtchd wide & kept on for press fnl 2f, not pace to threaten wnr.	1½	106
FAINT HEART [1] D Wachman 2-8-9 T Jarnet 22/1: 2213: Held up, swtchd wide & kept on, no impress.	2	102

6 Ran   Time 1m 38.90()   Owned: Sheikh Mohammed   Trained: France

1429

Official Going Good/Soft

4729 1.15 Gr 3 Prix des Chenes 2yo ()
£25704 £10282 £7711 **1m rnd** **Good/Soft**

HELIOS QUERCUS [1] C Diard 2-9-2 A Roussel 98/10: 1141411: br c Diableneyev - Criss Cross **108**
(Crystal Palace) Mid-div, pshd along & hdwy to chall over 1f out, led ins last, all out, gamely: a winner 4 times
prev in career at up to 7f: appreciated step up to 1m: acts on gd/sft & v soft ground: smart & game.
  MUSKETIER [3] P Bary 2-9-2 T Thulliez 8/5 FAV: 412: Held up, styd on from over 1f out, nrst fin. snk **107**
  VATORI [7] P Demercastel 2-9-2 S Pasquier 15/2: 613: Held up in tch, styd on for press, not btn far. nk **106**
  CAPABLE GUEST 7 [6] M R Channon 2-9-2 (100) S Hitchcott 142/10: 33321434: Pushed along chasing snk **105**
ldrs early, drvn to lead over 1f out, hdd just ins last, kept on, btn less than 1L in a tight fin: see 4003, 3811 (mdn).
4429* **HYPNOTIC** 14 [4]2-9-2 (96) J B Eyquem 11/2: 411317: Led 1f, chsd ldr, rdn & slightly hampered 12 **84**
over 2f out, sn btn: much btr 4429.
7 Ran Time 1m 40.60 () Owned: T Maudet Trained: France

4730 2.20 Gr 3 Prix du Prince d'Orange 3yo ()
£25704 £10282 £7711 **1m2f** **Good/Soft**

4158 **DELFOS** 28 [4] C Laffon-Parias 3-9-0 M Blancpain 33/10: 1110221: Trkd ldr, rdn to chall over 1f **116**
out, led ins last & styd on strongly: suited by 10f, tried 12f, may yet suit: likes good/soft & soft ground: v smart.
4835* **APSIS** 340 [2] A Fabre 3-8-12 C Soumillon 11/10 FAV: 11-2: b c Barathea - Apogee (Shirley 1½ **111**
Heights) Trkd ldrs, styd on for press, not pace to chall but nrst fin: belated reapp: unbeaten juv, 2nd of 2
victories came at Saint Cloud (Gr 3): both wins at 1m, styd 10f well today, 12f will suit: acts on gd & gd/sft:
smart. 1 Oct'03 Sain 8g/s 97- :
3507 **LYONELS GLORY** [9] U Suter 3-9-0 C P Lemaire 118/10: -233613: Led till ins last, no extra: see 3507. 1½ **110**
9 Ran Time 2m 09.40 () Owned: L Marinopoulos Trained: France

4731 3.00 Gr 3 Prix du Pin 3yo+ ()
£25704 £10282 £7711 **7f rnd** **Good/Soft**

  COMETE [1] M Cesandri 5-8-12 D Bonilla 133/10: 0303511: b m Jeune Homme - Cocooning (Galetto) **110**
Mid-div, hdwy & chsd ldr 2f out, led over 1f out, rdn out: Italian trained raider: suited by 7f/1m on gd & soft.
2139* **PUPPETEER** [11] A de Royer Dupre 4-9-5 C Soumillon 7/2: 1-621442: Held up rear, styd on for press. 2 **112**
4386 **MILLENNIUM FORCE** 14 [8] M R Channon 6-9-1 (106) S Hitchcott 19/10 FAV: 04233883D: Mid-div, hdwy hd **107**
& led over 2f out, drvn & hdd over 1f out, edged right under press close home: finished 3rd, disqualified & placed 4th.
4311 **KELTOS** 20 [4] C Laffon Parias 6-9-1 M Blancpain 22/1: 11-12224: Rear, hdwy to chall dist, no hd **106**
extra when short of room nr fin: finished 4th, btn a hd, placed 3rd: see 4311.
4311* **AUTUMN GLORY** 20 [6]4-9-5 (102) S Drowne 109/10: 0-1100615: Chsd ldrs, kept on but not able to 1 **108**
chall: not disgraced under topweight, ahead of today's 3rd in 4311 (hvy).
12 Ran Time 1m 20.10() Owned: Mme J C Bouret Trained: Italy

Official Going Good/Soft

4732 3.05 Gr 3 Ballygallon Stakes 3yo+ ()
£32663 £21269 £4523 **6f str** **Good/Soft**

4384 **ROYAL MILLENNIUM** 14 [6] M R Channon 6-9-5 (111) T E Durcan 7/2 FAV: 1425-1041: Held up, hdwy 2f **116**
out, led ins last, rdn out: op 3/1: eff at 6/7f, does stay 1m: acts on firm, suited by v smart performer.
4060 **MOSS VALE** 30 [8] B W Hills 3-9-0 (112) M Hills 6/1: 3-4111092: Trkd ldrs, swtchd & kept on ins ½ **111**
last, not pace of wnr: back to smart best: see 2421.
4152 **GRAND REWARD** 13 [9] A P O'Brien 3-9-0 tBL J P Spencer 7/1: 5-2501U33: Held up, styd on from over nk **110**
1f out, not able to chall: smart run in blnks: see 4152, 1559.
4526 **RUBY ROCKET** 7 [2]3-8-11 (105) K Fallon 9/2: 4-5232327: Chsd ldrs till over 1f out: see 2769, 2240. 4 **95**
4226 **MILLYBAA** 21 [4]4-8-13 (97) J P Murtagh 16/1: 20-240048: Chsd ldrs, btn 2f out: see 1773 (Listed). 3 **86**
12 Ran Time 1m 13.10 () Owned: Jackie & George Smith Trained: West Ilsley

4733 3.40 Gr 1 Irish St Leger 3yo+ ()
£112560 £38592 £18492 **1m6f** **Good**

4019 **VINNIE ROE** 34 [5] D K Weld 6-9-8 bl P J Smullen 7/2 JT FAV: 1154-221: Trkd ldrs, smooth hdwy to **121**
lead over 2f out, in command over 1f out, readily: op 11/4: 4th successive victory in this race: eff at 12f, suited
by 14f+, stays 2m4f: acts on fast & hvy grnd, stiff/gall trks: reportedly has various options, including the
Melbourne Cup and the Arc: see 4019, 2138.
4161 **BRIAN BORU** 27 [14] A P O'Brien 6-9-8 t J P Spencer 7/2 JT FAV: 3-1555522: Mid-div, hdwy to chse 2½ **116**
ldr over 2f out, kept on but always well held: op 5/1: gd run from this smart colt: see 4161, 994.
4000* **FIRST CHARTER** 32 [13] Sir Michael Stoute 5-9-8 (112) K Fallon 10/1: 120-01213: Handy & chsd ldr ½ **115**
6f out, rdn & led 3f out, hdd over 2f out, kept on for press: op 4/1: just btr 4000 (2m).
3958 **DUBAI SUCCESS** 35 [10] B W Hills 4-9-8 (112) M Hills 10/1: D3-140224: Chsd ldrs, chsd front pair ¾ **114**
over 2f out, kept on onepace: needs drop to Gr 3/Listed: see 3958, 2817 & 1230 (12f, Gr 3).
2518 **ALCAZAR** 93 [9]9-9-8 (115) M Fenton 14/1: 024-1205: Trkd ldrs, outpcd 3f out, kept on late. hd **113**
3315 **TWO MILES WEST** 34 [7]3-8-12 t J A Heffernan 10/1: 12246: Held up, nvr able to land a blow: abs. 2 **111**

4230* **ORANGE TOUCH** 21 [4]4-9-8 (112) J P Murtagh 9/2: 51/54-6118: Led till 3f out, sn btn: btr 4230 (List).   6½   100
4391 **JAGGER** 14 [3]4-9-8 (101) D P McDonogh 33/1: D11-03040: 11th: Always bhd & no chance fnl 2f.   13¼   82
13 Ran   Time 3m 03.90 ()   Owned: S Sheridan   Trained: The Curragh

CURRAGH   SUNDAY 19.09.04   Righthand, Galloping Track

Official Going Good (Yielding Places)

4734	**3.45 Gr 1 National Stakes 2yo** ()
	£118858 £38458 £18358 **7f str** **Good**

3060* **DUBAWI** 73 [2] Saeed bin Suroor 2-9-0 L Dettori 8/13 FAV: 111: Trkd ldrs trav well, led over 1f   121+
out & sn qcknd clr, readily: 10 wk abs: eff over a stiff 7f, strong mid-dist pedigree & 1m+ looks sure to suit: acts
on fast & gd grnd: heads the betting for next year's Epsom Derby & this high-class/unbtn colt must be followed.
BERENSON 29 [1] T Stack 2-9-0 T Stack 12/1: 12: b c Entrepreneur - On Air (Chief Singer) Held   3   112
up, rdn & styd on to take 2nd ins last, no threat to easy wnr: well regarded colt who made a winning debut over C/D
last month: eff over a stiff 7f on fast & gd grnd: smart, must win a Gr race sn.
4159 **RUSSIAN BLUE** 28 [3] A P O'Brien 2-9-0 J P Spencer 5/1: 1112333: Led till over 1f out, sn outpcd   1½   109
by ready wnr: longer 7f trip: btr 4159, 3841.
4154 **DEMOCRATIC DEFICIT** 29 [6] J S Bolger 2-9-0 K J Manning 9/2: 1124: Chsd ldrs, btn 2f out: btr 4154.   3   103
2578 **IN EXCELSIS** 92 [5]2-9-0 J P Murtagh 16/1: 155: Dwelt, rear, efft over 1f out, sn btn: 3 mth abs: see 2578. 2½   98
4154 **ELUSIVE DOUBLE** 29 [4]2-9-0 P J Smullen 16/1: 1136: Trkd ldrs, pshd along halfway & btn 2f out.   nk   97
7 Ran   Time 1m 24.80 ()   Owned: Godolphin   Trained: Newmarket

4735	**4.15 Gr 2 Blandford Stakes Fillies & Mares 3yo+** ()
	£56615 £16549 £7839 **1m2f** **Good**

4160 **MONTURANI** 28 [13] G Wragg 5-9-3 (104) T E Durcan 12/1: 2-3624451: Handy & led over 2f out, held   114
on most gamely for press ins last: eff at 1m/10.5f on firm & gd/sft ground: tough & smart mare, deserved this 1st
success of the season: see 2487 & 57.
3836 **KINNAIRD** 47 [9] P C Haslam 3-8-11 t (110) K Darley 10/1: 11-45222: Handy, rdn to chall ins last,   ½   113
just held close home: 7 wk abs: tough, deserves to find a race: see see 3836, 3089.
3321 **ALL TOO BEAUTIFUL** 63 [2] A P O'Brien 3-8-11 J P Spencer 11/2: 11243: Held up, styd on well for   shd   113
press from over 1f out, nrst fin: 2 mth abs: see 2210.
4323* **RED BLOOM** 18 [3] Sir Michael Stoute 3-8-11 (113) K Fallon 13/8 FAV: 311-4314: Mid-div, outpcd   2   110
over 2f out, late gains: btr 4323 (Gr 3).
4020 **TROPICAL LADY** 35 [12]4-9-3 K J Manning 10/1: 11111255: Held up, efft over 2f out, no extra dist.   1½   107
3866+ **NEW MORNING** 39 [10]3-8-11 (104) P Robinson 12/1: 4-214516: Led/dsptd lead till over 2f out, sn btn.   3½   103
13 Ran   Time 2m 05.40 ()   Owned: Mrs R Phillips   Trained: Newmarket

4736	**4.45 Listed Blenheim Stakes 2yo** ()
	£23989 £7038 £3354 **6f str** **Good/Soft**

AD VALOREM 14 [5] A P O'Brien 2-9-0 J P Spencer 9/4 JT FAV: 11: b c Danzig - Classy Women   116
(Relaunch) Trkd ldrs, led over 1f out & styd on strongly: earlier made a winning debut in a C/D maiden: dam a useful
winning juvenile: dam a winning US sprinter: eff at 6f, 7f could suit: acts on fast & gd grnd, likes a gall trk:
unbeaten & smart, will be wng in Gr grade sn.
4431 **INDESATCHEL** 14 [1] D Wachman 2-9-0 M J Kinane 9/4 JT FAV: 413232: Trkd ldrs, swtchd & kept on   1   111
fnl 1f, not pace of wnr: see 4431, 4153.
4177* **CUPIDS GLORY** 24 [4] Sir Mark Prescott 2-9-0 (97) D P McDonogh 5/2: 61113: Handy & led over 1f   ½   109
out, hdd over 1f out, no extra: acts on polytrack, gd & soft ground: just btr 4177 (7f, AW h'cap).
6 Ran   Time 1m 13.90 ()   Owned: Mrs John Magnier   Trained: Ballydoyle

4737	**5.15 Irish Breeders Foal Levy Stakes 2yo** ()
	£66330 £26130 £16080 **6f63y str** **Good**

4432 **SLIP DANCE** 14 [1] E Tyrell 2-8-10 J F Egan 11/4: 31416261: Trkd ldrs, hdwy & led ins last, rdn   108
clr: op 7/2: eff at 6/7f on fast & gd/sft ground: likes a stiff/gall trk: tough & v useful filly: see 2763.
2883 **ALL NIGHT DANCER** 39 [7] D Wachman 2-8-4 W M Lordan 14/1: 1520002: Handy & led over 2f out, hdd 2   95
ins last, not pace of wnr: gd run from this useful filly: see 2883.
MAKUTI 15 [4] M J Grassick 2-8-4 N G McCullagh 14/1: U613: b f Monashee Mountain - Lady Anna   ¾   93
Livia (Ahonoora) Trkd ldr, kept on onepace fnl 2f: recent wnr of a Down Royal clmr: eff at 6f, winning form at 7f:
acts on firm & gd grnd: handles a gall or sharp trk.
4533 **TOURNEDOS** 8 [8]2-9-1 (100) T E Durcan 14/1 FAV: 22010325: Trkd ldrs, no extra fnl 1f: just btr 4533.   1   101
4551 **NOVA TOR** 6 [2]2-8-7 p (87) P J Smullen 14/1: 15401306: Chsd ldrs, swtchd & onepace dist: qk reapp.   shd   93$
3869 **WAVERTREE WARRIOR** 39 [9]2-8-12 J P Guillambert 10/1: 0320: 10th: Chsd ldrs 3f, btn/eased ins last. 16½   44
10 Ran   Time 1m 18.40()   Owned: M McLoughlin   Trained: Ireland

Official Going Standard

4738 2.10 Rose Maiden Auction Stakes Div 1 2yo (E3)
£3455 £1063 £532 **1m aw rnd** **Going 24** **-33 Slow** Outside

4522 **RAISE A TUNE 11** [6] J A Osborne 2-8-10 S W Kelly 33/1: 01: ch c Raise A Grand - Magic Melody — **80a**
(Petong) Led & dictated pace, rdn & held on well ins last, well judged ride: left debut bhd: Apr foal, £45,000
purchase: half-brother to a 6f 3yo wnr: eff forcing the pace over a sharp 1m on polytrack.

4444 **WATCHMYEYES 15** [8] N P Littmoden 2-8-10 (77) J P Guillambert(3) 11/10 FAV: 64422: Keen rear, — nk — **79a**
smooth hdwy wide 2f out, styd on, just failed: hvly bckd, AW bow: stays 1m on firm, soft & polytrack.

4490 **LORD OF DREAMS 12** [7] D W P Arbuthnot 2-8-11 (68) K McEvoy 4/1: 0503: Trkd wnr, rdn & no extra — 1½ — **77a$**
well ins last: op 6/1: stays a sharp 1m, rtn to 7f could suit: handles polytrack & gd/soft grnd: see 4233.

4233 **KRASIVIS BOY 25** [11] G L Moore 2-8-9 I Mongan 4/1: 024: Trkd ldr, no extra fnl 1f: op 3/1: — ½ — **73a**
handles polytrack & gd/soft grnd: see 4233.

4233 **KATANA 25** [5]2-8-2 F Norton 25/1: 005: b f Spectrum - Karlaska (Lashkari) Cl-up, onepace for — 1¼ — **64a**
press fnl 2f: clr rem: 10,000gns Feb foal, half-sister to 2 mid-dists wnrs abroad: dam a useful 12f wnr abroad.

INDIAN DOVE [2]2-8-5 E Ahern 11/1: 6: b f Indian Danehill - African Dance (El Gran Senor) — 6 — **57a**
Rear, sn pushed along & no impress over 2f out: £32,000 May foal, half-sister to a 6f juv wnr, also mid-dist wnrs,
incl multiple 3yo scorer Shaka Zulu.

MOONSTRUCK [9]2-8-9 J Tate 20/1: 7: Rear,sn pshd along, nvr dngr. — 1¼ — **58a**

4450 **LEGEND OF DANCE 15** [3]2-8-3 J F McDonald(3) 33/1: 008: Rear, struggling fnl 3f. — 1¼ — **49a**

2851 **AFRICAN EMPEROR 84** [4]2-8-8 N Callan 33/1: 69: Chsd ldrs, btn 2f out, abs. — ¾ — **53a**

4250 **FLY ME TO DUNOON 24** [1]2-8-3 vis R Mullen 50/1: 060: 10th: Mid-div, struggling fnl 3f. — shd — **48a**

4316 **SECRET DIVA 21** [10]2-8-1 (40) D Kinsella 66/1: 000000: 11th: Wide & strug early, t.o: hung right. — 9 — **30a**

11 Ran Time 1m 40.77 (4.57) Owned: H Rosenblatt and D Margolis Trained: Upper Lambourn

Official Going Good/Firm

4739 2.45 Air Harrods Handicap Stakes 3yo+ 46-55 (F4) **[69]**
£3000 £857 £429 **5f str** **Good/Firm** **Inapplicable** Stands Side

4603 **BETTYS PRIDE 7** [19] M Dods 5-8-11 (52) S W Kelly 13/2: 6601061: Dwelt, sn trkd ldrs, led ins — **58**
last, drvn out: suited by 5/6f on firm & gd grnd, likes a sharp trk, handles any: see 3527, 1973.

4548 **PULSE 9** [20] J M Bradley 6-9-0 p (55) P Fitzsimons 7/1: 4006052: Held up, styd on for press ins — 1 — **58**
last, not reach wnr: on a fair mark & threatening to find similar: handles soft, likes firm & fast grnd: see 4070.

4253 **VALIANT ROMEO 24** [18] R Bastiman 4-8-13 p (54) R Ffrench 5/1 FAV: 4052033: Led, hdd ins last, no — hd — **56**
extra nr line: nicely bckd: see 4253 & 3561.

2951 **CERTA CITO 81** [14] D Flood 4-8-12 BL (53) F Norton 12/1: 0-005004: b f Mind Games - Bollin — shd — **55**
Dorothy (Rambo Dancer) Mid-div, hdwy over 2f out, chall dist, no extra ins last: 12 wk abs, imprvd eff in first
time blnks: prev with T D Easterby: lightly rcd '03, mdn scorer (AW h'cap unplcd, rtd 8a): winning form over a
sharp 6f on fast grnd: can go well fresh. 1 Mar'03 Catt 6.0g/f 71- D:

4636 **YORKIES BOY 6** [8]9-8-12 p (53) M Savage(2) 25/1: 0311005: Mid-div, short of room 2f out, switched — ½ — **53**
& kept on, not able to chall: qck reapp: apprec drop to 5f, gd run: see 4370.

4636 **ENJOY THE BUZZ 6** [15]5-8-10 (51) C Catlin 9/1: 0325506: Well bhd, late gains, nrst fin, qck reapp. — nk — **50**

4485 **MILLFIELDS DREAMS 13** [9]5-8-11 (52) D Nolan(3) 33/1: 0006007: Cl-up, rdn & no extra from dist. — 1 — **48**

4452 **ELLIOTS CHOICE 15** [11]3-8-11 (53) L Keniry(3) 33/1: 0240508: Chsd ldrs, no impress dist, new yard. — hd — **48**

4603 **HES A ROCKET 7** [12]3-8-13 bl (55) Hayley Turner(3) 20/1: 0602009: Mid-div, nvr able to chall. — ¾ — **48**

4489 **CORANGLAIS 13** [4]4-9-0 bl (55) R Miles(3) 14/1: 0050050: 10th: Bhd, mod gains for press, nrst fin. — nk — **47**

4508 **FLYING TACKLE 11** [6]6-8-12 p (53) D Tudhope(4) 12/1: 1000020: 11th: Slow away & rear, short of — nk — **44+**
room 2f out, hmpd ins last when no impress: stablemate of wnr: closer with a clr run: see 4508.

4335 **CHANTELLE 20** [16]4-8-12 BL (55) T P Queally 8/1: 1005000: 12th: Dwelt, nvr on terms: blnks. — ¾ — **42**

4595* **FOX COVERT 8** [5]3-8-13 (6ex)vis (55) L Enstone 10/1: 0400310: 13th: Cl-up 3f, sn btn: btr 4595. — ¾ — **42**

4548 **Formalise 9** [7]4-8-13 p(54) S Drowne 20/1:0 4595 **Turkish Delight 8** [13]3-8-13 (55) A Culhane 25/1:0

4317 **Smokin June 21** [2]3-8-11 BL(53) G Baker 25/1:0 3645* **Rehia 51** [17]3-8-11 (53) Derek Nolan(7) 20/1:0

4404 **Song Koi 16** [10]3-8-11 (55) M Fenton 33/1:0 4043 **The Baroness 34** [3]4-8-10 (51) D Corby(3) 33/1:0

19 Ran Time 58.12 (1.32) Owned: Betty's Brigade Trained: Darlington

4740 3.20 Dahlia Handicap Stakes 3yo 56-70 (E3) **[77]**
£3675 £1131 £565 **6f str** **Good/Firm** **Inapplicable** Stands Side

3995* **GLENCALVIE 37** [5] J Noseda 3-9-5 vis (68) E Ahern 5/1 FAV: 050411: Pushed along towards rear, — **72**
styd on for press to lead cl-home, all out: eff at 6f, return to 7f will surely suit: acts on fast & gd grnd: imprvd
for visor last twice: see 3995.

804 **FISSION 202** [13] Mrs Stef Liddiard 3-9-7 (70) F Norton 33/1: 13-63102: Sn handy trav well & led — hd — **73**
2f out, hdd over 1f out, just held: 7 month abs: prev with J Osborne: acts on both AWs & fast grnd: see 671 (AW).

3977 **PICCLEYES 37** [3] R Hannon 3-8-11 bl (60) R Hughes 20/1: 1003603: Mid-div, drvn & led over 1f out, — hd — **62**
hdd cl-home: see 3589 & 2586.

4465 **LANDUCCI 14** [6] J W Hills 3-9-2 t (65) S Drowne 13/2: 0-206134: Rear, styd on well for press ins — shd — **67**
last, nrst fin & just held: eff at 6f, crying out for rtn to 7f: acts on fast, soft & gd/f/sand: see 4144 (sft).

4452* **TORQUEMADA 15** [8]3-8-11 (60) K McEvoy 9/1: 0030015: Rear, short of room over 1f out, styd on — hd — **61+**
strongly cl-home, lkd unlucky: op 12/1: lkd the likely wnr with a clr passage, remains one to keep on side.

3920 **CYFRWYS 40** [17]3-8-11 T (60) D Kinsella 16/1: 4-022606: Keen & trkd ldrs, short of room over 1f — shd — **61**
out, switched & chall ins last, no extra fnl strides: only btn around 1L in a v tight fin: reportedly struck into:

6 wk abs, gd run in first time t-strap: see 3095 & 2849.

4582 **RUSSIAN SYMPHONY** 8 [14]3-9-6 bl (69) T E Durcan 20/1: 05-067: Held up, outpcd over 2f out, 1 67
switched & kept on in last, not pace to chal: rtn to 7f+ could suit: lightly rcd, again hinted more to come.
3910 **WHISTFUL** 40 [10]3-9-2 (65) R Mullen 10/1: 3035048: Dwelt, mid-div, no impress dist, abs. 1 60
3610* **MOON LEGEND** 53 [4]3-9-3 (66) Hayley Turner(3) 25/1: 06-03019: Dwelt, switched wide & mod prog. nk 60
4528 **SIMPSONS MOUNT** 11 [12]3-9-3 (66) S W Kelly 20/1: 0501500: 10th: Dwelt, mid-div, no impress fnl 1f. shd 60
4646 **DARLA** 5 [9]3-9-6 (69) T P Queally 14/1: 6-052600: 11th: Cl-up, btn dist, qck reapp: btr 3870. ½ 61
4317 **ACE CLUB** 21 [20]3-9-1 (64) A Culhane 8/1: 5004200: 12th: Trkd ldrs, lost pl halfway, no ch after. hd 55
4709 • **DANIFAH** 2 [19]3-9-6 (6ex) (69) F P Ferris(3) 6/1: 6113010: 13th: Led till 2f out, sn btn: qck reapp. ¾ 58
4335 **ILTRAVITORE** 20 [18]3-8-11 (60) L Keniry(3) 33/1: 00500: 14th: Dwelt, short of room 2f out, sn btn. nk 48
4548 **INNSTYLE** 9 [2]3-9-1 (64) A Daly 20/1: 0-600300: 15th: Held up, rdn & btn over 1f out: btr 4412. shd 52
4262* **GROWLER** 24 [15]3-9-7 vis (70) I Mongan 7/1: 0-030210: 16th: Held up, short of room 2f out, sn ½ 56
btn: reportedly hung right thr'out: btr 4262 (soft, mdn).
3952 **BELLA TUTRICE** 39 [16]3-9-4 (67) N Callan 33/1: 3403000: 17th: Cl-up till 2f out, sn btn: btr 3198. 5 40
17 Ran   Time 1m 12.06 (3.26)   Owned: Mrs Susan Roy   Trained: Newmarket

---

4741   3.55 Polyanthus Nursery Handicap Stakes 2yo 0-75 (E4)   [82]
£3367 £962 £481   **7f str**   **Good/Firm**   **Inapplicable**   Stands Side

4635* **REBEL REBEL** 6 [7] N A Callaghan 2-9-6 (6ex) (74) O Urbina 4/5 FAV: 005411: Handy trav well & led 88+
2f out, readily asserted under hand riding, val 4L+: hvly bckd under a 6lb pen, qck reapp: eff at 7f/1m on fast &
gd/soft grnd: progressive juv, keep on side: see 4635.
4193 **TUMBLEWEED GALORE** 26 [1] B J Meehan 2-9-5 (73) J F McDonald(3) 16/1: 033362: Pushed along rear, 2 82
styd on wide halfway, nvr able to chal wnr: eff at 7f/1m, shown enough to find a race: see 3925, 3500 & 3342.
4337 **TYBALT** 20 [4] P W Harris 2-8-8 VIS (62) I Mongan 40/1: 25003: Bmpd start, mid-div, eff over 2f 1 69
out, kept on, no ch with wnr: gd run in first time visor: eff at 6/7f, handles fast & gd grnd: see 3020.
4296 **RESISTANCE HEROINE** 23 [17] E A L Dunlop 2-9-5 (73) S Drowne 16/1: 00304: Mid-div trav well, kept ¾ 79
on onepace ins last, no threat: see 3770.
4344 **ROYAL PARDON** 20 [20]2-8-3 (57) J Mackay 10/1: 00445: Chsd ldrs, no extra fnl 1f: prob styd shd 63
longer 7f trip: see 4344 & 3722.
3627 **HES A STAR** 52 [3]2-8-7 (61) R Smith 33/1: 04066: Bmpd start, late gains, nrst fin: abs. shd 66
4444 **THREE ACES** 15 [12]2-8-4 bl (58) N Chalmers(4) 66/1: 05607: Rear, late gains, nrst fin, improve. 1 61+
4396 **SOCIETY MUSIC** 17 [5]2-9-6 BL (74) S W Kelly 16/1: 3136058: Led/dsptd lead 5f, fdd: blnks. ¾ 76
4207 **COCONUT SQUEAK** 26 [18]2-8-9 (63) M Fenton 25/1: 3609: Led/dsptd lead 5f, fdd ins last. nk 64
4444 **IVANA ILLYICH** 15 [16]2-9-4 (72) C Catlin 7/1: 0403300: 10th: Mid-div, staying on when no room nk 72+
fnl 1f, pos accepted: much better than finishing position suggests, remains interesting at 1m.
4509 **TRANSVESTITE** 11 [6]2-9-4 VIS (72) E Ahern 20/1: 54360: 11th: Chsd ldrs, ch dist, no extra. ½ 71
4273 **MABELLA** 23 [10]2-8-9 (63) T P Queally 40/1: 050400: 12th: Mid-div, sn rdn, nvr a factor. shd 62
4503 **WEMBURY POINT** 11 [19]2-8-8 (62) S Whitworth 40/1: 00060: 13th: Cl-up, sn btn: btr 4503. nk 60
4363 **LADY LUISA** 19 [14]2-8-6 (60) R Mullen 50/1: 05000: 14th: Rear, nvr a factor: flattered 3467. 2½ 53
4576 **MERRYMADCAP** 8 [15]2-8-9 (63) F Norton 16/1: 0566060: 15th: Mid-div, btn 2f out: btr 4576 (sft). hd 55
4666 **GRAND OPTION** 4 [2]2-9-1 bl (69) A Daly 33/1: 2500460: 16th: Rcd alone towards centre, cl-up 4f, nk 60
sn btn: qck reapp: btr 4666 & 4269.
4545 **ATSOS** 9 [17]2-9-0 (68) R Hughes 20/1: 660560: 17th: Mid-div, hmpd over 2f out, sn btn. nk 58
reportedly hung left thr'out: btr 3962 (5f).
4072 **SHUJUNE AL HAWAA** 33 [9]2-8-10 (64) T E Durcan 50/1: 563000: 18th: Rear, rdn 3f out, no hdwy. ¾ 53
4289 **CHICKEN SOUP** 23 [8]2-9-7 (75) K McEvoy 25/1: 6300: 19th: Chsd ldrs 5f, eased down over 1f out: ¾ 63
reportedly stumbled & lost action: h'cap bow: btr 4178 (AW).
4420 **MISS COTSWOLD LADY** 16 [11]2-9-2 (70) N Callan 10/1: 542000: 20th: Prom till halfway, sn strug. 9 42
20 Ran   Time 1m 24.5 (4.1)   Owned: Six Star Racing   Trained: Newmarket

---

Official Going Standard

4742   4.30 Pansy Classified Stakes 3yo+ 0-75 (D2)
£6988 £2150 £1075   **1m2f aw**   **Going 24**   **+12 Fast**   Inside

4643 **COMPTON DRAKE** 5 [13] G A Butler 5-9-4 (72) E Ahern 3/1 FAV: 1-021241: Rear, smooth hdwy wide 2f 82a+
out & led ins last, stayed on strongly: fast AW time, bckd, qck reapp: eff at 1m/10f, stays 14f: acts on fast,
soft & both AWs: in fine form, can win again: see 4643, 4057.
4336 **MA YAHAB** 20 [4] L M Cumani 3-8-12 (72) N Mackay(3) 8/1: 0-330442: Mid-div, rdn & briefly led 1¼ 78a
dist, no extra ins last: encouraging AW bow, shown enough to find a race: handles firm, gd/soft & polytrack.
4473 **KATIYPOUR** 13 [5] Miss B Sanders 7-9-4 (75) S Carson 11/1: 0345003: Trkd ldrs, led over 2f out, 3 74a
drvn & hdd dist, no extra: op 9/1: see 1691 (1m).
3990 **DOCTORED** 37 [9] P D Evans 3-8-12 bl (75) F P Ferris(3) 33/1: 1130604: Rear, outpcd over 2f out, 1¾ 72a
kept on for press, no threat: acts on firm, gd/soft & both AWs: see 3471.
4502 **SECRET FLAME** 12 [10]3-8-9 (74) A Culhane 7/1: 5-331065: Held up wide, eff 3f out, hung left 1 68a
under press over 1f out & no extra: btr 2709 (9f).
4607 **KRYSSA** 7 [2]3-8-9 (75) I Mongan 8/1: 1313106: Rear, short of rm 2f out, sn hung & no impress. hd 67a
3862 **LOVE TRIANGLE** 42 [8]3-8-12 (74) R Hughes 20/1: 3000457: Trkd ldr, no extra dist, eased, abs. 2½ 66a
4656 **OPENING CEREMONY** 5 [6]5-9-1 (75) T Hamilton(3) 7/1: 1515248: Mid-div, no impress fnl 2f, qck reapp. shd 63a
4392 **ELECTRIQUE** 18 [7]4-9-4 (72) S W Kelly 33/1: 3221-009: Sn handy wide & led 6f out till over 2f 3½ 61a
out, wknd: reportedly lost action: see 3892.
4227 **SILVALINE** 25 [14]5-9-4 (72) D Tudhope(5) 11/2: 1030260: 10th: Mid-div wide, no impress fnl 3f. nk 60a
3961 **CONVINCE** 39 [11]3-8-12 (74) S Drowne 50/1: 0056500: 11th: Rear/wide, strug fnl 3f: abs. 5 53a
4469 **WHITGIFT ROCK** 14 [3]3-8-12 (73) T P Queally 50/1: 0320000: 12th: Led 4f, btn 2f out, prefer 7f/1m. 2½ 49a
4254 **INTERNATIONALGUEST** 24 [1]5-9-4 bl (75) N Pollard 12/1: 0555000: 13th: Prom, rdn halfway & sn bhd. ¾ 48a
4254 **MAGIC AMIGO** 24 [12]3-8-12 (74) T E Durcan 33/1: 0436260: 14th: Trkd ldrs, btn 2f out: btr 3914. 5 41a
14 Ran   Time 2m 05.40 (1.2)   Owned: Mr Erik Penser   Trained: Blewbury

---

4743

5.05 Marigold Handicap Stakes Fillies & Mares 3yo+ 56-70 (E3) [81]
£3519 £1083 £541 **1m aw rnd** **Going 24** **-12 Slow** Outside

4440* **RIVER OF BABYLON 15** [7] M L W Bell 3-9-3 (70) R Mullen 6/1: 50-26511: Keen, mid-div wide, hdwy 74a
to chall over 2f out, led dist, drvn out: eff at 7f/1m on fast, gd & polytrack: took well to this surface, prog mare.
4295 **ISLAND RAPTURE 23** [8] J A R Toller 4-9-6 (69) E Ahern 13/2: 4032602: Dwelt, rear, short of room 1 70a
over 2f out, drvn & kept on, not able to chall: eff at 1m/10f: see 1891.
4642 **KINDLELIGHT DEBUT 5** [11] D K Ivory 4-9-5 (68) N Callan 16/1: 0300003: Held up wide, eff to chase hd 68a+
ldrs 2f out, onepace ins last: qck reapp: acts on fast, gd & polytrack: spot on at 7f: see 3257.
3364 **MORNING AFTER 62** [5] J R Fanshawe 4-9-5 (68) R Hughes 5/1: 2/43-0664: Handy & led over 3f out ½ 67a
till dist, no extra, abs: op 7/1: stays 1m, 7f poss ideal: see 3364 & 2840.
4683 **VONADAISY 4** [6]3-9-3 BL (70) A Culhane 14/1: 0344-105: Trkd ldrs, short of room over 2f out, drvn nk 68a
& kept on, nrst fin: qck reapp, imprvd eff in blnks: stays a sharp 1m: acts on fast, gd & polytrack: see 4275.
2419 **GRAND APOLLO 101** [9]3-9-3 (70) K McEvoy 7/1: 6-256: Led/dsptd lead wide till over 3f out, rdn & shd 68a
outpcd sn after, kept on ins last: 3 month abs: looks worth a try a 10f: handles firm grnd & polytrack: see 2031.
4669 **CUDDLES 4** [10]5-9-5 vis (68) T P Queally 25/1: 3000607: Rear, kept on wide, no threat, qck reapp. ½ 65a
4479 **STARBECK 13** [2]6-9-3 (66) P McCabe 9/1: 5400408: Slow away, mod gains for press, nrst fin. shd 63a
4510 **AND TOTO TOO 11** [12]4-9-7 bl (70) P Ferris(3) 7/2 FAV: 4214069: Chsd ldrs, rdn & btn over 2f 3½ 60a
out: subs reportedly to be coughing: see 3456.
4268 **EFRHINA 24** [1]4-9-5 P (68) S Drowne 14/1: 0030200: 10th: Led till 3f out, sn btn: cheekpieces. 5 49a
3749 **LILLI MARLANE 47** [3]4-9-6 (69) W Ryan 11/1: 0010050: 11th: Rear, little room but no obvious 2 46a+
attempt to improve position & eased ins last: 7 wk abs: much better than this, strangly in enquiry.
3791 **BLONDE EN BLONDE 46** [4]4-9-4 bl (67) I Mongan 16/1: 0305600: 12th: Mid-div, rdn & btn 2f out. ½ 43a
12 Ran Time 1m 39.1 (2.9) Owned: Mr C Wright & The Hon Mrs J M Corbett Trained: Newmarket

---

4744

5.35 Rose Maiden Auction Stakes Div 2 2yo (E3)
£3455 £1063 £532 **1m aw rnd** **Going 24** **-18 Slow** Outside

4271 **RAFFISH 23** [4] J M P Eustace 2-8-7 J Tate 9/2: 041: Chsd ldr, rdn to lead over 1f out, just 78a
held on: AW bow: eff at 7f, styd longer 1m trip well: acts on polytrack & gd grnd: see 4271.
4078 **RAGGED GLORY 33** [10] R Hannon 2-8-10 VIS (76) R Hughes 6/1: 46202: Mid-div, hdwy over 2f out, shd 80a
drvn & hung left ins last, styd on, just denied: op 7/1: gd run in first time visor: AW bow: stays a sharp 1m:
acts on fast, gd & polytrack: see 3285 & 1816.
4289 **POLLITO 23** [7] B J Meehan 2-8-10 (77) J F McDonald(3) 7/4 FAV: 5643: Trkd ldrs, hung left & ½ 79a
onepace for press fnl 1f: AW bow: stays a sharp 1m: prob handles firm, gd & polytrack: see 4289, 3981.
4369 **AMIGRA 18** [8] Miss Jacqueline S Doyle 2-8-1 BL J Doyle(7) 50/1: 004: b f Grand Lodge - Beaming ½ 69a
(Mtoto) Keen & led, sn clr, hdd over 1f out, kept on for press: AW bow, much imprvd eff with forcing tactics &
first time blnks: cheaply bght Feb foal, dam a 6f juv wnr: stays a sharp 1m on polytrack.
 KANGRINA [5]2-8-5 J Mackay 7/2: 5: b f Acatenango - Kirona (Robellino) Mid-div, outpcd 2 69a+
halfway, kept on late, nrst fin: op 3/1: Jan first foal, dam a useful dual 7f/1m wnr abroad: expect improvement.
4363 **PRINCE VETTORI 19** [1]2-8-9 E Ahern 33/1: 006: Rear, outpcd 3f out, mod late prog. 2 69a
 SOFT FOCUS [11]2-8-2 C Catlin 14/1: 7: b f Spectrum - Creme Caramel (Septieme Ciel) Mid-div, ¾ 61a
no impress fn 2f: 6,000gns May foal, half-sister to a 7f juv wnr, dam a 7f juv scorer.
4576 **MONAD 8** [3]2-8-2 Amy Baker(7) 33/1: 0008: Prom, btn 2f out, AW bow. ¾ 60a
4484 **YARDSTICK 13** [9]2-8-8 S Whitworth 14/1: 069: Mid-div, struggling fnl 1f: AW bow. ½ 65a
 ROYAL GAME [6]2-8-9 T P Queally 10/1: 0: 10th: Dwelt & al bhd, no ch 2f out. 7 54a
3818 **AUTUMN DAZE 44** [2]2-8-1 M Henry 50/1: 00: 11th: Dwelt, keen & chsd ldrs till halfway, sn bhd. dist 0a
11 Ran Time 1m 39.58(3.38) Owned: Blue Peter Racing 5 Trained: Newmarket

---

Official Going GOOD.

4745

2.20 Macphie Foodservice Classified Stakes 3yo+ 0-75 (D2)
£6874 £2115 £1058 **1m4f** **Good 50** **-13 Slow** Outside

4361 **BELLE ROUGE 19** [13] C A Horgan 6-9-0 (74) L Dettori 3/1 FAV: 1212121: In tch, styd on to lead 76
bef 2f out, rdn out to hold on ins fnl 1f: well bckd: eff btwn 12f/2m on fast, hvy grnd & both AWs: tough,
versatile & most progressive this term: see 4361 & 4203.
4643 **NAWOW 5** [11] P D Cundell 4-9-3 (74) D Holland 16/1: 6-035602: Rear, prog 4f out, styd on to ½ 77
chase wnr well fnl 1f, nrst fin: qck reapp: back to form here: see 1003 (2m).
4274 **DR CERULLO 23** [4] C Tinkler 3-8-9 (73) S Sanders 14/1: 3302443: Held up, prog wide 3f out, styd shd 77
on ins fnl 1f, just held for 2nd: gd eff in defeat & worth a try over 14f on this evidence: see 2984 & 238.
4292 **WASTED TALENT 23** [15] J G Portman 4-9-0 vis (75) P Hanagan 14/1: 31-12004: Keen handy, led after 1¼ 72
5f, hdd bef 2f out, no extra fnl 1f: fin 2nd in this race 12 months ago: see 2114 & 1399.
3625 **MAD CAREW 53** [14]5-9-3 bl (73) R L Moore 14/1: 4055405: Rear, prog when short of room well over 2 72
1f out, kept on late, no ch with principals: 8 wk abs: see 816 (clmr).
4441 **GANYMEDE 15** [16]3-8-9 (75) K Fallon 12/1: 2220436: Led 5f, styd cl-up, no extra bef 1f out: btr 4441. ½ 71
4468 **PAGAN MAGIC 14** [9]3-8-9 (75) P Robinson 7/1: 3010507: Handy 10f, sn hung right & wknd: btr 4468. 1¼ 69
4360 **ALBAVILLA 19** [3]4-9-0 (74) T Quinn 8/1: 556-3258: Keen chsd ldrs 1m, sn outpcd, mod late gains. 1½ 64
4395 **VELVET WATERS 18** [5]3-8-6 (71) S Carson 10/1: 1221339: Handy 10f, wknd: btr 4395 & 4080. shd 64
4473 **SILVER CITY 13** [2]4-9-3 (73) P Dobbs 25/1: 10-20000: 10th: Missed break, nvr a factor: btr 2874. hd 66
4473 **MAYSTOCK 13** [6]4-9-0 (73) J Fortune 9/1: 1030030: 11th: Missed break, nvr a factor: btr 4473. 1 61
4196 **BUKIT FRASER 26** [1]3-8-9 (75) M Hills 14/1: 4000500: 12th: Bhd, nvr able to chall: btr 1756 & 1140. 4 58
4097 **Miss Pebbles 32** [12]4-9-0 (73) Martin Dwyer 16/1:0
4315* **Abington Angel 21** [7]3-8-6 h bl(75) R Winston 16/1:0
147 **Mumbling 291** [10]6-9-3 (69) A Hindley(7) 50/1:0 2192 **Linens Flame 111** [8]5-9-3 (73) D Sweeney 50/1:0

GOODWOOD WEDNESDAY 22.09.04 Righthand, Sharpish, Undulating Track

16 Ran Time 2m 39.43 (7.63) Owned: Mrs B Woodford Trained: Ogbourne Maizey

4746

2.55 Rich's Products Corporation E B F Maiden Stakes 2yo (D2)
£5551 £1708 £854 **1m rnd** **Good 50** **-07 Slow** Inside

4326 **WINGMAN 21** [2] J W Hills 2-9-0 K Fallon 16/1: 051: b c In The Wings - Precedence (Polish Precedent) Held up, prog halfway, styd on to lead cl-home, pushed out, val more: May foal, half-brother successful at 9f: dam plcd at mid-dists: sire decent performer at 12f: apprec today's step up to 1m, will relish 10f: acts on gd: v pleasing eff, looks sure to rate higher. **99+**

4355 **FOXHAVEN 19** [5] P R Chamings 2-9-0 Martin Dwyer 7/2: 322: Led 3f, styd cl-up & led again 3f out, clr dist, hdd under press cl-home: op 9/2, clr rem: useful, can find a minor trk mdn: see 4355. *nk* **95**

4355 **BERTROSE 19** [10] J L Dunlop 2-9-0 S Sanders 12/1: 453: Rear, prog 3f out, onepace. *7* **81**

4462 **SPEAR THISTLE 14** [9] J H M Gosden 2-9-0 J Fortune 2/1 FAV: 44: Handy, no extra bef 1f out: bckd: shade disapp & failed to build on promise shown in 4462 (debut). *¾* **79**

4410 **CHAPTER 16** [4]2-9-0 (77) R L Moore 16/1: 22035: In tch, prog 3f out, no extra ins fnl 1f: btr 4410. *shd* **79**

4363 **WATER PISTOL 19** [6]2-9-0 P Robinson 66/1: 006: Rear, nvr nrr than mid-div: see 4363. *1½* **76**

4356 **ART ELEGANT 19** [11]2-9-0 M Hills 20/1: 057: b c Desert Prince - Elegant (Marju) Held up, prog wide halfway, no impress fnl 2f: Apr foal, dam unplcd: sire Gr 1 wnr at 1m: with B W Hills. *shd* **76**

4522 **LOCH QUEST 11** [7]2-9-0 L Dettori 6/1: 58: Handy 6f, fdd: tchd 8/1: showed more in 4522 (debut). *6* **66**

4544 **SPILL A LITTLE 9** [8]2-9-0 S Hitchcott 16/1: 659: Handy, led after 3f, hdd 3f out, sn wknd: btr 4544. *nk* **65**

4464 **INCA WOOD 14** [1]2-8-9 D Holland 7/1: 220: 10th: In tch, fdd bef 1f out: btr 4464 & 4147. *3* **54**

HUBOOB [3]2-9-0 R Hills 16/1: 0: 11th: b c Almutawakel - Atnab (Riverman) Missed break, al in rear on debut: Jan foal, just 200,000gns: dam successful at 12f: sire high-class mid-dist performer on dirt. *1¾* **56**

11 Ran Time 1m 42.01 (4.61) Owned: Mr D M Kerr Trained: Lambourn

4747

3.30 Sharp Commercial Microwave Oven Stakes Handicap 3yo+ 71-85 (D2) **[87]**
£7072 £2176 £1088 **6f str** **Good 50** **+03 Fast** Stands Side

4700+**ENDLESS SUMMER 2** [8] A W Carroll 7-9-9 (6ex) (82) P Doe 11/2: 0460211: Held up, prog when short of room bef 1f out, pushed & styd on to lead ins fnl 1f, pushed out, val further: qck reapp under 6lb pen: eff at 5/6f on firm & soft grnd, any trk: thriving at present & h'capped to land hat-trick: see 4700 & 921. **93**

4496 **MARSHALLSPARK 12** [12] R A Fahey 5-8-12 (71) P Hanagan 12/1: 0510162: In tch, styd on to lead 1f out, sn hdd, kept on but no pace wnr: gd run on rtn to 6f: see 4496 & 3763. *1* **76**

4394 **NAJEEBON 18** [20] M R Channon 5-9-5 (78) S Hitchcott 11/2: 6300023: Chsd ldrs, prog after halfway, ev ch 1f out, sn no extra: another gd run & is h'capped to find similar (won this off 80 in '03). *1¼* **79**

4700 **TURIBIUS 2** [16] T E Powell 5-9-0 vis (73) A Quinn(5) 33/1: 0000004: Handy till dist, no extra: qck reapp: encouraging eff & rtn to 5f will suit: btr 755 (5f, polytrack). *1* **71**

4496 **CURRENCY 12** [6]7-9-4 (77) R L Moore 8/1: 0052145: Rear, prog 2f out, nrst fin: btr 3966. *½* **74**

4350 **KINGSCROSS 19** [5]6-9-7 (80) D Sweeney 14/1: 1050226: Held up, prog when short of room well over 1f out, sn no impress: likes easy grnd: just btr 4350 & 4184. *hd* **77**

4496 **FYODOR 12** [10]3-8-13 (74) R Hills 50/1: 12-06007: Held up, nvr nrr than mid-div: btr 2137. *½* **70**

4184 **CANTERLOUPE 26** [18]6-9-3 (76) S Sanders 12/1: 0000108: In tch, led after 4f, hdd 1f out, wknd. *1½* **68**

4713 **SKYHARBOR 2** [9]3-9-1 vis (76) Martin Dwyer 33/1: 0523409: In tch 3f, sn outpcd, rallied late. *hd* **68**

3643 **HIGH RIDGE 51** [11]5-8-12 p (71) L Dettori 5/1 FAV: 3412240: 10th: Missed break, nvr nrr than mid-div: op 7/1: rider reported mount was nvr travelling: btr 3643 & 3569. *½* **62**

4394* **THURLESTONE ROCK 18** [14]4-9-5 (78) J Fortune 14/1: 01-05010: 11th: Handy over 4f, wknd: btr 4394. *¾* **66**

4604 **IVORY LACE 7** [13]3-9-2 (77) K Fallon 20/1: 1141500: 12th: Rear, modest late gains: qck reapp. *½* **64**

3569 **UNDETERRED 54** [4]8-9-2 (75) D Mernagh 20/1: 0444100: 13th: In tch stands side, led that group ins fnl 1f, no ch with far side: 8 wk abs; prob at disadvantage racing with small stands side group: btr 3461. *1½* **58**

2717* **SWINBROOK 89** [1]3-9-5 (80) Lisa Jones 25/1: 52-00210: 14th: In tch stands side, led that group 2f out, no ch with far side: long abs: showed more in 2717. *¾* **60**

4394 **SEMENOVSKII 18** [3]4-8-13 (72) D Holland 12/1: 3601000: 15th: Handy over 4f, wknd: bckd from 33/1. *nk* **51**

4184 **Michelle Ma Belle 26** [7]4-9-1 bl(74) M Hills 25/1:0

4642 **Danehill Stroller 5** [2]4-9-7 p(80) N De Souza(5) 25/1:0

4465* **Peruvian Style 14** [17]3-8-13 (74) R Winston 16/1:0 4496 **Zarzu 12** [19]5-9-4 (77) R Thomas(3) 20/1:0

19 Ran Time 1m 12.86 (2.86) Owned: Seasons Holidays Trained: Alcester

4748

4.05 Listed Merbury Catering Consultants Foundation Stakes 3yo+ (A1)
£17400 £6600 £3300 **1m1f192y** **Good 50** **-24 Slow** Inside

4538+**ALKAADHEM 10** [6] M P Tregoning 4-9-3 bl (107) R Hills 6/4 FAV: 4104311: Mid-div, prog bef 2f out, styd on to lead 1f out, qcknd clr, v readily: bckd: eff at 1m, suited by 10f, prob stays 12f: acts on firm & gd grnd: loves Goodwood: imprvd for recent fitting of blnks & looks a horse to follow, win more Gr races. **118**

2825 **PRIVY SEAL 87** [1] J H M Gosden 3-8-8 (107) J Fortune 12/1: 1223042: In tch, styd on to lead 2f out, hdd 1f out, kept on but no ch with easy wnr: long abs: encouraging eff after being gelded: useful. *3½* **107**

4538 **BATTLE CHANT 10** [4] Mrs A J Perrett 4-9-0 (102) R L Moore 11/2: 30-30223: Mid-div, prog 2f out, kept on ins fnl 1f, just held for 2nd: poss tricky customer now: see 4538, 4290. *nk* **106**

4530* **COLISAY 11** [3] E F Vaughan 5-9-0 (102) K Fallon 15/2: 10-36414: Cl-up, no extra bef 1f out: up in class. *1¼* **104**

4219* **NAHEEF 25** [8]5-9-0 vis t (109) L Dettori 2/1: 25-35015: Led, hdd 2f out, wknd from dist: well bckd: disapp on rtn to 10f: inconsistent, btr 4219. *¾* **103**

1685 **SKIDMARK 133** [2]3-8-8 (97) S Sanders 33/1: 2113406: Keen bhd, nvr a factor: long abs: btr 1040 (AW). *¾* **102**

3754+**CORRIOLANUS 11** [7]4-9-0 (103) D Holland 33/1: 6061007: Al in rear: recently unplcd abroad. *nk* **101**

4296} **BAYADERE 371** [5]4-8-9 M Henry 100/1: 312/30-8: br f Lavirco - Brangane (Anita's Prince) Chsd ldrs over 6f, fdd: reapp & new stable: 3rd of 6 on 1 of only 2 '03 starts (rtd 100, stks, Sir M Stoute): juv wnr in '02 in native Germany: eff at 7f, stays 10.5f: acts on firm & gd grnd. *27* **61**

8 Ran Time 2m 11.62 (7.42) Owned: Mr Hamdan Al Maktoum Trained: Lambourn

4749   4.40 Crosse & Blackwell Stakes Handicap 3yo 71-85 (D2)   [92]
£7066 £2174 £1087   **1m3f**   **Good 50**   **-34 Slow**   Outside

4468* **NORDWIND** 14 [1] P W Harris 3-9-5 (83) L Dettori 2/1 FAV: 3411211: Cl-up, led 3f out, sn clr,   **95**
pushed out to assert: well bckd: bckd at 1m/10f, suited by 11/12f: acts on fast, gd/ soft & polytrack:
progressive performer who can land qck-fire hat-trick & another fine positive L Dettori ride.
4281* **QUDRAAT** 23 [7] E F Vaughan 3-9-2 (80) R Hills 7/1: 5012: Held up, still plenty to do when short   1½   **89+**
of room 3f out, switched wide & styd on to chase wnr ins fnl 1f, kept on, nvr getting to wnr: clr rem: imprvd eff &
poss unlucky (jock does not excel here or on hld up horses), can find similar.
4267 **GOODWOOD FINESSE** 24 [5] J L Dunlop 3-8-10 (74) S Sanders 20/1: 55-1563: Chsd ldrs, no impress   5   **75**
bef 1f out: more encouraging back at 11f: see 3255 & 2536.
4293 **PRIME POWERED** 23 [9] G L Moore 3-9-7 p (85) R L Moore 15/2: 1-550204: Missed break, prog 3f out,   hd   **86**
no impress ins fnl 1f: clr rem: btr 2930 (10f).
4502 **JAKARMI** 12 [2]3-8-9 (73) P Hanagan 20/1: 3211005: Nvr nrr than mid-div: btr 2930 (10f).   6   **66**
2621 **GJOVIC** 93 [4]3-8-8 (72) R Winston 20/1: 5043306: Handy 1m, sn wknd: long abs.   4   **59**
4553 **MR TAMBOURINE MAN** 9 [10]3-9-6 (84) N De Souza(5) 5/1: 0131427: Rear, wknd bef 1f out: btr 4553.   hd   **71**
4080 **QUARTINO** 33 [11]3-9-5 BL (83) J Fortune 33/1: 521-008: Rear, styd on to lead 6f out, hdd 3f out, fdd.   3   **65**
3893 **ABSOLUTELYTHEBEST** 41 [3]3-9-2 (80) D Holland 25/1: 2264509: Al in rear: 6 wk abs.   ½   **61**
4314+ **WEDDING CAKE** 21 [12]3-8-9 (73) K Fallon 9/1: 03410: 10th: Handy 1m, fdd: btr 4314 (mdn, a/w).   ½   **53**
4183 **MICHABO** 26 [8]3-9-2 (80) T Quinn 9/1: 3262130: 11th: Led, rcd keenly, hdd 6f out, fdd ins fnl 4f.   2½   **57**
4188 **LOMAPAMAR** 26 [6]3-9-0 (78) P Robinson 20/1: 030-30: 12th: Handy, fdd bef 3f out: btr 4188.   ¾   **54**
12 Ran   Time 2m 27.15 (9.25)   Owned: Mrs P W Harris   Trained: Berkhamstead

4750   5.15 Premier Foods Claiming Stakes Handicap 3yo+ 46-55 (F4)   [67]
£3543 £1090 £545   **1m rnd**   **Good 50**   **+04 Fast**   Inside

4506 **BABY BARRY** 11 [8] Mrs G S Rees 7-8-8 (47) S Sanders 8/1: 0302021: Mid-div, prog 3f out, styd on   **54**
to lead ins fnl 1f, rdn out: prev suited by 5/6f, now stays 1m: acts on firm, gd grnd, handles soft & fibresand:
made gd use of drop down h'cap & this was a confidence boost: see 4506 & 3670.
4485 **MOBO BACO** 13 [14] R J Hodges 7-8-13 (52) K Fallon 13/2: 5060432: Mid-div, prog when short of   nk   **58**
room bef 1f out, switched & styd on well ins fnl 1f, just denied: rider rec a 1 day whip ban: see 2909.
4241 **COLEMANSTOWN** 25 [17] B Ellison 4-9-0 (53) P Hanagan 15/2: 0000003: Handy, styd on to lead 1f   ¾   **57**
out, sn hdd & no extra: eff at 6f/1m: signs of encouragement drpd in grade: see 3872.
4488 **CAPTAIN CLOUDY** 13 [16] M Madgwick 4-8-12 (51) G Baker 33/1: 0030404: In tch, ev ch bef 1f out, wknd.1   **53**
4539 **ICANNSHIM** 10 [18]4-9-2 (55) D Holland 7/1: 0304265: Led, hdd 1f out, no extra: btr 4419.   nk   **56**
4299 **MIDSHIPMAN** 23 [15]6-9-0 vis t (53) R L Moore 9/1: 0222406: Held up, prog 3f out, staying on when   shd   **53**
badly hmpd dist, not recover: closer with clr run: btr 2998.
4488 **ARMENTIERES** 13 [2]3-8-9 bl (52) B Swarbrick(5) 16/1: 0062347: Rear, prog 3f out, no impress fnl   nk   **52**
1f.
4419 **COMPTON AVIATOR** 16 [13]8-8-10 t P (49) P Dobbs 33/1: 6050658: Handy over 6f, wknd: cheek pieces.   nk   **48**
4616 **LUCEFER** 7 [10]6-8-13 (52) Dean Williams(7) 11/1: 4031059: Nvr nrr than mid-div: qck reapp: btr 4141.   ¾   **49**
4342 **BERTOCELLI** 20 [12]3-8-12 (55) A McCarthy 12/1: 4006000: 10th: Nvr nrr than mid-div.   5   **42**
4299 **BLUE QUIVER** 23 [3]4-9-0 (53) L Dettori 14/1: 06-62000: 11th: Rear, prog when short of room 2f   shd   **40**
out, sn btn: has been gelded: btr 820.
4262 **CAFE AMERICANO** 24 [6]4-8-9 e (48) D Sweeney 40/1: 0502200: 12th: Keen rear, nvr a dngr: btr 4055.   nk   **34**
4354 **SMART BOY PRINCE** 19 [7]4-8-10 (53) P Makin(5) 33/1: 5030060: 13th: Handy, fdd 2f out.   11   **19**
3512 **LEARNED LAD** 57 [4]6-8-9 (48) P Doe 33/1: 0000000: 14th: In tch, fdd 2f out.   4   **6**
4367 **MEELUP** 19 [7]4-8-12 p (51) V Slattery 40/1: 2200000: 15th: Al in rear.   4   **0**
4366 **LAND OF NOD** 19 [11]3-8-10 vis (53) J Fortune 14/1: 0-400560: 16th: Rear, nvr able to chall.   10   **0**
4132 **PRIVATE JESSICA** 30 [5]3-8-7 (50) R Winston 33/1: 00400: 17th: Handy, fdd 2f out.   5   **0**
4272 **MACS TALISMAN** 23 [9]4-8-8 t P (47) T Quinn 4/1 FAV: 002300W: Withdrawn at start on vets   **0**
certificate: well bckd from morning at odds of 20/1: see 3232.
18 Ran   Time 1m 41.13 (3.73)   Owned: S B Partnership   Trained: Preston

4751   5.45 Westler Foods Apprentice Stakes Handicap 3yo+ 56-70 (E3)   [75]
£3463 £1065 £533   **5f str**   **Good 50**   **-01 Slow**   Stands Side

4489* **INCH BY INCH** 13 [7] P J Makin 5-8-13 bl (60) A Quinn(3) 9/1: 00-04011: Held up, prog when short of   **68**
room bef 1f out, styd on to lead cl-home, pushed out, val bit more: rider rec a 1 day careless riding ban: eff at
5/6f on firm, gd & polytrack: acts on any trk: eff with blnks: in form 5yo & can land hat-trick: see 4489.
4335 **ONE WAY TICKET** 20 [8] J M Bradley 4-9-7 p (68) L Fletcher 14/1: 0004502: Led, hdd under press   ¾   **72**
cl-home: gd effort & can find similar: see 3984.
4126 **FLARAN** 30 [11] E F Vaughan 4-8-10 (57) N De Souza(3) 12/1: 1504-003: In tch, prog & ev ch well   shd   **61**
ins fnl 1f, no extra: eff at 5/6f on fast & gd grnd: can find a race off this mark: see 3984.
4335 **BYO** 20 [13] M Quinn 6-9-7 (68) Dean Williams(5) 14/1: 0013404: Cl-up, ev ch dist, sn no extra.   nk   **71**
4605 **BORZOI MAESTRO** 7 [3]3-9-7 p (69) A Beech 16/1: 0506055: Chsd ldrs, onepcd fnl 1f: qck reapp.   1   **69**
4184 **MADRASEE** 26 [2]6-9-1 (62) D Nolan 7/1: 5000606: Rear, prog bef 1f out, nrst fin: see 329.   ½   **61**
4548 **DOUBLE M** 9 [16]7-9-4 vis (65) R Thomas(3) 9/4 FAV: 1200037: Mid-div, prog bef 1f out, staying on   nk   **63**
when short of room ins fnl 1f, not recover: bckd: shade closer with clr run: btr 4548.
4528 **KING EGBERT** 11 [9]3-8-8 (54) T Dean(7) 10/1: 000-0408: Rear, nvr nrr than mid-div: btr 4528 (fast).   hd   **54**
4489 **MAROMITO** 13 [15]7-9-2 (63) A Mullen(5) 5/1: 0030149: Missed break, prog halfway, wknd fnl 1f.   2   **55**
3888 **GOLDEN BOUNTY** 41 [5]5-9-0 (61) P Gallagher(5) 25/1: 00-06000: 10th: Missed break, nvr a factor.   shd   **53**
3341 **MARGALITA** 63 [14]4-8-13 bl t (60) Lisa Jones 33/1: 0060000: 11th: Handy 3f, wknd: 9 wk abs.   ½   **51**
4496 **PALAWAN** 12 [10]8-9-2 P (63) R J Killoran(7) 16/1: 0000000: 12th: Handy 3f, sn wknd: cheek pieces.   1¼   **50**
4528 **URBAN ROSE** 11 [6]3-8-10 t p (58) P Makin(5) 16/1: 0304040: 13th: Al in rear stands side: btr 4528.   ½   **44**
4489 **Indian Bazaar** 13 [1]8-8-7 (6oh)(48) M Halford(5) 25/1:0 3849   **Avit** 43 [4]4-8-7 (14oh)(40) Kirsty Milczarek(7) 28/1:0
15 Ran   Time 59.26 (2.56)   Owned: Mrs Anna L Sanders   Trained: Marlborough

PONTEFRACT THURSDAY 23.09.04 Lefthand, Undulating Track, Stiff Uphill Finish

Official Going Firm

4752

2.30 European Breeders Fund Poppin Lane Maiden Stakes 2yo (D2)
£5733 £1764 £882 **6f rnd** **Firm 03** **-17 Slow** Inside

4223 **WISE OWL 26** [10] M Johnston 2-9-0 K Darley 8/15 FAV: 241: Handy & led over 2f out, in command over 1f out, val 5L+: hvly bckd at odds-on, confirmed prev promise: eff at 6f, bred to relish further: acts on firm & gd grnd: likes a stiff/undul or gall trk: useful, win more races: see 4223 & 2408. **92+**

CIRCUMSPECT 0 [4] P C Haslam 2-9-0 G Faulkner 66/1: 2: b g Spectrum - Newala (Royal Academy) Dwelt, mid-div, jmpd faller halfway, styd on to chase wnr over 1f out, no impress: 11,000gns Mar foal, half-brother to a 7f juv wnr, dam plcd at 7f/1m: 7f+ shld suit, handles fm: gd start. *4* **76**

4447 **ZONIC 16** [5] Sir Michael Stoute 2-8-9 K Fallon 4/1: 003: b f Zafonic - Ferber's Follies (Saratoga Six) Chsd ldrs, kept on fnl 2f, nvr any impress on wnr: 100,000gns Mar foal, half-sister to a multiple US wnr, also a 6f juv scorer: dam a juv wnr in US: shld improve over further. *3½* **60**

GRAND SHOW 0 [8] P W Harris 2-9-0 I Mongan 12/1: 4: b c Efisio - Christine Daae (Sadler's Wells) Dwelt, trkd ldrs, no impress fnl 2f: Apr foal, half-brother to a dual 5f juv & subs 1m scorer Risque Lady, also smart sprinter To The Roof: dam a 10f scorer. *1¼* **61**

4670 **ON ACTION 5** [2]2-9-0 A Beech(3) 20/1: 35: Led till over 2f out, fdd under press, qck reapp: btr 4670. *¾* **59**
4436 **KNOT IN WOOD 16** [6]2-9-0 P Hanagan 40/1: 06: Trkd ldrs, struggling from halfway. *10* **33**
4338 **ISLE DREAM 21** [7]2-8-9 K Pierrepont(7) 100/1: 07: Cl-up, rdn & btn 2f out. *6* **12**
CLIFFIE 0 [3]2-9-0 S Righton 66/1: 8: Al outpcd rear. *1¾* **12**
BAILEYS HONOUR 0 [9]2-8-9 R Ffrench 22/1: B: Rdn rear when b.d. halfway. **0**
MATSUNOSUKE 0 [1]2-9-0 Dean McKeown 66/1: F: Dwelt, chsd ldrs when stumbled & fell halfway. **0**
10 Ran Time 1m 15.27 (1.17) Owned: Sheikh Mohammed Trained: Middleham

4753

3.00 Racing Uk On Channel 432 Nursery Handicap Stakes Fillies 2yo 0-85 (D2) **[92]**
£5603 £1724 £862 **1m rnd** **Firm 03** **-18 Slow** Inside

4157 **GLORIOUS STEP 33** [8] J H M Gosden 2-9-7 (85) J Fortune 7/2: 3101: Dwelt, rear, short of room 2f out, switched & rdn/qcknd ins last to lead cl-home, val further: nicely bckd, op 4/1: h'cap bow: eff at 1m, get further: relishes firm grnd, disapp on hvy latest: handles any trk: nice turn of foot here. **95+**
4457 **DANCE FLOWER 15** [3] M R Channon 2-8-13 (77) A Culhane 7/2: 23542: Trkd ldrs, rdn & led over 1f out, drvn & hdd well ins last: progressive filly, styd longer 1m trip well: shown enough to find similar: see 4457. *nk* **82**
4285 **PATXARAN 24** [10] P C Haslam 2-8-2 (66) Rory Moore(5) 25/1: 05463: Chsd ldrs, drvn & kept on, not pace of front pair: stays a stiff 1m, acts on firm grnd: shown enough to find a race: see 3202. *2* **67**
4418 **LOTTIE DUNDASS 17** [13] P W Harris 2-8-9 (73) E Ahern 12/1: 5204: Mid-div, rdn when joc lost whip over 1f out, kept on ins last: h'cap bow: styd longer 1m trip, handles firm & gd/soft grnd: see 3046. *½* **73**
3908* **RATUKIDUL 41** [5]2-9-2 (80) K Fallon 6/4 FAV: 15: Held up in tch, short of room over 2f out, onepace for press ins last: hvly bckd on h'cap bow, 6 wk abs: longer 1m trip likely to suit, handles firm & gd grnd. *shd* **80**
4552 **BLACKCOMB MOUNTAIN 10** [2]2-8-4 (68) A Nicholls 28/1: 5344036: Led/dsptd lead till over 1f out, no extra when eased nr fin: caught the eye latest, may impr on this if rdn with a shade more restraint: see 4552. *1* **66**
4436 **STREET BALLAD 16** [9]2-8-3 (67) T P Queally 16/1: 4037: Mid-div, drvn & no impress fnl 1f, h'cap bow. *1¼* **62**
4518 **FADAEL 12** [6]2-8-1 (65) R Ffrench 22/1: 06338: Mid-div, eff 3f out, rdn & no extra ins last, eased. *2* **56**
4337 **BURTON ASH 21** [1]2-8-8 (72) M Fenton 25/1: 043409: Led/dsptd lead till 2f out, fdd under press. *2½* **58**
3988 **SAHARA MIST 38** [4]2-7-12 (17oh) (45) Hayley Turner(3) 150/1: 06500: 10th: Chsd ldrs, rdn & btn 2f out. *¾* **47**
2845 **KASHMAR FLIGHT 85** [7]2-7-12 (3oh) (59) Dale Gibson 25/1: 00650: 11th: Al bhd, abs: btr 2845 (7f). *3* **41**
11 Ran Time 1m 43.46 (1.66) Owned: Mr Saif Ali Trained: Manton

4754

3.30 S B Honda Handicap Stakes 3yo+ 56-70 (E3) **[77]**
£4243 £1306 £653 **5f rnd** **Firm 03** **+12 Fast** Inside

4339 **BLUE MAEVE 21** [4] J Hetherton 4-8-9 (58) S Righton 16/1: 4215001: Led & rdn clr over 1f out, drvn & held on well: fast time: suited by 5f on fm & gd/soft, prob any trk: best when able to dominate: see 3667. **67**
4696 **TROJAN FLIGHT 4** [2] Mrs J R Ramsden 3-9-3 (67) K Fallon 5/2 FAV: 2121042: Pushed along towards rear, switched wide & styd on well for press, not reach wnr: qck reapp & imprvd eff, see 4339 (6f). *½* **73**
4603 **TUSCAN FLYER 8** [3] R Bastiman 6-8-9 bl (58) Darren Williams 14/1: 4040003: Chsd wnr, styd on for press, no extra well ins last: nicely h'capped, sharper trk may suit, likes Musselburgh: see 1600. *hd* **63**
4618 **BALLYBUNION 7** [6] D Nicholls 5-8-7 (1oh) (55) A Nicholls 15/2: 5103204: Mid-div, styd on for press, nrst fin: likes this trk, return to form: see 4408 & 3966. *¾* **59**
4652 **OBE ONE 6** [5]4-9-4 (67) F Lynch 7/1: 4044505: Towards rear, drvn & kept on, not pace to threaten. *1¼* **66**
4339 **FITZWARREN 21** [8]3-8-9 (59) E Ahern 66/1: 3003606: Chsd ldrs, outpcd fnl 2f: btr 3684 (6f). *1* **55**
4603 **MIDNIGHT PARKES 8** [9]5-9-7 (70) M Henry 10/1: 3100307: Rdn towards rear, kept on wide, no dngr. *nk* **65**
4603 **ONLINE INVESTOR 8** [14]5-8-13 (62) S Sanders 10/1: 0002448: Dwelt & towards rear, only mod prog. *1* **54**
4380 **ROAN RAIDER 19** [1]4-8-8 vis (57) M Fenton 40/1: 5020259: Chsd ldrs, no impress fnl 1f: new yard. *¾* **47**
4636* **KEW THE MUSIC 7** [17]4-8-7 (6ex)(1oh)vis (55) S Hitchcott 16/1: 0000010: 10th: Dwelt, bhd, mod prog. *¾* **44**
4548 **STAGNITE 10** [10]4-8-8 p (57) N Chalmers(5) 40/1: 1006500: 11th: Chsd ldrs, struggling fnl 2f: btr 4412. *1* **42**
4514 **CHICO GUAPO 12** [13]4-9-1 (64) R Winston 25/1: 0000000: 12th: Cl-up, fdd over 1f out: see 1476. *½* **47**
4618 **STRAWBERRY PATCH 7** [11]5-8-8 p (57) N Mackay(3) 11/2: 0210620: 13th: Dwelt & al bhd: btr 4618. *2½* **32**
4496 **CALYPSO DANCER 13** [12]4-9-4 (67) K Darley 33/1: 0424000: 14th: b f Celtic Swing - Calypso Grant (Danehill) Mid-div wide, btn over 2f out: ex-French, h'cap wnr in '03: winning form at 5f, acts on gd & gd/soft. *2½* **34**
4585 **GONENDUNNETT 9** [16]5-8-11 p (60) Hayley Turner(3) 33/1: 3105200: 15th: Al rear: btr 4140. *3½* **16**
3984 **ERRACHT 52** [15]6-8-11 (60) G Baker 50/1: 6000500: 16th: Al bhd, abs: see 1371. *2½* **8**
16 Ran Time 1m 0.84 (u0.46) Owned: Mr R G Fell Trained: Malton

PONTEFRACT
THURSDAY 23.09.04 Lefthand, Undulating Track, Stiff Uphill Finish

4755
4.00 Dalby Screw-Driver Handicap Stakes 3yo+ 86-100 (C1) [95]
£12006 £4554 £2277 **1m2f** **Firm 03** **-19 Slow** Inside

4609 **GO TECH 8** [3] T D Easterby 4-8-7 (1oh) (74) G Gibbons 7/1: 2460421: Held up in tch, briefly **84**
outpcd 2f out, led ins last, drvn out: eff at 7f/1m, now suited by 10f: acts on firm & gd grnd, handles gd/soft:
likes a stiff/undul trk: gd confidence boost: see 2483.

4463 **JAMES CAIRD 15** [5] M H Tompkins 4-9-5 (87) J Fortune 3/1: 2220032: Held up, drvn & kept on for 1¼ **93**
press, not pace of wnr ins last: bckd: tough & genuine, deserves a race: see 4463, 2860 & 2101.

4516 **PARKVIEW LOVE 12** [2] M Johnston 3-8-12 (86) K Darley 18/1: 0000453: Led, hdd over 1f out, kept hd **91**
on for press: stays 10f: slipped to a handy mark, gd run with forcing tactics & turn may not be far away.

3615 **ADAIKALI 54** [8] Sir Michael Stoute 3-8-13 (87) K Fallon 85/40 FAV: 0-021204: Trkd ldrs, rdn & hd **91**
briefly led dist, sn drvn & hdd, no extra: bckd: abs: bckd: see 3358 & 2277.

4728† **TORCELLO 696** [4]6-9-7 (89) R Ffrench 50/1: 340030/-5: b g Royal Academy - Vanya (Busted) Trkd 2 **90**
ldrs & chall over 2f out, briefly led over 1f out, sn hdd & no extra: reapp/long abs: missed '03: unplcd in '02
(tried blnks, rtd 104 at best, reapp, cond stks): '01 mdn scorer: eff at 10/12f on firm & soft, stiff/gall or sharp
trks. 1 Jun'01 Sand 10sft 86- D:

4231 **SELECTIVE 26** [7]5-9-6 (88) E Ahern 20/1: 4004046: Rear, eff when hmpd over 2f out, no impress after. hd **88**
3694 **MASAFI 50** [1]3-9-4 (92) S Sanders 14/1: 1111157: Trkd ldrs, rdn & btn 2f out: well bckd, abs: see 3546. 1½ **90**
4613 **GREY CLOUDS 8** [6]4-8-11 (79) D Allan 18/1: 2322508: Al bhd: btr 3435. 14 **58**
8 Ran Time 2m 10.3 (2.2) Owned: Ryedale Partners No 4 Trained: Malton

4756
4.30 European Breeders Fund Frier Wood Maiden Stakes 2yo (D2)
£5577 £1716 £858 **1m rnd** **Firm 03** **-26 Slow** Inside

3803 **LITTLE MISS GRACIE 33** [1] A B Haynes 2-8-9 (85) K Fallon 11/8 FAV: 33241: Went on after 1f, **88+**
pulled clr fnl 2f, val 8L+: prev trnd by P Burgoyne: hvly bckd, 4th in a Frnch Lstd last mth: suited by 1m, will get
further: acts on firm & gd/soft grnd, sharp or stiff/undul trk: enjoyed forcing tactics today: looks useful.

AMAZING VALOUR 0 [9] M Johnston 2-9-0 K Darley 14/1: 2: b c Sinndar - Flabbergasted (Sadler's 5 **77**
Wells) Chsd ldrs, kept on for press ins last, no threat to wnr: op 12/1: May foal, half-brother to a smart 10f
French wnr, dam a 10f 3yo French scorer: stays 1m & handles firm grnd, will get further & can progress.

MUJAZAF 0 [2] M R Channon 2-9-0 A Culhane 11/4: 3: b c Grand Lodge - Decision Maid (Diesis) nk **76**
Chsd front pair halfway, rdn & no impress fnl 2f but kept on: nicely bckd, op 9/2: 150,000gns Apr first foal, dam a
7f juv wnr: this 1m trip shld suit, prob handles firm grnd.

TRAVEL TIP 0 [8] J H M Gosden 2-9-0 J Fortune 7/1: 4: ch c Gone West - Cap Beino (Lyphard) 3½ **69**
Dwelt, rear, late prog wide, nvr a threat: Mar foal, half-brother to a multiple US wnr, also a 1m scorer Torchlight.

4455 **OPTIMUM 16** [5]2-9-0 T P Queally 25/1: 05: Mid-div, rdn & no impress over 2f out, longer trip. 1 **67**
4483 **SOVEREIGN SPIRIT 14** [4]2-9-0 I Mongan 25/1: 006: Rear halfway, little hdwy, longer trip. 2½ **62**
RED OPERA 0 [3]2-9-0 S Sanders 9/2: 7: Dwelt & held up, no prog: op 11/4. 2½ **57**
4242 **CARIBBEAN DANCER 26** [7]2-8-9 R Ffrench 25/1: 08: Led early, remained cl-up till over 2f out. 2½ **47**
8 Ran Time 1m 44.09 (2.29) Owned: AbacusAliciaHardenAndrewHaynesRacing Ltd Trained: Marlborough

4757
5.00 Betfair Com Apprentice Series Classified Stakes Final Round 3yo+ 0-60 (F3)
£4202 £1293 £647 **1m2f** **Firm 03** **-12 Slow** Inside

4623 **LUCAYAN DANCER 7** [16] D Nicholls 4-9-0 (57) P J Benson(2) 5/1: 6550141: Settled rear, smooth hdwy **66**
to chase ldr dist, hung left & rdn to lead well ins last: eff at 7f, now suited by 10/10.5f: acts on firm & soft,
any trk: appears suited by waiting tactics off a decent pace in amat/appr events: see 4145 & 1049.

4650 **COTTINGHAM 6** [2] M C Chapman 3-8-8 (59) W Hogg 20/1: 0206662: Cl-up & led 3f out, sn rdn clr, ¾ **64**
hdd well ins last & no extra: op 25/1: qck reapp: styd this stiff 10f well under an enterprising ride: see 3835.

4456 **SNOWED UNDER 16** [3] J D Bethell 3-8-8 (58) J Cavanagh(5) 10/1: 5500163: Trkd ldrs, eff to chase 2½ **60**
ldr 2f out, onepace for press: acts on firm & gd/soft grnd: see 4243 & 2322.

4650 **MAMBINA 6** [9] M R Channon 3-8-5 (59) T O'Brien(7) 4/1: 4022324: Held up, chsd ldrs 2f out, ¾ **56**
onepace for press: bckd, op 13/2: qck reapp: prob handles firm grnd but btr 4650 (g/s).

4584* **OUR EMMY LOU 9** [13]3-8-11 (60) S Archer(7) 11/4 FAV: 6-245615: Mid-div, onepace & held over 2f 3 **58**
out: op 15/8: well clr of rem: btr 4584 (g/s, clmr).

4456 **ACTIVE ACCOUNT 16** [1]7-9-0 BL (57) A Mullen 33/1: 6630006: Chsd ldrs, rdn & btn 3f out, tried blnks. 11 **39**
4613* **TATA NAKA 8** [12]4-9-3 (45) Laura Pike(5) 8/1: 0223417: Rear, eff 3f out, no impress: btr 4613. 3½ **37**
4624* **TIME MARCHES ON 7** [7]6-9-6 t (40) Neil Brown(5) 12/1: 6/20-4018: Rear, eff wide, no prog fnl 2f. 1½ **38**
4624 **TURFTANZER 7** [14]5-9-0 t (30) Janice Webster(7) 100/1: 0450059: Mid-div wide, btn 3f out: btr 4624. 3½ **27**
4419 **MANDINKA 17** [6]4-9-0 (35) J Brennan(7) 100/1: 500-0400: 10th: Rider lost iron start, al bhd: see 4243. hd **24**
4719 **LEGAL SET 2** [8]8-9-0 t (60) Suzanne France 25/1: 5002400: 11th: Led 7f, sn btn: qk reapp, needs 6f/1m. 1¼ **24**
4694 **RABITATIT 4** [10]3-8-5 (60) D Fentiman 12/1: 5562040: 12th: Prom, rdn & btn 2f out: qk reapp: btr 4694. 6 **12**
12 Ran Time 2m 09.58(1.48) Owned: Lucayan Stud Trained: Thirsk

BRIGHTON
THURSDAY 23.09.04 Lefthand, V Sharp, Undulating Track

Official Going Firm (Good/Firm Places)

4758
2.10 Djmt Magnotherapy Horse Rug Nursery Handicap Stakes 2yo 0-85 (D3) [91]
£4173 £1284 £642 **5f213y rnd** **Firm** **All times slow** Inside

4551 **MOTH BALL 10** [6] J A Osborne 2-9-7 (84) D Holland 4/5 FAV: 231031: Al cl-up, styd on to lead **99**
dist, pushed out to assert, val 3L+: well bckd: eff at 5f, apprec return to 6f: acts on firm & gd grnd: improving
performer who won with authority under top-weight: useful, see 4551 & 3951.

4471 **ELISHA 14** [2] D M Simcock 2-8-5 (68) C Catlin 4/1: 5106622: Led, hdd under press dist, styd on, 1½ **74**
not pace of wnr: continues to run well & deserves to go one btr: see 4471 & 2020.

4273 **SAFENDONSEABISCUIT 24** [1] S Kirk 2-8-7 (70) J F Egan 16/1: 3342003: Trkd ldrs, hung left & sltly   *1*   **73**
outpcd well over 1f out, kept on ins fnl 1f, well clr of rem: back to form today after a couple of disapp efforts.
3297 **RONNIES LAD 66** [7] Andrew Reid 2-8-0 (63) F Norton 33/1: 5012204: Rear, prog bef 1f out, onepace.   *6*   **50**
4679 **CORNICHE DANCER 5** [8]2-8-10 (73) T E Durcan 12/1: 0002105: Handy 4f, no extra when hung left dist.   *¾*   **58**
4114 **GURRUN 32** [3]2-8-4 (67) R L Moore 20/1: 00006: Nvr nrr than mid-div: see 3005.   *1*   **49**
3671 **MULBERRY LAD 51** [9]2-8-5 bl T (68) Martin Dwyer 12/1: 52427: Sn cl-up, fdd bef 1f out: 7 wk abs.   *1½*   **46**
4483 **ASTEEM 14** [5]2-7-12 (6oh) (55) C Haddon(6) 40/1: 05008: Al in rear.   *1*   **36**
4509 **GORTUMBLO 12** [4]2-9-3 BL (80) T Quinn 12/1: 130009: Chsd ldrs over 3f, fdd: first time blnks.   *3*   **46**
9 Ran   Time 1m 10.30 (2.50)   Owned: Mountgrange Stud   Trained: Upper Lambourn

---

4759   **2.40 Boc Sureflow Selling Stakes 2yo (G4)**
         £2583 £738 £369   **5f59y rnd**   **Firm**   **All times slow**   Inside

4608 **WILTSHIRE 8** [1] M R Channon 2-8-11 L Harman(7) 16/1: 00001: Cl-up, styd on for press to lead   **59**
dist, drvn out to hold on: no bid: eff around 5f on firm grnd: acts on a v sharp/undul trk: apprec drop in grade.
4218 **VON WESSEX 26** [7] G M Turner 2-9-2 P (58) A Quinn(5) 12/1: 3314662: Led, hung right after   *hd*   **62**
halfway, hdd dist, ev ch well in fnl 1f, just held: back to form with fitting of cheek pieces: see 2321 & 2110.
3897 **QUEENS GLORY 42** [6] W R Muir 2-8-6 (57) Martin Dwyer 7/2: 5500663: V slow away, prog halfway, ev   *2*   **46**
ch 1f out, sn no extra: bckd from 8/1: 6 wk abs: eff at 5/6f on firm & fast grnd: btr 1937.
3943 **BAILEYS APPLAUSE 40** [5] C A Dwyer 2-8-6 bl (63) F Norton 7/4 FAV: 5360064: Cl-up, short of room   *2½*   **39**
after halfway, ev ch dist, wknd: 6 wk abs: better expected on drop in grade: btr 1652.
      EIDSFOSS 0 [4]2-8-11 D Holland 2/1: 5: b g Danehill Dancer - Alca Egeria (Shareef Dancer)   *1¾*   **39**
Missed break, prog when short of room well over 1f out, sn no impress: tchd 6/4 on debut: clmd for 5,600: Feb
first foal, dam unrcd: sire useful performer at sprint dists: with N A Callaghan.
4316 **IMPERATRICE 22** [3]2-8-6 C Catlin 20/1: 066: Missed break, nvr nrr than mid-div: btr 4316.   *2*   **28**
3896 **SARTAENA 42** [9]2-8-6 BL F P Ferris(3) 33/1: 007: Sn cl-up, short of room & fdd well over 1f out.   *2*   **22**
4121 **JONNY FOXS 31** [8]2-8-11 bl (48) T E Durcan 40/1: 60608: V slow away, nvr a factor.   *11*   **1**
8 Ran   Time 1m 3.46 (3.46)   Owned: Mr M Channon   Trained: West Ilsley

---

4760   **3.10 European Breeders Fund Maiden Stakes 2yo (D3)**
         £4872 £1499 £750   **6f209y rnd**   **Firm**   **All times slow**   Inside

4192 **LOLA SAPOLA 27** [1] N A Callaghan 2-8-9 R L Moore 25/1: 0001: b f Benny The Dip - Cutpurse Moll   **79**
(Green Desert) Sn well outpcd in rear, prog well over 1f out, styd on to lead cl-home, pushed out, val bit more:
Feb foal, half-sister to wnrs at 5/7f, incl useful sprinter Colonel Cotton: dam successful at 7f: sire Gr 1 wnr at
12f: eff at 7f, furthest will suit on this evidence: acts on firm grnd & a v sharp/undul trk.
4393 **GITCHE MANITO 19** [4] A King 2-9-0 (76) J D Smith 14/1: 3052: Cl-up, led after 2f, under press   *1*   **80**
well over 1f out, hdd cl-home: acts on firm & gd grnd: see 3883.
4422 **MISS TRIAL 17** [7] M A Jarvis 2-8-9 P Robinson 11/8: 633: Led, hdd after 1f, styd in tch & ev ch   *2*   **71**
dist, no extra well ins fnl 1f: clr rem: well bckd: stays 7f, return to 6f will suit: acts on firm & fast grnd.
4470 **WINGSPEED 14** [5] Mrs A J Perrett 2-9-0 D Holland 1/1 FAV: 524: Prom over 5f, sn hung left &   *7*   **64**
fdd: well bckd: disapp run & did not appear to enjoy today's trk: showed more in 4470.
4330 **PUSSY CAT 21** [3]2-8-9 (50) C Catlin 66/1: 0605: Rear, nvr a factor.   *9*   **43**
      SERGEANT LEWIS 0 [6]2-9-0 S W Kelly 12/1: 6: gr c Mind Games - Silver Blessings (Statoblest)   *2*   **44**
Mid-div 5f, fdd: op 20/1 on debut: Feb foal, cost 9,000gns: half-brother to wnrs at sprint dists: dam unrcd.
6 Ran   Time 1m 24.21 (4.41)   Owned: Mr Jeremy Gompertz   Trained: Newmarket

---

4761   **3.40 Betdaq Com Global Betting Exchange Classified Stakes 3yo 0-60 (F3)**
         £3476 £1070 £535   **7f214y rnd**   **Firm**   **All times slow**   Inside

4542 **OTAGO 11** [1] J R Best 3-9-0 (58) T Quinn 4/1: 5042101: Mid-div, prog 2f out, styd on to lead   **66**
well ins fnl 1f, rdn out: prev suited by 5/6f, now suited by 1m: acts on firm & gd/soft grnd: see 4346 & 4202.
4649 **BEAUTIFUL NOISE 6** [4] D Morris 3-8-11 bl (49) M Tebbutt 10/1: 6555552: Mid-div, prog & ev ch   *nk*   **60**
dist, styd on ins fnl 1f, just denied: acts at 1m on firm grnd: eff with blnks: see 3711 & 1825.
4057 **MISTER TRICKSTER 35** [8] R Dickin 3-9-0 (60) Lisa Jones 16/1: 0010003: In tch, styd on to lead   *2½*   **58**
dist, hdd ins fnl 1f, no extra: stays 1m, return to 7f may prove ideal: acts on firm & gd grnd: btr 2199.
4546 **BEAUTY OF DREAMS 10** [7] M R Channon 3-8-11 (57) C Catlin 7/1: 0530604: Bhd, prog over 1f out,   *nk*   **54**
nrst fin: op 11/2: acts on firm & fast grnd: see 3963.
4440 **NEW YORK 16** [6]3-8-11 t (60) D Holland 7/1: 324-0035: Led, hdd dist, no extra: see 4440 (7f).   *1*   **52**
4487 **OFF BEAT 14** [10]3-9-0 (60) S Carson 16/1: 0000006: Nvr nrr than mid-div: btr 729.   *½*   **54**
4452 **CARTE NOIRE 16** [12]3-8-11 P (54) F P Ferris(3) 25/1: 0-510007: Cl-up till halfway, sn outpcd,   *1½*   **48**
rallied late: first time cheek pieces: btr 2216.
4475 **LADY TAVERNER 14** [5]3-8-11 (54) S Whitworth 20/1: 00508: Rear, modest late prog: see 3038.   *nk*   **47**
4366 **ARCHERFIELD 20** [9]3-8-111 (58) R L Moore 7/2 FAV: 0233449: Rear, prog 3f out, no impress fnl 2f: *nk*   **46**
op 5/1: reportedly did not handle today's firm grnd: showed more in 3219 (gd) & 2873 (fast).
4334 **FISBY 21** [2]3-9-0 (60) J F Egan 12/1: 0-55000: 10th: Sn cl-up, fdd bef 1f out.   *6*   **38**
4504* **MEGABOND 12** [3]3-9-0 p (60) D Fox(5) 12/1: 5040010: 11th: Cl-up, fdd 2f out: op 7/1: new stable.   *nk*   **37**
3950 **TRIFTI 40** [11]3-9-0 (56) N Callan 20/1: 0004200: 12th: Handy 6f, sn fdd & hung left: 6 wk abs.   *1½*   **34**
12 Ran   Time 1m 36.07 (4.07)   Owned: Mrs L M Askew   Trained: Maidstone

---

4762   **4.10 Betdaq Co Uk Maiden Stakes 3yo+ (D3)**
         £3513 £1081 £541   **7f214y rnd**   **Firm**   **All times slow**   Inside

2261 **SOUTHERN BAZAAR 109** [6] B W Hills 3-8-13 T R Hughes 5/4 FAV: 5-21: Cl-up, led 3f out, pushed out   **79**
ins fnl 1f to hold on, val bit more: bckd: long abs: eff at 1m, bred to apprec further: acts on firm grnd & a
sharp/undul or stiff trk: goes well fresh: got off the mark with fitting of first time t-strap: see 2261.
2385 **OLIVANDER 103** [7] R M Beckett 3-8-13 bl T (74) N Callan 4/1: 2U6-0302: Keen cl-up, led halfway,   *1*   **73**
hdd 3f out, kept on ins fnl 2f, not pace wnr: bckd: long abs & new stable: eff at 6/7f, now stays 1m: ran to form
after being gelded with fitting of first time t-strap: see 2259 (G A Butler).

BRIGHTON THURSDAY 23.09.04 Lefthand, V Sharp, Undulating Track

4578 **ELUSIVE KITTY 9** [9] G A Butler 3-8-9 (1ow)t (68) D Holland 9/2: 5-6R3353: Led till halfway, no extra dist. ¾ **67**

2495 **GROUND PATROL 99** [5] G L Moore 3-8-13 T (62) R L Moore 12/1: 3436004: Chsd ldrs over 6f, no extra: clr rem: long abs & first time t-strap: see 676 (10f, polytrack). 1¼ **69$**

4445 **POLISH ROSE 16** [1]3-8-8 Martin Dwyer 5/1: 05: Chsd ldrs 6f, wknd: see 4445. 6 **53**

2536 **ROYAL LOGIC 97** [8]3-8-8 T E Durcan 33/1: 006: Chsd ldrs, wknd 3f out: long abs. 10 **35**

4661 **DARK PARADE 5** [3]3-8-13 J Jones(7) 66/1: 5057: Keen mid-div 4f, fdd. 13 **18**

LITTLE MISS LILI 0 [2]3-8-8 A McCarthy 25/1: 8: Missed break, nvr a factor on debut. 14 **0**

8 Ran Time 1m 36.79 (4.79) Owned: Mr K Abdulla Trained: Lambourn

4763

4.40 Betdaq Com Handicap Stakes 3yo 46-55 (F4) **[61]**
£2643 £755 £378 **1m1f209y** **Firm** **All times slow** Outside

3982* **DAYDREAM DANCER 38** [5] C G Cox 3-9-2 bl (49) R Smith 7/2: 0003011: Chsd ldrs, short of room 2f out, switched & styd on to lead ins fnl 1f, pushed out, val 4L+: eff around 10f on firm & fast grnd: eff with blnks & likes Brighton: see 3982. **62**

4202 **COBALT BLUE 27** [8] W J Haggas 3-9-4 P (51) J F Egan 5/1: 1550302: Cl-up, led 5f out, sn clr, hdd under press ins fnl 1f, no extra: acts on firm & gd grnd: ran to form with visor left off & pieces fitted: see 3982. 2½ **57**

4612* **LENWADE 8** [7] G G Margarson 3-8-13 (6ex) (46) A McCarthy 15/2: 0452213: Bhd, prog 3f out, no impress ins fnl 1f: op 5/1: acts on firm & gd grnd: see 4612 (seller). 1¼ **50**

4202 **HANA DEE 27** [4] M R Channon 3-9-2 (49) T E Durcan 14/1: 0453004: Rear, nvr nrr than mid-div. 5 **46**

3916 **LARAD 41** [2]3-8-13 bl (46) Laura Reynolds(7) 14/1: 6106065: Missed break, nvr nrr than mid-div: 6 wk abs. 2 **40**

1529 **MELINDAS GIRL 143** [1]3-9-2 (49) N Callan 16/1: 0650-06: Rcd keenly & led 5f, hung left & fdd fnl 2f. 6 **35**

4372 **FIDDLES MUSIC 19** [10]3-8-13 (46) C Catlin 11/1: 5650167: Keen cl-up 1m, fdd: btr 4165 (1m, soft). 1¼ **30**

4113 **MR BELVEDERE 33** [3]3-9-4 (51) J Mackay 7/1: 0032048: Handy 6f, fdd: btr 2431 (1m). 9 **23**

4268 **AFRICAN STAR 25** [6]3-9-3 p (50) R L Moore 3/1 FAV: 5-656409: In tch, lost action around 3f out, eased & returned lame: op 5/1: btr 2868. 15 **0**

4037 **BREAKING THE RULE 36** [9]3-9-0 (47) Dane O'Neill 40/1: 06500: 10th: Al in rear: see 3422. 1¼ **0**

10 Ran Time 2m 4.97 (7.17) Owned: The Grey Lady Partnership Trained: Hungerford

4764

5.10 Alexander Catering Amateur Riders' Maiden Handicap Stakes 3yo+ 46-55 (F4) **[41]**
£2587 £739 £370 **1m3f196y** **Firm** **All times slow** Outside

3727 **TOM BELL 49** [10] J G M O'Shea 4-10-8 (49) Mr E Dehdashti 11/2: 0442401: In tch, styd on to lead 3f out trav well, pushed out, val 6L+: 7 wk abs: eff at 12f/2m1f on firm & hvy grnd: see 2937 & 1064. **61**

4624 **ISLANDS FAREWELL 7** [8] D Nicholls 4-10-8 (49) Miss Kelly Harrison(3) 3/1 FAV: 0250322: Mid-div, prog to chase wnr dist, kept on but al held ins fnl 1f: tchd 9/4, clr rem: eff at 1m/10f, now stays 12f. 4 **53**

4372 **PRINCESS BANKES 19** [11] Miss Gay Kelleway 3-9-11 (45) Miss E J Tuck(7) 25/1: 0600043: Bhd, prog 6f out, styd on to chase wnr 2f out, wknd ins fnl 1f: see 2049. 6 **41**

4319 **MADAME MARIE 22** [3] S Dow 4-10-7 (48) Mr D Hutchison(5) 12/1: 0600004: Missed break, no dngr. 5 **36**

3768} **EACHY PEACHY 399** [7]5-10-5 (11oh) (35) Miss K Manser(5) 12/1: 002536-5: ch f Perugino - Miss Big John (Martin John) Nvr nrr than mid-div: reapp: plcd 3 time in '03 (med auct mdn & sell h'caps, rtd 34 & 54$): plcd in early '02 (rtd 56a & 53, h'cap & class stks): eff at 1m/10f, stays a slowly run 2m: acts on fast, gd grnd & both AWs: tried eye-shield: with J R Best. 4 **28**
2 Jul'03 Folk 16.4g/f 34-33 F: 2 Sep'01 Beve 7.4gd 55-50 F:

3618 **GREEK STAR 54** [6]3-9-11 (45) Miss S Harler(7) 20/1: 0-4006: Handy, wknd 3f out: 8 wk abs. 7 **18**

1396 **COLONNADE 150** [9]5-10-5 (46) Mrs N Wilson(3) 16/1: 00-20307: Al bhd: long abs. 7 **8**

4319 **WALTZING BEAU 22** [5]3-9-11 (45) Mr S Walker 100/30: 0023668: In tch 6f, wknd: disapp: btr 3300. *shd* **7**

3145 **KARAKUM 74** [12]5-10-5 (6oh) (40) Mr G Tumelty(7) 33/1: 000/0-409: Missed break, al bhd. ¾ **5**

3845 **AUTUMN FLYER 44** [1]3-10-5 (54) Miss N Forde(5) 15/2: 00-00050: 10th: Cl-up 1m, sn wknd. ¾ **11**

4188 **LASSER LIGHT 27** [4]4-11-0 (55) Miss E J Jones 20/1: 0-0050: 11th: Prom 6f, sn wknd. 4 **6**

4584 **DUKES VIEW 9** [2]3-10-4 bl (53) Miss L J Harwood(3) 14/1: 5506060: 12th: Sn led, hdd 3f out, fdd. 4 **0**

12 Ran Time 2m 35.74(7.54) Owned: Mr K W Bell Trained: Westbury On Severn

HAYDOCK FRIDAY 24.09.04 Lefthand, Flat, Galloping Track

Official Going Heavy (Soft Places) Times Suggest Straight Course much softer

4765

1.50 Barry Case North West Ltd Nursery Handicap Stakes 2yo (C1) **[102]**
£10868 £3344 £1672 **6f str** **Soft** **Inapplicable** Centre

4490* **TAGULA SUNRISE 14** [4] R A Fahey 2-8-3 (77) P Hanagan 9/2 FAV: 2203211: Mid-div, short of room over 1f out, rdn to lead ins last, decisively: nicely bckd: eff at 5f, suited by 6f & shld get further: acts on firm & soft, likes a gall trk: well regarded & prog filly, keep on side: see 4490. **88+**

3221 **HARVEST WARRIOR 71** [15] T D Easterby 2-9-7 (95) D Allan 16/1: 22152: Mid-div, hdwy & led 2f out, drvn & hdd ins last, no extra: fine run, returned to form after 10 wk abs: acts on gd & hvy: useful: see 2902. 1¾ **101**

4509 **DAHTEER 13** [3] M R Channon 2-9-4 (92) A Culhane 10/1: 1160233: Unruly bef start, trkd ldrs, onepace for press from dist: see 4105, 2367. ¾ **97**

3735* **THROW THE DICE 50** [14] K A Ryan 2-8-13 (87) N Callan 11/2: 214: Held up, smooth hdwy to chall over 1f out, no extra for press ins last: bckd: 7 wk abs, h'cap bow: lightly rcd & prog: see 3735 (C/D, mdn). ½ **91**

4443* **MISSED A BEAT 17** [2]2-8-2 (76) W Supple 33/1: 04015: Chsd ldrs, drvn & kept on onepace: handles firm & soft: see 4443. *hd* **79**

4692 **MAKE US FLUSH 5** [9]2-8-0 (74) F Norton 12/1: 1021006: Rear, styd on for press, nrst fin: quick reapp: see 3902 (gd/soft, C/D). 1¼ **74**

4153 **CELTIC SPA 34** [6]2-8-9 (83) K Darley 8/1: 1053047: Mid-div, onepcd fnl 2f: bckd: btr 4153 (g/f). ½ **82**

4385 **SYDNEYROUGHDIAMOND 20** [8]2-8-1 (75) S Righton 50/1: 0508: Led/dsptd lead 4f, fdd under press. 5 **64**

4490 **FLYING DANCER 14** [7]2-7-12 (2oh) (70) D Kinsella 50/1: 3409: In tch, no impress fnl 2f, h'cap bow. *nk* **60**

4396 **SELKIRK STORM 19** [12]2-7-12 (72) Dale Gibson 12/1: 1250000: 10th: Mid-div, no impress on ldrs. *nk* **59**

4490 **DANCING ROSE 14** [1]2-8-2 (76) P Robinson 6/1: 23150: 11th: Chsd ldrs, btn 2f out: btr 4490 & 4200. ½ **62**

4545 **CROSS MY SHADOW 11** [5]2-7-12 (9oh)t (63) R Thomas(1) 100/1: 05000: 12th: Cl-up, btn over 2f out. ½ **57**

3931 **MITCHELLAND 42** [10]2-7-12 (5oh)vis (67) D Mernagh 50/1: 6635550: 13th: Cl-up, strugg halfway. ½ **56**
4396 **TIVISKI 19** [11]2-7-13 (1ow)(2oh) (70) J Quinn 33/1: 0450000: 14th: Chsd ldrs, rdn & btn 2f out. 1¼ **54**
4458 **TRANSACTION 16** [13]2-9-1 (89) J Tate 10/1: 3211600: 15th: Chsd ldrs, strug fnl 2f: btr 3614 (g/f). 7 **56**
15 Ran Time 1m 17.89 (6.59) Owned: Mr David M Knaggs & Mel Roberts Trained: Malton

4766 **2.20 Vale Uk Handicap Stakes 3yo+ 71-85 (D2)** **[99]**
£11003 £3386 £1693 **1m2f120y** **Good/Soft** **Fair** Outside

4656* **STRAW BEAR 7** [11] Sir Mark Prescott 3-8-12 (6ex) (83) S Sanders 15/8 FAV: 31-23511: Trkd ldrs, smooth prog & led 3f out, pulled clr under hand riding from over 1f out, val 7L+: hvly bckd, op 5/2: eff at 1m/9f, significant prog at 10f last twice, 12f will suit: acts on fast & fibresand, loves gd/soft grnd & a gall trk: useful performance, remains one to follow: see 4656. **99+**
4499 **SEWNSO CHARACTER 14** [9] M Blanshard 3-9-0 (85) N Callan 20/1: 4404602: Trkd ldrs travelling well 4f out, chsd wnr 2f out, rdn & no impress dist; stays a gall 10.5f well: well h'capped, can find a race this autumn. 5 **90**
4656 **TROUBLE MOUNTAIN 7** [16] M W Easterby 7-8-7 (71) P Mulrennan(3) 11/2: 4021423: Rear, styd on wide for press despite hanging left, not able to chall: aslo bhd today's wnr in 4656, see 3904. 1¼ **74**
1668 **CRUISE DIRECTOR 136** [4] W J Musson 4-9-7 (85) R Mullen 14/1: 3010024: Rear, late gains when short of room dist, nvr threat: 5 month abs: see 1668, 1056. 2½ **84**
4515 **MCQUEEN 13** [3]4-8-7 (5oh) (66) A Mullen(7) 20/1: 6021105: Dwelt, mid-div, eff wide, mod prog for press: likes to dominate, fair run after slow start: see 4299. 2½ **66**
4629 **INTRICATE WEB 8** [5]8-9-2 (80) D Allan 25/1: 0100056: Rear, mod gains, no threat. 1 **74**
4399 **SANTIBURI LAD 19** [1]7-8-7 (4oh) (67) D Tudhope(5) 33/1: 2112007: Led 4f, btn 2f out: btr 3139. 1½ **63**
625 **BROOKLYNS GOLD 223** [19]9-9-0 (78) L Enstone 50/1: 332///40-68: b g Seeking The Gold - Brooklyn's Dance (Shirley Heights) Rear, only mod prog: abs: lightly rcd in '03 (h'cap plcd, rtd 78): won 3 h'cap hdles in 02/03 (rtd 126h, 2m1f, fast & soft): former List wnr in France: eff arnd 10f on fast & hvy grnd. 1¼ **68**
4579+ **FORT CHURCHILL 10** [7]3-8-6 (6ex)bl (77) P Hanagan 6/1: 5342019: Handy & led after 4f till 3f out, fdd: new yard: btr 4579 (clmr). shd **67**
3802 **SAFIRAH 47** [2]3-8-2 (1ow) (72) P Robinson 20/1: 3550: 10th: Mid-div, strug fnl 3f: h'cap bow, abs. 1¼ **61**
4346 **TEMPLET 22** [10]4-8-8 bl (72) T Eaves(3) 33/1: 3002140: 11th: Trkd ldrs, fdd fnl 2f: btr 4346 & 4135. hd **59**
1235 **DOWER HOUSE 160** [15]9-8-12 (76) D Mernagh 66/1: 6540500: 12th: Rear, nvr a factor: 5 mth abs. 2½ **59**
4353 **GOLANO 21** [6]4-8-12 VIS (76) Dane O'Neill 33/1: 10-20060: 13th: Dwelt, chsd ldrs, btn 3f out: visor. 1 **58**
4609 **DREAM MAGIC 9** [18]6-8-13 (77) M Henry 14/1: 0323330: 14th: Struggling halfway: btr 4609, 4097. 1 **58**
4071 **TRIPLE JUMP 35** [17]3-8-4 (75) W Supple 12/1: 4-2130: 15th: Held up, hdwy 3f out, btn 2f out. 12 **40**
2762 **Sunny Glenn 90** [8]6-9-2 (80) P McCabe 66/1:0 4305 **Akash 24** [14]4-9-7 (85) K Darley 40/1:0
3945 **Adjawar 41** [12]6-9-2 (80) R Winston 100/1:0 3084 **Kings Empire 77** [13]3-8-11 T(82) K McEvoy 66/1:0
19 Ran Time 2m 17.25 (7.25) Owned: Mr Chris Jenkins Trained: Newmarket

4767 **2.50 Betfred In-Running On Sports Handicap Stakes 3yo+ 86-100 (C1)** **[103]**
£18740 £7108 £3554 **1m30y rnd** **Good/Soft** **Fast** Inside

3775 **ST ANDREWS 48** [6] M A Jarvis 4-9-5 (94) P Robinson 9/4 FAV: 4/-262501: Chsd ldrs, smooth prog & led 2f out, rdn clr, easily: hvly bckd, op 3/1: 7 wk abs: eff at 7f, suited by 1m: acts on fast & gd, relishes gd/soft grnd, stiff/gall trks: v useful display, keep on side with ease in the grnd this autumn: see 2915, 1962. **111+**
4386 **EXCELSIUS 20** [1] J L Dunlop 4-9-7 bl (96) K Darley 11/1: 1-030042: Dwelt, held up in tch & rcd keenly, styd on for press fnl 2f, no ch with wnr: see 4386 & 108. 7 **101**
4279 **IMPERIALISTIC 25** [8] K R Burke 3-9-0 p (93) S Sanders 3/1: 4110553: Held up, kept on for press fnl 3f, nvr able to threaten: well bckd tho' op 9/4: just btr 4279. 1¼ **95**
3001 **GIFT HORSE 80** [5] J R Fanshawe 4-8-11 (86) R Winston 6/1: 16-02304: Held up, switched wide & mod gains for press: bckd, abs: btr 2679 & 2172 (7f). 1 **86**
4685* **YOUNG MR GRACE 6** [10]4-8-11 (6ex) (86) D Allan 5/1: 6213015: Trkd ldr, ch 3f out, wknd: bckd under a 6lb pen, quick reapp: btr 4685 (dictated). 3½ **80**
4515 **YOUNG ROONEY 13** [2]4-8-7 (12oh)BL (70) L Enstone 25/1: 4-403226: Led & sn clr racing freely, hdd 2f out & wknd: 1st time blnks: stiff task, see 4515, 4347. 1¾ **73**
4531 **WILL HE WISH 13** [9]8-9-0 bl (89) T Eaves(3) 20/1: 0136207: Chsd ldrs, btn 2f out: btr 4279. 1½ **77**
3620 **RESPLENDENT ONE 55** [3]3-9-4 (97) K McEvoy 16/1: 01-60448: Chsd ldrs, strug when hmpd 3f out: abs. 3½ **79**
4928} **CAMILLE PISSARRO 332** [4]4-9-0 (89) Dane O'Neill 40/1: 255053-9: b g Red Ransom - Serenity (Selkirk) Al bhd on reapp: reapp wnr in '03 (AW mdn, P Cole, subs val h'cap rnr-up, disapp in blnks): unplcd '02 (rtd 79, lightly rcd, mdn): wng form at 8.5f, stays gall 10.4f well: acts on firm, fast & fibresand, prob any trk can go well fresh. 2 Aug'03 Folk 9.7g/f 93-(93) C: 2 May'03 York 10.4g/f 93-89 B: 1 Mar'03 Wolv 8.5af 89a- D: 6 **61**
1616} **NORTHERN DESERT 493** [7]5-9-7 (96) Darren Williams 100/1: 20554/0-0: 10th: b g Desert Style - Rosie's Guest (Be My Guest) Chsd ldrs, rdn & struggling fnl 3f: reapp: unplcd sole '03 start (rtd 85, h'cap): '02 mdn wnr on reapp, subs dual rnr-up, incl a val h'cap (rtd 106 at best, G Wragg): best at 7f/1m on firm & soft, prob any trk: has gone well fresh. 2 May'02 Ches 7.5fm 96-90 C: 2 Apr'02 Newm 7fm 92- C: 1 Mar'02 Nott 8.2sft 84- D: 2 Oct'01 Ling 6sft 75- D: 2 Sep'01 Ling 6gd 81- F: 9 **53**
10 Ran Time 1m 44.37 (3.87) Owned: Team Havana Trained: Newmarket

4768 **3.25 Subscribe To Racing Uk On 08700 860432 Maiden Stakes 3yo+ (D3)**
£3679 £1132 £566 **1m30y rnd** **Good/Soft** **Slow** Inside

2248 **MUSICANNA 111** [17] J R Fanshawe 3-8-9 T R Winston 5/2 FAV: 21: Rear, hdwy halfway, switched/rdn to lead well ins last, going away: hvly bckd, 4 month abs: eff at 1m on fast & gd/soft, stiff/gall trks: goes well fresh & suited by t-strap today: lightly rcd & can progress, particularly over further: see 2248. **78**
3634 **FOOLISH GROOM 54** [10] R Hollinshead 3-9-0 (66) W Supple 11/2: 4563502: Trkd ldrs, briefly led ins last, no extra nr line: op 7/1, clr rem, 8 wk abs: t-strap & cheek pieces omitted: imprvd, off rtd 66. 1¾ **79$**
4388 **SANTA CATERINA 20** [13] J L Dunlop 3-8-9 (69) S Sanders 11/4: 0-452003: Held up, styd on onepace for press fnl 2f: btr 3108 (10f). 3 **68**
4547 **TENNYS GOLD 11** [2] B W Hills 3-8-9 (70) A Culhane 9/2: 02-4354: Trkd ldrs, rdn & ch over 1f out, no extra ins last: bckd, op 11/2: just btr 2378. shd **68**
3697 **THE LOOSE SCREW 51** [4]6-9-4 p (35) K Darley 100/1: 0000055: b g Bigstone - Princess of Dance 2 **69$**

(Dancing Dissident) Led after 2f, hdd ins last & wknd: h'cap rnr-up in '03: unplcd '02 (tried blnks, rtd 32, no sand form): stays a stiff 10f, handles fast & gd/soft grnd: off rtd 35, treat this rating with caution.
2 Sep'03 Newc 10.1g/f 50-37 D:

3175 **DANCES WITH ANGELS 73** [16]4-8-13 (35) P M Quinn 66/1: 0300P06: Mid-div, edged left & no impress fnl 2f: abs, new yard: off rtd 35.	2½	59
DOVEDALE [9]4-8-13 V Slattery 100/1: 7: b f Groom Dancer - Peetsie (Fairy King) Dwelt & held up, mod gains, nvr a factor: Flat debut, 12 wk jumps abs (mod).	1	57
2886 **WARBRECK 85** [15]3-9-0 BL P Hanagan 33/1: 008: Dwelt & bhd, mod prog in 1st time blnks, abs.	1½	59
4674 **AGGI MAC 6** [6]3-8-9 e (35) Suzanne France(7) 100/1: 5-500009: Dwelt, mid-div, struggling fnl 2f.	2	50$
ALGHAAZY [14]3-9-0 N Mackay(3) 10/1: 0: 10th: Held up, eff 3f out, little hdwy, debut.	¾	54
BODFARI DREAM [18]3-8-9 L Enstone 100/1: 0: 11th: Slow away & al bhd, rider reported he was hit in the face by mount as the gates opened, debut.	3½	42

Delta Star [8]4-8-13 N Callan 25/1:0   **4921} Carnt Spell 332** [7]3-9-0 A Nicholls 100/1:0
Jacks Check [12]3-9-0 R Mullen 100/1:0   4042 **Classic Expression 36** [1]3-8-9 (45) G Gibbons 33/1:0
4667 **Pearl Island 6** [3]3-9-0 M Tebbutt 100/1:0   **Marburyanna** [5]4-8-13 S Righton 100/1:0
17 Ran   Time 1m 47.43 (6.93)   Owned: Mr Abdulla BuHaleeba   Trained: Newmarket

---

4769   4.00 Visitsthelens Com Maiden Stakes Fillies 2yo   (D3)
£3679   £1132   £566   **6f str**   **Soft**   **Inapplicable**   Centre

4625 **ALEXIA ROSE 8** [13] A Berry 2-8-11 (73) F Lynch 4/1: 604321: Handy & led halfway, flashed tail under press ins last but styd on strongly: nicely bckd: eff at 5f, imprvd for forcing tactics at 6f today: acts on fast & gd, relished soft grnd: likes a stiff/gall trk: prog of late, interesting for nurs: see 4625 & 4497.		85
4490 **MOLLY MARIE 14** [10] T D Easterby 2-8-11 (77) D Allan 6/4 FAV: 4620002: Chsd ldrs, rdn & kept on fnl 1f, al held: hvly bckd: lkd unlucky latest: prob handles firm & soft grnd: see 4490 & 3736.	2½	77
3975 **SQUAW DANCE 39** [5] W J Haggas 2-8-11 P Hanagan 15/8: 63: Towards rear, kept on for press to take 3rd ins last, nvr lkd dangerous: well bckd, op 9/4: imprvd from intro & handles soft: could improve at 7f+.	1	75
4447 **SAND IRON 17** [3] S L Keightley 2-8-11 R Fitzpatrick 25/1: 64: b f Desert Style - Mettlesome (Lomond) Chsd ldrs, rdn & kept on onepace fnl 2f: turf bow: Apr foal, half sister to 2 1m 3yo scorers, also a dual 10/14f 4yo wnr: dam a multiple 1m wnr abroad: handles soft grnd & a gall trk, stay further.	1½	72
4349 **DANZATRICE 21** [7]2-8-11 T Eaves(3) 50/1: 05: b f Tamure - Miss Petronella (Petoski) Held up, kept on from halfway under hand riding, nrst fin: left debut bhd: Apr foal, sister to prog mid-dist/staying h'capper Lets Roll: handles soft grnd: caught the eye late on, breeding suggests 1m+ will suit in time.	shd	72+
4442 **JOYEAUX 17** [2]2-8-11 R Havlin 50/1: 06: b f Mark of Esteem - Divine Secret (Hernando) Led till halfway, no extra over 1f out: 25,000gns Mar 1st foal: dam unrcd: clr of rem today.	shd	71
TARAGAN [4]2-8-7 R Winston 50/1: 7: Dwelt & rear, mod late prog.	6	55
4556 **KILMOVEE 11** [8]2-8-11 (67) A Culhane 33/1: 5055008: Cl-up, struggling fnl 2f, longer trip.	hd	58
STEVMARIE STAR [9]2-8-7 F Norton 33/1: 9: Dwelt & al towards rear.	½	53
3633 **SWALLOW FALLS 54** [1]2-8-11 L Enstone 33/1: 050: 10th: Chsd ldrs, no impress from halfway, abs.	1	55
4511 **POLAR PASSION 13** [14]2-8-11 W Supple 50/1: 50: 11th: In tch, wknd fnl 2f: dropped in trip.	5	45
LIRAGE [12]2-8-7 S Righton 100/1: 0: 12th: Al bhd.	2	37

Just Elizabeth [6]2-8-7 P Mulrennan(2) 40/1:0   **Witchy Vibes** [11]2-8-7 G Gibbons 100/1:0
14 Ran   Time 1m 17.92 (6.62)   Owned: Pisani PLC   Trained: Cockerham

---

4770   4.35 Telindus Maiden Stakes Colts & Geldings 2yo   (D3)
£3523   £1084   £542   **6f str**   **Soft**   **Inapplicable**   Centre

1531 **DRAMATICUS 143** [7] D R Loder 2-8-11 S Sanders 7/2 JT FAV: 31: Held up, prog & led over 1f out, pushed out, cosily: hvly bckd tho' op 5/2: 5 month abs: apprec step up to 6f, 7f+ could suit: acts on soft & prob handles hvy grnd, likes a gall trk & goes well fresh: well regarded & can rate higher: see 1531.		90+
RIO RIVA [6] Miss J A Camacho 2-8-11 R Winston 14/1: 2: b c Pivotal - Dixie Favor (Dixieland Band) Slow away & towards rear, styd on eye-catchingly from over 1f out, not rch wnr: op 20/1: Mar foal, half brother to a smart 6f juv River Belle, also a useful 7f performer abroad: dam a wnr btwn 6f/1m: eff at 6f, get further: handles soft grnd & a gall trk: gd intro, has ability & looks likely to progress.	1¾	85+
4223 **BREATHING FIRE 27** [5] W J Musson 2-8-11 R Mullen 9/2: 53: Trkd ldrs, onepace for press fnl 1f: nicely bckd tho' op 7/2: confirmed promise of debut, handles gd & soft grnd: see 4223.	2½	80
4385 **SACRANUN 20** [11] L M Cumani 2-8-11 N Mackay(3) 9/2: 2304: Mid-div, kept on, not able to chall: bckd, h'cap company shld now suit, poss over further: see 3272 (C/D).	2	76
4596 **PRIMARILY 9** [10]2-8-11 F Lynch 100/1: 05: b c Mind Games - Prim N Proper (Tragic Role) Dwelt & rear, late hdwy under hand riding, nvr a threat but imprvd from mod intro: 8,000 gns Feb 1st foal, dam unplcd: sire high-class juv/sprint performer.	3	70
4591 **LORD MAYFAIR 10** [3]2-8-11 P Hanagan 7/2 JT FAV: 256: Led till over 2f out, fdd: nicely bckd.	nk	69
4617 **HITS ONLY CASH 8** [8]2-8-11 P Bradley 100/1: 6057: Held up, nvr threatened ldrs.	½	68
4443 **GLAD BIG 17** [1]2-8-11 M Fenton 13/2: 38: Prom, led 2f out till dist, fdd under min press.	¾	67
GOLDEN SQUARE [2]2-8-11 W Supple 20/1: 9: ch g Tomba - Cherish Me (Polar Falcon) Slow away & sn pushed along, al rear: op 25/1: Apr foal, dam a dual 6f 3yo scorer.	3½	60
3178 **DIAMOND HERITAGE 73** [4]2-8-11 F Norton 100/1: 00: 10th: Trkd ldrs, rdn & btn over 1f out, abs.	5	50
RUMAN [12]2-8-11 N Callan 100/1: 0: 11th: Went right start, mid-div, struggling over 1f out.	nk	49
4303 **EL POTRO 24** [9]2-8-11 G Gibbons 25/1: 00: 12th: Trkd ldrs, btn over 1f out.	13	27

12 Ran   Time 1m 17.41 (6.11)   Owned: Derek and Jean Clee   Trained: Newmarket

4771
5.10 Racing Uk On Channel 432 Handicap Stakes 3yo+ 56-70 (E3)   **[83]**
£3886 £1196 £598   1m3f200y   Good/Soft   Slow Outside

2203 **IVY LEAGUE STAR 112** [7] B W Hills 3-8-7 (62) A Culhane 50/1: 06-501: Mid-div, prog/short of room   **70**
over 2f out, switched & styd on for press to lead cl-home: 4 month abs, h'cap bow: eff at 12f, shld get 14f+:
enjoyed gd/soft grnd & a gall trk today: goes well fresh: did well to overcome trouble in rng, shld progress.
4623* **ARTISTIC STYLE 8** [14] B Ellison 4-9-13 (6ex) (74) T Eaves(3) 11/4: 0131112: Mid-div, hdwy & led   nk **82**
over 1f out, drvn & hdd cl-home: hvly bckd under a 6lb pen: styd longer 12f trip & continues on an upward curve.
4388 **MISS INKHA 20** [10] R Guest 3-8-6 (61) J Quinn 66/1: 0066203: Handy, lost place 5f out, rallied   3½ **62**
for press & briefly led over 1f out, not pace of front pair: stays 12f: see 4167.
4672* **CIRCASSIAN 6** [13] Sir Mark Prescott 3-9-4 (6ex) (73) S Sanders 7/4 FAV: 00-02114: Mid-div wide,   ½ **75**
hung left under press & onepace fnl 2f: hvly bckd under a 6lb pen: quick reapp: see 4672.
4456 **BRAMANTINO 17** [6]4-9-4 bl (65) P Hanagan 11/1: 0551135: Mid-div, styd on onepace fnl 2f.   ½ **66**
3997 **ONWARD TO GLORY 39** [3]4-9-4 (65) K McEvoy 66/1: 5/60-0046: Held up, hdwy 4f out, rdn & no extra   ¾ **63**
fnl 2f: prob handles gd & soft grnd: see 3997, 3114.
4439 **CAN CAN FLYER 17** [16]3-8-13 (68) R Ffrench 7/1: 006-1227: Chsd ldrs, no extra dist: btr 4259.   hd **67**
1542 **KARATHAENA 143** [4]4-8-8 (55) P Mulrennan(3) 100/1: 3-000008: b f Barathea - Dabtara (Kahyasi)   1¾ **52**
Mid-div, no impress dist: 5 month abs: visor omitted: lightly rcd '03 (mdn plcd, rtd 75, J Hills): rnr-up in '02
(fills mdn): stays 1m on soft grnd. 2 Oct'02 Ayr 8sft 79- D:
4033 **SUDDEN FLIGHT 37** [19]7-9-6 (67) R Havlin 11/1: 3165039: Held up, some hdwy fnl 3f, nvr threat.   nk **63**
4215 **GENERAL GB 28** [1]7-9-5 (66) R Thomas(3) 14/1: 0005320: 10th: Led/dsptd lead till dist, sn btn.   ½ **61**
4388 **ESTEPONA 20** [5]3-8-8 (63) G Parkin 66/1: 40000: 11th: Rear, only mod late prog, longer trip.   5 **52**
4672 **RED SKELTON 6** [12]3-8-5 (60) A Nicholls 50/1: 0000300: 12th: Rear when short of room over 2f   1 **48**
out, only mod late prog, quick reapp: see 4448.
4203 **DANEBANK 28** [8]4-8-7 p (54) Dale Gibson 22/1: 0-051230: 13th: Mid-div, btn 2f out: btr 4203, 3056.   3 **38**
1772 **SUN HILL 132** [18]4-9-6 (67) D Sweeney 50/1: 1100500: 14th: Al rear, 5 month abs, likes f/sand.   8 **41**
4327 **ARCHIE BABE 23** [2]8-9-5 (66) R Winston 16/1: 0-015000: 15th: Cl-up, rdn & btn 3f out: btr 1064.   2½ **36**
4406 **FLIGHT COMMANDER 18** [17]4-9-3 (64) D Allan 66/1: 55-500: 16th: Mid-div, strug fnl 3f: see 4135.   9 **23**
4182 **ANDURIL 29** [9]3-8-5 BL (60) J Tate 100/1: 6400400: 17th: Keen in mid-div, rapid prog to dispute   2½ **15**
lead over 5f out, hdd over 2f out & sn btn, blnks: rcd too freely in headgear: btr 3906 (1m).
4228 **CELEBRE CITATION 27** [15]3-8-5 t (60) R Mullen 50/1: 0500: 18th: Al rear on h'cap bow, longer trip.   10 **3**
4286 **Super King 25** [20]3-8-11 (66) F Norton 50/1:0   4592} **Desert City 709** [11]5-9-4 (65) Dane O'Neill 100/1:0
20 Ran Time 2m 36.84(9.04) Owned: Mr D M James   Trained: Lambourn

Official Going GOOD/FIRM (GOOD places).

4772
2.00 Sodexho European Breeders Fund Classified Stakes 3yo+ 0-90 (C1)
£15167 £5753 £2877   1m2f   Good/Firm 23   -14 Slow Inside.

4463 **DESTINATION DUBAI 16** [2] Saeed bin Suroor 3-8-10 vis t (90) L Dettori 9/1: 2-130001: Trkd ldrs,   **96**
imprvd to lead dist, held on all-out: apprec this return to a RH'd trk, likes Ascot: stays 12f, suited by 10f: acts
on gd & fast grnd: wears a t-strap & visor, can run well fresh: see 2519 (R Ascot) & 1489.
4530 **COURAGEOUS DUKE 13** [7] J Noseda 5-9-6 (94) E Ahern 8/1: 3502322: Chsd ldrs, prog & ev ch dist,   ½ **98**
kept on well & only just btn: op 13/2, top-weight: another tough & useful run: see 4530.
4467* **IMPELLER 16** [8] W R Muir 5-9-4 (92) S Drowne 9/1: 6052213: Mid-div, kept on fnl 1f, nvr nrr: ¾ **95**
nicely bckd: another typical run from this in-from sort, tho' does apprec a stronger pace: see 4467.
4467 **BOULE DOR 16** [11] R Ingram 3-8-10 (89) N Day 25/1: 1420144: Held up, styd on well fnl 1f, nvr   nk **92**
nrr: gd run under hold up tactics - not favoured today: see 3945.
4467 **MUHAREB 16** [3]5-9-2 (90) T P Queally 40/1: 004-5005: Led till dist, no extra.   hd **92**
4463 **MOCCA 16** [6]3-8-7 (88) Martin Dwyer 16/1: 2-451626: Mid-div wide, not pace to chall.   ¾ **88**
4227+ **BORDER CASTLE 27** [1]3-8-10 (89) K Fallon 7/4 FAV: 441-17: Chsd ldrs wide, eff over 2f out, sn   ½ **90**
onepcd: hvly bckd: much more expected, but this was tougher than 4227 (sharp trk, gd grnd).
4525* **GOLD HISTORY 13** [12]3-9-0 (94) D Holland 11/1: 5006518: Rear, eff 2f out, sn onepcd.   nk **93**
4502* **TOP SPEC 14** [13]3-8-10 (80) R L Moore 25/1: 0201219: Held up, nvr nr ldrs: see 4502.   ¾ **88$**
4467 **MANGO MISCHIEF 16** [4]3-8-7 (90) R Hughes 9/2: 10-12420: 10th: Held up, nvr dngrs: btr 4467.   1 **83**
789} **SHARMY 559** [9]8-9-6 (94) T E Durcan 66/1: 30/1100-0: 11th: b g Caerleon - Petticoat Lane (Ela   nk **89**
Mana Mou) Keen in rear, nvr dngrs on reapp: mod chase form this summer: won a beg & h'cap chase in 03/04 (rtd
121c, eff at 2m on gd & soft): dual &w h'cap wnr early in '03: suited by a sharp 12f on fm & soft, loves polytrack
at Lingfield: with Ian Williams. 1 Feb'03 Ling 12ap 100a-100 B: 1 Jan'03 Ling 12ap 102a-95 C:
4467 **FOODBROKER FOUNDER 16** [10]4-9-2 (90) J Fortune 66/1: 0660600: 12th: Chsd ldrs, wknd fnl 1f.   3 **80**
4684} **SAILING THROUGH 349** [5]4-9-4 (92) R Miles 66/1: 111140-0: 13th: b g Bahhare - Hopesay (Warning)   ¾ **81**
Mid-div, wkng when short of room 2f out: mod hdle form this summer: completed a 4-timer in h'caps for T Mills in
'03: eff at 8.5/10f on firm, gd & polytrack: v prog last season, now with R Dickin. 1 Aug'03 Newb 10.0fm 93-81 D:
1 Aug'03 Wind 10.0g/f 87-76 D: 1 Jul'03 Wind 10.0g/f 77-70 E: 1 Jul'03 Epso 8.5gd 75-64 E: 2 Mar'03 Ling 10ap 69a-(67) D:
13 Ran Time 2m 07.70 (3.70) Owned: Godolphin   Trained: Newmarket

4773
2.30 Pricewaterhousecoopers Stakes Handicap 3yo 86-100 (C1)   **[107]**
£15788 £5988 £2994   6f110y rnd   Good/Firm 23   +13 Fast Inside.

4322 **KHABFAIR 23** [10] Mrs A J Perrett 3-9-2 (95) J Murtagh 9/2 FAV: 2-413601: Chsd ldrs, eff &   **102**
wandered ins fnl 1f, strong run to lead on line: gamble from 7/1, gd time: confirmed promise of last couple of
starts, top-weight: v eff at 6/6.5f, acts on fast & polytrk, sharp or gall trks: lightly rcd, useful & improving.
4048 **COMPTONS ELEVEN 36** [8] M R Channon 3-9-0 (93) S Hitchcott 6/1: 5212222: Keen & disputed lead,   hd **99**
led dist till collared dying strides: nicely bckd: tough gelding, imprvd again in defeat: see 4048
4318* **MAJORS CAST 23** [6] J Noseda 3-8-12 (91) E Ahern 15/2: 31313: Rear, styd on strongly wide fnl   1¼ **93+**

1.5f, nrst fin: op 11/2: fine run with tactics that are proving hard to execute today: eff at 6.5f, crying out for a return to 7f: see 4318 (AW).
3941 **BENTLEYS BALL 41** [13] R Hannon 3-8-9 (88) R L Moore 8/1: 2-600344: Led till dist, no extra: *½* **89**
tchd 12/1, 6 wk abs: see 3941.
4638 **OASIS STAR 7** [11]3-8-10 (89) D Holland 13/2: 1512055: Chsd ldrs, kept on under press, not pace *nk* **89**
of ldrs: nicely bckd tho' op 11/2: return to 7f will suit: see 4638 (List) & 3006.
4604 **OUT AFTER DARK 9** [3]3-8-7 (5oh) (81) R Smith 14/1: 2-511326: Mid-div wide, not pace to chall. *hd* **85**
627 **MR LAMBROS 223** [14]3-8-7 (1oh) (85) Martin Dwyer 16/1: 3-127: Rear, styd on late, nvr dngrs: *hd* **84+**
long abs: return to further will suit: handles fast grnd: gd eff after slow start & will improve on this: see 627.
4099 **RYDAL 6** [9]3-8-8 bl (87) J Fortune 25/1: 2401458: Chsd ldrs, onepcd fnl 2f. *1* **82**
1847 **BRAVO MAESTRO 128** [12]3-9-0 (93) T Quinn 14/1: 011-6059: Slow away & keen, nvr in it: long abs. *½* **87**
4322 **APEX 23** [2]3-8-9 (88) K Fallon 12/1: 5032100: 10th: Slow away, mod late prog: btr 3920. *nk* **81**
4225 **DOITNOW 27** [7]3-8-9 (88) T Hamilton(3) 16/1: 122660: 11th: Held up, nvr a factor. *1* **78**
4585 **TONY THE TAP 10** [4]3-8-7 (4oh) (82) F P Ferris(3) 14/1: 2100520: 12th: Slow away, al rear: btr 4585. *1¼* **72**
4627* **SARISTAR 8** [5]3-8-9 (6ex) (88) N De Souza(5) 14/1: 0-100510: 13th: Trkd ldrs 5f, wknd: op 11/1. *nk* **73**
13 Ran Time 1m 20.21 (0.71) Owned: Star Pointe Ltd & Arlington Bloodstock Trained: Pulborough

4774

3.05 Gr3 Princess Royal John Doyle Stakes Fillies & Mares 3yo+ (A1)
£29000 £11000 £5500 **1m4f** **Good/Firm 23** **+13 Fast** Inside.

4460 **MAZUNA 16** [3] C E Brittain 3-8-6 (97) R L Moore 14/1: 6-123221: Held up, prog 2f out, strong run **108**
to lead on line: gd time: vastly imprvd last 2 starts, btn in a h'cap off 68 2 runs ago: eff at 12/14f on fast grnd, handles a sharp or gall trk: developed into a smart filly & reportedly needs to come late: see 4460.
2138 **MY RENEE 53** [6] M J Grassick 4-9-0 N G McCullagh 5/2 FAV: 3151-312: b f Kris S - Mayenne *shd* **107**
(Nureyev) Mid-div, prog to lead dist, collared on line: well bckd Irish chall, 8 wk abs: earlier won a List event at Cork: List wnr again in '03: wng form at 12f, stays 14f: acts on gd & fast grnd: runs well fresh: v useful filly, may now be campaigned in the US. 1 Sep'03 Asco 12g/f 104- A:
3837 **HIDDEN HOPE 48** [4] G Wragg 3-8-6 (109) T E Durcan 9/2: 0-215423: Chsd ldrs, ev ch dist, kept on *1½* **104**
but not pace of front 2: nicely bckd, 7 wk abs: acts on fast & gd/soft grnd: see 3837 & 1568.
3619 **SUMMITVILLE 33** [2] J G Given 4-9-0 (102) D Holland 10/1: 2-326364: Prom, led over 2f out till *1½* **102**
dist, no extra: nicely bckd, well clr rem: see 2946.
4460 **ASTROCHARM 16** [8]5-9-3 (103) L Dettori 7/1: 5121105: Rear, nvr nr ldrs: btr 3619 (14f). *6* **96**
4614+ **POLAR JEM 9** [7]4-9-0 (98) A McCarthy 8/1: 1163216: Led till 2f out, wknd: btr 4614. *1½* **91**
3837 **BENEVENTA 48** [10]4-9-3 (110) R Hughes 7/2: 1120107: Keen & chsd ldrs, btn 2f out: well bckd, 7 *2½* **90**
wk abs: reportedly ran flat: btr 3278 (List).
4058 **CASTAGNA 36** [9]3-8-6 (85) W Ryan 50/1: 0-4108: Chsd ldrs till halfway: see 3422 (fill mdn). *2* **84**
8 Ran Time 2m 30.24 (1.24) Owned: Mr Saeed Manana Trained: Newmarket

4775

3.40 Bollinger Champagne Series Final Hcap Gentleman Amateur Riders 3yo+ 71-85 (D2) **[58]**
£7033 £2164 £1082 **1m4f** **Good/Firm 23** **-23 Slow** Inside.

4292 **SKYLARKER 25** [4] W S Kittow 6-11-2 (74) Mr L Jefford 20/1: 0441551: Prom, went on dist, pushed **84**
clr for a surprise win: eff btwn 1m/12f on firm, gd/soft & both AWs: gets on well with Mr L Jefford: see 2912 & 273.
4647 **GENGHIS 7** [10] H Morrison 5-11-8 (80) Mr J J Best(3) 5/1: 2520332: Trkd ldr, led 5f out till hdd *3* **84**
dist, kept on but no ch with wnr: bckd from 13/2: another consistent run: see 4647.
4292* **TENDER FALCON 25** [8] R J Hodges 4-11-10 (82) Mr James White(3) 9/2: 5102113: Mid-div, prog when *1¾* **84**
short of room 2f out & barged thro', styd on well & nrst fin: well bckd tho' op 7/2, top-weight: rider given a 7-day ban: bt today's wnr in 4292.
4377* **NIGHT SIGHT 20** [7] Mrs S Lamyman 7-10-13 (71) Mr J Morgan(3) 11/1: 3441514: Mid-div, chsd ldrs 2f *1¾* **71**
out, onepcd fnl 1f: see 4377.
4609 **JACARANDA 9** [5]4-10-13 (71) Mr S Walker 33/1: 2413605: Held up, prog halfway, bmpd 2f out, nrst *¾* **70**
fin: back to form & stays 12f: see 3404.
4473 **SCOTTISH RIVER 15** [9]5-11-8 (80) Mr L Newnes(3) 20/1: 1240406: Mid-div, no impress fnl 1.5f. *¾* **78**
4354 **IBERUS 21** [13]6-10-10 (68) Mr T Woodside(7) 20/1: 0005427: Chsd ldrs, btn dist: see 4354. *½* **65**
4647 **BUCKS 7** [2]7-11-7 (79) Mr Michael Murphy 14/1: 5022568: V wide mid-div, nvr a factor. *nk* **75**
4377 **SMART JOHN 20** [14]4-11-0 (72) Mr C Davies(5) 13/2: 1354139: Keen in mid-div, nvr in it: btr 4377. *1* **66**
4327 **KYLKENNY 23** [1]9-10-12 t (70) Mr J Rees 25/1: 5344400: 10th: Dwelt, al towards rear: longer *1¼* **62**
priced stablemate of rnr-up: see 3867.
4361 **ROME 21** [3]5-10-10 (6oh) (62) Mr J Pemberton(5) 40/1: 0355400: 11th: Al rear: see 3340. *4* **54**
4415* **POLAR TRYST 18** [16]5-11-0 (72) Mr T Greenall 4/1 FAV: 54/022-10: 12th: Led till 5f out, wknd: *8* **46**
nicely bckd: puzz run over this shorter trip: made just about all in 4415 & much better expected.
4292 **Danakil 25** [15]9-11-2 (74) Mr D Hutchison(5) 14/1:0
4529} **Constantine 360** [12]4-11-4 (76) Mr E Dehdashti 25/1:0
14 Ran Time 2m 34.54 (5.54) Owned: Midd Shire Racing Trained: Cullompton

4776

4.15 Allied Irish Bank Gb Maiden Stakes 2yo (D2)
£7475 £2300 £1150 **7f rnd** **Good/Firm 23** **No Standard Time** Inside.

4591 **DAVID JUNIOR 10** [2] B J Meehan 2-9-0 R Hills 1/1 FAV: 31: Made all, rdn & styd on strongly fnl **92**
1f: hvly bckd from 6/4 & made gd use of prev experience: eff over a gall 7f on fast grnd, 1m will suit: potentially useful, see 4591 (debut).
MACABRE [1] Saeed bin Suroor 2-9-0 L Dettori 9/4: 2: b c Machiavellian - Lady In Waiting *¾* **90**
(Kylian) Trkd ldr, ran green & ev ch 2f out, rdn & kept on well on debut: nicely bckd, clr of rem: 280,000gns March 1st foal: dam a 5/6f juv wnr: sire a top-class miler: eff at 7f on fast grnd: v green today, will win races.
GIANTS ROCK [3] G A Butler 2-9-0 J Fortune 12/1: 3: ch c Giant's Causeway - En Garde (Irish *6* **78**
River) Chsd ldrs, left bhnd fnl 1f on debut: 58,000gns April foal: half brother to 1m juv wnr Rifleman: dam a 6f 2yo wnr, sire a top-class 1m/10f performer: sure to learn from this.
BONFIRE [4] M Johnston 2-9-0 D Holland 10/1: 4: b c Machiavellian - Forest Express (Kaaptive *nk* **77**
Edition) Chsd ldrs, outpcd fnl 1f under handls & heels on debut: op 7/1: 140,000gns Feb 1st foal: sire a top-class miler, dam high-class in Australia: will learn from this.
DART ALONG [5]2-9-0 R Hughes 7/1: 5: Dwelt, rdn & al rear on debut: Apr foal, half brother to *1¼* **74**

ASCOT   FRIDAY 24.09.04   Righthand, Stiff, Galloping Track

1m juv wnr Fantastic View: dam a 6f wnr, site a top-class miler: with R Hannon & better expected.
5 Ran   Time 1m 29.69 ()   Owned: Roldvale Limited   Trained: Upper Lambourn

4777   4.50 West End & Metropolitan Ltd Handicap Stakes 3yo 71-85 (D2)   [92]
£7181 £2210 £1105   1m rnd   Good/Firm 23   -12 Slow   Inside.

4482 GRANSTON 15 [15] J D Bethell 3-8-11 (75) T Quinn 10/1: 6602531: Keen in mid-div, switched wide & 83
prog 1.5f out, strong run to lead cl home: op 14/1: eff at 7f/1m on gd & firm grnd: game effort today, hit over
head by rivals whip: see 1176.
4122 EVALUATOR 32 [4] T G Mills 3-9-7 (85) K Fallon 6/1: 6122022: Trkd ldrs, went on dist, collared   nk   91
cl home: well bckd, top-weight: fine run, deserves to go one better: see 4122.
4185 CELLO 28 [16] R Hannon 3-9-0 t (78) P Dobbs 25/1: 1600423: Keen in rear, prog wide over 1f out,   1½   81
nrst fin: carried head high, poss unhappy on this much faster grnd: see 4185 (soft).
4502 BORDER MUSIC 14 [11] A M Balding 3-9-2 (80) D Holland 11/2: 0032234: Held up, short of room 2f   shd 83+
out & again dist, fin well but too late: al strug for a run & lkd unlucky: see 4502 & 4362.
3598 ALEKHINE 55 [12]3-9-4 e (82) E Ahern 14/1: 2300605: Held up, fin strongly fnl 1.5f, nvr nrr: 8   shd 85+
wk abs: set plenty to do on a day when it was hard to come from off the pace: stays 10f: keep an eye on, see 2040.
4263* NEW ORDER 26 [13]3-9-0 (78) R Hughes 5/1: 3116: Early ldr, rem prom & ev ch dist, no extra when   ½   80
short of room cl home: nicely bckd tho' op 3/1: lightly rcd & prog prev on softer grnd than this: see 4263.
4445* KODIAC 17 [2]3-9-4 (82) L Dettori 7/1: 1-17: Trkd ldrs, slightly hmpd 2f out, ev ch dist,   ¾   82
sn no extra: gamble from 9/2: longer 1m trip & h'cap bow: better clearly expected, but not disgraced.
4148* JATH 31 [6]3-9-2 (80) Lisa Jones 20/1: 1-060618: Dwelt, styd on late: btr 4148 (sft).   nk   79
4318 FORTHRIGHT 23 [17]3-9-5 BL (83) R Hills 20/1: 5600069: Dwelt, keen in rear, styd on late wide,   hd   82
nvr dngrs: tried blnks (prev cheek pieces): see 325 (AW).
1756 GRAVARDLAX 132 [9]3-9-4 (82) J Fortune 33/1: 42-0400: 10th: Held up, nvr dngrs: long abs.   1¾   78
4352 ZWEIBRUCKEN 21 [8]3-9-5 (83) J F Egan 66/1: 20-00100: 11th: Trkd ldrs, hmpd 1.5f out, wkng when   nk   78
hmpd ins fnl 1f: did not get the run of today's race: twice below 3885.
4469 HERMITAGE COURT 16 [18]3-9-6 (84) S W Kelly 25/1: 1460: 12th: Held up, al bhnd: btr 3961.   1   77
4607 TAMINOULA 9 [5]3-8-13 (77) J Murtagh 14/1: 311-0060: 13th: Rear, prog to chase ldrs when bmpd 2f   2½   65
out, sn wknd: see 4607.
4499 BARATHEA DREAMS 14 [7]3-9-3 (81) Martin Dwyer 20/1: 4130050: 14th: Led after 1f till dist, wknd.   nk   68
4465 MALIBU 16 [1]3-8-12 (76) P Doe 66/1: 5015000: 15th: Prom 6f, wknd.   1¼   60
4482 Overdrawn 15 [3]3-9-2 (80) T P Queally 50/1:0   4469 Habanero 16 [14]3-9-0 (78) R L Moore 33/1:0
17 Ran   Time 1m 41.28(2.78)   Owned: The Four Players Partnership   Trained: Middleham

HAYDOCK   SATURDAY 25.09.04   Lefthand, Flat, Galloping Track

Official Going SOFT (HEAVY places).

4778   2.15 Betfred The Bonus King Handicap Stakes 3yo+ 86-100 (C1)   [109]
£15097 £5727 £2863   1m6f   Soft 90   +17 Fast   Inside

4647+ REGAL SETTING 8 [6] Sir Mark Prescott 3-8-1 (82) J Mackay 6/5 FAV: 21-611: Chsd ldrs, imprvd to 92
lead over 2f out, held on well drvn out: well bckd, fast time: suited by 14f now, worth a try at 2m+: acts on
gd/soft & f/sand: fast improving for a highly shrewd yard: see 4647.
3510 BIG MOMENT 60 [3] Mrs A J Perrett 6-9-10 (95) S W Kelly 15/2: 440-3562: Rear, hdwy 3f out, chsd   ¾   103
wnr fnl 1.5f, not btn far: 9 wk abs: ran nr to best, acts on firm & soft grnd: spot on next time, see 1569.
4647 TRANCE 8 [1] T D Barron 4-8-13 (84) P Makin(5) 20/1: 4110003: Chsd ldrs, onepcd fnl 1f: well clr   2   89
of rem: acts on fast, soft & fibresand: see 4647.
4183 HEZAAM 29 [7] J L Dunlop 3-8-3 (84) W Supple 11/4: 0501124: Led till over 2f out, wknd: well   13   74
bckd: prob not stay this longer 14f trip in these testing conds, reportedly fin wrong bhnd: see 4183 & 3940 (12f).
4383 BENDARSHAAN 21 [4]4-9-1 (86) S Chin 20/1: 1120505: Chsd ldrs, btn 2f out: see 3510.   nk   75
4383 CROW WOOD 21 [5]5-9-10 (95) I Mongan 9/1: 3352066: Keen & prom, ev ch till wknd 1.5f out: too   3   81
keen today: faster grnd suits: see 4383.
3026] BOLLIN THOMAS 434 [2]6-8-10 (1oh) (80) G Gibbons 14/1: 006103-7: b g Alhijaz - Bollin Magdalene   dist 37
(Teenoso) Hedl up, al bhnd, t.o. on reapp: '03 h'cap wnr: '02 h'cap wnr, rnr-up 3 times: eff over 14f/2m on fm &
hvy: handles a sharp or gall trk: better than this. 1 Jun'03 Donc 14.6g/f 82-77 D: 2 Aug'02 Hayd 14hvy 80-77 D:
2 Jul'02 Ches 15.8fm 77-71 D: 1 Jun'02 Hayd 14sft 74-68 D: 2 May'02 Hayd 14gd 70-66 D: 2 Oct'01 Redc 14gd 66-63 E:
2 Oct'01 Catt 12g/s 65-63 E: 2 Aug'01 Beve 12gf 64-59 E: 2 Jul'01 Beve 12g/f 63-59 E: 1 Jul'01 Beve 12g/f 61-55 E:
7 Ran   Time 3m 08.26 (10.26)   Owned: W E Sturt - Osborne House   Trained: Newmarket

4779   2.45 Akzo Nobel Handicap Stakes 3yo 86-100 (C1)   [100]
£20553 £6324 £3162   6f str   Soft 90   -16 Slow   Centre

4652+ EISTEDDFOD 8 [8] P F I Cole 3-9-7 (93) N De Souza(5) 7/4 FAV: 1331111: Prom, went on dist, held 105
on well despite drifting left, rdn out: well bckd: 5th win of season, incl Ayr Silver Cup: eff btwn 6/7f on firm &
soft, any trk: thriving 3yo who is well worth a chance in List/Gr 3 company now: see 4652.
4350* SOLAR POWER 22 [3] J R Fanshawe 3-8-12 (84) J D Smith 9/2: 2444312: Rear, gd hdwy to chall fnl   ½   93
1f, just btn in a cl fin: well clr rem: met a potentially smart rival: imprvd in defeat & can win more races.
4278* IMPERIAL ECHO 26 [7] T D Barron 3-8-12 (84) P Fessey 20/1: 2203413: Slow away, gd hdwy to lead   6   81
briefly dist, wknd cl home: met two v prog rivals & not disgraced after missing break: prob acts on soft grnd.
4322* PARTNERS IN JAZZ 24 [10] T D Barron 3-9-3 (89) P Makin(5) 8/1: 1-500514: Front rank, led over 2f   1¾   83
out till dist, wknd: shorter priced stablemate of 3rd: btr 4322 (gd).
4604* BO MCGINTY 10 [11]3-9-0 (86) G Parkin 14/1: 2004515: Chsd ldrs, onepcd when short of room dist.   ½   79
4048 DANZIG RIVER 37 [5]3-9-3 (89) R Mullen 14/1: 0000046: Held up, nvr nr ldrs: btr 4048 (fast).   1¼   79
4048 COMMANDO SCOTT 37 [6]3-9-5 (91) F Lynch 10/1: 2611507: Led early, prom till wknd dist.   ½   80
4667* MORSE 7 [12]3-8-11 (83) S W Kelly 16/1: 0600018: Prom, led halfway till 2f out, wknd: btr 4667.   shd   72
4562 JILLY WHY 12 [9]3-8-10 (1ooh) (72) C Haddon(7) 50/1: 0-041109: Led till halfway: stiff task.   8   53

4454 **EFISTORM** 18 [1]3-9-2 (88) W Supple 50/1: 11-14000: 10th: b c Efisio - Abundance (Cadeaux   3½   51
Genereux) Held up, al bhnd: prev trained in Italy, earlier won at San Siro: dual '03 wnr: wng form at 5/6f on
gd/soft & hvy grnd: with M Quinlan.
4537 **SPLIFF** 13 [2]3-9-3 (89) D Sweeney 10/1: 1000050: 11th: Held up, nvr in it.   2½   46
4459 **HIGH VOLTAGE** 17 [4]3-9-10 t (96) I Mongan 16/1: 6000100: 12th: Prom 4f, wknd: top-weight.   ¾   51
12 Ran   Time 1m 17.64 (6.34)   Owned: Elite Racing Club   Trained: Whatcombe

---

4780	3.15 Betfred Com Handicap Stakes 4yo+ 86-100 (C1)	[107]
	£20176 £6208 £3104 5f str Soft 90 +11 Fast Centre	

4686 **JONNY EBENEEZER** 7 [8] D Flood 5-8-10 bl e (89) Hayley Turner(3) 14/1: 4110001: Hld up, hdwy 1.5f   101
out, led ins fnl 1f, going away: gd time: back to form for 7th win of season: suited by 5/7f, stays 1m on fm, soft &
f/sand: best hld up, loves Newmarket: wears an eyehood & blnks, has tried cheek pieces: goes esp well for L
Dettori: thriving this term & can win more races: see 3827.
4459 **WHISTLER** 17 [9] J M Bradley 7-8-11 p (90) P Fitzsimons 8/1: 4034042: Held up, styd on well fnl 1f   2   96
despite hanging left, no ch with wnr: another fine run: see 4459.
4459 **CORRIDOR CREEPER** 17 [4] J M Bradley 7-9-1 p (94) P Makin(5) 11/2: 3603503: Prom, went on halfway   1   98
till ins fnl 1f, no extra: has not won for 12 months, but still 9lbs above last wmg mark.
4686 **RIVER FALCON** 7 [1] J S Goldie 4-8-9 (88) W Supple 9/1: 0301004: Chsd ldrs, onepcd fnl 1f.   1   90
4605 **FURTHER OUTLOOK** 10 [6]10-8-7 (4oh) (82) D Sweeney 12/1: 6515035: Led till halfway, no extra.   1   86
4652 **JOHNSTONS DIAMOND** 8 [11]6-8-7 (1oh) (89) J Quinn 6/1: 0000036: Chsd ldrs, onepcd fnl 1f.   hd   85
4459 **PTARMIGAN RIDGE** 17 [10]8-8-8 (87) M Fenton 7/2 FAV: 6510337: Trkd ldrs, wknd fnl 1f: op 9/2.   5   76
4481 **BISHOPS COURT** 16 [3]10-9-7 (100) I Mongan 13/2: 0025658: Chsd ldrs, wknd: 'broke blood vessel'.   1¾   84
4588 **WHITBARROW** 11 [7]5-8-11 bl (90) S W Kelly 14/1: 0000549: Chsd ldrs 3f: s/mate 2nd & 3rd.   hd   73
4291 **HENRY HALL** 26 [5]8-8-10 (89) Kim Tinkler 25/1: 0300000: 10th: Nvr btr than mid-div.   1¾   69
4718 **ABSENT FRIENDS** 4 [2]7-8-7 (3oh) (83) R Mullen 25/1: 0000400: 11th: Prom 3f, wknd & eased, t.o.   22   26
11 Ran   Time 1m 02.75 (3.95)   Owned: Mrs Ruth M Serrell   Trained: Hungerford

---

4781	3.50 European Breeders Fund 'reprocolor' Handicap Stakes Fillies & Mares 3yo+ 86-100 (C1)	[86]
	£19828 £6101 £3050 1m2f120y Soft 90 -17 Slow Inside	

4305 **LA SYLPHIDE GB** 25 [7] G M Moore 7-9-10 (82) S W Kelly 9/2: 0-256021: Made all, styd on well fnl   90
1f, drvn out: 1st win since landed this race last year (9lbs lower mark): eff btwn 7f & 10.5f on gd, soft &
fibresand: likes Hamilton & Southwell & goes well from the front: tough & game.
4463* **TARTOUCHE** 1 [1] Lady Herries 3-9-12 (91) J Quinn 10/3: 1112: Chsd ldrs, went after wnr 2f out,   ¾   96
kept on & not btn far: bckd, top-weight: acts on fm & soft, 12f may now suit: useful & progressive.
3938 **CHARNOCK BATES ONE** 42 [3] T D Easterby 3-8-7 (72) G Gibbons 13/2: 6012223: Dwelt & rear, styd on   ¾   74
fnl 2f, nvr nrr: 6 wk abs: another consistent run: see 3938.
3926 **FLING** 43 [2] J R Fanshawe 3-9-4 (83) R Mullen 11/4 FAV: 15224: Dwelt, outpcd till styd on fnl   1¾   85
1.5f, nvr nrr: 6 wk abs: return to 12f will suit: acts on fm, prob soft: see 3926.
4607 **NOUVEAU RICHE** 10 [5]3-8-12 (77) I Mongan 15/2: 231235: Chsd ldrs, onepcd fnl 1.5f: softer grnd.   nk   78
3629 **LIGHT WIND** 55 [4]3-9-7 (86) W Supple 8/1: 51156: Prom, onepcd fnl 2f: 8 wk abs: better prev   shd   87
over 12f on fast grnd: see 2972.
4547 **UIG** 12 [6]3-8-9 (74) M Fenton 20/1: 0320427: Keen & prom, lost place halfway, no ch fnl 1.5f.   5   67
7 Ran   Time 2m 21.39 (11.39)   Owned: Geoff & Sandra Turnbull   Trained: Middleham

---

4782	4.20 European Breeders Fund Sodexho Maiden Stakes Fillies 2yo (D2)	
	£5574 £1715 £858 1m30y rnd Soft 90 -25 Slow Inside	

4480 **TCHERINA** 16 [8] T D Easterby 2-8-11 (73) G Gibbons 11/2: 002301: Chsd ldrs, imprvd to lead 3f   76
out till 2f out, regained lead dist, rdn out: op 9/2: deserved win: eff at 1m on fast & soft.
4450 **HIGHER LOVE** 18 [2] M L W Bell 2-8-11 R Mullen 5/2 FAV: 62: Dwelt, hdwy to lead 2f out till   1¾   72
dist, not pace of wnr ins fnl 1f: well bckd: imprvd form on this soft grnd: stays a gall 1m: see 4450.
        LIMIT [6] M R Channon 2-8-11 J Quinn 7/2: 3: b f Barathea - Orlena (Gone West) Slow away,   3   67
hdwy & ev ch 2f out, onepcd fnl 1f: op 7/1, clr of rem on debut: E38,000gns May 1st foal: dam a juv wnr in France.
4035 **SIDESHOW** 38 [4] D R Loder 2-8-11 VIS D R McCabe 12/1: 04: ch f In The Wings - Sheer Harmony   6   57
(Woodman) Dspt lead till halfway, wknd fnl 1f: tried a visor: Jan 1st foal: dam a 1m wnr.
3991 **HILL FAIRY** 40 [5]2-8-11 J Mackay 9/1: 645: Dsptd lead, went on halfway till 3f out, wknd dist: abs.   ¾   55
4511 **LAKE WAKATIPU** 14 [1]2-8-11 (57) L Enstone 25/1: 0436: Chsd ldrs, hmpd 2f out & wknd qckly.   10   37
4192 **NAPAPIJRI** 29 [7]2-8-11 W Supple 8/1: 57: Slow away, al bhnd.   2½   33
4418 **ORLAR** 19 [3]2-8-11 S W Kelly 6/1: 58: Keen & prom, hmpd 2f out, no ch after & eased: op 9/2:   6   23
forgive fst: see 4418 (debut).
8 Ran   Time 1m 49.83 (9.33)   Owned: Mr & Mrs W J Williams   Trained: Malton

---

4783	4.55 E B F Betfred In-Shop On-Phone On-Line Maiden Stakes Colts & Geldings 2yo (D2)	
	£5720 £1760 £880 1m30y rnd Soft 90 -22 Slow Inside	

4591 **MOZAFIN** 11 [2] M R Channon 2-8-11 vis (82) J Quinn 11/10 FAV: 2432021: Made all, clr halfway,   87
held on fnl 1f, drvn out: hvly bckd: plcd numerous times prev: eff at 7f/1m on fast & soft grnd: handles a gall or
sharp trk, likes to force the pace: wears a visor: see 4591.
3005 **LOVE BEAUTY** 81 [6] M Johnston 2-8-11 S Chin 8/1: 402: Chsd wnr tho'out, kept on well: 12 wk   1¼   84
abs: stays a gall 1m on soft grnd: see 2316 (debut).
4484 **SOLARIAS QUEST** 16 [5] A King 2-8-11 J D Smith 3/1: 33: Chsd ldrs, kept on under press fnl 1f: shd   84
clr of rem: acts on gd & soft grnd: failed to build on 4484 (debut).
        KONG [3] J L Dunlop 2-8-11 I Mongan 4/1: 4: b c Sadler's Wells - Hill of Snow (Reference   4   77
Point) Slow away & green, nrst fin on debut: nicely bckd: Feb foal, half brother to smart 7f juv performers
Preseli & Snowfire: dam a 10f wnr, sire a top-class mid-dist performer: bred to apprec mid-dists next term.
        EMERALD DESTINY [4]2-8-11 W Supple 22/1: 5: b g Key of Luck - Green Belt (Tirol) Keen & prom   9   62
5f, wknd on debut: Apr foal, cost 16,000gns: dam unrcd, sire smart over 1m/10f: with D Carroll.

HAYDOCK SATURDAY 25.09.04 Lefthand, Flat, Galloping Track

4511 **LAYED BACK ROCKY 14** [1]2-8-11 (62) L Enstone 25/1: 6026: Chsd ldrs, wknd 3f out: btr 4511. ¾ 60
6 Ran   Time 1m 49.61(9.11)   Owned: Mr Jaber Abdullah   Trained: West Ilsley

RIPON SATURDAY 25.09.04 Righthand, Sharpish Track

Official Going Good/Firm

4784
1.50 Weatherbys Bank Nursery Handicap Stakes 2yo 0-85 (D2) [87]
£10335 £3180 £1590 **5f str**   **Good 46**   -17 Slow   Inside

4551 **TALCEN GWYN 12** [14] M F Harris 2-9-3 (76) A Nicholls 11/1: 4045041: Chsd ldrs, switched & rdn to 85
lead well ins last: eff at 5f on fast & gd grnd, prob handles soft: likes a sharp/undul trk: see 4551, 4187 & 2430.
4437* **MELANDRE 18** [10] M Brittain 2-8-10 (69) T Williams 10/1: 604512: Al handy & led over 1f out, nk 76
drvn & hdd well in last: remains on the up-grade after 4437.
3756 **CHILLY CRACKER 50** [11] R Hollinshead 2-8-6 (65) Dale Gibson 33/1: 261003: Led/dsptd lead till 1¾ 67
over 1f out, kept on for press, 7 wk abs: acts on fibresand, gd & gd/soft grnd: see 2498 (AW).
3374 **SKIDDAW WOLF 65** [2] B Smart 2-8-4 (63) T P Queally 22/1: 03654: Reportedly v free to post, dwelt nk 64+
& pushed along towards rear, styd on from halfway, nvr threatened front pair: 2 month abs, gd run from awkward
low draw: eff at 5f, rtn to 6f in similar could suit: worth noting for similar: see 2671.
4551 **WONDERFUL MIND 12** [12]2-9-0 bl (73) D Allan 12/1: 1563205: Handy, fdd ins last: btr 4172. nk 73
4551* **OCEANICO DOT COM 12** [15]2-9-1 (74) F Norton 7/2 FAV: 0021316: Chsd ldrs, no extra dist: btr 4551. 1¼ 70
4258 **BAYMIST 27** [13]2-8-8 (67) T Lucas 20/1: 5614167: Chsd ldrs, hung left & btn over 1f out: btr 3756. ½ 61
4551 **ANNATALIA 12** [8]2-9-5 (78) J F McDonald(3) 4/1: 461008: Dwelt, towards rear, mod prog, no dngr. ½ 70
4517 **HOWARDS PRINCESS 14** [1]2-8-10 (69) T Eaves(3) 16/1: 52249: Went left start, bhd, mod gains. nk 60
4545 **MONASHEE ROSE 12** [5]2-9-4 (77) Dane O'Neill 15/2: 01120: 10th: Al rear, op 13/2: btr 4545 & 4172. nk 67
4509 **BOLTON HALL 14** [6]2-9-7 (80) P Hanagan 13/2: 165650: 11th: Al towards rear: bckd, op 9/1: btr 4004. 2 64
4549 **HYMN OF VICTORY 12** [3]2-8-7 (66) S Drowne 20/1: 052620: 12th: Always bhd, op 9/1: see 4549. 1¼ 46
4670 **MAS O MENOS 7** [4]2-8-6 (65) P Mulrennan(2) 33/1: 20020: 13th: Chsd ldrs, struggling from halfway. 1¾ 40
4596 **LUCY PARKES 10** [9]2-7-12 (6oh) (51) D Mernagh 50/1: 04000: 14th: Sn struggling: see 3755. ½ 30
4596 **HAMBURG SPRINGER 10** [16]2-7-13 (1ow)(12oh) (45) S Righton 66/1: 0500: 15th: Al outpcd rear. 1½ 27
15 Ran   Time 1m 0.95 (3.15)   Owned: Mr D K Watkins   Trained: Banbury

4785
2.20 Homesale Network Handicap Stakes 3yo+ 56-70 (E3) [82]
£5096 £1568 £784 **6f str**   **Good 46**   -02 Slow   Stands Side

4452 **BLYTHE SPIRIT 18** [7] R A Fahey 5-8-8 p (62) P Hanagan 7/1: 5000661: Held up stands side, hdwy to 74
lead ins last, rcn clr, going away: eff at 6f/1m on firm & gd/soft, any trk: well h'capped, follow-up.
3680 **VIGOROUS 52** [3] M Todhunter 4-8-9 (63) A Mullen(7) 33/1: 0-050062: Chsd ldrs stands side, overall 2½ 66
ldr over 1f out, hdd ins last & no ch with wnr: 7 wk abs: see 1749.
4719 **PRINCE OF GOLD 4** [11] R Hollinshead 4-8-8 p (62) S Drowne 25/1: 0000053: Held up far side, rdn & shd 65+
styd on to lead that group ins last, not pace of wnr stands side: qck reapp: first home far side, gd run: eff at
6f, h'capped rto win shortly at 7f/1m: see 2324.
4582 **DR SYNN 11** [6] J Akehurst 3-8-10 (66) P Doe 25/1: 6502034: Rear stands side, switched & styd on ½ 67
for press, nrst fin: eff at 6f, rtn to 7f in similar will suit: acts on fast, gd & enjoys soft grnd: see 4582, 4029.
4676* **BINT ROYAL 7** [17]6-8-4 (58) F Norton 11/1: 0021015: Trkd ldrs far side, onepcd dist: see 4676. 1 56
4562+ **BOWLING ALONG 12** [13]3-8-4 (60) T Dean(7) 18/1: 4320016: Chsd ldrs far side, kept on onepace. nk 57
4475 **MAGIC AMOUR 16** [4]6-8-3 BL (57) S Righton 22/1: 0400107: Chsd ldrs stands side 5f, blnks. 1 51
4592 **WESSEX 11** [18]4-8-11 VIS (65) D Mernagh 50/1: 6005008: Held up far side, switched & mod gains: vis. ½ 57
4603* **COMPTON PLUME 10** [9]4-8-13 (67) Dale Gibson 20/1: 2100019: Towards rear far side, rdn & late gains. ½ 57
3109 **DESERT ARC 77** [5]6-8-10 (64) D Allan 50/1: 0116000: 10th: Chsd ldrs stands side 4f, 11 wk abs. nk 53
4272 **VAL DE MAAL 26** [20]4-8-13 (67) T Eaves(3) 12/1: 3040460: 11th: Led far side 4f, fdd under press. hd 55
4700 **NEVER WITHOUT ME 5** [14]4-8-11 (65) P Mulrennan(3) 13/2 JT FAV: 1242260: 12th: Cl-up far side, led nk 52
that group over 2f out, sn hdd & fdd: best at 5f.
4603 **TALLY 10** [10]4-8-9 (63) Dane O'Neill 28/1: 1400600: 13th: Chsd ldrs far side, struggling fnl 3f. 1 47
4562 **BANJO BAY 12** [16]6-8-9 (63) A Nicholls 13/2 JT FAV: 6000050: 14th: Held up far side, no impress. ½ 45
4562 **WINTHORPE 12** [15]4-9-0 (69) Darren Williams 15/2: 2054430: 15th: Chsd ldrs far side till over 1f out. 1 47
4618 **SHARP HAT 9** [1]10-8-9 (63) A Culhane 12/1: 0302450: 16th: Led/dsptd lead stands side till over nk 41
1f out, fdd qckly: btr 3350 (5f).
4240 **Mynd 28** [2]4-8-7 (2ow)P(59) V Halliday 25/1:0   4278 **Attacca 26** [12]3-8-4 bl(60) D Fentiman(7) 100/1:0
4093 **Mister Sweets 36** [8]5-9-2 (70) D Tudhope(5) 33/1:0   4603 **Torrent 10** [19]9-8-3 bl(57) Rory Moore(5) 14/1:0
20 Ran   Time 1m 12.87 (2.87)   Owned: The Matthewman Partnership   Trained: Malton

4786
2.55 Sportingoptions Co Uk Commission Cutters Handicap Stakes 3yo+ 86-100 (C1) [106]
£12255 £4649 £2324 **6f str**   **Good 46**   +06 Fast   Stands Side

4459 **PIC UP STICKS 17** [2] M R Channon 5-9-1 (93) A Culhane 6/1: 6360001: Chsd ldrs stands side, led 102
dist, drvn out: op 15/2: stays 7f, best at 5/6f on firm & gd/soft, any trk: inconsistent but back to best.
4652 **ELLENS ACADEMY 8** [3] E J Alston 9-8-7 (1oh) (84) F Norton 20/1: 2235602: Held up rear stands 1 89
side, styd on well from over 1f out, not reach wnr: btr run: see 386.
4693 **SMART HOSTESS 6** [8] J J Quinn 5-8-13 (91) T Eaves(3) 25/1: 011-0003: Sn prom, styd on for press, nk 94
qck reapp: imprvd eff, coming to hand & won thrice in Oct '03: see 3422.
4654 **ARTIE 8** [13] T D Easterby 5-8-7 (2oh) (83) Dane O'Neill 20/1: 1000004: Led far side, hung left & ½ 86
kept on for press: qck reapp: fair run, 1st home from far side group: see 3073 (5f).
4394 **AVERSHAM 21** [6]4-8-9 (87) S Drowne 11/2 JT FAv: 30-00035: Trk ldrs stand side, led over 1f out, nk 87
sn hdd & onepace: just btr 4394 (firm).
4686 **FANTASY BELIEVER 7** [7]6-9-6 (98) P Hanagan 11/2 JT FAV: 0120026: Chsd ldrs stands side, onepace. 1 95
4627 **IMPRESSIVE FLIGHT 9** [11]5-8-7 (3oh) (82) D Mernagh 20/1: 6-000657: Held up far side, prog & chall hd 81

1447

over 1f out, sn no extra.
4322 **MARSAD 24** [4]10-8-9 (87) P Doe 12/1: 0200028: Stands side, chsd ldrs, no impress fnl 1f: btr 4322. *shd* **83**
4686 **HIDDEN DRAGON 7** [10]5-8-12 P (90) G Faulkner 8/1: 2006409: Handy stands side 5f, chkpcs. *1½* **81**
4496 **INTER VISION 15** [9]4-8-7 (4oh)P (81) P Mulrennan(3) 20/1: 0042000: 10th: Dsptd lead stands side 4f. *shd* **76**
4652 **PIETER BRUEGHEL 8** [1]5-8-8 (86) A Nicholls 8/1: 0133200: 11th: Hung right thr'out, hung right/dpstd lead stands side 4f, fdd: btr 3937. *½* **75**
4537 **PERUVIAN CHIEF 13** [12]7-9-0 bl (92) T P Queally 16/1: 00U0030: 12th: Chsd ldr far side, wknd ins last. *2* **75**
1627 **RAYMONDS PRIDE 140** [5]4-8-7 (3oh)bl (82) A Mullen(7) 50/1: 0511450: 13th: Al rear stands side. *3* **59**
4718 **DAZZLING BAY 4** [14]4-9-7 bl (99) D Allan 15/2: 3520030: 14th: Reluctant to go to post, chsd ldrs far side till halfway, eased: qck reapp: see 4718, 2949. *5* **58**
14 Ran Time 1m 12.4 (2.4) Owned: A Ball & W Harrison-Allan Trained: West Ilsley

4787

3.25 Ark De Triumph Maiden Auction Stakes Fillies 2yo (E3)
£4103 £1262 £631 **5f str** **Good 46** **-16 Slow** Inside

4049 **ANGELOFTHENORTH 37** [12] J D Bethell 2-8-4 (63) T P Queally 8/1: 3433301: Sn led stands side & rdn clr over 1f out, held on for press cl-home: eff at 5f on fast & soft, likes a sharp trk & forcing tactics. **71**
4517 **THORNBER COURT 14** [10] A Berry 2-8-4 (56) F Norton 100/1: 0402: Dwelt, held up in tch stands side, drvn & styd on well ins last, just failed: eff at 5f on gd grnd, rtn to 6f in similar may suit: see 4277. *nk* **70**
3224 **PIVOTALS PRINCESS 72** [4] B A McMahon 2-8-6 Dane O'Neill 3/1 JT FAV: 33: Held up stands side, no room when switched 2f out, hdwy/switched dist & styd on well ins last, nrst fin: well bckd, op 9/2: 10 wk abs: gone close with a clear passage: handles gd & gd/soft grnd, 6f in similar could suit: see 3224. *shd* **72**
4549 **BOBS FLYER 12** [11] J G Given 2-8-8 (67) P Hanagan 8/1: 040244: Pushed along towards rear, late prog, no threat: see 4517. *1¾* **69**
3245 **LADY HOPEFUL 71** [1]2-8-4 (62) T Eaves(3) 20/1: 5422055: Chsd wnr stands side, btn over 1f out: abs. *1¾* **60**
4358 **DAISYS GIRL 22** [9]2-8-6 S Drowne 6/1: 06: b f Inchinor - Andbell (Trojan Fen) Pushed along towards rear stands side, only mod prog for press: op 4/1: 8,500gns Jan foal, half-sister to a 7f/1m wnr. *2½* **54**
4617 **SWEET MARGUERITE 9** [16]2-8-6 (55) D Allan 20/1: 5446007: Led far side, no impress on ldrs stands side fnl 1f: first home from smaller far side group: see 2275. *½* **52**
3431 **BAHAMIAN BAY 63** [8]2-8-2 T Williams 80/1: 008: b f Bahamian Bounty - Moly (Inchinor) Chsd ldrs stands side, no impress fnl 2f, 2 month abs, clr rem: cheaply bght Feb foal: dam plcd at 10f. *¾* **46**
TIME FOR MEE 0 [2]2-8-2 J F McDonald(3) 33/1: 9: ch f Timeless Times - Heemee (On Your Mark) Al bhd stands side: 2,000gns May foal: half-sister to wnrs at 5f/9f: dam 5f juv wnr. *5* **32**
1974 **ASHES 123** [7]2-8-4 BL (64) Darren Williams 10/1: 0540: 10th: Chsd ldrs stands side, struggling fnl 2f. *1* **31**
4596 **BOPPYS DREAM 10** [5]2-8-2 D Mernagh 28/1: 60: 11th: Al outpcd stands side. *½* **27**
4503 **BRAVE TARA 14** [13]2-8-4 P M Quinn 100/1: 000: 12th: Chsd ldr far side, struggling from halfway. *1¼* **25**
1880 **COURTINTIME 127** [3]2-8-4 Paul Eddery 50/1: 00: 13th: Mid-div stands side, no ch with hmpd 2f out. *1½* **20**
4401 **WOODFORD WONDER 20** [14]2-8-2 P Mulrennan(3) 100/1: 00: 14th: Bhd halfway far side. *hd* **17**
4303 **AGREAT DAYOUTWITHU 25** [15]2-8-2 J McAuley 100/1: 000: 15th: Sn bhd far side, broke blood vessel. *15* **0**
4343 **LADY DAN 23** [6]2-8-4 (65) Dale Gibson 3/1 JT FAV: 320603P: Chsd ldrs, struggling halfway & lost action/p.u. lame over 1f out: op 7/2: see 4343. **0**
16 Ran Time 1m 0.91 (3.11) Owned: Mr J Hamilton Trained: Middleham

4788

4.00 A Rhodes Haulage Maiden Stakes Div 1 3yo+ (D3)
£4072 £1253 £626 **6f str** **Good 46** **-25 Slow** Stands Side

2372 **KENSINGTON 106** [10] R Guest 3-9-0 (64) S Drowne 2/1 FAV: 64-63261: Trkd ldrs trav well, led dist & rdn clr, decisively: op 9/4: gelded, abs: eff at 6f: acts on fast & soft grnd, gall or sharp trk: see 1876, 1607. **67**
4407 **FORREST GUMP 19** [2] C J Teague 4-9-2 T Eaves(3) 80/1: 00-02: ch g Zilzal - Mish Mish (Groom Dancer) Towards rear, late gains for press, no impress on wnr: bckd at long odds: drpd in trip: unplcd in both '03 starts (rtd 3a, tried blnks & a visor): eff at 6f on gd grnd. *4* **54**
4237 **BRAIN WASHED 28** [1] T D Easterby 3-8-9 (67) D Allan 3/1: 042533: Handy, drvn & onepcd/held dist. *¾* **47**
2897} **AEGEAN MIST 439** [9] M Mullineaux 4-8-11 (40) S Righton 50/1: 400050-4: ch f Prince Sabo - Dizzydaisy (Sharpo) Led till dist, no extra: reapp: unplcd '03 (rtd 45a & 40, P Howling): plcd '02 (rtd 66, T D Easterby, auct mdn): best eff at 5f on fast grnd & a stiff/undul trk. *½* **45**
4561 **M FOR MAGIC 12** [3]5-9-2 (45) K Pierrepont(7) 9/1: 045-5245: Chsd ldrs, no impress bef dist: see 4561. *¾* **48$**
3610 **PAY TIME 56** [12]5-8-11 (35) P Mulrennan(3) 33/1: 00-60056: Dwelt, held up in tch, nvr pace to chall. *nk* **42$**
3575 **CARIBBEAN BLUE 57** [8]3-8-9 VIS (40) J F McDonald(3) 14/1: 00-50007: Chsd ldrs 5f, visor, abs. *1* **39$**
4740 **RUSSIAN SYMPHONY 3** [13]3-9-0 bl (65) A Culhane 9/4: 05-0608: Chsd ldrs, outpcd fnl 2f: nicely bckd, gelded: qck reapp: see 4740, 4582. *shd* **44**
4237 **DESIGNER CITY 28** [11]3-8-9 (35) F Norton 33/1: 0000409: Rdn rear & nvr a factor. *6* **21**
4404 **SECRET OF SECRETS 19** [5]3-9-0 J McAuley 22/1: 00: 10th: Sn rdn rear & outpcd, no form. *dist* **0**
10 Ran Time 1m 14.28 (4.28) Owned: Mr M Sakal Trained: Newmarket

4789

4.35 Nidderdale Novice Stakes 2yo (D2)
£8770 £2506 £1253 **6f str** **Good 46** **-03 Slow** Stands Side

4513 **COUNTRY RAMBLER 14** [1] B W Hills 2-9-5 (94) K May(7) 9/4: 01031: Made all, rdn & in command over 1f out: bckd: eff at 6/7f on firm & gd grnd, sharp/easy trks: likes to force the pace: useful: see 2597. **96**
4577* **LOADERFUN 11** [2] H Candy 2-9-5 (100) Dane O'Neill 2/5 FAV: 4212: Trkd wnr, rdn & btn over 1f out, eased: hvly bckd but ran as if something amiss today: btr 4577 (soft). *16* **82**
2 Ran Time 1m 12.94 (2.94) Owned: Mr Ahmed BuHaleeba Trained: Lambourn

4790   5.05 A Rhodes Haulage Maiden Stakes Div 2 3yo+   (D3)
£4064 £1250 £625   6f str   Good 46   -17 Slow   Stands Side

4562 **FLYING BANTAM 12** [3] R A Fahey 3-9-0 (68) P Hanagan 9/4: 4024041: Made all, rdn & asserted from   74
dist, styd on strongly: nicely bckd: eff at 5f, suited by 6f on firm & gd/soft grnd, any trk: eff in cheek pieces,
best without: tough & consistent, deserved this: see 1639.
4413 **DEUXIEME 19** [2] R Charlton 3-8-9 (72) S Drowne 7/4 FAV: 33522: Held up, switched for eff 2f out,   1¾   63
kept on but al well held: bckd: see 4413, 3921 & 3048.
4275 **BLUEBOK 26** [9] D R Loder 3-9-0   T P Queally 7/2: 5-23: Trkd ldrs, no impress over 1f out: bckd.   4   56
2080} **ROSE OF YORK 471** [5] T D Walford 4-8-11   T Eaves(3) 66/1: 00-4: b f Emarati - True Ring (High   ½   49
Top) Outpcd rear, mod gains, no threat: Flat reapp, 7 months jumps abs (unplcd, rtd 82h, juv nov, prob flattered, J
G Portman): unplcd both '03 starts on the level (rtd 45).
4504 **NICHOLAS NICKELBY 14** [12]4-9-2 p (52) Dane O'Neill 10/1: 0434425: Swerved right start, chsd ldrs,   2½   46
btn over 1f out: btr 4504.
4404 **JUNIPER BANKS 19** [10]3-9-0 (46) A Culhane 25/1: 60420-66: Chsd ldrs, btn dist: see 4404.   ½   44
4216 **GREY FORTUNE 29** [1]5-8-11 M Lawson(5) 50/1: 047: Cl-up till over 1f out.   5   26
4340} **DORISIMA 372** [6]3-8-9 e P Mulrennan(3) 50/1: 0-8: ch f Mark of Esteem - Suhaad (Unfuwain) Al   2   20
outpcd rear, eye-shield, reapp: unplcd sole '03 start (rtd 38).
      KUSSHARRO 107 [8]3-9-0   D Mernagh 16/1: 59: Cl-up, outpcd when hmpd halfway, sn btn, abs.   1½   20
4595 **SEA FERN 11** [7]3-9-0 (45) A Nicholls 66/1: 0-500060: 10th: Sn outpcd & struggling, eased over 1f out.   8   0
10 Ran   Time 1m 13.75(3.75)   Owned: The Matthewman Partnership   Trained: Malton

Official Going Good/Firm (Good Places)

4791   11.25 Book Now For The Christmas Festival Banded Stakes 3yo+ 0-45 (H5)
£1565 £447 £224   1m2f   Good/Firm 32   -25 Slow   Inside

4659 **ENNA 7** [1] Mrs Stef Liddiard 5-9-4 (45) T Quinn 12/1: 2060431: Keen in mid-div, hdwy to lead   51
over 1f out, rdn & sn asserted: eff at 6f in native Poland prev, suited by 1m/11f: acts on firm, soft & polytrack.
4505* **DANCING TILLY 14** [15] R A Fahey 6-9-5 p (46) T Hamilton(3) 11/2: 4246412: Mid-div, styd on for press.   2   48
4373 **MY MAITE 21** [17] R Ingram 5-9-5 vis t (46) N Day 9/2: 0450333: Mid-div, drvn & kept on, not pace wnr.   ½   47
4372* **CUNNING PURSUIT 21** [13] M L W Bell 3-9-3 (50) K Fallon 2/1 FAV: 5620014: Chsd ldrs, onepace dist.   3½   43
4145 **MISTER COMPLETELY 32** [2]3-9-0 (47) Martin Dwyer 12/1: 0160105: Mid-div wide, no extra fnl 1f.   shd   43
4202 **MAID THE CUT 29** [4]3-8-12 (45) A Daly 20/1: 00-40056: Held up, eff over 2f out, btn dist.   ½   40
3746 **ARTZOLA 50** [14]4-9-8 (49) D Holland 25/1: 050-0007: Mid-div, no impress fnl 1f, abs: see 917.   ½   43
4373 **PIQUET 21** [10]6-9-4 (50) G Baker 33/1: 3010008: Mid-div, no prog fnl 1f, abs: likes   nk   38
Brighton/Lingfield.
3373 **NUZZLE 65** [8]4-9-4 (45) S Hitchcott 20/1: 0303009: Trkd ldr, btn 2f out: abs: btr 2993 (1m).   nk   37
4708 **FIZZY LADY 5** [19]3-9-3 t (50) M Savage(5) 16/1: 0000240: 10th: V slow away, mod late prog, lost ch   nk   41
start, qck reapp: reportedly resented t-strap: see 4485.
3370 **ROJABAA 65** [16]5-9-7 (48) S Haddon(7) 20/1: 11-65550: 11th: Al bhd, abs: btr 2548.   ½   38
2955 **GLENDALE 83** [6]3-9-3 (50) M Howard(7) 33/1: 0000500: 12th: Handy, no impress fnl 1f, abs, new yard.   ½   39
2064 **SUNSET DREAMER 119** [5]3-9-2 (49) R L Moore 33/1: 60000: 13th: Handy/dsptd lead till over 1f out: abs.½   37
4669 **FAIRLAND 7** [9]5-9-5 (46) L Smith(7) 20/1: 0-340600: 14th: Went left start & badly hmpd early when   hd   33
rider lost iron, nvr factor.
4616 **INDIAN LILY 10** [11]3-8-12 (45) C Catlin 33/1: 0600000: 15th: Prom, btn 2f out, longer trip.   ¾   31
3145 **PISTE BLEU 76** [7]4-9-7 (48) Joanna Badger 20/1: 0016400: 16th: Al bhd, abs.   8   24
3487 **JADE STAR 61** [3]4-9-8 p (49) Derek Nolan(7) 25/1: 6440300: 17th: Led 1m, wknd qckly, abs, new yard.   7   16
4228 **TREGENNA 28** [12]3-9-0 (47) M Henry 33/1: 4500: 18th: Rear, hung left & btn over 1f out, eased.   12   0
18 Ran   Time 2m 08.03 (5.73)   Owned: Valley Fencing   Trained: Hungerford

4792   11.55 Jump Racing Here 23rd October Maiden Auction Stakes 2yo (H5)
£1523 £435 £218   1m rnd   Good/Firm 32   -27 Slow   Inside

4658 **BOLD COUNSEL 7** [11] B J Meehan 2-8-12 (65) C Catlin 8/1: 5261: Trkd ldr & led over 3f out,   67
narrowly hdd dist, gamely rallied to lead again cl-home, all out: eff at 7f/1m: handles firm, fast & polytrack.
      GHAILL FORCE 0 [2] J G Portman 2-8-12   N Callan 66/1: 2: b g Piccolo - Coir 'a' Ghaill (Jalmood)   nk   66
Dwelt & held up, rdn & hdwy to lead over 1f out, just hdd cl-home: cheaply bght Mar foal, half-brother to a dual
3yo wnr abroad, dam plcd at 6s as a juv & subs plcd over hdles: eff at 1m, could get further: handles fast.
4316 **CABIN FEVER 24** [7] J C Fox 2-8-6 (55) D Fox(5) 5/1: 05003: Mid-div, hdwy/hung right when chall   hd   59
dist, no extra cl-home: styd longer 1m trip but lkd a tricky ride: acts on fast grnd: see 3848.
4297 **MAKTU 26** [8] P F I Cole 2-8-11   K Fallon 10/11 FAV: 534: Prom, ch 2f out, onepace for press: well bckd.   hd   61
4369 **SUNNY TIMES 21** [16]2-8-6 (51) J F Egan 16/1: 5005: Rear, mod late prog, nrst fin: stays 1m on fast.   1½   55
4658 **BONNABEE 7** [9]2-8-5   Lisa Jones 20/1: 006: Slow away & rear, late gains under hand riding, nrst   nk   52+
fin: gave impression last twice of more to come, interesting for low-grade h'caps: see 4658.
4233 **TRANQUILIZER 28** [12]2-8-6 t E Ahern 12/1: 6U7: Chsd ldrs, no impress fnl 1f.   1   52
4114 **KAPAJE 34** [4]2-8-5 (70) Joanna Badger 6/1: 0538: Held up, eff 3f out, no prog dist: btr 4114.   hd   48
4575 **WHITLAND 11** [20]2-8-12 t R Havlin 50/1: 009: Prom, sn pushed along & nvr land a blow.   1¼   52
4436 **LADY VEE 18** [10]2-8-5   T Hamilton(3) 20/1: 050: 10th: Prom, wknd fnl 1f: btr 4436 (6f).   1¼   43
4316 **BEAU MARCHE 24** [3]2-8-11 P (61) Martin Dwyer 16/1: 50020: 11th: Rear, rdn & little prog, chkpcs.   1   46
4576 **MANORSHIELD MINX 11** [13]2-8-6 D Holland 14/1: 0000: 12th: Mid-div, struggling fnl 2f.   1½   35
2939 **COIS NA TINE EILE 84** [14]2-8-4 (51) N Chalmers(5) 33/1: 3030: 13th: Al rear, new yard: abs: new yard.   3   28
3750 **BLUE SPECTRUM 50** [5]2-8-12 Derek Nolan(7) 33/1: 0000: 14th: Mid-div, struggling over 2f out, abs.   2½   28
4316 **TIGER HUNTER 24** [18]2-8-9 Kristin Stubbs(7) 100/1: 000: 15th: Mid-div, struggling fnl 2f: longer trip.   4   18
4658 **TOUCH OF SPICE 7** [6]2-8-9 W Ryan 100/1: 000: 16th: Led till over 3f out, sn btn.   3½   7
      MILLQUISTA DOR 0 [19]2-8-6 R Thomas(3) 50/1: 0: 17th: Slow away & al rear.   7   0

Miss Dinamite 0 [17]2-8-3 A McCarthy 66/1:0   **Charlieslastchance** 0 [1]2-8-3 A Daly 66/1:0
19 Ran   Time 1m 41.69 (4.69)   Owned: Racegoers Club Owners Group   Trained: Upper Lambourn

---

4793

12.25 Racing Uk On Channel 432 Banded Stakes 3yo+ 0-40 (H5)
£1491 £426 £213   **6f str**   Good/Firm 32   +13 Fast   Centre

4660 **SPINETAIL RUFOUS** 7 [2] D Flood 6-9-0 bl (40) J F Egan 12/1: 06/000-01: Went left start, hdwy to   53
lead overall over 1f out, rdn out: op 10/1: eff at 5/6f on both AWs & fast grnd: likes a sharp/easy trk: see 4660.
4659 **CRIMSON STAR** 7 [4] C Tinkler 3-8-12 (40) C Catlin 11/2: 0003222: Handy stands side, styd on for   1   49
press, not pace to beat wnr: eff at 6f/1m: see 4659, 4371.
3545 **ANGEL ISA** 58 [5] R A Fahey 4-9-0 VIS (40) T Hamilton(3) 9/1: 0-000033: Led stands side till over   3½   38
3f out, styd on onepace for press: op 7/1: 2 month abs, first time visor: see 2445.
3763 **DANAKIM** 21 [17] J R Weymes 7-9-0 (40) D Holland 7/1: 0042004: Handy far side, led that group   1¼   34
over 1f out, no ch with ldrs stands side ins last: 7 wk abs: see 3609.
4371 **MR UPPITY** 21 [3]5-9-0 e (40) T Quinn 9/2 FAV: 3654205: Chsd ldrs stands side, no impress fnl 1f: op 6/1.1   31
4371 **ZINGING** 21 [6]5-9-0 vis (40) A Daly 20/1: 5600406: Chsd ldrs stands side, nvr pace to chall: btr 4168 (7f). 2½ 23
4751 **AVIT** 3 [12]4-9-0 (40) R Price 14/1: 1450207: Mid-div far side, no impress dist: qk reapp: btr 3849 (5f).   shd   23
3790 **OLD HARRY** 49 [20]4-9-0 (40) Martin Dwyer 20/1: 000-0008: Overall ldr far side till over 1f out, fdd: abs. nk 22
4116 **JASMINE PEARL** 34 [8]3-8-12 (40) S Whitworth 33/1: 0256609: Handy stands side & led that group   ½   20
over 3f out till over 1f out, fdd.
4595 **SUITCASE MURPHY** 11 [18]3-8-12 (45) N Callan 7/1: 004-0630: 10th: Chsd ldrs far side, btn dist.   ½   18
4489 **ZAMBEZI RIVER** 16 [19]5-9-0 (40) R L Moore 16/1: 0060000: 11th: Chsd ldrs far side, btn over 1f out. shd   18
4371 Badou 21 [13]4-9-0 (40) P Dobbs 25/1:0   3301 **Bahamian Belle** 68 [14]4-9-0 (40) J Brennan(7) 33/1:0
4116 Pardon Moi 34 [16]3-8-12 (40) A McCarthy 16/1:0   4662 **Daimajin** 7 [1]5-9-0 vis(40) D Nolan(3) 33/1:0
4202 Lady Predominant 29 [9]3-8-12 (40) B Reilly(3) 66/1:0   3651 **Beaver Diva** 54 [11]3-8-12 (40) B Swarbrick(5) 25/1:0
3000 Sotonian 81 [7]11-9-0 (40) Lisa Jones 20/1:0   4081 **Society Pet** 36 [10]5-9-0 (40) Derek Nolan(7) 66/1:0
19 Ran   Time 1m 12.25 (1.15)   Owned: Miss J Wickens   Trained: Hungerford

---

4794

12.55 Kempton For Christmas Parties Tri-Banded Stakes 3yo 0-45 (H5)
£1505 £430 £215   **7f rnd**   Good/Firm 32   -29 Slow   Inside

3737 **DANTES DEVINE** 51 [15] A Bailey 3-9-5 (45) V Slattery 20/1: 6504001: Handy & led dist, drvn out: 49
7 wk abs: first win: eff at 7f on fast grnd & an easy trk in banded company: see 2205.
4587 **ELSINORA** 11 [17] H Morrison 3-9-5 bl (45) L Fletcher(3) 11/2: 2635242: Prom & ch dist, drvn & not   nk   48
pace of wnr nr fin: shown enough to find similar: see 4587 & 4370.
4587 **DAVIDS GIRL** 11 [8] D Morris 3-9-0 (40) B Reilly(3) 20/1: 6500663: Held up, styd on from over 1f   1¾   40
out, nrst fin: eff over an easy 7f on fast grnd in banded company: see 1416.
4140 **EMARADIA** 32 [13] A W Carroll 3-9-5 (45) D Nolan(3) 12/1: 2660304: Led/dsptd lead till dist, no extra.   ¾   44
4474 **FABULOSO** 16 [1]3-9-5 (45) N Callan 1/1: 00-56065: Mid-div, onepace fnl 2f: op 6/1.   ¾   43
3895 **SILVER ISLAND** 44 [16]3-9-5 (45) M Henry 33/1: 00-0006: Towards rear, mod prog, nvr a factor, 7 wk abs. ½   42
4707 **AMBER FOX** 5 [10]3-9-5 (45) F P Ferris(3) 7/1: 4-565037: Chsd ldrs, no prog fnl 1f, qck reapp: see 4705. hd   41
4662* **STAGECOACH RUBY** 7 [5]3-9-5 (45) R Brisland 12/1: 3300518: Mid-div, no impress fnl 2f: op 8/1.   nk   40
4202 **WHIPLASH** 29 [14]3-9-5 bl (45) C Catlin 20/1: 0600609: Hmpd start, rear, mod late prog.   nk   39
4347 **ROYALTEA** 23 [12]3-9-5 (45) N Chalmers(3) 25/1: 6640000: 10th: Chsd ldrs, btn over 1f out.   1   37
4368 **PAPPY** 22 [11]3-9-5 (45) P Dobbs 6/1: 00-40300: 11th: Al towards rear: btr 3900.   nk   36
4371* **SAVERNAKE BRAVE** 21 [3]3-9-5 (45) G Baker 11/4 FAV: 0400010: 12th: Dwelt, sn prom racing wide,   1¼   33
led 4f out till 2f out, fdd: op 5/1: btr 4371.
4116 **JOANS JEWEL** 34 [6]3-9-5 P (45) A McCarthy 33/1: 5560000: 13th: Mid-div, hung left & btn over 1f out. hd   32
4413 Imperial Wizard 19 [7]3-9-5 (45) A Daly 50/1:0   4367 **Welsh Empress** 22 [9]3-9-5 (45) R Price 20/1:0
4508 Hi Darl 14 [2]3-9-5 (45) B Swarbrick(5) 25/1:0   3603 **Court Chancellor** 56 [4]3-9-5 bl(45) J F Egan 33/1:0
17 Ran   Time 1m 28.37 (4.27)   Owned: Mr Raymond Gomersall   Trained: Tarporley

---

4795

1.25 Subscribe To Racing Uk On 08700 860432 Banded Stakes 3yo+ 0-45 (H5)
£1589 £454 £227   **1m rnd**   Good/Firm 32   -19 Slow   Inside

4488 **CAERPHILLY GAL** 16 [7] P L Gilligan 4-9-6 (47) D Fox(5) 16/1: 40-00001: Chsd ldrs, hdwy to lead   50
over 1f out, rdn out: eff at 7f/1m on fast grnd, easy or gall trk: see 2768.
4659* **LEVANTINE** 7 [12] Miss J Feilden 7-9-7 (48) Kirsty Milczarek(7) 10/1: 33-35612: Handy, styd on for   1½   48
press ins last, al held: see 4659 (AW).
4449 **SONDERBORG** 18 [3] Miss A M Newton Smith 3-9-4 bl (49) Lisa Jones 33/1: 0006663: Dwelt & towards   ½   48
rear, kept on late, nrst fin: stays 1m: see 662.
       IDLE JOURNEY 32 [6] M Scudamore 3-9-3 (48) V Slattery 14/1: 0-001204: b c Mujadil - Camassina   nk   46
(Taufan) Dwelt, mid-div & keen, kept on onepace fnl 2f: ex Irish, h'cap wnr at Down Royal earlier in '04: eff at
7f/1m on fast & gd grnd.
4676 **TOKEWANNA** 7 [2]4-9-7 t (48) B Swarbrick(5) 12/1: 3045435: Mid-div wide, kept on onepace.   nk   45
3963 **MARNIE** 41 [19]7-9-6 (47) S Hitchcott 12/1: 2255506: Held up, styd on onepace for press, abs.   2½   39
4411 **CITY GENERAL** 19 [4]3-9-4 p (45) Derek Nolan(7) 25/1: 5105607: Chsd ldr, led 3f out till over 1f out, wknd. shd 41
4707 **WOOD FERN** 5 [20]4-9-6 (47) C Catlin 8/1: 0610048: Held up, nvr land a blow: qck reapp: btr 4707 (7f). shd 38
4542 **MYTHICAL CHARM** 13 [14]5-10-0 t (55) A Daly 7/1 FAV: 3500229: V slow away & rear, little hdwy.   2   42
3733 **MAGIC WARRIOR** 51 [9]4-9-9 (50) P McCabe 33/1: 5-346000: 10th: Al bhd, 7 wk abs: btr 622 (AW).   nk   36
4698 **RUSSALKA** 5 [8]3-9-2 (49) M Halford(7) 20/1: 6060050: 11th: Towards rear, no impress fnl 2f: qck reapp. 2   29
4373 **GRAN CLICQUOT** 21 [18]9-9-6 (47) S Whitworth 16/1: 0102000: 12th: Al bhd: btr 2857.   ½   28
4676 **GEMINI LADY** 7 [17]4-9-6 bl (47) A McCarthy 16/1: 0200040: 13th: Mid-div, no impress fnl 2f: btr 4676. 2½   23
4145 **PRINCE VALENTINE** 32 [15]3-9-4 bl (49) N Pollard 33/1: 5404000: 14th: Mid-div, no prog fnl 2f.   2   21

KEMPTON SATURDAY 25.09.04 Righthand, Flat, Fair Track

3823 **INDIAN BLAZE 47** [13]10-9-8 (49) J F Egan 10/1: 0360600: 15th: Mid-div, struggling fnl 2f: 'lost action'. *5* **12**
4720 **HIRAYNA 4** [5]5-9-7 (48) G Baker 9/1: 3044000: 16th: Prom, btn 2f out: 'disliked ground'. *5* **2**
3718 **FAITH HEALER 51** [11]3-9-5 bl (50) N Callan 12/1: 0461060: 17th: Led till 3f out, sn btn: 'nvr trav'. *3* **0**
2812 **St Tropez 89** [16]3-9-3 bl(48) L Keniry(3) 50/1:0 3490 **Albadi 61** [1]3-9-5 bl(50) J P Guillambert(3) 20/1:0
19 Ran Time 1m 40.86 (4.06) Owned: Mr T Williams Trained: Newmarket

4796

2.00 Buy Your Jump Membership Now Banded Stakes 3yo+ 0-45 (H5)
£1572 £449 £225 **1m4f** **Good/Firm 32** **-13 Slow** Inside

3703 **THEATRE LADY 52** [3] P D Evans 6-9-8 (47) F P Ferris(3) 20/1: 0151061: Mid-div, hdwy to lead over 1f out, rdn clr, decisively: 7 wk abs: eff btwn 7f/12f on firm, hvy & polytrack: see 3398, 539. **53**
4119 **MAKE MY HAY 34** [9] J Gallagher 5-9-6 (45) Martin Dwyer 6/1: 1255562: Mid-div, styd on for press fnl 2f, nrst fin: op 8/1: see 1645 (C/D). *1¾* **48**
4663 **OPEN BOOK 7** [15] H Morrison 3-9-1 (48) L Fletcher(3) 20/1: 0000303: Chsd ldrs 2f out, onepce dist. *½* **50**
4665 **TASNEEF 7** [7] T D McCarthy 5-9-10 (49) S Whitworth 8/1: 0-066044: Handy & led 4f out till over 1f out. *¾* **50**
4665 **BANNINGHAM BLAZE 7** [14]4-9-11 (50) D Nolan(3) 9/2 FAV: 3222325: Held up, eff over 2f out, onepace. *1* **50**
4720 **FAIRY MONARCH 4** [12]5-9-8 p (47) R Fitzpatrick 25/1: 0-202006: Rear, eff 3f out, onepace: qck reapp. *nk* **46**
4374 **VANDENBERGHE 21** [5]5-9-7 (46) R Keogh(7) 12/1: 6333407: Held up, nvr pace to threaten ldrs. *3* **41**
4594 **CHEVIN 11** [13]5-9-6 (45) T Hamilton(3) 10/1: 0-501008: Handy, no impress fnl 2f: btr 3669. *¾* **39**
4374* **LYSANDERS QUEST 21** [8]6-9-7 (46) N Day 20/1: 00-00519: Rear, mod late prog: btr 4374. *¾* **39**
4319 **MONTOSARI 24** [1]5-9-7 (46) J F Egan 12/1: 6312030: 10th: Chsd ldrs, lost pl over 3f out, sn no prog. *½* **38**
4675 **RHETORICAL 7** [10]3-9-2 (49) J P Guillambert(3) 10/1: 00-50600: 11th: Led after 1f till 4f out, sn btn. *nk* **40**
4665 **LUNAR LORD 7** [20]8-9-7 (46) R Price 25/1: 0422060: 12th: Mid-div, no impress fnl 3f: btr 3420. *shd* **37**
4661 **RICKY MARTAN 7** [2]3-8-12 (45) L Keniry(3) 66/1: 0006060: 13th: Prom, struggling fnl 3f, longer trip. *hd* **35**
4419 **AMBERSONG 19** [16]6-9-10 (49) P Dobbs 14/1: 3014360: 14th: Slow away & al bhd: flattered 4181. *¾* **38**
4716* **REGENCY RED 4** [6]6-9-13 (46) B Swarbrick(5) 8/1: 100/-4010: 15th: Led mid-div, strugging fnl 3f. *nk* **40**
4581 **GIKO 11** [18]10-9-8 (47) Lisa Jones 20/1: 2300020: 16th: Al bhd: see 4581 (led, 1m). *6* **26**
4660 **SPRING WHISPER 7** [4]3-8-12 (45) D Fox(5) 50/1: 000-000: 17th: Mid-div, rdn & btn 2f out, qck reapp. *12* **9**
4669 **HAVANTADOUBT 7** [19]4-9-6 t (45) G Baker 50/1: 0-000500: 18th: Al bhd: btr 3473. *hd* **8**
4374 **TINTAWN GOLD 21** [11]4-9-8 p (47) C Catlin 20/1: 0042020: 19th: Al bhd: btr 3474. *12* **0**
4594 **MISTER MERLIN 11** [17]3-8-12 (45) N Pollard 66/1: 350-00: 20th: Keen & led 1f, remained handy till halfway, wknd qckly, t.o.: see 4594. *dist* **0**
20 Ran Time 2m 35.43(5.43) Owned: Waterline Racing Club Trained: Abergavenny

ASCOT SATURDAY 25.09.04 Righthand, Stiff, Galloping Track

Official Going Good/Firm (Firm places)

4797

1.55 Gr2 Hackney Empire Royal Lodge Stakes Colts & Geldings 2yo (A1)
£58000 £22000 £11000 **1m rnd** **Good/Firm 37** **-05 Slow** Inside

3865* **PERFECTPERFORMANCE 45** [1] Saeed bin Suroor 2-8-11 (100) L Dettori 4/6 FAV: 1211: Handy, gd hdwy to lead over 1f out, edged right for press but styd on strongly ins last: hvly bckd after abs: stays 1m well, shld get further next term: acts on fast & gd grnd, stiff trks: runs well fresh: smart & improving, win more Gr races. **111**
SCANDINAVIA 56 [6] A P O'Brien 2-8-11 J P Spencer 8/1: 2212: b c Fusaichi Pegasus - Party Cited (Alleged) Held up, hdwy well over 1f out, styd on to chase ldr dist, no extra well ins last: 8 wk abs: May foal, cost $725,000: half-brother to several wnrs: dam useful juv: earlier won a mdn at Galway: stays 8.5f on gd & firm: clearly useful & must be winning a List/Gr 3 shortly. *1½* **107**
4493 **WILKO 15** [8] J Noseda 2-8-11 (100) E Ahern 7/1: 3321243: Handy, eff to chall well over 1f out, sn rdn, sltly short of room & kept on same pace over 1f out: proving most tough & consistent but needs drop into stks/List: stays 1m: see 4493, 3919. *1¼* **104**
4493 **ELLIOTS WORLD 15** [7] M Johnston 2-8-11 K Darley 9/1: 1164: Set pace till over 1f out, no extra: sweating: shld stay 1m but prob needs return to List as in 4003. *½* **103**
3582 **FRITH 57** [5]2-8-11 M Hills 25/1: 235: Held up, eff well over 1f out, onepace, no dngr: 8 wk abs: will stay at least 1m & would apprec a confidence boosting mdn win: see 3582. *1¾* **99**
3774 **KANDIDATE 49** [3]2-8-11 (90) S Sanders 80/1: 0306: Held up, eff 2f out, sn no extra: wants mdns. *¾* **97**
4493 **GRAND MARQUE 15** [4]2-8-11 (96) K Fallon 14/1: 511257: In tch, wknd 2f out: too highly tried. *1¾* **93**
4156* **BERKHAMSTED 35** [2]2-8-11 (100) D Holland 20/1: 162518: With ldrs, wkng when hmpd over 1f out: up in class after List win on hvy in 4156. *nk* **92**
8 Ran Time 1m 41.89 (3.39) Owned: Godolphin Trained: Newmarket

4798

2.30 Gr1 Meon Valley Stud Mile Fillies 2yo (A1)
£116000 £44000 £22000 **1m rnd** **Good/Firm 37** **-09 Slow** Inside

4476* **PLAYFUL ACT 16** [2] J H M Gosden 2-8-10 (90) J Fortune 11/4: 2111: Made all, clr over 1f out, drvn out ins last: well bckd: stays 1m well, looks sure to apprec 10f+ next term: acts on firm & gd grnd, likes stiff trks: v smart, tough & progressive filly, strong classic candidate for '05: see 4476. **112**
4476 **MAIDS CAUSEWAY 16** [8] B W Hills 2-8-10 (100) M Hills 7/1: 212132: Cl-up, eff to chase wnr over 2f out, kept on but al held: similar distance bhd this wnr on 3lb worse terms in 4476: tough & smart, win a Gr 2/3. *1* **110**
4450* **DASH TO THE TOP 18** [6] L M Cumani 2-8-10 D Holland 16/1: 213: In tch, hdwy & short of room 2f out, sn rdn, rallied ins last: coped well with step up in class & looks to be crying out for 10f: type to win Gr races & one for the notebook over mid-dists next term: see 4450. *¾* **108+**
MONA LISA 41 [4] A P O'Brien 2-8-10 J P Spencer 14/1: 424: ch f Giant's Causeway - Colorsnap (Shirley Heights) Handy, eff & badly hmpd over 2f out, rallied over 1f out, kept on: 6 wk abs: Mar foal, cost 1,250,000gns: half-sister to smart juv wnrs: eff at 1m, shld stay further: earlier mdn rnr-up: clearly useful, prob 2nd with a clr run here & must be winning Gr races. *shd* **107+**
3386* **SHOHRAH 64** [1]2-8-10 R Hills 10/1: 15: Dwelt, sn bhd, eff over 1f out, kept on same pace: 2 mth abs: stays 1m: would enjoy a drop into List/Gr 3: see 3386. *2* **103**

4359* **JOINT ASPIRATION 22** [7]2-8-10   T E Durcan 20/1: 116: Dwelt, bhd, eff over 1f out, sn onepace: *shd*   102
prob stays 1m but needs a drop into List/stks: see 4359.
4223* **ECHELON 28** [5]2-8-10   K Fallon 15/8 FAV: 17: Dwelt, held up, short of room 2f out, held when   1¾   98
short of room again over 1f out: prob btr than this & shld stay 1m: impressed on debut in 4223 (debut).
4264* **DUBAI SURPRISE 27** [3]2-8-10 (100) L Dettori 7/1: 3118: Chsd wnr to over 2f out, no extra: Gr 3   3   92
wnr on soft grnd & over 7f in 4264.
4457 **GHASIBA 17** [9]2-8-10 (82) S Sanders 100/1: 62009: Bhd, wknd over 2f out: see 3908, 3386.   7   78
9 Ran   Time 1m 42.22 (3.72)   Owned: Sangster Family   Trained: Manton

---

4799   **3.00 Gr2 Gner Diadem Stakes 3yo+   (A1)**
£58000 £22000 £11000   **6f rnd   Good/Firm 37   Inapp** Inside

4678 **PIVOTAL POINT 7** [6] P J Makin 4-9-0 (100) S Sanders 11/2: 0121151: Keen cl-up, led trav well   120
over 1f out, sn rdn clr, readily: well bckd: eff over 5/6f on firm & gd grnd, any trk: right back to form & a
career best/high-class eff: still unexposed for a sprinter & would enjoy a sound surface in the Prix L'Abbaye.
4678 **AIRWAVE 7** [4] H Candy 4-8-11 (108) J P Spencer 4/1 FAV: 6016032: Held up, hdwy 2f out, sn short   3   108
of room, switched & styd on to chase wnr ins last, nvr getting there: well bckd: ran to current best: see 4678, 3304.
4678+**THE TATLING 7** [12] J M Bradley 7-9-4 (116) R L Moore 6/1: 1032213: Handy, trav well 2f out, rdn   1¼   111
& onepace over 1f out: best at 5f as in 4678, 3rd in Prix L'Abbaye last term: see 4678.
4678 **CELTIC MILL 7** [2] D W Barker 6-9-0 p (104) D Holland 12/1: 1006104: Set pace till over 1f out,   hd   106
onepace: wants List/Gr 3: see 4481 (5f).
4588 **COUNTRY REEL 11** [10]4-9-0 t (110) L Dettori 7/1: 0440025: Handy, no extra dist: nicely bckd.   1¾   102
4686 **CAPRICHO 7** [7]7-9-0 (99) R Hughes 40/1: 4000006: Held up, eff dist, no impress: stiff task.   1   99
4433* **RINGMOOR DOWN 20** [1]5-8-11 (108) T Quinn 9/1: 3424117: Held up, brief eff over 1f out, no   ¾   94
impress: poor draw: btr 4433 (Gr 3), 3551.
4693 **SIMIANNA 6** [3]5-8-11 p (97) T E Durcan 50/1: 5032158: Keen, wide in tch, no impress over 1f out.   ½   92
4472* **MAC LOVE 16** [11]3-8-12 (103) G Carter 12/1: 2661019: In tch, wkng when sltly short of room over   nk   94
1f out: btr 4472 (List, 7f).
4477 **GOLDEN NUN 16** [9]4-8-11 bl (104) R Winston 25/1: 1050540: 10th: In tch, wknd over 1f out.   1¾   86
4384 **RATIO 21** [8]6-9-0 t P Robinson 11/2: 1010-100: 11th: In tch, short of room after 1f, al bhd.   nk   88
3062 **STEENBERG 79** [5]5-9-0 (111) N Callan 12/1: 1-212000: 12th: In tch 4f, wknd: 11 wk abs: btr 1667.   3½   78
12 Ran   Time 1m 13.55 ()   Owned: Mr R A Bernard   Trained: Marlborough

---

4800   **3.35 Totejackpot On Saturday Stakes Heritage Handicap 3yo+   (B1)**   [115]
£40600 £15400 £7700   **7f rnd   Good/Firm 37   Inapp** Inside

3555 **KEHAAR 58** [12] M A Magnusson 3-8-6 (93) E Ahern 13/2: 1101: Handy, hdwy over 1f out, led ins   105
last, sn rdn clr, v readily: bckd after abs: eff over 7f/1m on fast grnd & likes a stiff trk, has disapp on a
sharp/undul one: runs well fresh: useful, progressive & has a turn of foot, more val prizes to be won.
4523 **KOOL 14** [6] P F I Cole 5-8-5 (89) R L Moore 12/1: 5402362: Held up, hdwy over 2f out, chall   1¾   95
dist, not pace of wnr: some gd effs in defeat this term: see 4231, 3954.
4531 **MINE 14** [5] J D Bethell 6-9-10 vis (108) T Quinn 9/1: 1152053: Held up, hdwy over 1f out, styd on ins   1   112
last, nrst fin: v tough & smart, relishes coming off a fast pace: see 4531, 2489.
3941 **TRAYTONIC 42** [7] J R Fanshawe 3-9-0 (101) J Murtagh 12/1: 5013004: In tch, eff well over 1f out,   shd   104
no impress till styd on late: 6 wk abs: enjoyed step up to 7f & continues to hint at more to come: see 2407.
4477 **NAAHY 16** [15]4-9-9 (107) S Hitchcott 25/1: 0446005: Set pace, kept on till collared ins last, no   ½   109
extra: ran well for a long way: see 2455.
4523+**ETTRICK WATER 14** [9]5-9-1 (5ex)vis (99) N Mackay(3) 4/1 FAV: 3-511016: Held up, eff well over 1f   ½   100
out, onepace: hvly bckd: most progressive earlier & shade more expected after 4523.
4499* **FREE TRIP 15** [8]3-8-7 (5ex) (94) R Hughes 6/1: 2555217: Handy, outer, eff well over 1f out, sn no   nk   94
extra: not disgraced but shade more expected after 4499 (1m).
4638 **BAHIANO 8** [3]3-9-3 (104) D Holland 50/1: 0040008: Held up, late gains: reportedly struck into.   nk   103
4731 **MILLENNIUM FORCE 7** [14]6-9-8 (106) T E Durcan 16/1: 2330049: Dwelt, bhd, eff & short of room   nk   104
over 1f out, kept on late: see 4731.
3954 **GREENSLADES 42** [10]5-8-9 (93) S Sanders 12/1: 2030660: 10th: In tch, eff & short of room 2f out   ½   89
till over 1f out, no extra: 6 wk abs: see 3775, 3061.
4523 **BOSTON LODGE 14** [2]4-8-12 vis (96) J Fortune 12/1: 4000320: 11th: Dwelt, held up, eff & short of   1¾   88
room over 1f out, no extra: reportedly reared in stalls: btr 4523, 3555.
4523 **UHOOMAGOO 14** [4]6-8-10 bl (94) N Callan 16/1: 1003000: 12th: Sn rdn bhd, hdwy & short of room   1½   83
over 1f out, no extra: no luck in running: see 3565, 3441.
4523 **GRIZEDALE 14** [16]5-8-6 t (90) J F Egan 25/1: 20-50000: 13th: Keen, cl-up, short of room over 2f   2   75
out, sn challenging, wknd over 1f out: reportedly lost action.
4638* **ROYAL STORM 8** [13]5-9-6 (5ex) (104) M J Kinane 10/1: 0020010: 14th: Handy, wknd appr fnl 1f: 1½   86
reportedly struck into: btr 4638.
4638 **MATERIAL WITNESS 8** [11]7-9-7 (105) Martin Dwyer 25/1: 2041600: 15th: Handy, wknd qckly over 1f   3½   80
out: been busy: likes to force the pace: see 4231.
15 Ran   Time 1m 27.15 ()   Owned: East Wind Racing Ltd   Trained: Upper Lambourn

---

4801   **4.10 Gr1 Queen Elizabeth Ii Stakes Sponsored By Netjets 3yo+   (A1)**
£145000 £55000 £27500   **1m rnd   Good/Firm 37   +21 Fast** Inside

4571 **RAKTI 14** [13] M A Jarvis 5-9-1 (122) P Robinson 9/2: 212-1051: Trkd ldr trav strongly, went on   125
2f out, clr dist, held on drvn out: hvly bckd, fast time: back to best & settled btr dropped to 1m, eff at 10f, stays
12f: acts on fast & gd/soft, runs well fresh: top-class when settling & may bid to repeat last season's win the
Champion stks: see 4571 & 2488.
4434 **LUCKY STORY 20** [6] M Johnston 3-8-11 (118) D Holland 16/1: 1111-202: Nvr far away, rdn 2f out,   ½   123+
styd on v strongly fnl 1f, not btn far: eff at 1m, 10f in the Champion stks looks sure to suit: career best run,
top-class & prob even more to come: see 3886.
3533 **REFUSE TO BEND 59** [3] Saeed bin Suroor 4-9-1 t (121) L Dettori 4/1: 0-001103: Held up, prog to   2½   118
chase ldrs 1.5f out, not qckn fnl 1f: well bckd, 8 wk abs: better run but rated higher earlier in 2916, 2470.
4232 **NAYYIR 28** [5] G A Butler 6-9-1 (120) J Fortune 11/1: 02-30224: Dwelt, hdwy from rear wide 2f   1½   115

out, nrst fin: clr of rem: just below best: see 4232.
4020* **ACE 41** [1]3-8-11 J P Spencer 12/1: 1115: Mid-div & wide, no impress fnl 2f: Irish challenger, 6 wk abs: only lightly rcd & this was a big step up in class: see 4020 (Gr 3). *4* **107**
4572* **SOVIET SONG 14** [8]4-8-12 (120) J Murtagh 5/2 FAV: 3121116: Mid-div, eff 2f out, no impress fnl 1f: hvly bckd: ran flat & this was prob a race too far after a busy season: top-class earlier: see 4572. *1¼* **101**
4477 **FONGS THONG 16** [4]3-8-11 T (108) P J Smullen 50/1: 321-1157: Chsd ldrs, short of room & lost place halfway, hmpd 2f out, no ch after: tried a t-strap: up in grade & did not get the run of today's race. *1¼* **101**
4434 **DIAMOND GREEN FR 20** [11]3-8-11 C Soumillon 8/1: 1-322228: Held up, nvr a factor: French challenger: much btr than this, see 4434. *4* **93**
4434 **ANTONIUS PIUS 20** [12]3-8-11 t K Fallon 14/1: 4530539: Keen & prom, wknd 2f out: see 4434. *2½* **88**
4571 **NORSE DANCER 14** [14]4-9-1 (121) J F Egan 11/1: 0441220: 10th: Nvr trav & well btn fnl 2f: puzzling run, this is clearly not his form: beat today's wnr in 4571 & today's 2nd in 3886. *4* **80**
4747} **BLATANT 198** [7]5-9-1 vis t (112) K McEvoy 100/1: 042-0560: 11th: ch c Machiavellian - Negligent (Ahonoora) Led till 2f out, wknd: long abs, stablemate of 3rd & pacemaker: Gr 1 rnr-up in Italy in '03: List wnr for J Oxx in '02: eff around 1m on fast & soft grnd: wears a t-strap & visor: btr than this. *3* **74**
2 Oct'03 San 8g/f 114- : 2 Sep'02 Curr 8g/f 112- :
11 Ran Time 1m 39.82 (1.32) Owned: Mr Gary A Tanaka Trained: Newmarket

4802

4.45 Listed Kleenex Rosemary Stakes Handicap Fillies & Mares 3yo+ 96-110 (A1) **[112]**
£17400 £6600 £3300 **1m rnd** **Good/Firm 37** **-08 Slow** Inside

4071 **TARFAH 36** [9] G A Butler 3-8-6 (90) S Sanders 4/1: 1121: Keen & prom, went on 2f out, held on gamely cl-home: well bckd: returned to winning ways on this drop back to 1m, does stay 10f: acts on fast & soft: handles a sharp or gall trk, likes to run up with the pace: useful & progressive filly, see 4071 & 3826. **100**
4331 **GOLDEN ISLAND 23** [1] J W Hills 3-8-3 (2oh) (85) R L Moore 25/1: 2151032: Dwelt, hdwy from rear 2f out, fin strongly & only just btn: apprec this return to 1m & a career best run: see 4331 & 3780. *hd* **96**
4495 **MANSFIELD PARK 15** [10] Saeed bin Suroor 3-9-2 (100) L Dettori 13/8 FAV: 21-33: Trkd ldrs, went after wnr 2f out, caught for 2nd cl-home: hvly bckd from 9/4: fine h'cap bow & this was a v useful effort. *1* **107**
4160 **SOLDERA 34** [4] J R Fanshawe 4-9-7 (101) J Murtagh 14/1: 140-3404: Held up, prog 2f out, ev ch fnl 1f, prob just held when short of room cl-home: fine run under top-weight: eff at 10f, poss best arnd 1m. *hd* **106**
4149 **FLOWERDRUM 32** [11]4-8-8 (88) K Darley 12/1: 1410505: Mid-div, styd on fnl 1f, nrst fin. *3* **88**
3965 **MOON DAZZLE 41** [13]3-9-6 (104) D Holland 8/1: 145526: Prom, wknd dist: 6 wk abs: see 3965. *3½* **97**
3965* **BRINDISI 41** [7]3-9-2 (100) M Hills 16/1: 4144617: Held up, prog wide 2f out, btn fnl 1f: 6 wk abs. *1* **91**
4331 **CONVENT GIRL 23** [5]4-8-7 (2oh) (85) R Havlin 20/1: 0000068: Dwelt, mid-div, btn dist. *2½* **73**
4933} **TREASURE THE LADY 27** [3]3-8-12 T (96) M J Kinane 14/1: 13-4549: b f Indian Ridge - Kasora (Darshaan) Held up, nvr nr ldrs: tried a t-strap: '03 wnr at the Curragh: eff at 7/9f on fast & gd/soft. *½* **81**
4607* **PORTHCAWL 10** [6]3-8-3 (8oh) (79) P Robinson 11/1: 0-110: 10th: Hmpd & lost place early, no ch when short of room 2f out: stiff task: btr 4607 (fills h'cap). *1¼* **70**
4095 **THREE SECRETS 35** [12]3-8-8 (92) A McCarthy 33/1: 20-01230: 11th: Chsd ldr, no impress. *shd* **74**
3965 **COTE QUEST 41** [8]4-8-10 (90) K Fallon 50/1: 0443600: 12th: Trkd ldrs 6f, wknd: 6 wk abs. *5* **62**
4290 **CRYSTAL CURLING 26** [2]3-8-13 T (97) Martin Dwyer 50/1: 1-330550: 13th: Keen & led 6f, wknd qckly: tired a t-strap: rider reportedly given a 3-day careless riding ban: btr 4290. *7* **55**
13 Ran Time 1m 42.12 (3.62) Owned: Mr Abdulla Al Khalifa Trained: Blewbury

4803

5.20 Caplan Gordon Carter Stakes Handicap 3yo+ 86-100 (C1) **[95]**
£13650 £4200 £2100 **2m45y** **Good/Firm 37** **-12 Slow** Inside

4527 **ESCAYOLA 14** [14] W J Haggas 4-9-7 vis (88) J F Egan 7/1: 1-020021: Mid-div, imprvd 2f out, switched wide & strong run to lead cl-home, cosily: eff at 14f/2m2f on gd & firm grnd, handles any trk: suited by blnks/visor & a gd weight-carrier: prog & heads for the Cesarewitch, but must have fast grnd. **98**
4647 **MAMCAZMA 8** [8] D Morris 6-8-13 (80) T E Durcan 33/1: 0400002: Nvr far away, went on dist, collared cl-home: clr of rem: back to form, has tumbled down the ratings & will win if repeating this: see 3119. *½* **88**
4491 **MIDAS WAY 15** [2] P R Chamings 4-9-12 (93) L Dettori 16/1: 6320-203: Prom, sltly outpcd 2f out, kept on fnl 1f: top-weight: only lightly rcd this season, seemed to stay this longer 2m trip: see 4104. *3* **98**
4383 **ITS THE LIMIT 21** [5] Mrs A J Perrett 5-9-10 (91) M J Kinane 16/1: 31/42-404: Held up, styd on strongly fnl 1f, nrst fin: held up to get this longer 2m trip & set plenty to do: lightly rcd, see 3444 (12f here). *hd* **96**
1689 **TEMPSFORD 136** [13]4-9-5 (86) S Sanders 15/2: 1511-505: Keen & prom, led 2f out till dist, no extra: nicely bckd, long abs: sharper next time & shld be plcd to advantage: see 856 (12f, AW). *¾* **90**
4527 **CORTON 14** [12]5-9-1 (82) J Fortune 16/1: 20250-36: Mid-div, not pace to chall: see 4527. *nk* **85**
3531 **MANA DARGENT 59** [3]7-9-7 (88) D Holland 4/1: 5000157: Held up, kept on late wide, nvr nr ldrs: bckd from 6/1, 8 wk abs: real Ascot specialist (6 wins here), see 3387 (C/D). *1¼* **90**
4062 **PEAK OF PERFECTION 37** [10]3-8-11 (90) P Robinson 7/2 FAV: 3511128: Led till 2f out, wknd: well bckd: most progressive prev, not stay this longer 2m trip? see 4062 & 3359 (14f). *1¼* **90**
4383 **ALMAH 21** [4]6-9-4 BL (85) R Hughes 100/1: 30-00609: Dwelt, recovered to dispute lead halfway till 2f out, wknd: tried blnks: see 3776 (C/D). *nk* **84**
4383 **LODGER 21** [1]4-9-7 (88) E Ahern 20/1: 14-06400: 10th: Held up, nvr nr ldrs. *1½* **85**
4634 **THEWHIRLINGDERVISH 9** [16]6-8-13 (80) T Quinn 14/1: 3132600: 11th: Prom 12f, sn strug: btr 3635. *¾* **76**
4527 **THEATRE 14** [9]5-8-12 (4oh) (75) A McCarthy 33/1: 2230000: 12th: Held up, nvr a factor. *2½* **72**
4400 **VALANCE 20** [7]4-9-0 (81) J Murtagh 16/1: 3514020: 13th: Mid-div, btn 2f out, eased: btr 4400. *5* **69**
3531 **STANCE 59** [15]5-8-12 p (79) R L Moore 10/1: 5023-020: 14th: Al towards rear: 8 wk abs. *5* **62**
4079} **MAC 385** [11]4-9-9 BL (90) K McEvoy 33/1: 601150-0: 15th: ch g Fleetwood - Midnight Break (Night Shift) Dwelt, al bhd, t.o. on reapp: tried blnks: dual Newbury h'cap wnr in '03: suited by racing up with the pace around 13f on firm grnd: likes Newbury: with M Tregoning. *2½* **70**
1 Aug'03 Newb 13.3fm 89-82 C: 1 Jul'03 Newb 13.3fm 88-72 D:
4491 **HIGHLAND GAMES 15** [6]4-9-8 (89) K Darley 25/1: 245330P: P.u. bef halfway. **0**
16 Ran Time 3m 34.03(8.03) Owned: Mrs M Findlay Trained: Newmarket

Official Going Good/Firm (Good Places)

4804 2.25 Criterion Pub Challenge Maiden Auction Stakes 2yo (E3)
£4095 £1260 £630 5f str Good 49 -24 Slow Stands side

4556 **HILLSIDE HEATHER** 13 [10] A Berry 2-8-3 p (61) P Hanagan 9/2: 0245061: Held up, prog 2f out, styd **76**
on to lead ins fnl 1f, rdn out: eff at 5f, rtn to 6f will suit: acts on fast & gd: eff with cheek pieces.
4436 **TURN ON THE STYLE** 19 [8] R P Elliott 2-8-8 S Chin 33/1: 002: In tch, prog to lead dist, hdd ins 1½ **75**
fnl 1f, not pace wnr: eff at 5f on gd grnd: imprvd eff on drop to min trip, now quals for h'caps: see 4436.
4409 **FARTHING** 20 [2] G C Bravery 2-8-8 (74) D Holland 5/4 FAV: 2423: Prom, ev ch well over 1f out, sn 1 **72**
no extra: well bckd: showed more in 4409 & 3488.
3272 **ORPHAN** 71 [1] K R Burke 2-8-7 Darren Williams 9/2: 054: Led, hdd bef 1f out, no extra: 10 wk ½ **70**
abs: eff at 5f on gd grnd: see 3272.
4599 **BEVERLEY BEAU** 11 [9]2-8-7 (68) Kristin Stubbs(7) 11/1: 554445: Chsd ldrs wide over 3f, onepcd. nk **69**
4599 **MS THREE** 11 [4]2-8-3 Joanna Badger 10/1: 0656: Bhd, nvr nrr than mid-div: see 4129. ½ **64**
4338 **DUCAL DIVA** 24 [6]2-8-2 (60) D Fentiman(7) 20/1: 02607: Cl-up, ev ch dist, fdd 3525. 4 **51**
3361 **IN RHUBARB** 66 [7]2-8-8 Natalia Gemelova(7) 50/1: 68: ch g Piccolo - Versami (Riverman) Missed ½ **56**
break, nvr a factor: 9 wk abs: Mar foal, cost 5,000gns: half-brother to wnrs at 7/8f: dam unplcd: sire Gr 1 wnr
at sprint dists: with I W McInnes.
4596 **WAGGLEDANCE** 11 [5]2-8-10 p (66) T Eaves(3) 14/1: 500029: Prom 4f, fdd: btr 4596. 3½ **48**
4549 **PROCRASTINATE** 13 [3]2-8-10 (68) R Winston 16/1: 3052030: 10th: Prom 3f, fdd: btr 4549. 1½ **44**
10 Ran Time 1m 1.15 (3.65) Owned: Hillside Racing Trained: Cockerham

4805 3.00 Royal Scots 'premier' Claiming Stakes 3yo+ (D3)
£5395 £1660 £830 1m4f Good 49 -60 Slow Inside

4620 **YENALED** 10 [6] K A Ryan 7-9-5 (72) N Callan 7/2: 2421041: Mid-div, prog to lead 2f out, rdn out: **72**
eff at 7/10f, apprec step up to 12f: acts on firm, soft & f/sand: likes claim grade & Musselburgh: see 4173.
4720 **DONNAS DOUBLE** 5 [2] D Eddy 9-9-1 p (52) K Darley 11/1: 4346202: Mid-div, prog & ev ch trav well 1¾ **63**
2f out, kept on, not pace wnr ins fnl 1f: qck reapp: clr rem: faced a stiff task at the weights & ran well.
4406 **SANDY BAY** 20 [1] A R Dicken 5-9-0 (30) P Fessey 10/1: 0000403: In tch, eff 2f out, onepcd dist. 7 **52$**
4690 **PERELANDRA** 8 [4] M J Wallace 4-9-2 (71) D Holland 4/5 FAV: 610-1044: Led, edged left & hdd 2f ¾ **52**
out, hung badly left & fdd: well bckd: disapp eff drpd in grade: has shown best form on softer grnd.
4364* **ON CLOUD NINE** 23 [3]3-8-5 (62) B Swarbrick(5) 9/2: 6004315: Keen cl-up, ev ch 3f out, fdd bef 1f nk **48**
out: op 7/2, new stable (prev with M Bell): btr 4364 (gd/soft).
4255 **WINSLOW BOY** 28 [5]3-8-13 (59) L Enstone 16/1: 6126366: Chsd ldrs 10f: btr 3893 (14f, g/s). 1¼ **54**
6 Ran Time 2m 43.70 (13.1) Owned: The Fishermen Trained: Hambleton

4806 3.35 Musselburgh News Handicap Stakes 3yo+ 71-85 (D2) [86]
£6781 £2086 £1043 7f30y rnd Good 49 -11 Slow Outside

4689 **SEA STORM** 8 [8] D R MacLeod 6-9-7 (79) R Winston 7/1: 5643021: In tch, prog over 1f out, styd on **87**
to lead cl-home, rdn out: eff at 7f/sharp 1m on firm, soft grnd & polytrack: likes Musselburgh: in form 6yo who
remains well h'capped & more prizes await: see 4689.
4341+**HARTSHEAD** 24 [12] G A Swinbank 5-9-6 (78) P Mulrennan(3) 5/1: 6114112: Handy, staying on when ½ **83**
short of room & switched inside, kept on ins fnl 1f, not btn far: gd eff in defeat on hat-trick bid: see 4341 & 3574.
4652 **KIRKBYS TREASURE** 9 [1] A Berry 6-9-3 (75) K Darley 8/1: 2022603: Held up, prog wide 2f out, ev hd **79**
ch dist, kept on despite hanging badly left ins fnl 1f, not btn far: op 3942 & 3562.
3305 **BALLYHURRY** 69 [6] J S Goldie 7-8-9 (67) T Eaves 14/1: 4-064604: Bhd, prog 3f out, kept on ins ½ **70**
fnl 1f, nrst fin: op 10/1: 10 wk abs: encouraging eff & is on a winning mark: see 2086.
4389 **TRANQUIL SKY** 22 [10]3-9-5 (80) D Holland 8/1: 0520405: Held up, prog 2f out, staying on when ½ **82**
short of room ins fnl 1f, nrst fin: btr 2040 (1m).
4482 **CLOUD DANCER** 17 [9]5-9-3 (75) N Callan 4/1 FAV: 1350456: Rear, prog 3f out, no impress fnl 1f. nk **76**
4695 **STOIC LEADER** 7 [3]4-9-5 (77) P Hanagan 16/1: 5640447: In tch, ev ch 1f out, no extra ins fnl 1f. shd **77**
4615 **H HARRISON** 11 [4]4-9-6 (78) T Hamilton(3) 16/1: 3500658: Mid-div, prog wide 3f out, sn no impress. nk **77**
4516 **MISTER MARMADUKE** 15 [13]3-9-3 (78) D Allan 33/1: 0-043509: Cl-up, led 2f out, hdd under press nk **76**
well ins fnl 1f, wknd: clr rem: rtn to 6f shld suit: btr 4048 (6f).
4341 **SAMUEL CHARLES** 24 [7]6-9-3 (75) B Swarbrick(5) 25/1: 3420160: 10th: Prom over 5f, fdd: btr 3696. 9 **57**
4516 **REDWOOD ROCKS** 15 [11]3-9-6 (81) F Lynch 16/1: 00-01060: 11th: Led 5f, wkng when short of room dist.8 **49**
4562 **FINGER OF FATE** 13 [14]4-8-7 (20oh)bl (45) J F McDonald(3) 100/1: 0030300: 12th: Dwelt, al bhd. 12 **12**
4719 **ALCHEMIST MASTER** 5 [5]5-8-12 p (70) A Culhane 7/1: 463003P: Rear, prog halfway, wknd under press **0**
& p.u. & dismounted dist, lame: qck reapp: returned distressed: btr 4719.
13 Ran Time 1m 29.11 (4.21) Owned: Mr Maurice W Chapman Trained: Lauder

4807 4.10 Royal Scots Club Cup Nursery Handicap Stakes 2yo 0-85 (D2) [92]
£5502 £1693 £846 1m rnd Good 49 +14 Fast Outside

4583* **SUCCESSION** 12 [5] Sir Mark Prescott 2-8-12 (76) D Holland 4/5 FAV: 0006111: Made all, pushed out **88**
to hold ins fnl 1f, val bit more: well bckd, gd time: eff at 7f/1m, further will suit: acts on gd & gd/soft grnd:
progressive performer who can win again: see 4583 & 4519.
3053* **IM SO LUCKY** 80 [4] M Johnston 2-9-7 (85) K Darley 7/2: 012: Chsd ldrs, styd on to chase wnr 1¾ **90**
dist, kept on but al held: 11 wk abs, top-weight, h'cap bow: eff at 7f, apprec step up to 1m: see 3053.
4673 **CAITLIN** 8 [3] B Smart 2-8-11 (75) F Lynch 7/1: 2413123: Cl-up, ev ch 2f out, no extra fnl 1f: 1 **78**
stays 1m, prob suited by rtn to 7f: acts on firm, gd & fibresand: see 4673 & 4337 (7f).
4673 **ALGORITHM** 8 [7] T D Easterby 2-7-12 (3oh) (59) D Mernagh 14/1: 0656234: Mid-div, nvr able to chall. 6 **53**
4283* **JUST WAZ** 27 [6]2-8-6 (70) A Culhane 14/1: 015: Rear, nvr able to chall: step up to 1m: btr 4283. 4 **53**
4597 **MAUREENS LOUGH** 11 [1]2-7-12 (9oh) (53) S Righton 50/1: 1050026: Chsd ldrs 6f, fdd: btr 4597. 7 **32**
3349 **MOUNT EPHRAM** 67 [8]2-8-8 (72) P Hanagan 50/1: 5641427: Missed break, prog halfway, fdd dist. 2½ **37**

MUSSELBURGH SUNDAY 26.09.04 Righthand, Sharp Track

4619 **FENRIR 10** [2]2-9-5 (83) R Winston 20/1: 01538: Chsd ldrs, fdd bef 1f out, eased ins fnl 1f. **11 27**
8 Ran Time 1m 40.34 (2.84) Owned: Dr Catherine Wills Trained: Newmarket

4808
4.45 Sunday Mail Joe Punter Handicap Stakes 3yo+ 71-85 (D2) **[79]**
£6887 £2119 £1060 **2m** **Good 49** **-13 Slow** Stands side

4634 **ASTYANAX 10** [6] Sir Mark Prescott 4-9-12 (77) D Holland 3/1: 0501021: Made all, went clr over 1f **89**
out, rdn out: op 4/1: eff at 12/14f, now suited by 2m: acts on fast, gd/soft & fibresand: still progressing & more
h'caps await: see 4634 & 3703.
4657 **KRISTENSEN 9** [1] D Eddy 5-9-10 p (75) J F McDonald(3) 7/1: 2500302: Rear, prog 7f out, styd on but **7 78**
no ch with easy wnr fnl 2f: has slipped to a fair mark: see 3999.
4657* **STRANGELY BROWN 9** [3] S C Williams 3-8-13 (76) P Hanagan 1/1 FAV: 0021113: In tch, prog to chase **1¾ 77**
wnr 2f out, sn no extra: well bckd: disapp on bid for 4-timer & perhaps came too soon after recent win in 4657.
4657 **TONI ALCALA 9** [5] R F Fisher 5-9-3 (68) P Mulrennan(3) 10/1: 1155604: Prog 4f out, onepcd fnl 2f. **nk 68**
4138 **PILGRIMS PROGRESS 34** [4]4-9-7 (72) R Winston 33/1: 0130-405: Bhd, nvr a factor: btr 3760. **7 65**
4634 **HATHLEN 10** [2]3-8-10 (73) A Culhane 14/1: 5615606: Cl-up 14f, fdd: btr 2376. **2 64**
6 Ran Time 3m 32.50 (10.0) Owned: Lady Katharine Watts Trained: Newmarket

4809
5.15 Rsp Consulting Classified Stakes 3yo+ 0-75 (D2)
£6864 £2112 £1056 **1m rnd** **Good 49** **+08 Fast** Outside

4469* **MR VELOCITY 18** [11] E F Vaughan 4-9-2 (75) D Holland 7/4 FAV: 2106311: Chsd ldrs, styd on to **82**
chase ldr ins fnl 1f, rdn out to lead cl-home: bckd: eff at 7f/8.5f on firm, gd/soft & polytrack: in form 4yo.
3978 **SUMMER SHADES 41** [4] W M Brisbourne 6-8-13 (71) B Swarbrick(5) 20/1: 3561252: In tch, hdwy to **nk 77**
lead 2f out, edged right under press ins fnl 1f, hdd cl-home: 6 wk abs: see 3780 & 3579.
4378 **MILLAGROS 22** [3] I Semple 4-8-13 p (74) P Hanagan 8/1: 4633133: Rear, prog wide 3f out, kept on **½ 76**
ins fnl 1f, not btn far: continues to run well: see 4378 & 4086.
4642 **JUSTE POUR LAMOUR 9** [6] P L Gilligan 4-9-2 (74) Hayley Turner(3) 6/1: 0015264: Held up, prog wide **hd 78**
3f out, kept on ins fnl 1f, nrst fin: btr 4469.
4702 **HONEST INJUN 6** [8]3-8-12 (72) R Winston 14/1: 0545225: Prom, led halfway, fdd 2f out, styd on **¾ 76**
cl-up & ev ch dist, no extra when short of room cl-home: qck reapp: btr 4702 & 4195.
3428 **TOP DIRHAM 64** [1]6-9-2 (72) Dale Gibson 6/1: 3200166: Rear, prog halfway, kept on fnl 1f: 9 wk abs. **shd 75**
4609 **ARRY DASH 11** [10]4-9-2 VIS (75) A Culhane 9/2: 2323257: Cl-up, no extra dist: first time visor. **hd 74**
4622 **ANTHEMION 10** [5]7-9-2 (58) D McGaffin 100/1: 1320008: In tch over 6f, wknd: btr 3593 & 3250. **¾ 72**
4246 **RAREFIED 29** [9]3-8-12 (74) D Allan 33/1: 0100009: Bhd, prog halfway, wknd bef 1f out: btr 1382. **3 66**
4694 **ISKANDER 7** [7]3-8-12 bl (72) N Callan 16/1: 0064050: 10th: Nvr nrr than mid-div: qck reapp. **1 64**
4408 **SILVER SEEKER 20** [2]4-9-2 (45) P Fessey 150/1: 2060000: 11th: Bhd, nvr a factor. **11 42**
4694 **DEVINE LIGHT 7** [12]4-8-13 (50) P Mulrennan(3) 100/1: 1-006000: 12th: Led 3f, wknd 2f out, eased. **dist 9**
12 Ran Time 1m 40.78(3.28) Owned: Mr A M Pickering Trained: Newmarket

ASCOT SUNDAY 26.09.04 Righthand, Stiff, Galloping Track

Official Going Good/Firm

4810
2.00 Riggs Bank Nursery Handicap Stakes 2yo (B1) **[102]**
£12644 £4796 £2398 **7f rnd** **Good/Firm 34** **Inapplicable** Inside

4387 **WISE DENNIS 22** [3] A P Jarvis 2-8-6 (80) K McEvoy 10/1: 003331: Held up wide, hdwy 3f out, styd **93**
on to lead dist, pushed clr despite hanging left, val bit more: eff at 6f/1m on firm, fast grnd & polytrack:
improving, gd confidence boost: see 4387 & 4177.
4741* **REBEL REBEL 4** [9] N A Callaghan 2-8-10 (5ex) (84) A Mullen(7) 15/8 FAV: 0054112: Sn rdn along bhd, **1¾ 91**
prog well over 1f out, kept on ins fnl 1f for 2nd, no ch with wnr: v well bckd on qck reapp: imprvd eff in defeat
on bid for hat-trick under 5lb pen: eff at 7f in 1m shld suit: see 4741 & 4635.
3820 **SKY CRUSADER 48** [12] R Ingram 2-8-9 (83) S Drowne 40/1: 1653: Cl-up, ev ch dist, sn no extra: abs. **3 84**
4387 **IM SPARTACUS 22** [8] I A Wood 2-8-1 P (75) Martin Dwyer 33/1: 0654154: Handy 5f, sn outpcd, **½ 75**
rallied late: cheek pieces: worth another try at 1m: see 4387 & 4410.
4470* **GOODWOOD SPIRIT 17** [4]2-8-7 (81) T Quinn 12/1: 22315: Stumbled start, nvr nrr than mid-div. **hd 80**
4666 **BROOKLIME 8** [10]2-8-6 (80) S W Kelly 16/1: 6410526: Cl-up, wknd ins fnl 1f: btr 4666 (7f, gd/soft). **¾ 77**
4396* **DIAMONDS AND DUST 21** [2]2-8-8 (82) P Robinson 10/1: 43417: Led, hdd dist, wknd: btr 4396 (7f). **shd 78**
4458 **PERSIAN ROCK 18** [11]2-9-0 (88) L Dettori 9/2: 21108: Missed break, sn mid-div, prog 2f out, wknd **¾ 82**
ins fnl 1f: tchd 7/1: disapp run on step up in trip: btr 3897 & 3478 (6f).
4606 **EASY MOVER 11** [5]2-8-3 (77) N Mackay(3) 16/1: 55129: Mid-div, prog 2f out, wknd ins fnl 1f: btr 4606. **¾ 69**
3800 **AL QUDRA 49** [7]2-9-7 (95) J Fortune 20/1: 510520: 10th: Mid-div, gd 5f, sn wknd: 7 wk abs. **2½ 82**
4480 **The Coires 17** [13]2-8-12 (86) R Hughes 12/1:0 4471 **Cusoon 17** [1]2-8-6 (80) R L Moore 14/1:0
12 Ran Time 1m 28.95 () Owned: Quadrillian Partnership Trained: Twyford

4811
2.35 Listed Miles And Morrison October Stakes Fillies & Mares 3yo+ (A1)
£17400 £6600 £3300 **7f rnd** **Good/Firm 34** **Inapplicable** Inside

4556} **BADMINTON 360** [6] Saeed bin Suroor 3-8-8 T (107) L Dettori 11/4 FAV: 123-1: b f Zieten - Badawi **109+**
(Diesis) Mid-div, hdwy 3f out, styd on to lead dist, rdn clr, val 5L+: well bckd on reapp: mdn wnr on 1 of 3 '03
starts (also plcd in Gr 2 & Gr 1's, rtd 109, C E Brittain): eff at 6f, suited by 7f: acts on firm & fast grnd: goes
well fresh: apprec fitting of t-strap: impressive, win Gr races.
2 Aug'03 York 6.0fm 104- A: 1 Jun'03 Donc 6g/f 91- D:
4510 **PEARL GREY 15** [2] Saeed bin Suroor 3-8-8 t (104) K McEvoy 7/1: 3112-32: Mid-div, prog wide 3f **3 101**
out, styd on to chase wnr ins fnl 1f, al held: stablemate of wnr: eff at 5/6f, ran to form on step up to 7f.

4479 **TAHIRAH 17** [1] R Guest 4-8-11 (85) S Drowne 50/1: 0000003: Bhd, hdwy wide 3f out, kept on ins fnl 1f: worth another try at 1m on this evidence: see 2532. ¾ **99**
4479 **LUCKY PIPIT 17** [5] B W Hills 3-8-8 (100) M Hills 20/1: 3-521004: Led, hdd dist, no extra: again bolted bef start: see 4479 & 3365. ¾ **97**
5032*}**THAMINAH 323** [4]3-8-8 (87) R Hills 9/2: 01-5: b f Danzig - Bashayer (Mr Prospector) Cl-up, wknd ins fnl 1f: op 10/3 on reapp: mdn wnr on 1 of only 2 '03 starts: eff at 6f, bred to apprec further: acts on gd grnd & a gall trk: encouraging eff & can impr for today's run. 1 Nov'03 Donc 6gd 92- D: 1½ **95**
3113* **DELPHIE QUEEN 78** [11]3-8-8 (102) J F Egan 7/2: 0-431216: Keen rear, hdwy well over 1f out, sn carried hd high & onepcd: 11 wk abs: btr 3113 (gd/soft). ½ **94**
4556} **VOILE 360** [9]3-8-8 (105) Dane O'Neill 25/1: 124345-7: b f Barathea - Samriah (Wassl) Mid-div, outpcd after halfway, rallied late: reapp: fills mdn wnr in '03 (also List & group plcd, rtd 106 at best): eff at 6f, bred to get further: acts on firm & gd grnd: has gone well fresh: with R Hannon. ½ **93**
2 Jun'03 Newm 6fm 93- A: 1 Jun'03 Newb 6.0fm 86- D:
4510 **BLUE DREAM 15** [3]4-8-11 p J Murtagh 12/1: 0243428: Cl-up 5f, wknd: Irish raider, btr 4510 (6f). *7* **80**
4743 **STARBECK 4** [7]6-8-11 (79) S W Kelly 100/1: 4004009: Missed break, sn in mid-div, wknd 2f out. *shd* **79**
4479 **LOOK HERES CAROL 17** [12]4-8-11 (92) K Fallon 12/1: 3105200: 10th: Missed break & al in rear, eased ins fnl 1f: below par eff: btr 4331. *6* **68**
4479 **CAVERAL 17** [10]3-8-8 (94) R L Moore 25/1: 0103060: 11th: Mid-div 4f, sn wknd, eased ins fnl 1f. ¾ **66**
4495 **MISS CHILDREY 16** [8]3-8-8 T Quinn 66/1: 5300000: 12th: Cl-up over halfway, sn wknd, eased fnl 1f. *6* **55**
12 Ran Time 1m 27.06 () Owned: Godolphin Trained: Newmarket

4812

3.10 Gr3 Barnardo's Cumberland Lodge Stakes 3yo+ (A1)
£29000 £11000 £5500 **1m4f Good/Firm 34 -01 Slow** Inside

4478 **HIGH ACCOLADE 17** [8] M P Tregoning 4-9-0 vis t (114) Martin Dwyer 3/1: 4230241: Sn cl-up, led 4f out, hdd 2f out, hmpd 1f out, rallied for press to lead cl-home: bckd tho' op 5/2: successful in this race 12 mths ago: eff at 12/14.6f, has tried further: acts on firm & gd grnd: eff with/without t-strap & visor: smart & tough. **116**
4023 **SELF DEFENSE 39** [9] P R Chamings 7-9-0 (102) K Fallon 9/1: 50/-06552: Handy, styd on to lead 2f out, sn hung right, hdd cl-home: eff at 14f/2m, imprvd on drop back to 12f: acts on fast & v soft: smart. *nk* **114**
4391 **BANDARI 22** [5] M Johnston 5-9-5 (119) R Hills 7/4 FAV: 1101033: Mid-div, hdwy under press 2f out, kept on despite hanging right ins fnl 1f, just held by front 2: clr rem: bckd: smart run conceding weight. ¾ **117**
4639 **COMPTON BOLTER 9** [6] G A Butler 7-9-0 (106) J Fortune 11/1: 6533234: Led, hdd 4f out, styd cl-up, no extra bef 1f out: fin 2nd bhd today's wnr in this race 12 mths ago: showed more in 4639 & 4494. *4* **106**
4538 **MUQBIL 14** [3]4-9-0 (114) W Supple 9/1: 4-011245: Bhd, prog 3f out, onepcd bef 1f out: first try at 12f: btr 3793 & 3264 (10f). 1¼ **104**
4494 **FRANKLINS GARDENS 16** [2]4-9-0 (105) P Robinson 33/1: 10-44066: Mid-div, outpcd 3f out, rallied late. *nk* **103**
THE KHAMSIN 15 [7]5-9-0 E Ahern 100/1: 2635027: b c Kateb - Medinova (Mas Media) Chsd ldrs, wkng when short of room 2f out: Scandinavian raider, 6 time wnr at trips from 9-14f: with Miss C Erichsen. 1½ **100**
ALPINO CHILENO 14 [4]5-9-0 BL Fernando Diaz 66/1: 1156448: gr c Alpino Fitz - Fairyland (Lode) Mid-div, no impress bef 3f out: Scandinavian raider, earlier won 3 times in native country (12/14f, gd). *shd* **99**
3563 **PERSIAN MAJESTY 58** [1]4-9-0 BL (113) J Murtagh 6/1: 1-633549: Missed break, al in rear, wknd bef 1f out: bckd in first time blnks: bolted to post & prob lost race bef start: showed more in 3030 & 2579. 1½ **96**
9 Ran Time 2m 33.21 (4.21) Owned: Lady Tennant Trained: Lambourn

4813

3.45 Nick Cheyne Farewell Stakes Handicap 3yo+ 86-100 (C1) **[101]**
£12792 £4852 £2426 **1m rnd Good/Firm 34 -07 Slow** Inside

4531 **WELCOME STRANGER 15** [3] J M P Eustace 4-9-5 (92) L Fletcher(3) 16/1: 2121201: Mid-div, prog wide 3f out, styd on to lead dist, pushed out, val 3L+: eff at 7.5f/1m, has tried further: acts on firm, fast grnd & polytrack: progressive & useful: see 3689 & 3523. **102**
4495 **THAJJA 16** [6] J L Dunlop 3-9-7 (98) R Hills 16/1: 1-102: Bhd, prog wide & ev ch bef 1f out, kept on but not pace of wnr: gd eff in defeat on only 4th ever start & is unexposed in h'caps: see 1317. *2* **102**
4531 **FLIGHTY FELLOW 15** [1] T D Easterby 4-9-7 bl (94) G Carter 14/1: 0624043: Held up, prog 2f out, kept on ins fnl 1f: remains in gd form: see 4531 & 3077. 1¼ **96**
4499 **ROYAL PRINCE 16** [10] J R Fanshawe 3-8-12 T (89) J Murtagh 9/2: 4-411334: Mid-div, prog well over 1f out, sn no extra: op 7/2: first time t-strap: btr 4499 & 3814. 1¼ **89**
4681 **LANGFORD 8** [4]4-8-13 (86) P Robinson 40/1: 0014005: Keen cl-up, led 2f out, hdd dist, wknd. *1* **84**
2987* **GRAND BUT ONE 83** [14]3-8-10 (87) M Hills 12/1: 622316: Cl-up, ev ch bef 1f out, wknd: abs. *nk* **84**
4525 **ALRAFID 15** [12]5-8-11 (84) I Mongan 25/1: 5620067: Mid-div, short of room 3f out, sn onepcd. 1½ **78**
4523 **NASHAAB 15** [7]7-9-3 (90) F P Ferris(3) 20/1: 0231508: Nvr nrr than mid-div: btr 3634. ½ **83**
4615 **RAFFERTY 11** [8]5-8-7 (1oh)bl (79) E Ahern 25/1: 0-053409: Keen handy over 6f, no extra: btr 3641. ½ **72**
4523 **PANGO 15** [11]5-8-13 (86) S Drowne 6/1: 2111240: 10th: Chsd ldrs 6f, sn wknd: well bckd: btr 4523. *3* **72**
4525 **TUNING FORK 15** [5]4-8-13 P (86) L Dettori 12/1: 0030000: 11th: Led 6f, sn fdd, eased ins fnl 1f: first time cheek pieces: btr 3565. *8* **58**
4642 **SERIEUX 9** [9]5-8-7 p (80) R L Moore 4/1 FAV: 0000040: 12th: Held up, nvr a factor: well bckd: btr 4642. *5* **43**
3253 **PSYCHIATRIST 72** [13]3-9-7 (98) R Hughes 14/1: 2-324060: 13th: Cl-up 6f, sn wknd & eased: 10 wk abs. *7* **48**
4067* **NORTON 37** [2]7-9-7 (94) J Fortune 7/1: 0400310: 14th: Chsd ldrs over 5f, sn wknd, eased ins fnl 1f: bckd: something amiss? btr 4067. *7* **31**
14 Ran Time 1m 41.85 (3.35) Owned: Mr H R Moszkowicz Trained: Newmarket

4814

4.20 Totesport Ascot Final Fling Stakes Heritage Handicap 3yo+ (B1) **[114]**
£34800 £13200 £6600 **1m4f Good/Firm 34 +06 Fast** Inside

4463 **FORT 18** [9] M Johnston 3-8-2 (88) N Mackay(3) 16/1: 3032051: Keen prom, styd on to lead 3f out, sn pushed clr, eased cl-home, val 4L+: suited by around 12f on fast & soft grnd: likes Ascot: useful. **102**
4690* **ELUSIVE DREAM 8** [7] Sir Mark Prescott 3-7-13 (4ex) (85) J Mackay 9/4 FAV: 1111312: Cl-up, chsd wnr well over 1f out, kept on but al held ins fnl 1f: bckd: clr rem: v progressive & tough. 2½ **92**
4491 **SERGEANT CECIL 16** [12] B R Millman 5-9-1 (93) J Fortune 11/2: 3512223: Held up, hdwy 3f out, no impress ins fnl 1f: continues to run well & return to 14f+ will suit: btr 4491 & 4383. *3* **96**
4534 **PAGAN DANCE 15** [14] Mrs A J Perrett 5-9-0 p (92) R L Moore 15/2: 2260024: Mid-div, hung right under press 2f out, sn onepcd: btr 4534. 1¾ **92**

ASCOT SUNDAY 26.09.04 Righthand, Stiff, Galloping Track

4333 **GRAMPIAN 24** [2]5-9-10 (102) T Quinn 25/1: 2623025: Held up, nvr nrr than mid-div: btr 4333 (14f). *1¼* **100**
4219 **OVAMBO 29** [5]6-9-8 (100) D Sweeney 33/1: 36243/-46: Held up, prog wide 3f out, onepcd dist: btr 4219. *shd* **97**
4491 **TRUST RULE 16** [4]4-8-12 t p (90) M Hills 14/1: 5000047: Nvr nrr than mid-div: btr 4491. *1½* **84**
4023 **TOP SEED 39** [10]3-9-2 (102) T E Durcan 50/1: 2403208: Handy 10f, fdd: btr 3027. *¾* **94**
4614 **WEECANDOO 11** [3]6-8-6 (84) G Carter 50/1: 54-00509: Al in rear: see 4530. *1¼* **74**
4643 **FLOTTA 9** [13]5-8-5 (83) S Hitchcott 25/1: 4301650: 10th: Held up, no impress when hmpd 2f out. *hd* **72**
3926* **TAWNY WAY 44** [6]4-8-13 (91) S Drowne 8/1: 1260110: 11th: Led, hdd 3f out, fdd: bckd: 6 wk abs. *4* **74**
3510 **NAWAMEES 61** [11]6-8-10 p (88) R Hughes 25/1: 36-42200: 12th: Chsd ldrs 10f, wknd & sn eased. *1¼* **69**
4530 **ROEHAMPTON 15** [8]3-8-11 vis (97) K Fallon 12/1: 01-6530: 13th: Keen cl-up, fdd 3f out: btr 4530. *7* **68**
4383 **LOVES TRAVELLING 22** [15]4-8-12 (90) L Dettori 6/1: 23-21200: 14th: Mid-div over 1m, fdd: v well bckd: twice below 3076 (gd/soft) & 2673 (gd). *12* **45**
14 Ran Time 2m 32.38 (3.38) Owned: Highclere Thoroughbred Racing IX Trained: Middleham

4815

4.55 Listed Tom Mcgee Fenwolf Stakes 3yo+ (A1)
£17400 £6600 £3300 **2m45y** **Good/Firm 34** **-26 Slow** Inside

4383* **DEFINING 22** [4] J R Fanshawe 5-9-3 (105) J Murtagh 2/1 FAV: 3-030411: Handy, styd on to lead dist, rdn out: bckd: eff at 12/14f, imprvd on step up to 2m: acts on firm, gd/soft & both AWs: progressing with racing & more List/Gr prizes await: see 4383. **113**
4494 **SWIFT TANGO 16** [5] E A L Dunlop 4-9-6 (106) L Dettori 5/2: 6431232: Missed break, bhd, prog 4f out, styd on to chase wnr trav well dist, kept on but not pace of wnr ins fnl 1f: bckd: stays 2m. *2½* **112**
4491 **SUPREMACY 16** [6] Sir Michael Stoute 5-9-3 (103) K Fallon 4/1: 1-040403: Led, hdd under press dist, no extra: won this race 12 mths ago: see 4230 & 3233. *2½* **107**
4628* **CORRIB ECLIPSE 10** [2] Jamie Poulton 5-9-3 (106) J F Egan 9/2: 166614: Cl-up, no extra over 3f out. *2½* **105**
4534 **TOTAL TURTLE 15** [1]5-9-3 (100) J Fortune 12/1: 12011/-65: Missed break, al in rear, eased ins fnl 1f. *dist* **75**
5 Ran Time 3m 35.71 (9.71) Owned: Mrs V Shelton Trained: Newmarket

HAMILTON MONDAY 27.09.04 Righthand, Undulating Track, Stiff Uphill Finish

Official Going Soft (Good/Soft Places)

4816

2.20 Famous Grouse E B F Median Auction Maiden Stakes 2yo (E3)
£4274 £1315 £658 **1m65y rnd** **Good/Soft 67** **-23 Slow** Inside

3214 **KISWAHILI 74** [5] Sir Mark Prescott 2-8-9 S Sanders 2/5 FAV: 21: Trkd ldrs, led over 2f out & sn pulled clr, val further: hvly bckd at odds on: 10 wk abs & confirmed debut promise: apprec step up to 1m, sure to relish mid-dists: acts on gd & gd/soft: goes well fresh: useful, win better races: see 3214. **92+**
4396 **AIRE DE MOUGINS 22** [3] P C Haslam 2-9-0 (75) G Faulkner 8/1: 04442: Chsd ldrs, styd on for press to take 2nd, nvr any ch with wnr: longer 1m trip shld suit, handles fast & gd/soft: apprec rtn to h'caps: see 4396. *9* **79**
4483 **FINE LADY 18** [8] M Johnston 2-8-9 D Holland 4/1: 623: Led, hdd over 2f out, no impress fnl 2f: op 7/2. *3½* **67**
4204 **LAST PIONEER 31** [2] T P Tate 2-9-0 P Hanagan 66/1: 004: b g New Frontier - Toordillon (Contract Law) Rear, mod late gains: clr rem: Mar foal, 10,000gns purchase: half-brother to a multiple 6f wnr: dam a 12f 3yo scorer: shapes as if further could suit. *1¼* **69**
4213 **EASTERN MANDARIN 31** [4]2-9-0 P Mulrennan(3) 50/1: 55: Chsd ldrs, no impress 2f out, new yard. *5* **61**
4207 **JEFFSLOTTERY 31** [1]2-9-0 R Winston 100/1: 06: b g Rock City - Thieves Welcome (Most Welcome) Rear, lost tch fnl 3f: cheaply bght Mar first foal, dam a 6f plcd juv. *7* **49**
4503 **CASALESE 16** [7]2-9-0 F Lynch 100/1: 07: ch g Wolfhound - Little Redwing (Be My Chief) Al bhd: longer trip: May foal, half-brother to a plcd bmpr performer, dam plcd at 1m7f as a 4yo & over hdles. *¾* **48**
4247 **FORPETESAKE 30** [6]2-9-0 (58) A Nicholls 100/1: 066068: Prom, rdn & struggling from halfway. *2½* **43**
8 Ran Time 1m 51.25 (7.45) Owned: Miss K Rausing Trained: Newmarket

4817

2.50 Sam Collingwood-Cameron Conditions Stakes 3yo+ (B1)
£12174 £4618 £2309 **6f str** **Good/Soft 67** **+20 Fast** Centre

4384 **WELSH EMPEROR 23** [6] T P Tate 5-9-5 bl (107) D Holland 2/1: 1465201: Made all, drvn out: well bckd: fast time: eff at 5/7f on fast, loves gd/soft & hvy: loves to force the pace: tough, v useful & genuine. **109**
4384 **CARTOGRAPHY 23** [8] Saeed bin Suroor 3-8-7 t (106) K McEvoy 15/8 FAV: 10-33202: Trkd ldrs, styd on for press, not pace to chall wnr: hvly bckd: also bhd this wnr latest: btr 3268 (fast). *1¾* **95**
4780 **JOHNSTONS DIAMOND 2** [1] E J Alston 6-8-9 (85) D Allan 20/1: 0000363: Prom, rdn & ch 2f out, kept on for press, not pace of wnr: gd run, qck reapp: see 4652 & 687 (h'caps). *nk* **94**
4686 **CIRCUIT DANCER 9** [4] A Berry 4-8-9 (89) F Lynch 33/1: 0504004: Dwelt, rear, styd on from halfway for press, not able to chall: best prev in h'caps on fast grnd: see 2357. *¾* **92**
4686 **PHILHARMONIC 9** [7]3-8-7 (98) P Hanagan 8/1: 114-4005: Rdn towards rear, mod late gains. *1½* **87**
4686* **FUNFAIR WANE 9** [2]5-8-9 (98) A Nicholls 4/1: 4006016: Cl-up/dsptd lead till halfway, fdd tamely: op 7/2: best when able to dominate as in 4686 (val h'cap, made all). *5* **74**
4618 **MUTAYAM 11** [3]4-8-12 t (50) J McAuley 200/1: 6060107: Sn outpcd & struggling: see 4404 (mdn). *11* **47**
4618 **LAS RAMBLAS 11** [9]7-8-9 bl e t (45) P Makin 500/1: 0640-008: Al well bhd, needs modest company. *12* **11**
4348} **SECOND WIND 373** [5]9-8-9 t P (40) C Haddon 500/1: 000000-9: ch g Kris - Rimosa's Pet (Petingo) Sn outpcd & struggling: reapp: chkpces: unplcd in '03 (rtd 45, class stks, prog flattered): rnr-up in '02 (C Dwyer, clmr): stays 1m, suited by 7f: acts on firm, soft & polytrack, any trk: has gone well fresh & eff in a t-strap. 2 Jul'02 Yarm 8g/f 60- F: *5* **0**
9 Ran Time 1m 12.62 (2.82) Owned: Mrs Sylvia Clegg Trained: Tadcaster

HAMILTON MONDAY 27.09.04 Righthand, Undulating Track, Stiff Uphill Finish

4818 **3.20 Hamilton Park Apprentice Series Final Handicap Stakes 4yo+ 56-70 (E3)** **[77]**
£4271 £1314 £657 **6f str** **Good/Soft 67** **-10 Slow** Centre

4241 **YORKER 30** [7] Ms Deborah J Evans 6-8-8 BL (57) Natalia Gemelova 33/1: 0003601: Made all, hung right under press over 2f out, drvn & styd on well: stays 9.4f, suited by 6f/1m on fast, gd/soft & loves fibresand: imprvd for first time blnks & forcing tactics today: see 241. **66**
4622* **LOCOMBE HILL 11** [12] N Wilson 8-9-6 (69) D Tudhope 11/4 FAV: 4015312: Chsd ldrs, styd on for press, al held by wnr: hvly bckd: eff at 6f, forcing tactics at 7f poss ideal: see 4622. *1¾* **73**
4618 **VIEWFORTH 11** [5] J S Goldie 6-8-7 (4oh)bl (52) J Currie(8) 15/2: 0000003: Dwelt, sn chsd ldrs, styd on for press, not pace to chall wnr: imprvd eff: see 1120. *½* **58**
3796 **FLYING EDGE 51** [4] E J Alston 4-8-7 (4oh) (52) J D O'Reilly 12/1: 6500044: Sn handy, styd on onepace for press: 7 wk abs: see 3796, 585. *½* **56**
4582 **SUNDRIED TOMATO 13** [6]5-9-5 (68) P Makin 9/2: 4606005: Cl-up, no extra bef dist: see 419. *¾* **66**
4676 **MICKLEDOR 9** [1]4-8-7 (4oh)p (52) C Haddon 20/1: 1003656: Towards rear, kept on late, nrst fin. *½* **52**
4622 **BUNDY 11** [9]8-8-12 (61) Rory Moore 7/1: 3204407: Mid-div, nvr plcd to chall: see 2315. *½* **55**
4622 **FAIR SHAKE 11** [2]4-9-6 p (69) A Mullen 5/1: 5026208: Dwelt, sn rdn & little hdwy: btr 4339. *hd* **62**
4087 **PAYS DAMOUR 38** [8]7-8-7 (4oh) (52) Leanne Kershaw 50/1: 0302009: Chsd ldrs, strugg from halfway. *1¾* **44**
4211 **INDIAN MUSIC 31** [10]7-8-7 (11oh) (45) C Ely(7) 33/1: 6200650: 10th: Mid-div, rdn & struggling halfway. *1¾* **39**
4689 **ULYSEES 9** [3]5-9-7 VIS (70) W Hogg 12/1: 0500400: 11th: Chsd ldrs, strugg halfway: poor run in vis. *6* **38**
11 Ran Time 1m 14.42 (4.62) Owned: Men Behaving Badly Trained: Lydiate

4819 **3.50 Totesport Buttonhook Handicap Stakes 3yo+ 86-100 (C1)** **[113]**
£12012 £4556 £2278 **1m5f9y** **Good/Soft 67** **-10 Slow** Stands Side

3534 **ZEITGEIST 61** [2] L M Cumani 3-8-2 (87) N Mackay(3) 2/1: 1-412501: Held up, hdwy halfway, drvn & styd on to lead line, all out: hvly bckd: 2 month abs: eff at 11/13f, shapes as if 14f+ would suit: acts on fast & soft: goes well fresh: lightly rcd, genuine & on the upgrade: see 2318. **96**
4534 **ALBANOV 16** [5] M Johnston 4-9-2 (92) D Holland 7/1: 2-004002: Handy, rdn over 3f out, styd on for press to lead well ins last, hdd line: much imprvd eff under a most forceful ride: see 3531. *shd* **100**
4324 **PROTECTIVE 26** [7] J G Given 3-8-0 (85) P Hanagan 20/1: 4014003: Held up, hdwy 3f out & rdn/led over 1f out, hdd well ins last & no extra: rest well covered: apprec rtn to easy grnd, stays 13f: see 2230 (mdn). *nk* **92**
4023 **GOLD RING 40** [3] G B Balding 4-9-7 (97) S Carson 15/8 FAV: 6531624: Led, hdd over 1f out & sn no extra: hvly bckd: 6 wk abs: just btr 4023 (val h'cap). *4* **98**
4628 **PUSHKIN 11** [1]6-9-6 (96) S Chin 7/1: 526-3025: Trkd ldrs, rdn & ch 2f out, sn outpcd: see 4628 (2m). *½* **96**
4553 **SAHEM 14** [6]7-8-7 (83) T Eaves(3) 9/1: 0331036: Rear, rdn & btn 3f out: btr 4138 (C/D). *5* **76**
4657 **ALAM 10** [4]5-8-7 (13oh) (70) L Enstone 66/1: 0346/0-67: Trkd ldrs, rdn & struggling fnl 4f: see 4657. *6* **68**
7 Ran Time 2m 55.55 (10.05) Owned: Mr L Marinopoulos Trained: Newmarket

4820 **4.20 Famous Grouse Handicap Stakes 3yo+ 71-85 (D2)** **[92]**
£7055 £2171 £1085 **1m65y rnd** **Good/Soft 67** **-00 Slow** Inside

4656 **APERITIF 10** [7] W J Haggas 3-8-13 (77) P Hanagan 7/2 FAV: 4331031: Hld up, smooth hdwy halfway to join ldrs 2f out, led dist & rdn clr, readily: hvly bckd, op 4/1: stays 10f, suited by 1m: acts on fast & polytrack, poss firm, clrly relishes gd/soft & a stiff/gall trk: settled well here, follow-up: see 4656. **88+**
4656 **STRONG HAND 10** [8] M W Easterby 4-8-12 (72) P Mulrennan(3) 7/1: 6300062: Trkd ldrs trav well, smooth prog & narrow lead over 2f out, hdd dist, not pace of wnr but pulled clr of rem: nicely h'capped on turf, shown enough to find similar: see 1066 & 127. *5* **77**
4620 **CHERISHED NUMBER 11** [2] I Semple 5-8-10 BL (70) R Winston 12/1: 0530433: Towards rear & rdn over 3f out, styd on for press, not threatened front pair: not disgraced in first time blnks but btr 4620 & 4397. *4* **68**
4520* **JUST A FLUKE 16** [11] M Johnston 3-8-7 (71) K Darley 11/1: 2305214: Rdn towards rear halfway, late hdwy for press, nvr posed a threat: see 4520 (gd grnd, mdn). *1¾* **66**
4656 **QUALITAIR WINGS 10** [10]5-8-12 (72) D McGaffin 14/1: 0206305: Dwelt, chsd ldrs, rdn & chall over 2f out, sn no impress: btr 4246. *¾* **66**
3074* **BLONDE STREAK 80** [9]4-9-4 (78) P Makin(5) 6/1: 04-44016: Led/dsptd lead, fdd under press fnl 2f: abs. *hd* **71**
4685 **TONY TIE 9** [1]8-9-6 (80) N Mackay(3) 25/1: 6106057: Bhd, only mod late prog: see 3152. *3½* **67**
4656 **NEVADA DESERT 10** [5]4-8-12 p (72) Hayley Turner(3) 14/1: 5201008: Chsd ldrs, ch over 2f out, wknd. *1¼* **56**
4656 **UROWELLS 10** [12]4-9-4 vis (78) S Sanders 20/1: 41-00009: Cl-up, btn 3f out: see 3076. *6* **52**
4629 **LES ARCS 11** [13]4-9-0 (74) D Holland 33/1: 2136060: 10th: Led till 2f out, sn btn: see 2890 & 2828. *½* **47**
4702* **ZAMEYLA 7** [6]3-9-11 (6ex) (89) N Callan 7/1: 022110: 11th: Chsd ldrs, hdwy to lead 3f out, hdd over 2f out & sn btn: nicely bckd under a 6lb pen but much btr 4702. *2* **58**
4500 **GREAT SCOTT 17** [4]3-8-13 (77) S Chin 33/1: 0534000: 12th: Mid-div, rdn & btn 4f out: btr 3647 (10f). *2½* **41**
4685 **DUKE OF MODENA 9** [14]7-9-10 (84) S Carson 16/1: 20400-00: 13th: Sn bhd & no ch 3f out: see 4685. *nk* **47**
4246 **CRESKELD 30** [3]5-8-10 (2oh) (68) F Lynch 20/1: 0000140: 14th: Chsd ldrs wide early, lost pl qckly from halfway & eased right down fnl 2f: ran as if something amiss: btr 4008 (made most). *dist* **0**
14 Ran Time 1m 49.4 (5.6) Owned: Stretton Manor Stud Trained: Newmarket

4821 **4.50 Scottish Racing Maiden Stakes 3yo (D3)**
£5610 £1726 £863 **1m1f36y** **Good/Soft 67** **-28 Slow** Inside

REEM ONE 0 [7] M A Jarvis 3-8-9 N Callan 100/30 FAV: 1: b f Rainbow Quest - Felona (Caerleon) Trkd ldrs, smooth prog to chall over 2f out, sn rdn & styd on for press to lead well ins last: hvly bckd: debut: eff at 9f, will relish 10f+: acts on gd/soft: goes well fresh: rate higher. **77**
3772 **BUBBLING FUN 51** [4] E A L Dunlop 3-8-9 (66) S Sanders 7/2: 0433262: Led, rdn & joined 2f out, wandered under press & hdd ins last, no extra: nicely bckd, 7 wk abs: acts on fast & gd/soft grnd: see 3299. *1½* **73**
4502 **ANTIGIOTTO 17** [3] L M Cumani 3-9-0 VIS (76) N Mackay(3) 7/2: 0422003: Trkd ldrs, rdn & styd on onepace for press in first time visor: well bckd & clr of rem but btr 3208 (fast). *3½* **72**
4407 **LAKE DIVA 21** [8] J G Given 3-8-9 (61) D Holland 12/1: 00-34: Chsd ldr, fdd under press fnl 2f: btr 4407. *7* **55**
4249 **ASTON LAD 30** [5]3-9-0 (50) P Mulrennan(3) 25/1: 4662505: Rear, only mod prog: flattered 3263. *1½* **57**

HAMILTON MONDAY 27.09.04 Righthand, Undulating Track, Stiff Uphill Finish

2319 **PAR INDIANA 110** [9]3-8-9 (57) P Hanagan 14/1: 43-3366: Held up in tch, no tch fnl 3f: 4 month abs.   *5*   **43**
4453 **BIJOU DAN 20** [2]3-9-0   R Winston 33/1: 467: Al bhd: see 4453 & 3246.   *3½*   **42**
    TREBELLO 0 [6]3-9-0   K Darley 9/2: 8: b c Robellino - Trempkate (Trempolino) Sn struggling   *2*   **38**
rear: op 7/2, debut: half-brother to a Gr 2 1m US wnr.
8 Ran   Time 2m 02.86 (8.76)   Owned: Sheikh Ahmed Al Maktoum   Trained: Newmarket

---

4822	5.20 Racing Uk On Channel 432 Classified Stakes 3yo 0-70 (E3)

£4144 £1275 £638   **5f str**   **Good/Soft 67**   **+02 Fast**   Centre

4048 **JADAN 39** [3] E J Alston 3-9-2 (74) D Allan 16/1: 6615001: Trkd ldrs trav well, styd on for press   **80**
to lead cl-home: eff at 5f on firm & gd/soft grnd, likes a stiff/gall trk: see 3135.
4779 **JILLY WHY 2** [1] Ms Deborah J Evans 3-8-11 (72) N Callan 20/1: 0411002: Handy/dsptd lead & went   *nk*   **74**
on 2f out, drvn & hdd cl-home: apprc drop to 5f, loves to race with/force the pace: see 4514.
4099 **MORGAN LEWIS 37** [7] G B Balding 3-8-12 (69) D Holland 9/4 FAV: 00-01323: Held up in tch & sn   *1*   **72**
rdn, hung left but kept on for press, not able to reach front pair: eff at 5f, 6f ideal: see 3920 & 3737 (6f).
4027 **ICENASLICE 40** [4] J J Quinn 3-8-9 (70) D Tudhope(5) 14/1: 1410404: Rdn chasing ldrs, not pace to   *1¾*   **64**
chall: 6 wk abs: see 3567 & 2731.
4236 **WUNDERBRA 30** [2]3-8-13 t (74) Hayley Turner(3) 3/1: 1311125: Keen early, trkd ldrs trav well, no   *1*   **65**
extra from dist: hvly bckd tho' op 5/2: see 4169.
4654 **MR WOLF 10** [5]3-9-1 (73) T Eaves(3) 9/2: 6000526: Led till 2f out, fdd under press: nicely bckd.   *hd*   **66**
4604 **FOUR AMIGOS 12** [8]3-9-3 (75) S Sanders 5/1: 3000407: Sn towards rear & no impress fnl 2f: well bckd.   *7*   **51**
4318 **FINDERS KEEPERS 26** [6]3-9-0 (72) K Darley 20/1: 1000108: Dwelt, sn strugg: btr 3744 (6f, AW).   *6*   **33**
8 Ran   Time 1m 01.33(3.23)   Owned: Mr Derrick Mossop   Trained: Preston

---

BATH MONDAY 27.09.04 Lefthand, Turning Track with Uphill Finish

Official Going GOOD (GOOD/FIRM IN PLACES)

4823	2.10 University And Literary Club/European Breeders Fund Maiden Stakes 2yo (D3)

£4433 £1364 £682   **5f161y**   **Good**   **Slow**   Far side

4385 **MUNADDAM 23** [8] Saeed bin Suroor 2-9-0   L Dettori 4/9 FAV: 221: Rcd in 2nd, hdwy to lead well   **95**
over 1f out, easily, val further: nicely bckd at odds on: eff at 5.5/6f, 7f will suit: acts on firm & gd: useful,
type to rate higher: see 3709 (debut).
4497 **RUBIES 17** [15] R F Johnson Houghton 2-8-9   J Fortune 12/1: 262: Handy, hdwy into 2nd ins fnl 1f,   *5*   **73**
not pace of wnr: met a useful rival: see 4200.
4466 **REGAL DREAM 19** [12] J W Hills 2-9-0   R Hills 14/1: 033: Rear, hdwy 2f out, onepcd fnl 1f: see 4466.   *1¾*   **73**
4543 **INKA DANCER 14** [1] B Palling 2-8-9   F P Ferris(3) 12/1: 34: Cl-up, onepcd fnl 1f: btr 4543.   *¾*   **66**
4543 **CHINALEA 14** [9]2-9-0   R Smith 9/1: 55: Cl-up, onepcd over 1f out: see 4543.   *½*   **69**
4490 **RUSKY DUSKY 17** [11]2-9-0 vis (77) R L Moore 10/1: 0325566: Led till well over 1f out, no   *2½*   **61**
extra/btn when not much room ins fnl 1f: see 2970.
4497 **WINDWOOD 17** [10]2-9-0 S Drowne 100/1: 07: Nvr btr than mid-div: see 4497.   *½*   **59**
4575 **GOLD MAJESTY 13** [16]2-8-9 (45) C Catlin 100/1: 00008: b f Josr Algarhoud - Calcutta Queen (Night   *1¾*   **49**
Shift) Rear, nvr nr ldrs: cost E58,000 Apr foal: half-sister to 2/3yo Majestic Desert: dam plcd over 1m.
3728 **WILL THE TILL 53** [3]2-9-0   D Corby(3) 100/1: 09: b g Fraam - Prim Ajwaad (Bin Ajwaad) Rear, nvr   *shd*   **53**
nr ldrs: 8 wk abs: Mar foal, cost 5,000gns: dam unrcd, sire smart over 7f/1m: with J Bradley.
3394 **AMALGAM 66** [14]2-8-9 (40) B Swarbrick(5) 100/1: 000500: 10th: Nvr a factor: 9 wk abs: see 3209.   *¾*   **46**
4418 **GYPSY ROYAL 21** [6]2-8-9 N Day 125/1: 000: 11th: b f Desert Prince - Menominee (Soviet Star)   *2½*   **38**
Nvr a factor: Feb foal, cost E50,000: half-sister to wnrs at 1m/12f: dam unrcd, sire a smart miler.
    MOONSIDE 0 [13]2-8-9 R Thomas(3) 100/1: 0: 12th: Al bhd on debut.   *1½*   **33**
4052 **BLADE RUNNER 39** [4]2-8-9 M Fenton 33/1: 000: 13th: Mid-div, hmpd on inner over 3f out, sn btn.   *4*   **21**
3097 **OPEN VERDICT 79** [7]2-9-0 T Darren Williams 33/1: 040: 14th: Keen/handy, no impress 2f out: t-strap.   *¾*   **24**
4218 **OUR NIGEL 30** [5]2-9-0 T E Durcan 100/1: 0000: 15th: Bhd, stumbled after 1f, nvr a factor.   *3½*   **13**
4575 **RUM CREEK 13** [2]2-9-0 J F Egan 66/1: 0000: 16th: Slow away, outpcd, t.o.: lame.   *dist*   **0**
16 Ran   Time 1m 12.84 (3.74)   Owned: Godolphin   Trained: Newmarket

---

4824	2.40 Letheby & Christopher Handicap Stakes 3yo+ 56-70 (E3)

£3578 £1101 £550   **2m1f34y**   **Good**   **Slow**   Inside   **[86]**

4512 **DARN GOOD 16** [8] R Hannon 3-8-7 bl (65) R L Moore 16/1: 1206601: Rear, hdwy to lead 2f out, drvn   **75**
out ins fnl 1f: prev eff at 12f, now suited by 15f/2m3f: acts on firm, gd & polytrack, stiff or sharp/undul trks,
likes a turning one, esp Warwick: back to form: see 915.
4512 **TEORBAN 16** [14] D J S ffrench Davis 4-9-5 (55) A Daly 50/1: 0-610002: Rear, hdwy 3f out,   *2*   **62**
styd on into 2nd fnl 1f, not pace to reach wnr: suited by 2m, stays 2m1f: back to form: see 3400.
4527 **MOONSHINE BEACH 16** [13] P W Hiatt 6-9-10 (70) Darren Williams 8/1: 1031103: Cl-up, hdwy to lead   *5*   **71**
over 8f out, hdd 2f out, no extra ins fnl 1f: btr 4276.
4512 **HENRY ISLAND 16** [16] Mrs A J Bowlby 11-8-11 (57) S Drowne 14/1: 0400204: Mid-div, hdwy over 6f   *2½*   **55**
out, no impress ins fnl 1f: see 4276.
4512 **NORTHERN NYMPH 16** [18]5-9-4 (64) J Fortune 14/1: 6234055: Mid-div, hdwy/ev ch 3f out, no impress.   *½*   **61**
4527 **RIYADH 16** [17]6-9-6 (66) R Ffrench 8/1: 2026046: Rear, hdwy 7f out, no impress.   *5*   **58**
4415 **LORD NELLSSON 21** [19]8-8-10 (56) V Slattery 33/1: 400507: Rear, hdwy 9f out, no impress over 2f   *½*   **47**
out: hdles fit (h'cap rnr-up, rtd 96h), stys 2m5f/2m6.5f on firm & gd/soft, tried cheek pieces): see 2668.
3868 **ANYHOW 47** [9]7-9-3 (63) P D Nolan(3) 22/1: 3210558: Rear, hdwy over 3f out, no impress over 1f out.   *3*   **51**
4319* **MOST SAUCY 26** [11]8-8-10 (56) B Swarbrick(5) 12/1: 0433019: Rear, some hdwy 4f out, not pace to chall.*14*   **30**
4170 **CLARADOTNET 32** [7]4-9-2 (62) T E Durcan 12/1: 6303200: 10th: Bhd, hdwy 6f out, no impress 3f out.   *10*   **26**
4319 **CIRCUS MAXIMUS 26** [22]7-8-10 (3oh)p (53) C Catlin 16/1: 0402300: 11th: Nvr a factor.   *¾*   **19**
4512 **RED SUN 16** [3]7-8-10 t (56) T P Queally 9/2: 1260630: 12th: Led 5f, led again over 9f out till   *13*   **6**
over 8f out, no extra 6f out: bckd from 7/1: much btr 2009.
3492} **KALUANA COURT 415** [12]8-9-8 (68) R Thomas(3) 16/1: 021410-0: 13th: b f Batshoof - Fairfields Cone   *3*   **15**

(Celtic Cone) Rear, hdwy over 8f out, no impress over 3f out: reapp: won 2 of 7 '03 starts (h'caps): h'cap scorer in '02: suited by 14f/2m1f on firm & gd, handles any trk: now an 8yo. 1 Jul'03 Newm 14.8g/f 68-62 D: 1 Jul'03 Newm 14.8fm 57-47 D: 2 Jul'03 Warw 15.0fm 49-46 E: 1 Jul'02 Sand 14g/f 53-50 D: 1 Aug'01 Pont 17.1gd 55-52 F: 1 Aug'01 Warw 15gd 50-48 F: 1 Jul'01 Bath 17.1fm 43-36 E:

4663 **CODY 9** [15]5-8-10 (11oh) (45) S Righton 50/1: 00/040-30: 14th: Cl-up, no impress 4f out: stiff task. *2½* **0**

1403} **BLAU GRAU 508** [6]7-8-10 (16oh) (40) M Halford(7) 100/1: 5/10500-0: 15th: gr g Neshad - Belle Orfana (Orfano) Nvr a factor on reapp: nov sell/claim hdle unplcd both 03/04 starts (rtd 62h, stays 2m on fast, K Morgan): won first of 5 '03 starts (seller, with H Hiller, later R Wilman & P Blockley): eff around 1m on gd, hvy & fibresand, sharp trk: tried blnks: now with N Berry & a v stiff task at these weights. 1 Jan'03 Sout 8af 47a- G: *20* **0**

4415 **OLYMPIAS 21** [5]3-7-12 (3oh)bl (53) F P Ferris(3) 20/1: 0064030: 16th: Nvr a factor. *1½* **0**

4166 **KOMOTO 33** [20]3-8-2 BL (60) Martin Dwyer 50/1: 10040: 17th: Cl-up, wknd 5f out: 'hung right': blnks. *12* **0**

4559 **ETCHING 14** [1]4-9-0 (60) L Dettori 7/2 FAV: 10-10050: 18th: Bhd, nvr nr ldrs: 'breathing problem'. *13* **0**

616 **ROYAL PRODIGY 227** [10]5-8-13 (59) M Fenton 25/1: 311-0420: 19th: In tch, rear & btn halfway. *10* **0**

4364 **ROLEX FREE 24** [4]6-8-10 (5oh)vis (51) J F Egan 22/1: 1410430: 20th: Rcd in 2nd till led after 5f, hdd over 9f out, fdd over 6f out, t.o.. *dist* **0**

20 Ran Time 3m 53.01 (12.11) Owned: Mr J E Garrett Trained: Marlborough

4825

3.10 Workplace Solutions/European Breeders Fund Maiden Stakes 2yo (D3)
£4537 £1396 £698 **1m2f46y** **Good** **Slow** Inside

4558 **HAATMEY 14** [2] M R Channon 2-9-0 (76) T E Durcan 5/1: 3421: Rear, hdwy over 3f out, led just over 2f out, rdn out: prev eff at 7/9f, relished this step up to 10f: acts on firm & gd, turning trk: deserved win. **86**

3323 **MASTER COBBLER 69** [6] G A Butler 2-9-0 J Fortune 4/1: 422: Slow away in rear, hdwy over 2f out, not pace of wnr over 1f out: 10 wk abs, clr of rem: prob stays 10f: shld find a race: see 3323. *3½* **79**

4631 **GIDAM GIDAM 11** [1] C E Brittain 2-9-0 R Hills 40/1: 663: Slow away, rear, hdwy over 1f out, no impress. *8* **67**

4544 **BATTLEDRESS 14** [4] M P Tregoning 2-9-0 Martin Dwyer 7/2: 034: Slow away, sn in mid-div, hdwy & ev ch over 2f out, no impress over 1f out: tchd 11/2: see 4544. *shd* **66**

3337 **NORTHANGER ABBEY 68** [3]2-9-0 R L Moore 25/1: 005: ch c In The Wings - Glenstal Priory (Glenstal) Rear, hdwy over 5f out, no impress over 1f out: 10 wk abs: Mar foal, cost 90,000gns: half-brother to 5/6f wnrs at 2: dam won thrice at 14/18f, sire smart over 12f: with J Gosden & shld stay this trip in time. *nk* **65**

4194 **THE DUKE OF DIXIE 31** [10]2-9-0 L Dettori 9/4 FAV: 336: Rear, hdwy 6f out, wknd 4f out: 'nvr trav'. *9* **51**

4558 **TIMBER SCORPION 14** [11]2-9-0 R Ffrench 14/1: 57: Led till just over 2f out, sn no extra: op 11/1. *1½* **49**

4483 **BACK TO REALITY 18** [7]2-9-0 F P Ferris(3) 100/1: 08: ch g Magic Ring - Arian Da (Superlative) Al bhd: Apr foal: dam a 5f 2yo scorer, sire speedy: with B Palling. *hd* **48**

4464 **RED RIOT 19** [8]2-9-0 T P Queally 16/1: 539: Cl-up, no impress over 2f out. *nk* **47**

4297 **INCHCAPE ROCK 28** [5]2-9-0 (78) I Mongan 20/1: 00020: 10th: Cl-up, hdwy to chall 5f out, wknd 2f out. *5* **39**

4544 **MOUNT ARAFAT 14** [9]2-9-0 T A Daly 150/1: 000: 11th: b g Erhaab - Cache (Bustino) Cl-up till 5f out, t.o.: Mar foal, cost 4,800gns: half-brother to a wnr at 11/14f: dam unplcd, sire a smart juv, later won Derby. *dist* **0**

11 Ran Time 2m 12.22 (6.22) Owned: Sheikh Ahmed Al Maktoum Trained: West Ilsley

4826

3.40 Letheby & Christopher Maiden Stakes Fillies & Mares 3yo+ (D3)
£3552 £1093 £547 **1m2f46y** **Good** **Slow** Inside

4336 **NAMAT 25** [2] M P Tregoning 3-8-10 R Hills 5/2 FAV: 21: Mid-div, hdwy over 3f out, drvn ins fnl 1f, led last strides: relished step up to 10f, shld stay further: acts on firm & gd, turning trk: imprvd from debut. **76**

4547 **PRINCIPESSA 14** [11] B Palling 3-8-10 (70) F P Ferris(3) 6/1: 2202432: Led, hdd last strides: clr of rem: found one too gd again: see 3845. *hd* **74**

4743 **EFRHINA 5** [3] Mrs Stef Liddiard 4-9-2 (68) S Drowne 9/1: 0302003: Rear, hdwy over 2f out, not pace of first 2: qck reapp, op 20/1: see 4743. *5* **66**

ANGRY BARK 99 [7] H S Howe 3-8-10 R Smith 40/1: 424: Cl-up, hdwy into 2nd 7f out, no impress fnl 1f. *1½* **64**

46[illegible]**AN THOMAS 10** [13]3-8-10 Martin Dwyer 33/1: 305: Rear, hdwy over 1f out, not pace to chall. *hd* **63**

4474 **PAINTBOX 18** [14]3-8-10 (69) R L Moore 5/1: 6326: Rear, hdwy over 2f out, not pace of ldrs. *nk* **62**

4228 **PLAY BOUZOUKI 30** [15]3-8-10 L Dettori 4/1: 347: Rear, hdwy 3f out, no impress fnl 1f: see 4228. *3½* **57**

4414 **MRS PHILIP 21** [1]5-9-2 V Slattery 66/1: 08: b f Puissance - Lightning Legacy (Super Concorde) Slow away, hdwy 7f out, wknd 4f out: h'cap hdle unplcd sole start in 04/05 (rtd 60h, eff at 2m3f on fast & gd). *6* **48**

4228 **WAIT FOR SPRING 30** [10]3-8-10 (69) J Fortune 12/1: 5209: Rear, hdwy 5f out, no impress 2f out. *1½* **46**

4182 **AL SHUUA 32** [12]3-8-10 (70) T E Durcan 25/1: 36-20400: 10th: Cl-up, no impress over 2f out. *3* **41**

1810 **FAVOURABLE 133** [5]3-8-10 T P Queally 50/1: 00: 11th: b f Mark of Esteem - Top Society (High Top) Cl-up, no impress 3f out: long abs: half-sister to wnrs at 7/10f: dam unrcd: now with A Carroll. *8* **29**

4125 **PLEASANT 35** [4]3-8-10 I Mongan 9/1: 420: 12th: Slow away, nvr a factor: 'hung left'. *shd* **28**

2066 **PINS N NEEDLES 121** [8]3-8-10 J F Egan 66/1: 060: 13th: gr f Mark of Esteem - Khalisiyn (Shakapour) Nvr a factor: long abs: cost 10,000gns: half-sister to Gr 3 wnr at 12f, dam a wnr at 3: with C Cyzer. *5* **20**

4612 **GOLDEN QUEEN 12** [9]3-8-10 Ashleigh Horton(7) 100/1: 030: 14th: Rear, nvr a factor. *6* **11**

1258 **OBSERVATION 161** [6]3-8-10 A Daly 66/1: 000: 15th: Mid-div, not much room/lost pl 5f out, sn btn: abs. *15* **0**

15 Ran Time 2m 12.47 (6.47) Owned: Mr Hamdan Al Maktoum Trained: Lambourn

4827

4.10 Bet365 Call 08000 322 365 Handicap Stakes 3yo 56-70 (E3) **[76]**
£3522 £1084 £542 **1m5y** **Good** **Slow** Inside

4474 **SACHIN 18** [14] J R Boyle 3-9-0 (62) Martin Dwyer 33/1: 40-06041: Rear, hdwy over 2f out, led over 1f out, all out to hold on ins fnl 1f: first win: eff at 1m on gd, prob handles fast & polytrack, turning trk. **69**

4709 **DESERT HAWK 7** [11] R Hannon 3-9-4 (66) R L Moore 11/1: 4006202: Rear, hdwy 3f out, ev ch over 1f out, kept on: qck reapp: gd eff, back to form: see 4546. *½* **72**

2877 **BARONS SPY 88** [16] A W Carroll 3-9-3 (65) R Hills 20/1: 00-4203: Bhd, hdwy over 2f out, ev ch over 1f out, onepcd ins fnl 1f: long abs: eff at 7f/1m on firm & gd: back to form: see 2092. *½* **70**

4520 **FIVE YEARS ON 16** [6] W J Haggas 3-9-2 (64) M Fenton 7/1: 024-44: Rear, hdwy over 2f out, ev ch over 1f out, onepcd ins fnl 1f: op 16/1: stays 1m: acts on gd & polytrack: see 76. *shd* **68**

3516 **THE FUN MERCHANT 61** [15]3-9-6 (68) L Dettori 9/2 J FAV: 0-011205: Rear, hdwy 2f out, kept on under hands & heels ins fnl 1f: 9 wk abs: interesting back in claiming grade: see 3410. *2½* **67**

4546* **MASTER MAHOGANY 14** [4]3-8-13 (61) S Drowne 11/2: 4603016: Cl-up, hdwy to lead 2f out till over 1f out, sn no extra: btr 4546. *½* **59**

4044	**FIT TO FLY 39** [13]3-9-3 (65) I Mongan 16/1: 5605007: Mid-div, hdwy & ev ch 2f out, sn no impress.	¾	61
4342	**DAN DI CANIO 25** [12]3-8-13 t (61) D Corby(3) 33/1: 505508: In tch, hdwy 3f out, no impress 1f out.	1½	54
4445	**TEXT 20** [1]3-9-3 VIS (65) J F Egan 16/1: 0-023569: Cl-up, no impress 2f out: tried visor.	1¾	54
3875	**SCRIPTORIUM 47** [9]3-9-0 (62) T P Queally 7/1: 6024200: 10th: Dsptd lead till led over 4f out, hdd 2f out, no extra over 1f out: 7 wk abs.	1¾	47
3732	**ZAZOUS 53** [8]3-9-1 (63) J D Smith 40/1: 03-6300: 11th: In tch, rear & btn after 3f: 8 wk abs.	¾	46
4452	**TICERO 20** [3]3-9-1 bl (63) T E Durcan 12/1: 4-000040: 12th: Nvr a factor: op 8/1: see 2403.	nk	45
3455	**THE WAY WE WERE 65** [10]3-9-7 (69) J Fortune 9/2 J FAV: 31-65030: 13th: Led over 3f, no extra 2f out.	11	29
4502	**LIVE WIRE LUCY 17** [2]3-9-3 (65) C Catlin 66/1: 3000000: 14th: Al bhd.	3	19
4448	**SEA OF GOLD 20** [5]3-9-6 (68) F P Ferris(3) 20/1: 062640: 15th: Chsd ldrs, no impress 3f out.	2	18
	15 Ran Time 1m 43.77 (5.47) Owned: Epsom Sorts Trained: Epsom		

4828   4.40 Letheby & Christopher Apprentice Maiden Handicap Stakes 3yo+ 46-55 (F4)   [71]
£2680 £766 £383   **1m5y**   **Good**   **Slow**   Inside

4195	**BLAKE HALL LAD 31** [12] Miss J Feilden 3-8-12 (55) Dean Williams(3) 16/1: 0051: b g Cape Cross - Queen of Art (Royal Academy) Rear, hdwy over 3f out, led & edged left ins fnl 1f, pushed out: h'cap bow/first win: cost 5,500gns: dam wnr over 7f: relished step up to 1m, acts on gd, turning trk: lightly rcd.		62
4520	**GRACEFUL AIR 16** [5] J R Weymes 3-8-9 p (52) D Fentiman 6/1: 4450032: Chsd ldrs, kept on ins fnl 1f.	½	56
4504	**MAGARI 16** [2] J G Given 3-8-7 (50) R Kingscote(7) 25/1: 3-40053: Slow away, sn handy, kept on ins fnl 1f: stays 1m: see 3610.	nk	53
4412	**MUSICAL TOP 21** [9] H Morrison 4-9-2 (55) T Block(5) 12/1: 0-003004: Rear, hdwy over 1f out, styd on ins fnl 1f: stays 7f/1m on fast & gd: see 3654.	hd	57
3449	**ASK THE DRIVER 65** [16]3-8-8 BL (51) Derek Nolan 9/1: 2433005: Rear, hdwy 2f out, kept on: blnks.	nk	52
976]	**DARK SOCIETY 898** [3]6-8-13 (52) T Dean(5) 25/1: 0000/00/-6: b g Imp Society - No Candles Tonight (Star Appeal) Slow away in rear, hdwy 1f out, not pace to chall on reapp: nov claim hdle 4th 1 of 2 02/03 starts (rtd 49h, eff around 2m on gd & hvy): missed '03: unplcd both '02 starts (h'caps, rtd 50): stays 1m, prob stays 10f: acts on gd & soft: has tried a visor.	½	52
4373	**KINDNESS 23** [1]4-8-11 (50) P Gallagher 7/1: 2202007: Led early, remained in 2nd, led again 4f out till ins fnl 1f, no extra: op 9/1: see 3540.	shd	49
2453	**DORINGO 105** [13]3-8-9 (52) R J Killoran(5) 25/1: 0-0008: b c Prince Sabo - Mistral's Dancer (Shareef Dancer) Chsd ldrs, hdwy & ev ch over 1f out, onepcd ins fnl 1f: long abs: unplcd sole '03 start.	1	49
3711	**HOLD UP 53** [7]3-8-10 (53) Kirsty Milczarek(5) 12/1: 0-000009: Slow away, hdwy over 3f out, no impress.	2½	45
4412	**NINAH 21** [15]3-8-10 (53) Jemma Marshall(5) 25/1: 40-00000: 10th: Rear, hdwy 3f out, no impress fnl 1f.	¾	43
4504	**NICHOLAS NICKELBY 2** [4]4-8-13 p (52) Kristin Stubbs 5/1 FAV: 4344250: 11th: Cl-up, wknd over 1f out.	1½	39
4402	**IMPERIAL ROYALE 22** [10]3-8-8 p (51) M Halford(3) 14/1: 0600000: 12th: Rear, nvr a factor.	hd	37
4649	**ROYAL FLIGHT 10** [6]3-8-7 (50) M Coumbe(5) 10/1: 5-000: 13th: In tch, wknd 3f out.	12	12
4546	**MY SUNSHINE 14** [14]3-8-7 BL (50) K May(5) 11/1: 0-000000: 14th: Sn led to 4f out, no extra 2f out: blnks.	nk	11
4669	**WHISPERING VALLEY 9** [8]4-8-8 (47) Thomas Yeung 20/1: 0-00000: 15th: In tch, rear & btn halfway.	2	4
4260	**MAID FOR LIFE 29** [11]4-9-1 (54) M Lawson 12/1: 0464-660: 16th: Slow away, nvr a factor.	1½	8
	16 Ran Time 1m 44.75(6.45) Owned: Blake Hall Lad Partnership Trained: Newmarket		

Official Going Good/Firm

4829   2.00 European Breeders Fund Maiden Stakes Div 1 2yo (D3)
£5239 £1612 £806   **1m67y rnd**   **Good/Firm**   **Inapplicable**   Inside

4648	**SPEIGHTSTOWN 10** [6] P F I Cole 2-9-0 T Quinn 5/4 FAV: 031: Cl-up, ran wide on bend halfway & lost pl, styd on for press to lead 1f out, drvn out to hold on: well bckd: eff around 1m, further will suit in time: acts on fast & gd/soft grnd: acts on a sharp or gall trk: deserved win, see 4648 & 4069.		84
	MR AITCH [9] J A Osborne 2-9-0 Dane O'Neill 16/1: 2: b c Soviet Star - Welsh Mist (Damister) Rear, left cl-up on bend halfway, sn led, hung left under press & hdd 1f out, kept on, just held by wnr: debut: Apr foal, cost 77,000gns: half-brother to wnrs at 6/8f: dam List wnr at 6f: sire decent performer around 6f/1m: eff around 1m, looks as tho' further will suit: acts on fast grnd: gd eff & can find similar.	nk	82
4455	**GINGIEFLY 20** [8] J L Dunlop 2-9-0 S W Kelly 33/1: 03: b c Sinndar - Native Ring (Bering) Handy, left in lead halfway, sn hdd, styd prom till dist, no extra: dam first foal, cost 15,000gns: dam a mid-dist wnr, sire top-class at 12f: eff arnd 1m on fst, further will suit: encouraging effort.	2	78
4723	**OUR KES 6** [1] P Howling 2-9-0 K Fallon 33/1: 0004: Keen cl-up 4f, sn ran wide on bend, ev ch 2f out, sn no extra: qck reapp: eff around 1m on fast grnd: see 2213.	½	72
4677	**PIRAN 9** [12]2-9-0 J F McDonald(3) 16/1: 005: b g Orpen - Dancing At Lunasa (Dancing Dissident) Keen handy, no extra bef 1f out: Apr foal, half-brother successful at 6/7f: dam successful at 5f: sire high-class juv performer at 6f: eff around 1m on fast grnd: with B J Meehan.	shd	76$
	GABANNA [4]2-9-0 E Ahern 9/2: 6: Chsd ldrs, outpcd after halfway, modest late gains: debut.	2	72
	DIZZY FUTURE [10]2-9-0 W Ryan 20/1: 7: Dwelt, prog when short of room dist, sn onepcd.	2	68
4417	**OVERJOY WAY 21** [11]2-8-9 J Quinn 25/1: 08: Cl-up, badly impeded & carr v wide bend halfway, eased when ran wide fnl 1f: forgive this, see 4417.	½	62
4611	**MAMBAZO 12** [7]2-9-0 W Supple 66/1: 0009: Missed break, nvr a factor.	nk	66
	SOLAR FALCON [5]2-8-9 S Whitworth 33/1: 0: 10th: Missed break, nvr able to chall.	11	39
4179	**TAKEMETOYOURHEART 32** [2]2-8-9 F Norton 66/1: 00: 11th: Cl-up when ran wide bend halfway, fdd.	dist	0
4416	**CROIX ROUGE 21** [3]2-9-0 R Hughes 3/1: 30: 12th: Led, not handle bend & nrly ran off crse on bend at halfway, t.o.: op 9/4: reportedly cocked jaw & looks one to avoid: btr 4416.	25	0
	12 Ran Time 1m 46.01 () Owned: Sir Martyn Arbib Trained: Whatcombe		

4830	2.30 Dine In The Castle Restaurant Today Nursery Handicap Stakes 2yo 0-85 (D2)	[91]
	£5769 £1775 £888 5f10y str Good/Firm Inapplicable Inside	

4458 **FORZEEN** 19 [5] J A Osborne 2-9-3 (80) E Ahern 14/1: 2314001: In tch, styd on to lead 1f out, rdn **89**
out: eff at 5f, has tried 6f but shld suit: acts on firm, gd & both AWs: likes a sharp trk: see 3284.

4409 **STAR DUSTER** 21 [6] B R Millman 2-8-2 (65) R Mullen 25/1: 0202: Dwelt, sn in tch wide, ev ch when ¾ **71**
hung left dist, kept on & only just btn: imprvd eff nr h'cap bow: acts on feast & gd: slow start prob cost him this.

4471 **LOUPHOLE** 18 [2] P J Makin 2-9-1 (78) D Sweeney 25/1: 341003: Cl-up, led after 2f out, hdd 1f nk **83**
out, no extra: gd run in defeat: see 3296.

4198 **WITHERING LADY** 31 [8] Mrs P N Dutfield 2-8-12 (75) R Havlin 25/1: 6201054: Mid-div, hdwy wide 2f ½ **79**
out, no impress ins fnl 1f: see 3504.

4517* **FOLGA** 16 [7]2-8-7 (70) J Mackay 33/1: 3015: Led despite hanging badly, hdd 2f out, no extra. hd **73**

4679 **MISS CASSIA** 9 [13]2-8-10 (73) P Dobbs 16/1: 32S3106: Mid-div, staying on when short of room hd **75**
cl-home: worth a try over further: see 4187.

4545 **MAJESTICAL** 14 [11]2-7-12 (10h) (60) Lisa Jones 20/1: 4004247: In tch, eff when no room dist, sn btn. ½ **62**

3943 **EMPIRES GHODHA** 44 [18]2-9-7 bl (84) J F McDonald(3) 14/1: 1534608: Short of room after 1f & sn ½ **84**
bhd, prog when short of room dist, switched & kept on late: not get run of race: btr 2895 & 2415.

4556 **CLOVE** 14 [19]2-9-1 (78) R Hughes 7/2 FAV: 4129: Keen rear, hdwy halfway, no impress fnl 1f: ½ **77**
reportedly missed the break: btr 4556 & 3476.

4784 **MONASHEE ROSE** 2 [17]2-9-0 (77) Derek Nolan(7) 12/1: 011200: 10th: Keen bhd, nvr nrr than mid-div. ¾ **74**

4338* **DANZILI BAY** 25 [14]2-9-3 (80) N Chalmers(5) 5/1: 4410: 11th: Nvr nrr than mid-div: btr 4338 (fm). 1¼ **74**

3517 **RUBYS DREAM** 61 [4]2-8-6 (69) S W Kelly 50/1: 3435400: 12th: Cl-up, wknd bef 1f out: 9 wk abs. ½ **62**

4536 **KEMPSEY** 15 [10]2-8-0 p (63) S Whitworth 50/1: 0644460: 13th: Mid-div when no room over 2f out, sn btn. 1¾ **51**

4471 **KING AFTER** 18 [9]2-8-4 (67) W Supple 20/1: 6655000: 14th: Keen rear, nvr a factor. 2½ **48**

4679 **HIGH CHART** 9 [12]2-8-4 t (67) A McCarthy 20/1: 0306000: 15th: Rear, nvr able to chall. hd **47**

4645 **ROSIELLA** 10 [20]2-8-9 (72) F Norton 8/1: 0513460: 16th: Bhd, eff when short of room dist, sn btn. 2 **46**

4645 **AVERTING** 10 [15]2-7-13 (1ow) (5oh)bl (56) J Quinn 40/1: 520000: 17th: Dwelt, nvr a factor. 1 **33**

4179 **BEAUTIFUL MOVER** 32 [16]2-8-10 (73) K Fallon 4/1: 23040: 18th: Sn bhd, hmpd 2f out, sn btn: op 2 **38**
6/1: reportedly lost action: showed more in 4179 & 2297.

18 Ran Time 59.63 () Owned: Cavendish Racing Trained: Upper Lambourn

4831	3.00 European Breeders Fund Maiden Stakes Div 2 2yo (D3)	
	£5226 £1608 £804 1m67y rnd Good/Firm Inapplicable Inside	

4522 **EVA SONEVA SO FAST** 16 [6] J L Dunlop 2-9-0 (80) J Quinn 5/4 FAV: 0521: Cl-up, ev ch halfway, **84**
styd on to lead dist, rdn out: bckd: apprec recent step up to 1m, further will suit: acts on fast & gd grnd.

4611 **PHI** 12 [1] Sir Michael Stoute 2-9-0 K Fallon 13/8: 02: b c Rahy - Salchow (Nijinsky) Led, hdd ½ **81**
under press dist, kept on well ins fnl 1f, just held: clr rem, well bckd: Feb foal, half-brother Gr 1 wnr at 1m:
dam unrcd: sire useful performer abroad on dirt: apprec 1m on fast grnd: lost little in defeat.

KINRANDE 11 [11] P J Makin 2-9-0 D Sweeney 25/1: 3: b c Sri Pekan - Pipers Pool (Mtoto) Held up, 5 **71**
styd on fnl 1f, no ch with front 2: debut: Jan foal, half-brother to wnrs at 6/10f: dam plcd at 10f: sire decent
juv performer: eff around 1m, further will suit: acts on fast grnd: encouraging eff & can improve.

4191 **HOH MY DARLING** 31 [7] M L W Bell 2-8-9 R Mullen 12/1: 04: Chsd ldrs, outpcd halfway, rallied late. nk **65**

4576 **ZEENA** 13 [8]2-8-9 N De Souza(5) 10/1: 545: Keen handy 6f, no extra: shade more in 4576 (7f). ¾ **63**

WAR PENNANT 2 [2]2-9-0 S Hitchcott 25/1: 6: b g Selkirk - Bunting (Shaadi) Handy over 5f, wknd. 7 **55**
debut: Apr foal, half-brother to 6f wnrs at 2, also decent mid-dists performers: dam successful at 1m/10f: sire
Gr 1 wnr at 1m: with M R Channon.

HAWRIDGE SENSATION [10]2-9-0 W Supple 33/1: 7: Keen handy 6f: hung right & ran green. 2 **51**

4664 **SAVOY CHAPEL** 9 [9]2-9-0 S W Kelly 100/1: 0008: Chsd ldrs 5f, wknd. 2½ **46**

STUNNING SPARK [4]2-8-9 R Miles(3) 100/1: 9: Al adrift on debut. 7 **28**

DUNLOWS MINSTREL [3]2-9-0 O Urbina 33/1: 0: 10th: Al bhd, nvr a factor on debut. 4 **25**

10 Ran Time 1m 45.87 () Owned: Eurostrait Ltd Trained: Arundel

4832	3.30 National Hunt Racing Returns To Windsor Handicap Stakes 3yo+ 56-70 (E3)	[80]
	£3636 £1119 £559 1m67y rnd Good/Firm Inapplicable Inside	

4642 **OMAHA CITY** 10 [12] B Gubby 10-9-3 (69) F Norton 11/1: 1000001: In tch, prog bef 1f out, rdn out **78**
to lead cl-home: eff at 7f/sharp 1m on firm, gd/soft & any trk, loves Goodwood: well h'capped but inconsistent
10yo: see 2540.

4714 **JUST FLY** 7 [13] S Kirk 4-9-4 (70) K Fallon 5/4 FAV: 0000022: Held up, hdwy 3f out, styd on to nk **77**
lead ins fnl 1f, hdd well ins last, just denied: qck reapp: deserves to go one btr: see 4714.

4643 **PETROSA** 10 [10] D R C Elsworth 4-9-3 (69) T Quinn 8/1: 323-4503: Held up, hdwy wide 3f out, kept ¾ **74**
on ins fnl 1f: encouraging effort: see 3535.

4388 **HILLTOP RHAPSODY** 23 [14] D J Daly 3-8-13 (69) N Pollard 14/1: 00104: Cl-up, ev ch well over 1f ¾ **72**
out, no extra ins fnl 1f: see 2974 (firm).

4500 **LOCKSTOCK** 17 [1]6-9-4 p (70) Dane O'Neill 16/1: 0010005: Cl-up, ev ch over 1f out, sn no extra. hd **72**

3821 **KABEER** 49 [8]6-8-11 (63) D R McCabe 33/1: 430056: Led, hdd ins fnl 1f, no extra: 7 wk abs: btr 2575. ½ **64**

2647 **DUELLING BANJOS** 97 [6]5-8-11 (63) S Hitchcott 16/1: 01-04007: Bhd, nvr nrr than mid-div: abs. ½ **63**

1872 **CHARLIE BEAR** 130 [7]3-8-12 (68) E Ahern 10/1: 500-028: Keen in tch, prog dist, wknd ins fnl 1f. hd **67**

4475 **MISTER CLINTON** 18 [4]7-8-9 (61) D Sweeney 20/1: 1201609: Nvr nrr than mid-div. ½ **59**

4475 **HAIL THE CHIEF** 18 [3]7-9-1 (67) S Whitworth 25/1: 3060000: 10th: Nvr nrr than mid-div. nk **64**

4300 **MAMORE GAP** 28 [5]6-8-12 (69) R Hughes 16/1: 0050550: 11th: Rear, hdwy 3f out, onepcd fnl 2f. ½ **60**

4334 **ZARIANO** 25 [9]4-8-13 (65) L Keniry(3) 33/1: 60-20000: 12th: Mid-div 6f, sn wknd. 1½ **58**

4615 **TIBER TIGER** 12 [11]4-9-4 P (70) J P Guillambert(3) 10/1: 5556000: 13th: Mid-div over 5f, wknd. 2½ **58**

4469 **INVADER** 19 [2]8-9-3 bl t (69) J Quinn 16/1: 0106600: 14th: Bhd, nvr a factor: btr 3708. nk **56**

14 Ran Time 1m 43.51 () Owned: Brian Gubby Ltd Trained: Bagshot

4833   4.00 Tangerine Handicap Stakes 3yo 71-85 (D2)   [92]
£7101 £2185 £1092   1m3f135y   Good/Firm   Inapplicable   Inside

4239 **RINGSIDER 30** [9] G A Butler 3-9-5 (83) R Hughes 11/2: 1-002101: Missed break, sn mid-div, hdwy   **94**
bef 1f out, styd on to lead ins fnl 1f, rdn out: op 7/1: eff around 1m/9f, imprvd for today's step up to 11.6f:
acts on firm & fast grnd: progressive 3yo who is unexposed around mid-dists: see 3625.
4288 **QUARRYMOUNT 28** [10] Sir Mark Prescott 3-8-7 (1oh) (70) J Mackay 100/30 FAV: 0212122: Led, hdd ins ¾   **79**
fnl 1f, not pace wnr: bckd: continues in gd form: see 4288 & 4166.
4613 **VAMP 12** [11] R M Beckett 3-8-11 (75) R Mullen 6/1: 2315043: Mid-div, prog 2f out, kept on but no 1¾   **80**
impress on front 2 ins fnl 1f: op 8/1: eff at 9.7/10f, ran to form on step up to 11.6f: see 4613 & 2980.
2956 **SUNNY LADY 85** [1] E A L Dunlop 3-8-13 (77) E Ahern 14/1: 2222144: Mid-div, prog 2f out, no   1   **80**
impress ins fnl 1f: 12 wk abs: btr 2642.
2567 **GRAHAM ISLAND 100** [6]3-9-5 (83) F Norton 20/1: 05-16605: Held up, hdwy 3f out, kept on ins fnl   hd   **85**
1f: long abs: has been gelded: btr 1211 (mdn).
4613 **TREW CLASS 12** [4]3-8-13 (77) T Quinn 16/1: 0011306: Cl-up, wknd dist: btr 2994 (10f).   shd   **78**
4613 **VANTAGE 12** [12]3-8-11 bl (75) J P Guillambert(3) 20/1: 1450467: Keen mid-div, no impress dist.   5   **69**
3619 **DARING AIM 58** [5]3-9-0 (85) K Fallon 4/1: 4-5158: Reluctant to start, hdwy & cl-up halfway,   ¾   **77**
onepcd over 2f out: 8 wk abs: looks to have own ideas: see 3619 & 3405.
4553 **RUTTERS REBEL 14** [7]3-8-7 (71) Kim Tinkler 16/1: 2401069: Al in rear: btr 3765.   ¾   **61**
4749 **MR TAMBOURINE MAN 5** [3]3-9-7 (85) N De Souza(5) 7/1: 1314200: 10th: Keen mid-div, hdwy 3f out,   ½   **74**
wknd dist: qck reapp: btr 4553.
4749 Jakarmi 5 [8]3-8-9 (73) R Miles(3) 33/1:0   4449* Dundry 20 [2]3-9-7 p(85) Dane O'Neill 16/1:0
12 Ran Time 2m 28.36 () Owned: Mr S A O'Donoghue & Mr M V Deegan   Trained: Blewbury

4834   4.30 Windsor-Racecourse Co Uk Selling Stakes 3yo (E3)
£3533 £1087 £544   1m2f7y   Good/Firm   Inapplicable   Inside

4612 **SOVIET SCEPTRE 12** [13] Miss D Mountain 3-9-0 (60) R Miles(3) 12/1: 3046001: Held up, hdwy after   **65**
6f, styd on to lead 2f out, sn clr, pushed out, val 5L+: bght in for 6,400gns: eff at 1m/10f on fast & gd grnd.
4501 **TIZI OUZOU 17** [1] J L Dunlop 3-8-9 T Quinn 8/1: U0-62: Held up, hdwy wide 3f out, styd on to   3   **55**
chase wnr ins fnl 1f, al held: eff at 10f, further shld suit: acts on fast grnd: encouraging run drpd in grade.
4661 **BONUS POINTS 9** [5] B J Meehan 3-9-0 (57) J F McDonald(3) 14/1: 0603: In tch, outpcd after 7f,   nk   **59**
rallied bef 1f out, no ch with front 2: clr reen: blnks left off: eff at 10f on fast grnd: see 4042.
4750 **BERTOCELLI 5** [3] G G Margarson 3-9-0 (55) J Mackay 9/2 JT FAV: 0060004: Led, rcd wide on bend   7   **49**
after halfway, hdd 2f out, wknd: bckd on qck reapp: btr 2272.
4698 **LA CALERA 7** [11]3-9-1 P (45) O Urbina 14/1: 0533005: Cl-up 1m, wknd: qck reapp & cheek pieces.   1   **48**
4698 **VITTORIOSO 7** [7]3-9-0 (40) B Reilly(3) 20/1: 2005006: In tch, hdwy halfway, fdd dist: qck reapp.   nk   **46**
4560* **DEFANA 14** [2]3-9-6 P (53) S W Kelly 9/2 JT FAV: 5330617: Cl-up, ev ch 4f out, wknd bef 2f out: nk   **51**
disapp with first time cheek pieces: showed more in 4560.
4541 **MONTGOMERY 15** [10]3-9-0 (48) S Whitworth 25/1: 6658: Nvr nrr than mid-div: showed more in 3967.   ¾   **43**
4612 **PORT SODRICK 12** [15]3-9-0 (60) K Fallon 5/1: 66459: Missed break, nvr able to chall: btr 4612.   hd   **42**
4612 **ROMEOS DAY 12** [4]3-9-0 vis (40) S Hitchcott 13/2: 0000540: 10th: Cl-up 7f, wknd: bckd from 11/1.   2   **39**
4539 **REGULATED 15** [12]3-9-6 (54) M Tebbutt 33/1: 6050000: 11th: Al in rear: btr 2107.   nk   **44**
4112 **ANOTHER CON 37** [8]3-9-1 VIS (48) E Ahern 10/1: 0020500: 12th: Cl-up till halfway, fdd 3f out.   ¾   **37**
4366 **HARRY CAME HOME 24** [9]3-9-0 bl (30) L Keniry(3) 66/1: 0000000: 13th: Al in rear.   5   **29**
4445 Charlie Masters 20 [6]3-9-0 A McCarthy 66/1:0   4661 Jimmy Hay 9 [14]3-9-0 D Fox(5) 66/1:0
15 Ran Time 2m 6.96 () Owned: Mr David Fremel   Trained: Newmarket

4835   5.00 Windsor Fireworks Extravaganza Sat 6th November Maiden Stakes Div 1 3yo+ (D3)
£4160 £1280 £640   6f rnd   Good/Firm   Inapplicable   Inside

4683 **PINE BAY 9** [1] B Gubby 3-8-7 (63) F Norton 9/1: 60001: Handy, prog to lead ins fnl 1f, rdn out: **68**
eff at 6f on fast grnd: acts on a sharp trk: gd confidence boost: see 1929.
  SOUL DANCE [7] P J Makin 3-8-7 T D Sweeney 15/2: 2: b f Imperial Ballet - Piccante (Wolfhound)   ½   **65**
Bhd, hdwy halfway, ev ch ins fnl 1f, sn hung left & just held by wnr: op 11/2 on debut: sprint bred: eff at 6f on
fast grnd: gd eff on debut with t-strap fitted & can rate higher.
4646 **BALLINGER EXPRESS 10** [6] A M Balding 4-8-9 bl (57) W Ryan 11/4 FAV: 0020003: Hood not taken off 1¾   **60+**
in time & lost over 7L, prog to handy 3f out, onepcd from dist: bckd: lost ch at start, see 3479.
3331 **CALLED UP 68** [2] H Candy 3-8-12 (68) Dane O'Neill 5/1: 400504: Cl-up, led after 4f, hdd ins fnl   nk   **64**
1f, no extra: 10 wk abs: see 2756.
4667 **PENEL 9** [5]3-8-12 (62) P Fitzsimons 100/30: 540-6025: Led 4f, sn wknd: btr 4467 (7f, g/s).   2   **58**
76 **CLEARING SKY 310** [11]3-8-7 E Ahern 25/1: 00-6d: Handy, no extra bef 1f out: reapp: new stable.   hd   **52**
4485 **DIAPHANOUS 18** [8]6-8-9 (30) Liam Jones(7) 66/1: 0000007: Keen mid-div, wknd bef 1f out.   1   **49**
  DUXFORD [10]3-8-12 J Quinn 16/1: 8: Al in rear on debut.   1½   **50**
4413 **SUPERFLING 21** [3]3-8-12 P Dobbs 6/1: 069: Cl-up 4f, fdd: showed more 4413.   1   **47**
4586 **TERENURE GIRL 13** [9]3-8-7 Lisa Jones 33/1: 60: 10th: Keen rear, nvr a factor.   6   **26**
10 Ran Time 1m 12.68 () Owned: Brian Gubby Ltd   Trained: Bagshot

4836   5.30 Windsor Fireworks Extravaganza Sat 6th November Maiden Stakes Div 2 3yo+ (D3)
£4160 £1280 £640   6f rnd   Good/Firm   Inapplicable   Inside

4674 **INDIANA BLUES 9** [6] A M Balding 3-8-7 (63) N Chalmers(5) 4/1: 3534321: Prom, styd on to lead bef   **67**
1f out, rdn out: tchd 5/1: eff at 5.7f/7f on fast & soft grnd: deserved success: see 4674 & 4413.
4335 **MILLINSKY 25** [4] R Guest 3-8-7 (56) K Fallon 11/8 FAV: 63232: In tch, hdwy & ev ch over 1f out,   ¾   **63**
kept on fnl 1f, not pace wnr: bckd: eff at 5f, imprvd for step up to 6f: see 4335 & 3687.
3921 **FUTURE DEAL 45** [10] C A Horgan 3-8-7 T Quinn 4/1: 43: Mid-div, hdwy after halfway, hung left &   ¾   **61**

WINDSOR   MONDAY 27.09.04   Sharp, Figure 8 Track

no impress from dist: op 11/2: 6 wk abs: eff at 6f, rtn to 7f shld suit: acts on fast & gd grnd: see 3921.

4616 **CHARLOTTEBUTTERFLY** 12 [11] T T Clement 4-8-9 (52) J F McDonald(3) 16/1: 0400304: Handy over 4f.	2½	54
4029 **IMTALKINGGIBBERISH** 40 [1]3-8-12 (79) W Ryan 7/1: 050205: Cl-up, led halfway, hdd dist, wknd.	1¾	54
4445 **APPOLONIOUS** 20 [9]3-8-12 T (55) N Pollard 66/1: 00006: Rear, nvr nrr than mid-div: t-strap.	nk	53
4445 **ALL QUIET** 20 [5]3-8-7 (67) R Hughes 8/1: 3235557: Handy over 4f, wknd: btr 2352.	1¼	44
4413 **MISS MONZA** 21 [7]3-8-7 (62) W Supple 50/1: 00308: Bhd, nvr a factor: btr 4081.	¾	42
4595 **WESTBOROUGH** 13 [8]3-8-12 t (52) Kim Tinkler 33/1: 2006029: Al in rear.	nk	46
4413 **BERESFORD BOY** 21 [2]3-8-12 Dane O'Neill 66/1: 06-P0: 10th: Bhd, nvr able to chall.	11	16
4275 **TANNE BLIXEN** 28 [3]3-8-7 L Keniry(3) 66/1: 000: 11th: b f Great Dane - Night Transaction (Tina's Pet) Led 3f, wknd bef 1f out: modest form to date.	1¾	6

11 Ran   Time 1m 12.16()   Owned: Mr J C Smith   Trained: Kingsclere

MAISONS LAFFITTE   TUESDAY 21.09.04   Righthand, Sharpish Track

Official Going Good

4837	2.50 Gr 3 La Coupe de Maisons Laffitte 3yo+ () £25704 £10282 £7711 **1m2f Good**

2459 **FAIR MIX** M Rolland 6-9-1 S Pasquier 47/10: 5-163261: Mid-div wide, rdn to lead over 1f out, held on all out: Gr 1 Prix Ganay wnr in '03: suited by 10f, stays 12f well: acts on good & hvy: v smart entire.		118
1914) **MARSHALL** C Laffon Parias 4-8-12 M Blancpain 21/1: 0020102: Rear, styd on wide for press from over 1f out, ch ins last, just held.	snk	115
4016* **SPECIAL KALDOUN** 38 D Smaga 5-9-1 D Boeuf 46/10: 00-00313: Mid-div, kept on for press, not pace of front pair: btr 4016 (hvy).	2½	114

10 Ran   Time 1m 59.40()   Owned: Mme J Shalam   Trained: France

COLOGNE   SATURDAY 25.09.04   Righthand, Fair Track

Official Going Soft

4838	3.35 Listed Europa Steher Preis 3yo+ () £9168 £2817 £1408 **1m7f Soft**

4425 **NO REFUGE** 24 Sir Mark Prescott 4-9-2 BL (94) T Hellier 28/10: 311213231: Mid-div, hdwy to chall over 2f out, led over 1f out, styd on strongly: eff btwn 12/15f on fast, soft & both AWs: useful, apprec blnks.		106
LE ROYAL H J Groschel 4-9-2 O Peslier : 2: b g Royal Solo - Liebste (Nebos)	2	103
adrift **LIQUIDO** H Steinmetz 5-9-4 A de Vries : 3: br h Lomitas - Lolli Pop (Cagliostro)	2	103

7 Ran   Time 3m 22.83 ()   Owned: W E Sturt - Osborne House III   Trained: Newmarket

4839	4.05 Gr 2 Grosse Europa Melle 3yo+ () £28169 £10563 £4225 **1m rnd Soft**

3664 **EAGLE RISE** 55 A Schutz 4-9-1 T Hellier 29/10: 21: b c Danehill - Evening Breeze (Surumu) Chsd ldrs, swtchd to lead over 1f out, drvn to hold on: Gr 3 wnr here at Cologne in '03: stays 10f, suited by 1m on good & v soft ground: smart colt. 2 Aug'04 Colo 8gd 113- :		114
4386 **PUTRA PEKAN** 21 M A Jarvis 6-9-1 bl (110) O Peslier 33/10: 010-11072: Led till over 1f out, styd on gamely ins last, just held: better run: see 1649 (soft).	nk	113
4424 **ASSIUN** 25 P Schiergen 3-8-9 Filip Minarik 24/10 FAV: 13233: Held up, some late gains.	1	109

7 Ran   Time 1m 41.06 ()   Owned: Baron G Von Ullmann   Trained: Germany

COLOGNE   SATURDAY 26.09.04   Righthand, Fair Track

Official Going Soft

4840	3.05 Gr 3 Oppenheim Stuten Melle Fillies & Mares 3yo+ () £22535 £7042 £3521 **1m rnd Soft**

SECRET MELODY H A Pantall 3-8-12 C P Lemaire 15/2: 1: b f Inchinor - Secret Music (Dixieland Band) Trkd ldr, drvn to lead close home: dual Listed plcd earlier this term: eff at 1m on good & v soft.		104
3866 **SNOW GOOSE** 46 J L Dunlop 3-8-12 (103) S Sanders 42/10: 12-042332: Led, hdd line: see 3876.	shd	103
KITCAT P Schiergen 3-8-12 A Schikora 17/10 FAV: 3: b f Monsun - Kittiwake (Barathea) Held up, styd on to take 3rd, no threat to front pair.	2½	98

11 Ran   Time 1m 40.07 ()   Owned: Lady O'Reilly   Trained: France

COLOGNE   SATURDAY 26.09.04   Righthand, Fair Track

4841   4.20 Gr 1 IVG Preis von Europa 3yo+ ()
£66901 £24648 £11972   **1m4f**   **Soft**

4018* **ALBANOVA 42** Sir Mark Prescott 5-9-2 (111) S Sanders 14/10 FAV: /1026-111: Held up in tch, hdwy   **116**
to chse ldr 2f out, drvn to lead well ins last: 6 wk abs: eff at 10/12f, has tried 2m: acts on good & hvy grnd:
superbly placed to land 3 German Gr 1 events this term: see 4018, 3497.
　　　　SALDENTIGERIN P Schiergen 3-8-6   A Starke 29/10: 2: b f Tiger Hill - Salde (Alkalde) Led   ½   **112**
after 1f, hdd close home.
4532 **DARSALAM 15** A Shavuyev 3-8-10   A Boschert 87/10: 21111163: Led early, trkd ldr after 1f, styd   ¾   **115**
on for press, not pace of wnr.
9 Ran   Time 2m 36.12()   Owned: Miss K Rausing   Trained: Newmarket

NOTTINGHAM   TUESDAY 28.09.04   Lefthand, Galloping Track

Official Going Good/Firm (Good Places) All Times Slow

4842   2.10 European Breeders Fund Maiden Stakes Fillies 2yo (D2)
£6370 £1960 £980   **1m54y rnd**   **Good/Firm**   **Inapplicable**   Centre

4600 **SHARAIJI BLOSSOM 13** [12] Saeed bin Suroor 2-8-11 L Dettori 11/8 FAV: 31: Made all, rdn & al   **84**
holding rivals from dist: well bckd, op 7/4: eff at 7.5f/1m, shld get further on this evidence: acts on fast grnd,
gall trks: progressing, win more races: see 4600.
4450 **ZAYN ZEN 21** [17] M A Jarvis 2-8-11 M Hills 4/1: 642: Chsd ldrs, rdn to press wnr over 1f out,   1½   **79**
kept on, al held: eff around 1m, handles fast & gd grnd: now qual for h'caps: see 4450 & 4191.
4617 **ORPENDONNA 12** [2] K A Ryan 2-8-11 N Callan 22/1: 03: b f Orpen - Tetradonna (Teenoso) Al prom   ½   **78**
& chall 3f out, rdn & no extra ins last: op 16/1, left debut bhd: E30,000 Jan foal, half-sister to wnrs at 1m/13f,
also a 7f juv wnr: dam styd up to 12f: eff at 1m, shld get further: handles fast: win a race.
　　　　RILL 0 [13] J H M Gosden 2-8-11   R Hughes 33/1: 4: ch f Unfuwain - River Cara (Irish River)   1¾   **75**
Trkd ldrs, rdn & kept on onepace, nvr a threat: Apr foal, half-sister to wnrs at 9f/hdls: dam smart 1m juv wnr:
stays 1m, mid-dists will suit: encouraging.
　　　　FEARLESS SPIRIT 0 [4]2-8-11 J Fortune 15/2: 5: ch f Spinning World - Hot Princess (Hot Spark)   3   **69**
Dwelt, rear, hdwy on wide nr fin, nrst fin: op 12/1, stablemate of 4th: Feb foal, half-sister to high-class dual
Guineas wnr Roderigo de Triano: dam a juv sprint wnr: learn from this.
3721 **MANSIYA 54** [5]2-8-11 S Sanders 13/2: 26: Chsd wnr, hung right on bend after 3f, rdn & btn 2f out.   nk   **68**
　　　　NATALIE JANE 0 [16]2-8-11 P Hanagan 40/1: 7: Dwelt, rear, late gains, nrst fin: likely improver.   ¾   **67**
　　　　KIAMA 0 [9]2-8-11 K Fallon 20/1: 8: Trkd ldrs, short of room when hmpd on bend after 3f, no impress.   1¼   **64**
　　　　LUJAIN ROSE 0 [7]2-8-11 S Drowne 50/1: 9: Pushed along mid-div, no impress 2f out.   nk   **63**
4329 **JENNA STANNIS 26** [6]2-8-11 N Chalmers(5) 40/1: 000: 10th: Mid-div, btn 3f out: btr 4329 & 3944 (7f).   1¾   **60**
　　　　GAMBLING SPIRIT 0 [3]2-8-11 Dane O'Neill 16/1: 0: 11th: Towards rear & sn pushed along, mod prog.   1   **58**
　　　　DANITA DANCER 0 [10]2-8-11 D Holland 40/1: 0: 12th: Towards rear, little hdwy.   2½   **53**
4450 **ALULA 21** [8]2-8-11 R L Moore 33/1: 000: 13th: Mid-div, fdd fnl 3f.   1   **51**
4610 **ASSURED 13** [18]2-8-11 P T Quinn 100/1: 000: 14th: Held up in tch, no impress fnl 2f, chkpcs.   1   **49**
4242 **Calamari 31** [11]2-8-11 J Quinn 40/1:0　　　4462 **Whoopsie 20** [14]2-8-11 F Norton 100/1:0
　　Treasury 0 [15]2-8-11 T P Queally 66/1:0　　　　**Glads Image 0** [1]2-8-11 C Catlin 100/1:0
18 Ran   Time 1m 45.84 (4.04)   Owned: Godolphin   Trained: Newmarket

4843   2.40 Midlands Racing - 9 Great Venues Maiden Stakes Div 1 Fillies 2yo (D3)
£4752 £1462 £731   **6f str**   **Good/Firm**   **Inapplicable**   Far Side

4600 **ECOLOGICALLY RIGHT 13** [6] Mrs J R Ramsden 2-8-11 T Quinn 6/1: 061: b f Entrepreneur - Logic   **79**
(Slip Anchor) Chasing ldrs, switched & briefly rdn to lead ins last, styd on strongly under hand riding: op 7/1:
Feb foal, half-sister to a 6/7f juv wnr Logsdail, dam plcd at 7f/1m as a juv: eff at 6f, 7f/1m shld suit: handles
fast grnd & a gall trk: progressive filly, shld make her mark in h'cap company.
3908 **ENTERTAINING 46** [13] H Candy 2-8-11 Dane O'Neill 11/4 FAV: 652: Led, rdn & hung left/hdd ins   1½   **73**
last, not pace of wnr: rest well covered, nicely bckd: 6 wk abs: eff at 6/7f on fast & gd grnd: see 3908.
3103 **MIDNIGHT LACE 80** [8] R Hannon 2-8-11 R L Moore 16/1: 003: ch f Tomba - Royal Passion (Ahonoora)   2½   **65**
Prom, rdn & no extra from dist: 12 wk abs, much imprvd eff: Mar foal, half-sister to a multiple winning sprinter
Tadeo, also a 6/10f wnr Attache: dam a 2m3f wnr: eff at 6f, get further in time: acts on fast grnd.
2603 **E BRIDE 100** [4] J G Given 2-8-11 M Fenton 14/1: 54: gr f Runaway Groom - Fast Selection   2½   **57**
(Talinum) Dwelt, held up in tch, rdn & some late gains, nvr a dngr: 3 mth abs: Apr foal: bred for 1m.
4726 **BORN FOR DIAMONDS 7** [11]2-8-11 M Hills 11/2: 05: Dwelt & pushed along towards rear, hdwy when   1½   **52**
hung left ins last, nvr a factor.
　　　　TURKANA GIRL 0 [1]2-8-11 S Drowne 18/1: 6: Outpcd early, some hdwy halfway, no dngr.   nk   **51**
4610 **QAWAAFIL 13** [7]2-8-11 R Hills 15/2: 507: Chsd ldrs till over 1f out: see 2399.   1   **48**
3517 **LADY HEN 62** [9]2-8-11 E Ahern 14/1: 068: Held up, no impress fnl 2f, 2 mth abs.   2½   **40**
4517 **PEDLAR OF DREAMS 17** [10]2-8-11 P Hanagan 9/1: 359: Prom till lost place after 2f, sn struggling.   3   **31**
4644 **TEMPLE BELLE XPRES 11** [3]2-8-11 S W Kelly 100/1: 00: 10th: Chsd ldrs, btn 2f out.   2   **25**
　　　　LA CYGNE BLANCHE 0 [5]2-8-11 Joanna Badger 100/1: 0: 11th: Slow away, hung left & al rear.   ½   **23**
4303 **Mochaccino 28** [12]2-8-11 Hayley Turner(3) 50/1:0　　　**Snowdrift 0** [2]2-8-11 K Fallon 11/1:0
13 Ran   Time 1m 15.6 (4.8)   Owned: Mr W J Gredley   Trained: Thirsk

---

4844 3.10 Midlands Racing - 9 Great Venues Maiden Stakes Div 2 Fillies 2yo (D3)
£4752 £1462 £731   6f str   Good/Firm   Inapplicable   Far Side

BON NUIT 0 [9] G Wragg 2-8-11   S Drowne 25/1: 1: b f Night Shift - Pray (Priolo) Dwelt & sn
pushed along towards rear, hdwy from halfway, led ins last, sn asserted under hand riding: E65,000 Feb foal,
half-sister to wnrs at 6f/hdls: eff at 6f, 7f shld suit: acts on fast: rate higher.   87

4466 **NAN JAN 20** [5] R Ingram 2-8-11 T N Callan 50/1: 002: Al prom, rdn & led over 1f out, hdd & not   1¾   81
pace of wnr ins last: much imprvd in first time t-strap: eff at 6f on fast grnd: see 4466.

4457 **INDIENA 20** [12] B J Meehan 2-8-11   (77) J Fortune 1/1 FAV: 452423: Sn handy, ev ch 2f out, not   ½   79
pace of wnr ins last: hvly bckd: just btr 4457 (firm).

GIMASHA 0 [2] M R Channon 2-8-11   T E Durcan 5/1: 4: b f Cadeaux Genereux - First Waltz (Green   2½   71
Dancer) Handy & led over 3f out till over 1f out, no extra: bckd tho' op 5/2: Mar foal, half-sister to a 1m wnr: dam
smart 6f juv wnr: handles fast grnd: ran well for a long way.

4557 **MUSARDIERE 15** [8]2-8-11 L Goncalves 66/1: 05: Towards rear, switched & mod late prog under   3½   60
minimal press: some improvement from intro, bred to relish mid-dists, impr further in time: see 4557.

4557 **RASSEEM 15** [11]2-8-11 (76) L Dettori 7/2: 2036: Chsd ldrs, outpcd halfway: bckd: btr 4557 & 3576.   shd   60

AROUS 0 [1]2-8-11 S Sanders 12/1: 1: br f Desert King - Moneefa (Darshaan) Towards centre &   ¾   58
mid-div, no impress over 1f out: Apr foal, half-sister to smart performer Dandoun, a winning miler: dam 10f wnr.

4596 **AMAZING GRACE MARY 13** [7]2-8-11 BL S W Kelly 100/1: 08: Led till over 3f out, wknd, blnks.   9   33

JOLIE 0 [10]2-8-11 Lisa Jones 80/1: 9: Dwelt & bhd, nvr on terms with ldrs.   1¾   29

PETITE GIRL 0 [3]2-8-11 C Catlin 50/1: 0: 10th: Hmpd start & al bhd.   1¾   24

4590 **KIMBERLEY HALL 14** [13]2-8-11 M Henry 100/1: 0000: 11th: Sn outpcd & struggling rear.   nk   23

4442 **SWIFT DAME 21** [4]2-8-11 R Hughes 33/1: 050: 12th: Prom centre, hung badly left after 2f & sn   dist   0
bhd, reportedly became unrideable.

12 Ran   Time 1m 15.76 (4.96)   Owned: Mr Howard Spooner   Trained: Newmarket

---

4845 3.40 Racing Uk On Channel 432 Classified Stakes 3yo+ 0-60 (F3)
£3874 £1192 £596   6f str   Good/Firm   Inapplicable   Far Side

4751* **INCH BY INCH 6** [8] P J Makin 5-8-11 bl (60) A Quinn(5) 3/1 FAV: 0-040111: Sn cl-up stands side   76
trav well, led over 1f out, rdn clr & eased nr line, val 3L: nicely bckd: completed hat-trick: eff at 5/6f on
firm, gd & polytrack: progressive mare, keep on side: see 4751.

4740 **PICCLEYES 6** [18] R Hannon 3-8-12 bl (60) R L Moore 10/1: 0036032: Held up stands side, styd on   1¾   69
for press, no threat to wnr: see 3599, 2586.

4592 **GRANDMA LILY 14** [20] M C Chapman 6-8-11 (60) D Tudhope(5) 33/1: 0000303: Held up stands side,   1½   61
switched & kept on late, no threat to wnr: see 1465 & 85.

4294 **FIREWORK 29** [13] J Akehurst 6-9-0 p (57) T Quinn 33/1: 5010044: Sn prom stands side, no extra ins   nk   63
last: cheek pieces reapplied: see 2715 (clmr).

4438 **HEADLAND 21** [12]6-9-0 bl e (58) A Culhane 40/1: 2155105: Held up stands side, late gains, no threat.   1¼   59

4667 **SWEET PICKLE 10** [11]3-8-9 (58) T P Queally 33/1: 0-246006: Chsd ldrs stands side, styd on onepace.   hd   55

3696 **ZIET DALSACE 55** [15]4-8-11 (59) L Dettori 14/1: 2010467: Held up stands side, not pace to chall.   nk   54

4334 **TUSCARORA 26** [4]5-8-11 (60) J Fortune 5/1: 0513348: Unruly stalls, held up stands side, nvr dngr.   1¼   50

4438 **RENE BARBIER 21** [19]3-8-12 (59) F Norton 50/1: 4156009: Chsd ldrs stands side, no impress.   ¾   51

4785 **BOWLING ALONG 3** [9]3-8-9 (60) T Eaves(3) 22/1: 3200160: 10th: In tch stands side, no impress fnl 2f.   ¾   46

4754 **GONENDUNNETT 5** [14]5-9-0 p (60) Dane O'Neill 33/1: 1052000: 11th: Prom stands side till over 1f out.   1¼   45

4475 **JAZZY MILLENNIUM 19** [7]7-9-0 (59) D Holland 7/1: 3041220: 12th: Held up, no impress.   ½   43

4335 **KALLISTAS PRIDE 26** [17]4-8-11 vis (58) K Fallon 16/1: 1060500: 13th: Swerved left start, led   1¼   36
stands side till over 1f out, wknd.

3737 **SHAMROCK TEA 54** [16]3-8-12 (59) P Hanagan 16/1: 0-051400: 14th: Slow away, bhd stands side.   2   33

4237 **VICTORIANA 31** [3]3-8-9 (57) J Quinn 40/1: 6450: 15th: Prom far side & led that group well ins   1¾   25
last, no ch with ldrs stands side: rcd on unfav'd side: see 4029.

4412 **St Austell 22** [5]4-9-0 (58) S Sanders 16/1:0   4398 **Zap Attack 23** [6]4-9-0 (58) M Lawson(5) 50/1:0
4754 **Fitzwarren 5** [2]3-8-12 vis(59) E Ahern 40/1:0   1660 **Mrs Spence 141** [1]3-8-9 (58) T Lucas 14/1:0

19 Ran   Time 1m 14.19 (3.39)   Owned: Mrs Anna L Sanders   Trained: Marlborough

---

4846 4.10 Roseland Group Autumn Handicap Stakes 3yo 71-85 (D2)
£10514 £3235 £1618   2m9y   Good/Firm   Inapplicable   Inside   [90]

4405* **TRILEMMA 22** [1] Sir Mark Prescott 3-8-10 (72) S Sanders 1/1 FAV: 6-006111: Held up in tch,   83
smooth hdwy over 3f out & led over 1f out, sn asserted, rdn out: hvly bckd to complete hat-trick: imprvd last
thrice at 2m, acts on fast & gd grnd, stiff/gall or sharpish trk: progressive, win again: see 4405.

4235* **RACE THE ACE 31** [6] J L Dunlop 3-9-1 (77) L Dettori 15/8: 4523312: Trkd ldrs, prog & led over 3f   2½   83
out, hdd over 1f out, not pace of wnr but rest well covered: nicely bckd: met a fast improving rival, can win again.

4634 **MARINE CITY 12** [5] M A Jarvis 3-8-10 p (72) D Fox(5) 7/1: 0-166343: Held up, kept on despite   3   75
hanging left 2f out, not pace of front pair but well clr of rem: see 4634, 1272.

4634 **TUDOR BELL 12** [3] J G M O'Shea 3-9-5 (81) D Sweeney 33/1: 1621304: Chsd ldr, rdn & btn 3f out.   16   71

4449 **GARNETT 21** [7]3-8-8 (70) D Holland 33/1: 433035: Held up in tch, hdwy & briefly led 4f out, no impress.   2   58

4288 **RICHTEE 29** [2]3-8-10 (72) P Hanagan 14/1: 2513146: Rear, eff over 3f out, no impress: btr 3881 (12f).   4   56

4749 **QUARTINO 6** [4]3-9-7 bl (83) J Fortune 50/1: 521-0007: Led & sn clr, hdd 4f out, wknd qckly, qck reapp.   dist   0

7 Ran   Time 3m 30.04 (5.84)   Owned: Mrs Sonia Rogers   Trained: Newmarket

NOTTINGHAM TUESDAY 28.09.04 Lefthand, Galloping Track

4847 **4.40 Letheby & Christopher Maiden Stakes 3yo+ (D3)**
£4986 £1534 £767 **1m54y rnd** **Good/Firm** **Inapplicable** Centre

3973 **BABOOSH 44** [4] J R Fanshawe 3-8-9 L Dettori 11/4: 2-21: Trkd ldrs, rdn & led well ins last: op 13/8: 6 wk abs: eff at 1m on fast & gd/soft grnd: goes well fresh: see 3973. **79**
4407 **THISTLE 22** [1] J H M Gosden 3-9-0 (76) J Fortune 11/4: 0222: Dwelt, sn led till well ins last: see 4407. 1½ **80**
2907 **ADMIRAL COMPTON 88** [10] E F Vaughan 3-9-0 (77) K Fallon 11/8 FAV: 0-223: Held up, rdn & hdwy when short of room 2f out, not pace to chall ins last: clr of rem: well bckd, op 2/1: closer to front pair without interference: 12 wk abs: see 2907 & 2378. 2 **76**
4485 **LYNS RESOLUTION 19** [8] D Burchell 4-9-4 R Price 200/1: 04: Prom, no extra over 1f out: see 4485. 5 **67**
1810 **EVA JEAN 134** [7]3-8-9 R L Moore 20/1: 0-05: b f Singspiel - Go For Red (Thatching) Mid-div, no impress fnl 2f, abs: unplcd sole '03 start (rtd 42, mdn). 1¼ **59**
4649 **CIRRIOUS 11** [5]3-8-9 F P Ferris(3) 40/1: 06: Dwelt, sn handy, btn over 1f out. nk **58**
4561 **SPEED RACER 15** [2]3-8-9 (45) Kim Tinkler 66/1: 0503637: Chsd ldrs, struggling fnl 2f: needs sellers. ¾ **57$**
4414 **MOON SPINNER 22** [11]7-8-13 S Drowne 66/1: 08: Dwelt, sn struggling, drpd in trip. 2½ **52**
3828 **RABBIT 50** [3]3-8-9 S Righton 100/1: 09: b f Muhtarram - Ninia (Affirmed) Chsd ldrs early, hung left & btn 2f out, abs. nk **51**
4586 **NOPLEAZINU 14** [9]4-8-13 Joanna Badger 200/1: 50: 10th: Slow away & al rear, longer trip. ½ **50**
4578 **SHES A FOX 14** [12]3-8-9 A Culhane 150/1: 0-00: 11th: Unruly start, dwelt, al rear. 1¾ **47**
4315 **CONSTRUCTOR 27** [13]3-9-0 D Sweeney 66/1: 0000: 12th: Unruly stalls, bhd halfway, drpd in trip. 6 **42**
4630 **SILLOTH SPIRIT 12** [6]4-9-4 N Pollard 250/1: 040: 13th: Dwelt & sn bhd. 8 **29**
13 Ran Time 1m 44.58 (5.18) Owned: Lord Halifax Trained: Newmarket

4848 **5.10 Betting With Ibetx Com Nursery Handicap Stakes 2yo 0-75 (E3)** **[79]**
£3949 £1215 £608 **1m1f213y** **Good/Firm** **Inapplicable** Inside

4356 **PENALTY KICK 25** [12] N A Callaghan 2-9-3 (68) K Fallon 9/2 FAV: 0601: Trkd ldrs, briefly rdn & qckned to lead over 1f out, styd on strongly under hand riding, eased cl-home, val 3L+: h'cap bow: blnks omitted & much imprvd: apprec step up to 10f, 12f+ likely to suit: acts on fast grnd & a gall trk: decisive wnr, keep on side. **80+**
4410 **FLYING PASS 22** [4] D J S ffrench Davis 2-9-7 (72) T Quinn 11/1: 0225642: Held up, styd on for press fnl 2f, no threat to wnr: styd longer 10f trip well: see 4410, 3330. 1½ **79**
4410* **CLINET 22** [14] P M Phelan 2-9-4 (69) C Catlin 10/1: 2050013: Rear, switched & styd on for press ins last, not pace to chall: styd longer 10f trip, remains on the upgrade: see 4410 (1m). shd **76**
4444 **HIDDEN CHANCE 21** [7] R Hannon 2-9-2 (67) R Hughes 11/1: 01004: Handy & led 3f out, hdd over 1f out & no extra: styd longer 10f trip: acts on fast & gd grnd: see 3381. ½ **73**
4325 **CAVA BIEN 27** [8]2-9-5 (70) M Fenton 33/1: 03305: Held up in tch, lost place 4f out, switched wide & kept on late for press, no threat: styd longer 10f trip: see 3559 & 2810 (7f). shd **76**
4753 **PATXARAN 5** [6]2-9-1 (66) Rory Moore(5) 9/1: 054636: Chsd ldrs halfway, hung left & no impress over 1f out: qck reapp: longer 10f trip may yet suit: see 4753 & 4285 (1m). 1½ **70**
4480 **CELESTIAL ARC 19** [16]2-9-3 (68) R L Moore 8/1: 30007: Rear, late gains for press, nrst fin: longer trip. 1¼ **70**
4635 **BONGOALI 12** [1]2-8-12 (63) S Hitchcott 14/1: 452508: Held up in tch, not pace to chall: see 4410. 1¼ **63**
4296 **YOU FOUND ME 29** [2]2-9-2 (67) E Ahern 15/2: 0639: Mid-div, onepace for press when short of room 2f out, h'cap bow & longer trip: see 4296. ¾ **66**
3425 **DANCERS SERENADE 66** [9]2-9-5 (70) P Hanagan 66/1: 3500: 10th: Rear, little prog for press, abs. 1 **68**
4648 **SILSONG 11** [5]2-9-0 (65) R Smith 33/1: 5000: 11th: Chsd ldrs, btn over 1f out, h'cap bow. hd **62**
4632* **LORNA DUNE 12** [11]2-9-1 VIS (66) D Sweeney 20/1: 6060310: 12th: Chsd ldrs, rdn & ch over 1f out, fdd: first time visor: btr 4632 (1m, sell h'cap, g/s). 1 **62**
4444 **SHAHEER 21** [15]2-9-6 (71) J Fortune 5/1: 62060: 13th: Chsd ldrs, rdn & btn over 2f out. 1¾ **65**
4558 **LUNAR SKY 15** [10]2-9-7 (72) S Sanders 12/1: 0640: 14th: Chsd ldrs 3f out, sn hung left & btn. nk **65**
4204 **COMICAL ERRORS 32** [3]2-9-5 (70) G Faulkner 28/1: 0450: 15th: Dwelt, bhd, nvr a factor: h'cap bow. ½ **62**
4518 **SCORPIO SALLY 17** [13]2-8-12 (63) A Culhane 66/1: 056550: 16th: Led till 3f out, sn btn, longer trip. 8 **43**
16 Ran Time 2m 12.71 (10.41) Owned: John Livock Bloodstock Limited Trained: Newmarket

4849 **5.40 Back Or Lay With Ibetx Com Handicap Stakes 3yo+ 56-70 (E3)** **[77]**
£4196 £1291 £646 **1m1f213y** **Good/Firm** **Inapplicable** Inside

4473 **KIRKHAM ABBEY 19** [8] M A Jarvis 4-9-6 (69) K Darley 10/1: 3265101: Held up in tch, rdn & hdwy/hung left over 1f out, led ins last, drvn out: op 12/1: eff at 8.5f, stays 12f, prob suited by 10f: acts on firm, fast & fibresand, any trk: tough, progressive profile: see 3695, 2433 & 1895. **77**
4182 **PLANTERS PUNCH 33** [3] R Hannon 3-8-13 (68) K Fallon 11/2: 0100032: Trkd ldr, rdn & led 2f out, hdd ins last & not pace of wnr cl-home: see 4182, 2135. ¾ **74**
4293 **FACTUAL LAD 29** [6] B R Millman 6-9-7 (70) G Baker 28/1: 0010003: Chsd ldrs, styd on for press. ¾ **75**
4539 **BARTON SANDS 16** [2] Andrew Reid 7-9-6 t (69) S Drowne 16/1: 00-11244: Rear, late gains for press. hd **73**
4623 **CHAMPION LION 12** [4]5-9-4 (67) S Hitchcott 7/2 FAV: 0506335: Held up, hdwy when short of room over 1f out, styd on ins last, no threat: bckd, op 9/2: closer with a clr run: well h'capped: see 4623. hd **70+**
4589 **KIND EMPEROR 14** [9]7-9-1 (64) A Mackay 12/1: 50-04026: Led 1m, btn ins last: btr 4589. 1 **66**
4364 **SAHAAT 25** [16]6-9-2 (65) R Thomas(3) 40/1: 0250467: Keen & prom, onepace fnl 2f: see 4124. ½ **66**
4538 **SIR HAYDN 16** [10]4-8-13 vis (62) L Dettori 12/1: 0530008: Held up, eff over 2f out, no impress: op 10/1. 1 **62**
4515 **MARKET AVENUE 17** [7]5-9-0 (63) P Hanagan 9/2: 0505109: In tch, eff 3f out, no extra when hmpd over 1f out: op 7/2: btr 4406. 1½ **61**
4589 **PIRI PIRI 14** [12]4-9-4 (67) S Whitworth 10/1: 3032000: 10th: Dwelt, rear, little prog: btr 3785. 3 **60**
3785 **DARAB 52** [1]4-9-0 p (63) E Ahern 100/1: 13300-00: 11th: Chsd ldrs, lost place from 4f out: abs, chkpcs. ¾ **55**
4415 **ONCE 22** [14]4-9-2 bl (65) S W Kelly 66/1: 0-300000: 12th: Pushed along towards rear: 'lost action'. 1 **56**
4406 **DERWENT 22** [15]5-8-13 vis (62) S Sanders 9/1: 0466030: 13th: Held up wide, no impress fnl 2f. shd **53**
4274 **Caroubier 29** [11]4-9-3 (66) T E Durcan 40/1:0 493 **Big Bertha 244** [5]6-9-4 (67) M Fenton 33/1:0
15 Ran Time 2m 09.78(7.48) Owned: Mr P D Savill Trained: Newmarket

Official Going Good/Soft (Good Places)

4850
2.30 Axminster Carpets Apprentice Handicap Stakes 3yo+ 56-70 (E3)
£3951 £1216 £608 1m1f198y Good 49 -04 Slow Inside
[82]

4388 **AMERICAN DUKE 25** [11] B J Meehan 3-8-11 (65) D Fox 10/1: 0-002051: Led/dsptd lead, went on over 1f out, sn rdn clr, eased cl-home, readily: op 8/1: first win: suited by 10f on firm, fast & gd grnd, handles a sharp/turning of gall trk: decisive success, old follow up: see 3690, 2619. **74**

4456 **RANI TWO 22** [17] W R Muir 5-9-7 (69) N Chalmers 8/1: 6544022: Chsd ldrs 4f out, kept on for press but no ch with wnr bef dist: confirmed improvement of 4456. 5 **70**

4327 **DICKIE DEADEYE 28** [10] G B Balding 7-9-7 (69) Frances Harper(10) 12/1: 3113403: Led/dsptd lead 6f, no extra fnl 2f: see 3222. nk **69**

3733 **CRITICAL STAGE 55** [16] J D Frost 5-8-13 (61) M Halford(5) 14/1: 5-313064: Rear, kept on late for press, nrst fin: jumps fit: likes Southwell: see 595 (AW). nk **60**

4456 **BLUEGRASS BOY 22** [6]4-9-1 (63) P Gallagher(3) 14/1: 0003105: Bhd when hmpd 4f out, late gains. 1¼ **60**

4609 **COMPETITOR 14** [8]3-8-9 P (63) A Quinn 25/1: 0-200506: Chsd ldrs, no impress fnl 2f: chkpcs. ½ **59**

4589 **BILLY BATHWICK 15** [2]7-8-10 (58) Liam Jones(5) 33/1: 3105007: Handy & led over 4f out till over 1f out. ¾ **53**

4111 **ROLLSWOOD 39** [7]4-9-0 (62) M Savage 14/1: 5668: Mid-div, rdn & nvr able to threaten, h'cap bow. 1¼ **55**

4456* **SMOOTHIE 22** [18]6-8-12 p (60) C Haddon(3) 9/1: 04-06019: Dwelt, rear, only mod prog wide: btr 4456. ¾ **52**

4222 **FARRIERS CHARM 32** [15]3-8-12 (66) N De Souza 10/1: 4-100150: 10th: Chsd ldrs & ch 2f out, wknd. 1¾ **56**

4589 **BLAZING THE TRAIL 15** [13]4-8-13 (61) K May(5) 7/1 FAV: 3230660: 11th: Mid-div, no impress fnl 3f. ¾ **50**

4033 **SECRET JEWEL 42** [12]4-9-5 P (67) M Lawson 50/1: 0/0-60500: 12th: Dwelt & bhd, hmpd over 4f out, no impress, ld wk abs, cheek pieces. 1½ **54**

4456 **KERNEL DOWERY 22** [14]4-9-0 e (62) M Coumbe(8) 14/1: 1100450: 13th: Chsd ldrs, struggling fnl 2f. 1¼ **47**

4601 **KYTHIA 14** [4]3-8-13 (67) T Block(5) 20/1: 4320600: 14th: Mid-div halfway, sn struggling: btr 4274. 2 **49**

4650 **MILK AND SULTANA 12** [1]4-9-0 (62) Dean Williams(5) 10/1: 0241140: 15th: Al rear: much btr 4515. 5 **37**

4609 **UNSUITED 14** [9]5-9-6 (68) Natalia Gemelova(3) 12/1: 4111300: 16th: Al bhd: btr 2680. 8 **33**

4623 **Tarawan 1** [5]8-9-5 vis(67) R J Killoran(8) 33/1:0

4542 **Kelseas Kolby 17** [3]4-8-9 (57) Kristin Stubbs(3) 33/1:0

18 Ran Time 2m 09.78 (5.28) Owned: Grays Jaye & Connolly Trained: Upper Lambourn

---

4851
3.00 E B F /Subscribe To Racing Uk On 08700 860432 Maiden Stakes Div 1 2yo (D2)
£5805 £1786 £893 1m str Good 49 -10 Slow Far Side

4712 **THE COMPOSER 9** [13] M Blanshard 2-9-0 K Fallon 7/4 FAV: 41: Chsd ldrs halfway, eff to chall from 2f out & styd on for press to lead well ins last: confirmed debut promise: eff at 1m: acts on fast & gd grnd, stiff/easy trk: looks potentially useful & should relish further: see 4712. **85**

4576 **WOTCHALIKE 15** [8] D R C Elsworth 2-9-0 (79) T Quinn 3/1: 5022: Handy & led over 3f out, sn strongly prsd, hdd well ins last & no extra: rest well covered: stays 1m: acts on gd & soft: win a race. ½ **83**

PLEA BARGAIN 0 [15] J H M Gosden 2-9-0 R Havlin 20/1: 3: b c Machiavellian - Time Saved (Green Desert): Pushed along in tch, switched & kept on eyecatchingly fnl 2f, no threat: 425,000gns Feb first foal, dam a 10f scorer: eff at 1m, shapes as if mid-dists will suit: acts on gd & a stiff/gall trk: clr of rem, will improve. 2½ **78+**

2618 **MISTER ELEGANT 100** [14] J L Spearing 2-9-0 S Whitworth 50/1: 04: b c Fraam - Risky Valentine (Risky Me): Mid-div, prog over 2f out, sn no impress: 3 month abs: cheaply by Mar first foal: dam 5/6f wnr. 5 **69**

4664 **ROYAL MOUGINS 11** [7]2-9-0 S Drowne 15/2: 055: Slow away, held up, late prog under hand riding: bred to apprec this longer 1m trip: see 4664. shd **69**

MT DESERT 0 [11]2-9-0 J Fortune 10/1: 6: b c Rainbow Quest - Chief Bee (Chief's Crown): Slow away, in tch, no impress fnl 2f, stablemate of 3rd: 30,000gns Jan foal, half-brother to smart stayer Beekeeper, also a 7f juv & 10f mdn wnr, dam a 9/14f scorer: sure to relish mid-dists & shld improve gvn time. 3½ **62**

4703 **OAKLEY ABSOLUTE 9** [2]2-9-0 Dane O'Neill 66/1: 07: Led till over 3f out, rdn & fdd. 1 **60**

MARHABA MILLION 0 [3]2-9-0 S Hitchcott 20/1: 8: Chsd ldrs, no impress fnl 2f. 3½ **53**

PALACE WALK 0 [1]2-9-0 Martin Dwyer 20/1: 9: V slow away & nvr a factor. ½ **52**

4576 **BACKSTREET LAD 15** [10]2-9-0 G Baker 50/1: 000: 10th: Al rear & no impression. nk **51**

4356 **SILVER SONG 26** [9]2-9-0 I Mongan 66/1: 00: 11th: Mid-div, no impression fnl 2f. nk **50**

BARBIROLLI 0 [5]2-9-0 T R L Moore 12/1: 0: 12th: Dwelt, al rear, op 9/1, t.o. 1¾ **47**

EMERALD DANCER 0 [12]2-8-9 M Fenton 25/1: 0: 13th: Sn bhd, nvr factor. 5 **33**

4710 **SMART DAWN 9** [6]2-8-9 P Hanagan 100/1: 000: 14th: Mid-div, struggling rear halfway. 7 **21**

4355 **NIGHT GUEST 26** [4]2-9-0 P Dobbs 66/1: 000: 15th: Al bhd. 9 **10**

15 Ran Time 1m 43.85 (4.75) Owned: Mrs C J Ward Trained: Upper Lambourn

---

4852
3.30 E B F /Subscribe To Racing Uk On 08700 860432 Maiden Stakes Div 2 2yo (D2)
£5785 £1780 £890 1m str Good 49 -09 Slow Far Side

4356 **NIGHT HOUR 26** [3] M P Tregoning 2-9-0 Martin Dwyer 3/1: 41: Trk ldr, chall 3f out, led over 2f out, rdn & styd on strongly to assert nr fin: confirmed debut promise: eff at 1m on fast & gd grnd, easy or stiff/gall trk: sure to relish further & shld prove useful: see 4356. **89**

TOP GEAR 0 [10] D R C Elsworth 2-9-0 T Quinn 10/1: 2: b c Robellino - Bundle (Cadeaux Genereux): Slow away, rear, stdy hdwy fnl 3f, nrst fin : op 12/1: 30,000gns Mar first foal, dam unrcd: stays 1m, 10f will suit: handles gd: fine start, improve & win sn. 1½ **85+**

4677 **TOP THE CHARTS 11** [8] R Hannon 2-9-0 R L Moore 11/4: 443: Led/dsptd lead 6f, no extra well ins last: nicely bckd, op 7/2: stays 1m: now equals for h'caps, shld find a race: see 4677 & 4190. shd **85**

BUREAUCRAT 0 [5] J H M Gosden 2-9-0 R Havlin 50/1: 4: b c Machiavellian - Lajna (Be My Guest): Dwelt, rear, rdn & styd on from over 1f out, not able to chall: Mar foal, half-brother to sev wnrs at up to 10f, dam unplcd juv: stays a stiff 1m & shld get further: pleasing start, rate higher. ¾ **84**

4264 **SUBYAN DREAMS 31** [14]2-8-9 (95) K Fallon 9/4 FAV: 53305: Keen chasing ldrs, chall over 2f out, sn edged right & no impress when eased cl-home: nicely bckd & clr of rem but btr 3919 (7f, comb stks). 2½ **74**

4355 **INDIAN PIPE DREAM 26** [15]2-9-0 P Dobbs 10/1: 06: Rear, late hdwy under hand ride: clr rem. 6 **68**

4522 **HONOUR HIGH 18** [9]2-9-0 I Mongan 50/1: 07: gr g Cloudings - Meant To Be (Morston): Keen, sn towards rear, mod prog: Feb foal, half-brother to a dual hdles wnr, dam a dual 12f wnr & plcd at 14f. 8 **54**

4078 **VOIR DIRE 40** [7]2-9-0 N Pollard 66/1: 0008: Rear, sn pushed along & only mod prog, abs. 6 **42**

3582 **KRISTINOR 61** [12]2-9-0 M Fenton 7/1: 69: Keen & chsd ldrs till over 2f out, fin distressed, abs. *4* **34**
4069 **ONEIRO WAY 40** [11]2-9-0 E Ahern 50/1: 00: 10th: Chsd ldrs 5f, abs, longer trip. *4* **26**
4511 **TAVALU 18** [1]2-9-0 S Drowne 20/1: 60: 11th: Dwelt, sn chsd ldrs, wknd 3f out, longer trip. *1½* **23**
4704 **FLOWER SEEKER 9** [2]2-8-9 P Hanagan 100/1: 000: 12th: Prom early, sn bhd, longer trip. *3½* **11**
4069 **SOUTH OTHE BORDER 40** [13]2-9-0 G Carter 100/1: 0000: 13th: Al bhd, 6 wk abs & longer trip. *2½* **11**
4296 **GARANCE 30** [4]2-8-9 Dane O'Neill 66/1: 0000: 14th: Keen, sn struggling rear. *8* **0**
14 Ran Time 1m 43.76 (4.66) Owned: Greenbay Stables Ltd Trained: Lambourn

4853

4.00 Portway E B F Novice Stakes 2yo (D2)
£5668 £1744 £872 **7f str** **Good 49** **-20 Slow** Far Side

4390 **SUDDEN DISMISSAL 25** [8] G A Butler 2-9-2 (95) P Hanagan 5/2 JT FAV: 4101: Chsd ldrs, qcknd & led **95**
over 1f out, rdn & styd on strongly: well bckd: eff at 6f, imprvd for step up to 7f today: acts on gd: useful.
3975* **SANT JORDI 44** [7] B J Meehan 2-9-5 (80) J F McDonald(3) 5/1: 312: Led till over 1f out, kept on, *1¾* **94**
not pace of wnr: 6 wk abs & styd longer 7f trip well: acts on fast, gd & polytrack: useful: see 3975.
4416 **NOTNOWCATO 23** [3] Sir Michael Stoute 2-8-12 K Fallon 5/2 JT FAV: 23: Chsd ldrs, drvn & kept on *1½* **84**
onepace: nicely bckd tho' op 2/1: handles fast & gd grnd: see 4416.
4576* **PALATINATE 15** [9] H Candy 2-9-2 (80) Dane O'Neill 8/1: 4314: Dwelt, held up in tch, switched & *1½* **85**
kept on fnl 2f, nvr pace to chall: see 4576.
4540 **AVIATION 17** [5]2-8-12 (78) R L Moore 14/1: 0355: Mid-div, kept on onepace: stays 7f & rtn to *½* **80**
mdn company wld suit: acts on firm & gd grnd: see 4385.
3927 **FAIRMILE 47** [2]2-8-12 E Ahern 5/1: 336: Keen early, trkd ldrs, outpcd from dist: abs. *3* **74**
4416 **COMPTON QUAY 23** [6]2-8-12 J D Smith 33/1: 67: ch c Compton Place - Roonah Quay (Soviet Lad) *3* **68**
Keen, mid-div, no impress fnl 2f: Mar foal, half-brother to a 5f juv wnr, dam unplcd as a 3yo.
4575 **FINAL PROMISE 15** [11]2-8-12 S Carson 100/1: 08: b c Lujain - Unerring (Unfuwain) Prom, btn 2f *1* **66**
out: cheaply bght Apr foal, dam unrcd half-sister to sev wnrs incl a multiple 2yo French wnr.
4576 **MISTER TROUBRIDGE 15** [12]2-8-12 S Drowne 66/1: 09: ch c Mister Baileys - So True (So Blessed) *5* **57**
Al rear: May foal, half-brother to a 1m 3/4yo wnr Bomb Alaska, also 6f wnr Sabrina Brown: dam plcd at 12f.
4483 **DESERT MOONBEAM 20** [10]2-8-7 N Pollard 100/1: 600: 10th: Al bhd. *nk* **51**
4443 **APRIL SHANNON 22** [4]2-8-7 Natalia Gemelova(7) 100/1: 00: 11th: Chsd ldrs till halfway, sn bhd. *12* **30**
11 Ran Time 1m 30.30 (4.8) Owned: The Schtum Partnership Trained: Blewbury

4854

4.30 Averti Conditions Stakes 2yo (C1)
£9831 £3729 £1865 **6f str** **Good 49** **+04 Fast** Far Side

4471* **YAJBILL 20** [2] M R Channon 2-9-1 vis (95) K Fallon 5/2: 2322111: Dwelt, sn led & pushed clr over **103**
3f out, rdn & al holding rival fnl 1f, eased cl-home, val 1L: bckd tho' op 7/4: gd juv time: completed hat-trick:
suited by forcing tactics: on fast & gd/soft grnd, stiff or sharp/undul trk: best in visor: useful & progressive.
4458 **CLARET AND AMBER 21** [5] R A Fahey 2-8-12 (97) P Hanagan 15/8 FAV: 3551152: Chsd ldrs, styd on *nk* **97**
for pressure to press wnr fnl 1f, al held: nicely bckd, rest well covered: rtn to 7f shld now suit: see 4458 & 4074.
4330 **MONTECITO 27** [3] R Hannon 2-8-7 P Dobbs 80/1: 003: b f Montjeu - Dancing Fire (Dayjur) Rear, *4* **80**
kept on late to take, nvr threat to front pair: 34,000gns Feb foal, dam unrcd daughter of a French 1,000gns wnr:
eff at 6f, handles gd grnd: imprvd eff, win a mdn.
4217* **ANGEL SPRINTS 32** [1] L G Cottrell 2-8-13 (90) A Daly 20/1: 336114: Led early, chsd wnr, no *nk* **85**
impress over 1f out: btr 4217 (made all).
4224 **MARCHING SONG 32** [6]2-9-1 (91) R L Moore 6/1: 3242125: Dwelt & rear, switched for eff 3f out, sn *3½* **76**
no impress: btr 4224 & 3722.
3975 **SOMETHING 44** [4]2-8-12 G Carter 11/4: 26: Chsd ldrs, wandered under press fnl 2f & no impress: *shd* **73**
6 wk abs: btr 3975 (fast, debut).
6 Ran Time 1m 14.82 (2.72) Owned: Sheikh Ahmed Al Maktoum Trained: West Ilsley

4855

5.00 Catisfield Hinton & Stud Handicap Stakes 3yo+ 71-85 (D2) **[95]**
£9516 £3610 £1805 **6f str** **Good 49** **+08 Fast** Far Side

4500 **GOODENOUGH MOVER 19** [10] J S King 8-8-13 (80) Hayley Turner(3) 33/1: 1152001: Cl-up & went on **92**
over 2f out, drvn & al holding rivals ins last: fast time: eff at 6/7f, stays 1m: acts on firm, soft & polytrack,
best dominating: v tough: see 2880, 2470 & 1723 (7f).
4713 **TOTALLY YOURS 9** [17] W R Muir 3-8-13 (82) E Ahern 66/1: 4050002: Chsd ldrs, styd on for press *1¾* **88**
ins last, nvr able to threaten: rtn to form: nicely bckd: see 2136.
4700 **OK PAL 9** [4] T G Mills 4-9-0 (81) G Carter 25/1: 0606123: Led till over 2f out, kept on but no *hd* **86**
extra ins last: stays 6f, rtn to 5f could suit: see 4700 & 4605 (clmr, made all).
4747 **KINGSCROSS 7** [16] M Blanshard 6-8-13 (80) K Fallon 9/1: 0502264: Rear, hdwy when short of room *hd* **84+**
over 1f out till ins last: gone v close with clr run: see 4350, 4184 & 1523.
4747 **DANEHILL STROLLER 7** [18]4-8-10 (77) M Fenton 20/1: 0400005: Rear, no room & switched over 1f *½* **79+**
out, switched & kept on well cl-home: poss unlucky, h'capped to win sn: see 2070.
4350 **CAUSTIC WIT 26** [11]6-9-3 p (84) S Drowne 25/1: 2200466: Chsd ldrs, onepace from dist: btr 4098 (5f). *hd* **85**
4747* **ENDLESS SUMMER 7** [20]7-9-1 (6ex) (82) P Doe 7/2 JT FAV: 4602117: Held up, hdwy 2f out, onepace. *½* **81**
4652 **FONTHILL ROAD 12** [12]4-9-1 (82) P Hanagan 7/2 JT FAV: 3221168: Mid-div, short of room 2f out, *1* **78**
rdn & kept on late: reportedly hung: just btr 4652 & 4229.
4652 **GOLDEN DIXIE 12** [15]5-8-11 (78) Martin Dwyer 25/1: 0255009: Chsd ldrs, no impress dist: btr 4005. *¾* **72**
4747 **NAJEEBON 7** [7]5-8-11 (78) S Hitchcott 11/1: 3000230: 10th: Rear, short of room 2f out, only mod prog. *1* **69**
4713 **BATHWICK BILL 9** [8]3-8-12 (81) G Baker 66/1: 0623000: 11th: Cl-up, btn dist: btr 2797. *2* **66**
3827 **PRESTO SHINKO 51** [19]3-9-0 (83) R L Moore 7/1: 6321340: 12th: Mid-div, no impress when bmpd & *1½* **63**
veered left ins last: gelded, abs.
4747 **CURRENCY 7** [1]7-8-10 (77) P Fitzsimons 25/1: 0521450: 13th: Rear, nvr a factor: btr 3966. *2½* **49**
4917*)**GREAT FOX 337** [9]3-8-10 T (79) R Price 33/1: 321-0: 14th: b c Foxhound - Good Enough (Simply *2* **45**
Great) Chsd ldrs, hung left & btn dist: t-strap on reapp, h'cap bow: won on fnl start '03 (lightly rcd, auct mdn):
eff at 6f, winning from at 5f: acts on fast grnd & a stiff/gall trk: showed a tendency to hang as a juv.
1 Oct'03 Redc 5g/f 82- F: 2 Oct'03 Newm 6g/f 81- D:
4747 **SWINBROOK 7** [3]3-8-11 (80) Dane O'Neill 40/1: 2-002100: 15th: Al outpcd rear, btr 2717 (firm). *½* **44**
4700 **LAW BREAKER 9** [14]6-9-4 (85) B Reilly(3) 25/1: 5200000: 16th: Mid-div, no impress fnl 2f. *3* **40**

SALISBURY   WEDNESDAY 29.09.04   Righthand, Galloping Track, Stiff Finish

4867} **AVENING 23** [5]4-9-0 BL t (81) P Dobbs 9/1: 0010420: 17th: br c Averti - Dependable (Formidable)   5   23
Chsd ldrs, struggling fnl 3f: blnks, new yard: recent rnr-up in a Chantilly h'cap, earlier won twice in France (J
Hammond): unpicd '03 for current yard (rtd 89, h'cap): eff at 5/6f on firm & gd/soft, handles hvy & any trk.
2 Sep'02 Sain 6g/s 98- : 1 Aug'02 Good 5g/f 93-84 C: 2 Jul'02 Bath 5g/f 92- D: 1 Jun'02 Leic 5g/f 87- F:
4713 **Big Bradford 9** [6]3-9-2 bl(85) D Kinsella 66/1:0   4446 **Taranaki 22** [2]6-9-4 (85) S Carson 18/1:0
19 Ran   Time 1m 14.58 (2.48)   Owned: D Goodenough Removals & Transport   Trained: Swindon

---

4856	**5.30 Sovereign Windows & Conservatories Handicap Stakes 3yo+ 56-70 (E3)**		**[84]**
	£4078 £1255 £627 **1m6f15y** **Good 49** -20 Slow Flag Start		

4512 **IRISH BLADE 18** [6] H Candy 3-8-13 (69) S Dweeney 12/1: 3000321: Chsd ldrs & led over 3f out, rdn   80+
clr fnl 2f, readily: eff at 14f/2m on fast & gd/soft grnd, prob any trk: most impressive today: lightly rcd &
progressive stayer, keep on side this autumn: see 4512 & 4235.
4589 **PERFECT PUNCH 15** [10] C F Wall 5-9-5 (65) S Drowne 50/1: 40-20002: Mid-div, styd on for press,   3½   70
no impress on wnr: styd longer 14f trip: imprvd effort: see 1777.
4361 **MAJESTIC VISION 26** [4] P W Harris 3-8-11 (67) R L Moore 8/1: 34-06253: Led till over 3f out, onepace.   1¼   70
3970 **PENNY STALL 45** [9] J L Dunlop 3-8-7 (63) T Quinn 11/1: 44-04264: Mid-div, styd on for press, nvr   1½   64
able to land blow: 6 wk abs: see 3275, 2905.
4274 **AONINCH 30** [20]4-9-1 (61) S Whitworth 25/1: 0262605: Held up, kept on onepace, nrst fin: see 3868.   1¼   60
4274 **SILVER PROPHET 30** [17]5-9-6 (66) G Baker 33/1: 5500156: Chsd ldrs, no impress fnl 2f: btr 4033.   3   61
4745 **NAWOW 7** [3]4-9-9 (69) K Fallon 11/4 FAV: 0356027: Held up, eff & hdwy 3f out, no prog fnl 2f: bckd.   2½   60
4601 **ARGENTUM 14** [7]3-8-3 (59) P Hanagan 15/2: 00-05128: Mid-div, no impress fnl 2f: btr 4601 & 4037.   1   49
4400 **TILLA 24** [8]4-9-9 (69) L Fletcher(3) 7/1: 6022659: Rear, mod prog: btr 3887.   1½   57
4120 **INNOCENT REBEL 38** [5]3-8-12 (68) E Ahern 25/1: 0430: 10th: Keen in mid-div, eff 3f out, sn btn.   shd   56
3688 **FLAMENCO BRIDE 56** [12]4-9-10 (70) Dane O'Neill 14/1: 500-0030: 11th: Mid-div, btn 2f out, abs.   hd   57
4033 **WESTERN 42** [16]4-9-0 (60) G Carter 25/1: 2000000: 12th: Rear & al bhd, 6 wk abs: likes polytrack.   3   43
4203 **SAXE COBURG 33** [1]7-8-10 (1oh) (55) A Daly 33/1: 5340460: 13th: Reluctant to race & al bhd: btr 4033.   hd   38
4276 **SNOWS RIDE 30** [13]4-9-0 (60) Martin Dwyer 9/1: 0000640: 14th: Mid-div, no ch fnl 2f: btr 4276.   ¾   41
4542} **SHUSH 364** [11]6-9-1 (61) S Hitchcott 50/1: 044120-0: 15th: b g Shambo - Abuzz (Absalom) Al   2½   38
rear, reapp: '03 AW h'cap & h'cap scorer: h'cap plcd '02 (rtd 69, also rtd 66a, AW h'cap, disapp in blnks): suited
by 10/12f, stays 13f: acts on fast, hvy & both AWs, likes Chepstow. 2 Sep'03 Newb 11.0g/f 62-59 D:
1 Aug'03 Chep 10.2g/f 62-55 E: 1 Mar'03 Ling 12ap 62a-56 E: 2 Feb'03 Wolv 12af 56a-53 F:
1 Sep'01 Chep 10.1g/f 73-70 D:
4235 **Blue Hills 32** [2]3-8-7 (63) R Miles(3) 100/1:0   4361 **Simonovski 26** [15]3-8-3 (59) P Doe 66/1:0
4584 **Hinode 15** [14]3-8-4 (60) N Pollard 50/1:0   4361 **San Hernando 26** [19]4-9-8 (68) M Fenton 14/1:0
19 Ran   Time 3m 07.60(9.6)   Owned: Thurloe Thoroughbreds V   Trained: Wantage

---

NOTTINGHAM   WEDNESDAY 29.09.04   Lefthand, Galloping Track

Official Going GOOD/FIRM

4857	**2.20 Ibetx Com - Life Is A Gamble Apprentice Selling Handicap Stakes 3yo 46-55 (G4)**		**[67]**
	£2666 £762 £381 **1m1f213y** **Good 52** -19 Slow Inside		

4791 **FIZZY LADY 4** [13] N E Berry 3-8-11 (50) Thomas Yeung(5) 8/1: 0002401: Rear, hdwy & hung left over   55
2f out, rdn to lead well ins fnl 1f: no bid: quick reapp: eff at 7f/10f on fast, gd/soft & fibresand, acts on a
sharp or gall trk: improved without t-strap, goes well in sell grade: back to form of 613.
4750 **SMART BOY PRINCE 7** [10] M J Attwater 3-9-0 (53) W Hogg(5) 25/1: 0300602: Led, hdd & no extra well   ½   57
ins fnl 1f: quick reapp: eff forcing the pace at 7f/10f: acts on gd, likes fibresand: back to form: see 486.
4791 **MISTER COMPLETELY 4** [8] J R Best 3-8-8 (47) L Keniry 9/2: 1601053: Chsd ldrs, hdwy & ev ch ins   1   49
fnl 1f, onepace nr fin: quick reapp: acts on firm, gd & polytrack: see 4113.
4671 **ZULETA 11** [9] J G M O'Shea 3-8-8 VIS (47) B Swarbrick(3) 4/1 FAV: 0062224: Cl-up, hung left over   hd   48
2f out, kept on ins fnl 1f: clr of rem: quick reapp: btr in sell div: continues in decent form: see 4671.
2790 **VALIANT AIR 93** [16]3-8-5 (4oh)bl (40) P Mulrennan 14/1: 5240045: Bhd, mod late gains: quick reapp.   3   40
4560 **ACCA LARENTIA 16** [15]3-8-6 (45) Lisa Jones 14/1: 0300656: Rear, hdwy/hung left 2f out, onepace.   nk   40
4671 **MYANNABANANA 11** [6]3-8-5 (4oh)vis (40) D Fentiman(5) 28/1: 0000007: Bhd, hdwy over 3f out, onepace   1   37
when hmpd over 1f out: see 95.
4698 **NAMED AT DINNER 9** [5]3-8-11 VIS (50) A Beech 20/1: 0000008: Chsd ldrs, no impress when hung left   2   40
over 1f out: tried a visor: see 4504.
4763 **LARAD 6** [2]3-8-7 bl (46) Laura Reynolds(7) 8/1: 1060659: Slow away in rear, mod late gains: op 11/1.   1   34
4698 **BULBERRY HILL 9** [1]3-8-6 (45) D Corby 10/1: 05500: 10th: Rear, nvr nr ldrs: see 4587.   nk   32
4665 **LORD GREYSTOKE 11** [11]3-8-6 BL (45) P Mathers(5) 66/1: 00-00000: 11th: Chsd ldrs, hung left over   hd   31
2f out, sn no impress: tried blnks: see 4366.
4507 **GRELE 18** [12]3-8-6 (45) Stephanie Hollinshead(5) 10/1: 0-056400: 12th: Rear, nvr a factor: see 3079.   7   20
4624 **REIGN OF FIRE 13** [14]3-8-9 VIS (48) Derek Nolan(5) 33/1: 46-00000: 13th: b f Perugino - White Heat   6   14
(Last Tycoon) Al bhd: mdn reapp both '03 starts (rtd 71): eff around 1m on fast & polytrack: tried a visor here.
2667 **LIVIA 98** [7]3-8-6 VIS (45) F P Ferris 40/1: 4060000: 14th: Handy, wknd over 3f out: tried a visor.   nk   10
4053 **BUCHANAN STREET 41** [4]3-8-6 bl t (45) T Eaves 20/1: 0662500: 15th: Slow away, nvr a factor: 6 wk abs. 8   0
4142 **PRINCE RENESIS 36** [3]3-8-9 (48) P Makin(3) 66/1: 00060: 16th: Al bhd: see 1539.   1   0
16 Ran   Time 2m 9.44 (7.14)   Owned: Leeway Group Limited   Trained: Earlswood

NOTTINGHAM WEDNESDAY 29.09.04 Lefthand, Galloping Track

4858 **2.50 City Life Magazine Novice Auction Stakes Fillies 2yo (F3)**
£3718 £1144 £572 **6f15y str** **Good 52** **-01 Slow** Stands side

4064 **ROCKBURST 41** [8] K R Burke 2-8-10 (75) Darren Williams 10/1: 521301: Handy, hdwy to lead over 3f out, rdn out ins fnl 1f: 6 wk abs, op 12/1: eff at 6f, tried 7f: acts on fast & gd, reportedly unsuited by soft: acts on gall trks: back to form on drop back to 6f: more races to be won at this trip: see 2178. **86**
4625 **SAMS SECRET 13** [2] J A Glover 2-8-6 F Norton 9/2: 232: Slow away, hdwy over 2f out, hung left over 1f out, kept on: clr of rem: acts on fast & gd: shown enough to find a race: see 4625. *1½* **75**
3825 **ENCANTO 51** [11] J S Moore 2-8-12 (82) J F Egan 9/2: 2221453: Chsd ldrs, hung left over 2f out, onepcd. *5* **66**
4455 **HEARTSONFIRE 22** [5] P W D'Arcy 2-8-2 (67) J Quinn 20/1: 3304004: Cl-up, wknd over 1f out. *2½* **48**
4466* **AMICA 21** [7]2-8-10 (82) S Sanders 15/8 FAV: 2215: Handy, wknd over 2f out: btr 4466 (mdn). *1¼* **52**
3915 **TANZANITE 47** [4]2-8-4 W Supple 66/1: 06: b f Revoque - Resume (Lahib) Chsd ldrs, wknd 2f out: 7 wk abs: Jan foal, cost E4,500: half sister to a wnr at 9f: dam a dual wnr over 12/16f. *2½* **38**
3509 **SPREE 64** [9]2-9-0 (92) R Hughes 7/2: 61007: Led till over 3f out, sn no extra: 9 wk abs. *7* **27**
4596 **DANETHORPE LADY 14** [10]2-8-4 Lisa Jones 150/1: 648: Cl-up, wknd over 2f out: see 4303. *hd* **16**
3600 **DANCING MOONLIGHT 60** [1]2-8-6 (35) B Swarbrick(5) 250/1: 60009: b f Danehill Dancer - Silver Moon (Environment Friend) Nvr a factor: 9 wk abs: Jan foal, cost 15,000 gns: half sister to a 1m wnr: dam unplcd. *3* **9**
SMALL TIME BLUES 0 [6]2-8-4 R Fitzpatrick 100/1: 0: 10th: b f Danetime - Barinia (Corvaro) Nvr a factor on debut: May foal, cost 9,800 gns: half sister to wnrs over 1m/2m. *25* **0**
10 Ran Time 1m 13.99 (3.19) Owned: Mrs Sally L Jones Trained: Leyburn

4859 **3.20 European Breeders Fund Maiden Stakes 2yo (D2)**
£5974 £1838 £919 **5f13y str** **Good 52** **+07 Fast** Stands side

ROCK DOVE 0 [9] Sir Mark Prescott 2-8-9 S Sanders 11/4 J FAV: 1: b f Danehill - Littlefeather (Indian Ridge) Slow away, sn handy, rdn ins fnl 1f, styd on to lead post on debut: nicely bckd: Mar 1st foal: dam smart sprinter: sire a top class sprinter/miler: eff at 5f, 6f will suit: acts on gd, gall trk: runs well fresh: fine start to racing, entitled to come on for this. **75**
4543 **DISGUISE 16** [12] B W Hills 2-9-0 T (78) R Hughes 11/4 J FAV: 5242: Prom, hdwy to lead 2f out, hdd post: bckd: eff at 5/6f: acts on fast & gd: tried a t-strap: must find a race: see 3473. *shd* **79**
4422 **VAGUE STAR 23** [1] R Ingram 2-9-0 N Day 66/1: 03: b c Soviet Star - Simova (Vaguely Noble) Chsd ldrs, hdwy & ev ch over 1f out, onepcd nr fin: 8,000 gns Apr foal: half brother to a 2yo wnr over 7f: dam plcd in France, sire a Gr1 scorer at 3/4 over 6f/1m: eff at 5f, will stay further: acts on gd: improved from debut. *1½* **74**
4307 **MALAIKA 29** [5] R Hollinshead 2-8-9 Stephanie Hollinshead(5) 20/1: 54: Trkd ldrs, onepcd ins fnl 1f: stays 5f on gd: imprvd from debut: see 4307. *¾* **67**
4409 **LITTLE WARNING 23** [16]2-8-9 J Quinn 25/1: 005: Rear, hdwy & edged left over 1f out, styd on well ins fnl 1f: stays 5f on gd: see 3962 (debut). *¾* **65**
4557 **MERCARI 16** [4]2-8-9 T Eaves(3) 50/1: 0006: ch f Bahamian Bounty - Aonach Mor (Anabaa) Chsd ldrs, onepcd over 1f out: Mar 1st foal: dam unrcd, sire top class 2yo over 6f: with G Moore. *½* **63**
4536 **PEEPTOE 17** [7]2-8-9 (72) L Dettori 3/1: 32547: Chsd ldrs, no impress fnl 1f. *1* **60**
4644 **ITALIAN TOUCH 12** [8]2-9-0 F Norton 50/1: 008: Cl-up till over 3f out, kept on again ins fnl 1f: 6f suit. *1* **62**
4599 **DISTINCTIVE MIND 14** [14]2-9-0 J F Egan 66/1: 009: Slow away, not a factor. *shd* **61**
4644 **LEIGHTON BUZZARD 12** [17]2-9-0 Thomas Yeung(5) 14/1: 00: 10th: Outpcd in rear, some late gains. *nk* **60**
4497 **ELMS SCHOOLBOY 19** [3]2-9-0 J Tate 66/1: 00: 11th: In tch, wknd after halfway. *2½* **52**
2911 **ANFIELD DREAM 89** [15]2-9-0 W Ryan 14/1: 630: 12th: Cl-up, wknd over 2f out: long abs. *½* **50**
3517 **KATIE KILLANE 63** [2]2-8-9 V Slattery 100/1: 000: 13th: Led & hung left, hdd 2f out, no extra. *½* **43**
CRUX 0 [11]2-9-0 P Mulrennan(3) 25/1: 0: 14th: Slow away, nvr a factor on debut. *2* **42**
WATERFRONT DANCER 0 [6]2-9-0 W Supple 20/1: 0: 15th: Slow away, nvr a factor on debut. *6* **24**
15 Ran Time 1m 0.76 (2.26) Owned: Sir Edmund Loder Trained: Newmarket

4860 **3.50 Eric Potter Clarkson Handicap Stakes 3yo+ 71-85 (D2)** **[90]**
£12125 £3731 £1865 **1m1f213y** **Good 52** **-07 Slow** Inside

4362 **HONORINE 26** [9] J W Payne 4-8-13 (75) J F Egan 33/1: 243-6051: Rear, hdwy over 2f out, hung left from over 1f out, drvn out to lead well ins fnl 1f: prev suited by 1m, relished this step up to 10f: acts on fast & gd, gall or easy trk: op to further improvement at this trip: see 2091. **85**
4453* **ONE SO MARVELLOUS 22** [2] L M Cumani 3-8-7 (75) O Urbina 8/1: 0012: Chsd ldrs, hdwy to lead 1f out, hdd well ins fnl 1f: h'cap bow: acts on fast & gd: lightly rcd & progressive: see 4453 (mdn). *1* **82**
4766* **STRAW BEAR 5** [4] Sir Mark Prescott 3-9-7 (6ex) (89) S Sanders 4/6 FAV: 1-235113: Rcd in 2nd, hdwy to lead over 2f out, hdd 1f out, sn onepcd: bckd under joint top weight, quick reapp: acts on fast, gd & fibresand, loves gd/soft: been busy, but another useful run: shade btr 4766 (gd/soft). *nk* **95**
4467 **NUNKI 21** [13] H R A Cecil 3-9-3 VIS (85) W Ryan 33/1: 31004: Led over 7f, no extra when hmpd nr fin: back to form in a visor: see 1922 (mdn). *1¼* **88**
4473 **RYANS FUTURE 20** [16]4-8-13 (75) L Dettori 8/1: 0052045: Rear, hdwy 6f out, onepace over 1f out. *1½* **77**
3683* **CLIPPERDOWN 56** [5]3-8-6 (74) N Callan 16/1: 3016: Chsd ldrs, onepcd over 1f out: 8 wk abs. *½* **75**
4742 **DOCTORED 7** [1]3-8-7 bl (75) F P Ferris(3) 25/1: 1306047: Chsd ldrs, onepcd over 1f out: quick reapp. *shd* **75**
4473 **REALISM 20** [11]4-9-6 (82) Darren Williams 33/1: 1101568: Mid-div & keen, outpcd over 2f out, late gains. *½* **81**
519 **STAR OF NORMANDIE 242** [10]5-9-3 (79) A McCarthy 100/1: 2112-009: Rear, nvr a factor: long abs. *½* **77**
2972 **DONT SIOUX ME 86** [7]6-9-4 (80) Lisa Jones 100/1: 0/00/4-050: 10th: Slow away in rear, nvr nr ldrs. *1¾* **75**
4614 **OLIVIA ROSE 14** [3]5-9-7 (83) J Quinn 33/1: 1413000: 11th: Rear, hdwy over 2f out, sn edged left, btn. *shd* **77**
4613 **LIQUID FORM 14** [12]4-8-11 (73) R Hughes 10/1: 0006050: 12th: Cl-up, wknd over 2f out: see 2185. *3½* **62**
4629 **HUMID CLIMATE 13** [14]4-9-2 (78) T Eaves(3) 50/1: 0/130-000: 13th: Al bhd: see 4073. *nk* **66**
4500 **GEMS BOND 19** [6]4-8-11 (73) Derek Nolan(7) 33/1: 0000050: 14th: Slow away in rear, hdwy over 3f out, no impress over 1f out: see 3898. *4* **55**
ZALAM 28 [15]4-8-12 (74) P Bradley 50/1: 05-00: 15th: b g Alzao - Zarlana (Darshaan) Al bhd: Brit bow: mdn unplcd sole earlier '04 start in native Ireland (10f, gd): mdn unplcd both '03 starts (1m, gd & soft). *2½* **52**
15 Ran Time 2m 8.23 (5.93) Owned: Mrs R A C Vigors Trained: Newmarket

NOTTINGHAM   WEDNESDAY 29.09.04   Lefthand, Galloping Track

4861
4.20 Racing Uk On Channel 432 Maiden Stakes 3yo+   (D3)
£5064 £1558 £779   **1m1f213y**   **Good 52**   **-16 Slow**   Inside

4501 **BARATHEA BLUE 19** [5] P W Harris 3-9-0 S Sanders 7/4 FAV: 521: Chsd ldrs, hdwy to lead 3f out,   67
hdd over 1f out, rallied to lead 1f out, hard drvn ins fnl 1f to hold on: bckd: eff at 10f on gd, acts on a gall
trk: game eff, imprvd for prev experience: see 3243 (debut).

4612 **SKIBEREEN 14** [15] Mrs A M Thorpe 4-9-6 (57) J F Egan 33/1: 3500022: Rear, hdwy & hung left from   ¾   64$
over 2f out, kept on: imprvd run for new yard (prev with I McInnes): see 1006 & 476.

4668 **ZONIC BOOM 11** [4] J R Fanshawe 4-9-6 (61) O Urbina 11/2: 00-5303: Chsd ldrs, hdwy & ev ch 1f   hd   63
out, kept on: stays 10f: see 1385.

4649 **ALL BLUE 12** [12] Saeed bin Suroor 3-9-0 t L Dettori 15/8: 44: Chsd ldrs, hdwy to lead over 1f   hd   62
out to 1f out, no extra: stays 10f on gd, prob acts on gd/soft: see 4649.

4111 **MOUFTARI 39** [1]3-9-0 BL (80) M Hills 8/1: 0-545235: Sn led to 3f out, no extra fnl 1f: tried   2   59
blnks: acts on fast, gd & polytrack: see 4111.

4421 **MY MICHELLE 23** [6]3-8-9 (57) F P Ferris(3) 33/1: 3-004546: In tch, outpcd over 3f out, kept on ins fnl 1f.   1¾   51

     FENDER 0 [2]3-9-0 BL R Hughes 16/1: 7: b c Rainbow Quest - Rockfest (Stage Door Johnny) In tch,   3   51
hdwy over 6f out, no impress 2f out on debut: tried blnks.

     CUMBRIAN KNIGHT 0 [11]6-9-6 T Eaves(3) 80/1: 8: b g Presenting - Crashrun (Crash Course) Slow   5   43
away in rear, nvr nr ldrs on Flat debut: long hdles abs: h'cap hdle unplcd sole 04/05 start (rtd 72h, eff at
2m1f/2m4f on gd & hvy, acts on any trk): with J Jefferson.

4671 **PARISI PRINCESS 11** [7]3-8-9 J Edmunds 150/1: 009: ch f Shaddad - Crambella (Red Sunset) Bhd,   ½   37
hdwy 4f out, sn no impress: dam a mdn: with G P Kelly.

4402 **IFTIKHAR 24** [13]5-9-6 (52) N Callan 50/1: 4-000400: 10th: Bhd, nvr nr ldrs.   2   39

     PILCA 577 [9]4-9-6 L Vickers 100/1: 0-0: 11th: Handy, wknd over 2f out on reapp.   7   28

     RAMBO BLUE 0 [14]4-9-6 W Supple 100/1: 0: 12th: Slow away in rear, nvr a factor on debut.   9   14

4762 **LITTLE MISS LILI 6** [10]3-8-9 A McCarthy 100/1: 00: 13th: Dwelt, nvr a factor: qck reapp.   dist   0

13 Ran   Time 2m 9.12 (6.82)   Owned: David & Elaine Long   Trained: Berkhamsted

4862
4.50 Fastest Growing Exchange Ibetx Com Handicap Stakes 3yo+ 56-70 (E3)
£4511 £1388 £694   **1m54y rnd**   **Good 52**   **+01 Fast**   Centre   [77]

4542 **SPIRITS AWAKENING 17** [1] J Akehurst 5-8-9 (58) F P Ferris(3) 11/2: 3242601: Made all, drvn & kept   67
on gamely to hold on ins fnl 1f: suited by 1m on firm & hvy, prob any trk: enjoyed forcing tactics.

4252 **DONT CALL ME DEREK 31** [10] S C Williams 3-8-12 (65) S Sanders 9/2 FAV: 0002132: Rear, hdwy over   ½   72
1f out, styd on: remains in gd form: see 4044.

4282 **GAY ROMANCE 30** [2] B W Hills 3-8-9 (62) M Hills 18/1: 00653: Chsd ldrs, hdwy & ev ch over 1f   nk   68
out, onepace nr fin: clr of rem: stays 1m on gd: gd eff: see 2659 (debut).

4542 **LITTLE ENGLANDER 17** [6] H Candy 4-8-8 (57) L Keniry(3) 16/1: 0051004: Rear, hdwy 1f out, kept on.   3½   56

4366* **ZAFARSHAH 26** [12]5-9-1 (64) B Swarbrick(5) 22/1: 3004015: Rear, hdwy over 3f out, not pace of ldrs.   hd   62

4674* **FASCINATION STREET 11** [7]3-8-12 (65) M Henry 12/1: 5023216: Chsd ldrs, onepcd over 1f out.   shd   62

4399 **GARDEN SOCIETY 24** [14]7-9-0 (63) F Norton 20/1: U06-0007: Bhd, hdwy 2f out, not pace to chall.   1¼   57

4438 **MISSION AFFIRMED 22** [3]3-8-8 (61) J Quinn 8/1: 0405238: Slow away, hdwy 4f out, wknd 1f out.   ¾   53

4832 **MISTER CLINTON 2** [8]7-8-12 (61) J F Egan 16/1: 2016009: Chsd ldrs, no impress: qk reapp.   nk   52

4398 **PHLUKE 24** [16]3-8-12 (65) Lisa Jones 33/1: 2040600: 10th: Handy, wknd over 1f out.   ¾   54

3846 **DAGOLA 50** [9]3-8-13 (66) R Smith 10/1: 0034240: 11th: Cl-up, no impress over 1f out.   nk   54

3542 **SCIENTIST 62** [13]3-9-2 (69) L Dettori 7/1: 5-003060: 12th: Rear, hdwy 3f out, no impress.   ½   56

4668 **ADOBE 11** [4]9-8-11 (60) P Mathers(5) 16/1: 4050000: 13th: Rear, hdwy 4f out, no impress 2f out.   2½   42

     KAYMICH PERFECTO 109 [15]4-9-0 (63) S Chin 100/1: 0132200: 14th: Al bhd: long abs.   ½   44

3579 **BLUE MARINER 61** [11]4-9-4 (67) N Callan 40/1: 0322000: 15th: Bhd, stumbled over 5f out, nvr a factor.   hd   47

4622 **MERDIFF 13** [17]5-8-11 (60) R Hughes 12/1: 1204200: 16th: Cl-up, no impress over 1f out.   4   32

4721 **CAYMAN CALYPSO 8** [5]3-8-11 (64) T Eaves(3) 100/1: 0622000: 17th: Rear, hdwy 3f out, wknd 2f out.   1½   33

17 Ran   Time 1m 43.5(4.1)   Owned: Canisbay Bloodstock   Trained: Epsom

NEWCASTLE   WEDNESDAY 29.09.04   Lefthand, Galloping, Stiff Track

Official Going Good/Firm

4863
2.10 Benfield Motors Renault Maiden Auction Stakes Div 1 2yo (F4)
£2961 £846 £423   **7f str**   **Firm 16**   **-17 Slow**   Centre

4519 **DAVY CROCKETT 18** [4] B Smart 2-8-8 (1ow) (67) D McGaffin 8/1: 005601: Cl-up far side, hdwy to   76
lead dist, drvn out to hold on: imprvd on 2nd start for current trainer & firm: game run: see 3544.

4163 **GRAND WELCOME 35** [7] C Tinkler 2-8-7 bl (71) S W Kelly 14/1: 00022: Led far side till dist,   hd   74
rallied ins last, just held: prob ran to form of 4163 & acts on firm & soft grnd: shld find a race.

4503 **PLENTY CRIED WOLF 18** [10] R A Fahey 2-8-10 (68) T Hamilton(3) 12/1: 00403: Led stands side trio,   shd   76
kept on fnl 1f, just held in a tight fin: ran to form of 4381 & shld find a small race.

4375 **ABSTRACT FOLLY 25** [6] J D Bethell 2-8-10 K McEvoy 7/2: 44: Cl-up, onepace fnl 2f: stays 7f on fm.   2   72

4381 **VANCOUVER GOLD 25** [5]2-8-5 Dale Gibson 2/1 FAV: 35: Handy far side, onepcd over 1f out: well   ¾   65
bckd: clrly btr expected after 4381 (in front of this 3rd).

4325 **LIABILITY 28** [2]2-8-2 Kim Tinkler 20/1: 066: In tch far side, wknd well over 1f out: see 3831.   8   46

     MAYNOOTH PRINCE [8]2-8-13 J Carroll 40/1: 7: b g Spectrum - Muffle (Sadler's Wells) Held up   4   49
far side, wknd 2f out: Feb foal, cost £20,000: bred to apprec 1m+ in time.

3831 **CONTINENTAL FLYER 51** [1]2-8-8 BL V Halliday 66/1: R8: b f Piccolo - Sunshine Coast (Posse)   1   42
Handy far side, wknd 2f out: 7 wk abs, ref to race at debut: Apr foal, cost 13,000gns: dam 7f wnr: tried blnks.

     SHOWTIME FAYE [11]2-8-3 (1ow) R Mullen 30/1: 9: Handy stands side, wknd 2f out.   3   31

2492 **FRAAMBUOYANT 105** [9]2-8-2 R Ffrench 100/1: 00: 10th: Handy, wknd over 2f out.   1½   27

     SERGEANT SHINKO [3]2-8-7 L Enstone 33/1: 0: 11th: Slow away & al bhd far side.   17   0

11 Ran   Time 1m 26.7 (2.6)   Owned: J M & Mrs E E Ranson   Trained: Thirsk

4864   **2.40 Benfield Motors Renault Maiden Auction Stakes Div 2 2yo** (F4)
£2954 £844 £422   **7f str**   **Firm 16**   **-27 Slow**   Centre

4591 **BRONZE DANCER 15** [5] G A Swinbank 2-8-7   R Winston 5/1: 0001: Held up, hdwy & short of room 2f 71
out, switched & styd on fnl 1f to lead cl-home, drvn out: imprvd run & clrly eff over a stiff 7f on firm grnd, 1m
shld suit: gd confidence boost: see 4171.
4557 **NEPAL 16** [8] T D Barron 2-8-5   D Mernagh 10/1: 62: In tch, hdwy to lead over 1f out, drvn ins   hd   68
last, collared cl-home: clr of rem: encouraging run & clrly stays a stiff 7f on firm grnd: shld find similar.
4250 **RUDAKI 31** [3] M G Quinlan 2-8-10   M Tebbutt 7/2: 043: Held up, hdwy 2f out, onepace fnl 1f: 3   67
stays 7f on firm: see 4250.
4271 **TAHLAL 30** [10] Mrs A Duffield 2-8-10 (63) A Culhane 9/1: 5004: Led after 1f till dist, no extra.   2½   62
4381 **SADIES STAR 25** [2]2-8-6 (1ow) S W Kelly 33/1: 05: Bhd, some late gains: see 4381.   1¼   55
2119 **AZA WISH 120** [9]2-8-2 (60) S Righton 14/1: 05006: In tch, wknd over 1f out: see 1458.   1   49
4552 **GEORDIE DANCER 16** [7]2-8-13 F Lynch 12/1: 057: Handy, wknd over 1f out: see 4343.   ¾   58
4617 **BLACKNYELLO BONNET 13** [1]2-8-8 K Darley 25/1: 08: b f Seeking The Gold - Salt It (Salt Lake)   ½   52
Cl-up, wknd over 1f out: Mar foal, cost $30,000: dam mid-dist wnr.
4602 **PAPARAAZI 14** [6]2-8-7 T Hamilton(3) 100/30 FAV: 59: b c Victory Note - Raazi (My Generation)   2½   46
Slow away & al bhd: well bckd: Feb foal, cost 3,200: dam plcd at 6f: btr 4602.
4401 **SEASON TICKET 24** [4]2-8-2 J Mackay 4/1: 0000: 10th: In tch, wknd 2f out.   5   31
10 Ran   Time 1m 27.4 (3.3)   Owned: Mr J Yates   Trained: Richmond

4865   **3.10 Reg Vardy Stoneygate Renault E B F Maiden Stakes 2yo** (D3)
£4557 £1402 £701   **6f str**   **Firm 16**   **-01 Slow**   Centre

4403 **CROSSPEACE 23** [13] M Johnston 2-9-0   R Ffrench 4/5 FAV: 21: Handy, hdwy to lead ins last, styd   85
on well, rdn out: hvly bckd: eff at 6f, 7f sure to suit: acts on firm & fast grnd: going the right way, type to
rate more highly & win more races: see 4403.
  DESERT CHIEF [12] Saeed bin Suroor 2-9-0   R Hills 5/2: 2: b c Green Desert - Oriental Fashion   1¾   79
(Marju) Handy, hdwy to lead over 1f out, rdn & hdd ins last, not pace of wnr: nicely bckd: Mar foal: half-brother
to a 6/7f juv wnr: acts on firm grnd: shld come on for this & win a mdn.
3755 **KOOL OVATION 54** [8] A Dickman 2-9-0   D Allan 25/1: 033: Cl-up, hdd over 1f out, onepace: 8 wk   2½   72
abs & eff at 6f on firm grnd: see 3755.
4436 **FLAXBY 22** [5] J D Bethell 2-9-0   J Carroll 100/1: 004: Chsd ldrs, onepace dist: btr run: see 4436.   3   63
4590 **MOSSMANN GORGE 15** [3]2-9-0   R Winston 40/1: 065: b g Lujain - North Pine (Import)   Bhd, some   nk   62
late gains, nvr dngrs: Apr foal, cost 9,000gns: half-brother to sev sprint wnrs: may do btr in h'caps.
4401 **NAVIGATION 24** [6]2-9-0 K McEvoy 25/1: 06: ch c Bahamian Bounty - Bridge Pool (First Trump) Led   ¾   60
to halfway, wknd 2f out: Apr foal, cost 7,000gns: half-brother to a 7f juv wnr: dam 5f scorer.
4344 **KAGGAMAGIC 27** [9]2-9-0 (65) S W Kelly 33/1: 54007: In tch, no impress over 1f out.   1½   56
4705 **DEVILS ISLAND 9** [10]2-9-0 J Mackay 14/1: 58: Slow away & al bhd: see 4705.   1¾   51
4557 **BRANSTON LILY 16** [11]2-8-9 A Culhane 10/1: 349: In tch, wknd 2f out: btr 376.   shd   45
  PEBBLE MILL [14]2-9-0 K Darley 12/1: 0: 10th: b c Cape Cross - Mill Path (Mill Reef)   Dwelt,   1¾   45
al bhd: stablemate of wnr: Mar foal, half-brother to wnrs over 6f/10f: bred to apprec 1m in time.
4617 Enborne Again 13 [7]2-9-0 G Parkin 66/1:0   Champagne Lujain [4]2-9-0 T Lucas 100/1:0
4590 Komreyev Star 15 [2]2-9-0 T Hamilton(3) 33/1:0   Cayman King [1]2-9-0 D Mernagh 100/1:0
14 Ran   Time 1m 12.35 (1.05)   Owned: Favourites Racing   Trained: Middleham

4866   **3.40 Renault Trafic E B F Maiden Stakes 2yo** (D3)
£4615 £1420 £710   **1m rnd**   **Firm 16**   **-02 Slow**   Inside

4351 **GLEN IDA 26** [11] M L W Bell 2-9-0   R Mullen 3/1: 321: Handy, hdwy to lead over 1f out, kept on,   91+
rdn out: stays 1m well on firm, handles gd/soft & stiff trks: useful, going the right wasy: see 4069.
4522 **TAMATAVE 18** [3] Saeed bin Suroor 2-9-0 t K McEvoy 5/1: 642: Set pace till over 1f out, rallied   ¾   88
ins last, just held: clr of rem: acts on firm grnd: looks sure to relish a step up in trip & shld be winning sn.
4608 **GOLDEN FURY 14** [2] J L Dunlop 2-9-0 (85) K Darley 6/4 FAV: 43423: Handy, onepace over 1f out: 5   78
hvly bckd: plcd again: see 4608 (gd).
4325 **GLOBE TREKKER 28** [8] James Moffatt 2-8-9   R Ffrench 12/1: 044: Handy, onepace dist: btr 4325.   1   71
4470 **CHASM 20** [5]2-9-0 R Hills 9/1: 35: In tch, wknd over 1f out: see 4470 (7f).   nk   75
  BLUE BAJAN [9]2-8-9 D Mernagh 14/1: 6: b c Montjeu - Gentle Thoughts (Darshaan)   Dwelt, hmpd   2½   70
after 1f, nvr a factor: Feb foal: dam styd 9f as a 2yo: bred for mid-dists.
  VOCATIVE [6]2-8-9 Rory Moore(5) 50/1: 7: gr f Acatenango - Vadinaxa (Linamix) Al bhd on debut: nk   64
Jan foal, cost 19,000gns: dam 10f wnr: bred to apprec 10f next term.
4325 **ARTIC FOX 28** [4]2-9-0 BL (52) R Winston 100/1: 50008: Held up, hung left & wknd dist: blnks.   3   63$
4756 **RED OPERA 6** [9]2-9-0 J Mackay 25/1: 09: Held up, wknd over 2f out.   8   47
  OUR WILDEST DREAMS [12]2-8-9 T Williams 100/1: 0: 10th: Al bhd.   1   40
4600 **TETRA SING 14** [1]2-8-9 G Faulkner 100/1: 000: 11th: Handy, wknd over 2f out.   2½   35
  SAKE [10]2-9-0 T A Culhane 100/1: 0: 12th: Al bhd: t-strap.   3½   33
12 Ran   Time 1m 41.91 (2.91)   Owned: Mr Andrew Buxton & Mr B J Warren   Trained: Newmarket

4867   **4.10 Renault Clio Handicap Stakes 3yo+ 56-70** (E3)
£3759 £1157 £578   **1m3y str**   **Firm 16**   **-08 Slow**   Centre   [72]

4554 **NEWCORP LAD 16** [16] Mrs G S Rees 4-9-1 P (59) A Culhane 8/1: 4424031: Made all stands side, clr   72
fnl 2f, easily: eff at 7f/1m on firm & hvy: improved for cheekpieces & front running.
3737 **INTAVAC BOY 55** [15] C W Thornton 3-8-9 (57) G Faulkner 20/1: 66402: ch g Emperor Fountain -   5   63
Altaia (Sicyos) Prom stands side, kept on fnl 1f but no ch with wnr: 8 wk abs: best eff to date on this step up to
1m: acts on firm grnd: clrly runs well fresh: see 2945 & 1639.

4554* **MOBANE FLYER 16** [13] R A Fahey 4-9-5 (63) T Hamilton(3) 5/1 JT FAV: 0063313: Chsd lds to stands side, kept on onepcd fnl 1f: nicely bckd: just btr 4554. *2½* **64**
4620 **SARRAAF 13** [19] J S Goldie 8-9-5 (63) V Halliday 16/1: 2034604: Chsd ldrs stands side, onepcd fnl 2f. *nk* **63**
4598 **APACHE POINT 14** [4]7-8-7 (51) Kim Tinkler 20/1: 3555505: Prom far side, led that group fnl 1f, no ch with stands side: first home on far side: rtn to 10f may suit: see 3325. *1½* **48+**
4520 **THE NUMBER 18** [3]3-9-2 (64) A Nicholls 16/1: 56-33526: Mid-div far side, styd on fnl 1f, no ch with stands side: btr than fin position suggests: see 4520. *hd* **60**
2322 **BEACON BLUE 112** [6]3-9-1 (63) K Darley 20/1: 5055-67: Rear far side, styd on late: long abs: big drop in trip & on the wrong side: see 2322. *shd* **59**
4554 **BOND MILLENNIUM 16** [1]6-9-4 (62) F Lynch 6/1: 455-0028: Rear far side, nrst fin: btr 4554. *1* **56**
4721 **DARK DAY BLUES 8** [20]3-8-11 (59) M Tebbutt 50/1: 6550009: Held up stands side, nvr dngrs. *½* **52**
4488 **PEPPER ROAD 20** [7]5-8-10 P (54) R Ffrench 5/1 JT FAV: 0012220: 10th: Prom far side, led that group 2f out till ins fnl 1f, wknd: nicely bckd, first time cheek pieces: on the wrong side, prev in fine form. *½* **46**
4592 **HULA BALLEW 15** [17]4-9-4 p (62) S W Kelly 12/1: 0155230: 11th: Switched far side, nvr ldrs: btr 4592. *2½* **49**
4621 **Showtime Annie 13** [5]3-9-6 (68) R Winston 12/1:0 4438 **Aragons Boy 22** [10]4-9-7 (65) D Allan 14/1:0
4008 **Ace Coming 43** [11]3-9-1 bl(63) J Mackay 33/1:0
4721 **Joshuas Gold 8** [8]3-8-9 vis(57) D Tudhope(5) 16/1:0
4408 **Lord Baskerville 23** [14]3-8-4 (52) D R McCabe 20/1:0 4438 **Washbrook 22** [2]3-8-9 (57) J Carroll 33/1:0
17 Ran Time 1m 38.96 (1.96) Owned: Red Rose Partnership Trained: Preston

4868

4.40 Renault Vans H B L B Handicap Stakes 3yo 56-70 (E3) **[73]**
£3480 £1071 £535 **2m19y** **Firm 16** **-12 Slow** Centre

3312* **PRINCESS KIOTTO 72** [11] T D Easterby 3-9-3 (62) D Allan 3/1 FAV: 00-52311: Mid-div, prog to lead 2f out, styd on strongly fnl 1f, drvn out: 10 wk abs: well bckd: eff at 12/14f, imprvd over 2m last twice: acts on gd, firm grnd & fibresand: clrly runs well fresh: thorough stayer who can complete hat-trick, see 3312. **71**
4340 **RESTART 27** [4] P C Haslam 3-8-13 (58) G Faulkner 20/1: 30-00102: Chsd ldrs, ev ch fnl 2f, not btn far: clr of rem: decent run, clrly stays 2m: acts on gd, firm grnd & fibresand: see 4249 (14f). *1* **65**
4308 **VICARIO 29** [12] M L W Bell 3-9-1 (60) R Mullen 10/1: 3326543: Chsd ldrs, ev ch 2f out, onepcd fnl 1f: prob stays 2m: see 3051. *3½* **63**
4612 **OKTIS MORILIOUS 14** [8] C R Dore 3-8-10 (55) R Thomas(3) 25/1: 1040104: Held up, hdwy 2f out, nrst fin: longer 2m trip for new stable (prev with A Carroll): seems to stay 2m, see 4199 (12f seller). *nk* **57**
4594 **LET IT BE 15** [13]3-8-10 (4oh) (51) A Culhane 12/1: 5115205: Held up, switched & styd on fnl 2f, nrst fin: longer 2m trip: see 4249 (14f). *3* **54**
4675* **SPRING BREEZE 11** [9]3-9-1 vis (60) D Tudhope(5) 7/2 FAV: 2325216: Led 3f out till 2f out, onepcd. *2½* **56**
4601 **QUICKSTYX 14** [7]3-9-8 (67) K McEvoy 8/1: 1454467: Chsd ldrs, ev ch 2f out, sn onepcd. *1* **62**
4663* **HABITUAL 11** [10]3-9-1 (60) J Mackay 9/2: 0-004518: Chsd ldrs, wknd qckly 2f out: btr 4663 (AW). *14* **41**
4439 **SIEGFRIEDS NIGHT 22** [1]3-9-5 (64) J P Guillambert(3) 25/1: 5300259: Held up, nvr a factor: btr 3703. *2½* **42**
3934 **KYBER 47** [5]3-9-3 (62) D Nolan(3) 33/1: 54330: 10th: Held up, nvr a factor: 7 wk abs: longer trip. *3* **37**
4243 **LUCKY PISCEAN 32** [3]3-8-10 (3oh) (52) R Ffrench 100/1: 50000: 11th: Al rear: longer trip. *9* **22**
4594 **GRANDE TERRE 15** [2]3-8-10 (5oh) (50) R Winston 66/1: 0-P00000: 12th: Al bhd, t.o. *28* **0**
4415 **SUNDAY CITY 23** [6]3-9-10 (69) K Darley 11/1: 335520: 13th: Led till 3f out, wknd qckly, eased. *1¾* **6**
13 Ran Time 3m 30.01 (4.51) Owned: Mr Roy Matthews Trained: Malton

4869

5.10 European Breeders Fund Renault Master Classified Stakes 3yo+ 0-70 (D3)
£5551 £1708 £854 **7f str** **Firm 16** **+07 Fast** Centre

4500 **PINTLE 19** [10] J L Spearing 4-9-0 (73) K McEvoy 2/1 FAV: 5-411641: Led till halfway, remained prom & regained lead 2f out, pushed clr fnl 1f: well bckd, gd time: prob stays 1m, ideally suited by 7f: likes fast & firm grnd, best up with/forcing the pace: career best eff today, see 3210. **81**
4667 **REIDIES CHOICE 11** [9] J G Given 3-9-0 (73) J Mackay 8/1: 0420352: Dwelt, gd hdwy to chase wnr fnl 1f, no impress cl-home: tchd 12/1: gd eff, worth another try at 1m: 4341 & 3016. *2½* **78**
4642 **IN THE PINK 12** [4] M R Channon 4-8-12 (71) A Culhane 4/1: 2020453: Held up, prog 2f out, onepcd. *2½* **68**
4652 **ZOOM ZOOM 12** [3] Mrs L Stubbs 4-9-1 (71) J P Guillambert(3) 16/1: 31/-10504: Chsd ldrs wide, onepcd. *¾* **69**
4689 **BANDOS 11** [8]4-9-3 t (73) D Allan 10/1: 20-30045: Prom, led halfway till 2f out, wknd fnl 1f: btr 4689. *1¾* **67**
3229 **MENAI STRAIGHTS 75** [6]3-8-11 (63) D Nolan(1) 100/1: 6351306: Nvr a factor after 11 wk abs. *2½* **59**
4740 **GROWLER 7** [7]3-8-11 vis (70) K Darley 8/1: 0302107: Chsd ldrs, btn 2f out: btr 4262 (6f, sft). *1½* **56**
4714 **BORREGO 9** [1]4-9-5 bl (75) R Hills 13/2: 6004108: Held up, nvr nr ldrs: twice below 4482. *hd* **60**
3797 **ACOMB 53** [5]4-9-5 (75) Dale Gibson 14/1: 0110069: Chsd ldrs, wknd 2f out: 8 wk abs. *1½* **57**
4615 **RED SAHARA 14** [2]3-8-13 BL (75) S W Kelly 11/1: 6624000: 10th: Chsd ldrs till halfway, wknd & eased, t.o.: tried blnks: btr 3885. *21* **12**
10 Ran Time 1m 24.78 (0.68) Owned: Mr Robert Heathcote Trained: Kinnersley

4870

5.40 Renault Kangoo Handicap Stakes 3yo+ 56-70 (E3) **[76]**
£4012 £1234 £617 **5f str** **Firm 16** **+00 Fast** Centre

4339 **PLAYFUL DANE 27** [8] W S Cunningham 7-9-6 (68) D Tudhope(5) 4/1 FAV: 0-150131: Prom, led halfway, clr fnl 1f, readily: stays 7f, seems best at 5/6f: acts on gd & firm grnd, handles a flat or gall trk: in fine form. **83**
4603 **ABELARD 14** [14] R A Fahey 3-8-7 VIS (56) T Hamilton(3) 14/1: 3-650502: Dwelt, imprvd 2f out, fin well but no ch with wnr: back to form in first time visor: eff at 5f on fast & firm grnd: can find similar, see 2227. *2½* **62**
4754+ **BLUE MAEVE 6** [10] J Hetherton 4-9-2 (6ex) (64) S Righton 13/2: 2150013: Led till after halfway, onepcd fnl 1f: qck reapp: see 4754. *1* **67**
4754 **BALLYBUNION 6** [2] D Nicholls 5-8-7 (55) A Nicholls 5/1: 1032044: Chsd ldrs, kept on under press fnl 1f: qck reapp: again bhd today's 3rd in 4754. *2½* **51**
4785 **VIGOROUS 4** [6]4-9-1 (63) A Mullen(7) 13/2: 0500625: Rdn rear, styd on late, nrst fin: qck reapp. *nk* **58**
4618 **COLLEGE MAID 13** [13]7-8-8 bl (56) J Currie(7) 25/1: 6653006: Rear, late gains: see 4087. *¾* **49**
4038 **LADY PROTECTOR 42** [12]5-8-9 (57) Dale Gibson 12/1: 1133307: Front rank, wknd dist: 6 wk abs. *hd* **49**
4754 **ROAN RAIDER 6** [11]4-8-9 vis (57) M Tebbutt 33/1: 0202508: Chsd ldrs 3.5f, wknd. *1½* **45**
4696 **MIND ALERT 10** [15]3-9-1 bl (64) D Allan 33/1: 6-020009: Chsd ldrs, btn dist. *nk* **51**

NEWCASTLE WEDNESDAY 29.09.04 Lefthand, Galloping, Stiff Track

4627 **CONSENSUS 13** [3]5-9-7 (69) T Williams 14/1: 0046000: 10th: Rcd alone far side, prom till   ½ **54**
halfway, wknd: top-weight, on the wrong side: see 3680.
4627 **FAVOUR 13** [7]4-9-5 (67) R Winston 8/1: 2060030: 11th: Nvr btr than mid-div: btr 4627.   shd **51**
4739* **BETTYS PRIDE 7** [9]5-8-11 (6ex) (59) S W Kelly 7/1: 6010610: 12th: Dwelt, nvr a factor: btr 4739.   1¼ **39**
925 **FAYRZ PLEASE 187** [4]3-8-6 (55) Joanna Badger 100/1: 03-44000: 13th: Chsd ldrs 3f, wknd: abs.   1¼ **31**
4398 **PERFECT LOVE 24** [5]4-9-0 (62) L Enstone 100/1: 00-00000: 14th: Al rear.   4 **26**
4404 **SELF BELIEF 23** [1]3-8-13 (62) J P Guillambert(3) 100/1: 4340-000: 15th: Slow away, al bhd & fin last.   17 **0**
15 Ran   Time 59.02(0.82)   Owned: Ann and David Bell   Trained: Yarm

GOODWOOD THURSDAY 30.09.04 Righthand, Sharpish, Undulating Track

Official Going Good (Good/Firm Places)

4871
2.05 3663 Nursery Stakes Handicap 2yo 0-85 (D2)   **[87]**
£5200 £1600 £800   **1m rnd**   **Good 50**   **-08 Slow**   Inside

4580* **SOMETHING EXCITING 16** [12] D R C Elsworth 2-9-5 (78) T Quinn 14/1: 40011: Towards rear, pushed   **93**
along & hdwy 3f out, styd on for press to lead well ins last, going away: suited by 1m last twice, get further:
acts on gd & soft grnd, sharp or stiff/undul trk: progressive filly: see 4580, 3252.
4673* **SECRET PACT 12** [18] M Johnston 2-9-6 (79) R Ffrench 15/2: 4230112: Led, rdn & hdd well ins last,   1½ **89**
no extra: gd front running eff from fav'ble high draw: styd longer 1m trip well: progressive: see 4673.
4807+ **SUCCESSION 4** [6] Sir Mark Prescott 2-9-10 (7ex) (83) S Sanders 3/1 FAV: 0061113: Sn trkd ldr &   1 **91**
chall 2f out, no extra for press ins last: hvly bckd: qck reapp: gd run from awkward low draw: see 4807.
4535 **DOVE COTTAGE 19** [4] W S Kittow 2-8-8 (67) D Kinsella 20/1: 6531254: Sn handy, styd on for press: 1¼ **72**
styd longer 1m trip, fine run from awkward low draw: see 4064, 3729 (6/7f).
4600* **VERBIER 15** [11]2-9-2 (75) F Norton 9/2: 615: Chsd ldrs, short of room & switched 2f out,   hd **79**
onepace: nicely bckd, op 7/1: h'cap bow: stays 1m but just btr 4600 (7.5f, mdn).
4741 **SHUJUNE AL HAWAA 8** [5]2-8-5 VIS (64) C Catlin 66/1: 5630006: Rdn chasing ldrs over 3f out, kept   hd **67**
on onepace: ndd strong handling but an imprvd eff in first time visor: shown ability earlier this term: see 3302.
4114* **INNOCENT SPLENDOUR 39** [14]2-9-7 (80) L Dettori 4/1: 217: Rdn & bhd early, kept on late, no threat.   nk **82**
4483* **PRESS EXPRESS 21** [10]2-9-6 (79) S Hitchcott 25/1: 0618: Keen & prom, btn over 1f out: btr 4483 (7f).   nk **78**
4741 **HES A STAR 8** [20]2-8-2 (61) R Smith 16/1: 040669: Mid-div, nvr able to chall: btr 4741 & 3627 (7f).   ½ **61**
4575 **TOHAMA 16** [7]2-9-1 (74) J Quinn 25/1: 6050: 10th: Rear, mod late prog for press: h'cap bow.   1 **72**
4115 **FLAG POINT 39** [17]2-9-2 (75) Dane O'Neill 50/1: 3000: 11th: Al towards rear: h'cap bow: btr 2695.   ½ **72**
4606 **KALMINI 15** [13]2-9-2 VIS (75) T E Durcan 33/1: 021540: 12th: Mid-div, rdn & btn 2f out: visor: btr 4606.   1½ **69**
4600 **PEARLS A SINGER 15** [2]2-8-12 (71) R Mullen 33/1: 0550: 13th: Al rear, h'cap bow: btr 4600 & 4035.   6 **55**
4233* **Jamaaron 33** [9]2-9-4 (77) R Hughes 16/1:0
4576 **Election Seeker 16** [16]2-8-7 (1ow)(65) P Dobbs 66/1:0
4444 **Mulberry Wine 23** [19]2-8-7 (66) D Sweeney 33/1:0
4483 **Knightsbridge Hill 21** [15]2-9-4 (77) D Holland 16/1:0
17 Ran   Time 1m 42.07 (4.67)   Owned: Setsquare Recruitment   Trained: Whitsbury

4872
2.35 European Breeders Fund Kent Reliance Building Society Classified Stakes 3yo+ 0-80 (C2)
£6960 £2640 £1320   **1m rnd**   **Good 50**   **+11 Fast**   Inside

4607 **DESERT CRISTAL 15** [10] J R Boyle 3-8-9 (78) L Dettori 7/1: 3132301: Trkd ldr trav well, led 2f   **89**
out, rdn & clr: fast time: eff at 7f/1m on fast & hvy grnd, likes a sharp/undul trk: progressive filly.
4473 **WOODY VALENTINE 21** [3] M Johnston 3-8-12 (80) S Chin 12/1: 6120052: Mid-div, drvn & styd on, not   2 **86**
able to reach wnr: relish a return to 10f: see 2874 (10f).
4629* **JAY GEES CHOICE 14** [1] M R Channon 4-9-7 (85) S Hitchcott 10/1: 0404613: Led till 2f out, no   1½ **88**
extra ins last: another gd run, confirmed improvement of 4629 under top-weight.
4714 **ARKHOLME 10** [7] P Winkworth 3-9-1 bl (83) P Doe 12/1: 1203144: Pushed along rear, late gains.   1 **84**
4813 **SERIEUX 4** [6]5-9-2 p (80) S Drowne 7/1: 0000405: Keen & trkd ldrs, btn over 1f out: see 4642, 4482.   1 **79**
4607 **ENFORD PRINCESS 15** [2]3-8-11 (82) R Hughes 10/1: 4034046: Mid-div, no impress dist: btr 4607, 3885.   ½ **77**
4500 **BINANTI 20** [12]4-9-3 (81) J Quinn 8/1: 6005537: Held up, prog over 2f out, btn dist: btr 4500 (7f).   1¼ **76**
4714 **SATTAM 10** [9]5-9-2 vis (79) W Supple 5/1: 3210-238: Keen, al rear: btr 4714 & 4500.   nk **74**
4642 **CALEDONIAN 13** [4]3-8-12 (79) T Quinn 50/1: 010-09: Al towards rear: btr 119 (AW).   2½ **69**
1602 **NAJAABA 146** [5]4-9-1 (82) B Reilly(3) 33/1: 1515650: 10th: Mid-div, struggling fnl 2f: abs: btr 1491.   ½ **67**
3059 **TARUSKIN 84** [11]3-9-2 dbl (84) D Holland 25/1: 1-313000: 11th: Chsd ldrs, btn/eased dist: abs: btr 1498 (6f).   1½ **69**
4615 **SALINOR 15** [8]4-9-2 (79) S Sanders 7/2 FAV: 23-11060: 12th: Al bhd, reportedly nvr trav: btr 1915.   3½ **58**
12 Ran   Time 1m 40.49 (3.09)   Owned: John Hopkins (T/A South Hatch Racing)   Trained: Epsom

4873
3.10 Anglo Irish Bank Stakes Handicap 3yo+ 71-85 (D2)   **[92]**
£6500 £2000 £1000   **7f rnd**   **Good 50**   **-10 Slow**   Inside

4446+ **IDLE POWER 23** [2] J R Boyle 6-8-13 p (77) L Dettori 4/1: 2300211: Chsd ldrs & led over 1f out,   **84**
rdn & held on well: op 5/1: eff at 6/7f on firm, gd/soft & polytrack: in great heart: see 4446, 4189 & 3069.
4615 **CONCER ETO 15** [13] S C Williams 5-8-9 p (73) W Supple 10/1: 4120042: Keen in mid-div, styd on for   nk **79**
press ins last, al just held by wnr: tough: see 3813 & 3490.
4482 **BI POLAR 21** [10] D R C Elsworth 4-8-8 (72) C Catlin 7/1: 0220363: Held up, pushed along over 2f   1½ **75**
out, styd on for press, not pace to chall: see 4030, 3034 & 2272.
4855 **TARANAKI 1** [16] P D Cundell 6-9-7 (85) N De Souza(5) 8/1: 00036504: Handy, ch 2f out, no extra   ¾ **87**
from dist: poor run yesterday, much imprvd today: see 3954, 1817.
4683 **STEVEDORE 12** [5]3-8-5 (72) G Carter 25/1: 4151505: Mid-div, onepace for press: see 4110.   1¼ **71**
4642 **QUANTUM LEAP 13** [3]7-8-7 (1oh)vis (70) D Holland 33/1: 6424006: Rear, mod late prog: see 2063.   hd **69**
4523 **MASTER ROBBIE 19** [9]5-9-6 (84) S Hitchcott 10/1: 0000007: Bhd, prog over 2f out, btn dist: see 2090.   hd **81**
4642 **BORDER EDGE 13** [4]6-8-13 vis (77) G Baker 40/1: 0-000008: Chsd ldrs, no impress dist: see 4122.   1¼ **71**
4482 **HEY PRESTO 21** [7]4-8-8 (1ow) Dane O'Neill 33/1: 5610009: Rear, prog over 2f out, btn dist: see 3443.   1¾ **63**
2129 **INSTRUCTOR 121** [14]3-8-8 (75) R Hughes 33/1: 42-21000: 10th: Led till over 1f out, fdd: abs, gelded.   ½ **65**

4615 **STAR SENSATION 15** [8]4-8-11 (75) S Sanders 14/1: 5600400: 11th: Slow away, al rear: btr 4141.   *shd* 65
4500 **ANUVASTEEL 20** [11]3-8-6 (73) F Norton 7/2-FAV: 32-60060: 12th: Mid-div, rdn & btn over 1f out: bckd.   1½ 60
4500 **Waterside 20** [1]5-9-2 (80) E Ahern 16/1:0   4263 **Sabrina Brown 32** [6]3-8-6 (1ow)(72) R Havlin 12/1:0
1817 **Just A Glimmer 135** [12]4-9-4 (82) L Keniry(3) 14/1:0   4331 **Betty Stogs 28** [15]3-8-10 (77) R Smith 50/1:0
16 Ran   Time 1m 28.72 (4.22)   Owned: The Idle B'S   Trained: Epsom

---

4874   **3.40 Gr3 Citigroup Charlton Hunt Supreme Stakes 3yo+   (A1)**
£29000 £11000 £5500   **7f rnd**   **Good 50**   **-03 Slow**   Inside

4799 **MAC LOVE 5** [7] J Akehurst 3-8-9 (106) G Carter 14/1: 6610101: Keen in rear, hdwy to lead over 1f   113
out, rdn & sn asserted: qck reapp: eff at 5/6f, imprvd last twice over a sharp/undul 7f: acts on firm & gd, prob
handles soft: v tough & progressive, developed into a smart performer: see 4472, 3596 & 2421.
4472 **VANDERLIN 21** [9] A M Balding 5-8-12 (105) L Keniry 16/1: 5310332: Held up, styd on for press fnl   2   108
2f, not pace of wnr ins last: consistent type, drop to List company suit: see 4063 & 3098 (cond stks).
4270* **POLAR WAY 31** [2] Mrs A J Perrett 5-8-12 (114) R Hughes 5/1: 1-032013: Rear, hdwy 2f out, not   *shd* 108
pace of wnr ins last: btr 4270 (stks).
4526 **SO WILL I 19** [11] M P Tregoning 3-8-9 P (106) W Supple 11/1: 1040534: Mid-div, styd on onepace   1   106
for press: fair run in first time cheek pieces: see 1732.
4017 **KHELEYF 46** [4]3-8-13 (111) L Dettori 2/1-FAV: 10-10365: Keen, trkd ldrs trav well 3f out,   2   106
briefly led over 1f out, wknd tamely ins last: well bckd, op 5/2: 6 wk abs: found less than lkd likely today.
4477 **COURT MASTERPIECE 21** [6]4-8-12 (110) S Sanders 11/1: 5421436: Rear, hdwy when short of room &   1   100
forced to switch over 1f out, onepace & sn held: nicely bckd: btr 4477 & 3441 (firm & fast).
4638 **KINGS POINT 13** [3]3-8-9 BL (100) Dane O'Neill 50/1: 0403007: Trkd ldrs, btn over 1f out: blnks: btr 3620. ½ 99
4638 **SUGGESTIVE 13** [10]6-8-12 bl (110) D Holland 7/1: 4022668: Held up, rdn & no impress fnl 2f: btr 3957. *hd* 98
4800 **ROYAL STORM 5** [8]5-8-12 (105) S Drowne 16/1: 0200109: Led after 1f till over 1f out, sn btn: qck reapp. *shd* 98
4063 **ROCKETS N ROLLERS 19** [1]4-8-12 (102) P Dobbs 50/1: 1454000: 10th: Al rear, btn/eased bef dist.   20   62
4526 **ATAVUS 19** [5]7-8-12 (92) J Mackay 50/1: 0500260: 11th: Led 1f, remained prom, btn when short of   5   53
room over 1f out, eased: btr 4226.
11 Ran   Time 1m 28.19 (3.69)   Owned: Mr Vimal Khosla   Trained: Epsom

---

4875   **4.15 Lloyds Tsb Dress Rehearsal Stakes Handicap 3yo+ 56-70 (E3)**
£3250 £1000 £500   **2m**   **Good 50**   **-14 Slow**   Inside   **[81]**

4559 **MASTERMAN READY 17** [1] P W Harris 3-8-13 (66) E Ahern 7/1: 0601361: Held up, prog & led over 6f   75
out trav well, hdd over 2f out, rallied for press to lead again dist, narrowly asserted fnl 100y: eff at 14f, imprvd
for step up to 2m: acts on gd/soft grnd, gall or sharp/easy trks: unexposed at this trip, game run.
4512 **ISAAF 19** [5] P W Hiatt 5-9-10 (65) P Makin(5) 7/2: 4160042: Trkd ldrs & led over 2f out, hdd   ½ 72
dist, just held well ins last: bckd, op 13/2: rest well covered: stays 2m well: tough & genuine, win more races.
4487 **MEDICA BOBA 21** [6] H Morrison 3-8-2 (55) J Mackay 33/1: 000003: b f Dr Fong - Silly View   4   58
(Scenic) Held up, late gains for press, not threaten front pair: imprvd eff, styd longer 2m trip well: handles gd
grnd & a sharp trk: well held prev 5 starts.
4824* **DARN GOOD 3** [8] R Hannon 3-9-4 (6ex)bl (71) R Hughes 5/2-FAV: 2066014: Rear, rdn 3f out, only mod   2½ 72
prog: qck reapp: clr of rem under a pen: btr 4824.
4663 **CANTRIP 12** [7]4-8-10 (6oh) (45) J Quinn 16/1: 1300505: Keen in mid-div, no impress fnl 3f.   10   44
4092 **GARSTON STAR 41** [9]3-8-9 (62) Derek Nolan(7) 12/1: 2205166: Led till over 6f out, btn over 2f out, abs.   11   46
4449 **SCARRABUS 23** [3]3-8-12 (65) T Quinn 11/1: 0634357: Rear, sn pushed along & struggling fnl 3f.   12   39
3580 **ILLEANA 62** [2]3-8-0 (53) F Norton 16/1: 0010308: Held up, bhd fnl 3f: abs: btr 3026 (12f).   1½ 26
4314 **CHAMPAGNE SHADOW 29** [4]3-8-12 bl (65) L Dettori 7/2: 0202329: Rear & lost tch over 3f out, eased: *dist* 0
reportedly lost action: longer trip: btr 4314, 2740 & 2393 (AW).
9 Ran   Time 3m 34.56 (10.26)   Owned: The Mastermen   Trained: Berkhamsted

---

4876   **4.50 European Breeders Fund Paddy Power Median Auction Maiden Stakes Fillies 2yo   (D3)**
£3250 £1000 £500   **6f str**   **Good 50**   **-18 Slow**   Stands Side

4679 **LOVE THIRTY 12** [7] M R Channon 2-8-11 (94) T E Durcan 5/6-FAV: 6251: Handy & led 2f out, edged   89
right under press ins last, held on all out: hvly bckd to confirm promise of latest: eff at 6/6.5f on fast & gd/soft.
       CAPE COLUMBINE 0 [2] D R C Elsworth 2-8-11 T Quinn 11/2: 2: b f Diktat - Cape Merino (Clantime)   *shd* 88
Held up, styd on well from over 1f out, just failed: bckd, op 8/1: 11,000gns Jan foal, half-sister to 6/7f 3yo
wnrs, dam a 5f wnr: eff at 6f, shaped as if 7f will suit: acts on gd grnd & a sharp trk: encouraging start.
4444 **CHUTNEY MARY 23** [10] J G Portman 2-8-11 (68) E Ahern 16/1: 2252503: Led till 2f out, not pace of   2   82
front pair: improved run from the front: see 3716 (fast).
4679 **HONEY RYDER 12** [11] D R Loder 2-8-11 (83) S Sanders 7/2: 2204: Trkd ldrs, no extra from dist.   2   76
4726 **SILVER BARK 9** [5]2-8-11 L Dettori 10/1: 05: b f Royal Applause - Argent du Bois (Silver Hawk)   3½ 65
Mid-div, outpcd fnl 2f: 56,000gns Jan foal, sister to a 6.5f/7f juv & subs Gr 1 10f 3yo wnr in the US.
       TAPA 0 [8]2-8-11 L Keniry(3) 40/1: 6: b f Tagula - Tweed Mill (Selkirk) Outpcd, nvr land a   *nk* 64
blow: cheaply bght Jan first foal, dam a 9f 3yo wnr.
       FLYING HEART 0 [3]2-8-11 C Catlin 25/1: 7: Al outpcd.   3½ 53
4577 **BELLE CHANSON 16** [9]2-8-11 D Sweeney 40/1: 08: Dwelt, sn handy till over 1f out.   1   50
       FLAUNT N FLIRT 0 [4]2-8-11 W Supple 12/1: 9: Slow away, went right start, sn bhd.   4   38
4637 **JUBILEE COIN 13** [1]2-8-11 S Drowne 66/1: 00: 10th: Keen & held up, no impress from halfway.   5   24
10 Ran   Time 1m 14.10 (4.1)   Owned: John Livock Bloodstock Limited   Trained: West Ilsley

4877 5.20 Sutton Business Centre Maiden Stakes 3yo (D2)
£6500 £2000 £1000 1m1f192y Good 50 -23 Slow Inside

DOUBLE DEPUTY 0 [7] Saeed bin Suroor 3-9-0 T L Dettori 7/4: 1: b c Sadler's Wells - Janaat 73+
(Kris) Led 1f, sn trkd ldrs, led going well over 2f out, rdn & asserted from dist, readily: hvly bckd, op 9/4:
half-brother to v smart 6/7f performer Lend A Hand: eff at 10f, could get further: acts on gd grnd & a sharp/undul
trk: goes well fresh & suited by a t-strap: tidy success, can rate higher.

DAY CARE 0 [4] Mrs A J Perrett 3-9-0 R Hughes 5/4 FAV: 2: gr c Daylami - Ancara (Dancing Brave) 4 63
Dwelt, sn chsd ldr, chall trav well 2f out, not pace of wnr bef dist but kept on:
mid-dist pedigree: stays 10f, 12f+ could suit: handles gd grnd.

4541 **POLAR DANCER 18** [2] Mrs A J Perrett 3-8-9 (55) S Drowne 14/1: 3-030033: Mid-div, styd on onepace 1 57
fnl 2f, no threat to wnr: op 10/1: see 3201 & 120.

3979 **DANZE ROMANCE 45** [1] J L Dunlop 3-8-9 (64) T Quinn 16/1: 0054: Rear, late gains for press, no threat. ¾ 56

4541 **ROYAL LUSTRE 18** [8]3-9-0 (67) R Havlin 6/1: 03025: Keen & led halfway, sn clr, hdd over 2f out & 1½ 59
no extra: bckd tho' op 9/2: clr of rem: see 4541.

4579 **CHARING CROSS 16** [6]3-9-0 R Brisland 50/1: 0006: Bhd, no ch fnl 2f. 17 35

TANK 0 [9]3-9-0 N Chalmers(5) 33/1: 7: Al bhd on debut, op 16/1. 5 28

428 **ELZEES 257** [5]3-9-0 V Venkaya 66/1: 08: Sn bhd, abs, gelded. 3½ 23

4541 **KWAI BABY 18** [3]3-8-9 (35) A Daly 100/1: 000-09: Al bhd. 12 3

1935 **KINGS MINSTREL 131** [10]3-9-0 P Doe 66/1: 000: 10th: Slow away, rcd keenly & led after 1f till 3½ 3
5f out, sn btn: abs, new yard & has been gelded.

10 Ran Time 2m 11.45(7.25) Owned: Godolphin Trained: Newmarket

Official Going Good (Rain throughout afternoon)

4878 1.15 Listed Unicoin Homes Noel Murless Stakes 3yo (A1)
£17400 £6600 £3300 1m6f Good/Firm Inapp Centre

3779 **TUNGSTEN STRIKE 54** [4] Mrs A J Perrett 3-8-12 (86) Martin Dwyer 22/1: 0-011321: Led, hit rails 104
after 3f, hdd over 2f out, led again dist, drvn out, gamely: abs: eff at 14f/2m on fast & gd: goes well fresh: tough,
much improved stepped up in class & well weighted in Cesarewitch: see 3200.

3076* **CARTE DIAMOND 83** [2] M Johnston 3-8-12 (96) K Darley 7/1: 112: Chsd wnr, narrow lead over 2f 2 101
out, drvn & hdd dist, hung left & no extra fnl 100y: rest well covered: 12 wk abs: imprvd over this longer 14f
trip: acts on fast & gd/soft grnd: lightly rcd & progressive colt: see 3076 & 2549.

4383 **LOCHBUIE 26** [5] G Wragg 3-8-12 (98) J F Egan 9/2: 1131443: Held up, rdn & styd on fnl 2f, not 3 97
pace of front pair: see 4383, 3556.

4491* **LOST SOLDIER THREE 20** [3] L M Cumani 3-8-12 (104) K Fallon 8/11 FAV: 1542114: Held up, pushed nk 97
along 4f out, no prog over 1f out: v hvly bckd at odds-on: shade bit 4491.

3507 **MASSIF CENTRALE 65** [7]3-8-12 (98) R L Moore 20/1: 020105: Chsd ldrs, btn 2f out: 2 mth abs. 5 90

4239 **MUTAFANEN 33** [6]3-8-12 (103) R Hills 9/1: 3304406: Held up, rdn & btn 2f out: btr 3794 & 3553 (10f). 5 83

4196 **ANOUSA 34** [1]3-9-1 (91) J Murtagh 50/1: 0310407: Chsd ldrs, btn 3f out: btr 3556. dist 0

7 Ran Time 2m 56.93 (1.43) Owned: Mr John Connolly Trained: Pulborough

4879 1.50 Listed Rolls-Royce Motor Cars London Rous Stakes 3yo+ (A1)
£17400 £6600 £3300 5f str Good/Firm Inapp Far Side

4313 **NIGHTS CROSS 32** [13] M R Channon 3-8-11 vis (101) A Culhane 11/1: 0333001: Trkd ldr, drvn to lead 109
well ins last: op 12/1: eff at 5/6f on firm & gd/soft, prob handles soft & any trk: smart back to best.

3100 **STEVES CHAMP 18** [16] Rune Haugen 4-9-4 bl J Murtagh 12/1: 1066112: Dwelt, led till well ins ½ 113
last, no extra: nicely bckd, op 20/1: Norwegian raider: smart run under top-weight: see 3100.

4718* **BALTIC KING 9** [8] H Morrison 4-8-12 t (104) R L Moore 5/2 FAV: 6013613: Held up, eff when short 1½ 103
of room over 1f out, styd on: gone closer with a clr run: hvly bckd: win again: see 4718.

4678 **TEXAS GOLD 12** [9] W R Muir 6-8-12 (106) Martin Dwyer 11/2: 6022144: Trkd ldrs, edged right & 1 100
onepace dist: bckd: see 4678 & 4537.

4604 **RED SOVEREIGN 15** [15]3-8-6 (74) M Fenton 100/1: 66-00105: Chsd ldrs, edged left & no extra in last. ½ 93$

4479 **THE CATS WHISKERS 21** [14]4-8-7 P Robinson 33/1: 0210206: Held up, short of room over 1f out, nk 92
kept on: see 4479 (7f).

4693 **DRAGON FLYER 11** [11]5-8-7 (98) J F Egan 25/1: 4304107: Chsd ldrs, short of room 2f out, no extra ½ 91
dist, saddle slipped.

4732 **MILLYBAA 12** [4]4-8-7 (93) R Winston 25/1: 2400408: Rear, prog halfway, no prog from dist. shd 90

4459+ **HALMAHERA 22** [3]9-8-12 (101) N Callan 9/1: 0506019: Rdn towards rear, nrst fin: see 4459. nk 94

4678 **HIGH REACH 12** [12]4-8-12 (94) K Fallon 6/1: 3630300: 10th: Chsd ldrs, btn ins last: btr 3622. 2 88

3773 **PROUD BOAST 18** [1]6-8-7 (90) K Darley 16/1: 2300650: 11th: Al outpcd: see 1162. shd 82

4291 **GREEN MANALISHI 31** [5]3-8-11 (87) K McEvoy 25/1: 1550000: 12th: Held up & nvr a factor: see 2593. ¾ 85

4747 **ZARZU 8** [10]5-8-12 (77) R Thomas 100/1: 6500500: 13th: Chsd ldrs, btn 3f out: see 2968 (h'cap). ½ 84

4604 **Silver Prelude 15** [2]3-8-11 (80) I Mongan 66/1:0 4718 **Colonel Cotton 9** [7]5-8-12 vis(97) W Ryan 11/1:0

15 Ran Time 59.46 (1.26) Owned: Ridgeway Downs Racing Trained: West Ilsley

NEWMARKET THURSDAY 30.09.04 Righthand, Stiff, Galloping Track

4880

2.25 Gr1 Sky Bet Cheveley Park Stakes Fillies 2yo (A1)
£110606 £41954 £20977 **6f str** **Good/Firm** **Inapp** Far Side

4697* **MAGICAL ROMANCE 10** [4] B J Meehan 2-8-11 (83) R Winston 40/1: 41611: Chsd ldr, rdn to chall over **114**
1f out, drvn & prevailed cl-home, all out: eff up with/forcing the pace at 6f on fast & gd grnd, stiff/gall trks: v
smart & much imprvd filly: see 4697, 3183.

4332* **SUEZ 28** [7] M A Jarvis 2-8-11 (100) P Robinson 4/1: 112: Led, rdn & hdd well ins last, just *nk* **113**
held: well bckd: tough & v smart, likes to dominate: win Gr races: see 4332.

3841* **DAMSON 53** [5] D Wachman 2-8-11 K Fallon 10/11 FAV: 11113: Chsd ldrs, rdn to chall over 1f out, *nk* **112**
kept on, just held: hvly bckd, 7 wk abs: will relish 7f/1m next term & can rate higher: Gr 1 wnr in 3841.

4684* **GOLDEN LEGACY 12** [2] R A Fahey 2-8-11 P Hanagan 16/1: 2011314: Held up, styd on for press, nrst *½* **110**
fin: smart eff, on the upgrade: see 4684 (List).

4737* **SLIP DANCE 11** [6]2-8-11 J F Egan 40/1: 4162615: Trkd ldrs, chall when short of room ins last, *hd* **109**
just held cl-home: only btn around 1L in a v tight fin: may have got even closer with more room: v useful.

4059* **SOAR 42** [3]2-8-11 (100) J Murtagh 4/1: 12116: Unruly stalls, dwelt & held up, no impress fnl 1f: *3½* **99**
nicely bckd, 6 wk abs: much btr 4059 (Gr 2), rate higher next term.

4432 **JEWEL IN THE SAND 25** [1]2-8-11 (100) R L Moore 12/1: 11107: Held up, btn 2f out: btr 3003. *3½* **89**

7 Ran Time 1m 12.71 (1.81) Owned: Mr F C T Wilson Trained: Upper Lambourn

4881

3.00 Gr3 Somerville Tattersall Stakes Colts & Geldings 2yo (A1)
£34800 £13200 £6600 **7f str** **Good** **Inapp** Far Side

4069* **DIKTATORIAL 41** [9] A M Balding 2-8-9 Martin Dwyer 3/1: 011: Led, hdd over 2f out, led again ins **104**
last, drvn out, most game: hvly bckd, op 7/2: 6 wk abs: eff at 7f, shld get 1m: acts on fast & gd/soft grnd,
stiff/gall trk: enjoys forcing tactics: still green but v useful & open to more improvement: see 4069, 3585.

4022 **CRIMSON SUN 43** [1] Saeed bin Suroor 2-8-9 (97) R Hills 12/1: 21102: Trkd ldrs, led over 2f out *nk* **103**
till ins last, just held: op 9/1: 6 wk abs, left latest bhd: styd longer 7f trip well: win a Listed.

4493 **MISTER GENEPI 20** [4] W R Muir 2-8-9 (95) P Hanagan 33/1: 522303: Held up, styd on well for press *shd* **102**
ins last, nrst fin: useful eff, mdn a formality on this evidence: see 4289, 3927 & 3594.

4455* **SANTA FE 23** [6] Sir Michael Stoute 2-8-9 (91) K Fallon 11/2: 514: Handy, chall ins last but just *½* **100**
held when short of room: up in grade & progressed again: see 4455 (mdn).

4458 **MOSCOW MUSIC 22** [8]2-8-9 (100) R Winston 16/1: 2126235: Dwelt & held up, rdn to press ldrs over *¾* **98**
1f out, no extra well ins last: styd longer 7f trip & fin clr of rem, only btn around 2L: see 4458 & 4025 (5/6f).

3919* **KINGS QUAY 48** [5]2-8-12 (100) R L Moore 9/1: 10216: Prom, rdn & btn fnl 1f: 7 wk abs: btr 3919. *5* **91**

4326* **SUBPOENA 29** [2]2-8-9 P Robinson 7/4 FAV: 17: Held up & keen, rdn & btn over 1f out: hvly bckd. *2* **84**

4190* **CHIEF SCOUT 34** [7]2-8-9 (83) M Hills 25/1: 0418: Chsd ldr, ch over 2f out, wknd: see 4190. *shd* **83**

4416* **WALKONTHEWILDSIDE 24** [3]2-8-9 (83) K Darley 12/1: 5419: Held up & keen, btn over 1f out: btr 4416. *15* **53**

9 Ran Time 1m 26.0 (3.2) Owned: Tweenhills Thurloe Trained: Kingsclere

4882

3.30 Ngk Spark Plugs Nursery Stakes Handicap 2yo 0-95 (B1) **[100]**
£13806 £4248 £2124 **6f str** **Good** **Inapp** Far Side

4529 **OBE GOLD 19** [4] M R Channon 2-9-4 vis (90) A Culhane 20/1: 424U331: Chsd ldrs, hdwy to lead over **104**
3f out, drvn out: eff at 5/6f on fast & gd, likes a stiff/gall trk: imprvd for drop back into h'cap company, this
was a career best effort: see 1632 (debut).

4727 **ELGIN MARBLES 9** [12] R Hannon 2-8-8 (80) R L Moore 10/1: 16022: Cl-up, hdwy into 2nd 2f out, *1¾* **87**
kept on: gd run, consistent: see 4727.

4536* **CYCLICAL 18** [11] G A Butler 2-9-6 (92) J Murtagh 9/4 FAV: 113: Slow away in rear, hdwy/slt short *1¾* **94**
of room over 1f out, kept on ins fnl 1f: hvly bckd: progressive, win again sn: see 4536.

4535 **ZOMERLUST 19** [9] J J Quinn 2-8-7 (79) R Winston 14/1: 31244: Chsd ldrs, onepcd fnl 1f. *shd* **80**

4490 **ROYAL ORISSA 20** [1]2-8-8 t (80) Martin Dwyer 12/1: 453025: Slow away in rear, styd on well fnl *nk* **80**
1f: clr of rem: return to 7f? see 4490.

4490 **BREAKING SHADOW 20** [7]2-8-6 (78) P Hanagan 14/1: 233106: Rear, some late gains. *3* **69**

4645* **VIKING SPIRIT 13** [3]2-9-7 (93) I Mongan 4/1: 022117: Cl-up, no impress fnl 1f under top-weight. *½* **82**

4535 **TURNAROUND 19** [2]2-8-9 (81) J F Egan 12/1: 321028: Rear, hdwy 3f out, no impress over 1f out. *½* **68**

4224* **COLEORTON DANCER 33** [10]2-9-3 (89) N Callan 13/2: 4011119: Cl-up till over 4f out, rallied when *¾* **74**
hmpd over 1f out, no impress fnl 1f: been busy: btr 4224.

4737 **NOVA TOR 11** [8]2-9-1 P (87) P Robinson 33/1: 4013060: 10th: Led to over 3f out, no extra over 1f out. *1½* **68**

4471 **TOBYS DREAM 21** [6]2-8-7 (79) K Darley 33/1: 01060: 11th: Cl-up, no impress 1f out. *5* **45**

4543* **BAHAMIAN MAGIC 17** [5]2-8-11 (83) K Fallon 12/1: 4310: 12th: Cl-up, lost place 2f out, btn: 'felt wrong'. *17* **15**

12 Ran Time 1m 13.05 (2.25) Owned: BDR Partnership Trained: West Ilsley

4883

4.05 Jra Golden Jubilee Maiden Stakes Colts & Geldings 2yo (D2)
£8499 £2615 £1308 **1m str** **Good** **Inapp** Far Side

3682 **PEVENSEY 57** [6] J H M Gosden 2-8-11 BL K Darley 50/1: 601: b g Danehill - Champaka (Caerleon) **85**
Cl-up, hdwy to lead 2f out, drvn out ins fnl 1f: 8 wk abs: Mar foal: full brother to smart 10/11f filly Steel
Princess: dam unrcd, sire top-class sprinter/miler: eff at 1m on gd, stiff/gall trk: runs well fresh: imprvd
dramatically here for first time blnks & has been gelded: relish mid-dists next term.

4576 **SALINJA 16** [8] Mrs A J Perrett 2-8-11 J Murtagh 6/1: 332: Mid-div, hdwy over 2f out, kept on: *nk* **84**
op 8/1: stays 1m: now quals for h'caps & deserves to find a race: see 4576.

4631 **CLUELESS 14** [12] W J Haggas 2-8-11 K Fallon 9/4 FAV: 43: Chsd ldrs, kept on ins fnl 1f: well *1¼* **81**
bckd: acts on gd & gd/soft: ran to form of debut in 4631.

ALRAFIDAIN 0 [5] M Johnston 2-8-11 R Hills 14/1: 4: b c Monsun - Demeter (Diesis) Rear, hdwy *1* **79+**
over 3f out, rcd in 2nd over 1f out, onepcd ins fnl 1f on debut: Jan first foal, cost 110,000gns: dam plcd at 1m on
sole start, sire top-class German performer at 10/12f: eff at 1m, will stay further: acts on gd: pleasing start,
not given a hard time once ch gone, entitled to come on for this & can find similar.

4648 **GIVEN A CHOICE 13** [2]2-8-11 A Culhane 5/1: 405: Trkd ldrs, hdwy to lead over 2f out, sn hdd, no *2* **75**

impress ins fnl 1f: tchd 7/1: see 3752.

4575 **MELS MOMENT** 16 [15]2-8-11 I Mongan 100/1: 06: b c Storm Creek - One Moment In Time nk 74
(Magesterial) Led till over 6f out, remained chasing ldrs, still ev ch 2f out, no extra ins fnl 1f: clr of rem:
cost $40,000: Apr foal: half-brother to a US wnr at 8.5f: dam wnr of 4 races, incl at 2, sire a useful juv, later
smart dirt miler: improvement from debut, shld find similar sn.

4575 **ASTRONOMICAL** 16 [9]2-8-11 M Hills 7/2: 37: Chsd ldrs, outpcd over 2f out, btn: well bckd. 3 68
4722 **SWORDS** 9 [7]2-8-11 S Whitworth 100/1: 08: Rear, outpcd over 3f out, nvr a factor. 1½ 65
6 **CAVAN GAEL** 0 [11]2-8-11 R Winston 50/1: 9: Rear, hdwy/not much room 4f out, no impress over 2f out. 53
4699 **ORPEN WIDE** 10 [3]2-8-11 T A Beech(3) 100/1: 0330: 10th: Led over 6f out, hdd over 2f out, no 1¼ 50
extra over 1f out: tried a t-strap.
 SANDYS LEGEND 0 [13]2-8-11 W Ryan 25/1: 0: 11th: Nvr a factor on debut. 2 46
 SPARKFORD 0 [10]2-8-11 J Fortune 8/1: 0: 12th: Dwelt, nvr dngrs on debut. nk 45
4704 **SOUTHERN TIDE** 10 [4]2-8-11 M Fenton 100/1: 0000: 13th: Slow away, nvr a factor. 4 37
 GOLD GUN 0 [1]2-8-11 P Robinson 12/1: 0: 14th: Dwelt, nvr a factor on debut: tchd 16/1. hd 36
 DREAM ALONG 0 [14]2-8-11 Martin Dwyer 25/1: 0: 15th: Slow away, al bhd on debut. 3 30
15 Ran Time 1m 39.9 (3.4) Owned: Jumeirah Racing Trained: Manton

4884 4.40 Newmarket Racecourses Handicap Stakes Fillies & Mares 3yo+ 86-100 (C1) [107]
£11957 £4536 £2268 **6f str Good Inapp** Far Side

4510 **PARADISE ISLE** 19 [8] C F Wall 3-9-7 (100) K Darley 14/1: 1-042101: Dsptd lead till led over 2f 109
out, drvn out ins fnl 1f: stays 5f, prob best at 6f: likes firm & fast, acts on gd, poss handles gd/soft: prob
acts on any trk, likes a stiff/gall one: back to form on drop in grade, enjoys forcing tactics: smart run: see 2593.
4779 **SOLAR POWER** 5 [6] J R Fanshawe 3-8-5 (84) O Urbina 5/6 FAV: 4443122: Rear, hdwy over 1f out, ½ 91
styd on ins fnl 1f, nrst fin: hvly bckd on qck reapp: fine eff tho' a shade btr expected: progressive: see 4350.
4693 **FOREVER PHOENIX** 11 [3] R M H Cowell 4-9-7 (98) A Quinn(5) 10/1: 0361663: Chsd ldrs, kept on ins ½ 103
fnl 1f: op 8/1: fine eff, back to form: win again sn: see 4382.
4498* **DAME DE NOCHE** 20 [7] J G Given 4-8-8 (85) K Fallon 6/1: 0530014: Cl-up, kept on ins fnl 1f: see 4498. nk 89
3941 **VALJARV** 47 [10]3-8-12 bl (91) I Mongan 20/1: 0442005: Dwelt & outpcd in rear, hdwy over 1f out, ½ 93
kept on: 7 wk abs: try 7f? see 1933.
4773 **SARISTAR** 6 [11]3-8-10 (89) A Culhane 12/1: 1005106: Led over 3f, no extra ins fnl 1f: tchd 14/1. ½ 89
4510 **FRUIT OF GLORY** 19 [1]5-9-3 (94) W Ryan 12/1: 1422547: Chsd ldrs, no impress ins fnl 1f. 2½ 87
4786 **IMPRESSIVE FLIGHT** 5 [2]5-8-7 (2oh)BL (82) P Hanagan 14/1: 0006508: Rear, hdwy over 3f out, hung 2 71
right & no impress over 1f out: qck reapp: faded blnks.
4331 **CUSCO** 28 [4]3-8-9 (88) R L Moore 16/1: 6020209: Bhd, hdwy 4f out, no impress 2f out. 7 61
3814 **FIREBELLY** 53 [9]3-8-11 vis (90) N Callan 33/1: 1311-500: 10th: Cl-up, lost place over 3f out, sn btn. dist 0
10 Ran Time 1m 13.1(2.21) Owned: The Equema Partnership Trained: Newmarket

Official Going Good

4885 1.15 Beech House Stud E B F Maiden Stakes 2yo (D2)
£8629 £2655 £1328 **7f str Good/Firm 20 -26 Slow** Centre

 ROB ROY 0 [8] Sir Michael Stoute 2-9-0 K Fallon 4/1 FAV: 1: b c Lear Fan - Camanoe (Gone West) 91+
Held up, gd hdwy over 2f out, led over 1f out, qcknd clr, v readily on debut: Mar first foal, cost $300,000: eff
over a stiff 7f on fast grnd, will relish 1m: runs well fresh: v useful prospect with a turn of foot, likely to
develop into a Group class performer, keep on side.
 FORTUNATE ISLE 0 [11] B W Hills 2-9-0 A Medeiros(5) 66/1: 2: ch c Swain - Isla Del Rey (Nureyev) 2½ 82
Cl-up, eff over 1f out, kept on but not pace of wnr on debut: May foal, half-brother to a useful 7f/10f scorer: dam
6/7f wnr: eff over a stiff 7f, 1m will suit: acts on fast grnd: v pleasing start, looks sure to win races.
 THARUA 0 [17] E A L Dunlop 2-9-0 E Ahern 66/1: 3: b f Indian Danehill - Peig Sayers (Royal ½ 76+
Academy) Held up, kept on nicely over 1f out, nrst fin on debut, not gvn hard time: Mar foal, cost 5,000gns: dam
1m/13f scorer: eff over a stiff 7f, 1m sure to suit: acts on fast grnd, will learn plenty from this educational
start, expect improvement & for her to win soon.
3959 **SAREM** 48 [7] M P Tregoning 2-9-0 R Hills 7/1: 04: Held up, hdwy over 1f out, kept on nicely ins ¾ 79
last, hand-and-heels: 7 wk abs: plenty to like about this, looks sure to relish 1m & win races.
4776 **DART ALONG** 7 [22]2-9-0 R Hughes 25/1: 55: Led till over 1f out, no extra: stays 7f on fast shd 78
grnd: imprvd for debut with forcing tactics: see 4776.
 BRAVEMORE 0 [21]2-9-0 K Darley 14/1: 6: b c Diesis - Private Indy (A P Indy) In tch, eff over 1 76
1f out, onepace on debut: Mar first foal: bred to apprec 1m in time & shaped with some promise here.
 MPENZI 0 [18]2-8-9 S Carson 50/1: 7: b f Groom Dancer - Muschana (Deploy) U.r. to post, dwelt, 1¾ 67
bhd, some late gains on debut: Jan first foal: dam 9/12f scorer: bred to relish mid-dist next term: improve.
4677 **BARBARY COAST** 13 [14]2-9-0 J F Egan 20/1: 68: Held up, no impress over 1f out. ½ 71
4648 **FEN GAME** 14 [6]2-9-0 R L Moore 15/2: 69: In tch, wknd over 1f out. 1 69
 GOOSE CHASE 0 [3]2-9-0 D Holland 20/1: 0: 10th: Handy, wknd over 2f out. shd 68
 MISS PARTICULAR 0 [9]2-8-9 M Hills 12/1: 0: 11th: Slow away, modest late gains on debut. hd 62
 HARLESTONE LINN 0 [1]2-9-0 Paul Eddery 66/1: 0: 12th: Held up, wknd over 1f out on debut. 5 57
 DANIELLA 0 [20]2-8-9 W Ryan 66/1: 0: 13th: In tch, wknd 2f out on debut. ¾ 50
 BACHELOR AFFAIR 0 [2]2-9-0 Martin Dwyer 50/1: 0: 14th: Slow away, al bhd on debut. shd 54
 CROWN OF MEDINA 0 [4]2-9-0 J Murtagh 25/1: 0: 15th: Al bhd. ½ 53
4326 **SUGITANI** 30 [10]2-9-0 t L Dettori 50/1: 00: 16th: In tch, wknd 2f out. ½ 52
 CAUSEWAY GIRL 0 [16]2-8-9 S Whitworth 66/1: 0: 17th: In tch, wknd halfway. bk 46
4455 **ART ROYAL** 24 [10]2-9-0 S Sanders 9/2: 50: 18th: Handy, wknd over 2f out: well bckd: btr 4455. 1¼ 48
 QUEEN OF ICENI 0 [5]2-8-9 I Mongan 50/1: 0: 19th: Slow away & al bhd. nk 42
 Rainbow Sky 0 [23]2-8-9 K May(7) 66/1:0 4462 **High Treason** 23 [24]2-9-0 A Culhane 50/1:0
 Expeditious 0 [13]2-8-9 t K McEvoy 20/1:0 4610 **Four Pleasure** 16 [12]2-8-9 F Norton 100/1:0

23 Ran Time 1m 26.57 (3.27) Owned: Mr Philip Newton Trained: Newmarket

4886 1.50 Listed Fishpools Furnishings Godolphin Stakes 3yo+ (A1)
£17400 £6600 £3300 1m4f Good/Firm 20 -07 Slow Centre

4494 **PRIVATE CHARTER 21** [5] B W Hills 4-9-0 P (102) M Hills 16/1: 5-020601: Made all, left to race
alone far side over 5f out, kept on well for press ins last: imprvd for forcing tactics, cheekpieces & a gd ride:
eff over 10/12f on gd & fast grnd, any trk: useful: see 1843.   **108**

4491 **FANTASTIC LOVE 21** [4] Saeed bin Suroor 4-9-0 t (103) K McEvoy 100/30: 121-0032: Chsd wnr, rcd   hd **107**
centre over 5f out, hung left over 1f out & right ins last but kept on, just held for press: ran to useful best but
did hang under press: see 4491.

2095 **SHANTY STAR 123** [1] M Johnston 4-9-0 (105) K Darley 20/1: 1/131-0P3: Slow away, sn in tch, came   ½ **106**
centre over 5f out, eff & sltly hmpd over 1f out, kept on, not btn far: 4 month abs & imprvd for recent gelding op:
eff at 12f, looks sure to relish a rtn to 14f/2m: useful, prob more to come.

4460 **LIGHT OF MORN 23** [3] R Guest 3-9-0 (93) Martin Dwyer 12/1: 231464: Held up, rcd centre over 5f   2½ **97**
out, onepace over 1f out: ran to best, wants h'caps: see 3335.

990 **RAZKALLA 188** [2]6-9-0 (113) L Dettori 4/7 FAV: 124-1445: Handy, rcd centre over 5f out, no extra   ¾ **101**
fnl 2f: hvly bckd: prev with D Loder: long abs, btr 990.

5 Ran Time 2m 31.51 (3.31) Owned: Sangster Family & Partners Trained: Lambourn

4887 2.25 Gr3 Shadwell Stud Joel Stakes 3yo+ (A1)
£29000 £11000 £5500 1m str Good/Firm 20 +10 Fast Centre

2765 **POLAR BEN 97** [2] J R Fanshawe 5-9-0 (111) J Murtagh 16/1: 100-2201: Held up, hdwy over 2f out,   **113**
styd on well to lead ins last, rdn out: fast time: 3 month abs right back to best & runs well fresh: eff over 7f/1m
on fast grnd, likes gd & soft, any trk: best held up: tough & smart: see 1356.

4538 **SALSELON 19** [5] L M Cumani 5-9-0 bl (116) L Dettori 11/2: 2305232: Slow away, bhd, strong hdwy to   ¾ **111**
lead over 1f out, sn rdn clr, idled badly ins last & allowed wnr to pass: nicely bckd: has a turn of foot & plenty
of ability but extremely quirky: looks to have to put head in front on the line: see 4538, 4323.

4531 **FUNFAIR 20** [1] Mrs A J Perrett 5-9-0 (104) R L Moore 11/1: 0/1020-23: Held up, hdwy over 1f out,   1¼ **108**
kept on same pace: smart & lightly rcd: ran to form of 4531 (h'cap).

3886 **TOUT SEUL 50** [3] R F Johnson Houghton 4-9-0 (105) S Carson 33/1: 5-100604: Held up, eff 2f out,   ¾ **106**
onepace: 7 wk abs: btr run: best 1356.

4495* **SECRET CHARM 21** [11]3-8-8 (110) M Hills 8/1: 11-55015: Chsd ldr till led over 3f out till over   2 **99**
1f out, no extra: shade btr expected after 4495 (stks).

4020 **GRAND PASSION 47** [9]4-9-0 (106) J F Egan 16/1: 0042136: In tch, eff 2f out, wknd over 1f out: 7 wk abs.1 **100**

4682 **CHECKIT 13** [7]4-9-0 (110) A Culhane 7/1: 4036227: Handy, eff to chase ldr over 2f out, wknd fnl 1f.   hd **99**

4682* **PENTECOST 13** [6]5-9-0 (110) Martin Dwyer 10/1: 4010018: Held up, wknd over 1f out: much btr 4682.   11 **77**

4572 **RED FEATHER 20** [13]3-8-11 T N G McCullagh 25/1: 0-213149: Led over 4f, wknd over 2f out: t-strap.   2½ **72**

4479* **ATTUNE 22** [12]3-8-8 (99) K Darley 16/1: 1001110: 10th: In tch, wknd over 1f out: best 4479.   ¾ **67**

4386 **TROUBADOUR 12** [10]3-8-11 J P Spencer 9/1: 135-1210: 11th: Handy, wknd over 1f out: well   ½ **69**
bckd: btr expected after 4386 (List).

4386 **SHOT TO FAME 27** [4]5-9-3 (111) E Ahern 16/1: 1121550: 12th: Handy, wknd over 2f out: twice   nk **71**
below 3886, 3124: been busy.

4531 **DESERT STAR 20** [8]4-9-0 (99) K Fallon 15/2: 310/-30: 13th: Slow away, sn handy, wknd over 2f   hd **67**
out: something amiss?: see 4531.

13 Ran Time 1m 37.33 (0.83) Owned: Mr Simon Gibson Trained: Newmarket

4888 3.00 Gr1 Shadwell Stud Middle Park Stakes Colts 2yo (A1)
£110606 £41954 £20977 6f str Good/Firm 20 -03 Slow Centre

4736* **AD VALOREM 12** [4] A P O'Brien 2-8-11 J P Spencer 9/2: 111: Handy, hdwy to lead over 1f out,   **121**
styd on strongly for press to hold on: well bckd: unbtn: v eff at 6f, shld stay 7f: acts on fast & gd grnd, gall
trks: smart & genuine, shld win more Group races: see 4736.

4680 **REBUTTAL 13** [1] B J Meehan 2-8-11 P J Smullen 9/1: 2132: Held up, hdwy over 2f out, chall ins   ¾ **118**
last, kept on, not btn far: progressing with every start & must win a Gr 2/3: see 4680, 4028.

4493 **ICEMAN 21** [6] J H M Gosden 2-8-11 (100) K Fallon 9/4 FAV: 21123: Held up, rdn & outpcd over 2f   2½ **111**
out, styd on strongly ins last, nrst fin: well bckd: most progressive & smart earlier, crying out for rtn to 7f.

4390+ **SATCHEM 27** [9] C E Brittain 2-8-11 L Dettori 9/2: 21114: In tch, eff over 1f out, onepace: up   nk **110**
in class & shade below form of 4390 (Gr 3), 3065.

4734 **RUSSIAN BLUE 12** [7]2-8-11 J Murtagh 9/1: 1123335: Trkd ldr, led over 2f out till over 1f out,   ½ **108**
no extra: btr 4734, 4159.

4633* **JOSH 15** [5]2-8-11 P Robinson 33/1: 13016: Held up, btn over 1f out: stiff task, needs stks as in 4633. 1 **105**

4770* **DRAMATICUS 7** [3]2-8-11 S Sanders 14/1: 317: Held up, eff & short of room over 1f out, no dngr: 1 **102**
prob best to forgive this: big step up in class after mdn win in 4770, more to come.

4651* **PRINCE CHARMING 14** [8]2-8-11 (98) K McEvoy 14/1: 110618: Led over 3f, wknd over 1f out: showed   shd **102**
much more 4651 (5f, gd/soft, List).

4533* **CHATEAU ISTANA 20** [5]2-8-11 t (98) K Darley 16/1: 611019: Handy, wknd fnl 1f: showed much more   hd **101**
over 5f in 4533 (Gr 2, first time t-strap).

9 Ran Time 1m 12.19 (1.39) Owned: Mrs John Magnier Trained: Ireland

4889 3.35 Greene King Ipa Champions Beer Handicap Stakes 3yo+ 86-100 (C1)   **[114]**
£12301 £4666 £2333 1m4f Good/Firm 20 +06 Fast Centre

4715 **VINANDO 11** [16] C R Egerton 3-8-8 t (94) L Dettori 12/1: 5-10151: Handy, hdwy over 2f out, led   **103**
just ins last, styd on well for press: suited by 12f now on fast or gd/soft, gall or sharp trks: wears a t-strap:
lightly rcd & progressive/useful stayer: see 3468.

2255 **MANORSON 118** [17] M A Magnusson 5-8-7 (1oh)t (85) E Ahern 12/1: 2/115/-002: ch g Desert King -   nk **94**
Familiar (Diesis) Cl-up, led 4f out, rdn & hdd ins last, kept on for press, just held: 4 month abs: missed '03,

'02 mdn & h'cap wnr: clrly stays 12f well on fast, soft & polytrack, any trk: gd weight carrier: runs well fresh: useful, game eff & can win shortly.
1 Mar'02 Donc 10.2sft 88-83 D: 1 Mar'02 Ling 10ap 83a- D: 2 Dec'01 Ling 10ap 79a- D:

4643* **SOLO FLIGHT** 14 [4] H Morrison 7-8-8 (87) R L Moore 20/1: 2602013: Held up, hdwy 2f out, kept on same pace: ran to form of 4643.	1½	92
4814 **OVAMBO** 5 [12] P J Makin 6-9-7 (100) S Sanders 20/1: 6243/-464: Held up, hdwy over 2f out, onepace.	2½	101
4681 **PAGAN SKY** 13 [14]5-8-7 (3oh) (83) Lisa Jones 20/1: 61-00645: Held up, eff over 2f out, onepace: longer trip: see 4392.	1	85
4814* **FORT** 5 [3]3-8-7 (6ex) (93) N Mackay(3) 4/1 FAV: 0320516: In tch, eff over 2f out, sn no impress: shade too sn after 4814?	nk	92
4715 **LARKWING** 11 [11]3-8-2 (88) F Norton 12/1: 23125S7: Handy, no extra over 1f out: see 4324, 3534.	½	86
4715 **VAUGHAN** 11 [8]3-8-5 (1ow) (90) K Darley 12/1: 01-048: In tch, wknd over 1f out: see 4715.	nk	88
4634 **KING EIDER** 15 [13]5-8-7 (3oh) (83) P Hanagan 50/1: 2/5603-09: Keen, handy, lost pl 3f out, some late gains: needs further: see 4634.	¾	82
4643 **TIP THE DIP** 14 [15]4-8-7 (1oh) (85) K McEvoy 13/2: 2131-20: 10th: Chsd ldr, wknd over 2f out: see 4643.	1¾	79
4491 **HEISSE** 21 [5]4-8-12 (91) R Hughes 66/1: 20-50000: 11th: Slow away, sn handy, wknd over 1f out.	5	77
3999 **PRINS WILLEM** 45 [1]5-8-8 VIS t (87) K Fallon 12/1: 0-234500: 12th: Held up, btn over 2f out: abs, vis.	1½	71
4383 **MILLVILLE** 27 [10]4-8-7 (1oh) (85) P Robinson 9/2: 1105450: 13th: Held up, btn over 3f out: btr 4383.	4	64
4530 **FAMOUS GROUSE** 20 [6]4-9-5 (98) D Holland 40/1: 020-0460: 14th: Al bhd.	3½	71
4534 **BAGAN** 20 [9]5-8-7 (86) W Ryan 25/1: 5-444040: 15th: Al bhd.	9	47
4715 **LUNAR EXIT** 11 [2]3-8-6 BL (92) J F Egan 50/1: 315-6060: 16th: Handy, wknd over 3f out: hung left.	nk	52
4772 **MUHAREB** 7 [7]5-8-11 (90) J Murtagh 16/1: 04-50050: 17th: In tch, wknd over 2f out: 'breathing prob'.	8	38

17 Ran   Time 2m 30.5 (1.7)   Owned: Mrs Evelyn Hankinson   Trained: Chaddleworth

---

4890   4.10 Taittinger Champagne E B F Classified Stakes 3yo+ 0-90 (C1)
£11971 £4541 £2270   1m str   Good/Firm 20   +07 Fast   Centre

4813 **ROYAL PRINCE** 5 [2] J R Fanshawe 3-8-11 (89) J P Murtagh 13/2: 4113341: Held up, hdwy to lead centre group dist, kept on well for press to lead overall cl-home: well bckd: shade below best in a t-strap last time, back to form here & stays 1m well on firm, gd/soft & polytrack, gall trks: useful, genuine & progressive.		99
4208* **DAWN SURPRISE** 35 [10] Saeed bin Suroor 3-8-11 t (93) L Dettori 5/4 FAV: 3-215112: Led far side duo, clr over 1f out, rdn & collared cl-home: hvly bckd: proving tough, useful: see 4208.	½	97
4279 **ACE OF HEARTS** 32 [4] C F Wall 5-9-0 (90) E Ahern 12/1: 2111003: Handy centre, led that group over 1f out, sn hdd & onepace: back to form: see 2606.	1¾	93
4685 **JAZZ SCENE** 13 [1] M R Channon 3-9-0 (93) A Culhane 8/1: 0224524: Sn rdn centre, outpcd halfway, some late gains: worth a try over further now: see 4685, 2749.	2	92
3814 **APPALACHIAN TRAIL** 54 [3]3-8-11 (87) P Hanagan 14/1: 010465: In tch, wknd over 1f out: abs.	2½	84
4607 **OUR JAFFA** 16 [8]3-8-8 (83) P Robinson 33/1: 4112506: Led centre over 6f, wknd.	2½	76
4389 **STATE DILEMMA** 27 [5]3-8-11 (90) M Hills 14/1: 5100047: In tch centre, wknd over 1f out: btr 4389.	nk	78
4516 **UNITED NATIONS** 20 [7]3-8-13 vis (92) S Sanders 11/1: 1348: Chsd ldrs centre, wknd over 1f out.	9	62
4773 **BRAVO MAESTRO** 7 [6]3-9-0 (93) K Fallon 12/1: 11-60509: Slow away & al bhd: 'breathing prob'.	20	23
MARKO JADEO 22 [11]6-9-1 (91) R Hughes 25/1: 3003310: 10th: Chsd ldr far side till wknd 3f out: reportedly free to post: Irish import, claim wnr earlier: stays 7.5f on firm, gd & sand.	¾	19

10 Ran   Time 1m 37.59 (1.09)   Owned: Mr Abdulla BuHaleeba   Trained: Newmarket

---

4891   4.45 Reg Day Memorial Handicap Stakes 3yo+ 86-100 (C1)
£12277 £4657 £2328   7f str   Good/Firm 20   -11 Slow   Centre   [107]

4208 **WIZARD OF NOZ** 35 [6] J Noseda 4-9-0 BL (93) E Ahern 12/1: 6055551: Handy, hdwy to lead dist, styd on well, rdn out: v eff at 7f on firm & soft grnd, likes a gall trks: useful, sharpened up by blnks, also ran well in first time visor earlier: see 2489.		101
4392 **LEOBALLERO** 27 [2] D J Daly 4-8-7 (7oh)t (79) J F Egan 20/1: 1-535402: Held up, hung right & hdwy over 1f out, kept on: btr run dropped back to 7f: see 2532, 1891.	1	90
4780+ **JONNY EBENEEZER** 6 [16] D Flood 5-9-2 (6ex)bl e (95) Hayley Turner(3) 12/1: 1100013: Held up, eff over 1f out, kept on, in fine heart: see 4784 (5f, soft).	1	98
4873 **MASTER ROBBIE** 1 [3] M R Channon 5-8-7 (2oh) (84) S Hitchcott 16/1: 00000004: Handy, eff over 1f out, kept on: tough: unplcd at Goodwood yesterday: see 3782, 2090.	¾	87
4800 **GREENSLADES** 6 [15]5-9-0 (93) S Sanders 7/2 FAV: 0306605:	dht	94
4523 **DIGITAL** 20 [1]7-8-9 (88) A Culhane 12/1: 0002205: Held up, some late gains: likes soft.	hd	88
951 **FREMEN** 188 [5]3-9-2 (93) K Fallon 8/1: 23110-07: ch c Rahy - Northern Trick (Northern Dancer). In tch, eff & short of room over 1f out, kept on ins last: won 2 of 5 '03 starts, mdn & h'cap: stays 1m well on firm & fast grnd: encouraging eff, closer with a clr run.	nk	91
1 Aug'03 Ripo 8g/f 93-88 C: 1 Aug'03 Wind 8.3g/f 93-88 D: 2 Apr'03 Beve 8.5g/f 88- D:		
4683* **DOCTORATE** 13 [14]3-8-5 (86) K Darley 11/1: 1253018: In tch, hdwy to lead over 1f out, rider dropped rein & hdd dist: no extra: shade more expected after 4683.	1	83
4523 **VINDICATION GB** 20 [13]4-8-8 t (87) N Mackay(3) 10/1: 0-066009: Held up, eff over 1f out, no impress.	1½	81
3338 **COLOUR WHEEL** 72 [11]3-8-8 VIS t (89) R Hughes 40/1: 2-602000: 10th: Chsd ldr, ch when hmpd over 1f out, sn no extra: abs, vis.	hd	82
4331 **ASIA WINDS** 29 [5]3-8-9 (90) M Hills 33/1: 155-5000: 11th: Nvr a factor.	shd	82
4686 **POMFRET LAD** 13 [7]6-8-13 (92) J Murtagh 25/1: 2-000000: 12th: Made most till over 5f, wknd: see 4459.	½	83
4523 **JEDBURGH** 20 [12]3-9-2 (97) I Mongan 8/1: 3320250: 13th: In tch, eff & hung left over 1f out, no extra.	shd	87
4523 **GOLDEN SAHARA** 20 [4]3-9-4 t (99) L Dettori 5/1: 22-03130: 14th: Held up, wknd over 1f out: btr 4532.	2	85
1957 **MAZEPA** 130 [8]4-9-0 (93) R L Moore 33/1: 00-63050: 15th: In tch, wknd over 2f out.	1½	76

15 Ran   Time 1m 25.38(2.18)   Owned: Mr C Fox & Mr J Wright   Trained: Newmarket

LINGFIELD **Polytrack FRIDAY 01.10.04 Lefthand, V Sharp Track**

Official Going Standard

4892 **1.30 Joe Hollywood 50th Birthday Maiden Stakes Div 1 3yo+ (D3)**
£3819 £1175 £588 **1m5f aw Going 20 -00 Slow** Inside

3243 **SHASTYE 77** [10] J H M Gosden 3-8-8 (73) R Havlin 10/1: 0341: Rear, smooth hdwy 3f out & led over 1f out, readily asserted, val 8L+: AW bow: eff at 10f, relished this step up to 13f: acts on gd grnd & enjoyed polytrack today, handles a sharp or stiff/undul trk: much imprvd, lightly rcd & interesting for h'caps: see 3243. **76a+**
4501 **PARLIAMENT SQUARE 21** [3] D R Loder 3-8-13 W Supple 11/2: 352: Trkd ldrs, smooth prog to briefly lead over 1f out, sn no ch with wnr: AW bow: styd longer 13f trip well: acts on polytrack & gd/soft grnd: see 1148. *7* **69a**
4547 **KEY IN 18** [11] B W Hills 3-8-8 T Quinn 50/1: 063: Rear, pushed along & hdwy 4f out, not pace of wnr over 1f out: AW bow: imprvd over longer 13f trip, acts on polytrack: see 4547. *shd* **64a**
4501 **KIPSIGIS 21** [2] Lady Herries 3-8-13 J Quinn 16/1: 044: Mid-div, keeping on when short of room ins last, closer to 2nd with clr run: AW bow, longer 13f will suit, prob get further: handles polytrack: a likely improver in mid-dist/staying h'caps: see 4501. *2* **66a+**
4449 **ALEXEI 24** [13]3-8-13 O Urbina 12/1: 025: Mid-div wide, handy 2f out, no extra over 1f out: see 4449. *hd* **65a**
4111 **DALISAY 41** [4]3-8-8 (74) R Winston 9/4 FAV: 0-3326: Led, reluctant on bend & hanging 2f out, sn hdd & no extra: 6 wk abs: btr 4111 & 2793. *hd* **59a**
330} **RED RACKHAM 633** [8]4-9-7 T E Durcan 14/1: 0/5-7: b g Groom Dancer - Manarah (Marju) Handy till lost pl after 6f, sn bhd in rear, mod gains: gelded, long abs: unplcd sole '03 start (rtd 69a, mdn, unplcd sole '02 start (rtd 65a, mdn): lkd a hard ride today. *¾* **63a**
4151 **SIMONS SEAT 38** [7]5-9-7 (58) S W Kelly 33/1: 30-66608: Slow away & rdn rear early, only mod prog. *½* **62a**
4111 **SUNSHINE ON ME 41** [5]3-8-8 R Mullen 33/1: 059: Dwelt, rear, some hdwy over 2f out, sn hmpd & position accepted: 6 wk abs: not gvn hard time, likely improver in low-grade h'cap company. *nk* **56a**
4353 **CHANTELOUP 28** [9]3-8-8 (80) Dane O'Neill 3/1: 244350: 10th: Chsd ldr 3f out, wknd qckly over 1f out. *3½* **51a**
EXPLOSIVE FOX 61 [12]3-8-13 (67) M Tebbutt 20/1: 0035020: 11th: gr c Foxhound - Grise Mine (Crystal Palace) Al bhd & no ch fnl 2f: 2 month abs, ex Irish: appr h'cap rnr-up earlier this term: eff around 11/13f on firm & gd/soft grnd, sharp trks. *nk* **55a**
3899 **LYES GREEN 50** [1]3-8-13 N Chalmers(3) 40/1: 40: 12th: Prom, btn 2f out, abs, AW bow, gelded. *nk* **54a**
3732 **Irish Playwright 57** [14]4-9-7 V Slattery 66/1:0 4579 **Pagan Ceremony 17** [6]3-8-13 S Drowne 66/1:0
14 Ran Time 2m 44.84 (2.54) Owned: Skara Glen Stables Trained: Manton

LINGFIELD **Polytrack FRIDAY 01.10.04 Lefthand, Sharp, Undulating Track**

Official Going Good/Firm

4893 **2.00 European Breeders Fund Turf Maiden Stakes 2yo (D3)**
£4251 £1308 £654 **5f str Good/Firm Inapplicable** Stands Side

3987 **DANES CASTLE 46** [10] B J Meehan 2-9-0 bl (75) J F McDonald(3) 9/2: 322331: Hanging left but made all, rdn & asserted fnl 2f, styd on well: 6 wk abs: stays 6f, suited by forcing tactics at 5f: acts on fast, gd & both AWs, gall or sharp trk: eff with/without blnks: most consistent & genuine, deserved this: see 3987, 3817. **86**
4409 **BORN FOR DANCING 25** [9] B W Hills 2-8-9 Dane O'Neill 8/1: 252: Hung left thr'out & chsd wnr, no impress on wnr from over 1f out but kept on: handles firm & fast grnd: now quals for h'caps: see 2437. *1¼* **76**
4617 **CAPTAIN JOHNNO 15** [8] D R Loder 2-9-0 VIS W Supple 11/2: 033: Went left start & sn hanging left, switched towards centre & styd on for press fnl 2f, nvr land a blow: eff at 5f, rtn to 6f shld suit: handles fast & gd/soft grnd: fair run in first time visor: see 4617. *¾* **79**
4823 **RUSKY DUSKY 4** [7] R Hannon 2-9-0 BL (77) P Dobbs 11/2: 3255664: Chsd ldrs, outpcd fnl 2f, blnks. *1¾* **74**
4422 **NODINA 25** [6]2-9-0 N Callan 33/1: 05: br c Primo Dominie - Princess Tara (Prince Sabo) Reluctant to enter stalls & sn outpcd, mod hdwy: May foal, 28,000gns purchase, half-brother to a smart 2yo wnr, also useful 5/7f performer Compton Eleven: dam a 5/6f juv scorer & subs 1m 3yo wnr. *¾* **72**
4787 **DAISYS GIRL 6** [2]2-8-9 BL S Drowne 20/1: 066: Reluctant to enter stalls, dwelt & sn outpcd, only mod prog: first time blnks: now quals for h'caps: see 4787. *3* **58**
4599 **GOLDEN ASHA 16** [1]2-8-9 R Mullen 9/4 FAV: 37: Chsd ldrs, struggling from halfway. *½* **56**
4121 **FOREST DELIGHT 39** [4]2-8-9 C Catlin 14/1: 08: Chsd ldrs, no impress fnl 2f. *½* **54**
4859 **WATERFRONT DANCER 2** [3]2-9-0 G Baker 66/1: 09: Sn outpcd & nvr a factor, qck reapp. *5* **45**
4599 **PRETTY WOMAN 16** [5]2-8-9 N Pollard 10/1: 00: 10th: Dwelt, al outpcd. *shd* **40**
10 Ran Time 58.96 (2.16) Owned: Mr Ed McCormack Trained: Upper Lambourn

4894 **2.35 Book A Box At Lingfield Nursery Handicap Stakes 2yo 0-75 (E3)** **[82]**
£3777 £1162 £581 **7f str Good/Firm Inapplicable** Stands Side

4444 **SEASONS ESTATES 24** [9] B R Millman 2-8-8 (62) P Doe 10/1: 40431: Handy & led 2f out, drvn & held on well: first win: suited by 7f on fast & gd grnd, sharp/undul or gall trk: likes to race with/force the pace. **71**
4697 **ABERDEEN PARK 11** [14] Mrs H Sweeting 2-8-12 (66) G Baker 6/1 JT FAV: 5004522: Dwelt, sn mid-div, chall over 1f out, no extra fnl 100yds: eff at 6/7f on firm, gd & prob handles gd/soft grnd: - *½* **73**
4635 **CAPTAIN MARGARET 15** [15] J Pearce 2-8-7 t (61) J Quinn 25/1: 05003: Twds rear, outpcd over 2f out, short of room & swtchd over 1f out, drvn & finished well: wants further. *1¼* **65+**
4437 **STARLIGHT RIVER 24** [10] W R Muir 2-8-8 (62) D Kinsella 33/1: 00304: Cl-up, onepace for press fnl 1f: stays 7f: handles fast & gd/soft grnd: see 3896. *shd* **66**
4666 **ELTIZAAM 13** [3]2-9-7 (75) W Supple 7/1: 65635: Dwelt, held in mid-div, kept on onepace: see 4666. *½* **78**
4418 **MIDCAP 25** [11]2-9-2 (70) Dane O'Neill 12/1: 06036: Dwelt, rear, hdwy to chase ldrs dist, no extra. *hd* **72**
4610 **LADY PILOT 16** [13]2-9-2 (70) T E Durcan 11/1: 0067: Chsd ldrs, onepace & held bef dist: h'cap bow. *nk* **71**
4178 **GO MO 36** [6]2-9-3 (71) M Fenton 16/1: 0668: Rear & rdn early, mod gains for press, h'cap bow. *1¼* **69**
4410 **DREEMON 25** [17]2-8-13 (67) S W Kelly 25/1: 030009: Cl-up, rdn & no extra over 1f out. *shd* **65**
4079 **FORTNUM 42** [18]2-8-7 (61) R Thomas(3) 6/1 JT FAV: 530530: 10th: Cl-up, rdn & btn over 1f out: abs. *nk* **58**
4471 **STORM FURY 22** [20]2-8-10 (64) Thomas Yeung(5) 16/1: 030000: 11th: Chsd ldrs, short of room 2f out *1¾* **58**

LINGFIELD   Polytrack   FRIDAY 01.10.04   Lefthand, Sharp, Undulating Track

& lost pl, no impress after.

4576	**BYRON BAY 17** [19]2-9-0 (68) R Miles(3) 25/1: 0050: 12th: Dwelt, mid-div, eff 2f out, sn wknd.	nk	61
3127	**LILY LENAT 83** [16]2-9-4 P (72) D Sweeney 14/1: 04300: 13th: Led 5f, fdd, cheek pieces, abs: btr 2395.	nk	64
4369	**TANNING 27** [5]2-8-11 (65) S Drowne 15/2: 6230: 14th: Chsd ldrs, struggling from halfway, h'cap bow.	½	56
4204	**NORTHERN SECRET 35** [12]2-9-2 (70) R Mullen 14/1: 0300: 15th: Al bhd & no ch halfway, h'cap bow.	nk	60
3818	**GUYANA 53** [1]2-9-3 (71) C Catlin 20/1: 0030: 16th: Chsd ldrs till halfway, sn wknd, 8 wk abs: btr 3818.	15	34
4645	**PEOPLETON BROOK 14** [2]2-8-9 (63) J F McDonald(3) 50/1: 56000: 17th: Rcd alone far side, prom 5f.	1½	23

17 Ran   Time 1m 25.24 (4.84)   Owned: Seasons Holidays   Trained: Cullompton

---

4895
3.10 Enterprise Inns 'premier' Claiming Stakes 2yo   (D2)
£6061 £1865 £933   **6f str**   **Good/Firm**   **Inapplicable**   Stands Side

4741	**COCONUT SQUEAK 9** [15] J G Given 2-8-1 (63) J Mackay 14/1: 36001: Made all, in command over 1f		69
	out, rdn & al holding rivals ins last: stay 7f, apprec drop to 6f in claim grade: acts on fast & gd grnd, stiff/gall		
	or sharp/undul trk: likes to race with/force the pace: see 3425.		
4677	**ATACAMA STAR 13** [18] B G Powell 2-9-5 A Hindley(7) 33/1: 02: ch g Desert King - Aunty (Riverman)	2	82
	Mid-div, styd on for press, not able to chall: gelded & left debut bhd: Apr foal, 10,000gns 2yo purchase:		
	half-brother to a smart 5f/1m juv Dame Laura: eff at 6f, 7f suit: win sn.		
4645	**ARBORS LITTLE GIRL 14** [10] B R Millman 2-8-8 (66) A Daly 5/2 FAV: 1153: Mid-div, styd on for	¾	70
	press, nrst fin: worth a try at 7f: see 4545 & 3847.		
4633	**ISLAND SWING 15** [1] J L Spearing 2-9-0 (81) S Drowne 7/1: 1140034: Sn chsd ldrs, onepace for	½	75
	press from dist: gd run from awkward low draw: see 4633, 2358.		
4645	**PENNESTAMP 14** [3]2-8-6 (65) R Havlin 20/1: 6644305: Handy, outpcd over 1f out: see 4123 & 3686.	1¾	64
4583	**LATERAL THINKER 17** [12]2-8-9 (68) S W Kelly 7/1: 1052606: Mid-div, onepace for press fnl 2f.	½	66
4706	**MISS MALONE 11** [2]2-8-6 (71) P Dobbs 10/1: 0240057: Mid-div, not pace to chall: see 3183.	1¾	60
4545	**PERIANTH 18** [9]2-8-11 (62) J F McDonald(3) 10/1: 400038: Towards rear & outpcd early, mod prog.	1	63
3994	**GOLDHILL PRINCE 46** [5]2-8-9 p (63) C Haddon(7) 20/1: 1136539: Cl-up, btn 2f out: 6 wk abs: see 3994.	½	60
4503	**BODDEN BAY 20** [19]2-8-8 (1ow) N Callan 66/1: 000: 10th: Rear, only mod prog.	2	55
4741	**MERRYMADCAP 9** [4]2-8-13 BL (65) Dane O'Neill 25/1: 5660600: 11th: Dwelt, mid-div, btn 2f out, blnks.	1	58
4127	**HIAMOVI 39** [16]2-8-13 (64) A Quinn(5) 20/1: 0520: 12th: Cl-up till over 2f out, fdd: btr 4127 (AW).	3	52
4422	**RED MARTEENEY 25** [8]2-9-5 T Quinn 20/1: 060: 13th: Al bhd.	½	57
4759*	**WILTSHIRE 8** [13]2-8-9 (60) L Harman(6) 20/1: 000010: 14th: Mid-div & sn pushed along, btn when no	1¼	44
	room over 1f out: btr 4759 (5f, seller).		
4218*	**RUBY MUJA 34** [6]2-8-4 (62) M Fenton 12/1: 00310: 15th: Chsd ldrs 4f: new yard: btr 4218 (5f).	1¾	36

	After The Snow 0 [17]2-8-0 (1ow) C Catlin 33/1:0		**4759**	**Imperatrice 8** [7]2-8-0 P M Henry 33/1:0
4760	**Sergeant Lewis 8** [20]2-8-9 V Slattery 25/1:0		**4178**	**Killington 36** [14]2-8-11 R Winston 12/1:0

19 Ran   Time 1m 12.07 (3.27)   Owned: Moneyleague Ltd   Trained: Gainsborough

---

LINGFIELD   Polytrack   FRIDAY 01.10.04   Lefthand, V Sharp Track

Official Going Standard

4896
3.45 European Breeders Fund Awt Maiden Stakes 2yo   (D3)
£4381 £1348 £674   **6f aw rnd**   **Going 20**   **-11 Slow**   Outside

4349	**EMERALD LODGE 28** [4] J Noseda 2-9-0 VIS S W Kelly 12/1: 351: Led/dsptd lead & went on after 2f,		86a
	in command over 1f out, rdn out: AW bow: eff at 5f, imprvd for step up to 6f: handles fast & gd grnd, enjoyed		
	polytrack today & forcing tactics: much imprvd for first time visor: see 4349, 3993.		
3824	**BOLODENKA 53** [9] W J Musson 2-9-0 R Mullen 8/1: 02: b c Soviet Star - My Lorraine (Mac's Imp)	2½	77a
	Twds rear, briefly rdn & styd on take 2nd ins last, nvr threat: 7 wk abs, AW bow: £35,000 Mar foal,		
	half-brother to a 5f wnr, dam a 5/6f 3yo scorer: eff at 6f on polytrack & a sharp trk: not knocked about, shapes as		
	the type to progress & find a race.		
	EL REY DEL MAMBO 0 [11] G A Butler 2-9-0 S Drowne 13/8 FAV: 3: b c Kingmambo - Scarab Bracelet	1¾	72a
	(Riverman) Sn trkd ldrs, shkn up & onepace/held dist: nicely bckd on debut: 95,000gns 2yo, May foal, dam a		
	multiple US wnr: sire smart juv & subs top-class miler: eff at 6f on polytrack.		
	SCRIPTED 0 [5] Sir Mark Prescott 2-9-0 J Mackay 16/1: 4: b g Diktat - Krameria (Kris) Pushed	½	70a
	along chasing ldrs, not able to chall but kept on, clr of rem: weak in mkt on debut: May foal, half-brother to		
	multiple sprint wnr Palawan, dam a 5f juv wnr: eff at 6f, handles polytrack.		
4443	**RIGHT TO ROAM 24** [6]2-9-0 J Quinn 25/1: 405: Outpcd towards rear, mod prog, nvr factor.	5	56a
4200	**WORLD MUSIC 35** [3]2-8-9 T E Durcan 2/1: 36: Handy, rdn & btn over 1f out: btr 4200.	nk	50a
4677	**CHIRACAHUA 13** [2]2-9-0 R Winston 33/1: 07: Led 2f, btn over 1f out.	5	41a
	WIZ IN 0 [8]2-9-0 M Henry 33/1: 8: Slow away & al outpcd rear.	¾	39a
	SILVER SWING 0 [7]2-9-0 Dane O'Neill 20/1: 9: Dwelt,wide & al outpcd.	nk	38a
	GIRLSWEEKEND 0 [10]2-8-9 P Doe 33/1: 0: 10th: U.r. bef start, slow away & al bhd.	4	22a
	JUST CLIFF 0 [1]2-9-0 N Callan 66/1: 0: 11th: Chsd ldrs till halfway, sn bhd.	1¼	23a
	MISS HERMIONE 0 [12]2-8-9 J McAuley 50/1: 0: 12th: Dwelt & sn outpcd, t.o.	11	0a

12 Ran   Time 1m 12.24 (1.84)   Owned: Hesmonds Stud   Trained: Newmarket

---

4897
4.20 H B L B Ladbrokes Com Handicap Stakes 3yo 71-85 (D2)
£7046 £2168 £1084   **7f aw rnd**   **Going 20**   **-00 Slow**   Inside   [91]

4110	**POLAR MAGIC 41** [1] J R Fanshawe 3-8-10 (73) Dane O'Neill 3/1 FAV: 121: Dwelt, rear, hdwy over 2f		84a
	out & led over 1f out, soon asserted : 6 wk abs on an AW bow: eff at 7f on gd, soft & polytrack: goes well fresh:		
	progressive, lightly rcd & can win again see 4110 & 2692.		
1879	**OUTER HEBRIDES 134** [4] D R Loder 3-8-13 T (76) W Supple 14/1: 221-0042: Chsd ldrs, rdn & hdwy to	2	81a
	lead over 1f out, sn hdd & not pace of wnr: 4 month abs, imprvd in t-strap: eff at 6/7f on fast grnd & both AWs.		
4713	**WYATT EARP 11** [5] J A R Toller 3-8-11 (74) T E Durcan 6/1: 0100023: Rear, styd on well for press	shd	79a

1483

ins last, nrst fin: styd longer 7f trip: handles fast, gd & polytrack, sharp or stiff trk: see 1734 (6f).

4683	**KALI 13** [3] R Charlton 3-8-13 (76) D Sweeney 13/2: 2-332164: Mid-div, switched & eff 2f out, onepace.	1	79a
4362	**MOSCOW TIMES 28** [9]3-8-9 (72) L Keniry(3) 20/1: 6501305: Rear, kept on wide, nvr land blow.	2½	70a
3954	**FANCY FOXTROT 48** [7]3-9-7 P (84) J F McDonald(3) 8/1: 0300006: Dwelt, rear, eff when short of room	shd	82a

over 1f out, onepce after: first time cheek pieces, 7 wk abs: see 2212 & 1021.

4561 +	**MOORS MYTH 18** [6]3-8-10 (73) S Drowne 10/1: 0-365617: Sn handy, wknd over 1f out: btr 4561 (mdn).	5	62a
4278	**BRIDGEWATER BOYS 32** [10]3-8-12 bl (75) N Callan 10/1: 1121508: Twds rear & wide, no impress.	nk	63a
4394	**MIDNIGHT BALLARD 27** [11]3-8-13 bl (76) T Quinn 33/1: 4201009: Led 2f, prom 5f, gelded.	nk	63a
2137	**BENNY THE BALL 122** [13]3-8-12 (75) M Fenton 20/1: 261-0000: 10th: Dwelt, mid-div wide, wknd 2f out.	1¼	59a
4465	**GLEBE GARDEN 23** [12]3-9-1 (78) R Mullen 25/1: 6001200: 11th: Chsd ldrs, btn over 1f out: btr 4251.	shd	62a
4350	**LITTLE RIDGE 28** [2]3-9-0 (77) L Fletcher(3) 50/1: 6011-000: 12th: Led after 2f till over 2f out, wknd qckly.	2¼	56a
4740*	**GLENCALVIE 9** [8]3-8-11 (6ex)vis (74) S W Kelly 5/1: 0504110: 13th: Sn pushed along in rear, btn	nk	52a

2f out: much btr 4740 & 3995 (turf).

13 Ran Time 1m 24.20 (1.4) Owned: Mr R C Thompson Trained: Newmarket

---

4898

4.55 Joe Hollywood 50th Birthday Maiden Stakes Div 2 3yo+ (D3)
£3799 £1169 £585 1m5f aw Going 20 +01 Fast Inside

2862	**MEISSEN 93** [5] E F Vaughan 3-8-8 (76) T Quinn 11/4 FAV: 60-221: Led/dsptd lead, went on over 2f		77a

out, drvn out: abs: eff at 10f, suited by 12/13f & could get further: acts on fast grnd & polytrack, sharp/undul or stiff trk: goes well fresh: see 2862 & 2386.

4415	**SEEKING A WAY 25** [11] J H M Gosden 3-8-8 (66) R Havlin 7/1: 21-23062: Rear, hdwy over 4f out &	½	75a

pressed wnr dist, drvn & al just held: AW bow: handles firm, fast & polytrack, stiff/gall or sharp trk: stays 13f.

4281	**SAMARIA 32** [4] C F Wall 3-8-8 VIS (72) J Quinn 4/1: 04243: Led/dsptd lead till over 2f out, no	4	69a

extra from dist: first time visor: prob stays 13f tho' rtn to 10/11f may suit: see 3997, 3802.

1358	**HELM 160** [1] R Rowe 3-8-13 P Doe 40/1: 04: Dwelt & held up, hdwy wide over 4f out, not able to	2½	70a

chall fnl 2f: gelded, 5 mth abs: longer trip: prev with L M Cumani.

4414	**RUGGTAH 25** [14]3-8-8 T E Durcan 7/1: 035: Held up, rdn & mod hdwy fnl 4f, nvr factor: see 4414.	2½	61a
	JONANAUD 0 [9]5-9-7 F P Ferris(3) 16/1: 6: b g Ballet Royal - Margaret Modes (Thatching) Dwelt,	1	65a

chsd ldrs, btn over 2f out, Flat debut, 6 month jumps abs (03/04 h'cap hdle & nov hdle scorer, rtd 114h, 2m/3m, fast & hvy, likes Chepstow).

2576	**VERASI 104** [2]3-8-13 (64) R Mullen 16/1: 000-4007: Chsd ldrs, btn 2f out, 3 month abs & new yard.	6	56a
3783	**RIVIERA RED 55** [10]4-9-7 A McCarthy 33/1: 08: Chsd ldrs, btn 3f out, 8 wk abs.	1	55a
4541	**MARIDAY 19** [12]3-8-13 Paul Eddery 16/1: 69: Rear & no ch fnl 4f, longer trip.	shd	55a
3783	**GRAND MUSIC 55** [8]4-9-7 BL A Quinn(5) 66/1: 00: 10th: Dwelt & al bhd, gelded, blnks, abs.	17	30a
4449	**MOANING MYRTLE 24** [7]3-8-8 Dane O'Neill 11/2: 40: 11th: Keen & trkd ldrs, wknd from halfway.	30	0a
4449	**CZECH SUMMER 24** [6]3-8-13 BL D Sweeney 100/1: 00: 12th: Dwelt, mid-div, t.o. from halfway, blnks.	dist	0a
4749	**LOMAPAMAR 9** [13]3-8-8 (78) S Drowne 9/1: 030-300: 13th: Mid-div wide, t.o. fnl 5f, eased.	dist	0a
	HELIXALOT 0 [3]3-8-13 D Corby(3) 66/1: 0: 14th: Dwelt & al bhd, drvn & btn halfway, t.o., debut.	dist	0a

14 Ran Time 2m 44.82 (2.52) Owned: Mr B H Voak Trained: Newmarket

---

4899

5.25 Lingfield-Racecourse Co Uk Apprentice Classified Stakes 3yo+ 0-60 (F3)
£3533 £1087 £544 1m4f aw Going 20 -03 Slow Inside

4594	**BROUGHTON KNOWS 17** [12] Miss Gay Kelleway 7-9-3 bl (54) A Kirby(7) 14/1: 1124641: Dwelt, keen in		63a

rear, hdwy 3f out, styd on for press to lead well ins last: eff at 10f/2m on both AWs & fast grnd: see 4594, 722.

4252	**KING OF KNIGHT 33** [8] G Prodromou 3-8-10 (59) A Beech 20/1: 4500042: Mid-div, hdwy 3f out & led	1	61a

over 1f out, hdd well in last & no extra: styd longer 12f trip: handles polytrack & gd/soft grnd: see 4252, 2530.

4634	**KING FLYER 15** [15] Miss J Feilden 8-9-3 e (60) B Reilly 11/2: 0200053: Mid-div, hdwy to lead over	2	58a

2f out till over 1f out, not pace of front pair: btr 4634 & 3032 (turf).

4092*	**SCOTT 42** [11] J Jay 3-8-10 (60) C Haddon(5) 7/1: 0060314: Mid-div, hdwy wide to chall 2f out, sn	1¼	56a

onepace: abs: see 4092 (fibresand).

4182*	**WILLHEGO 36** [7]3-8-10 (60) R Thomas 6/1: 0-002315: Trkd ldrs, no extra for press dist: btr 4182 (10f).	½	55a
4623	**JOLIZERO 15** [13]3-8-10 (60) Thomas Yeung(5) 5/1 JT FAV: 4032506: Rcd keenly & led after 2f till	1¼	53a

over 2f out, sn btn: btr 3856.

2433	**CHOCOLATE BOY 109** [16]5-9-3 (60) A Quinn(3) 16/1: 4102567: Rear, mod late hdwy, nvr a threat: abs.	2	50a
4320	**STATE OF BALANCE 30** [3]6-9-0 (60) L Keniry 14/1: 40-04168: Dwelt & towards rear, nvr able to chall.	½	46a
4757	**OUR EMMY LOU 8** [2]3-8-7 (58) S Archer(7) 5/1 JT FAV: 2456159: Led 2f, remained handy till over 1f out.	nk	45a
4486	**DANCING BEAR 22** [6]3-8-10 BL (57) M Halford(5) 50/1: 0-40340: 10th: Keen in mid-div, btn over 1f	2	45a

out: blnks: btr 4486 & 1871.

4320	**RAHEEL 30** [14]4-9-3 t (58) M Savage(3) 33/1: 4300000: 11th: Dwelt, rear, eff 3f out, sn btn.	1½	43a
4388	**TURTLE PATRIARCH 27** [10]3-8-10 (59) R Miles 10/1: 0004260: 12th: Chsd ldr 5f out, btn when no	3	38a

room over 2f out: btr 4119.

4415 **Embassy Sweets 25** [4]3-8-7 (55) N De Souza(3) 33/1:0 3727 **Chanfron 57** [5]3-8-10 (52) D Fox(3) 50/1:0
3741 **Our Little Rosie 57** [9]3-8-7 (56) A Putland(7) 50/1:0   4856 **Saxe Coburg 2** [1]7-9-3 (55) D Nolan 20/1:P
16 Ran Time 2m 31.99(2.79) Owned: Mr A J Clarke Trained: Newmarket

---

Official Going Good All Times Slow

4900   11.05 Betfred Com In-Running Maiden Auction Stakes 2yo (H5)
£1453 £415 £208   6f rnd   Good   Inapplicable   Inside

4792 **BEAU MARCHE 7** [3] I A Wood 2-8-10 (61) I Mongan 28/1: 500201: Trkd ldr, chall wnr over 1f out &   72
prevailed on the nod, all out: eff at 6f on fast & gd ground: jockey given a 3 day whip ban: see 4316.
4658 **PINAFORE 14** [2] H Morrison 2-8-3 (1ow) R L Moore 1/2 FAV: 322: Led, duelled with wnr over 1f   shd 64
out, just denied on line: handles fast, gd & polytrk: jockey given a 1-day whip ban: btr 4658.
3311 **MOONFLEET 75** [1] M F Harris 2-8-4   A Nicholls 50/1: 03: b f Entrepreneur - Lunasa (Don't Forget   3   56
Me) Hld up, onepace fnl 1f: 11 wk abs: cheaply bought Mar foal: dam a 14f wnr.
4369 **AVERTIGO 28** [6] W R Muir 2-8-11 (73) T E Durcan 3/1: 532024: Chsd ldrs, rdn & btn dist: btr 4369.   6   47
3981 **VINO VENUS 47** [5]2-8-3 N Chalmers(2) 16/1: 05: b f Tipsy Creek - Galaxy Glow (Kalaglow) Dwelt,   nk   38
sn rdn & no impress fnl 2f: 7 wk abs: cheaply bought May foal, half sister to a placed 5f juv abroad: dam unplaced.
4704 **DEWIN COCH 12** [4]2-8-7 S Whitworth 12/1: 006: Keen, rear, rdn & bhd fnl 2f.   ¾   40
6 Ran   Time 1m 13.21 (5.41)   Owned: Mr Christopher Shankland   Trained: Upper Lambourn

4901   11.35 Betfred Com Now Online Maiden Claiming Stakes 3yo+ (H5)
£1523 £435 £218   7f rnd   Good   Inapplicable   Inside

4794 **ELSINORA 7** [18] H Morrison 3-8-6 vis (45) R L Moore 5/2 JT FAV: 6352421: Swtchd start & held up,   47
hdwy to lead dist, rdn clr, decisively: claimed by A G Juckes for 3000: vis reapp: 1st win: eff at 6f/1m, 7f ideal:
acts on firm, soft & any trk: eff in chkpcs, blnks or vis: consistent & deserved this: see 4794, 4370 & 798.
4485 **WODHILL BE 23** [12] D Morris 4-9-2 (40) Paul Eddery 16/1: 3000002: Rear, kept on late to take 2nd: mdn. 5   44
4659 **CATCH THE FOX 14** [17] J J Bridger 4-9-7 (35) Hayley Turner(3) 10/1: 4000403: Rear, kept on wide   nk   48$
fnl 2f, no dngr: handles good & soft: see 1334.
4793 **BAHAMIAN BELLE 7** [9] P S McEntee 4-8-12 (35) J Brennan(7) 25/1: 0005004: Led 2 out till dist, wknd.   1½   36
3706 **ROVING VIXEN 59** [1]3-8-6 (40) R Miles(3) 14/1: 0334005: Led 5f, no extra: 2 mth abs: see 2667.   hd   31
1593 **SHAAMITS ALL OVER 149** [5]5-9-2 (30) M Savage(5) 20/1: 600-0036: Dwelt, chsd ldrs 5f, abs.   1¾   35
4616 **BLAKESEVEN 17** [2]4-9-7 BL (46) S Whitworth 20/1: 3223007: Keen chasing ldrs, found little over 1f out.   1½   38
4507 **LORD WISHINGWELL 21** [6]3-9-5 (30) P McCabe 5/2 JT FAV: 3046008: Prom, btn over 1f out: btr 3687. 5   29
480} **DANGEROUS DAVE 614** [10]5-9-5 (40) P Doe 16/1: 0/000-9: b g Superpower - Lovely Lilly (Arrasas)   nk   26
Chsd ldrs, no impress bef dist: long abs: unplcd '03 (rtd 35a).
4794 **COURT CHANCELLOR 7** [11]3-9-5 bl (40) J Mongan 33/1: 00-00000: 10th: Sn rdn mid-div, no impress.   ½   27
2218 **Military Two Step 120** [7]3-9-1 (50) L Enstone 66/1:0   3372 **Till There Was You 72** [15]3-8-6 C Haddon(7) 12/1:0
4504 **Mazram 21** [16]5-8-12 bl R Ffrench 66/1:0   4762 **Royal Logic 9** [13]3-9-0 (45) T E Durcan 50/1:0
4411 **Magico 26** [4]3-9-5 (48) Derek Nolan(7) 12/1:0   **Dunlea 141** [14]8-9-3 vis(35) B Reilly(3) 66/1:0
16 Ran   Time 1m 26.23 (6.43)   Owned: Mr John R Goddard and Mr John Steel   Trained: East Ilsley

4902   12.05 Betfred 'the Bonus King' Banded Stakes 3yo+ 0-45 (H5)
£1673 £478 £239   1m rnd   Good   Inapplicable   Inside

4165 **MAGIC VERSE 38** [5] R Guest 3-8-12 (46) R L Moore 13/2: 0444541: Chsd ldrs, rdn to lead ins last,   55
drvn clr: eff arnd 1m, tried 10f: acts on gd & fibresand, sharp/undul trks: 1st win today: see 2805, 2383.
4795* **CAERPHILLY GAL 7** [14] P L Gilligan 4-9-5 (50) D Fox(5) 4/1 FAV: 0-000012: Handy & briefly led   4   50
over 1f out, no extra ins last: prob ran to form of 4795.
4720 **SHAMWARI FIRE 11** [6] I W McInnes 4-9-4 (49) R Ffrench 8/1: 0013603: Mid-div, kept on for press,   ¾   48
not pace of wnr: likes banded company: eff at 1m, 9/10f poss ideal: see 4373 (9.7f).
4795 **LEVANTINE 7** [3] Miss J Feilden 7-9-3 (48) Kirsty Milczarek(7) 11/2: 3-356124: Reared start, led   2   43
after 1f, hdd over 1f out & wknd ins last: just btr 4795 & 4659.
4626 **ENCOUNTER 16** [1]8-9-0 (45) R Miles(3) 9/2: 2500535: Held up, taken wide & little prog fnl 2f: btr 4626.   3   34
4411 **PERERIN 26** [13]3-8-11 (45) L Enstone 16/1: 1000306: Held up, only mod prog: btr 4248.   1½   31
4676 **SUSIEDIL 14** [10]3-8-11 (45) M Coumbe(7) 25/1: 0066007: Always rear: btr 2432.   ¾   30
4698* **INESCAPABLE 12** [8]3-9-5 (53) T P Queally 14/1: 004018: Led 1f, rdn & wknd over 1f out: btr 4698 (7f).   1½   25
4366 **BELTANE 29** [12]6-9-1 (46) P Doe 22/1: 2000509: Slow away & always rear: flattered 3806.   1¼   25
4795 **WOOD FERN 7** [9]4-9-1 (46) T O'Brien(7) 11/1: 6100400: 10th: Always rear: btr 4707.   nk   24
3651 **LOVE OF LIFE 61** [15]3-9-1 (49) Lisa Jones 12/1: 006020: 11th: V slow away & always bhd: abs: btr 3651.   hd   26
4662 **Lady Liesel 14** [11]4-9-0 (45) Hayley Turner(3) 40/1:0
4720 **Sheer Focus 11** [2]6-9-2 p(47) Natalia Gemelova(5) 20/1:0
13 Ran   Time 1m 40.07 (8.07)   Owned: Mr Eugene Lismonde   Trained: Newmarket

4903   12.35 Betfred 'we Pay Double Result' Banded Stakes 3yo+ 0-45 (H5)
£1498 £428 £214   1m2f   Good   Inapplicable   Inside

4834 **ROMEOS DAY 5** [17] M R Channon 3-8-9 vis (40) T O'Brien(6) 12/1: 0005401: Mid-div, rdn & hdwy to   47
lead over 2f out, duelled with rnr up ins last, prevailed line, all out: 1st win: eff at 10/11.5f, tried 2m: acts on
fast & gd grnd. easy or sharp/undul trk: eff in a visor: see 1724.
4763 **LENWADE 9** [1] G G Margarson 3-8-9 (40) D Fox(5) 7/1: 4522132: Dwelt, keen & sn chsd ldrs, hmpd   shd 46
over 2f out, drvn to chall ins last, just denied: op 5/1: see 4763 & 4612.
4372 **ANISETTE 28** [7] Julian Poulton 3-8-9 (40) Lisa Jones 16/1: 0063653: Slow away & pshd along rear,   2   43
late gains to take 3rd, nvr threatened front pair: acts on fast, gd & fibresand: stays 10f: see 3706.
4708 **TARTIRUGA 12** [2] L G Cottrell 3-8-13 (49) S Whitworth 11/2: 0005624: Keen & prom, no impress   ½   46
over 1f out: acts on gd & hvy grnd: see 4708.
4669 **MIGHTY PIP 14** [9]8-9-0 (45) G Baker 5/1 FAV: 10200-05: Rear, late prog, nrst fin: clr rem: see 4669. shd 42
4505 **MERLINS PROFIT 21** [13]4-9-0 (40) L Enstone 10/1: 420U436: Mid-div, btn 2f out: see 4505, 4133. 5   35
4364 **MR WHIZZ 29** [11]7-9-0 p (40) Derek Nolan(7) 6/1: 2051047: Mid-div, no prog bef dist: see 3692. 2½   31
4547 **ZARNEETA 19** [18]3-8-9 (40) P Doe 40/1: 0-000008: Handy 7f: see 2742.   7   22

BRIGHTON
SATURDAY 02.10.04 Lefthand, V Sharp, Undulating Track

4659	**TAP DANCER** 14 [20]6-9-0 (35) A Hindley(7) 33/1: 10060/-09: Led halfway till over 2f out, sn btn: see 4659.	nk	21
4824	**BLAU GRAU** 5 [10]7-9-0 (40) M Savage(4) 33/1: 10500-00: 10th: Bhd & nvr a factor, qck reapp: see 4824.	1¾	19
4302	**MORNING HAWK** 33 [4]3-8-9 bl (35) D Sweeney 25/1: 5604040: 11th: Reuctant to enter stalls, al rear.	¾	18
4716	**COOLFORE JADE** 11 [12]4-9-0 (40) A Beech(3) 9/1: 3000640: 12th: Trkd ldr, strugg halfway: btr 4716.	shd	18
4374	**HILARIOUS** 28 [15]4-9-0 (40) R Thomas(3) 16/1: 6406000: 13th: Mid-div, no ch fnl 2f: btr 3895 (sft).	1½	16
4662	**TSHUKUDU** 14 [14]3-8-9 (35) D Kinsella 66: 0302000: 14th: In tch 7f, sn strugg: btr 4142 (sft).	1¾	14
4661	**MARGERY DAW** 14 [16]4-9-0 bl (40) J Brennan(7) 25/1: 0050000: 15th: Mid div, rdn & btn over 2f out.	1¼	12
1373	**GEOGRAPHY** 160 [5]4-9-0 p (40) D Nolan(3) 33/1: 5-P06000: 16th: Always bhd, t.o.: 5 mth jmps abs.	11	0
2643	**BONTADINI** 102 [3]5-9-0 (40) Paul Eddery 14/1: 0-500300: 17th: Mid-div, no ch from 3f out, t.o: abs.	9	0
4796	**SPRING WHISPER** 7 [19]3-8-9 vis (40) J P Guillambert(3) 33/1: 000-0000: 18th: Led till halfway, sn bhd.	10	0
4662	**PRINCE IVOR** 14 [6]4-9-0 vis t (35) B Reilly(3) 50/1: 000-0000: 19th: Tailed off halfway: see 4662 & 1026.	25	0

19 Ran Time 2m 09.80 (12.0) Owned: Heart of the South Racing Trained: West Ilsley

---

4904
1.05 Betfred In Shops On Phone And Online Banded Stakes 3yo+ 0-45 (H5)
£1498 £428 £214 **1m rnd** **Good** **Inapplicable** Inside

3547	**DELCIENNE** 65 [12] G G Margarson 3-8-11 (45) A Beech(3) 7/2: 3021501: Mid-div, rdn to lead dist, rdn clr, decisively: op 4/1: 2 mth abs: eff at 1m on firm, good & polytrk: see 2834.		51
4660	**LABELLED WITH LOVE** 14 [2] J R Boyle 4-9-0 t (45) D Sweeney 3/1 FAV: 0-256052: Cl up & led 5f out till dist, sn no ch with wnr: op 9/2: handles firm & gd grnd: eff in t-strap: see 2107.	5	44
4659	**RATHMULLAN** 14 [10] E A Wheeler 5-9-0 (35) James Jones(7) 18/1: 5000403: Rear, late prog to take 3rd, nvr danger: flattered 3298.	¾	43$
4793	**ZINGING** 7 [4] J J Bridger 5-9-0 (40) G Baker 5/1: 6004064: Chsd ldrs, no extra dist: clr rem: best at 6/7f.	1	41
1548	**KUMAKAWA** 151 [6]6-9-0 (40) M Howard(7) 12/1: 0260005: Mid-div, no impress fnl 2f: new yard: 5 mth abs	6	29
1838	**DUNDONALD** 136 [11]5-9-0 t (35) S Righton 12/1: 5033306: Mid-div, rcd stands side fnl 3f, no impress.	nk	28
4507	**NOBLE DESERT** 21 [1]3-8-11 (40) R Mills(7) 33/1: 0-05007: Mid-div, badly hmpd halfway, in tch till 2f out.	6	16
4485	**LYRICAL LADY** 23 [5]3-8-11 (40) R Thomas(3) 25/1: 46-00008: Held up, btn when hmpd over 1f out.	shd	16
2372	**MAHLSTICK** 113 [7]6-9-0 (40) R Marks(3) 14/1: 6-634409: Mid-div, rdn & strugg over 2f out, 4 mth abs.	½	15
3806	**THWAAB** 55 [9]12-9-0 vis (40) L Enstone 20/1: 600/-0000: 10th: Sn bhd, rcd stands side fnl 3f, 8 wk abs.	1½	12
1045	**VIZULIZE** 182 [3]5-9-0 (45) D Nolan(3) 11/2: 6500400: 11th: Led till over 5f out, strugg stands side fnl 2f.	4	4
2347	**CRUSTY LILY** 114 [8]8-9-0 (30) A Quinn(5) 22/1: 000-3000: 12th: Dwelt, in tch till over 3f out, t.o: abs.	dist	0

12 Ran Time 1m 42.2 (10.2) Owned: The Del Boys Trained: Newmarket

---

4905
1.40 Betfred Com Early Prices From 10am Banded Stakes 3yo+ 0-45 (H5)
£1516 £433 £217 **6f rnd** **Good** **Inapplicable** Inside

4793+	**SPINETAIL RUFOUS** 7 [14] D Flood 6-9-3 bl (48) P Doe 9/2: 6/000-011: Trkd ldr, came stands side fnl 3f, rdn/led dist & in command ins last: eff at 5/6f on both AWs, fast & gd grnd: see 4793, 4660.		57
4370	**CARGO** 28 [7] B A Pearce 5-9-1 bl t (46) R Miles(3) 16/1: 0022002: Led, came stands side fnl 3f, hdd dist, no extra: blnks reapp: see 544.	2	48
4707	**CHATSHOW** 12 [13] A W Carroll 3-8-13 (45) D Nolan(3) 20/1: 4050003: Rdn mid-div, kept on for press fnl 2f, no threat to wnr: eff over a sharp 6f on gd grnd in banded company: see 3091.	2½	39
3232	**TUSCAN TREATY** 78 [11] T T Clement 4-9-0 vis (45) B Reilly(3) 25/1: 0406004: Slow away, mod late prog.	3	30
4489	**TAPPIT** 23 [12]5-9-0 (45) M Halford(7) 33/1: 5000605: Handy, btn over 1f out: see 1963.	nk	29
4595	**YAMATO PINK** 18 [9]3-9-4 (50) G Baker 5/1: 1253046: Held up, strugg fnl 2f: btr 2439.	shd	34
4370	**OTYLIA** 28 [10]3-9-4 VIS (45) A Quinn(5) 66/1: 44-54007: Chsd ldrs till over 1f out: vis: btr 750.	hd	28
3790	**NIGHT CAP** 56 [5]5-9-0 (45) J P Guillambert(3) 13/2: 0203048: Held up & nvr a factor: abs: btr 3790.	hd	27
4508	**ASTRAC** 21 [15]3-9-3 (48) Paul Eddery 10/1: 2400049: Held up, no impress fnl 2f, finished lame: op 7/1.	2	24
4636	**DOCTOR DENNIS** 16 [16]7-9-5 vis (50) A Beech(3) 4/1 FAV: 6010600: 10th: Held up, no impress fnl 2f.	2½	18
4118	**FLAPDOODLE** 41 [6]6-9-0 bl (45) L Enstone 11/1: 0-500030: 11th: Handy till halfway: abs: btr 4118 (5f).	3	4
1413	**Gentle Response** 158 [8]4-9-0 VIS(45) S Whitworth 20/1:0		
3380	**Queen Of Bulgaria** 72 [3]3-8-13 (45) P McCabe 33/1:0		
4413	**Scarlett Breeze** 26 [2]3-8-13 (45) Derek Nolan(7) 10/1:0 3720 **Run On** 58 [4]6-9-0 BL(45) S Righton 25/1:0		

15 Ran Time 1m 13.14(5.34) Owned: Miss J Wickens Trained: Hungerford

---

EPSOM
SATURDAY 02.10.04 Lefthand, Very Sharp, Undulating Track

Official Going GOOD (GOOD/SOFT IN PLACES)

4906
2.05 Rht 40th Anniversary Conditions Stakes 2yo (C2)
£9118 £3458 £1729 **1m114y** **Good 54** **-22 Slow** Inside

4688*	**COMIC STRIP** 14 [2] Sir Mark Prescott 2-8-11 (100) J Mackay 2/5 FAV: 14111: Slow away, sn handy, rcd far side straight, hdwy to lead 2f out, readily: bckd, landed hat-trick: eff at 7f, now suited by around 1m: acts on fast, soft & fibresand, prob any trk: smart juv, win a List/Gr 3: see 4688.		111
4619	**ROCAMADOUR** 16 [3] M R Channon 2-8-11 (87) T E Durcan 10/1: 5122: Rcd in 2nd, rcd nr side straight, onepaced 2f out: met a smart rival: consistent: see 4257.	2½	101
3412	**FIEFDOM** 71 [1] M Johnston 2-8-11 (98) R Ffrench 8/1: 541243: Led, rcd far side straight, hdd 2f out, no extra: abs: not disgraced: see 3412.	1½	98
4540	**ABERDEEN** 20 [5] P Mitchell 2-8-11 R L Moore 16/1: 624: Rear, rcd nr side straight, onepaced 2f out: mdns & gall trk will suit: see 4540.	nk	97
4522*	**EMILE ZOLA** 21 [4]2-9-0 Hayley Turner(3) 8/1: 15: Dwelt, bhd, rcd far side straight, btn over 2f out.	15	70

5 Ran Time 1m 48.27 (6.47) Owned: Neil Greig - Osborne House Trained: Newmarket

EPSOM SATURDAY 02.10.04 Lefthand, Very Sharp, Undulating Track

4907

2.40 Icon Display Nursery Handicap Stakes 2yo 0-85 (D2) **[91]**
£10348 £3184 £1592 **5f** **Good/Firm** **Inapplicable** Stands side

4830 **LOUPHOLE 5** [1] P J Makin 2-9-0 (77) D Sweeney 8/1: 3410031: Trkd ldrs, hdwy to lead ins fnl 1f, rdn out: qck reapp: eff around 5f on fast, likes a sharp/undul trk: gd run, back to form of 3296. **87**
4830 **STAR DUSTER 5** [5] B R Millman 2-8-2 (65) D Fox(5) 7/1: 02022: Rear/wide, hdwy over 2f out, no impress fnl last: qck reapp: 6f now suit: see 4830. *1* **70**
4551 **SMIDDY HILL 19** [4] R Bastiman 2-9-7 (84) R Ffrench 8/1: 1451023: Cl up, hdwy to lead over 1f out, hdd and no extra ins fnl 1f: shade btr 3488. *¾* **87**
4706* **CREE 12** [7] W R Muir 2-8-1 (64) Hayley Turner(3) 7/1: 5252314: Trkd ldrs, onepaced 1f out: see 4706. *shd* **66**
4645 **GRAND PLACE 15** [9]2-8-11 (74) R L Moore 4/1 FAV: 4010445: Handy, kept on fnl 1f but not pace of ldrs. *½* **74**
4717 **BOLD MINSTREL 11** [6]2-9-6 (83) I Mongan 14/1: 1242556: Led to over 1f out, no extra. *1½* **78**
4784 **WONDERFUL MIND 7** [10]2-8-9 bl (72) T P Queally 12/1: 5632057: Prom, wkng/not much room 1f out. *1¼* **63**
4830* **FORZEEN 5** [2]2-9-9 (6ex) (86) D Corby(3) 9/1: 3140018: Outpaced in rear, some late gains: qck reapp. *½* **75**
4784 **MELANDRE 7** [11]2-8-10 (73) T Williams 7/1: 6045129: Slow away, sn handy, hung over 1f out, sn btn. *1¼* **58**
4784* **TALCEN GWYN 7** [3]2-9-5 (82) A Nicholls 10/1: 0450410: 10th: Slow away, nvr a factor: qck reapp. *1½* **62**
4679 **TOP FORM 14** [8]2-9-0 (77) T E Durcan 20/1: 051500: 11th: Al bhd. *1½* **52**
11 Ran Time 55.8s (1.5) Owned: Ten of Hearts Trained: Marlborough

4908

3.10 Sodexho Prestige Handicap Stakes 3yo+ 86-100 (C1) **[102]**
£17400 £6600 £3300 **5f** **Good/Firm** **Inapplicable** Stands side

4291 **JAYANJAY 33** [11] Miss B Sanders 5-8-7 (3oh) (81) R Thomas(3) 17/2: 1522501: Bmpd start, rear, not clr run 2f out, styd on well ins fnl 1f to lead fnl strides: eff at 5/6f on fm, soft & both AWs, loves Epsom: tough. **93**
4780 **CORRIDOR CREEPER 7** [4] J M Bradley 7-9-3 p (94) R L Moore 11/2: 6035032: Prom, hdwy/narrow lead just over 1f out, hdd fnl strides: qck reapp: most consistent: see 1594. *nk* **102**
4879 **DRAGON FLYER 2** [3] M Quinn 5-9-7 (98) I Mongan 12/1: 3041003: Made most to just over 1f out, no extra: qck reapp: back to wng form of 4454. *1¼* **102**
4678 **CARIBBEAN CORAL 14** [5] J J Quinn 5-9-7 (98) T Hamilton(3) 3/1 FAV: 1100304: Dwelt, handy, onepace. *½* **100**
4537 **CORPS DE BALLET 20** [1]3-8-7 (84) T P Queally 25/1: 1-010005: Slow away, sn handy, onepaced 1f out. *½* **84**
4585 **MALAPROPISM 18** [13]4-8-7 (2oh) (82) T Dean(7) 10/1: 4066106: Dsptd lead to over 1f out, wknd quickly. *1* **81**
4718 **BLUE CRUSH 11** [7]3-8-7 (2oh) (82) D Sweeney 25/1: 0000067: Dsptd lead, no extra fnl 1f. *½* **79**
4780 **HENRY HALL 7** [9]8-8-9 (86) Kim Tinkler 7/1: 3000008: Trkd ldrs, not clr run 2f out to 1f out, sn onepaced. *shd* **80**
4780 **WHITBARROW 7** [12]5-8-12 (89) P Doe 7/1: 0005409: Dsptd lead to over 1f out, wknd 2f out. *¾* **81**
4693 **FRASCATI 13** [6]4-8-7 (2oh) (82) T E Durcan 14/1: 1200430: 10th: Stall op fraction early, al bhd. *½* **74**
4588 **BOLEYN CASTLE 18** [10]7-8-7 (4oh)bl (80) J Brennan(7) 20/1: 0040060: 11th: Nvr a factor. *1* **71**
1767 **NO TIME 140** [2]4-8-10 (87) L Fletcher 25/1: 2110000: 12th: Handy & wide, wknd over 2f out: abs. *4* **62**
12 Ran Time 55.69s (1.39) Owned: Mr Peter Crate Trained: Epsom

4909

3.45 Bms Group Handicap Stakes 3yo 71-85 (D2) **[89]**
£9433 £3578 £1789 **1m114y** **Good 54** **-28 Slow** Inside

4334 **RIDGE BOY 30** [4] R Hannon 3-8-11 (72) R L Moore 4/1 J FAV: 6010321: Made most, styd on well for press ins fnl 1f: eff around 1m, prob stays 10f: acts on fm & gd, sharp or undul trks: game, imprvd for rtn to forcing tactics: also won from the front in 2971. **80**
3690 **DESERT REIGN 59** [1] A P Jarvis 3-8-10 (71) D Sweeney 4/1 J FAV: 000-5142: In tch, hdwy over 2f out, kept on but not pace of wnr: tchd 6/1, 8 wk abs: consistent: see 3690. *1½* **76**
4683 **LORD LINKS 14** [9] R Hannon 3-9-2 (77) R Thomas(3) 12/1: 0000403: Keen in 2nd, onepaced over 1f out: wng form at 5f, stays 7f/1m: handles fm & gd: see 1847. *hd* **81**
4607 **PICKLE 17** [11] S C Williams 3-9-5 (80) R Miles(3) 7/1: 6111204: Rear & wide, came nr side straight, hdwy 2f out, hung left fnl 1f, styd on: btr 3410. *¾* **82**
4539 **JACKIE KIELY 20** [2]3-8-7 (3oh)t (65) J Brennan(7) 14/1: 0304035: Bhd, outpaced over 2f out, styd on 1f out: rtn to further will suit: see 4539. *1¾* **66**
4318 **DAVORIN 31** [10]3-9-5 (80) T P Queally 25/1: 1606: Dwelt, sn in tch, onepaced 2f out. *shd* **77**
4469 **CARRY ON DOC 24** [7]3-9-3 (78) S Whitworth 8/1: 6153107: Keen in rear, nvr dngrs: see 1152. *shd* **74**
4621 **BRIGHT SUN 16** [5]3-8-11 (72) Kim Tinkler 12/1: 0341068: Keen in tch, nvr nrr. *1¾* **64**
4502 **WYCHBURY 22** [12]3-8-12 (73) D Corby(3) 20/1: 2201509: Cl up, btn over 2f out. *½* **64**
4683 **ASK THE CLERK 14** [8]3-8-11 (72) A Nicholls 10/1: 3054200: 10th: Al bhd. *2½* **58**
4225 **BURLEY FLAME 35** [3]3-9-3 (78) M Fenton 10/1: 0316000: 11th: Keen & cl up, no impress over 1f out. *1½* **61**
4714 **MAREN 12** [6]3-9-7 t (82) T E Durcan 10/1: 31-000: 12th: Al bhd: see 4500. *1¼* **62**
12 Ran Time 1m 48.78 (6.98) Owned: Mrs Chris Harrington Trained: Marlborough

4910

4.20 International Mortgage Plans Apprentice Derby Handicap Stakes 3yo+ 56-70 (E3) **[84]**
£6958 £2141 £1071 **1m4f10y** **Good 54** **-08 Slow** Centre

4119 **NOUNOU 41** [8] D J Daly 3-8-7 (63) M Halford(5) 20/1: 0500151: In tch, hdwy 3f out, led over 1f out, kept on well for press: op 14/1, 6 wk abs: eff at 9.7/12f on gd, likes a sharp/undul trk: unexposed. **70**
4690 **LENNEL 14** [9] A Bailey 6-9-4 bl (67) L Enstone 14/1: 2330562: Bhd, styd on ins fnl 1f to go 2nd. *2* **69**
4669 **DUCS DREAM 14** [10] D Morris 6-8-7 (5oh) (51) B Reilly 20/1: 1005033: Trkd ldrs, hdwy to lead over 2f out till over 1f out, no extra: clr of rem: gd eff from 5lbs out of the h'cap: see 4669. *2½* **54**
4589 **CARROWDORE 18** [13] G A Huffer 4-9-7 p (70) T Block(7) 13/2: 3422434: Handy, wknd 2f out. *5* **60**
4669* **BOJANGLES 14** [15]5-8-9 (58) D Nolan 10/1: 3412515: Led to halfway, no extra over 2f out. *2* **45**
4542 **BURGUNDY 20** [1]7-9-1 bl (64) A Beech 12/1: 1212546: Bhd, hdwy 3f out, no impress fnl 1f. *½* **50**
4672 **DONASTRELA 14** [3]3-8-10 vis (66) N Chalmers(3) 12/1: 4133547: Trkd ldrs to halfway, no impress str. *¾* **51**
4861 **SKIBEREEN 3** [4]4-8-8 (57) J P Guillambert 8/1: 5000228: Dwelt, sn in tch, no impress over 2f out. *5* **34**
4589 **GREAT VIEW 18** [7]5-9-3 bl (66) Hayley Turner 12/1: 0230249: Cl up, btn over 2f out. *½* **42**
4506 **TOUCH OF EBONY 21** [6]5-8-7 (11oh) (45) A Medeiros(3) 50/1: 00002-00: 10th: b g Darshaan - Cormorant Wood (Home Guard) Cl up, no impress 3f out: 4th at best in '03 (h'cap, rtd 56): h'cap rnr-up for J *3* **27**

EPSOM SATURDAY 02.10.04 Lefthand, Very Sharp, Undulating Track

Neville in '02: eff at 1m, suited by 12f/easy 14f on fm, soft & fibresand, prob handles any trk, likes a sharp one: tried blinks: stiff task at these weights.
2 Jun'02 Good 14g/s 64-62 E: 2 May'02 Wind 11.6sft 60-59 E:
4266 **KNOCKTOPHER ABBEY 34** [12]7-8-7 bl (56) Dean Williams(5) 20/1: 4050/-000: 11th: Dwelt, al bhd. *1* **25**
4650* **INCROYABLE 15** [14]3-8-10 (66) T P Queally 6/4 FAV: 0006-210: 12th: Cl up, hdwy to lead halfway, hdd/faded over 2f out: hvly bckd: much btr 4650 (10f). *5* **27**
4806*]**TASS HEEL 350** [5]5-8-7 (2oh) (54) Thomas Yeung(5) 25/1: 011001-0: 13th: b g Danehill - Mamouna (Vaguely Noble) Al bhd on reapp: won 4 h'caps & a class stks in '03 (M Channon): dual h'cap rnr-up in '02: suited by 14f/2m on fm, fast & both AWs, prob any trk: now with W Jarvis. *2* **14**
1 Oct'03 Catt 13.8g/f 57-(53) F: 1 Oct'03 Catt 15.8g/f 56-51 F: 1 Sep'03 Muss 16g/f 53-45 E:
2 Jun'03 Nott 16.0gd 52-(53) F: 2 May'03 Muss 14g/f 55-(55) F: 1 May'03 Beve 16.2gd 55-50 E:
2 Jan'03 Wolv 14.7af 67a-62 E: 1 Jan'03 Sout 14af 63a-52 F: 2 Dec'02 Ling 13ap 51a-50 F: 2 Oct'02 Newc 16g/f 49-51 E:
4446 **BLACKMAIL 25** [11]6-8-8 bl (57) R Thomas 33/1: 05000-00: 14th: Al bhd: see 4446. *1½* **13**
14 Ran Time 2m 42.33 (7.53) Owned: Miss Anita Farrell Trained: Newmarket

4911

4.55 Woodhurst Construction Maiden Stakes 3yo (D3)
£5369 £1652 £826 **1m2f18y** **Good 54** **-37 Slow** Inside

4757 **MAMBINA 9** [2] M R Channon 3-8-9 (63) T E Durcan 4/1: 0223241: Trkd ldrs, hdwy to lead over 2f out, sn idled, kept on: stays 10f on fast & soft, prob handles fm, sharp/undul trk: deserved win: see 1124. **75**
4781 **UIG 7** [7] H S Howe 3-8-9 (72) P Doe 7/2: 3204202: Led till over 2f out, no extra: qck reapp. *1¾* **71**
3648 **NEWS SKY 61** [3] B W Hills 3-9-0 (79) R L Moore 5/2 FAV: 02233: Prom, onepaced & btn 2f out: abs. *hd* **75**
4440 **REVENIR 25** [1] E F Vaughan 3-9-0 (72) D Corby(3) 4/1: 02224: Bhd, onepaced & btn over 2f out. *2½* **71**
4762 **ELUSIVE KITTY 9** [4]3-8-9 t (66) R Ffrench 7/1: 6R33535: Nvr a factor. *½* **65**
4252 **MY PENSION 34** [5]3-9-0 (60) I Mongan 20/1: 043006: Prom, no impress over 2f out. *2* **67$**
4448 **LAWAAHEB 25** [6]3-9-0 P (63) S Whitworth 33/1: 056-0007: Rcd in 2nd, no impress ent straight, t.o. *dist* **17**
7 Ran Time 2m 12.97 (9.17) Owned: Mr R A Scarborough Trained: West Ilsley

4912

5.30 Ibetx Com Classified Stakes 3yo+ 0-80 (D2)
£10452 £3216 £1608 **7f** **Good 54** **+07 Fast** Inside

3860 **BETTALATETHANNEVER 52** [9] S Dow 3-9-0 (82) J Mackay 14/1: 0026001: Rear/wide, hdwy to lead over 1f out, kept on: 7 wk abs: stays 7f/1m on gd & polytrack, sharp/undul trks, esp Lingfield: fine run, back to form. **95**
3326 **MANAAR 74** [8] J Noseda 4-9-3 (83) T E Durcan 10/1: 0-0502B2: Rear, styd on well ins fnl 1f to go 2nd cl home: abs: gd run: see 3068. *6* **84**
4806 **H HARRISON 6** [7] I W McInnes 4-9-0 p (78) R Ffrench 16/1: 5006503: Trkd ldrs, hdwy to chall over 2f out, found little over 1f out, lost 2nd cl home: qck reapp: shade btr 4615 (1m). *nk* **80**
4872 **JAY GEES CHOICE 2** [3] M R Channon 4-9-5 (85) S Whitworth 11/2: 4046134: Led for 1f, led again over 3f out till over 1f out, no extra: qck reapp: btr 4872, 4629. *1¾* **81**
4714 **DR THONG 12** [6]3-9-1 (83) R L Moore 11/4 FAV: 4104205: Handy, onepaced over 2f out: clr of rem. *hd* **78**
4352 **BRIEF GOODBYE 29** [4]4-9-0 (79) D Corby(3) 25/1: 1401406: Handy, no impress over 2f out. *5* **65**
4773 **MR LAMBROS 8** [10]3-9-3 (85) N Chalmers(3) 4/1: 3-1207: Keen in rear, nvr a factor: btr 627. *1* **68**
4689 **TRUE NIGHT 14** [1]7-9-2 (82) P Doe 7/1: 1300208: In tch, hdwy to lead after 1f till over 3f out, no extra. *8* **49**
3947 **DUMNONI 49** [2]3-8-9 (80) I Mongan 6/1: 0413229: Slow away, t.o.: 7 wk abs: much btr 3947. *19* **6**
4482 **SAWWAAH 23** [5]7-9-5 (85) A Nicholls 9/1: 3021040: 10th: Rear, t.o.: something amiss? *4* **6**
10 Ran Time 1m 23.43(3.33) Owned: Mr J R May Trained: Epsom

NEWMARKET SATURDAY 02.10.04 Righthand, Stiff, Galloping Track

Official Going Good (Good/Soft places)

4913

2.00 European Breeders Fund Jersey Lily Nursery Handicap Stakes Fillies 2yo (B1) **[88]**
£25269 £7775 £3888 **7f str** **Good/Firm** **Slow** Centre

4177 **WEDDING PARTY 37** [11] Mrs A J Perrett 2-9-5 (79) J Murtagh 9/1: 3141: Handy centre, led over 1f out, hung left ins last but styd on, rdn out: eff over 6/7f on fast, gd & polytrack, any trk: lightly rcd, useful & prog. **89**
4490 **LOVE AFFAIR 22** [13] R Hannon 2-8-11 (71) K Darley 20/1: 2002: Prom centre, eff over 1f out, kept on: apprec step up to 7f & shown enough to win a race: see 3554. *1½* **77**
4648* **CATCH A STAR 15** [10] N A Callaghan 2-9-6 (80) N Mackay(3) 7/1: 350313: Slow away centre, held up, eff dist, kept on ins last: well bckd: acts on fast & gd/soft: shld win again with a return to 1m as in 4648. *shd* **86**
4679 **MUSICAL DAY 14** [15] B J Meehan 2-9-4 (78) S Sanders 25/1: 000204: In tch far side, eff over 1f out, styd on: first home on his side, v encouraging: acts on fast & gd/soft: see 4242. *hd* **83**
4679 **SHOSOLOSA 14** [8]2-8-10 (70) J F McDonald(3) 14/1: 022305: In tch, eff to chall over 1f out centre, kept on: gd run: see 3848, 2927. *hd* **74**
4664 **BELLY DANCER 14** [6]2-9-0 (74) N De Souza(5) 16/1: 6426: Led stands side group, kept on: gd run. *nk* **77**
4679 **LADY LE QUESNE 14** [14]2-9-6 (80) Martin Dwyer 25/1: 621107: Led centre over 5f, no extra: poss stays 7f: see 3369 (5f). *¾* **81**
4420 **GODSEND 26** [16]2-9-2 (76) R Hughes 12/1: 21238: In tch centre, wknd over 1f out: see 3729 (6f). *2* **73**
4490 **TOFFEE VODKA 22** [9]2-8-13 (73) R Hills 12/1: 63109: Bhd centre, eff dist, no dngr: best 4178. *½* **69**
4457 **ABERDOVEY 24** [1]2-9-3 (77) R Mullen 11/1: 51350: 10th: Held up stands side, hmpd halfway, eff over 2f out, no extra: see 4457. *1½* **70**
4447* **ICING 25** [7]2-9-1 (75) P Hanagan 20/1: 6410: 11th: Held up stands side, hmpd halfway, no dngr. *½* **67**
4535* **MALINSA BLUE 21** [5]2-9-6 (80) F Norton 16/1: 6226210: 12th: Nvr a factor stands side: best 4535. *¾* **70**
4655* **JE SUIS BELLE 15** [3]2-8-11 (71) M Hills 10/1: 03210: 13th: Al bhd stands side: btr 4655 (6f, g/s). *2* **57**
4697 **CEREBUS 12** [4]2-9-0 (74) D Holland 20/1: 6423360: 14th: Chsd ldrs stands side, wknd dist: btr 4337. *shd* **59**
4753 **DANCE FLOWER 9** [12]2-9-7 (81) K Fallon 6/1 FAV: 235420: 15th: In tch centre, wknd & virtually p.u. over 1f out: well bckd: surely something amiss: much btr 4753 (1m). *dist* **0**
4807 **CAITLIN 6** [2]2-9-1 (75) D McGaffin 10/1: 413123P: With ldr stands side, p.u. lame over 5f out. **0**
16 Ran Time 1m 27.18 (3.98) Owned: Cheveley Park Stud Trained: Pulborough

4914 **2.35 Listed Finnforest Oh So Sharp Stakes Fillies 2yo (A1)**
£14500 £5500 £2750 **7f str** **Good/Firm** **Slow** Centre

4727 **PENKENNA PRINCESS 11** [9] R M Beckett 2-8-9 (84) P Hanagan 25/1: 0131: Held up, gd hdwy to lead dist, styd on, rdn out: imprvd stepped up in class & at 7f: acts on firm & fast grnd, easy or stiff trks: lightly rcd, useful & progressive: see 4358. **104**
4476 **FAVOURITA 23** [1] C E Brittain 2-8-9 (99) T Quinn 10/1: 1452: In tch, short of room & lost pl dist, rallied fnl 1f, kept on: poss not straightforward but this was encouraging back at 7f, return to 1m suit. *½* **102**
3357 **BORTHWICK GIRL 27** [10] B J Meehan 2-8-9 M Hills 16/1: 1403: With ldrs, led 2f out till dist, onepace. *1¾* **98**
4679 **BALTIC DIP 14** [3] R Hannon 2-8-9 (94) R Hughes 7/1: 1404: Led 5f, no extra fnl 1f: stays 7f. *½* **97**
4679 **UMNIYA 14** [5]2-8-9 vis (100) K Fallon 9/2: 4566435: Slow away, sn rdn bhd, hdwy late, nrst fin: well bckd: gd run with a return to 7f: see 4679. *nk* **96**
4679* **SALAMANCA 14** [8]2-8-9 (94) J F Egan 4/1 FAV: 116: In tch, eff over 1f out, sn no extra: well bckd: not disgraced: see 4679 (val sales race). *nk* **95**
4679 **ALTA PETENS 14** [12]2-8-9 (85) R Mullen 50/1: 1004567: Held up, eff dist, no dngr: wants nurseries. *2½* **90**
4332 **ALL FOR LAURA 30** [2]2-8-9 (95) Martin Dwyer 10/1: 41558: Chsd ldrs, wknd dist: see 4332 (6f). *nk* **89**
4610* **DIVINELY DECADENT 17** [7]2-8-9 A McCarthy 7/1: 19: Held up, short of room over 2f out, no dngr. *hd* **88**
4264 **MISS LAUGEVAL 34** [13]2-8-9 (77) D Holland 33/1: 4100: 10th: In tch, wknd over 1f out: btr 3554. *2½* **83**
4264 **JANE JUBILEE 34** [4]2-8-9 (93) K Darley 25/1: 2211500: 11th: With ldr, wknd dist: best 3560. *½* **82**
4330 **ELIZABETHAN AGE 30** [14]2-8-9 S Sanders 12/1: 220: 12th: Held up, btn dist: btr 4330, 3616. *1¾* **78**
4680 **ROYAL ALCHEMIST 14** [11]2-8-9 (94) A Daly 20/1: 120050: 13th: Nvr a factor: see 2763. *1¾* **74**
4684 **GOLDEN ANTHEM 14** [6]2-8-9 (92) J Quinn 50/1: 103660: 14th: Held up, btn over 1f out: see 2763. *½* **73**
14 Ran Time 1m 26.22 (3.02) Owned: Mrs H M Chamberlain Trained: Lambourn

4915 **3.15 Gr1 Kingdom Of Bahrain Sun Chariot Stakes Fillies & Mares 3yo+ (A1)**
£116000 £44000 £22000 **1m str** **Good/Firm** **Fast** Centre

4572 **ATTRACTION 21** [3] M Johnston 3-8-11 (119) K Darley 11/4: 1112021: Made all, kept on most gamely for press when pressed ins last: suited by a stiff 1m: likes to dominate on fm & fast, has disapp on soft: 4th Gr 1 success this term, top-class, most tough & thoroughly genuine filly who typifies her stables runners. **121**
4232+ **CHIC 35** [1] Sir Michael Stoute 4-9-0 (117) K Fallon 9/4 FAV: 1-603112: Held up, hdwy to chase wnr over 1f out, styd on to chall ins last, al just held: ran to high-class best & hard to pass this most game wnr: tough, still improving, more Gr races to be won: see 4232. *nk* **120**
3659 **NEBRASKA TORNADO 62** [5] A Fabre 4-9-0 R Hughes 5/2: 161-5433: Trkd wnr, hdwy well over 1f out, styd on same pace: 2 mth abs: smart French raider, ran to best: see 2470. *1½* **116**
4017 **MAJESTIC DESERT 48** [4] M R Channon 3-8-11 (113) D Holland 11/2: 0022244: Handy, eff well over 1f out, sn no extra: needs Gr 3: see 3659, 3011. *5* **106**
2306 **MISS MAMBO 13** [2]3-8-11 J Murtagh 14/1: 3-113225: Al bhd: rnr-up in List & Gr 2 since 2306. *14* **78**
5 Ran Time 1m 36.27 (u0.23) Owned: Duke of Roxburghe Trained: Middleham

4916 **3.55 Totesport Cambridgeshire Heritage Handicap 3yo+ (B1)** **[113]**
£75400 £28600 £14300 **1m1f str** **Good/Firm** **Fast** Centre

4681 **SPANISH DON 14** [3] D R C Elsworth 6-8-10 (95) L Keniry(3) 100/1: 0511501: Held up stands side, hdwy over 1f out, styd on strongly ins last to lead cl-home: shock 100/1 wnr of this famous h'cap: suited by 1m/9f on fast or soft grnd, stiff or easy trk, likes Kempton: v useful gelding, has a turn of foot & career best eff here. **106**
4499 **TAKE A BOW 22** [7] P R Chamings 3-8-9 (98) J Quinn 25/1: 1141222: Handy stands side, hdwy to lead dist, styd on well, collared cl-home: thriving this term & stays 9f: see 4499, 3860. *nk* **108**
3553 **FINE SILVER 65** [5] P F I Cole 3-8-7 (96) T Quinn 25/1: 4014223: Chsd ldrs stands side, led that group over 3f out till dist, kept on: 2 mth abs: enjoyed return to a gall trk & a fine eff: see 3553, 2521. *1¼* **103**
4681 **BLUE SPINNAKER 14** [18] M W Easterby 5-9-3 (102) P Mulrennan(3) 16/1: 4104634: Handy centre, eff over 1f out, kept on: fine run: see 4681, 2101. *nk* **108**
4061 **UNSHAKABLE 44** [29]5-8-8 (93) F Norton 33/1: 0130545: In tch far side, hdwy over 1f out, styd on to lead that group ins last: excellent eff on "wrong" side: v tough: see 2915, 1351. *¾* **97**
4021 **BLYTHE KNIGHT 45** [26]4-9-3 P (102) R Hills 100/1: 4630006: Chsd ldrs centre, led that group & edged left over 1f out, hdd ins last: back to form: tried cheekpieces: see 2556. *hd* **105**
4681 **GATWICK 14** [31]3-9-4 (107) S Hitchcott 9/1: 0605157: Held up far side, eff over 1f out, kept on: another fine run: see 4681, 4239 (10f). *hd* **109**
4714* **BLUE TROJAN 12** [34]4-8-2 (3ex)(1ow) (86) J F Egan 16/1: 2000218: Led far side over 2f, led again over 3f out till ins last, no extra: up in class after 4714. *½* **88**
4061 **EL COTO 44** [14]4-9-1 bl (100) G Gibbons 40/1: 0040409: Held up centre, eff dist, kept on, lame. *¾* **99**
4531 **LUNDYS LANE 21** [2]4-8-9 (94) M Hills 20/1: 0-400000: 10th: In tch stands side, onepcd dist. *¾* **91**
4772 **IMPELLER 8** [27]5-8-10 (5ex) (95) S Drowne 33/1: 0522130: 11th: Led far side group over 7f out till over 3f out, no extra: btr with waiting tactics: see 4772, 4467. *hd* **91**
4525 **KINGS COUNTY 21** [33]6-8-8 (93) N Mackay(3) 16/1: 3030020: 12th: Held up far side, eff over 2f out, sn no extra: btr 4525. *1¾* **85**
3565 **PUTRA KUANTAN 64** [20]4-8-13 (98) O Urbina 66/1: 6310600: 13th: Led centre over 7f, no extra. *shd* **89**
4813 **NASHAAB 6** [17]7-8-5 vis (90) Lisa Jones 100/1: 2315000: 14th: Slow away centre, nvr a factor: btr 3634. *nk* **80**
4279 **VICIOUS WARRIOR 33** [35]5-8-1 (86) B Swarbrick(5) 33/1: 5302230: 15th: Keen, handy far side, no extra. *hd* **75**
3265 **ABLE BAKER CHARLIE 77** [28]5-8-8 (93) K Fallon 14/1: 110-4200: 16th: Handy far side, no extra over 1f out: reportedly nvr trav, 11 wk abs: btr 2489. *hd* **81**
4149 **ICE PALACE 39** [24]4-8-11 (96) J Murtagh 14/1: 40-32140: 17th: Handy centre, wknd over 1f out: nicely bckd: btr 4149, 2772. *1¼* **82**
4767* **ST ANDREWS 8** [23]4-9-0 (5ex) (99) P Robinson 10/1: 2625010: 18th: Handy centre, wknd over 2f out: nicely bckd: btr 4767 (gd/soft). *nk* **84**
4813 **LANGFORD 6** [21]4-8-1 (86) F P Ferris(3) 100/1: 0140050: 19th: Keen centre, handy, wknd dist. *¾* **69**
44 **DIAMOND MAX 63** [10]6-8-0 Joanna Badger 100/1: 050-0130: 20th: b g Nicolotte - Kawther (Tap On Wood) Led stands side over 5f, wknd over 1f out: now with J Eyre, 2 mth abs, earlier won in minor race in Spain: '03 class stks & h'cap wnr for P Evans: stays up to 9f well & likes gd or softer grnd, acts on fibresand & any trk: has run well fresh & tried a visor. 1 Jun'03 Wind 6gd 92-85 D: 1 May'03 Chep 8.1g/s 88-(79) D: *1¾* **64**

2 Apr'03 Hami 9.2g/s 80-(84) E: 2 Mar'02 Wolv 8.4af 101a-100 B: 1 Oct'01 Long 8sft 100- :
1 Aug'01 Chep 8sft 92-84 C: 2 Jul'01 Ayr 7g/s 85-83 C:
4685 **WING COMMANDER 14** [12]5-8-9 vis (94) P Hanagan 80/1: 1030500: 21th: In tch stands side, wknd. *shd* **72**
4695* **PEDRILLO 13** [16]3-8-3 (5ex) (92) S Sanders 7/2 FAV: 321-310: 22th: In tch, centre, keen, hung right & wknd 2f out: massive gamble: much btr expected after 4695 (soft), prog earlier in much smaller fields. *3* **64**
4386 **AUDIENCE 28** [6]4-8-13 p (98) D Holland 25/1: 0246130: 23th: Held up stands side, wknd 2f out. *3* **64**
4525 **CHINKARA 21** [25]4-8-4 (89) J F McDonald(3) 25/1: 0004030: 24th: Nvr a factor centre: btr 4525. *1¾* **51**
4467 **ZONERGEM 24** [32]6-8-7 p (92) R Hughes 22/1: 03-06330: 25th: Nvr a factor far side: see 4467. *1* **52**
4538 **PAWN BROKER 20** [22]7-9-10 (109) P Fitzsimons 100/1: 25-01460: 26th: Slow away & al bhd centre. *½* **68**
4525 **KRUGERRAND 21** [8]5-8-4 (89) R Mullen 66/1: 3605150: 27th: Slow away & al bhd stands side. *1* **46**
1231 **THIHN 168** [19]9-8-9 (94) A Daly 50/1: 011-0100: 28th: Keen held up, nvr a factor centre: abs. *shd* **50**
4767 **CAMILLE PISSARRO 8** [9]4-8-4 (89) D Kinsella 100/1: 55053-00: 29th: Held up stands side, wknd 2f out. *3* **39**
4767 **GIFT HORSE 8** [13]4-8-1 (86) A McCarthy 50/1: 6-023040: 30th: Handy centre, wknd over 2f out. *2½* **31**
4685 **EVEREST 14** [30]7-8-1 (1ow) (85) Martin Dwyer 16/1: 0011040: 31th: Held up centre, wknd over 2f out: reportedly broke a blood vessel: see 4685. *3* **25**
4681 **DUMARAN 14** [15]6-8-5 (90) A Mullen(7) 50/1: 0235060: 32th: Reared & hit hd on stalls, took no part. **0**
32 Ran Time 1m 49.8 (0.6) Owned: Mr Richard J Cohen Trained: Whitsbury

4917

4.30 Kennett Handicap Stakes 3yo 86-100 (C1) **[100]**
£12138 £4604 £2302 **1m2f** **Good/Firm** **Fair** Centre

4630* **FLAMBOYANT LAD 16** [16] B W Hills 3-8-8 (80) M Hills 11/2 JT FAV: 2-333211: With ldr far side, led that group 2f out, styd on strongly, rdn out: nicely bckd: v eff at 10f, shld stay further: acts on firm & gd/soft, likes stiff trks: progressing with each run, genuine: see 4630. **91**
4541* **CORSICAN NATIVE 20** [17] Mrs A J Perrett 3-9-4 (90) R Hughes 8/1: 3-12: In tch far side, eff dist, kept on till no extra cl-home, just btn: excellent eff on step up in class: lightly rcd, useful & can win again. *½* **100**
4772 **BOULE DOR 8** [5] R Ingram 3-9-3 (89) N Day 17/2: 4201443: Handy stands side, hdwy to lead that group just ins last, kept on, no ch with far side pair: won race on "wrong" side & a fine run: poised to win again. *1¾* **95+**
4629 **NAMROC 16** [14] E F Vaughan 3-9-1 (87) R Mullen 11/2 JT FAV: 1424: Held up far side, eff well over 1f out, kept on: nicely bckd: stays 10f, further may suit: see 4629, 3112. *nk* **92**
4523 **BARBAJUAN 21** [3]3-9-1 (87) N Mackay(3) 25/1: 0000005: Held up stands side, eff dist, kept on. *1* **90**
4347* **COUNTRYWIDE LUCK 30** [6]3-9-1 (87) D Holland 20/1: 6216: In tch far side, wknd 2f out: best 4347. *shd* **89**
4614 **DAMI 17** [9]3-8-8 p (80) S Sanders 25/1: 2211557: With ldrs stands side, led that group 3f out, hdd just ins last, no extra: best 3540. *hd* **81**
3029 **MOTIVE 87** [4]3-9-4 (90) K Fallon 6/1: 51208: Held up stands side, eff & short of room over 2f out, staying on when hmpd ins last, not recover: well bckd: no luck in running, 3 mth abs: best to forgive this. *nk* **90**
4499 **MASTER MARVEL 22** [1]3-9-0 (86) J Murtagh 16/1: 2110069: Led stands side till 3f out, wkng when hmpd ins last: best 1496. *½* **85**
3912 **DANCING LYRA 50** [2]3-9-2 (88) S Drowne 25/1: 1124060: 10th: In tch stands side, some late gains. *1* **85**
4755 **PARKVIEW LOVE 9** [12]3-9-0 (86) K Darley 14/1: 0004530: 11th: Led far side group till 2f out, wknd. *shd* **82**
4534 **HELLO ITS ME 21** [10]3-9-1 (87) J Quinn 14/1: 0254350: 12th: Held up far side, wknd over 1f out. *2½* **78**
1924 **IKTITAF 133** [8]3-8-13 (85) R Hills 16/1: 03100: 13th: In tch stands side, wknd dist: abs. *¾* **74**
4531 **ISIDORE BONHEUR 21** [7]3-9-7 (93) Martin Dwyer 50/1: 4-444400: 14th: With ldrs stands side, wknd. *1* **80**
4682 **SGT PEPPER 14** [11]3-9-3 (89) J F Egan 33/1: 0-004650: 15th: In tch far side, wknd over 1f out. *nk* **75**
4463 **INCHLOSS 24** [13]3-8-11 (83) T Quinn 25/1: 6122400: 16th: Held up far side, wknd over 1f out. *1* **67**
4681 **KEELUNG 14** [15]3-9-0 P (86) P Robinson 20/1: 1320000: 17th: In tch far side, wknd over 2f out: not take to cheek pieces? btr 2127, 1500. *¾* **68**
17 Ran Time 2m 03.4 (1.3) Owned: Maktoum Al Maktoum Trained: Lambourn

4918

5.05 Suffolk Insulation And Renovation Services E B F Maiden Stakes Fillies 2yo (D2)
£8206 £2525 £1263 **6f str** **Good/Firm** **Slow** Centre

4358 **LOYAL LOVE 29** [12] Saeed bin Suroor 2-8-11 J Murtagh 12/1: 61: Made all far side, styd on well over 1f out, rdn out: enjoyed forcing tactics & clearly eff at 6f, 7f sure to suit: acts on fast grnd: useful, plenty more to come, win btr races: see 4358. **96**
DISCUSS [2] Sir Michael Stoute 2-8-11 K Fallon 5/2 FAV: 2: b f Danzig - Private Line (Private Account) Slow away, held up centre, qcknd to lead that group just ins last, styd on, no ch with far side wnr: hvly bckd: May foal: half-sister to 10f wnrs: dam 7f/1m scorer: eff at 6f, sure to relish a step up to 7f: acts on fast grnd: v nice debut, showed a neat turn of foot & must be kept in mind. *2½* **87+**
4679 **DIAMOND KATIE 14** [9] R Guest 2-8-11 T Quinn 10/1: 003: Chsd ldrs centre, led that group over 1f out till ins last, onepace: encouraging eff, win a less well contested mdn: see 4679. *2* **81**
3418 **AHDAAF 70** [4] J L Dunlop 2-8-11 P Robinson 14/1: 334: Cl-up stands side, onepcd over 1f out: 10 wk abs: shld win a minor trk mdn: see 3064. *½* **79**
ARCHEOLOGY [13]2-8-11 K Darley 16/1: 5: b f Seeking The Gold - Caress (Storm Cat) Chsd wnr far side, no extra over 1f out: stablemate of wnr: Feb foal: dam useful in the US: bred to relish 1m in time. *½* **78**
4679 **COUNTY CLARE 14** [6]2-8-11 (86) Martin Dwyer 14/1: 02306: In tch centre, no extra over 1f out. *1½* **74**
4726 **ENCOURAGEMENT 11** [8]2-8-11 (75) R Hughes 16/1: 030437: Led centre over 4f, no extra: see 4726. *nk* **73**
LADY DORIS WATTS [10]2-8-11 S Hitchcott 50/1: 8: b f Emarati - Wrong Bride (Reprimand) Held up centre, nvr a factor on debut: Mar foal: half-sister to an 11/12f wnr: bred for speed. *½* **71**
ALHAADH [7]2-8-11 R Hills 7/4 FAV: 9: b f Diesis - Wishah (Red Ransom) Slow away centre, held up, btn over 1f out on debut: hvly bckd: Mar foal, dam 7f juv wnr: clearly held in high regard. *1* **68**
2610 **ROCK FEVER 104** [3]2-8-11 S Drowne 80/1: 00: 10th: Al bhd centre. *1½* **64**
3290 **LILTING PROSE 75** [5]2-8-11 D Holland 33/1: 50: 11th: Held up centre, btn 2f out: 10 wk abs. *1½* **60**
4611 **TREBLE SEVEN 17** [11]2-8-11 S Sanders 16/1: 60: 12th: In tch far side, wknd over 2f out. *5* **45**
4357 **RUBY MURRAY 29** [1]2-8-11 L Keniry(3) 66/1: 000: 13th: Centre, in tch, wknd 2f out. *1* **42**
13 Ran Time 1m 12.6 (1.8) Owned: Godolphin Trained: Newmarket

---

| **4919** | 5.35 Ngk Spark Plugs Handicap Stakes 3yo 71-85 (D2) | | [87] |
| | £8245 £2537 £1269   1m6f   Good/Firm   Fast   Centre | | |

4833 **QUARRYMOUNT 5** [10] Sir Mark Prescott 3-8-11 (70) S Sanders 7/2 FAV: 2121221: In tch, hdwy to   86
lead on bit over 2f out, sn clr, cmftbly: relished step up to 14f & acts on fast, soft & polytrack, any trk: tough
& progressive, more wins to come over 14f+: see 4166.

4766 **FORT CHURCHILL 8** [7] B Ellison 3-9-3 bl (76) J Murtagh 11/1: 3420102: Led till over 2f out, not   6   80
pace of wnr: stays 14f: would certainly win another clmr as in 4579, see 3929.

4555* **SHARADI 19** [9] V Smith 3-8-12 (71) D Holland 9/2: 0022213: Held up, hdwy over 2f out, onepace: .   2½   71

4643 **DAZE 15** [8] Sir Michael Stoute 3-9-1 (74) K Fallon 6/1: 3104: Trkd ldr, chall well over 1f out,   nk   73
sn no extra: longer trip, see 4075 (mdn, 12f, soft).

4808 **STRANGELY BROWN 6** [1]3-9-3 (76) Martin Dwyer 4/1: 0211135: Handy, wknd well over 1f out: 5   68
progressive earlier, see 4808, 4657.

4613 **WINNERS DELIGHT 17** [2]3-9-7 (80) K Darley 14/1: 5530036: Held up, btn 2f out: see 4613, 2919.   5   65

4468 **MAN AT ARMS 24** [11]3-8-13 p (72) R Hughes 25/1: 0046007: In tch, wknd over 2f out: see 2538.   1¾   54

2827 **BILL BENNETT 95** [6]3-9-7 (80) O Urbina 20/1: 1250148: Held up, btn 2f out: 3 mth abs: see 2621.   hd   61

4395 **MASKED 28** [12]3-9-6 (79) T Quinn 12/1: 4152209: Held up, btn over 2f out: see 3688.   ¾   59

4860 **DOCTORED 3** [5]3-9-2 bl (75) F P Ferris(3) 33/1: 3060400: 10th: Held up, wknd 2f out: see 4742.   15   37

4657 **LATE OPPOSITION 15** [4]3-8-12 vis (71) S Drowne 9/1: 0031220: 11th: In tch, wknd 3f out: btr 4657.   24   0

11 Ran   Time 2m 55.9(0.4)   Owned: Lady Fairhaven   Trained: Newmarket

---

Official Going Standard

| **4920** | 7.00 Parkstone Group Quality Assured Claiming Stakes 3yo+ (F3) | | |
| | £3458 £1064 £532   7f32y aw rnd   Standard   Inapplicable   Outside | | |

4806 **SAMUEL CHARLES 6** [7] W M Brisbourne 6-9-2 (75) B Swarbrick(5) 6/1: 4201601: Trkd ldrs, rdn to   76a
lead well ins last, all out: op 11/1: qck reapp: eff at 7/8.5f on firm, gd/soft & both AWs, any trk.

4779 **MORSE 7** [11] J A Osborne 3-9-8 (78) S W Kelly 5/1: 6000102: Broke well & led till well ins last,   nk   83a
just held: fine run from awkward wide draw, can win again after 4667.

4446 **MALLARD 25** [8] J G Given 6-9-6 (75) M Fenton 3/1 FAV: 2600043: Chsd ldrs, no impress on front pair.   3½   72a

4180 **TRE COLLINE 37** [10] N Tinkler 5-9-10 (76) G Baker 10/1: 4610604: Rear, eff wide over 3f out, mod prog.   2½   71a

4714 **ILE MICHEL 12** [6]7-9-6 (72) D Sweeney 20/1: 0043005: Held up, hdwy over 2f out, no prog bef dist.   2   63a

3550 **DVINSKY 65** [9]3-9-8 (85) P Hanagan 6/1: 61-006: Rear, eff wide, btn dist: breathing prob, abs.   3   61a

1743 **CASHEL MEAD 141** [5]4-9-1 (75) A Daly 20/1: 5006007: Led early, chsd ldr, btn 2f out, 5 month abs.   ¾   51a

4266 **LINNING WINE 34** [4]8-9-6 (94) S Carson 6/1: 0645558: Held up, lost pl over 2f out, lost action.   1½   53a

4847 **MOON SPINNER 4** [2]7-8-3   F Norton 33/1: 009: Sn pushed along & al bhd.   hd   35a

4689 **HURRICANE FLOYD 14** [1]6-9-10 bl (74) T P Queally 10/1: 0004200: 10th: Dwelt, al rear, saddle slipped.   6   46a

10 Ran   Time 1m 29.51 (No Std Time)   Owned: Mr J F Thomas   Trained: Nesscliffe

---

| **4921** | 7.30 Guinness Median Auction Maiden Stakes 2yo (F3) | | |
| | £4310 £1326 £663   6f aw rnd   Standard   Inapplicable   Inside | | |

3445 **MANIC 70** [3] Andrew Reid 2-8-9   G Gibbons 33/1: 01: Trkd ldrs, styd on for press to lead well   76a
ins last: abs, AW bow: eff at 6f, get further in time: acts on polytrack: goes well fresh.

4369 **PINK BAY 28** [5] W S Kittow 2-8-9   F Norton 9/1: 42: Sn handy, outpcd bef halfway, styd on for   1½   70a
press ins last, not able to reach wnr: op 7/1: eff at 6f on fast & polytrack, 7f in similar could suit: see 4369.

4610 **DEPRESSED 17** [4] Andrew Reid 2-8-9   J F Egan 14/1: 003: Led, rdn clr over 2f out, hdd & no extra   ¾   68a
well ins last: shorter priced stablemate of wnr: eff at 6f on polytrack: imprvd eff with forcing tactics: see 4178.

2275 **FIRST RHAPSODY 117** [13] T J Etherington 2-8-9   Kristin Stubbs(7) 100/1: 004: b f Rossini - Tinos   1   65a
Island (Alzao) Bhd, late gains, nrst fin: 4 month abs: AW bow: E5,500 Apr foal, half-sister to a 7f juv plc juv,
dam unplcd as a juv at 5/7f: eff at 6f on polytrack: imprvd eff despite awkward high draw, one to note at 7f.

4518 **MANGROVE CAY 21** [9]2-9-0   T P Queally 9/2: 045: Handy wide, no extra fnl 1f: see 4518.   hd   69a

4543 **EDGE OF ITALY 19** [10]2-8-9   D Sweeney 20/1: 066: Held up, some hdwy halfway, no prog dist.   1¾   59a

4670 **MISSIN MARGOT 14** [12]2-8-9   F Norton 40/1: 57: Bhd, al outpcd, awkward high draw: see 4670.   4   47a

4631 **PROPHETS CALLING 16** [1]2-9-0   Lisa Jones 100/1: 008: b g Brave Act - Arbitration (Bigstone)   ¾   50a
Chsd ldrs early, sn lost pl & struggling: 8,000gns 2yo, Apr foal: dam unrcd: sire smart juv.

4644 **PRESKANI 15** [11]2-9-0 P C Haddon(7) 100/1: 0009: Prom, hung right & lost pl early, sn bhd, chkpcs.   5   37a

4704 **MISS SUDBROOK 12** [2]2-8-9   M Fenton 6/1: 040: 10th: Led early, lost pl from halfway: btr 4704 (hvy).   5   19a

4704 **SPECTAIT 12** [7]2-9-0   S W Kelly 8/11 FAV: 20: 11th: Unruly stalls & reportedly banged head,   3½   13a
dwelt & al outpcd in rear: well bckd, see 4704 (hvy, 7f).

4349 **RANDALLS TOUCH 29** [6]2-9-0   B Swarbrick(5) 100/1: 00: 12th: Prom, strugg from over 3f out, sn bhd.   9   0a

12 Ran   Time 1m 17.10 (No Std Time)   Owned: Mr A S Reid   Trained: Mill Hill London

---

| **4922** | 8.00 Dine At Dunstall Park Selling Stakes 2yo (G4) | | |
| | £2597 £742 £371   5f20y aw rnd   Standard   Inapplicable   Inside | | |

4787 **BOBS FLYER 7** [9] J G Given 2-8-7 (1ow) (65) K Fallon 5/2 FAV: 0402441: Sn chsd ldrs, led ins last   72a
& rdn clr, decisively: sold to J G M O'Shea for 7,000gns: first win: eff at 5f on fast, gd & polytrack,
sharp/turning trks: apprec drop to sell grade: see 4517, 4303.

4673 **LLAMADAS 14** [3] M Dods 2-8-11 VIS (64) J F Egan 7/1: 4036602: Bhd, switched & kept on well from   3½   66a
over 1f out, nrst fin: op 10/1: gd run in first time visor: eff at 5/6f, tried 7f: acts on fast, gd/soft &
polytrack, sharp/turning of gall trk: eff in blnks/visor: clmd by Mrs S Liddiard for 6,000: see 4172 & 2995.

4549 **OUR LITTLE SECRET 19** [11] A Berry 2-8-6   F Norton 14/1: 53: Chsd ldr, chance dist, no extra.   1   58a

---

WOLVERHAMPTON **Polytrack SATURDAY 02.10.04 Lefthand, Sharp Track**

4804 **DUCAL DIVA 6** [1] J R Weymes 2-8-6 (60) D Fentiman(7) 14/1: 026004: Led till ins last, no extra: qck reapp: handles fast grnd & polytrack: see 3525. ½ **57a**
4765 **MITCHELLAND 8** [4]2-8-11 (65) P Hanagan 6/1: 6355505: Towards rear, only mod prog: see 1037 (hvy). *nk* **61a**
4289 **WILLIAM JAMES 33** [5]2-8-11 S W Kelly 25/1: 506: Went right start, sn hmpd & outpcd, mod prog: reportedly hung left thr'out: see 3993. *3* **52a**
4617 **MOUNT KELLET 16** [10]2-8-11 M Fenton 20/1: 07: ch g Bluebird - Antinnaz (Thatching) Chsd ldrs, btn 2f out: E25,000 Feb first foal, dam a 5f juv wnr & smart 3yo at 5/6f. *nk* **51a**
4625 **AYNSLEY 16** [8]2-8-7 (1ow) N Callan 11/2: 458: In tch, no impress fnl 2f: see 4349. 1½ **43a**
4471 **BOGAZ 23** [2]2-8-11 (61) G Gibbons 9/2: 20009: Prom, lost pl qckly bef halfway, sn bhd: new yard. ½ **46a**
3376 **WILFORD MAVERICK 72** [12]2-8-11 A McCarthy 40/1: 0000: 10th: Prom, btn 2f out, 10 wk abs. ¾ **43a**
4741 **MISS COTSWOLD LADY 10** [7]2-8-6 VIS (65) T P Queally 10/1: 5420000: 11th: Sn rdn & bhd in visor. *3* **29a**
4590 **INDEPENDENT SPIRIT 18** [6]2-8-11 P Mulrennan(3) 50/1: 000: 12th: ch g Wolfhound - Kigema (Case Law) Bmpd start & al outpcd: cheaply bght Mar first foal, dam a 6f juv wnr & subs 1m 3yo scorer. 1¾ **29a**
12 Ran Time 1m 03.44 (No Std Time) Owned: Mr D Maloney Trained: Gainsborough

4923 **8.30 Martin Collins Enterprises Handicap Stakes 3yo+ 56-70 (E3)** **[76]**
£5113 £1573 £787 **1m141y aw rnd** **Standard** **Inapplicable** Inside

4702 **RISKA KING 12** [9] R A Fahey 4-9-3 (65) P Hanagan 4/1: 3361541: Held up, hdwy 3f out & led ins last, drvn out: op 7/1: eff at 7f/8.5f on fast, soft & polytrack, handles hvy & an trk: well h'capped on AW. **73a**
4321 **ALMOND WILLOW 31** [13] J Noseda 3-9-2 (68) S W Kelly 10/1: 61-02062: Sn cl-up, flashed tail, led 4f out, hdd ins last & no extra: op 7/1: fine run with forcing tactics from awkward wide draw: acts on fast, gd/soft & both AWs: can find similar: see 3138 & 423. ½ **74a**
4743 **ISLAND RAPTURE 10** [4] J A R Toller 4-9-7 (69) J F Egan 6/1: 0326023: Rear, hdwy wide over 2f out, hung left under press but kept on: see 4743 & 1891. ¾ **74a**
4581 **HAZEWIND 18** [6] P D Evans 3-9-4 vis t (70) F P Ferris(3) 7/1: 1164164: In tch, styd on for press, no dngr. *nk* **74a**
4135 **MOONSHAFT 40** [11]3-9-1 (67) S Sanders 20/1: 004045: Bhd, kept on wide, nvr able to chall: 6 wk abs: handles polytrack, eff around 1m, tried up to 12f previously. 1½ **68a**
4702 **THE BONUS KING 12** [5]4-9-5 (67) G Baker 20/1: 2400506: Handy, wknd over 2f out: see 1066. 1¾ **65a**
4546 **ALI DEO 19** [8]3-9-1 p (67) T P Queally 14/1: 1306007: Held up, hdwy halfway, chsd ldr over 2f out, sn no extra: op 20/1: see 1832. ½ **64a**
4721 **CHARLIE TANGO 11** [7]3-9-0 (66) M Fenton 16/1: 3500048: Dwelt, held up, eff 3f out, no impress. *7* **51a**
4743 **VONADAISY 10** [3]3-9-2 bl (68) A Culhane 9/1: 344-1059: Handy when short of room & lost pl 3f out. ½ **52a**
4827 **TEXT 5** [2]3-9-2 P (68) F Norton 20/1: 0235600: 10th: Rear, short of room over 3f out, no impress. 1½ **49a**
4809 **SUMMER SHADES 6** [12]6-9-1 (63) K Fallon 11/4 FAV: 5612520: 11th: Held up, hdwy 5f out, btn 3f out. 2½ **39a**
4448 **WESTERN ROOTS 25** [1]3-9-3 (69) N Callan 40/1: 6155000: 12th: Led till 4f out, sn hmpd & struggling. *15* **17a**
12 Ran Time 1m 51.47 (No Std Time) Owned: Market Avenue Racing Club Ltd Trained: Malton

4924 **9.00 Weatherbys Bank Handicap Stakes 3yo+ 56-70 (E3)** **[74]**
£5205 £1601 £801 **1m4f50y aw** **Standard** **Inapplicable** Inside

4690 **MERRYMAKER 14** [4] W M Brisbourne 4-9-9 (69) K Fallon 9/2: 1003551: Held up, rdn & hdwy to lead ins last, rdn clr: op 7/1: eff at 12/14f on firm, gd/soft & polytrack: handles any trk: see 3270, 2546. **78a**
4473* **RESONATE 23** [9] A G Newcombe 6-9-4 (64) Dane O'Neill 4/1 JT FAV: 006-4012: Keen, chsd ldrs, rdn & hdwy to lead over 1f out, hdd ins last & no response to wnr: nicely bckd: handles firm, soft & polytrack. *5* **65a**
4850 **MILK AND SULTANA 3** [1] G A Ham 4-9-6 (66) A Daly 14/1: 2411403: Held up, rdn & kept on fnl 2f, not pace to threaten: acts on firm, soft & both AWs: see 4515. ½ **66a**
4826 **EFRHINA 5** [6] Mrs Stef Liddiard 4-9-4 (64) F Norton 20/1: 3020034: Bhd, styd on wide from over 1f out, nrst fin: qck reapp: poss stays a sharp 12f: acts on firm, gd & polytrack: see 4826, 3867. *hd* **63a**
4771* **IVY LEAGUE STAR 8** [10]3-9-3 (70) A Culhane 8/1: 06-5015: Mid-div when jinked right & lost pl on bend after 5f, styd on onepace for press fnl 3f: op 3/1: handles polytrack & gd/soft grnd: see 4771. *nk* **68a**
1875 **JADEERON 135** [2]5-9-4 p (64) Lisa Jones 14/1: 2344006: Led 2f, btn 3f out: 5 month abs: see 342. *1* **61a**
4170 **ALPINE SPECIAL 37** [11]3-9-3 (70) G Faulkner 12/1: 6042207: Held up, eff 2f out, no impress: btr 4012. *1* **66a**
4620 **CRATHORNE 16** [3]4-9-9 p (69) T P Queally 20/1: 3400008: Handy & led over 3f out till over 1f out, fdd. 1¾ **63a**
4589 **ZEIS 18** [5]4-9-5 t (65) J F Egan 20/1: 0011009: Sn rdn & al bhd: see 3211 (clmr). *4* **53a**
3531 **QUEDEX 66** [8]8-9-4 (64) R Miles(3) 5/1: 1521100: 10th: Prom, btn 3f out: btr 3275 (2m, soft). 1½ **50a**
4487* **NUTS FOR YOU 23** [12]3-9-2 (69) D Sweeney 4/1 JT FAV: 002-10: 11th: Led after 2f till over 2f out, sn btn. *5* **48a**
4188 **PORT N STARBOARD 36** [7]3-9-1 (68) S Sanders 25/1: 45440: 12th: Held up from bhd, eff wide 4f out, sn but hung badly right & t.o. over 1f out: btr 4188 & 4034. *dist* **0a**
12 Ran Time 2m 42.12 (No Std Time) Owned: The Blacktoffee Partnership Trained: Nesscliffe

4925 **9.30 Wood Brothers Handicap Stakes 3yo 46-55 (F4)** **[67]**
£2936 £839 £419 **1m1f103y aw rnd** **Standard** **Inapplicable** Inside

4598 **BOPPYS PRINCESS 17** [5] R A Fahey 3-9-2 (55) P Hanagan 4/1: 0-121151: Bhd, hdwy over 2f out & styd on for press to lead line, all out: eff at 1m/9.5f on firm, hvy & polytrack: tough & progressive: see 4085. **63a**
4421 **VELOCITAS 26** [8] H J Collingridge 3-9-1 (54) J F Egan 33/1: 0-400052: Rear, eff wide from over 3f out, styd on well ins last for press, just held: eff around 1m/9.5f on fast, gd & polytrack: see 4421 & 2243. *nk* **61a**
4421 **RUBAIYAT 26** [11] G Wragg 3-9-2 (55) F Norton 7/2 FAV: 0432533: Held up, rdn & hdwy to lead over 1f out, hdd line: op 9/2: acts on fast & both AWs: clr of rem: see 4421. *hd* **61a**
4660 **CALCULAITE 14** [4] Mrs G S Rees 3-9-2 (55) S Sanders 13/2: 6450134: Led till over 1f out, no extra. 3½ **54a**
3906 **MR LEWIN 51** [6]3-9-1 (54) Darren Williams 14/1: 005-005: Prom, btn dist: 7 wk abs: see 2506. *1* **51a**
3207 **TURKS AND CAICOS 79** [3]3-9-2 (55) G Faulkner 10/1: 40-22106: Mid-div, nvr pace to chall: abs. ½ **51a**
4828 **IMPERIAL ROYALE 5** [1]3-8-12 p (51) G Gibbons 50/1: 6000007: Mid-div, outpcd fnl 3f: qck reapp. *nk* **46a**
4669 **BE WISE GIRL 14** [10]3-9-1 (54) M Fenton 14/1: 03-3108: Keen, dsptd lead 1m, flashed tail/wknd. ½ **48a**
4515 **INFIDELITY 21** [12]3-8-13 (52) V Slattery 8/1: 0635049: Held up, hdwy 5f out, btn over 2f out: btr 4515. *10* **30a**
4546 **TROIS ETOILES 19** [7]3-9-1 VIS (54) K Fallon 9/2: 5055360: 10th: Keen early in mid-div, btn when lost action & eased over 1f out: visor. ½ **31a**
2804 **BLUE VIKING 96** [13]3-8-12 (51) D Fentiman(7) 50/1: 4-0500: 11th: Al rear, abs: btr 2383 (fibresand). 1½ **25a**
4720 **GRAND RAPIDE 11** [9]3-9-1 (54) N Callan 11/1: 6004100: 12th: Al bhd: btr 4202 (g/s). ¾ **27a**
4367 **POKER 29** [2]3-9-0 (53) A Culhane 16/1: 060-1000: 13th: Prom, strugg fnl 3f: btr 656 (fbsd, gamble). *12* **6a**

13 Ran   Time 2m 03.34(No Std Time)   Owned: Mrs S Bond   Trained: Malton

REDCAR   SATURDAY 02.10.04 Lefthand, Flat, Galloping Track

Official Going GOOD/FIRM (FIRM places).

4926	1.45 Tetley's Smooth Handicap Stakes 3yo+ 56-70 (E3)	[82]
	£8382 £2579 £1290 **1m str Firm 01 -02 Slow** Centre	

4321 **MISTRESS TWISTER 31** [16] T D Barron 3-8-13 (67) P Fessey 33/1: 3-330301: Mid-div, prog 2f out, **79**
strong run to lead cl-home: first success: eff at 6/7f, apprec this gall 1m: acts on fast & firm grnd: unexposed
over 1m & open to further improvement: see 3548 & 2463.

4452 **MOUNT VETTORE 25** [14] Mrs J R Ramsden 3-8-13 (67) Dane O'Neill 11/2: 0006632: Held up, gd hdwy   ½   **77**
wide to lead dist, collared cl-home: nicely bckd: tumbled down the h'cap & back to gd early season form here:
wandered in the closing stages & that may have cost him this race: stays a gall 1m well: see 955 & 481 (AW).

4554 **REGENTS SECRET 19** [20] J S Goldie 4-8-5 p (56) W Supple 25/1: 0330603: Held up, gd hdwy when   1½   **63**
short of room dist, kept on & nrst fin: has been gelded: see 4399.

4867* **NEWCORP LAD 3** [18] Mrs G S Rees 4-9-0 (6ex)p (65) A Culhane 4/1 FAV: 4240314: Mid-div, hdwy when   nk   **71**
short of room dist, nrst fin: nicely bckd: qck reapp & 6lb pen for 4867.

4542 **ALCHERA 20** [5]3-8-6 (60) S Carson 25/1: 4404005: Nvr far away, led briefly dist, no extra: see 3995.   2½   **61**

4696 **BEST DESERT 13** [26]3-8-8 (62) Darren Williams 33/1: 0515006: Dwelt, outpcd, styd on fnl 2f, nrst   ½   **62**
fin: seems to stay 1m: see 3654 (7f).

4613 **FLAME QUEEN 17** [2]3-8-6 (60) J McAuley 40/1: 0040407: Led till dist, no extra.   2   **56**

4719 **ATLANTIC ACE 11** [10]7-8-8 p (59) F Lynch 20/1: 6000008: Mid-div, nvr nr ldrs: v well h'capped.   nk   **54**

4719 **DARA MAC 11** [17]5-8-10 (61) Suzanne France(5) 50/1: 1060409: Rear, late gains, nvr dngrs.   1   **54**

4336 **HEARTS DESIRE 30** [9]3-9-0 (68) W Ryan 33/1: 52-6260: 10th: Prom 6f, grad wknd: btr 3079.   3   **55**

4672 **TEDSDALE MAC 14** [24]5-8-8 (59) C Catlin 12/1: 3225200: 11th: Held up, nvr a factor: btr 4399.   nk   **45**

4452 **BLAEBERRY 25** [8]3-8-10 bl (64) S W Kelly 20/1: 4151200: 12th: Prom 6f, wknd: btr 3806.   1½   **47**

4867 **LORD BASKERVILLE 3** [27]3-8-2 (4oh) (52) J Bramhill 66/1: 2404400: 13th: Held up, nvr a factor.   nk   **38**

4809 **ANTHEMION 6** [15]7-8-7 (58) T Eaves(3) 20/1: 3200000: 14th: Chsd ldrs till halfway, sn bhd: qck reapp.   ¾   **38**

4719* **GIFTED FLAME 11** [6]5-9-7 (72) P Makin(5) 14/1: 1436010: 15th: Bmpd start, prog halfway, btn 1.5f   nk   **51**
out: top-weight & shorter priced stablemate of wnr: lost all real ch at the start, see 4719.

6   **PEARSON GLEN 327** [25]5-8-6 (1ow)(2oh) (54) R Winston 50/1: 2/00546-0: 16th: ch g Dolphin Street -   1   **34**
Glendora (Glenstal) Held up, nvr a factor on belated reapp: lightly rcd & modest h'cap form in '03: mdn wnr in
'02, h'cap rnr-up: eff at 9/10f on fast & firm grnd: with G Swinbank.

2 Sep'02 Redc 10fm 60-57 E: 1 Apr'02 Muss 9g/f 63- D:

4598 **GOLDEN SPECTRUM 17** [3]5-8-5 (5oh) (51) P M Quinn 28/1: 0300030: 17th: Nvr btr than mid-div.   1   **31**

4144 **PRIME OFFER 39** [21]8-9-0 (65) N Pollard 12/1: 1215420: 18th: Chsd ldrs 6f, wknd: btr 4144 (7f, sft).   nk   **39**

4598 **Splodger Mac 17** [23]5-8-5 (3oh)(53) A Reilly(7) 28/1:0 4346 **Zarin 30** [12]6-8-5 (4oh)(52) N Pollard 50/1:0

4009 **Orangino 46** [11]6-8-5 (11oh)(45) R Kennemore(7) 100/1:0785 **Mister Sweets 7** [13]5-9-3 T(68) D Tudhope(5) 20/1:0

4721 **Heversham 11** [1]3-8-12 (66) M Tebbutt 14/1:0   3088 **Cashneem 85** [4]6-8-11 (62) D Allan 20/1:0

4719 **Gala Sunday 11** [7]4-8-5 (1oh)(55) Dale Gibson 50/1:0 1253 **Rahjel Sultan 166** [19]6-8-8 t(59) G Carter 50/1:0

26 Ran   Time 1m 35.06 (0.26)   Owned: Mr Dave Scott   Trained: Thirsk

4927	2.20 European Breeders Fund Maiden Stakes Fillies 2yo (D3)	
	£4550 £1400 £700 **7f str Firm 01 -23 Slow** Centre	

4358 **SHEBOYGAN 29** [1] J G Given 2-8-11   J Bramhill 4/1: 31: Made all, styd on strongly despite   **86**
drifting left fnl 1f, rdn out: clearly benefitted from recent debut: apprec this gall 7f, may stay 1m: acts on
fast & firm grnd: likes to force the pace: see 4358.

HER OWN KIND [6] Saeed bin Suroor 2-8-11   K McEvoy 3/1 FAV: 2: b f Dubai Millennium - The   ¾   **83**
Caretaker (Caerleon) Dwelt, imprvd halfway, kept on fnl 1f & not btn far: nicely bckd: Feb foal, half-sister to
top-class mid-dist performer Mutafaweq & 10f US performer Dimitrova: dam a useful miler, sire a top-class 1m/10f
performer: eff over a gall 7f on firm, 1m will suit: runs well fresh: sure to find similar.

4575 **VILLARRICA 18** [2] Sir Michael Stoute 2-8-11   R Winston 100/30: 43: Dwelt, recovered to chase   2   **79**
ldrs, ev ch 2f out, not qckn fnl 1f: op 5/1: acts on firm & soft grnd: 1m will now suit, see 4575.

4557 **KINDLING 19** [12] M Johnston 2-8-11   S Chin 22/1: 54: Trkd ldrs, ev ch 1.5f out, onepace fnl 1f: ½   **78**
imprvd in defeat, prob met a couple of fair rivals here: see 4557.

4418 **HEAT OF THE NIGHT 26** [4]2-8-11 (75) Dane O'Neill 13/2: 4025: Nvr far away, ev ch till onepcd fnl   shd   **77**
1f: ran to form of 4418.

MADGE [7]2-8-11   R Havlin 12/1: 6: b f Marju - Aymara (Darshaan) Outpcd, styd on late, nrst   3½   **70**
fin on debut: ran green: Jan first foal: dam a mid-dist wnr, sire top-class over mid-dists: bred to apprec 1m +
next term & sure to learn from this.

4648 **MOONMAIDEN 15** [10]2-8-11 (77) A Culhane 7/1: 0557: Prom 5f, grad wknd: see 4648.   1   **68**

4244 **SWEET POTATO 35** [8]2-8-11 P Fessey 66/1: 58: Keen in rear, nvr nr ldrs: see 4244.   2   **64**

4610 **NEFERURA 17** [9]2-8-11 S W Kelly 66/1: 09: b f Mister Baileys - Boadicea's Chariot (Commanche   1¼   **61**
Run) Nvr nr ldrs: Mar foal, half-sister to 7f juv wnr Agrippina: dam a mid-dist/hdle wnr, sire a top-class miler.

4670 **KATIES BISCUIT 14** [5]2-8-11 N Pollard 150/1: 60: 10th: Prom 4f, sn wknd.   shd   **60**

4844 **MUSARDIERE 4** [3]2-8-11 L Goncalves 28/1: 050: 11th: Held up, al rear: qck reapp.   1½   **57**

4591 **KEYALZAO 18** [11]2-8-11 D Fentiman(7) 200/1: 0000: 12th: Dwelt, recovered to chase ldrs 4f, sn btn.   10   **37**

2492 **KALIKA 108** [13]2-8-11 (35) N Callan 150/1: 6000: 13th: Chsd ldrs 4f, wknd qckly, t.o.: abs.   dist   **0**

13 Ran   Time 1m 23.53 (1.73)   Owned: Mr D Eiffe   Trained: Gainsborough

---

4928

2.55 Listed Betfair Com Two-Year-Old Trophy 2yo (A1)
£128412 £48708 £24354   **6f str   Firm 01   +02 Fast**   Centre

4882* **OBE GOLD 2** [24] M R Channon 2-8-3 vis (89) C Catlin 15/2: 24U3311: Made just about all, held on   **105**
well fnl 1f despite drifting left, drvn out: well bckd, juv crse rec time: eff at 5/6f on gd & firm grnd: likes
forcing tactics on a stiff/gall trk: suited by a visor: fast improving & a useful colt, see 4882.

4458* **CAESAR BEWARE 24** [8] H Candy 2-8-9 Dane O'Neill 4/7 FAV: 1112: Nvr far away, ev ch fnl 1f, just   *1*   **107**
btn in a driving fin: hvly bckd at odds-on: first defeat, tho' far from disgraced conceding wnr 6lb: acts on gd & fm:
rtd just higher in 4458 (val sales race).

4458 **DARIO GEE GEE 24** [2] K A Ryan 2-8-7 (1ow) (95) N Callan 33/1: 2021503: Prom, kept on fnl 1f but   *1½*   **101**
not pace of front 2: career best run, acts on fm & soft: likes to run up with the pace: again bhd today's 2nd in 4458.

4758* **MOTH BALL 9** [25] J A Osborne 2-9-0 (83) S W Kelly 33/1: 2310314: Chsd ldrs, onepcd fnl 1f: rcd   *½*   **106**
away from main pace & an excellent eff conceding plenty of weight to the 3 that beat him: much imprvd form.

4153* **BEAVER PATROL 42** [16]2-8-9 (100) S Carson 11/1: 2106215: Prom, onepcd fnl 1f: 6 wk abs: btr 4153.   *½*   **99**

4699* **PIVOTAL FLAME 12** [10]2-9-2 (100) G Carter 18/1: 15416: Dwelt, hdwy from rear 2f out, nrst fin: *¾*   **104**
sound run under jt top-weight: crying out for a return to 7f: see 4699.

4655 **WORD PERFECT 15** [21]2-8-7 (85) Dale Gibson 100/1: 3115057: Chsd ldrs, onepcd fnl 1f: see 4655.   shd   **94**

4369 + **BAHIA BREEZE 28** [3]2-8-4 (89) W Ryan 12/1: 418: Prom, onepcd fnl 1.5f: only 3rd start & this   nk   **90**
was a big step up in grade: see 4369 (mdn auct).

4651 **SENTIERO ROSSO 15** [20]2-8-9 (96) K McEvoy 66/1: 421309: Front rank 4.5f, wknd: much btr 4280.   2½   **88**

4533 **BOND CITY 21** [9]2-8-9 (95) F Lynch 50/1: 1335250: 10th: Nvr btr than mid-div: btr 4307 (gd).   shd   **87**

4692 **GIFTED GAMBLE 13** [11]2-8-9 P (80) R Winston 66/1: 2215020: 11th: Held up, nvr nr ldrs: cheekpieces.   hd   **86**

4765 **HARVEST WARRIOR 8** [15]2-8-9 (95) D Allan 22/1: 221520: 12th: Chsd ldrs, btn 1.5f out: btr 4765 (sft).   hd   **85**

4633 **ROODEYE 16** [18]2-8-7 (96) W Supple 33/1: 2156340: 13th: Prom 4f, grad wknd.   1½   **79**

4684 **WORLD AT MY FEET 14** [23]2-8-1 (87) P Fessey 25/1: 2130400: 14th: Nvr btr than mid-div.   shd   **72**

4727 Monsieur Mirasol 11 [14]2-8-9 BL(79) J Carroll 125/1:04533   Amazin 21 [7]2-8-12 (95) P Dobbs 25/1:0
3743 Russian Rocket 57 [5]2-8-6 (79) J McAuley 100/1:0   4349 Cillas Smile 29 [12]2-7-12 P M Quinn 200/1:0
4089 Second Reef 43 [19]2-8-6 G Parkin 125/1:0   4645 Gogetter Girl 15 [4]2-8-1 p(66) J Bramhill 250/1:0
3445 Lowestoft Playboy 70 [6]2-9-2 (67) S Chin 200/1:0   3431 Forest Viking 70 [22]2-8-9 (58) D Mernagh 200/1:0
4403 Ross Is Boss 26 [17]2-8-4 (1ow) T Eaves 250/1:0   4481 Komac 23 [13]2-8-12 (72) A Culhane 200/1:P
24 Ran   Time 1m 08.84 (u0.06)   Owned: BDR Partnership   Trained: West Ilsley

---

4929

3.25 Listed Betfair Com Guisborough Stakes 3yo+ (A1)
£17400 £6600 £3300   **7f str   Firm 01   (+12 Fast)**   Centre

4479 **GONFILIA 23** [10] Saeed bin Suroor 4-9-0 t (102) K McEvoy 2/1 FAV: 2110421: Prom, led halfway,   **110**
styd on strongly fnl 1f, rdn out: well bckd, fast time: eff up with/forcing the pace over 7f/1m on firm, soft grnd
& dirt: handles a sharp/undul or gall trk: tough & smart filly who wears a t-strap: see 4479 & 2211.

2913 **TWILIGHT BLUES 91** [3] J Noseda 5-9-0 (103) S W Kelly 11/2: 000-5052: Held up, hdwy to chase wnr   1¾   **106**
2f out, ev ch fnl 1f, not qckn cl-home: 3 mth abs & fine run for new stable (prev with B Meehan): lightly rcd this
season & could win bef season's end, see 1958.

4472 **IQTE SAAB 23** [2] J L Dunlop 3-8-12 (100) W Supple 8/1: 12-16053: Held up, switched & prog 2f   *1*   **104**
out, nrst fin: see 4472 & 1150 (reapp).

4573* **VORTEX 20** [5] Miss Gay Kelleway 5-9-3 e t (105) N Cordrey 7/2: 3024214: Prom, onepcd fnl 1f: 1¾   **103**
well bckd under top-weight: see 4573.

4479 **ITHACA 23** [8]3-8-7 (98) W Ryan 7/1: 3653435: Prom, wknd fnl 1f: btr 4479.   2½   **90**

3253 **ORCADIAN 78** [9]3-8-12 (101) J Tate 25/1: 1220-306: Chsd ldrs, btn fnl 1f: best 2069.   shd   **90**

4799 **SIMIANNA 7** [4]5-8-12 p (97) R Winston 16/1: 0321507: Held up, nvr nr ldrs: btr 4510 (6f).   *1*   **90**

4811 **LUCKY PIPIT 6** [6]3-8-7 (98) A Culhane 10/1: 5210048: Led till bef halfway, wknd: qck reapp.   3½   **80**

4495 **MOONLIGHT MAN 22** [1]3-8-12 (100) P Dobbs 20/1: 0024269: Prom till halfway, sn btn: btr 3814.   *½*   **84**

4743 **KINDLELIGHT DEBUT 10** [7]4-8-9 (70) N Callan 150/1: 3000030: 10th: Prom till halfway: highly tried.   8   **63**

10 Ran   Time 1m 21.04 (u0.76)   Owned: Godolphin   Trained: Newmarket

---

4930

4.00 Shepherd Construction Classified Stakes 3yo+ 0-70 (E3)
£7228 £2224 £1112   **5f str   Firm 01   -05 Slow**   Centre

4585 **POLISH EMPEROR 18** [13] P W Harris 4-9-2 e (73) N Callan 8/1: 1000601: Front rank, went on   **82**
halfway, styd on strongly fnl 1f, drvn out: stays 6f, suited by 5f: acts on firm, gd/soft & both AWs: suited by
blnks/eye shield & loves to run up with/force the pace: handles a sharp/easy or gall trk: tough sprinter, see 1765.

4870* **PLAYFUL DANE 3** [2] W S Cunningham 7-9-5 (68) D Tudhope(5) 15/8 FAV: 1501312: Prom, kept on well   *¾*   **82**
fnl 1f & just btn in a close fin: hvly bckd from 5/2: qck reapp & remains in fine form, see 4870.

3833 **NANNA 54** [1] R Hollinshead 3-8-10 (68) F Lynch 14/1: 6211603: Dsptd lead till halfway, kept on   1¼   **69**
fnl 1f but not pace of front 2: 8 wk abs: gd run after short break, spot on next time: see 3193.

4747 **FYODOR 10** [5] W J Haggas 3-9-0 (71) S W Kelly 14/1: 2-060004: Mid-div, kept on under press fnl   *1*   **70**
1f, nrst fin: slipped down the h'cap this term, showed a bit more today: see 2137.

4585 **FOLEY MILLENNIUM 18** [4]6-9-2 (73) R Winston 10/1: 2142055: Led till halfway, wknd fnl 1f: has   *½*   **70**
had a fine season & high in the h'cap now: see 4039 & 3577.

3833 **LUALUA 54** [14]3-9-1 (72) P Makin(5) 12/1: 3043006: Dwelt, styd on late, nvr dngrs: 8 wk abs.   2   **63**

4652 **INDIAN SPARK 15** [10]10-9-0 (71) W Supple 12/1: 0006007: Outpcd, styd on late, nvr dngrs: see 4005.   *1*   **59**

4126 **SMIRFYS PARTY 40** [6]6-8-13 vis (48) P M Quinn 25/1: 0003508: Speed till halfway, sn btn: abs.   hd   **57**

4604 **MIRASOL PRINCESS 17** [8]3-9-0 (74) Dane O'Neill 10/1: 6401039: Outpcd & nvr a factor: btr 4604.   *½*   **56**

3924 **SCOTTISH EXILE 50** [15]3-8-10 vis (70) Darren Williams 25/1: 2103400: 10th: Nvr btr than mid-div.   2   **46**

4603 **COUNT COUGAR 17** [7]4-8-13 (50) Dale Gibson 200/1: 3006000: 11th: Chsd ldrs 3.5f, sn btn.   1½   **45**

3974 **SMIRFYS NIGHT 48** [9]5-8-13 (49) J Bramhill 33/1: 5/-000540: 12th: Al outpcd: 7 wk abs: see 3974.   *¾*   **43**

3852 **MISS CEYLON 52** [3]4-8-10 (35) J McAuley 200/1: 0-000000: 13th: Slowly away, al rear: 7 wk abs.   7   **26**

REDCAR SATURDAY 02.10.04 Lefthand, Flat, Galloping Track

4174 **CATCH THE CAT 37** [16]5-9-1 vis (72) T Eaves(3) 14/1: 0010000: 14th: Al struggling: btr 3561. ½ **29**
14 Ran Time 56.82 (0.32) Owned: Edrich Graves Harris Trained: Berkhamsted

4931

4.35 Book Your Christmas Party At Redcar Racecourse Handicap Stakes 3yo+ 71-85 (D2) **[92]**
£9516 £2928 £1464 **1m2f** **Firm 01** **-06 Slow** Inside

4755* **GO TECH 9** [6] T D Easterby 4-9-0 (78) D Allan 7/2 FAV: 4604211: Mid-div, gd hdwy to lead entering fnl 1f, pushed clr: bckd from 9/2: eff at 7f/1m, suited by 10f: acts on gd & firm grnd, handles gd/soft: likes a stiff/undul or gall trk: confidence at a high & remains on a fair mark: see 4755. **89**
4702 **ST SAVARIN 12** [9] J R Best 3-8-4 (73) Dale Gibson 33/1: 3100052: Held up, switched & hdwy 2f out, not reach wnr: styd this longer 10f trip: back to form, see 3562. *3* **78**
4767 **YOUNG ROONEY 8** [4] M Mullineaux 4-8-7 (1oh) (70) S Chin 20/1: 4032263: Led till entering fnl 1f, no extra: yet to win: see 4515. *shd* **76**
4809 **RAREFIED 6** [1] T D Easterby 3-8-5 (74) W Supple 14/1: 1000004: Held up, switched & hdwy 2f out, not qckn fnl 1f: op 20/1, longer priced stablemate of wnr: qck reapp: see 1382 (12f). *1½* **76**
4775 **NIGHT SIGHT 8** [2]7-8-7 (1oh) (70) R Winston 7/1: 4415145: Trkd ldrs, onepcd fnl 1.5f: btr 4377 (12f). *nk* **72**
4672 **STALLONE 14** [8]7-8-7 (5oh)t (66) D Tudhope(4) 12/1: 4360066: Dwelt, hdwy from rear 3f out, no impress. *3½* **66**
4550 **BARKING MAD 19** [3]6-9-7 (85) A Culhane 5/1: 1626127: Front rank, wknd 2f out: top-weight. *9* **64**
4643 **CAUSE CELEBRE 15** [7]3-8-8 (77) W Ryan 14/1: 4-101608: Nvr nr ldrs: btr 2780. *3½* **51**
4613 **RIVER TREAT 17** [11]3-8-11 (80) Dane O'Neill 11/1: 1650429: Held up, chsd ldrs 3f out, sn btn. *1¼* **52**
4766 **DREAM MAGIC 8** [5]6-9-1 (79) G Carter 15/2: 3233300: 10th: Chsd ldrs 1m, wknd. *1* **49**
3972* **DOUBLE VODKA 48** [10]3-8-4 (73) D Mernagh 4/1: 2401110: 11th: Prom wide & v keen, wknd over 3f out, eased: 7 wk abs: most disapp, rcd much too keenly, prev progressive, see 3972 (1m, gd/soft). *6* **33**
11 Ran Time 2m 03.06 (0.76) Owned: Ryedale Partners No 4 Trained: Malton

4932

5.10 Redcar Racecourse Conference & Banqueting Centre Handicap Stakes 3yo+ 56-70 (E3) **[75]**
£4271 £1314 £657 **1m6f19y** **Firm 01** **-16 Slow** Inside

4259 **RED FOREST 34** [8] J Mackie 5-9-6 t (67) Dale Gibson 11/2: 0333161: Trkd ldrs, prog to lead 4f out, clr 2f out, styd on strongly, pushed out: tchd 13/2: eff at 12/14f on gd, firm grnd & fibresand: suited by a t-strap: positively rdn & in gd form: see 4170. **77**
4559 **MOST DEFINITELY 19** [5] T D Easterby 4-9-3 (64) D Allan 4/1 FAV: 2062322: Held up, prog to chase wnr 2f out, no impress ins fnl 1f: nicely bckd: another consistent run: see 4559. *2½* **69**
4559 **BEST PORT 19** [1] J Parkes 8-9-2 (63) M Lawson(5) 5/1: 0161043: Held up, prog 3f out, nrst fin. *2* **65**
4360 **DOVEDON HERO 29** [7] P J McBride 4-9-9 bl (70) G Carter 11/2: 4602034: Chsd ldrs, ev ch till onepcd fnl 1f: clr of rem: see 3475. *shd* **72**
4672 **COLWAY RITZ 14** [2]10-9-2 (63) J Bramhill 6/1: 422-0225: Trkd ldrs, wknd 2f out: does stay 14f, tho' btr recently over 10/12f: see 4672 & 4402. *6* **57**
4601 **GOLDEN DRIFT 17** [6]3-8-3 (59) C Catlin 9/1: 5025036: Chsd ldrs, btn 2f out: see 4601 (12f). *nk* **53**
4308 **SPITTING IMAGE 32** [3]4-9-0 (61) A Culhane 9/2: 4123167: Led till 4f out, wknd: btr 3810 (2m). *6* **47**
4559 **DISTANT COUSIN 19** [4]7-8-9 vis (56) Dane O'Neill 10/1: 5300438: Prom, wknd after 1m, t.o. *15* **18**
8 Ran Time 3m 0.17(2.37) Owned: Mr P Riley Trained: Church Broughton

PONTEFRACT MONDAY 04.10.04 Lefthand, Undulating Track, Stiff Uphill Finish

Official Going Good/Firm

4933

2.20 European Breeders Fund Claxton Bay Maiden Stakes 2yo (D2)
£5590 £1720 £860 **1m2f6y** **Good/Firm 39** **-22 Slow** Inside

4723 **AYAM ZAMAN 13** [4] M A Jarvis 2-8-9 P Robinson 5/4 FAV: 51: Trkd ldrs trav well, qcknd to lead over 1f out, eased, val 4L+: hvly bckd to confirm debut promise: eff at 1m, relished this step up to 10f & 12f shld suit: acts on firm & fast grnd, stiff/undul trks: lightly rcd & progressive, keep on side. **90+**
4722 **ROYAL JET 13** [15] M R Channon 2-9-0 VIS A Culhane 5/1: 362: Chsd ldrs, rdn to chase wnr over 1f out, al well held by wnr but pulled clr of rem: op 15/2: back to form in visor: stays 10f: win sn. *2½* **85**
4102 **MAJESTIC MOVEMENT 44** [7] J H M Gosden 2-9-0 R Havlin 12/1: 503: Chsd ldrs wide, no impress on front pair fnl 2f: 6 wk abs: see 3890. *9* **72**
4519 **DOVER STREET 23** [13] P W D'Arcy 2-9-0 (59) N Callan 50/1: 50004: Chsd ldrs wide, onepace. *1¼* **68**
4648 **MUTAMAASEK 17** [12]2-9-0 (84) R Hills 5/1: 5045: Prom & led 2f out, sn hdd & fdd: btr 4698 (1m, g/s). *3½* **65**
NUMERO DUE 0 [9]2-9-0 P M Quinn 50/1: 6: b c Sinndar - Kindle (Selkirk) Bhd, late gains wide, nvr a factor: 10,000gns Mar first foal, dam plcd thrice abroad: sire high-class mid-dist performer. *1¼* **63**
4597 **MR MAXIM 19** [5]2-9-0 (57) F Lynch 50/1: 050047: Led/dsptd lead 1m, fdd: see 4597 (7.5f). *1¾* **61**
4756 **AMAZING VALOUR 11** [8]2-9-0 K Darley 7/1: 28: Dwelt & rear, sn rdn, little prog: btr 4756 (1m). *shd* **61**
4722 **THREE BOARS 13** [6]2-9-0 R Winston 50/1: 009: Chsd ldrs till over 2f out: see 3869. *3½* **56**
4792 **COIS NA TINE EILE 9** [11]2-8-9 (51) A Nicholls 100/1: 30300: 10th: Dwelt & al towards rear: see 2939. *1½* **49**
4744 **YARDSTICK 12** [3]2-9-0 (65) M Hills 33/1: 0600: 11th: Mid-div, drvn/hung left & btn 3f out: longer trip. *¾* **53**
4825 **NORTHANGER ABBEY 7** [2]2-9-0 J Carroll 20/1: 0050: 12th: Led till 3f out, sn struggling: btr 4825. *¾* **44**
4591 **SOOYOU SIR 20** [14]2-9-0 J Quinn 100/1: 00: 13th: b g Orpen - Naivement (Doyoun) Al bhd: Mar foal, cheaply bght juv: dam unrcd, half-sister to a minor 9f 3yo scorer. *6* **42**
4783 **Emerald Destiny 9** [1]2-9-0 D Tudhope(5) 66/1:0 4816 **Forpetesake 7** [10]2-9-0 (58) D Corby(3) 125/1:0
15 Ran Time 2m 14.18 (6.08) Owned: Mr Saif Ali Trained: Newmarket

4934
2.50 Maraval Nursery Handicap Stakes 2yo 0-75 (E3)   [80]
£4417 £1359 £680   6f rnd   Good/Firm 39   -12 Slow   Inside

4758 SAFENDONSEABISCUIT 11 [9] S Kirk 2-9-4 (70) M Hills 8/1: 3420031: Led & rdn clr over 1f out, in   83
command dist, styd on strongly: eff at 6/7f on firm & gd grnd, sharp or stiff/undul trk, best without blnks: well
suited by forcing tactics & landed first success today, could make a qk follow-up.
4645 RANCHO CUCAMONGA 17 [17] T D Barron 2-8-12 VIS (64) K Darley 14/1: 1005502: In tch wide, styd on 4   67
for press ins last, nrst fin: gd run in first time visor despite awkward passage from high draw: acts on fast & gd.
4697 XEERAN 14 [6] M A Jarvis 2-8-9 (61) P Robinson 11/2: 55543: Trkd ldrs, outpcd by wnr from over 1f out.   shd   64
4583 AZUREE 20 [5] R Hannon 2-8-13 bl (65) P Dobbs 16/1: 3043054: Held up in tch, smooth hdwy halfway,   ¾   66
rdn & no extra ins last: stays 6/7f, stiff 5f in similar could prove ideal: see 3691, 3183 & 1499.
4285 MING VASE 35 [11]2-8-8 (60) D Tudhope(5) 66/1: 625605: Mid-div, styd on for press, nvr able to chall.   ½   59
4655 FAVOURING 17 [10]2-8-10 VIS (62) T Hamilton(3) 7/1: 4002406: Cl-up, fdd under press over 1f out: vis.   1½   56
4396 GAME LAD 29 [7]2-9-7 (73) D Allan 9/2 FAV: 34037: Pushed along towards rear, nvr pace to threaten.   hd   66
4673 PRO TEMPORE 16 [3]2-8-12 (64) F Norton 8/1: 4166308: Held up, short of room early, no impress.   ¾   55
3483 PAULINES PRINCE 70 [16]2-9-4 (70) N Callan 25/1: 6149: Sn handy & chsd wnr over 1f out, wknd fnl 1f.   ¾   54
4895 PERIANTH 3 [14]2-8-10 (62) J F McDonald(3) 12/1: 4000300: 10th: Mid-div, btn/short of room 2f out.   nk   50
4688 APETITE 16 [4]2-8-8 (60) J Quinn 25/1: 0021000: 11th: Drvn rear, mod prog: see 4277 (seller).   1¼   44
4403 PEE JAYS DREAM 28 [15]2-8-7 (59) Dale Gibson 50/1: 6000: 12th: Went right start, al towards rear.   hd   42
4673 LODGICIAN 16 [8]2-9-0 (66) R Winston 20/1: 430400: 13th: Sn bhd & nvr a factor: btr 4519 (1m).   1   46
4590 SOUND AND VISION 20 [12]2-8-11 bl (63) S W Kelly 25/1: 565650: 14th: Al bhd: btr 4590 & 2511.   ½   41
4517 Bond Puccini 23 [2]2-8-11 (63) F Lynch 16/1:0
4617 High Petergate 18 [13]2-8-10 (62) P Mulrennan(3) 25/1:0
4673 Paris Heights 16 [1]2-8-11 (63) A Culhane 50/1:0
3713 Mill By The Stream 60 [18]2-8-4 (56) A Nicholls 20/1:0
18 Ran   Time 1m 17.16 (3.06)   Owned: J B R Leisure Ltd   Trained: Upper Lambourn

4935
3.20 Toteplacepot Handicap Stakes 3yo 71-85 (D2)   [95]
£9670 £3668 £1834   1m4y rnd   Good/Firm 39   +00 Fast   Inside

4607 ZERLINA 19 [8] W J Musson 3-8-8 (75) J Quinn 7/1: 1-000421: Dwelt, held up in tch, switched wide   85
& rdn/qcknd to lead best time of day: eff at 7f/1m on fast, gd & polytrack, stiff or sharp/undul trk.
4465 LITTLE JIMBOB 26 [4] R A Fahey 3-8-8 (75) T Hamilton(3) 9/2: 2-124352: Led, qcknd from halfway,   2   80
hdd ins last, kept on for press: see 2705 & 2443.
4931 DOUBLE VODKA 2 [1] Mrs J R Ramsden 3-8-6 (73) P Robinson 15/8 FAV: 4011103: Trkd ldrs, switched   1   76
to chall over 1f out, sn no extra for press: well bckd, op 5/2, qck reapp: imprvd eff but jst btr 3972 & 3647.
4407* BACKGAMMON 28 [2] D R Loder 3-8-11 (78) T P Queally 9/2: 2314: Trkd ldrs, no extra over 1f out.   3   75
3938 SAFFRON FOX 51 [7]3-8-12 P (79) A Culhane 16/1: 4042005: Rear, sn pushed along, mod prog, abs.   nk   75
4649* CANTARNA 17 [12]3-8-7 (1ow) (73) N Callan 7/1: 55-23516: Cl-up till lost place qckly over 1f out: 7   58
op 9/2: btr 4649 (mdn, g/s).
4683 ASHWAAQ 16 [11]3-8-9 (76) R Hills 9/1: 4-107: Dwelt, chsd ldrs, btn over 2f out: btr 1177.   shd   60
7 Ran   Time 1m 44.92 (3.12)   Owned: Mr G Howard-Spink   Trained: Newmarket

4936
3.50 Trinidad & Tobago Handicap Stakes 3yo+ 56-70 (E3)   [74]
£4183 £1287 £644   2m1f22y   Good/Firm 39   -22 Slow   Inside

4824 MOONSHINE BEACH 7 [5] P W Hiatt 6-9-10 (70) P Makin(5) 11/1: 0311031: Sn handy & led 3f out, rdn   79
clr over 1f out, al holding rivals for press ins last: eff at 2m/2m2f, shapes as a thorough stayer: acts on fast,
gd/soft & polytrack, any trk: likes to race with/force the pace: v tough & progressive gelding: see 4276, 3853.
4361 CROCOLAT 31 [8] Mrs Stef Liddiard 3-8-9 (66) F Norton 5/1: 5241132: Rear, hdwy from 4f out,   ¾   73+
short of room over 1f out, styd on for press ins last, not reach wnr: op 7/2: unlucky, would have gone close with a
clr run at a crucial stage: keep in mind for similar: progressive: see 4361 & 4128.
4628 VICARS DESTINY 18 [6] Mrs S Lamyman 6-9-4 (64) R Winston 10/1: 6433233: Rear, styd on for press   1   68
fnl 2f, not pace to chall: mdn: see 4628, 4209 & 1069.
4824 RIYADH 7 [11] M Johnston 6-9-6 (66) K Darley 8/1: 0260464: Mid-div, styd on for press, not pace of wnr.   1½   70
4675 SUPER FELLOW 16 [7]10-8-10 (11oh) (45) M Halford(7) 16/1: 00///-31155: Dwelt & rear, hdwy into   5   55
mid-div halfway, sn rdn & outpcd but kept on fnl 2f: appeared to run in snatches: handles fast & soft grnd.
4868 OKTIS MORILIOUS 5 [14]3-7-13 (1oh) (55) Lisa Jones 20/1: 0401046: Trkd ldrs halfway, rdn & fdd fnl 2f.   1   54
3970 CRACKLEANDO 50 [9]3-8-2 (59) J Bramhill 16/1: 0310327: Led till 3f out, fdd under press, abs: btr 3970.   3   54
4675 BUSHIDO 16 [13]5-8-10 (1oh) (55) L Enstone 15/2: 500/-6028: Chsd ldrs, rdn & lost place from 4f out.   shd   51
4415 RAWALPINDI 28 [3]3-7-13 (1oh) (55) Dale Gibson 25/1: 0-000259: Mid-div, struggling fnl 3f: btr 4092 (AW).13   41
2807 ACCEPTING 98 [1]7-8-10 (3oh)bl (53) N Callan 14/1: 10-50240: 10th: In tch, btn 3f out: jumps   1¾   39
fit: won this race in '03: btr 2577.
2807 MUZIO SCEVOLA 98 [4]3-8-5 (62) S Hitchcott 28/1: 255630: 11th: Al bhd, 3 mth abs: btr 2807.   5   40
4868 RESTART 5 [12]3-8-1 (58) J Quinn 7/2 FAV: 0-001020: 12th: Trkd ldrs, hdwy to chall 3f out, wknd   1¾   34
qckly over 1f out, eased: nicely bckd, op 4/1, qck reapp: drpd out as if something amiss in the closing stages.
4808 TONI ALCALA 8 [2]5-9-8 (63) P Mulrennan(3) 16/1: 1556040: 13th: Chsd ldrs till lost place over 4f out.   17   30
4675 LITTLE TOBIAS 16 [10]5-8-10 (3oh) (53) D Mernagh 16/1: 0-601330: 14th: Chsd ldrs, strugg fnl 4f.   5   13
14 Ran   Time 3m 50.75 (10.45)   Owned: Mr Ken Read   Trained: Banbury

4937
4.20 Buccoo Reef 'premier' Claiming Stakes 3yo (D3)
£5564 £1712 £856   1m4y rnd   Good/Firm 39   -12 Slow   Inside

4813 GRAND BUT ONE 8 [12] B W Hills 3-9-5 (87) M Hills 9/2: 6223161: Trkd ldrs wide, styd on for   85
press to lead wide ins last: op 3/1: suited by 1m on fast & gd grnd: can force the pace on any trk.
4465 PATTERDALE 26 [13] W J Haggas 3-8-12 (74) K Darley 9/1: 200-2102: Towards rear, styd on well for   1¼   74
press ins last, nrst fin: styd longer 1m trip in claim grade: see 3985 (6f, mdn).
4768 FOOLISH GROOM 10 [6] R Hollinshead 3-8-4 (68) J Quinn 16/1: 5635023: Dwelt, chsd ldrs & led   hd   65

dist, hdd well ins last & no extra: shown enough to find a race: handles fast & soft grnd: see 4768 & 1108.

4809 **ISKANDER 8** [15] K A Ryan 3-8-9 bl (71) J Carroll 20/1: 0640504: Rear, styd on wide for press, not   *nk* **69**
pace to chall: back to form on drop to claim grade: see 3738 & 1665.

4820 **GREAT SCOTT 7** [4]3-8-4 (77) P Robinson 7/1: 5340005: Chsd ldrs, no extra over 1f out: see 3598.   ½ **63**

4777 **FORTHRIGHT 10** [1]3-6-11 bl (81) Dale Gibson 4/1 FAV: 6000606: Pushed along mid-div early, hdwy &   *1* **68**
led over 2f out, hdd dist & no extra: clr rem: btr 4777.

4676 **PASSION FRUIT 16** [9]3-7-13 (50) Lisa Jones 80/1: 0630-007: Rear, only mod prog wide, nvr a factor.   *6* **46**

4656 **GO SOLO 17** [16]3-8-9 (74) A Culhane 12/1: 3353008: Towards rear, eff wide, btn dist: btr 3542.   *5* **47**

4827 **DESERT HAWK 7** [8]3-8-4 (66) N Pollard 14/1: 0062029: Mid-div, btn 2f out: btr 4827 & 4546.   *6* **32**

4270 **ROMARIC 35** [5]3-9-0 vis (84) J Bramhill 33/1: 103-40: 10th: Chsd ldrs 4f out, sn strugg: flattered 4270.   ½ **41**

4694 **FAMILIAR AFFAIR 15** [7]3-8-10 (78) N Callan 6/1: 14-00130: 11th: Led/dsptd lead 6f, sn btn: btr 4694.   *1* **35**

4875} **ON THE WING 346** [10]3-8-9 (78) R Winston 18/1: 55515-0: 12th: b f Pivotal - Come Fly With Me   *3* **28**
(Bluebird) Bhd & drvn, no impress, reapp: auct mdn scorer in '03, AW unplcd (rtd 66a, debut): eff at 6f, winning
form at 7f: acts on firm & fast grnd, prob handles polytrack, sharp or stiff/gall trk.

1 Oct'03 Newc 7fm 78- E:

4321 **Cheverak Forest 33** [11]3-8-4 (55) Kim Tinkler 50/1:0   4582 **Kings Rock 20** [2]3-8-4 bl(58) T P Queally 33/1:0

14 Ran   Time 1m 45.9 (4.1)   Owned: Enton Thoroughbred Racing 2   Trained: Lambourn

---

4938	4.50 Blanchisseuse Handicap Stakes 3yo+ 46-55 (F4)				[67]
	£3640 £1120 £560 **1m4f8y** **Good/Firm 39** **-01 Slow** Inside				

4419* **HEATHYARDS PRIDE 28** [5] R Hollinshead 4-8-13 (52) N Callan 12/1: 4-104511: Held up inner, hdwy   **61**
over 3f out & drvn to lead well ins last: eff at 1m/9f, imprvd of late at 11/12f: acts on firm, fast & fibresand,
stiff/undul or sharp trks: best held up, given a well judged ride today: see 4419, 1954 & 299.

4771 **DANEBANK 10** [16] J Mackie 4-8-13 p (52) Dale Gibson 7/1: 0512302: Held up, hdwy wide & rdn/led 2f   1½ **58**
out, clr over 1f out, drvn & hdd well ins last: op 9/1: gd run under an enterprising ride: see 4203, 3056.

4235 **WYOMING 37** [18] J A R Toller 3-8-9 (55) A Culhane 11/1: 3000303: Held up, styd on onepace for   *3* **57**
press fnl 2f: acts on fast & gd grnd: see 4189 & 1617.

4589 **FIELD SPARK 20** [17] J A Glover 4-9-2 (55) P Mulrennan(3) 12/1: 2302004: Rear, late gains for   2½ **53**
press, nrst fin: imprvd eff: see 3222, 2465 & 2217.

4910 **DUCS DREAM 2** [11]6-8-12 (51) Paul Eddery 13/2 FAV: 0050335: Chsd ldrs, styd on onepace fnl 2f.   *nk* **48**

4579 **PERSIAN GENIE 20** [2]3-8-9 (55) R Havlin 20/1: 0000026: Held up, eff wide 3f out, sn btn: btr 4579.   *5* **45**

4720 **SENOR EDUARDO 13** [15]7-9-2 (55) A Nicholls 12/1: 1623037: Held up, no impress fnl 2f: btr 4720 (10f).   ¾ **44**

4805 **DONNAS DOUBLE 8** [6]9-8-13 p (52) K Darley 8/1: 3462028: Held up, eff wide 4f out, fdd under press.   *2* **38**

4665* **LAZZAZ 16** [8]6-9-1 (54) P Gallagher(7) 8/1: 2655119: Trkd ldrs, btn 2f out: btr 4665.   *5* **33**

4771 **KARATHAENA 10** [9]4-9-2 (55) T Eaves(3) 33/1: 0000000: 10th: In trch, led over 3f out, hdd 2f out, wknd.   1¾ **32**

4675 **ZAN LO 16** [1]4-8-10 (49) R Winston 33/1: 0004100: 11th: Held up, struggling fnl 3f: much btr 4340.   *10* **14**

4716 **ELLWAY HEIGHTS 13** [12]7-8-12 (51) F Norton 12/1: 2530600: 12th: Mid-div, lost place from over 3f out.   ½ **15**

4720 **ELLOVAMUL 13** [3]4-8-11 (50) P Makin(5) 25/1: 0100000: 13th: Towards rear & nvr a factor.   *2* **11**

4720 **BENEKING 13** [4]4-8-10 (49) Stephanie Hollinshead(5) 33/1: 6050000: 14th: Chsd ldrs 2f out, sn wknd.   *hd* **9**

1105} **IRON WARRIOR 536** [14]4-9-2 (55) N Pollard 50/1: D/26200-0: 15th: b g Lear Fan - Robalana (Wild   *9* **4**
Again) Chsd ldrs, struggling fnl 3f, abs: dual AW mdn rnr up '03, mod turf form (rtd 18): unplcd '02 (rtd 51): eff
at 11/12f on fibresand, sharp trks: eff in chkpcs, tried blnks.

2 Mar'03 Wolv 12af 58a-(58) D: 2 Jan'03 Sout 11af 58a- D:

4366 **DREAMS FORGOTTEN 31** [13]4-9-2 (55) A Beech(3) 40/1: 200-4000: 16th: Prom, drvn & btn 2f out.   *2* **1**

4106 **BRAVELY DOES IT 44** [10]4-9-2 (55) S W Kelly 16/1: 006200: 17th: Led till 4f out, sn bhd, abs: btr 3549.   1½ **0**

4669 **MY LAST BEAN 16** [7]7-9-0 (53) F Lynch 10/1: 55436-60: 18th: Handy & briefly led 4f out, sn hdd & wknd.   7 **0**

18 Ran   Time 2m 38.94 (4.84)   Owned: Mr L A Morgan   Trained: Upper Longdon

---

4939	5.20 Caroni Maiden Stakes 3yo (D3)			
	£5616 £1728 £864 **1m4y rnd** **Good/Firm 39** **-20 Slow** Inside			

4649 **MISS POLARIS 17** [3] P W Harris 3-8-9 M Fenton 10/1: 61: Trkd ldrs, short of room & hmpd over 1f   **73**
out, switched & shaken up to lead nr line, val more: imprvd from debut: eff at 1m, dam a 10f wnr & that trip could
suit: acts on fast grnd & a stiff/undul trk: lightly rcd & progressing: see 4649.

3237 **PINCHING 80** [7] H R A Cecil 3-8-9 vis (73) W Ryan 6/1: 432302: Cl-up, ev ch ins last, just hdd &   ½ **71**
no extra cl-home: 12 wk abs: see 2962 & 1810.

4649 **MENEEF 17** [4] M P Tregoning 3-9-0 (76) R Hills 7/4 FAV: 4-323: Led, rdn & edged left over 1f   *shd* **76**
out, hdd well ins last: hvly bckd, fin ahd of today's wnr latest: see 4649 & 3366.

4719 **MRS SHILLING 13** [11] J R Fanshawe 3-8-9 (67) R Winston 11/4: 6-3424: Trkd ldrs racing keenly,   *nk* **70**
chall dist, drvn when bmpd nr line: op 10/3: btn less than 1L in a tight fin & stays a stiff 1m.

4721 **TRUE 13** [9]3-8-9 (56) T Eaves(3) 28/1: 4060205: Keen in rear, little prog: see 4593.   *5* **62**

4520 **HARRYCAT 23** [10]3-9-0 J Quinn 25/1: 056: Mid-div, not pace to chall fnl 2f, low grade h'caps will suit.   ½ **66**

2225 **SLAVONIC 122** [12]3-9-0 bl (73) N Callan 7/1: 4-544647: Trkd ldrs, btn over 1f out: abs & new stable.   1¾ **63**

    MTILLY 0 [5]3-8-9 K Darley 33/1: 8: br f Mtoto - Corn Lily (Aragon) Chsd ldrs till lost place   *2* **54**
early, no ch fnl 2f, debut: half-sister to winning h'capper Fisio Therapy.

4761 **BEAUTIFUL NOISE 11** [6]3-8-9 bl (60) A Culhane 14/1: 5555529: Trkd ldrs, lost place fnl 2f, op 12/1.   2½ **49**

4768 **JACKS CHECK 10** [1]3-9-0 P Mulrennan(3) 100/1: 00: 10th: Dwelt, rear, no ch fnl 2f.   *11* **37**

10 Ran   Time 1m 46.54(4.74)   Owned: Cool Customers   Trained: Berkhamsted

WINDSOR **MONDAY 04.10.04 Sharp, Fig 8 Track**

Official Going SOFT.

4940

2.30 Canons Stoke Poges Nursery Handicap Stakes 2yo 0-75 (E3) **[82]**
£3630 £1117 £559 **1m67y rnd** **Good/Soft** **Inapp** Inside

4403 **COME ON JONNY 28** [9] R M Beckett 2-9-4 (72) D Holland 14/1: 0341: Keen cl-up, led over 3f out, styd on, drvn out: first win: much imprvd stepped up to 8.3f: acts on gd/soft grnd & a sharp trk: see 4205. **83**
4535 **SECRET HISTORY 23** [3] M Johnston 2-9-3 (71) R Ffrench 14/1: 235102: Handy, eff 2f out, sn chall, kept on ins last, not btn far: stays 8.3f & right back to best: see 4207. *½* **80**
4396 **DARKO KARIM 29** [4] D R Loder 2-9-6 (74) S Sanders 40/1: 40003: Bhd, eff over 2f out, onepace: visor discarded & a btr run stepped up to 8.3f on gd/soft: see 1934. *2½* **78**
4738 **LORD OF DREAMS 12** [11] D W P Arbuthnot 2-9-2 (70) R L Moore 11/1: 05034: Held up, hmpd over 2f out, onepace: see 4738. *2* **70**
4848* **PENALTY KICK 6** [10]2-9-6 (6ex) (74) L Dettori 6/4 FAV: 06015: Handy, wknd 2f out: hvly bckd: shade too sn after 4848 (10f, gd/firm)? *1½* **71**
4679 **OASIS WAY 16** [2]2-9-4 (72) Martin Dwyer 20/1: 5506: Bhd, eff 2f out, sn no extra: see 4114. *1¾* **65**
4848 **FLYING PASS 6** [14]2-9-2 (70) S Whitworth 10/1: 2256427: Bhd, eff 2f out, sn no impress: see 4848. *shd* **62**
4894 **GO MO 3** [13]2-9-3 (71) J F Egan 9/1: 06608: In tch, wknd 2f out: see 4297, best 4078. *½* **62**
4673 **JUST DO IT 16** [7]2-8-12 (66) T E Durcan 25/1: 62509: Slow away, in tch, wknd/hung left 2f out. *nk* **56**
4725 **GRANDMAS GIRL 13** [1]2-8-13 (67) E Ahern 16/1: 04500: 10th: In tch, wknd 3f out. *3* **51**
4410 **LADY CHEF 28** [6]2-9-7 (75) A McCarthy 40/1: 051300: 11th: In tch, btn 2f out: see 3624, 2584 (7f). *1½* **56**
4490 **MUSICO 24** [5]2-9-5 (73) S Drowne 8/1: 4642300: 12th: Keen in tch, wknd 2f out: see 3897 (6f). *8* **38**
4725 **SWELL LAD 13** [12]2-9-1 bl (69) T Quinn 14/1: 006200: 13th: Led till over 3f out, wknd over 2f out: reportedly lost action: see 4410, 2578. *5* **24**
13 Ran Time 1m 46.96 (3.96) Owned: Mr A E Frost Trained: Lambourn

4941

3.00 European Breeders Fund Maiden Stakes Div 1 2yo (D3)
£5213 £1604 £802 **6f str** **Good/Soft** **Inapp** Inside

3968 **HANSEATIC LEAGUE 50** [4] M Johnston 2-9-0 (82) L Dettori 3/1 FAV: 2261: Made virtually all, kept on, pushed out: 7 wk abs: apprec step up to 6f: acts on fast & gd/soft: see 2241, 1974. **85**
PUYA [8] H Candy 2-8-9 Dane O'Neill 7/1: 2: b f Kris - Pervenche (Latest Model) Slow away, hdwy 2f out, styd on strongly ins last, just failed: debut, op 11/2: May foal: half-sister to multiple sprint wnr Gorse: eff over a sharp 6f, 7f will suit: acts on gd/soft: will learn plenty from this encouraging start. *nk* **79**
4610 **PESQUERA 19** [1] J Noseda 2-8-9 E Ahern 9/1: 03: b f Green Desert - Rose des Andes (Royal Academy) Cl-up, rdn & onepcd over 1f out: Apr foal, cost 60,000gns: eff over a sharp 6f on gd/soft. *1¾* **74**
3399 **GUILDENSTERN 73** [12] H Morrison 2-9-0 S Drowne 6/1: 04: b c Danetime - Lyphard Abu (Lyphard's Special) Bhd, eff 2f out, no impress: abs: Apr foal, cost 13,000gns: dam 12/13f scorer. *2½* **72**
4522 **IN DREAMS 23** [3]2-9-0 L Keniry(3) 25/1: 0005: In tch, wknd 2f out. *1¾* **68**
BABE MACCOOL [11]2-9-0 S Sanders 13/2: 6: In tch, wknd 2f out on debut. *nk* **67**
4664 **BRIANNIE 16** [2]2-8-9 Martin Dwyer 20/1: 667: In tch, wknd 2f out: see 4466. *1½* **58**
4830 **KEMPSEY 7** [9]2-9-0 (63) A Daly 25/1: 6444608: Handy, wknd over 1f out: see 3284. *1¾* **58**
4462 **NORTH SHORE 26** [7]2-9-0 R L Moore 7/2: 659: In tch, wknd 2f out: see 4462. *3* **49**
4644 **EFORETTA 17** [5]2-8-9 V Slattery 50/1: 00: 10th: Al bhd. *6* **26**
FORMIDABLE WILL [10]2-9-0 R Smith 20/1: 0: 11th: Slow away & al bhd. *9* **4**
11 Ran Time 1m 15.0 (4.7) Owned: Sheikh Mohammed Trained: Middleham

4942

3.30 Morelli Classified Stakes 3yo+ 0-70 (D3)
£4966 £1528 £764 **1m3f135y** **Good/Soft** **Inapp** Inside

4745* **BELLE ROUGE 12** [9] C A Horgan 6-9-5 (75) L Dettori 11/4: 2121211: Chsd ldrs, hdwy 2f out, styd on well to lead ins last, going away: eff over 12f/2m on fast, hvy & both AWs, any trk, likes a sharp one: most tough, versatile & progressive this term: see 4745. **84**
4919 **QUARRYMOUNT 2** [12] Sir Mark Prescott 3-9-2 (70) S Sanders 10/11 FAV: 1212212: Handy, led over 3f out till ins last, not pace of wnr: hvly bckd: continues in fine heart & most progressive: see 4919. *2* **85**
4745 **ALBAVILLA 12** [2] P W Harris 4-9-2 (72) R L Moore 16/1: 56-32503: Cl-up, eff dist, onepace. *2* **75**
4856 **NAWOW 5** [10] P D Cundell 4-9-8 (75) D Holland 14/1: 3560204: Chsd ldrs, btn dist: qck reapp. *5* **74**
4609 **HATCH A PLAN 19** [3]3-8-10 P (70) R Mullen 33/1: 1224005: Bhd, some late gains when hmpd over 1f out: tried cheek pieces stepped up in trip: see 3084, 2800 (10f, fast grnd). *nk* **68**
4183 **ROYAL BATHWICK 38** [6]4-9-3 (73) G Baker 18/1: 106-3346: Slow away, bhd, nvr a factor: see 4183. *2* **65**
2673 **MONTECRISTO 103** [8]11-9-4 (71) R Mills(7) 66/1: 5323-007: Al bhd: 3 mth abs: see 2673. *1¼* **64**
4850 **DICKIE DEADEYE 5** [7]7-9-3 (69) S Drowne 12/1: 1134038: Handy, wknd 2f out: qck reapp, see 4850. *1* **61**
4512 **GALLANT BOY 23** [5]5-9-3 vis t (63) I Mongan 25/1: 5444409: In tch, wknd 2f out: see 3964, 549. *1¼* **59**
4775 **JACARANDA 10** [4]4-9-3 (70) D Sweeney 20/1: 4136050: 10th: In tch, wknd 2f out: see 4775, 3404. *4* **53**
4620 **SOLLER BAY 18** [1]7-9-3 (67) J F Egan 25/1: 2004000: 11th: Led till wknd 3f out: see 1059. *17* **23**
11 Ran Time 2m 32.0 (5.2) Owned: Mrs B Woodford Trained: Ogbourne Maizey

4943

4.00 National Hunt Racing Returns To Windsor Handicap Stakes 3yo 71-85 (D2) **[95]**
£7077 £2178 £1089 **1m2f7y** **Good/Soft** **Inapp** Inside

4265 **DAY TO REMEMBER 36** [2] E F Vaughan 3-9-4 (85) D Holland 4/1 JT FAV: 43-5131: Led after 2f, hard pressed ins last but kept on for press: apprec step up to 10f: acts on gd & soft: useful, genuine & prog. **95**
4609 **ANOTHER CHOICE 19** [5] N P Littmoden 3-8-11 t (78) T E Durcan 9/1: 0004162: Handy, eff to chall dist, kept on, just held: another fine run: see 4254. *nk* **87**
4607 **FLYING ADORED 19** [8] J L Dunlop 3-8-13 (80) T Quinn 5/1: 0-301153: Handy, eff over 1f out, kept on ins last, no threat to front 2: ran to best: stays 10f: see 4265 (1m). *1¼* **86**
4609* **DIEGO CAO 19** [12] G L Moore 3-9-3 (84) R L Moore 9/2: 21614: Handy, onepace dist: see 4609. *2½* **86**
4694 **MAGIC STING 15** [9]3-8-8 (75) Hayley Turner(3) 4/1 JT FAV: 0332125: Keen bhd, hdwy on bit 3f out, *2* **74**

WINDSOR   MONDAY 04.10.04   Sharp, Fig 8 Track

wknd over 2f out: see 4694, 4365.

4709 **SMOOTHLY DOES IT 14** [11]3-8-4 (2oh) (69) J F Egan 7/1: 6040126: In tch, outpcd halfway, modest *1* **68**
late gains: shld stay 10f: see 4709, 4300.

4293 **OVER THE RAINBOW 35** [6]3-8-13 P (80) S Sanders 9/1: 0-100067: In tch, wknd 2f out: cheek pieces. *1¼* **75**

2491 **BUZZ BUZZ 110** [7]3-8-4 (3oh) (68) J Mackay 25/1: 02040-08: Al bhd: see 2491. *15* **46**

5034} **ENGLISH ROCKET 331** [1]3-8-6 (73) E Ahern 25/1: 025323-9: b g Indian Rocket - Golden Charm *6* **39**
(Common Grounds) Keen, led 2f, handy till wknd over 2f out on reapp: plcd on 4 of 6 '03 starts (h'caps): eff at
7f, shld stay further: acts on fast & fibresand.
2 Oct'03 Newb 7g/f 74-67 D: 2 Aug'03 Wolv 6af 71a- F:
9 Ran   Time 2m 12.03 (6.03)   Owned: Racing For Gold   Trained: Newmarket

---

4944   4.30 Attheraces Com Maiden Stakes 3yo+   (D3)
£4485 £1380 £690   **1m2f7y**   **Good/Soft**   **Inapp**   Inside

4315 **MIKAO 33** [5] M H Tompkins 3-9-0 (78) D Holland 4/1: 532421: Led early, remained prom & regained **69**
lead 2f out, collared dist, rallied well to regain lead ins fnl 1f, all out: bckd from 6/1: deserved win, eff at
10f, prob stays 12f: acts on firm, gd/soft grnd & polytrack: battled well today, see 4315 (AW).

4286 **ZAKFREE 35** [11] N P Littmoden 3-9-0 bl (66) T E Durcan 14/1: 4030-222: Chsd ldrs, imprvd to lead *nk* **68**
dist, worn down cl-home: well clr rem: rnr-up again, deserves a change of luck: see 4286.

4903 **ZARNEETA 2** [4] W de Best Turner 3-8-9 (40) P Doe 100/1: 0000003: Prom, left bhd by front 2 fnl *9* **48**
1.5f: qck reapp: modest, btr off in sell h'cap grade: prob stays 10f on gd/soft grnd: see 2742.

4228 **RESIDENTIAL 37** [9] Mrs A J Perrett 3-9-0 (64) R Hughes 8/1: 5-464: Keen & chsd ldrs, btn fnl 2f: *1¼* **51**
longer 10f trip: more expected after 4228 & 3446.

4832 **PETROSA 7** [3]4-9-0 (69) T Quinn 5/2 FAV: 23-45035: Mid-div, wide into straight, sn chsd ldrs *½* **45**
till left bhd fnl 2f: well bckd from 4/1: much btr on fast grnd in 4832 (AW).

4662 **MACS ELAN 16** [1]4-9-5 (35) L Dettori 25/1: 0-0506: b g Darshaan - Elabella (Ela Mana Mou) Chsd *shd* **49$**
ldrs, btn 2f out: offic rtd just 35: little form to date.

4228 **RIVER OF DIAMONDS 37** [15]3-9-0 Martin Dwyer 16/1: 07: b g Muhtarram - City Gambler (Rock City) *5* **42**
Nvr btr than mid-div: only 2nd start: with R Guest & no form yet.

4826 **PLEASANT 7** [7]3-8-9 S Drowne 14/1: 4208: Chsd ldrs, wknd 3f out: twice below 4125. *2½* **33**

4578 **DANDYGREY RUSSETT 20** [19]3-8-9 (63) R L Moore 8/1: 0449: Mid-div, hmpd & lost place halfway, no *¾* **32**
ch after: op 6/1: see 4578 (1m).

4407 **NADIR 28** [18]3-9-0 (65) E Ahern 14/1: 3-060: 10th: Nvr btr than mid-div: longer 10f trip: see 4407. *1½* **35**

4826 **MRS PHILIP 7** [13]5-9-0 V Slattery 66/1: 000: 11th: Bhd, modest progress. *1¼* **28**

PACIFIC RUN [8]3-9-0 L Keniry(3) 20/1: 0: 12th: b c Gone West - Miss Union Avenue (Steinlen) *shd* **33**
Led after 2f till 2f out, wknd on debut: related to a wnr in the US: bred to apprec 1m: with B Meehan.

4125 **DIEQUEST 42** [2]3-9-0 J F Egan 33/1: 0-000: 13th: Al rear: 6 wk abs. *2* **30**

4649 **DESIREE 17** [16]3-8-9 Frances Pickard(7) 66/1: 00: 14th: Al bhd: no form. *3* **21**

4502 **TREE TOPS 24** [10]3-8-9 (69) J Fortune 7/1: 5233600: 15th: Prom 7f, sn wknd: btr 3255. *3.6* **16**

3603 **JUST DASHING 65** [14]5-9-5 H Poulton(7) 100/1: 000: 16th: Al bhd: 9 wk abs. *6* **12**

852} **ZORN 558** [17]5-9-5 R Mullen 100/1: 0/50000-0: 17th: Speed till halfway, sn btn: reapp. *3* **8**

MISTER CHALK [12]3-9-0 J P Guillambert(3) 66/1: 0: 18th: Slowly away, al bhd, t.o. on debut. *dist* **0**
18 Ran   Time 2m 11.0 (5)   Owned: Mr Ben Allen   Trained: Newmarket

---

4945   5.00 European Breeders Fund Maiden Stakes Div 2 2yo   (D3)
£5213 £1604 £802   **6f str**   **Good/Soft**   **Inapp**   Inside

4457 **ON THE WATERLINE 26** [5] P D Evans 2-8-9 VIS (72) S Drowne 12/1: 3042001: Made all, clr fnl 1f, **77**
styd on strongly, pushed out: clearly apprec first time visor: first win on 8th start, rnr-up twice prev: eff at
5/6f on gd & gd/soft, likes to run up with/force the pace: handles a sharp or gall trk: deserved win, see 3987.

4418 **DALIYA 28** [11] Sir Michael Stoute 2-8-9 VIS D Holland 9/1: 62: Chsd ldrs, styd on late into 2nd *3* **66**
under hands & heels, no ch with wnr: imprvd showing: tried a visor, blnkd on debut: eff over an easy 6f on gd/soft
grnd, return to 7f shld suit: see 4418.

4726 **PAMIR 13** [7] L M Cumani 2-9-0 A Hamblett(7) 33/1: 03: b g Namid - Mijouter (Coquelin) Chsd *1* **68**
ldrs, onepcd fnl 1.5f: £30,000 Apr foal: half-brother to a juv wnr abroad, also 6f scorer Hopeful Star: dam unrcd,
sire a high-class sprinter: handles gd/soft grnd, 7f shld suit.

MARHOON [1] E F Vaughan 2-9-0 T E Durcan 50/1: 4: ch c Lion Cavern - United Kingdom (Danzig) *2* **62**
Chsd ldrs, onepcd fnl 1.5f on debut: Feb foal, half-brother to a wnr Hakeyma: dam a mid-dist wnr, sire a smart
6/7f performer: looks sure to apprec 7f/1m given time & shld learn from this.

4540 **DR ZALO 22** [3]2-9-0 S Sanders 5/2: 35: Prom, wknd fnl 1f: well bckd: btr on debut in 4540 (g/f). *½* **60**

PATTERNMAKER [2]2-9-0 T Quinn 40/1: 6: b g Elnadim - Attasliyah (Marju) Dwelt, some late *1¼* **56**
hdwy, nvr dngrs on debut: 30,000gns Mar first foal: dam unrcd, sire a top-class sprinter: with W Jarvis.

4577 **ANCHOR DATE 20** [12]2-9-0 R Hughes 10/1 FAV: 27: Stdd start, switched far side, nvr nr ldrs: *2½* **49**
hvly bckd from 11/8: puzzling run, showed much more on debut in 4577.

HALCYON EXPRESS [4]2-9-0 L Dettori 16/1: 8: Chsd ldrs till halfway, wknd on debut. *2½* **42**

4363 **LAUROLLIE 31** [6]2-8-9 A Daly 100/1: 0009: Nvr a factor: highly tried. *nk* **36**

4896 **SILVER SWING 3** [8]2-9-0 Dane O'Neill 33/1: 00: 10th: Dwelt, al rear: qck reapp, no form. *5* **26**

4544 **CIENDRA GIRL 21** [9]2-8-9 Hayley Turner(3) 100/1: 000: 11th: Al towards rear: no form. *12* **0**

1779 **STANS GIRL 141** [10]2-8-9 (60) P Doe 25/1: 0320: 12th: Rcd alone stands side & al bhd: long abs *5* **0**
& new stable: btr 1779 (fast grnd).
12 Ran   Time 1m 13.96 (3.66)   Owned: Mr M W Lawrence   Trained: Abergavenny

---

4946   5.30 Windsor Fireworks Extravaganza On Sat 6th November Handicap Stakes 3yo+ 56-70 (E3)   [80]
£3648 £1122 £561   **6f str**   **Good/Soft**   **Inapp**   Inside

4548* **OEUF A LA NEIGE 21** [20] G C H Chung 4-9-2 (68) O Urbina 16/1: 0615011: Mid-div, stdy prog to **77**
lead entering fnl 1f, held on gamely, all out: stays 1m, suited by 5/6f: acts on fast & gd/soft grnd: handles a
stiff or sharp trk: in gd form, see 4548.

4548 **ROMAN QUINTET 21** [1] D W P Arbuthnot 4-8-10 (62) T Quinn 10/1: 2-000322: Held up, prog when *hd* **70**
short of room dist, fin strongly & just btn: acts on fast, gd/soft & polytrk: again just btn by wnr in 4548.

4622 **BRANSTON TIGER 18** [7] P D Evans 5-8-11 vis (63) T E Durcan 8/1: 0014303: Nvr far away, not pace *1½* **67**

1499

WINDSOR   MONDAY 04.10.04   Sharp, Fig 8 Track

of front 2 cl-home: see 4272.
2661 **MISSUS LINKS 103** [15] R Hannon 3-9-3 (70) R Hughes 33/1: 1-525064: Chsd ldrs, sltly short of room dist, kept on & nrst fin: long abs: gd run from outsider & back to form: did not get run of today's race. — nk 73
4646* **STOKESIES WISH 17** [3]4-8-13 (65) B Swarbrick(5) 16/1: 6330015: Chsd ldrs, went on 2f out till collared entering fnl 1f, no extra: see 4646. — hd 67
4099 **EXTREMELY RARE 44** [18]3-8-11 (64) E Ahern 50/1: 0100066: Nvr far away, onepcd fnl 1f: 6 wk abs. — hd 65
1540* **GO GO GIRL 153** [13]4-9-3 (69) S Drowne 16/1: 65330-17: Held up, styd on fnl 1f, nrst fin: long abs: gd return, spot on next time: see 1540. — 1¼ 66
4696* **PURE IMAGINATION 15** [4]3-8-12 (65) R L Moore 7/1: 6040018: Rear, prog 2f out, onepcd fnl 1f. — nk 61
4197 **SIRAJ 38** [12]5-8-10 (62) J Brennan(7) 50/1: 025-0109: Chsd ldrs, onepcd fnl 1f: see 4041 (AW). — nk 57
4818 **SUNDRIED TOMATO 7** [11]5-9-2 (68) L Fletcher(3) 8/1: 6060050: 10th: Chsd ldrs, onepcd fnl 1f. — shd 62
4747 **HIGH RIDGE 12** [8]5-9-4 p (70) Dane O'Neill 20/1: 4122400: 11th: Rear, late hdwy, nvr dngrs. — shd 63
4272 **FULL SPATE 35** [14]9-9-3 (69) J F Egan 16/1: 0216000: 12th: Nvr btr than mid-div. — ½ 60
4475 **WHIPPASNAPPER 25** [17]4-8-11 (63) L Keniry(3) 9/1: 2000400: 13th: Dwelt, nvr trbld ldrs. — ¾ 52
4586* **INSTINCT 20** [10]3-8-7 (60) R Smith 20/1: 0033210: 14th: Chsd ldrs, onepcd when short of rm dist. — nk 48
3976 **AFTER THE SHOW 49** [9]3-9-2 (69) Martin Dwyer 33/1: 6060200: 15th: Led till 2f out, wknd: 7 wk abs. — 2½ 50
4740 **ACE CLUB 12** [2]3-8-10 (63) L Dettori 6/1 FAV: 0042000: 16th: Chsd ldrs, onepcd when hmpd dist, no ch after: btr 4169. — 1 41
4646 **CEFIRA 17** [16]3-8-12 (65) D Holland 20/1: 0-30100: 17th: Mid-div, btn dist: btr 1908 (firm). — ¾ 41
4785 **DR SYNN 9** [5]3-8-13 (66) P Doe 12/1: 5020340: 18th: Slowly away, al rear. — hd 41
4646 **GOJO 17** [6]3-8-10 (63) S Sanders 25/1: 0-420000: 19th: Al in rear. — ½ 36
4197 **CERULEAN ROSE 38** [19]5-9-3 (69) J Fortune 10/1: 2030240: 20th: Rcd alone stands side, bhd halfway. — 9 24
20 Ran   Time 1m 13.95(3.65)   Owned: Mr G C H Chung   Trained: Newmarket

LONGCHAMP   SATURDAY 02.10.04   Righthand, Stiff, Galloping Track

Official Going GOOD

4947 1.15 Group 2 Prix Chaudenay 3yo (A)
£42148 £16268 £7764   1m7f   Good/Firm

4565 **REEFSCAPE 23** [2] A Fabre 3-9-2 T Gillet 13/2: 25-311021: gr c Linamix - Coraline (Sadlers Wells) Held up, rdn & qcknd to lead ins last, styd on strongly: won twice prev this term, incl a Listed contest: eff at 12/15f, 2m shld suit: acts on fast & soft ground: v smart stayer who could prove a Cup contender for '05. 2 Sep'04 Long 15gd 109- : — 120
4566 **LORD DU SUD 20** [3] J C Rouget 3-9-2 I Mendizabal 7/4 FAV: 1-111642: Held up hdwy to lead 2f out, hdd & no extra ins last: clr rem: acts on fast & sft, stays 15f: see 1852 (Gr 2, 12f). — 2 117
4687 **PERCUSSIONIST 14** [1] J H M Gosden 3-9-2 (118) L Dettori 28/1: 32-114023: Trkd ldrs, no impress on front pair over 1f out: btr 4687 (soft) & 2254 (11/12f). — 5 112
7 Ran   Time 3m 08.1 ()   Owned: Trained: France

4948 2.20 Group 2 Prix de Royallieu Hotel de Golf Barriere 3yo+ Fillies & Mares (A)
£42148 £16268 £7764   1m4f110y   Good/Firm

1699 **SAMANDO 19** [8] F Doumen 4-9-1 S Pasquier 16/1: 6376641: ch f Hernando - Samshu (Nashwan) Mid-div, hdwy to lead over 1f out, briefly hdd ins last, rallied gamely to lead line, all out: 3 wins last term, including a Listed contest: suited by 11/13f on fast & hvy ground: v smart filly. — 115
1699 **RUSSIAN HILL 5** [5] A Fabre 4-9-1 T Gillet 12/1: 4-2220722: Held up, drvn to briefly ins last, just denied: ahead of this wnr earlier this term: eff btwn 10/13f on fast & hvy grnd. — snk 114
4934} **BEHKARA 7** [7] A de Royer Dupre 4-9-1 C Soumillon 11/4 FAV: 441113-63: Held up, rdn to chse ldrs over 1f out, kept on, not able to chall: 6 wk abs. — 1½ 112
4460* **ECHOES IN ETERNITY 24** [11]4-9-8 (106) L Dettori 3/1: 011-44510: 11th: Trkd ldr, rdn & led briefly 2f out, sn fdd under press: much btr 4460 (14f). — 0
11 Ran   Time 2m 39.4 ()   Owned: Trained: France

4949 2.50 Group 2 Prix Daniel Wildenstein 3yo+ (A)
£42148 £16268 £7764   1m   Good/Firm

4002 **CACIQUE 46** [9] A Fabre 3-8-12 C Soumillon 6/4 FAV: 1122141: b c Danehill - Hasili (Kahyasi) Rear, hdwy wide 2f out, led ins last, drvn out: 6 wk abs: eff at 1m/10f on fast & gd/sft ground: eff held up or forcing the pace: goes well fresh: tough & v smart colt: see 4002, 3657. 1 Jul'04 Chan 9gd 118- : 2 Jun'04 Long 10g/s 116- : 2 Jun'04 Chan 9g/s 114- : — 118
4232 **HURRICANE ALAN 35** [1] R Hannon 4-9-3 (114) L Dettori 8/1: 15030332: Held up, hdwy & rdn to lead over 1f out till dist, not pace of wnr: tough & smart: see 1349. — ½ 117
4311 **MISTER SACHA 34** [6] J C Rouget 3-8-12 I Mendizabal 7/1: 111533: Rear, hdwy to trk wnr 2f out, kept on for press, nrst fin: acts on fast & soft: eff at 1m, return to 9f+ shld suit: see 1851 (Gr 3). — hd 115
4063* **POLAR BEAR 44** [4]4-9-1 (103) P J Smullen 21/1: 3/11-30117: Rear, kept on late for press, not able to land a blow: ideally suited by a softer surface: see 4063 (Listed, g/s). — 2 111
11 Ran   Time 1m 37.5 ()   Owned: Trained: France

4950 3.20 Group 2 Prix Dollar 3yo+ (A)
£42148 £16268 £7764   1m2f   Good/Firm

4570 **TOUCH OF LAND 21** [3] H A Pantall 4-9-4 C P Lemaire 16/1: 03112403131: b c Lando - Touch Of Class (Be My Guest) Held up, hdwy wide over 1f out, rdn & chall over 1f out, led ins last, drvn out: eff at 10/12f on firm & soft ground: high class performance from this German trained colt: see 4570, 2141. 1 May'04 Bade 11gd 115- : 2 May'03 Long 12sft 108- : — 121

LONGCHAMP SATURDAY 02.10.04 Righthand, Stiff, Galloping Track

4220 **GATEMAN 35** [4] M Johnston 7-9-0 (114) T Jarnet 11/2: 20312222: Always handy, rdn & led over 1f **nk** **116**
out, hdd ins last, just held: most consistent, game & smart: see 4220, 3306.
4837 **SPECIAL KALDOUN 11** [1] D Smaga 5-9-0 D Boeuf 11/2: 00-003133: Mid-div, hdwy & drvn to chall **1** **114**
dist, not pace of wnr close home: acts on fast & hvy grnd: see 4016 (Gr 3, hvy).
4639* **SIGHTS ON GOLD 15** [7]5-9-0 (114) L Dettori 7/4 FAV: 2/2612-117: Mid-div, no extra fnl 1f: btr 4639. **6** **105**
12 Ran Time 1m 58.3() Owned: Trained: France

LONGCHAMP SUNDAY 03.10.04 Righthand, Stiff, Galloping Track

Official Going GOOD.

4951 1.15 Group 1 Prix du Cadran 4yo+ (A)
£80479 £32197 £16099 **2m4f** Good/Firm

4569* **WESTERNER 21** [3] E Lellouche 5-9-2 O Peslier 8/13 FAV: 11-122011: Chsd ldrs, prog to lead 2f **122**
out, pushed clr fnl 1f, readily: well bckd: also won this race last year: suited by 15f+, stays stiff 2m4f well:
acts on fast, loves gd/sft & soft: high class stayer who will be hard to beat in the Cup races next season.
4569 **CUT QUARTZ 21** [5] R Gibson 7-9-2 T Jarnet 12/1: -01114322: Waited with, prog 2f out, styd on **3** **117**
into 2nd, no ch with wnr: stays 2m4f on fast & soft: 3rd in this 2 yrs ago: again bhnd today's wnr in 4569.
987* **LE CARRE 21** [7] A de Royer Dupre 6-9-2 I Mendizabal 40/1: -214443: Chsd ldrs, styd on under **1** **116**
press fnl 1.5f but not pace to chall wnr: clearly stays 2m4f well: acts on fast & soft grnd: smart stayer.
4478 **DANCING BAY 24** [6] N J Henderson 7-9-2 (116) K Fallon 7/1: 0/31/-12234: Rear, late hdwy: likes soft. **2** **114**
4162* **HOLY ORDERS 42** [2]7-9-2 bl (110) D J Condon 25/1: 6U0-44615: Held up, nvr nr ldrs: 6 wk abs. **3** **111**
4478 **DARASIM 24** [1]6-9-2 vis (115) K Darley 7/2: 30-613156: Prom, led 3f out till 2f out, no extra: **2½** **108**
unable to front run today: 3rd in this race last year: see 3552 (Gr 2).
3552 **ANAK PEKAN 66** [8]4-9-2 (105) P Robinson 20/1: 222-11387: Led till 3f out, wknd: 10 wk abs, stiff task. **10** **98**
4569 **CLEAR THINKING 21** [4]4-9-2 C Soumillon 25/1: 153333038: Chsd ldrs, wknd 2f out. **10** **88**
8 Ran Time 4m 19.8 () Owned: Ecurie Wildenstein Trained: France

4952 1.55 Group 1 Prix de l'Abbaye 2yo+ (A)
£80479 £32197 £16099 **5f** Good/Firm

4678 **VAR 15** [13] C E Brittain 5-9-11 bl L Dettori 8/1: 4016-1121: Made all, trav well, held on well **121**
fnl 1f, drvn out: eff at 5/6f on fm & gd, any trk: likes to force the pace: suited by blnks & goes well fresh: much
improved this term & thriving, top sprint performance in Europe this term: see 4678 & 4526.
4799 **THE TATLING 8** [14] J M Bradley 7-9-11 (116) R L Moore 5/1: 10322132: Mid-div, strong run wide **½** **119**
fnl 1f, not btn far: ran to high-class best, close 3rd in this race last year: most tough & consistent, beat today's
wnr on 5lbs worse terms in 4678.
4732* **ROYAL MILLENNIUM 15** [4] M R Channon 6-9-11 (111) T E Durcan 10/1: 1425-10413: Held up, imprvd **1** **115**
halfway, fin strongly but too late: ran to best over this shorter 5f trip, will relish a return to 6/7f & can win sn
in slightly easier grade: see 4732 (6f).
4433 **OSTERHASE 28** [8] J E Mulhern 5-9-11 bl (94) F M Berry 16/1: -06111434: Prom, caught for 2nd cl **nk** **114**
home: fine run form this Irish chall: loves to run up with/force the pace & v speedy: win a Gr race.
4060 **AVONBRIDGE 45** [9]4-9-11 bl (114) J Fortune 9/1: 43-215445: Nvr far away, no extra cl home. **1½** **110**
4384 **ORIENTOR 29** [5]6-9-11 (115) J P Murtagh 28/1: 50531576: Trkd ldrs, onepcd fnl 1f: likes soft. **nse** **109**
4384 **PATAVELLIAN 29** [10]6-9-11 bl (114) S Drowne 7/2 FAV: 5111-3037: Mid-div, some late gains under **½** **108**
kind ride: well bckd: won this last year & much better expected, but prob ideally suited by softer grnd: see 4384.
4799 **RINGMOOR DOWN 8** [6]5-9-8 (108) T Quinn 12/1: 34241178: Rear, hdwy when short of room halfway, **hd** **105**
nrst fin: did not get the run of today's race: bt today's 4th in 4433.
4384 **BAHAMIAN PIRATE 29** [7]9-9-11 (110) S Sanders 20/1: 00016109: Nvr btr than mid-div: prefers **1** **105**
softer grnd: 6th in this in '03, 4th in '02 & rnr-up in '01 (hvy grnd): see 4060.
4686 **CONTINENT 15** [2]7-9-11 (108) D Holland 20/1: 0-3010530: 10th: Nvr a factor: btr 4686. **snk** **104**
4384 **THE TRADER 29** [1]6-9-11 bl (114) K Fallon 8/1: 6-1301500: 14th: Held up, al bhnd: 1L 2nd in this **5½** **89**
race last year: this is clearly not his form: btr 3167.
11 Ran Time 55.0 () Owned: Mohammed Rashid Trained: Newmarket

4953 2.30 Group 1 Prix de l'Opera 3yo+ Fillies & Mares (A)
£100599 £40246 £20123 **1m2f** Good/Firm

2816 **ALEXANDER GOLDRUN 99** [3] J S Bolger 3-8-12 K Manning 6/1: 1221-112421: Waited with, prog 2f **119**
out, styd on to lead well ins fnl 1f, won going away: long abs: deserved Gr 1 win, rnr-up in Irish 1000 Guineas &
4th in French Oaks: eff at 1m, stays 10f well: acts on fast & hvy grnd, runs v well fresh: high-class filly.
4434* **GREY LILAS 28** [10] A Fabre 3-8-12 E Legrix 10/11 FAV: 62-1123112: Nvr far away, went on 2f out, **1** **117**
collared ins fnl 1f & no extra: well bckd: fine run on grnd faster than ideal: see 4434 (gd/soft).
57* **WALKAMIA 27** [7] A Fabre 4-9-2 C Soumillon 14/1: 1-55433: Sn led till 2f out, onepace: longer **1½** **115**
priced stablemate of rnr-up: eff at 10f on fast & gd/soft grnd: v smart filly, see 57.
4572 **YESTERDAY 22** [2] A P O'Brien 4-9-2 J P Spencer 6/1: 124223-54: Mid-div, styd on under press fnl **1½** **113**
1f, nvr nrr: only 2nd run of injury this season: rnr-up in this race last yr: encouraging & a return to 12f will suit.
4024 **MENHOUBAH 46** [6]3-8-12 (106) R L Moore 50/1: 30210688: Nvr btr than mid-div: 6 wk abs. **4½** **106**
5 Ran Time 2m 02.3 () Owned: Mrs N O'Callaghan Trained: Co Carlow

4954   3.05 Group 1 Prix Marcel Boussac 2yo Fillies (A)
£100599 £40246 £20123   1m   Good/Firm

4159* **DIVINE PROPORTIONS** 42 [4] P Bary 2-8-11 C P Lemaire 8/11 FAV: 11111: Trkd ldrs, rdn to lead ent   **118+**
fnl 1f, v readily: well bckd, 6 wk abs: unbtn filly, eff at 6f, apprec this step up to 1m: acts on fast & soft
grnd, runs well fresh: top-class filly with fine turn of foot, leading 1000 Guineas claims.

4723* **TITIAN TIME** 12 [3] J H M Gosden 2-8-11 J Fortune 25/1: 2312: Led till ent fnl 1f, just held on   2   112
for 2nd: vastly imprvd form, fillies mdn wnr prev: stays 1m well, acts on fast & firm: clearly v smart, see 4723.

    FRALOGA 25 [10] A Fabre 2-8-11 C Soumillon 10/1: -413: b f Grand Lodge - Fragrant Hill (Shirley   nse 111
Heights) Prom, styd on under press fnl 1f, just failed to take 2nd: lightly rcd & imprvd form, recent Chantilly
wnr: eff at 1m on gd & fast grnd: bred to be a 3yo & open to more improvement: clearly smart.

4464* **INTRIGUED** 25 [7] Sir Mark Prescott 2-8-11 S Sanders 9/1: 314: Held up, styd on fnl 1f, nvr nrr: ½   109
imprvd in defeat, acts on fast & gd grnd: lightly rcd, win in Gr class: see 4464.

4728 **PORTRAYAL** 20 [9]2-8-11 O Peslier 18/1: 313425: Chsd ldrs, onepcd fnl 1f.   snk 108

4476 **QUEEN OF POLAND** 24 [1]2-8-11 L Dettori 5/1: 1126: Chsd ldrs, onepcd fnl 1f: wants List.   nk 107

4157 **GORELLA** 43 [2]2-8-11 E Legrix 33/1: 2137: Held up, nvr a factor: 6 wk abs: see 4157.   snk 106

    NEW LARGUE 11 [6]2-8-11 T Jarnet 66/1: -2228: b f Distant View - New Story () Prom 6f, grad   1½ 103
wknd: mdn rnr-up on prev 3 starts: eff at 1m on gd & v soft grnd: with R Collet.

    MIRABILIS 24 [5]2-8-11 R Hughes 11/1: -319: Al rear: s/mate of 3rd.   2½ 98

4157* **COURS DE LA REINE** 43 [8]2-8-11 K Fallon 16/1: 3010: 10th: Nvr a factor: 6 wk abs: disapp   3   92
thrice at fast grnd, best form by some way was on hvy in 4157.

10 Ran   Time 1m 36.7 ()   Owned: Niarchos Family   Trained: France

4955   3.45 Group 1 Priz Jean Luc Legardere 2yo (A)
£140838 £56345 £28173   7f   Good/Firm

4154* **ORATORIO** 43 [1] A P O'Brien 2-9-0 J P Spencer 5/2: 101211: Prom, slightly outpcd & short of   **120+**
room 2f out, styd on well fnl 1f to get up cl home: bckd, abs: eff at 7f, 1m sure to suit: acts on gd & fast, runs
well fresh: top-class juv with a turn of foot, ideal sort for Racing Post Trophy.

4564* **EARLY MARCH** 24 [6] Mme C Head Maarek 2-9-0 O Peslier 11/4: 112: Sn led till 1.5f out, rallied   snk 118
to regain lead ent fnl 1f, caught cl home: nicely bckd: 1st defeat, eff at 7f on gd & fast grnd, 1m shld suit:
clearly v smart & shld gain Gr 1 success: see 4564.

4159 **LAYMAN** 42 [4] A Fabre 2-9-0 C Soumillon 7/4 FAV: 1123: Led early, remained prom & led again   nse 117
briefly 1.5f out, ev ch ins fnl 1f & just btn in a cl fin: well bckd, clr of rem, 6 wk abs: apprec this step up to
7f, 1m shld suit: acts on fast & soft grnd: v smart, see 4159.

3566* **MONTGOMERYS ARCH** 65 [3] P W Cahpple Hyam 2-9-0 J Fortune 10/1: 114: Chsd ldrs, styd on under   2½ 112
press fnl 1f, nvr not pace of front 3: 9 wk abs: gd run in this top-class company, imprvd in defeat: see 3566.

4734 **DEMOCRATIC DEFICIT** 14 [5]2-9-0 K Manning 20/1: 11245: Waited with, prog 2f out & sn ev ch, wknd   1   110
fnl 1f: again bhnd today's wnr in 4154.

4022* **TONY JAMES** 46 [2]2-9-0 (100) S Sanders 14/1: 14516: Chsd ldrs, wknd fnl 1f: 7 wk abs: stiff task.   ¾ 108

6 Ran   Time 1m 19.3 ()   Owned: Mrs John Magnire & M Tabor   Trained: Ballydoyle, Co Tippe

4956   4.30 Group 1 Prix de l'Arc de Triomphe 3yo+ (A)
£643831 £257577 £128789   1m4f   Good/Firm

4566 **BAGO** 21 [5] J E Pease 3-8-11 T Gillet 10/1: 1111-11331: Rear, gd hdwy 2f out, strong run to   128
lead ins fnl 1f for a famous victory: eff at 10/12f on fast & soft: likes a gall trk: top-class colt with a fine turn
of foot off a strong pace: career best effort & must be kept on the right side: see 4566 & 2825.

4312* **CHERRY MIX** 35 [1] A Fabre 3-8-11 C Soumillon 33/1: 2-3232112: Nvr far away, imprvd to lead 1.5f   ½   126
out, not pace to repel wnr cl home: suited by 12f on fast & hvy: top-class, progressive & career best here: see 4312.

3321* **OUIJA BOARD** 77 [9] E A L Dunlop 3-8-8 (110) J P Murtagh 7/1: 313-1113: Hld up, prog when short   1   **121+**
of room 2f out, switched wide & fin strongly but too late: 11 wk abs: tremendous run in the circumstances, wld have
gone v close if able to start run earlier: tough & high-class filly, remains in training next year & sure to win more
Group 1 races: see 3321.

5003* **ACROPOLIS** 22 [19] A P O'Brien 3-8-11 J P Spencer 100/1: 7163-14: b c Sadler's Wells - Dedicated   2   121
Lady (Pennine Walk) Held up, styd on fnl 2f & nrst fin: much imprvd form, recent wnr of a List contest at
Leopardstown: eff at 10/12f on fast & gd/soft grnd: only lightly rcd & nailed on to win in Group company.

2822 **NORTH LIGHT** 98 [12]3-8-11 (115) K Fallon 9/2 FAV: 1-1125: Led/dsptd lead at v fast pace till   shd 121
1.5f out, onepace: well bckd, abs: fine front running eff on unsuitably fast grnd & being forced to go quicker than
he wld prob like: top-class Epsom Derby wnr.

3442 **VALLEE ENCHANTEE** 71 [16]4-9-2 S Pasquier 14/1: 1411-4356: Held up wide, styd on fnl 2f, nvr   ½   118
nrr: 10 wk abs: lightly rcd & yet to win this season, but clearly v smart: see 3442 & 2209.

4567 **LATICE** 21 [13]3-8-8 I Mendizabal 66/1: 11-1187: Mid-div, not much room & switched twice ins fnl   snk 116
2f, nrst fin: did not get the run of today's race: see 2460.

4567 **SILVERSKAYA** 21 [6]3-8-8 I Mendizabal 66/1: 11110168: Held up, styd on late, nvr nrr: see 4310 (soft).   2½ 111

4428* **WARRSAN** 28 [8]6-9-5 (120) K McEvoy 9/1: 33-5312919: Held up, late prog, nvr dngrs: btr 4428.   ½   114

4566* **VALIXIR** 21 [20]3-8-11 E Legrix 9/1: 12-133110: 10th: Nvr btr than mid-div: shorter priced   shd 113
stablemate of rnr-up: bt today's wnr in 4566 (soft).

1558* **EXECUTE** 154 [17]7-9-5 D Boeuf 66/1: 25326-210: 11th: Prom, wknd fnl 1f: long abs: btr 1558.   nk 113

2308* **BLUE CANARI** 21 [3]3-8-11 C P Lemaire 40/1: 31-343150: 12th: Held up, nvr dngrs: btr 2308.   ½   111

4567 **PRIDE** 21 [10]4-9-2 (80) T Jarnet 33/1: 0-4135230: 13th: Nvr btr than mid-div: see 4567.   ½   108

4639 **IMPERIAL DANCER** 16 [15]6-9-5 (110) T E Durcan 100/1: 00303620: 14th: Held up, nvr in it.   snk 110

4391* **MAMOOL** 29 [14]5-9-5 (118) L Dettori 11/1: 53110-310: 15th: Prom wide, wknd fnl 1f: btr 4391.   hd 110

4566 **PROSPECT PARK** 21 [2]3-8-11 O Peslier 10/1: 3-1122120: 16th: Prom till wknd 1.5f out.   ½   108

    TAP DANCE CITY 98 [18]7-9-5 T Sato 10/1: 118-110: 17th: b h Pleasant Tap - All Dance () Dsptd   8   97
lead till 3f out, wknd: 3 mnth abs: unbtn in native country this term (Gr 1 & 2): eff at 10/12f on firm & gd/soft.

4571 **GREY SWALLOW** 22 [11]3-8-11 P J Smullen 5/1: -143140: 18th: Mid-div wide, rdn & btn 2f out: nvr   1½ 94
really trav & not given a hard time: this is not his form, see 4571 & 2822 (Irish Derby).

4568* **POLICY MAKER** 21 [4]4-9-5 T Thulliez 33/1: 110-51210: 19th: Prom 10f, wknd & eased.   10   80

19 Ran   Time 2m 25.0()   Owned: Niarchos Family   Trained: France

CHANTILLY   FRIDAY 01.10.04   Righthand, Galloping Track

Official Going Good

4957   **1.50 Gr 3 Prix Eclipse 2yo** ()
£25704 £10282 £7711   **6f str**   **Good**

4390 **TREMAR 27** T G Mills 2-8-11 (90) G Carter 12/1: 432141: Trkd ldr, led halfway, asserted ins **109**
last, readily: eff at 6f, 7f will suit: acts on fm, soft & polytrk: smart.
4563 **CROSSOVER 23** H A Pantall 2-8-8 T Jarnet 52/10: 5222: Cl up, kept on, not pace of wnr.   1½   **98**
     NIPPING R Collet 2-8-8 O Peslier 23/10: 2013: Trkd ldrs, kept on for press, not pace of wnr.   nk   **97**
7 Ran   Time 1m 11.20()   Owned: T Jacobs   Trained: Headley

CURRAGH   SATURDAY 02.10.04   Righthand, Galloping Track

Official Going Yielding To Soft

4958   **4.00 Gr 3 Weld Park Stakes 2yo Fillies** ()
£52080 £10238 £4878   **7f**   **Soft**

     JAZZ PRINCESS 26 Mrs J Harrington 2-8-11 N G McCullagh 12/1: 111: b f Bahhare - Jazz Up   **113**
(Cadeaux Genereux) Made all, rdn clr over 1f out, styd on strongly: op 10/1: remains unbeaten, earlier landed
auction events at Sligo & Galway: eff at 7f/1m on gd & soft: smart & improving, win more Gr races.
4432 **SAOIRE 27** Ms F M Crowley 2-8-11 M J Kinane 100/30: 2132: Trkd ldrs, rdn & kept on fnl 2f, no dngr.   3   **105**
     VIRGINIA WATERS 14 A P O'Brien 2-8-11 J A Heffernan 4/1: 013: Trkd ldrs, chsd ldr 3f out, onepace.   1½   **102**
4760 **DONGERIE 12** 2-8-11 E Ahern 5/2 FAV: 19: Rdn early & always bhd: up in grade but much btr 4703.   **0**
9 Ran   Time 1m 26.70 ()   Owned: T Curran   Trained: Stud Moone

4959   **4.30 Listed Stanleybet Diamond Stakes 3yo+** ()
£23989 £7038 £3353   **1m2f**   **Soft**

4532 **MIKADO 21** A P O'Brien 3-9-0 (106) C O'Donoghue 100/30: -44351: Led, rdn & briefly hdd ins last,   **115**
sn led again & asserted for press nr fin, styd on strongly: eff btwn 9f/14f on fast & soft ground, loves a stiff/gall
trk: likes to force the pace: tough, smart & versatile colt: see 4532, 4023 & 10.
1148* **ECOMIUM 172** J Noseda 3-9-0 E Ahern 9/2: 12: Trkd ldrs, smooth prog & briefly led ins last, sn   1½   **111**
hdd & no extra nr fin: 6 mth abs: acts on good & soft ground: up in grade & a v useful performance, poss undone by
inexperience close home: looks sure to win more races: see 1148.
3721} **MINGUN 410** A P O'Brien 4-9-5 J A Heffernan 6/1: 1114-3: b c A P Indy - Miesque (Nureyev) Trkd   1½   **109**
ldr, chall over 2f out, not pace of front pair bef dist, kept on & clr rem on reapp: lightly raced '03, mdn, Listed &
Gr 3 scorer bef most creditable 4th in Gr 1 International stakes at York (rtd 118): stays 10f & acts on soft & hvy, v
smart form last term on firm & gd grnd: likes a gall trk: can go well fresh.
1 Jul'03 Leop 10g/f 117- A: 1 Jun'03 Curr 8gd 118- A:
14 Ran   Time 2m 11.40()   Owned: Mrs J Magnier   Trained: Ballydoyle

TIPPERARY   SUNDAY 03.10.04   Lefthand, Sharp Track

Official Going Heavy

4960   **2.15 Listed Tipperary Stakes 2yo** ()
£26170 £7678 £3658   **5f str**   **Heavy**

1994 **KAY TWO 45** Ms F M Crowley 2-9-0 D P McDonogh 3/1 FAV: 2241511: ch c Monashee Mountain - Tricky   **106**
(Song) Handy & led over 1f out, rdn, readily: 6 wk abs: dual C/D wnr earlier this term, in btwn Gr 3 unplcd:
suited by a sharp 5f on fast & hvy ground: goes well fresh: loves Tipperary: v useful. 2 May'04 Curr 5g/f 99- :
4737 **TOURNEDOS 14** M R Channon 2-9-7 (100) S Hitchcott 4/1: 220103252: Chsd ldrs, styd on for press   2   **104**
to go 2nd ins last, no chance with wnr: op 9/4: acts on hvy grnd, poss prefers gd or faster: see 3509.
     DANCING DUCHESS 17 O Weldon 2-8-11 C O'Donoghue 6/1: 0222513: Chsd ldrs, styd on for press.   hd   **93**
4830 **MONASHEE ROSE 6** 2-8-11 (77) E Ahern 10/1: 0112006: Chsd ldrs, btn over 2f out: qck reapp.   5½   **82**
9 Ran   Time 1m 03.40 ()   Owned: H B McGahon   Trained: Curragh

4961   **3.15 Gr 3 Concorde Stakes 3yo+** ()
£34840 £10184 £4824   **7f100yds rnd**   **Heavy**

4020 **HAMAIRI 49** J M Oxx 3-8-12 T P O'Shea 7/2 FAV: 421221: Trkd ldrs, went over 1f out & rdn clr,   **111**
decisvely: 7 wk abs: C/D mdn wnr earlier this term: suited by 7f/1m, on fast & hvy, any trk: smart.
     FEARN ROYAL 9 P Casey 5-8-11 C O'Donoghue 12/1: 30202272: b m Ali Royal - Sparrowhawk (Doyoun)2½   **102**
Mid-div, styd on for press fnl 2f, nvr able to threaten wnr: dual Listed rnr up earlier this term: not won since
'02 (h'cap): suited by 7f/1m on good, loves soft & hvy ground.
4479 **POETICAL 24** M J Grassick 3-8-9 N G McCullagh 14/1: 222-3103: Led & clr over 2f out, hdd over   ½   **101**
1f out, kept on: rest well covered: acts on fast & hvy ground: see 4479.
4800 **MILLENNIUM FORCE 8** 6-9-0 (106) S Hitchcott 13/2: 23300495: Held up, efft 3f out, no prog bef   6   **95**
dist: conditions ideal: btr 2826, 2184.
12 Ran   Time 1m 43.50()   Owned: H H Aga Khan   Trained: Currabeg

Official Going GOOD - Pace Figures Inapplicable Due To Rain

4962
2.10 Lancashire Maiden Stakes Div 1 2yo (D3)
£3426 £1054 £527 **5f str** **Good** **Inapplicable** Inside

4503 **HARRYS HOUSE 24** [6] J J Quinn 2-9-0 (67) R Winston 9/1: 40431: Sn cl-up & led over 1f out, rdn & in command ins last, eased cl-home: eff at 5f, stays a stiff 7f: acts on firm & soft grnd, sharp or stiff trk: showed plenty of speed dropping down in trip, interesting for nurseries: see 4503, 4283. **75**

4645 **GAUDALPIN 18** [8] M J Attwater 2-8-9 (61) A McCarthy 22/1: 3404002: Chsd ldrs, hung left & kept on, no threat to wnr: eff at 5/6f on gd grnd & polytrack: see 2927, 1170 & 1071. 1¼ **65**

4787 **THORNBER COURT 10** [11] A Berry 2-8-9 (66) F Norton 14/1: 04023: Chsd ldrs, took 3rd ins last, nvr a threat: see 4787. nk **64**

4804 **ORPHAN 9** [2] K R Burke 2-9-0 Darren Williams 20/1: 0544: Led till dist, no extra: see 4804. 3 **60**

4717 **CUTLASS GAUDY 14** [7]2-9-0 (82) D Sweeney 7/2: 4025: Mid-div, nvr a pace to threaten: btr 4717. 3½ **49**

3431 **UNDERTHEMISTLETOE 73** [10]2-8-9 (55) F Lynch 50/1: 6306: Chsd ldrs, no impress over 1f out: abs. 1¼ **40**

1190 **CAVORTING 173** [5]2-9-0 S Sanders 8/11 FAV: 47: Mid-div, rdn & hung right over 2f out, no impress when eased ins last: well bckd at odds-on, 6 mth abs, has been gelded: see 1190. ½ **43**

PASSIONATELY ROYAL [1]2-9-0 P Hanagan 20/1: 8: b c Royal Applause - Passionelle (Nashwan) Dwelt & bhd, mod prog: 24,000gns Feb foal, half-brother to a plcd hdles performer, dam unplcd & related to several smart stayers: could well get much further in time. nk **42**

4599 **GRANDMA RYTA 20** [3]2-8-9 Lisa Jones 100/1: 09: br f Cyrano de Bergerac - Tamara (Marju) Sn outpcd & bhd: Apr foal, dam a 5f 2yo scorer. ½ **35**

4040 **SERENE PEARL 47** [4]2-8-9 t (53) D Allan 150/1: 0066400: 10th: Al bhd: 7 wk abs: btr 3484 (AW). 3 **27**

LADY EDGE [12]2-8-9 P Mulrennan(3) 50/1: 0: 11th: ch f Bold Edge - Lady Sheriff (Taufan) Slow away & sn well bhd: Apr foal, dam a prolific sprint wnr. 5 **13**

11 Ran Time 1m 0.09 (2.79) Owned: Mr N Bulmer Trained: Malton

4963
2.40 Toteexacta Nursery Stakes Handicap Fillies 2yo 0-85 (D2) [89]
£7261 £2234 £1117 **7f rnd** **Good** **Inapplicable** Inside

4692 **HANSOMELLE 16** [6] B Mactaggart 2-9-0 (75) Dale Gibson 10/1: 41241: Chsd ldrs, rdn & led ins last, styd on well for press: eff at 6f, now stays a sharp 7f well: acts on fast & soft grnd, sharp or stiff/undul trk: consistent filly, progressive profile: see 4692, 4344 & 3589. **84**

4418 **USHINDI 29** [15] M L W Bell 2-8-8 (69) J Mackay 20/1: 0042D: Chsd ldrs wide, rdn & hdwy to lead over 1f out, sn hung badly left under press & hdd ins last, kept on: fin 2nd, disqual & plcd 3rd: acts on fast & gd grnd: fine run from awkward wide draw: see 4418. ½ **76**

4480 **MY PRINCESS 26** [9] N A Callaghan 2-9-0 (75) K Fallon 4/1 FAV: 5310553: Mid-div, rdn & keeping on when badly hmpd ins last, rallied well cl-home: promoted to 2nd: acts on firm & gd grnd: unlucky, see 4480. nk **81 +**

4692 **TEQUILA SHEILA 16** [12] K R Burke 2-9-6 (81) Darren Williams 25/1: 0161604: Held up, styd on wide for press fnl 2f, nrst fin: stays a sharp 7f: see 3825. nk **86**

4655 **DISPOL ISLE 18** [3]2-8-4 (65) P Fessey 11/1: 444435: Chsd ldrs, pushed along over 2f out, kept on ins last, no threat: stays a sharp 7f: see 4655, 4343 & 3988. 1 **68**

4876 **CHUTNEY MARY 5** [2]2-8-7 (1ow) (67) N Callan 17/2: 2525036: Led till over 1f out, no extra when short of room ins last: qck reapp: see 3716, 2652. nk **70**

4653* **MARKET TREND 18** [17]2-9-7 (82) K Darley 5/1: 217: Mid-div, eff wide, not pace to chall: nicely bckd, h'cap bow: acts on gd & gd/soft grnd: prob to form of 4653. ½ **83**

4697 **EPIPHANY 15** [10]2-9-7 T (82) S Sanders 8/1: 2108: Rear, nvr nr ldrs: see 3761. 1¼ **80**

4807 **ALGORITHM 9** [7]2-7-13 (1ow) (59) R Ffrench 10/1: 6562349: Chsd ldrs, rdn & no impress fnl 1f. ¾ **57**

4673 **IGNITION 1** [14]2-7-13 (60) B Swarbrick(3) 33/1: 543400: 10th: Mid-div & wide, nvr able to chall. 1½ **54**

4753 **STREET BALLAD 12** [13]2-8-3 (64) F Norton 20/1: 40300: 11th: Bhd, mod late prog: btr 4436. 1¾ **55**

3981 **Missed Turn 50** [18]2-7-12 (12oh)(47) F P Ferris(3) 100/1:0

4437 **Evanesce 28** [1]2-8-6 (67) S Hitchcott 22/1:0

4787 **Lady Hopeful 10** [4]2-8-0 (61) D Fentiman(7) 33/1:0   4655 **Dorn Dancer 18** [8]2-9-4 (79) L Enstone 16/1:0

4163* **Daisy Bucket 41** [11]2-8-9 (70) C Catlin 16/1:0

4337 **Summer Silks 33** [5]2-7-12 (2oh)(57) Lisa Jones 50/1:0

17 Ran Time 1m 28.29 (5.29) Owned: Corsby Racing Trained: Hawick

4964
3.10 Cumbria Median Auction Maiden Stakes Div 1 3yo (F4)
£1881 £1881 £418 **6f rnd** **Good** **Inapplicable** Inside

4618 **SESSAY 19** [6] D Nicholls 3-9-0 (65) A Nicholls 1/1 FAV: 3506061: Cl-up & led over 1f out, drvn & joined on line: hvly bckd: eff at 5/6f, tried 7f: acts on fast & gd/soft, reportedly suited by latter, prob handles any trk: see 1570 & 1473. **71**

4740 **CYFRWYS 13** [10] P Palling 3-8-9 (60) F P Ferris(3) 15/8: 0226061: Cl-up & rdn to chall fnl 1f, joined ldr line: nicely bckd: eff at 6f, tried 7f: acts on fast, gd & fibresand, prob any trk: see 3095 & 2849. dht **66**

1509 **SHAYMEES GIRL 156** [1] Ms Deborah J Evans 3-9-0 (52) B Swarbrick(5) 12/1: 0-53303: Led till over 1f out, sn no ch with front pair: 5 mth abs: handles gd grnd & fibresand: see 863 & 795. 7 **45**

4598 **WEAKEST LINK 20** [5] E J Alston 3-9-0 (51) D Allan 14/1: 2330004: Mid-div, nvr able to chall. 2 **44**

4595 **FAITES VOS JEUX 21** [2]3-8-9 (40) M Halford(7) 50/1: 4430-005: b f Foxhound - Desert Bloom (Last Tycoon) Chsd ldrs, outpcd from halfway: AW mdn plcd '03 (rtd 56a, turf unplcd, rtd 53): eff around a sharp 6f on fibresand, prob handles fast grnd. shd **39**

4507 **SVENSON 24** [9]3-9-0 (30) D R McCabe 100/1: 0000006: Chsd ldrs, no impress over 1f out. shd **43$**

4445 **GOLDEN BANKES 28** [4]3-8-9 D Sweeney 16/1: 07: Bhd, little hdwy: no form prev. 2 **32**

3610 **MISS CHANCELOT 66** [7]3-8-9 J McAuley 100/1: 008: Al bhd & no ch halfway, abs. 11 **0**

4870 **FAYRZ PLEASE 6** [8]3-9-0 (55) S Chin 33/1: 3-440009: Sn strug rear: qck reapp: btr 197 (AW). 9 **0**

2613 **QUINTILLION 106** [3]3-9-0 (40) P Hanagan 40/1: 00-0000: 10th: Slow away & sn bhd, eased, abs. 13 **0**

10 Ran Time 1m 14.16 (3.86) Owned: Derek and Jean Clee Trained: Cowbridge

4965 **3.40 Skyram Handicap Stakes 3yo+ 46-55 (F4)** **[57]**
£3053 £872 £436 **1m7f177y** **Good** **Inapplicable** Inside

4045 **MERCURIOUS 47** [13] J Mackie 4-9-2 (45) Dale Gibson 12/1: 5421251: Bhd, hdwy 5f out, rdn/chsd ldrs over 2f out, styd on for press to lead cl-home, all out: 7 wk abs: eff at 14f, suited by 2m, shapes as a thorough stayer: acts on both AWs & gd grnd, sharp/turning trks: see 3397, 1263. **53**
4675 **DOCTOR JOHN 17** [9] Andrew Turnell 7-9-2 (45) D Corby(3) 20/1: 2202402: Mid-div, hdwy halfway, rdn to lead well ins last, hdd cl-home: acts on gd grnd & fibresand: see 690 & 612. *hd* **52**
1285 **TOTALLY SCOTTISH 168** [17] K G Reveley 8-9-2 (45) S Sanders 8/1: 00/4/42-33: Held up, hdwy wide 5f out, rdn/led over 2f out, hdd well ins last, no extra nr line: 6 mth abs, clr of rem: see 1285. *½* **51**
4796 **BANNINGHAM BLAZE 10** [18] A W Carroll 4-9-5 (48) D Nolan(3) 10/1: 2223254: Held up, hdwy 5f out, kept on fnl 2f tho' no impress ins last: tough type, stays 2m, poss best over sltly shorter: see 4423, 4364 & 3983. *6* **48**
3896} **SIMLET 406** [12]9-9-2 (45) G Faulkner 50/1: /0/40//50-5: b g Forzando - Besito (Wassl) Held up, hdwy 4f out, no extra ins last: Flat reapp, 5 mth jumps abs (nov h'cap chase rnr-up, eff btwn 2m/3m1f on firm, gd/soft & any trk, rtd 101c): unplcd in '03 (rtd 39, h'cap): prev eff btwn 1m/10f on firm, gd & f/sand. *nk* **44**
4405 **MADIBA 29** [3]5-9-11 (54) K Fallon 13/2 FAV: 000P526: Mid-div, smooth prog 5f out, edged right under press over 2f out & sn no extra: see 4405, 1753, 690 & 306. *4* **49**
4249 **NODS STAR 38** [1]3-8-5 (45) R Ffrench 16/1: 5000037: Chsd ldrs, hdwy to lead over 5f out, hdd over 2f out & wknd: not convince over longer 2m trip: btr 4249 (14f). *3½* **37**
2785} **LAKE O GOLD 453** [4]5-9-4 (47) T Williams 80/1: 650500-8: ch f Karinga Bay - Ginka (Petoski) Rear, late hdwy for press, nvr a factor: 4 mth jumps abs, nov hdle rnr-up (rtd 94h, 2m5f, fast): unplcd in '03 (J W Mullins, rtd 53 & 23a, h'caps): plcd in '02 (rtd 70a, AW mdn): eff btwn 10/13f on fast grnd & polytrk. *1¾* **37**
4675 **OOPS 17** [2]5-9-3 (46) D Allan 7/1: 6232449: Chsd ldrs, btn 4f out: btr 4675 & 4423. *nk* **35**
4594 **MUNAAWESH 21** [8]3-9-0 bl (54) A Culhane 12/1: 4220450: 10th: Mid-div trav well, no prog fnl 3f. *2½* **41**
4771 **RED SKELTON 11** [14]3-8-12 (52) I Mongan 20/1: 0003000: 11th: Rear, eff wide halfway to dispute lead, wknd qckly 2f out: see 4448 (10f, AW). *5* **34**
4796 **REGENCY RED 10** [7]6-9-5 (48) B Swarbrick(5) 16/1: 00/-40100: 12th: Dwelt, rear: btr 4716 (12f). *3* **27**
3360} **OWN LINE 428** [20]5-9-2 (45) T Hamilton(3) 20/1: 400130-0: 13th: Mid-div, btn 4f out, reapp. *1* **23**
4555 **DANCE LIGHT 22** [11]5-9-10 VIS (53) E Ahern 16/1: 0530050: 14th: Mid-div, strugg halfway: vis. *14* **20**
4276 **ASTROMANCER 36** [10]4-9-6 (49) N Callan 7/1: 0031030: 15th: Cl-up wide, lost place from halfway. *5* **11**
4720 **AMALFI COAST 14** [6]5-9-2 (45) D Tudhope(5) 100/1: 40U-0000: 16th: Prom till halfway. *1¼* **6**
4151 **SEATTLE PRINCE 42** [5]6-9-8 (51) A Nicholls 33/1: 31/004-00: 17th: Al bhd: 6 wk abs. *3* **9**
4628 **JAMAICAN FLIGHT 19** [19]11-9-2 (45) R Winston 16/1: 4444550: 18th: Led till over 5f out, sn bhd. *10* **0**
2062} **Ensemble 482** [15]4-9-2 (5oh)(40) C Catlin 100/1:0 3263 **Bien Good 80** [16]3-8-5 (45) T Eaves 50/1:0
20 Ran Time 3m 34.74 (13.94) Owned: Gwen K DotCom Trained: Church Broughton

4966 **4.10 Nottinghamshire Handicap Stakes 3yo 56-70 (E3)** **[74]**
£3628 £1116 £558 **1m3f214y** **Good** **Inapplicable** Inside

4862 **DONT CALL ME DEREK 6** [20] S C Williams 3-9-5 (65) S Sanders 4/1 FAV: 0021321: Held up, smooth hdwy to lead 2f out, held on all out: hvly bckd: eff at 1m, imprvd for step up to 12f: acts on firm, gd/soft & both AWs, prob any trk: trav well & unexposed at this trip, keep on side: see 4044. **79**
4594* **EGO TRIP 21** [12] M W Easterby 3-8-12 bl (58) Dale Gibson 10/1: 0130412: Mid-div, rdn & hdwy to chall over 1f out, just denied: well clr of rem: imprvd again, keep on side: see 4594. *shd* **71**
4589 **ELLINA 21** [10] J Pearce 3-9-3 (63) K Fallon 12/1: 6401003: Rear, smooth hdwy to chase ldrs over 3f out, no impress on front pair ins last: see 3334. *9* **65**
4757 **COTTINGHAM 12** [7] M C Chapman 3-8-13 (59) S Chin 16/1: 2066624: Chsd ldrs, ch 2f out, no extra: yet to fully convince beyond 10f: see 4757, 3835 & 355. *nk* **60**
4487 **SAIDA LENASERA 26** [1]3-9-3 (63) A Culhane 33/1: 0-066055: Chsd ldrs, outpcd & lost place over 2f out, kept on ins last: 14f+ in similar may suit: see 1708. *hd* **63**
4868 **QUICKSTYX 6** [6]3-9-7 (67) C Catlin 14/1: 4544606: Mid-div, eff 2f out, sn no impress: qck reapp. *1¾* **65**
4771 **CAN CAN FLYER 11** [5]3-9-6 (66) R Ffrench 5/1: 06-12207: Led early, sn trkd ldrs, btn dist. *shd* **64**
3573 **LUCKY ARTHUR 67** [19]3-8-10 (56) D Sweeney 25/1: 5032308: Rear, hdwy to chase ldrs over 2f out, sn no impress: 2 mth abs: btr 3085 & 2978. *½* **53**
4282 **MUSIC MIX 36** [15]3-9-2 VIS (62) E Ahern 22/1: 0014409: Cl-up/dsptd lead 10f, sn no extra: visor. *2½* **55**
4601 **PRELUDE 20** [11]3-9-1 (61) S W Kelly 16/1: 0666150: 10th: Mid-div, btn 2f out: btr 4282 (10f). *1¼* **52**
4111 **ABBEYGATE 45** [16]3-9-0 T (60) J P Guillambert(3) 66/1: 006-0000: 11th: Al rear: abs, t-strap. *2* **48**
4593 **THE RIP 21** [14]3-8-11 (57) D Allan 33/1: 004-030: 12th: Mid-div, strug fnl 3f: btr 4593 (1m). *3* **41**
4701 **GO GREEN 15** [8]3-8-10 (2oh)t (54) N Callan 12/1: 3260320: 13th: Al towards rear: btr 4701 (10f). *6* **31**
2919 **BAAWRAH 94** [3]3-9-5 (65) R Winston 14/1: 2-214060: 14th: Al rear: abs, new yard, gelded. *4* **34**
4721 **IT MUST BE SPEECH 14** [13]3-8-11 (57) R Fitzpatrick 50/1: 00-52500: 15th: Al bhnd. *2* **23**
4826 **PRINCIPESSA 8** [2]3-9-10 (70) F P Ferris(3) 8/1: 2024320: 16th: Led/dsptd lead 5f: btr 4826. *1¾* **34**
1528 **Crociera 155** [4]3-9-3 (63) P Robinson 16/1:0 4674 **Jonnyem 17** [9]3-8-10 (4oh)(52) P Hanagan 25/1:0
4709 **Suchwot 15** [18]3-8-10 (56) K Darley 40/1:0 **Cambo 158** [17]3-8-10 (1oh)(55) Joanna Badger 50/1:F
20 Ran Time 2m 41.57 (10.37) Owned: The Chummy Northerners Trained: Newmarket

4967 **4.40 Derbyshire Apprentice Handicap Stakes 3yo+ 46-55 (F4)** **[69]**
£2961 £846 £423 **6f rnd** **Good** **Inapplicable** Inside

4636 **ON THE TRAIL 19** [2] D W Chapman 7-8-13 (54) P Makin(3) 7/1: 1145201: Led, rdn & prsd dist, styd on strongly to assert ins last: eff at 5/6f on firm, gd/soft & both AWs: loves to force the pace: see 4562. **63**
4508* **LOUGHLORIEN 24** [7] R E Barr 5-8-13 (54) D Tudhope(5) 8/1: 0334012: Chsd ldrs, rdn & pressed wnr over 1f out, no extra ins last: stays 6f, stiff 5f poss ideal: see 4508 (banded). *1¾* **57**
4636 **LAUREL DAWN 19** [13] I W McInnes 6-8-13 (54) Natalia Gemelova(5) 8/1: 0000033: Rear, hdwy wide from halfway, onepace ins last: stays 6f, 5f prob ideal: see 2657. *1½* **52**
3667 **AMANDAS LAD 63** [10] M C Chapman 4-8-12 (53) D Nolan 16/1: 4563304: Bhd, switched & kept on late, nrst fin, abs: longstanding mdn: see 999, 487. *1¼* **47**

CATTERICK TUESDAY 05.10.04 Lefthand, Undulating, Very Tight Track

4618 **WILLIAMS WELL 19** [8]10-9-0 bl (55) P Mulrennan 8/1: 5063305: Bhd, late gains, wants a stiffer trk. *¾* **47**
4739 **YORKIES BOY 13** [6]9-9-0 p (55) R Thomas 10/1: 3110056: Rear, mod hdwy for press, nvr land blow. *1¼* **43**
4870 **ROAN RAIDER 6** [5]4-8-13 vis (54) R Miles 16/1: 2025007: Chsd ldrs till over 1f out: qck reapp. *1* **39**
4438 **KISS THE RAIN 28** [14]4-8-13 vis (54) M Lawson(5) 33/1: 334-6008: Bhd, switched & only mod prog. *¾* **37**
4603 **BRIGADIER MONTY 20** [12]6-8-12 (53) S Hitchcott 9/1: 2550309: Nvr nr ldrs. *2* **30**
4489 **MORITAT 26** [1]4-8-13 (54) F P Ferris 6/1: 6356300: 10th: Cl-up, btn over 1f out: btr 4368. *nk* **30**
4438 **CROSS ASH 28** [3]4-8-12 (53) R Kennemore(7) 40/1: 00-00000: 11th: Chsd ldrs, outpcd from halfway. *½* **27**
4592 **TIME TO REMEMBER 21** [4]6-9-0 (55) T Hamilton 11/2 FAV: 0020000: 12th: Chsd ldrs, btn 2f out. *nk* **28**
4126 **Highland Lass 43** [11]3-8-13 (55) N Chalmers(3) 16/1:0 4562 **Global Achiever 22** [9]3-8-13 T(55) A Quinn(3) 16/1:0
14 Ran Time 1m 14.97 (4.67) Owned: Mr J M Chapman Trained: York

4968

5.10 Lancashire Maiden Stakes Div 2 2yo (D3)
£3416 £1051 £526 **5f str** **Good** **Inapplicable** Inside

4804 **TURN ON THE STYLE 9** [11] R P Elliott 2-9-0 S Chin 9/2: 0021: Unruly start, cl-up & led over 1f out, wandered under press & swerved left ins last, just prevailed: nicely bckd, op 6/1: confirmed recent improvement: suited by 5f last twice on gd grnd, sharp/turning trk: see 4804 & 4436. **71**
4006 **BENNY THE BUS 49** [3] Mrs G S Rees 2-9-0 A Culhane 33/1: 0002: b g Komaite - Amy Leigh (Imperial Frontier) Chsd ldrs, chall when badly bmpd ins last, just held: 7 wk abs: left prev bhd on this return to 5f: May foal, brother to a 5/6f AW juv wnr, dam a 5f juv & subs 5/6f AW wnr: eff at 5f on gd grnd & a sharp/turning trk. *nk* **70**
REVIEN [9] G A Huffer 2-9-0 I Mongan 3/1: 3: b g Rossini - Kazimiera (Polish Patriot) Chsd ldrs, outpcd halfway, kept on ins last, not threaten front pair: nicely bckd tho' op 7/4: 25,000gns 2yo, Mar foal: dam plcd at up to 1m & half-sister to a multiple 5/6f wnr: eff at 5f, shaped as if 6f will suit: handles gd grnd. *2½* **62**
4535 **TIFFIN DEANO 24** [7] P C Haslam 2-9-0 (56) G Faulkner 16/1: 50004: Outpcd towards rear, hung left but kept on ins last: op 25/1: see 1161. *nk* **61$**
4596 **BEN CASEY 20** [1]2-9-0 (66) F Lynch 6/4 FAV: 06335: Led, hung right & hdd over 1f out, no extra ins last: hvly bckd, op 9/4: btr 4596 & 4438 (firm & fast). *½* **59**
4921 **MISSIN MARGOT 3** [8]2-8-9 B Swarbrick(5) 33/1: 506: Chsd ldrs, btn over 1f out, qck reapp. *4* **42**
4804 **IN RHUBARB 9** [4]2-9-0 Natalia Gemelova(5) 50/1: 607: Swerved right start, sn outpcd: see 4804. *1¾* **42**
AMMIRARE [10]2-8-9 R Winston 11/1: 8: b f Diktat - Mathaayl (Shadeed) Slow away & bhd, little hdwy: Mar foal, half-sister to 1m/9f 3yo wnrs, dam a 6/10f 3yo scorer. *shd* **37**
3141 **GLORIA NIMBUS 86** [6]2-8-9 (50) S Righton 80/1: 00609: Hmpd start & keen, chsd ldrs till halfway. *3½* **26**
4706 **LADY ERICA 15** [2]2-8-9 VIS (57) Darren Williams 12/1: 254300: 10th: Chsd ldr, hung right & lost place over 1f out, eased: tried a visor. *3* **17**
10 Ran Time 1m 01.80 (4.5) Owned: The Haydock Badgeholders Trained: Formby

4969

5.40 Cumbria Median Auction Maiden Stakes Div 2 3yo (F4)
£2918 £834 £417 **5f212y** **Good** **Inapplicable** Inside

4836 **WESTBOROUGH 8** [7] N Tinkler 3-9-0 t (52) Kim Tinkler 16/1: 0060201: Chsd ldrs, rdn to lead dist, styd on strongly: eff at 5/6f on firm & hvy grnd, any trk: imprvd of late in t-strap: see 4595, 1682. **64**
4667 **KNEAD THE DOUGH 17** [3] D E Cantillon 3-9-0 (55) A McCarthy 8/1: 2602: Led, hdd dist, no extra: handles gd grnd & polytrack: see 706. *2* **57**
4696 **KAMENKA 16** [8] R A Fahey 3-8-9 (65) P Hanagan 5/2: 4-444003: Chsd ldrs, no extra dist: bckd. *2½* **44**
4740 **WHISTFUL 13** [10] C F Wall 3-8-9 (63) S Sanders 6/4 FAV: 0350404: Chsd ldrs wide, no extra over 1f out: nicely bckd: had an awkward passage today: btr 3910. *1* **41**
4561 **COMIC TALES 22** [9]3-9-0 P (40) L Enstone 50/1: 0-66065: Dwelt, nvr a pace to threaten: chkpcs. *1½* **41**
4788 **BRAIN WASHED 10** [6]3-8-9 (59) R Winston 9/2: 0425336: Sn outpcd: op 7/2: btr 4788. *1¾* **31**
4440 **GOVERNMENT 28** [1]3-9-0 (45) S Chin 40/1: 0457: Outpcd early & nvr a threat: btr 2523 (10f). *3* **27**
MISS PRIM 0 [4]3-8-9 J Edmunds 40/1: 8: Slow away, sn outpcd. *1½* **17**
8 Ran Time 1m 15.32(5.02) Owned: Mr Venning Mr Parks & Mr Raybould Trained: Malton

LINGFIELD Polytrack WEDNESDAY 06.10.04 Lefthand, V Sharp Track

Official Going Standard

4970

1.50 Menzies Distribution E B F Maiden Stakes Div 1 2yo (D3)
£4251 £1308 £654 **7f aw rnd** **Going 25** **-06 Slow** Inside

4664 **BLUE TORPEDO 18** [1] Mrs A J Perrett 2-9-0 R L Moore 25/1: 01: Chsd ldrs, pushed along over 2f out, rdn & led well ins last: AW bow, left debut bhd: eff at 7f, 1m will suit: acts on polytrack & a sharp trk. **82a**
4179 **OPTIMUS 41** [11] G A Butler 2-9-0 J Fortune 4/1: 52: Dwelt & settled rear, drvn & stayed on well fnl 1f, not able to rch wnr: 6 wk abs: imprvd over this longer 7f trip, get further: acts on polytrack: win similar. *¾* **80a**
3818 **MUTANABI 58** [4] Saeed bin Suroor 2-9-0 L Dettori 4/7 FAV: 23: Led, rdn & hdd ins last, jinked right & no extra: hvly bckd at odds-on, 2 mth abs: styd longer 7f trip: see 3818. *1¼* **77a**
ANGEL RAYS 0 [5] G A Butler 2-8-9 D Holland 16/1: 4: ch f Unfuwain - Success Story (Sharrood) Trkd ldrs, kept on onepace: longer priced stablemate of rnr-up: Jan foal, half-sister to a dual 6/7f juv wnr & a multiple 10/12f 3yo scorer: dam a dual 10f 3yo wnr: eff at 7f, relish 1m+: encouraging start. *1* **70a**
POSTGRADUATE 0 [8]2-9-0 S Drowne 33/1: 5: b c Almutawakel - Institutrice (College Chapel) Chsd ldrs wide over 2f out, no extra dist: Apr foal, E50,000 purchase: half-brother to a 5f juv wnr, dam plcd at 7f as a 2/3yo: eff at 7f on polytrack: ran well for a long way, can improve. *1¼* **72a**
4853 **COMPTON QUAY 7** [12]2-9-0 R Hughes 33/1: 606: Slow away & rear, late gains under hand ride, nrst fin: not knocked about, likely type for nursery company. *1½* **69a**
3330 **MEDITATION 77** [9]2-8-9 F Norton 33/1: 007: ch f Inchinor - Trojan Desert (Troy) Pushed along mid-div, nvr able to chall: 11 wk abs: Apr foal, half-sister to a 10f wnr. *shd* **64a**
HIGH CARD 0 [7]2-9-0 J Tate 66/1: 8: Dwelt, pushed along mid-div, no impress fnl 2f. *1¼* **66a**
AGGRAVATION 0 [6]2-9-0 A Nicholls 50/1: 9: Dwelt & rcd keen early, mid-div, no impress fnl 2f. *3½* **59a**
3722 **LAMA ALBARQ 62** [10]2-9-0 R Hills 33/1: 060: 10th: Mid-div, wide, nvr land blow, abs, new yard. *½* **58a**

LAKE CHINI 0 [3]2-9-0 P Robinson 12/1: 0: 11th: Slow away & rear, no impression. 1¼ 55a
4866 RED OPERA 7 [14]2-9-0 S Sanders 40/1: 000: 12th: Sn rdn in rear, al bhd. 5 45a
4711 IN THE SHADOWS 16 [13]2-8-9 N Callan 100/1: 000: 13th: Al rear & no ch fnl 3f. 3 34a
4121 ARAMAT 44 [2]2-8-9 Natalia Gemelova(5) 100/1: 00: 14th: Led/dsptd lead 4f, wknd qckly, 6 wk abs. 11 12a
14 Ran Time 1m 24.95 (2.15) Owned: Mr A D Spence Trained: Pulborough

4971

2.20 Menzies Distribution E B F Maiden Stakes Div 2 2yo (D3)
£4238 £1304 £652 **7f aw rnd** **Going 25** **-10 Slow** Inside

2221 **QADAR 124** [9] M P Tregoning 2-9-0 t R Hills 10/11 FAV: 231: Trkd ldr, led over 1f out, hung left under press but sn asserted: hvly bckd, op 5/4: 4 mth abs & AW bow: eff at 6f, styd longer 7f trip well: acts on fast, gd & polytrack, sharp/undul trk: goes well fresh: see 2221 & 1848. **86a**
4670 **BALKAN LEADER 18** [10] Saeed bin Suroor 2-9-0 L Dettori 5/1: 42: Led, rdn & hdd over 1f out, no extra: op 7/1, AW bow: imprvd from intro with forcing tactics applied: stays 7f & acts on polytrack: see 4670. 2½ **80a**
DESERT LIGHTNING 0 [2] J Noseda 2-9-0 E Ahern 3/1: 3: ch c Desert Prince - Saibhreas (Last Tycoon) Chsd ldrs, styd on onepace from dist: nicely bckd tho' op 2/1: Mar foal, 120,000gns purchase: dam a 10f 3yo scorer: eff at 7f, 1m+ could suit: handles polytrack & a sharp/undul trk: clr of rem, encouraging start. hd **79a**
4611 **MISSY CINOFAZ 21** [4] I A Wood 2-8-9 F Norton 100/1: 04: ch f Zafonic - Dancing Wolf (Wolfhound) Chsd ldrs, no extra bef dist: AW bow: Apr foal, half-sister to a 10f 3yo wnr: dam plcd at 5f/1m. 4 **66a**
3047 **PRECIOUS SAMMI 90** [12]2-9-0 N Callan 100/1: 05: b c Mark of Esteem - Night Over Day (Most Welcome) Dwelt, in tch, hdwy wide over 2f out, no extra over 1f out: imprvd from intro on AW bow: Apr foal, cheaply bght: half-brother to a dual wnr abroad, dam unplcd as a 2/3yo. 2 **67a**
4610 **MAGIC FLO 21** [7]2-8-9 S Whitworth 50/1: 06: Keen & trkd ldrs, btn over 1f out, longer trip. nk **61a**
DAYBREAKING 0 [3]2-9-0 S Carson 66/1: 7: Mid-div, no impress fnl 2f. shd **66a**
4677 **PLANET 18** [5]2-9-0 K Fallon 14/1: 08: Dwelt, towards rear, no impress fnl 2f, AW bow. 1¾ **63a**
HEATHWOOD 0 [1]2-9-0 J Fortune 25/1: 9: Slow away & rear, late gains, kind ride, improve. nk **62a**
4756 **OPTIMUM 13** [6]2-9-0 T P Queally 40/1: 050: 10th: Held up, no impress fnl 2f. 1½ **59a**
4865 **DEVILS ISLAND 7** [8]2-9-0 S Sanders 28/1: 500: 11th: Dwelt & held up rear, wide, nvr a factor. ½ **58a**
SONG SPARROW 0 [14]2-8-9 D Holland 66/1: 0: 12th: Al bhd & no ch fnl 3f. 1 **51a**
BLUE HEDGES 0 [11]2-9-0 J Quinn 100/1: 0: 13th: Slow away & always bhd. hd **55a**
CELTIC PROMISE 0 [13]2-8-9 R L Moore 25/1: 0: 14th: Sn struggling rear, al bhd. 2½ **45a**
14 Ran Time 1m 25.22 (2.42) Owned: Mr Hamdan Al Maktoum Trained: Lambourn

4972

2.50 Sun Nursery Handicap Stakes 2yo 0-85 (D2) **[90]**
£5655 £1740 £870 **6f aw rnd** **Going 25** **-03 Slow** Inside

4179 **FANTAISISTE 41** [2] Sir Mark Prescott 2-8-13 (75) S Sanders 2/1 FAV: 0321: Made all, strongly pressed over 1f out, drvn & held on well: well bckd tho' op 13/8: 6 wk abs, h'cap bow: stays 7f, suited by forcing tactics at 6f: acts on fast grnd & polytrack, sharp/undul trks: goes well fresh: type to prog: see 4179 & 3716. **86a**
4882 **BAHAMIAN MAGIC 6** [1] D R Loder 2-9-7 (83) L Dettori 11/4: 43102: Handy & drvn to chall over 1f out, al held fnl 100y: well bckd, op 4/1: qck reapp: eff at 5/6f: see 4543. ½ **91a**
4741 **TRANSVESTITE 14** [6] J W Hills 2-8-8 vis (70) E Ahern 8/1: 543603: Chsd ldrs, styd on well for press ins last, nrst line: eff at 6f, worth another try at 7f on this evidence: eff in vis: acts on polytrk & gd. ½ **76a**
4444 **FASYLITATOR 29** [8] J A Osborne 2-8-7 (69) S W Kelly 9/2: 63604: Rear, switched & kept on for press, nrst fin: AW bow: handles fast grnd & polytrack, worth another try at 7f: see 3975. ¾ **73a**
4894 **LILY LENAT 5** [5]2-8-10 p (72) D Sweeney 33/1: 043005: Chsd wnr, no extra fnl 1f, qck reapp: eff at 5/6f on gd grnd & polytrack, eff in cheek pieces: see 2395. nk **75a**
4758 **MULBERRY LAD 13** [10]2-8-3 bl (65) D Kinsella 33/1: 524206: Dwelt, sn trkd ldrs on rail, poised to chall when short of room ins last, sn no extra: shade closer without interference: see 3671. nk **67a**
4653 **NASSEEM DUBAI 19** [11]2-9-2 (78) J Quinn 12/1: 062537: Held up, onepace/short of room ins last. ½ **78a**
4443 **SAN DENG 29** [3]2-7-13 (1ow) (60) F Norton 66/1: 03008: Dwelt & held up, nvr able to chall. 4 **49a**
4108 **GENERAL HAIGH 46** [7]2-8-10 (72) W Supple 16/1: 6449: Mid-div wide, btn over 1f out, abs. 5 **47a**
4637 **SIR BLUEBIRD 19** [4]2-8-6 (68) R L Moore 12/1: 0060: 10th: ch c Bluebird - Persian Tapestry (Tap On Wood) Sn rdn, drpd rear & nvr trav: 38,000gns Apr foal, brother to a sprint scorer: dam 10f scorer. 2 **37a**
3521 **GEE BEE EM 70** [9]2-8-13 (75) L P Keniry(3) 33/1: 214400: 11th: Wide & prom till 2f out, wknd: abs. 1 **41a**
11 Ran Time 1m 12.10 (1.7) Owned: Miss K Rausing Trained: Newmarket

4973

3.20 Sport Newspapers Ltd Handicap Stakes 3yo+ 56-70 (E3) **[84]**
£3681 £1133 £566 **1m4f aw** **Going 25** **-33 Slow** Inside

3855* **MITH HILL 56** [9] E A L Dunlop 3-8-12 (68) E Ahern 10/1: 011: Trkd ldrs, outpcd over 2f out, rdn to lead ins last: nicely bckd: AW/h'cap bow, 8 wk abs: eff at 10f, imprvd for step up to 12f & shld get further: acts on gd/soft grnd & polytrack: goes well fresh: lightly rcd & progressive type: see 3855. **77a**
4647 **REDI 19** [7] L M Cumani 3-9-0 (70) N Mackay(3) 6/1: 0463102: Mid-div, styd on for press from over 1f out, not able to reach wnr: acts on firm, gd/soft & polytrack, sharp or gall/undul trk: see 3899. ½ **76a**
3740 **BARANOOK 62** [16] P W Harris 3-8-11 (67) J Fortune 20/1: 0053: Led & dictated pace, rdn & hdd well ins last, no extra: 2 mth abs & AW/h'cap bow: styd longer 12f trip: acts on polytrack. ¾ **72a**
3026 **REGAL GALLERY 91** [2] C A Horgan 6-9-7 (70) L Dettori 2/1 FAV: 1-113424: Held up, switched & styd on from over 1f out, not able to reach wnr: nicely bckd, op 3/1, 2 mth abs: stays 12f, best at 10f. hd **74a**
4385} **STRATHSPEY 380** [12]5-9-6 (69) L Keniry(3) 50/1: 534234-5: ch f Dancing Spree - Diebiedale (Dominion) Trkd ldrs wide & chall 2f out, no extra dist: reapp: h'cap rnr-up '03 (C Wall, plcd on 2 other starts, h'caps): '02 mdn scorer: winning form at 8.5f, stays sharp 12f: acts on firm, gd/soft & polytrack, prob any trk: v consistent profile, gd return & could be spot on at 10f next time. 1 **72a**
2 Aug'03 Sali 9.9 g/f 70-68 E: 1 Sep'02 Epso 8.5 g/f 72- D: 2 Aug'02 Pont 8 g/f 72- D: 2 Aug'02 Pont 8 g/s 74- D: 2 Jun'02 Yarm 8 fm 76- D: 2 Jun'02 Yarm 7 fm 76- D: 2 Jun'02 Sout 7 g/f 68- F:
4924 **JADEERON 4** [13]5-9-1 p (64) Lisa Jones 20/1: 3440066: Keen early, prom wide till over 1f out. ½ **66a**
4850 **ROLLSWOOD 7** [4]4-8-13 T p (62) S Whitworth 16/1: 56607: Rear, late prog for press, t-strap. 1 **63a**
4942 **GALLANT BOY 2** [10]5-8-10 vis t (59) F P Ferris(3) 9/1: 4444008: Held up, rdn & only mod hdwy. 1½ **58a**
4448 **SEWMORE CHARACTER 29** [8]4-9-5 (68) D Sweeney 12/1: 6250029: Dwelt, rear, mod late gains. ¾ **66a**
4649 **EIJAAZ 19** [15]3-8-9 (65) C Catlin 50/1: 00400: 10th: Chsd ldr, btn over 1f out: btr 2953 (1m). ½ **62a**
4899 **RAHEEL 5** [5]4-8-9 BL t (58) D Holland 20/1: 3000000: 11th: Slow away & rear, well bhd halfway, hd **54a**

only mod prog: reportedly ran too free in first time blnks: qck reapp: see 757 (10f).

4143 **PRECIOUS MYSTERY** 43 [6]4-8-11 (60) K Fallon 7/1: 2016-420: 12th: Keen & prom, btn 2f out, reportedly hung right in the fnl furlong: 6 wk abs: btr 4143, 3638 (firm & soft).		1½	54a
1385 **SURDOUE** 163 [11]4-9-2 (65) N Pollard 40/1: 2420000: 13th: Wide & rear, nvr a factor, 5 mth abs.		½	58a
4850 **BILLY BATHWICK** 7 [1]7-8-9 (58) R L Moore 20/1: 1050000: 14th: Trkd ldrs inner, wknd qckly 2f out.		2½	47a
4449 **DISPARITY** 29 [3]3-8-9 t (65) W Ryan 25/1: 04200: 15th: Al bhd, btr 3787 (10f).		5	47a
4578 **CEMGRAFT** 22 [14]3-8-9 (65) S Drowne 20/1: 5060: 16th: Chsd ldrs, no ch fnl 3f: AW & h'cap bow.		nk	46a

16 Ran   Time 2m 36.11 (6.91)   Owned: Mr Mohammed Jaber   Trained: Newmarket

---

4974   3.50 Dawson News Selling Stakes 3yo+   (G4)
£2688 £768 £384   1m aw rnd   Going 25   +06 Fast   Outside

3216 **ANALYZE** 83 [8] B G Powell 6-9-0 (67) R L Moore 4/1: 6-235401: Held up, smooth hdwy over 2f out & stalked wnr ins last, rdn to lead cl-home, fine ride: gd time: no bid: 2 mth jumps abs (mod form): eff at 1m/10f on firm, soft or polytrack: goes well fresh: apprec drop to sell grade: see 1691.			73a
4832* **OMAHA CITY** 9 [9] G Gubby 10-9-5 (69) F Norton 11/4 FAV: 0000012: Trkd ldrs wide & led over 1f out, rdn & hdd well ins last: nicely bckd, clr of rem: acts on firm, gd/soft & polytrack: will win a seller.		nk	77a
4411 **CHANDELIER** 30 [5] M S Saunders 4-9-5 (50) L P Keniry(3) 25/1: 16006R3: Slow away & bhd, hung left but kept on from over 1f out, nvr a threat: tricky ride: see 3087 (sell h'cap).		5	68a$
4713 **EXTRA COVER** 16 [6] N A Callaghan 3-9-2 bl (67) L Dettori 13/2: 3166004: Dwelt & cl-up, led over 2f out till over 1f out, wknd: op 5/1: clmd by Ms D J Evans for 5,500: return to 6f shld suit: see 3095 (6f, mdn).		1¾	65a
4582 **GALLERY BREEZE** 22 [5]5-9-0 bl (65) V Slattery 14/1: 0-100005: Led/dsptd lead 6f, fdd: 7f prob ideal.		1	58a
3482 **ITS ECCO BOY** 72 [10]6-9-5 (53) S W Kelly 40/1: 0000006: Rear & sn pushed along, mod prog, abs.		6	53a
4368 **ROCKLEY BAY** 33 [2]3-8-11 t (57) D Sweeney 25/1: 0000207: Chsd ldrs, no impress over 2f out: btr 4116.		3½	41a
4485+ **ALAFZAR** 27 [7]6-9-5 bl t (62) K Fallon 3/1: 4044018: Chsd ldrs, wknd 2f out & eased, made a noise.		1	44a
4626 **DANCING KING** 20 [1]8-9-5 (46) P Makin(5) 20/1: 2555559: Led 2f, prom till 2f out: see 754 (fibresand).		2	40a
4612 **SOVIET SPIRIT** 21 [4]3-8-6 BL (48) D Fox(5) 50/1: 3504000: 10th: Slow away, sn handy till 3f out, blnks.		10	15a
4667 **PICO ALTO** 18 [12]3-8-6 T F P Ferris(3) 100/1: 000: 11th: Al bhd, t-strap, AW bow.		¾	14a
4827 **TICERO** 9 [11]3-8-11 bl (63) S Sanders 16/1: 0000400: 12th: Chsd ldrs wide till halfway, wknd qckly.		3	13a

12 Ran   Time 1m 37.72 (1.52)   Owned: The Arkle Bar Partnership   Trained: Winchester

---

4975   4.20 Higg's International Maiden Stakes Div 1 3yo+   (D3)
£3809 £1172 £586   1m aw rnd   Going 25   +03 Fast   Outside

4847 **ADMIRAL COMPTON** 8 [4] E F Vaughan 3-9-0 VIS (77) K Fallon 1/1 FAV: 0-2231: Trkd ldrs & led over 3f out, rdn clr fnl 2f, readily: fair time: nicely bckd: AW bow: eff at 7f, suited by 1m, dam styd 12f: acts on fast, gd & polytrack: any trk: gd confidence booster & enjoyed visor: see 4847, 2907.			82a
4835 **DUXFORD** 9 [6] D K Ivory 3-9-0 J Quinn 50/1: 02: Dwelt, mid-div, styd on to chase wnr, nvr any threat: AW bow & left debut bhd over this longer 1m trip: acts on polytrack.		4	73a
4321 **HUNTERS VALLEY** 35 [10] R Hannon 3-8-9 (65) R Hughes 7/1: 0240443: Rear, hdwy wide 3f out, not able to chall: handles firm, gd & polytrack: btr 4321 (led, h'cap).		2	64a
3947 **SONG OF VALA** 53 [8] R Charlton 3-9-0 t (74) S Drowne 11/4: 2-050634: Trkd ldrs wide, no extra over 1f out: nicely bckd, 8 wk abs: btr 3947 & 3339 (fast).		nk	68a
4768 **WARBRECK** 12 [9]3-9-0 N A Callaghan 33/1: 0005: Rdn rear, mod late prog: wants further?		½	67a
4275 **MAGIC SPIN** 37 [7]4-8-12 S Carson 25/1: 656: Held up, short of room over 2f out, sn no impress.		1	60a
4826 **ANGRY BARK** 9 [5]3-8-9 R Smith 14/1: 4247: Trkd ldrs, btn 2f out: see 4826.		3	54a
3705] **KING AT LAST** 774 [12]5-9-3 D Sweeney 50/1: 0/-8: b g Zamindar - Louis' Queen (Tragic Role) Wide, mid-div, btn 3f out: long abs: missed '03: no form sole '02 start (Mrs A J Perrett, mdn).		1½	56a
4578 **MAD 22** [1]3-8-9 A Nicholls 66/1: 009: Led till over 4f out, sn fdd.		1¼	48a
4180] **BEBOPSKIDDLY** 391 [11]3-9-0 E Ahern 40/1: 000-0: 10th: b c Robellino - Adarama (Persian Bold) Dwelt, al bhd, reapp: unplcd '03 (rtd 41a & 65$).		2	49a
4827 **SEA OF GOLD** 9 [3]3-9-0 VIS (68) C Catlin 14/1: 0626400: 11th: Led till over 4f out, wknd qckly in vis.		5	35a
SON AND HEIR 0 [2]3-9-0 Paul Eddery 50/1: 0: 12th: b c Princely Heir - Margarets Memory (Imperial Frontier) Slow away, pulled hard & sn handy, btn halfway, debut.		7	27a

12 Ran   Time 1m 37.98 (1.78)   Owned: Racing For Gold   Trained: Newmarket

---

4976   4.50 W H Smith News Apprentice Handicap Stakes 3yo 56-70 (E3)   [77]
£3482 £1071 £536   6f aw rnd   Going 25   +03 Fast   Inside

4740 **SIMPSONS MOUNT** 14 [6] R M Flower 3-9-2 (65) D Tudhope(3) 16/1: 5015001: Rear, hdwy when short of room & switched over 1f out, styd on for press to lead well ins last, going away: eff at 5/6f on fast & polytrack.			73a
4683 **SAVIOURS SPIRIT** 18 [2] T G Mills 3-9-7 (70) A Mullen(3) 4/1: 3-221002: Chsd ldrs, rdn to lead ins last, hdd well ins last: bckd: back to form at 6f on polytrack: see 691 (C/D mdn).		1	74a
4740 **DARLA** 14 [8] J W Payne 3-9-4 (67) N Chalmers 12/1: 0526003: Trkd ldrs & led over 1f out, hdd ins last & not pace of wnr: acts on firm, gd & polytrack: see 3218.		1	68a
4747 **IVORY LACE** 14 [1] S Woodman 3-9-5 (68) A Kirby(5) 8/1: 1415004: Rear, hdwy over 1f out, onepace.		hd	68a
4646 **LA VIE EST BELLE** 19 [4]3-9-0 (63) Stephanie Hollinshead(3) 15/2: 0061045: Led till over 1f out, wknd.		2½	55a
4788* **KENSINGTON GB** 11 [3]3-9-1 (64) P Makin 7/2 FAV: 4-632616: Mid-div, no extra over 1f out: bckd.		hd	55a
4368 **MULTIPLE CHOICE** 33 [7]3-9-1 BL C t (64) Steven Harrison(5) 25/1: 0246407: Mid-div, outpcd fnl 2f: blnks.		1	52a
835 **EVER CHEERFUL** 207 [5]3-9-3 p (66) S Haddon(7) 20/1: 2105268: Chsd ldr till 2f out, sn wknd, 7 mth abs.		½	52a
4528 **DOLCE PICCATA** 25 [11]3-9-5 (68) N De Souza 10/1: 0000069: Wide & sn struggling: see 1809.		1½	49a
4740 **BELLA TUTRICE** 14 [10]3-9-1 P (64) B Swarbrick 25/1: 4030000: 10th: In tch wide 4f, sn bhd, chkpcs.		½	43a
3910 **DANDOUCE** 54 [7]3-9-5 (68) Thomas Yeung(3) 11/2: 3-634030: 11th: Chsd ldrs wide, no ch fnl 2f: abs.		1¾	42a
4946 **GOJO** 2 [12]3-9-0 P (63) R Mills(5) 33/1: 420000F: Wide, rear, stumbled & fell over 1f out, chkpcs.			0a

12 Ran   Time 1m 11.69 (1.29)   Owned: CSimpson ZMount TJLowe RMFlower   Trained: Jevington

LINGFIELD Polytrack WEDNESDAY 06.10.04 Lefthand, V Sharp Track

4977 5.20 Higg's International Maiden Stakes Div 2 3yo+ (D3)
£3809 £1172 £586 1m aw rnd Going 25 -16 Slow Outside

4101 **NOORA** 46 [8] M P Tregoning 3-8-9 (69) R Hills 13/2: 0-202431: Held up wide, rdn to lead well ins
last, going away: nicely bckd: 6 wk abs, AW bow: eff at 7f/1m on gd, gd/soft & polytrack, stiff or sharp/undul trk. **72a**
4925 **RUBAIYAT** 4 [7] G Wragg 3-9-0 (55) S Drowne 9/1: 4325332: Trkd ldrs, led over 1f out, hdd well 1¼ **73a$**
ins last & not pace of wnr: qck reapp: see 4925 & 4421.
3595 **KAURI FOREST** 67 [4] J R Fanshawe 3-9-0 t (83) L Dettori 6/4 FAV: 3223: Mid-div, hdwy over 1f out, 1¼ **70a**
onepace for press ins last: hvly bckd tho' op 5/4: 2 mth abs, AW bow: acts on polytrack but btr 3595, 3237 (fast).
4702 **MASTER THEO** 16 [6] H J Collingridge 3-9-0 (73) J Quinn 6/1: 3333034: Chsd ldrs wide, short of ¾ **69a**
room over 1f out, onepace: see 4702, 2106.
3031} **AUTHORITY** 445 [1]4-9-3 S Sanders 14/1: 24-5: b g Bluebird - Persian Tapestry (Tap On Wood) 1¾ **66a+**
Dwelt, rear, hdwy to press ldrs over 1f out, no impress ins last under a v kind ride: AW bow: mdn rnr up '03 (W
Haggas, subs mdn 4th, rtd 74): eff at 7f, this longer 1m trip likely to suit: handles firm grnd & polytrack: now
qual for h'cap, expect improvement. 2 Jul'03 Newm 7 fm 71- D:
4649 **SUBTLE BREEZE** 19 [3]3-8-9 J Fortune 7/2: 306: Led, hung right from halfway & hdd over 1f out, wknd. 1 **59a**
4542 **LORD OF THE SEA** 24 [10]3-9-0 (59) P Doe 33/1: 0040607: Chsd ldr till over 1f out, sn btn. nk **63a**
4546 **ZURI** 23 [12]3-8-9 (58) N Mackay(3) 40/1: 6400008: Rear & no ch fnl 2f. 5 **49a**
4834 **CHARLIE MASTERS** 9 [11]3-9-0 Lisa Jones 66/1: 009: Al bhd, modest form. 1¼ **51a**
3884 **KAJUL** 55 [5]3-8-9 Paul Eddery 100/1: 00: 10th: Dwelt, keen in rear, btn 3f out, 8 wk abs & AW bow. 4 **38a**
2224 **KINISKA** 124 [2]3-8-9 (60) F P Ferris(3) 40/1: 40-00: 11th: Keen & prom, wknd qckly 3f out, 30 **0a**
virtually p.u., lost action, abs.
11 Ran Time 1m 39.48(3.28) Owned: Mr Khalil Alsayegh Trained: Lambourn

WOLVERHAMPTON Polytrack THURSDAY 07.10.04 Lefthand, Sharp Track

Official Going Standard

4978 1.50 Holiday Inn Garden Court Maiden Auction Stakes Div 1 2yo (E4)
£2947 £842 £421 1m141y aw rnd Inapplicable Inside

4738 **WATCHMYEYES** 15 [7] N P Littmoden 2-8-12 (77) K Fallon 7/4 FAV: 644221: Trkd ldrs trav well & led **86a**
over 2f out, rdn clr but hung badly right dist, just prevailed: nicely bckd: eff at 7f/1m on polytrack, gd & soft,
sharp or gall/undul trk: headgear may suit: see 4738, 4444 & 4052.
4724 **LINDAS COLIN** 16 [4] P W D'Arcy 2-8-9 M Fenton 50/1: 02: b c Xaar - Capable Kate (Alzao) Chsd shd **82a**
ldrs, rdn & short of room over 1f out, styd on well ins last, just denied: AW bow & left debut bhd: Mar foal,
half-brother to wnrs btwn 5/7f: eff at 8.5f on polytrk, sharp trk, cld get further: going the right way.
4913 **MUSICAL DAY** 5 [3] B J Meehan 2-8-7 (1ow) (78) D Holland 15/8: 0002043: Trkd ldrs, rdn & outpcd ½ **79a**
over 2f out, rallied well for press, fin best of all: nicely bckd & would have won this in a few more strides:
crying out for 9f+: acts on fast, gd/soft & polytrack: see 4913, 4242.
4744 **KANGRINA** 15 [2] Sir Mark Prescott 2-8-7 S Sanders 4/1: 54: Led/dsptd lead till over 2f out, 2 **75a**
edged right & no ch press ldr dist: clr of rem: nicely bckd: see 4744.
4375 **MR MARUCCI** 33 [5]2-8-10 T Eaves(3) 50/1: 505: Dwelt & pushed along rear, mod late gains, nvr 6 **68a**
threatened front quartet: see 4207.
  KERGOLAY 3 [8]2-8-9 S Drowne 50/1: 6: b c King's Theatre - Trim Star (Terimon) Dwelt, nvr on 2½ **62a**
terms: Mar foal, E10,000 purchase: half-brother to an unplcd juv & subs 7f 3yo wnr: dam plcd at 12f as a 3yo.
4744 **SOFT FOCUS** 15 [6]2-8-4 C Catlin 25/1: 07: Held up, no impress fnl 2f. 3 **52a**
4703 **MONICAS REVENGE** 17 [11]2-8-4 T P Queally 66/1: 008: Held up, eff over 2f out, sn no impression. 3 **47a**
4325 **DIXIE QUEEN** 36 [12]2-8-6 (1ow)BL (62) S W Kelly 50/1: 500309: Dwelt, hmpd early, nvr a factor. 1¼ **46a**
4242 **MOUNTAIN BREEZE** 40 [1]2-8-3 Lisa Jones 100/1: 00: 10th: Pushed along & handy, btn 4f out, abs. hd **42a**
4083 **GOOD INVESTMENT** 48 [8]2-8-10 (69) G Faulkner 10/1: 3500: 11th: Led 5f out till 3f out, wknd. ¾ **48a**
11 Ran Time 1m 52.42 () Owned: V and J Properties Trained: Newmarket

4979 2.20 Holiday Inn Garden Court Maiden Auction Stakes Div 2 2yo (E4)
£2940 £840 £420 1m141y aw rnd Inapplicable Inside

4484 **CLOONAVERY** 28 [4] J A Osborne 2-8-11 L Dettori 2/1 FAV: 41: Held up, smooth hdwy & led over 1f **81a**
out, edged right, drvn out: hvly bckd, confirmed debut promise: eff at 1m/8.7f, get further: acts on polytrack & gd
grnd, sharp or gall/undul trk: lightly rcd, entitled to prog: see 4484.
4283 **DESPERATION** 38 [13] K R Burke 2-8-8 Darren Williams 10/1: 052: Chsd ldrs, rdn & chall over 2f ¾ **76a**
out, kept on, not pace of wnr: clr of rem: stays 8.7f on polytrack & soft: see 4283.
4600 **TAMORA** 22 [10] A P Jarvis 2-8-4 (65) F Norton 16/1: 6003: Chsd ldrs & led over 2f out till over 3½ **65a**
1f out, not pace of wnr: styd longer 8.7f trip, acts on polytrack: see 3071.
4711 **DANZARE** 17 [11] M P Tregoning 2-8-5 N De Souza(5) 6/1: 04: Mid-div, hmpd after 2f, kept on late, ½ **65a**
nvr a pace to threaten: op 4/1: handles polytrack: see 4711.
4753 **FADAEL** 14 [6]2-8-6 (64) M Fenton 6/1: 063305: Chsd ldrs, short of room after 2f, rdn & hung left 1¾ **63a**
over 1f out, no impress: op 9/1: just btr 4518 & 3798.
4863 **PLENTY CRIED WOLF** 8 [1]2-8-10 (68) T Hamilton(3) 8/1: 004036: Led till over 2f out, sn btn. 1 **65a**
4271 **OVERTOP WAY** 38 [5]2-8-9 T P Queally 66/1: 07: b c Denebola Way - Dada (Ice Reef) Dwelt, rear, ½ **63a**
mod prog, nrst fin: 9,000gns Mar foal, half-brother to wnrs abroad, dam a multiple wnr abroad.
4635 **KERRYS BLADE** 21 [2]2-8-9 (66) G Faulkner 4/1: 056268: Mid-div, btn 2f out: btr 4519. 1½ **60a**
4484 **STOLEN** 28 [3]2-8-8 S Drowne 100/1: 009: b c Groom Dancer - Jezyah (Chief's Crown) Chsd ldrs, 10 **41a**
no impress fnl 3f: cheaply bght May foal, half-brother to a dual French wnr at 6/9f, dam a 7f juv wnr.
3735 **HARRYS SIMMIE** 63 [7]2-8-3 Dale Gibson 100/1: 000: 10th: Strug early & al bhd: abs. ¾ **35a**
4863 **SERGEANT SHINKO** 8 [8]2-8-8 BL L Enstone 100/1: 00: 11th: Pushed in rear, no ch fnl 3f: blnks. nk **39a**
4035 **Magdelaine** 50 [12]2-8-6 J F Egan 80/1:0 4705 **Inagh** 17 [9]2-8-4 C Catlin 25/1:0
13 Ran Time 1m 51.87 () Owned: Mr David N Reynolds and Mr Chris Watkins Trained: Upper Lambourn

---

4980   **2.50 Come Floodlit Racing This Saturday 'premier' Claiming Stakes 2yo (D2)**
£5616 £1728 £864   **6f aw rnd**   Inapplicable   Inside

4907 **FORZEEN** 5 [12] J A Osborne 2-9-7 (80) L Dettori 11/4 FAV: 1400101: Handy & led over 1f out, rdn   **88a**
& hdd ins last, rallied for press & led again cl-home, all out: bckd, op 10/3: qck reapp: eff at 5f/sharp 6f on
firm, gd & both AWs: see 4830 & 3284.
4758 **CORNICHE DANCER** 14 [13] M R Channon 2-8-6 (70) A Culhane 6/1: 0021052: Held up, smooth hdwy   hd   72a
wide to chall over 1f out, rdn & led ins last, hdd cl-home: apprec return to polytrack: see 4436.
4645 **APOLOGIES** 20 [7] B A McMahon 2-9-2 bl (73) G Gibbons 11/2: 0603633: Chsd ldrs, rdn & ch dist, no   1½   77a
extra well ins last: op 7/1: clr of rem: acts on polytrack, gd/soft & soft grnd: see 4645, 4258 & 1107.
4722 **CHIEF DIPPER** 16 [1] P J McBride 2-8-5   T P Queally 100/1: 04: b c Benny The Dip - Cuban Reef   5   51a
(Dowsing) Chsd ldrs & led 4f out till over 2f out, no impress bef dist: cheaply bght Apr foal, half-brother to a 2m
wnr, dam a multiple 7/10f scorer.
4823 **WINDWOOD** 10 [9]2-8-11   S Drowne 66/1: 005: Prom, btn over 1f out: see 4497.   nk   56a
4645 **INDIBRAUN** 20 [6]2-8-4 (70) N Pollard 12/1: 4403406: Led 2f, cl-up till dist: btr 4171 & 4072.   nk   48a
1631 **BOND FINESSE** 152 [8]2-8-8   C Catlin 20/1: 447: Dwelt, mod prog: abs: see 1631.   1   49a
4738 **AFRICAN EMPEROR** 15 [10]2-8-3   F P Ferris(3) 66/1: 608: gr g Highest Honor - Land of Ivory (The   2   38a
Minstrel) Chsd ldrs, btn 2f out: 15,000gns Apr foal, half-brother to a high-class 7f juv wnr, dam a 5f juv wnr &
subs dual 1m 3yo scorer.
4536 **PIDDIES PRIDE** 25 [11]2-7-12 (69) Hayley Turner(3) 7/1: 3204059: Sn rdn & al towards rear, op 5/1.   ½   31a
4644 **BEAUNE** 20 [2]2-9-7   K Fallon 7/2: 360: 10th: Chsd ldrs & led over 2f out till over 1f out, wknd   shd   54a
qckly, eased: nicely bckd: btr 4644 & 4349.
4765 **MAKE US FLUSH** 13 [4]2-8-7 (72) F Norton 10/1: 0210060: 11th: Mid-div, sn outpcd, eased.   5   26a
   Val Disere [5]2-8-11   J F McDonald(3) 33/1:0   4895 **Bodden Bay** 6 [3]2-8-3 D Fox(5) 100/1:0
13 Ran   Time 1m 15.81 ()   Owned: Cavendish Racing   Trained: Upper Lambourn

---

4981   **3.20 Wolverhampton-Racecourse Co Uk Novice Stakes 2yo (D3)**
£4212 £1296 £648   **5f20y aw rnd**   Inapplicable   Inside

4928 **BOND CITY** 5 [1] B Smart 2-9-2 (94) F Lynch 2/1 FAV: 3352501: Trkd ldrs, drvn & led well ins   **94a**
last: nicely bckd, qck reapp: eff at 5f on firm, gd & polytrack, sharp/turning or stiff/gall trk: useful gelding.
4907 **BOLD MINSTREL** 5 [11] M Quinn 2-9-2 (83) F Norton 10/1: 2425562: Al cl-up & rdn/led dist, hdd   ¾   91a
well ins last: qck reapp: v speedy, can win more races: acts on firm, gd/soft & polytrack: see 4907, 4198 & 3097.
4727 **CONNOTATION** 16 [5] P W D'Arcy 2-8-11 BL (72) L Dettori 10/1: 2230163: Held up, kept on late to   3   77a
take 3rd, no pace of front pair: blnks, op 7/1: see 4556 (h'cap).
4921 **DEPRESSED** 5 [2] Andrew Reid 2-8-7   J F Egan 16/1: 0034: Led till dist, no extra: op 20/1, qck   1½   68a
reapp: h'cap company shld suit: see 4921.
4563 **COUNTDOWN** 29 [8]2-9-10 (92) S Sanders 11/4: 3211205: Slow away & sn pushed along, mod gains   2½   77a
wide, nrst fin: well bckd but lost ch with tardy start: blnks omitted after latest: see 4123 & 4065.
4385 **COOL SANDS** 33 [12]2-8-12   Darren Williams 100/1: 006: Slow away, mod gains, nrst fin.   1½   60a
4129* **PARIS TAPIS** 45 [3]2-8-7 (60) J Brennan(7) 20/1: 042217: Prom, btn 2f out: abs: btr 4129 (f/sand).   1¾   50a
4784 **ANNATALIA** 12 [7]2-9-0 (76) K Fallon 100/30: 4610008: Chsd ldrs early, sn outpcd: op 4/1.   nk   56a
3374 **ETERNALLY** 77 [6]2-8-12 VIS (57) R L Moore 25/1: 0353109: Dwelt & sn outpcd: visor, abs.   9   29a
3607 **TOWN HOUSE** 68 [4]2-8-7 (70) A Culhane 40/1: 0210000: 10th: Chsd ldrs, strugg from halfway, abs.   ½   22a
4893 **WATERFRONT DANCER** 6 [10]2-8-12   T P Queally 100/1: 000: 11th: Al outpcd, qck reapp.   ½   25a
4859 **KATIE KILLANE** 8 [9]2-8-7 P J Quinn 100/1: 0000: 12th: Sn struggling & no ch halfway, chkpieces.   1¼   16a
12 Ran   Time 1m 02.41 ()   Owned: Mr R C Bond   Trained: Thirsk

---

4982   **3.50 Sponsor A Race Handicap Stakes 3yo+ 46-55 (F4)**   **[69]**
£3038 £868 £434   **1m141y aw rnd**   Inapplicable   Inside

4367* **NAUTICAL** 34 [8] A W Carroll 6-9-0 (55) L Dettori 4/1 JT FAV: 4302011: Held up, smooth hdwy to   **70a+**
lead over 1f out, readily asserted, val 4L+: op 7/2: recent jumps runner (p.u., nov): eff btwn 7/10f on firm,
gd/soft & polytrack, any trk: see 4367, 2589.
4845 **ZIET DALSACE** 9 [9] A W Carroll 4-8-12 (53) R L Moore 12/1: 0104602: Dwelt, rear, smooth hdwy to   3   59a
chase wnr dist, sn no extra: stays a sharp 8.7f, ideally suited to sltly shorter trips: see 3176 (7f).
4616 **TEMPER TANTRUM** 22 [12] J R Best 6-8-13 p (54) T P Queally 7/1: 0546503: Rear, smooth hdwy from   1¼   57a
over 2f out, onepace for press ins last: rest well covered: stays 8.7f, 7f ideal: see 151 (7f).
4345 **DUBONAI** 35 [6] Andrew Turnell 4-8-13 (54) C Catlin 10/1: 0300104: Led/dsptd lead, went on after   3   51a
2f till over 1f out, no extra: op 14/1: acts on fast & both AWs: see 4132.
4554 **COMMITMENT LECTURE** 24 [2]4-9-0 t (55) S W Kelly 12/1: 00-51465: Trkd ldrs, no extra dist.   2   48a
3395 **DANGER BIRD** 76 [4]4-9-0 (55) K Fallon 8/1: 2441506: Chsd ldrs, btn dist: abs: btr 1223.   5   39a
4378 **SHARP SECRET** 33 [3]6-8-12 (53) Lisa Jones 14/1: 65-51007: Led/dsptd lead early, btn 2f out.   6   26a
4750* **BABY BARRY** 15 [10]7-8-13 (54) S Sanders 4/1 JT FAV: 3020218: Held up in tch, rdn & btn 2f out.   1½   24a
4539 **PHRED** 25 [1]4-8-13 t (54) S Carson 25/1: 2005009: Chsd ldrs, drpd rear from halfway: btr 3922.   2   20a
4539* **FANTASY CRUSADER** 25 [11]5-9-0 p (55) Dane O'Neill 11/2: 0031310: 10th: Sn handy, btn 2f out.   ¾   20a
4707 **PHAROAHS GOLD** 17 [5]6-9-0 BL e (55) Darren Williams 20/1: 0000000: 11th: Bhd 4f out, blnks.   2   16a
4452 **Senior Minister** 30 [13]6-9-0 (55) R Miles(3) 66/1:0   4515 **Killala** 26 [7]4-8-13 (54) L Keniry(3) 33/1:0
13 Ran   Time 1m 51.02 ()   Owned: Mr Gary J Roberts   Trained: Alcester

WOLVERHAMPTON Polytrack THURSDAY 07.10.04 Lefthand, Sharp Track

4983 **4.20 Dine At Dunstall Park Handicap Stakes 3yo+ 56-70 (E3)** **[84]**
£3558 £1095 £547 **1m4f50y aw** **Inapplicable** Inside

4966* **DONT CALL ME DEREK 2** [7] S C Williams 3-9-1 (6ex) (71) R L Moore 5/4 FAV: 0213211: Held up, smooth hdwy to lead 2f out, readily pulled clr despite edging left: nicely bckd, qck reapp: eff at 1m, improvement last twice on step up to 12f: acts on firm, gd/soft & both AWs, any trk: progressive, keep on side. **83a+**
4932 **DOVEDON HERO 5** [8] P J McBride 4-9-7 bl (70) S Sanders 9/2: 6020342: Held up, smooth hdwy to chase wnr dist, sn rdn & no impress but well clr of rem: op 11/2: qck reapp: see 3475, 1889. *4* **73a**
4924 **EFRHINA 5** [9] Mrs Stef Liddiard 4-9-1 (64) F Norton 11/1: 0200343: Rear, rdn & hdwy 3f out, no threat to wnr: qck reapp: see 4924, 4826 & 3867. *6* **58a**
4623 **GIUNCHIGLIO 21** [2] W M Brisbourne 5-9-4 (67) K Fallon 10/1: 6041604: Held up, eff over 2f out, sn no impress: see 4076. *nk* **60a**
4377 **PARTY PLOY 33** [6]6-9-6 (69) Darren Williams 7/1: 1210445: Led till 2f out, sn btn: see 3345. *¾* **61a**
SWEETWATER 129 [1]4-9-7 (70) S Drowne 33/1: 3-306626: b f Goofalik - Safrane (Mister Rock's) Trkd ldr, btn 2f out: jumps fit (p.u., sell h'cap): ex-French, rnr-up earlier in '04: dual wnr '03: all 3 wins at 10f, stays 12f: acts on gd & hvy grnd. *¾* **61a**
4924 **ZEIS 5** [3]4-9-2 t (65) L Fletcher(3) 33/1: 0110007: Held up, nvr nr ldrs: qck reapp. *1¾* **54a**
4623 **MARITIME BLUES 21** [11]4-8-12 (61) A Culhane 14/1: 0010508: Chsd ldrs, no impress when hmpd 3f out. *1½* **48a**
4512 **ARABIAN MOON 26** [12]8-9-6 (69) D Nolan(3) 25/1: 060-1009: Held up wide, btn 3f out: see 3983. *hd* **55a**
4276 **VIN DU PAYS 38** [10]4-9-7 (70) D Sweeney 33/1: 6-000000: 10th: Handy, wknd 2f out: recent jmps rnr. *shd* **56a**
2323 **MISTER ARJAY 120** [5]4-9-7 (70) T Eaves(3) 40/1: 5200-060: 11th: Held up, strug fnl 3f: abs. *½* **55a**
744 **MODESTY BLAISE 224** [4]4-9-3 (66) L Dettori 8/1: 00-1050: 12th: Dwelt, al bhd: nicely bckd, abs. *6* **42a**
12 Ran Time 2m 43.04 () Owned: The Chummy Northerners Trained: Newmarket

4984 **4.50 Come Racing Saturday Night At Dunstall Park Handicap Stakes 3yo+ 56-70 (E3)** **[82]**
£3449 £1061 £531 **6f aw rnd** **Inapplicable** Inside

4785* **BLYTHE SPIRIT 12** [12] R A Fahey 5-9-1 p (69) K Fallon 11/8 FAV: 0006611: Held up, hdwy over 2f out, rdn to lead ins last & in command when eased fnl strides: hvly bckd, op 15/8: eff at 6f/1m on firm, gd/soft & polytrack: well h'capped & in gd heart: see 4785, 1977. **79a**
4452 **BOBS BUZZ 30** [2] S C Williams 4-9-2 (70) S Sanders 9/2: 5352052: Slow away, sn in tch & hdwy to lead over 1f out, not pace of wnr when hdd ins last: op 8/1: see 3791 & 2855. *1¼* **76a**
4091 **SILENT STORM 48** [7] H J Cyzer 4-8-13 (67) F Lynch 14/1: 5/-330023: Al prom & styd on for press fnl 2f, not pace of front pair: clr of rem: 7 wk abs: handles firm, fast & both AWs: shown enough to find a race. *1¼* **69a**
4412 **WILLHECONQUERTOO 31** [5] Andrew Reid 4-9-1 t (69) F Norton 12/1: 5100544: Led/dsptd lead 4f. *5* **56a**
4751 **BORZOI MAESTRO 15** [9]3-8-12 p (67) R Miles(3) 14/1: 5060555: Chsd ldrs, eff dist, sn no extra. *1¾* **49a**
4946 **WHIPPASNAPPER 3** [10]4-8-12 (66) L Dettori 8/1: 0004006: Dwelt, in tch, outpcd fnl 2f: btr 4051. *¾* **46a**
4140 **LANDING STRIP 44** [3]4-8-12 (66) F P Ferris(3) 25/1: 0050007: Led/dsptd lead till dist: abs. *3½* **35a**
4339 **CHAIRMAN BOBBY 35** [11]6-8-10 (64) L Enstone 25/1: 5000008: Chsd ldrs, no impress from halfway. *¾* **31a**
4785 **VAL DE MAAL 12** [13]4-8-11 (65) O Urbina 12/1: 0404609: Held up, rdn & btn 2f out: btr 4126. *½* **30a**
4785 **TALLY 12** [8]4-8-10 (64) G Gibbons 14/1: 4006000: 10th: Chsd ldrs till 3f out. *hd* **28a**
1984 **PHRENOLOGIST 135** [1]4-8-11 (65) S Drowne 50/1: 5613-000: 11th: Prom, btn 2f out, 4 mth abs. *2½* **21a**
4339 **RONNIE FROM DONNY 35** [4]4-8-12 (66) Dane O'Neill 6/1: 5550000: 12th: Dwelt & sn outpcd rear. *5* **7a**
12 Ran Time 1m 15.04() Owned: The Matthewman Partnership Trained: Malton

YORK FRIDAY 08.10.04 Lefthand, Flat,Galloping Track

Official Going GOOD.

4985 **2.05 Acorn Web Offset Stakes Nursery Handicap 2yo (C2)** **[102]**
£9698 £2984 £1492 **6f str** **Good 58** **-13 Slow** Centre

4617* **INGLETON 22** [9] B A McMahon 2-8-3 (77) G Gibbons 9/1: 0411: Al handy trav well, went on halfway & rdn clr over 1f out, decisively: nicely bckd, h'cap bow: eff at 6f, handles fast, likes gd/soft & gd grnd, gall trks: likes to race with/force the pace: progressive colt, looks useful. **94**
4705* **DALDINI 18** [10] J A Osborne 2-8-6 (80) T P Queally 11/1: 412: Pushed along towards rear, styd on from halfway, not pace to trouble wnr: h'cap bow: handles gd & hvy grnd, win more races: see 4705 (mdn, hvy). *3* **87**
4928 **WORD PERFECT 6** [11] M W Easterby 2-8-11 (85) Dale Gibson 11/2: 1150503: Chsd ldrs, styd on for press, not pace of wnr: qck reapp: now stays a gall 6f well: see 4655, 3224 (5f). *1* **89**
4727 **ROWAN LODGE 17** [14] M H Tompkins 2-8-10 (84) P Robinson 16/1: 1210204: Mid-div, kept on for press: return to 7f could suit: see 4509. *1½* **83**
4692 **RAINBOW IRIS 19** [8]2-7-12 (6oh) (66) F P Ferris(3) 33/1: 452065: Led till halfway, no extra over 1f out: stiffish task, gd run: see 4205. *hd* **70**
4717 **BOLD MARC 17** [4]2-8-12 (86) Darren Williams 33/1: 1210646: Mid-div, no extra fnl 1f: prefer 5f. *1½* **79**
4784 **BOLTON HALL 13** [5]2-8-4 (78) P Hanagan 12/1: 1656507: Rear, hdwy halfway, no prog fnl 1f: btr 4509. *shd* **71**
4784 **OCEANICO DOT COM 13** [6]2-8-0 (74) F Norton 14/1: 0213168: Chsd ldrs till btn dist: btr 4551 (5f). *1¼* **63**
4765 **DAHTEER 14** [13]2-9-4 (92) A Culhane 15/2: 1602339: Mid-div, outpcd halfway: btr 4765 (sft). *2½* **73**
4551 **GRAZE ON 25** [2]2-8-9 (83) R Winston 6/1: 21250: 10th: Al rear & little prog: btr 4258 & 3968. *½* **62**
4688 **JOHN FORBES 20** [7]2-8-8 BL (82) T Eaves(3) 66/1: 010000: 11th: Dwelt & al bhd in first time blnks. *½* **59**
3082 **PIPER LILY 91** [12]2-8-4 (78) W Supple 66/1: 51600: 12th: Mid-div, btn 2f out: btr 2241. *nk* **54**
4727 **PROSPECT COURT 17** [15]2-8-2 BL (76) C Catlin 33/1: 3010000: 13th: Mid-div trav well, rdn & btn qckly over 1f out: blnks. *½* **50**
4752* **WISE OWL 15** [3]2-9-0 (88) K Darley 9/2 FAV: 2410: 14th: Chsd ldrs & sn pushed along, no impress over 1f out: hvly bckd on h'cap bow but much btr 4752 (firm). *6* **47**
4810 **AL QUDRA 12** [1]2-9-7 BL (95) J Fortune 20/1: 5105200: 15th: Chsd ldrs, struggling from over 2f out: blnks, top-weight: btr 3800 (stks, firm). *½* **52**
15 Ran Time 1m 13.65 (4.25) Owned: Mr J C Fretwell Trained: Tamworth

YORK FRIDAY 08.10.04 Lefthand, Flat,Galloping Track

4986 **2.40 Garbutt & Elliott Stakes Handicap 3yo+ 71-85 (C2)** **[91]**
£11047 £3399 £1700 **1m2f88y** **Good 58** **-01 Slow** Inside

4931* **GO TECH 6** [13] T D Easterby 4-9-7 (6ex) (84) D Allan 4/1 FAV: 6042111: Mid-div, smooth hdwy over 2f out & led over 1f out, styd on strongly to assert: well bckd, op 9/2: eff at 7f/1m, now suited by 10f on firm & gd grnd, handles gd/soft: gd weight-carrier: useful gelding who has regained best form: see 4931. **93**
4664} **BEAT THE HEAT 365** [12] Jedd O'Keeffe 6-9-0 (77) Leanne Kershaw(7) 66/1: 04/2000-2: b g Salse - Summer Trysting (Alleged) Al handy & led 3f out, rdn & hdd over 1f out, kept on: Flat reapp, 5 mth jmps abs (mdn & h'cap hdle scorer 03/04, rtd 122h at best, 2m, gd & soft): AW rnr-up '03, turf h'cap unplcd, (rtd 76): turf h'cap rnr-up '02: eff at 10/11f, acts on fast, gd/soft & fibresand, any trk: win similar if repeating. *1½* **83**
2 Feb'03 Sout 11 af 81a-80 D: 2 Aug'02 Newm 10 fm 83-80 C: 2 Jul'02 Newc 10.1 g/f 80- D:
4613 **STRETTON 23** [7] J D Bethell 6-9-3 (80) P Robinson 8/1: 3440103: Held up, hdwy when short of room over 2f out, switched & kept on well for press: in gd heart: see 4305. *¾* **85**
4647 **SKI JUMP 21** [9] R A Fahey 4-9-2 vis (79) P Hanagan 10/1: 6060004: Mid-div, styd on onepace for press: imprvd for this drop back to 10f, on a fair mark: see 2197. *¾* **83**
4377 **CRIPSEY BROOK 34** [20]6-9-2 (79) Kim Tinkler 20/1: 2560005: Rear, switched & kept on late, nrst fin: slipped to a handy mark, signs of a revival today: see 1704. *½* **82**
4360 **TRUENO 35** [11]5-9-4 (81) N Mackay(3) 11/1: 1205506: Mid-div, smooth prog 2f out, onepace dist. *shd* **84**
4656 **PETRULA 21** [5]5-9-0 bl (77) N Callan 16/1: 34-26007: Chsd ldrs, no extra over 1f out: see 1586. *nk* **79**
4860 **RYANS FUTURE 9** [19]4-8-12 (75) G Carter 16/1: 0520458: Slow away & rear, eff wide, late gains. *1¼* **75**
4766 **INTRICATE WEB 14** [17]8-8-12 (75) W Supple 16/1: 1000569: Dwelt, sn chsd ldrs, no impress fnl 2f. *hd* **74**
DARGHAN 102 [1]4-9-4 t (81) S Drowne 25/1: 1-466620: 10th: b g Air Express - Darsannda (Kahyasi) Mid-div, no impress over 1f out, t-strap: 3 mth abs, rnr-up in US earlier in '04: ex-Irish, '03 auct mdn wnr for J Oxx at Listowel: winning form at 7f, stays 9f well: acts on gd grnd: wore a t-strap today. *3½* **75**
470} **ALTAY 622** [8]7-9-0 (77) T Hamilton(3) 20/1: 016/116-0: 11th: b g Erins Isle - Aliuska (Fijar Tango) Chsd ldrs, no impress fnl 2f: 7 mth jmps abs (h'cap hdle rnr up 03/04, rtd 135h): dual AW h'cap wnr early '03: dual turf h'cap wnr '02, AW h'cap plcd (rtd 63a): eff btwn 10/14f on fast, soft & polytrk, any trk, likes Lingfield: suited by chkpieces: likes to force the pace. *2* **68**
1 Jan'03 Ling 12 ap 76a-65 C: 1 Jan'03 Ling 13 ap 75a-65 E: 1 Oct'02 Ayr 10 sft 72-70 D: 2 May'02 Ayr 10 g/s 73-72 C: 1 Apr'02 Beve 10 g/f 73-64 D: 1 Jun'01 Beve 10 g/f 62-59 E:
4992*}**TALLDARKNANDSOME 340** [18]5-8-13 bl (76) T E Durcan 50/1: 520661-0: 12th: Rear, eff over 3f out, no impress: reapp. *1½* **65**
4656 **LEWIS ISLAND 21** [10]5-8-12 (75) R L Moore 40/1: 16630/-00: 13th: Slow away, in tch, btn 3f out. *1¾* **62**
2317 **LOVE IN SEATTLE 121** [2]4-8-12 (75) K Darley 25/1: 2-010000: 14th: Dsptd lead 7f, 4 mth abs. *1* **61**
4400 **FOURTH DIMENSION 33** [4]5-9-3 (80) A Nicholls 25/1: 00-04000: 15th: Al towards rear: needs 12f+. *5* **59**
2662 **MEZUZAH 107** [14]4-9-0 (77) Dale Gibson 50/1: 406-0500: 16th: Chsd ldrs 1m: abs, new yard. *3* **52**
4613 **BALTIC BLAZER 23** [16]4-8-12 VIS (75) J Fortune 25/1: 21-500: 17th: Led/dsptd lead 7f, visor. *¾* **49**
4681 **JABAAR 20** [15]6-9-7 (84) K Fallon 9/2: 6250020: 18th: Dwelt, rear, switched wide & no hdwy. *1¼* **56**
4222 **Czarina Waltz 41** [3]5-9-4 (81) R Mullen 20/1:0 4643 **Rasid 21** [6]6-9-0 (77) D Holland 33/1:0
20 Ran Time 2m 13.46 (6.16) Owned: Ryedale Partners No 4 Trained: Malton

4987 **3.15 Betfair Com Handicap Stakes 3yo+ 86-100 (C1)** **[111]**
£13584 £5152 £2576 **7f205y rnd** **Good 58** **+11 Fast** Inside

4916 **NASHAAB 6** [4] P D Evans 7-8-7 vis (90) K Fallon 14/1: 3150001: Pushed along towards rear, hdwy over 2f out & styd on for press to lead well ins last: fast time: qck reapp: eff at 7f/1m on firm, hvy & fibresand, any trk: see 3634, 1598. **98**
4755 **ADAIKALI 15** [1] Sir Michael Stoute 3-8-1 (87) F Norton 10/1: 0212042: Trkd ldrs & smooth prog to lead over 1f out, hdd well ins last & no extra: acts on firm & gd grnd, eff at 1m/10f: can win again: see 4755. *¾* **93**
4463 **LITERATIM 30** [15] L M Cumani 4-8-3 (86) N Mackay(3) 7/1 JT FAV: 41203: Mid-div, hdwy & rdn to chall over 1f out, hung right under press & no extra nr fin: nicely bckd: see 4463, 4067 & 3595. *½* **91**
4516 **PENRITH 27** [14] M Johnston 3-8-0 (86) R Ffrench 20/1: 0350234: Dwelt & hmpd by loose horse at start, rear, styd on wide for press fnl 2f, nrst fin: unlucky after interference early, keep in mind: see 4136. *1* **89+**
4755 **SELECTIVE 15** [8]5-8-5 (88) E Ahern 14/1: 0040465: Chsd ldrs trav well over 2f out, rdn & no extra when hmpd ins last, prob plcd with a clr run: see 4231, 3199. *nk* **90**
4916 **VICIOUS WARRIOR 6** [12]5-8-3 (86) B Swarbrick(5) 11/1: 3022306: Mid-div, styd on onepace fnl 2f. *3* **82**
4531* **CALCUTTA 27** [16]8-9-3 (100) M Hills 10/1: 2030117: Hmpd start & held up, styd on late for press. *¾* **95**
4813 **PANGO 12** [7]5-8-3 (86) R L Moore 14/1: 1112408: Rear, switched & late prog, nvr a threat. *shd* **81**
4652 **MYSTIC MAN 21** [17]6-8-5 (88) P Fessey 16/1: 3043009: Hmpd start, mid-div, btn dist: btr 4322. *2½* **78**
4813 **FLIGHTY FELLOW 12** [13]4-8-11 bl (94) G Carter 10/1: 6240430: 10th: Hmpd by loose horse start, rear, mod late prog. *2½* **79**
4021* **DUNASKIN 51** [18]4-9-1 (98) K Darley 8/1: 5631110: 11th: Hmpd by loose horse start, sn handy & led after 1f till 3f out, sn btn, 7 wk abs: btr 4021. *shd* **83**
4550 **DARK CHARM 25** [19]5-8-3 (86) P Hanagan 33/1: 00-30050: 12th: Rear, rdn 4f out, mod late prog. *1¾* **68**
4208 **VICIOUS KNIGHT 42** [3]6-8-5 (88) A Nicholls 14/1: 0000530: 13th: Led/dsptd lead 5f, sn btn. *shd* **70**
4813* **WELCOME STRANGER 12** [11]4-9-1 (6ex) (98) L Fletcher(3) 7/1 JT FAV: 1212010: 14th: Hmpd start & al bhd: v progressive on firm & fast ground this summer: see 4813 (fast). *nk* **79**
1620 **MISS IVANHOE 153** [9]4-9-3 (100) D Holland 25/1: 2612-060: 15th: Chsd ldrs, btn 3f out: 5 mth abs. *1¼* **78**
4516 **Kelucia 27** [2]3-8-4 (90) C Catlin 40/1:0 2491 **Crafty Fancy 114** [5]3-8-1 (87) J F McDonald(3) 66/1:0
4767 **Northern Desert 14** [6]5-8-7 (90) Darren Williams 100/1:04695 **Mrs Moh 19** [10]3-8-0 (86) Dale Gibson 20/1:U
19 Ran Time 1m 39.59 (3.79) Owned: Mr M W Lawrence Trained: Abergavenny

4988   3.50 Betfair Com E B F Maiden Stakes 2yo (D3)
£5489 £1689 £845   **6f str**   **Good 58**   **-21 Slow**   Centre

MAFAHEEM 0 [3] M Johnston 2-9-0 R Hills 10/1: 1: b c Mujahid - Legend of Aragon (Aragon) Al   87
prom & led over 1f out, rdn & asserted ins last: op 8/1: Feb foal, dam a 5f juv wnr: eff at 6f, 7f+ could suit:
handles gd grnd & a gall trk, goes well fresh: could prove useful.
4787 PIVOTALS PRINCESS 13 [8] B A McMahon 2-8-9 D Holland 5/2 FAV: 332: Led till over 1f out, no   1   78
extra fnl 100y: well bckd & rest well covered: styd longer 6f trip, shld find a race: see 4787 & 3224.
4752 KNOT IN WOOD 15 [10] R A Fahey 2-9-0 T Hamilton (3) 50/1: 063: b c Shinko Forest - Notley Park   5   68
(Wolfhound) Chsd ldrs, not pace of front pair over 1f out: much imprvd eff: 10,000gns Feb foal, half-brother to a
7f 3yo wnr, dam plcd at 7f as a 3yo: eff at 6f, 7f could suit: handles gd grnd: now qual for h'caps.
REAL COOL CAT [4] M Johnston 2-8-9 K Darley 11/4: 4: gr f Storm Cat - Hail Kris (Kris S)   ½   61
Dwelt, sn chsd ldrs, no impress over 1f out: nicely bckd, shorter priced stablemate of wnr: $100,000 Feb foal,
half-sister to a US Gr 2 6.5f wnr, dam a multiple US scorer.
LAKE CAREZZA [5]2-9-0 E Ahern 5/1: 5: b c Stravinsky - May Wedding (French Deputy) Towards   1   63+
rear, late hdwy under kind ride, nvr a threat: nicely bckd, op 7/1: 110,000gns Apr first foal, dam a US mid-dist
wnr: looks sure to apprec 7f+ & rate higher.
4770 GOLDEN SQUARE 14 [9]2-9-0 J Fortune 12/1: 06: Trkd ldrs, no impress over 1f out.   1¾   58
4770 RUMAN 14 [1]2-9-0 N Callan 66/1: 07: Trkd ldrs trav well, hmpd halfway, no extra dist.   1   55
XEBEC [12]2-9-0 N De Souza(5) 10/1: 8: Swerved right start, chsd ldrs, no impress over 1f out.   shd   54
TELEGRAM SAM [11]2-9-0 P Hanagan 16/1: 9: Dwelt, sn outpcd & al rear.   1¼   51
LOBENGULA [7]2-9-0 C Catlin 100/1: 0: 10th: Slow away & al bhd.   ½   49
4670 LOVE FROM RUSSIA 20 [2]2-9-0 F Lynch 100/1: 0000: 11th: Cl-up, btn over 1f out.   6   32
RUSSIANNIGHTINGALE [13]2-9-0 J D O'Reilly(7) 66/1: 0: 12th: Swerved right start & sn strug.   21   0
MOONLIGHT APPEAL [6]2-8-9 T Eaves(3) 66/1: 0: 13th: Dwelt & al well bhd.   28   0
13 Ran   Time 1m 14.12 (4.72)   Owned: Mr Hamdan Al Maktoum   Trained: Middleham

4989   4.25 Parsonage Country House Hotel Handicap Stakes 3yo+ 56-70 (E3)   [77]
£6037 £1858 £929   **5f str**   **Good 58**   **-09 Slow**   Centre

4930 PLAYFUL DANE 6 [18] W S Cunningham 7-9-11 (6ex) (74) D Tudhope(5) 5/2 FAV: 5013121: Sn led, rdn   82
clr dist, held on well cl-home: hvly bckd under a 6lb pen, op 3/1, qck reapp: stays 7f, best at 5/6f on firm & gd,
loves a flat/gall trk: best up with/forcing the pace: fast improving, keep on side.
4785 PRINCE OF GOLD 13 [14] R Hollinshead 4-9-0 p (63) K Fallon 8/1: 0000532: Dwelt, hdwy from halfway   nk   70
& styd on well for press ins last, just failed: imprvd last twice at 5/6f, could win soon: see 4785, 2324.
4751 BYO 16 [8] M Quinn 6-9-5 (68) F Norton 16/1: 0134043: Al handy & ch 2f out, kept on for press,   nk   74
not pace of wnr: see 3372, 1886.
4654 KINGS COLLEGE BOY 21 [4] R A Fahey 4-9-5 vis (68) Dale Gibson 12/1: 0102404: Rdn towards rear,   1   71
styd on well for press, nrst fin: see 4107.
4946* OEUF A LA NEIGE 16 [16]4-9-11 (6ex) (74) O Urbina 8/1: 6150115: Pushed along in rear, hdwy when   nk   76
forced to switch 2f out, nrst fin: edged under 6lb pen, qck reapp: eff at 5f, stiffer trk/6f will suit: see 4946.
4785 WINTHORPE 13 [6]4-9-4 P (67) R Winston 11/1: 0544306: Chsd ldrs, onepace for press dist: chkpcs.   hd   68
4700 PARKSIDE PURSUIT 18 [7]6-9-7 (70) R L Moore 16/1: 1310007: Pushed along towards rear, kept on.   2½   63
4700 PRINCE CYRANO 18 [9]5-9-7 (70) R Mullen 25/1: 0352008: Dwelt, late gains, nvr a dngr: btr 4070.   hd   62
4618 ROMAN MISTRESS 22 [12]4-9-3 bl (66) D Allan 33/1: 5041009: Led 1f, no extra fnl 1f: btr 4038.   nk   57
4754 CALYPSO DANCER 15 [10]4-8-13 VIS (62) K Darley 33/1: 4240000: 10th: Trkd ldrs, edged right & btn   1   50
dist: visor: see 4754.
4870 BLUE MAEVE 9 [2]4-8-13 (62) S Righton 14/1: 1500130: 11th: Dwelt, mod prog: best dominating.   ½   48
4603 HARRISONS FLYER 23 [1]3-9-1 P (64) P Hanagan 25/1: 0202U00: 12th: Mid-div, btn over 1f out: ½   48
cheek pieces: btr 4380 (mdn).
4946 CERULEAN ROSE 4 [15]5-9-6 (69) J Fortune 16/1: 0302400: 13th: Dwelt & bhd, no impress.   nk   52
4785 Sharp Hat 13 [19]10-8-13 (62) A Culhane 33/1:0   4618 Aahgowangowan 22 [3]5-9-0 t(63) P Makin(5) 18/1:0
4646 College Queen 21 [17]6-8-12 (61) A Nicholls 28/1:0   4984 Tally 1 [20]4-8-12 (61) L Fletcher(1) 40/1:0
4514 Izmail 27 [13]5-9-4 vis(67) S Drowne 25/1:0   1572 Demolition Molly 156 [5]3-9-7 t p(70) P McCabe 50/1:0
19 Ran   Time 1m 0.16 (3.36)   Owned: Ann and David Bell   Trained: Yarm

4990   5.00 Green Howards Cup Apprentice Handicap Stakes 3yo+ 56-70 (E3)   [84]
£4781 £1471 £736   **1m3f198y**   **Good 58**   **-21 Slow**   Inside

4899 SCOTT 7 [3] J Jay 3-8-4 (60) D Fox 12/1: 0603141: Trkd ldrs & led over 2f out, held on well for   68
press ins last: eff around 12f on fast & fibresand, prob handles polytrack: handles a sharp or gall trk: see 4092.
4931 NIGHT SIGHT 6 [16] Mrs S Lamyman 7-9-7 (70) D Tudhope(3) 11/1: 4151452: Trkd ldrs trav well & ch   1   76
over 1f out, not pace of wnr ins last: qck reapp: see 4377.
4931 STALLONE 6 [4] N Wilson 7-9-3 (66) P Mathers(3) 12/1: 3600663: Swerved badly right start & rear,   ¾   71
hdwy when short of room over 2f out, kept on well ins last: imprvd eff, qck reapp: see 1781.
4623 DANCE TO MY TUNE 22 [13] M W Easterby 3-8-11 (67) D Fentiman(3) 13/2 JT FAV: 0412424: Mid-div,   hd   71
hdwy to chall dist, no extra ins last: bckd: styd longer 12f trip: remains in fine form: see 4623.
4623 CALATAGAN 22 [14]5-9-6 (69) M Savage 16/1: 3155205: Handy, led 3f out till 2f out, no extra.   2   70
4775 SMART JOHN 14 [5]4-9-7 (70) B Swarbrick 7/1: 3541306: Mid-div, onepace fnl 2f: see 4274.   2½   67
4771 ARCHIE BABE 14 [8]8-8-13 (62) P Makin 16/1: 0150007: Chsd ldrs, no extra dist: loves soft/hvy.   1   58
4721 CHARMATIC 17 [11]3-8-7 (63) Rory Moore(3) 16/1: 1545068: Keen in rear, mod late gains, no threat.   hd   58
3929 PONT NEUF 56 [15]4-9-4 t (67) Natalia Gemelova(3) 13/2 JT FAV: 5110239: Mid-div, hdwy over 3f out,   ½   61
no prog over 1f out: bckd, abs: btr 3929 & 3829.
4327 MIDDLETHORPE 37 [7]7-9-2 bl (65) N De Souza 7/1: 55-15600: 10th: Chsd ldrs, btn over 1f out.   ½   58
4327 DRAMATIC QUEST 37 [10]7-9-2 p (65) A Mullen(3) 16/1: 224-0000: 11th: Towards rear, nvr a threat.   shd   58
4899* BROUGHTON KNOWS 7 [1]7-8-9 (6ex)bl (58) A Kirby(5) 7/1: 1246410: 12th: Dwelt & bhd, little hdwy.   ¾   50
4867 DARK DAY BLUES 9 [6]3-8-0 (56) M Halford 50/1: 5500000: 13th: Mid-div, eff 4f out, btn 2f out.   1¾   46

YORK FRIDAY 08.10.04 Lefthand, Flat,Galloping Track

4630 **JIDIYA 22** [2]5-9-3 (66) N Chalmers 33/1: 0020330: 14th: Trkd ldrs, strug fnl 3f: btr 4630. ½ 55
4406 **Melodian 32** [9]9-9-1 bl(64) M Lawson(3) 25/1:0
4132 **Disabuse 46** [12]4-8-7 (7oh)P(49) Stacey Renwick(5) 66/1:0
16 Ran Time 2m 36.19(9.39) Owned: Mr Keith Wills Trained: Newmarket

WARWICK SATURDAY 09.10.04 Lefthand, Sharp, Turning Track

Official Going Good/Soft

4991

11.25 Hannah's Late Birthday Bash Maiden Claiming Stakes 3yo+ (H5)
£1498 £428 £214 **1m4f134y** **Good/Soft 75** **-20 Slow** Inside

4300 **RICHIE BOY 40** [10] V Smith 3-8-13 (58) Dane O'Neill 11/2: 0-06001: Made all, rdn & press over 1f out, drvn & styd on strongly: 6 wk abs, new stable, bckd: claimed for 5,000: apprec step up to 12.6f, acts on gd/sft ground: goes well fresh: see 3480. 57
4857 **ZULETA 10** [5] J G M O'Shea 3-8-8 vis (47) B Swarbrick(5) 100/30 FAV: 0622242: Handy, chsd wnr over 3f out & chall over 1f out, drvn & no extra ins last: claimed for 5,000: see 4857, 4671. *1* 50
4671 **CALOMERIA 21** [4] R M Beckett 3-8-8 (50) N Chalmers(3) 11/2: 4030033: Chsd wnr 1m, styd on onepace for press fnl 2f: also bhd this wnr latest: claimed for 5,000: see 4671, 3275 (blnks, 2m). ¾ 49
4828 **DARK SOCIETY 12** [3] A W Carroll 6-9-7 (52) P Doe 9/2: 000/00/-64: Dwelt, held up, styd on for press fnl 2f: clr rem: stays 12f in banded company: see 4828. ¾ 53
4791 **MAID THE CUT 14** [6]3-8-8 (45) N Pollard 22/1: 0-400565: Prom, rdn & btn over 1f out, longer trip. *8* 37
4364 **BLACK LEGEND 36** [12]5-9-3 (45) J F Egan 4/1: 2/0-24056: Held up, rdn & btn over 1f out: see 4045. *hd* 37
4834 **PORT SODRICK 12** [2]3-8-10 (55) Ashleigh Horton(7) 16/1: 664507: Held up, only mod prog & nvr dngr. *1¾* 36
3055 **CLOUDINGSWELL 93** [13]3-8-8 (48) N De Souza(5) 20/1: 6-066448: Chsd ldrs, rdn & btn over 2f out. *9* 22
3452] **CIRCLE OF WOLVES 789** [11]6-9-7 (45) S Whitworth 20/1: 00/50/00/-9: ch g Wolfhound - Misty Halo (High Top) Slow away & always rear: long abs, 5 mth jmps abs (mod form, h'cap hdle). *1¾* 25
4826 **OBSERVATION 12** [9]3-8-8 A Daly 100/1: 0000: 10th: Dwelt & held up, al rear & no ch fnl 3f, lngr trip. *dist* 0
Diwan 1446 [8]6-9-7 M Lawson(5) 80/1:0 4834 **Jimmy Hay 12** [7]3-8-7 A Nicholls 100/1:0
12 Ran Time 2m 51.42 (12.12) Owned: Mr Tony Stafford Trained: Newmarket

4992

11.55 Ascott Tri-Banded Stakes 3yo 0-45 (H5)
£1523 £435 £218 **1m22y rnd** **Good/Soft 75** **-24 Slow** Inside

1246 **BACKLASH 173** [9] A W Carroll 3-8-9 (40) S W Kelly 11/2: 0-000551: Hld up, hdwy to lead ins last, drvn out: abs, well bckd: apprec step up to 1m on gd/soft ground & goes well fresh. 48
4857 **LIVIA 10** [8] J G Portman 3-9-0 vis (45) C Catlin 66/1: 0600002: Sn pshd along in tch, styd on for press fnl 2f, not pace of wnr: eff at 1m on polytrk & gd/sft ground: see 815. *1¾* 49
4901* **ELSINORA 7** [10] A G Juckes 3-9-0 vis (45) Dane O'Neill 3/1 FAV: 3524213: Trkd ldr, rdn & led over 2f out, hung right under press over 1f out & looked reluctant, hdd ins last: new yard: stays 1m, best at 7f. *hd* 48
4372 **JAOLINS 35** [14] P G Murphy 3-8-9 (40) D Kinsella 25/1: 0006504: Mid-div, styd on onepace for press fnl 2f, nvr threat: stays 1m in banded company: acts on polytrk & gd/sft ground: see 606. *2½* 38
4113 **NINA FONTENAIL 49** [13]3-9-0 (45) R Havlin 14/1: 0005425: Mid-div, styd on for press, nvr pace to chall. ¾ 42
4901 **ROVING VIXEN 7** [1]3-8-9 bl (40) R Miles(3) 25/1: 3340056: Slow away & bhd, mod prog: qck reapp. *shd* 37
4847 **SPEED RACER 11** [15]3-9-0 (45) Kim Tinkler 33/1: 5036307: Rear, late gains, nvr a threat to ldrs. *1½* 39
4794 **PAPPY 14** [3]3-8-9 (40) B Swarbrick(5) 9/1: 0-403008: Handy, rdn & btn dist: btr 3900 (g/s). *hd* 33
4507 **PRIMATECH 28** [7]3-9-0 p (45) P Makin(5) 33/1: 0000049: Trkd ldrs, btn 2f out: see 4507. ½ 37
4507 **ROMAN THE PARK 28** [2]3-9-0 (45) P M Quinn 9/1: 3134320: 10th: Dwlet, held up, efft wide, btn dist. *nk* 36
4834 **LA CALERA 12** [5]3-9-0 bl (45) O Urbina 33/1: 5330050: 11th: Rdn to lead, hdd over 2f out, fdd: btr 4834. *hd* 35
4904 **NOBLE DESERT 7** [12]3-8-9 (40) J F Egan 7/1: 0-050000: 12th: Mid-div, btn over 1f out. *1¼* 27
4370 **MOSCOW MARY 35** [4]3-8-9 (40) S Whitworth 8/1: 0-000000: 13th: Always bhd, longer trip. *1½* 24
4794 **Fabuloso 14** [16]3-8-9 (40) I Mongan 22/1:0
4793 **Suitcase Murphy 14** [11]3-9-0 (45) N Chalmers(3) 25/1:0
32 **Reckless Moment 330** [6]3-9-0 (45) L Enstone 8/1:0 4707 **Seven Shirt 19** [17]3-9-0 (45) P Doe 18/1:0
17 Ran Time 1m 44.79 (7.99) Owned: One Under Par Racing Trained: Alcester

4993

12.25 World Cargo Banded Stakes 3yo+ 0-45 (H5)
£1505 £430 £215 **1m22y rnd** **Good/Soft 75** **-18 Slow** Inside

4660 **BALLARE 21** [7] Bob Jones 5-9-2 vis (45) T Williams 11/4 FAV: 0400021: Chsd ldrs, edged right & chall over 1f out sn led, drvn out: recent jmps rnr (t.o., nov hdle): eff btwn 7f/10f on fast, gd & polytrk. 50
4902 **ENCOUNTER 7** [13] J Hetherton 8-9-2 (45) L Keniry(3) 6/1: 5005352: Held up, drvn & styd on fnl 2f. *nk* 49
4904 **VIZULIZE 7** [14] A W Carroll 5-9-2 (40) D Nolan(3) 18/1: 5004003: Prom, led over 2f out, edged right & hdd over 1f out, kept on: acts on fast, gd/sft & polytrk: see 969. *nk* 48
1755 **PRINTSMITH 147** [8] J R Norton 7-9-2 (45) J Bramhill 14/1: 2105004: Twds rear, late gains. *2½* 43
2589 **HAPPY CAMPER 112** [6]4-9-2 (45) S Whitworth 28/1: 0653005: Held up & keen, late gains, nrst fin: abs. *4* 35
4768 **THE LOOSE SCREW 15** [10]6-9-2 p (45) S W Kelly 7/1: 0000556: Led/dsptdlead till over 2f out, hung left over 1f out & btn ins last. ½ 34
4036 **SINJAREE 52** [4]6-9-2 (40) R Thomas(3) 9/2: 1060007: Mid-div, rdn & nvr pace to chall ldrs, 7 wk abs. ½ 33
3487 **ROCKY REPPIN 75** [16]4-9-2 (45) K Pierrepont(7) 33/1: 0003408: Held up, rdn 3f out, btn over 1f out. *hd* 32
2503 **KING OF MEZE 114** [17]3-8-13 T (40) A Beech(3) 22/1: 06009: Held up, rdn & btn 2f out, abs, t-strap. *1¾* 29
1285 **MURAQEB 172** [2]4-9-2 bl (45) R Havlin 50/1: 0005000: 10th: Hled up, rdn & no impress fnl 2f: 6 mth abs. *3* 23
4902 **PERERIN 7** [1]3-8-13 VIS (45) G Gibbons 12/1: 0003060: 11th: Keen & prom, btn 2f out: vis: btr 3712. *2½* 18
4261 **ST JUDE 41** [5]4-9-2 (45) J Edmunds 33/1: 00-000: 12th: Led early, strugg fnl 3f, 6 wk abs: btr 4261 (mdn) *hd* 17
4090 **Jamestown 50** [15]7-9-2 (45) L Fletcher(3) 20/1:0 4809} **Green Ginger 355** [11]8-9-2 (45) C Catlin 33/1:0
457 **Fridays Takings 261** [3]5-9-2 bl(40) Paul Eddery 16/1:0

4595 **Big Tom** 25 [9]3-8-13 BL(40) D Tudhope(5) 20/1:0

16 Ran   Time 1m 44.34 (7.54)   Owned: The Ballare Partnership   Trained: Newmarket

4994   **12.55 Nash Mcdermott Banded Stakes 3yo+ 0-45 (H5)**
£1575 £450 £225   **7f26y rnd**   **Good/Soft 75**   **+09 Fast**   Inside

4707 **ZHITOMIR** 19 [7] M Dods 6-9-7 (50) S W Kelly 5/2 FAV: 6164021: Held up, hdwy & tkn wide over 2f   **60**
out, led dist & rdn to assert: eff at 6/7f on firm & soft: apprec drop to banded grade: see 3324.
4408 **THE OLD SOLDIER** 33 [1] A Dickman 6-9-7 (50) A Beech(3) 11/2: 00-00202: Led after 2f out, rdn &   2½   **54**
hdd dist, not pace of wnr ins last: acts on firm & gd/sft ground: see 2615.
4902 **CAERPHILLY GAL** 7 [14] P L Gilligan 4-9-7 (50) D Fox(5) 9/2: 0000123: Chsd ldrs, styd on onepace   2   **50**
for press: acts on fast & gd/sft ground: see 4902, 4795.
4739 **CHANTELLE** 17 [11] S Kirk 4-9-7 (50) J F Egan 12/1: 0050004: Mid-div, mod prog, no dngr.   3½   **43**
4739 **MILLFIELDS DREAMS** 17 [13]5-9-7 P (50) D Nolan(3) 10/1: 0060005: Led till over 5f out, fdd fnl 2f: chkpcs.   1   **41**
4739 **ELLIOTS CHOICE** 17 [2]3-9-5 (50) L Keniry(3) 11/1: 2405006: Chsd ldrs, lost place from halfway.   nk   **40**
3672 **TICTACTOE** 67 [8]3-9-5 VIS (50) M Halford(7) 33/1: 361-6607: Dwelt, rear, wide over 3f out, sn btn: abs.   4   **32**
4587 **SAINTLY PLACE** 25 [12]3-9-5 (50) R Fitzpatrick 14/1: 0-00528: Chsd ldrs, btn 3f out, new stable.   ½   **31**
4408 **REDOUBTABLE** 33 [5]13-9-6 (49) A Nicholls 12/1: 0400409: Chsd ldrs till over 1f out: btr 4211 (6f).   ½   **29**
4041 **GO FREE** 51 [3]3-9-4 (49) P Makin(5) 22/1: 00-25050: 10th: Bhd from halfway, 7 wk abs: btr 2997 (AW).   3   **23**
4709 **INK IN GOLD** 19 [10]3-9-5 (50) G Parkin 33/1: 05000: 11th: Slow away, sn strugg.   nk   **23**
4504 **Sophrano** 28 [9]4-9-7 (50) P Bradley 16/1:0   4546 **Romantic Drama** 26 [6]3-9-4 T(49) S Righton 50/1:0
13 Ran   Time 1m 27.05 (4.65)   Owned: Mr M J K Dods   Trained: Darlington

4995   **1.25 Shipston Banded Stakes 3yo+ 0-45 (H5)**
£1484 £424 £212   **5f rnd**   **Good/Soft 75**   **-41 Slow**   Inside

3667 **JOYCES CHOICE** 67 [11] J S Wainwright 5-9-0 VIS (45) P Mathers(5) 12/1: 4000261: Prom, drvn & led   **49**
well ins last, all out: 2 mth abs: eff at 5f on firm & soft ground, any trk: goes well fresh: see 1179.
3974 **FAIRGAME MAN** 55 [13] J S Wainwright 6-9-0 p (45) G Parkin 8/1: 5100002: Chsd ldrs, drvn to chall   nk   **48**
when short of room dist, styd on, just held: 8 wk abs, stablemate of wnr: see 3180.
3974 **WHINHILL HOUSE** 55 [5] D W Barker 4-9-0 (45) L Enstone 50/1: 630-0003: ch g Paris House -   nk   **47**
Darussalam (Tina's Pet) Chsd ldrs, rdn & led over 1f out, hdd well ins last: 8 wk abs; AW h'cap wnr '03, turf plcd
(rtd 45): AW mdn plcd '02 (rtd 61a): eff at 5f on fibresand & gd/sft ground.
1 Feb'03 Sout 5 af 61a-54 E:
4370 **LITTLE FLUTE** 35 [10] T Keddy 3-9-0 (45) J P Guillambert(3) 10/1: 0001664: Sn pushed along, kept   shd   **47**
on well from over 1f out: acts on fibresand & gd/sft ground: not btn far in a tight fin: see 1312.
4905 **FLAPDOODLE** 7 [4]6-9-0 bl (45) Dane O'Neill 8/1: 5000305: Led 3f, rdn & no extra well ins last.   ¾   **45**
4038 **RED LEICESTER** 52 [12]4-9-0 vis (45) S W Kelly 22/1: 1605006: Cl up, ch/bmpd dist, no extra ins last.   1   **42**
4905 **CHATSHOW** 7 [1]3-9-0 (45) D Nolan(3) 5/1 FAV: 0500037: Chsd ldrs till over 1f out, no extra fnl 100yds.   nk   **41**
4368 **DIAMOND RING** 36 [7]5-9-0 (45) I Mongan 11/2: 0362408: Pushed along towards rear, late prog.   shd   **41**
2720 **PLAYFUL SPIRIT** 106 [6]5-9-0 vis (45) J Edmunds 0/1: 0300009: Chsd ldrs, outpcd fnl 2f: 3 mth abs.   1¼   **37**
4368 **CHORUS** 36 [9]7-9-0 bl (45) R Havlin 16/1: 06-03000: 10th: Mid-div, lost pl halfway, no impress.   shd   **37**
2756 **RADLETT LADY** 105 [8]3-9-0 (45) M Howard(7) 40/1: 00000: 11th: Chsd ldrs 3f: 3 mth abs: see 3667.   nk   **36**
4618 **MYSTERY PIPS** 23 [3]4-9-0 vis (45) Kim Tinkler 7/1: 4004300: 12th: Chsd ldrs, no impress over 1f out.   ½   **34**
4508 **John Ogroats** 28 [16]6-9-0 bl(45) L Keniry(3) 20/1:0   3974 **Lakelands Lady** 55 [15]4-9-0 (45) P Makin(5) 28/1:0
4043 **Levelled** 51 [14]10-9-0 (45) A Nicholls 25/1:0   889 **Rellim** 201 [2]5-9-0 (45) L Fletcher(3) 16/1:0
16 Ran   Time 1m 03.09 (5.99)   Owned: Mrs Jean Neilson   Trained: Malton

4996   **1.55 Rht 40th Anniversary Median Auction Maiden Stakes 2yo (H5)**
£1537 £439 £220   **7f26y rnd**   **Good/Soft 75**   **-09 Slow**   Inside

4617 **MOON FOREST** 23 [6] P W Chapple Hyam 2-9-0 Paul Eddery 8/11 FAV: 241: Led/dsptd lead, went on   **82**
over 2f out, rdn & asserted ins last, styd on strongly: suited by return to 7f, shld get 1m: acts on gd & gd/sft.
4918 **LADY DORIS WATTS** 7 [11] M R Channon 2-8-9 C Catlin 7/2: 02: Chsd wnr, chall 2f out, outpvcd by   2   **72**
wnr ins last: styd longer 7f trip & will get further: acts on gd/sft ground: see 4918 (6f).
4704 **VALIANT ACT** 19 [4] D M Simcock 2-8-9 L Keniry(3) 10/1: 63: b f Brave Act - Jungle Story (Alzao)   shd   **72**
Chsd ldrs, rdn & kept on fnl 2f: Apr foal, 18,000gns Mar foal: half sister to a plcd 7f 3yo performer: dam a 7f juv
wnr & subs plcd at 10f: eff at 7f, shld apprec 1m on this evidence: acts on gd/sft ground: going the right way.
4896 **JUST CLIFF** 8 [1] W R Muir 2-9-0 J F Egan 66/1: 04: b c Handsome Ridge - Justfortherecord   3½   **70**
(Forzando) In tch, keen, styd on for press fnl 2f, no threat: 5,000gns Feb foal, hlaf brother to a wnr abroad: dam
unplcd: handles gd/sft grnd: improved effort on this turf bow.
4852 **HONOUR HIGH** 10 [7]2-9-0 Dane O'Neill 14/1: 005: Chsd ldrs, no impress fnl 2f, drop in trip.   7   **58**
4842 **GLADS IMAGE** 11 [12]2-8-9 S W Kelly 50/1: 06: Mid-div, rdn & btn over 2f out, drop in trip.   ¾   **52**
PIPER GENERAL 0 [5]2-9-0 Derek Nolan(7) 40/1: 7: Slow away & always bhd, debut.   shd   **57**
3600 **A QUI LE TOUR** 70 [3]2-9-0 S Whitworth 100/1: 008: Pshd along twds rear, only mod prog, 10 wk   ½   **56**
abs.
BRUMAIRE 0 [2]2-9-0 I Mongan 12/1: 0: Slow away & nvr a factor.   1¼   **53**
SO ELEGANT 0 [13]2-8-9 O Urbina 33/1: 0: 10th: Mid-div, no impress fnl 2f.   1¼   **45**
PADDY OLIVER 0 [14]2-9-0 A Nicholls 28/1: 0: 11th: Prom 4f, sn strugg.   3½   **43**
2287 **DAVALA** 123 [8]2-9-0 N Pollard 80/1: 000: 12th: Chsd ldrs 4f, sn btn, 4 mth abs.   5   **34**
4769 **WITCHY VIBES** 15 [9]2-8-9 S Righton 100/1: 00: 13th: Bhd halfway, longer trip.   5   **20**
13 Ran   Time 1m 28.39(5.99)   Owned: Collins Deal Harrison-Allan Chapple-Hyam   Trained: Newmarket

YORK SATURDAY 09.10.04 Lefthand, Flat, Galloping Track

Official Going GOOD.

4997 **1.35 Symphony Group Median Auction Maiden Stakes Div 1 2yo (E3)**
£5346 £1645 £823 **7f205y rnd** **Good 43** **-31 Slow** Inside

4722 **MAIDANNI 18** [3] Saeed bin Suroor 2-9-0 L Dettori 4/5 FAV: 41: Made most, held on gamely fnl 1f, drvn out: hvly bckd: made most of prev experience, eff over 1m on gd & firm grnd: shld progress further. **85**
AYLMER ROAD [1] P F I Cole 2-9-0 K Fallon 6/1: 2: b c Groom Dancer - Pekan's Pride (Sri Pekan) Chsd ldrs, imprvd to chase wnr 2f out, styd on well & only just btn on debut: op 5/1: Feb first foal, dam a 7f juv wnr: sire a high-class mid-dists performer: eff at 1m on gd grnd, clrly runs well fresh: decent debut. ½ **83**
TICKI TORI [11] Julian Poulton 2-8-9 N Callan 33/1: 3: b f Vettori - Lamees (Lomond) Held up, imprvd halfway, styd on well fnl 1f & nrst fin on debut: May foal, cost 4,800gns: half-sister to 7f juv wnrs Lomberto & Dumoni: sire a top-class miler: eff at 1m on gd grnd: pleasing start, will learn from this & win races. 1½ **75**
4611 **SELIKA 24** [5] M H Tompkins 2-9-0 BL P Robinson 25/1: 004: ch c Daggers Drawn - Hint of Romance (Treasure Kay) Dwelt, keen & recovered to chase ldrs, onepcd fnl 1f on h'cap qual run: tried in blnks: E7,000 Apr foal: half-brother to hdle wnr Dottie Digger: dam a 6/7f wnr, sire a high-class juv: eff at 1m on gd grnd. 2 **76**
4558 **INDONESIA 26** [16]2-9-0 K Darley 28/1: 005: Front rank, ev ch till left bhd 1.5f out: clr rem. 1¾ **73**
4722 **PENNY WEDDING 18** [14]2-8-9 W Ryan 14/1: 06: b f Pennekamp - Eilean Shona (Suave Dancer) Chsd ldrs, wknd 1.5f out: Feb first foal: dam a 9f winning juv, subs scored over 2m: sire a top-class miler. 7 **54**
VIRGINS TEARS [12]2-8-9 A McCarthy 20/1: 7: Chsd ldrs 6.5f, wknd on debut. *nk* **53**
WOODFORD CONSULT [7]2-8-9 P Mulrennan(3) 100/1: 8: Nvr btr than mid-div on racecourse bow. 1¾ **49**
4381 **MISS BEAR 35** [13]2-8-9 D McGaffin 40/1: 09: Keen & trkd ldrs 6f, sn wknd. *hd* **49**
NAVAL ATTACHE [10]2-9-0 T P Queally 40/1: 0: 10th: Nvr btr than mid-div on debut. *nk* **53**
4376 **LIGHTENING FIRE 35** [15]2-9-0 T E Durcan 100/1: 0000: 11th: Rdn in rear, nvr nr ldrs. 1¼ **50**
4866 **SAKE 10** [8]2-9-0 Dale Gibson 100/1: 00: 12th: Chsd ldrs 5f, sn wknd. 1½ **47**
4829 **OUR KES 12** [9]2-8-9 (65) A Culhane 7/1: 00040: 13th: Al rear: btr 4829. ¾ **40**
MISTERS SISTER [2]2-8-9 M Fenton 33/1: 0: 14th: Slowly away, al rear on debut. 2½ **35**
Madame Fatale [4]2-8-9 P Hanagan 66/1:0 4784 **Hamburg Springer 14** [6]2-9-0 (45) J Quinn 100/1:0
16 Ran Time 1m 41.75 (5.95) Owned: Godolphin Trained: Newmarket

4998 **2.05 Listed Newton Investment Management Rockingham Stakes 2yo (A1)**
£16250 £5000 £2500 **6f str** **Good 43** **-02 Slow** Centre

4928 **MOTH BALL 7** [2] J A Osborne 2-8-11 (92) D Holland 15/2: 3103141: Chsd ldr, imprvd to lead ent fnl 1f, styd on strongly, rdn out: bckd from 10/1: eff at 5/6f on gd & firm grnd: continues rapid improvement. **111**
4684 **NUFOOS 21** [8] M Johnston 2-8-6 (98) R Hills 6/1: 3100122: Chsd ldrs, kept on well for press fnl 1f, not pace of wnr: clr of 3rd: tough & useful performer: see 4684 & 4258. 1¼ **100**
4121* **WOODCOTE 47** [4] C G Cox 2-8-11 (93) L Dettori 10/1: 13: Chsd ldrs, kept on fnl 1f, not pace of front 2: 7 wk abs: fine run on only 2nd start over this longer 6f trip: clrly useful, see 4121 (mdn, debut). 2½ **98**
1466+**JOSEPH HENRY 162** [3] M Johnston 2-8-11 (100) K Darley 9/1: 114: Hmpd start, recovered to chase ldrs, ev ch till onepcd ins fnl 1f: long abs & an encouraging rtn after injury problems: stays 6f: showed a deal of promise in 1466 & one to keep in mind. ½ **97**
4854* **YAJBILL 10** [10]2-8-11 vis (95) K Fallon 11/4 FAV: 3221115: Led till ent fnl 1f, no extra: well bckd. ½ **96**
4004 **THE CROOKED RING 53** [9]2-8-11 (94) R Winston 25/1: 3411236: Slowly away, styd on late, nrst fin. 5 **81**
4637* **NEWSROUND 22** [5]2-8-11 (96) P Robinson 3/1: 217: Chsd ldrs, onepcd fnl 1.5f: well bckd tho' drifted from 2/1: only lightly rcd & more expected after impressive mdn wnr in 4637. 1 **78**
4928 **SENTIERO ROSSO 7** [1]2-8-11 (96) T Eaves 100/1: 4213008: Al outpcd: see 4280. 1½ **74**
4684 **MADAME TOPFLIGHT 21** [6]2-8-6 (93) N Mackay 66/1: 0215209: Nvr nr ldrs: btr 4155 (5f hvy). 3 **60**
4651 **SUNDANCE 22** [7]2-8-11 (97) J Quinn 25/1: 12160: 10th: Al rear: much btr 4307. 8 **41**
4651 **NEXT TIME AROUND 22** [11]2-8-11 (98) M Fenton 40/1: 135040: 11th: Nvr nr ldrs, fin last. 2½ **35**
11 Ran Time 1m 12.08 (2.68) Owned: Mountgrange Stud Trained: Upper Lambourn

4999 **2.35 Davis Langdon Stakes Handicap 3yo+ 71-85 (D2)** **[94]**
£12149 £3738 £1869 **1m208y** **Good 43** **+05 Fast** Inside

4620* **THE PRINCE 23** [7] Ian Williams 10-8-13 (79) L Dettori 6/1 JT FAV: 1121111: Held up, stdy hdwy to lead dist, rdn well clr: gd time, op 8/1: unbtn in 5 claim races prev, clrly in fine form & this was impressive upped in grade: eff at 1m/9f on firm, soft grnd & both AWs: tough & thriving 10yo: see 4620. **94**
4689 **KHANJAR 21** [12] K R Burke 4-8-10 (76) Hayley Turner(3) 33/1: 2401202: Chsd ldrs, imprvd to lead 2f out till collared dist, sn left bhd by wnr: acts on gd, fast grnd & fibresand: back to form, see 4304 & 4093. 5 **81**
4609 **FREELOADER 24** [8] J W Hills 4-8-12 (78) R Hills 12/1: 3014543: Rear, hdwy wide over 2f out, kept on well & just failed to take 2nd: see 3187. *hd* **82**
4714 **PAGAN PRINCE 19** [14] J A R Toller 7-8-11 (77) Lisa Jones 9/1: 10-01464: Mid-div, kept on under press fnl 1f, nrst fin: won this race from a 10lb lower mark last term: see 4362 & 4221. ½ **80**
4502 **RONDELET 29** [16]3-8-10 (80) N Callan 33/1: 3210455: Rear, styd on fnl 2f, nrst fin. *nk* **82**
4629 **ANNA PALLIDA 23** [3]3-8-11 VIS (81) Martin Dwyer 11/1: 2312036: Dwelt, styd on fnl 2f, nvr nrr: vis. 1¾ **80**
4352+**GOODBYE MR BOND 36** [11]4-8-11 (77) D Allan 8/1: 1132617: Mid-div, hdwy to chall 2 out, btn fnl 1f. 1¼ **73**
4820 **BLONDE STREAK 12** [13]4-8-12 (78) D Holland 16/1: 4-440168: Front rank, led 3f out till 2f out, wknd. 1¾ **71**
4473 **DANELOR 30** [18]6-9-4 (84) P Hanagan 20/1: 5010509: Trkd ldrs, onepcd fnl 2f: see 4227. *nk* **76**
4742+**COMPTON DRAKE 17** [4]5-8-13 (79) E Ahern 6/1 JT FAV: 0212410: 10th: Trkd ldrs, wknd 1.5f out. 1½ **68**
1304* **CESARE 170** [2]3-8-10 (80) K Darley 12/1: 210: 11th: Trkd ldrs, ev ch 2f out, wknd fnl 1f: long abs & has been gelded: lightly rcd & h'cap bow: see 1304 (soft grnd mdn). ½ **68**
4550 **TEDSTALE 26** [1]6-8-11 bl (77) T E Durcan 22/1: 4530400: 12th: Nvr nr ldrs: btr 4305. 2 **62**
4122 **BEST BEFORE 47** [15]4-8-13 (79) K Fallon 14/1: 3331600: 13th: Nvr btr than mid-div: 7 wk abs. *shd* **64**
4685 **HARRY POTTER 21** [6]5-8-11 vis (77) Darren Williams 33/1: 1150300: 14th: Rear, nvr nr ldrs: btr 4397. 2 **59**
4149 **ULTIMATA 46** [5]4-9-1 (81) W Ryan 25/1: 1-02200: 15th: Chsd ldrs 6f, sn wknd: 7 wk abs. ½ **62**
4592* **HUXLEY 25** [10]5-8-12 t (78) R L Moore 10/1: 0004010: 16th: Al rear: much btr 4592. 1 **57**
4820 **Tony Tie 12** [17]8-8-11 (77) T Eaves(3) 33/1:0 2247 **Maganda 126** [19]3-8-10 (80) P Robinson 50/1:0

4689 **Hills Of Gold** 21 [20]5-8-10 (76) Dale Gibson 33/1:0   4482 **Threezedzz** 30 [9]6-9-1 t(81) R Winston 33/1:0
20 Ran   Time 1m 52.25 (3.45)   Owned: Mr Patrick Kelly   Trained: Alvechurch

---

5000	3.05 Four High Petergate Hotel And Sawfish Software Stakes Handicap 3yo+ 71-85 (D2)		[95]
	£11476 £3531 £1766 **6f217y rnd** **Good 43** -04 Slow Inside		

4689 **MARSHMAN** 21 [16] M H Tompkins 5-8-12 (79) R Hills 14/1: 0003351: Held up, smooth hdwy to lead **94**
dist, rdn well clr: made most of fav'able h'cap mark: eff at 6f, suited by 7f, acts on fast, soft & polytrack:
seems to handle any trk: has tried blnks, btr without: see 4301 & 1151.
4652 **CD FLYER** 22 [9] B Ellison 7-9-3 (84) P Mulrennan(3) 20/1: 0435602: Rear, gd hdwy when short of **5 89**
room & switched dist, styd on into 2nd but wnr had flown: stays 7f, best at 6f: see 2561.
4806 **HARTSHEAD** 13 [3] G A Swinbank 5-8-12 (79) K Fallon 9/2 FAV: 1141123: Chsd lrds, prog to lead **shd 84**
briefly dist, sn onepcd: well bckd: continues in fine form: see 4806 & 4341.
4855 **KINGSCROSS** 10 [17] M Blanshard 6-8-13 (80) D Sweeney 16/1: 5022644: Rear, prog 2f out, styd on **hd 84**
fnl 1f & nrst fin: see 4350 (6f).
4642 **ARMAGNAC** 22 [5]6-9-2 (83) A Culhane 20/1: 2300105: Chsd lrds, short of room dist, onepcd fnl 1f. **½ 86**
4482 **HARRISON POINT** 30 [12]4-9-3 (84) A McCarthy 7/1: 1220106: Mid-div, prog to chall 2 out, onepcd. **1 85**
3088 **SOYUZ** 92 [10]4-9-2 (83) P Robinson 25/1: 2315007: Chsd lrd, onepcd fnl 1.5f: 3 month abs. **1 82**
4817 **JOHNSTONS DIAMOND** 12 [15]6-9-8 (89) K Darley 25/1: 0003638: Prom, wknd fnl 1.5f. **1 86**
4642 **ARCTIC DESERT** 22 [1]4-8-11 (78) Martin Dwyer 12/1: 0616209: Keen & prom, ev ch till wknd fnl 1f. **¾ 73**
4689 **PRESUMPTIVE** 21 [20]4-9-1 (82) L Dettori 9/1: 3-530100: 10th: Wide in rear, mod gains: btr 3891. **hd 76**
4689 **WATCHING** 21 [7]7-9-2 (83) P Hanagan 10/1: 0002330: 11th: Rear, nvr nr ldrs: btr 4184 & 4005 (6f). **shd 77**
4777 **JATH** 15 [11]3-8-11 (80) N Callan 25/1: 0606100: 12th: Slowly away, prog to chase ldrs 2f out, sn wknd. **1 72**
4800 **GRIZEDALE** 14 [18]5-9-4 t (85) D Holland 25/1: 0-500000: 13th: Chsd lrds wide, wknd 1.5f out. **½ 76**
4683 **PRIMO WAY** 21 [13]3-9-0 (83) M Hills 14/1: 1363030: 14th: Dwelt, nvr nr ldrs: btr 4683. **hd 73**
4891 **MASTER ROBBIE** 8 [14]5-9-3 (84) S Hitchcott 10/1: 0000040: 15th: Mid-div, btn 2f out. **nk 73**
4767 **YOUNG MR GRACE** 15 [6]4-9-4 (85) D Allan 25/1: 2130150: 16th: Chsd lrd wide, wknd 2f out. **shd 74**
4689 **KING HARSON** 21 [4]5-9-4 vis (85) T P Queally 50/1: 0601500: 17th: Led till dist, wknd, eased. **2 70**
4912 **MANAAR** 7 [19]4-9-2 BL (83) E Ahern 12/1: 0502B20: 18th: Chsd lrds wide, wknd 2f out: blnks. **6 56**
18 Ran   Time 1m 24.62 (3.32)   Owned: Mr J H Ellis   Trained: Newmarket

---

5001	3.40 Coral Sprint Trophy Handicap 3yo+ 86-100 (C1)		[110]
	£19500 £6000 £3000 **6f str** **Good 43** +01 Fast Centre		

4891 **JONNY EBENEEZER** 8 [14] D Flood 5-9-0 bl e (96) L Dettori 13/2: 1000131: Held up, hdwy & short of **105**
room over 1f out, switched right & styd on strongly to lead cl-home, rdn out: suited by 5/7f, acts on firm, soft
& fibresand: best held up & loves Newmarket: wears an eye hood & blnks, tried cheek pieces: v useful & has thrived
this term (8th win): credit to connections: see 4780, 3827.
4678 **TALBOT AVENUE** 21 [1] M Mullineaux 6-9-4 (100) K Fallon 16/1: 0202202: Chsd lrd far side, led **½ 106**
overall over 2f out, rdn & hdd cl-home: 6th rnr-up placing this term, proving tough & useful: see 4481, 4454.
4786 **FANTASY BELIEVER** 14 [3] J J Quinn 6-9-2 (98) T Hamilton(3) 16/1: 1200263: Chsd lrds far side, eff **½ 103**
over 1f out, kept on, not btn far: v tough, ran right up to best: see 4686, 3622.
4686 **CONNECT** 21 [2] M H Tompkins 7-8-8 bl (90) P Robinson 66/1: 1400004: Handy far side, onepace. **1¼ 91**
4780 **RIVER FALCON** 14 [16]4-8-5 (87) W Supple 25/1: 3010045: In tch, kept on over 1f out, no threat. **1¼ 84**
4718 **BONUS** 18 [13]4-8-11 (93) R L Moore 25/1: 5-600056: In tch, onepace over 1f out: nicely bckd: **nk 89**
gd run, back on a handy mark: see 1187.
4779 **DANZIG RIVER** 14 [9]3-8-6 (1ow) (88) M Hills 25/1: 0000467: Held up far side, late gains, no dngr. **hd 85**
4686 **TOM TUN** 21 [12]9-9-1 bl (97) T Lucas 25/1: 4203508: In tch, no extra over 1f out: likes soft grnd. **shd 93**
4786* **PIC UP STICKS** 14 [19]5-9-1 (97) A Culhane 10/1: 3600019: Held up, some late gains, nvr dngrs. **¾ 90**
4779 **PARTNERS IN JAZZ** 14 [5]3-8-5 (88) K Darley 25/1: 5005140: 10th: Led far side group till over 2f **½ 80**
out, wknd: see 4322.
4773 **COMPTONS ELEVEN** 15 [7]3-8-13 (96) S Hitchcott 12/1: 2122220: 11th: In tch, wknd over 1f out. **hd 88**
4700 **MINE BEHIND** 19 [11]4-8-6 (88) Martin Dwyer 12/1: 1000140: 12th: In tch, no extra dist: see 4585. **1 77**
4884 **VALJARV** 9 [4]3-8-8 (91) D Holland 25/1: 4420050: 13th: Al bhd. **hd 80**
4786 **MARSAD** 14 [10]10-8-4 (86) F P Ferris(3) 20/1: 2000200: 14th: Al bhd: see 4322. **nk 74**
4686 **CARDINAL VENTURE** 21 [17]6-8-10 (92) N Callan 22/1: 0010000: 15th: Led stands side, wknd 2f out. **1 77**
4817 **PHILHARMONIC** 12 [6]3-8-12 (95) P Hanagan 16/1: 14-40050: 16th: In tch, wknd well over 1f out. **2 74**
4891 **POMFRET LAD** 8 [15]6-8-5 (87) J Quinn 25/1: 0000000: 17th: Al bhd. **2½ 59**
4786 **SMART HOSTESS** 14 [8]5-8-10 (92) R Winston 8/1: 11-00030: 18th: In tch, wknd well over 1f out: **nk 63**
nicely bckd: btr expected after 4786.
4686 **MUTAWAQED** 21 [18]6-8-6 t (88) E Ahern 4/1 FAV: 0102040: 19th: Dwelt, in tch, hdwy over 2f out, **4 47**
wknd & eased ins last, broke a blood vessel: well bckd: see 4686.
4686 **ZILCH** 21 [20]6-8-13 (95) R Mullen 20/1: 4010000: 20th: Al bhd: see 4686, 2758. **1¾ 50**
20 Ran   Time 1m 11.92 (2.52)   Owned: Mrs Ruth M Serrell   Trained: Hungerford

---

5002	4.15 Symphony Group Median Auction Maiden Stakes Div 2 2yo (E3)		
	£5324 £1638 £819 **7f205y rnd** **Good 43** -32 Slow Inside		

4881 **MISTER GENEPI** 9 [12] W R Muir 2-9-0 (100) Martin Dwyer 8/13 FAV: 5223031: Held up, gd hdwy over **98**
2f out, led over 1f out, sn rdn clr, v readily: hvly bckd: enjoyed step up to 1m & acts on firm & gd: useful &
improving, more to come all this trip.
4580 **WILLIAM TELL** 25 [3] M R Channon 2-9-0 (78) A Culhane 7/1: 64522: In tch, sltly outpcd over 2f **5 83**
out, rallied over 1f out, no threat to wnr: acts on gd & soft: can find a minor trk mdn: see 4580.
4724 **MINERAL STAR** 18 [10] M H Tompkins 2-9-0 (?) P Robinson 50/1: 03: b c Monashee Mountain - Summit **1 81**
Talk (Head For Heights) In tch, gd hdwy to chall over 2f out, sn onepcd: Apr foal, cost E13,000: half-brother to
wnrs over 1m/10f: dam 7.5f scorer: encouraging run at 1m on gd grnd: shld find a mdn.
4376 **TRUCKLE** 35 [7] M Johnston 2-9-0 K Darley 20/1: 064: Chsd lrds, onepcd fnl 2f: see 43k76. **2½ 75**
4738 **KATANA** 17 [5]2-8-9 (62) T P Queally 40/1: 0055: Set pace till 2f out, no extra: 4738. **¾ 68**
4842 **ORPENDONNA** 11 [8]2-8-9 N Callan 7/1: 036: In tch, no extra dist: nicely bckd: see 4842. **nk 67**
4722 **ROYAL SAILOR** 18 [11]2-9-0 J Tate 40/1: 07: b c Bahhare - Old Tradition (Royal Academy) In tch, **nk 71**

wknd over 2f out: May foal, cost 5,000gns: half-brother to wnrs over 5/6f.
4900 **MOONFLEET 7** [14]2-8-9 S Hitchcott 50/1: 038: Al bhd. *1* **64**
4691 **ALANI 20** [9]2-8-9 P Hanagan 25/1: 259: In tch, wknd over 2f out. *nk* **63**
QUEEN NEFITARI [1]2-8-9 Dale Gibson 100/1: 0: 10th: Al bhd. *hd* **63**
4484 **NOBBLER 30** [6]2-9-0 M Hills 20/1: 00: 11th: Al rear. *5* **58**
4752 **Baileys Honour 16** [13]2-8-9 R Ffrench 40/1:0 2408 **Mount Butler 119** [2]2-9-0 M Fenton 50/1:0
Another Plan [16]2-9-0 R L Moore 25/1:0 4590 **Avizandum 25** [15]2-9-0 T E Durcan 100/1:0
15 Ran Time 1m 41.80 (6.00) Owned: Mike Caddy & Brian Moss Trained: Lambourn

5003 4.45 Shirley Heights E B F Maiden Stakes 2yo (D3)
£5415 £1666 £833 **7f205y rnd** **Good 43** **-38 Slow** Inside

DARING RANSOM [11] J Noseda 2-9-0 E Ahern 25/1: 1: b c Red Ransom - Young and Daring (Woodman) **89+**
Slow away, in tch, eff well over 1f out, kept on to lead ins last, rdn out: Apr foal: stays 1m on gd grnd, shld get further: v pleasing start, potentially useful, win more races.
TARRAMAN [1] M Johnston 2-9-0 K Darley 7/2: 2: b c Fusaichi Pegasus - Gerri N Jo Go (Top Command) In tch, hdwy to chall dist, kept on, not btn far: well bckd, debut: Apr foal, cost $50,000: half-brother to a 6f wnr: dam won in US: stays 1m on gd grnd: learn plenty from this & must be winning sn. *1¼* **85**
4640 **NOBLE DUTY 22** [6] Saeed bin Suroor 2-9-0 L Dettori 8/13 FAV: 23: Set pace, rdn & hdd ins last, no extra: hvly bckd: shld find a race: see 4640. *1* **83**
BLUE TRAIN [9] Sir Michael Stoute 2-9-0 K Fallon 6/1: 4: b c Sadler's Wells - Igreja (Southern Halo) Bhd, modest late gains, not gvn hard time on debut: Apr foal, cost 50,000gns: dam 1m wnr. *4* **75**
PERFECT TONE [4]2-8-9 P Hanagan 25/1: 5: In tch, onepcd fnl 2f. *hd* **70**
4851 **PALACE WALK 10** [12]2-9-0 Martin Dwyer 100/1: 06: Held up, nvr a factor. *5* **65**
4522 **TIAMO 28** [10]2-9-0 P Robinson 50/1: 067: In tch, wknd over 2f out. *hd* **65**
4591 **LILLAS FOREST 25** [2]2-9-0 G Faulkner 100/1: 08: In tch, wknd over 2f out. *1* **63**
ELLERSLIE TOM [7]2-9-0 J Quinn 66/1: 9: Slow away, al bhd on debut. *1¼* **60**
MAHMJRA [8]2-9-0 T E Durcan 50/1: 0: 10th: In tch, wknd over 3f out on debut. *1½* **57**
4885 **HIGH TREASON 8** [3]2-9-0 A Culhane 66/1: 0000: 11th: Al bhd. *2½* **52**
11 Ran Time 1m 42.27 (6.47) Owned: Mr R Bates Newton Trained: Newmarket

5004 5.20 Coldstream Guards Association Handicap Stakes 3yo+ 56-70 (D3) [84]
£5433 £1672 £836 **1m5f197y** **Good 43** **-14 Slow** Inside

4361 **TREASON TRIAL 36** [11] Mrs Stef Liddiard 3-8-2 (58) N Mackay(3) 14/1: 4313341: Held up, hdwy over 2f out, styd on to lead ins last, rdn out: apprec 14f/2m last 2 starts, won earlier at 10f: acts on fast & gd grnd, fair or gall trks: improving, unexposed at this trip. **66**
4824 **NORTHERN NYMPH 12** [3] R Hollinshead 5-9-1 (62) W Supple 16/1: 2340552: Handy, hdwy to lead over 3f out till rdn & hdd ins last, not btn far: gd run: 1 win in 28: see 2887, 743. *½* **68**
4601 **HEARTHSTEAD DREAM 24** [6] J D Bethell 3-8-13 (69) T Quinn 10/1: 1213343: In tch, eff over 1f out, onepace: see 3649. *¾* **74**
4647 **SKYES FOLLY 22** [1] J G Given 4-9-9 bl (70) M Fenton 10/1: 0033344: In tch, eff 2f out, onepace. *5* **67**
3760 **SALAMBA 64** [12]3-8-10 (66) P Robinson 33/1: 53-5005: Keen bhd, some late gains: 2 month abs. *2½* **60**
4555 **GARGOYLE GIRL 26** [13]7-8-9 (56) T Eaves(3) 20/1: 5106046: In tch, no impress 2f out: see 1551. *1¾* **48**
4875 **ISAAF 9** [8]5-9-6 (67) P Makin(5) 7/1: 1600427: With ldrs, led 7f till 4f out, wknd: btr 4875 (2m). *3* **54**
3437 **INCHNADAMPH 77** [14]4-9-1 t (62) K Fallon 5/2 FAV: 6221158: In tch, wknd over 2f out: hvly bckd. *½* **48**
4601 **ROYAL DISTANT 24** [5]3-8-7 (63) P Mulrennan(3) 25/1: 0020009: Bhd, modest late gains: see 3459. *1¾* **47**
4824 **CLARADOTNET 12** [15]4-8-12 (59) T E Durcan 25/1: 3032000: 10th: In tch, modest late gains. *hd* **43**
4672 **SOVEREIGN DREAMER 21** [4]4-9-7 t (68) P Hanagan 40/1: 0600000: 11th: Al bhd: see 4672, 1969. *1* **51**
4287 **WELKINOS BOY 40** [20]3-8-6 (62) Dale Gibson 14/1: 056330: 12th: Keen in tch, wknd 2f out: see 4287. *3* **40**
3856 **ITS BLUE CHIP 59** [2]3-8-3 e (59) J F Egan 33/1: 6410000: 13th: In tch, btn 2f out: abs. *2* **34**
4938 **ZAN LO 5** [16]4-8-9 (7oh) (49) R Fitzpatrick 50/1: 0041000: 14th: In tch, wknd over 2f out. *5* **23**
4990 **PONT NEUF 1** [10]4-9-6 t (67) N Callan 12/1: 51102390: 15th: Al bhd: see 3929. *7* **24**
4856 **PERFECT PUNCH 10** [7]5-9-7 (68) E Ahern 11/1: 0-200020: 16th: Handy, led over 4f out till over 3f out. *3* **20**
4932 **Distant Cousin 7** [17]7-8-9 (2oh)BL(54) A Culhane 33/1:0 4671 **Bold Blade 21** [18]3-8-0 (6oh)(50) J Quinn 66/1:0
4824 **Kaluana Court 12** [19]8-9-5 (66) Martin Dwyer 16/1:0 4559 **Dr Cool 26** [9]7-8-9 (4oh)(52) F P Ferris(3) 33/1:0
20 Ran Time 3m 01.40(8.00) Owned: Simon Mapletoft Racing I Trained: Hungerford

WOLVERHAMPTON Polytrack SATURDAY 09.10.04 Lefthand, Sharp Track

Official Going STANDARD

5005 7.00 Zongalero Maiden Handicap Stakes 3yo+ 46-55 (F4) [69]
£3016 £862 £431 **1m141y aw rnd** **Inapplicable** Inside

REBEL RAIDER 709 [7] B N Pollock 5-8-9 (50) Lisa Jones 25/1: 0/30300/-1: b g Mujadil - Emily's Pride (Shirley Heights) Cl-up, hdwy to lead 1f out, rdn out: reapp: hdles rnr in 03/04 (mdn/nov rnr-up, rtd 102h, eff at 2m1.5f on fast & gd): missed '03: h'cap plcd twice in '02 in native Ireland (1m/9f, gd & gd/soft): eff around 1m/9f on gd/soft & polytrack, sharp trk: runs well fresh: gd start to Brit career. **59a**
4088 **IRUSAN 50** [1] Jedd O'Keeffe 4-8-13 BL (54) I Mongan 14/1: 0046502: Led to 1f out, no extra: 7 wk abs: stays 1m & handles both AWs: back to form here in first time blnks: see 1518. *1¾* **59a**
3982 **SEMELLE DE VENT 54** [9] J H M Gosden 3-8-10 vis (55) Dane O'Neill 6/1: 3300203: Mid-div, hdwy 6f out, ev ch dist, sn onepcd: 7 wk abs: eff at 1m/12f: back to form of 3605. *¾* **59a**
3823 **MRS BROWN 61** [13] Sir Mark Prescott 3-8-9 (54) J Mackay 9/1: 3560504: Rear, hdwy over 2f out, not pace to chall: 9 wk abs: back to form of 3605. *1½* **56a**

4828 **MUSICAL TOP 12** [11]4-9-0 (55) L Fletcher(3) 100/30: 0030045: Cl-up 6f, sn no extra: op 6/1. ½ **56a**

3737 **ORCHESTRATION 65** [2]3-8-9 (54) S W Kelly 25/1: 6-440006: Mid-div, hmpd after 2f, lost pl & btn. 3½ **51a**

4202 **QUEEN LUCIA 43** [6]3-8-10 (55) K Fallon 3/1 FAV: 4540237: Nvr nrr than mid-div: 6 wk abs. 2 **50a**

4320 **CARLBURG 38** [5]3-8-10 BL (55) J P Guillambert(3) 33/1: 00-00008: Slow away, nvr a factor: tried blnks. 1½ **49a**

4720 **DANCE PARTY 18** [10]4-9-0 BL (55) G Gibbons 12/1: 0400009: In tch, wknd 2f out: tried blnks: btr 1082. 1 **48a**

3642 **CEYLON ROUND 68** [3]3-8-10 (55) D Corby(3) 16/1: 0060: 10th: Rcd in 2nd, no impress over 3f out. 9 **39a**

4672 **SMIRFYS DANCE HALL 21** [4]4-8-12 (53) B Swarbrick(5) 12/1: 06-400: 11th: Nvr a factor: btr 3572 (mdn). 3 **34a**

4650 **SAHARAN SONG 22** [12]3-8-10 (55) A Culhane 12/1: 4-00000: 12th: Rear, hdwy over 4f out, sn wknd. 10 **26a**

ANY NEWS 763 [8]7-9-0 t (55) S Righton 100/1: 304020/-0: 13th: ch g Karinga Bay - D'Egliere (Port Etienne) Rear, t.o. on reapp: hdles fit (p.u., h'cap, P Blockley): missed '03: mdn rnr-up on the Flat in '02 in native Ireland (9f, fast): eff at 7/9f on fast & hvy grnd: with Miss M Rowland & wears a t-strap. dist **0a**

13 Ran Time 1m 51.08 () Owned: Mr S G B Morrison Trained: Market Harborough

5006

7.30 Stars In Their Eyes Night Claiming Stakes 3yo+ (F3)
£4222 £1299 £650 **7f32y aw rnd** **Inapplicable** Outside

4681 **CAMP COMMANDER 21** [7] C E Brittain 5-9-9 t (89) L Dettori 2/1 FAV: 5000001: Bhd, hdwy over 3f out, styd on well for press ins fnl 1f to lead nr fin: clmd for £11,000: suited by 7f/1m, stays 10f: acts on fast, gd & polytrack, any trk: relished this drop into claim grade: see 1624. **91a**

4974 **GALLERY BREEZE 3** [4] J L Spearing 5-8-3 bl (65) Lisa Jones 7/1: 1000052: Rcd in 2nd till led 3f out, hdd nr fin: qck reapp, op 20/1: clmd for £6,000: back to form: just btr 2755. ¾ **68a**

4446 **POINT OF DISPUTE 32** [11] P J Makin 9-9-3 vis (76) D Sweeney 9/2: 2-520403: Mid-div, hdwy over 2f out, ev ch ins fnl 1f, onepcd cl-home: clr of rem: back to form: see 2280. hd **81a**

4920* **SAMUEL CHARLES 7** [8] W M Brisbourne 6-9-6 (75) B Swarbrick(5) 3/1: 2016014: Chsd ldrs, no impress. 7 **77a**

3670 **SMITH N ALLAN OILS 67** [3]5-9-3 p (65) S W Kelly 11/1: 5224605: Mid-div, nvr nrr: op 9/1, 10 wk abs. 1¼ **73a$**

4920 **ILE MICHEL 7** [6]7-9-9 (67) D Fentiman(7) 25/1: 0430056: Nvr a factor: qck reapp. ½ **78a$**

4667 **COMMANDER BOND 21** [2]3-8-12 (67) D McGaffin 33/1: 0000507: Led to 3f out, no extra well over 1f out. shd **68a**

4051 **RISK FREE 51** [12]7-8-8 bl (65) I Mongan 25/1: 5-060008: Mid-div, outpcd & btn 3f out: 7 wk abs. 5 **57a**

4347 **BOBERING 37** [10]4-9-0 P Mathers(5) 100/1: 0-09: Bhd, nvr nr ldrs: see 4347. 6 **57a**

4984 **RONNIE FROM DONNY 2** [5]4-9-6 (66) Dane O'Neill 14/1: 5500000: 10th: Cl-up, wknd 3f out: qck reapp. 3½ **59a**

4768 **MARBURYANNA 15** [1]4-8-3 S Righton 100/1: 00: 11th: b f Classic Cliche - Lake Mistassiu (Tina's Pet) Slow away, nvr a factor: mdn unplcd sole earlier start: with M Mullineaux. 9 **33a**

4030 **OAKLEY RAMBO 52** [9]5-9-6 (66) R L Moore 11/1: 2060000: 12th: Al bhd: 7 wk abs, op 15/2. 2 **48a**

12 Ran Time 1m 29.29 () Owned: A J Richards & S A Richards Trained: Newmarket

5007

8.00 Holiday Inn Garden Court Novice Auction Stakes 2yo (F3)
£3380 £1040 £520 **1m141y aw rnd** **Inapplicable** Inside

4978* **WATCHMYEYES 2** [2] N P Littmoden 2-9-1 P (77) K Fallon 7/4 FAV: 6442211: Trkd ldrs, kept on well for press ins fnl 1f to lead nr fin: bckd, qck reapp: eff around 7f/1m on polytrack, gd & soft, sharp or gall/undul trks, likes W'hampton: tough, took well here to first time cheek pieces: see 4978. **88a**

4461 **LE CORVEE 31** [7] A King 2-9-6 (94) J D Smith 9/4: 1342: Rear, hdwy 4f out, led over 1f out, hdd nr fin: nicely bckd, not btn far under top-weight: acts on fast, gd & polytrack: see 3991. hd **92a**

4741 **TUMBLEWEED GALORE 17** [8] B J Meehan 2-8-12 BL (76) L Dettori 5/2: 0333623: Rear, prog 4f out, no impres on first 2 ins fnl 1f: nicely bckd, clr of rem: acts on fast & polytrack: gd eff in 1st blnks. 2 **82a**

3698 **HERES THE PLAN 66** [5] M G Quinlan 2-8-10 (79) R L Moore 12/1: 10604: Cl up, led over 3f out till dist 1f out, sn no extra: 9 wk abs: btr 3407 (7f). 4 **76a**

4697 **THREE PENNIES 19** [6]2-8-13 (64) S W Kelly 50/1: 0130005: Rear, nvr nr ldrs. 2 **77a$**

4744 **RAGGED GLORY 17** [3]2-8-12 vis (77) Dane O'Neill 11/1: 462026: Led till over 3f out, no extra 2f out. 3½ **72a**

4632 **SHERBOURNE 23** [1]2-8-3 (1ow) (45) Paul Eddery 100/1: 0600007: Bhd, nvr a factor: just btr 3488. 9 **54a$**

4697 **THE KEEP 19** [4]2-8-2 (54) R Smith 100/1: 000408: Cl-up, wknd over 3f out: btr 4271. 1¾ **51a**

8 Ran Time 1m 51.88 () Owned: V and J Properties Trained: Newmarket

5008

8.30 Sue Cleary 50th Birthday Handicap Stakes 3yo 56-70 (E3) **[77]**
£4570 £1406 £703 **7f32y aw rnd** **Inapplicable** Outside

4646 **STORMY NATURE 22** [9] P W Harris 3-9-3 (66) S Carson 16/1: 0-300001: Prom, led well over 2f out, rdn out ins fnl 1f: eff at 5/6f, relished this step up to 7f: acts on fast, gd/soft & polytrack, sharp trk: gd confidence boost & is unexposed over this trip: see 1116. **74a**

4788 **RUSSIAN SYMPHONY 14** [8] C R Egerton 3-9-4 bl (67) A Culhane 25/1: 05-06002: Mid-div, hdwy 3f out, kept on ins fnl 1f, not pace wnr: stays 7f on polytrack: gd run: see 4582. ¾ **72a**

4832 **CHARLIE BEAR 12** [4] E A L Dunlop 3-9-5 (68) E Ahern 11/2: 500-0203: Cl-up, onepcd ins fnl 1f: tchd 7/1: eff at 7f/stiff 1m, tried 11f, may suit: acts on gd & polytrack: back to form of 1872. 1¼ **72a**

4923 **HAZEWIND 7** [2] P D Evans 3-9-7 vis t (70) K Fallon 11/4 FAV: 1641644: In tch, lost pl over 3f out, kept on again over 1f out but not pace of ldrs: qck reapp: remains in gd form, see 4398. nk **73a**

4827 **FIVE YEARS ON 12** [5]3-9-4 (67) S W Kelly 3/1: 024-445: Bhd, hdwy over 1f out, sn onepcd. shd **69a**

4740 **MOON LEGEND 17** [12]3-9-3 (66) Hayley Turner(3) 25/1: 6-030106: Slow away in rear, modest late gains. 2½ **65a**

4790 **BLUEBOK 14** [1]3-9-4 T (67) L Dettori 7/1: 5-237: Al rear: op 5/1, t-strap: reportedly 'hung right'. nk **65a**

4668 **HERE TO ME 21** [10]3-9-7 (70) R L Moore 13/2: 2135628: Cl-up, no impress ins fnl 1f. 2 **66a**

2463 **THREE SHIPS 116** [3]3-9-6 (69) B Reilly(3) 40/1: 0-059: ch g Dr Fong - River Lullaby (Riverman) Led till well over 2f out, no extra over 1f out: op 20/1, long abs: mdn unplcd sole '03 start (rtd 65, B Hills): has been gelded: with Miss J Feilden. 1 **64a**

4398 **OH GOLLY GOSH 34** [6]3-9-3 p (66) J P Guillambert(3) 16/1: 2053100: 10th: Sn mid div, wknd over 1f out: btr 4131 (mdn). ½ **60a**

4117 **GO YELLOW 48** [7]3-9-4 (67) N Callan 14/1: 4614020: 11th: Rear, hdwy wide over 2f out, sn wknd. 1 **60a**

4967 **GLOBAL ACHIEVER 4** [11]3-9-4 t (67) O Urbina 20/1: 0000000: 12th: Mid-div/wide, no impress over 1f out. 3½ **56a**

12 Ran Time 1m 28.9 () Owned: The Herts Desire Trained: Berkhamsted

WOLVERHAMPTON Polytrack SATURDAY 09.10.04 Lefthand, Sharp Track

5009 **9.00 Hotel And Conferencing At Dunstall Park Selling Handicap Stakes 3-5yo 46-55 (G4)** **[73]**
£2596 £742 £371 **1m4f50y aw** **Inapplicable** Inside

4903* **ROMEOS DAY 7** [10] M R Channon 3-8-0 (45) T O'Brien(2) 9/1: 0054011: Rear, hdwy 4f out, chall 2f out, sn led, all out to hold on ins fnl 1f: clmd for £6,000: qck reapp, op 11/2: eff at 10/12f, tried 2m: acts on fast, gd & polytrack, easy, sharp or undul trks: tough, in fine form at present. **54a**
4675 **LORD LAHAR 21** [6] M R Channon 5-8-7 (45) C Catlin 16/1: 0050402: Slow away, bhd, hdwy over 3f out, kept on ins fnl 1f: op 10/1: stays 1m/12f on gd/soft & polytrack in claim/sell grade: see 1894. *nk* **53a**
4584 **BROOKLANDS LODGE 25** [8] M J Attwater 3-8-7 (52) G Gibbons 50/1: 6000003: Mid-div, hdwy & ev ch 2f out, onepcd fnl 1f: stays 12f on polytrack: just btr 2529. *2½* **56a**
4512 **DIAMOND ORCHID 28** [1] P D Evans 4-8-9 p (47) K Fallon 5/4 FAV: 1510204: Slow away, hdwy & hmpd 4f out, hdwy wide over 2f out, onepcd fnl 1f: bckd, NH fit, clr of rem: btr 3822. *2* **48a**
4354 **KING HALLING 36** [2]5-9-2 p (54) V Slattery 14/1: 00/-06045: Led to 2f out, sn no extra: see 2088. *8* **43a**
4903 **COOLFORE JADE 7** [7]4-8-7 (45) L Keniry(3) 14/1: 0006406: Rcd in 2nd, no impress over 2f out. *6* **25a**
4721 **SPES BONA 18** [9]3-8-9 (54) A Culhane 9/2: 04007: In tch, hdwy 7f out, no impress 2f out: btr 2987. *¾* **33a**
4834 **DEFANA 12** [12]3-8-5 (1ow) (49) S W Kelly 7/1: 3306108: Rear, no impress over 2f out. *½* **28a**
4624 **BANNERS FLYING 23** [3]4-8-7 (5oh)BL (40) A Nicholls 50/1: 0400009: Handy 7f, no extra over 4f out. *25* **0a**
4319 **QUEENSBERRY 38** [4]5-8-12 (50) I Mongan 10/1: 20412-00: 10th: Mid-div 5f, wknd: see 4319. *3½* **0a**
4661 **DAMASK DANCER 21** [11]5-8-7 bl (45) R L Moore 25/1: 55000-00: 11th: b g Barathea - Polish Rhythm (Polish Patriot) Mid-div over 1m, wknd: 5th at best in '03 (mdn, h'cap, rtd 51a, part with F Murphy): mdn unplcd on sole '02 start (rtd 70a): stays 7f on polytrack: wears blnks, tried cheek pieces. *9* **0a**
11 Ran Time 2m 41.55 () Owned: Heart of the South Racing Trained: West Ilsley

5010 **9.30 Dine In Style Handicap Stakes 3yo+ 56-70 (E3)** **[82]**
£3485 £1072 £536 **5f216y aw rnd** **Inapplicable** Inside

4984 **SILENT STORM 2** [5] H J Cyzer 4-8-13 (67) C Catlin 15/2: 3300231: Rear, hdwy 2f out, styd on well for press ins fnl 1f to lead nr fin: qck reapp: eff at 6f, tried further: acts on firm, fast & both AWs, sharp trk: improving 4yo: see 2722. **76a**
4605 **WILLHEWIZ 24** [1] R M Stronge 4-9-2 (70) L Keniry(3) 33/1: 0004002: Rcd in 2nd, hdwy to lead just ins fnl 1f, hdd nr fin: loves firm & gd, acts on gd/soft & both AWs: back to form here: just btr 2591. *½* **76a**
4548 **SEWMUCH CHARACTER 26** [13] M Blanshard 5-9-0 (68) K Fallon 16/1: 4201063: Mid-div, hdwy over 1f out, kept on: acts on fast, gd/soft & polytrack: back to winning form of 3910. *1¾* **70a**
4475* **MANDARIN SPIRIT 30** [10] G C H Chung 4-8-12 bl (66) O Urbina 8/1: 0550514: In tch, hdwy 2f out, styd on: stays 6f, rtn to 7f/8.5f will suit: acts on fast, gd & both AWs: shade btr 4475. *hd* **67a**
3220 **LARKYS LOB 86** [7]5-8-9 (63) J D O'Reilly(4) 14/1: 2216235: Led to just ins fnl 1f, no extra: long abs: acts on gd/soft & both AWs: see 2201. *nk* **63a**
4984 **BOBS BUZZ 2** [2]4-9-2 (70) L Dettori 11/8 FAV: 3520526: Bhd, outpcd, some late gains: qck reapp,wel blckd: disappointing effort: btr 4984. *shd* **69a**
4754 **OBE ONE 16** [11]4-8-11 BL (65) A Culhane 4/1: 0445057: Bhd, hdwy 2f out, no impress ins fnl 1f. *2* **58a**
4368 **MR PERTEMPS 36** [3]6-8-9 p (63) E Ahern 14/1: 0-312508: Handy, outpcd & btn over 2f out. *1* **53a**
4946 **FULL SPATE 5** [4]9-9-1 (69) R L Moore 16/1: 2160009: Slow away, nvr nr ldrs: qck reapp. *¾* **57a**
4618* **BLUEBERRY RHYME 23** [8]5-8-11 vis (65) N Callan 20/1: 1500010: 10th: Chsd ldrs, fdd ent fnl 1f. *1½* **48a**
4070 **CREWES MISS ISLE 50** [12]3-8-10 (65) S Whitworth 66/1: 5000500: 11th: Al bhd: 7 wk abs: btr 1338. *4* **36a**
4984 **PHRENOLOGIST 2** [6]4-8-11 BL (65) A Nicholls 66/1: 613-0000: 12th: In tch, no impress over 1f out. *shd* **35a**
4984 **WILLHECONQUERTOO 2** [9]4-9-1 t p (69) G Gibbons 20/1: 1005440: 13th: Slow away, nvr a factor. *2½* **31a**
13 Ran Time 1m 15.46() Owned: Mrs Charles Cyzer Trained: Newmarket

NEWCASTLE SUNDAY 10.10.04 Lefthand, Galloping, Stiff Track

Official Going Good (Good/Firm Places)

5011 **1.50 Npower Maiden Auction Stakes Div 1 2yo (E3)**
£3543 £1090 £545 **7f str** **Good/Firm 24** **-05 Slow** Stands side

4247 **AZAHARA 43** [6] K G Reveley 2-8-4 Dale Gibson 100/1: 001: Rear, prog bef 1f out, rdn to get up on line: 6 wk abs: eff at 7f, will apprec further: acts on fast grnd & a stiff/gall trk: goes well fresh: see 4247. **77**
4455 **WESTER LODGE 33** [12] J M P Eustace 2-8-13 J Tate 14/1: 02: ch c Fraam - Reamzafonic (Grand Lodge) Cl-up, styd on to lead ins fnl 1f, sn hung right under press, hdd on line: rider received 7 day whip ban: Feb foal, half-brother plcd at 5f: dam unplcd: sire useful performer around 1m: eff at 7f, further will suit: acts on fast grnd: can find similar on this evidence. *nk* **84**
4600 **HANNAHS DREAM 25** [13] M Johnston 2-8-5 K Darley 100/30: 623: Led, hdd bef 1f out, rallied when hung left ins fnl 1f, held when short of room cl-home: bckd: now quals for h'caps: see 4600. *¾* **74**
4896 **SCRIPTED 9** [9] Sir Mark Prescott 2-8-13 S Sanders 6/4 FAV: 44: Prom, ev ch well over 1f out, sn no extra: v well bckd: eff at 6f, prob stays 7f: handles fast grnd & polytrack: see 4896 (debut). *2½* **77**
4866 **ARTIC FOX 11** [10]2-8-12 bl (55) D Allan 66/1: 500005: Cl-up over 5f, no extra: see 2682. *2½* **71$**
DAMBURGER XPRESS 0 [11]2-8-11 M Fenton 33/1: 6: b c Josr Algarhoud - Upping The Tempo (Dunbeath) Nvr nrr than mid-div: debut: Apr foal, cost 20,000gns: half-brother to sprint wnrs: dam unrcd. *2½* **65**
4692 **INVERTIEL 21** [14]2-8-11 (75) R Winston 8/1: 42007: Cl-up over 5f, hung left & wknd: btr 3589. *1½* **62**
3582 **MINK MITTEN 72** [8]2-8-4 t P Hanagan 12/1: 08: Handy 5f, wknd: 10 wk abs. *5* **46**
4726 **PACIFIC PIRATE 19** [2]2-8-11 G Faulkner 14/1: 069: Keen handy over 5f, fdd: see 4726. *shd* **52**
VILLA CHIGI 0 [5]2-8-10 D McGaffin 50/1: 0: 10th: Chsd ldrs, wknd bef 2f out: debut. *1¾* **49**
4325 **BOSCHETTE 39** [1]2-8-5 T P Queally 9/1: 50: 11th: Cl-up wide till halfway, fdd: showed more in 4325. *1¾* **40**
4933 **EMERALD DESTINY 6** [7]2-8-9 D Tudhope(4) 100/1: 500: 12th: Keen prom till halfway, fdd: qck reapp. *17* **12**
12 Ran Time 1m 26.15 (2.05) Owned: Mr J Stevenson Trained: Saltburn

5012

2.20 Npower Maiden Auction Stakes Div 2 2yo (E3)
£3543 £1090 £545 **7f str** **Good/Firm 24** **+01 Fast** Stands side

4617 **REAL QUALITY 24** [9] I Semple 2-8-13 R Winston 6/4 FAV: 21: Bhd, prog to lead 2f out, rdn out to assert: bckd: eff at 6f, apprec step up to 7f: acts on fast & gd/soft grnd: eff on a stiff/gall trk: bright future. **90**
4644 **THREE DEGREES 23** [14] R M Beckett 2-8-6 M Fenton 11/4: 32: In tch, ev ch dist, kept on, not pace of wnr: well clr of rem: eff at 6f, imprvd for step up to 7f: acts on fast & gd/soft grnd: can find a mdn. *¾* **80**
LE CHIFFRE 0 [3] D R Loder 2-8-13 T P Queally 7/1: 3: br c Celtic Swing - Implicit View (Persian Bold) Bhd, prog bef 1f out, styd on, no ch with clr front 2: debut: May foal, cost E40,000: half-brother to multiple wnr abroad: dam unrcd: sire Gr 1 wnr at 2, subs 12f Gr 1 wnr at 3: imprve for today. *9* **70**
4864 **AZA WISH 11** [10] Ms Deborah J Evans 2-8-3 (58) Rory Moore(5) 50/1: 050064: Led 5f, wknd: see 1458. *1¼* **58**
4864 **NEPAL 11** [12]2-8-3 P Fessey 10/1: 625: Nvr nrr than mid-div: showed more in 4864 (firm). *dht* **58**
2360 **KUDBEME 121** [1]2-8-2 J Bramhill 100/1: 06: b f Forzando - Umbrian Gold (Perugino) Nvr nrr than mid-div: long abs: Jan first foal, cost 2,000gns: dam successful at 7f: sire useful performer around 1m. *1¾* **53**
HAYRAAN 0 [4]2-8-9 J Carroll 14/1: 7: b c Bluebird - Alma Latina (Persian Bold) Al hanging left in tch, wknd bef 1f out: bckd on debut: Mar foal, dam plcd at 5f: sire decent performer at sprint dists. *nk* **59**
4617 **HAENERTSBURG 24** [2]2-8-3 G Gibbons 28/1: 008: Handy 5f, wknd: see 4617. *6* **42**
4653 **VICTOR BUCKWELL 23** [13]2-8-12 T Eaves(3) 25/1: 09: Al bhd: see 4653. *1½* **48**
4787 **WOODFORD WONDER 15** [6]2-8-4 (2ow) P Mulrennan 100/1: 000: 10th: Al bhd. *¾* **38**
4351 **CALA FONS 37** [8]2-8-4 Kim Tinkler 100/1: 0000: 11th: In tch 4f, fdd. *hd* **37**
3554 **MARY GRAY 73** [5]2-8-4 S Chin 14/1: 500: 12th: In tch, hung badly left & fdd 2f out. *3* **31**
4617 **STANLEY ARTHUR 24** [11]2-8-10 A Nicholls 66/1: 00: 13th: Missed break & al in rear. *1½* **34**
13 Ran Time 1m 25.71 (1.61) Owned: Mr David McKenzie Trained: Carluke

5013

2.55 Saint Gobain Pipelines Selling Nursery Handicap Stakes 2yo 0-65 (F4) **[69]**
£2688 £768 £384 **6f str** **Good/Firm 24** **-27 Slow** Stands side

4277 **HOWS THAT 41** [2] K R Burke 2-8-12 (53) Darren Williams 6/1 FAV: 000021: In tch far side group, styd on to lead that group dist, rdn out: 6 wk abs: new stable, no bid: eff at 6f, tried further: acts on fast & gd grnd: goes well fresh: enjoys sell grade: see 4277 (P J McBride). **64**
4673 **STRATHTAY 22** [5] P C Haslam 2-9-0 VIS (55) K Darley 10/1: 3056002: Missed break & sn bhd far side, prog bef 1f out, kept on, not pace of wnr: eff at 5/6f on fast grnd: apprec fitting of first time vis. *1½* **60**
4895 **WILTSHIRE 9** [7] M R Channon 2-9-4 (59) J Carroll 9/1: 0000103: Bhd far side group, prog 2f out, kept on ins fnl 1f: clmd for 6,000: eff at 5/6f on firm & fast grnd: see 4759. *nk* **63**
4859 **MERCARI 11** [8] G M Moore 2-9-6 (61) T Eaves(3) 16/1: 00064: Chsd ldrs far side, onepcd ins fnl 1f: eff at 6f on fast grnd: see 4859. *½* **64**
4591 **DANCING DEANO 26** [16]2-8-11 VIS (52) V Halliday 16/1: 0605: Prom stands side group, led that group after halfway, kept on fnl 1f but no ch with far side: first time visor: eff at 6f on fast grnd: won race on unfav'd stands side & is worth keeping in mind: see 4244. *nk* **54+**
4597 **DESERT BUZZ 25** [1]2-8-12 p (53) T P Queally 16/1: 0500006: Prom far side group, led that group 3f out, hdd bef 1f out, no extra: btr 2933. *nk* **54**
4787 **SWEET MARGUERITE 15** [10]2-9-0 (55) D Allan 10/1: 4460007: In tch far side over 4f, sn onepcd. *¾* **54**
4632 **LAKESDALE 24** [15]2-9-1 (56) P Makin(5) 14/1: 2361008: Nvr nrr than mid-div stands side: btr 4316. *1½* **51**
4503 **SINGHALONGTASVEER 29** [4]2-9-4 (59) J Bramhill 20/1: 0530059: Rear far side, prog 2f out, onepcd when short of room ins fnl 1f: btr 4503. *shd* **53**
4804 **MS THREE 14** [11]2-9-0 (55) P Hanagan 10/1: 06560: 10th: Cl-up stands side group, wknd bef 1f out. *1* **46**
4451 **CHICAGO NIGHTS 33** [20]2-8-10 (51) G Faulkner 12/1: 4005200: 11th: Led stands side group over 3f. *1* **39**
4635 **TIT FOR TAT 24** [13]2-9-1 BL (56) M Fenton 16/1: 05400: 12th: Missed break, nvr a factor stands side. *¾* **42**
3994 **ALZARMA 55** [14]2-9-7 (62) R Winston 12/1: 03060: 13th: Chsd ldrs stands side 4f, wknd: op 7/1. *½* **47**
4934 **APETITE 6** [18]2-9-5 (60) A Reilly(7) 16/1: 0210000: 14th: Al in rear stands side. *2* **39**
4602 **SATIN ROSE 25** [17]2-8-13 (54) G Gibbons 14/1: 56060: 15th: Prom 4f stands side, fdd. *½* **32**
4792 **LADY VEE 15** [9]2-9-0 (55) T Hamilton(3) 14/1: 0500: 16th: Missed break, nvr a factor far side. *1* **30**
4784 **MAS O MENOS 15** [6]2-9-7 (62) A Nicholls 20/1: 200200: 17th: Led 3f far side, fdd. *19* **0**
4617 **SHATIN LEADER 24** [12]2-8-11 (52) P Fessey 20/1: P634000: 18th: Al in rear stands side. *20* **0**
18 Ran Time 1m 14.39 (3.09) Owned: Mr D Wigglesworth & Mr J Harthen Trained: Leyburn

5014

3.30 Northumbrian Water Handicap Stakes 3yo+ 56-70 (E3) **[83]**
£5426 £1670 £835 **7f str** **Good/Firm 24** **+06 Fast** Stands side

4683 **SENESCHAL 22** [16] M R Channon 3-8-12 (67) T O'Brien(7) 12/1: 0000051: Mid-div stands side, prog centre 2f out, led ins fnl 1f, pushed out, val 3L+: eff at 5f, suited by around 7f: acts on fast & gd grnd: apprec recent switch to inexperienced rider & is h'capped to follow up: see 4683. **77**
4719 **NO GROUSE 19** [14] R A Fahey 4-8-10 p (63) P Hanagan 7/1 JT FAV: 0050542: Chsd ldrs stands side, styd on to lead stands side group 1f out, kept on, not pace wnr in centre: on a winning mark. *1¾* **68**
4818* **YORKER 13** [20] Ms Deborah J Evans 6-8-9 bl (62) S Sanders 12/1: 0036013: Led stands side group 6f, onepcd: ran to form of win in 4818 (6f, first time blnks). *nk* **66**
4806 **BALLYHURRY 14** [17] J S Goldie 7-9-0 (67) T Eaves(3) 7/1 JT FAV: 0646044: In tch stands side, kept on ins fnl 1f, no ch with principals: encouraging eff & is on a winning mark: see 4806 & 2086. *¾* **69**
4719 **MOUNT HILLABY 19** [15]4-8-10 (63) T Lucas 16/1: 0020105: Handy stands side over 5f, no extra. *¾* **63**
4869 **MENAI STRAIGHTS 11** [18]3-8-8 (63) R Winston 25/1: 3513066: In tch stands side over 5f, no extra. *½* **62**
4719 **JUBILEE STREET 19** [1]5-8-9 (62) A Beech(3) 12/1: 0612107: In tch far side group, styd on to lead that group ins fnl 1f, no ch with stands side: won race on unfav'd far side: btr 4438. *¾* **59+**
4581 **BLUE PATRICK 26** [8]4-9-0 (67) J Tate 20/1: 2065058: Missed break far side, nvr nrr than mid-div. *1¾* **60**
4926 **MISTER SWEETS 8** [19]5-8-13 t (66) D Tudhope(5) 8/1: 5006009: Nvr nrr than mid-div stands side. *½* **58**
4740 **LANDUCCI 18** [4]3-8-10 t (65) T P Queally 8/1: 2061340: 10th: In tch far side over 5f, wknd: btr 4465. *1½* **54**
4592 **QUEEN CHARLOTTE 26** [9]5-8-9 (62) Dale Gibson 16/1: 2000560: 11th: Led far side group over 6f, wknd. *shd* **50**
3242 **ASWAN 86** [11]6-8-7 t (60) P Makin(3) 33/1: 0-530000: 12th: Handy stands side over 5f, wknd: long abs. *nk* **47**
4696 **VADEMECUM 21** [3]3-8-10 (65) D McGaffin 25/1: 3-600000: 13th: Nvr a factor far side. *2* **48**
4721 **Kingsmaite 19** [2]3-8-11 bl(66) J Bramhill 16/1:0 4818 **Fair Shake 13** [6]4-9-1 p(68) K Darley 12/1:0

3375 **Grey Cossack** 80 [10]7-9-1 (68) R Fitzpatrick 28/1:0   4622 **Downland** 24 [7]8-8-11 (64) Kim Tinkler 20/1:0
4926 **Cashneem** 8 [13]6-8-6 (59) D Allan 25/1:0   4926 **Dara Mac** 8 [12]5-8-8 (61) T Hamilton(3) 25/1:0
19 Ran   Time 1m 25.39 (1.29)   Owned by Mr Peter Taplin   Trained: West Ilsley

---

5015   4.05 Orange Maiden Stakes Fillies & Mares 3yo+   (D3)
£3741 £1151 £576   **1m2f32y**   **Good/Firm 24**   **-67 Slow**   Centre

1747 **INTO THE SHADOWS** 149 [1] K G Reveley 4-9-3 (72) T Eaves(3) 11/4: 3341: In tch, prog trav well to   **75**
lead dist, pushed out, val 5L+: bckd from 5/1: long abs: eff at 1m/12f on fast & gd/soft grnd: acts on a
stiff/gall trk & goes well fresh: imprvd eff since mid-season break & can prog: see 1507.
4821 **BUBBLING FUN** 13 [6] E A L Dunlop 3-8-12 (66) S Sanders 2/1 FAV: 4332622: Chsd ldrs, prog to lead   3   **69**
bef 1f out, sn hdd, kept on but not pace of wnr fnl 1f: bckd: another plcd effort: see 4821 & 3299.
4336 **LADY KARR** 38 [5] M Johnston 3-8-12   K Darley 12/1: 03: Mid-div over 6f, sn outpcd, rallied late.   ¾   **67**
4321 **ROSIE MAC** 39 [4] N Bycroft 3-8-12 (54) A Reilly(7) 33/1: 6346604: Dsptd lead over 1m, no extra.   ¾   **65**
4501 **RED SAIL** 30 [9]3-8-12 (4) R Winston 11/4: 3305: Cl-up over 1m, no extra: bckd, btr 3631.   shd   **64**
     BOTTOMLESS WALLET 0 [7]3-8-12   T Hamilton(3) 40/1: 6: Nvr nrr than mid-div on debut.   ½   **63**
     AWAKEN 84 [3]3-8-12   P Hanagan 8/1: 67: Handy over 7f, wknd.   3   **59**
4408 **GAIETY GIRL** 34 [8]3-8-12 (46) D Allan 28/1: 0650008: Led, hdd bef 1f out, wknd.   5   **52**
4790 **DORISIMA** 15 [10]3-8-12   P Mulrennan(3) 66/1: 0-09: Al in rear.   2   **49**
9 Ran   Time 2m 15.06 (9.1)   Owned: Mr R C Mayall   Trained: Saltburn

---

5016   4.40 Lumsden And Carroll Construction Handicap Stakes 3yo+ 56-70   (E3)   [82]
£4059 £1249 £624   **1m2f32y**   **Good/Firm 24**   **-16 Slow**   Centre

4911* **MAMBINA** 8 [3] M R Channon 3-8-12 (66) D Allan 5/1: 2232411: Mid-div, short of room 2f out, prog   **75**
to lead well ins fnl 1f, rdn out: suited by around 10f on fast & soft, prob handles firm, any trk.
4757* **LUCAYAN DANCER** 17 [13] D Nicholls 4-8-12 (61) S Sanders 3/1 FAV: 5501412: Chsd ldrs, prog over   ½   **68**
3f out, ev ch ins fnl 1f, just held by wnr: tchd 9/1 in defeat: ran to form of win in 4757 (apprs, class stks).
4553 **EASIBET DOT NET** 27 [4] I Semple 4-9-6 p (69) T Eaves(3) 12/1: 0531343: In tch, styd on to lead   ¾   **74**
despite hanging left 2f out, hdd ins fnl 1f, no extra: see 3588 (12f).
4849 **SAHAAT** 12 [8] C R Dore 6-9-1 (64) Darren Williams 20/1: 2504604: Missed break, prog 3f out, ev   shd   **68**
ch ins fnl 1f, sn no extra: eff at 8.5f/10f: signs of encouragement today & is well h'capped: see 2628.
4932 **COLWAY RITZ** 8 [14]10-8-12 (61) J Bramhill 12/1: 22-02255: Held up, prog 3f out, staying on when   1¾   **63**
short of room ins fnl 1f, sn no impress: shade closer with clr passage: showed more in 4672 (12f).
4849 **MARKET AVENUE** 12 [6]5-9-0 P (63) P Hanagan 9/1: 5051006: Missed break, prog 4f out, ev ch dist,   shd   **64**
no extra ins fnl 1f: clr rem: first time cheek pieces: btr 4406.
4407 **MEDALLA** 34 [7]4-9-7 (70) M Lawson(5) 50/1: 3507: Nvr nrr than mid-div: btr 3973.   7   **61**
4406 **FUTOO** 34 [9]3-9-2 (70) K Darley 20/1: 0134208: Led, hdd after 1f, styd in tch, wknd bef 1f out.   2   **58**
4771 **SUPER KING** 16 [15]3-8-11 (65) P Makin(5) 28/1: 0052309: Nvr nrr than mid-div.   2½   **49**
4650 **JAKE BLACK** 23 [5]4-9-0 (63) R Winston 33/1: 0441000: 10th: In tch when short of room 2f out, wknd.   2   **44**
4515 **HAVETOAVIT** 29 [2]3-8-11 (65) T P Queally 11/1: 4041200: 11th: Led 9f out, hdd 2f out, fdd: btr 4342.   ½   **45**
4592 **INCHDURA** 26 [17]6-9-1 (64) Kim Tinkler 25/1: 00-00600: 12th: Al in rear.   8   **33**
4862 **KAYMICH PERFECTO** 11 [1]4-8-11 (60) W Halliday 66/1: 1322000: 13th: Chsd ldr over 7f, fdd.   2½   **25**
4766 **SANTIBURI LAD** 16 [12]7-9-2 (65) T Hamilton(3) 14/1: 1120000: 14th: Cl-up till halfway, fdd.   7   **20**
4867 **BOND MILLENNIUM** 11 [16]6-8-13 (62) D McGaffin 12/1: 55-00200: 15th: Chsd ldrs over 7f, fdd.   7   **7**
4347 **DREAM EASY** 38 [10]3-8-13 BL (67) R Price 25/1: 054530: 16th: In tch over 6f, fdd.   6   **3**
2673 **SILVERTOWN** 109 [11]9-9-3 (66) P Mulrennan(3) 12/1: 3/11-0000: 17th: Handy over 5f, sn lost place   7   **0**
& eased: surely something amiss: recently p.u. over hdles: see 2162.
17 Ran   Time 2m 10.54 (4.04)   Owned: Mr R A Scarborough   Trained: West Ilsley

---

5017   5.15 Conor Sadler Uts Classified Stakes 3yo+ 0-60   (F3)
£3504 £1078 £539   **1m3y str**   **Good/Firm 24**   **-05 Slow**   Stands side

4926 **TEDSDALE MAC** 8 [15] N Bycroft 5-9-3 (57) P Makin(5) 8/1: 2252001: Bhd stand side, prog halfway,   **66**
styd on to lead ins fnl 1f, pushed out, val bit more: prev eff at 5f, now suited by 1m/10f: acts on firm & gd/soft
grnd: deserved success: see 4399 & 3598.
4709 **NIGHT FROLIC** 20 [20] J W Hills 3-8-11 (58) T P Queally 12/1: 3066042: Mid-div stands side, prog   ¾   **60**
to lead 2f out, hdd ins fnl 1f, not pace of wnr: find similar on this evidence: see 1953.
4926 **REGENTS SECRET** 8 [14] J S Goldie 4-9-3 p (56) S Sanders 11/2: 3306033: Bhd stands side, prog bef   1   **61**
1f out, nrst fin: clr rem: op 7/1: see 4926.
4650 **WRENLANE** 23 [16] R A Fahey 3-9-0 (60) P Hanagan 10/1: 6504034: Chsd ldrs stands side over 4f, no   5   **51**
extra bef 1f out: op 7/1: recent hdles unplcd.
4757 **LEGAL SET** 17 [18]8-9-3 t (60) Ann Stokell 25/1: 0024005: Prom stands side, ev ch bef 1f out, wknd.   ½   **50**
2726 **EVERY NOTE COUNTS** 107 [5]4-9-3 (60) R Winston 28/1: 0-000666: Sn switched to stands side, prog   3   **44**
3f out, onepcd bef 1f out: op 20/1: recent hdles unplcd, btr 2448.
4926 **NEWCORP LAD** 8 [12]4-9-3 p (60) J Carroll 11/10 FAV: 2403147: Led stands side group 6f, fdd: v   3   **38**
well bckd: disappointing effort: btr 4867.
4721 **ALWAYS FLYING** 19 [13]3-9-0 (57) T Hamilton(3) 40/1: 6602008: Prom stands side 6f, fdd.   3½   **31**
4488 **PAGAN STORM** 31 [11]4-9-3 (52) Kristin Stubbs(7) 50/1: 0030009: Nvr nrr than mid-div stands side.   4   **23**
4407 **SHARDDA** 34 [17]4-9-0 (55) P Mulrennan(3) 33/1: 30-30000: 10th: Nvr nrr than mid-div stands side.   1¾   **16**
4398 **NEW WISH** 35 [6]4-9-3 (60) Dale Gibson 16/1: 000-5000: 11th: Sn switched stands side, nvr a factor.   1   **17**
4926 **LORD BASKERVILLE** 8 [8]3-9-0 (52) M Lawson(5) 100/1: 4044000: 12th: Cl-up over 4f, wknd.   nk   **16**
4131 **Aliba** 48 [10]3-9-0 (60) D McGaffin 66/1:0   4406 **Jordans Spark** 34 [7]3-9-0 p(57) D Allan 16/1:0
4085 **Miskina** 51 [3]3-8-11 (58) B Swarbrick(5) 40/1:0   4621 **Glencairn Star** 24 [9]3-9-0 (60) T Eaves(3) 100/1:0
4674 **Danettie** 21 [1]3-8-11 (60) M Fenton 40/1:0   4668 **Bonsai** 22 [4]3-8-11 t(60) K Darley 50/1:0
18 Ran   Time 1m 39.33(2.33)   Owned: Mr Barrie Abbott   Trained: Malton

BATH **SUNDAY 10.10.04 Lefthand, Turning Track with Uphill Finish**

Official Going Good/Soft (Good Places)

5018

2.10 107 9 Bath Fm Maiden Stakes Div 1 2yo (D3)
£3965 £1220 £610 **1m5y rnd** **Good 55** **-58 Slow** Inside

3959 **MAYADEEN 57** [4] M P Tregoning 2-9-0 R Hills 1/1 FAV: 31: Cl-up, styd on to lead dist, rdn out: eff at 7f, apprec step up to 1m, further will suit: acts on fast grnd & goes well fresh: can impr with experience. **80**

4792 **TRANQUILIZER 15** [14] D J Coakley 2-8-9 t Hayley Turner(3) 66/1: 6U02: Cl-up, chsd wnr ins fnl 1f, al held: eff at 1m on gd grnd: best eff to date & can find a race on this evidence: see 3803. *¾* **72**

SKYSCAPE [8] Mrs A J Perrett 2-8-9 Martin Dwyer 10/1: 3: b f Zafonic - Aquarelle (Kenmare) Chsd ldrs over 5f, sn outpcd, rallied late, no ch with front 2: debut: Mar foal, half-sister successful at 7f/1m: dam successful at 1m abroad: sire Gr 1 wnr at 1m: eff at 1m on gd, further shld suit: encouraging start. *1¼* **70**

4782 **NAPAPIJRI 15** [9] D P Keane 2-8-9 D Sweeney 100/1: 504: gr f Highest Honor - Les Marettes (Baillamont) Cl-up, led 2f out, hdd dist, no extra: Apr foal, cost E28,000: half-sister to wnrs at 1m & mid-dists: dam successful at 1m: sire decent performer around 1m/10f: quals for h'caps. *nk* **69**

4724 **COST ANALYSIS 19** [1]2-9-0 P Robinson 12/1: 065: Led 6f, no extra dist: now quals for h'caps. *shd* **73**

KEY OF SOLOMON [10]2-9-0 T S Drowne 33/1: 6: ch c Machiavellian - Minerva (Caerleon) Nvr nrr than mid-div on debut: Jan first foal, cost 50,000gns: sire high-class miler: with H Morrison. *1* **71**

4484 **VOLITIO 31** [12]2-9-0 L Keniry(3) 100/1: 0007: Chsd ldrs over 6f, wknd. *3½* **64**

4746 **LOCH QUEST 18** [5]2-9-0 I Mongan 14/1: 508: Chsd ldrs over 5f, wknd. *2* **60**

3925 **LEGALLY FAST 58** [16]2-9-0 J F Egan 66/1: 09: Rear, nvr a factor: 8 wk abs. *½* **59**

ANCIENT EGYPT [11]2-9-0 F Norton 14/1: 0: 10th: Mid-div over 5f, wknd. *3½* **52**

ALFRED THE GREAT [2]2-9-0 R Ffrench 12/1: 0: 11th: Missed break, nvr a factor. *1¾* **48**

3824 **REFERENCE 62** [6]2-9-0 M Hills 100/1: 000: 12th: Rear, nvr a factor. *28* **3**

4699 **COURT RULER 20** [15]2-9-0 R Thomas(3) 100/1: 5U: Rear when stumbled & u.r. halfway. **0**

4776 **GIANTS ROCK 16** [13]2-9-0 J Fortune 9/2: 3R: Withdrawn at start, ref to enter stalls: btr 4776. **0**

14 Ran Time 1m 47.41 (9.11) Owned: Mr Hamdan Al Maktoum Trained: Lambourn

5019

2.45 107 9 Bath Fm Maiden Stakes Div 2 2yo (D3)
£3955 £1217 £609 **1m5y rnd** **Good 55** **-26 Slow** Inside

4611 **NOTABILITY 25** [11] M A Jarvis 2-9-0 P Robinson 4/1: 021: Led 2f, styd cl-up, styd on to lead over 1f out, pushed out, val 3L+: eff at 7f on gd, now suited by 1m: improving with racing, see 4611. **90**

4677 **RAIN STOPS PLAY 22** [6] M R Channon 2-9-0 S Hitchcott 16/1: 302: Led after 2f, hdd over 1f out, kept on but not pace of easy wnr: eff at 7f/1m on firm & gd: gd eff in defeat & can find a race: see 4393. *1½* **84**

4842 **NATALIE JANE 12** [8] G A Butler 2-8-9 J Fortune 20/1: 03: ch f Giant's Causeway - Kirk (Selkirk) Rear, prog halfway, kept on but no ch with front 2 ins fnl 1f: Mar first foal, dam successful at 1m: sire multiple Gr 1 wnr at 7/10f: eff at 1m on gd, further will suit: promising effort & can rate higher. *1¼* **77**

4544 **RIGHTFUL RULER 27** [16] B W Hills 2-9-0 M Hills 10/1: 44: Chsd ldrs, no extra dist: needs further. *1* **80**

4677 **ALFIE NOAKES 22** [1]2-9-0 S Drowne 9/4 FAV: 35: Mstk, sn mid-div, no impress dist: btr 4677. *3* **74**

4483 **MONTJEU BABY 31** [14]2-8-9 R Smith 100/1: 0006: Handy over 6f, wknd: see 3103. *2* **65**

4640 **PITTSBURGH 23** [2]2-9-0 Martin Dwyer 7/2: 47: Handy 6f, wknd: btr 4640 (debut, fast). *1¼* **68**

4710 **SHINY THING 20** [15]2-8-9 D Kinsella 33/1: 58: Chsd ldrs 6f, fdd. *3½* **56**

4648 **RED RIVER ROCK 23** [9]2-9-0 J F McDonald(3) 33/1: 309: Al in rear: btr 4115. *2* **57**

3798 **SEA MAP 63** [3]2-9-0 J F Egan 50/1: 00U0: 10th: Rear, nvr a factor. *1½* **54**

FRENCH GOLD [12]2-8-9 I Mongan 50/1: 0: 11th: Missed break, nvr a factor on debut. *nk* **48**

4575 **HAWRIDGE STAR 26** [4]2-9-0 L Keniry(3) 15/2: 620: 12th: Chsd ldrs till halfway, wknd. *1* **51**

Tiger Dawn [5]2-9-0 BL R Hills 33/1:0 — 4699 **Silver Court 20** [10]2-9-0 R Thomas(3) 100/1:0

4829 **Solar Falcon 13** [7]2-8-9 F P Ferris(3) 100/1:0 — 4637 **Speedy Spirit 23** [13]2-8-9 A Daly 100/1:0

16 Ran Time 1m 44.78 (6.48) Owned: Sheikh Mohammed Trained: Newmarket

5020

3.20 Oval Motor Group Claiming Stakes 3yo (F4)
£3066 £876 £438 **5f161y rnd** **Good 55** **+11 Fast** Far side

4740 **INNSTYLE 18** [10] J L Spearing 3-8-4 (61) Lisa Jones 16/1: 6003001: Missed break, prog halfway, styd on to lead dist, drvn out: fast time: eff at 5/6f on fast & gd: enjoyed drop to claim grade & first win. **66**

4976 **LA VIE EST BELLE 4** [19] B R Millman 3-8-9 (63) A McCarthy 11/2: 0610452: Missed break, prog halfway, ev ch 1f out, kept on but not pace of wnr: qck reapp: gd eff from poor wide draw: see 4646 & 4236. *1* **67**

4835 **CALLED UP 13** [4] H Candy 3-8-7 (65) D Sweeney 20/1: 4005043: Bhd, prog dist, nrst fin: see 2756. *1* **62**

4496 **TRICK CYCLIST 30** [14] A M Balding 3-9-3 (71) Martin Dwyer 11/2: 0213504: Cl-up, led 2f out, hdd dist, no extra: not disgraced under top-weight: btr 3720. *nk* **71**

4210 **SHIELALIGH 44** [5]3-8-8 p (66) I Mongan 12/1: 0306655: Dwelt, styd on fnl 1f, nrst fin: 6 wk abs. *hd* **61**

2369 **DESERT DAISY 121** [9]3-8-0 (47) J F McDonald(3) 66/1: 60-00006: Rear, prog when short of room dist, switched & sn no impress: long abs. *¾* **51**

4646 **MISS JUDGEMENT 23** [12]3-8-2 (62) R Ffrench 14/1: 0010007: Handy over 4f, no extra: btr 4317. *nk* **52**

4879 **RED SOVEREIGN 10** [6]3-8-10 (81) R Mullen 3/1 FAV: 6-001058: Chsd ldrs 3f, no extra: btr 3036. *¾* **58**

4976 **EVER CHEERFUL 4** [17]3-8-11 p (66) S Haddon(7) 40/1: 1052609: Nvr nrr than mid-div: qck reapp. *nk* **58**

4976 **BELLA TUTRICE 4** [1]3-8-2 p (64) F P Ferris(3) 25/1: 0300000: 10th: Cl-up 3f, wknd: qck reapp. *3* **40**

4740 **ILTRAVITORE 18** [11]3-8-4 (57) J F Egan 25/1: 005000: 11th: Nvr nrr than mid-div. *½* **41**

4698 **MELODY KING 20** [3]3-8-6 (1ow)bl (55) S Drowne 8/1: 5U06040: 12th: Mid-div 3f, wknd. *1¾* **38**

4317 **BLACK SABBETH 39** [7]3-8-5 (59) R Smith 50/1: 0006400: 13th: Bhd, nvr a factor. *¾* **35**

3844 **JAVA GOLD 61** [13]3-7-13 C Haddon(7) 100/1: 00: 14th: Led, hdd 2f out, fdd. *1¼* **25**

4739 **HES A ROCKET 18** [16]3-8-9 bl (52) Hayley Turner(3) 16/1: 6020000: 15th: Cl-up wide till halfway. *nk* **34**

4236 **Arfinnit 43** [8]3-8-10 vis(55) S Hitchcott 12/1:0 — 4605 **Master Rat 25** [15]3-8-9 D Kinsella 100/1:0

17 Ran Time 1m 11.62 (2.52) Owned: The Square Milers Trained: Kinnersley

BATH SUNDAY 10.10.04 Lefthand, Turning Track with Uphill Finish

5021 3.55 Grosvenor Casinos Nursery Handicap Stakes 2yo 0-75 (E3) [79]
£4930 £1517 £759 **5f11y rnd** **Good 55** **+06 Fast** Far side

4784 **CHILLY CRACKER 15** [13] R Hollinshead 2-8-13 (64) D Sweeney 12/1: 2610031: Made all, rdn out ins fnl 1f: fast time: eff at 5f on gd, gd/soft grnd & fibresand: still only lightly rcd & can rate higher. **74**
4907 **STAR DUSTER 8** [16] B R Millman 2-9-2 (67) G Baker 3/1 FAV: 020222: Handy, chsd wnr 2f out, kept on but not pace of wnr ins fnl 1f: continues to run well & deserves to go one btr: see 4907 & 4830. *1½* **72**
4577 **AUWITESWEETHEART 26** [18] B R Millman 2-9-3 (68) S Drowne 14/1: 5553: Rear, prog halfway, kept on despite on hanging left ins fnl 1f, nrst fin: eff at 5f, worth another try over 6f on this evidence: acts on gd grnd: imprvd eff on h'cap bow & can progress: see 2373. *shd* **72**
4543 **IL PRANZO 27** [12] S Kirk 2-9-5 (70) J F Egan 7/1: 063504: Chsd ldrs, no extra dist: btr 3361. *1¾* **69**
4420 **LUCKY EMERALD 34** [14]2-9-7 T (72) S Hitchcott 25/1: 20105: Rear, prog halfway, btn when hmpd ins fnl 1f: first time t-strap: shade closer with clr run: btr 3728. *¾* **69**
4830 **MAJESTICAL 13** [6]2-8-8 (59) L Keniry(3) 11/1: 0042406: Handy over 3f, wknd: btr 3847. *2* **50**
4765 **CROSS MY SHADOW 16** [11]2-8-6 BL t (57) C Haddon(7) 50/1: 050007: In tch, fdd dist: tried blnks. *1½* **44**
4706 **ROBMANTRA 20** [10]2-8-8 p (59) D Corby(3) 16/1: 6536048: Nvr nrr than mid-div. *½* **45**
4679 **AGENT KENSINGTON 22** [3]2-9-2 (67) J Fortune 10/1: 3242009: Chsd ldrs over 3f, wknd: btr 3848. *½* **52**
3745 **CONCERT TIME 65** [19]2-7-12 (2oh) (47) Hayley Turner(3) 33/1: 0365330: 10th: Handy 3f, wknd. *½* **33**
4369 **BEFORE THE DAWN 36** [9]2-7-13 (50) D Kinsella 20/1: 00000: 11th: In tch 3f, wknd. *hd* **33**
3271 **LITTLE BISCUIT 85** [4]2-8-9 (60) R Ffrench 14/1: 2542640: 12th: Missed break, nvr a factor. *2* **37**
4830 **RUBYS DREAM 13** [1]2-8-13 (64) P Fitzsimons 33/1: 4354000: 13th: In tch 3f, wknd: btr 3258. *1* **38**
4545 **MISTER BELL 27** [17]2-8-3 (54) J F McDonald(3) 33/1: 36000: 14th: Missed break, nvr a factor. *hd* **27**
4706 **KNOCK BRIDGE 20** [8]2-9-0 (65) J Dekeyser 6/1: 42030: 15th: Missed break, al in rear. *nk* **37**
4337 **TOWN END TOM 38** [7]2-8-7 BL (58) Martin Dwyer 33/1: 56600: 16th: In tch when stumbled 4f out, wknd halfway: first time blnks. *1½* **26**
4123 **WATERLINE LOVER 48** [20]2-8-6 VIS (57) Natalia Gemelova(5) 33/1: 0040640: 17th: In tch wide 3f. *1* **22**
3896 **Ms Polly Garter 59** [5]2-7-13 (4oh)(45) R Thomas 66/1:01808 **Little Wizzy 146** [15]2-9-7 (72) F P Ferris(3) 20/1:0
19 Ran Time 1m 2.76 (2.46) Owned: Mr John L Marriott Trained: Upper Longdon

5022 4.30 Bet365 Call 08000 322365 Handicap Stakes 3yo+ 56-70 (E3) [80]
£4729 £1455 £728 **1m5y rnd** **Good 55** **-00 Slow** Inside

4581 **PARNASSIAN 26** [13] G B Balding 4-9-4 (70) R Thomas(3) 8/1: 1543031: Missed break, prog 3f out, styd on to lead dist, drvn out to hold on: acts on firm & fast, loves gd & gd/soft grnd: enjoys being held up off a strong pace: progressive 4yo: see 4067 & 3225. **79**
4452 **WELCOME SIGNAL 33** [6] J R Fanshawe 4-9-1 p (67) M Hills 5/1 FAV: 0550322: Rear, prog wide dist, kept on ins fnl 1f, just denied: eff at 7f, ran to form on return to 1m: another consistent run: see 4452. *nk* **74**
4668* **TAGULA BLUE 22** [8] J A Glover 4-9-4 t (70) D Kinsella 6/1: 3654013: Missed break, prog wide 3f out, kept on ins fnl 1f, nrst fin: 6lb higher than recent win in 4668 (gd/soft). *2* **73**
4832 **LOCKSTOCK 13** [7] M S Saunders 6-9-4 p (70) N Mackay(3) 7/1: 0100054: Cl-up, led bef 1f out, hdd dist, no extra: btr 1542 (soft). *1¾* **69**
4719 **NEARLY A FOOL 19** [2]6-9-1 vis (67) N Pollard 28/1: 1340505: Mid-div, no impress dist: btr 3423. *2* **62**
3465 **J R STEVENSON 77** [1]8-9-3 (69) I Mongan 12/1: 2046506: Nvr nrr than mid-div: 11 wk abs: btr 1736. *nk* **63**
4740 **DANIFAH 18** [4]3-9-0 (69) F P Ferris(3) 16/1: 1130107: Led till dist, no extra: btr 4709 (hvy). *1½* **60**
4709 **PREMIER ROUGE 20** [15]3-8-12 (67) P Robinson 10/1: 443238: Cl-up 6f, sn wknd: btr 4709 & 4252. *1* **56**
4943 **SMOOTHLY DOES IT 6** [5]3-9-0 (69) J F Egan 8/1: 0401269: Nvr nrr than mid-div: qck reapp. *nk* **57**
4581 **LAKOTA BRAVE 26** [11]10-9-3 (69) S Drowne 25/1: 4000640: 10th: Nvr nrr than mid-div. *½* **56**
3535 **DARK RAIDER 74** [16]3-9-1 (70) D Corby(3) 50/1: 2551000: 11th: Cl-up 6f, fdd. *1* **55**
1273 **DEL MAR SUNSET 173** [10]5-8-13 (65) R Hills 14/1: 3-450100: 12th: Al rear: long abs: btr 942. *1* **48**
4620 **Travelling Band 24** [9]6-9-4 BL(70) L Keniry(3) 16/1:0 4334 **Priors Dale 38** [12]4-8-13 T(65) Martin Dwyer 40/1:0
4975 **Hunters Valley 4** [3]3-8-10 (65) J Fortune 20/1:0 4399 **Fen Gypsy 35** [14]6-9-4 (70) Natalia Gemelova(5) 20/1:0
16 Ran Time 1m 42.70 (4.4) Owned: Miss B Swire Trained: Andover

5023 5.05 Coast Spas Maiden Stakes 3yo+ (D3)
£3689 £1135 £568 **1m2f46y** **Good 55** **-17 Slow** Inside

MARIAS MAGIC 126 [10] John M Oxx 3-8-7 Martin Dwyer 5/2 FAV: 61: b f Mtoto - Majoune (Take Risks) Led, hdd after 1f, styd on to lead bef 1f out, rdn out: Irish raider, long abs: earlier unplcd on debut in native Ireland: eff at 10f on gd grnd: acts on a turning trk & goes well fresh: now will be trained in Britain. **79**
4766 **SAFIRAH 16** [7] M A Jarvis 3-8-7 (69) P Robinson 9/2: 35502: Chsd ldrs, styd on fnl 1.5f, not pace of wnr: op 6/1: eff at 10f, further shld suit: acts on gd grnd: see 2843. *1½* **75**
SWIFT SAILOR [2] M Johnston 3-8-12 R Ffrench 16/1: 3: Cl-up, led 4f out, hdd bef 1f out, no extra: debut: eff at 10f, further shld suit: acts on gd grnd: encouraging debut. *hd* **79**
4768 **DOVEDALE 16** [9] Mrs Mary Hambro 4-8-12 V Slattery 80/1: 04: Handy, prog 2f out, onepace fnl 1f. *1¾* **71**
1832 **STAR MAGNITUDE 145** [15]3-8-12 (75) J Fortune 9/2: 0225: Handy 1m, no extra: long abs: btr 1832. *1½* **73**
4861 **RAMBO BLUE 11** [12]4-9-3 D Sweeney 100/1: 06: Nvr nrr than mid-div. *2½* **69**
4898 **JONANAUD 9** [13]5-9-3 F P Ferris(3) 16/1: 67: Nvr nrr than mid-div. *½* **68**
4911 **NEWS SKY 8** [6]3-8-12 P (75) M Hills 4/1: 022338: Handy 1m, wknd. *1* **66**
4944 **MRS PHILIP 6** [19]5-8-12 S Drowne 66/1: 0009: Rear, nvr a factor. *1* **59**
ISLEOFHOPEANTEARS 68 [16]5-9-3 D Kinsella 50/1: 500: 10th: Rear, prog 4f out, fdd 2f out. *2* **61**
4768 **ALGHAAZY 16** [3]3-8-12 N Mackay(3) 20/1: 00: 11th: Handy 1m, fdd. *1¼* **59**
4081 **GENTLE RAINDROP 51** [5]3-8-7 (58) J F Egan 40/1: 0500000: 12th: Al in rear. *1¼* **52**
WOOLSTONE BOY [17]3-8-12 G Baker 50/1: 0: 13th: Missed break, nvr a factor. *3* **53**
4541 **TYUP POMPEY 28** [4]3-8-12 L Keniry(3) 20/1: 3-40: 14th: Led after 1f, hdd 4f out, fdd 2f out. *5* **46**
4764 **Princess Bankes 17** [11]3-8-7 (45) I Mongan 40/1:0 4826 **Favourable 13** [18]3-8-7 R Hills 100/1:0
2337 **Bijou Dancer 122** [1]4-9-3 (46) Hayley Turner(3) 50/1:0

2099 **Deewaar 132** [14]4-9-3 (45) P Fitzsimons 80/1.0

18 Ran   Time 2m 13.27 (7.27)   Owned: Newsells Park Stud   Trained: Ireland

5024	5.40 Biffa Waste Services Handicap Stakes 3yo+ 56-70 (E3)			[77]
	£4568 £1406 £703 1m3f144y Good 55 -27 Slow Inside			

4983* **DONT CALL ME DEREK** 3 [18] S C Williams 3-9-11 (6ex) (74) Martin Dwyer 5/4 FAV: 2132111: In tch, **83**
styd on to lead 2f out, pushed out, val 3L+: bckd, qck reapp, 6lb pen: eff at 1m, imprvd for recent step up to
11/12f: acts on firm, gd/soft & both AWs: v prog, wng run may not yet be at an end: see 4983.

4623 **MOUNT BENGER** 24 [15] R M Beckett 4-9-5 VIS (61) R Mullen 33/1: 0410302: Rear, prog wide to chase 1 **66**
wnr ins fnl 1f, al held: eff at 7f, below mark: eff at 1m, improving run pieces left off & visor fitted: see 4248.

4182 **CARRIACOU** 45 [16] P W D'Arcy 3-8-12 (61) J F Egan 25/1: 0530403: Rear, prog wide 4f out, kept on nk **65**
ins fnl 1f: 6 wk abs: now stays 11.6f: on a fair mark: see 3492.

4850 **CRITICAL STAGE** 11 [7] J D Frost 5-9-5 (61) M Halford(7) 20/1: 3130644: Handy, styd on to chase nk **64**
wnr dist, no extra ins fnl 1f: btr 595.

4771 **MISS INKHA** 16 [11]3-8-13 (62) N Mackay(3) 22/1: 0662035: Rear, styd on fnl 1f, nrst fin: btr 4771. 2 **62**

4402 **GOLD GUEST** 35 [6]5-9-6 (62) J Dekeyser 33/1: 1-100456: Nvr nrr than mid-div. hd **61**

4924 **MILK AND SULTANA** 8 [3]4-9-4 (60) A Daly 14/1: 4114037: Nvr nrr than mid-div: btr 4924. 1 **57**

4849 **CHAMPION LION** 12 [1]5-9-11 (67) S Hitchcott 5/1: 5063358: Chsd ldrs, wknd dist: btr 4623 (10f). 1 **62**

2311 **CHIVITE** 123 [17]5-9-11 (67) R Thomas(3) 22/1: 4555/0-09: Chsd ldrs over 1m, wknd: jumps fit. 1½ **59**

4771 **ONWARD TO GLORY** 16 [14]4-9-7 (63) S Drowne 28/1: 60-00460: 10th: Cl-up 9f, fdd: see 2114. nk **54**

4584 **ZAFFEU** 26 [13]3-8-11 (60) V Slattery 25/1: 1060000: 11th: Chsd ldrs, fdd bef 1f out: btr 2413. 3 **46**

4973 **GALLANT BOY** 4 [10]5-9-7 vis t (63) J Mongan 25/1: 4440000: 12th: Chsd ldrs 7f, wknd: btr 4119. nk **46**

4487 **MUSTANG ALI** 31 [9]3-9-0 (63) L P Keniry(3) 16/1: 5535660: 13th: Mid-div over 7f, wknd. 1¼ **46**

4456 **SWIFT ALCHEMIST** 33 [8]4-9-0 p (56) G Baker 33/1: 0000100: 14th: Missed break, nvr a factor. 9 **26**

4850 **COMPETITOR** 11 [2]3-9-0 (63) D Sweeney 50/1: 2005060: 15th: Bhd, nvr a factor. 3½ **28**

4594 **THEATRE TINKA** 26 [20]5-9-0 p (56) R Ffrench 14/1: 0520430: 16th: Led, hdd 2f out, fdd. nk **20**

4973 **BILLY BATHWICK** 4 [19]7-9-1 (57) P Fitzsimons 33/1: 0500000: 17th: Cl-up 1m, wknd. 1¾ **18**

4856 **WESTERN** 11 [5]4-9-0 p (56) N Pollard 50/1: 0000000: 18th: Cl-up, fdd 3f out: btr 288. 15 **0**

4268* **POLISH SPIRIT** 42 [12]9-9-7 (63) J Fortune 6/1: 5///5-00610: 19th: Cl-up wide halfway, wknd: op 5 **0**
10/1: 6 wk abs: btr 4628 (soft).

19 Ran   Time 2m 34.69(9.69)   Owned: The Chummy Northerners   Trained: Newmarket

---

Official Going GOOD/SOFT

5025	2.00 Ucello Ii And Ubu Iii Trophy Stakes Handicap For National Hunt Jockeys 3yo+ 56-70 (E3)			[42]
	£3513 £1081 £541 2m Good 51 -62 Slow Inside			

4856 **SAN HERNANDO** 11 [3] D R C Elsworth 4-11-9 (65) R Young 11/1: 0420001: Rear, hdwy to lead after **75**
6f, styd on well for press ins fnl 1f: stays 12f/2m on firm & gd, prob any trk: see 948.

4965 **MADIBA** 5 [10] P Howling 5-10-12 (54) M A Fitzgerald 16/1: 00P5262: In tch, hdwy over 3f out, 1½ **61**
chall 1f out, found little for press: qck reapp: back to winning form of 306.

4276 **ROSSALL POINT** 41 [9] J L Dunlop 3-10-8 (61) T Scudamore 16/1: 450403: Bhd, hdwy over 2f out, shd **67**
onepcd ins fnl 1f: 6 wk abs: eff at 14f/2m: back to form of 3998.

4856 **SNOWS RIDE** 11 [8] W R Muir 4-11-2 (58) J M Maguire 11/1: 0006404: Trkd ldrs, no impress over 1f out. 5 **59**

4856* **IRISH BLADE** 11 [4]3-11-11 (78) R Johnson 2/1 FAV: 0003215: Cl-up, hdwy into 2nd over 4f out to 2½ **76**
2f out, sn btn: nicely bckd: shade btr 4856.

3822* **TOMMY CARSON** 62 [16]9-10-11 (13oh) (40) S Curran 33/1: 26/5-3016: Led till over 10f out, no extra. ¾ **50**

4361 **MOON EMPEROR** 37 [15]7-11-11 (67) R Hughes 11/1: 0466007: Bhd, hdwy over 3f out, wknd over 1f out. 6 **58**

1291 **SUNGIO** 172 [12]6-10-11 (8oh) (45) C Studd 33/1: 3123358: In tch, outpcd 3f out, sn btn: long abs. 3 **41**

4423 **HEART SPRINGS** 34 [2]4-10-11 (8oh) (45) A Thornton 50/1: 0045209: Dwelt in rear, hdwy over 3f out, shd **40**
wknd over 2f out: stiff task at weights: btr 4056 (soft).

4512 **REDSPIN** 29 [14]4-11-3 (59) S Durack 14/1: 4000300: 10th: Cl-up, hdwy into 2nd over 6f out till 1½ **44**
over 4f out, no impress 3f out: see 4112.

2340 **PIPSSALIO** 122 [6]7-10-11 (8oh)t (45) M Batchelor 33/1: 3-626200: 11th: Bhd, nvr a factor: long abs. 2½ **35**

4771 **SUN HILL** 16 [13]4-11-9 (65) C Llewellyn 10/1: 1005000: 12th: Rcd in 2nd till over 10f out, wknd 5f out. 2 **45**

4824 **HENRY ISLAND** 13 [7]11-10-13 (55) L Fletcher 9/1: 4002040: 13th: In tch, wknd 4f out. 1¼ **34**

1629 **KAPAROLO** 155 [11]5-11-10 (66) J Crowley 14/1: 30650-00: 14th: Cl-up, fdd over 3f out: long abs. 1¼ **44**

1271 **MISTER PUTT** 173 [1]6-11-4 bl (60) L Aspell 20/1: 300//60-20: 15th: Nvr a factor: long NH abs. 7 **31**

15 Ran   Time 3m 42.43 (18.13)   Owned: The Madding Crowd   Trained: Whitsbury

5026	2.35 Royal Navy Claiming Stakes 3yo (E3)		
	£6841 £2105 £1053 1m3f Good 51 -79 Slow Outside		

4261 **ST BARCHAN** 42 [7] W Jarvis 3-9-3 (72) T Quinn 5/1: 4231: Rcd in 2nd 2f, remained cl-up, hdwy 3f **77**
out, led ins fnl 1f, cosily: clmd for 18,000: first win: 6 wk abs: eff at 9/10f, relished this step up to 11f:
acts on fast & soft, sharp trk: sure to win again in this grade: see 2843 (debut).

4315 **ZUMA** 39 [5] R Hannon 3-9-5 (72) R Hughes 10/1: 3055442: Bhd, hdwy 3f out, styd on ins fnl 1f: 1½ **73**
eff at 1m, clearly stays 11f well: acts on firm & gd: back to form of 2072.

4584 **MARIA BONITA** 26 [3] Mrs Stef Liddiard 3-8-12 (60) S Whitworth 12/1: 4040433: Rear, not clr run ½ **65**
3f out, hdwy 2f out, styd on well ins fnl 1f: gd run on first start for new yard (prev R Beckett): eff at
10/11f on gd & polytrack: see 4112.

3914 **KEEPERS KNIGHT** 58 [9] P F I Cole 3-9-0 (62) N De Souza(5) 20/1: 5000354: Rear, hdwy over 3f out, shd **66**
onepcd fnl 1f: 8 wk abs: stays 10/11f on gd & polytrack, prob fm: gd run, back to winning form of 365.

4834* **SOVIET SCEPTRE** 13 [2]3-8-10 (66) R Miles 9/2: 0460015: Rcd in 2nd after 2f, hdwy to lead over nk **61**
4f out till ins fnl 1f, no extra: clr of rem: poss stays 11f: see 4834 (10f).

4579 **PANGLOSS** 26 [4]3-9-0 bl (60) R L Moore 7/1: 0504566: In tch, hung right & wknd 2f out: shade btr 1260. 3 **60**

4857* FIZZY LADY 11 [6]3-8-4 (52) C Catlin 10/1: 0024017: Trkd ldrs, no impress over 1f out.   5   42
4877 POLAR DANCER 10 [8]3-9-0 (63) W Supple 6/1: 0300338: Trkd ldrs, no impress over 1f out: op 9/1.   5   44
4453 KABIS BOOIE 33 [1]3-8-9 (70) W Ryan 4/1 FAV: 24-39: Led till over 4f out, fdd 2f out, t.o.: bckd.   18   12
9 Ran   Time 2m 32.26 (14.36)   Owned: The Phantom House Partnership   Trained: Newmarket

---

5027   3.10 Gordon's Of Yiewsley Stakes Handicap 3yo 71-85 (D2)   [94]
£6744   £2075   £1038   1m   Good 51   +06 Fast   Inside

4909 LORD LINKS 8 [8] R Hannon 3-8-11 (77) R L Moore 3/1: 0004031: Rcd in 2nd, hdwy to lead over 2f   86
out, chall over 1f out, drvn out to hold on ins fnl 1f: nicely bckd from 5/1: winning form btwn 5f/1m, handles firm
& gd, sharp/undul or stiff/gall trk: another gd run, see 1847.
4977 MASTER THEO 4 [7] H J Collingridge 3-8-7 (73) T Quinn 12/1: 3330342: Trkd ldrs, hdwy to chall   nk   80
fnl 1f, found little for press: qck reapp: v consistent: see 2325.
4266 CARTRONAGEERAGHLAD 42 [9] J A Osborne 3-8-8 bl (74) Dane O'Neill 20/1: 4454003: Keen & handy,   2   77
hdwy over 2f out, not pace of first 2 fnl 1f: 6 wk abs: back to form of 2024.
4607 MRS PANKHURST 25 [4] B W Hills 3-8-3 (69) J Quinn 12/1: 0-505604: Keen in rear, not clr run 2f   ½   71
out, switched over 1f out, kept on: op 9/1: handles fast & gd: see 923.
4806 TRANQUIL SKY 14 [2]3-9-0 (80) W Supple 13/2: 5204055: Bhd, some late gains.   1¼   79
4613 LADYS VIEW 25 [6]3-9-2 (82) T E Durcan 25/1: 41-3006: Slow away, sn in tch, wknd over 1f out.   nk   80
4872 ENFORD PRINCESS 10 [5]3-9-0 (80) R Hughes 8/1: 0340467: Trkd ldrs, hdwy over 2f out, wknd 1f out.   hd   77
4777 BORDER MUSIC 16 [1]3-9-0 (80) N Chalmers(3) 5/2 FAV: 0322348: Wide in rear, nvr nr ldrs: nicely bckd.   1½   74
4683 FREAK OCCURENCE 22 [3]3-8-8 (74) R Havlin 12/1: 3060009: Bhd, hmpd 2f out, sn btn.   3½   61
4709 FLEET ANCHOR 20 [10]3-8-2 (55) C Catlin 50/1: 0025350: 10th: Al bhd.   1½   52
4777 OVERDRAWN 16 [11]3-8-9 bl (75) S W Kelly 20/1: 0000000: 11th: Dwelt, sn led, hdd over 2f out, no   25   9
extra when sn hmpd, t.o.: much btr 1315.
11 Ran   Time 1m 41.07 (3.67)   Owned: Coriolan Links Partnership VI   Trained: Marlborough

---

5028   3.45 EBF Racing Uk On Sky 432 Stakes Handicap Fillies & Mares 3yo+ 86-100 (C1)   [101]
£13280   £4086   £2043   1m4f   Good 51   -42 Slow   Outside

4467 NUZOOA 32 [3] M P Tregoning 3-9-3 (90) W Supple 6/1: 2-1501: Rear, hdwy over 2f out, led over 1f   100
out, styd on well for press ins fnl 1f: eff at 10/12f, may stay further: acts on firm & gd, gall or sharp/undul
trks: back to form with blnks left off: useful, win again at this trip: see 2349.
4468 SAND AND STARS 32 [1] M H Tompkins 3-8-9 (82) J Mackay 2/1 FAV: 5212032: In tch, styd on to go   3½   84
2nd ins fnl 1f, no ch with wnr: acts on gd: see 4468.
4781 LIGHT WIND 15 [6] Mrs A J Perrett 3-8-13 (86) R L Moore 7/2: 511563: Led for 4f, no extra 2f out.   ½   87
4360 BLAZE OF COLOUR 37 [7] Sir Michael Stoute 3-8-5 vis (78) J Quinn 3/1: 4231424: Keen & led after   2½   75
4f, hdd over 1f out, no extra: shade btr 3299.
4149 CARINI 47 [2]3-9-7 (94) Dane O'Neill 11/1: 11-36305: Dwelt, sn in mid-div, no impress over 4f out.   5   83
4966 QUICKSTYX 5 [4]3-8-0 VIS (65) T Dean(7) 20/1: 5446066: Keen, in tch, hdwy into 2nd 7f out to 4f   dist 12
out, sn fdd, t.o.: qck reapp, tried a visor: much btr 4966.
6 Ran   Time 2m 42.98 (11.18)   Owned: Mr Hamdan Al Maktoum   Trained: Lambourn

---

5029   4.20 Autumn Extended Maiden Stakes 3yo (D3)
£3474   £1069   £535   1m6f   Good 51   -13 Slow   Inside

4395 TURNSTILE 36 [7] R Hannon 3-9-0 (73) R L Moore 3/1: 2032061: In tch, hdwy to lead over 2f out,   75
sn chall, styd on gamely for press ins fnl 1f: nicely bckd: stays 14f well, further may suit: acts on fast &
gd/soft, sharp/undul trk: confidence boosted, see 1211.
3894 NIOBES WAY 59 [6] P R Chamings 3-8-9 (66) W Ryan 14/1: 0432: Bhd, hdwy 4f out, chall 2f out,   shd   69
just held nr fin: clr of rem, 8 wk abs: stays 14f on gd & gd/soft: shown enough to find a race: see 3894.
4486 MARKET LEADER 31 [4] Mrs A J Perrett 3-8-9 (67) Dane O'Neill 9/1: 502-3333: Trkd ldrs, hdwy over   9   55
2f out, sn no impress: op 7/1: btr 4267.
4414 TASHREEFAT 34 [2] E F Vaughan 3-8-9 T (68) W Supple 8/1: 3424: Cl-up, hdwy to lead over 3f out   nk   54
till over 2f out, sn no extra: t-strap: longer trip: btr 4414.
3783 DAY ONE 64 [5]3-9-0 T Quinn 4/1 FAV: 0-35: In tch, hdwy over 4f out, no impress 2f out: nicely bckd.   ½   58
4898 HELM 9 [12]3-9-0 P Doe 33/1: 046: Bhd, outpcd over 4f out, modest late gains: btr 4898.   ¾   57
4861 FENDER 11 [11]3-9-0 bl R Hughes 14/1: 07: b c Rainbow Quest - Rockfest (Stage Door Johnny) Keen   8   45
& cl-up, hdwy to lead over 4f out till over 3f out, sn no extra: dam a smart 2/3yo: half-brother to wnrs at 10/12f.
4861 ALL BLUE 11 [13]3-9-0 T E Durcan 7/1: 448: Trkd ldrs, not clr run 3f out, sn no impress: btr 4861.   4   39
4898 VERASI 9 [9]3-9-0 bl (60) S W Kelly 66/1: 00-40009: Bhd, nvr a factor: much btr 1514 (1m).   ¾   38
4898 RUGGTAH 9 [10]3-8-9 (65) C Catlin 16/1: 0350: 10th: Chsd ldrs, wknd 4f out.   3½   28
4579 SILKEN JOHN 26 [3]3-9-0 R Miles(3) 50/1: 050: 11th: ch g Grand Lodge - Lady Ela (Ela Mana Mou)   dist 0
Led till over 4f out, no extra, t.o.: cost 18,000gns: dam unrcd: with J Portman.
11 Ran   Time 3m 7.76 (8.96)   Owned: The Queen   Trained: Marlborough

---

5030   4.55 Cocked Hat Maiden Stakes 3yo+ (D3)
£3455   £1063   £532   6f   Good 51   +05 Fast   Stands side

4946 DR SYNN 6 [6] J Akehurst 3-9-0 (66) M Tebbutt 5/1: 0203401: Prom, hdwy to lead over 2f out, styd   77
on well for press to hold on ins fnl 1f: qck reapp: eff at 6f on fast, gd & enjoys soft, sharp/undul trk: see 1722.
4445 GREAT EXHIBITION 33 [10] Saeed bin Suroor 3-9-0 t (77) T E Durcan 2/1 J FAV: 32-00322: Trkd ldrs,   hd   75
hdwy to chall ins fnl 1f, not pass wnr: bckd: found one too gd again: worth a try in maidenage: see 4445.
RUSSIAN CAFE 0 [11] M A Magnusson 3-8-9 T Dane O'Neill 14/1: 3: b f Stravinsky - Bistro   2   64
(Strawberry Road) Mid-div & wide, hdwy over 2f out, not pace of first 2 ins fnl 1f & eased nr fin on debut: clr of
rem: cost 50,000gns: dam unrcd: eff at 6f, 7f may suit: acts on gd: should learn from this.
4836 IMTALKINGGIBBERISH 13 [8] J R Jenkins 3-9-0 (75) W Ryan 8/1: 0502054: In tch, no impress.   5   54
4847 RABBIT 12 [4]3-8-9 S Righton 33/1: 005: b f Muhtarram - Ninia (Affirmed) Led till over 2f out,   ½   47
no extra over 1f out: cost 6,800gns: half-sister to a French 1m wnr: dam wnr over 7f/10f: with Mrs A King.

GOODWOOD SUNDAY 10.10.04 Righthand, Undulating, Sharpish Track

4835 **DIAPHANOUS 13** [9]6-8-10 (30) S Carson 66/1: 0000006: Keen in rear, hdwy over 2f out, wknd 1f out. *1¼* **43**
3920 **BEE MINOR 58** [2]3-8-9 (70) R L Moore 2/1 J FAV: 0200247: Dwelt, sn handy, found little over 2f out, wkng/hung over 1f out: 8 wk abs, nicely bckd: btr 3452. *1* **40**
2575 **TOP PLACE 113** [1]3-8-9 (35) W Supple 33/1: 0055068: In tch, fdd fnl 1f: long abs: see 1075. *1* **37**
146 **LADY KORRIANDA 309** [5]3-8-9 (60) R Miles(3) 20/1: 002-9: Prom, wknd 2f out: now with Lady Herries. *nk* **36**
4091 **LADY FRANPALM 51** [7]4-8-10 (40) J Quinn 100/1: 40-00000: 10th: b f Danehill Dancer - Be Nimble (Wattlefield) Al bhd: 7 wk abs: h'cap, nov & mdn unplcd all '03 starts (rtd 57): '02 unplcd (rtd 68, mdn): eff at 5/6f, handles gd & polytrack, sharp/undul or turning trk. *3* **27**
4845 **VICTORIANA 12** [3]3-8-9 (54) T Quinn 20/1: 64500: 11th: Cl-up early, wknd halfway, t.o. fnl 1f. *28* **0**
11 Ran Time 1m 12.79 (2.79) Owned: Canisbay Bloodstock Trained: Epsom

5031 5.30 Finale Nursery Stakes Handicap 2yo 0-85 (D2) [92]
£7231 £2225 £1113 **7f** **Good 51** **-21 Slow** Inside

4396 **ENFORCER 35** [5] W R Muir 2-9-0 (78) R Miles(3) 16/1: 45201: Bhd, switched to nr side & gd hdwy over 1f out, styd on well ins fnl 1f to lead fnl stride: first win: eff at 6/7f on gd, acts on a sharp/undul trk: lightly rcd, can impr further & shld stay 1m. **88**
4726* **KING MARJU 19** [7] P W Chapple Hyam 2-9-7 (85) J Quinn 9/4 FAV: 6212: Keen & handy, hdwy to lead just over 1f out, hdd fnl stride: tchd 4/1: suited by 6f, stays 7f: acts on firm & gd: continues in gd form. *shd* **94**
4737 **WAVERTREE WARRIOR 21** [6] N P Littmoden 2-8-13 (77) J P Guillambert(3) 20/1: 03203: In tch, hdwy over 1f out, styd on ins fnl 1f: stays 7f: back to form: see 3120. *1* **84**
3927 **COUP DETAT 58** [13] J L Dunlop 2-9-6 (84) T Quinn 9/1: 4264: Dwelt, hdwy 3f out, hung over 1f out, styd on: 8 wk abs: back to form, see 3927. *½* **90**
4078 **RIVER BISCUIT 51** [18]2-8-6 (70) R L Moore 25/1: 0505: In tch, hdwy over 2f out, not pace of ldrs: 7 wk abs: back to form on this drop back to 7f, acts on gd grnd: see 3390. *shd* **75**
4727 **KEEP BACCKINHIT 19** [16]2-9-0 (78) A Quinn(5) 10/1: 0315046: Trkd ldrs, rcd far side straight, onepcd. *shd* **82**
4810 **BROOKLIME 14** [12]2-9-2 (80) S W Kelly 9/1: 4105267: Rcd in 2nd, hdwy & ch 1f out, sn no impress. *½* **83**
4894 **ABERDEEN PARK 9** [9]2-8-5 (69) P Doe 7/1: 0045228: Rcd in 2nd, hdwy to dspt lead 1f out, no impress. *nk* **71**
4753 **RATUKIDUL 17** [11]2-9-2 (80) Dane O'Neill 8/1: 159: In tch, onepcd over 1f out. *¾* **80**
4725 **PENNY ISLAND 19** [17]2-8-8 (72) J D Smith 12/1: 06350: 10th: Led till just over 1f out, no extra fnl 1f. *hd* **71**
4580 **BRIANNSTA 26** [4]2-8-12 (76) T E Durcan 20/1: 652100: 11th: Bhd, modest late gains. *1½* **72**
4580 **BENEDICT BAY 26** [14]2-8-2 (1ow)VIS (65) S Carson 100/1: 60000: 12th: Dwelt, nvr a factor: see 2696. *2* **58**
4471 **SIMPLIFY 31** [1]2-8-13 bl (77) R Hughes 16/1: 3250100: 13th: Bhd, hdwy over 2f out, sn btn. *2½* **64**
4810 **CUSOON 14** [15]2-8-12 (76) S Whitworth 25/1: 314400: 14th: Al bhd. *1* **61**
4552 **MANEKI NEKO 27** [8]2-8-11 (75) J Mackay 14/1: 4220: 15th: Chsd ldrs, hung throughout, no impress 2f out *1½* **57**
4697 **ELLENS PRINCESS 20** [10]2-8-1 (65) C Catlin 25/1: 54000: 16th: Chsd ldrs, wknd over 3f out: btr 3908. *2* **43**
16 Ran Time 1m 29.54(5.04) Owned: D G Clarke & C L A Edginton Trained: Lambourn

AYR MONDAY 11.10.04 Lefthand, Galloping Track

Official Going Soft (Good/Soft places)

5032 2.00 Racing Uk On Sky 432 Handicap Stakes 3yo+ 56-70 (E3) [86]
£3406 £1048 £524 **1m7f** **Soft** **Inapp** Inside

4308 **HABITUAL DANCER 41** [3] Jedd O'Keeffe 3-7-13 (57) P Hanagan 7/1: 1230501: Handy, hdwy to lead 2f out, hung left & kept on fnl 1f, rdn out: abs: stays 2m1f & likes gd/soft & soft, any trk. **66**
4805 **WINSLOW BOY 15** [10] P Monteith 3-7-12 (56) D Fentiman(7) 10/1: 1263662: Held up, hdwy & short of room dist, styd on well ins last, not pace of wnr: clr of rem & imprvd for step up to 1m7f: acts on fast & soft. *1¼* **63**
4868 **SPRING BREEZE 12** [7] M Dods 3-8-1 vis (59) P Fessey 11/2: 3252163: Led after 1f till 2f out, no extra: not disgraced & poss acts on soft, won on fast grnd in 4675. *6* **60**
4936 **LITTLE TOBIAS 7** [1] Andrew Turnell 5-8-8 (3oh) (53) A Nicholls 12/1: 6013304: Held up, some late gains, nvr dngrs: see 3549. *1¼* **56**
4819 **ALAM 14** [5]5-9-8 (70) R Winston 9/2: 346/0-605: Cl-up, wknd over 1f out: see 4657. *1¼* **69**
3929 **PLATINUM CHARMER 59** [8]4-8-8 (3oh)p (53) Rory Moore(5) 8/1: 0325106: In tch, wknd over 2f out. *3½* **51**
1238 **FLAME OF ZARA 177** [11]5-8-8 (3oh) (53) T Eaves(3) 14/1: 0460-047: Held up, wknd over 2f out: now with J Moffatt: long abs: see 1238. *5* **46**
4808 **PILGRIMS PROGRESS 15** [4]4-9-8 (70) T Williams 25/1: 130-4058: Keen in tch, wknd 2f out. *6* **54**
4936 **CRACKLEANDO 7** [9]3-8-1 (59) J Bramhill 4/1 FAV: 3103209: In tch, wknd over 2f out: btr 3970. *¾* **42**
4406 **GRAN DANA 35** [6]4-9-4 (66) R Ffrench 20/1: 1000000: 10th: In tch, wknd over 2f out. *12* **39**
4771 **FLIGHT COMMANDER 17** [2]4-9-0 (62) D Allan 66/1: 55-5000: 11th: Held up, wknd 3f out: see 4135. *18* **21**
11 Ran Time 3m 28.9 (19.1) Owned: The Country Stayers Trained: Leyburn

5033 2.30 European Breeders Fund Linfern Maiden Stakes Fillies 2yo (D2)
£5470 £1683 £842 **1m rnd** **Soft** **Inapp** Inside

4723 **RUSSIAN REVOLUTION 20** [4] Saeed bin Suroor 2-8-11 t K McEvoy 8/13 FAV: 31: Cl-up, led 2f out, kept on for press, drvn out: well bckd: stays 1m, 10f will suit: acts on firm & soft: wears a t-strap: rate higher. **84**
4769 **SQUAW DANCE 17** [1] W J Haggas 2-8-11 P Hanagan 16/1: 632: Keen cl-up, eff over 1f out, kept on ins last, just held: stays 1m: imprvd again & will be winning shortly: see 4769, 3975. *shd* **83**
4653 **CONSIDER THIS 24** [5] W M Brisbourne 2-8-11 (79) S W Kelly 12/1: 2532023: Led till 2f out, kept on same pace: consistent in defeat & stays 1m on fast & soft: see 4653. *1* **81**
4746 **INCA WOOD 19** [2] M Johnston 2-8-11 (74) R Ffrench 33/1: 2204: Held up, outpcd over 2f out, rallied late: shapes likes mid-dists will suit next term: see 4464, 4147. *1¼* **78**
3761 **MINTLAW 65** [9]2-8-11 R Winston 9/2: 25: Keen, held up, hung left & no extra dist: abs. *2½* **72**
4842 **ZAYN ZEN 13** [6]2-8-11 (80) P Robinson 16/1: 6425: In tch, no extra dist: btr 4842 (fast). *5* **62**
4866 **GLOBE TREKKER 12** [7]2-8-11 (71) J Carroll 50/1: 0447: Al bhd. *5* **50**
WHIRLING [3]2-8-11 N Callan 100/1: 8: ch f Groom Dancer - Supersonic (Shirley Heights) In tch, wknd over 2f out on debut: Feb first foal, cost 4,000gns: dam styd 10f: bred to want mid-dists. *7* **36**

AYR   MONDAY 11.10.04   Lefthand, Galloping Track

4782 **LIMIT 16** [8]2-8-11   A Culhane 10/1: 39: In tch, wknd over 2f out: see 4782. *dist* **0**
9 Ran   Time 1m 47.96 (11.36)   Owned: Godolphin   Trained: Newmarket

5034 3.00 Daily Record Punter 'premier' Claiming Stakes 3yo (D3)
£5398 £1661 £830   **1m2f**   **Soft**   **Inapp** Inside

TRICKSTEP 60 [1] I Semple 3-9-1 (47) Darren Williams 16/1: 0000261: b c Imperial Ballet - Trick   **72**
of Ace (Clever Trick) Handy, hdwy to lead 2f out, hdd briefly ins last, kept on gamely, all out: 2 month abs,
earlier rnr-up in a clmr in native Ireland: eff over 10/13f on gd & soft: eff with/without blnks & goes well fresh.
4923 **CHARLIE TANGO 9** [3] N Tinkler 3-8-12 (63) R Winston 6/1: 5000402: Held up, hdwy over 2f out, led   *shd* **68**
briefly ins last, just held for press: clr of rem & acts on fast, soft & polytrack: ran to best: see 2565.
4701* **PLATINUM PIRATE 21** [7] K R Burke 3-9-1 bl (65) Rory Moore(5) 11/4: 6540113: Held up, eff to chase   **6**   **61**
wnr 2f out, no extra fnl 1f: well bckd: shade more expected after win in 4701 (gd).
4505 **CAMPBELLS LAD 30** [5] A Berry 3-8-8 (45) P Hanagan 25/1: 0053024: Keen in tch, wknd over 1f out.   ¾   **53**
4821 **BIJOU DAN 14** [8]3-8-12 (58) T Eaves(3) 40/1: 4605: Handy, wknd over 2f out: see 4453, 3246.   **4**   **54**
4944 **ZAKFREE 7** [9]3-9-1 bl (66) J Brahill(3) 11/4: 030-2226: Held up, wknd 2f out: btr 4944, 4286.   *nk*   **53**
4937 **GREAT SCOTT 7** [2]3-9-7 P (74) R Ffrench 5/2 FAV: 3400057: Led till 2f out, wknd: bckd: see 3598.   **3**   **49**
4593 **FIFTH COLUMN 27** [6]3-8-5 (53) T Williams 66/1: 0-0005P: In tch, wknd 3f out, p.u. & dismounted.   **0**
8 Ran   Time 2m 18.58 (14.18)   Owned: Market Avenue Racing Club Ltd   Trained: Carluke

5035 3.30 Racinguk Tv Joe Carr Memorial Nursery Handicap Stakes 2yo 0-85 (DD)   [92]
£5574 £1715 £858   **6f str**   **Soft**   **Inapp** Stands Side

4556 **PARIS BELL 28** [7] T D Easterby 2-7-12 (62) P M Quinn 33/1: 3500401: Chsd ldrs, hdwy to lead ins   **72**
fnl 1f, kept on, rdn out:—first win: eff over 5/6f & likes soft grnd: see 1143.
4882 **ZOMERLUST 11** [11] J J Quinn 2-9-1 (79) R Winston 9/4 FAV: 312442: Held up, short of room   *nk*   **88**
halfway, switched & kept on fnl 1f, just held: hvly bckd: acts on firm & soft: running well: see 4535, 4306.
4765 **SELKIRK STORM 17** [4] M W Easterby 2-8-1 (65) Dale Gibson 16/1: 2500003: Cl-up, led over 3f out   ½   **72**
till ins last, kept on, not btn far: best 1677 (auct mdn, debut).
3935 **PROPELLOR 58** [12] A Dickman 2-9-6 (84) D Allan 11/1: 31344: Bhd, hdwy over 1f out, kept on late,   ½   **89**
nrst fin: 2 month abs: well worth a try over 7f now: see 3202.
4244* **TSAROXY 44** [9]2-9-0 (78) P Mulrennan(3) 5/1: 3315: Handy, trav well till rdn & onepace fnl 1f: 6   *shd*   **82**
wk abs: acts on gd & soft: clr of rem: see 4244 (auct mdn).
4963 **DISPOL ISLE 6** [14]2-8-1 (65) P Fessey 7/1: 4444356: Handy, short of room 2f out, sn no extra.   **3**   **60**
4972 **NASSEEM DUBAI 5** [15]2-9-0 (78) A Culhane 12/1: 0625307: Led till 2f out, wknd: see 4653, 4204.   ½   **71**
4688 **CATWALK CLERIC 23** [5]2-9-7 (85) N Callan 10/1: 4120448: Handy, wknd over 1f out: see 4688.   1¼   **74**
4741 **SOCIETY MUSIC 19** [8]2-8-10 bl (74) S W Kelly 20/1: 1360509: In tch, wknd over 2f out.   **2**   **57**
4765 **SYDNEYROUGHDIAMOND 17** [6]2-8-6 (70) S Righton 6/1: 05000: 10th: Al bhd: seek 4385 (fast), 4083.   **7**   **32**
4172 **AFRICAN GIFT 46** [3]2-8-2 (66) P Hanagan 33/1: 30600: 11th: Bhd, hung left & wknd dist: abs.   3½   **18**
4617 **COMPTON CLASSIC 25** [2]2-7-13 (1ow)(6oh) (56) R Ffrench 40/1: 0660: 12th: Al bhd: see 3323.   *shd*   **14**
3944 **ROMANTIC GIFT 58** [13]2-8-0 (64) A Nicholls 14/1: 00000: 13th: b f Cadeaux Genereux - Last   1¾   **10**
Romance (Last Tycoon) In tch, wknd over 2f out: 2 month abs: Feb third foal, cost 13,000gns: bred to apprec 7f.
4490 **STRIKING ENDEAVOUR 31** [1]2-8-12 (76) J Bramhill 20/1: 1600: 14th: Bhd, btn 2f out: best 1574 (debut).4   **10**
14 Ran   Time 1m 14.98 (5.68)   Owned: Ryedale Partners No 8   Trained: Malton

5036 4.00 Doctor Bill Morris Handicap Stakes 3yo 56-70 (E3)   [76]
£3400 £1046 £523   **5f str**   **Soft**   **Inapp** Stands Side

4969* **WESTBOROUGH 6** [11] N Tinkler 3-8-10 (6ex)t (58) Kim Tinkler 20/1: 0602011: Prom, led halfway,   **67**
styd on strongly, rdn out: eff at 5/6f on firm, hvy & any trk: suited by a t-strap: in fine form, see 4969.
4528 **SIR LOIN 30** [10] N Tinkler 3-8-12 vis (60) A Culhane 8/1: 5260222: Led till halfway, kept on well   **1**   **66**
fnl 1f but not quite pace of wnr: acts on fast & soft grnd: in fine form, deserves a change of luck.
4528 **SHORT CHORUS 30** [1] J Balding 3-8-7 p (55) D Allan 14/1: 1242403: Nvr far away, kept on under   ¾   **59**
press fnl 1f & not btn far: acts on firm & soft grnd: see 3599 & 1605.
4754 **TROJAN FLIGHT 18** [12] Mrs J R Ramsden 3-9-7 (69) R Winston 2/1 FAV: 1210424: Held up, styd on   ½   **71**
fnl 1f, nrst fin: hvly bckd: got going too late, see 4754 & 4339.
4278 **GEORGE THE BEST 42** [3]3-9-0 (62) P Hanagan 25/1: 4060005: Chsd ldrs, switched far side, kept on   *nk*   **63**
fnl 1f, nrst fin: 6 wk abs: see 1745.
4696 **SWEET CANDO 22** [5]3-8-10 p (58) R Ffrench 16/1: 5003006: Chsd ldrs, onepcd fnl 1f.   1¼   **55**
4508 **OL LUCY BROON 30** [7]3-8-7 (45) P Fessey 66/1: 600-0007: Rear, some late gains, nvr dngrs: no   **1**   **49**
form this term, incl in a visor: stiff task here, see 1457.
4085 **MUSIOTAL 52** [9]3-8-7 (54) T Eaves(3) 16/1: 5021048: Rear, nvr nr ldrs: 7 wk abs.   *hd*   **48**
4964* **SESSAY 6** [6]3-9-9 (6ex) (71) P Makin(5) 8/1: 5060619: Chsd ldrs, btn 2f out: top-weight: qck   ½   **62**
reapp under a pen & btr 4964 (6f, gd grnd, mdn auct).
4790 **JUNIPER BANKS 16** [8]3-8-9 (57) P Mathers(5) 50/1: 0420-660: 10th: Held up, nvr nr ldrs.   1½   **44**
1951 **MADRA RUA 140** [2]3-8-7 (55) P Mulrennan(2) 50/1: 0050-000: 11th: b g Foxhound - Fun Fashion   **3**   **33**
(Polish Patriot) Chsd ldrs till halfway, long abs: ex Irish, modest form in native country, has tried cheek pieces.
4930 **FYODOR 9** [14]3-9-7 (69) S W Kelly 4/1: 0600040: 12th: Chsd ldrs till halfway, wknd: well bckd.   ½   **45**
4618 **BLUE POWER 25** [4]3-8-12 (60) Darren Williams 14/1: 1020200: 13th: Bhd halfway: btr 4094 (AW).   *hd*   **35**
4696 **TROODOS JET 22** [13]3-8-11 (59) F Lynch 40/1: 4441000: 14th: Prom 3f, wknd: see 3936.   3½   **24**
4845 **MRS SPENCE 13** [15]3-8-7 BL (52) T Lucas 33/1: 25-06000: 15th: Speed till halfway, wknd & eased, t.o. 13   **0**
15 Ran   Time 1m 0.9 (4.3)   Owned: Mr Venning Mr Parks & Mr Raybould   Trained: Malton

5037 4.30 Subscribe To Racing Uk On 08700 860432 Lochranza Handicap Stakes 3yo+ 71-85 (D2) [87]
£6830 £2102 £1051 **1m2f** Soft **Inapp** Inside

4771 **ARTISTIC STYLE** 17 [1] B Ellison 4-9-7 (80) T Eaves(3) 4/1 FAV: 1311121: Chsd ldrs, imprvd to lead **96**
dist, pushed well clr, v easily: well bckd under top-weight, most progressive this term, this was his 5th win: eff
at 1m, suited by 10/12f & acts on both firm & hvy grnd: handles an easy or gall trk: most progressive & type to run
well in the Nov h'cap, esp if the grnd comes up soft: see 4771 & 4623.
4821* **REEM ONE** 14 [5] M A Jarvis 3-8-9 (73) P Robinson 9/2: 12: Keen & prom, left bhd by wnr fnl 1f: 9 **78**
nicely bckd: only 2nd start, met a most progressive rival here: prob acts on soft grnd: see 4821.
    KARELIAN 107 [8] K A Ryan 3-8-9 BL (73) N Callan 9/1: 0-004123: gr g Linamix - Kalikala 2½ **74**
(Darshaan) Led till 2f out, no extra: bckd from 16/1, long abs: ex French, won a h'cap at Lyon Parilly in June
'04: eff at 11/12f on gd grnd, poss handles soft: sharper next time.
4809 **MILLAGROS** 15 [6] I Semple 4-9-0 p (73) D Allan 25/1: 6331334: Prom, led 2f out till dist, wknd. shd **74**
4766 **TROUBLE MOUNTAIN** 17 [14]7-9-2 (75) P Mulrennan(3) 11/2: 0214235: Rear, styd on late, nvr dngrs. shd **75**
4781 **CHARNOCK BATES ONE** 16 [9]3-8-8 (72) G Gibbons 6/1: 0122236: Slow away, nvr nr ldrs: btr 3938. 2 **69**
4656 **ROTUMA** 24 [10]5-9-2 bl (75) S W Kelly 20/1: 1251007: Chsd ldrs 1m, sn btn: btr 3815 (firm grnd). ½ **71**
4620 **YORK CLIFF** 25 [7]6-9-3 (76) A Culhane 33/1: 0-054508: Held up, nvr nr ldrs. ¾ **70**
4656 **LITTLE BOB** 24 [2]3-8-8 (72) K McEvoy 25/1: 2301009: Keen in rear, nvr dngrs: btr 3697. 2½ **62**
4766 **DOWER HOUSE** 17 [3]9-9-1 t (74) F Lynch 33/1: 5405000: 10th: Held up, nvr a factor. 1¾ **61**
4935 **DOUBLE VODKA** 7 [4]3-8-9 (73) P Hanagan 8/1: 0111030: 11th: Chsd ldrs, btn 2f out: btr 4935. 1¾ **57**
4694* **LAURO** 22 [13]4-9-1 (74) R Winston 14/1: 3244010: 12th: Al bhd, t.o.: op 10/1. 19 **28**
4621 **TYTHEKNOT** 25 [11]3-8-9 p (73) Darren Williams 33/1: 3643150: 13th: Prom 1m, wknd, t.o.: btr 4286. 5 **20**
1602 **LYFORD LASS** 157 [15]3-8-6 (70) P Fessey 66/1: 2100: 14th: Slowly away, recovered to chase ldrs 10 **0**
halfway, wknd 3f out, t.o. in last: long abs: longer 1m trip, twice below 1279.
14 Ran Time 2m 17.07 (12.67) Owned: Mr & Mrs D A Gamble Trained: Malton

5038 5.00 Dawn Construction Conditions Stakes 3yo (C2)
£5997 £2275 £1137 **1m rnd** Soft **Inapp** Inside

4638 **SABBEEH** 24 [5] Saeed bin Suroor 3-8-9 t (110) K McEvoy 5/4 FAV: 1016-01: Keen & made most, sn **99**
clr, held on gamely, all out: well bckd: eff at 6/7f, just stays a gall 1m: acts on gd & soft grnd, handles a
sharp or gall trk: runs well fresh in a t-strap: useful, see 4638.
4890 **JAZZ SCENE** 10 [3] M R Channon 3-8-9 VIS (93) A Culhane 6/4: 2245242: Chsd wnr thr'out, sltly shd **98**
outpcd halfway, rallied well fnl 1f & just btn in thrilling fin: well bckd in first time visor, clr of rem:
deserves a win, see 4685 (C/D, h'cap).
4694 **BANANA GROVE** 22 [1] A Berry 3-8-12 (66) P Mathers(5) 100/1: 0P14063: Chsd ldrs till halfway, left 18 **65**
well bhd: highly tried: see 3805 (mdn auct).
1113 **DIVINE GIFT** 184 [4] M A Jarvis 3-9-5 (102) P Robinson 7/2: 2021-144: Prom till halfway, sn bhd, 6 **60**
t.o.: tchd 9/2, long abs: something clrly amiss, not handle soft grnd?: much btr 949 (gd).
    KATIE KAI [2]3-8-4 T Eaves 200/1: 5: b f Cayman Kai - Yemaail (Shaadi) Al bhd, t.o. in last 23 **0**
on debut: highly tried.
5 Ran Time 1m 46.91(10.31) Owned: Godolphin Trained: Newmarket

Official Going Good (Good/Soft Places)

5039 2.10 Shelduck Handicap Stakes Fillies & Mares 3yo+ 56-70 (E3) [82]
£3613 £1112 £556 **5f21 8y str** Good 43 -06 Slow Stands side

3796 **INDIAN MAIDEN** 65 [10] M S Saunders 4-8-8 (62) S Whitworth 25/1: 00-04001: Bhd, prog 2f out, rdn **72**
out to lead cl-home: 9 wk abs, suited by 6f on fibresand & gd, prob handles firm: acts on a stiff/gall or
sharp/turning trk: goes well fresh: apprec draw down weights & can win again on this evidence: see 2760.
4582 **EMERALD FIRE** 27 [15] A M Balding 5-8-3 (57) Martin Dwyer 7/1: 5-600052: Cl-up, led despite hd **65**
hanging left dist, hdd under press cl-home: op 10/1: gd run in defeat & is on a wng mark: see 3109.
3408 **INDIAN STEPPES** 80 [1] Julian Poulton 5-8-12 (66) J Mongan 20/1: 6643063: Mid-div, prog bef 1f 1 **71**
out, kept on, not btn far in 3rd: 11 wk abs: see 2760.
4646 **RIQUEWIHR** 24 [9] D R Loder 4-8-6 (62) L Dettori 9/2 FAV: 10-434: Handy, onepcd dist: see 4646. 1½ **63**
4785 **BINT ROYAL** 16 [13]6-8-5 (1ow) (58) J F Egan 12/1: 0210155: Mid-div, prog 2f out, onepcd fnl 1f. ½ **59**
4646 **ASBO** 24 [8]4-8-3 (57) F Norton 14/1: 00-54356: In tch 4f, sn hung left & no extra: btr 4262. 1¼ **53**
4870 **FAVOUR** 12 [5]4-8-12 (66) K Fallon 5/1: 0600307: Held up, prog halfway, onepcd fnl 1f: op 13/2. nk **61**
4946 **MISSUS LINKS** 7 [18]3-9-1 (70) R Hughes 11/1: 5250648: Cl-up over 4f, no extra: quick reapp. nk **64**
4109* **FAIR COMPTON** 51 [12]3-8-3 (58) R Smith 14/1: 6545519: Cl-up over 4f, wknd: 7 wk abs: btr 4109. 1 **49**
4245 **KARMINSKEY PARK** 44 [17]5-8-4 (58) W Supple 20/1: 0000050: 10th: In tch, ev ch dist, wknd: abs. hd **48**
4622 **SHAROURA** 25 [11]8-8-10 (64) T Hamilton(3) 12/1: 4240030: 11th: Cl-up, fdd bef 1f out: btr 4622. ½ **53**
3456 **PINK SAPPHIRE** 79 [20]3-9-1 BL (70) K Darley 20/1: 0-024640: 12th: In tch, wknd dist: blnks. 1¾ **54**
4964* **CYFRWYS** 6 [4]3-8-11 (6ex)VIS t (66) F P Ferris(3) 14/1: 2260610: 13th: In tch 4f, fdd: qck reapp ½ **49**
& 1st time visor: btr 4964.
4210 **MARABAR** 45 [16]6-8-2 (56) J Quinn 20/1: 2266040: 14th: Al in rear: reportedly in season. 1¾ **34**
3849 **INNCLASSIC** 62 [19]3-8-5 bl (60) B Swarbrick(5) 66/1: 0312000: 15th: Led, hung right & hdd dist, fdd. 2½ **31**
1655 **SOMEWHERE MY LOVE** 154 [7]3-8-9 (64) R Miles(3) 33/1: 50-10030: 16th: Cl-up 4f, fdd. 1 **32**
1423 **Red Galaxy** 166 [2]4-9-2 (70) J Murtagh 50/1:0 4251 **Emsam Ballou** 43 [6]3-8-9 (64) S Sanders 14/1:0
18 Ran Time 1m 12.77 (2.97) Owned: Chris Scott & Peter Hall Trained: Wells

LEICESTER MONDAY 11.10.04 Righthand, Stiff, Galloping Track

5040 2.40 E B F **Hare Maiden Stakes Div 1 Fillies 2yo (D2)**
£5707 £1756 £878 **7f9y str** **Good 43** **-39 Slow** Stands side

CORCORAN [16] Mrs A J Perrett 2-8-11 R Hughes 16/1: 1: b f Lear Fan - Corsini (Machiavellian) **82+**
Handy al trav well, styd on to lead well ins fnl 1f, pushed out, val bit more: debut: Mar foal, sister 10f wnr: dam successful at 7f: sire decent performer at 1m: eff at 7f, 1m/10f will suit next term: acts on gd grnd & a stiff/gall trk: goes well fresh: defied greeness to win a shade cosily & can rate higher.
4631 **KAHIRA 25** [11] M L W Bell 2-8-11 R Mullen 66/1: 02: ch f King's Best - Sine Labe (Vaguely Noble) Rear, prog wide 2f out, kept on ins fnl 1f, just denied: Apr foal, half sister to a useful sprinter: sire Gr1 wnr at 1m: eff at 7f on gd, 1m will suit: sound run, can go one better. *nk* **80**
TEMPESTAD [8] H R A Cecil 2-8-11 W Ryan 11/4: 3: b f Giant's Causeway - Arutua (Riverman) *nk* **79**
Cl-up, kept on ins fnl 1f, not btn far in 3rd: op 9/4, debut: Apr foal, cost 240,000gns: half sister to 6/7f juv wnrs, also 2 mid-dist wnrs: sire top-class 7/10f performer: eff at 7f on gd, further will suit: gd start.
TAJAATHUB [15] E F Vaughan 2-8-11 R Hills 14/1: 4: ch f Aljabr - Tajannub (Dixieland Band) In tch, styd on to lead dist, hdd ins fnl 1f, just held when short of room cl-home: clr rem on debut: Apr foal, half sister wng miler: dam a useful sprinter, sire a smart miler: eff at 7f on gd grnd. *½* **78**
ARIAN [1]2-8-11 R Smith 66/1: 5: Sn in mid-div, prog when short of room 2f out, switched & kept on late under hands & heels: debut: shaped with encouragement & can rate higher with experience. *3* **72**
HASHIMIYA [19]2-8-11 L Dettori 15/8 FAV: 6: b f Gone West - Touch of Greatness (Hero's Honor) *2* **68**
Sn handy, wknd dist: bckd on debut: Feb foal, cost 3,800,000: sister to high-class miler Elusive Quality: dam unrcd, sire fine performer arnd 1m: with Saeed bin Suroor.
4417 **TARABUT 35** [13]2-8-11 W Supple 66/1: 07: In tch when short of room 2f out, wknd: see 4417. *1¾* **64**
4600 **SHAMROCK BAY 26** [12]2-8-11 M Fenton 20/1: 048: Led, hdd dist, wknd: btr 4600. *nk* **63**
TOQUE [20]2-8-11 S Drowne 50/1: 9: Nvr nrr than mid-div on debut. *1* **61**
4918 **RUBY MURRAY 9** [3]2-8-11 S Whitworth 66/1: 0000: 10th: Rear, mod late gains: rcd too freely. *1¾* **57**
4723 **QUEEN TOMYRA 20** [2]2-8-11 N Mackay(3) 50/1: 00: 11th: Missed break, nvr a factor. *shd* **56**
HOH HEDSOR [17]2-8-11 J F Egan 100/1: 0: 12th: Nvr nrr than mid-div. *hd* **55**
4417 **ROMANOVA 35** [14]2-8-11 S Sanders 10/1: 040: 13th: Handy 5f, sn wknd. *nk* **54**
4710 **TI ADORA 21** [7]2-8-11 K Fallon 9/1: 00: 14th: Handy 5f, wkng when short of room dist. *nk* **53**
4329 **MAGGIE TULLIVER 39** [4]2-8-11 T E Durcan 25/1: 000: 15th: Bhd, nvr a factor. *1* **51**
Missella [9]2-8-11 K Darley 28/1:0 **Creek Dancer** [5]2-8-11 J Quinn 100/1:0
2714 **Fantasias Forest 108** [10]2-8-11 I Mongan 100/1:0 4711 **Roma Valley 21** [18]2-8-11 Martin Dwyer 100/1:0
19 Ran Time 1m 27.77 (5.77) Owned: Mr K Abdulla Trained: Pulborough

5041 3.10 **Dormouse Maiden Stakes 3yo (D3)**
£3601 £1108 £554 **7f9y str** **Good 43** **-38 Slow** Stands side

4683 **STAR PUPIL 23** [6] A M Balding 3-9-0 BL (73) Martin Dwyer 5/2: 0055541: In tch, led after 2f, sn clr, drvn out to hold on despite hanging left ins fnl 1f: eff at 6/7f, has tried 1m: acts on gd & gd/soft grnd: finally got off mark with visor left off & first time blnks fitted: see 4683 & 1498. **76**
4827 **BARONS SPY 14** [7] A W Carroll 3-9-0 (65) S Sanders 14/1: 00-42032: Rear, prog 3f out, styd on to chase wnr fnl 1f, al held: see 4827 (h'cap). *1½* **72**
4768 **TENNYS GOLD 17** [3] B W Hills 3-8-9 (66) M Hills 9/1: 02-43543: In tch, kept on ins fnl 1f, just held for 2nd: see 4768 & 2378 (1m). *shd* **66**
4586 **ANTIGUA BAY 27** [9] J A R Toller 3-8-9 (66) Lisa Jones 11/1: 002634: Missed break, prog 3f out, no impress ins fnl 1f: eff at 6/7f: see 4586 & 3873. *1¼* **64**
4578 **WOODLAND GLADE 27** [2]3-8-9 R Hughes 13/8 FAV: 225: Missed break, prog 3f out, wknd dist: bckd: v disapp on rtn to 7f: showed more in 4578 (1m, soft) & 3921. *3½* **57**
3208 **ELECTRAS DREAM 88** [8]3-8-9 I Mongan 100/1: 0006: Dwelt, prog 3f out, wknd dist: long abs. *nk* **56**
4827 **SCRIPTORIUM 14** [1]3-9-0 VIS (61) N Mackay(3) 20/1: 0242007: Led 2f, wknd 2f out: 1st visor. *2½* **56**
4561 **ESHAADEH 28** [5]3-8-9 t L Dettori 8/1: 58: Handy till halfway, wknd: broke blood vessel. *5* **41**
966 **BABA 196** [4]3-9-0 J Quinn 40/1: 09: Keen cl-up 4f, sn fdd, eased fnl 1f: long abs: found to have tounge over bit & rcd too freely. *19* **12**
9 Ran Time 1m 27.70 (5.7) Owned: Mr J C Smith Trained: Kingsclere

5042 3.40 **Stoat Selling Stakes 3yo (G4)**
£2982 £852 £426 **1m1f218y** **Good 43** **-16 Slow** Inside

4587 **YASHIN 27** [14] M H Tompkins 3-8-11 (53) L Dettori 11/2: 3204031: In tch, led trav well dist, pushed clr, eased cl-home, val 11L+: sold for 12,000gns: eff at 7f/1m, imprvd for step up to 10f: acts on fast & gd/soft grnd: more races await over this trip: see 4587 & 3218. **64**
4857 **SMART BOY PRINCE 12** [1] M J Attwater 3-9-2 (54) K Fallon 7/1: 3006022: Led, hdd dist, sn no ch with easy wnr: another gd effort: see 4857 & 486. *8* **56**
4698 **RED ROCKY 21** [9] R Hollinshead 3-8-6 p (45) Stephanie Hollinshead(5) 16/1: 0203533: Keen in tch, onepcd from dist: first try at 10f: showed more in 4698 (7f). *½* **45**
4834 **BERTOCELLI 14** [17] G G Margarson 3-8-11 (50) S Sanders 7/1: 0600044: Mid-div, onepcd fnl 1f. *shd* **49**
4834 **VITTORIOSO 14** [7]3-8-11 (45) B Reilly(3) 50/1: 0050065: Mid-div, prog 3f out, kept on late: btr 742. *hd* **48**
4584 **AUROVILLE 27** [2]3-8-11 (55) Martin Dwyer 9/2 FAV: 0062P56: Handy 1m, onepcd: bckd: btr 3874. *1¼* **46**
4903 **ANISETTE 9** [4]3-8-6 (40) M Halford(7) 11/1: 0636537: Dwelt, nvr nrr than mid-div: btr 4903. *1¼* **39**
4991* **RICHIE BOY 2** [3]3-9-2 (58) I Mongan 8/1: 0-060018: Missed break, nvr nrr than mid-div: new stable, showed more in 4991 (12.6f, V Smith). *shd* **48**
4249 **VENETIAN ROMANCE 44** [8]3-8-6 VIS (35) N Mackay(3) 50/1: 0000309: Nvr nrr than mid-div: 6 wks abs. *3* **34**
4507 **CHIQITITA 30** [13]3-8-6 (40) B Swarbrick(5) 66/1: 0006050: 10th: Chsd ldrs 7f, wknd: jumps fit. *nk* **33**
4857 **VALIANT AIR 12** [11]3-8-11 bl (40) J Quinn 33/1: 2400450: 11th: Rear, nvr a factor: btr 2790. *3½* **33**
4364 **KELTIC RAINBOW 38** [5]3-8-6 vis (35) J F Egan 33/1: 6004500: 12th: Mid-div over 7f, wknd. *1¾* **25**
4721 **KALISHKA 20** [16]3-8-11 (55) K Darley 7/1: 0-650000: 13th: Missed break, nvr a factor: op 12/1. *shd* **29**
4862 **CAYMAN CALYPSO 12** [6]3-8-11 (58) T Hamilton(3) 16/1: 6220000: 14th: Rear, nvr a factor. *nk* **28**
4560 **MR MOON 28** [15]3-8-11 (30) M Lawson(4) 50/1: 0060500: 15th: Handy 1m, fdd. *1¾* **25**

4249 **SES SELINE 44** [18]3-8-6 BL (40) F P Ferris(3) 100/1: 45000: 16th: Mid-div over 7f, fdd. *7* **10**
4671 **WEAVER SPELL 23** [12]3-8-11 vis (35) A Mullen(7) 66/1: 6-564000: 17th: Mid-div over 6f, wknd. *3* **11**
4372 **BROTHER CADFAEL 37** [10]3-8-11 (35) S Whitworth 100/1: 6600000: 18th: Rear, nvr a factor. *14* **0**
18 Ran Time 2m 08.40 (5.9) Owned: Roalco Limited Trained: Newmarket

5043

4.10 Toteplacepot Handicap Stakes 3yo 86-100 (C1) **[102]**
£13917 £4282 £2141 **1m3f183y** **Good 43** **+21 Fast** inside

4878 **MASSIF CENTRALE 11** [9] D R C Elsworth 3-9-8 (96) J F Egan 28/1: 0201051: In tch, led 2f out, sn clr, pushed out, eased cl home, val 2L+: fast time: eff at 10/12f, tried further: acts on fast & gd grnd: apprec rtn to 12f in h'cap grade: see 2879. **105**
4819* **ZEITGEIST 14** [3] L M Cumani 3-9-2 (90) N Mackay(3) 12/1: 4125012: Missed break, prog 4f out, short of room bef 1f out, kept on fnl 1f, not pace wnr: remains in gd form & is worth a try over 14f, see 4819. *1¼* **95**
4878 **CARTE DIAMOND 11** [8] M Johnston 3-9-8 (96) K Darley 9/4 FAV: 1123: In tch, ev ch 2f out, hung left & onepcd from dist: bckd: gd run but will apprec rtn to 14f: fin in front of today's wnr in 4878 (List, 14f). *½* **100**
4690 **LETS ROLL 23** [7] C W Thornton 3-8-10 (84) Martin Dwyer 14/1: 2311524: Rear, prog bef 1f out, nrst fin: continues to run well: see 4690 & 4602. *nk* **87**
4324 **ODIHAM 40** [13]3-8-13 (87) S Drowne 16/1: 02-10405: Bhd, prog bef 1f out, nrst fin: 6 wk abs: rider reported mount hung left, see 3534 & 2127. *hd* **89**
4486* **DUNE RAIDER 32** [14]3-8-10 (2oh) (82) A Mullen(7) 50/1: 0016: In tch, no room & lost pl 2f out, rallied late. *¾* **84**
4749 **QUDRAAT 19** [6]3-9-0 (88) R Hills 10/1: 50127: Cl-up, no extra dist: failed to build on 4749. *shd* **87**
4681 **THYOLO 23** [4]3-9-9 (97) R Smith 66/1: 2030008: Nvr nrr than mid-div: first try at 12f, btr 2521 (1m). *½* **95**
4917 **MOTIVE 9** [2]3-9-2 (90) K Fallon 9/2: 512009: Rear, prog 3f out, wknd fnl 1f: op 7/1: btr 2406 (10f). *1¼* **86**
4715* **CAMROSE 21** [5]3-9-6 (94) L Dettori 12/1: 4325210: 10th: Handy over 1m, hung right & wknd fnl 2f. *5* **83**
4715 **SECRETARY GENERAL 21** [10]3-9-6 (94) S Sanders 40/1: 5012200: 11th: Missed break, prog 4f out, wknd fnl 2f: btr 4324 & 3912. *1¼* **81**
4749* **NORDWIND 19** [1]3-9-5 (93) I Mongan 14/1: 4112110: 12th: Cl-up, led after 5f, hdd 2f out, wknd: disapp on bid for hat-trick: 10lb higher than last win in 4749. *1½* **77**
4917 **CORSICAN NATIVE 9** [11]3-9-5 (93) R Hughes 7/1: 3-120: 13th: Led 5f, ev ch 2f out, fdd: btr 4917 (10f). *1¾* **74**
2948 **Haadef 100** [15]3-9-10 BL(98) W Supple 33/1:0 3534 **Settlement Craic 75** [12]3-9-2 (90) J P Murtagh 66/1:0
15 Ran Time 2m 31.01 (2.71) Owned: Mr Raymond Tooth Trained: Whitsbury

5044

4.40 Racecourse Video Services Conditions Stakes 2yo (C2)
£6078 £2306 £1153 **1m1f218y** **Good 43** **-22 Slow** Inside

4376* **SUNDAY SYMPHONY 37** [7] Saeed bin Suroor 2-9-1 (83) L Dettori 11/10 FAV: 211: Handy, styd on to lead well ins fnl 1f, pushed out, val more: bckd: eff at 1m, apprec step up to 10f: acts on firm & gd grnd: lightly rcd performer who has a good future: see 4376 & 3925. **91**
4078* **BAYEUX DE MOI 52** [1] Mrs A J Perrett 2-9-1 (81) J Murtagh 100/30: 412: Cl-up, led 3f out, hdd dist, kept on, just held by wnr: 7 wk abs: eff at 1m, apprec step up to 10f: acts on gd & gd/soft grnd: see 4078. *½* **89**
4883* **PEVENSEY 11** [2] J H M Gosden 2-9-1 bl (87) K Darley 14/1: 6013: In tch, ev ch over 3f out, led dist, hdd ins fnl 1f, not btn far in 3rd: eff at 1m, stays 10f: see 4883. *shd* **88**
4825* **HAATMEY 14** [5] M R Channon 2-9-1 (87) T E Durcan 5/1: 34214: In tch, hung badly under press bef 1f out, kept on late: see 4825. *½* **87**
4883 **SWORDS 11** [6]2-8-11 S Whitworth 100/1: 005: b c Vettori - Pomorie (Be My Guest) Rear, nvr nrr than mid-div: Jan foal, half-brother to wnrs at 6/10f: dam successful at 10f on level, also wnr over hdles: sire Gr 1 wnr at 1m: with D J Daly. *6* **74**
4351* **SAADIGG 38** [3]2-8-13 (87) K Fallon 7/1: 3416: Led 7f, wknd fnl 2f: btr 4351 (1m, fast). *1½* **73**
4807 **FENRIR 15** [4]2-8-13 (83) J Quinn 50/1: 015307: Al in rear. *15* **52**
7 Ran Time 2m 9.04 (6.54) Owned: Godolphin Trained: Newmarket

5045

5.10 E B F Hare Maiden Stakes Div 2 Fillies 2yo (D2)
£5694 £1752 £876 **7f9y str** **Good 43** **-21 Slow** Stands side

SAYWAAN [8] Saeed bin Suroor 2-8-11 L Dettori 7/4 FAV: 1: ch f Fusaichi Pegasus - Sharp Cat (Storm Cat) Rear, prog 3f out, led dist, pushed clr, val 5L+: bckd on debut: Apr foal, E1,500,000: dam won numerous Gr 1 contests abroad: sire high-class mid-dist performer in US: eff at 7f, further will suit next term: acts on gd grnd & a stiff/gall trk: goes well fresh: impressive success & can rate higher. **87+**
4885 **QUEEN OF ICENI 10** [12] J L Dunlop 2-8-11 I Mongan 125/1: 02: b f Erhaab - Princess Genista (Ile de Bourbon) Missed break, sn cl-up, led over 1f out, sn hdd, kept on not pace easy wnr: Apr foal, half-sister to decent staying performer Give Notice, also half-sister to a useful miler: dam eff from 1m/2m: sire Gr 1 wnr at 12f: eff at 7f, further will suit next term: acts on gd grnd: signs of encouragement & can rate higher. *3½* **78**
ART EYES [1] D R C Elsworth 2-8-11 S Sanders 8/1: 3: ch f Halling - Careyes (Sadler's Wells) Dwelt, prog when short of room dist, switched & kept on, just held for 2nd: op 11/1, debut: Jan first foal, cost 48,000gns: sire mulitple Gr 1 wnr at 10f: eff at 7f on gd, 1m/10f will suit: pleasing effort. *hd* **77+**
4823 **RUBIES 14** [6] R F Johnson Houghton 2-8-11 (77) N Mackay(3) 25/1: 2624: In tch, kept on ins fnl 1f: eff at 5f, imprvd for step up to 7f: see 4823 & 4200. *shd* **76**
ALWAYS MINE [10]2-8-11 Martin Dwyer 40/1: 5: ch f Daylami - Mamoura (Lomond) Missed break, prog bef 1f out, nrst fin: debut: Mar foal, half-sister to wnrs at 1m/12f: dam successful over mid-dists: sire Gr 1 wnr at 1m/12f: imprve for today. *1½* **73**
4710 **ABIDE 21** [11]2-8-11 R Hughes 12/1: 626: Handy, short of room dist, switched & kept on late. *¾* **71**
4524 **NICE TUNE 30** [2]2-8-11 M Hills 3/1: 347: In tch over 5f, sn onepcd: btr 4524 (1m, fast). *shd* **70**
4710 **ROYAL JELLY 21** [17]2-8-11 R Havlin 66/1: 08: In tch, led 2f out, hdd dist, wknd: see 4710. *shd* **69**
ALSHARQ [18]2-8-11 R Hills 16/1: 9: In tch, ev ch 2f out, sn wknd: debut. *2½* **64**
4191 **BLUEBERRY TART 45** [13]2-8-11 S Drowne 14/1: 540: 10th: Handy over 5f, sn wknd: 6 wk abs. *shd* **63**
DESERT GLORY [7]2-8-11 W Supple 66/1: 0: 11th: Rear, prog 3f out, wkng when no room fnl 1f. *1* **61**
KATHRYN JANEWAY [9]2-8-11 J F Egan 80/1: 0: 12th: Rear, nvr able to chall. *hd* **60**
FIGGYS BREW [5]2-8-11 R Smith 125/1: 0: 13th: Cl-up over 5f, fdd. *hd* **59**
MAMBOS MELODY [14]2-8-11 J Quinn 40/1: 0: 14th: Cl-up, fdd bef 1f out. *10* **41**
4823 **MOONSIDE 14** [19]2-8-11 R Thomas(3) 125/1: 00: 15th: Missed break, nvr a factor. *1¼* **39**

LEICESTER MONDAY 11.10.04 Righthand, Stiff, Galloping Track

FANTASTIC NIGHT [16]2-8-11 K Darley 125/1: 0: 16th: Mid-div 5f, sn fdd. *nk* **38**
4191 **MAKE IT SNAPPY 45** [3]2-8-11 T E Durcan 66/1: 00: 17th: Al in rear. *10* **20**
4401 **BOWLED OUT 36** [15]2-8-11 M Fenton 80/1: 400: 18th: Led 5f, wkng when short of room bef 1f out. *26* **0**
MARITIMA [4]2-8-11 K Fallon 8/1: U: Dwelt, prog halfway, prob held when b hmpd & u.r. dist. **0**
19 Ran Time 1m 26.50 (4.5) Owned: Godolphin Trained: Newmarket

5046 **5.40 Teletext Racing 'hands And Heels' Apprentice Series Handicap Stakes 3yo+ 56-70 (E3)** **[80]**
£3621 £1114 £557 **7f9y str** **Good 43** **-22 Slow** Stands side

4562 **SNOW BUNTING 28** [6] Jedd O'Keeffe 6-8-7 (59) T Block(3) 9/1: 5334061: Rear, prog to chase ldr 2f out, styd on to lead 1f out, rdn clr, eased cl-home, val 3L+: op 12/1: suited by 6/7f on firm & gd, prob handles polytrack: likes a stiff/gall trk: deserved success: see 3751, 3584 & 3424. **66**
4984 **BOBS BUZZ 2** [19] S C Williams 4-9-0 (66) S O'Hara(3) 5/1: 5205262: Missed break, prog halfway, kept on ins fnl 1f, al held by wnr: tchd 13/2: qck reapp: h'capped to find similar: see 4984 & 3791. *1¼* **70**
4909 **ASK THE CLERK 9** [17] V Smith 3-9-2 (70) Steven Harrison 20/1: 0542003: Rear, prog halfway, kept on ins fnl 1f, just held for 2nd: back to form after a couple of recent disapp efforts: see 4465. *hd* **73**
4862 **LITTLE ENGLANDER 12** [12] H Candy 4-8-5 (57) J Doyle(5) 10/1: 0510044: Rear, kept on fnl 1f. *1½* **57**
4582* **FEARBY CROSS 27** [11]8-9-0 (66) Laura Pike(3) 8/1: 0054615: Mid-div, prog 2f out, onepcd fnl 1f. *nk* **65**
4168 **HAND CHIME 47** [8]7-8-13 (65) Danielle Deverson(5) 20/1: 5002006: Handy 5f, no extra & hung right dist. *1½* **61**
4036 **OUT FOR A STROLL 54** [13]5-9-4 (70) J Brennan(5) 10/1: 10-00007: Nvr nrr than mid-div: 8 wk abs. *nk* **65**
4367 **ARRAN 38** [5]4-8-4 (4oh) (52) K May(3) 12/1: 0210508: Bhd, nvr nrr than mid-div: btr 3821. *½* **50**
4241 **OASES 44** [4]5-8-4 (5oh)p (51) Stacey Renwick(3) 20/1: 0356049: Reluctant to start, nvr nrr than mid-div. *shd* **49**
4750 **COLEMANSTOWN 19** [7]4-8-4 (3oh) (53) Donna Caldwell(3) 8/1: 0000030: 10th: Handy over 5f, no extra. *hd* **48**
4702 **FIVEOCLOCK EXPRESS 21** [16]4-9-3 p (69) A Kirby(3) 22/1: 0520000: 11th: Rear, modest late gains. *1½* **58**
4366 **CRAIC SA CEILI 38** [15]4-8-6 (58) Kirsty Milczarek(3) 14/1: 0004050: 12th: Led after 2f, sn clr, hung right & hdd 1f out, wknd: btr 4366. *1½* **44**
1806 **PHECKLESS 147** [1]5-8-5 (57) Liam Jones(3) 50/1: 4000300: 13th: Handy 5f, wknd. *1* **41**
4321 **BOOK MATCHED 40** [10]3-8-4 (58) M Stainton(3) 40/1: 0601300: 14th: In tch 5f, wknd. *1* **40**
4539 **MORAG 29** [14]3-8-4 (58) R Keogh(3) 50/1: 6620000: 15th: Bhd, nvr a factor. *1* **38**
4562 **SIMPLY THE GUEST 28** [2]5-8-4 (2oh)t (54) Janice Webster(5) 100/1: 2114000: 16th: Bhd, nvr a factor. *¾* **34**
5022 **DANIFAH 1** [3]3-9-1 (69) R J Killoran(3) 14/1: 11301000: 17th: Led, hdd after 2f, wknd 2f out. *2½* **42**
4683 **PICK OF THE CROP 23** [9]3-9-1 (69) A Hamblett(3) 100/1: 5-120000: 18th: Chsd ldrs 5f, fdd. *nk* **41**
4582 **YOUNG ALEX 27** [20]6-9-2 vis (68) H Poulton 4/1 FAV: 6343-520: 19th: Rear, nvr a factor: bckd from 9/1: failed to build on promising effort in 4582 (soft, first time visor). *3½* **33**
4845 **SHAMROCK TEA 13** [18]3-8-3 (57) N Lawes(5) 40/1: 0514000: 20th: Mid-div till halfway, wknd. *7* **9**
20 Ran Time 1m 26.58(4.58) Owned: WRB Racing 49 (wrbracingcom) Trained: Leyburn

WINDSOR MONDAY 11.10.04 Sharp, Figure 8 Track

Official Going GOOD (GOOD/FIRM IN PLACES)

5047 **1.50 Davies Collison Cave E B F Maiden Stakes Div 1 2yo (D3)**
£5278 £1624 £812 **6f** **Good/Firm 24** **-59 Slow** Inside

3863 **NOTA BENE 61** [12] D R C Elsworth 2-9-0 L Keniry(3) 7/4 FAV: 21: Made all, drvn out to hold on ins fnl 1f: 9 wk abs: eff at 6f, 7f/1m shld suit in time: acts on fast grnd, sharp trk: built on prev experience, can improve in future & shld win more races: runs well fresh: see 3863 (debut). **85**
4844 **GIMASHA 13** [9] M R Channon 2-8-9 S Hitchcott 6/1: 42: Chsd wnr, hung left over 1f out, onepcd ins fnl 1f: stays 6f: imprvd from debut & shld find similar: see 4844. *1* **75**
4823 **INKA DANCER 14** [2] B Palling 2-8-9 J Fortune 10/1: 343: Chsd ldrs, onepcd over 1f out: stays 6f, acts on fast & gd: see 4543. *1¼* **71**
3476 **GREAT BELIEF 77** [14] T D McCarthy 2-9-0 T Quinn 18/1: 364: Chsd ldrs, hdwy over 1f out, sn onepcd: long abs: stays 6f on fast: back to form of 3160. *nk* **75**
PEACE LILY 0 [8]2-8-9 S Carson 33/1: 5: b f Dansili - Shall We Run (Hotfoot) Slow away in rear, hdwy 2f out, styd on fnl 1f on debut: 54,000 gns Apr foal: half sister to wnr of the Gimcrack: dam a mdn, sire a high-class miler: pleasing start to racing, entitled to come on for this next time. *1* **67+**
4941 **BABE MACCOOL 7** [13]2-9-0 A Medeiros(5) 12/1: 66: ch c Giant's Causeway - Kotama (Shahrastani) In tch, outpcd 3f out, onepcd & btn 2f out: op 16/1, quick reapp: May foal, cost 50,000 gns: half brother to a dual Norway wnr at 3: dam useful at 7/9f, sire v smart at 7/10f: with B Hills. *2½* **64**
4575 **TIGGERS TOUCH 27** [10]2-8-9 (73) Dane O'Neill 12/1: 4067: Chsd ldrs, outpcd over 2f out, sn btn. *¾* **57**
4705 **ARCHIE GLENN 21** [7]2-9-0 (79) P McCabe 8/1: 00428: Rear, outpcd 3f out, btn 2f out: op 10/1. *1½* **57**
4853 **AVIATION 12** [4]2-9-0 (78) R L Moore 13/2: 03559: Al bhd. *nk* **56**
4893 **NODINA 10** [3]2-9-0 E Ahern 25/1: 050: 10th: Dwelt, nvr a factor: see 4893. *1¾* **51**
4557 **SORCERESS 28** [11]2-8-9 D Sweeney 100/1: 00: 11th: b f Wizard King - Aonia (Mummy's Pet) In tch, wknd over 2f out: 8,000 gns Apr foal: half sister to a 6f 3yo wnr: dam a dual 5f 2yo wnr, sire v smart at 7f/1m. *2½* **38**
ATHBOY NIGHTS 0 [5]2-8-9 A McCarthy 33/1: 0: 12th: Dwelt, nvr nr ldrs on debut. *2½* **30**
MAD MARTY WILDCARD 0 [6]2-9-0 D Nolan(3) 66/1: 0: 13th: Bhd, nvr a factor on debut. *3½* **24**
13 Ran Time 1m 15.28 (4.98) Owned: WV & Mrs ES Robins Trained: Whitsbury

5048 **2.20 Davies Collison Cave E B F Maiden Stakes Div 2 2yo (D3)**
£5278 £1624 £812 **6f** **Good/Firm 24** **-80 Slow** Inside

4121 **TRACTOR BOY 49** [2] W J Haggas 2-9-0 T Quinn 33/1: 01: b c Mind Games - Day Star (Dayjur) In tch, hdwy 2f out, drvn into lead ins fnl 1f: 7 wk abs: Mar foal, cost 30,000 gns: dam wnr at 6f, sire a top class 2yo/sprinter: relished step up to 6f: acts on fast, sharp trk: imprvd from debut, win again. **90**
4679 **HOLLY SPRINGS 23** [10] J H M Gosden 2-8-9 J Fortune 5/6 FAV: 202: Dwelt, sn handy, hdwy to lead well over 1f out, sn hung left & hdd ins fnl 1f, no extra: well bckd: shld win a race: see 4357 (debut). *½* **82**
4710 **MISS TOLERANCE 21** [14] Sir Michael Stoute 2-8-9 S Carson 25/1: 03: ch f Mt Livermore - Acquiesce (Generous) Trkd ldrs, kept on ins fnl 1f: clr of rem: Feb foal: half sister to 2yo wnrs at 7f: dam *1* **79**

WINDSOR MONDAY 11.10.04 Sharp, Figure 8 Track

unrcd, sire a top class dirt sprinter in the US: eff at 6f, 7f will suit: acts on fast: imprvd from debut, find sim.

4885	**DART ALONG 10** [13] R Hannon 2-9-0 R L Moore 4/1: 554: Made most till well over 1f out, no extra fnl 1f.	4	72
4843	**ENTERTAINING 13** [9]2-8-9 (70) Dane O'Neill 8/1: 6525: Dsptd lead to well over 1f out, no extra fnl 1f.	¾	65
	HIGH RHYTHM 0 [3]2-8-9 N Pollard 33/1: 6: b f Piccolo - Slave To The Rythm (Hamas) Dwelt in	2	59

rear, outpcd, dsptd 2f out on debut: Jan 1st foal: dam unplcd both 2yo starts, sire a high-class sprinter.

4543	**ROSIE MUIR 28** [11]2-8-9 S Hitchcott 100/1: 07: In tch, wknd qckly over 1f out.	1¾	54
4876	**FLYING HEART 11** [7]2-8-9 C Catlin 20/1: 08: In tch, wknd qckly 2f out.	nk	53
4759	**EIDSFOSS 18** [1]2-9-0 J Mackay 50/1: 59: Dwelt, hdwy over 2f out, no impress 1f out: with T Clement.	shd	57
	KITCHEN SINK 0 [8]2-9-0 D Sweeney 25/1: 0: 10th: Slow away in rear, nvr nr ldrs on debut.	1½	52
	TYCHEROS 0 [12]2-9-0 D Fox(5) 33/1: 0: 11th: In tch, no impress 2f out on debut.	½	50
	SOL ROJO 0 [4]2-9-0 T P Queally 40/1: 0: 12th: Dwelt, al bhd on debut.	nk	49
4981	**WATERFRONT DANCER 4** [6]2-9-0 G Baker 80/1: 0000: 13th: Al bhd: quick reapp.	2½	41

13 Ran Time 1m 16.54 (6.24) Owned: Simon and Holly Turner Trained: Newmarket

---

5049 — 2.50 Haines Watts Chartered Accountants Selling Stakes 2yo (F3)
£3445 £1060 £530 **1m67y** Good/Firm 24 **-42 Slow** Inside

4711	**MISSIE BAILEYS 21** [2] D R C Elsworth 2-8-7 (70) T Quinn 5/1: 6501: Mid-div, hdwy into 2nd after		70

1f, led 2f out, rdn out fnl 1f: bought in for 10,400 gns: 1st win: relished this step up to 1m, further shld suit in time: acts on fast grnd, sharp trk: made most of this drop into sell grade: see 4447 (mdn).

4316	**FERRARA FLAME 40** [5] J A Osborne 2-8-7 T P Queally 25/1: 0002: In tch, hdwy over 2f out, hung	1¾	65

left from over 1f out, not pace of wnr: claimed for 6,000: 6 wk abs: eff around 1m on fast: much imprvd.

4355	**PICOT DE SAY 38** [12] John Berry 2-8-12 L Fletcher(1) 33/1: 0003: Bhd, hdwy over 1f out, not clr	2	66

run just over 1f out, kept on: stays 1m on fast: shade closer with a clr run: see 3981.

4895	**LATERAL THINKER 10** [6] J A Osborne 2-8-13 (65) J Fortune 7/2 FAV: 0526064: In tch, styd on fnl	1½	64

1f, not pace of ldrs: see 4895.

4848	**LORNA DUNE 13** [13]2-8-13 vis (66) D Sweeney 9/2: 0603105: Trkd ldrs, not clr run/lost place 2f out.	1	62
4635	**PON MY SOUL 25** [10]2-9-4 (60) R L Moore 8/1: 1606: Trkd ldrs, hdwy 2f out, no impress fnl 1f.	¾	65
4544	**EDITH BANKES 28** [3]2-8-7 C Haddon(7) 66/1: 07: ch f Woodborough - Mayday Kitty (Interrex) Bhd,	1½	51

mod late gains: clr of rem: Apr foal: dam plcd at 10/12f, sire a top class 2yo: much imprvd from debut.

4895	**PENNESTAMP 10** [14]2-8-12 (62) N Pollard 9/2: 6443058: Led to 2f out, no extra over 1f out: op 7/1.	4	48
	RAVEN 0 [7]2-8-7 E Ahern 10/1: 9: b f Alzao - Eman's Joy (Lion Cavern) Keen in tch, hdwy 3f	1	41

out, fdd over 1f out, eased: debut: clmd for 6,000: 28,000 gns Feb 1st foal: dam 6f wnr, sire useful at 1m/7f.

4830	**HIGH CHART 14** [1]2-8-13 t (62) A McCarthy 7/1: 3060000: 10th: In tch, ran wide bend 5f out, sn btn.	¾	45
1097	**BERHAM MALDU 186** [4]2-8-7 Hayley Turner(3) 66/1: 000: 11th: b f Fraam - Corniche Quest (Salt	3½	32

Dome) Keen in tch, no impress over 2f out: long abs: Apr foal: half sister to a couple of wnrs at 5f at 2: dam a wnr btwn 5f/1m, sire smart at 7f/1m.

4831	**STUNNING SPARK 14** [11]2-8-7 P Doe 66/1: 00: 12th: Slow away, nvr nr ldrs.	11	10
3864	**JULES LEE 61** [9]2-8-12 P A Quinn(5) 100/1: 00: 13th: Chsd ldrs, fdd over 3f out, t.o.: tried cheek pieces.	21	0
4792	**CHARLIESLASTCHANCE 16** [8]2-8-7 C Catlin 66/1: 00: 14th: Rear, t.o.	5	0

14 Ran Time 1m 48.65 (5.65) Owned: Mrs J Wotherspoon Trained: Whitsbury

---

5050 — 3.20 Toteexacta Handicap Stakes 3yo+ 71-85 (D2) [92]
£7222 £2222 £1111 **1m2f7y** Good/Firm 24 **+07 Fast** Inside

4392	**BEST BE GOING 37** [18] P W Harris 4-8-9 VIS (73) T Quinn 14/1: 0054001: Trkd ldrs, hdwy 2f out,		83

drvn into lead fnl 1f: eff at 1m/12f on firm & fast, sharp or undul trks: apprec visor, back to form of 2099.

4943	**DIEGO CAO 7** [2] G L Moore 3-9-1 (84) R L Moore 8/1: 216142: In tch, hdwy to lead well over 1f	nk	92

out, hdd ins fnl 1f, no extra: quick reapp, clr of rem: op 6/1: acts on fast & gd/soft: most consistent: see 4609.

4656	**BURNING MOON 24** [8] J Noseda 3-8-12 vis (81) E Ahern 20/1: 0-510003: Trkd ldrs, onepcd.	3	84
4392	**STREET LIFE 37** [15] W J Musson 6-8-8 (72) Dane O'Neill 8/1: 3435444: Dwelt, hdwy 2f out, onepcd.	shd	74
4392	**SANGIOVESE 37** [12]5-8-11 (75) P Dobbs 11/1: 3110505: Cl-up, hdwy into 2nd 4f out, led over 2f	shd	76

out till well over 1f out, sn no extra: back to form of 3964.

4937	**PATTERDALE 7** [10]3-8-5 (74) T P Queally 9/1: 00-21026: Cl-up, hdwy to chall over 2f out, wknd	1¼	73

qckly over 1f out: quick reapp: see 4937.

4745	**MAYSTOCK 19** [17]4-8-8 vis (74) Hayley Turner(3) 12/1: 0300307: Dwelt, short of room on inner 4f	1	69

out, hdwy over 2f out, sn onepcd: btr 4473.

4809	**ARRY DASH 15** [20]4-8-9 vis (73) S Hitchcott 8/1: 3232508: Dwelt, sn cl-up, hung left over 1f out, wknd.	2½	66
4873	**BORDER EDGE 11** [6]6-8-10 vis (74) G Baker 33/1: 0000009: Bhd, hdwy over 2f out, sn onepcd: btr 4122.	hd	66
4766	**BROOKLYNS GOLD 17** [1]9-8-11 (75) C Catlin 6/1: 32///40-600: 10th: Bhd, hdwy over 2f out, sn wknd.	¾	66
4360	**DESERT ISLAND DISC 38** [19]7-8-10 (74) A Beech(3) 14/1: 5116300: 11th: Chsd ldrs to 4f out, btn 2f out.	hd	64
4777	**TAMINOULA 17** [9]3-8-5 (74) S Carson 16/1: 11-00600: 12th: Dwelt in rear, not clr run 2f out,	½	63

btn: shade closer with a clr run: just btr 3535 (9f).

3738	**GOLDEN GRACE 67** [3]3-9-2 (85) J Fortune 20/1: 1-044000: 13th: Rear, nvr a factor: 10 wk abs.	7	63
4441*	**SPACE COWBOY 382** [4]4-9-0 (78) A Quinn(5) 25/1: 341-0: 14th: b c Anabaa - Lady Moranbon	3	51

(Trempolino) Bhd, nvr a factor on reapp: hcks rnr-up sole 04/05 start (nov, rtd 113h, eff at 2m on firm, poss gd, blnks): won last of 3 '03 starts (mdn, with A Perrett): eff at 10f on fast, sharp/undul trks: lightly rcd on the level. 1 Sep'03 Good 9.9 fm 79- D:

4482	**THREEZEDZZ 2** [7]6-9-3 t (81) L Keniry(3) 20/1: 1331000: 15th: Dsptd lead at fast pace, hdd & no	2½	50

extra just over 2f out: quick reapp: paid penalty for going off too fast.

4916	**CAMILLE PISSARRO 9** [13]4-9-7 (85) Frances Pickard(7) 33/1: 5053-000: 16th: In tch, wknd 3f out.	nk	53
4220	**A ONE 44** [14]5-9-5 (83) Derek Nolan(7) 20/1: 0115000: 17th: Dsptd lead at fast pace, lost pl 4f	dist	1

out, sn fdd, t.o.: 6 wk abs: paid penalty for going off too fast.

17 Ran Time 2m 7.7 (1.7) Owned: Mrs P W Harris Trained: Berkhamsted

---

5051　3.50 Quality Heating Services Nursery Handicap Stakes 2yo 0-85 (D2)　　　　[89]
£7222 £2222 £1111　　1m67y　　Good/Firm 24　　-15 Slow　　Inside

4725 **ALRIGHT MY SON** 20 [11] R Hannon 2-9-6　(81) R L Moore　9/2: 4524021: Chsd ldrs, hdwy to lead 2f　　　　　92
out, drvn out ins fnl 1f: 1st win: eff around 7f/1m on firm & soft, sharp trk: deserved win: see 1646.
4810 **IM SPARTACUS** 15 [9] A Wood 2-8-13 p (74) P Doe　16/1: 6541542: In tch, hdwy over 2f out, not　　2　　79
pace of wnr ins fnl 1f: stays 1m: back to form of 4387.
4703 **MYSTERY LOT** 21 [10] A King 2-8-13　(74) J D Smith　14/1: 6223: Bhd, hdwy over 2f out, onepace.　1¼　76
4269 **TUVALU** 42 [14] A M Balding 2-8-7　(68) N Chalmers(3) 16/1: 0564: Dwelt, sn in tch, onepcd over 1f out.　hd　69
4940 **DARKO KARIM** 7 [7]2-8-13　(74) T P Queally 12/1: 400035: Rear, hdwy over 2f out, onepace over 1f out.　2　　71
4913 **CATCH A STAR** 9 [5]2-9-6　(81) L Keniry(3)　4/1 FAV: 3503136: Keen in tch, nvr nrr: btr 4913.　1　　76
4829* **SPEIGHTSTOWN** 14 [1]2-9-7　(82) T Quinn　7/1: 0317: With ldr till led 4f out, hdd 2f out, no extra.　1　　75
4250 **SIGN WRITER** 43 [6]2-9-2　(77) E Ahern 13/2: 62458: Keen & handy, no impress over 1f out: 6 wk abs.　5　　60
4193 **FAIR ALONG** 45 [3]2-8-11　(72) M Tebbutt 33/1: 000409: Keen & cl-up, no impress over 1f out: 6 wk abs.　1½　52
4193 **EMERALD PENANG** 45 [4]2-9-0　(75) J Fortune 25/1: 541000: 10th: Led to 4f out, no extra 2f out: 6 wk abs　hd　54
4746 **BERTROSE** 19 [2]2-9-3　(78) Dane O'Neill 14/1: 4530: 11th: Al bhd: btr 4746.　　　1　　55
4738 **KRASIVIS BOY** 19 [13]2-8-9　(70) P Dobbs 50/1: 0240: 12th: Chsd ldrs, wknd over 2f out.　　1¾　43
4940* **COME ON JONNY** 7 [8]2-9-3 (6ex) (78) J Mackay 13/2: 03410: 13th: Keen in rear, nvr a factor: qck reapp. 1½　48
13 Ran　Time 1m 46.33 (3.33)　Owned: Mr James Crickmore　Trained: Marlborough

---

5052　4.20 Windsor Fireworks Extravaganza Sat 6th November Maiden Stakes Div 1 3yo+ (D3)
£4147 £1276 £638　　1m67y　　Good/Firm 24　　-15 Slow　　Inside

4847 **THISTLE** 13 [3] J H M Gosden 3-9-0　(76) J Fortune　4/9 FAV: 02221: Made all, pushed clr ins fnl　　　　76
1f, eased nr fin, val 8L+: bckd: stays 8.5f on fast & gd, acts on a sharp trk: deserved win: see 3973 (debut).
4944 **MACS ELAN** 7 [8] A B Coogan 4-9-3　(35) E Ahern 33/1: 0-05062: In tch, hdwy over 2f out, not pace　5　　63$
to go with wnr ins fnl 1f: quick reapp: prob flattered by this: see 4944.
4901 **CATCH THE FOX** 9 [9] J J Bridger 4-9-3　(40) G Baker 33/1: 0004033: Chsd ldrs, onepcd ins fnl 1f.　1¾　59
4674 **ZWADI** 23 [1] H Candy 3-8-9　(70) Dane O'Neill 6/1: 5032434: Keen in chd, wknd 2f out: clr of rem.　¾　52
2117 **ROOD BOY** 133 [10]3-9-0　(55) Hayley Turner(3) 14/1: 43-45505: Keen & handy, no impress 2f out.　6　　45
2709 **JUST DANCE ME** 109 [2]3-8-9　D Sweeney 10/1: 0-26: Chsd ldrs, no impress 2f out: now with R Charlton.1¾　36
4294 **CHAIN OF HOPE** 42 [11]3-9-0　(49) A Beech(3) 50/1: 006-007: Cl-up, no impress 2f out: NH fit: see 4054. nk　40
4901 **SHAAMITS ALL OVER** 9 [7]5-8-12　(30) D Kinsella 100/1: 00-00368: Slow away, nvr a factor.　½　　34
CASPIAN LAKE 6 [6]3-9-0　V Slattery 100/1: 9: ch g Lake Coniston - Hardtimes (Distinctly North)　1　　37
Al bhd on debut: cost £2,400: dam unplcd: with Mrs L Jewell.
4944 **ZORN** 7 [5]5-9-3　(35) J Mackay 100/1: 50000-00: 10th: br c Dilum - Very Good (Noalto) Keen in　6　　25
rear, nvr nr ldrs: quick reapp: mdn & h'cap unplcd in '03 (rtd 50a): mdn & nurs unplcd in '02 (rtd 53a): mod.
4120 **SANDOKAN** 50 [4]3-9-0　T P Queally 33/1: 00: 11th: b g Tiger Hill - Suivez (Fioravanti) Rear,　6　　13
ran wide over 5f out & over 4f out, btn 3f out: 7 wk abs: half brother to a 9f wnr: half brother to an 11f scorer.
11 Ran　Time 1m 46.33 (3.33)　Owned: Duke of Devonshire　Trained: Manton

---

5053　4.50 National Hunt Racing Returns To Windsor Handicap Stakes 3yo+ 56-70 (E3)　　[80]
£3786 £1165 £583　　6f　　Good/Firm 24　　-39 Slow　　Inside

4646 **YOMALO** 24 [12] R Guest 4-9-1　(67) C Catlin 12/1: 5625621: Bhd, gd hdwy 2f out, led ins fnl 1f,　　　79
rdn out: eff at 5/6f, stays 7f: acts on fast, gd/soft & fibresand, any trk: confirmed recent improvement: see 2034.
4946 **ROMAN QUINTET** 7 [18] D W P Arbuthnot 4-8-10 p (62) T Quinn　7/2 FAV: 0003222: Mid-div, hdwy to　1½　68
chall over 1f out, not pace of wnr ins fnl 1f: quick reapp, nicely bckd: rng well, see 4946.
4751 **FLARAN** 19 [4] E F Vaughan 4-8-6　(58) E Ahern 12/1: 504-0033: Cl-up, hdwy to lead over 2f out,　1¼　60
hdd ins fnl 1f, no extra: see 4751.
4946 **FULL SPATE** 2 [9] J M Bradley 9-9-3　(69) R L Moore 12/1: 1600004: Mid-div, not pace of ldrs.　nk　70
4582 **MAJIK** 27 [10]5-8-6　(58) J F McDonald(3) 14/1: 3404045: Bhd, hdwy 2f out, sn onepcd.　2½　51
4109 **I WISH** 51 [7]6-8-5　(57) N Chalmers(3) 16/1: 5530226: Rear, hdwy 2f out, sn onepcd: 7 wk abs.　hd　49
4946 **BRANSTON TIGER** 7 [15]5-8-11 vis (63) L Keniry(3) 8/1: 0143037: In tch, onepcd over 1f out: tchd 10/1.　hd　54
4989 **OEUF A LA NEIGE** 3 [8]4-9-8 (6ex) (74) O Urbina 7/1: 1501158: Slow away in rear, nvr clr run 2f　½　　63
out till over 1f out, bmpd 1f out, kept on ins fnl 1f: quick reapp: did not get run of the race, closer with a clr run.
4754 **KEW THE MUSIC** 18 [3]4-8-5 (1ow)vis (56) S Hitchcott 20/1: 0000109: Rear, not clr run 2f out, some　hd　45+
hdwy when not clr run over 1f out, sn switched left, not clr run ins fnl 1f, no ch after: much closer with a clr run.
4946 **SUNDRIED TOMATO** 7 [13]5-9-0　(66) L Fletcher(3) 14/1: 0600500: 10th: Made most till over 2f out,　2　　48
no extra over 1f out: quick reapp: btr 4946.
4562 **MIMIC** 28 [14]4-9-1　(67) P Doe 33/1: 0001500: 11th: Bhd, not clr run 2f out, squeezed out ins fnl　½　　47
1f, no ch after: closer with a clr run: btr 3888.
4946 **EXTREMELY RARE** 7 [16]3-8-11　(64) A Daly 28/1: 1000660: 12th: Cl-up, hdwy into 2nd 2f out, lost　nk　43
place & wknd over 1f out: quick reapp.
4646 **GENEROUS GESTURE** 24 [19]3-8-8　(61) J Mackay 20/1: 0656000: 13th: Slow away, not clr run 2f out,　nk　39
staying on when not clr run over 1f out, nvr a factor: much btr 1441.
4976 **HIGH RIDGE** 7 [20]5-9-4 p (70) Dane O'Neill 12/1: 1224000: 14th: Mid-div, wkng when hmpd over 1f out.　½　　46
3687* **ELVINA** 68 [2]3-8-4　(57) D Kinsella 20/1: 4-10: 15th: In tch, no impress when bmpd over 1f out.　3　　24
4976 **DANDOUCE** 5 [11]3-8-12　(65) J Fortune 14/1: 6340300: 16th: Chsd ldrs, wknd/short of room over 1f out.　1　　29
2423 **JOY AND PAIN** 120 [6]3-8-13　(66) T P Queally 33/1: 0162300: 17th: Handy, no impress 2f out: long abs.　2　　24
2053 **BLAKESHALL QUEST** 136 [5]4-8-5 vis (57) S Carson 33/1: 5101000: 18th: Dsptd lead till over 2f out,　6　　0
no extra when bmpd sn after: long abs.
4969 **KNEAD THE DOUGH** 6 [17]3-8-3　(55) D Fox(5) 25/1: 26020: 19th: Handy to 3f out, wkng/hmpd after.　2　　0
19 Ran　Time 1m 14.08 (3.78)　Owned: Mr F Nowell　Trained: Newmarket

---

5054	**5.20 Windsor Fireworks Extravaganza Sat 6th November Maiden Stakes Div 2 3yo+ (D3)**
	£4134 £1272 £636 **1m67y** **Good/Firm 24** **-08 Slow** Inside

SLEEPING INDIAN 0 [4] J H M Gosden 3-9-0   J Fortune 1/1 FAV: 1: b c Indian Ridge - Las Flores   **82**
(Sadler's Wells) In tch, hdwy to lead well over 1f out, pushed clr ins fnl 1f, eased nr fin, val 8/9L: debut, bckd:
half brother to wnrs at 1m/10f: dam a 10f wnr: eff around 1m on fast, sharp trk: runs well fresh: gd start.
4392 **LASANGA 37** [3] Lady Herries 5-9-3 (75) T P Queally 9/2: 4/32-002: Led after 2f, hdd well over 1f   6   **67**
out, not pace of wnr: clr of rem: met a useful rival: see 4122.
4868} **MISTER RIGHT 353** [6] K Bell 3-9-0   C Catlin 25/1: 00-3: ch g Baratheca - Broken Spirit (Slip   4   **59**
Anchor) Dwelt in rear, some late gains on reapp: mdn unplcd both '03 starts (rtd 62, debut with M Quinn).
4898} **BLUEFIELD 352** [1] R F Johnson Houghton 3-9-0   S Carson 4/1: 03-4: b c Second Empire - Imco   1¼   **56**
Reverie (Grand Lodge) Chsd ldrs, hung left over 5f out, found little 2f out on reapp: plcd last of 2 '03 starts
(mdn, rtd 80): shld stay 1m, handles gd grnd: lightly rcd.
4275 **RUSSIAN APPLAUSE 42** [9]4-9-3 (65) S Hitchcott 10/1: 0045: Rcd in 2nd over 5f out, chall over 2f   hd   **55**
out, no impress over 1f out: 6 wk abs.
4828 **KINDNESS 14** [2]4-8-12 (49) Dane O'Neill 16/1: 2020006: Chsd ldrs, btn over 2f out.   1½   **47**
4877 **KINGS MINSTREL 11** [10]3-9-0 P Doe 20/1: 0007: Slow away, rear, nvr dangerous.   5   **42**
SUSTAINABLE STYLE 190 [7]3-8-9   V Slattery 33/1: 008: Slow away, al bhd: long abs.   2   **33**
4877 **KWAI BABY 11** [11]3-8-9 (35) Hayley Turner(3) 50/1: 000-009: Slow away, rear, t.o.   18   **0**
4898 **CZECH SUMMER 10** [5]3-9-0 bl A Daly 50/1: 000: 10th: Slow away, al t.o.   8   **0**
4593 **UNPRECEDENTED 27** [8]3-9-0 vis (48) J Mackay 33/1: 0-004000: 11th: Led for 2f, fdd 5f out, t.o.   28   **0**
11 Ran   Time 1m 45.79(2.79)   Owned: Mr George Strawbridge   Trained: Manton

---

Official Going Good (Good/Soft Places)

5055	**1.50 E B F Ladbrokes Com Reference Point Maiden Stakes Colts & Geldings 2yo (D2)**
	£5980 £1840 £920 **7f9y str** **Good 51** **-14 Slow** Stands side

3594 **EQDAAM 73** [7] J H M Gosden 2-8-11   R Havlin 11/1: 331: Led, hdd dist, rallied to lead cl-home,   **86+**
pushed out, val bit more: 10 wk abs: eff over a stiff/gall 7f, 1m+ will suit: acts on fast, gd grnd & goes well
fresh: game & tough performer who can rate higher: see 3594 & 2766.
FLAG LIEUTENANT 0 [11] Sir Michael Stoute 2-8-11   Martin Dwyer 12/1: 2: b c Machiavellian -   ½   **84**
Fairy Godmother (Fairy King) In tch, styd on for press well ins fnl 1f, just denied: debut: Feb first foal, dam
successful at 10f: sire decent performer around 1m: eff at 7f, will relish 1m+: win races.
TRAGEDIAN 0 [5] J H M Gosden 2-8-11   J Fortune 16/1: 3: ch c Theatrical - Foreign Courier (Sir   hd   **83**
Ivor) Handy, kept on ins fnl 1f, not btn far in 3rd: debut: stablemate of wnr: Apr foal, half-brother to decent
wnrs at 5f/1m: dam unrcd: sire top-class performer over mid-dists: eff at 7f, 1m will suit next term: acts on gd
grnd: promising effort & looks sure to impr for the experience.
4483 **WORLD REPORT 33** [14] R Hannon 2-8-11   R L Moore 40/1: 464: Prom, led dist, hdd well in fnl 1f,   shd   **82**
no extra: eff at 7f on gd grnd: back to form after disapp last time in 4483, see 4026 (debut).
3811 **MOSTASHAAR 65** [20]2-8-11   R Hills 6/1: 05: Cl-up, no extra ins fnl 1f: 9 wk abs: eff at 7f on gd.   1¼   **80**
FIRESONG 0 [3]2-8-11   D Holland 20/1: 0: b c Dansili - Leaping Flame (Trempolino) Dwelt, prog   2   **76+**
2f out, nrst fin under hands & heels: debut: Mar foal, half-brother successful at mid-dists: dam wnr at 7f: sire
decent performer around 1m: pleasing start, relish 1m/10f+.
4970 **LAKE CHINI 6** [9]2-8-11   P Robinson 66/1: 07: Cl-up 5f, sn outpcd, rallied late: qck reapp.   nk   **75**
JABBRAAN 0 [17]2-8-11   L Dettori 4/5 FAV: 8: b c Aljabr - Miss Zafonic (Zafonic) In tch over 5f,   nk   **74**
no extra: well supported on debut: Mar first foal, dam successful at 6/7f: sire Gr 1 wnr as a juv, developed into
high-class performer around 1m: clearly btr expected today & rider reported mount had a breathing problem.
4829 **CROIX ROUGE 15** [10]2-8-11   R Hughes 40/1: 309: Cl-up over 5f, wknd: btr 4416.   ¾   **72**
4895 **ATACAMA STAR 11** [6]2-8-11   T E Durcan 33/1: 020: 10th: Slow away, nvr a factor.   hd   **71**
PRINCE VECTOR 0 [2]2-8-11   J D Smith 100/1: 0: 11th: Nvr nrr than mid-div.   shd   **70**
NEUTRINO 0 [19]2-8-11   N Mackay(3) 66/1: 0: 12th: Mid-div 5f, sn btn.   hd   **69**
SHORTBREAD 0 [12]2-8-11   I Mongan 100/1: 0: 13th: Al in rear.   1¾   **65**
   Seattle Robber 0 [1]2-8-11 J F Egan 33/1:0   2802 **Reaching Out 106** [18]2-8-11 S Drowne 100/1:0
4244 **Interwoven 45** [16]2-8-11 S Chin 100/1:0   4823 **Will The Till 15** [4]2-8-11 P Fitzsimons 200/1:0
4724 **Spanish Ridge 21** [15]2-8-11 T Quinn 14/1:0   **Valet 0** [13]2-8-11 L Keniry(3) 150/1:0
19 Ran   Time 1m 26.56 (4.56)   Owned: Mr Hamdan Al Maktoum   Trained: Manton

---

5056	**2.20 Ladbrokes Com Selling Handicap Stakes 3-4yo 46-55 (G4)**	**[71]**
	£3018 £862 £431 **7f9y str** **Good 51** **-14 Slow** Stands side	

4750 **ARMENTIERES 20** [20] J L Spearing 3-8-9 bl (62) S Drowne 13/2: 0623401: Held up, prog 3f out, rdn   **58**
out to lead cl-home: bght in for 4,000gns: eff around 7f/1m on gd, soft grnd & firesand: eff with blnks.
3737 **DISCO DIVA 68** [17] M Blanshard 3-8-9 (52) F Norton 33/1: 2-000002: Missed break, prog 2f out,   ½   **56**
styd on to lead well ins fnl 1f, hdd cl-home: 10 wk abs: acts on firm & gd grnd: gd run in defeat.
3796 **CALUSA LADY 66** [12] G B Balding 4-8-11 (52) S Carson 14/1: 05-50203: Handy, styd on to lead bef   ½   **55**
1f out, hdd well ins fnl 1f, no extra: 9 wk abs: eff at 6/7f: see 3109.
4548 **CAYMAN BREEZE 29** [7] J M Bradley 4-9-0 (55) R L Moore 16/1: 4105004: Bhd, prog 3f out, kept on   nk   **57**
ins fnl 1f: not disgraced under top-weight: see 708.
2633 **LIGHT THE DAWN 113** [14]4-8-6 (47) B Swarbrick(5) 16/1: 0-0005: Keen rear, hdwy 2f out, staying on   nk   **48**
when short of room bef 1f out, switched & kept on late: long abs: eff at 7f on gd grnd: see 1527.
4967 **CROSS ASH 7** [13]4-8-12 (53) H Fellows(7) 40/1: 0-000006: Bhd, prog & ev ch bef 1f out, no extra.   1½   **51**
4739 **CERTA CITO 20** [19]4-8-12 (53) L Dettori 100/30 FAV: 0050047: In tch, led bef 3f out, hdd over 1f   1¾   **47**

LEICESTER   TUESDAY 12.10.04   Righthand, Stiff, Galloping Track

out, wknd: first attempt at 7f: btr 4739 (5f).

4626	**NAUGHTY GIRL 26** [11]4-8-7 vis t (48) F P Ferris(3) 9/1: 4020108: Keen cl-up over 5f, wknd: btr 4411.	hd	41
4605	**MAN CRAZY 27** [1]3-8-7 (50) J F Egan 11/1: 0040049: Keen cl-up 3f, sn outpcd, mod late gains.	shd	42
4974	**CHANDELIER 6** [18]4-8-6 (47) L Keniry(2) 7/1: 6006R30: 10th: ln tch, led over 1f out, sn hdd & wknd.	hd	38
4587*	**ZALEBE 28** [3]3-8-12 (55) J Quinn 9/1: 0010: 11th: Nvr nrr than mid-div: btr 4587 (gd/soft).	½	45
4275	**OLLIJAY 43** [10]3-8-7 (50) G Gibbons 50/1: 6600: 12th: ln tch over 5f, wknd.	1¾	36
4994	**GO FREE 3** [9]3-8-6 (49) T P Queally 25/1: 0-250500: 13th: Cl-up 5f, fdd.	nk	34
4902	**INESCAPABLE 10** [4]3-8-10 (53) Martin Dwyer 16/1: 0040100: 14th: Cl-up 5f, fdd.	½	37
2054	**IAMBACK 137** [2]4-8-12 p (53) D Holland 22/1: 3011000: 15th: Handy over 4f, wknd.	1¼	35
3830	**BLUNHAM 64** [8]4-8-5 (46) B Reilly(3) 20/1: 0062000: 16th: Led over 3f, wknd fnl 2f.	2	24
3974	**PALVIC MOON 58** [5]3-8-7 P (50) R Fitzpatrick 50/1: 6-536000: 17th: Al in rear: reportedly struck into.	4	20

17 Ran   Time 1m 26.57 (4.57)   Owned: Mr J Spearing   Trained: Kinnersley

---

5057   2.50 Ladbrokes Com Wreake Conditions Stakes Fillies 3yo   (C2)
£6096 £2312 £1156   **1m9y rnd**   **Good 51**   **+11 Fast**   Inside

4802	**MANSFIELD PARK 17** [5] Saeed bin Suroor 3-8-9 (102) L Dettori 4/9 FAV: 21-331: Made all, went clr bef 1f out, eased cl-home, val 8L+: bckd at odds-on: fast time: eff at 7f/1m, further could suit: acts on firm & gd grnd: gd confidence boost for lightly rcd 3yo with ability: can find a fills listed/Gr race: see 4802 & 4495.		109
1702	**COQUETERIA 156** [3] G Wragg 3-8-9 (102) S Drowne 15/2: 0441-232: ln tch, prog bef 1f out, styd on to take 2nd cl-home, no ch with wnr: long abs: encouraging eff after long lay-off: see 1702 & 1110.	5	96
4341	**MARINAITE 40** [8] S R Bowring 3-8-13 (73) J Bramhill 80/1: 5220303: Al cl-up, no extra ins fnl 1f: prob flattered by today: see 2153 (h'cap).	1	98$
4614	**SILK FAN 27** [1] P W Harris (95) Martin Dwyer 7/2: 1-164444: Sn handy, wknd fnl 2f: btr 4095.	2½	89
4892*	**MILLY WATERS 353** [2]3-8-9 (85) S Sanders 25/1: 100011-5: b f Danzero - Chilly Waters (Polar Falcon) Nvr nrr than mid-div: reapp: progressive in '03 winning mdn, val auct stks & h'cap: eff at 5/6f on gd, fast grnd & fibresand: handles a sharp/undul or stiff trk: best with waiting tactics: with W M Brisbourne. 1 Oct'03 Newb 6.0 gd 87-78 D: 1 Oct'03 Newm 6 g/f 78-(78) B: 1 May'03 Warw 5 g/f 79- D: 2 Apr'03 Sout 5 af 78a- F: 2 Mar'03 Folk 5 gd 80- F:	4	81
1611	**SUMMERISE 158** [7]3-8-9 (51) P Robinson 200/1: 10-06306: Al in rear: long abs: btr 1529.	3	75$
4709	**PRIMESHADE PROMISE 22** [6]3-8-9 (53) J Tate 150/1: 00307: Handy over 5f, fdd.	1½	72$
4926	**FLAME QUEEN 10** [4]3-8-9 (57) T P Queally 150/1: 0404008: Keen handy over 5f, fdd.	½	71$

8 Ran   Time 1m 41.46 (3.26)   Owned: Godolphin   Trained: Newmarket

---

5058   3.20 E B F Ladbrokes Com Soar Maiden Stakes Div 1 2yo   (D2)
£5668 £1744 £872   **1m9y rnd**   **Good 51**   **-01 Slow**   Inside

4608	**LUIS MELENDEZ 27** [3] P F I Cole 2-9-0 R L Moore 5/2 FAV: 431: Made all, rdn out ins fnl 1f to assert: eff around 1m, further will suit: acts on fast & gd grnd: see 4608 & 4355.		84
4885	**BARBARY COAST 11** [1] W R Muir 2-9-0 Martin Dwyer 16/1: 602: Cl-up, styd on to chase wnr bef 1f out, just held ins fnl 1f: imprvd eff on step up to 1m: acts on gd grnd: now quals for h'caps & can find a race.	¾	81
4783	**KONG 17** [7] J L Dunlop 2-9-0 T Quinn 14/1: 43: Trkd ldrs, kept on but no ch with front 2 fnl 1f: eff at 1m, mid-dists will suit next term: acts on gd grnd: encouraging effort: see 4783.	1¼	79
	GROOMSMAN 0 [4] H Morrison 2-9-0 L Fletcher(3) 16/1: 4: b g Groom Dancer - Trois Heures Apres (Soviet Star) Mid-div, prog halfway, no impress fnl 1f: debut: Mar foal, cost 40,000gns: half-brother successful at 9/10f: dam plcd at Gr 1 level over 12f: sire top-class performer around 10f: eff at 1m, further will suit next term: acts on gd grnd: sharper for this.	2	75
4831	**PHI 15** [9]2-9-0 S Sanders 3/1: 025: Cl-up, no extra from dist: op 4/1: showed more in 4831 (fast).	nk	74
4611	**MONT SAINT MICHEL 27** [13]2-9-0 D Holland 66/1: 06: b c Montjeu - Band of Angels (Alzao) Bhd, prog 4f out, wknd dist: Mar foal, half-brother successful at 7f: dam unrcd: sire multiple Gr 1 wnr at 12f.	3½	67
4522	**GROUNDCOVER 31** [8]2-9-0 R Hughes 33/1: 07: b c Zafonic - Moss (Alzao) Missed break, nvr nrr than mid-div: Mar foal, half-brother to wnrs at 1m/2m1f: dam successful abroad: sire Gr 1 wnr at 1m.	1¾	63
	TILT 0 [11]2-9-0 J Murtagh 16/1: 8: Mid-div over 5f, wknd bef 1f out: debut.	nk	62
	KABIS AMIGOS 0 [6]2-9-0 T W Ryan 20/1: 9: Nvr nrr than mid-div on debut.	½	61
	SEEKING AN ALIBI 0 [12]2-9-0 L Dettori 5/1: 0: 10th: Slow away, prog 3f out, wknd fnl 2f.	1½	58
4355	**My Portfolio 39** [5]2-9-0 S Drowne 16/1:0		4842	**Danita Dancer 14** [2]2-8-9 F P Ferris(3) 125/1:0
	Hiddensee 0 [14]2-9-0 S Chin 40/1:0		4756	**Travel Tip 19** [10]2-9-0 J Fortune 16/1:P

14 Ran   Time 1m 42.41 (4.21)   Owned: Richard Green (Fine Paintings)   Trained: Whatcombe

---

5059   3.50 E B F Ladbrokes Com Soar Maiden Stakes Div 2 2yo   (D2)
£5668 £1744 £872   **1m9y rnd**   **Good 51**   **-11 Slow**   Inside

4416	**RIVER ALHAARTH 36** [9] P W Chapple Hyam 2-9-0 M Hills 6/1: 51: Prom, led 2f out, hdd dist, rallied for press to lead cl-home: eff at 1m, further will suit: acts on gd grnd & a stiff/gall trk: lightly rcd & game.		80
4724	**REGISTRAR 21** [10] Mrs A J Perrett 2-9-0 S Sanders 6/1: 52: Slow away, sn in tch, led dist, edged left under press & hdd cl-home: op 9/2: imprvd eff on step up to 1m: acts on gd: see 4724.	¾	77
4726	**HAWKES BAY 21** [2] M H Tompkins 2-9-0 R Hills 25/1: 03: b c Vettori - Nordico Princess (Nordico) Held up, prog wide 3f out, kept on fnl 1f: Jan first foal, cost 27,000gns: dam unrcd: sire fine performer around mid-dists: eff at 1m, looks in need of further: acts on gd grnd: signs of encouragement & can progress.	2	73
4677	**BULWARK 24** [6] Mrs A J Perrett 2-9-0 J Murtagh 12/1: 04: b c Montjeu - Bulaxie (Bustino) Handy 6f, sn onepcd: March foal, half-brother to numerous decent wnrs around 1m/10f: dam successful in List/group company at 7f/10f: sire multiple Gr 1 wnr at 12f: eff at 1m, further will suit: acts on gd grnd.	shd	72
3824	**ONE GOOD THING 64** [14]2-9-0 L Dettori 5/1: 05: b c Touch Gold - Once To Often (Raise A Native) Led 6f, no extra dist: op 4/1, 9 wk abs: Feb foal, cost $550,000: half-brother to wnrs abroad: dam wnr in US: sire useful performer around 1m/12f abroad: with Saeed bin Suroor.	½	71
4851	**MT DESERT 13** [4]2-9-0 J Fortune 7/1: 66: Rear, prog bef 2f out, kept on late: op 12/1: see 4851.	1½	68
	HAWK ARROW 0 [1]2-9-0 S Drowne 33/1: 7: Handy 6f, no extra: debut.	½	67
4355	**AMPELIO 39** [3]2-9-0 Martin Dwyer 12/1: 08: Nvr nrr than mid-div.	3	61
4608	**CAVE OF THE GIANT 27** [7]2-9-0 T Quinn 4/1 FAV: 59: Rear, nvr a factor, returned lame: btr 4608.	6	49

4710 **ZAVILLE 22** [11]2-8-9 P Robinson 25/1: 00: 10th: Handy over 6f, wknd.   ½   **43**
    Finnegans Rainbow 0 [5]2-9-0 R L Moore 16/1:0   **4865** **Pebble Mill 13** [13]2-9-0 D Holland 25/1:0
4703 **Turnover 22** [12]2-8-9 T E Durcan 33/1:0   **4722** **Fantastic Luck 21** [8]2-9-0 I Mongan 66/1:0
14 Ran   Time 1m 43.23 (5.03)   Owned: Mr R J Arculli   Trained: Newmarket

5060   4.20 Ladbrokes Com Claiming Stakes 3-4yo (E3)
          £3543 £1090 £545   **1m3f183y**   **Good 51**   **+03 Fast**   Inside

4414 **SOVIETTA 36** [4] R M Beckett 3-8-0 (65) N Mackay(3) 14/1: 4301: Rear, prog 5f out, styd on to lead   **62**
1f out, rdn cl: clmd for 6,000: eff at 12f on gd & fast grnd: lightly rcd 3yo who apprec drop to claim grade.
4850 **SECRET JEWEL 13** [5] Lady Herries 4-8-9 BL (65) R L Moore 16/1: 0-605002: Bhd, prog bef 1f out,   3½   **57**
nrst fin: tried blnks: eff at 12f, further will suit on this evidence: acts on gd: see 3222.
4702 **WEET A HEAD 22** [3] R Hollinshead 3-9-5 (72) R Hughes 10/1: 6346003: Bhd, prog 5f out, styd on to   ½   **73**
lead dist, sn hdd & no extra: eff at 1m/10f, ran to form on step up to 12f: see 2040 & 1877.
4745 **SILVER CITY 20** [2] Mrs A J Perrett 4-9-12 (70) L Dettori 11/2: 0-200004: Bhd, prog halfway, styd   1½   **70**
on to lead 2f out, hdd dist, no extra: clr rem: btr 2874.
4441 **CHESTALL 35** [6]3-8-11 R Kennemore(7) 66/1: 445: Cl-up 10f, fdd: see 4441 & 2515.   5   **55**
4966 **GO GREEN 7** [1]3-8-4 t (54) F P Ferris(3) 14/1: 2603206: In tch, wknd fnl 2f: jumps fit.   1¼   **46**
4856 **HINODE 13** [12]3-8-4 (57) J Quinn 25/1: 0035407: Cl-up, led 4f out, hdd 2f out, wknd: btr 4584.   1   **44**
4966 **CROCIERA 7** [11]3-8-11 BL (63) P Robinson 33/1: 00-4008: Nvr nrr than mid-div in first time blnks.   1¾   **48**
4665 **WODHILL HOPE 24** [14]4-8-11 (40) M Tebbutt 80/1: 430009: Missed break, nvr a factor.   3   **37**
2596 **ARRESTING 115** [16]4-9-12 (84) J Murtagh 6/5 FAV: 22-10650: 10th: Cl-up 10f, sn fdd: long abs: 2½   **48**
disapp effort dropped in grade: btr 1016.
4827 **ZAZOUS 15** [7]3-9-5 (58) J D Smith 80/1: 03-63000: 11th: Al in rear: btr 3595.   3   **44**
4669 **KILLING ME SOFTLY 24** [9]3-9-0 (51) R Fitzpatrick 33/1: 01-2040: 12th: Led, hdd after 1f, wknd fnl 3f.   ½   **38**
3182 **AIREDALE LAD 91** [10]3-8-5 (30) J Bramhill 100/1: 0-64500: 13th: Al bhd: reportedly lost action.   26   **0**
4559 **LAWRENCE OF ARABIA 29** [8]4-8-13 (56) S Sanders 7/1: 4/-066000: 14th: Led after 1f, hdd 4f out, wknd. 1   **0**
170 **TORZAL 308** [15]4-9-2 (45) L Fletcher(3) 125/1: 40/0000-0: 15th: Rear, nvr a factor: reapp   *dist* **0**
modest form in '03 (rtd 50, 38a, R F Marvin): with Miss M E Rowland.
15 Ran   Time 2m 34.08 (5.78)   Owned: Mr J H Richmond-Watson   Trained: Lambourn

5061   4.50 Ladbrokes Com Conditions Stakes 2yo (C2)
          £6148 £2332 £1166   **7f9y str**   **Good 51**   **-73 Slow**   Stands side

4746 **FOXHAVEN 20** [3] P R Chamings 2-8-10 (88) Martin Dwyer 6/1: 3221: Grabbed rail & made all, pushed   **100+**
out to assert, val 3L+: stays 1m, apprec drop back to 7f: acts on fast & gd grnd: progressive & useful.
4476 **RED PEONY 33** [1] Sir Mark Prescott 2-8-10 (99) S Sanders 10/11 FAV: 1362: Cl-up, styd on ins fnl   1½   **95**
1f, not pace of wnr: bckd: more encouraging after sltly disapp run in 4476, see 4264 & 3539.
4455 **SILENT JO 35** [2] Saeed bin Suroor 2-8-10 L Dettori 6/4: 323: Rcd last of 3, eff over 2f out,   1   **93**
onepcd fnl 1f: acts on firm & gd grnd, poss would have apprec stronger gallop & can lose mdn tag: see 4455 & 3568.
3 Ran   Time 1m 30.69 (8.69)   Owned: Mrs Ann Jenkins   Trained: Basingstoke

5062   5.20 Ladbrokes Com Handicap Stakes 3yo+ 56-70 (E3)
          £5130 £1578 £789   **1m1f218y**   **Good 51**   **-03 Slow**   Inside   **[78]**

4832 **DUELLING BANJOS 15** [4] J Akehurst 5-8-11 (61) S Sanders 5/1: 1-040001: Rear, prog 4f out, rdn   **71**
out to lead cl-home: eff at 1m, apprec step up to 10f: acts on gd, hvy grnd & both AWs: can win again: see 1385.
4849 **PLANTERS PUNCH 14** [1] R Hannon 3-9-0 (69) R Hughes 12/1: 1000322: Cl-up, styd on to lead dist,   hd   **77**
hdd under press cl-home: continues to run well & deserves to go one btr: see 4849 & 4182.
4392 **FUEL CELL 38** [7] R Hannon 3-9-0 bl (69) R L Moore 25/1: 3013503: In tch, ev ch dist, kept on, not btn far. ¾   **75**
4850 **BLAZING THE TRAIL 13** [5] J W Hills 4-8-11 (61) R Hills 20/1: 2306604: Rear, prog when short of   1¼   **65**
room bef 1f out, kept on late: btr 1913.
4862 **GARDEN SOCIETY 13** [8]7-8-10 (60) F Norton 9/1: 06-00005: Rear, prog 4f out, ev ch 1f out, sn no extra.½   **63**
4668 **ELIDORE 24** [2]4-9-2 (66) L Dettori 9/1: 0502456: Led, hdd 3f out, onepcd: btr 4057 (1m).   hd   **63**
4321 **ADORATA 41** [12]3-8-12 (67) M Tebbutt 25/1: 2302107: Nvr nrr than mid-div: 6 wk abs: btr 4042.   2½   **65**
4775 **KYLKENNY 18** [16]9-9-3 t (67) L Fletcher(3) 16/1: 3444008: Cl-up, led 3f out, hdd dist, wknd: btr 3867.   2   **62**
4861 **ZONIC BOOM 13** [3]4-8-12 (62) J Murtagh 9/1: 00-53039: Handy, wknd bef 1f out: btr 4861.   ¾   **55**
4775 **IBERUS 18** [18]6-9-3 (67) D Holland 20/1: 0054200: 10th: Rear, prog & ev ch dist, wknd: btr 4354.   1   **58**
4352 **MISS MONICA 38** [17]3-8-12 (67) W Ryan 50/1: 64300: 11th: Bhd, hdwy 4f out, wknd fnl 2f: btr 2835.   1   **56**
4832 **KABEER 15** [10]6-8-12 (62) L Keniry(3) 22/1: 4300560: 12th: Nvr nrr than mid-div.   hd   **50**
4487 **STEPHANO 33** [9]3-9-0 (69) M Hills 9/4 FAV: 0501120: 13th: Bhd, prog 3f out, wknd fnl 2f: btr 4487.   ½   **56**
4771 **General Gb 18** [13]7-9-2 (66) J Bramhill 16/1:0   4709 **Waziri 22** [6]3-8-13 VIS(68) S Drowne 50/1:0
4515} **Sharp Rigging 379** [19]4-9-5 (69) T P Queally 40/1:0   1823 **Reap 147** [11]6-9-1 (65) J Quinn 40/1:0
17 Ran   Time 2m 7.95(5.45)   Owned: E & S Racing III   Trained: Epsom

Official Going Good/Soft (Soft places)

5063   2.00 Racinguk Tv Handicap Stakes 3yo+ 56-70 (E3)   [73]
£3607 £1110 £555   **7f50y rnd   Soft   Inapp** Inside

1348} **WIZARD OF US** 526 [14] M Mullineaux 4-8-5 (5oh) (50) S Righton 100/1: 05005/0-1: b g Wizard King - Sian's Girl (Mystiko) Cl-up, styd on despite wandering fnl 1f, rdn to lead cl-home: sweating: well btn sole start for B Smart last term: mod form in '03 for E Alston: eff at 7f on soft grnd: clearly goes well fresh.   62

4818 **LOCOMBE HILL** 15 [15] N Wilson 8-9-5 (69) D Tudhope(5) 9/2 JT FAV: 0153122: Set pace, kept on till ¾ collared ins last: in fine heart: see 4622.   74

4346 **ABLE MIND** 40 [4] A C Whillans 4-8-7 (57) P Fessey 16/1: 33-00633: Chsd ldrs, eff over 1f out, ½ kept on: 6 wk abs: mdn: acts on firm, soft & fibresand: see 4346, 2726.   61

4820 **CHERISHED NUMBER** 15 [18] I Semple 5-9-4 bl (68) R Winston 10/1: 5304334: Held up, gd hdwy over 1f ½ out, kept on ins last & no threat to ldrs: see 4820.   71

4246 **FAIR SPIN** 45 [9]4-8-10 (60) K Darley 12/1: 00-03005: Held up, hdwy well over 1f out, keeping on nk when short of room cl-home: 6 wk abs: see 2947 (1m), 2542.   62

5014* **SENESCHAL** 2 [6]3-9-7 (6ex) (73) T O'Brien(7) 9/2 JT FAV: 0000516: Chsd ldrs, onepcd over 1f out: hd qck reappr: prob acts on fast & soft: see 5014.   74

4622 **SCOTLAND THE BRAVE** 26 [7]4-9-5 p (69) K McEvoy 10/1: 0414207: In tch, no extra fnl 2f: btr 4086.   2   66

1678* **INSUBORDINATE** 153 [2]3-8-9 (61) T Eaves(3) 16/1: 1006-018: Held up, nvr a factor: gelded & abs.   3   52

4622 **RARE COINCIDENCE** 26 [12]3-8-8 p (60) P Hanagan 16/1: 4003409: Handy, wknd over 1f out: see 1872. nk   50

3593 **FRANCIS FLUTE** 73 [11]6-8-5 (6oh) (49) R Ffrench 25/1: 0240000: 10th: Chsd ldrs, wknd over 1f out. shd   44

4246 **PARISIAN PLAYBOY** 45 [8]4-8-5 (6oh) (49) Leanne Kershaw(7) 12/1: 0121000: 11th: In tch, no extra ½ over 1f out: 6 wk abs: see 3700.   43

2990 **Pop Up Again** 98 [17]4-9-4 (68) W Supple 50/1:0   3768 **Pawan** 66 [10]4-9-3 (67) Ann Stokell 40/1:0
5036 **Musiotal** 1 [3]3-8-3 (1oh) (54) C Catlin 14/1:0   4867 **Washbrook** 13 [1]3-8-3 T(55) A Nicholls 50/1:0
4867 **Showtime Annie** 13 [16]3-9-0 (66) M Fenton 20/1:0   4845 **Headland** 14 [13]6-8-7 bl e(57) A Culhane 25/1:0
17 Ran   Time 1m 34.92 (11.12)   Owned: Mr P Currey   Trained: Tarporley

---

5064   2.30 European Breeders Fund Kirkoswald Maiden Stakes 2yo (D2)
£5606 £1725 £862   **7f50y rnd   Soft   Inapp** Inside

4691 **KAMES PARK** 23 [4] I Semple 2-9-0 R Winston 16/1: 421: Keen, chsd ldr, hdwy to lead & hung left ins last, styd on, rdn out: eff at 7f, 1m will suit: acts on soft grnd: going the right way: see 4691, 4351.   84

4883 **ALRAFIDAIN** 12 [8] M Johnston 2-9-0 W Supple 4/5 FAV: 42: Set pace, rdn & hdd ins last, not pace 1 of wnr: well bckd: eff at 7f, will apprec a return to 1m: acts on gd & soft grnd: can find similar: see 4883.   81

4283 **ONYERGO** 43 [2] J R Weymes 2-9-0 P Mulrennan(3) 33/1: 33: Handy, onepace over 1f out: 6 wk abs.   3½   75

4247 **IL COLOSSEO** 45 [9] Mrs L Stubbs 2-9-0 D Allan 12/1: 34: In tch, no extra dist: abs, btr 4247.   4   68

SCRIPTWRITER [3]2-9-0 K McEvoy 5/2: 5: b c Sadler's Wells - Dayanata (Shirley Heights) Slow 1¾   64
away, rdn bhd, styd far side, btn & flashed tail 2f out: nicely bckd on debut: Mar foal: half-brother to wnrs at 6f/12f: mid-dist bred.

4782 **LAKE WAKATIPU** 17 [7]2-8-9 (57) S Righton 66/1: 04366: In tch, wknd over 2f out: see 4006.   1¾   55

4866 **BLUE BAJAN** 13 [6]2-9-0 C Catlin 25/1: 67: In tch, btn 2f out: see 4866.   1¼   57

4863 **SHOWTIME FAYE** 13 [5]2-8-9 P Hanagan 150/1: 08: b f Overbury - Rebel County (Maelstrom Lake) In 9   34
tch, wknd over 2f out: Jan foal, cost 1,800gns: half-sister to a 6f/1m wnr: dam 1m/10f scorer.

4518 **ANSELLS LEGACY** 31 [1]2-9-0 (53) A Culhane 150/1: 0069: Al bhd.   5   29

9 Ran   Time 1m 37.36 (13.56)   Owned: Mrs June Delaney   Trained: Carluke

---

5065   3.00 Daily Record Gary Owen Nursery Handicap Stakes 2yo 0-85 (D2)   [89]
£5616 £1728 £864   **1m rnd   Soft   Inapp** Inside

4602* **KINGS ACCOUNT** 27 [4] M Johnston 2-9-7 (82) K Darley 9/2: 22211: Cl-up, led over 2f out, held on   91
gamely for press ins last: stays 1m well on fast & soft grnd, any trk: genuine & progressing with each start.

4602 **STANCOMB WILLS** 27 [5] M H Tompkins 2-9-0 (75) N Callan 10/1: 0022: In tch, eff over 1f out, kept nk   83
on, just held: stays 1m on fast & soft: also rnr-up to this wnr in 4602, deserves similar.

4580 **GUINEA A MINUTE** 28 [6] M L W Bell 2-8-1 (62) Hayley Turner(3) 5/1: 0366533: Keen cl-up, eff over nk   69
1f out, kept on ins last, just held: nicely bckd: gd run: see 4580.

4816 **LAST PIONEER** 15 [3] T P Tate 2-8-4 (65) R Ffrench 40/1: 0044: Held up, eff over 2f out, no 2½   67
impress: acts on soft: see 4816.

4285 **LADY MISHA** 43 [10]2-8-12 (73) P Hanagan 4/1 FAV: 5503125: In tch, hdwy & short of room over 1f 1   73
out, kept on ins last, no impress: nicely bckd: see 4285, 3698.

4673 **ALONG THE NILE** 24 [11]2-8-9 (70) A Culhane 7/1: 0360046: Held up, some late gains, nvr dngrs. shd   69

4381 **ROBINZAL** 38 [7]2-8-8 (69) D Allan 25/1: 03267: Keen in tch, wknd dist: longer trip: see 4207.   2   64

4583 **VELVETEEN RABBIT** 28 [2]2-8-11 (72) K McEvoy 16/1: 03208: Handy, wknd dist: see 3909 (7f).   1¼   65

4864* **BRONZE DANCER** 13 [8]2-8-9 (70) R Winston 14/1: 00019: Chsd ldrs, hung left & wknd over 1f out.   ½   62

4871 **SHUJUNE AL HAWAA** 12 [12]2-8-2 vis (63) C Catlin 16/1: 6300060: 10th: Al bhd: see 4871.   6   43

4741 **THREE ACES** 20 [9]2-7-12 (3oh)bl (56) J Mackay 50/1: 056000: 11th: Slow away & al bhd.   1¼   37

4375 **BLUSHING RUSSIAN** 38 [1]2-7-13 (60) D Fentiman(7) 10/1: 0030: 12th: Led till over 2f out, wknd.   12   14

12 Ran   Time 1m 47.66 (11.06)   Owned: Brian Yeardley Continental Ltd   Trained: Middleham

---

5066   3.30 Subscribe To Racing Uk On 08700 860432 Maiden Stakes 3yo+   (E3)
£5491 £1690 £845   **1m2f**   **Soft**   **Inapp**   Inside

4392 **OUNINPOHJA** 38 [9] G A Swinbank 3-9-0 (72) R Winston 10/11 FAV: 43251: Hld up, hdwy & hung left   75
over 1f out, led, rdn clr: bckd: confirmed promise of 4392 & stays 10f well on fm & soft: confidence boost.
4931 **YOUNG ROONEY** 10 [7] M Mullineaux 4-9-5 (70) K Darley 3/1: 0322632: Sn clr ldr, rdn & hdd over 1f   4   63
out, not pace of wnr: mdn after 17 but in fair form: see 4931.
4623 **LOADED GUN** 26 [11] W M Brisbourne 4-9-5 (53) S W Kelly 12/1: 00-02403: In tch, eff 2f out, onepace.   2   60
964 **SHARES** 197 [10] P Monteith 4-9-5 (60) R Ffrench 9/1: 0/0330-24: Held up, btn 2f out: long abs.   6   52
4135 **STRAVONIAN** 50 [2]4-9-5 P Mathers(5) 150/1: 005: b g Luso - In The Evening (Distinctly North) In   5   46
tch, wknd 2f out.
4868 **KYBER** 13 [1]3-9-0 (60) P Hanagan 40/1: 543306: In tch, wknd over 2f out: btr 3697.   14   28
4768 **BODFARI DREAM** 18 [5]3-8-9 S Righton 100/1: 07: ch f Environment Friend - Al Reet (Alzao)   3   19
Dwelt, al bhd.
4407 **QUEENS ECHO** 36 [4]3-8-9 (57) L Enstone 33/1: 5-258: Handy, wknd over 2f out: btr 4216.   ½   18
1275} **SPECTRUM STAR** 530 [13]4-9-5 (40) P Mulrennan(3) 100/1: 030/0-9: b g Spectrum - Persia (Persian   3½   18
Bold) Al bhd: changed stable, modest form.
4286 **RHUM** 43 [3]4-9-5 T Eaves(3) 66/1: P50: 10th: Handy, wknd over 2f out.   2   15
2410 **ARRAN SCOUT** 122 [14]3-9-0 BL (74) N Callan 12/1: 04-300: 11th: Chsd clr ldr, wknd over 2f out: 14   0
blnks, changed stable, long abs: see 1636 (gd).
513} **OCOTILLO** 619 [8]4-9-5 K McEvoy 50/1: 5-0: 12th: Dwelt, al bhd.   dist   0
4216 **PERRYWINKLE BOY** 46 [12]3-9-0 T (40) M Fenton 100/1: 400P: Bhd, p.u. over 1f out, reportedly lame.   0
13 Ran   Time 2m 16.03 (11.63)   Owned: Am No Havin That   Trained: Richmond

---

5067   4.00 Family Day At Ayr On 7th November Selling Stakes 3yo+   (F3)
£4251 £1308 £654   **1m1f20y**   **Soft**   **Inapp**   Inside

1118 **FIDDLERS CREEK** 184 [11] R Allan 5-9-4 p (54) D Tudhope(5) 9/2: 60-60001: Chsd ldrs, styd on to   50
lead ins fnl 1f, held on gamely, all out: bckd: unplcd in a nov hdle 11 days ago: eff at 9/12f, has tried 2m:
acts on gd, soft & f/sand, any trk: wears cheekpieces, has tried t-strap/visor: apprec drop to sell grade.
3487 **REVERSIONARY** 78 [6] M W Easterby 3-9-5 bl (48) R Winston 14/1: 0001032: Prom, led 3f out till ins   hd   54
fnl 1f, rallied & only just failed: 11 wk abs: apprec return to sell grade, acts on gd, soft & f/sand.
4626 **RYMERS RASCAL** 26 [4] E J Alston 12-9-9 (49) D Allan 9/2: 0206123: Keen & chsd ldrs, kept on   ½   53
under press fnl 1f, not btn far in a close fin: op 3/1: eff at 7/9f: 12yo who continues in fine form: see 4626.
4695 **KING SUMMERLAND** 23 [12] B Mactaggart 7-9-4 (50) R Ffrench 10/1: 42160-54: Chsd ldrs, onepcd fnl   2½   44
1f: drpd in grade: see 4695.
3764 **THE SPOOK** 66 [8]4-9-4 (35) P Fessey 100/1: 300-0005: Dwelt, late hdwy despite flashing tail,   hd   43
nrst fin: 10 wk abs & new stable (prev with W Brisbourne): prob stays 9f & acts on soft grnd: see 2811.
4499*)**DUBAI LIGHTNING** 607 [7]4-9-4 P (80) D Sweeney 5/2 FAV: 11-0: b g Seeking The Gold - Heraklia   8   29
(Irish River) Keen & chsd ldrs, btn over 1f out: hvly bckd from 5/1 in first time cheek pieces, reapp: trained by
D Loder & unplcd sole '03 start: prev term won an AW mdn: $2,000,000 foal, eff at 7f on fast grnd & polytrack:
dropped in grade & better expected, should be noted: with J O'Shea.
1 Oct'02 Ling 7 ap 88a- D: 2 Sep'02 York 6.9 g/f 88- D:
1223 **PRINCE PROSPECT** 178 [1]8-9-9 (40) Kristin Stubbs(7) 50/1: 0122007: Rear, nvr nr ldrs: long abs.   1¼   32
4903 **MERLINS PROFIT** 10 [2]4-9-4 BL (40) S W Kelly 16/1: 20U4368: Led till 3f out, wknd: tried blnks.   3   23
4284 **ASH BOLD** 43 [3]7-9-4 (45) T Eaves(3) 10/1: /000///-429: Prom 7f, sn wknd: 6 wk abs.   ¾   21
4189 **OPEN HANDED** 46 [5]4-9-9 (47) P Hanagan 6/1: 1055000: 10th: Chsd ldrs till halfway: 7 wk abs.   9   12
3651 **BLACKPOOL JACK** 71 [9]3-9-0 P Mulrennan(3) 100/1: 00: 11th: b g Mtoto - Endearing Val (Entitled)   dist   0
Prom early, sn bhd, t.o: 10 wk abs, no form.
11 Ran   Time 2m 05.54 (15.24)   Owned: I Flannigan R Allan & A Grant   Trained: Cornhill-On-Tweed

---

5068   4.30 Racing Uk On Sky 432 Stakes Handicap 3yo+ 71-85 (D2)   [94]
£8185 £2518 £1259   **1m5f13y**   **Soft**   **Inapp**   Inside

1318 **WINGED DARGENT** 172 [9] M Johnston 3-8-10 (76) K Darley 7/1: 151: Chsd ldrs, outpcd after 1m,   87
rallied well to lead ins fnl 1f, drvn out: long abs: eff at 10f, stays 13f well & shld get further: acts on
gd/soft, clearly revels in soft & hvy grnd: runs v well fresh: only lightly rcd & a promising young stayer.
4771 **CIRCASSIAN** 18 [5] Sir Mark Prescott 3-8-11 (77) J Mackay 2/1 FAV: 0-021142: Nvr far away, led 3f   1   86
out till ins fnl 1f, kept on & only just btn: hvly bckd, clr of rem: typically tough & progressive Sir M Prescott
performer, stays 13f & acts on fast & soft grnd: see 4672.
3918 **SHREDDED** 60 [6] J H M Gosden 4-9-6 t (78) W Supple 14/1: 4-021063: Chsd ldrs, chall 2f out, left   5   80
bhd by front 2 ins fnl 1f: 9 wk abs: see 2192.
4634 **PATRIXPRIAL** 26 [7] M H Tompkins 3-8-10 (76) N Callan 9/1: 0-55104: Chsd ldrs, onepcd fnl 2f.   3½   73
3749 **FIRST CENTURION** 67 [4]3-9-0 (80) S Whitworth 25/1: 6-10045: Held up, nvr reach ldrs: 10 wk abs.   2½   73
3881 **CHARLOTTE VALE** 62 [3]3-8-8 (74) M Fenton 16/1: 2131236: Chsd ldrs, wknd 2f out: 9 wk abs.   2   64
4919 **FORT CHURCHILL** 10 [1]3-8-12 bl (78) P Hanagan 100/30: 4201027: Keen & led, hdd 3f out, wknd,   16   44
t.o: well bckd: rcd much too keenly today: btr 4919.
4657 **MASTER WELLS** 25 [2]3-9-1 (81) K McEvoy 7/1: 2002148: Chsd ldrs, btn over 2f out: btr 4209 (2m).   3   43
1679*)**CAKE IT EASY** 508 [8]4-9-3 (75) A Culhane 33/1: 3324/21-9: ch f Kendor - Diese Memory (Diesis)   dist   0
Chsd ldrs till halfway, sn btn, t.o on reapp: trained by M Johnston to win fnl of 4 '03 starts (fills mdn): mod nov
hdle form (rtd 106h): likes to force the pace over 12f on soft, acts on gd/soft & f/sand: now with K Reveley.
1 May'03 Hayd 11.9 sft 74-(75) D: 2 May'03 Hami 12.1 g/s 75-(75) E: 2 Dec'02 Wolv 8.4 af 68a- F:
9 Ran   Time 3m 02.16 (17.56)   Owned: Mr Daniel A Couper   Trained: Middleham

5069 5.00 Serendipity Interactive Ticketing Handicap Stakes 3yo+ 56-70 (E3)   [79]
£4228 £1301 £651   6f str   Soft   Inapp   Stands Side

4622 **NORTHERN GAMES 26** [14] K A Ryan 5-9-0 bl (65) N Callan 4/1 FAV: 0142421: Prom, went on dist,   **80**
pushed clr fnl 1f, cmftbly: nicely bckd: eff at 6/7f on fast, soft grnd & fibresand: handles a sharp/turning or
gall trk: eff in blnks & cheek pieces: see 4622 & 3352.
4967* **ON THE TRAIL 7** [12] D W Chapman 7-8-5 (2oh) (54) R Ffrench 7/1: 1452012: Led till dist, held on   5   **59**
for 2nd but no ch with wnr: tchd 9/1: acts on firm, soft grnd & both AWs: in-form front runner, see 4967.
4754 **MIDNIGHT PARKES 19** [19] E J Alston 5-9-4 (69) D Allan 22/1: 1003003: Prom, outpcd halfway, styd   nk **71**
on well fnl 1f & just failed to take 2nd: prev best on fast & firm grnd, clearly handles a soft surface: see 3241.
4654 **HIGHLAND WARRIOR 25** [8] J S Goldie 5-9-5 (70) W Supple 12/1: 6630264: Held up, prog when short   ½   **70**
of room 2f out, nrst fin: see 4087 (C/D).
4818 **ULYSEES 15** [18]5-9-3 (68) P Hanagan 14/1: 5004005: Chsd ldrs, sltly outpcd halfway, kept on fnl 1f.   1¼ **65**
4754 **ONLINE INVESTOR 19** [16]5-8-10 (61) A Nicholls 14/1: 0024406: Keen in rear, hdwy to chase ldrs   nk **57**
dist, sn no impress.
5036 **TROJAN FLIGHT 1** [5]3-9-3 (69) R Winston 5/1: 12104247: Switched stands side & rear, styd on   ¾   **63**
late, nvr dngrs: well bckd: ran similarly over C/D yesterday: see 4754.
4818 **PAYS DAMOUR 15** [6]7-8-5 (5oh) (51) T Eaves(1) 50/1: 3020008: Rear, late prog, nvr dngrs.   1½ **47**
4989 **SHARP HAT 4** [21]10-8-11 (62) A Culhane 16/1: 0245009: Held up, no room from halfway, nvr a   1¾ **49**
factor: qck reapp: forgive this: see 3350.
3796 **INDIAN SHORES 66** [9]5-8-5 (11oh) (45) S Righton 100/1: 6000000: 10th: Nvr a factor: 9 wk abs.   1¼ **40**
4818 **FLYING EDGE 15** [13]4-8-5 (2oh) (54) Natalia Gemelova(5) 10/1: 5000440: 11th: Chsd ldrs, btn 1.5f out.   shd **39**
4562 **HAULAGE MAN 29** [11]6-8-6 p (57) T Hamilton(3) 20/1: 0202000: 12th: Chsd ldrs 4f, wknd.   nk **39**
4618 **ROBWILLCALL 26** [15]4-8-5 (10oh)p (46) P Mathers(5) 50/1: 1550500: 13th: Chsd ldrs, wknd 2f out.   hd **37**
4869 **ZOOM ZOOM 13** [4]4-9-4 (69) M Fenton 16/1: 1/-105040: 14th: Prom till halfway: see 4869.   3½ **43**
4870 **COLLEGE MAID 13** [3]7-8-5 (2oh)bl (54) J Currie(7) 25/1: 6530060: 15th: Speed 4f, sn btn.   1¼ **27**
333 **Foxies Future 280** [1]3-8-4 (56) D Fentiman(7) 66/1:0   4754 **Strawberry Patch 19** [20]5-8-9 p(60) J Mackay 14/1:0
4696 **Thornaby Green 23** [2]3-8-11 (63) P Makin(5) 16/1:0
3129 **Speedfit Free 94** [7]7-8-5 (16oh)vis(40) T O'Brien(7) 100/1:0
19 Ran   Time 1m 13.51(4.21)   Owned: Mr R E Robinson   Trained: Hambleton

Official Going Soft

5070 3.00 Group 1 Prix de la Foret 3YO+ (A)
£80479 £32197 £16099   7f rnd   Soft   Inapplicable

4384 **SOMNUS 35** [6] T D Easterby 4-9-2 (118) M J Kinane 26/10 FAV: 0-025121: Bhd, prog & ev ch bef 1f   **121**
out, styd on to lead nr line, pushed out, val bit more: eff at 6/7f on firm & fast, just prefers gd/soft & soft grnd:
high class performer who relished today's conditions: top-class & tough, see 4384.
4434 **DENEBOLA 34** [3] P Bary 3-8-11 C-P Lemaire 41/10: 31-32042: Mid div, hdwy 2f out, kept on ins   ¾   **115**
fnl 1f, not pace wnr: fine run on drop back to 7f & lost little in defeat: see 4434.
4434 **LE VIE DEI COLORI 34** [7] L M Cumani 4-9-2 C Soumillon 64/10: 1-114303: In tch, slightly outpcd   1   **116**
over 2f out, rallied fnl 1f: back to form on return to 7f: see 3533.
4384 **MONSIEUR BOND 35** [1] B Smart 4-9-2 bl (115) F Lynch 165/10: 51106054: Cl up, led bef 3f out, sn   nk **115**
clr, hdd & no extra well ins fnl 1f: back to form with give in the ground: see 3062 & 1667 (Gr 2).
4477+ **PASTORAL PURSUITS 30** [5]3-9-0 (110) S Drowne 41/10: 111-2115: Bhd, nvr able to challenge: below   1   **113**
par on first try on soft grnd: most prog earlier, see 4477 (firm, Gr 2).
4801 **NAYYIR 14** [2]6-9-2 (120) J Fortune 39/10: 2-302246: Rear, nvr a factor: poor run: btr 4801.   3   **107**
2826* **CHARMING GROOM 104** [4]5-9-2 O Peslier 56/10: 14642107: Led over 3f, wknd fnl 2f.   6   **95**
7 Ran   Time 1m 22.30()   Owned: Legard Sidebottom   Trained: Germany

Official Going Rnd Course - Good/Soft, Str Course - Soft

5071 3.00 Group 2 Juddmonte Beresford Stakes 2YO (A)
£54925 £16055 £7605   1m rnd   Good/Soft   Inapplicable

ALBERT HALL 21 [2] A P O'Brien 2-9-0 J P Spencer 4/5 FAV: 21: b c Danehill - Al Theraab   **113**
(Roberto) Led 6f, rallied to lead ins fnl 1f, rdn out to hold on: earlier 2nd in a mdn here at The Curragh: cost
510,000 gns: eff at 7f/1m, further will suit: acts on gd/soft grnd & a gall trk: game & smart, win more Gr races.
MERGER 10 [3] D K Weld 2-9-0 P J Smullen 9/2: 12: gr c Mr Greeley - Toledo Queen (El Gran   ½   **110**
Senor) Cl up, led & edged right 2f out, hdd ins fnl 1f, kept on when slightly short of room cl home, just held:
earlier mdn wnr at Thurles: eff at 1m, further will suit: acts on gd/soft grnd: smart, win a Gr race.
4853 **SANT JORDI 11** [5] B J Meehan 2-9-0 (80) M J Kinane 16/1: 3123: Handy, eff bef 1f out, onepcd fnl   4½ **101**
1f: longer trip & up in grade.
5 Ran   Time 1m 43.80 ()   Owned: Mrs John Magnier   Trained: Ireland

CURRAGH SUNDAY 10.10.04 Righthand, Galloping Track

5072 3.30 Listed EBF Fillies Flame of Tara Stakes 2YO (A)
£31736 £9311 £4436 **6f str Soft Inapplicable**

4679 **BIBURY FLYER 22** [12] M R Channon 2-8-11 (81) A Culhane 12/1: 03332451: Handy, styd on to lead **104**
bef 1f out, rdn out: stays 7f, prob suited by 5/6f on firm, improved on soft: useful.
4958 **VIRGINIA WATERS 8** [3] A P O'Brien 2-8-11 t J P Spencer 9/4: 0132: In tch, prog to lead bef 1f ½ **101**
out, hdd ins fnl 1f, not pace wnr: see 4958.
GOUACHE 11 [6] Kevin Prendergast 2-8-11 D P McDonogh 20/1: 30221043: bl f Key Of Luck - Sketch 4½ **88**
Pad (Warning) Bhd, prog 2f out, styd on, no ch with front 2.
10 Ran Time 1m 17.30() Owned: Ridgeway Downs Racing Trained: West Ilsley

5073 5.00 Listed Leinster Leader Waterford Testimonal Stakes 3YO+ (A)
£23273 £6828 £7700 **6f str Soft Inapplicable**

4313 **STRIKING AMBITION 42** [4] R Charlton 4-9-1 (113) J P Murtagh 4/1 FAV: 000-0031: Made all, clr bef **117+**
2f out, eased ins fnl 1f, val 5L+: 6 wk abs: eff at 6f on fast & hvy grnd: back to smart best.
4732 **GRAND REWARD 22** [5] A P O'Brien 3-9-0 tbl J P Spencer 5/1: 01L36302: Chsd ldrs, styd on for 2nd 3½ **107**
ins fnl 1f, no ch with wnr: see 4732.
2947] **SENOR BENNY 813** [2] M McDonagh 5-9-1 E Ahern 14/1: 01212113: br c Benny The Dip - Senora Tippy ½ **106**
(El Gran Senor) In tch, prog 3f out, onepcd fnl 1f.
4879 **MILLYBAA 10** [17]4-8-12 BL (93) M J Kinane 12/1: 24004009: Bhd, prog 2f out, wknd & eased fnl 1f. 12 **70**
4879* **NIGHTS CROSS 10** [7]3-9-4 bl (101) A Culhane 6/1: 03330010: 14th: Cl up 3f, sn wknd & eased: 5 **64**
reportedly lost action: btr 4879 (5f, fast).
17 Ran Time 1m 15.10() Owned: Peter Webb Trained: Beckhampton

SAN SIRO SUNDAY 10.10.04 Righthand, Stiff, Galloping Track

Official Going Good

5074 4.20 Group 1 Premio Vittorio di Capua 3YO+ (A)
£129085 £64067 £37077 **1m Good Inapplicable**

4220* **ANCIENT WORLD 43** [4] Saeed Bin Suroor 4-8-13 (110) L Dettori 1/09/1 FAV: 1-221011: Made all trav **119**
well, pushed out to assert: 6 wk abs: eff at 1m on firm & soft grnd: progressed into v smart 4yo & well plcd
to land this val event: stays in training next term: see 4220 & 3565.
4915 **MAJESTIC DESERT 8** [3] M R Channon 3-8-6 (113) D Holland 4/1: 00222442: Bhd, prog wide 3f out, 1½ **111**
chsd wnr ins fnl 1f, al held: back to smart best today: see 3659 & 1349.
4949 **HURRICANE ALAN 8** [7] R Hannon 4-8-13 (114) P Dobbs 32/10: 50303323: Mid div, outpcd 2f out, 1½ **112**
rallied fnl 1f: again ran with credit: see 4949 & 1349.
SCABIUN [2] A Botti 6-8-13 E Botti 15/1: 4131114: Bhd, prog bef 1f out, no impress fnl 1f. snk **111**
7 Ran Time 1m 37.80() Owned: Godolphin Trained: Newmarket

DUSSELDORF SUNDAY 10.10.04

Official Going Soft

5075 3.05 Group 3 Grosser Preis der Landeshauptstadt Dusseldorf 3YO+ (A)
£22535 £9155 £4577 **1m100y rnd Soft Inapplicable**

4524*)**PEPPERCORN FR 378** [2] U Ostmann 7-9-0 P Heugl 89/10: 4311-611: b h Big Shuffle - Pasca **110**
(Lagunas) Bhd, prog 3f out, led ins fnl 1f, readily: won this race for the 3rd time: eff at 1m on soft grnd.
1 Sep'03 Colo 8sft 110- A:
GLAD LION [1] U Ostmann 3-8-9 I Ferguson 9/10 FAV: 2: b c Dashing Blade - Glady Beauty (Big 1¾ **101**
Shuffle) Led, hdd ins fnl 1f, not pace wnr.
4839 **PUTRA PEKAN 15** [7] M A Jarvis 6-9-0 (110) N Callan 5/1: 010-110723: Prom, ev ch 1f out, sn onepcd. ½ **102**
8 Ran Time 1m 45.21() Owned: Stall Biovita Trained: Germany

LINGFIELD Polytrack WEDNESDAY 13.10.04 Lefthand, V Sharp Track

Official Going Standard

5076 1.15 Bet Direct At Lingfield Park Maiden Stakes Div 1 2yo (D3)
£4238 £1304 £652 **7f aw rnd Going 34 -00 Slow Inside**

HAPPY AS LARRY [3] Saeed bin Suroor 2-9-0 T L Dettori 5/1: 1: b c Yes It's True - Don't Be Blue **86a+**
(Henbane) Missed break, prog 3f out, styd on to lead dist, pushed clr fnl 1f, val: Mar foal,
sire decent sprint performer in US: eff at 7f, shld get further: acts on polytrack & a v sharp trk: goes well
fresh: eff in a t-strap: won in gd style & looks to have a bright future.
KARENS CAPER [14] J H M Gosden 2-8-9 J Fortune 7/1: 2: b f War Chant - Miss Caerleona 2½ **72a**
(Caerleon) Slow away, hdwy wide 3f out, kept on for 2nd well ins fnl 1f, no ch with wnr: tchd 5/1 on debut: May

foal, half-sister successul at 1m: dam a smart mid-dist performer, sire high-class over 1m: eff at 7f, further will suit: acts on polytrack, encouraging eff after losing grnd at start, can improve.
4416 **KINGS KAMA 37** [7] Sir Michael Stoute 2-9-0 Martin Dwyer 13/8 FAV: 443: Al cl-up, no extra dist: bckd on AW bow: back on fast grnd & polytrack: now quals for h'caps: see 4416 & 3869. ½ **76a**
4121 **THREE DEUCES 51** [10] B J Meehan 2-8-9 D Holland 5/1: 54: Led, rcd keenly, hdd dist, wknd: op 4/1, 7 wk abs: rtn to sprinting shld suit: see 4121. 3½ **64a**
4829 **OVERJOY WAY 16** [4]2-8-9 T P Queally 20/1: 005: Keen in tch 5f, no extra: quals for h'caps. 1¼ **62a**
4470 **BOLD DIKTATOR 34** [8]2-9-0 S Drowne 50/1: 066: In tch over 5f, wknd: now quals for h'caps. 1 **65a**
4416 **MY RASCAL 37** [2]2-9-0 A McCarthy 100/1: 0007: b c Imperial Ballet - Derena (Crystal Palace) Handy 5f, wknd: Mar foal, half-brother useful 1m wnr: sire a useful miler: with M J Wallace. 3½ **58a**
4941 **IN DREAMS 9** [6]2-9-0 F Norton 33/1: 00058: Mid-div over 5f, wknd: btr 4941. nk **57a**
LEKKA DING [12]2-8-9 J Quinn 50/1: 9: Missed break, nvr a factor: debut. ¾ **50a**
GALLANTIAN [13]2-9-0 P Hanagan 25/1: 0: 10th: Slow away, al bhd: debut. shd **54a**
4876 **BELLE CHANSON 13** [5]2-8-9 T Quinn 50/1: 000: 11th: Handy 5f, fdd: debut. ¾ **47a**
OBLIQUE [1]2-8-9 S Sanders 14/1: 0: 12th: Slow away & nvr a factor. 1¼ **45a**
Petticoat Hill [9]2-8-9 R Havlin 20/1:0 4843 **La Cygne Blanche 15** [11]2-8-9 C Haddon(7) 100/1:0
14 Ran Time 1m 25.20 (2.4) Owned: Godolphin Trained: Newmarket

5077

1.45 Bet Direct 'red To Bet' On Itv Classified Stakes 4yo+ 0-55 (F4)
£2912 £832 £416 **1m aw rnd** **Going 34** **-08 Slow** Outside

4982 **FANTASY CRUSADER 6** [12] J A Gilbert 5-8-12 p (55) Dane O'Neill 14/1: 0313101: Held up wide, hdwy 2f out, rdn out to lead cl-home: qck reapp: eff at 7f, suited by 1m/10f: acts on firm, fast grnd & polytrack: eff with cheek pieces & likes Lingfield: see 4539 & 3748. **61a**
4542 **OH SO ROSIE 31** [5] J S Moore 4-8-9 p (54) Martin Dwyer 8/1: 1004252: Held up, plenty to do bef 1f out, styd on wide ins fnl 1f, post came too sn: gd eff & can rtn to winning ways on this evidence: see 4077 & 3363. ½ **55a**
4661* **RYANS BLISS 25** [3] T D McCarthy 4-8-11 (57) C Catlin 20/1: 0005613: Chsd ldrs, styd on to lead ins fnl 1f, hdd cl-home, no extra: eff at 1m, rtn to 10f will suit: btr 4661 (mdn clmr). nk **56a**
3524 **HOLLYWOOD HENRY 77** [6] J Akehurst 4-8-12 p (55) J Quinn 20/1: 000-1604: Bhd, prog when short of room dist, switched & kept on ins fnl 1f: 11 wk abs: acts on firm, soft grnd & polytrack: see 2440. nk **56a**
1198 **GALLOWAY MAC 181** [8]4-9-0 (57) D Holland 25/1: 0124605: Cl-up, ev ch 2f out, no extra fnl 1f. ¾ **56a**
4867 **PEPPER ROAD 14** [4]5-8-12 (54) R Ffrench 11/2: 0122206: In tch when short of room bef 1f out till ins fnl 1f, sn no impress: op 8/1: just btr 4488 & 3650. ½ **53a**
4668 **SISTER SOPHIA 25** [2]4-8-9 T (55) R Mullen 33/1: 0036007: Slow away, prog from rear when short of room dist, kept on late: first time t-strap: did not get run of today's race & showed encouragement, see 3490. ¾ **48a**
4982* **NAUTICAL 6** [10]6-9-4 (55) L Dettori 1/1 FAV: 3020118: Rear, prog & ev ch trav well bef 1f out, sn no extra: bckd from qck reapp: disapp on hat-trick bid: showed more in 4982 & 4367 (h'caps). shd **56a**
3142 **MUYASSIR 94** [1]9-8-12 (54) S Sanders 16/1: 0100009: Al in rear: long abs. 3 **44a**
DARLING RIVER 352 [11]5-9-0 (60) T Quinn 66/1: 343/000-0: 10th: b f Double Bed - Oh Lucky Day (Balidar) Led 1f, led again 2f out, hdd ins fnl 1f, sn wknd: reapp: long abs & Brit bow, ex French, plcd in 6 of 13 career starts in native France: with S Dow. hd **45a**
4982 **ZIET DALSACE 6** [9]4-8-9 (53) J Fortune 9/1: 1046020: 11th: Led after 3f till 2f out, wknd. 1½ **37a**
4974 **ITS ECCO BOY 7** [7]6-8-12 (53) Lisa Jones 66/1: 0000060: 12th: Led 3f, no room dist, wknd. 1¼ **38a**
12 Ran Time 1m 39.59 (3.39) Owned: The Fantasy Fellowship Trained: Bury St Edmunds

5078

2.15 Bet Direct At Lingfield Park Maiden Stakes Div 2 2yo (D3)
£4238 £1304 £652 **7f aw rnd** **Going 34** **-38 Slow** Inside

4970 **MEDITATION 7** [6] I A Wood 2-8-9 N Callan 10/1: 0001: Made all, went clr 2f out, rdn out to hold on cl-home: qck reapp: eff at 7f, further will suit: acts on polytrack & easy sharp trk: imprvd eff today for switched to front running tactics: see 3330. **75a**
4724 **KINGS MAJESTY 22** [2] Sir Michael Stoute 2-9-0 D Holland 11/10 FAV: 02: b c King's Best - Tiavanita (J O Tobin) Missed break, prog when hung left dist, flew ins fnl 1f, just failed: well bckd: Mar foal, cost E240,000: half-brother to wnrs at 7f/1m, incl Gr 1 wnr: dam unrcd: sire Gr 1 wnr at 1m: eff at 7f, will apprec further: acts on polytrack: unsuited by today's slow run race & can go one better. shd **78a+**
BODHI TREE [12] J H M Gosden 2-8-9 J Fortune 7/1: 3: b f Southern Halo - Dharma (Zilzal) Sn cl-up, no extra ins fnl 1f: op 4/1 on debut: Mar foal, dam plcd over 1m: sire decent performer on dirt: eff at 7f, further shld suit: acts on polytrack: encouraging debut eff & can progress. 1¼ **71a**
MISSATACAMA [3] D J Daly 2-8-9 R Ffrench 33/1: 4: b f Desert Style - Delta Town (Sanglamore) Mid-div, hdwy 2f out, no impress ins fnl 1f: debut: Mar foal, half-sister to wnrs at 7/10f: sire decent performer around 7f: eff at 7f on polytrack: signs of promise & shld come on for today. 1 **69a**
CONTENTED [14]2-9-0 R Mullen 33/1: 5: Dwelt, held up wide, nvr nrr than mid-div: debut. 3½ **67a**
4971 **SONG SPARROW 7** [11]2-8-9 P Hanagan 50/1: 06: Nvr nrr than mid-div: qck reapp. 4 **54a**
CAPE ENTERPRISE [13]2-9-0 M Hills 16/1: 7: Missed break, modest late gains. nk **58a**
4970 **RED OPERA 7** [10]2-9-0 S Sanders 33/1: 0008: Mid-div over 5f, onepcd. 1¼ **56a**
4544 **LAMBRIGGAN LAD 30** [7]2-9-0 V Slattery 33/1: 09: Keen cl-up over halfway, fdd. 2½ **51a**
4970 **ARAMAT 7** [5]2-8-9 T Quinn 100/1: 000: 10th: Handy 5f, wknd: reportedly hung left in straight. 1 **44a**
LIVVIES LADY [9]2-8-9 Martin Dwyer 33/1: 0: 11th: Missed break, nvr a factor. 5 **35a**
MON PLAISIR [1]2-8-9 J Quinn 33/1: 0: 12th: Slow away, al bhd: reportedly ran green. 3 **29a**
HUGO THE BOSS [4]2-9-0 Dane O'Neill 50/1: 0: 13th: Slow away & al bhd. ½ **33a**
4883 **MELS MOMENT 13** [8]2-9-0 S Drowne 4/1: 06U: Stumbled & u.r. after start: btr 4883. **0a**
14 Ran Time 1m 27.90 (5.1) Owned: Mr Paddy Barrett Trained: Upper Lambourn

5079

2.50 Bet Direct On Super League Grand Final Handicap Stakes 3yo+ 56-70 (E3) **[81]**
£3523 £1084 £542 **1m aw rnd** **Going 34** **-02 Slow** Outside

4974 **OMAHA CITY 7** [9] B Gubby 10-9-3 (70) F Norton 5/1: 0000121: Keen mid-div, hdwy 2f out, rdn out to lead well ins fnl 1f: qck reapp: eff at 7f/sharp 1m on firm, gd/soft & polytrack: see 4974 & 4832. **79a**
4974* **ANALYZE 7** [6] B G Powell 6-9-6 (6ex) (73) J Fortune 14/1: 2354012: Chsd ldrs, styd on to lead dist, hdd well ins fnl 1f, not pace wnr: qck reapp: gd run: fin just ahd of today's wnr on 8lb btr terms in 4974. ¾ **79a**

4873 **CONCER ETO 13** [11] S C Williams 5-9-3 p (70) L Dettori 5/2 FAV: 1200423: Held up, hdwy 3f out, ev ch well ins fnl 1f, onepcd: bckd: 4873 & 3813. *nk* **75a**
4743 **LILLI MARLANE 21** [8] N A Callaghan 4-9-2 (69) J F Egan 16/1: 0100504: Mid-div, hdwy 2f out, staying on when short of room ins fnl 1f, not recover: would have gone v close with clr run: see 4743. *nk* **73a**
4254 **PURE MISCHIEF 45** [2]5-9-3 (70) R Thomas(3) 25/1: 1324655: Bhd, prog wide & still plenty to do dist, kept on ins fnl 1f, nrst fin: 6 wk abs: apprec rtn to 10f: btr 3276 (10.5f, soft). *1¼* **72a**
4929 **KINDLELIGHT DEBUT 11** [1]4-9-1 (68) D Holland 16/1: 0000306: Cl-up, led briefly dist, no extra. *nk* **69a**
4923* **RISKA KING 11** [12]4-9-1 (68) P Hanagan 5/1: 3615417: Bhd, nvr nrr than mid-div: btr 4923. *1¾* **65a**
4392 **VOICE MAIL 39** [4]5-9-3 vis (70) L Keniry(3) 6/1: 0340308: Handy 6f, no extra: bckd, btr 3964 (11.7f). *nk* **66a**
4668 **LIBERTY ROYAL 25** [7]5-9-1 p (68) S Sanders 8/1: 3034109: Rear, hdwy 3f out, wknd dist: op 11/1. *½* **63a**
4910 **BLACKMAIL 11** [5]6-9-3 bl (70) S Carson 50/1: 5000-000: 10th: Bhd, nvr a factor. *nk* **64a**
4742 **ELECTRIQUE 21** [3]4-9-3 BL (70) Martin Dwyer 16/1: 221-0000: 11th: Handy, prog 2f out, no extra under press when short of room ins fnl 1f: first time blnks. *½* **63a**
128 **HARRY THE HOOVER 319** [10]4-9-3 (70) B Reilly(3) 50/1: 01/00-0: 12th: b g Fayruz - Mitsubishi Style (Try My Best) Led till dist, fdd: reapp: unplcd in '03 (rtd 62, h'cap): mdn wnr on last of only 2 '02 starts: eff over a stiff 6f, revels in hvy grnd: has gone well fresh. *3* **57a**
1 Nov'02 Donc 6 hvy 73- D:
12 Ran Time 1m 39.12 (2.92) Owned: Brian Gubby Ltd Trained: Bagshot

5080

3.25 Betdirect Co Uk Claiming Stakes 3yo+ (F4)
£3080 £880 £440 **7f aw rnd** **Going 34** **+02 Fast** Inside

4920 **LINNING WINE 11** [12] B G Powell 8-9-6 (93) T Quinn 7/1: 6455501: Held up, hdwy halfway, led well ins fnl 1f, pushed out, val 3L+: clmd for 12,000: eff at 7f/10f, stays 12f: acts on firm, gd/soft & polytrack/Lingfield: has been disapp of late but returned to form on fav trk: see 547. **82a**
4923 **WESTERN ROOTS 11** [9] K A Morgan 3-8-10 (67) S Drowne 25/1: 1550002: Handy, prog bef 1f out, kept on, not pace wnr: gd eff in defeat & can find similar on this evidence: see 2133. *1½* **70a**
4743 **BLONDE EN BLONDE 21** [10] N P Littmoden 4-9-1 bl (64) N Callan 16/1: 3056003: Handy, prog 2f out, no extra ins fnl 1f: see 3508 & 562. *1¼* **71a**
4469 **TAKES TUTU 35** [3] K R Burke 5-9-10 vis (76) S Whitworth 5/1: 2003504: Held up, hdwy 3f out, onepcd fnl 1f. *shd* **79a**
4642 **AMMENAYR 26** [11]4-9-10 (67) J Fortune 13/2: 0353605: Cl-up, led 3f out till ins fnl 1f, no extra. *½* **78a$**
4622 **PERTEMPS MAGUS 27** [7]4-8-3 VIS (62) P Hanagan 7/2: 0-316366: Keen in tch, prog bef 1f out, hung left, no extra fnl 1f: disapp in first time visor: showed more in 4251. *nk* **56a**
4652 **CHEESE N BISCUITS 26** [6]4-9-5 (75) A Quinn(5) 12/1: 0540007: Nvr nrr than mid-div: btr 1616. *3* **66a**
4646 **WALL STREET RUNNER 26** [1]3-8-9 (62) D Fox(5) 50/1: 685-088: ch f Kirkwall - Running Tycoon (Last Tycoon) Handy over 5f, wknd: plcd all 3 '03 starts (rtd 68, fill mdn): with C A Dwyer. *nk* **57a**
4855 **GOLDEN DIXIE 14** [2]5-9-10 (75) Martin Dwyer 3/1 FAV: 2550009: Cl-up over 5f, wknd: bckd from 11/2: disapp & rider reported mount hung right thr'out: btr 3408 & 3136. *1½* **67a**
4976 **MULTIPLE CHOICE 7** [8]3-9-0 bl e t (64) T E Durcan 25/1: 2464000: 10th: Al bhd: qck reapp. *3* **53a**
4709 **GREEN RIDGE 23** [4]3-8-13 (62) Hayley Turner(3) 50/1: 6-240000: 11th: Led, hdd bef 3f out, sn fdd. *16* **22a**
4370 **SUPERCHIEF 39** [13]9-9-2 bl t (64) S Sanders 16/1: 5525000: 12th: Missed break, nvr a factor. *1¾* **19a**
4587 **Mannyman 29** [5]3-8-3 C Catlin 50/1:0 4930} **Sahara Scirocco 351** [14]3-8-4 (61) T P Queally 66/1:0
14 Ran Time 1m 25.10 (2.3) Owned: Favourites Racing Trained: Winchester

5081

4.00 Bet Direct 1/4 First Five At Newmarket Conditions Stakes 2yo (C2)
£5476 £1685 £843 **6f aw rnd** **Going 34** **+04 Fast** Inside

4896* **EMERALD LODGE 12** [4] J Noseda 2-9-4 vis (79) L Dettori 11/8 FAV: 3511: Made all, rd out to assert ins fnl 1f: bckd: eff at 5f, apprec recent step up to 6f: handles fast & gd, enjoys polytrack: likes to force the pace & has apprec recent fitting of visor: progressive performer: see 4896. **89a**
4028 **MIDDLE EARTH 56** [1] A M Balding 2-8-11 T Martin Dwyer 3/1: 202: Handy, styd on to chase wnr dist, kept on but al held fnl 1f: bckd, 8 wk abs: eff at 5f, now stays 6f: acts on firm & polytrack: eff with a t-strap. *1¼* **76a**
4859 **VAGUE STAR 14** [5] R Ingram 2-8-11 N Day 12/1: 033: Mid-div, hung under press bef 1f out, kept on late: eff at 5f, now stays 6f: acts on gd grnd & polytrack: now quals for h'caps: see 4859. *1½* **72a**
4928 **LOWESTOFT PLAYBOY 11** [8] Mrs C A Dunnett 2-8-11 (62) Hayley Turner(3) 25/1: 065004: Trkd ldrs over 4f, no extra: see 2858. *2½* **65a**
4697 **KWAME 23** [9]2-8-9 vis (77) K Fallon 5/1: 2025305: Rear, nvr nrr than mid-div: btr 4471 (fast). *shd* **62a**
4945* **ON THE WATERLINE 9** [6]2-8-13 vis (72) S Drowne 6/1: 0420016: Cl-up, ev ch dist, sn wknd. *2½* **59a**
DEFINITELY ROYAL [3]2-8-4 P Hanagan 66/1: 7: b f Desert Prince - Specifically (Sky Classic) Al bhd on bhd: Mar foal, half-sister successful at 9/10f: dam successful abroad: sire Gr 1 wnr at 1m. *6* **34a**
PRIDE OF POONA [7]2-8-4 T P Queally 40/1: 8: b f Indian Ridge - Scandalous (Warning) Al bhd on debut: May foal, dam unrcd: sire decent performer at sprint dist: with R M H Cowell. *3* **26a**
8 Ran Time 1m 12.20 (1.80) Owned: Hesmonds Stud Trained: Newmarket

5082

4.35 Littlewoods Bet Direct Handicap Stakes 3yo+ 46-55 (F4) **[63]**
£2926 £836 £418 **2m aw** **Going 34** **-11 Slow** Inside

4796 **VANDENBERGHE 18** [7] J A Osborne 5-9-1 (50) R Keogh(7) 10/1: 3334001: Mid-div, prog 2f out, styd on to lead ins fnl 1f, pushed out: rider rec a 3 day ban for careless riding: eff at 9/12f, suited by sharp 2m: acts on firm, gd grnd & both AWs: goes well for today's pilot: see 3822 & 2436. **58a**
4319 **PEAK PARK 42** [6] J A R Toller 4-8-13 vis (48) J F Egan 7/2 FAV: 0020322: Bhd, hdwy 4f out, styd on to lead 1f out, hdd ins fnl 1f, not pace wnr: 6 wk abs: continues in gd form: fin ahd of today's wnr in 4319. *1½* **53a**
3948 **PRIVATE BENJAMIN 60** [2] Jamie Poulton 4-9-4 (53) P Doe 18/1: 1050053: Bhd, hdwy over 2f out, kept on ins fnl 1f: recently u.r. over hdles (h'caps): eff t 10/12f, now stays 2m: see 2293. *1¼* **57a**
4966 **CAMBO 8** [14] R Ford 3-8-9 (55) P Hanagan 50/1: 00-06F4: b g Mansonnien - Royal Lie (Garde Royale) Bhd, prog wide 3f out, outpcd dist, rallied late: ex French, modest form in native country: eff at 2m on polytrk. *1¼* **58a**
4453 **SURFACE TO AIR 36** [12]3-8-7 (1ow) (52) R Havlin 100/1: 00005: Mid-div, hdwy 3f out, no impress dist. *½* **55a**
4938 **LAZZAZ 9** [10]6-9-5 (54) P Makin(5) 12/1: 6551106: Led, hdd 3f out, no extra dist: btr 4665. *shd* **55a**
4663 **GALANDORA 25** [13]4-8-13 (48) A Daly 20/1: 0330057: In tch, led 3f out, hdd 1f out, wknd. *shd* **48a**

LINGFIELD Polytrack WEDNESDAY 13.10.04 Lefthand, V Sharp Track

4834	**ANOTHER CON** 16 [9]3-8-9 (55) Lisa Jones 33/1: 0205008: Handy, prog 2f out, wknd fnl 1f: btr 2065.	½	54a
4824	**MOST SAUCY** 16 [1]8-9-6 (55) L Dettori 4/1: 4330109: Held up, nvr a factor: op 3/1: btr 4319.	2	52a
4663	**INDIAN CHASE** 25 [4]7-8-11 (46) R Thomas(3) 10/1: 0040120: 10th: Held up, nvr a factor: btr 4663.	nk	42a
4594	**MUSLIN** 29 [3]3-8-7 (53) Dane O'Neill 7/1: 3002560: 11th: Mid-div, eff when short of room 3f out, again short of room bef 2f out, sn btn: btr 3367.	1¼	48a
4796	**MONTOSARI** 18 [11]5-9-6 (55) D Holland 7/1: 3120300: 12th: Handy, wknd when short of room 2f out.	11	40a
4875	**Medica Boba** 13 [8]3-8-9 (1ow)(54) J Fortune 14/1:0 4056 **Bakhtyar** 55 [5]3-8-9 bl(55) S Sanders 12/1:0		

14 Ran Time 3m 27.28 (7.28) Owned: Mr D Marks Trained: Upper Lambourn

---

5083 5.10 Bet Direct On 0800 329393 Handicap Stakes 3yo 56-70 (E3) [79]
£3543 £1090 £545 **1m2f aw rnd** Going 34 -10 Slow Inside

4911	**REVENIR** 11 [4] E F Vaughan 3-9-3 (68) S Drowne 8/1: 022241: Held up, prog wide 4f out, styd on for press cl-home: rider received 2 day whip ban: eff at 7f/1m, now stays 10f: acts on fast, gd grnd & polytrack: unexposed at this trip in h'cap grade: see 4440.		76a
4468	**THE VIOLIN PLAYER** 35 [5] H J Collingridge 3-9-1 (66) D Holland 9/2: 0000502: Cl-up, ev ch over 1f out, kept on, just denied: op 6/1: eff at 7f/10f on firm, gd grnd & polytrack: encouraging eff & on a fair mark.	nk	72a
4923	**ALMOND WILLOW** 11 [6] J Noseda 3-9-4 (66) L Dettori 11/4 FAV: 1-020623: Led, flashed tail under press ins fnl 1f, hdd cl-home: tchd 4/1: eff at 1m/10f on fast, gd/soft & both AWs: see 4923 & 3138.	½	74a
4923	**ALI DEO** 11 [13] W J Haggas 3-9-1 (66) T P Queally 20/1: 3060004: Rear, hdwy wide over 2f out, kept on ins fnl 1f, nrst fin: eff at 7.5f/10f on fast, gd grnd & polytrack: encouraging eff: see 2116.	nk	70a
5024	**COMPETITOR** 3 [8]3-9-3 p (68) T Quinn 20/1: 0050605: In tch, eff dist, held when no room ins fnl 1f.	hd	71a
4762	**GROUND PATROL** 20 [2]3-9-1 t (66) J Fortune 16/1: 4360046: Mid-div, prog dist, no impress fnl 1f.	nk	68a
4761	**OFF BEAT** 20 [11]3-9-4 (69) S Carson 33/1: 0000067: Nvr nrr than mid-div: btr 729.	¾	69a
4321	**CHIGORIN** 42 [9]3-9-0 (65) T E Durcan 7/1: 3-060038: Handy, outpcd over 3f out, rallying when short of room ins fnl 1f: 6 wk abs: see 4321.	hd	64a
4827	**THE FUN MERCHANT** 16 [12]3-9-2 (67) J Quinn 10/1: 0112059: Bhd, hdwy when no room dist.	2½	61a
4650	**JOMUS** 26 [1]3-9-1 (66) A McCarthy 20/1: 0040350: 10th: Bhd, nvr a factor.	1½	57a
4924	**PORT N STARBOARD** 11 [10]3-9-0 VIS (65) C Catlin 50/1: 454400: 11th: Al bhd: first time visor.	1¼	54a
4826	**PAINTBOX** 16 [3]3-9-3 (68) S Sanders 10/1: 63260: 12th: Handy, trav well 2f out, sn wknd: op 7/1.	4	49a
4044	**Come What July** 55 [7]3-9-3 bl(68) K Fallon 14/1:0 4448 **Belisco** 36 [14]3-9-4 (69) D Fox(5) 20/1:0		

14 Ran Time 2m 7.20(4.4) Owned: Mr M A Whelton Trained: Newmarket

---

NEWMARKET THURSDAY 14.10.04 Righthand, Stiff, Galloping Track

Official Going Soft

5084 1.40 Robert Sangster Memorial E B F Maiden Stakes 2yo (D2)
£7072 £2176 £1088 **6f str** Good 48 +10 Fast Far side

	TOMOOHAT 0 [18] Sir Michael Stoute 2-8-9 W Supple 12/1: 1: b f Danzig - Crystal Downs (Alleged) Cl-up, styd on for press to lead ins fnl 1f, drvn out: debut: Feb foal, cost $650,000: dam smart performer around 7f/1m: sire rel related: eff at 6f, 7f/1m will suit: acts on gd/soft grnd & a stiff/gall trk: goes well fresh: useful start in a fast time, win better races.		92+
4726	**KENMORE** 23 [2] B W Hills 2-9-0 M Hills 4/1: 42: In tch, led 3f out, hdd ins fnl 1f, not pace of wnr: bckd: eff at 6f on firm & gd/soft: left prev eff bhd with a useful display & will lose mdn tag: see 4726.	1¼	91
4223	**RIVER ROYALE** 47 [3] P W Chapple Hyam 2-9-0 J Fortune 7/2 FAV: 33: Cl-up, onepcd from dist: bckd, 7 wk abs: gd eff in defeat tho' looks in need of further: see 4223 (debut).	¾	89
	TEEBA 0 [11] J L Dunlop 2-8-9 R Hills 16/1: 4: ch f Seeking The Gold - Shadayid (Shadeed) Dwelt, prog when no room 3f out, sn outpcd, rallied fnl 1f under hands & heels: debut: Apr foal, half-sister to Group/List wnrs at 7/10f: dam Gr 1 wnr at 1m: sire decent performer on dirt abroad: eff at 6f, looks sure to impr over further, acts on gd/soft: v pleasing start, will improve & win races over further.	1½	80+
	POKER PLAYER 0 [1]2-9-0 D Holland 20/1: 5: ch g Raise A Grand - Look Nonchalant (Fayruz) Slow away, prog halfway, kept on fnl 1f: debut: Mar foal, half-brother successful at 5f, also half-brother to wnr over Flat & hdles: dam plcd at 7f: plenty to like about this, win races over 7f+.	2½	78
4865	**DESERT CHIEF** 15 [16]2-9-0 L Dettori 4/1: 26: Led 3f, styd cl-up & ev ch dist, no extra: bckd: see 4865.	hd	77
2348	**WAATHEB** 126 [24]2-9-0 Dane O'Neill 50/1: 07: Cl-up, no extra from dist: long abs.	shd	76
	TUCKER 0 [15]2-9-0 T Quinn 16/1: 8: Nvr nrr than mid-div on debut: encouraging & can rate higher.	3	67
3686	**RED FINESSE** 73 [7]2-8-9 P Robinson 20/1: 09: Handy over 4f, sn edged right & wknd: 10 wk abs.	1¼	58
4752	**MATSUNOSUKE** 21 [22]2-9-0 T Williams 100/1: F0: 10th: Cl-up, wknd bef 1f out.	1¼	59
	SHAREB 0 [20]2-9-0 A Culhane 50/1: 0: 11th: Nvr nrr than mid-div on debut.	½	58
	MUNSEF 0 [12]2-9-0 T E Durcan 50/1: 0: 12th: Missed break, modest late gains.	½	57
	CHIEF EXEC 0 [21]2-9-0 N Callan 66/1: 0: 13th: Mid-div, prog halfway, wknd fnl 2f.	1¾	58
4543	**LATIN EXPRESS** 31 [17]2-9-0 S Drowne 50/1: 00: 14th: Cl-up, fdd bef 1f out.	½	51
	BANJO PATTERSON 0 [8]2-9-0 S Sanders 20/1: 0: 15th: In tch over 4f, wknd on debut.	2½	44

Diamond Dan 0 [9]2-9-0 J Dekeyser 10/1:0	**Petite Spectre** 0 [23]2-8-9 R L Moore 25/1:0
4637 **Pagan Quest** 27 [5]2-9-0 Lisa Jones 25/1:0	**Woolfall Joanna** 0 [19]2-8-9 A McCarthy 100/1:0
Horningsheath 0 [6]2-9-0 R Mullen 66/1:0	**Krullind** 0 [10]2-9-0 J Quinn 50/1:0
4854 **Montecito** 15 [13]2-8-9 (82) P Dobbs 9/1:0	**Whispering Death** 0 [4]2-9-0 S W Kelly 25/1:0

23 Ran Time 1m 13.10 (2.3) Owned: Mr Hamdan Al Maktoum Trained: Newmarket

5085
2.15 Rht 40th Anniversary Handicap Stakes 3yo+ 86-100 (C1)   [111]
£12533 £4754 £2377   1m4f   Good 48   -09 Slow   Far side

4917* **FLAMBOYANT LAD 12** [22] B W Hills 3-8-1 (84) P Hanagan 13/2: 3332111: Mid-div, gd prog to lead   94
ins fnl 1f, sn idled, drvn out to hold on: eff at 10f, imprvd for step up to 12f: acts on firm & soft grnd: likes
a stiff trk, esp Newmarket: v progressive performer who can land a big h'cap next term: see 4917 & 4630.
4778 **BIG MOMENT 19** [17] Mrs A J Perrett 6-9-6 (96) S W Kelly 8/1: 40-35622: Hld up, hdwy trav well 2f   hd   104
out, styd over 1f out, nrst fin: fine eff on drop back to 12f & v likely wnr if asked for effort earlier: last win
in '01, but poised to strike: see 4778 (14f) & 1569.
4062 **SOULACROIX 56** [11] Mrs A J Perrett 3-8-7 (90) S Sanders 12/1: 221-2103: Cl-up, ev ch dist, sn   2   95
onepcd: 8 wk abs: back to form today with solid display: see 3918 & 3468.
4889 **MANORSON 13** [20] M A Magnusson 5-8-13 t (89) Dane O'Neill 11/2 FAV: 115/-0024: Led, went 2L clr   ½   93
over 2f out, hdd ins fnl 1f, no extra: clr rem: well bckd: another gd run: see 4889.
4681 **SWAGGER STICK 26** [18]3-8-3 bl (86) J Quinn 14/1: 6006005: Rear, prog 5f out, no impress from   5   83
dist: has been disapp of late but this was more encouraging: see 2519 & 1355.
4527 **ENHANCER 33** [7]6-8-7 (13oh) (70) J F McDonald(3) 66/1: 00356: Cl-up over 10f, sn hung right & no extra.   shd   79
4889 **SOLO FLIGHT 13** [12]7-8-12 (88) R L Moore 12/1: 6020137: Rear, prog after halfway, wknd dist.   3½   79
4778 **BENDARSHAAN 19** [23]4-8-9 (85) K Darley 33/1: 1205058: Rear, hdwy/short of room 2f out, no dngr.   1¼   74
4814 **TAWNY WAY 18** [13]4-9-1 (91) T Quinn 16/1: 2601109: Handy 10f, wknd: showed more in 3926 (gd).   7   70
4814 **FLOTTA 18** [3]5-8-7 (2oh) (81) T O'Brien(7) 33/1: 3016500: 10th: Missed break, nvr nrr than mid-div.   11   47
4772 **SHARMY 20** [19]8-9-0 (90) C Catlin 50/1: 0/1100-00: 11th: Nvr nrr than mid-div.   nk   53
4715 **CREDIT 24** [8]3-8-8 (1ow) (90) D Holland 16/1: 0413330: 12th: In tch when short of room after 2f,   6   45
styd in tch, wknd 2f out: btr 4715 (fast grnd) & 4324.
4819 **GOLD RING 17** [6]4-9-7 (97) S Carson 14/1: 5316240: 13th: Handy when hmpd after 2f, wknd 3f out.   1½   48
2759 **PERFECT STORM 110** [5]5-9-1 (91) F Norton 25/1: 2-005400: 14th: Bhd, prog 5f out, wknd fnl 2f.   6   33
4491 **STAR MEMBER 34** [9]5-9-6 (96) N Callan 20/1: 1412660: 15th: Al in rear: btr 3119.   23   8
4715 **ELMUSTANSER 24** [14]3-9-1 t (98) L Dettori 6/1: 21220: 16th: Al bhd: disapp eff: btr 4715 & 3749 (fast).   1   8
4803 **MAC 19** [15]4-8-9 (85) Martin Dwyer 25/1: 01150-00: 17th: Cl-up 1m, fdd: see 4803.   15   0
4803 **Corton 19** [5]5-8-7 (2oh)(81) A Culhane 40/1:0   4889 **Muhareb 13** [16]5-9-0 (90) K McEvoy 50/1:0
19 Ran   Time 2m 32.75 (6.95)   Owned: Maktoum Al Maktoum   Trained: Lambourn

5086
2.50 Listed Lanwades Stud Severals Stakes Fillies & Mares 3yo+ (A1)
£17400 £6600 £3300   1m2f   Good 48   -10 Slow   Far side

2210 **SUNDROP 132** [11] Saeed bin Suroor 3-8-9 (115) L Dettori 11/8 FAV: 12-261: Bhd, prog when short   107
of room 2f out, prog wide bef 1f out, hung left ins fnl 1f, pushed out to lead cl-home, val bit more: well bckd
after long abs: eff at 7f/1m, stays 10f, tried 12f: acts on firm, gd/soft & polytrack, goes well fresh: smart.
I HAD A DREAM 56 [4] M A Jarvis 3-8-9 (92) N Callan 10/1: 25-33102: b f Bering - Dirigeante   ½   104
(Lead On Time) Keen cl-up, ev ch ins fnl 1f, just held by wnr: op 16/1: 8 wk abs: Brit bow, ex-French, earlier
wnr at Longchamp (10f, v soft): eff at 10f on gd/soft grnd: useful start, can find similar.
4781* **LA SYLPHIDE GB 19** [2] G M Moore 7-9-0 (85) S W Kelly 9/1: 2560213: Dictated slow pace, hdd under   ½   103
press well ins fnl 1f: career best eff on step up in grade tho' did have race run to suit: see 4781 (fills h'cap).
3866 **TAHTHEEB 64** [5] M P Tregoning 3-8-9 (100) R Hills 3/1: 124: Slow away, sn mid-div, kept on ins   1½   100
fnl 1f, no ch with principals: 9 wk abs: acts on firm & gd/soft grnd: prob unsuited by slow pace & looks sure to
impr when stepped up to 12f: showed more in 3866.
2772 **BLUE OASIS 12** [1]3-8-9 (92) T Quinn 20/1: 152005: Held up, prog bef 1f out, nrst fin: see 1636 (mdn).   2½   96
4614 **SHAMARA 29** [9]4-9-0 (92) K Darley 13/2: 0-224026: Nvr nrr than mid-div: op 10/1: btr 4614.   1¼   94
4860* **HONORINE 15** [8]4-9-0 (80) J F Egan 25/1: 43-60517: Bhd, prog when short of room 2f out, sn onepcd.   hd   93
4814 **WEECANDOO 18** [13]6-9-0 (82) G Carter 50/1: 4-005008: Handy 1m, no extra: btr 2898.   ½   92
4860 **STAR OF NORMANDIE 15** [7]5-9-0 (78) A McCarthy 50/1: 112-0009: Handy 1m, wknd: btr 134 (h'cap).   5   85
4757 **TATA NAKA 21** [6]4-9-0 (68) Hayley Turner 66/1: 2234100: 10th: In tch wide over 7f, fdd: see 4613.   8   74$
10 Ran   Time 2m 7.92 (5.82)   Owned: Godolphin   Trained: Newmarket

5087
3.25 #100000 Tattersalls Autumn Auction Stakes 2yo (B1)
£70300 £28120 £14060   6f str   Good 48   -01 Slow   Far side

4876 **CAPE COLUMBINE 14** [17] D R C Elsworth 2-8-8   T Quinn 5/1 JT FAV: 21: Hld up centre, prog 2f out,   102+
styd on well to lead ins fnl 1f, pushed out, val bit more: bckd: eff at 6f, 7f shld suit: acts on gd & gd/soft
grnd: eff on a stiff/gall or sharp trk: lightly raced, useful & improving, more to come & looks up to List/Gr class.
4928* **OBE GOLD 12** [1] M R Channon 2-9-5 vis A Culhane 5/1 JT FAV: 4U33112: In tch centre, switched   2   105
stands side after 2f, styd on to lead stands side group dist, hdd well ins fnl 1f, not pace of wnr: acts on fm &
gd/soft: fine eff conceding weight all round: useful & consistent.
4928 **GIFTED GAMBLE 12** [26] K A Ryan 2-8-9   N Callan 14/1: 2150203: Mid-div far side, styd on to lead   shd   94
that group 1f out, kept on, just held cl-home for overall 2nd: imprvd eff with pieces left off: see 4692 & 3445.
4679 **ARABIAN DANCER 26** [24] M R Channon 2-8-0 C Catlin 7/1: 6535124: Held up far side, prog halfway,   hd   84
kept on fnl 1f: gd eff in defeat: acts on fast & gd/soft: see 4679.
4914 **ALTA PETENS 12** [8]2-8-2 J Mackay 12/1: 0045605: In tch stands side over 4f, onepcd from dist.   nk   85
4810 **DIAMONDS AND DUST 18** [20]2-8-9 P Robinson 33/1: 434106: Handy 4f far side, sn outpcd, rallied   shd   91
late: acts on fast & gd/soft: return to 7f will suit: see 4396.
4651 **MARY READ 27** [27]2-8-10 F Lynch 9/1: 1312027: Led far side 2f, led again over 1f out, hdd 1f   1   89
out, no extra when short of room cl-home: first try at 6f & will apprec return to 5f: btr 4651 (List, 5f).
4697 **HIGHLAND CASCADE 24** [6]2-8-2 J Tate 16/1: 132038: Led stands side, hdd bef 1f out, wknd.   2½   72
4533 **PITCH UP 33** [30]2-9-1 G Carter 25/1: 3611509: In tch stands side over 4f, no extra: btr 3743.   1   84
4907* **LOUPHOLE 12** [13]2-8-7 S Sanders 16/1: 4100310: 10th: In tch stands side, wknd fnl 1f: btr 4907 (fast).   1   73
4271* **POLAR DAWN 45** [7]2-8-0 Lisa Jones 25/1: 26410: 10th: Nvr nrr than mid-div stands side: 6 wk abs.   dht   66
4583 **WHATATODO 30** [28]2-8-2 J Quinn 100/1: 3012040: 12th: Handy far side 4f, wknd.   hd   67
4914 **JANE JUBILEE 12** [3]2-8-4 K Darley 25/1: 2115000: 13th: Handy stands side over 4f, wknd.   hd   68
3003 **POLLY ALEXANDER 67** [23]2-8-10 R L Moore 25/1: 1321000: 14th: In tch far side 4f, hung left & wknd.   1¼   70
4858* **ROCKBURST 15** [14]2-8-2 A Nicholls 14/1: 5213010: 15th: Sn switched to stands side, wknd bef 1f out.   hd   61

4535 **TREAT ME WILD 33** [21]2-8-0 R Smith 66/1: 1651400: 16th: Al bhd far side: btr 3686.	*shd*	**58**
4679 **MADHAVI 26** [22]2-8-8 bl Dane O'Neill 66/1: 035000: 17th: Al rear far side: btr 3536.	*hd*	**65**
4934* **SAFENDONSEABISCUIT 10** [15]2-8-11 D Holland 33/1: 4200310: 18th: Led centre 4f, wknd.	*1*	**65**
4666 **FONG SHUI 26** [19]2-8-9 VIS Martin Dwyer 40/1: 40140: 19th: Al in rear far side.	*2*	**57**

4679 **Persian Carpet 26** [18]2-8-0 F Norton 100/1:0   4876 **Tapa 14** [11]2-8-2 R Mullen 66/1:0
4787* **Angelofthenorth 19** [10]2-8-2 T P Queally 100/1:0   4443 **Purple Door 37** [9]2-8-2 N Mackay 100/1:0
4864 **Rudaki 15** [4]2-8-9 R Winston 66/1:0   4900 **Avertigo 12** [1]2-8-7 BL S Drowne 100/1:0
4602 **Killena Boy 29** [29]2-8-9 J Fortune 100/1:0   4177 **Time For You 49** [2]2-8-0 F P Ferris 100/1:0
4744* **Raffish 22** [5]2-8-9 T E Durcan 100/1:0   4829 **Dizzy Future 17** [16]2-8-9 W Ryan 100/1:0
29 Ran   Time 1m 13.76 (2.96)   Owned: Mrs R F Lowe   Trained: Whitsbury

---

5088   4.00 Listed E B F Christo Philipson Boadicea Stakes Fillies & Mares 3yo+   (A1)
£20300 £7700 £3850   6f str   Good 48   +04 Fast   Far side

4732 **RUBY ROCKET 26** [4] H Morrison 3-8-11 (105) S Drowne 6/1: 2323201: In tch stands side, led that group bef 1f out, kept on to lead overall well ins fnl 1f, rdn out: bckd: eff at 6f, has tried 7f: acts on firm & gd/soft grnd: smart & tough: see 4526.		**111**
4952 **RINGMOOR DOWN 11** [2] D W P Arbuthnot 5-9-3 (108) T Quinn 7/1: 2411002: Slow away stands side, prog halfway, kept on ins fnl 1f, not pace of wnr: gd eff in defeat but prob prefers 5f on sltly faster grnd.	1½	**110**
4884* **PARADISE ISLE 14** [12] C F Wall 3-8-11 (105) K Darley 6/1: 0421013: Led far side group, hdd overall ins fnl 1f, no extra: bckd: prob best on faster grnd: btr 4884 (h'cap).	2½	**98**
5001 **VALJARV 5** [8] N P Littmoden 3-8-11 (91) N Callan 33/1: 4200504: In tch far side 4f, sn outpcd, rallied fnl 1f: qck reapp: btr 3235 (h'cap, fast).	1¾	**93**
4331 **FANNYS FANCY 42** [11]4-8-12 (87) S Sanders 16/1: 0003555: In tch far side 4f, sn outpcd, rallied late.	½	**92**
4811 **DELPHIE QUEEN 18** [9]3-8-11 (102) J F Egan 5/1 FAV: 4312166: Handy far side over halfway, sn hung right & outpcd, rallied late: well bckd: wants 7f: btr 3113 (7f).	½	**91**
4510 **TYCHY 33** [3]5-8-12 (95) Martin Dwyer 16/1: 5104007: Led stands side, hdd dist, wknd: btr 4291.	nk	**90**
4811 **VOILE 18** [14]3-8-11 (100) R L Moore 33/1: 24345-08: Handy far side over 4f, onepcd: btr 4811.	1	**87**
4743 **DANGLE 4** [5]3-8-11 VIS F M Berry 20/1: 4025459: Nvr nrr than mid-div stands side: 1st time visor.	¾	**85**
4588* **DOWAGER 30** [16]3-8-11 (90) Dane O'Neill 20/1: 3000010: 10th: Cl-up far side over 4f, wknd: btr 4588.	hd	**84**
4585 **FIDDLE ME BLUE 30** [2]3-8-11 vis (76) J Fortune 50/1: 0001360: 11th: Handy stands side over 4f, fdd.	hd	**83**
4811 **THAMINAH 18** [7]3-8-11 (89) R Hills 8/1: 01-50: 12th: In tch stands side 4f, fdd: showed more in 4811.	3½	**73**
4450 **IMSHY 31** [6]3-8-11 D Holland 33/1: 0-062440: 13th: on f Daggers Drawn - Paganina (Galetto) Al bhd stands side: French raider, best eff to date this term when h'cap 2nd in native country (5.5f, gd/soft): won twice in native country back in '03, also 6th in fills auct race in Brit (rtd 83): eff at 6/7f on gd/soft & fast grnd: tried cheek pieces: with R Pritchard-Gordon.	3	**64**
4811 **PEARL GREY 18** [10]3-8-11 f (100) L Dettori 11/2: 3112-320: 14th: In tch far side over halfway, sn short of room & wknd: tchd 13/2: showed more in 4811 & 4510 (fast).	¾	**62**
4693 **ENCHANTED 25** [13]5-8-12 (94) F Norton 40/1: 0000400: 15th: Al in rear far side.	13	**27**

15 Ran   Time 1m 13.46 (2.66)   Owned: Thurloe Thoroughbreds IX   Trained: East Ilsley

---

5089   4.35 Ngk Spark Plugs Nursery Handicap Stakes 2yo 0-95 (C2)   [94]
£7046 £2168 £1084   1m str   Good 48   -13 Slow   Far side

4666* **DANEHILL WILLY 26** [10] N A Callaghan 2-8-12 (78) D Holland 15/2: 20011: Sn rdn bhd, prog 2f out, rdn out to lead cl-home: bckd: prev eff at 5/7f, apprec step up to 1m, mid-dists will suit next term: acts on gd & gd/soft grnd: progressive performer who enjoyed today's stamina test: see 4666.		**88**
4289* **ATLANTIC STORY 45** [9] Saeed bin Suroor 2-9-4 (84) L Dettori 9/2: 012: Led, clr ins fnl 2f, edged right for press & hdd cl-home: bckd tho' op 7/2: 6 wk abs: eff at 7f/1m on gd & gd/soft grnd: lost little in defeat on h'cap bow & can return to winning ways: see 4289 (med auct mdn).	hd	**92**
4591 **HALLA SAN 30** [6] Mrs J R Ramsden 2-8-4 (70) C Catlin 20/1: 00543: Bhd, prog over 1f out, nrst fin: apprec today's step up to 1m on h'cap bow: can prog next term for shrewd yard: see 4591.	½	**77**
4480 **SEA HUNTER 35** [4] M R Channon 2-9-4 (84) T E Durcan 16/1: 1423504: Handy, onepcd from dist: clr rem: prev eff at 5f, now suited by 7f/1m: see 3407.	½	**90**
4079* **CALY DANCER 55** [11]2-9-6 (86) J Fortune 14/1: 0533315: Rear, prog 3f out, fdd dist: 8 wk abs: disapp on first try at a mile: btr 4079 (6f).	9	**76**
4191* **THAKAFAAT 48** [13]2-9-7 (87) W Supple 11/1: 516: Handy, wknd bef 1f out: 7 wk abs: btr 4191 (7f, gd).	1¾	**73**
4664* **RED AFFLECK 26** [12]2-9-3 (83) A McCarthy 13/2: 3217: Cl-up 6f, wkng when short of room dist.	hd	**68**
4509 **LANGSTON BOY 33** [7]2-8-7 (73) R Mullen 50/1: 4230248: In tch over 6f, fdd: btr 4177.	¾	**56**
4635 **MOBARHEN 28** [8]2-8-10 (76) R Hills 7/2 FAV: 55239: Slipped after start, bhd, prog 3f out, fdd bef 1f out: bckd: disapp: showed more in 4635.	1¾	**55**
4963 **MARKET TREND 9** [2]2-9-2 (82) K Darley 7/1: 2100: 10th: Cl-up 6f, wknd: btr 4653.	1	**59**

4710 **Rosapenna 24** [3]2-8-4 (70) J Quinn 20/1:0   4580 **Scarlet Invader 30** [5]2-9-0 (80) S Sanders 50/1:0
12 Ran   Time 1m 41.39 (4.89)   Owned: Mr T Mohan   Trained: Newmarket

---

5090   5.10 Thoroughbred Breeders Handicap Stakes 3yo+ 96-110 (B1)   [113]
£12041 £4567 £2284   5f str   Good 48   -05 Slow   Far side

4908 **CORRIDOR CREEPER 12** [11] J M Bradley 7-8-11 p (96) R L Moore 7/1: 0350321: Cl-up, styd on to lead 1f out, rdn out to assert: eff at 6f, suited by 5f: acts on firm & soft grnd: eff with cheek pieces: ultra consistent performer who has been a credit to connections, gained deserved 1st win of term: see 4908 & 4780.		**105**
4718 **IF PARADISE 23** [13] R Hannon 3-8-13 (98) Dane O'Neill 20/1: 0600022: Led, hdd 1f out, kept on, just held: useful, on a fair mark: see 4718 & 1106.	½	**104**
4884 **FRUIT OF GLORY 14** [10] J R Jenkins 5-8-7 (92) W Ryan 9/1: 4225403: Trkd ldrs, ev ch ins fnl 1f, not btn far in 3rd: gd run in defeat: see 4510 & 3971.	nk	**97**

4908 **CARIBBEAN CORAL** 12 [9] J J Quinn 5-8-12 (97) R Winston 5/1 JT FAV: 1003044: Missed break, eff   hd   101+
when short of room bef 1f out, switched when hmpd ins fnl 1f, kept on late: well bckd: not get run of today's race
& would have fin at least 2nd wth clr passage: see 4481 & 2727.
4884 **FOREVER PHOENIX** 14 [5]4-9-0 (99) A Quinn(5) 8/1: 3616635: Missed break, prog halfway, kept on late.   hd   102
4780 **WHISTLER** 19 [3]7-8-7 (1oh)p (91) P Fitzsimons 8/1: 0340426: Nvr nrr than mid-div: stablemate of wnr.   ½   94
4780 **BISHOPS COURT** 19 [6]10-8-12 (97) P Hanagan 11/1: 0256507: Mid-div, no impress ins fnl 1f,   1   96
reportedly broke blood vessel: btr 3989 & 2638.
4526 **LYDGATE** 33 [2]4-9-7 t (106) L Dettori 6/1: 4421048: Al bhd: showed more in 4526 (6f, fast).   1   102
4908 **DRAGON FLYER** 12 [4]5-8-13 (98) J F Egan 16/1: 0410039: Handy over 4f, wkng/short of room fnl 1f.   ½   93
4454 **FROMSONG** 37 [8]6-8-7 (2oh) (90) S Drowne 5/1 JT FAV: 4400660: 10th: Handy, wknd bef 1f out: bckd.   1¾   82
10 Ran   Time 1m 0.85(2.65)   Owned: Mr G & L Johnson   Trained: Chepstow

Official Going Soft

5091
2.25 Bbi Insurance E B F Median Auction Maiden Stakes 2yo (F3)
£4261 £1311 £656   7f214y rnd   Soft 92   -19 Slow   Inside

4631 **OLIGARCH** 29 [9] N A Callaghan 2-9-0 (86) O Urbina 11/10 FAV: 2031: Made virtually all, clr over   81
2f out, hands & heels: stays 1m & likes gd/soft & soft, poss handles fm: enjoyed positive ride.
4325 **SHINGLE STREET** 44 [3] M H Tompkins 2-9-0 P Doe 16/1: 0002: b g Bahhare - Sandystones (Selkirk)   ¾   78
In tch, eff to go 2nd 3f out, hung left & kept on same pace fnl 1f: 6 wk abs: Feb foal, cost E21,000: half brother
to a couple of 5f juv wnrs: imprvd for gelding op & stays 1m on soft grnd: clr of rem.
4522 **SOLE AGENT** 34 [6] G L Moore 2-9-0 A Quinn(5) 33/1: 03: b g Trans Island - Seattle Siren (Seattle   3½   73
Slew) Held up, eff 2f out, onepace: Apr foal, cost 5,000 gns: half brother to wnrs over 6f/2m: stays 1m on soft.
4704 **MAXAMILLION** 25 [7] S Kirk 2-9-0 M Fenton 4/1: 54: b c Mujadil - Manazil (Generous) Held up,   2   70
keen hdwy over 2f out, sn no extra: Feb foal, cost 10,000 gns: half brother to a 6f wnr: dam 1m/10f scorer.
4664 **EMPANGENI** 27 [5]2-9-0 Dane O'Neill 33/1: 05: Sn bhd, some late gains: will need 10f+.   shd   69
4575 **BEST GAME** 31 [12]2-9-0 S Whitworth 25/1: 006: Bhd, some late gains.   hd   69
     TANGIBLE 0 [11]2-8-9 J Mackay 10/1: 7: Missed break, nvr a factor.   1½   62
5003 **MAHMJRA** 6 [1]2-9-0 C Catlin 25/1: 08: Al bhd.   hd   66
4741 **WEMBURY POINT** 23 [2]2-9-0 (56) L Keniry(3) 40/1: 000609: In tch, wknd over 2f out.   1½   64
4738 **INDIAN DOVE** 23 [4]2-8-9 S Chin 20/1: 60: 10th: Al bhd.   1¾   56
4928 **GOGETTER GIRL** 13 [13]2-8-9 p (60) F P Ferris(3) 25/1: 4600000: 11th: In tch, wknd over 2f out.   1¾   53
4829 **PIRAN** 18 [8]2-9-0 (70) J F McDonald(3) 10/1: 0050: 12th: Al bhd: see 4829.   1½   56
4704 **BREGO** 25 [10]2-9-0 P Dobbs 33/1: 0000: 13th: Cl-up, wknd over 2f out.   15   34
13 Ran   Time 1m 40.93 (8.93)   Owned: Team Havana   Trained: Newmarket

5092
3.00 32red Online Casino Maiden Stakes 3yo (D3)
£5504 £1694 £847   1m3f196y   Soft 92   +09 Fast   Outside

4630 **MAGNETIC POLE** 29 [5] Sir Michael Stoute 3-9-0 (77) Dane O'Neill 100/30: 3-230221: Made all, drew   91
clr over 3f out, v easily by huge dist: stays 12f & acts on fast grnd, imprvd on this soft surface: handles any trk
& blnks discarded: shade frustrating earlier but did nothing run here with forcing tactics & an imprvd run.
4944 **RIVER OF DIAMONDS** 11 [2] R Guest 3-9-0 M Fenton 8/1: 002: Held up, hdwy over 2f out, wnr had   21   74
flown: btr run stepped up to 12f on soft grnd: see 4944.
4898 **SEEKING A WAY** 14 [8] J H M Gosden 3-9-0 (70) P Dobbs 100/30: 1-230623: With wnr, outpcd 3f out.   3   65
2230 **CHAPLIN** 133 [4] B W Hills 3-9-0 P (84) C Catlin 2/1 FAV: 0-204: Chsd ldrs, wknd over 3f out: ¾   69
tried cheek pieces after long abs: now twice well below reapp in 1153.
4347 **SARENNE** 43 [1]3-8-9 S Chin 10/1: 665: In tch, wknd over 3f out: see 4347.   7   54
4898 **MARIDAY** 14 [3]3-9-0 Paul Eddery 20/1: 606: br g Trifolio - Classic Hand (Some Hand) Dwelt, al bhd.   9   47
873 **MR DINGLAWI** 210 [7]3-9-0 T (70) M Tebbutt 50/1: 0057: Dwelt, al bhd: long abs, t-strap: btr 873.   28   17
4944 **PACIFIC RUN** 11 [6]3-9-0 J F McDonald(3) 25/1: 08: Handy, wknd qckly over 2f out: see 4944.   dist   0
8 Ran   Time 2m 38.2 (10)   Owned: The Queen   Trained: Newmarket

5093
3.35 32red Com Handicap Stakes 3yo+ 56-70 (E3)   [68]
£4831 £1486 £743   1m3f196y   Soft 92   -00 Slow   Outside

4973 **PRECIOUS MYSTERY** 9 [10] A King 4-9-6 (60) A Quinn(5) 8/1: 016-4201: Handy, hdwy to lead ins last,   70
drvn out: stays 12f on firm & soft, prob any trk: see 3638.
4990* **SCOTT** 7 [5] J Jay 3-8-11 (58) D Fox(5) 9/4 FAV: 6031412: Handy, hdwy to lead 2f out till ins   hd   67
last, kept on, just held: clr of rem & in fine form: acts on fast, fibresand & soft, prob polytrack: see 4990.
4166 **RUMBLING BRIDGE** 51 [1] J L Dunlop 3-8-6 (53) P Doe 20/1: 546-0023: Slow away, hdwy to lead 3f   5   56
out till 2f out, onepace: 7 wk abs: see 4166.
4796 **MAKE MY HAY** 20 [2] J Gallagher 5-8-7 (1oh) (46) L Keniry(3) 6/1: 2555624: In tch, eff 2f out, onepace.   1¾   48
4910* **NOUNOU** 13 [8]3-9-7 (68) M Halford(7) 4/1: 5001515: Held up, eff over 2f out, sn no impress.   2½   66
4708* **COTTON EASTER** 25 [3]3-8-8 (55) R Thomas(3) 7/1: 6000316: Slow away, held up, hung left & wknd   5   48
over 1f out: btr 4708 (10f).
4856 **SHUSH** 16 [6]6-9-4 (58) Dane O'Neill 33/1: 44120-07: In tch, hung left & wknd over 2f out: see 4856.   3½   48
5024 **MUSTANG ALI** 5 [12]3-9-2 (63) S Whitworth 22/1: 5356608: In tch, wknd over 2f out.   13   41
4892 **ALEXEI** 14 [9]3-9-2 (63) O Urbina 20/1: 0259: Al bhd, eased: see 4449 (polytrack).   3   38
3690 **MIDSHIPMAN EASY** 72 [4]3-9-4 (65) M Fenton 20/1: 3200600: 10th: Led till 3f out, wknd: abs.   5   35
4877 **DANZE ROMANCE** 15 [11]3-9-1 (62) C Catlin 16/1: 00540: 11th: Handy, wknd over 2f out: see 3979.   3½   29
4877 **CHARING CROSS** 15 [7]3-8-7 BL (54) R Brisland 33/1: 00060: 12th: In tch, wknd over 4f out: blnks.   7   15
12 Ran   Time 2m 39.3 (11.1)   Owned: The Dunnkirk Partnership   Trained: Barbury Castle

BRIGHTON   FRIDAY 15.10.04   Lefthand, Very Sharp, Undulating Track

5094   4.10 Michael Tonks Family & Friends Memorial Handicap Stakes 3yo 46-55 (F4)   [68]
£3367 £962 £481   7f214y rnd   Soft 92   -18 Slow   Inside

2740 **CLARE GALWAY 111** [7] S Kirk 3-8-9 (49) M Fenton 20/1: 0500401: Held up, hdwy over 2f out, styd   **58**
on to lead ins last, rdn out: 4 month abs: 1st win: apprec drop back to 1m, stays 10f: acts on polytrack, enjoyed
this soft grnd: runs well fresh: imprvd for new stable (prev with T D McCarthy): see 2064.

4828 **DORINGO 18** [5] J L Spearing 3-8-10 (50) R J Killoran(7) 14/1: 0-00002: Handy, hdwy to lead over   nk **58**
2f out till ins last, kept on, just held: btr eff & stays 1m, imprvd on soft grnd: see 4828.

4761 **BEAUTY OF DREAMS 22** [10] M R Channon 3-9-0 VIS (55) C Catlin 11/2: 5306043: Handy, eff to chall   shd **61**
ins last, kept on, just held: acts on firm & soft: improved for vis: well clr of rem: see 4761.

4660* **SYLVA ROYAL 27** [8] C E Brittain 3-9-0 (54) Dane O'Neill 8/1: 446014: Dwelt, keen in tch, eff 2f   8 **49**
out, sn wknd: not see out this longer trip on more testing grnd: btr 4660 (banded stks, 7f, polytrack).

5005 **MRS BROWN 6** [1]3-9-0 (54) J Mackay 6/1: 5605045: Keen, handy, short of room over 1f out, sn wknd   nk **48**

4937 **PASSION FRUIT 11** [13]3-8-10 (50) P Doe 8/1: 630-0006: Dwelt, in tch, wknd over 2f out: see 4676.   1 **42**

4367 **JUST ONE LOOK 42** [4]3-8-13 (53) R Thomas(3) 7/1: 0006057: Sn rdn bhd, eff 2f out, sn wknd & eased.   1¾ **42**

4902* **MAGIC VERSE 13** [12]3-9-0 (54) J F McDonald(3) 7/2 FAV: 4445418: Dwelt, nvr a factor: btr 4902 (gd).   2 **40**

4763 **MELINDAS GIRL 22** [6]3-8-7 VIS (49) L Keniry 33/1: 0650-069: Led till 3f out, wknd: vis, see 1529.   8 **21**

4925 **MR LEWIN 13** [11]3-8-13 (53) T Hamilton(3) 7/1: 005-0050: 10th: in tch, wknd over 2f out: see 2506.   1¾ **24**

3480 **MONASH GIRL 81** [9]3-8-5 (30) N Chalmers(3) 50/1: 00-600: 11th: Dwelt, al bhd: 11 wk abs: see 2834.   4 **10**

4593 **THE NIBBLER 31** [3]3-8-9 (49) O Urbina 20/1: 46060: 12th: In tch, wknd over 2f out: see 2854.   7 **4**
12 Ran   Time 1m 40.79 (8.79)   Owned: Mrs M Devine   Trained: Upper Lambourn

5095   4.45 Wkd Builders & Decorators In Essex Classified Stakes 3yo+ 0-70 (E3)
£4183 £1287 £644   1m1f209y   Soft 92   -23 Slow   Outside

5050 **ARRY DASH 4** [3] M R Channon 4-9-3 (73) C Catlin 5/2 FAV: 2325001: Held up, hdwy & short of room   **85**
over 2f out, switched & styd on to lead ins last, rdn clr: eff over 1m/10f on fast, soft & both AWs: tried visor
earlier, btr here without: deserved win after sev plcd effs this term: on a handy mark: see 758.

4846 **QUARTINO 17** [2] J H M Gosden 3-8-9 (70) P Dobbs 16/1: 21-00002: Held up, hdwy to lead over 1f   2½ **78**
out till just ins last, not pace of wnr: stays 10f on firm & soft: tried blnks: on a handy mark.

5050 **DESERT ISLAND DISC 4** [6] J J Bridger 7-9-1 (74) A Beech(3) 7/2: 1163003: Cl-up, lost place over   2 **76**
2f out, rallied fnl 1f, no impress: back to form: best over 12f: see 3674.

4745 **MAD CAREW 23** [4] G L Moore 5-9-3 bl (73) S Whitworth 9/1: 0554054: In tch, hdwy to lead 3f out   2½ **74**
till over 1f out, sn wknd & hung left: see 4745, 816.

4973 **STRATHSPEY 9** [5]5-8-11 (69) L Keniry 10/1: 34234-55: In tch, wknd over 1f out: see 4973.   1¾ **65**

4468 **PAYOLA 37** [1]3-8-6 (70) Dane O'Neill 6/1: 0-1656: Handy, wknd over 1f out: see 4058, 3648.   1 **64**

4473 **PRAIRIE WOLF 36** [7]8-9-3 (73) M Fenton 10/1: 0510007: Rdn early, led till 3f out, wknd over 1f out.   shd **70**

4702 **TADAWUL 25** [8]3-8-8 (72) J Mackay 7/1: 0168: Cl-up, wknd & hung left fnl 2f: btr 4474 (fast grnd, mdn).   1 **64**
8 Ran   Time 2m 09.32 (11.52)   Owned: Mike & Denise Dawes   Trained: West Ilsley

5096   5.15 32redpoker Com Handicap Stakes 3yo+ 56-70 (E3)   [80]
£4044 £1244 £622   5f59y rnd   Soft 92   +02 Fast   Inside

4989 **HARRISONS FLYER 7** [4] R A Fahey 3-8-12 p (64) G Parkin 16/1: 202U001: In tch, hdwy to lead dist,   **74**
rdn clr: 1st win: eff at 5/6f on firm & soft: wears cheek pieces, has tried blnks: handles any trk: see 2849.

4751 **MADRASEE 23** [2] L Montague Hall 6-8-8 (60) Dane O'Neill 9/2: 0006062: Chsd ldr, led 2f out till   2½ **64**
dist, not pace of wnr: gd run: loves Brighton & well h'capped: see 329.

4739 **PULSE 23** [8] J M Bradley 6-8-4 p (56) P Fitzsimons 9/2: 0060523: Handy, hdwy 3f out, onepace.   ½ **59**

3599 **SMART STARPRINCESS 76** [3] M J Attwater 3-8-4 (2oh)P (54) F P Ferris(3) 25/1: 2350004: Led till 2f   ¾ **57**
out, no extra: 11 wk abs, tried cheek pieces: see 405 (sell, polytrack).

4548 **TABOOR 32** [1]6-8-7 h bl t (59) M Fenton 10/1: 0601205: Sn bhd, eff over 2f out, no impress: see 4197.   ½ **58**

4253 **WHITE LEDGER 47** [6]5-8-6 vis (58) T Hamilton(3) 7/2: 0031106: Slow away & nvr a factor: 7 wk abs.   ½ **55**

4905* **SPINETAIL RUFOUS 13** [7]6-8-4 (1oh)bl (55) P Doe 11/4 FAV: 000-0117: Handy, wknd 2f out: best 4905.   1 **51**

4989 **PARKSIDE PURSUIT 7** [5]6-9-4 (70) C Catlin 14/1: 3100008: Al bhd: see 2838.   18 **29**
8 Ran   Time 1m 04.51(4.51)   Owned: P D Smith Holdings Ltd   Trained: Malton

NEWMARKET   FRIDAY 15.10.04   Righhand, Stiff, Galloping Track

Official Going Soft

5097   1.10 Federation Of Bloodstock Agents Maiden Stakes 2yo (D2)
£7163 £2204 £1102   1m str   Soft   Inapplicable   Far side

PROCLAMATION 0 [13] J Noseda 2-9-0   E Ahern 12/1: 1: gr c King's Best - Shamarra (Zayyani)   **96+**
Cl-up, led 2f out, sn hung left, rdn out fnl 1f, val bit more: back from 25/1 on debut: May foal, cost 84,000 gns:
half brother successful at 6/15f: dam unrcd: sire Gr1 wnr at 1m: eff at 1m, further will suit next term: acts on
soft grnd & a stiff/gall trk: goes well fresh: v useful start, has a bright future.

4712 **UNFURLED 25** [9] J L Dunlop 2-9-0   T Quinn 20/1: 62: ch c Unfuwain - Peony (Lion Cavern) Al   3½ **88+**
cl-up, kept on under hands & heels, not pace wnr fnl 1f: Apr 1st foal, cost 8,500 gns: dam successful at 1m: sire
decent performer at mid-dists: eff at 1m, further will suit: acts on soft grnd: win races.

MURAABET 0 [8] J L Dunlop 2-9-0   J Fortune 25/1: 3: b c Dubai Millennium - Mahasin (Danzig)   1 **86**
Cl-up, led 3f out, hdd 2f out, no extra dist: clr rem: debut: Mar foal, half brother to decent performers at 6/8f:
sire fine performer around 1m/10f: eff at 1m, 10f shld suit: acts on soft grnd: promising debut.

ECHO OF LIGHT 0 [23] Saeed bin Suroor 2-9-0 T L Dettori 7/2 FAV: 4: b c Dubai Millennium -   3½ **79**
Spirit of Tara (Sadler's Wells) Bhd, prog over 3f out, hung left & no impress bef 1f out: bckd tho' op 3/1 on
debut: Mar foal, cost £1,200,000: half brother to a couple of smart performers around 1m/9f: dam smart mid-dist

performer: sire fine performer around 1m/10f: well regarded, relish 10f next term.
HARD TOP 0 [22]2-9-0 M Hills 20/1: 5: Slow away, prog 3f out, kept on late: debut: apprec further. *1¾* **75**
WELL ESTABLISHED 0 [10]2-9-0 P Robinson 16/1: 6: Missed break, prog halfway, kept on late under hands & heels: debut: ran with promise & can improve. *½* **74+**
AZIZAM 0 [5]2-8-9 A McCarthy 66/1: 7: Cl-up over 6f, wknd on debut. *nk* **68**
4680 **OCEAN GIFT 27** [19]2-9-0 (88) R Hughes 15/2: 6408: Led 2f, wknd bef 1f out: showed more in 3955. *hd* **72**
4723 **BASSERAH 24** [3]2-8-9 W Supple 11/2: 09: Handy over 6f, wknd: see 4723. *1¼* **65**
4971 **BLUE HEDGES 9** [17]2-9-0 J Quinn 100/1: 00: 10th: In tch, wknd bef 1f out. *2* **66**
POLISH EAGLE 0 [21]2-9-0 R L Moore 25/1: 0: 11th: Mid-div, 6f, wknd on debut. *1¼* **64**
BOLD EAGLE 0 [16]2-9-0 K Fallon 7/1: 0: 12th: Missed break, nvr a factor on debut. *1¼* **62**
CASH ON 0 [25]2-9-0 Martin Dwyer 20/1: 0: 13th: Al rear on debut. *½* **61**
TAWQEET 0 [6]2-9-0 T E Durcan 50/1: 0: 14th: Bhd, nvr a factor: debut. *½* **60**
TREW STYLE 0 [14]2-9-0 K Darley 66/1: 0: 15th: Mid-div 6f, wknd. *1½* **57**
4883 **GOLD GUN 15** [24]2-9-0 N Mackay(3) 100/1: 00: 16th: Cl-up, fdd bef 2f out. *3* **51**
LIBERTY RUN 0 [1]2-9-0 D Holland 14/1: 0: 17th: Al bhd. *1¾* **47**
4691 **IMPERIOLI 26** [4]2-9-0 P Bradley 100/1: 060: 18th: Led after 2f, hdd 3f out, fdd. *7* **34**
TREW FLIGHT 0 [15]2-9-0 N Callan 66/1: 0: 19th: Mid-div 6f, fdd. *16* **4**
Westfield Boy 0 [2]2-9-0 G Gibbons 100/1:0 **Obezyana 0** [20]2-9-0 S Sanders 33/1:0
21 Ran Time 1nm 41.78 (5.28) Owned: Abdullah Saeed BelHab Trained: Newmarket

5098

1.40 Prestige Nursery Handicap Stakes 2yo 0-95 (C2) **[95]**
£8190 £2520 £1260 **6f str** **Soft** **Inapplicable** Far side

4985* **INGLETON 7** [9] B A McMahon 2-9-3 (7ex) (84) G Gibbons 15/8 FAV: 04111: Cl-up, styd on press to lead well ins fnl 1f, just held on: well bckd on quick reapp: eff at 6f, handles fast, likes gd & soft: prog & useful. **96**
4298* **OUR FUGITIVE 46** [6] A W Carroll 2-9-0 (81) D Holland 12/1: 403212: Led, hdd under press well ins fnl 1f, just held: clr rem: 7 wk abs: eff around 5f, imprvd for step up to 6f: acts on firm & soft grnd: fine eff in defeat & can return to wng ways if reappearing bef seasons end: see 4298. *nk* **91**
4179 **PRINCE SAMOS 50** [10] R Hannon 2-8-13 (80) K Fallon 16/1: 40533: Held up, prog 2f out, kept on fnl 1f: 7 wk abs: looks in need of further: btr 4179 (polytrack). *5* **80**
4332 **GHURRA 43** [13] E A L Dunlop 2-9-6 (87) W Supple 16/1: 104: Mid-div, eff 2f out, no impress dist: 6 wk abs & h'cap bow: btr 3709 (fast, mdn). *¾* **85**
4882 **ELGIN MARBLES 15** [3]2-9-3 (84) R L Moore 6/1: 160225: Handy over 4f, wknd: disapp in today's soft grnd: shown more in 4882 (gd) & 4727 (firm). *2½* **75**
4830 **EMPIRES GHODHA 18** [15]2-9-1 bl (82) J Fortune 25/1: 5346006: Rear, nvr nrr than mid-div. *shd* **72**
5081 **ON THE WATERLINE 2** [5]2-8-12 (7ex)vis (79) S Drowne 20/1: 4200167: Cl-up over 4f, wknd: qck reapp. *5* **56**
4883 **ORPEN WIDE 15** [4]2-8-4 (71) N Mackay(3) 40/1: 03308: Cl-up over 4f, wknd: btr 4699 (7f). *2* **42**
4513 **PERSONIFY 34** [1]2-9-5 VIS T (86) L Dettori 8/1: 149: Handy over 4f, wknd: btr 2851 (fast). *2½* **50**
4655 **GENEROUS OPTION 28** [12]2-9-2 (83) K Darley 14/1: 513440: 10th: Nvr nrr than mid-div: btr 3303. *hd* **46**
4680 **Doctors Cave 27** [11]2-9-7 (88) S Sanders 40/1:0 4490 **My Gacho 35** [14]2-8-13 (80) R Havlin 20/1:0
4871 **Press Express 15** [8]2-8-11 (78) A Culhane 20/1:0 4577 **Drum Dance 31** [7]2-8-13 (80) S Carson 18/1:0
14 Ran Time 1m 14.20 (3.4) Owned: Mr J C Fretwell Trained: Tamworth

5099

2.15 Heathavon Stud Houghton Conditions Stakes 2yo (C1)
£9013 £3419 £1709 **1m str** **Soft** **Inapplicable** Far side

4871* **SOMETHING EXCITING 15** [5] D R C Elsworth 2-9-3 (87) T Quinn 8/1: 400111: Held up, prog 3f out, styd on to lead dist, pushed clr, val 5L+: suited by 1m, further will suit: acts on gd & soft grnd: acts on a sharp or stiff/gall trk: v prog filly who relished today's stamina test: can rate higher & win a Listed/Gr race. **110+**
4461 **EMBOSSED 37** [1] R Hannon 2-9-3 (100) R L Moore 11/4 FAV: 616222: Rear, prog 3f out, ev ch dist, sn outpcd by easy wnr, clr rem: bckd: eff at 7f, ran to form of step up to 1m: acts on firm & soft: consistent. *3* **105**
4212 **SKIDROW 49** [9] M L W Bell 2-8-12 (89) S Sanders 25/1: 01223: Led 2f, styd in tch, short of room & wknd bef 1f out: 7 wk abs: see 4212 & 4046. *5* **91**
4325* **XTRA TORRENTIAL 44** [7] D M Simcock 2-9-1 N Callan 12/1: 14: Missed break, sn cl-up, fdd dist: 6 wk abs: not disgraced on only 2nd ever run: see 4325 (debut, gd). *nk* **93**
4691* **LOVE PALACE 26** [3]2-9-3 (95) K Darley 9/2: 22415: Cl-up, led bef 1f out, hdd dist, wknd: bckd. *1* **93**
4723 **HALLOWED DREAM 24** [8]2-8-7 (80) K Fallon 25/1: 00026: Led after 2f, hdd bef 1f out, fdd: btr 4723 (fm). *hd* **82**
4852* **NIGHT HOUR 16** [2]2-9-3 (88) Martin Dwyer 11/2: 417: Cl-up over 6f, sn wknd & eased: bckd: reportedly unsuited by today's grnd: btr 4852 (gd). *6* **81**
4688 **HALLHOO 27** [4]2-9-3 (89) T E Durcan 7/1: 31228: Cl-up 6f, sn fdd & eased: rider reported mount was unsuited by soft grnd: btr 4688 & 4387. *20* **46**
4328 **SUN KISSED 43** [6]2-9-3 (93) L Dettori 15/2: 129: Missed break, al adrift: rider reported mount was unhappy on today's soft grnd: btr 4328 (gd) & 3586 (fast). *1¾* **42**
9 Ran Time 1m 41.99 (5.49) Owned: Setsquare Recruitment Trained: Whitsbury

5100

2.50 Gr3 Igloos Bentinck Stakes 3yo+ (A1)
£29000 £11000 £5500 **6f str** **Soft** **Inapplicable** Far side

4952 **ROYAL MILLENNIUM 12** [4] M R Channon 6-9-2 (111) T E Durcan 7/2 FAV: 5-104131: Cl-up stands side group, kept on for press to lead well ins fnl 1f, rdn out: bckd: eff at 5f, just best at 6/7f: acts on firm & soft grnd: in-form tough & v smart performer: see 4952 & 4732. **117**
4732 **MOSS VALE 27** [1] B W Hills 3-8-11 (110) M Hills 9/2: 1110022: Led stands group, hdd under press well ins fnl 1f, just held: bckd: smart & tough: see 4732. *shd* **111**
4686 **QUITO 27** [12] D W Chapman 7-8-12 bl (105) A Culhane 8/1: 0651653: Held up, prog far side over 1f out, nrst fin: op 13/2: another fine run: see 2949 (gd). *2* **105**
4799 **COUNTRY REEL 20** [9] Saeed bin Suroor 4-8-12 t (105) L Dettori 11/1: 4400254: Led far side group 4f, sn no extra: not disgraced but has not won since '02: see 4588 & 2580. *1½* **101**
4879 **BALTIC KING 15** [15]4-8-12 t (106) S Drowne 12/1: 0136135: Cl-up, led far side group 2f out, no *¾* **99**

extra dist: best recent form has come at 5f on faster grnd: btr 4879 & 4718.
5001* **JONNY EBENEEZER 6** [2]5-8-12 bl e (96) R L Moore 11/1: 0001316: Cl-up stands side over 4f, no extra. *1* **96**
4879 **HALMAHERA 15** [8]9-8-12 (101) N Callan 25/1: 5060107: Cl-up, wknd dist: btr 4459 (val h'cap, firm). *hd* **95**
4929 **TWILIGHT BLUES 13** [18]5-8-12 (103) E Ahern 20/1: 00-50528: Cl-up, wknd dist: btr 4929 (7f, firm). *hd* **94**
4510 **GOLDEVA 34** [11]5-8-9 (104) R Hughes 16/1: 5054159: Missed break, nvr a factor: btr 3971. *1¼* **87**
4879 **COLONEL COTTON 15** [6]5-8-12 (95) J Fortune 33/1: 0653400: 10th: Al bhd stands side: btr 4588. *1* **87**
4384 **ASHDOWN EXPRESS 12** [14]5-8-12 (116) S Sanders 10/1: 2024000: 11th: Al in rear: best form has come on faster grnd: btr 3062. *½* **86**
4799 **CAPRICHO 20** [13]7-8-12 (96) T Quinn 20/1: 0000060: 12th: Mid-div, wknd bef 1f out: btr 2140. *4* **75**
4786 **Ellens Academy 20** [17]9-8-12 (86) F Norton 66/1:0 1621 **Petardias Magic 145** [16]3-8-11 (88) K Fallon 20/1:0
14 Ran Time 1m 13.71 (2.91) Owned: Jackie & George Smith Trained: West Ilsley

5101

3.25 Bellwinch Homes Handicap Stakes 3yo+ 86-100 (C1) **[112]**
£12486 £4736 £2368 **7f str** **Soft** **Inapplicable** Far side

4499 **STREAM OF GOLD 35** [7] Sir Michael Stoute 3-8-3 (87) F Norton 8/1: 5141: Cl-up, styd on travelling well to lead dist, pushed clr, val 5L+: eff at 1m/10f, imprvd dramatically for drop to 7f: acts on firm & gd/soft, enjoyed today's soft: lightly rcd 3yo, more h'caps await: see 4499. **103+**
4686 **KINGS CAPRICE 27** [15] G B Balding 3-8-4 (88) S Carson 16/1: 0441502: Cl-up, prog & ev ch dist, kept on, not pace easy wnr: clr rem: back to best on return to 7f in the mud: can return to wng ways: see 4231. *3½* **94**
4531 **BAYEUX 34** [5] Saeed bin Suroor 3-9-0 VIS t (98) L Dettori 12/1: 02-53003: Keen rear, prog 2f out, no impress fnl 1f: visor: first try on soft grnd: see 1888. *4* **97**
4800 **ETTRICK WATER 20** [6] L M Cumani 5-9-4 vis (100) N Mackay(3) 12/1: 5110164: Handy over 5f, no extra. *nk* **98**
5000* **MARSHMAN 6** [16]5-8-4 (6ex)(1oh) (85) P Robinson 7/2 FAV: 0033515: Held up, prog 2f out, mod late gains: quick reapp: shade btr expected under a pen after recent win in 5000 (gd). *shd* **83**
EMPIRICAL POWER 34 [20]3-8-11 (95) D P McDonogh 16/1: 4-531116: b c Second Empire - Rumuz (Marju) Led, hdd dist, fdd: Irish raider, earlier landed hat-trick in native country, wng 2 h'caps & a mdn: eff around 7f on firm & fast grnd: with Edward Lynam. *2* **88**
4891 **DIGITAL 14** [8]7-8-5 (87) T Quinn 7/1: 0022057: Keen rear, prog 2f out, no impress dist: bckd. *nk* **79**
4811 **STARBECK 19** [2]6-8-4 (9oh) (77) A McCarthy 66/1: 0040008: Nvr nrr than mid-div: 'not handle grnd'. *1¼* **76**
4773 **OASIS STAR 21** [11]3-8-8 (92) Martin Dwyer 11/1: 5120559: Nvr nrr than mid-div: btr 3421. *¾* **80**
4873 **TARANAKI 15** [19]6-8-4 (2oh) (84) N De Souza(5) 33/1: 0365040: 10th: Keen cl-up over 5f, wknd: btr 4873. *nk* **73**
4891* **WIZARD OF NOZ 14** [21]4-9-1 bl (97) E Ahern 9/1: 0555510: 11th: Cl-up 6f, fdd: btr 4891 (fast). *3½* **77**
3061 **GOLDEN CHALICE 99** [12]5-8-8 (90) D Holland 14/1: 6001000: 12th: Al in rear: long abs. *1* **68**
4773 **Apex 21** [18]3-8-3 (87) W Supple 14/1:0
2389 **Moayed 125** [17]5-8-4 (1oh)bl t(85) G Gibbons 20/1:0
4531 **Always Esteemed 34** [13]4-9-0 bl(96) T E Durcan 33/1:02593 **Oro Verde 118** [14]3-8-3 (1ow)(86) R L Moore 40/1:0
16 Ran Time 1m 27.25 (4.05) Owned: Ballymacoll Stud Trained: Newmarket

5102

4.00 Sporting Index 'premier' Claiming Stakes 3-5yo (D2)
£6838 £2104 £1052 **1m4f** **Soft** **Inapplicable** Far side

4324 **ALWAYS WAINING 44** [1] M Johnston 3-8-10 (93) J Fanning 11/10 FAV: 5316041: Cl-up, led 3f out, sn pushed clr, eased cl-home, val 7L+: 6 wk abs: well bckd: clmd for 30,000: eff at 12f, has tried further: acts on fast & soft grnd: v easy wnr on drop to clmg grade & more prizes await: see 4324 & 3444. **97**
4939 **HARRYCAT 11** [5] V Smith 3-8-5 J Quinn 50/1: 0562: Bhd, prog after 4f, kept on ins fnl 2f, no ch with easy wnr: imprvd for step up to 12f: acts on soft grnd: lightly rcd & imprvg 3yo who can win in this grade. *4* **81**
4889 **PRINS WILLEM 14** [8] J R Fanshawe 5-9-4 (85) L Dettori 11/4: 2345003: Cl-up, no extra from 1f out. *½* **86**
4772 **TOP SPEC 21** [4] R Hannon 3-8-12 (82) R Hughes 6/1: 2012104: Rear, prog 3f out, wknd bef 1f out. *5* **80**
4601 **PATRIXTOO 30** [9]3-8-5 (58) P Robinson 25/1: 0502405: Led 9f, wknd: btr 3875 (10f). *2½* **69**
5026 **ZUMA 5** [6]3-8-10 (72) R L Moore 14/1: 0554426: Nvr nrr than mid-div: quick reapp: btr 5026. *2½* **70**
4983 **SWEETWATER 8** [3]4-8-9 (70) S Drowne 33/1: 3066267: Mid-div, wknd 3f out. *14* **42**
5024 **GALLANT BOY 5** [2]5-8-10 BL t (63) J Fortune 25/1: 4400008: Al adrift: quick reapp & 1st blnks. *½* **42**
2654 **INDIAN SOLITAIRE 115** [7]5-8-10 p (72) E Ahern 33/1: 00-30609: Mid-div 1m, fdd: rider reported mount was unsuited by grnd: btr 1668. *3½* **37**
2230 **WOOLLY BACK 133** [10]3-8-9 (80) W Supple 20/1: 2260: 10th: Keen cl-up 1m, fdd: long abs. *21* **17**
10 Ran Time 2m 37.30 (9.5) Owned: The Always Trying Partnership Trained: Middleham

5103

4.35 George Winsor Lifetime In Racing Handicap Stakes 3yo+ 86-100 (C1) **[110]**
£14019 £4314 £2157 **1m str** **Soft** **Inapplicable** Far side

2705* **KAMANDA LAUGH 113** [7] B W Hills 3-8-1 (83) Martin Dwyer 10/1: 60-12111: Cl-up, led after 3f, hdd dist, rallied well to lead cl-home: tchd 14/1, long abs: eff at 6/7f, now suited by around 1m: acts on fast, soft grnd & polytrack: likes a stiff/gall trk: goes well fresh: prog & game 3yo who may not be at end of wng run. **93**
4917 **BOULE DOR 13** [23] R Ingram 3-8-8 (90) N Day 16/1: 2014432: Handy, styd on to lead ins fnl 1f, sn edged right for press, hdd cl-home: eff at 1m/10f on fast & soft grnd: continues to run well but is not a easy ride. *nk* **98**
2240 **BLAISE CASTLE 132** [14] G A Butler 4-8-11 (90) E Ahern 50/1: 042-4203: In tch, led dist, hdd ins fnl 1f, not btr far: long abs: decent eff after lay-off & can be plcd to find similar: see 1925 & 1620. *½* **97**
4067 **FINISHED ARTICLE 56** [12] D R C Elsworth 7-8-6 (85) T Quinn 16/1: 5300004: Held up, prog bef 1f out, nrst fin: 8 wk abs: back to form today with strong pace that suits: see 2096 & 1812. *1* **90**
4987 **SELECTIVE 7** [17]5-8-9 P (88) D Holland 16/1: 0404655: Rear, prog 2f out, hung left & onepcd ins fnl 1f: quick reapp in 1st time cheek pieces: handles soft, could apprec return to faster surface: see 3199. *½* **92**
4999 **GOODBYE MR BOND 6** [13]4-8-4 (6oh) (77) G Gibbons 33/1: 1326106: Trkd ldrs, onepcd dist: qck reapp. *1¼* **85**
4916 **UNSHAKABLE 13** [8]5-9-1 (94) F Norton 13/2: 1305457: Rear, prog 2f out, no impress fnl 1f. *½* **95**
4282} **MOMBASSA 5** [2]4-8-13 (92) D J Condon(3) 11/2 FAV: 0005418: Missed break, bhd, prog when no room 2f out till ins fnl 1f, swtch & kept on late: well bckd Irish raider, recent h'cap wnr at the Curragh (1m, soft): Listed rnr-up in '03: stks wnr at Tipperary in '02: prev eff at 5/6f, now suited by 1m: acts on fast & soft grnd: not get run of race & is better than this. *1¼* **91+**
2313 **DAFORE 128** [10]3-8-2 (84) R L Moore 50/1: 109: Nvr nrr than mid-div: long abs: btr 1497. *shd* **82**

NEWMARKET FRIDAY 15.10.04 Righhand, Stiff, Galloping Track

4820* **APERITIF 18** [21]3-8-4 (86) J Quinn 7/1: 3310310: 10th: Missed break, prog when short of room over 1f out, kept on under kind ride: did not get run of race & is worth another chance: btr 4820. *shd* **83+**
4917 **BARBAJUAN 13** [16]3-8-4 (86) N Mackay(3) 20/1: 0000050: 11th: Rear, prog 2f out, no impress fnl 1f. *shd* **82**
4916 **PUTRA KUANTAN 13** [1]4-9-4 (97) P Robinson 20/1: 3106000: 12th: Led 3f, wknd dist: disapp. *1¼* **91**
4987 **PENRITH 7** [20]3-8-4 (86) J Fanning 16/1: 3502340: 13th: Cl-up over 6f, wknd: quick reapp: btr 4987. *shd* **79**
4987+ **NASHAAB 7** [19]7-9-2 (6ex)vis (95) N Callan 33/1: 1500010: 14th: Al rear: btr 4987 (gd). *1¼* **86**
5038 **JAZZ SCENE 4** [4]3-8-11 vis (93) A Culhane 16/1: 2452420: 15th: Handy, wknd bef 1f out: quick reapp. *2½* **79**
4890 **ACE OF HEARTS 14** [25]5-8-11 (90) S Sanders 20/1: 1110030: 16th: Rear, prog halfway, wknd fnl 2f. *nk* **75**
4813 **Thajja 19** [18]3-9-4 (100) W Supple 14/1:0 2026 **Oman Gulf 141** [6]3-8-1 (83) K May(7) 66/1:0
4891 **Fremen 14** [26]4-8-13 (92) K Fallon 14/1:0
3760} **Faithful Warrior 421** [3]6-8-12 (91) A Medeiros(5) 66/1:0
4891 **Leoballero 14** [5]4-8-9 t(88) J F Egan 33/1:0 4638 **Lago Dorta 28** [15]4-9-4 (97) L Dettori 20/1:0
22 Ran Time 1m 42.36 (5.86) Owned: Mr John Sillett Trained: Lambourn

5104 5.05 Newmarket Challenge Whip A Handicap 3yo+ 0-85 (G4) [95]
£0 £0 £0 **1m2f** **Soft** **Inapplicable** Far side

4999 **ULTIMATA 6** [1] J R Fanshawe 4-9-0 (81) L Dettori 11/4: 1-022001: Made all, rdn out ins fnl 1f to hold on: op 9/4, quick reapp: eff at 1m, now stays 10f: acts on fast & soft grnd: see 3978 & 2620. **86**
4833 **VAMP 18** [2] R M Beckett 3-8-3 (75) N Mackay(3) 2/1: 3150432: Cl-up, ev ch over 3f, kept on, not pace wnr fnl 1f: just btr 4833 (12f, fast). *1¼* **77**
4609 **IMPERSONATOR 30** [3] J L Dunlop 4-8-9 (76) T Quinn 11/10 FAV: 0-043303: Keen cl-up, wknd dist: v well bckd: disapp: btr 4221 & 3797. *5* **70**
3 Ran Time 2m 10.83(8.73) Owned: Mr J H Richmond-Watson Trained: Newmarket

REDCAR FRIDAY 15.10.04 Lefthand, Flat, Galloping Track

Official Going GOOD

5105 1.30 'become A Redcar Annual Member 2005!' Claiming Stakes 2yo (F4)
£3556 £1016 £508 **7f** **Good/Soft 90** **-02 Slow** Centre

4519 **EXIT SMILING 34** [7] M Johnston 2-8-13 (67) R Ffrench 11/2: 230501: Made most, pushed clr ins fnl 1f: clmd for 10,000: stays 7f on gd & gd/soft, gall trk: made most of this drop in grade: see 1386. **71**
4552 **BELLA PLUNKETT 32** [2] W M Brisbourne 2-8-3 (3ow) (51) R Mullen 33/1: 00062: Chsd ldrs, outpcd 3f out, kept on again ins fnl 1f to go 2nd but no ch with wnr: poss stays 7f on gd/soft: see 4050. *4* **53**
4450 **IFIT 38** [14] M R Channon 2-8-4 (58) S Hitchcott 10/1: 00003: In tch, outpcd 3f out, styd on ins fnl 1f. *½* **53**
4980 **BOND FINESSE 8** [10] B Smart 2-8-12 F Lynch 10/1: 4404: Slow away in rear, hdwy 3f out, onepcd fnl 1f. *1* **59**
4895 **AFTER THE SNOW 14** [4]2-7-12 D Kinsella 40/1: 05: b f Danetime - State (Dominion) Trkd ldr, onepcd over 2f out: Mar foal: half sister to an Italian sprint wnr: dam unrcd, sire high-class sprinter: with I Wood. *1* **43**
4934 **PRO TEMPORE 11** [6]2-8-12 (64) P Hanagan 9/2 FAV: 1663006: Trkd ldrs, hdwy 3f out, sn onepcd. *nk* **56**
4206 **FILEY BUOY 49** [1]2-8-3 VIS B Swarbrick(5) 40/1: 0007: Chsd ldrs, no impress: 7 wk abs: tried visor. *2* **43**
4927 **SWEET POTATO 13** [5]2-8-8 P Makin(5) 5/1: 508: In tch, hdwy over 3f out, s btn: btr 4244 (6f). *1* **46**
5013 **SINGHALONGTASVEER 5** [8]2-8-5 (59) J Bramhill 16/1: 5300509: Outpcd in rear, some late gains. *1¼* **40**
3864 **MUESTRA 65** [11]2-7-12 (45) Amy Baker(5) 66/1: 0005300: 10th: In tch, hdwy 2f out, no impress fnl 1f. *3½* **26**
QUEENS HAND 0 [20]2-8-8 R Winston 16/1: 0: 11th: b f Lend A Hand - Winchester Queen (Persian Bold) Handy, hung left over 2f out, sn wknd on debut: May foal, cost 3,000 gns: half sister to a mod juv wnr over 5f: dam unrcd, sire high-class 2yo, later high-class sprinter/miler: with G Swinbank. *1¼* **33**
4597 **RIVERWELD 30** [15]2-8-5 (55) P M Quinn 20/1: 642500: 12th: Handy till 2f out, sn btn. *4* **22**
4865 **BRANSTON LILY 16** [17]2-8-12 (63) K McEvoy 6/1: 3400: 13th: In tch, outpcd & btn 3f out. *shd* **28**
4670 **EKATERINA 27** [9]2-7-13 (1ow) Dale Gibson 50/1: 00: 14th: b f Merdon Melody - Hsian (Shantung) Nvr a factor: 5,000 gns Apr foal: sister to a dual 6f 2yo scorer: half sister to wnrs at 7f/1m: dam unplcd. *hd* **14**
4635 **COUNTRYWIDE SUN 29** [16]2-9-3 p (56) T P Queally 14/1: 0002400: 15th: Chsd ldrs till hmpd 2f out. *shd* **31**
4072 **NORTHERN REVOQUE 56** [3]2-8-0 (45) S Righton 66/1: 0500400: 16th: Prom till over 3f out, sn btn. *6* **0**
4316 **PIPS PEARL 44** [19]2-8-0 vis t (45) D Fentiman(7) 33/1: 000050: 17th: Slow away, al bhd: 6 wk abs. *½* **0**
17 Ran Time 1m 28.24 (6.44) Owned: Kennet Valley Thoroughbreds VI Trained: Middleham

5106 2.00 European Breeders Fund Maiden Stakes Fillies 2yo (D3)
£4810 £1480 £740 **6f** **Good/Soft 90** **-09 Slow** Centre

4610 **DESERT IMP 30** [6] B W Hills 2-8-11 (78) R Winston 9/2: 0331: Trkd ldrs, hdwy to lead well over 1f out, pushed clr ins fnl 1f: stays 6f on fast & gd/soft, acts on a gall trk: deserved win, see 4357. **82**
4610 **FASHION HOUSE 30** [9] Saeed bin Suroor 2-8-11 J Carroll 9/1: 52: Led till well over 1f out, sn no extra: stays 6f on gd/soft: imprvd from debut & shld find a race: see 4610. *1½* **75**
4760 **MISS TRIAL 22** [1] M A Jarvis 2-8-11 (71) R Mullen 4/1: 6333: Rear, hdwy 3f out, kept on ins fnl 1f: acts on firm & gd/soft: consistent, 7f prob suit best now: see 4760. *nk* **74**
GILDAS FORTUNA 0 [7] P C Haslam 2-8-11 G Faulkner 50/1: 4: b f Fort Wood - Gleaming Sky (Badger Land) Dwelt, sn in tch, hdwy over 2f out, onepcd over 1f out on debut: Mar foal, cost 5,000 gns: half sister to a 5f 2yo wnr: dam useful sprinter: sire prog into a top class sprinter: stays 6f on gd/soft: gd start. *½* **72**
WESTLAKE BOND 0 [14]2-8-11 F Lynch 28/1: 5: b f Josr Algarhoud - Rania (Aragon) Mid-div, hdwy over 2f out, kept on ins fnl 1f: debut: Feb 1st foal, cost E29,000: dam unrcd, sire v smart juv, later v smart over 7f/1m: fair start, will come on for this & can rate higher next time. *2½* **64+**
LA VIOLA 0 [12]2-8-11 Darren Williams 40/1: 6: b f Fraam - Arasong (Aragon) Dwelt, sn in tch, hdwy 3f out, no impress 2f out on debut: 2,800 gns Apr foal: half sister to a 7f juv wnr: dam 5f wnr. *1* **61**
4996 **LADY DORIS WATTS 6** [13]2-8-11 S Hitchcott 11/1: 027: Rcd in 2nd, wknd over 1f out: qck reapp. *shd* **60**
3939 **SHEKAN STAR 62** [15]2-8-11 Dale Gibson 100/1: 0008: Nvr btr than mid-div: 9 wk abs. *3* **51**
4918 **ARCHEOLOGY 13** [10]2-8-11 K McEvoy 13/8 FAV: 59: Chsd ldrs, no impress 2f out. *2* **45**

4200 **SOME NIGHT 49** [11]2-8-11 N Pollard 33/1: 500: 10th: Handy, wknd over 2f out: 7 wk abs. *6* **27**
CELTIC CARISMA 0 [5]2-8-11 P Hanagan 50/1: 0: 11th: Slow away, al bhd on debut. *1¼* **23**
4653 **RAINBOW TREASURE 28** [2]2-8-11 T Eaves(3) 80/1: 060: 12th: Mid-div, wknd over 2f out. *2½* **15**
MADAME GUILLOTINE 0 [8]2-8-11 J Edmunds 66/1: 0: 13th: In tch till halfway, sn btn on debut. *½* **13**
GIFTED LASS 0 [3]2-8-11 D Allan 50/1: 0: 14th: Slow away, al bhd on debut. *9* **0**
14 Ran Time 1m 14.88 (5.98) Owned: Maktoum Al Maktoum Trained: Lambourn

5107

2.35 Redcarracing Co Uk Median Auction Maiden Stakes 2yo (F4)
£3318 £948 £474 **1m Good/Soft 90 -15 Slow** Centre

4704 **DUROOB 25** [12] E A L Dunlop 2-9-0 (72) P Hanagan 3/1: 0331: Prom, slt lead over 1f out, drvn out ins fnl 1f: relished this step up to 1m, further will suit in time: acts on gd/soft & hvy, gall trk: deserved win. **82**
5002 **WILLIAM TELL 6** [6] M R Channon 2-9-0 (78) S Hitchcott 7/4 FAV: 645222: Led after 2f, hung left 2f out & sn hdd, no extra ins fnl 1f: quick reapp, clr of rem: plcd again: see 5002. *½* **79**
THREE WRENS 0 [7] D J Daly 2-8-9 S W Kelly 9/1: 3: b f Second Empire - Three Terns (Arctic Tern) Cl-up early, sn outpcd, hdwy over 3f out, sn onepcd on debut: 26,000 gns Apr foal: half sister to wnrs btwn 5/10f: dam a French 3yo wnr, sire a 1m Gr1 wnr at 2: pleasing start, will come on for this & can improve next time. *3½* **67**
4577 **WOOD SPIRIT 31** [10] Mrs P N Dutfield 2-8-9 N Pollard 25/1: 664: Slow away, hdwy over 2f out, onepace. *nk* **66**
WOODBURY LANE 0 [5]2-8-9 K McEvoy 9/2: 5: br f Wild Wonder - Maximum Blue (Blue Ensign) Handy, onepcd 2f out on debut: Jan foal: dam unrcd, sire prog btwn 6f/1m: fair start. *1* **64**
4193 **OUR CHOICE 49** [3]2-9-0 (59) T P Queally 20/1: 040606: Handy, onepcd 2f out: 7 wk abs: see 1149. *1* **67**
4831 **HOH MY DARLING 18** [8]2-8-9 R Mullen 8/1: 047: Chsd ldrs, outpcd & btn 2f out: btr 4191. *1¾* **58**
4934 **PARIS HEIGHTS 11** [11]2-9-0 VIS (63) B Swarbrick(5) 25/1: 064008: Led 2f, rem prom, no extra over 2f out: tried visor: much btr 2959. *10* **43**
4558 **BE BOP 32** [9]2-9-0 Kim Tinkler 50/1: 009: ch g Groom Dancer - Norpella (Northfields) Chsd ldrs, wknd over 3f out: 16,000 gns Apr foal: half brother to wnrs at 6f/10f: dam unrcd. *8* **27**
4752 **CLIFFIE 22** [4]2-9-0 S Righton 100/1: 00: 10th: Hmpd start, nvr a factor in rear. *3½* **20**
4863 **MAYNOOTH PRINCE 16** [1]2-9-0 J Carroll 100/1: 00: 11th: In tch till over 3f out, sn btn. *1¾* **16**
3939 **JUDGE DAMUSS 62** [2]2-9-0 L Enstone 100/1: 00: 12th: Mid-div, wknd over 3f out: 9 wk abs. *11* **0**
12 Ran Time 1m 43.23 (8.43) Owned: Mr Hamdan Al Maktoum Trained: Newmarket

5108

3.10 Weatherbys Insurance Services Handicap Stakes 3yo+ 56-70 (E3) **[74]**
£7787 £2396 £1198 **1m6f19y Good/Soft 90 +00 Fast** Inside

4932 **MOST DEFINITELY 13** [9] T D Easterby 4-9-5 (65) D Allan 8/1: 0623221: Rear, hdwy over 3f out, led & hung right well over 1f out, rdn out fnl 1f: eff at 14f, poss best at 2m/2m1f: acts on firm & gd/soft, likes a stiff/gall trk: well deserved win, consistent prev: see 2444. **75**
4601* **WING COLLAR 30** [3] T D Easterby 3-9-0 (69) F Lynch 9/1: 3204312: Mid-div, lost place 6f out, hdwy 3f out, no run well over 1f out, hdwy 1f out, not pace to reach wnr: poss wnr with a clr run: eff at 10f/14f, poss stays 2m: remains in gd form, ran to wng form of 4601. *¾* **76+**
4938 **DANEBANK 11** [15] J Mackie 4-8-9 (3oh)p (52) Dale Gibson 15/2: 5123023: Trkd ldrs, hdwy over 3f out, kept on: eff around 12/12.5f, clrly stays 14f: gd eff from 3lbs out of the h'cap: see 4203. *2½* **58**
5016 **SILVERTOWN 5** [12] L Lungo 9-9-6 (66) P Mulrennan(3) 20/1: 11-00004: In tch, hdwy 3f out, not clr run & switched 2f out, kept on ins fnl 1f: quick reapp: suited by 12f, stays 14f: shade closer with a clr run, prob 3rd. *1* **67**
4924 **IVY LEAGUE STAR 13** [4]3-9-0 (69) R Winston 5/1 FAV: 06-50155: Trkd ldrs, hdwy 4f out, ch when sltly hmpd well over 1f out, sn onepcd. *hd* **69**
4361 **MACARONI GOLD 42** [10]4-8-12 (58) D Tudhope(5) 7/1: 4503366: Bhd, hdwy 5f out, onepcd 2f out. *1* **56**
5004 **SALAMBA 6** [1]3-8-11 (66) S Hitchcott 7/1: 53-50057: Handy, hdwy to lead 3f out, hdd well over 1f out, sn no extra: quick reapp: see 1462. *3* **59**
5004 **HEARTHSTEAD DREAM 6** [14]3-9-0 bl (69) T P Queally 6/1: 2133438: In tch, hdwy & ev ch 3f out, sn btn. *½* **61**
4559 **EAST CAPE 32** [8]7-8-9 (10oh) (45) Kim Tinkler 33/1: 6352409: Rear, hdwy 3f out, sn btn: stiff task. *3* **42**
4856 **MAJESTIC VISION 16** [5]3-8-13 (68) K McEvoy 6/1: 4-062530: 10th: Led to 3f out, no extra. *1¼* **53**
5004 **ZAN LO 6** [6]4-8-9 (6oh) (49) T Eaves(3) 33/1: 0410000: 11th: Chsd ldrs, wknd over 3f out: quick reapp. *2* **37**
4647 **WEET FOR ME 28** [7]8-9-9 (69) R Ffrench 20/1: 0265600: 12th: Rcd in 2nd, wknd over 3f out. *5* **43**
12 Ran Time 3m 10.47 (12.67) Owned: Mr B Batey Trained: Malton

5109

3.45 'book Your Wedding Reception At Redcar Racecourse!' Handicap Stakes 3yo 56-70 (E3) **[80]**
£5213 £1604 £802 **7f Good/Soft 90 -02 Slow** Centre

4862 **SCIENTIST 16** [12] J H M Gosden 3-9-0 (66) K McEvoy 7/1: 0030601: Led after 2f, clr over 3f out, rdn out nr fin: eff at 7f on fast & gd/soft, acts on a gall trk: 1st win & imprvd for this drop back to 7f: see 2314. **76**
5063 **SENESCHAL 3** [11] M R Channon 3-9-7 (6ex) (73) T O'Brien(7) 2/1 FAV: 0005162: Rear, hdwy 2f out, hung left fnl 1f, kept on but not pace of wnr: qk reapp: acts on fast, prob soft: back to wng form of 5014. *1½* **78**
4595 **UHURU PEAK 31** [4] M W Easterby 3-8-4 (6oh)bl (50) Dale Gibson 20/1: 0320603: Slow away, sn handy, kept on fnl 1f: stays 7f: gd run: see 3262. *nk* **60**
4937 **CHEVERAK FOREST 11** [13] Don Enrico Incisa 3-8-4 (1oh)T (55) Kim Tinkler 40/1: 0-000004: Dwelt in rear, hdwy over 2f out, onepcd over 1f out: suited by 6f, stays 7f: imprvd run with application of t-strap. *½* **59**
4870 **MIND ALERT 16** [1]3-8-8 (60) D Allan 25/1: 0200005: Trkd ldrs far side, onepcd 2f out: stays 6/7f on fast & gd/soft: now with Miss J Camacho: see 1881. *1* **61**
5008 **GO YELLOW 6** [6]3-9-1 (67) D Nolan(3) 9/1: 6140206: Trkd ldrs, outpcd 2f out, kept on again over 1f out. *1* **66**
5014 **MENAI STRAIGHTS 5** [9]3-8-11 (63) R Ffrench 11/1: 5130667: Led 2f, rem handy, no extra over 1f out. *shd* **61**
4304 **FOSSGATE 45** [14]3-9-2 p (68) J Cavanagh(7) 8/1: 0364448: Chsd ldrs stands side, outpcd & btn 2f out. *1¼* **63**
4845 **RENE BARBIER 17** [3]3-8-6 (2ow) (56) S Hitchcott 16/1: 1560009: Chsd ldrs far side, wknd qckly 1f out. *3* **47**
4465 **SWEET REPLY 37** [10]3-9-2 P (68) T P Queally 14/1: 5100500: 10th: Rear, hdwy 3f out, sn hung right, wknd 2f out: cheek pieces. *1* **55**
4621 **NEON BLUE 29** [5]3-9-4 (70) S W Kelly 8/1: 3316000: 11th: Chsd ldrs till outpcd over 2f out, sn wknd. *1* **55**
4845 **FITZWARREN 17** [8]3-8-4 (4oh) (52) A Reilly(7) 20/1: 0360600: 12th: Slow away & keen, no impress. *¾* **39**
3528 **ALICE BLACKTHORN 79** [7]3-8-4 (2oh) (54) R Mullen 20/1: 0-005000: 13th: Rear, hdwy over 3f out, wknd over 2f out: long abs: btr 1477 (6f). *1* **37**
4037 **COMPTON MICKY 58** [2]3-8-4 p (53) J Edmunds 33/1: 0560500: 14th: Keen & handy far side, btn 2f out. *½* **36**
14 Ran Time 1m 28.28 (6.48) Owned: Highclere Thoroughbred Racing XII Trained: Manton

---

5110 4.20 Anne Webster - Lifetime In Racing Maiden Stakes 3yo+ (D3)
£3803 £1170 £585 6f **Good/Soft 90** +04 Fast Centre

4709 **LIGNE DEAU 25** [19] P D Evans 3-9-0 BL (53) D Nolan(3) 16/1: 5366061: Prom, led after 1f, wandered
over 1f out, drvn out ins fnl 1f: eff at 6f on fast & gd/soft: improved for blnks. 66

5030 **RUSSIAN CAFE 5** [10] M A Magnusson 3-8-9 † R Winston 6/5 FAV: 32: Rear, hdwy over 2f out, hmpd &
switched over 1f out, styd on well fnl 1f, nrst fin: quick reapp: acts on gd & gd/soft: try 7f now? see 5030 (debut). nk 59

4969 **KAMENKA 10** [20] R A Fahey 3-8-9 VIS (65) P Hanagan 4/1: 4440033: Prom, chall over 1f out, onepcd
ins fnl 1f: imprvd in visor: see 3833. ½ 57

4211 **DARK CHAMPION 49** [11] R E Barr 4-9-1 (50) B Swarbrick(5) 22/1: 4500004: Chsd ldrs, hdwy 2f out,
ch over 1f out, onepcd ins fnl 1f: 7 wk abs: see 313. nk 61$

COME ON 0 [9]5-9-1 J Dekeyser 66/1: 5: b g Aragon - All On (Dunbeath) Mid-div, hdwy 2f out, ev
ch over 1f out, onepcd ins fnl 1f on debut: stays 6f on gd/soft. nk 60

YOUNG KATE 0 [16]3-8-9 T P Queally 11/1: 6: b f Desert King - Stardyn (Star Appeal) Slow away,
hdwy 3f out, kept on on debut: should be able to wnr at 7f/1m: dam plcd: stays 6f on gd/soft. hd 54

4101 **POETRY N PASSION 55** [17]3-8-9 R Ffrench 20/1: 07: Chsd ldrs, no impress over 1f out: 8 wk abs. 3 45

4761 **NEW YORK 22** [2]3-8-9 S W Kelly 8/1: 24-00358: Cl-up alone far side, no impress fnl 1f: blnks. nk 44

4788 **FORREST GUMP 20** [13]4-9-1 (52) T Eaves(3) 25/1: 00-029: In tch, nvr nrr. 1½ 44

4790 **ROSE OF YORK 20** [18]4-8-10 (53) P Mulrennan(3) 33/1: 00-40: 10th: Chsd ldrs, wknd over 2f out. ½ 37

4133 **NEVER FORGET BOWIE 53** [15]8-9-1 (40) D Tudhope(5) 80/1: 30404/-00: 11th: Chsd ldrs, wknd 2f out. 2 36

5036 **JUNIPER BANKS 4** [7]3-9-0 (57) L Fletcher(2) 50/1: 420-6600: 12th: Chsd ldrs, wknd 2f out: quick reapp. ½ 34

4964 **SVENSON 10** [1]3-9-0 (30) D Allan 100/1: 0000060: 13th: ch c Dancing Spree - Bella Bambola (Tate
Gallery) Led 1f, rem cl-up, no extra over 2f out: well btn sole '03 start (mdn, rtd 48, J Matthias): mod. 1¼ 30

4788 **M FOR MAGIC 20** [5]5-9-1 bl (45) K Pierrepont(7) 40/1: 45-52450: 14th: In tch to halfway, sn btn. 1½ 25

4788 **PAY TIME 20** [6]5-8-10 (40) M Lawson(4) 66/1: 0-600560: 15th: Slow away, al bhd. ½ 18

4595 **YORKES FOLLY 31** [8]3-8-9 vis (45) L Enstone 25/1: 0000350: 16th: In tch to halfway, sn btn. 2½ 10

4901 **LORD WISHINGWELL 13** [3]3-9-0 p (30) P Mathers(5) 40/1: 0460000: 17th: In tch, wknd halfway. 3½ 4

CARMARTHEN BELLE 0 [1]4-8-10 T Williams 66/1: 0: 18th: Slow away, al bhd on debut. 2 0

MERLINS CITY 0 [12]4-8-10 Dale Gibson 66/1: 0: 19th: Slow away, nvr a factor on debut. 17 0

19 Ran Time 1m 14.1 (5.2) Owned: Mr M W Lawrence Trained: Abergavenny

---

5111 4.55 Redcar Racecourse Conference Centre Handicap Stakes 3yo+ 46-55 (F4) [69]
£3962 £1219 £610 1m1f **Good/Soft 90** +09 Fast Inside

4720 **TIME TO REGRET 24** [3] J S Wainwright 4-8-10 (51) P Hanagan 8/1: 1000251: Mid-div, not clr run
over 2f out, hdwy to lead over 1f out, drvn out ins fnl 1f: best time of day: stays 7/10f on fast & gd/soft,
stiff/undul or gall trk: imprvd rdn closer to the pace: back to form of 3242. 65

3759 **EXPLODE 70** [10] Miss L C Siddall 7-8-11 (52) T Williams 12/1: 000-4022: In tch, hdwy 4f out, led
over 2f out till over 1f out, no extra: long abs: stays 9f on gd & soft. 5 56

4408 **THE WIZARD MUL 39** [11] W Storey 4-8-10 (51) J Bramhill 33/1: 0000003: Rear, hdwy 3f out, onepace. ½ 54

4598 **SEDGE 30** [12] P T Midgley 4-8-11 (52) L Enstone 16/1: 100004: Chsd ldrs, onepcd 2f out. hd 54

4867 **APACHE POINT 16** [5]7-8-10 (51) Kim Tinkler 3/1 FAV: 5555055: Bhd, some late gains: clr of rem. hd 52

4925 **CALCULATE 13** [4]3-8-10 (55) K McEvoy 8/1: 4501346: Trkd ldrs, switched wide 2f out, styd on. 3 50

3328 **ARAWAN 87** [2]4-8-12 (53) Dale Gibson 16/1: 0000007: In tch till after 2f, rear, some late gains: abs. 1¼ 45

4594 **WESTCOURT DREAM 31** [16]4-8-8 (49) P Mulrennan(3) 20/1: 3-310608: Chsd ldrs, outpcd & btn 2f out. hd 40

4828 **GRACEFUL AIR 18** [1]3-8-8 p (53) D Fentiman(7) 14/1: 4500329: In tch, hmpd over 4f out, outpcd 3f out. nk 43

4926 **GOLDEN SPECTRUM 13** [7]5-8-10 (51) T Eaves(3) 20/1: 3000300: 10th: Rear, hdwy 4f out, btn 2f out. 5 31

4506* **PENWELL HILL 34** [14]5-8-10 (51) P Makin(5) 6/1: 0600310: 11th: Rcd in 2nd till led 3f out, sn hdd, wknd. 4 23

4938 **SENOR EDUARDO 11** [15]7-9-0 (55) N Pollard 16/1: 6230300: 12th: Chsd ldrs, wknd over 2f out. 3 21

3487 **ROCINANTE 84** [8]4-8-12 (53) R Winston 4-8-10 20/1: 0110060: 13th: Mid-div, wknd over 2f out: long abs. 7 5

4861 **IFTIKHAR 16** [6]5-8-11 BL (52) S W Kelly 25/1: 0004000: 14th: Chsd ldrs till 2f out, sn
wknd/eased, broke a blood vessel: tried blnks. 6 0

4720 **ROYAL RACER 24** [13]6-8-11 bl (52) T P Queally 10/1: 3600160: 15th: Led to 3f out, hung left, no extra. 1 0

15 Ran Time 1m 56.1(7.3) Owned: Denison Arms Trained: Malton

WOLVERHAMPTON Polytrack SATURDAY 16.10.04 Lefthand, Sharp Track

Official Going Standard

5112 7.00 Ladbrokescasino Com Handicap Stakes 3yo+ 46-55 (F4) [69]
£3038 £868 £434 7f32y aw rnd **Inapplicable** Inside

5005 **IRUSAN 7** [3] Jedd O'Keeffe 4-9-0 bl (55) M Fenton 12/1: 0465021: Cl up, styd on for press to lead
well ins fnl 1f: qck reapp: eff at 7f/8.6f on both AW's: imprvd for recent fitting of blnks: see 5005 & 1518. 65a

5077 **NAUTICAL 3** [4] A W Carroll 4-9-8 (63) L Dettori 11/4 FAV: 0201102: Held up, prog 3f out, led 1f
out, hdd well ins fnl 1f: clr rem: qck reapp: back to best today & can return to winning ways: see 4982 & 4367. shd 71a

4926 **BEST DESERT 14** [6] J R Best 3-9-3 (60) J Quinn 8/1: 5150063: Bhd, prog 2f out, kept on late:
acts on polytrack & fast grnd: see 4926 & btr 3654. 3½ 61a

5069 **ON THE TRAIL 4** [2] D W Chapman 7-9-1 (56) P Makin(5) 9/2: 4520124: Led, hdd 1f out, sn no extra:
qck reapp: prob stays 7f, return to 6f will suit: btr 5069 & 4967 (6f). nk 56a

4739 **SMOKIN JOE 24** [1]3-9-1 bl (58) G Baker 25/1: 0000005: Handy over 5f, onepcd: btr 3774. 3 52a

4994+ **ZHITOMIR 7** [9]6-9-0 (55) S W Kelly 6/1: 1640216: Missed break, nvr nrr than mid div: qck reapp. 3½ 42a

4946 **SIRAJ 12** [10]5-9-4 T (59) J Brennan(7) 20/1: 25-01007: Nvr nrr than mid div: btr 4041 (6f). 1¼ 44a

5063 **PAWAN 4** [5]4-9-4 (59) Ann Stokell 33/1: 1050008: Al in rear: qck reapp: btr 2962. nk 43a

4794 **EMARADIA 21** [7]3-9-0 (57) D Nolan(3) 25/1: 6603049: Cl up 5f, wknd. nk 40a

5014 **YORKER 6** [8]6-9-7 bl (62) B Swarbrick(5) 9/1: 0360130: 10th: Cl up 5f, wknd: qck reapp, btr 5014 (fast). 1½ 42a

4438 **SAROS 39** [12]3-9-4 (61) D McGaffin 8/1: 2030100: 11th: Al bhd: btr 4175 (fast). 10 23a

4636 **WARLINGHAM 30** [11]6-9-5 (60) R Winston 25/1: 0500000: 12th: Mid div over 5f, fdd. 5 12a

12 Ran   Time 1m 29.14 (2.94)   Owned: Highbeck Racing   Trained: Leyburn

5113   7.30 Ladbrokes Com Selling Stakes 2yo (G4)
£2660 £760 £380   **7f32y aw rnd**   Inapplicable   Inside

5019 **TIGER DAWN 6** [8] W J Haggas 2-8-11   S W Kelly 7/2 JT FAV: 01: b g Anabaa - Armorique (Top Ville)   **70a+**
In tch, led trav well dist, pushed clr, val 5L+: qck reapp & AW bow: bought in for 9,500 gns: Apr foal, half
brother 6f wnr: Sire Gr 1 wnr at 6f: eff at 7f on polytrack: acts on a sharp trk, tried blnks: enjoyed drop in grade.
4726 **BRANSTON PENNY 25** [12] J G Given 2-8-6   M Fenton 5/1: 02: ch f Pennekamp - Branston Jewel   3   **56a**
(Prince Sabo) Mid div, prog to chase wnr ins fnl 1f, al held: Mar foal, cost 13,000 gns: half-sister won numerous
times at sprint dists: dam 5f wnr, also Gr 3 plcd: eff at 7f on polytrack.
4792 **TIGER HUNTER 21** [2] P Howling 2-8-11   R Winston 12/1: 0003: Led after 1f, hdd dist, wknd.   3½   **54a**
      PROSPECT POINT 0 [6] C A Dwyer 2-8-6   D Fox(5) 10/1: 4: Missed break, nvr nrr than mid div on debut.   2½   **44a**
47**GRAND GIRL 26** [10]2-8-6   A Daly 7/2 JT FAV: 0005: Bhd, mod late gains: AW bow.   5   **35a**
      LOVE ATTACK 0 [7]2-8-6   Y Houben 10/1: 6: Al in rear on debut.   5   **26a**
4658 **ROOKS BRIDGE 28** [9]2-8-11   J Quinn 25/1: 007: Chsd ldrs 5f, wknd.   nk   **30a**
4921 **RANDALLS TOUCH 14** [5]2-8-11   B Swarbrick(5) 50/1: 008: Mid div over 5f, fdd: 'lost action'.   9   **14a**
4863 **FRAAMBUOYANT 17** [1]2-8-6   R Ffrench 12/1: 009: Cl up till halfway, fdd.   1   **7a**
4922 **INDEPENDENT SPIRIT 14** [3]2-8-11   P Hanagan 13/2: 0000: 10th: Wknd halfway: 'lost action'.   1½   **9a**
4484 **CHESTMINSTER GIRL 37** [11]2-8-6 P   A Nicholls 33/1: 00: 11th: Al adrift.   9   **0a**
11 Ran   Time 1m 32.17 (5.97)   Owned: M S Bloodstock Ltd   Trained: Newmarket

5114   8.00 Ladbrokes Com Handicap Stakes 3yo 56-70 (E3)
£3410 £1049 £525   **5f216y aw rnd**   Inapplicable   Inside   [77]

4909 **BURLEY FLAME 14** [8] J G Given 3-10-0 (77) M Fenton 20/1: 3160001: Chsd ldrs, led dist, all out   **86a**
to hold on: AW bow: eff at 7f/1m, appreciated drop to 6f: acts on fast, gd/soft & polytrack: see 3179.
4713 **CHEROKEE NATION 26** [12] P W D'Arcy 3-9-3 (66) J F Egan 20/1: 1035002: Cl up, ev ch ins fnl 1f,   nk   **73a**
just held: acts on fast, gd & both AW's: back to form today & is weighted to find similar: see 2985 & 2855.
4790* **FLYING BANTAM 21** [9] R A Fahey 3-9-10 (73) P Hanagan 6/1: 0240413: Bhd, prog halfway, kept on,   2   **74a**
not pace front 2 fnl 1f: AW bow: acts on firm, gd/soft & polytrack: 5lb higher than win in 4790 (gd).
4822 **JILLY WHY 19** [13] Ms Deborah J Evans 3-9-9 (72) A Nicholls 12/1: 4110024: In tch, led 2f out,   ¾   **71a**
hdd dist, no extra: AW bow: acts on firm, gd & polytrack: btr 4822 (5f).
4976 **SAVIOURS SPIRIT 10** [11]3-9-9 (72) K Fallon 2/1 FAV: 2210025: Mid div, onepcd bef 1f out: btr 4976.   1¾   **66a**
4897 **BRIDGEWATER BOYS 15** [4]3-9-10 bl (73) R Ffrench 11/1: 1215006: Nvr nrr than mid div: btr 2482 (fast).   2½   **60a**
4604 **BEEJAY 31** [2]3-9-9 (72) L Dettori 6/1: 1-100067: Rear, mod gains: btr 4604.   1   **56a**
4683 **SOLINIKI 28** [5]3-9-7 BL (70) S W Kelly 50/1: 1-0008: Bhd, mod late gains: 1st time blnks.   1¾   **49a**
5020+ **INNSTYLE 6** [6]3-9-4 (6ex) (67) Lisa Jones 16/1: 0030019: Al in rear: qk reapp: btr 5020 (clmr, gd).   1   **43a**
4984 **BORZOI MAESTRO 9** [1]3-9-3 p (66) D Nolan(3) 10/1: 0605550: 10th: Led 1f, fdd bef 1f out: see 2048.   hd   **41a**
4897 **MIDNIGHT BALLARD 15** [10]3-9-10 bl (73) S Carson 50/1: 2010000: 11th: Led 5f out, hdd 2f out, fdd.   3½   **38a**
4604 **MARYSIENKA 31** [7]3-9-5 (68) J Edmunds 50/1: 0503400: 12th: In tch 3f, wknd.   2   **27a**
4806 **MISTER MARMADUKE 20** [3]3-9-13 (76) R Winston 7/1: 0435000: 13th: Mid div over 4f, fdd: btr 4048.   7   **16a**
13 Ran   Time 1m 15.43 (2.63)   Owned: Burley Appliances Ltd   Trained: Gainsborough

5115   8.30 Ladbrokes Com Maiden Stakes 2yo (D3)
£4271 £1314 £657   **1m141y aw rnd**   Inapplicable   Inside

3601 **JAZRAWY 77** [5] L M Cumani 2-9-0   N Mackay(3) 100/30: 441: Prom, led halfway, pushed out ins fnl   **79a**
1f, val 4L+: 11 wk abs & AW bow: eff at 7.6f, imprvd for step up to 8.6f: acts on fast gnd & polytrack: goes well
fresh: can rate higher with racing: see 3601 & 2522.
4971 **PLANET 10** [3] Sir Michael Stoute 2-9-0   K Fallon 3/1 JT FAV: 002: b c Soviet Star - Laurentia   2   **73a**
(St Jovite) Cl up, kept on, not pace wnr fnl 1f: Feb first foal, dam wnr at mid dists: sire Gr 1 performer at
sprint dists & 1m: imprvd for step up to 8.6f: acts on polytrack: can find a race.
4921 **SPECTAIT 14** [3] Sir Mark Prescott 2-9-0   S Sanders 3/1 JT FAV: 203: Chsd ldrs, no extra bef 1f out.   2   **69a**
4648 **IRISH BALLAD 29** [10] P W Harris 2-9-0   M Fenton 25/1: 004: Handy over 6f, onepcd: see 4648.   ¾   **67a**
4883 **SANDYS LEGEND 16** [1]2-9-0   L Dettori 5/1: 05: ch c Tale of The Cat - Avasand (Avatar) Led till   ½   **66a**
halfway, no extra bef 1f out: AW bow: Jun foal, half brother to decent performers at 6/8f: dam wnr at 3 abroad.
4970 **HIGH CARD 10** [6]2-9-0   J F Egan 12/1: 06: Chsd ldrs 6f, no extra: clr rem.   hd   **65a**
4792 **MILLQUISTA DOR 21** [8]2-9-0   A Daly 80/1: 07: Bhd, nvr a factor.   6   **49a**
4356 **FIGAROS QUEST 43** [9]2-9-0   N De Souza(5) 25/1: 608: Cl up 6f, wknd: 6 wk abs.   5   **45a**
4831 **WAR PENNANT 19** [7]2-9-0   J Quinn 12/1: 69: Bhd, nvr a factor.   3½   **38a**
4851 **BACKSTREET LAD 17** [2]2-9-0   G Baker 66/1: 0000: 10th: Rear, nvr a factor.   3   **32a**
4703 Patrician Dealer 26 [4]2-9-0   V Slattery 66/1:0:0   Soumillon 0 [11]2-8-9 A Nicholls 50/1:0:0
12 Ran   Time 1m 51.44 (5.24)   Owned: Sheikh Mohammed Obaid Al Maktoum   Trained: Newmarket

5116   9.00 Ladbrokespoker Com Maiden Handicap Stakes 3yo+ 56-70 (E3)
£3433 £1056 £528   **1m141yaw rnd**   Inapplicable   Inside   [72]

4862 **BLUE MARINER 17** [12] P W Harris 4-9-5 (63) M Fenton 14/1: 3220001: In tch, styd on to lead ins   **70a**
fnl 1f, drvn out to hold on: eff at 7f/10f on fast grnd & polytrack: back to form on switch to AW: see 2694 & 2401.
4683 **TRUMAN 28** [11] J A R Toller 3-9-5 (67) S Sanders 10/1: 5-03502: Held up, outpcd 2f out, rallied   nk   **72a**
dist, kept on well, just held: eff at 6f, now stays 8.6f: acts on fast grnd & polytrack: unexposed at this trip.
4939 **MRS SHILLING 12** [13] J R Fanshawe 3-9-5 (67) L Dettori 3/1 FAV: 6-34243: Bhd, prog wide 3f out,   hd   **71a**
kept on ins fnl 1f, not btn far: eff at 7.4/8.6f on fast grnd & polytrack: proving consistent: see 4719.
4542 **JARVO 34** [4] N P Littmoden 3-8-12 (60) K Fallon 7/1: 4002304: Prom, led after 2f, hdd ins fnl   1   **62a**
1f, no extra: acts on fast, gd grnd & polytrack: btr 4542 (7f).
4743 **GRAND APOLLO 24** [5]3-9-6 (68) R Havlin 7/1: 2-2565: Bhd, prog bef 1f out, nrst fin: btr 4743.   1½   **67a**
4826 **PLAY BOUZOUKI 19** [3]3-9-7 (69) N Mackay(3) 10/1: 3406: Cl up till dist, no extra: AW bow: see 4228.   nk   **67a**

4867	**THE NUMBER** 17 [2]3-9-1 P (63) R Winston 9/2: 6-335267: Handy 6f, no extra: cheek pieces: btr 4520.	3½	54a
4636	**MUTASSEM** 30 [7]3-8-10 (58) B Reilly(3) 14/1: 0000028: Cl up over 6f, wknd: btr 4636 (6f, gd/soft).	4	41a
4578	**SUPAMACH** 32 [9]3-9-6 P (68) P Hanagan 20/1: 3440009: Mid div, wknd bef 1f out.	½	50a
5023	**GENTLE RAINDROP** 6 [6]3-8-10 bl (58) J F Egan 33/1: 5000000: 10th: Cl up over 5f, wknd: qck reapp.	22	4a
5080	**SAHARA SCIROCCO** 3 [1]3-8-13 (61) A Daly 100/1: 05040-00: 11th: Led 2f, fdd halfway.	11	0a
4937	**FOOLISH GROOM** 12 [8]3-9-6 (68) J Quinn 8/1: 635023P: Chsd ldrs till halfway, sn fdd, p.u. bef 1f out: prob something amiss: btr 4937.		0a

12 Ran Time 1m 51.29 (5.09) Owned: Graham & Lynn Knight Trained: Berkhamsted

---

5117   9.30 Ladbrokesgames Com Handicap Stakes 3yo+ 46-55 (F4)   **[67]**
£2992 £855 £427   **1m4f50y aw**   **Inapplicable**   Inside

4938*	**HEATHYARDS PRIDE** 12 [7] R Hollinshead 4-9-5 (58) K Fallon 5/4 FAV: 1045111: Bhd, prog wide over 1f out, led cl home, pushed out, val bit more: eff at 1m/9f, imprvd for recent step up to 11/12f: acts on firm, fast & both AW's: hold up performer who is progressing with racing: see 4938 & 4419.		67a+
4938	**FIELD SPARK** 12 [6] J A Glover 4-9-1 p (54) P Hanagan 6/1: 3020042: Rear, prog 3f out, kept on well ins fnl 1f, held by wnr: acts on firm, gd/soft & polytrack: h'capped to find similar: see 4938 & 3222.	½	59a
4708	**UNCLE JOHN** 26 [1] S Kirk 3-9-0 BL (60) J F Egan 33/1: 4240003: Handy, led 3f out, hdd well ins fnl 1f, no extra: back to form in blnks: see 3173 & 2024.	½	64a
4850	**KERNEL DOWERY** 17 [12] P W Harris 4-9-7 e (60) M Fenton 16/1: 1004504: Held up, prog 3f out, onepcd.	1¾	61a
4750	**MIDSHIPMAN** 24 [4]6-9-4 vis t (57) S W Kelly 6/1: 2224065: In tch, prog 2f out, no extra fnl 1f.	shd	57a
5062	**ZONIC BOOM** 4 [5]4-9-9 (62) L Dettori 11/2: 0-530306: Nvr nrr than mid div: AW bow: btr 4861 (10f).	3½	57a
4672	**TRUSTED MOLE** 28 [10]6-9-1 (54) B Swarbrick(5) 16/1: 6210007: Bhd, hdwy halfway, wknd bef 1f out.	6	40a
1396	**LAMPOS** 173 [9]4-9-1 p (54) R Winston 33/1: 1250008: Bhd, nvr a factor.	2	37a
4868	**HABITUAL** 17 [3]3-9-0 (60) S Sanders 10/1: 0045109: Handy over 1m, grad wknd: btr 4663 (2m).	1½	40a
4982	**DANGER BIRD** 9 [8]4-9-1 (54) R Kennemore(7) 25/1: 4415060: 10th: Led 9f, fdd: first try at 12f.	1¼	32a
4827	**FIT TO FLY** 19 [2]3-9-2 (62) B Reilly(3) 20/1: 6050000: 11th: Keen prom, fdd 3f out.	13	22a

11 Ran Time 2m 43.14(9.54) Owned: Mr L A Morgan Trained: Upper Longdon

---

Official Going Good/Soft

5118   11.15 Custom Kitchens Maiden Auction Stakes 2yo (H5)
£1498 £428 £214   **1m3y str**   **Good/Soft 80**   **-06 Slow**   Stands side

4848	**CAVA BIEN** 18 [1] J G Given 2-8-8 (70) M Fenton 8/1: 033051: Made all, hung left ins fnl 1f, all out to hold on: eff at 7/10f on fast & gd/soft grnd: see 3559 & 2810.		77
4792	**SUNNY TIMES** 21 [9] J W Payne 2-8-5 (57) F Norton 16/1: 50052: Held up, prog 2f out, kept on ins fnl 1f, post came too sn: eff around 1m on fast & gd/soft grnd: see 4792.	nk	72
4885	**THARUA** 15 [15] E A L Dunlop 2-8-6 K Fallon 1/3 FAV: 33: Cl-up, ev ch 2f out, hung right & onepcd bef dist: clr rem: handles today's gd/soft grnd on step up to 1m: see 4885 (fast).	1¼	71
4410	**SIRCE** 40 [5] D J Coakley 2-8-5 J Quinn 100/1: 06004: Show away, prog bef 1f out, nrst fin.	3½	63$
4451	**SLITE** 39 [12]2-8-5 (54) P Makin(1) 33/1: 02555: Cl-up, wknd dist: btr 3864 (fast).	hd	62$
4851	**MISTER ELEGANT** 17 [6]2-8-9 S Whitworth 25/1: 046: Handy over 6f, no extra: btr 4851.	½	65
4363	**ARCH FOLLY** 43 [14]2-8-9 A Beech(3) 25/1: 067: Handy over 6f, wkng when short of room ins fnl 1f.	¾	63
4632	**TIP TOES** 30 [16]2-8-3 (45) C Catlin 33/1: 0450648: Cl-up, wknd 2f out: see 4632.	shd	56$
	ROSE BIEN 0 [8]2-8-2 R Mullen 100/1: 9: b f Bien Bien - Madame Bovary (Ile de Bourbon) Bhd, nvr a factor on debut: Mar foal, cost 100,000gns: half-sister to numerous wnr: dam successful at 1m/12f.	3	49
4896	**MISS HERMIONE** 15 [7]2-8-3 Hayley Turner(3) 100/1: 00: 10th: ch f Bahamian Bounty - Try Vickers (Fuzzbuster) Mid-div till halfway, wknd: May foal, half-sister to wnrs at sprint/staying dists: dam plcd around 1m/10f: sire Gr winning performer at 6f as a juv: with Mrs C A Dunnett.	5	41
4971	**Precious Sammi** 10 [11]2-8-8 Lisa Jones 20/1:0	**Sign Of Promise** 0 [10]2-8-5 A McCarthy 25/1:0
4602	**Yankey** 31 [3]2-8-10 S Hitchcott 100/1:0	**Mishap** 0 [13]2-8-6 P Doe 16/1:0

14 Ran Time 1m 42.00 (6.9) Owned: Lovely Bubbly Racing Trained: Gainsborough

---

5119   11.45 Saltwell Signs Banded Stakes 3yo+ 0-45 (H5)
£1568 £448 £224   **1m3y str**   **Good/Soft 80**   **-02 Slow**   Stands side

4994	**CAERPHILLY GAL** 7 [5] P L Gilligan 4-9-5 (50) D Fox(5) 5/1: 0001231: Cl-up, styd on to lead despite hanging right dist, eased clr, pushed clr, eased: eff at 7f/1m on fast & gd/soft grnd.		58
4794*	**DANTES DEVINE** 21 [20] A Bailey 3-8-12 (46) V Slattery 7/1: 5040012: Mid-div, prog bef 1f out, kept on, not pace wnr: eff at 7f, now stays 1m: acts on fast & gd/soft grnd: remains in gd form: see 4794.	2	46
4902	**WOOD FERN** 14 [1] M R Channon 4-9-0 (45) S Hitchcott 12/1: 1004003: Cl-up, onepcd fnl 1f: see 4707.	½	44
4828	**MAGARI** 19 [18] J G Given 3-9-2 (50) M Fenton 20/1: 3-400534: In tch, onepcd dist: see 4828.	nk	48
4346	**FLYING SPUD** 44 [11]3-9-0 (48) D Nolan(3) 7/1: 0002005: Led 3f, no extra bef 1f out: 6 wk abs.	1	44
4901	**BLAKESEVEN** 14 [12]4-9-0 P (45) S Whitworth 16/1: 2230006: Dwelt, prog when no room dist, sn onepcd.	shd	40
4795	**CITY GENERAL** 21 [15]3-8-13 p (47) Derek Nolan(7) 9/1: 1056007: Cl-up, led 5f out, hdd bef 1f out, wknd.	½	41
4904*	**DELCIENNE** 14 [6]3-9-1 (49) A Beech(3) 13/2: 0215018: Nvr nrr than mid-div: op 5/1: btr 4904 (gd).	1¼	41
4660	**PIROUETTES** 28 [16]4-9-0 (45) D Corby(3) 40/1: 0-000049: Cl-up over 6f, wknd: btr 215 (AW).	¾	35
4795	**TOKEWANNA** 21 [8]4-9-3 t (48) W Supple 12/1: 0454350: 10th: Never nrr, nvr a factor: btr 4676 (7f, fast).	hd	37
4993	**ROCKY REPPIN** 7 [7]4-9-0 (45) J Edmunds 33/1: 0034000: 11th: Mid-div 6f, wknd: qck reapp.	1	32
4750	**LUCEFER** 24 [9]4-9-6 (50) N Chalmers(3) 9/2 FAV: 0310500: 12th: Al in rear: btr 4141.	1	35
4795	**SONDERBORG** 21 [10]3-9-1 bl (49) Lisa Jones 20/1: 0066630: 13th: Al bhd: btr 4795.	2½	29
4993	**ENCOUNTER** 7 [3]8-9-0 (45) L Keniry(3) 5/1: 0053520: 14th: Cl-up, fdd bef 1f out: qck reapp.	3	19
4828	**HOLD UP** 19 [17]3-9-2 (50) B Reilly(3) 20/1: 0000000: 15th: Mid-div 6f, wknd: btr 3711.	2½	19
2805	**Muqarrar** 110 [2]5-9-0 t(45) A McCarthy 40/1:0		

4371 **Brandywine Bay 42** [14]4-9-0 p(40) Hayley Turner(3) 20/1:0
4791 **Sunset Dreamer 21** [4]3-8-13 (47) I Mongan 40/1:0   4902 **Beltane 14** [13]6-9-0 (45) P Doe 50/1:0
19 Ran   Time 1m 41.71 (6.61)   Owned: Mr T Williams   Trained: Newmarket

5120 12.15 Futters Bookmakers Manager Of The Year Award Tri-Banded Stakes 3yo 0-45 (H5)
£1498 £428 £214   7f3y str   Good/Soft 80   -02 Slow   Stands side

4992 **ELSINORA 7** [2] A G Juckes 3-9-0 vis (45) C Catlin 11/4 FAV: 5242131: Held up, prog 3f out, styd   49
on to lead ins fnl 1f, rdn out: qck reapp: stays 1m, apprec rtn to 7f: acts on firm & soft grnd: eff in cheek
pieces, blnks or visor: in-form 3yo who can win again in this grade: see 4992 & 4901.
4794 **DAVIDS GIRL 21** [10] D Morris 3-8-9 (40) B Reilly(3) 8/1: 5006632: Bhd, prog 3f out, kept on ins   ½   42
fnl 1f, just denied: acts on fast & gd/soft grnd: can find similar: see 4794 & 1416.
4992 **PRIMATECH 7** [19] K A Morgan 3-8-9 p (40) P Fitzsimons 25/1: 0000403: Handy, ev ch well over 1f   1½   39
out, no extra fnl 1f: qck reapp: eff at 7f on gd/soft grnd: see 3900.
4992 **LA CALERA 7** [20] G C H Chung 3-9-0 bl (45) Dean Williams(7) 16/1: 3300504: In tch, led bef 3f out,   ½   43
hdd ins fnl 1f, no extra: qck reapp: btr 4165.
4992 **ROVING VIXEN 7** [5]3-8-9 (40) S Hitchcott 12/1: 3400565: Led, hdd bef 3f out, styd cl-up & ev ch   1¼   36
dist, sn no extra: op 9/1 on qck reapp: btr 2052 (fibresand).
4595 **TSARBUCK 32** [4]3-9-0 P (45) G Faulkner 9/1: 5233006: In tch over 5f, sn onepcd: cheek pieces.   2   37
4587 **TARDIS 32** [11]3-8-9 vis (40) J Quinn 14/1: 0000607: Cl-up, ev ch dist, sn wknd: 1st time visor.   ¾   30
4993 **PERERIN 7** [15]3-8-9 vis (40) M Fenton 8/1: 0030606: Nvr nrr than mid-div: qck reapp: btr 2339.   nk   29
4507 **CELLINO 35** [17]3-8-4 (35) N Chalmers(3) 33/1: 0400009: Nvr nrr than mid-div.   2   20
4616 **ZONNEBEKE 31** [7]3-9-0 (45) Hayley Turner(3) 6/1: 4120600: 10th: Rear, prog 3f out, wknd bef fnl   1½   27
1f, saddle slipped: op 9/1: btr 3706 & 3414.
4794 **JOANS JEWEL 21** [3]3-8-9 p (40) J Tate 50/1: 5600000: 11th: Cl-up alone far side over 5f, wknd.   3½   15
2852 **BOOKIESINDEXDOTCOM 108** [12]3-8-9 vis (40) W Supple 25/1: 6605560: 12th: Nvr nrr than mid-div.   1   13
4243 **BOPPYS BABE 49** [18]3-8-4 (30) P Doe 66/1: 00000-00: 13th: Al in rear: 7 wk abs.   1¾   4
4901 **MILITARY TWO STEP 14** [13]3-9-0 p (45) I Mongan 16/1: 2-000000: 14th: Handy 5f, wknd.   nk   13
4794 Silver Island 21 [6]3-8-9 T(40) R Mullen 16/1:0   2613 Petrion 117 [16]3-9-0 (45) D Corby(3) 33/1:0
4195 Shebaan 50 [9]3-8-9 (40) J Brennan(7) 66/1:0   4793 Pardon Moi 21 [14]3-8-9 (40) Lisa Jones 14/1:0
4216 La Fonteyne 50 [1]3-9-0 (45) S Whitworth 20/1:0   2274 Miss St Albans 131 [8]3-8-9 (40) A Kirby(7) 100/1:0
20 Ran   Time 1m 28.36 (5.76)   Owned: Mr R T Juckes   Trained: Abberley

5121 12.45 Custom Kitchens Banded Stakes 3yo+ 0-45 (H5)
£1512 £432 £216   6f3y str   Good/Soft 80   +03 Fast   Stands side

4905 **TAPPIT 14** [9] N E Berry 5-9-0 (45) R Mullen 25/1: 0006051: In tch, led 2f out, hung right for   49
press ins fnl 1f, styd on well: eff btwn 5.8f/7f on firm, soft & fibresand: win again in banded grade: see 963.
2347 **POLAR HAZE 128** [8] J Pearce 7-9-0 vis (40) M Fenton 14/1: 4550402: In tch, ev ch dist, not pace   1½   44
of wnr ins fnl 1f: long abs: gd eff in defeat but all wins have come on fibresand: see 1989 & btr 533 (AW).
1992 **INDIAN WARRIOR 144** [11] J Jay 8-9-0 bl (40) Liam Jones(7) 25/1: 4055003: Missed break, prog 2f   2   38
out, nrst fin: long abs: acts on firm, gd/soft & both AWs: btr 310 (7f, fibresand).
4995 **LAKELANDS LADY 7** [12] J Balding 4-9-0 (45) P Makin(5) 25/1: 00000004: In tch, onepcd dist: qck reapp. hd 37
4995 **LITTLE FLUTE 7** [2]3-8-13 (45) S Whitworth 8/1: 0016645: Mid-div, prog halfway, no impress fnl 1f. 1¼   33
4793 **AVIT 21** [18]4-9-0 (40) S Hitchcott 20/1: 4502006: In tch, ev ch dist, no extra: btr 3849 (5f, fast). hd   32
4793 **DANAKIM 5** [7]-9-0 (40) I Mongan 6/1 JT FAV: 0420047: In tch over 4f, hung right & no extra.   shd 31
4901 **WODHILL BE 14** [19]4-9-0 (40) Paul Eddery 8/1: 0000028: Missed break, prog & short of room bef 1f nk   30
out, eased ins fnl 1f: btr 4901 (7f).
4793 **ANGEL ISA 21** [3]4-9-0 vis (40) G Parkin 6/1 JT FAV: 0000339: In tch, outpcd halfway, rallied late. ½   29
4901} **TOM FROM BOUNTY 355** [1]4-9-0 (45) P Doe 66/1: 000000-0: 10th: ch g Opera Ghost - Tempus Fugit   1   26
(Timeless Times) Nvr nrr than mid-div on reapp: unplcd in '03 (rtd 60, mdn): has tried a t-strap.
3655 **ROYAL NITE OWL 75** [13]3-8-13 (40) W Supple 11/1: 0-004430: 11th: Led, hdd 2f out, wknd: new stable. 3   17
4995 **WHINHILL HOUSE 7** [16]4-9-0 (45) B Reilly(3) 8/1: 30-00030: 12th: In tch, wknd bef 1f out: qck reapp. hd 16
4995 **PLAYFUL SPIRIT 7** [4]5-9-0 vis (45) J Edmunds 10/1: 3000000: 13th: In tch, wknd bef 1f out: qck reapp. ½ 15
4256 **BANK GAMES 48** [14]3-8-13 BL (40) T Lucas 25/1: 006500: 14th: In tch 4f, wknd: 7 wk abs & 1st blnks. nk 14
4905 Scarlett Breeze 14 [10]3-8-13 (45) M Tebbutt 20/1:0   4794 Hi Darl 21 [20]3-8-13 (40) Rory Moore(5) 25/1:0
4370 Tamarella 42 [6]4-9-0 bl(45) A Beech(3) 20/1:0
4788 Caribbean Blue 21 [15]3-8-13 BL(40) Hayley Turner(3) 33/1:0
4905 Queen Of Bulgaria 14 [17]3-8-13 (40) P McCabe 25/1:0 4793 Sotonian 21 [7]11-9-0 (40) Lisa Jones 25/1:0
20 Ran   Time 1m 15.07 (4.67)   Owned: Mrs Jan Adams   Trained: Earlswood

5122 1.15 Advision Advertising Services Banded Stakes 3yo+ 0-45 (H5)
£1526 £436 £218   1m2f21y   Good/Soft 80   +04 Fast   Inside

4938 **ELLOVAMUL 12** [4] W M Brisbourne 4-9-1 (46) B Swarbrick(5) 14/1: 1000001: Held up, prog 3f out,   53
styd on to lead ins fnl 1f, pushed out, val bit more: eff at 1m/10f, stays a sharp 12f: acts on firm, gd/soft &
fibresand: apprec drop to banded grade with refitting of blnks: see 3492.
4903 **LENWADE 14** [7] G G Margarson 3-8-9 (45) A Beech(3) 13/2: 5221322: In tch, ev ch ins fnl 1f, not pace wnr2 48
4373 **MISS GLORY BE 42** [6] E R Oertel 6-9-0 p (45) Lisa Jones 16/1: 5233063: In tch, led 2f, hdd well   1½   45
ins fnl 1f, no extra: clr rem: 6 wk abs: btr 3823 (polytrack).
4857 **LARAD 17** [12] J S Moore 3-8-9 bl (45) Derek Nolan(7) 20/1: 0606504: In tch 1m, wknd: btr 1946 (fast). 6   36
4796 **TASNEEF 21** [13]5-9-3 (48) S Hitchcott 4/1 FAV: 0660445: Led 1m, sn wknd: btr 4796 (12f).   1¾   36
4791 **DANCING TILLY 21** [5]6-9-1 p (46) G Parkin 6/1: 2464126: Rear, prog 4f out, wknd fnl 2f: btr 4791 (fast). nk 33
5023 **PRINCESS BANKES 6** [14]3-8-9 (45) A Kirby(7) 50/1: 0004307: Bhd, hdwy 3f out, wknd bef 1f out.   1   30
4795 **IDLE JOURNEY 21** [9]3-8-12 (48) V Slattery 10/1: 0012048: Missed break, prog 4f out, wknd fnl 2f.   2   30

4008 **NO CHANCE TO DANCE** 60 [15]4-9-0 t (45) W Supple 13/2: 0436609: Nvr nrr than mid-div: 9 wk abs.   3½   22
4791 **FAIRLAND** 21 [1]5-9-1 (46) L Smith(7) 33/1: 3406000: 10th: Al bhd.   1¼   21
4348 **DEE PEE TEE CEE** 44 [3]10-9-0 (45) T Lucas 10/1: 0500/-030: 11th: Al in rear: 6 wk abs: btr 4348.   nk   19
4973 **RAHEEL** 10 [10]4-9-5 t (50) I Mongan 20/1: 0000000: 12th: Al in rear.   11   9
4411 **CONFUZED** 40 [8]4-9-0 e (45) R Mullen 5/1: 0400330: 13th: Keen cl-up, fdd: 6 wk abs: rcd far too keenly.   1   0
4261 Mount Cottage 48 [11]3-8-12 (48) M Fenton 33/1:0   4944 **Zarneeta** 12 [16]3-8-9 (45) M Tebbutt 50/1:0
15 Ran   Time 2m 11.81 (7.61)   Owned: Clayfields Racing   Trained: Nesscliffe

---

5123	1.45 Desira Motors Banded Stakes 3yo+ 0-45 (H5)
	£1505 £430 £215 1m6f17y Good/Soft 80 -19 Slow Inside

4965 **BANNINGHAM BLAZE** 11 [2] A W Carroll 4-9-8 bl (46) D Nolan(3) 7/2: 2232541: Held up, prog 3f out,   50
styd on to lead ins fnl 1f, rdn out, val bit more: eff at 12f/2m on firm, gd/soft & polytrack: eff with blnks:
tough 4yo who rarely runs a bad race: see 4965 & 4665.
4910 **TOUCH OF EBONY** 14 [6] C Roberts 5-9-7 p (45) A Medeiros(5) 25/1: 0002-002: In tch, led dist, hdd   nk   48
ins fnl 1f, styd on, just held by wnr: clr rem: left recent efforts bhd on rtn to 14f in banded grade: see 4910.
4255 **ANNAKITA** 48 [3] W J Musson 4-9-7 (45) Lisa Jones 3/1 FAV: 0004123: Rear, prog 4f out, onepcd.   3   45
4965 **REGENCY RED** 11 [7] W M Brisbourne 6-9-8 (46) B Swarbrick(5) 8/1: 0/-401004: Cl-up, led 2f out,   2½   44
hdd dist, wknd: btr 4716 (12f, fast).
4669 **RIBBONS AND BOWS** 28 [1]4-9-12 VIS (50) H Mongan 8/1: 0400455: In tch, led 3f out, hdd 2f out,   5   43
fdd: first time visor: rider reported mount did not stay: btr 4299.
5009 **LORD LAHAR** 7 [16]5-9-11 (49) S Hitchcott 8/1: 0504026: Nvr nrr than mid-div: 'hung right'.   6   37
4662 **SMARTER CHARTER** 28 [13]11-9-7 (35) Kristin Stubbs(7) 16/1: 0456437: Nvr nrr than mid-div: btr 4662.   2½   31
5042 **VENETIAN ROMANCE** 5 [5]3-8-12 (35) M Halford(7) 25/1: 0003008: Rear, nvr a factor: qck reapp.   ½   30
473} **WHO CARES WINS** 630 [8]8-9-7 (45) P McCabe 12/1: 0000//00-9: ch g Kris - Anne Bonny (Ajdal) Bhd,   11   20
nvr a factor: long jumps abs: fin 2nd of 10 in amat h'cap hdle (rtd 101h, stays 2m6f on gd & soft): amat hdle wnr
in 03/04 (rtd 111h): modest Flat form in both '03 starts (h'caps): 4th of 15 at best in '01 (rtd 68, h'cap): eff
at 14f, prob stays 2m: acts on fast & hvy grnd, tried blnks & visor.
1563 **LITTLE RICHARD** 164 [4]5-9-7 p (40) V Slattery 25/1: 4023540: 10th: Handy, fdd 3f out: long abs.   4   16
4423 **VANBRUGH** 40 [14]4-9-7 vis t (40) M Fenton 11/1: 000600: 11th: Cl-up, led 6f out, hdd 3f out, fdd.   5   11
3901} **RENS MAGIC** 417 [11]6-9-7 (35) W Supple 33/1: 000404-0: 12th: gr g Petong - Bath (Runnett) Al   3½   8
bhd: rnr-up on 1 of 3 03/04 hdle starts (rtd 86h, nov, stays 2m on firm): rnr-up on Flat once in '03 (rtd 47a, med
auct mdn): eff at 10/13f on fast, gd & polytrack: best without visor, tried t-strap.
2 Jan'03 Ling 12 ap 47a- E: 2 Aug'02 Wind 11.6 gd 45-43 E: 2 May'02 Yarm 10 g/f 44-43 F:
3679} **Yaheska** 426 [10]7-9-7 (35) R Mullen 20/1:0   3400 **Jazil** 85 [9]9-9-7 vis t(45) P Fitzsimons 25/1:0
14 Ran   Time 3m 11.69(13.89)   Owned: Mr Dennis Deacon   Trained: Alcester

---

Official Going GOOD/SOFT (SOFT after 4.10) - Rain through Afternoon.

5124	1.50 Racing Uk Live On 432 E B F Novice Stakes 2yo (D4)
	£3461 £1065 £532 5f rnd Soft Inapplicable Inside

4332 **REGINA** 44 [5] Sir Michael Stoute 2-9-0 (88) R Winston 15/8 FAV: 3161: Broke well & made all,   91
held on well fnl 1f, rdn out: hvly bckd, 6 wk abs: tried 6f, apprec return to 5f: acts on gd & soft grnd: runs
well fresh: likes to force the pace, useful filly, see 3993.
4981* **BOND CITY** 9 [7] B Smart 2-9-9 (91) F Lynch 2/1: 3525012: Chsd ldrs, went after wnr 2f out, kept   1   96
on & not btn far: well bckd, clr of rem: fine run conceding wnr 9lb: acts on firm, soft & polytrack.
4893 **BORN FOR DANCING** 14 [6] B W Hills 2-8-7 (73) A Culhane 7/2: 2523: Chsd ldrs, left bhd by front 2   10   58
fnl 2: disapp on this soft grnd: much btr 4893 (gd/firm).
4928 **WORLD AT MY FEET** 14 [2] N Bycroft 2-9-0 BL (81) N Callan 17/2: 1304004: Prom till halfway: tried   1¾   61
blnks, op 10/1: closer to today's 2nd in 4307 (gd grnd).
4962 **THORNBER COURT** 11 [1]2-8-7 (64) P Mathers(5) 12/1: 040235: Slowly away, nvr a factor.   1½   51
4928 **CILLAS SMILE** 14 [3]2-8-7 (55) Dale Gibson 50/1: 0606: Speed till halfway, sn bhd: highly tried.   7   36
4549 **MISS JELLYBEAN** 33 [4]2-8-7 P Mulrennan(3) 66/1: 007: Chsd ldrs, btn halfway: highly tried.   2   32
7 Ran   Time 1m 01.86 (4.56)   Owned: Cheveley Park Stud   Trained: Newmarket

5125	2.25 Totescoop6 Catterick Dash A Handicap Stakes 3yo+ 71-85 (D2)	[89]
	£13943 £4290 £2145 5f rnd Soft Inapplicable Inside	

4908 **MALAPROPISM** 14 [3] M R Channon 4-9-7 (82) A Culhane 14/1: 0661061: Chsd ldrs & remained far   91
side, led ent fnl 1f, styd on strongly, drvn out: best at 5/5.7f, stays 6f: acts on firm & soft grnd, any trk.
4780 **FURTHER OUTLOOK** 21 [14] D K Ivory 10-9-7 P (82) N Callan 6/1: 5150352: Led & came stands side,   ½   89
just btn in a close fin: excellent eff in first time cheek pieces, revels in soft & hvy grnd: see 4031 & 944.
4700 **DANCING MYSTERY** 26 [15] E A Wheeler 10-9-4 bl (79) S Carson 8/1: 0020033: Nvr far away stands   1   83
side, kept on well fnl 1f, not btn far: fine run on fav'd soft grnd, see 4700.
4652 **SIR DESMOND** 29 [4] R Guest 6-9-1 p (76) T P Queally 12/1: 1350404: Chsd ldrs & remained far side,   ¾   77
kept on under press fnl 1f: back to form on this rtn to soft grnd: see 4184.
4786 **ARTIE** 21 [10]5-9-10 (85) R Winston 11/2 FAV: 0000045: Prom stands side, onepcd fnl 1f: well bckd.   1¼   83
4822* **JADAN** 19 [13]3-9-3 (78) D Allan 6/1: 6150016: Held up stands side, styd on fnl 1f, nrst fin.   hd   76
4604 **HANDSOME CROSS** 31 [9]3-9-4 (79) L Fletcher(3) 16/1: 5560307: Prom stands side, onepcd fnl 1f.   1   74
4686 **BOND BOY** 28 [2]7-9-11 (68) F Lynch 11/1: 3000408: 2nd far side, onepcd fnl 1f.   nk   80
4652 **SIERRA VISTA** 29 [5]4-9-2 (77) L Enstone 14/1: 1600509: Prom far side, led briefly dist, onepcd.   1   68
4693 **BARON RHODES** 27 [12]3-9-5 (80) T Eaves(3) 14/1: 5130000: 10th: Prom stands side, btn dist.   nk   70
4855 **CURRENCY** 17 [11]7-9-1 (76) D Tudhope(5) 25/1: 5214500: 11th: Al bhd stands side: btr 3966 (gf).   ½   65
2841 **TAG TEAM** 108 [1]3-9-1 (76) Dane O'Neill 12/1: 3051320: 12th: Led till dist far side, wknd: abs.   1   62

4654 **PAX** 29 [7]7-9-3 (78) A Nicholls 33/1: 0000000: 13th: Dwelt, al bhd stands side: btr 2059.   2   59
4604 **SNOW WOLF** 31 [8]3-9-3 (78) Dale Gibson 33/1: 1200400: 14th: Held up stands side, al bhd.   2   54
3792 **AWAKE** 70 [16]7-9-9 (84) S W Kelly 16/1: 1620100: 15th: Trkd ldrs stands side, wknd 1.5f out: 10 wk abs.   ½   59
15 Ran   Time 1n 01.68 (4.38)   Owned: Mr Michael A Foy   Trained: West Ilsley

---

5126   3.00 Catterickbridge Co Uk Nursery Handicap Stakes 2yo 0-85 (D2)   [90]
£7183 £2210 £1105   7f rnd   Soft   Inapplicable   Inside

5021 **KNOCK BRIDGE** 6 [2] P D Evans 2-8-3 (65) T P Queally 14/1: 420301: Prom switched stands side   74
dist, sn led, styd on strongly, drvn out: first win: eff at 5/6f, apprec this step up to 7f: acts on firm, likes hvy.
4934 **GAME LAD** 12 [15] T D Easterby 2-8-11 (73) D Allan 9/1: 340302: Nvr far away, switched stands   nk   80
side 2f out & sn led, collared ins fnl 1f, only just btn: op 12/1: acts on fast, soft grnd & fibresand.
2612 **FORFEITER** 117 [14] T D Barron 2-9-0 (76) N Callan 50/1: 26223: Front rank, led stands side 2f   1½   80
out, hdd dist, no extra ins fnl 1f: long abs & has been gelded: acts on firm & soft grnd, clrly runs well fresh:
blnks omitted today, see 2612 & 2462.
4673 **WAYWARD SHOT** 28 [8] M W Easterby 2-7-12 (2oh) (58) Dale Gibson 22/1: 50054: Mid-div, stands side,   nk   63
kept on fnl 1f, nrst fin: imprvd form, stays 7f on soft grnd, 1m will suit: see 4673.
4670* **LESLINGTAYLOR** 28 [1]2-8-13 (75) R Winston 12/1: 5315: Held up, imprvd to chase ldrs 2f out, onepcd. 1¼   76
5031 **BROOKLIME** 6 [13]2-9-4 (80) S W Kelly 11/1: 1052606: Led till 2f out, switched stands side & sn onepcd. shd 81
4882 **BREAKING SHADOW** 16 [9]2-9-1 (77) T Hamilton(3) 8/1: 2331067: Rear stands side, nvr nr ldrs.   shd 80
4934 **PAULINES PRINCE** 12 [6]2-8-3 (65) Stephanie Hollinshead(5) 40/1: 61408: Trkd ldrs stands side, onepcd. nk 65
4691 **BOO** 27 [10]2-8-6 (68) L Enstone 25/1: 4649: Trkd ldrs stands side, wknd fnl 1f: h'cap bow: see 4691.   ½   67
4480 **FOLLOWING FLOW** 37 [4]2-9-7 (83) F Lynch 16/1: 031200: 10th: Nvr a factor: jt top-weight: btr 4074.   1¼   80
4894 **ELTIZAAM** 15 [16]2-8-12 (74) O Urbina 9/1: 656350: 11th: Trkd ldrs stands side, wknd dist.   1¼   69
4591* **HADRIAN** 32 [7]2-9-7 (83) S Chin 7/2 FAV: 6210: 12th: Outpcd, nvr a factor: jt top-weight & well   2½   74
bckd: not handle this soft grnd, much btr on fast & firm in 4591 & 3935.
4725 **SHIVAREE** 25 [5]2-9-7 (83) A Culhane 16/1: 3140300: 13th: Chsd ldrs, wknd dist: jt top-weight.   nk   73
4963 **MY PRINCESS** 11 [3]2-9-2 (78) A Mullen(7) 5/1: 3105520: 14th: Sn outpcd, fin last: btr 4963 (gd).   2   65
14 Ran   Time 1m 32.17 (9.17)   Owned: Diamond Racing Ltd   Trained: Abergavenny

---

5127   3.35 Goracing Co Uk Median Auction Maiden Stakes Div 1 2yo (E4)
£2976 £850 £425   7f rnd   Soft   Inapplicable   Inside

4726 **KANAD** 25 [1] B Hanbury 2-9-0 BL t (75) N Callan 9/2: 320251: Trkd ldrs, went on dist, rdn clr fnl   80
1f: tchd 11/2, first time blnks: apprec this longer 7f trip, acts on fast, clrly relishes soft grnd: handles a
sharp trk & wears a t-strap, suited by blnks today: see 4443 & 1987.
4417 **FOXY GWYNNE** 40 [2] A M Balding 2-8-9 Dane O'Neill 5/2 FAV: 032: Led till dist, kept on fnl 1f   2½   70
but not pace of wnr: well bckd, 6 wk abs: acts on fast & soft grnd: shld find a small race: see 4417.
4741 **CHICKEN SOUP** 24 [6] J A Osborne 2-9-0 (73) S W Kelly 11/2: 63003: Held up, styd far side & late   ½   74
hdwy, nrst fin: op 9/2, well clr rem: acts on soft grnd & polytrack, poss gd: stays 7f: see 4178.
4691 **PETER ROUGHLEY** 27 [10] A Berry 2-9-0 P Bradley 66/1: 00: Chsd ldrs, wknd dist: see 4691.   9   58
4673 **ZANTERO** 28 [3]2-9-0 (57) T Hamilton(3) 9/1: 4646065: Chsd ldrs, wkng when short of room dist: op 14/1. hd   57
4769 **STEVMARIE STAR** 22 [9]2-9-0 R Winston 14/1: 06: b f Muhtarram - Cabaret Artiste (Shareef Dancer)   2½   48
Chsd lds 5f, sn btn: 5,700gns Apr foal: half-sister to sev wnrs, incl 7f juv scorer Misalliance: dam unrcd, sire
a top-class mid-dist performer: with J Glover.
4816 **JEFFSLOTTERY** 19 [7]2-9-0 P Mulrennan(3) 100/1: 067: Chsd ldrs 5f, sn btn: see 4816.   4   47
4711 **FRANELA** 26 [5]2-8-9 T P Queally 11/1: 08: b f Dansili - Pernilla (Tate Gallery) Al rear: Apr   4   36
foal, half-sister to sev wnrs, incl 7f scorer Hunting Tiger: dam a useful 7f wnr, sire a high-class miler.
      WATERLOO CORNER [8]2-9-0 T Eaves(3) 80/1: 9: b g Cayman Kai - Rasin Luck (Primitive Rising)   20   11
Slowly away, al bhd, t.o. on debut: Mar first foal, sire a high-class 6f/1m performer: with R Craggs.
4653 **BRANDEXE** 29 [4]2-8-9 (69) A Culhane 3/1: 0540: 10th: Rdn in rear, t.o. from halfway & virtually   dist 0
p.u.: well bckd: something clrly amiss.
10 Ran   Time 1m 33.30 (10.30)   Owned: Mr Ibrahim Belselah   Trained: Newmarket

---

5128   4.10 Moulton Apprentice Claiming Stakes 3yo+ (F4)
£3044 £870 £435   1m3f214y   Soft   Inapplicable   Inside

4805* **YENALED** 20 [12] N Wilson 7-9-9 (70) Donna Caldwell(7) 10/3: 4210411: Keen in rear, gd hdwy to   83
lead ent fnl 1f, pushed clr: well bckd: eff at 7/12f on firm, soft & fibresand: suited by claim grade: fine start
for new yard (prev wth K Ryan), see 4805 & 4173.
5024 **GOLD GUEST** 6 [3] P D Evans 5-8-13 (62) T P Queally 11/4 FAV: 1004562: Trkd ldrs, led after 1m &   5   63
sn clr, collared ent fnl 1f, no extra: nicely bckd, well clr rem: stays 12f, suited by 9/10f: acts on fast & soft,
likes Lingfield/polytrack: gd run but met an in-form rival: see 339 (AW).
4675 **PETERS IMP** 28 [2] A Berry 9-8-13 (45) P Mathers(5) 9/1: 0-153403: Rear, mod hdwy, nvr dngrs.   17   43
521   **NEWTONIAN** 259 [9] J Parkes 5-8-13 (69) M Lawson(5) 14/1: 6/23-304: Keen in rear, nvr a factor: 2½   40
long abs: sharpener for AW campaign? see 388 & 194.
4092 **SILVER RHYTHM** 57 [11]3-8-3 (46) A Elliott(7) 20/1: 0-350005: Chsd ldrs 10f, sn wknd: 8 wk abs.   1   36
3632 **KINGS WELCOME** 787 [10]6-9-9 (92) P Mulrennan 3/1: 22/4210/-6: b g Most Welcome - Reine de   9   37
Thebes (Darshaan): Prom, wknd 2f out on comeback: missed '03 & has been gelded: prev term won an Ascot h'cap:
eff at 12f on fast & hvy grnd, handles any trk: runs well fresh: formerly useful, clrly had his problems.
1 Aug'02 Asco 12 g 94-88 B: 2 Jul'02 Leic 11.8 g/f 94-88 C: 2 Jun'01 Hayd 12 gd 100-90 B:
2 May'01 York 10.3 g/f 90-84 B: 2 Apr'01 Pont 10 hvy 87- C:
5042 **VALIANT AIR** 5 [7]3-8-4 (1ow) (40) T Eaves 25/1: 4004507: Prom, wknd 3f out: qck reapp.   7   15
4766 **ADJAWAR** 22 [6]6-9-9 (75) T Hamilton 12/1: 0610-008: Trkd ldrs 1m, sn btn: see 3945.   6   18
4716 **SHAMELESS** 25 [4]7-8-10 t R Keogh(5) 80/1: 0009: ch g Prince Daniel - Level Edge (Beveled) Led   16   0
1m, wknd qckly: no form: see 3824.
4716 **MODULOR** 25 [8]12-8-12 (20w) L Fletcher 100/1: ////////-00: 10th: Al bhd, t.o.: see 4716.   2½   0
464} **ZAMIR** 15 [5]5-8-10 VIS (30) D Tudhope(5) 50/1: 0000/P0-0: 11th: b g Zaminder - Fairy Flax   dist 0
(Dancing Brave) Al bhd, t.o.: tried a visor: p.u. in a nov hdle 8 days ago (t-strap): no Flat form, incl for A Crook in '03.
11 Ran   Time 2m 48.20 (17.00)   Owned: Watson Wilson Mckinnon   Trained: York

5129

4.45 Course With Character Classified Stakes 3yo+ 0-60 (F3)
£3435 £1057 £529   1m5f175y   **Soft**   **Inapplicable**   Inside

4966 **EGO TRIP 11** [7] M W Easterby 3-8-9 bl (65) Dale Gibson 11/4 FAV: 1304121: Prom, came stands side,   **71**
went on over 1f out, styd on strongly, drvn out: well bckd: continues in fine form, eff at 12f, apprec this step up
to 14f: acts on firm & soft grnd: suited by blnks now & in top form, see 4966 & 4594.
5025 **SNOWS RIDE 6** [5] W R Muir 4-9-4 (58) T P Queally 7/2: 0064042: Trkd ldrs, led 3f out till over   2½   **66**
1f out, kept on but not pace of wnr: bckd from 5/1, clr of rem: met an in-form rival: see 4276.
4721 **CAPITOLE 25** [6] E F Vaughan 3-8-9 (60) Dane O'Neill 16/1: 045403: Rear, prog to chase ldrs 3f   6   **58**
out, onepcd fnl 1.5f: remains a mdn, prob stays an easy 14f on soft grnd: see 4546 (1m, first time visor).
4348 **SCURRA 44** [1] A C Whillans 5-9-4 (58) D Tudhope(5) 13/2: 1246524: Chsd ldrs, wknd fnl 1.5f: 6 wk abs.   9   **46**
5032 **PLATINUM CHARMER 5** [8]4-9-4 p (53) Darren Williams 12/1: 3251065: Chsd ldrs, outpcd 3f out.   8   **36**
4892 **KEY IN 15** [4]3-8-6 (60) A Culhane 11/2: 0636: Chsd ldrs, lost pl halfway, no ch after: op 7/1.   ½   **32**
701 **VIVRE SA VIE 236** [2]3-8-6 (60) N Callan 5/1: 43257: Led till 3f out, wknd: well bckd after long abs.   21   **7**
4475▶ **SIR EDWARD BURROW 1092** [3]6-9-4 (35) J Bramhill 66/1: 306000//-8: b g Distinctly North - Alalja   5   **4**
(Entitled) Chsd ldrs till halfway, sn btn & t.o. on comeback: last rcd in '01 (with R Fisher) & has since been
gelded: h'cap plcd in '01 (rtd 90): prob stays a sharp 2m & acts on fast grnd: mdn, now with W Storey.
4764 **COLONNADE 23** [10]5-9-1 (45) P Mathers(5) 66/1: 0-203009: Held up, al bhd, t.o.   2½   **0**
4966 **ABBEYGATE 11** [11]3-8-9 t (55) O Urbina 40/1: 06-00000: 10th: Chsd ldrs till halfway, t.o.   5   **0**
4045 **TIOGA GOLD 58** [9]5-9-4 (30) T Williams 100/1: 400-5000: 11th: Rdn in rear, t.o. fnl 4f: 8 wk abs.   10   **0**
11 Ran   Time 3m 17.85 (22.45)   Owned: Mr K Hodgson & Mrs J Hodgson   Trained: Sheriff Hutton

5130

5.20 Tote Big Screen Is Here Handicap Stakes 3yo+ 56-70 (E3)   **[80]**
£3582 £1102 £551   **7f rnd**   **Soft**   **Inapplicable**   Inside

5069* **NORTHERN GAMES 4** [14] K A Ryan 5-9-5 (6ex)bl (71) A Mullen(7) 7/2 FAV: 1424211: Front rank, sn   **83**
led, styd on strongly fnl 1f, won pushed out: nicely bckd, qck reapp: eff at 6/7f on fast, soft grnd & fibresand:
likes a sharp/turning or gall trk: wears blnks or cheek pieces: in fine form & could complete hat-trick, see 5069.
5017 **LEGAL SET 6** [6] Miss A Stokell 8-8-8 t (60) T P Queally 10/1: 0240052: Chsd ldrs, kept on under   3   **65**
press, not reach wnr: qck reapp: acts on firm, soft grnd & polytrack: see 2713.
4652 **BOND PLAYBOY 29** [8] B Smart 4-9-0 (66) F Lynch 20/1: 0031103: Led early, remained prom & styd   3   **66**
far side str, no extra fnl 1f: stays 7f, all wins at 6f: see 4245 (6f).
4820 **STRONG HAND 19** [15] M W Easterby 4-9-6 (72) P Mulrennan(3) 8/1: 3000624: Chsd ldrs, onepcd.   nk   **71**
5014 **NO GROUSE 6** [18]4-8-11 p (63) T Hamilton(3) 12/1: 0505425: Chsd ldrs wide, not pace to chall.   2   **59**
5109 **SENESCHAL 1** [1]3-9-5 (6ex) T O'Brien(7) 10/1: 00051626: Held up, prog when short of room   1¼   **67**
halfway, nvr rchd ldrs: qck reapp: rnr-up at Redcar yesterday: see 5109 & 5014.
4168▶ **PLUM 52** [4]4-9-4 (70) Dane O'Neill 4/1: 443-17: Chsd ldrs, onepcd fnl 2f: bckd from 11/2, 7 wk abs.   1¼   **62**
4820 **QUALITAIR WINGS 19** [7]5-9-4 (70) N Callan 12/1: 2063058: Rear, late prog, nvr dngrs.   1   **60**
4989 **PRINCE OF GOLD 8** [13]4-8-13 p (65) A Culhane 8/1: 0005329: Nvr btr than mid-div: btr 4989 (5f).   2½   **52**
4986 **MEZUZAH 8** [12]4-9-8 (74) Dale Gibson 40/1: 06-05000: 10th: Rear, nvr ldrs ldrs: see 4986.   ½   **60**
4867 **SARRAAF 17** [2]8-8-9 (61) T Eaves(3) 20/1: 0346040: 11th: Slowly away, nvr nr ldrs: new stable.   2½   **44**
4999 **HILLS OF GOLD 7** [13]5-9-9 (75) P Fessey 25/1: 2146600: 12th: Al rear: see 4051.   ½   **57**
4747 Semenovskii 24 [10]4-9-4 (70) Darren Williams 33/1:0   5057 **Marinaite 4** [3]3-9-7 (73) J Bramhill 16/1:0
2235 Aventura 133 [5]4-9-6 (72) L Fletcher(3) 50/1:0.0   5014 **Jubilee Street 6** [9]5-8-10 (62) D Allan 12/1:0
16 Ran   Time 1m 32.07 (9.07)   Owned: Mr R E Robinson   Trained: Hambleton

5131

5.50 Goracing Co Uk Median Auction Maiden Stakes Div 2 2yo (E4)
£2976 £850 £425   **7f rnd**   **Soft**   **Inapplicable**   Inside

4843 **QAWAAFIL 18** [5] E A L Dunlop 2-8-9 (64) O Urbina 5/1: 5001: Chsd ldrs, kept on under press to   **74**
lead ins fnl 1f, drvn out: tchd 13/2: apprec this step up to 7f & first try on soft grnd: handles a sharp trk.
4816 **FINE LADY 19** [6] M Johnston 2-8-9 (69) S Chin 2/1 FAV: 6232: Led till ins fnl 1f, no extra: ¾   **72**
well bckd & clr of rem: eff at 7f/1m on gd & soft grnd: deserves a small race, see 4816 & 4483.
4417 **PONENTE 40** [8] B W Hills 2-8-9 A Culhane 9/2: 603: b f Robellino - Polmara (Polish Precedent)   8   **60**
Trkd ldrs, led bhd by front 2 fnl 1.5f: op 7/2, 6 wk abs: Apr first foal: sire a high-class juv: mod form to date.
 BOND CAT [2] B Smart 2-8-10 (1ow) F Lynch 11/1: 4: ch f Raise A Grand - Merrily (Sharrood)   3½   **56**
Slow away, nvr nr ldrs on debut: Feb foal, cost £50,000: half-sister to sprint wnr Vigorous: sire a high-class juv.
4865 **CHAMPAGNE LUJAIN 17** [4]2-9-0 P Mulrennan(3) 50/1: 05: b g Lujain - Brief Glimpse (Taufan) Trkd   2   **57**
ldrs 6f, wknd qckly: Jan foal, half-brother to 1m scorer Once Seen: dam a 5/6f juv wnr, sire a top-class sprinter.
4443 **BEAUCHAMP TURBO 39** [9]2-9-0 N Callan 10/3: 556: Chsd ldrs 5f: well bckd: best 4178 (AW).   5   **49**
4859 **ITALIAN TOUCH 17** [10]2-9-0 Dane O'Neill 7/1: 0007: Front rank till halfway, sn bhd, t.o.: op 20/1.   8   **37**
4769 **JUST ELIZABETH 22** [7]2-8-9 T Eaves(3) 50/1: 08: Chsd ldrs 5f, wknd qckly.   16   **12**
4988 **RUSSIANNIGHTINGALE 8** [1]2-9-0 J D O'Reilly(7) 80/1: 09: Slowly away, al bhd, t.o. in last.   6   **9**
9 Ran   Time 1m 36.13(13.13)   Owned: Mr Hamdan Al Maktoum   Trained: Newmarket

Official Going Soft (Heavy places)

5132　1.05 Gr3 Cornwallis Stakes 2yo　(A1)
£17400　£6600　£3300　5f str　Soft　Slow　Stands Side

4684　**CASTELLETTO 28** [6] B A McMahon 2-8-9 (98) G Gibbons 15/2: 2125231: Led 1f, cl-up, led over 1f　　　**106**
out, rdn to hold on: eff at 5/6f on fast, enjoys soft grnd & gall trks: proving tough, useful, genuine & prog.

1422　**CORNUS 171** [3] R Hannon 2-8-12 (95) R L Moore 12/1: 1122: Hld up, hdwy over 1f out, styd on ins　¾　**107**
last, al just held: long abs & excellent return stepped up in class: likes gd/soft & soft: relish 6f.

4960* **KAY TWO 13** [9] Ms F M Crowley 2-9-1　M J Kinane 5/1: 2415113: Cl-up, eff over 1f out, onepace.　1½　**107**

4998　**JOSEPH HENRY 7** [5] M Johnston 2-8-12 (100) K Darley 9/2: 1144: Dwelt, hdwy to lead after 1f till　hd　**103**
over 1f out, onepace: well bckd: ran to best, List will suit: see 4998, 1466.

4888　**PRINCE CHARMING 15** [14]2-9-1 (100) L Dettori 100/30 FAV: 1106105: In tch, eff dist, onepace.　1　**104**

4960　**TOURNEDOS 13** [4]2-9-3 (100) T E Durcan 9/1: 1032526: In tch, onepace over 1f out: big weight.　1　**103**

4533　**BUNDITTEN 35** [13]2-8-9 (93) J F Egan 50/1: 134407: In tch, no extra dist: see 2490, 2094.　nk　**94**

4533　**SUMORA 35** [11]2-8-12 (100) J Fortune 8/1: 1168: Dwelt, held up, no impress: btr 3956 (5f, fast).　1½　**94**

4928　**AMAZIN 14** [2]2-8-12 (99) R Hughes 33/1: 2125409: Slow away & nvr a factor.　1½　**91**

4458　**RIGHT ANSWER 38** [8]2-8-9 (97) K Fallon 20/1: 1225300: 10th: Dwelt, in tch, wknd 2f out.　¾　**86**

5087　**PITCH UP 2** [10]2-8-12 (87) G Carter 50/1: 6115000: 11th: In tch, wknd 2f out: see 4533, 3743.　nk　**88**

11 Ran　Time 1m 01.79 (3.59)　Owned: Mr J C Fretwell　Trained: Tamworth

5133　1.35 Gr2 Owen Brown Rockfel Stakes Fillies 2yo　(A1)
£40600　£15400　£7700　7f str　Soft　Slow　Stands Side

4798　**MAIDS CAUSEWAY 21** [1] B W Hills 2-8-12 (100) M Hills 3/1 FAV: 2121321: Chsd ldr, led over 2f out　　　**110**
till ins last, rallied most gamely to get up again on line: hvly bckd: stays 1m well, clearly v eff at 7f: acts on
firm & soft grnd, fair or gall trks: yet to run a below par race: smart, v genuine & tough, more to come: see 4476.

4914* **PENKENNA PRINCESS 14** [11] R M Beckett 2-8-9 (100) S Sanders 7/1: 01312: Chsd ldrs, eff well over　shd　**106**
1f out, styd on to lead just ins last, hdd on line: excellent run stepped up in class & acts on firm & soft grnd:
progressing with every run & can win a Gr race: see 4914.

4914　**FAVOURITA 14** [7] C E Brittain 2-8-9 (100) T Quinn 7/1: 14523: Handy, eff over 1f out, kept on,　¾　**104**
not btn far: bckd, clr rem: another progressive filly: shaped like she will relish 1m+ next term: see 4914.

5072* **BIBURY FLYER 6** [3] M R Channon 2-8-9 (89) T E Durcan 12/1: 3324514: In tch, eff & hung right 2f　3½　**98**
out, kept on same pace: qck reapp, shade btr 5072 (6f).

4431* **CHEROKEE 41** [4]2-8-12　J P Spencer 4/1: 15: In tch, eff over 1f out, no extra: 6 wk abs:　2　**98**
btr expected after Gr 3 win on fast grnd in 4431 but reportedly not handle this testing grnd.

4679　**JUSTAQUESTION 28** [5]2-8-9 (93) J Fortune 16/1: 0321506: Dwelt, nvr a factor: see 4679, 3774.　2½　**91**

4484* **SHES MY OUTSIDER 37** [9]2-8-9 (82) F Norton 40/1: 0317: Keen, bhd, no impress: see 4484 (mdn).　4　**84**

4710* **FEN SHUI 26** [8]2-8-9　L Dettori 7/2: 18: Led till 2f out, wknd: stiff task: see 4710 (mdn, g/f).　9　**68**

8 Ran　Time 1m 28.93 (5.73)　Owned: Mr Martin S Schwartz　Trained: Lambourn

5134　2.05 Gr2 Victor Chandler Challenge Stakes 3yo+　(A1)
£58000　£22000　£11000　7f str　Soft　Fair　Stands Side

4477　**FIREBREAK 37** [9] Saeed bin Suroor 5-9-4 t (116) L Dettori 11/2: 005-1421: Made all, styd on well　　　**119**
over 1f out, drvn out: v eff at 7f, stays 1m well on firm, soft & dirt, any trk: v tough, smart & genuine: see 988.

4731　**KELTOS 14** [13] C Laffon Parias 6-9-0　O Peslier 6/1: 1222352: In tch, hdwy over 1f out, styd on　1　**113**
ins last, al just held by wnr: still smart & likes soft grnd: see 4311.

4949　**POLAR BEAR 14** [7] W J Haggas 4-9-0 (108) K Fallon 5/1 FAV: 1-301103: In tch, hdwy over 1f out,　nk　**112**
kept on ins last, not btn far: relished return to soft surface: tough & smart: see 4063.

4874　**POLAR WAY 16** [14] Mrs A J Perrett 5-9-0 (114) R Hughes 11/1: 0320134: Handy trav well, no extra　2½　**108**
fnl 1f: gd run, prob prefer a sounder surface as in 4270 (stks).

4060　**BALMONT 58** [8]3-8-12 (112) J P Spencer 9/1: 110-3205: Held up, hdwy over 1f out, sn no impress:　1¾　**105**
well bckd: 2 mth abs: up in trip, prob best at 6f & on a sounder surface: smart efforts in 3409 & 3062 (6f, fast).

　　　CARADAK 27 [2]3-8-12　M J Kinane 20/1: 41136: b c Desert Style - Caraiyma (Shahrastani) Handy,　½　**104**
wknd over 1f out: Irish raider, earlier won a mdn & List: stays 1m on fast grnd.

4874　**VANDERLIN 16** [1]5-9-0 (105) Martin Dwyer 20/1: 3103327: In tch, wknd dist: see 4874 (Gr 3, gd).　3½　**98**

4811* **BADMINTON 20** [4]3-8-9 t (107) K McEvoy 10/1: 123-18: Chsd wnr, wknd 2f out: not handle soft?　3½　**89**

4887 + **POLAR BEN 15** [10]5-9-0 (111) J Murtagh 11/2: 00-22019: Held up, hdwy trav well & short of room　shd　**92**
over 2f out, sn rdn & no extra: btr expected after 4887 & does handle this testing grnd.

4797} **CAPE FEAR 364** [5]3-8-12 (110) J Fortune 33/1: 132510-0: 10th: Slow away, nvr a factor.　1½　**90**

4799　**GOLDEN NUN 21** [6]4-8-11 bl (104) T Quinn 25/1: 0505400: 11th: Handy, wknd 2f out: lost action.　18　**59**

4811　**TAHIRAH 20** [3]4-8-11 (85) S Sanders 66/1: 0000030: 12th: Al bhd: see 4811, 2532.　8　**45**

12 Ran　Time 1m 27.22 (4.02)　Owned: Godolphin　Trained: Newmarket

5135　2.45 Totesport Cesarewitch Heritage Handicap 3yo+　(B1)
£75400　£28600　£14300　2m2f　Soft　Fair　Far Side　　　**[109]**

4106　**CONTACT DANCER 56** [18] M Johnston 5-8-2 (83) R Ffrench 16/1: 12/56-641: Cl-up, led over 2f out,　　　**94**
held on gamely for press ins last: suited by 2m2f & loves gd/soft & hvy, acts on fast: likes gall trks: useful,
lightly rcd this term: goes well fresh: more to come for outstanding trainer: see 3181.

4647　**MR ED 29** [12] P Bowen 6-7-13 p (80) J Quinn 10/1 JT FAV: 00-22122: Keen in tch, hdwy over 1f out,　½　**90**
kept on ins last, just btn: excellent run up in class & stays 2m2f well on fast & soft grnd: see 3688.

4634 + **HIGH POINT 30** [32] G P Enright 6-7-12 (3ex)(1oh) (78) S Whitworth 50/1: 3360513: Held up, hdwy　hd　**88**
over 3f out, kept on to chall ins last, not btn far: at the top of his form: stays 2m2f on fm, soft & polytrack.

4924　**QUEDEX 14** [19] R J Price 8-7-12 (5oh) (74) C Haddon(7) 33/1: 5211004: In tch, eff over 1f out,　½　**87**
kept on same pace: joc received a 3-day whip ban: excellent run from 5oh: see 3275.

4803* **ESCAYOLA 21** [35]4-8-9 (5ex)vis (90) J F Egan 20/1: 0200215: Held up, hdwy 2f out, kept on, not　1　**97**

btn far: progressive young stayer: acts on firm & soft: more to come, see 4803.
4634 **LAND N STARS 30** [20]4-8-2 (3ex)(1ow) (82) P Doe 33/1: 0154136: Held up, eff over 2f out, kept on, ½ **89**
no threat: thorough stayer: acts on firm & soft: see 4634, 4527.
2771* **MIRJAN 112** [29]8-8-12 bl (93) P Hanagan 14/1: 404////-317: In tch, hdwy on bit over 2f out, ½ **98**
onepace for press over 1f out: 4 mth abs & ran right up to winning form of 2771 (2m): stays 2m2f.
3531 **DISTANT PROSPECT 80** [3]7-8-11 (92) L Dettori 10/1 JT FAV: 3-420038: In tch, onepace over 2f out. *nk* **97**
4778 **TRANCE 21** [16]4-8-6 (87) P Makin(4) 50/1: 1100039: Bhd, late gains, nvr dngrs: prob stays 2m2f. *1* **91**
4808 **KRISTENSEN 20** [26]5-7-12 (2oh)p (77) J F McDonald(2) 33/1: 5003020: 10th: Handy, eff to chall over *hd* **83**
2f out, sn no extra: see 4808, 3999.
1502* **THE LAST CAST 167** [7]5-7-12 (3oh) (76) F P Ferris(3) 16/1: 00226/-10: 11th: Handy, led 10f out *1¼* **82**
till over 2f out, wknd: nicley bckd: long abs: longer trip: see 1502 (14f).
4634 **HALLAND 30** [10]6-8-1 (82) N Mackay(3) 66/1: 12//00-000: 12th: Held up, mod late gains, no dngr. *nk* **84**
4803 **THEATRE 21** [5]5-7-12 (2oh) (77) A McCarthy 66/1: 2300000: 13th: In tch, wknd 2f out: see 2899. *1¼* **80**
4796} **DUBAI SEVEN STARS 364** [36]6-7-12 (9oh) (70) D Fox(5) 66/1: 526000-0: 14th: In tch, wknd 2f out. *2* **78**
4657 **HISTORIC PLACE 29** [31]4-7-13 (80) R Thomas(3) 20/1: 24030: 15th: Nvr a factor: see 4657. *1¾* **77**
2567 **MONOLITH 119** [33]6-7-13 (80) N De Souza(1) 14/1: 4361//-30: 16th: In tch, wknd 2f out: long abs. *2½* **75**
4527 **ALMIZAN 35** [30]4-8-1 vis (82) C Catlin 33/1: 0404300: 17th: Al bhd: btr 4106, see 3531. *2½* **75**
4838* **NO REFUGE 21** [9]4-9-12 (7ex)BL (107) S Sanders 16/1: 2132-310: 18th: In tch, wknd over 2f out: *nk* **99**
tried blnks: best 4838.
4196 **LAGGAN BAY 50** [34]4-7-12 (7oh)vis (72) D Fentiman(7) 100/1: 12-06000: 19th: Al bhd. *4* **67**
3776 **PENNY PICTURES 70** [21]5-8-6 (87) R L Moore 16/1: 2234/-350: 20th: Slow away & lost many lengths, *2½* **73**
nvr a factor: rcd in a h'cap hdle since 3776.
4808* **ASTYANAX 20** [13]4-7-12 (3ex) (79) J Mackay 33/1: 5010210: 21th: Handy, wknd 3f out: btr 4808. *5* **60**
4623 **NAKWA 30** [11]6-8-1 (3ow)(14oh) (65) A Daly 100/1: 1260000: 22th: Keen in tch, wknd over 3f out. *½* **63**
4803 **MIDAS WAY 21** [4]4-9-0 (95) J Murtagh 20/1: 320-2030: 23th: In tch, wknd 4f out: btr 4803 (fast). *1½* **85**
4889 **KING EIDER 15** [23]5-8-5 (86) T E Durcan 16/1: 5603-000: 24th: In tch, wknd over 3f out. *14* **52**
4796} **ITS DEFINITE 364** [24]5-7-13 (1ow)(4oh)p (75) F Norton 33/1: 103200-0: 25th: In tch, wknd 4f out. *16* **36**
4803 **STANCE 21** [2]5-7-12 p (79) J Jones(7) 50/1: 023-0200: 26th: In tch, wknd 4f out. *1¾* **33**
864] **MUJALINA 1229** [22]6-7-13 D Kinsella 40/1: 063/560//-0: 27th: Handy, wknd over 3f out. *3* **31**
4878* **TUNGSTEN STRIKE 16** [14]3-8-1 (7ex) (93) Martin Dwyer 14/1: 0113210: 28th: In tch, wknd over 3f *nk* **44**
out: much btr 4878 (fast grnd).
2754* **Glory Quest 112** [17]7-7-12 (2oh)(77) B Reilly(1) 100/1:0 4803 **Mana Dargent 21** [6]7-8-7 (88) J Fanning 50/1:0
4803 **Tempsford 21** [27]4-8-5 (86) D Holland 20/1:0 4803 **Its The Limit 21** [8]5-8-11 (92) M J Kinane 25/1:0
5004 **Kaluana Court 7** [28]8-7-12 (11oh)(68) Natalia Gemelova(5) [illegible] **Pushkin 19** [25]6-9-10 K Darley 50/1:0
34 Ran Time 3m 58.52 (9.02) Owned: Mr Michael H Watt Trained: Middleham

5136

3.25 Gr1 Emirates Airline Champion Stakes 3yo+ (A1)
£215064 £81576 £40788 **1m2f** **Soft** **Fair** Stands Side

3533 **HAAFHD 80** [9] B W Hills 3-8-11 (122) R Hills 12/1: 33-11401: In tch, hdwy to lead over 1f out, **125**
rdn out: 11 wk abs: eff at 1m, relished step up to 10f: acts on firm & soft, loves Newmarket: goes well fresh:
right back to top-class form of earlier 2,000 Guineas success in 1480.
4160 **CHORIST 55** [4] W J Haggas 5-8-13 (112) K Fallon 20/1: 13-11332: Led 2f, led over 3f out till *2½* **118**
over 1f out, not pace of wnr: 8 wk abs: v tough & smart mare who ran right up to best: see 3621, 2816.
4571* **AZAMOUR 35** [10] John M Oxx 3-8-11 M J Kinane 6/1: 11-32113: Held up, eff over 2f out, kept on *1* **120**
same pace: well bckd, well clr of rem: high-class run & handles soft grnd, capable of racing a few lbs higher on
fast grnd as in 4571: tough & top-class.
4801 **NORSE DANCER 21** [7] D R C Elsworth 4-9-2 (121) J F Egan 12/1: 4412204: Held up, modest late *6* **113**
gains, nvr a factor: twice below 4571, see 4002 & 3886 (gd grnd).
4801 **REFUSE TO BEND 21** [8]4-9-2 t (121) K McEvoy 7/1: 0011035: In tch, wknd over 2f out: reportedly *½* **112**
not handle this testing grnd: btr 4801, 2916.
4887 **SALSELON 15** [2]5-9-2 bl (116) J Murtagh 16/1: 3052326: Held up, eff & veered badly right 2f out, *nk* **112**
no impress: tricky ride: see 4887.
4571 **DOYEN 35** [5]4-9-2 (127) L Dettori 3/1 FAV: 24-21107: Held up, brief eff well over 2f out, sn *1¾* **110**
wknd: hvly bckd: not appear to handle this testing grnd: twice well below 3442 (fine turn of foot on fast grnd).
4959 **MINGUN 14** [11]4-9-2 J P Spencer 33/1: 2/1114-38: Handy, wknd over 2f out: see 4959. *6* **104**
4801 **LUCKY STORY 21** [3]3-8-11 (123) D Holland 9/2: 111-2029: In tch, wknd over 2f out: much btr *dist* **4**
expected after high-class run in 4801 (1m, fast grnd): much btr than this, see 3886.
4748 **NAHEEF 24** [1]5-9-2 vis t T E Durcan 100/1: 5-350150: 10th: Missed break, hdwy to lead after 2f *dist* **4**
till over 3f out, wknd.
4158* **MISTER MONET 56** [6]3-8-11 (117) K Darley 5/1: 1-21111P: In tch, sadly broke down 5f out. **0**
11 Ran Time 2m 06.9 (4.8) Owned: Mr Hamdan Al Maktoum Trained: Lambourn

5137

4.00 Gr1 Darley Dewhurst Stakes Colts 2yo (A1)
£152772 £57948 £28974 **7f str** **Soft** **Fair** Stands Side

3532* **SHAMARDAL 80** [4] M Johnston 2-9-0 K Darley 9/2: 111: Made all, powered clr over 1f out, **122+**
impressive: 11 wk abs, bckd tho' op 3/1: v eff at 7f, sure to relish 1m: acts on firm & soft grnd, prob any trk:
unbeaten, top-class & progressive, plenty more to come & must have outstanding claims for next year's 2,000 Guineas.
4955* **ORATORIO 13** [10] A P O'Brien 2-9-0 J P Spencer 15/2: 1012112: Handy, hdwy over 1f out, kept on *2½* **116**
but not pace of wnr: nicely bckd: not disgraced bhd a potential champion: acts on fast & soft grnd: shld apprec
1m & more Gr races to come: see 4955.
4955 **MONTGOMERYS ARCH 13** [1] P W Chapple Hyam 2-9-0 (100) M J Kinane 10/1: 1143: Held up, hdwy *nk* **115**
well over 1f out, kept on, no threat: acts on fm, imprvd on this soft: stays 7f well, will relish a drop into Gr 2.
4888 **ICEMAN 15** [11] J H M Gosden 2-9-0 (100) J Fortune 7/1: 211234: Handy, onepace well over 1f out: *½* **114**
not disgraced but prob much more to come on faster grnd: see 4493.
4461* **LIBRETTIST 38** [9]2-9-0 (100) K McEvoy 10/1: 115: Handy, wknd well over 1f out, hvly bckd: poss *¾* **112**
not enjoy soft grnd: promising 4461 (firm).
4957* **TREMAR 15** [5]2-9-0 G Carter 33/1: 4321416: Handy, wknd over 2f out: see 4957 (Gr 3). *8* **100**
4797* **PERFECTPERFORMANCE 21** [8]2-9-0 (100) L Dettori 8/1: 12117: In tch, wknd 2f out: btr 4797 (fast). *4* **94**

4493* **ETLAALA 36** [6]2-9-0 (100) R Hills 9/4 FAV: 118: Dwelt, held up, wknd well over 2f out: hvly   4   **88**
bckd: prob not handle this testing grnd & lkd potentially top-class on fast grnd earlier: btr than this, see 4493.
4611* **HOME AFFAIRS 31** [7]2-9-0 (88) K Fallon 12/1: 519: Dwelt, in tch, wknd over 2f out: reportedly   1¼   **86**
not handle soft grnd: see 4611 (mdn, gd).
9 Ran   Time 1m 27.16 (3.96)   Owned: Gainsborough Stud   Trained: Middleham

---

5138   4.35 Gr3 Persian Punch Jockey Club Cup 3yo+   (A1)
£34800 £13200 £6600   **2m**   **Soft**   **Fair**   Far Side

4478* **MILLENARY 37** [6] J L Dunlop 7-9-5 bl (119) T Quinn 7/2 JT FAV: 42-31311: Keen, held up, hdwy on   **120**
bit 2f out, led ins last, rdn out: hvly bckd: just tchd off in this race last term: eff over 14f/2m2f on firm &
soft: v tough, high-class & genuine (10 wins from 29 starts): see 4478.
4812 **FRANKLINS GARDENS 20** [9] M H Tompkins 4-9-0 (105) D Holland 20/1: 0-440662: Chsd ldr, led 6f out   1¼   **113**
till ins last, kept on but not pace of wnr: relished step up to 2m: acts on firm & soft grnd: unexposed at this
trip & the type to win in List/group class at 2m+: see 1350: clr of rem.
      TRUE LOVER 1116 [14] J W Mullins 7-9-0 S Drowne 66/1: 1/56106//-3: b g Winged Love - Truneba   4   **110**
(Nebos) Handy, onepace over 2f out: last rcd over hdles back in Apr, won 2 novs (rtd 127h, stays 3m on gd): former
wnr in Scandinavia: stays 2m on gd, soft & dirt: smart run, poised for a successful hdles campaign.
4951 **DANCING BAY 13** [3] N J Henderson 7-9-0 (116) W Ryan 7/2 JT FAV: 1/-122344: Held up, hdwy over 2f   1   **109**
out, onepace: well bckd: more expected on fav'd soft grnd: see 4478, 4000.
4569 **GOLD MEDALLIST 34** [4]4-9-5 (112) R Hughes 12/1: 3-604155: Led till 6f out, wknd 2f out: best 4161.   1   **113**
4815* **DEFINING 20** [5]5-9-0 (107) J Murtagh 9/1: 0304116: In tch, wknd 2f out: prefers faster grnd?   5   **104**
4951 **ANAK PEKAN 13** [15]4-9-0 (105) P Robinson 8/1: 2-113007: Handy, wknd well over 1f out: btr 2771.   5   **100**
4162 **MKUZI 55** [8]5-9-3 M J Kinane 10/1: 0511328: In tch, wknd dist: 8 wk abs: see 4162, 4019.   5   **99**
4886 **SHANTY STAR 15** [10]4-9-0 (104) K Darley 12/1: 131-0P39: Slow away & al bhd: see 4886, 2095 (fast).   6   **91**
4174} **POLE STAR 401** [12]6-9-0 (115) M Hills 16/1: 1/32306-0: 10th: b g Polar Falcon - Ellie Ardensky   1¾   **89**
(Slip Anchor) Held up, wknd over 3f out on reapp: plcd in Ascot Gold Cup in '03 (rtd 114): '02 stks wnr: eff at
2m/2m4f on firm & hvy, likes gall trks.
2 May'03 Sand 16.4 g/f 112-(109) A: 1 Nov'02 Donc 14.6 hvy 105- C: 2 Aug'02 York 13.8 g/f 104-98 B:
2 May'02 Newm 10 fm 98-92 B: 2 Apr'02 Pont 10 fm 95- C: 1 May'01 Leic 8 fm 75- F:
4478* **KASTHARI 37** [1]5-9-5 (115) P Hanagan 7/1: 20/303-10: 11th: Slow away, sn in tch, wknd over 3f   5   **90**
out, reportedly not handle soft grnd: btr 4478 (firm).
11 Ran   Time 3m 21.1 (9.3)   Owned: Mr L Neil Jones   Trained: Arundel

---

5139   5.10 Gr3 Rolls-Royce Motor Cars London Darley Stakes 3yo+   (A1)
£34800 £13200 £6600   **1m1f**   **Soft**   **Fair**   Stands Side

4731 **AUTUMN GLORY 28** [7] G Wragg 4-9-4 (106) S Drowne 9/2 JT FAV: 1006151: Made all, styd on well   **118**
over 1f out, rdn out: eff over 1m/9f & acts on fast grnd, loves soft & hvy, gall trks: relished forcing tactics here
& a career best run: tough, smart now: see 4311, 1686.
4950 **SIGHTS ON GOLD 14** [3] Saeed bin Suroor 5-9-4 t (114) L Dettori 6/1: 612-1102: Handy, eff to go   2   **115**
2nd over 1f out, kept on, not pace of wnr: right back to smart best: see 4639.
4323 **BABODANA 45** [4] M H Tompkins 4-9-0 (107) D Holland 9/1: 3554643: Handy, onepace over 1f out: 1¾   **108**
blnks discarded: gd run & stays 9f: likes easy grnd: wants List: see 4063, 951.
4220 **FRUHLINGSSTURM 13** [20] M A Jarvis 4-9-0 (112) P Robinson 8/1: 1-510344: Handy, onepace dist.   1½   **106**
4748 **BATTLE CHANT 24** [18]4-9-0 (106) R L Moore 20/1: 0-302235: In tch, wknd over 1f out: see 4748.   hd   **106**
4929 **ORCADIAN 14** [16]3-8-10 (99) J F Egan 100/1: 220-3066: Handy, outpcd over 2f out, rallied dist.   dht   **106**
1188 **IMPERIAL STRIDE 184** [9]3-8-10 (113) K Fallon 7/1: 116-47: Keen, handy, wknd dist: see 1188.   1¾   **103**
4916 **PAWN BROKER 14** [13]7-9-0 (108) R Hughes 25/1: 5-014608: Held up, nvr a factor: see 3613.   nk   **102**
4687 **BONECRUSHER 28** [17]5-9-0 vis (103) S Sanders 20/1: 5536439: Dwelt, bhd, nvr a factor: see 4687.   nk   **102**
1888+ **ALMURAAD 148** [6]3-8-10 (105) R Hills 16/1: 16-10: 10th: Nvr a factor: long abs: btr 1888 (gd).   2½   **98**
4916 **GATWICK 14** [12]3-8-10 (108) T Quinn 9/2 JT FAV: 6051500: 11th: In tch, wknd 2f out: see 4681.   1   **97**
4802 **SOLDERA 21** [2]4-8-11 (103) W Ryan 25/1: 40-34040: 12th: Al bhd: see 4802, 2487 (fast grnd).   ¾   **93**
4802 **BRINDISI 21** [19]3-8-7 (98) M Hills 50/1: 1446100: 13th: Al bhd: twice below 3965, see 2491.   2   **90**
2520 **MUTAHAYYA 121** [10]3-8-10 (102) T E Durcan 66/1: 212-2500: 14th: In tch, wknd 2f out: see 1814.   1¾   **90**
2864} **ETESAAL 462** [11]4-9-0 (106) K McEvoy 20/1: 53/1142-0: 15th: b c Danzig - Electric Society (Law   3   **86**
Society) With wnr, wknd over 2f out: reapp: '03 mdn & h'cap wnr, rnr-up in John Smith Cup h'cap: stays 12f, v eff
at 10.5f: acts on firm, soft & fibresand, any trk: with D Loder last term, now with S bin Suroor.
2 Jul'03 York 10.4 fm 108-97 B: 1 May'03 York 10.4 g/f 97-90 B: 1 Apr'03 Wolv 8.5 af 90a- D:
4626} **DANDOUN 378** [14]6-9-0 (111) I Mongan 0/1: 0/11000-0: 16th: Held up, wknd 2f out, virtually p.u.   *dist*   **0**
16 Ran   Time 1m 54.96(5.76)   Owned: Mollers Racing   Trained: Newmarket

---

Official Going GOOD/SOFT (SOFT IN PLACES IN HOME STRAIGHT)

5140   2.30 European Breeders Fund Maiden Stakes 2yo   (E3)
£5463 £1681 £841   **1m1f**   **Good/Soft 77**   **-10 Slow**   Outside

4927 **KINDLING 15** [4] M Johnston 2-8-9 J Fanning 7/2: 541: Prom, led 7f out, clr bef 1f out, pushed   **80+**
out, val 5L+: op 5/2: eff at 7f, imprvd today at 9f, further will suit next term: acts on firm & gd/soft grnd:
improving performer who enjoyed today's stamina test: see 4927 & 4557.
4756 **CARIBBEAN DANCER 24** [3] M Johnston 2-8-9 R Ffrench 40/1: 002: b f Theatrical - Enticed (Stage   3½   **71**
Door Johnny) Led, hdd after 2f, styd prom, not pace of wnr bef 1f out: stablemate of wnr: Feb foal, cost $55,000:
half-sister to a couple of wnrs abroad: dam smart performer around 1m abroad: sire top-class mid-dist performer:
eff at 9f, further will suit next term: acts on gd/soft grnd: encouraging eff & now quals for h'caps.
4979 **DESPERATION 10** [1] K R Burke 2-9-0 (75) L Enstone 10/1: 0523: In tch, prog & ev ch bef 1f out,   1   **74**
sn no extra: clr rem: just btr 4979 (polytrack).
4825 **MASTER COBBLER 20** [5] G A Butler 2-9-0 (84) L Dettori 1/2 FAV: 4224: Mid-div, prog 4f out, hung   5   **64**

right for press 2f out, wknd: bckd at odds-on: below form eff on today's gd/soft grnd: showed more in 4825 (gd).
5012 **AZA WISH 7** [7]2-8-9 (58) Rory Moore(5) 66/1: 0500655: Chsd ldrs over 6f, wknd: qck reapp. 4 **51**
4753 **BLACKCOMB MOUNTAIN 24** [6]2-8-9 (66) A Nicholls 20/1: 3440366: Cl-up 6f, wknd: btr 4552 (1m, fast). 2½ **46**
4511 **THE TERMINATOR 36** [8]2-9-0 (50) F Lynch 100/1: 0000047: Bhd, nvr a factor: see 4511. 1 **49**
4933 **COIS NA TINE EILE 13** [2]2-8-9 (51) S Hitchcott 100/1: 303008: Bhd, prog 4f out, fdd fnl 2f: btr 2939. 2½ **39**
8 Ran Time 1m 58.55 (7.85) Owned: The Duchess of Roxburghe Trained: Middleham

5141 **3.00 Weatherbys Bank Sprint Conditions Stakes 2yo (C1)**
£12018 £4558 £2279 **5f str** **Good/Soft 77** **-13 Slow** Stands side

4458 **BIGALOS BANDIT 39** [6] J J Quinn 2-9-4 (95) R Winston 6/4 FAV: 4043301: In tch, prog halfway, **100**
styd on to lead trav well dist, pushed clr, val 4L+: has tried 6f, suited by around 5f: acts on fast, best on gd or soft grnd: acts on a gall or sharp trk: fine eff conceding weight all round: see 4307 & 4025.
4769* **ALEXIA ROSE 23** [3] A Berry 2-8-13 (78) F Lynch 9/2: 6043212: Prom, led bef 1f out, hdd dist, not 2½ **85**
pace of wnr fnl 1f: clr rem: continues in gd form: see 4769 (6f, soft) & 4625.
4651 **HANDSOME LADY 30** [4] I Semple 2-8-7 (75) P Hanagan 10/1: 6056403: Prom over 3f, no extra. 5 **64**
4907 **TALCEN GWYN 15** [2] M F Harris 2-8-12 (81) A Nicholls 8/1: 4504104: Led, hdd over 1f out, fdd. 1¾ **64**
4307 **STEAL THE THUNDER 47** [5]2-8-12 (54) P Mathers(5) 200/1: 0550005: Bhd, nvr a factor: 7 wk abs. ¾ **62**
4907 **SMIDDY HILL 15** [7]2-8-11 (84) R Ffrench 5/2: 4510236: Prom 3f, fdd: btr 4907 & 4551 (fast). 4 **49**
6 Ran Time 1m 2.03 (4.53) Owned: Mr Ian Buckley Trained: Malton

5142 **3.30 East Lothian News Selling Stakes 2yo (E3)**
£6916 £2128 £1064 **7f30y rnd** **Good/Soft 77** **-31 Slow** Outside

5013 **STRATHTAY 7** [9] A Berry 2-8-6 vis (55) F Norton 14/1: 0560021: In tch, prog halfway, styd on to **64**
lead dist, drvn out: qck reapp & new stable: eff at 5/6f, now stays 7f: acts on fast & gd/soft grnd: apprec recent fitting of visor: gd start for new yard: see 5013 (P C Haslam).
4865 **MOSSMANN GORGE 18** [7] G A Swinbank 2-8-11 (62) F Lynch 6/1: 0652: Keen in tch, prog halfway, ev ½ **66**
ch ins fnl 1f, sn edged right for press, just held by wnr: imprvd eff on step up to 7f: acts on gd/soft grnd.
4617 **MYTTONS BELL 31** [10] A Bailey 2-8-6 (65) D Allan 16/1: 3030503: Led & sn clr, hdd bef 1f out, no 2½ **56**
extra: eff at 6/7f on firm, gd/soft grnd & fibresand: btr 3632 & 2051.
3601 **BEAUCHAMP TWIST 78** [3] G A Butler 2-8-6 bl (61) N Mackay(3) 20/1: 00064: Cl-up, no extra bef 1f out. 1½ **53**
2194 **VENEER 136** [2]2-8-11 (55) R L Moore 5/1: 4005: b g Woodborough - Sweet Lass (Belmez) In tch, hd **57**
prog after 2f, no extra bef 1f out: tchd 4/1 on long abs: May first foal, dam wnr at mid-dists.
5011 **INVERTIEL 7** [13]2-8-11 VIS (75) P Hanagan 12/1: 420006: Nvr nrr than mid-div: 1st time visor. ½ **56**
4963 **STREET BALLAD 12** [14]2-8-6 (62) J Fanning 8/1: 403007: Chsd ldrs 5f, wknd: btr 4436 (6f, fast). 1½ **48**
4807 **MOUNT EPHRAM 21** [6]2-9-2 bl (70) D Nolan(3) 33/1: 6414208: Al in rear: btr 3349 (fast). 1¾ **54**
4980 **CORNICHE DANCER 10** [12]2-8-11 (68) L Dettori 9/4 FAV: 0210529: Mid-div when hmpd bef 5f out, 1½ **46**
carried wide turning for home, onepcd fnl 2f: bckd: best form at come at 6f.
4631 **RIVER CARD 31** [11]2-8-6 P Robinson 10/1: 00: 10th: Al in rear: see 4631. ½ **40**
4040 **SPINNAKERS GIRL 59** [8]2-8-6 (69) R Winston 10/1: 032400: 11th: Mid-div 4f, wknd: 8 wk abs. 4 **32**
DAVIDS CHOICE 0 [5]2-8-11 P Mathers(5) 100/1: 0: 12th: b g Wizard King - Welch's Dream (Brief dist **0**
Truce) Missed break, nvr a factor on debut: Apr first foal, cost 500gns: dam successful at 5f: sire useful performer around 1m: with A Berry.
12 Ran Time 1m 32.51 (7.61) Owned: Mr E Nisbet Trained: Cockerham

5143 **4.00 Racing Uk Channel 432 Handicap Stakes 3yo+ 86-100 (C1)** **[104]**
£12083 £4583 £2292 **5f** **Good/Soft 77** **+10 Fast** Stands side

5125* **MALAPROPISM 1** [10] M R Channon 4-8-12 (6ex) (88) D Allan 8/1: 06610611: Cl-up, ev ch over 1f out, **99**
styd on to lead ins fnl 1f, pushed out, val 3L+: won yesterday at Musselburgh: eff btwn 5/5.7f, stays 6f: acts on firm or soft grnd: thriving with racing & easily landed qck-fire double under 6lb pen: see 5125 & 4496.
5090* **CORRIDOR CREEPER 3** [9] J M Bradley 7-9-12 (6ex)p (102) R L Moore 5/1: 3503212: Prom, led dist, 1¾ **106**
hdd ins fnl 1f, not pace of wnr: qck reapp & top-weight; ultra consistent performer who ran well under pen.
4908 **WHITBARROW 15** [15] J M Bradley 5-8-11 (87) F Norton 20/1: 0054003: Chsd ldrs wide, prog bef 1f ½ **89**
out, nrst fin: stablemate of 2nd: encouraging eff & is back on a winning mark: see 4459 & btr 1845.
5125 **FURTHER OUTLOOK 1** [5] D K Ivory 10-8-7 (1oh)P (82) J Fanning 9/1: 51503524: Led, hdd bef 1f out, nk **84**
no extra: gd eff in first time cheek pieces: fin closer bhd today's wnr only yesterday in 5125 (soft).
5090 **WHISTLER 3** [7]7-9-1 p (91) P Fitzsimons 9/1: 3404265: Bhd, prog halfway, kept on fnl 1f: qck ½ **90**
reapp.
5001 **CONNECT 8** [12]7-8-13 bl (89) P Robinson 12/1: 4000046: Held up, prog halfway, staying on when nk **87**
short of room ins fnl 1f, sn no impress: btr 3279 (fast).
5001 **PIC UP STICKS 8** [13]5-9-7 (97) S Hitchcott 11/1: 6000107: Bhd, prog when short of room bef 1f nk **94**
out, switched & kept on late: talented but needs everything to fall right: btr 4786 (6f).
4773 **RYDAL 23** [1]3-8-10 vis (86) S Sanders 10/1: 4014508: Handy over 3f, wknd: btr 3889. ¾ **81**
4908 **FRASCATI 15** [11]4-8-7 (3oh) (80) P Mathers(5) 20/1: 2004309: Handy 4f, wknd: btr 4693. nk **77**
5001 **RIVER FALCON 8** [2]4-8-9 (85) R Winston 4/1 FAV: 0100450: 10th: Handy over 3f, wknd: well bckd. 1¼ **75**
4780 **PTARMIGAN RIDGE 22** [4]8-8-11 (87) N Mackay(3) 9/1: 5103300: 11th: In tch over 3f, wknd: btr 3 **68**
4459.
4908 **Henry Hall 15** [3]8-8-7 (83) Kim Tinkler 16/1:0 3561 **Alfie Lee 80** [16]7-8-7 bl e t(45) P Hanagan 200/1:0
13 Ran Time 1m 0.89 (3.39) Owned: Mr Michael A Foy Trained: West Ilsley

5144 4.30 Famous Grouse Handicap Stakes 3yo+ 71-85 (D2) [93]
£7112 £2188 £1094 7f30y rnd Good/Soft 77 -16 Slow Outside

4987*]GO PADERO 349 [7] M Johnston 3-9-4 (83) J Fanning 16/1: 651-1: ch c Night Shift - Watch The Clock (Mtoto) Cl-up, styd on to lead ins fnl 1f, sn hung right then left, all out: reapp: mdn wnr on fnl '03 start: eff at 7f, further shld suit: acts on fast, seems suited by gd/soft & soft grnd: acts on a gall or sharp trk & goes well fresh: defied greenness to win on h'cap bow, only lightly rcd & can rate higher. **92**
1 Nov'03 Redc 7 sft 86- D:

4689* AZREME 29 [2] D K Ivory 4-8-13 (76) L Dettori 4/1 J FAV: 4302012: Held up, prog bef 1f out, styd on well ins fnl 1f, just held: continues in gd form: 4lb higher than narrow win in 4689. shd **84**

4820 LES ARCS 20 [8] R C Guest 4-8-9 T (72) F Norton 40/1: 1360603: Bhd, prog 2f out, staying on when no room ins fnl 1f, again short of room cl home: eff at 7f, return to 1m/10f will suit: lkd likely wnr with clr run & can find similar: see 2890 & 2828. 1 **78+**

4891 DOCTORATE 16 [14] E A L Dunlop 3-9-7 (86) S Sanders 5/1: 2530104: Stumbled start, rear, prog 3f out, kept on ins fnl 1f, not btn far: gd eff under top-weight: 5lb higher than win in 4683. shd **91**

4806 KIRKBYS TREASURE 21 [5]6-8-13 (76) F Lynch 9/2: 0226035: Rear, prog & ev ch dist, sn onepcd. ¾ **79**

4689 NAMROUD 29 [11]5-8-9 (72) P Hanagan 12/1: 0000406: In tch, prog & ev ch dist, no extra when short of room cl-home: btr 4103. shd **74**

3880* DIZZY IN THE HEAD 48 [3]5-9-1 bl (78) A Nicholls 16/1: 1000127: Led, hdd ins fnl 1f, wknd: 7 wk abs. 1½ **77**

4806* SEA STORM 21 [13]6-9-4 (81) R Winston 4/1 J FAV: 6430218: Handy, ev ch dist, wknd: bckd: btr 4806. hd **79**

4341 ABBAJABBA 45 [9]8-8-9 (72) P Robinson 10/1: 0002059: Mid-div 5f, wknd: 6 wk abs: btr 3880. 1½ **67**

4999 TONY TIE 8 [1]8-8-12 (75) N Mackay(3) 20/1: 0605000: 10th: Bhd, rcd alone stands side in straight, nvr a factor: btr 3152. 3 **64**

4912 BRIEF GOODBYE 15 [4]4-8-13 (76) R L Moore 16/1: 4014060: 11th: Cl-up over 5f, wknd: btr 2313. shd **64**
11 Ran Time 1m 31.44 (6.54) Owned: Pagodero Partnership Trained: Middleham

5145 5.00 Musselburgh News Maiden Stakes 3yo+ (D3)
£4849 £1492 £746 1m4f Good/Soft 77 -28 Slow Inside

5023 SWIFT SAILOR [10] M Johnston 3-9-0 J Fanning 13/8 FAV: 31: Prom, led 3f out, sn clr, eased cl-home, val 10L+: bckd on qck reapp: eff at 10f, imprvd for step up to 12f: acts on gd & gd/soft grnd: acts on a sharp trk: lightly rcd performer who won in gd style, can rate higher: see 5023. **83**

5029 DAY ONE 7 [5] G Wragg 3-9-0 S Sanders 3/1: 0-352: In tch, prog bef 2f out, no impress on wnr fnl 1f: clr rem: qck reapp: showed more in 3783 (fast). 7 **70**

4486 NEWNHAM 38 [7] L M Cumani 3-9-0 N Mackay(3) 15/8: 2423: Handy, styd on to chase wnr well over 1f out, no extra: bckd: disapp in today's gd/soft grnd: showed more in 4486 (gd). 5 **62**

5066 KYBER 5 [2] R F Fisher 3-9-0 D Nolan(3) 50/1: 5433064: Led, hdd 3f out, wknd: qck reapp. ½ **61**

4805 SANDY BAY 21 [9]5-9-7 (30) P Fessey 50/1: 0004035: Nvr nrr than mid-div: recently unplcd over hdles. shd **60$**

5066 STRAVONIAN 5 [1]4-9-7 P Mathers(5) 100/1: 0056: Missed break, nvr a factor: qck reapp. 12 **42**

5015 AWAKEN 7 [4]3-8-9 R Winston 16/1: 607: Chsd ldrs till halfway, wknd. 17 **11**

1121 EYES DONT LIE 189 [3]6-9-7 p (35) D Allan 200/1: 05620-08: Rear, nvr a factor: long abs. 1¼ **14**

4441 TAILI 40 [6]3-8-9 BL (30) T Eaves(3) 200/1: 000-069: Mid-div 6f, wknd: first time blnks: jumps fit. 18 **0**

THROWMEUPSOMETHING 0 [8]3-9-0 P Bradley 66/1: 0: 10th: Missed break, nvr a factor on debut. 22 **0**
10 Ran Time 2m 43.26 (12.66) Owned: Maktoum Al Maktoum Trained: Middleham

5146 5.30 Live Racing On Racing Uk Channel 432 Classified Stakes 3yo+ 0-50 (G4)
£2996 £856 £428 5f str Good/Soft 77 -13 Slow Stands side

4636 MOLOTOV 31 [13] I W McInnes 4-8-12 (50) Natalia Gemelova(5) 5/1 J FAV: 0413341: Prom, led bef 2f out, sn clr, pushed out, val bit more: eff at 5/6f, has tried further: acts on firm, gd/soft & fibresand: in-form. **62**

4739 CORANGLAIS 25 [9] J M Bradley 4-9-0 bl (52) R L Moore 12/1: 0500502: Bhd, prog wide 2f out, kept on ins fnl 1f, nrst fin: gd eff & can return to winning ways over further: btr 3143. 1 **59**

4739 VALIANT ROMEO 25 [16] R Bastiman 4-9-2 vis (54) R Ffrench 8/1: 0520333: In tch, styd on to chase wnr bef 1f out, no extra fnl 1f: tchd 6/1: just btr 4739 & 4253. 2 **55**

5020 ARFINNIT 7 [14] M R Channon 3-9-3 (55) S Hitchcott 16/1: 0024604: Chsd ldrs over 3f, onepcd. hd **55**

4994 THE OLD SOLDIER 8 [10]6-8-12 (50) R Winston 5/1 J FAV: 0-002025: Bhd, prog halfway, onepcd dist. ½ **48**

5010 MR PERTEMPS 8 [2]6-9-0 (52) D Allan 16/1: 3125006: Handy over 3f, no extra: btr 551 & 385 (AW). ¾ **48**

5069 ROBWILLCALL 5 [11]4-8-9 p (46) P Mathers(5) 16/1: 5505007: Nvr nrr than mid-div: qck reapp. 1¼ **39**

3974 TELEPATHIC 63 [8]4-9-0 (52) F Lynch 33/1: 4000508: Al in rear: 9 wk abs. 1½ **39**

5010 LARKYS LOB 8 [7]5-8-12 (47) J D O'Reilly(7) 7/1: 2162359: Prom 3f, wknd: btr 3220. 2½ **29**

4636 TOMTHEVIC 31 [17]6-8-12 (50) P Fitzsimons 20/1: 0405000: 10th: Led, hdd bef 2f out, wknd: btr 4335. 2½ **21**

4345 FENWICKS PRIDE 45 [4]6-8-12 vis (50) P Hanagan 14/1: 0-300000: 11th: Bhd, nvr a factor. hd **20**

5096 SMART STARPRINCESS 2 [1]3-8-13 P (54) A Nicholls 7/1: 23500040: 12th: In tch over 3f, wknd. 1¾ **16**

4618 REGAL SONG 31 [6]8-8-13 (51) J Fanning 50/1: 0000000: 13th: b g Anita's Prince - Song Beam (Song) Chsd ldrs 3f, fdd: h'cap wnr in '03: h'cap wnr in '02: eff at 6f, suited by 5f: acts on fast & fibresand, loves gd/soft or softer, any trk: eff with blnks: with T J Etherington. hd **15**
1 Jul'03 Beve 5 g/s 74-68 C: 2 May'03 Thir 5 g/s 70-70 D: 1 Jul'02 Hami 5 sft 82-75 D: 1 Oct'01 Wind 5 hvy 84-76 C: 2 Oct'01 Catt 5 sft 78-75 D: 2 May'01 Thir 5 g/s 85-84 D: 1 Apr'01 Muss 5 hvy 86-79 D: 1 Mar'01 Muss 5 hvy 82-68 E:
13 Ran Time 1m 2.02(4.52) Owned: Cloak And Dagger Racing Club Trained: Catwick

Official Going Good/Soft

5147   2.20 Trevor Woods Memorial Nursery Handicap Stakes 2yo 0-75 (E3)   [82]
£4319 £1329 £665   1m4y rnd   Good/Soft 67   -26 Slow   Inside

4213* **TOLDO** 52 [16] G M Moore 2-8-13 (67) L Dettori 9/1: 0402111: In tch, hdwy outer over 2f out, led   77
over 1f out, rdn out: 7 wk abs & prev with A Berry: eff over 7f/1m on fast & hvy, easy or gall trks: runs well
fresh: tough & v progressive: see 4213.
4940 **LORD OF DREAMS** 14 [18] D W P Arbuthnot 2-8-13 (67) S W Kelly 14/1: 050342: In tch, eff to chase   2   73
wnr & wandered over 1f out, kept on, not pace of wnr: shown enough to win a race: see 4738.
4851 **ROYAL MOUGINS** 19 [2] G Wragg 2-9-0 (68) D Holland 15/2: 0553: In tch, hdwy & short of room over   ½   73
2f out till over 1f out, kept on ins last: clr 2nd with an uninterrupted run: stays 1m on gd/soft, apprec further.
4760* **LOLA SAPOLA** 25 [19] N A Callaghan 2-9-7 (75) A Mullen(7) 18/1: 00014: Held up, kept on late, nrst   ¾   78
fin: stays 1m, shaped like even further will suit: acts on firm & gd/soft: encouraging run stepped up in class.
4703 **SCENT** 28 [13]2-8-12 (66) S Sanders 16/1: 5035: Held up, hdwy wide over 2f out, some late gains, no   2½   65
threat: prob stays 1m on gd/soft: see 3915.
4848 **YOU FOUND ME** 20 [17]2-8-11 (65) C Catlin 50/1: 06306: In tch, onepace over 1f out: see 4296.   hd   63
4673 **BRACE OF DOVES** 30 [20]2-9-0 (68) P Makin(5) 28/1: 3323007: Held up, some late gains, no dngr.   1¾   64
4997 **SELIKA** 9 [10]2-9-5 (73) P Robinson 10/1: 0048: Slow away & bhd, nvr a factor: see 4997.   hd   68
4933 **DOVER STREET** 14 [5]2-8-11 (65) A Culhane 28/1: 500049: Held up, nvr a threat: see 4519.   ½   59
4580 **TORRENS** 34 [15]2-9-7 (75) J Fanning 10/1: 4100: 10th: Led over 3f till over 1f out, wknd.   2½   65
4848 **HIDDEN CHANCE** 20 [3]2-8-13 (67) R L Moore 10/1: 010040: 11th: Nvr a factor: see 4848, 3381.   1¾   54
4810 **EASY MOVER** 22 [6]2-9-7 (75) N Mackay(3) 8/1: 551200: 12th: Held up, hmpd over 2f out, no extra.   nk   61
4455 **ROAD TO HEAVEN** 41 [14]2-8-11 T (65) W Supple 28/1: 3000: 13th: Slow away & al bhd: see 2897.   1   49
4979 **Tamora** 11 [4]2-8-11 (65) K Darley 25/1:0   3935 **El Rey Royale** 65 [12]2-9-7 (75) T Eaves(3) 40/1:0
4396 **English Fellow** 43 [8]2-8-11 (65) G Gibbons 28/1:0   4271 **Geisha Lady** 49 [7]2-9-3 (71) P Hanagan 20/1:0
4004 **Rich Albi** 62 [11]2-9-2 (70) D Allan 50/1:0   4688 **Young Thomas** 30 [1]2-9-1 (69) R Winston 16/1:0
19 Ran   Time 1m 49.24 (7.44)   Owned: Mr J W Armstrong   Trained: Middleham

---

5148   2.50 Sponsor A Race At Pontefract Handicap Stakes 3yo+ 56-70 (E3)   [77]
£4354 £1340 £670   1m2f6y   Good/Soft 67   -10 Slow   Inside

5016 **SAHAAT** 8 [16] C R Dore 6-9-1 (64) R Winston 16/1: 5046041: Held up, hdwy well over 1f out, styd   73
on lead ins last, rdn out: eff at 1m/10f on gd, soft & fibresand: regained enthusiasm & on a handy mark.
5062 **PLANTERS PUNCH** 6 [9] R Hannon 3-9-1 (69) R L Moore 11/2 FAV: 0003222: In tch, hdwy to lead &   1¾   75
hung till over 1f out, hdd ins last, no extra: deserves similar: see 5062.
5016 **COLWAY RITZ** 8 [4] W Storey 10-8-12 (61) J Bramhill 20/1: 2-022553: Hld up, hdwy over 2f out, onepace.   ½   66
4935 **LITTLE JIMBOB** 14 [15] R A Fahey 3-9-7 (75) P Hanagan 16/1: 1243524: Set pace till over 1f out,   nk   79
onepace: consistent: acts on firm & gd/soft: see 2705, 2443.
5027 **MRS PANKHURST** 8 [2]3-9-1 (69) M Hills 10/1: 5056045: Chsd ldrs, short of room over 2f out, kept   3½   68
on ins last: see 5027, 923.
5016* **MAMBINA** 8 [8]3-9-4 (6ex) (72) A Culhane 6/1: 2324116: In tch, some late gains, no threat: btr 5016 (fast).   1½   69
5062* **DUELLING BANJOS** 6 [6]5-9-4 (6ex) (67) S Sanders 15/2: 0400017: In tch, nvr a factor: qck reapp.   5   57
5017* **TEDSDALE MAC** 8 [3]5-9-0 (6ex) (63) P Makin(5) 16/1: 2520018: Held up, nvr a factor: btr 5017 (1m).   ¾   51
4377 **NORTHSIDE LODGE** 44 [13]6-9-6 (69) S W Kelly 9/1: 5200059: In tch, wknd over 1f out: abs: see 2538.   1   55
4931 **RAREFIED** 16 [18]3-9-5 (73) D Allan 25/1: 0000040: 10th: Held up, nvr a factor: see 4931, 1382.   nk   59
4850 **RANI TWO** 19 [7]5-9-6 (69) L Dettori 6/1: 5440220: 11th: In tch, bhd from halfway: bckd from 9/1.   5   48
4742 **INTERNATIONALGUEST** 26 [14]5-9-3 p (66) N Pollard 40/1: 5550000: 12th: In tch, wknd over 2f out.   nk   44
3904 **SLALOM** 67 [11]4-9-7 (70) G Faulkner 25/1: 1005050: 13th: In tch, not clr run over 2f out & over   1½   46
1f out, no threat: ignore this: 2 month abs & now with J Poulton: best to forgive this: see 3107, 939.
4850 **Bluegrass Boy** 19 [12]4-9-0 (63) R Thomas(3) 25/1:0   4515 **Secluded** 37 [5]4-9-5 bl(68) D Holland 16/1:0
4983 **Giunchiglio** 11 [19]5-9-2 (65) K Darley 50/1:0   4924 **Crathorne** 16 [10]4-9-2 p(65) W Supple 33/1:0
4860 **Humid Climate** 19 [17]4-9-11 (74) T Eaves(3) 66/1:0   4609 **Lord Eurolink** 33 [1]10-9-7 (70) P Robinson 50/1:0
19 Ran   Time 2m 15.78 (7.68)   Owned: Mr G D J Linder   Trained: Spalding

---

5149   3.20 Packsaddle Handicap Stakes 3yo+ 71-85 (D2)   [99]
£7183 £2210 £1105   5f rnd   Good/Soft 67   +11 Fast   Inside

4855 **OK PAL** 19 [12] T G Mills 4-8-11 (82) G Carter 10/1: 6061231: Handy, led dist, styd on well, drvn   92
out: gd time: stay 6f, all 3 wins at 5f & likes a stiff trk: acts on gd, gd/soft & fibresand: best up
with/forcing the pace & has tried blnks: useful & in fine heart: see 4605.
4908 **CORPS DE BALLET** 16 [13] J L Dunlop 3-8-12 (83) J Quinn 25/1: 0100052: In tch, hdwy over 1f out,   ½   91
kept on ins last, not pace of wnr: shld find similar: see 2155.
5125 **BARON RHODES** 2 [16] J S Wainwright 3-8-9 (80) T Eaves(3) 28/1: 1300003: Held up, hdwy wide over   nk   87
1f out, styd on ins last, not btn far: unplcd 2 days ago: back to form: see 2591.
5001 **MINE BEHIND** 9 [4] J R Best 4-9-3 (88) L Dettori 5/1 FAV: 0001404: Held up, hdwy 2f out, chall   hd   94
ins last, just held: best 4585.
4498 **DOMIRATI** 38 [5]4-8-11 (82) R L Moore 8/1: 4202045: Slow away, held up, hdwy over 1f out, sn   2½   83
short of room, kept on late: see 4498.
4654* **HOUT BAY** 31 [18]7-8-4 (75) P Hanagan 6/1: 2411316: Held up, some late gains, no threat: tough.   nk   75
4496 **TRUE MAGIC** 38 [6]3-8-1 (72) N Mackay(3) 14/1: 2211007: In tch, some late gains: best 3833.   shd   71
4855 **BATHWICK BILL** 19 [9]3-8-6 (77) R Winston 20/1: 6230008: In tch, nvr a factor: see 1901.   ½   75
4654 **BRAVE BURT** 31 [14]7-8-5 (76) A Nicholls 16/1: 0200009: Led till dist, no extra: see 4107, 3060.   ¾   72
4496 **MATTY TUN** 38 [11]5-8-10 (81) W Supple 7/1: 0005000: 10th: In tch, some late gains: see 1479.   shd   76

PONTEFRACT **MONDAY 18.10.04 Lefthand, Undulating Track, Stiff Uphill Finish**

5114 **JILLY WHY 2** [7]3-8-1 (72) B Swarbrick(4) 16/1: 1100240: 11th: Bhd, some late gains. ½ **65**
3889 **CATCH THE WIND 67** [1]3-8-12 p (83) S Sanders 12/1: 5561220: 12th: In tch, wknd over 1f out. ¾ **74**
4700 **Treasure House 28** [15]3-8-4 (75) D Fox(5) 33/1:0
4930 **Foley Millennium 16** [3]6-8-0 (71) C Catlin 25/1:0
4718 **Beyond The Clouds 27** [2]8-8-4 p(75) P Mathers(5) 16/1:0
5125 **Awake 2** [10]7-8-13 vis(84) K Darley 16/1:0
4604 **Celtic Thunder 33** [8]3-8-11 (82) D Holland 25/1:0
5001 **Pomfret Lad 9** [17]6-8-12 bl(83) J Fanning 25/1:0
18 Ran Time 1m 04.11 (2.81) Owned: Sherwoods Transport Ltd Trained: Epsom

5150

3.50 Listed Totesport Silver Tankard Stakes 2yo (A1)
£20300 £7700 £3850 **1m4y rnd** **Good/Soft 67** **+09 Fast** Inside

4906* **COMIC STRIP 16** [3] Sir Mark Prescott 2-8-11 (100) S Sanders 4/5 FAV: 141111: In tch, hdwy over 2f out, styd on to lead over 1f out, rdn clr ins last: hvly bckd, gd time: suited by 1m now, shld appr further: acts on fast, soft & fibresand, any trk: smart juv, plenty more to come in List/Gr class: see 4906. **111**
4810* **WISE DENNIS 22** [7] A P Jarvis 2-8-11 (89) K Darley 14/1: 0033312: Dwelt, in tch, hdwy to lead briefly over 1f out, sn hdd & hmpd, switched left & kept on, not pace of wnr: useful/imprvd run on this gd/soft grnd, acts on firm & polytrack: clr of rem, win similar with repeat of this: see 4810. 3½ **104**
4699 **HAUNTING MEMORIES 28** [2] M A Jarvis 2-8-11 (97) P Robinson 10/1: 4123: Led after 1f till over 3f out, onepace: useful & consistent, needs an ease in grade: see 4699 (7f), 4026. 4 **97**
4756* **LITTLE MISS GRACIE 25** [1] A B Haynes 2-8-6 (85) R L Moore 14/1: 332414: In tch, hdwy to lead over 3f out, hdd over 1f out, no extra: see 4756 (mdn, firm). ¾ **90**
4147* **FANTASY RIDE 55** [4]2-8-11 (94) J Quinn 16/1: 015: Held up, hdwy 2f out, sn no extra: 8 wk abs. 1½ **93**
4854 **CLARET AND AMBER 19** [10]2-8-11 (97) P Hanagan 10/1: 5511526: Nvr a factor: see 4854 (6f), 4458. 1¾ **90**
4906 **FIEFDOM 16** [8]2-8-11 (95) J Fanning 25/1: 5412437: Led early, wknd over 1f out: see 4906. 2 **87**
4692 **PROFITS REALITY 29** [5]2-8-11 (84) G Gibbons 66/1: 5543138: In tch, wknd over 2f out: see 4692 (6f). 2½ **83**
4356* **HUMOUROUS 45** [9]2-8-11 t (92) L Dettori 4/1: 519: In tch, wknd over 2f out: 6 wk abs: btr 4356 (mdn, fast). 13 **57**
9 Ran Time 1m 46.45 (4.65) Owned: Neil Greig - Osborne House Trained: Newmarket

5151

4.20 Bluff Cove Handicap Stakes 3yo+ 56-70 (E3) **[74]**
£4120 £1268 £634 **2m1f216y** **Good/Soft 67** **-37 Slow** Inside

4936* **MOONSHINE BEACH 14** [10] P W Hiatt 6-9-13 (73) P Makin(5) 11/2: 3110311: Made just about all, styd on gamely fnl 1f, rdn out: op 13/2, top-weight: recent C/D wnr & 6th win of campaign: eff at 2m/2m2f on fast, gd/soft grnd & polytrack: handles any trk, likes Pontefract: tough & progressive: see 4936. **82**
4868* **PRINCESS KIOTTO 19** [2] T D Easterby 3-8-9 (66) D Allan 7/4 FAV: 0-523112: Trkd ldrs, styd on under press fnl 1f but not pace to chall wnr: well bckd: fine run on hat-trick bid, acts on firm, gd/soft & f/sand. 1½ **73**
4936 **RIYADH 14** [11] M Johnston 6-9-4 (64) K Darley 6/1: 2604643: Trkd ldrs, kept on under press fnl 1f, not pace to chall: v well h'capped but has not won since June '02: again bhd today's wnr in 4936 (C/D). nk **70**
5004 **ISAAF 9** [8] P W Hiatt 5-9-6 (66) R L Moore 20/1: 6004204: Held up, prog to chase ldrs 2f out, onepcd. 2 **70**
4932 **BEST PORT 16** [5]8-9-2 (62) M Lawson(5) 14/1: 1610435: Rear, styd on late under press, nrst fin: best on fast/firm grnd, see 3611. 1 **65**
5004 **CLARADOTNET 9** [9]4-8-10 (56) A Culhane 20/1: 0320006: Trkd ldrs, onepcd fnl 2f. ¾ **58**
5108 **SALAMBA 3** [6]3-8-8 (65) P Robinson 10/1: 3-500507: Prom, ev ch 5f out till wknd 2f out: op 14/1, qck reapp: longer 2m trip: still a mdn, see 1462. 1¾ **66**
4657] **ROBBO 728** [1]10-8-10 T Eaves(3) 16/1: /64/51/4/-8: b g Robellino - Basha (Chief's Crown) Al rear: won a h'cap chase in Apr '04 (rtd 131c, eff at 3m/4m1f on gd & hvy, cheek pieces): missed '03 on the Flat, h'cap 4th on sole start prev term: '01 h'cap wnr here at Pontefract: eff at 2m/2m2f on fast, soft & f/sand: eff with/without blnks on a stiff trk: sharper back over fences next time. ¾ **56**
1 Oct'01 Pont 18 sft 58-50 E:
4936 **VICARS DESTINY 14** [4]6-9-4 (64) R Winston 7/1: 4332339: Held up, nvr troubled ldrs. 5 **60**
4936 **TONI ALCALA 14** [7]5-9-6 (66) S Sanders 16/1: 5560400: 10th: Chsd ldrs, btn 4f out: see 4808. dist **0**
10 Ran Time 4m 10.82 (18.82) Owned: Ken Read And Jill Harmsworth Trained: Banbury

5152

4.50 Thanks To Cheryl Hibbert And Andrea Hall Maiden Auction Stakes Div 1 2yo (F3)
£3445 £1060 £530 **6f str** **Good/Soft 67** **-29 Slow** Inside

4741 **GRAND OPTION 26** [2] B W Duke 2-8-10 (63) A Daly 11/2: 5004601: Chsd ldrs, kept on well for press to lead cl-home, drvn out: op 7/1: first win on 12th attempt: eff at 5/6f, stays 7f: acts on fast & soft grnd: tried blnks, seems btr without: handles a flat or gall trk: see 1716 & 943. **75**
4784 **SKIDDAW WOLF 23** [3] B Smart 2-8-3 (63) C Catlin 4/1: 036542: Chsd ldrs, went on 2f out, worn down cl-home: op 5/2, clr of rem: lkd all over the wnr till wrn down cl-home: caught the eye in 4784. ½ **66**
4893 **DAISYS GIRL 17** [4] B Hanbury 2-8-5 (55) C Haddon(7) 10/1: 0663: Hmpd start, styd on late, nvr dngrs: lost all realistic ch at the start: blnks omitted today: see 4893. 6 **54**
4784 **HYMN OF VICTORY 23** [9] T J Etherington 2-8-9 (61) D Holland 6/1: 0526204: Switched start & front rank wide, wknd fnl 1f: btr 4549 (5f). 2 **53**
4787 **ASHES 23** [6]2-8-5 (1ow) (64) T Eaves 20/1: 05405: Hmpd start, chsd ldrs, wknd fnl 1f: btr 1974 (g/f). nk **48**
4344 **ZENDARO 46** [5]2-8-10 (54) S W Kelly 33/1: 46006: Hmpd start, recovered to chase ldrs 4.5f, wknd. 2 **48**
4464 **ARCHIE WRIGHT 40** [11]2-8-9 (56) R L Moore 12/1: 0047: Outpcd & wide thr'out, nvr dngrs: 6 wk abs. 5 **35**
4688 **TURKS WOOD 30** [10]2-8-11 (68) P Robinson 3/1 FAV: 455008: Hmpd start, nvr a factor: nicely bckd: lost all ch at the start over this shorter 6f trip: blnks left off & much btr expected: see 1981. 1¾ **34**
4978 **MOUNTAIN BREEZE 11** [1]2-8-4 D Allan 100/1: 009: b f Monashee Mountain - Breezy Louise (Dilum) Al outpcd: 1,500gns Mar first foal: dam a 5f wnr, sire a high-class 7f performer: with D Shaw. 1¾ **24**
4894 **PEOPLETON BROOK 17** [7]2-8-11 BL (63) L Dettori 11/1: 560000: 10th: Swerved start, led till 2f out, wknd & eased: tried blnks: see 2415. 16 **0**
4787 **TIME FOR MEE 23** [12]2-8-3 P Hanagan 66/1: 00: 11th: Al outpcd, t.o.: see 4787. 3½ **0**
SCARBOROUGH FLYER [8]2-8-12 J Edmunds 40/1: 0: 12th: b c Almaty - Calamanco (Clantime) Al outpcd, fin last on debut: 14,500gns Apr foal: half-brother to sprint wnrs Artie & Kings Cross: dam a 5f wnr. ½ **0**
12 Ran Time 1m 19.87 (5.77) Owned: The G S M Group Trained: Lambourn

5153

5.20 Subscribe To Racing Uk On 08700 860432 Classified Stakes 3yo 0-60 (F3)
£3484 £1072 £536 1m4y rnd Good/Soft 67 -11 Slow Inside

5017 **WRENLANE** 8 [13] R A Fahey 3-8-12 (60) P Hanagan 12/1: 5040341: Chsd ldrs wide, went on 1.5f out, **67**
held on well cl-home, drvn out: first success: eff around 1m, stays 10f: acts on fast & gd/soft grnd, handles well.
4867 **INTAVAC BOY** 19 [12] C W Thornton 3-8-12 (57) G Faulkner 16/1: 664022: Prom, led 2f out till 1.5f nk **66**
out, rallied gamely fnl 1f & only just btn: clr of rem: acts on firm & gd/soft grnd: deserves similar, see 4867.
4827* **SACHIN** 21 [5] J R Boyle 3-9-3 (65) K Darley 16/1: 0-060413: Rdn in rear, styd on well fnl 1f, no dngr. 4 **64**
4721* **PELLA** 27 [4] M Blanshard 3-9-0 (65) L Dettori 4/1 FAV: 2301014: Pushed in rear, styd on fnl 1f, 1 **59**
nvr nrr: nicely bckd: btr on fast grnd in 4721.
4032 **DEIGN TO DANCE** 61 [9]3-8-11 (62) R L Moore 12/1: 5103255: Rear, prog 2f out, sn no impress: abs. 3 **51**
4668 **MOTU** 30 [8]3-9-1 bl (63) S Sanders 11/2: 0000036: Rear, imprvd halfway, btn dist: btr 4668. ¾ **54**
4845 **BOWLING ALONG** 20 [2]3-8-9 (58) T Eaves(3) 50/1: 2001607: Rdn rear, nvr nr ldrs: btr 4562 (6f, fm). nk **47**
4926 **ALCHERA** 16 [1]3-8-12 (58) S Carson 14/1: 4040058: Chsd ldrs, btn 1.5f out. 2½ **46**
4721 **SION HILL** 27 [3]3-9-2 (64) J D O'Reilly(7) 25/1: 02-00009: Prom, wknd 2f out. 1¾ **47**
4821 **LAKE DIVA** 21 [7]3-8-10 (61) A Culhane 50/1: 00-340: 10th: Chsd ldrs, wkng when short of room 2f out. 4 **35**
4966 **COTTINGHAM** 13 [11]3-8-12 (58) D Holland 11/2: 0666240: 11th: Prom, hmpd 2f out & sn wknd: bckd ½ **36**
from 8/1: drop in trip & did not get the run of today's race: btr 4757 (10f, firm grnd).
4761* **OTAGO** 25 [10]3-9-2 (64) W Supple 7/1: 0421010: 12th: Trkd ldrs 6f, wknd: btr 4761 (firm). 1 **38**
4899 **WILLHEGO** 17 [6]3-8-12 (59) J Fanning 13/2: 0023150: 13th: Led till 2f out, sn wknd: btr 4182. 3 **30**
13 Ran Time 1m 48.05 (6.25) Owned: Mr Keith Taylor Trained: Malton

5154

5.50 Thanks To Cheryl Hibbert And Andrea Hall Maiden Auction Stakes Div 2 2yo (F3)
£3445 £1060 £530 6f str Good/Soft 67 -35 Slow Inside

4409 **DOITFORREEL** 42 [12] I A Wood 2-8-4 (68) W Supple 6/4 FAV: 0031: Held up, gd hdwy to lead dist, **68**
rdn clr fnl 1f: hvly bckd, 6 wk abs: eff at 5f, apprec this step up to 6f: acts on fast & gd/soft grnd: see 4409.
4770 **PRIMARILY** 24 [3] A Berry 2-8-10 R Winston 12/1: 052: Chsd ldrs, styd on under press fnl 1f & 2 **68**
took 2nd cl-home, not reach wnr: 7f shld now suit: could find a small race, poss a sell: see 4770.
4934 **MING VASE** 14 [8] D Carroll 2-8-10 (57) D Tudhope(5) 6/1: 6256053: Chsd ldrs, outpcd halfway, 1 **65**
switched wide & styd on fnl 1f: op 8/1: return to 7f will suit, as in 2802 (AW).
4963 **LADY HOPEFUL** 13 [7] R P Elliott 2-8-5 BL (59) J Fanning 14/1: 2205504: Front rank, led 2f out ½ **58**
till dist, no extra: tried blnks & clr of rem: btr 2810 (7f, fast grnd).
4787 **BOPPYS DREAM** 23 [2]2-8-3 P Hanagan 16/1: 605: Held up, nvr nr ldrs: see 4596. 7 **40**
4945 **SILVER SWING** 14 [5]2-8-9 S W Kelly 20/1: 006: gr c Celtic Swing - Poetry In Motion (Ballad ¾ **44**
Rock) Chsd ldrs 4f, sn lost place: 5,500 gns Feb foal: dam a 5f wnr, sire a top class mid-dist performer.
4590 **MONKEY MADGE** 34 [10]2-8-5 C Catlin 11/4: 27: Chsd ldrs 4f, sn btn: drifted from 7/4: disapp nk **39**
run, much btr on debut in 4590 (fast grnd).
IROQUOIS PRINCESS [9]2-8-4 Stacey Renwick(7) 66/1: 8: ch f Polish Precedent - Chelsea (Miswaki) 8 **22**
Slowly away, al bhd on debut: Feb foal, cost 3,200 gns: half sister to 6f juv wnr Cedar Rangers: dam a 1m wnr in
France, sire a top class miler: with D Shaw.
4934 **MILL BY THE STREAM** 14 [6]2-8-12 VIS (52) K Darley 16/1: 000609: Led till 2f out, wknd & eased, 3 **24**
fin last: tried a visor & has been gldd: mod.
9 Ran Time 1m 20.25(6.15) Owned: Mr Jim Browne Trained: Upper Lambourn

Official Going Standard

5155

2.00 Bet Direct On Itv Page 367 Classified Stakes 3yo+ 0-60 (F4)
£2989 £854 £427 5f216y aw rnd Inapplicable Inside

5130 **PRINCE OF GOLD** 2 [12] R Hollinshead 4-9-1 p (57) D Sweeney 5/1: 0053201: Held up, prog when short **69a**
of room bef 1f out, styd on to lead ins fnl 1f, rdn out: qck reapp: eff at 7f/1m, best form recently has come at
5/6f: acts on firm, gd/soft & polytrack with cheek pieces: see 4989 & 4785.
4646 **WOODBURY** 31 [7] Mrs H Sweeting 5-8-12 (57) G Baker 5/1: 1041062: Led, hdd after 1f, led again 1 **62a**
halfway, hdd ins fnl 1f, not pace wnr: gd eff in defeat: btr 4412.
5039 **ASBO** 7 [6] Dr J D Scargill 4-8-12 (57) S Drowne 14/1: 0-543563: Held up, prog & short of room 1 **59a**
bef 1f out, switched & kept on late: qck reapp & polytrack bow: acts on fast, gd/soft & polytrack: see 4646.
5112 **SIRAJ** 2 [5] P S McEntee 5-9-3 (59) Dane O'Neill 25/1: 5-010004: Cl-up, no extra dist: qck reapp. 1¼ **61a**
5130 **LEGAL SET** 2 [10]8-9-4 t (60) L Fletcher(3) 11/1: 2400525: Bhd, prog 3f out, hmpd & lost pl 2f out, 2 **56a**
kept on late: qck reapp: shade closer with clr run & will apprec rtn to 7f: btr 5130 (7f, soft).
3333 **ZAGALA** 89 [9]4-9-1 t (60) L Keniry(3) 16/1: 2020006: Handy over 4f, wknd: long abs. 1 **50a**
4845 **KALLISTAS PRIDE** 20 [2]4-8-11 vis (56) T Quinn 16/1: 0605007: Cl-up 5f, wknd: btr 3109 (gd/soft). ½ **45a**
4408* **ROMAN EMPIRE** 42 [13]4-9-2 bl (58) N Callan 7/2 FAV: 3354018: In tch over 4f, wknd: tchd 9/2: 6 nk **49a**
wk abs & blnks refitted: showed more in 4408 (fast).
4870 **ABELARD** 19 [1]3-9-0 vis (57) T Hamilton(3) 6/1: 6505029: In tch over 4f, wknd: btr 4870 (5f, firm). 1¼ **44a**
4272 **FULL PITCH** 49 [3]8-9-2 (58) V Slattery 33/1: 6100000: 10th: Missed break, nvr nrr than mid-div. 2½ **38a**
4253 **BOISDALE** 50 [8]6-9-1 (57) R Fitzpatrick 20/1: 5010350: 11th: Led after 1f, hdd halfway, wknd. 7 **19a**
4646 **SILVER CHIME** 31 [11]4-9-1 (60) M Fenton 25/1: 6000000: 12th: Cl-up 4f, fdd. 5 **5a**
12 Ran Time 1m 15.73 () Owned: Horne Hollinshead Johnson Trained: Upper Longdon

---

5156　2.30 Holiday Inn Garden Court Dunstall Park Handicap Stakes 3yo+ 46-62 (F4)　　[69]
£2989 £854 £427　　5f20y aw rnd　　Inapplicable Inside

5096* **HARRISONS FLYER** 3 [9] R A Fahey 3-9-11 (6ex)p (66) G Parkin 9/2: 02U0011: In tch, styd on to lead　**75a**
dist despite hanging left, rdn out to assert: qck reapp: AW bow: eff at 5/6f on firm, soft grnd & polytrack: eff
with cheek pieces: did well to defy a 6lb pen & can land hat-trick: see 5096 & 2849.
5096　**WHITE LEDGER** 3 [6] R A Fahey 5-9-3 vis (58) T Hamilton(3) 6/1: 0311062: Mid-div, prog & short of　½　**65a**
room over 1f out, kept on ins fnl 1f, just held: qck reapp: back to form on switch to AW & can find similar.
5110　**JUNIPER BANKS** 3 [3] Miss A Stokell 3-9-2 (57) L Fletcher(3) 40/1: 20-66003: Cl-up when no room　1¾　**59a**
bef 1f out, kept on & not pace front 2: qck reapp: AW bow: acts on fast grnd & polytrack: only lightly rcd.
5069　**SHARP HAT** 6 [11] D W Chapman 10-9-4 (59) A Quinn(5) 13/2: 2450004: Held up, outpcd over 2f out,　½　**60a**
rallied well fnl 1f: op 11/2 on qck reapp: btr 3350 & 2846.
1605　**DESERT LIGHT** 164 [2]3-9-0 vis (55) Lisa Jones 16/1: 1300225: In tch, ev ch when hung left dist, onepcd.　1　**53a**
4751　**KING EGBERT** 26 [8]3-9-0 (55) M Fenton 4/1 FAV: 00-40306: Missed break, prog bef 1f out, nrst　nk　**52a**
fin: op 6/1 on AW bow: could nvr get competitive: btr 4528 (fast).
5039　**INNCLASSIC** 7 [10]3-9-4 bl (59) L Enstone 20/1: 3120007: Handy over 3f, sn hung left & no extra.　shd　**55a**
2702　**LADY PEKAN** 116 [13]5-9-3 bl (58) I Mongan 14/1: 5300008: In tch over 3f, onepcd: long abs.　hd　**53a**
4140　**MULTAHAB** 55 [5]5-9-0 t (55) N Callan 20/1: 0000069: Handy over 3f, short of room bef 1f out, sn btn.　1　**47a**
4964　**SHAYMEES GIRL** 13 [1]3-9-1 (56) N Chalmers(3) 25/1: 0-533030: 10th: Led, hdd dist, wknd: btr 4964 (6f).　nk　**47a**
4489　**DAVIDS MARK** 39 [4]4-9-0 (55) W Ryan 6/1: 4441200: 11th: In tch, wknd bef 1f out: btr 3974 & 3640.　3　**37a**
1787　**BEAU JAZZ** 154 [7]3-9-5 (60) P Doe 66/1: 3060000: 12th: Bhd, nvr a factor.　½　**41a**
4603　**MALAHIDE EXPRESS** 33 [12]4-9-5 (60) J D O'Reilly(7) 9/1: 5410030: 13th: Al in rear: btr 4603 (fast).　2½　**34a**
13 Ran　Time 1m 3.38 ()　Owned: P D Smith Holdings Ltd　Trained: Malton

---

5157　3.00 Gordon Hodgetts Lifetime In Racing Median Auction Maiden Stakes Div 1 3yo (F4)
£2919 £834 £417　　5f216y aw rnd　　Inapplicable Inside

4836　**FUTURE DEAL** 21 [3] C A Horgan 3-8-9　T Quinn 9/4 FAV: 431: Held up, prog 2f out, styd on to lead　**61a**
ins fnl 1f, rdn out: well bckd on AW bow: eff at 6f, rtn to 7f will suit: acts on fast, gd grnd & polytrack.
5030　**IMTALKINGGIBBERISH** 8 [12] J R Jenkins 3-9-0 (75) W Ryan 5/1: 5020542: Missed break, prog　1　**62a**
halfway, kept on ins fnl 1f, not pace wnr: AW bow: acts on fast grnd & polytrack: see 5030 & 784.
4262　**HEAVENS WALK** 50 [5] P J Makin 3-9-0 (50) D Sweeney 8/1: 5043: Rear, prog to lead 2f out, hdd ins　shd　**61a**
fnl 1f, no extra: clr rem: 7 wk abs & AW bow: imprvd eff on switch to polytrack: see 3687.
4636　**STAR FERN** 32 [2] R M H Cowell 3-9-0 (47) E Ahern 33/1: 5500004: Missed break, nvr nrr than mid-div.　5　**47a**
182　**SAFFRON RIVER** 311 [1]3-9-0 (56) Dane O'Neill 16/1: 4304-5: b c Polar Prince - Cloudy Reef　2　**41a**
(Cragador) Missed break, nvr a factor: reapp: plcd once in '03 (rtd 64a, AW mdn): eff at 5f on fibresand.
5110　**KAMENKA** 3 [13]3-8-9 vis (62) T Hamilton(3) 4/1: 4400336: In tch, ev ch bef 1f out, fdd: qck　3　**27a**
reapp: v disapp eff: showed more in 5110 (6f, gd/soft, visor) & 4969.
4413　**SOKOKE** 42 [8]3-9-0 (58) M Fenton 10/1: 23007: In tch, led 3f out, hdd 2f out, wknd: 6 wk abs.　2½　**25a**
4969　**MISS PRIM** 13 [10]3-8-9　Hayley Turner(3) 100/1: 08: Led 3f, wknd bef 1f out.　nk　**19a**
4404　**RAETIHI** 42 [6]3-8-9 (40) N Callan 20/1: 0409: In tch over 3f, wknd: 6 wk abs.　1　**16a**
1392　**FRABROFEN** 175 [4]3-8-9　R Ffrench 13/2: 20: 10th: In tch 4f, wknd: long abs & AW bow: btr 1392.　2½　**9a**
4788　**Designer City** 23 [11]3-8-9 (35) T E Durcan 66/1:0　　4413　**Dane Rhapsody** 42 [7]3-8-9 (45) S Hitchcott 16/1:0
12 Ran　Time 1m 16.20 ()　Owned: Mr Mohammed Al-Gaoud　Trained: Ogbourne Maizey

---

5158　3.30 Wolverhampton-Racecourse Co Uk Selling Stakes 2yo (G4)
£2709 £774 £387　　7f32y aw rnd　　Inapplicable Outside

5049　**LATERAL THINKER** 7 [8] J A Osborne 2-8-12 (68) E Ahern 9/4 JT FAV: 5260641: Cl-up, led after 2f,　**67a**
rdn out: qck reapp: bought in for 4,250 gns: eff at 5/7f on fast, gd/soft & polytrack: see 3820 & 3521.
4922　**MITCHELLAND** 16 [5] James Moffatt 2-8-12 (69) R French 10/1: 3555052: Cl-up, ev ch ins fnl 1f,　nk　**65a**
just held: handles gd, hvy grnd & polytrack: can find similar: see 3698.
4725　**NORCROFT** 29 [9] N A Callaghan 2-9-3 (69) J F Egan 9/4 JT FAV: 0004003: Keen in tch, styd on　hd　**69a**
despite hanging left dist, not btn far in 3rd: bckd: eff at 5/7f on gd, gd/soft & polytrack: see 4100 & 1237.
4403　**WHITE STAR MAGIC** 42 [7] J R Weymes 2-8-11 (69) I Mongan 14/1: 0064: Bhd, prog 3f out, kept on　2　**59a**
late: clr rem: 6 wk abs: eff at 7f on polytrack: see 4083.
4706　**WORTH A GRAND** 28 [3]2-8-11 (62) P Doe 14/1: 055065: Led 2f, wknd bef 1f out: btr 4706.　5　**50a**
5013　**ALZARMA** 8 [12]2-8-13 (2ow) (62) J Dekeyser 16/1: 030606: Handy, wknd bef 2f out.　nk　**51a**
4922　**MOUNT KELLET** 16 [2]2-8-11　M Fenton 33/1: 007: In tch till halfway, wknd: see 4922.　3　**43a**
　　　　CHICKS BABE 0 [4]2-8-7 (1ow) S Hitchcott 40/1: 8: Missed break, prog after 2f, fdd halfway:　2½　**34a**
debut: Apr first foal, dam unplcd: sire useful performer as a juv, was successful over hdles: with B Palling.
4635　**GOOD WEE GIRL** 32 [1]2-8-12 (68) Hayley Turner(3) 13/2: 1510009: Missed break, nvr a factor.　nk　**38a**
4842　**ASSURED** 20 [10]2-8-7 (1ow)BL N Callan 33/1: 0000: 10th: Sn cl-up, fdd 3f out: first time blnks.　11　**12a**
4171　**La Providence** 53 [11]2-8-6 bl e P M Quinn 100/1:0　　4540　**Chek Oi** 36 [6]2-8-11 BL(60) S Drowne 14/1:P
12 Ran　Time 1m 32.22 ()　Owned: Colin G R Booth And Patricia Hughes　Trained: Upper Lambourn

---

5159　4.00 Ladbrokes Com Handicap Stakes 3yo+ 71-85 (D2)　　[94]
£7147 £2199 £1100　　7f32y aw rnd　　Inapplicable Outside

4912　**JAY GEES CHOICE** 16 [2] M R Channon 4-9-4 (84) T E Durcan 6/1: 0461341: In tch, styd on to lead　**93a**
dist, rdn out: bckd from 11/1: AW bow: eff at 7f/1m on firm, soft grnd & polytrack: h'capped to win again.
4446　**MISS GEORGE** 41 [1] D K Ivory 6-9-3 (83) Dane O'Neill 16/1: 3030032: Rear, prog 2f out, kept on　1½　**88a**
to chase wnr ins fnl 1f, al held: stays well: continues to run well & can find similar: see 4446 & 4031.
4689　**FLUR NA H ALBA** 30 [9] I Semple 5-9-0 p (80) T Hamilton(3) 33/1: 0-103403: In tch, led 2f out, hdd　1　**83a**
dist, no extra: AW bow: acts on firm, soft grnd & polytrack: encouraging eff: see 4350 & 3326.
4642* **CHATEAU NICOL** 31 [7] B G Powell 5-9-3 (83) T Quinn 9/2: 1566014: Rear, prog 3f out, kept on　shd　**85a**

late: acts on fast, hvy grnd & both AWs: btr 4642.
5000 **SOYUZ 9** [12]4-9-2 (82) N Callan 11/1: 3150005: Rear, hdwy 3f out, kept on late: btr 1616 (gd/soft). *hd* **83a**
4318 **ECCENTRIC 47** [8]3-9-2 (84) J F Egan 10/1: 0422026: In tch 3f, sn outpcd, rallied & ev ch bef 1f out, wknd: 7 wk abs: best when able to front run: btr 4318 & 3331. *1¼* **83a**
5000 **PRIMO WAY 9** [5]3-9-0 P (82) K May(7) 12/1: 3630307: In tch 4f, sn outpcd, rallied late: cheek pieces. *½* **80a**
4469 **FLINT RIVER 40** [10]6-9-3 (83) L Fletcher(3) 5/1: 4002258: Bhd, prog 4f out, wknd fnl 2f: 6 wk abs: prefers fibresand: btr 4141, 3694 & 940. *3* **75a**
4891 **VINDICATION GB 17** [11]4-9-2 t (82) A Quinn(5) 16/1: 0660009: Al in rear: new stable. *½* **73a**
4642 **WINNING VENTURE 31** [6]7-9-0 (80) M Fenton 11/1: 3200200: 10th: Led after 2f, hdd 2f out, wknd. *hd* **70a**
4873* **IDLE POWER 18** [3]6-9-2 p (82) E Ahern 4/1 FAV: 3002110: 11th: Led 2f, styd cl-up, wknd ins fnl 1f, sn eased: disapp on hat-trick bid & reportedly ran flat: btr 4873 & 4446. *1* **70a**
4873 **JUST A GLIMMER 18** [4]4-9-3 (83) S Drowne 20/1: 1201000: 12th: Cl-up 5f, wknd: btr 1525 (soft). *3* **65a**
12 Ran Time 1m 29.72 () Owned: Mr John Guest Trained: West Ilsley

5160

4.30 Tie The Knot At Dunstall Park Handicap Stakes 3yo+ 56-70 (E3) **[77]**
£3458 £1064 £532 **1m5f194y aw** **Inapplicable** Inside

4942 **ALBAVILLA 14** [10] P W Harris 4-9-7 (70) E Ahern 5/1 CO FAV: 6-325031: Cl-up, led 5f out, all out ins fnl 1f to hold on: eff around 12f, imprvd for step up to 14f: acts on firm, gd/soft & poss soft, apprec switch to polytrack: confidence boosting first win, unexposed at this trip: see 4942. **80a**
5004 **SKYES FOLLY 9** [7] J G Given 4-9-6 bl (69) M Fenton 5/1 CO FAV: 0333442: Rear, prog 4f out, staying on when short of room 2f out, switched & ev ch ins fnl 1f, just held: acts on fm, gd/soft & polytrack. *shd* **78a**
4973 **JADEERON 12** [2] Miss D A McHale 5-8-11 p (60) Lisa Jones 11/1: 4400663: Mid-div, prog 4f out, wknd. *10* **60a**
4983 **DOVEDON HERO 11** [12] P J McBride 4-9-7 bl (70) L Keniry(3) 5/1 CO FAV: 0203424: Bhd, prog 5f out, short of room 2f out, sn wknd: disapp: btr 4983 & 4360. *hd* **69a**
INDALO GREY 64 [13]8-9-4 (67) R Havlin 33/1: 3//-6455: b g Toca Madera - Pollyfaster (Polyfoto) Missed break, prog 5f out, wknd fnl 2f: Brit bow: earlier unplcd in h'cap hdle at Galway: unplcd all 3 Flat starts to date in native Ireland (14f/2m, mdns & h'cap): Mrs Stef Liddiard. *3½* **63a**
4973 **REGAL GALLERY 12** [6]6-9-7 (70) Paul Eddery 11/2: 1134246: Bhd, prog after halfway, wknd bef 1f out, sn eased: op 9/2: first try at 14f: btr 4973 & 3026 (12f). *nk* **65a**
4849 **ONCE 20** [5]4-8-13 (62) Dane O'Neill 14/1: 3000007: Handy 12f, wknd: btr 1923 (fast). *nk* **56a**
5024 **MILK AND SULTANA 8** [9]4-9-1 (64) S Drowne 12/1: 1140308: Al in rear: btr 4924. *21* **40a**
4983 **ZEIS 11** [11]4-8-11 t (60) L Fletcher 40/1: 1100009: Bhd, nvr a factor. *8* **29a**
107* **HEFIN 327** [3]7-9-1 (64) T Quinn 5/1 CO FAV: 033131-0: 10th: Handy, wknd 5f out: new stable, btr 107. *11* **23a**
4983 **VIN DU PAYS 11** [1]4-8-11 (60) N Callan 33/1: 0000000: 11th: In tch, wknd 5f out. *10* **10a**
5123 **VANBRUGH 2** [8]4-9-2 vis (65) I Mongan 33/1: 0000600: 12th: Led & sn clr, hdd 5f out, wknd: qck reapp. *5* **10a**
12 Ran Time 3m 4.25 () Owned: Mrs P W Harris Trained: Berkhamsted

5161

5.00 Sponsor A Race At Dunstall Park Handicap Stakes 3yo 56-70 (E3) **[80]**
£3858 £1187 £594 **1m1f103y aw** **Inapplicable** Inside

4055* **GENTLEMANS DEAL 60** [5] E A L Dunlop 3-9-9 (75) E Ahern 7/4 FAV: 411: In tch, led 2f out, pushed clr, val 5L+: 9 wk abs: AW bow: eff at 7f, imprvd for step up to 9.4f: acts on fast, soft grnd & polytrack: goes well fresh: fine win on h'cap bow & more prizes await: see 4055 (mdn). **88a+**
4939* **MISS POLARIS 14** [4] P W Harris 3-9-8 (74) M Fenton 7/1: 612: Rear, prog 2f out, kept on, not pace wnr: eff around 1m, ran to form on step up to 9.5f: acts on fast grnd & polytrack: gd run, win again. *3* **79a**
5008 **HAZEWIND 9** [2] P D Evans 3-9-4 vis t (70) S Drowne 11/2: 6416443: In tch, under press when carr right over 1f out, sn onepcd: btr 4398 (7f). *¾* **73a**
5083 **ALI DEO 5** [1] W J Haggas 3-9-0 (66) J F Egan 10/1: 0600044: Keen rear, eff when short of room over 1f out, switched & kept on late: qck reapp: see 5083. *nk* **68a**
4931 **ST SAVARIN 16** [12]3-9-7 (73) T Quinn 15/2: 1000525: Rear, hdwy 3f out, edged left & no impress fnl 1f. *shd* **74a**
5027 **CARTRONAGEERAGHLAD 8** [3]3-9-4 bl (70) Dane O'Neill 14/1: 4540036: Cl-up over 7f, no extra: btr 5027. *nk* **70a**
5083 **THE FUN MERCHANT 5** [6]3-9-1 (67) N Callan 20/1: 1120507: Handy, wknd bef 1f out: qck reapp. *1½* **64a**
5050 **TAMINOULA 7** [10]3-9-8 BL (74) I Mongan 16/1: 1-006008: Nvr nrr than mid-div: qck reapp, blnks. *1½* **68a**
4634 **CHERUBIM 32** [8]3-9-8 (74) T P Queally 20/1: 5512009: Led, hdd 5f out, wknd fnl 2f: btr 3287 (10f). *3½* **62a**
4909 **JACKIE KIELY 16** [11]3-8-13 t (65) J Brennan(7) 16/1: 3040350: 10th: Al in rear: btr 4539 (fast). *1½* **50a**
4897 **BENNY THE BALL 17** [13]3-9-4 (70) T E Durcan 22/1: 61-00000: 11th: Cl-up, wkng when no room dist. *7* **44a**
5026 **SOVIET SCEPTRE 8** [9]3-9-0 (66) S Hitchcott 25/1: 4600150: 12th: Cl-up, led 5f out, hdd 2f out, wknd. *¾* **38a**
4937 **ISKANDER 14** [7]3-9-3 bl (69) J Carroll 16/1: 6405040: 13th: Missed break, prog 4f out, wknd 2f out. *1¼* **39a**
13 Ran Time 2m 1.39 () Owned: Khalifa Sultan And Mohammed Jaber Trained: Newmarket

5162

5.30 Gordon Hodgetts Lifetime In Racing Median Auction Maiden Stakes Div 2 3yo (F4)
£2912 £832 £416 **5f216y aw rnd** **Inapplicable** Inside

4790 **DEUXIEME 23** [11] R Charlton 3-8-9 (67) S Drowne 8/11 FAV: 335221: In tch, styd on to lead ins fnl 1f despite hanging left, drvn out: bckd: eff at 5.5/7f on fast, gd/soft grnd & polytrack: see 4790 & 4413. **60a**
4836 **BERESFORD BOY 21** [3] D K Ivory 3-9-0 (49) D Sweeney 80/1: 06-P02: Handy, kept on fnl 1f, not pace wnr: imprvd on modest form to date: eff at 6f on polytrack: can find a banded race or a seller. *2* **58a**
4116 **LAKESIDE GUY 57** [5] P S McEntee 3-9-0 (54) N Callan 14/1: 0356203: Cl-up, led dist, hdd ins fnl 1f, no extra: 8 wk abs: acts on firm, fast grnd & polytrack: see 3725. *1½* **54a**
4739 **SONG KOI 26** [4] J G Given 3-8-9 (50) M Fenton 9/1: 44-0204: In tch, outpcd halfway, rallied dist. *2* **43a**
5053 **KNEAD THE DOUGH 7** [12]3-9-0 P (55) J F Egan 4/1: 260205: Cl-up, led over 1f out, hdd dist, edged left & sn wknd: qck reapp & cheek pieces: btr 4969 (gd). *½* **47a**
4054 **EIGHT ELLINGTON 60** [8]3-9-0 (55) I Mongan 14/1: 0-046006: Nvr nrr than mid-div. *¾* **45a**
1607 **ONYX 164** [1]3-9-0 P Doe 66/1: 607: Rear, prog 2f out, nrst fin: long abs. *shd* **44a**
4366 **INDIAN EDGE 45** [2]3-9-0 (51) S Hitchcott 12/1: 5200008: Handy, outpcd 3f out, staying on when hmpd dist: 6 wk abs: btr 1607 (soft). *3* **35a**
4836 **TANNE BLIXEN 21** [13]3-8-9 L Keniry(3) 100/1: 0009: Al in rear: mod form to date. *shd* **29a**
4964 **FAITES VOS JEUX 13** [6]3-8-9 (45) M Halford(7) 66/1: 430-0050: 10th: In tch, led 2f out, hdd over 1f out, fdd: btr 4964. *2* **23a**
4964 **MISS CHANCELOT 13** [7]3-8-9 S Whitworth 100/1: 0000: 11th: Al bhd: mod form to date. *6* **7a**

WOLVERHAMPTON Polytrack MONDAY 18.10.04 Lefthand, Sharp Track

2493 **VELVET TOUCH 124** [9]3-8-9 (46) W Ryan 16/1: 6065000: 12th: Led till halfway, fdd: long abs.   6   0a
12 Ran   Time 1m 15.96()   Owned: Beckhampton Stables Ltd   Trained: Beckhampton

NAAS SUNDAY 17.10.04 Lefthand, Galloping Track, Uphill Finish

Official Going GOOD/SOFT.

| 5163 | 2.15 Tifrums EBF Maiden 2yo Colts & Geldings ()
£8333 £1941 £856   6f   Good/Soft |

    FOOTSTEPSINTHESAND [1] A P O'Brien 2-9-0   C O'Donoghue 3/1 FAV: 1: b c Giants Causeway -   100+
Glatisant (Rainbow Quest) Made all, clr halfway, eased fnl 1f, val 6L+: debut: well bckd: Feb foal, cost 170,000
gns: half brother to wnrs at 6/16f: dam decent at 7f: sire multiple Gr 1 wnr at 7f/10f: eff at 6f, 7f/10f shld
suit: acts on gd/soft & a gall trk: goes well fresh: won in fine style & has a bright future.
    OLYMPIC [7] A P O'Brien 2-9-0   J P Spencer 7/2: 2: b c Danzig - Queena (Mr Prospector) Cl up,   4½   85
outpcd halfway, kept on ins fnl 1f, no ch with wnr: debut: op 2/1: stablemate of wnr: May foal, brother/half
brother to decent performers abroad: dam succesful in US: eff at 6f, further will suit: acts on gd/soft grnd.
    KAWAASER 29 [19] K Prendergast 2-9-0   D P McDonoh 10/1: -2603: br c Dixie Union - Thunderous   hd   84
Return (Thunder Gulch) Prom, no extra ins fnl 1f.
20 Ran   Time 1m 13.10()   Owned: Mr M Tabor   Trained: Ballydoyle

LONGCHAMP SUNDAY 17.10.04 Righthand, Stiff, Galloping Track

Official Going HEAVY.

| 5164 | 1.10 Gr 3 Prix de Conde 2yo ()
£25704 £10282 £7711   1m1f   Heavy |

4729 **MUSKETIER 29** [3] P Bary 2-8-11   C P Lemaire 9/10 FAV: 4121: Cl up, led 2f out, sn clr, eased cl   113
home, val 9L+: earlier won at Deauville: eff at 1m, apprec step up to 9f, 10f will suit: acts on gd/soft & hvy
grnd: lightly rcd juvenile who relished today's testing conditions: see 4729.
4156 **DOCTOR DINO 57** [4] R Gibson 2-8-11   T Jarnet 19/10: 1312: Held up, prog to chall 2f out, kept   6   103
on, no ch with wnr: see 4156.
4746* **WINGMAN 25** [1] J W Hills 2-8-11   C Soumillon 66/10: 0513: In tch, outpcd over 2f out, mod late   4   97
gains: showed more in 4747 (mdn, gd).
    FIXATEUR [2] F Head 2-8-11   O Peslier 7/2: -0114: b c Anabaa - Fabulous Account (Private   5   89
Account) Led, hdd 2f out, fdd.
4 Ran   Time 1m 59.60 ()   Owned: Ecurie J L Bouchard   Trained: France

| 5165 | 2.15 Gr 2 Prix du Conseil de Paris 3yo+ ()
£42148 £16268 £7764   1m4f   Heavy |

4956 **PRIDE 14** [2] A de Royer Dupre 4-9-1 (80) D Bonilla 33/10: 0-41352301: Held up, prog 3f out, styd   119
on to lead dist, pushed out, val 7L+: eff at 10/12f on gd & soft, imprvd today on hvy: v smart 4yo who enjoyed
today's testing conditions: see 4956 & 4160.
9}   **SIMPLEX 344** [6] C Laffon Parias 3-8-9   O Peslier 29/10: 212-512: Bhd, prog 3f out, kept on late.   5   112
    GEORDIELAND [3] J M Beguigne 3-8-9   C P Lemaire 61/10: 12123123: Led after 4f, hdd dist, no extra.   hd   111

4532 **FRANK SONATA 36** [8]3-8-9 (105) D Boeuf 23/1: 0-6131197: Bhd, under press over 4f out, btn &   15   89
eased fnl 1f: first try on hvy grnd: btr 3274 (listed, soft).
8 Ran   Time 2m 39.10()   Owned: Np Bloodstock Ltd   Trained: France

SAN SIRO SUNDAY 17.10.04 Righthand, Stiff, Galloping Track

Official Going SOFT.

| 5166 | 2.20 Gr 3 Premio Sergio Cumani 3yo+ Fillies & Mares ()
£37852 £17474 £9771   1m   Soft |

4840 **SNOW GOOSE 21** [1] J L Dunlop 3-8-9 (103) J Fortune 7/2: 12-0423321: Led 6f, rallied to lead ins   106
fnl 1f, rdn out: stays 1m, stays well fresh: acts on firm & gd grnd: has been in gd form this term, deserved win.
4840 **KITCAT 21** [2] P Schiergen 3-8-9   A Suborics 12/1: 32: Mid div, led 2f out, hdd ins fnl 1f, not pace wnr.   ¾   102
4840* **SECRET MELODY 21** [8] H A Pantall 3-8-12   M Blancpain 11/4: 13: Cl up, ev ch over 1f out, sn onepcd.   ½   104
8 Ran   Time 1m 40.80 ()   Owned: Sir Thomas Pilkington   Trained: Arundel, W Sussex

SAN SIRO   SUNDAY 17.10.04   Righthand, Stiff, Galloping Track

5167
3.0 Gr 1 Gran Criterium 2yo ()
£130880 £65414 £37975   **1m**   **Soft**

KONIGSTIGER [2] P Schiergen 2-8-11 Filip Minarik 12/1: -11: b c Tiger Hill - Kittiwake **109**
(Barathea) Bhd, prog bef 1f out, rdn out to lead nr fin: eff at 1m on soft grnd: useful.
　　　IDEALIST [3] P Schiergen 2-8-11 A Suborics 9/1: -12: Prom, led ins fnl 1f, hdd nr fin: eff at 1m on soft. *hd* **108**
45**BEARTHSTEAD WINGS** 36 [10] M Johnston 2-8-11 (99) K Darley 7/2 FAV: 14613: Rear, prog halfway, ¾ **105**
led 2f out, hdd ins fnl 1f, no extra: acts on firm & soft grnd: ran to form of 4524.
4640* **MERCHANT** 30 [7] M L W Bell 2-8-11 (99) R Mullen 9/2: 53211114: Al prom, no extra dist: acts on ½ **104**
firm & soft: up in grade: see 4640.
4797 **BERKHAMSTED** 22 [4]2-8-11 (100) Martin Dwyer 7/1: 1625185: Nvr nrr than mid div: see 4156 (listed). 1½ **101**
4914 **UMNIYA** 15 [5]2-8-8 vis (100) A Culhane 11/2: 56643536: Bhd, hdwy 3f out, onepcd fnl 1f: see 4679. ½ **97**
4462 **SHANNON SPRINGS** 39 [8]2-8-11 M Hills 11/2: 2327: Al in rear: btr 4462 (mdn, firm). 3½ **93**
10 Ran   Time 1m 42.30 ()   Owned: Gestut Schienderhan   Trained: Germany

5168
4.10 Gr 1 Gran Premio del Jockey Club 3yo+ ()
£151056 £80546 £48063   **1m4f**   **Soft**

4428 **SHIROCCO** 42 [3] A Schutz 3-8-13 A Suborics 11/4 FAV: -213131: Led 10f out, drvn out ins fnl 1f: **119**
6 wk abs: eff at 11/12f on soft & hvy grnd: v smart mid dist performer in the mud: see 4428 & 3010.
　　　ELECTROCUTIONIST [6] V Valiani 3-8-13 E Botti 10/1: -1112: Chsd ldrs, ev ch over 1f out, kept on. *nse* **118**
49**IMPERIAL DANCER** 14 [2] M R Channon 6-9-4 (110) T E Durcan 14/1: 003036203D: Held up, prog wide 5 **110**
3f out, hung right ins fnl 1f, no impress, fin 3rd, disqualified & plcd 5th: consistent 6yo who was harshly demoted.
4567* **SWEET STREAM** 35 [5] J E Hammond 4-9-1 T Gillet 9/1: 3311-0313: Bhd, prog over 2f out, onepcd 1¼ **105**
fnl 1f, fin 4th, plcd 3rd: btr 4567.
4837* **FAIR MIX** 26 [4] M Rolland 6-9-4 S Pasquier 6/1: 5-1632614: Led, hdd 10f out, styd prom, onepcd ½ **107**
when hmpd ins fnl 1f, fin 5th, plcd 4th: btr 4837 (10f, gd).
4947 **PERCUSSIONIST** 15 [1]3-8-13 (118) J Fortune 10/1: 32-1140236: Sn cl up, outpcd 3f out, rallied late. *shd* **109**
3711} **WITHOUT CONNEXION** 428 [7]5-9-4 D Vargiu 20/1: 6-418717: Bhd, nvr a factor. *nk* **106**
4733 **DUBAI SUCCESS** 29 [9]4-9-4 (112) M Hills 6/1: D3-1402248: Mid div 10f, sn wknd: disappointing in 5 **98**
today's soft grnd: btr 4733 (14f, gd) & 3958 (13.3f, fast).
4812 **BANDARI** 21 [8]5-9-4 (119) W Supple 10/3: 11010339: Cl up, wknd bef 2f out: poor display on 3 **93**
today's soft grnd & perhaps had enough for the year: btr 4812 (fast) & 4391 (firm).
9 Ran   Time 2m 31.60 ()   Owned: Baron G Von Ullmann   Trained: Germany

BATH   TUESDAY 19.10.04   Lefthand Turning Track with Uphill Finish

Official Going Soft

5169
2.00 Trianglecasino Co Uk/E B F Maiden Stakes 2yo   (D3)
£4238 £1304 £652   **5f11y rnd**   **Soft 102**   **+03 Fast**   Far Side

4625 **CESAR MANRIQUE** 33 [8] B W Hills 2-9-0 (75) M Hills 6/1: 0541: Chsd ldrs, hdwy to lead over 1f **82**
out, styd on strongly ins last, rdn out: eff at 5f on gd & fast grnd, imprvd here on soft: gd confidence boost.
5021 **AUWITESWEETHEART** 9 [5] B R Millman 2-8-9 (68) S Drowne 3/1: 55532: In tch, eff over 1f out, kept 1½ **72**
on to chase wnr ins last, onepace: acts on gd & soft grnd: shld find a race: see 5021.
4859 **MALAIKA** 20 [2] R Hollinshead 2-8-9 Stephanie Hollinshead(5) 11/1: 543: Slow away, sn handy, led 1½ **68**
over 2f out till over 1f out, no extra: acts on soft grnd: see 4859, 4307.
　　　KEEP ME WARM [7] W G M Turner 2-9-0 C Haddon(7) 66/1: 4: ch g Atraf - Little Greenbird 1¼ **70**
(Ardkinglass) Slow away, bhd, eff 2f out, onepace: joc received a 2-day whip ban: Mar first foal, cost 3,000gns.
2109 **THREE STRIKES** 141 [6]2-8-9 Martin Dwyer 14/1: 05: b f Selkirk - Special Oasis (Green Desert) 1½ **62**
In tch, wknd over 1f out: long abs: now with S Williams: Apr foal, cost 85,000gns: full sister to a 1m scorer.
　　　JENNVERSE [12]2-8-9 T Quinn 33/1: 6: b f Opening Verse - Jennelle (Nomination) Slow away & 2 **57**
bhd, nvr a factor on debut: Feb first foal: dam 5f wnr.
4844 **SWIFT DAME** 21 [1]2-8-9 (63) R L Moore 25/1: 0507: In tch, wknd over 1f out. *nk* **56**
　　　BEFITTING [10]2-9-0 T P Queally 16/1: 8: Nvr a factor on debut. ¾ **59**
4187 **AFRICAN STORM** 53 [3]2-9-0 (71) J F Egan 14/1: 522069: In tch, wknd qckly over 1f out, abs. *nk* **58**
5048 **KITCHEN SINK** 8 [11]2-9-0 D Sweeney 25/1: 00: 10th: Al bhd: gelded. ½ **57**
4893 **FOREST DELIGHT** 18 [9]2-8-9 E Ahern 33/1: 000: 11th: In tch, wknd over 2f out. 1½ **49**
5047 **GIMASHA** 8 [4]2-8-9 T E Durcan 15/8 FAV: 420: 12th: Led till over 2f out, wknd: reportedly fin *shd* **48**
distressed.
12 Ran   Time 1m 05.25 (4.95)   Owned: Mr Philip G Harvey   Trained: Lambourn

5170
2.30 European Breeders Fund Maiden Stakes Div 1 2yo   (D3)
£4537 £1396 £698   **1m5y**   **Soft 102**   **-26 Slow**   Inside

4851 **WOTCHALIKE** 20 [8] D R C Elsworth 2-9-0 (82) T Quinn 1/2 FAV: 50221: Led after 1f, pushed clr fnl **84**
1f, cmftbly: stays 1m on gd & soft grnd: deserved win, gd confidence boost & shld apprec further: see 4851.
4416 **WUJOOD** 43 [10] J L Dunlop 2-9-0 R Hills 10/1: 0002: b c Alzao - Rahayeb (Arazi) Held up, hdwy 1½ **79**
to chase wnr over 1f out, kept on: clr of rem after 6 wk abs: Mar first foal: dam 12f scorer: imprvd for step up
to 1m & soft grnd: v encouraging, plenty more to come over further.
4894 **BYRON BAY** 18 [3] J J Bridger 2-9-0 (64) T P Queally 33/1: 00503: Chsd ldrs, onepcd dist: see 4576. 7 **67**
　　　GRASP [1] R M Beckett 2-9-0 T N Chalmers(3) 33/1: 4: b c Kayf Tara - Circe (Main Reef) Slow ¾ **65**
away & bhd, hung left & some late gains: Apr foal: half-brother to wnrs over 1m/12f: dam 1m scorer.
4971 **DAYBREAKING** 13 [6]2-9-0 S Carson 25/1: 05: br c Daylami - Mawhiba (Dayjur) Led early, cl-up 1½ **63**
till wknd over 2f out: Apr foal, cost E18,000: half-brother to a 1m juv wnr: bred to apprec mid-dists next term.

ALAMIYAN [4]2-9-0 D Holland 6/1: 6: Slow away, in tch, wknd well over 1f out.	½	62
4712 MOTHECOMBE DREAM 29 [7]2-9-0 L Keniry(3) 66/1: 007: In tch, outpcd over 2f out, hung left.	1¼	60
4979 STOLEN 12 [13]2-9-0 S Drowne 66/1: 0008: Al bhd.	3½	55
4677 OVER TIPSY 31 [1]2-9-0 R L Moore 20/1: 0009: In tch, wknd over 2f out.	9	39
4760 PUSSY CAT 26 [2]2-8-9 (50) Dane O'Neill 66/1: 06050: 10th: Al bhd.	1¼	32
4988 XEBEC 11 [12]2-9-0 J Fortune 20/1: 00: 11th: Handy, wknd over 2f out.	nk	37
4883 DREAM ALONG 19 [9]2-9-0 Martin Dwyer 25/1: 00: 12th: Unruly stalls, u.r. just after start.		0
12 Ran Time 1m 48.56 (10.26) Owned: Mr D R C Elsworth Trained: Whitsbury		

5171   3.00 European Breeders Fund Maiden Stakes Div 2 2yo (D3)
£4524 £1392 £696   1m5y   Soft 102   -10 Slow   Inside

5019 RAIN STOPS PLAY 9 [12] M R Channon 2-9-0 S Hitchcott 3/1: 3021: Held up, hdwy over 2f out, styd on to chall ins last, led cl-home, drvn out: eff over 7f/1m on firm & soft grnd: gd confidence boost: see 5019.		85
4205 JAAMID 53 [8] M Johnston 2-9-0 J Fanning 14/1: 402: Led early, led again 5f out till 2f out, led again btn till cl-home, just btn: 7 wk abs: eff over 7f/1m on fast & soft grnd: deserves similar: see 3665.	hd	84
5018 KEY OF SOLOMON 9 [7] H Morrison 2-9-0 t S Drowne 20/1: 63: Held up, hdwy over 2f out, styd on to chall ins last, not btn far: stays 1m on soft grnd: see 5018.	¾	82
4866 TAMATAVE 20 [11] Saeed bin Suroor 2-9-0 t (85) L Dettori 2/1 FAV: 6424: Led after 1f till 5f out, led again 2f out till dist, no extra: well bckd: softer grnd & clearly btr expected after 4866 (firm grnd).	2½	77
UNDERGRADUATE [4]2-9-0 J Fortune 10/1: 5: b c Unfuwain - Starlet (Teenoso) Slow away & bhd, some late gains on debut: Apr foal: half-brother to wnrs over 1m/13f: bred to relish mid-dists next term.	1¼	75
4677 KING GABRIEL 31 [13]2-9-0 Dane O'Neill 50/1: 06: b g Desert King - Broken Spirit (Slip Anchor) Slow away, sn in tch, wknd over 1f out: Apr foal, cost 11,000gns: half-brother to wnrs over 6f/2m.	shd	75
4885 HARLESTONE LINN 18 [2]2-9-0 Paul Eddery 40/1: 07: Bhd, nvr a factor.	8	63
5019 FRENCH GOLD 9 [10]2-8-9 T Quinn 66/1: 08: Al bhd.	3	54
4296 MADAM CAVERSFIELD 50 [5]2-8-9 (70) R L Moore 16/1: 0344629: Nvr a factor: see 4296.	2½	50
4455 SECRET AFFAIR 42 [1]2-9-0 J D Smith 25/1: 000: 10th: In tch, wknd over 2f out.	shd	55
5058 BARBARY COAST 7 [3]2-9-0 Martin Dwyer 11/4: 6020: 11th: In tch, wknd 2f out: btr 5058 (gd).	1½	53
11 Ran Time 1m 47.25 (8.95) Owned: John Livock Bloodstock Limited Trained: West Ilsley		

5172   3.30 Weatherbys Insurance Services Handicap Stakes 3yo+ 71-85 (D2)
£6965 £2143 £1072   1m5y   Soft 102   + 05 Fast   Inside   [96]

4777 CELLO 25 [15] R Hannon 3-8-10 t (78) R Hughes 7/1: 6004231: In tch, hdwy to lead 2f out, carried hd high but kept on: stays 1m & handles fm, likes soft & hvy, any trk: carries hd high but did nothing wrong.		88
4621 ALFONSO 33 [13] B W Hills 3-8-9 (77) M Hills 6/1: 4-100242: Held up, hdwy over 2f out, chall over 1f out, no extra ins last: gd run: see 4621, 4225.	2	83
4872+DESERT CRISTAL 19 [7] J R Boyle 3-9-2 (84) L Dettori 6/1: 1323013: Led after 1f till 2f out, onepace.	nk	89
5103 APERITIF 4 [10] W J Haggas 3-9-4 (86) Martin Dwyer 2/1 FAV: 3103104: Held up, hdwy over 1f out, onepace: back to form of 4820.	hd	90
4999 PAGAN PRINCE 10 [11]7-8-12 (77) E Ahern 7/1: 0-014645: In tch, wknd fnl 1f: see 4362, 4221.	3	76
4714 GIOCOSO 29 [16]4-8-13 (78) T Quinn 20/1: 0145406: In tch, wknd over 1f out: see 3813.	1½	75
4777 ZWEIBRUCKEN 25 [4]3-9-0 (82) J F Egan 25/1: 0-001007: Al bhd: see 4777, 3885.	4	73
4909 DAVORIN 17 [6]3-8-10 (78) T P Queally 66/1: 16068: In tch, wknd over 2f out: see 4318, 1152.	10	54
3128 PASS THE PORT 101 [9]3-8-10 (78) D Holland 16/1: 5169: In tch, wknd 2f out: long abs, see 2383.	nk	53
4820 ZAMEYLA 22 [1]3-9-1 (83) P Robinson 20/1: 0221100: 10th: In tch, wknd over 3f out: reportedly nvr trav.	½	57
4935 BACKGAMMON 15 [5]3-8-8 (76) N Pollard 16/1: 23140: 11th: In tch, wknd 3f out: best 4407.	½	49
4802 CONVENT GIRL 24 [8]4-9-4 (83) R Havlin 20/1: 0000600: 12th: Al bhd: see 4331.	1	54
5050 THREEZEDZZ 8 [2]6-9-1 t (80) L Keniry(3) 20/1: 3310000: 13th: Led 1f, wknd over 3f out: see 4301.	2	48
13 Ran Time 1m 46.11 (7.81) Owned: Mr Louis Stalder Trained: Marlborough		

5173   4.00 M J Church Plant Maiden Stakes Fillies & Mares 3yo+ (D3)
£3562 £1096 £548   1m2f46y   Soft 102   -04 Slow   Inside

3237 RADISH 95 [14] E F Vaughan 3-8-11 T E Durcan 9/1: 0-01: b f Alhaarth - Nichodoula (Doulab) Trkd ldrs, went on entering fnl 1f, rdn clr: 3 mth abs: unplcd on sole juv start: eff at 10f on soft grnd, clearly runs well fresh: still signs of greenness here, open to more improvement on fav'd soft grnd.		74
4768 SANTA CATERINA 25 [13] J L Dunlop 3-8-11 (66) L Dettori 3/1: 4520032: Sn led, collared entering fnl 1f, kept on but no ch with wnr: nicely bckd: acts on gd & soft grnd: see 4768 & 3108.	5	67
WHIRLY BIRD [12] Mrs A J Perrett 3-8-11 R L Moore 9/1: 3: b f Nashwan - Inchyre (Shirley Heights) Rear, styd on fnl 1.5f, nvr nrr: debut: half-sister to mid-dist performer Inchberry: bred to apprec mid-dists & shld learn from this.	2	64
4768 DANCES WITH ANGELS 25 [6] J W Unett 4-9-2 (35) P M Quinn 100/1: 300P064: Rear, modest gains, nvr dngrs: offic rtd just 35, treat this rating with caution: see 1547 (banded).	4	59$
4847 CIRRIOUS 21 [4]3-8-11 D Sweeney 25/1: 065: Nvr btr than mid-div: see 4649.	3½	54
4911 ELUSIVE KITTY 17 [2]3-8-11 (66) D Holland 8/1: R335356: Chsd ldrs 1m, wknd.	5	48
4501 NEATH 39 [7]3-8-11 R Hughes 2/1 FAV: 537: Chsd ldrs, rdn & wknd 3f out: well bckd & shorter priced stablemate of 3rd: btr expected after 4501 (gd grnd).	2½	44
4975 ANGRY BARK 13 [1]3-8-11 Dane O'Neill 33/1: 42408: ch f Woodman - Polemic (Roberto) Chsd ldrs till halfway: prev trained in France & rnr-up in a minor event (9f, soft grnd): with H Howe.	12	28
2368 SINGITTA 130 [5]3-8-11 P Doe 100/1: 009: Nvr nr ldrs: long abs.	4	22
3292 BLAZE THE TRAIL 92 [15]3-8-11 BL (35) Martin Dwyer 100/1: 0600: 10th: Chsd ldrs till halfway, sn bhd: 3 mth abs, tried blnks.	3½	17
4944 TREE TOPS 15 [11]3-8-11 (65) J Fortune 9/1: 2336000: 11th: Led early, remained prom, wknd qckly 3f out & eased: see 3630.	4	12
3546 GWEN JOHN 82 [16]3-8-11 (70) S Drowne 14/1: 5-53000: 12th: Al rear: 12 wk abs.	4	7
STARJESTIC [8]3-8-11 L Keniry(3) 50/1: 0: 13th: Slowly away, al bhd & t.o. on debut.	dist	0
13 Ran Time 2m 16.64 (10.64) Owned: De La Warr Racing Trained: Newmarket		

5174   4.30 Levy Board Handicap Stakes 3yo+ 71-85 (D2)   [96]
£7015 £2158 £1079   1m3f144y   Soft 102   -12 Slow   Inside

4261* **AUTUMN WEALTH 51** [3] Mrs A J Perrett 3-8-6 (74) Martin Dwyer 5/1: 2211: Chsd ldrs, imprvd to   **84**
lead ins fnl 1f, styd on strongly, drvn out: 7 wk abs: eff at 10/12f on fast & soft grnd: clearly runs well fresh:
fast improving filly who can complete hat-trick, see 4261 (mdn).

4775* **SKYLARKER 25** [6] W S Kittow 6-9-2 (77) L Dettori 5/1: 4415512: Chsd ldrs, went on 2f out till   1½   **85**
ins fnl 1f, kept on but not pace of wnr: acts on firm, soft grnd & both AWs: in gd form, see 4775 (amat).

4856 **SILVER PROPHET 20** [1] M R Bosley 5-8-5 (1oh) (65) Hayley Turner(3) 12/1: 5001563: Chsd ldrs, ev ch   1   **73**
fnl 2f, no extra cl-home: see 4033.

4942 **MONTECRISTO 15** [4] R Guest 11-8-9 (70) R L Moore 20/1: 323-0004: Rear, styd on fnl 2f, nrst fin: nk   **76**
gd run from this old timer on fav'd soft grnd: see 2673.

4924* **MERRYMAKER 17** [5]4-8-10 (71) J F Egan 10/1: 0035515: Rear, prog to chase ldrs 2f out, sn onepcd.   5   **70**

4615} **FAME 379** [13]4-9-5 (80) P Doe 7/1: 432-6: ch g Northern Amethyst - First Sapphire (Simply Great)   5   **72**
Led till 2f out, wknd on reapp: thrice rcd for Mrs A Perrett in '03, mdn rnr-up on fnl start, has since been
gelded: eff at 10/12f on fast grnd: now with P Hobbs & sharper next time.
2 Oct'03 Wind 10.0 g/f 81- D:

3992 **FIRST DYNASTY 64** [12]4-8-11 p (72) J F McDonald(3) 33/1: 23-10637: Rear, styd on late, nvr nr   ¾   **63**
ldrs: u.r. in a h'cap hdle 10 days ago: see 3992.

4942 **ROYAL BATHWICK 15** [7]4-8-9 (70) S Drowne 14/1: 06-33468: Chsd ldrs, btn 2f out.   1½   **59**

4778 **HEZAAM 24** [14]3-9-0 (82) R Hills 11/4 FAV: 5011249: Chsd ldrs, wknd over 3f out: well bckd: 9   **58**
prev in decent form & something clearly amiss: much btr 4183 & 3940.

4943 **OVER THE RAINBOW 15** [10]3-8-10 T (78) M Hills 20/1: 1000600: 10th: Chsd ldrs 1m, wknd: t-strap.   1½   **52**

5050 **MAYSTOCK 8** [11]4-8-11 vis (72) J Fortune 12/1: 3003000: 11th: Chsd ldrs 1m, sn wknd: op 9/1.   9   **34**

2612} **PARACHUTE 474** [2]5-9-4 (79) E Ahern 33/1: 111330-0: 12th: ch g Hector Protector - Shortfall   9   **29**
(Last Tycoon) Al bhd, t.o. on reapp: trained by Sir M Prescott to complete a hat-trick in '03 (mdn, h'cap & class
stks, all on the AW): eff at 13f on both AWs, likes a sharp trk: gd weight-carrier: now with J Old.
1 Feb'03 Ling 13 ap 75a- E: 1 Jan'03 Wolv 12 af 79a-71 E: 1 Jan'03 Sout 12 af 70a- D:

4602} **NOT AMUSED 381** [9]4-9-2 (77) R Thomas(3) 16/1: 102246-0: 13th: ch g Indian Ridge - Amusing Time   20   **0**
(Sadler's Wells) Chsd ldrs till halfway, wknd & t.o. in last on reapp: reapp mdn wnr for B Hills in '03, also h'cap
rnr-up: eff at 1m/10f on firm & gd/soft, handles a sharp or gall trk & runs well fresh: now with Ian Williams.
2 Aug'03 Ches 10.3 gd 78-75 C: 2 Aug'03 Newb 10.0 fm 78-75 D: 1 Mar'03 Donc 8 g/s 77- D:
13 Ran   Time 2m 38.2 (13.2)   Owned: Mr D J Burke   Trained: Pulborough

---

5175   5.00 Betfred Com Now On Line Handicap Stakes 3yo 56-70 (E3)   [77]
£3420 £1052 £526   2m1f34y   Soft 102   -41 Slow   Inside

4919 **SHARADI 17** [5] V Smith 3-9-7 (70) D Holland 11/8 FAV: 0222131: Trkd ldr, went on 4f out, sn clr,   **81**
cmftbly: well bckd: eff at 14f, apprec this return to 2m: acts on fast & soft grnd, prob any trk: gd
weight-carrier: progressive young stayer, see 4555.

4991 **PORT SODRICK 10** [4] M D I Usher 3-8-7 (6oh) (50) Ashleigh Horton(7) 50/1: 6645002: Prom, lost   6   **60**
place halfway, styd on strongly fnl 2f into 2nd cl-home, no ch with wnr: gd run from out of the h'cap, met a
progressive rival: clearly apprec this step up to 2m, acts on soft grnd: see 4612.

5025 **ROSSALL POINT 9** [2] J L Dunlop 3-8-12 (61) T Quinn 4/1: 4504033: Prom, left bhd fnl 2f & caught   5   **61**
for 2nd cl-home: clr of rem: see 5025.

4919 **STRANGELY BROWN 17** [1] S C Williams 3-9-12 (75) L Dettori 7/2: 2111354: Chsd ldrs, wknd 3f out: 9   **67**
op 5/2, top-weight: see 4657.

5082 **CAMBO 6** [8]3-8-7 (1oh) (55) E Ahern 11/1: 00-06F45: Held up, imprvd to chase ldrs halfway, btn 3f   7   **42**
out: qck reapp: see 5082.

5029 **NIOBES WAY 9** [3]3-9-3 (66) R L Moore 4/1: 04326: Held up, nvr nr ldrs: much btr 5029 (gd grnd).   9   **44**

4892 **EXPLOSIVE FOX 18** [6]3-9-2 (65) M Tebbutt 40/1: 0350207: Led till 4f out, wknd, t.o.: see 4892.   dist   **0**

5054 **KWAI BABY 8** [7]3-8-7 (21oh) (35) Hayley Turner(3) 100/1: 000-0008: Al bhd, t.o. v stiff task.   26   **0**
8 Ran   Time 4m 05.33 (24.43)   Owned: Mr R J Baines   Trained: Newmarket

---

5176   5.30 Wick Apprentice Handicap Stakes 3yo+ 46-55 (F4)   [69]
£2706 £773 £387   5f161y rnd   Soft 102   +05 Fast   Far Side

4995 **CHATSHOW 10** [16] A W Carroll 3-8-4 (1oh) (50) D Fentiman 25/1: 5000301: Mid-div, imprvd halfway,   **56**
styd on strongly to lead cl-home, drvn out: first success: eff at 5/6f, has tried 1m: acts on fast & soft grnd,
handles a gall/undul trk: has tried a t-strap, btr without: see 4905.

5146 **CORANGLAIS 2** [6] J M Bradley 4-8-11 bl (52) Rory Moore 3/1 FAV: 5005022: Chsd ldrs, led 2f out   1¼   **58**
till collared cl-home: nicely bckd: qck reapp since 5146.

5053 **MAJIK 8** [4] D J S ffrench Davis 5-9-3 (58) Liam Jones(5) 5/1: 4040453: Rear, imprvd halfway, styd   1½   **61**
on fnl 1f & nrst fin: bckd from 7/1: see 1393.

5056 **CALUSA LADY 7** [11] G B Balding 4-8-11 (52) T Block(5) 8/1: 5-502034: Chsd ldrs, ev ch entering   nk   **54**
fnl 1f, no extra cl-home: return to 6/7f shld suit: see 5056.

5121* **TAPPIT 3** [5]5-8-10 (6ex) (51) Thomas Yeung 7/1: 0060515: Chsd ldrs, led briefly 2f out, no extra fnl 1f.   hd   **52**

5020 **DESERT DAISY 9** [14]3-8-5 (47) Donna Caldwell(5) 16/1: 0-000066: Rear, prog 2f out, nrst fin.   ¾   **46**

5096 **SPINETAIL RUFOUS 4** [12]6-9-0 bl (55) J Doyle(7) 15/2: 00-01107: Chsd ldrs, onepcd fnl 1f: qck reapp.   nk   **53**

4408 **A TEEN 43** [1]6-8-7 (48) Kristin Stubbs 25/1: 0056008: Slow away, styd on late, nvr dngrs: abs.   1½   **43**

4168 **HARBOUR HOUSE 55** [3]5-8-5 (1oh) (45) C Haddon 16/1: 3026659: Chsd ldrs, onepcd fnl 1.5f: abs.   1¼   **38**

4967 **YORKIES BOY 14** [2]9-8-13 p (54) Jemma Marshall(5) 14/1: 1100560: 10th: Rear, mod gains, nvr dngrs.   nk   **45**

4836 **APPOLONIOUS 22** [13]3-8-13 (55) T Dean(5) 20/1: 000060: 11th: b c Case Law - Supreme Thought   shd   **45**
(Emarati) Nvr btr than mid-div: t-strap left off: modest form to date.

4210 **ELA FIGURA 53** [9]4-8-5 p (46) Natalia Gemelova 12/1: 5000530: 12th: Led till 2f out, wknd: 8 wk abs.   1¾   **32**

2053 **ITALIAN MIST 144** [18]5-8-8 e (49) M Halford 14/1: 1310400: 13th: Chsd ldrs till halfway: long abs.   1   **33**

4905 *Otylia 17* [10]4-8-5 (1oh)vis(45) Dean Williams 33/1:0   4828 *Ninah 22* [19]3-8-6 (48) S O'Hara(5) 50/1:0

4365 *Among Friends 46* [15]4-8-11 (52) Joanne Thomas(7) 40/1:0

4835 *Clearing Sky 22* [17]3-8-10 (52) Stephanie Hollinshead 40/1:0

4262 **Silver Reign 51** [7]3-8-6 (48) R J Killoran(4) 40/1:0
3757 **Cloudless 74** [8]4-8-5 (6oh)(40) Leanne Kershaw 50/1:0
19 Ran   Time 1m 14.57(5.47)   Owned: Mr Dennis Deacon   Trained: Alcester

WOLVERHAMPTON Polytrack TUESDAY 19.10.04 Lefthand, Sharp Track

Official Going Standard

5177	1.50 Dine In Style At Dunstall Park E B F Median Auction Maiden Stakes Div 1 2yo (F4) £3346 £956 £478 5f216y aw rnd Inapplicable Inside

4893 **CAPTAIN JOHNNO 18** [13] D R Loder 2-9-0 vis (76) W Supple 9/4 FAV: 0331: Mid-div, prog wide   **73a**
halfway, styd on to lead despite hanging left ins fnl 1f, eased cl-home: tchd 3/1 on AW bow: eff at 5f, apprec
return to 6f: acts on fast, gd/soft grnd & polytrack: eff in a visor: see 4893 & 4617.
4829 **MAMBAZO 22** [3] S C Williams 2-9-0 (54) S W Kelly 25/1: 00002: Missed break, sn in mid-div, kept   2½   **64a**
on for 2nd ins fnl 1f, no ch with wnr: Mar first foal, cost 60,000gns: dam successful at 7f in List grade: sire
decent performer around 1m: eff at 6f, has tried further: acts on polytrack: needs low grade h'caps.
4968 **REVIEN 14** [5] G A Huffer I Mongan 9/2: 33: Led 5f out, hung left & hdd ins fnl 1f, no   ¾   **62a**
extra: AW bow: eff at 5f, ran to form on step up to 6f: acts on gd grnd & polytrack: see 4968.
4769 **JOYEAUX 25** [6] S L Keightley 2-8-9 N Callan 25/1: 064: Cl-up, ev ch dist, no extra: see 4769.   ½   **56a**
4497 **SMALL STAKES 39** [7]2-9-0 J Quinn 3/1: 05: Nvr nrr than mid-div: bckd tho' op 5/2, AW bow.   1½   **57a**
4972 **MULBERRY LAD 13** [2]2-9-0 bl (64) D Kinsella 14/1: 5242066: Chsd ldrs 4f, no extra: btr 3671 (fm).   ½   **56a**
4442 **ALL A DREAM 42** [8]2-8-9 (71) C Catlin 14/1: 6037: Nvr nrr than mid-div: 6 wk abs: btr 4442 (7f).   1½   **47a**
4556 **BOND BABE 36** [12]2-8-9 (66) F Lynch 10/1: 423358: In tch over 4f, fdd: btr 4303 (5f, gd).   3   **38a**
4645 **HAROLDINI 32** [4]2-9-0 P (73) J Edmunds 10/1: 4262009: Led 1f, wknd halfway: cheek pieces.   2½   **36a**
4895 **HIAMOVI 18** [9]2-9-0 (60) M Henry 50/1: 05200: 10th: Al in rear: btr 4127.   3   **27a**
   Annibale Caro [10]2-9-0 S Sanders 12/1:0   1987 Belle Largesse 147 [1]2-8-9 R Winston 66/1:0
12 Ran   Time 1m 15.64 ()   Owned: The Valais Boys   Trained: Newmarket

5178	2.20 Come Floodlight Racing At Dunstall Park Selling Stakes 3yo (G4) £2590 £740 £370 7f32y aw rnd Inapplicable Outside

4256 **TWO OF CLUBS 51** [3] P C Haslam 9/5-9-5 p (62) G Faulkner 9/2: 54-33151: Handy, styd on to lead well   **71a**
over 1f out, rdn out: sold for 6,750gns: 7 wk abs: eff at 5/7f, poss stays 1m: acts on gd/soft grnd & both AWs:
eff with cheek pieces: enjoyed drop to sell grade: see 779.
3724 **LA PUCE 75** [6] Miss Gay Kelleway 3-9-0 (71) I Mongan 7/1: 1460002: Dwelt, prog 2f out, styd on   1¾   **61a**
fnl 1f, no ch with wnr: bght for 6,000, 11 wk abs: back to form & will apprec return to further.
5112 **EMARADIA 3** [11] A W Carroll 3-9-0 bl (57) D Nolan(3) 10/1: 6030403: Led, hdd over 1f out, no   2   **57a**
extra: qck reapp: return to 5/6f will suit: btr 835 & 703.
4923 **VONADAISY 17** [2] W J Haggas 3-9-0 (68) S W Kelly 5/2 FAV: 44-10504: Bhd, prog over 2f out, no   1¼   **55a**
impress dist: bckd: btr 4275 (mdn, gd).
4761 **MEGABOND 26** [10]3-9-5 p (60) N Callan 14/1: 0400105: Held up, prog wide 3f out, onepcd dist.   2½   **55a**
4795 **FAITH HEALER 24** [8]3-9-0 bl (57) J Quinn 12/1: 4610606: Cl-up wide 5f, wknd: btr 3094 (mdn h'cap).   1½   **47a**
5010 **CREWES MISS ISLE 10** [12]3-9-0 (60) S Whitworth 18/1: 0005007: Chsd ldrs 5f, wknd: btr 1338 (5f).   nk   **46a**
4646 **DIAMOND SHANNON 32** [5]3-9-0 (58) D Tudhope(5) 10/1: 0512008: Al in rear: btr 2497 (1m).   2½   **41a**
5017 **ALIBA 9** [1]3-9-0 (61) D McGaffin 20/1: 4-400209: Missed break, nvr a factor: rider reported   6   **30a**
mount was nvr trav: btr 4131 (fibresand).
5046 **MORAG 8** [7]3-9-0 (58) M Fenton 7/1: 620000: 10th: Al in rear: btr 3995.   ½   **24a**
5020 **BLACK SABBETH 9** [4]3-9-0 VIS (59) S Sanders 16/1: 0064000: 11th: Cl-up 5f, fdd: tried visor.   1¼   **27a**
11 Ran   Time 1m 31.23 ()   Owned: Blue Lion Racing II   Trained: Middleham

5179	2.50 Enjoy Themed Race Nights Maiden Auction Stakes 2yo (F4) £3101 £886 £443 7f32y aw rnd Inapplicable Outside

   MAJOR FAUX PAS [11] J A Osborne 2-8-13 S W Kelly 12/1: 1: b g Barathea - Edwina (Caerleon) In   **87a+**
tch, kept on to lead ins fnl 1f, pushed out, val 3L+: debut: Mar foal, cost £35,000: half-brother to wnrs at
7f/1m: dam mdn: sire Gr 1 wnr around 1m: eff at 7f, further will suit: acts on polytrack & a sharp trk: goes
well fresh: fine start to career & looks sure to progress.
4913 **BELLY DANCER 17** [1] P F I Cole 2-8-9 (1ow) (75) S Sanders 5/4 FAV: 64262: Cl-up, led 3f out, hdd   1¾   **77a**
ins fnl 1f, not pace of wnr: bckd: continues ch gd form & deserves to get head in front: see 4664 & 2498.
5040 **QUEEN TOMYRA 8** [12] L M Cumani 2-8-8 N Mackay(3) 25/1: 003: b f Montjeu - Kama Tashoof (Mtoto)   2   **72a**
Missed break, sn in mid-div, styd on for press fnl 1f, no ch with front 2: AW bow: May foal, cost 25,000gns:
half-sister to wnrs at 7/10f: dam plcd at mid-dists: sire multiple Gr 1 wnr at 12f: eff at 7f, will impr next term
over further: acts on polytrack: now quals for h'caps.
5078 **MELS MOMENT 6** [9] Mrs A J Perrett 2-8-13 I Mongan 7/1: 06U4: Sn bhd, prog halfway, kept on late.   1¾   **73a**
4963 **CHUTNEY MARY 14** [6]2-8-7 (1ow) (71) N Callan 15/2: 5250365: Led 4f, wknd bef 1f out: op 11/2.   2½   **62a**
4885 **CROWN OF MEDINA 18** [5]2-8-9 W Supple 12/1: 06: ch c Fraam - Medina de Rioseco (Puissance) Nvr   ¾   **62a**
nrr than mid-div: Feb first foal, cost 10,000gns: dam plcd at 5f: sire useful performer around 1m.
5045 **BLUEBERRY TART 8** [8]2-8-6 R Winston 4/1: 5407: Handy 5f, wknd: disapp on AW bow: btr 4191.   ¾   **57a**
4769 **SAND IRON 25** [4]2-8-2 R Fitzpatrick 12/1: 648: In tch over 5f, wkng when short of room dist.   nk   **52a**
5048 **SOL ROJO 8** [10]2-8-9 R Keogh(7) 33/1: 09: Mid-div 5f, wknd.   nk   **58a**
4997 **WOODFORD CONSULT 10** [2]2-8-2 Dale Gibson 66/1: 00: 10th: Rear, nvr a factor.   1¼   **49a**
4941 **Formidable Will 15** [3]2-8-11 R Smith 50/1:0   4979 Magdelaine 12 [7]2-8-8 C Catlin 66/1:0
12 Ran   Time 1m 30.47 ()   Owned: Mr Martin Collins   Trained: Upper Lambourn

---

5180

3.20 Zongalero Restaurant Handicap Stakes 3yo+ 46-55 (F4) **[69]**
£3088 £882 £441 1m4f50y aw Inapplicable Inside

5123 **LORD LAHAR 3** [1] M R Channon 5-8-8 (49) C Catlin 8/1: 5040261: Held up, prog after halfway, rdn **58a**
out to lead cl-home: qck reapp: eff at 10/12f on gd/soft grnd & polytrack: first win: see 5009.
4487 **CAPTAIN MARRYAT 40** [8] P W Harris 3-8-12 (60) W Supple 9/2 FAV: 0223232: Chsd ldrs, styd on to *hd* **67a**
lead trav travl 2f out, hung right under press ins fnl 1f, hdd cl-home: 6 wk abs: eff at 1m/10f, ran to form on step
up to 12f: acts on firm, gd/soft & polytrack: continues to run well but is proving frustrating: see 4487 & 4388.
4203 **TRAVELLERS TALE 53** [9] P G Murphy 5-8-13 (54) Derek Nolan(7) 14/1: 6062203: Rear, prog wide 3f *2½* **57a**
out, kept on fnl 1f, no ch with frond 2: 8 wk abs: acts on fast, soft grnd & polytrack, poss fibresand: has
slipped to a fair mark & is worth keeping in mind for similar: btr 4033 & 3948.
5042* **YASHIN 8** [12] P A Blockley 3-8-11 (6ex) (59) N Callan 15/2: 2040314: Cl-up 10f, wkng when hmpd *5* **55a**
bef 1f out: new stable: appeared not to stay on first try at 12f: showed more in 5042 (10f, M H Tompkins).
4938 **BRAVELY DOES IT 15** [3]4-8-11 (52) S W Kelly 33/1: 0062005: Cl-up, led 5f out, hdd 3f out, wknd. *nk* **47a**
4515 **HEAD TO KERRY 38** [6]4-9-0 (55) S Sanders 5/1: 4245406: Keen mid-div, wknd fnl 2f: btr 4268. *1* **48a**
4128 **HEATHERS GIRL 57** [5]5-8-9 (50) S Whitworth 10/1: 2422427: Cl-up, led 3f out, hdd 2f out, wknd. *2½* **39a**
4849 **FACTUAL LAD 21** [7]6-9-7 (62) G Baker 10/1: 0100038: Led, hdd 5f out, wknd fnl 3f: btr 4849 (10f). *1* **49a**
5004 **PONT NEUF 10** [10]4-9-1 t (56) D Nolan(3) 7/1: 1023009: Al in rear: btr 3929 (soft). *2½* **39a**
5024 **CARRIACOU 9** [4]3-8-12 (60) M Fenton 6/1: 5304030: 10th: Al bhd: polytrack bow: btr 5024 (gd). *9* **30a**
1777 **MYTHICAL KING 157** [11]7-8-11 (52) B Swarbrick(5) 10/1: 6/350-060: 11th: Al in rear: long abs. *7* **12a**
11 Ran Time 2m 42.79 () Owned: Barry Walters Catering Trained: West Ilsley

---

5181

3.50 Racing Welfare Handicap Stakes 3yo+ 56-70 (E3) **[80]**
£3836 £1180 £590 5f216y aw rnd Inapplicable Inside

4984* **BLYTHE SPIRIT 12** [8] R A Fahey 5-9-10 p (76) P Hanagan 9/4 FAV: 0066111: Handy, styd on to lead **85a**
dist, rdn out to hold on: stays 1m, suited by 6f: acts on firm, gd/soft & polytrack: eff with cheek pieces: in
form 5yo who is making full use of fav'ble mark: see 4984 & 4785.
3924+ **MISTRAL SKY 67** [10] Mrs Stef Liddiard 5-9-6 vis (72) I Mongan 6/1: 4012212: Sn bhd, prog wide *nk* **80a**
halfway, styd on well fnl 1f, just denied: 10 wk abs: op 9/2: continues in gd form: see 3924 & 3518.
5053 **MIMIC 8** [2] R Guest 4-9-1 (67) C Catlin 20/1: 0015003: In tch, prog & ev ch dist, kept on, not *½* **74a**
btn far in 3rd: apprec return to polytrack: see 3880 & 3751.
4446 **ANOTHER GLIMPSE 42** [7] Miss B Sanders 6-9-11 t (77) N Callan 11/1: 0232004: Rear, prog when short *1¼* **80a**
of room after halfway, no impress on fnl 1f: 6 wk abs & top-weight: just btr 2051.
4585 **MUSICAL FAIR 35** [9]4-9-9 (75) R Winston 10/1: 6003035: Chsd ldr 5f, no extra: AW bow, btr 4585. *nk* **77a**
5080 **AMMENAYR 6** [11]4-9-1 (67) A Mullen(7) 11/2: 3536056: Nvr nrr than mid-div: qck reapp: op 7/1. *2* **63a**
5046 **BOBS BUZZ 8** [13]4-9-7 (73) S Sanders 5/1: 2052627: Chsd ldrs over 4f, wknd: btr 5046 (7f, gd). *½* **68a**
2084 **IF BY CHANCE 143** [4]6-9-3 (69) T Eaves(3) 25/1: 2441008: Chsd ldrs till halfway, wknd bef 1f out. *3* **55a**
3966 **PLAYTIME BLUE 65** [5]4-9-5 (71) G Baker 25/1: 5330009: Led, hdd dist, wknd: 9 wk abs. *2* **51a**
5053 **BLAKESHALL QUEST 8** [6]4-9-5 vis (71) D Nolan(3) 40/1: 1010000: 10th: Cl-up 4f, wknd: btr 1465. *nk* **50a**
5096 **PARKSIDE PURSUIT 4** [12]6-9-2 (68) P Fitzsimons 25/1: 1000000: 11th: Prom & ev ch dist, fdd. *nk* **46a**
3710 **Blue Knight 75** [1]5-9-6 (72) S W Kelly 20/1:0
4989 **Demolition Molly 11** [3]3-9-3 t p(70) L Fletcher(3) 50/1:0
13 Ran Time 1m 16.01 () Owned: The Matthewman Partnership Trained: Malton

---

5182

4.20 Dine In Style At Dunstall Park E B F Median Auction Maiden Stakes Div 2 2yo (F4)
£3339 £954 £477 5f216y aw rnd Inapplicable Inside

4858 **HEARTSONFIRE 20** [8] P W D'Arcy 2-8-9 (63) M Fenton 15/2: 3040041: Bhd, prog halfway, styd on for **68a**
press to lead cl-home: AW bow: eff at 6f on fast grnd & polytrack: gd confidence boost: see 3517.
4962 **GAUDALPIN 14** [7] M J Attwater 2-8-9 (64) A McCarthy 7/1: 4040022: Cl-up, led halfway, sn clr, *½* **66a**
hdd cl-home: op 11/2: continues to run well: see 4962, 2927 & 1071.
SWEET NAMIBIA 4 [4] J W Hills 2-8-9 S Whitworth 10/1: 3: ch f Namid - Almond Flower (Alzao) *hd* **65a**
Mid-div, prog over 1f out, kept on late: debut: op 7/1: Apr foal, cost 130,000gns: half-sister to numerous wnrs:
dam successful at 5f, sire useful sprinter: eff at 6f on polytrk, shld get 7f: encouraging eff.
4980 **CHIEF DIPPER 12** [9] P J McBride 2-9-0 J Quinn 25/1: 044: Sn in rear, prog bef 1f out, nrst fin: *nk* **69a**
eff at 6f, looks sure to apprec further: acts on polytrack: see 4980.
4921 **MANGROVE CAY 17** [2]2-9-0 VIS (67) S Sanders 7/1: 0455: Chsd ldrs over 4f, onepcd: clr rem: *shd* **68a**
first time visor: just btr 4921.
5076 **LA CYGNE BLANCHE 6** [12]2-8-9 P Makin(5) 66/1: 006: Sn outpcd, modest late gains: qck reapp. *5* **50a**
4922 **LLAMADAS 17** [1]2-9-0 vis (64) I Mongan 5/1: 0366027: Nvr nrr than mid-div: btr 4922. *shd* **54a**
4985 **RAINBOW IRIS 11** [10]2-8-9 (68) F Lynch 5/2 FAV: 4520658: Handy over 4f, wknd: disapp on AW bow. *½* **48a**
4703 **LITTLE INDY 29** [11]2-9-0 (60) D Nolan(3) 10/1: 00069: Chsd ldrs 4f, wknd. *5* **40a**
4703 **CRYSTAL MYSTIC 29** [3]2-9-0 bl F P Ferris(3) 20/1: 040: 10th: Led 3f, wknd: btr 4703. *1¾* **35a**
4859 **ELMS SCHOOLBOY 20** [13]2-9-0 L Fletcher(3) 25/1: 000: 11th: Cl-up 4f, fdd. *1½* **31a**
5021 **Rubys Dream 9** [6]2-8-9 (64) P Fitzsimons 12/1:0 4970 **Aggravation 13** [5]2-9-0 G Gibbons 16/1:0
13 Ran Time (1m 17.15) Owned: Mrs Jean Mitchell Trained: Newmarket

---

5183

4.50 Wolverhampton-Racecourse Co Uk Handicap Stakes 3yo+ 46-55 (F4) **[69]**
£3032 £866 £433 1m141y aw rnd Inapplicable Inside

4241 **KING NICHOLAS 52** [8] J Parkes 5-9-0 t p (55) M Lawson(5) 7/1: 4106061: Mid-div, eff when short of **64a**
room 3f out, styd on well to lead ins fnl 1f, rdn out: tchd 10/1, 7 wk abs: equally eff at 6f/8.5f: acts on firm,
soft & both AWs: eff with t-strap & cheek pieces: goes well fresh: more prizes await: see 1606 & 851.
4252 **LA LANDONNE 51** [12] P M Phelan 3-8-13 (58) C Catlin 16/1: 4366002: Chsd ldrs wide, led 2f out *1* **63a**
till dist, sn regained lead, hdd well ins fnl 1f: 7 wk abs: eff at 6f/8.5f: unexposed around this trip.
4911 **MY PENSION 17** [5] P Howling 3-9-1 (60) R Winston 14/1: 0430063: Cl-up, styd on bef 1f out, not *hd* **64a**

WOLVERHAMPTON **Polytrack TUESDAY 19.10.04 Lefthand, Sharp Track**

btn far in 3rd: AW bow: eff at 8.4f on polytrack: see 1907.
5016 **BOND MILLENNIUM 9** [7] B Smart 6-9-6 (61) F Lynch 13/2: 5-002004: Held up, prog 2f out, kept on late. *hd* **64a**
5077 **ZIET DALSACE 6** [3]4-9-0 (55) D Nolan(3) 5/1: 0460205: Missed break, eff when short of room over 2f out, pushed & kept on late, nrst fin: qck reapp: shade btr 4982. *shd* **57a**
2128 **EASTER OGIL 140** [4]9-9-4 (59) L Enstone 11/1: 0265006: Mid-div, prog to lead bef 1f out, sn hdd & no extra: long abs: btr 1083 (gd/soft). *½* **60a**
5080 **WALL STREET RUNNER 6** [11]3-9-3 (62) J Quinn 33/1: 0652007: Bhd, prog wide 3f out, wknd fnl 1f. *2* **59a**
4320 **BLUE JAVA 48** [13]3-9-0 (59) L Fletcher(3) 3/1 FAV: 0002528: Chsd ldrs over 6f, wknd: 7 wk abs. *hd* **55a**
4598 **MON SECRET 34** [10]6-9-4 (59) D McGaffin 13/2: 0606109: Bhd, prog wide 3f out, wknd dist: btr 4345. *1½* **53a**
5112 **PAWAN 3** [6]4-9-4 (59) Ann Stokell 16/1: 0500000: 10th: Chsd ldrs 6f, wknd: qck reapp. *4* **45a**
4750 **MEELUP 27** [2]4-9-1 p (56) V Slattery 20/1: 2000000: 11th: Led, hdd 2f out, wknd: btr 1748. *1* **40a**
5056 **Iamback 7** [1]4-8-12 p(53) I Mongan 14/1:0 4835 **Penel 22** [9]3-9-3 bl(62) G Baker 16/1:0
13 Ran Time 1mn 51.90 () Owned: Mr M Wormald Trained: Malton

5184

5.20 Bet Direct On 0800 32 93 93 Classified Stakes 3yo+ 0-50 (G4)
£2996 £856 £428 **1m141y aw rnd** **Inapplicable** Inside

4982 **TEMPER TANTRUM 12** [7] J R Best 6-9-6 p (54) W Supple 11/4 FAV: 5465031: Bhd, prog 3f out, rdn out to lead cl-home: eff at 6f, suited by 7f/8.5f on firm, gd & both AWs: eff with cheek pieces: on a winning mark. **63a**
4926 **ATLANTIC ACE 17** [4] B Smart 7-9-7 p (55) F Lynch 10/1: 0000002: Bhd, prog 3f out, styd on to lead dist, sn hung right & hdd cl-home: acts on firm, soft & both AWs: encouraging return to AW & well h'capped. *shd* **62a**
5094 **JUST ONE LOOK 4** [10] M Blanshard 3-8-12 (53) N Callan 20/1: 0060503: Mid-div, prog when short of room bef 1f out, switched & kept on late: qck reapp: eff at 6/7f, now stays 8.5f: see 2495. *1½* **55a**
3759 **QOBTAAN 74** [5] M R Bosley 5-9-3 (51) G Baker 16/1: 1000004: Held up, prog when short of room 2f out, switched & kept on late: 11 wk abs: btr 387. *2* **52a**
1198 **SMART SCOT 187** [2]5-9-4 (52) M Savage(5) 20/1: 1111205: In tch, led 2f out, hdd dist, no extra. *hd* **52a**
4719 **CRYFIELD 28** [1]7-9-4 vis (52) Kim Tinkler 6/1: 4340066: Handy 6f, no extra: tchd 8/1: btr 2890. *¾* **50a**
5077 **MUYASSIR 6** [6]9-9-6 (54) S Sanders 11/1: 1000007: Nvr nrr than mid-div: qck reapp. *nk* **51a**
5094 **BEAUTY OF DREAMS 4** [11]3-8-13 vis (54) C Catlin 7/2: 3060438: Cl-up, wknd bef 1f out: op 4/1: disappointing on AW bow: btr 5094 (soft). *1½* **46a**
5005* **REBEL RAIDER 10** [3]5-9-7 (55) Lisa Jones 11/2: 30300/-19: Cl-up when bmpd & nrly lost rider after 1f, sn no impress: lost all ch with incident after 1f & is worth another ch: btr 5005. *¾* **48a**
1196 **BUNDABERG 187** [9]4-9-7 (55) P Makin(5) 16/1: 05-42230: 10th: Rear, nvr a factor: long abs. *shd* **47a**
3829 **SIR ALFRED 71** [12]5-9-4 vis (52) A Nicholls 20/1: 630-0400: 11th: Led, hdd 2f out, wknd: jumps fit. *1* **42a**
4488 **Filliemou 40** [8]3-8-12 (53) F P Ferris(3) 16/1:0 4320 **Lady Blade 48** [13]3-9-0 (55) A McCarthy 33/1:0
13 Ran Time 1m 51.82() Owned: The Little House Partnership Trained: Maidstone

NOTTINGHAM **WEDNESDAY 20.10.04 Lefthand, Galloping Track**

Official Going Heavy

5185

2.15 Ibetx Com Sports Betting Exchange Novice Auction Stakes 2yo (F4)
£3248 £928 £464 **6f15y str** **Heavy 162** **-02 Slow** Inside

4895 **ISLAND SWING 19** [9] J L Spearing 2-9-0 (78) S Drowne 100/30 FAV: 1400341: Held up, prog halfway, styd on to lead dist, pushed clr, val 7L+: eff at 6f on fast grnd & hvy: likes a gall trk: easily defied top-weight & relished today's conditions: see 4895, 4633 & 2358. **87**
5098 **ORPEN WIDE 5** [1] M C Chapman 2-8-9 (71) A Beech(3) 9/2: 033002: Led, hdd dist, no extra: op 9/1: qck reapp: acts on fast & hvy grnd: see 4699 & 4590. *5* **71**
4921* **MANIC 18** [8] Andrew Reid 2-8-7 (70) J F Egan 9/2: 013: Rear, prog halfway, no impress bef 1f out: below form in today's hvy grnd: showed more in 4921 (polytrack). *1½* **65**
3994 **TIPSY LILLIE 65** [6] Julian Poulton 2-8-8 (59) K Fallon 10/1: 0014144: Cl-up over 4f, no extra. *shd* **65**
4770 **DIAMOND HERITAGE 26** [2]2-8-11 F Norton 33/1: 005: ch c Compton Place - Eccolina (Formidable) Mid-div, prog & ev ch well over 1f out, fdd: Apr foal, dam plcd at 7f: sire decent performer at spirnt dists. *6* **54**
2110 **FAITHISFLYING 142** [10]2-8-9 (50) D Fox(5) 66/1: 06066: Handy 4f, fdd: long abs: see 2110. *8* **33**
4900* **BEAU MARCHE 18** [5]2-8-8 (73) I Mongan 11/2: 5002017: Prom 4f, fdd: op 9/2: btr 4900 (gd). *½* **31**
4611 **MUDDY 35** [3]2-8-10 (65) Martin Dwyer 11/2: 5008: Chsd ldrs till halfway, wknd: see 4250. *3* **25**
4945 **STANS GIRL 16** [7]2-8-6 (56) W Supple 20/1: 03209: Keen bhd, nvr a factor: btr 1779 (fast). *1½* **17**
9 Ran Time 1m 20.66 (9.86) Owned: Mr J Spearing Trained: Kinnersley

5186

2.50 Eversheds Royal Standard Novice Stakes 2yo (D3)
£4596 £1414 £707 **1m54y rnd** **Heavy 162** **-09 Slow** Outside

PUBLIC FORUM 0 [1] Sir Michael Stoute 2-8-8 K Fallon 9/4: 1: b c Rainbow Quest - Valentine Girl (Alzao) Cl-up, styd on to lead dist, rdn out, val bit more: debut: Jan first foal, dam smart performer around 1m/11f: sire high-class performer around 1m/10f: eff at 1m, mid-dists will suit next term: acts on hvy grnd & a gall trk: goes well fresh: sure to improve for today's experience & rate higher. **79**
4914 **MISS LAUGEVAL 18** [4] G Wragg 2-9-0 (81) D Holland 11/8 FAv: 41002: Prom, styd on to lead 3f out, hdd under press dist, kept on well ins fnl 1f, just denied: well clr of rem: well bckd: eff at 6/7f, ran to form on step up to 1m: acts on firm & hvy grnd: see 3554 (7f, mdn) & 3251 (debut). *nk* **83**
4933 **NUMERO DUE 16** [5] G M Moore 2-8-12 P M Quinn 14/1: 63: Rear, prog 3f out, no impress bef 1f out: will apprec further next term: see 4933. *8* **68**
4393 **MOLEM 46** [2] Sir Michael Stoute 2-8-12 R Hills 11/4: 64: br c Green Desert - Injaad (Machiavellian) Handy, prog halfway, hung left & wknd bef 1f out: 7 wk abs: Apr first foal, dam unrcd: sire find performer around 6f/1m: disapp in today's hvy grnd & can show more back on faster ground. *¾* **66**
5003 **ELLERSLIE TOM 11** [3]2-8-12 A Culhane 25/1: 05: br g Octagonal - Tetravella (Groom Dancer) Rcd keenly & led 7f out, ran wide turning for home, hdd 3f out, fdd: Mar first foal, cost 10,000gns: dam successful at *18* **36**

NOTTINGHAM   WEDNESDAY 20.10.04   Lefthand, Galloping Track

15f: sire won 10 Grade 1 races abroad around mid-dists: with O Brennan.
5 Ran   Time 1m 53.13 (13.73)   Owned: Mr K Abdulla   Trained: Newmarket

5187   3.25 Browne Jacobson Stakes Handicap 3yo 86-100 (C1)
£13796 £4245 £2122   1m1f213y   Heavy 162   +11 Fast   Inside   [110]

4525 **EXTERIOR 39** [5] Mrs A J Perrett 3-8-9 (91) R Hughes 2/1 FAV: 3-1141: Cl-up, led trav well dist, pushed clr, val 9L+: well bckd: fast time: eff at 9/10f, further shld suit: acts on fast grnd & polytrack, suited by soft & hvy grnd: acts on a sharp/undul or gall trk: lightly rcd 3yo who relished today's testing conditions.   102+
5043 **HAADEF 9** [3] J H M Gosden 3-9-2 bl (98) W Supple 20/1: 314002: Led after 1f, trav well till rdn & hdd dist, found little: better run drpd back to 10f, acts on gd/soft & hvy grnd: see 2554 & 2131.   6   101
4860 **NUNKI 21** [2] H R A Cecil 3-8-3 vis (85) J Quinn 12/1: 310043: Handy over 1m, no extra: btr 4860 (gd).   3   84
4766 **SEWNSO CHARACTER 26** [6] M Blanshard 3-8-5 (87) F Norton 7/2: 4046024: Nvr nrr than mid-div: disapp in today's hvy grnd: btr 4766 (gd/soft) & 3277 (fast).   7   76
4917 **DANCING LYRA 18** [1]3-8-4 (86) T P Queally 8/1: 1240605: In tch, wknd bef 2f out: not handle hvy.   1½   72
4324 **ETMAAM 49** [8]3-8-8 (90) R Hills 4/1: 2130066: Cl-up, fdd 3f out: 7 wk abs: disapp: btr 2519 (fast).   11   61
3597 **HAVE FAITH 81** [7]3-8-2 (81) Martin Dwyer 33/1: 210-3667: Rear, nvr a factor: long abs.   20   28
4814 **ROEHAMPTON 24** [4]3-9-0 BL (96) K Fallon 13/2: 01-65308: Handy 6f, fdd: blnks, not handle hvy.   26   7
8 Ran   Time 2m 17.48 (15.18)   Owned: Mr K Abdulla   Trained: Pulborough

5188   4.00 David Ashley Construction Limited Maiden Stakes Div 1 2yo (D3)
£4615 £1420 £710   1m1f213y   Heavy 162   -38 Slow   Inside

3820 **LOUISE RAYNER 72** [6] M L W Bell 2-8-9 (56) D Holland 28/1: 54001: Cl-up, led 3f out, drvn out ins fnl 1f to hold on: 10 wk abs: imprvd for today's step up to 10f on hvy grnd: acts on a gall trk & goes well fresh: enjoyed today's stamina test: see 2652 & 2343.   75
4147 **SAND REPEAL 57** [10] Miss J Feilden 2-9-0 B Reilly(3) 14/1: 032: Keen handy, prog 2f out, kept on ins fnl 1f, just held by wnr: 8 wk abs: eff at 10f on hvy grnd: now quals for h'caps: see 4147.   1   77
4829 **GABANNA 23** [9] Saeed bin Suroor 2-9-0 L Dettori 11/4: 63: b c Kingmambo - Star Begonia (Sadler's Wells) Cl-up, ev ch dist, sn no extra: bckd: eff at 10f on hvy grnd: Feb foal, cost £1,200,000: half-brother to a number of fine performers at mid-dists: dam fine performer around 12f: sire Gr 1 wnr at 1m: eff at 10f, further shld suit: acts on hvy grnd.   1½   74
4450 **KRISTALCHEN 43** [7] J G Given 2-8-9 S Chin 12/1: 0004: Led, hdd 3f out, wknd bef 1f out: 6 wk abs.   5   62
4933 **ROYAL JET 16** [8]2-9-0 vis (83) A Culhane 10/11 FAV: 3625: In tch, prog & ev ch well over 1f out, sn fdd: bckd: disapp in today's hvy grnd: showed more in 4933 (fast, 1st time visor): & 4522.   ½   66
4971 **CELTIC PROMISE 14** [4]2-8-9 S Drowne 33/1: 06: b f Celtic Swing - Tainted Halo (Halo) Chsd ldrs over 6f, wknd: Apr foal, half-sister plcd at 10f: sire Gr 1 at 1m/12f: with Mrs A J Perrett.   4   55
4933 **AMAZING VALOUR 16** [2]2-9-0 K Darley 10/1: 207: Rear, nvr a factor: btr 4756 (1m, firm).   21   32
5078 **LAMBRIGGAN LAD 7** [3]2-9-0 V Slattery 200/1: 008: Handy 6f, fdd: qck reapp.   1¼   30
4979 **SERGEANT SHINKO 13** [5]2-9-0 bl J F Egan 200/1: 009: Missed break, nvr a factor.   9   17
5018 **COURT RULER 10** [1]2-9-0 R Thomas(3) 150/1: 5U0: 10th: Al adrift.   7   7
10 Ran   Time 2m 22.39 (20.09)   Owned: Richard Green (Fine Paintings)   Trained: Newmarket

5189   4.35 David Ashley Construction Limited Maiden Stakes Div 2 2yo (D3)
£4596 £1414 £707   1m1f213y   Heavy 162   -26 Slow   Inside

5019 **NATALIE JANE 10** [3] G A Butler 2-8-9 D Holland 9/4: 031: Prom, led after 4f, kept on for press fnl 1f: tchd 11/4: eff at 1m, relished today's step up to 10f & shld get further: acts on gd & hvy grnd: improving with ev start & relished today's test of stamina: see 5019.   84
4783 **SOLARIAS QUEST 25** [9] A King 2-9-0 J D Smith 5/1: 332: Prom wide, ev ch well over 2f out, not pace wnr ins fnl 1f: clr rem: eff at 1m, ran to form of step up to 10f: acts on gd & hvy grnd: can find a race.   2½   84
4852 **VOIR DIRE 21** [4] Mrs P N Dutfield 2-9-0 (63) R Havlin 3/1: 00003: Dwelt, prog over 5f out, onepcd.   12   67
4997 **AYLMER ROAD 11** [5] P F I Cole 2-9-0 K Fallon 11/10 FAV: 24: Cl-up, ev ch over 3f out, wknd fnl 2f: below form on step up to 10f in today's hvy grnd: btr 4997 (1m, gd, debut).   3   63
4635 **SHARP N FROSTY 34** [2]2-9-0 (57) S W Kelly 20/1: 4044U05: Rear, nvr nrr than mid-div.   ½   62
5002 **MOUNT BUTLER 11** [1]2-9-0 A Culhane 66/1: 006: Chsd ldrs over 6f, wknd.   8   51
4997 **MISTERS SISTER 11** [6]2-9-0 M Fenton 50/1: 07: Missed break, nvr a factor.   11   31
SENIOR WHIM 0 [7]2-9-0 Dane O'Neill 33/1: 8: b c Lahib - Euphorie (Feenpark) Led, hdd 6f out, styd prom, fdd 3f out: debut: Mar foal, cost 10,000gns: half-brother success at 10f: dam 1m wnr.   12   30
5019 **SILVER COURT 10** [8]2-9-0 R Thomas(3) 200/1: 609: Bhd, prog after halfway, wknd 3f out.   11   5
9 Ran   Time 2m 21.16 (18.86)   Owned: Woodcote Stud Ltd   Trained: Blewbury

5190   5.10 Freeth Cartwright Llp Maiden Stakes 3yo (D3)
£4927 £1516 £758   1m1f213y   Heavy 162   -45 Slow   Inside

4898 **LOMAPAMAR 19** [2] Mrs A J Perrett 3-8-9 (70) S Drowne 9/1: 030-3001: Mid-div, prog 2f out, rdn out to led cl-home: eff at 1m/10f, has tried further: acts on fast & hvy grnd: acts on a gall trk: see 4188.   72
STAGE LEFT 0 [9] H R A Cecil 3-8-9 R Hughes 4/1: 2: ch f Nashwan - Interval (Habitat) Cl-up, short of room 2f out, styd on to lead ins fnl 1f, hdd cl-home: debut: well related: eff at 10f, will apprec further on breeding: acts on hvy grnd: sure to improve for today's experience & rate higher.   ¾   70
4701 **INDIANS LANDING 30** [6] K A Morgan 3-9-0 P Fitzsimons 150/1: 00003: Missed break, sn tch, prog & ev ch dist, no extra: new stable: eff at 10f on hvy grnd: ex Irish, mod form prev with M Cunningham.   2½   71
DESIGN 0 [1] Sir Michael Stoute 3-9-0 K Fallon 7/2 FAV: 4: ch g Machiavellian - Vitaba (Northern Baby) Prom, led 6f out, hdd 1f out, fdd: tchd 11/2 on debut: cost 220,000: half-brother successful abroad: prob stays 10f in hvy grnd: improve for today's experience.   1¾   68
5023 **WOOLSTONE BOY 10** [4]3-9-0 G Baker 33/1: 05: In tch, prog to lead 1f out, sn hdd & wknd: see 5023.   1   66
ILL DO IT TODAY 0 [5]3-9-0 I Mongan 25/1: 6: b g Mtoto - Knayton Lass (Presidium) Missed break, prog bef 1f out, nrst fin: debut: further looks sure to suit on this evidence.   3½   61
5052 **SANDOKAN 9** [3]3-9-0 T P Queally 25/1: 007: Nvr nrr than mid-div.   1¾   58

5029 **ALL BLUE 10** [7]3-9-0 VIS t L Dettori 9/2: 4408: Handy 1m, wknd: first time visor: btr 4861 (gd). ½ 57
      HIGH CHARTER 0 [12]3-9-0 Dane O'Neill 5/1: 9: In 1m, wknd: op 10/3 on debut: cost 6 49
78,000gns: half-brother to v smart First Charter who was successful over 2m: with J R Fanshawe.
4939 **MTILLY 16** [11]3-8-9 K Darley 6/1: 00: 10th: Keen prom till halfway, fdd. 21 18
2339 **JUDDA 132** [8]3-9-0 T P J Quinn 150/1: 0000: 11th: Led 6f, wknd 4f out. 2½ 19
2419 **APRON 129** [10]3-8-9 M Tebbutt 50/1: 0000: 12th: Handy 6f, fdd: long abs. 2½ 10
12 Ran   Time 2m 23.06 (20.76)   Owned: Wickham Stud   Trained: Pulborough

---

5191   5.45 Back Or Lay With Ibetx Com Apprentice Handicap Stakes 3yo+ 56-70 (E3)   [83]
           £3955 £1217 £609   1m54y rnd   Heavy 162   +00 Fast   Outside

5042 **RICHIE BOY 9** [5] P A Blockley 3-8-3 (58) R J Killoran(1) 50/1: 0600101: Mid-div, prog 3f out, 67
styd on for press to lead cl-home: stays 10.6f, imprvd back at 1m: acts on gd/soft, relished today's hvy grnd.
4867 **MOBANE FLYER 21** [11] R A Fahey 4-8-11 (63) N Lawes(8) 6/1: 0633132: Prom, styd on to lead dist, ½ 70
hdd cl-home: acts on firm & hvy grnd: see 4554 & 3850.
4668 **DIDNT TELL MY WIFE 32** [4] C F Wall 5-8-13 (65) Rebecca Bird(8) 11/1: 4313063: Keen rear, prog 3f 2½ 67
out, kept on late: acts on firm, hvy grnd & both AWs: see 4399 & 3922.
5062 **IBERUS 8** [9] S Gollings 6-9-1 (67) Kirsty Milczarek(3) 22/1: 0542004: Handy, no extra dist: btr 4354. ¾ 67
5046 **LITTLE ENGLANDER 9** [6]4-8-5 (57) J Doyle(5) 9/2 FAV: 5100445: Rear, hdwy 3f out, kept on late. 1½ 54
4346 **BAND 48** [8]4-8-5 (57) Steven Harrison 9/1: 0405106: In 1ch, styd on to lead 3f out, hdd dist, wknd. hd 53
5079 **PURE MISCHIEF 7** [3]5-9-4 (70) H Poulton 9/1: 3246557: Bhd, hdwy halfway, no impress fnl 1f: qk reapp. 3 60
4862* **SPIRITS AWAKENING 21** [13]5-8-10 (62) M Coumbe(3) 15/2: 2426018: Handy 6f, wknd: btr 4862 (gd). shd 51
5063 **FAIR SPIN 8** [17]4-8-8 (60) T Block 13/2: 0-030059: Nvr nrr than mid-div: btr 5063. 2 45
4721 **PRINCESS GALADRIEL 29** [2]3-8-6 (61) T O'Brien(3) 9/1: 0636130: 10th: Rear, mod late gains. ¾ 44
5062 **ADORATA 8** [18]3-8-12 (67) Liam Jones(3) 18/1: 3021000: 11th: Mid-div, prog 4f out, wknd fnl 2f. nk 49
5037 **YORK CLIFF 9** [15]6-9-10 (76) T Dean(3) 16/1: 0545000: 12th: Handy 5f, wknd: btr 695. 2 54
4943 **ENGLISH ROCKET 16** [14]3-9-1 (70) A Hindley(3) 66/1: 25323-00: 13th: Mid-div over 5f, wknd. 25 3
441} **DOLLAR LAW 638** [1]8-8-8 t (60) W Hogg 50/1: 00300/0-0: 14th: ch g Selkirk - Western Heights 5 0
(Shirley Heights) Led 5f, fdd: reapp: nov hdle wnr in 02/03 (rtd 109h, stays 2m on gd/soft & hvy, eff in cheek
pieces & t-strap): unplcd sole '03 Flat start (rtd 32a, h'cap): won 2 h'caps in '02: eff at 7f, suited by 1m/10f
on fast & soft grnd: eff with a t-strap: with R J Price.
1 Jun'02 Sout 10 g/f 67-61 E: 1 Apr'02 Wind 8.3 gd 63-58 E: 2 Nov'01 Nott 8.2 g/s 60-55 F:
1849 **AMNESTY 154** [12]5-8-10 bl e (62) Jemma Marshall(6) 25/1: 6115200: 15th: Missed break, nvr a factor. 1¾ 0
15 Ran   Time 1m 52.40(13.0)   Owned: Mr Clive Whiting   Trained: Cockerham

---

Official Going SOFT (HEAVY PLACES). Abandoned due to High Winds

5192   2.20 Solstone Plus Median Auction Maiden Stakes 2yo (E3)
           £4703 £1447 £724   6f209y rnd   Soft   Inapplicable   Inside

5091 **MAXAMILLION 6** [16] S Kirk 2-9-0 J F Egan 12/1: 541: Chsd ldrs, styd on strongly to lead ins fnl 88
1f, rdn clr: op 8/1: eff over a sharp 7f on soft grnd, handles a sharp/undul trk: settled btr today & a much
imprvd eff, see 5091 (1m here).
4945 **MARHOON 17** [15] E F Vaughan 2-9-0 T T E Durcan 8/1: 42: Chsd ldrs, led 2f out till ins fnl 1f, 3½ 78
kept on for 2nd but no ch with wnr: tchd 12/1: imprvd for first time t-strap over this longer 7f trip on soft grnd.
5031 **COUP DETAT 11** [2] J L Dunlop 2-9-0 (84) T Quinn 11/10 FAV: 42643: Prom, led briefly entering fnl ½ 77
1f, sn no extra: well bckd: handles soft, poss just btr on gd & fast grnd: see 5031.
4375 **SECRET CAVERN 47** [3] J A Osborne 2-9-0 E Ahern 20/1: 604: Chsd ldrs, onepcd fnl 1.5f: abs. 2 72
5091 **SHINGLE STREET 6** [14]2-9-0 N Callan 7/1: 00025: Chsd ldrs, wknd 2f out: much btr & beat 9 52
today's wnr in 5091 (1m here).
4885 **GOOSE CHASE 20** [10]2-9-0 D Holland 5/1: 06: b g Inchinor - Bronzewing (Beldale Flutter) Led nk 51
till 2f out, wknd: op 7/1: Feb foal, half-brother to numerous wnrs, notably useful mid-dist performer Merry Merlin:
dam a 1m scorer, sire a high-class 7f performer: with M Bell, not handle this soft grnd?
4918 **ROCK FEVER 19** [13]2-9-0 K Fallon 25/1: 007: ch f Desert Sun - Icefern (Moorestyle) Chsd ldrs 5 34
till after halfway, wknd: £25,000 May foal: half-sister to several wnrs, incl sprinter Mac The Knife: dam a useful
sprinter, sire a smart 6f/1m performer: with M Wallace.
5076 **GALLANTIAN 8** [17]2-9-0 J Fortune 33/1: 08: gr g Turtle Island - Galletina (Persian Heights) 2½ 33
Dwelt, nvr a factor: has been gelded: Jan foal, half-brother to 10f wnr Gondolin: dam a 2m Flat scorer & hdles
wnr, sire a top-class miler: with G Butler.
4853 **MISTER TROUBRIDGE 22** [8]2-9-0 S Drowne 100/1: 009: Nvr btr than mid-div. ¾ 31
5091 **SOLE AGENT 6** [5]2-9-0 A Quinn(5) 25/1: 030: 10th: At outpcd: btr 5091 (1m here). hd 31
4996 **BRUMAIRE 12** [7]2-9-0 I Mongan 66/1: 00: 11th: Dwelt, nvr a factor. nk 30
      Generous Measure [4]2-9-0 L Fletcher(3) 66/1:0   **Dont Call Me Babe** [9]2-9-0 P Doe 33/1:0
5040 **Fantasias Forest 10** [1]2-9-0 G Carter 80/1:0   **Als Glennmay** [12]2-8-9 A Daly 66/1:0
15 Ran   Time 1m 29.55(9.75)   Owned: Mr N Hartery   Trained: Upper Lambourn

NEWBURY   FRIDAY 22.10.04   Lefthand, Flat, Galloping Track

Official Going SOFT (HEAVY places).

5193   1.15 Cantorodds Com Nursery Handicap Stakes 2yo 0-85 (D3)   [92]
   £5389 £1658 £829   **7f str**   **Soft 90**   **-00 Slow**   Centre

4996* **MOON FOREST** 13 [8] P W Chapple Hyam 2-8-12 (76) Thomas Yeung(5) 6/1: 2411: Made all, held on **86**
gamely fnl 1f despite drifting left: well bckd: eff at 7f, shld get 1m: acts on gd & soft grnd: lightly rcd &
improving, battled well in these testing conds: see 4996 (mdn auct).
4688 **LOOKS COULD KILL** 34 [9] G A Butler 2-9-7 (85) J Fortune 9/2 FAV: 21432: Trkd ldrs, went after   *hd*   **94**
wnr 2f out, ev ch fnl 1f & just btn: bckd from 11/2: fine run under top-weight: eff at 7f, return to 1m will suit.
4940 **SECRET HISTORY** 18 [11] M Johnston 2-8-11 (75) J Fanning 6/1: 2351023: Chsd ldrs, ev ch 2f out,   *½*   **83**
no extra ins fnl 1f: fine run, btn under 1L: tough & in-form, see 4940.
4853 **FAIRMILE** 23 [3] P W Harris 2-9-1 (79) T Quinn 11/1: 3364: Held up, prog to chase ldrs when   *2*   **83**
flashed tail 1.5f out, onepcd ins fnl 1f: acts on gd & soft grnd: see 3927.
5007 **TUMBLEWEED GALORE** 13 [6]2-8-12 (76) J F McDonald(3) 14/1: 3336235: Chsd ldrs, onepcd fnl 1f.   *1½*   **77**
4972 **FASYLITATOR** 16 [12]2-8-5 (69) S Hitchcott 10/1: 636046: Chsd ldrs, not pace to chall.   *½*   **69**
4940 **OASIS WAY** 18 [5]2-8-6 (70) T P Queally 50/1: 55067: Rear, late prog, nvr nrr: see 4114 (debut).   *1*   **68**
4535 **DRY ICE** 41 [4]2-9-4 (82) Dane O'Neill 14/1: 51568: Chsd ldrs 5f, wknd: 6 wk abs.   *5*   **72**
4746 **WATER PISTOL** 30 [7]2-8-8 (72) Martin Dwyer 20/1: 0069: Al rear on h'cap bow: see 4363.   *5*   **54**
5031* **ENFORCER** 12 [13]2-9-5 (7ex) (83) S Drowne 6/1: 452010: 10th: Nvr nr ldrs: btr 5031 (gd).   *2½*   **61**
4064 **TOM FOREST** 14 [1]2-8-13 (77) E Ahern 14/1: 622500: 11th: Mid-div wide, btn 2f out: tchd 25/1:   *1½*   **53**
9 wk abs & new stable (prev with A Crook).
4363 **GROUP CAPTAIN** 49 [2]2-9-2 (80) R L Moore 11/1: 4220230: 12th: Al rear: 7 wk abs: btr 4363.   *shd*   **56**
4224 **Naval Force** 55 [10]2-8-13 t(77) J F Egan 50/1:0   5170 **Byron Bay** 3 [14]2-8-0 (64) C Catlin 25/1:0
14 Ran   Time 1m 30.65 (6.35)   Owned: Collins Deal Harrison-Allan Chapple-Hyam   Trained: Newmarket

---

5194   1.45 Sodexho Prestige Handicap Stakes 3yo+ 71-85 (D2)   [82]
   £7560 £2326 £1163   **2m**   **Soft 90**   **-28 Slow**   Outside

4527 **STOOP TO CONQUER** 41 [11] J L Dunlop 4-9-8 (76) T Quinn 6/1: 0014101: Chsd ldrs, prog to lead   **86**
1.5f out, rdn clr fnl 1f: bckd from 8/1, 6 wk abs: eff at 14f/2m1f on fast & soft grnd: game & tough 4yo who
enjoyed today's stamina test: gd weight carrier: type to make a decent hdler: see 4267.
4647 **TERESA** 35 [13] J L Dunlop 4-9-2 (70) R L Moore 20/1: 6600002: M-div wide, prog halfway & chsd   *3½*   **75**
ldrs, ev ch 2f out, kept on but left bhnd by wnr: longer priced stablemate of wnr: acts on fast & soft grnd:
reportedly hung right thro'out: see 1112 (reapp).
4919 **BILL BENNETT** 20 [9] J Jay 3-9-0 (78) G Baker 16/1: 2501403: Chsd ldrs, kept on under press fnl   *½*   **82**
2f: longer 2m trip & seemed to stay in these testing conds: see 2621 (12f).
4745 **LINENS FLAME** 30 [5] B G Powell 5-9-3 (71) P J Smullen 14/1: 1120004: Led till 1.5f out, no extra   *shd*   **75**
cl home: well clr of rem: front runner, back to form on fav soft grnd: see 1516.
4846 **MARINE CITY** 24 [3]3-8-7 p (71) M Henry 12/1: 1663435: Rear, prog to chase ldrs 4f out, btn 3f out.   *18*   **60**
5025 **IRISH BLADE** 12 [1]3-8-13 (77) Dane O'Neill 9/1: 0032156: Prom, wknd 3f out: btr 4856.   *8*   **60**
4846* **TRILEMMA** 24 [6]3-9-1 (79) S Sanders 7/4 FAV: 0061117: Mid-div, prog wide 5f out, btn 3f out: *15*   **50**
hvly bckd on 4-timer bid: prev in fine form on gd & fast grnd: see 4846.
4745 **DR CERULLO** 30 [2]3-8-9 (73) J Fortune 7/1: 3024438: Chsd ldrs, wknd 3f out, eased: op 10/1:   *2½*   **42**
longer 2m trip: see 4745 (12f gd grnd).
5095 **DESERT ISLAND DISC** 7 [12]7-9-6 (74) T P Queally 33/1: 1630039: Al rear, t.o.: btr 5095 (9f).   *2½*   **41**
4643 **SEEYAAJ** 35 [7]4-9-9 (77) S Hitchcott 25/1: 1300-500: 10th: Al rear, t.o.: see 3816.   *10*   **36**
1232 **TOMINA** 188 [8]4-9-7 (75) S Drowne 9/1: 0/6143-20: 11th: Mid-div, rdn & btn 4f out: long abs,   *11*   **26**
new yard (prev with N Graham): see 1232.
3783 **Jayer Gilles** 76 [10]4-9-10 (78) C Catlin 50/1:0   5025 **Sun Hill** 12 [4]4-8-11 (65) R Havlin 40/1:0
13 Ran   Time 3m 44.91 (18.91)   Owned: I H Stewart-Brown & M J Meacock   Trained: Arundel

---

5195   2.20 Gr3 Stan James Horris Hill Stakes Colts & Geldings 2yo (A1)
   £23200 £8800 £4400   **7f str**   **Soft 90**   **+24 Fast**   Centre

4736 **CUPIDS GLORY** 33 [8] Sir Mark Prescott 2-8-9 (100) S Sanders 2/1 FAV: 611131: Mid-div, prog to   **112+**
lead ent fnl 1f, pushed clr, impressive: fast time, well bckd: fast improving & now a v smart soft grnd performer:
eff at 6/7f on gd, soft grnd & polytrack: see 4736 & 4177.
4513* **JOHNNY JUMPUP** 41 [7] R M Beckett 2-8-9 (96) J F Egan 12/1: 11012: Chsd ldrs, prog & led briefly   *4*   **102**
dist, kept on but no ch with wnr: 6 wk abs: eff at 7/7.6f on fast & soft: gd run on this step up in grade.
5031 **KING MARJU** 12 [13] P W Chapple Hyam 2-8-9 (85) T Quinn 11/1: 62123: Mid-div & keen, kept on well   *2½*   **98**
fnl 1f, nvr nrr: tchd 14/1: clearly acts on firm & soft grnd: cld prove v smart if learning to settle: see 5031.
3919 **BRECON BEACON** 70 [10] P F I Cole 2-8-9 (100) S Drowne 10/1: 112144: Rear, prog 2f out, no   *2*   **94**
impress fnl 1f: 10 wk abs: earlier in fine form, see 3585 (fast grnd).
4325 **WOODSLEY HOUSE** 51 [11]2-8-9 (88) R Havlin 66/1: 2225: Rear, hung left & styd on fnl 1f, nvr nrr: *½*   **93**
7 wk abs: mdn, promise in this tougher grade: acts on fast & soft grnd: see 4325.
5061* **FOXHAVEN** 10 [12]2-8-9 (88) Martin Dwyer 20/1: 32216: Chsd ldrs, wknd 2f out.   *3*   **88**
4853* **SUDDEN DISMISSAL** 23 [5]2-8-9 (95) E Ahern 16/1: 41017: Mid-div, outpcd fnl 2f: rider reportedly   *½*   **87**
given a 1-day careless riding ban: btr 4853 (gd).
3254 **ST ANDREWS STORM** 98 [9]2-8-9 (100) Dane O'Neill 25/1: 1448: Chsd ldrs, rdn halfway, outpcd 2f   *1¼*   **85**
out: 3 month abs: longer 7f trip & softer grnd: see 3028.
4511* **DHAULAR DHAR** 41 [6]2-8-9 (90) M Hills 11/2: 219: Prom, led 2f out, sn hdd & wknd: well bckd   *¾*   **84**
tho' op 4/1, 6 wk abs: btr 4511 (fast grnd).
5099 **EMBOSSED** 7 [2]2-8-9 (100) R L Moore 9/2: 6162220: 10th: Front rank 5.5f, wknd: op 7/1.   *1¾*   **82**
3786* **RUSSIAN CONSORT** 76 [3]2-8-9 (88) J D Smith 33/1: 210: 11th: Dwelt, nvr nr ldrs: 11 wk abs.   *½*   **81**
4727* **THE PHEASANT FLYER** 31 [4]2-8-9 (88) J Fortune 20/1: 3110: 12th: Led till 2f out, wknd: *9*   **67**
reportedly ran flat: btr 4727 (6f).
4385* **ZOHAR** 48 [1]2-8-9 P J Smullen 22/1: 10: 13th: Chsd ldrs, lost place halfway, sn t.o. & eased: *20*   **37**

1579

7 wk abs & reportedly unsuited by this soft grnd: btr 4385 (6f firm grnd).
13 Ran Time 1m 28.95 (4.65) Owned: Hesmonds Stud Trained: Newmarket

5196

2.55 Q Associates Handicap Stakes 3yo+ 86-100 (C1) **[107]**
£12550 £4760 £2380 **6f8y str** **Soft 90** **+08 Fast** Centre

4686 **ONLYTIME WILL TELL 34** [3] D Nicholls 6-8-11 (90) J Fanning 5/1: 4201461: Prom, went on 2f out, styd on strongly, rdn out: well bckd, gd time: stays 1m, suited by 6f on firm, hvy & fibresand, any trk: in-form 6yo, nr career best today: see 3977 (clmr). **99**
5001 **DANZIG RIVER 13** [6] B W Hills 3-8-6 (86) M Hills 9/1: 0004602: Mid-div, prog 2f out, styd on well fnl 1f but not rch wnr: acts on firm & soft grnd: gd run, see 1154 (reapp). *¾* **92**
5159 **CHATEAU NICOL 4** [10] B G Powell 5-8-4 bl (83) T Quinn 6/1: 5660143: Chsd ldrs, ev ch ent fnl 1f, no extra cl home: nicely bckd, qck reapp: eff at 6f, best at 7f & stays 1m: see 4642 (7f here). *1¾* **86**
5001 **MARSAD 13** [8] J Akehurst 10-8-5 (84) P Doe 10/1: 0002004: Held up, slightly short of room 2f out, switched wide & fin well, nvr nrr: op 8/1: see 4322. *1½* **84**
5143 **PIC UP STICKS 5** [2]5-9-4 (97) S Hitchcott 10/1: 0001005: Chsd ldrs, kept on under press fnl 1f: top-weight, qck reapp: acts on firm & gd/soft, handles soft: btr 4786. *shd* **97**
5000 **GRIZEDALE 13** [12]5-8-4 (1oh)t (82) S Whitworth 25/1: 5000006: Rear, badly hmpd 1.5f out, fin v well: better over 7f & did not get the run of today's race: dropping down the h'cap & poised to strike: see 3061. *shd* **83+**
5101 **KINGS CAPRICE 7** [9]3-8-8 (88) S Carson 10/3 FAV: 4415027: Prom rail, wknd fnl 1f: well bckd: better expected after 5101 (7f). *nk* **87**
5090 **IF PARADISE 8** [4]3-9-4 (98) Dane O'Neill 12/1: 6000228: Prom, ev ch 2f out, wknd dist. *5* **87**
4884 **SARISTAR 22** [7]3-8-8 (88) S Drowne 20/1: 0051069: Prom, lost place halfway, rear. *6* **65**
4855 **TOTALLY YOURS 23** [5]3-8-3 (83) R L Moore 14/1: 0500020: 10th: Led till 2f out, wknd: btr 4855. *hd* **60**
4912 **MR LAMBROS 20** [11]3-8-4 (84) Martin Dwyer 10/1: 3-12000: 11th: Chsd ldrs 4f, sn btn. *1¾* **58**
4891 **MAZEPA 21** [1]4-8-11 (90) J F Egan 33/1: 0-630500: 12th: Mid-div, btn after halfway. *2½* **58**
12 Ran Time 1m 16.53 (4.93) Owned: Mr D Faulkner & Mr J Hair Trained: Thirsk

5197

3.30 James & Cowper Maiden Stakes 2yo (D2)
£5980 £1840 £920 **6f8y str** **Soft 90** **-20 Slow** Centre

4358 **BAILEY GATE 49** [13] R Hannon 2-8-9 R L Moore 13/2: 001: b f Mister Baileys - Floppie (Law Society) Mid-div, prog to lead 2f out, rdn clr: nicely bckd, 7 wk abs: Apr foal, half sister to sev wnrs, notably smart sprinter Ringmoor Down: dam a 1m wnr in France, sire a high-class miler: eff at 6f on soft grnd, handles a gall trk: made most of prev experience. **89**
WESTLAND [8] Mrs A J Perrett 2-9-0 S Sanders 7/1: 2: gr c Cozzene - Cherie Yvonne (Vice Regent) Dwelt, prog 2f out, styd on fnl 1f under handls-&-heels, not pace of wnr: tchd 9/1: $180,000 Feb 1st foal: dam a sprint wnr in the US, sire a top-class miler: eff at 6f on soft grnd, 7f will suit: promising start. *3½* **85**
HOLIDAY CAMP [7] B W Hills 2-9-0 M Hills 11/4 FAV: 3: b c Chester House - Arewehavingfunyet (Sham) Chsd ldrs, ev ch 1.5f out, onepcd under hands-&-heels fnl 1f: well bckd from 6/1 on debut: Feb foal, half brother to wnrs abroad (sprint - mid-dists): dam a high-class juv in USA, sire a top-class 10f performer: eff at 6f on soft grnd, 7f will suit: sure to learn from this encouraging start. *2½* **79**
4853 **FINAL PROMISE 23** [14] G B Balding 2-9-0 S Carson 33/1: 004: Rear, styd on nicely under hands-&-heels fnl 1f, nrst fin: clr rem: handles soft, return to 7f will suit judged on this: now qual for h'caps. *2½* **73**
5055 **WORLD REPORT 10** [6]2-9-0 Dane O'Neill 3/1: 4645: Chsd ldrs, ev ch 2f out, sn left bhnd by ldrs: well bckd tho' op 9/4: shorter priced stablemate of wnr & better expected after 5055 (7f gd grnd). *4* **63**
DARSHARP [9]2-8-9 B Reilly(3) 33/1: 6: Prom, wknd over 2f out on debut. *3* **51**
PRIME CONTENDER [1]2-9-0 J Fortune 16/1: 7: Rear, mod late prog on debut. *½* **55**
5048 **FLYING HEART 11** [5]2-8-9 C Catlin 25/1: 008: Chsd ldrs, outpcd fnl 1.5f. *1¾* **47**
PHYSICAL [10]2-9-0 Martin Dwyer 11/1: 9: Slow away, al rear on debut: op 7/1, s/mate 2nd. *1* **49**
4997 **VIRGINS TEARS 13** [12]2-8-9 A McCarthy 8/1: 00: 10th: Front rank 4.5f, wknd: op 11/2. *5* **32**
5019 **SPEEDY SPIRIT 12** [2]2-8-9 S Whitworth 100/1: 000: 11th: Chsd ldrs wide, wknd 1.5f out. *¾* **30**
YOUNG VALENTINO [4]2-9-0 T P Queally 50/1: 0: 12th: Chsd ldrs 4f, sn btn on debut. *½* **34**
5047 **Mad Marty Wildcard 11** [3]2-9-0 D Nolan(3) 100/1:0 1531 **Clipper Hoy 171** [11]2-9-0 G Baker 100/1:0
14 Ran Time 1m 18.25 (6.65) Owned: Mr Timothy N Chick Trained: Marlborough

5198

4.00 Jack Colling Polar Jest Apprentice Handicap Stakes 3yo+ 56-70 (E3) **[79]**
£4033 £1241 £620 **1m1f** **Soft 90** **-29 Slow** Centre

4766 **MCQUEEN 28** [3] Mrs H Dalton 4-9-0 (65) N Chalmers 13/2: 0211051: Held up, gd hdwy to lead 2f out, styd on strongly fnl 1f, rdn out: stays 12f, suited by 1m/10f: acts on gd & fast, revels in gd/soft, soft grnd & on both AWs: handles a sharp/undul or gall trk: type to do well over hdles this winter, see 4299. **77**
4539 **CORMORANT WHARF 40** [17] T E Powell 4-9-0 (65) Jemma Marshall(5) 25/1: 0064322: Held up, prog 3f out, styd on strongly with wnr fnl 1f but al held: clr of rem, 6 wk abs: acts on fast, soft grnd & polytrack: v well h'capped & sn go one btr, see 4539. *1½* **73**
4421 **COUNT BORIS 46** [1] G B Balding 3-8-3 (58) T Block(5) 33/1: 00003: b g Groom Dancer - Bu Hagab (Royal Academy) Rear, styd on under press fnl 2f, not reach front 2: 7 wk abs: h'cap debut & imprvd form over 9f on soft grnd: clrly runs well fresh: modicum of promise mdns previously. *4* **58**
5066 **LOADED GUN 10** [12] W M Brisbourne 4-8-4 (2oh) (53) L Jones(5) 14/1: 0-024034: Rear, prog 2f out, no impress fnl 1f: op 11/1, clr of rem: prob flattered 5066 (mdn). *2½* **51**
1650 **PEQUENITA 165** [11]4-9-4 bl (69) J Jones(5) 40/1: 00421-65: Chsd ldrs, btn 2f out: long abs: dropped in trip, see 1650 (10f). *5* **57**
5062 **GENERAL GB 10** [16]7-9-1 (66) M Savage 12/1: 0532006: Chsd ldrs, btn 2f out: btr 4215. *3½* **50**
4365 **CORNISH GOLD 49** [13]3-8-8 (63) N De Souza 16/1: 0056-027: Held up, prog to chase ldrs 3f out, sn btn: 7 wk abs: btr 4365. *nk* **46**
5191 **DIDNT TELL MY WIFE 2** [4]5-9-0 (65) S O'Hara(5) 7/2: 3130638: Prog from rear to chase ldrs 3f out, sn btn: bckd from 9/2: qck reapp & too sn after 5191? *¾* **47**
5022 **DARK RAIDER 12** [5]3-9-1 (70) W J Lee 66/1: 5510009: Chsd ldrs 7f, sn wknd. *1¾* **50**
5052 **ROOD BOY 11** [9]3-8-0 (55) R Kingscote(1) 66/1: 3-455050: 10th: Prom, led 4f out till 2f out, wknd. *2* **32**
4650 **SIENNA SUNSET 35** [6]5-8-7 (58) Rory Moore(3) 20/1: 2413000: 11th: Chsd ldrs 7f, sn btn. *10* **20**

NEWBURY FRIDAY 22.10.04 Lefthand, Flat, Galloping Track

4795 **MYTHICAL CHARM 27** [2]5-8-4 t (55) M Halford(3) 33/1: 5002200: 12th: Chsd ldrs, wknd 2f out. *2* **14**
4850* **AMERICAN DUKE 23** [10]3-9-4 (73) D Fox 7/1: 0020510: 13th: Chsd ldrs 5f, wknd: btr 4850 (gd). *1½* **30**
5062 **ELIDORE 10** [7]4-9-1 (66) A Quinn 33/1: 5024560: 14th: Led till 4f out, wknd. *nk* **22**
4763 **MR BELVEDERE 29** [8]3-8-0 (5oh) (50) J Doyle(7) 66/1: 0320400: 15th: Al rear: btr 4113. *3* **7**
MATOURAKA 61 [14]3-9-0 (69) Thomas Yeung(3) 9/4 FAV: 3-01010: 16th: b f Great Palm - Madragoa *10* **7**
(Kaldoun) Chsd ldrs 6f, wknd qckly & eased: hvly bckd, 9 wk abs & reportedly fin lame: prev trained in France & a dual wnr at Deauville: eff at 12f on AW: with P Chapple-Hyam & capable of much btr.
5052 **CATCH THE FOX 11** [15]4-8-4 (15oh) (40) Stephanie Hollinshead(3) 66/1: 0040330: 17th: Chsd ldrs, *9* **0**
btn bef halfway, fin last: stiff task.
17 Ran Time 1m 59.74(10.74) Owned: Mr R Edwards and Mr W J Swinnerton Trained: Shifnal

DONCASTER FRIDAY 22.10.04 Lefthand, Flat, Galloping Track

Official Going Soft (Heavy Places on Rnd Course)

5199

1.05 Dransfield Novelty Company E B F October Maiden Stakes Div 1 2yo (D3)
£3543 £1090 £545 **7f str** **Heavy 123** **+02 Fast** Stands side

BALLINTENI [10] Saeed bin Suroor 2-9-0 T L Dettori 5/1: 1: b c Machiavellian - Silabteni **96+**
(Nureyev) Handy, styd on to lead ins fnl 1f, pushed out, val 4L+: bckd on debut: Mar foal, half-brother to wnrs at 6/10f: dam unrcd: sire decent performer around 1m: eff at 7f, will apprec further: acts on hvy grnd & a gall trk: goes well fresh: eff with a t-strap: gd start to career & can rate higher.
FULL OF ZEST [3] Mrs A J Perrett 2-8-9 A Culhane 8/1: 2: ch f Pivotal - Tangerine (Primo *2½* **84**
Dominie) Led, hdd dist, kept on, not pace wnr: debut: Apr first foal, dam successful at 5f: sire decent performer at sprint dists: eff at 7f on hvy grnd: encouraging start & can improve for today's experience.
CASHIER [6] J H M Gosden 2-9-0 R Hughes 6/1: 3: gr c Alhaarth - Cashew (Sharrood) Cl-up, led *2½* **84**
despite hanging left 1f out, hdd ins fnl 1f, no extra: debut: Feb foal, cost 360,000gns: half-brother to numerous wnrs at 5/8f: dam successful at 8f: sire decent Group performer around 1m: signs of promise & can improve.
5055 **NEUTRINO 10** [14] L M Cumani 2-9-0 N Mackay 14/1: 04: Bhd, prog halfway, kept on late. *½* **83**
5147 **ROYAL MOUGINS 4** [2]2-9-0 (68) D Holland 4/1 FAV: 05535: Prom, ev ch 2f out, sn wknd: qck reapp. *1* **81$**
4883 **CAVAN GAEL 22** [12]2-9-0 R Winston 33/1: 06: Keen in tch over 5f, no extra. *1¾* **77**
KINGDOM OF DREAMS [5]2-9-0 R Hills 6/1: 7: Mid-div over 5f, wknd on debut. *3½* **70**
GREATCOAT [8]2-9-0 W Supple 50/1: 8: Mid-div, nvr a factor. *4* **62**
DINNER DATE [4]2-9-0 K Fallon 13/2: 9: Al bhd on debut: op 9/1. *shd* **61**
PITCAIRN ISLAND [13]2-8-9 R Ffrench 20/1: 0: 10th: Cl-up, fdd 2f out: debut. *9* **40**
5084 **WHISPERING DEATH 8** [7]2-9-0 S W Kelly 33/1: 00: 11th: Al bhd. *hd* **44**
1424 **Beacon Star 177** [1]2-9-0 K Darley 33/1:0 **Cream Of Esteem** [11]2-9-0 T Kim Tinkler 100/1:0
13 Ran Time 1m 31.69 (8.49) Owned: Godolphin Trained: Newmarket

5200

1.35 Dransfield Novelty Company E B F October Maiden Stakes Div 2 2yo (D3)
£3543 £1090 £545 **7f str** **Heavy 123** **-07 Slow** Stands side

TASDEED [13] E F Vaughan 2-9-0 T E Durcan 12/1: 1: ch c Cadeaux Genereux - Miss Universe **95+**
(Warning) Held up, prog 2f out, styd on to lead ins fnl 1f, pushed clr, val 4L+: op 9/1 on debut: Apr foal, cost 100,000gns: half-brother successful at 1m/10f: dam decent sprinter: sire fine performer at sprint dists: eff at 7f, further will suit: acts on hvy & a gall trk: goes well fresh: imprressive win & has a bright future.
4028 **DANIEL THOMAS 65** [2] Mrs A J Perrett 2-9-0 (92) A Culhane 15/8 FAV: 2232: In tch, styd on for *2½* **88**
press to lead dist, hdd ins fnl 1f, not pace wnr: 9 wk abs: acts on fast & hvy grnd: continues to run well & deserves to get head in front: see 4028 (6f) & 2766.
GOLDEN FEATHER [14] J H M Gosden 2-9-0 L Dettori 3/1: 3: ch c Dr Fong - Idolize (Polish *1* **86**
Precedent) In tch, kept on bef 1f out, no ch with front 2: bckd from 13/2 on debut: Feb first foal, dam a 1m/10f wnr, sire decent 1m turf performer: eff at 7f, looks sure to apprec further: acts on hvy grnd: just come on for today's experience & rate higher.
SHARP REPLY [5] Sir Michael Stoute 2-9-0 R Hughes 12/1: 4: b c Diesis - Questonia (Rainbow *nk* **85**
Quest) Held up, prog halfway, kept on fnl 1f, just held for 3rd: debut: Apr foal, half-brother a 10f wnr: dam successful at 1m, sire fine performer as a juv: eff at 7f, sure to apprec further: acts on hvy grnd: signs of encouragement & can rate higher,
WOOLSACK [12]2-9-0 D Holland 18/1: 5: Led, hdd dist, no extra: debut. *¾* **83**
GAMBLE OF THE DAY [8]2-9-0 K Fallon 9/1: 6: Nvr nrr than mid-div: op 12/1 on debut. *¾* **81**
KEON [4]2-9-0 D Sweeney 100/1: 7: Rear, prog & ev ch over 1f out, wknd: debut. *2* **77**
5076 **LEKKA DING 9** [11]2-8-9 J Quinn 100/1: 08: Al bhd. *½* **71**
ROYAL SAPPHIRE [3]2-9-0 R Ffrench 20/1: 9: Chsd ldrs far side alone over 5f, wknd. *¾* **74**
4988 **REAL COOL CAT 14** [9]2-8-9 K Darley 13/2: 40: 10th: Cl-up 5f, fdd: op 9/2: see 4988. *1* **67**
3713 **SPENCE APPEAL 78** [6]2-9-0 P Fessey 100/1: 000: 11th: Mid-div 4f, wknd: has been gelded. *3½* **65**
Vettorious [10]2-9-0 M Fenton 40/1:0 5018 **Cost Analysis 12** [7]2-9-0 P Robinson 14/1:0
13 Ran Time 1m 32.34 (9.14) Owned: Sheikh Ahmed Al Maktoum Trained: Newmarket

5201

2.10 Persimmon Homes Handicap Stakes 3yo 71-85 (D2) **[90]**
£7296 £2245 £1122 **1m2f60y** **Soft 111** **+12 Fast** Inside

4877* **DOUBLE DEPUTY 22** [13] Saeed bin Suroor 3-9-4 t (80) L Dettori 6/1: 11: Made all, drvn out fnl 1f **89**
to hold on: h'cap bow: fast time: eff around 10f, shld get further: acts on gd & hvy: eff on a sharp/undul or gall trk: suited by a t-strap: unbtn 3yo who showed battling qualities here, see 4877.
4943 **ANOTHER CHOICE 18** [5] N P Littmoden 3-9-4 t (80) T E Durcan 16/1: 0041622: Held up, prog when *nk* **87**
short of room 2f out, switched wide & kept on well ins fnl 1f, post came too sn: another gd eff & would have won in another couple of strides: can find similar: see 4943 & 4254.
4917 **IKTITAF 20** [16] J H M Gosden 3-9-7 (83) R Hills 25/1: 031003: In tch, prog trav well & ev ch *1¾* **88**

over 1f out, kept on, not pace front 2 cl-home: acts on gd & soft grnd: imprvd eff today & is unexposed in h'caps.

4872 **WOODY VALENTINE** 22 [7] M Johnston 3-9-6 (82) S Chin 13/2: 1200524: Chsd ldrs, short of room 2f hd **86**
out, switched & kept on late, nrst fin: op 8/1, clr rem: see 4872 & 2874.

4392 **SUNISA** 48 [2]3-9-6 (82) D Holland 50/1: 2130205: In tch, no extra dist: 7 wk abs: btr 2680. 4 **80**

5148 **MAMBINA** 4 [1]3-8-10 (6ex) (72) T O'Brien(7) 12/1: 3241166: Bhd, prog when short of room bef 2f 2 **67**
out, sn no impress: qck reapp: btr 5016 (fast).

5102 **TOP SPEC** 7 [9]3-9-6 (82) P Dobbs 33/1: 0121047: Missed break, eff when short of room over 2f 2½ **73**
out, kept on late: qck reapp: showed more in 5102 (12f) & 4503.

4643 **CELLARMASTER** 35 [11]3-9-3 (79) K Darley 7/1: 52-31438: Nvr nrr than mid-div: btr 3108 (gd). ½ **69**

4939 **SLAVONIC** 18 [4]3-8-8 (70) P Fessey 40/1: 5446409: Mid-div, short of room 3f out, sn onepcd. ½ **59**

4777 **ALEKHINE** 28 [18]3-9-6 e (82) M Fenton 12/1: 3006050: 10th: Held up, prog 3f out, onepcd dist. nk **70**

4909 **BRIGHT SUN** 20 [10]3-8-10 T (72) Kim Tinkler 66/1: 3410600: 11th: keen bhd, nvr a factor. 1 **58**

5037 **CHARNOCK BATES ONE** 11 [6]3-8-10 (72) G Gibbons 20/1: 1222360: 12th: Handy over 7f, wknd. ¾ **56**

3238 **GHANTOOT** 98 [3]3-8-11 vis (73) N Mackay 18/1: 0003130: 13th: In tch, wknd bef 2f out. 1½ **54**

4766 **KINGS EMPIRE** 28 [14]3-9-4 t (80) D Tudhope(5) 40/1: 31-4400: 14th: Prom 6f, wknd. 5 **54**

5037 **TYTHEKNOT** 11 [8]3-8-11 (73) P Hanagan 33/1: 6431500: 15th: Mid-div 1m, wknd. 1¼ **45**

4943 **FLYING ADORED** 18 [19]3-9-4 (80) K Fallon 10/1: 3011530: 16th: Prog wide 5f out, wknd fnl 2f. 18 **27**

4777 **NEW ORDER** 28 [12]3-9-2 (78) R Hughes 9/2 FAV: 31160: 17th: Chsd ldrs 1m, fdd: well bckd: yet 1 **23**
to convince at 10f: btr 4263 (7f) & 2886 (1m).

4935 **Saffron Fox** 18 [15]3-9-0 p(76) A Culhane 20/1:0 4694 **On Every Street** 33 [17]3-8-13 (75) R Ffrench 100/1:0
19 Ran Time 2m 16.60 (10.2) Owned: Godolphin Trained: Newmarket

---

5202	**2.45 Dbs October Yearling Stakes 2yo** (B1)			
	£25914 £9830 £4915	**6f str**	**Heavy 123**	**+05 Fast** Stands side

4928 **PIVOTAL FLAME** 20 [10] B A McMahon 2-8-11 G Carter 6/4 FAV: 154161: Bhd far group, prog over 2f **95**
out, rdn out to lead cl-home: well bckd: eff at 6/7f on fast & hvy grnd: in form juv: see 4928 & 4699.

4381 **HIDDEN JEWEL** 48 [13] B A McMahon 2-8-11 G Gibbons 100/1: 06602: Prom far side, led bef 2f out, hd **93$**
hdd under press cl-home: 7 wk abs: much imprvd on first try on hvy grnd: eff at 6f: see 2802.

5035 **DISPOL ISLE** 11 [3] T D Barron 2-8-6 K Darley 50/1: 4443563: Cl-up far side, styd on ins fnl 1f, 1½ **84$**
not btn far in 3rd: acts on fast & hvy grnd: prob shade flattered: see 4655.

4625* **SEAMUS SHINDIG** 36 [4] H Candy 2-8-11 D Sweeney 12/1: 14: Bhd far side, prog 2f out, kept on shd **88**
late: eff at 5f, ran to form on step up to 6f: acts on fast & hvy grnd: only 2nd start: see 4625.

4998 **THE CROOKED RING** 13 [8]2-8-11 (81) L Dettori 11/2: 4112365: Bhd far side, prog halfway, kept on hd **87**
late: acts on hvy grnd: showed more in 4004 (8f, h'cap).

4658 **OCEANCOOKIE** 34 [1]2-8-7 (1ow) D Holland 66/1: 556: In tch far side over 4f, wknd: see 4401. 5 **70**

4980 **PIDDIES PRIDE** 15 [18]2-8-6 (70) Hayley Turner 100/1: 2040507: In tch stands side, kept on to 1½ **65+**
lead that group ins fnl 1f, no ch with far side: won race on unfav'd stands side: see 3614 & 3382.

4865 **FLAXBY** 23 [15]2-8-11 P Robinson 100/1: 0048: Led stands side, hdd ins fnl 1f, no extra. nk **69$**

4895* **COCONUT SQUEAK** 21 [16]2-8-6 F Norton 66/1: 360019: In tch stands side 4f, onepcd: btr 4895. 2 **58**

4004 **MELALCHRIST** 66 [19]2-8-11 (94) P Hanagan 25/1: 1221300: 10th: Chsd ldrs stands side 4f, wknd. 1½ **59**

4985 **GRAZE ON** 14 [21]2-8-11 R Winston 20/1: 212500: 11th: Al bhd stands side. ¾ **57**

4280* **SPACE SHUTTLE** 53 [7]2-9-3 (85) K Fallon 7/2: 1333110: 12th: Bhd far side, prog halfway, fdd ¾ **61**
dist: bckd: disapp in today's hvy grnd: showed more in 4280 (gd) & 4004.

4882 **COLEORTON DANCER** 22 [2]2-8-11 (65) P Fessey 11/1: 0111100: 13th: Ride slow in taking hood off & 2 **49**
v slow away, nvr a factor far side: lost any ch at start & is worth another ch: btr 4224.

5035 **SELKIRK STORM** 11 [22]2-8-11 (81) P Mulrennan 25/1: 5000030: 14th: Al bhd stands side. ½ **48**

4863* **DAVY CROCKETT** 23 [17]2-8-11 D McGaffin 100/1: 0056010: 15th: Cl-up stands side 4f, fdd. 1¼ **44**

5124 **World At My Feet** 6 [14]2-8-6 (55) J Quinn 80/1:0 4859 **Little Warning** 23 [6]2-8-6 N Mackay 100/1:0
4258 **Tartatartufata** 54 [12]2-8-6 R P Cleary 100/1:0 4928 **Forest Viking** 20 [9]2-8-11 G Parkin 150/1:0
4617 **Slate Grey** 36 [11]2-8-11 vis Darren Williams 200/1:0 4645 **Marcela Zabala** 35 [5]2-8-6 (55) M Fenton 100/1:0
21 Ran Time 1m 17.92 (7.12) Owned: Mr R L Bedding Trained: Tamworth

---

5203	**3.20 Racing Post #1 Million Totetentofollow Nursery Handicap Stakes 2yo 0-90 (C2)**			
	£10686 £3288 £1644	**1m rnd**	**Soft 111**	**-02 Slow** Outside **[95]**

4296* **ALPINE GOLD** 53 [3] J L Dunlop 2-8-8 (75) I Mongan 14/1: 0011: Chsd ldrs, prog & ev ch dist, drvn **84**
out to lead cl-home: 8 wk abs: h'cap bow: eff at 1m, further will suit in time: acts on gd/soft & soft grnd:
acts on undul or gall trk: imprvng with racing & enjoyed today's stamina test: see 4296.

4484 **MOKARABA** 43 [10] J L Dunlop 2-8-13 (80) R Hills 16/1: 4422: Held up, prog wide halfway, styd on hd **87**
to lead 1f out, hdd under press cl-home: 6 wk abs, s/mate of wnr: acts on fast & soft grnd: see 4035.

4871 **SECRET PACT** 22 [12] M Johnston 2-9-3 (84) K Darley 10/1: 2301123: Led, hdd under press 1f out, ½ **90**
rallied & sn ev ch, just held by front 2: game performer who continues in gd form: see 4871 & 4673.

4807 **IM SO LUCKY** 26 [7] M Johnston 2-9-6 (87) R Ffrench 10/1: 0124: Bhd, prog halfway, kept on wide ¾ **91**
fnl 1f, nrst fin: acts on gd & soft: best work at fin & is sure to apprec further next term: see 4807.

5051 **IM SPARTACUS** 11 [8]2-8-7 p (74) C Haddon(7) 8/1: 5415425: In tch when short of room 2f out, 1¼ **76**
switched & sn no impress: btr 5051 (fast).

5051* **ALRIGHT MY SON** 11 [4]2-9-6 (6ex) (87) R Hughes 9/2 JT FAV: 5240216: Prom, ev ch over 1f out, fdd: 6 **78**
well bckd: disappointing under 6lb pen: btr 5051 (fast).

4387 **NIGHT OF JOY** 48 [6]2-9-7 (88) P Robinson 10/1: 441107: Nvr nrr than mid-div: 7 wk abs: btr 4285. ½ **78**

4997* **MAIDANNI** 13 [5]2-9-3 (84) L Dettori 9/2: 418: In tch, prog halfway, ev ch 2f out, sn fdd: h'cap 1¼ **72**
bow: showed more in 4997 (gd).

5031 **WAVERTREE WARRIOR** 12 [9]2-8-10 P (77) J P Guillambert(3) 14/1: 032039: Prom 5f: cheek pieces. 9 **49**

4807 **JUST WAZ** 26 [13]2-8-1 (68) F Norton 25/1: 0150: 10th: Rear, nvr a factor: btr 4283. nk **39**

5065 **LADY MISHA** 10 [2]2-8-6 (73) J Mackay 14/1: 5031250: 11th: Handy over 5f, wknd. 2 **40**

4985 **JOHN FORBES** 14 [1]2-8-8 bl (75) P Mulrennan(3) 66/1: 0100000: 12th: Keen mid-div, wknd 3f out. ½ **41**

5051 **DARKO KARIM** 11 [11]2-8-6 (73) W Supple 25/1: 4000030: 13th: Bhd, nvr a factor. hd **38**

4580 **BATHWICK FINESSE** 38 [14]2-8-13 (80) S W Kelly 10/1: 0140: 14th: Rear, prog wide 4f out, wknd bef 10 **28**
1f out, sn eased: btr 4580 & 4363.

DONCASTER   FRIDAY 22.10.04   Lefthand, Flat, Galloping Track

14 Ran   Time 1m 45.19 (9.09)   Owned: Windflower Overseas Holdings Inc   Trained: Arundel

5204
3.50 Racing Post/Sis Betting Shop Manager Of The Year Handicap Stakes 3yo+ 71-85 (D2) [97]
£7179 £2209 £1104   1m6f132y   Soft 111   +02 Fast   Inside

5068* **WINGED DARGENT** 10 [10] M Johnston 3-8-13 (6ex) (82) K Darley 9/4 FAV: 1511: Rcd wide over 6f, 97+
styd prom, led 2f out, drvn clr ins fnl 1f: bckd: eff at 10f, suited by 13/14.5f, shld get further: acts on
gd/soft, revels in soft & hvy grnd: v progressive 3yo who relished today's stamina test: see 5068.

4553* **JEEPSTAR** 39 [2] T D Easterby 4-9-6 (80) M Fenton 20/1: 6221012: Led, hdd 2f out, not pace ready 8 85
wnr: eff at 10/12f, poss stays 14f: handles soft, prob apprec rtn to faster surface: btr 4553 (12f, fast).

4942* **BELLE ROUGE** 18 [5] C A Horgan 6-9-6 (80) L Dettori 5/1: 1212113: Rcd wide 6f, bhd, prog 3f out, hd 84
no impress fnl 1f: showed more in 4942 (gd/soft).

3783* **MANDATUM** 76 [8] L M Cumani 3-8-10 (79) K Fallon 11/2: 2214: Bhd, eff when short of room 3f out, 1¾ 81
switched & kept on late: 11 wk abs: bckd from 9/1: showed more in 3783 (12f, fast).

4942 **QUARRYMOUNT** 18 [3]3-8-12 (81) J Mackay 3/1: 2122125: Nvr a factor in mid-div: well bckd: ¾ 82
disapp in today's soft grnd: see 4919 (fast).

4803 **PEAK OF PERFECTION** 27 [1]3-9-7 (90) P Robinson 10/1: 5111206: Rcd wide over 6f, wknd fnl 2f. ¾ 90

4932* **RED FOREST** 20 [9]5-8-12 t (72) Dale Gibson 20/1: 3331617: Handy, wknd 3f out. 5 67

1569 **GRACILIS** 170 [7]7-9-1 (75) R Winston 66/1: 0000/-008: Chsd ldrs 6f, fdd: jumps fit. dist 40

8 Ran   Time 3m 18.95 (15.95)   Owned: Mr Daniel A Couper   Trained: Middleham

5205
4.25 Auker Rhodes Plue Parrot E B F Maiden Stakes Fillies 2yo   (D3)
£4380 £1348 £674   1m rnd   Soft 111   -25 Slow   Outside

4927 **HER OWN KIND** 20 [10] Saeed bin Suroor 2-8-11 L Dettori 4/5 FAV: 21: Cl-up, led trav well 3f 90+
out, sn pushed clr, eased cl-home, val 5L+: well bckd: eff at 7f, improve for step up to 1m: acts on firm & soft
grnd: acts on a gall trk: won with authority & can progress: see 4927.

4035 **TWYLA THARP** 65 [2] J H M Gosden 2-8-11 R Hughes 5/1: 02: b f Sadler's Wells - Sumoto (Mtoto) 3 82
Prom, ev ch over 2f out, kept on, not pace wnr fnl 1f: w wk abs: Mar foal, half-sister to numerous wnrs at 7/10f:
dam successful at 6/7f: sire decent performer around 1m/12f: eff at 1m, further will suit next term: acts on soft
grnd: left debut eff bhd with encouraging display & can rate higher.

ASAWER [8] Sir Michael Stoute 2-8-11 R Hills 13/2: 3: b f Darshaan - Sassy Bird (Storm Bird) nk 81
Missed break, sn mid-div, prog 2f out, onepcd dist: tchd 10/1 on debut: clr rem: Apr foal, cost 600,000gns:
half-brother to smart sprint performer abroad: sire Gr 1 wnr at 12f: eff at 1m on soft, shld apprec further.

5040 **MISSELLA** 11 [1] M Johnston 2-8-11 K Darley 33/1: 04: gr f Danehill - Delage (Bellypha) Prom 8 67
6f, wknd: Apr foal, half-sister successful numerous times at mid-dists: dam won numerous times at mid-dists: sire
useful performer around 1m: improve next term.

ENAMOURED [9]2-8-11 A Culhane 14/1: 5: Bhd, prog over halfway, wknd bef 1f out on debut. 1½ 64

5045 **KATHRYN JANEWAY** 11 [6]2-8-11 K Fallon 10/1: 06: Mid-div, hdwy & ev ch over 2f out, fdd. 5 55

MINNESINGER [3]2-8-11 P Hanagan 80/1: 7: Bhd, nvr a factor on debut. 3½ 48

5140 **AZA WISH** 5 [7]2-8-11 T Eaves(3) 100/1: 5006558: Led 5f, fdd: qck reapp: btr 5012. 3½ 41

WOOD SPRITE [4]2-8-11 M Fenton 40/1: 9: Rear, nvr a factor. nk 40

ANISSATI [5]2-8-11 D Holland 25/1: 0: 10th: Chsd ldrs 4f, fdd. 12 19

4842 **WHOOPSIE** 24 [11]2-8-11 R Winston 100/1: 000: 11th: Missed break, nvr a factor. 19 0

11 Ran   Time 1m 47.40 (10.9)   Owned: Godolphin   Trained: Newmarket

5206
5.00 Weatherbys Bank European Racing Schools Apprentice Stakes Handicap 3yo+ 56-70 (E3) [76]
£7342 £2259 £1130   1m2f60y   Soft 111   -12 Slow   Inside

4589 **WELLINGTON HALL** 38 [3] P W Chapple Hyam 6-9-4 (66) A Mullen(5) 9/2 CO FAV: 0-101351: In tch, prog 78
trav well 4f out, styd on to lead dist, rdn clr: stays 12.5f, suited by around 10/11f: acts on fast & hvy grnd:
goes well fresh: see 4274 & 3785.

5191 **MOBANE FLYER** 2 [9] R A Fahey 4-9-1 (63) A Baroni(3) 9/2 CO FAV: 6331322: Mid-div, prog over 2f 3½ 69
out, ev ch dist, not pace wnr: op 7/2 on qck reapp: continues in gd form & deserves to rtn to winning ways.

5016 **LUCAYAN DANCER** 12 [7] D Nicholls 4-8-13 (61) S Breux(3) 9/2 CO FAV: 5014123: Held up, prog wide 2 64
3f out, kept on late: btr 5016 (fast).

5148 **TEDSDALE MAC** 4 [1] N Bycroft 5-9-1 (6ex) (63) A Bonnefoy 14/1: 5200104: Led, hdd dist, fdd: qck reapp.1½ 63

5026 **KEEPERS KNIGHT** 12 [6]3-8-9 (62) Hayley Turner 16/1: 0003545: Rear, prog 4f out, kept on late. ¾ 60

4993 **MURAQEB** 13 [8]4-8-4 (12oh) (40) C Hayes(5) 100/1: 0050006: Chsd ldrs over 7f, wknd. 1 48

4623 **ZANDEEL** 36 [5]6-8-9 (57) A Sanna(3) 12/1: 0314057: Cl-up, wknd 2f out: btr 4406. ¾ 51

5062 **GARDEN SOCIETY** 10 [2]7-8-12 (60) P B Beggy(5) 9/2 CO FAV: 6/-000058: Held up, nvr a factor. ¾ 52

4757 **SNOWED UNDER** 29 [11]3-8-5 (58) R Fradet 12/1: 5001639: Handy 1m, fdd. 3 45

5083* **REVENIR** 9 [10]3-9-9 (6ex) (76) J O'Dwyer(3) 14/1: 0222410: 10th: Bhd, nvr a factor: btr 5083 (Aw). 9 51

10 Ran   Time 2m 19.07(12.67)   Owned: Allan Darke & Tom Matthews   Trained: Newmarket

WOLVERHAMPTON   Polytrack   SATURDAY 23.10.04   Lefthand, Sharp Track

Official Going Standard

5207
11.15 Dunstall Park Maiden Auction Stakes 2yo   (H5)
£1477 £422 £211   5f20y aw rnd   Inapplicable   Inside

5021 **IL PRANZO** 13 [5] S Kirk 2-8-10 (68) M Fenton 11/4 FAV: 0635041: In tch, prog to lead dist, drvn 76a
out to hold on: eff at 5f, improved on polytrack: acts on a sharp trk: see 3361.

4981 **DEPRESSED** 16 [8] Andrew Reid 2-8-5 (1ow) (64) G Gibbons 100/30: 00342: Handy, ev ch dist, kept ½ 68a
on, not pace wnr: eff at 5/6f: continues to run well & can find a race: see 4981 & 4921.

4922 **OUR LITTLE SECRET** 21 [7] A Berry 2-8-4 F Norton 25/1: 533: Led, hung right & hdd dist, no 1 64a

extra: eff at 5f on polytrack: see 4549.
4900 **PINAFORE 21** [9] H Morrison 2-8-3 (1ow) (65) T P Queally 100/30: 3224: In tch, onepcd fnl 1f: eff at 5f. *¾* **61a**
5081 **LOWESTOFT PLAYBOY 10** [11]2-8-11 (68) Hayley Turner(3) 9/1: 0650045: Cl up, hung left & no extra dist.*nk* **68a**
4804 **BEVERLEY BEAU 27** [6]2-8-9 (67) S Whitworth 20/1: 5544456: Mid div, prog 2f out, onepcd dist. *1* **63a**
4865 **NAVIGATION 24** [2]2-8-11 Kristin Stubbs(7) 14/1: 067: Missed break, nvr nrr than mid div. *nk* **64a**
4922 **DUCAL DIVA 21** [13]2-8-3 P (54) D Fentiman(7) 40/1: 0260048: Nvr nrr than mid div. *3* **47a**
5113 **ROOKS BRIDGE 7** [3]2-8-7 J Quinn 100/1: 0009: Al bhd: qck reapp. *1½* **47a**
5182 **GAUDALPIN 4** [12]2-8-4 (64) A McCarthy 5/1: 0400220: 10th: In tch till halfway, wknd: btr 5182. *¾* **42a**
4843 **MOCHACCINO 25** [1]2-8-7 (2ow)VIS Darren Williams 66/1: 0000: 11th: Al in rear. *6* **29a**
5013 **Ms Three 13** [4]2-8-5 (55) Joanna Badger 50/1:0 4752 **Isle Dream 30** [10]2-8-5 J Edmunds 100/1:0
13 Ran Time 1m 4.91 () Owned: Mr David P Moss Trained: Upper Lambourn

5208

11.45 Wolverhampton-Racecourse Co Uk Banded Stakes 3yo+ 0-40 (H5)
£1460 £417 £209 **1m4f50y aw** **Inapplicable** Inside

2988 **MELOGRANO 109** [6] Mark Campion 4-9-2 (40) D Nolan(3) 7/1: 60-20001: Bhd, prog after halfway, led 2f out, sn clr, eased cl home, val 7L+: tchd 9/1: long abs: eff at 1m, now stays 12f: handles fast, soft grnd & both AW's: goes well fresh: first win on drop in class: see 1589. **50a**
4663 **BRETTON 35** [8] B A Pearce 3-8-9 p (40) T P Queally 5/1: 0250002: Rear, hdwy 5f out, kept on for 2nd, no ch with easy wnr: clr rem: eff at 9/12f: see 3025. *5* **40a**
5128 **VALIANT AIR 7** [3] J R Weymes 3-8-9 bl (40) P Mulrennan(3) 14/1: 0045003: Mid div, prog to lead 5f out, hdd 2f out, wknd: qck reapp: see 2790. *3½* **35a**
3486 **SPANISH STAR 89** [7] Mrs N Macauley 7-9-2 (40) Sarah Sayer(7) 10/1: 3300004: Bhd, nvr nrr than mid div.*1¾* **32a**
1313 **VITELUCY 184** [2]5-9-2 vis (40) A Quinn(5) 11/4 FAV: 00-55355: In tch 1m, fdd: jumps fit, earlier h'cap hdle wnr (rtd 96h, stays 2m5.5f on fast & gd): btr 984 (2m, fibresand). *19* **7a**
3899 **BENS REVENGE 72** [9]4-9-2 (40) V Slattery 50/1: 6056: Bhd, hdwy halfway, fdd 3f out: 10 wk abs. *6* **0a**
3085 **BEN KENOBI 106** [11]6-9-2 (40) Dean Williams(7) 10/1: 5220207: Keen rear, nvr a factor. *2* **0a**
GREEN MASTER 118 [5]4-9-2 (40) N Chalmers(3) 18/1: 24-10008: bl g Who Knows - Green Fee (Windwurf) Mid div 1m, fdd: Brit bow, ex Polish, earlier won twice at 6f in native country (hvy & gd). *½* **0a**
4796 **RICKY MARTAN 28** [10]3-8-9 (40) S Whitworth 12/1: 0060609: Keen cl up 1m, fdd. *shd* **0a**
3982 **MARY CARLETON 68** [12]3-8-9 (40) M Henry 25/1: 06000: 10th: ch f Halling - Anne Bonny (Ajdal) Missed break, prog to lead after 3f, hdd 5f out, fdd: 10 wk abs: mod form to date. *2½* **0a**
4675 **CAPER 35** [4]4-9-2 (40) Stephanie Hollinshead(5) 16/1: 60-00000: 11th: Led 3f, fdd halfway. *25* **0a**
244 **BRIOS BOY 306** [1]4-9-2 (40) Darren Williams 9/2: 00/0600-0: 12th: ch g My Best Valentine - Rose Elegance (Bairn) Mid div 1m, fdd: reapp & new stable: unplcd all 3 '03 starts (rtd 44, R Bastiman): with K R Burke. *3½* **0a**
12 Ran Time 2m 45.13 () Owned: Faulkner West Trained: Malton

5209

12.15 Holiday Inn Garden Court Tri-Banded Stakes 3yo 0-45 (H5)
£1474 £421 £211 **1m1f103y aw** **Inapplicable** Inside

5122 **LARAD 7** [6] J S Moore 3-8-9 bl (40) Derek Nolan(7) 3/1 FAV: 6065041: Missed break, prog 4f out, led dist, pushed out, val 3L+: qck reapp: eff at 1m/10f on both AW's, fast & soft: enjoys banded grade: see 1946. **47a**
4302 **KNIGHT OF HEARTS 54** [12] P A Blockley 3-9-0 (45) M Lawson(5) 8/1: 5500402: Keen mid div, prog to lead 2f out, hdd dist, no extra: 8 wk abs: eff at 9.5f on polytrack: encouraging & can find similar: see 4011. *1¾* **46a**
5034 **CAMPBELLS LAD 12** [1] A Berry 3-9-0 (45) P Mathers(5) 7/1: 0530243: Cl up, no extra fnl 1f: acts on firm, fast & polytrack: see 4505. *¾* **44a**
4994 **INK IN GOLD 14** [3] P A Blockley 3-9-0 (45) V Slattery 33/1: 050004: Bhd, prog 3f out, short of room bef 1f out, sn no impress: see 4216. *1¾* **41a**
5119 **FLYING SPUD 7** [9]3-9-0 (45) D Nolan(2) 9/2: 0020055: Rear, nvr nrr than mid div: qck reapp: polytrack bow: btr 3182 (gd/soft). *¾* **39a**
4624 **SIXTILSIX 37** [7]3-9-0 (45) J Carroll 16/1: 00-00306: Led 7f, wknd dist: btr 4113. *1* **37a**
1675 **SECRET BLOOM 165** [2]3-9-0 vis (45) Darren Williams 8/1: 5424137: Cl up, wknd fnl 2f: long abs. *1¾* **34a**
5042 **RED ROCKY 12** [4]3-9-0 p (45) Stephanie Hollinshead(5) 15/2: 2035338: Keen handy 7f, wknd: btr 5042. *½* **33a**
4857 **ACCA LARENTIA 24** [10]3-9-0 (45) Hayley Turner(3) 14/1: 3006569: Cl up, fdd 2f out. *3* **29a**
4793 **LADY PREDOMINANT 28** [11]3-9-0 (45) Frances Pickard(7) 33/1: 1050000: 10th: Al in rear. *2* **26a**
2065 **WARIF 147** [5]3-9-0 (45) T Hamilton(3) 66/1: 000-5000: 11th: Rear, nvr a factor. *3½* **21a**
4256 **GAME FLORA 55** [8]3-9-0 (45) P Mulrennan(3) 9/1: 0506020: 12th: Keen cl up, ev ch 2f out, fdd: 8 wk abs.*7* **11a**
12 Ran Time 2m 7.21 () Owned: Mr A P Crook Trained: Hungerford

5210

12.45 Andrew Higginbottom 40th Birthday Banded Stakes 3yo+ 0-45 (H5)
£1502 £429 £215 **7f32y aw rnd** **Inapplicable** Outside

5119 **TOKEWANNA 7** [6] W M Brisbourne 4-9-2 t (45) P Mathers(5) 9/2: 4543501: Mid div, prog when hmpd bef 2f out, styd on to lead well ins fnl 1f, rdn out: qck reapp: eff at 5/7f on firm, gd/soft & polytrack: 1st win. **50a**
4626 **ACE MA VAHRA 37** [11] S R Bowring 6-9-2 bl (45) J Bramhill 12/1: 3350502: Mid div, prog & ev ch ins fnl 1f, onepcd when hmpd cl home: acts on firm, fast & both AW's: see 4130 & 3609. *1* **47a**
4707 **DEXILEOS 33** [12] A D W Pinder 5-9-2 t (45) N Chalmers(3) 10/1: 0036003: In tch, prog to lead 1f out, hdd well ins fnl 1f, no extra: see 3301. *1* **45a**
4794 **SAVERNAKE BRAVE 28** [8] Mrs H Sweeting 3-9-0 (45) G Baker 9/2: 4000104: Missed break, prog 3f out, onepcd dist: btr 4371 (fast). *1½* **42a**
3830 **EASTERN SCARLET 75** [7]4-9-2 p (45) J Quinn 11/2: 555-0505: Bhd, prog after 2f, onepcd fnl 1f: abs. *½* **41a**
5017 **PAGAN STORM 13** [10]4-9-2 (45) Kristin Stubbs(7) 7/2 FAV: 0300006: Led after 1f, hdd 1f out, fdd. *1¼* **39a**
4676 **SPRING DANCER 35** [9]3-9-0 t (45) P Mulrennan(3) 7/1: 0536067: Cl up, fdd bef 1f out. *1½* **36a**
4795 **GEMINI LADY 28** [4]4-9-2 bl (45) J Carroll 10/1: 2000408: Al bhd: btr 4676. *shd* **35a**
4371 **BALMACARA 49** [3]5-9-2 (45) T P Queally 20/1: 0060509: In tch, wknd over 2f out: 7 wk abs. *9* **19a**
3746 **BAHAMA BELLE 78** [2]3-9-0 (45) O Urbina 25/1: 0-040000: 10th: Cl up 4f, fdd: 11 wk abs & new stable. *nk* **18a**
4243 **SONEARSOFAR 56** [1]4-9-2 (45) G Gibbons 40/1: 06000: 11th: Led 1f, styd in tch, fdd 2f out: 8 wk abs. *11* **0a**
11 Ran Time 1m 32.80 () Owned: Merryland Properties Ltd Trained: Nesscliffe

WOLVERHAMPTON Polytrack SATURDAY 23.10.04 Lefthand, Sharp Track

5211 **1.15 Civil Weddings At Dunstall Park Banded Stakes 3yo+ 0-45 (H5)**
£1495 £427 £214 **5f216y aw rnd** **Inapplicable** Inside

5146 **REGAL SONG 6** [4] T J Etherington 8-9-5 bl (49) O Urbina 16/1: 0000001: In tch, styd on to lead dist, rdn out: qck reapp: eff at 5/6f on fast, hvy grnd & both AW's: apprec drop to banded grade: see 5146. **60a**
4995 **CHORUS 14** [12] B R Millman 7-9-5 vis (49) A Quinn(5) 12/1: 6-030002: Cl up when hmps after 1f, prog 2f out, kept on, not pace wnr fnl 1f: acts on firm, gd & both AW's: can find similar: see 483. 2½ **53a**
2634 **BREEZIT 124** [13] S R Bowring 3-9-3 (48) P Makin(5) 20/1: 00-44503: Rear, prog bef 1f out, hung left & onepcd fnl 1f: long abs; btr 2439. 2 **46a**
3569 **LONG WEEKEND 85** [3] D Shaw 6-9-6 (50) Darren Williams 10/1: 0600004: Missed break, prog when short of room bef 1f out, nrst fin: long abs. ¾ **46a**
5036 **OL LUCY BROON 12** [9]3-9-4 (49) P Fessey 10/1: 00-00005: Bhd, prog 2f out, nrst fin. nk **44a**
5176 **TAPPIT 4** [7]5-9-4 (48) M Savage(5) 4/1 FAV: 0605156: Led after 1f, hdd 4f out, wknd fnl 1f: qck reapp. shd **42a**
4636 **BAYTOWN FLYER 37** [5]4-9-6 (50) T P Queally 6/1: 2112007: Led 1f, styd in tch, led over 1f out, sn hdd & wknd: btr 1452. 1¼ **40a**
835 **AMBER LEGEND 224** [10]3-9-5 (50) S Chin 33/1: 26020-08: Al in rear: long abs: see 835. 2½ **33a**
4043 **SCARY NIGHT 65** [2]4-9-6 p (50) J Edmunds 10/1: 0602009: Cl up, led 4f out, hdd over 1f out, fdd. ½ **32a**
4739 **REHIA 31** [11]3-9-4 (49) R Smith 20/1: 3503100: 10th: In tch, wknd bef 1f out: btr 3645 (fast, 5f). 3 **22a**
4676 **LINDENS LADY 35** [6]4-9-5 bl (49) D Fentiman(7) 6/1: 5054300: 11th: Keen mid div, nvr a factor. ½ **21a**
3289 **STRIKE LUCKY 98** [8]4-9-5 (49) J Quinn 5/1: 400-1000: 12th: In tch 3f, sn hmpd/wknd: btr 313 (a/w). 1½ **17a**
2928 **SOUNDS LUCKY 112** [1]8-9-6 bl (50) G Gibbons 20/1: 6040000: 13th: Al adrift: long abs. dist **0a**
13 Ran Time 1m 18.23 () Owned: Mr J Brierley Trained: Malton

5212 **1.45 Ringside Banded Stakes 4yo+ 0-45 (H5)**
£1481 £423 £212 **1m141y aw rnd** **Inapplicable** Inside

4862 **ADOBE 24** [2] W M Brisbourne 9-9-5 (50) M Savage(5) 13/2: 0500001: Handy, led bef 1f out, rdn out: best around 1m on any trk, likes Bath: acts on firm, gd/soft & both AW's, handles soft: enjoyed return to AW. **57a**
4488 **EXTEMPORISE 44** [13] T T Clement 4-9-5 (50) G Baker 25/1: 3511602: Bhd, prog 3f out, styg on when short of room dist, not pace wnr: 6 wk abs: acts on gd/soft, soft & both AW's: not get the best of runs. 1¾ **53a**
5056 **CROSS ASH 11** [3] R Hollinshead 4-9-5 (50) P Makin(5) 28/1: 0000063: Bhd, prog bef 1f out, nrst fin: eff at 7f/8.5f on firm, fast grnd & polytrack: see 2920. 1¼ **51a**
5054 **KINDNESS 12** [10] A D W Pinder 4-9-4 (49) J Quinn 25/1: 0200064: Led 6f out, hung left & hdd 1f out. ½ **49a**
5119 **LUCEFER 7** [11]6-9-3 (48) O Urbina 10/1: 3105005: Nvr nrr than mid div: qck reapp. nk **47a**
5111+**TIME TO REGRET 8** [8]4-9-6 (51) T Hamilton(3) 100/30 FAV: 0002516: Led, hdd 6f out, no extra dist. 1 **48a**
5119* **CAERPHILLY GAL 7** [4]4-9-3 e (48) D Fox(5) 9/2: 0012317: Rear, mod late gains: op 7/2: btr 5119. 1½ **42a**
4990 **DISABUSE 15** [12]4-9-3 VIS (48) Darren Williams 20/1: 5450008: Nvr nrr than mid div: 1st time visor. shd **41a**
4616 **SCARROTTOO 38** [6]6-9-3 bl e (48) Esther Remmerswaal 11/1: 3150309: Al in rear: btr 4475. ¾ **39a**
4993* **BALLARE 14** [5]5-9-5 vis (50) T Williams 13/2: 4000210: 10th: Keen cl up up 6f, wknd: btr 4993 (gd/soft). 1¼ **39a**
4132 **SORBIESHARRY 61** [1]5-9-3 p (48) P McCabe 12/1: 0140500: 11th: Keen cl up 6f, fdd. 2 **33a**
4764 **LASSER LIGHT 30** [7]4-9-5 (50) D Nolan(3) 50/1: 0-00500: 12th: Rear, nvr a factor. 1¼ **33a**
5063* **WIZARD OF US 11** [9]4-9-13 (58) S Righton 12/1: 5005/0-10: 13th: Keen cl up, fdd 2f out: btr 5063. nk **40a**
13 Ran Time 1m 53.66() Owned: Mr P R Kirk Trained: Nesscliffe

DONCASTER SATURDAY 23.10.04 Lefthand, Flat, Galloping Track

Official Going Soft (Heavy places on Rnd Crse)

5213 **1.50 'jock Murray Memorial' Nursery Handicap Stakes 2yo 0-95 (C1)** **[96]**
£14443 £4444 £2222 **7f str** **Soft** **Slow** Stands Side

4865* **CROSSPEACE 24** [1] M Johnston 2-9-2 (84) R Ffrench 5/1: 211: Made most, styd on well fnl 1f, rdn out: eff at 6f, enjoyed this step up to 7f & 1m will suit next term: winning form on firm & soft grnd, gall trks: useful & progressive, just the type to win more races next term: see 4865, 4403. **95**
4852 **TOP THE CHARTS 24** [3] R Hannon 2-9-1 (83) R L Moore 11/1: 4432: Dwelt, sn handy, hdwy to chall dist, kept on ins last, not pace of wnr: acts on gd & fast, imprvd here on soft: useful, can win a race. ¾ **92**
4963* **HANSOMELLE 18** [12] B Mactaggart 2-8-9 (77) Dale Gibson 14/1: 412413: Handy, hdwy 2f out, onepcd fnl 1f: another fine run: see 4963. 2 **83**
5089 **RED AFFLECK 9** [11] P W Chapple Hyam 2-9-1 (83) A McCarthy 14/1: 32104: In tch, eff over 1f out, no extra ins last: well clr of rem & back to form at 7f on soft grnd, acts on fast: see 4664 (mdn). 1 **87**
4590* **TARAS TREASURE 39** [9]2-8-4 (72) P Hanagan 25/1: 2643515: Went right start, held up, eff over 1f out, no impress: not enjoy soft?: btr 4590 (6f, fast grnd). 5 **68**
4247* **COOL PANIC 56** [14]2-9-1 (83) K Fallon 15/2: 02516: Handy, wknd dist: abs: not handle soft? 1¾ **76**
5098 **PRESS EXPRESS 8** [6]2-8-7 (75) A Culhane 40/1: 061007: Sn bhd, some late gains, nvr dngrs. nk **67**
4205* **ENTAILMENT 57** [13]2-8-8 (76) P Robinson 16/1: 018: Nvr a factor: 8 wk abs: btr 4205 (6f, mdn). 1½ **66**
4985 **DALDINI 15** [5]2-9-0 (82) S Sanders 4/1 FAV: 4129: Nvr a factor: well bckd: btr 4985, 4705 (6f). 1½ **70**
5105* **EXIT SMILING 8** [2]2-8-4 (72) A Nicholls 33/1: 2305010: 10th: Cl-up, wknd 2f out: new yard. shd **59**
5147* **TOLDO 5** [4]2-8-5 (6ex) (73) J Mackay 9/1: 4021110: 11th: Handy, wknd well over 1f out: too sn? 2½ **56**
4858 **SAMS SECRET 24** [10]2-8-4 (72) F Norton 9/1: 2320: 12th: In tch, wknd 2f out: see 4858 (gd). 1¼ **53**
4998 **SENTIERO ROSSO 14** [7]2-9-4 (86) T Eaves(3) 25/1: 2130000: 13th: In tch, wknd 2f out: see 4280. ½ **66**
4480 **BUDDY BROWN 44** [8]2-9-7 (89) R Winston 12/1: 1200: 14th: Al bhd: abs, btr 3877, see 2570. 1½ **67**
14 Ran Time 1m 30.89 (7.69) Owned: Favourites Racing Trained: Middleham

---

5214   2.25 Racing Post Weekender Conditions Stakes 3yo+   (B2)
£7524 £2854 £1427   **7f str**   **Soft**   **Fair**   Stands Side

4638 **MESHAHEER 36** [2] Saeed bin Suroor 5-8-9 t (105) W Supple 100/30: 0241-021: Keen in tch, gd hdwy   **108**
2f out, qcknd to lead ins last, cmftbly: suited by 7f on firm or soft, loves gall trks, esp Newbury & Doncaster:
lightly rcd this term, v useful: see 1486.
4961 **MILLENNIUM FORCE 20** [7] M R Channon 6-8-9 (104) K Fallon 3/1 FAV: 3004052: Cl-up, led over 1f   2   **104**
out, hdd & not pace of wnr ins last: ran close to useful best on fav'd soft grnd: see 2826, 2184.
5100 **QUITO 8** [1] D W Chapman 7-9-2 bl (105) A Culhane 100/30: 6516533: Sltly hmpd start, held up, hdwy   nk   **110**
2f out, kept on ins last, nrst fin: nicely bckd: v tough & smart, loves to come late off a fast pace: see 5100.
1685 **MUTAWAFFER 164** [9] B W Hills 3-8-7 (99) K Darley 14/1: 1510-04: Set pace till over 1f out,   nk   **102**
onepace: long abs & a useful rtn: poss handles firm, acts on soft grnd: lightly rcd: see 1685.
2555 **CAIRNS 127** [5]3-8-8 (107) T E Durcan 9/1: 11-0605: In tch, onepace over 1f out: 4 month abs.   hd   **102**
4800 **TRAYTONIC 28** [4]3-9-0 (101) R Winston 8/1: 0130046: Held up, hdwy dist, no extra: btr 4800.   5   **101**
5038 **DIVINE GIFT 12** [6]3-9-0 (102) P Robinson 33/1: 021-1447: Handy, wknd 2f out: see 5038, 949 (gd).   5   **93**
4795} **MEMBERSHIP 226** [8]4-8-9 R L Moore 12/1: 14-05528: ch c Belong To Me - Shamisen (Diesis) 12/1:   5   **79**
tch, wknd over 2f out: rnr-up in Dubai last spring: '03 stks, List & Gr 3 wnr: stays 1m, 7f specialist on firm,
gd/soft & fibresand: best without blnks: has run well bhks: has run well before: smart at best.
1 Oct'03 Redc 7 g/f 112-(110) A: 1 Jun'03 Asco 7 g/f 112-(109) A: 2 May'03 Newm 7 g/f 110-(108) A:
2 Apr'03 Ling 8 ap 108a- A: 1 Mar'03 Ling 7 ap 110a-(106) B: 2 Sep'02 Ayr 5 g/s 101- A:
2 Jul'02 Yarm 5.1 fm 99- C: 1 May'02 Yarm 6 g/f 103- D:
4395} **TYPHOON GINGER 1106** [10]9-8-4 (60) P Hanagan 200/1: 311502//-9: Lost iron start, keen in tch,   18   **46**
wknd over 2f out.
9 Ran Time 1m 29.53 (6.33)   Owned: Godolphin   Trained: Newmarket

---

5215   2.55 Racing Post #1 Million Totetentofollow Handicap Stakes 3yo+ 86-100 (C1)   **[97]**
£14100 £4338 £2169   **1m4f**   **Soft**   **Inapp**   Inside

5135 **TEMPSFORD 7** [3] Sir Mark Prescott 4-9-3 (86) S Sanders 10/1: 11-50501: Made all, styd on well   **96**
over 1f out, rdn out: back to best with a rtn to 12f, prob stays 2m: acts on fast & soft, both AWs: see 856.
4889 **MILLVILLE 22** [12] M A Jarvis 4-9-2 (85) P Robinson 9/1: 1054502: In tch, hdwy over 2f out, chsd   1¼   **92**
wnr over 1f out, onepcd ins last: gd run: eff over 12/14f on firm, soft & polytrack: see 4383, 3999.
5085 **BENDARSHAAN 9** [2] M Johnston 4-9-0 (83) K Darley 20/1: 2050503: Trkd wnr, eff over 1f out, kept   ½   **89**
on same pace: on a fair mark: acts on fast & soft grnd: see 3281 (14.7f).
5043 **ODIHAM 12** [8] H Morrison 3-8-11 (87) R L Moore 11/2: 2-104054: Held up, hdwy over 2f out, onepcd   2½   **90**
fnl 1f, no threat: nicely bckd: clr of rem & acts on firm, soft & polytrack: see 3534, 2127.
4766 **CRUISE DIRECTOR 29** [7]4-9-2 (85) K Fallon 5/1: 0100245: Held up, eff over 2f out, sn no extra.   5   **83**
5085 **FLOTTA 9** [6]5-8-12 (81) T E Durcan 40/1: 0165006: Held up, btn 2f out: see 3681 (gd grnd).   ¾   **78**
4917 **COUNTRYWIDE LUCK 21** [11]3-8-10 (86) J P Guillambert(3) 10/1: 62167: Held up, eff & hung left 2f   1½   **81**
out, no extra: btr 4347 (9f, fast grnd).
4491 **SANTANDO 43** [9]4-9-5 (88) S Carson 40/1: 0040008: In tch, eff over 2f out, no extra: 6 wk abs.   1½   **81**
4819 **PROTECTIVE 26** [1]3-8-11 (86) D Allen 14/1: 0140039: In tch, wknd over 2f out: btr 4819.   2½   **76**
5085 **SOULACROIX 9** [10]3-9-0 (90) A Culhane 9/2 FAV: 21-21030: 10th: Rcd wide, cl-up, wknd 2f out.   2½   **77**
4986 **JABAAR 15** [4]6-9-1 (84) R Winston 20/1: 2500200: 11th: In tch, wknd over 2f out: see 4681.   1½   **69**
5043 **QUDRAAT 12** [13]3-8-11 (87) W Supple 9/1: 501200: 12th: In tch, wknd 2f out: see 4749, 4281 (gd).   14   **58**
4467 **COLD TURKEY 45** [5]4-9-7 (90) S Whitworth 9/1: 2412400: 13th: In tch, wknd 2f out: 6 wk abs.   1½   **59**
13 Ran Time 2m 40.89 (11.09)   Owned: Syndicate 2001   Trained: Newmarket

---

5216   3.30 Gr1 Racing Post Trophy Colts 2yo (A1)
£120000 £46000 £23000   **1m str**   **Soft**   **Fast**   Far Side

3925* **MOTIVATOR 71** [5] M L W Bell 2-9-0   K Fallon 6/4 FAV: 11: Handy, hdwy to lead over 2f out, styd   **121+**
on strongly fnl 1f, cmfbly: hvly bckd, abs: stays 1m well, sure to relish mid-dists next term: acts on gd & soft,
gall trks: only twice rcd, already top-class & open to plenty of further improvement: just the type to win Gr 1
mid-dist events next term, esp on easy grnd: see 3925.
5071* **ALBERT HALL 13** [7] A P O'Brien 2-9-0 J P Spencer 5/2: 212: Held up, gd hdwy over 2f out,   2½   **117**
wandered over 1f out, kept on but not pace of wnr: nicely bckd: acts on soft grnd: v smart colt, looks sure to win
more Group races: see 5071.
3060 **HENRIK 107** [2] M R Channon 2-9-0   T E Durcan 12/1: 123: In tch, eff to chase wnr 2f out, onepcd   1   **115**
abs, clr rem: imprvd/smart eff stepped up in class: stays 1m on soft, acts on fast: win a Gr 3.
      HILLS OF ARAN 46 [1] A P O'Brien 2-9-0   C O'Donoghue 11/1: 314: b c Sadler's Wells - Danefair   8   **103**
(Danehill) Led till over 4f out, no extra over 2f out: 6 wk abs: stablemate of rnr-up: Apr foal: half-brother to
a high-class 7f wnr: dam 10/12f scorer: earlier won a Galway mdn: eff at 8.5f on gd, bred to relish mid-dists.
4928 **BEAVER PATROL 21** [6]2-9-0 (100) S Carson 25/1: 1062155: In tch, eff 2f out, sn wknd: btr 4153.   6   **94**
5167 **BERKHAMSTED 6** [4]2-9-0 (100) R L Moore 20/1: 6251056: Int ch, wknd over 2f out: see 5167.   6   **85**
4797 **ELLIOTS WORLD 28** [3]2-9-0 (100) K Darley 13/2: 11647: Led over 4f out till over 2f out, wknd: 17   **61**
needs an ease in grade: see 4003 (List, gd).
4797 **FRITH 28** [8]2-9-0 (100) S Sanders 18/1: 2358: Handy, wknd 2f out: see 4797, 3582 (g/f, mdn).   shd **61**
8 Ran Time 1m 41.62 (5.12)   Owned: The Royal Ascot Racing Club   Trained: Newmarket

---

5217   4.05 Listed At The Races Red Button Betting Doncaster Stakes 2yo (A1)
£16250 £5000 £2500   **6f str**   **Soft**   **Fair**   Stands Side

4680 **ANDRONIKOS 35** [2] P F I Cole 2-8-9 T (100) K Fallon 100/30 CO FA: 1201: In tch, hdwy to lead   **108**
dist, styd on, rdn out: nicely bckd: back to best in first time t-strap & v eff at 6f, shld stay further: acts on
firm, clrly enjoys soft grnd & gall trks: useful up: see 3247.
4928 **HARVEST WARRIOR 21** [7] T D Easterby 2-8-9 (97) D Allan 10/1: 2215202: Sltly hmpd & sn bhd, hdwy   2   **103**
over 1f out, switched & styd on well ins last, no threat to wnr: ran to useful best: see 4765, 2906.

DONCASTER SATURDAY 23.10.04 Lefthand, Flat, Galloping Track

5132 **JOSEPH HENRY 7** [4] M Johnston 2-8-9 (100) K Darley 4/1: 11443: Led till dist, no extra: fine run. 1¼ 101
5087 **GIFTED GAMBLE 9** [1] K A Ryan 2-8-9 (84) R Winston 16/1: 1502034: In tch, eff to chall over 1f out, no extra ins last: clr of rem: see 4692. ¾ 99
2895 **LADY FILLY 113** [5]2-8-4 (94) A Daly 25/1: 111055: Chsd ldr, wknd well over 1f out: 4 month abs. 9 76
4843* **ECOLOGICALLY RIGHT 25** [6]2-8-4 (75) P Hanagan 25/1: 0616: Al bhd: btr 4843 (fast grnd, mdn). nk 75
5132 **CORNUS 7** [8]2-8-9 (95) R L Moore 100/30 CO FA: 11227: In tch, wknd 2f out: btr 5132, 1422. 9 62
4888 **DRAMATICUS 22** [9]2-8-9 (100) S Sanders 100/30 CO FA: 3108: In tch, wknd over 2f out: well bckd. 15 32
8 Ran Time 1m 15.82 (5.02) Owned: Mr C Shiacolas Trained: Whatcombe

5218 4.40 Rectangle Group Handicap Stakes 3yo+ 86-100 (C1) [102]
£12101 £4590 £2295 **5f str** **Soft** **Fair** Stands Side

5149 **MATTY TUN 5** [13] J Balding 5-8-7 (4oh) (81) W Supple 16/1: 0050001: Keen held up, hdwy 2f out, styd on well to lead ins last, rdn out: qck reapp: eff at 5f on firm, soft & fibresand: see 1479. 92
5143 **WHITBARROW 6** [6] J M Bradley 5-8-9 (87) F Norton 12/1: 0540032: Cl-up, led over 1f out, rdn & hdd ins last, kept on: running well: see 4459, 1845. ¾ 92
5001 **TOM TUN 14** [4] J Balding 9-9-2 bl (94) T Lucas 11/1: 2035003: Chsd ldrs, eff over 1f out, onepcd ins last: loves easy grnd: v tough: see 4005 (6f), see 248. 1¼ 96
5125 **BOND BOY 7** [11] B Smart 7-8-7 (1oh) (84) K Darley 12/1: 0004004: Held up, hdwy dist, kept on. ½ 86
5143 **CORRIDOR CREEPER 6** [9]7-9-7 p (99) R L Moore 5/1: 5032125: Handy, eff to chall dist, onepace. ½ 98
5090 **BISHOPS COURT 9** [5]10-9-3 (95) S Sanders 20/1: 2565006: In tch, eff dist, no extra: see 5090. 1¼ 92
5143 **FURTHER OUTLOOK 6** [3]10-8-7 p (85) N Callan 12/1: 5035247: Led till dist, no extra: see 5143. 1¼ 79
4652 **NATIVE TITLE 36** [2]6-8-8 (86) A Nicholls 14/1: 1003008: Nvr a factor. nk 79
5090 **CARIBBEAN CORAL 9** [12]5-9-5 (97) R Winston 9/2 FAV: 0030449: Held up, btn dist: nicely bckd. ¾ 88
5143+**MALAPROPISM 6** [1]4-9-3 (6ex) (95) A Culhane 11/2: 6106110: 10th: In tch, wknd dist: btr 5143. ¾ 84
5100 **PETARDIAS MAGIC 8** [8]3-8-7 (85) K Fallon 8/1: 1302400: 11th: In tch, wknd dist: see 1621. nk 73
4786 **DAZZLING BAY 28** [7]4-9-6 e (98) D Allan 50/1: 5200300: 12th: Al bhd: see 4718, 2949. ½ 84
5001 **SMART HOSTESS 14** [10]5-9-0 (92) T Eaves(3) 16/1: 1-000300: 13th: In tch, wknd 2f out: see 4786. hd 77
13 Ran Time 1m 01.51 (3.31) Owned: Mrs O Tunstall Trained: Doncaster

5219 5.15 Teletext Racing 'hands And Heels' Apprentice Series Final Handicap Stakes 3yo 71-85 (E2) [95]
£6839 £2104 £1052 **7f str** **Soft** **Slow** Stands Side

5130 **SENESCHAL 7** [9] M R Channon 3-8-5 (72) T O'Brien(3) 9/2 FAV: 0516261: Dwelt, in tch, gd hdwy to lead 2f out, sn rdn clr, v easily: well bckd: suited by around 7f & acts on fast grnd, much imprvd here on soft. 87
5066 **ARRAN SCOUT 11** [2] K A Ryan 3-8-5 (72) Donna Caldwell(3) 50/1: 04-3002: In tch, eff over 1f out, not pace of wnr: blnks discarded & a btr run: acts on gd & soft grnd: eff over 7f/1m: see 5066, 1636. 11 75
5046 **ASK THE CLERK 12** [6] V Smith 3-8-4 (1oh) (70) M Stainton(3) 11/2: 5420033: Sltly hmpd start, held up, eff over 1f out, nvr dngrs: see 5046, 3543. 1¼ 72
4987 **MRS MOH 15** [5] T D Easterby 3-9-5 (86) J D O'Reilly 8/1: 13122U4: Slow away, sn handy, wknd 2f out. ¾ 85
4920 **MORSE 21** [3]3-9-0 (81) R Keogh(3) 13/2: 0001025: Cl-up, led 3f out till 2f out, wknd: see 4920. ¾ 79
4897 **KALI 22** [11]3-8-8 (75) R Kingscote(5) 6/1: 3321646: Led till 3f out, wknd: see 4683, 2575 (mdn, fm). ½ 72
4607 **CITRINE SPIRIT 38** [10]3-8-4 (71) R J Killoran(3) 8/1: 0-613007: Cl-up 5f: best 1610 (mdn). 1 66
4683 **KEYAKI 35** [1]3-8-11 (78) Natalie Jankiewicz(5) 20/1: 6114408: Slow away & al bhd: see 4148. 1 71
1417 **MUY BIEN 178** [7]3-8-11 (78) T Block(3) 12/1: 2031239: Al bhd: long abs: see 1417 (6f), 1088. 8 59
4714 **MOLCON 33** [8]3-9-1 (82) W Hogg 11/1: 4010000: 10th: In tch, wknd over 2f out. 2 60
4917 **PARKVIEW LOVE 21** [4]3-9-4 BL (85) A Elliott(5) 9/1: 0045300: 11th: Slow away & al bhd: blnks. shd 62
11 Ran Time 1m 30.17(6.97) Owned: Mr Peter Taplin Trained: West Ilsley

NEWBURY SATURDAY 23.10.04 Lefthand, Flat, Galloping Track

Official Going Soft (Heavy Places) HEAVY RAIN THROUGH AFTERNOON

5220 1.00 Cantorodds Com E B F Maiden Stakes Div 1 2yo (D2)
£6734 £2072 £1036 **1m str** **Heavy** **Inapplicable** Centre

4746 **SPEAR THISTLE 31** [2] J H M Gosden 2-9-0 J Fortune 11/4 FAV: 441: Made all, strongly pressed fnl 2f, drvn & held on all out: eff at 1m on firm & hvy grnd, gall trks: lightly rcd colt, can progress again. 87
GENERAL JUMBO 0 [6] B J Meehan 2-9-0 D Holland 16/1: 2: b c Dansili - Aunt Jemima (Busted) Chsd ldrs, rdn to chall ins last, just held nr line: 17,000gns Apr foal, half-brother to a 6f juv wnr & subs multiple 12f scorer: eff at 1m, stay further: acts on hvy & a gall trk: v pleasing start, clr rem, win races. nk 86
4858 **TANZANITE 24** [11] D W P Arbuthnot 2-8-9 D Sweeney 66/1: 063: Keen tracking ldrs, eff to chase wnr 2f out, no impress ins last: styd longer 1m trip well & imprvd on this hvy grnd: see 4858. 3½ 76
BAYARD 0 [8] D R C Elsworth 2-9-0 T Quinn 8/1: 4: gr c Lord Avie - Mersey (Crystal Palace) Rear, late gains for press, nvr threatened front trio: Apr foal, half-brother to a 12f 3yo scorer abroad, also a 10f 3yo wnr: dam high-class French performer: sure to apprec mid-dists & will improve. 4 75
5059 **BULWARK 11** [14]2-9-0 S W Kelly 7/1: 045: Prom in smaller group stands side, no impress on ldrs towards centre fnl 2f: first home from unfav'd stands side group, fair eff in circumstances: prob handles gd & hvy. 2 72
CROSS TIME 0 [12]2-9-0 C Catlin 16/1: 6: b c Cape Cross - Reine Maid (Mr Prospector) Rdn & bhd early, late gains, nvr factor: E7,000 Mar foal, half-brother to wnrs at 6f/1m & a wnr over hdles. 5 65
TRITONVILLE LODGE 0 [10]2-9-0 L Keniry(3) 50/1: 7: Slow away & bhd, chsd ldrs halfway till 2f out. ½ 64
505 **SHORTBREAD 11** [5]2-9-0 I Mongan 16/1: 08: Sn pushed along in rear, mod late gains. 2 61
5058 **KABIS AMIGOS 11** [16]2-9-0 t W Ryan 16/1: 09: Stands side group & struggling from halfway. 3 57
4851 **OAKLEY ABSOLUTE 24** [13]2-9-0 P Dobbs 40/1: 000: 10th: Led stands side group & cl-up 5f, sn fdd. shd 57
5058 **GROOMSMAN 11** [1]2-9-0 L Fletcher(3) 8/1: 40: 11th: Cl-up, wknd qckly fnl 2f, op 13/2: btr 5058 (gd). 1 56
5040 **HOH HEDSOR 12** [7]2-8-9 J F Egan 33/1: 00: 12th: Chsd ldrs, struggling from halfway. 1 50
INTREPID JACK 0 [9]2-9-0 S Drowne 25/1: 0: 13th: Al towards rear. 2½ 51
4885 **MPENZI 22** [4]2-8-9 Dane O'Neill 7/2: 00: 14th: Slow away & bhd halfway. shd 46
5003 **Palace Walk 14** [3]2-9-0 Martin Dwyer 33/1:0

NEWBURY SATURDAY 23.10.04 Lefthand, Flat, Galloping Track

~~4455 City Trader 46 [15]2-9-0 M Hills 50/1.0~~

16 Ran Time 1m 49.58 (12.78) Owned: Duke of Devonshire Trained: Manton

5221

1.35 Cantorodds Com E B F Maiden Stakes Div 2 2yo (D2)
£6734 £2072 £1036 **1m str** **Heavy** **Inapplicable** Centre

DESCARTES 0 [14] Saeed bin Suroor 2-9-0 L Dettori 1/1 FAV: 1: b c Dubai Millennium - Gold's Dance (Goldneyev) Dwelt, rear, smooth hdwy stands side halfway & led over 2f out, hands & heels, cmftbly: hvly bckd: Feb foal, half-brother to a top-class 10f Italian juv wnr, dam a mid-dist French scorer: eff at 1m, sure to apprec 10f+: acts on hvy grnd & a gall trk: goes well fresh: impressive, one to follow. **90+**

5115 **HIGH CARD 7** [4] J M P Eustace 2-9-0 S W Kelly 33/1: 062: b g So Factual - High Cut (Dashing Blade) Chsd ldrs, rdn to chase wnr dist, al held: rest well covered: half-brother to a plcd 6f/1m 3yo, dam plcd at 5/7f: stays a gall 1m & imprvd on this hvy grnd: win similar. *1¼* **83**

LOS ORGANOS 0 [9] P W Chapple Hyam 2-8-9 R Havlin 9/1: 3: br f Turtle Island - Spicebird (Ela Mana Mou) Chsd ldrs, hdd over 2f out & no extra dist: mkt support, op 16/1: Mar first foal, dam a 12f 3yo scorer: eff at 1m, will apprec further: handles hvy grnd & a gall trk: improve for this. *4* **72**

GIFTED MUSICIAN 0 [7] J L Dunlop 2-9-0 Dane O'Neill 10/1: 4: b c Sadler's Wells - Photogenic (Midyan) Bhd, hdwy over 2f out, kept on well ins last, no threat: 190,000gns Mar foal, half-brother to a 2 1m plcd 3yos: dam at 6/7f as a 2yo: encouraging late hdwy, handles hvy grnd & shld progress from this. *3* **73**

4723 **QUEENS DANCER 32** [2]2-8-9 C Catlin 100/1: 05: Rear, late gains for press, nvr a threat. *nk* **67**
4842 **KIAMA 25** [6]2-8-9 Martin Dwyer 14/1: 06: Led till over 2f out, fdd. *hd* **66**
4722 **ELOQUENT KNIGHT 32** [1]2-9-0 S Drowne 16/1: 07: Prom, rdn halfway, sn no impression. *9* **58**
5012 **VICTOR BUCKWELL 13** [3]2-9-0 J Fanning 33/1: 008: Mid-div, eff to chase ldrs 3f out, sn btn. *2½* **54**
2348 **DREAM TONIC 135** [12]2-9-0 S Hitchcott 12/1: 69: Rear, eff 3f out, no impression. *9* **43**
OPHISTROLIE 0 [10]2-9-0 J F Egan 33/1: 0: 10th: Chsd ldrs 4f, sn bhd. *14* **24**
TOP MARK 0 [13]2-9-0 L Fletcher(3) 50/1: 0: 11th: Cl-up, wknd over 2f out. *1¼* **22**
CLIMATE CHANGE 0 [8]2-9-0 R Hughes 10/1: 0: 12th: Slow away, sn mid-div, btn 3f out. *1¾* **20**
CHRISTOM 0 [11]2-9-0 D Holland 16/1: 0: 13th: Chsd ldrs 5f. *10* **8**
ALONG CAME MOLLY 0 [5]2-8-9 J Fortune 20/1: 0: 14th: Slow away & al bhd. *1½* **1**
PRINCESS LINKS 0 [15]2-8-9 P Dobbs 25/1: 0: 15th: Chsd ldrs, struggling from halfway. *3* **0**

15 Ran Time 1m 50.11 (13.31) Owned: Godolphin Trained: Newmarket

5222

2.10 Listed Stanjamesuk Com Radley Stakes Fillies 2yo (A1)
£14500 £5500 £2750 **7f str** **Heavy** **Inapplicable** Centre

5133 **BIBURY FLYER 7** [6] M R Channon 2-8-11 (89) S Hitchcott 3/1 JT FAV: 3245141: Rear, rdn & hdwy to lead over 1f out, drvn out: op 7/2: eff at 5f, suited by 6/7f on firm, likes soft & hvy: v tough, useful & progressive. **103**

4913* **WEDDING PARTY 21** [4] Mrs A J Perrett 2-8-8 (83) S Drowne 3/1 JT FAV: 31412: Chsd ldrs, rdn & chall over 1f out, not pace of wnr: confirmed rtn to form of latest: acts on fast, hvy & polytrack: see 4913. *2* **95**

4927* **SHEBOYGAN 21** [7] J G Given 2-8-8 (84) L Dettori 7/2: 313: Al prom, led over 1f out, sn hdd & no extra ins last: up in grade, gd run: acts on firm & hvy grnd: see 4927 (mdn). *2* **92**

4575* **BRECON 39** [2] D R C Elsworth 2-8-8 T Quinn 6/1: 14: Keen in rear, outpcd 2f out, kept on for press ins last, nrst fin: op 3/1: acts on soft & hvy grnd, crying out for 1m: see 4575 (1m). *¾* **91**

5045 **NICE TUNE 12** [3]2-8-8 D Holland 16/1: 3405: Chsd ldrs, btn 2f out: see 4329. *3* **87**
4641 **SHARP AS A TACK 36** [5]2-8-8 bl (88) J Fortune 16/1: 021026: Led till over 1f out, sn btn: btr 4641 (fast). *7* **78**
4711 **CLARA BOW 33** [1]2-8-8 M Hills 8/1: 67: Bhd & no ch over 2f out: highly tried after 4711. *8* **67**

7 Ran Time 1m 35.94 (11.64) Owned: Ridgeway Downs Racing Trained: West Ilsley

5223

2.40 Stan James 08000 383384 Handicap Stakes 3yo+ 86-100 (C1) **[112]**
£13305 £5047 £2523 **1m2f rnd** **Heavy** **Inapplicable** Centre

3661 **TIGER TIGER 83** [1] Jamie Poulton 3-7-13 (83) J F McDonald(3) 5/1 CO FAV: 1200421: Chsd ldrs, rdn to lead dist, drvn out: op 8/1, 12 wk abs: eff btwn 1m/12f: handles fast, acts on gd & polytrack, relishes hvy grnd, any trk: goes well fresh: progressive colt, see 3661, 2660 & 1298. **94**

4681 **TURBO 35** [2] G B Balding 5-8-7 p (89) R Thomas(3) 10/1: 0400002: Rear, hdwy to lead over 2f out, hdd dist, not pace of wnr: look to have to come to hand, landed the November h'cap in '03 off today's mark.. *2* **93**

4889 **PAGAN SKY 22** [14] J A R Toller 5-8-4 (3oh) (83) Lisa Jones 12/1: 1-006453: Chsd ldrs & ch 2f out, not pace of wnr: acts on fast & hvy grnd: see 4392. *1¼* **89**

4755 **TORCELLO 30** [3] G Wragg 6-8-6 (1ow) (87) S Drowne 16/1: 40030/-54: Mid-div, styd on onepace for press fnl 2f: clr rem: acts on firm & hvy grnd: see 4755. *2* **89**

4916 **BLYTHE KNIGHT 21** [8]4-9-7 p (103) L Dettori 11/2: 6300065: Keen in rear, hdwy over 3f out, btn dist. *7* **97**
4021 **SHAHZAN HOUSE 66** [12]5-9-1 p (97) D Holland 5/1 CO FAV: 3233336: Chsd ldrs, btn 2f out: 2 mth abs. *1¼* **90**
4917 **NAMROC 21** [11]3-8-0 (87) Martin Dwyer 5/1 CO FAV: 14247: Handy & ch over 2f out, sn wknd: btr 4629. *2½* **78**
3464 **BOURGAINVILLE 90** [6]6-8-8 (90) L Keniry(3) 25/1: 5500008: Rear, little hdwy for press, 3 month abs. *2½* **79**
4715 **TIZZY MAY 33** [13]4-8-8 (90) Dane O'Neill 25/1: 4005509: Led/dsptd lead till over 2f out, sn btn. *¾* **78**
5085 **PERFECT STORM 9** [9]5-8-8 (90) D Sweeney 10/1: 0054000: 10th: Chsd ldrs, btn 2f out: flattered 1746. *1¾* **76**
1398* **SOLOR 179** [10]3-8-2 (89) P Doe 20/1: 410: 11th: Sn bhd & no ch when hung right 4f out, fin lame. *dist* **0**
2896 **MILLAFONIC 113** [7]4-8-11 (93) N Mackay 16/1: 150-6000: 12th: Al rear & t.o. fnl 3f, 4 month abs. *3* **0**

598 **CARTE SAUVAGE 261** [5]3-9-0 (101) J Fanning 25/1: 41233-60: 13th: gr c Kris S - See You (Gulch) Led till over 3f out, sn t.o., abs: mdn scorer '03, subs dual List plcd (rtd 100): winning form at 7f, stays a stiff 10f well: acts on firm & gd grnd, stiff/undul or gall trks. *9* **0**
2 Sep'03 Ayr 8 fm 100- D: 1 Jul'03 Ayr 7.2 gd 97- D:

4749 **PRIME POWERED 31** [4]3-7-13 BL (85) C Catlin 16/1: 5502040: 14th: Sn bhd & t.o. fnl 3f: blnks. *11* **0**

14 Ran Time 2m 22.73 (19.93) Owned: Mr R W Huggins Trained: Lewes

5224

3.10 Gr3 Stan James St Simon Stakes 3yo+ (A1)
£29000 £11000 £5500   **1m4f rnd**   **Heavy**   **Inapplicable**   Centre

5139 **ORCADIAN 7** [8] J M P Eustace 3-8-7 (99) Martin Dwyer 33/1: 20-30651: Made all & pulled clr fnl   **114**
2f, unchall: prev eff at 1m, clrly relished longer 12f trip: acts on firm, gd & loved this hvy grnd today:
enjoyed forcing tactics: revelation in these testing conditions: see 2069.
5165 **FRANK SONATA 6** [4] M G Quinlan 3-8-7 (105) S Drowne 12/1: 1311002: Rear, hdwy for press fnl 3f,   *15*   **104**
nvr threatened wnr: qck reapp: not disgraced: see 3274 (soft).
4812 **SELF DEFENSE 27** [6] P R Chamings 7-9-0 (112) L Dettori 5/2 FAV: 0/-065523: Rear, hdwy to chase   *8*   **96**
wnr over 2f out, no impress fnl 1f: btr 4812 (fast).
2817 **THE WHISTLING TEAL 119** [5] G Wragg 8-9-0 (112) J F Egan 7/2: 52-02154: Led/dsptd lead, btn 2f   *2*   **94**
out: 4 month abs: see 1757.
4574* **COLLIER HILL 41** [7]6-9-3 (106) J Fortune 8/1: 0143015: Al rear & t.o. fnl 2f: abs: see 4574.   *dist*   **0**
5043+ **MASSIF CENTRALE 12** [2]3-8-7 (101) Dane O'Neill 7/1: 2010516: Chsd ldr, wknd qckly from 4f out.   *27*   **0**
1408* **ASIAN HEIGHTS 534** [1]6-9-0 D Holland 100/30: 1/110/21-7: b c Hernando - Miss Rinjani (Shirley   *dist*   **0**
Heights) Chsd wnr, btn 6f out, t.o.: mkt drifter on reapp/long abs, op 5/2: lightly rcd '03, Gr3 scorer: '02
List & Gr3 wnr: eff at 12/13f on firm or hvy grnd, any trk.
1 May'03 Ches 13.4 g/f 118-(114) A: 2 Apr'03 Newb 12.01 hvy 118-(109) A: 1 Sep'02 Kemp 12 fm 112- A:
1 May'02 Wind 11.6 sft 108- A: 1 May'01 Good 11 fm 117- A: 2 Apr'01 Sand 10 hvy 111- A:
4814 **TOP SEED 27** [3]3-8-7 (98) S Hitchcott 16/1: 403200P: Al rear & t.o./p.u .over 1f out, dismounted.   **0**
8 Ran   Time 2m 53.11 (23.81)   Owned: Mr J C Smith   Trained: Newmarket

5225

3.45 Sir Gerald Whent Memorial Nursery Handicap Stakes 2yo 0-85 (D2)   **[90]**
£7300 £2246 £1123   **6f str**   **Heavy**   **Inapplicable**   Centre

5035* **PARIS BELL 12** [8] T D Easterby 2-8-3 (65) P M Quinn 9/1: 5004011: Rear, hdwy from halfway & led   **78**
over 1f out, rdn clr, decisively: eff at 5/6f on soft & hvy grnd, loves a gall trk: progressive juv: see 5035.
4940 **GO MO 19** [14] S Kirk 2-8-6 (68) J F Egan 40/1: 066002: Al prom & led 3f out till over 1f out, sn   *3½*   **73**
no impress on wnr: dropped in trip & imprvd on this hvy grnd: see 3824.
5031 **ABERDEEN PARK 13** [10] Mrs H Sweeting 2-8-6 (68) P Doe 12/1: 0452203: Dwelt, sn chsd ldrs, no   *3½*   **66**
impress fnl 1f: handles fast & hvy grnd: well clr of rem: see 4894 (7f).
4100 **LITTLE DALHAM 63** [9] P W Chapple Hyam 2-9-6 (82) D Holland 15/2: 42164: Mid-div, rdn & mod prog,   *10*   **62**
no threat: 2 month abs: btr 3431 (fast).
4907 **CREE 21** [13]2-8-2 (64) Martin Dwyer 7/1: 2523145: Led/dsptd lead till over 2f out: see 4706 (5f).   *hd*   **43**
4108 **CROCODILE KISS 63** [4]2-8-8 (70) L Dettori 16/1: 5506: Mid-div, no impress fnl 2f: abs, h'cap bow.   *2½*   **44**
4602 **RED RUDY 38** [11]2-8-6 (68) T P Queally 14/1: 6307: Chsd ldrs 4f, sn btn, h'cap bow: btr 4204.   *¾*   **41**
5142 **CORNICHE DANCER 6** [12]2-8-6 (68) S Hitchcott 33/1: 2105208: Trkd ldrs & ch 2f out, wknd under press.   *1*   **39**
4765 **CELTIC SPA 29** [16]2-9-7 (83) R Havlin 20/1: 0530409: Chsd ldrs, no impress fnl 2f: flattered 4153.   *1½*   **51**
4387 **ADORATION 49** [15]2-8-11 (73) J Fanning 20/1: 325000: 10th: Nvr a factor, 7 wk abs.   *11*   **23**
4697 **ALEXANDER CAPETOWN 33** [20]2-8-6 (68) M Hills 12/1: 2564400: 11th: Bhd & no ch fnl 2f: btr 4224.   *2½*   **13**
4843 **MIDNIGHT LACE 25** [17]2-8-1 (63) D Kinsella 14/1: 0030: 12th: Sn rdn & struggling halfway, h'cap bow.   *¾*   **7**
4934 **AZUREE 19** [3]2-8-2 bl (64) J F McDonald(3) 25/1: 0430540: 13th: Chsd ldrs, btn over 2f out: btr 4934.   *2*   **4**
4928 **MONSIEUR MIRASOL 21** [7]2-8-11 (73) T Quinn 13/2 FAV: 0240500: 14th: Al bhd: btr 4727 (firm).   *2½*   **8**
5185* **ISLAND SWING 3** [5]2-9-9 (7ex) (85) S Drowne 7/1: 4003410: 15th: Mid-div, wknd qckly 2f out: qck reapp.   *5*   **12**
5126 **BROOKLIME 7** [6]2-9-2 (78) S W Kelly 8/1: 0526060: 16th: Mid-div, struggling fnl 2f.   *3*   **0**
4894 **GUYANA 22** [19]2-8-3 (65) C Catlin 33/1: 00300: 17th: Sn rdn & bhd.   *2½*   **0**
5021 **LITTLE WIZZY 13** [18]2-8-4 (66) F P Ferris(3) 50/1: 3013600: 18th: Dwelt & al bhd: btr 1646 (5f).   *nk*   **0**
4637 **METHODICAL 36** [1]2-8-5 (67) L Keniry(1) 33/1: 4050: 19th: Chsd ldrs 4f, sn struggling, h'cap bow.   *5*   **0**
4765 **MISSED A BEAT 29** [2]2-8-13 (75) D Sweeney 25/1: 040150: 20th: In tch till halfway, btr 4443 (gd).   *12*   **0**
20 Ran   Time 1m 20.88 (9.28)   Owned: Ryedale Partners No 8   Trained: Malton

5226

4.20 Mike Lester & Friends - Bulldog Takes The Biscuit Maiden Stakes 3yo (D3)
£5688 £1750 £875   **1m2f rnd**   **Heavy**   **Inapplicable**   Centre

4899 **JOLIZERO 22** [9] P W Chapple Hyam 3-9-0 (58) R Havlin 6/1: 0325061: Made all & rdn clr fnl 2f,   **85**
drvn out: op 8/1: eff at 10/12f, tried 14f: acts on fast & gd/soft, relished hvy today with forcing tactics applied.
1959 **NIETZSCHE 152** [3] J Noseda 3-9-0 (85) S W Kelly 9/1: 0252: Chsd wnr, rdn & chall over 3f out, sn   *17*   **70**
no impress on wnr: 5 month abs: btr 1384 (10f, gd).
2678 **MAID TO TREASURE 122** [8] J L Dunlop 3-8-9 (76) L Dettori 2/1 FAV: 2-463: Chsd ldr 6f out, rdn &   *3*   **62**
no impress over 2f out: 4 month abs: not handle hvy? btr 2678 & 2131 (10f).
     SHESHALAN 0 [4] Sir Michael Stoute 3-9-0   J Fortune   9/2: 4: ch c Indian Ridge - Sheshara   *2*   **65**
(Kahyasi) Chsd ldrs, rdn & no impress fnl 2f: dam a 12/15f French wnr.
5023 **TYUP POPPY 13** [5]3-9-0 (60) L Keniry(3) 25/1: 3-405: Bhd, little hdwy for press, longer trip.   *9*   **56**
     FUSS 0 [6]3-8-9   T Quinn 9/1: 6: b f Unfuwain - First Sapphire (Simply Great) Slow away & al   *2½*   **49**
bhd: mid-dist pedigree.
     MAJESTIC STAR 0 [2]3-8-9   R Price 20/1: 7: b f Fraam - Fun While It Lasts (Idiot's Delight)   *12*   **37**
Chsd ldrs, no ch fnl 4f: dam plcd over hdles.
4762 **POLISH ROSE 30** [1]3-8-9   Dane O'Neill 16/1: 058: Chsd ldrs, no ch 3f out, longer trip.   *3½*   **34**
8 Ran   Time 2m 27.40 (24.6)   Owned: Norcroft Park Stud   Trained: Newmarket

5227

4.55 Mentor Lady Jockeys' Championship Handicap Stakes 3yo+ 71-85 (D2)   **[71]**
£7233 £2226 £1113   **1m str**   **Heavy**   **Inapplicable**   Centre

5050 **SANGIOVESE 12** [6] H Morrison 5-10-3 (74) Mrs S Bosley 6/1 CO FAV: 1105051: Towards rear,   **85**
switched to far rail & hdwy to lead narrowly ins last, just prevailed, all out: eff btwn 1m/12f on fast, hvy & both AWs.
4809 **MR VELOCITY 27** [1] E F Vaughan 4-10-5 (76) Miss Joanna Rees(3) 8/1: 1063112: Led, hung left under   *shd*   **86**
press & hdd over 1f out, rallied gamely, just denied: clr of rem: acts on firm, hvy & polytrack: progressive.
4909 **DESERT REIGN 21** [10] A P Jarvis 3-9-12 (72) Miss Kelly Burke(5) 8/1: 00-51423: Chsd ldrs, styd on   *5*   **75**

for press, not pace of front pair: acts on gd & hvy grnd: see 3690 & 3219.

3428 **TIDY 91** [8] M D Hammond 4-10-7 (78) Miss E J Jones 6/1 CO FAV: U030044: Rear, hdwy halfway, drvn & no impress on front pair from dist: 3 month abs: stays 1m, 7f prob ideal: see 1035.		*shd*	**81**
4986 **DARGHAN 15** [3]4-10-7 t (78) Miss A Bevan(7) 33/1: 4666205: Chsd ldrs, no impress fnl 1f.		2½	77
5050 **PATTERDALE 12** [2]3-9-13 (73) Ms C Williams 12/1: 0-210266: Chsd ldrs till ov 2f out: btr 4937.		6	63
4987 **VICIOUS KNIGHT 15** [5]6-11-0 (85) Miss Kelly Harrison(3) 11/1: 0005307: Rear, hung right & btn 2f out.		2	72
5022* **PARNASSIAN 13** [9]4-10-3 (74) Miss J Hannaford(7) 6/1 CO FAV: 5430318: Mid-div, btn 2f out: btr 5022.		2	58
5063 **LOCOMBE HILL 11** [11]8-10-0 (1oh) (70) Mrs N Wilson(3) 7/1: 1531229: Chsd ldrs, no impress fnl 2f.		13	38
4909* **RIDGE BOY 21** [7]3-10-2 (76) Mrs S Moore(3) 10/1: 0103210: 10th: Mid-div, btn 3f out: btr 4909 (gd).		2½	39
4615 **JOHANNIAN 38** [13]6-10-0 (71) Miss Faye Bramley(5) 10/1: 4632120: 11th: Mid-div, struggling halfway.		8	23
4999 **BEST BEFORE 14** [4]4-10-5 (76) Miss E Folkes(3) 20/1: 3316000: 12th: Chsd ldrs till halfway, sn bhd.		6	20
4036 **NIMELLO 66** [12]8-10-7 (78) Miss C Hannaford 8/1: 0010100: 13th: Al well bhd, abs: see 3042.		8	11
5050 **CAMILLE PISSARRO 12** [14]4-10-9 (80) Miss H M Lewis(7) 66/1: 053-0000: 14th: Chsd ldrs till 3f out.		6	5

14 Ran   Time 1m 57.73(21.93)   Owned: Kentisbeare Quartet   Trained: East Ilsley

Official Going Standard

5228   2.20 Ringside Maiden Auction Stakes 2yo (H5)
£1477 £422 £211   7f32y aw rnd   Inapplicable   Outside

4658 **BIRD OVER 37** [6] R M Beckett 2-8-2 N Mackay 11/10 FAV: 41: Keen & trkd ldrs, qcknd to lead over 1f out, rdn clr: op 6/4 & confirmed debut promise: eff at 7f, shld get 1m: acts on polytrack & a sharp trk.			**71a**
FULLANDBY [2] T J Etherington 2-8-11 J Fanning 9/1: 2: b c Monashee Mountain - Ivory Turner (Efisio) Slow away, rdn & styd on to take 2nd cl-home, no threat to wnr: cheaply bght Mar foal, dam a mulitple Italian wnr: eff over a sharp 7f on polytrack.		2	75a
4864 **PAPARAAZI 26** [5] R A Fahey 2-8-9 P Hanagan 7/1: 503: Sn trkd ldrs trav well, rdn & onepace bef dist: op 7/2, AW bow: handles fast grnd & polytrack: type to improve in h'cap company: see 4864 & 4602.		*shd*	73a
4996 **JUST CLIFF 16** [12] W R Muir 2-8-11 F Norton 10/1: 044: In tch, rdn & no extra bef dist, clr rem: handles polytrack & gd/soft grnd: see 4996.		3	69a
4996 **SO ELEGANT 16** [11]2-8-4 D Fox(5) 16/1: 05: b f Bahhare - Soignee (Night Shift) Held up, edged left & only mod prog: AW bow: cheaply bght Apr foal, half-sister to a 1m juv wnr & 9f/hdles scorer.		5	52a
5113 **LOVE ATTACK 9** [8]2-8-5 D Allan 16/1: 66: Mid-div, outpcd fnl 2f.		¾	52a
HIGHEST REGARD [4]2-8-9 R Price 14/1: 7: Led/dsptd lead till over 1f out, fdd.		½	55a
5064 **SHOWTIME FAYE 13** [7]2-8-3 J Mackay 80/1: 008: Dwelt, al towards rear.		11	29a
5154 **IROQUOIS PRINCESS 7** [9]2-8-5 S Whitworth 100/1: 09: Al bhd.		4	23a
5106 **GIFTED LASS 10** [10]2-8-6 J Edmunds 100/1: 00: 10th: Keen & prom, btn 2f out, longer trip.		3½	17a
4744 **AUTUMN DAZE 33** [3]2-8-2 A Nicholls 80/1: 000: 11th: Led till halfway, sn bhd.		28	0a

11 Ran   Time 1m 32.37 (No Std Time)   Owned: Mrs Robert Langton   Trained: Lambourn

5229   2.50 Zongalero Banded Stakes Div 1 3yo+ 0-45 (H5)
£1474 £421 £211   7f32y aw rnd   Inapplicable   Outside

5109 **COMPTON MICKY 10** [8] J Balding 3-9-2 p (49) J Edmunds 50/1: 5605001: Keen & handy, led over 1f out, drvn out: first win, unplcd from 10 starts prev: eff around a sharp 7f, tried 10f: acts on polytrack, handles firm & gd/soft grnd: eff in cheek pieces.			**55a**
5146 **THE OLD SOLDIER 8** [9] A Dickman 6-9-5 (50) A Beech(3) 11/4 FAV: 0020252: Mid-div, rdn & chase wnr ins last, al just held: clr of rem: acts on firm, gd/soft & polytrack: see 4994 & 2516.		¾	54a
509 **NOW AND AGAIN 269** [2] I W McInnes 5-9-3 (48) Natalia Gemelova(5) 25/1: 3433: Dwelt, sn handy, rdn & outpcd 2f out, kept on ins last: new yard, abs: prob handles both AWs: see 509, 416 & 334 (1m).		5	43a
5069 **FLYING EDGE 13** [7] E J Alston 4-9-5 (50) D Allan 5/1: 0004404: Led/dsptd lead till dist, fdd.		*shd*	45a
5211 **BAYTOWN FLYER 2** [5]4-9-5 (50) Hayley Turner(3) 10/1: 1120005: Prom, no extra bef dist, qck reapp.		3	39a
5077 **ITS ECCO BOY 12** [6]6-9-4 (49) J Fanning 16/1: 0000606: Led/dsptd lead, wknd fnl 1f: prefer 6f.		*shd*	38a
4994 **CHANTELLE 16** [12]4-9-3 (48) A Culhane 8/1: 0500047: Held up, rdn & nvr pace to chall: btr 4994.		1¼	34a
5094 **MR LEWIN 10** [4]3-9-3 (50) P Hanagan 5/1: 05-00508: Mid-div, rdn over 3f out, btn bef dist.		½	35a
4994 **SAINTLY PLACE 1** [3]3-9-1 (48) R Fitzpatrick 10/1: 0005209: Slow away & al bhd: flattered 4587.		1½	30a
4708 **UNINTENTIONAL 35** [11]3-9-1 BL (48) D Nolan(3) 66/1: 6060P00: 10th: Dwelt, sn strug, tried blnks.		2½	25a
4090 **BULAWAYO 66** [10]7-9-5 bl (50) B Swarbrick(5) 5/1: 4210440: 11th: Al outpcd & & struggling, abs.		nk	26a
5005 **CEYLON ROUND 16** [1]3-9-3 (50) D Corby(3) 16/1: 00000: 12th: Chsd ldrs, btn 2f out.		14	1a

12 Ran   Time 1m 31.88 (No Std Time)   Owned: Mr J M Lacey   Trained: Doncaster

5230   3.20 Holiday Inn Garden Court Maiden Claiming Stakes 3yo+ (H5)
£1488 £425 £213   1m141y aw rnd   Inapplicable   Inside

3150} **TYNEHAM 353** [4] W G M Turner 4-9-2 P (59) C Haddon(7) 16/1: 002/000-1: b c Robellino - Diamond Wedding (Diamond Shoal) Handy & led halfway, duelled with rnr-up ins last, prevailed all out: reapp: unplcd sole '03 start (G C Bravery, 'cap): well btn mdn rnr-up '02: eff around 8.5f: acts on polytrack & prob handles soft grnd, likes a sharp trk & goes well fresh: suited by cheek pieces today. 2 Oct'02 Donc 7 sft 75- D:			**57a**
4977 **CHARLIE MASTERS 19** [10] P Howling 3-8-12 J Fanning 14/1: 0002: Handy & rdn to chall dist, ev ch ins last, just denied line: op 10/1: eff arnd 8.5f on polytrk in banded company: mod form prev.		*shd*	56a
5067 **ASH BOLD 13** [12] B Ellison 7-8-10 (45) T Eaves(3) 3/1: 000///-4203: Held up, drvn & styd on to take 3rd ins last, nvr threat to front pair: handles polytrack, gd/soft & soft grnd: see 4284 & 3850.		2	46a
4992 **LIVIA 16** [5] J G Portman 3-8-7 vis (52) A Culhane 11/8 FAV: 6000024: Prom, led over 5f out till over 3f out, no extra for press dist: bckd: see 4992, 815.		2½	42a
4857 **PRINCE RENESIS 26** [2]3-8-12 (45) P Mulrennan(3) 33/1: 000605: Mid-div, nvr pace to land blow.		3	41a
2260 **BOLD RIDGE 141** [8]4-8-10 bl (52) P Hanagan 9/1: 00-0006: Chsd ldrs, btn 2f out: 5 month abs.		1¼	32a
4991 **CLOUDINGSWELL 16** [3]3-8-7 (45) N De Souza(5) 16/1: 0664407: Led 3f, btn over 2f out: btr 2798.		5	24a
4365 **DUAL PURPOSE 52** [9]9-9-2 BL (55) S Whitworth 20/1: 064008: Chsd ldrs, btn 3f out, blnks: jumps fit.		¾	28a

4991 **DIWAN 16** [13]6-9-2 M Lawson(5) 33/1: 00///-09: Al outpcd & strug: mod form. *5* **19a**
4698 **NIPPY NIPPER 35** [11]3-8-3 T J Mackay 66/1: 00: 10th: Held up & keen, btn 3f out, t-strap. *¾* **9a**
4974 **PICO ALTO 19** [7]3-8-2 (1ow) A Nicholls 66/1: 0000: 11th: Slow away & al bhd. *3½* **1a**
A DOUBLE EWE BEE [1]3-8-7 P Makin(4) 12/1: 0: 12th: Held up & sn struggling, op 8/1. *8* **0a**
12 Ran Time 1m 54.85 (No Std Time) Owned: Mr T Lightbowne Trained: Sherborne

5231

3.50 Wolverhampton-Racecourse Co Uk Banded Stakes 3yo+ 0-45 (H5)
£1453 £415 £208 **5f20y aw rnd** **Inapplicable** Inside

4905 **CARGO 23** [3] B A Pearce 5-9-0 bl t (45) P Doe 7/2: 0220021: Fly jmpd start & missed break, held up, switched wide & hdwy to lead over 1f out, drvn out: op 4/1: eff at 5/7f on fast, gd/soft & both AWs, any trk: suited by blnks/t-strap, eff in cheek pieces: enjoys banded company: see 544. **51a**
5176* **CHATSHOW 6** [10] A W Carroll 3-9-0 (45) D Fentiman(7) 3/1 FAV: 0003012: Held up, styd on well fnl 1f, nrst fin: qck reapp: eff at 5f, ideally suited by stiffer trk &/or further: acts on polytrk, fast & soft. *1* **47a**
4995 **RED LEICESTER 16** [13] J A Glover 4-9-0 vis (45) F Norton 12/1: 6050063: Held up, rdn to chall dist, not pace of wnr: acts on fast, gd/soft & polytrack: see 2152. *nk* **46a**
4210 **ESTOILLE 59** [2] Mrs S Lamyman 3-9-0 t (45) T P Queally 25/1: 0000604: Chsd ldrs & ch over 1f out, hung left & btn ins last: 2 month abs: eff at 5f on polytrack in a t-strap. *1* **43a**
4660 **HAGLEY PARK 37** [11]5-9-0 (45) J Fanning 16/1: 0000505: Chsd ldrs, not pace to chall. *1½* **38a**
4130 **TRAVELLING TIMES 63** [7]5-9-0 vis (45) D Allan 4/1: 0040266: Outpcd, nrst fin, needs 6f: abs. *¾* **36a**
2262 **PLEASURE TIME 141** [4]11-9-0 vis (45) R Fitzpatrick 50/1: 5001607: Chsd ldr, hung right under press & btn dist: abs: see 981. *¾* **34a**
4995 **FLAPDOODLE 16** [8]6-9-0 bl (45) N Callan 8/1: 0003058: Chsd ldrs, outpcd fnl 2f: btr 4118. *3* **25a**
4043 **THE LEATHER WEDGE 67** [1]5-9-0 (45) P Bradley 8/1: 5255039: Led, hung right & hdd dist, fdd. *nk* **24a**
4905 **RUN ON 23** [6]6-9-0 (45) D Nolan(2) 33/1: 0005500: 10th: Mid-div, sn outpcd & nvr land blow. *nk* **23a**
5121 **TAMARELLA 9** [5]4-9-0 vis (45) A Beech(3) 25/1: 0050000: 11th: Chsd ldrs, btn 2f out. *1¼* **19a**
4995 **Mystery Pips 16** [12]4-9-0 vis(45) Kim Tinkler 20/1:0 4995 **Rellim 16** [9]5-9-0 (45) J Edmunds 16/1:0
13 Ran Time 1m 03.00 (No Std Time) Owned: Mr Noel Lawless Trained: Lingfield

5232

4.20 Hospitality At Dunstall Park Banded Stakes 3yo+ 0-45 (H5)
£1495 £427 £214 **1m141y aw rnd** **Inapplicable** Inside

5210 **TOKEWANNA 2** [5] W M Brisbourne 4-9-6 t (45) P Mathers(5) 3/1 FAV: 5435011: Trkd ldrs & led over 1f out, drvn out: qck reapp: eff at 7/8.5f on firm, gd/soft & polytrack, likes W'hampton & banded company. **54a**
4904 **LABELLED WITH LOVE 23** [2] J R Boyle 4-9-0 t (45) A Culhane 14/1: 2560522: Dwelt & held up, hdwy wide & rdn/chsd wnr ins last, lkd reluctant & hung left under press, al held: handles firm, gd & polytrack. *1¼* **44a**
5209 **INK IN GOLD 2** [1] P A Blockley 3-8-10 (45) V Slattery 6/1: 0500043: b g Intikhab - Your Village (Be My Guest) Dwelt, chsd ldrs, styd on onepace for press fnl 2f: qck reapp: stays 8.5f in banded company on polytrack, little form previously. *2* **40a**
3830 **EASTERN SCARLET 2** [12] V Smith 4-9-0 VIS (45) S Carson 20/1: 55-05054: Held up, hdwy & chall 2f out, onepace ins last: qck reapp & imprvd eff in first time visor: see 3830. *nk* **39a**
4791 **NUZZLE 30** [6]4-9-0 vis (45) F Norton 12/1: 3030005: Led/dsptd lead till dist, no extra: btr 3099. *¾* **38a**
4620 **PAS DE SURPRISE 39** [7]6-9-0 (45) N Callan 4/1: 5400006: Chsd ldrs, btn fnl 1f. *½* **37a**
4902 **LEVANTINE 23** [10]7-9-0 (45) Kirsty Milczarek(7) 4/1: 3561247: Sn handy & ch 2f out, no extra ins last, eased cl-home: btr 4795 & 4659. *3½* **30a**
5210 **ACE MA VAHRA 2** [13]6-9-0 bl (45) J Bramhill 10/1: 3505028: In tch, ch 2f out, no extra: qck reapp. *5* **21a**
4413 **DINE N DASH 49** [8]3-8-10 (45) S Whitworth 50/1: 0609: Held up, no ch fnl 3f, 7 wk abs. *11* **2a**
917 **HAITHEM 215** [9]7-9-0 t (45) P Hanagan 22/1: 0561000: 10th: Dwelt & sn struggling: abs: btr 786. *1½* **0a**
4974 **DANCING KING 19** [3]8-9-0 (45) P Makin(5) 16/1: 5555500: 11th: Led till halfway, sn btn: btr 4626. *2½* **0a**
4902 **SUSIEDIL 23** [4]3-8-10 (45) P Doe 33/1: 0660000: 12th: Held up & al towards rear. *1½* **0a**
2873 **SINGLE TRACK MIND 116** [11]6-9-0 p (45) N De Souza(5) 33/1: 0064000: 13th: Dwelt & sn bhd, abs. *25* **0a**
13 Ran Time 1m 52.49 (No Std Time) Owned: Merryland Properties Ltd Trained: Nesscliffe

5233

4.50 Zongalero Banded Stakes Div 2 3yo+ 0-45 (H5)
£1474 £421 £211 **7f32y aw rnd** **Inapplicable** Inside

4587 **MOLINIA 41** [6] R M Beckett 3-9-3 t (50) T P Queally 20/1: 4040301: Hmpd early, sn chsd ldrs, led over 1f out, drvn out: 6 wk abs, first win: eff at 7f: acts on polytrack, fast & gd grnd, gall or sharp trk: eff in a t-strap: see 3995, 2314. **56a**
4370 **LILY OF THE GUILD 51** [8] W S Kittow 5-9-3 P (48) F Norton 10/1: 4450002: Held up trav well, rdn to chase wnr ins last, al held: fair run in first time cheek pieces, 7 wk abs: see 270. *2* **49a**
5211 **LONG WEEKEND 2** [12] D Shaw 6-9-5 (50) S Whitworth 10/1: 6000043: Dwelt & held up, styd on onepace for press fnl 2f: clr of rem: op 5/1, qck reapp: see 3569, 832. *1* **49a**
4164 **FULVIO 61** [4] P D Evans 4-9-5 (50) N Callan 9/2: 0050004: Handy trav well & led over 2f out till over 1f out, wknd qckly: abs, op 10/1: prev with Jamie Poulton: found less than lkd likely today: see 2394. *5* **40a**
5212 **SCARROTTOO 2** [1]6-9-3 (48) D Allan 7/2 JT FAV: 1503005: Chsd ldrs, btn over 1f out, qck reapp. *¾* **37a**
4624 **DUBAI DREAMS 39** [11]4-9-5 (50) P Makin(5) 10/1: 5000606: Handy, btn 2f out: see 138. *½* **38a**
5120* **ELSINORA 9** [10]3-9-2 vis (49) D Sweeney 7/2 JT FAV: 2421317: Dwelt, nvr a factor: btr 5120. *shd* **37a**
5094* **CLARE GALWAY 10** [5]3-9-3 (50) A Culhane 7/1: 5004018: Handy till lost pl over 2f, btn dist. *1¼* **35a**
4708 **FARNBOROUGH 35** [7]3-9-1 (48) A McCarthy 20/1: 0000459: Prom, btn 2f out: btr 4708 & 4202. *2* **29a**
4905 **DOCTOR DENNIS 23** [3]7-9-5 vis (50) N Pollard 16/1: 0106000: 10th: Led 4f, btn dist, prefer 6f. *½* **30a**
4994 **Elliots Choice 16** [9]3-9-1 (48) L Keniry(3) 16/1:0 2325 **Phoenix Eye 138** [2]3-9-3 (50) L Enstone 33/1:0
12 Ran Time 1m 30.99 (No Std Time) Owned: Larksborough Stud Limited Trained: Lambourn

WOLVERHAMPTON Polytrack MONDAY 25.10.04 Lefthand, Sharp, Oval Track

5234
5.20 Civil Weddings At Dunstall Park Banded Stakes 4yo+ 0-45 (H5)
£1488 £425 £213   1m1f103y aw rnd   Inapplicable   Inside

MONTARA 118 [4] Lindsay Woods 5-9-0 P (45) A Culhane 8/1: 0/0-63201: b c Perugino - Tatra **49a**
(Niniski) Held up, hdwy & rdn to lead ins last, styd on strongly: 4 month abs, Irish raider, first win: eff at
9.5f/10.5f on gd & polytrack, likes a sharp trk & goes well fresh.
2583} **VRUBEL 56** [10] V Smith 5-9-0 VIS T (45) M Tebbutt 7/1: 5002502: ch g Entrepreneur - Renzola   1½ **45a**
(Dragonara Palace) Chsd ldrs, rdn & styd on, not pace of wnr: abs: h'cap plcd '03 (rtd 47 & 50a, H Collingridge):
amat h'cap wnr for N Callaghan in '02: eff at 7f, suited by 9/10f: acts on fast, soft & polytrack, prob any trk:
eff in chkpieces, vis & t-strap.   1 Jun'02 Good 9 sft 65-63 E: 2 May'02 Ling 7 ap 64a- E:
4665 **LAHOB 37** [12] P Howling 4-9-0 (45) F Norton 12/1: 6-060003: Led after 1f, hdd ins last & no   nk **44a**
extra: op 10/1: handles polytrack: see 2530.
4993 **SINJAREE 16** [3] Mrs S Lamyman 6-9-0 (45) T P Queally 12/1: 0600004: Led 1f, no extra dist.   shd **44a**
5122 **DANCING TILLY 9** [1]6-9-0 p (45) P Hanagan 9/4 JT FAV: 4641265: Trkd ldrs, onepace fnl 2f.   1¼ **41a**
3486 **ELA RE 91** [13]5-9-0 (45) J Bramhill 9/4 JT FAV: 6/0-40446: Held up, no pace to chall: op 3/1, abs.   ½ **40a**
429 **SUMMER STOCK 282** [9]6-9-0 t P (45) M McCabe 33/1: 04000-07: Chsd ldrs, btn dist, jumps fit.   1 **38a**
1838 **MISTY MAN 159** [2]6-9-0 bl (45) S Whitworth 33/1: 3514558: Nvr a factor: 5 mnth abs.   nk **37a**
3502 **LITTLE TASK 90** [6]6-9-0 (45) T Eaves(3) 25/1: 4104609: Pushed along & al rear: btr 2892 (12f).   2½ **32a**
3270} **RESCIND 452** [7]4-9-0 (45) J Fanning 14/1: 656/000-0: 10th: Held up & al bhd, reapp.   2½ **27a**
2340 **EUROLINK ARTEMIS 137** [11]7-9-0 p (45) N Callan 11/1: 40113P0: 11th: Held up, eff over 2f out, sn   3½ **20a**
hung left & btn: op 8/1, long abs.
4902 **SHEER FOCUS 23** [8]6-9-0 (45) Natalia Gemelova(5) 16/1: 4303-000: 12th: Cl-up 7f, btn 2f out.   8 **7a**
12 Ran   Time 2m 05.01(No Std Time)   Owned: White Heather Syndicate   Trained: Ireland

LINGFIELD Polytrack MONDAY 25.10.04 Lefthand, V Sharp Track

Official Going Standard

5235
1.40 Bet Direct On 0800 329393 Maiden Auction Stakes Div 1 2yo (E3)
£4186 £1288 £644   1m aw rnd   Going 35   -11 Slow   Outside

4635 **GRYSKIRK 39** [2] P W D'Arcy 2-8-8 (62) T Quinn 10/1: 0030501: In tch trav well, styd on to lead **78a**
ins fnl 1f, pushed out, val 2L+: eff at 6/7f, stays 1m: acts on fast grnd & polytrack: appreciated return to AW &
won in gd style: see 3820 & 1728.
4797 **KANDIDATE 30** [4] C E Brittain 2-8-11 (95) R L Moore 8/15 FAV: 03062: Cl-up, led 2f out, hdd   ¾ **77a**
under press ins fnl 1f, not pace wnr: clr rem: bckd at odds on: AW bow: eff at 7f, now stays 1m: acts on fast,
prob polytrack: shld have won this on prev ratings: see 3267.
5078 **CONTENTED 12** [8] E A L Dunlop 2-8-8 J Quinn 14/1: 53: b c Orpen - Joyfullness (Dixieland Band)   3 **68a**
Sn bhd, prog bldle 3f out, kept on late: Mar first foal, dam unrcd: sire Gr 1 wnr at sprint dists: eff at 1m,
further will suit on this evidence: acts on polytrack: encouraging.
CROSS THE LINE 0 [9] A P Jarvis 2-8-12 D Holland 11/2: 4: b c Cape Cross - Baalbek (Barathea)   shd **71a**
In tch wide, ran green, onepace bef 1f out: bckd from 9/1 on debut: Apr first foal, cost 34,000gns: dam successful
at 7f: sire high-class around 1m: showed promise despite greeness & looks sure to improve for today.
5091 **WEMBURY POINT 10** [1]2-8-10 VIS (56) R Winston 100/1: 0006005: Held up, prog 3f out, no impress.   1¼ **67a$**
4941 **KEMPSEY 21** [7]2-8-7 (59) Martin Dwyer 33/1: 4446006: Cl-up over 6f, wknd: btr 3284.   4 **56a**
CHRISTOM 2 [11]2-8-12 J Fortune 33/1: 07: b c Groom Dancer - Throw Away Line (Assert) Rear,   ¾ **59a**
nvr nrr than mid-div: qck reapp: Apr foal, cost 31,000gns: half-brother to wnrs on level at 7/12f, also successful
over fences: dam successful abroad: sire decent performer around 10f: with G A Butler.
4894 **STARLIGHT RIVER 24** [5]2-8-7 (1ow) (62) S Drowne 14/1: 003048: Keen in tch, prog over 2f out, sn wknd. ¾ **52a**
4997 **OUR KES 16** [3]2-8-6 (2ow) (62) S W Kelly 40/1: 000409: Led 6f, sn fdd: btr 4829.   1¼ **49a**
5002 **BAILEYS HONOUR 16** [6]2-8-3 R Ffrench 50/1: B00: 10th: Bhd & hmpd after 1f, sn drpd to rear, no dngr.   4 **38a**
4978 **SOFT FOCUS 18** [10]2-8-2 C Catlin 33/1: 000: 11th: Missed break, sn handy, fdd 2f out.   1½ **34a**
11 Ran   Time 1m 39.88 (3.68)   Owned: Charnwood Boy Partnership & Mrs J Harris   Trained: Newmarket

5236
2.10 Bet Direct On 0800 329393 Maiden Auction Stakes Div 2 2yo (E3)
£4173 £1284 £642   1m aw rnd   Going 35   -09 Slow   Outside

4978 **MUSICAL DAY 18** [11] B J Meehan 2-8-5 BL (75) R L Moore 7/2: 0020431: Cl-up wide, led bef 1f out, **80a**
drvn out: first time blnks: eff at 7/8.6f, further will suit: acts on fast, gd/soft & polytrack: has been running
well & this was a deserved success: enjoyed fitting of 1st time blnks: see 4978.
5033 **LIMIT 14** [8] M R Channon 2-8-6 C Catlin 12/1: 302: Keen bhd, hdwy 3f out, styd on to chase wnr   ¾ **78a**
ins fnl 1f, held: eff at 1m, further will suit next term: acts on polytrack: gd run after v disapp last time in
5033 (soft), can lose mdn tag: see 4782 (debut).
5019 **ALFIE NOAKES 15** [1] Mrs A J Perrett 2-8-12 S Drowne 11/10 FAV: 353: Handy, rear & short of room   1¼ **82a**
bef 2f out, switched & kept on, not pace front 2: bckd on AW bow: eff at 7f/1m, will apprec further: acts on fast
grnd & polytrack: shade closer with clr run & sure to improve & win a race: see 4677.
5097 **BLUE HEDGES 10** [10] H J Collingridge 2-8-10 J Quinn 33/1: 004: b c Polish Precedent - Palagene   ½ **79a**
(Generous) Keen bhd, prog wide trav well after halfway, onepcd dist: Mar first foal, dam plcd at 10f: sister 12f
List wnr abroad: eff at 1m, shld get 10f: acts on polytrack: now quals for h'caps.
4635 **SILVER VISAGE 39** [7]2-8-8 P (60) Dean Williams(7) 33/1: 55505: Led, hdd bef 1f out, no extra: see 2584. ½ **76a$**
PERSIAN KHANOOM 0 [6]2-8-4 J F McDonald(3) 33/1: 6: b f Royal Applause - Kshessinskaya (Hadeer)   1 **70a**
Held up, trav well 3f out, prog when short of room bef 1f out, switched & kept on late: debut, Mar foal, half-sister
plcd at 7f: dam successful at mid-dists: sire Gr 1 wnr at 6f: signs of encouragement & shld rate higher for today.
5179 **SOL ROJO 6** [5]2-8-8 S W Kelly 66/1: 007: Missed break, hdwy 3f out, onepcd bef 1f out: qck   hd **73a**
reapp: Feb foal, cost 12,000gns: half-brother to wnrs at 7f/1m: dam wnr at 6f.
5084 **WAATHEB 11** [9]2-8-12 P Dobbs 7/1: 008: Cl-up over 6f, wknd: op 9/2 on AW bow.   1 **75a**
5097 **CASH ON 10** [2]2-8-10 Martin Dwyer 15/2: 09: Missed break, nvr a factor: AW bow.   nk **72a**
4978 **KERGOLAY 18** [4]2-8-8 J F Egan 25/1: 60: 10th: Keen in tch 6f, fdd.   8 **55a**

4864 **TAHLAL 26** [3]2-8-8 P (61) R Ffrench 33/1: 50040: 11th: Keen cl-up, fdd 3f out: btr 4864.   9   **39a**
11 Ran   Time 1m 39.78 (3.58)   Owned: Mr T G Holdcroft   Trained: Upper Lambourn

---

5237   2.40 Littlewoods Bet Direct Novice Stakes 2yo (D3)
£5096 £1568 £784   **6f aw rnd**   **Going 35**   **-04 Slow**   Inside

4970 **POSTGRADUATE 19** [9] H Morrison 2-8-12   S Drowne 6/1: 51: Mid-div wide, hdwy 3f out, styd on to   **87a+**
lead cl-home, pushed out, val 2L+: op 8/1: eff at 6f, will apprec rtn to 7f: acts on polytrack: gd turn of foot.
   EXCUSEZ MOI 0 [8] C E Brittain 2-8-9 (1ow)   S Sanders 12/1: 2: b c Fusaichi Pegasus - Jiving   ¾   **81a+**
(Generous) Held up, hdwy wide 3f out, styd on to lead dist, hdd cl-home: debut: Feb first foal, cost $410,000:
dam plcd at 6f: sire high-class mid-dist performer in US: eff at 6f, 7f+ will suit next term: acts on polytrack:
gd eff in defeat racing so wide & looks sure to improve with experience & find similar.
4985 **BOLD MARC 17** [4] K R Burke 2-9-4 (83) Darren Williams 12/1: 2106463: Cl-up, styd on to lead over   1   **87a**
1f out, hdd dist, no extra: AW bow: stay 6f, prob just apprec rtn to min trip: acts on fast, gd/soft & polytrack:
gd run conceding weight all round: btr 2100 & 1091 (5f).
4401 **JOHN ROBIE 50** [7] G A Butler 2-8-12   J Fortune 3/1: 634: Missed break, outpcd & bhd over 2f out,   ¾   **79a**
pushed & styd on well ins fnl 1f, nrst fin: 7 wk abs & AW bow: eff at 6f, looks sure to apprec further: acts on
fast grnd & polytrack: did not get run of race & is open to more improvement: see 4401.
5098 **ELGIN MARBLES 10** [5]2-9-0 (83) R L Moore 15/8 FAV: In tch, outpcd over 2f out, hung   shd   **80a**
left over 1f out, late rally under hand ride: well bckd: not knocked about & looks in need of 7f: btr 4882 (h'cap).
5076 **THREE DEUCES 12** [2]2-8-7   D Holland 8/1: 546: Led, hdd over 1f out, no extra: quals for h'caps.   ½   **72a**
5048 **MISS TOLERANCE 14** [3]2-8-7   R Winston 8/1: 037: Bhd, short of room after 1f, prog bef 1f out,   1¼   **68a**
kept on late: AW bow: showed more in 5048 (fast).
4726 **PERFECT SOLUTION 34** [1]2-8-7   J F Egan 40/1: 08: ch f Entrepreneur - Pearl Barley (Polish   1   **65a**
Precedent) Bhd, nvr a factor: Feb first foal, dam successful at 6f: sire Gr 1 wnr at 1m: with J A R Toller.
5021 **LUCKY EMERALD 15** [6]2-8-11 t (70) F P Ferris(3) 25/1: 201059: Cl-up over 4f, fdd: disapp on AW bow.   6   **53a**
9 Ran   Time 1m 12.74 (2.34)   Owned: Thurloe Thoroughbreds XII   Trained: East Ilsley

---

5238   3.10 Bet Direct Predictor Com Handicap Stakes 3yo+ 56-70 (E3)
£3517 £1082 £541   **1m aw rnd**   **Going 35**   **+08 Fast**   Outside   **[83]**

4378 **SHARP NEEDLE 51** [12] J Noseda 3-9-4 (73) S W Kelly 8/1: 0251141: Mid-div, hdwy 3f out, styd on   **83a**
to lead cl-home: 7 wk abs: AW bow: eff at 1m/9f, further shld suit: acts on fast, gd grnd & polytrack: goes well
fresh: in form 3yo who is open to more improvement in h'cap grade: see 3806 & 2475.
5148 **SLALOM 7** [11] Julian Poulton 4-9-2 (68) G Faulkner 25/1: 0050502: In tch v wide, hdwy to lead 2f   ½   **75a**
out, hdd under press cl-home: qck reapp: acts on gd/soft grnd & both AWs: apprec rtn to 1m & can find similar.
5191 **PURE MISCHIEF 5** [7] C R Dore 5-9-4 (70) R Thomas(3) 16/1: 2465503: Held up, plenty to do over 2f   1½   **74a**
out, styd on bef 1f out, nrst fin: eff at 1m, rtn to 10/12f will suit: see 3276 & 2499.
5079 **ANALYZE 12** [8] B G Powell 6-9-8 (74) T Quinn 11/4: 3540124: Held up, prog 3f out, hung left for   shd   **77a**
press dist, no impress on ldrs: op 7/2: showed sltly more in 5079 & 4974 (C/D).
4923 **ISLAND RAPTURE 23** [10]4-9-3 (69) S Sanders 9/2: 3260235: Bhd, hdwy 4f out, no extra dist: op 6/1.   1½   **69a**
4714 **FRANKSALOT 35** [1]4-9-10 (76) S Drowne 13/2: 5415306: Sn handy, no extra bef 1f out: op 5/1.   ½   **75a**
2045 **GREENWOOD 150** [6]6-9-7 (73) D Kinsella 16/1: 3006627: Keen cl-up, led trav well over 2f out, hit   5   **62a**
2f out, sn wknd: long abs: showed more in 2045 (7f).
5079 **LILLI MARLANE 12** [5]4-9-3 (69) J F Egan 7/2 FAV: 1005048: Bhd & nvr trav, eased & btn fnl 1f: btr 5079. 10   **40a**
5079 **ELECTRIQUE 12** [3]4-9-4 bl (70) Martin Dwyer 11/1: 21-00009: Cl-up over 5f, wknd: btr 3892.   ¾   **39a**
4642 **CORKY 38** [4]3-9-7 (76) R L Moore 14/1: 4310300: 10th: Bhd, nvr a factor: btr 4110 (7f, gd).   1¼   **43a**
4860 **GEMS BOND 26** [9]4-9-6 (72) Derek Nolan(7) 33/1: 0000500: 11th: Bhd, nvr a factor.   1½   **36a**
5080 **CHEESE N BISCUITS 12** [2]4-9-4 (70) A Quinn(5) 16/1: 5400000: 12th: Led, hdd bef 2f out, fdd: btr 1616. 16   **4a**
12 Ran   Time 1m 38.36 (2.16)   Owned: Mr Arashan Ali   Trained: Newmarket

---

5239   3.40 Ladbrokes Com Handicap Stakes 3yo 71-85 (D2)
£6855 £2109 £1055   **1m4f aw**   **Going 35**   **+10 Fast**   Inside   **[92]**

4919 **WINNERS DELIGHT 23** [6] A P Jarvis 3-9-0 (78) R Winston 16/1: 5300361: Held up, hdwy wide over 2f   **88a**
out, hung for press bef 1f out, rdn out to lead cl-home: eff at 10f, now stays 12f: acts on fast, gd/soft grnd &
polytrack: op to more improvement as stays this trip & more races await on this surface: see 4613 & 2919.
4615 **KING OF DIAMONDS 40** [9] J R Best 3-8-12 (76) Martin Dwyer 25/1: 0010402: Keen bhd, hdwy 4f out,   nk   **84a**
styd on to lead 2f out, hdd under press cl-home: 6 wk abs: prev eff at 6f/1m, suited by step up to 12f.
4745 **PAGAN MAGIC 33** [7] J A R Toller 3-8-10 (74) Lisa Jones 10/1: 0105403: Keen bhd, prog bef 1f out,   2   **79a**
kept on late, nrst fin: clr rem: acts on gd, soft grnd & polytrack: just btr 2175.
4833 **GRAHAM ISLAND 28** [5] G Wragg 3-9-5 (83) D Holland 12/1: 5-166054: In tch, prog over 3f out,   3½   **83a**
sltly lost pl 2f out & sn short of room, no impress bef 1f out: AW bow: just btr 4833 & 1211.
5068 **CIRCASSIAN 13** [8]3-9-3 (81) S Sanders 1/1 FAV: 0211425: Cl-up wide, led 4f out, hdd over 2f out,   ½   **80a**
wknd bef 1f out: well bckd: polytrack bow: disapp & did not help cause by racing so wide: btr 5068 & 4672.
4833 **SUNNY LADY 28** [10]3-8-13 (77) J Fortune 16/1: 2221446: In tch wide, no room over 2f out, onepcd dist. 1   **74a**
4861* **BARATHEA BLUE 26** [4]3-8-11 (75) T Quinn 13/2: 5217: Keen cl-up, led halfway, hdd 4f out, grad wknd. 2½   **68a**
5050 **DIEGO CAO 14** [1]3-9-10 (88) R L Moore 11/2: 2161428: Nvr nrr than mid-div: btr 5050 (10f).   6   **72a**
5068 **FIRST CENTURION 13** [2]3-9-0 (78) M Hills 16/1: 6-100459: Sn handy, wknd 3f out.   5   **55a**
4966 **PRINCIPESSA 20** [3]3-8-8 (72) F P Ferris(3) 33/1: 0243200: 10th: Led, hdd halfway, sn fdd.   dist   **19a**
10 Ran   Time 2m 32.27 (3.07)   Owned: Breckland Bingo   Trained: Twyford

---

5240   4.10 Bet Direct On The Breeders Cup Maiden Stakes 3yo+ (D3)
£3877 £1193 £597   **7f aw rnd**   **Going 35**   **-10 Slow**   Inside

4275 **MISTER MUJA 56** [5] P W Harris 3-9-5 t   R L Moore 20/1: 061: Mid-div, prog & short of room bef 2f   **82a**
out, styd on to lead cl-home, rdn out: 8 wk abs & AW bow: eff at 7f, 1m shld suit: acts on polytrack & goes well
fresh: eff with a t-strap: only lightly rcd & can progress.
4797 **GRAND IDEAS 720** [7] Julian Poulton 5-9-7   Dale Gibson 66/1: 35/-2: br g Grand Lodge - Afrafa   ¾   **79a**

LINGFIELD Polytrack MONDAY 25.10.04 Lefthand, V Sharp Track

(Lashkari) Cl-up, kept on ins fnl 1f, not pace wnr: reapp: AW bow: missed '03: plcd on 1 of only 2 '02 starts
(rtd 76, mdn, C P Tate): eff at 7f, rtn to 10f shld suit: acts on soft grnd & polytrack: gd eff after a long abs.

4029	PEARL FARM 68 [8] C A Horgan 3-9-0 D Holland 50/1: 03: Held up, short of room 2f out, switched & kept on well ins fnl 1f, nrst fin: 10 wk abs: apprec step up to 7f, shld apprec 1m: acts on polytrack.	nk	73a
4977	KAURI FOREST 19 [14] J R Fanshawe 3-9-5 t (77) M Hills 3/1: JT FAV: 32234: Led, still trav well over 1f out, hdd under press cl-home: looked set to collect for a long way bef tiring & is proving frustrating.	shd	77a
	KATAVI 0 [4]3-9-0 S W Kelly 3/1: JT FAV: 5: b f Stravinsky - Halholah (Secreto) In tch, hdwy wide over 2f out, kept on late: debut: sire Gr 1 wnr at 6f: signs of encouragement & shld improve with experience.	1	70a
4975	MAD 19 [13]3-9-0 J F Egan 100/1: 0006: Bhd, prog wide over 2f out, nrst fin: see 4315.	1¼	68a
4975	KING AT LAST 19 [1]5-9-7 D R McCabe 66/1: 0/-07: Cl-up over 5f, wknd: see 4975.	1½	70a
4977	AUTHORITY 19 [9]4-9-7 (70) S Sanders 7/2: 24-58: In tch, outpcd over 2f out, kept on late under hands riding: tchd 11/2: reportedly hung left; see 4977.	½	69a
1235	SHAMDIAN 191 [3]4-9-7 t (83) T Quinn 4/1: 32262-09: b g Indian Ridge - Shamadara (Kahyasi) Mid-div, eff when hmpd bef 1f out, wknd: op 7/1: jumps fit, earlier wnr at Hereford (rtd 116h, stays 2m1f on fast & gd/soft): ex French, plcd at up to 10f on Flat in native country (gd & gd/soft): with N J Henderson.	3	63a
5110	POETRY N PASSION 10 [11]3-9-0 R Ffrench 33/1: 000: 10th: Cl-up wide 5f, wknd.	3½	51a
	RED LANTERN 0 [6]3-9-5 M Henry 100/1: 0: 11th: Missed break, nvr a factor.	6	45a
5110	YOUNG KATE 10 [2]3-9-0 Martin Dwyer 12/1: 60: 12th: Held up, trav well when short of room over 2f out, sn eased: reportedly moved badly in race: btr 5110.	shd	39a
4923	MOONSHAFT 23 [10]3-9-5 VIS (66) S Drowne 10/1: 0040450: 13th: Handy 5f, wknd.	2	40a
4835	TERENURE GIRL 28 [12]3-9-0 Lisa Jones 100/1: 600: 14th: Rear, nvr a factor.	nk	34a

14 Ran Time 1m 26.01 (3.21) Owned: The Mint Trained: Berkhamsted

---

5241 | 4.40 Bet Direct 'red To Bet' On Itv Apprentice Handicap Stakes 3yo+ 46-55 (F4)
£2995 £856 £428 6f aw rnd Going 35 -08 Slow inside [70]

4646	PARTY PRINCESS 38 [6] J A Glover 3-9-1 (57) A Mullen 14/1: 4000001: Led, hdd bef halfway, styd cl-up & led again dist, pushed out, val 3L+: eff at 5/6f, has tried further: acts on fast grnd or polytrack: back to form today with easy success & is poised to find more h'caps: see 2268 & 2011.		69a+
5096	TABOOR 10 [9] J W Payne 6-9-6 h bl t (61) Rory Moore 10/1: 6012052: Held up, hdwy wide halfway, kept on ins fnl 1f, not pace easy wnr: gd eff in defeat: see 4197 & 3673.	2	63a
5156	DAVIDS MARK 7 [7] J R Jenkins 4-9-0 (55) R J Killoran(5) 10/1: 4412003: Mid-div, hdwy to lead 2f out, hdd dist, no extra: quick reapp: just btr 3974 & 3640 (5f).	¾	55a
5120	TSARBUCK 9 [2] R M H Cowell 3-9-3 p (59) G Bartley(7) 20/1: 2330064: Cl-up, outpcd halfway, rallied 2f out, onepace fnl 1f: btr 3485 (fibresand, 1st time visor).	¾	57a
5155	WOODBURY 7 [12]5-9-2 (57) D Tudhope 5/2 FAV: 0410625: Handy wide over 4f, no extra: op 7/4 on quick reapp: poor high draw: showed more in 5155.	nk	54a
4582	BEN LOMAND 41 [11]4-9-0 c (55) A Kirby(5) 16/1: 0030006: Bhd, hdwy halfway, kept on late: 6 wk abs.	½	51a
5112	WARLINGHAM 3 [3]6-9-3 (58) Derek Nolan 14/1: 5000007: Bhd, prog when no room bef 1f out, sn btn.	1	51a
5053	KEW THE MUSIC 14 [5]4-9-1 vis (56) T O'Brien(5) 3/1: 0001008: Missed break, eff when short of room bef 1f out, kept on late: lost all ch with tardy start: showed more in 4636.	¾	47a
1054	STAMFORD BLUE 203 [1]3-9-2 (58) Laura Reynolds(5) 12/1: 2060129: Cl-up 4f, wknd: long abs.	nk	48a
5156	MULTAHAB 7 [4]5-9-0 t (55) M Halford 8/1: 0000600: 10th: Nvr nrr than mid-div: btr 4140.	1	42a
2644	GOODWOOD PRINCE 125 [10]4-9-0 vis (55) L Smith(7) 33/1: 0000000: 11th: Keen cl-up, led bef halfway, hdd 2f out, fdd: long abs: btr 2262.	2	36a
4169	CHEEKY CHI 61 [8]3-9-0 (56) Dean Williams 25/1: 4000060: 12th: Cl-up 4f, fdd: se 4169.	2½	30a

12 Ran Time 1m 12.98 (2.58) Owned: Mr Derrick Bloy Trained: Worksop

---

5242 | 5.10 Bet Direct At Lingfield Park Classified Stakes 3yo 0-55 (F4)
£2905 £830 £415 1m aw rnd Going 35 -04 Slow Outside

5183	MY PENSION 6 [6] P Howling 3-9-3 (60) R Winston 8/1: 4300631: Mid-div, hdwy to chase ldr over 1f out, styd on to lead cl-home, rdn out: quick reapp: eff around 1m on polytrack: in gd form: see 5183.		67a
4252	KING OF MUSIC 57 [1] G Prodromou 3-8-12 (52) O Urbina 12/1: 350-0062: In tch, styd on to lead 2f out, hdd under press cl-home: 8 wk abs: eff at 7f/1m on fast grnd & polytrack: see 3872.	1	58a
5094	SYLVA ROYAL 10 [8] C E Brittain 3-8-9 (54) S Sanders 7/2 JT FAV: 4460143: Held up, hdwy 3f out, kept on ins fnl 1f, not btn far in 3rd: showed more in 4660 (7f).	½	54a
5112	BEST DESERT 9 [5] J R Best 3-9-2 (59) J Quinn 7/2 JT FAV: 1500634: Mid-div, prog 2f out, onepcd dist.	nk	60a
4763	HANA DEE 32 [9]3-8-9 (54) S Hitchcott 33/1: 4530045: Bhd, prog halfway, onepcd bef 1f out: btr 3679.	2	49a
4828*	BLAKE HALL LAD 28 [7]3-9-1 (58) Dean Williams(7) 8/1: 00516: Held up, nvr nrr than mid-div.	1½	52a
5041	ANTIGUA BAY 14 [4]3-9-0 (60) J F Egan 6/1: 0026347: Handy over 5f, sn outpcd, mod gains: btr 4586.	2	47a
5184	BEAUTY OF DREAMS 6 [3]3-8-9 vis (54) C Catlin 12/1: 0604308: Led 6f, fdd: quick reapp: btr 5094.	3	36a
4546	KINBRACE 42 [2]3-8-11 (57) Martin Dwyer 4/1: 050-6559: Cl-up 6f, wknd & hung badly bef 1f out: 6 wk abs: v disapp on AW bow: showed more in 4546 (gd 2098).	5	28a

9 Ran Time 1m 39.34 (3.14) Owned: Mr David Andrew Brown Trained: Newmarket

---

DEAUVILLE TUESDAY 19.10.04 Righthand, Galloping Track

Official Going SOFT.

5243 | 1.50 Gr 3 Prix des Reservoirs 2yo ()
£25704 £10282 £7711 1m rnd Soft

4958	SONGERIE 17 [5] Sir Mark Prescott 2-8-9 J B Eyquem 243/10: 191: Chsd ldrs, hdwy to chse ldr dist, drvn & led well ins last: back to form after reportedly suffering major trouble in running in 495: eff at 7f, imprvd for step up to 1m & will get further: acts on soft & hvy, gall trks: lightly rcd, useful filly.		108
	SOIGNEE [2] A Wohler 2-8-9 A Suborics 14/10 FAV: 112: b f Dashing Blade - Sulvez (Fioravanti) Led till caught cl home: prev unbtn German filly, incl a List event at Baden Baden: eff at 1m on soft grnd: useful.	½	106
	YSOLDINA [9] A de Royer Dupre 2-8-9 T Jarnet 4/1: 2213: Held up, styd on for press, not pace of wnr.	shd	105

DEAUVILLE   TUESDAY 19.10.04   Righthand, Galloping Track

9 Ran   Time 1m 44.40()   Owned: Miss K Rausing   Trained: Newmarket

CAPANNELLE   SUNDAY 24.10.04   Righthand, Flat, Galloping Track

Official Going GOOD/SOFT.

5244   3.30 Gr 1 Premio Lydia Tesio Darley Fillies And Mares 3yo+ ()
£136690 £69771 £40880   1m2f   Good/Soft

3837* **LUNE DOR** [4] R Gibson 3-8-10   T Jarnet   758/100: 2-311101: Held up, smooth prog & led over 1f   **120**
out, drvn out: eff at 10/12f on gd/soft & soft grnd: high class filly: see 3837 (Gr 2).
4953 **WALKAMIA 21** [12] A Fabre 4-8-13   E Legrix   5/2: 1-554332: Handy, drvn & ev ch dist, kept on but   2   **115**
not pace of wnr: smart filly: see 4953, 57.
   SUPER BOBBINA [1] I Bugattella 3-8-10   D Vargiu   107/10: 120-1213: b f Daggers Drawn - Lucky   ½   **116**
Coin (Hadeer) Held up, hdwy to chall over 1f out, not pace of wnr ins last: Gr 2 rnr-up earlier: eff at 1m/10f on
gd/sft & hvy grnd: smart.
4774+ **MAZUNA 30** [14]3-8-10 (97) R Moore   103/10: 6-1232216: Held up, kept on fnl 2f, nvr pace to   5   **108**
threaten: up in grade, eff at 10f, return to 12f will suit: handles fast & gd/sft grnd: see 4774 (Gr 3, 12f, g/f).
4149 **WINDY BRITAIN** [5]5-8-13 (88) P Agus   176/10: 1-0426077: Mid-div, efft wide & nvr able to chall: nse **105$**
big step up in grade, offic rtd 87: see 3072, 179.
4735* **MONTURANI 35** [16]5-8-13 (104) T E Durcan   82/10: 2-36244510: 11th: Trkd ldr, btn 2f out.   10   **91**
14 Ran   Time 2m 02.40()   Owned: Mme P de Moussac   Trained: France

LONGCHAMP   SUNDAY 24.10.04   Righthand, Stiff, Galloping Track

Official Going HEAVY.

5245   2.20 Gr 1 Prix Royal Oak 3yo+ ()
£80479 £32197 £16099   1m7f110y   Heavy

4951* **WESTERNER 21** [4] E Lellouche 5-9-4   S Pasquier   2/5 FAV: 11-1220111: Held up, hdwy to lead dist,   **122**
styd on strongly, readily: suited by 15f+, stays stiff 2m4f well: acts on fast, loves gd/sft & hvy grnd: high-class
stayer who is hard to beat in these conditions: see 4951.
4948 **BEHKARA 22** [3] A de Royer Dupre 4-9-1   C Soumillon   48/10: 113-632: b f Kris - Behera (Mill Reef)   2½   **113**
Keen & trkd ldrs, swtchd & styd on for press, not rch wnr: Gr 2 wnr in '03, subs 3rd in this race (rtd 112): eff at
12f, suited by 2m on gd/sft & hvy grnd: smart stayer. 1 Oct'03 Long 15sft 111- A:
4733 **ALCAZAR 36** [6] H Morrison 9-9-4 (115) M Fenton   21/1: 024-12053: Chsd ldrs, hdwy to chall 2f out,   ½   **115**
rdn & no extra ins last: rnr-up to today's wnr in this race last term: see 1705.
5168 **PERCUSSIONIST 7** [9]3-8-9 bl (118) J Fortune   27/1: 11402365: Led till 4f out, wknd fnl 2f: see 5168.   7   **109**
5138 **FRANKLINS GARDENS 8** [1]4-9-4 (105) D Holland   25/1: 0-4406626: Trkd ldr, led 4f out, hdd 2f out, fdd.   2   **106**
8 Ran   Time 3m 28.90()   Owned: Ecurie Wildenstein   Trained: France

WOODBINE   SUNDAY 24.10.04

Official Going GOOD.

5246   8.26 Gr 1 E P Taylor Stakes Fillies & Mares 3yo+ ()
£194805 £64935 £35714   1m2f   Good

4936} **COMMERCANTE** [6] R J Frankel 4-8-11   J R Velazquez   51/20: 002-1021: b f Marchand de Sable -   **119**
Deception (Tropular) Prevailed in the closing stages: v smart filly, eff at 10f on gd grnd.
2 Oct'03 Sain 10.5sft 113- : 1 Aug'03 Deau 10g/s 113- A:
4024 **PUNCTILIOUS 67** [10] Saeed bin Suroor 3-8-6 (110) L Dettori   11/10 FAV: 3-131242: Chsd ldrs, led   ½   **116**
ins last, caught cl home: 2 mth abs: back to form, see 4424, 3321 & 2517.
   CLASSIC STAMP [2] C Hopmans Jr 4-8-11   P Husbands   105/10: 231321-3: Just btn in a cl fin.   nk   **115**
8 Ran   Time 2m 04.02 ()   Owned: A Falourd, H Guy & R Trussel   Trained: Usa

5247   10.07 Gr 1 Canadian International 3yo+ ()
£389610 £129870 £71429   1m4f   Good

4002* **SULAMANI 68** [3] Saeed bin Suroor 5-9-0 (124) L Dettori   17/20 FAV: 15-42311: Held up, swtchd wide   **126**
& hdwy over 2f out, led ins last & sn asserted under hand riding, readily: eff at 10/12f on firm, likes gd & soft
grnd: top class entire who will now reportedly be retired: see 4002 (Gr 1).
   SIMONAS [10] A Wohler 5-9-0   K Fallon   214/10: 1116442: gr h Sternkoenig - Sistadari (Shardari)   1½   **121**
Held up, hdwy to lead over 1f out, hdd ins last & not pace to repel: German raider, Gr 2 wnr in Italy earlier: eff
at 12/14f on gd & hvy grnd: high-class effort.
4733 **BRIAN BORU 36** [5] A P O'Brien 4-9-0   J P Spencer   49/10: 3-15555223: Rear, styd on for press, nvr   2   **117**
able to chall: Irish chall, see 4733, 4161 & 994.
4428 **MUBTAKER 49** [1] M P Tregoning 7-9-0 (130) R Hills   11/2: 21/1112-174: Dwelt, sn trkd ldrs, rdn &   ¾   **116**
no extra dist: 7 wk abs & a return to form but below top-class best: see 3958.
10 Ran   Time 2m 28.64()   Owned: Godolphin   Trained: Newmarket

Official Going SOFT.

5248   2.30 Gr 3 Kilavullan Stakes 2yo   ()
£30532 £8958 £4268   7f rnd   Soft

5163* **FOOTSTEPSINTHESAND 8** [6] A P O'Brien 2-9-0   J P Spencer   4/5 FAV: 11: Trkd ldr, qcknd to lead 2f   **108+**
out & sn in command, readily: remains unbtn: apprec step up to 7f, 1m+ shld suit: acts on gd/sft & soft grnd:
likes a stiff trk: potentially smart colt, well regarded & shld prove a classic prospect for '05.

     GAFF 26 [3] D K Weld 2-9-0   P J Smullen   100/30: 012: b c Maria's Mon - Ionlyhaveeyesforu   2   101
(Tunerup) Chsd ldrs, edged right & styd on for press fnl 2f, no impress on easy wnr: well clr of rem: recent List
wnr at Fairyhouse: acts at 7f, 1m shld suit: acts on gd/soft & soft grnd, likes a stiff/ gall trk: useful.

2454 **CLASH OF THE ASH 138** [7] J S Bolger 2-9-0   K J Manning   12/1: 5133: Chsd ldrs, no impress on   7   90
front pair fnl 2f: 5 mth abs: see 2454.

6 Ran   Time 1m 32.90()   Owned: M Tabor   Trained: Ballydoyle

Official Going Soft

5249   1.10 Weatherill Brothers Marquees Selling Stakes 3-4yo   (G4)
£2506 £716 £358   1m6f17y   Soft 98   -34 Slow   Inside

4965 **ENSEMBLE 22** [5] D M Simcock 4-9-5   (40) N Callan   33/1: 000/00-01: b g Polish Precedent - Full   55
Orchestra (Shirley Heights) Sn chsd ldr, led 4f out, hung left ins last, drvn out: no bid: unplcd '03 (rtd 13,
tried blnks, M W Easterby): unplcd '02 (rtd 50): eff over 14f on soft grnd in v modest sell company.

5060 **SECRET JEWEL 15** [6] Lady Herries 4-9-0 ld (60) R L Moore   8/15 FAV: 6050022: Rear, pushed along   3   46
over 5f out, chsd wnr from 2f out, hung left & no impress ins last: hvly bckd at odds on, clr of rem: stays 14f in
sell grade: acts on gd & soft grnd: see 5060 & 3222.

4857 **MISTER COMPLETELY 28** [3] J R Best 3-9-2   (47) T P Queally   11/2: 6010533: Held up, rdn & btn 3f out.   10   47
4374 **PURR 53** [2] T T Clement 3-8-10   (49) Hayley Turner(3) 20/1: 6000004: Led 1f & handy till over 2f   6   35
out: jumps fit (mod): see 2222.

     KATIE MERNAGH 416 [1]4-9-0 BL S W Kelly   28/1: 000-5: b f Danetime - White Jasmin (Jalmood) Slow   hd   30
away & led after 1f till 4f out, sn btn: blnks: reapp: Brit bow, ex Irish: no form 3 mdn starts '03.

4671 **SIGNORA PANETTIERA 39** [4]3-8-6 (1ow) (40) S Hitchcott   6/1: 0600046: Prom till over 2f out, wknd qckly.   1¼   30

6 Ran   Time 3m 16.32 (18.52)   Owned: Mr David Sugars & Mr Bob Parker   Trained: Newmarket

5250   1.40 E B F /Potters Leisure Resort Maiden Stakes Div 1 2yo   (D3)
£4193 £1290 £645   7f str   Soft 98   -04 Slow   Stands Side

     ZALONGO 0 [7] Sir Michael Stoute 2-9-0   R Winston   20/1: 1: ch c Zafonic - Tamassos (Dance In   **84+**
Time) Held up, hdwy 2f out & styd on for press to lead well ins last: op 12/1: half-brother to sev wnrs, incl
top-class 11/12f performer Posidonas, dam a 12f wnr: eff at 7f, 1m+ sure to suit: acts on soft grnd & a fair trk:
goes well fresh: type to progress & rate higher.

     PARADISE MILL 0 [15] J H M Gosden 2-8-9   J Fortune   17/2: 2: b f Horse Chestnut - Eaton Place   ½   77
(Zafonic) Dwelt & held up, prog & led over 1f out, rdn & hdd well ins last: Mar first foal, dam a 10f 3yo scorer:
eff at 7f, strong mid-dist pedigree: acts on soft grnd: promising debut, improve over further.

4997 **TICKI TORI 18** [6] Julian Poulton 2-8-9   N Callan   12/1: 33: Prom, rdn & styd on onepace fnl 1f: hd   76
confirmed promise of debut: eff at 7f/1m on gd & soft grnd: see 4997.

     RED RACKETEER 0 [4] E A L Dunlop 2-9-0   R L Moore   16/1: 4: b c Red Ransom - Furajet (The   3   77
Minstrel) Held up, rdn to chase ldrs over 1f out, no extra ins last: op 12/1: May foal, half-brother to a 6f/1m
scorer, also a 1m juv wnr: dam a 5f juv scorer: eff at 7f, handles soft grnd.

4664 **DANTES DIAMOND 39** [9]2-9-0   (75) G Baker   20/1: 2255045: Led till over 1f out, no extra.   1½   75
5097 **MURAABET 12** [8]2-9-0   R Hills   4/6 FAV: 36: Chsd ldr, edged left & no impress over 1f out: hvly bckd.   2   72
5192 **GALLANTIAN 6** [13]2-9-0   D Holland   66/1: 007: Held up, late gains, imprve in h'caps at 1m+.   ¾   71
     BARCARDERO 0 [10]2-9-0   K Darley   14/1: 8: Prom till lost pl 4f out, sn short of room, mod late rally.   1   70
5192 **DOSE CHASE 6** [3]2-9-0   J Mackay   25/1: 069: Chsd ldrs, btn over 2f out.   2   67
5084 **HORNINGSHEATH 13** [11]2-8-9   J Quinn   10/1: 00: 10th: Keen & prom, btn 2f out.   nk   61
4843 **BORN FOR DIAMONDS 29** [14]2-8-9   M Hills   20/1: 050: 11th: Prom till over 2f out, longer trip.   1   60
     TAXMAN 0 [1]2-9-0   S Sanders   28/1: 0: 12th: Slow away & sn struggling.   5   58
     FOREHAND 0 [2]2-8-9   Dane O'Neill   25/1: 0: 13th: Dwelt, al outpcd in rear.   2½   49
     ANGEL RIVER 0 [12]2-8-9   R Price   100/1: 0: 14th: Held up & rdn halfway, sn struggling.   9   36

14 Ran   Time 1m 29.77 (7.17)   Owned: Mr Athos Christodoulou   Trained: Newmarket

5251   2.15 E B F /Potters Leisure Resort Maiden Stakes Div 2 2yo   (D3)
£4193 £1290 £645   7f str   Soft 98   -15 Slow   Stands Side

4851 **PLEA BARGAIN 28** [4] J H M Gosden 2-9-0   J Fortune   2/1 FAV: 31: Led/dsptd lead & al trav well,   **83+**
shkn up & pulled clr from over 1f out, val 7L+: well bckd, op 5/2: confirmed promise of debut: eff at 7f/1m, rtn
to further shld suit: acts on gd & soft grnd, stiff/gall or fair trk: decisive success, potentially useful colt.

5097 **POLISH EAGLE 12** [6] E A L Dunlop 2-9-0   S Sanders   14/1: 02: b c Polish Precedent - Tinashaan   5   75
(Darshaan) Handy, eff to chase wnr over 1f out, sn no impress: imprvd from intro: 60,000gns Jan foal, half-brother
to Pantone, a dual 1m/11f 3yo scorer: dam an 11/12f 3yo wnr: eff at 7f, 1m+ shld suit: handles soft grnd.

5084 **MUNSEF 13** [8] J L Dunlop 2-9-0   R Hills   7/1: 03: b c Zafonic - Mazaya (Sadler's Wells) Hld up,   3   71
late gains, no threat: longer trip & imprvd from intro: Mar foal, dam a 12f 3yo scorer: apprec 1m+.

     VIP 0 [14] Saeed bin Suroor 2-9-0   D Holland   11/2: 4: ch c Dubai Millennium - Danish (Danehill)   1¼   69
Led/dsptd lead 4f, no extra over 1f out: op 7/2: Mar foal, half-brother to a useful 6f juv wnr & a 12f wnr abroad:

dam a 6f juv wnr & subs 9f Gr 1 US scorer: faster grnd could suit.
DIAMOND CIRCLE 0 [11]2-8-9 M Hills 14/1: 5: Slow away & held up, prog halfway, no impress dist. *¾* **63**
ARTURIUS 0 [12]2-9-0 R L Moore 7/1: 6: Dwelt, in tch, no impress fnl 2f, op 9/1. *2½* **64**
5012 **HAYRAAN 17** [7]2-9-0 P Robinson 40/1: 07: Handy, btn over 2f out. *1¼* **62**
5011 **WESTER LODGE 17** [15]2-9-0 S W Kelly 8/1: 028: Chsd ldrs, rdn & btn 2f out: btr 5011. *1* **61**
5182 **AGGRAVATION 8** [13]2-9-0 J F Egan 100/1: 009: In tch, keen, btn over 2f out, turf bow. *3* **57**
5078 **MON PLAISIR 14** [3]2-8-9 J Quinn 100/1: 00: 10th: Keen & prom, no impress fnl 2f, turf bow. *2½* **48**
5199 **WHISPERING DEATH 5** [5]2-9-0 A Culhane 40/1: 000: 11th: Dwelt & sn outpcd. *1* **52**
4217 **COME TO DADDY 60** [2]2-9-0 G Baker 100/1: 050: 12th: Chsd ldrs, no impress fnl 2f, abs, longer trip. *4* **46**
4710 **ROCKYS GIRL 37** [10]2-8-9 M Henry 150/1: 0000: 13th: Dwelt & sn outpcd in rear. *7* **31**
FALLUJAH 0 [1]2-8-9 J Fanning 14/1: 0: 14th: Chsd ldrs, no ch fnl 3f. *20* **3**
14 Ran Time 1m 29.24 (7.94) Owned: Sheikh Mohammed Trained: Manton

5252

2.50 Great Yarmouth And Caister Golf Club Maiden Stakes 2yo (D3)
£3595 £1106 £553 **1m str** **Soft 98** **-20 Slow** Stands Side

VERY WISE 0 [3] W J Haggas 2-9-0 A Culhane 50/1: 1: b c Pursuit of Love - With Care (Warning) **84**
Dwelt & held up, hdwy over 2f out & edged right ins last, rdn & led cl-home: half-brother to a dual 9/11f 3yo wnr & also v useful sprint peformer Forever Phoenix: dam a 7f 3yo wnr: eff at 1m on soft grnd & goes well fresh: shld learn plenty & can rate higher.
5064 **SCRIPTWRITER 15** [19] Saeed bin Suroor 2-9-0 T P Queally 16/1: 52: Chsd ldrs, led & hung left *hd* **83**
over 1f out, swerved left ins last & just hdd cl-home: left debut bhd: eff over longer 1m trip, mid-dist pedigree: acts on soft grnd: win a race: see 5064.
FORGERY 0 [4] G A Butler 2-9-0 R Winston 16/1: 3: ch c Dr Devious - Memory Green (Green Forest) *hd* **82**
Held up, hdwy to chall ins last, just held on line: well clr rem: 130,000gns Apr foal, pedigree success mid-dists will suit, dam a dual 3yo US wnr: eff at 1m, get further: acts on soft grnd: will improve.
PRINCELET 0 [1] M A Jarvis 2-9-0 P Robinson 14/1: 4: b c Desert Prince - Soeur Ti (Kaldoun) *6* **73**
Held up, switched right & kept on fnl 2f, no threat to front trio: E80,000 Mar foal, dam a 7f/1m juv wnr.
QUIZZENE 0 [10]2-9-0 K Darley 33/1: 5: Outpcd, late gains, nvr a factor. *1½* **71**
4852 **BUREAUCRAT 28** [14]2-9-0 J Fortune 9/4 FAV: 46: Prom & led over 2f out, hdd when hmpd over 1f *nk* **70**
out, wandered under press & fdd: bckd, op 11/4: btr 4852 (gd).
DOOIE DANCER 0 [20]2-9-0 W Ryan 20/1: 7: In tch, no impress over 1f out. *hd* **69**
BREAMORE 0 [8]2-9-0 S Sanders 25/1: 8: Held up, eff over 2f out, sn no extra. *3* **65**
SUN AND SHOWERS 0 [15]2-9-0 R Havlin 33/1: 9: Slow away & outpcd, late gains, nvr factor. *shd* **65**
5059 **FANTASTIC LUCK 15** [9]2-9-0 G Carter 100/1: 000: 10th: Pushed along rear & nvr a factor. *3* **61**
SILBER MOND 0 [18]2-9-0 Dane O'Neill 40/1: 0: 11th: Slow away, nvr on terms. *½* **60**
5059 **ONE GOOD THING 15** [2]2-9-0 D Holland 10/1: 050: 12th: Mid-div, rdn & btn 2f out: see 5059. *nk* **59**
4927 **NEFERURA 25** [12]2-8-9 S W Kelly 66/1: 000: 13th: Prom, no impress fnl 2f. *1¾* **52**
5019 **RIGHTFUL RULER 17** [6]2-9-0 M Hills 10/1: 440: 14th: Prom, no impress over 2f out. *1½* **55**
4712 **KERASHAN 37** [7]2-9-0 R L Moore 100/30: 420: 15th: Chsd ldrs, pushed along halfway & btn 2f out. *3* **51**
GOLDEN GATE 0 [16]2-9-0 J Mackay 22/1: 0: 16th: Dwelt & al outpcd in rear. *5* **44**
4997 **NAVAL ATTACHE 18** [13]2-9-0 J P Guillambert(3) 66/1: 00: 17th: Chsd ldrs, btn 2f out. *5* **37**
FIRST FOUGHT 0 [11]2-9-0 J Fanning 33/1: 0: 18th: Chsd ldrs, no impress fnl 3f. *1½* **35**
COLOUR BLIND 0 [17]2-9-0 P Fitzsimons 50/1: 0: 19th: Al outpcd in rear. *3½* **30**
LOVE AND HONOUR 0 [5]2-8-9 N Callan 100/1: 0: 20th: Mid-div, struggling from halfway. *18* **0**
20 Ran Time 1m 44.50 (9.4) Owned: Mr J M Greetham Trained: Newmarket

5253

3.25 Halls Group Nursery Handicap Stakes 2yo 0-85 (D2) **[88]**
£6708 £2064 £1032 **5f43y str** **Soft 98** **-19 Slow** Stands Side

4928 **RUSSIAN ROCKET 25** [2] Mrs C A Dunnett 2-9-5 (79) Hayley Turner(3) 11/2: 5212501: Handy & led over **88**
1f out, rdn out: suited by 5f on firm, soft & polytrack, sharp or fair trk: see 3284 & 2839.
5202 **PIDDIES PRIDE 5** [7] P S McEntee 2-8-6 (66) S W Kelly 4/1: 0405002: Sn pushed along chasing ldrs, *1½* **70**
switched & short of room over 1f out, kept on: not pace of wnr: qck reapp: acts on fast & soft, handles hvy.
5207* **IL PRANZO 4** [3] S Kirk 2-9-1 (7ex) (75) J F Egan 3/1 FAV: 6350413: Handy, onepace for press from *nk* **78**
dist: qck reapp under a pen: acts on polytrack & soft grnd: see 5207.
4770 **HITS ONLY CASH 33** [4] P A Blockley 2-8-3 (63) J Quinn 4/1: 60504: Keen trkg ldrs, briefly outpcd *½* **65**
when of room ins last, switched & kept on cl-home: h'cap bow: closer with a clr run: handles soft grnd.
4725 **ASHARON 36** [6]2-8-10 (70) S Sanders 11/1: 06605: Dwelt, in tch, outpcd over 1f out. *hd* **71**
4981 **PARIS TAPIS 20** [1]2-8-0 (60) F P Ferris(3) 10/1: 0422106: Led 1f, no extra fnl 1f: btr 4129. *¾* **60**
5141 **TALCEN GWYN 10** [8]2-9-7 (81) A Nicholls 10/1: 5041047: Led/dsptd lead till over 1f out: btr 4784 (gd). *3½* **74**
4985 **PIPER LILY 19** [5]2-8-13 (73) D Sweeney 10/1: 516008: Chsd ldrs, btn over 1f out: btr 2241 (gd). *nk* **65**
8 Ran Time 1m 06.20 (6.1) Owned: Mrs Christine Dunnett Trained: Norwich

5254

4.00 Listed Toteexacta Lady Godiva Stakes Fillies & Mares 3yo+ (A1)
£17400 £6600 £3300 **1m6f17y** **Soft 98** **+07 Fast** Inside

4460 **MODESTA 49** [3] H R A Cecil 3-8-5 (95) W Ryan 3/1: 4120651: Chsd ldrs, led over 1f out, rdn & **104**
styd on strongly: nicely bckd, op 4/1: 7 wk abs: eff at 11.5f, now stays 14f well & shld get 2m: handles firm & soft grnd, prob any trk: goes well fresh: tough filly with a progressive profile: see 4460, 2238 & 1725.
CORRINE 48 [10] S E Lilja 5-9-3 M Larsen 25/1: 1102122: gr f Spectrum - La Luna (Lyphard) *1½* **104**
Handy & led 2f out, sn hdd, kept on for press: Norwegian raider, won thrice in native land this term (incl Listed): eff at 12/14f on gd & soft grnd: v useful mare.
4460 **BOWSTRING 49** [6] J H M Gosden 3-8-5 (97) P Robinson 2/1 FAV: 0-122333: Chsd ldrs & led over 3f *1¾* **99**
out till 2f out, no extra ins last: nicely bckd tho' op 2/1: 7 wk abs: ahd of today's wnr latest: see 4460, 4149.
4058 **GOSLAR 69** [8] H Candy 3-8-5 (90) D Sweeney 8/1: 31444: Handy, rdn & no extra over 1f out: op *¾* **98**
13/2: 10 wk abs: prob styd longer 14f trip: handles fast & soft grnd: see 3278, 2368.
4781 **FLING 32** [7]3-8-5 (83) R Winston 10/1: 152245: Dwelt & held up, hung left & not able to chall *2½* **96$**
over 1f out: longer 14f trip may yet suit, not lkd entirely straightforward on occasions: headgear may help.
5028 **LIGHT WIND 17** [12]3-8-5 (85) R L Moore 11/1: 5115636: Handy & led after 3f till over 3f out, clr of rem. *shd* **96$**
4898 **SAMARIA 26** [4]3-8-5 (70) J Quinn 66/1: 042437: Held up, no ch fnl 4f: highly tried: see 3997 (mdn). *14* **84$**

5160* **ALBAVILLA** 9 [2]4-9-0 (70) J Fortune 14/1: 3250318: Led 3f, cl-up till over 3f out: btr 5160 (AW h'cap).	4	80
4892* **SHASTYE** 26 [5]3-8-6 (1ow) (73) R Havlin 20/1: 03419: Dwelt & held up, no ch fnl 4f.	3½	78
4460 **OPERA COMIQUE** 49 [1]3-8-5 t D Holland 11/1: 13-600: 10th: Prom, btn 3f out, 7 wk abs: see 4460.	¾	76
4188* **TRULLITTI** 31 [11]3-8-5 bl (84) K Darley 33/1: 5-35P130: 11th: Held up, hung right after 3f, btn 4f out.	19	60
4920 **MOON SPINNER** 25 [9]7-9-0 J F Egan 300/1: 0000: 12th: Held up, rdn & bhd fnl 3f.	7	53
12 Ran Time 3m 10.50 (12.7) Owned: Mr K Abdulla Trained: Newmarket		

5255   4.35 Weatherbys Insurance Classified Stakes 3yo+ 0-85   (C2)
£6812 £2096 £1048   **1m2f21y**   **Soft 98**   **+01 Fast**   Inside

4227 **OFARABY** 60 [3] M A Jarvis 4-9-5 (88) P Robinson 7/2: 6425031: Chsd ldrs, led ins last, hung left, rdn out: op 9/2: 2 month abs: eff at 9/10f & prob stays a sharp 12f: acts on both AWs, gd & hvy grnd, any trk: goes well fresh: see 964.		95
4293+ **WIGGY SMITH** 58 [4] H Candy 5-9-2 (85) Dane O'Neill 9/2: 5/41-5012: Hmpd start & held up, rdn & styd on from over 1f out, not able to reach wnr: see 4293.	¾	90
4889 **TIP THE DIP** 26 [6] J H M Gosden 4-9-2 T (85) J Fortune 9/2: 2131-203: Chsd ldrs & led over 2f out, rdn/hung left over 1f out & hdd ins last, no extra: fair run in first time t-strap: acts on fast & soft grnd.	1	89
5223* **TIGER TIGER** 4 [8] Jamie Poulton 3-9-3 (83) J F Egan 5/2 FAV: 2004214: Held up, styd on for press fnl 2f, not pace of wnr: qck reapp: see 5223.	shd	95
4463 **SILENT HAWK** 49 [2]3-8-11 vis t (85) T P Queally 16/1: 4104005: Held up, eff over 2f out, onepace.	3	86
5104* **ULTIMATA** 12 [5]4-8-13 (82) R Winston 14/1: 0220016: Prom & led over 3f out till over 2f out, fdd.	3½	80
4931 **BARKING MAD** 25 [7]6-9-2 (84) D Holland 18/1: 6261207: Led till over 3f out, sn btn: btr 4124.	3½	80
4748 **BAYADERE** 35 [12]4-8-13 (85) M Henry 50/1: 312/30-08: Chsd ldrs, btn 3f out: see 4748.	6	71
4931 **DREAM MAGIC** 25 [10]6-9-2 VIS (77) M Halford 25/1: 2333009: Dwelt & held up, hung right & struggling fnl 2f: poor run in visor: see 4609.	nk	73
5128 **KINGS WELCOME** 11 [1]6-9-2 (85) J Fanning 50/1: 2/4210/-60: 10th: Bhd halfway: see 5128 (clmr).	dist	0
10 Ran Time 2m 13.97 (9.77) Owned: Mr T G Warner Trained: Newmarket		

5256   5.10 Eventguard Handicap Stakes 3yo+ 56-70   (E3)
£4317 £1328 £664   **7f str**   **Soft 98**   **-04 Slow**   Stands Side   [84]

5219 **ASK THE CLERK** 4 [9] V Smith 3-9-0 (70) D Holland 6/1 FAV: 4200331: Held up, hdwy when short of room over 1f out, drvn to lead well ins last: bckd, op 15/2: qck reapp: eff at 1m, suited by 6/7f on firm, soft & fibresand, prob any trk: tough & genuine: see 975.		80
4897 **OUTER HEBRIDES** 26 [4] D R Loder 3-9-6 t (76) R L Moore 8/1: 21-00422: Held up, hdwy to lead dist, rdn & hdd well ins last: op 10/1: acts on fast, soft & both AWs: see 4897.	½	84
5010 **MANDARIN SPIRIT** 18 [7] G C H Chung 4-8-12 bl (66) O Urbina 14/1: 5505143: Prom, led over 1f out, sn hdd & no extra ins last: acts on fast, soft & fibresand.	3½	69
4845 **GRANDMA LILY** 29 [10] D Carroll 6-8-5 (59) J Quinn 9/1: 0003034: Chsd ldrs, no extra ins last: new yard: stays 7f, rtn to 5/6f could suit: see 1465 & 85.	2½	58
5130 **SEMENOVSKII** 11 [2]4-9-0 (68) R Ffrench 33/1: 0100005: Rear, late gains, nrst fin: handles firm, soft & polytrack: see 3751 (6f).	shd	67
3870 **MUGEBA** 77 [8]3-8-5 (61) A Kirby(7) 33/1: 5512206: Held up, eff over 2f out, no impress dist: see 3380.	1¾	58
5077 **OH SO ROSIE** 14 [12]4-8-3 p (57) J F Egan 8/1: 0042527: Held up, hdwy trav well, outpcd over 1f out.	½	53
5046 **FEARBY CROSS** 16 [17]8-8-12 bl (66) J Fortune 8/1: 0546158: Held up, hdwy & led stands side group over 2f out, no impress on ldrs towards centre: first home from unfav'd stands side group, prob worth another look.	2½	58+
5144 **NAMROUD** 10 [6]5-9-4 (72) T Hamilton(3) 10/1: 0004069: Chsd ldrs, no impress fnl 2f: btr 4103.	hd	63
4221 **LIZARAZU** 60 [5]5-8-9 (63) A Culhane 33/1: 52-00000: 10th: Held up, nvr a factor, 2 month abs.	3	50
5046 **HAND CHIME** 16 [1]7-8-9 (63) Danielle Deverson(7) 12/1: 0020060: 11th: Held up, rdn & btn 2f out.	2½	46
3872 **WARDEN WARREN** 77 [11]6-9-6 bl (74) Hayley Turner(3) 16/1: 0410020: 12th: Led in centre 5f, abs.	nk	56
3898 **TOPTON** 76 [13]10-9-6 bl (74) R Winston 14/1: 2654050: 13th: Held up stands side & no ch fnl 2f, abs.	3	52
5191 **SPIRITS AWAKENING** 7 [19]5-8-8 (62) F P Ferris(3) 9/1: 4260100: 14th: Prom stands side, btn 2f out.	nk	39
4946 **AFTER THE SHOW** 23 [18]3-8-11 (67) W Ryan 33/1: 0602000: 15th: Struggling stands side halfway.	2½	40
5053 **JOY AND PAIN** 16 [15]3-8-7 (63) T P Queally 40/1: 1623000: 16th: Chsd ldrs stands side 5f.	2½	32
5030* **DR SYNN** 17 [14]3-9-0 (70) M Tebbutt 14/1: 2034010: 17th: Sn rdn prom stands side, btn 3f out.	3	35
4943 **BUZZ BUZZ** 23 [20]3-8-10 (66) S Sanders 33/1: 2040-000: 18th: Prom stands side 4f.	9	19
5036 **FYODOR** 16 [16]3-8-11 (67) S W Kelly 25/1: 6000400: 19th: Led stands side, btn over 2f out: btr 4930.	5	13
5014 **MISTER SWEETS** 17 [3]5-8-10 t (64) M Halford(7) 20/1: 0060000: 20th: Stumbled badly start & al bhd.	1¾	8
20 Ran Time 1m 29.72(7.12) Owned: Mr R J Baines Trained: Newmarket		

Official Going Standard

5257   1.50 Shirley Oaks E B F Maiden Stakes Div 1 Fillies 2yo   (D3)
£5265 £1620 £810   **7f aw rnd**   **Going 30**   **-17 Slow**   Inside

5045 **ROYAL JELLY** 17 [10] J H M Gosden 2-8-11 J Fortune 7/2 JT FAV: 001: b f King's Best - Baked Alaska (Green Desert) Keen trckg ldrs, rdn & chald over 1f out, drvn to lead well ins last: imprvd on this AW bow: Mar foal, half-sister to a multiple 6/7f wnr, dam a 6f juv wnr: eff over a sharp 7f, 1m shld suit: acts on polytrack & a sharp trk: going the right way.		80a
5106 **ARCHEOLOGY** 13 [5] Saeed bin Suroor 2-8-11 E Ahern 7/2 JT FAV: 502: b f Seeking The Gold - Caress (Storm Cat) Handy & led halfway, shaken up & hdd well ins last: clr of rem: eff at 6/7f, handles fast grnd & polytrack: return to form, noticeably less vigorous ride than the wnr: can find a race: see 4918.	¾	78a
5045 **MAKE IT SNAPPY** 17 [6] P W Harris 2-8-11 T Quinn 20/1: 003: b f Mujadil - Snap Crackle Pop (Statoblest) Trckd ldrs, outpcd over 2f out, shaken up & styd on ins last, no threat: AW bow: 24,000gns Mar foal, half-sister to 5/6f juv wnrs, dam a 5f juv wnr: prob handles polytrack.	5	68a
3909 **HASHIMA** 76 [14] C E Brittain 2-8-11 M Hills 4/1: 34: Sn handy, no impress over 1f out: 11 wk abs.	nk	67a
5091 **TANGIBLE** 13 [1]2-8-11 S Sanders 7/1: 05: Mid-div, not pace of front pair fnl 2f: need further.	2	63a

4723 **SHADES OF GREEN 37** [7]2-8-11 J F Egan 16/1: 06: Towards further, late gains, wants further. ¾ **62a**
4896 **GIRLSWEEKEND 27** [2]2-8-11 I Mongan 50/1: 07: Led till halfway, btn over 1f out. ¾ **61a**
5081 **PRIDE OF POONA 15** [9]2-8-11 M Henry 33/1: 08: Keen, chsd ldrs, btn 2f out. *6* **49a**
XAARA DOON 0 [12]2-8-11 S Righton 25/1: 9: Dwelt & bhd, mod late prog. *hd* **48a**
2676 **JUST BEWARE 127** [4]2-8-11 N Chalmers(3) 100/1: 000: 10th: Dwelt & al towards rear, 4 mth abs. *hd* **47a**
BELLA MIRANDA 0 [11]2-8-11 T P Queally 10/1: 0: 11th: Dwelt, al bhd. ¾ **46a**
4941 **EFORETTA 24** [8]2-8-11 Frances Pickard(7) 100/1: 000: 12th: Slow into stride & al rear. *3½* **39a**
1161 **GEORGIE BELLE 197** [13]2-8-11 C Catlin 10/1: 330: 13th: Keen, sn cl-up, wknd qckly & hung dist. ¾ **38a**
5078 **LIVVIES LADY 15** [3]2-8-11 Dane O'Neill 40/1: 00: 14th: Slow away, sn mid-div, struggling halfway. *12* **17a**
14 Ran Time 1m 26.10 (3.3) Owned: Cliveden Stud Trained: Manton

5258

2.20 Shirley Oaks E B F Maiden Stakes Div 2 Fillies 2yo (D3)
£5265 £1620 £810 **7f aw rnd** **Going 30** **-33 Slow** Inside

4611 **ALLIED CAUSE 43** [4] L M Cumani 2-8-11 N Mackay 5/1: 051: ch f Giant's Causeway - Alligram (Alysheba) Led 1f, trkd ldrs, led again ins last, rdn out: 6 wk abs, AW bow: Feb foal, half-sister to a high-class multiple 1m/10f 3yo scorer: dam unplcd: eff at 7f, shld get 1m+: handles polytrack & gd grnd, sharp/easy trk. **77a**
4450 **CELTIQUE 51** [11] Sir Michael Stoute 2-8-11 R Winston 2/1 FAV: 232: Sn handy, rdn & outpcd over 1f out, rallied well ins last, just held: nicely bckd tho' op 7/4: 7 wk abs: AW bow: handles fast, gd & polytrack. *nk* **76a**
4782 **ORLAR 33** [1] J A Osborne 2-8-11 S W Kelly 11/1: 503: Mid-div trav well, briefly short of room over 1f out, styd on well cl-home, nrst fin: AW bow: handles fast grnd & polytrack: eff at 7f, crying out for 1m. *nk* **75a**
4711 **SIGN OF LUCK 38** [6] C E Brittain 2-8-11 M Hills 40/1: 04: ch f Daylami - Ascot Cyclone (Rahy) Rear, switched wide & styd on well fnl 1f, nrst fin: AW bow: Apr foal, half-sister to juv wnrs btwn 5/7f, dam a 6f juv wnr: eff over a sharp 7f, 1m looks sure to suit: handles polytrack: progressing. *shd* **75a**
4970 **ANGEL RAYS 22** [13]2-8-11 D Holland 4/1: 45: Keen & led after 1f, hdd ins last & no extra: op 7/2. *1* **73a**
IRREVERSIBLE 0 [3]2-8-11 J Fortune 10/1: 6: Dwelt, held up in tch, kept on fnl 2f, not able to chall. *shd* **73a**
ELLE NINO 0 [7]2-8-11 S Drowne 12/1: 7: Mid-div, outpcd fnl 2f. ¾ **72a**
5084 **PETITE SPECTRE 14** [8]2-8-11 Dane O'Neill 50/1: 08: Mid-div wide, no impress over 1f out. *1¼* **69a**
ARRIVATO 0 [9]2-8-11 Martin Dwyer 28/1: 9: V slow away & rear, short of room over 1f out, no impress: lost ch start, leave this debut bhd. *nk* **68a**
4876 **FLAUNT N FLIRT 28** [2]2-8-11 T Quinn 50/1: 00: 10th: Mid-div, no impress over 1f out. *nk* **67a**
5076 **OBLIQUE 15** [12]2-8-11 S Sanders 50/1: 00: 11th: Rear, eff wide halfway, sn no impress. ½ **66a**
SUTURIA 0 [14]2-8-11 E Ahern 25/1: 0: 12th: Keen & chsd ldr 5f out till over 1f out, sn btn. *4* **58a**
4035 **Creme De La Creme 71** [5]2-8-11 T P Queally 14/1:0 **Rosablanca 0** [10]2-8-11 A Culhane 50/1:0
14 Ran Time 1m 27.19 (4.39) Owned: Helena Springfield Ltd Trained: Newmarket

5259

2.50 Nicholas Hall E B F Maiden Stakes Div 1 Colts & Geldings 2yo (D3)
£5148 £1584 £792 **7f aw rnd** **Going 30** **-14 Slow** Inside

5200 **DANIEL THOMAS 6** [3] Mrs A J Perrett 2-8-11 (92) A Culhane 4/6 FAV: 22321: Sn cl-up & led 2f out, in command fnl 1f, hand riding: nicley bckd at odds-on, qck reapp: AW bow: eff at 6/7f on fast, hvy & polytrack, sharp/undul or stiff trk: useful & consistent, deserved this: see 5200, 4028 & 2766. **92a**
5084 **CHIEF EXEC 14** [4] C A Cyzer 2-8-11 D Sweeney 20/1: 02: br g Zafonic - Shot At Love (Last Tycoon) Led early, sn trkd ldrs, eff to chase wnr fnl 1f, kept on but al held: rest well covered: left debut bhd: Feb foal, half-brother to a plcd 6/7f performer, also a 7f 2/3yo scorer: dam a 1m 3yo wnr: eff at 7f on polytrack. *2½* **85a**
5097 **LIBERTY RUN 13** [2] N A Callaghan 2-8-11 J F Egan 7/2: 03: ch c Grand Lodge - Bathe In Light (Sunshine Forever) Rdn mid-div, styd on for press fnl 2f, nvr threatened front pair: bckd, op 7/1: imprvd from soft grnd debut: 160,000gns Mar foal, dam a multiple 12/14f 4yo wnr: sure to apprec 1m+. *2½* **80a**
5048 **DART ALONG 17** [9] R Hannon 2-8-11 (78) Dane O'Neill 15/2: 5544: Trkd ldrs wide, no extra fnl 1f. *2* **76a**
5177 **ANNIBALE CARO 9** [10]2-8-11 S Sanders 20/1: 05: Pushed along rear, late gains, shld improve. *2½* **71a**
4885 **EXPEDITIOUS 27** [5]2-8-11 BL t E Ahern 12/1: 06: Led/dsptd lead 5f, sn wknd: blnks. *5* **61a**
READY TEDDY GO 0 [8]2-8-11 A Nicholls 66/1: 7: Dwelt & al towards rear, little hdwy. *6* **49a**
5078 **HUGO THE BOSS 15** [7]2-8-11 Martin Dwyer 66/1: 08: Chsd ldrs 4f. *1¾* **46a**
CANADIAN DANEHILL 0 [6]2-8-11 M Henry 33/1: 9: Slow away & al rear. ½ **45a**
4896 **CHIRACAHUA 27** [1]2-8-11 R Winston 33/1: 000: 10th: Mid-div, struggling & eased over 1f out. *11* **23a**
10 Ran Time 1m 25.89 (3.09) Owned: Mr J H Richmond-Watson Trained: Pulborough

5260

3.20 Eleanor Harrington Conditions Stakes 2yo (C2)
£4872 £1848 £924 **5f aw rnd** **Going 30** **-08 Slow** Inside

5124 **BOND CITY 12** [5] B Smart 2-9-5 (94) F Lynch 11/4: 5250121: Trkd ldr, qcknd to lead over 1f out, drvn out: op 7/2: eff at 5f on firm, gd & polytrack, sharp or stiff trk: tough gelding with a useful turn of foot. **103a**
4882 **CYCLICAL 28** [2] G A Butler 2-9-2 (93) J Fortune 7/4: 1132: Trkd ldrs, outpcd over 1f out, rallied well for press ins last, nrst fin: eff at 5f, crying out for stiffer trk &/or 6f: acts on fast, gd/soft & polytrack. *1¼* **95a**
4717* **SHARPLAW STAR 37** [4] W J Haggas 2-9-2 (100) M Hills 6/4 FAV: 1313: Trkd ldrs, not pace of front pair from dist: nicely bckd but btr 4717, 2490. *3½* **84a**
CASHEL HOUSE 46 [3] D Loughnane 2-8-11 A Culhane 25/1: 23054: b c Bishop of Cashel - Forest Treasure (Green Forest) Led & qcknd over 2f out, hdd & no extra over 1f out: 6 wk abs, Irish raider: unplcd in mdn & cond events earlier: eff at 5f, handles firm, gd & polytrack. *shd* **79a**
4843 **SNOWDRIFT 30** [6]2-8-6 BL S W Kelly 50/1: 05: b f Desert Prince - Snowing (Tate Gallery) Dwelt, rear, no impress over 1f out: tried blnks, highly tried after debut: 38,000gns Apr foal, half-sister to smart sprinter The Trader: dam a dual 5f wnr. *6* **58a**
5 Ran Time 59.70 (1.9) Owned: Mr R C Bond Trained: Thirsk

LINGFIELD Polytrack THURSDAY 28.10.04 Lefthand, V Sharp Track

5261 3.50 **Barclaycard Business Handicap Stakes 3yo+ 56-70 (E3)** **[84]**
£3515 £1082 £541 **1m4f aw** **Going 30** **-05 Slow** Inside

4973* **MITH HILL 22** [13] E A L Dunlop 3-9-0 (70) E Ahern 5/2 FAV: 0111: Trkd ldrs, rdn & led over 1f out, sn asserted, decisively: nicely bckd: completed hat-trick: eff at 10f, imprvd last twice at 12f, get further: acts on gd/soft grnd, loves polytrack & Lingfield: lightly rcd & progressive, keep on side: see 4973 & 3855. **81a+**
5160 **DOVEDON HERO 10** [2] P J McBride 4-9-7 bl (70) S Sanders 11/2: 2034242: Mid-div, hdwy to chase ldrs ins last, al held: on a long losing run but shown enough to find similar: acts on firm, gd & polytrack. *2½* **74a**
674 **GINGKO 253** [7] P R Webber 7-9-5 (68) Dane O'Neill 25/1: 066-1503: Mid-div wide, eff to chall when wide on bend 2f out, onepace for press ins last: 5 mth jumps abs (modest): likes this trk, can find a race. *¾* **71a**
4986 **LEWIS ISLAND 20** [12] B Ellison 5-9-7 (70) J F Egan 16/1: 6630/-004: Slow away & rear, styd on well from over 1f out, nrst fin: lost winning ch at start but caught the eye late on: acts on fast, soft & polytrack: nicely h'capped, shld be noted for similar with a level break: see 4656. *½* **72a+**
5079 **BLACKMAIL 15** [11]6-9-4 bl (67) S Carson 25/1: 000-0005: b g Twining - Black Penny (Private Account) Mid-div, styd on onepace for press: '03 h'cap scorer, turf h'cap unplcd (rtd 61): unplcd in '02 (N Hamilton, rtd 83a & 73): stays 12f, suited by 10f: acts on polytrack & gd/soft grnd: eff in blnks, tried t-strap & visor. 2 Mar'03 Ling 10 ap 80a-79 D: 1 Feb'03 Ling 10 ap 80a-74 E: *nk* **68a**
5025 **MADIBA 18** [9]5-9-0 (63) R Winston 14/1: 0P52626: Keen in rear, kept on for press, not pace to chall: 14f+ poss ideal: see 5025 & 4405. *shd* **64a**
4875 **CHAMPAGNE SHADOW 28** [10]3-9-0 bl (70) J Fortune 10/1: 2023207: Handy, wknd dist: btr 4314. *½* **70a**
3144 **EASTBOROUGH 109** [3]5-9-2 (65) J Fanning 16/1: 4662328: Held up, keeping on when short of room ins last, nvr dngrs: closer with a clr run: kind ride, can impr: 4 mth abs: see 978, 714 & 480. *½* **64a+**
4856 **AONINCH 29** [8]4-8-11 (60) S Whitworth 14/1: 2626059: Bhd, late prog, nvr a threat. *¾* **58a**
5024 **WESTERN 18** [5]4-9-2 p (65) T Quinn 12/1: 0000000: 10th: Dwelt, rear/wide, switched & mod prog. *shd* **63a**
2523 **ATLANTIC CITY 133** [16]3-8-12 e (68) N Callan 33/1: 622-250: 11th: Handy trav well, wknd fnl 1f: eye-shield: abs: new yard. *¾* **65a**
4986 **RASID 20** [14]6-9-11 (74) D Holland 16/1: 5310000: 12th: Led after 1f till over 1f out, fdd: 10f prob ideal. *½* **70a**
5160 **REGAL GALLERY 10** [1]6-9-7 (70) Paul Eddery 7/1: 1342460: 13th: Chsd ldrs, btn/short of room ins last. *1¼* **64a**
4668 **SCALLOWAY 40** [15]4-9-2 (65) V Slattery 40/1: 04/144-00: 14th: b g Marju - Zany (Junius) Prom, wknd fnl 3f: jumps fit, June '04 mdn hdles scorer (rtd 108h, 2m/2m1f, fast & gd): '03 h'cap wnr for J Osborne: eff at 10f on firm & fast grnd, without blnks: sharp or stiff trk. *7* **49a**
1 Jun'03 Bath 10.2 fm 67-65 E: 2 Jun'02 Sout 6 g/f 74- D:
4973 **Sewmore Character 22** [6]4-9-4 (67) D Sweeney 20/1:0 4892 **Red Rackham 27** [4]4-9-0 (63) M Tebbutt 20/1:0
16 Ran Time 2m 33.43 (4.23) Owned: Mr Mohammed Jaber Trained: Newmarket

5262 4.20 **Ladbrokes Com Stakes Handicap 3yo+ 86-100 (C1)** **[110]**
£13520 £4160 £2080 **7f aw rnd** **Going 30** **+10 Fast** Inside

4855+**GOODENOUGH MOVER 29** [10] J S King 8-8-4 (86) Hayley Turner(3) 20/1: 1520011: Cl-up wide, rdn & led over 1f out, drvn out: fast time: op 25/1: eff at 6/7f, stays 1m: acts on firm, soft & polytrack: eff up with/forcing the pace: v tough & useful, overcame awkward passage, keep on side: see 4855. **95a+**
4773+**KHABFAIR 34** [8] Mrs A J Perrett 3-9-1 (99) Dane O'Neill 7/1: 4136012: Mid-div, styd on well for press cl-home, just denied: stays a sharp 7f: see 4773. *hd* **107a**
4891 **GREENSLADES 27** [3] P J Makin 5-8-8 (90) J Quinn 15/2: 3066053: Trkd ldrs inner trav well, ev ch ins last, just held cl-home: stays 7f, all wins at 6f: acts on firm, soft & polytrack: see 1151. *nk* **97a**
4884 **DAME DE NOCHE 28** [7] J G Given 4-8-4 (86) E Ahern 14/1: 5300144: Sn cl-up, no extra fnl 1f: acts on firm, gd & polytrack: see 4498. *1¼* **90a**
3872 **LYGETON LAD 78** [4]6-9-6 t (102) S Drowne 8/1: 0000465: Trkd ldrs, styd on for press: abs: see 1043. *nk* **105a**
5101 **MARSHMAN 13** [13]5-8-7 (89) P Robinson 7/1: 0335156: Rear, eff wide, kept on, nrst fin: see 5000. *nk* **91a**
5101 **ETTRICK WATER 13** [11]5-9-4 vis (100) N Mackay 6/1 FAV: 1101647: Chsd ldrs, onepace dist: op 8/1. *nk* **101a**
5090 **FRUIT OF GLORY 14** [1]5-8-10 (92) D Holland 16/1: 2254038: Trkd ldrs trav well, no extra dist: 5/6f ideal. *¾* **91a**
4800 **UHOOMAGOO 33** [9]6-8-4 (1oh)bl (85) P Hanagan 10/1: 0030009: Pushed along rear, only mod prog. *shd* **85a**
4879 **HIGH REACH 28** [5]4-8-12 (94) G Carter 10/1: 6303000: 10th: Led till over 1f out, fdd: btr 3622 (6f). *½* **92a**
4471} **LITTLE GOOD BAY 397** [2]4-9-2 vis (98) J Fortune 8/1: 431316-0: 11th: b c Danehill - Brave Kris (Kris) Slow away & rear, btn over 1f out: reapp: '03 dual h'cap scorer, AW mdn wnr late '02: eff at 7f/1m on firm, gd & polytrack, sharp or stiff trk, loves Chester: eff in a visor. *1¼* **93a**
1 Aug'03 Ches 7.0 gd 100-92 B: 1 Jun'03 Ches 7.0 g/f 92-84 C: 2 Apr'03 Wind 8.3 g/f 86-81 D: 1 Nov'02 Ling 8 ap 84a- D: 2 Oct'02 Ling 7 ap 75a- D:
3942 **TE QUIERO GB 75** [6]6-9-4 e t (100) A Culhane 40/1: 0000000: 12th: Mid-div, btn 2f out, abs, fibresand. *shd* **95a**
4508 **Massey 47** [12]8-8-13 (95) P Makin(5) 50/1:0 4573 **Hanzano 9** [14]6-9-4 (100) C Catlin 33/1:0
14 Ran Time 1m 24.19 (1.39) Owned: D Goodenough Removals & Transport Trained: Swindon

5263 4.50 **Formark Scaffolding Classified Stakes 3yo+ 0-60 (F3)**
£3543 £1090 £545 **7f aw rnd** **Going 30** **-01 Slow** Inside

5022 **NEARLY A FOOL 18** [14] G G Margarson 6-9-0 vis (60) N Pollard 7/1: 3405051: Rear, hdwy wide 3f out, styd on for press to lead cl-home, going away: eff at 6/7f on firm, soft & both AWs, loves Lingfield: see 1049. **73a**
5053 **ROMAN QUINTET 17** [8] D W P Arbuthnot 4-9-0 (60) T Quinn 3/1 FAV: 0032222: Led, hdd cl-home: ran well with forcing tactics applied, stays 7f well: deserves to find a race: see 5053, 4946 & 231. *1¼* **69a**
4740 **TORQUEMADA 36** [12] W Jarvis 3-8-12 (60) P Doe 7/2: 0300153: Mid-div, rdn & hdwy to chall dist, wknd. *1½* **66a**
5053 **I WISH 17** [5] M Madgwick 6-8-11 (59) G Baker 8/1: 5302264: Keen in mid-div, kept on fnl 2f, no threat. *1* **61a**
4845 **JAZZY MILLENNIUM 30** [6]7-9-0 bl (59) S Drowne 12/1: 0412205: Trkd ldrs, onepace dist: see 4168. *1* **62a**
5062 **KABEER 16** [7]6-9-0 T (59) D R McCabe 16/1: 3005606: Rear, switched & late gains, nrst fin: t-strap. *shd* **62a**
5155 **LEGAL SET 10** [13]8-9-0 t (60) T P Queally 12/1: 4005257: Chsd ldrs, no extra bef dist: btr 5130. *1* **60a**
4977 **LORD OF THE SEA 22** [9]3-8-12 BL (59) J F Egan 14/1: 0406008: Rear, mod hdwy in blnks. *1* **58a**
5178 **MEGABOND 9** [11]3-8-12 VIS (60) F Lynch 50/1: 4001059: Rear & wide, no impress: visor: see 4504. *2* **54a**
5183 **WALL STREET RUNNER 9** [3]3-8-9 (59) D Fox(5) 25/1: 6520000: 10th: Prom, wknd 2f out. *nk* **50a**
4984 **CHAIRMAN BOBBY 21** [4]6-9-0 (60) D Holland 10/1: 0000000: 11th: Keen in mid-div, btn over 1f out, *2* **49a**

LINGFIELD **Polytrack THURSDAY 28.10.04 Lefthand, V Sharp Track**

new stable: prefer 5/6f: see 1120.
4835 **SUPERFLING 31** [2]3-8-12 (60) Dane O'Neill 33/1: 0400: 12th: Al bhd & no ch fnl 2f: btr 4413. *5* **40a**
5039 **EMSAM BALLOU 17** [1]3-8-9 (60) N Callan 20/1: 333000: 13th: Trkd ldrs, btn/hmpd over 2f out. *½* **36a**
5077 **DARLING RIVER 15** [10]5-8-11 (58) J Mackay 25/1: 43/000-00: 14th: Chsd ldr till 2f out, sn wknd. *3* **30a**
14 Ran Time 1m 24.95 (2.15) Owned: Mr J Burns Trained: Newmarket

5264 **5.20 Nicholas Hall E B F Maiden Stakes Div 2 Colts & Geldings 2yo (D3)**
£5135 £1580 £790 **7f aw rnd** **Going 30** **-02 Slow** Inside

5078 **KINGS MAJESTY 15** [7] Sir Michael Stoute 2-8-11 D Holland 13/8 FAV: 021: Trkd ldrs trav well, briefly short of room over 1f out, rdn to lead well ins last, styd on strongly: well bckd, confirmed recent promise: eff at 7f, 1m shld suit: acts on polytrack & sharp trk: going the right way, more to come at 1m: see 5078. **86a**
DUBAI DREAMER 0 [5] Saeed bin Suroor 2-8-11 E Ahern 7/2: 2: gr c Stephen Got Even - Blacktie Bid (Black Tie Affair) Trkd ldrs, hdwy wide to lead over 1f out, hdd ins last & not pace of wnr: bckd, op 5/1: Mar foal, half-brother to a US sprint wnr, also a UW 2yo scorer: dam a US juv wnr: eff at 7f, 1m may suit: acts on polytrack & a sharp trk: most promising intro, can find a race. *1½* **82a**
MACAULAY 0 [6] R Charlton 2-8-11 S Drowne 33/1: 3: Rear, styd on well from over 1f out, nrst fin: op 20/1: Feb foal, 60,000gns 2yo: dam a 7f 3yo wnr & well related: eff at 7f, 1m shld suit: acts on polytrack & a sharp trk: most encouraging start, looks sure to win races. *hd* **81a**
4970 **OPTIMUS 22** [11] G A Butler 2-8-11 J Fortune 2/1: 524: Sn handy wide & dsptd lead over 1f out, rdn & no extra ins last: clr of rem & not btn far: suffered an awkward passage today, can find a race: see 4970. *½* **80a**
DON PASQUALE 0 [3]2-8-11 S Sanders 25/1: 5: Held up in tch, not pace of front quartet fnl 2f. *5* **71a**
CROON 0 [2]2-8-11 N Mackay 33/1: 6: Rear, no impress fnl 2f. *2½* **66a**
5002 **ROYAL SAILOR 19** [10]2-8-11 S W Kelly 40/1: 007: Cl-up till 2f out, sn btn. *1¼* **63a**
5081 **VAGUE STAR 15** [8]2-8-11 (74) N Day 12/1: 0338: Led till over 1f out, fdd, op 10/1. *1¼* **60a**
5118 **PRECIOUS SAMMI 12** [4]2-8-11 (60) N Callan 66/1: 0509: Keen & prom, wknd over 2f out. *7* **48a**
FOLLOW THE GAME 0 [1]2-8-11 T Quinn 20/1: 0: 10th: V slow away, al well bhd. *hd* **47a**
10 Ran Time 1m 25.04(2.24) Owned: Mr Saeed Suhail Trained: Newmarket

NEWMARKET **FRIDAY 29.10.04 Righthand, Stiff, Galloping Track**

Official Going Soft

5265 **1.00 E B F George Colling Maiden Stakes Div 1 2yo (D3)**
£4755 £1463 £732 **6f str** **Soft 91** **-10 Slow** Far Side

5084 **TUCKER 15** [3] D R C Elsworth 2-9-0 T Quinn 5/2 FAV: 01: b c Inchinor - Tender Moment (Caerleon) Held up, hdwy to lead dist, hung left, rdn out: Apr foal, half-brother to numerous wnrs btwn 6/9f: dam a multiple 7f wnr: eff at 6f on soft grnd, likes a stiff/gall trk: learnt plenty from intro & can rate higher. **86**
5055 **LAKE CHINI 17** [4] M A Jarvis 2-9-0 P Robinson 9/1: 002: b c Raise A Grand - Where's The Money (Lochnager) Chsd ldrs, edged right & kept on: 70,000gns Mar foal, half-brother to wnrs at 5/7f: dam a dual 5f juv wnr: eff at 6f, tried 7f, shld suit: handles soft grnd & a stiff/gall trk: qual for h'caps. *1¾* **80**
4896 **BOLODENKA 28** [6] W J Musson 2-9-0 C Catlin 7/2: 023: Trkd ldrs, rdn & kept on onepace fnl 1f: nicely bckd: handles polytrack & soft grnd: see 4896. *1¼* **77**
JESSIAUME [1] H Candy 2-8-9 Dane O'Neill 14/1: 4: gr f Mister Baileys - Jucinda (Midyan) In tch, edged right & kept on onepace fnl 1f: Mar foal, half-sister to a dual 6f juv wnr & a dual 1m 3yo scorer: dam a stayer: eff at 6f, shld get further: handles soft, could apprec a faster surface. *1* **70**
4752 **GRAND SHOW 36** [7]2-9-0 Martin Dwyer 7/1: 45: Cl-up 4f, no extra ins last: not btn far, prob handles soft grnd: rest well covered: see 4752. *hd* **74**
4369 **DIAMOND JOSH 137** [9]2-9-0 Lisa Jones 8/1: 36: Led 4f, btn dist, 4 mth abs. *3½* **67**
HELEN HOUSE [2]2-8-9 N Callan 40/1: 7: Slow away, in tch till over 1f out. *1¼* **59**
4191 **LOVE ME TENDER 63** [10]2-8-9 W Ryan 13/2: 058: Chsd ldrs, no impress fnl 2f: op 5/1, abs. *2* **55**
4723 **CUP OF LOVE 38** [8]2-8-9 S Sanders 40/1: 009: Held up, rdn & btn 2f out. *nk* **54**
BINTY [11]2-8-9 L Keniry(3) 25/1: 0: 10th: Slow away & al towards rear. *1¾* **51**
CARA SPOSA [5]2-9-0 F Norton 40/1: 0: 11th: Slow away, sn struggling. *8* **40**
11 Ran Time 1m 16.88 (6.08) Owned: Mr Ray Richards Trained: Whitsbury

5266 **1.30 E B F George Colling Maiden Stakes Div 2 2yo (D3)**
£4745 £1460 £730 **6f str** **Soft 91** **-23 Slow** Far Side

MAGGIE JORDAN [5] B J Meehan 2-8-9 J Fortune 7/2: 1: b f Fusaichi Pegasus - Pharapache (Lyphard) Mid-div, hdwy to lead ins last, hung left but sn asserted, styd on strongly: nicely bckd: $120,000 Mar foal, half-sister to a high-class 7/9f US performer: dam a mid-dist French wnr: eff at 6f, shld stay further: acts on soft grnd & a stiff/gall trk: goes well fresh: well regarded, potentially useful. **89**
4941 **PUYA 25** [4] H Candy 2-8-9 Dane O'Neill 5/2: 22: Al handy & rdn/narrow lead over 1f out, edged left & hdd ins last, not pace of wnr: nicely bckd: acts on soft & gd/soft grnd: see 4941. *2* **82**
TOPATOO [1] M H Tompkins 2-8-9 P Robinson 50/1: 3: ch f Bahamian Bounty - Topatori (Topanoora) Slow away & rear, hdwy halfway, styd on under hand riding fnl 1f, no threat: Apr foal, half-sister to a 1m 3yo scorer: dam a 7/10f wnr: eff at 6f, shld get further: handles soft grnd: lost winning ch start but caught the eye late on, expect improvement. *3* **76+**
SOUND BREEZE [2] M Johnston 2-9-0 J Fanning 12/1: 4: ch c Giant's Causeway - Madame Est Sortie (Longleat) Sn prom, rdn & no extra dist: op 14/1: Mar foal, 54,000gns 2yo: half-sister to a high-class 1m/10f scorer: dam a multiple wnr abroad: prob handles soft grnd: ran well for a long way & a likely improver. *1¾* **78**
4941 **GUILDENSTERN 25** [9]2-9-0 R Hughes 12/1: 045: Chsd ldrs, no extra & hung left ins last: op 10/1. *4* **70**
4637 **ORANMORE CASTLE 42** [7]2-9-0 M Hills 6/4 FAV: 26: Led 4f, wknd ins last: btr 4637 (gd). *shd* **70**
QUATRE SAISONS [8]2-9-0 P Fitzsimons 66/1: 7: Slow away & al bhd. *5* **60**
5182 **ELMS SCHOOLBOY 10** [3]2-9-0 L Fletcher(3) 66/1: 0008: Cl-up 2f, struggling from halfway. *nk* **59**
TITO GOFIRST [6]2-9-0 J Quinn 40/1: 9: Dwelt & held up, nvr a factor. *½* **58**
5045 **FANTASTIC NIGHT 18** [10]2-8-9 K Darley 100/1: 00: 10th: Held up, struggling fnl 2f. *11* **32**

10 Ran   Time 1m 17.61 (6.81)   Owned: Mr Andy J Smith   Trained: Upper Lambourn

5267
2.05 Listed E B F Bosra Sham Stakes Fillies 2yo (A1)
£17400 £6600 £3300   **6f str**   **Soft 91**   -04 Slow   Far Side

4928 **BAHIA BREEZE 27** [2] R Guest 2-8-8 (86) C Catlin 11/1: 4101: Held up in tch, styd on for press to   **97**
lead well ins last: op 9/1: eff at 6f on fast & soft grnd, sharp/undul or stiff trk: useful filly: see 4369.
4264 **NANABANANA 61** [8] Mme C Head Maarek 2-8-8 K Darley 4/5 FAV: 421222: Trkd ldrs, rdn to chall ins   hd   **96**
last, just denied: hvly bckd, 2 mth abs: French raider: eff at 6/7f: see 4264 (Gr 3).
4563 **SIENA GOLD 51** [1] B J Meehan 2-8-8 (93) J Fortune 11/1: 1010403: Cl-up rang well, led dist,   ¾   **95**
edged left & hdd well ins last: 7 wk abs: stays a stiff 6f, acts on fast & hvy: tough, held form well.
4914 **ALL FOR LAURA 27** [6] D R Loder 2-8-8 (95) S Sanders 17/2: 415504: Chsd ldrs, onepace for press   1¾   **92**
fnl 2f: op 7/1: handles fast & soft grnd: see 4332, 3956 & 3576 (5f).
5154* **DOITFORREEL 11** [3]2-8-8 (68) W Supple 50/1: 00315: In tch, eff 2f out, no extra dist: offic rtd   2   **88$**
68, up in grade, fine eff but treat rating with caution: handles fast & soft grnd: see 5154.
5132 **BUNDITTEN 13** [9]2-8-8 (90) J F Egan 33/1: 1344006: Trkd ldrs & keen, hmpd & lost place over 1f   1   **86**
out: sn btn: too free early stages, likes to dominate & a return to 5f shld suit: see 2490, 2094 & 882.
5141 **ALEXIA ROSE 12** [5]2-8-8 (78) J Fanning 25/1: 0432127: Led 4f, btn dist: btr 5141 & 4769.   2½   **81**
5222* **BIBURY FLYER 6** [7]2-8-11 (94) E Ahern 4/1: 2451418: Chsd ldrs, eff over 1f out, sn no extra &   nk   **83**
position accepted when short of room ins last: qck reapp, prev with M Channon: been v busy this term: btr 5222.
8 Ran   Time 1m 16.41 (5.61)   Owned: Mr F Nowell   Trained: Newmarket

5268
2.40 Tnt Express E B F Handicap Stakes Fillies & Mares 3yo+ 71-85 (D2)
£8381 £3179 £1590   **1m4f**   **Soft 91**   -07 Slow   Centre   [92]

5015* **INTO THE SHADOWS 19** [5] K G Reveley 4-8-8 (72) T Eaves(3) 4/1: 33411: Held up, smooth hdwy over   **78**
2f out & led ins last, drvn out: nicely bckd, op 5/1: eff at 1m, suited by 10/12f & may get further: acts on fast
& soft grnd, lightly rcd filly, open to further improvement: see 5015.
5037 **REEM ONE 18** [6] M A Jarvis 3-8-4 (75) P Robinson 15/8 FAV: 122: Trkd ldrs, led 3f out, rdn/edged   ½   **79**
left under press & hdd ins last, kept on: stays 12f: lightly rcd & can win again: see 5037.
1382 **MISS LANGKAWI 186** [3] G Wragg 3-8-0 (71) F Norton 12/1: 31-003: gr f Daylami - Miss Amanpuri   nk   **74**
(Alzao) Led 1f, remained handy till outpcd over 2f out, rallied ins last: 6 mth abs: lightly rcd in '03, mdn wnr:
wng form at 6f, clearly stays a stiff 12f: acts on gd & soft, stiff or sharp trk: sharper next time.
1 Nov'03 Donc 6 gd 74- D:
4849 **BIG BERTHA 31** [8] John Berry 6-8-5 (3oh) (66) J F Egan 16/1: 23-42004: Rear, hdwy over 3f out &   hd   **71**
rdn to chall dist, no extra well ins last: op 25/1: gd run, spot on now for an AW campaign: see 424 & 147.
4547+ **BATIK 46** [2]3-8-6 (77) N Mackay 5/2: 315: In tch, outpcd over 2f out, kept on ins last, no   ¾   **78**
threat: well bckd, 6 wk abs & h'cap peep: stays 12f on gd & soft, further may suit: see 4547.
4749 **GOODWOOD FINESSE 37** [7]3-8-3 (74) J Quinn 8/1: 55-15636: Trkd ldrs & led over 3f out, sn hdd,   ½   **74**
outpcd fnl 2f: only btn around 2L in a tight fin: prob stays 12f & handles fast & soft grnd: see 4749 & 2536.
5135 **KALUANA COURT 13** [1]8-8-5 (5oh) (64) R Thomas(3) 25/1: 410-0007: Led after 1f till 3f out, sn btn.   dist0
7 Ran   Time 2m 40.54 (11.74)   Owned: Mr R C Mayall   Trained: Saltburn

5269
3.15 Listed James Seymour Stakes 3yo+ (A1)
£17400 £6600 £3300   **1m2f str**   **Soft 91**   -09 Slow   Far Side

4916* **SPANISH DON 27** [1] D R C Elsworth 6-9-0 (100) L Keniry 4/1: 5115011: Cl-up & led over 7f out,   **109**
strongly pressed fnl 2f, edged left, drvn & held on gamely: nicely bckd: suited by 1m/10f on fast or soft grnd, any
trk, likes Kempton & Newmarket: most progressive gelding: see 4916 (val h'cap).
4678} **MENOKEE 384** [2] Sir Michael Stoute 3-8-9 (95) K Darley 13/2: 512-2: Held up racing keenly, rdn   ¾   **107**
to press wnr over 1f out, kept on, al just held: reapp: lightly rcd '03, mdn scorer, subs Gr 3 rnr-up: eff at 1m,
styd longer 10f trip well & may get further: acts on gd & soft grnd, stiff or easy trk: lightly rcd colt, smart.
5139 **BONECRUSHER 13** [6] D R Loder 5-9-0 vis (103) S Sanders 9/4 JT FAV: 5364303: Trkd ldrs racing   1   **106**
keenly, trav well till rdn & wandered under press from over 1f out, not land blow: hvly bckd.
5223 **CARTE SAUVAGE 6** [4] M Johnston 3-8-9 (101) J Fanning 12/1: 1233-604: Led, hdd after 3f, out rdn   2½   **103**
& outpcd over 3f out, late rally, no impress: much imprvd from latest, qck reapp: handles firm & soft grnd.
4593* **IKTIBAS 45** [5]3-8-9 t R Hills 9/4 JT FAV: 15: Trkd ldrs, rdn & btn 2f out: hvly bckd, 6 wk abs   8   **95**
& significant rise in grade: see 4593 (weak mdn, fast).
5086 **WEECANDOO 15** [3]6-8-9 (82) G Carter 16/1: 0050006: Held up, eff 3f out, sn btn: see 2898.   hd   **89$**
6 Ran   Time 2m 12.05 (9.95)   Owned: Mr Richard J Cohen   Trained: Whitsbury

5270
3.50 Burwell Conditions Stakes 2-3yo (C1)
£12110 £4594 £2297   **6f str**   **Soft 91**   -05 Slow   Far Side

5047* **NOTA BENE 18** [10] D R C Elsworth 2-8-6 (84) L Keniry(2) 7/1: 211: Trkd ldrs trav well & led/hung   **99**
right dist, drvn out: op 5/1: eff at 6f on fast grnd, relished soft today: handles a sharp or stiff trk: lightly
rcd, useful & progressive colt: see 5047.
4985 **WORD PERFECT 21** [8] M W Easterby 2-8-1 (86) Dale Gibson 4/1: 1505032: Al prom & narrow lead 2f   nk   **93**
out, edged left & hdd dist, drvn & styd on well, just held: op 11/2: acts on firm & soft grnd: both wins
at 5f, now seems suited by 6f: tough & useful: see 4985, 4655 & 3224.
5149 **BARON RHODES 11** [2] J S Wainwright 3-9-3 (78) T Eaves(3) 14/1: 3000033: Trkd ldrs trav well, styd   1½   **87**
on onepace for press ins last: stays a stiff 6f, spot on back at 5f: see 3591 (h'cap, 5f).
5088 **VALJARV 15** [6] N P Littmoden 3-9-6 (90) N Callan 4/1: 2005044: Slow away, hdwy from halfway &   ½   **89**
pressed ldrs over 1f out, no extra ins last: poss lost winning ch with a slow start: on a long losing run but shown
enough to find a race: handles firm & soft grnd: see 1933.
5217 **JOSEPH HENRY 6** [9]2-8-6 (100) J Fanning 9/4 FAV: 114435: Led 4f, remained handy, no extra ins   hd   **93**
last: nicely bckd, again shaped as if a return to 5f would suit: see 5217, 5132.
4855 **GREAT FOX 30** [12]3-9-8 (73) R Price 33/1: 321-06: Cl-up 3f, hung left & no extra dist: see 4855.   2½   **85$**
4914 **GOLDEN ANTHEM 27** [11]2-7-12 (90) J Quinn 10/1: 1036607: Held up, nvr able to land blow.   1½   **77**

4452 **FOOLS ENTIRE** 52 [5]3-9-8 e (55) Dane O'Neill 100/1: 0034508: Chsd ldrs, btn 2f out: abs, offic rtd 55.   3½   75$
5196 **TOTALLY YOURS** 7 [4]3-9-3 P (83) Martin Dwyer 16/1: 5000209: Mid-div, struggling fnl 2f: btr 4855.   shd   70
4740 **FISSION** 37 [7]3-9-3 (71) F Norton 33/1: 3-631020: 10th: Dwelt & held up, btn 2f out: see 671 (A/W).   ¾   69
5056 **MAN CRAZY** 17 [3]3-9-3 (48) J F Egan 150/1: 0400400: 11th: Prom till lost place after 2f.   nk   68$
11 Ran   Time 1m 16.55 (5.75)   Owned: WV & Mrs ES Robins   Trained: Whitsbury

---

5271   4.25 Subscribe To Racing Uk On 08700 860432 Handicap Stakes 3yo+ 71-85 (D2)   [101]
£6078 £2306 £1153   2m   Soft 91   +04 Fast   Centre

4846 **RACE THE ACE** 31 [6] J L Dunlop 3-8-6 (79) T Quinn 3/1 FAV: 5233121: Chsd ldrs, hdwy to lead over   93
2f out, rdn clr from over 1f out, decisively in a fast time: nicely bckd: eff at 2m: acts on fast, loves gd/soft &
soft grnd, any trk: progressive 3yo stayer, keep on side in these conds: see 4235, 3861.
5135 **LAGGAN BAY** 13 [2] J S Moore 4-8-8 (1oh) Martin Dwyer 33/1: 2-060002: Held up, hdwy to   7   76
press wnr over 1f out, sn no impress: stays a stiff 2m: handles firm, soft & polytrack: see 1759.
5025* **SAN HERNANDO** 19 [5] D R C Elsworth 4-8-8 (3oh) (68) J F Egan 10/1: 4200013: Held up, hdwy over 2f   ¾   75
out, hung right & no impress over 1f out: clr of rem: well bckd, op 12/1: prob handles firm & soft: see 5025.
4383 **DR SHARP** 55 [3] T P Tate 4-9-4 (81) P Hanagan 9/2: 2106104: Trckd ldrs & keen, led over 6f out   10   77
till over 2f out, sn no impress: nicely bckd, op 6/1: 8 wk abs: btr 4106.
5135 **LAND N STARS** 13 [8]4-9-8 (85) P Doe 9/2: 1541365: Held up, eff over 4f out, no prog fnl 3f: bckd.   3½   78
5068 **PATRIXPRIAL** 17 [4]3-8-2 (75) J Fanning 12/1: 0-551046: Chsd ldr, btn 3f out: btr 4255 (14f).   3   65
5194 **BILL BENNETT** 7 [10]3-8-5 (78) D Fox(5) 14/1: 5014037: Chsd ldrs, no ch fnl 3f: btr 5194.   3   65
2444 **BID FOR FAME** 137 [1]7-8-13 (76) P Robinson 28/1: 21-00008: In tch, hung right & btn 4f out: 5 mnth abs   nk   52
5194 **TERESA** 7 [7]4-8-8 (1oh) (70) J Quinn 10/1: 6000029: Held up, rdn & btn 3f out.   nk   45
5194 **LINENS FLAME** 7 [9]5-8-8 (71) D Holland 8/1: 1200040: 10th: Led 9f, btn 3f out: bckd, op 10/1.   2   43
4803 **MAMCAZMA** 34 [11]6-9-4 (81) T E Durcan 12/1: 4000020: 11th: Chsd ldrs, no ch fnl 3f: btr 4803 (g/f).   24   35
11 Ran   Time 3m 35.10 (12.3)   Owned: I H Stewart-Brown & M J Meacock   Trained: Arundel

---

5272   5.00 Ella & White Limited Apprentice Handicap Stakes 3yo 56-70 (E3)   [80]
£3441 £1059 £529   1m str   Soft 91   -07 Slow   Far Side

5178 **LA PUCE** 10 [19] M J Attwater 3-8-4 (56) C Haddon(3) 25/1: 4600021: Held up in tch, hdwy over 1f   65
out & drvn to lead line, all out: new yard: eff at 7f, suited by 1m/8.5f: acts on fast, soft & fibresand, stiff or
sharp trk: best without t-strap: well h'capped on turf: see 5178, 809.
5191 **PRINCESS GALADRIEL** 9 [16] J R Best 3-8-9 (61) Thomas Yeung(3) 14/1: 6361302: Held up, rdn & hdwy   nk   69
to lead dist, just hdd line: rest well covered, op 11/1: tough filly, back to form, could win again: see 4721 & 4251.
5161 **THE FUN MERCHANT** 11 [18] J Pearce 3-9-0 P (66) M Lawson(3) 16/1: 1205003: Keen & prom, ch over 1f   3½   69
out, no extra ins last: gd run in firm time cheek pieces: acts on firm & soft grnd: see 3410 & 2732.
5034 **CHARLIE TANGO** 18 [14] N Tinkler 3-8-8 T (60) N De Souza 7/1: 0004024: Chsd ldrs, styd on onepace   nk   62
for press, no threat to front pair: ran to form in first time t-strap: see 5034, 2565.
5017 **NIGHT FROLIC** 19 [20]3-8-6 (58) Derek Nolan(3) 6/1 FAV: 0660425: Handy & led after 2f till dist, no extra.   1   59
5191 **ADORATA** 9 [12]3-8-13 (65) D Fox 10/1: 0210006: Held up, hmpd early, hdwy to press ldrs over 1f   nk   65
out, edged right & no extra: acts on firm, soft & fibresand: see 4042 (AW mdn).
4935 **CANTARNA** 25 [17]3-8-4 (70) B Swarbrick 10/1: 5-235167: Keen & prom, kept on onepace.   ¾   69
5153 **SACHIN** 11 [13]3-8-13 (65) P Makin 10/1: 0604138: Prom, edged right & btn dist: btr 5153 & 4827.   3   60
4939 **TRUE** 25 [1]3-8-4 (56) A Mullen(3) 16/1: 0602059: Slow away & held up, no impress fnl 2f: btr 4593.   1   50
4862 **GAY ROMANCE** 30 [10]3-8-12 (64) K May(5) 13/2: 006530: 10th: Led 2f, prom till over 1f out: btr 4862.   1¾   56
5027 **FLEET ANCHOR** 19 [6]3-8-4 (1oh) (55) Rory Moore(5) 33/1: 0253500: 11th: Held up & keen, btn 2f out.   nk   47
4926 **HEVERSHAM** 27 [11]3-9-0 (66) D Tudhope(3) 14/1: 0002200: 12th: Reared start, held up & keen, rear.   2   54
5242 **BLAKE HALL LAD** 4 [2]3-8-6 (58) Dean Williams(7) 20/1: 005160: 13th: Hmpd start & held up, no impress.   5   39
5094 **MRS BROWN** 14 [7]3-8-4 (5oh) (51) Stephanie Hollinshead(3) 14/1: 6050450: 14th: Keen & prom, hung   2½   33
right & btn 2f out.
5184 **Filliemou** 10 [5]3-8-4 (3oh)VIS(53) D Fentiman(3) 33/1:05080   **Western Roots** 16 [3]3-8-13 (65) P Mathers 14/1:0
5016 **Dream Easy** 19 [8]3-8-11 (63) Nicol Polli(3) 40/1:0   848   **Chariot** 229 [9]3-8-12 (64) M Savage 50/1:0
18 Ran   Time 1m 44.3(7.8)   Owned: Brooklands Racing   Trained: Wysall

---

Official Going Soft ALL TIMES SLOW

5273   11.00 Racing Uk On Sky 432 Median Auction Maiden Stakes 2yo (H5)   £1449 £414 £207   1m rnd   Soft   Inapplicable   Inside

5107 **THREE WRENS** 15 [2] D J Daly 2-8-9 S W Kelly 6/4 JT FAV: 31: Keen, trckd ldrs, led over 1f out,   67
edged right & just held on for press: eff at 1m on soft & gd/sft ground: likes a gall trk: see 5107.
5127 **JEFFSLOTTERY** 14 [6] J R Weymes 2-9-0 BL (45) R Winston 25/1: 0602: Dwelt, held up, styd on well   nk   71
for press fnl 1f, just held: imprvd in 1st time blnks: stays a gall 1m on soft ground: see 4816.
5179 **WOODFORD CONSULT** 11 [4] M W Easterby 2-8-9 T Lucas 25/1: 003: b f Benny The Dip - Chicodove (In   2½   62
The Wings) Held up, efft & hung left fnl 2f, kept on to take 3rd: cheaply bought Mar foal: dam a 11/12f 3yo wnr:
stays a gall 1m on soft ground.
5142 **SPINNAKERS GIRL** 13 [5] J R Weymes 2-8-9 (64) P Mulrennan(3) 7/1: 0324004: Led 2f, btn 2f out.   1½   60
4769 **DANZATRICE** 36 [3]2-8-9 T Eaves(3) 6/4 JT FAV: 055: Chsd ldrs, pushed along over 3f out, no prog.   hd   59
5105 **EKATERINA** 15 [7]2-8-9 J Bramhill 33/1: 006: Led after 2f till over 1f out, sn btn: see 5105.   2½   55
5105 **NORTHERN REVOQUE** 15 [8]2-8-9 (45) P Mathers(5) 20/1: 5004007: Chsd ldrs, btn 2f out: modest.   9   42
4816 **CASALESE** 33 [1]2-9-0 Darren Williams 33/1: 008: In tch, rdn & lost tch from over 2f out: see 4816.   9   34
8 Ran   Time 1m 57.48 (20.88)   Owned: Mrs James Wigan   Trained: Newmarket

---

5274	11.30 Simpson And Shaw Maiden Claiming Stakes 3yo+ (H5)
	£1474 £421 £211 7f50y rnd Soft Inapplicable Inside

5094 **PASSION FRUIT** 15 [7] C W Fairhurst 3-8-7 BL (47) P Mulrennan(3) 5/1: 30-00061: Handy, pushed along **46**
3f out, rdn to lead ins last, styd on best: eff at 7f on fast & soft ground: likes a gall trk: apprec blnks.
4993 **THE LOOSE SCREW** 21 [3] G M Moore 6-9-0 p (40) N Pollard 11/4 FAV: 0005562: Led, hung left under 5 **43**
press over 1f out, hdd ins last & no extra: eff at 7/10f on fast & soft ground: see 4768.
3677 **BLADES EDGE** 88 [2] A Bailey 3-8-12 (40) R Winston 14/1: 0000003: Held up, hdwy over 2f out, 2½ **39**
onepace & held in last: 12 wk abs: handles fast & soft ground, stays 7f: see 673.
5120 **LA FONTEYNE** 14 [4] C B B Booth 3-8-8 (1ow) (45) G Parkin 8/1: 2050304: Held up, no impress. 6 **26**
5110 **NEVER FORGET BOWIE** 15 [14]8-8-12 (40) P Mathers(5) 7/1: 0404/-005: Dwelt & held up, no impress. 5 **21**
4560 **CANLIS** 47 [9]5-8-8 (40) T Williams 5/1: 0050006: Handy, chsd ldr over 3f out, sn rdn & fdd, 7 wk abs. 1½ **15**
5066 **PERRYWINKLE BOY** 18 [8]3-8-12 t (40) Darren Williams 33/1: 400P7: Cl up, btn 2f out: dropped in trip. 5 **14**
2055 **LADY OF THE LINKS** 155 [10]3-8-7 T (45) Kim Tinkler 7/1: 00-40508: Mid-div, strugg fnl 2f: 5 mth abs. 2 **6**
3370} **LADY TILLY** 453 [5]7-8-9 t (30) J McAuley 50/1: 500/65/0-9: b f Puissance - Lady of Itatiba (King nk **5**
of Macedon) Dwelt & al rear, long abs, new yard: lightly raced & v modest form in recent seasons.
2767 **GOLDEN SHELL** 841 [13]5-8-7 (35) D Tudhope(1) 16/1: 0/0000/-0: 10th: Handy, btn over 2f out: jmps fit. 17 **0**
5067 **Blackpool Jack** 18 [6]3-8-6 T Eaves 50/1:0   4347 **Transkei** 58 [12]3-8-5 (35) D Allan 33/1:0
12 Ran   Time 1m 41.87 (15.07)   Owned: G H & S Leggott   Trained: Middleham

---

5275	12.00 Ferguson Media Banded Stakes 3yo+ 0-45 (H5)
	£1470 £420 £210 1m rnd Soft Inapplicable Inside

5119 **MUQARRAR** 14 [9] T J Fitzgerald 5-9-0 VIS t (40) P Mulrennan(3) 20/1: 06-66001: ch c Alhaarth - **50**
Narjis (Blushing Groom) Held up, prog to chall over 1f out, duelled with rnr up & just prev for press close home:
1st win: unplcd '03 (rtd 65): eff at 1m on soft ground: suited by vis today in banded comp, has tried blnks.
5209 **CAMPBELLS LAD** 7 [5] A Berry 3-8-11 (45) P Mathers(5) 4/1: 5302432: Held up, smooth hdwy & led nk **49**
over 1f out, rdn & sn duelled with wnr, just hdd close home: acts on firm, soft & polytrk: see 5209, 4505.
5119 **ENCOUNTER** 14 [4] J Hetherton 8-9-0 (45) D Allan 7/2 FAV: 0535203: Hld up, hdwy 2f out, onepace. 3½ **44**
4659 **DESERT FURY** 42 [13] R Bastiman 7-9-0 T (40) R Winston 5/1: 0065064: Chsd ldrs, hdwy to lead over 8 **32**
2f out, hdd over 1f out, wknd: 6 wk abs: 1st time t-strap: see 1750.
4466} **THE COUNT** 754 [10]5-9-0 (40) T Eaves(3) 33/1: 000656/-5: b g Sillery - Dear Countess (Fabulous 6 **23**
Dancer) Chsd ldrs, btn 2f out, kept on: missed '03: AW h'cap rnr up & turf sell h'cap '03:
eff arnd 1m on fast ground & fibresand, sharp or gall trk: best without blnks.
2 May'02 Nott 8.2 g/f 50-50 G: 2 Apr'02 Beve 9.9 g/f 47- F:
4626 **DISPOL VERITY** 44 [8]4-9-0 (35) S W Kelly 25/1: 0/-000006: Held up, mod hdwy fnl 2f: 6 wk abs. 5 **16**
3159 **MEXICAN** 110 [11]5-9-0 t (40) Darren Williams 6/1: 0-003527: Handy, led over 3f out till over 2f out, fdd. 3 **12**
4505 **NEVER PROMISE** 49 [7]6-9-0 vis (40) A Medeiros(5) 16/1: 00/600-68: Rear, little hdwy fnl 3f, jmps fit. ½ **11**
3668 **CEZZARO** 88 [3]6-9-0 p (40) Dale Gibson 12/1: 2200059: Led till over 3f out, sn btn: 12 wk abs, new yard. 3½ **6**
4088 **ZAHUNDA** 71 [12]5-9-0 (40) B Swarbrick(5) 7/1: 4024500: 10th: Cl up, hung left & btn over 2f out: abs. 6 **0**
2544 **ANDREYEV** 134 [2]10-9-0 (40) J Currie(7) 10/1: 0-600050: 11th: Handy, wknd 2f out: best at 5/7f. 5 **0**
4817 **Second Wind** 33 [6]9-9-0 t(40) D Tudhope(5) 50/1:0   4256 **Tiz Wiz** 62 [1]3-8-11 (40) J Bramhill 25/1:0
13 Ran   Time 1m 53.14 (16.54)   Owned: Kramo Racing   Trained: Malton

---

5276	12.30 Daily Record Good Morning Banded Stakes 3yo+ 0-45 (H5)
	£1509 £431 £216 1m2f Soft Inapplicable Inside

1244 **TOP STYLE** 194 [13] J Howard Johnson 6-9-0 (40) P Mulrennan(3) 4/1: 004/-0221: Sn pshd along **52**
chasing ldrs, rdn to lead ins last, hung left, rdn out: 6 mth abs, prev with M J Wallace: eff btwn 7f/10f on polytrk
& soft ground, sharp or gall trk: goes well fresh: see 1244, 1181.
5067 **REVERSIONARY** 18 [9] M W Easterby 3-9-0 bl (40) R Winston 3/1 FAV: 0010322: Handy trav well, rdn & 3 **53**
led over 1f out, hung left & hdd ins last, kept on: see 5067, 3487.
5108 **EAST CAPE** 15 [3] Don Enrico Incisa 7-9-0 (45) Kim Tinkler 8/1: 3524003: Rear, late gains for press. 1¾ **46**
4620 **SPREE VISION** 44 [2] P Monteith 8-9-2 vis (47) D Fentiman(7) 6/1: 4224564: Dwelt & held up, hdwy & 1¾ **46**
handy over 1f out, sn no extra: jmps fit: see 4620, 3588.
5111 **THE WIZARD MUL** 15 [7]4-9-5 (50) J Bramhill 8/1: 0000035: Hld up, hdwy to chse ldrs 2f out, wknd dist. 5 **44**
3726 **KYLE OF LOCHALSH** 86 [5]4-9-0 (45) T Eaves(3) 16/1: 0005506: Mid-div, rdn & btn 2f out: 12 wk abs. ½ **38**
4348 **DANEFONIQUE** 58 [8]3-9-0 (50) D Tudhope(5) 10/1: 6040267: Rear, sn pshd along, only mod late prog. ½ **42**
4137 **KOODOO** 68 [4]3-8-9 (45) G Parkin 8/1: 0600058: Prom, rdn & btn 2f out, new yard, 10 wk abs. ¾ **36**
4667 **FIVE GOLD** 42 [1]3-9-0 (50) N Pollard 20/1: 10-00009: Led till over 1f out, wknd qckly: abs, new yard. ½ **40**
4821 **ASTON LAD** 33 [12]3-9-0 (50) Darren Williams 8/1: 6625050: 10th: Mid-div, rdn & btn over 2f out: btr 4560.7 **33**
4857 **MYANNABANANA** 31 [11]3-8-9 bl (40) D Allan 33/1: 0000000: 11th: Keen & trkd ldrs, btn over 2f out. 1 **27**
5111 **Iftikhar** 15 [6]5-9-7 (52) S W Kelly 16/1:0   4809 **Devine Light** 34 [10]4-9-0 (45) P Fessey 50/1:0
13 Ran   Time 2m 26.35 (21.95)   Owned: Mr Thomas Harty   Trained: Crook

---

5277	1.00 African Dancer Banded Stakes 3yo+ 0-45 (H5)
	£1467 £419 £210 1m5f13y Soft Inapplicable Inside

4282 **BORIS THE SPIDER** 61 [5] M D Hammond 3-9-2 (48) Darren Williams 11/2: 0055461: Keen early, sn **52**
close up, led over 1f out, duelled with rnr up, rdn & asserted twds fin: 2 mth abs: 1st win: eff at 6f/1m, now stays
13f in banded company: acts on good & soft ground: see 1426.
5129 **SIR EDWARD BURROW** 14 [6] W Storey 6-9-7 (30) J Bramhill 20/1: 06000//-02: Led, hdd over 1f out & 2 **45$**
no extra wk ins last: clr rem: handles fast & soft ground: see 5129.
5123 **TOUCH OF EBONY** 14 [3] C Roberts 5-9-8 (46) A Medeiros(5) 6/4 FAV: 002-0023: Held up, no dngr. 8 **38**
4716 **STAFF NURSE** 39 [4] Don Enrico Incisa 4-9-7 (35) Kim Tinkler 11/2: 4053324: Held up, mod late 2 **35**

prog for press, nvr threat: see 4716, 4128.

5123 **SMARTER CHARTER 14** [1]11-9-7 (35) Kristin Stubbs(7) 10/1: 4564305: Rear, btn dist: btr 4662. *1½* **34**

4243 **DANCER KING 63** [9]3-9-4 (50) R Winston 4/1: 500306: Trkd ldrs, btn over 1f out, 2 mth abs. *5* **34**

5066 **SPECTRUM STAR 18** [8]4-9-7 (35) T Eaves(3) 33/1: 030/0-07: Cl up, btn over 2f out: see 5066. *1* **28**

4687 **HOWARDS DREAM 42** [10]6-9-7 t (30) D Allan 10/1: 6000548: Rear, no hdwy fnl 3f: 6 wk abs: btr 4687. *26* **6**

1840 **MARAVEDI 164** [2]4-9-7 (35) S W Kelly 16/1: 000-0009: Mid-div, rdn & btn over 3f out: new stable: abs. *3* **3**

9 Ran Time 3m 17.57 (32.97) Owned: The Adbrokes Partnership Trained: Middleham

5278

1.35 Laughing Zebra At African Interiors Banded Stakes 3yo+ 0-45 (H5)
£1477 £422 £211 **6f str** **Soft** **Inapplicable** Stands Side

4995 **JOHN OGROATS 21** [9] B Mactaggart 6-9-0 (45) J McAuley 9/1: 0000001: Made all, hung left from over 1f out but held on well: prev with D W Chapman: eff at 5/6f on firm & hvy ground: suited by change of stable. **47**

4088 **STELLITE 71** [6] J S Goldie 4-9-0 (45) T Eaves(3) 5/2 FAV: 0-010002: Chsd wnr fnl 2f, hung left under press, nrst fin: 10 wk abs: eff at 6/7f on gd/sft & soft ground: see 1448 (7f). *nk* **46**

5121 **DANAKIM 14** [2] J R Weymes 7-9-0 (40) D Fentiman(7) 11/2: 4200403: Chsd wnr, rdn & no extra fnl 1f. *3* **40**

3650 **HEBENUS 89** [7] T A K Cuthbert 5-9-0 (45) Dale Gibson 6/1: 250-2004: Prom, outpcd 2f out, kept on late. *¾* **39**

5121 **HI DARL 14** [10]3-8-13 (35) N Pollard 20/1: 0000005: Held up, no impress fnl 2f. *nk* **38**

3562 **PROCREATE 87** [8]4-9-0 (45) R Winston 14/1: 0-000006: Held up, rdn & nvr landed a blow: jumps fit. *2* **34**

2812 **BE MY ALIBI 124** [4]3-8-13 (35) B Swarbrick(5) 20/1: 00-05007: Rear, rdn & nvr landed a blow: 4 mth abs. *2* **30**

4676 **MISS WIZZ 42** [5]4-9-0 p (45) Rory Moore(5) 4/1: 5100008: Mid div, rdn & btn 2f out, 6 wk abs: btr 2730. *2* **26**

4817 **LAS RAMBLAS 33** [1]7-9-0 t p (45) D Allan 28/1: 640-0009: Chsd ldrs, btn over 2f out: see 4618. *7* **12**

4818 **INDIAN MUSIC 33** [3]7-9-0 (45) P Mathers(5) 9/2: 2006500: 10th: Held up, rdn & btn over 1f out. *6* **0**

10 Ran Time 1m 18.55(9.25) Owned: Miss E Johnston Trained: Hawick

NEWMARKET **SATURDAY 30.10.04 Righthand, Stiff, Galloping Track**

Official Going Good/Soft (Soft places)

5279

1.00 European Breeders Fund Maiden Stakes Div 1 Fillies 2yo (D3)
£4882 £1502 £751 **7f str** **Good/Soft 76** **-41 Slow** Stands Side

READ FEDERICA 0 [11] Sir Michael Stoute 2-8-11 D Holland 14/1: 1: ch f Fusaichi Pegasus - Reading Habit (Half a Year) Pushed along in tch centre, outpcd over 2f out, rdn & strong run ins last to lead cl-home: $140,000 Feb first foal, dam a US List sprint wnr & half-sister to sev wnrs: eff at 7f, relish 1m+ on this evidence: acts on gd/soft grnd & a stiff/gall trk: goes well fresh: potentially useful. **83+**

4242 **SHARABY 63** [5] E A L Dunlop 2-8-11 (70) E Ahern 25/1: 3002: Led, rdn & hdd cl-home, 2 month abs: acts on fast & gd/soft grnd: imprvd for forcing tactics today: see 3035. *nk* **82**

MY DUBAI 0 [1] Saeed bin Suroor 2-8-11 T T E Durcan 6/1: 3: ch f Dubai Millennium - Pastorale (Nureyev) Cl-up, led stands side group over 1f out, kept on, just held cl-home: nicely bckd, first home from stands side group: Mar foal, half-sister to wnrs at 7f/1m, dam a dual 7f/1m 3yo scorer: eff at 7f, get 1m: acts on gd/soft grnd & a stiff/gall trk: promising start. *¾* **80**

GULCHINA 0 [13] D R C Elsworth 2-8-11 T Quinn 15/2: 4: b f Gulch - Harda Arda (Nureyev) Sn prom centre, lost pl around halfway, kept on fnl 2f, not pace to chall: Mar first foal, dam a 9f 3yo scorer: eff at 7f, will relish 1m+: handles gd/soft grnd: sure to improve. *1* **78+**

NAWAAEM 0 [3]2-8-11 R Hills 8/1: 5: Chsd ldr stands side & led that group halfway till over 1f, out. *hd* **77**

ANTOINETTE 0 [18]2-8-11 K Darley 14/1: 6: Chsd ldr centre, not pace to chall. *½* **76**

HEART STOPPING 0 [8]2-8-11 M Hills 16/1: 7: Cl-up centre 5f, no extra fnl 1f. *½* **75**

MINEKO 0 [10]2-8-11 S Sanders 33/1: 8: Sn trkd ldrs centre, outpcd fnl 2f. *shd* **74**

CAMERON ORCHID 0 [4]2-8-11 P Robinson 10/1: 9: Led stands side till halfway, hung right & no impress *½* **73**

50[illegible] **QUEEN OF ICENI 19** [7]2-8-11 I Mongan 11/2 FAV: 020: 10th: Chsd ldrs stands side, no impress. *2½* **68**

SWALLOW SENORA 0 [14]2-8-11 J Quinn 33/1: 0: 11th: Held up centre, nvr a factor. *1¼* **66**

LET SLIP 0 [12]2-8-11 Martin Dwyer 33/1: 0: 12th: Dwelt, held up centre, no impress. *2½* **61**

SAVOIE 0 [19]2-8-11 W Ryan 9/1: 0: 13th: Chsd ldrs centre 5f. *1* **59**

5045 **MOONSIDE 19** [9]2-8-11 VIS R Thomas(3) 100/1: 000: 14th: Prom centre till over 2 fout, visor. *9* **41**

PRAKARA 0 [16]2-8-11 A Hamblett(7) 66/1: 0: 15th: Dwelt, held up centre, no impress fnl 2f. *6* **29**

MRS CHIPPY 0 [6]2-8-11 N Callan 66/1: 0: 16th: Slow away & al bhd centre. *2½* **24**

4885 **CAUSEWAY GIRL 29** [15]2-8-11 S Whitworth 50/1: 00: 17th: Held up centre, nvr a factor. *5* **14**

3927 **CAYUSE 78** [2]2-8-11 M Tebbutt 100/1: 00: 18th: Slow away stands side, bhd halfway. *4* **6**

SUNNY NATURE 0 [17]2-8-11 R Hughes 7/1: 0: 19th: Slow away in centre, sn bhd & eased halfway. *5* **0**

19 Ran Time 1m 31.39 (8.19) Owned: Mrs R J Jacobs Trained: Newmarket

5280

1.30 European Breeders Fund Maiden Stakes Div 2 Fillies 2yo (D3)
£4882 £1502 £751 **7f str** **Good/Soft 76** **-32 Slow** Stands Side

SONGTHRUSH 0 [1] P F I Cole 2-8-11 S Sanders 20/1: 1: gr f Unbridled's Song - Virgin Michael (Green Dancer) Rcd alone stands side, made all, rdn out: $120,000 Mar foal, related to sev US wnrs, dam a useful 3/4yo US turf performer: eff at 7f, shld get 1m: acts on gd/soft: fine start. **87**

LADEENA 0 [10] J L Dunlop 2-8-11 W Supple 12/1: 2: b f Dubai Millennium - Aqaarid (Nashwan) Trkd ldr centre & led that group over 1f out, kept on well, not pace of wnr stands side: Feb foal, half-sister to a 1m juv wnr, dam top-class 1m scorer: acts on gd/soft: will relish 1m+ & win races. *2½* **80+**

SHARED DREAMS 0 [7] L M Cumani 2-8-11 Dane O'Neill 16/1: 3: b f Seeking The Gold - Coretta (Caerleon) Held up centre, styd on strongly from over 1f out, nrst fin: Apr foal, dam plcd at 7f as a juv, subs 10f 3yo scorer: eff at 7f, sure to relish 1m+: acts on gd/soft grnd: most eye-catching closing stages, will improve. *1* **78+**

4417 **LYSANDRA 54** [14] Sir Michael Stoute 2-8-11 K Darley 5/1 FAV: 24: Led/dsptd lead centre till over 1f out, kept on: bckd, 8 wk abs: handles fast & gd/soft grnd: see 4417. *½* **77**

VILLAROSI 0 [15]2-8-11 A McCarthy 16/1: 5: Mid-div centre, no impress over 1f out. *2* **73**

LINNET 0 [3]2-8-11 D Holland 14/1: 6: Slow away in centre, hdwy from halfway, onepace dist. *hd* **72**

PRITHEE 0 [4]2-8-11 R Hughes 8/1: 7: Held up centre, nvr able to chall ldrs. *1½* **69**

5045 **ALSHARQ 19** [12]2-8-11 R Hills 11/2: 08: Cl-up centre, fdd dist. *1* **67**
5047 **PEACE LILY 19** [8]2-8-11 S Carson 8/1: 59: Led/dsptd lead centre 5f, fdd: bckd, op 12/1: see 5047. *1¼* **64**
4971 **MAGIC FLO 24** [18]2-8-11 S Whitworth 100/1: 060: 10th: Mid-div, no impress fnl 2f. *2½* **59**
HELEN SHARP 0 [2]2-8-11 P Robinson 7/1: 0: 11th: Mid-div centre, no impress over 1f out. *1* **57**
LA BELLA GRANDE 0 [17]2-8-11 S Drowne 16/1: 0: 12th: Dwelt, in tch centre till over 2f out. *3* **51**
CIEL BLEU 0 [9]2-8-11 M Hills 20/1: 0: 13th: Slow away centre & al rear. *5* **41**
5084 **WOOLFALL JOANNA 16** [16]2-8-11 J Mackay 66/1: 00: 14th: Prom centre 5f, sn btn. *4* **33**
KATY JEM 0 [13]2-8-11 L Keniry(3) 33/1: 0: 15th: Slow away & al rear centre, hung left halfway. *3½* **26**
SNOW LYNX 0 [5]2-8-11 T E Durcan 8/1: 0: 16th: Prom centre 4f, reportedly unsuited by grnd. *½* **25**
16 Ran Time 1m 30.74 (7.54) Owned: Mr CWright & The Hon Mrs JMCorbett Trained: Whatcombe

5281

2.05 Listed William Claridge Memorial Zetland Stakes 2yo (A1)
£14500 £5500 £2750 **1m2f** **Good/Soft 76** **-08 Slow** Stands Side

4933* **AYAM ZAMAN 26** [1] M A Jarvis 2-8-6 (86) P Robinson 3/1: 511: Trkd ldrs trav well & led over 2f out, rdn clr ins last, decisively: nicely bckd tho' op 9/4: stays 10f well, 12f+ suit next term: acts on firm & gd/soft grnd, loves a stiff/undul trk: useful, plenty more to come: see 4933. **100+**
5150 **FANTASY RIDE 12** [5] J Pearce 2-8-11 (94) J Quinn 16/1: 0152: Slow away & held up in tch, short of room 2f out, switched & kept on well ins last, wnr had flown: much closer to this wnr with more positive tactics: styd longer 10f trip well: see 5150 & 4147. *5* **96+**
5189* **NATALIE JANE 10** [3] G A Butler 2-8-6 P Hanagan 12/1: 0313: Trkd ldrs, rdn & outpcd over 2f out, kept on well ins last to snatch 3rd: set to apprec 12f+ next term: see 5189. *2* **88**
5222 **BRECON 7** [4] D R C Elsworth 2-8-6 T Quinn 6/1: 144: Held up & keen, hdwy when hung left over 1f out, no extra ins last: well bckd: longer 10f trip likely to suit: see 5222 & 4575 (7f). *shd* **88**
5044* **SUNDAY SYMPHONY 19** [8]2-8-11 (89) T E Durcan 9/4 FAV: 2115: Held up, rdn & hung left over 2f out, sn no impress: well bckd: reportedly unsuited by the soft ground: see 5044 (gd). *1¼* **91**
5170* **WOTCHALIKE 11** [9]2-8-11 (82) A McCarthy 22/1: 502216: Dwelt, sn trkd ldrs, btn 2f out: new stable. *5* **84**
5089* **DANEHILL WILLY 16** [6]2-8-11 (81) D Holland 6/1: 200117: Chsd ldr & led over 3f out till hdd/hmpd over 2f out, sn btn: nicely bckd, op 15/2: up in grade & trip: btr 5089 (gd). *3* **80**
3859 **ACTIVE ASSET 80** [7]2-8-11 (89) A Culhane 12/1: 2128: Chsd ldrs, hmpd when struggling over 2f out: 12 wk abs: btr 3859 (7f, fast). *dist* **0**
5158 **NORCROFT 12** [2]2-8-11 (69) Hayley Turner 100/1: 0040039: Led 6f, sn btn: new stable: highly tried. *13* **0**
9 Ran Time 2m 10.53 (8.43) Owned: Mr Saif Ali Trained: Newmarket

5282

2.35 Listed Best Bet John 0800 587 7086 E B F Montrose Stakes Fillies 2yo (A1)
£14500 £5500 £2750 **1m str** **Good/Soft 76** **-37 Slow** Stands Side

5033 **SQUAW DANCE 19** [8] W J Haggas 2-8-8 (81) P Hanagan 16/1: 6321: Made all & dictated pace, increased tempo from 3f out, rdn & al holding on ins last: eff at 1m, stay further: acts on gd/soft & soft grnd, stiff/gall trks: much improved under a fine ride: see 5033 & 4769. **103**
5099* **SOMETHING EXCITING 15** [7] D R C Elsworth 2-8-8 (100) T Quinn 1/1 FAV: 4001112: Held up, rdn & outpcd 3f out, styd on despite hanging right ins last, nrst fin: hvly bckd: crying out for 10f+ now: btr 5099 (C/D). *1½* **99**
4914 **BORTHWICK GIRL 28** [2] B J Meehan 2-8-8 (98) J Fortune 13/2: 14033: Chsd wnr & ch over 2f out, sn no extra: nicely bckd: styd longer 1m trip: acts on fast & gd/soft grnd: see 4914 & 2733. *2½* **94**
5133 **JUSTAQUESTION 14** [1] I A Wood 2-8-8 (93) N Callan 14/1: 3215064: Trkd ldrs, styd on onepace for press: stays 1m: tough: see 3774. *hd* **93**
5040 **TEMPESTAD 19** [3]2-8-8 W Ryan 15/2: 35: Handy, rdn & no extra over 1f out: bckd: longer trip. *1½* **90**
5045 **ALWAYS MINE 19** [5]2-8-8 Martin Dwyer 22/1: 56: Held up, rdn & outpcd from over 2f out. *nk* **89**
5203* **ALPINE GOLD 8** [6]2-8-8 (75) I Mongan 7/1: 00117: Handy & keen, rdn & wknd fnl 1f: see 5203. *nk* **88**
5221 **LOS ORGANOS 7** [4]2-8-8 R Havlin 25/1: 38: Held up, rdn & struggling fnl 2f: see 5221. *½* **87**
8 Ran Time 1m 45.55 (9.05) Owned: Mr Tony Hirschfeld Trained: Newmarket

5283

3.10 Listed Best Bet John 0800 587 7086 Ben Marshall Stakes 3yo+ (A1)
£17400 £6600 £3300 **1m str** **Good/Soft 76** **+16 Fast** Stands Side

5054* **SLEEPING INDIAN 19** [1] J H M Gosden 3-8-10 J Fortune 9/2 FAV: 11: Trkd ldrs, trav well when short of room over 1f out, switched & strong run/carr right nr fin, just denied, fin 2nd, plcd 1st: fast time: bckd, op 7/1: eff around 1m, stay further: acts on fast, relished gd/soft today: handles a stiff or sharp trk: lightly rcd & v useful, prob have won this decisively with a clr passage. *shd* **110+**
5139 **BABODANA 14** [3] M H Tompkins 4-8-13 (107) D Holland 5/1: 5546432: Chsd ldrs, short of room over 1f out, rdn to lead & hung right ins last, held on all out: fin 1st, plcd 2nd: nicely bckd: joc gvn 2 day whip ban: unlucky to lose this in stewards room: loves easy grnd: see 5139, 4063 & 951. **111**
4916 **TAKE A BOW 28** [4] P R Chamings 3-8-10 (102) J Quinn 5/1: 1412223: Chsd ldr, rdn to chall over 1f out, edged right & not pace of front pair ins last: nicely bckd: reportedly struck into: tough & consistent. *1* **108**
4887 **TOUT SEUL 29** [9] R F Johnson Houghton 4-9-2 (105) S Carson 12/1: 1006044: Held up, hdwy to press ldrs over 1f out, onepace ins last: see 1356. *1* **109**
5214 **QUITO 7** [6]7-8-13 bl (104) A Culhane 11/2: 5165335: Held up, styd on for press fnl 2f, not able to chall. *1½* **103**
4887 **FUNFAIR 29** [7]5-8-13 (106) S Sanders 15/2: 1020-236: Held up, hdwy when hmpd ins last, not able to recover: closer with a clr passage: see 4531. *½* **102**
5134 **CAPE FEAR 14** [10]3-8-10 (107) E Ahern 33/1: 32510-07: b c Cape Cross - Only In Dreams (Polar Falcon) Prom & led over 2f out till ins last, no extra: mdn & val cond stks wnr in '03: eff at 5/6f, shld stay this 1m trip: acts on fast & gd/soft grnd. *½* **101**
1 Sep'03 Donc 6 gd 110- B: 2 Jul'03 Newm 6 g/f 108- A: 1 May'03 Kemp 5 g/f 91- D:
5075 **PUTRA PEKAN 20** [2]6-9-2 bl (109) P Robinson 10/1: 1100238: Led 5f, btn when hmpd over 1f out. *1½* **101**
5139 **IMPERIAL STRIDE 14** [11]3-8-10 (109) K Darley 8/1: 116-409: Chsd ldrs, wknd ins last: btr 1188. *½* **97**
4916 **AUDIENCE 28** [8]4-8-13 p (105) M Tebbutt 20/1: 2461300: 10th: Held up, struggling fnl 2f: btr 4061. *1¼* **94**
4866} **JOSEPHUS 372** [5]3-8-10 (104) S Drowne 33/1: 412-0: 11th: ch c King of Kings - Khulasah (Affirmed) Held up, no impress fnl 2f: reapp: lightly rcd '03, mdn scorer, subs Gr 3 rnr-up: eff at 7f on fast grnd & a stiff/gall trk. 2 Oct'03 Newb 7 g/f 105- A: 1 Jul'03 Newm 7 g/f 97- D: *8* **80**
11 Ran Time 1m 41.32 (4.82) Owned: Mr George Strawbridge Trained: Manton

5284 3.45 Best Bet John 0800 587 7086 Mile Handicap 3yo+ 86-100 (C1) [101]
£17400 £6600 £3300 1m str Good/Soft 76 +07 Fast Stands Side

4227 **ZERO TOLERANCE 63** [9] T D Barron 4-9-7 (94) P Hanagan 9/1: 4000221: Switched to stands rail & made all, qcknd over 1f out, rdn out: good time: abs: eff at 1m/10f, tried 12f: acts on fast, likes gd/soft & soft grnd: goes well fresh: another fine front running ride from P Hanagan: see 4227 & 4021 & 1104. **105**
4916 **IMPELLER 28** [3] W R Muir 5-9-5 (92) S Drowne 20/1: 5221302: Held up, short of room over 1f out, styd on well ins last, not able to reach wnr: acts on firm & gd/soft grnd: see 4467. ¾ **101**
4999* **THE PRINCE 21** [6] Ian Williams 10-9-1 (88) A Mullen(7) 6/1: 1211113: Slow away & bhd, hdwy when short of room over 1f out, styd on strongly ins last, nrst fin: lost winning ch start, eye-catching eff in defeat. 1½ **94+**
5144* **GO PADERO 13** [12] M Johnston 3-8-9 (85) J Fanning 6/1: 651-14: Chsd wnr, edged left & onepace dist: well bckd: styd longer 1m trip but btr 5144 (7f). 1½ **88**
5103* **KAMANDA LAUGH 15** [10]3-8-11 (87) M Hills 7/2 FAV: 0-121115: Chsd ldrs, no extra fnl 1f: hvly bckd. nk **89**
1862 **WAKE 163** [7]4-9-3 (90) R Hughes 50/1: 2/-1606: Handy, rdn & no extra ins last: 5 month abs, new yard: ran well for a long way: see 881 (AW). 1¾ **88**
5223 **PERFECT STORM 7** [11]5-9-0 (87) D Sweeney 16/1: 0540007: Chsd ldrs, no extra fnl 1f: drpd in trip. ½ **84**
5103 **FINISHED ARTICLE 15** [2]7-8-12 (85) P Makin(5) 6/1: 3000048: Held up, no impress dist, new yard. ½ **81**
5103 **ACE OF HEARTS 15** [13]5-9-3 (90) S Sanders 22/1: 1100309: Held up, rdn & btn 2f out: btr 4890 (fast). 1 **84**
5103 **DAFORE 15** [1]3-8-6 (82) J F McDonald(3) 16/1: 1000: 10th: Held up, btn 2f out: btr 1497 (6f). ½ **75**
4813 **NORTON 34** [8]7-9-7 (94) J Fortune 20/1: 4003100: 11th: Trkd ldrs, hmpd over 1f out & no extra. 2½ **82**
5103 **UNSHAKABLE 15** [4]5-9-6 (93) F Norton 15/2: 3054500: 12th: Held up & al bhd: btr 4061. 3½ **74**
4916 **KRUGERRAND 28** [5]5-9-2 (89) Laura Pike(7) 40/1: 6051500: 13th: Slow away & al rear: btr 4122 (gd). 3 **64**
13 Ran Time 1m 42.02 (5.52) Owned: The Hornsey Warriors Racing Syndicate Trained: Thirsk

5285 4.20 European Breeders Fund Maiden Stakes Colts & Geldings 2yo (D3)
£4999 £1538 £769 7f str Good/Soft 76 -15 Slow Stands Side

CENTAURUS 0 [14] Saeed bin Suroor 2-8-11 T E Durcan 3.1: 1: gr c Daylami - Dandanna (Linamix) Handy & chsd ldr over 2f out, led dist, rdn out: hvly bckd, op 4/1: Jan first foal, dam a 6f juv wnr on debut: eff at 7f, 1m+ shld suit: acts on gd/soft grnd & a stiff trk: goes well fresh: looks useful. **94**
MASTER OF THE RACE 0 [20] Sir Michael Stoute 2-8-11 D Holland 7/1: 2: ch c Selkirk - Dust Dancer (Suave Dancer) Al handy, rdn & styd on fnl 2f, not pace of wnr: bckd, op 8/1: 200,000gns Apr foal, half-brother to a useful 7f/1m juv wnr Spotlight: dam a high-class 10f wnr as a 3yo: eff at 7f, get further: acts on gd/soft grnd & a stiff trk: useful start, shld win races. 1½ **91**
5084 **RIVER ROYALE 16** [12] P W Chapple Hyam 2-8-11 A McCarthy 11/4 FAV: 333: Handy & keen, switched to lead halfway, hdd dist, no extra ins last: clr rem: hvly bckd: styd longer 1m trip well, acts on gd & gd/soft. 2 **87**
5097 **TREW STYLE 15** [17] M H Tompkins 2-8-11 Dane O'Neill 25/1: 04: ch c Desert King - Southern Psychic (Alwasmi) Held up, styd on fnl 3f, nvr threatened front trio: bckd at long odds, op 66/1: Feb foal, 26,000gns purchase: half-brother to useful 1m/10f h'capper Wing Commander: dam a 4yo US wnr. 5 **79**
ZADALRAKIB 0 [1]2-8-11 M Hills 12/1: 5: ch c Machiavellian - Party Doll (Be My Guest) Dwelt, sn handy, rdn & no extra over 1f out: longer priced stablemate of rnr-up: op 8/1: 240,000gns Feb foal: half-brother to smart 6f juv wnr Titus Livius, also wnr at up to 7f: 6/7f may suit next term, promising start. 1½ **77**
5084 **KRULLIND 16** [9]2-8-11 Thomas Yeung(5) 66/1: 06: Led till over 3f out, sn hung left & no extra. 3½ **71**
4776 **BONFIRE 36** [11]2-8-11 J Fanning 14/1: 47: Prom, no impress fnl 2f: btr 4776 (fast). 4 **63**
PAGAN SWORD 0 [15]2-8-11 S Sanders 16/1: 8: Dwelt, in tch till over 1f out. 1½ **61**
GOODBYE BEN 0 [2]2-8-11 J Fortune 12/1: 9: Chsd ldrs, btn 2f out. ½ **60**
4885 **BACHELOR AFFAIR 29** [4]2-8-11 Martin Dwyer 50/1: 00: 10th: Keen & prom, btn 2f out. 1 **58**
NATIONAL TRUST 0 [13]2-8-11 K Darley 12/1: 0: 11th: Mid-div, no impress fnl 2f, stablemate of rnr-up. hd **57**
RAISON DETRE 0 [6]2-8-11 J Quinn 66/1: 0: 12th: Slow away & bhd, mod late prog. ½ **56**
TAAKEED 0 [8]2-8-11 P Robinson 20/1: 0: 13th: Chsd ldrs, btn 3f out. nk **55**
NEW REALM 0 [18]2-8-11 S Drowne 33/1: 0: 14th: Slow away & al bhd. 3 **50**
BEN BACCHUS 0 [5]2-8-11 P Doe 66/1: 0: 15th: Dwelt & al rear. ½ **49**
LAST CHAPTER 0 [10]2-8-11 V Slattery 66/1: 0: 16th: Slow away, al well bhd. 7 **37**
BLOOD MONEY 0 [7]2-8-11 J F Egan 20/1: 0: 17th: Slowly to stride & al rear. 2 **33**
BULLSEYE 0 [19]2-8-11 T Quinn 50/1: 0: 18th: Dwelt, in tch 4f. 2 **29**
JOHNNY CHI 0 [3]2-8-11 A Culhane 33/1: 0: 19th: Dwelt, sn struggling rear. 13 **9**
19 Ran Time 1m 29.61 (6.41) Owned: Godolphin Trained: Newmarket

5286 4.55 Racing Uk On Sky 432 Handicap Stakes 3yo+ 71-85 (D2) [94]
£6989 £2150 £1075 7f str Good/Soft 76 -34 Slow Stands Side

5172 **ALFONSO 11** [18] B W Hills 3-8-11 (77) M Hills 5/1: 1002421: Al prom in centre & led over 2f out, drvn out: nicely bckd: stays 1m, both wins at 7f: acts on gd, likes gd/soft, soft & fibresand, stiff or sharp trk. **88**
5000 **ARCTIC DESERT 21** [17] A M Balding 4-8-13 (77) P Hanagan 25/1: 6162002: Held up centre, styd on from over 1f out, not pace of wnr: see 4117. 2½ **82**
4652 **QUEENS RHAPSODY 43** [14] A Bailey 4-9-2 (80) J Fortune 14/1: 0400053: Chsd ldrs centre, styd on for press: nicely h'capped, gd run: handles firm, gd/soft & both AWs: see 431. ½ **84**
5001 **CARDINAL VENTURE 21** [1] K A Ryan 6-9-11 (89) A Mullen(7) 16/1: 0100004: Led stands side group, styd on for press, no ch with front trio centre ins last: gd run: see 2187. ½ **92**
5227 **TIDY 7** [19]4-8-13 (77) T E Durcan 14/1: 0300445: Held up centre, styd on onepace fnl 2f: see 1035. 2 **77**
5101 **DIGITAL 15** [6]7-9-7 (85) S Hitchcott 10/1: 0220506: Held up stands side, late gains, nrst fin. ½ **84**
2247 **SYDNEY STAR 147** [16]3-9-4 (84) Martin Dwyer 33/1: 2-107: Led centre group 4f, btn dist: abs. ¾ **81**
4642 **MUTAMARED 43** [4]4-9-5 (83) R Hills 7/2 FAV: 226-138: Stands side, prom till dist: bckd, op 9/2, abs. hd **79**
5196 **CHATEAU NICOL 8** [9]5-9-5 bl (83) T Quinn 12/1: 6601439: Held up stands side, not land a blow. ½ **78**
4702 **CRAIL 40** [20]4-8-10 (74) Lisa Jones 50/1: 0-304100: 10th: Held up centre, no impress 2f out, abs. ½ **68**
4683 **SURF THE NET 42** [8]3-8-13 vis (79) R Hughes 50/1: 0034000: 11th: Chsd ldrs stands side, btn 2f out, abs. ½ **72**
5144 **AZREME 13** [3]4-8-13 (77) A Culhane 7/1: 3020120: 12th: Held up stands side, btn over 1f out. 2½ **65**
4362 **CAMBERWELL 57** [13]3-8-12 (78) G Carter 66/1: 150000: 13th: Prom centre 4f, 8 wk abs. ½ **65**
3942* **MIDDLETON GREY 77** [10]6-8-7 bl (71) L Keniry(3) 20/1: 2035210: 14th: Held up stands side, btn dist. ¾ **56**
4500 **Serre Chevalier 50** [12]3-8-12 (78) D Holland 33/1:0

NEWMARKET   SATURDAY 30.10.04   Righthand, Stiff, Galloping Track

4713 **Tregarron 40** [15]3-8-5 (71) P Norton 66/1:0
4777 **Kodiac 36** [2]3-9-2 (82) P Robinson 12/1:0
4195* **Viennas Boy 64** [11]3-8-13 (79) Dane O'Neill 25/1:0
5159 **Winning Venture 12** [5]7-9-1 (79) W Supple 25/1:0
5000 **Kingscross 21** [7]6-9-2 (80) D Sweeney 12/1:0
20 Ran   Time 1m 30.91(7.1)   Owned: Mr Guy Reed   Trained: Lambourn

WOLVERHAMPTON   Polytrack   SATURDAY 30.10.04   Lefthand, Sharp Track

Official Going STANDARD.

5287   7.00 Ladbrokes Com Median Auction Maiden Stakes 2yo (F3)
£3465 £1066 £533   5f216y aw rnd   No Standard Time   Inside

4945 **PAMIR 26** [10] L M Cumani 2-9-0 S Drowne 7/2 JT FAV: 031: Trkd ldrs, led dist, drvn out: AW   77a
bow: confirmed improvement of latest: eff at 6f on gd/soft & polytrack, get further: see 4945.
5169 **KEEP ME WARM 11** [1] W G M Turner 2-9-0 P Makin(5) 5/1: 42: Al handy & led 2f out till over 1f   ½   74a
out, styd on well for press: AW bow: styd longer 6f trip well: acts on polytrack & soft grnd: see 5169.
5182 **SWEET NAMIBIA 11** [4] J W Hills 2-8-9 S Sanders 7/2 JT FAV: 33: Dwelt, sn trkd ldrs trav well,   1½   65a
led over 1f out till dist, no extra: op 11/4: see 5182.
  DASH OF LIME [5] S Kirk 2-8-9 J F Egan 7/1: 4: b f Bold Edge - Green Supreme (Primo Dominie)   nk   64a+
Dwelt, sn mid-div, styd on well from over 1f out, nrst fin: Feb foal, half-sister to high-class sprinter Sampowe
Star, also useful multiple sprint wnrs Absent Friends & Fire Up The Band: dam unrcd: eff at 6f on polytrack.
2902 **SEAMLESS 120** [9]2-9-0 S W Kelly 5/1: 55: Trkd ldrs, onepace over 1f out: 4 mth abs, AW bow: nk   68a
handles polytrack & gd grnd: looks sure to relish 7f+ on breeding: see 2902.
  ROSSIN GOLD [6]2-9-0 BL V Slattery 20/1: 6: b g Rossini - Sacred Heart (Catrail) V slow away,   7   47a
late prog, nvr a factor: blnks: 21,000gns 2yo, Apr first foal: dam unplcd: half-sister to a multiple 1m wnr.
5105 **QUEENS HAND 15** [12]2-8-9 T Hamilton(3) 33/1: 07: Sn outpcd & nvr a factor.   ½   41a
5113 **PROSPECT POINT 14** [11]2-8-9 P D Fox(5) 14/1: 48: Chsd ldrs wide till halfway: cheek pieces.   2½   34a
4596 **LUGANA POINT 45** [7]2-9-0 C Catlin 33/1: 09: Led till 2f out, sn btn, 6 wk abs.   3   30a
5152 **SCARBOROUGH FLYER 12** [8]2-9-0 D Allan 66/1: 00: 10th: Dwelt & al outpcd.   6   12a
  COMPTON SPARK [3]2-9-0 T Eaves(3) 28/1: 0: 11th: Slow away & al outpcd rear.   1¾   7a
5127 **Stevmarie Star 14** [13]2-8-9 J Quinn 66/1:0   5106 **Madame Guillotine 15** [2]2-8-9 J Edmunds 50/1:0
13 Ran   Time 1m 17.41 ()   Owned: Mrs E H Vestey   Trained: Newmarket

5288   7.30 Ladbrokescasino Com Maiden Auction Stakes 2yo (E3)
£3413 £1050 £525   1m141y aw rnd   No Standard Time   Inside

4978 **KANGRINA 23** [5] Sir Mark Prescott 2-8-8 S Sanders 5/1: 541: Chasing ldrs when hmpd inner after   79a
2f, switched wide & styd on for press to lead well ins last: op 11/4: eff at 1m/8.5f, 9f+ shld suit: acts on
polytrack & a sharp trk: progressing with racing: see 4978 & 4744.
4978 **LINDAS COLIN 23** [7] P W D'Arcy 2-8-10 N Callan 2/1 FAV: 022: Al handy, rdn & briefly led ins   ¾   78a
last, not pace of wnr cl-home: nicely bckd: ahd of today's wnr latest: see 4978 (C/D).
5018 **TRANQUILIZER 20** [4] D J Coakley 2-8-2 (69) J Quinn 9/1: 6U023: Sn handy trav well, rdn to chall   ½   69a
ins last, just held cl-home: confirmed improvement of latest: eff around 1m/8.6f on gd & polytrack: see 5018.
5019 **RED RIVER ROCK 20** [1] C Tinkler 2-8-13 (75) C Catlin 10/1: 3004: Led, hdd & no extra ins last: hd   79a
op 12/1: stays 8.6f: acts on polytrack & gd grnd: imprvd eff with forcing tactics applied: see 4115.
5236 **SOL ROJO 5** [6]2-8-10 V Slattery 20/1: 0005: Mid-div, outpcd over 2f out, keeping on when short   1   74a
of room ins last, qck reapp: type to impr in h'cap company: handles polytrack: see 5236.
5179 **MELS MOMENT 11** [8]2-8-13 (74) S W Kelly 7/2: 06U46: Trkd ldr, rdn & fdd ins last: op 9/2.   2½   72a
  INNPURSUIT [2]2-8-10 S Drowne 14/1: 7: b c Inchinor - Quest For The Best (Rainbow Quest)   1¾   65a
Mid-div, nvr able to threaten: 16,000gns Feb foal, half-brother to a dual 7f 3yo scorer: dam unplcd.
  INN FOR THE DANCER [12]2-8-7 J F Egan 40/1: 8: b g Groom Dancer - Lady Joyce (Galetto) Dwelt,   5   52a
sn rdn & al bhd: cheaply bght Apr foal, half-brother to a multiple 1m/9f scorer, also a 6f juv wnr: dam unrcd.
5081 **DEFINITELY ROYAL 17** [3]2-8-8 M Henry 50/1: 09: Dwelt, sn rear.   ½   52a
4997 **MADAME FATALE 21** [11]2-8-3 (1ow) T P Queally 50/1: 00: 10th: Mid-div, btn 3f out.   3   41a
5033 **WHIRLING 19** [10]2-8-2 J Mackay 66/1: 00: 11th: Prom wide, sn bhd.   6   28a
4864 **Sadies Star 31** [9]2-8-5 Lisa Jones 20/1:0   **Suncliff** [13]2-8-7 BL D Allan 66/1:0
13 Ran   Time 1m 53.61 ()   Owned: Mr Faisal Salman   Trained: Newmarket

5289   8.00 Ladbrokes Com Handicap Stakes 3yo+ 56-70 (E3)
£3432 £1056 £528   7f32y aw rnd   No Standard Time   Outside   [82]

2409 **UP TEMPO 140** [1] K A Ryan 6-9-4 bl (72) N Callan 11/2: 4200501: Mid-div, sn pushed along, rdn to   81a
lead well ins last: 5 mth abs: eff at 6/7f on firm, hvy & both AWs: goes well fresh: tough & genuine: see 1142.
5008* **STORMY NATURE 21** [12] P W Harris 3-9-0 (70) S Drowne 9/2 FAV: 3000012: Rear, hdwy wide from   1½   75a
over 1f out, not pace of wnr: confirmed improvement of 5008 (C/D).
5006 **SAMUEL CHARLES 21** [9] W M Brisbourne 6-9-7 (75) B Swarbrick(5) 7/1: 0160143: Chsd ldrs & led 2f   shd   80a
out, drvn & hdd well ins last: see 4920 (clmr).
4766 **TEMPLET 36** [11] I Semple 4-9-2 bl (70) R Winston 10/1: 0021404: Dwelt & outpcd rear, late gains,   2½   70a
nrst fin: eff at 7f, crying out for return to 1m+: acts on fast, hvy & polytrack: worth another look over further.
4621 **WEST HIGHLAND WAY 44** [3]3-9-5 (75) T Eaves(3) 20/1: 502-1505: Rear, late gains for press, no threat.   2   71a
4912 **H HARRISON 28** [10]4-9-6 p (74) L Vickers 13/2: 0065036: Chsd ldrs trav well, wknd dist: btr 4912.   1¼   67a
1059 **MUSICAL GIFT 208** [8]4-9-1 (69) T P Queally 14/1: 0-144507: Rear, rdn & little prog, abs, new yard.   3   56a
5181 **BLUE KNIGHT 11** [2]5-9-2 (70) S W Kelly 33/1: 0620408: Held up, no impress fnl 2f: see 5181 & 655.   1¾   54a
4832 **ZARIANO 33** [5]4-9-2 (70) S Drowne 25/1: 0-200009: Led after 1f till 5f out, btn 2f out: btr 3286.   1¾   51a
5010 **SEWMUCH CHARACTER 21** [6]5-9-0 (68) D Sweeney 8/1: 2010630: 10th: Trkd ldr & led 5f out, hdd 2f   1¼   46a

1608

out, sn wknd: btr 5010.

5130 **AVENTURA** 14 [4]4-9-0 (68) P Makin(5) 10/1: 0000000: 11th: Led 1f, btn over 2f out: btr 800.   **8**   **30a**

4086 **ZANJEER** 71 [7]4-9-1 (69) T Hamilton(3) 9/1: 1631050: 12th: Trkd ldr early, wknd qckly 2f out: btr 3310 (gd) 5   **21a**

12 Ran   Time 1m 31.00 ()   Owned: Yorkshire Racing Club & Derek Blackhurst   Trained: Hambleton

---

5290   8.30 Ladbrokes Com Maiden Stakes 3yo+   (D3)
£3432 £1056 £528   1m1f103y aw   **No Standard Time**   Inside

5173 **WHIRLY BIRD** 11 [6] Mrs A J Perrett 3-8-9 S Sanders 1/1 FAV: 31: Dwelt & towards rear, switched   **75a**
wide & rapid hdwy over 2f out, rdn & led ins last, going away: nicely bckd to confirm debut promise: eff around
9/10f, could get further: acts on polytrack & soft grnd: lightly rcd, entitled to prog: see 5173.

2716 **TROMP** 127 [13] D J Coakley 3-9-0   T P Queally 12/1: 562: ch c Zilzal - Sulitelma (The Minstrel)   **2**   **75a**
Held up, hdwy wide to lead 2f out, hdd ins last & no extra: rest well covered, op 14/1, 4 mth abs: styd longer 9.5f
trip well: acts on polytrack, mod at 7f previously.

4892 **IRISH PLAYWRIGHT** 29 [10] D G Bridgwater 4-9-4 BL D Nolan(3) 25/1: 003: b g King's Theatre -   **5**   **67a**
Marino Waltz (Thatching) Trkd ldr & led after 2f till 2f out, no extra dist: some improvement in first time blnks
with forcing tactics: handles polytrack: unplcd previously.

2274 **MISS MERENDA** 145 [9] D E Cantillon 3-8-9   J F Egan 10/1: 0004: Rear, mod hdwy wide fnl 3f, no   1½   **60a**
threat: op 18/1, 5 mth abs: unplcd on turf at up to 11.5f previously.

5023 **DOVEDALE** 20 [11]4-8-13 V Slattery 6/1: 045: Dwelt & bhd, prog/no room over 1f out, kept on late.   1¼   **58a**
4847 **NOPLEAZINU** 32 [2]4-8-13 G Gibbons 33/1: 506: Mid-div, btn 2f out.   3½   **53a**
BOLDINI 129 [5]3-9-0 S Drowne 5/1: 037: Chsd ldrs till 2f out, jumps fit.   nk   **57a**
5052 **CASPIAN LAKE** 19 [7]3-9-0 L Keniry(3) 66/1: 08: Chsd ldr 3f out, btn over 1f out.   1¼   **55a**
WON OF A FEW [4]4-9-4 A Kirby(7) 33/1: 9: Slow away & rear, nvr a factor on debut.   nk   **54a**
5023 **RAMBO BLUE** 20 [8]4-9-4 J Quinn 12/1: 060: 10th: Mid-div wide, btn 3f out.   nk   **53a**
CELTIC TANNER [12]5-9-4 S Hitchcott 40/1: 0: 11th: Led 2f, btn 3f out, jumps fit.   ¾   **52a**
4768 **Delta Star** 36 [1]4-8-13 N Callan 20/1:0   **Archie Clarke** [3]4-9-4 D Sweeney 33/1:0

13 Ran   Time 2m 05.17 ()   Owned: Woodcote Stud Ltd   Trained: Pulborough

---

5291   9.00 Ladbrokespoker Com Handicap Stakes 3yo+ 56-70 (E3)   [81]
£3444 £1060 £530   5f216y aw rnd   **No Standard Time**   Inside

5114 **FLYING BANTAM** 14 [3] R A Fahey 3-9-6 (73) P Hanagan 5/1: 2404131: Mid-div, rdn halfway, drvn to   **82a**
lead well ins last: eff at 5f, suited by 6f on firm, gd/soft & polytrack, any trk: see 5114 & 4790.

5014 **KINGSMAITE** 20 [5] S R Bowring 3-9-5 bl (72) P Makin(5) 16/1: 5130502: Trkd ldrs trav well & led   nk   **79a**
over 1f out, hdd well ins last: rest well covered: acts on fast, gd & both AWs: see 2551.

5114 **BRIDGEWATER BOYS** 14 [8] K A Ryan 3-9-3 bl (70) N Callan 7/1: 2150063: Hmpd early, switched right   3½   **67a**
& kept on fnl 2f, no threat to front pair: acts on fast, gd & both AWs: see 2482 & 2055.

5114 **CHEROKEE NATION** 14 [1] P W D'Arcy 3-9-2 (69) J F Egan 11/2: 0350024: Trkd ldr & led 2f out till   1¼   **62a**
over 1f out, wknd: ahd of today's wnr latest: see 5114 (C/D).

5149 **JILLY WHY** 12 [9]3-9-3 (70) B Swarbrick(5) 10/1: 1002405: Chsd ldrs, no extra ins last: see 4822 (5f).   ½   **62a**
4652 **HILITES** 43 [12]3-9-4 p (71) S Whitworth 22/1: 3040006: Slow into stride & bhd, nrst fin, 6 wk abs.   ½   **62a**
5181 **BLAKESHALL QUEST** 11 [2]4-9-3 vis (69) D Nolan(3) 28/1: 0100007: Rear, mod prog for press.   nk   **59a**
4689 **SMIRFYS SYSTEMS** 42 [13]5-9-7 (73) S W Kelly 10/1: 0500208: Trkd ldrs, btn dist, abs: btr 3574.   1   **60a**
5010 **WILLHEWIZ** 21 [11]4-9-7 (73) L Keniry(3) 8/1: 0040029: Led till 2f out, sn wknd: btr 5010.   shd   **60a**
4920 **CASHEL MEAD** 28 [7]4-9-4 (70) Lisa Jones 18/1: 0060000: 10th: Chsd ldrs till halfway, btn/eased fnl 1f.   3½   **47a**
5114 **BEEJAY** 14 [4]3-9-4 (71) N De Souza(5) 16/1: 1000000: 11th: Hmpd bef halfway, sn struggling: btr 4604.   nk   **47a**
5181 **MISTRAL SKY** 11 [6]5-9-8 vis (74) S Drowne 3/1 FAV: 0122120: 12th: Sn bhd & btn/eased over 1f out.   9   **25a**

12 Ran   Time 1m 15.81 ()   Owned: The Matthewman Partnership   Trained: Malton

---

5292   9.30 Ladbrokesgames Com Handicap Stakes 3yo+ 46-55 (F4)   [69]
£3023 £864 £432   1m1f103y aw   **No Standard Time**   Inside

5017 **REGENTS SECRET** 20 [8] J S Goldie 4-9-3 (58) T Eaves(3) 9/2: 3060331: Rear, hdwy to lead ins last,   **65a**
drvn out: op 13/2: first win: eff btwn 7/9f on firm, gd & polytrack, handles gd/soft, any trk: eff with/without
cheek pieces, tried visor: see 1092.

4990 **CHARMATIC** 22 [1] J A Glover 3-9-3 (62) J Quinn 8/1: 5450602: Trkd ldrs trav well, rdn to chall   1¾   **66a**
dist, not pace of wnr: acts on fast, soft & polytrack: eff btwn 1m/10f: on a handy mark: see 2277 & 1628.

5153* **WRENLANE** 12 [12] R A Fahey 3-9-5 (64) P Hanagan 4/1 FAV: 0403413: Chsd ldrs & led 2f out till   1   **66a**
ins last, not pace of front pair: op 7/2: stays 9.5f: see 5153.

4719 **ZAWRAK** 39 [4] I W McInnes 5-9-2 P (57) J F McDonald(3) 22/1: 0520004: Rear, rdn & styd on fnl 2f,   nk   **58a**
nrst fin: imprvd eff in first time cheek pieces: see 194.

5016 **INCHDURA** 20 [3]6-9-6 (61) Kim Tinkler 22/1: 0-006005: Chsd ldrs, onepcd dist.   ¾   **61a**
5183 **EASTER OGIL** 11 [13]9-9-3 (58) L Enstone 9/1: 2650066: Rear, mod gains for press, nvr a threat.   ½   **57a**
5183 **BOND MILLENNIUM** 11 [5]6-9-6 (61) F Lynch 11/2: 0020047: Held up, eff wide, no impress fnl 1f.   ¾   **59a**
4983 **EFRHINA** 23 [11]4-9-5 (60) S Drowne 9/1: 2003438: Mid-div, not pace to land blow: see 4924 (12f).   ½   **57a**
5130 **SARRAAF** 14 [7]8-9-4 (59) S W Kelly 7/1: 3460409: Rear, prog/switched over 1f out, no impress.   hd   **56a**
4973 **SURDOUE** 24 [2]4-9-5 (60) N Pollard 22/1: 4200000: 10th: Led 1f & trkd ldrs after, btn over 1f out.   hd   **57a**
5112 **YORKER** 14 [10]6-9-5 (60) N Callan 14/1: 3601300: 11th: Held up, nvr land a blow, eased.   2   **54a**
4668 **QUINTOTO** 42 [6]4-9-2 (57) T Hamilton 33/1: 00-60000: 12th: Led after 1f till 2f out, sn btn, 6 wk abs.   3½   **46a**
4528 **DAVE** 49 [9]3-9-2 (61) G Baker 20/1: 50-10000: 13th: Keen & prom, btn over 1f out, eased, abs.   27   **5a**

13 Ran   Time 2m 04.47()   Owned: Mrs M Craig   Trained: Glasgow

LINGFIELD **Polytrack SUNDAY 31.10.04 Lefthand, V Sharp Track**

Official Going Standard

5293 **12.25 Testers Of Edenbridge All New Discovery 3 Maiden Stakes Div 1 2yo (D3)**
£4329 £1332 £666 **1m aw rnd Going 21 -04 Slow** Outside

5076 **KARENS CAPER 18** [4] J H M Gosden 2-8-9 J Fortune 4/5 FAV: 21: Al cl-up trav well & led 2f out, readily pulled clr, val 7L+: hvly bckd to confirm debut promise: apprec step up to 1m: acts on polytrack, sharp trk: potentially useful: see 5076. **85a+**
5097 **OBEZYANA 16** [6] G A Huffer 2-9-0 N Callan 50/1: 02: ch c Rahy - Polish Treaty (Danzig) Keen chasing ldrs, short of room 2f out, styd on for press to take 2nd cl-home, no ch with easy wnr: left soft grnd debut bhd: 46,000gns 2yo, Feb foal: eff at 1m, shapes like further will suit: handles polytrack. *5* **77a**
4831 **KINRANDE 34** [9] P J Makin 2-9-0 D Sweeney 16/1: 33: Trkd ldrs, styd on for press, no threat: handles fast grnd & polytrack: see 4831. *nk* **76a**
4829 **MR AITCH 34** [5] J A Osborne 2-9-0 Dane O'Neill 9/1: 24: Keen in mid-div, short of room 2f out, switched & kept on, nrst fin: op 7/1: handles polytrack & fast grnd: see 4829. *hd* **75a**
5078 **MISSATACAMA 18** [8]2-8-9 S W Kelly 20/1: 45: Mid-div wide, outpcd over 2f out, kept on ins last for press: styd longer 1m trip, shaped as if further will suit: see 5078. *¾* **68a**
1717 **NANTON 171** [2]2-9-0 T Quinn 6/1: 06: gr c Spinning World - Grab The Green (Cozzene) Led 6f, btn dist: op 12/1, 6 mth abs: $75,000 Mar foal: half-brother to wnrs abroad, dam a useful performer at 1m/9f. *¾* **71a**
5059 **REGISTRAR 19** [1]2-9-0 S Drowne 9/2: 527: Dwelt, chsd ldrs, btn dist: btr 5059. *1¾* **67a**
5058 **SEEKING AN ALIBI 19** [11]2-9-0 T T E Durcan 16/1: 08: Chsd ldrs wide, btn 2f out, t-strap. *1¼* **65a**
ZABADANI 0 [7]2-8-9 Martin Dwyer 33/1: 9: Dwelt, pushed along rear, only mod late prog. *nk* **59a**
5091 **EMPANGENI 16** [12]2-9-0 T P Queally 33/1: 050: 10th: Al towards rear & no ch fnl 2f. *2½* **59a**
5091 **MAHMJRA 16** [10]2-9-0 C Catlin 66/1: 000: 11th: Rear, t.o. fnl 3f. *10* **41a**
5002 **ANOTHER PLAN 22** [3]2-9-0 G Baker 100/1: 00: 12th: Dwelt & al bhd, t.o.. *3½* **34a**
12 Ran Time 1m 38.22 (2.02) Owned: Stonerside Stables LLC Trained: Manton

5294 **12.55 Bet Direct 'red To Bet' On Itv Classified Stakes 3yo+ 0-55 (F4)**
£2954 £844 £422 **7f aw rnd Going 21 -07 Slow** Inside

4750 **MACS TALISMAN 62** [8] V Smith 4-9-1 t p (56) D Holland 5/2 JT FAV: 0023001: Chsd ldrs, smooth prog wide to lead over 1f out, asserted under hand riding: well bckd, op 11/4: 2 mth abs: eff at 6/7f on both AWs, fast & gd grnd: now eff in t-strap/cheek pieces: decisive success, can win again: see 1806. **63a+**
5263* **NEARLY A FOOL 3** [3] G G Margarson 6-9-11 vis (60) N Pollard 5/2 JT FAV: 4050512: Trkd ldrs, eff to chase wnr fnl 1f, kept on, al held: qck reapp: see 5263 (C/D). *1* **69a**
5112 **SMOKIN JOE 15** [13] J R Best 3-8-12 bl (55) G Baker 16/1: 0000053: Rear, hdwy wide over 2f out & styd on for press, not threaten front pair: eff at 6/7f: see 258, 217 & 182. *¾* **56a**
5155 **ASBO 13** [5] Dr J D Scargill 4-8-11 (55) S Drowne 6/1: 5435634: Mid-div, mod prog for press, no threat: longer 7f trip may yet suit: see 5155 & 4646. *2* **49a**
3788 **KINSMAN 85** [9]7-9-0 bl (55) J P Guillambert(3) 33/1: 5460005: Slow away & rear, late gains, nrst fin. *shd* **51a**
3966 **ADANTINO 77** [6]5-9-2 bl (57) J Fortune 10/1: 3631606: Rear, eff wide, btn dist: abs: see 3289 (6f). *1½* **50a**
5116 **MUTASSEM 15** [2]3-8-12 (55) M Henry 16/1: 0000207: Mid-div, short of room over 2f out & again over 1f out, no impress, op 25/1: see 4636. *2* **44a**
4791 **GLENDALE 36** [12]3-9-0 (57) Dane O'Neill 33/1: 0005008: Handy & led over 2f out till over 1f out. *hd* **45a**
5030 **LADY KORRIANDA 21** [7]3-8-11 (57) T P Queally 20/1: 002-09: Mid-div, btn 2f out: btr 146 (6f). *3* **36a**
4751 **MARGALITA 39** [14]4-8-11 bl t (55) Lisa Jones 33/1: 0600000: 10th: Led till over 2f out, saddle slipped. *½* **33a**
5046 **Pheckless 20** [11]5-9-5 (60) P Fitzsimons 20/1:0 3092 **Noble Mount 114** [4]3-8-12 (55) Derek Nolan(7) 33/1:0
3155 **Arogant Prince 111** [10]7-9-0 (55) T Quinn 40/1:0 2280 **Captain Darling 146** [1]4-9-5 p(60) A Quinn(5) 12/1:0
14 Ran Time 1m 24.78 (1.98) Owned: Mr V Smith Trained: Newmarket

5295 **1.25 Testers Of Edenbridge All New Discovery 3 Maiden Stakes Div 2 2yo (D3)**
£4316 £1328 £664 **1m aw rnd Going 21 -10 Slow** Outside

5192 **MARHOON 10** [3] E F Vaughan 2-9-0 t T E Durcan 11/4 JT FAV: 421: Sn handy & chsd ldr over 1f out, led ins last, rdn out: nicely bckd: eff at 7f, apprec step up to 1m: acts on soft grnd & polytrack, sharp/undul trks: progressing with racing: see 5192. **80a**
ROLLERBIRD 0 [8] A M Balding 2-8-9 Martin Dwyer 11/4 JT FAV: 2: b f Sinndar - Speedybird (Danehill) Handy & led over 2f out, hdd ins last & not pace of wnr: rest well covered: bckd: 60,000gns Apr foal, half-sister to a plcd 7f 3yo, dam a 7f 3yo wnr: eff at 1m on polytrack & a sharp trk: encouraging start. *3* **66a**
MARIA DELFINA 0 [11] J H M Gosden 2-8-9 J Fortune 4/1: 3: ch f Giant's Causeway - Photographie (Trempolino) Dwelt, rear, switched wide & styd on well fnl 2f, nrst fin under a kind ride: 180,000gns Mar foal, dam unplcd, well related to high-class French performers: stays 1m, shld get further on this evidence: handles polytrack: eye-catching late hdwy, expect significant progress. *3* **60a+**
THE GEEZER 0 [10] D R C Elsworth 2-9-0 L Keniry(3) 13/2: 4: Pushed along towards rear, styd on. *nk* **64a**
CHOCOLATE CARAMEL 0 [9]2-9-0 S W Kelly 16/1: 5: Mid-div, outpcd halfway, rdn & kept on fnl 2f. *½* **63a**
3691 **BUSACO 88** [4]2-9-0 T Quinn 20/1: 046: Chsd ldrs, hung left & outpcd fnl 2f, abs. *nk* **62a**
4664 **MR MAYFAIR 43** [6]2-9-0 P Fitzsimons 16/1: 07: Chsd ldrs, btn over 1f out, abs. *3* **56a**
MAAM 0 [7]2-8-9 N Callan 66/1: 8: Dwelt, pushed along in rear, little hdwy. *3½* **44a**
5040 **TOQUE 20** [5]2-8-9 S Drowne 14/1: 09: Towards rear & no ch fnl 2f. *¾* **42a**
5259 **HUGO THE BOSS 3** [12]2-9-0 Dane O'Neill 66/1: 000: 10th: Held up wide, struggling fnl 2f, qck reapp. *4* **39a**
4896 **WIZ IN 30** [2]2-9-0 M Henry 66/1: 00: 11th: U.r. & unruly bef start, led till over 2f out, sn btn. *hd* **38a**
4722 **LA MUSIQUE 40** [1]2-9-0 S Whitworth 100/1: 00: 12th: Dwelt, cl-up, wknd qckly 3f out, abs. *14* **12a**
12 Ran Time 1m 38.72 (2.52) Owned: Sheikh Ahmed Al Maktoum Trained: Newmarket

5296

2.00 Chris Davies Classified Stakes 3yo+ 0-60 (F3)
£3572 £1099 £550   1m4f aw   Going 21   -23 Slow Inside

4414 **STORMY DAY 55** [9] Mrs A J Perrett 4-9-1 e (60) S Drowne 16/1: 60-61: b f Rainbow Quest - Broken 66a
Peace (Devil's Bag) Rear, hdwy wide 2f out & drvn to lead well ins last, going away: 8 wk abs & AW bow: first win:
unplcd '03 (rtd 59, M Jarvis): eff at 12f, shaped as if 14f+ will suit: took well to polytrack & fitting of
eye-shield: likes a sharp trk & goes well fresh: lightly rcd & can progress.
5117 **UNCLE JOHN 15** [8] S Kirk 3-8-11 bl (60) J F Egan 14/1: 2400032: Trkd ldrs, rdn & led ins last, sn 1 65a
hdd & not pace of wnr: confirmed return to form of latest: see 5117, 3173 & 2024.
4850 **SMOOTHIE 32** [6] Ian Williams 6-9-4 p (60) L Enstone 16/1: 4-060103: Rear, late gains for press, 1½ 62a
nrst fin: handles fast, soft & both AWs: see 6.
4899 **KING OF KNIGHT 30** [13] G Prodromou 3-8-11 (60) A Beech(3) 9/2 FAV: 5000424: Keen & trkd ldrs, led nk 61a
over 2f out till hdd ins last, no extra: see 4899.
4966 **ELLINA 26** [16]3-8-8 (60) T Quinn 12/1: 4010035: Rear, late gains under hand riding, nrst fin: ¾ 56a
eff around 10/12f on gd, soft & polytrack: not given a hard time here, can impr: see 4966 & 3334.
4899 **KING FLYER 30** [15]8-9-4 (58) B Reilly(3) 9/1: 2000536: Rear, late prog for press, no threat. ½ 58a
4966 **SAIDA LENASERA 26** [12]3-8-8 (60) T E Durcan 25/1: 0660557: Keen & cl-up, lost place 4f out, sn nk 54a
hmpd & towards rear, late rally.
5153 **WILLHEGO 13** [5]3-8-11 (58) Martin Dwyer 16/1: 0231508: Pulled hard early, trkd ldrs, rdn to shd 56a
chall 2f out, wknd dist: not see out this 12f trip, spot on back at 10f: see 4182.
4650 **AIRGUSTA 44** [10]3-8-11 (57) A Daly 66/1: 00-00009: Keen & trkd ldrs, btn over 1f out, 6 wk abs. 2½ 52a
5077* **FANTASY CRUSADER 18** [7]5-9-4 p (58) Dane O'Neill 10/1: 3131010: 10th: Keen, rear, hdwy wide 2f nk 51a
out, btn dist: btr 5077 (1m).
5194 **DESERT ISLAND DISC 9** [14]7-9-1 (59) G Baker 10/1: 6300300: 11th: Rear, little prog: btr 5095. 1¼ 46a
4892 **SUNSHINE ON ME 30** [2]3-8-8 (60) T P Queally 11/2: 0500: 12th: Cl-up, wknd 2f out: btr 4892 & 4111. 2½ 42a
4824 **ANYHOW 34** [11]7-9-1 (60) D Nolan(3) 10/1: 2105500: 13th: Held up, hdwy wide halfway & led 4f out 4 36a
till over 2f out, sn btn: btr 3481.
5117 **KERNEL DOWERY 15** [1]4-9-4 e (59) D Holland 15/2: 0045040: 14th: Led/dsptd lead 1m, fdd: btr 5117. 5 32a
4973 **Disparity 25** [3]3-8-8 t(60) R Winston 25/1:0   4965 **Red Skelton 26** [4]3-8-11 (60) N Callan 25/1:0
16 Ran   Time 2m 34.58 (5.38)   Owned: Sir Eric Parker   Trained: Pulborough

5297

2.35 Ladbrokes Com Handicap Stakes 3yo+ 71-85 (D2) [97]
£7034 £2164 £1082   6f aw rnd   Going 21   +13 Fast Inside

5101 **MOAYED 16** [7] N P Littmoden 5-9-1 bl t (84) J P Guillambert(3) 8/1: 3310401: Slow away & rear, 96a+
smooth hdwy wide over 2f out & led ins last, hand riding, cosily: op 14/1, fast time: stays 10f, suited by 6f on
fast, hvy & polytrack: loves Lingfield: eff in visor/blnks & t-strap: useful, can win again: see 1481, 1035 & 571.
1638 **QUIET TIMES 176** [4] K A Ryan 5-9-5 bl (88) N Callan 25/1: 4155002: Handy & rdn to lead 2f out, 1¾ 91a
hdd ins last & not pace of wnr: 6 mth abs & a fine return: loves both AWs: see 834.
5181* **BLYTHE SPIRIT 12** [12] R A Fahey 5-8-11 p (80) P Hanagan 6/1: 0661113: Chsd ldrs, styd on for press. 1 80a
4786 **AVERSHAM 36** [9] R Charlton 4-8-11 (80) S Drowne 5/1 FAV: 0-000354: Mid-div, rdn & hmpd over 1f shd 79a
out, styd on late for press, no threat: acts on firm, soft & polytrack: see 4394.
4832 **JUST FLY 34** [5]3-8-13 J Fortune 8/1: 0000225: Held up, late gains for press, no threat: see 4832. 1 78a
4908* **JAYANJAY 29** [11]5-8-13 (82) R Thomas(3) 11/1: 5225016: Held up, short of room 2f out, onepace. 1¾ 73a
4713+ **WHOS WINNING 44** [8]3-8-11 (81) T Quinn 11/2: 0212117: Led/dsptd lead wide, wknd bef dist, abs. 1¼ 68a
5149 **CORPS DE BALLET 13** [2]3-9-1 (85) T P Queally 11/1: 1000528: Mid-div, btn over 1f out: btr 5149 (5f). ½ 71a
5159 **IDLE POWER 13** [3]6-8-13 p (82) D Sweeney 9/1: 0021109: Led till 2f out, sn btn: btr 4873 (7f). 1¼ 64a
5218 **MALAPROPISM 8** [6]4-9-11 (94) T O'Brien(7) 14/1: 1061100: 10th: Chsd ldrs, lost place from 2f out. 2½ 69a
4855 **LAW BREAKER 32** [1]6-9-6 (89) B Reilly(3) 14/1: 2000000: 11th: Sn rdn in mid-div & struggling halfway. 2 58a
       AUENTRAUM 91 [10]4-8-11 (80) P Makin(5) 25/1: 1612-300: 12th: or c Big Shuffle - Auenglocke 11 21a
(Surumu) AI bhd, t.o. halfway: 3 mth abs & Brit bow: ex-German, dual '03 wnr: both wins at 6.5f, acts on gd & soft.
12 Ran   Time 1m 10.90 (0.50)   Owned: Mr Nigel Shields   Trained: Newmarket

5298

3.10 Listed Littlewoods Bet Direct E B F Fleur De Lys Stakes Fillies & Mares 3yo+ (A1)
£17400 £6600 £3300   1m aw rnd   Going 21   -02 Slow Outside

5159 **MISS GEORGE 13** [10] D K Ivory 6-8-13 (83) Dane O'Neill 16/1: 0300321: Dwelt, rear, switched wide 99a
& strong run for press to lead well ins last: eff at 5/6f, now seems suited by 7f/1m: acts on firm, fast &
polytrack, handles fibresand, loves Lingfield: useful mare with a fine turn of foot: see 879.
5134 **TAHIRAH 15** [5] R Guest 4-8-13 (92) Martin Dwyer 20/1: 0000302: Rear, switched wide & styd on 1 95a
well for press cl-home, nrst fin: stays a sharp 1m well: handles firm, gd & polytrack: see 2289.
4331 **ZIETORY 59** [9] P F I Cole 4-9-2 (95) T Quinn 8/1: 2-503103: Cl-up, rdn to lead over 1f out, hdd shd 97a
well ins last: 2 mth abs: rnr-up in this race '03: see 4095.
3550 **PEERESS 94** [1] Sir Michael Stoute 3-8-10 (96) D Holland 5/6 FAV: 3-11134: Missed break & settled shd 93a
rear, short of room over 2f out & again over 1f out, switched & styd on ins last, nrst fin: well bckd but missing
break proved crucial in what was a messy race: acts on firm, gd & polytrack: see 3550 & 3006.
5057 **MILLY WATERS 19** [4]3-8-10 (83) S W Kelly 50/1: 00011-55: Trkd ldrs, kept on onepace: handles 1½ 90a
fast, gd & both AWs: prob stays a sharp 1m: see 5057.
2555 **ARICIA 92** [8]3-8-10 (94) J Fortune 12/1: 01006: Led 1f & remained handy, outpcd fnl 2f, abs. nk 89a
4872 **NAJAABA 31** [6]4-8-13 (80) B Reilly 33/1: 5156507: Rear, smooth hdwy wide 2f out, sn no prog. hd 88a
5086 **STAR OF NORMANDIE 17** [12]5-8-13 (82) A McCarthy 40/1: 12-00008: Mid-div wide, no impress dist. hd 87a
5088 **VOILE 17** [3]3-8-10 (95) F Norton 16/1: 4345-009: Mid-div, btn over 1f out, prefers 6/7f. 1½ 84a
5057 **COQUETERIA 19** [7]3-8-10 (100) S Drowne 5/1: 441-2320: 10th: Keen early, trkd ldrs, btn over 1f out. ½ 83a
4935* **ZERLINA 27** [11]3-8-10 (80) C Catlin 18/1: 0004210: 11th: Led after 1f, qcknd over 2f out, hdd over 1f out. nk 82a
5270 **VALJARV 2** [2]3-8-10 (90) N Callan 14/1: 2005040: 12th: Slow away & bhd, in tch halfway, btn over ¾ 80a
1f out: qck reapp: lost chance start, 6/7f ideal.
12 Ran   Time 1m 38.10 (1.90)   Owned: Mrs A Shone   Trained: Radlett

---

5299   3.45 Bet Direct On Itv Page 367 Handicap Stakes 3yo 56-70 (E3)   [77]
£3527 £1085 £543   1m2f aw   Going 21   -04 Slow   Inside

5083 **THE VIOLIN PLAYER 18** [5] H J Collingridge 3-9-3 (66) D Holland 11/2: 0005021: Trkd ldrs & led   **76a**
over 2f out, rdn & styd on strongly when pressed ins last: eff at 7f, suited by 10f on firm, gd & polytrack: see 5083.
5239 **KING OF DIAMONDS 6** [14] J R Best 3-9-13 (76) Martin Dwyer 7/2 FAV: 0104022: Keen early, trkd   1¾   **82a**
ldrs wide, smooth hdwy to press wnr 2f out, no extra ins last: bckd: qck reapp: rest well covered: eff at 10/12f:
suffered an awkward passage today, can find similar: see 5239, 3947.
5153 **DEIGN TO DANCE 13** [3] J G Portman 3-9-2 (65) C Catlin 25/1: 1032553: Rear, short of room over 1f   3   **67a**
out, styd on well ins last, nrst fin: longer 10f trip may yet suit: see 3799, 2394 (1m).
5083 **GROUND PATROL 18** [11] G L Moore 3-9-2 t (65) T P Queally 14/1: 3600464: Rear, mod gains for press.   nk   **66a**
5153 **PELLA 13** [13]3-9-2 (65) D Sweeney 14/1: 3010145: Held up, eff wide 2f out, sn no prog: btr 4721 (1m).   shd   **65a**
4777 **HABANERO 37** [9]3-9-13 (76) F Norton 25/1: 3316006: Keen & handy, wknd over 1f out: prefer 1m.   1¾   **73a**
4143 **SCIENCE ACADEMY 68** [6]3-9-4 (67) N De Souza(5) 14/1: 5621167: Mid-div, outpcd fnl 2f: abs.   hd   **63a**
5148 **LITTLE JIMBOB 13** [8]3-9-12 (75) P Hanagan 9/2: 2435248: Led till over 2f out, sn btn: btr 5148, 4935.   3½   **66a**
5083 **COMPETITOR 18** [2]3-9-5 p (68) T Quinn 10/1: 0506059: Chsd ldrs, sn pushed along, btn over 1f out.   1½   **56a**
4667 **TETCOTT 43** [12]3-9-5 (68) L Keniry(3) 33/1: 53430: 10th: Rear, hdwy wide over 3f out, btn 2f out.   1¼   **53a**
5109 **SWEET REPLY 16** [10]3-9-2 (65) N Callan 5/1: 1005000: 11th: Rear, rdn & btn 2f out: btr 4110 (7f).   1¼   **48a**
5148 **MRS PANKHURST 13** [1]3-9-4 (67) S Drowne 8/1: 0560450: 12th: Mid-div, lost place from 3f out.   shd   **49a**
5116 **GRAND APOLLO 15** [4]3-9-3 (66) J Fortune 8/1: 6-25650: 13th: Cl-up, wknd fnl 2f: btr 5116 & 2419.   5   **41a**
13 Ran   Time 2m 5.2 (2.5)   Owned: Mr Peter Webb   Trained: Newmarket

---

5300   4.20 John Whittington 65th Birthday & Retirement Apprentice Handicap Stakes 3yo+ 46-55 (F4) [72]
£3023 £864 £432   7f aw rnd   Going 21   -17 Slow   Inside

5109 **MIND ALERT 16** [8] Miss J A Camacho 3-8-13 (57) D Allan 10/1: 2000051: Sn handy & led over 1f   **67a**
out, drvn out: eff at 6/7f on fast, gd/soft & polytrack, sharp/undul or stiff trk: best without blnks: see 5109, 1881.
5109 **MENAI STRAIGHTS 16** [11] R F Fisher 3-8-12 (56) D Nolan 9/1: 1306602: Chsd ldrs, eff to chase   2½   **59a**
wnr dist, kept on, al held: also bhd today's wnr latest: acts on firm, gd/soft & polytrack: see 2936 & 2081.
3034 **FRANKS QUEST 116** [7] A B Haynes 4-9-4 (60) S Hitchcott 25/1: 0211003: Pushed along rear,   nk   **62a**
switched wide & styd on well from over 1f out, nrst fin: 4 mth abs: prev with P Burgoyne, gd run: acts on both
AWs, fast & gd/soft grnd: see 2495, 2052 & 718.
5080 **PERTEMPS MAGUS 18** [2] R A Fahey 4-9-2 vis (58) T Hamilton 7/2 FAV: 3163664: Pulled hard trkg   shd   **59a**
ldrs, onepcd for press dist.
4488 **ICED DIAMOND 52** [12]5-9-1 (57) B Swarbrick(3) 5/1: 0440265: Keen & wide, prom till no extra dist, abs.   1   **56a**
4989 **CALYPSO DANCER 23** [3]4-9-1 (57) P Makin(3) 16/1: 2400006: Dwelt & held up, mod prog.   shd   **55a**
5241 **WARLINGHAM 6** [6]6-9-2 (58) J P Guillambert 11/1: 0000007: Keen & prom, hung right & btn over 1f out. nk   **55a**
5263 **LEGAL SET 3** [13]8-9-0 t (56) T P Queally 8/1: 0052508: Sn handy & led after 2f till over 1f out,   nk   **52a**
wknd: qck reapp: poor high draw for forcing tactics: see 5130.
5155 **SIRAJ 13** [1]5-9-0 (56) L Keniry 14/1: 0100049: Rear, little prog fnl 2f: btr 5155 (6f).   shd   **51a**
5080 **SUPERCHIEF 18** [10]9-9-6 bl t (62) B Reilly 16/1: 5250000: 10th: Dwelt, rear, drvn & little prog.   ¾   **55a**
4616 **FEAST OF ROMANCE 46** [4]7-9-2 bl (54) R J Killoran(7) 9/1: 3064020: 11th: Mid-div, btn over 1f out.   hd   **46a**
5039 **SHAROURA 20** [9]8-9-2 p (58) N Lawes(7) 9/1: 2400300: 12th: Keen, wide, nvr a factor: btr 4622.   hd   **49a**
4452 Scarlett Rose 54 [5]3-9-4 (62) M Savage(3) 25/1:0   2435 Ashstanza 139 [14]3-9-4 (62) R Thomas 50/1:0
14 Ran   Time 1m 25.46(2.66)   Owned: Mr David W Armstrong   Trained: Malton

---

Official Going Soft (Heavy Places)

5301   1.00 Manny Bernstein Freephone 0800 821 821 E B F Maiden Stakes 2yo (D3)
£4729 £1455 £728   7f str   Soft 94   -42 Slow   Centre

5126 **GAME LAD 16** [4] T D Easterby 2-9-0 (76) D Allan 5/4 FAV: 3403021: Sn led, edged right over 1f   **80**
out, drvn out: hvly bckd: suited by 7f on fast & soft grnd, handles fibresand, gall or sharp trks.
      RESTORATION 0 [5] J H M Gosden 2-9-0 J Fortune 9/2: 2: gr c Zafonic - Restless Mixa (Linamix)   2   **75**
Led early, remained handy, rdn & no extra over 1f out: op 3/1: £110,000 Mar foal, half-brother to wnrs btwn 6/10f,
dam plcd at 10f as a 3yo: eff at 7f, 1m+ shld suit: handles soft grnd & a gall trk: encouraging start.
      BLUE OPAL 0 [9] Miss S E Hall 2-8-9 N Callan 25/1: 3: b f Bold Edge - Second Affair (Pursuit of   hd   **69**
Love) Led/dsptd lead, rdn & outpcd halfway, styd on well for press cl-home: Mar first foal, dam a 12f 4yo scorer:
eff at 7f, 1m+ looks sure to suit: acts on soft grnd & a gall trk: promising start, improve further over.
4843 **E BRIDE 34** [3] J G Given 2-8-9 A Culhane 12/1: 544: Dwelt, sn chsd ldrs, rdn & kept on, nvr   2½   **65**
threat to wnr: op 9/1: longer 7f trip looks likely to suit: handles fast & soft grnd: see 4843.
4988 **LOBENGULA 24** [7]2-9-0 J Carroll 66/1: 05: b g Spectrum - Playwaki (Miswaki) Chsd ldrs, outpcd   ½   **69**
over 2f out, kept on ins last: £15,000 Feb foal, dam unrcd half-sister to a multiple US wnr.
4927 **KATIES BISCUIT 30** [1]2-8-9 N Pollard 50/1: 606: Towards rear, late gains for press, no threat.   1½   **62**
4503 **CALFRAZ 51** [13]2-9-0 Darren Williams 66/1: 07: Mid-div, no prog fnl 2f, abs.   3½   **62**
4864 **BLACKNYELLO BONNET 33** [2]2-8-9 K Darley 16/1: 008: Prom early, rdn & btn 2f out.   nk   **56**
      BRUT FORCE 0 [14]2-9-0 J F Egan 33/1: 9: In tch, no impress fnl 2f.   nk   **60**
5106 **CELTIC CARISMA 17** [6]2-8-9 T Eaves(3) 10: 00: 10th: Dwelt, chsd ldrs 5f, longer trip.   3   **51**
4988 **TELEGRAM SAM 24** [8]2-9-0 P Hanagan 10/1: 00: 11th: Trkd ldrs, struggling from halfway.   3   **52**
5131 **CHAMPAGNE LUJAIN 16** [11]2-9-0 P Mulrennan(3) 20/1: 050: 12th: Dwelt & al towards rear.   1¾   **50**
      Cascade Lakes 0 [10]2-8-9 S W Kelly 25/1:0   5107 Cliffie 17 [12]2-9-0 S Righton 200/1:0
14 Ran   Time 1m 31.28 (9.48)   Owned: Mrs J B Mountifield   Trained: Malton

5302 1.30 Manny Bernstein 1st For Telephone Betting Nursery Handicap Stakes 2yo 0-75 (E3)   [82]
£5103 £1570 £785   1m str   Soft 94   -21 Slow   Centre

4337 **THE PEN 60** [8] P C Haslam 2-8-4 (58) N Pollard 9/1: 0121: Al handy & led over 1f out, drvn out: 68
2 month abs: eff at 6/7f, imprvd again for step up to 1m: acts on firm & soft grnd, loves Redcar: goes well fresh:
lightly rcd & progressive: see 4337 & 3769.
5049 **PICOT DE SAY 21** [18] John Berry 2-8-6 (60) K Darley 16/1: 00032: Mid-div, styd on for press from   1¾ 66
over 1f out, nrst fin: h'cap bow: eff around 1m on fast & soft grnd, confirmed improvement of 5049.
5147 **TORRENS 14** [13] S P Griffiths 2-9-3 (71) A Nicholls 25/1: 41003: Al handy & led over 2f out, hdd   hd 76
over 1f out, kept on: gd run for new yard: acts on gd/soft & soft grnd: see 4297.
5142* **STRATHTAY 15** [20] A Berry 2-8-5 vis (59) F Norton 7/1: 5600214: Chsd ldrs, rdn to chall over 1f   ½ 63
out, no extra well ins last: styd longer 1m trip: acts on fast, enjoyed gd/soft & soft last twice: see 5142.
4933 **MAJESTIC MOVEMENT 28** [15]2-9-0 (68) J Fortune 7/1: 5035: Handy, drvn & no extra dist: h'cap bow.   1¼ 70
4451 **HERENCIA 55** [17]2-8-0 p (54) S Righton 12/1: 000426: Towards rear, late gains for press, nrst   ¾ 55
fin: abs: longer 1m trip looks likely to suit: handles fast & soft grnd: see 4451 (7f).
5065 **THREE ACES 20** [11]2-7-13 bl (53) J Quinn 33/1: 0560007: Mid-div halfway, no impress fnl 1f: btr 4741.   2 51
5126 **BREAKING SHADOW 16** [1]2-9-7 (75) P Hanagan 5/1 FAV: 3310608: Trkd ldrs, rdn & btn over 1f out.   2 70
5012 **MARY GRAY 22** [19]2-8-10 (64) J Fanning 33/1: 5009: Chsd ldrs till over 2f out, h'cap bow.   1 58
4344 **MISTER BUZZ 60** [12]2-8-3 (57) N Mackay 50/1: 0004400: 10th: Mid-div, rdn & nvr a factor, abs.   4 45
5011* **AZAHARA 22** [16]2-9-4 (72) Dale Gibson 14/1: 0010: 11th: Towards rear, rdn & little prog: btr 5011.   ½ 59
4863 **GRAND WELCOME 33** [2]2-8-12 bl (66) C Catlin 11/1: 000220: 12th: Led 6f, fdd under press: btr 4863.   2 50
4535 **VISION VICTORY 51** [3]2-8-1 (55) R Ffrench 50/1: 40000: 13th: Chsd ldrs till halfway, sn btn, abs.   ¾ 38
5091 **BEST GAME 17** [9]2-8-8 (62) D Holland 10/1: 0060: 14th: Prom till over 2f out, h'cap bow: btr 5091.   hd 44
4963 **ALGORITHM 27** [6]2-8-4 (1ow) (57) D Allan 12/1: 5623400: 15th: Went left start, in tch till 2f out: btr 4807.   2½ 36
4631 **King Zafeen 46** [7]2-8-13 (67) P Mulrennan(3) 20/1:0   5142 **Mount Ephram 15** [5]2-8-8 (62) R Winston 50/1:0
4848 **Patxaran 34** [4]2-8-12 (66) G Faulkner 20/1:0   5002 **Moonfleet 23** [10]2-8-5 (59) T Eaves(1) 33/1:0
19 Ran   Time 1m 43.98 (9.18)   Owned: Middleham Park Racing XXVIII   Trained: Middleham

5303 2.00 Manny Bernstein Free #20 Bet New Accounts Selling Stakes 3-5yo (G4)
£3122 £892 £446   1m2f   Soft 94   -33 Slow   Inside

5191* **RICHIE BOY 12** [8] P A Blockley 3-9-3 (63) N Callan 4/7 FAV: 6001011: Sn cl-up & led 4f out,   66+
readily pulled clr & eased cl-home, wld 5L+: bght in for 12,500gns: nicely bckd at odds on: eff at 1m/10.6f on
gd/soft & hvy grnd: win again in similar company: see 5191, 4991.
3354 **MISS FLEURIE 103** [7] R Craggs 4-8-10 (30) R Winston 33/1: 0026002: Chsd ldrs, rdn to chase wnr   3 47
2f out, kept on, al held: 3 month abs: handles soft grnd & fibresand: see 1592 (banded).
4716 **GOLDEN FIELDS 41** [9] Mrs J Candlish 4-8-10 bl (40) S Hitchcott 20/1: 020-0003: Rdn towards rear,   4 43
styd on for press to take 3rd nr fin, nvr a threat: 6 wk abs: see 3834.
5017 **ALWAYS FLYING 22** [10] N Wilson 3-9-3 (54) T Hamilton(3) 13/2: 6020004: Led till 4f out, no extra dist.   ½ 53
5017 **SHARDDA 22** [11]4-8-10 t (50) P Robinson 14/1: 0-300005: Chsd ldrs, rdn to chall over 2f out: t-strap reapp.   1½ 40
4757 **TURFTANZER 39** [2]5-9-1 t (30) Kim Tinkler 28/1: 4500506: Mid-div, eff 4f out, no prog fnl 2f.   7 38
5067 **THE SPOOK 20** [4]4-9-1 (40) J Fanning 20/1: 00-00057: Dwelt & held up, eff over 3f out, no impression.   4 34
4965 **BIEN GOOD 27** [1]3-8-6 (45) T Eaves(2) 25/1: 0-3508: Dwelt & rear, little hdwy: btr 3019.   1 28
2509 **INDI ANO STAR 137** [6]3-8-11 (52) D Tudhope 14/1: 6660559: Dwelt, rear, nvr a factor, 5 month abs.   3 30
5110 **MERLINS CITY 17** [3]4-8-10 T Williams 200/1: 00: 10th: Dwelt, held up, rdn & btn 3f out, longer trip.   8 17
778 **QUEEN LOUISA 245** [5]4-8-10 P Mulrennan(3) 200/1: 00-00: 11th: Mid-div, drvn & btn over 2f out, abs.   3½ 13
11 Ran   Time 2m 15.02 (12.72)   Owned: Mr Clive Whiting   Trained: Wolverhampton

5304 2.30 Manny Bernstein Don't Be Disqualified Again Handicap Stakes 3yo+ 71-85 (D2)   [92]
£10816 £3328 £1664   6f str   Soft 94   +14 Fast   Centre

5125 **SIR DESMOND 16** [14] R Guest 6-8-12 p (76) C Catlin 14/1: 3564041: Held up, hdwy & switched over   85
1f out, rdn to lead well ins last: best time of day: eff at 5/6f on firm, hvy & both AWs, any trk: see 292.
5291 **FLYING BANTAM 2** [6] R A Fahey 3-9-1 (6ex) (79) P Hanagan 12/1: 4041312: Chsd ldrs, short of room   nk 87
dist, switched & kept on well cl-home, nrst fin: qk reapp & remains in fine form: acts on fm, soft & polytrack.
5000 **JOHNSTONS DIAMOND 23** [11] E J Alston 6-9-10 (88) D Allan 12/1: 0036303: Handy & led over 1f out,   nk 95
rdn & hdd well ins last: fine run under top-weight: see 687.
4779 **IMPERIAL ECHO 37** [12] T D Barron 3-9-6 (84) P Fessey 25/1: 2034134: Trkd ldrs, rdn to chall   nk 90
dist, no extra well ins last: see 4779 & 4278.
5125 **ARTIE 16** [13]5-9-6 (84) R Winston 12/1: 0000455: Led/dsptd lead till over 1f out, no extra well   shd 90
ins last: eff at 6f, 5f poss ideal: see 3073 & 1627.
5144 **ABBAJABBA 15** [16]8-8-7 (1oh) (70) J Fanning 14/1: 0020506: Chsd ldrs, kept on onepace: see 834.   1½ 74
5027 **FREAK OCCURENCE 22** [4]3-8-7 (1oh) (70) N Callan 16/1: 0600007: Cl-up, rdn & outpcd fnl 2f.   2 70
5114* **BURLEY FLAME 16** [15]3-9-4 (82) A Culhane 25/1: 1600018: Rdn towards rear, not pace to chall.   1 79
4930 **INDIAN SPARK 30** [9]10-8-7 (3oh) (68) T Eaves(5) 16/1: 0060009: Rear, mod late prog, no threat.   ½ 67
4184* **MARKER 66** [5]4-9-0 (78) R Thomas(2) 4/1 FAV: 0400410: 10th: Chsd ldrs, rdn & btn dist: abs: btr 4184.   5 64
4817 **CIRCUIT DANCER 35** [2]4-9-11 (89) F Lynch 33/1: 5040040: 11th: Mid-div, eff 2f out, no impress.   nk 74
5000 **CD FLYER 23** [1]7-9-6 (84) P Mulrennan(3) 9/1: 4356020: 12th: Mid-div, btn 2f out: btr 5000.   2½ 64
5130 **MARINAITE 16** [10]3-8-9 (73) P Makin(5) 100/1: 2030300: 13th: Chsd ldrs till over 1f out: see 5057 (1m).   1 51
5143 **RIVER FALCON 16** [3]4-9-5 (83) N Mackay 12/1: 1004500: 14th: Prom early, struggling fnl 2f: btr 4780.   1¾ 58
5130* **NORTHERN GAMES 16** [7]5-9-1 bl (79) A Mullen(7) 9/2: 4242110: 15th: Dwelt & al bhd: bckd: btr 5130.   1 52
5053 **OEUF A LA NEIGE 21** [8]4-8-9 (73) O Urbina 11/1: 5011500: 16th: Dwelt & al rear: btr 4946.   1½ 43
16 Ran   Time 1m 13.69 (4.79)   Owned: Mr A P Davies   Trained: Newmarket

---

5305

3.00 Manny Bernstein Stable Staff Appreciation Classified Stakes 3yo+ 0-70 (E3)
£7215 £2220 £1110   **5f str   Soft 94   +02 Fast**   Centre

4897 **LITTLE RIDGE 31** [11] H Morrison 3-9-0 (72) L Fletcher(3) 12/1: 011-0001: Sn led, carr right but   **81**
asserted ins last, rdn out: apprec rtn to 5f, stays 6f: acts on fast & soft grnd, gall or sharp trk.
5069 **HIGHLAND WARRIOR 20** [8] J S Goldie 5-8-12 (69) N Mackay 9/2: 6302642: Dwelt & held up, hdwy when 1¾   **73**
short of room over 1f out, nrst fin: nicely bckd: gd run: see 1898 (6f).
4585 **PRIME RECREATION 48** [2] P S Felgate 7-8-12 (70) Lisa Jones 16/1: 0400103: Rcd far side & led   ½   **72**
that pair, dsptd lead & drifted to stands side from halfway, no extra fnl 1f: abs: see 4253, 660.
5181 **IF BY CHANCE 13** [7] R Craggs 6-9-1 bl (73) T Eaves(3) 20/1: 4410004: Chsd wnr stands side, onepace.   ½   **74**
4700 **PADDYWACK 42** [3]7-9-0 bl (72) A Culhane 5/1: 6330455: Pushed along towards rear, late gains, nrst fin. ½   **72**
4700 **LETS GET IT ON 42** [6]3-8-10 (71) R Winston 20/1: 2005306: Held up, short of room over 1f out,   1   **66**
mod late prog: abs: acts on fast & soft grnd: see 1360.
5149 **HOUT BAY 14** [10]7-9-3 (75) P Hanagan 5/2 FAV: 4113167: Dwelt, pushed along rear, hdwy/short of   1   **71**
room over 1f out, sn no impress: nicely bckd, op 3/1: btr 4654.
4989 **KINGS COLLEGE BOY 24** [5]4-8-12 vis (68) Dale Gibson 11/2: 1024048: Mid-div, rdn & no prog bef dist.   nk   **65**
4785 **MYND 37** [9]4-8-12 (57) V Halliday 33/1: 6405009: Chsd ldrs, btn over 1f out: prefer faster grnd.   1   **63**
4605 **HELLO ROBERTO 47** [4]3-8-9 (69) Kim Tinkler 25/1: 0004000: 10th: Al towards rear, abs: new yard.   1¼   **57**
4718 **STRENSALL 41** [12]7-9-3 (75) P Mathers(5) 16/1: 0552000: 11th: Chsd ldrs, btn 2f out: abs: btr 4174. 1½   **62**
2747 **A LITTLE BIT YARIE 128** [1]3-9-1 vis (74) Darren Williams 20/1: 3-304000: 12th: Chsd ldr far side   11   **40**
& struggling halfway, abs: see 1229.
12 Ran   Time 1m 01.09 (4.59)   Owned: Lady Margadale   Trained: East Ilsley

---

5306

3.30 Manny Bernstein Hedging For Bookmakers Maiden Stakes 3yo (D3)
£3526 £1085 £543   **1m2f   Soft 94   -29 Slow**   Inside

5023 **SAFIRAH 22** [2] M A Jarvis 3-8-9 (69) P Robinson 15/8: 355021: Handy & led over 1f out, asserted   **73**
ins last under hand riding: well bckd: eff around 10f on firm & soft grnd, sharp or gall trk: see 5023, 3802 & 2843.
4899 **TURTLE PATRIARCH 31** [1] Mrs A J Perrett 3-9-0 (58) D Holland 7/2: 0042602: Held up & keen, styd   1½   **75**
on for press fnl 2f, not able to chall wnr: bckd, op 4/1: acts on gd & soft grnd: see 4119.
5102 **HARRYCAT 17** [7] V Smith 3-9-0 (70) J Quinn 13/8 FAV: 05623: Handy & led over 2f out, drvn & hdd   1½   **73**
over 1f out, sn held: clr of rem: hvly bckd, op 15/8: eff at 10/12f: see 5102 (clmr, 12f).
5015 **BOTTOMLESS WALLET 22** [5] F Watson 3-8-9   T Hamilton(3) 33/1: 64: Held up, mod late prog.   8   **60**
5190 **INDIANS LANDING 12** [8]3-9-0 K Darley 16/1: 000035: Chsd ldrs, btn over 2f out: btr 5190.   1   **64**
4243 **INMOM 65** [4]3-8-9 (52) P Makin(3) 33/1: 0466006: Led till over 2f out, sn btn, 2 month abs.   ½   **58**
5190 **ILL DO IT TODAY 12** [3]3-9-0 P Hanagan 16/1: 67: Held up & keen, btn over 2f out.   3   **60**
3905 **WHITKIRK STAR 81** [6]3-9-0 A Nicholls 200/1: 0-68: Sn well bhd & t.o., abs & longer trip.   dist 0
8 Ran   Time 2m 14.57 (12.27)   Owned: Sheikh Ahmed Al Maktoum   Trained: Newmarket

---

5307

4.00 Manny Bernstein 1st For Prices Daily Handicap Stakes 3yo+ 56-70 (E3)
£5381 £1656 £828   **1m2f   Soft 94   -15 Slow**   Inside   **[77]**

5198* **MCQUEEN 10** [5] Mrs H Dalton 4-9-8 (71) J F Egan 9/4 FAV: 2110511: Dwelt, pushed along rear, hdwy   **80**
to lead 2f out, rdn out: stays 12f, suited by 1m/10f: acts on gd & fast, loves gd/soft & soft grnd, both AWs.
4983 **MARITIME BLUES 25** [4] J G Given 4-8-11 (60) A Culhane 25/1: 0105002: Mid-div, drvn & styd on fnl   1¾   **66**
2f, not able to reach wnr: see 4084 & 1164.
5191 **FAIR SPIN 12** [12] M D Hammond 4-8-9 (58) K Darley 12/1: 0300503: Mid-div, styd on for press fnl   ½   **63**
2f, nrst fin: stays 10f: see 2947 & 2542.
5206 **LUCAYAN DANCER 10** [3] D Nicholls 4-8-13 (62) D Holland 3/1: 0141234: Mid-div, eff to chase ldrs   ¾   **66**
over 2f out, onepace fnl 1f: well bckd, op 9/2: remains in gd heart: see 5206, 4757.
4820 **CRESKELD 35** [11]5-9-5 (68) F Lynch 25/1: 0001405: Rear, hdwy wide to chase ldrs over 1f out, no   1   **71**
extra in last: poss stays 10f, best prev at 1m/9f: see 4008.
5066 **YOUNG ROONEY 20** [2]4-9-7 (70) T P Queally 9/1: 3226326: Led till 2f out, fdd under pressure.   1½   **71**
3741 **PHONE TAPPING 88** [8]3-8-3 (10h) (55) P Robinson 7/1: 06607: Mid-div, lost pl halfway, kept on late.   ¾   **56**
5037 **ROTUMA 21** [6]5-9-10 (73) S W Kelly 20/1: 2510008: Chsd lds, no extra over 1f out, top-weight.   shd   **73**
5004 **ROYAL DISTANT 23** [17]3-8-7 (60) P Mulrennan(3) 25/1: 0200009: Rear, only mod late prog, no threat.   3½   **56**
4990 **MELODIAN 24** [16]9-8-11 bl (60) T Williams 14/1: 2160000: 10th: Chsd ldrs, btn 2f out, likes to dominate. 1   **55**
4983 **MISTER ARJAY 25** [15]4-9-7 (70) T Eaves(3) 25/1: 200-0600: 11th: Mid-div, rdn & btn 2f out: btr 2323.   ½   **64**
5037 Lyford Lass 21 [9]3-9-1 (60) R Winston 33/1:0   5130 Mezuzah 16 [14]4-9-7 (70) Dale Gibson 25/1:0
4867 Ace Coming 33 [1]3-8-8 bl(61) J Quinn 33/1:0   5201 On Every Street 10 [13]3-9-3 (70) R Ffrench 100/1:0
4847 Eva Jean 34 [7]3-8-7 (60) J Fanning 25/1:0   4719 Captain Saif 41 [10]4-9-1 (64) T Hamilton(3) 50/1:0
17 Ran   Time 2m 13.18(10.88)   Owned: Mr R Edwards and Mr W J Swinnerton   Trained: Shifnal

LONE STAR PARK   SATURDAY 30.10.04   Lefthand, Oval Track

Official Going AW - FAST; Turf - GOOD/SOFT.

5308   7.35 Gr 1 Netjets Breeders' Cup Mile 3yo+   ()
£488045 £187709 £103240   1m   Good/Soft

SINGLETARY 21 [10] D Chatlos Jnr 4-9-0   D Flores 16/1: 5-121231: b c Sultry Song - Joiskis Star   **123**
(Star de Naskra) Made all against stands rail, rdn out: eff at 1m on firm & gd/soft: top-class.
4801 **ANTONIUS PIUS 35** [7] A P O'Brien 3-8-10   J P Spencer 16/1: 5375392: Rear, prog to chase ldrs   ½   **121**
1.5f out, ev ch & hard drvn ins fnl 1f, no extra: notoriously tricky customer who is high-class when in the mood.
4017 **SIX PERFECTIONS 76** [11] P Bary 4-8-11   J D Bailey 9/2 JT FAV: 211-2623: Mid-div, prog when hmpd   1½   **117**
1.5f out, fin well but too late: 11 wk abs: won this race last yr when the gaps came, not so lucky here: see 4017.
4801 **DIAMOND GREEN FR 35** [8]3-8-10 L Dettori 12/1: 3222288: Rear, nvr a factor in 8th: btr 4434.   2   **114**
4434 **WHIPPER 55** [1]3-8-10 C Soumillon 6/1: 1-152150: 10th: Chsd ldrs, wknd fnl 1f: 8 wk abs.   1   **112**
8 Ran   Time 1m 36.90 ()   Owned: Little Red Feather Racing   Trained: Usa

5309   8.45 Gr 1 Alberto VO5 Breeders' Cup Filly & Mare Turf 3yo+   ()
£409609 £157542 £86648   1m3f   Good/Soft

4956 **OUIJA BOARD 27** [5] E A L Dunlop 3-8-6 (110) K Fallon 10/11 FAV: 13-11131: Chsd ldrs, strong run   **123**
to lead dist, styd on strongly, rdn out: well bckd: suited by 11/12f on firm & gd/soft grnd: runs well fresh:
handles any trk: top-class filly who has had an exceptional season, remains in training next year & will prove a
major force in all the top mid-dist events: see 4956 & 3321.
FILM MAKER 28 [3] H G Motion 4-8-11 bl J R Velazquez 20/1: 8-621342: br f Dynaformer - Miss Du   1½   **119**
Bois (Mr Prospector) Prom, styd on well fnl 1f but not pace of wnr: eff at 9/11f on firm & gd/soft: high-class.
WONDER AGAIN 28 [12] J J Toner 5-8-11 E Prado 12/1: 14-61163: Rear, styd on late into 3rd.   nk   **118**
4953 **YESTERDAY 27** [11]4-8-11 VIS J P Spencer 8/1: 4223-545: Mid-div, not pace to chall fnl 1f: visor.   4   **112**
14 Ran   Time 2m 18.25 ()   Owned: Lord Derby   Trained: Newmarket

5310   9.20 Gr 1 Bessemer Trust Breeders' Cup Juvenile Dirt 2yo   ()
£435754 £167598 £92179   1m110y Dirt   Fast

4797 **WILKO 35** [8] J Noseda 2-8-10 (100) L Dettori 20/1: 33212431: Prom wide, eff over 2f out, battled   **120**
on v gamely to lead cl home, all-out: eff at 7f/1m on firm, fast & dist, poss hvy: v tough, tho' well held numerous
times in List/Gr 2 company in Europe: massively improved on dirt & this was a top-class run.
AFLEET ALEX 21 [3] T F Ritchey 2-8-10   J Rose 10/3: 111122: b c Northern Afleet - Maggy Hawk   ¾   **118**
(Hawkster) Rear, prog wide to lead 2f out, hdd cl home, in a close fin: well bckd: high-class juv.
SUN KING USA 21 [1] N Zito 2-8-10 E Prado 15/2: 4133: br c Charismatic - Clever But Costly   nk   **117**
(Clever Trick) Rear, prog to lead 3f out, worn down cl home: fine run & a v smart juv.
4797 **SCANDINAVIA 35** [5]2-8-10 J P Spencer 12/1: 22128: Dwelt, chsd ldrs wide, lost place halfway.   15   **87**
12 Ran   Time 1m 42.09 ()   Owned: J Paul Reddam & Susan Roy   Trained: Newmarket

5311   9.55 Gr 1 John Deere Breeders' Cup Turf 3yo+   ()
£581006 £223464 £122905   1m4f   Good/Soft

BETTER TALK NOW 49 [5] H G Motion 5-9-0 R A Dominguez 33/1: 8922141: b g Talkin Man - Bendita   **125**
(Baldski) Rear, imprvd 3f out, hung & led ent fnl 1f, styd on strongly, drvn out: 7 wk abs: top-class.
4015* **KITTENS JOY 28** [4] D Romans 3-8-9 J R Velazquez 4/5 FAV: 1121112: Chsd ldrs, short of room   1¾   **124**
dist, fin well & not btn far: well bckd: poss a shade unlucky: see 4015.
4571 **POWERSCOURT 49** [1] A P O'Brien 4-9-0 vis J P Spencer 11/4: -12521D33: Dwelt, rapid prog to lead   1   **120**
over 3f out, collared ent fnl 1f, no extra cl home: abs: poss went for home too soon but another high-class run.
8 Ran   Time 2m 29.70()   Owned: Bushwood Stables   Trained: Usa

MAISONS LAFFITTE   FRIDAY 29.10.04   Left & Righthand, Sharpish Track

Official Going Very Soft

5312   1.50 Gr 2 Criterium de Maisons Laffitte 2yo   ()
£76268 £29437 £14049   6f   Soft

CENTIFOLIA R Collet 2-8-11 I Mendizabal 13/10 CO FAV: 10111: gr f Kendor - Djayapura   **114**
(Fabulous Dancer) Made all against stands rail, rdn out: eff at 5/6f on gd & hvy: v smart.
4563 **SALUT THOMAS** R Collet 2-9-0 bl S Maillot 13/10 CO FAV: 5363422: Mid-div, kept on fnl 2.   2   **111**
CAMPO BUENO X Nakkachdji 2-9-0 G Benoist 144/10: 0114413: Held up, rdn & styd on fnl 2f.   hd   **110**
5132 **PRINCE CHARMING 13** J H M Gosden 2-9-0 (100) R Havlin 15/1: 11061054: Cl up, wknd over 1f out.   2½   **105**
5087 **OBE GOLD 15** 2-9-0 vis (89) A Culhane 33/10: 4U331125: Pshd along rear, only mod prog for press.   1   **103**
4955 **TONY JAMES 26** 2-9-0 (100) D Boeuf 34/10: 145169: Always strugg rear: much btr 4022.   10   **83**
9 Ran   Time 1m 12.00 ()   Owned: S Berland   Trained:

MAISONS LAFFITTE   FRIDAY 29.10.04   Left & Righthand, Sharpish Track

5313   2.50 Gr 3 Prix de Seine et Oise 3yo+   ()
£25704 £10282 £7711   6f   Soft

2212} **MISS EMMA** J E Hammond 4-8-9 F Spanu 303/10: 1522-1131: b f Key Of Luck - Disregard That   116
(Don't Forget Me) Made all, styd on strongly, pushed out nr fin: dual Listed rnr up earlier this term: Listed & Gr
3 wnr '03 in native Ireland (M Halford): eff at 5/6f on good & soft ground, prob any trk: smart sprinter.
1 May'03 Curr 6sft 116- A: 2 Oct'02 Curr 6.2g/s 87- :
5073* **STRIKING AMBITION 19** R Charlton 4-8-13 (113) T Thulliez 22/1: 000-00312: Chsd ldrs, rdn to   ½   117
chall ins last, no extra nr fin: smart, fine run: see 5073.
4952 **PATAVELLIAN 26** R Charlton 6-8-13 bl (114) S Drowne 24/10 FAV: 5111-30373: Handy, chsd ldr over   1   115
1f out, no extra ins last: below high-class best last twice: see 4952, 3062.
4817+ **WELSH EMPEROR 32** 5-8-13 bl (107) R Winston 185/10: 14652018: Trkd ldr, rdn & btn 2f out: see 4817.   9½   95
4693 **AUTUMN PEARL 40** 3-8-8 (97) D Boeuf 31/1: 1-1236020: 10th: Mid-div, strugg fnl 2f: abs: btr 1513.   1½   88
11 Ran Time 1m 12.10() Owned: T Wada Trained:

LEOPARDSTOWN   FRIDAY 31.10.04   Lefthand, Galloping Track

Official Going Soft To Heavy (Heavy Places)

5314   3.15 Listed Eyrefiled Stakes 2yo   ()
£22134 £6399 £3049   1m1f   Heavy

YEHUDI 18 A P O'Brien 2-9-0 J P Spencer 7/4 JT FAV: 11: b c Sadlers Wells - Bella Vitessa   108+
(Thatching) Led/dsptd lead, pulled clr from over 2f out, eased nr line, readily: earlier landed a Navan mdn: eff at
1m, mid- dists will suit next term: acts on soft & hvy ground, gall trks: goes well fresh: unbeaten colt, looks
potentially smart & likely to emerge as a classic prospect for '05.
IMPERIAL BRIEF 7 K Prendergast 2-9-0 D P McDonogh 7/4 JT FAV: 00112: br g Imperial Ballet -   3   100
Lyphards Goddess (Lyphard's Special) Held up, hdwy to take 2nd over 1f out, nvr any impress on easy wnr: unbeaten
prev, landing a Curragh mdn & Galway cond stks: stays 9f on gd/soft & hvy: useful type.
IN THE RIBBONS 41 J J Murphy 2-8-11 D M Grant 33/1: 540543: Held up, rdn & styd on fnl 2f.   2½   93
9 Ran Time 2m 02.20() Owned: Mrs John Magnier Trained:

SAINT CLOUD   SUNDAY 31.10.04   Lefthand, Galloping Track

Official Going Very Soft

5315   2.25 Gr 1 Criterium International 2yo   ()
£100599 £40246 £20123   1m rnd   Very Soft

4729* **HELIOS QUERCUS 43** C Diard 2-9-0 A Roussel 51/10: 11414111: Led early, remained close up & led   95
again over 1f out, drvn out: 6 wk abs: suited by 1m, could get further: acts on good/soft & v soft ground: likes a
stiff/gall trk: goes well fresh: tough & smart colt: see 4729 (Gr 3).
4798 **DUBAI SURPRISE 36** D R Loder 2-8-11 (100) T Jarnet 26/1: 31102: Held up, styd on for press to   1½   88
take 2nd well ins last, nvr threat to wnr: stays 1m well & loves give: see 4264 (Gr 3).
WALK IN THE PARK J E Hammond 2-9-0 T Gillet 41/10: 33213: b c Montjeu - Classic Park   snk   91
(Robellino) Rear & pulled hard, kept on late, nvr threat: earlier landed a C/D event: eff at 1m on good & soft.
5195+ **CUPIDS GLORY 9** Sir Mark Prescott 2-9-0 (100) S Sanders 89/10: 6111314: Chsd ldrs, drvn & chall   ¾   90
dist, no extra: stays 1m: btr 5195 (Gr 3, 7f).
5167 **MERCHANT 14** 2-9-0 (99) K Darley 19/10: 532111147: Trkd ldr, wknd over 1f out: btr 5167, 4640.   7½   79
5167 **UMNIYA 14** 2-8-11 vis (100) A Culhane 50/1: 566435368: Always rear: btr 4914.   3   72
8 Ran Time 1m 45.30() Owned: T Maudet Trained:

CATTERICK   TUESDAY 02.11.04   Lefthand, Undulating, Very Tight Track

Official Going Soft ALL TIMES SLOW EXCEPT 3.30

5316   1.00 Robin Hood's Bay Maiden Auction Stakes Div 1 2yo   (E4)
£2926 £836 £418   7f rnd   Soft   Slow   Inside

4692 **MCELDOWNEY 44** [1] M Johnston 2-8-11 (76) J Fanning 7/2: 2300251: Made all, in command ins last,   80$
pushed out: 6 wk abs: eff at 6/7f on firm & soft grnd, sharp or stiff trk: best without blnks: goes well fresh.
4597 **OUTRAGEOUS FLIRT 48** [6] A Dickman 2-8-4 (47) J Mackay 14/1: 000332: Keen & chsd ldrs, drvn to   3   66$
chase wnr over 1f out, kept on, al held: 7 wk abs: handles fast & soft grnd: see 4597 & 4277.
4979 **PLENTY CRIED WOLF 26** R A Fahey 2-8-9 (69) P Hanagan 10/1: 0040363: Chsd ldrs, kept on for   3   66
press, not pace of wnr: handles firm & soft grnd: see 4381.
5033 **CONSIDER THIS 22** [2] W M Brisbourne 2-8-2 (79) D Allan 4/7 FAV: 5320234: Handy, rdn & btn over   1   58
1f out: hvly bckd at odds-on but much btr 5033 & 4653.
5097 **TREW FLIGHT 18** [8]2-9-0 P Robinson 12/1: 05: b c Rahy - Magdala (Sadler's Wells) Towards rear,   5   63
hdwy halfway, no prog fnl 2f: bred to apprec mid-dists.
5141 **STEAL THE THUNDER 16** [10]2-8-7 (54) P Mathers(5) 66/1: 5500056: Mid-div, no impress from halfway.   7   46
WITH HONOURS 0 [7]2-8-2 A Nicholls 50/1: 7: b f Bien Bien - Fair Test (Fair Season) Dwelt, al   5   34
bhd: half sister to 2 1m juv wnrs, dam a 5f 3yo wnr.

4933 **SOOYOU SIR 29** [4]2-8-7   A Culhane 66/1: 008: Sn struggling in rear.   5   32
     GRASS WIDOW 0 [3]2-8-4   R Ffrench 20/1: 9: Dwelt & al towards rear.   2½   25
9 Ran   Time 1m 34.82 (11.82)   Owned: Mr C G Maybury   Trained: Middleham

---

5317	1.30 Robin Hood's Bay Maiden Auction Stakes Div 2 2yo (E4)
	£2919 £834 £417 **7f rnd** Soft Slow Inside

5142 **MYTTONS BELL 16** [8] A Bailey 2-8-2 (58) D Fox(5) 100/30 FAV: 0305031: Made all, rdn clr over 1f   67
out, in command ins last & eased nr fin: eff at 6/7f on firm, soft & fibresand, any trk: see 5142.
5127 **PETER ROUGHLEY 17** [7] A Berry 2-8-7   P Bradley 16/1: 042: Sn chsd wnr, kept on, al held: eff at   4   64
7f on soft grnd & a sharp trk: see 4691.
5154 **PRIMARILY 15** [5] A Berry 2-8-9 (68) R Winston 7/2: 0523: Chsd front pair, kept on for press, al   shd   66
held: longer 7f trip may yet suit: handles gd/soft & soft grnd: see 5154, 4770.
4401 **BOLD HAZE 58** [1] Miss S E Hall 2-8-9   Leanne Kershaw(7) 9/2: 304: Slow away & bhd, late gains for   2½   62
press, no threat: clr rem: 2 mth abs: longer 7f trip likely to suit: see 3939.
5011 **ARTIC FOX 23** [2]2-8-11 bl (60) D Allan 11/2: 5000055: Chsd ldrs, rdn & btn 2f out: flattered 5011.   7   54
5113 **FRAAMBUOYANT 17** [6]2-8-2 VIS R Ffrench 50/1: 0: 0006: b f Fraam - River Maiden (Riverman) Chsd   1½   43
ldrs till halfway, sn struggling, visor: cheaply bought Feb foal: half sister to a 9f 3yo wnr & subs hdles scorer.
3178 **BREEDERS FOLLY 112** [10]2-8-6   P Hanagan 20/1: 07: b f Mujahid - Wynona (Cyrano de Bergerac)   ½   46
Dwelt, al bhd, 4 mth abs: dam a dual 7f juv wnr.
5273 **SPINNAKERS GIRL 3** [9]2-8-2 BL (64) C Catlin 9/1: 3240048: Chsd ldrs till halfway, sn bhd, blnks.   1   41
4769 **TARAGAN 39** [3]2-8-4   K Ghunowa(6) 8/1: 09: Slow away & al bhd: btr 4769 (debut).   16   19
4503 **DEMOLITION FRANK 52** [4]2-8-7   P M Quinn 33/1: 00: 10th: Slow away, sn bhd, abs, gelded.   3½   17
10 Ran   Time 1m 34.44 (11.44)   Owned: Mr Gordon Mytton   Trained: Tarporley

---

5318	2.00 Thomas Darley Nursery Handicap Stakes 2yo 0-85 (D2)	[86]
	£6832 £2102 £1051 **6f rnd** Soft Slow Inside	

5225* **PARIS BELL 10** [2] T D Easterby 2-9-3 (75) P M Quinn 3/1: 0040111: Dwelt, rear, smooth hdwy bef   83
halfway & rdn to lead well ins last: eff at 5/6f & loves soft & hvy: most progressive in the mud.
5225 **GO MO 10** [9] S Kirk 2-8-12 (70) J F Egan 11/2: 0660022: Held up in tch, hdwy to lead over 1f   shd   77
out, hdd well ins last, just denied: also bhd today's wnr latest: imprvd last twice on soft/hvy grnd: see 5225.
3303 **MONASH LAD 106** [7] M H Tompkins 2-9-2 (74) P Robinson 11/1: 053343: Held up, styd on for press,   2½   76
not pace of front pair: abs, gelded: acts on fast & soft grnd: see 3021.
5182 **RAINBOW IRIS 14** [4] B Smart 2-8-10 (68) F Lynch 16/1: 5206504: Handy, rdn & no extra over 1f out.   3½   63
5185 **ORPEN WIDE 13** [1]2-8-6 (64) Lisa Jones 16/1: 0330025: Handy, fdd over 1f out: btr 5185.   3   53
5106 **LADY DORIS WATTS 18** [3]2-8-6 (64) C Catlin 11/1: 0206: Broke well but outpcd bef halfway, no dngr.   ½   52
5203 **JOHN FORBES 11** [5]2-8-12 (70) T Eaves(3) 25/1: 1000007: Dwelt & rear, little hdwy: btr 2774.   ½   52
4962* **HARRYS HOUSE 28** [6]2-9-5 (77) R Winston 8/1: 404318: Mid-div, hung left & btn over 1f out.   5   54
4963 **DORN DANCER 28** [10]2-9-7 (79) L Enstone 28/1: 1500609: Towards rear & bhd, stumbled badly 2f out   3   50
when no impress: much btr 4655.
5035 **TSAROXY 22** [8]2-9-6 BL (78) P Mulrennan(3) 2/1 FAV: 33150: 10th: Led & clr halfway, hdd over 1f   1¼   46
out & wknd qckly: hvly bckd but ran too freely in first time blnks: much btr 5035 & 4244.
10 Ran   Time 1m 20.28 (9.98)   Owned: Ryedale Partners No 8   Trained: Malton

---

5319	2.30 Hambleton Maiden Stakes 3yo+ (D3)
	£3513 £1081 £541 **1m3f214y** Soft Slow Inside

5015 **LADY KARR 23** [6] M Johnston 3-8-9   J Fanning 4/1: 031: Made all, edged left but in full command   71+
fnl 2f, val 9L+: bckd tho' op 7/2: eff at 10f, relished this step up to 12f & shld get further: handles fast grnd,
imprvd on soft with forcing tactics: enjoyed a sharp trk: unexposed, win more races.
5052 **MACS ELAN 22** [8] A B Coogan 4-9-6 (46) A Culhane 16/1: 0-050622: Chsd ldrs, eff to chase wnr 3f   6   64
out, no impress fnl 2f: longer 12f trip may yet suit: prob handles fast & soft grnd: see 5052.
3415 **CLASSIC EVENT 102** [2] T D Easterby 3-9-0 (62) D Allan 9/1: 350-0023: Slow away & well bhd, hdwy   1¾   62
for press from halfway, took 3rd over 1f out but nvr any threat: lost ch start, poss 2nd with a level break: 3 mth
abs, bened, gelded: handles fast & soft grnd: see 3415 & 1000.
4701 **SELKIRK GRACE 43** [4] K A Morgan 4-9-6   P Hanagan 5/1: 3/-54: Mid-div, rdn & no impress fnl 2f: 7   55
6 wk abs & longer trip: see 4701.
5173 **DANCES WITH ANGELS 14** [7]4-9-1 (40) P M Quinn 25/1: 00P0645: Cl-up, fdd fnl 3f: flattered 5173.   5   45
5180 **CARRIACOU 14** [5]3-8-9 (61) J F Egan 7/2: 3040306: Held up, no prog fnl 3f: bckd: btr 5024.   7   38
321 **CALCAR 302** [3]4-9-6 (45) L Vickers 100/1: 00500-07: b g Flying Spur - Poscimur (Prince Rupert)   3½   40
Chsd ldrs, btn 3f out: abs: class stks rnr-up '03 (J Hills, AW h'cap unplcd, rtd 44a): unplcd '02 (rtd 65, mdn):
stays a gall 13f on gd/soft grnd. 2 May'03 Ayr 13.1 g/s 52-(52) F:
5190 **SANDOKAN 13** [11]3-9-0   T P Queally 20/1: 0008: Mid-div, lost tch from 4f out, longer trip.   23   17
5034 **BIJOU DAN 22** [1]3-9-0 (54) R Winston 50/1: 46059: Chsd ldrs, drvn & struggling from halfway.   5   12
     EXPRESS LILY 0 [12]5-9-1   Darren Williams 33/1: 0: 10th: Well bhd fnl 5f on Flat debut, lng jmps abs.   10   0
36 **RED MOUNTAIN 90** [9]3-9-0   T Eaves(3) 100/1: 0-000: 11th: Sn bhd & no ch 4f out, 3 mth abs.   5   0
5226 **MAID TO TREASURE 10** [10]3-8-9 (75) K Darley 3/1: 2-4630: 12th: Handy, rdn & btn 3f out, eased   3   0
from dist, t.o.: nicely bckd tho' op 5/2: much btr 2678 & 2131 (10f, g/s).
12 Ran   Time 2m 49.97 (18.77)   Owned: Iona Equine   Trained: Middleham

---

5320	3.00 Toteplacepot Stakes Handicap 3yo+ 71-85 (D2)	[96]
	£6984 £2149 £1074 **7f rnd** Soft Slow Inside	

5284 **GO PADERO 3** [1] M Johnston 3-9-3 (85) J Fanning 9/4 FAV: 651-141: Handy, drvn & led well ins   92
last: nicely bckd, qck reapp: stays 1m, suited by 7f: acts on fast, enjoys gd/soft & soft grnd, gd or sharp trk.
5000 **KING HARSON 24** [8] J D Bethell 5-9-1 vis (82) P Robinson 16/1: 6015002: Led, hdd well ins last &   ¾   87
no extra: loves to dominate, gd run: see 4073.
5144 **KIRKBYS TREASURE 16** [11] A Berry 6-8-9 (1ow) (75) F Lynch 8/1: 2260353: Rear, hdwy to press ldrs   hd   80

CATTERICK TUESDAY 02.11.04 Lefthand, Undulating, Very Tight Track

ins last, no extra fnl 100y: gd run, loves Musselburgh: see 5144, 2809.
5286 **DIGITAL 3** [5] M R Channon 7-9-4 (85) A Culhane 9/2: 2205064: Trkd ldrs, drvn & onepace dist: see 945. *2½* **85**
5000 **YOUNG MR GRACE 24** [9]4-9-3 (84) D Allan 20/1: 1301505: Handy, fdd fnl 2f: see 4685. *1½* **82**
4820 **NEVADA DESERT 36** [4]4-8-4 p (71) B Swarbrick(5) 20/1: 2010006: Mid-div, rdn & nvr able to chall. *5* **62**
5286 **AZREME 3** [2]4-8-10 (77) R Ffrench 11/2: 0201207: Mid-div, hmpd on bend & lost place over 3f out. *¾* **67**
5069 **ULYSEES 21** [7]5-8-4 (5oh) (66) P Hanagan 16/1: 0040058: Struggling halfway: see 2542. *1* **60**
4786 **RAYMONDS PRIDE 38** [6]4-8-13 bl (80) N Callan 11/1: 5114509: Al towards rear: btr 1476 (5f). *1* **68**
5000 **JATH 24** [3]3-8-10 (78) K Darley 8/1: 6061000: 10th: Dwelt, mid-div, struggling halfway: btr 4148. *10* **51**
10 Ran Time 1m 33.82 (10.82) Owned: Pagodero Partnership Trained: Middleham

5321

3.30 Boroughbridge Claiming Stakes 3yo+ (F4)
£3024 £864 £432 **5f rnd** **Soft** **Fair** Inside

4654 **TRINCULO 46** [14] D Nicholls 7-9-10 (75) A Nicholls 4/1: 0600051: Made all stands rail, drvn clr over 1f out, val 10L+: bckd, abs: prev with N Littmoden: eff at 5/6f on fast, soft & fibresand, with/without chkpcs: goes well fresh: apprec drop to claiming grade but formerly useful & revitalised for new yard. **87+**
5146 **ROBWILLCALL 16** [8] A Berry 4-8-1 p (45) P Hanagan 14/1: 5050002: Mid-div, styd on for press to take remote 2nd ins last, nvr a threat: handles fast & soft grnd: see 2476 & 1797. *8* **48**
4967 **LOUGHLORIEN 28** [11] R E Barr 5-8-8 (56) D Tudhope(5) 9/2: 3340123: Bhd, mod gains for press. *2½* **50**
5231 **THE LEATHER WEDGE 8** [10] A Berry 5-8-4 (40) P Mathers(4) 25/1: 2550304: Cl-up, btn over 1f out. *nk* **45**
2944 **BOND ROMEO 122** [2]3-8-8 (67) D McGaffin 20/1: 55020-05: Cl-up, fdd fnl 1f, 4 mth abs: see 2944. *2* **45**
5036 **GEORGE THE BEST 22** [1]3-8-12 (62) A Culhane 8/1: 0600056: Slow away & rcd alone far side, no dngr. *1¼* **46**
4785 **TORRENT 38** [13]9-8-4 bl (56) Lisa Jones 9/1: 2000207: Chsd ldrs, no impress dist: btr 4603. *nk* **37**
5110 **PAY TIME 18** [6]5-8-0 (1ow) (40) C Catlin 66/1: 6005608: Chsd ldrs till halfway: flattered 3610. *hd* **32**
5157 **FRABROFEN 15** [9]3-8-13 R Ffrench 25/1: 209: Al outpcd in rear: btr 1392 (debut). *9* **29**
4967 **BRIGADIER MONTY 28** [12]6-8-12 (52) R Winston 7/1: 5503000: 10th: Sn struggling rear: bckd, op 14/1. *1* **26**
4930 **MISS CEYLON 31** [15]4-8-5 (35) D Allan 80/1: 0000000: 11th: Al outpcd in rear. *8* **5**
5041 **BABA 22** [5]3-8-12 K Darley 28/1: 000: 12th: Mid-div, struggling from halfway, drop in trip. *2½* **7**
4514 **BEAUVRAI 52** [4]4-9-4 bl (77) O Urbina 7/2 FAV: 0231130: 13th: Chsd ldrs till halfway, sn bhd & eased dist: nicely bckd, op 5/1: 8 wk abs: much btr 4294 & 4150. *3* **7**
13 Ran Time 1m 02.35 (5.05) Owned: Mr D Nicholls Trained: Thirsk

5322

4.00 Oliver Cromwell Handicap Stakes 3yo+ 56-70 (E3) **[74]**
£3548 £1092 £546 **1m5f175y** **Soft** **Slow** Inside

5024 **ONWARD TO GLORY 23** [3] J L Dunlop 4-9-0 (60) W Ryan 13/2: 0-004601: Rear, hdwy 4f out & led over 1f out, drvn out: first win: eff at 11.5f, suited by return to 14f & 2m could suit: handled gd, enjoyed soft grnd/sharp trk today: unexposed at this trip, may progress. **68**
5004 **INCHNADAMPH 24** [5] T J Fitzgerald 4-9-1 t (61) K Darley 7/1: 2211502: Held up, hdwy halfway & led over 3f out till over 1f out, not pace of wnr: acts on gd & soft grnd: see 3134. *1* **67**
5093 **SCOTT 18** [2] J Jay 3-8-10 (64) G Baker 100/30 FAV: 0314123: Held up, smooth hdwy over 3f out, sn chall, no extra bef dist: stays 14f, return to 12f could suit: see 5093 & 4990. *3½* **67**
5174 **MONTECRISTO 14** [8] R Guest 11-9-10 (70) C Catlin 9/2: 23-00044: Held up, styd on for press fnl 3f, not able to land blow: return to 12f could suit: well clr of rem: see 5174 & 2673. *1¼* **72**
5145 **KYBER 16** [4]3-8-2 (1oh) (55) R Ffrench 25/1: 4330645: Led till over 3f out, wknd qckly: btr 5145. *10* **49**
5093* **PRECIOUS MYSTERY 18** [1]4-9-7 (67) A Quinn(5) 4/1: 16-42016: Mid-div, struggling fnl 3f: btr 5093. *1* **59**
4623 **THE FAIRY FLAG 47** [9]6-8-10 (1oh)p (55) D Fox(5) 16/1: 436-4007: Chsd ldrs, drvn & btn 2f out: 7 wk abs. *4* **44**
5032 **PILGRIMS PROGRESS 22** [6]4-9-5 P (65) T Williams 81: 30-40508: Handy & narrow lead over 3f out, hdd over 2f out & wknd, cheek pieces. *10* **44**
4990 **ARCHIE BABE 25** [7]8-9-0 (60) R Winston 13/2: 1500009: Cl-up, wknd qckly from over 3f out: btr 1034. *19* **23**
3225} **WIN ALOT 462** [10]6-8-10 (11oh) (45) Lisa Jones 66/1: 044100-0: 10th: b g Aragon - Having Fun (Hard Fought) Struggling rear fnl 5f: Flat reapp, jumps fit (p.u., h'cap hdle): '03 appr h'cap wnr on the level: unplcd '02 (rtd 32a, S Bowring, tried blnks & t-strap): winning form at 10f, stays 12f: acts on fibresand & gd/soft grnd, sharp or stiff/undul trk. 1 Jun'03 Pont 10.0 g/s 44-39 E: *dist* **0**
10 Ran Time 3m 17.64(22.24) Owned: Mr Michael H Watt Trained: Arundel

FLEMINGTON TUESDAY 02.11.04

Official Going Good/Soft

5323

4.10 Gr 1 Melbourne Cup (Handicap) 3yo+ () **[129]**
£1176471 £306723 £140756 **2m** **Good/Soft**

5012*}**MAKYBE DIVA 17** L Freedman 7-8-11 (112) G Boss 26/10 FAV: 2142021: Held up inner, smooth prog 3f out & led over 1f out, rdn out: won this race last year: smart & tough stayer. **120**
4733* **VINNIE ROE 45** D K Weld 6-9-2 bl (117) P J Smullen 5/1: 1154-2212: Held up, rdn & hdwy to briefly lead over 1f out, not pace of wnr ins last: abs: brave effort under topweight: plcd in this in '02: high class. *1¼* **123**
ZAZZMAN 3 T Vasil 6-8-4 bl (105) N Ryan 100/1: 0003003: Led 7f, led 2f out till over 1f out. *2½* **109**
4494* **DISTINCTION 53** 5-8-7 (108) D Beadman 12/1: 15-05116: Twrds rear, effort wide to chase ldrs over 2f out, onepace: abs: connections reportedly felt gelding was set too much to do: see 4494. *3* **109**
4956 **MAMOOL 30** 5-9-0 (115) L Dettori 25/1: 15-05117: Held up, short of room 4f out, swtchd wide & onepace: jockey banned for a month for careless riding: see 4956, 4391. *shd* **116**
4886 **RAZKALLA 32** 6-8-10 (111) K McEvoy 40/1: 24-14459: Mid-div, not able to chall fnl 2f: see 4886. *½* **111**
4805*]**MEDIA PUZZLE 45** 7-8-11 bl (112) D M Oliver 20/1: 0311/500: 12th: Held up, effort wide over 4f out, btn 2f out: 6 wk abs: just 2 starts since winning this race in '02 (finished lame). *1½* **111**
24 Ran Time 3m 28.55() Owned: Emily Kristina Pty Ltd Syndicate Trained: Australia

WOLVERHAMPTON **Polytrack WEDNESDAY 03.11.04 Lefthand, Sharp, Oval Track**

Official Going Standard - No Standard Times

5324 **4.15 Littlewoods Bet Direct Maiden Stakes 2yo (D3)**
£3614 £1112 £556 **7f32y aw rnd Going Inapplicable** Outside

5064 **IL COLOSSEO 22** [3] Mrs L Stubbs 2-9-0 Dane O'Neill 7/1: 341: Made all & pulled clr from halfway, readily, val 7L+: eff at 7f, handles soft, likes gd & polytrack, relished forcing tactics tonight: see 5064. **87a+**
5258 **FLAUNT N FLIRT 6** [7] M P Tregoning 2-8-9 N De Souza(5) 14/1: 002: b f Erhaab - Lets Fall In Love (Northern Baby) Chsd ldrs, hmpd early, styd on to take 2nd, nvr threat to wnr: Apr foal, half-sister to 2 yo wnrs at 5f/1m: dam a US wnr: handles polytrack: now quals for h'caps. *5* **70a**
5078 **CAPE ENTERPRISE 21** [8] J W Hills 2-9-0 M Hills 14/1: 03: b c Cape Canaveral - Principessa (Alydeed) In tch, styd on onepace fnl 2f, no threat: $60,000 Apr foal, dam unrcd, related to a high-class US 3yo. *1¼* **72a**
5199 **NEUTRINO 12** [10] L M Cumani 2-9-0 N Mackay 13/8 FAV: 044: Held up, late gains, nvr a threat: op 2/1: btr 5199 (hvy). *nk* **71a**
BLUE AZURE 0 [6]2-8-9 D Holland 12/1: 5: Dwelt & towards rear, late gains, nrst fin. *1* **64a**
5236 **LIMIT 9** [12]2-8-9 A Culhane 9/2: 3026: Chsd wnr over 2f out, hung left & btn dist: btr 5236. *1¼* **61a**
5251 **AGGRAVATION 7** [1]2-9-0 J F Egan 40/1: 0007: Chsd ldrs, hmpd early, btn over 1f out. *2½* **61a**
5259 **ANNIBALE CARO 6** [4]2-9-0 S Sanders 7/1: 058: Dwelt, pushed along towards rear, nvr factor. *3* **55a**
SEA LARK 0 [5]2-9-0 S W Kelly 20/1: 9: Dwelt & al towards rear. *2* **51a**
SWEET SIOUX 0 [2]2-8-9 E Ahern 10/1: 0: 10th: Dwelt, sn struggling rear. *7* **34a**
4653 **DEGREE OF HONOR 47** [9]2-8-9 K Fallon 14/1: 00: 11th: Chsd ldr, btn/hmpd over 2f out, eased. *5* **24a**
BLUE OTIS 0 [11]2-8-9 G Baker 40/1: 0: 12th: Held up, rdn & struggling halfway. *4* **16a**
12 Ran Time 1m 32.04 (No Std Time) Owned: Mr Des Thurlby Trained: Malton

5325 **4.40 Bet Direct On Itv Page 367 Classified Stakes 3yo 0-60 (F3)**
£3497 £1076 £538 **7f32y aw rnd Going Inapplicable** Outside

5041 **TENNYS GOLD 23** [3] B W Hills 3-8-9 (60) M Hills 7/2: 2-435431: Held up, prog 3f out & led ins last, rdn out: reportedly broke a blood vessel latest: eff around 7f/1m on fast, gd/soft & polytrack: see 4768. **68a**
5014 **LANDUCCI 24** [11] J W Hills 3-9-3 t (65) K Fallon 5/2 FAV: 0613402: Chsd ldr 3f out, rdn to lead ins last, sn hdd & not pace of wnr: acts on both AWs, fast & soft grnd: see 4465, 4144. *2* **71a**
4251 **DOUBLE DAGGER LADY 66** [6] J Noseda 3-8-9 (60) E Ahern 3/1: 64563: Chsd ldrs & led over 2f out till ins last, no extra: op 5/2, 2 month abs: eff around 7f on polytrack, unplcd on turf previously. *nk* **62a**
5017 **MISKINA 24** [4] W M Brisbourne 3-8-9 (58) B Swarbrick(5) 12/1: 0301504: Chsd ldrs, rdn & keeping on when short of room ins last, kept on to the line: prob plcd with a clr run: acts on fast grnd & both AWs. *nk* **61a+**
1647 **THE JOB 177** [8]3-8-12 (59) A Culhane 10/1: 14-62505: Held up, eff when short of room over 2f out, styd on onepace ins last: 6 month abs: eff at 7f, rtn to 1m could suit: see 933. *1¼* **61a**
4974 **EXTRA COVER 28** [10]3-9-1 bl (63) D Sweeney 16/1: 1660046: Held up, eff 2f out, no impress: see 4974. *1* **62a**
5153 **SION HILL 16** [9]3-8-12 (60) J D O'Reilly(7) 12/1: 2-000007: Held up, little hdwy for press fnl 2f. *½* **58a**
5263 **WALL STREET RUNNER 6** [2]3-8-9 (59) J Quinn 33/1: 5200008: Towards rear & nvr a factor, qck reapp. *1½* **52a**
5117 **FIT TO FLY 18** [1]3-8-12 P (58) A Nicholls 33/1: 0500009: Chsd ldr 3f, sn rdn & btn, tried cheekpieces. *4* **47a**
5241 **TSARBUCK 9** [7]3-8-12 p (59) G Faulkner 11/1: 3300640: 10th: Chsd ldrs, hung left & btn 2f out. *½* **46a**
5014 **Vademecum 24** [5]3-8-12 (60) D McGaffin 14/1:0
4587 **Wings Of Morning 50** [12]3-8-12 (60) Danielle McCreery(7) 33/1:0
12 Ran Time 1m 32.23 (No Std Time) Owned: Mr Rick Barnes Trained: Lambourn

5326 **5.05 Bet Direct On At The Races Handicap Stakes 3yo 56-70 (E3)** **[80]**
£3437 £1058 £529 **5f20y aw rnd Going Inapplicable** Inside

5008 **GLOBAL ACHIEVER 25** [13] G C H Chung 3-8-12 (64) O Urbina 25/1: 0000001: Dwelt & held up, styd on for press to lead well ins last: eff at 6f, stays 7f: acts on both AWs, appears v modest on turf: imprvd for omission of t-strap today, also tried blnks: likes W'hampton: see 750. **73a**
4713 **KOSTAR 44** [7] C G Cox 3-9-8 (74) R Smith 12/1: 41042: Held up, hdwy to chase ldr over 2f out, led & edged left ins last, hdd nr fin: 6 wk abs: acts on firm, gd & polytrack: see 4173, 3252. *hd* **82a**
5305* **LITTLE RIDGE 2** [6] H Morrison 3-9-12 (6ex) (78) L Fletcher(3) 11/4 FAV: 11-00013: Led & clr halfway, hung right & hdd well ins last: qck reapp: nicely bckd: acts on fast, soft & polytrack. *3* **77a**
3599 **ONLY IF I LAUGH 95** [3] P A Blockley 3-9-1 (67) M Lawson(5) 20/1: 2305304: Chsd ldrs, rdn & kept on, not pace to chall: 3 month abs: see 1902 & 914. *shd* **66a**
4528 **MALUTI 53** [11]3-8-4 (1oh) (55) C Catlin 9/1: 6314205: Held up, late gains, no dngr: prefer stiffer trk or 6f. *¾* **53a**
5291 **JILLY WHY 4** [9]3-9-4 (70) A Nicholls 8/1: 0024056: Chsd ldrs wide, onepcd for pressure. *2½* **59a**
4747 **SKYHARBOR 42** [12]3-9-8 (74) K Fallon 11/2: 5234007: Pushed along rear, mod late gains: btr 4604. *½* **61a**
4930 **NANNA 32** [4]3-8-7 (59) A Culhane 9/2: 2116038: Chsd ldrs, short of room when struggling over 1f out. *¾* **44a**
5125 **SNOW WOLF 18** [8]3-9-10 (76) Dane O'Neill 33/1: 2004009: Led 1f, btn over 1f out: btr 3976. *1¾* **56a**
5156 **INNCLASSIC 16** [2]3-8-4 (1oh)bl (55) Lisa Jones 16/1: 1200009: Chsd ldrs 3f, reportedly struck into. *dht* **36a**
2784 **Laconia 129** [1]3-8-12 (64) Derek Nolan(7) 25/1:0 5156 **Juniper Banks 16** [5]3-8-5 (57) D Fox(5) 20/1:0
12 Ran Time 1m 03.66 (No Std Time) Owned: Dr Johnny Hon Trained: Newmarket

5327 **5.30 Bet Direct On Sky Active Classified Stakes 3yo+ 0-60 (F3)**
£3510 £1080 £540 **6f aw rnd Going Inapplicable** Inside

4862 **MERDIFF 35** [4] W M Brisbourne 5-9-1 (63) K Fallon 11/2: 2042001: Trkd ldrs, led over 1f out, hung left, rdn to hold on: eff btwn 6/9f on fast, both AWs & loves a sharp/turning trk: eff with/without t-strap. **71a**
5155* **PRINCE OF GOLD 16** [2] R Hollinshead 4-9-1 p (63) D Sweeney 13/8 FAV: 0532012: Held up, hdwy when short of room ins last, rdn & styd on strongly, just failed: shade unlucky, remains in fine form & can win again. *nk* **70a**
4622 **ROMAN MAZE 48** [9] W M Brisbourne 4-9-3 (65) S W Kelly 7/1: 0424203: ch g Lycius - Maze Garden (Riverman) Towards rear, switched when short of room over 1f out, styd on well, nrst fin: stablemate of wnr: 7 wk *¾* **70a**

WOLVERHAMPTON Polytrack WEDNESDAY 03.11.04 Lefthand, Sharp, Oval Track

abs: acts on both AWs, firm & soft grnd: on a long losing run but hinting turn not far away: eff at 6/7.6f: see
3634. 2 Sep'04 York 7.0 g/f 67-61 E: 2 Aug'04 Ches 7.6 fm 66-60 C: 1 Nov'03 Wolv 7 af 71a- D:

5010	**WILLHECONQUERTOO** 25 [7] Andrew Reid 4-9-3 t p (65) J F Egan 20/1: 0054404: Held up, hdwy wide to chall when hung left over 1f out & no extra ins last, ran well despite awkward passage: on a fair mark: see 2975.	2		64a
4976	**KENSINGTON GB** 28 [3]3-9-0 (62) S Sanders 8/1: 6326165: Mid-div, wide, not pace to chall.	1¾	56a
4984	**VAL DE MAAL** 27 [10]4-9-1 P (63) O Urbina 14/1: 4046006: Chsd ldrs, onepace for press dist.	½	55a
2214*	**TAYIF** 152 [12]8-9-3 t (65) S Carson 9/1: 0205317: Held up, nvr able to chall: 5 month abs.	1¼	53a
4696	**OBE BOLD** 45 [13]3-8-13 (64) F Norton 20/1: 0100408: Held up, no impress fnl 2f: 6 wk abs.	¾	47a
5053	**BRANSTON TIGER** 23 [6]5-9-1 bl (63) D Nolan(3) 12/1: 1430309: Mid-div & sn rdn, nvr a factor.	1	46a
4227	**BRAGADINO** 55 [11]5-9-3 VIS T (65) A Culhane 20/1: 0060060: 10th: Al onepce: abs, vis/ t-strap.	½	46a
2599	**SHOLTO** 136 [8]6-9-1 bl (63) J D O'Reilly(7) 25/1: 000-0200: 11th: Led early, cl-up till over 1f out, abs.	3½	33a
1635	**MOUNT ROYALE** 179 [5]6-9-2 vis t (64) Kim Tinkler 20/1: 0622230: 12th: Chsd ldrs, sn outpcd, 6 mth abs.	1¼	30a
4438	**WEET WATCHERS** 57 [1]4-9-2 (64) G Gibbons 20/1: 3051P00: 13th: Led after 1f till over 1f out, wknd.	7	13a

13 Ran   Time 1m 16.91 (No Std Time)   Owned: Team Racing   Trained: Nesscliffe

5328   5.55 Betdirect Co Uk Handicap Stakes 4yo+ 46-55 (F4)   [69]
£2610 £746 £373   1m4f50y aw   Going   Inapplicable   Inside

4672	**GREENWICH MEANTIME** 46 [4] Mrs J R Ramsden 4-9-3 (58) L Goncalves 4/1: 0560431: Led 2f & remained cl-up, rdn clr, flashed tail but val 10L+: 6 wk abs: eff at 10f/2m, poss best suited by 12f: acts on firm & gd/soft & polytrack, prob any trk: took well to this surface, win again if repeating: see 4672, 1361.			71a+
5184	**REBEL RAIDER** 15 [7] B N Pollock 5-9-0 (55) J Quinn 14/1: 0300/-102: Chsd ldr after 2f & led over 2f out, hdd over 1f out & no ch with wnr: back to form after latest: stays 12f: see 5005 (8.6f).	8	58a
5117	**FIELD SPARK** 18 [5] J A Glover 4-9-0 p (55) D Holland 3/1 FAV: 0200423: Held up, eff to chase ldrs over 2f out, onepace for press: see 5117, 4938 & 3222.	1¼	56a
5180	**TRAVELLERS TALE** 15 [10] P G Murphy 5-8-13 (54) Derek Nolan(7) 11/1: 0622034: Dwelt & held up, eff wide, not pace to threat: see 5180, 4033 & 3948.	nk	54a
4669	**OUR DESTINY** 46 [9]6-9-0 (55) P Makin(5) 16/1: 5660005: Held up, hdwy halfway, short of room over 1f out, onepace: 6 wk abs: see 2844, 1940.	1½	53a
5292	**EFRHINA** 4 [1]4-9-5 (60) F Norton 16/1: 0034306: Held up, eff 3f out, onepace, qck reapp, op 10/1.	¾	57a
5123*	**BANNINGHAM BLAZE** 18 [2]4-9-4 vis (59) D Nolan(3) 10/1: 2325417: Held up, short of room over 1f out, no impress: see 5123 (banded).	2½	52a
5082	**LAZZAZ** 21 [12]6-8-12 (53) Joanna Badger 15/2: 5511068: Led after 2f till over 2f out, sn btn: btr 4665.	3	42a
768	**TROPICAL SON** 248 [6]5-8-6 BL e (47) S Whitworth 25/1: 1025059: Dwelt & held up, nvr factor: blnks, abs.2½	32a
5180*	**LORD LAHAR** 15 [11]5-8-13 (54) C Catlin 11/2: 0402610: 10th: Held up & pulled hard, hdwy wide 5f out, btn 8f out: new stable: btr 5180 (C/D).	19	11a
5180	**Pont Neuf** 15 [3]4-9-0 t(55) K Fallon 11/1:0	**Alaipour** 21 [8]5-8-12 (53) A Culhane 20/1:P

12 Ran   Time 2m 43.25 (No Std Time)   Owned: Mr J D Martin   Trained: Thirsk

5329   6.20 Bet Direct Football Cashbacks Classified Stakes 3yo 0-50 (G4)
£2716 £776 £388   1m14ly aw rnd   Going   Inapplicable   Inside

4761	**FISBY** 41 [6] S Kirk 3-9-3 (55) J F Egan 16/1: 0-550001: Dwelt & held up, styd on for press to lead well ins last: first win: 6 wk abs: eff around 1m/8.6f: handles firm grnd & polytrack, sharp trk: goes well fresh.			64a
5056	**DISCO DIVA** 22 [9] M Blanshard 3-8-12 (53) F Norton 12/1: 0000022: Held up, hdwy to chall ins last, not pace of wnr: acts on firm, gd & polytrack: stays sharp 8.6f: see 933.	1½	55a
5111	**CALCULAITE** 19 [3] Mrs G S Rees 3-9-2 (54) S Sanders 15/8 FAV: 5013463: Led, hdd well ins last & no extra: op 11/4: see 4660, 4507.	nk	58a
5242	**BEAUTY OF DREAMS** 9 [2] M R Channon 3-8-9 (50) A Culhane 11/2: 6043004: Trkd ldr & not settle early, eff to chall over 1f out, no extra fnl 1f: op 7/1: acts on firm, soft & polytrack: visor omitted: see 5094, 4761.	2	47a
5229*	**COMPTON MICKY** 9 [8]3-9-4 p (49) F Edmunds 10/1: 6050015: Keen & handy, rdn & no extra dist: stays 8.6f, rtn to 7f could suit: see 5229 (7f, banded).	1¼	53a
4925	**TROIS ETOILES** 32 [7]3-8-13 (54) M Hills 7/1: 0553606: Prom, rdn & no extra from dist: handles polytrack: visor omitted after latest: see 2922, 2650.	nk	47a
5005	**ORCHESTRATION** 25 [10]3-8-13 (51) S Whitworth 20/1: 4400067: Chsd ldrs, no impress over 1f out.	3	41a
5119	**DELCIENNE** 18 [4]3-8-9 (50) A McCarthy 8/1: 2150108: Chsd ldrs, btn 2f out: see 4904 (banded).	1	35a
5066	**QUEENS ECHO** 22 [12]3-9-0 (55) S W Kelly 20/1: 5-2509: Stumbled start, held up in tch, nvr a factor.	1	38a
4594	**DIAL SQUARE** 50 [5]3-9-2 (54) K Fallon 7/1: 1110000: 10th: Held up & no impress thr'out, 7 wk abs.	nk	39a
5230	**LIVIA** 9 [1]3-8-9 vis (50) C Catlin 14/1: 0000240: 11th: Chsd ldrs till lost pl 3f out: much btr 4992.	¾	31a
3414	**WEET AN HAUL** 103 [13]3-9-0 vis (52) G Gibbons 16/1: 120-0030: 12th: Held up & keen, strugg fnl 3f.	9	21a

12 Ran   Time (No Std Time)   Owned: Mr Peter Valentine   Trained: Upper Lambourn

MUSSELBURGH   WEDNESDAY 03.11.04   Righthand, Sharp Track

Official Going GOOD/SOFT (GOOD places).

5330   1.30 Toteplacepot E B F Median Auction Maiden Stakes 2yo (E3)
£4222 £1299 £650   7f30y rnd   Good/Soft 90   -19 Slow   Outside

5033	**MINTLAW** 23 [7] I Semple 2-8-9 R Winston 5/1: 261: Trkd ldrs, imprvd to lead ins fnl 1f, pushed clr despite drifting left: eff at 6/7f, has tried 1m: acts on fast, clrly gd/soft: handles a sharp trk: see 3761.			88
5033	**CONSIDER THIS** 23 [11] W M Brisbourne 2-8-9 (79) P Mathers(5) 4/1: 5320232: Led till ins fnl 1f, kept on but left bhd by ready wnr: nicely bckd: another consistent run, bt today's wnr in 5033.	3½	81
	PICCOLOMINI [3] M Johnston 2-9-0 K Darley 12/1: 3: b c Diktat - La Dama Bonita (El Gran Senor) Mid-div, styd on well fnl 1f, nrst fin on debut: op 7/1: 18,000gns Mar foal, half-brother to useful miler Conflict: dam a 7f scorer, sire a top-class sprinter: eff at 7f on gd/soft grnd, sure to learn from this.	¾	84
4945	**HALCYON EXPRESS** 30 [4] P F I Cole 2-9-0 T Martin Dwyer 10/1: 04: b c Mujadil - Hakkaniyah (Machiavellian) Front rank, outpcd fnl 1f in first time t-strap: Apr foal, cost 17,000gns: dam a 6f juv wnr, sire	½	83

1620

a speedy juv: imprvd run tho' struggled to stay 7f in these conditions.
5106 **LA VIOLA 19** [2]2-8-9 Darren Williams 10/1: 65: Trkd ldrs, outpcd fnl 1.5f: see 5106. 1¾ **74**
5200 **WOOLSACK 12** [1]2-9-0 S Drowne 10/3 FAV: 56: ch c Spinning World - Rich And Famous (Deep Roots) 1½ **76**
Trkd ldrs, ev ch till wknd 1.5f out: well bckd: $40,000 May foal: half-brother to a decent sprinter in the US: dam a high-class 2yo scorer in France, sire a top-class miler: with H Morrison.
4968 **AMMIRARE 29** [5]2-8-9 P Mulrennan(3) 66/1: 07: Slowly away, nvr a factor. 3½ **65**
4375 **LINZIS LAD 60** [13]2-9-0 A Mullen(7) 66/1: 08: Nvr btr than mid-div: 9 wk abs. ½ **69**
3831 **HANNAHS TRIBE 86** [14]2-8-9 F Lynch 50/1: 009: Al rear: 12 wk abs. shd **64**
PORT DARGENT [10]2-8-9 J Fanning 10/1: 0: 10th: Chsd ldrs 5f on debut: stablemate 3rd. nk **63**
BRADS HOUSE [8]2-9-0 T Eaves(3) 66/1: 0: 11th: Slowly away, al bhd on racecourse bow. ½ **67**
5235 **CHRISTOM 9** [6]2-9-0 P Hanagan 16/1: 000: 12th: Slowly away, nvr a factor. nk **66**
Bold Pursuit [12]2-9-0 D Allan 50/1:0 4338 **Tyrone Sam 62** [9]2-9-0 G Parkin 66/1:0
14 Ran Time 1m 32.57 (7.67) Owned: Evelyn Duchess of Sutherland Trained: Carluke

5331

2.00 Totesport 0800 221 221 E B F Maiden Stakes 2yo (D2)
£5486 £1688 £844 **1m rnd** **Good/Soft 90** **+03 Fast** Outside

5221 **DREAM TONIC 11** [5] M R Channon 2-9-0 S Hitchcott 20/1: 601: b c Zafonic - Dream On Deya **87**
(Dolphin Street) Chsd ldrs, led 2f out, styd on strongly fnl 1f, rdn out: Feb foal, half-brother to a 7f juv wnr, sire a top-class miler: eff over a sharp 1m on gd/soft: recorded a decent time & this was an imprvd effort.
5171 **KEY OF SOLOMON 15** [2] H Morrison 2-9-0 S Drowne 7/2: 632: Mid-div, prog to chase wnr fnl 1f, no 1¾ **82**
impress cl-home: tchd 5/1: acts on gd/soft & soft grnd: has shown enough to win a small race, see 5171.
5064 **ONYERGO 22** [10] J R Weymes 2-9-0 R Winston 14/1: 333: Chsd ldrs, onepcd fnl 1f: tchd 20/1. 3½ **76**
4466 **CORDAGE 56** [4] G A Butler 2-9-0 (80) P Hanagan 9/2: 5444: Trkd ldrs, onepcd when short of room & 1 **74**
switched dist, no impress: op 10/3, clr of rem, 8 wk abs: longer 1m trip: see 4466 (gd grnd).
4783 **LOVE BEAUTY 39** [6]2-9-0 (79) J Fanning 2/1 FAV: 4025: Front rank, hmpd 2f out & no ch after: 5 **64**
bckd from 10/3: btr expected after 4783.
5131 **BOND CAT 18** [9]2-8-9 F Lynch 25/1: 46: Led till 2f out, wknd: see 5131. nk **58**
3399 **ARTHURS DREAM 103** [3]2-9-0 T Eaves(3) 66/1: 07: b c Desert Prince - Blueprint (Shadeed) Slowly 1 **61**
away, nvr a factor: long abs: 60,000gns Apr foal: dam unrcd, sire a top-class miler: with J O'Shea.
5220 **BAYARD 11** [1]2-9-0 L Keniry(3) 5/1: 48: Al rear: nicely bckd. 1 **59**
5055 **VALET 22** [7]2-9-0 P Mulrennan(3) 66/1: 09: Slowly away, al bhd, t.o. in last. 16 **29**
9 Ran Time 1m 44.48 (6.98) Owned: The National Stud Owner-Breeders' Club Trained: West Ilsley

5332

2.35 Totequadpot Handicap Stakes 3yo+ 71-85 (D2) **[91]**
£6799 £2092 £1046 **5f str** **Good/Soft 90** **+05 Fast** Stands Side

5156* **HARRISONS FLYER 16** [7] R A Fahey 3-8-9 (72) P Hanagan 7/1: 2U00111: Trkd ldrs, went on ent fnl **81**
1f, styd on strongly, rdn out: op 11/2: completed qck hat-trick of h'cap wins: eff at 5/6f on firm, soft grnd & polytrack: eff with/without cheek pieces, likes a sharp trk: in fine form, see 5156.
5088 **FIDDLE ME BLUE 20** [9] H Morrison 3-8-13 (76) S Drowne 12/1: 0013602: Chsd ldrs, kept on under 1¼ **80**
press fnl 1f but not pace of wnr: solid run, see 3849.
5270 **GREAT FOX 5** [2] P L Gilligan 3-8-10 (73) K Darley 7/1: 321-063: Led till ent fnl 1f, no extra: 1 **74**
qck reapp: only lightly rcd this term, acts on fast & gd/soft grnd: see 4855.
5218 **BOND BOY 11** [11] B Smart 7-9-7 (84) F Lynch 7/1: 0040044: Rear, staying on when short of room nk **84**
dist, nrst fin: top-weight: see 4382.
5304 **IMPERIAL ECHO 2** [6]3-9-7 (84) P Fessey 5/1: 0341345: Chsd ldrs, onepcd fnl 1f: qck reapp. ½ **83**
5305 **HIGHLAND WARRIOR 2** [4]5-8-7 (1oh) (69) R Winston 4/1 FAV: 3026426: Slowly away, styd on fnl 1f, 2½ **63**
nrst fin: qck reapp: btr 5305.
3628 **KATHOLOGY 94** [5]7-9-1 (78) L Keniry(3) 8/1: 0600357: Front rank 4f, wknd: 3 month abs. 1¾ **66**
5020 **TRICK CYCLIST 24** [8]3-8-8 (71) Dale Gibson 16/1: 2135048: Nvr btr than mid-div: new stable. 1¼ **55**
5270 **BARON RHODES 5** [3]3-9-4 P (81) T Eaves(3) 9/1: 0000339: Front rank, wknd fnl 1f: cheek pieces. 2½ **59**
5305 **STRENSALL 2** [12]7-8-12 (75) P Mathers(5) 25/1: 5520000: 10th: Slow away, nvr a factor: qck reapp. nk **52**
4642 **TRIBUTE 47** [10]3-8-8 (71) A Mullen(7) 33/1: 0055500: 11th: Slowly away, al rear: 7 wk abs. 1¼ **44**
11 Ran Time 1m 01.77 (4.27) Owned: P D Smith Holdings Ltd Trained: Malton

5333

3.05 Totepool Handicap Stakes 3yo+ 56-70 (E3) **[77]**
£3486 £1073 £536 **1m4f** **Good/Soft 90** **-05 Slow** Inside

2285* **SHAPE UP 148** [10] R Craggs 4-8-9 bl (58) R Winston 12/1: 0-324111: Mid-div, hdwy to lead over 1f **66**
out, drvn out: op 10/1, 5 month abs, prev with T Keddy: eff at 10f, suited by 12f on firm, soft & polytrack, any trk: goes well fresh: progressive profile: see 2285.
5016 **EASIBET DOT NET 24** [2] I Semple 4-9-6 p (69) T Eaves(3) 10/1: 5313432: Trkd ldrs & led over 3f 1 **74**
out, hung left under press & hdd over 1f out, kept on: see 3588.
4986 **ALTAY 26** [6] R A Fahey 7-10-0 (77) P Hanagan 5/1: 16/116-03: Mid-div, drvn & styd on well ins 1 **80**
last, not pace to chall & nrst fin: prob a sharpener for hdles but lkd in need of 14f+ on the level today.
5067* **FIDDLERS CREEK 22** [7] R Allan 5-8-7 (4oh)p (52) P Mathers(5) 14/1: 0-600014: Rear, styd on for 1 **57**
press fnl 2f, no threat: see 5067 (9f, seller).
4990 **STALLONE 26** [5]7-9-3 (66) T Hamilton(3) 10/1: 6006635: Mid-div, kept on onepace for press fnl 2f: nk **66**
op 8/1: stays 12f, poss best at 10f: see 1781.
5129* **EGO TRIP 18** [12]3-8-10 bl (65) Dale Gibson 7/2 FAV: 3041216: Keen & led 3f, remained handy, rdn & 3 **60**
btn over 1f out: nicely bckd: btr 5129.
5129 **SCURRA 18** [1]5-8-8 (57) D Tudhope(5) 16/1: 2465247: Chsd ldrs wide early, btn 2f out: btr 4348. 1¾ **50**
5083 **OFF BEAT 21** [11]3-8-1 (56) P Fessey 20/1: 0000608: Rear, eff 3f out, little prog: new yard. nk **48**
4521* **MINIVET 53** [9]9-8-8 (57) P Mulrennan(3) 6/1: 54-05419: Led after 3f till 3f out: jumps fit. ½ **48**
4966 **LUCKY ARTHUR 29** [4]3-8-1 (2oh)VIS (54) R Ffrench 33/1: 0323000: 10th: Dwelt, eff wide 3f out, sn btn. nk **46**
5201 **SLAVONIC 12** [3]3-8-12 P (67) G Parkin 25/1: 4464000: 11th: Chsd ldrs till 3f out: cheek pieces. 1½ **55**
5032 **FLIGHT COMMANDER 23** [13]4-8-9 VIS (58) D Allan 50/1: 55-50000: 12th: Chsd ldrs, strug fnl 3f: visor. 1½ **44**
4867 **BEACON BLUE 35** [8]3-8-7 (62) K Darley 12/1: 5055-600: 13th: Al bhd & eased from 2f out: op 9/1. dist **18**
13 Ran Time 2m 42.06 (11.46) Owned: Mr Ray Craggs Trained: Sedgefield

MUSSELBURGH   WEDNESDAY 03.11.04   Righthand, Sharp Track

5334
3.40 Listed Totesport Willie Park Stakes 3yo+   (A1)
£23200 £8800 £4400   2m   Good/Soft 90   +01 Fast   Stands Side

5245 **ALCAZAR 10** [3] H Morrison 9-9-6 (113) S Drowne 11/8 FAV: 4-120531: Trkd ldrs, led going well 3f   **113**
out, asserted fnl 1f, readily: hvly bckd, gd time: eff at 14f/2m on firm, likes gd & soft grnd: apprec drop to List
company, smart stayer: see 5245 & 1005.

5204* **WINGED DARGENT 12** [6] M Johnston 3-8-7 (96) K Darley 13/8: 15112: Chsd ldrs, chsd wnr over 2f   5   **99**
out, al held but well clr rem: nicely bckd: ran to best, stays 2m: see 5204.

5254 **FLING 7** [1] J R Fanshawe 3-8-2 (83) P Hanagan 8/1: 1522453: Keen & chsd ldrs, no impress on   7   **86**
front pair fnl 2f: flattered latest: see 4781 & 3926 (10/12f).

4951 **HOLY ORDERS 10** [4] W P Mullins 7-9-6 bl D J Condon 5/1: 4461504: Dwelt, rear, eff to chase ldrs   3   **92**
over 3f out, sn no impress: see 4162.

4846 **TUDOR BELL 36** [2]3-8-7 (79) R Winston 66/1: 6213045: Led till 3f out, btn & eased: highly tried.   16   **73**

5004 **GARGOYLE GIRL 25** [5]7-8-11 (55) T Eaves 150/1: 1060466: Trkd ldrs, lost pl halfway: jumps fit.   8   **53**

6 Ran   Time 3m 36.75 (14.25)   Owned: JRepard FMelrose OPawle MStokes RBlack   Trained: East IIsley

5335
4.10 Totesport Com Stakes Handicap 3yo+ 71-85 (D2)   [90]
£8411 £2588 £1294   2m   Good/Soft 90   -06 Slow   Stands Side

4383 **SENDINTANK 60** [10] S C Williams 4-9-9 (85) Martin Dwyer 6/5 FAV: 3111131: Held up, smooth hdwy   **97**
over 3f out & led over 1f out, duelled with rnr-up but asserted fnl 100yds: hvly bckd, 2 month abs: eff at 12f/2m
on fast, hvy & fibresand: goes well fresh: v prog stayer, started wng run from a mark of 50: see 4383 & 4353.

5108* **MOST DEFINITELY 19** [2] T D Easterby 4-8-10 (72) D Allan 8/1: 6232212: Reared start, smooth prog   2   **78**
to lead over 2f out, hdd dist, no extra: well clr rem: see 5108.

5135 **KRISTENSEN 18** [7] D Eddy 5-9-0 p (76) P Fessey 7/1: 0030203: Mid-div, prog & led over 3f out till   6   **76**
over 2f out, sn outpcd by front pair: see 4808, 1361

4986 **SKI JUMP 26** [5] R A Fahey 4-9-2 vis (78) P Hanagan 12/1: 0600044: Rear, prog 3f out, onepcd fnl 2f.   2   **76**

5135 **ALMIZAN 18** [8]4-9-4 (80) S Hitchcott 10/1: 4043005: Chsd ldrs, onepace fnl 3f: see 4106.   4   **74**

5037 **KARELIAN 23** [9]3-8-1 (72) R Ffrench 10/1: 0041236: Led 2f, btn 2f out: btr 5037 (10f, sft).   3   **63**

4634 **TYPHOON TILLY 48** [1]7-8-11 (73) K Darley 14/1: 4032167: Keen rear, chsd ldrs halfway, btn 2f out.   hd   **64**

4623 **KIDZPLAY 48** [3]8-8-9 (8oh) T Eaves(3) 33/1: 1534568: Led/dsptd lead, btn 3f out: jumps fit.   10   **52**

5085 **CORTON 20** [6]5-9-4 P (80) J Fanning 20/1: 250-3609: Led after 2f till 4f out, wknd: cheekpieces.   25   **36**

2757† **MARBLE ARCH 483** [11]8-9-8 (84) S Drowne 25/1: 100304-0: 10th: b g Rock Hopper - Mayfair Minx (St   6   **35**
Columbus) al rear, t.o.: reapp: AW mdn wnr in '03, subs turf h'cap plcd (rtd 87, cheek pieces): former high-class
hdler (Champion Hdle 2nd): wng from at 12f, stays 2m: acts on firm, fast & polytrack, stiff or sharp trk: prob a
sharpener for hdles campaign. 1 Feb'03 Ling 12 ap 77a- D:

1389 **ACCELERATION IRE 191** [4]4-8-9 (9oh)p (62) P Mulrennan(3) 50/1: 040-1600: 11th: Chsd ldrs,   dist0
struggling from 4f out, eased, t.o.: stiff task, jumps fit: see 965.

11 Ran   Time 3m 37.97(15.47)   Owned: Steve Jones and Phil McGovern   Trained: Newmarket

WOLVERHAMPTON   Polytrack   THURSDAY 04.11.04   Lefthand, Sharp, Oval Track

Official Going Standard

5336
4.10 Bet Direct At Dunstall Park Classified Stakes 3yo 0-60 (F3)
£3562 £1096 £548   1m141y aw rnd   Going   Inapplicable   Inside

5292 **WRENLANE 5** [5] R A Fahey 3-9-2 (64) T Hamilton(3) 3/1 FAV: 4034131: Handy & led 2f out, held on   **67a**
all out: qck reapp: eff around 1m, stays 10f: acts on fast, gd/soft & fibresand, handles soft: tough & genuine.

LYTHAM 15 [2] M J Wallace 3-9-3 (65) S Drowne 12/1: 0400032: b g Spectrum - Nousaiyra (Be My   hd   **67a**
Guest) Chsd ldrs, rdn & styd on strongly ins last, just failed: op 7/1: Brit bow, ex-Irish: recent Navan h'cap
plcd: eff around 1m/8.6f on polytrack & soft grnd, sharp or gall trk.

5112 **SAROS 19** [10] B Smart 3-8-12 (58) F Lynch 16/1: 0301003: Led 6f, kept on onepace for press: 1¾   **59a**
stays 8.6f, return to 7f could suit: acts on fast & both AWs: see 4175.

4925 **INFIDELITY 33** [6] A Bailey 3-8-9 (52) J Quinn 25/1: 6350404: Chsd ldrs, kept on onepace: ¾   **55a**
handles fast, polytrack & a stiff or sharp trk: see 568.

5153 **OTAGO 17** [8]3-9-2 (64) G Baker 12/1: 4210105: Held up, late gains for press, not able to chall: nk   **61a**
handles firm, gd/soft & polytrack: see 4761.

5083 **JOMUS 22** [13]3-8-13 (61) R Winston 8/1: 0403506: Held up, eff wide 2f out, not able to chall.   ½   **57a**

5272 **SACHIN 6** [4]3-9-3 (65) Dane O'Neill 12/1: 6041307: In tch, no impress fnl 2f: qck reapp: btr 5153.   2½   **56a**

3690 **IFFY 92** [11]3-9-1 (63) C Catlin 9/2: 0-404138: Dwelt & held up, no impress: abs: btr 3391 (fast).   ¾   **53a**

4708 **AMWELL BRAVE 45** [12]3-9-0 (62) W Ryan 33/1: 5000609: Chsd ldrs, btn 3f out, 6 wk abs.   2   **48a**

4175 **SON OF THUNDER 70** [9]3-8-13 (61) S W Kelly 16/1: 1620100: 10th: Al bhd, 10 wk abs: btr 3526.   2½   **42a**

4042 **NOBLE MIND 77** [3]3-9-2 (64) D Kinsella 25/1: 20030: 11th: Slow away & hit rails halfway, sn strugg, abs.   ½   **44a**

5272 **PRINCESS GALADRIEL 6** [7]3-8-10 (61) Thomas Yeung(5) 5/1: 3613020: 12th: Held up, struggling from   nk   **37a**
halfway & sn bhd, reportedly nvr trav: qck reapp: much btr 5272 & 4721.

4448 **ONE UPMANSHIP 58** [1]3-9-3 (65) D Sweeney 20/1: 2612300: 13th: Chsd ldrs till over 2f out: jumps fit.   ¾   **43a**

13 Ran   Time 1m 53.10 (No Std Time)   Owned: Mr Keith Taylor   Trained: Malton

5337
4.35 Bet Direct Red To Bet On Itv Classified Stakes 4yo+ 0-50 (G4)
£2625 £750 £375   1m141y aw rnd   Going   Inapplicable   Inside

5184 **QOBTAAN 16** [13] M R Bosley 5-8-13 (51) G Baker 9/1: 0000041: Dwelt & held up, hdwy to lead over   **60a**
1f out, hung left, rdn out: suited by 1m/9.4f on both AWs, loves a sharp trk: see 387 & 300.

4750 **MOBO BACO 43** [4] R J Hodges 7-9-1 (53) S Drowne 7/2 FAV: 0604322: Chsd ldr & led over 1f out, sn   1¾   **59a**
hdd & not pace of wnr when short of room ins last: 6 wk abs: acts on firm, soft & both AWs: remains in gd heart.

WOLVERHAMPTON Polytrack THURSDAY 04.11.04 Lefthand, Sharp, Oval Track

5183 **ZIET DALSACE 16** [9] A W Carroll 4-9-0 (55) D Nolan(3) 9/2: 4602053: Held up, rdn to chall over 1f out, not pace of wnr when short of room ins last: see 4982, 3176. *nk* **57a**
3354 **MIDDLEHAM PARK 106** [2] P C Haslam 4-9-2 (54) G Bartley(7) 25/1: 60-20004: Held up, hmpd over 2f out, kept on late, nrst fin: 7 wk jumps abs: handles both AWs & fast grnd: see 677. *2½* **54a**
5212* **ADOBE 12** [6]9-9-2 (54) M Savage(5) 4/1: 5000015: Chsd ldrs, no extra dist: btr 5212. *1½* **51a**
4967 **TIME TO REMEMBER 30** [7]6-9-0 (52) T Hamilton(3) 14/1: 0200006: Held up, prog & led over 2f out till over 1f out, wknd: btr 3537. *¾* **48a**
556 **MISTER BENJI 273** [5]5-9-3 (55) A Culhane 20/1: 0010-057: Chsd ldrs, styd on onepace: 9 mth abs. *¾* **50a**
5184 **CRYFIELD 16** [12]7-8-13 vis (51) Kim Tinkler 16/1: 3400668: Held up, btn 2f out: btr 4719. *1½* **43a**
5256 **OH SO ROSIE 8** [1]4-8-13 p (54) Derek Nolan(7) 4/1: 0425209: Held up, hmpd over 2f out & sn btn. *8* **29a**
3726 **BURNT COPPER 91** [3]4-9-0 (52) N Pollard 25/1: 0-010000: 10th: Slow away, in tch 6f, 6 wk jmps abs. *2* **26a**
5183 **Pawan 16** [11]4-9-2 (54) Ann Stokell 33/1:0 4993 **Fridays Takings 26** [10]5-8-12 bl(50) F Lynch 33/1:0
12 Ran Time 1m 53.12 (No Std time) Owned: Inca Financial Services Trained: Wantage

5338

5.00 Bet Direct On Itv Page 367 Classified Stakes 4yo+ 0-55 (F4)
£2618 £748 £374 **1m1f103y aw rnd** **Going** **Inapplicable** Inside

5123 **RIBBONS AND BOWS 19** [12] C A Cyzer 4-8-9 vis (48) D Sweeney 16/1: 4004551: Chsd ldrs & led 3f out, sn rdn clr, in command fnl 1f, rdn out: unplcd at up to 2m prev this term: apprec drop to sharp 9.5f, stays 10f: acts on fast, gd/soft & polytrack: now eff in visor, has tried blnks: see 1721. **65a**
5180 **FACTUAL LAD 16** [5] B R Millman 6-9-3 (60) G Baker 4/1: 1000302: Chsd ldrs, styd on for press. *4* **64a**
5198 **SIENNA SUNSET 13** [13] W M Brisbourne 5-8-10 (56) B Swarbrick(5) 8/1: 4130003: Held up, eff to chase wnr over 2f out, no impress bef dist: acts on firm, soft & polytrack: see 3938. *nk* **56a**
5077 **HOLLYWOOD HENRY 22** [4] J Akehurst 4-8-12 p (55) J Quinn 11/2: 00-16044: Held up, mod gains. *4* **50a**
5234* **MONTARA 10** [1]5-9-4 p (45) A Culhane 2/1 FAV: 0-632015: Mid-div, rdn for eff over 2f out, no impress. *1* **54a$**
5183 **MON SECRET 16** [6]6-9-0 (57) D McGaffin 12/1: 6061006: Held up, eff 3f out, no impress: prefers 7f. *shd* **50a**
5122* **ELLOVAMUL 19** [9]4-8-9 (50) P Mathers(5) 9/1: 0000017: Held up, little prog fnl 2f: btr 5122 (gd/soft). *1¾* **42a**
4926 **ZARIN 33** [10]6-9-2 (59) A Nicholls 14/1: 6215008: Held up, eff when hung left over 1f out, sn btn. *½* **48a**
5117 **DANGER BIRD 19** [8]4-8-9 (50) W Ryan 12/1: 4150609: Chsd ldr & led over 3f out, sn hdd & fdd. *4* **33a**
4904 **KUMAKAWA 33** [7]6-8-12 (47) A Quinn(4) 40/1: 2600050: 10th: Held up, rdn halfway & sn struggling. *5* **27a**
5232 **PAS DE SURPRISE 10** [11]6-8-12 p (45) D Nolan(3) 12/1: 4000060: 11th: Chsd ldrs, btn 3f out. *hd* **26a**
3306} **MUJKARI 461** [2]8-8-12 bl (46) J F Egan 16/1: 522414-0: 12th: In tch, pulled hard early, strugg halfway. *1¼* **23a**
5292 **QUINTOTO 5** [3]4-9-0 P (57) T Hamilton(3) 20/1: 0-600000: 13th: Led 6f, sn bhd, qck reapp, cheek pieces. *5* **16a**
13 Ran Time 2m 03.51 (No Std Time) Owned: Mrs Charles Cyzer Trained: Horsham

5339

5.30 Bet Direct Football Cashbacks Handicap Stakes 3yo 46-55 (F4) **[69]**
£2662 £761 £380 **1m4f50y aw** **Going** **Inapplicable** Inside

5082 **ANOTHER CON 22** [3] P Howling 3-8-13 (54) R Winston 10/1: 2050001: Made all & rdn clr over 2f out, in command fnl 1f, readily: eff at 10/12f, tried 2m latest: likes polytrack & a sharp trk with forcing tactics applied: eff with/without cheek pieces, tried visor: see 676. **67a**
4361 **PAPEETE 62** [12] Miss B Sanders 3-9-1 (56) S Drowne 11/2: 4400102: Handy & chsd wnr over 1f out, kept on, al held: pulled clr of rem: acts on fast, soft & polytrack: see 4143. *4* **62a**
5026 **MARIA BONITA 25** [9] Mrs Stef Liddiard 3-9-6 (61) S Whitworth 13/2: 0404333: Held up, late gains for press to take 3rd, no threat: see 5026 & 4112. *5* **60a**
4763* **DAYDREAM DANCER 42** [6] C G Cox 3-8-13 bl (54) R Smith 6/1: 0030114: Chsd ldr 3f out, no impress fnl 2f: yet to convince beyond 10f: see 4763. *1* **52a**
5034* **TRICKSTEP 24** [5]3-9-3 BL (58) Darren Williams 8/1: 0002615: Chsd ldrs, no impress fnl 2f, blnks. *2* **53a**
4925 **TURKS AND CAICOS 33** [10]3-9-0 (55) G Bartley(7) 7/1: 0-221066: Held up, btn 2f out: btr 658 (fbsd). *1½* **48a**
5004 **ITS BLUE CHIP 26** [4]3-9-0 (55) S W Kelly 100/30 FAV: 4100007: V slow away, bhd. *5* **41a**
4601 **CHARA 50** [11]3-9-4 (59) F Lynch 22/1: 0555008: Dwelt, held up in tch, btn 2f out, 7 wk abs. *¾* **44a**
4805 **ON CLOUD NINE 39** [8]3-9-4 (59) R Havlin 20/1: 0043159: Dwelt, rdn & bhd fnl 3f: btr 4364. *7* **34a**
4826 **PINS N NEEDLES 38** [2]3-9-3 (58) D Sweeney 33/1: 0600: 10th: Chsd ldrs till over 2f out, h'cap bow. *1¾* **31a**
5296 **Red Skelton 4** [7]3-9-5 (60) A Nicholls 25/1:0
5173 **Elusive Kitty 16** [1]3-9-7 BL(62) Thomas Yeung(5) 16/1:0
12 Ran Time 2m 43.69 (No Std Time) Owned: Mr D C Patrick Trained: Newmarket

5340

5.55 Bet Direct On Sky Active Classified Stakes 3yo+ 0-65 (E3)
£3523 £1084 £542 **7f32y aw rnd** **Going** **Inapplicable** Inside

5069 **ZOOM ZOOM 23** [4] Mrs L Stubbs 4-9-0 (66) R Winston 4/1 JT FAV: 1050401: Keen & sn led trav well, rdn clr over 1f out, styd on strongly: bckd, op 12/1: eff at 5/6f, now stays a sharp 7f well: acts on firm, gd/soft & polytrack, sharp or stiff trk: enjoyed forcing tactics: see 1345. **76a**
4300 **HOWS THINGS 66** [10] D Haydn Jones 4-9-1 (67) R Havlin 25/1: 23-60002: Dwelt & held up, styd on wide for press, not able to reach wnr: 2 mth abs: much imprvd, likes both AWs: see 93. *1¼* **73a**
5161 **HAZEWIND 17** [12] P D Evans 3-9-2 vis t (69) D Nolan(3) 4/1 JT FAV: 4164433: Handy, onepace. *nk* **74a**
5256 **GRANDMA LILY 8** [3] D Carroll 6-8-12 (67) D Tudhope(5) 8/1: 0030344: Held up, rdn & lost place early, short of room over 2f out, kept on late & clr of rem: acts on fast, gd/soft & both AWs: see 5256 & 85. *1½* **66a**
5014 **BALLYHURRY 25** [7]7-9-0 (66) N Mackay 5/1: 6460445: Chsd ldrs, btn dist: btr 5014. *5* **59a**
5054 **LASANGA 24** [9]5-9-4 (70) T P Queally 8/1: 4/32-0026: Slow away & held up, only mod prog: btr 5054. *½* **62a**
KALANI STAR 56 [11]4-9-4 (70) T Eaves(3) 16/1: 6030457: b c Ashkalani - Bellissi (Bluebird) Held up, rdn & no impress: 8 wk abs, Brit bow: landed a Tipperary mdn back in '03: winning form at 7.5f on gd grnd. *shd* **62a**
4622 **CONSTABLE BURTON 49** [2]3-9-2 (69) D Allan 20/1: 000-0108: Chsd ldrs till over 1f out, abs: btr 1196. *1* **59a**
5006 **ILE MICHEL 26** [6]7-9-1 (67) D Sweeney 25/1: 4300569: Held up & al rear. *½* **56a**
5289 **BLUE KNIGHT 5** [8]5-9-4 (70) S W Kelly 20/1: 6204000: 10th: Al bhd, qck reapp. *nk* **58a**
5079 **KINDLELIGHT DEBUT 22** [5]4-8-12 (67) Dane O'Neill 6/1: 0003060: 11th: Trkd ldr, wknd 2f out. *hd* **51a**
5304 **ABBAJABBA 3** [1]8-9-4 (70) J Fanning 9/1: 0205060: 12th: Led early, remained cl-up till 2f out. *3½* **50a**
12 Ran Time 1m 30.71 (No Std Time) Owned: Mr H Conlon Trained: Malton

5341 6.20 Betdirect Co Uk Handicap Stakes 4yo+ 56-70 (E3)   [80]
£3429 £1055 £528   5f20y aw rnd   Going   Inapplicable   Inside

4548 **JAGGED** 52 [4] J R Jenkins 4-8-11 vis (63) F Lynch 7/2 FAV: 6312241: Led 1f & remained cl-up, led   **71a**
again last, held on all out: 7 wk abs: eff btwn 5/sharp 7f on firm, gd/soft & both AWs: see 4043, 1533.
4989 **BYO** 27 [10] M Quinn 6-8-11 (63) F Norton 5/1: 1340432: Al handy & rdn to chall ins last, just   *shd* **70a**
denied: tough & consistent, can win again: see 1886.
5181 **ANOTHER GLIMPSE** 16 [3] Miss B Sanders 6-9-11 t (77) S Drowne 8/1: 2320043: Held up, short of room   ½   **82a**
halfway, hdwy to chall ins last, not pace of wnr cl-home: see 2053, 1615.
4394 **SAVILES DELIGHT** 61 [2] R Brotherton 5-9-1 bl (67) C Catlin 14/1: 0114304: Held up, styd on for   *nk*   **71a**
press, not pace to chall: 2 mth abs, gd run: return to 6f/7f could suit: see 4186, 3402.
5181 **PARKSIDE PURSUIT** 16 [11]6-8-11 (63) P Fitzsimons 20/1: 0000005: Mid-div, rdn & kept on onepace.   1¾   **62a**
5125 **CURRENCY** 19 [8]7-9-4 (70) J F Egan 10/1: 2145006: Dwelt, late gains, nrst fin.   *shd*   **69a**
4930* **POLISH EMPEROR** 33 [13]4-9-11 e (77) J Fanning 11/2: 0006017: Dwelt, chsd ldrs, no extra dist,   *nk*   **75a**
saddle slipped.
5146 **LARKYS LOB** 18 [12]5-8-13 (65) J D O'Reilly(7) 14/1: 1623508: Led after 1f & clr halfway, hdd ins last.   ¾   **61a**
5181 **PLAYTIME BLUE** 16 [7]4-9-3 (69) G Baker 16/1: 3300009: Chsd ldrs, no impress dist, likes to lead.   2   **59a**
4989 **IZMAIL** 27 [5]5-8-13 BL (65) D Nolan(3) 10/1: 0000500: 10th: Chsd ldrs, rdn & btn over 1f out, blnks.   *nk*   **54a**
5336 **BRAGADINO** 1 [6]5-8-13 (61) A Culhane 20/1: 00600600: 11th: Sn outpcd: abs, vis/t-strap.   5   **41a**
5181 **MUSICAL FAIR** 6 [1]4-9-8 (74) R Winston 8/1: 0030350: 12th: Chsd ldrs, struggling fnl 2f.   1¾   **45a**
4201 **SEVEN NO TRUMPS** 69 [9]7-9-8 (74) S W Kelly 16/1: 020040P: Dwelt & held up, p.u. halfway, 10 wk abs.   **0a**
13 Ran   Time 1m 03.14(No Std time)   Owned: The Jagged Partnership   Trained: Royston

Official Going HEAVY (SOFT places).

5342 1.25 City Life Magazine Maiden Stakes 2yo (D3)
£6175 £1900 £950   6f15y str   Heavy 153   -18 Slow   Inside

STARCHY [5] M Johnston 2-8-9   J Fanning 12/1: 1: b f Cadeaux Genereux - Sahara Star (Green   **88**
Desert) Mid-div, imprvd halfway, led entering fnl 1f, pushed well clr: op 8/1, debut: Jan foal, half-sister to 5f
juv wnr Land Of Dreams & 12f wnr Edraak: dam a 5f juv wnr, sire a top-class sprinter: eff at 6f on hvy grnd: runs
well fresh, handles a gall trk: decent start, clearly revels in the mud & potentially useful.
ALLEGRETTO [14] S Kirk 2-9-0   J F Egan 20/1: 2: b c Anabaa - Aimores (Persian Heights) Rear,   6   **80**
styd on well into 2nd fnl 1f, no ch with wnr on debut: 24,000gns Feb foal: half-brother to 1m juv scorer Lonely
Place: dam a 7f wnr abroad, sire a top-class sprinter: eff at 6f on hvy grnd: sure to learn from this.
5202 **HIDDEN JEWEL** 13 [1] B A McMahon 2-9-0 (82) G Gibbons 5/4 FAV: 066023: Led till entering fnl 1f,   *nk*   **79**
no extra: well bckd, clr of rest: eff expected after imprvd run in 5202 (prob flattered)
5258 **OBLIQUE** 7 [7] Sir Mark Prescott 2-8-9 S Sanders 16/1: 004: b f Giant's Causeway - On Call   6   **60+**
(Alleged) Dwelt, styd on late, nvr dngrs on h'cap qual run: Apr foal, half-sister to mid-dist/stayer One Off & 10f
wnr Optimal: dam a mid-dist/staying wnr, sire a top-class 7/10f performer: made late hdwy over this inadequate
trip, shld impr considerably over further in h'caps for shrewd stable next term.
4590 **STREET DANCER** 51 [8]2-9-0 R Winston 50/1: 0005: Mid-div, nvr nr ldrs: 7 wk abs.   *nk*   **64**
4783 **LAYED BACK ROCKY** 40 [9]2-9-0 (60) C Catlin 40/1: 60266: Nvr nr ldrs: 6 wk abs: see 4511.   *hd*   **63**
MIRACLE BABY [3]2-8-9 S Carson 40/1: 7: Al rear on debut.   *shd*   **58**
4865 **KOMREYEV STAR** 36 [10]2-9-0 N Lawes(7) 80/1: 008: Nvr a factor.   6   **51**
5228 **IROQUOIS PRINCESS** 10 [13]2-8-9 S Whitworth 125/1: 009: Al rear.   2½   **41**
4962 **PASSIONATELY ROYAL** 30 [4]2-9-0 P Hanagan 25/1: 00: 10th: Nvr nr ldrs.   4   **38**
5182 **CRYSTAL MYSTIC** 16 [11]2-9-0 (60) F P Ferris(3) 50/1: 0400: 11th: Prom till halfway: see 4703.   ¾   **36**
5235 **SOFT FOCUS** 10 [2]2-8-9 S W Kelly 80/1: 0000: 12th: Al bhd.   *nk*   **30**
4934 **XEERAN** 31 [6]2-8-9 (61) P Robinson 2/1: 555430: 13th: Prom till halfway, wknd & eased: well   3½   **24**
bckd: much btr clearly expected: see 4934 (fast grnd).
5047 **ATHBOY NIGHTS** 24 [12]2-8-9 K Fallon 16/1: 00: 14th: Prom 4f, wknd & eased.   *hd*   **24**
14 Ran   Time 1m 21.10 (10.30)   Owned: Maktoum Al Maktoum   Trained: Middleham

5343 1.55 Bhb/Rca Season Finale Lunch Nursery Handicap Stakes 2yo 0-75 (E3)   [81]
£4193 £1290 £645   5f13y str   Heavy 153   +10 Fast   Inside

4443 **PENANG SAPPHIRE** 58 [12] G A Butler 2-8-1 (54) C Catlin 40/1: 6001: b g Spectrum - Penang Pearl   **63**
(Bering) Rear, prog wide halfway, strong run to lead cl-home, drvn out: 8 wk abs, fast time: Apr first foal, dam a
1m wnr: sire a top-class 1m/10f performer: eff over a gall 5f on hvy grnd, clearly runs well fresh.
5225 **CREE** 12 [6] W R Muir 2-8-11 (64) Martin Dwyer 4/1: 5231452: Chsd ldrs, led ins fnl 1f till   ½   **71**
caught cl-home: back to form: see 4706.
5267 **DOITFORREEL** 6 [2] I A Wood 2-9-1 (68) S Sanders 9/2: 003153: Dwelt, imprvd halfway, sltly short   1   **72**
of room dist, nrst fin: qck reapp: acts on fast & hvy: flattered 5267, see 5154.
4545 **TASKS MUPPET** 52 [14] J A Osborne 2-8-4 (57) J F McDonald(3) 66/1: 55504: Mid-div, kept on under   1½   **58**
press fnl 1f: 7 wk abs.
5253 **HITS ONLY CASH** 8 [8]2-8-10 (63) K Fallon 3/2 FAV: 605045: Chsd ldrs, onepcd fnl 1f: well bckd.   *shd*   **64**
5152 **ASHES** 17 [3]2-8-4 (57) P Hanagan 33/1: 054056: Rear, prog 2f out, onepcd fnl 1f.   ¾   **56**
5021 **ROBMANTRA** 25 [11]2-8-5 p (58) S Whitworth 33/1: 5360407: Rear, some late hdwy: see 4706.   *shd*   **57**
5021 **LITTLE BISCUIT** 25 [15]2-8-6 (1ow) (58) V Halliday 50/1: 5426408: Chsd ldrs, wknd fnl 1f: btr 3271.   2½   **53**
5152 **SKIDDAW WOLF** 17 [10]2-8-10 (63) F Lynch 14/1: 0365429: Prom, ev ch when hmpd dist, sn eased: no   2   **53+**
luck today & must be given another chance after imprvd run at this encouraging run: stable do well on the AW, keep in mind.
5317* **MYTTONS BELL** 2 [16]2-8-12 (7ex) (65) D Fox(5) 8/1: 3050310: 10th: Prom, led briefly dist, wknd fnl   *nk*   **54**
1f: too sn after 5317 (7f)?
5021* **CHILLY CRACKER** 25 [17]2-9-3 (70) D Sweeney 12/1: 6100310: 11th: Led till dist: btr 5021 (gd).   1¾   **56**
5253 **PIDDIES PRIDE** 8 [4]2-8-13 (66) F P Ferris(3) 14/1: 4050020: 12th: Chsd ldrs, btn dist.   1¼   **49**

4706 **Roko** 45 [7]2-8-1 vis(54) Lisa Jones 40/1:0
4692 **Kristikhab** 46 [5]2-8-0 (53) P Fessey 66/1:0
16 Ran   Time 1m 05.65 (7.15)   Owned: Mrs A K H Ooi   Trained: Blewbury

5154 **Lady Hopeful** 17 [9]2-8-6 bl(59) J Fanning 20/1:0
4172 **Wizardmicktee** 70 [1]2-9-7 (74) R Winston 33/1:0

5344   2.25 Fastest Growing Betting Exchange Ibetx Com Maiden Stakes 2yo   (D3)
£6390 £1966 £983   **1m54y rnd**   **Heavy 153**   **-40 Slow**   Outside

5097 **TAWQEET** 20 [14] J L Dunlop 2-9-0   R Hills 11/2: 01: ch c Kingmambo - Caerless (Caerleon)   78
Mid-div, prog to lead 1.5f out, styd on well fnl 1f, rdn out: 100,000gns Apr foal: dam a mid-dist wnr, sire a
top-class miler: eff over a gall 1m on hvy grnd: clearly benefitted from recent debut.
5221 **QUEENS DANCER** 12 [4] M R Channon 2-8-9   C Catlin 4/1: 052: b f Groom Dancer - Special Beat   1   70
(Bustino) Chsd ldrs, styd on under press fnl 1f, not pace of wnr: op 6/1: Apr foal, half-sister to 1m wnr Samba
Beat: dam a thorough stayer, scored over hdles: sire a high-class 10f performer: eff over a gall 1m on hvy grnd.
       CONSULAR [2] M A Jarvis 2-9-0   P Robinson 6/1: 3: br c Singspiel - Language of Love (Rock City)   ¾   73
Trkd ldrs, kept on under press fnl 1f on debut: op 9/2: Apr foal, half-brother to 5f wnr Tregarron: dam unrcd,
sire a top-class mid-dist performer: eff at 1m on hvy grnd, bred to stay further next term.
       CRETE [13] W J Haggas 2-9-0   A Culhane 3/1 FAV: 4: Trkd ldrs, went on after halfway till   ½   72
collared dist, wknd on debut: nicely bckd, clr of remainder.
       ROMAN ARMY [11]2-9-0   Martin Dwyer 16/1: 5: Slowly away, styd on fnl 1f, nvr nrr on debut.   5   64
5019 **SEA MAP** 25 [12]2-9-0   J F Egan 33/1: 00U06: Rear, nvr nr ldrs.   2½   60
5205 **ENAMOURED** 13 [8]2-8-9   D R McCabe 14/1: 57: Bhd, nvr a factor: new stable.   1½   53
4825 **BACK TO REALITY** 38 [10]2-9-0   F P Ferris(3) 50/1: 008: Led till after halfway, wknd.   1½   56
3968 **ALLIZAM** 81 [6]2-9-0 (53) S Sanders 22/1: 0409: Al towards rear: see 3513.   ½   55
       MICHAELS PRIDE [1]2-8-9   J Fanning 12/1: 0: 10th: Slow away, sn chsd ldrs, btn 2f out: debut.   5   42
5264 **ROYAL SAILOR** 7 [5]2-9-0   K Darley 10/1: 0000: 11th: Prom, led briefly halfway, sn wknd.   4   41
       Briar Ghyll [3]2-8-9 D Fox(5) 66/1:0   5252 **Golden Gate** 8 [15]2-9-0 J Mackay 28/1:0
5113 **Chestminster Girl** 19 [7]2-8-9 p D Corby(3) 100/1:0   5252 **Colour Blind** 8 [9]2-9-0 P Fitzsimons 66/1:0
15 Ran   Time 1m 54.84 (15.44)   Owned: Mr Hamdan Al Maktoum   Trained: Arundel

---

5345   3.00 Betting With Ibetx Com Handicap Stakes 3yo+ 56-70 (E3)   [80]
£4462 £1373 £687   **1m1f213y**   **Heavy 153**   **-17 Slow**   Inside

4986 **RYANS FUTURE** 27 [6] J Akehurst 4-9-7 (73) S Sanders 11/2: 5204501: Mid-div, hdwy to lead over 1f   83
out, rdn out: eff at 1m/10f on firm, hvy & polytrack, any trk: see 174.
5307* **MCQUEEN 3** [14] Mrs H Dalton 4-9-11 (6ex) (77) J F Egan 9/4 FAV: 1105112: Sn pushed along mid-div,   4   81
styd on wide for press, not able to reach wnr: nicely bckd under a 6lb pen, qck reapp: imprvd again in defeat:
acts on fast & gd, both AWs & loves gd/soft/hvy grnd: see 5307.
5201 **MAMBINA** 13 [7] M R Channon 3-8-12 (68) S Hitchcott 11/1: 2411663: Led till 3f out, styd on for   1¾   70
press: acts on fast & hvy: see 5016.
5191 **BAND** 15 [8] B A McMahon 4-8-4 (56) G Gibbons 16/1: 4051064: Held up, switched & kept on for   ¾   57
press, not able to chall: prob stays 10f, btn prev at 1m: see 3996.
5022 **TAGULA BLUE** 25 [3]4-9-4 f (70) J Crowley 11/1: 6540135: Held up rear, hdwy for press over 2f out,   1¼   69
not able to chall: bckd: prob stays 10f, 1m poss ideal: see 5022, 4668 (1m).
5206 **MOBANE FLYER** 13 [15]4-8-12 (64) P Hanagan 4/1: 3313226: Handy, led 3f out till dist, fdd.   hd   63
5173 **SANTA CATERINA** 16 [4]3-8-7 (63) K Darley 10/1: 5200327: Chsd ldrs, no extra short of room dist.   hd   62
5206 **KEEPERS KNIGHT** 13 [13]3-8-6 T (62) J Fanning 33/1: 0035458: Mid-div, not pace to chall: t-strap.   2   58
2078 **MR LEAR** 159 [10]5-9-2 (68) N Lawes(7) 100/1: 1040-009: Handy, btn 2f out, abs, likes to dominate.   3½   60
5034 **PLATINUM PIRATE** 24 [11]3-8-8 bl (64) T Eaves(3) 28/1: 5401130: 10th: Al bhd: btr 5034 & 4701.   3½   52
5261 **RASID** 7 [1]6-9-9 (75) K Fallon 14/1: 3100000: 11th: Chsd ldrs 7f: poss start dominating.   1½   61
5191 **AMNESTY** 15 [12]5-8-8 bl e (60) E Ahern 28/1: 1152000: 12th: Chsd ldrs, strug fnl 4f: btr 1542 (1m).   1¾   44
5093 **Danze Romance** 20 [16]3-8-4 (60) Martin Dwyer 50/1:0 5227 **Camille Pissarro** 12 [5]4-9-4 (70) M Tebbutt 100/1:0
2650} **Irie Rasta** 489 [9]5-9-0 (66) S Whitworth 33/1:0   4668 **Bold Phoenix** 47 [2]3-8-9 (65) T P Queally 50/1:0
16 Ran   Time 2m 19.36 (17.06)   Owned: Mr Vimal Khosla   Trained: Epsom

---

5346   3.35 Ibetx Com - The Punters Choice Conditions Stakes 3yo+   (C2)
£12087 £4585 £2292   **1m54y rnd**   **Heavy 153**   **-11 Slow**   Outside

4916 **ST ANDREWS** 33 [2] M A Jarvis 4-8-10 (104) P Robinson 10/11 FAV: 6250101: Chsd ldrs, smooth prog   104
& led over 3f out, al in command from over 1f out under hand riding: nicely bckd: eff at 7f, suited by 1m: acts on
fast & gd, loves gd/soft & hvy grnd: v useful in these conds: see 4767.
4916 **FINE SILVER** 33 [4] P F I Cole 3-9-2 (98) K Fallon 10/3: 0142232: Chsd ldrs, rdn to chase wnr fnl   3½   103
2f, kept on, al held: acts on firm & hvy grnd: see 3553, 2026 & 1665.
5139 **DANDOUN** 19 [7] J L Dunlop 6-8-10 (105) S Sanders 7/1: 11000-03: Held up, rdn over 3f out, styd   3   90
on to take 3rd, no threat: see 5139.
4220 **DUCK ROW** 68 [8] J A R Toller 9-8-10 (102) E Ahern 6/1: 0-205064: Held up, strug fnl 2f: op 4/1, abs.   3   84
5198 **ELIDORE** 13 [5]4-8-5 (63) D Fox(5) 100/1: 0245605: Cl-up, rdn & btn 3f out, highly tried.   7   63
5232 **DANCING KING** 10 [1]8-8-13 (45) P Makin(5) 300/1: 5555006: Led till 3f out, sn btn: highly tried.   3   63$
       LEGACY 130 [3]4-8-10 (103) M Tebbutt 100/1: 143-0007: Dwelt & al bhd, 4 mth abs.   4   54
5109* **SCIENTIST** 20 [6]3-8-8 (69) K Darley 40/1: 0306018: Chsd ldrs, struggling fnl 3f: new yard.   27   24
8 Ran   Time 1m 52.54 (13.14)   Owned: Team Havana   Trained: Newmarket

---

5347

4.05 Back Or Lay With Ibetx Com Handicap Stakes 3yo+ 46-55 (F4)   [74]
£3562 £1018   £509   **1m54y rnd**   **Heavy 153**   **-21 Slow**   Outside

4925* **BOPPYS PRINCESS** 33 [15] R A Fahey 3-8-13 (59) P Hanagan 5/1: 1211511: Held up wide, hdwy stands   71
rail & led over 1f out, rdn clr: op 10/3: eff at 1m/9.5f on firm, hvy & polytrack: progressive.
5212 **WIZARD OF US** 12 [4] M Mullineaux 4-9-0 (58) Liam Jones(7) 25/1: 005/0-102: Led after 1f, hdd 3f   3½   62
out but remained handy, not pace of wnr from dist: eff at 7f/1m, loves soft/hvy grnd: see 5063.
4982 **COMMITMENT LECTURE** 28 [13] M Dods 4-8-8 t (52) K Darley 5/1: 0-514653: Held up, wide into str,   hd   56
short of room 3f out, switched & styd on: clr rem: acts on fast, likes gd/soft & hvy.
5212 **TIME TO REGRET** 12 [3] J S Wainwright 4-9-1 (59) K Fallon 7/2 FAV: 0025164: Handy & led 3f out,   7   53
hung left & hdd over 1f out, sn btn: btr 5111 (g/s).
4057 **CADORO** 77 [11]11-8-11 (55) R Thomas(3) 20/1: 02040///-05: Held up, late gains for press, abs.   5   41
1319 **ACORAZADO** 195 [16]5-8-9 bl (53) S Sanders 15/2: 0162046: Mid-div, hdwy wide to chall over 2f out,   3½   35
sn no extra: return to 6/7f may suit.
5056* **ARMENTIERES** 23 [12]3-8-9 bl (55) E Ahern 9/1: 6234017: Handy & chall wide 3f out, sn no extra.   2   34
5212 **CAERPHILLY GAL** 12 [5]4-8-11 (55) D Fox(5) 16/1: 0123108: Led 1f & remained prom till over 2f out.   2½   31
5111 **ROCINANTE** 20 [17]4-8-7 (55) R Ffrench 11/1: 1100609: Handy wide, btn 2f out.   2   24
5111 **EXPLODE** 20 [6]7-8-8 (52) T Williams 11/1: 00-40220: 10th: Chsd ldrs, strug halfway: btr 5111.   5   17
1472 **ALBEE** 187 [10]4-8-10 (54) P Fitzsimons 50/1: 66400: 11th: Bhd halfway, 6 mth abs.   2   16
5184 **BUNDABERG** 16 [7]4-8-11 (55) P Makin(5) 33/1: 5-422300: 12th: Struggling halfway: btr 1196 (AW).   1   15
2891 **Jakeal** 125 [1]5-8-9 (53) V Halliday 33/1:0   5292   **Yorker** 5 [14]6-9-4 bl(62) Natalia Gemelova(5) 33/1:0
4562 **Pride Of Kinloch** 52 [8]4-8-11 (55) M Tebbutt 40/1:0   1028   **Mutarafaa** 216 [9]5-8-7 vis(51) Lisa Jones 50/1:0
16 Ran   Time 1m 53.37(13.97)   Owned: Mrs S Bond   Trained: Malton

---

Official Going SOFT (GOOD/SOFT places).

5348

1.00 Sharp Minds Betfair Claiming Stakes 3yo+   (F4)
£3108 £888   £444   **1m3y str**   **Good/Soft 89**   **+13 Fast**   Inside

5022 **J R STEVENSON** 26 [4] M Wigham 8-8-13 (67) K Fallon 15/8 FAV: 0465061: Rear, gd hdwy to lead 1.5f   68
out, held on despite drifting right, all-out: well bckd from 9/4, gd time, clmd for 8,000: eff at 1m, stays sharp
10f well: acts on firm, likes gd/soft, soft & polytrack, handles any trk: can go well fresh, eff with/without a
visor: apprec this drop to claim grade, see 265 (AW).
5022 **LAKOTA BRAVE** 26 [12] Mrs Stef Liddiard 10-9-1 (66) E Ahern 9/1: 0006402: Chsd ldrs, styd on well   ½   68
fnl 1f & only just btn: clr of rem: fine run in the circumstances, rider dropped reins ins fnl 1f: see 4581 & 5.
5120 **PERERIN** 20 [3] I A Wood 3-8-5 vis (40) J F McDonald(3) 5/1: 0306003: Led till dist, no extra: gd run.   5   48
5095 **STRATHSPEY** 21 [13] P J McBride 5-8-12 (66) L Keniry(3) 7/1: 4324-554: Prom, left bhnd fnl 1f.   ¾   52
4560 **ESPERANCE** 53 [2]4-8-9 p (46) J Quinn 14/1: 5055245: Dwelt, styd on late, nvr dngrs: 8 wk abs.   1   47
5234 **SINJAREE** 11 [5]6-8-13 (40) F P Ferris(3) 40/1: 6000046: Trkd ldrs, outpcd fnl 1.5f: flattered.   hd   51$
4284* **EASTERN HOPE** 67 [9]5-9-3 (59) Kristin Stubbs(7) 11/1: 3003017: Slow away, nvr nr ldrs: 9 wk abs.   2   52
4925 **GRAND RAPIDE** 34 [8]3-8-2 (54) S Whitworth 10/1: 0041008: Chsd ldrs 3f, short of room 2f out.   1   37
5230 **A DOUBLE EWE BEE** 11 [7]3-8-2 D Fox(5) 100/1: 09: b f Kingsinger - Some Dream (Vitiges) Chsd   3   32
ldrs 6f, wknd: no form yet.
5094 **MAGIC VERSE** 21 [18]3-8-6 (53) C Catlin 11/1: 4454100: 10th: Al rear: btr 4902 (gd).   ¾   35
5230* **TYNEHAM** 11 [1]4-8-9 p (59) C Haddon(5) 11/1: 02/000-10: 11th: Trkd ldrs 4f, sn wknd: btr 5230 (AW). 4   30
472   **Claranete Princess** 286 [17]3-9-6 D Corby(3) 25/1:0   3929   **Eight** 84 [15]8-8-9 (45) K Darley 20/1:0
5230 **Nippy Nipper** 11 [10]3-8-2 t M Halford(7) 80/1:0   4974   **Alafzar** 30 [14]6-8-9 vis t(57) T P Queally 14/1:0
5054 **Sustainable Style** 25 [6]3-9-0 S Hitchcott 66/1:0   5110   **Carmarthen Belle** 21 [16]4-9-2 J Fanning 100/1:0
17 Ran   Time 1m 41.19 (6.09)   Owned: Claret & Blue Army   Trained: Newmarket

---

5349

1.30 Sharp Minds Winners Welcome Nursery Handicap Stakes 2yo 0-75 (E3)   [82]
£4141 £1274   £637   **1m3y str**   **Good/Soft 89**   **-03 Slow**   Inside

5045 **BOWLED OUT** 25 [13] P J McBride 2-8-6 (60) T P Queally 25/1: 4001: Hmpd start, gd hdwy 2f out &   69
led dist, styd on strongly, drvn out: back to form on h'cap bow: eff at 1m on gd/soft grnd: see 4192 (debut).
4257 **AKRAAN** 68 [10] E A L Dunlop 2-8-10 (64) R Hills 11/1: 0052: Chsd ldrs, led 2f out till dist,   1¼   69
kept on well fnl 1f on h'cap bow: confirmed earlier promise, eff at 1m on gd/soft & soft grnd: see 4257.
4271 **BADDAM** 67 [17] J L Dunlop 2-8-11 (65) K Darley 10/1: 4063: Outpcd, styd on strongly fnl 1f, nvr   nk   69
nrr: 10 wk abs & h'cap bow: apprec this step up to 1m, handles fast & gd/soft grnd: see 4271 & 3811.
4635 **UNION JACK JACKSON** 50 [18] J G Given 2-8-8 (62) P Robinson 16/1: 400644: Chsd ldrs, onepcd fnl 1f. ½   65
5302 **PICOT DE SAY** 4 [1]2-8-6 (60) N Mackay 8/1: 000325: Rear, styd on fnl 1f, nrst fin: op 13/2, qck reapp. hd   63
4635 **UNCLE BULGARIA** 50 [3]2-8-7 (61) S Whitworth 25/1: 30056: Dwelt, recovered to chase ldrs & ev ch   ½   63
2f out, onepcd after: 7 wk abs: see 4635.
5147 **LOLA SAPOLA** 18 [2]2-9-7 (75) D Holland 7/1 FAV: 000147: Prom, slightly outpcd after halfway,   ¾   75
rallied fnl 1f: nicely bckd, top-weight: see 4760 (firm grnd).
5118 **SUNNY TIMES** 20 [16]2-8-9 (63) P Cosgrave 16/1: 500528: Rear, nvr nr ldrs: btr 5118.   1¾   61
5185 **MANIC** 16 [20]2-8-10 (64) J F Egan 25/1: 0139: Rear, mod late prog: see 5185 & 4921 (6f).   ½   61
5018 **VOLITIO** 26 [14]2-8-6 (60) E Ahern 33/1: 00000: 10th: Prom, ev ch till wknd 1.5f out.   ½   56
4871 **FLAG POINT** 36 [9]2-9-3 (71) Dane O'Neill 25/1: 30000: 11th: Chsd ldrs 6.5f, wknd.   ¾   66
4894 **CAPTAIN MARGARET** 35 [8]2-8-8 t (62) J Quinn 14/1: 050030: 12th: Chsd ldrs 6f, wknd: btr 4894 (g/f). 1   55
5140 **CARIBBEAN DANCER** 19 [5]2-9-4 (72) J Fanning 14/1: 0020: 13th: Led after 3f till 2f out, wknd.   nk   64

4963	**DAISY BUCKET 31** [11]2-8-11 (65) C Catlin 20/1: 03100: 14th: Nvr a factor: btr 4163.	½	56
5044	**SWORDS 25** [12]2-9-4 (72) K Fallon 8/1: 0050: 15th: Hmpd start, nvr a factor: h'cap bow: see 5044.	1	61
4848	**BONGOALI 38** [7]2-8-4 (58) T Dean(7) 14/1: 4525000: 16th: Slow away, al rear.	1¼	45
4741	**TYBALT 44** [15]2-8-10 vis (64) Martin Dwyer 12/1: 250030: 17th: Keen & chsd ldrs 6f: 6 wk abs.	¾	50
5065	**GUINEA A MINUTE 24** [6]2-8-10 (64) J Fortune 15/2: 3665330: 18th: Chsd ldrs 3f, wknd: new yard.	1¼	48
4933	**Yardstick 32** [19]2-8-6 (60) O Urbina 33/1:0		
5207	**Lowestoft Playboy 13** [4]2-8-11 (65) Leanne Kershaw(7) 20/1:0		

20 Ran   Time 1m 42.50 (7.40)   Owned: The Silver-Lining Cricketers Syndicate   Trained: Newmarket

---

5350 2.00 European Breeders Fund Sharp Minds At Betfair Maiden Stakes 2yo (D3)
£4950 £1523 £762   **6f3y str**   **Good/Soft 89**   **-04 Slow**   Inside

5197	**WESTLAND 14** [6] Mrs A J Perrett 2-9-0 K Fallon 11/10 FAV: 21: Chsd ldrs, imprvd to lead dist, rdn clr fnl 1f despite flashing tail: well bckd: eff at 6f on gd/soft & soft, 7f+ will suit: see 5197.		90
	STAGE SCHOOL [8] M Johnston 2-8-9 J Fanning 10/1: 2: b f Sunday Silence - Danseur Fabuleux (Northern Dancer) Chsd ldrs, ev ch dist, kept on but left bhnd by wnr fnl 1f on debut: Apr foal, half sister to sev wnrs, notably top-class juv Arazi: eff at 6f on gd/soft grnd: sure to learn from this & find similar.	3	75
5265	**HELEN HOUSE 7** [12] M H Tompkins 2-8-9 P Robinson 12/1: 03: b f Tipsy Creek - Tiempo (King of Spain) Led 2f, remained prom, onepcd fnl 1f: May foal, half sister to 1m juv wnr Ten Bob: sire a smart sprinter: eff at 6f on gd/soft grnd.	shd	75
	LEGAL BELLE [18] J L Spearing 2-8-9 S Hitchcott 50/1: 4: ch f Superpower - Legal Sound (Legal Eagle) Rear, styd on fnl 1f, nvr nrr on debut: Mar foal, half sister to 5f juv wnr Brias & wng sprinter Zucchero: dam a sprinter, sire a high-class juv: handles gd/soft grnd, 7f looks sure to suit judged on this.	2	70
5118	**MISS HERMIONE 20** [9]2-8-9 Dane O'Neill 80/1: 005: Led after 2f tilt dist, no extra.	nk	69
5285	**KRULLIND 6** [1]2-9-0 A McCarthy 12/1: 066: Held up, styd on late, nvr nrr.	1½	71
5228	**HIGHEST REGARD 11** [14]2-9-0 D Fox(5) 33/1: 07: Chsd ldrs, outpcd halfway, rallied fnl 1f.	½	70
5197	**PHYSICAL 14** [13]2-9-0 D Holland 14/1: 08: Prom, wknd fnl 1f: s/mate of wnr.	hd	70
4988	**LAKE CAREZZA 28** [5]2-9-0 E Ahern 7/2: 59: Nvr a factor: see 4988 (gd).	1½	67
5250	**ANGEL RIVER 9** [15]2-8-9 Martin Dwyer 100/1: 00: 10th: Nvr btr than mid-div.	nk	61
5265	**BINTY 7** [3]2-8-9 L Keniry(3) 20/1: 00: 11th: Chsd ldrs 4f, wknd.	¾	59

Suivez Moi [10]2-9-0 J Quinn 18/1:0		**Red Apache 59** [7]2-9-0 J F Egan 40/1:0	
5192 **Rock Fever 15** [11]2-8-9 D Corby(3) 25/1:0		5251 **Rockys Girl 9** [2]2-8-9 S Whitworth 66/1:0	
Chillin Out [17]2-9-0 M Tebbutt 40/1:0		5228 **Autumn Daze 11** [16]2-8-9 M Henry 100/1:0	

17 Ran   Time 1m 15.98 (5.58)   Owned: Mr & Mrs R Scott   Trained: Pulborough

---

5351 2.30 Sharp Minds Betfair: Best Odds Selling Stakes 3yo (G4)
£2590 £740 £370   **1m3f101y**   **Good/Soft 89**   **-31 Slow**   Inside

5092	**RIVER OF DIAMONDS 21** [5] R Guest 3-8-12 (60) K Fallon 11/4 JT FAV: 0021: Nvr far away, ev ch 2f out, went on ins fnl 1f & just prevailed drvn out in a tight fin: well bckd tho' op 2/1: eff at 12f on gd/soft & soft grnd: apprec this drop to sell grade: see 5092 (mdn).		54
5024	**ZAFFEU 26** [4] N P Littmoden 3-9-5 (55) P Cosgrave 11/2: 0600002: Waited with, fin v strongly & just btn in a thrilling fin: tchd 13/2: back to form on drop to sell grade: see 2413.	shd	60
3862	**HAT TRICK MAN 86** [2] J Akehurst 3-8-12 (70) J Quinn 3/1: 00-603: Rear, prog to lead 2f out, worn down ins fnl 1f, not btn far: nicely bckd, 3 mnth abs: eff at 12f on gd/soft: apprec drop to sell grade: see 3292.	¾	51
5060	**GO GREEN 24** [3] P D Evans 3-9-0 t (50) J Fortune 11/4 JT FAV: 6032064: Dwelt, styd on fnl 1.5f.	¾	52
5240	**POETRY N PASSION 11** [7]3-8-7 J F Egan 14/1: 0005: b f Polish Precedent - Ghassanah (Pas de Seul) Prom, led 2f out till 2f out, no extra: big step up in trip, poss stays 12f & drop in grade: with C Cyzer.	1¼	43
4975	**BEBOPSKIDDLY 30** [1]3-8-12 (55) E Ahern 14/1: 000-06: b c Robellino - Adarama (Persian Bold) Led 2f, remained prom till wknd 2f out: no form: longer 12f trip.	13	32
5190	**APRON 16** [6]3-8-7 (50) Martin Dwyer 25/1: 00007: Led after 2f till 3f out, wknd.	2½	24

7 Ran   Time 2m 36.67 (13.87)   Owned: Mr J J May   Trained: Newmarket

---

5352 3.00 Sharp Minds Betfair: Back And Lay Maiden Stakes 2yo (D3)
£3465 £1066 £533   **1m2f21y**   **Good/Soft 89**   **-25 Slow**   Inside

5252	**QUIZZENE 9** [6] M Johnston 2-9-0 K Darley 9/2: 51: gr c Cozzene - Company Binness (Seattle Dancer) Trkd ldrs, forged ahd cl home, rdn out: op 7/2: confirmed debut promise: $65,000 Mar foal: half brother to 1m wnr Itemise: dam unrcd: eff at 10f on gd/soft grnd.		83
5331	**CORDAGE 2** [4] G A Butler 2-9-0 P (80) J Fortune 11/2: 54442: Tried to make all, just btn in a thrilling fin: qck reapp & tried cheek pieces: stays 10f well, acts on gd & gd/soft grnd: see 5331.	shd	82
4462	**SUBTLE AFFAIR 58** [13] M G Quinlan 2-8-9 T P Queally 20/1: 03: b f Barathea - Uncertain Affair (Darshaan) Mid-div, styd on well fnl 1f, not btn far: 8 wk abs: Apr foal, cost 60,000gns: half sister to sev wnrs, incl mid-dist scorers Lochbuie & Euro Pressure: dam a 14f wnr, sire a top-class miler: eff at 10f on gd/soft, bred to stay well next term: promising run & shld win similar.	¾	75
3925	**ROSECLIFF 84** [2] A M Balding 2-9-0 Martin Dwyer 15/8 FAV: 44: Chsd ldrs, onepcd fnl 1f: well bckd from 11/4, 12 wk abs: stays 10f on gd/soft grnd: see 3925.	1¼	78
5188	**CELTIC PROMISE 16** [8]2-8-9 P Robinson 66/1: 065: Chsd ldrs, onepcd fnl 1f.	nk	72
5002	**NOBBLER 27** [10]2-9-0 S Whitworth 33/1: 006: Mid-div, styd on fnl 1f, nvr nrr.	3	72
	SELF RESPECT [5]2-9-0 E Ahern 3/1: 7: b c Lear Fan - Cap of Dignity (Shirley Heights) Chsd ldrs, onepcd fnl 1.5f: Jan foal, cost $85,000: half brother to US wnr Beret: dam unrcd, sire a top-class miler.	1	70
5040	**TI ADORA 25** [9]2-8-9 A McCarthy 50/1: 008: Waited with, nvr a factor.	3	60
5330	**CHRISTOM 2** [14]2-9-0 J F Egan 66/1: 0009: Nvr in it: qck reapp.	1½	63
5252	**SILBER MOND 9** [12]2-9-0 K Fallon 20/1: 00: 10th: Chsd ldrs, wknd 1.5f out.	¾	62

4851 **Silver Song 37** [7]2-9-0 Dane O'Neill 66/1:0		5097 **Westfield Boy 21** [3]2-9-0 Steven Harrison(7) 100/1:0	
5189 **Misters Sister 16** [1]2-8-9 BL J Mackay 100/1:0		5170 **Grasp 17** [11]2-9-0 t D Holland 16/1:0	

4418 **Winter Mist** 60 [16]2-8-9 P Cosgrave 100/1:0 5220 **City Trader** 13 [15]2-9-0 BL J Quinn 100/1:0
16 Ran Time 2m 15.61 (11.41) Owned: Favourites Racing Trained: Middleham

5353	3.30 Sharp Minds Betfair Handicap Stakes 3yo+ 56-70 (E3)	[82]
	£3983 £1225 £613 1m2f21y Good/Soft 89 -06 Slow Inside	

5050 **STREET LIFE** 25 [8] W J Musson 6-9-3 (71) A Rutter(7) 3/1: 4354441: Mid-div, smooth prog when **80**
short of room 1f out, qcknd to lead ins fnl 1f, easily: well bckd, rdier given 3-day careless riding ban: eff at
10/12f on fast & gd, loves gd/soft, hvy & f/sand: handles any trk, loves Windsor: see 4392 & 391.
5198 **COUNT BORIS** 14 [1] G B Balding 3-8-0 (58) Martin Dwyer 10/1: 000032: Dwelt, prog 2f out, styd on 1¼ **61**
well fnl 1f, not pace of easy wnr: eff at 9/10f on gd/soft & soft grnd: see 5198.
5261 **GINGKO** 8 [5] P R Webber 7-8-9 (63) Dane O'Neill 7/1: 66-15033: Chsd ldrs, imprvd to lead dist, shd **66**
not pace to repel wnr cl home: see 5261 (AW).
5062 **REAP** 24 [6] J Pearce 6-8-8 (62) J Quinn 33/1: 2-030604: Chsd ldrs, slight short of room 2f out, hd **64**
kept on well: back to form, best when able to dominate: see 1036.
4008 **DOUBLE RANSOM** 80 [10]5-8-11 bl (65) K Fallon 5/1: 2162165: Rear, styd on fnl 1f, not pace to 2½ **63**
chall: op 7/2, 12 wk abs: sharper next time, see 3759.
4849 **KIND EMPEROR** 38 [11]7-8-8 (62) A Mackay 12/1: 0-040266: Set pace till dist, wkng when slightly ½ **59**
hmpd ins fnl 1f: btr 4989.
3785 **RAJAYOGA** 90 [9]3-7-13 (57) M Henry 40/1: 40-00407: Trkd ldrs, btn 2f out: 3 month abs. 6 **46**
5086 **TATA NAKA** 22 [7]4-9-0 (68) Joanna Badger 25/1: 2341008: Keen in rear, btn 2f out: btr 4613. 1 **55**
5023* **MARIAS MAGIC** 26 [2]3-9-3 (75) J Fanning 7/4 FAV: 619: Trkd ldr, wkng when hmpd 1.5f outt: bckd 1¾ **60**
from 5/2: prev trained in Ireland by J Oxx & better expected on first start for M Johnston: see 5023 (gd).
5054 **MISTER RIGHT** 25 [3]3-8-5 (63) C Catlin 25/1: 00-30: 10th: Keen in rear, nvr a factor. 1¼ **46**
4832 **TIBER TIGER** 39 [4]4-8-13 (67) P Cosgrave 16/1: 5560000: 11th: Al rear & fin last. 2½ **47**
11 Ran Time 2m 13.79 (9.59) Owned: Mr W J Musson Trained: Newmarket

5354	4.00 Sharp Minds Phone 0870 90 80 121 Handicap Stakes 3yo 46-55 (F4)	[63]
	£3340 £954 £477 6f3y str Good/Soft 89 -09 Slow Inside	

5231 **ESTOILLE** 11 [9] Mrs S Lamyman 3-8-5 (6oh)t (40) F P Ferris(3) 20/1: 0006041: Prom, led 2f out, **52**
styd on well fnl 1f, rdn out: first win: eff at 5/6f on gd/soft & polytrack: suited by a t-strap: see 5231.
5231 **CHATSHOW** 11 [7] A W Carroll 3-8-11 (52) D Fentiman(7) 7/2 FAV: 0030122: Rear, gd hdwy to chase ½ **55**
wnr fnl 1f, nrst fin: op 9/2: continues in fine form: see 5231 & 5176.
     MARGARETS DREAM 16 [16] Ms Caroline Hutchinson 3-8-6 (47) E Ahern 7/1: 4-000043: b f Muhtarram - nk **49**
Acidanthera (Alzao) Outpcd, styd on well fnl 1f, nrst fin: nicely bckd: Irish chall, eff at 6f on gd/soft grnd.
5270 **MAN CRAZY** 7 [14] C A Dwyer 3-8-7 (48) P Cosgrave 14/1: 4004004: Keen & prom, onepcd fnl 1f. 2 **45**
5156 **KING EGBERT** 18 [12]3-9-0 (55) T Dean(7) 15/2: 0-403065: Rear, styd on fnl 1f, nvr nrr. shd **52**
2331 **VENDORS MISTAKE** 148 [18]3-8-6 (47) J F Egan 25/1: 0-063366: Rear, prog 2f out, onepcd fnl 1f. 2 **39**
4660 **BOLD WOLF** 48 [5]3-8-5 (1oh) (45) S Whitworth 25/1: 0000407: Chsd ldrs, onepcd fnl 1f: 7 wk abs. nk **37**
5294 **MUTASSEM** 5 [2]3-9-3 (58) D Holland 8/1: 0002008: Rear, nvr nr to chall: qck reapp. shd **49**
5053 **GENEROUS GESTURE** 25 [10]3-9-3 (58) J Mackay 9/1: 6560009: Slow away, nvr nr ldrs. nk **48**
5020 **MELODY KING** 26 [15]3-8-12 bl (52) J Fortune 16/1: U060400: 10th: Chsd ldrs 4f, wknd: see 4698. 1 **40**
4698 **ABSOLUTELY SOAKED** 46 [11]3-8-6 bl (47) N Mackay 10/1: 5600020: 11th: Held up, nvr dngrs: abs. nk **33**
4091 **SHIFTY NIGHT** 77 [6]3-8-5 (1oh) (45) A McCarthy 25/1: 1060040: 12th: Prom, led briefly halfway: abs. 1½ **29**
5241 **Cheeky Chi** 11 [8]3-9-1 (56) J Brennan(7) 66/1:0 5162 **Velvet Touch** 18 [17]3-8-11 (52) T P Queally 40/1:0
5120 **Zonnebeke** 20 [4]3-8-5 (1oh)(45) C Catlin 20/1:0
4211 **Sam The Sorcerer** 70 [13]3-8-5 (1oh)(45) J Quinn 20/1:0
5270 **Fools Entire** 7 [1]3-9-0 e(55) Dane O'Neill 14/1:0 5176 **Desert Daisy** 17 [3]3-8-6 (47) J F McDonald(3) 11/1:0
18 Ran Time 1m 16.29(5.89) Owned: Mr B C S Kemp Trained: Louth

Official Going Standard

5355	4.15 Bet Direct On 0800 32 93 93 Maiden Stakes 2yo (D3)	
	£3621 £1114 £557 1m141y aw rnd Inapplicable Inside	

5040 **MAGGIE TULLIVER** 25 [2] P W Harris 2-8-9 S W Kelly 11/4: 0001: b f Spectrum - Eliza Acton **76a**
(Shirley Heights) Chsd ldrs, went on 2f out, pushed well clr, easily: bckd from 9/2: Apr foal, dam a 1m winning
juv: sire a top-class 1m/10f performer: apprec this step up to 8.5f, clrly likes polytrack & a sharp trk.
5115 **SANDYS LEGEND** 20 [7] J H M Gosden 2-9-0 VIS R Havlin 8/1: 052: Led till 2f out, held on for 2nd 5 **67a**
but no ch with wnr: tried a visor: eff at 8.5f on polytrack: see 5115 (C/D).
     NOVELINA 10 [10] W J Haggas 2-8-9 A Culhane 9/1: 3: b f Fusaichi Pegasus - Novelette (Darshaan) nk **61a**
Mid-div, styd on under press fnl 1f, not pace to chall on debut: May foal, dam a 1m wnr in France, sire a high-class
performer in the US: eff at 8.5f on polytrack, sure to learn from this.
5250 **TAXMAN** 9 [3] C E Brittain 2-9-0 S Carson 25/1: 04: Chsd ldr, onepcd fnl 2f. shd **65a**
     BRIDEGROOM 8 [2]2-9-0 P Hanagan 13/2: 5: Chsd ldrs, lost pl halfway, no ch after: debut, op 4/1. ¾ **63a**
5091 **GOGETTER GIRL** 21 [11]2-8-9 p (55) N Callan 25/1: 6000006: Chsd ldrs 6f, wknd. ¾ **56a**
     RUSTLER 4 [2]2-9-0 D Sweeney 10/1: 7: Nvr btr than mid-div on racecourse bow. shd **60a**
     RAMSGILL 1 [2]2-9-0 Lisa Jones 14/1: 8: Nvr a factor on debut. 5 **51a**
4632 **ZOLASH** 50 [9]2-9-0 (59) Derek Nolan(7) 25/1: 0443609: Nvr a factor: 7 wk abs. 1¾ **47a**
5257 **TANGIBLE** 8 [13]2-8-9 S Sanders 2/1 FAV: 050: 10th: Slowly away, rcd wide & nvr a factor in ¾ **40a**
h'cap qual run: bred to apprec mid-dists next term & shld leave this bhd in h'cap company for shrewd stable.
5049 **FERRARA FLAME** 25 [12]2-8-10 (1ow) (58) D Nolan 25/1: 00020: 11th: Al rear: new stable. 5 **32a**
     GERMANICUS 6 [2]2-9-0 R Kingscote(7) 33/1: 0: 12th: Slowly away, al rear on debut. 9 **20a**

5259 **CANADIAN DANEHILL 8** [5]2-9-0 F Lynch 66/1: 00: 13th: Prom wide, wknd 2f out. *5* **11a**
13 Ran Time 1m 53.83 () Owned: Mrs P W Harris Trained: Berkhamsted

5356

4.40 Bet Direct At Dunstall Park Classified Stakes 3yo 0-55 (F4)
£2653 £758 £379 **1m141y aw rnd** **Inapplicable** Inside

5153 **LAKE DIVA 18** [12] J G Given 3-8-11 (57) A Culhane 12/1: 00-3401: Rear, gd hdwy to lead ent fnl 1f, styd on strongly, rdn out: eff over a sharp 8.5f on polytrack: lightly rcd & set for a decent AW campaign. **61a**
5242* **MY PENSION 11** [5] P Howling 3-9-9 (60) R Winston 7/4 FAV: 3006312: Nvr far away, led 2f out till dist, kept on but not pace of wnr: in gd form: see 5242. *2* **67a**
5184 **JUST ONE LOOK 17** [8] M Blanshard 3-8-9 (51) N Callan 3/1: 0605033: Rear, styd on under press fnl 1f. *½* **52a**
4365 **PETITE COLLEEN 63** [6] D Haydn Jones 3-8-11 VIS (57) D Kinsella 8/1: 4060504: Rdn in rear, styd on late, nrst fin: 9 wk abs & tried a visor (has prev worn cheek pieces): see 3161 & 2452. *½* **53a**
5211 **BREEZIT 13** [11]3-8-9 (47) P Makin(5) 14/1: 0-445035: Chsd ldr, onepcd fnl 2f. *½* **50a**
5017 **JORDANS SPARK 26** [4]3-9-0 BL (57) T Eaves(3) 9/1: 0061606: Led early, again 3f out till 2f out, wknd. *3* **49a**
5242 **HANA DEE 11** [9]3-8-9 (47) T O'Brien(7) 11/2: 5300457: Nvr btr than mid-div. *1* **42a**
5176 **NINAH 17** [3]3-8-9 (45) S W Kelly 50/1: 0000008: Chsd ldrs 6f, wknd. *7* **29a**
4448 **DEVIOUS AYERS 59** [10]3-9-1 (58) L Fletcher(3) 25/1: 3-400609: Chsd ldrs 6f: 8 wk abs, new yard. *2* **31a**
5060 **KILLING ME SOFTLY 24** [1]3-8-12 (48) R Fitzpatrick 25/1: 01-20400: 10th: Led, hdd 3f out, fdd. *6* **17a**
3967 **CLOUD CATCHER 82** [7]3-8-9 T (30) S Righton 100/1: 0-00000: 11th: Al rear: abs, t-strap. *¾* **12a**
11 Ran Time 1m 52.90 () Owned: Mr P B Doyle Trained: Gainsborough

5357

5.05 Betdirect Co Uk Classified Stakes 3yo 0-65 (E3)
£3416 £1051 £526 **7f32y aw rnd** **Standard** Outside

1617 **NIGHT STORM 182** [9] S Dow 3-8-9 (65) S Sanders 14/1: 5333601: Held up wide, imprvd halfway, strong run to lead cl-home: long abs, 1st win: eff at 7f/1m on fast & polytrack: likes a sharp trk, runs well fresh. **68a**
5180 **YASHIN 17** [7] P A Blockley 3-8-12 (64) D Sweeney 10/1: 0403142: Rear, imprvd 2f out, fin strongly & only just btn: big drop in trip, prob failed to stay 12f in 5180: acts on polytrk: see 5042 (sell). *nk* **69a**
4836* **INDIANA BLUES 39** [4] A M Balding 3-8-9 (63) N Chalmers(3) 9/2: 5343213: Led & sn clr, worn down cl-home: clr of rem: bold front running eff on AW bow, clrly acts on polytrack: see 4836 (turf mdn). *½* **65a**
5340 **CONSTABLE BURTON 1** [3] Mrs A Duffield 3-9-2 (69) D Allan 22/1: 000-0104: Prom, sn rdn along, left bhd fnl 1f: unplcd yesterday: see 1196 (mdn auct). *4* **64a**
5027 **OVERDRAWN 26** [1]3-9-3 bl (70) S W Kelly 9/2: 0000005: Prom, onepcd fnl 2f. *shd* **64a**
4873 **STEVEDORE 36** [2]3-9-3 (70) G Baker 3/1 JT FAV: 1515056: Slowly away, modest late gains, nvr dngrs: gamble from 7/1: much btr clrly expected, first run on polytrack: see 4110 (turf). *1* **62a**
2840 **CERTIFIABLE 128** [5]3-9-3 (70) B Swarbrick(5) 25/1: 1150507: Chsd ldrs, wknd dist: long abs. *1¼* **60a**
5291 **BRIDGEWATER BOYS 6** [6]3-9-3 bl (70) N Callan 3/1 JT FAV: 1500638: Nvr btr than mid-div. *¾* **58a**
5046 **DANIFAH 25** [10]3-8-11 (67) D Nolan(3) 10/1: 3010009: Prom, wknd 2f out. *5* **42a**
5114 **INNSTYLE 20** [11]3-8-9 (63) Lisa Jones 25/1: 0300100: 10th: Chsd ldrs wide 4f, wknd: btr 5020 (turf). *nk* **39a**
4902 **LOVE OF LIFE 34** [8]3-8-9 VIS (47) G Faulkner 66/1: 006020R: Ref to race: tried visor. **0a**
11 Ran Time 1m 31.36 () Owned: Anderson Connolly and Thornton Trained: Epsom

5358

5.30 Bet Direct On At The Races Classified Stakes 3yo+ 0-50 (G4)
£2625 £750 £375 **7f32y aw rnd** **Inapplicable** Outside

4836 **CHARLOTTEBUTTERFLY 39** [4] T T Clement 4-8-12 (52) G Baker 16/1: 4003041: Held up, hdwy to lead over 1f out, styd on, rdn out: first win: apprec step up to 7f: acts on firm, gd & both AWs: gd confidence boost. **57a**
5112 **ZHITOMIR 20** [5] M Dods 6-9-1 (52) S W Kelly 6/1: 6402162: Slow away, in tch, hdwy to chase wnr over 1f out, kept on, not btn far: acts on firm, soft & polytrack: in gd form: see 4994 (banded), 3324. *¾* **58a**
4667 **HEAD BOY 48** [3] S Dow 3-9-1 (53) S Sanders 8/1: 4200063: In tch, eff over 1f out, kept on, no threat: clr of rem, 7 wk abs: acts on fast, gd/soft & polytrack: see 1054. *1½* **56a**
5121 **LAKELANDS LADY 20** [7] J Balding 4-9-0 (54) J Edmunds 20/1: 0000044: In tch, wknd fnl 1f: see 859. *5* **45a**
5046 **OASES 25** [2]5-9-0 p (51) P Hanagan 4/1 FAV: 3560405: Slow away, bhd, modest late gains. *1* **43a**
5176 **A TEEN 17** [1]6-9-1 (52) R Winston 9/1: 0560006: In tch, wknd over 1f out: see 4368 (6f), 740. *nk* **43a**
5178 **EMARADIA 17** [12]3-8-12 vis (53) D Nolan 11/1: 0304037: Led till dist, wknd: see 5178, 835. *2* **37a**
5039 **MARABAR 25** [6]6-9-0 bl e (54) A Culhane 10/1: 2660408: Al bhd: see 5039. *1¾* **34a**
5077 **PEPPER ROAD 23** [8]5-9-3 (54) R Ffrench 5/1: 1222069: Handy, wknd dist: btr 4488 (turf), 3229. *1¼* **35a**
5017 **DANETTIE 26** [11]3-9-0 (55) N Pollard 25/1: 0545400: 10th: Handy, wknd over 2f out: see 4674. *6* **22a**
5184 **SMART SCOT 17** [9]5-9-1 (52) Darren Williams 8/1: 1112050: 11th: Handy, wknd 2f out: see 847. *3* **16a**
5056 **CAYMAN BREEZE 24** [10]4-9-0 (51) P Doe 12/1: 1050040: 12th: In tch, wknd 2f out: see 5056, 708. *1* **13a**
12 Ran Time 1m 31.17 () Owned: Future Electrical Services Ltd Trained: Newmarket

5359

5.55 Littlewoods Bet Direct Classified Stakes 3yo+ 0-50 (G4)
£2660 £760 £380 **5f216y aw rnd** **Inapplicable** Inside

4845* **INCH BY INCH 38** [5] P J Makin 5-9-0 bl (55) A Quinn(5) 9/4 FAV: 0401111: Held up, hdwy to lead over 1f out, styd on well, rdn out: eff over 5/6f on firm, gd & polytrack: thriving: see 4845, 4751. **62a**
3920 **CHICKADO 84** [4] D Haydn Jones 3-9-0 (55) R Havlin 11/1: 13-36062: Chsd ldrs, eff over 1f out, kept on but not pace of wnr: 3 month abs: acts on fibresand & polytrack: see 69. *1¾* **55a**
5112 **ON THE TRAIL 20** [12] D W Chapman 7-9-3 (55) A Culhane 4/1: 5201243: Led till dist, onepace. *shd* **57a**
3670 **MR BOUNTIFUL 94** [2] M Dods 6-9-3 t (55) S W Kelly 16/1: 4006404: Bhd, late gains, nvr dngrs: abs. *¾* **55a**
4845 **ST AUSTELL 38** [8]4-9-2 (54) S Sanders 9/1: 21-00005: Slow away, in tch, late gains, nvr dngrs: stay 6f & acts on firm, gd & polytrack: see 3924. *¾* **52a**
5039 **KARMINSKEY PARK 25** [6]5-9-0 (55) G Baker 10/1: 0000506: Nvr a factor, broke a blood vessel. *2½* **43a**
5096 **PULSE 21** [1]6-9-1 p (53) P Fitzsimons 11/1: 0605237: Handy, wknd over 1f out: see 4739 (turf). *½* **43a**
5294 **MARGALITA 5** [3]4-9-0 bl t (55) G Gibbons 40/1: 6000008: Nvr a factor. *½* **41a**
2755 **PARK STAR 132** [9]4-9-0 (55) R Winston 20/1: 00U4409: Al bhd: 4 month abs: see 740, 587. *1½* **37a**
5241 **GOODWOOD PRINCE 11** [7]4-9-3 vis (55) Lisa Jones 40/1: 0000000: 10th: Nvr a factor: see 2262. *1¼* **37a**

4754 **STAGNITE 43** [10]4-9-3 p (55) N Chalmers(3) 20/1: 0065000: 11th: Handy, wknd dist: 6 wk abs. ½ 36a
5146 **VALIANT ROMEO 19** [11]4-9-1 vis (53) R Ffrench 10/1: 5203330: 12th: In tch, wknd 2f out: btr 5146. 1 31a
5294 **AROGANT PRINCE 5** [13]7-9-3 bl (55) N Callan 25/1: 1006000: 13th: Chsd ldr, wknd 2f out: see 1267. 9 8a
13 Ran Time 1m 16.27 () Owned: Mrs Anna L Sanders Trained: Marlborough

---

5360 6.20 Bet Direct Football Cashbacks Classified Stakes 3yo 0-55 (F4)
£2597 £742 £371 **1m1f103y aw** Inapplicable Inside

5005 **SEMELLE DE VENT 27** [5] J H M Gosden 3-8-9 vis (55) R Havlin 11/2: 3002031: Chsd ldr, led over 3f 61a
out, eased cl-home: eff over 1m/12f on gd/soft & polytrack: see 3605, 1165.
4925 **VELOCITAS 34** [1] H J Collingridge 3-9-0 VIS (57) P Hanagan 3/1: 4000522: Chsd wnr, kept on ins ¾ 62a
last, al held: gd run in a visor: deserves a race: see 4925.
4515 **MR MIDASMAN 55** [8] R Hollinshead 3-8-13 (56) D Sweeney 3/1: 0046333: Chsd ldrs to 3f out, 3½ 56a
onepcd: 8 wk abs: acts on firm, soft & polytrack: see 4388, 923.
4899 **DANCING BEAR 35** [9] Julian Poulton 3-8-12 bl (55) N Callan 9/1: 0-403404: Led till 3f out, wknd. 11 40a
2741 **ALIANNA 132** [2]3-8-9 J Lisa Jones 40/1: 000005: Al bhd: long abs. 3½ 32a
5122 **ZARNEETA 20** [3]3-8-9 (35) P Doe 33/1: 0000306: Al bhd. 5 25a
5056 **OLLIJAY 24** [4]3-8-12 (47) G Gibbons 16/1: 66007: In tch, wknd over 2f out: see 3595. nk 27a
5242 **BEST DESERT 11** [7]3-9-2 (59) S Sanders 9/4 FAV: 5006348: Handy, wknd over 3f out: see 5112. nk 30a
4485 **PRINCESS ISMENE 57** [6]3-9-9 VIS (48) S Righton 40/1: 546R0RR: Slow away, ref to race: visor. 0a
9 Ran Time 2m 2.99() Owned: Skara Glen Stables Trained: Manton

---

Official Going Standard

5361 4.30 Bet Direct Football Cashbacks Handicap Stakes 3yo+ 46-55 (F4) [65]
£3069 £877 £438 **1m1f103y aw** Inapplicable Inside

5117 **MIDSHIPMAN 21** [7] A W Carroll 6-9-5 vis t (56) S W Kelly 9/2: 2240651: Held up, prog 2f out, styd 65a
on to lead well ins fnl 1f, rdn out: eff at 1m/12f on soft, hvy & both AW's: eff in blnks, visor or t-strap: gd
confidence boost & is h'capped to win more races: see 4750 & 2998.
5292 **CHARMATIC 7** [9] J A Glover 3-9-10 (64) J Quinn 4/1: 4506022: Rcd keenly, led 7f out, clr ins fnl 2 68a
2f, hdd well ins fnl 1f, no extra: op 6/1: qck reapp: continues in gd form & can find similar: see 5292.
5328 **OUR DESTINY 3** [2] A W Carroll 6-9-4 (55) D Fentiman(7) 16/1: 6604053: Bhd, hdwy when no room bef 1 57a
1f out, kept on, nrst fin: qck reapp: stablemate of wnr: encouraging eff & can return to winning ways: see 4485.
4791 **MY MAITE 42** [6] R Ingram 5-9-2 vis t (53) J Loveridge(7) 16/1: 4503334: Cl up, no extra dist: 6 wk abs. shd 54a
5294 **GLENDALE 6** [1]3-9-3 (57) A Nicholls 50/1: 0050005: Led, hdd bef 7f out, styd prom, no extra bef 1f out. 1½ 55a
5016 **MARKET AVENUE 27** [5]5-9-11 p (62) Darren Williams 9/1: 0510066: Keen mid div, prog 3f out, wknd dist. 1¾ 56a
5292 **ZAWRAK 7** [8]5-9-5 p (56) L Fletcher(3) 12/1: 5200047: Nvr nrr than mid div: qck reapp: btr 5292. hd 49a
5338* **RIBBONS AND BOWS 2** [4]4-9-3 (6ex)vis (54) D Sweeney 9/4 FAV: 0045518: Cl up, wknd fnl 1f: qck ½ 46a
reapp, poss came too sn after win here in 5338.
5337 **BURNT COPPER 2** [10]4-9-1 (52) N Pollard 20/1: 0100009: Missed break, al bhd. ½ 43a
4321 **ORION EXPRESS 66** [3]3-9-1 (55) P Mulrennan(3) 25/1: 4646600: 10th: Cl up till halfway, wknd: abs. 3 41a
4861 **MY MICHELLE 38** [11]3-9-1 (55) F P Ferris(3) 25/1: 0045460: 11th: Mid div, prog halfway, fdd bef 1f out. 3½ 36a
4333 **HERODOTUS 65** [12]6-9-4 (55) L Keniry(3) 20/1: 50-00000: 12th: Rear, nvr a factor. 3 32a
5198 **LOADED GUN 15** [13]4-9-4 (55) B Swarbrick(5) 15/2: 0240340: 13th: Bhd, nvr a factor: btr 5066. ½ 31a
13 Ran Time 2m 2.75 () Owned: Langwood Racing Trained: Alcester

---

5362 5.00 Bet Direct Red To Bet On Itv Claiming Stakes 3yo+ (F4)
£3038 £868 £434 **5f20y aw rnd** Inapplicable Inside

1867 **PANJANDRUM 170** [5] N E Berry 6-9-1 (61) M Savage(5) 14/1: 6004001: Made all, hung right from 2f 68a
out, drvn out: long abs: eff at 5/6f on firm, fast, loves both AW's: goes well fresh: likes claiming grade.
5327 **WILLHECONQUERTOO 3** [7] Andrew Reid 4-9-5 t p (65) B Swarbrick(5) 6/1: 0544042: Bhd, prog halfway, 1½ 66a
kept on ins fnl 1f, not pace wnr: qck reapp: can find similar back at 6f: see 5327.
3602 **ST IVIAN 98** [3] Mrs N Macauley 4-9-1 (61) L Fletcher(3) 25/1: 0000003: Bhd, prog when short of 1½ 58a
room halfway, kept on, no ch with front 2: long abs: see 864.
4920 **DVINSKY 35** [8] G A Butler 3-8-5 t (78) E Ahern 7/2 FAV: 61-0064: Rear, hdwy halfway, no impress nk 47a
dist: clmd for 5,000: well bckd: disappointing back at 5f: btr 4920 & 3550.
4747 **CANTERLOUPE 45** [11]6-9-0 (81) D Fox(5) 11/2: 0001005: Slow away, prog 2f out, nrst fin: 6 wk abs 1 53a
& new stable: btr 3952 (h'cap, P J Makin).
5178 **DIAMOND SHANNON 18** [10]3-8-10 (58) D Tudhope(5) 25/1: 5120006: Nvr nrr than mid div. 2 43a
5020 **RED SOVEREIGN 27** [6]3-8-10 (79) J Quinn 11/2: 0010507: Cl up over 3f, no extra: btr 4879. nk 42a
5321 **BOND ROMEO 4** [4]3-8-9 (67) D McGaffin 25/1: 5020-058: Prom, wknd dist: qck reapp. shd 40a
5149 **BRAVE BURT 19** [9]7-9-5 (72) A Nicholls 9/2: 2000009: Cl up over 3f, wknd dist: op 3/1: btr 3960. 1½ 46a
5020 **JAVA GOLD 27** [1]3-8-0 C Haddon(5) 50/1: 000: 10th: Cl up 4f, fdd. 1½ 23a
5050 **A One 26** [12]5-9-1 (70) F P Ferris(3) 11/1:0 5341 **Izmail 2** [13]5-8-11 (65) J P Guillambert(3) 16/1:0
12 Ran Time 1m 2.46 () Owned: Leeway Group Limited Trained: Earlswood

5363

5.25 Bet Direct On 0800 32 93 93 Maiden Stakes 3yo+ (D3)
£3435 £1057 £529 **5f20y aw rnd** **Inapplicable** Inside

4094 **DUTCH KEY CARD 78** [5] G A Butler 3-9-0 (61) E Ahern 7/2: 5050051: Cl up, led ins fnl 1f, pushed **69a+**
out, val 4L+: long abs: eff at 5f on polytrack & goes well fresh: won in gd style & can progress.
5156 **SHAYMEES GIRL 19** [1] Ms Deborah J Evans 3-8-9 (52) N Chalmers(3) 20/1: 5330302: Led, hdd under 2½ **55a**
press rls fnl 1f, not pace wnr: eff at 5/6f on gd & both AW's: see 4964.
5155 **ABELARD 19** [7] R A Fahey 3-9-0 (54) Dale Gibson 9/2: 5050203: Mid div, prog 2f out, kept on late. 1½ **56a**
5162 **LAKESIDE GUY 19** [2] P S McEntee 3-9-0 (55) S W Kelly 11/1: 3562034: Cl up, wknd dist: btr 5162. 1¼ **53a**
5110 **COME ON 22** [3]5-9-0 M Tebbutt 8/1: 55: in tch over 3f, sn onepcd: AW bow: btr 5110 (6f, gd/soft). ¾ **51a**
5326 **JUNIPER BANKS 3** [8]3-9-0 (57) Ann Stokell 20/1: 6600306: In tch over 3f, no extra: qck reapp. 2½ **44a**
5290 **WON OF A FEW 7** [4]4-9-0 A Kirby(7) 66/1: 07: Al in rear: qck reapp. 2½ **37a**
5240 **YOUNG KATE 12** [11]3-8-9 J Quinn 12/1: 608: Bhd, nvr a factor. 1¼ **28a**
       BIG MYSTERY 0 [10]3-8-9 N Pollard 11/1: 9: Al in rear on debut: with J R Best. ¾ **26a**
2152 **RADMORE SPIRIT 157** [12]4-8-9 S Whitworth 100/1: 000: 10th: Missed break, nvr a factor: long abs. 5 **13a**
4835 **SOUL DANCE 40** [6]3-8-9 t D Sweeney 9/4 FAV: 2W: Refused to enter stalls & withdrawn at star. **0a**
11 Ran Time 1m 3.27 () Owned: Mr M Berger Trained: Blewbury

5364

5.55 Littlewoods Bet Direct Handicap Stakes Fillies & Mares 3yo+ 56-70 (E3) [77]
£4159 £1280 £640 **1m141y aw rnd** **Inapplicable** Inside

5014 **MOUNT HILLABY 27** [2] M W Easterby 4-8-13 (62) P Mulrennan(3) 9/2: 0201051: Mid div, eff over 1f **70a**
out, drvn out to get up cl home: eff at 7f/8.5f, tried 10f: acts on fast, gd/soft & both AW's: see 4399.
5219 **KALI 14** [5] R Charlton 3-9-8 (74) D Sweeney 9/1: 3216462: Cl up, led dist, hdd cl home: op 7/1: shd **80a**
lost little in defeat & can find similar: see 2575.
4806 **CLOUD DANCER 41** [4] K A Ryan 5-9-11 (74) A Mullen(7) 6/1: 3504563: Bhd, prog 3f out, ev ch ins nk **79a**
fnl 1f, just held: 6 wk abs: in gd form: see 4482 & 2409.
5346 **ELIDORE 22** [13] B Palling 4-9-0 (63) F P Ferris(3) 33/1: 2456054: Led, hdd 2f out, no extra well 1¼ **66a**
ins fnl 1f: qck reapp: polytrack bow: acts on fast, soft & polytrack: dropped to a fair mark.
5037 **LAURO 26** [7]4-9-9 (72) R Winston 9/1: 2440105: Held up, prog 2f out, onepcd dist: btr 4694 (soft). ¾ **73a**
4999 **BLONDE STREAK 28** [6]4-10-0 (77) P Makin(5) 7/1: 4401606: Cl up, led 2f out, hdd dist, no extra. 1 **76a**
5325* **TENNYS GOLD 3** [10]3-9-0 (6ex) (66) M Hills 7/2 FAV: 4137: Nvr nrr than mid div: qck reapp. 1¼ **63a**
4743 **AND TOTO TOO 45** [3]4-9-7 bl (70) D Nolan(3) 14/1: 2140608: Al in rear: 6 wk abs. hd **66a**
5037 **MILLAGROS 26** [1]4-9-9 (72) P Hanagan 11/1: 3313349: Mid div over 5f, wknd: btr 4809 (gd). ½ **67a**
4850 **FARRIERS CHARM 38** [12]3-9-2 (68) E Ahern 14/1: 1001500: 10th: Mid div over 6f, wknd: btr 4032. 5 **53a**
4923 **SUMMER SHADES 35** [9]6-9-0 (63) B Swarbrick(5) 10/1: 6125200: 11th: Rear, nvr a factor: btr 4809. ¾ **46a**
4743 **Cuddles 45** [8]5-9-2 bl(65) L Keniry(3) 20/1:0 5039 **Red Galaxy 26** [11]4-9-0 e(63) S W Kelly 50/1:0
13 Ran Time 1m 51.26 () Owned: The Woodford Group Limited Trained: Sheriff Hutton

5365

6.20 Bet At The Races On 0800 083 83 83 Handicap Stakes 3yo+ 46-55 (F4) [66]
£3178 £908 £454 **1m141y aw rnd** **Inapplicable** Inside

5294* **MACS TALISMAN 6** [12] V Smith 4-9-10 (6ex) t p (62) N Callan 2/1 FAV: 0230011: In tch, prog 3f out, **71a**
led ins fnl 1f, rdn out: qck reapp: eff at 6/7f, now stays 8.5f: acts on fast, gd & both AW's: eff in t-strap &
cheek pieces: in-form 4yo who did well to defy top-weight under pen: see 5294.
5184 **ATLANTIC ACE 18** [4] B Smart 7-9-6 p (58) F Lynch 15/2: 0000022: Rear, prog 3f out, ev ch ins fnl nk **65a**
1f, just held: another gd eff & is h'capped to go one better: see 5184.
5184* **TEMPER TANTRUM 18** [9] J R Best 6-9-6 p (58) E Ahern 7/1: 4650313: Bhd, prog halfway, ev ch ins 1¾ **61a**
fnl 1f, sn no extra: beat today's 2nd in 5184.
5183* **KING NICHOLAS 18** [13] J Parkes 5-9-5 t p (57) M Lawson(5) 8/1: 1060614: Held up, prog after 2f, ev ½ **59a**
ch ins fnl 1f, no extra: btr 5183.
5300* **MIND ALERT 6** [5]3-9-2 (57) D Allan 7/1: 0000515: Keen prom, led 5f out till halfway, led again 3f 1½ **56a**
out, hdd ins fnl 1f, no extra: qck reapp: btr 5300 (7f).
5292 **SARRAAF 7** [8]8-9-5 (57) R Winston 7/1: 4604006: Nvr nrr than mid div: qck reapp. 3 **50a**
4539 **WIND CHIME 55** [10]7-8-13 (51) L Keniry(3) 12/1: 2013007: Cl up, no extra fnl 2f: 8 wk abs: btr 3034. nk **43a**
465 **ROCK CONCERT 288** [1]6-9-10 (62) Natalia Gemelova(5) 14/1: 132-1238: Cl up 6f, sn btn: long abs. 1 **52a**
5329 **DIAL SQUARE 3** [6]3-8-13 (54) S W Kelly 25/1: 1100009: Mid div 4f, wknd: qck reapp. 3 **38a**
5232* **TOKEWANNA 12** [11]4-9-1 t (53) P Mathers(5) 15/2: 4350110: 10th: Keen early & saddle sn slipped, 5 **27a**
led halfway, hdd 3f out, sn wknd: worth another ch: btr 5232 & 5210.
2801 **EAGER ANGEL 131** [7]6-9-2 (54) L Fletcher(3) 50/1: 1030000: 11th: Al bhd: long abs. 2½ **23a**
1125 **INDIAN CALL 208** [3]3-9-0 (55) G Gibbons 33/1: 400-0000: 12th: Cl up 4f, wknd: long abs. 1¼ **22a**
2664 **HSI WANG MU 136** [2]3-9-7 (62) D Nolan(3) 66/1: 2505000: 13th: Led, hdd 5f out, fdd 3f out. 4 **22a**
13 Ran Time 1m 52.22 () Owned: Mr V Smith Trained: Newmarket

5366

6.50 Bet Direct On At The Races Handicap Stakes 4yo+ 46-55 (F4) [65]
£2918 £834 £417 **2m119y aw** **Inapplicable** Inside

5025 **SUNGIO 27** [2] B G Powell 6-9-1 bl (52) Dale Gibson 12/1: 1233501: Slow away, prog 6f out, led **59a**
dist, drvn out: eff at 12f/2m on fast, soft grnd & both AW's: eff with/without blnks: see 896.
5151 **BEST PORT 19** [12] J Parkes 8-9-0 (51) D Allan 4/1: 6104352: Rear, prog 4f out, ev ch when ¾ **56a**
carried left ins fnl 1f, just held: polytrack bow: acts on polytrack & soft, likes firm & fast: well h'capped.
5082 **PEAK PARK 24** [6] J A R Toller 4-8-13 vis (50) P Hanagan 7/2 FAV: 0203223: Mid div, eff 4f out, 1¾ **53a**
onepcd dist: proving consistent: see 5082 & 4319.
4659J **ELLWAY PROSPECT 747** [3] Miss I E Craig 4-9-1 (52) N Chalmers(3) 33/1: 6000/-4: ch f Pivotal - 2½ **53a**
Littlemisstrouble (My Gallant) Rear, outpcd 5f out, rallied late: long jumps abs, plcd once (rtd 93h, mdn hdle):
unplcd on level in '02 (G A Butler, rtd 63, mdn): poss stays 2m on polytrack: gd run after long lay off.

WOLVERHAMPTON **Polytrack SATURDAY 06.11.04 Lefthand, Sharp Track**

5180 **BRAVELY DOES IT 18** [11]4-8-13 (50) B Swarbrick(5) 12/1: 0620055: Mid div, led 3f out, hdd dist, wknd. *shd* **50a**
4892 **SIMONS SEAT 36** [9]5-9-7 (58) S W Kelly 16/1: 0-666006: Bhd, eff when no room 4f out, kept on late. *shd* **57a**
5117 **LAMPOS 21** [8]4-9-0 (51) R Winston 8/1: 2500007: Nnvr nrr than mid div: btr 491 (fibresand). *3½* **47a**
5102 **SWEETWATER 22** [1]4-9-9 (60) D Sweeney 25/1: 0662608: Nvr nrr than mid div: btr 4983. *1½* **54a**
5249* **ENSEMBLE 10** [10]4-8-13 (50) N Callan 12/1: 00/00-019: Cl up, led 4f out, hdd 3f out, wknd: btr 5249. *14* **32a**
4910 **BOJANGLES 35** [7]5-9-7 (58) D Nolan(3) 9/1: 4125150: 10th: Cl up, fdd 6f out: btr 4669 (11f, gd/soft). *8* **32a**
5160 **VANBRUGH 19** [5]4-9-4 vis t (55) F Lynch 25/1: 0006000: 11th: Cl up, fdd 4f out. *2* **27a**
5328 **LAZZAZ 3** [4]6-9-2 (53) P Makin(5) 4/1: 5110600: 12th: Led, hdd 4f out, fdd: qck reapp: btr 4665 (12.6f). *3½* **22a**
TANIA DI SCEPTRE 37 [13]4-9-0 P (51) E Ahern 10/1: 02-00400: 13th: b f King's Theatre - Timarete *28* **0a**
(Green Dancer) Mid div, fdd 5f out: Irish raider, plcd at best in of 7 starts (11f, gd).
13 Ran Time 3m 43.51() Owned: Mrs Rachel A Powell Trained: Winchester

DONCASTER **SATURDAY 06.11.04 Lefthand, Flat, Galloping Track**

Official Going Good/Soft (Good places)

5367

12.15 Robin Hastings Memorial Fund Apprentice Stakes Handicap 3yo+ 71-85 (D2) **[94]**
£7089 £2181 £1091 **7f str** **Soft 105** **-09 Slow** Stands Side

5159 **SOYUZ 19** [16] K A Ryan 4-9-1 (81) A Mullen(5) 8/1: 1500051: Chsd ldr, led over 3f out, clr over 1f out, cmftbly: eff at 6f/1m on fast, loves soft grnd: acts on any trk: useful in the mud: see 1616, 1057. **92**
5320 **KIRKBYS TREASURE 4** [17] A Berry 6-8-9 (75) P Mathers(3) 10/1: 2603532: Hld up, hdwy & switched 2f out, styd on well, not pace of wnr: qk reapp: in gd form: see 5320. *3* **80**
5286 **QUEENS RHAPSODY 7** [11] A Bailey 4-9-0 (80) S Hitchcott 6/1: 4000533: In tch, hdwy 2f out, kept on: acts on fm, soft & polytrack: gd run: see 5286, 431. *nk* **84**
4916 **DIAMOND MAX 35** [18] John Berry 6-9-1 (81) Lisa Jones 11/1: 50-01304: Hld up, kept on late, nrst fin: prev with J Eyre: on a fair mark: see 4916. *1¼* **83**
4777 **BARATHEA DREAMS 43** [14]3-8-12 (79) Derek Nolan(5) 14/1: 1300505: With ldrs, wknd fnl 1f: abs: acts on soft & polytrack: see 1315. *1½* **79**
5227 **MR VELOCITY 14** [2]4-8-13 (79) T P Queally 5/1 FAV: 0631126: In tch far side, led that group over 1f out, no ch with stands side: fine run on 'wrong side': v progressive: see 5227, 4809 (1m). *2½* **75+**
4227 **ST PANCRAS 70** [21]4-9-2 (82) P Makin(3) 12/1: 0153207: Slow away, bhd, late gains: 10 wk abs: now with D Chapman: see 4082, 3210. *3½* **72**
5103 **OMAN GULF 22** [6]3-8-11 (78) K May(7) 33/1: 1-0408: Led far side till 2f out: see 2026 (fast). *hd* **67**
3574 **CLIMATE 99** [19]5-8-11 (77) Donna Caldwell(7) 33/1: 0216309: Chsd ldrs, onepace fnl 2f: abs. *shd* **65**
5289 **H HARRISON 7** [4]4-8-11 (77) Natalia Gemelova(5) 25/1: 0650360: 10th: Led far side gr over 2f out till over 1f out, no extra: see 4912, 4615. *1¾* **62**
4279 **RETIREMENT 68** [9]5-8-10 (76) B Reilly 14/1: 1300000: 11th: In tch, btn 2f out: see 1598, 1423. *½* **60**
4987 **NORTHERN DESERT 29** [12]5-9-2 (82) L Keniry 66/1: 554/0-000: 12th: Chsd ldrs, no impress: see 4767. *¾* **64**
5227 **DARGHAN 14** [1]4-8-10 t (76) Amy Myatt(7) 33/1: 6662050: 13th: Nvr a factor: see 4986. *3½* **52**
5304 **CD FLYER 5** [15]7-9-4 (84) P Mulrennan 14/1: 3560200: 14th: Al bhd: see 5000, 2561. *1¼* **58**
4937 **ROMARIC 33** [7]3-8-13 vis (80) T Hamilton 66/1: 103-400: 15th: In tch 5f far side: see 4270. *1* **53**
5286 **TIDY 7** [10]4-8-10 (76) N Mackay 9/1: 3004450: 16th: In tch, wknd 2f out: see 1035. *1* **47**
5227 **Best Before 14** [8]4-8-11 (1ow)(76) D Nolan 50/1:0
5256 **Warden Warren 10** [22]6-8-7 p(73) B Swarbrick(3) 25/1:0
645 **Marcus Eile 264** [20]3-8-13 (80) L Enstone 66/1:0 5159 **Vindication Gb 19** [5]4-9-3 (83) A Quinn(3) 33/1:0
20 Ran Time 1m 31.18 (7.98) Owned: The Fishermen Trained: Hambleton

5368

12.45 European Breeders Fund Freeclaim Idc Maiden Stakes 2yo (D3)
£4473 £1376 £688 **6f str** **Soft 105** **-55 Slow** Stands Side

BOW WAVE [7] H Candy 2-9-0 Dane O'Neill 11/1: 1: b c Danzero - Moxby (Efisio) Dwelt, hld up, gd hdwy 2f out, styd on to lead ins last, rdn out: Feb first foal, cost 18,000 gns: eff over a gall 6f, 7f will suit: acts on soft & goes well fresh: has a bright future. **86+**
5106 **WESTLAKE BOND 22** [16] B Smart 2-8-9 F Lynch 10/1: 52: Led over 3f out till ins last, not pace of wnr: sharper for debut & eff at 6f on soft: win a race: see 5106. *1¾* **75**
OATCAKE [19] G A Butler 2-8-9 D Holland 10/1: 3: ch f Selkirk - Humble Pie (Known Fact) In tch, eff over 1f out, kept on: Apr foal: half sister to 1m wnrs: dam sprinter: eff at 6f, 7f will suit: acts on soft: fine start, learn plenty from this & win races. *nk* **74+**
4823 **CHINALEA 40** [22] C G Cox 2-9-0 R Smith 13/2 JT FAV: 554: Unruly stalls, led till over 3f out, onepace: abs: eff at 6f on soft: see 4543. *shd* **78**
5197 **PRIME CONTENDER 15** [14]2-9-0 M Hills 11/1: 05: b c Efisio - Gecko Rouge (Rousillon) Hld up, kept on late: Apr foal, cost E30,000: eff at 6f on soft. *hd* **77**
5049 **RAVEN 26** [6]2-8-9 P Mulrennan(3) 66/1: 06: With ldrs, onepace: with M Sowersby: eff at 6f on sft. *nk* **71**
DABBERS RIDGE [15]2-9-0 Martin Dwyer 33/1: 7: In tch, some late gains. *2* **71**
5199 **CAVAN GAEL 15** [1]2-9-0 R Winston 16/1: 068: In tch, onepace fnl 2f. *½* **69**
OVER THE LIMIT [17]2-8-9 S Sanders 12/1: 9: In tch, no impress on debut. *1¼* **61**
ATRIFFIC STORY [4]2-9-0 B Reilly(3) 33/1: 0: 10th: In tch, no impress on debut. *shd* **65**
IN THE KNOW [20]2-9-0 J Fortune 13/2 JT FAV: 0: 11th: Slow away, bhd, no dngr. *1½* **61**
5199 **PITCAIRN ISLAND 15** [18]2-8-9 R Ffrench 25/1: 00: 12th: No dngr. *nk* **55**
5199 **CREAM OF ESTEEM 15** [3]2-9-0 t Kim Tinkler 100/1: 00: 13th: Slow away, al bhd. *¾* **58**
GRANDE ROCHE [11]2-9-0 R Hills 18/1: 0: 14th: Al bhd. *hd* **57**
NELLIE GWYN [21]2-8-9 K Fallon 12/1: 0: 15th: Slow away, al bhd. *3* **46**
4349 **GUADIARO 64** [5]2-9-0 K Darley 20/1: 00: 16th: In tch, wknd 2f out. *shd* **50**
ITS PEGGY SPEECH [8]2-8-9 R Fitzpatrick 66/1: 0: 17th: Al bhd. *nk* **44**
5228 **LOVE ATTACK 12** [9]2-9-1 (6ow) J Dekeyser 66/1: 660: 18th: With ldrs, wknd 2f out. *shd* **49**
5197 **DARSHARP 15** [2]2-8-9 A Culhane 33/1: 60: 19th: In tch, wknd 2f out. *hd* **42**
MANRIQUE [12]2-9-0 J Fanning 8/1: 0: 20th: Chsd ldrs, wknd 2f out. *6* **35**
5131 **JUST ELIZABETH 21** [13]2-8-9 T Eaves(3) 100/1: 000: 21th: In tch, btn 3f out. *8* **14**
21 Ran Time 1m 20.43 (9.63) Owned: Henry Candy & Partners Trained: Wantage

5369   1.20 Listed Ciu Serlby Stakes 3yo+   (A1)
£19500 £6000 £3000   1m4f   Soft 111   +00 Fast   Inside

5085 **BIG MOMENT 23** [5] Mrs A J Perrett 6-8-13 (99) S W Kelly 2/1: 0-356221: Slow away, in tch, hdwy **109**
on bit 2f out, led ins last, rdn clr, cmtbly: lkd unlucky last time: eff at 12f/2m2f on fm & soft, any trk: v useful,
at the top of his form: see 5085, 1569.
4574 **FOREIGN AFFAIRS 55** [2] Sir Mark Prescott 6-9-4 (109) S Sanders 11/10 FAV: 3451122: Cl up, led   5   **107**
over 2f out till ins last, onepace: bckd, abs: tough & smart, gd run conceding weight: see 4574.
5307 **YOUNG ROONEY 5** [1] M Mullineaux 4-8-13 (70) D Holland 50/1: 2263263: Led till over 2f out,   2½   **98$**
onepace: offic rtd 70 & this effort must be treated with caution: mdn after 19: stays 12f: see 4084.
5086 **LA SYLPHIDE GB 23** [6] G M Moore 7-8-8 (90) K Fallon 5/1: 5602134: In tch 10f, wknd: best at 10f.   6   **87**
4614 **CRYSTAL 52** [4]3-8-2 BL (90) J F McDonald 25/1: 0-215005: Chsd ldr, wknd 4f out: 7 wk abs, blnks.   9   **78**
5224 **TOP SEED 14** [3]3-8-7 T (98) A Culhane 14/1: 03200PP: Al bhd, p.u. over 5f out: tried t-strap but   **0**
something amiss: see 3027 (fast), 2557.
6 Ran   Time 2m 43.2 (13.4)   Owned: R Doel A Black Dr J Howells R & P Scott   Trained: Pulborough

5370   1.50 Listed E B F Gillies Stakes Fillies & Mares 3yo+   (A1)
£19500 £6000 £3000   1m2f60y   Soft 111   -83 Slow   Inside

4772 **MANGO MISCHIEF 43** [6] J L Dunlop 3-8-10 (90) Dane O'Neill 12/1: 0-124201: Hld up, hdwy 3f out, **102**
styd on to lead over 1f out, rdn out: 6 wk abs: stays 10.5f well on fm & soft, any trk: goes well fresh: useful.
5298 **STAR OF NORMANDIE 6** [8] G G Margarson 3-8-10 (78) A McCarthy 100/1: 2-000002: Hld up, hdwy over 3½   **97**
2f out, styd on, nrst fin: qk reapp: back to form: h'capped to win on a/w: see 134.
5174* **AUTUMN WEALTH 18** [1] Mrs A J Perrett 3-8-10 (79) Martin Dwyer 6/1: 22113: in tch, hdwy 2f out, shd   **97**
sn rdn, kept on ins last: continues in fine heart: see 5174 (12f).
2211 **GLEN INNES 35** [5] D R Loder 3-8-10 (101) S Sanders 12/1: 1220P4: In tch, hdwy on bit over 2f   ½   **96**
out, onepace: recently p.u. at Longchamp, back to form here on soft: clr rem: see 1666, 1419.
4772 **MOCCA 20** [12]3-8-10 (88) K Darley 14/1: 5162635: In tch, led over 2f out, hdd & wknd over 1f   3   **92**
out: acts on fm & soft: see 4463, 2366.
4767 **IMPERIALISTIC 20** [7]3-8-10 (91) Darren Williams 16/1: 1055306: Hld up, hdwy 2f out, wknd dist.   ½   **91**
5086 **I HAD A DREAM 23** [13]3-8-10 (92) P Robinson 9/2 JT FAV: 5-331027: In tch, led over 3f out till   5   **84**
over 2f out, wknd: btr 5086.
5086 **HONORINE 23** [9]4-9-0 (80) J F Egan 25/1: 3-605108: Hld up, btn 3f out: best 4860 (h'cap, gd).   2   **81**
5254 **BOWSTRING 10** [10]3-8-10 BL (97) J Fortune 9/2 JT FAV: 1223339: Cl up, led after 3f till over 3f   8   **71**
out, wknd: tried blnks: btr 5254.
5086 **BLUE OASIS 23** [11]3-8-10 (92) K Fallon 11/1: 1520050: 10th: Al bhd: see 1636 (1m, gd).   3½   **66**
4847* **BABOOSH 39** [14]3-8-10 (76) R Winston 14/1: 2-210: 11th: In tch 7f, wknd: btr 4847 (mdn, g/f).   14   **50**
5268 **MISS LANGKAWI 8** [4]3-8-10 (71) D Holland 20/1: 31-0030: 12th: Led 3f, wknd 3f out: see 5268.   1½   **48**
4757] **TAWOOS 27** [2]5-9-3 BL A Culhane 11/1: 1302110: 13th: In tch, wknd 2f out: blnks: Scandinavian.   6   **43**
3321 **MARINNETTE 27** [3]3-8-10 T P Queally 20/1: 5045160: 14th: In tch, wknd 2f out: 7   **32**
14 Ran   Time 2m 18.16 (11.76)   Owned: Antoniades Family   Trained: Arundel

5371   2.20 Listed Totescoop6 Wentworth Stakes 3yo+   (A1)
£19500 £6000 £3000   6f str   Soft 105   +08 Fast   Stands Side

5283 **QUITO 7** [5] D W Chapman 7-8-11 bl (104) A Culhane 7/2: 1653351: Held up, gd hdwy 2f out, strong **112**
run to lead cl home, won going away: well bckd, gd time: eff at 5f, best at 6/7f: acts on firm, loves gd/sft, soft
& f/sand: handles any trk: loves to come late in a big field/off a fast pace & showed customary turn of foot today.
5214 **MILLENNIUM FORCE 14** [10] M R Channon 6-8-11 (103) K Fallon 13/2: 0040522: Dwelt, styd on   1¼   **108**
strongly fnl 1f, just failed: op 8/1: eff at 6f, 7f specialist: see 5214.
5088* **RUBY ROCKET 23** [3] H Morrison 3-8-9 (105) J Fortune 3/1 FAV: 3232013: Prom, led 1.5f out & went shd   **106**
for home, not pace to repel wnr cl home: well bckd: acts on fm & soft: gd run & in-form: see 5088.
4874 **ROYAL STORM 37** [8] Mrs A J Perrett 5-9-0 (105) D Holland 14/1: 2001004: Led till halfway,   ¾   **109**
remained prom & ev ch till no extra ins fnl 1f: acts on fm, soft & polytrack: gd run: see 4638 (7f).
5283 **CAPE FEAR 7** [2]3-8-11 (107) E Ahern 9/1: 2510-005: Prom, lead halfway till 1.5f out, no extra.   2   **102**
5100 **GOLDEVA 22** [7]5-8-9 (103) W Ryan 10/1: 0541506: Dwelt, styd on late, nvr nrr.   2½   **95**
5218 **TOM TUN 14** [4]9-8-11 bl (94) T Lucas 16/1: 0350037: Trkd ldrs, wknd fnl 1f.   1   **95**
5196+ **ONLYTIME WILL TELL 15** [11]6-8-11 (95) J Fanning 12/1: 2014618: Prom 4.5f, wknd: see 5196.   2   **91**
5100 **HALMAHERA 22** [9]9-8-11 (100) N Callan 14/1: 0601009: Chsd ldrs 4.5f, wknd: 4th in this last yr.   1¼   **89**
5073 **MILLYBAA 27** [1]4-8-6 (90) C Catlin 50/1: 0040000: 10th: Chsd ldrs 4f: stiff task.   16   **52**
4879 **TEXAS GOLD 37** [6]6-8-11 (104) Martin Dwyer 14/1: 0221440: 11th: Keen & chsd ldrs, wknd 2f out.   2   **53**
3646 **ROMANY NIGHTS 96** [12]4-8-11 bl (79) S Sanders 100/1: 6020530: 12th: Chsd ldrs 3f: abs, new yard.   5   **43**
12 Ran   Time 1m 16.64 (5.84)   Owned: Mr Michael Hill   Trained: York

5372   2.55 Enter The #1 Million Totetentofollow November Stakes Heritage Handicap 3yo+ 0-110 (B1) [105]
£35425 £10900 £5450   1m4f   Soft 111   +00 Fast   Inside

5043 **CARTE DIAMOND 26** [3] B Ellison 3-9-6 (97) K Fallon 12/1: 11231: Chsd ldrs, imprvd to lead 2f **108**
out, rdn clr ent fnl 1f, styd on strongly, drvn out: fine start for new stable, prev with M Johnston: eff at 12/14f
on fast & soft grnd: v smart: a stiff/gall trk: only lightly rcd & open to useful improvement: see 5043 & 3076.
5135 **DISTANT PROSPECT 21** [6] A M Balding 7-9-7 (92) L Dettori 20/1: 4200302: Held up, gd hdwy 2f out, 2½   **99**
styd on well fnl 1f, but not quite rch wnr: gd run over this inadequate trip: see 3531 (2m5f).
5215 **BENDARSHAAN 14** [1] M Johnston 4-8-13 BL (84) J Fanning 20/1: 0505033: Trkd ldrs, short of room 2f   3   **87**
out, switched & styd on under press fnl 1f: gd run in first time blnks: see 5215.
5204 **JEEPSTAR 15** [4] T D Easterby 4-8-9 (80) G Gibbons 28/1: 2210124: Keen & led till 2f out, kept on   1¼   **81**
but not pace of ldrs: see 5204 (14f) & 4553.
5215 **CRUISE DIRECTOR 14** [7]4-8-13 (84) P Makin(5) 20/1: 1002455: Rear, styd on fnl 2f, nvr nrr.   hd   **85**
5037* **ARTISTIC STYLE 26** [21]4-9-10 (95) T Eaves(3) 14/1: 3111216: Rear, prog 2f out, no impress fnl 1f: 6   **90**

DONCASTER   SATURDAY 06.11.04   Lefthand, Flat, Galloping Track

top-weight: btr 5037 (10f).

5201 **ANOTHER CHOICE** 15 [2]3-8-5 t (82) P Cosgrave 14/1: 0416227: Held up, prog 2f out, sn no impress.		3	74
4775 **TENDER FALCON** 43 [9]4-8-11 (82) P Hanagan 12/1: 1021138: Chsd ldrs, btn 2f out: 6 wk abs.		1¾	72
5223 **PAGAN SKY** 14 [24]5-9-0 (85) Lisa Jones 25/1: 0064539: Rear, late prog, nvr dngrs.		3½	71
5215 **MILLVILLE** 14 [19]4-9-2 (87) P Robinson 12/1: 0545020: 10th: Rear, prog wide 3f out, nvr a factor.		¾	72
5215 **JABAAR** 14 [12]6-8-10 vis (81) T P Queally 33/1: 5002000: 11th: Nvr a factor: btr 4681 (10f gd).		2½	63
5223 **TURBO** 14 [20]5-9-5 p (90) S Carson 4/1 FAV: 4000020: 12th: Rear, prog wide 3f out, nvr nr ldrs:		5	67
gamble from 7/1: won this race from a 1lb lower mark last year: see 5223.			
5215* **TEMPSFORD** 14 [14]4-9-7 (92) S Sanders 8/1: 1-505010: 13th: Trkd ldr, wknd 2f out: well bckd.		3½	65
5068 **SHREDDED** 25 [17]4-8-7 t (78) K Darley 22/1: 0210630: 14th: Chsd ldrs, btn 2f out.		6	45
4986 **TALLDARKNANDSOME** 29 [13]5-8-5 bl (76) N Mackay 66/1: 20661-00: 15th: b g Efisio - Fleur du Val		1¼	42
(Valiyar) Nvr a factor: p.u. in a mdn hdle 11 days ago: ended '03 with a h'cap win: suited by 10f on firm, likes			
gd/soft & soft, polytrack: wears blnks: with N Littmoden.			
1 Nov'03 Redc 10 sft 77-71 E: 2 Jul'03 Newm 10 g/f 75-74 C: 2 Oct'02 Wind 10 g/s 84-78 C: 2 Jul'02 Ling 10 ap 77a- E:			
1 Jul'02 Brig 10 g/s 82-74 E: 1 Jul'02 Chep 10.1 gd 75-68 D: 2 Jun'02 Redc 9 fm 70-67 E:			
5215 **PROTECTIVE** 14 [11]3-8-8 (85) E Ahern 66/1: 1400300: 16th: Nvr btr than mid-div.		4	47
5261* **MITH HILL** 9 [15]3-8-1 (78) J F McDonald(3) 9/1: 01110: 17th: Chsd ldrs 9f, wknd: btr 5261.		½	39
4986* **GO TECH** 29 [18]4-9-5 (90) D Allan 20/1: 0421110: 18th: Nvr a factor: btr 4986.		shd	51
4695 **Bessemer** 48 [5]3-8-7 T(84) P Fessey 50/1:0		5255 **Bayadere** 10 [22]4-8-6 VIS(77) M Henry 100/1:0	
5043 **Dune Raider** 26 [23]3-8-6 (83) N Callan 33/1:0		4819 **Albanov** 40 [16]4-9-9 bl(94) D Holland 33/1:0	
5255 **Tip The Dip** 10 [8]4-9-0 t(85) J Fortune 14/1:0			
5102* **Always Waining** 22 [10]3-9-2 (93) A Culhane 33/1:0			
24 Ran Time 2m 43.16 (13.36) Owned: Mr Ashley Carr Trained: Malton			

5373   3.25 Totesport Com Nursery Handicap Stakes 2yo 0-85 (D2)   [92]
£7202 £2216 £1108   **7f str**   **Soft 105**   **-39 Slow**   Stands Side

5302 **BREAKING SHADOW** 5 [5] R A Fahey 2-8-11 P (75) P Hanagan 16/1: 3106001: Chsd ldrs, styd on			85
strongly to forge ahd cl home, drvn out: qck reapp & first time cheek pieces: eff at 5/7f: handles fast, acts on gd			
& soft grnd: likes a stiff/gall trk: tough, see 4306.			
4882 **ROYAL ORISSA** 37 [9] D Haydn Jones 2-9-1 t (79) L Dettori 5/1 FAV: 4530252: Trkd ldrs, went on		½	87
dist, worn down by wnr cl home: bckd from 7/1: eff at 6/7f on firm & soft grnd: mdn, shown enough to win.			
5035 **ZOMERLUST** 26 [7] J J Quinn 2-9-3 (81) R Winston 8/1: 3124423: Held up, fin strongly fnl 1f, not		½	88
btn far: tough & consistent: see 5035 (6f).			
5301* **GAME LAD** 5 [18] T D Easterby 2-9-5 (7ex) (83) D Allan 14/1: 4030214: Chsd ldrs stands side,		1¾	87
wandered & kept on under press fnl 1f: qck reapp & gd run racing away from rivals: see 5301.			
5318 **JOHN FORBES** 4 [4]2-8-6 (70) J Fanning 50/1: 0000005: Chsd ldrs, kept on under press fnl 1f: qck		shd	74
reapp: has tried blnks, btr without: mainly out of form since 2774.			
5192* **MAXAMILLION** 16 [12]2-9-3 (81) J F Egan 11/1: 5416: Chsd ldrs, onepcd fnl 1f: btr 5192.		2½	81
5091* **OLIGARCH** 22 [6]2-9-7 (85) D Holland 9/1: 20317: Led till dist, no extra: see 5091.		1	83
5213 **RED AFFLECK** 14 [13]2-9-4 (82) A McCarthy 12/1: 321048: Chsd ldrs, ev ch 2f out, wknd fnl 1f.		shd	79
5065 **ALONG THE NILE** 25 [19]2-8-5 (69) L Goncalves 33/1: 3600469: Chsd ldrs stands side, btn 1.5f out.		1¼	64
5250 **DANTES DIAMOND** 10 [24]2-8-5 (69) G Baker 50/1: 2550450: 10th: Chsd ldrs 5f: btr mdn.		hd	36
5126 **LESLINGTAYLOR** 21 [10]2-8-9 (73) T Hamilton(3) 20/1: 53150: 11th: Rear, styd on late despite not		shd	67
much room: see 4670.			
5126* **KNOCK BRIDGE** 21 [3]2-8-5 (69) T P Queally 12/1: 4203010: 12th: Front rank 5.5f: btr 5126.		3½	58
5131 **BEAUCHAMP TURBO** 21 [14]2-8-1 (65) N Mackay 33/1: 5560: 13th: Chsd ldrs, btn 2f out.		10	38
5302 **TORRENS** 5 [11]2-8-7 T (71) Dale Gibson 33/1: 410030: 14th: Nvr nr ldrs: tried t-strap.		1½	42
5131* **QAWAAFIL** 21 [22]2-8-7 (71) R Hills 14/1: 50010: 15th: Front rank 5f stands side.		2½	38
4913 **SHOSOLOSA** 35 [20]2-8-6 (70) J F McDonald(3) 14/1: 0223050: 16th: Chsd ldrs 4f stands side.		hd	36
5253 **ASHARON** 10 [1]2-8-4 (68) S Carson 20/1: 066050: 17th: Dwelt, al bhnd.		1¾	31
4490 **SUPERSTITIOUS** 57 [15]2-8-1 (65) C Catlin 33/1: 00600: 18th: Slow away, al bhnd: 8 wk abs.		nk	27
5126 **FORFEITER** 21 [16]2-8-12 VIS (76) K Darley 16/1: 262230: 19th: Al rear: visor.		shd	38
5078* **MEDITATION** 24 [17]2-8-7 (71) K Fallon 33/1: 00010: 20th: Chsd ldrs 5f, wknd & eased: tchd 14/1.		3	29
20 Ran Time 1m 33.29 (10.09) Owned: Mr G Morrill Trained: Malton			

5374   4.00 Merlin New Discovery 3 Handicap Stakes 3yo+ 86-100 (C1)   [96]
£13437 £4134 £2067   **2m110y**   **Soft 111**   **-59 Slow**   Inside

5335* **SENDINTANK** 3 [5] S C Williams 4-9-9 (6ex) (91) Martin Dwyer 10/11 FAV: 1111311: Trkd ldrs, styd			102
on under press to lead well ins fnl 1f, drvn out: hvly bckd, qck reapp, 10th win of this season: 12f/2m on fast, hvy			
& f/sand: goes well fresh: v prog stayer, started wng run from a mark of 50: credit to all concerned, see 5335.			
5271 **DR SHARP** 8 [2] T P Tate 4-8-12 (80) R Winston 14/1: 1061042: Tried to make all, worn down cl		½	90
home: well clr of rem: fine front running effort bhnd a most prog triple: see 4106.			
5135* **CONTACT DANCER** 21 [7] M Johnston 5-9-7 (89) R Ffrench 4/1: 2/56-6413: Trkd ldrs, left bhnd fnl		8	92
1.5f: see 5135.			
5334 **FLING** 3 [3] J R Fanshawe 3-8-10 (87) K Fallon 7/1: 5224534: Chsd ldrs 12f, sn btn: qck reapp.		9	82
5135 **TRANCE** 21 [6]4-9-3 (85) P Makin(5) 14/1: 1000305: Al rear: btr 4778 (14f).		3	77
5135 **HISTORIC PLACE** 21 [4]4-8-11 (79) S Sanders 8/1: 240306: Held up, al bhnd.		5	66
5068 **MASTER WELLS** 25 [1]3-8-3 (80) C Catlin 25/1: 0021407: Al strug rear: btr 4209.		4	63
7 Ran Time 5m 56.95(28.15) Owned: Steve Jones and Phil McGovern Trained: Newmarket			

A To Z Index

With the A To Z Index, you can see at a glance where each horse performed best, and pinpoint it's optimum distance, going and track preferences.

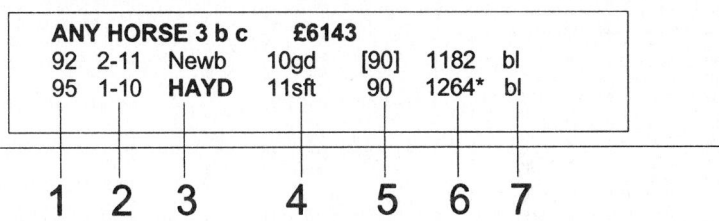

```
ANY HORSE 3 b c      £6143
92  2-11  Newb   10gd   [90]  1182   bl
95  1-10  HAYD   11sft   90   1264*  bl
```

1   2   3   4   5   6   7

The first line in **bold type** provides the horse's name, age, sex and total season win and place prize money.

1   Superform performance rating in that race.
a = all weather rating
Each time a horse runs, Superform's experienced handicappers award a rating which indicates the "worth" of the performance. The Scale used is 0-140, as used by the official handicappers.

2   Finishing position - Number of runners in race.   F=fell
U=unseated   R=refused   B=brought down   P=pulled up

3   Track name. **Bold type & Capitals** indicates a win.

4   Distance of the race and state of the ground on the day.

5   The official BHB rating going into the race is shown here. Figures [in brackets] denote non handicaps. This figure also includes any pounds out of the handicap. For example a horse rated officially 80 may be allotted 7-3 in a handicap. However, the race conditions state that the minimum weight to be carried is 7-12. Thus the horse is said to be 9lbs out of the handicap and in effect runs off an official mark of 89.

6   The race reference number * indicates a win + indicates a win in a time of +10 Fast or greater.

7   Any headgear worn. (Capitals indicate first time worn)
bl=blinkers   vis=visor   t=tongue strap   p=cheekpieces   hd=hood

A BEETOO 3 b f £0
40a	5-13	Ling	6ap [63]	219
42a	7-15	Ling	7ap [60]	263
36a	9-14	Ling	10ap 55	498

A BID IN TIME 3 b f £830
36a	8-9	Ling	5ap [48]	405
26a	8-11	Sout	5af 45	609
50	2-8	Folk	5g/s [48]	1268
41	9-14	Bath	5gd 48	1404
46	6-10	Hami	5g/s 49	1605
45	6-19	Beve	5g/s 47	2326
41	6-13	Newc	6sft 45	2683
37	8-14	Catt	6g/f 45	3018

A BIT OF FUN 3 ch g £1822
30a	5-12	Wolv	8.5af [35]	584
34a	2-12	Wolv	9.4af [35]	782
15a	7-9	Ling	8ap [35]	1185
43a	1-6	WOLV	9.4af [35]	1675*
33	8-13	Beve	8.5g/f [45]	1947
7	11-15	Beve	8.5g/s 40	3182

A DOUBLE EWE BEE 3 b f £0
0	12-12	Wolv	8.6ap	5230
32	9-17	Yarm	8g/s	5348

A LITTLE BIT YARIE 3 b g £2260
85	3-13	Thir	5sft 84	1229
50	7-9	Hayd	5g/s 84	1344
62	4-6	Hami	5gd [84]	1387
59	7-11	Hami	6gd 80	1745 VIS
10	11-11	Ches	5.1g/s 77	2747 vis
40	12-12	Redc	5sft [73]	5305 vis

A MONK SWIMMING 3 br g £440
28	4-7	Muss	8g/f 35	2613
40	3-14	Folk	12gd 32	3383
26	7-14	Yarm	11.5g/f 35	3714

A ONE 4 b g £27206
41a	10-16	Sout	7af [45]	61
44a	4-8	Ling	7ap [45]	1413
53	3-9	Ling	7g/f [51]	1984
59	1-16	CHEP	7.1gd [51]	2369*
72	1-7	WIND	8.3fm 56	2787*
77	1-8	WIND	10fm 62	2973*
59	8-20	Chep	7.1g/s 61	3088
84	1-10	SAND	10g/f 73	3336*
86	1-17	WIND	10fm 73	3477+
81	5-8	Wind	8.3fm 85	3641
64	10-15	Bath	11.7g/f 83	3964
91	7-8	Wind	10g/s [83]	4220
1	17-17	Wind	10g/f 83	5050
36a	11-12	Wolv	5.1ap [70]	5362

A QUI LE TOUR 2 b c £0
39	10-11	Wind	5gd	3160
22a	8-8	Ling	5ap	3600
52	8-13	Warw	7.1g/s	4996

A TEEN 5 ch h £3842
51a	10-15	Ling	7ap [55]	117
29a	11-13	Ling	6ap [52]	271
49a	5-13	Ling	6ap [52]	340
50a	2-13	Ling	6ap 49	451
37a	7-13	Ling	6ap [50]	544
53a	1-13	LING	6ap 50	740*
52a	6-14	Ling	6ap 53	897
57	6-20	Wind	6g/s 63	1255
26	13-13	Yarm	6ap 62	1726
30	16-16	Good	6gd 60	2023
59	6-18	Donc	6gd 58	2752
32	10-17	Wind	6fm 57	2975
48	10-14	Leic	6g/f 57	3213
51	10-15	Newc	6gd 54	3424
31	5-9	Newm	6gd 54	3924
54	6-11	Sand	5sft 54	4070
47	7-20	Chep	6.1g/s 50	4368
14	18-20	Newc	6gd 50	4408
43	8-19	Bath	5.7sft 48	5176
43a	6-12	Wolv	7.1ap [52]	5358

A TWO 4 ch f £0
0	14-15	Sout	16af 48	67
0	10-11	Sout	11af [44]	191

A WOMAN IN LOVE 4 gr f £17306
53a	6-16	Ling	7ap 56	55
55a	4-15	Ling	7ap [55]	117
49a	11-16	Ling	7ap 55	144
52a	6-12	Ling	7ap 53	1024
67	1-10	BRIG	7g/f 58	1941*
71	1-16	BRIG	7fm 63	2258*
79	1-8	BRIG	8g/f 69	2432*
84	1-13	LING	7.6g/f 72	2587*
82	4-13	Asco	7gd 79	3068
76	7-9	Asco	8gd 79	3465
43	15-15	Brig	8fm 79	3694

AAHGOWANGOWAN 5 b m £11874
46	12-20	Ripo	5gd 60	1179 t
55	7-13	Newc	5sft 60	1276 t
56	5-13	Hami	5g/f 58	2320 t
66	2-6	Hami	5gd 58	2712 t
65	1-8	HAMI	5g/s 58	2830* t
64	5-10	Ayr	5gd 63	3150 t
52	9-12	Newc	5gd 63	3427 t
56	5-10	Hami	5g/s [62]	4010 t
67	2-9	Thir	5g/s 62	4210 t
54	11-26	Ayr	5g/s 63	4618 t
43	15-19	York	5gd 63	4989 t

AASTRAL MAGIC 2 b f £7685
70	1-19	KEMP	6g/f	1911*
87	1-6	WIND	6fm	2783*
84	4-6	Wind	6fm [87]	3800
56	6-8	Bath	5.7g/s [87]	4198

ABANINETOES 3 b f £0
26a	7-10	Wolv	7af [44]	4
8a	11-16	Sout	8af 41	86

ABBAJABBA 8 b g £1644
37a	10-10	Wolv	6af 82	834
71	10-22	Donc	6gd 85	921
68	11-20	Kemp	6gd 83	1138
23	13-15	Pont	6hvy 83	1251
67	2-8	Hami	6g/s [78]	3880
66	8-19	Ripo	6g/s 78	3937
75	5-13	Redc	7fm [74]	4341
67	9-11	Muss	7.1g/s 72	5144
74	6-16	Redc	6sft 70	5304
50a	12-12	Wolv	7.1ap [70]	5340

ABBEYGATE 2 b c £0
67a	6-12	Ling	10ap	120
48	10-15	Nott	10gd 64	3108
11	11-12	Beve	9.9g/s 64	3854
58a	10-15	Ling	12ap [64]	4111
48	11-20	Catt	12gd 60	4966 T
2	10-11	Catt	13.8sft [55]	5129 t

ABBIEJO 7 b m £0
28a	6-12	Wolv	5af [40]	889 P
35a	5-12	Wolv	7af 40	956 p
15a	6-8	Sout	8af [40]	1200 p
23a	6-9	Wolv	7af [40]	1266
21	7-10	Warw	6.1g/s [40]	1327
3	14-17	Bath	10.2sft 30	1541

ABELARD 3 b g £2298
59	6-10	Hayd	5g/s 67	2227
63	5-16	Leic	5g/f 65	2400
34	10-11	Donc	6g/s 65	3379
56	5-8	Redc	6g/f 62	3808
35	15-17	Beve	5g/f 60	4603
62	2-15	Newc	5fm 56	4870 VIS
44a	9-12	Wolv	6ap [57]	5155 vis
56a	3-11	Wolv	5.1ap [54]	5363

ABERDEEN 2 b c £2490
74a	6-8	Ling	7ap	4176
81	2-8	Good	6g/f	4540
97	4-5	Epso	8.5gd	4906

ABERDEEN PARK 2 gr f £4335
61	5-14	Bath	5sft	1538
47	10-13	Newb	6g/f	1760
67	8-11	Ling	5gd	2395
68	4-10	Bath	5.7fm	2666
58	5-9	Warw	7.1g/s 68	4666
74	2-13	Leic	6gd 68	4697
71	2-17	Ling	7g/f 66	4894
71	8-16	Good	7gd 69	5031
67	3-20	Newb	6hvy 68	5225

ABERDOVEY 2 b f £4624
71	5-10	Newm	6gd	1887
79	1-12	REDC	6g/f	2119*
80	3-6	Ling	6gd 78	3022
78	5-21	Donc	6.5fm 77	4457
70	10-16	Newm	7g/f 77	4913

ABIDE 2 ch f £1620
77	6-16	Sali	7gd	4329
80	2-15	Kemp	7g/f	4710
73	6-19	Leic	7gd	5045

ABIGAIL ADAMS 3 ch f £0
49	8-8	Sand	8.1g/s	4101
7	10-13	Leic	10g/f	4453

ABINGTON ANGEL 2 ch f £3780
70a	7-11	Ling	8ap 78	54 t
59	15-20	Newb	7g/f 78	1761
47	13-14	Nott	8.2g/f 75	2153
58	8-12	Kemp	9sft 70	4032 H Bl
78a	1-9	LING	12ap [67]	4315* h bl
42	14-16	Good	12gd [75]	4745 h bl

ABLAJ 3 ch g £272
48	8-16	Leic	8g/s 60	1359
55	4-9	Thir	7g/f [57]	2218 VIS
51	4-8	Brig	7g/f 53	2434 vis
52a	5-15	Ling	12ap 51	2741

ABLE BAKER CHARLIE 5 b g £22770
96	4-18	Good	8g/f 91	1812
97	2-31	Asco	8g/f 91	2489
88	8-18	Newb	8g/f 93	3265
81	16-32	Newm	9g/f 93	4916

ABLE CHARLIE 2 ch g £1138
80	2-18	Donc	6g/s	3376
69	6-14	Thir	7g/s	3831
50	7-13	Thir	6g/f	4590

ABLE MIND 4 b g £1375
39	12-13	Hami	6g/f 69	2315
17	10-11	Newc	10.1g/s 65	2726
49	6-10	Hayd	7.1g/s 62	3137
61	3-15	Carl	7.9g/f 57	4346
61	3-17	Ayr	7.2sft 57	5063

ABOUSTAR 4 b g £0
35a	5-16	Sout	8af [40]	442
15a	8-11	Sout	7af [40]	771
25a	5-12	Sout	6af [35]	982
47	5-14	Newc	5g/f [35]	4404

ABOVE BOARD 8 b g £2508
14a	10-15	Sout	6af [43]	172
24a	13-15	Sout	7af [38]	253 P
32a	5-10	Sout	6af [35]	352
17a	8-12	Sout	6af [35]	377 bl
59a	2-9	Sout	6af [35]	487 t
24a	8-15	Sout	6af 35	550 t
44a	3-13	Wolv	6af [45]	582 t p
0	14-15	Sout	6af [45]	773 t
52a	1-10	SOUT	6af [45]	907* t
23a	14-16	Sout	5ap 50	1046 t
20a	6-9	Sout	6af [50]	1194 t
15	14-17	Nott	6.1sft 35	1606
6	11-11	Redc	6sft [35]	1662 t

ABRACADABJAR 6 b g £0
9a	8-9	Sout	11af 30	331

ABRAXAS 5 b g £596
53a	2-16	Sout	5af 50	183 p
37a	6-8	Wolv	5af 53	274 p
48a	5-11	Sout	5af 52	418 p
21a	9-9	Ling	5ap 52	435 p
13a	7-8	Sout	5af [51]	742 p
18	16-17	Kemp	5sft 40	944 p
51	7-8	Folk	5g/s [40]	1269 p
7	9-10	Kemp	5hvy [40]	1644 p

ABRAXAS ANTELOPE 2 b c £30793
90	1-6	HAMI	6g/f	2316*
106	1-7	DONC	6g/s	3221*
104	3-11	York	6g/s	4022
102	2-6	Ripo	6gd [100]	4280

ABROGATE 2 b g £1094

49a	3-10	Sout	8af	52	189
11a	12-12	Ling	8ap	50	402
49a	2-8	Sout	8af	48	490
46a	4-12	Sout	8af	49	656
39	5-8	Muss	8gd	49	1798
36	9-16	Thir	8g/f	47	3414 P

ABSENT FRIENDS 7 b g £804

23	8-8	Beve	5sft	[98]	1626
92	6-15	Hayd	5g/f	95	1917
79	13-17	Muss	5fm	94	2082
86	6-11	Sand	5g/s	92	2894
74	10-12	York	5g/s	92	3073
88	10-11	Beve	5g/s	[89]	4238
77	8-16	Hayd	5fm	86	4382
9	9-12	Leic	5g/f	[86]	4454
84	4-12	Yarm	5.2g/s	83	4585
81	7-10	Beve	5g/f	[83]	4718
26	11-11	Hayd	5sft	83	4780

ABSINTHER 7 b g £7165

40	8-11	Folk	12g/f	46	2273
49	2-16	Folk	12fm	45	2718
55	1-7	**BRIG**	11.9fm	45	2836*
52	4-15	Wind	11.6fm	50	3481
51	3-14	Brig	11.9fm	50	3674
50	3-16	Wind	11.6gd	49	3829
11	12-19	Brig	9.9sft	49	4145
43	8-15	Folk	12g/f	[49]	4374

ABSOLUT EDGE 2 ch g £0

10	11-11	Warw	5g/f		2911
5a	6-6	Sout	5af		3093

ABSOLUT POWER 3 ch c £1408

98	3-7	Colo	11gd		3663

ABSOLUTE UTOPIA 10 b g £8060

62a	1-12	LING	10ap	[63]	267*
47a	7-10	Ling	10ap	[63]	370
59a	2-10	Ling	10ap	[63]	540
65a	2-10	Ling	10ap	[63]	738
65a	3-14	Ling	10ap	63	803
65a	4-9	Ling	10ap	63	903
61a	1-6	LING	10ap	[63]	972*
63	1-10	BATH	10.2gd	[63]	1402*
0	P-11	Bath	10.2fm	63	1899

ABSOLUTELY FAB 3 ch f £0

29	14-14	Yarm	7fm	[35]	2148
2a	14-15	Ling	12ap	35	2741
11a	10-11	Sout	8af	[31]	3091

ABSOLUTELY SOAKED 3 b f £1120

69	5-17	Leic	10g/s		1019
48	6-10	Pont	10sft	64	1427
47	8-20	Wind	11.6sft	62	1648
44	9-13	Yarm	10.1gd	59	3492
46	10-11	Yarm	10.1gd	[57]	3875
48	2-18	Leic	7gd	[54]	4698 BL
33	11-18	Yarm	6g/s	47	5354 bl

ABSOLUTELYTHEBEST 2 b c £8857

72a	4-12	Ling	10ap		116
77a	1-14	LING	10ap	[71]	367*
83	2-11	Ripo	12.3gd	73	1174
88	2-14	York	11.9g/s	78	1708
41	6-6	Good	12g/f	82	2021
84	4-5	Sali	14.1fm	82	2418 VIS
77	5-12	Wind	11.6gd	80	3161
58	8-9	Sand	14g/s	80	3893
61	9-12	Good	11gd	80	4749

ABSTRACT FOLLY 2 b g £270

58	4-11	Thir	7fm		4375
70	4-11	Newc	7fm		4863

ABUELOS 5 b g £241

39a	3-15	Ling	7ap	[40]	411
42a	4-11	Ling	8ap	[45]	535
34a	10-14	Ling	6ap	[45]	652
5a	12-12	Ling	7ap	[45]	1074
45	5-8	Catt	15.8g/f	[43]	3666
13	10-12	Hami	8.3g/s	[43]	4007
28	6-8	Hami	9.2g/s	[43]	4133
40	6-15	Thir	8fm	[40]	4379
36	5-15	Carl	9.3fm	[40]	4505

ACADEMY 8 ch g £2169

49a	8-14	Ling	16ap	58	107
59	2-9	Newc	16.1gd	56	1870
17	11-13	Pont	17.1g/f	57	2276
24	9-10	Thir	16fm	57	3611
61	2-14	Warw	16.2g/f	55	4423
0	P-19	Catt	15.8g/f	58	4675

ACCA LARENTIA 3 gr f £562

23	14-15	Ripo	10g/f	57	1976
35	10-11	Redc	8fm	52	2296
52	3-8	Thir	7sft	48	269ᴼ
29	10-14	Beve	7.5g/s	[50]	3177
14	9-12	Pont	8gd	50	3679
43	6-8	Catt	7g/f	[47]	4440
42	5-14	Redc	10fm	47	4560
40	6-16	Nott	10gd	45	4857
29a	9-12	Wolv	9.5ap	[45]	5209

ACCELERATION IRE 4 b g £3614

67	1-12	NEWC	16.1sft	60	965* vis
60	6-10	Muss	16g/f	65	1093 vis
39	13-14	Hami	12.1gd	63	1389 vis
1	11-11	Muss	16g/s	62	5335 p

ACCENDERE 3 b g £4191

30a	12-15	Ling	7ap		670
50a	14-15	Ling	7ap		875
57	5-12	Warw	7.1gd		1125
40	7-14	Warw	8.1sft	52	1529
59	1-18	SALI	7fm	52	2292*
50	7-16	Ling	7gd	55	3024
58	3-20	Chep	7.1gd	55	4488

ACCEPTING 7 b g £1534

39	5-13	Pont	18hvy	53	1069 BL
4	13-13	Pont	21.6hvy	51	1252 bl
56	2-12	Warw	19.1fm	51	2577 bl
49	4-6	Muss	16g/f	54	2807 bl
39	14-14	Pont	17.1g/f	53	4936 bl

ACCLAMATION 4 £26400

113	5-14	Sha	5g/f		210

ACE 3 b c £36735

118	1-5	LEOP	8g/f		4020*
106	5-11	Asco	8g/f		4801

ACE CLUB 3 ch g £1352

71	5-14	Ches	6.1g/s	75	1570
60	9-13	Hayd	6g/f	73	1881
65a	7-11	Ling	6ap	70	2841
65	4-7	Brig	6fm	67	3693
67	2-7	Brig	5.3sft	[64]	4169
52	11-20	Ling	6g/f	64	4317
55	12-17	Ling	6gd	64	4740
41	16-20	Wind	6g/s	63	4946

ACE COMING 3 b g £7793

35	12-14	Donc	10.3gd	57	923 bl
56	3-16	Redc	8sft	55	1147 bl
64	1-11	NEWC	8sft	55	1395* bl
74	1-8	HAMI	9.2g/s	61	1603* bl
53	13-14	Hami	8.3gd	67	1748 bl
21	8-8	Hami	9.2fm	70	3250
45	10-12	Hayd	8.1gd	69	3738 bl
7	16-17	Hami	9.2g/s	66	4008 bl
40	14-17	Newc	8fm	63	4867 bl
35	14-17	Redc	10sft	61	5307 bl

ACE IN THE HOLE 4 br f £0

0	20-20	Warw	10.9gd	46	1128 P
11	17-18	Nott	8.2gd	[45]	1992 p

ACE MA VAHRA 6 b m £4838

35a	6-8	Sout	8af	[45]	577
9a	7-8	Sout	8af	45	597
29a	6-9	Sout	7af	[45]	639
49a	1-10	SOUT	8af	45	677*
18a	6-8	Sout	11af	[40]	722
14a	13-15	Sout	8af	48	1028 P
31	12-17	Nott	6.1sft	47	1606 BL
32	10-20	Beve	5g/f	[45]	1948 bl
38a	5-12	Wolv	7af	47	2049
35	9-19	Beve	5g/s	43	2326 bl
42	3-15	Leic	6g/f	43	2398 bl
17	14-19	Beve	5gd	40	2657 bl
32a	6-16	Sout	6af	46	2806 bl

ACE OF HEARTS 5 b g £30069

66	14-24	Donc	8gd	84	928
79	5-13	Wind	8.3g/s	[83]	1057
68	15-17	Sand	8.1g/s	81	1351
83	2-10	Beve	8.5g/f	79	1833
88	1-7	NEWM	8fm	[80]	2091+
93	1-8	DONC	8g/f	83	2425*
93	1-8	PONT	8g/f	86	2606+
91	9-15	Sand	8.1g/s	91	2915
68	13-13	Ripo	8gd	91	4279
93	3-10	Newm	8g/f	[90]	4890
75	16-22	Newm	8sft	90	5103
94	9-13	Newm	8g/s	90	5284

ACHILLES RAINBOW 4 ch g £0

22a	9-12	Wolv	8.5af	[39]	47
43a	6-16	Sout	7af	[39]	66
0	15-15	Sout	8af	39	84
36a	4-13	Ling	10ap	[40]	539
1a	12-12	Ling	8ap	[40]	649
51a	6-10	Ling	10ap	[40]	738
0	S-10	Ling	10ap	[40]	784

ACOLA 4 ch f £0

54	8-15	Beve	9.9sft	60	1307
39a	10-14	Ling	10ap	56	1618
31	13-16	Yarm	10.1fm	54	2146 P
27	10-14	Yarm	8gd	52	3363 VIS

ACOMB 4 b g £9344

54	12-18	Catt	8gd	65	998
60	6-12	Thir	7g/s	64	1215
51	9-12	Hayd	8.1g/f	62	1485
70	1-18	THIR	8g/f	62	1972*
82	1-12	SAND	8.1g/s	67	2129*
69	7-11	Hami	8.3g/f	75	2317
65	8-15	Epso	10.1gd	[77]	3216
69	6-8	Hayd	8.1fm	77	3797
57	9-10	Newc	7fm	[75]	4869

ACORAZADO 4 b g £7494

51a	5-16	Ling	7ap	53	55
57a	1-16	SOUT	8af	53	94* bl e
42a	5-15	Sout	6af	56	168 bl e
55a	3-16	Sout	7af	56	208
55a	5-16	Ling	7ap	56	270
50a	7-15	Ling	7ap	[56]	366
60a	2-14	Ling	7ap	55	499 e
55a	7-13	Ling	7ap	58	565 e
65a	1-12	LING	8ap	58	607*
55a	6-11	Ling	8ap	64	714
65a	2-12	Ling	8ap	[64]	878 bl e
51	7-19	Yarm	7g/f	55	1132 bl e
63a	4-10	Wolv	7af	[64]	1319 bl e
35	6-16	Nott	8.2hvy	53	5347 bl

ACROPOLIS 3 b c £64338

121	4-19	Long	12g/f		4956

ACT OF THE PACE 4 b f £8555

56	4-8	Hami	11.1gd		1390
76	1-4	RIPO	12.3g/f		2484*
81	2-8	Hayd	11.9gd	76	2881
71	6-10	Hami	13fm	78	3249
82	3-17	Newm	14.8gd	78	4196

ACTION FIGHTER 3 ch c £1363

64a	13-13	Ling	6ap	98	235
51a	10-10	Ling	7ap	93	262
85a	3-8	Wolv	8.5af	[93]	360 P
64a	14-16	Sout	7af	88	419 p

ACTIVE ACCOUNT 7 b g £2773

69a	2-9	Wolv	8.5af	66	809
71a	2-7	Wolv	8.5af	66	942
61a	5-10	Wolv	8.5af	69	1322
59	6-12	Hayd	8.1g/f	66	1485
63	6-13	Carl	7.9fm	63	2447
64	3-8	Nott	10g/s	61	2929

37 9-10 Hayd 10.5g/s 61 3139
53 8-8 Leic 10g/f 60 3514
43 14-19 Leic 10g/f 59 4456
39 6-12 Pont 10fm [57] 4757 BL

ACTIVE ASSET 2 ch c £6595
86 2-11 Yarm 6g/f 1727
85 1-14 YARM 7gd 3489*
91 2-4 Sand 7.1g/f [85] 3859
0 8-9 Newm 10g/s [89] 5281

ACTRICE 4 b f £49148
112 1-5 SAIN 10.5g/s 2143*
104 4-10 Asco 8g/f 2487

ACUZIO 3 b c £0
56 6-8 Hayd 10.5g/f 1489
75 6-9 Hayd 8.1g/f 1882
50 8-14 Hayd 8.1g/s 2231
57 4-8 Ayr 7.2gd [65] 2506
53 8-10 Hayd 8.1g/s 63 3138
52 8-13 Ling 7g/f 61 3604
49 5-10 Hayd 8.1g/s 58 3906
17 8-12 Chep 10.2hvy 55 4708

AD VALOREM 2 b f £134595
117 1-6 CURR 6g/s 4736*
121 1-9 NEWM 6g/f 4888*

ADAIKALI 3 b c £18130
42 7-15 Thir 7g/s 1473
86 2-9 Hayd 8.1g/f 1882
91 1-12 PONT 10g/f 79 2277*
91 2-6 Sand 10g/f 86 3358
80 9-10 Newm 10g/f 87 3615
91 4-8 Pont 10fm 87 4755
93 2-19 York 7.9gd 87 4987

ADALAR 3 b r g £2334
52a 11-11 Ling 8ap [85] 273
55a 9-16 Ling 12ap 80 475
72a 9-14 Ling 10ap 75 625
1a 11-11 Ling 10ap 73 716 VIS
57a 11-14 Ling 12ap 73 731
68a 6-9 Ling 10ap 68 903
58 10-14 Nott 10g/s 67 1777
62 7-14 Leic 10g/f 67 1828
47 10-14 Ches 12.3gd 63 2285
60 4-9 Yarm 10.1fm 60 2866
54 7-11 Bath 8gd 60 3142
59 2-14 Chep 8.1gd 58 3733
62 2-12 Brig 8g/f 58 3986
39 9-19 Chep 8.1g/s [58] 4366

ADALPOUR 5 b g £2044
54a 1-10 WOLV 12af 50 243*
27a 7-10 Wolv 16.2af 52 358
23a 8-12 Wolv 12ap 52 469

ADANTINO 4 b g £6959
45a 12-16 Ling 7ap 54 55
49a 5-15 Ling 7ap [51] 216
58a 3-15 Ling 7ap [48] 263
49a 6-13 Ling 6ap [48] 340
51a 3-12 Sout 7af [52] 416
42a 4-7 Wolv 9.4af [52] 509
59a 1-12 LING 8ap [52] 536* bl
60a 3-16 Ling 7ap 54 600 bl
60a 3-10 Ling 7ap [57] 765 bl
52 6-16 Ling 7g/f 54 2063 bl
54 3-13 Yarm 6g/f 53 2347 bl
60 1-14 LING 6gd 54 3289* bl
56 6-17 Wind 6fm 57 3643 bl
51 8-15 Bath 5.7g/f 57 3966 bl
50a 6-14 Ling 7ap [57] 5294 bl

ADAPTABLE 3 b f £0
54 8-18 Wind 8.3g/f 1810
31 9-11 Chep 10.2gd [75] 2196

ADEEBA 3 b f £0
32a 6-9 Wolv 9.4af 1340
43a 13-14 Ling 10ap 55 2064

ADEES DANCER 3 b f £0
34 10-11 Beve 8.5sft 1304
40 11-11 Beve 9.9g/f 1835
52 5-12 Beve 9.9gd 58 2893
49 8-20 Beve 16.2gd 55 3312

4 16-16 Thir 12g/f 55 3573

ADIEMUS 6 b g £32681
106 1-12 NAD 10g/f 98 789* vis

ADJAWAR 6 b g £0
53 8-8 Newm 10g/f [83] 3945
9 18-19 Hayd 10.5g/s 80 4766
18 8-11 Catt 12sft [75] 5128

ADJIRAM 8 b g £1847
23a 3-12 Ling 10ap [30] 654
30a 5-15 Ling 12ap [30] 707
26a 4-12 Wolv 9.4af [30] 782 VIS
38 1-5 BRIG 8gd [30] 1546* vis
40a 2-10 Ling 12ap [30] 1714 vis
21 12-16 Folk 12fm 37 2718 vis

ADMIRAL 3 b c £40836
75 9-19 Newb 8gd 1236
85 1-6 GOOD 12g/f 76 2021*
87 3-13 Hayd 11.9gd 80 2238
90 1-17 ASCO 12g/f 82 2519*
77 11-16 Good 12fm 86 3534

ADMIRAL COMPTON 3 ch c £7716
75 2-10 Good 8gd 2378
79 2-14 Warw 7.1g/f 2907
76 3-13 Nott 8.2g/f [77] 4847
82a 1-12 LING 8ap [77] 4975* VIS

ADMITTANCE 2 b f £0
47 8-18 Donc 6g/s 3376
54 8-14 Hayd 6gd 3735
46 11-18 Ripo 6g/s 3939
45 11-14 Thir 7g/s 4204
44 10-16 Beve 7.5g/f 58 4597

ADOBE 9 b g £5040
12 15-15 Warw 8.1sft 69 1530
62 7-13 Ripo 8g/f 69 2010
67 3-8 Wind 8.3g/f 67 2448
67 4-11 Warw 8.1fm 67 2600
67 4-8 Bath 8fm 67 2665
70 2-11 Bath 8gd 66 3142
60 9-12 Ayr 8gd 66 3328
57 7-9 Nott 8.2g/f [67] 3423
67 4-8 Thir 8fm 66 3608
56 8-12 Leic 8fm 65 3813
62 5-12 Brig 8g/f 65 3986
56 10-19 York 7.9g/f 64 4399
63 7-16 Thir 8g/f 64 4592
46 11-17 Warw 8.1g/s 62 4668
41 13-17 Nott 8.2gd 60 4862
57a 1-13 WOLV 8.6ap [50] 5212*
51a 5-12 Wolv 8.6ap [54] 5337

ADORATA 3 b f £8407
34a 10-15 Sout 6af 795
33a 11-12 Ling 6ap 1044
57 7-13 Nott 6.1sft 1464
66 3-15 Leic 6g/f 1829
65 2-14 Redc 7fm 63 2295
51 12-20 Newb 7fm 64 2650
68 2-11 Carl 6.9gd 64 2936
61a 3-8 Sout 6af 64 3092
57 9-16 Epso 8.5gd 68 3219
69 2-11 Newm 8gd [67] 3923
67a 1-10 SOUT 8af [63] 4042*
59 12-20 York 7.9gd 69 4321
65 7-17 Leic 10gd 67 5062
49 11-15 Nott 8.2hvy 67 5191
65 6-18 Newm 8sft 65 5272

ADORATION 2 b c £3096
84 3-8 York 5sft 1670
83 2-10 Donc 6g/f 2077
75 5-8 Epso 6fm 2251
75 12-13 Newm 7g/f 80 3065
76 8-11 Hayd 8.1fm 78 4387
24 10-20 Newb 6hvy 73 5225

ADRIATIC ADVENTURE 2 ch f £0
5a 9-9 Wolv 6af 247
12a 10-11 Wolv 6af [45] 466
3a 12-12 Ling 8ap [40] 538

AEGEAN MIST 4 ch f £313
45 4-10 Ripo 6gd [40] 4788

AESCULUS 2 b f £24484
75a 1-8 LING 6ap 49*
32 12-16 Leic 8g/s 72 1359
60 5-17 Yarm 7g/f [70] 1729
69 3-8 Bath 5.7fm 67 2034
18 20-20 Newb 7g/f 67 2314
68 3-12 Beve 9.9gd 67 2893
74 2-14 Yarm 8gd 67 3363
76 1-15 BRIG 8fm 68 3694*

AETHELING 3 b f £0
0 9-10 Ling 12ap 4314

AFADAN 5 br g £0
58a 15-16 Ling 12ap 79 218

AFLEET ALEX 2 b c £167598
118 2-14 Lone 8.5Fast 5310

AFRASHAD 2 ch c £4303
111a1-7 LING 6ap 3196+

AFRICAN BREEZE 2 b f £5041
65 7-10 Thir 5g/f 1764
83 4-12 Beve 5g/f 2165
80 1-7 REDC 5gd 2547*
83 4-7 Hayd 6gd 2883
82 5-10 Thir 5fm 81 3607
68 11-21 Donc 6.5fm 80 4457
55 8-10 Ayr 8gd 80 4655

AFRICAN DAWN 6 b g £0
49 6-11 Sali 12fm 53 2293 t
29 14-16 Folk 12fm 52 2718 t
40 9-13 Warw 12.6gd 50 3056 t
39a 4-6 Sout 16af 46 3397 t P

AFRICAN DREAM 3 b g £95405
75a 3-12 Ling 8ap 623
84a 1-11 LING 8ap 696*
106 1-9 KEMP 9sft [81] 947*
116 1-15 NEWB 8gd 94 1206*
115 1-5 SAND 10g/s [94] 1316*
110 1-3 CHES 10.3gd[113] 1595*
105 10-12 Sand 10g/s [113] 2916
111 4-9 Mais 10sft [113] 3316
108 7-12 Sali 8gd [112] 3886

AFRICAN EMPEROR 2 gr g £0
18 6-6 Yarm 6g/f 2851
53a 9-11 Ling 8ap 4738
36a 8-13 Wolv 6ap 4980

AFRICAN GIFT 2 b f £901
71 3-10 Hayd 6g/s 2228
62 7-8 Asco 6gd 3071
64 6-7 Redc 7g/f 3770
62 7-12 Muss 5g/f 68 4172
18 11-14 Ayr 6sft 66 5035

AFRICAN SAHARA 5 br h £44031
69a 6-12 Wolv 9.4af 78 513 t
80a 1-14 LING 10ap 76 625* t
66a 11-14 Ling 10ap 79 758 t
83a 1-11 LING 8ap [79] 800* t
75a 6-12 Ling 8ap 80 888 t
79 6-13 Wind 8.3g/s [85] 1057 t
64 15-20 Newb 10gd 85 1235 t
59 17-17 Sand 8.1g/s 82 1351 t
78 6-13 Donc 8gd [80] 2753 t
80 9-20 Newm 8fm 79 3001 t
83 3-9 Donc 8gd 79 3225 t
83 4-9 Asco 8gd 78 3465 t
79 3-8 Newm 8g/f 78 3583 t
83 1-16 REDC 8g/f 78 3768* t
84 4-10 Sand 8.1g/s 82 4067 t
85 2-13 Wind 8.3g/s 82 4221 t
88 2-15 Hayd 8.1g/f 82 4352 t

AFRICAN SPUR 3 b g £1565
64a 8-13 Wolv 6af 75 113
42a 9-9 Sout 7af 72 193
50a 9-10 Sout 5af 69 390
66a 7-16 Sout 5af 69 461
64a 2-9 Sout 5af [66] 533
50a 2-11 Sout 5af [64] 775
1 15-19 Newc 6sft 73 967 T

45 10-13 Redc 7sft [70] 1142 t
42 14-16 Newc 6sft 70 1277 t
33 19-20 Newc 6sft 65 1393 t
29 13-13 Muss 7.1gd 65 1553 t
39 16-20 Thir 6gd 63 1638 t
2 19-20 Thir 5g/f 58 1765 t
31 6-13 Yarm 5g/f 55 2347
51 5-14 Muss 7.1g/f 51 2615
30a 10-16 Sout 6af 51 2720 P
38 10-13 Muss 8gd [49] 2967
3a 11-13 Ling 10ap [49] 3025
36 7-9 Catt 5g/f [47] 3353
53 4-7 York 6g/f [47] 3436 VIS
35 6-18 Thir 6fm 47 3609 vis
26 16-20 Redc 6g/f 45 3767 vis

AFRICAN STAR 2 b c £0
67a 5-14 Sout 7af 98
57a 6-16 Ling 7ap 290
51 5-7 Warw 10.9fm 57 2576
52 6-13 Yarm 11.5fm 55 2868
51a 4-14 Ling 10ap 53 3449
0 11-12 Good 9.9sft 52 4268 P
2 9-10 Brig 9.9fm 50 4763 p

AFRICAN STORM 2 b c £2748
63 5-6 Sand 5gd 2364
76 2-7 Ling 5g/f 2738
79 2-8 Kemp 5g/f 2858
50 7-11 Sali 6g/f [81] 3863
58 6-6 Good 5sft 74 4187
58 9-12 Bath 5sft [71] 5169

AFRICAN SUNSET 4 b g £848
60 3-6 Ayr 10g/f 1894
53 5-6 York 10.4g/f 2356

AFTER ALL 2 grf £1415
60a 5-9 Ling 5ap [62] 76
64a 2-9 Ling 6ap 62 105
57a 6-10 Ling 6ap [64] 258 BL
58a 3-5 Ling 5ap [64] 289
46a 5-7 Ling 6ap [61] 706

AFTER LENT 3 b g £0
67 8-12 Leic 8fm 2106
39 6-8 Hami 9.2g/f 3592
36 9-10 Newc 7hvy 4216

AFTER THE SHOW 3 b c £1204
63 6-16 Kemp 6g/s 69 1116
58 10-14 Bath 5g/f 69 1404
68 6-11 Newb 6gd 68 1734
60 7-9 Sand 5g/f 67 2387
70 2-18 Hayd 6gd 66 3737
59 8-9 Wind 5g/f 69 3976
50 15-20 Wind 6g/s 69 4946
40 15-20 Yarm 7sft 67 5256

AFTER THE SNOW 2 b f £0
28 16-19 Ling 6g/f 4895
43 5-17 Redc 7g/s 5105

AGAIN JANE 4 ch f £0
0 7-7 Sout 12af 679

AGATA 3 b f £16099
114 3-7 Long 10gd 2001
113 5-17 Chan 12.5g/s 2460

AGE OF KINGS 2 b c £1315
86 3-10 Sali 5g/f 1717
95 6-15 Asco 5g/f 2472

AGENT KENSINGTON 2 b f £5424
74 2-15 Wind 5gd 1380
65 2-7 Folk 5sft 1574
70 5-19 Newb 6g/f 2310
69 3-17 Nott 6.1gd 2927
74 2-9 Sand 5g/f 3355
70 4-12 Chep 5.1gd [67] 3728
70 2-11 Bath 5.7g/f [67] 3848
60 9-11 Bath 6g/f [69] 4409
39 24-26 Newb 6.5g/f 4679
52 9-19 Bath 5gd 67 5021

AGGI MAC 3 b f £0
29a 5-5 Sout 7af [45] 682
6 17-20 Thir 6g/f 44 3575

34a 7-11 Sout 8af [40] 4090 e
33 8-15 Carl 7.9fm [40] 4507
42 8-9 Catt 7g/f [35] 4674 e
50 9-17 Hayd 8.1g/s [35] 4768 e

AGGRAVATION 2 b g £0
58a 9-14 Ling 7ap 4970
18a 13-13 Wolv 6ap 5182
57 9-14 Yarm 7sft 5251
61a 7-12 Wolv 7.1ap 5324

AGILETE 2 b c £1240
48 9-14 Bath 5sft 1538
61 3-7 Bath 5.7fm 1900
76 3-7 Warw 5fm 2573
72 5-11 Wind 5gd 3160
55 13-14 Warw 6.1g/f 75 4420

AGILIS 3 b g £579
62a 13-15 Ling 7ap 83 81
74a 8-16 Ling 7ap 80 181
86a 4-12 Ling 8ap [80] 234
76a 6-11 Ling 8ap [79] 273
59a 11-12 Ling 8ap 78 517
69a 6-11 Ling 8ap 78 547 BL
72a 11-11 Ling 7ap [74] 627 bl
55a 9-12 Ling 8ap [70] 1042
58a 9-12 Ling 8ap 67 1613 VIS
39 12-15 Brig 8fm 62 1691 bl
50 10-18 Good 8g/f 59 1849 bl
52 7-10 Brig 7g/f 55 1941 bl
35 6-7 Brig 7g/f 55 2045 bl

AGOUTI 3 b f £0
30 16-18 Wind 8.3g/f 1810
41 10-13 Wind 10g/f 2453

AGREAT DAYOUTWITHU 2 ch f £0
3 8-8 Pont 6g/f 2603
23 11-13 Ripo 5gd 4303
0 15-16 Ripo 5gd 4787

AGUILA LOCO 4 ch g £6506
33a 10-15 Sout 5af [36] 253
53a 3-10 Sout 6af [36] 308
39a 2-10 Sout 6af [40] 352
27a 6-16 Sout 6af [40] 374
50a 2-13 Sout 6af 45 500
47a 5-8 Sout 6af [50] 577
44a 3-12 Wolv 6af [50] 646
55a 1-10 WOLV 7af 50 685* p
52a 4-13 Ling 7ap 54 739 p
48a 7-13 Ling 7ap 54 761 p
48a 6-13 Ling 6ap 54 767 p
57a 2-12 Wolv 7af 53 956 p
27 10-13 Sout 6g/s 53 1052 p
57a 3-13 Wolv 6af 55 1221 p
55a 7-10 Wolv 7af [55] 1319 p
57 3-5 Yarm 7g/f [56] 1731 p
55 6-18 Wind 6g/f [56] 1806 p
50a 8-12 Ling 6ap [56] 2016 p
51 8-16 Brig 7fm 55 2258 p
29 10-11 Brig 7fm 55 2334 p
49a 4-16 Sout 6af 52 3000 p

AGUILERA 3 ch f £291
24 7-9 Redc 5sft 1146
38 8-14 Donc 6g/f 2428
28 10-13 Muss 7.1g/f 45 2812 P
19 4-4 Hami 5gd [43] 3133 p
11 13-14 Catt 6g/f [43] 3191
25 9-12 Carl 5.9g/f 40 3655
21 12-16 Catt 5sft [40] 3932
34 8-14 Newc 5g/f [30] 4404

AHAZ 2 b c £0
43 14-14 Bath 5gd 1401
46 6-7 Hami 6gd 1744
52 12-17 Ling 7g/f 2584
44 5-5 Brig 6fm 2833 BL
52 4-8 Yarm 6gd 3491 bl
43 6-13 Sali 7g/f [55] 3864 P
6 16-17 Ling 6g/f [55] 4316 bl

AHDAAF 2 b f £2637
81 3-10 Newm 6g/f 3064
76 3-10 Nott 6.1g/f 3418
79 4-13 Newm 6g/f 4918

AIMEES DELIGHT 4 b f £0
65 9-13 Wind 8.3g/s [80] 1057
66 9-14 Yarm 8g/f 80 1131
62 6-8 Muss 8g/s [78] 1461
64 8-12 Kemp 8g/f [74] 1915
56 10-13 Ripo 8g/f 74 2010
58 7-11 Redc 8fm 70 2296
24 12-12 Nott 8.2g/s 67 2931 BL
56 9-14 Pont 8g/f 67 2993

AINTNECESSARILYSO 5 ch g £18175
51a 5-10 Ling 6ap [42] 133
43a 4-15 Sout 6af [42] 167
50a 6-15 Sout 5af [43] 253
40a 5-9 Wolv 5af 43 275
44a 5-10 Wolv 7af 45 379
37a 5-15 Ling 7ap [45] 411 p
54a 1-14 SOUT 6af 45 501*
55a 4-12 Sout 6af [50] 610
51a 3-13 Ling 6ap 51 740
49a 6-11 Sout 5af 52 859
53a 3-14 Ling 6ap 52 874
60a 3-6 Wolv 6af [51] 941
45 3-12 Chep 5.1sft [45] 1336
46 2-10 Brig 5.3gd [45] 1544
49 2-18 Good 5g/f 45 1867
64a 2-12 Ling 6ap [58] 2016
47 3-16 Brig 6fm 47 2262
40 6-18 Ling 6gd 47 2396
56 1-11 GOOD 6gd 47 2535*
60 1-18 DONC 6gd 51 2752*
57 5-17 Pont 6g/f 56 2990
56 3-12 Bath 5.7gd 55 3146
53 6-17 Sand 5g/f 55 3341
51 8-17 Wind 6fm 55 3643
47 10-20 Hayd 6fm 55 3796

AIR MAIL 7 b g £984
80a 4-12 Wolv 9.4af 79 513
51a 8-10 Sout 7af 79 611
66a 9-12 Wolv 8.5af 79 632
45a 12-12 Wolv 7af 76 840 p
62a 4-8 Sout 7af 72 1195 vis
65a 6-8 Wolv 8.5af 72 1219 vis
42a 8-10 Wolv 8.5af 72 1322 vis
52a 6-10 Sout 8af 67 3395
63a 4-8 Sout 7af [64] 4093

AIR OF ESTEEM 7 b g £715
36a 5-13 Wolv 8.5af [50] 46
57a 5-13 Sout 8af [48] 188
46a 3-13 Sout 8af 48 228
36a 5-10 Wolv 8.5af [48] 311
40a 5-12 Wolv 8.5af 47 564
20a 6-9 Wolv 9.4af 45 647
31a 7-13 Sout 8af [45] 776
43a 2-8 Sout 8af [40] 1200
37a 4-7 Sout 8af [45] 1590
37a 5-12 Sout 7af [43] 2337
22a 9-16 Sout 8af 41 3159 P

AIR OF SUPREMACY 3 gr c £0
55a 7-15 Ling 7ap 472
59a 6-12 Ling 8ap 734
75 7-17 Donc 8gd 919

AIRE DE MOUGINS 2 b c £2390
87 8-11 York 6g/s 1687
63 4-13 Donc 6gd 2236
79 4-10 Redc 7g/s 2959
77 4-17 York 7g/f 75 4396
79 2-8 Hami 8.3g/s [75] 4816

AIREDALE LAD 3 b g £0
16a 6-9 Sout 8af 983
36a 4-7 Sout 7af 1196
0 5-7 Sout 8af [35] 1591
0 13-15 Beve 8.5g/s 32 3182
0 13-15 Leic 11.8gd [30] 5060

AIRGUSTA 3 b c £0
59a 8-11 Ling 7ap 1008
54 10-18 Nott 8.2sft 64 1470
50 7-20 Wind 11.6sft 61 1648
42 10-13 Nott 10g/s [59] 4650
52a 9-16 Ling 12ap [57] 5296

AIRWAVE 4 b f £53150
102 6-15 York 6sft [117] 1667
104 6-14 Asco 6fm [115] 2580
104 9-20 Newm 6g/f [115] 3062
107 1-10 AYR 5g/f [110] 3304*
109 6-12 York 5g/s [110] 4060
99 11-19 Hayd 6fm [110] 4384
107 3-11 Newb 5.2g/f [108] 4678
108 2-12 Asco 6g/f [108] 4799

AITANA 4 b f £0
15a 6-9 Ling 12ap [58] 324
34a 4-5 Wolv 12af [53] 583
0 9-9 Wolv 9.4af 53 620 BL e

AJEEL 5 b g £0
66 8-11 Newm 7g/f 80 2532

AKASH 4 b g £13554
95 1-9 PONT 10hvy [90] 1068*
92 2-13 Diel 11.5 [90] 1437
78 12-19 Newm 10g/f 91 1478
58 10-10 Asco 12gd 91 3777
72 11-14 Ripo 10gd 88 4305
32 17-19 Hayd 10.5g/s 85 4766

AKIMBO 3 b c £960
87 3-19 Newb 8gd 1236

AKIRAMENAI 4 br f £279
14a 9-9 Ling 5ap 572
58 4-8 Redc 6sft 1659
37 10-12 Thir 7g/f 1971
49 6-10 Redc 6gd [58] 2559
24 7-9 Beve 5sft [55] 2945
27 14-14 Ling 6gd 53 3289
27 10-12 Folk 6g/s 48 3911 BL
3a 13-14 Ling 10ap [45] 4661

AKRAAN 2 ch f £1274
61 9-16 Newm 7g/f 3582
68 7-12 Folk 7gd 3909
68 5-12 Beve 8.5sft 4257
69 2-20 Yarm 8g/s 64 5349

AKRITAS 3 b c £3534
90 4-9 Ches 12.3gd 90 1582
89 4-6 Good 12g/f 88 2021
87 5-13 Hayd 11.9gd 88 2238
89 3-13 Asco 16.2g/f 84 3387

AKSHAR 5 b h £5427
103 3-7 Curr 10g/s [103] 1560 BL
92 11-14 Asco 10g/f 107 2556 BL

AL AZHAR 10 b g £1056
35a 6-10 Sout 11af [68] 2499
34 3-6 Beve 12.1gd [68] 2653
45 3-11 Catt 12g/f [60] 3190

AL BEEDAA 3 ch f £1701
73 4-8 Folk 12sft 1272
75 3-7 Donc 14.6g/s 74 1521
74 3-7 Brig 11.9g/f [73] 1939
18 10-10 Good 14gd 73 2376 VIS

AL GARHOUD BRIDGE 2 b c £5095
76 5-13 Newb 6g/f 1760
60 7-18 Chep 6.1gd 2194
95 1-10 CATT 7g/f 2845*
90 4-9 Good 7fm 90 3624

AL MABROOK 9 b g £0
14a 7-13 Sout 14af 30 2494

AL MUALLIM 9 b g £0
44a 9-16 Ling 7ap [50] 180 t

AL QUDRA 2 b c £6625
74 5-14 Bath 5gd 1401
88a 1-10 SOUT 6af 2382*
60 12-12 Newm 7g/f 3060
87 5-8 Newb 6g/f 3254
96 2-6 Wind 6fm [90] 3800
82 10-12 Asco 7g/f 95 4810
52 15-15 York 6gd 69 4985 BL

AL SHUUA 3 b f £1958
78 2-11 Good 9g/f 1864
43 12-12 Pont 10g/f 79 2277

67 4-6 Brig 9.9fm [79] 2835
50 13-13 Ling 10g/s 74 4182
41 10-15 Bath 10.2gd [70] 4826

AL SIFAAT 3 ch f £757
47 7-7 Good 9.9g/f [90] 1844 T
77 4-4 Newm 8g/f [90] 2533 t

ALAARED 4 b g £412
50 3-5 Brig 11.9g/f [83] 3983 c

ALAFDAL 4 b c £0
24 8-8 Ayr 13.1fm 68 1905

ALAFZAR 6 b g £10836
56a 4-14 Ling 7ap 52 344 vis
53a 7-16 Ling 7ap 52 600 vis t
59a 1-11 LING 8ap 52 669* BL t
61a 3-11 Ling 8ap 58 732 bl t
64a 1-13 LING 7ap 56 761* bl t
62 3-10 Brig 7g/f 59 1941 bl t
32 14-16 York 7sft 59 2057 vis t
58 4-16 Brig 7fm 59 2258 bl t
26 9-11 Chep 7.1gd 59 2370 vis t
59 4-11 Muss 8g/f [58] 3558 t
65a 4-13 Ling 7ap 62 3791 vis t
28 10-11 Brig 8g/s 57 4141 bl t
62 1-18 CHEP 8.1gd [55] 4485+ vis t
44a 8-12 Ling 8ap [62] 4974 bl t
13 15-17 Yarm 8g/s [57] 5348 vis t

ALAIPOUR 5 b h £0
0 P-12 Wolv 12.2ap 53 5328

ALALOOF 3 b f £0
66 6-14 Bath 10.2gd 67 1403
62 6-15 Ripo 12.3g/f 67 1785
60 8-11 Ling 11.5g/f 66 2842

ALAM 5 b g £0
66 6-8 Ayr 17.5g/s 74 4657
67 7-7 Hami 13g/s 70 4819
69 5-11 Ayr 15sft 70 5032

ALAMIYAN 2 b c £0
62 6-12 Bath 8sft 5170

ALANI 2 b f £1393
66 2-8 Newc 7sft 4283
52 5-7 Hami 8.3sft 4691
61 9-15 York 7.9gd 5002

ALASTAIR SMELLIE 8 ch g £3037
24a 10-16 Sout 5af [40] 720
4a 8-8 Sout 7af [40] 847
48 2-17 Pont 6hvy [45] 1065 vis
35a 2-11 Wolv 6af [35] 1261 vis
48a 1-5 LING 6ap [35] 1452* vis
3a 15-15 Sout 6af 48 1750 vis
22a 12-16 Sout 6af 47 2720
28a 10-15 Sout 6af 47 3000 vis
19 15-16 Catt 5sft [45] 3932 vis

ALBADI 3 b c £3533
46 11-12 York 7g/s 1688
38 9-9 Asco 7g/f 1929
50 7-11 Newm 8g/f 2248 BL
54 1-8 BRIG 7g/f 49 2434* bl
7 17-17 Newm 7g/f 52 2768 bl
0 12-12 Yarm 7gd 50 3490 bl
0 19-19 Kemp 8g/f [50] 4795 bl

ALBANOV 4 b g £6556
74 15-19 Good 21fm 95 3531 BL
87 8-10 Asco 16.2gd 95 3776
98 4-6 Ches 13.4sft 94 4104
76 19-20 Hayd 14fm 94 4383
76 8-8 Donc 12fm 93 4534
99 2-7 Hami 13g/s 92 4819
45 22-24 Donc 12sft 94 5372 bl

ALBANOVA 5 gr m £197182
116 1-7 DUSS 12sft [111] 3497*
112 1-7 COLO 12gd [111] 4018*
116 1-9 COLO 12sft [111] 4841*

ALBASHOOSH 6 b g £8520
55 6-12 Hami 6g/s [67] 1600
65 5-12 Ayr 7.2fm 65 1909

56 6-9 Muss 7.1fm 64 2086
71 1-15 PONT 6g/f 63 2280*
61 8-16 Carl 5.9fm 69 2445
59 3-4 Hami 6g/s [70] 2831
69 4-26 Good 6fm 70 3569
71 3-8 Ayr 6g/f 69 3763
76 2-9 Newm 6gd 69 3924
0 15-18 Ayr 7.2sft 71 4689

ALBAVILLA 4 b f £7212
77 3-10 Bath 11.7gd 74 1399
77 2-7 Leic 8.1fm [75] 3816
75 5-9 Kemp 12g/f 75 4360
64 8-16 Good 12gd [74] 4745
75 3-11 Wind 11.6g/s [72] 4942
80a 1-12 WOLV 13.9ap 70 5160*
80 8-12 Yarm 14.1sft [70] 5254

ALBEE 4 b g £261
24a 6-7 Wolv 9.4af 509
31a 6-7 Wolv 9.4af 561 P
56a 4-12 Wolv 9.4af 939 p
26 7-8 Thir 12g/s [54] 1472 p
16 11-16 Nott 8.2hvy 54 5347

ALBERT HALL 2 b c £100925
113 1-5 CURR 8g/s 5071*
116 2-8 Donc 8sft 5216

ALBERTINE 4 b f £0
31 9-12 Ling 6g/f 2586
6 8-8 Yarm 8g/f 2854
24a 8-9 Ling 8ap 3195 T

ALBINUS 2 gr c £25736
73a 3-12 Ling 8ap 175
74 10-19 Newb 8gd 1236
80 2-13 Bath 10.2g/f [71] 1791 BL
92 1-6 RIPO 12.3g/f 71 1980* bl
99 1-10 SALI 12gd 80 2660* bl
108 3-7 Hayd 11.9sft [90] 3274 bl
106 5-8 Newb 11g/f [104] 4639 bl

ALBURY HEATH 4 b g £0
22a 12-14 Ling 6ap [40] 652
14a 11-12 Ling 8ap [40] 710

ALCAIDESA 3 b g £0
71 4-11 Newc 8sft 1279
49 11-20 Donc 7g/s 1518

ALCAZAR 9 b g £87499
116 1-6 NOTT 14.1fm [118] 1005*
114 2-10 York 13.9g/s [118] 1705
52 13-13 Asco 20g/f [115] 2518
114 5-13 Curr 14gd [115] 4733
115 3-8 Long 15.5hv [115] 5245
113 1-6 MUSS 16g/s [113] 5334*

ALCHARINGA 2 b g £424
68 5-8 Muss 5gd 1795
60 9-18 Leic 5fm 2109
66 4-6 Beve 5gd 2513

ALCHEMIST MASTER 5 b g £16364
52 6-18 Thir 8g/f 55 1972
60 2-15 Beve 7.5g/s 54 2324
63 2-14 Thir 7fm 54 2466
61 2-8 Redc 8gd 54 2550 P
72 1-18 CATT 7g/f 57 2848+ p
73 1-11 RIPO 8gd 53 2986* p
63 4-10 York 7.9g/s 63 3074 p
70 6-11 Leic 7g/f 74 3210 p
74 3-8 Thir 8fm 72 3608 p
66 10-13 Ripo 8gd 72 4279 p
71a 7-14 Ling 7ap 72 4446 p
73 3-15 Beve 7.5g/f 70 4719 p
0 P-13 Muss 7.1gd 70 4806 p

ALCHERA 3 b c £1137
51 13-16 Kemp 6g/s 75 1116 bl
22 13-17 Asco 6sft 73 1417 bl
67 6-12 Wind 5g/f 70 1809 bl
61 4-9 Chep 5.1gd 68 2195 bl
63 4-10 Carl 5gd 66 2675 bl
52 10-12 Kemp 5g/f 64 3036 bl
61 4-14 Yarm 7gd 62 3995
62 7-13 Wind 8.3g/s 60 4221
57 7-14 Good 8g/f 60 4542

61 5-26 Redc 8fm 60 4926
47 8-13 Pont 8g/s [58] 5153

ALDENTE 2 gr f £1336
76 2-7 Redc 7g/f 3770
0 P-14 Ches 7sft 4102

ALDERNEY RACE 3 ch c £71812
63a 5-12 Ling 6ap 1044
84 2-17 Sali 6g/s 1497
101 1-15 LEIC 6g/f [84] 1829*
98 4-20 York 6g/f 90 2407
103 1-19 NEWM 6fm 91 3002*
105 2-10 Asco 6gd 97 3778
108 1-11 NEWM 6g/f 99 3941*

ALEKHINE 3 b g £3586
87 2-7 Thir 8g/f [83] 1770
88 3-11 Pont 8g/f 85 2040
69 16-18 Epso 10.1fm 87 2250
79 8-14 Hayd 8.1gd 86 2903
88 6-11 Newm 10g/f 84 3236
81 9-15 Donc 10.3g/f 82 3598 e
85 5-17 Asco 8g/f 82 4777 e
70 10-19 Donc 10.3sft 82 5201 e

ALENUSHKA 3 b f £2024
65 9-11 Newb 10g/f 2349
62 6-14 Wind 8.3fm 2974
70 4-17 Wind 8.3fm 3480
70 2-8 Sand 8.1g/f [65] 3858

ALERON 6 b h £11865
76 2-12 Ches 12.3gd 68 1599
72 1-9 NEWC 10.1sft [68] 1681* P
74 2-7 Ripo 10g/f [72] 1979
69 10-19 Carl 11.9gd 72 2673
70 4-7 Redc 9g/s [72] 2962
78 3-15 Ches 10.3g/f 72 3099 p
65 5-10 Ripo 12.3g/s 72 3261 p
77 2-8 Ches 12.3fm 71 3637 p
46 8-9 Pont 12g/s 72 3969 p

ALESHANEE 2 b f £0
15 10-10 Ripo 5gd 2983
0 7-7 Folk 5gd 3907
1 18-18 Ling 6gd 4108
0 17-17 Ling 6gd 4443

ALETHEA GEE 6 b m £0
38 11-16 Ripo 9gd 2987
15 8-10 Carl 6.9g/f 3230
0 6-6 Ripo 10g/f 3648

ALEUTIAN 4 gr g £15470
81a 1-14 LING 6ap 449*
96a 1-11 LING 7ap [85] 627*
106a1-8 WOLV 7af 838*
101a6-8 Ling 7ap [104] 1043
87 11-11 Leic 7g/s [104] 1356
73 13-13 York 6gd 100 4322

ALEXANDER AMBITION 3 b f £5597
63a 4-14 Ling 10ap [75] 367
66a 3-12 Sout 8af [67] 460
52a 4-12 Ling 7ap [65] 566
68a 2-12 Ling 8ap 63 798
69a 1-15 LING 7ap 64 901*

ALEXANDER ANAPOLIS 3 b f £2247
66a 1-10 WOLV 12af [80] 154*

ALEXANDER CAPETOWN 2 b f £2964
74 2-12 Warw 5sft 1524
69 5-10 York 5g/s 1709
73 6-12 Newb 6g/f 3251
71 4-16 Newm 6gd 70 4224
67 4-14 Warw 6.1g/f 70 4420
62 8-13 Leic 6gd 69 4697
14 11-20 Newb 6hvy 68 5225

ALEXANDER DUCHESS 3 b f £0
65 7-9 Ches 11.4gd 1568

ALEXANDER GOLDRUN 3 b f £255207
107 1-10 CURR 8hvy 895*
110 1-9 LEOP 7g/s 1701*
118 2-15 Curr 8g/f 2005
115 4-17 Chan 12.5g/s 2460

116 2-6 Curr 10gd 2816
119 1-10 LONG 10g/f 4953*

ALEXANDER ICEQUEEN 2 b f £6399
100 2-6 Leop 6g/s 3314

ALEXEI 3 ch g £826
36 7-9 Warw 8.1sft 1089
68a 2-9 Ling 12ap 4449
65a 5-14 Ling 13ap 4892
38 9-12 Brig 11.9sft 63 5093

ALEXIA ROSE 2 b f £11044
39 6-6 Hami 6g/f 2316
13 13-13 Carl 5gd 2670
60 4-18 Pont 5g/s 3968
76 3-9 Sand 5gd [61] 4497
81 2-5 Pont 5g/f [63] 4625
83 1-14 HAYD 6sft [73] 4769*
85 2-6 Muss 5g/s [78] 5141
83 7-8 Newm 6sft [78] 5267

ALEYAH 2 ch f £0
0 13-13 Kemp 6g/f 4358

ALFELMA 4 gr f £0
34 9-19 Donc 6g/f [47] 1876
0 15-16 Nott 6.1gd [47] 1988
0 18-19 Beve 5g/s 41 2326

ALFHALA 3 b f £0
47 18-20 Newm 8g/f 3237

ALFIE LEE 7 ch g £536
37 7-8 Muss 5g/f [43] 3527 t p
40 4-15 Muss 5g/f 43 3561 t p
0 13-13 Muss 5g/s 45 5143 bl e

ALFIE NOAKES 2 b c £1602
83 3-16 Newb 7g/f 4677
74 5-16 Bath 6g/f 5019
77a 3-11 Ling 8ap 5236

ALFONSO 3 ch c £17393
83a 1-7 WOLV 7af 617*
62 7-11 Ripo 8gd 79 1176
61 12-20 Newm 8fm 76 1496
81 2-12 Newm 7gd 73 4225
78 4-11 Ayr 8sft 77 4621
84 2-13 Bath 8sft 77 5172
88 1-20 NEWM 7g/s 77 5286*

ALFRED THE GREAT 2 b c £0
48 11-14 Bath 8gd 5018

ALFRIDINI 3 ch c £11490
15a 10-11 Ling 8ap 322 BL
54a 8-15 Ling 7ap 472
71a 2-15 Ling 7ap 670
72a 2-9 Ling 7ap [65] 764
70a 1-10 LING 10ap 65 817*
70a 4-8 Ling 8ap [70] 934
0 12-12 Wind 11.6g/s 70 1260
76 1-14 SALI 8fm 70 2423*
74 3-6 Sali 9.9gd 70 2663
73 5-9 Sali 8g/s 73 3112
47 5-7 Folk 9.7gd 73 3384

ALGHAAZY 3 b g £0
54 10-17 Hayd 8.1g/s 4768
59 11-18 Bath 10.2gd 5023

ALGORITHM 2 b f £3394
57 8-11 Ripo 5g/s 3258
52 6-12 Thir 5g/f 3411
53 5-10 Thir 5fm 3606
58 6-20 Redc 7fm 58 4337
62 2-17 York 7g/f 58 4396
62 3-18 Catt 7g/f 59 4673
53 4-8 Muss 8gd 59 4807
57 9-17 Catt 7gd 59 4963
36 15-19 Redc 8sft 57 5302

ALHAADH 2 b f £0
68 9-13 Newm 6g/f 4918

ALI BRUCE 4 b g £4932
49 5-13 Leic 10fm 2107
69 2-15 Ayr 8gd 2504
60a 1-9 SOUT 7af 2801*

66a 3-14 Ling 7ap 64 3821
64 4-17 Warw 8.1g/s 64 4668

ALI DEO 3 ch c £5663
78 1-10 BEVE 7.5g/f 1832*
74 3-7 Chep 8.1gd [77] 2116
65 11-13 Newc 8g/s 77 2773
73 6-8 Asco 10g/f 76 3391
42 12-14 Yarm 7gd 73 3995
62 7-13 Bath 8gd 70 4546 P
64a 7-12 Wolv 8.6ap 67 4923 p
70a 4-14 Ling 10ap 66 5083
68a 4-13 Wolv 9.5ap 66 5161

ALI PASHA 5 b g £0
6a 6-6 Wolv 9.4af [35] 1262

ALIABAD 9 b g £0
0 5-6 Wolv 16.2af [30] 395 vis

ALIANNA 3 b f £0
46a 12-15 Ling 7ap 814
36a 11-12 Ling 8ap 881
17 9-9 Folk 9.7sft 980
36 14-16 Sand 10g/s 2131
28a 11-15 Ling 12ap 40 2741
32a 5-9 Wolv 9.5ap [35] 5360

ALIBA 3 ch g £834
62a 4-6 Wolv 7af [66] 1321
54 10-11 Redc 7g/f [66] 1822
3a 11-12 Sout 7af [62] 2339
62a 2-9 Sout 7af [60] 4131
10 13-18 Newc 8g/f [60] 5017
30a 9-11 Wolv 7.1ap [61] 5178

ALIBONGO 3 ch g £0
0 13-13 Wolv 6af [40] 582
24a 9-9 Sout 7af [40] 613

ALICE BLACKTHORN 3 b f £0
48 15-20 Nott 6.1gd 69 1239
46 7-9 Thir 6g/s [67] 1477
22 5-5 Carl 6.9fm 64 2446
39 10-12 Catt 7g/f [64] 3017
46 8-8 Muss 7.1g/f 59 3528
37 13-14 Redc 7g/s 54 5109

ALICE BRAND 5 b m £0
14a 11-14 Sout 8af 49 62
5a 16-16 Sout 7af 46 208

ALICE KING 2 b f £999
38 4-10 Thir 5sft 1224
37 4-7 Newc 5sft 1394
9 9-11 Beve 5g/f 1831
59a 2-10 Ling 5ap 2017
36 5-5 Yarm 6fm 2145
1a 7-8 Ling 6ap [50] 3745

ALIMISTE 4 b f £0
39a 9-14 Ling 10ap 430
34a 9-10 Ling 10ap 540
51a 9-13 Ling 10ap 715
28a 8-10 Ling 12ap 916
21a 10-13 Ling 13ap [40] 1076
0 8-8 Chep 10.2sft [35] 1333

ALINDA 3 b f £12194
84 1-10 LEIC 7g/f [70] 2920*
79 1-7 CHEP 7.1g/f [75] 3402*

ALISA 4 b f £541
44a 8-12 Ling 8ap 401
59a 3-15 Ling 12ap 521 T
41a 5-11 Ling 12ap 672 t
58a 5-14 Ling 10ap 58 801
46a 6-14 Ling 10ap 57 1618 t
26 11-18 Wind 11.6g/f 55 1960 t

ALIZAR 2 b f £12491
58a 1-10 SOUT 5af [45] 139*
59a 1-12 SOUT 6af [54] 200*
48a 5-8 Sout 6af 61 223
57a 3-9 Wolv 6af 60 247
49a 9-15 Ling 7ap 58 295
63a 2-10 Ling 5ap 56 371
59a 3-11 Wolv 6af [59] 466
61a 1-14 LING 6ap [59] 495*

49a	4-12	Sout	5af	[59]	587
59a	2-10	Ling	5ap	58	712
58a	3-11	Ling	6ap	58	735
55	6-10	Brig	5.3fm	59	1694
39	7-8	Brig	5.3g/f	58	1942
47	6-12	Chep	6.1gd	58	2118
21	18-18	Wind	6g/f	57	2268
61	1-12	**BRIG**	6g/f	55	2435*
40	11-12	Brig	5.3g/f	58	2645
40a	9-11	Ling	6ap	59	3198
21	9-9	Epso	6fm	58	3543
36	7-10	Ling	6gd	57	4109
17	19-20	Ling	6gd	55	4317
35	11-12	Sand	5gd	[53]	4605

ALJAAREH 3 b c £0

64	12-17	Newb	8g/f		1762

ALJAFLIYAH 3 ch f £0

0	U-13	Newm	8fm		2595
41	8-9	York	7gd		3121
49	7-9	Newm	7g/f		3282
49	9-10	Newm	7gd		3921
40	15-17	Newm	8gd		4228

ALJOMAR 4 b g £0

36a	7-9	Sout	11af	[41]	224 p
25a	9-9	Sout	7af	[39]	303 p
25a	6-10	Sout	11af	[40]	375 p
0	10-16	Sout	8af	[35]	719
0	12-12	Wolv	8.5af	[35]	777

ALKA INTERNATIONAL 11 b g £0

23a	10-13	Ling	16ap	40	137

ALKAADHEM 4 b c £70600

102	5-24	Donc	8gd	100	951
103	4-27	Newb	8gd	100	1231
107	1-10	**GOOD**	9.9g/f	[102]	1862*
99	11-16	Asco	8g/f	[108]	2470
106	4-7	Sand	10g/s	[108]	2898
109	3-9	Good	12fm	[108]	3563
114	1-7	**GOOD**	9.9g/f	[107]	4538+ BL
119	1-8	**GOOD**	9.9gd	[107]	4748* bl

ALKAASED 4 b c £71832

100	2-9	Newm	12g/f	[93]	2246
110	1-15	**HAYD**	11.9gd	94	2948+
117	1-9	**GOOD**	12fm	[105]	3563*
115	2-4	Kemp	12fm	[113]	4391

ALL A DREAM 2 b r f £800

46a	6-6	Sout	5af		3484
29a	10-15	Sout	5af		4089
67a	3-10	Ling	7ap		4442
47a	7-12	Wolv	6ap	[71]	5177

ALL BLEEVABLE 7 b g £0

42	6-9	Pont	12g/f		2992
32	6-10	Ripo	12.3g/f	45	3649
45	7-19	Thir	12g/f	40	4594

ALL BLUE 3 b g £772

71	4-15	Nott	8.2g/s		4649 T
62	4-13	Nott	10gd		4861 t
39	8-11	Good	14gd		5029 t
57	8-12	Nott	10hvy		5190 VIS

ALL FOR LAURA 2 ch f £8957

82	4-9	Newm	6g/f		2245
92	1-4	**NOTT**	5.1g/f		3576*
95	5-12	Newb	5.2g/f		3956
94	5-11	Sali	6gd	[95]	4332
89	8-14	Newm	7g/f	[95]	4914
94	4-8	Newm	6sft	[95]	5267

ALL NIGHT DANCER 2 b f £27668

86	2-7	Hayd	6gd		2883
95	2-10	Curr	6.3gd		4737

ALL ON MY OWN 8 ch g £590

0	15-15	Sout	16af	38	67
2a	8-9	Wolv	14.8af	[35]	301 bl
32a	4-9	Wolv	9.4af	[35]	399 bl
35a	2-12	Wolv	8.5af	[35]	584 bl
18a	4-12	Ling	10ap	[35]	654 bl
21a	8-12	Wolv	8.5af	[40]	777 bl
11a	12-12	Ling	8ap	[35]	971 p
0	5-5	Wolv	8.5af	[35]	1264 bl

37	3-10	Warw	8.1g/s	[35]	1328 bl
35	4-13	Kemp	10hvy	[35]	1643 bl
23	9-10	Beve	8.5g/f	[35]	1943 bl

ALL QUIET 3 b f £3295

65	3-14	Brig	6fm		1690
75	2-12	Good	7g/f		1846
68	3-11	Bath	8fm	[67]	2031
67	5-12	Newb	7g/f	[78]	2352
60	5-10	Sali	6g/s	[75]	4081
64	5-15	Ling	7gd	[70]	4445
44	7-11	Wind	6g/f	[67]	4836

ALL TOO BEAUTIFUL 3 b f £114576

112	1-9	**NAVA**	10g/s		1435*
114	2-7	Epso	12g/f		2210
99	4-7	Curr	12g/f		3321
113	3-13	Curr	10gd		4735

ALLEGRETTO 2 b c £1900

80	2-14	Nott	6.1hvy		5342

ALLEGRINA 3 b f £0

49a	6-13	Wolv	8.5af	65	40
37a	9-14	Sout	8af	62	195 BL

ALLERTON BOY 5 ch g £0

39a	4-10	Wolv	5af	[37]	286
21a	7-10	Sout	6af	[40]	352
37a	6-11	Wolv	5af	40	507
29a	8-10	Ling	5ap	[40]	653

ALLEZ MOUSSON 6 b g £0

12	11-14	Donc	18gd	58	926 P
0	13-13	Pont	18hvy	56	1069
18	9-10	Hayd	16.2sft	52	3275 bl
38	7-10	Newc	16.1g/s	45	3701 bl
28	9-17	Pont	17.1g/s	41	3970

ALLIED CAUSE 2 ch f £5265

69	8-14	Newm	7g/f		3944
73	5-14	Yarm	7gd		4611
77a	1-14	**LING**	7ap		5258*

ALLIED VICTORY 4 b c £8662

66a	1-7	**SOUT**	8af	[73]	334*
52a	11-13	Wolv	8.5af	73	439
37a	9-12	Sout	11af	69	534
62	2-9	Hayd	10.5gd	[69]	2901
59	8-10	Hayd	10.5g/s	75	3139
65	3-7	Hami	9.2g/s	73	3879
70	7-12	Beve	12.1sft	72	4259 T
74	4-8	Hayd	11.9g/f	72	4353 t

ALLIZAM 7 b c £419

58	12-12	Hayd	6sft		3272
55	4-6	Leic	6g/f		3513
0	18-18	Pont	5g/s		3968
55	9-15	Nott	8.2hvy	[53]	5344

ALLODARLIN 2 b f £0

38a	9-11	Ling	8ap	[56]	77
34	8-12	Brig	9.9g/f	53	3300
31	12-14	Yarm	11.5g/f	50	3714
28	11-12	Brig	8g/f	45	3986

ALLSTAR PRINCESS 2 b f £0

49	7-9	Carl	5.9gd		2671
46	11-12	York	6gd		3122
55	7-12	Newc	7gd		3425
40	12-14	Thir	7g/s		4207

ALLY MAKBUL 3 b f £4879

52a	1-12	**WOLV**	6af	[55]	33*
45a	7-11	Sout	6af	55	91
29a	10-16	Sout	6af	55	94
33a	13-16	Ling	7ap	[53]	180
55a	1-10	**WOLV**	8.5af	[51]	311*
49a	4-8	Wolv	8.5af	[51]	362
50a	4-12	Wolv	12af	55	469
48a	8-13	Wolv	8.5af	55	559
51a	1-9	**WOLV**	8.5af	[53]	664*

ALMAH 6 b m £1804

73	14-17	Asco	16.2gd	95	3125
85	12-15	Good	14g/f	90	3510
88	6-10	Asco	16.2gd	90	3776
72	17-20	Hayd	14fm	86	4383
84	9-16	Asco	16.2g/f	85	4803 BL

ALMANAC 3 b c £0

49a	7-13	Sout	8af		553
37a	11-12	Ling	8ap		734
14a	10-10	Sout	8af		4042
25	10-10	Warw	8.1g/f	[49]	4421

ALMANSHOOD 2 b c £935

54	5-7	Sand	7.1g/s		2897
73	3-14	Sali	6gd		4078

ALMANSOORA 2 b f £13183

85	2-10	Newm	6g/f		3064
90	1-16	**SALI**	7gd		4330*

ALMARA 4 b f £0

14a	15-15	Ling	7ap	[40]	411 T p
22a	4-11	Sout	5af	[35]	578 t p
8a	11-14	Sout	6af	[35]	637 t p
18a	5-6	Ling	6ap	[30]	1415 t

ALMATY EXPRESS 2 b g £4308

71	3-6	Newc	5sft		1274
54	8-10	Newc	6sft		1677
66	7-13	Carl	5fm		1950
59	3-8	Muss	5g/f		2611
67	4-7	Muss	5g/s		2965
64	1-6	**CATT**	5g/f		3014*

ALMAVIVA 4 b f £0

73	7-8	Kemp	8g/s	[92]	1115
64	15-19	Newm	10g/f	90	1478

ALMENDRADOS 2 b f £729

84	3-9	Newm	6g/f		2245

ALMIZAN 4 b c £3524

79	10-17	Ches	18.7gd	88	1569
75	9-12	Good	14g/f	86	1861
84	4-13	Chep	18gd	82	2198
79	8-29	Asco	20g/f	82	2471
86	4-19	Good	21fm	80	3531 VIS
87	3-12	Ches	15.9sft	82	4106 vis
73	10-13	Good	16g/f	82	4527 vis
75	17-34	Newm	18sft	82	5135 vis
75	5-11	Muss	16g/s	80	5335

ALMNADIA 5 b m £0

48	9-12	Newc	16.1sft	51	965
48	5-9	Newc	16.1gd	50	1870 P
34	6-9	Redc	14.1g/f	48	2105 p

ALMOND BEACH 4 ch g £0

31a	7-10	Wolv	7af	[65]	298
11a	10-11	Ling	8ap	[65]	343 bl

ALMOND WILLOW 2 b f £6140

71a	1-13	**WOLV**	8.5af	[66]	43*
53	9-12	Wind	10g/f	[68]	2800
67	2-10	Hayd	8.1g/s	66	3138
53	7-10	Hayd	8.1g/s	66	3906
62	6-20	York	7.9gd	65	4321
74a	2-12	Wolv	8.6ap	68	4923
74a	3-14	Ling	10ap	69	5083

ALMOST PERFECT 2 ch f £615

37a	6-12	Sout	5af		1439
70	3-12	Hami	6gd		2178

ALMOST ROYAL 2 b f £0

11a	9-11	Wolv	6af	[47]	73

ALMOST WELCOME 2 b c £582

64a	10-12	Ling	10ap	[39]	116
38a	10-12	Ling	7ap	[50]	566
36a	9-12	Ling	8ap	[45]	649
67a	3-13	Ling	10ap	[45]	715
59a	5-10	Ling	10ap	[50]	843
65	7-10	Kemp	11.1gd	[45]	1140
36	10-10	Bath	11.7g/f	55	2978
28a	10-12	Ling	10ap	49	4113

ALMURAAD 3 b c £8398

107	1-6	**NEWM**	8gd		1888+
98	10-16	Newm	9sft	[105]	5139

ALNAJA 5 b g £0

0	P-15	Newc	12.4hvy	70	1034
0	9-9	Folk	15.4sft	70	1271 VIS

ALNITAK 3 br c £40246
111 3-4 Long 10g/s 2825

ALONG CAME MOLLY 2 ch f £0
1 14-15 Newb 8hvy 5221

ALONG THE NILE 2 b g £1445
70 7-15 Pont 6gd 3239
75 3-13 Pont 6gd 3682
65 6-18 Ripo 6g/s 3939
57 9-10 Ripo 6gd 75 4306
51 10-14 Donc 7fm 70 4535
72 4-18 Catt 7g/f 70 4673
69 6-12 Ayr 8sft 70 5065
64 9-20 Donc 7sft 69 5373

ALPAGA LE JOMAGE 2 b c £17000
87 3-8 Newm 5g/f 1190
88 3-6 Asco 5sft 1422
81 2-7 Ches 5.1g/s 1573
91 4-8 Sand 5g/f 2094
76 5-8 Sand 5gd 2188 BL
91 8-15 Asco 5g/f 2472
82 5-8 Newb 5.2fm 2646
88 1-7 MUSS 5g/s 2965*
88 4-24 Newb 5.2g/f 3266
77 7-8 Good 6fm 3566

ALPH 7 b g £280
74a 4-15 Ling 12ap 4111
0 W-10 Ling 12ap 4314

ALPHA ECHO 5 b h £0
46a 7-12 Wolv 9.4af 939

ALPHA JULIET 3 b f £0
46 6-14 Thir 7sft 2692
37 6-8 Redc 9g/f 3805
46 6-11 Ripo 12.3gd 4281

ALPHA ZETA 3 b g £0
34 10-16 Hayd 6g/f 2182
15 9-14 Newc 6g/s 2730
28 10-10 Beve 5sft 2944
27 10-16 Thir 8g/f 40 3414
32 9-18 Carl 7.9fm 40 3547
0 13-14 Redc 10fm 40 4560

ALPHECCA 3 b c £6412
88 1-6 LING 10g/f 2843*
97 3-7 Asco 10gd [93] 3464
96 6-6 Epso 10.1gd [95] 4290

ALPINE GOLD 2 b f £14258
53 12-13 Kemp 7g/f 3520
70 7-14 Newm 7g/f 3944
80 1-11 CHEP 8.1g/s 4296*
84 1-14 DONC 8sft 75 5203*
88 7-8 Newm 8g/s [75] 5282

ALPINE HIDEAWAY 11 b g £3572
20 14-18 Donc 7g/f 49 2080
41 6-16 Beve 7.5gd 47 2891 p
34 10-17 Thir 8g/s 45 3830 p
51 1-16 BEVE 8.5g/s [45] 3850* p
39 7-17 Pont 8g/f 49 4626 p
47 7-19 Beve 9.9g/f 49 4720 p

ALPINE SPECIAL 3 gr g £3197
71 6-22 Donc 7gd 72 955
59 10-12 Pont 10g/f 71 2277
69a 4-10 Sout 12af 69 2998
71 2-5 Hayd 10.5g/s 67 3904
69 2-5 Hami 12.1sft 67 4012
34 12-12 Muss 14g/f 67 4170
66a 7-12 Wolv 12.2ap 70 4924

ALPINO CHILENO 5 gr h £0
99 8-9 Asco 12g/f 4812 BL

ALQAAHIR 2 b c £809
84 3-14 Yarm 7gd 4611

ALQWAH 3 b f £5688
84 1-10 SALI 7gd 2659* T

ALRAFID 4 ch c £11718
83a 4-13 Ling 10ap 83 26
85a 2-13 Ling 10ap 83 134
84a 6-10 Ling 10ap [83] 179

65 14-20 Newb 10gd 84 1235
91 5-19 Newm 10g/f 82 1478
87 6-18 Good 8g/f 85 1812
88 2-13 Epso 8.5g/f 85 2207
78 7-13 Sali 8gd 88 2662
79 12-15 Good 9.9g/f 86 3506
83 6-11 Good 9g/f 85 4525
78 7-14 Asco 8g/f 84 4813

ALRAFIDAIN 2 b c £2379
79 4-15 Newm 8gd 4883
81 2-9 Ayr 7.2sft 5064

ALRIDA 5 b g £23994
69 4-13 Newc 16.1sft 67 2685
75 1-19 GOOD 21fm 65 3531*

ALRIGHT MY SON 2 b c £15139
53 8-14 Bath 5sft 1538
78 2-5 Wind 5sft 1646
73 4-8 Brig 6g/f 2043
77 5-11 Newm 7fm 75 3407
78 2-7 Newm 9g/f 76 3753
79 4-13 Newm 8g/f 77 4193
78 7-17 Donc 8fm 77 4480
86 2-13 Newm 8fm 76 4725
92 1-13 WIND 8.3g/f 81 5051*
78 6-14 Donc 8sft 87 5203

ALS ALIBI 10 b g £1182
58a 2-12 Wolv 12af [41] 114
57a 2-10 Sout 11af [41] 142

ALS GLENNMAY 2 b f £0
0 15-15 Brig 7sft 5192

ALSHARQ 2 b f £0
66 9-19 Leic 7gd 5045
67 8-16 Newm 7g/s 5280

ALSHAWAMEQ 3 b g £15867
85 3-7 Thir 8g/f [81] 1770
90 1-13 NEWM 8g/f 83 2247*
88 7-27 Asco 8g/f 86 2521
83 5-16 Newm 8g/f 86 3059
90 3-6 Newm 8g/f 86 3472
90 2-10 Pont 8g/s 86 3972

ALSU 2 b f £5583
76 3-14 Bath 5gd 1401
70 1-7 HAMI 6gd 1744*
55 10-13 Curr 6.3gd 2815
69 6-9 Asco 6gd 74 3127
71 3-7 Leic 5g/f 72 3343
72 3-12 Hayd 5gd 71 3756
65 6-7 Sand 5sft 72 4065

ALTA PETENS 2 b f £17350
69 4-8 Pont 5hvy 1249
82 1-11 YARM 6g/f 1728*
83 10-17 Asco 6g/s 2553
68 12-24 Newb 5.2g/f 3266
81 4-11 Newb 7fm 78 3627
92 5-6 Good 8g/f [77] 4524
76 6-26 Newb 6.5g/f 4679
90 7-14 Newm 7gd [85] 4914
85 5-29 Newm 6gd 5087

ALTARES 2 b c £0
0 4-10 Sout 8af 54 190
17a 10-10 Ling 10ap [48] 291
33a 9-12 Ling 8ap [45] 648
0 13-13 Wolv 8.5af [40] 894
1 9-9 Good 11g/f 35 2019
15 9-9 Wind 11.6gd [35] 3164

ALTAY 7 b g £536
68 11-20 York 10.4g/f 77 4986
80 3-13 Muss 12g/s 77 5333

ALTIERI 5 ch h £263283
111 2- Capa 10g/s 59
119 1-7 CAPA 10g/s 1858*

ALTITUDE DANCER 4 b g £4812
59a 3-10 Sout 16af 59 491
66a 2-7 Sout 16af 59 529
65a 1-8 SOUT 16af 59 554*
37a 4-10 Sout 16af 64 743

51 8-14 Donc 18gd 63 926
56 11-12 Newc 16.1sft 63 965

ALULA 2 ch f £0
45 10-11 Newb 6gd 3915
59 9-13 Leic 8g/f 4450
51 13-18 Nott 8.2g/f 4842

ALVARINHO LADY 2 b f £5900
76 1-5 NOTT 5.1fm 1001*
63 5-6 Asco 5sft 1422
74 4-10 Sali 6gd 2697
73 4-12 Wind 6gd 74 3825
38 13-13 Warw 6.1gd 74 4273
31 19-21 Donc 6.5fm 74 4457

ALWAYS BELIEVE 8 b g £0
21a 9-12 Wolv 7af [48] 512 t
14a 9-9 Wolv 9.4af [45] 821

ALWAYS DARING 5 b m £0
15 14-14 Muss 7.1g/f 40 2615
3a 11-13 Sout 7af 35 3155
8 9-10 Carl 5.9fm [31] 3545 P

ALWAYS ESTEEMED 4 b g £15989
99 2-17 Sand 8.1g/s 95 1351
89 7-14 York 10.4g/s 97 1704
87 14-15 Redc 10g/f 97 2101
94 4-8 Pont 8g/f 95 2606
100a 1-12 LING 8ap [94] 3199*
103 4-5 Newm 8g/f [95] 3613
64 13-15 York 7.9g/s 100 4061
83 13-15 Donc 8fm 98 4531
66 15-16 Newm 6sft 96 5101 bl

ALWAYS FIRST 3 b c £19500
98 8-9 Wind 8.3fm 2757
105 2-4 Hami 9.2g/f [95] 3204
100 3-16 Good 12fm 95 3534
112 4-7 York 11.9gd [95] 4001
0 8-8 Newb 11g/f [110] 4639

ALWAYS FLYING 3 ch g £5955
70a 1-11 WOLV 9.4af [64] 438*
60a 5-10 Ling 10ap 69 568
71 2-14 Donc 10.3gd 69 923
47 6-8 Hami 9.2g/s 70 1603
67 6-15 Ripo 10g/f 70 1976
46 8-11 Redc 9g/s 69 2565
65 2-10 Muss 9g/f [67] 2811
52 7-14 Beve 7.5g/s [64] 3177
17 17-17 Beve 8.5g/f 61 4721
31 8-18 Newc 8g/f [57] 5017
53 4-11 Redc 10sft [54] 5303

ALWAYS KING 3 b c £4754
87 3-6 Mais 7sft 1155

ALWAYS MINE 2 ch f £375
75 5-19 Leic 7gd 5045
89 6-8 Newm 8g/s 5282

ALWAYS RAINBOWS 6 b g £0
51 16-17 Ripo 16g/s 75 1361 vis
47 8-12 Ches 12.3gd 70 1599 p

ALWAYS WAINING 3 b c £27327
63 3-12 Ripo 9g/f 1784
82 3-10 Hayd 10.5g/f 1922
90 1-8 CHEP 12.1gd 2113*
83 5-9 Hayd 11.9gd 85 2900
93 3-15 Newm 12g/f 85 3066
99 1-10 ASCO 12g/f 86 3444*
93 6-16 Good 12fm 93 3534
81 9-13 York 13.9g/s 96 4062
95 4-10 York 11.9gd 94 4324
98 1-10 NEWM 12sft [93] 5102*
0 24-24 Donc 12sft 93 5372

ALYOUSUFEYA 3 ch f £274
52 4-10 Bath 8g/s 1100

ALZARMA 2 b g £458
47 11-18 Chep 6.1gd 2194
66 3-20 Hayd 6gd 2882
48 7-15 Beve 5g/s 3178
62 6-7 Yarm 6g/f [63] 3994
47 13-18 Newc 6g/f 62 5013

51a 6-12 Wolv 7.1ap [62] 5158

AMALFI COAST 5 b g £0
30 8-18 Beve 9.9g/s 49 4243
40 11-19 Thir 12g/f 48 4594
27 17-19 Beve 9.9g/f 48 4720
6 16-20 Catt 15.8gd 45 4965

AMALGAM 2 ch f £0
23 14-14 Bath 5sft 1538
24 16-19 Kemp 6g/f 1911
33 11-11 Warw 7.1gd 3053
47 5-6 Leic 5g/f 3209
37a 7-12 Sout 7af 3394
46 10-18 Bath 5.7gd [40] 4823

AMALIE 2 b f £3926
75 7-16 Sali 7gd 4330
93 1-12 REDC 6fm 4557*

AMANDAS LAD 3 b g £4176
20a 11-16 Sout 6af 43 166
6a 6-8 Sout 8af [40] 355
59a 3-9 Sout 6af [40] 487
41a 4-13 Sout 6af 40 551
36a 9-12 Sout 5af [45] 587
44a 6-13 Sout 6af [45] 659
43a 4-10 Sout 8af 45 678
51a 6-9 Sout 5af [45] 793
19a 6-10 Sout 6af [45] 851
69 3-11 Catt 6gd [45] 999
65 5-14 Thir 6g/s [49] 1216
60 5-20 Donc 7g/s [65] 1518
47 10-20 Thir 5g/f 65 1765
66 4-19 Donc 6g/f [65] 1876
62 2-9 Thir 7g/f [60] 2216
53 7-20 York 6g/f 60 2409
51 3-8 Ripo 5g/f [60] 2527
59 5-12 Thir 5g/s 58 2690
57 4-17 Catt 5g/f 56 2846
50 5-9 Beve 5sft [56] 2945
53 6-13 Catt 5g/f 55 3350
55 3-14 Thir 5g/f 55 3417
54 3-20 Thir 6g/f 55 3575
46 9-17 Catt 5g/f 53 3667
47 4-14 Catt 6gd 53 4967

AMANDERICA 2 b f £0
0 10-10 Thir 5g/f 1764
0 10-10 Beve 7.5gd 2652
13 14-14 Beve 7.5sft 2939
21 10-10 Yarm 8g/f 3713 T

AMANDUS 4 b g £8080
0 9-9 Pont 10hvy [95] 1068
95 7-17 Sand 8.1g/s 95 1351
100 2-18 Good 8g/f 94 1812
99 4-31 Asco 8g/f 94 2489
94 7-19 Newm 7g/f 95 3061
87 12-21 Good 8fm 95 3565

AMANKILA 3 b f £3677
57 9-17 Leic 10g/s 1019
60 3-9 Sout 10gd 1283
62 1-9 FOLK 9.7sft 1581*
46a 6-12 Wolv 12af 68 2203
61 4-7 Hami 8.3g/f [66] 2474
26 13-13 Newc 8g/s 63 2773

AMANPURI 5 b g £452
33a 9-11 Wolv 12af [52] 6 e
35a 12-15 Ling 7ap [46] 366
27a 4-9 Wolv 9.4af [45] 522
0 9-12 Wolv 9.4af [40] 668
19a 6-12 Wolv 9.4af [35] 782
37 2-9 Warw 15g/s [35] 1329
30 7-9 Ayr 13.1g/s [35] 1449

AMAR 3 ch g £0
0 14-14 Sout 7af [35] 573
19a 7-9 Sout 11af 35 608
0 11-11 Catt 13.8g/f [35] 4671

AMARETTO EXPRESS 5 b g £0
0 14-14 Redc 10fm 40 4560

AMARULA RIDGE 3 b c £6005
106 3-7 Curr 7sft 1063
101 3- Leop 8sft 1301

AMAZIN 2 b c £15967
87 2-18 Wind 6gd 2618
95 1-4 KEMP 6g/f 2859*
95 2-8 Ches 5.1g/f 3081
91 5-8 Good 6fm 3566
97 4-11 Donc 5fm [97] 4533
65 16-24 Redc 6fm [95] 4928
91 9-11 Newm 5sft [99] 5132

AMAZING GRACE MARY 2 b f £0
5 12-12 Beve 5g/f 4596
33 8-12 Nott 6.1g/f 4844 BL

AMAZING VALOUR 2 b c £1716
77 2-8 Pont 8fm 4756
61 8-15 Pont 10g/f 4933
32 7-10 Nott 10hvy 5188

AMAZONIC 3 b f £0
0 13-13 Ling 10ap 2066

AMBER FOX 3 b f £441
45 5-6 Ayr 6fm [54] 1908
36 6-13 Hami 5gd 54 2181
20 5-8 Ripo 6g/f [52] 2527 P
28 10-12 Bath 8g/f 47 3846
49 3-16 Chep 7.1hvy [45] 4707
42 7-17 Kemp 7g/f [45] 4794

AMBER LEGEND 3 b f £0
10a 9-9 Wolv 5af [60] 835
30a 8-13 Wolv 6ap [50] 5211

AMBERSONG 5 ch g £6246
49a 2-12 Wolv 12af 47 75
11a 8-10 Wolv 12af 51 243
54a 3-13 Ling 13ap 51 342
49a 3-11 Wolv 12af 51 380
42a 8-12 Ling 16ap 51 478
40a 6-13 Sout 14af 50 590
25a 4-8 Wolv 12af 48 1342
42 3-11 Folk 12g/f 41 2273
42 3-9 Yarm 14.1g/f 41 2856
25 11-17 Bath 11.7gd 41 3145
48 1-9 WIND 11.6fm [41] 3294*
47 4-11 Chep 10.2gd [51] 3730
56 3-8 Ling 11.5g/s [51] 4181
48 6-13 Warw 10.9g/f 51 4419
38 14-20 Kemp 12g/f [49] 4796

AMBITIOUS ANNIE 4 b f £1176
41a 2-15 Sout 16af 39 67
30a 4-16 Sout 16af 40 206
43a 2-12 Wolv 12af 40 244

AMBUSHED 8 b g £0
33 6-10 Ayr 8g/s [59] 2544
55 4-10 Muss 9g/f [57] 2811
48 8-8 Ayr 10gd [52] 3151
45 10-11 Muss 9g/f [50] 4550

AMEEQ 2 b c £1782
84 2-10 Newb 7g/f 3955
88 3-13 Kemp 8g/f 4355
65 9-10 Kemp 8g/f 4712

AMELIA 5 b m £9005
20a 6-12 Wolv 6af [51] 33
43a 11-16 Sout 6af [50] 227
49a 2-10 Wolv 6af 50 246
47a 5-10 Wolv 6af 48 282
50a 2-12 Wolv 6af 48 385
37a 5-14 Sout 6af 50 501
49a 5-14 Ling 6ap 49 897
43a 5-11 Wolv 5af 49 958
49a 3-12 Ling 7ap 49 1024
27a 10-13 Wolv 6af 48 1221
58 1-16 NOTT 6.1sft 50 1465*
58 3-16 Bath 5.7sft 56 1540
58 2-15 Leic 6g/f 56 2398
52 5-8 Newb 6fm 58 2648
59 3-11 Warw 5.5gd 57 3054
63 3-14 Thir 5g/f 58 3416
0 8-8 Hami 5g/f 59 3591

AMERICAN COUSIN 9 b g £6878
65 1-8 NEWC 6sft [60] 963*
0 17-17 Pont 6hvy [60] 1065

AMERICAN COUSIN (cont.)
63 1-9 MUSS 5gd [58] 1797*
21 16-20 York 6g/f 64 2059
60 2-10 Newc 5g/f [64] 2161
50 5-10 Hami 5g/f [62] 2476
31 8-14 Newc 6g/s [62] 2730
49 14-18 Carl 5sft 58 3228
53 6-14 Thir 5g/f 58 3417
45 6-8 Muss 5sft [55] 3527
37 5-13 Hayd 6gd [55] 3757
38 7-16 Catt 5sft [52] 3932

AMERICAN DUKE 3 b g £5247
44 14-20 Newb 7g/f 70 2314
64 8-16 Sand 10g/s 66 2919
72 2-14 Kemp 10g/f 64 3690
60 7-7 Wind 10fm 64 3801
66 5-17 Hayd 10.5fm 66 4388
76 1-18 SALI 9.9gd 65 4850*
30 13-17 Newb 9sft 73 5198

AMERICAN POST 3 br c £203183
119 1-5 SAIN 8gd 1060*
121 1-4 LONG 8g/s 1433*
121 1-7 LONG 8g/s 1855*
112 6-14 Epso 12fm 2254

AMETHYST ROCK 6 b g £2060
9a 11-14 Ling 12ap [40] 968
37a 3-6 Wolv 9.4af [35] 1262
38a 1-10 SOUT 8af [35] 1406*
26a 6-7 Sout 8af [35] 1593
40a 2-10 Wolv 8.5af [40] 1801
10 9-11 Newm 12g/f 40 2244
1a 16-16 Sout 8af 40 3487

AMEYRAH 2 b f £0
59a 7-11 Ling 8ap 21
58a 7-14 Ling 10ap 759
41 7-9 Leic 11.8g/s 1016
30 11-11 Sout 10gd 55 1280

AMICA 2 b f £8000
74 2-13 Wind 6fm 3639
75 2-8 Chep 5.1g/s 3896
82 1-7 EPSO 6gd 4466*
52 5-10 Nott 6.1gd [82] 4858

AMID THE CHAOS 4 ch c £0
72 16-29 Asco 20g/f 88 2471 VIS

AMIGRA 2 b f £266
34 16-18 Ling 6gd 4108
27 12-15 Folk 6g/f 4369
69a 4-11 Ling 8ap 4744 BL

AMIR ZAMAN 6 ch g £2884
80a 1-6 SOUT 12af 77 388*
71a 6-8 Sout 11af 80 595

AMMENAYR 3 b g £1698
72a 8-11 Ling 8ap [80] 273
67a 9-12 Ling 8ap 77 369
68 8-13 Kemp 7sft 77 945
82 3-17 Leic 7g/s 77 1020
74 5-6 Folk 7g/s [75] 1079
78 3-7 Yarm 7gd 78 3872
70 6-7 Sali 7g/s [78] 4082 VIS
60 15-24 Newb 7g/f 75 4642
78a 5-14 Ling 7ap [67] 5080
61a 6-13 Wolv 6ap 67 5181

AMMIRARE 2 b f £0
37 8-10 Catt 5gd 4968
62 7-14 Muss 7.1g/s 5330

AMNESTY 5 ch g £7949
8a 8-9 Ling 12ap [60] 324
55a 4-14 Ling 10ap [60] 477 BL e
57a 5-7 Ling 13ap [56] 546 b l e
48a 8-14 Ling 10ap 54 718 b l e
45a 11-13 Ling 10ap 54 805 b l e
45a 6-12 Ling 8ap 49 1013 b l e
56 1-14 WIND 8.3g/s [56] 1058* b l e
64 1-12 FOLK 9.7sft 62 1273* b l e
64 5-18 Wind 8.3gd 63 1385 b l e
64 2-13 Bath 8sft 62 1542 b l e
50 13-18 Good 8g/f 62 1849 b l e
0 15-15 Nott 8.2hvy 62 5191 b l e
44 12-16 Nott 10hvy 60 5345 b l e

AMONG DREAMS 2 ch f £298
64a 3-11 Wolv 7af 64 29
39a 15-15 Ling 7ap 66 337
31 15-17 Warw 7.1sft 66 1526
37 13-14 Wind 8.3g/f 63 1956

AMONG EQUALS 7 b g £0
0 18-18 Bath 10.2g/s 75 1098

AMONG FRIENDS 4 b g £0
49 6-6 Folk 7g/s [72] 1079
43 9-16 Nott 6.1sft [70] 1743
55 8-12 Folk 5g/f 67 2269 BL
44 7-9 Chep 6.1g/f 63 2626
19 11-12 Nott 8.2g/s 58 2931
21 14-16 Chep 10.2g/s 54 4365
27 16-19 Bath 5.7sft 52 5176

AMORAS 6 b m £2723
71a 7-12 Ling 8ap 72 17
74a 2-11 Ling 8ap 70 80

AMPELIO 2 ch c £0
26 13-13 Kemp 8g/f 4355
61 8-14 Leic 8gd 5059

AMPHITHEATRE 2 b g £4858
71 5-11 Hayd 5g/f 1880
31 16-18 Chep 6.1gd 2194
66 3-13 York 6g/f 2358
62 11-13 Newm 7g/f 66 3065
65a 3-11 Sout 6af 66 3393
67 3-12 Newm 7g/f [66] 3750
43a 11-13 Sout 7af 64 4040
70 1-20 LEIC 7g/f 62 4451*

AMSTERDAM 2 b c £11771
91 5-11 York 6g/s 1687
95 1-6 LEOP 6gd 2300*
102 3-7 Leop 7g/f 3494

AMUSEMENT 8 ch g £413
41a 4-7 Wolv 14.8af 2200
41a 6-11 Ling 12ap 2588
3a 12-13 Ling 10ap 3025
44a 3-6 Sout 16af 44 3397

AMWELL BRAVE 2 b c £5048
68a 4-11 Ling 8ap 71 54
72a 5-16 Sout 8af [69] 192
71a 2-7 Ling 10ap 69 325
73a 2-6 Ling 10ap 69 403
70a 3-14 Ling 10ap [71] 473
70a 3-13 Ling 10ap [70] 601
72a 5-14 Ling 10ap [68] 759
63 10-17 Donc 8gd [68] 919
55 5-9 Sout 10gd [65] 1283 vis
58 8-18 Nott 8.2sft 65 1470
44 8-18 Wind 8.3sft 62 1647 vis
28a 7-12 Wolv 12af 65 2203
53 6-13 Ling 10g/s 56 4182
28 7-12 Chep 10.2hvy 55 4708
48a 9-13 Wolv 8.6ap [62] 5336

ANABAA REPUBLIC 3 b f £7711
105 3-10 Deau 12.5Ver 4310

ANACAPRI 4 b f £0
0 8-12 Sout 8af 460
33a 6-7 Sout 7af 531
0 11-12 Sout 11af [35] 640
13 7-7 Ayr 10g/s [35] 1450

ANAK PEKAN 4 ch g £99274
94 1-18 KEMP 16g/s 80 1112*
105 1-17 CHES 18.7gd 90 1569*
109 3-19 Newc 16.1g/s 101 2771
99 8-9 Good 16fm [105] 3552
98 7-8 Long 20g/f [105] 4951
100 7-11 Newm 16sft [105] 5138

ANALYZE 5 b g £6207
72a 6-14 Ling 10ap 72 122
74 2-15 Brig 8fm 72 1691
74 3-12 Kemp 8g/f [73] 1915
71 5-11 Warw 8.1fm 73 2600
69 4-5 Sali 9.9gd 73 2694
57 11-15 Epso 10.1gd [72] 3216

73a 1-12 LING 8ap [67] 4974*
79a 2-12 Ling 8ap 73 5079
79a 4-12 Ling 8ap 74 5238

ANANI 4 ch c £24477
102 3-12 Nad 10g/f 105 789
108a2-14 Ling 10ap [104] 884
84 13-17 Newb 12gd [106] 1230
100 6-10 Good 9.9g/f [106] 1862
98 7-14 Asco 10g/f 104 2556
106 4-15 Good 9.9g/f 102 3506
58 15-15 York 7.9g/s 102 4061

ANATOLIAN QUEEN 3 b f £6823
65 3-11 Kemp 8hvy 1514
72 4-14 Wind 8.3g/s 2622
75 1-9 YORK 7gd 3121*

ANATOM 2 ch f £122
41a 6-6 Ling 6ap [40] 79
1a 8-8 Sout 5af [40] 197
7a 7-7 Wolv 5af [35] 703
23a 5-7 Ling 6ap [35] 1453 T
26 4-9 Kemp 6hvy [35] 1641 t
0 9-9 Wolv 6af [35] 1803 VIS

ANCHOR DATE 2 b c £1798
85 2-8 Sali 6sft 4577
54 7-12 Wind 6g/s 4945

ANCIENT EGYPT 2 b c £0
52 10-14 Bath 8gd 5018

ANCIENT WORLD 4 b c £226749
101 2-4 Wind 8.3sft 1649 T
110 2-6 Nott 8.2g/f [100] 2154
114 1-21 GOOD 8fm 103 3565+
103 8-12 Sali 8gd [110] 3886
115 1-8 WIND 10g/s [110] 4220*
119 1-7 SAN 8gd [110] 5074*

AND TOTO TOO 3 br f £17674
70a 1-16 LING 7ap 66 270* VIS
54a 5-8 Wolv 7ap 66 280 VIS
45a 11-11 Ling 8ap 70 547 vis
71a 6-14 Ling 7ap 70 604 bl
71a 2-11 Ling 8ap 69 760 bl
68a 4-10 Ling 7ap 69 799 bl
69a 4-12 Ling 7ap 69 1024 bl
71 2-19 Sali 7g/f 66 1723 bl
67 4-16 Ling 7g/f 67 2063 bl
61 8-9 Leic 8fm 67 2108 bl
72 2-10 Newb 7g/f 67 2312 bl
55 10-13 Ling 7.6g/f 68 2587 bl
71 4-12 Yarm 7fm 67 2864 bl
68 4-17 Newb 7g/f 67 3257 bl
71 2-11 Yarm 7gd 67 3364 bl
73 1-9 SALI 7gd 67 3456* bl
66 4-7 Yarm 7gd 69 3872 vis
91 7-12 Bath 8g/f [69] 3965 bl
71 6-11 Ches 6.1g/f [75] 4510 bl
60a 9-12 Ling 8ap 70 4743 bl
66a 8-13 Wolv 8.6ap 70 5364 bl

ANDAAD 4 b f £255
51a 5-14 Ling 10ap 430
42a 4-8 Wolv 12af 644
34a 7-14 Ling 10ap 50 757

ANDALUZA 3 b f £4152
61a 4-12 Ling 8ap 1044
72a 1-6 WOLV 7af 1321*
74 3-20 Newb 7g/f 1761
71 8-12 Sand 7.1g/f 72 2098

ANDEAN 3 b c £7077
92 1-19 YARM 8g/f 1130*
104 5-10 York 10.4g/s 1685

ANDREYEV 10 ch g £0
28 6-9 Ayr 6g/s [45] 1447
29 11-12 Hami 6g/s [45] 1600 p
17 10-11 Redc 6sft [40] 1662 vis
14 14-18 Ayr 7.2g/f 40 1897
34 5-10 Ayr 8g/s [39] 2544
0 11-13 Ayr 8sft [40] 5275

ANDRONIKOS 2 ch c £50473
94 1-3 HAMI 5fm 3247*

106 2-11 York 6g/s 4022
91 7-9 Newb 6g/f 4680
108 1-8 DONC 6sft [100] 5217* T

ANDURIL 3 ch c £1573
63a 6-8 Ling 8ap [71] 934
67 7-16 Beve 7.5g/s 70 1163
69 3-5 Brig 8g/f 69 1370
53 6-18 Wind 8.3sft 69 1647
65 4-10 Leic 10g/f 68 1965
48 10-14 Wind 10g/f 67 2452 P
59 8-14 Kemp 10g/f 64 3690
58 4-10 Hayd 8.1g/s 64 3906
56 8-13 Ling 10g/s 63 4182
15 17-20 Hayd 11.9g/s 60 4771 BL

ANDY MAL 2 b f £0
44 8-14 Thir 7g/s 3831
51 6-14 Thir 7g/s 4204
39 8-11 Thir 7fm 4375

ANEMOS 8 ch g £0
24a 14-14 Ling 10ap 57 101
50a 10-14 Ling 10ap 55 174 ble
43a 10-14 Ling 10ap 51 265 h

ANFIELD DREAM 2 b g £583
66 6-8 Kemp 5gd 2171
72 5-11 Warw 5g/f 2911
50 12-15 Nott 5.1gd 4859

ANGE GARDIEN 3 b c £0
113 5-15 Chan 12g/s 2308

ANGEL ISA 4 b f £673
11 14-16 Carl 5.9fm 50 2445
39 11-14 Yarm 6g/f 48 2855
42 12-12 Yarm 7fm 48 2864
29 7-14 Ayr 7.2gd [44] 3324
45 3-10 Carl 5.9fm [44] 3545
38 3-19 Kemp 6g/f [40] 4793 VIS
29 9-20 Yarm 6g/s [40] 5121 vis

ANGEL MAID 3 b f £0
2 9-9 Kemp 5g/f 3687

ANGEL RAYS 2 ch f £327
69a 4-14 Ling 7ap 4970
73a 5-14 Ling 7ap 5258

ANGEL RIVER 2 ch f £0
36 14-14 Yarm 7sft 5250
61 10-17 Yarm 6g/s 5350

ANGEL SPRINTS 2 b f £12523
77 3-10 Sali 5g/f 1716
81 3-8 Bath 5fm 2033
71 6-11 Sali 5gd 2658
89 1-10 WIND 6fm 3290*
93 1-6 WIND 6g/f [86] 4217*
85 4-6 Sali 6gd [90] 4854

ANGELAS GIRL 2 gr f £0
41 7-9 Brig 5.3fm 2257
0 9-9 Chep 5.1g/f 2625
3 10-10 Brig 6g/s 4139

ANGELICA GARNETT 4 ch f £1663
49a 10-14 Ling 7ap 52 344
46a 6-12 Ling 8ap [52] 401
40a 10-11 Ling 8ap 49 669 e
31a 10-10 Ling 8ap 45 770
50a 1-14 LING 12ap [45] 827*
0 10-10 Folk 12g/s 47 1082
1 17-17 Bath 11.7sft 47 1543

ANGELOFTHENORTH 2 b f £7423
58 3-5 Ripo 5g/s 1362
54 4-6 Carl 5fm 2442
70 3-8 Catt 5g/f 2847
58 3-6 Hami 6fm 70 3931
68 3-9 Catt 6sft 68 4049
16 10-10 Ches 5.1g/f 68 4049
71 1-16 RIPO 5gd [63] 4787*
40 22-29 Newm 6g/s 5087

ANGELOS PRIDE 3 ch c £4110
53a 3-8 Wolv 9.4af 299
40a 7-11 Wolv 7af 396

53a 2-9 Wolv 9.4af [57] 665
42a 3-7 Sout 8af [57] 721
57a 3-12 Sout 8af [59] 848
56a 3-8 Wolv 9af [59] 892
63a 1-7 WOLV 9.4af 55 1324*
40a 5-8 Sout 12af 61 1444

ANGELS VENTURE 8 ch g £0
25a 11-12 Ling 13ap 50 762

ANGIOLINI 7 ch g £0
0 11-11 Wolv 12af [35] 666

ANGLO SAXON 4 b c £838
71 11-13 Wind 8.3g/s [84] 1057
75 9-19 Ripo 10g/f 84 1781
82 3-8 Chep 10.2gd [82] 2197
45 6-7 Ayr 10gd 81 2507

ANGRY BARK 3 ch f £273
64 4-15 Bath 10.2gd 4826
54a 7-12 Ling 8ap 4975
29 8-13 Bath 10.2sft 5173

ANICAFLASH 3 b f £0
7 14-16 Newc 7sft 966
32 8-9 Ripo 8gd 1178

ANIMAL LOVER 3 b f £0
3a 11-12 Wolv 7af 55 74 T

ANISETTE 2 b f £1659
59a 2-13 Wolv 6af 126
42a 3-6 Wolv 6af 313
39a 7-9 Wolv 7af 381
45a 6-12 Wolv 6af 55 1374
4 16-20 Yarm 6g/f 52 1730 VIS
31a 6-12 Wolv 8.5af 49 2205
42 4-11 Yarm 11.5g/f 49 2346
30 9-11 Leic 10g/f [46] 2924
37a 8-12 Ling 8ap [45] 3286
28 6-14 Brig 9.9g/f 45 3300
42 3-11 Yarm 8g/f 41 3706
26 6-14 Good 8sft 41 4189
35 5-13 Folk 9.7g/f [40] 4372
43 3-19 Brig 9.9gd [40] 4903
39 7-18 Leic 10gd [40] 5042

ANISSATI 2 ch f £0
19 10-11 Donc 8sft 5205

ANNA GAYLE 3 ch f £0
39 12-13 Kemp 10gd 3186
44 14-17 Wind 8.3fm 3480
44 5-7 Bath 11.7g/f 3967
17 11-13 Folk 9.7g/f [45] 4372
30a 9-14 Ling 10ap [40] 4661

ANNA PALLIDA 3 b f £15629
43 18-19 Newb 8gd 1236
81 2-9 Sali 9.9g/f 1719
82 2-6 Newm 10gd 1892
70 3-13 Hayd 11.9g/s [81] 2230
84 1-13 KEMP 10g/f [80] 3038*
84 2-7 Newm 10g/f 80 3474
48 8-10 Ches 10.3sft 82 4071
82 3-7 Pont 8g/f [82] 4629
80 6-20 York 8.9gd 81 4999 VIS

ANNA PANNA 2 b f £3496
59a 3-8 Wolv 7af 276
62 6-10 Sali 7gd 2659
74 2-9 Warw 6.1g/f 2906
64 5-10 Sali 6gd [71] 3452
68 5-11 Wind 8.3fm 71 3799
75 2-8 Sand 8.1g/s [69] 4101
65 8-11 Wind 8.3g/s 72 4222

ANNA WALHAAN 5 b g £1724
27 14-15 Warw 8.1sft 75 1530
68 7-12 Kemp 8g/f [73] 1915
71 2-12 Sand 8.1g/s 70 2129
63 5-5 Leic 10g/f [70] 2401
42 12-17 Warw 8.1g/s 70 4668

ANNAKITA 3 b f £4929
1a 7-12 Wolv 12af 53 244
17 9-17 Pont 12hvy 48 1064
29a 7-9 Ling 16ap [45] 1414

37 10-13 Nott 14.1gd [45] 1990
37 4-9 Yarm 14.1g/f 40 2856
43 1-12 YARM 16gd 37 3493*
42 2-10 Yarm 14.1g/s 40 4255
46 3-14 Yarm 14.1g/s [45] 5123

ANNALS 2 b f £5897
88 1-5 GOOD 6sft 4234*
80 4-4 Newb 7g/f 4641

ANNAMBO 4 ch c £0
74 11-20 Newm 12gd 85 1172 vis
70 8-9 Thir 12g/f 83 1969 vis

ANNATALIA 2 ch f £4815
70 4-6 Sand 5gd 2364
79 6-13 Curr 6.3gd 2815
82 1-7 BATH 5g/f 2976*
62 21-24 Newb 5.2g/f 3266
75 8-13 Muss 5gd 81 4551
70 8-15 Ripo 5gd 78 4784
56a 8-12 Wolv 5.1ap [76] 4981

ANNIBALE CARO 2 b c £0
24a 11-12 Wolv 6ap 5177
71a 5-10 Ling 7ap 5259
55a 8-12 Wolv 7.1ap 5324

ANNIE HARVEY 3 ch f £1054
39 20-20 Nott 6.1gd 75 1239
61 8-15 Redc 7sft 73 1660
72a 2-8 Sout 8af 70 2495
53 5-9 Beve 8.5sft 70 2940

ANNIE MILLER 3 b f £0
47 9-19 Leic 6g/f 65 2925
59 7-11 Yarm 7g/f 65 3711

ANNIJAZ 7 b m £4209
60 2-16 Bath 5.7sft 54 1540
56 2-15 Redc 7sft 54 1660
57 4-19 Redc 7g/f 57 1820
49 7-8 Bath 5.7fm 57 2034
40 14-17 Ling 7gd 55 2397
52 4-6 Good 7gd 55 2539
46 6-18 Donc 7gd 53 2755
54 7-12 Yarm 7fm 53 2864
54 7-20 Chep 7.1g/s 52 3088
36 14-19 Chep 7.1gd 52 3401
31 8-8 Chep 8.1gd 51 3731
25 14-14 Bath 8g/f 48 3963
8 16-20 Chep 7.1g/s 46 4367 P

ANNISHIRANI 3 b f £619
74a 4-11 Ling 8ap 74 80
30a 12-12 Ling 8ap 74 369
71a 6-13 Ling 7ap 74 474

ANNIVERSARY GUEST 5 b m £420
12a 8-10 Ling 16ap [35] 650
37a 3-14 Ling 12ap [35] 968
27 4-9 Warw 15g/s [40] 1329
43a 3-9 Ling 16ap [40] 1414 P
32a 7-9 Ling 13ap [40] 1456
39 9-10 Bath 13.1g/f 40 1789
42 5-13 Nott 14.1gd [40] 1990
30 7-11 Thir 12g/f 37 2217

ANOLITAS 4 br c £9155
107 2-11 Dort 9.3gd 2637 bl

ANOTHER BOTTLE 3 b g £22831
68 8-22 Donc 7gd 72 955
87 1-5 AYR 9.1g/f [70] 2025*
87 1-10 NEWB 8g/f 78 2877*
81 3-6 Ayr 8gd [83] 3152
90 1-13 RIPO 8gd 83 4279+

ANOTHER CHOICE 3 ch c £18378
69 3-18 Nott 8.2fm 65 1007 t
78 1-12 BEVE 9.9sft 66 1306* t
78 1-14 BATH 10.2gd 72 1403* t
42 10-11 Newb 11g/f 78 1756 t
66 10-15 Newm 12g/f 78 3066 t
65 11-11 Newm 10g/f 78 3236 t
65 4-4 Sand 10g/s [73] 4068 t
80 1-9 YARM 10.1g/s [73] 4254* t
78 6-16 Sand 10gd 78 4609 t
87 2-9 Wind 10g/s 78 4943 t

87 2-19 Donc 10.3sft 80 5201 t
74 7-24 Donc 12sft 82 5372 t

ANOTHER CON 2 b f £7811
64a 3-10 Ling 8ap 232
61a 4-14 Ling 10ap 473
67a 1-10 LING 10ap 59 676*
68a 4-10 Ling 10ap 66 817
63a 5-6 Ling 12ap 66 915
43 11-19 Warw 10.9gd 66 1124
48 12-14 Bath 10.2gd 62 1403
62a 2-8 Ling 12ap [66] 2065 P
34 8-15 Wind 11.6g/f [58] 2267
42a 5-12 Ling 12ap [60] 3819
43a 8-13 Ling 10ap [60] 4112
37 12-15 Wind 10g/f [48] 4834 VIS
54a 8-14 Ling 16ap 55 5082
67a 1-12 WOLV 12.2ap 54 5339*

ANOTHER DEAL 5 ch g £0
37 9-11 Brig 7g/f [67] 3298
41 9-15 Chep 8.1sft 60 4057
19 11-15 Chep 10.2g/s 55 4299

ANOTHER EXPLETIVE 3 b f £0
30a 8-11 Wolv 7af [47] 396
2a 6-6 Ling 8ap [45] 651

ANOTHER FAUX PAS 3 b f £5512
76 1-12 GOOD 7g/f 1846*
61 11-13 Sand 8.1g/s [79] 2126

ANOTHER GLIMPSE 6 b g £9546
73a 4-10 Ling 5ap 72 755 t
77a 1-12 LING 6ap 71 880* t
56a 9-14 Ling 6ap 73 1025 t
64 9-13 Epso 5sft 69 1293 t
77 2-11 Folk 6sft 67 1578 t
67 3-12 Ling 5g/s 67 1615 t
81a 2-13 Wolv 6af 73 2053 t
0 9-9 Wind 6fm [69] 2760 t
70a 8-14 Ling 7ap 78 4446 t
78a 4-13 Wolv 6af 77 5181 t
82a 3-13 Wolv 5.1ap 77 5341 t

ANOTHER PLAN 2 b g £0
46 14-15 York 7.9gd 5002
34a 12-12 Ling 8ap 5293

ANOTHER SECRET 5 b m £429
47a 7-14 Ling 10ap 56 101
48a 4-14 Ling 10ap 53 236 BL e
52a 3-12 Ling 10ap 50 542 bl
48a 5-14 Ling 10ap 49 718 bl e
49a 4-14 Ling 10ap 49 757 bl e

ANOTHER VICTIM 10 ch g £0
37 6-12 Ling 5g/f 50 2743
12 15-15 Wind 5gd 46 3165

ANOUSA 3 b c £25347
59 12-13 Kemp 9gd 79 1141
84 1-13 KEMP 9hvy 77 1515* VIS
24 11-14 York 11.9g/s 82 1708 vis
63 8-11 Sand 10g/s 83 2127 vis
82 7-17 Asco 12g/f 81 2519
84 3-8 Ches 12.3g/s 81 2746
98 1-4 NEWM 14.8g/f [82] 3027*
92 7-7 Hayd 11.9sft [82] 3274
98 4-9 Good 14fm 95 3556
40 17-17 Newm 14.8gd 93 4196
0 7-7 Newm 14g/f [91] 4878

ANSELLS LEGACY 2 b c £0
54 8-9 Warw 7.1fm 2776
45 12-14 Ches 7sft 4102
57 6-7 Muss 7.1gd 4518
29 9-9 Ayr 7.2sft [53] 5064

ANSWER DO 4 b f £0
9 6-6 Ayr 6fm 1908

ANSWERED PROMISE 4 ro g £2592
4a 12-13 Sout 8af [58] 188
47a 7-14 Ling 10ap 55 236
46a 9-12 Ling 8ap 54 406
24a 7-9 Wolv 9.4af [51] 480
46a 6-14 Ling 10ap 51 498
54a 2-12 Ling 10ap 51 542

56 3-11 Warw 8.1fm 54 2600
49 3-7 Yarm 8g/f 54 2853
38 8-11 Bath 8gd 54 3142

ANTEDILUVIAN 3 b f £28072
107 1-6 HAMI 8.3gd 2710*
106 1-9 SAND 8.1g/s 2917*

ANTHEMION 7 ch g £8936
43 10-13 Muss 7.1g/f 62 1122
64 2-14 Hami 8.3gd 60 1504
48 11-14 Hami 8.3gd 60 1748
0 10-10 Newc 8g/f 60 2159
48 9-12 Ayr 8g/s [58] 2543
23 10-12 Hami 9.2g/s 55 2832
70 5-6 Ayr 8gd [50] 3152
81 3-6 Hami 8.3g/f [50] 3205
64 1-8 HAMI 9.2fm 50 3250*
59 3-12 Ayr 8gd 56 3328
64 2-9 Hami 9.2g/f 60 3593
25 15-17 Hami 9.2g/s 60 4008
52 9-13 Muss 8g/f [60] 4554
49 7-18 Ayr 7.2sft 60 4622
72 8-12 Muss 8gd [58] 4809
38 14-26 Redc 8fm 58 4926

ANTHOS 3 b f £358
74 5-6 Newm 6g/f [93] 2736
78 8-8 Newm 6g/f 90 3235

ANTICIPATING 4 b g £4120
80a 9-12 Ling 13ap 84 877
87 4-13 Epso 12fm 84 2255
82 7-13 Asco 12fm 85 2582
87 2-6 Wind 11.6fm [84] 2972
59 14-15 Good 14g/f 85 3510
51 7-9 Newm 12gd 85 3926
75 8-12 Epso 12gd 83 4292
75 12-15 Newb 11g/f 81 4643

ANTIGIOTTO 3 ch g £3989
52a 8-10 Ling 8ap 1021
34 11-15 Thir 7g/s 1473
61 11-20 Wind 10sft 1651
78 4-11 Folk 9.7g/f 2274
77 2-6 Sali 9.9gd [76] 2663
77 2-11 Leic 10g/f [76] 3208
69 8-14 Brig 11.9fm 78 3674
56 10-12 Sand 10gd 78 4502 BL
72 3-8 Hami 9.2g/s [76] 4821 VIS

ANTIGUA BAY 3 b f £1947
73 11-17 Newm 7gd 1171
43 8-13 Newm 8g/f 1935
70 2-8 Yarm 6gd 3873
37a 6-9 Sout 7af [74] 4131
50 3-6 Yarm 6g/s [70] 4586
64 4-9 Leic 7gd [66] 5041
47a 7-9 Ling 8ap [60] 5242

ANTLEY COURT 2 ch c £0
0 13-13 Carl 5fm 1950

ANTOINETTE 2 b f £0
76 6-19 Newm 7g/s 5279

ANTONIO CANOVA 8 ch g £3702
67 9-15 Folk 6sft 80 976
57 10-15 Pont 6hvy 75 1251
80 1-16 NOTT 6.1sft [70] 1743+
68 11-18 Donc 6gd 78 2752
65 7-11 Newm 6fm 78 3408
69 5-7 Yarm 7gd 76 3872
49 15-17 Wind 6gd 74 4126 VIS
59 11-12 Newm 6gd 74 4229

ANTONIO STRADIVARI 2 b c £0
64 7-8 Asco 6g/f 3438
73a 7-8 Ling 7ap 4176
68 5-10 Newc 6g/f 4403 VIS

ANTONIUS PIUS 3 b c £256170
114 2d-4 Long 8g/s 1433
118 5-7 Long 8g/s 1855
120 3-11 Asco 8g/f 2469 T
109 7-20 Newm 6gd 3062 t
112 5-11 Good 8fm 3533 VIS
119 3-11 Long 8g/s 4434
87 9-11 Asco 8g/f 4801 t

121 2-5 Lone 8g/s 5308

ANTONY EBENEEZER 5 ch h £4247
26a 5-10 Sout 11af [40] 375 t
39a 3-11 Sout 12af 40 458 t
20a 9-13 Sout 14af 40 590 t
28a 10-12 Ling 13ap 35 762 t
41a 1-15 SOUT 12af 35 867* t
34a 5-14 Ling 12ap [40] 968 t
18a 11-13 Ling 13ap [40] 1076 t
21 12-12 Ling 10g/f 35 2844
42a 2-14 Sout 12af 35 3486
34 6-14 Redc 10fm 40 4560

ANUVASTEEL 2 gr c £3885
76a 5-13 Ling 7ap 79 15
85a 1-10 LING 8ap 76 132*
85a 3-15 Ling 7ap 82 177
86a 2-10 Ling 8ap [83] 229
78 6-9 Kemp 9sft [82] 947
72 8-20 Newm 8fm 78 1496
65 9-12 Good 7g/f 76 1847
72 6-15 Sand 7.1gd 74 4500
60 12-16 Good 7gd 73 4873

ANY NEWS 7 ch g £0
2a 13-13 Wolv 8.6ap 55 5005 t

ANYHOW 7 b m £17010
44a 9-14 Ling 10ap [60] 477
56a 11-16 Ling 12ap 60 493
64a 2-11 Ling 12ap 57 624
67a 1-14 LING 12ap 59 801*
65a 4-9 Ling 10ap 64 876
59a 5-10 Ling 12ap 64 936
62 4-10 Bath 11.7gd 60 1399
65a 2-14 Ling 10ap 64 1618
68 1-10 BATH 13.1g/f 61 1789*
53 5-10 Chep 12.1gd 62 2114
64 3-11 Sali 12fm 62 2293
67 2-5 Sali 12fm 61 2422
68 1-11 NEWB 13.3fm 63 2651*
45a 8-8 Ling 12ap 68 3026
63 5-15 Wind 11.6fm 67 3481
55 5-12 Sali 12g/f 65 3868
51 8-20 Bath 17.2gd 63 4824
36a 13-16 Ling 12ap [60] 5296

AONINCH 4 ch f £3356
61a 6-14 Ling 12ap 62 801
45 11-14 Kemp 14.4sft 62 948
57 5-10 Folk 12g/s 61 1082
59 8-10 Bath 13.1g/f 59 1789
58 6-15 Sand 10g/f 56 2099
51 8-11 Sali 12fm 56 2293
66 2-14 Sali 12g/s 56 3114
58 6-6 Leic 11.8g/f 61 3345
65 2-12 Sali 12g/f 60 3868
66 6-17 Kemp 12sft 60 4033
50 10-13 Warw 12.6gd 62 4274
60 5-19 Sali 14.1gd 61 4856
60a 9-16 Ling 12ap 60 5261

APACHE POINT 7 ch g £2128
25 10-16 Newc 8hvy 60 1036
35 8-14 Pont 8hvy [60] 1253
56 5-14 Nott 10g/s 58 1776
55 4-15 Redc 9g/f 57 2120
57 5-8 Redc 8gd 56 2550
55 5-17 Hayd 8.1gd 54 2947
57 2-9 Hami 9.2gd 53 3132
57 3-13 Ayr 10gd 54 3325
53 5-17 Hayd 8.1gd 54 3759
55 5-17 Hami 9.2g/s 54 4008
52 5-12 Newc 9hvy 54 4215
53 5-14 Carl 6.9g/f 54 4345
45 9-15 Beve 8.5g/f 53 4598
48 5-17 Newc 8fm 51 4867
51 5-15 Redc 9g/s 51 5111

APEIRON 3 b c £5176
111 4-9 Deau 10hvy 4158

APERITIF 2 ch c £18124
80a 3-10 Ling 5ap 13
70 7-14 York 7.9g/s 75 1707
75 4-13 Sand 8.1gd 73 2365
81 3-16 Newm 8g/f 73 3059

59 3-10 Carl 6.9g/f [73] 3230
79 1-6 HAYD 8.1g/s [77] 3905*
73 7-15 Hayd 8.1g/f 77 4352
80 3-20 Ayr 10g/s 77 4656
89 1-14 HAMI 8.3g/s 77 4820*
83 10-22 Newm 8sft 86 5103
91 4-13 Bath 8sft 86 5172

APETITE 2 ch g £4200
29 10-10 Pont 5gd 3457
39 9-15 Redc 6g/f 3769
51 10-18 Pont 5g/s 3968
64 2-14 Thir 7g/s 4206
66 1-9 RIPO 6gd 4277*
54 10-17 York 6g/f 64 4396
46 10-11 Ayr 8sft 60 4688
44 11-18 Pont 6g/f 60 4934
39 14-18 Newc 6g/f 60 5013

APEX 3 ch c £16389
79 1-17 WARW 7.1sft 73 1526*
82 5-14 Newm 8g/f 78 1930
50 12-13 Newm 8g/f 78 2247
83 3-9 Sali 8g/s 78 3112
85 2-9 Ling 7gd 78 3447
92 1-15 NEWB 6gd 80 3920+
68 11-13 York 8g/f 89 4322
81 10-13 Asco 6.5g/f 88 4773
63 13-16 Newm 7sft 87 5101

APOLLO GEE 3 b g £0
8a 13-13 Sout 8af [64] 1193
9a 8-8 Wolv 7af [64] 1222 BL

APOLOGIES 2 b c £7231
70 7-13 Donc 5gd 954
80 1-10 HAYD 5sft 1107*
81 4-5 Donc 5g/s 1517
49 13-13 Newm 7g/f 78 3065
64 6-9 Hayd 5sft 78 3271
49 10-12 Hayd 5gd 76 3756
73 3-10 Beve 5sft 71 4258 BL
68 6-14 Catt 5g/f 71 4437 bl
73 3-19 Nott 6.1g/s 72 4645 bl
75a 3-13 Wolv 6ap [73] 4980 bl

APPALACHIAN TRAIL 3 b c £27005
83 3-17 Donc 8gd 919
81 1-9 RIPO 8gd [76] 1178*
90 2-8 Sand 8.1g/s 81 1315
32 14-15 Ches 7.6gd 86 1583
92 4-18 Hayd 8.1g/f 86 1919
95 1-4 NEWM 8g/f [89] 2533*
92 6-11 Sand 7.1g/s 90 2918
86 6-13 Newm 8g/f 90 3277
86 5-7 Leic 7fm 89 3814 VIS
84 5-10 Newm 8g/f [87] 4890

APPETINA 3 b f £425
67 5-12 Good 9g/f [77] 1864
65 5-11 Folk 9.7g/f [75] 2274
54 4-9 Folk 7fm [73] 2716
60 4-5 Donc 10.3g/s 65 3377
34 14-17 Catt 12sft 62 3929
27 10-14 Yarm 8g/s [60] 4252
24 14-19 Thir 6g/f 55 4595 BL

APPLE OF MY EYE 2 b f £5852
46 10-11 Ling 5gd 2395
67 4-10 Wind 6fm 3290
78 1-13 WIND 6fm 3639*
34 10-12 Sali 6g/s 79 4079
40 18-21 Donc 6.5fm 75 4457

APPLEACRE 4 b f £0
39a 9-10 Ling 12ap [85] 24

APPOLONIOUS 3 b c £0
59a 7-11 Ling 8ap 841
57a 7-10 Ling 8ap 1021
44 7-10 Wind 6g/f 3977
57 9-15 Ling 7gd 4445
53 6-11 Wind 6g/f [55] 4836 T
45 11-19 Bath 5.7sft 55 5176

APRIL ACE 8 ch g £0
2a 7-9 Ling 12ap [35] 414

APRIL SHANNON 2 b f £0

15 16-17 Ling 6gd 4443
30 11-11 Sali 7gd 4853

APRON 3 b f £0
70 9-10 Newb 10gd 1209
58 9-10 Sali 9.9g/f 1718
53 11-11 Sali 8fm 2419
10 12-12 Nott 10hvy 5190
24 7-7 Yarm 11.5g/s [50] 5351

APSARA 3 br f £8105
78 2-14 Kemp 10g/s 2678 VIS
87 1-11 **PONT** 10g/f 2991* vis
81 4-10 Newb 10fm 80 3630 vis

APSIS 3 b c £10282
111 2-9 Long 10g/s 4730

AQRIBAA 6 b g £0
36 13-15 Beve 8.5g/f 52 4598
36 15-19 Beve 9.9g/f 52 4720

AQUA PURA 5 b g £0
2a 8-9 Sout 16af 52 612

AQUALUNG 3 b c £4805
64 12-20 Bath 10.2gd 1398
92 1-12 **RIPO** 9g/f 1783*
68 8-8 York 10.4g/f 92 2406
63 15-15 Donc 8fm 92 4531

ARABIAN ANA 2 b c £4454
63 6-6 Hami 6g/f 3202
82 1-11 **NEWC** 7gd 3429*
72 4-11 Ches 7sft [83] 4072
74 4-9 Newc 8sft 79 4285

ARABIAN DANCER 2 b f £74105
78 2-12 Redc 6g/f 2119
92 6-17 Asco 6g/f 2553
84 5-10 Newm 6fm 3003
76 3-10 Yarm 8g/f [88] 3713
72 5-17 Chep 6.1sft [88] 4052
79 1-11 **BATH** 5g/f [82] 4409*
84 2-26 Newb 6.5g/f 4679
84 4-29 Newm 6gd 5087

ARABIAN KNIGHT 4 ch g £0
35a 12-14 Ling 6ap [62] 819
39a 8-12 Wolv 5af [60] 960
66 7-16 Bath 5.7g/s [57] 1103
47 9-20 Wind 6g/s 60 1255
35 8-11 Folk 6sft 58 1578
39 13-18 Bath 5.7g/f 55 1788
7 20-20 Chep 7.1gd 51 4488

ARABIAN MOON 8 ch g £2884
73 1-5 **BRIG** 11.9g/f [71] 3983*
40 8-9 Good 12sft 76 4183
70 7-15 Ches 15.9g/f 70 4512
55a 9-12 Wolv 12.2ap 69 4983

ARABIE 6 b g £313
31 17-17 Kemp 10g/s 92 1111
63 4-9 Epso 7gd [86] 3215
24a 11-14 Sout 8af 3392

ARAGON DANCER 3 b g £0
2a 8-9 Ling 6ap [40] 327

ARAGONS BOY 4 ch g £3153
48 17-19 Newb 10gd 71 1736
63 11-15 Beve 7.5g/s 70 2324
71 1-5 **BRIG** 8g/f [66] 2641*
58 7-10 Brig 8gd 72 2954
70 4-9 Nott 8.2g/f [70] 3423
46 11-15 Brig 8fm 69 3694
61 7-18 Catt 7g/f 67 4438
46 13-17 Newc 8fm 65 4867

ARAKAN 4 br c £67584
113 1-8 **NEWM** 6g/f [111] 1187*
109 3-15 York 6sft [111] 1667
111 2-10 Curr 6g/f [111] 1996
89 12-16 Asco 8g/f [111] 2470
111 1-8 **NEWM** 7g/f [111] 2765+

ARAMAT 2 b f £0
26 14-14 Wind 5gd 4121
11a 14-14 Ling 7ap 4970

46a 10-14 Ling 7ap 5078

ARAWAN 4 b g £0
0 10-10 Hayd 10.5g/s 86 1346
6 20-20 Donc 10.3g/s 84 1519
16 19-19 Ripo 10g/f 77 1781
5 14-15 Redc 9g/f 70 2120
53 8-11 Ripo 10g/f 65 2483
41 10-12 Beve 8.5gd 62 2890
49 10-12 Ayr 8gd 57 3328 BL
44 7-15 Redc 9g/s 53 5111

ARBELLA 2 ch f £4796
82 2-16 Kemp 7g/f 3035
79 4-13 Kemp 7g/f 3520
97 4-11 Newm 7g/f 3781
83 3-15 Leic 7g/f [98] 4455

ARBORS LITTLE GIRL 2 b f £6589
72 1-9 **BATH** 5g/f 3847*
70 1-12 **BATH** 5.7gd 58 4545*
58 5-19 Nott 6.1g/s 64 4645
70 3-19 Ling 6g/f [66] 4895

ARC EL CIEL 5 b h £7966
74a 1-10 **WOLV** 7af [66] 152*
63a 6-11 Wolv 7af 74 241
78a 2-8 Wolv 7af 74 280 vis
77a 1-11 **WOLV** 7af 73 363* vis
80a 3-13 Wolv 8.5af 78 439 vis
78a 3-10 Wolv 8.5af [78] 511 vis
66a 9-11 Ling 8ap 78 547 vis
73a 7-12 Wolv 8.5af 78 632 vis
78a 3-7 Wolv 8.5af 77 700 vis
59a 11-11 Ling 8ap [77] 800 vis
69a 6-12 Wolv 7af 76 840 vis

ARC EN CIEL 5 b g £0
42a 14-14 Ling 10ap 66 265
56a 4-8 Ling 16ap 66 288
25a 8-11 Ling 13ap [60] 515

ARC OF LIGHT 2 b c £0
77 5-8 Newm 6g/f 1934
70 7-15 Wind 6gd 3163
49 11-16 Leic 7fm 3811

ARCALIS 4 gr g £99607
97 1-8 **AYR** 10g/f 88 1895+
107 1-21 **YORK** 10.4gd 95 3118+

ARCH FOLLY 2 b g £0
67 7-10 Wind 8.3fm 3803
69 6-11 Chep 8.1g/s 4363
59 7-14 Yarm 8g/s 5118

ARCHDUKE FERDINAND 6 ch g £4875
62 13-17 Ches 18.7gd 88 1569
89 2-12 Good 14g/f 86 1861
0 14-14 Hayd 16.2gd 86 2239

ARCHENKO 4 b g £0
30 8-9 Muss 12g/f 1121
38 7-8 Hami 11.1gd 1390
55 6-9 Hami 12.1gd 1507
34 5-10 Beve 9.9g/f [45] 1946

ARCHEOLOGY 2 b f £1620
78 5-13 Newm 6g/f 4918
45 9-14 Redc 6g/s 5106
78a 2-14 Ling 7ap 5257

ARCHERFIELD 3 ch f £5550
69a 2-10 Ling 8ap 67 455
70a 2-12 Ling 8ap 69 603
63a 3-12 Ling 8ap [70] 734
57 11-15 Bath 8g/s 69 1099
29 17-17 Kemp 7gd 66 2174
60 2-5 Brig 8g/f [63] 2641 T
57 3-8 Epso 8.5g/f [63] 2873 t
65 3-16 Epso 8.5gd 59 3219 t
60 4-6 Epso 8.5fm 62 3540
48 4-19 Chep 8.1g/s [60] 4366 t
46 9-12 Brig 8fm [58] 4761 t

ARCHIAS 5 b g £0
59 7-7 Newc 16.1g/f 65 4405

ARCHIE BABE 8 ch g £5129

35 10-22 Donc 12gd 62 918
68 1-15 **NEWC** 12.4hvy 61 1034*
67 5-17 Pont 12hvy 67 1064
54 13-14 Nott 10g/s 66 1777
32 11-14 York 11.9gd 66 4327
36 15-20 Hayd 11.9g/s 66 4771
58 7-16 York 11.9gd 62 4990
23 9-10 Catt 13.8sft 60 5322

ARCHIE CLARKE 4 b g £0
15a 13-13 Wolv 9.5ap 5290

ARCHIE GLENN 2 b c £1525
63 7-8 Wind 5g/f 1955
39 15-15 Wind 6g/f 2263
79 4-8 Good 6g/f 4540
79 2-7 Chep 6.1hvy 4705
59 8-13 Wind 6g/f [79] 5047

ARCHIE WRIGHT 2 ch c £418
45 17-18 Newm 7gd 3927
58 7-17 Warw 7.1gd 4269
36 4-5 Epso 8.5gd 4464
35 7-12 Pont 8g/f [56] 5152

ARCHIRONDEL 6 b g £8309
53a 6-14 Ling 10ap 55 339
44a 10-14 Ling 10ap 55 718
0 U-22 Donc 12gd 52 918
0 14-15 Newc 12.4hvy 52 1034
40 8-19 Beve 9.9g/s 50 1164
50 2-19 Redc 8sft 46 1661
57 1-15 **REDC** 12g/f 47 2120*
34 10-14 Leic 8g/f 54 2402
61 2-8 Muss 12g/f 54 2616
62 1-10 **MUSS** 12g/f 54 2813*
56 5-8 Hami 11.1g/f 60 3207
58 5-10 Ripo 12.3g/f 58 3649

ARCTIC BLUE 4 b g £0
37 9-13 Yarm 11.5fm 52 2868
34a 10-11 Ling 16ap 50 3450 P

ARCTIC BURST 4 b g £0
56 12-13 Beve 5g/s [90] 1162 t
2 15-15 Pont 6hvy 90 1251 t
16 30-30 Newm 6g/f 85 1481 VIS
32a 12-12 Ling 6ap [78] 2016 vis
8 18-19 Beve 5gd 70 2512 vis
33 11-12 Catt 6g/f [63] 3017 vis
32 14-15 Chep 5.1gd 55 3403 vis
35 12-18 Pont 5gd 55 3463 vis
37 12-18 Pont 5g/s 49 3974 vis

ARCTIC COVE 3 b g £0
0 17-17 Newm 8gd 4228

ARCTIC DESERT 4 b g £8869
85a 13-15 Ling 7ap 90 887
77 18-20 Newm 7gd 90 1151
28 28-28 Asco 7g/f 88 2558
24 14-16 Wind 6fm 84 2758 VIS
58 18-20 Chep 7.1g/s 82 3088 vis
69 11-25 Asco 7g/f 78 3443
69a 6-14 Ling 7ap 75 3821 vis
80 1-8 **FOLK** 7gd [72] 4117*
73 6-13 Wind 8.3g/s 75 4221
82 2-21 Donc 7fm 77 4482
73 9-24 Newb 7g/f 77 4642
73 9-18 York 7gd 78 5000
82 2-20 Newm 7g/s 77 5286

ARCTIC QUEEN 2 br f £0
22a 14-14 Sout 8af 226

ARCTIC SILK 3 ch f £2540
63 10-14 Kemp 10g/s 2678
79 3-20 Newm 8gd 3237 T
79 2-7 Asco 8gd 3469 t
32 9-9 Sand 9g/s [77] 3892 t

ARDASNAILS 2 b g £0
46 12-14 Folk 7fm 2714
18 12-13 Sali 7g/f 3864

ARDERE 3 ch f £0
39 7-9 Sand 10gd 4501

ARDKEEL LASS 3 ch f £1093

23	9-9	Chep	5.1gd	66	2195
42	14-14	Ling	5g/f	62	2585
61	2-13	Wind	5fm	57	2784
43	4-13	Bath	5gd	[59]	3143
49	5-7	Brig	5.3sft	[58]	4169
42	12-18	Bath	5.7g/f	57	4412
52	6-15	Chep	5.1gd	57	4489

ARE YOU THERE 2 b f £0

10a	9-13	Sout	6af	[64]	63
40a	6-10	Sout	5af	[57]	139 VIS
26a	7-12	Sout	6af	[52]	200 BL
29a	9-15	Sout	7af	[47]	462
48a	6-10	Ling	6ap	[45]	606 bl
42a	4-5	Sout	7af	[45]	682
31a	9-11	Ling	8ap	[45]	696

AREIAS 6 b h £7746

108	3-13	Hamb	6hvy		3009

ARFINNIT 3 b g £8735

36	19-22	Donc	7gd	75	955
70	3-15	Wind	6g/s	72	1054
50	12-17	Warw	7.1sft	70	1526
46	6-14	Sali	7g/f	[70]	1720
59	5-8	Bath	5.7fm	67	1903 vis
67	1-6	RIPO	6g/f	[64]	1975* vis
54	6-12	Thir	6g/f	[64]	2215 vis
55	6-8	Good	6gd	64	2375 vis
63	1-5	AYR	6gd	[63]	2541* vis
56	6-9	Warw	6.1fm	[61]	2778
60	4-11	Brig	5.3gd	61	2957 vis
41	8-13	Bath	6gd	[60]	3143 vis
47	8-12	Folk	6gd	60	3380 vis
53	7-18	Hayd	6gd	58	3737 vis
62	2-13	Bath	5.7g/f	[58]	3844 vis
53	4-7	Brig	5.3sft	[58]	4169 vis
44	6-7	Good	5sft	58	4236 vis
10	16-17	Bath	5.7gd	[55]	5020 vis
55	4-13	Muss	5g/s	[55]	5146

ARGENT 3 b c £3429

0	P-7	Wolv	12af	[62]	959
30	8-12	Catt	12gd	62	1000
49	2-6	Beve	9.9sft	[58]	1630
34	7-8	Muss	8gd	53	1798
0	15-15	Ayr	8gd	[50]	2504 P
47	8-12	Ayr	8gd	50	3328 p
66	2-8	Hami	9.2g/f	[48]	3592 p
49	3-6	Hami	9.2g/s	48	4137 p

ARGENTUM 3 b g £5290

42	10-14	Wind	8.3g/s		2622
49	5-11	Folk	7g/s		3048
62	1-15	NOTT	10g/s	52	4037*
63	2-12	Beve	12.1g/f	56	4601
49	8-19	Sali	14.1g/d	59	4856

ARGONAUT 3 b g £3033

56	6-9	Pont	10hvy	[88]	1068
88	3-10	Asco	12g/f	88	3444
83	7-8	Newm	12g/f	[89]	3617
92	4-17	Newm	14.8gd	89	4196

ARIAN 2 b f £0

72	5-19	Leic	7gd		5040

ARIANE STAR 2 b f £0

59	9-18	Wind	6gd		2618
52	11-17	Nott	6.1gd		2927
54	5-6	Yarm	5.2gd		3488
35	11-12	Newm	7g/f		3750

ARIANS LAD 3 b g £536

55	8-17	Bath	5g/f		1787
36	12-15	Nott	5.1g/f		2152
31a	7-12	Sout	7af		2339
65	3-8	Chep	7.1sft		4055

ARICIA 3 b f £6027

78	8-17	Newm	7g/f		1171
90	1-16	NEWM	7fm		2092*
91	10-11	Asco	8g/f		2555
89a	6-12	Ling	8ap	[94]	5298

ARIES 4 ch f £0

54	9-18	Thir	8g/f	70	1972
48a	14-14	Ling	10ap	68	2392

ARIESANNE 3 ch f £729

38	3-4	Ripo	5g/s	3936
37	7-11	Beve	6gd	4237
26	6-9	Thir	6fm	4380

ARIODANTE 2 b g £4655

81	3-18	Wind	6gd		2618
86	1-8	LING	6gd		3021*
79	4-8	Asco	7gd		3467
50	12-12	York	7g/s	80	4064

ARJAY 6 b g £971

40a	12-13	Ling	10ap	[59]	912
19	15-20	Ripo	8g/s	56	1366 bl
44a	3-8	Wolv	9.4af	51	1657
33a	5-12	Wolv	9.4af	48	2054
48	3-15	Redc	9g/f	48	2120
15a	12-16	Sout	12af	45	2340
35	10-16	Hayd	10.5sft	47	3276

ARK ADMIRAL 5 b g £0

50	12-20	Kemp	9g/f	67	2857
55	10-13	Sali	6g/s	63	3109 t
38	11-14	Chep	8.1gd	61	3733

ARKHOLME 3 b g £23502

79	4-8	Sali	9.9g/s	82	1500
46	13-13	Hayd	11.9gd	80	2238
79	2-10	Newm	8g/f	[78]	2732 BL
82	1-10	ASCO	8gd	[76]	3067* bl
44	9-9	Sand	10g/f	80	3523 bl
84	3-14	Wind	8.3gd	[80]	4122 bl
87	1-15	KEMP	8g/f	80	4362* bl
81	4-18	Kemp	8g/f	83	4714 bl
84	4-12	Good	8gd	[83]	4872 bl

ARMAGNAC 6 b g £19274

52	19-22	Donc	6gd	81	921
71	7-20	Kemp	6gd	79	1138
67	8-17	Donc	6g/s	77	1523
80	3-13	Yarm	6g/f	77	1726
62	6-14	Ayr	6gd	77	1898
62	8-11	Ripo	6gd	79	1977
72	10-18	Donc	6gd	77	2752
83	2-11	Asco	6.5gd	75	3069
83	3-16	Newb	6g/f	77	3269
81	2-11	Donc	6g/f	[77]	3375
82	3-20	Newm	7g/f	79	3782
80	7-16	Newb	7g/f	80	3954
68	11-19	Kemp	6fm	80	4394
86	1-15	SAND	7.1gd	80	4500*
86	7-24	Newb	7g/f	85	4642
86	5-18	York	7gd	83	5000

ARMATORE 4 b g £0

64	11-14	Ling	11.5gd		3335
31	13-16	Ches	10.3g/f	68	4515

ARMENTIERES 2 b f £4880

54a	3-12	Wolv	8.5af	[59]	28 bl
52a	5-11	Ling	8ap	[55]	77 bl
52a	3-16	Sout	8af	[54]	164 bl
24a	9-11	Wolv	8.5af	[53]	279 bl
30a	6-10	Ling	10ap	[53]	291 bl
32	8-8	Brig	11.9g/f	58	3299 P
54	7-12	Beve	9.9g/s	55	3854 bl
50	6-15	Nott	10g/s	55	4037 bl
53	2-9	Brig	8sft	53	4165 bl
56	3-20	Chep	7.1g/s	53	4367 bl
54	4-20	Chep	7.1gd	52	4488 bl
52	7-18	Good	8gd	52	4750 bl
58	1-17	LEIC	7gd	52	5056* bl
34	7-16	Nott	8.2hvy	55	5347 bl

ARMS ACROSSTHESEA 5 b g £10001

53	2-8	Muss	12gd	[40]	1552
54	1-10	REDC	11g/f	[50]	1819*
64a	1-12	WOLV	9.4af	56	2054*
59	4-11	Leic	10gd	59	2135
50	10-11	Warw	12.6fm	61	2601
43a	7-10	Sout	8af	61	3395
62	1-7	YARM	10.1g/f	[57]	3704*
60	6-11	Yarm	10.1gd	[57]	3875
23	17-19	Leic	10g/f	60	4456
1	13-13	Nott	10g/s	[60]	4650

ARMY OF ANGELS 2 ch c £10249

90	2-6	Newm	6g/f		3031 T
98	1-6	LEIC	6g/f		3513+ t
98	2-4	Yarm	6g/s		4633 t

AROGANT PRINCE 7 ch g £9080

46a	4-10	Wolv	7af	[60]	298 p
51a	4-13	Wolv	6af	55	384 VIS
26a	7-13	Wolv	6af	[53]	483
47a	6-12	Wolv	7af	[53]	512 bl
50a	3-12	Wolv	6af	[53]	524 bl
60a	1-8	WOLV	5af	[51]	619* bl
26a	10-12	Wolv	6af	[49]	646 bl
60a	1-11	WOLV	5af	51	748* bl
47a	7-13	Wolv	6af	57	807 bl
46	8-17	Kemp	5sft	54	944 bl
46a	7-12	Wolv	5af	[59]	960 bl
62	1-15	FOLK	6g/s	52	1267*
31a	11-12	Sout	5af	58	1442 bl
36	19-18	Good	5g/f	60	1867 bl
48	6-6	Folk	6fm	[59]	2715
9a	12-13	Sout	7af	57	3155 bl
29a	13-14	Ling	7ap	[55]	5294
8a	13-13	Wolv	6ap	[55]	5359 bl

AROUND ALONE 7 b h £10845

108	2-7	San	15gd		1998

AROUS 2 b r f £0

58	7-12	Nott	6.1g/f		4844

ARRAN 3 ch c £4872

46a	10-14	Ling	6ap		23
54	9-14	Yarm	7fm		2148
53	3-9	Newm	6g/f	54	2529
48	9-13	Kemp	7g/f	53	3034
61a	2-10	Sout	8af	52	3395
62a	1-16	SOUT	8af	52	3487*
44a	9-14	Ling	7ap	52	3821
56	5-16	Nott	8.2g/s	53	4036
28	13-20	Chep	7.1g/s	53	4367
50	8-20	Leic	7gd	52	5046

ARRAN SCOUT 3 b g £2996

77	3-14	Thir	8gd		1636
54	10-12	York	7.9g/f	[77]	2410
0	11-13	Ayr	10sft	[74]	5066 BL
75	2-11	Donc	7sft	72	5219

ARRESTING 4 b g £4765

86	1-9	LEIC	11.8g/s	[85]	1016*
0	11-13	Kemp	14.4hvy	85	1516
85	6-9	Newm	12g/f	[85]	2246
82	5-9	Newm	14.8fm	85	2596
48	10-15	Leic	11.8gd	[84]	5060

ARRGATT 3 gr c £10584

82	3-13	Newm	10sft		1935
84	2-8	Redc	10g/f		2124
84	2-4	Redc	11gd	[83]	2549
77	1-8	HAMI	8.3fm	[83]	3246*
85	4-7	Wind	10fm	83	3801

ARRIVATO 2 b f £0

68a	9-14	Ling	7ap		5258

ARRJOOK 3 b c £425

73	4-13	Newm	8fm		2595

ARROW 5 b g £0

42a	9-13	Ling	10ap	49	805

ARRY DASH 4 b g £16475

90a	4-14	Ling	10ap	87	758
80	9-24	Donc	8gd	86	928
87	2-10	Hayd	10.5sft	[85]	1104
34	13-16	Epso	10.1hvy	87	1296
82	7-15	Kemp	10fm	86	2067
82	3-8	Newb	8gd	[84]	2313
74	7-13	Redc	10gd	83	2560
63	6-6	Epso	10.1g/f	[80]	2874
57	11-12	Kemp	10gd	79	3185
68	6-10	Nott	8.2g/f	75	3579
74	2-9	Newb	9gd	72	3922
74	3-5	Ayr	8hvy	[72]	4086
77	2-12	Good	9.9sft	73	4268
76	3-19	Kemp	9.0fm	73	4392
76	2-13	Epso	10.1g/f	73	4473
77	5-16	Sand	10gd	75	4609
74	7-12	Muss		[75]	4809 VIS

66	8-17	Wind	10g/f	73	5050	vis
85	**1-8**	**BRIG**	**9.9sft**	**[73]**	**5095***	

ART ELEGANT 2 b c £0
59	10-12	Good	7fm		3568
79	5-14	Kemp	8g/f		4356
76	7-11	Good	8gd		4746

ART EXPERT 6 b g £0
25a	7-9	Sout	12af	2724

ART EYES 2 ch f £876
79	3-19	Leic	7gd	5045

ART LEGEND 2 b g £404
70	4-5	Kemp	5g/s	1114
32	12-13	Newb	6g/f	1760
46	10-11	Sand	8.1g/s	3890

ART MASTER 3 b c £25704
116	**1-5**	**CHAN**	**8g/s**	**2639***

ART MODERNE 4 ch c £10282
113	2-12	Sain	8sft	993 BL

ART ROYAL 2 b c £0
82	5-15	Leic	7g/f	4455
48	18-23	Newm	7g/f	4885

ART TRADER 3 b c £46749
100	2-11	Newm	10g/f	88	3236
106	**1-16**	**GOOD**	**9.9fm**	**93**	**3553***

ARTADI 2 b f £532
48	7-9	Warw	5sft		1084
58	3-7	Folk	5sft		1574
44	5-6	Brig	5.3g/f		3296
35	6-6	Folk	7g/f	57	3723 e
40a	5-10	Sout	5af	[50]	4129 BL
49	4-17	Ling	6g/f	[50]	4316 bl
50	6-20	Leic	7g/f	50	4451 bl
38	6-16	Yarm	8g/s	50	4632 bl

ARTE ET LABORE 4 b f £0
2a	8-9	Wolv	9.4af	[45]	522

ARTHUR WARDLE 2 b c £1702
75	2-6	Hami	6g/f		2316
76	5-10	Leic	6gd		2703
47	13-20	Wind	6fm		2970
71	6-10	Kemp	6g/f	72	3521
61	13-20	Ling	7g/f	70	4444 VIS

ARTHURS DREAM 2 b c £0
43	13-13	Chep	6.1gd	3399
61	7-9	Muss	8g/s	5331

ARTIC FOX 2 b g £0
64	5-20	Newc	6sft		2682
40	12-13	York	6gd		3120
41	13-18	Ripo	6g/s		3939
48	9-13	York	7.9gd		4325
63	8-12	Newc	8fm	[52]	4866 BL
69	5-12	Newc	7g/f	[55]	5011 bl
54	5-10	Catt	7sft	[60]	5317 bl

ARTICULATION 3 b c £8084
77	4-8	Newm	10fm	3007
84	2-7	Newm	12fm	3405
89	1-12	HAYD	10.5gd	3740*

ARTIE 5 b g £21127
61	13-22	Donc	6gd	79	921
57	7-19	Redc	6sft	76	1145
77	2-20	Thir	5g/s	73	1476
86	**1-19**	**BEVE**	**5sft**	**75**	**1627***
50	18-20	York	5g/s	81	1683
49	15-15	Beve	5sft	83	2942
90	**1-12**	**YORK**	**5g/s**	**83**	**3073***
88	7-28	Good	6fm	86	3622
70	16-20	Hayd	5fm	87	3792
80	7-19	Ripo	6gd	86	3937
73	14-19	York	6gd	86	4005
79	7-15	Ayr	5g/s	84	4654
86	4-14	Ripo	6gd	83	4786
83	5-15	Catt	5sft	85	5125
90	5-16	Redc	6sft	84	5304

ARTIES LAD 3 ch g £0
63	5-14	Sout	6gd	1281

ARTIST RIFLE 3 b g £0
29	12-13	Newm	8fm	2595

ARTISTIC LAD 4 ch c £500
91	5-6	Donc	10.3fm	4492

ARTISTIC STYLE 4 b c £23427
44	8-11	Pont	6sft	[70]	1426
66	6-14	Thir	8gd	[68]	1636
55	8-18	Nott	8.2g/s	67	1778
62	7-12	Redc	8g/f	[67]	1823
59	**1-13**	**MUSS**	**8gd**	**[63]**	**2967***
66	3-12	Good	9fm	63	3625
75	**1-13**	**NOTT**	**10gd**	**63**	**3992***
72	**1-12**	**NEWC**	**9hvy**	**63**	**4215+**
81	**1-18**	**AYR**	**10.9sft**	**68**	**4623***
83	2-20	Hayd	11.9g/s	74	4771
103	**1-13**	**AYR**	**10sft**	**80**	**5037***
90	6-24	Donc	12sft	95	5372

ARTISTICIMPRESSION 3 b c £0
44a	10-11	Ling	8ap		841
0	11-12	Redc	10sft	68	1144

ARTISTRY 4 b f £4647
63a	**1-12**	**LING**	**7ap**	**57**	**1024***
57	5-14	Yarm	8g/f	62	1131
52	10-15	Sout	7gd	62	1282
52	10-16	Kemp	7gd	60	3184
57	1-12	Yarm	7gd	58	3490
64a	2-14	Ling	7ap	61	3821

ARTISTS RETREAT 5 ch m £0
0	11-11	Chep	10.2gd	[37]	3730
0	10-10	Beve	9.9sft	37	4260

ARTURIUS 2 b c £0
64	6-14	Yarm	7sft	5251

ARTZOLA 4 b f £0
38a	9-10	Ling	8ap	52	917
26a	12-14	Ling	10ap	50	3605
42a	7-14	Ling	7ap	50	3746
43	7-18	Kemp	10g/f	[49]	4791

AS HANDSOME DOES 2 ch g £916
70	2-20	Hayd	6gd		2882 T
30	13-13	York	6gd		3120 t
44	13-18	Newc	6g/s		3699 t
62	7-20	Redc	7fm	65	4337 t

ASAATEEL 2 br c £273
71	10-15	Ling	7gd		3285
70	8-11	Sand	8.1g/s		3890
66	4-9	Chep	8.1g/s		4297
60	9-9	Warw	7.1g/s	73	4666

ASADARA 2 ch f £0
55	6-10	Pont	5gd	3457

ASALEEB 3 b f £12583
84	2-11	Newb	10g/f		2349
70	**1-3**	**YARM**	**11.5fm**	**[80]**	**2867***
89	**1-12**	**SALI**	**12g/f**	**80**	**3868***
70	15-17	Thir	12fm	85	4377

ASAWER 2 b f £674
81	3-11	Donc	8sft	5205

ASBO 4 b f £1699
61	5-14	Leic	6g/f	60	3213
59	4-9	Yarm	6g/f	60	3705
59	3-9	Good	6sft	[59]	4262
59	5-20	Nott	6.1g/s	58	4646
53	6-18	Leic	6gd	57	5039
59a	3-12	Wolv	6ap	[57]	5155
49a	4-14	Ling	7ap	[55]	5294

ASCERTAIN 2 ch g £55397
85a	**1-12**	**LING**	**8ap**		**100***
94a	**1-6**	**LING**	**10ap**	**85**	**403***
102a	2-10	Ling	10ap	92	568
103a	**1-9**	**LING**	**8ap**	**[98]**	**756***
100	5-9	Nad	9af	[98]	989

ASH BOLD 7 ch g £1332
40	4-16	Beve	8.5g/s	[28]	3850
44	2-12	Newc	8sft	[40]	4284
22	9-11	Ayr	9.1sft	[45]	5067

46a	3-12	Wolv	8.6ap	[45]	5230

ASH HAB 6 b g £0
43	10-13	Sali	14.1gd	60	3454
9a	11-14	Ling	16ap	55	4319 P
0	14-14	Ling	16ap	[45]	4663 bl

ASH LADDIE 4 ch g £0
1	20-20	Donc	7g/s	[63]	1518
38	11-15	Redc	9g/f	58	2120
31	12-17	Warw	8.1fm	53	2440 P
22a	13-16	Sout	8af	49	3159 p
0	16-17	Carl	7.9fm	[45]	4506 BL

ASHARON 2 b c £0
33	7-7	Nott	8.2gd		3991
56	6-9	Yarm	8sft		4147
73	6-11	Donc	8fm		4462
33	13-13	Newm	8fm	80	4725
68	5-8	Yarm	5.2sft	70	5253
31	17-20	Donc	7sft	68	5373

ASHDOWN EXPRESS 5 ch g £72942
114	3-8	Newm	6g/f	[111]	1187
76	12-15	York	6g/f	[111]	1667
112	2-9	Wind	6g/f	[111]	1958
106	7-14	Asco	6fm	[111]	2580
119	2-20	Newm	6g/f	[111]	3062
117	4-12	Deau	6.5g/s	[111]	3838
105	9-19	Hayd	6fm	[117]	4384
86	11-14	Ling	6fm	[116]	5100

ASHES 2 b f £430
54	11-15	Wind	5gd		1380
63	5-6	York	6sft		1669
62	4-12	Ripo	5g/f		1974
31	10-16	Ripo	5gd	[64]	4787 BL
48	5-12	Pont	6g/s	[64]	5152
56	6-16	Nott	5.1hvy	57	5343

ASHKAL WAY 2 ch c £0
82	5-10	Kemp	8g/f	4712

ASHSTANZA 3 gr g £731
64a	4-11	Ling	8ap		322
65a	3-8	Sout	11af	63	614
56a	4-10	Sout	12af	63	796 P
29	13-18	Leic	10g/s	63	1017 p
35	10-17	Hayd	8.1gd	58	2243
38	9-12	Brig	6g/f	55	2435 BL
26a	14-14	Ling	7ap	62	5300

ASHTAROUTE 3 b f £0
37a	8-15	Sout	12af	[46]	89
35a	6-10	Sout	16af	[40]	307
45	9-13	Thir	12g/f	[49]	1768
37	5-7	Beve	16.2sft	49	2941

ASHTREE BELLE 4 b f £4614
79a	**1-9**	**WOLV**	**7af**	**72**	**27***
78a	4-9	Sout	7af	76	193
80a	2-8	Wolv	7af	76	285

ASHWAAQ 3 b f £4040
72	**1-11**	**RIPO**	**8gd**		**1177***
65	15-25	Newb	8g/f	78	4683
60	7-7	Pont	8g/f	76	4935

ASIA WINDS 3 ch f £1375
87	5-6	York	10.4sft	[93]	1666
90	9-18	Hayd	8.1g/f	93	1919
80	12-14	Sali	7gd	93	4331
82	11-15	Newm	7g/f	90	4891

ASIAN HEIGHTS 6 b h £0
0	7-8	Newb	12hvy	5224

ASIAN TIGER 2 b c £8307
88	2-8	York	5sft		1670
88	2-8	Good	5g/f		1816
80	5-8	Wind	5g/f		1955
87	3-10	Sali	6gd		2697
91	5-13	Newm	7g/f	86	3065
76a	8-13	Ling	7ap		3329
81	**1-9**	**BRIG**	**7g/f**	**[83]**	**3981***

ASIATIC 3 ch c £3740
90	2-9	Ches	12.3gd	80	1582
5	13-14	York	11.9g/s	80	1708

```
82  10-17  Asco   12g/f    86     2519
78   4-6   Wind   11.6fm [85]     2972
```

ASK FOR RAIN 2 gr f £1023
```
66  12-16  Sali   7gd             4329
70   3-10  Newb   6g/f            4637
```

ASK FOR THE MOON 3 b f £106183
```
116  1-6    SAIN   10.5g/s         1157*
116  1-7    LONG   10gd           2001*
```

ASK THE CLERK 2 b g £18836
```
67a  7-10   Ling   5ap              13
51a 12-15  Ling   7ap      72     337 P
71a  3-11   Wolv   6af     [67]    481
64a  5-9    Ling   5ap     [70]    572
37a 11-11  Sout   5af      70     609
73   1-12   FOLK   6sft     66     975*
44  13-19  Newm   6g/s     71    1154
78   2-17   Asco   6sft     71    1417
47   8-16   Nott   6.1sft  [73]   1743
71   3-10   Brig   6g/f    [73]   2048
65   4-9    Folk   6gd      73    2271
66   6-13   Newm   7fm      72    2590
72   4-9    Wind   6g/f     71    2797
73   3-11   Newm   7g/f     71    3283
72   3-9    Epso   6fm      71    3543
31   7-8    Pont   7gd     [71]   3684
68   5-15   Newb   6gd      71    3920
70   4-20   Ling   6g/f     70    4317
74   2-14   Epso   7gd      70    4465
48  20-25  Newb   7gd      72    4683
58  10-12  Epso   8.5gd    72    4909
73   3-20   Leic   7gd      70    5046
72   3-11   Donc   7sft     70    5219
80   1-20   YARM   7sft     70    5256*
```

ASK THE DRIVER 3 b g £1983
```
57   2-13   Nott   8.2gd    54    1242
48   4-11   Newc   8sft     54    1395
57a  3-14   Ling   10ap     54    2064
54   3-8    Sali   8gd      54    2701
40   7-9    Brig   9.9gd    53    2955
3a  13-14  Ling   10ap     53    3449
52   5-16   Bath   8gd      51    4828 BL
```

ASKWITH 2 b g £562
```
71   5-11   Newc   7gd             3429
71   3-14   Thir   7g/s            4207
54   8-10   Beve   7.5g/f          4602
```

ASPEN RIDGE 2 ch f £0
```
63   9-15   Wind   5gd             1380
66   7-19   Wind   5g/f            1805
51a  7-10   Ling   6ap             3818
41  10-17  Chep   6.1sft          4052
62   5-13   Leic   6gd       57   4697
```

ASPIRED 3 b f £314
```
56   7-15   Wind   10fm            3292
1    P-4    Beve   9.9g/s          3855
```

ASSIUN 3 b c £39436
```
112  3-9    Colo   8gd            1860
112  2-6    Hopp   8g/f           3166
106  3-16   Bade   8sft           4424
108  3-7    Colo   8sft           4839
```

ASSOON 5 b g £644
```
59   7-10   Ling   7gd            3446
63   3-15   Chep   18sft    58   4056 P
```

ASSURED 2 ch f £0
```
21  16-16  Newm   7g/f           3582
17  17-17  Yarm   6gd            4610
49  14-18  Nott   8.2g/f         4842 P
12a 10-12  Wolv   7.1ap          5158 BL
```

ASTEEM 2 b g £0
```
50  14-18  Wind   6gd            2618
57   5-6    Epso   6g/s           3041
57   8-17   Chep   6.1sft         4052
52  10-15  Chep   7.1gd   [55]   4483
36   8-9    Brig   6fm      55   4758
```

ASTI 3 b f £42479
```
112  2-6    Long   9.3hvy         1557
115  2-7    Long   10gd           2001
```


ASTON LAD 3 b c £1571
```
50   4-7    Newc   10.1gd         1871
40   6-8    Ripo   10g/f          2523
9    6-7    Catt   13.8g/f        3019
57   2-7    Ripo   9g/s    [45]   3263
53   5-12   Beve   9.9g/s         3854
42   8-13   Redc   14.1gd   50   4249
53   5-8    Hami   9.2g/s  [50]   4821
33  10-13  Ayr    10sft   [50]   5276
```

ASTRAC 13 b g £2119
```
49   5-19   Warw   5gd      51   1127
38a  9-11   Wolv   6af      50   1337
0   17-17  Nott   6.1sft   50   1606
52   2-11   Chep   7.1gd    48   2370
50   4-10   Kemp   6g/f     49   2861
39   9-11   Leic   7g/f     49   3210
47   8-16   Ling   6g/f     49   3602
49   7-18   Bath   5.7g/f   48   4412
48   4-15   Carl   5fm     [48]   4508
24   9-15   Brig   6gd     [48]   4905
```

ASTRAL PRINCE 6 ch g £0
```
42   5-11   Pont   8sft     48   1425 bl
30   6-8    Muss   12gd    [48]   1552 bl
```

ASTROCHARM 4 b f £54979
```
63a 14-14  Ling   12ap     75     83 bl
61   5-8    Muss   8g/s    [75]   1461 bl
81   1-8    NEWM   12gd     73   1889*
49   7-9    Donc   12g/f    76   2078
75   5-10   Newm   10fm     76   2592
85   1-8    HAYD   11.9gd   74   2881*
91   2-15   Newm   12g/f    80   3066
92   1-6    PONT   12gd    [83]   3458*
106  1-7    GOOD   14fm    [83]   3619*
96   7-10   Donc   14.6fm[103]   4460
96   5-8    Asco   12g/f  [103]   4774
```

ASTROMANCER 3 b f £5208
```
57a  2-11   Ling   13ap     50     11
54a  4-14   Ling   16ap     54    107
52a  4-13   Ling   16ap     54    137
50a 10-16  Ling   12ap     53    493
49a  4-8    Ling   16ap     52    733
51   5-17   Nott   14.1gd   50   1238
18   8-10   Muss   16gd     50   1551
37   7-8    Ayr    13.1fm   49   1905 BL
50   3-14   York   13.9g/f  49   2060
54   1-10   REDC   14.1g/s  49   2562*
39   7-9    Yarm   14.1g/f  50   2856
54   3-16   Warw   16.2gd   49   4276
11  15-20  Catt   15.8gd   49   4965
```

ASTRONOMIC 4 b g £0
```
63  13-13  York   11.9g/s  99   3076
```

ASTRONOMICAL 2 b c £564
```
82  14-14  Sali   7sft            4677
68   7-15   Newm   8gd             4883
```

ASTYANAX 4 b c £13291
```
1   18-18  Nott   14.1g/s  74   1772
73   5-9    Beve   16.2g/s  73   3181
66   9-13   Asco   16.2g/f  73   3387
79   1-9    YARM   14.1g/f  72   3703*
49   8-12   Ches   15.9sft  76   4106
84   2-13   Yarm   16g/s    76   4634
89   1-6    MUSS   16gd     77   4808*
60  21-34  Newm   18sft    79   5135
```

ASWAN 6 ch g £632
```
62   5-8    Nott   10g/f    64   2157
70   3-6    Beve   8.5gd   [64]   2514 t
31  12-12  Beve   8.5gd    66   2890 t
37   9-10   Hayd   7.1g/s   65   3137 t
19  18-18  Pont   8gd      65   3242 t
47  12-19  Newc   7g/f     60   5014 t
```

AT YOUR REQUEST 3 gr g £1725
```
74   3-8    Pont   10hvy           1067
56   3-4    Beve   12.1sft         1308
71   3-8    Chep   12.1g/f         2623
```

ATACAMA STAR 2 ch c £1865
```
37  15-16  Newm   7g/f            4677
82   2-19   Ling   6g/f            4895
71  10-19  Leic   7gd             5055
```


ATAHUELPA 4 b g £1500
```
61a 10-12  Ling   8ap      82    888
74   3-7    Sali   8gd     [77]   3453
75   3-8    Ling   11.5fm   73   3747
```

ATAVUS 7 b h £8381
```
73  12-17  York   7.9g/s   97   1686
96   6-20   Asco   7g/f     95   1926
46  22-28  Asco   7g/f     93   2558
90   5-11   Warw   7.1fm   [91]   2777
74  15-19  Newm   7g/f     91   3061
74  18-20  Newm   7g/f     88   3782
98   2-8    Newm   6gd     [85]   4226
92   6-7    Good   6g/f    [92]   4526
53  11-11  Good   7gd     [92]   4874
```

ATHBOY 3 ch c £6811
```
28a 11-14  Ling   10ap            473
64a  1-12   LING   8ap      55    603* VIS
72a  1-12   LING   7ap      63    729* vis
64a  9-12   Ling   8ap     [70]   798 vis
61a  8-12   Ling   8ap     [70]   2840 vis
0   13-13  Chep   8.1hvy   68   4709 vis
```

ATHBOY NIGHTS 2 b f £0
```
32  12-13  Wind   6g/f            5047
24  14-14  Nott   6.1hvy          5342
```

ATHOLLBROSE 3 b g £2984
```
48   4-12   Redc   10sft    56   1144
57   2-12   Beve   9.9sft   56   1306
48   4-11   Warw   12.6sft  56   1528
56   5-11   Beve   9.9g/f   56   1834
54   4-9    Beve   8.5g/f   55   2168
34  10-13  Redc   8gd      53   2552
11  12-15  Beve   8.5g/s   52   3182 BL
50   3-14   Redc   10fm     49   4560 bl
```

ATLANTIC ACE 7 b g £1764
```
59  18-24  Donc   8gd      82    928
61  11-17  Thir   8g/s     80   1475
68   7-14   Donc   8g/f    [78]   1877
65   6-9    Muss   8fm     [76]   2087
58   8-12   Beve   8.5gd    73   2890
23   9-9    Donc   8g/s     70   3225
58  11-19  Good   8g/f     65   3512
51  12-16  Thir   8gd      63   4592
12  15-15  Beve   7.5g/f   63   4719 p
54   8-26   Redc   8fm      59   4926 p
63a  2-13   Wolv   8.6ap   [55]   5184 p
65a  2-13   Wolv   8.6ap    58   5365 p
```

ATLANTIC BREEZE 2 br f £2630
```
67a  1-11   SOUT   8af            159*
43a  7-11   Sout   8af      68    252
20a  7-9    Wolv   9.4af    66    441 VIS
19a  7-8    Sout   11af     60    614
0    9-10   Sout   7af      56    794
34   7-14   Sout   10g/s    52   1051
40   7-11   Sout   10gd     47   1280
42a  3-8    Sout   12af     47   1444
25   9-16   Nott   10hvy    45   1611 P
```

ATLANTIC CITY 3 ch g £1085
```
73   2-7    Newc   10.1gd  [71]   1871
43   5-8    Ripo   10g/f   [71]   2523 P
67a 11-16  Ling   12ap     68   5261 e
```

ATLANTIC QUEST 5 b g £6907
```
68  14-18  Catt   7gd      83    998
81   5-16   Thir   7g/s     82   1474
72   7-20   Donc   10.3g/s  82   1519
67  12-19  Redc   7g/f     80   1820
83   1-10   THIR   8g/f    [80]   1970* p
77   5-8    Donc   8g/f     82   2425 p
72  16-20  Newm   8fm      82   3001 vis
0    B-7    Ayr    7.2gd   [80]   3326 p
50  10-10  Beve   8.5g/f   80   3501
77   4-16   Redc   8g/f     77   3768 p
```

ATLANTIC STORY 2 b c £7836
```
68   8-18   Newm   7gd             3927
93   1-11   EPSO   7gd            4289*
92   2-12   Newm   8gd      84    5089
```

ATLANTIC TERN 2 b c £0
```
46a  9-10   Ling   8ap             229
62a  6-14   Ling   10ap            367
```

ATLANTIC VIKING 9 b g £28546
```
27a 11-14 Ling 10ap   [53]  759
18  10-11 Donc 10.3gd [53]  930

62 13-15 Hayd 5g/f   96        1917
90 10-20 Epso 5fm    96        2253
95  4-13 York 5g/f   94        2359
90  8-15 Newc 5g/s   94        2727
84 16-24 Asco 5gd    93        3466
76  1-13 BATH 5.7g/f [91]      3844*
73  4-10 Wind 6g/f   [91]      3977
93  1-14 EPSO 5gd    88        4291*
88 17-22 Donc 5.6fm  98        4459
```

ATLANTIC WALTZ 4 b g £0
```
0 15-15 Leic 10g/s              1358 T
```

ATRIFFIC STORY 2 ch c £0
```
65 10-21 Donc 6sft              5368
```

ATSOS 2 b c £0
```
55  6-8 Kemp 5hvy               1510
69 6-10 Sali 5g/f               1717
38 13-13 Sali 6fm               2287
68 5-11 Bath 5g/f               3962
62 6-12 Bath 5.7gd   68         4545
58 17-20 Ling 7g/f   68         4741
```

ATTACCA 3 b c £221
```
62  6-11 Ripo 8gd    78         1176 p
40 10-10 Hayd 6g/f   77         1488 p
0  11-11 Hami 6gd    75         1745 BL
53  7-9 Redc 8g/f    [70]       3806
26 16-20 Ripo 6gd    65         4278
35 18-20 Ripo 6gd    60         4785 bl
```

ATTACK MINDED 3 ch g £0
```
24 8-9 Thir 8g/f                4593
```

ATTILA THE HUN 4 b g £0
```
16a 12-15 Sout 6af  [38]  167
30a 13-16 Sout 6af  [38]  227
26a 4-10 Wolv 5af   [30]  781 VIS
23  6-9 Muss 5g/f   [40]  1797 vis
28 11-20 Beve 5g/f  [40]  1948 P
21 5-13 Hami 5gd    35    2181
```

ATTISHOE 2 b f £0
```
54 8-14 Wind 5gd                4121
45 11-17 Ling 6gd               4443
```

ATTORNEY 5 ch g £6591
```
47a 3-12 Wolv 6af   [45]   33 e
46a 7-16 Sout 7af   [45]   66 e
22a 11-15 Sout 6af  47     168 e
29a 11-16 Sout 7af  47     208 e
55a 7-16 Sout 6af   [47]   227 e
38a 4-10 Wolv 6af   45     246 e
38a 3-11 Wolv 6af   [43]   296 e
31a 7-13 Wolv 6af   45     384 e
46a 1-13 WOLV 6af   [45]   397* e
18a 10-13 Ling 6ap  51     448 vis
20a 7-13 Sout 6af   47     500 e
47a 4-12 Wolv 6af   [47]   524 e
39a 7-11 Wolv 6af   46     643 e
25a 11-13 Sout 6af  46     741 e
51a 6-11 Sout 6af   [45]   775 e
23a 5-10 Wolv 6af   45     822 e
47a 3-12 Ling 6ap   45     844 vis
19a 9-10 Sout 6af   [45]   907 vis
34a 7-9 Ling 6ap    [46]   1012 vis
48a 1-8 SOUT 6af    [45]   1199* vis
52a 1-9 LING 6af    [45]   1248* vis
52 2-12 Chep 5.1sft [45]   1336 vis
50a 8-12 Sout 5af   56     1442 vis
52 3-18 Bath 5.7g/f 50     1788 vis
49 6-16 Good 6gd    50     2023 vis
42 6-7 Hayd 6g/s    50     2187 vis
43 5-18 Ling 6gd    49     2396 vis
1  16-20 Nott 6.1g/f 48    2630 vis
44a 9-15 Sout 5af   [54]   2803 vis
46a 8-15 Sout 5af   54     3000 e
37 6-10 Epso 6g/s   46     3045 vis
34 11-19 Donc 5g/s  46     3220 vis
44 13-26 Good 6fm   46     3569 vis
9a 15-15 Sout 5af   50     4043 vis
```

ATTRACTION 3 b f £671000
```
120 1-16 NEWM 8fm   [119]  1492*
122 1-15 CURR 8g/f  [119]  2005*
122 1-11 ASCO 8g/f  [119]  2555+
117 2-7 Newm 8fm    [119]  3004
75 10-10 Deau 8sft  [119]  4017
121 2-6 Leop 9g/f   [119]  4572
121 1-5 NEWM 8g/f   [119]  4915*
```

ATTUNE 3 br f £47576
```
83  4-17 Newm 7gd               1171
35 10-11 Asco 8sft              1419
81  1-7 THIR 8g/f    [80]       1770*
57 13-13 Sand 8.1g/s [80]       2126
72  8-8 Nott 8.2g/f  80         3421
88  1-8 NEWM 7g/f    77         3612+ BL
96  1-14 SALI 9gd    83         4331*
104 1-15 DONC 7fm    [82]       4479*
67 10-13 Newm 8g/f   [99]       4887
```

AUBONNE 4 ch f £25704
```
113 1-10 LONG 10g/s             2635*
```

AUDIENCE 4 b g £27001
```
51 10-10 Donc 8gd   [101]  922
92 12-20 Newm 7g/s  99     1151
73 7-14 Kemp 8hvy   95     1512
91 7-20 Asco 7g/f   92     1926 P
92 8-31 Asco 8gd    90     2489 p
100 2-20 Newm 8fm   90     3001 p
97 4-18 Newb 8g/f   93     3265 p
89 6-21 Good 8fm    90     3565 p
103 1-15 YORK 7.9g/s 92    4061+ p
108 3-8 Hayd 8.1fm  [98]   4386 p
64 23-32 Newm 9g/f  98     4916 p
94 10-11 Newm 8g/s  [105]  5283 p
```

AUDITORIUM 3 b c £1500
```
104 4-8 Newm 7g/f   [113]  1932
74 12-15 Asco 7g/f  [113]  2486
81 8-9 Good 8fm     [109]  3620
```

AUENTRAUM 4 br c £0
```
21a 12-12 Ling 6ap  80     5297
```

AUNT DORIS 6 b m £0
```
4a 12-12 Sout 6af   39     85 e
4a 10-10 Sout 6af   [35]   352 P
0  11-11 Sout 8af   [35]   372 p
```

AUNT JULIA 2 b f £810
```
83 3-14 Kemp 7g/f              4711
```

AUNTY EURO 2 br f £2677
```
69a 4-9 Ling 5ap              931
62 3-9 Warw 5sft              1084
68 3-7 Ayr 6g/f               1893
68a 2-10 Sout 6af             2382
52 9-9 Brig 7g/f    70        3297
63a 6-10 Sout 7af   70        3483
```

AURELIA 3 b f £888
```
78 3-5 Carl 11.9g/f  76        3653
74 8-13 Good 16g/f   77        4527
```

AUROVILLE 3 b c £1130
```
62 8-16 Beve 7.5g/s  68        1163
68 4-18 Nott 8.2sft  66        1470
61 7-18 Thir 8g/f    66        1769
62 5-9 Beve 8.5g/f   65        2168
56 7-14 Wind 10g/f   63        2452
53 7-15 Nott 10gd    62        3108 VIS
44 6-6 Thir 12g/f    60        3415 vis
56 2-10 Yarm 10.1gd  [57]      3874
0  P-13 Ling 10ap    [57]      4112
57 5-11 Yarm 11.5g/s [57]      4584
46 6-18 Leic 10gd    [55]      5042
```

AUSTRALIAN 2 b c £5304
```
87 1-10 KEMP 8g/f              4712*
```

AUSTRALIE 3 b f £0
```
110 6-7 Long 10gd              2001
```

AUTHENTICATE 2 b f £465
```
70 4-16 Nott 6.1gd             3103
75 6-18 Nott 8.2g/s            4035
72 10-16 Sali 7gd              4329
67 18-26 Newb 6.5g/f           4679
```

AUTHORITY 4 b g £0
```
66a 5-11 Ling 8ap              4977
65a 8-14 Ling 7ap    [70]      5240
```

AUTUMN DAZE 2 b f £0
```
8a 10-10 Ling 6ap              3818
0  11-11 Ling 8ap              4744
0  11-11 Wolv 7.1ap            5228
29 17-17 Yarm 6g/s             5350
```

AUTUMN FANTASY 5 b h £519
```
52 4-5 Muss 14g/s    67        1459 t
2  12-12 Thir 16gd   64        1637 t
51 7-9 Newc 16.1gd   60        1870
3  8-9 Ripo 16g/f    60        2009
```

AUTUMN FLYER 3 ch g £0
```
57 9-16 Bath 10.2g/f           1790
47 9-14 Wind 10g/f   65        2452
52 8-11 Ling 10gd    [62]      3201
54 5-12 Bath 11.7g/f 57        3845
11 10-12 Brig 11.9fm 54        4764
```

AUTUMN GLORY 4 b c £96224
```
99 1-24 DONC 8gd     82        928*
103 1-17 YORK 7.9g/s 94        1686+
56 28-31 Asco 8g/f   103       2489
67 16-21 Asco 7g/f   103       3441
105 6-12 Sali 8gd    [102]     3886
108 1-4 DEAU 8hvy    [102]     4311*
108 5-12 Long 7g/s   [102]     4731
118 1-16 NEWM 9sft   [106]     5139*
```

AUTUMN MELODY 2 b f £0
```
77 5-16 Kemp 7g/f              3035 T
71 6-13 Kemp 7g/f              3520 t
67 5-7 Redc 7g/f               3770 t
```

AUTUMN PEARL 3 b f £42830
```
95 1-7 KEMP 6hvy     [87]      1513*
100 2-12 Epso 5g/f   [93]      2206
102 3-9 Newm 5fm     98        2593
93 6-10 Ayr 5g/f     [98]      3304
78 13-13 Good 5fm    [98]      3551
99 2-11 Hami 5sft    [97]      4693
88 10-11 Mais 6sft   [97]      5313
```

AUTUMN WEALTH 3 ch f £17104
```
79 2-13 Kemp 10g/f             3038
68 2-7 Nott 10g/f              3422
79 1-11 BEVE 9.9sft            4261*
83 1-13 BATH 11.7sft 74        5174*
97 3-14 Donc 10.3sft [79]      5370
```

AUWITESWEETHEART 2 b f £2063
```
66 5-6 Good 6gd               2373
65 5-11 Bath 5g/s             4200 T
66 5-8 Sali 6sft             4577
72 3-19 Bath 6gd    68        5021
72 2-12 Bath 5sft   [68]      5169
```

AVEIRO 7 b g £10525
```
24a 9-10 Ling 13ap   34        11 bl
39a 4-12 Wolv 12af   [34]      114 bl
42a 1-9 SOUT 11af    [31]      204* bl
38a 4-12 Wolv 12af   38        244 bl
29a 7-10 Wolv 12af   [31]      250 P
50a 2-10 Sout 12af   45        321 bl
51a 1-16 SOUT 11af   [45]      445* bl
52a 3-7 Sout 12af    51        504 bl
49a 3-7 Sout 12af    [51]      679 bl
52a 3-10 Wolv 16.2af 52        812 vis
54a 2-9 Ling 12ap    52        842 vis
65a 1-7 WOLV 16.2af  52        866*
63a 2-11 Wolv 12af   62        937
17 8-13 Pont 21.6hvy 52        1252
0 10-12 Newc 14.4sft 52        1396
40 7-11 Leic 11.8fm  47        2112
44a 5-7 Wolv 14.8af  [62]      2200
27 8-10 Hami 13g/f   45        2479
```

AVENING 4 br c £0
```
23 17-19 Sali 6gd    81        4855 BL t
```

AVENTURA 4 b c £318
```
72a 14-14 Ling 10ap  85        625
26a 9-12 Wolv 8.5af  85        688
83a 4-11 Ling 8ap    [80]      800
57 19-24 Donc 8gd    85        928
```

58	10-10	Hayd	10.5sft	[83]	1104
74	9-30	Newm	6g/f	80	1481
60	7-10	Warw	7.1sft	[80]	1525
70	7-12	Donc	7gd	75	2235
51	15-16	Catt	7sft	72	5130
30a	11-12	Wolv	7.1ap	68	5289

AVERAMI 2 b f £0

64a	6-10	Ling	5ap		13
66a	5-10	Ling	5ap		176
55a	4-10	Ling	6ap	[68]	260
49a	9-15	Ling	7ap	[68]	671
57a	5-14	Ling	7ap	[64]	804 VIS
23	11-12	Folk	6sft	59	975 vis
36	13-16	Ling	7gd	55	3024 vis
47a	6-10	Ling	6ap	55	3332 vis
35	10-20	Thir	6g/f	50	3575 vis
21	11-12	Folk	6g/f	47	3911
35a	6-14	Ling	7ap	[50]	4660 BL

AVERLLINE 3 b f £0

58	7-10	Brig	6g/f	[73]	2048
32	8-8	Good	6gd	70	2375
51	8-10	Brig	7fm	65	3672
9	10-10	Ling	6ap	60	4109 T

AVERSHAM 4 b c £2163

88	3-19	Kemp	6fm	85	4394
87	5-14	Ripo	6g/f	87	4786
79a	4-12	Ling	6ap	80	5297

AVERTAINE 3 b f £846

57a	9-15	Ling	7ap		814
52a	12-15	Ling	7ap		875
56	5-10	Folk	9.7sft		977
51	2-11	Sout	10gd	50	1280
49	7-13	Beve	12.1g/f	53	1836
49a	6-14	Ling	10ap	52	2064
47	5-13	Bath	8fm	50	2667 BL
33	8-17	Chep	8.1g/s	49	3087 bl

AVERTIGO 2 b c £2585

68	5-9	Ling	6gd		3020
76	3-6	Brig	6g/f		3171
73	2-6	Leic	6g/f		3513
26	11-12	Sali	6g/s	74	4079
74	2-15	Folk	6g/f	[74]	4369
47	4-6	Brig	6gd	[73]	4900
37	25-29	Newm	6gd		5087 BL

AVERTING 2 br c £1284

55	5-7	Bath	5g/f		2976
65	2-7	Folk	5g/f		3722
54	7-9	Good	6gd		3951
55	7-14	Warw	6.1g/f	65	4420
7	19-19	Nott	6.1g/s	65	4645 BL
33	17-18	Wind	5g/f	56	4830 bl

AVESOMEOFTHAT 3 b g £0

60	6-16	Bath	10.2g/f	[74]	1790
45	9-9	Kemp	12gd	72	2175

AVESSIA 3 b f £439

65	4-10	Sali	6gd		3452

AVIATION 2 b c £880

73	7-8	Kemp	6sft		4028
86	3-14	Hayd	6fm		4385
69	5-8	Good	6g/f		4540
80	5-11	Sali	7gd	[78]	4853
58	9-13	Wind	6g/f	[78]	5047

AVIT 4 ch f £4897

22a	8-9	Ling	5ap	[45]	572 BL
23a	11-14	Ling	6ap	[45]	652
41a	2-10	Ling	5ap	[40]	832
33a	3-8	Ling	5ap	[40]	1290
0	9-10	Brig	5.3gd	[40]	1544
22a	6-12	Wolv	5ap	[40]	1799
10a	8-10	Sout	6af	[40]	1837
40	1-10	BRIG	5.3fm	35	2331*
42	4-14	Ling	5g/f	39	2585
35	5-15	Chep	5.1gd	39	3403
25	11-16	Wind	5fm	38	3640
38	2-11	Bath	5g/f	38	3849
15	15-15	Good	5gd	40	4751
23	7-19	Kemp	6ap	[40]	4793
32	6-20	Yarm	6g/s	[40]	5121

AVIZANDUM 2 b g £0

5	12-13	Thir	6g/f		4590
34	15-15	York	7.9gd		5002

AVONBRIDGE 4 b c £75926

118	2-13	Newm	5g/f	[113]	1479
117	1-8	CHAN	5g/f	[113]	2305*
111	5-14	Asco	6fm	[113]	2580
115	4-13	Good	5fm	[114]	3551
115	4-12	York	6g/f	[114]	4060 BL
110	5-15	Long	5g/f	[114]	4952 bl

AVONDALE LAD 3 ch g £0

0	11-13	Wolv	6af	[48]	30 VIS

AWAASER 2 ch f £511

68	4-10	Newb	6g/f		4637

AWAKE 7 ch g £15694

59	12-20	Donc	5gd	76	927
69	6-15	Pont	6hvy	72	1251
74	5-13	Epso	5sft	72	1293
51	11-19	Beve	5sft	71	1627
83	1-11	CHES	5.1gd	70	2286*
79	6-12	Thir	5g/f	78	2690
83	2-16	Newm	5g/f	78	3033
66	9-17	Pont	5gd	78	3241
87	1-12	NEWC	5gd	79	3427*
74	13-20	Hayd	5fm	85	3792
59	15-15	Catt	5sft	84	5125
72	14-18	Pont	5g/s	84	5149 vis

AWAKEN 3 b f £0

59	7-9	Newc	10.1g/f		5015
11	7-10	Muss	12g/s		5145

AWARDING 3 ch g £157

68a	9-14	Ling	6ap	80	149
73a	6-10	Ling	7ap	78	262 t
65a	5-10	Sout	6af	75	390 t
67a	8-10	Ling	5ap	72	755 t
33a	14-14	Ling	6ap	70	874 t
46	17-19	Thir	6g/f	78	1767
62	8-8	Chep	10.2gd	[74]	2197 t
18	7-7	Sali	8gd	[70]	3453
9	15-15	Sali	6gd	63	3888 BL t

AWESOME LOVE 3 br c £5960

87	3-9	Asco	7g/f		1929
83	2-7	Muss	8fm		2081
74	2-11	Beve	7.5g/s	[83]	2325
74	2-11	Beve	8.5gd	[79]	2656
65	6-7	Pont	10g/f	[77]	2994
34	12-12	Ayr	8gd	74	3328 BL
46	5-6	Hami	11.1sft	[70]	4011

AWWAL MARRA 4 ch f £1078

42	7-13	Thir	12g/f		1768
43	3-8	Hami	8.3fm		3246
30	14-19	Beve	9.9g/f	45	3505
24	9-18	Beve	9.9g/s	44	4243
17	16-19	Thir	12g/f	45	4594

AXFORD LORD 4 gr g £0

0	6-6	Newc	10.1gd	[60]	3430
40	8-8	Hami	6g/s	[55]	3880
0	15-15	Ayr	7.2hvy	55	4088
0	16-17	Ayr	9.1g/s	[45]	4620 vis

AYAM ZAMAN 2 b f £20090

84	5-15	Newm	8fm		4723
90	1-15	PONT	10g/f		4933*
102	1-9	NEWM	10g/s	[86]	5281*

AYLMER ROAD 2 b c £1999

85	2-16	York	7.9gd		4997
63	4-9	Nott	10hvy		5189

AYNSLEY 2 ch f £383

63	4-11	Hayd	5g/f		4349
52	5-5	Pont	5g/f		4625
43a	8-12	Wolv	5.1ap		4922

AZA WISH 2 b f £273

59	7-9	Muss	5g/s		1458
59	5-7	Ches	5.1g/s		1571
2	16-16	Ripo	6g/f		1780
8	8-12	Redc	6g/f		2119
49	6-10	Newc	7fm	[60]	4864

58	4-13	Newc	7g/f	[58]	5012
56	5-8	Muss	9g/s	[58]	5140
41	8-11	Donc	8sft	[58]	5205

AZAHARA 2 b f £3543

0	16-18	Newc	6g/s		3699
48	7-8	Redc	7gd		4247
75	1-12	NEWC	7g/f		5011*
59	11-19	Redc	8sft	72	5302

AZAMOUR 3 b c £653338

119	3-14	Newm	8g/f		1480
118	2-8	Curr	8g/f		1995
123	1-11	ASCO	8g/f		2469*
124	1-8	LEOP	10g/f		4571*
120	3-11	Newm	10sft		5136

AZAROLE 3 b c £3750

105	5-11	Newm	7gd	108	1167
103	4-8	Kemp	8fm	[108]	2069
105	4-14	Newb	7g/f	[106]	4638

AZIZAM 2 ch f £0

68	7-21	Newm	8sft		5097

AZREME 3 ch c £23527

46a	14-16	Ling	7ap	71	20 vis
35a	6-8	Wolv	9.4af	68	157 e
72	1-13	WARW	7.1hvy	[68]	1537*
62	5-8	Nott	8.2g/s	[70]	1775
67	7-16	Ling	7g/f	70	2063
56a	4-12	Sout	7af		2496
53a	5-14	Sout	6af	[65]	2502
73	4-14	Wind	8.3g/f	69	2799
75	3-13	Asco	7g/s	69	3068
51	12-17	Newb	7g/f	69	3257
74	2-13	Kemp	7sft	70	4030
50	7-8	Folk	7gd	[70]	4117
81	1-10	AYR	7.2sft	72	4689*
85	2-11	Muss	7.1g/s	76	5144
65	12-20	Newm	7g/s	77	5286
67	7-10	Catt	7sft	77	5320

AZUREE 3 b f £4831

73	2-6	Sali	6g/f		1499
3	6-6	York	6sft		1669
73	3-6	Leic	6g/f		2399
53	8-11	Sali	5gd		2658
70	4-13	Kemp	6gd		3183 BL
69	3-7	Brig	7fm	[77]	3691 bl
22	13-13	Newm	5g/f	71	3943 bl
67	5-14	Yarm	7g/s	67	4583 bl
66	4-18	Pont	6g/f	65	4934 bl
5	13-20	Newb	6hvy	64	5225 bl

B A HIGHFLYER 4 b g £279

33a	13-14	Ling	6ap	62	1025
63	5-15	Sout	7gd	66	1282
53	9-13	Bath	8sft	65	1542
42	12-16	Good	6gd	63	2023
48	13-16	Brig	7fm	61	2258
59	5-17	Wind	6fm	58	3643
49	4-15	Sali	6gd	58	3888
0	B-15	Bath	5.7g/f	58	3966

BA CLUBMAN 4 b g £0

0	14-15	Leic	10g/s		1358 BL
25	5-9	Folk	9.7sft		1581
0	9-9	Hayd	10.3g/f		1885 P

BAAWRAH 2 ch c £7558

74a	3-13	Wolv	9.4af		37
74a	2-12	Ling	10ap	[71]	120
76a	2-14	Ling	10ap	[72]	367
73a	1-14	LING	10ap	[71]	473*
64a	4-10	Ling	10ap	72	568
38	13-14	Donc	10.3gd	70	923
67	6-16	Sand	10g/s	65	2919
34	14-20	Catt	12gd	65	4966

BABA 3 ch g £0

51	8-16	Newc	7sft		966
12	9-9	Leic	7gd		5041
7	12-13	Catt	5sft		5321

BABE MACCOOL 2 ch c £0

70	6-11	Wind	6g/s		4941
66	6-13	Wind	6g/f		5047

BABODANA 3 ch c £90125
92a	9-14	Ling	10ap	[107]	82
113	1-24	DONC	8gd	107	951*
107	6-10	Sand	8.1g/s	[111]	1349
109	3-9	Hayd	7.1g/f	[111]	1486
109	5-9	Wind	8.3fm	[111]	2757
110	5-10	Asco	8gd	[110]	3124
109	4-13	Newb	7g/f	[108]	3957
103	6-11	York	7g/s	[108]	4063
113	4-4	York	8.9gd	[107]	4323 BL
108	3-16	Newm	9sft	[107]	5139
111	2-11	Newm	8g/s	[107]	5283

BABOOSH 3 b f £7731
70	2-13	Pont	8g/s		3973
82	1-13	NOTT	8.2g/f		4847*
50	11-14	Donc	10.3sft	[76]	5370

BABOUSHKA 3 b f £0
| 33 | 8-8 | Newc | 8hvy | | 1039 |
| 0 | 12-12 | Beve | 9.9sft | 59 | 1306 |

BABY BARRY 6 b g £5989
25a	11-12	Wolv	7af	60	68 vis
41a	8-15	Sout	6af	59	168 vis
29	11-12	Leic	6fm	57	2111 vis
24	13-16	Carl	5.9fm	54	2445 vis
32a	11-16	Sout	8af	55	2805 vis
52	3-15	Ches	7.6g/f	47	3102
42	10-19	Chep	7.1gd	47	3401
52	2-18	Catt	7af	46	3670
33	8-15	Catt	7sft	46	3933
49	2-17	Carl	7.9fm	[47]	4506
54	1-18	GOOD	8gd	47	4750*
24a	8-13	Wolv	8.6ap	54	4982

BACHELOR AFFAIR 2 b c £0
| 54 | 14-23 | Newm | 7g/f | | 4885 |
| 58 | 10-19 | Newm | 7g/s | | 5285 |

BACHELOR DUKE 3 b c £156244
113	7-14	Newm	8gd	[114]	1480
121	1-8	CURR	8g/f	[114]	1995*
112	7-11	Asco	8g/f	[120]	2469

BACHELORS TONIC 5 b g £0
| 0 | 9-9 | Wolv | 9.4af | | 239 |

BACK AT DE FRONT 2 b f £3290
66a	5-8	Sout	5af	76	169
58a	9-10	Ling	5ap	76	217
51a	4-9	Wolv	6af	[74]	247
65a	1-8	WOLV	6af	60	422*
58a	5-11	Wolv	6af	[60]	466
57a	5-11	Sout	6af	64	609
57a	4-11	Ling	6ap	63	735
60a	5-9	Wolv	5af	[60]	835
54a	6-11	Sout	6af	60	872
23a	13-15	Ling	7ap	[59]	935
38	18-20	Nott	6.1gd	70	1239
30	11-14	Leic	6g/f	[67]	1963
22a	8-11	Wolv	6af	[58]	2202
33a	6-9	Sout	6af	[55]	2493

BACK IN ACTION 3 b c £0
68a	12-14	Ling	12ap	79	83 t
14a	12-15	Ling	12ap	[75]	118 BL t
62	7-8	Wind	8.3g/f	75	2448 t
32.	14-15	Newm	12g/f	70	3066 t

BACK IN FASHION 3 b f £0
| 2 | 16-17 | Leic | 7gd | | 2704 |

BACK IN SPIRIT 4 ch g £829
24a	10-12	Wolv	6af	45	385 t
12a	10-14	Sout	6af	40	501 t
12a	10-12	Wolv	6af	[40]	1799 t
15a	7-16	Sout	6af	33	2806 t
39	2-19	Nott	6.1gd	[30]	3104 t
32a	4-15	Sout	5af	38	4043 t
1	14-16	Chep	7.1hvy	[40]	4707 t

BACK TO PARIS 2 b c £1219
| 85 | 3-7 | Curr | 6g/f | | 2003 |

BACK TO REALITY 2 ch g £0
44	13-15	Chep	7.1gd		4483
48	8-11	Bath	10.2gd		4825
56	8-15	Nott	8.2hvy		5344

BACKGAMMON 3 b c £7037
79	2-6	Pont	10sft		1428
82	3-7	Hami	9.2gd		1747
79	1-12	NEWC	8g/f		4407*
75	4-7	Pont	8g/f	78	4935
50	11-13	Bath	8sft	76	5172

BACKLASH 2 b f £1523
45a	11-11	Ling	6ap		135
45a	8-13	Ling	6ap		364
21a	13-14	Ling	6ap		449
32a	7-11	Sout	6af	51	591
44	5-14	Warw	7.1sft	45	1085
39a	5-6	Ling	8ap	[45]	1246
48	1-17	WARW	8.1g/s	[40]	4992*

BACKSTREET LAD 2 b c £0
23	15-16	Sali	7gd		3882
66	9-13	Sali	7sft		4576
52	10-15	Sali	8gd		4851
32a	10-12	Wolv	8.6ap		5115

BAD INTENTIONS 4 b f £0
46	6-8	Bath	5.7fm	[70]	2669
37	14-14	Yarm	6g/f	70	2855
55	10-11	Warw	5.5gd	70	3054
38	6-11	Epso	8g/f	[65]	3541
20	10-10	Yarm	7g/s	60	4251

BADDAM 2 b c £1045
46	4-7	Nott	6.1g/f		2629
71	8-16	Leic	7fm		3811
71	6-7	Warw	7.1gd		4271
69	3-20	Yarm	8g/s	65	5349

BADMINTON 3 b f £17400
| 109 | 1-12 | ASCO | 7g/f | [107] | 4811* T |
| 89 | 8-12 | Newm | 7sft | [107] | 5134 t |

BADOU 3 b g £3568
39a	15-16	Ling	7ap	55	55 vis
27a	11-12	Ling	8ap	[51]	150 vis
11a	14-16	Ling	7ap	[47]	214 vis
39a	6-10	Ling	8ap	[45]	410
44a	1-12	WOLV	7af	[40]	528*
43a	4-12	Ling	8ap	[45]	649
48a	1-14	LING	8ap	[45]	709*
40a	7-13	Ling	6ap	51	767
35a	7-14	Ling	7ap	[45]	783
35a	12-15	Ling	7ap	47	913
40a	2-9	Ling	6ap	[45]	1248 vis
36	4-10	Kemp	5hvy	[45]	1644 vis
29	9-11	Brig	7fm	43	2334
27	10-18	Ling	6gd	43	2396 vis
18	13-15	Folk	7g/f	[40]	4371 vis
15	12-19	Kemp	6g/f	[40]	4793

BADR 3 b c £0
56	6-7	Muss	9g/s		1462
63	7-11	Beve	9.9g/f	69	1834
55	5-6	Redc	11g/f	65	2103
42	17-18	Leic	10gd	62	2706
43	7-9	Hami	9.2gd	59	3132

BADRINATH 9 b g £0
| 10a | 12-12 | Ling | 10ap | [48] | 272 |

BAFFLE 3 b f £5902
73	1-12	HAYD	8.1sft	[77]	1108*
71	5-13	Kemp	9hvy	77	1515
61	7-12	Hayd	8.1gd	76	2904
75	6-12	Hayd	8.1gd	74	3738
52	13-15	Hayd	8.1g/f	73	4352

BAGAN 5 b h £3686
87	4-20	Newm	12gd	85	1172
82	4-19	Newm	12g/f	86	1484
90	4-14	York	10.4g/s	86	1704
50	18-21	York	11.9gd	88	3999
86	4-8	Donc	12fm	87	4534
47	15-17	Newm	12g/f	86	4889

BAGO 3 b/b r p £984241
123	1-8	CHAN	9g/s		2307*
121	1-4	LONG	10g/s		2825*
122	3-9	York	10.4gd		4002
119	3-8	Long	12sft		4566
128	1-19	LONG	12g/f		4956*

BAHAMA BELLE 3 b f £468
39	13-17	Sali	6g/f	62	1722
59	4-14	Sali	7fm	[57]	2291
29	12-19	Leic	6g/f	57	2925
47	7-7	Bath	5g/f	55	3371 BL
16a	14-14	Ling	7ap	52	3746 bl
18a	10-11	Wolv	7.1ap	[45]	5210

BAHAMA REEF 3 b g £2600
49a	8-10	Ling	7ap	[67]	911
62	9-10	Good	8g/f	[63]	1815
55a	5-12	Ling	6ap	[63]	2016
59	2-8	Brig	7g/f	55	2434
39	8-9	Brig	8gd	[57]	2953 P
51	3-11	Brig	7g/f	[57]	3298
56	3-13	Ling	7g/f	55	3604
57	3-15	Ling	7.6fm	55	3788
49	11-15	Ling	7gd	[55]	4445

BAHAMIAN BAY 2 b f £0
19	8-8	York	7g/s		3078
0	13-13	York	7gd		3431
46	8-16	Ripo	5gd		4787

BAHAMIAN BELLE 3 b f £322
40a	5-10	Wolv	7af	[52]	4 bl
49a	6-12	Ling	6ap	50	880
5a	9-10	Ling	6ap	[48]	973
54	4-20	Ripo	5gd	56	1179 T
46	7-16	Bath	5.7sft	56	1540 t
36	15-17	Nott	5.1g/s	55	1774 t
0	20-18	Good	5g/f	55	1867 bl
41	13-15	Ling	5g/f	54	2062 t
38	8-10	Brig	5.3fm	50	2331
31	9-12	Brig	5.3g/f	48	2645
17	5-5	Folk	5g/s	45	3050
26	7-12	Brig	6g/f	40	3301
7	13-19	Kemp	6g/f	[40]	4793
36	4-16	Brig	7gd	[35]	4901

BAHAMIAN BREEZE 3 b g £0
| 60 | 9-10 | Wind | 6gd | [81] | 1383 |
| 61 | 12-12 | Wind | 5g/f | 76 | 1809 VIS |

BAHAMIAN MAGIC 2 b c £6533
74	4-13	Ling	6gd		3120
89a	3-8	Ling	5ap		3600
83	1-11	BATH	5.7gd		4543*
15	12-12	Newm	6ap	83	4882
91a	2-11	Ling	6ap	83	4972

BAHAMIAN PIRATE 9 ch g £148920
104	1-7	NOTT	5.1fm	[114]	1004+
96	4-8	Newm	6g/f	[112]	1187
107	4-11	Leic	7g/s	[112]	1356
106	2-7	Hayd	6g/s	[110]	1487
107	1-8	BEVE	5sft	[108]	1626*
91	10-15	York	6sft	[110]	1667
111	7-19	Asco	5g/f	[105]	2468
103	8-14	Asco	6fm	[105]	2580
72	10-11	Newc	6g/s	[105]	2769
95	17-20	Newm	6g/s	[105]	3062
117	1-7	NEWM	5fm	[105]	3409+
105	6-13	Good	5g/f	[105]	3551
119	1-12	YORK	5g/s	[110]	4060+
101	12-19	Hayd	6fm	[110]	4384
105	9-15	Long	5g/f	[110]	4952

BAHAMIAN SPRING 2 b c £0
| 31 | 12-12 | Newm | 7gd | | 4194 |

BAHIA BREEZE 2 b f £19154
85	4-8	Kemp	5gd		4028
91	1-15	FOLK	6g/f		4369+
90	8-24	Redc	6fm	[89]	4928
99	1-8	NEWM	6sft	[86]	5267*

BAHIANO 2 ch c £22771
76a	2-8	Wolv	7af		276
79a	2-6	Wolv	8.5af		468
83a	1-8	LING	7ap	[72]	713*
96a	2-9	Ling	8ap	[72]	756
101a	3-15	Ling	7ap	[92]	885
104	6-10	Newb	7gd	[95]	1234
99	7-14	York	7sft	100	1665
76	17-18	Hayd	8.1g/f	98	1919
106	4-15	Asco	7g/f	[97]	2486

BAKHTYAR 3 gr g £657

60	19-21	Asco	7g/f	105	3441
0	9-9	Good	8fm	[105]	3620
89	12-14	Newb	7g/f	[104]	4218
103	8-15	Asco	7g/f	104	4800

BAHJA 2 ch f £2084

81	4-14	Newm	7g/f		3944
87	3-16	Sali	7gd		4330

BAILADOR 4 b c £9613

116	3-9	Deau	12.5hvy		4312

BAILAMOS 4 b c £12676

106	2-8	Bade	16gd		1993
103	8-10	York	15.9gd		4000

BAILAORA 3 b c £908

64	6-11	Kemp	8hvy	[79]	1514
70	8-17	Newb	8g/f	[79]	1762 bl
72	6-15	Ling	7g/f	75	1983 bl
71	3-10	Nott	10g/s	[73]	2930 bl
31	7-7	Folk	9.7gd	72	3384 bl
65	5-8	Newm	10g/f	[72]	3471 bl
46	12-12	Bath	11.7g/f	69	3845 bl
64	4-11	Folk	9.7gd	[66]	4120 T

BAILEY GATE 2 b f £5980

71	7-10	Newb	6gd		3917
57	9-13	Kemp	6g/f		4358
89	1-14	NEWB	6sft		5197*

BAILEYS APPLAUSE 2 b f £530

74	5-15	Wind	5gd		1380 P
45a	3-7	Wolv	5af		1652 p
65	6-10	Newm	6gd		1887
30	12-12	Ling	5gd	67	3284 BL
0	12-12	Wind	6gd	64	3825 bl
62	6-13	Newm	6g/f	64	3943 bl
39	4-8	Brig	5.3fm	[63]	4759 bl

BAILEYS DANCER 3 b f £8401

60	8-8	Sand	8.1g/s	87	1315
71	4-7	Nott	8.2sft	[85]	1741
73	9-14	Asco	10g/f	81	1924
55	12-14	Nott	8.2g/f	78	2153
77	2-8	Newm	10g/f	74	2735
20	10-10	Ripo	12.3g/s	75	3261 BL
83	1-5	CARL	11.9g/f	75	3653+
21	9-9	Muss	12gd	80	3926
77	8-9	Muss	12g/f	81	4553

BAILEYS HONOUR 2 b f £0

2	B-10	Pont	6fm		4752
50	12-15	York	7.9gd		5002
41a	10-11	Ling	8ap		5235

BAILIEBOROUGH 5 b g £17624

61	10-18	Catt	7gd	70	998
54	6-13	Redc	7sft	[69]	1142
57	7-17	Thir	8g/s	69	1214
67	3-13	Muss	7.1gd	67	1553
68	4-14	Hami	8.3gd	67	1748
61	8-12	Redc	8g/f	[68]	1823
73	1-6	PONT	8g/f	[68]	2037* vis
70	3-15	Beve	7.5g/s	67	2324 vis
54a	8-15	Sout	8af	67	2500 vis
74	1-10	MUSS	9g/f	[67]	2811+ vis
61	6-8	Ayr	10gd	[70]	3151 vis
50	5-15	Newc	7gd	[70]	3426 vis
71	1-11	MUSS	8g/f	[70]	3558* vis
70	1-9	AYR	7.2g/f	[68]	3764* vis
60	3-8	Hami	9.2g/s	[68]	4133 vis
68	2-8	Muss	9g/f	[68]	4173 vis
62	9-19	York	7.9g/f	68	4399 vis

BAJAN STORM 2 ch c £0

43a	10-13	Wolv	6af	61	1 BL

BAKER OF OZ 2 b c £5150

51a	8-10	Wolv	7af	72	112
73a	2-12	Ling	8ap	[67]	734
34a	6-10	Wolv	8.5af	[68]	839
72	4-6	Folk	5g/s	[72]	1079
74	1-7	WIND	8.3g/f	[70]	2264*
63	7-10	Leic	7g/f	[72]	2920
60	9-12	Good	9fm	72	3625
55	7-11	Newm	8gd	[72]	3923
41	9-13	Warw	7.1g/s	[72]	4667

BAKHTYAR 3 gr g £657

52	8-12	Wind	11.6g/s	63	1260
32	12-20	Wind	11.6sft	61	1648
59	4-16	Wind	11.6g/s	58	2621 BL
57a	5-11	Ling	16ap	58	3450 bl
59	4-15	Chep	18sft	55	4056 bl
31a	14-14	Ling	16ap	55	5082 bl

BAKIRI 6 b g £7055

15	13-18	Wind	8.3g/s	75	1059
62	4-9	Folk	15.4sft	70	1271
14	12-12	Ches	12.3gd	67	1599
61	5-18	Nott	14.1g/s	60	1772
60	2-8	Newc	12.4g/f	[59]	2163
62	3-11	Thir	12g/f	59	2217
66	2-9	Thir	12fm	60	2465
60	4-11	Warw	12.6fm	60	2601
53	7-10	Newb	11g/f	64	2875
49	9-15	Wind	11.6fm	60	3481
61	1-16	WIND	11.6gd	55	3829*

BAKKE 2 b c £0

63	9-13	Newb	6g/f		1760
59	14-15	Newb	7g/f		2876

BALAKIREF 5 b g £24994

67	1-13	SOUT	6g/s	53	1052*
36	9-19	Redc	6sft	59	1145
67	2-15	Sout	7gd	62	1282
66	2-10	Hami	6gd	62	1391
66	2-13	Warw	7.1hvy	[64]	1537
0	U-12	Donc	7gd	64	2235
72	1-13	AYR	7.2g/s	64	2568*
66	10-18	Newc	6g/s	69	2770
67	9-15	York	7gd	69	3117
65	8-13	Newc	7gd	69	3428
66	5-6	Hayd	6g/s	68	3903
79	1-7	AYR	6hvy	68	4087*
79	3-12	Newm	6gd	73	4229
79	4-26	Ayr	6g/s	73	4652

BALALAIKA TUNE 4 b f £1588

0	16-16	Sout	7af	48	202
29a	8-9	Sout	7af	[43]	303
22a	7-16	Sout	8af	[40]	442
3a	9-12	Sout	11af	[35]	640
30a	6-16	Sout	11af	[30]	852
0	15-16	Newc	10.1sft	40	1278
34	4-9	Ayr	13.1g/s	[40]	1449
22	7-10	Muss	16gd	40	1551
28	10-13	Ripo	12.3g/f	35	2008
43	4-9	Redc	16fm	[35]	2298
29	6-10	Redc	14.1g/s	35	2562
0	13-14	Carl	17.2gd	32	2937
38	3-7	Muss	12gd	32	2966
37	2-11	Catt	12g/f	[28]	3190 T
33	6-14	Catt	12g/f	[34]	3668 t

BALASHOVA 2 b f £0

51	5-5	Ripo	5g/s		1362
0	U-7	Newc	5sft		1394

BALAVISTA 3 br c £5629

90	1-11	HAYD	8.1gd		2885*
67	9-12	Hayd	8.1gd	84	3738

BALEARIC STAR 3 b c £11460

67	6-18	Nott	8.2fm	70	1007
53	7-13	Kemp	9hvy	68	1515
73	1-14	WIND	8.3g/f	66	1956*
68	7-12	Sand	9g/f	69	2385
53	14-16	Sand	10g/s	69	2919
56	6-11	Sali	8gd	69	3455
78	1-16	NOTT	8.2g/s	66	4036*

BALERNO 4 b g £10021

36a	11-14	Ling	10ap	53	101
36a	12-14	Ling	10ap	50	265
50a	1-11	LING	8ap	[45]	408*
55a	3-11	Ling	8ap	51	669
39a	11-11	Ling	8ap	51	732
45a	4-10	Ling	8ap	51	770
51a	5-11	Ling	8ap	51	820
46a	8-15	Ling	7ap	50	846
50a	5-15	Ling	7ap	50	913
52	2-19	Yarm	7g/f	47	1132
55	3-13	Muss	7.1g/s	51	1463
47	7-20	Yarm	8fm	51	2149

(BALERNO continued)

53	4-17	Ling	7gd	50	2397
42	7-11	Warw	8.1fm	50	2600
56	2-17	Newm	7g/f	50	2768
63	1-16	KEMP	7gd	54	3184*
63	2-12	Yarm	7gd	59	3490
58	5-11	Kemp	8g/f	59	3685
31	11-13	Kemp	7sft	62	4030
57	6-15	Epso	7g/f	61	4475

BALGARTH 2 b c £0

57	11-18	Newc	6g/s		3699

BALI ROYAL 6 b m £2200

95	6-10	Kemp	5fm	[104]	2068
83	4-8	Sali	6fm	[104]	2421
97	8-13	Chan	5g/s	[104]	2638
73	12-12	Sand	5g/s	[102]	2913
86	9-10	Ayr	5g/f	[98]	3304
53	10-10	Asco	6gd	98	3773

BALI STAR 8 b g £1967

38a	5-15	Sout	6af	[43]	167
10a	10-10	Wolv	5af	[43]	286
39a	2-16	Sout	5af	[40]	374
36a	4-10	Ling	5ap	[40]	653
32a	7-10	Ling	5ap	[40]	832
12	17-19	Warw	5gd	45	1127
30a	4-8	Ling	5ap	40	1290
49	1-12	CHEP	5.1sft	[45]	1336*
2	16-17	Nott	6.1sft	46	1606
36	9-18	Bath	5.7g/f	46	1788

BALIMAYA 3 b f £0

67	8-17	Newm	8gd		1166
68	6-8	Ches	10.3gd		1597

BALKAN KNIGHT 4 b c £11568

80	6-20	Newb	10gd	80	1235 vis
86	1-19	YORK	11.9sft	80	1668+ vis
71	12-15	Hayd	11.9gd	84	2948 vis
87	3-7	Newm	14.8g/f	83	3281 vis

BALKAN LEADER 2 b c £1628

65	4-9	Catt	6g/f		4670
80a	2-14	Ling	7ap		4971

BALL BOY 2 b c £1520

69	7-15	Newb	7g/f		2876
83	5-8	Epso	7g/f		3214
77	2-11	Beve	7.5g/f		3500
32	5-6	Hami	8.3g/s	[75]	3878

BALLARE 4 b g £4208

29a	7-14	Sout	8af	48	62
20a	9-13	Ling	10ap	[45]	412
46a	3-12	Ling	8ap	[40]	649
44a	4-10	Ling	8ap	45	766
44a	6-15	Ling	7ap	45	846 VIS
53a	1-12	LING	8ap	[45]	1073* vis
45	10-19	Yarm	7g/f	54	1132 vis
47	4-15	Sout	7gd	48	1282
24	14-20	Yarm	8fm	47	2149
43	9-19	Chep	7.1gd	47	3401 vis
29	11-15	Folk	9.7g/f	[45]	4373 P
50a	2-14	Ling	7ap	[50]	4660 vis
48	1-16	WARW	8.1g/f	45	4993* vis
39a	10-13	Wind	8.6ap	[50]	5212 vis

BALLERINA SUPREMA 4 b f £0

83	5-10	Wind	10fm	85	2761
0	7-7	Good	14fm	[85]	3619

BALLET BALLON 2 b f £0

59	11-14	Kemp	7g/f		4711

BALLET RUSE 3 ch f £0

32	16-17	Wind	8.3fm		3480
29	11-11	Thir	8g/f		3572
2	7-8	Chep	16.2g/s	48	4302

BALLETOMAINE 2 b f £0

67	8-13	Kemp	7g/f		3520
66	7-11	Beve	7.5g/s		3851
50a	8-8	Ling	7ap		4447

BALLETTO 2 b f £836

74	3-10	Pont	6g/f		2610
64	7-8	Asco	5g/f		3386

BALLIN ROUGE 3 ch f £0
40 10-10 Beve 7.5g/f 1832
9 7-7 Ripo 10gd 2982 T
30 6-15 Carl 7.9fm [35] 4507 t

BALLINGER EXPRESS 4 ch f £4333
50a 8-11 Ling 8ap 697
68a 5-12 Ling 8ap 881
73a 3-9 Ling 8ap 1022
69 2-11 Redc 7g/f [64] 1822 BL
37 9-13 Donc 6gd 64 2232 bl
10 15-20 Chep 6.1gd 64 2372 bl
68 2-13 Wind 6fm 62 3479 bl
49 9-16 Wind 5fm 62 3640 bl
46 10-11 Bath 5g/f 64 3849 bl
45 13-20 Nott 6.1g/s 62 4646 bl
60 3-10 Wind 6g/f [57] 4835 bl

BALLINGER RIDGE 5 b g £3566
64a 2-12 Ling 8ap [65] 401
51a 3-12 Ling 7ap [65] 536
60a 2-6 Ling 8ap [60] 651 P
63a 2-10 Ling 8ap [60] 785 BL
55a 1-8 LING 10ap [60] 829* VIS
60a 6-12 Ling 8ap [67] 878 vis

BALLINTENI 2 b c £3543
97 1-13 DONC 7hvy 5199* T

BALLY HALL 4 b c £0
65a 11-14 Ling 10ap 73 674

BALLYBORO 3 b f £0
47 6-6 Ches 7gd 1587
35 11-12 Thir 7g/f 1971
12 9-11 Yarm 11.5g/f 54 2346 VIS

BALLYBUNION 5 ch g £6983
53 10-15 Hami 6gd 68 1508
37 15-20 Thir 5g/f 65 1765
53 11-15 Muss 5fm 62 2084
48 11-20 York 6fm 59 2409
51 5-19 Beve 5gd 59 2512
51 3-19 Beve 5gd 55 2657
51 9-12 Thir 5g/s 55 2690
41 10-13 Hayd 6gd 55 2884
48 9-20 Beve 5g/s 52 3180
42 9-19 Donc 5g/s 52 3220
51 5-14 Catt 6g/f 52 3352
59 1-18 PONT 5gd 49 3463+
50 7-26 Good 6fm 53 3569
56 3-15 Bath 5.7g/f 54 3966
60 2-20 Newc 6g/f 54 4408
43 13-26 Ayr 5g/s 54 4618
59 4-16 Pont 5fm 54 4754
51 4-15 Newc 6gd 54 4870

BALLYCROY GIRL 2 ch f £6812
54 6-7 Ayr 1893
70 2-7 Ayr 7.2g/s 2570
63 5-8 York 7g/s 3078
78 1-7 AYR 7.2g/f 3302*
70 8-11 Newm 7fm 73 3407
67 6-17 York 7g/f 72 4396
55 7-11 Ayr 8sft 71 4688

BALLYGRIFFIN KID 4 gr g £1668
28a 8-14 Ling 7ap [45] 783
40a 3-12 Ling 6ap [45] 1075
32a 4-8 Sout 5af [45] 1199
44a 1-4 LING 7ap [40] 1710*
30 10-18 Nott 8.2gd [45] 1992

BALLYHURRY 7 b g £1457
52 11-13 Muss 7.1g/f 74 1122
71 6-12 Ayr 7.2fm 73 1909
70 4-9 Muss 7.1fm 72 2086
63 6-13 Ayr 7.2g/s 71 2568
59 8-9 Ayr 8g/f 69 3305
70 4-13 Muss 7.1gd 67 4806
69 4-19 Newc 7g/f 67 5014
59a 5-12 Wolv 7.1ap [66] 5340

BALLYLIFFIN 3 b g £844
46 11-20 Bath 10.2gd 1398
55 2-9 Folk 9.7sft 1581

BALLYRUSH 4 ch g £1862
51a 8-12 Wolv 9.4af 68 513

61a 5-7 Wolv 8.5af 67 700
31a 4-9 Wolv 8.5af [67] 751
44a 5-8 Sout 11af [60] 857
33 6-13 Wind 8.3g/s [57] 1058
32 5-8 Ripo 10g/s [53] 1363 P
40a 2-5 Wolv 9.4af [45] 1674 BL
48a 1-8 SOUT 8af [45] 1841* bl
31 12-18 Nott 8.2gd [45] 1992 bl

BALMACARA 4 b f £0
44a 5-16 Ling 7ap [50] 123 p
49a 4-12 Ling 8ap [50] 150 p
44a 7-12 Ling 8ap [48] 401 p
45a 9-11 Ling 8ap 48 669 p
40 6-17 Warw 8.1fm 47 2440
22 12-14 Pont 8g/f 45 2993
38 5-14 Yarm 8gd 41 3363
23 10-15 Folk 7g/f [40] 4371
19a 9-11 Wolv 7.1ap [45] 5210

BALMONT 3 b c £33192
113 3-20 Newm 6g/f [115] 3062
112 2-7 Newm 5fm [115] 3409
111 7-12 York 5g/s [113] 4060
105 5-12 Newm 7sft [112] 5134

BALTHASAR 2 b c £0
42 15-18 Leic 5fm 2109
25 6-6 Hami 8.3g/s 3878
52 7-11 Hami 6g/s 4006
30 6-9 Ripo 6gd 4277

BALTIC BLAZER 4 b g £0
72 5-9 Hayd 10.5g/s 76 2185
68 9-13 Yarm 10.1gd 75 4613
49 17-20 York 10.4gd 75 4986 VIS

BALTIC DIP 2 b f £14605
93 1-6 GOOD 6g/f 1866*
92 4-9 Newm 6g/f 2763
84 8-26 Newb 6.5g/f 4679
97 4-14 Newm 7g/f [94] 4914

BALTIC KING 4 b c £57946
102 6-13 Newm 5g/f [105] 1479 t
65 8-9 Wind 6g/f [104] 1958 t
111 1-24 ASCO 5gd 101 3466* t
107 3-11 Beve 5g/s [106] 4238 t
89 6-9 Donc 5fm [106] 4481 t
108 1-10 BEVE 5g/f [104] 4718* t
103 3-15 Newm 5g/f [104] 4879 t
99 5-14 Newm 6sft [106] 5100 t

BALTIC WAVE 3 b g £728
87 6-10 Donc 7g/f 95 2427
94 4-7 Ches 7g/s 92 2749
84 11-19 Newm 6fm 90 3002

BALWEARIE 3 b g £232
37 6-6 Hami 5gd [66] 1387
54 9-14 Ayr 8g/f [63] 1896 p
21 6-6 Redc 6g/f [62] 2104 p

BAMBOOZLED 2 b f £315
52a 6-10 Ling 5ap 882
37 9-11 Kemp 5hvy 1640
53a 7-10 Ling 5ap 2017 VIS
19 5-6 Folk 5ap 2270 BL

BAMFORD CASTLE 9 b g £0
13a 9-9 Ling 16ap [75] 454 P

BAMZOOKI 2 b f £264
67 4-9 Ling 6gd 3020
65 5-18 Ling 6gd 4108

BANANA GROVE 3 b g £6785
72 3-4 Hami 9.2g/f 3204
2 7-9 Pont 8gd 3462
0 P-10 Hayd 8.1gd 3739
72 1-8 REDC 9g/f 3805*
71 4-6 Hami 9.2g/s 71 4137
51 7-7 Ripo 8gd [71] 4304
26 6-8 Hami 9.2sft [68] 4694
65 3-5 Ayr 8sft [66] 5038

BANCHIERI 2 b c £3637
91 3-16 Leic 7fm 3811
88 3-8 York 7gd 4326

---

86 2-11 Nott 8.2g/s 4648

BAND 4 b g £4211
31 12-18 Asco 8sft 74 1423
57 12-12 Hayd 8.1g/f 72 1883
32a 12-15 Sout 8af 67 2500
52 10-12 Wind 10g/f [62] 2800
57 4-10 Hayd 10.5g/s 58 3139
57 8-16 Hayd 10.5sft 58 3276
55 5-14 Hayd 10.5gd 55 3741
62 1-20 YARM 8gd 54 3996*
58 7-15 Carl 7.9g/f 57 4346
53 6-15 Nott 8.2hvy 57 5191
57 4-16 Nott 10hvy 56 5345

BANDARI 5 b h £130567
90 11-17 Newb 12gd [114] 1230
113 1-10 NEWM 10g/f [114] 1483*
117 1-10 CHES 10.3gd[114] 1585*
119 1-9 SAND 10g/s [114] 2128+
97 9-10 Asco 12g/f [114] 2488
120 1-8 NEWM 12g/f [117] 3030*
119 7-11 Asco 12g/f [117] 3442
118 3-4 Kemp 12fm [119] 4391
117 3-9 Asco 12g/f [119] 4812
93 9-9 San 12sft [119] 5168

BANDBOX 9 ch g £418
29a 8-15 Sout 7af 35 2384
29a 5-15 Sout 7af 35 2501
14a 7-9 Sout 7af [32] 2801
26 3-7 Brig 6g/f 32 3717 P

BANDINI 3 b g £0
33a 9-13 Ling 6ap 219

BANDIT QUEEN 4 b f £5923
86 3-15 Ripo 6g/f 85 1782
83 4-11 Newm 6fm 86 2093
90 2-9 Ches 7gd 86 2282
60 9-11 Asco 6.5gd 86 3069

BANDOS 4 ch g £1608
65 3-4 Redc 6g/f [75] 2122 t
28 13-13 Ayr 7.2g/s 74 2568 t
3 18-18 Newc 7sft 74 2684 t
76 4-18 Ayr 7.2sft 74 4689 t
67 5-10 Newc 7fm [73] 4869 t

BANJO BAY 6 b g £848
77 8-18 Ches 7.6gd 86 1598
61 14-19 Thir 6g/f 84 1767
79 3-8 Donc 6gd [82] 2074
69 11-17 Epso 6fm 80 2256
54 18-28 Asco 7g/f 78 2558
70 6-8 Hami 5g/s 76 2830
32 8-11 Donc 6g/f [73] 3375
66 8-16 Redc 7g/f 70 3809
34 10-12 Brig 5.3g/s 68 4140
62 7-17 York 7g/f 65 4398
65 5-15 Redc 6fm 65 4562
45 14-20 Ripo 6gd 63 4785

BANJO PATTERSON 2 b c £0
44 15-23 Newm 6gd 5084

BANK GAMES 3 b g £0
43 8-9 Ripo 6g/f 2485
37a 8-12 Sout 6af 2722
46a 6-9 Sout 6af 3396
33 5-9 Ripo 5g/f 48 3645
16 11-14 Beve 7.5sft [43] 4256
14 14-20 Yarm 6g/s [40] 5121 BL

BANK ON HIM 9 b g £13915
57a 1-10 LING 10ap [56] 370*
57a 6-13 Ling 10ap [56] 429
62a 1-14 LING 10ap 53 498*
63a 2-12 Ling 8ap 60 607
64a 2-14 Ling 10ap 60 674
65a 2-13 Ling 10ap 62 726
64a 2-6 Ling 10ap 62 1027
57a 5-8 Wolv 8.5af 62 1219
51 1-12 BRIG 9.9fm 45 1695*
62a 3-13 Ling 12g/f 62 1986
50 4-16 Good 9gd 50 2220
68a 3-14 Ling 10ap 62 2392

BANKNOTE 2 b c £6013

73	4-7	Kemp	6fm		2071
65	4-9	Carl	5.9gd		2671
79	1-11	BEVE	7.5g/f		3500*
60	13-17	Donc	8fm	79	4480

BANNERS FLYING 4 ch c £0

48a	8-8	Sout	7af	74	1195
1a	13-13	Wolv	8.5af	[70]	2052
20a	4-9	Sout	12af	[64]	2381
35	11-13	Redc	8gd	66	2552
30a	4-11	Sout	12af	[55]	3154
8a	13-14	Sout	12af	50	3486
29	9-10	Thir	16sft	50	3834
1	12-13	Redc	14.1fm	45	4340
2	10-14	Pont	10g/f	45	4624
3a	9-11	Wolv	12.2ap	40	5009 BL

BANNINGHAM BLAZE 4 b f £14510

0	11-12	Sout	11af	66	534 vis
44	9-13	Catt	13.8gd	54	997 BL
49	4-13	Brig	11.9g/f	50	1373 vis
50	1-6	BRIG	11.9fm	[50]	1692* vis
52	2-7	Leic	11.8g/f	50	1967
53	2-6	Brig	11.9g/f	[50]	2047 vis
51	3-11	Warw	12.6fm	50	2601
45	6-7	Brig	11.9fm	50	2836
43	5-10	Leic	11.8g/f	[50]	3211
53	3-8	Brig	11.9g/f	50	3299 vis
51	1-12	NOTT	14.1g/f	46	3420* vis
50	3-8	Brig	11.9fm	50	3692 vis
50	2-7	Brig	11.9fm	50	3715
52	2-5	Brig	11.9g/f	[48]	3983 vis
63	2-12	Chep	12.1g/s	[48]	4364 vis
53	3-14	Warw	16.2g/f	48	4423
52	2-13	Warw	12.6g/s	[50]	4665
50	5-20	Kemp	12g/f	[50]	4796
48	4-20	Catt	15.8gd	48	4965
51	1-14	YARM	14.1g/s	[46]	5123* bl
52a	7-12	Wolv	12.2ap	59	5328 vis

BANNISTER 6 ch g £1058

60a	3-11	Ling	6ap	60	728
40a	9-13	Wolv	6af	60	807
62	3-15	Sout	7gd	60	1282
41	14-18	Wind	8.3gd	60	1385

BANSHA BRU 4 b g £526

66a	3-8	Wolv	8.5af		1220
0	S-9	Folk	9.7sft		1581

BANUTAN 3 b f £0

42a	8-14	Sout	8af	64	60
47a	9-11	Ling	8ap	60	131

BAQAH 3 ch f £64148

114	1-9	CHAN	8g/s	2306*
112	3-7	Newm	8fm	3004 T
99	7-10	Deau	8sft	4017

BAR OF SILVER 3 ch g £0

34a	8-13	Wolv	8.5af	[55]	39 p
23a	9-13	Wolv	9.4af	49	287
42a	5-12	Ling	8ap	[45]	649 VIS
0	11-11	Wolv	6af	[45]	778 vis
12a	5-5	Ling	7ap	[40]	1288 vis

BARABELLA 3 gr f £331

50	12-15	Bath	8g/s	66	1099
61	5-14	Bath	5gd	63	1404
36	14-16	Bath	5.7sft	63	1540
54	4-8	Bath	5.7fm	60	1903
59	5-11	Sali	6gd	58	2661
12	13-13	Bath	5gd	[58]	3143
45	4-11	Brig	7g/f	[58]	3298
49	5-7	Brig	6fm	55	3693
27	12-19	Chep	6.1sft	54	4054 P
38	15-20	Chep	6.1g/s	50	4368
24	11-16	Chep	7.1hvy	[47]	4707

BARADORE 2 ch f £4954

83	2-11	Newm	7g/f	3234
88	1-10	YARM	8g/f	3713*

BARAKA 3 b f £29750

114	1-5	LING	11.5sft	1619*

BARAKANA 6 b g £0

22a	10-11	Ling	10ap	[45]	970 bl

BARANCELLA 3 ch f £7711

109	3-10	Sain	10.5sft	1850
109	6-17	Chan	12.5g/s	2460

BARANOOK 3 b c £566

10	13-13	Wind	10g/f		2453
47	7-10	Pont	10gd		3243
67	5-12	Hayd	10.5gd		3740
72a	3-16	Ling	12ap	67	4973

BARATHEA BLUE 3 ch c £6776

73	5-10	Pont	10gd	3243
74	2-9	Sand	10gd	4501
67	1-13	NOTT	10gd	4861*
68a	7-10	Ling	12ap 75	5239

BARATHEA DREAMS 3 b c £24868

70a	1-13	LING	10ap		715*
74a	1-10	LING	10ap	[60]	843*
65a	4-6	Ling	12ap	63	915
83	1-8	SAND	8.1g/s	72	1315*
87	3-14	York	7.9g/s	79	1707
93	10-13	Asco	10g/f	[82]	2520
76	7-10	Newb	8g/f	85	2877
79	5-7	Sand	8.1gd	83	4499
68	14-17	Asco	8g/f	81	4777
79	5-20	Donc	7sft	79	5367

BARATI 3 b c £20284

107	3-5	Curr	10g/f	2006
100	3-5	Asco	12g/f	2554

BARBAJUAN 3 b c £1273

95	5-7	Kemp	8g/s	[110]	1113
84	12-14	Newm	8g/f	[110]	1480
90	8-10	York	10.4g/s	[110]	1685
97	7-8	Kemp	8fm	[102]	2069
92	13-19	Newm	6fm	100	3002 BL
72	10-13	Newm	8g/f	97	3277 bl
83	13-16	Good	7g/f	92	4523 bl
90	5-17	Newm	10g/f	87	4917
82	11-22	Newm	8sft	86	5103

BARBARY COAST 2 b c £1744

69	6-16	Newb	7g/f	4677
71	8-23	Newm	7g/f	4885
81	2-14	Leic	8gd	5058
53	11-11	Bath	8sft	5171

BARBILYRIFLE 3 b g £374

42a	9-10	Ling	5ap	67	712
22a	11-11	Sout	6af	67	872 BL
63	3-9	Leic	6g/s	[63]	1015 p
11	9-10	Bath	5.7sft	[62]	1539 p

BARBIROLLI 2 b c £0

48	12-15	Sali	8gd	4851 T

BARCARDERO 2 b c £0

70	8-14	Yarm	7sft	5250

BARCELONA 7 b g £0

41	9-12	Chep	12.1g/s	63	3085 bl

BARGAIN HUNT 3 b g £2075

0	10-12	Redc	10sft	53	1144 vis
48	2-8	Hami	9.2gd	[50]	1505
43	7-15	Ripo	12.3g/f	50	1785
48	7-14	Redc	10fm	47	2299
48	3-8	Carl	7.9gd	[46]	2932
28	6-11	Muss	9gd	46	2969 vis
28	10-14	Catt	6g/f	[46]	3191 vis
25	11-14	Ayr	7.2gd	[44]	3324 vis
45	4-16	Thir	9g/f	44	3414
45	3-15	Carl	7.9fm	[45]	4507

BARHOLM CHARLIE 3 b g £0

13	19-19	Donc	6g/f	1876
6	14-15	Nott	5.1g/f	2152
1	8-8	Warw	10.9gd	3055

BARKING MAD 6 b g £18547

79	6-13	Newm	10gd	[83]	1381
84	4-9	Newm	10gd	[83]	1890
84	3-14	Wind	10g/f	82	2265
85	2-4	Wind	10g/f	[82]	2798
87	1-8	CHES	10.3g/f	[82]	3083*
40	6-7	Newm	10g/f	84	3474
84	2-4	Ayr	10g/f	[84]	3762

77	6-8	Newm	10g/f	[84]	3945
85	1-11	WIND	10gd	[84]	4124*
79	2-11	Muss	9g/f	[85]	4550
64	7-11	Redc	10fm	85	4931
80	7-10	Yarm	10.1sft	[84]	5255

BARMAN 5 ch g £13183

64	10-11	Donc	12gd	81	2233
69	7-15	Bath	11.7g/f	80	3964 t
88	1-12	YORK	13.9g/f	80	4400* t

BARNBROOK EMPIRE 2 b f £551

33	14-18	Chep	6.1gd		2194
53	5-10	Beve	7.5gd		2652
72	3-13	Chep	6.1gd		3399
45	7-11	Bath	5.7g/f	[72]	3848

BAROLO 5 b g £43913

86	12-17	Newb	12gd	[98]	1230
109	1-12	GOOD	14g/f	98	1861*
87	17-19	Newc	16.1g/s	107	2771
108	1-12	LEOP	14g/s	[107]	3315*
113	1-7	SALI	14.1gd	[106]	4333*

BARON RHODES 3 b f £23940

72	2-13	Thir	5sft	68	1229
73	2-8	Hami	5gd	70	1509
77	2-10	Thir	5gd	72	1973
71	3-10	Hayd	5g/s	72	2227
82	1-9	SAND	5g/f	73	2387*
80	3-12	Ayr	5g/s	78	2566
74	7-11	Pont	6g/f	78	2791
77	5-10	Hayd	5g/s	77	3135
85	1-8	HAMI	5g/f	76	3591*
83	3-15	Thir	5g/s	80	3833
59	13-14	York	5g/s	80	4027
85	8-11	Beve	5g/s	[80]	4238
84	7-11	Hami	5sft	[80]	4693
70	10-15	Catt	5sft	80	5125
87	3-18	Pont	5g/s	80	5149
87	3-11	Newm	6sft	[78]	5270
59	9-11	Muss	5g/s	81	5332 P

BARONS PIT 4 b c £8343

108	1-7	KEMP	6gd	[114]	1137*

BARONS SPY 3 b c £3807

65	4-16	Newm	7fm		2092
69	2-4	Warw	7.1fm	[66]	2438
11	10-10	Newb	8g/f	65	2877
69	3-15	Bath	8gd	65	4827
72	2-9	Leic	7gd	[65]	5041

BAROQUE 3 b c £0

0	10-12	Sout	8af		848
21	8-9	Leic	11.8g/s		1016
11	13-14	Nott	10gd		1241
0	6-6	Beve	9.9sft		1630
2	14-14	Redc	14.1g/f	20	2123
0	10-11	Pont	12g/f	20	2790 BL

BARRANTES 6 b m £0

75a	7-10	Ling	10ap	[83]	179
60	9-11	Newm	6fm	81	3408
73	7-8	Wind	8.3fm	79	3641
47	9-10	Asco	6gd	81	3773
38	14-15	Bath	11.7g/f	74	3964
52	13-15	Kemp	8g/f	74	4362

BARRAS 3 b g £880

0	8-8	Wolv	6af	57	422 p
45a	8-14	Sout	5af	57	485 VIS
52a	3-11	Sout	6af	55	591 BL
40a	5-13	Sout	6af	53	797 vis
68a	4-9	Wolv	5af	[51]	835 vis
46a	7-11	Sout	5af	57	2380 vis
39	11-16	Ling	7gd	55	3024 vis
51	3-9	Ripo	5g/f	52	3645 vis

BARRISSIMO 4 b g £0

67	18-19	Newm	10g/f	96	1478
68	11-14	York	10.4g/s	92	1704

BARRY ISLAND 5 b g £25858

76a	1-13	LING	10ap	[75]	429*
73a	5-16	Ling	12ap	75	475
80a	2-10	Ling	12ap	73	570
82a	4-11	Ling	10ap	78	716
77a	4-6	Ling	10ap	78	1027

80	3-20	Newb	10gd	78	1235
82	10-19	Newm	10g/f	78	1478
75	9-19	Newb	10gd	78	1736
78	3-13	Kemp	12g/f	77	1916
73	8-15	Sand	10g/f	77	2099
75	6-11	Asco	12gd	76	3070
73	4-10	Sand	10g/f	74	3336
81	1-10	NEWM	10g/f	73	3615*
46	14-14	Sand	10g/s	77	4097

BARTON FLOWER 3 br f £0

36	7-8	Newc	8hvy		1039
30	8-11	Newc	8sft		1279
23	9-10	Beve	9.9gd	50	2510
6	11-14	Catt	12g/f	47	3192
28	14-20	Beve	16.2gd	47	3312
37	7-13	Redc	14.1gd	42	4249 BL

BARTON SANDS 7 b g £6296

63	1-7	WARW	10.9g/s	[61]	1326* vis t
73	1-11	YARM	10.1gd	[60]	3875+
69	2-8	Ling	11.5g/s	[69]	4181
69	4-12	Good	9g/f	69	4539 t
73	4-15	Nott	10g/f	69	4849 t

BARZAK 3 b c £2597

69a	1-14	SOUT	8af	65	60* t
42a	12-14	Sout	8af	71	93 t
47a	8-12	Sout	8af	68	141 P
59a	5-11	Sout	8af	68	255 p
52a	8-11	Wolv	7af	66	363 BL
57a	5-11	Sout	8af	64	457 bl t
60a	3-13	Sout	6af	62	551 bl t
58	10-17	Leic	7g/s	62	1020 bl t
50	8-20	Ripo	8g/s	60	1366 t
51	8-14	Muss	7.1gd	57	1794 t
0	15-15	Beve	7.5g/s	55	2324 t

BASIC SYSTEM 2 b c £0

70	8-12	Newm	6g/f		3280
79	5-9	Epso	7fm		3539

BASINET 6 b g £634

28	12-20	Ripo	8g/s	58	1366
43	12-14	Hami	8.3gd	56	1748
43	8-15	Redc	9g/f	54	2120 p
56	4-16	Redc	8g/s	54	2958
50	8-18	Pont	8gd	54	3242
50	6-9	Hami	9.2g/f	53	3593 p
51	4-15	Chep	8.1sft	53	4057 p
48	8-19	Leic	10g/f	53	4456
51	8-15	Beve	8.5g/f	53	4598 p

BASSERAH 2 b f £0

80	7-15	Newm	8fm		4723
65	9-21	Newm	8sft		5097

BATCHWORTH BEAU 3 ch g £0

49	11-17	Sali	6g/s		1497
40	16-17	Newb	8g/f		1762
41	9-10	Newb	6g/f		2309
45	10-10	Newb	5.2fm		2649

BATCHWORTH BREEZE 6 ch m £0

16a	9-10	Sout	6af	[30]	352

BATHWICK BILL 3 ch g £3525

74	9-16	Kemp	6g/s	85	1116
50	6-11	Sali	6g/s	83	1498
85	2-8	Bath	5fm	[80]	1901
83	3-9	Wind	6g/f	81	2797
50	8-10	Kemp	6g/f	[81]	3188
67	11-15	Kemp	6g/f	81	4713
66	11-19	Sali	6gd	81	4855
75	8-18	Pont	5g/s	77	5149

BATHWICK BRUCE 6 b g £0

55	7-15	Chep	8.1g/s	65	4300
57	7-17	Warw	8.1g/s	63	4668

BATHWICK DREAM 6 b m £0

0	11-12	Wolv	12af		114
18a	14-14	Ling	13ap	[40]	537

BATHWICK FINESSE 2 b f £3865

65	7-17	Chep	6.1sft		4052
80	1-11	CHEP	8.1g/s		4363*
84	4-12	Sali	8sft	79	4580
28	14-14	Donc	8sft	80	5203

BATIK 3 gr f £4745

69	3-8	Sand	8.1g/f		3858
81	1-9	BATH	10.2gd		4547+
78	5-7	Newm	12sft	77	5268

BATTLE BACK 2 b f £0

18a	12-15	Sout	7af		184
31a	12-16	Ling	7ap		290
0	9-9	Wolv	9.4af	[30]	399 BL e

BATTLE CHANT 4 b g £24798

106	3-18	Newb	8g/f	102	3265
81	18-21	Good	8fm	102	3565
104	2-6	Epso	10.1gd	[103]	4290
108	2-7	Good	9.9g/f	[102]	4538
106	3-8	Good	9.9gd	[102]	4748
106	5-16	Newm	9sft	[106]	5139

BATTLEDRESS 2 b c £913

72	8-12	Newm	7gd		4194
83	3-11	Bath	8gd		4544
66	4-11	Bath	10.2gd		4825

BAY HAWK 2 b c £935

82	3-16	Sali	7g/s		3111

BAY SOLITAIRE 3 b g £0

47	6-8	Redc	10g/f		2124
32	8-14	Catt	12g/f	48	3192
36	9-13	Redc	14.1gd	45	4249

BAY TREE 3 b f £6800

94	6-13	Newm	7gd	[105]	1169
99	3-6	York	10.4sft	[102]	1666
83	11-19	Asco	8g/f	99	2491
99	8-18	Deau	10g/s	[99]	3836

BAYADERE 4 br f £0

61	8-8	Good	9.9gd		4748
71	8-10	Yarm	10.1sft	[85]	5255
34	20-24	Donc	12sft	77	5372 VIS

BAYARD 2 gr c £518

75	4-16	Newm	8hvy		5220
59	8-9	Muss	8g/s		5331

BAYBERRY 4 ch f £9925

92	5-10	Sali	9.9g/f		3866
98	2-5	Sand	8.1g/s	[90]	4095
106	3-6	Donc	10.3fm	[93]	4492

BAYCHEVELLE 3 ch f £0

6	12-13	Nott	6.1sft		1464

BAYEUX 3 b c £4711

98	5-5	Newm	10g/f	[112]	1482 t
98	3-6	Newm	8gd	[112]	1888 t
78	7-8	Donc	10.3gd	[105]	2234 t
99	10-15	Donc	8fm	100	4531 t
97	3-16	Newm	7sft	98	5101 VIS

BAYEUX DE MOI 2 b c £8811

89	4-6	Asco	7g/f		3390
82	1-14	SALI	8g/s		4078*
89	2-7	Leic	10gd	[81]	5044

BAYHIRR 3 b c £10577

84	3-17	Leic	10g/s		1019
92	1-15	LEIC	10g/s		1358*
91	5-13	York	10.4sft	87	1664
92	2-7	Wind	8.3fm	85	2787
60	11-13	Newm	8g/f	86	3277

BAYLAW STAR 3 b c £1990

72	6-13	Thir	5sft	76	1229
73	3-6	Hami	5gd	[75]	1387
67	7-10	Leic	6gd	[75]	2137
72	4-10	Hayd	5g/s	72	2227
49	9-9	Sand	5g/f	73	2387
48	10-12	Ayr	5g/s	71	2566 P
65	6-15	Thir	5g/s	69	3833 p
29	15-20	Ripo	6gd	67	4278 p
49	11-16	Good	5g/f	62	4528 BL
48	6-15	Hami	6sft	61	4696

BAYMIST 2 b f £7310

52	5-10	Ripo	5gd		2983
45	6-15	Beve	5g/s		3178
69	1-7	BEVE	5gd		3308*

51	4-6	Hami	6g/f	63	3590
70	1-12	HAYD	5gd	63	3756*
57	6-10	Beve	5sft	67	4258
61	7-15	Ripo	5gd	67	4784

BAYONET 8 b m £0

40	8-9	Sali	7gd	40	3456
10	8-10	Ling	6gd	40	4109

BAYOU PRINCESS 3 ch f £415

45	7-10	Folk	9.7sft		1580
57	7-8	Chep	12.1gd		2113
58	5-11	Leic	10g/f		3208
51	3-7	Chep	12.1g/s	[62]	3899
53	6-12	Good	16g/s	58	4235

BAYREUTH 2 ch f £0

51	13-18	Nott	8.2g/s		4035

BAYTOWN FLYER 3 ch f £8768

0	13-13	Wolv	6af	[37]	30 P
37a	2-12	Sout	7af	[35]	909
38a	2-12	Ling	8ap	[35]	971
4a	10-12	Sout	8af	[35]	982
36a	1-10	LING	7ap	[35]	1181*
47a	1-11	WOLV	6af	[35]	1261*
49a	1-5	LING	7ap	[35]	1288*
47a	2-8	Wolv	7af	[35]	1314
53	1-10	WARW	6.1g/s	[35]	1327+
53a	1-8	LING	7ap	[40]	1413*
44a	2-5	Ling	6ap	[40]	1452
3a	14-15	Sout	6af	52	1750
12	15-19	Yarm	6g/s	51	4636
37a	7-13	Wolv	6ap	[50]	5211
39a	5-12	Wolv	7.1ap	[50]	5229

BAZELLE 2 ch f £1748

46	16-19	Newb	6g/f		2310
71	4-10	Folk	7g/s		3046
82	2-13	Leic	8g/f		4450
81	6-15	Newm	8fm	[83]	4723

BE BOP 2 ch g £0

50	11-14	Thir	8fm		4376
62	9-10	Redc	9fm		4558
27	9-12	Redc	8g/s		5107

BE BOP ALOHA 2 b f £420

26	15-15	Wind	5gd		1380
50	6-11	Yarm	6g/f		1727
54a	3-14	Sout	7af		2492
61	5-8	Brig	7gd		2952
51	11-14	Yarm	7gd		3489
60	8-10	Wind	8.3fm	[58]	3803 P
25	18-20	Leic	7g/f	57	4451
22	14-16	Beve	7.5g/f	57	4597

BE MY ALIBI 2 ch f £0

0	10-12	Wolv	8.5af	[58]	28
5a	11-16	Sout	8af	[51]	164
23	7-9	Folk	7sft	49	1577
34a	5-9	Wolv	6af	[40]	1803
7	10-13	Hami	5gd	40	2181
14	11-13	Muss	7.1g/f	35	2812
30	7-10	Ayr	6sft	[35]	5278

BE WISE GIRL 3 ch f £3336

41a	3-9	Sout	8af		983
56	1-16	NOTT	10gd	47	1240*
17	14-18	Warw	10.9g/s	55	4669
49a	8-13	Wolv	9.5ap	54	4925

BEACH PARTY 3 b f £415

65a	3-10	Ling	8ap		1021
20a	9-11	Wolv	8.5af	63	1339

BEACON BLUE 3 ch f £0

21	6-6	Beve	12.1g/s	68	2322
59	7-17	Newc	8fm	63	4867
18	13-13	Muss	12g/s	62	5333

BEACON STAR 2 ch c £0

40	8-9	Pont	5sft		1424
33	12-13	Donc	7hvy		5199

BEADY 5 b g £0

47	6-9	Redc	10gd	58	4248

BEAMISH PRINCE 5 ch g £0

56 7-9 Newc 10.1g/s [59] 3702
53 7-13 Muss 8g/f [57] 4554

BEAMSLEY BEACON 3 ch g £259
0 12-12 Redc 10sft 57 1144
0 9-11 Newc 8sft 53 1395 BL
46 4-13 Carl 5.9fm [49] 1949 bl
24 11-14 Redc 9g/f [49] 2102 P
38a 6-8 Sout 6af [59] 2379 bl
47a 4-9 Sout 6af [57] 2493 VIS
50a 4-10 Sout 8af [47] 4042
28 8-14 Beve 7.5sft [47] 4256
64 5-9 Catt 7g/f [45] 4674

BEAT THE HEAT 6 b g £3399
83 2-20 York 10.4gd 77 4986

BEAU JAZZ 3 br c £466
55a 5-9 Ling 5ap [68] 621
65a 3-10 Ling 5ap 65 712
59a 7-8 Ling 5ap 66 818
42 6-6 Leic 6g/s [62] 1018
48 13-16 Bath 5.7g/s [62] 1103
38 14-14 Bath 5gd 60 1404
36 14-17 Bath 5g/f [55] 1787
41a 12-13 Wolv 5.1ap 60 5156

BEAU MARCHE 2 b g £2299
50 5-6 Leic 6g/f 3513
56 8-11 Bath 6gd 3962
42 13-18 Ling 6gd 4108
62 2-17 Ling 6gd 4316
46 11-19 Kemp 8g/f [61] 4792 P
72 1-6 BRIG 6gd [61] 4900*
28 7-9 Nott 6.1hvy [73] 5185

BEAU WEST 2 b f £0
42a 6-13 Wolv 8.5af 43

BEAUCHAMP PILOT 6 ch g £2625
105 6-11 Epso 8.5fm 2252
0 16-16 Asco 6ap 2470
107 4-9 Wind 8.3fm [111] 2757

BEAUCHAMP RIBBON 4 b f £0
0 7-8 Wind 11.6g/f 67 2796
0 19-19 Chep 12.1gd 63 3398 P
22 9-9 Epso 10.1fm 63 3538 bl

BEAUCHAMP SPARK 2 ch g £0
0 13-13 Wolv 9.4af 37

BEAUCHAMP STAR 3 ch f £3289
57 9-14 Folk 7g/s 1080
65 3-12 Warw 7.1gd 1129
75 3-14 Warw 8.1sft 1527
56 8-13 Good 9g/f 74 2024
74 4-6 Donc 10.3g/f [72] 2426
70 2-5 Warw 10.9fm [72] 2602 BL

BEAUCHAMP SURPRISE 2 ch f £0
1a 13-13 Wolv 8.5af 111

BEAUCHAMP TRUMP 2 b g £428
68a 7-12 Ling 6ap 4179
64 10-11 Epso 7gd 4289
69 4-6 Epso 7g/f 4470

BEAUCHAMP TURBO 2 ch g £0
70a 5-12 Ling 6ap 4178
65 5-17 Ling 6gd 4443
50 6-9 Catt 7sft 5131
38 13-20 Donc 7sft 65 5373

BEAUCHAMP TWIST 2 b f £532
39 8-8 Newb 5.2fm 2646
35 10-11 Warw 6g/f 2911
48a 12-13 Ling 7ap 3329
62 6-14 Ling 7.6g/f 3601 BL
53 4-12 Muss 7.1g/s [61] 5142 bl

BEAUMONT GIRL 2 ch f £3255
42 7-10 Hayd 5g/s 3901
61 1-14 THIR 7g/s 4206*
13 15-16 Yarm 8g/s 55 4632
33 16-18 Catt 7g/f 55 4673

BEAUNE 2 b c £766
78 3-11 Hayd 5g/s 4349
59 6-15 Nott 6.1g/s 4644

52a 10-13 Wolv 6ap 4980

BEAUTEOUS 5 ch g £6431
34a 8-11 Wolv 7af 48 378
18a 8-9 Wolv 9.4af [45] 525
21a 6-11 Sout 7af [40] 771
62 4-13 Muss 7.1g/f 65 1122
29a 4-10 Ling 7ap [35] 1181
64a 1-8 SOUT 6af [35] 1201+
64a 1-5 WOLV 8.5af [35] 1264+
64a 1-6 LING 8ap [35] 1292*
59a 1-8 WOLV 7af [35] 1314*
65 4-14 Hami 8.3gd 63 1504

BEAUTIFIX 2 b f £15845
95 1-9 DEAU 5hvy 4155*

BEAUTIFUL MARIA 2 b f £0
54 7-8 Newm 5gd 1170

BEAUTIFUL MOVER 2 ch f £2293
77 2-10 Newm 6gd 1887
75 3-14 Redc 6fm 2297
24 8-9 Wind 5g/f 2795
76a 4-12 Ling 6ap [76] 4179
38 18-18 Wind 5g/f 73 4830

BEAUTIFUL NOISE 3 b f £1070
37 14-18 Nott 8.2sft [63] 1470
54 6-16 Leic 7g/f 60 1825
49 5-20 Newb 7g/f 57 2314
53 5-16 Ling 7gd 54 3024
48 5-11 Yarm 7g/f 52 3711
44 5-14 Yarm 6gd 52 3870 BL
63 5-15 Nott 8.2g/s [49] 4649 bl
60 2-12 Brig 8fm [49] 4761 bl
49 9-10 Pont 8g/f [60] 4939 bl

BEAUTY OF DREAMS 3 b f £1554
55 9-12 Hayd 8.1gd 74 2904
63 10-12 Hayd 6sft 71 3273
62 7-13 Leic 7f 71 3346
59 5-8 Folk 7g/f 65 3724
61 3-14 Bath 8g/f 61 3963
38 12-16 Brig 7sft [61] 4144
35 6-14 Beve 7.5sft [60] 4256
41 8-13 Bath 8gd 57 4546
54 4-12 Brig 8fm [57] 4761
59 3-12 Brig 8sft 54 5094 VIS
47a 8-13 Wolv 8.6ap [54] 5184 vis
36a 8-9 Ling 8ap [54] 5242 vis
47a 4-12 Wolv 8.6ap [50] 5329

BEAUVRAI 4 b g £14499
33a 12-12 Wolv 6af 90 361
53a 9-10 Ling 5ap 86 567
70 8-30 Newm 6g/f 75 1481
56 11-14 Kemp 5g/f 73 1914
65 5-12 Folk 5g/s 69 2269
74 3-8 Newm 6fm [67] 2591
61 13-16 Newm 5g/f 73 3033
55 12-12 Newm 5g/f 72 3279 P
78 2-10 Newm 6g/f 72 3584 p
55 3-5 Brig 5.3g/f [72] 3720 p
53 1-5 YARM 6sft [75] 4150* p
83 1-11 EPSO 6gd [75] 4294* BL
70 3-13 Ches 5.1g/f 77 4514 bl
7 13-13 Catt 5sft [77] 5321 bl

BEAVER DIVA 3 b f £2132
48 4-5 Newc 10.1sft 1275
22 7-8 Hami 9.2gd 1505
3a 7-10 Sout 7af [30] 1842
45 2-5 Ayr 6gd [23] 2541
47 2-6 Muss 5g/f [40] 2808
17 16-19 Ripo 6g/s 40 3262
10 9-11 Carl 6.9g/f [40] 3651
0 17-19 Kemp 6g/f [40] 4793

BEAVER PATROL 2 ch c £127017
89 1-9 WIND 5g/s 1256*
93 3-9 Ches 5.1gd 1567
97 2-6 Wind 5g/f 1808
104 1-7 KEMP 6fm 2071*
80 11-13 Asco 6g/f 2467
86 6-8 Newb 6g/f 3254
104 2-10 Asco 7gd [95] 3774
111 1-16 CURR 6g/f [95] 4153*

99 5-24 Redc 6fm [100] 4928
93 5-8 Donc 8sft [100] 5216

BEBOPSKIDDLY 3 b c £0
49a 10-12 Ling 8ap 4975
32 6-7 Yarm 11.5g/s [55] 5351

BECKERMET 2 b g £26783
75 3-6 Hami 5gd 1503
81 1-11 HAYD 5g/f 1880*
82 1-8 THIR 5g/f 2213*
96 2-5 Ripo 5g/f 2481
107 1-10 CHES 5.1g/s 2744*
105 1-8 CHES 5.1g/f 3081*
89 9-13 Good 5g/f 3509
94 4-5 York 5g/s [100] 4025
86 11-11 Donc 5g/f [100] 4533
93 5-12 Ayr 5g/s [100] 4651

BEDAZZLED 3 b f £0
22a 13-15 Ling 7ap 56 50
0 F-12 Wolv 7af 56 68 BL

BEDTIME BLUES 2 b f £0
63 9-13 Donc 5gd 954
31 8-15 Beve 5g/s 1161

BEE DEES LEGACY 3 b g £0
64a 8-13 Ling 10ap 2066
45a 10-15 Ling 12ap 2393
34 8-8 Good 9gd 2536
17 9-10 Folk 12g/s 59 3051 BL

BEE MINOR 3 b f £3950
58 8-12 Newm 7g/f 73 2249
78 2-8 Newb 6fm 70 2648
58 8-13 Newb 6g/f 70 2880
35 16-16 Newb 6g/f 74 3269
70 2-10 Sali 6gd [73] 3452
69 4-15 Newb 6g/f 71 3920
37 7-11 Good 6gd [70] 5030

BEE STINGER 2 b c £2815
38 10-13 Sali 6fm 2287
78 3-17 Ling 7g/f 2584
78 2-8 Ling 6gd 3021
55 2-12 Newc 7g/f 3425
74 4-13 Hayd 6gd [76] 3736

BEECHES THEATRE 2 b f £0
13 11-11 Nott 5.1g/f 2151
29 11-11 Ling 5gd 2395

BEECHY BANK 6 b m £669
60a 8-13 Ling 13ap 70 342
69 7-10 Bath 13.1g/f 69 1789
63 5-11 Newb 13.3fm 68 2651
66 3-7 Warw 16.2gd 65 3057
65 5-13 Asco 16.2g/f 63 3387
60 9-16 Kemp 16g/f 63 4361

BEEJAY 3 b f £3630
77 1-20 NOTT 6.1gd 71 1239*
37 20-20 Newb 7g/f 75 1761
25 12-12 Chep 6.1gd 75 2118
58 8-15 Newb 6gd 74 3920
72 6-15 Sand 5gd 73 4604
56a 7-13 Wolv 6ap 72 5114
47a 11-12 Wolv 6ap 71 5291

BEEKEEPER 6 b h £0
95 8-10 Newm 10g/f 1483

BEENABOUTABIT 6 b m £0
8a 9-13 Ling 6ap [35] 541 p
0 15-15 Ling 7ap [30] 935 p
26 5-12 Brig 5.3g/f 30 2645
10 16-19 Leic 5gd 30 2702

BEETLE BUG 3 b rf £0
0 13-14 Ling 13ap 47 264

BEFITTING 2 b c £0
59 8-12 Bath 5sft 5169

BEFORE THE DAWN 2 b f £0
57 7-17 Nott 6.1gd 2927
55 8-13 Chep 6.1gd 3399
41 12-18 Ling 6gd 4108
40 9-15 Folk 6g/f 4369

33 11-19 Bath 5gd 50 5021

BEHAN 4 ch g £0
17a 7-10 Sout 11af [27] 142 bl
22a 9-14 Sout 12af [24] 305 bl
21a 5-5 Sout 12af [30] 446 vis
0 7-8 Wolv 16.2af 30 563 bl

BEHKARA 4 b f £39961
112 3-11 Long 10.5g/f 4948
113 2-8 Long 15.5hvy 5245

BEIRUT 2 br f £14085
97 2-7 Bade 6gd 4427

BELENUS 2 ch c £8444
97 1-15 NEWM 7fm 3005*

BELISCO 3 b c £4225
72 7-20 Bath 10.2gd 1398
52 7-8 Newm 10g/f [73] 3471
66 6-9 Good 8gd 72 3950 T
70a 1-13 LING 10ap [69] 4112* BL t
33 13-14 Redc 10fm 69 4342 VIS
63a 8-14 Ling 10ap [69] 4448 bl t
43a 14-14 Ling 10ap 69 5083

BELLA BEGUINE 4 b f £2194
31a 8-9 Wolv 8.5af 69 2 bl
73a 2-9 Wolv 7af 69 27 VIS
50a 5-9 Sout 6af [70] 487 vis
26a 14-14 Ling 6ap [70] 516 vis
48a 2-4 Wolv 7af [67] 1378 vis
35 14-14 Muss 7.1gd 55 1794 vis
46 4-9 Ayr 7.2gd 50 2508 vis
49 4-20 Beve 5g/s 48 3180
44 5-14 Thir 5g/f 48 3417 bl
26 12-15 Catt 5ft 47 3933 bl
35 11-18 Pont 5g/s 47 3974 bl

BELLA BOY ZEE 3 b f £5627
54a 3-14 Sout 5af 57 485
53a 2-11 Sout 6af 55 591
37a 5-7 Wolv 5af [54] 703
61 1-12 DONC 5g/f 57 3599*
37 8-8 Redc 6g/f 60 3808
36 14-15 Thir 5g/s 60 3833

BELLA MIRANDA 2 ch f £0
46a 11-14 Ling 7ap 5257

BELLA PAVLINA 5 ch m £16876
39a 3-12 Wolv 12af [39] 114
29a 6-14 Sout 8af 35 165
38a 1-9 WOLV 9.4af [35] 399*
45a 2-11 Sout 12af 35 458
63a 1-12 WOLV 12af [40] 523*
50a 1-13 SOUT 12af [40] 575*
59a 4-12 Wolv 12af 62 634
67a 1-7 SOUT 12af [56] 679*
48a 5-6 Wolv 12af 69 752
72a 1-9 SOUT 12af 66 856*+
10 17-22 Donc 12gd 71 918
72a 3-7 Ling 12ap [74] 1009

BELLA PLUNKETT 2 ch f £1016
35 12-14 Hayd 6gd 3735
43 7-7 Ches 6.1g/f 4050
54 7-17 Warw 7.1gd 4271
34 6-6 Muss 8g/f 4552
53 2-17 Redc 7g/s [51] 5105

BELLA TUTRICE 3 b f £1795
49 15-16 Leic 5g/f 77 2400
73 3-9 Pont 5g/f 72 2609
65 4-12 Ling 5g/f 72 2743
45a 10-11 Ling 6ap 72 2841
67a 3-11 Ling 6ap 69 3198
55 9-12 Folk 6gd 69 3380
25 12-13 Good 6gd 69 3952
40 17-17 Ling 6g/f 67 4740
43a 10-12 Ling 6ap 64 4976 P
40 10-17 Bath 5.7gd [64] 5020 p

BELLALOU 2 b f £364
57 8-9 Newm 6g/f 2531
63 7-14 Folk 7fm 2714
55 3-8 Brig 6g/f 3172
31a 11-12 Ling 7ap 55 3820

BELLE ARTISTE 2 b f £0
103 5-12 Curr 7g/f 4432 BL

BELLE CHANSON 2 b f £0
63 7-8 Sali 6sft 4577
50 8-10 Good 6gd 4876
47a 11-14 Ling 7ap 5076

BELLE LARGESSE 2 b f £0
42 5-7 Newc 5sft 1394
32 13-13 Nott 5.1gd 1987
10a 12-12 Wolv 6ap 5177

BELLE ROUGE 6 b m £30010
59a 2-14 Ling 12ap 55 768
60 2-14 Kemp 14.4sft 52 948
60 1-10 FOLK 12g/s 54 1082*
65 2-11 Ling 16gd 59 3200
69a 1-11 LING 16ap 60 3450*
72 2-12 Sand 16.4g/f 65 3861
78 1-14 BATH 13.1g/s 66 4203*
78 2-16 Kemp 16g/f 72 4361
76 1-16 GOOD 12gd [74] 4745*
85 1-11 WIND 11.6g/s [75] 4942*
84 3-8 Donc 14.6sft 80 5204

BELLS BEACH 6 b m £10135
36a 6-16 Sout 6af [40] 447
50a 2-12 Wolv 6af [40] 524
24a 8-13 Wolv 6af [40] 582
51a 1-14 LING 6ap [45] 652*
28a 9-14 Ling 6ap [45] 709
57a 1-11 LING 6ap 51 728*
51a 5-13 Ling 6ap 56 767
48a 6-14 Ling 6ap [55] 819
55a 1-9 LING 6ap [54] 1012*
17 9-15 Folk 6g/s 48 1267
43a 4-6 Sout 6af [54] 1443
47 4-18 Wind 6g/f [45] 1806
56a 1-12 LING 6ap [53] 2016*
53 5-8 Sand 5gd [45] 2361
22 10-20 Nott 6.1gd 45 2928
44a 8-14 Ling 7ap 53 3746
51a 7-11 Sout 6af [51] 4041
9 9-10 Ling 6ap 45 4109

BELLS BOYS 4 b g £844
7a 9-12 Wolv 6af [40] 33
43a 5-15 Sout 6af [38] 172 P
30a 3-16 Sout 5af [40] 374 p
41a 3-16 Sout 5af [40] 447 p
25a 5-10 Wolv 6af [40] 667 BL
0 15-15 Sout 6af [40] 773 bl
39a 4-10 Sout 6af [40] 907 p
0 12-12 Sout 6af [40] 982 p
30a 3-12 Wolv 5af [40] 1799 p
40 3-16 Nott 6.1gd [40] 1989 p
8 14-19 Redc 6g/f 37 2125 p
10 14-20 Thir 6g/f 37 3575 p
1 15-18 Thir 6fm 37 3609 p

BELLY DANCER 2 gr f £2528
69 6-16 Leic 5fm 2109
69a 4-7 Sout 5af 2498
76 2-13 Warw 7.1g/s 4664
77 6-16 Newm 7g/f 74 4913
77a 2-12 Wolv 7.1ap [75] 5179

BELSHAZZAR 3 b c £374
51 9-12 Ripo 9g/f 1783
74 4-8 Ripo 10g/f 2012
47 7-11 Beve 8.5gd 2656
66 5-10 Hayd 8.1g/s 69 3138
0 13-14 Hayd 10.5gd 68 3741

BELT AND BRACES 2 b g £0
7a 9-10 Sout 8af [30] 162

BELTANE 6 b g £2303
40a 10-13 Ling 10ap [40] 569
0 11-11 Ling 10ap [40] 693
45a 1-12 LING 8ap [40] 710*
50a 2-7 Ling 8ap 45 910
38 12-19 Yarm 7g/f 48 1132
17 13-14 Wind 8.3g/f 46 2799
29 15-16 Redc 8g/f 42 3768
53 5-9 Redc 8g/f [42] 3806

42 7-19 Chep 8.1g/s [46] 4366
25 9-13 Brig 8gd [46] 4902
0 19-19 Yarm 8g/s [45] 5119

BELTON 2 b c £3147
20 13-14 Donc 6g/f 1874
33 8-10 Donc 6g/f 2077
36 7-15 Catt 7sft 3930
59 6-10 Newc 8hvy 4213
31 17-20 Leic 7g/f 55 4451
62 1-16 BEVE 7.5g/f 55 4597*

BEN BACCHUS 2 b c £0
49 15-19 Newm 7g/s 5285

BEN CASEY 2 b c £1073
40 18-18 York 7g/f 2360
67 6-15 Nott 5.1gd 3988
67 3-10 Redc 5fm 4338
65 3-12 Beve 5gd [66] 4596
59 5-10 Catt 5gd [66] 4968

BEN HUR 5 b g £14404
23 18-19 Beve 9.9g/s 58 1164
63 1-9 LEIC 8g/f [56] 1966*
25 13-15 Beve 7.5g/s 62 2324
68 2-13 Carl 7.9fm 62 2447
65 1-10 AYR 8g/s [62] 2544*
77 1-9 CHES 10.3g/s [63] 2745*
57 5-8 Epso 8.5g/f [63] 2873
78 4-8 Ches 10.3g/f [73] 3083
77 5-8 Ches 12.3fm 75 3637
73 6-9 Sand 9g/s [75] 3892
72 3-11 Wind 10gd [74] 4124
48 9-9 Good 9sft [74] 4266
35 14-17 Ayr 9.1g/s [72] 4620

BEN KENOBI 6 ch g £1720
31a 5-8 Wolv 7af [30] 1565
33a 2-8 Wolv 7af [30] 1676
29a 2-6 Wolv 9.4af [30] 1800
36 7-12 Warw 10.9fm 41 2436
39 2-7 Warw 12.6fm 37 2782
24 8-12 Chep 12.1g/s 37 3085
0 7-12 Wolv 12.2ap [40] 5208

BEN LOMAND 4 ch g £852
50 12-15 Folk 6sft 76 976 c
52 13-16 Good 6gd 74 2023 c
51 3-9 Newm 6gd 71 3924 c
54 9-13 Kemp 7sft 71 4030 c
54 9-13 Warw 6.1gd 65 4272 c
46 10-16 Sali 7sft 60 4582 c
53a 6-12 Ling 6ap 55 5241 c

BENBAUN 3 b c £39918
91 1-10 HAYD 6g/f 81 1488*
68 8-14 Ches 6.1g/s 87 1570
99 1-14 THIR 5g/f 87 1766* vis
106 2-13 Naas 5g/f [87] 2327 BL
100 1-6 SAND 5g/f [93] 2390* vis
105 3-15 Napl 5g/f [93] 3170
110 2-8 Curr 5g/f [93] 4433 bl

BENBYAS 7 b g £9975
51 6-22 Donc 12gd 65 918
76 1-17 PONT 12hvy 65 1064*
79 1-13 HAYD 14sft 65 1109*
49 5-6 Newc 10.1sft [75] 1397 vis

BENDARSHAAN 4 b c £21328
85 4-7 Newm 12g/f 83 2737
84 1-9 PONT 12g/f [81] 2992*
91 1-7 NEWM 14.8g/f 83 3281*
91 2-6 Pont 12gd [87] 3458
86 9-15 Good 14g/f 87 3510
88 5-8 Newb 13.3gd 90 3918
73 18-20 Hayd 14fm 89 4383
76 5-7 Hayd 14sft 86 4778
74 8-19 Newm 12gd 85 5085
89 3-13 Donc 12sft 83 5215
87 3-24 Donc 12sft 84 5372 BL

BENEDICT 2 b c £0
44 7-17 Wind 6g/f 3975
67 8-11 Epso 7gd 4289

BENEDICT BAY 2 b c £0
71 6-9 Sali 7gd 2696

61 10-16 Sali 7g/s   3111
70 7-8   Asco 7gd   3467
27 12-12 Sali 8sft   70   4580
58 12-16 Good 7gd   65   5031 VIS

BENEKING 3 b g £553
38a 11-14 Ling 6ap   [62]   23
24a 13-16 Sout 6af   59   92
27 9-11 Warw 8.1hvy 59 1536
57 3-18 Donc 7g/f   55 2080
38 8-11 Chep 7.1gd 55 2370
54 6-20 Nott 6.1g/f 54 3102 p
35 13-15 Ches 7.6g/f 53 3505
51 5-19 Beve 9.9g/f 51 4243
29 10-18 Beve 9.9g/s 51 4243
45 8-14 York 10.4g/f 51 4402
36 14-19 Beve 9.9g/f 49 4720
9   14-18 Pont 12g/f   49 4938

BENEVENTA 4 b f £74800
110 1-8   KEMP 8g/s   [95] 1115*
110 1-8   NEWM 9fm   [104] 1491*
115 2-6   York 10.4g/s[104] 1684
90 8-10 Asco 8g/f   [110] 2487
109 1-9   NEWM 12g/f [110] 3278+
86 10-12 Deau 12.5g/s[110] 3837
90 7-8   Asco 12g/f [110] 4774

BENJAMIN 6 b g £776
41a 2-9   Ling 8ap   [40] 1185 BL t
38a 2-5   Ling 8ap   [40] 1245 bl t
16a 5-5   Ling 8ap   [40] 1711 bl t
26 11-18 Nott 8.2gd [45] 1992 bl t
16 14-17 Warw 8.1g/f 42 2909 bl t
0   15-17 Bath 11.7gd 39 3145 t
27 5-12 Brig 7fm   35 3677 bl t

BENNANABAA 5 b g £0
7a 13-13 Ling 10ap   338 T
59a 5-12 Ling 8ap   514 T
39a 7-8   Ling 7ap   713 t
37 9-10 Bath 8g/s   [57] 1100 t
0   12-15 Sout 8af   55   1755 t
4   11-11 Chep 7.1gd   48   2370 t
40 8-17 Bath 5g/f   43   2981 t
62 5-11 Bath 5g/f   [40] 3372 t
14 13-13 Bath 5.7g/f [46] 3844 t
23 8-15 Sali 6gd   46   3888 t
36 8-15 Newc 6hvy   42   4211 t
38 13-15 Sali 5gd   45   4335 BL t

BENNY BATHWICK 3 b g £0
58 7-14 Sali 7fm   2291
39 12-14 Wind 8.3g/s   2622

BENNY THE BALL 2 b c £2331
82a 1-14 SOUT 7g/f   [88]   98*
65 15-20 Newm 7g/f   85   1186
72 11-18 Hayd 8.1g/f 83   1919
51 9-10 Leic 8gd   [80] 2137
59a 10-13 Ling 7ap   75   4897
44a 11-13 Wolv 9.5ap   70   5161

BENNY THE BUS 2 b g £1051
20 11-11 Ches 7fm   3633
47 10-10 Hayd 5gd   3755
5   11-11 Hami 6g/s   4006
70 2-10 Catt 5gd   4968

BENS REVENGE 4 b g £0
42 6-10 Leic 11.8g/f   3211
28 11-12 Hayd 10.5gd   3740
29 5-7   Chep 12.1g/s   3899
0   6-12 Wolv 12.2ap [40]   5208

BENTLEYS BALL 3 b g £4453
76 6-19 Newm 6g/s   92   1154
78 13-27 Asco 8g/f   92   2521
88 8-11 Sand 7.1g/s 90   2918
90 3-9   Sand 7.1g/f 88   3338
92 4-11 Newm 6g/f   88   3941
89 4-13 Asco 6.5g/f 88   4773

BENTLEYS BUSH 2 ch f £10652
75 5-6   Newb 5.2gd   1735
86 2-9   Newm 6gd   2245
82 1-8   GOOD 6gd   2537*
86 3-9   Asco 6gd   83   3127

96 3-9   Sand 7.1g/f   3357

BENVOLIO 7 br g £0
0   11-11 Beve 12.1g/f   4716

BERENSON 2 b c £38458
112 2-7   Curr 7gd   4734

BERESFORD BOY 2 b c £832
52a 6-8   Ling 6ap   49
2   P-13 Bath 5.7g/f   4413
16 10-11 Wind 6g/f   4836
58a 2-12 Wolv 6ap   [49]   5162

BERGAMO 8 b g £0
24a 7-9   Sout 16af [45]   576 bl
5a 7-9   Sout 14af [45]   849 bl

BERHAM MALDU 2 b f £0
19 15-15 Donc 5gd   920
6   10-10 Bath 5g/s   1097
30 11-14 Wind 8.3g/f   5049

BERKELEY HEIGHTS 3 b f £2060
41a 6-15 Sout 12af [66]   89
30a 5-9   Sout 11af [48]   204 BL
39a 4-10 Wolv 12af [45]   315 bl
28a 10-16 Sout 11af [40]   445 bl
12a 6-9   Sout 14af [40]   849
44a 2-10 Sout 16af [35]   984
32a 3-7   Wolv 16.2af [45]   1263 VIS
38a 4-7   Sout 14af [45]   1407
44a 1-8   SOUT 14af [45]   1840*
32 9-12 Warw 19.1fm 45   2847
0   12-12 Muss 16gd   42   2964

BERKHAMSTED 2 b c £50767
80 1-5   LEIC 5g/s   1014*
95 6-13 Asco 6g/f   2467
101 2-9   Asco 7gd   3126
100 5-10 Good 7fm   3532
101 1-7   DEAU 8hvy   4156*
93 8-8   Asco 8g/f   [100] 4797
101 5-10 San   8sft   [100] 5167
84 6-8   Donc 8sft   [100] 5216

BERRY RACER 3 ch f £0
24 11-13 Warw 6.1fm   50   2439

BERRYWHITE 6 ch g £1057
26a 7-15 Sout 12af   45   867
24 8-16 Newc 10.1sft 40   1278
40 3-12 Newc 14.4sft 40   1396
42 3-9   Newc 16.1gd 40   1870
58 5-9   Redc 16fm   [40] 2298

BERTOCELLI 3 ch c £1118
51 14-17 Sali 6g/f   75   1722
48 14-15 Ling 7g/f   73   1983
70 3-7   Folk 7g/f   [70] 2272
70 4-14 Nott 8.2g/f 69   2634
49 8-10 Leic 7g/f   [68] 2920
57 7-12 Newm 8fm   65   3410
56 6-8   Folk 7g/f   63   3724
37 8-9   Good 8gd   60   3950
53 7-14 Redc 10fm   56   4342
42 10-18 Good 8gd   55   4750
49 4-15 Wind 10g/f [55] 4834
49 4-18 Leic 10gd   [50] 5042

BERTROSE 2 ch c £1346
84 4-11 Newb 7g/f   3959
81 5-13 Kemp 8g/f   4355
81 3-11 Good 8g/f   4746
55 11-13 Wind 8.3g/f 78   5051

BESEEKA RUNNIN FOX 3 b f £0
0   7-8   Pont 12g/f   2608

BESPOKE 2 ch g £0
49 5-7   Ayr   6gd   3323
49 6-8   Newm 6g/f   3473
39 9-13 Pont 6gd   3682
43 8-12 Sali 8sft   62   4580

BESSEMER 3 b g £9491
84 5-8   Muss 7.1g/s 93   1460
84 3-4   Newm 8g/f   [90] 2533
75 6-8   Muss 7.1g/f 85   2809

86 1-4   AYR   10g/f   [81] 3762+
88 4-10 Ches 10.3sft 84   4071
2   19-20 Ayr   10g/s   84   4656
84 3-6   Hami 8.3sft [84] 4695
41 19-24 Donc 12sft   84   5372 T

BEST ABOUT 2 ch f £0
71 7-15 Kemp 7g/f   4710 T

BEST BE GOING 4 b g £7751
52 17-20 Newb 10gd   77   1235
76 7-15 Sand 10g/f   76   2099
75 5-12 Kemp 9g/f   76   2860
78 4-6   Leic 11.8g/f 76   3345
56 14-21 York 11.9gd 76   3999
55 16-19 Kemp 10fm   75   4392
83 1-17 WIND 10g/f   73   5050* VIS

BEST BEFORE 3 b g £16559
36a 5-8   Wolv 8.5af [68]   248
43a 7-13 Ling 6ap   60   471
58a 7-11 Ling 8ap   [56]   697
64a 1-10 LING 8ap   56   769*
69 2-18 Wind 8.3gd   61   1385
70 2-15 Warw 8.1sft 61   1530
37 16-18 Good 8g/f   65   1849
71 2-16 Good 9gd   65   2220
76 1-8   WIND 8.3g/f 67   2448+
76 3-9   Good 8gd   73   2540
76 3-13 Newb 8fm   73   2647
78 3-16 Kemp 9g/f   74   3039
83 1-20 NEWM 8g/f   74   3232*
79 6-9   Asco 8gd   80   3465
70 9-14 Wind 8.3gd [80] 4122
64 13-20 York 8.9gd   79   4999
20 12-14 Newb 8hvy   76   5227
45 17-20 Donc 7sft   76   5367

BEST DESERT 3 b g £5215
63 4-17 Yarm 7g/f   [65] 1729
67 2-16 Ling 7g/f   [65] 1982
44 14-20 Newb 7fm   66   2650
57 8-9   Sali 8g/s   66   3112
61 5-9   Ling 7gd   66   3447
68 1-8   CARL 6.9g/f [63] 3654*
64 5-8   Newm 8g/f   66   3947
32 12-14 Yarm 8g/s   [65] 4252
38 7-15 Hami 6sft   64   4696
62 6-26 Redc 8fm   62   4926
61a 3-12 Wolv 7.1ap   60   5112
60a 4-9   Ling 8ap   [59] 5242
30a 8-9   Wolv 9.5ap [59] 5360

BEST FLIGHT 4 gr g £425
51 11-20 Donc 10.3g/s 72   1519
54 15-19 Newb 10gd   72   1736
68 4-8   Wind 10fm   70   2973
54 11-13 Asco 16.2g/f 68   3387
39 9-13 Folk 12gd   66   4119
56 9-13 Warw 12.6gd 66   4274

BEST FORCE 3 b f £289
56 4-14 Bath 5gd   57   1404
48 7-10 Folk 6sft   57   1576

BEST GAME 2 b g £0
49 12-17 Ling 6gd   4443
66 7-14 Sali 7sft   4575
65 6-13 Brig 8sft   5091
44 14-19 Redc 8sft   62   5302

BEST LEAD 4 b g £5191
45a 6-16 Sout 5af   56   166 VIS
54a 5-15 Sout 5af   [53]   253 BL
64a 1-10 WOLV 5af   [53]   286* bl
54a 9-9   Sout 5af   65   415 bl
45a 4-13 Wolv 6af   [62]   483 bl
55a 4-11 Wolv 5af   60   643 bl
53a 3-8   Wolv 5af   55   1218 bl
52 4-15 Muss 5gd   52   1555 bl
49 3-9   Muss 5gd   [52] 1797 bl
57 3-10 Newc 5g/f   [52] 2161 bl
54 3-10 Hami 5g/f   [52] 2476 bl
46 3-14 Newc 6g/s   [52] 2730 bl
43 8-14 Hami 6gd   54   3129 bl

BEST PORT 8 b g £12839
40 10-13 Catt 13.8gd 54   997

59 1-17 **NOTT** 14.1gd 53 1238*
0 11-12 Sout 16af 53 1753
68 1-9 **REDC** 14.1g/f 58 2105*
60 6-13 Newc 16.1sft 64 2685
67 1-10 **THIR** 16fm 62 3611*
64 9-12 York 13.9g/f 64 4400
67 4-9 Redc 14.1fm 64 4559
65 3-8 Redc 14.1fm 63 4932
65 5-10 Pont 18g/s 62 5151
56a 2-13 Wolv 16.5ap 51 5366

BESTBYFAR 2 b c £0
63 7-11 Ayr 7.2g/s 4653

BESTSELLER 4 ch f £776
46a 4-10 Wolv 12af 359
47a 3-7 Sout 12af 588
21a 5-11 Wolv 12af 689

BETFRED 3 b g £0
0 8-8 Hami 9.2g/f 3592

BETHANYS BOY 2 ch g £2142
67a 5-10 Wolv 7af 76 112
82a 1-16 **SOUT** 8af [73] 192*
37 14-14 Donc 10.3gd 76 923
46 10-11 Ripo 8gd 75 1176
26 8-8 Nott 8.2g/s [72] 1775

BETTALATETHANNEVER 2 ch g £29408
69a 6-11 Ling 6ap 135
84a 1-11 **LING** 7ap 213*
95a 1-7 **LING** 7ap 82 368*
100a 4-15 Ling 7ap [88] 885
56 20-20 Newm 7g/f 95 1186
83 12-17 Epso 7g/f 92 2212
88 2-4 Newm 8af [87] 2533
91a 6-12 Ling 8ap [95] 3199
83 7-17 Good 7fm 85 3550
80 8-12 Sand 7.1g/f 84 3860
95 1-10 **EPSO** 7gd [82] 4912*

BETTER OFF 5 ch g £0
15a 16-16 Sout 7af [73] 161 p
22a 7-9 Wolv 9.4af [70] 239 VIS
40a 5-10 Wolv 7af [65] 298 p
47a 8-11 Wolv 7af 60 558 p
40a 6-7 Wolv 7af 57 860
27a 13-13 Wolv 9.4af 52 1223 p
19a 5-7 Wolv 8.5af [48] 1672

BETTER PAL 4 ch g £0
19a 15-16 Sout 7af [54] 61
0 14-15 Sout 8af 54 84
0 14-14 Sout 8af [45] 354

BETTER TALK NOW 5 b g £581006
125 1-3 **LONE** 12g/s 5311*

BETTERGETGONE 4 b f £0
5a 11-12 Wolv 8.5af [35] 47

BETTERTHEDEVILUNO 5 b g £0
0 12-12 Sout 8af 905

BETTERWARE BOY 3 ch g £0
64a 5-16 Ling 10ap 148
60a 7-11 Ling 16ap 66 3450
47 11-14 Wind 11.6fm 72 3638

BETTY STOGS 3 b f £0
54 9-9 Kemp 8g/s [84] 1110
77 5-5 Sali 8gd 84 3885
68 14-14 Sali 7gd 80 4331
46 16-16 Good 7gd 77 4873

BETTYS PRIDE 5 b m £6890
55 9-13 Newc 5gd 1873
57 4-10 Thir 5g/f 62 1973
12 16-18 Thir 6g/f 59 2214
51 6-10 Donc 5g/f 56 2429
47 13-18 Carl 5.5gd 53 3054
47 13-18 Carl 5g/f 53 3228 P
48 1-8 **MUSS** 5g/f [49] 3527*
54 7-8 Hami 5g/f 52 3591
52 6-17 Beve 5g/f 52 4603
58 1-19 **LING** 5g/f 52 4739*
39 12-15 Newc 5fm 59 4870

BETTYS VALENTINE 4 b f £0
0 4-5 Sout 11af 772
0 10-11 Newc 8sft [30] 1279
29 8-10 Ayr 8g/s [30] 1446 T
16 12-15 Beve 7.5g/f [30] 1944
20 9-10 Hami 5g/f [25] 2476
0 13-14 Newc 6g/s [25] 2730

BEVELLER 4 ch g £660
56a 2-16 Sout 6af [48] 65

BEVERLEY BEAU 2 b c £584
37 5-8 Muss 5g/f 1091
43 5-6 Ayr 5g/f 1445
64 4-6 Leic 5fm 2110
64 4-10 Catt 6g/f [60] 4436
76 4-11 Beve 5g/f [60] 4599
69 5-10 Muss 5gd [68] 4804
63a 6-13 Wolv 5.1ap [67] 5207

BEVIER 10 b g £654
26a 5-9 Wolv 9.4af [45] 522
44a 3-11 Wolv 12af [45] 666
45a 4-12 Wolv 9.4af 45 747
46a 2-9 Wolv 9.4af [45] 821
16 8-17 Pont 12hvy 40 1064
16a 4-6 Wolv 12af [45] 1313
28a 7-10 Wolv 9.4af [45] 1564
1 12-15 Chep 10.2g/s 40 4299
0 15-15 Carl 9.3fm [40] 4505

BEYOND CALCULATION 10 ch g £270
54 18-20 Thir 5g/s 67 1476
41 16-17 Nott 5.1g/s 64 1774
55 7-11 Hayd 5g/f 64 1886
27 10-10 Brig 5.3g/f 60 2044 P
57 4-11 Good 6gd 56 2535 p
31 7-14 Newc 6g/s [56] 2730 p
56 4-20 Nott 6.1gd 55 2928 BL
32 4-19 Nott 6.1gd [54] 3104 bl
49 5-9 Catt 5g/f [53] 3353 bl
29 11-18 Thir 6fm 51 3609 bl
35 8-11 Epso 6gd [48] 4294 bl

BEYOND THE CLOUDS 8 b g £5603
60 12-16 Muss 5g/f 82 1120
72 12-20 Thir 5g/s 79 1476
61 12-12 Ripo 5g/f 79 2524
78 2-8 Hami 5g/s 76 2830
63 9-15 Beve 5sft 76 2942
65 9-12 York 5g/s 76 3073
76 3-12 Newc 5gd 75 3427
67 7-18 Beve 5gd 75 3852
58 15-16 Muss 5g/f 75 4174
75 6-19 Beve 5g/s 75 4240 P
78 2-20 Donc 5fm 73 4496 p
76 7-16 Leic 5gd 74 4700 p
61 10-10 Beve 5g/f [76] 4718 p
51 17-18 Pont 5g/s 75 5149 p

BEYOND THE POLE 5 b g £5929
44a 8-10 Ling 13ap 60 11
59a 1-13 **LING** 13ap [55] 602*
18a 12-14 Ling 12ap 55 711
62a 1-14 **LING** 12ap 55 768*

BHUTAN 9 b g £870
17 10-11 Newm 12g/f 50 2244
49 2-16 Brig 9.9g/f 46 3175
28 8-14 Wind 11.6fm 46 3638

BI POLAR 4 b g £4460
57 23-30 Newm 6g/f 78 1481
25 19-19 Sali 7g/f 76 1723
77 2-7 Folk 7g/f [73] 2272
77 2-13 Kemp 7g/f 73 3034
52 13-17 Newb 7g/f 73 3257
74 3-13 Kemp 7sft 74 4030
72 6-21 Donc 7fm 73 4482
75 3-16 Good 7gd 72 4873

BIBI HELEN 2 b f £189
61 6-7 Kemp 6fm 2071
62 11-14 Newm 7gd 2766
40 11-11 Newm 8gd 3925

BIBURY FLYER 2 br f £88217
80 2-7 Kemp 5sft 943

67 2-4 Newc 5hvy 1037
69 3-8 Thir 5g/f 2213
79 3-4 Bath 5fm 2411
71 5-11 Sali 5gd 2658
74 2-8 Catt 5g/f 2847
82 2-4 Donc 5g/s 3224
86 6-24 Newb 5.2g/f 3266
85 1-8 **DONC** 5g/f 75 3374*
85 3-6 Good 6fm 82 3623
62 9-9 Redc 6g/f 84 3807
74 7-12 Sali 6g/s 84 4079
85 3-6 Good 5sft 83 4187
82 3-6 Chep 5.1g/s 82 4298
87 3-21 Donc 6.5fm 82 4457
89 2-14 Yarm 7g/s 81 4583
90 4-26 Newb 6.5g/f 4679
104 1-10 **CURR** 6sft [81] 5072*
98 4-8 Newm 7sft [89] 5133
103 1-7 **NEWB** 7hvy [89] 5222*
85 8-8 Newm 6sft [94] 5267

BID FOR FAME 6 b g £3992
89a 2-8 Sout 16af 80 140
93a 1-12 **SOUT** 14af 80 173+
56 15-18 Kemp 16g/s 86 1112
58 13-18 Newb 16gd 85 1232
41 14-18 York 13.9g/s 80 1689 P
0 10-10 Carl 14.1fm 76 2444
52 8-11 Newm 16sft 76 5271

BID SPOTTER 4 b g £0
36a 8-10 Sout 12af 45 138
7a 9-14 Sout 14af 45 185
34a 4-12 Wolv 12af [45] 891 P
9a 13-16 Sout 14af 45 1033 p
0 13-13 Yarm 11.5fm 35 2868

BIEN GOOD 3 b f £413
45 3-7 Catt 13.8g/f 3019
30 5-7 Ripo 9g/s 3263
0 20-20 Catt 15.8gd 45 4965
28 8-11 Redc 10sft [45] 5303

BIENHEUREUX 3 b g £4144
44a 9-13 Sout 8af 553
19a 8-10 Sout 8af 47 662
18a 13-14 Ling 7ap [45] 783
16 11-14 Sali 8fm 40 2423
46 2-11 Pont 12g/f 40 2790
54 1-14 **FOLK** 12gd 45 3383*
43 5-14 Nott 16g/f 50 3580

BIENVENUE 2 ch f £6803
70a 2-11 Ling 8ap 21
70a 3-12 Ling 8ap 102
67a 5-12 Ling 8ap 175
70 4-12 Sand 10gd 67 2366
69 1-17 **WIND** 11.6fm [67] 2788*
76 2-12 Wind 11.6gd 69 3161
69 6-12 Sand 14g/f 69 3359
61 6-11 Bath 11.7g/f 73 3845
62 6-11 Epso 12gd 73 4468

BIG BAD BOB 4 br c £20041
111 3-10 Good 9.9g/f [112] 1862
111 4-10 Long 10g/s [112] 2635
99 5-8 Leop 10g/f [112] 3496
114 1-6 **DONC** 10.3fm[110] 4492*

BIG BAD BURT 2 ch c £3073
63a 9-10 Ling 5ap 13
55a 14-16 Ling 8ap 64 455 VIS
66a 2-12 Ling 7ap 62 545 vis
66a 2-11 Ling 6ap 64 735 vis
64a 3-14 Ling 7ap [64] 804
54 7-11 Warw 8.1hvy 66 1534
64 3-18 Nott 8.2g/s 64 1778 P
64 4-16 Ling 7g/f [63] 1982 T p
60 6-7 Hami 8.3g/f [63] 2474 tp
0 9-10 Sout 8af [66] 2997 tp
42 9-11 Yarm 10.1gd [62] 3362
58 4-7 Yarm 10.1g/f [59] 3704
34 7-9 Ches 12.3sft 59 4076
25 4-7 Brig 9.9sft [59] 4142

BIG BAMBO 2 ch c £0
11 8-8 Wind 5g/s 1053
20 17-19 Kemp 6g/f 1911

BIG BERTHA 5 ch m £1982
69a	3-14	Ling	13ap	65	147
67a	4-13	Ling	13ap	66	342
69a	2-9	Wolv	12af	67	424 e
67a	8-16	Ling	12ap	68	493
56	15-15	Nott	10g/f	67	4849
71	4-7	Newm	12sft	66	5268

BIG BRADFORD 2 b g £8000
52a	11-13	Ling	7ap	87	15 bl
93	2-18	Newm	6g/f	85	1933 VIS
70	12-20	York	6g/f	90	2407 vis
78	16-19	Newm	6fm	90	3002 vis
71	12-12	Newm	7ap	88	4225 vis
77a	6-14	Ling	7ap	82	4446 bl
63	14-15	Kemp	6g/f	85	4713 bl
25	18-19	Sali	6gd	85	4855 bl

BIG HASSLE 2 b c £5244
70	5-13	Carl	5gd		2670
84	2-12	Carl	5gd		2933
87	1-15	BEVE	5g/s		3178*
1	9-11	York	6g/s	[89]	4022

BIG HOO HAH 2 ch f £275
44	16-16	Kemp	7g/f		3035
63	6-12	Folk	7gd		3908
67	4-11	Chep	8.1g/s		4296
50	7-20	Yarm	8g/s	67	4635

BIG HURRY 3 b f £0
54	11-14	Newb	9fm	3631

BIG MOMENT 6 ch g £44806
102	3-17	Ches	18.7gd	96	1569
99	5-12	Asco	22.2fm	[99]	2583
99	6-15	Good	14g/f	97	3510
104	2-7	Hayd	14sft	95	4778
104	2-19	Newm	12gd	96	5085
109	1-6	DONC	12sft	[99]	5369*

BIG MYSTERY 3 b f £0
26a	9-11	Wolv	5.1ap	5363

BIG SMOKE 4 gr g £436
50	11-11	Hami	8.3g/f	74	2317
58a	4-10	Sout	11af	[74]	2499 bl
59a	5-9	Sout	12af	[69]	2724 P
46	3-7	Carl	11.9g/f	[60]	3226 p

BIG TOM 3 ch c £0
25	9-10	Hayd	8.1gd	[62]	3739
0	11-11	Sout	5af	59	4094
21	10-11	Beve	5g/s	[54]	4237
0	19-19	Thir	6g/f	49	4595
0	16-16	Warw	8.1g/s	[40]	4993 BL

BIGALOS BANDIT 2 ch c £23460
78	1-6	REDC	5sft		1143*
96	2-5	Donc	5g/s		1517
89	4-7	Beve	5g/f		2167
42	8-8	Ches	5.1g/f		3081
96	4-13	Good	5g/f		3509
95	3-5	York	5g/s	[99]	4025
93	3-8	Ripo	5gd	[99]	4307
80	15-22	Donc	6fm	[91]	4458
99	1-6	MUSS	5g/s	[95]	5141*

BIJAN 5 b m £0
24a	5-12	Sout	6af	37	85
24a	8-10	Wolv	6af	35	282
37a	4-9	Sout	7af	[35]	304
21a	9-11	Wolv	7af	35	378 P

BIJOU DAN 3 ch g £539
48	4-8	Hami	8.3fm		3246
56	6-13	Leic	10g/f		4453
42	7-8	Hami	9.2g/s		4821
51	5-8	Ayr	10sft	[58]	5034
12	9-12	Catt	12sft	[54]	5319

BIJOU DANCER 4 ch g £0
46	12-18	Wind	8.3gd	59	1385
33	7-9	Leic	9g/f	[56]	1966
32a	6-12	Sout	7af	[51]	2337 P
41	17-18	Bath	10.2gd	[46]	5023

BILL BENNETT 2 b g £19344

77a	2-13	Wolv	9.4af	[71]	37
65a	9-12	Ling	10ap	[74]	116
72a	1-9	WOLV	9.4af	[73]	240*
61a	6-7	Ling	10ap	74	325
1a	9-9	Wolv	9.4af	74	441
60a	6-6	Sout	12af	71	683
64	5-12	Catt	12gd	68	1000
70	1-19	WARW	10.9gd	65	1124*
77	1-11	WARW	12.6sft	67	1528*
78	2-10	Nott	14.1hvy	73	1612
57	5-6	Good	12g/f	77	2021
78	7-11	Sand	14g/s	77	2130
82	1-16	WIND	11.6g/s	75	2621*
79	4-5	Hami	12.1g/s	81	2827
61	8-11	Newm	14g/f	80	4919
82	3-13	Newb	16sft	78	5194
65	7-11	Newm	16sft	78	5271

BILLY BATHWICK 7 ch g £5084
48	9-17	Kemp	10g/f	58	1913
38	8-12	Bath	10.2fm	58	2036
64	3-11	Chep	10.2gd	56	2371
59	3-8	Chep	10.2g/f	56	2628
63	1-9	YARM	10.1fm	56	2866*
41	7-13	Bath	10.2gd	[59]	3144
60	5-16	Chep	10.2g/s	59	4365
48	8-12	Good	9g/f	59	4539
25	12-16	Yarm	11.5g/s	59	4589
53	7-18	Sali	9.9gd	58	4850
47a	14-16	Ling	12ap	58	4973
18	17-19	Bath	11.7gd	57	5024

BILLY ONE PUNCH 2 b c £0
73	7-12	Newm	7gd	4194

BILLY TWO RIVERS 5 ch g £0
23	5-12	Muss	16gd	33	2964 p

BILLY WHISTLER 3 ch c £0
0	12-12	Sout	8af	848 BL

BINANTI 4 b g £1920
78	13-14	Sand	8.1g/f	91	2096
86	6-8	Sand	7.1g/f	90	2389
90	6-11	Warw	7.1fm	[88]	2777
70a	9-12	Ling	8ap	[88]	3199
48	17-21	Asco	7g/f	88	3441 VIS
82	5-8	Sand	7.1g/s	85	3891
79a	5-14	Ling	7ap	83	4180 vis
84	3-15	Sand	7.1gd	80	4500
76	7-12	Good	8gd	[81]	4872

BINARY VISION 3 ch c £6944
94	1-13	YORK	7.9g/f	2410*
105	6-9	Wind	8.3fm	2757

BINNION BAY 2 b c £0
72a	8-13	Ling	7ap	84	15
53	8-9	Kemp	6gd	[84]	2173
57	11-12	Leic	8g/f	78	2922
59	9-10	Asco	8gd	[78]	3067
46	6-11	Brig	7g/f	[67]	3298
44	7-12	Bath	8g/f	59	3846

BINT IL SULTAN 2 b f £718
69	3-6	Good	6gd	2373
56	7-13	Epso	6g/f	2870
35	12-13	Kemp	6gd	3183
54a	8-12	Ling	7ap	63 3820

BINT MAKBUL 4 b f £2072
52a	1-12	WOLV	7af	53	129*
58a	4-15	Ling	7ap	58	151

BINT ROYAL 6 ch m £10997
60a	5-11	Wolv	6af	67	1337 p
51	5-10	Donc	6g/f	60	1878 p
34	12-18	Donc	7g/f	58	2080 p
61	3-11	Newm	6fm	58	2093 p
61	4-9	Yarm	7fm	58	2150 p
33	7-13	Donc	6gd	58	2232 p
54	4-15	Leic	6g/f	60	2398 p
59	3-6	Good	7gd	60	2539 p
52	8-11	Pont	6gd	58	2791 p
57	9-12	Yarm	7fm	58	2864 p
52	5-10	Hayd	7.1g/s	55	3137 p
52	8-11	Donc	7g/f	55	3223 p
33	8-14	Yarm	8gd	55	3363

29	19-25	Asco	7g/f	53	3443
57	2-8	Muss	7.1g/f	53	3528
62	1-12	CARL	6.9fm	53	3548*
43	13-20	Chep	7.1gd	55	4488
61	1-16	CATT	7g/f	55	4676*
56	5-20	Ripo	6gd	58	4785
59	5-18	Leic	6gd	58	5039

BINTY 2 b f £0
51	10-11	Newm	6sft	5265
59	11-17	Yarm	6g/s	5350

BIRCHALL 5 b g £0
14	14-17	Newm	10g/f	54	3238

BIRD KEY 3 b f £0
28	8-8	Newm	6g/f	3784

BIRD OVER 2 b f £1477
61a	4-14	Ling	7ap	4658
68a	1-11	WOLV	7.1ap	5228*

BIRIKINA 2 b f £0
48a	9-13	Wolv	6af	57	1
26a	6-6	Sout	6af	57	316
4a	7-8	Wolv	6af	57	422

BIRIYANI 2 b f £403
76	4-15	Kemp	6g/f	4357

BIRTH OF THE BLUES 8 ch g £1840
40a	8-10	Ling	10ap	[40]	370
36a	8-14	Ling	13ap	[40]	537
10a	6-11	Wolv	12af	[35]	689
43a	3-10	Ling	12ap	[30]	916
44a	1-13	LING	13ap	[40]	1076*
38a	4-7	Ling	12ap	[45]	1243
41	6-13	Brig	11.9g/f	45	1373
16	6-6	Brig	11.9fm	[45]	1692

BIRTHDAY STAR 2 b c £0
49	14-20	York	6g/f	4401

BIRTHDAY SUIT 3 ch f £4924
87	3-5	Ripo	6gd	[102] 1175
69	3-4	Donc	8g/s	[102] 1520

BIRTHSTONE 2 ch f £25704
113	1-6	CHAN	8gd	4728*

BISCAR TWO 2 b g £5986
38a	8-13	Wolv	8.5af		43
39a	4-8	Sout	8af	45	490
34a	6-10	Sout	11af	45	658
50	2-16	Redc	8sft	45	1147
50	2-11	Newc	8sft	48	1395
52	2-8	Nott	8.2sft	49	1740 VIS
45	8-15	Ripo	10g/f	49	1976
56	1-7	RIPO	10gd	[48]	2982* BL
39	9-15	Nott	10g/s	52	4037 bl

BISH BASH BOSH 3 b f £0
24a	9-11	Wolv	6af	[45]	466
25a	8-9	Sout	7af	[40]	613 BL

BISHOP TO ACTRESS 3 ch f £0
0	13-13	Sout	8af	[52]	319
0	15-16	Sout	5af	[45]	720

BISHOPRIC 4 b g £10010
30	19-20	Donc	10.3g/s	88	1519
97	1-10	HAYD	8.1gd	88	2242*
71	14-14	Hayd	8.1gd	94	2903 VIS
37	10-11	York	10.4g/s	94	4021

BISHOPS BOUNCE 3 b g £0
0	14-15	Ayr	8gd	[60]	2504
28	8-10	Carl	5.9fm	[55]	3545

BISHOPS COURT 10 ch g £38486
112	1-11	NEWB	5.2gd	108	1207*
112	2-8	Beve	5sft	[111]	1626
106	7-20	York	5g/s	110	1683
102	3-12	Epso	5g/f	[110]	2206
105	3-13	Chan	5g/s	[110]	2638
80	7-9	Ches	5.1g/f	[107]	3100
99	10-13	Good	5fm	[107]	3551
105	2-7	Nott	5.1gd	[105]	3989
103	5-11	Beve	5gd	[105]	4238
100	6-14	Epso	5gd	103	4291

91	5-9	Donc	5fm	[102]		4481
84	8-11	Hayd	5sft	100		4780
96	7-10	Newm	5sgd	97		5090
92	6-13	Donc	5sft	95		5218

BISHOPSTONE MAN 7 b g £1743

0	18-18	Wind	8.3g/s	73	1059
64	7-12	Sand	8.1g/s	71	1352
68	4-12	Bath	8g/f	68	1792
62	8-8	Bath	8fm	68	2665
62	6-11	Bath	8gd	66	3142
74	2-19	Chep	7.1gd	66	3401

BLA SHAK 2 b c £0

2	P-13	Newb	6g/f	1760

BLACK COMBE LADY 2 br f £0

27	12-13	Carl	5fm	1950
5	7-7	Hami	6g/f	2473
19	7-7	Muss	7.1g/f	2810
15	13-13	Catt	7g/f	3349
13a	11-12	Sout	7af	3394

BLACK DRAFT 2 b g £0

66	9-10	Sali	5g/f	1716
69	8-12	Ling	5g/f	1981

BLACK LEGEND 5 b g £774

42	2-14	Chep	10.2g/s	42	3895	t
38a	4-16	Sout	14af	42	4045	t
25	9-15	Chep	10.2g/s	45	4299	t
44	5-12	Chep	12.1g/s	[45]	4364	
37	6-12	Warw	12.6g/s	[45]	4991	

BLACK OVAL 3 b f £684

60a	4-8	Ling	7ap	62	933	
58	4-12	Catt	5gd	[62]	995	
62	5-9	Bath	5g/s	61	1102	
53	11-20	Nott	6.1gd	59	1239	
45	3-8	Folk	5g/s	[59]	1268	
44	8-16	Ling	6g/f	55	1985	
42	12-17	Kemp	7gd	55	2174	
46	5-10	Brig	5.3fm	52	2331	
36	8-11	Sali	6gd	49	2661	
45	8-9	Epso	6fm	49	3543	
24	11-15	Ling	6fm	49	3790	VIS
46	9-12	Sand	5gd	[45]	4605	

BLACK SABBETH 3 br c £258

0	11-11	Kemp	8hvy		1514	
51	11-10	Newb	7g/f		2352	
55	10-14	Warw	7.1g/f		2907	
65	6-10	Sali	6gd		3452	
45	4-6	Folk	5g/f	[69]	3725	
30	18-20	Ling	6g/f	64	4317	
35	13-17	Bath	5.7gd	[59]	5020	
27a	11-11	Wolv	7.1ap	[59]	5178	VIS

BLACK SWAN 4 b g £0

18	13-19	Chep	12.1gd	40	3398
57	5-10	Ling	14fm	[35]	3742
27	8-15	Chep	18sft	40	4056
33	13-14	Warw	16.2g/f	35	4423

BLACK VELVET 2 br g £10148

96	1-10	SALI	5g/f		1717*
99	2-8	Newb	5g/f		3254
95	8-10	Good	7fm		3532 BL

BLACKBURN MEADOWS 7 b m £0

28	12-14	Thir	7sft	2692

BLACKCHURCH MIST 7 b m £0

47	11-12	Asco	22.2fm	2583 t

BLACKCOMB MOUNTAIN 2 b f £1844

68	5-11	Warw	7.1gd		3053
73	3-8	Beve	7.5gd		3311
66	4-8	Muss	7.1g/f		3559
70a	4-12	Ling	7ap	70	3820
49	9-12	York	7g/s	70	4064
62	3-6	Muss	8g/f	[68]	4552
66	6-11	Pont	8fm	68	4753
51	6-8	Muss	9g/s	[66]	5140

BLACKDOUN 3 gr c £15036

107	3-5	Sain	8gd	1060
110	2-4	Long	8g/s	1433

BLACKHEATH 8 ch g £29951

66	14-22	Donc	6gd	85	921	
77	4-9	Thir	5g/s	[84]	1217	
80	4-10	Wind	6gd	[82]	1383	
54	13-20	York	6g/f	80	2059	
77	6-17	Epso	6fm	78	2256	
83	2-20	York	6g/f	77	2409	
84	2-17	Redc	6gd	79	2561	
76	6-15	Beve	5sft	82	2942	
84	4-12	York	5g/s	82	3073	
93	1-11	HAMI	6fm	82	3248+	
75	4-5	Asco	6g/f	85	3388	
92	5-24	Asco	5gd	90	3466	
51	23-28	Good	6fm	87	3622	
78	12-20	Hayd	5fm	88	3792	
66	13-16	Hayd	5fm	87	4382	
15	26-26	Ayr	6g/s	87	4652	

BLACKMAIL 6 b g £0

49a	13-14	Ling	7ap	78	4446	bl
13	14-14	Epso	12gd	57	4910	bl
64a	10-12	Ling	8ap	70	5079	bl
70a	5-16	Ling	12ap	67	5261	bl

BLACKNYELLO BONNET 2 b f £0

42	9-18	Ayr	6g/s	4617
52	8-10	Newc	7fm	4864
56	8-14	Redc	7g/f	5301

BLACKPOOL JACK 3 b g £0

0	11-11	Carl	6.9g/f	3651
1	11-11	Ayr	9.1sft	5067
0	11-12	Ayr	7.2sft	5274

BLACKTHORN 5 ch g £1411

59	4-22	Donc	12gd	59	918
22	12-18	Nott	14.1sft	59	1469
57	3-11	Pont	12g/f	58	2041
58	3-8	Newc	12.4g/f	[58]	2163
49	6-10	Thir	16fm	57	3611

BLADE OF GOLD 2 ch f £0

48	10-14	Warw	6.1g/f	4422

BLADE RUNNER 2 ch f £0

22	10-11	Warw	5gd	1123
25	14-14	Chep	6.1sft	4052
21	13-16	Bath	5.7gd	4823

BLADES BOY 2 ch c £3387

50	8-10	Redc	6gd	4244
23	9-10	Catt	6gd	4436
69	1-7	MUSS	5g/f	4549*

BLADES DAUGHTER 3 gr f £0

0	6-10	Pont	6hvy		1070	
20a	11-12	Wolv	6af	45	1374	BL
32	7-9	Muss	5g/s	45	1457	P
17a	6-6	Wolv	6af	[40]	1671	

BLADES EDGE 3 b c £1049

26a	12-12	Ling	7ap	65	545	
50a	5-8	Ling	6ap	58	673	
61	3-8	Donc	6gd	[59]	953	
48	9-12	Catt	5gd	[59]	995	
47	8-8	Ayr	7.2gd	[59]	2506	
6	18-20	Nott	6.1gd	55	2928	BL
35	12-15	Ches	7.6g/f	53	3102	bl
20	12-14	Ayr	7.2gd	[50]	3324	bl
1	18-18	Thir	6fm	45	3609	VIS
17	10-12	Brig	7fm	45	3677	
39	3-12	Ayr	7.2sft	[40]	5274	

BLAEBERRY 3 b f £8876

38	11-17	Donc	8gd		919	
60	7-14	Nott	10gd		1241	
60	5-12	Redc	8g/f	[57]	1823	
51	5-10	Yarm	8g/f	57	2344	
55	4-14	Wind	10gd	55	2617	
65	1-16	LING	7gd	55	3024*	BL
58	5-13	Leic	7g/f	60	3346	bl
67	1-13	LING	7g/f	60	3604*	bl
67	2-9	Redc	8g/f	[65]	3806	bl
52	10-19	Leic	7g/f	55	4452	bl
47	12-26	Redc	8fm	64	4926	bl

BLAINA 3 ch f £0

16a	10-12	Wind	7af	[75]	71
65	5-17	Chep	8.1gd	[75]	2117

72	8-10	Newb	7g/f	75	2312

BLAISE CASTLE 3 b f £14514

95	2-	Mais	7fV		58	
97	4-11	Ling	7sft	[90]	1620	
91	2-7	Asco	7g/f	[90]	1925	
35	11-11	Hayd	6gd	[90]	2240	BL
97	3-2	Newm	8sft	90	5103	

BLAISE HOLLOW 2 b c £3484

60	8-12	Hayd	6gd		2902
74	5-15	Ling	7gd		3285
88	1-11	WIND	8.3fm		3798*
78	5-7	Nott	8.2gd		3991

BLAISE WOOD 3 b f £732

61	10-10	Good	8g/f		1815	
63	6-12	Sand	10g/f		2193	P
38	8-8	Brig	7g/f	65	2434	BL
47	2-9	Brig	8fm	[62]	2834	p
29	11-12	Brig	5g/f	53	3301	p
32	7-12	Brig	7fm	47	3677	bl
24a	11-13	Ling	10ap	47	3823	

BLAKE HALL LAD 3 b g £2680

62	9-12	Newm	7g/s		1152
36	14-17	Ling	7g/s		1617
44	5-14	Newm	7gd		4195
62	1-16	BATH	8gd	55	4828*
52a	6-9	Ling	8ap	[58]	5242
39	13-18	Newm	8sft	58	5272

BLAKESET 8 ch g £15708

75a	1-11	SOUT	6af	68	198*	VIS
79a	1-8	WOLV	7af	72	285*	vis
7a	16-16	Sout	7af	78	419	vis
76a	1-9	SOUT	6af	[78]	487*	vis
72a	1-6	SOUT	6af	[78]	593*	vis
61a	2-12	Sout	6af	78	610	vis
59a	3-8	Ling	7ap	[76]	730	vis
53a	11-12	Wolv	7af	74	840	vis
52a	5-6	Wolv	6af	[72]	941	
38a	3-9	Sout	6af	[68]	1194	vis
55a	2-6	Sout	6af	[63]	1443	

BLAKESEVEN 3 b g £2626

38a	12-16	Ling	7ap	50	270	
49a	3-10	Sout	8af	48	387	
50a	2-13	Sout	7af	48	556	
49a	2-10	Sout	8af	48	678	
51a	3-13	Ling	7ap	48	761	
46a	7-15	Ling	7ap	48	846	
41	7-16	Yarm	7gd	48	4616	
38	7-16	Brig	7gd	[46]	4901	BL
40	6-19	Yarm	8g/s	[45]	5119	P

BLAKESHALL BOY 5 b g £0

58a	4-16	Ling	7ap	58	22

BLAKESHALL GIRL 4 ch f £0

0	12-13	Wolv	6af	[53]	483	
0	8-8	Wolv	8.5af	[45]	630	BL

BLAKESHALL HOPE 2 ch g £816

61	3-7	Nott	6.1g/f		2629
46a	8-9	Sout	6af		3157
63	7-12	Chep	5.1gd		3728
56	4-9	Bath	5g/f		3847 VIS

BLAKESHALL QUEST 3 b f £7448

50a	10-13	Wolv	6af	74	41	
50a	13-13	Wolv	6af	74	113	
51a	8-10	Wolv	6af	70	245	
49a	9-10	Wolv	6af	66	349	
61a	4-10	Sout	6af	66	390	VIS
58a	4-15	Wolv	6af	62	550	vis
59a	4-10	Sout	6af	60	657	vis
45a	5-10	Wolv	6af	60	685	vis
68a	1-11	WOLV	5af	58	958*	vis
52	9-19	Warw	5gd	58	1127	vis
72a	1-11	WOLV	6af	55	1337*	vis
20	14-16	Nott	6.1sft	63	1465	vis
49a	8-13	Wolv	6af	57	2053	vis
1	18-19	Wind	6af	57	5053	vis
48a	10-13	Wolv	6ap	71	5181	vis
59a	7-12	Wolv	6af	69	5291	vis

BLATANT 5 ch h £0

73	11-11	Asco	8g/f	[112]	4801	vis t

BLAU GRAU 7 gr g £0
0 15-20 Bath 17.2gd 40 4824
19 10-19 Brig 9.9gd [40] 4903

BLAZE OF COLOUR 3 ch f £12455
61 3-6 Pont 10sft 1428
75 4-8 Chep 12.1gd 2113
73 2-16 Wind 11.6g/s 70 2621
74 3-8 Wind 10.2gd 70 2796
79 1-8 BRIG 11.9g/f 71 3299* VIS
77 4-14 Brig 11.9fm 77 3674 vis
80 2-9 Kemp 12g/f 77 4360 vis
75 4-6 Good 12gd 78 5028 vis

BLAZE THE TRAIL 3 b f £0
35 11-14 Wind 8.3g/s 2622
30 6-7 Newb 12g/f 2879
13 14-15 Wind 10fm 3292
18 10-13 Bath 10.2sft [35] 5173 BL

BLAZING SADDLES 5 b g £0
17a 6-7 Sout 14af [45] 638 p

BLAZING THE TRAIL 4 ch g £7659
54a 4-13 Ling 10ap [70] 338
49a 8-14 Ling 10ap [63] 430 bl
60a 2-14 Ling 10ap 57 622
61a 5-13 Ling 10ap 60 726
65a 1-13 LING 10ap [59] 912*
68 3-14 Folk 9.7g/s 65 1083
70 2-5 Nott 10sft 66 1609
69 3-17 Kemp 10g/f 67 1913
53 10-15 Sand 10g/f 67 2099
65 6-8 Newm 10g/f 65 2735
55 6-16 Yarm 11.5g/s 64 4589
50 11-18 Sali 9.9gd 61 4850
65 4-17 Leic 10gd 61 5062

BLAZING VIEW 2 b f £0
64 5-20 Wind 6fm 2970
56 9-13 Wind 6fm 3639
34 13-15 Kemp 6g/f 4357

BLESS EM ALL 2 b f £0
12a 12-12 Ling 8ap 102

BLESSED PLACE 4 ch g £4664
36a 8-9 Ling 5ap 55 435
1a 11-11 Wolv 5af 53 643 BL
41a 13-13 Ling 5ap 53 740 T
23 12-12 Ling 5g/s 50 1615
28a 8-13 Wolv 5af 50 2201
0 16-17 Warw 8.1fm 45 2440
48 3-17 Warw 5fm 45 2599
48 3-20 Nott 6.1g/f 45 2630 t
47 5-18 Hayd 5gd 47 2951 p
49 4-17 Bath 5g/f 47 2981 p
55 1-15 WIND 5gd 47 3165* t
52 5-18 Pont 5gd 51 3463 t
45 13-22 Good 5fm 51 3537 t
44 7-16 Wind 5fm 51 3640
46 6-15 Bath 5.7g/f 50 3966 t

BLESSINGINDISGUISE 10 b g £0
19a 11-16 Sout 6af 49 92 bl
7 9-9 Ripo 6g/f [49] 2007 bl
33 8-19 Beve 5gd 45 2657 bl
13 17-18 Hayd 5gd 43 2951 bl

BLISSPHILLY 2 b f £0
0 9-10 Beve 5g/f 3504
39 6-15 Redc 6g/f 3769
33 11-14 Muss 7.1g/f 4171

BLOFELD 2 b g £14832
51a 5-15 Ling 7ap [55] 52
70a 1-6 SOUT 6af 55 182*
72a 1-8 SOUT 6af 62 223*
76a 1-7 SOUT 6af 69 333*
61a 6-8 Wolv 6af 75 422

BLONDE EN BLONDE 3 ch f £6300
60a 5-9 Wolv 7af 69 31
62a 3-10 Wolv 7af [69] 152
58a 4-10 Wolv 7af 67 245
53a 6-8 Wolv 7af 67 285
57a 6-11 Wolv 7af 65 363
58a 8-13 Ling 7ap 63 474

70a 1-14 LING 7ap 63 499* BL
68a 2-11 Wolv 7af 66 562 bl
61a 13-14 Ling 7ap 68 604 bl
69a 3-11 Ling 6ap 68 760
68a 3-10 Ling 7ap 68 799 bl
47a 10-12 Ling 8ap [68] 878 bl
34 12-15 Leic 6g/f 55 2398 bl
54 3-9 Ayr 7.2gd 55 2508 bl
39 9-11 Warw 5.5gd 53 3054 bl
54 5-12 Carl 6.9fm 52 3548 bl
47 6-10 Brig 7fm 52 3672 bl
68a 7-13 Ling 7ap 68 3791 bl
43a 12-12 Ling 8ap 67 4743 bl
71a 3-14 Ling 7ap [64] 5080 bl

BLONDE STREAK 4 ch f £7285
79 4-13 Ripo 8g/f 77 2010
78 4-9 Leic 8fm 77 2108
79 7-17 Carl 7.9gd 77 2672
82 1-10 YORK 7.9g/s 75 3074*
71 6-14 Hami 8.3g/s 78 4820
71 8-20 York 8.9gd 78 4999
76a 6-13 Wolv 8.6ap 77 5364

BLOOD MONEY 2 b g £0
33 17-19 Newm 7g/s 5285

BLUE AZURE 2 b f £0
64a 5-12 Wolv 7.1ap 5324

BLUE BAJAN 2 b c £0
70 6-12 Newc 8fm 4866
57 7-9 Ayr 7.2sft 5064

BLUE BIJOU 4 b g £0
0 12-12 Wolv 7af 512
0 5-5 Sout 11af 772
4 10-10 Ayr 8g/s 1446

BLUE CANARI 3 ch c £442634
119 1-15 CHAN 12g/s 2308*
111 12-19 Long 12g/f 4956

BLUE CIRCLE 3 b c £0
23a 13-16 Sout 7af [34] 61 bl
0 10-11 Sout 6af 34 198 P
23a 11-12 Wolv 6af [34] 242 p
0 10-10 Wolv 6af 34 245
0 11-12 Wolv 6af [30] 297 bl
0 9-12 Sout 6af [30] 377 p

BLUE CRUSH 3 ch f £226
72 10-10 Ayr 5g/f 3304
78 10-14 York 5g/s 90 4027
80 10-16 Muss 5g/f 90 4174
77 6-10 Beve 5g/f [85] 4718
79 7-12 Epso 5g/f 82 4908

BLUE DAKOTA 2 b c £56880
104 1-8 NEWM 5sft 1190*
102 1-5 WIND 5g/f 1646*
110 1-6 WIND 5g/f 1808*
109 1-9 ASCO 5g/f 2516*
89 6-8 Good 6fm 3566

BLUE DAZE 3 b f £0
55 14-20 Newb 7g/f 74 1761
39 12-12 Newm 7g/f 72 2249
69 5-12 Sand 9g/f 68 2385
63 5-12 Hayd 8.1gd 68 2904
58 5-13 Warw 8.1gd 68 3058 BL
47 11-13 Leic 7g/f 65 3346
51 7-12 Kemp 9sft 61 4032
49 7-16 Sali 7sft 59 4582
50 6-18 Leic 7gd [59] 4698

BLUE DREAM 4 b f £7700
101 2-11 Ches 6.1g/f 4510 P
80 8-12 Asco 7g/f 4811 p

BLUE EMPEROR 3 b g £0
15a 14-15 Sout 8af [70] 795
43 7-7 Sout 6g/s [66] 1050
32a 5-7 Sout 7af [60] 1196
13a 7-8 Wolv 7af [60] 1222 BL
27 11-14 Donc 6g/f [52] 2428
0 11-12 Ayr 8g/s [52] 2543
0 12-13 Donc 8gd [45] 2753

BLUE EMPIRE 2 b g £8245
70a 2-10 Sout 8af 65 189
76a 1-10 SOUT 7af 65 203*
78a 4-7 Ling 8ap 75 341
77a 5-7 Ling 8ap 75 368
81a 1-12 WOLV 7af [75] 560*
70a 4-8 Ling 10ap [78] 626
77a 2-11 Ling 8ap [78] 696
60a 6-10 Sout 7af 77 794
56 15-18 Good 9g/f 75 1813
57 8-9 Beve 8.5g/f 72 2168

BLUE HEDGES 2 b c £321
55a 13-14 Ling 7ap 4971
66 10-21 Newm 8sft 5097
74a 4-11 Ling 8ap 5236

BLUE HILLS 3 br g £0
0 11-12 Wind 11.6g/s 73 1260
67 5-9 Hami 12.1gd [73] 1507
43 11-11 Sand 14g/s 70 2130
26 11-12 Good 16g/s 65 4235
39 16-19 Sali 14.1gd 63 4856

BLUE JAVA 2 ch c £2162
59a 4-14 Sout 8af 88
69a 8-12 Ling 8ap 175
48 9-20 Newb 7g/f 66 2314
59 8-20 Newb 7fm 63 2650
30 12-16 Epso 8.5gd 61 3219
63 2-15 Leic 7g/f [59] 3515
58a 5-11 Sout 8af 59 4044
63a 2-12 Ling 8ap [59] 4320
55a 8-13 Wolv 8.6ap 59 5183

BLUE KANDORA 2 b c £374
81 4-8 York 5sft 1670
59 7-10 Newm 7fm 2594

BLUE KNIGHT 5 ch g £3485
75a 2-11 Sout 5af 72 655
75a 4-13 Wolv 6af 73 807
70a 7-12 Ling 6ap 73 880
71 6-13 Epso 5sft 73 1293
73 2-14 Kemp 6gd 72 1914
53 11-16 Good 6gd 72 2023
43 4-6 Yarm 6g/f [73] 3710
44a 12-13 Wolv 6ap 72 5181
54a 8-12 Wolv 7.1ap 70 5289
58a 10-12 Wolv 7.1ap [70] 5340

BLUE LEADER 5 b g £0
0 15-16 Ling 12ap 77 475 p

BLUE LINE 2 gr f £0
43 17-19 Wind 5g/f 1805
66 5-9 Brig 5.3fm 2257
41 8-8 Brig 7g/f 3716

BLUE MAEVE 3 b g £12681
35a 9-16 Sout 6af 65
28a 6-15 Sout 6af 43 168
32a 4-9 Wolv 7af [40] 310
0 11-12 Wolv 8.5af [35] 584
24a 4-12 Wolv 7af [35] 663 BL
0 13-16 Sout 8af [30] 719
46 8-13 Pont 5g/f [27] 2279
49 4-12 Ripo 5g/f 27 2524
50 2-14 Newc 5g/s 50 2775
50 4-10 Beve 5sft [51] 2944
57 2-18 Pont 5gd 51 3463
64 1-17 CATT 5g/f 51 3667+
57 5-18 Beve 5g/s 61 3852
1 12-12 Ches 5.1sft 61 4107
47 15-18 Redc 6fm 60 4339
67 1-16 PONT 5fm 58 4754+
67 3-15 Newc 5fm 64 4870
48 11-19 York 5gd 62 4989

BLUE MARBLE 2 b c £4199
62 4-11 Good 5gd 2020
65 6-8 Epso 6fm 2251
46 16-18 Wind 6gd 2618
78 1-9 NOTT 5.1gd 2926*
57 7-10 York 5gd 78 3115
20 9-9 Good 6fm 75 3623

BLUE MARINER 3 b c £7723

28a 8-14 Sout 8af 170
55 9-14 Thir 8gd 1636
70 3-12 Thir 7g/f 1971
71 2-5 Leic 10g/f [70] 2401
71 2-5 Sali 9.9gd 70 2694
52 14-16 Kemp 9g/f 70 3039
48 9-10 Nott 8.2g/f 70 3579
46 15-17 Nott 8.2gd 67 4862
70a 1-12 WOLV 8.6ap 63 5116*

BLUE MOON HITMAN 2 ch c £1699
52a 6-10 Wolv 5af 56 69
48a 3-10 Sout 5af [53] 139
44a 6-9 Sout 5af [49] 256
62 3-7 Bath 5fm [55] 1902
44 7-20 Chep 6.1gd 60 2372
61 3-13 Wind 5fm 58 2784
57 3-6 Ling 5gd [58] 3023
45 8-9 Wind 5fm 60 3804
30 13-19 Chep 6.1sft 60 4054

BLUE NUN 3 b f £0
2 5-5 Newc 10.1sft 1275
49 8-12 Ripo 9g/f 1783
28 10-12 Ripo 8g/f 1978
37 5-6 Ripo 10g/f [47] 3648
8 8-9 Newc 9g/s [47] 3697
15 9-14 Beve 7.5sft [40] 4256
0 14-15 Thir 8fm [40] 4379 P

BLUE OASIS 3 b f £14398
75 1-14 THIR 8gd 1636*
88 5-8 Epso 8.5g/f [77] 2211
93 2-6 Newc 10.1g/s [87] 2772
96 5-10 Newm 10gd [92] 5086
66 10-14 Donc 10.3sft [92] 5370

BLUE OPAL 2 b f £728
69 3-14 Redc 7sft 5301

BLUE OTIS 2 ch f £0
16a 12-12 Wolv 7.1ap 5324

BLUE PATRICK 3 gr g £1320
82a 12-13 Ling 10ap 88 134
48a 10-12 Ling 8ap [86] 234
48a 10-16 Ling 12ap 82 475
42 11-12 Ches 10.3gd 86 1586
31 14-14 Donc 8g/f [80] 1877
76 2-15 Pont 6g/f 75 2280 P
59 11-17 Wind 6g/f 75 2451 p
75 6-13 Newb 7g/f 75 2880 p
66 5-13 Kemp 7sft 74 4030
51 12-15 Kemp 8g/f 72 4362
64 5-7 Sali 8sft [70] 4581
60 8-19 Newc 7g/f 67 5014

BLUE POWER 2 b c £10137
62a 4-13 Wolv 6af [59] 3
63a 2-10 Wolv 5af 59 69
68a 1-8 SOUT 5af 61 169*
59a 3-5 Wolv 5af 69 237
50a 10-14 Sout 5af 66 485
31a 9-10 Ling 5ap [66] 548
62a 3-8 Sout 5af 62 1031
48 5-8 Folk 5g/s [60] 1268
58 3-7 Carl 5fm 56 1951
68a 1-11 SOUT 5af 59 2380*
44 8-12 Ayr 5g/s 58 2566
64 2-8 Newc 5g/s 58 2731
21 16-16 Catt 5sft [60] 3932
68a 2-11 Sout 5af 65 4094
50 12-26 Ayr 5g/s 60 4618
35 13-15 Ayr 5sft 60 5036

BLUE PRINCE 2 ch c £1524
80 2-8 Beve 7.5gd 3311

BLUE QUIVER 4 b c £866
59a 6-13 Ling 10ap 715
59a 2-11 Ling 8ap 53 820
50 9-14 Chep 7.1gd 56 2199
1 15-15 Chep 10.2g/s 54 4299
40 11-18 Good 8g/f 53 4750

BLUE REEMA 4 ch f £9597
100 2-10 Curr 8hvy 895 TP

BLUE RONDO 3 b g £0

56a 7-13 Ling 10ap [65] 148
0 15-15 Sout 12af 60 257
12a 7-9 Ling 13ap [55] 787 VIS

BLUE SAVANNA 3 ch g £4795
47a 3-12 Ling 10ap [48] 267 bl
27a 6-9 Ling 16ap [48] 454 bl
43a 4-6 Wolv 8.5af [46] 526 bl
49a 2-8 Ling 10ap [45] 829 bl
47a 1-10 LING 12ap [47] 916* p
16 12-14 Sout 12g/s [47] 1047 p
40 5-15 Wind 11.6g/f [45] 2267 bl
62a 6-8 Ling 12ap [45] 2739 bl
62 4-9 Wind 11.6gd [40] 3164 bl
36 4-9 Wind 11.6fm [40] 3294 bl
45 2-8 Brig 11.9fm 40 3692 bl
22a 6-12 Ling 12ap [50] 3819 bl

BLUE SKY THINKING 4 b g £24387
99a 4-14 Ling 10ap [90] 82
102a1-13 LING 10ap 96 519*
103a5-11 Ling 10ap [102] 693
102a6-14 Ling 10ap [102] 884
88 13-24 Donc 8gd 97 951
96 3-8 Ayr 10g/f 95 1895
93 4-7 York 7.9g/s 93 3077
84 6-15 York 7.9g/s 92 4061
98 2-7 Thir 8g/s [92] 4208
86 7-8 Donc 10.3fm 92 4530

BLUE SPECTRUM 2 b g £0
57 12-15 Ling 7gd 3285
59 9-14 Ling 7.6g/f 3601
41 10-12 Newm 7g/f 3750
28 14-19 Kemp 8g/f 4792

BLUE SPINNAKER 5 b g £65915
86 7-24 Donc 8gd 90 951
102 1-17 THIR 8g/s 90 1475*
101 4-17 York 7.9g/s 98 1686
104 1-15 REDC 10g/f 98 2101+
92 10-21 York 10.4gd 102 3118
104 4-11 York 10.4g/s 102 4021
104 6-15 Donc 8fm 102 4531
106 3-18 Newb 10gd 102 4681
108 4-32 Newm 9g/f 102 4916

BLUE STREAK 7 ch g £0
29a 10-14 Ling 10ap 48 2589 bl
36 5-8 Brig 11.9fm 48 3692 bl
53 5-8 Ling 11.5g/s [45] 4181 bl

BLUE TOMATO 3 b c £0
79 9-11 Newm 7gd 104 1167

BLUE TORPEDO 2 ch c £4251
61 8-13 Warw 7.1g/s 4664
81a 1-14 LING 7ap 4970*

BLUE TRACK 3 b c £0
42 8-11 Leic 10g/f 3208
7 7-7 Newm 12fm 3405
2a 8-8 Ling 10ap 3787

BLUE TRAIN 2 b c £417
75 4-11 York 7.9gd 5003

BLUE TROJAN 3 b g £32468
66a 6-13 Wolv 8.5af 73 44
67a 4-11 Ling 8ap 70 131
70a 4-14 Ling 10ap 68 265
71a 2-8 Ling 10ap [68] 294
73a 2-14 Ling 10ap 67 434
54 7-18 Asco 8sft 78 1423
64 15-18 Good 8g/f 78 1849
89 1-12 HAYD 8.1g/f 78 1883+
85 4-14 Sand 8.1g/f 84 2096
75 12-13 Epso 8.5g/f 84 2207
66 15-28 Asco 7g/f 84 2558
92 4-20 Newm 8fm 83 3001
90 2-20 Chep 7.1g/s 83 3088
75 11-18 Newb 8g/f 86 3265
80 7-8 Sand 7.1g/s 86 3891
77 8-14 Wind 8.3gd [85] 4122
90 2-24 Newb 9g/f 84 4642
94 1-18 KEMP 9g/f 83 4714*
88 8-32 Newm 9g/f 86 4916

BLUE VENTURE 4 ch g £430

31a 8-10 Sout 8af 60 791
31 9-11 Beve 9.9sft 55 1633
34 9-14 Carl 7.9fm 53 1954
45 4-13 Ripo 12.3g/f 53 2008
36 13-20 Catt 12g/f 51 2850
9 14-14 Carl 17.2gd 51 2937
49 3-20 Catt 12g/f 48 3354

BLUE VIKING 3 b g £0
32 8-8 Ripo 10g/f 2012
49a 5-13 Sout 8af 2383
1a 10-11 Sout 12af 55 2804
26a 11-13 Wolv 9.5ap 51 4925

BLUE WATER 4 b f £0
2a 10-10 Wolv 12af [40] 780 p

BLUEBERRY JIM 3 ch g £0
41 8-9 Ches 10.3g/s [39] 2745
0 11-11 Hayd 8.1gd [39] 2886

BLUEBERRY RHYME 4 b g £16070
59a 4-12 Wolv 5af [66] 70 vis
69a 2-12 Wolv 5af 66 109 vis
51a 3-12 Wolv 5af [68] 242 vis
66a 2-7 Wolv 5af [68] 348 vis
68a 2-9 Ling 5ap [66] 572 vis
65a 1-8 SOUT 5af [65] 742* vis
59a 8-11 Sout 5af 65 859 vis
63a 1-12 WOLV 5af [65] 960* vis
56 5-12 Hami 6g/s [62] 1600 vis
56 8-16 Ayr 5g/f 60 2029 vis
25 14-14 Thir 5g/f 58 3417 vis
28 20-20 Hayd 6fm 56 3796 vis
62 1-26 AYR 5g/s 52 4618* vis
48a 10-13 Wolv 6ap 65 5010 vis

BLUEBERRY TART 2 b f £423
74 5-10 Newb 6gd 3917
73 4-10 Newm 7gd 4191
65 10-19 Leic 7gd 5045
57a 7-12 Wolv 7.1ap 5179

BLUEBOK 3 b c £1945
73 2-14 Warw 7.1gd 4275
64 3-10 Ripo 6gd 4790
65a 7-12 Wolv 7.1ap 67 5008 T

BLUEFIELD 3 b c £318
60 4-11 Wind 8.3g/f 5054

BLUEGRASS BOY 3 b g £5582
67a 3-13 Ling 10ap [63] 148
63a 8-16 Ling 12ap 67 218
60a 8-14 Ling 10ap 66 265
63 3-18 Bath 10.2g/s 63 1098
51 11-17 Kemp 10g/f 63 1913
48 8-12 Newb 10g/f 62 2354
48 8-10 Newb 11g/f 61 2875
59 3-10 Sand 10g/f 60 3336
68 1-14 SALI 9.9g/f 59 3867*
56 7-19 Leic 10g/f 63 4456
60 5-18 Sali 9.9gd 63 4850
33 14-19 Pont 10g/s 63 5148

BLUES AND ROYALS 2 b c £9246
95 1-8 YORK 6g/f 2408*
100 2-8 Newb 7g/f 3267
75 4-4 Sand 7.1g/f 3859

BLUES OVER 2 b f £0
0 12-16 Sout 8af 164
0 10-11 Ling 6ap 233
15a 8-10 Ling 10ap 291

BLUES PRINCESS 4 b f £0
23 13-13 Newc 5gd 56 1873
19 14-19 Beve 5g/s 52 2326
31 12-18 Hayd 5gd 48 2951 bl
5 14-18 Thir 6fm 44 3609 bl

BLUETORIA 3 b f £376
72 4-12 Ripo 8g/f 1978
49 7-13 Nott 8.2g/f 2633
70 5-14 Redc 10fm 68 4342
53 13-19 Leic 10g/f 68 4456

BLUNHAM 3 b g £1302
22a 9-14 Sout 8af 55 62

0	16-16	Sout	6af	55	94 BL
0	13-13	Sout	8af	48	228
23a	14-16	Sout	5af	[48]	253
29a	4-16	Sout	5af	[40]	374
37a	5-16	Sout	6af	[40]	447
15a	9-9	Sout	6af	[40]	487
38	14-18	Catt	7gd	[53]	996
49	6-16	Beve	7.5gd	48	2655
46	2-11	Ripo	8gd	47	2986
16	17-18	Catt	7g/f	47	3670
0	16-17	Thir	8g/s	47	3830
24	16-17	Leic	7gd	46	5056

BLUSHING PRINCE 6 b g £0
35a	5-7	Wolv	9.4af	[61]	862 t

BLUSHING RUSSIAN 2 b g £539
55	8-13	York	6g/f		3431
57	9-15	Nott	5.1gd		3988
61	3-11	Thir	7fm		4375
14	12-12	Ayr	8sft	60	5065

BLYTHE KNIGHT 4 ch c £27990
103	4-17	Kemp	10g/s	98	1111
106	1-16	EPSO	10.1hvy	99	1296*
109	4-19	Newm	10g/f	103	1478
100	6-11	Epso	10.1g/f	103	2208
105	3-14	Asco	10g/f	103	2556
80	15-21	York	10.4gd	103	3118
94	13-15	Good	9.9g/f	103	3506
94	8-11	York	10.4g/s	103	4021
105	6-32	Newm	9g/f	102	4916 P
97	5-16	Newb	10hvy	103	5223 p

BLYTHE SPIRIT 5 b g £13855
68	5-11	Ripo	6g/f	75	1977
57	13-20	York	6g/f	74	2409 p
55	9-17	Redc	6gd	72	2561
53	12-17	Pont	6g/f	69	2990
62	6-10	Muss	7.1g/f	66	3562
56	6-19	Leic	7g/f	64	4452 p
74	1-20	RIPO	6gd	62	4785* p
81a	1-12	WOLV	6ap	69	4984* p
83a	1-13	WOLV	6ap	76	5181* p
80a	3-12	Ling	6ap	80	5297 p

BO MCGINTY 3 ch g £22720
67	7-14	Ches	6.1g/s	79	1570
87	1-11	HAMI	6gd	79	1745*
89	2-12	Ripo	6g/f	85	2482
79	7-9	Pont	6g/f	85	2609
77	8-15	York	6g/f	87	3434
69	4-9	Ripo	6g/f	86	3646
83	5-16	Hayd	5fm	84	4382
89	1-11	SAND	5gd	83	4604*
79	5-12	Hayd	6sft	86	4779

BOANERGES 7 br g £1275
27	18-19	Warw	5gd	62	1127
54	5-17	Warw	5hvy	[59]	1532
51	6-11	Hayd	5g/f	57	1886
59	2-16	Brig	6fm	55	2262
54	4-12	Ripo	5g/f	55	2524
51	7-14	Ling	5g/f	58	2585
30	12-12	Thir	5g/s	58	2690
51	5-11	Brig	5.3gd	55	2957 P
48	11-17	Bath	5g/f	55	2981 p
35	15-19	Donc	5g/s	55	3220 p
15	15-16	Ling	6g/f	51	3602 BL
23	12-13	Brig	5.3g/f	48	3984
38	10-11	Sand	5sft	48	4070
36	9-11	Epso	6gd	[45]	4294

BOAVISTA 4 b f £12229
33a	9-13	Ling	6ap	[57]	544
54a	3-6	Sout	7af	[57]	593 T
59a	2-10	Sout	6af	53	657 t
57a	4-8	Ling	7ap	[54]	713 t
51a	5-7	Ling	5ap	[54]	737 t
56a	3-11	Sout	6af	[56]	869
53	4-13	Sout	6g/s	55	1052
55	4-19	Warw	5gd	55	1127
59a	2-11	Wolv	6af	55	1337
64	2-17	Bath	5g/f	[54]	1787
63	1-8	BATH	5.7fm	54	2034*
60	10-15	Ling	5g/f	66	2062
48	9-15	Leic	6g/f	60	2398

34	8-9	Chep	6.1g/f	59	2626
65	2-11	Warw	5.5gd	58	3054
61	2-13	Bath	5gd	[58]	3143
57	8-13	Catt	5g/f	62	3350
63	3-10	Beve	5g/f	[62]	3503
59	3-12	Nott	5.1g/f	[62]	3577
55	6-11	Bath	5g/f	61	3849

BOB BAILEYS 2 b g £273
62a	4-10	Ling	6ap	3818
51	10-17	Warw	7.1gd	4269

BOBBIE LOVE 2 ch c £0
62	6-10	Newm	7fm	2594
60	8-13	Epso	7g/f	2870

BOBBY CHARLES 3 ch g £0
60	9-15	Nott	8.2g/s	4649

BOBERING 4 b g £0
17	9-14	Carl	9.3g/f	4347
57a	9-12	Wolv	7.1ap	5006

BOBS BUZZ 4 ch g £4832
59	11-19	Leic	6g/s	70	1354
69	5-14	Yarm	6g/f	69	2855
71	3-11	Yarm	7gd	68	3364
56	5-6	Yarm	7g/f	68	3708
73a	2-13	Ling	7ap	68	3791
46	14-17	York	7g/f	68	4398
63	5-19	Leic	7g/f	68	4452
76a	2-12	Wolv	6ap	70	4984
69a	6-13	Wolv	6ap	70	5010
70	2-20	Leic	7gd	66	5046
66a	7-13	Wolv	6ap	73	5181

BOBS FLYER 2 b rf £4747
37	15-18	Ling	6gd		4108
57	4-13	Ripo	5gd		4303
64	8-11	Bath	5g/f		4409
71	2-8	Muss	5g/f		4517
57	4-7	Muss	5g/f		4549
69	4-16	Ripo	5gd	[67]	4787
72a	1-12	WOLV	5.1ap	[65]	4922*

BOBSLEIGH 5 b g £1430
73	6-14	Donc	18gd	79	926
57	13-18	Kemp	16g/s	76	1112
73	4-7	Newm	14.8g/f	72	3281
73	6-19	Good	21fm	71	3531
68	3-9	Yarm	14.1g/f	71	3703

BODDEN BAY 2 b g £0
54	9-14	Thir	8fm	4376
61	8-14	Carl	6.9fm	4503
55	10-19	Ling	6g/f	4895
17a	13-13	Wolv	6ap	4980

BODFARI DREAM 3 ch f £0
42	11-17	Hayd	8.1g/s	4768
19	7-13	Ayr	10sft	5066

BODHI TREE 2 b f £652
73a	3-14	Ling	7ap	5078

BOGAZ 2 b c £1296
69	2-4	Ling	5g/s		1614
62	8-18	Leic	5fm		2109
68a	7-10	Ling	6ap		3817
10	14-14	Epso	5g/f	64	4471 VIS
46a	9-12	Wolv	5.1ap	[61]	4922

BOHOLA FLYER 3 b f £17736
75a	1-12	LING	6gd	[74]	1044*
71	4-16	Kemp	6g/s	73	1116
59	6-17	Asco	6sft	73	1417
69	4-10	Folk	6sft	73	1576
77	1-18	WIND	6g/f	71	2268*
82	1-9	WIND	6gd	75	2619*
77	4-15	Hayd	6gd	78	2950
78	5-8	Newm	6g/f	78	3235
80	2-7	Wind	6fm	[78]	3293
70	11-13	Wind	6fm	78	3479
73	5-6	Sand	5gd	[78]	4498
69	6-15	Kemp	6g/f	78	4713

BOING BOING 4 b g £0
26	15-18	Donc	7g/f	56	2080
48	6-13	Warw	12.6gd	54	3056

41	5-8	Hayd	10.5g/f	52	4354

BOISDALE 5 b g £5107
24a	12-16	Sout	6af	55	92
39a	9-15	Sout	6af	[52]	172
34a	15-16	Sout	6af	[52]	227 t
39a	6-11	Wolv	6af	47	1337
58a	1-8	SOUT	6af	[45]	1588*
53a	6-12	Ling	6ap	[53]	2016
42a	5-13	Wolv	5af	53	2201
6	19-19	Leic	5gd	49	2702
60a	1-16	SOUT	6af	52	2806*
49a	9-15	Sout	6af	58	3000
48	3-15	Catt	7sft	49	3933
40	5-9	Yarm	5.2g/s	48	4253
19a	11-12	Wolv	6ap	[57]	5155

BOJANGLES 5 b g £11265
1a	7-11	Wolv	12af	[55]	689
35	8-19	Warw	10.9sft	50	1090
49	1-10	CHEP	8.1sft	[45]	1334+
44	3-14	Warw	8.1hvy	48	1535
33	10-17	Warw	8.1fm	48	2440
50	3-17	Warw	8.1fm	48	2572
47a	4-15	Sout	8af	48	2725
45	5-20	Kemp	9g/f	48	2857
53	3-13	Warw	12.6gd	48	3056
52	4-19	Chep	12.1gd	49	3727
57	1-12	NEWB	10gd	49	3916*
57	2-15	Chep	10.2g/s	53	4299
55	5-14	Warw	16.2g/f	53	4423
61	1-18	WARW	10.9g/s	53	4669*
45	5-14	Epso	12gd	58	4910
32a	10-13	Wolv	16.5ap	58	5366

BOLD BLADE 2 b g £8191
68a	4-14	Sout	7af	[48]	98 bl
73a	1-10	SOUT	8af	60	190* bl
68a	3-11	Sout	8af	70	252 bl
75a	2-9	Wolv	9.4af	70	441 bl
26a	5-6	Wolv	8.5af	70	470 bl
16	16-16	Beve	7.5g/s	70	1163 bl
0	14-16	Leic	8g/s	65	1359 bl
73a	1-7	WOLV	12af	[70]	2050* bl
9	8-8	Ches	12.3g/s	65	2746 bl
20a	10-10	Sout	8af	72	3395 bl
62	2-8	Catt	15.8g/f	[60]	3666
59	4-4	Hami	12.1g/s	60	3881
56	9-12	Muss	14g/f	60	4170
53	9-16	Warw	16.2gd	60	4276
50	7-8	Catt	13.8g/f	60	4439
41	6-11	Catt	13.8g/f	[55]	4671
1	18-20	York	13.9gd	50	5004

BOLD BUNNY 3 b f £1100
61	3-14	Donc	6g/f	2428
58	3-10	Ling	6g/f	3603
49	7-12	Kemp	6g/f	4029

BOLD COUNSEL 2 b c £2601
65	5-7	Brig	7fm		3691
66	2-11	Thir	7fm		4375
65a	6-14	Ling	7ap		4658 BL
67	1-19	KEMP	8g/f	[65]	4792*

BOLD DIKTATOR 2 b c £0
61	10-10	Newb	7g/f	3955
56	6-6	Epso	7g/f	4470
65a	6-14	Ling	7ap	5076

BOLD EAGLE 2 ch c £0
62	12-21	Newm	8sft	5097

BOLD EFFORT 11 b g £0
21a	11-16	Sout	7af	[40]	66 bl
0	14-14	Sout	8af	40	99 bl
0	9-9	Wolv	7af	[30]	310 b le
0	10-10	Wolv	6af	[30]	822 b le

BOLD HAZE 2 ch g £773
63	3-18	Ripo	6g/s	3939
41	16-20	York	6g/f	4401
62	4-10	Catt	7sft	5317

BOLD JOE 2 b c £0
66a	5-11	Ling	8ap	72	54

BOLD MAGGIE 2 ch f £0
55	6-6	Sand	5g/f	3857

BOLD MARC 2 b c £10080
77	4-9	Newc	5sft		962
88	1-8	MUSS	5g/f		1091*
84	2-7	Thir	5g/s		1471
92	1-7	REDC	5g/f		2100*
81	11-15	Asco	5g/f		2472
72	6-8	Ayr	6g/f	90	3303
90	4-6	Beve	5g/f	[88]	4717
79	6-15	York	6gd	86	4985
87a	3-9	Ling	6ap	[83]	5237

BOLD MINSTREL 2 br c £9182
43	7-11	Hayd	5g/f		1880
75	3-7	Bath	5fm		2415
77	2-11	Warw	5g/f		2911
72	1-9	CHES	5.1g/f		3097*
86	2-4	Bath	5g/f		3369
86	4-11	Nott	5.1gd	84	3987
84	2-8	Bath	5.7g/s	[84]	4198
78	5-14	Epso	5g/f	83	4471
86	5-6	Beve	5g/f	[83]	4717
78	6-11	Epso	5g/f	83	4907
91a	2-12	Wolv	5.1ap	[83]	4981

BOLD PHOENIX 3 b c £0
45	10-13	Newm	8g/f		1935
58	8-10	Sand	10g/f		2386
71	6-8	Newm	10fm		3007
54	8-9	Thir	8sft	73	3835
54	10-17	Warw	8.1g/s	69	4668
6	16-16	Nott	10hvy	65	5345

BOLD PURSUIT 2 br c £0
61	13-14	Muss	7.1g/s		5330

BOLD RIDGE 3 b g £0
54a	8-13	Ling	10ap		148
34a	7-9	Ling	10ap		269
37	10-11	Bath	8g/s		1101
53	8-14	Brig	6fm		1690
0	11-11	Brig	9.9fm	53	2260 bl
32a	6-12	Wolv	8.6ap	[53]	5230 bl

BOLD TRUMP 3 b g £0
50a	4-12	Ling	7ap		536
48	12-17	Sali	6g/s		1497
11	15-18	Chep	7.1g/s	55	3900
41	10-13	Bath	5.7g/f	[52]	4413 VIS

BOLD WOLF 3 b g £287
54a	4-11	Ling	6ap	[54]	898
52	4-14	Warw	7.1sft	54	1085
54a	4-12	Wolv	6af	54	1374
30	14-16	Ling	6g/f	52	1985
0	18-20	Chep	6.1gd	50	2372
27	9-12	Beve	6g/f	47	3301 P
33	8-15	Ling	6fm	44	3790
49a	4-14	Sout	6af	49	4130
29a	10-14	Ling	7ap	[48]	4660
37	7-18	Yarm	6g/s	45	5354

BOLDINI 3 ch g £0
55a	7-13	Wolv	9.5ap		5290

BOLEYN CASTLE 7 ch g £969
70	10-10	Kemp	5fm	[96]	2068
43	28-29	Asco	5fm	96	2581
66	7-7	Newm	5fm	[89]	3409 P
88	4-10	Newm	6g/f	89	3584
68	9-16	Wind	6gd	87	3827
68	10-12	Leic	5g/f	[86]	4454
74	6-8	Yarm	6g/s	[86]	4588 BL
71	11-12	Epso	5g/f	80	4908 bl

BOLLIN ANNABEL 3 b f £1664
60	2-6	Thir	12g/s		1213
51	5-6	Pont	10sft		1428
48	10-13	Beve	12.1g/f	55	1836
55	4-14	Redc	14.1g/f	53	2123
36	9-18	Hayd	14gd	53	2905
36	12-20	Beve	16.2gd	50	3312

BOLLIN ARCHIE 3 b c £432
53	5-8	Donc	6gd		953
33	11-14	Thir	6g/f		1216
51	4-11	Pont	6sft		1426

BOLLIN EDWARD 5 b g £5083
59	6-20	York	6g/f	63	2059
56	5-15	Pont	6g/f	61	2280
66	3-14	Thir	7fm	61	2466
68	2-18	Donc	6gd	60	2752 bl
58	7-17	Pont	6g/f	64	2990 vis
69	2-13	Thir	7g/f	63	3571 vis
63	7-16	Redc	7g/f	65	3809 vis
66	2-12	Redc	6gd	[64]	4245 vis
50	11-17	York	7g/f	64	4398 vis
60	4-18	Ayr	7.2sft	64	4622 vis

BOLLIN JANET 4 b f £0
48	11-15	Pont	6hvy	76	1251
8	15-15	Ripo	6g/f	74	1782 BL
56	10-12	Ripo	5g/f	72	2524
33	12-13	Hayd	6gd	69	2884
43	9-9	Nott	5.1gd	65	3106 bl

BOLLIN RUTH 2 gr f £0
48	8-11	Thir	7fm		2462

BOLLIN THOMAS 6 b g £0
38	7-7	Hayd	14sft	80	4778

BOLODENKA 2 b c £2080
67	8-18	Wind	6gd		3824
77a	2-12	Ling	6ap		4896
77	3-11	Newm	6sft		5265

BOLSHEVIK 3 b g £0
0	11-11	Pont	6sft		1426
30	10-14	Carl	7.9fm	50	1954
11	11-12	Thir	7g/f	[50]	2215

BOLSHOI BALLET 6 b g £0
41	11-13	Catt	13.8gd	56	997 BL
46	6-8	Donc	14.6gd	55	2754 bl

BOLTON HALL 2 b g £12270
90	1-7	BEVE	5g/f		2167*
87	6-11	Asco	7fm		2578
81	5-13	York	6gd	87	4004
81	6-16	Newm	6gd	85	4224
77	5-7	Ches	7g/f	83	4509
64	11-15	Ripo	5gd	80	4784
71	7-15	York	6gd	78	4985

BON NUIT 2 b f £4752
87	1-12	NOTT	6.1g/f		4844*

BOND BABE 2 b f £2770
60	4-6	Muss	5g/f		3525
73	2-6	Carl	5g/f		3652
69	3-4	Hami	5g/s		4134
63	3-13	Ripo	5gd		4303
63	5-14	Redc	5fm	68	4556
38a	8-12	Wolv	6ap	[66]	5177

BOND BOY 6 b g £7117
87a	7-15	Sout	5af	93	64
91a	4-12	Wolv	6af	90	361
58a	7-10	Sout	6af	[90]	532
80a	8-13	Wolv	6af	90	618
83a	4-10	Wolv	6af	87	834
83	7-20	Donc	5gd	93	927
85	6-13	Beve	5g/s	[92]	1162
73	8-9	Newm	6fm	92	1490
94	3-15	Beve	5sft	90	2942
62	8-10	York	6gd	92	3116
74	11-19	Ripo	6g/s	90	3937
75	10-12	Good	6sft	88	4184
87	4-16	Hayd	5fm	86	4382
69	14-24	Ayr	6af	88	4686
80	8-15	Catt	5sft	86	5125
86	4-13	Donc	5sft	84	5218
84	4-11	Muss	5g/s	84	5332

BOND BROOKLYN 2 b c £759
67a	3-13	Wolv	6af	[67]	3 VIS
67a	3-12	Wolv	6af	[67]	42 vis
27a	10-10	Wolv	7af	70	112 bl

BOND CAT 2 ch f £0
57	4-9	Catt	7sft		5131
58	6-9	Muss	8g/s		5331

BOND CITY 2 b g £34197
50	8-14	Donc	6g/f		1874
88	1-13	CARL	5gd		2670*
86	3-5	Beve	5gd		2888
94	3-24	Newb	5.2g/f		3266
84	5-5	York	5g/s	[95]	4025
96	2-8	Ripo	5gd	[95]	4307
92	5-11	Donc	5fm	[95]	4533
87	10-24	Redc	6fm	[95]	4928
94a	1-12	WOLV	5.1ap	[94]	4981*
99	2-7	Catt	5sft	[91]	5124
103a1-5		LING	5ap	[94]	5260*

BOND DOMINGO 4 b g £205
39a	7-15	Sout	6af	[40]	172 bl
9a	11-15	Sout	6af	[40]	773 bl
17a	12-12	Wolv	5af	[40]	889 bl
28a	3-9	Sout	5af	[40]	981 vis
30a	6-8	Sout	5af	[35]	1201 bl
19a	4-7	Wolv	5af	[35]	1309 vis

BOND FINESSE 2 b f £344
62	4-6	Ayr	5g/s		1445
65	4-12	Beve	5sft		1631
47a	7-13	Wolv	6ap		4980
59	4-17	Redc	7g/s		5105

BOND MAY DAY 4 b f £290
36	18-19	Ripo	10g/f	72	1781
58	7-9	Thir	12fm	70	2465
63	4-7	Warw	12.6fm	66	2782
63	4-5	Beve	9.9sft	66	2943
46	8-11	Bath	10.2g/f	63	3373
25	13-14	Catt	12g/f	62	4672

BOND MILLENNIUM 5 ch g £1084
61a	5-14	Sout	8af	69	93
51a	5-6	Wolv	9.4af	67	249
48a	10-12	Sout	8af	64	530
41	11-13	Newc	10.1g/f	59	4406
65	2-13	Muss	8g/f	[59]	4554
56	8-17	Newc	8fm	62	4867
7	15-17	Newc	10.1g/f	62	5016
64a	4-13	Wolv	8.6ap	61	5183
61a	7-13	Wolv	9.5ap	61	5292

BOND MOONLIGHT 3 ch g £3470
60a	2-10	Sout	8af	60	662
63a	2-8	Wolv	12af	[63]	808
55a	3-10	Wolv	8.5af	64	839
61a	2-7	Wolv	12af	[63]	959
6	9-12	Redc	10sft	63	1144
21	8-11	Redc	10sft	60	1663 P

BOND PLAYBOY 3 b g £14616
89a	1-13	WOLV	6af	84	45*
90a	2-16	Sout	5af	87	171
85a	5-12	Wolv	6af	89	361
87a	6-16	Sout	5af	89	461
79a	7-13	Wolv	6af	88	618
76a	6-10	Wolv	6af	86	834
64	10-17	Kemp	5sft	77	944
23	16-19	Redc	6sft	72	1145
59	8-15	Pont	6hvy	72	1251
47	17-19	Redc	7g/f	67	1820
27	14-16	Beve	7.5gd	62	2655
65	3-17	Newc	7g/s	60	3700
70	1-16	HAMI	6g/s	60	4009*
70	1-12	REDC	6gd	[66]	4245+
39	19-26	Ayr	6g/s	66	4652
66	3-16	Catt	7sft	66	5130

BOND PUCCINI 2 b c £1253
18	7-7	Muss	5g/s		2965
67	2-13	Ripo	5gd		4303
63	7-8	Muss	5gd		4517
39	15-18	Pont	6g/f	63	4934

BOND ROMEO 2 ch g £0
40a	7-10	Wolv	5af	70	69
29	2-10	Beve	5af	[70]	2944
45	5-13	Catt	5sft	[67]	5321
40a	8-12	Wolv	5.1ap	[67]	5362

BOND ROYALE 3 ch f £1245
79a	4-13	Wolv	6af	79	41
18a	12-12	Ling	6ap	[79]	106
79a	2-10	Wolv	6af	79	390
44a	13-13	Wolv	6af	79	482
65a	8-13	Wolv	6af	77	687

BOND SHAKIRA 3 ch f £827

53	3-9	Redc	5sft			1146
31	14-14	Sout	6gd			1281
54	4-19	Beve	5g/s	55		2326
44a	8-11	Sout	5af	55		2380
25	16-19	Beve	5gd	54		2657
27a	4-10	Sout	5af	[52]		3156
44a	5-13	Sout	6af	[49]		3482
23	11-16	Catt	5sft	[47]		3932

BOND SOLITAIRE 3 ch f £0

12a	13-16	Sout	7af	[46]	66

BONECRUSHER 5 b g £25006

105a4-11		Ling	10ap		693	vis
91a	8-12	Wolv	8.5af	104	836	vis
108	5-17	Kemp	10g/s	105	1111	vis
110	2-16	Epso	10.1hvy	104	1296	
79	9-12	Hami	12.1gd	107	1746	
106	5-14	Asco	10g/f	107	2556	
80	5-6	Epso	10.1g/g	105	3043	
110	3-15	Good	9.9g/f	104	3506	vis
105	6-20	Hayd	10.5fm	106	3794	vis
106	4-8	Donc	10.3fm	105	4530	vis
106	3-6	Ayr	10.9sft	[105]	4687	vis
102	9-16	Newm	9sft	[103]	5139	vis
104	3-6	Newm	10sft	[103]	5269	vis

BONFIRE 2 b c £575

77	4-5	Asco	7g/f		4776
63	7-19	Newm	7g/s		5285

BONGOALI 2 b f £1274

67	4-15	Folk	7gd		3381
67	5-8	Brig	7g/f		3716
68	2-10	Newc	8hvy		4213
63	5-12	Bath	8g/f	67	4410
8	17-20	Yarm	8g/s	67	4635
63	8-16	Nott	10g/f	63	4848
45	16-20	Yarm	8g/s	58	5349

BONJOUR BOND 3 ro g £905

35a	4-9	Sout	8af	[67]		983
18	7-9	Sout	10gd	[64]		1283
0	11-11	Warw	12.6sft	62		1528
48	3-6	Beve	9.9sft	[62]		1630 BL
46	11-13	Beve	12.1g/f	54		1836 bl
44	3-7	Ripo	10gd	[51]		2982 bl
28	10-15	Beve	8.5g/s	51		3182 bl
41	5-10	Beve	12.1g/f	47		3499 VIS
21	8-12	Hami	8.3g/s	[44]		4007 vis
36	5-11	Catt	13.8g/f	[45]		4671 P

BONJOUR DIRECTA 3 ch c £0

6a	7-11	Sout	11af		191

BONNABEE 2 b f £0

50	11-15	Folk	7gd		4114
48a	7-14	Ling	7ap		4658
52	6-19	Kemp	8g/f		4792

BONNE DE FLEUR 3 b f £18303

96	1-5	RIPO	6gd	[78]		1175*
83	10-20	York	6g/f	97		2407
55	13-15	Hayd	6gd	94		2950
69	5-9	Ripo	6g/f	90		3646
77	7-14	York	5g/s	85		4027
58	9-11	Hayd	6g/f	[80]		4350

BONNETTS 3 ch f £0

50	11-12	Good	7g/f		1846
50	17-20	Newm	8g/f		3237
51	8-10	Newb	7gd		3921
56	10-17	Newm	8gd		4228

BONSAI 3 b f £0

64	7-18	Wind	8.3g/f			1810
65	9-16	Sand	10g/s			2131
55	10-14	Newb	9fm			3631
35	14-17	Warw	8.1g/s	65		4668 T
0	18-18	Newc	8g/f	[60]		5017 t

BONTADINI 4 b g £366

0	10-11	Wolv	8.5af	[60]		128
56a	5-13	Ling	10ap	[48]		429 vis
35a	11-13	Ling	10ap	[48]		569 vis
0	7-9	Wolv	9.4af	[45]		633 vis
53	3-7	Brig	9.9fm	[34]		2332
29	7-9	Brig	9.9g/f	[42]		2643

0	17-19	Brig	9.9gd	[40]	4903

BONUS 4 b c £827

96	6-8	Newm	6g/f	[108]		1187
81	11-15	York	6sft	[108]		1667
57	9-9	Wind	6g/f	[105]		1958
84	9-16	Wind	6fm	102		2758 T
86	5-10	Beve	5g/f	[98]		4718
89	6-20	York	6gd	93		5001

BONUS POINTS 3 b c £544

30a	9-10	Sout	8af			4042
56a	6-14	Ling	10ap			4448
24a	10-14	Ling	10ap			4661 BL
59	3-15	Wind	10g/f	[57]		4834

BOO 2 b c £837

66	4-18	Ripo	6g/s		3939
72	6-20	York	6g/f		4401
66	4-7	Hami	8.3sft		4691
67	9-14	Catt	7sft	68	5126

BOOGIE MAGIC 3 b f £1581

36a	12-13	Ling	10ap	68		215
48	10-14	Yarm	7fm	[68]		2148
56	2-3	Yarm	11.5fm	[62]		2867
56	3-9	Wind	11.6gd	[62]		3164
7	13-13	Yarm	10.1gd	60		3492
41a	4-12	Ling	12ap	[57]		3819 P

BOOGIE STREET 3 b c £45100

106	3-13	Newm	5g/f	[107]		1479 t
111	2-9	Hayd	6g/f	[107]		1918 t
113	1-10	KEMP	5fm	[107]		2068* t
113	6-19	Asco	6g/f	[107]		2468
100	4-12	Sand	5g/s	[111]		2913
112	2-13	Good	5fm	[110]		3551 t
98	10-11	Newb	5.2g/f	[110]		4678 t

BOOK MATCHED 2 b g £8188

69a	14-14	Sout	7af			98
71a	3-8	Wolv	8.5af	65		645
76a	1-9	WOLV	8.5af	[65]		751*
64a	4-7	Sout	8af	70		855
29	18-18	Nott	8.2fm	70		1007
54a	6-15	Sout	8af	70		2338
38	10-11	Redc	9g/s	65		2565
76a	1-14	SOUT	8af	[67]		3392*
74a	3-11	Sout	8af	71		4044
40	19-20	York	7.9gd	62		4321
40	14-20	Leic	7gd	58		5046

BOOK OF KINGS 3 b c £0

113	6-10	Curr	12g/f		2822

BOOKIESINDEXDOTCOM 2 b f £1173

65a	2-12	Wolv	7af	[65]		42 vis
16a	9-9	Wolv	7af	63		510 vis
57a	3-7	Wolv	7af	[63]		617 vis
28a	7-8	Ling	6ap	[60]		691 vis
42a	6-13	Sout	6af	57		797 bl
0	6-9	Sout	7af	[54]		871 bl
31	8-14	Warw	8.1sft	50		1529 vis
30a	5-10	Sout	7af	[45]		1842 vis
31a	5-8	Sout	6af	[41]		2379 vis
29	6-11	Yarm	7g/f	[39]		2852 P
13	12-20	Yarm	7g/s	[40]		5120 vis

BOOM OR BUST 5 ch g £0

32a	8-13	Ling	10ap	[40]		539 p
19a	7-15	Ling	12ap	[40]		707 p
3a	13-13	Ling	10ap	[35]		3025 p

BOOT N TOOT 3 b f £4701

15	9-10	Folk	9.7sft			977
78	1-11	WIND	10fm			3802*
59	9-12	Sand	10gd	76		4502
90	6-11	Yarm	10.1gd	[76]		4614

BOOZY DOUZ 4 ch f £0

4	8-8	Epso	8.5hvy			1297
11a	6-8	Wolv	7af	[30]		1676 P
21	8-15	Nott	10gd	[30]		1991

BOPPYS BABE 3 ch f £0

5	11-18	Beve	9.9g/s	30		4243
4	13-20	Yarm	7g/s	[30]		5120

BOPPYS DREAM 2 ch f £0

35	6-12	Beve	5g/f		4596
27	11-16	Ripo	5gd		4787
40	5-9	Pont	6g/s		5154

BOPPYS PRINCESS 3 b f £19941

46	1-15	BEVE	8.5g/s	38		3182*
50	2-18	Carl	7.9fm	43		3547
59	1-10	HAYD	8.1g/s	45		3906*
61	1-5	AYR	8hvy	51		4085*
56	5-15	Beve	8.5g/f	55		4598
66a	1-13	WOLV	9.5ap	59		4925*
71	1-16	NOTT	8.2hvy	59		5347*

BORACAY BEAUTY 2 b f £0

0	10-10	Thir	5sft		1224
33	9-11	Thir	5gd		1634
0	11-11	Thir	6g/f		1968
20	8-8	Muss	5g/f		2611 BL

BORACAY DREAM 2 ch c £0

57	8-16	Sali	7gd		3882

BORDER ARTIST 5 ch g £5560

19	11-19	Newc	6sft	64		967
29	11-17	Thir	8g/s	61		1214
66	1-14	MUSS	7.1gd	59		1794*
61	7-18	Thir	8g/f	65		1972
52	9-11	Hami	8.3g/f	64		2317
69	4-14	Thir	7fm	64		2466
69	3-16	Beve	7.5gd	64		2655
68	4-10	Brig	8gd	65		2954
64	5-14	Carl	6.9g/f	65		3229
56	5-7	York	6g/f	[64]		3436

BORDER CASTLE 3 b c £15428

95	1-9	NEWM	10gd	81		4227+
90	7-13	Asco	10g/f	[89]		4772

BORDER EDGE 5 b g £0

82a	8-15	Ling	7ap	86		81 vis
68a	9-11	Ling	8ap	[84]		273 vis
75a	11-14	Ling	7ap	82		518 vis
74a	10-11	Wind	8.3gd	[85]		4122 vis
73	10-14	Wind	8.3gd	[85]		4122 vis
72	9-15	Kemp	8g/f	85		4362 vis
65	16-24	Newb	7g/f	82		4642 vis
71	8-16	Good	7gd	77		4873 vis
66	9-17	Wind	10g/f	74		5050 vis

BORDER MUSIC 3 b g £7322

80a	7-8	Ling	7ap	[81]		879
73	8-15	Newb	8gd	80		1206
82	3-12	Hayd	8.1gd	77		3738
82	2-9	Good	8gd	77		3950
82	2-15	Kemp	8g/f	78		4362
83	3-12	Sand	10gd	78		4502
83	4-17	Asco	8g/f	80		4777
74	8-11	Good	8gd	80		5027

BORDER SAINT 3 b g £1048

77a	3-13	Ling	12ap			873
4a	7-7	Sout	12af			1030
76	4-8	Newm	12g/s			1153
5	14-14	York	11.9g/s	79		1708

BORDER SUBJECT 7 b g £312

91	6-9	Newm	6fm	107		1490
88	9-10	Kemp	5fm	[105]		2068 BL
30	15-15	York	6g/f	100		3434

BORDER TALE 4 b g £2877

78a	8-16	Ling	12ap	80		404
82a	1-7	WOLV	12af	78		642*
68a	7-10	Wolv	12af	81		810

BORDER TERRIER 6 b g £733

0	16-16	Newc	10.1sft	55		1278
38	8-10	Muss	12gd	53		1796
40	9-11	Hayd	10.5g/s	50		2226
44	3-5	Ayr	10.9g/s	45		2545 BL
28	12-20	Catt	12g/f	40		2850 bl
41	4-7	Ayr	10.9gd	37		3149 bl
38	4-12	Nott	14.1g/f	39		3420 bl
23	12-16	Catt	11.9g/f	40		4348 VIS

BORDERLESCOTT 2 b c £5826

64	6-18	York	5g/f		2360
57	10-13	Carl	5gd		2670
62	5-9	Beve	5g/s		3178

77 1-6 HAMI 6g/f 61 3590*

BORIS THE SPIDER 3 b g £3195
54	2-11	Pont	6sft	[62]	1426
48	9-14	Thir	6gd	[61]	1639
36	8-13	Carl	5.9fm	[58]	1949
48	5-8	Leic	7g/f	55	2403
47	5-13	Redc	8gd	55	2552
47	4-15	Beve	8.5g/s	52	3182
47	6-12	Ripo	10gd	50	4282
53	1-9	AYR	13.1sft	[48]	5277*

BORN FOR DANCING 2 b f £3523
75	2-6	Warw	5fm		2437
72	5-11	Bath	5g/f		4409 BL
76	2-10	Ling	5g/f		4893
61	3-7	Catt	5sft	[73]	5124

BORN FOR DIAMONDS 2 b f £0
59	7-13	Newm	6fm	4726
52	5-13	Nott	6.1g/f	4843
60	11-14	Yarm	7sft	5250

BORODINSKY 3 b g £3067
45	5-6	Redc	6g/f		2104
56	7-11	Thir	7fm	[45]	2463
46	4-13	Newc	6sft	45	2683
38	7-11	Carl	6.9gd	44	2936
59	2-9	Thir	7g/f	[44]	3413
55	4-8	Redc	9g/f	[44]	3805
52	8-10	Newc	7hvy	[47]	4216
59	2-7	Redc	7fm	[47]	4561

BORREGO 4 br c £9844
78	2-12	Donc	7gd	74	2235
36	8-8	Sand	7.1g/f	78	2389
68	6-7	Yarm	8g/f	78	2853
66	11-14	Hayd	8.1gd	78	2903
44	14-15	Brig	8fm	76	3694
76	4-13	Redc	7fm	[72]	4341 BL
77	1-21	DONC	7fm	72	4482* bl
68	8-18	Kemp	8g/f	75	4714 bl
60	8-10	Newc	7fm	[75]	4869 bl

BORTHWICK GIRL 2 b f £11745
88	1-7	NEWM	6g/f		2733*
95	4-9	Sand	7.1g/f		3357
98	3-14	Newm	7g/f		4914
94	3-8	Newm	8g/s	[98]	5282

BORZOI MAESTRO 3 ch g £6308
69	2-10	Bath	5.7sft	[77]	1539
74	3-12	Wind	5g/f	73	1809
75	1-10	BRIG	6g/f	[73]	2048* p
70	9-11	Redc	5g/f	78	2121 p
76	4-9	Sand	5g/f	77	2387
78	3-10	Kemp	6gd	[76]	3188 p
65	8-10	Sand	5gd	76	3356 p
72	5-9	Wind	5fm	75	3804 p
54	12-15	Newb	6gd	75	3920
69	6-9	Wind	5g/f	75	3976
55	7-11	Epso	6gd	[72]	4294
58	5-12	Sand	5gd	[69]	4605 p
69	5-15	Good	5gd	69	4751 p
49a	5-12	Wolv	6ap	67	4984 p
41a	10-13	Wolv	6ap	66	5114 p

BOSCHETTE 2 b f £0
66	5-13	York	7.9gd	4325
38	11-12	Newc	7g/f	5011

BOSCO 3 br c £2562
56	9-12	Wind	11.6g/s	67	1260
55	10-10	Wind	11.6gd	67	1382
32	13-17	Kemp	10g/f	62	1913 BL
57	1-7	BRIG	9.9fm	[59]	2332*
44	6-11	Leic	10g/f	[52]	2924 T
46	8-9	Wind	11.6gd	[52]	3164 t
16	13-17	Newm	10g/f	52	3238 t

BOSPHORUS 5 b g £1666
40a	3-7	Ling	12ap	[45]	1243 vis
51a	1-6	WOLV	12af	[45]	1313* vis

BOSTON LODGE 4 ch c £18180
96	3-9	Nad	6.5g/f	95	790
99	4-12	Epso	5g/f	[97]	2206 BL
89	13-20	Epso	5fm	97	2253 bl
93	9-29	Asco	6fm	97	2581

97	8-15	Sand	8.1g/s	96	2915 bl
100	3-12	Good	7fm	[95]	3555 VIS
100	2-16	Good	7g/f	96	4523 vis
88	11-15	Asco	7g/f	96	4800 vis

BOTANICAL 3 b c £750
99	5-11	Newb	6gd		1732 T
73	15-17	Epso	7g/f	98	2212 t
96	8-11	Newm	6g/f	97	3941 t

BOTTOMLESS WALLET 3 ch f £271
63	6-9	Newc	10.1g/f	5015
60	4-8	Redc	10sft	5306

BOUGHT DIRECT 5 b h £0
0	12-12	Wolv	9.4af	63	513
35a	11-12	Sout	8af	63	530
36a	6-10	Sout	8af	57	791
50a	5-13	Wolv	9.4af	52	1223
49a	4-12	Wolv	8.5af	51	1379
57	6-14	Chep	7.1gd	57	2199
51	8-17	Hayd	8.1gd	55	2947

BOULE DOR 3 b c £25674
74	4-16	Leic	7g/f	75	1825
84	1-13	GOOD	9g/f	75	2024*
78	4-6	Newb	12g/f	81	2353
90	2-16	Sand	10g/s	81	2919
71	9-11	Asco	8gd	[85]	3128
92	1-8	NEWM	10g/f	[85]	3945*
97	4-11	Epso	10.1gd	[89]	4467
92	4-13	Asco	10g/f	[89]	4772
5	3-17	Newm	10g/f	89	4917
98	2-22	Newm	8sft	90	5103

BOUMAHOU 4 b c £5725
73a	3-12	Ling	16ap	70	478
67a	3-7	Ling	13ap	[71]	546
78a	1-11	LING	16ap	71	605*
56	7-14	Kemp	14.4sft	69	948

BOUNCER 2 ch g £0
16a	11-11	Ling	8ap	[46]	77

BOUND TO PLEASE 9 b g £0
0	10-10	Warw	6.1g/s	[40]	1327 vis
0	6-6	Sout	6af	[47]	1443 vis
0	7-7	Wolv	8.5af	[40]	1672 vis

BOUNDLESS PROSPECT 5 b g £7979
68a	7-12	Ling	8ap	75	369
58a	10-12	Ling	8ap	72	517
63	11-12	Kemp	8g/f	[72]	1915
0	10-10	Newb	8g/f	70	2350
73	2-6	Redc	7g/s	[70]	2564
74	3-13	Newb	7g/f	70	2880
80	1-17	NEWB	7g/f	71	3257*
69	6-8	Newm	8g/f	77	3583
75	11-16	Newb	7g/f	77	3954
67	8-15	Kemp	8g/f	77	4362

BOUNTIFUL 2 gr f £0
69	7-12	Newm	6g/f	3251

BOUNTY QUEST 2 b c £2198
85	3-8	Newb	5.2fm	2646
73	4-12	Hayd	6gd	2902
86	3-9	Epso	7fm	3539

BOURGAINVILLE 6 b g £5875
95a	8-11	Ling	10ap	[109]	693
104a	4-14	Ling	10ap	[102]	884
106	5-11	Sand	10g/s	[107]	1350
105	5-10	Ches	10.3gd	[107]	1585
73	14-14	Good	12g/f	[105]	1843
93	13-15	Redc	10g/f	102	2101
74	17-21	York	10.4gd	99	3118
68	7-7	Asco	10gd	[94]	3464 P
79	8-14	Newb	10hvy	90	5223

BOURGEOIS 7 ch g £16834
99	2-9	Pont	10hvy	[95]	1068
98	3-12	Hami	12.1gd	95	1746
102	1-9	THIR	12g/f	95	1969*
96	10-15	Hayd	11.9gd	98	2948
77	12-14	York	13.9gd	98	3119
71	9-11	York	10.4g/s	99	4021
83	12-15	Donc	14.6fm	96	4491

BOW SPRIT 4 ch g £0
0	9-9	Ling	12ap	[60]	324

BOW STRADA 7 ch g £654
75	3-11	Ling	16gd	70	3200

BOW WAVE 2 b c £4473
86	1-21	DONC	6sft	5368*

BOWING 4 b g £0
29a	13-13	Wolv	8.5af	75	439
58a	5-15	Ling	12ap	[70]	521
56a	13-14	Ling	10ap	66	803
25	17-20	Wind	11.6g/s	72	1056
29	12-12	Bath	10.2fm	60	2036
9a	9-9	Sout	12af	[55]	2724

BOWLAND BRIDE 2 b f £3875
20	5-10	Thir	5sft		1224
30	10-11	Thir	5gd		1634
45	4-11	Ripo	6g/f		1779
17	4-4	Ayr	6fm		1906
55	1-11	THIR	6g/f		1968*
24	7-8	Hayd	6g/f		2183
23a	7-7	Sout	7af		2721
36	5-6	Catt	5g/f		3014 BL
28a	10-12	Sout	7af		3394 bl

BOWLED OUT 2 b f £4564
65	4-9	Newm	7gd		4192
44	12-20	York	6g/f		4401
0	18-19	Leic	7gd		5045
69	1-20	YARM	8g/s	60	5349*

BOWLEGS BILLY 4 gr g £0
31	12-19	Beve	5gd	52	2657
39	8-10	Beve	5sft	[48]	2944 P
33	10-18	Catt	7g/f	45	3670
20	16-20	Yarm	8gd	42	3996 p

BOWLING ALONG 3 b f £5845
54	5-16	Nott	6.1sft	60	1465
32	8-10	Donc	6g/f	58	1878
46	8-19	York	6gd	58	2055
53	9-11	Pont	6g/f	53	2791
54	4-10	Catt	7g/f	53	3016
56	3-14	Leic	6g/f	53	3213
61	2-12	Carl	5.9g/f	54	3655
40	14-20	Redc	6g/f	54	3767
48	10-14	Muss	7.1g/f	58	4175
65	1-15	REDC	6fm	57	4562+
57	6-20	Ripo	6gd	60	4785
46	10-19	Nott	6.1g/f	[60]	4845
48	7-13	Pont	8g/s	[58]	5153

BOWMANS CROSSING 4 b g £339509
118	2-14	Sha	8g/f		211
111	3-16	Kran	10gd		1859
112	7-16	Asco	8g/f		2470 VIS
108	6-10	Asco	8gd		3124

BOWSTRING 3 b f £37291
88	1-9	FOLK	9.7sft		980*
99	2-4	Epso	10.1hvy	[95]	1294
98	2-5	Ling	11.5sft	[95]	1619
101	3-12	Yarm	10.1sft	95	4149
102	3-10	Donc	14.6fm	[97]	4460
99	3-12	Yarm	14.1sft	[97]	5254
71	9-14	Donc	10.3sft	[97]	5370 BL

BOX BUILDER 7 ch g £4164
67a	1-9	SOUT	16af	58	612*
68a	2-7	Sout	14af	64	681

BOXGROVE 2 gr g £3487
80a	3-12	Ling	8ap		100
71a	6-12	Ling	8ap		175
80a	1-10	LING	8ap		232*
50a	7-7	Ling	8ap	80	341
0	6-6	Wolv	8.5af	79	470

BOXHALL 2 b f £0
75	6-11	Newm	7gd	4190
68	10-14	Yarm	7gd	4611

BRACE OF DOVES 2 b c £5937
0	14-15	Beve	5g/s	1161
51a	5-11	Sout	6af	2336
71	2-20	Newc	6sft	2682

67 3-9 Pont 6g/f 68 2989
67 3-12 Catt 7g/f 69 3351
74 2-6 Muss 7.1g/f 69 3560
71 3-13 Newc 7g/s 69 3698
49 10-14 Muss 8gd 71 4519
67 7-18 Catt 7g/f 70 4673
64 7-19 Pont 8g/s 68 5147

BRADS HOUSE 2 b c £0
64 11-14 Muss 7.1g/s 5330

BRAG 2 b f £7694
82 2-10 Sali 5g/f 1717
69 4-8 Bath 5fm 2033
68 7-11 Sali 5gd 2658
82 1-7 LEIC 5g/f 73 3343*
82 3-10 Thir 5fm 80 3607
64 9-13 Newm 5g/f 81 3943

BRAGADINO 5 b h £0
46a 10-13 Wolv 6ap [65] 5327 VIS
41a 11-13 Wolv 5.1ap 65 5341 VIS

BRAHMINY KITE 2 b c £10118
91 2-11 Beve 7.5g/s 3851
104 1-3 SAND 8.1g/s 4066*

BRAIN WASHED 3 b f £2592
7 16-16 Hayd 6g/f 2182
60 4-10 Redc 6gd 2559
69 2-7 Newc 6g/s 2728
43 5-7 Catt 7g/f [72] 3194
57 3-11 Beve 5g/s [70] 4237
47 3-10 Ripo 6gd [67] 4788
31 6-8 Catt 6gd [59] 4969

BRAMANTINO 4 b g £15745
48a 5-12 Sout 8af 55 530 bl
50a 3-9 Wolv 9.4af 53 647 VIS
57a 1-11 SOUT 11af 53 746* P
47a 12-14 Ling 12ap 58 801 p
61 2-15 Newc 12.4hvy 59 1034 bl
56 5-10 Hayd 14g/f 59 1923 bl
48 7-11 Pont 12g/f 58 2041 bl
54 5-8 Hayd 14g/s 56 3140 bl
53 5-17 Catt 12sft 53 3929 bl
62 1-12 BEVE 12.1sft 52 4259* bl
68 1-14 YORK 11.9gd 58 4327* bl
60 3-19 Leic 10g/f 58 4456 bl
66 5-20 Hayd 11.9g/s 56 4771 bl

BRANDEXE 2 b f £424
68 11-16 Sali 7gd 4330
60 5-15 Chep 7.1gd 4483
71 4-11 Ayr 7.2g/s 4653
0 10-10 Catt 7sft [69] 5127

BRANDY COVE 6 b g £1112
67a 4-14 Sout 8af 66 93
60a 5-12 Sout 8af 66 141
64a 2-14 Sout 8af 65 195
69a 3-11 Sout 8af 65 255
59a 4-10 Sout 8af 65 387
9a 13-14 Sout 8af 64 1198
56a 5-15 Sout 8af 62 2500
60a 5-15 Sout 8af 62 2725
52a 5-10 Sout 8af 61 3395

BRANDYWINE BAY 3 b f £2975
50a 4-10 Wolv 7af [41] 8 p
36a 8-12 Ling 8ap [45] 1073 p
30a 4-5 Ling 8ap [40] 1711 p
41 1-12 BRIG 7fm 38 3677* p
33 5-12 Folk 6g/s 38 3911 p
29 9-15 Folk 7g/f [40] 4371 p
1 17-19 Yarm 8g/s [40] 5119 p

BRANSTON LILY 2 ch f £1142
67 3-7 Ayr 6g/f 3761
64 4-12 Redc 6fm 4557
45 9-14 Newc 6fm 4865
28 13-17 Redc 7g/s [63] 5105

BRANSTON NELL 5 b m £0
2a 12-12 Wolv 12af 46 634 BL
32a 5-9 Ling 13ap [45] 787

BRANSTON PENNY 2 ch f £760
16 13-13 Newm 6fm 4726

56a 2-11 Wolv 7.1ap 5113

BRANSTON TIGER 5 b h £4711
70a 5-12 Wolv 7af 73 840
65 11-22 Donc 6gd 79 921
32 14-19 Redc 6sft 77 1145
70 8-19 Leic 6g/s 76 1354
65 6-17 Donc 6g/s 73 1523
66 5-19 Redc 7g/f 70 1820
43 15-17 Newm 7g/f 68 2768 BL
50 7-10 Hayd 7.1g/s 65 3137
66a 1-13 SOUT 6af [62] 3482* bl
67 4-12 Newm 6gd 62 4229 VIS
67 3-13 Warw 6.1gd 62 4272 vis
52 8-18 Ayr 7.2sft 64 4622 vis
67 3-20 Wind 6g/s 63 4946 vis
54 7-19 Wind 6g/f 63 5053 vis
46a 9-13 Wolv 6ap [63] 5327 bl

BRANTWOOD 4 b g £2970
43 14-16 Bath 5.7g/s [70] 1103 T
39 16-19 Warw 5gd 70 1127
50 9-17 Warw 5hvy [63] 1532 t
61 4-17 Nott 5.1g/s 58 1774 tP
59 3-12 Leic 6fm 58 2111 t
61a 2-14 Sout 6af [58] 2502 t
61 3-13 Hayd 6gd 59 2884 t
45 10-11 Leic 7g/f 59 3210 t
58 6-11 Thir 6gd 59 3574 t
33 18-20 Hayd 6fm 58 3796 t
57 5-19 Beve 5g/s 56 4240 t
51 8-26 Ayr 5g/s 55 4618 t

BRAVE BURT 7 ch g £1992
68 18-20 Epso 5fm 83 2253
61 10-11 Ches 5.1g/s 83 2747
68 14-16 Newm 5g/f 82 3033
86 2-13 Newb 5.2g/f 80 3960
59 17-19 York 6gd 80 4005
24 11-12 Ches 5.1sft 83 4107
71 11-14 Epso 5g/s 82 4291
72 10-15 Ayr 5g/s 80 4654
72 9-18 Pont 5g/s 76 5149
46a 9-12 Wolv 5.1ap [72] 5362

BRAVE CHIEF 2 ch c £572
0 12-13 Wolv 6af 3
55a 2-9 Sout 5af 256
49a 7-13 Sout 5af [53] 319
21 17-18 Bath 5.7g/f 53 1788
33a 5-11 Wolv 6af [51] 2202
48a 6-11 Sout 5af 51 2380
0 15-15 Sout 5af [48] 2803
31a 5-10 Sout 5af [46] 3156

BRAVE DANE 6 b g £12125
62a 1-12 LING 10ap 51 542*
69a 1-14 LING 10ap 51 622*
71a 5-11 Ling 10ap 68 716
67a 6-14 Ling 10ap 68 803
75 1-19 DONC 10.3gd 68 924*
77a 2-12 Ling 8ap 73 1613
67a 10-14 Ling 10ap 74 2392
67 10-25 Asco 7g/f 74 3443
76 2-6 Brig 7fm [74] 3696
60 7-10 Wind 10g/f [74] 3980

BRAVE KNIGHT 7 b g £0
42 8-11 Beve 12.1g/s [32] 3856

BRAVE TARA 2 b f £0
19 14-14 Thir 7g/s 4204
23 12-14 Carl 6.9fm 4503
25 12-16 Ripo 5gd 4787

BRAVELY DOES IT 4 gr g £928
50 9-13 Hayd 11.9g/s 2230
51 10-16 Donc 10.3gd 2751
56 6-11 Pont 10g/f 2991
57 2-10 Carl 14.1fm 52 3549
0 12-12 Ches 15.9sft 56 4106
0 17-18 Pont 12g/f 55 4938
47a 5-11 Wolv 12.2ap 52 5180
50a 5-13 Wolv 16.5ap 50 5366

BRAVEMORE 2 b c £0
76 6-23 Newm 7g/f 4885

BRAVO DANCER 3 ch f £2838
79a 2-7 Ling 10ap 77 16

BRAVO MAESTRO 2 b c £6258
100a1-13 LING 7ap 86 15*
98a 6-15 Ling 7ap [96] 885
96a 7-9 Ling 8ap [95] 1040
92 5-12 Good 7g/f 95 1847
87 9-13 Asco 6.5g/f 93 4773
23 9-10 Newm 8g/f [93] 4890

BRAZIL NUT 3 b g £0
0 15-15 Chep 16.2gd 3400

BRAZILIAN TERRACE 4 ch f £16505
76a 3-11 Ling 8ap [76] 800
59a 4-12 Ling 8ap [74] 878
60 10-14 Yarm 8g/f 75 1131
77 1-8 NOTT 8.2g/s [73] 1775*
78 1-6 BATH 8fm 73 2414*
79 3-8 Bath 8fm 75 2665
62a 9-12 Ling 8ap [75] 2840
76 2-9 Nott 8.2g/f [75] 3423
77 2-14 Bath 8g/f 75 3963
42 9-11 Wind 8.3g/s 75 4222
81 3-11 Yarm 8gd 75 4615

BREAD OF HEAVEN 3 b f £0
0 7-7 Kemp 6hvy [81] 1513
58 6-7 Chep 7.1gd [77] 3402 BL

BREAKING SHADOW 2 br c £15855
72 2-15 Beve 5g/s 3178
73 3-6 Carl 5gd 3652
76 3-15 Nott 5.1gd 3988
83 1-10 RIPO 6gd 72 4306*
68 10-21 Donc 6fm [72] 4490
69 6-12 Newm 6gd 78 4882
78 7-14 Catt 7sft 77 5126
70 8-19 Redc 8sft 75 5302
85 1-20 DONC 7sft 75 5373* P

BREAKING THE RULE 3 ch f £0
56a 10-13 Ling 10ap 2066
32 6-6 Bath 11.7fm 2668
46 5-7 Nott 10g/f 3422
1 15-15 Nott 10g/s 50 4037
2 10-10 Brig 9.9fm 47 4763

BREAMORE 2 b c £0
65 8-20 Yarm 8sft 5252

BREATHING FIRE 2 b c £542
81 5-13 Newm 6gd 4223
79 3-12 Hayd 6sft 4770

BREATHING SUN 3 b c £1073
52 14-14 Newm 10g/f 78 1192
57 10-14 York 7.9g/s 78 1707 t
72 9-16 Sand 10g/s 76 2919 t
80 3-7 Wind 10fm 76 3801 t
57 12-14 Sand 10g/s 75 4097 t

BRECON 2 ch f £6166
80 1-14 SALI 7sft 4575*
91 4-7 Newb 7hvy 5222
88 4-9 Newm 10g/s 5281

BRECON BEACON 2 b c £27891
91 1-8 YORK 5sft 1670*
86 1-5 BRIG 6g/f 1937*
104 2-11 Asco 7fm 2578
105 1-8 NEWM 7g/f 3585*
99 4-5 Newb 7gd [100] 3919
94 4-13 Newb 7sft [100] 5195

BREEDERS FOLLY 2 b f £0
40 11-15 Beve 5g/s 3178
46 7-10 Catt 7sft 5317

BREEZER 4 b g £364
35 7-10 Bath 10.2gd [57] 1402
0 12-12 Sali 8g/s 52 4077
37 3-10 Bath 11.7g/s [52] 4199

BREEZIT 3 b f £214
54 4-13 Nott 8.2gd 54 1242
51 4-8 Muss 8gd 53 1798
46 5-13 Warw 6.1fm 52 2439

21 12-14 Nott 8.2g/f 52   2634
43a 3-13   Wolv 6ap   [48] 5211
50a 5-11   Wolv 8.6ap [47] 5356

BREGAGLIA 2 ch f £363
1   14-14 Folk 7fm   2714
22 15-16 Newm 7g/f   3582
60 14-14 Newm 7g/f   3944
42a 3-10   Sout 5af   4129 VIS
23 13-17 Ling 6g/f   4316 vis

BREGO 2 b g £0
29 14-14 Kemp 8g/f   4356
67 8-14   Chep 8.1gd   4484
0   11-11 Chep 7.1hvy   4704 BL
31 13-13 Brig 8sft   5091 bl

BRESSBEE 5 ch g £4187
45a 9-10   Wolv 8.5af   78   5 vis
34a 10-13 Wolv 9.4af   76   127 bl
64a 8-13   Wolv 8.5af   72   439 vis
69a 2-12   Sout 11af   70   534 vis
67a 4-8   Sout 11af   70   595 vis
65a 8-14   Ling 12ap   68   731 vis
71a 1-7   WOLV 9.4af [66]   862* vis
50a 12-12 Ling 8ap   72   932 bl
0   P-14   Folk 9.7g/s 53   1083 vis

BRETTON 2 b g £2581
37a 7-13   Wolv 9.4af [45]   37 P
47a 5-15   Sout 7af   [45]   184 p
38a 4-9   Wolv 9.4af [45]   238 p
44a 4-11   Wolv 8.5af [45]   279 BL
49a 2-9   Wolv 9.4af   45   351 bl
19a 6-9   Wolv 9.4af   47   441 bl
23a 6-9   Wolv 8.5af [47]   865 bl
8   4-8   Pont 12hvy [45]   1250 bl
38a 4-5   Sout 8af   [45]   1440 p
40 4-6   Beve 9.9sft [45]   1630 bl
33a 3-6   Wolv 12af   [45]   1673
0   7-8   Sout 8af   [45]   1841 bl
47a 2-13   Ling 10ap   [35]   3025
34 5-12   Brig 9.9g/f 43   3300
56a 9-13   Ling 10ap   [44]   4112
3   13-13 Folk 9.7g/f [40]   4372 p
35a 9-14   Ling 16ap   [45]   4663
40a 2-12   Wolv 12.2ap [40]   5208 p

BREVITY 9 b g £0
0   10-10 Hami 5g/f   [60]   2476 VIS
2   16-17 Chep 8.1g/s 55   3087

BRIAN BORU 4 b c £160377
118 1-8   LEOP 10g/s   994* t
106 5-7   Curr 10g/s   1560 t
116 5-11   Epso 12g/f   2209 t
113 5-13   Asco 20g/f   2518 t
112 5-7   Duss 12sft   3497
115 2-9   Deau 15sft   4161
117 2-13   Curr 14gd   4733 t
116 3-10   Wood 12gd   5247

BRIANNIE 2 b f £0
61 6-7   Epso 6gd   4466
62 6-13   Warw 7.1g/s   4664
61 7-11   Wind 6g/s   4941

BRIANNSTA 2 b c £5103
63 6-18   Donc 6g/s   3376
79 5-10   Wind 8.3fm   3803
78 2-15   Folk 7gd   4114
78 1-17   WARW 7.1g/f   4269*
57 10-12 Sali 8sft   80   4580
72 11-16 Good 7gd   76   5031

BRIAR 4 b c £0
0   12-15 Sout 12af   89
24a 6-7   Sout 8af   334 p

BRIAR GHYLL 2 ch f £0
28 12-15 Nott 8.2hvy   5344

BRIAREUS 4 ch g £5445
71a 10-16 Ling 12ap   80   293
76a 10-16 Ling 12ap   80   404
70 10-20 Newb 10gd   80   1235
80 2-20   Donc 10.3g/s 78   1519
76 7-19   Newb 10gd   78   1736
80 3-9   Hayd 10.5g/s 79   2185

76 6-13   Asco 12fm   78   2582
74 7-11   Asco 12gd   77   3070
65 6-11   Newb 11g/f   77   3256

BRIDEGROOM 2 b c £0
63a 5-13   Wolv 8.6ap   5355

BRIDEWELL 4 b g £0
0   8-10   Wolv 12af   [38]   154
0   15-16 Sout 11af   [35]   852
23 8-10   Muss 14g/f   40   1118
15 6-7   Ayr   10g/s [30]   1450
11a 8-10   Ling 12ap   [30]   1714 P

BRIDGE PAL 4 ch f £0
0   6-6   Hami 12.1g/f 56   3588
11 9-9   Muss 14gd   52   4521

BRIDGE PLACE 2 b c £5336
63 7-7   Kemp 5sft   943
73 3-5   Brig 6g/f   1937
85 2-15   Wind 6g/f   2263 BL
83 1-8   BEVE 7.5gd   2511* bl

BRIDGE TTHE STARS 2 b f £3353
76 1-12   BATH 5.7gd   3141*
76 5-5   Hayd 6fm   3795
64a 10-14 Ling 7ap   76   4177

BRIDGEWATER BOYS 2 b g £27555
69a 2-13   Wolv 6af   58   1 bl
73a 1-12   WOLV 6af   [58]   42* bl
63a 5-6   Sout 6af   69   182 bl
49a 4-7   Sout 6af   69   333 bl
73a 1-9   WOLV 7af   65   510* P
66a 3-6   Wolv 7af   71   615 p
72 1-17   SALI 6g/f   62   1722* bl
79 1-13   HAYD 6g/f   67   1881* bl
76 2-19   York 6g/f   73   2055 bl
83 1-12   RIPO 6g/f   73   2482* bl
51 5-5   Hami 6gd   [80]   3131 bl
56 9-20   Ripo 6gd   60   4278 bl
63a 8-13   Ling 7ap   75   4897 bl
60a 6-13   Wolv 6ap   73   5114 bl
67a 3-12   Wolv 6ap   70   5291 bl
58a 8-11   Wolv 7.1ap [70]   5357 bl

BRIEF GOODBYE 4 b g £12189
78 1-6   MUSS 8g/f   72   1092*
76 4-20   Donc 10.3g/s 76   1519
49 8-9   Muss 8fm   [76] 2087
81 1-8   NEWB 8g/f   [76] 2313*
72 4-6   Ayr   8gd   [81] 3152
72 10-15 Hayd 8.1g/f   81   4352
65 6-10   Epso 7gd   [79] 4912
64 11-11 Muss 7.1g/s   76   5144

BRIERY MEC 9 b g £0
18a 7-9   Sout 11af   35   331 p
20a 6-9   Ling 12ap   [35]   414 p
0   15-16 Brig 9.9g/f   31   3175

BRIGADIER MONTY 6 b g £2016
49 11-16 Sout 7g/s   61   1049
53 6-17   Warw 5hvy   [59] 1532
39 7-18   Thir 6g/f   57   2214
40 9-19   Beve 5gd   54   2512
55 2-17   Catt 5g/f   50   2846
56 5-15   Beve 5sft   50   2942
55 5-15   Wind 5g/f   53   3165
40 10-18 Pont 5gd   53   3463
56 3-19   Beve 5g/s   52   4240
46 10-17 Beve 5g/f   53   4603
30 9-14   Catt 6gd   53   4967
26 10-13 Catt 5sft   [52] 5321

BRIGADORE 5 b g £884
67 6-20   Thir 5g/s   68   1476
64 3-20   Thir 5g/f   67   1765
65 6-16   Ayr   5g/f   66   2029
53 12-15 Muss 5fm   66   2084

BRIGHT FIRE 3 b f £1342
30a 5-8   Wolv 6af   750
48 4-12   Newm 8fm   52   3410
50 6-14   Kemp 10g/f   50   3690
56 2-15   Nott 10g/s   50   4037

BRIGHT GREEN 4 b g £0

71a 9-10   Ling 10ap   [76]   179

BRIGHT MIST 5 b m £0
0   12-12 Chep 5.1sft [45] 1336
26a 4-12   Wolv 5af   [40] 1799
31a 7-16   Sout 7af   38   2335
0   16-16 Sout 6af   36   2806

BRIGHT MOLL 2 b f £12432
86 1-6   FOLK 5sft   974*
86 2-4   Nott 5.1sft   1608
87 2-10   Thir 5g/f   1764
91 5-17   Asco 5g/f   2490
93 1-7   HAYD 6gd   2883*

BRIGHT SKY 5 ch m £10282
118 2-10   Sain 10g/s   833
107 7-11   Nad   9g/f   991

BRIGHT SUN 3 b c £6964
75 8-14   Ripo 6g/s   86   1360
57 10-15 Ches 7.6gd   82   1583
73 10-14 York 7sft   82   1665
75 4-11   Nott 6.1g/f   78   2155
74 3-6   Redc 6gd   76   2551
63 7-11   Ripo 6gd   74   2985
77 3-9   Donc 8g/s   72   3378
73 4-8   Newm 7g/f   72   3612
77 1-11   NEWM 8gd   [72] 3923+
74 8-12   Newm 7g/f   75   4225
70 6-11   Ayr   8sft   73   4621
64 8-12   Epso 8.5gd   72   4909
58 11-19 Donc 10.3sft 72   5201 T

BRILLIANT RED 10 b g £1154
86a 9-14   Ling 12ap   91   83 t
87a 7-13   Ling 10ap   89   134 t
88a 3-10   Ling 10ap   [89]   179 t
59a 16-16 Ling 12ap   87   293 t
60a 9-13   Ling 10ap   80   519 t
77a 6-11   Ling 16ap   82   605 t
83a 4-7   Ling 12ap   80   695 t
79a 7-12   Ling 13ap   79   877 t
76a 5-6   Ling 9ap   79   1027 t
48 15-19 Newm 12g/f   78   1484 t

BRILLIANT WATERS 3 ch g £0
0   15-15 Ling 7ap   55   50
10a 15-15 Ling 7ap   52   913

BRILLIANTRIO 5 ch m £5967
45a 5-16   Sout 7af   [49]   66 t
36a 3-16   Sout 8af   49   86 t
39a 5-16   Sout 7af   46   202
41a 2-9   Sout 7af   [44]   303
36a 4-13   Sout 7af   [45]   356
18a 9-16   Sout 8af   [40]   442
35a 6-13   Sout 7af   40   556
2a U-11   Sout 7af   40   585
37a 3-8   Sout 7af   [40]   847
21a 6-12   Sout 6af   [40]   982
56 2-20   Yarm 8fm   51   2149
59 1-11   REDC 8fm   51   2296*

BRILLYANT DANCER 6 b m £0
21a 6-9   Sout 7af   [40]   661
1a 11-11 Sout 7af   [35]   771 BL

BRINDISI 3 b f £29916
71 3-11   Bath 8g/s   1101
100 4-9   Newm 10fm   1494
85 1-9   HAYD 8.1g/f [89] 1882*
98 4-9   Asco 8g/f   95   2491
93 4-9   Sand 8.1g/s [95] 2917
96 6-7   Asco 8g/f   [95] 3389
102 1-12   BATH 8g/f   [95] 3965*
91 7-13   Asco 8g/f   100   4802
90 13-16 Newm 9sft   [98] 5139

BRIOS BOY 3 ch g £0
1a 9-12   Wolv 12af   39   244 p
0   12-12 Wolv 12.2ap [40] 5208

BRIOSO 3 b c £0
11a 12-12 Wolv 5af   57   109 BL
31a 12-14 Sout 6af   54   501

BROADWAY SCORE 6 b g £0
68 7-12   Pont 8hvy   90   1066

42	9-10	Hayd	10.5g/s	88	1346
66	9-20	Donc	10.3g/s	83	1519
59	13-19	Ripo	10g/f	80	1781
43	9-10	Beve	9.9g/s	80	2323
59	10-13	Redc	10gd	80	2560
50	11-12	Beve	8.5gd	75	2890
45	8-9	Ripo	10g/s	70	3260 BL

BRONWEN 2 b f £0

| 67 | 6-9 | Newm | 7gd | | 4192 |

BRONX BOMBER 6 ch g £2892

40a	1-7	LING	6ap	[35]	1715* BL
50a	1-10	SOUT	7af	[35]	1839* bl
46a	7-15	Sout	7af	51	2384 bl
30	13-14	Leic	6g/f	51	3213

BRONZE DANCER 2 b g £2954

37	12-14	Muss	7.1g/f		4171
64	8-14	Thir	8fm		4376
71	7-12	Thir	7g/f		4591
71	1-10	NEWC	7fm		4864*
62	9-12	Ayr	8sft	70	5065

BROOKLANDS LODGE 3 ch f £371

59	6-9	Newm	8g/f	70	2529
41	9-12	Nott	8.2g/s	67	2931
55	9-13	Nott	10g/f	63	3419
13	8-8	Ling	11.5fm	60	3747
0	19-19	Leic	10g/f	56	4456
0	10-11	Yarm	11.5g/s	[56]	4584 P
56a	3-11	Wolv	12.2ap	52	5009

BROOKLANDS TIME 3 b f £0

31a	7-13	Sout	6af	[63]	659
24a	7-8	Wolv	6af	[63]	750
30a	11-11	Sout	6af	[63]	869
14a	12-15	Ling	7ap	[45]	969
18	16-18	Catt	7gd	[45]	996

BROOKLIME 2 b c £5435

59a	6-10	Ling	6ap		3818
74	4-17	Wind	6g/f		3975
83	1-17	CHEP	6.1sft		4052*
64	10-16	Newm	6gd	78	4224
75	5-10	Ripo	6gd	78	4306
83	2-9	Warw	7.1g/s	76	4666
77	6-12	Asco	7g/f	80	4810
83	7-16	Good	7gd	80	5031
81	6-14	Catt	7sft	80	5126
2	16-20	Newb	6hvy	78	5225

BROOKLYNS GOLD 9 b g £391

79a	6-14	Ling	10ap	79	625
68	8-19	Hayd	10.5g/s	78	4766
66	10-17	Wind	10g/f	75	5050

BROTHER CADFAEL 2 ch g £1497

35a	4-14	Sout	8af	[47]	95
47a	5-11	Sout	7af	[42]	207
42a	6-11	Wolv	8.5af	[45]	279
48a	3-8	Wolv	8.5af	[45]	383
11a	8-9	Sout	8af	49	486
49a	3-12	Sout	8af	47	656
41	2-7	Folk	7g/s	40	1081
38	6-13	Nott	8.2gd	40	1242
25	6-6	Warw	7.1g/s	[40]	1330
33	6-7	Brig	7gd	[40]	1549
21	7-8	Nott	8.2sft	40	1740
33a	7-11	Sout	8af	[47]	3091 p
21	7-10	Yarm	8g/f	36	3712
12	10-13	Folk	9.7g/f	[35]	4372 T
0	18-18	Leic	10gd	[35]	5042

BROUGH SUPREME 3 b g £749

74	5-16	Wind	10gd		1384
64	4-10	Nott	14.1sft		1742
58	6-6	Warw	10.9fm	72	2780
66	8-12	Nott	14.1gd	67	3105
68a	3-8	Ling	10ap	[65]	3787

BROUGHTON BOUNTY 3 b f £0

| 40 | 12-12 | Newm | 8fm | 68 | 3410 |

BROUGHTON KNOWS 6 b g £12068

17a	6-12	Wolv	16.2af	35	156
35a	2-10	Wolv	12af	32	243
51a	1-10	SOUT	12af	35	321* bl
48a	1-9	LING	12ap	[35]	414* bl

52a	1-7	SOUT	14af	[45]	638*
53a	1-8	SOUT	11af	[45]	722* bl
53a	2-9	Sout	12af	[46]	774 bl
54a	4-16	Sout	14af	54	1033 bl
34	6-12	Newc	14.4sft	54	1396 bl
55	4-19	Thir	12g/f	52	4594 bl
63a	1-16	LING	12ap	[54]	4899* bl
50	12-16	York	11.9gd	58	4990 bl

BROUGHTON MELODY 4 ch f £472

42a	6-10	Sout	11af		142
44a	3-7	Sout	14af	[46]	376
26a	8-13	Sout	14af	45	590
37a	4-10	Wolv	16.2af	45	812
39a	4-13	Sout	14af	40	2494
28a	5-10	Sout	14af	40	3158

BROUGHTONS FLUSH 6 b g £3474

39a	7-8	Ling	16ap	47	733
23a	8-16	Sout	14af	45	1033
36a	5-7	Sout	14af	[45]	1407
50a	1-13	SOUT	14af	40	2494* vis

BROUGHTONS MILL 9 gr g £0

48a	5-10	Ling	10ap	[30]	540
25a	6-15	Ling	12ap	[35]	707
30a	6-14	Ling	10ap	[35]	784
14a	8-13	Wolv	8.5af	[35]	826
27a	6-7	Ling	12ap	[30]	1287 p

BROWN DRAGON 3 ch g £2064

64a	6-11	Wolv	6af		481
65a	2-6	Wolv	6af	[65]	631
65a	2-7	Wolv	6af	[63]	863
39	12-14	Sout	6gd	[60]	1281
43	10-13	Wind	6fm	[60]	2756
42a	6-8	Sout	6af	63	3092

BRUMAIRE 2 b c £0

| 49 | 9-13 | Warw | 7.1g/s | | 4996 |
| 30 | 11-15 | Brig | 7sft | | 5192 |

BRUNEL 3 b c £95353

115	1-11	NEWM	7gd	105	1167*
117	1-9	COLO	8gd	[105]	1860*
116	5-11	Asco	8g/f	[115]	2469
104	11-12	Deau	6.5g/s	[115]	3838
102	6-7	Good	8g/f	[113]	4232

BRUT 2 b c £1030

59	10-13	Donc	5gd		954
35	6-8	Muss	5gd		1091
66	2-8	Ayr	5gd		2505
13	17-20	Newc	6sft		2682
58	5-9	Hayd	5sft	68	3271
66	5-7	York	5g/f	65	3432

BRUT FORCE 2 b g £0

| 60 | 9-14 | Redc | 7sft | | 5301 |

BRUZELLA 5 b m £0

| 31a | 9-9 | Ling | 10ap | | 476 |
| 33a | 11-11 | Ling | 12ap | | 816 |

BUBBLING FUN 3 b f £5605

72	4-8	Ripo	10g/s		1365
66	7-10	Sali	9.9g/f		1718
67	4-8	Brig	9.9g/f	65	2046
68	3-14	Wind	10gd	64	2617
69	3-11	Ling	11.5g/f	64	2842
69	2-8	Brig	11.9g/f	66	3299
52	6-10	Redc	10g/f	66	3772
73	2-8	Hami	9.2g/s	[66]	4821
69	2-9	Newc	10.1g/f	[66]	5015

BUCHANAN STREET 2 b c £930

42a	6-10	Sout	8af	60	189 BL T
0	16-16	Bath	8fm	[56]	2032 bl
42	6-9	Brig	8g/f	[49]	2431
42	6-13	Bath	8fm	49	2667
46	2-7	Ripo	10gd	[44]	2982
52	5-15	Chep	16.2gd	[44]	3400
0	7-7	Chep	12.1sft	44	4053
0	15-16	Nott	10gd	45	4857 bl t

BUCKENHAM STONE 4 ch f £0

27a	14-16	Ling	7ap		180
18	11-13	Folk	7g/s		1270
16	9-13	Leic	10fm		2107

17a	7-13	Sout	8af	30	2497
20a	7-13	Ling	10ap	[30]	3025
38	8-11	Yarm	10gd	[30]	3362
0	9-12	Ling	12ap	[30]	3819

BUCKEYE WONDER 3 b c £7443

85	2-11	Newm	10gd		1148
84	1-12	SAND	10g/f	[92]	2193*
69	13-13	Asco	10g/f	[92]	2520

BUCKS 6 b g £31794

73a	2-14	Ling	12ap	[64]	14
76a	1-15	SOUT	12af	[65]	89*
71a	2-13	Ling	16ap	70	137
71a	5-5	Sout	14af	75	201
65a	14-16	Ling	12ap	75	493
70	3-20	Wind	11.6g/s	71	1056
58	11-20	Epso	12hvy	71	1295
75	2-17	Sali	14.1g/s	69	1502
79	1-18	NOTT	14.1g/s	70	1772+
84	1-11	NEWM	12g/f	74	2244*
84	2-19	Carl	11.9gd	78	2673
80	5-7	Kemp	14.4g/f	80	3037
72	8-10	Asco	12g/f	80	3444
84	2-6	Pont	10gd	79	3678
83	2-15	Bath	11.7g/f	79	3964
77	5-9	Ches	12.3sft	79	4076
77	6-17	Nott	14.1g/s	79	4647
75	8-14	Asco	14g/f	79	4775

BUDDY BROWN 2 b c £5885

76	1-7	AYR	7.2g/s		2570*
92	2-5	Hami	6g/s		3877
20	17-17	Donc	8fm	89	4480
67	14-14	Donc	7sft	89	5213

BUGLE CALL 3 b g £0

28a	8-12	Wolv	7af	[43]	71
3a	7-12	Wolv	12af	[43]	114
6a	10-10	Wolv	12af	[35]	581 BL e
45a	7-8	Ling	7ap	[35]	730 bl e
15a	8-11	Wolv	8.5af	35	806 bl e
0	13-13	Wolv	8.5af	[35]	826 bl e

BUKIT FRASER 3 b c £6429

87	1-10	KEMP	11.1gd		1140*
96	4-11	Newb	11g/f	86	1756
78	7-9	Kemp	12gd	84	2175
77	9-10	Sali	12gd	83	2660
77	9-12	Sand	14g/f	81	3359
75	5-12	Newm	14.4g/f	79	3688
65	10-17	Newm	14.8gd	77	4196 T
58	12-16	Good	12gd	[75]	4745

BULAWAYO 6 b g £7780

58a	2-16	Sout	7af	[57]	66
2a	16-16	Ling	7ap	[57]	123
62a	3-16	Sout	7af	[57]	161
35a	8-16	Sout	7af	57	202
30a	5-8	Sout	7af	55	320
50a	3-11	Wolv	7af	[53]	440 vis
43a	7-12	Wolv	7af	[53]	512 vis
49a	3-9	Wolv	8.5af	[48]	664
24a	8-10	Wolv	8.5af	48	754
31a	6-10	Sout	8af	[49]	868 vis
51a	1-12	WOLV	7af	46	956* BL
42a	7-15	Sout	6af	49	1750 bl
42	6-9	Ling	7af	[49]	1984 bl
49a	4-12	Wolv	7af	49	2204 bl
52a	2-15	Sout	7af	49	2501 bl
54a	1-9	SOUT	8af	47	2996* BL
38a	8-16	Sout	8af	54	3159 bl
52a	4-16	Sout	8af	52	3487 bl
51a	4-11	Sout	8af	[51]	4090 bl
26a	11-12	Wolv	7.1ap	[50]	5229 bl

BULBERRY HILL 2 b g £0

2a	8-9	Wolv	8.5af		751
32a	5-12	Sout	8af		848
40	5-15	Yarm	7g/s		4587
42	8-18	Leic	7gd		4698
32	10-16	Nott	10gd	45	4857

BULGARIA MOON 4 ch g £0

11	7-12	Newc	14.4sft	40	1396
30	9-14	York	13.9g/f	40	2060
46	7-9	Redc	16fm	[35]	2298
19	8-14	Carl	17.2gd	39	2937

BULL RUN 3 ro c £16852

108	1-14	WIND	10g/s	1055*
118	1-4	EPSO	10.1hvy	1294*

BULLSEYE 2 b c £0

29	18-19	Newm	7g/s	5285

BULWARK 2 b c £436

56	10-16	Newb	7g/f	4677
72	4-14	Leic	8gd	5059
72	5-16	Newb	8hvy	5220

BUMPTIOUS 3 b c £11911

90	3-18	Leic	10g/s	75	1017
80	3-11	Ripo	12.3gd	75	1174
82	1-9	HAMI	12.1gd	[75]	1507*
79	4-11	Sand	14g/s	75	2130
91	4-10	Asco	16.2g/f	[75]	2557 BL
91	3-4	Newm	14.8g/f	[90]	3027 bl
69	14-17	Newm	14.8gd	90	4196 bl

BUNDABERG 4 b c £1242

19a	4-6	Sout	8af		503
52a	2-7	Sout	7af	[40]	636
64a	2-8	Wolv	7af	[45]	892
58a	3-7	Sout	7af	[55]	1196
48a	10-13	Wolv	8.6ap	[55]	5184
15	12-16	Nott	8.2hvy	55	5347

BUNDITTEN 2 gr f £20130

80a	1-10	LING	5ap		882*
94	3-8	Sand	5g/f		2094
95	4-17	Asco	5g/f		2490
78	4-5	Sand	5g/s		2895
86	8-11	Donc	5fm	[96]	4533
94	7-11	Newm	5sft	[93]	5132
88	6-8	Newm	6sft	[90]	5267

BUNDY 8 b g £5500

51	8-12	Thir	7g/s	66	1215
45	13-20	Newc	6sft	65	1393
24	10-13	Warw	7.1hvy	[65]	1537
64	2-13	Hami	6g/f	61	2315
64	2-11	Hami	6g/f	61	2477
67	3-8	Hami	6gd	63	2713
68	2-4	Hami	6g/s	[63]	2831
54	8-17	Pont	6g/s	63	2990
63	4-14	Hami	6gd	64	3129
52	4-7	Pont	6gd	[64]	3244
44	11-18	Ayr	7.2sft	63	4622
55	7-11	Hami	6g/s	61	4818

BUNINO VEN 3 gr g £0

38a	8-9	Ling	10ap		899
50	4-6	Yarm	10.1g/f		1134 VIS
0	7-8	Pont	12hvy		1250 vis
23	5-8	Brig	11.9gd	[40]	1547 BL e
27a	4-6	Wolv	12af	[40]	1673

BUNKHOUSE 4 ch g £0

43	8-16	Hayd	6g/f		2182
41	7-12	Ling	6g/f		2586
27	13-14	Warw	7.1g/f		2907
35a	8-9	Ling	8ap		3197
28	8-12	Brig	7fm	47	3677 P
0	14-14	Chep	10.2g/s	47	3895 VIS

BUNNY RABBIT 2 b c £15845

64	3-7	Pont	6g/f		2792
90	5-8	Newm	7ap		3585
86a	4-8	Ling	7ap		4176
87	8-17	Donc	8fm	87	4480
98	1-13	NEWM	8fm	87	4725*

BUNYAH 3 ch f £0

43a	9-10	Ling	7ap	911

BUOYANT 3 b f £16268

111	2-7	Sain	12g/s	3013

BUREAUCRAT 2 b c £445

86	4-14	Sali	8gd	4852
70	6-20	Yarm	8sft	5252

BURGUNDIAN 2 b c £404

82	4-14	Yarm	7gd	4611

BURGUNDY 6 b g £21364

61a	11-14	Ling	10ap	67	122 vis
62a	1-11	LING	8ap	[65]	145*
60a	7-14	Ling	10ap	65	265
61a	6-14	Ling	10ap	60	434
58a	3-12	Ling	8ap	59	607
57a	4-10	Ling	8ap	57	769
62a	2-9	Ling	10ap	57	903 BL
53	7-20	Warw	10.9gd	58	1128
40	9-12	Brig	9.9fm	55	1695 vis
54	8-19	Brig	9.9g/f	55	1940 bl
60	3-16	Yarm	10.1fm	55	2146 bl
48	6-12	Newb	10g/f	53	2354 bl
60	1-8	EPSO	8.5g/f	[57]	2873* bl
63a	1-13	LING	10ap	[58]	3025* bl
68a	1-13	LING	10ap	[58]	3288* bl
66	2-9	Epso	10.1fm	59	3538 bl
64	1-11	KEMP	8g/f	59	3685* bl
67	2-6	Leic	10fm	59	3815 bl
66	5-11	Epso	10.1gd	64	4293 bl
65	4-14	Good	12gd	64	4542 bl
50	6-14	Epso	12gd	64	4910 bl

BURKEES GRAW 2 ch g £1667

0	11-11	Sout	7af	[60]	207
33a	7-9	Sout	5af	[60]	256 BL
25a	7-9	Sout	7af	[45]	555
20a	7-8	Wolv	5af	[45]	619
18a	9-12	Sout	5af	[35]	904
17	14-16	Leic	7g/f	47	1825
49	2-9	Thir	5g/f	47	2219
27	17-20	Beve	5g/s	47	3180
49	2-9	Ripo	5g/f	45	3645
14a	10-11	Sout	5af	32	4094

BURLEY FIREBRAND 4 b g £0

0	19-20	Warw	10.9gd	60	1128
51	8-14	Nott	10g/s	57	1777 VIS
3	15-15	Ayr	10.9g/s	55	2545 BL

BURLEY FLAME 3 b g £20527

66	4-12	Warw	7.1gd		1129
67	3-15	Thir	7g/s		1473
73	3-18	Thir	8g/f	72	1769
81	1-8	BEVE	7.5g/f	72	2166+
44	22-27	Asco	8g/f	77	2521
81	3-12	Leic	8g/f	77	2922
82	1-13	BEVE	7.5g/s	77	3179*
79	6-8	Nott	8.2g/f	80	3421
77	7-12	Sand	7.1g/f	80	3860
80	7-12	Newm	7gd	79	4225
61	11-12	Epso	8.5gd	78	4909
86a	1-13	WOLV	6ap	77	5114*
79	8-16	Redc	6sft	82	5304

BURLINGTON PLACE 2 b g £3122

55a	11-12	Ling	8ap		19
71a	2-11	Ling	6ap		51
63a	4-9	Ling	6ap	63	105
45a	6-6	Sout	6af	68	182
53	10-20	Newb	7fm	63	2650
51a	7-11	Ling	6ap	65	3198
59	2-11	Leic	8g/f	60	3516
0	8-8	Brig	8fm	[60]	3676
0	18-19	Chep	8.1g/s	[60]	4366

BURN 3 ch f £860

70	7-11	Newb	10g/f		2349
62	3-4	Hami	9.2gd		2709
49	11-14	Wind	8.3fm		2974
22	12-12	Wind	8.3fm	64	3291

BURNING MOON 3 b c £6987

64	5-12	Hayd	8.1sft		1108
86	1-8	NEWC	10.1sft	[80]	2687*
46	15-15	Newm	12g/f	86	3066
79	11-11	Beve	9.9g/s	86	4239
67	10-20	Ayr	10g/s	85	4656 VIS
84	3-17	Wind	10g/f	81	5050 vis

BURNING TRUTH 10 ch g £0

29	9-12	Nott	14.1g/f	53	3420

BURNLEY AL 2 ch g £0

74	5-9	York	6g/s	4026
51	10-20	York	6gd	4401

BURNT COPPER 4 b g £5057

45	10-16	Folk	12fm		2718
56	1-18	PONT	10g/f	50	2988*
47	8-17	Bath	11.7gd	55	3145
41	9-19	Chep	12.1gd	54	3398
45	9-13	Folk	9.7g/f	52	3726 VIS
26a	10-12	Wolv	8.6ap	[52]	5337
43a	9-13	Wolv	9.5ap	52	5361

BURTON ASH 2 b f £1603

59	7-10	York	5g/s		1709
73	4-12	Redc	6g/f		2119
73	3-16	Nott	6.1gd		3103
73	4-7	Newm	7g/f	74	3753
65	9-20	Redc	7fm	72	4337
58	9-11	Pont	8fm	72	4753

BUSACO 2 b c £263

47	15-18	Wind	6gd	2618
67	4-7	Brig	7fm	3691
62a	6-12	Ling	8ap	5295

BUSCADOR 4 ch g £2135

71a	1-8	WOLV	9.4af	65	157+
52a	8-12	Wolv	9.4af	70	382
0	9-9	Pont	10sft	58	1430
15	13-14	Nott	10g/s	55	1776
40	9-15	Redc	9g/f	53	2120
1	9-10	Ayr	9.1gd	50	2571
35	8-8	Ches	10.3g/f	[47]	3083

BUSHIDO 5 br g £883

56	6-8	Hayd	14g/s	59	3140
46	8-17	Catt	12sft	56	3929
56	2-19	Catt	15.8g/f	53	4675
51	8-14	Pont	17.1g/f	55	4936

BUSINESS MATTERS 4 b f £0

21a	11-11	Ling	12ap	53	624
22	10-16	Newc	10.1sft	50	1278
14	12-19	Redc	8sft	46	1661
69	5-9	Redc	9fm	[45]	4336
25	15-17	Ayr	9.1g/s		4620

BUSINESS TRAVELLER 4 ch g £0

0	15-16	Warw	16.2gd	45	4276

BUST 2 b c £0

49	13-18	York	5g/f	2360
54	6-7	Muss	7.1g/f	2810

BUSTAN 5 b h £15620

105a	3-14	Ling	10ap	[107]	884
107	2-12	Kemp	10gd	[107]	1139
101	9-11	Sand	10g/s	[107]	1350 BL
94	4-6	Epso	10.1g/s	[107]	3043

BUSTLING RIO 8 b g £2884

64a	4-10	Wolv	16.2af	63	358
58a	7-12	Ling	16ap	61	478
71a	1-7	SOUT	16af	60	529*
0	8-13	Pont	18hvy	65	1069

BUTHAINA 4 b f £0

13	12-12	Hayd	8.1g/f	70	1485
49	9-15	Redc	7sft	67	1660
33	15-18	Thir	8g/f	63	1972
29	10-10	Hayd	8.1gd	59	2242
31	9-9	Ches	10.3g/s	[55]	2745
34	11-17	Hayd	8.1gd	50	2947
11	10-13	Hayd	6gd	[45]	3757

BUY ON THE RED 3 b c £33689

76a	2-10	Ling	6ap	[72]	973
74	2-8	Thir	5sft	[72]	1228
88	1-14	BRIG	6fm	[72]	1690+
88	1-18	NEWM	6g/f	77	1933*
73	7-10	Kemp	6gd	[84]	3188
90	2-10	Sand	5g/f	84	3356
75	12-21	Good	5fm	84	3567
35	12-14	Ches	6.1g/f	86	4048

BUYING A DREAM 7 ch g £2749

21a	5-10	Wolv	12af	[35]	780
0	13-16	Sout	11af	[35]	852
40a	1-7	LING	12ap	[35]	1287*
36a	3-6	Sout	11af	[35]	1409
36a	1-10	Ling	12ap	[35]	1714*

BUZ KIRI 6 b g £7076

37a	3-9	Ling	12ap	[35]	414
42a	2-14	Ling	13ap	[35]	537

43a 1-10 **WOLV** 12af [35] 581*
39a 2-12 Sout 11af [35] 640
37a 2-7 Sout 14af [40] 724
45a 1-10 **WOLV** 12af [40] 780*
45a 2-6 Wolv 16.2af [40] 824
45a 2-12 Wolv 12af [45] 891
31a 6-11 Wolv 12af 45 937
35 2-8 Chep 10.2sft [35] 1333
42 1-8 **BRIG** 11.9gd [35] 1547*

BUZZ BUZZ 3 b f £0
57 13-19 Asco 8g/f 68 2491
46 8-9 Wind 10g/s 68 4943
19 18-20 Yarm 7sft 66 5256

BUZZ MAITE 2 b c £0
30 5-5 Good 6gd 2221

BY ALL MEN 3 b g £0
30a 9-10 Sout 11af 142
0 11-14 Sout 12af [50] 194

BY DEFINITION 6 gr m £0
2a 8-9 Wolv 9.4af [30] 399
0 15-16 Sout 8af [30] 719 VIS
0 9-10 Ling 8ap 30 769

BYGONE DAYS 3 ch g £23449
86 1-9 **KEMP** 6sft 946*
86 3-14 York 7sft 83 1665
84 4-18 Newm 6g/f 85 1933
87 5-18 Newc 6g/s 85 2770
93 1-9 **RIPO** 6g/f 84 3646*
92 3-14 York 5g/s 89 4027

BYINCHKA 3 br g £0
32a 11-14 Ling 12ap [50] 14
17a 9-14 Sout 8af [45] 354 VIS

BYO 5 gr g £11846
57a 11-15 Ling 7ap 68 50
55a 4-11 Ling 6ap [67] 130
63a 4-10 Ling 5ap 65 231
60a 4-13 Ling 6ap [65] 271
59a 7-10 Ling 6ap 65 329
63 6-17 Kemp 5sft 69 944
72 2-8 Folk 5g/s [67] 1269
44 10-12 Ling 5g/s 70 1615
74 1-11 **HAYD** 5g/f 69 1886*
62 7-10 Brig 5.3g/f 69 2044
52 6-6 Bath 5.7fm 72 2416
62 6-7 Warw 6.1fm [71] 2598
46 7-8 Bath 5.7fm [71] 2669
6 12-12 Bath 5.7gd 70 3146
73 1-11 **BATH** 5g/f [70] 3372*
72 3-9 Brig 5.3fm 69 3673
60 4-13 Bath 5.7g/f [69] 3844
63 8-15 Sali 5gd 69 4335
71 4-15 Good 5gd 68 4751
74 3-19 York 5gd 68 4989
70a 2-13 Wolv 5.1ap 63 5341

BYRD ISLAND 3 b f £0
27 14-17 Donc 8gd 919
11 17-19 Yarm 8gd 1130
0 10-10 Yarm 10.1g/f 1724

BYRON 3 b c £86173
118 3-7 Long 8g/s [100] 1855
109 8-11 Asco 8g/f [111] 2469 T
117 1-8 **GOOD** 7g/f [111] 3508* t
96 9-10 Deau 8sft [111] 4017

BYRON BAY 2 b c £698
41 9-9 Good 6gd 3951
56 9-14 Kemp 8g/f 4356
73 5-13 Sali 7sft 4576
59 12-17 Ling 7g/f 68 4894
67 3-12 Bath 8sft [64] 5170
37 14-14 Newb 7sft 64 5193

CABIN FEVER 2 b f £218
60 8-12 Newb 6g/f 3251
56 5-11 Bath 5.7g/f 3848
55 7-18 Ling 6gd 4108
32 8-17 Ling 6gd 4316
59 3-19 Kemp 8g/f [55] 4792

CABOPINO LAD 2 b g £0

---

57 10-10 Redc 9fm 4558

CACHE CREEK 6 b m £15678
104 2-9 Cork 10.2g/f [89] 1857
101 3-8 Leop 10g/f [89] 3496

CACIQUE 3 b c £203542
114 2-8 Chan 9g/s 2307
118 2-4 Long 10g/s 2825
118 1-6 **CHAN** 9gd 3657*
115 4-9 York 10.4gd 4002
118 1-11 **LONG** 8g/f 4949*

CADEAUX ROUGE 3 ch f £271
59 4-12 Wind 11.6g/s 65 1260
41 7-10 Nott 14.1hvy 63 1612
22 15-15 Leic 11.8gd 60 2134
0 19-19 Beve 9.9g/f 55 3505

CADOGEN SQUARE 2 ch f £0
27 12-13 Beve 5gd 2889
15 7-7 Donc 6g/s 3221
0 10-10 Nott 6.1g/f 3418
52 4-15 Redc 8g/f 3769
34 8-14 Catt 5g/f 49 4437
39 10-14 Redc 5fm 49 4556
46 7-16 Beve 7.5g/f 49 4597

CADORO 11 ch g £0
15 12-15 Chep 8.1sft 55 4057
41 5-16 Nott 8.2hvy 55 5347

CADWALLADER 3 ch g £0
34a 12-14 Ling 12ap [58] 103 T
16a 4-5 Sout 12af [58] 723
30a 6-9 Ling 12ap 52 842
22a 5-7 Ling 12ap [45] 1243 P
0 U-9 Ling 16ap [45] 1414
35 8-8 Muss 16gd 40 1793
16 13-13 Nott 14.1gd [40] 1990

CAERPHILLY GAL 4 b f £3860
43 9-20 Yarm 6g/f 55 1730
24 13-14 Chep 7.1gd 54 2199
47 9-17 Newm 7g/f 52 2768
44 9-20 Chep 7.1gd 50 4488
50 1-19 **KEMP** 8g/f [47] 4795*
50 2-13 Brig 8gd [50] 4902
50 3-13 Warw 7.1g/s [50] 4994
58 1-19 **YARM** 8g/s [50] 5119*
42a 7-13 Wolv 8.6ap [48] 5212 e
31 8-16 Nott 8.2hvy 55 5347

CAESAR BEWARE 2 b g £232726
106 1-18 **CHEP** 6.1gd 2194*
112 1-6 **WIND** 6fm 3800*
112 1-22 **DONC** 6fm 4458*
107 2-24 Redc 6fm 4928

CAFE AMERICANO 4 b g £2108
29 7-10 Brig 7g/f [49] 1938
45 5-20 Nott 6.1g/f 45 2630 e
39 9-17 Brig 7g/f 44 3176 e
49 2-7 Brig 6g/f [42] 3985 e
68 2-8 Chep 7.1sft [42] 4055 e
28 7-9 Good 6sft [48] 4262 e
34 12-18 Good 8gd 48 4750 e

CAIRDEAS 3 b c £10237
108 2-5 Curr 10g/f 2006

CAIRNS 3 b f £324
102 10-16 Newm 8fm 1492
107 6-13 Long 8g/s 1854
92 9-11 Asco 8g/f [107] 2555
102 5-9 Donc 7sft [107] 5214

CAITLIN 2 ch f £13289
45 6-9 Pont 5sft 1424
64a 2-11 Sout 6af 2336
63a 4-9 Sout 6af 3157
72a 1-10 **SOUT** 7af 65 3483*
76a 3-13 Sout 7af 68 4040
78 1-20 **REDC** 7fm 70 4337*
77 2-18 Catt 7g/f 73 4673
78 3-8 Muss 8gd 75 4807
0 P-16 Newm 7g/f 75 4913

CAKE IT EASY 4 ch f £0

---

2 9-9 Ayr 13.1sft 75 5068

CAL MAC 5 b g £828
41 18-18 Good 8g/f 77 1812
3a 11-13 Wolv 8.5af [77] 2052
34 7-9 Brig 8g/f [70] 2431 P
53 2-9 Brig 9.9g/f [70] 2643
43 7-8 Epso 10.1g/s 59 3044
15a 10-13 Ling 10ap [57] 3288

CALA FONS 2 b f £0
28 16-18 Donc 6g/s 3376
46 10-14 Thir 7g/s 4207
44 7-8 Hayd 8.1g/f 4351
37 11-13 Newc 7g/f 5012

CALAMARI 2 ch f £433
41 10-12 Thir 6g/f 3411
68 4-12 Beve 7.5g/s 4242
45 15-18 Nott 8.2g/f 4842

CALAMINTHA 4 b f £7398
67 2-18 Nott 14.1sft 60 1469
66 6-10 Bath 13.1g/f 64 1789
69 1-13 **CHEP** 18gd 63 2198*
59 3-6 Nott 16g/f [65] 2632
67 5-16 Warw 16.2gd 64 4276

CALARA HILLS 3 ch f £705
36 11-16 Nott 10gd 52 1240
49 3-11 Warw 12.6sft 50 1528
37 12-13 Beve 12.1g/f 49 1836

CALATAGAN 5 ch g £6300
64 3-13 Catt 13.8gd 58 997
68 1-19 **BEVE** 9.9g/s 58 1164*
63 5-14 Hami 12.1gd 63 1389
62 5-14 Nott 10g/s 63 1777
71 2-14 York 11.9gd 63 4327
5 18-18 Ayr 10.9sft 69 4623
70 5-16 York 11.9gd 69 4990

CALCAR 3 b g £0
51a 5-15 Sout 12af [44] 89
40a 7-8 Sout 16af 44 140
19a 9-15 Sout 11af 48 196 VIS
3a 9-10 Sout 12af 45 321
40 7-12 Catt 12sft [45] 5319

CALCULAITE 2 b g £2437
25a 11-12 Wolv 6af 42
13a 11-13 Wolv 8.5af 111
50a 7-11 Sout 8af 159
64 9-9 Hayd 8.1g/f 1882
44 6-14 Catt 6g/f 50 3018
42 6-10 Hami 6g/f 50 3203
48 4-18 Hayd 6gd 47 3737
39 5-16 Hami 6g/s 46 4009
27a 7-14 Sout 6af 46 4130
61 1-15 **CARL** 7.9fm [45] 4507+
51a 3-14 Ling 7ap [55] 4660
55a 4-13 Wolv 9.5ap 55 4925
49 6-15 Redc 9g/s 55 5111
58a 3-12 Wolv 8.6ap [54] 5329

CALCUTTA 8 b h £30646
95 10-20 Newm 7g/s 100 1151
71 13-17 York 7.9g/s 99 1686
92 10-20 Asco 7g/f 98 1926
80 19-31 Asco 8g/f 96 2489
97 2-8 Pont 8g/f 96 2606
70 12-15 Sand 8.1g/s 97 2915
99 3-10 Pont 8gd 97 3460
83 9-10 Asco 8gd 97 3775
93 1-8 **YORK** 8.9g/f [95] 4397*
105 1-15 **DONC** 8fm 98 4531*
95 7-19 York 7.9gd 100 4987

CALDY DANCER 3 ch f £0
0 10-11 Curr 9g/f [96] 3322
83 11-12 Bath 12.1g/f [105] 3965

CALEDONIAN 2 b c £3248
83a 1-13 **LING** 7ap 119*
48a 9-10 Ling 8ap [82] 232
57 22-24 Newb 7g/f 82 4642
69 9-12 Good 8gd [79] 4872

CALENDAR GIRL 3 b f £0
40a 10-10 Ling 6ap [48] 133
19a 10-13 Wolv 5af [45] 312
34a 6-10 Ling 5ap [40] 653 BL

CALFRAZ 2 b g £0
60 9-14 Carl 6.9fm 4503
62 7-14 Redc 7sft 5301

CALIBAN 6 ch g £613
1a 7-9 Wolv 14.8af 49 1654
33 10-17 Nott 14.1g/f 46 2156
49 3-12 Warw 19.1fm 45 2577
33 10-16 Warw 16.2gd 47 4276
30 8-13 Warw 12.6g/s [46] 4665

CALIBRE 4 b c £450
96 6-7 Newm 12g/f [98] 2762
0 14-14 York 13.9gd 98 3119

CALL ME MAX 2 b c £1091
79 4-14 Yarm 7gd 3489
86 3-10 Wind 8.3fm 3803
82 5-14 Folk 9gd 4115
83 3-8 Hayd 8.1g/f 4351

CALL ME SUNSHINE 4 b f £4155
58a 1-7 WOLV 9.4af [70] 561*
31a 7-7 Wolv 12af 65 642
9a 5-6 Sout 12af 63 870
2 17-17 Pont 12hvy 65 1064
61 3-10 Muss 12gd 60 1796
39 7-9 Redc 14.1g/f 59 2105

CALL OF THE WILD 4 ch g £2061
33a 8-10 Sout 12af 55 421
52a 3-12 Wolv 9.4af 52 747 p
48a 3-10 Sout 8af [51] 868 p
54a 3-7 Wolv 9.4af 51 961 VIS
47 6-19 Warw 10.9sft 54 1090 vis
36a 4-8 Wolv 9.4af 51 1657 p
43a 4-15 Sout 8af 51 1755 BL
52a 2-12 Wolv 9.4af 50 2054 p
41 12-13 Carl 7.9fm 51 2447 p
27a 12-16 Sout 8af 51 2805 vis

CALLED UP 3 b g £1046
67 4-13 Nott 6.1sft 1464
63 7-15 Leic 6af 1829
49 9-14 Sali 7fm 2291
69 5-13 Wind 6fm [64] 2756
17a 11-11 Ling 7ap [68] 3331
64 4-10 Wind 6g/f [68] 4835
62 3-17 Bath 5.7gd [65] 5020

CALOMERIA 3 b f £1470
48 11-17 Leic 10g/s 1019
67 8-10 Newb 10gd 1209
30 14-15 Ripo 12.3g/f 66 1785
64 4-8 Thir 12g/s 60 2691
44 10-12 Nott 14.1gd 59 3105
61 3-10 Hayd 16.2sft 57 3275 BL
54 8-10 Newc 16.1g/s 62 3701 bl
53 7-15 Chep 18sft 57 4056 bl
44 3-11 Catt 13.8g/f [54] 4671 bl
49 3-12 Warw 12.6g/s [50] 4991

CALONNOG 4 ch f £1700
63 2-8 Thir 12g/s 1472
53 9-11 Beve 9.9g/f 1835

CALUKI 7 b h £43500
110a1-14 LING 10ap 884*

CALUSA LADY 3 ch f £1531
48a 7-14 Ling 6ap [59] 23 VIS
52a 9-16 Ling 7ap 59 55 vis
53a 5-15 Ling 7ap 55 151
50 5-16 Bath 5.7sft 58 1540
48 9-10 Newb 7g/f 55 2312
55 2-13 Sali 6g/s 52 3109
30 17-20 Hayd 6fm 53 3796
55 3-17 Leic 7gd 52 5056
54 4-19 Bath 5.7sft 52 5176

CALVADOS 5 b h £1020
68a 2-5 Wolv 12af 701 BL

CALY DANCER 2 ch g £5856

59 9-9 Wind 5g/s 1256
79 5-10 Sali 5g/f 1717
82 3-8 Sand 5gd 2188
80 3-13 Sali 6fm 2287
82 3-11 Newb 7fm 76 3627
88 1-12 SALI 6g/s 77 4079*
76 5-12 Newm 8gd 86 5089

CALYPSO DANCER 4 b f £0
53 19-20 Donc 5fm 72 4496
34 14-16 Pont 5fm 67 4754
50 10-19 York 5gd 62 4989 VIS
55a 6-14 Ling 7ap 57 5300

CAMACHO 2 b c £6077
90 1-12 NEWM 6g/f 3280*
99 3-5 Donc 7fm 4461

CAMBERLEY 7 b g £3553
96 2-13 Kemp 7sft 90 945
94 5-20 Newm 7g/s 92 1151
66 26-30 Newm 6g/f 92 1481

CAMBERWELL 3 b g £6722
86 1-14 SALI 7fm 2291*
87 5-6 Sali 7g/s [90] 3113
70 9-9 Sand 7.1g/f 88 3338
74 9-12 Sand 7.1g/f 85 3860
57 14-15 Kemp 8g/f 83 4362
65 13-20 Newm 7g/s 78 5286

CAMBO 3 b g £0
3 F-20 Catt 12gd 55 4966
58a 4-14 Ling 16ap 55 5082
42 5-8 Bath 17.2sft 55 5175

CAMERON ORCHID 2 b f £0
73 9-19 Newm 7g/s 5279

CAMILLE PISSARRO 4 b g £0
61 9-10 Hayd 8.1g/s 89 4767
39 29-32 Newm 9g/f 89 4916
53 16-17 Wind 10g/f 85 5050
5 14-14 Newb 8hvy 80 5227
38 14-16 Nott 10hvy 70 5345

CAMMIES FUTURE 2 gr c £18495
78 3-10 Hayd 5sft 1107
89 1-18 DONC 6g/s 3376*
95 2-9 Deau 5hvy 4155
95 6-22 Donc 6fm 4458

CAMP COMMANDER 4 gr c £11223
97a 3-15 Ling 7ap 93 81 t
94a 4-10 Ling 7ap 95 262 t
85 9-14 Ling 7sft 96 1624 t
100 4-20 Asco 7g/f 94 1926 t
99 5-31 Asco 8g/f 95 2489 t
98 7-15 Sand 8.1g/s 96 2915 t
57 17-18 Newb 8g/f 95 3265 t
83 8-10 Asco 8gd 94 3775 t
48 7-8 Good 7g/s 92 4231
22 18-18 Newb 10gd 92 4681 t
91a 1-12 WOLV 7.1ap [89] 5006* t

CAMPBELLS LAD 3 b c £2011
11a 5-7 Wolv 5af [45] 1320
40a 4-10 Sout 7af [45] 1842
31 8-17 Hayd 8.1gd 42 2243
12 12-13 Redc 8gd 42 2552
45 5-8 Carl 7.9gd [40] 2932
40 3-10 Beve 12.1g/f 40 3499
3 14-18 Beve 9.9g/s 39 4243
42 2-15 Carl 9.3fm [40] 4505
53 4-8 Ayr 10sft [45] 5034
44a 3-12 Wolv 9.5ap [45] 5209
49 2-13 Ayr 8sft [45] 5275

CAMPBELLS TALE 5 gr g £0
0 11-12 Sout 8af 460
0 12-12 Wolv 6af 524 T

CAMPEON 2 b c £5225
52 12-13 Donc 5gd 954
77 5-8 Newm 5g/s 1149
60 9-9 Muss 5g/s 1458
67 5-11 Wind 5gd 2450
77 2-8 Brig 7gd 2952
71 4-6 Brig 6g/f 3171

76 3-13 York 6g/f 3431
69 5-12 Hayd 5gd 74 3756
71 2-7 Yarm 6gd [74] 3994
57a 4-14 Sout 6af [74] 4127 VIS
64 2-8 Wind 5g/s [71] 4218 vis

CAMPO BUENO 2 b c £14049
110 3-9 Mais 6sft 5312

CAMROSE 3 ch c £20856
88 4-9 Sand 10g/s 83 1318
88 3-10 Good 11g/f 83 1865
92 2-4 Sali 9.9fm [85] 2290
90 5-12 Wind 11.6fm 87 2759
93 2-11 Epso 10.1gd 87 4293
96 1-13 KEMP 12g/f [89] 4715*
83 10-15 Leic 11.8gd 94 5043

CAN CAN FLYER 2 ch c £6916
2a 11-13 Wolv 9.4af 37
39a 6-10 Sout 8af 162
70 1-12 BEVE 9.9g/s 59 3854*
72 2-12 Beve 12.1sft 63 4259
69 2-8 Catt 13.8g/f 63 4439
67 7-20 Hayd 11.9g/s 68 4771
64 7-20 Catt 12gd 66 4966

CANADIAN DANEHILL 2 b c £0
45a 9-10 Ling 7ap 5259
11a 13-13 Wolv 8.6ap 5355

CANADIAN STORM 3 gr c £4446
59 5-8 Muss 7.1gd [70] 1554
54 7-17 Yarm 7g/f [70] 1729
61 4-15 Leic 11.8gd 60 2134
45 5-7 Brig 9.9g/f [60] 2433
69 1-11 LEIC 10g/f [58] 2924*

CANARY DANCER 2 b f £1619
38 11-13 Redc 6g/f 1818
59 4-8 Hami 5gd 2177
65 2-16 Pont 6g/f 2275
51 8-12 Catt 7g/f 63 3351
22 9-9 Ches 7sft 63 4074
42 7-14 Thir [63] 4206

CANATRICE 4 gr f £0
1 15-17 Bath 11.7sft 55 1543 p

CANDLERIGGS 8 ch g £0
50 13-19 Beve 5sft 72 1627
47 13-20 Thir 5g/f 68 1765
56 7-16 Carl 5.9fm 63 2445
0 13-13 Catt 5g/f 60 3350

CANDY ANCHOR 5 b m £415
41a 2-14 Ling 10ap [35] 1072 bl
29a 7-9 Ling 10ap [45] 1289 bl
26a 7-13 Sout 8af 41 3094 bl

CANLIS 5 b g £1362
48 7-9 Thir 7g/f [45] 2216
50 2-14 Leic 8g/f 45 2402
27 12-16 Beve 7.5gd 47 2891
33 12-13 Muss 8g/f 47 3526
34 7-14 Catt 12g/f [47] 3668
40 5-17 Thir 8g/s 45 3830
32 7-16 Carl 11.9g/f 45 4348 P
38 9-15 Thir 8fm [45] 4379 p
29 8-14 Redc 10fm 40 4560
15 6-12 Ayr 7.2sft [40] 5274

CANNI THINKAAR 3 b g £973
62 6-8 Brig 9.9g/f [70] 1369
27 15-15 Ripo 12.3g/f 67 1785
25 7-9 Yarm 14.1g/f 66 2345 e
59 4-15 Nott 10gd 63 3108
53 10-13 Nott 10g/f 62 3419
53a 3-13 Ling 10ap [59] 4112
36 12-12 Good 9g/f 59 4539 P

CANTARA 3 ch f £7660
78 2-14 Hayd 8.1g/s [78] 2231
76 3-11 Chep 8.1g/f [76] 2627
55 5-11 Pont 10g/f [76] 2991
74 1-15 NOTT 8.2g/s [73] 4649*
58 6-7 Pont 8g/f 73 4935
69 7-18 Newm 8sft 70 5272

CANTEMERLE 3 b f £974
29a 5-12 Wolv 12af 54 75 bl
23a 8-12 Wolv 16.2af 51 156 bl
56 2-12 Newc 12.4sft 51 1680 bl
2 7-7 Leic 11.8g/f 55 1967
34 7-8 Thir 12g/s 54 2691 bl
47 6-8 Hayd 11.9gd 54 2881 bl
25 7-10 Hayd 16.2sft 50 3275 bl
31 9-16 Carl 11.9g/f 46 4348 bl

CANTERLOUPE 5 b m £10227
83a 1-13 WOLV 6af 76 41*
78a 6-11 Sout 6af 82 198
63a 8-12 Wolv 6af 82 361
72 10-19 Kemp 6fm 78 2070 T
70 7-10 Kemp 6g/f 76 2861 t
68 7-16 Newb 6g/f 73 3269
80 1-13 GOOD 6gd 71 3952*
67 8-12 Good 6sft 76 4184
68 8-19 Good 6gd 76 4747
53a 5-12 Wolv 5.1ap [81] 5362

CANTON 2 b c £10836
70 6-7 Kemp 5sft 943
89a 1-5 LING 5ap 1041*
88 4-9 Ches 5.1gd 1567
89 4-9 Asco 6gd 87 3127
93 5-24 Newb 5.2g/f 3266
90a 3-10 Ling 5ap [95] 3743
90 3-13 Newm 5g/f 90 3943
86 3-6 Wind 6g/s [89] 4217
81 13-22 Donc 6fm [87] 4458

CANTORIS 4 b g £0
27 12-14 Bath 18.2fm 53 2417 bl

CANTRIP 3 b f £3896
0 14-14 Ling 13ap 62 264 T
48a 8-8 Ling 16ap 62 288 t
8a 14-14 Ling 12ap 57 711 BL t
45 7-16 Brig 11.9fm 53 1693
8 17-18 Wind 11.6g/f 49 1960
52 1-11 FOLK 12g/f 45 2273*
53 3-11 Sand 14g/f 50 2391
23 9-12 Kemp 14.4g/f 51 3688
10a 12-13 Ling 16ap 51 3822
47 5-15 Folk 12g/f [49] 4374
25a 11-14 Ling 16ap [49] 4663
44 5-9 Good 16gd 45 4875

CAONA 2 b f £0
58 8-8 Asco 6g/f 3386
64 5-13 Wind 6fm 3639
63 10-10 Newb 6gd 3917

CAPABLE GUEST 2 b c £20685
96 3-11 York 6g/s 1687
95 3-8 Newm 6g/f 1934
105 3-13 Asco 6gd 2467
95 2-6 Asco 7g/f 3390
97 1-16 LEIC 7fm [100] 3811*
100 4-7 York 7gd [100] 4003
101 3-6 Good 6g/f [100] 4524
107 4-7 Long 8g/s [100] 4729

CAPE CANAVERAL 5 b g £0
38a 7-11 Ling 12ap 672

CAPE COLUMBINE 2 b f £71300
88 2-10 Good 6gd 4876
102 1-29 NEWM 6gd 5087*

CAPE ENTERPRISE 2 b c £556
60a 7-14 Ling 7ap 5078
72a 3-12 Wolv 7.1ap 5324

CAPE FEAR 3 b c £0
90 10-12 Newm 7sft [110] 5134
101 7-11 Newm 8g/s [107] 5283
102 5-12 Donc 6sft [107] 5371

CAPE GREKO 2 ro c £7266
96 2-8 Sali 7gd 2695
105 1-9 ASCO 7gd 3126*

CAPE OF GOOD HOPE 5 ch g £150800
120 3-14 Sha 5g/f 210 vis
116 2-19 Asco 6sft 2468 VIS
115 3-14 Asco 6fm 2580 vis t

112 4-20 Newm 6g/f 3062 vis t

CAPE QUEST 2 b c £6728
71 10-15 Newm 7fm 3005
84 3-13 Wind 6fm 3478
90 1-11 SALI 6g/f 3863*
70 8-14 Donc 7fm 83 4535

CAPE ROYAL 4 b g £16602
69 9-20 Donc 5gd 83 927
80 6-16 Muss 5gd 82 1120
91 1-11 EPSO 5sft 82 1293*
80 7-14 Ches 5.1gd 88 1594
85 6-20 York 5g/s 88 1683
80 11-20 Epso 5fm 87 2253
91 2-11 Ches 5.1g/s 85 2747
78 8-12 York 5g/s 87 3073
91 3-12 Newm 5g/f 87 3279
92 2-14 Newb 5.2fm 88 3628
70 17-20 Hayd 5fm 88 3792

CAPE ST VINCENT 4 gr c £6220
43 10-16 Nott 6.1sft [72] 1743
79a 1-13 WOLV 6af 70 2053+ VIS
76 2-9 Warw 5.5fm 72 2779 vis
60 7-9 Epso 6g/f 72 2871 vis
56 8-11 Newm 6fm 74 3408 vis

CAPE TIA 2 b f £0
17a 14-14 Ling 6ap 146

CAPE VINCENT 3 b c £5805
91 1-11 SALI 7gd 3884*
66 5-5 Good 9sft 90 4185

CAPER 4 b g £0
11 9-10 Carl 14.1fm 45 3549
0 15-16 Sout 14af 41 4045
25 11-16 Carl 11.9g/f 40 4348
17 14-19 Catt 15.8g/f 40 4675
0 11-12 Wolv 12.2ap [40] 5208

CAPESTAR 3 b f £7671
80 6-17 Newm 7gd 1171
82 2-12 York 7g/s 1688
77 1-13 KEMP 8fm 2072*
75 4-8 Ling 7g/f 79 2742

CAPETOWN GIRL 3 b f £5473
71 1-10 PONT 6hvy [67] 1070*
24 12-14 Hayd 8.1g/s 75 1348
63 8-12 Donc 7g/f 73 1899
52 7-9 Ayr 7.2gd 70 2508
49 10-11 Carl 8g/f 67 2936 P
45 12-14 Thir 6g/f 62 3416 VIS
16 13-15 Ayr 7.2hvy 57 4088
38 11-18 Leic 7gd [52] 4698

CAPITOLE 3 b g £1261
37 11-13 Newm 8fm 2595
69 4-11 Pont 10g/f 2991
60 5-13 Pont 8g/s 3973
64 4-13 Bath 8gd 61 4546 VIS
50 11-17 Beve 8.5g/f 61 4721 vis
58 3-11 Catt 13.8sft [60] 5129

CAPLAW SONG 2 ch f £0
0 11-11 Wolv 6af [32] 73

CAPPED FOR VICTORY 3 b c £1784
77 2-14 Thir 8gd [100] 1636
88 7-18 Hayd 8.1g/f 88 1919
74 12-25 Asco 7g/f 86 3443

CAPRICHO 7 gr g £4669
75 17-17 Donc 6gd [110] 952
93 4-10 Bade 6gd [110] 2140
80 11-21 Asco 7g/f 104 3441
99 10-20 Newm 7g/f 102 3782
75 11-11 York 7g/s [100] 4063
95 16-19 Hayd 6fm [100] 4384
91 9-20 Ayr 6sft 99 4686
99 6-12 Asco 6g/f [99] 4799
75 12-14 Newm 6sft [96] 5100

CAPTAIN CLIPPER 4 b g £4450
76 3-14 Newc 10.1sft 72 964
81 1-7 THIR 12sft [75] 1226*
8 17-19 York 11.9sft 79 1668

CAPTAIN CLOUDY 3 b g £698
35a 9-14 Ling 6ap 60 121
55a 5-15 Ling 6ap [57] 366
53a 6-12 Ling 8ap 57 607
48a 6-13 Ling 7ap 54 739
35 14-15 Brig 5.3g/f 62 1371
51 10-11 Bath 6g/f [57] 3372
54 3-12 Brig 7fm 53 3677
34 12-12 Brig 8g/f 53 3986
53 4-20 Chep 6.1g/s 53 4368
50 7-20 Chep 7.1gd 53 4488
53 4-18 Good 8gd 51 4750

CAPTAIN CRUSOE 6 b g £364
58a 3-8 Sout 11af 857
1a 10-10 Ling 12ap 916

CAPTAIN DARLING 3 b g £1594
51a 5-14 Sout 8af 66 99
61a 5-11 Ling 8ap 66 131
65a 4-11 Wolv 7af 64 241
63a 3-15 Ling 7ap 64 266
36a 6-10 Wolv 7af 63 685
61a 7-9 Ling 10ap 62 903
67 2-16 Sout 7g/s 61 1049 p
40 9-17 Thir 8g/s 61 1214 p
53 7-15 Brig 8fm 65 1691 p
63 5-16 Ling 7g/f 63 2063 VIS
47 7-15 Pont 6g/f 62 2280 vis
28a 14-14 Ling 7ap [60] 5294 p

CAPTAIN FEARLESS 3 ch g £0
0 13-13 Sout 8af 553
1a 8-8 Ling 10ap 626
14 6-6 Yarm 10.1g/f 1134

CAPTAIN GINGER 3 ch g £0
62a 7-11 Ling 8ap 72 131
22a 12-15 Sout 11af 69 196

CAPTAIN HURRICANE 2 b c £56457
86 2-5 Yarm 6g/f 2341
97 2-10 Sali 6gd 2697
111 1-7 NEWM 6g/f 3028*
103 4-9 Deau 6g/f 4159
86 16-22 Donc 6fm 4458

CAPTAIN JOHNNO 2 b c £4532
62 7-11 Sali 7gd 3883
82 3-18 Ayr 6g/s 4617 BL
79 3-10 Ling 5g/f 4893 VIS
73a 1-12 WOLV 6ap [76] 5177* vis

CAPTAIN MARGARET 2 b f £581
0 10-10 Newm 6g/f 3063
70 5-14 Yarm 7gd 3489 T
62 10-17 Warw 7.1gd 4271 t
26 12-20 Newm 8g/s 68 4635 P
63 3-17 Ling 7g/f 61 4894 t
55 12-20 Yarm 8g/s 62 5349 t

CAPTAIN MARRYAT 3 ch g £7508
61 2-10 Bath 8hvy 1100
2 11-12 Kemp 8hvy 1511
63 2-14 Sali 8fm 57 2423
64 2-14 Nott 8.2g/f 57 2634
64 3-14 Wind 8.3g/f 59 2799
64 2-17 Hayd 10.5fm 59 4388
62 3-14 Chep 10.2gd 59 4487
67a 2-11 Wolv 12.2ap 60 5180

CAPTAIN MILLER 8 b g £5562
73 2-18 York 13.9g/s 67 1689
74 2-13 Kemp 12g/f 70 1916
38 15-17 Newm 14.8gd 72 4196 T

CAPTAIN SAIF 4 b c £946
79 14-18 Good 8g/f 92 1812
73 16-20 Asco 7g/f 92 1926 bl
58 11-13 Sali 8gd 87 2662
57 4-8 Epso 8.5g/f [87] 2873
62 3-9 Epso 7gd [75] 3215 T
49 14-15 Beve 7.5g/f 70 4719
18 17-17 Redc 10sft 64 5307

CARA BELLA 3 ch f £1393
79 7-17 Warw 7.1gd 1171
63 5-14 Warw 8.1sft 1527

75 3-12 Newm 7g/f 75 2249
76 6-12 Yarm 7fm 74 2864

CARA FANTASY 4 b f £2103
82 4-13 Hayd 14sft 80 1109
76 7-12 Good 14g/f 80 1861
84 2-7 Newm 14.8g/f 79 3281

CARA SPOSA 2 b c £0
40 11-11 Newm 6sft 5265

CARACARA 3 ch f £0
3 13-13 York 10.4sft 85 1664

CARADAK 3 b c £1500
104 6-12 Newm 7sft 5134

CARDINAL VENTURE 5 b g £23438
91a 1-9 WOLV 8.5af 80 2+
94a 1-13 WOLV 8.5af 86 44*
97a 1-12 SOUT 8af 92 141*
97a 2-8 Wolv 7af [95] 838
79 11-24 Donc 8gd 87 928
86 7-16 Thir 8g/s 87 1474
59 15-18 Ches 7.6gd 87 1598
97 1-7 HAYD 6g/s 85 2187*
88 8-29 Asco 6fm 90 2581
74 16-19 Newm 7g/f 95 3061
73 15-24 Ayr 8sft 93 4686
77 15-20 York 6gd 92 5001
92 4-20 Newm 7g/s 89 5286

CARGO 4 b g £5619
41a 7-16 Ling 7ap [48] 180
51a 5-13 Ling 6ap [47] 271
15a 11-13 Ling 6ap [47] 340
36a 4-13 Ling 6ap [47] 544
47a 2-14 Ling 6ap [45] 709 BL T
34a 11-11 Ling 6ap 45 728 BL T
46a 2-8 Ling 7ap [45] 1413 t P
47a 3-8 Sout 6af [45] 1588 t p
50 2-9 Ling 7g/f [48] 1984 t p
40 8-17 Warw 8.1fm 48 2572 t p
44 7-20 Nott 6.1gd 48 2928 t p
51 2-11 Brig 6g/f [46] 3298 t p
49 2-7 Brig 6gd 46 3717 t p
37 9-12 Brig 8g/f 47 3986 t
8 9-16 Folk 6g/f [47] 4370 t p
48 2-15 Brig 6gd [46] 4905 bl t
54a 1-13 WOLV 5.1ap [45] 5231* bl t

CARIBBEAN BLUE 3 b f £0
44 5-13 Ripo 6g/f 52 2011
35 8-9 Thir 7g/f [52] 2218
22 9-13 Newc 6af 47 2683
0 19-20 Thir 6g/f 45 3575
39 7-10 Ripo 6gd [40] 4788 VIS
3 18-20 Yarm 6g/s [40] 5121 BL

CARIBBEAN CORAL 5 ch g £68840
78 8-20 Donc 5gd 90 927
94 2-13 Beve 5gd [90] 1162
99 1-20 EPSO 5fm 92 2253*
105 1-15 NEWC 5g/s 96 2727+
98 13-28 Good 6fm 103 3622
84 11-11 Beve 5g/s [102] 4238
100 3-9 Donc 5fm [101] 4481
97 11-11 Newb 5.2g/f [100] 4678
100 4-12 Epso 5g/f 98 4908
101 4-10 Newm 5gd 97 5090
88 9-13 Donc 5sft 97 5218

CARIBBEAN DANCER 2 b f £1681
58 10-12 Beve 7.5g/s 4242
47 8-8 Pont 8fm 4756
77 2-8 Muss 9g/s 5140
64 13-20 Yarm 8g/s 72 5349

CARIBBEAN DIAMOND 2 b f £0
33 9-10 Yarm 8g/f 3713

CARIBE 5 b h £220
61 6-7 Thir 8sft 1225
8 12-12 Ayr 7.2fm 65 1909
41 10-13 Hami 6gd 60 2315
29a 8-14 Sout 6af [60] 2502
33a 10-13 Sout 7af 50 3155

CARINI 3 b f £5113

---

96 3-7 Good 9.9g/f 1844
90 6-9 Newm 12g/f [94] 3233
93 3-6 Newm 12g/f [94] 3754
81 8-12 Yarm 10.1sft 94 4149
83 5-6 Good 12gd 94 5028

CARK 5 b g £2935
43a 4-12 Wolv 5af 47 109
44a 12-16 Sout 6af [45] 227
37a 8-15 Sout 5af [45] 253
32a 6-13 Wolv 5af [45] 312 p
50a 1-9 SOUT 5af [45] 335* p
49a 2-9 Ling 5ap [45] 413 p
22a 8-12 Wolv 5af 52 641
39a 7-11 Sout 5af [50] 775 p
24a 13-16 Sout 5ap 49 1046 p
31 14-17 Warw 5hvy [47] 1532 p

CARLA MOON 3 b f £0
40 11-17 Yarm 7g/f [65] 1729
10 19-19 Leic 6g/f 60 2925
28 12-13 Yarm 10.1gd 60 3492
39 10-11 Yarm 7g/f 60 3711

CARLBURG 3 b g £0
35 10-10 Good 11g/f 71 1865
55 11-11 Newm 7g/f 68 3283
33 12-13 Ling 7g/f 64 3604
24a 12-12 Ling 8ap [60] 4320
49a 8-13 Wolv 8.6ap 55 5005 BL

CARLTON 10 ch g £4585
58a 8-13 Ling 7ap 62 565
57a 4-12 Ling 6ap 60 628
57a 4-9 Wolv 7af 60 684
34a 10-13 Ling 6ap 57 902
58 2-13 Sout 6g/s 54 1052
54 4-19 Yarm 7g/f 54 1132
39a 5-8 Sout 7af 54 1195
61 2-16 Newc 6sft 56 1277
59 2-20 Newc 6sft 55 1393
61 2-10 Warw 6.1hvy 59 1533
54 7-14 Ling 7sft 59 1625
33a 8-12 Wolv 7af 52 2204
57 5-9 Beve 7.5gd 59 3310
51 9-17 Newc 7g/s 58 3700
39 9-16 Hami 6g/s 56 4009
44 10-14 Beve 7.5g/s 54 4241

CARLYS QUEST 10 ch g £0
10 27-29 Asco 20g/f 82 2471 vis t

CARMANIA 2 b g £0
23 16-20 Hayd 6gd 2882
56 5-9 Ches 5.1g/f 3097
31 9-10 Hayd 5g/s 3901
20 13-14 Catt 5g/f 53 4437
29 12-14 Redc 5fm 53 4556

CARMARTHEN BELLE 4 b f £0
0 18-19 Redc 6g/s 5110
3 17-17 Yarm 8g/s 5348

CARNEGIE HALL 2 b c £2535
105 4-5 Curr 7g/f 4154

CARNIVORE 2 ch c £1912
72 2-10 Thir 5fm 3606

CARNT SPELL 3 b g £0
44 13-17 Hayd 8.1g/s 4768

CAROLINA MORNING 3 gr f £0
0 15-15 Ling 12ap 118

CAROLINES ROSE 5 b r m £0
29a 9-12 Ling 10ap [20] 267

CAROLS CHOICE 6 ch m £293
33a 6-9 Wolv 7af 45 27
41a 3-12 Sout 5af 45 85
37a 8-13 Wolv 5af 45 110
14a 14-16 Sout 6af 43 166
39a 9-16 Sout 6af [43] 227
1a 10-10 Wolv 6af 39 246
23a 6-11 Wolv [36] 296
34a 5-13 Wolv 5af [40] 312
20a 10-16 Sout 5af [35] 374

CARONTE 4 b g £1453
0 10-13 Sout 7af [40] 356 bl
18a 12-16 Sout 5af [40] 374 bl
6a 12-14 Sout 6af 35 501 bl
0 13-14 Sout 7af [35] 573 bl
26a 10-15 Ling 7ap 830 H
34a 1-12 SOUT 5af [30] 904+ h bl
0 8-8 Sout 6af [40] 1201 h bl
11a 8-10 Sout 5af [40] 1408 h bl
27 7-9 Muss 5gd [40] 1797 bl

CAROUBIER 3 ch g £10456
69a 2-11 Sout 11af [83] 191
70a 4-10 Wolv 9.4af 80 278
76a 5-12 Wolv 9.4af 78 382 bl
74a 2-9 Wolv 9.4af [75] 480 VIS
75a 1-6 SOUT 8af [73] 586*
79a 2-7 Wolv 8.5af 73 700
58a 9-12 Ling 8ap 76 888 vis
77 1-18 WIND 8.3g/s 68 1059*
74 9-13 Wind 10gd [76] 1381
68 9-18 Good 8g/f 76 1849
61 14-15 Kemp 10fm 76 2067
70 15-17 Carl 7.9gd 74 2672
62a 6-10 Sout 12af 75 2998
52 12-13 Warw 12.6gd 69 4274
56 14-15 Nott 10g/f 66 4849

CARRIACOU 2 b f £2622
39a 8-14 Sout 8af [80] 88
71a 2-16 Sout 8af [72] 192 e
70 6-13 Kemp 9gd 75 1141
68a 4-11 Wolv 8.5af 69 1339 e
71 5-14 Ling 7sft 73 1625
38 9-9 Leic 8gd 70 2705
64 5-11 Newm 7g/f 67 3283
68 3-13 Yarm 10.1gd 64 3492
53 7-11 Yarm 10.1gd [64] 3875
63 4-12 Kemp 9sft 64 4032
58 7-13 Ling 10g/s 63 4182
65 3-19 Bath 11.7gd 61 5024
30a 10-11 Wolv 12.2ap 60 5180
38 6-12 Catt 12sft [61] 5319

CARRIZO CREEK 3 b c £0
95 7-11 Newm 7gd 110 1167
102 7-13 Newb 7g/f [109] 3957

CARROWDORE 3 b c £6706
66a 10-14 Ling 10ap 71 122
67a 2-11 Ling 12ap [71] 816
56 4-9 Donc 12g/f 68 2078 p
70 3-15 Wind 13.3g/f 65 2311 p
71 4-9 Newm 14.8fm 68 2596 p
75 2-9 Yarm 10.1fm 68 2866
75 2-8 Ling 11.5fm 70 3747
71 4-19 Leic 10g/f 70 4456 p
71 3-16 Yarm 11.5g/s 70 4589 p
60 4-14 Epso 12gd 70 4910 p

CARRY ON DOC 3 b c £17058
73a 3-6 Wolv 7af [75] 1321
77 6-11 Bath 8fm [73] 1904
81 1-9 BRIG 8gd [73] 2953*
74 5-11 York 7g/f 75 3433
76 3-6 Brig 7fm [75] 3696
82 1-14 EPSO 8.5gd 74 4295*
49 11-13 Epso 8.5gd 80 4469
74 7-12 Epso 8.5gd 78 4909

CARRY ON KATIE 3 b r f £4841
112 6-16 Newm 8fm 1492
104 9-13 Long 8g/s 1854

CARTE DIAMOND 3 ch c £60590
97 1-4 REDC 11gd 2549*
101 1-13 YORK 11.9g/s 90 3076*
101 2-7 Newm 12g/f [96] 4878
100 3-15 Leic 11.8gd 96 5043
108 1-24 DONC 12sft 97 5372*

CARTE NOIRE 3 b f £3059
62 5-15 Bath 8g/s 62 1099
61 1-9 THIR 7g/f [60] 2216*
36a 8-12 Sout 7af [60] 2496
43 11-14 Wind 8.3fm 59 2971
41 11-19 Leic 7g/f 57 4452
48 7-12 Brig 8fm [54] 4761 P

CARTE ROYALE 2 ch c £5071

93	1-13	CARL	5fm	1950*	
93	2-4	Bath	5fm	2411	
62	6-6	Hami	6gd	2711	

CARTE SAUVAGE 3 gr c £1500

93a	6-14	Nad	8af		598
1	13-14	Newb	10hvy	101	5223
101	4-6	Newm	10sft	[101]	5269

CARTOGRAPHY 3 b c £21668

108	3-8	Newm	7g/f	[104]	1932
108	3-15	Asco	7g/f	[106]	2486 T
109	2-11	Newb	6g/f	[106]	3268 t
92	18-19	Hayd	6fm	[106]	4384 t
95	2-9	Hami	6g/s	[106]	4817 t

CARTRONAGEERAGHLAD 2 b c £4129

70a	6-13	Ling	7ap	74	15 bl
15a	9-10	Sout	8af	74	189 bl
76	10-22	Donc	8gd	82	955 bl
66	12-16	Kemp	6g/s	80	1116
69	9-17	Warw	7.1sft	78	1526 bl
67	9-12	Kemp	8g/f	[75]	1915 bl
77	2-13	Good	9g/f	75	2024
71	4-8	Nott	10g/f	72	2157
81	4-12	Sand	9g/f	77	2385
79	5-16	Sand	10g/s	77	2919
78	4-7	Pont	10g/f	[77]	2994
63	12-14	Kemp	10g/f	75	3690
58	8-9	Good	9sft	[75]	4266 bl
77	3-11	Good	8gd	74	5027 bl
70a	6-13	Wolv	9.5ap	70	5161 bl

CASALESE 2 ch c £0

27	13-14	Carl	6.9fm	4503
48	7-8	Hami	8.3g/s	4816
34	8-8	Ayr	8sft	5273

CASANTELLA 2 b f £292

12a	11-13	Wolv	8.5af	[50]	43
25a	9-15	Sout	7af	[50]	87 VIS
40a	8-14	Sout	7af	38	158
45a	3-11	Sout	7af	[38]	207
21a	6-9	Wolv	9.4af	[38]	238
3a	8-8	Sout	8af	[47]	355 vis
41a	4-8	Sout	7af	[47]	389
47a	5-12	Sout	8af	[45]	460
23a	7-9	Sout	8af	45	486
38a	5-9	Sout	8af	[45]	596
0	10-10	Sout	8af	45	662
38a	8-14	Ling	7ap	[40]	804
43a	9-10	Ling	10ap	[40]	843

CASCADE LAKES 2 ch f £0

44	13-14	Redc	7sft	5301

CASEYS HOUSE 4 gr f £0

0	12-13	Muss	7.1g/f	1119
33	8-10	Newc	5sft	1682
7	10-10	Redc	6gd	2559
0	11-11	Sout	6af	4041

CASH 5 b g £8506

43a	9-12	Wolv	5af	62	35
47a	7-16	Sout	6af	59	94
56a	5-12	Wolv	5af	59	124
15a	16-16	Sout	6af	57	166
63a	1-16	SOUT	5af	57	183* P
42a	6-10	Wolv	6af	61	246 p
62a	4-9	Wolv	5af	61	275 p
33a	7-13	Sout	6af	61	551 p
65a	1-12	WOLV	5af	60	641* p
63a	3-10	Wolv	5af	66	749 p
59a	5-12	Sout	5af	65	853 p
21	18-20	Ripo	5gd	56	1179 VIS
28	11-13	Newc	5sft	56	1276 p
34	14-20	Newc	6sft	55	1393 p
61	1-15	MUSS	5gd	55	1555* p
18	18-20	Thir	5g/f	59	1765 p
30	13-16	Catt	5sft	[59]	3932 p

CASH ON 2 ch c £0

61	13-21	Newm	8sft	5097
67a	9-11	Ling	8ap	5236

CASH TIME 2 ch f £0

25	6-8	Hayd	6g/f	2183

21	14-20	Hayd	6gd		2882
47	4-6	Catt	5g/f		3014
12	12-15	Catt	7sft	[44]	3930

CASHBAR 3 b f £4138

68a	2-9	Ling	8ap		3197
80	1-9	NOTT	8.2g/f		3581*
64	8-8	Newm	8g/f	77	3947

CASHEL HOUSE 2 b c £420

79a	4-5	Ling	5ap	5260

CASHEL MEAD 3 b f £1358

69a	6-13	Wolv	6af	78	45
81a	2-13	Wolv	6af	78	113
81a	3-11	Sout	8af	80	198
81a	5-14	Ling	6ap	80	292
42a	9-11	Sout	6af	80	386
76a	8-11	Ling	7ap	[79]	627
70	6-15	Folk	6sft	77	976
57	15-19	Leic	6g/s	73	1354
36	12-16	Nott	6.1sft	[72]	1743
51a	7-10	Wolv	7.1ap	[75]	4920
47a	10-12	Wolv	6ap	70	5291

CASHEMA 3 b f £0

60	8-18	Wind	8.3g/s		1258
2	16-16	Nott	10hvy	55	1611
36	8-10	Leic	8gd	[52]	2133 P
0	16-16	Wind	11.6g/s	47	2621

CASHIER 2 gr c £545

82	3-13	Donc	7hvy	5199

CASHNEEM 6 b g £4071

59	4-13	Warw	7.1hvy	[61]	1537
55	6-19	Redc	7g/f	60	1820
64	1-9	YARM	7fm	58	2150*
64	4-12	Donc	7g/f	64	2235
49	7-8	Redc	8gd	64	2550
59	9-16	Redc	8g/s	64	2958
52	14-20	Chep	7.1g/s	64	3088
25	24-26	Redc	8fm	62	4926
22	18-19	Newc	7g/f	59	5014

CASPIAN DUSK 3 b g £6507

60a	2-12	Sout	8af	[53]	848
61a	3-9	Ling	10ap	[53]	899
72a	1-9	SOUT	8af	[58]	983+
66a	2-5	Sout	8af	[70]	1440
64a	1-6	SOUT	11af	[70]	1754*
61a	3-7	Wolv	12af	[70]	2050
36a	7-10	Sout	11af	[65]	2499

CASPIAN LAKE 3 ch g £0

37	9-11	Wind	8.3g/f	5052
53a	8-13	Wolv	9.5ap	5290

CASSANOS 2 b c £470

59a	8-16	Sout	8af	[60]	192
46a	3-9	Wolv	9.4af	57	351
40a	6-10	Sout	8af	57	662 P

CASSYDORA 2 b f £9557

75	6-13	Newb	7g/f	3252
97	1-14	NEWM	7g/f	3944*
97	4-8	Donc	8fm	4476

CASTAGNA 3 ch f £5435

76	4-13	Kemp	10g/f		3038
81	1-7	NOTT	10g/f		3422*
74	7-9	York	11.9g/s	[87]	4058
84	8-8	Asco	12g/f	[85]	4774

CASTAIGNE 4 ch f £866

50a	8-16	Ling	7ap	54	55 t
57a	2-14	Ling	10ap	54	101 t
41a	10-13	Ling	10ap	56	215 t
50a	7-14	Ling	10ap	54	339 t
16a	13-14	Ling	10ap	54	498
52	6-17	Kemp	10g/f	57	1913
38	7-12	Bath	10.2fm	57	2036
50	4-15	Warw	10.9g/f	52	2910
52	4-14	Folk	9.7g/s	52	3052
38	11-16	Brig	9.9g/f	50	3175

CASTANET 5 b m £0

41	5-12	Sout	16gd	45	1285
22	9-10	Chep	12.1gd	44	2114

CASTAWAY QUEEN 5 ch m £1836

62	2-18	Bath	10.2g/s	61	1098
39a	13-14	Ling	10ap	62	1618
53	8-17	Kemp	10g/f	62	1913 BL
62	3-8	Brig	8g/f	60	2432 bl
80	9-10	Chep	10.2g/s	[59]	3089

CASTELLETTO 2 b f £46132

70	3-4	Nott	5.1sft		1608
89	2-11	Nott	5.1g/f		2151
69	16-17	Asco	5g/f		2490
87	2-9	Wind	5g/f		2795
87	1-10	RIPO	5g/f		2983*
99	2-12	Newb	5.2g/f	[85]	3956
92	5-8	York	6g/s	[85]	4059
99	2-11	Sali	6gd	[99]	4332
103	2-9	Ayr	6sft	[98]	4684
106	1-11	NEWM	5sft	[98]	5132*

CASTEROSSA 2 ch f £800

51	6-6	Good	6gd		2373
73	4-10	Nott	6.1g/f		3418
68	4-13	Wind	6fm		3639
69	6-13	Warw	6.1gd	72	4273
64	19-26	Newb	6.5g/f		4679

CASTLESHANE 7 b g £0

82	11-15	Redc	10g/f	89	2101

CASTLETON 3 b c £13852

91	2-17	Ling	7g/s		1617
101	3-6	Newm	10g/f	[100]	1931
94	1-11	NEWM	8g/f	[100]	2248*
115	6-11	Asco	8g/f	[100]	2469

CASUAL GLANCE 2 b f £0

55	13-13	Good	7fm	3554
59	9-14	Sali	6g/f	4078

CATALINI 3 ch c £946

67a	2-11	Ling	8ap	[75]	841
74a	5-8	Ling	8ap	[75]	934
71	5-8	Brig	7fm	[75]	2259
56	6-6	Hami	8.3g/s	[73]	2828

CATCH A STAR 2 ch f £12178

74	3-10	Newm	6gd		1887
81	5-9	Newm	6g/f		2245
71	8-14	Newm	7g/f		2766
84	3-10	Newm	6g/f		3063
83	1-11	NOTT	8.2g/s	[80]	4648*
86	3-16	Newm	7g/f	80	4913
76	6-13	Wind	8.3g/f	81	5051

CATCH THE CAT 4 b g £20618

43a	5-16	Sout	6af	52	92 vis
41a	8-15	Sout	5af	50	187 vis
68	3-20	Ripo	5gd	68	1179 bl
65	7-20	Newc	6sft	69	1393 bl
71	2-19	Beve	5sft	68	1627 bl
67	8-17	Nott	5.1g/s	69	1774 bl
77	1-15	MUSS	5fm	69	2084* bl
68	6-13	York	7g/f	72	2359 bl
51	5-9	Wind	6fm	[72]	2760 bl
65	7-15	Beve	5sft	72	2942 bl
66	7-12	York	5g/s	72	3073 vis
58	10-17	Pont	5gd	71	3241 p
77	1-15	MUSS	5gd	72	3561* vis
61	8-15	Pont	5gd	76	3680 bl
56	8-8	Nott	5.1gd	[74]	4039 vis
59	14-16	Muss	5g/f	74	4174 vis
29	14-14	Redc	5sft	[72]	4930 vis

CATCH THE FOX 4 b g £1842

46	12-17	Kemp	7gd	[45]	1136
45	2-10	Chep	8.1sft	[45]	1334
23	7-17	Kemp	7hvy	[45]	1642
34	10-17	Kemp	10g/f	45	1913
44	4-15	Newm	9gd	43	2170
41	12-16	Kemp	9g/f	42	3039
28	9-11	Kemp	9g/f	42	3685
1	10-12	Newb	10gd	42	3916
31	4-14	Good	8sft	40	4189
29a	7-12	Ling	8ap	[40]	4655
48	3-16	Brig	7gd	[35]	4901
59	3-11	Wind	8.3g/f	[40]	5052
0	17-17	Newb	9sft	40	5198

CATCH THE WIND 3 b f £7384

43	13-14	Ches	6.1g/s			1570
65	5-8	Bath	5fm	[79]		1901
75a	5-11	Ling	6ap	76		2841
57	6-10	Hayd	5g/s	73		3135
84	1-7	**BATH**	5g/f	73		3371* P
75	2-12	Nott	5.1g/f	[70]		3577 p
84	2-8	Sand	5g/s	80		3889 p
74	12-18	Pont	5g/s	83		5149 p

CATCHTHEBATCH 7 b g £667

54a	7-12	Wolv	5af	[53]	70
46a	7-13	Wolv	5af	53	110
42a	9-12	Wolv	5af	53	124
43a	6-11	Wolv	6af	[50]	153
48a	3-15	Sout	6af	[50]	172
31a	13-16	Sout	5af	50	183
32a	7-8	Wolv	5af	50	274
43a	4-9	Ling	5ap	48	435
54a	3-8	Wolv	5af	[47]	619
19a	11-12	Sout	5af	47	853
38	11-14	Ling	5g/f	50	2585
28a	11-15	Sout	5af	[47]	2803
14	16-16	Wind	5fm	47	3640
0	10-10	Wind	6g/f	[39]	3977 bl
26	15-15	Sali	5gd	40	4335 bl

CATERHAM COMMON 5 b g £0

0	11-11	Sout	8af	30	457
8a	6-14	Sout	7af	[30]	573
12a	8-16	Sout	8af	[30]	719
7a	10-13	Wolv	8.5af	[30]	826 bl
30a	5-12	Sout	7af	[30]	909 bl

CATHERINE HOWARD 3 b f £1196

68	4-11	Ripo	8gd	74	1176
62	9-18	Thir	8g/f	74	1769
73	4-14	Nott	8.2g/f	71	2153
59	5-6	Beve	8.5gd	[71]	2514

CATHERINE WHEEL 3 b f £14621

74	2-14	Thir	6g/s		1216
70	1-8	**DONC**	5g/f		2075*
79	1-8	**NEWB**	6fm	68	2648*
76a	1-11	**LING**	6ap	73	3198*

CATS WHISKERS 5 b g £5869

73	7-10	Hayd	10.5sft	[84]	1104
81	3-17	Thir	8g/s	81	1475
81	4-13	Donc	8gd	[81]	2753
43	15-15	Ches	10.3g/f	80	3099
82	2-12	Redc	8gd	79	4246
77	7-14	Ripo	10gd	79	4305
73	5-17	Ayr	9.1g/s	[79]	4620

CATSTAR 3 b f £92282

110a	1-8	**NAD**	8af		599* t
72	5-6	Sand	7.1g/f	[107]	2190 T
94	5-11	Warw	7.1fm	[107]	2574 t

CATTIVA GENEROSA 3 b f £10282

103	2-7	Chan	9g/s	2814

CATWALK CLERIC 2 b c £20765

80	4-9	Wind	5g/s		1256
83	1-7	**CHES**	5.1g/s		1571*
88	2-8	Capa	5.5gd		2303
55	13-13	Asco	6g/f		2467
87	4-13	Warw	6.1gd	88	4273
87	4-11	Ayr	8sft	86	4688
74	8-14	Ayr	6sft	85	5035

CAUSE CELEBRE 3 gr f £9432

79	1-16	**BATH**	10.2g/f	[78]	1790*
59	10-13	Hayd	11.9gd	78	2238
79	1-6	**WARW**	10.9fm	76	2780*
70	6-12	Newb	10gd	80	3255
72	13-15	Newb	11g/f	78	4643
51	8-11	Redc	10fm	77	4931

CAUSEWAY GIRL 2 br f £0

46	17-23	Newm	7g/f	4885
14	17-19	Newm	7g/s	5279

CAUSTIC WIT 5 b g £43013

48a	3-13	Wolv	6af	[52]	30
15a	13-16	Sout	6af	52	94
59a	1-13	**WOLV**	6af	50	384*
0	13-13	Wolv	6af	56	1221

68	1-11	FOLK	6sft	56		1578+ P
72	1-12	LEIC	6fm	60		2111* p
82	1-12	SALI	6fm	66		2289* p
90	1-17	WIND	6g/f	72		2451* p
89	2-16	Wind	6fm	83		2758 p
86	2-11	Newb	6g/f	83		2878 p
78	9-16	Newb	6g/f	86		3269 p
45	12-16	Wind	6gd	85		3827 p
86	4-6	Sand	5g/s	85		4098 p
75	6-11	Hayd	6g/f	[85]		4350 p
85	6-19	Sali	6gd	84		4855 p

CAVA BIEN 2 b c £2535

54	7-11	Thir	7fm		2462
63	3-7	Muss	7.1g/f		2810
72	3-8	Muss	7.1g/f		3559
62	7-13	York	7.9gd	[70]	4325
76	5-16	Nott	10g/f	70	4848
73	1-14	**YARM**	8g/s	[70]	5118*

CAVALARRA 2 b c £0

53	8-11	Hayd	5g/s	4349
63	5-15	Nott	6.1g/s	4644

CAVAN GAEL 2 b c £0

53	9-15	Newm	8gd	4883
75	6-13	Donc	7hvy	5199
69	8-21	Donc	6sft	5368

CAVARADOSSI 2 gr c £0

0	P-20	Wind	6fm	2970
0	15-17	Wind	6g/f	3975

CAVE OF THE GIANT 2 b c £0

78	5-8	Sand	8.1gd	4608
49	9-14	Leic	8gd	5059

CAVERAL 3 ch f £13040

72	8-11	Asco	8sft		1419
66	7-7	Good	7g/f	[88]	1811
101	1-5	**WIND**	6g/f	[88]	1957*
40	10-11	Hayd	6gd	[85]	2240
96	3-10	Asco	6gd	95	3773
87	10-14	Sali	7gd	95	4331
97	6-15	Donc	7fm	[95]	4479
66	11-12	Asco	7g/f	[94]	4811

CAVORTING 2 ch c £367

86	4-8	Newm	5g/f	1190
43	7-11	Catt	5gd	4962

CAYENNE GER 2 ch f £0

40	5-7	Folk	5gd	3907
60	5-11	Thir	7fm	4375

CAYMAN BREEZE 3 b g £1612

66a	3-15	Ling	7ap	65	151
51a	12-16	Ling	7ap	65	181
52a	13-16	Ling	7ap	65	270
53a	12-16	Ling	7ap	65	323
46a	5-7	Sout	7af	[62]	589
43a	4-14	Ling	6ap	[62]	652 VIS
56a	1-15	**LING**	7af	[59]	708*
51	8-14	Redc	7g/f	[60]	2102
57	5-13	Bath	5.7g/f	[57]	3844
34	9-18	Chep	8.1gd	[57]	4485
48	10-13	Bath	5.7gd	57	4548
57	4-17	Leic	7gd	55	5056
13a	12-12	Wolv	7.1ap	[51]	5358

CAYMAN CALYPSO 3 ro g £1959

47	9-13	Newm	8g/f		1935
67	8-12	Newb	7.1g/f		2352
66	6-14	Warw	7.1g/f		2907
55	7-11	Ling	10gd	[65]	3201
59	6-12	Newm	8fm	65	3410
63	2-10	Hayd	8.1gd	[62]	3739
60	2-16	Beve	8.5g/s	[62]	3850
19	12-12	Ripo	10gd	64	4282
49	12-17	Beve	8.5g/f	64	4721
32	17-17	Nott	8.2gd	64	4862
28	14-18	Leic	10gd	[58]	5042

CAYMAN KING 2 b g £0

2	14-14	Newc	6fm	4865

CAYMAN MISCHIEF 4 b f £0

0	7-8	Wolv	9.4af	299
0	14-14	Newc	6g/s	2730

32	6-10	Carl	5.9fm	[25]	3545
26	8-16	Catt	5sft	[27]	3932

CAYMAN SUNRISE 3 gr f £0

58a	6-13	Ling	10ap	[65]	148
43a	6-15	Ling	7ap	[61]	263
51a	8-12	Wolv	9.4af	58	427

CAYMANS GIFT 4 ch g £828

71	4-9	Hami	12.1gd		1507
60	5-7	Hami	9.2gd		1747
49	7-7	Muss	8fm		2081
60	3-7	Ayr	13.1g/s	60	2546
34	10-10	Muss	12g/f	58	2813

CAYUSE 2 b f £0

10	18-18	Newm	7gd	3927
6	18-19	Newm	7g/s	5279

CAZENOVE 3 b g £269

57	4-11	Folk	7g/s		3048
60	6-9	Newm	7g/f		3282
50	7-10	Chep	7.1gd		3732
9	13-14	Yarm	7gd	92	3995 P

CAZISA STAR 3 ch f £0

51	11-12	Sand	10gd	62	2366
45	8-9	Yarm	10.1fm	60	2866
33	9-14	Folk	12gd	55	3383

CD EUROPE 6 ch g £13128

87	8-19	Thir	6g/f	92	1767
56	25-29	Asco	6fm	92	2581 p
68	17-18	Newc	6g/s	91	2770 p
84	10-15	York	7gd	89	3117 BL
86	6-11	Hami	6fm	89	3248 bl
87	10-28	Good	6fm	89	3622 p
71	10-19	Ripo	6gd	87	3937 p
90	2-9	Good	6g/f	85	4537 p
93	2-26	Ayr	6g/s	85	4652 p

CD FLYER 7 ch g £25792

83	5-22	Donc	6gd	83	921
89	2-15	Pont	6hvy	83	1251
71	19-30	Newm	6g/f	85	1481
73	7-14	York	6g/s	85	1703
80	4-7	Hayd	6g/s	85	2187
90	1-17	**REDC**	6gd	83	2561*
80	13-18	Newc	6g/s	85	2770
92	4-15	York	7gd	87	3117
88	3-8	Pont	6gd	87	3461
85	5-19	Ripo	6gd	87	3937
86	6-12	Good	6sft	86	4184
60	18-26	Ayr	6gd	86	4652
89	2-18	York	7gd	84	5000
64	12-16	Redc	6sft	84	5304
58	14-20	Donc	7sft	84	5367

CEASAR 2 b g £7857

28a	12-14	Sout	8af	[58]	88
40a	4-10	Sout	7af	52	203
53a	2-9	Sout	8af	47	486
57a	1-8	**SOUT**	11af	51	614* P
0	10-10	Sout	12af	55	796 p
60	1-8	**PONT**	12hvy	[55]	1250* p
58	3-13	Beve	12.1g/f	55	1836
1	9-9	Yarm	14.1g/f	59	2345 p

CEDAR MASTER 7 b g £0

52	10-11	Sand	14g/f	66	2391 bl t
64	7-11	Ling	16gd	65	3200 bl t

CEDRIC COVERWELL 4 ch g £0

35a	4-10	Ling	6ap		973
14	17-17	Kemp	7gd		1136
46	13-17	Sali	6g/s		1497
36	11-15	Nott	5.1g/f	[51]	2152
24	12-12	Brig	5.3g/f	49	2645
7	16-20	Nott	6.1gd	45	2928
41	5-6	Ling	5gd	[45]	3023
19	9-15	Ling	6fm	41	3790 BL

CEFIRA 3 b f £4329

58	3-10	Pont	6hvy		1070
61	8-10	Newm	6g/f		1191
67	1-6	**AYR**	6fm	[67]	1908*
64	7-20	Nott	6.1g/s	67	4646
41	17-20	Wind	6g/s	65	4946

CEIRIOG VALLEY 2 b f £7280
70	8-13	Good	7fm		3554
89	1-14	CHES	7sft		4102*
76	11-11	Hayd	8.1fm	85	4387

CELADON 2 b c £1244
| 4a | 13-13 | Wolv | 6af | [73] | 126 |
| 58a | 2-9 | Ling | 5ap | [66] | 621 |

CELEBRE CITATION 3 ch c £0
47	12-19	Yarm	8g/f		1130
65	5-9	Wind	10fm		3642 T
51	12-17	Newm	8gd		4228 t
3	18-20	Hayd	11.9g/s	60	4771 t

CELESTIAL ARC 2 b c £848
77	3-9	Sali	7gd		2696
60	11-16	Sali	7g/s		3111
67	7-8	Sali	6gd		3451
65	12-17	Donc	8fm	72	4480
70	7-16	Nott	10g/f	68	4848

CELLARMASTER 3 ch g £6396
74	3-16	Wind	11.6g/s	72	2621
81	1-16	NOTT	10gd	72	3108*
80	4-8	Newm	10g/f	[79]	3945
83	3-15	Newb	11g/f	79	4643
69	8-19	Donc	10.3sft	79	5201

CELLINO 3 b f £0
12a	12-12	Sout	5af	54	853
45	4-9	Thir	5g/f	47	2219
32	10-14	Thir	5g/f	45	3417
33	7-20	Thir	6g/f	45	3575
23	10-19	Chep	6.1sft	41	4054
25	10-15	Carl	7.9fm	[40]	4507
20	9-20	Yarm	7g/s	[35]	5120

CELLO 3 gr c £18783
81	2-12	Warw	7.1gd	[78]	1125
86	1-8	EPSO	8.5hvy	[78]	1297*
69	6-15	Ches	7.6gd	82	1583
76	9-17	Epso	7g/f	82	2212
41	25-27	Asco	8g/f	80	2521
79	4-9	Sand	9g/s	[78]	3892 T
80	2-5	Good	9sft	78	4185 t
81	3-17	Asco	8g/f	78	4777 t
89	1-13	BATH	8sft	78	5172* t

CELTIC BLAZE 5 b m £860
58	3-9	Beve	16.2g/s	56	3181 t p
24	8-10	Thir	16fm	56	3611 t p
38	7-9	Ripo	16gd	54	4308 t p
52	5-7	Newc	16.1g/f	54	4405 t p

CELTIC CARISMA 2 b f £0
| 23 | 11-14 | Redc | 6g/s | | 5106 |
| 51 | 10-14 | Redc | 7sft | | 5301 |

CELTIC HEROINE 2 ch f £58679
73a	4-13	Ling	7ap	74	15
78a	1-10	SOUT	8af	72	189*
81	2-13	Kemp	9gd	78	1141
90	1-15	HAMI	8.3g/s	81	1602*
95	2-4	Ayr	8g/f	[89]	2026
103	1-19	ASCO	8g/f	89	2491*
104	2-6	Hami	8.3gd	[89]	2710
93	5-11	Newm	10g/f	97	3029
108	2-7	Asco	8g/f	[97]	3389

CELTIC MILL 6 b g £58048
91a	1-13	WOLV	6af	85	482+
88a	4-13	Wolv	6af	89	618
75	15-30	Newm	6g/f	85	1481
97	1-19	THIR	6g/f	84	1767*
109	1-9	WIND	6g/f	[91]	1958*
82	9-11	Newc	6g/s	[107]	2769
104	7-13	Good	5fm	[107]	3551
95	6-8	Newm	6gd	[106]	4226
109	1-9	DONC	5fm	[104]	4481* P
100	8-11	Newb	5.2g/f	[107]	4678 p
106	4-12	Asco	6g/f	[104]	4799 p

CELTIC PROMISE 2 b f £0
45a	14-14	Ling	7ap		4971
55	6-10	Nott	10hvy		5188
72	5-14	Yarm	10.1g/s		5352

CELTIC ROMANCE 5 b m £268

0	14-16	Newc	8hvy	63	1036
45	8-13	Redc	7sft	[59]	1142
24	8-14	Hayd	8.1g/s	55	1348
49	5-15	Redc	7sft	50	1660
36	8-11	Redc	8fm	49	2296
35	6-9	Ayr	7.2gd	49	2508 P
39	7-16	Beve	7.5gd	46	2891
34	4-11	Catt	12g/f	[44]	3190

CELTIC SOLITUDE 2 b f £0
47a	12-14	Sout	7af		98
10	12-12	Ripo	9g/f		1783
10	13-14	Redc	14.1g/f	46	2123

CELTIC SPA 2 gr f £19441
69	7-15	Wind	5gd		1380
84	1-4	NOTT	5.1sft		1608*
82	7-8	Sand	5g/f		2094
92	5-15	Asco	5g/f		2472
82	3-6	Wind	5fm		2786
67	13-24	Newb	5.2g/f		3266
88	4-16	Curr	6g/f		4153
82	7-15	Hayd	6sft	83	4765
52	9-20	Newb	6hvy	83	5225

CELTIC STAR 6 b g £0
47	11-11	Warw	12.6fm	63	2601 p
55	6-7	Bath	10.2g/f	60	2979
33	15-17	Wind	10fm	58	3477 BL

CELTIC TANNER 5 b g £0
| 50a | 11-13 | Wolv | 9.5ap | | 5290 |

CELTIC THATCHER 6 b g £746
| 57a | 2-13 | Wolv | 8.5af | | 2052 vis |

CELTIC THUNDER 3 b g £6026
82	2-6	Hami	5gd	[84]	1387
74	9-14	Thir	5g/f	84	1766
87	5-11	Redc	5g/f	84	2121
77	8-16	Leic	5g/f	83	2400
88	2-8	Kemp	6g/s	[82]	2677
70	7-15	Hayd	6gd	84	2950
78	4-10	Kemp	6gd	[84]	3188
82	4-8	Redc	6g/f	83	3808
56	18-19	Kemp	6fm	83	4394
82	5-15	Sand	5gd	82	4604
16	16-18	Pont	5g/s	82	5149

CELTIC VISION 8 b g £450
86	6-6	Nott	14.1fm		1005 t
37	6-8	Newc	12.4hvy		1038 t
77	10-10	Warw	7.1gd		1126
45	14-17	Ripo	16g/s	60	1361 t
45	4-10	Muss	16gd	50	1551 t
17a	6-9	Wolv	14.8af	50	1654 t
42	5-5	Warw	10.9fm	[45]	2602 t p

CELTIQUE 2 b f £4186
80	2-10	Newm	7gd		4191
76	3-13	Leic	8g/f		4450
76a	2-14	Ling	7ap		5258

CEMGRAFT 3 b f £0
68	5-14	Ling	11.5gd		3335
0	9-12	Newm	12g/f		3783
48	6-10	Sali	8sft		4578
46a	16-16	Ling	12ap	65	4973

CENTAURUS 2 gr c £4999
| 94 | 1-19 | NEWM | 7g/s | | 5285* |

CENTIFOLIA 2 gr f £76268
| 114 | 1-9 | MAIS | 6sft | | 5312* |

CEREBUS 2 b f £3563
69	6-10	Newm	6g/f		3064
64	4-12	Thir	6g/f		3411
76	2-14	Leic	6g/f		3517
77	3-20	Redc	7fm	72	4337
73	7-14	Donc	7fm	73	4535
74	6-13	Leic	6gd	74	4697
59	14-16	Newm	7g/f	74	4913

CERTA CITO 3 b f £0
35a	9-12	Sout	6af	62	85
25	10-19	Newc	6sft	64	967
17	13-19	Redc	6sft	61	1145
56	5-16	Redc	6g/f	56	1824

1	13-13	Donc	6gd	56	2232
43	10-18	Hayd	5gd	55	2951
55	4-19	Ling	5g/f	53	4739 BL
47	7-17	Leic	7gd	53	5056

CERTAIN JUSTICE 5 gr g £427
80a	4-13	Wolv	8.5af	85	44
78a	10-15	Ling	7ap	85	81
77	8-17	Sand	8.1g/s	82	1351
64	6-10	Warw	7.1sft	[80]	1525
71	5-7	Chep	8.1gd	[77]	2116
62a	10-12	Ling	8ap	[75]	2840 P
68	5-9	Epso	7gd	[70]	3215
62a	7-14	Sout	8af	[70]	3392

CERTIFIABLE 3 b g £8353
21a	4-9	Wolv	9.4af		665
75a	1-12	LING	8ap		734*
76a	1-12	LING	8ap	[68]	934*
71	5-8	Sand	8.1g/s	74	1315
27	12-14	York	7.9g/s	73	1707
58	5-6	Donc	10.3g/f	[70]	2426
55a	11-12	Ling	8ap	[74]	2840
60a	7-11	Wolv	7.1ap	[70]	5357

CERULEAN ROSE 5 ch m £4540
66	4-12	Ling	5g/s	68	1615
65	9-18	Good	5g/f	68	1867
73	2-10	Donc	5g/f	67	2429
24	8-8	Newb	6fm	67	2648
69	3-15	Chep	5.1gd	68	3403
59	15-22	Good	5fm	68	3537
68	2-11	Nott	5.1gd	68	4038
70	4-12	Newm	5gd	68	4197
24	20-20	Wind	6g/s	69	4946
52	13-19	York	5gd	69	4989

CESAR MANRIQUE 2 ch c £4555
56	9-14	Wind	5gd		4121
78	5-9	Sand	5gd		4497
79	4-5	Pont	5g/f		4625
82	1-12	BATH	5sft	[75]	5169*

CESARE 3 b c £5316
73	2-8	Warw	8.1sft		1086
83	1-11	BEVE	8.5sft		1304*
68	11-20	York	8.9gd	80	4999

CEYLON ROUND 3 b f £0
36	7-9	Brig	8gd		2953
57	7-17	Wind	8.3fm		3480
52	6-9	Wind	10fm		3642
39a	10-13	Wolv	8.6ap	55	5005
1a	12-12	Wolv	7.1ap	[50]	5229

CEZZARO 6 ch g £1887
27a	5-8	Sout	8af	[35]	1200
10a	6-10	Sout	8af	[35]	1406
17	11-13	Beve	12.1g/f	[45]	1945
43	2-8	Redc	10gd	[40]	2548
37	2-6	Beve	12.1gd	[40]	2653
30	12-15	Thir	8g/s	[40]	2688
26	15-20	Catt	12g/f	39	3354
12a	9-14	Sout	12af	30	3486 T
41	5-14	Catt	12g/f	[36]	3668
6	9-13	Ayr	8sft	[40]	5275 p

CHABIBI 4 br f £602
| 55a | 4-13 | Sout | 8af | [40] | 188 |
| 51a | 2-13 | Sout | 8af | 40 | 221 |

CHAIN OF HOPE 3 ch g £0
25	16-19	Chep	6.1sft	59	4054
37	10-11	Epso	6gd	[54]	4294
40	7-11	Wind	8.3g/f	[49]	5052

CHAIRMAN BOBBY 6 ch g £3589
69	5-16	Muss	5g/f	70	1120
66	7-20	Thir	5g/s	70	1476
38	19-20	Thir	6gd	69	1638
74	3-8	Hami	5gd	[69]	1749
71	2-9	Ripo	5gd	[70]	2007
15	19-20	York	6g/f	70	2059
73	2-13	Hami	5g/f	70	2320
68	5-11	Hami	5g/f	70	2477
68	8-17	Catt	5g/f	72	2846
61	11-17	Pont	6g/f	72	2990
49	9-13	Catt	5g/f	69	3350

41	17-19	Beve	5g/s	67	4240
60	10-18	Redc	6fm	67	4339
31a	8-12	Wolv	6ap	64	4984
48a	11-14	Ling	7ap	[60]	5263

CHAIRMAN RICK 2 b c £258

69	7-10	Folk	7g/s		3046
58a	6-7	Ling	6ap		3196
64	4-6	Yarm	5.2gd		3361
22	7-7	Kemp	6g/f	66	3686 VIS
55	7-19	Carl	5.9g/f	65	4344

CHAKA ZULU 6 b g £0

26a	4-10	Wolv	14.8af	53	34

CHAKRA 10 gr g £206

10a	6-6	Ling	6ap	[30]	1184
39	5-10	Bath	10.2gd	[40]	1402
31	3-8	Brig	8gd	[40]	1548
0	8-8	Wolv	7af	[30]	1676
16	10-11	Bath	10.2fm	40	1899

CHALISON 2 b c £1788

87	2-9	Wind	5g/s		1256
93	3-7	Good	6g/f		1848
90	5-9	Asco	7gd		3126

CHAMBRAY 3 b f £0

53	8-11	Bath	8g/s		1101
59	8-17	Chep	8.1gd		2117
55	5-8	Wind	11.6g/f	58	2796

CHAMPAGNE BRANDY 2 ch f £0

41	13-13	Donc	5gd		954
36	13-18	Chep	6.1gd		2194
44	12-15	Wind	6g/f		2263

CHAMPAGNE CRACKER 3 ch f £4307

5	8-8	Redc	6sft	[65]	1659
58	3-6	Ayr	6fm	[63]	1908
69	1-10	HAYD	5g/s	60	2227*
54	5-12	Ayr	5g/s	66	2566
56	9-14	Catt	6g/f	66	3018
57	9-15	Muss	5g/s	65	3561
26	6-7	Ayr	6hvy	64	4087
0	25-26	Ayr	5g/s	62	4618

CHAMPAGNE IN PARIS 2 gr f £0

18	11-11	Warw	5g/s		1123

CHAMPAGNE LUJAIN 2 b g £0

41	12-14	Newc	6fm		4865
58	5-9	Catt	7sft		5131
50	12-14	Redc	7sft		5301

CHAMPAGNE RIDER 7 b g £1716

37a	8-16	Sout	7af	[42]	66 vis
31a	9-14	Sout	8af	42	93 vis
37a	7-15	Sout	6af	[36]	167 e
38a	3-9	Sout	7af	[36]	303 e
33a	5-13	Sout	7af	[40]	356 e
45a	1-16	SOUT	6af	[40]	447* e

CHAMPAGNE ROSSINI 2 b g £0

51	9-11	Wind	5gd		3160
57	5-10	Yarm	8g/f		3713
57a	6-14	Sout	6af		4127
24	12-16	Yarm	8g/s	60	4632

CHAMPAGNE SHADOW 3 b c £4211

54a	8-11	Ling	8ap		322
69a	4-13	Ling	10ap		601
19a	12-14	Ling	10ap		759 BL
69a	2-6	Ling	12ap	65	915 bl
59	8-10	Wind	11.6gd	66	1382 bl
74a	2-15	Ling	12ap	[64]	2393 bl
68a	3-14	Ling	10ap	[69]	2740 bl
72a	2-10	Ling	12ap	[69]	4314 bl
0	9-9	Good	16gd	65	4875 bl
72a	7-16	Ling	12ap	70	5261 bl

CHAMPAIN SANDS 5 b g £2386

50a	3-13	Wolv	9.4af	48	1223
58	4-14	Nott	10g/s	57	1776
59	2-7	Ayr	10g/f	57	2030
47	5-8	Hami	9.2gd	57	2179
13	7-7	Ayr	10gd	57	2507
28	9-9	Ripo	10g/s	55	3260
41	9-14	York	10.4g/f	53	4402

53	6-15	Beve	8.5g/f	53	4598

CHAMPION LION 5 b g £1750

25	15-22	Donc	12gd	77	918
66	10-13	Hayd	14sft	75	1109
72	5-20	Epso	12hvy	70	1295
64	7-19	Newm	12g/f	69	1484
71	6-12	Ches	12.3gd	69	1599
69	3-14	Nott	10g/s	66	1776
70	3-18	Ayr	10.9sft	67	4623
70	5-15	Nott	10g/f	67	4849
62	8-19	Bath	11.7gd	67	5024

CHANCE FOR ROMANCE 3 ch f £1726

84	2-10	Leic	6gd	[83]	2137
71	6-8	Kemp	6g/s	[83]	2677
72	5-7	Wind	6fm	[82]	3293
48	7-7	Brig	6fm	80	3693 VIS
37	10-13	Good	6gd	79	3952

CHANCELLOR 6 ch h £29975

90	9-12	Kemp	10gd	[110]	1139
113	1-11	SAND	10g/s	[110]	1350*
110	8-8	Long	10.5hv	[110]	1558
52	9-9	Sand	10g/s	[112]	2128
71	12-12	Sand	10g/s	[110]	2916
105	6-6	Hayd	10.5fm	[110]	3793

CHANDELIER 4 ch g £4531

40a	5-11	Wolv	7af	[58]	440
56a	3-12	Ling	8ap	[54]	571 BL
54a	6-11	Ling	8ap	54	732 bl
42a	7-10	Ling	8ap	54	769 bl
50a	3-4	Wolv	7af	[51]	1378
49a	2-8	Wolv	7af	[48]	1656 p
0	15-16	Bath	8fm	[45]	2032 p
56	1-17	CHEP	8.1g/s	42	3087*
45	6-17	Newb	7g/f	48	3257
30	10-14	Chep	8.1gd	51	3733
33	8-12	Chep	8.1g/s	51	3898
44	6-15	Chep	8.1g/s	49	4300
0	R-14	Bath	9g/f	49	4411
68a	3-12	Ling	8ap	[50]	4974
38	10-17	Leic	7gd	47	5056

CHANFRON 3 ch g £0

61	7-15	Leic	11.8gd	65	2134
59	5-16	Wind	11.6g/s	60	2621
50	5-7	Warw	16.2gd	58	3057
50	9-19	Chep	12.1gd	55	3727
26a	14-16	Ling	12ap	[52]	4899

CHANGARI 3 b f £390

70	5-6	Sand	5g/f	[90]	2390

CHANTACO 2 b c £4557

69	5-18	Leic	7g/f		3342
74	2-7	Brig	7fm		3691
78	1-11	THIR	7fm		4375*

CHANTELLE 4 b f £0

51	7-15	Sali	5gd	56	4335
42	12-19	Ling	5g/f	53	4739 BL
43	4-13	Warw	7.1g/s	[50]	4994
34a	7-12	Wolv	7.1ap	[48]	5229

CHANTELLES DREAM 2 ch f £0

14a	10-10	Ling	5ap		3743
12	6-7	Folk	5gd		3907

CHANTELOUP 3 ch f £5347

70	2-11	Beve	8.5sft		1304
90	4-6	York	10.4sft		1666
71	4-6	Pont	10g/f		2793
74	3-12	Hayd	10.5gd	[89]	3740
82	5-8	Hayd	11.9g/f	80	4353
51a	10-14	Ling	13ap	[80]	4892

CHANTERELLE 3 ch f £441

87	6-8	Newm	6g/f	87	3235
78	6-8	Newm	7gd	86	3928
66	17-25	Newb	7gd	84	4683

CHANTEUSE 3 b f £0

15a	8-9	Sout	8af	54	163
0	10-10	Wolv	6af	49	282
15a	6-6	Wolv	6af	[49]	313 BL
12a	11-12	Wolv	7af	[40]	528 bl

CHANTILLY BEAUTY 2 b f £0

76	14-17	Asco	6g/f		2553 P

CHANTILLY GOLD 5 ch m £0

0	10-10	Wolv	7af	[30]	298 p
25a	5-6	Wolv	6af	[30]	313 p
0	10-11	Sout	8af	[30]	372 BL

CHANTILLY SUNSET 3 b f £0

0	8-9	Thir	6fm		4380
0	15-15	Yarm	7g/s		4587

CHANTRESS 4 b f £4400

67	8-8	Newm	9fm	[92]	1491
95	3-7	Hayd	11.9g/f	[92]	1921 P
89	7-8	Hayd	11.9gd	[92]	2946

CHANTRY FALLS 4 br g £0

33a	8-12	Wolv	7af	49	956
20a	6-8	Wolv	9.4af	48	1657
29	11-19	Redc	6af	48	2125
33	12-17	Ling	7gd	45	2397 BL

CHAPEL ROYALE 7 gr g £0

29a	6-9	Wolv	9.4af	[47]	480 t
11a	5-5	Wolv	12af	[45]	616 t P

CHAPELCO 3 b g £0

59	6-7	Newm	10g/f		2534
28	7-7	Newb	12g/f		2879
0	P-7	Chep	12.1g/s		3899

CHAPLIN 3 b c £2059

83	2-8	Newm	12g/s		1153
56	8-13	Hayd	11.9g/s		2230
68	4-8	Brig	11.9sft	[84]	5092 P

CHAPPEL CRESENT 4 ch c £15651

59a	8-10	Wolv	8.5af		511
44a	12-13	Wolv	6af	90	618
80	8-22	Donc	6gd	90	921
80	5-13	Newc	7hvy	87	1035
90	2-20	Newm	7g/s	85	1151
84	5-17	Thir	8g/s	87	1475
98	1-18	CHES	7.6gd	87	1598*
77	5-14	York	6g/s	90	1703
29	17-18	Newc	7sft	94	2684
32	19-19	York	6gd	94	4005
71	10-10	Ayr	8sft	93	4685

CHAPTER 2 ch c £4146

80	2-12	Sand	7.1g/f		2388
81	2-9	Sali	7gd		2696
70	7-11	Sand	8.1g/s		3890
78	3-12	Bath	8gd	77	4410
79	5-11	Good	8gd	[77]	4746

CHAPTER HOUSE 5 b g £0

67a	6-15	Sout	8af	70	2725 bl
60	7-10	Warw	12.6g/f	70	2912 bl
39	15-17	Catt	12sft	68	3929
38	7-8	Hayd	10.5g/f	65	4354

CHARA 2 ch f £5668

67a	4-12	Ling	10ap		120
50a	5-14	Sout	8af	[66]	226
69	3-10	Folk	9.7sft	[64]	977
68	1-10	BEVE	12.1g/s	64	1165*
60	7-10	Wind	11.6gd	66	1382
73	5-5	Ling	11.5sft	[66]	1619
62	5-13	Nott	10g/f	65	3419
63	5-17	Newm	12g/f	65	3618
16	9-9	Sand	14g/s	64	3893
33	12-12	Beve	12.1g/f	62	4601
44a	8-12	Wolv	12.2ap	59	5339

CHARING CROSS 3 ch c £0

37a	13-15	Ling	12ap		4111
53a	7-9	Ling	12ap		4315
44	9-10	Sali	12sft		4579
35	6-10	Good	9.9gd		4877
15	12-12	Brig	11.9sft	54	5093 BL

CHARIOT 2 ch c £736

65a	2-10	Sout	8af	64	190
0	9-12	Sout	8af	[64]	848
9	18-18	Newm	8sft	64	5272

CHARLATAN 6 b g £0

| 5 | 16-19 | Redc | 6g/f | 30 | 2125 |

CHARLESTON 3 ch c £4197

74	2-11	Kemp	8hvy		1514
75	2-16	Bath	10.2g/f		1790
75	2-11	Chep	10.2gd		2196
71a	4-15	Ling	12ap	[73]	2393
33	11-17	Wind	11.6fm	[73]	2788 BL

CHARLIE BEAR 3 ch c £1950

47	10-19	Warw	10.9gd	69	1124
71	2-14	Newc	8gd	67	1872
67	8-14	Wind	8.3g/f	68	4832
72a	3-12	Wolv	7.1ap	68	5008

CHARLIE GEORGE 3 ch g £0

39	9-15	Ayr	8gd		2504
43	6-9	Hayd	10.5gd		2901
34	5-5	Hami	9.2g/s		3876

CHARLIE MASTERS 3 b g £425

42	13-15	Ling	7gd		4445
16	14-15	Wind	10g/f		4834
51a	9-11	Ling	8ap		4977
56a	2-12	Wolv	8.6ap		5230

CHARLIE PARKES 6 ch g £0

| 57 | 12-20 | Thir | 7ff | 77 | 1765 |
| 55 | 11-15 | Hayd | 5g/f | 73 | 1917 |

CHARLIE TANGO 3 b g £8939

73a	3-10	Ling	10ap	70	817
78	7-18	Leic	10g/s	71	1017
43	10-16	Beve	8.5sft	70	1628
66	11-13	Bath	10.2g/f	[67]	1791
74	3-5	Ayr	9.1g/f	[67]	2025
44	9-11	Sand	10g/s	65	2127
56	4-14	Sali	8fm	62	2423
69	1-11	REDC	9g/s	62	2565*
68	3-5	Brig	9.9fm	67	2837
58	4-8	Ayr	10gd	[68]	3151
69	3-6	Muss	9g/f	68	3529
66	5-7	Ayr	10.9g/f	68	3765
66	7-10	Nott	10gd	67	3990
59	9-20	York	7.9gd	66	4321
14	12-13	Bath	8gd	64	4546 BL
65	4-17	Beve	8.5g/f	64	4721
51a	8-12	Wolv	8.6ap	66	4923
68	2-8	Ayr	10sft	[63]	5034
62	4-18	Newm	8sft	60	5272 T

CHARLIEISMYDARLING 2 b g £0

52a	8-11	Ling	6ap		51
54a	5-13	Wolv	6af		126
51a	6-8	Sout	5af	65	169
31a	7-8	Sout	5af	[65]	197
41	4-14	Leic	6g/f	[55]	1963
43	8-18	Sali	7fm	51	2292
28	10-13	Bath	8fm	48	2667

CHARLIES PROFIT 3 ch f £0

| 2a | 13-14 | Ling | 10ap | | 367 |

CHARLIESLASTCHANCE 2 b f £0

| 0 | 19-19 | Kemp | 8g/f | | 4792 |
| 0 | 14-14 | Wind | 8.3g/f | | 5049 |

CHARLOTTE VALE 3 ch f £15264

64	6-14	York	7.9g/s	68	1707
67	5-17	Hayd	8.1gd	66	2243
68	2-7	Ayr	9.1gd	65	2509
73	1-8	THIR	12g/s	65	2691*
75	3-13	Redc	11g/s	68	2960
78	1-10	PONT	12gd	68	3240*
76	2-5	Carl	11.9g/f	73	3653
72	3-4	Hami	12.1g/s	73	3881
64	6-9	Ayr	13.1sft	74	5068

CHARLOTTEBUTTERFLY 4 b f £4132

46	11-16	Bath	5.7sft	61	1540
53	4-12	Leic	6fm	58	2111
53	9-14	Yarm	6g/f	56	2855
49	8-16	Kemp	7gd	55	3184
54	3-17	Wind	6gd	53	4126
32	15-16	Yarm	7gd	53	4616
54	4-11	Wind	6g/f	[52]	4836
57a	1-12	WOLV	7.1ap	[52]	5358*

CHARLOTTINE 3 b f £478

| 48 | 3-12 | Chep | 10.2hvy | 54 | 4708 P |

CHARMANTE FEMME 5 b m £0

| 35a | 6-9 | Ling | 13ap | 50 | 18 |
| 20a | 11-13 | Ling | 16ap | 46 | 137 |

CHARMATIC 3 br f £9759

58	5-8	Newc	8hvy		1039
64	2-14	Pont	8hvy	[60]	1253
66	2-18	Nott	8.2sft	60	1470
69	1-16	BEVE	8.5sft	62	1628*
66	5-14	Nott	8.2g/f	65	2153
69	4-12	Pont	10g/f	65	2277
65	5-18	Leic	10gd	65	2706
62	6-17	Beve	8.5g/f	65	4260
58	8-16	York	11.9gd	63	4990
68a	2-13	Wolv	9.5ap	62	5292
68a	2-13	Wolv	9.5ap	64	5361

CHARMED BY FIRE 3 b c £0

62	11-13	Kemp	10gd		3186
68	7-14	Newb	9fm		3631
70	5-5	Sand	10g/s		3894
17	11-11	Wind	10gd	[68]	4125 T

CHARMING ADMIRAL 11 b g £2115

| 10 | 6-13 | Pont | 18hvy | 50 | 1069 |
| 56 | 2-13 | Pont | 21.6hvy | 48 | 1252 bl |

CHARMING GROOM 5 gr h £35986

112	2-10	Chan	8g/s		2458
112	1-6	LONG	7g/s		2826*
95	7-7	Long	7sft		5070

CHARMO 3 gr c £15422

| 106 | 3-7 | Long | 9.3sft | | 1851 |
| 107 | 3-5 | Chan | 8g/f | | 2639 |

CHARNOCK BATES ONE 3 b f £15516

65	4-16	Beve	7.5g/s	64	1163
63	6-18	Nott	8.2sft	65	1470
58	8-13	Newc	8g/s	64	2773
75	1-9	BEVE	8.5sft	63	2940+
75	2-9	Donc	8g/s	70	3378
75	2-6	Donc	8g/f	70	3597
74	2-8	Ripo	10g/s	70	3938
74	3-7	Hayd	10.5sft	72	4781
70	6-14	Ayr	10sft	72	5037
56	12-19	Donc	10.3sft	72	5201

CHARNWOOD PRIDE 3 gr g £0

57	12-18	Wind	10g/f		1959 T
46	11-12	Sand	10g/f		2193 t
0	9-9	Pont	12g/f		2992 t

CHARNWOOD STREET 4 b g £0

20a	9-15	Sout	16af	42	67 e
5a	5-7	Sout	14af	[40]	357 vis
25a	5-12	Sout	14af	[35]	443 e

CHASE THE RAINBOW 2 gr f £831

37a	9-11	Wolv	7af	64	29
56a	2-15	Sout	7af	[59]	417
33a	6-11	Wolv	8.5af	56	1339
33	6-8	Hami	9.2gd	[62]	1505
34	12-14	Ayr	8g/f	[59]	1896
73	6-6	Leic	7gd	[55]	2136
45	11-18	Sali	7fm	55	2292
30	11-13	Bath	8fm	52	2667

CHASING THE DREAM 3 b f £6468

73a	1-11	LING	8ap		322*
84a	2-3	Ling	10ap		727
67	6-8	Sali	9.9g/s	74	1500
51	10-13	Good	9g/f	72	2024
67	3-7	Wind	8.3g/f	[69]	2264
64	4-8	Sali	8gd	65	2701

CHASM 2 b c £856

| 70 | 3-6 | Epso | 7g/f | | 4470 |
| 75 | 5-12 | Newc | 8fm | | 4866 |

CHATEAU ISTANA 2 ch c £70699

76	6-9	Wind	5g/s		1256
95	1-10	LEIC	5g/f		1826*
108	1-15	ASCO	5g/f		2472*
73	7-7	Newm	6g/f		3028
108	1-11	DONC	5fm	[98]	4533* T

| 101 | 9-9 | Newm | 6g/f | [98] | 4888 t |

CHATEAU NICOL 4 b g £43405

39a	11-11	Ling	8ap	58	12 bl
62a	1-16	LING	7ap	58	55* vis
75a	1-16	LING	7ap	[62]	123* vis
72a	7-16	Ling	7ap	74	144 vis
64a	7-12	Ling	8ap	[72]	234 bl
80a	1-14	LING	6ap	72	292* vis
80a	3-7	Ling	6ap	[77]	431 vis
66a	13-14	Ling	7ap	77	518 vis
83a	1-14	LING	7ap	77	604* vis
82a	4-8	Ling	7ap	[80]	879 bl
78	1-6	FOLK	7g/s	[68]	1079* vis
81	3-15	Pont	6hvy	76	1251 vis
79	3-10	Warw	7.1sft	[77]	1525 vis
81	3-19	Sali	7g/f	77	1723 vis
81	4-13	Kemp	7gd	78	2172 vis
88	1-12	KEMP	7g/s	78	2679* vis
80	5-11	Newb	8g/f	81	2878 vis
84	6-13	Asco	7gd	84	3068 vis
81	6-16	Newb	6g/f	83	3269 vis
79	7-25	Asco	7g/f	82	3443
89	1-24	NEWB	7g/f	81	4642*
85a	4-12	Wolv	7.1ap	83	5159
86	3-12	Newb	6sft	83	5196 bl
78	9-20	Newm	7g/s	83	5286 bl

CHATER FLAIR 7 b g £0

| 0 | 12-12 | Wolv | 12af | 50 | 484 |

CHATSHOW 3 br g £4570

57	10-15	Leic	6g/f		1829
18	15-17	Chep	8.1gd		2117
58	4-14	Donc	6g/f		2428
38	12-14	Yarm	6g/f	60	2855
54a	5-11	Sout	8af	[60]	3091
39	8-12	Brig	6g/f	55	3301
30	10-15	Ling	6fm	53	3790 T
22	12-16	Chep	7.1hvy	[50]	4707
39	3-15	Brig	6gd	[45]	4905
41	7-16	Warw	5g/s	[45]	4995
55	1-19	BATH	5.7sft	45	5176*
50a	2-13	Wolv	5.1ap	[45]	5231
55	2-18	Yarm	5g/s	52	5354

CHECKIT 4 br c £48804

115	6-11	Nad	9g/f	[113]	991
106	8-10	Sand	8.1g/s	[112]	1349
114	7-15	Newb	8g/f	[112]	1758
115	3-5	Long	9.3gd	[112]	2002
108	4-11	Epso	8.5fm	[112]	2252
109	8-16	Asco	8g/f	[112]	2470
113	3-6	Hopp	8gd	[112]	3166
114	4-7	Ayr	10g/f	[112]	3306
103	8-11	Good	8fm	[112]	3533
108	3-6	Hayd	10.5fm	[112]	3793
111	2-16	Bade	8sft	[112]	4424
109	2-5	Newb	9gd	[110]	4682
99	7-13	Newm	9g/f	[110]	4887

CHEEKY CHI 3 b f £4624

67a	4-15	Ling	7ap		875
67a	4-10	Ling	7ap		911
66a	3-12	Ling	6ap		1044
66	1-9	REDC	5sft	[66]	1146*
51a	4-8	Sout	6af		1441
56	13-15	Ches	5.1g/s	66	1572
60	7-10	Brig	5.3fm	66	1694
52	11-12	Wind	5g/f		1809
37	8-8	Brig	5.3g/f	64	1942
24	6-7	Brig	5.3sft	[60]	4169
32a	12-12	Ling	6ap	56	5241
38	13-18	Yarm	6g/s	56	5354

CHEESE N BISCUITS 4 b f £2432

64	11-14	Yarm	8g/f	82	1131
62	20-30	Newm	6g/f	79	1481
77	2-4	Ling	7.6g/s	[79]	1616
64	8-20	Asco	9g/f	76	1927
53	11-13	Kemp	7gd	75	2172 P
67a	11-13	Ling	7ap	80	3791 p
67	5-8	Newm	7gd	76	3928 p
61	4-8	Folk	7gd	[68]	4117 p
59a	12-14	Ling	7ap	78	4180 p
49	11-16	Sali	7sft	65	4582 p

21 25-26 Ayr 6g/s 68 4652 p
66a 7-14 Ling 7ap [75] 5080
6a 12-12 Ling 8ap 70 5238

CHEK OI 2 b c £0
48 8-11 Good 5gd 2020
57 9-13 Epso 7g/f 2870
56a 7-7 Ling 6ap 3196
58 6-8 Good 6ap 4540
0 P-12 Wolv 7.1ap [60] 5158 BL

CHELSEA ROSE 2 ch f £120801
96 3-8 Curr 7g/f 3843
109 1-12 CURR 7g/f 4432*

CHELSEAS DIAMOND 4 b f £0
39 5-6 Bath 11.7fm 2668 BL
45 13-14 Ling 11.5gd 3335 bl
23 9-11 Epso 7fm 3541 P

CHEMS LEGACY 4 b g £429
17 12-12 Ling 6g/f 2586
52 4-5 Sand 8.1g/f 3360
55 8-10 Ling 7gd 3446

CHERISHED NUMBER 4 b g £8562
58a 4-9 Wolv 8.5af 67 2
51 9-12 Pont 8hvy 81 1066
77 4-17 Thir 8g/s 79 1475
74 9-12 Hayd 8.1g/f 79 1883
77 6-13 Ripo 8g/f 79 2010 VIS
79 3-11 Hami 8.3g/f 77 2317 vis
78 3-7 Ayr 10gd 77 2507 vis
76 10-17 Carl 7.9gd 76 2672 vis
76 4-10 Nott 8.2gd [75] 3107 vis
70 4-9 Ayr 8g/f 74 3305 vis
55 7-9 Hami 9.2g/f 72 3593 vis
64 5-12 Leic 8fm 70 3813
74 3-17 Hami 9.2g/s 70 4008
63 7-10 Hami 8.3g/s 69 4136
72 4-8 York 8.9g/f [70] 4397 p
73 3-17 Ayr 9.1g/s [70] 4620 p
68 3-14 Hami 8.3g/s 70 4820 BL
71 4-17 Ayr 7.2sft 68 5063 bl

CHEROKEE 2 b f £36644
108 1-11 CURR 6g/f 4431*
98 5-8 Newm 7sft 5133

CHEROKEE BAY 4 b f £235
43a 4-10 Ling 10ap [51] 370
45a 3-11 Ling 8ap [45] 535 e
23a 12-12 Ling 8ap [45] 648 e
25a 12-14 Ling 10ap [45] 705 e

CHEROKEE NATION 3 br c £21236
56 4-16 Nott 10gd 54 1240
50a 4-7 Wolv 9.4af 54 1324 e
59 1-16 LING 6g/f 53 1985*
39 7-9 Folk 6g/f 57 2271
63 2-9 Wind 6gd 57 2619
65 1-14 YARM 6g/f 57 2855*
76 1-11 RIPO 6gd 64 2985*
53 10-14 Catt 6g/f 64 3018
70 3-11 Donc 6g/s 70 3379
56 6-7 Leic 6g/f [70] 3518
55a 9-13 Sout 6af 70 4091 e
42 15-15 Kemp 6g/f 70 4713
73a 2-13 Wolv 6ap 66 5114
62a 4-12 Wolv 6ap 69 5291

CHERRY MIX 3 gr c £333793
108 2-9 Long 11sft 1158
112 3-6 Long 12sft 1852
123 1-9 DEAU 12.5hvy 4312*
126 2-19 Long 12g/f 4956

CHERTSEY 3 ch f £936
64 3-6 Yarm 7g/f 2342
50 3-5 Brig 8g/f 2641
55 5-9 Warw 6.1g/f 2906
40 9-14 Yarm 8gd 62 3363
56 5-10 Brig 7fm 59 3672
51 6-14 Yarm 6gd 59 3870
38a 5-9 Sout 7af [56] 4131

CHERUBIM 3 ch f £5130
75 5-10 Newb 10gd 1209
74 5-11 Chep 8.1g/f [78] 2627

CHESNUT CRACKER 3 ch f £0
13a 12-16 Sout 7af [40] 66 T

CHESNUT RIPPLE 4 ch f £902
51a 2-10 Sout 8af [53] 143
43a 5-13 Sout 8af [53] 199
42a 4-7 Sout 8af [48] 334

CHESTALL 3 b c £538
66 4-8 Beve 12.1gd 2515
58 4-6 Catt 12g/f 4441
55 5-15 Leic 11.8gd 5060

CHESTMINSTER GIRL 2 ch f £0
0 14-14 Chep 8.1gd 4484
0 11-11 Wolv 7.1ap 5113 P
21 14-15 Nott 8.2hvy 5344 p

CHETAK 3 ch f £186
83a 6-11 Ling 8ap 86 80

CHEVERAK FOREST 3 ch g £401
55 10-16 Beve 7.5g/s 66 1163
51 12-13 Nott 10g/f 64 3419
30 9-9 Thir 8sft 62 3835
42 16-20 York 7.9gd 60 4321
19 13-14 Pont 8g/f [55] 4937
59 4-14 Redc 7g/s 55 5109 T

CHEVIN 5 ch m £4251
40 5-10 Muss 12g/f 42 2813
30 14-20 Catt 12g/f 42 3354
49 1-10 CATT 13.8g/f 41 3669*
42 7-13 Redc 14.1fm 46 4340
40 9-19 Thir 12g/f 46 4594
39 8-20 Kemp 12g/f [45] 4796

CHEVRONNE 3 b g £904
47a 10-12 Ling 12ap 70 56
16 17-19 Wind 10sft [70] 1650 BL
27 10-12 Sali 7fm [68] 2288 P
60 2-16 Chep 7.1gd [68] 2369
36 16-20 Kemp 9g/f 59 2857
39 16-20 Chep 7.1g/s 59 3088

CHIASSO 3 ch f £0
19a 12-13 Wolv 9.4af 57 38
3a 9-10 Sout 8af [52] 143

CHIC 4 ch f £136950
89 6-8 Good 8g/f [97] 1863
91 7-10 Asco 8g/f [97] 2487
105 3-12 Good 7fm [97] 3564
115 1-13 NEWB 8g/f [101] 3957+
120 1-7 GOOD 8g/s [101] 4232+
120 2-5 Newm 8g/f [117] 4915

CHICA 3 gr f £0
29a 11-15 Ling 7ap 45 295

CHICA ROCA 3 ch f £0
64 9-17 Newb 8g/f [80] 1762
50 16-17 Kemp 7gd 75 2174
50 6-10 Newb 6g/f [75] 2309
3 9-9 Ripo 6g/f [70] 2485 BL T
40a 10-12 Ling 8ap [60] 4320 t

CHICAGO BOND 3 b f £0
53 7-8 Thir 7sft 65 2693
24 11-12 Beve 9.9gd 65 2893
27 6-7 Ripo 9g/s [63] 3263
21 9-9 Redc 8g/f [60] 3806

CHICAGO NIGHTS 2 ch f £1045
52 4-5 Ripo 5g/s 1362
48 7-9 Muss 5fm 2083
50 10-12 Hami 6gd 2178
32a 5-11 Sout 6af 49 3393
53 2-9 Yarm 6sft 49 4146
35 14-20 Leic 7g/f 52 4451 P
39 11-18 Newc 6g/f 51 5013

CHICKADO 2 b f £1549
71a 3-10 Wolv 5af 68 69

67a 3-8 Wolv 6af 67 422
41 6-7 Sout 6g/s [65] 1050
57 7-14 Leic 6g/f 62 3213
53 6-15 Newb 6gd 60 3920
55a 2-13 Wolv 6ap [55] 5359

CHICKASAW TRAIL 5 ch m £1442
10a 10-14 Sout 8af 34 160
7a 9-12 Wolv 9.4af [30] 302 P
0 10-12 Wolv 9.4af [30] 782
8a 9-13 Wolv 8.5af [30] 826
12a 6-7 Wolv 9.4af [30] 862
28 5-10 Warw 8.1g/s [40] 1328
45 1-8 BRIG 8gd [40] 1548*
12 11-13 Kemp 10hvy [40] 1643
43 5-18 Nott 8.2gd [45] 1992
11 15-16 Chep 7.1gd [43] 2369
17 14-17 Warw 8.1fm 43 2440 VIS

CHICKEN SOUP 2 br c £964
70 6-14 Hayd 6gd 3735
78a 3-12 Ling 6ap 4178
74 7-11 Epso 7gd 4289
63 19-20 Ling 7g/f 75 4741
74 3-10 Catt 7sft [73] 5127

CHICKS BABE 2 br f £0
34a 8-12 Wolv 7.1ap 5158

CHICO GUAPO 4 b g £5707
63a 8-10 Ling 5ap 79 692
76a 5-10 Ling 5ap 77 755
44 16-20 Donc 5gd 77 927 p
71 8-13 Epso 5sft 75 1293 p
79 1-20 THIR 5g/s 73 1476*
54 17-20 York 5g/s 77 1683
68 5-20 Thir 5g/f 77 1765
63 9-15 Hayd 5g/f 76 1917
36 11-11 Ches 5.1gd 75 2286
23 17-17 Warw 5fm 73 2599 BL
62 12-17 Catt 5g/f 73 2846 bl
52 13-18 Beve 5g/f 72 3852
55 13-16 Muss 5g/f 69 4174 p
33 13-13 Ches 5.1g/f 67 4514 bl
47 12-16 Pont 5fm 64 4754

CHIEF DIPPER 2 b c £432
26 15-18 Newm 8fm 4722
49a 4-13 Wolv 6ap 4980
69a 4-13 Wolv 6ap 5182

CHIEF EXEC 2 b g £1584
52 13-23 Newm 6gd 5084
85a 2-10 Ling 7ap 5259

CHIEF SCOUT 2 br c £5846
71 7-12 Hayd 6sft 3272
81 4-18 Newm 7gd 3927
88 1-11 NEWM 7gd 4190*
83 8-9 Newm 7gd [83] 4881

CHIGORIN 3 b g £871
66 9-13 Kemp 8fm 2072
69 6-13 Sand 8.1gd 70 2365
66 7-13 Newc 8g/s 70 2773
56 8-12 Newm 8fm 68 3410
68 3-20 York 7.9gd 65 4321
64a 8-14 Ling 10ap 65 5083

CHILALI 2 b f £3275
61 5-9 Muss 5g/s 1458
26a 7-7 Wolv 5af 1652
58 3-9 Muss 5gd 2083
56 3-8 Ayr 5gd 2505
49 9-13 Beve 5gd 2889
60 3-9 Ches 5.1g/f 3097
55 6-8 Donc 5gd 63 3374
59 4-10 Thir 5fm [60] 3606
48 9-11 Nott 5.1gd 60 3987
57a 2-10 Sout 5af [60] 4129

CHILLIN OUT 2 ch c £0
37 16-17 Yarm 6g/s 5350

CHILLY CRACKER 2 ch f £11062
72 2-11 Warw 5gd 1123
52 6-7 Ches 5.1g/s 1571
71a 1-7 SOUT 5af 2498*
45 10-14 Leic 6g/f 72 3212

53 8-12 Hayd 5gd 71 3756
67 3-15 Ripo 5gd 65 4784
73 1-19 BATH 5gd 64 5021*
56 11-16 Nott 5.1hvy 70 5343

CHIMALI 3 b g £9410
64 1-9 BEVE 5sft 2945*
57 4-10 Hayd 5g/s 67 3135
71a 3-11 Ling 6ap 67 3333
77 1-20 LING 6g/f 67 4317* VIS
70 3-15 Kemp 6g/f 73 4713 vis

CHIMES AT MIDNIGHT 7 b h £0
46 24-29 Asco 20g/f 95 2471 bl
63 11-13 Asco 20g/f 2518 bl

CHIMES EIGHT 2 b f £0
39a 9-15 Sout 7af 184
40a 7-8 Wolv 7af 276
33a 8-11 Wolv 9.4af 438

CHIN DANCER 2 ch f £0
12 17-17 Ling 7g/f 2584
37 10-11 Warw 7.1gd 3053
40a 6-12 Sout 7af 3394 BL t
26 10-13 Sali 7g/f 3864 bl t

CHINALEA 2 b c £344
73 5-11 Bath 5.7gd 4543
69 5-16 Bath 5.7gd 4823
78 4-21 Donc 6sft 5368

CHINESE PUZZLE 2 b c £1482
77 6-16 Sali 7g/s 3111 T
66 6-11 Beve 7.5g/f 3500 t
67 9-16 Leic 7fm 3811 t
75 3-14 Thir 8fm 4376 t
78 3-10 Redc 9fm [71] 4558 t

CHINEUR 3 b c £23556
111 1-13 CHAN 5g/s 2638*
105 3-9 Long 5g/s 4435

CHINKARA 4 ch g £2870
69 19-27 Newb 8gd 92 1231
84 10-14 Sand 8.1g/f 92 2096
64 23-31 Asco 8g/f 92 2489
92 4-12 Kemp 9g/f 90 2860
85 10-15 Good 9.9g/f 90 3506
92 3-11 Good 9g/f 89 4525
51 24-32 Newm 9g/f 89 4916

CHIQITITA 3 b f £0
36a 11-12 Ling 7ap 61 545
32a 10-11 Ling 6ap 55 735
46 13-20 Nott 6.1gd 58 1239 BL
13 10-10 Folk 6sft 55 1576 bl
28a 9-13 Sout 8af 49 3094
39 7-15 Leic 7g/f [51] 3515
36 6-10 Leic 7fm [47] 3812
34 8-13 Folk 9.7g/f [45] 4372
37 5-15 Carl 7.9fm [40] 4507
33 10-18 Leic 10gd [40] 5042

CHIRACAHUA 2 ch g £0
17 16-16 Newb 7g/f 4677
41a 7-12 Ling 6ap 4896
23a 10-10 Ling 7ap 5259

CHIRU 3 b f £0
0 14-14 Ling 13ap 65 259

CHISEL 3 ch g £0
56 8-10 Beve 7.5g/f 1832
58 10-12 Leic 8fm 2106
51 6-11 Beve 7.5g/s 2325
38 8-12 Hami 9.2g/s 60 2832
48 10-13 Beve 9.9gd 57 3309
23 8-10 Redc 10g/f 55 3772
33 5-8 Hami 9.2g/s [50] 4133
10 11-12 Newc 8sft [50] 4284

CHISELLED 2 b c £4441
74 4-10 Hayd 5sft 1107
81 2-10 Muss 5g/s 1458
82 2-10 Leic 5g/f 1826
82 9-24 Newb 5.2g/f 3266
68 4-12 Thir 5g/s [85] 3832
81 2-12 Carl 5g/f [80] 4343 T

CHISPA 5 b m £2707
66a 2-12 Sout 6af 58 85
65a 1-16 SOUT 6af 60 166*
57a 10-16 Sout 5af 67 183
54a 8-11 Sout 6af 66 198

CHIVALRY 5 b g £0
77 18-24 Donc 8gd 95 951

CHIVITE 5 b g £0
40 9-15 Newb 13.3g/f 67 2311
59 9-19 Bath 11.7gd 67 5024

CHOCOLATE BOY 4 b g £4065
13a 12-12 Ling 8ap [48] 150
40a 7-12 Ling 10ap [43] 267
42a 5-12 Ling 8ap [45] 538 P
47a 2-12 Ling 8ap [45] 649 BL e
46a 4-14 Ling 10ap [45] 705 b|e
46a 4-14 Ling 12ap [45] 827 b|e
56a 1-9 LING 12ap 45 842* b|e
30a 10-13 Ling 13ap 50 896 b|e
59 2-6 Brig 11.9fm [57] 1692 bl
49 5-6 Brig 11.9g/f [60] 2047 bl
25 6-7 Brig 9.9g/f [60] 2433
50a 7-16 Ling 12ap [60] 4899

CHOCOLATE CARAMEL 2 b c £0
63a 5-12 Ling 8ap 5295

CHOIR LEADER 3 b c £7268
47 13-15 Leic 10g/s 1358
87 1-9 PONT 8gd 3462*
87 3-10 Pont 8g/s 85 3972

CHOOKIE HEITON 6 br g £19420
102 4-17 Donc 6gd [106] 952
97 5-9 Newm 6fm 104 1490
86 14-19 Newm 7g/f 102 3061
77 11-11 Hami 8fm 102 3248
112 1-11 BEVE 5g/s [98] 4238+
88 12-24 Ayr 6sft 105 4686

CHOREOGRAPHIC 2 b c £592
61 7-13 Beve 5gd 2889
64 3-8 Catt 6g/f 3348
56 10-13 Hayd 6gd 3736
47 8-19 Carl 5.9g/f 61 4344

CHORIST 5 ch m £236160
115 1-7 PONT 8g/f [111] 2278*
117 1-6 CURR 10gd [111] 2816*
116 3-6 Good 9.9fm [112] 3621
117 3-13 Deau 10sft [112] 4160
118 2-11 Newm 10sft [112] 5136

CHORISTAR 3 ch g £1303
49 6-8 Leic 7g/f 60 2403
59 2-16 Ling 7gd 55 3024
57 5-14 Ling 6gd 55 3289
61 3-12 Ling 7.6gd [55] 3448

CHORUS 7 b m £797
35a 9-10 Wolv 7af 55 379
36a 3-13 Wolv 6af [54] 483 vis
0 13-14 Good 8sft 48 4189
10 20-20 Chep 6.1g/s 48 4368
37 10-16 Warw 5g/s [45] 4995 bl
50a 2-13 Wolv 6ap [49] 5211 vis

CHORUS BEAUTY 2 b f £6376
41a 12-14 Ling 6ap 146
66a 1-10 LING 6ap 260*
49 14-20 Nott 6.1gd 66 1239
10 11-11 Warw 8.1hvy 64 1534
58 7-16 Ling 7g/f [61] 1982
64a 3-12 Ling 8ap [63] 2394
65a 1-15 SOUT 7af [63] 2999*

CHRISTINAS DREAM 3 b f £0
71 5-10 Catt 7g/f 73 3016
44a 8-11 Ling 7ap [72] 3331

CHRISTMAS TRUCE 5 b g £0
3a 10-10 Sout 11af 65 330 p
18a 9-10 Wolv 16.2af 65 358 p

CHRISTOM 2 b c £0
8 13-15 Newb 8hvy 5221

62a 7-11 Ling 8ap 5235
63 12-14 Muss 7.1g/s 5330
63 9-16 Yarm 10.1g/s 5352

CHUBBES 2 b c £4566
77a 2-11 Ling 8ap 74 54 vis
67a 3-10 Wolv 7af 74 112 vis
67a 8-10 Ling 8ap 78 132 vis
46 13-15 Brig 8fm 74 1691 vis
34 10-10 Leic 10g/f 71 1965 vis
52 4-17 Leic 7gd [69] 2704 P
46 4-8 Carl 7.9gd [60] 2932 vis
46 7-16 Thir 8g/f 50 3414 BL
48 1-11 CARL 6.9g/f [48] 3651* bl
12 13-19 Brig 9.9sft 51 4145 bl
23 10-14 Bath 8g/f 51 4411 bl

CHUTNEY MARY 2 b f £3780
56 12-15 Wind 5gd 1380
37 6-6 Sand 5g/f 2097
72 2-10 Beve 7.5gd 2652
73a 2-11 Sout 7af 2995
72a 5-10 Sout 7af 72 3483
73 2-8 Brig 7g/f [72] 3716
64 5-12 Sali 6g/s 71 4079
64 11-20 Ling 7gd 70 4444
82 3-10 Good 6gd [68] 4876
70 6-17 Catt 7gd 67 4963
62a 5-12 Wolv 7.1ap [71] 5179

CIACOLE 2 b f £3645
46a 8-8 Sout 5af 70 169
49a 13-13 Ling 7ap 70 474
40a 4-9 Sout 8af [60] 596
41 10-10 Beve 12.1g/s 64 1165
33 3-8 Pont 12hvy [64] 1250
47 1-6 BEVE 9.9sft [50] 1630*
2 13-13 Beve 12.1g/f 50 1836
1 8-11 Pont 12g/f 50 2790
25 5-7 Ripo 10gd [50] 2982

CICATRICE 2 ch c £0
41a 14-15 Ling 7ap 52

CIEL BLEU 2 ch f £0
41 13-16 Newm 7g/s 5280

CIENDRA GIRL 2 ch f £0
13 12-12 Warw 7.1g/f 4418
0 11-11 Bath 8gd 4544
0 11-12 Wind 6g/s 4945

CILLAS SMILE 2 b f £0
46 8-8 Newm 5gd 1170
59 6-11 Hayd 5g/f 4349
48 18-24 Redc 6fm 4928
39 6-7 Catt 5sft [55] 5124

CIMYLA 3 b c £21346
91 3-9 Kemp 5gd [83] 947
62 12-14 Newm 10g/f 83 1192
89 1-7 NOTT 8.2sft [83] 1741*
63 10-13 Newm 8g/f 88 2247
98 1-12 SAND 9g/f 86 2385*

CINNAMON RIDGE 3 b g £0
53 8-13 Folk 5g/f 1575
46 9-14 Brig 6fm 1690 BL
10 7-7 Bath 5fm 1902 bl

CIRCASSIAN 3 b g £18348
53 9-14 Kemp 10g/f 61 3690
73 2-11 Sali 12g/s 61 4080
81 1-16 YARM 11.5g/s 67 4589+
81 1-14 CATT 12g/f 73 4672*
75 4-20 Hayd 11.9g/s 73 4771
86 2-9 Ayr 13.1sft 77 5068
80a 5-10 Ling 12ap 81 5239

CIRCLE OF WOLVES 6 ch g £0
25 9-12 Warw 12.6g/s [45] 4991

CIRCUIT DANCER 4 b g £17253
81 3-7 Thir 6sft [89] 1227
92 4-7 Hayd 6gd [92] 1487
23 14-14 York 6g/s 92 1703
98 1-10 YORK 6g/f 92 2357*
87 16-29 Asco 6fm 100 2581
95 5-8 Hayd 6gd [96] 2949

70 22-28 Good 6fm 96 3622
92 4-8 Ches 7sft 94 4073
87 7-13 York 6gd 93 4322
75 13-24 Ayr 6sft 93 4686
92 4-9 Hami 6g/s [89] 4817
74 11-16 Redc 6sft 89 5304

CIRCUMSPECT 2 b g £1764
76 2-10 Pont 6fm 4752

CIRCUS MAXIMUS 7 b g £1579
39 9-10 Hayd 14g/f 58 1923 bl
51 4-10 Redc 14.1g/s 55 2562 p
28 12-15 Folk 16.4g/s 50 3049 bl
54 2-19 Bath 17.2gd 50 3147 p
56 3-12 Yarm 16gd 53 3493 p
26a 9-14 Ling 16ap 53 4319 p
19 11-20 Bath 17.2gd 53 4824 p

CIRRIOUS 3 gr f £0
57 8-15 Nott 8.2g/s 4649
58 6-13 Nott 8.2g/f 4847
55 5-13 Bath 10.2sft 5173

CITRINE SPIRIT 3 gr f £6074
68 6-8 Ripo 10g/s 1365
73 1-7 NOTT 8.2hvy 1610*
74 3-20 Asco 8g/f 74 1927
54 9-14 Nott 8.2g/f 74 2153
64 10-13 Sand 8.1gd 74 4607
66 7-11 Donc 7sft 71 5219

CITRUS MAGIC 7 b g £1681
47a 1-9 WOLV 14.8af [33] 301* P
40a 2-12 Sout 14af [45] 443 p
24a 7-9 Sout 12af 45 456 p

CITY AFFAIR 2 b g £0
0 14-14 Sout 8af [62] 88 bl
58a 5-10 Ling 6ap [57] 260
46a 10-10 Ling 5ap 62 371 P
46a 9-11 Wolv 6af [60] 481 p
61a 4-15 Ling 7ap [55] 671 p
8 14-14 Sali 7g/f [60] 1720

CITY GENERAL 2 ch g £4707
58a 5-13 Ling 6ap [58] 25 p
51a 5-11 Wolv 6af [58] 73 p
29a 8-16 Sout 8af [58] 164 p
54 3-18 Catt 7gd [57] 996 p
57 3-7 Folk 7g/s 57 1081 p
55 4-14 Sali 7g/f [56] 1720 p
49 3-10 Brig 7g/f 1938 p
41 5-9 Leic 8g/f [55] 1966 p
32 7-12 Sali 7fm 2288 p
54 2-11 Yarm 7g/f [49] 2852 p
49 7-13 Kemp 7g/f 3034 p
45 5-14 Leic 8g/f [50] 3344 p
57 1-10 YARM 8g/f 49 3712* p
15 14-18 Chep 7.1g/s 55 3900 p
50 5-11 Brig 9.9g/f 52 3982 p
41 6-15 Bath 8g/s 52 4202 p
42 7-14 Bath 8g/f 50 4411 p
41 7-19 Kemp 8g/f [49] 4795 p
41 7-19 Yarm 8g/s [47] 5119 p

CITY LASS 4 b f £0
0 12-13 Pont 8g/s 3973

CITY PALACE 3 ch c £3656
81 1-9 WARW 8.1sft 1089*
72 9-13 York 10.4sft 78 1664

CITY TORQUE 2 ch f £0
63 6-7 Muss 5g/f 1117
0 8-8 Hami 5gd 2177

CITY TRADER 2 ch c £0
42 15-15 Leic 7g/f 4455
0 16-16 Newb 8hvy 5220
15 16-19 Yarm 10.1g/s 5352 BL

CLANN A COUGAR 4 ch g £0
25a 7-7 Wolv 8.5af 66 942 p
41a 7-8 Sout 7af 60 1195
57 6-13 Bath 8sft 63 1542 BL
55 8-14 Hami 8.3gd 63 1748 bl
48 6-12 Sali 7fm [60] 2288
39 11-16 Beve 7.5gd 55 2891 bl

48 7-17 Bath 11.7gd 53 3145 p

CLAPTRAP 3 b c £2899
48a 7-11 Wolv 12af 54 72
60a 1-10 WOLV 14.8af [54] 125*
46a 5-14 Sout 14af 61 185
51a 2-8 Wolv 12af [59] 347
39a 5-12 Wolv 12af 53 469
31a 6-8 Wolv 16.2af 53 563

CLARA BOW 2 b f £0
78 6-14 Kemp 7g/f 4711
67 7-7 Newb 7hvy 5222

CLARADOTNET 4 b f £2267
39 16-20 Wind 11.6g/s 82 1056
51 9-10 Bath 11.7gd 80 1399
69 8-10 Sali 12g/f 75 1721
64 6-10 Hayd 14g/f 70 1923
62 3-6 Hami 11.1gd [67] 2180
57 8-10 Carl 14.1fm 64 2444
61 3-13 Sali 14.1gd 62 3454
65 2-6 Redc 16g/f 62 3810
58 10-12 Muss 14g/f 63 4170
26 10-20 Bath 17.2gd 62 4824
43 10-20 York 13.9gd 59 5004
58 6-10 Pont 18g/s 56 5151

CLARANETE PRINCESS 3 b f £0
51a 6-15 Ling 7ap 472
41 12-17 Yarm 8g/s 5348

CLARE GALWAY 3 b f £3367
26a 9-11 Ling 6ap 543
56a 5-12 Ling 8ap 734
14a 9-10 Ling 10ap 886
30 10-14 Ling 11.5g/f 50 2014
52a 4-14 Ling 10ap 50 2064
48a 9-14 Ling 10ap [49] 2740
57 1-12 BRIG 8sft 49 5094*
37a 8-12 Wolv 7.1ap [50] 5233

CLARET AND AMBER 2 b c £32570
70 3-13 Beve 5gd 2889
65 5-13 York 6gd 3120
71 5-13 York 6g/f 3431
86 1-14 REDC 6g/f 71 3807*
93 1-9 CHES 7sft 77 4074*
96 5-22 Donc 6fm 4458
97 2-6 Sali 6gd [97] 4854
90 6-9 Pont 8g/s [97] 5150

CLARINCH CLAYMORE 8 b g £9081
77 2-18 Nott 14.1g/s 69 1772
53 12-12 Muss 14fm 73 2085
71 5-14 Hayd 16.2gd 72 2239
75 3-8 Donc 14.6gd 71 2754
76 1-9 BEVE 16.2g/s 71 3181*
74 5-6 Beve 16.2g/s 72 3853

CLASH OF THE ASH 2 b c £7317
94 3-14 Leop 6g/f 2454
90 3-6 Leop 7sft 5248

CLASP 2 ch c £1569
79 8-9 Asco 7gd 3126
86 2-10 Yarm 8g/s 4631

CLASSIC EVENT 3 ch c £2253
48 7-12 Catt 12gd 65 1000
42 10-15 Ripo 12.3g/f 63 1785
63 2-6 Thir 12g/f 62 3415
62 3-12 Catt 12sft [62] 5319

CLASSIC EXPRESSION 3 ch f £0
36a 6-12 Sout 6af 2722
37 7-8 Newm 6g/f 3784
35a 7-10 Sout 8af 4042
32 15-17 Hayd 8.1g/s [45] 4768

CLASSIC GUEST 2 b f £359
68 4-6 Good 6gd 2373
59 6-8 Newb 5.2m 2646
45 15-16 Sali 7gd 4329
41 12-13 Newm 6fm [60] 4726

CLASSIC LEASE 3 b g £870
49 10-11 Hayd 8.1gd 2885
53 5-9 Thir 7g/f 3413

64 3-6 Hayd 8.1g/s 3905
54 10-17 Hayd 10.5fm 61 4388

CLASSIC LIN 4 gr f £0
0 8-8 Wolv 12af 808

CLASSIC MILLENNIUM 5 b m £2012
36a 5-9 Ling 13ap 49 18
40a 7-13 Ling 13ap 46 896
48a 2-11 Sout 12af 46 1197
48a 2-8 Wolv 12af 46 1342
62 5-10 Bath 13.1g/f 58 1789
57 7-15 Newb 13.3g/f 58 2311
56 4-11 Newb 13.3fm 57 2651

CLASSIC ROLE 4 b g £8410
71a 8-13 Ling 10ap 75 26
74a 3-16 Sout 11af 72 97
67a 8-13 Ling 10ap 72 178
74a 4-16 Ling 12ap 72 404
64a 12-16 Ling 12ap 72 493
78a 3-15 Ling 12ap 72 549
73a 4-14 Ling 12ap 71 731
79a 1-10 LING 12ap 70 936* VIS
80 2-20 Wind 11.6g/s 75 1056 vis
78 2-20 Warw 10.9gd 75 1128 vis
48 10-16 Epso 10.1hvy 79 1296 vis
69 10-19 Newb 10gd 77 1736 vis
68 8-14 Wind 10gd 77 2265 vis

CLASSIC STAMP 4 b f £35714
113 3-8 Wood 10gd 5246

CLASSIC STYLE 2 b f £0
45a 5-7 Sout 5af 2498
42 9-20 Newc 6sft 2682
47a 7-11 Sout 7af 2995
68 5-12 Newc 7gd 3425

CLASSIC VISION 4 b f £8114
61a 1-13 SOUT 6af 319*
21a 9-9 Sout 6af [60] 459
45a 10-12 Ling 6ap 58 628
54a 4-11 Ling 6ap 56 760
52 5-15 Thir 7gd 55 1635
45 11-20 Yarm 8fm 53 2149 P
56 1-14 LEIC 8g/f 51 2402* BL
45 7-9 Pont 8g/f 54 2604 bl
54 6-14 Wind 8.3g/f 54 2799 bl
45 8-11 Ripo 8gd 54 2986 bl
43 11-20 Newm 8g/f 53 3232 bl
0 14-14 Yarm 8gd 53 3363 bl

CLASSICAL DANCER 3 ch f £14190
84 1-18 WIND 8.3g/s 1258*
102 2-8 Good 8g/f [84] 1863
100 3-6 Newb 10g/f [95] 2351
82 8-10 Chep 10.2g/s [99] 3089

CLASSICAL WALTZ 6 ch m £206
25a 4-8 Wolv 9.4af [35] 1561
25a 3-6 Wolv 9.4af [30] 1800
19 9-15 Nott 10gd [30] 1991
29 7-11 Folk 12g/f 30 2273

CLASSICISM 2 b f £0
78 5-16 Sali 7gd 4329

CLEAR IMPRESSION 2 b f £3210
88 2-8 Good 6fm 3536

CLEAR THINKING 4 b c £23239
116 5-6 Long 15.5gd 2000
110 3-4 Mais 15.5g/s 3317
111 3-8 Long 15.5sft 4569
88 8-8 Long 20g/f 4951

CLEARING SKY 2 gr f £0
54a 8-9 Ling 5ap 76
52 6-10 Wind 6g/f 4835
26 17-19 Bath 5.7sft 52 5176

CLEAVER 3 ch c £0
67 5-10 Kemp 11.1gd 1140
55 9-10 Yarm 11.5g/f 1725

CLEO COLLINS 2 b f £0
23 13-14 Bath 5sft 1538

CLEVELAND WAY 3 b g £4781

44a 8-16 Sout 6af [52] 65 vis
31a 9-16 Sout 6af 49 166 vis
49a 1-11 WOLV 6af [45] 296* vis
45a 2-9 Sout 7af [45] 304 vis
37a 6-13 Wolv 6af 48 384 vis
35a 5-13 Sout 6af 47 500 vis
48a 6-12 Sout 6af [46] 610 vis
42a 4-11 Wolv 5af 46 748 vis
44a 5-11 Sout 6af 46 859 vis
19 11-13 Sout 6g/s 52 1052 vis
44a 2-8 Sout 6af [45] 1201 vis
48a 2-6 Sout 6af [45] 1405 vis
26a 6-7 Sout 7af [45] 1590 vis
43a 2-12 Wolv 5af [40] 1799 vis
49a 1-10 SOUT 6af [40] 1837* vis
0 14-15 Pont 6g/f 48 2280 vis
17 15-17 Catt 5g/f 44 3667 vis
31 13-20 Redc 6g/f 44 3767 vis

CLIFFIE 2 ch g £0
12 8-10 Pont 6fm 4752
20 10-12 Redc 8g/s 5107
42 14-14 Redc 7sft 5301

CLIMATE 4 ch g £6048
72a 8-14 Ling 10ap 75 122
63a 5-12 Ling 8ap [72] 878
76 4-13 Wind 8.3g/s [77] 1057 VIS
44 11-18 Asco 8sft 77 1423 vis
78 2-12 Kemp 8g/f [74] 1915 vis
79a 1-11 LING 8ap 68 2018* vis
79 6-13 Ling 7.6g/f 77 2587 vis
81 3-8 Wind 8.3g/s [77] 2620 vis
73 9-11 Thir 6g/f 77 3574 bl
65 9-20 Donc 7sft 77 5367

CLIMATE CHANGE 2 ch c £0
20 12-15 Newb 8hvy 5221

CLINET 2 b f £7881
65 8-15 Wind 5gd 1380
41 5-11 Yarm 5gd 1728
64 2-11 Good 5gd 2020
41 13-17 Nott 6.1gd 2927
64 5-9 Asco 66 3127
48 10-11 Newm 7fm 68 3407
60a 7-14 Ling 7ap 65 4177
71 1-12 BATH 8g/f 63 4410*
76 3-16 Nott 10g/f 69 4848

CLIPPER HOY 2 ch c £0
39 6-6 Warw 5hvy 1531
26 14-14 Newb 6sft 5197

CLIPPERDOWN 3 b c £6261
71 3-11 Hayd 8.1gd 2886
72 7-20 Newm 8g/f 3237
83 1-5 PONT 8gd 3683*
75 3-16 Nott 10gd 74 4860

CLIQUEY 5 b g £0
18a 11-12 Wolv 9.4af 62 464
0 11-11 Wolv 12af 55 557 bl
33a 9-14 Ling 12ap 51 711 T

CLOANN 2 b f £2884
59 5-19 Kemp 6g/f 1911
45 11-18 Leic 5fm 2109
64 1-8 WIND 6g/f 2449*

CLOG DANCE 2 b f £3136
76a 1-13 WOLV 9.4af [73] 37*

CLOON 3 b f £15422
100 3-7 Chan 9g/s 2814 bl
109 3-18 Deau 10g/s 3836 bl

CLOONAVERY 2 b c £3222
82 4-14 Chep 8.1gd 4484
81a 1-13 WOLV 8.6ap 4979*

CLOUD CATCHER 3 br f £0
29 7-14 Sali 7g/f 1720
1a 12-13 Wolv 8.5af 2052
23 11-11 Wind 10fm 3802
6 7-7 Bath 11.7g/f 3967
12a 11-11 Wolv 8.6ap [30] 5356 T

CLOUD DANCER 4 b f £15876

77a 3-9 Wolv 7af 74 27
76a 1-16 SOUT 7af [74] 161*
68a 7-11 Sout 6af 80 198
75a 3-13 Ling 7ap 74 474
70a 8-14 Ling 7ap 74 518
73a 2-6 Sout 7af [73] 593
62a 2-13 Wolv 8.5af [73] 699
80 1-20 YORK 6g/f 71 2409*
80 3-11 Pont 6g/f 76 2791
76 5-10 York 6gd 77 3116
57 17-25 Asco 7g/f 77 3443
77 4-19 York 6gd 76 4005
75 5-21 Donc 7fm 75 4482
76 6-13 Muss 7.1gd 75 4806
79a 3-13 Wolv 8.6ap 74 5364

CLOUDINGSWELL 3 b f £535
62 10-10 Newb 10gd [63] 1209
33 6-11 Warw 12.6sft 63 1528
44 6-7 Wind 8.3g/f [60] 2264
50 4-4 Wind 10g/f [57] 2798
37 4-8 Warw 10.9gd [57] 3055 VIS
22 8-12 Warw 12.6g/s [48] 4991
24a 7-12 Wolv 8.6ap [45] 5230

CLOUDLESS 3 b f £4285
0 10-13 Wolv 6af [64] 30
61a 1-12 WOLV 5af [55] 242+
52a 5-8 Wolv 5af 61 274
8a 11-13 Wolv 6af [60] 483
54a 2-8 Wolv 8.5af [57] 630
54a 4-7 Sout 7af 57 680
39a 10-10 Ling 7ap 57 799
55a 3-10 Wolv 7af 55 864
52a 3-11 Wolv 5af 55 958
40 6-14 Hayd 8.1g/s 55 1348
44 6-16 Bath 5.7sft 53 1540
3 19-20 Yarm 6g/f 53 1730
33a 9-12 Wolv 7af 54 2049
10 18-19 Leic 5gd 47 2702
0 12-13 Hayd 6gd [43] 3757
17 19-19 Bath 5.7sft 40 5176

CLOUDS OF GOLD 3 b f £864
35 10-13 Muss 7.1g/f 1119
47 3-11 Pont 6sft 1426
2 11-12 Ripo 9g/f 1784
5 18-19 Redc 6g/f 50 2125

CLOUDY SKY 8 b g £0
70 14-17 Sali 14.1g/s 80 1502

CLOVE 2 b f £6850
72 4-11 Sali 5gd 2658
76 1-10 WIND 5fm 3476*
81 2-14 Redc 5fm 75 4556
77 9-18 Wind 5g/f 78 4830

CLUELESS 2 b c £1700
84 4-10 Yarm 8g/s 4631
81 3-15 Newm 8gd 4883

COALITION 5 b g £5922
68 9-11 Donc 12gd 77 2233
84 2-10 Sali 14.1gd 75 2699
83 2-11 Sand 14g/f 78 3340
86 3-11 Newm 16.1g/f 81 3779

COAT OF HONOUR 4 gr g £45500
68 16-21 York 10.4gd 92 3118 bl
101 1-15 GOOD 9.9g/f 92 3506*
106 2-20 Hayd 10.5fm 97 3794

COBALT BLUE 3 b g £4140
40 8-14 Newc 8gd 55 1872
49 6-17 Hayd 8.1gd 52 2243 BL
57 1-7 MUSS 8g/f 50 2613* bl
48 5-15 Nott 10gd 54 3108 bl
48a 5-14 Ling 10ap 52 3449 bl
0 4-12 Folk 12g/s 52 3913 bl
56 3-11 Brig 9.9g/f 52 3982 VIS
25 11-15 Bath 8g/s 51 4202 vis
57 2-10 Brig 9.9fm 51 4763 P

COBALT RUNNER 3 b c £0
10a 8-9 Ling 5ap 621
0 14-14 Donc 5gd 2237

COBRA 3 b c £3048

104 3-10 Leop 10g/f 2456
71 9-10 Curr 12g/f 2822

COCO POINT BREEZE 3 b f £0
34a 7-9 Ling 8ap 3195
40 8-11 Thir 8g/f 3572
37 7-8 Sand 8.1g/f 3858
28 10-11 Folk 9.7gd 4120
0 14-15 Carl 9.3fm [40] 4505 BL

COCO REEF 3 b f £0
40 6-17 Leic 7gd [57] 2704
30a 12-15 Sout 6af 55 3000
52a 5-9 Sout 6af [50] 3396
28 10-13 Bath 5.7g/f [47] 3844

COCONUT COOKIE 3 ch f £0
38 18-20 Newb 7g/f 72 1761
46 11-14 Nott 8.2g/f 69 2153
23 7-8 Brig 8g/f 65 2432

COCONUT MOON 2 b f £0
60 6-12 Thir 5g/s 3832

COCONUT PENANG 4 b c £18350
84 14-17 Donc 6gd [98] 1162
87 1-3 Beve 5g/s [95] 1162
99 2-29 Asco 6fm 93 2581
69 18-19 Newm 7g/f 96 3061
44 25-28 Good 6fm 96 3622 BL
94 5-8 Newm 6gd [95] 4226
1 P-7 Good 6g/f [93] 4526

COCONUT SQUEAK 2 b f £6531
68 3-12 Newc 7gd 3425
59 6-12 Ayr 7.2hvy 4083
49 7-14 Thir 7g/s 4207
64 9-20 Ling 7g/f 63 4741
69 1-19 LING 6g/f [63] 4895*
58 9-21 Donc 6hvy 5202

COCTAIL LADY 3 ch f £0
18a 12-13 Ling 16ap 45 137 t

CODE ORANGE 2 b f £3340
85 2-6 Leic 6g/f 2399
88 2-13 Kemp 6g/f 4358

CODY 5 ch g £214
45a 3-14 Ling 16ap [45] 4663 t
0 14-20 Bath 17.2gd 45 4824

COEUR COURAGEUX 2 b c £0
63 7-10 Donc 7g/f 3594

COHN BLUE 2 b c £0
80 10- Sain 10g/s 9

COIS NA TINE EILE 2 br f £1052
46 3-11 Ripo 6g/f 1779
25a 10-14 Sout 7af 2492
53 3-14 Beve 7.5sft 2939
28 13-19 Kemp 8g/f [51] 4792
49 10-15 Pont 10g/f [51] 4933
44 8-8 Muss 9g/s [51] 5140

COLD CLIMATE 8 ch g £6033
56a 2-16 Ling 7ap [56] 123
67a 1-16 LING 7ap 58 144*
63a 9-15 Ling 7ap 65 698
67a 4-14 Ling 7ap 65 1010
54 7-14 Yarm 6g/f 56 2855
55 5-16 Kemp 7gd 55 3184
59 2-16 Ling 6g/f 54 3602
59 2-12 Newm 6gd 54 3751
13 9-9 Newm 6gd 55 3924
59 4-15 Epso 7g/f 57 4475

COLD ENCOUNTER 9 ch g £0
19a 13-14 Ling 16ap [50] 4663

COLD TURKEY 3 b g £55983
80a 1-9 LING 13ap 68 18*
75a 1-12 LING 12ap 67 56*
82a 2-14 LING 13ap 75 147
86a 1-16 LING 12ap 79 404*
92a 1-16 LING 12ap 84 475+
90a 3-10 Ling 12ap 88 570
92a 2-12 Ling 13ap 88 877
82 4-18 Kemp 16g/s 79 1112

91 1-20 EPSO 12hvy 79 1295*
95 2-17 Newb 12g/f 85 1759
87 4-12 Good 14g/f 85 1861
59 10-11 Epso 10.1gd [90] 4467
59 13-13 Donc 12sft 90 5215

COLEMANSTOWN 4 b g £545
32 11-13 Newc 7hvy 74 1035
63 7-12 Thir 7g/s 72 1215
21 18-20 York 6g/f 70 2059
49 12-12 Newc 6g/f 70 2160
60 8-13 Hami 6g/f 66 2315
19 16-18 Newc 7sft 64 2684
21 10-10 Epso 7g/f 64 2872
45 14-25 Asco 7g/f 60 3443
57 7-14 Beve 7.5g/s 56 4241
57 3-18 Good 8gd 53 4750
48 10-20 Leic 7gd 53 5046

COLEORTON DANCER 2 ch c £29824
52 8-11 Nott 5.1gd 1237
68 4-10 Muss 5gd 1550
64a 4-11 Sout 5af 1752
69 4-7 Warw 5fm 2573
63 7-8 Ches 5.1g/f 68 3082
86 1-12 THIR 5g/s [65] 3832*
89 1-11 NOTT 5.1gd 71 3987*
87 1-10 CHES 5.1g/f 71 4049*
91 1-16 NEWM 6gd 82 4224*
74 9-12 Newm 6gd 89 4882
49 13-21 Donc 6hvy [65] 5202

COLEORTON DANE 2 gr g £5788
87 6-11 York 6g/s 1687
72 3-9 Warw 7.1fm 2776
75 2-7 Catt 7g/f 3189
78 1-8 MUSS 7.1g/f 3559*
79 3-10 Ripo 6gd 78 4306
49 14-17 Donc 8fm 78 4480

COLEORTON PRINCE 2 b g £0
35a 7-10 Sout 5af 139
2a 11-12 Sout 6af [40] 200
2a 10-10 Ling 6ap [35] 606

COLISAY 5 b g £24382
68 3-4 Leic 7g/f [103] 1962
104 6-15 Sand 8.1g/s 101 2915
100 4-10 Asco 8gd 100 3775 VIS
105 1-8 DONC 10.3fm 99 4530*
104 4-8 Good 9.9gd [102] 4748

COLLADA 3 b f £0
0 18-18 Wind 8.3g/s 1258
7 12-12 Good 9g/f 1864
54 6-14 Sali 7fm 2291
3 16-18 Chep 7.1g/s 53 3900

COLLEGE DELINQUENT 4 br g £1575
68a 3-11 Ling 8ap 66 12 t
62a 9-14 Ling 10ap 66 122 t
67a 3-11 Ling 8ap 66 131 t
68a 3-12 Ling 8ap 66 517 t
66a 4-12 Ling 8ap [66] 1042 t
62a 6-12 Ling 8ap 66 1613 t
62a 7-11 Ling 8ap 65 2018 t

COLLEGE HIPPIE 4 b f £0
42a 6-15 Sout 5af 49 187
38a 9-15 Sout 5af [45] 253
23 12-19 Beve 5g/s 48 2326
5 16-17 Warw 5fm 45 2599 P
17 15-19 Beve 5gd 45 2657 p
26 14-19 Donc 5g/s 45 3220 BL

COLLEGE MAID 7 b m £7441
41 4-5 Muss 5gd 53 1096 bl
38 13-20 Ripo 5gd 53 1179 bl
46 6-15 Muss 5gd 50 1555 bl
46 7-13 Newc 5gd 48 1873 bl
46 7-16 Ayr 5gd 48 2029 VIS
55 2-13 Donc 6g/f 48 2232 bl
49 4-13 Hami 6g/f 47 2315 bl
62 1-9 AYR 7.2gd 54 2508*
64 3-11 Ayr 6gd 60 2542
53 5-6 Hami 5gd 60 2712
53 6-12 Catt 7g/f [62] 3017
57 6-9 Ayr 5g/f 61 3307

58 6-14 Thir 6g/f 61 3416 bl
57 6-8 Muss 7.1g/f 61 3528
55 5-8 Ayr 6g/f 59 3763 vis
60 3-7 Ayr 6hvy 57 4087 vis
46 13-18 Redc 6fm 57 4339 vis
42 17-26 Ayr 5g/s 57 4618 vis
49 6-15 Newc 5fm 56 4870 bl
27 15-19 Ayr 6sft 54 5069 bl

COLLEGE QUEEN 6 b m £2077
48 11-15 Ripo 6g/f 67 1782
66 7-13 Newc 5gd 67 1873 P
61 5-13 Donc 6gd 66 2232 bl
66 4-10 Donc 6g/f 65 2429 p
64 5-11 Pont 6g/f 64 2791 bl
65 2-5 Folk 5g/s 64 3050 bl
52 11-14 Thir 6g/f 64 3416 bl
57 7-8 Folk 5gd 63 4118 bl
63 5-18 Redc 6fm 63 4339
65 3-15 Chep 5.1gd 61 4489
40 15-20 Nott 6.1g/s 61 4646
40 16-19 York 5gd 61 4989

COLLEGE STAR 5 b g £0
30a 9-13 Sout 8af [29] 188 bl
11a 8-13 Sout 8af 29 228 bl
0 8-11 Sout 8af [30] 372 bl
21a 8-9 Sout 7af [30] 555 bl

COLLIER HILL 6 ch g £64906
87 11-17 Ches 18.7gd 96 1569
105 1-12 HAMI 12.1gd 96 1746+
106 4-19 Newc 16.1g/s 101 2771
105 3-14 York 13.9gd 104 3119
99 9-19 York 13.9g/s 103 4023
108 1-9 TABY 12gd [103] 4574*
0 5-8 Newb 12hvy [106] 5224

COLLOSEUM 3 b g £0
43 7-13 Muss 7.1g/f 1119
60 4-14 Ayr 8g/f [59] 1896
36 12-14 Redc 7fm 59 2295
40 16-18 Leic 10gd 58 2706
40 8-12 Ayr 9.1g/f 54 3766
36 6-6 Muss 8gd [52] 4520

COLNE VALLEY AMY 7 b m £429
41a 4-10 Ling 8ap [40] 410 bl
38a 2-13 Ling 10ap [40] 539 bl
0 8-8 Sout 8af [40] 635 bl
31a 8-12 Ling 8ap [40] 710 bl
2a 12-14 Sout 8af [39] 3392

COLONEL BILKO 2 b c £6457
77 2-6 Folk 5sft 974
48 10-11 Nott 5.1gd 1237
40 6-8 Brig 6g/f 2043 BL
68 1-14 LEIC 6g/f 65 3212*
62 10-10 Kemp 6g/f 72 3521

COLONEL COTTON 5 b g £12750
0 6-8 Cork 5g/s [109] 1159
94 10-13 Newm 5g/f [109] 1479
77 6-8 Beve 5sft [109] 1626
102 5-10 Kemp 5fm [103] 2068
96 5-12 Epso 5g/f [103] 2206 bl
89 16-19 Asco 5g/f [103] 2468 bl
100 3-12 Sand 5g/s [100] 2913
99 10-11 Newb 5g/f [100] 3268
89 6-7 Newm 5fm [100] 3409
98 5-7 Good 6g/f [98] 4526
97 3-8 Yarm 6g/s [98] 4588 vis
96 4-10 Beve 5g/f [97] 4718 vis
81 15-19 Newm 6sft [97] 4879 vis
87 10-14 Newm 6sft [95] 5100

COLONIAL GIRL 2 b f £2554
72 4-10 Thir 5g/f 1764
71 3-11 Nott 5.1g/f 2151
70a 2-7 Sout 5af 2498
73 4-10 Ripo 5gd 2983

COLONNADE 5 b m £644
45a 2-7 Sout 14af [45] 376
23a 7-9 Sout 16af 45 612
44a 3-9 Sout 14af [40] 849
9 9-12 Newc 14.4sft 50 1396
8 7-12 Brig 11.9fm 46 4764

2 9-11 Catt 13.8sft [45] 5129

COLOPHONY 4 ch g £426
63 12-13 Wind 10gd [79] 1381 t
74 4-5 Leic 10g/f [75] 2401 t
59 7-9 Hayd 11.9gd 74 2900 t
68 6-8 Leic 10g/f 71 3514 t

COLORADO FALLS 6 b g £10229
80 1-10 HAMI 13gd 72 1506*
81 5-8 Hami 12.1g/f 78 2318
73 4-9 Ayr 13.1g/s 78 2567
68 8-10 Hami 13fm 78 3249
71 4-10 Newc 16.1g/s 75 3701
74 3-8 Hami 13g/s 73 4138
69 4-6 Newc 14.4sft 73 4287

COLOUR BLIND 2 b c £0
30 19-20 Yarm 8sft 5252
21 15-15 Nott 8.2hvy 5344

COLOUR CODE 2 b c £863
68a 2-13 Wolv 6af 3
54a 11-14 Sout 7af 98
41 14-17 Kemp 7gd 1136

COLOUR WHEEL 3 ch c £3703
74 6-8 Sand 8.1g/s 90 1315
73 15-18 Hayd 8.1g/f 90 1919 T
94 2-11 Newm 7g/f 87 2532 t
66 11-13 Asco 7gd 90 3068 t
86 7-9 Sand 7.1g/f 90 3338 t
82 10-15 Newm 7g/f 89 4891 VIS

COLOURFUL LADY 3 b f £0
45a 9-13 Ling 10ap 58 104
32a 5-11 Wolv 12af 55 380

COLUMBIAN EMERALD 3 ch g £424
32 7-7 Muss 9g/s 1462
47 4-6 Ayr 10g/f 1894
52 5-8 Beve 12.1gd 2515
27 7-7 Ayr 10.9g/f 52 3765
4a 10-14 Ling 16ap 48 4319

COLWAY RITZ 10 b g £4381
54 11-12 Beve 12.1sft 61 4259
65 2-14 York 10.4g/f 61 4402
66 2-14 Catt 12g/f 61 4672
57 5-8 Redc 14.1fm 63 4932
63 5-17 Newc 10g/s 61 5016
67 3-19 Pont 10g/s 61 5148

COMANCHE WOMAN 3 b f £0
0 14-14 Ling 12ap [39] 103
2a 9-9 Wolv 14.8af [35] 301 T

COME AWAY WITH ME 4 b f £4957
59 2-20 Yarm 6g/f 52 1730
65 1-11 WARW 5.5gd 55 3054*

COME GOOD 2 ch c £4400
49 5-5 Wind 5sft 1646
76 2-7 Bath 5.7fm 1900
69 6-15 Wind 6g/f 2263
72 3-9 Good 6fm 70 3623
76 2-6 Chep 6.1g/s 70 3897
65 7-10 Brig 6g/s [73] 4139

COME ON 5 b g £0
60 5-19 Redc 6g/s 5110
51a 5-11 Wolv 5.1ap 5363

COME ON JONNY 2 b c £5126
55 12-18 Wind 6gd 3824
74 3-16 Thir 6g/f 4205
72 4-10 Newc 6g/f 4403
83 1-11 WIND 8.3g/s 72 4940*
48 13-13 Wind 8.3g/f 78 5051

COME TO DADDY 2 ch g £0
2 13-13 Pont 6gd 3682
57 5-6 Wind 6g/s 4217
46 12-14 Yarm 7sft 5251

COME WHAT JULY 2 b c £9886
66a 2-11 Wolv 7af 63 29 bl
68a 3-11 Sout 8af [67] 159 bl
75a 1-13 LING 10ap [67] 601* bl
77a 2-6 Wolv 9.4af 73 702 bl

74a 5-10 Ling 10ap 73 817 bl (continued)

74a	5-10	Ling	10ap	73	817 bl
65	6-12	Catt	12gd	73	1000 bl
29	6-6	Newc	10.1sft	[70]	1397 bl
49	11-14	Ayr	8g/f	[65]	1896 bl
60a	3-8	Ling	12ap	[73]	2065 VIS
21	5-8	Warw	10.9gd	[60]	3055 bl
62a	1-11	SOUT	8af	[70]	3091* bl
52	7-13	Beve	9.9gd	55	3309 bl
57	3-19	Beve	9.9g/f	55	3505 bl
56	6-12	Beve	9.9g/s	55	3854 bl
64a	7-11	Sout	8af	70	4044 vis
47a	13-14	Ling	10ap	68	5083 bl

COMERAINCOMESHINE 2 ch f £6273

64a	3-11	Ling	6ap		51
66a	8-13	Ling	7ap		119
66a	3-5	Ling	5ap	[64]	725
62	6-9	Bath	5g/s	62	1102
63	4-15	Ling	5g/f	60	2062
65	2-18	Wind	6g/f	60	2268
51	7-11	Sali	6gd	63	2661
25	15-15	Chep	5.1gd	63	3403
72	1-13	BATH	5.7g/f	[62]	4413*

COMETE 5 b m £25704

110	1-12	LONG	7g/s	4731*

COMFY 5 b h £1250

98	5-9	Sand	10g/s	[113]	2128
108	7-10	Asco	10g/f	[113]	2488

COMIC GENIUS 2 b f £939

37a	6-15	Sout	7af	[45]	87
43a	2-11	Wolv	8.5af	[42]	279 vis
43a	3-9	Sout	8af	[45]	596
28a	5-9	Wolv	8.5af	[45]	865 BL
33	9-11	Sout	10gd	40	1280
0	6-6	Chep	12.1sft	[40]	1331

COMIC STRIP 2 b g £53675

89a	1-9	SOUT	4af		3157*
76	4-8	Beve	7.5gd		3311
101	1-12	CHES	7g/f	88	4509*
110	1-11	AYR	8sft	96	4688*
111	1-5	EPSO	8.5gd	[100]	4906*
111	1-9	PONT	8g/s	[100]	5150+

COMIC TALES 3 b g £0

46	6-14	Donc	6g/f		2428
47	6-7	Catt	7g/f		3194
27	7-18	Chep	7.1g/s	49	3900 BL
42	6-7	Redc	7fm	[45]	4561 bl
41	5-8	Catt	6gd	[40]	4969 P

COMIC TIMES 4 b f £0

0	19-19	Beve	5g/s	40	2326

COMICAL ERRORS 2 b g £289

56	11-15	Pont	6gd		3239
73	4-14	Thir	7g/s		3831
59	5-14	Thir	7g/s		4204
62	15-16	Nott	10g/f	70	4848

COMING AGAIN 3 b c £1384

77	5-11	Newm	10gd	1148
85	2-18	Wind	10g/f	1959
73	12-14	Epso	12fm	2254

COMINTRUE 2 ch f £1046

56a	7-10	Ling	5ap		1071
54	7-8	Newm	5g/s		1149
36	11-12	Hami	6gd		2178
57	2-13	Beve	5g/s		2321
23	7-7	Leic	5g/f	60	3343
0	14-15	Folk	6g/f	[56]	4369

COMMANDER BOND 3 b g £5395

48	8-9	Thir	6g/s	[74]	1477
24	12-12	Donc	7g/f	72	1879
73a	1-8	SOUT	7af	67	2723*
58	9-11	Carl	6.9gd	71	2936
53a	8-9	Sout	6af	71	3485
16	8-8	Pont	6gd	[71]	3684
47a	7-8	Sout	7af	[70]	4093
49	5-7	Ripo	8gd	[68]	4304
27	11-13	Warw	7.1g/s	[60]	4667
68a	7-12	Wolv	7.1ap	[67]	5006

COMMANDER FLIP 4 ch g £261

44a 4-8 Wolv 12af [65] 808 (continued)

44a	4-8	Wolv	12af	[65]	808
6	14-17	Pont	12hvy	58	1064

COMMANDO SCOTT 3 b g £23056

80	1-14	THIR	6g/s	[80]	1216*
55	12-14	Ches	6.1g/s	78	1570
69	8-13	Hayd	6g/f	76	1881
77	2-6	Redc	6gd	73	2551
78	2-8	Thir	7sft	73	2693
79	2-11	Ripo	6gd	76	2985
72	6-13	Beve	7.5g/s	76	3179
95	1-12	HAYD	6sft	78	3273*
97	1-11	DONC	6g/s	84	3379*
90	5-10	Asco	6gd	90	3778
76	8-14	Ches	6.1g/f	92	4048
80	7-12	Hayd	6sft	91	4779

COMMEMORATION DAY 3 b g £0

61	6-14	Thir	8gd		1636
55	6-11	Pont	12g/f	64	2041
3a	8-11	Sout	12af	62	2804
16	15-15	Nott	10gd	60	3108

COMMENDABLE COUP 2 b c £0

72	5-13	Thir	6g/s	2689
63	7-13	York	6gd	3120
64	6-8	Hayd	8.1g/f	4351

COMMERCANTE 4 b f £194805

117	1-8	WOOD	10gd	5246*

COMMITMENT LECTURE 4 b f £4606

50	5-16	Newc	8hvy	51	1036 T
59	1-14	HAYD	8.1g/s	51	1348* t
49	4-14	Warw	8.1hvy	57	1535 t
53	6-13	Muss	8g/f	[57]	4554 t
48a	5-13	Wolv	8.6ap	55	4982 t
56	3-16	Nott	8.2hvy	52	5347 t

COMPASSION 2 b f £1768

22a	13-13	Wolv	6af	63	1
14a	10-11	Wolv	8.5af	58	1339
40	10-14	Brig	6fm	[62]	1690 P
29	7-10	Leic	8gd	[58]	2133 P
37	4-15	Ayr	8gd	[53]	2504 p
53	4-4	Hami	9.2gd	[53]	2709
42	5-5	Hami	12.1g/s	47	2827
46	3-11	Muss	9gd	47	2969 p
43	6-7	Ayr	7.2gd	47	3153 p
17	8-11	Carl	6.9g/f	[46]	3651 p
39	3-9	Ayr	7.2g/f	[46]	3764 p
0	F-12	Hami	8.3g/s	[43]	4007 p

COMPETITOR 2 b c £975

56a	7-10	Ling	8ap		229
73a	2-9	Ling	10ap	70	365
17	9-9	Good	12gd		2540
43	12-12	Wind	10g/f	[70]	2800
59	5-12	Good	9.9sft	65	4268
58	13-16	Sand	10gd	65	4609
59	6-18	Sali	9.9gd	63	4850 P
71a	5-14	Ling	10ap	68	5083 p
56a	9-13	Ling	10ap	68	5299 p

COMPLETE CIRCLE 3 ch f £0

80a	8-14	Ling	12ap	84	83 vis
75a	4-8	Sout	16af	82	140 e

COMPLICATION 4 b f £21226

57	7-13	Yarm	6g/f	67	1726 bl
58	6-11	Newm	6fm	63	2093 bl
70	2-12	Sali	6fm	63	2289 bl
62	4-17	Wind	6g/f	61	2451 bl
73	2-11	Pont	6g/f	65	2791 bl
73	1-17	PONT	6g/f	65	2990* bl
56	7-9	Pont	6g/f	70	4627 bl

COMPOS MENTIS 3 b g £0

18a	9-15	Sout	8af	[67]	96 BL

COMPTON ARROW 7 b g £0

33a	7-9	Wolv	7af	63	27
0	10-10	Warw	6.1hvy	47	1533
38	15-19	Sali	10g/f	63	1723
34	14-16	Ling	7g/f	59	2063
38	11-12	Donc	7gd	55	2235
6	18-18	Donc	6gd	51	2752
34	15-19	Chep	7.1gd	51	3401

COMPTON AVIATOR 8 ch g £0

54a	6-8	Ling	10ap	56	900 t
29	11-17	Bath	11.7sft	55	1543 t
50a	5-13	Ling	12g/f	53	1986 t
39	9-17	Bath	11.7gd	51	3145 t
51	6-11	Yarm	11.5gd	51	3367 t
47	5-13	Warw	10.9g/f	49	4419 t
48	8-18	Good	8gd	49	4750 t P

COMPTON BANKER 6 br g £8110

74a	1-16	LING	7ap	70	20* vis
79a	1-14	LING	7ap	74	149* vis
76a	5-10	Ling	7ap	78	262
54a	15-16	Sout	5af	78	461 vis
64	6-11	Chep	7.1gd	72	2370
67	5-7	Warw	6.1fm	[70]	2598 vis
70	2-4	Brig	5.3fm	70	2838
53	7-10	Epso	6g/s	68	3045
62	3-11	Bath	5g/f	[69]	3372 vis
24	15-16	Wind	6gd	67	3827
43	15-18	Bath	5.7g/f	63	4412 bl

COMPTON BAY 4 b g £0

28a	11-11	Wolv	7af	49	558
17a	9-15	Sout	6af	[45]	773
0	11-12	Sout	6af	[40]	982 BL
24a	5-7	Sout	7af	[35]	1202

COMPTON BOLTER 6 b g £59850

106a	1-14	LING	10ap	[103]	82*
103	10-13	Nad	12g/f	[103]	990 bl
96	3-9	Ches	13.4gd	[108]	1596
109	2-10	Good	9.9g/f	[108]	1862
108	5-11	Epso	10.1g/f	110	2208
96	10-14	Asco	10g/f	110	2556
99	6-7	Sand	10g/s	[109]	2898
107	5-9	Good	12fm	[107]	3563
111	3-4	Newb	13.3g/f	[107]	3958
106	3-7	Wind	11.6g/s	[109]	4219
109	2-7	Donc	12fm	[109]	4494
110	3-8	Newb	11g/f	[109]	4639
106	4-9	Asco	12g/f	[106]	4812

COMPTON CLASSIC 2 b c £0

31	7-7	Ayr	6gd	3323
48	6-7	Muss	5g/f	4549
65	6-18	Ayr	6g/s	4617
14	12-14	Ayr	6sft	56	5035

COMPTON COMMANDER 6 ch g £0

77a	11-13	Ling	10ap	87	433
47a	8-10	Wolv	12af	82	810 vis

COMPTON DRAGON 5 ch g £4353

77a	8-8	Ling	7ap	[80]	879
69	12-24	Donc	8gd	80	928
69	5-20	Donc	10.3g/s	77	1519
57	12-19	Ripo	10g/f	75	1781
79	5-11	Hayd	10.5g/f	75	1884
78	2-10	Newc	10.1g/f	73	2162 VIS
79	2-13	Ches	10.3gd	73	2284 vis
70	5-9	Thir	12fm	74	2465 vis
72	2-5	Beve	9.9sft	75	2943 vis
70	12-15	Ches	10.3gd	74	3099 vis
61	6-9	Carl	9.3fm	[74]	3546 vis
72	10-15	Donc	10.3g/f	74	3598 vis
70	4-8	Ayr	10hvy	74	4084 vis
65	10-14	Ripo	10gd	74	4305 vis

COMPTON DRAKE 4 b g £22041

61a	1-13	LING	10ap	52	104*
67a	1-6	WOLV	9.4af	59	249*
46	17-19	Good	8g/f	66	3512
73	2-14	Sali	9.9g/f	66	3867
75	1-15	CHEP	8.1sft	66	4057*
78	2-14	Epso	8.5gd	72	4295
75	4-15	Newb	11g/f	72	4643
82a	1-14	LING	10ap	[72]	4742+
68	10-20	York	8.9gd	79	4999

COMPTON EAGLE 4 b g £0

56	11-14	Folk	7g/s	1080
16a	6-8	Wolv	7af	1656

COMPTON ECLAIRE 3 ch f £12214

50a	1-10	LING	12ap	[57]	24* VIS
39a	9-14	Ling	12ap	[52]	103 vis

52a	3-10	Wolv	12af	52	243	bl
49a	4-14	Ling	13ap	52	259	
48a	3-9	Wolv	12af	52	424	vis
52	3-5	Muss	14g/s	57	1459	bl
53a	2-9	Wolv	14.8af	49	1654	vis
60	4-10	Bath	13.1g/f	55	1789	vis
41	6-10	Chep	12.1gd	55	2114	vis
60	1-11	**WARW**	12.6fm	54	2601*	vis
64	2-7	Brig	11.9fm	60	2836	vis
51	4-5	Leic	11.8g/f	58	2923	
59a	2-11	Ling	16ap	52	3450	vis
58	4-10	Sali	14.1gd	61	3887	vis
51a	7-14	Ling	16ap	55	4319	bl

COMPTON EMERALD 3 ch f £0

29a	9-12	Ling	8ap	[65]	150	bl

COMPTON MICKY 3 ch c £1474

52	8-13	Donc	7gd		925	
65	6-14	Thir	6g/s		1216	
20	12-13	Ripo	6g/f	60	2011	
54	5-9	Thir	7g/f	[60]	2218	P
56	6-14	Redc	7fm	58	2295	p
31	9-11	Donc	6g/s	56	3379	p
47	5-9	Thir	8sft	55	3835	p
22	12-15	Nott	10g/s	55	4037	p
36	14-14	Redc	7g/s	53	5109	p
55a	1-12	**WOLV**	7.1ap	[49]	5229*	p
53a	5-12	Wolv	8.6ap	[49]	5329	p

COMPTON PLUME 4 ch g £9329

55	7-14	Thir	6g/f	[55]	1639	
57	3-16	Redc	6g/f	55	1824	
57	19-19	Redc	6g/f	55	2125	
57	3-18	Thir	6g/f	55	2214	
71	2-10	Redc	6gd	55	2559	
72	1-12	**CATT**	6g/f	[55]	2849*	
59	7-14	Catt	6g/f	69	3352	
41	13-15	Pont	5gd	67	3680	
63	7-19	Beve	5g/s	65	4240	
70	1-17	**BEVE**	5g/f	62	4603*	
57	9-20	Ripo	6gd	67	4785	

COMPTON PRINCESS 4 b f £594

39	3-17	Pont	6hvy	[45]	1065	
11a	6-6	Sout	6af	[40]	1405	
11	10-14	Donc	6g/s	[40]	1522	
0	14-15	Beve	7.5g/f	[40]	1944	BL
36	9-14	Redc	7g/f	[39]	2102	
0	8-8	Ripo	6g/f	[37]	2527	

COMPTON QUAY 2 ch c £0

73	6-13	Warw	7.1g/f		4416
68	7-11	Sali	7gd		4853
68a	6-14	Ling	7ap		4970

COMPTON SPARK 2 ch g £0

7a	11-13	Wolv	6ap		5287

COMPTONS ELEVEN 3 gr g £31008

68	8-19	Newm	6g/s	90	1154
72	8-11	Sali	6g/s	89	1498
77	7-12	Good	7g/f	87	1847
73	8-13	Sand	8.1g/s	[83]	2126
78	5-13	Newm	7fm	80	2590
83	2-13	Newb	6gd	77	2880
92	1-5	**HAMI**	6gd	[80]	3131+
94	2-17	Good	7fm	86	3550
92	2-11	Hayd	6gd	[86]	3758
98	2-14	Ches	6.1g/f	90	4048
99	2-13	Asco	6.5g/f	93	4773
88	11-20	York	6gd	96	5001

COMTESSE LALANDE 2 ch f £0

61	6-7	Ling	5g/f		2738

CONCER ETO 5 ch g £11215

0	12-12	Ling	8ap	73	517	BL
68a	10-15	Ling	7ap	71	698	p
72a	2-12	Ling	8ap	68	932	p
73a	3-12	Ling	8ap	70	1613	p
63	4-15	Brig	8fm	70	1691	p
75	1-12	**YARM**	7gd	69	3490*	p
76	2-12	Leic	8fm	73	3813	p
59	10-16	Ches	7g/f	73	4051	p
68	10-21	Donc	7fm	73	4482	p
78	4-11	Yarm	8gd	73	4615	p
79	2-16	Good	7gd	73	4873	p

75a	3-12	Ling	8ap	70	5079	p

CONCERT HALL 3 b f £285

57	4-10	Folk	9.7sft	[75]	977
37	6-6	Sali	9.9gd	[75]	2663

CONCERT TIME 2 ch f £1359

50	7-9	Donc	5gd		929
48	3-11	Beve	5g/f		1831
38	6-11	Thir	6g/f		1968
34a	5-7	Sout	7af		2721
49	3-9	Leic	5g/f		2921
48a	3-8	Ling	6ap	[46]	3745
33	10-19	Bath	5gd	47	5021

CONCHONITA 3 b f £590

42a	2-13	Wolv	8.5af	[40]	46
38a	6-9	Sout	11af	[43]	224
0	9-9	Wolv	9.4af	[45]	480

CONCUBINE 5 b m £2996

59	3-7	Brig	7g/f	60	2045	
57	7-16	Brig	7fm	60	2258	
63	2-6	Good	7gd	60	2539	
55	4-8	Newb	6fm	58	2648	P
56	7-10	Epso	7g/f	62	2872	p
27	12-12	Ling	7.6gd	[60]	3448	
12	13-13	Good	6gd	58	3952	BL

CONFUZED 4 b g £1154

35a	9-14	Ling	6ap		652	
60a	3-7	Ling	5ap		737	e
33a	6-14	Ling	7ap	[45]	783	e
26a	14-14	Ling	6ap	[52]	819	e
51a	9-9	Ling	5ap	[45]	1023	e
4a	11-12	Ling	6ap	[45]	1075	e
41a	8-15	Sout	5af	[43]	2803	e
39	4-12	Brig	6g/f	43	3301	BL
29a	11-13	Sout	6af	[43]	3482	e
34	9-13	Bath	5.7g/f	[40]	3844	bl e
47	3-9	Brig	7sft	[40]	4164	e
46	3-14	Bath	6g/f	45	4411	e/s
4	13-15	Yarm	10.1g/s	[45]	5122	e

CONFUZION 2 b f £0

1a	14-14	Sout	8af		95	P

CONGO MAN 11 b g £0

4	10-10	Hami	13g/f	55	2479
16	8-10	Hayd	16.2sft	45	3275

CONJUROR 3 b c £5434

0	U-10	Sali	6gd		3452
86	1-8	**NEWM**	6g/f		3784*
19	11-11	Hayd	6g/f	[83]	4350

CONNECT 7 b g £22380

89	2-15	Hayd	6g/f	86	1917	bl
86	4-17	Muss	5fm	87	2082	bl
77	10-13	York	5g/f	87	2359	bl
83	4-11	Sand	5g/s	86	2894	bl
92	1-12	**NEWM**	5g/f	85	3279*	bl
98	4-24	Asco	5gd	94	3466	bl
84	8-14	Newb	5.2fm	87	3628	bl
85	11-20	Hayd	5fm	94	3792	bl
87	15-22	Donc	5.6fm	93	4459	bl
64	19-24	Ayr	6sft	93	4686	bl
91	4-20	York	6gd	90	5001	bl
87	6-13	Muss	5g/s	89	5143	bl

CONNOTATION GB 2 b f £7265

72	2-5	Brig	5.3g/f		2430	
75a	2-7	Ling	5ap		2839	
59	3-6	Brig	6fm		3671	
49a	13-14	Ling	7ap	69	4177	
75	1-14	**REDC**	5fm	66	4556*	VIS
62	6-10	Newm	6fm	72	4727	vis
77a	3-12	Wolv	5.1ap	[72]	4981	BL

CONQUERING LOVE 6 b g £0

65	11-13	York	11.9g/s	83	3076
0	R-6	Pont	12gd	[83]	3458
0	P-17	Thir	12fm	83	4377

CONSENSUS 4 b f £2179

42a	15-15	Sout	5af	80	64
6a	14-14	Ling	6ap	75	149
81	4-22	Donc	6gd	80	921
36	16-19	Beve	5sft	80	1627

38	13-15	Ripo	6g/f	79	1782
76	3-10	Donc	6g/f	79	1878
23	20-20	York	6g/f	79	2059
2	12-13	Donc	6gd	77	2232
74	4-15	Pont	5gd	75	3680
69	6-18	Beve	5g/s	75	3852
48	16-19	Beve	5g/s	72	4240
35	8-9	Pont	6g/f	71	4627
54	10-15	Newc	5fm	69	4870

CONSIDER THIS 2 b f £7783

75	2-8	Pont	6g/f		2603
60	5-17	Nott	6.1gd		2927
79	3-12	Thir	6g/f		3411
83	2-12	Wind	6gd	79	3825
80	7-21	Donc	6.5fm	82	4457
81	2-11	Ayr	7.2g/s	[82]	4653
82	3-9	Ayr	8sft	[79]	5033
58	4-9	Catt	7sft	[79]	5316
78	2-14	Muss	7.1g/s	[79]	5330

CONSIDINE 3 b c £13461

21a	8-13	Sout	8af	[60]	1193
69	1-6	**PONT**	12sft	59	1429*
73	2-11	Sand	14g/s	67	2130
76	1-9	**YARM**	14.1g/f	67	2345+
64	8-13	Newc	16.1sft	71	2685
75	2-12	Sand	14g/f	71	3359
62	6-9	Sand	14g/f	72	3893
74	4-13	Kemp	14.4fm	72	4395

CONSIGNIA 4 ch f £2065

49a	1-13	**WOLV**	8.5af	[48]	46*	VIS
25a	10-12	Wolv	7af	54	68	vis
38a	6-12	Ling	8ap	[49]	150	vis
28a	9-13	Sout	8af	49	221	vis
6a	11-13	Wolv	9.4af	49	281	bl
33a	9-12	Wolv	9.4af	45	427	P
11a	5-9	Wolv	8.5af	[45]	437	

CONSONANT 7 ch g £30362

69a	1-10	**WOLV**	8.5af		398+
82a	1-11	**WOLV**	8.5af	70	479*
90a	1-12	**WOLV**	8.5af	80	688*
94a	1-14	**LING**	10ap	86	758*
72	9-12	Ches	10.3gd	90	1586
89	6-14	Sand	8.1g/f	90	2096
88	8-15	York	8.9g/f	89	2404
95	2-13	Sali	8gd	89	2662
91	3-14	Hayd	8.1gd	89	2903
69	14-21	York	10.4gd	89	3118
76	7-15	York	7.9g/s	90	4061
86	7-11	Good	8.5g/f	89	4525

CONSTABLE BURTON 3 b g £3154

41	9-13	Muss	7.1g/f		1119
74a	1-7	**SOUT**	7af		1196*
0	18-18	Ayr	7.2sft	65	4622
59a	8-12	Wolv	7.1ap	[69]	5340
64a	4-11	Wolv	7.1ap	[69]	5357

CONSTANTINE 4 gr g £0

40	14-14	Asco	12g/f	76	4775

CONSTRUCTOR 3 b g £0

59	10-17	Wind	8.3fm		3480
57a	7-15	Ling	12ap		4111
48a	9-9	Ling	12ap		4315
42	12-13	Nott	8.2g/f		4847

CONSULAR 2 br c £983

73	3-15	Nott	8.2hvy		5344

CONTACT DANCER 5 b g £78007

81	6-9	Beve	16.2g/s	85	3181
88	4-12	Ches	15.9sft	84	4106
94	1-34	**NEWM**	18sft	83	5135*
92	3-7	Donc	16.5sft	89	5374

CONTENTED 2 b c £644

69a	5-14	Ling	7ap		5078
71a	3-11	Ling	8ap		5235

CONTINENT 7 ch g £23930

99	3-8	Hayd	6gd	[112]	2949
99	15-20	Newm	6g/f	[112]	3062
112	1-7	**NOTT**	5.1gd	[108]	3989+
96	7-11	Beve	5g/s	[108]	4238
102	5-12	Leic	5g/f	[107]	4454

111 3-24 Ayr 6sft 108 4686
104 10-15 Long 5g/f [108] 4952

CONTINENTAL FLYER 2 b f £0
0 R-14 Thir 7g/s 3831
40 8-11 Newc 7fm 4863 BL

CONTRARY MARY 8 b m £0
52a 13-16 Ling 7ap 64 55

CONVENT GIRL 4 b f £394
44 23-24 Donc 8gd 96 951
83 8-17 York 7.9g/s 95 1686
81 12-14 Sand 8.1g/f 94 2096
90 7-13 Epso 8.5g/f 94 2207
40 30-31 Asco 8g/f 94 2489
70 17-21 Good 8fm 91 3565
87 6-14 Sali 7gd 88 4331
73 8-13 Asco 8gd 85 4802
55 12-13 Bath 8sft 83 5172

CONVICTION 3 b g £0
60 5-7 Newm 10g/f 2534
40 14-16 Donc 10.3gd 2751

CONVINCE 3 ch g £314
67 9-19 Newm 6g/s 94 1154
85 8-14 York 7sft 90 1665
75 13-18 Hayd 8.1g/f 87 1919
83 5-7 Ches 7g/s 84 2749
75 6-9 Ling 7gd 82 3447 P
77 5-7 Kemp 7g/f 82 3522
67 12-14 Newb 10g/f 77 3961
53a 11-14 Ling 10ap [74] 4742

COODEN BEACH 4 b f £0
13a 11-12 Wolv 9.4af 48 427
43a 4-14 Ling 10ap [45] 828
42a 4-12 Ling 8ap [45] 1073
46 4-18 Nott 8.2g/s 48 1778
2 20-20 Yarm 8fm 46 2149

COOL BART 4 ch g £0
0 11-12 Sout 6af [30] 377

COOL BATHWICK 4 b g £4541
38a 10-14 Ling 13ap 56 259
60a 1-10 WOLV 12af [56] 359*
59a 2-11 Wolv 12af 57 380
40a 6-12 Wolv 12af 61 484
45 10-20 Warw 10.9gd 59 1128
45 7-17 Bath 11.7sft 55 1543 BL
44 7-18 Nott 10g/s 49 1777 bl
32 7-18 Wind 11.6g/f 47 1960 P
35 9-17 Nott 14.1g/f 47 2156 bl
45 4-19 Bath 17.2gd 44 3147
41 5-13 Sali 14.1gd 44 3454 T

COOL CLEAR WATER 3 b f £0
53a 11-15 Ling 7ap 875
49 11-14 Wind 10g/s 1055
53 8-12 Good 9g/f 1864
61 6-11 Chep 10.2gd 2196

COOL CRISTAL 2 ch f £0
23 12-13 Epso 7g/f 2870
13 10-11 Hayd 5g/f 4349
3 9-10 Newc 6g/f 4403

COOL PANIC 2 b c £6722
54 7-10 Newm 5fm 2089
88 2-13 Wind 6fm 3478
72 5-17 Wind 6g/f 3975
91 1-8 REDC 7gd [78] 4247*
76 6-14 Donc 7sft 83 5213

COOL SANDS 2 b c £0
23 8-8 Redc 7gd 4247
2 14-14 Hayd 6fm 4385
60a 6-12 Wolv 5.1ap 4981

COOL TEMPER 7 b g £4203
79a 3-12 Sout 8af 77 141 t
77a 3-11 Sout 8af 77 186 t
52a 6-10 Wolv 9.4af 78 278 t
67 5-6 Muss 8g/f 70 1092 t
68 3-9 Epso 8.5hvy [69] 1298
42 11-12 Hayd 8.1g/f 69 1485 P
56 8-10 Sand 10g/f 66 3336

56 10-12 Kemp 8g/f 66 3524 BL
66 2-12 Chep 8.1g/s 62 3898
28 13-15 Chep 8.1g/s 62 4300

COOLFORE JADE 3 ch f £6172
36a 13-16 Sout 7af 161
57a 4-14 Ling 10ap 60 230
50a 5-14 Ling 13ap 57 259
51a 9-14 Ling 10ap 57 339
60a 1-6 SOUT 12af [55] 392*
51a 4-6 Wolv 9.4af [55] 423
59a 1-9 SOUT 11af [57] 505*
52a 4-10 Sout 12af [57] 552
60a 3-7 Sout 12af [57] 594
45a 5-12 Wolv 12af 55 634
49a 8-14 Ling 12ap 52 801
61a 5-11 Ling 12ap [52] 816
15a 12-15 Sout 12af 52 867
28a 7-11 Wolv 12af 52 937
25 19-19 Brig 9.9g/f 49 1940
41 6-11 Folk 12g/f 45 2273
22a 3-9 Sout 12af [49] 2381
37a 8-8 Ling 12ap [47] 2739
5 10-14 Chep 10.2g/s 41 3895
23 9-19 Brig 9.9sft 41 4145
42 6-15 Folk 12g/f [40] 4374
37 4-11 Beve 12.1g/f [40] 4716
18 12-19 Brig 9.9gd [40] 4903
25a 6-11 Wolv 12.2ap 45 5009

COOLING CASTLE 8 ch g £0
13a 8-11 Wolv 12af [35] 666

COOMBE CENTENARY 2 b f £0
38 7-9 Ling 6gd 3020
56 10-13 Wind 6fm 3478
40 11-14 Folk 7ap 4115
51a 9-10 Ling 7ap 4442

COPPERFIELDS LASS 5 b m £0
2a 9-11 Sout 7af [40] 488 BL
13a 7-12 Wolv 7af [35] 663 P

COPPICE 3 ch c £1226
61 6-19 Yarm 8g/f 1130
74 4-14 Newb 9fm 3631
63 5-11 Folk 9.7gd 4120
74 3-15 Nott 8.2g/s [74] 4649

COPPINGTON FLYER 3 ch f £0
54a 10-12 Ling 8ap 58 17
33a 12-15 Ling 7ap 58 50
27a 15-15 Ling 7ap 54 151 BL
48a 4-13 Ling 7ap 50 474
46a 8-11 Ling 8ap 49 732
48a 4-10 Ling 8ap 49 766
23a 10-12 Ling 8ap 47 845
39a 4-10 Ling 8ap 47 917
26 12-14 Wind 8.3g/f 45 2799
2 17-17 Brig 7g/f 42 3176
34 4-15 Folk 7g/f [40] 4371 T

COPPLESTONE 8 b g £0
0 7-9 Sout 12af [30] 353 p
31 6-9 Ayr 13.1g/s [35] 1449 p
0 9-10 Redc 14.1g/s 33 2562 p

CORA 2 b f £0
54a 8-11 Ling 8ap 21

CORANGLAIS 4 ch g £5361
44 16-16 Thir 7g/s 76 1474
53 13-19 Sali 7g/f 73 1723
57 8-16 Good 6gd 69 2023
60 8-12 Sali 6fm 65 2289
57 9-18 Donc 6gd 61 2752 P
56 4-4 Brig 5.3fm 61 2838 bl
67 1-13 BATH 5gd [58] 3143* p
48 12-15 Chep 5.1gd 65 3403 p
48 7-9 Yarm 6g/f 63 3705 p
50 5-7 Folk 6g/s [63] 3910 p
35 12-15 Bath 5.7g/f 61 3966 p

51 8-18 Bath 5.7g/f 59 4412 bl
56 5-15 Chep 5.1gd 59 4489 bl
47 10-19 Ling 5g/f 55 4739 bl
59 2-13 Muss 5g/s [52] 5146 bl
58 2-19 Bath 5.7sft 52 5176 bl

CORBEL 4 b f £0
46 11-17 Newm 8gd [72] 4228
26 16-16 Sali 7sft 65 4582

CORCORAN 2 b f £5707
82 1-19 LEIC 7gd 5040*

CORDAGE 2 ch c £2277
71 5-9 Good 6gd 3951
78 4-10 Brig 6g/s 4139
74 4-7 Epso 6gd 4466
74 4-9 Muss 8g/s [80] 5331
82 2-16 Yarm 10.1g/s [80] 5352 P

CORDIER 2 b c £0
56 10-14 Ling 7.6g/f 3601

CORKER 2 ch c £0
65 6-10 Bath 5.7fm 2666
34 6-7 Ayr 5gd 3148

CORKY 3 b g £5487
74 4-12 Newb 7g/f 2352
75 3-13 Wind 6fm 2756
82 1-11 FOLK 7g/s 3048*
54 11-14 Sand 7.1g/f 78 3860
80 3-9 Sand 7gd 77 4110
65 14-24 Newb 7g/f 77 4642
45a 10-12 Ling 8ap 76 5238

CORMORANT WHARF 4 b c £4509
79a 7-14 Ling 6ap 80 292
75a 6-12 Ling 8ap 79 369
77a 5-14 Ling 7ap 77 518
75a 8-14 Ling 7ap 76 604
60a 10-11 Ling 8ap [75] 800
72a 5-14 Ling 6ap 74 874
55a 8-14 Ling 6ap 72 1017
31 7-9 Wind 6fm [70] 2760 P
65 6-13 Sali 6g/s 68 3109 VIS
68a 4-11 Ling 6ap 67 3333 BL
65 3-14 Chep 8.1gd 66 3733
71 2-12 Good 9g/f 65 4539
73 2-17 Newb 9sft 65 5198

CORNELIUS 6 b g £398
74a 13-14 Ling 10ap [100] 82
71a 12-12 Wolv 8.5af 100 836
40 9-14 Kemp 8hvy 98 1512
89 5-13 Sali 8gd 93 2662

CORNICHE DANCER 2 b f £5753
41 12-13 Newb 7g/f 3252
48 8-8 Good 6fm 3536
13 10-11 Wind 8.3fm 3798
74a 2-12 Ling 6ap 4178
72 1-10 CATT 6g/f [75] 4436*
5 26-26 Newb 6.5g/f 4679
58 5-9 Brig 7g/f 73 4758
69a 2-13 Wolv 6ap [70] 4980
46 9-12 Muss 7.1g/s [68] 5142
40 8-20 Newb 6hvy 68 5225

CORNISH GOLD 2 b f £1131
61a 6-14 Sout 7af [67] 98
38 12-14 Wind 10g/f 65 2452
66 2-16 Chep 10.2g/s 62 4365
46 7-17 Newb 9sft 62 5198

CORNUS 2 ch c £19969
90 1-8 WIND 5g/s 1053*
98 1-8 NEWM 5g/s 1149*
96 2-6 Asco 5sft 1422
107 2-11 Newm 5sft [95] 5132
62 7-8 Donc 6sft [95] 5217

CORNWALLIS 2 b c £4068
43a 10-13 Wolv 6af 126
54a 6-10 Ling 6ap 260
24a 14-11 Ling 6ap 543
68 1-10 BATH 5.7sft [55] 1539*
68 2-17 Sali 6g/f 61 1722
23 14-14 Wind 8.3fm 64 2971

46a 7-13 Sout 6af [57] 3482

CORONADO FOREST 4 b g £5120
51a	6-9	Wolv	7af	63	31
57a	9-14	Ling	10ap	61	174
60a	2-13	Ling	10ap	[58]	338
58a	4-14	Ling	10ap	[59]	430
65a	**1-9**	**LING**	10ap	[59]	476*
46a	10-14	Ling	10ap	65	520
44a	14-14	Ling	10ap	63	674
17	9-13	Folk	9.7sft	51	1273
33	6-9	Brig	9.9g/f	[49]	2643
7a	10-13	Ling	10ap	[59]	3025 BL

CORPS DE BALLET 3 b f £8761
51	7-8	Bath	5fm	[83]	1901
91	**1-11**	**NOTT**	6.1g/f	83	2155*
59	19-19	Newm	6fm	88	3002
75	10-10	Newm	6g/f	88	3584
80	9-9	Good	6g/f	87	4537
84	5-12	Epso	5g/f	84	4908
91	2-18	Pont	5g/s	83	5149
71a	8-12	Ling	6ap	85	5297

CORRAN ARD 3 b g £444
69	4-8	Hayd	10.5g/f	1489

CORRIB ECLIPSE 5 b g £32728
109	1-12	ASCO	22.2fm	2583*
93	6-8	Sand	16.4g/f[105]	2914
107	6-10	York	15.9gd[104]	4000
105	6-8	Donc	18fm [106]	4478
106	**1-5**	**PONT**	18g/f [106]	4628*
105	4-5	Asco	16.2g/f[106]	4815

CORRIDOR CREEPER 7 ch g £54704
90	5-14	Ches	5.1gd	90	1594 p
91	4-20	York	5g/s	90	1683 p
86	4-11	Good	5g/f	90	1845 p
93	2-17	Muss	5fm	89	2082 p
92	6-20	Epso	5fm	90	2253 p
65	24-29	Asco	6fm	89	2581 p
96	2-15	Newc	5g/s	92	2727 p
93	3-11	Sand	5g/s	91	2894 p
96	6-24	Asco	5gd	95	3466 p
78	18-28	Good	5fm	94	3622 p
99	3-20	Hayd	5fm	94	3792 p
94	5-14	Epso	5gd	95	4291 p
98	7-22	Donc	5.6fm	94	4459 p
98	3-11	Hayd	5sft	94	4780 p
102	2-12	Epso	5g/f	94	4908 p
105	**1-10**	**NEWM**	5gd	96	5090* p
106	2-13	Muss	5g/s	102	5143 p
98	5-13	Donc	5sft	99	5218 p

CORRINE 5 gr m £6600
104	2-12	Yarm	14.1sft	5254

CORRIOLANUS 4 b c £11807
102a	3-11	Ling	10ap		693
97a	11-14	Ling	10ap		884
95	7-12	Kemp	10gd	[104]	1139
0	16-16	Epso	10.1hvy	104	1296 BL
96	6-14	Good	12g/f	[100]	1843
86	9-14	Asco	10g/f	97	2556
91	6-7	Asco	10gd	[94]	3464
103	**1-6**	**NEWM**	10g/f	[94]	3754+
101	7-8	Good	9.9gd	[103]	4748

CORSICAN NATIVE 3 b c £11559
80	**1-7**	**GOOD**	9.9g/f		4541*
100	2-17	Newm	10g/f	90	4917
74	13-15	Leic	11.8gd	93	5043

CORTON 5 gr g £1068
84	3-13	Good	16g/f	80	4527
84	6-16	Asco	16.2g/f	82	4803
0	18-19	Newm	12gd	81	5085
37	9-11	Muss	16g/s	80	5335 P

CORTON DENHAM 2 ch c £0
32a	10-10	Ling	8ap	229
23a	12-14	Ling	10ap	473

CORYLUS 2 b f £0
13a	11-11	Wolv	7af	64	29

COSI FAN TUTTE 6 b g £2905
54	2-15	Wind	11.6g/f	2267 vis T

COSMIC CASE 9 b m £9167
65	3-12	Wind	10g/f	[65]	2800 vis t
8	7-7	Brig	11.9g/f	[65]	3173 vis t
57	7-17	Wind	10fm	63	3477 vis t
60	2-11	Chep	10.2gd	[63]	3730 vis t
55a	2-12	Ling	12ap	[63]	3819 vis t
47	1-8	AYR	13.1fm	45	1905*
44	7-9	Hami	13gd	47	2176
46	3-10	Hami	13g/f	46	2479
45	5-7	Hami	13gd	46	2708
49	2-7	Muss	12gd	45	2966
48	3-7	Hami	13gd	45	3134
42	7-10	Hami	13fm	45	3249
50	3-9	Ayr	15gd	45	3327
52	**1-7**	**MUSS**	13g/f	44	3530*
49	2-6	Hami	12.1g/f	51	3588
50	5-12	Muss	14g/f	49	4170
24	8-9	Muss	14gd	48	4521

COSMIC DESTINY 2 b f £0
63	7-20	York	6g/f	4401

COSMIC RANGER 6 b g £0
2a	9-11	Sout	12af	[32]	3154 bl t

COST ANALYSIS 2 ch c £0
68	10-12	Newm	7gd	4194
66	6-13	Newm	7fm	4724
73	5-14	Bath	8gd	5018
51	13-13	Donc	7hvy	5200

COSTA DEL SOL 2 ch g £0
41a	8-13	Ling	6ap	[53]	25
34a	9-12	Ling	8ap	[50]	78
34a	5-11	Ling	6ap	[47]	233 VIS
0	9-9	Ling	6ap	[45]	327
27a	11-15	Ling	7ap	[45]	411
34a	11-12	Ling	7ap	[40]	566
42a	4-6	Ling	8ap	[35]	651 bl
0	10-10	Brig	7g/f	[45]	1938
1	16-16	Kemp	9gd	40	3187
28	6-12	Brig	6g/f	40	3301 bl
15	9-12	Brig	7fm	37	3677 bl
19	8-14	Folk	6gd	32	4116
0	13-14	Ling	10ap	[35]	4662 P

COTE QUEST 3 b f £12794
93	3-	Mais	7fV		58
101	4-8	Kemp	8g/s		1115
61	14-17	York	7.9g/s	92	1686
99	4-8	Good	8g/f	[92]	1863
90	4-7	Pont	8g/f	[92]	2278
92	3-6	Newc	10.1g/s	[92]	2772
86	6-10	Chep	10.2g/s	[92]	3089
78	12-12	Bath	8g/f	[92]	3965
62	12-13	Asco	8g/f	90	4802

COTE SOLEIL 7 ch g £0
0	10-10	Sout	12af	49	421
22	8-12	Newb	10gd	53	3916
28	7-14	Good	8sft	50	4189

COTOSOL 3 b g £4581
74	7-22	Donc	7gd	76	955
81	**1-12**	**THIR**	7g/s	75	1215*
75	5-17	Warw	7.1sft	77	1526
69	8-14	York	7.9g/s	77	1707
79a	3-8	Sout	7af	76	2723

COTTAM GRANGE 3 b c £0
38a	4-12	Wolv	16.2af	46	156
9a	10-10	Wolv	12af	[45]	315

COTTAM KARMINSKI 3 b f £0
28	11-15	Beve	7.5g/f		1944
39	8-8	Beve	7.5g/f		2169
6	13-14	Donc	7hvy		2428
41	6-10	Beve	5sft		2944
0	14-15	Beve	8.5g/s	40	3182
13	14-16	Thir	8g/f	40	3414

COTTINGHAM 2 b c £4463
39a	9-14	Sout	8af	[67]	88
61a	4-14	Sout	8af	[60]	226
27a	8-11	Sout	8af	60	252
69a	**1-8**	**SOUT**	8af	[58]	355*
67	4-8	Thir	7sft	65	2693
47	6-9	Beve	8.5sft	65	2940
43	6-9	Donc	8g/s	63	3378
44	12-13	Thir	7g/f	63	3571
58	2-9	Thir	8sft	59	3835
44	15-20	York	7.9gd	60	4321
61	6-14	Redc	10fm	60	4342
57	6-18	Catt	7g/f	60	4438
49	6-13	Nott	10g/s	[59]	4650
64	2-12	Pont	10fm	[59]	4757
60	4-20	Catt	12gd	59	4966
37	11-13	Pont	8g/s	[58]	5153

COTTON EASTER 3 b f £3850
49	12-13	Newb	7gd		1210
56	9-17	Chep	8.1gd		2117
53	6-11	Chep	8.1g/f		2627
40	12-14	Wind	8.3fm	59	2971
45	12-19	Chep	7.1gd	55	3401
43	7-15	Nott	10g/s	51	4037
50	3-15	Chep	10.2g/s	49	4299
57	**1-12**	**CHEP**	10.2hvy	49	4708*
48	6-12	Brig	11.9sft	55	5093

COUGAR CAT 2 b c £12597
95	4-9	Asco	5g/f	2516
108	2-8	Curr	6.3gd	3319

COULD SHE BE MAGIC 2 b f £8159
58a	**1-15**	**SOUT**	7af	[56]	87*
62a	2-6	Sout	8af	57	506
61a	**1-6**	**WOLV**	7af	57	615*
34a	7-10	Sout	7af	61	794
63a	2-7	Wolv	7af	61	1376 BL
34	8-11	Newc	7sft	58	1678
23	5-6	Ripo	8g/f	[55]	1975 bl

COUNCELLOR 2 b c £3561
84	3-12	Newb	7g/f		2348
82	4-14	Newm	7g/f		2766
78	10-14	Good	6g/f		3511
82	2-13	Newm	7fm	[81]	4724

COUNCIL MEMBER 2 b c £43224
98	**1-10**	**NEWC**	5g/f		2158*
110	2-13	Asco	6g/f		2467
110	2-7	Newm	6g/f		3028
1	11-11	York	6g/s	[100]	4022
110	2-8	Kemp	6fm	[100]	4390

COUNSELS OPINION 7 ch g £15303
108	3-17	Kemp	10g/s	103	1111
104	4-11	Epso	10.1g/f	104	2208
88	11-13	Asco	12fm	104	2582
102	9-15	Hayd	11.9gd	103	2948
100	4-7	Asco	10gd	[100]	3464
105	2-10	Asco	12gd	100	3777
65	17-18	Newb	10gd	100	4681

COUNT BORIS 3 b g £1845
61	13-15	Newb	8g/f		1763
57	7-9	Wind	8.3g/f		3979
63	7-11	Wind	10gd		4125
44	7-10	Warw	8.1g/f		4421
58	3-17	Newm	9sft	58	5198
61	2-11	Yarm	10.1g/s	58	5353

COUNT COUGAR 3 b g £621
46a	12-16	Sout	5af	61	205
58a	3-11	Sout	5af	61	418
49a	10-10	Ling	5ap	61	453
22	17-19	Beve	5gd	60	2512
54	6-17	Catt	5g/f	56	2846
37	14-17	Catt	5g/f	54	3667
25	17-17	Beve	5g/f	53	4603
45	11-14	Redc	5fm	[50]	4930

COUNT DRACULA 3 b c £3311
69a	**1-11**	**LING**	8ap	[72]	841*
34	13-13	Kemp	7g/f	70	1141
48a	6-8	Sout	8af	67	2495 VIS
33	12-12	Bath	8g/f	64	3846

COUNT KRISTO 2 br c £1976
86	2-10	Newb	7g/f	3955
52	12-16	Newb	7g/f	4677

COUNT ON US 4 ch g £0
26a	13-14	Ling	10ap	[45]	828

COUNT WALEWSKI 4 b g £0

```
11 20-20 Newb 10gd    72  1235
18a 12-12 Ling 8ap    70  1613
```

COUNTDOWN 2 ch c £14973
```
85   3-3  Hami 5fm        3247
90a  2-8  Ling 5gd        3600
87   1-10 HAYD 5gd        3755*
92   1-7  SAND 5sft   81  4065*
91   2-6  Wind 5gd    87  4123
91   8-9  Chan 5.5gd [87]  4563 bl
77a  5-12 Wolv 5.1ap [92]  4981
```

COUNTESS ELTON 4 ch f £0
```
3a  12-12 Sout 8af [35]  309
```

COUNTRY RAMBLER 2 b c £13993
```
28  10-10 Donc 6g/f          2077
96  1-6   WARW 7.1fm         2597*
95  7-12  Newm 5gd           3060
94  3-4   Ches 7.6g/f [98]   4513
96  1-2   RIPO 6gd   [94]    4789*
```

COUNTRY REEL 4 b c £22432
```
96   8-15  York 6sft [110]  1667 VIS
94   4-9 . Wind 6g/f [107]  1958 vis t
113  4-14  Asco 6fm  [107]  2580 vis t
103  11-20 Newm 6g/f [104]  3062 vis t
87   12-13 Newb 7g/f [110]  3957 vis t
101  2-8   Yarm 6g/s [110]  4588 vis t
102  5-12  Asco 6g/f [110]  4799 t
101  4-14  Newm 6sft [105]  5100 t
```

COUNTRYWIDE DREAM 2 ch g £0
```
17  11-11 Hayd 5g/f   1880
18  14-14 Redc 6fm    2297
19  8-8   Beve 7.5gd  2511 P
9   5-5   Muss 7.1g/f 2612 p
```

COUNTRYWIDE FLYER 2 b g £10413
```
85a  1-14 SOUT 8af   [82]  88+
79a  4-11 Sout 8af    82   252
68a  5-7  Ling 8ap    81   341 BL
92a  1-6  WOLV 8.5af  80   470+
93a  2-10 Wolv 8.5af [80]  511
88a  3-3  Ling 10ap  [92]  727
```

COUNTRYWIDE GIRL 5 ch m £3079
```
0    10-11 Wolv 6af [32]  296
21a  3-11  Sout 8af [30]  372
30a  5-10  Wolv 7af [30]  394
25a  3-12  Wolv 7af [30]  663
22a  6-16  Sout 8af [30]  719
30a  4-7   Sout 7af [30]  1202
28a  3-11  Wolv 6af [30]  1261
38a  3-8   Wolv 7af [30]  1314
27a  2-7   Wolv 6af [35]  1566
36a  1-8   WOLV 7af [35]  1676*
24a  5-10  Sout 7af [35]  1839
39a  3-9   Sout 7af [39]  2801
26a  4-9   Sout 8af  39   2996
8    10-15 Newc 7gd [39]  3426
0    11-13 Hayd 6gd [35]  3757
```

COUNTRYWIDE LUCK 3 b g £5218
```
75  6-20 Newm 8g/f        3237
88  2-12 Hayd 10.5gd      3740
78  1-14 CARL 9.3g/f      4347*
89  6-17 Newm 10g/f   87  4917
81  7-13 Donc 12sft   86  5215
```

COUNTRYWIDE STAR 6 ch g £0
```
0  12-12 Wolv 9.4af [40]  668
```

COUNTRYWIDE SUN 2 b c £1427
```
60   8-8   Newm 6.1sft      1190
55   10-11 Nott 6.1sft      1739
64   7-9   Folk 7g/s        3047 BL
62   2-11  Thir 7g/f        3570 P
64a  4-13  Sout 7af     61  4040 p
4    18-20 Yarm 8g/s    61  4635 p
31   15-17 Redc 7g/s  [56]  5105 p
```

COUNTY CLARE 2 ch f £2782
```
57  10-13 Ling 6g/f         2061
82  2-14  Newb 6fm          3626
82  3-14  Newm 7g/f         3944
74  15-26 Newm 6.5g/f       4679
74  6-13  Newm 6g/f   [86]  4918
```

COUNTYKAT 3 b g £9963
```
76a  3-9   Wolv 8.5af   77      2 vis
36a  11-12 Sout 8af     77    141
73a  6-9   Wolv 12af    76    467 P
41a  13-15 Ling 12ap    75    549 vis
34   7-9   Newc 10.1sft [70]  1681
61   2-6   Pont 8g/f    [68]  2037
78a  1-12  SOUT 7af     [64]  2496* vis
77   2-17  Carl 7.9gd   69    2672 vis
35   7-7   Wind 8.3fm   73    2787 vis
62   7-9   Ayr 8g/f     72    3305 vis
```

COUP DE CHANCE 4 ch f £2248
```
64a  11-12 Ling 13ap    85   877 bl
84   5-14  Leic 10g/f   84   1828 bl
84   3-3   Ches 18.7fm  84   3635 bl
60   13-15 Bath 11.7g/f 84   3964 bl
```

COUP DETAT 2 b c £3766
```
87  4-9  Newm 6g/f        2531
88  2-12 York 6gd         3122
79  6-18 Newm 7gd         3927
90  4-16 Good 7gd    84   5031
77  3-15 Brig 7sft  [84]  5192
```

COURAGEOUS DUKE 5 b g £20425
```
74  20-31 Asco 8g/f    93   2489
99  2-9   Asco 10g/f   92   3439
94  3-6   Newm 10g/f   93   3749
98  2-8   Donc 10.3fm  93   4530
98  2-13  Asco 10g/f  [94]  4772
```

COURAGEOUSLY 2 b c £524
```
55  5-6  Wind 5g/f  1808
```

COURANT DAIR 3 b g £1841
```
31a  7-13 Wolv 8.5af  [45]  300
40a  3-9  Sout 8af     40   486
32a  6-8  Sout 11af    40   614
25a  5-10 Sout 8af     40   662
40   1-6  WARW 7.1g/s [40]  1330*
34   7-15 Carl 7.9fm  [40]  4507
```

COURS DE LA REINE 2 b f £26437
```
89   3-19  Newb 6g/f  2310
79   13-17 Asco 6g/f  2553
103  1-8   DEAU 7hvy  4157*
92   10-10 Long 8g/f  4954
```

COURT CHANCELLOR 3 b g £0
```
6   13-13 Kemp 8fm         2072
17  12-14 Sali 8fm    50   2423 VIS
48  7-10  Ling 6g/f  [43]  3603 BL
22  17-17 Kemp 7g/f  [45]  4794 bl
27  10-16 Brig 7gd   [40]  4901 bl
```

COURT EMPEROR 4 b g £0
```
0   9-9  Leic 11.8g/s  1016
54  9-15 Leic 10g/s    1358
55  9-10 Nott 14.1sft  1742
```

COURT MASTERPIECE 4 b c £122477
```
109  3-7  Good 7g/f  [106]  1811
103  5-11 Hayd 7.1gd [106]  2184
105  4-8  Newm 7g/f  [106]  2765
112  2-19 Newm 7g/f   105   3061
113  1-21 ASCO 7g/f   105   3441+
111  4-7  Good 8g/s  [110]  4232
109  3-8  Donc 7fm   [110]  4477
100  6-11 Good 7gd   [110]  4874
```

COURT MUSIC 4 b f £394
```
24a  8-11  Sout 6af  41     91 VIS
0    13-13 Sout 8af [36]   188 vis
7a   7-9   Sout 7af [32]   304 vis
33a  2-12  Sout 6af [35]   377 vis
22a  6-14  Sout 6af [35]   637 vis
0    9-11  Wolv 6af [35]   778 vis
```

COURT OF APPEAL 6 ch g £25280
```
67a  4-10  Sout 12af    70   138 t
70a  3-12  Sout 14af    70   173 t
66a  4-15  Sout 12af    67   257 t
84   1-13  CATT 13.8gd  70   997* t
91   1-12  CHES 12.3gd  78   1599* t
91   3-9   Thir 12g/f   85   1969 t
94   2-10  York 11.9g/f 86   2405 t
62   10-10 Asco 12g/f   87   3444 t
94   2-21  York 11.9gd  87   3999 t
```

```
0  6-6  Ayr 10.9sft [90]  4687 t
```

COURT ONE 6 b g £3245
```
0   14-15 Sout 12af     35   867
34  7-8   Yarm 11.5g/f  35   1135
40  1-9   WARW 15g/s   [35]  1329*
47  1-13  NOTT 14.1gd  [45]  1990*
15  11-11 Sand 14g/f    47   2391
42  7-10  Carl 14.1fm   47   3549
40  8-16  Warw 16.2gd   46   4276
39  11-14 Warw 16.2g/f  46   4423
```

COURT RULER 2 b g £0
```
0  5-6   Leic 7gd   4699
0  U-14  Bath 8gd   5018
7  10-10 Nott 10hvy 5188
```

COURTINTIME 2 b f £0
```
27  9-11  Hayd 5g/f  1880
20  13-16 Ripo 5gd   4787
```

COURTLEDGE 9 b g £0
```
13a  7-7  Ling 10ap [35]  1182 vis
```

COUSTOU 4 b g £1429
```
45  6-7   Muss 7.1g/f [75]  1094 p
32  10-10 Hami 6gd     69   1391
53  8-20  Thir 6gd     64   1638
59  4-14  Muss 7.1gd   59   1794
60  3-9   Ayr 7.2fm   [59]  1910
62  3-9   Hami 9.2gd   59   3132
52  7-8   Hami 9.2fm   59   3250 p
```

COVENTINA 3 gr f £18185
```
76  7-14 Donc 10.3gd   82  923
68  8-11 Ripo 12.3g/f  81  1174
86  2-9  Wind 11.6g/f  80  1807
91  3-5  Sali 14.1fm   82  2418
89  3-12 Sand 14g/f    85  3359
97  1-9  NEWM 16.1g/f  86  3779*
```

COY 3 b f £32000
```
92   5-6   Newm 8gd          1888
95   2-6   Leic 7gd   [92]   2136
106  2-19  Asco 8g/f   94    2491
107  1-7   ASCO 8g/f  [100]  3389+
```

CRACKLEANDO 2 ch c £7179
```
50a  10-11 Ling 8ap           21
67a  7-12  Ling 10ap         116
9a   7-9   Wolv 9.4af        240
60a  3-10  Ling 10ap  [62]   291
42a  9-10  Ling 10ap   59    676
60   3-6   Pont 12sft   57   1429
63   1-10  NOTT 14.1hvy 57   1612*
11   16-18 Hayd 14gd    62   2905
58   3-6   Redc 14.1g/f [60]  3771
60   2-17  Pont 17.1g/s 58   3970
54   7-14  Pont 17.1g/f 59   4936
42   9-11  Ayr 15sft    59   5032
```

CRACOW 7 b g £1389
```
49  2-11  Leic 11.8fm   45   2112
0   14-16 Sout 12af     45   2340
47  4-10  Leic 11.8g/f [46]  3211
43  5-12  Nott 14.1g/f  46   3420 P
2   8-8   Brig 11.9fm   45   3692 p
5   11-13 Folk 12gd     42   4119 p
```

CRAFTY CALLING 4 b c £0
```
51  9-9   Newm 6fm    96    1490
73  17-20 Asco 6fm    94    1926 t
51  11-11 Newm 7g/f   90    2532 BL
56  4-6   Folk 6fm   [90]   2715 t
29  8-8   Chep 7.1g/s [80]  4301
```

CRAFTY FANCY 3 ch f £9900
```
90  2-5   Hayd 5sft   85   1106
90  3-6   Asco 6sft  [88]  1421
68  8-11  Newb 6gd   [93]  1732
80  10-19 Asco 8g/f   93   2491
32  17-19 York 7.9gd  87   4987
```

CRAFTY POLITICIAN 6 ch h £1670
```
28a  13-16 Ling 7ap  [50]  123
40a  11-16 Ling 7ap  [47]  180 BL e
37a  10-12 Ling 10ap [42]  272 bl
41a  4-9   Sout 7af  [40]  639
45a  1-6   LING 6ap  [40]  1184+ bl
```

```
42a  2-5   Ling  7ap    [40]   1288 bl
41   5-7   Brig  6g/f   [47]   1368 bl
32   6-10  Brig  5.3gd  [45]   1544 bl
28   15-18 Good  5g/f    45    1867 bl
```

CRAIC SA CEILI 4 b f £454
```
46   10-18 Asco  8sft    75    1423
34   17-19 Sali  7g/f    72    1723 P
42   9-9   Leic  8fm     68    2108
63   4-13  Newb  7g/f    63    2880
48   8-13  Good  6gd     63    3952
47   5-19  Chep  8.1g/s [60]   4366
44   12-20 Leic  7gd     58    5046
```

CRAIGMOR 4 br g £0
```
24a  8-10  Wolv  8.5af  [52]   311
8a   8-9   Wolv  8.5af  [45]   437 BL
```

CRAIL 4 b g £5041
```
69   3-18  Asco  8sft    72    1423
63   7-12  Sand  8.1g/s  72    2129
71   4-13  Newb  8fm     70    2647
75   1-12  SALI  8g/s    70    4077*
63   10-10 Leic  8gd    [75]   4702
68   10-20 Newm  7g/s    74    5286
```

CRAIOVA 5 b h £800
```
77   16-24 Donc  8gd     90    951
59   22-27 Newb  8gd     90    1231 P
82   7-13  Kemp  7gd     87    2172
75   7-12  Kemp  7g/s    84    2679
76   9-14  Hayd  8.1gd   84    2903
73   9-13  Asco  7gd     80    3068
82   4-16  Newb  7g/f    77    3954
73   12-24 Newb  7g/f    80    4642
```

CRATHES 3 ch f £1996
```
59   2-10  Pont  6hvy          1070
55   4-8   Muss  7.1gd         1554
43a  6-13  Sout  8af           2383
```

CRATHORNE 4 b g £2101
```
82   4-19  York  11.9sft 80    1668 p
83   3-9   Donc  12g/f   80    2078 p
79   4-9   Thir  12fm    80    2465 p
49   13-15 Newm  12g/f   79    3066 p
63   11-21 York  11.9gd  77    3999 p
69   13-17 Thir  12fm    75    4377 p
52   13-17 Ayr   9.1g/s [71]   4620 p
63a  8-12  Wolv  12.2ap  69    4924 p
18   17-19 Pont  10g/s   65    5148 p
```

CRAZY LIKE A FOOL 5 b g £0
```
0    13-13 Muss  8gd           2967
```

CREAM OF ESTEEM 2 b c £0
```
26   13-13 Donc  7hvy          5199 T
58   13-21 Donc  6sft          5368 t
```

CREATIVE CHARACTER 2 b c £343
```
72   4-15  Ling  7gd           3285
56   9-11  Sand  8.1g/s        3890
55   9-15  Chep  7.1gd         4483
```

CREDIT 3 b c £21246
```
60   3-10  Bath  8g/s          1100
90   3-24  Newm  8fm           1495
86   1-15  NEWB  8g/f          1763*
84   10-27 Asco  8g/f    88    2521
79   7-16  Newm  8g/f    87    3059
87   4-7   Newm  10g/f   85    3474
94   1-7   WIND  10fm    84    3801+
92   3-14  Newb  10g/f   89    3961
92   3-10  York  11.9gd  90    4324
92   3-13  Kemp  12g/f  [90]   4715
45   12-19 Newm  12gd    90    5085
```

CREE 2 b c £9406
```
44   8-8   Newb  5.2gd         1205
49   13-14 Bath  5gd           1401
63   5-6   Carl  5g/f          3652 BL
61   2-7   Folk  5gd           3907 bl
60   5-6   Wind  5gd     59    4123 bl
63   2-6   Good  5sft    59    4187
62   3-8   Good  6g/f    59    4536
70   1-9   CHEP  5.1hvy  59    4706*
66   4-11  Epso  6g/s    64    4907
44   5-20  Newb  6hvy    64    5225
71   2-16  Nott  5.1hvy  64    5343
```


CREEK DANCER 2 b f £0
```
45   17-19 Leic  7gd           5040
```

CREME DE LA CREME 2 b f £0
```
70   8-18  Nott  8.2g/s        4035
56a  13-14 Ling  7ap           5258
```

CRESKELD 5 b g £14875
```
87a  3-12  Wolv  8.5af   87    836
18   12-16 Newc  8hvy    72    1036
29   14-17 Thir  8g/s    72    1214
51   14-14 Hami  8.3gd   72    1748
60   9-17  Hayd  8.1gd   70    2947
49   8-10  Hayd  7.1g/s  67    3137
71   1-17  HAMI  9.2g/s  64    4008*
67   4-12  Redc  8gd     68    4246
1    14-14 Hami  8.3g/s  68    4820
71   5-17  Redc  10sft   68    5307
```

CRESSEX KATIE 4 b f £0
```
0    15-15 Sout  5af     58    187
30a  13-13 Ling  7ap     58    565
```

CRETAN GIFT 12 ch g £0
```
76a  5-12  Ling  6ap    [85]   106 bl
51a  16-16 Sout  5af     80    205 vis
74a  9-13  Ling  6ap     80    235 vis
63a  5-8   Wolv  7af     76    285 vis
59a  4-13  Ling  6ap    [73]   400 vis
```

CRETE 2 b c £492
```
72   4-15  Nott  8.2hvy        5344
```

CREWES MISS ISLE 2 b f £3338
```
69a  8-13  Wolv  6af     75    1
57a  4-11  Wolv  6af    [70]   466
55   6-6   Warw  6.1sft [72]   1088
70a  1-4   WOLV  5af    [65]   1338*
61   5-10  Folk  6sft    69    1576
62   8-12  Wind  5g/f    67    1809
34   9-12  Chep  6.1gd   64    2118
28a  7-8   Sout  6af    [67]   2379
55   5-12  Folk  6gd     62    3380
56   8-11  Sand  5sft    60    4070
36a  11-13 Wolv  6ap     65    5010
46a  7-11  Wolv  7.1ap  [60]   5178
```

CRIMSON BOW 2 ch f £0
```
53   9-14  Hayd  6gd           3735
```

CRIMSON PALACE 5 b m £338362
```
111  4-11  Nad   9g/f          991
115  1-6   YORK  10.4g/s       1684*
94   6-10  Asco  8g/f   [110]  2487
118  1-11  ARLI  9.5fm  [110]  4013*
```

CRIMSON SILK 4 ch g £7872
```
99   8-17  Donc  6gd    [102]  952
57   8-8   Newm  6gd    [102]  1187
90   10-11 Leic  7g/s   [102]  1356
76   12-14 Ling  7sft    98    1624 P
82   9-11  Hayd  7.1gd  [94]   2184 p
95   3-16  Wind  6fm     90    2758 p
80   11-11 Newb  6g/f   [92]   3268 p
92   3-16  Wind  6gd     92    3827 BL
```

CRIMSON STAR 3 b f £1665
```
13   7-7   Nott  8.2hvy        1610
47a  11-13 Ling  10ap          2066
37   12-14 Sali  7fm           2291
39   15-17 Wind  8.3fm         3480
33   3-14  Folk  6gd     38    4116
45   2-15  Folk  7g/f   [40]   4371
43a  2-12  Ling  8ap    [40]   4659
49   2-19  Kemp  6g/f   [40]   4793
```

CRIMSON SUN 2 b c £24164
```
98   2-11  York  6g/s          1687
88   1-10  DONC  6g/f          2077*
103  1-4   NEWM  6fm           3406*
84   8-11  York  6g/f   [97]   4022
103  2-9   Newm  7gd    [97]   4881
```

CRIPSEY BROOK 6 ch g £4835
```
81   6-17  Thir  8g/s     86   1475
88   6-14  York  10.4g/s  86   1704
87   7-15  Redc  10g/f    86   2101
85   7-15  York  8.9g/f   85   2404
```


```
90   2-13  Redc  10gd     84   2560
85   5-13  Donc  8gd     [87]  2753
80   6-10  Pont  8gd      87   3460
74   12-20 Hayd  10.5fm   85   3794
81   7-9   Newm  10gd     84   4227
76   12-17 Thir  12fm     82   4377
82   5-20  York  10.4gd   79   4986
```

CRISPIN GIRL 2 ch f £0
```
56a  7-9   Ling  5ap     [52]  76
0    9-11  Ling  6ap     [54]  233
```

CRISPIN HOUSE 4 b f £0
```
0    12-12 Nott  14.1g/f  34   3420
```

CRISTOFORO 7 b g £19591
```
55   1-19  WARW  10.9sft  48   1090*
49   10-11 Leic  10g/s    56   1357
71   1-16  FOLK  12fm     55   2718*
79   1-8   EPSO  12g/f    60   2869*
77   1-9   EPSO  10.1fm   66   3538*
82   1-14  WIND  11.6fm   66   3638*
```

CRITICAL STAGE 4 b g £6105
```
60a  5-11  Sout  8af      61   186 e
63a  3-12  Wolv  9.4af    61   382 e
68a  1-8   SOUT  11af     61   595* e
65a  3-6   Sout  12af     67   683 e
51   4-11  Chep  12.1gd   66   3398
56   6-14  Chep  8.1gd    63   3733
60   4-18  Sali  9.9gd    61   4850
64   4-19  Bath  11.7gd   61   5024
```

CROCIERA 3 b c £314
```
58   4-8   Pont  10hvy         1067
1    9-11  Warw  12.6sft   68   1528
16   17-20 Catt  12gd      63   4966
48   8-15  Leic  11.8gd   [63]  5060 BL
```

CROCODILE DUNDEE 2 b c £64600
```
86a  5-13  Ling  7ap           119
97a  7-15  Ling  7ap     [88]  885
100a 6-9   Ling  8ap     [90]  1040
104  3-5   Newm  10g/f   [93]  1482
107  2-7   Good  11g/f   [96]  1814
110  2-13  Asco  10g/f  [105]  2520
112  1-1   SAND  10g/s  [105]  2898+
112  1-11  COPE  12gd   [105]  3660*
```

CROCODILE KISS 2 b f £0
```
72   5-13  Kemp  6gd           3183
72   5-12  Carl  5.9fm         3544
51   10-18 Ling  6gd           4108
45   6-20  Newb  6hvy     70   5225
```

CROCOLAT 3 ch f £9420
```
44   20-24 Newm  8fm           1495
57   9-20  Wind  10sft         1651
48   5-6   Yarm  7g/f          2342
61   2-5   Brig  11.9g/f   55   2642
59a  4-11  Sout  12af      55   2804
64a  1-11  SOUT  12af     [57]  3154*
72a  1-8   SOUT  12af      56   4128*
67   3-16  Kemp  16g/f     62   4361
73   2-14  Pont  17.1g/f   66   4936
```

CROIX DE GUERRE 4 gr g £443
```
53   3-13  Warw  12.6g/s [50]  4665 bl
```

CROIX ROUGE 2 b c £984
```
78   3-13  Warw  7.1g/f         4416
0    12-12 Wind  8.3g/f         4829
72   9-19  Leic  7gd            5055
```

CROMARTY BAY 3 b f £0
```
0    11-11 Leic  10g/f          3208
```

CRONKYVODDY 3 b g £281
```
62   6-14  Yarm  7fm            2148 T
7a   11-13 Sout  8af            2383 t
57   6-11  Hayd  8.1gd          2886 t
54   4-6   Newc  10.1sft [58]   4286 t
```

CROON 2 b c £0
```
66a  6-10  Ling  7ap            5264
```

CROSS ASH 4 ch g £212
```
39   7-8   Hayd  6gd     [76]   1345
38   10-10 Leic  7g/f    [72]   2920
```

CROSS MY SHADOW (continued)

10a	14-14	Sout	8af	[66]	3392 H
33	17-18	Catt	7g/f	60	4438
27	11-14	Catt	6gd	53	4967
51	6-17	Leic	7gd	53	5056
51a	3-13	Wolv	8.6ap	[50]	5212

CROSS MY SHADOW 2 b c £0

37	7-11	Wind	8.3fm		3798 T
56	5-6	Brig	7sft		4163 t
56	9-17	Warw	7.1gd		4269 t
56	7-12	Bath	5.7gd	63	4545 t
57	12-15	Hayd	6sft	63	4765 t
44	7-19	Bath	5gd	57	5021 BL t

CROSS THE LINE 2 b c £322

74a	4-11	Ling	8ap	5235

CROSS TIME 2 b c £0

65	6-16	Newb	8hvy	5220

CROSSED WIRE 5 ch m £0

23a	8-10	Sout	14af	67	90

CROSSOVER 2 b f £20564

107	2-9	Chan	5.5gd	4563
98	2-7	Chan	6gd	4957

CROSSPEACE 2 b c £20481

88	2-10	Newc	6g/f		4403
85	1-14	NEWC	6fm		4865*
95	1-14	DONC	7sft	84	5213*

CROSSWAYS 6 b g £6304

62a	4-14	Ling	10ap	63	520
70a	1-12	LING	13ap	63	762*
49a	9-10	Ling	12ap	68	936
72	4-18	Nott	14.1g/s	68	1772
75	2-17	Nott	14.1g/f	69	2156
74	2-15	Newb	13.3g/f	69	2311

CROW WOOD 5 b g £23442

77	8-16	Epso	10.1hvy	92	1296
93	3-12	Ches	10.3gd	92	1586
97	3-15	Redc	10g/f	92	2101
89	5-7	Pont	10g/f	[94]	2605
99	2-15	Hayd	11.9gd	94	2948
86	13-19	York	13.9g/s	95	4023
98	6-20	Hayd	14fm	95	4383
82	6-7	Hayd	14sft	95	4778

CROWN AGENT 4 b f £0

27a	10-11	Ling	12ap	[75]	672
66	5-22	Donc	12gd	75	918
60	8-20	Wind	11.6g/s	73	1056
66	9-17	Sali	14.1g/s	70	1502
68a	7-15	Ling	12ap	[61]	2393

CROWN CITY 4 b f £0

32a	7-10	Sout	8af	48	677
25a	2-10	Ling	10ap	[48]	738 t
6a	9-12	Sout	8af	[35]	905 t
5	10-10	Warw	8.1g/s	[40]	1328 t

CROWN OF MEDINA 2 ch c £0

53	15-23	Newm	7g/f	4885
62a	6-10	Wolv	7.1ap	5179

CRUISE DIRECTOR 3 b g £12516

75a	10-13	Ling	10ap	84	26
88a	3-16	Ling	12ap	83	293
35a	13-16	Ling	12ap	83	475
77a	3-7	Wolv	12af	82	642
41a	7-9	Sout	12af	81	856
87	1-20	WIND	11.6g/s	80	1056*
70	13-20	Newm	12gd	84	1172
68	11-14	Hami	12.1gd	85	1389
88	2-19	York	11.9sft	83	1668
84	4-19	Hayd	10.5g/s	85	4766
83	5-13	Donc	12sft	85	5215
85	5-24	Donc	12sft	84	5372

CRUNCHY 5 ch g £0

1a	16-16	Sout	11af	67	97 t
38	13-19	Donc	10.3gd	54	924 t p

CRUSOE 6 b g £2803

66a	5-10	Wolv	8.5af	67	5
38a	9-16	Sout	11af	66	97
64a	4-12	Sout	8af	66	141 bl
46a	4-8	Wolv	9.4af	65	157 bl
57a	8-11	Sout	8af	65	186 bl
61a	3-13	Wolv	8.5af	[61]	699 bl
9a	11-12	Wolv	9.4af	61	747 bl
21a	9-9	Wolv	8.5af	61	809 bl
47a	4-10	Sout	8af	[57]	868
0	18-19	Donc	10.3gd	57	924 bl
39a	8-15	Sout	8af	55	1028 bl
50a	4-13	Wolv	9.4af	51	1223 bl
52a	2-12	Wolv	8.5af	50	1379 bl
18a	7-8	Wolv	9.4af	51	1657 bl
8	11-11	Hayd	10.5g/s	51	2226 bl
53a	2-15	Sout	8af	51	2338 bl
35a	9-15	Sout	8af	51	2500 bl
33a	10-15	Sout	8af	51	2725 bl

CRUSTY LILY 8 gr m £206

19a	3-7	Ling	6ap	[30]	1715 P
19	13-16	Nott	6.1gd	[35]	1989 p
9	7-13	Yarm	6g/f	30	2347 p
0	12-12	Brig	8gd	[30]	4904

CRUX 2 b g £0

42	14-15	Nott	5.1gd	4859

CRUZSPIEL 4 br c £4824

111	3-7	Curr	14gd	2817 bl

CRY OF THE WOLF 2 ch c £0

52	9-11	Yarm	6g/f	1727
66	8-8	Newm	6g/f	1934

CRYFIELD 7 b g £9136

25	15-19	Donc	10.3gd	65	924
48	8-17	Thir	8g/s	62	1214
57	6-20	Ripo	8g/s	60	1366
59	2-5	Yarm	7g/f	[58]	1731
57	4-18	Thir	8g/f	57	1972
52	7-15	Beve	7.5g/s	57	2324
54	8-16	Beve	7.5g/s	56	2655
66	1-12	BEVE	8.5gd	56	2890*
56	6-10	York	7.9g/s	61	3074
59	4-10	Beve	8.5g/f	62	3501
59	3-12	Ayr	9.1g/f	60	3766
54a	4-15	Sout	8af	55	4132
58	9-15	Carl	7.9g/f	60	4346
41	11-13	Nott	10g/s	[59]	4650
58	6-15	Beve	7.5g/s	57	4719 vis
51a	6-13	Wolv	8.6ap	[52]	5184 vis
43a	8-12	Wolv	8.6ap	[51]	5337 vis

CRYPTOGAM 4 b f £0

0	8-9	Sout	12af	52	456
0	8-8	Sout	16af	47	554
4a	9-10	Sout	8af	47	678
30	10-15	Redc	9g/f	47	2120
20	11-11	Redc	8fm	47	2296
36	5-20	Catt	12g/f	40	2850
2	11-13	Pont	12gd	39	3240
23	16-20	Catt	12g/f	39	3354

CRYSTAL 3 b f £14781

95	2-10	Newb	10gd		1209
88	1-16	WIND	10gd		1384*
80	5-7	Epso	12g/f	[93]	2210
58	11-12	Yarm	10.1sft	93	4149
87	8-11	Yarm	10.1gd	[93]	4843
78	5-6	Donc	12sft	[90]	5369 BL

CRYSTAL CASTLE 6 b g £65211

109	3-10	Long	7g/s	[94]	2139
116	2-14	Asco	6gd		2580 T
107	5-8	Good	7g/f		3508 t

CRYSTAL CHOIR 3 b f £0

0	W-13	Wolv	8.5af		39
24	15-17	Leic	10g/s		1019
69	6-10	Sali	9.9g/f		1718
40	13-15	Kemp	9gd	65	2170

CRYSTAL CURLING 3 ch f £10073

98	3-9	Ches	11.4gd		1568
98	3-7	Newb	10gd		1733
94	7-9	Asco	12g/f	[99]	2517
88	5-6	Newc	10.1g/s	[99]	2772
96	5-6	Epso	10.1gd	[99]	4290
55	13-13	Asco	8g/f	97	4802 T

CRYSTAL MYSTIC 2 b c £0

CRYSTAL MYSTIC (continued)

49	11-15	Chep	7.1gd		4483 BL
64	4-11	Chep	7.1hvy		4703 bl
35a	10-13	Wolv	6ap		5182 bl
36	11-14	Nott	6.1hvy	[50]	5342

CRYSTALLINE 2 b f £741

79	3-7	Newm	7g/f	3616
47	11-12	Folk	7gd	3909

CTESIPHON 2 b f £418

45a	3-9	Wolv	9.4af		238
49	8-8	Ripo	10g/s		1365
28	10-16	Nott	10hvy	52	1611
6a	10-12	Wolv	8.5af	50	2205 BL

CUBIC CONFESSIONS 2 b f £1310

58a	4-10	Ling	5ap	882
52a	4-5	Ling	5ap	1041
13	4-4	Folk	5gd	3382

CUDDLES 5 b m £868

74a	7-9	Ling	10ap	77	876 p
58	5-9	Folk	9.7sft	[65]	978 p
47	9-10	Folk	12g/s	65	1082 p
60	4-10	Newb	8g/f	60	2350
53	5-8	Kemp	9g/s	59	2680
61	3-13	Bath	10.2gd	[59]	3144
51	8-12	Ling	7.6gd	[57]	3448
56	10-10	Sali	9.9g/f	[57]	3866
52	7-11	Wind	8.3g/s	57	4222
54	6-16	Chep	10.2g/s	57	4365
34	11-18	Warw	10.9g/s	54	4669 BL
65a	7-12	Ling	8ap	68	4743 vis
35a	12-13	Wolv	8.6ap	65	5364 bl

CUGINA NICOLA 3 b f £0

58	10-13	Kemp	10gd	3186
41	10-12	Hayd	10.5gd	3740
18	9-13	Leic	12g/f	4453

CULCABOCK 4 b g £0

36	7-9	Muss	14gd	50	4521

CULMINATE 7 ch g £0

0	11-12	Wolv	7af	[35]	663 P

CULTURED 3 b f £0

63	5-20	Wind	10sft	1651
55	6-12	Good	9g/f	1864

CUMBRIA 3 b f £1267

73	3-4	Hayd	11.9g/s	1347
70	4-13	Thir	12g/f	1768

CUMBRIAN KNIGHT 6 b g £0

43	8-13	Nott	10gd	4861

CUMBRIAN PRINCESS 6 gr m £3517

30a	8-14	Sout	8af	38	93
22a	5-13	Sout	8af	34	228
30a	4-9	Wolv	12af	35	424
7a	10-12	Wolv	8.5af	35	564
18a	8-13	Wolv	8.5af	[30]	894
42a	1-12	LING	8ap	[30]	971*
45a	1-12	LING	8ap	[40]	1185*
43a	3-5	Ling	8ap	[40]	1245
0	6-8	Sout	8af	[45]	1841
46a	3-14	Ling	10ap	45	2589
39a	6-14	Ling	10ap	45	3605
33	6-9	Newb	8g/s	45	3922
18	10-12	Sali	8g/s	45	4077

CUMMISKEY 2 b c £4485

71	5-8	Wind	5g/s		1053
76	3-13	Bath	5.7g/f		3368
75	4-10	Wind	5fm		3476
80	2-14	Warw	6.1g/f	77	4420
81	2-8	Good	6g/f	77	4536

CUMWHITTON 5 b m £1449

16a	5-12	Sout	11af	[35]	640
23a	9-16	Sout	11af	[30]	852
40a	1-9	SOUT	11af	[30]	906* P
10a	6-7	Sout	11af	[45]	1589 p

CUNNING PURSUIT 3 b g £2467

50	10-19	Yarm	8g/f	1130
42a	6-6	Wolv	8.5af	1377
49	5-11	Nott	6.1sft	1607

37 6-13 Beve 8.5g/f [45] 1947
48 2-11 Yarm 11.5g/f 43 2346
24 10-18 Hayd 14gd 47 2905
22 9-14 Nott 16g/f 46 3580
53 1-13 FOLK 9.7g/f [45] 4372*
46 4-18 Kemp 10g/f [50] 4791

CUP OF LOVE 2 ch f £0
59 8-13 Kemp 6g/f 4358
53 12-15 Newm 8fm 4723
54 9-11 Newm 6sft 5265

CUPIDS GLORY 2 b c £52882
79a 6-13 Ling 7ap 3329
98a 1-10 LING 6ap 3817*
103 1-5 CHES 6.1sft 4105*
111a1-14 LING 7ap 97 4177*
109 3-6 Curr 6g/s [97] 4736
112 1-13 NEWB 7sft [100] 5195+
90 4-8 Sain 8Very [100] 5315

CURATE 5 ch g £0
8 6-6 York 10.4g/f [40] 2356 t

CURFEW 5 b m £2250
93 4-14 Bath 5gd [95] 1400
84 5-9 Ches 5.1g/f [94] 3100
89 8-10 Ayr 5g/f [92] 3304

CURRAGH GOLD 4 b f £0
24 9-12 Wind 10fm 54 3295
17 11-13 Nott 10gd 50 3992
22a 12-14 Ling 16ap [47] 4663

CURRENCY 6 b g £9406
60a 10-13 Wolv 6af 76 45
60a 12-14 Ling 6ap 73 292
74a 3-10 Ling 5ap 73 329
75a 2-14 Ling 6ap 70 407
69a 4-10 Ling 5ap 73 453
73a 7-14 Ling 7ap 73 604
67a 12-15 Ling 7ap 72 698
55 14-16 Good 6gd 78 2023
77 4-13 Hami 5g/f 75 2320
26 9-9 Chep 6.1g/f 76 2626
72 6-10 Kemp 6gd 76 2861
80 3-16 Newm 5g/f 76 3033 P
71 9-17 Sand 5g/f 77 3341 p
62 11-26 Good 6fm 76 3569 BL
69 5-9 Yarm 6g/f 76 3705 p
79 2-15 Sali 6gd 74 3888
81 1-15 BATH 5.7g/f 72 3966*
74 4-20 Donc 5fm 77 4496
74 5-19 Good 6gd 77 4747
49 13-19 Sali 6gd 77 4855
65 11-15 Catt 5sft 76 5125
69a 6-13 Wolv 5.1ap 70 5341

CURZON LODGE 4 ch g £0
38a 9-13 Ling 10ap 338
42 10-16 Chep 7.1gd 2369 T
0 P-5 Sand 8.1g/f 3360

CUSCO 3 ch f £9584
91 2-7 Kemp 6hvy [87] 1513
63 6-7 Nott 8.2sft [87] 1741
78 9-19 Asco 8g/f 89 2491
93 2-6 Newm 6g/f [89] 2736
79 9-9 Newm 7fm 88 3006
93 2-8 Newm 7g/f 88 3928
85 9-14 Sali 7gd 90 4331
61 9-10 Newm 6gd 88 4884

CUSOON 2 b c £4933
75 3-9 Sand 5g/f 3355
82 1-6 BRIG 6fm 3671*
74 4-8 Bath 5.7g/s [83] 4198
78 4-14 Epso 6g/f 83 4471
63 12-13 Asco 7gd 80 4810
61 14-16 Good 7gd 76 5031

CUSP 4 b f £850
52 2-12 Newc 14.4sft 45 1396

CUT AND DRIED 3 ch g £7622
68a 1-9 LING 5ap [57] 621*
68a 1-10 LING 5ap 66 712*
67a 6-8 Ling 5ap 69 818
49a 9-9 Ling 5ap 68 914

67 5-10 Brig 5.3fm 68 1694
61 4-7 Bath 5fm [68] 1902
63 6-13 Wind 5fm 67 2784
64 4-12 Kemp 5g/f 67 3036
62a 5-11 Ling 6ap 66 3198
45a 11-11 Ling 6ap 65 3744
40 7-7 Ling 6fm [65] 3789
56 10-16 Good 5g/f 63 4528

CUT QUARTZ 7 b h £50243
110 3-9 Deau 15sft 4161
114 2-8 Long 15.5sft 4569
117 2-8 Long 20g/f 4951

CUT RIDGE 5 b m £6214
3 18-20 Yarm 6g/f 47 1730
33 9-20 Beve 5g/f [45] 1948
1 17-19 Beve 5g/s 43 2326
25 11-14 Pont 8g/f 40 2993
46 3-8 Muss 7.1g/f 38 3528
53 2-12 Carl 6.9fm 38 3548
56 1-15 LING 7.6fm 46 3788*
54 2-12 Folk 6g/s 52 3911
54 5-10 Ling 6gd 55 4109
50 7-14 Carl 6.9g/f 55 4345
40 13-16 Catt 7g/f 54 4676

CUT SHORT 3 b f £6422
69 5-12 Good 7g/f 1846
84 1-10 GOOD 8gd 2224+
79 3-7 Wind 8.3gd [80] 3826

CUT TO THE CHASE 2 b g £0
21 14-16 Thir 6g/s 4205 T

CUTE CAIT 3 b f £0
17a 13-15 Sout 7af 51 2501
20 6-8 Carl 7.9gd [49] 2932

CUTLASS GAUDY 2 br c £2107
70 4-9 Ches 5.1gd 2281
52 7-13 Pont 6gd 3682
84 2-6 Beve 5g/f 4717
49 5-11 Catt 5gd [82] 4962

CUTTHROAT 4 ch g £0
44 7-8 Ripo 10g/f 2012

CUTTING CREW 3 ch c £60571
87 3-9 Sand 10g/s 81 1318
99 1-14 YORK 11.9g/s 81 1708*
84 6-10 Good 11g/f 86 1865
99 2-11 Asco 12gd 90 3070
101 1-16 GOOD 12fm 92 3534*

CYBER SANTA 6 b g £1075
38 6-11 Newm 12g/f 48 2244
23 8-9 Beve 12.1gd 45 2892
50 2-9 Ches 12.3sft 45 4076
47 8-12 Beve 12.1sft 49 4259

CYCLICAL 2 b c £14431
86 1-4 HAMI 5g/s 4134*
95 1-8 GOOD 6g/f 85 4536*
94 3-12 Newm 6gd 92 4882
95a 2-5 Ling 5ap [93] 5260

CYCLONIC STORM 5 b m £1131
64 3-8 Hami 9.2g/f 60 2475
49 4-5 Carl 9.3gd 60 2674
46 10-14 Pont 8g/f 60 2993 BL

CYFRWYS 3 b f £3771
58 16-20 Newb 7g/f 78 1761
65 2-12 Catt 6g/f [75] 2849
63a 2-6 Sout 6af [75] 3095
64 6-19 Chep 7.1gd 65 3401
51 10-15 Newb 6gd 62 3920
61 6-17 Ling 6g/f 40 4740 T
66 1-10 CATT 6g/f [60] 4964*
49 13-18 Leic 6gd 66 5039 VIS

CZAR WARS 9 b g £0
22a 8-13 Wolv 6af [66] 483 bl
28a 6-9 Sout 6af [66] 533 bl
5a 7-7 Sout 6af [63] 1032 bl

CZARINA WALTZ 4 b f £1740
79a 12-14 Ling 10ap [86] 82

85 2-14 Wind 10g/f 82 2265
74 10-10 Wind 10fm 83 2761
79a 6-7 Ling 10ap 85 3287
79 6-11 Wind 8.3g/s 83 4222
52 19-20 York 10.4gd 81 4986

CZARS PRINCESS 2 b f £0
48a 8-15 Ling 7ap [60] 52

CZECH SUMMER 3 b g £0
0 8-9 Ling 12ap 4449
0 12-14 Ling 13ap 4898 BL
12 10-11 Wind 8.3g/f 5054 bl

DABBERS RIDGE 2 b c £0
71 7-21 Donc 6sft 5368

DABIROUN 3 b c £15089
107 2-7 Curr 7sft 1063
106 2- Leop 10sft 1302

DABUS 9 b g £0
33 8-14 Catt 12g/f [28] 3668

DAFA 8 b g £2888
41a 1-10 WOLV 7af [30] 394*
43a 1-14 LING 10ap [40] 784*
27a 6-12 Wolv 12af [45] 891
25a 8-9 Ling 10ap [40] 1289 BL
34a 6-9 Ling 13ap [40] 1456 bl
37a 4-10 Wolv 8.5af [40] 1801 P

DAFINA 4 b f £711
58 4-5 Warw 10.9fm 2602
63a 3-10 Sout 8af 2997

DAFORE 3 b c £5844
86 1-17 SALI 6g/s 1497*
44 7-8 Newb 8g/f [85] 2313
82 9-22 Newm 8sft 84 5103
75 10-13 Newm 8g/s 82 5284

DAGGERS CANYON 2 ch g £5152
72a 5-12 Ling 8ap 102
52a 4-15 Sout 7af 184
10a 8-8 Wolv 7af [65] 276
65 2-14 Sout 10g/s 55 1051
45 9-13 Nott 8gd 58 1242
67 1-15 RIPO 10gd 58 1976*

DAGOLA 3 b g £5655
64 1-13 NOTT 8.2gd 55 1242*
48 7-17 Hayd 8.1gd 62 2243
54 10-18 Leic 10gd 62 2706
65 3-14 Wind 8.3fm 62 2971
64 4-11 Sali 8gd 64 3455
69 2-12 Pont 8gd 64 3679
66 4-12 Bath 8g/f 64 3846
53 11-17 Nott 8.2gd 66 4862

DAHJEE 3 b c £428
78 4-9 Kemp 12g/f 2862 T

DAHLIYEV 2 b c £686
54 9-10 Leic 6gd 2703
78 3-15 Ling 7gd 3285
60 9-16 Sali 7gd 3882

DAHMAN 2 b c £376
82 4-12 Newm 7g/f 3470
0 11-11 Sand 8.1g/s 3890

DAHTEER 2 b c £13706
73 4-16 Ripo 6g/f 1780
92 1-8 BRIG 6g/f 2043*
94 1-6 CHEP 6.1gd 2367*
97 6-8 Deau 7sft 3169
85 10-10 Good 7fm 3532 VIS
95 2-5 Ches 6.1sft [90] 4105
89 3-7 Ches 7g/f 92 4509
97 3-15 Hayd 6sft 92 4765
73 9-15 York 6gd 92 4985

DAIMAJIN 5 b g £2947
58a 1-8 WOLV 8.5af [55] 362* T
11a 9-9 Wolv 8.5af [58] 437 t
32a 5-8 Wolv 8.5af [56] 630
44a 4-11 Wolv 12af [56] 689
20a 7-11 Sout 11af 53 746
38 12-19 Beve 9.9g/s 62 1164

0	9-9	Pont	10hvy	62	1254
7	11-14	Warw	8.1hvy	60	1535
11a	8-8	Wolv	9.4af	50	1657
49	7-12	Bath	8g/f	55	1792
24	9-9	Yarm	10.1fm	52	2866
43	10-10	Nott	8.2gd	[47]	3107
15	17-18	Pont	8gd	47	3242
45	7-11	Yarm	11.5gd	47	3367
39	6-7	Muss	13g/f	47	3530 P
23	10-12	Newm	10g/f	42	3785
20	13-20	Yarm	8gd	39	3996 p
3	12-15	Carl	9.3fm	[40]	4505
0	12-14	Ling	10ap	[35]	4662 VIS
0	15-19	Kemp	6g/f	[40]	4793 vis

DAINTREE AFFAIR 3 b g £500

47a	8-12	Wolv	5af	64	35
60a	5-11	Wolv	5af	63	155
62a	3-16	Sout	5af	62	205
46a	9-11	Sout	5af	63	655

DAISY BUCKET 2 b f £3852

52	9-17	Ling	7g/f		2584
72	3-14	Yarm	7gd		3489
68	1-6	BRIG	7sft		4163*
49	16-17	Catt	7gd	70	4963
56	14-20	Yarm	8g/s	65	5349

DAISY POOTER 2 b f £0

36	12-16	Thir	6g/s		4205

DAISYCUTTER 3 ch f £0

36a	8-14	Ling	12ap	[60]	14

DAISYS GIRL 2 b f £530

55	10-13	Kemp	6g/f		4358
54	6-16	Ripo	5gd		4787
58	6-10	Ling	5g/f	[55]	4893 BL
54	3-12	Pont	6g/s	[55]	5152

DALDINI 2 b c £6556

69	4-17	Ling	6gd		4443
84	1-7	CHEP	6.1hvy		4705*
87	2-15	York	6gd	80	4985
70	9-14	Donc	7sft	82	5213

DALIDA 2 ch f £0

53a	9-14	Sout	7af		98
3a	U-6	Sout	8af		503
57	5-13	Donc	7gd		925
46	5-16	Redc	8sft	52	1147
36	13-18	Sali	7fm	50	2292
38	10-18	Carl	7.9fm	47	3547

DALISAY 3 b f £2842

76	3-10	Sand	10g/f		2386
78	3-6	Pont	10g/f		2793
75a	2-15	Ling	12ap	[74]	4111
59a	6-14	Ling	13ap	[74]	4892

DALIYA 2 b f £1604

66	6-12	Warw	7.1g/f	4418 BL
71	2-12	Wind	6g/s	4945 VIS

DALKEYS LASS 3 gr f £476

21	8-8	Hami	8.3fm	3246
36	4-8	Hami	9.2g/f	3592
10	9-10	Hami	9.2g/s	4135

DALLAAH 3 b f £234

56	6-6	Sand	5g/f	[92]	2390

DALLINGTON BROOK 5 b g £0

0	7-7	Brig	6g/f	1368 bl

DALLOOL 3 b c £12718

75	5-8	Newm	12g/s		1153
82	1-4	HAYD	11.9g/s		1347*
86	4-14	York	11.9g/s	79	1708
83	4-13	Hayd	11.9gd	80	2238
90	1-12	HAYD	11.9gd	80	3734+
50	8-9	Newm	12gd	85	3926

DALMARNOCK 3 ch g £0

50	10-12	Ripo	10g/f	1783
43	9-11	Beve	8.5gd	2656
56	5-9	Pont	8gd	3462

DALON 5 b g £0

45	7-8	Folk	9.7sft	53	1579

45a	6-16	Sout	12af	50	2340 BL
26	11-15	Folk	16.4g/s	46	3049 bl

DALRIATH 5 b m £3938

12a	10-12	Sout	7af	[45]	416
24a	6-12	Sout	11af	40	534
28a	6-7	Sout	7af	40	680
27a	4-10	Sout	8af	35	791
37a	2-10	Sout	8af	40	1406
42a	1-7	SOUT	8af	[35]	1593*
42a	2-8	Sout	8af	[40]	1841
34	5-11	Redc	8fm	39	2296
0	9-9	Newm	8g/f	39	2529
43	3-8	Thir	12g/s	38	2691
37a	5-16	Sout	8af	39	2805
39	2-20	Catt	12g/f	38	3354
32	10-13	Beve	12.1g/f	38	3502
15	8-10	Ripo	12.3g/f	39	3649
26a	4-8	Sout	12af	32	4128

DALYAN 7 b g £0

14	10-10	Beve	8.5g/f	[30]	1943

DAMASK DANCER 5 b g £0

38a	7-14	Ling	10ap	[45]	4661 P
3a	11-11	Wolv	12.2ap	45	5009 bl

DAMBURGER XPRESS 2 b c £0

63	6-12	Newc	7g/f	5011

DAME DE NOCHE 4 b f £14799

83	6-8	Kemp	8g/s	[92]	1115
70	13-18	Ches	7.6gd	90	1598
90	3-7	Asco	7g/f	[88]	1925
67	9-9	Ches	7gd	88	2282
83	10-29	Asco	6fm	88	2581
47	11-11	Newb	6g/f	85	2878
86	5-10	Ayr	5g/f	[82]	3304
88	3-26	Good	5g/f	85	3569
53	9-9	Ripo	6g/f	85	3646
82	7-16	Muss	5g/f	87	4174
90	1-6	SAND	5gd	[85]	4498*
89	4-10	Newm	6gd	85	4884
90a	4-14	Ling	7ap	86	5262

DAME MARGARET 3 ch f £323

41a	3-9	Ling	13ap	43	18
4a	1-5	Wolv	12af	[45]	583
0	14-15	Ling	12ap	[40]	707

DAME NOVA 3 b f £0

0	13-14	Thir	6g/s		1216
40	6-7	Carl	9.3fm	47	1953
0	15-15	Sout	12af	45	2503
16	9-10	Beve	12.1g/f	42	3499
8	12-14	Redc	10fm	40	4560

DAMI 3 b f £14568

71	5-14	Wind	8.3g/f	68	1956
67	5-10	Yarm	11.5fm	68	2147
75	2-8	Brig	8g/f	68	2432 P
71	2-10	Chep	8.1g/f	68	2624 p
77	1-5	BRIG	9.9fm	70	2837* p
0	W-7	Ling	10ap	74	3287 p
82	1-6	EPSO	8.5fm	74	3540* p
79	5-10	Nott	10gd	77	3990 p
91	5-11	Yarm	10.1gd	[77]	4614 p
81	7-17	Newm	10g/f	80	4917 p

DAMSON 2 b f £215462

112	1-6	NAAS	6g/f	2328*
115	1-17	ASCO	5g/f	2490*
117	1-6	CURR	6g/f	3841*
112	3-7	Newm	6g/f	4880

DAN DI CANIO 3 b g £0

69	5-12	Leic	8fm		2106
45	9-14	Wind	8.3g/s		2622
60	5-11	Hayd	8.1gd		2885
60	5-12	Newm	8fm	65	3410 T
38	12-14	Redc	10fm	63	4342 t
53	8-15	Bath	8gd	61	4827 t

DANAATT 2 b f £0

17	15-15	Kemp	6g/f	4357

DANAKIL 8 b g £8363

65a	11-14	Ling	13ap	73	147
61a	12-14	Ling	10ap	70	674

43a	14-14	Ling	12ap	70	731
58	9-22	Donc	12gd	76	918
66	9-20	Epso	12hvy	73	1295
75	2-16	Brig	11.9fm	70	1693
71	4-13	Kemp	12g/f	70	1916
73a	1-13	LING	12g/f	63	1986*
78	2-11	Newm	12g/f	72	2244
76	2-6	Kemp	12g/s	74	2681
79	4-13	York	11.9g/f	75	3437
64	6-9	Newm	12gd	77	3926
51	11-12	Epso	12gd	75	4292
46	13-14	Asco	12g/f	74	4775

DANAKIM 7 b g £4569

24a	6-10	Wolv	5af	[35]	527
37a	1-11	SOUT	5af	[35]	578* bl e
24a	7-14	Sout	5af	[35]	637 bl e
27a	8-16	Sout	5af	[40]	720 bl e
26a	4-9	Sout	5af	[40]	981 bl e
28a	8-8	Sout	5af	[40]	1199 bl e
18a	7-10	Sout	5af	[40]	1408
50	1-16	NOTT	6.1gd	[35]	1988*
45	5-12	Leic	6fm	42	2111
29	12-18	Ling	6gd	50	2396
27	10-11	Ayr	6gd	50	2542
15	13-20	Nott	6.1gd	45	2928
38	9-14	Catt	6g/f	[42]	3191 bl e
36	7-14	Thir	5g/f	42	3417
48	4-8	Muss	5gd	40	3527
41	2-18	Thir	6fm	39	3609
25	10-15	Pont	5gd	39	3680
24	8-8	Ayr	6gd	40	3763
34	4-19	Kemp	6g/s	[40]	4793
31	7-20	Yarm	6g/s	[40]	5121
40	3-10	Ayr	6sft	[40]	5278

DANCE ANTHEM 2 ch c £4833

79	1-10	MUSS	5gd		1550*
89	2-7	Yarm	6fm		2144
83	10-13	Asco	6g/f		2467
45	8-9	Hayd	5sft	88	3271

DANCE AWAY 2 ch f £7323

81	2-8	Newm	5gd		1170
97	1-10	YORK	5g/s		1709*
32	12-12	Newb	5.2g/f		3956
93	5-9	Ayr	6sft	[97]	4684

DANCE FLOWER 2 b f £6258

81	2-8	Asco	6gd		3071
77	3-8	Asco	6g/f		3386
73	5-14	Newb	6fm		3626
79	4-21	Donc	6.5fm	77	4457
82	2-11	Pont	8fm	77	4753
0	15-16	Newm	7g/f	81	4913

DANCE IN THE SUN 3 ch f £21720

86a	1-7	LING	10ap	78	16*
83a	6-13	Ling	10ap	85	433
88a	4-16	Ling	12ap	85	475
91a	2-14	Ling	10ap	85	758
89a	1-9	LING	10ap	85	876*

DANCE LIGHT 4 b f £600

54a	10-14	Ling	16ap	65	107
1a	12-14	Sout	14af	60	185
45a	10-12	Ling	16ap	55	478
48	8-9	Newc	16.1gd	62	1870
59	5-12	Warw	19.1fm	62	2577
63	3-7	Beve	16.2sft	60	2941
0	19-19	Good	21fm	58	3531
54	10-16	Kemp	16g/f	58	4361
40	5-6	Muss	16g/f	56	4555
20	14-20	Catt	15.8gd	53	4965 VIS

DANCE NIGHT 2 b c £39834

88	2-15	Donc	5gd		920
89	1-15	BEVE	5g/s		1161*
97	1-9	CHES	5.1gd		1567*
71	6-9	Asco	5g/f		2516
91	7-8	Curr	6.3gd		3319
92	6-13	Good	5g/f		3509
103	1-5	YORK	5g/s	[94]	4025*
87	11-22	Donc	6fm	[92]	4458
101	3-12	Ayr	5g/s	[100]	4651

DANCE ON THE TOP 6 ch g £12427

91a	1-12	LING	8ap	80	369* t

96a 1-11 LING 8ap 87 547* t
92a 9-15 Ling 7ap 94 887 t
79 6-8 Bath 8fm 81 2665 t
91a 5-12 Ling 8ap [94] 3199 t
74 7-15 Brig 8fm 79 3694 t
50 14-14 Epso 8.5gd 77 4295 t
65 10-18 Kemp 8g/f 75 4714 t

DANCE PARTY 4 b f £1211
62a 3-13 Ling 10ap [62] 569
67a 3-11 Ling 12ap 62 624
47a 11-13 Ling 10ap 63 726
58 8-19 Donc 10.3gd 64 924
62 4-10 Folk 12g/s 64 1082
60 7-13 Pont 10g/f 63 2038 P
60a 7-14 Ling 10ap 62 2392 p
52 7-17 Wind 11.6fm [60] 2788 p
45 12-19 Beve 9.9g/f 55 4720
48a 9-13 Warw 8.6ap 55 5005 BL

DANCE TO MY TUNE 3 b f £12503
35a 6-13 Sout 8af [57] 1193
67 1-6 NEWC 8sft 54 1679*
47 7-14 Newc 8gd 60 1872
52 4-6 Carl 9.3g/f 60 3231
66 1-10 NOTT 10gd 60 3990*
67 2-9 Redc 10gd 62 4248
65 4-14 Redc 10fm 62 4342
72 2-18 Ayr 10.9sft 65 4623
71 4-16 York 11.9gd 67 4990

DANCE TO THE BLUES 3 br f £3903
49 9-17 Bath 5g/f 1787
50 3-15 Nott 5.1g/f 2152
62 1-6 FOLK 5g/f 3725+
50 8-8 Folk 5sft 57 4118

DANCE WORLD 4 b g £9162
70a 1-7 SOUT 12af 1030*
67 12-20 Newm 12gd 80 1172
66 3-13 Kemp 14.4hvy 78 1516
63 7-8 Chep 10.2gd [76] 2197
50a 7-10 Sout 12af 75 2998
59 5-13 Nott 10gd 70 3992
76 1-13 FOLK 12gd 70 4119*
46 13-13 Warw 12.6gd 74 4274

DANCEINTHEVALLEY 2 b c £0
34 10-12 Carl 5gd 2933
45 9-10 Carl 5g/f 3227

DANCER KING 3 b g £567
55 5-14 Thir 7sft 2692
48 9-16 Ripo 8gd 2987
43 9-9 Thir 7g/f 3413
48 3-9 Thir 8sft 51 3835
34 7-18 Beve 9.9g/s 51 4243
35 6-9 Ayr 13.1sft [50] 5277

DANCER POLISH 5 b g £0
0 7-10 Wolv 14.8af 42 34

DANCERS SERENADE 2 b c £644
72 3-7 Ayr 7.2g/s 2570
68 5-10 Redc 6gd 2959
58 9-12 Newc 7gd 3425
68 10-16 Nott 5g/f 70 4848

DANCES IN TIME 4 b f £206
0 8-8 Wolv 9.4af 299
53a 5-11 Wolv 7af 396
0 12-13 Sout 6af 444
23a 10-13 Ling 6ap [55] 544
0 12-12 Wolv 5af 50 641
36a 3-6 Wolv 5af [45] 779 BL
9a 9-12 Sout 6af [40] 982 bl

DANCES WITH ANGELS 4 b f £487
25a 11-14 Ling 10ap [35] 1072
5a 11-12 Ling 12ap [35] 1180 p
34 3-8 Brig 11.9gd [40] 1547
23 9-13 Beve 12.1g/f [40] 1945
28 12-13 Nott 14.1gd [40] 1990
0 P-15 Warw 10g/f 35 2910
22 12-16 Brig 9.9g/f 35 3175
59 6-17 Hayd 8.1g/s [35] 4768
60 4-13 Bath 10.2sft [35] 5173
45 5-12 Catt 12sft [40] 5319

DANCING BAY 7 b g £66120
103 1-14 HAYD 16.2gd 90 2239*
107 2-12 Asco 22.2fm[100] 2583
116 2-10 York 15.9gd[104] 4000
111 3-8 Donc 18fm [116] 4478
114 4-8 Long 20g/f [116] 4951
109 4-11 Newm 16sft [116] 5138

DANCING BEAR 3 b g £1241
61 4-11 Donc 10.3gd 930
55 9-14 Nott 10gd 1241
53 3-7 Newc 10.1gd [62] 1871
51 4-6 Chep 12.1gd [60] 4486
45a 10-16 Ling 12ap [57] 4899 BL
40a 4-9 Wolv 9.5ap [55] 5360 bl

DANCING DEANO 2 b c £0
45 9-16 Ripo 6g/f 1780
54 6-10 Redc 6gd 4244
33 12-12 Thir 7g/f 4591
54 5-18 Newc 6g/f 52 5013 VIS

DANCING DOLPHIN 5 b m £211
27 3-8 Chep 10.2sft [35] 1333
0 6-6 Sout 12af [30] 1592
32 6-13 Kemp 10hvy [30] 1643
2 12-15 Nott 10gd [30] 1991

DANCING DUCHESS 2 ch f £3658
93 3-9 Tipp 5hvy 4960

DANCING FOREST 3 br g £0
36a 7-16 Ling 7ap [68] 214
50a 11-15 Ling 7ap 66 266
17a 9-11 Ling 8ap [66] 343
54a 5-14 Ling 10ap [60] 477

DANCING KING 7 b g £7802
7a 10-13 Sout 8af 31 221
17a 5-12 Sout 8af [26] 309
0 11-11 Ling 8ap [30] 408
30a 4-9 Wolv 8.5af [30] 437
0 11-12 Wolv 8.5af 30 479
12a 5-14 Sout 7af [30] 573
31a 2-8 Sout 8af [30] 635
42a 1-12 WOLV 7af [30] 663*
40a 3-16 Sout 8af [30] 719
46a 1-10 WOLV 8.5af 36 754*
40a 5-10 Sout 8af 51 791
52a 4-9 Wolv 8.5af 51 809
27a 8-12 Ling 8ap 49 845
24a 8-10 Wolv 7af 49 864
36a 6-10 Wolv 7af [49] 890
47a 2-6 Wolv 8.5af [47] 957
95 6-10 Warw 7.1gd [46] 1126
50 2-14 Warw 8.1hvy 46 1535
30a 5-8 Wolv 9.4af 46 1657
32 5-6 Pont 8g/f [48] 2037
95 5-5 Warw 7.1gd [48] 4270
45 5-18 Chep 8.1gd [48] 4485
44 5-17 Pont 8g/f 48 4626
40a 9-12 Ling 8ap [46] 4974
0 11-13 Wolv 8.6ap [45] 5232
63 6-8 Nott 8.2hvy [45] 5346

DANCING LYRA 3 b c £34823
56a 6-11 Ling 8ap [86] 496
82a 1-14 LING 10ap [73] 759*
94 1-8 SALI 9.9g/s 78 1500*
94 2-18 Good 9g/f 87 1813
91 4-18 Epso 10.1fm 90 2250
75 11-16 Good 9.9fm 90 3553
77 6-8 Folk 9.7g/s [89] 3912
85 10-17 Newm 10g/f 88 4917
74 5-8 Nott 10hvy 86 5187

DANCING MOONLIGHT 2 b f £0
29 6-7 Leic 5gd 2132
17a 13-14 Sout 7af 2492
24 9-9 Ling 6gd 3020
42a 7-8 Ling 5ap 3600 P
9 9-10 Nott 6.1gd [35] 4858

DANCING MYSTERY 9 b g £25287
90a 3-15 Sout 5af 89 64 bl
90a 3-16 Sout 5af 89 171 bl
97a 1-16 SOUT 5af 90 461* bl
98a 3-10 Ling 5ap 94 567 bl

92a 5-10 Ling 5ap 94 692 bl
50 17-20 Donc 5gd 85 927 bl
63 12-13 Epso 5sft 84 1293 bl
59 8-12 Ling 5g/s 82 1615 bl
51 14-14 Wind 5g/f 80 2266 bl
85 1-9 SALI 5fm 80 2420*
83 4-9 Warw 5.5fm 83 2779
81 5-8 Asco 5gd 82 3123
78 9-14 Newb 5.2fm 82 3628
80 8-20 Hayd 5fm 82 3792
76 8-13 Newb 5.2g/f 80 3960
79 2-8 Kemp 5sft [80] 4031 bl
57 9-11 Bath 5g/s [78] 4201 bl
69 14-20 Donc 5fm 78 4496 bl
83 3-16 Leic 5gd 77 4700 bl
83 3-15 Catt 5sft 79 5125 bl

DANCING PEARL 6 ch m £438
46 12-17 Leic 10g/s 1019
53 5-13 Hayd 14sft 40 1109
35 7-12 Warw 19.1fm 45 2577
40 3-14 Carl 17.2gd 43 2937

DANCING PHANTOM 9 b g £1247
57a 3-8 Wolv 12af [77] 347
52a 2-10 Sout 12af [70] 552

DANCING PRINCE 3 b g £0
55a 5-11 Ling 6ap [46] 543
45a 4-10 Sout 8af 51 662
39a 9-13 Ling 7ap 50 761
31a 13-15 Ling 7ap 48 815
0 8-9 Sout 7af [48] 871 vis

DANCING RIDGE 6 b g £0
0 15-16 Sout 6af [45] 65 p
0 9-10 Wolv 6af [40] 822
0 15-17 Pont 6hvy [35] 1065
15a 5-7 Wolv 5af [30] 1309
22a 6-10 Sout 5af [30] 1408 vis
30a 7-7 Wolv 7af [30] 1562 vis

DANCING ROSE 2 b f £7121
76 2-11 Wind 5gd 3160
71 3-12 Chep 5.1gd 3728
78 1-11 BATH 5g/s 4200*
75 5-21 Donc 6fm [77] 4490
62 11-15 Hayd 6sft 76 4765

DANCING SHIRL 2 b f £2062
57 6-7 Thir 7g/f 3412
54 3-11 Thir 7g/f 3570
58 3-10 Newc 8hvy 4213
57 3-14 Muss 8gd 58 4519

DANCING TILLY 6 b m £2448
38a 4-12 Wolv 9.4af [38] 302 p
41a 2-10 Sout 11af [40] 375 p
39a 4-8 Sout 11af [40] 420
35a 6-13 Ling 10ap [40] 539
42 4-15 Thir 8fm [40] 4379 p
49 1-15 CARL 9.3fm [40] 4505* p
48 2-18 Kemp 10g/f [46] 4791 p
35 6-15 Yarm 10.1g/s [46] 5122 p
41a 5-12 Wolv 9.5ap [45] 5234 p

DANCINGINTHECLOUDS 2 b f £0
68 8-15 Newm 8fm 4723

DANCLARE 3 ch f £1983
75 12-13 Newm 7gd [84] 1169
84 6-10 Newb 7g/f 84 2312
89 5-19 Asco 8g/f 84 2491
80 4-10 Newm 8g/f 85 2767

DANDOUCE 2 b f £2469
75a 2-10 Ling 5ap 13 vis
72a 3-11 Ling 6ap 135
67 6-17 Warw 7.1sft 70 1526
71 3-17 Yarm 7g/f [70] 1729
72 4-14 Wind 8.3g/f 68 1956
60 9-17 Kemp 7gd 68 2174 BL
66 3-7 Folk 6g/s [67] 3910
42a 11-12 Ling 6ap 68 4976
29 16-19 Wind 6g/f 65 5053

DANDOUN 6 b h £2292
0 16-16 Newm 9sft [111] 5139
90 3-8 Nott 8.2hvy[105] 5346

DANDY JIM 2 b c £0
0	13-13	Sout	6af			63	
0	12-12	Sout	6af			200	
22a	6-9	Wolv	6af			247	
17a	8-10	Sout	6af	30		592	
26a	5-14	Sout	6af	[30]		637	
13a	9-11	Sout	7af	[30]		771	
13a	9-13	Sout	6af	30		797	
0	5-5	Sout	8af	[30]		986	
25	6-6	Newc	8sft	30		1679	
0	7-9	Wolv	6af	[30]		1803	BL
3a	8-10	Sout	7af	[30]		1842	bl
0	13-13	Beve	8.5g/f	[30]		1947	bl

DANDYGREY RUSSETT 3 gr f £873
68	11-19	Newb	8gd			1236	
55	4-12	Kemp	8hvy			1511	
60	4-10	Sali	8sft			4578	
32	9-18	Wind	10g/s	[63]		4944	

DANE RHAPSODY 3 b f £0
32a	10-11	Wolv	6af			481	
44	5-15	Nott	5.1g/f			2152	
28	13-13	Wind	6fm			2756	
44	5-17	Catt	5g/f	44		3667	
19	9-18	Chep	7.1g/s	44		3900	
61	5-13	Bath	5.7g/f	[45]		4413	
0	12-12	Wolv	6ap	[45]		5157	

DANEBANK 4 b g £7286
18	11-17	Bath	10.2sft	52		1541	
43	5-11	Leic	10gd	48		2135	
55	1-13	WARW	12.6gd	47		3056*	
58	2-19	Chep	12.1gd	51		3727	P
58	3-14	Bath	13.1g/s	54		4203	p
38	13-20	Hayd	11.9g/s	54		4771	p
58	2-18	Pont	12g/f	52		4938	p
60	3-12	Redc	14.1g/s	50		5108	p

DANECARE 4 b c £763
| 80 | 4-12 | Hayd | 6g/s | [95] | | 2186 | |

DANEFONIQUE 3 b f £3368
33	8-11	Donc	10.3gd	[53]		930	
57	3-14	Sout	10g/s	53		1051	
57	2-16	Nott	10gd	52		1240	
57	2-13	Beve	12.1g/f	54		1836	
57	5-15	Leic	11.8gd	57		2134	
43	6-9	Yarm	14.1g/f	57		2345	
48a	8-15	Ling	12ap	55		2741	
54	4-20	Catt	12g/f	55		3354	
0	12-12	Beve	9.9g/s	50		3854	
50	2-18	Beve	9.9g/s	50		4243	
38	6-16	Carl	11.9g/f	50		4348	
42	7-13	Ayr	10sft	[50]		5276	

DANEHILL ANGEL 2 ch f £0
| 33a | 7-12 | Sout | 5af | | | 1439 | |
| 42 | 12-17 | Donc | 6g/f | | | 2424 | |

DANEHILL DAZZLER 2 b f £409
| 82 | 4-8 | Kemp | 7g/s | | | 2676 | |

DANEHILL FAIRY 2 b f £3340
39	7-8	Pont	5hvy			1249	
50	2-7	Newc	5sft			1394	BL
0	15-15	York	5g/f			2056	bl
34	6-8	Hami	5gd			2177	
48	3-13	Beve	5g/s			2321	VIS
50	3-10	Thir	6fm			2461	vis
50	3-6	Catt	5g/f			3014	vis
47	2-7	Ripo	6g/s			3259	bl
16	12-15	Redc	6g/f	[47]		3769	bl
47	4-10	Hayd	5g/s	[47]		3901	vis
3	8-9	Ripo	6gd	[45]		4277	bl

DANEHILL LAD 3 b g £645
67a	2-9	Ling	13ap	67		18	
65a	6-16	Ling	12ap	66		218	
2a	P-13	Ling	13ap	66		342	

DANEHILL STROLLER 4 b g £1165
77	13-19	Kemp	6fm	88		2070	
73	17-29	Asco	6fm	88		2581	p
68	9-11	Newb	6g/f	86		2878	p
85	4-16	Newb	6gd	83		3269	p
71	12-14	Newb	5.2fm	83		3628	p
71	10-19	Kemp	6fm	82		4394	p

61	18-24	Newb	7g/f	80		4642	p
52	17-19	Good	6gd	80		4747	p
79	5-19	Sali	6gd	77		4855	

DANEHILL WILLY 2 b c £12700
72	2-6	Yarm	5.2gd			3361	
71	8-16	Newm	7g/f			3582	
70	9-12	Newm	7gd			4194	
80	1-9	WARW	7.1g/s	71		4666*	
89	1-12	NEWM	8gd	78		5089*	
80	7-9	Newm	10g/s	[81]		5281	

DANELISSIMA 3 br f £18987
107	2-12	Curr	12g/f	102		2821	
107	4-8	Hayd	11.9gd			2946	BL
87	6-7	Curr	12g/f	[102]		3321	b
85	6-8	York	11.9g/s			4024	VIS

DANELOR 6 b g £15104
86a	4-12	Wolv	8.5af	87		836	
88	5-24	Donc	8gd	87		928	
81	7-11	Epso	10.1g/f	86		2208	
71	8-10	York	11.9g/f	85		2405	
82	5-8	Pont	8g/f	85		2606	
68	8-10	York	7.9g/s	83		3074	
88	1-7	HAMI	9.2g/s	80		3879*	
79	8-10	Hami	8.3g/s	86		4136	
89	5-9	Newm	10gd	86		4227	
76	8-13	Epso	10.1g/f	85		4473	
76	9-20	York	8.9gd	84		4999	

DANES CASTLE 2 b g £8116
75	3-20	Wind	6fm			2970	
73a	2-9	Sout	6af			3157	
75	2-6	Brig	5.3g/f			3296	
83a	3-10	Ling	6ap	[75]		3817	
78	3-11	Nott	5.1gd	75		3987	BL
86	1-10	LING	5g/f	[75]		4893*	bl

DANES ROCK 2 b c £888
58a	4-8	Sout	5ap			1048	
57	7-11	Yarm	6g/f			1727	
55	6-9	Muss	5fm			2083	VIS
60	2-8	Hayd	6g/f			2183	BL
42a	7-11	Sout	6af	65		3393	
30	9-15	Catt	7sft	[65]		3930	bl
47	4-10	Newc	8hvy	[59]		4213	bl

DANESCOURT 2 b c £423
60a	5-10	Ling	6ap			3818	
50a	8-14	Sout	6af			4127	
62	3-17	Ling	6g/f			4316	

DANESMEAD 3 b c £0
| 96 | 6-14 | York | 7sft | 96 | | 1665 | |
| 82 | 11-18 | Newm | 6g/f | 95 | | 1933 | |

DANETHORPE LADY 2 b f £324
45	6-13	Ripo	5gd			4303	
44	4-12	Beve	6g/f			4596	
16	8-10	Nott	6.1gd			4858	

DANETTIE 3 b f £589
51	9-14	Warw	8.1sft			1527	
35	5-8	Hami	9.2g/f			3592	
61	4-13	Wind	8.3gd			3828	
0	5-5	Ches	12.3sft			4075	
62	4-9	Catt	7g/f	[62]		4674	
0	17-18	Newc	8g/f	[60]		5017	
22a	10-12	Wolv	7.1ap	[55]		5358	

DANGER BIRD 3 ch f £5773
51a	3-10	Wolv	7af	[53]		4	
36a	5-14	Sout	8af	[50]		170	
50a	3-8	Wolv	8.5af	[50]		248	
52a	2-13	Wolv	9.4af	50		281	
51a	3-12	Wolv	9.4af	48		427	
21a	8-9	Wolv	9.4af	[48]		480	
53a	2-9	Wolv	9.4af	48		620	
52a	4-10	Wolv	8.5af	51		753	
52a	4-7	Wolv	9.4af	51		961	P
59a	1-13	WOLV	9.4af	50		1223+	
50a	5-15	Sout	7af	[57]		2999	
25a	8-10	Sout	8af	57		3395	
39a	6-13	Wolv	8.6ap	55		4982	
32a	10-11	Wolv	12.2ap	54		5117	
33a	9-13	Wolv	9.5ap	[50]		5338	

DANGER ZONE 2 b c £213

56	12-15	Wind	6gd			3163	
64	8-14	Ling	7.6g/f			3601	
71	5-16	Sali	7gd			3882	
59	15-20	Ling	7gd	70		4444	
71a	3-14	Ling	7ap	[66]		4658	

DANGEROUS BEANS 3 b g £0
| 39a | 7-14 | Sout | 8af | 54 | | 60 | |
| 55a | 4-14 | Ling | 12ap | [54] | | 103 | |

DANGEROUS DAVE 5 b g £0
| 26 | 9-16 | Brig | 7gd | [40] | | 4901 | |

DANGLE 3 b f £0
| 85 | 9-15 | Newm | 6g/f | | | 5088 | VIS |

DANI RIDGE 6 b m £2754
84	4-11	Hayd	6gd	[81]		2240	
79	7-10	Donc	5g/f	85		2429	
86	4-11	Pont	6g/f	84		2791	
75	6-9	Ches	5.1g/f	[84]		3100	
49	15-16	Newb	6g/f	84		3269	

DANIEL THOMAS 2 b c £9930
87	2-14	Newm	7g/f			2766	
90	2-5	Newm	6g/f			3586	
92	3-8	Kemp	6sft			4028	
90	2-13	Donc	7hvy	[92]		5200	
92a	1-10	LING	7ap	[92]		5259*	

DANIELLA 2 b f £0
| 50 | 13-23 | Newm | 7g/f | | | 4885 | |

DANIELLES LAD 7 b g £6551
68a	3-9	Wolv	7af	72		31	bl
48a	8-10	Wolv	7af	[70]		152	bl
65a	7-16	Ling	7ap	70		181	bl
62a	5-13	Wolv	8.5af	67		251	bl
65a	4-11	Wolv	7af	65		363	bl
68a	2-13	Wolv	8.5af	65		439	bl
59a	9-14	Ling	7ap	65		499	bl
68a	4-12	Wolv	7af	66		704	bl
73a	1-11	WOLV	8.5af	66		806*	
67a	3-7	Wolv	8.5af	72		942	bl
67	7-16	Sout	7g/s	73		1049	bl
73a	3-10	Wolv	8.5af	72		1322	
70	7-19	Sali	7g/f	71		1723	bl
22	17-18	Good	8g/f	71		1849	bl

DANIFAH 3 b f £11259
48a	12-15	Ling	7ap	60		901	
53	7-9	Bath	5g/s	55		1102	
24	16-18	Bath	5.7g/f	51		1788	
34	8-12	Chep	6.1gd	47		2118	
46	4-13	Warw	6.1fm	47		2439	
26	10-19	Leic	6g/f	45		2925	
35	13-17	Bath	5g/f	45		2981	bl
39	4-11	Yarm	8g/f	42		3706	
36	4-8	Chep	8.1gd	42		3731	
47	6-12	Bath	8g/f	42		3846	
61	1-18	CHEP	7.1g/s	42		3900*	
62	1-14	FOLK	6gd	56		4116*	
64	3-20	Ling	6g/f	62		4317	
41	16-19	Leic	7g/f	62		4452	
70	1-13	CHEP	8.1hvy	63		4709+	
58	13-17	Ling	6g/f	69		4740	
60	7-16	Bath	8gd	69		5022	
42	17-20	Leic	7gd	69		5046	
42a	9-11	Wolv	7.1ap	[67]		5357	

DANISH MONARCH 3 b g £604
43	11-16	Leic	8g/s	74		1359	
53	13-16	Leic	7g/f	71		1825	
61	3-20	Chep	6.1gd	66		2372	
24	19-20	Newb	7fm	65		2650	
31	19-19	Chep	7.1gd	64		3401	
54	6-19	Chep	6.1sft	60		4054	
48	9-20	Ling	6g/f	57		4317	
41	12-15	Epso	7g/f	57		4475	

DANITA DANCER 3 b f £0
| 53 | 12-18 | Nott | 8.2g/f | | | 4842 | |
| 39 | 12-14 | Leic | 8gd | | | 5058 | |

DANNY LEAHY 4 b c £0
38a	5-11	Sout	12af	60		458	
61	10-12	Newc	16.1sft	65		965	
0	9-13	Pont	18hvy	65		1069	

DANS HEIR 2 b g £2362

37	8-11	Hayd	5g/f		1880
60	2-7	Redc	7fm		2294 P
64	7-10	Catt	7g/f		2845
60	2-12	Catt	7g/f	56	3351 p
47a	9-13	Sout	7af	58	4040 p
57	7-20	Leic	7g/f	58	4451 p

DANTES BATTLE 12 b g £0

2a	11-11	Sout	12af	[60]	3154

DANTES DEVINE 2 b g £1953

55a	5-11	Sout	8af	[65]	159
0	8-9	Wolv	9.4af	60	441
30a	6-8	Wolv	6af	[56]	750
58	5-8	Warw	8.1sft	[56]	1086
34	8-8	Muss	8gd	54	1798
36a	4-12	Wolv	8.5af	52	2205
38a	10-15	Sout	7af	52	2384
38	9-18	Hayd	6gd	47	3737
50	1-17	KEMP	7g/f	[45]	4794*
46	2-19	Yarm	8g/s	[46]	5119

DANTES DIAMOND 2 b c £3291

75	2-5	Nott	5.1fm		1001
81	2-12	Ripo	5gd		1173
70	5-7	Nott	6.1sft		1738
77	5-18	Leic	5fm		2109
65	11-13	Warw	6.1gd	79	4273
77	4-13	Warw	7.1g/s	[75]	4664
75	5-14	Yarm	7sft	[75]	5250
69	10-20	Donc	7sft	75	5373

DANUM 3 b c £0

33a	7-15	Sout	8af	[65]	96
47a	6-10	Wolv	12af	[60]	154
41a	6-15	Sout	11af	54	196 P
24a	4-6	Sout	11af	[49]	306 p
16a	5-9	Wolv	9.4af	[47]	665 p
2a	8-11	Sout	11af	47	746

DANZARE 2 b f £0

69	7-14	Kemp	7g/f		4711
65a	4-13	Wolv	8.6ap		4979

DANZATRICE 2 b f £0

28	9-11	Hayd	5g/f	4349
70	5-14	Hayd	6sft	4769
59	5-8	Ayr	8sft	5273

DANZE ROMANCE 3 b f £500

66	8-20	Newm	8g/f		3237
38	14-14	Newb	9fm		3631
61	5-9	Wind	8.3g/f		4262
56	4-10	Good	9.9gd	[64]	4877
29	11-12	Brig	11.9sft	62	5093
41	13-16	Nott	10hvy	60	5345

DANZIG RIVER 3 b c £8809

97	2-19	Newm	6g/s	93	1154
70	16-18	Newm	6g/f	96	1933
89	9-20	York	6g/f	96	2407
19	16-16	Wind	6fm	95	2758
87	13-24	Asco	5gd	93	3466
66	10-10	Asco	6gd	93	3778
91	4-14	Ches	6.1g/f	90	4048
79	6-12	Hayd	6sft	89	4779
85	7-20	York	6gd	88	5001
92	2-12	Newb	6sft	86	5196

DANZIG STAR 4 b f £0

0	6-6	Wolv	8.5af	526

DANZILI BAY 2 b c £3317

60	4-7	Bath	5g/f		2976
75	4-11	Bath	8g/f		3962
82	1-10	REDC	5fm		4338*
74	11-18	Wind	5g/f	80	4830

DAPHNES DOLL 9 b m £0

14a	10-12	Ling	8ap	[30]	971

DARA GIRL 2 b f £0

51	13-19	Newb	6g/f	2310
41	15-17	Ling	7g/f	2584
40	9-11	Sali	6g/s	3110 T

DARA MAC 5 b g £8788

5	14-19	Redc	8sft	50	1661 p

59	2-9	Thir	7g/f	[47]	2218
54	6-14	Thir	7fm	53	2466
58	3-8	Bad	8gd	53	2550
63	1-15	THIR	8g/s	[53]	2688*
55	7-16	Redc	8g/s		2958
32	13-18	Pont	8gd	55	3242
64	1-17	THIR	8g/f	59	3830*
46	9-16	Ches	7g/f	59	4051
58	6-12	Redc	8gd	62	4246
42	14-19	York	7.9g/f	61	4399
62	4-16	Thir	8g/f	61	4592
57	7-15	Beve	7.5g/f	59	4719
54	9-26	Redc	8fm	61	4926
23	19-19	Newm	7g/f	61	5014

DARAB 4 ch g £0

50	9-12	Newm	10g/f	65	3785
55	11-15	Nott	10g/f	63	4849 p

DARASIM 6 b g £112043

48	6-13	Asco	16.2sft	[114]	1418 vis
113	1-8	BADE	16gd	[114]	1993* vis
118	3-13	Asco	20g/f	[114]	2518 vis
117	1-9	GOOD	16fm	[115]	3552* vis
109	5-8	Donc	18fm	[115]	4478 vis
108	6-8	Long	20g/f	[115]	4951 vis

DARCIE MIA 2 ch f £0

0	11-13	Sout	6af	[42]	63 BL
3a	12-12	Wolv	9.4af	[38]	302 bl

DARENEUR 4 ch f £0

4a	7-9	Wolv	9.4af	1340
53	8-14	Warw	8.1sft	1527
64	5-11	Beve	9.9g/f	1835

DARGHAN 4 b g £0

75	10-20	Hurn	10.4gd	81	4986 t
77	5-14	Newb	8hvy	78	5227 t
52	13-20	Donc	7sft	76	5367 t

DARING AFFAIR 2 b f £12096

65a	2-8	Sout	6af	62	223
59a	6-11	Ling	7ap	64	261
62a	3-6	Sout	6af	64	316 VIS
59a	2-13	Sout	6af	[63]	444
65a	1-7	SOUT	7af	[63]	636*
53a	5-10	Sout	7af	63	794
70a	1-11	WOLV	8.5af	61	1339*
65	4-11	Warw	8.1hvy	66	1534
71a	1-5	WOLV	8.5af	66	1655*

DARING AIM 3 b f £6762

74	5-14	Kemp	10g/s		2678
82	1-7	NEWM	12fm		3405*
86	5-7	Good	14fm		3619
77	8-12	Wind	11.6g/f	85	4833

DARING GAMES 3 b f £0

50	5-6	York	11.9g/f	2058
3	6-6	Pont	10g/f	2793
21	15-16	Ripo	8gd	2987

DARING LOVE 2 b f £37324

101	1-7	BADE	6gd	4427*

DARING RANSOM 2 b c £5415

89	1-11	YORK	7.9gd	5003*

DARIO GEE GEE 2 ch c £43610

93	1-13	DONC	5gd		954*
92	2-8	Newm	5g/s		1149
100	2-6	Pont	6g/f		2039
92	8-13	Asco	6g/f		2467
99	2-7	Donc	6g/s		3221
99	1-7	RIPO	6g/s	[95]	3935*
90	5-6	Ripo	6gd	[95]	4280
76	19-22	Donc	6fm	[95]	4458
101	3-24	Redc	6fm	[95]	4928

DARK CHAMPION 3 b g £2056

51a	4-16	Sout	6af	[61]	65
41a	7-13	Ling	6ap	[56]	219
50a	5-13	Sout	6af	[56]	254
55a	2-6	Wolv	6af	[50]	313
40a	9-11	Wolv	7af	50	562 P
50a	4-13	Sout	6af	[48]	659
43a	6-7	Ling	6ap	[48]	706
57a	5-11	Sout	6af	[48]	869

71	3-14	Thir	6gd	[60]	1639
51	9-16	Redc	6g/f	64	1824
0	13-13	Pont	5g/f	[62]	2279
50	4-8	Ripo	6g/f	[62]	2527
58	5-12	Catt	6g/f	[59]	2849
53	12-18	Carl	5g/f	59	3228 p
21	16-20	Thir	6g/f	57	3575 p
33	14-18	Pont	5g/s	54	3974 VIS
44	10-15	Newc	6hvy	54	4211
61	4-19	Redc	6g/s	[50]	5110

DARK CHARM 5 b g £10000

93	3-24	Donc	8gd	90	951
58	12-15	York	7.9g/s	91	4061
73	8-8	York	8.9g/f	[90]	4397
74	5-11	Muss	9g/f	[90]	4550
68	12-19	York	7.9gd	86	4987

DARK CHEETAH 2 b c £0

96	7-15	Asco	5g/f	2472

DARK CUT 4 b g £0

17a	13-14	Ling	10ap	55	622
0	13-15	Newc	12.4hvy	50	1034
0	17-17	Nott	14.1gd	48	1238
39	7-7	Hami	13gd	45	2708
5	12-12	Hami	9.2g/s	45	2832
30	9-18	Pont	10g/f	42	2988
29	11-16	Carl	7.9g/f	37	3650
33	13-16	Beve	8.5g/s	[37]	3850

DARK DAY BLUES 3 ch c £3936

53	8-11	Ripo	8gd	71	1176
28	14-16	Beve	8.5sft	69	1628
37	11-14	Newc	8gd	60	1872
69	1-14	REDC	7fm	63	2295*
54	8-8	Thir	7sft	67	2693
65	6-11	York	7g/f	67	3433
64	5-10	Muss	7.1g/f	65	3562
56	5-12	Pont	8gd	66	3679
42	13-14	Muss	7.1g/f	64	4175
53	10-18	Catt	7g/f	62	4438
52	9-17	Beve	8.5g/f	59	4721
52	9-17	Newc	8fm	59	4867
46	13-16	York	11.9gd	56	4990

DARK DOLORES 5 b m £0

36a	6-10	Ling	12ap	[35]	24
11a	5-12	Ling	10ap	[35]	654

DARK EMPRESS 3 b r f £450

93	6-11	Warw	7.1fm	[90]	2574 BL

DARK PARADE 3 b c £0

34	14-15	Ling	7gd	4445
43a	5-14	Ling	10ap	4661
18	7-8	Brig	8fm	4762

DARK RAIDER 3 b r f £5006

64	2-7	Nott	8.2hvy		1610
74	5-11	Bath	8fm	[63]	1904
77	5-11	Newb	10g/f	[63]	2349
72	1-7	AYR	9.1gd	63	2509*
53	10-12	Newb	10g/f	70	3255
44	12-12	Good	9fm	70	3535
55	11-16	Bath	8gd	70	5022
50	9-17	Newb	9sft	70	5198

DARK SHAH 4 b g £0

43a	5-9	Ling	8ap	[60]	717 t
46a	11-15	Ling	7ap	55	913 P
31	10-16	Bath	8fm	[55]	2032 p
23	14-17	Warw	8.1fm	50	2572 tp

DARK SOCIETY 6 b g £0

52	6-16	Bath	8gd	52	4828
53	4-12	Warw	12.6g/s	[52]	4991

DARKO KARIM 2 b c £922

90	4-8	Newm	6g/f		1934
72	10-11	Asco	7fm		2578
71	9-13	Wind	6fm		3478
66	11-17	York	7g/f	78	4396 VIS
78	3-13	Wind	8.3g/s	74	4940
71	5-13	Wind	8.3g/f	74	5051
38	13-14	Donc	8sft	73	5203

DARLA 3 b f £1717

59	8-9	Epso	7gd	70	3218

```
70  5-13  Wind  6fm       68    3479
71  2-14  Yarm  6gd       67    3870
65  6-20  Ling  6g/f      69    4317
45  16-20 Nott  6.1g/s    69    4646
61  11-17 Ling  6g/f      69    4740
68a 3-12  Ling  6ap       67    4976

DARLING RIVER 5 b m £0
45a 10-12 Ling  8ap  [60]       5077
29a 14-14 Ling  7ap  [58]       5263

DARN GOOD 2 ch c £14380
63a 9-11  Ling  8ap       72      54
61a 9-12  Ling  10ap [69]        120
56a 9-14  Ling  10ap [65]        367
57a 8-13  Ling  10ap [62]        715
59a 3-6   Ling  12ap      52     915 VIS
32  14-19 Warw  10.9gd    69    1124 vis
64  6-15  Leic  11.8gd    66    2134 BL
56  7-10  Good  14gd      66    2376 bl
67  1-12  WARW  19.1fm    60    2577* bl
73  1-12  WARW  15g/f     64    2908* bl
79  2-7   Warw  16.2gd    70    3057 bl
37  10-12 Kemp  14.4g/f   71    3688 bl
71  6-12  Sand  16.4g/f   71    3861 bl
64  6-16  Warw  16.2gd    68    4276 bl
57  14-15 Ches  15.9g/f   67    4512 bl
76  1-20  BATH  17.2gd    65    4824* bl
72  4-9   Good  16gd      71    4875 bl

DARSALAM 3 ch c £11972
115 6-9   Donc  14.6fm          4532
115 3-9   Colo  12sft           4841

DARSHARP 2 b f £0
51  6-14  Newb  6sft            5197
42  19-21 Donc  6sft            5368

DART ALONG 2 b c £802
74  5-5   Asco  7g/f            4776
78  5-23  Newm  7g/f            4885
72  4-13  Wind  6g/f            5048
76a 4-10  Ling  7ap  [78]       5259

DARTANIAN 2 b g £3006
71  7-10  Sali  5g/f            1716
63  5-6   Warw  7.1fm           2597
46  6-8   Yarm  6fm             2865
53  3-13  Catt  7g/f            3349
54a 7-12  Ling  7ap       58    3820
63  1-15  CATT  7sft  [58]      3930*
24  8-9   Ches  7sft       63   4074
33  16-17 York  7g/f      60    4396

DARTING 2 b f £2300
76a 1-10  LING  5ap             13*

DASAR 3 ch f £834
30a 8-12  Wolv  7af       54      68
41a 7-14  Sout  8af       49     165
39a 6-16  Sout  7af       49     202
35a 6-9   Sout  7af  [45]        303
39a 4-13  Sout  6af       45     500 BL
33a 7-11  Wolv  7af  [45]        579 bl
45a 2-9   Wolv  7af  [45]       1266 VIS
51a 3-12  Wolv  7af       48    2049 vis
37a 9-15  Sout  7af       48    2384 vis
19  15-16 Beve  7.5gd     48    2891 vis

DASH FOR COVER 4 b g £1036
71  2-9   Folk  9.7sft [69]      978
42  11-18 Bath  10.2g/s  69     1098
65  7-18  Wind  8.3gd    66     1385
14  10-14 Warw  8.1hvy   66     1535
55  5-15  Brig  8fm      64     1691
61  6-9   Newm  8gd      64     1891
53  9-15  Kemp  9gd      62     2170
51  5-12  Sali  8g/s     59     4077
31  13-16 Sali  8gd      57     4334

DASH FOR GLORY 5 ch g £618
25a 9-13  Ling  13ap [40]       1076
5a  8-9   Sout  12af [40]       1204
27a 8-9   Ling  16ap [30]       1414
29  7-15  Warw  10.9g/f    30   2910
44  3-4   Brig  9.9fm  [29]     3675
10  11-12 Chep  12.1g/s [30]    4364

DASH OF LIME 2 b f £267
```

```
64a 4-13  Wolv  6ap             5287

DASH OF MAGIC 5 b m £6465
10a 7-10  Sout  14af      43       90
5a  8-14  Sout  14af      40      185
40a 1-14  SOUT  14af [36]        305*
24a 6-10  Sout  12af      40      321
39a 2-16  Sout  11af [40]        445
36a 5-13  Sout  12af [40]        575
41a 1-16  SOUT  11af [35]        852*
35  11-15 Beve  9.9sft    45     1307
34  6-13  Beve  12.1g/f [45]     1945
47  3-11  Hayd  10.5g/s  41      2226
48a 1-16  SOUT  12af      40     2340*
36  5-10  Redc  14.1g/s  41      2562
3a  W-10  Sout  14af      45     3096
27  10-17 Catt  12sft     40     3929
6a  7-8   Sout  12af      45     4128

DASH TO THE TOP 2 b f £29245
83  2-18  Nott  8.2g/s           4035
85  1-13  LEIC  8g/f             4450*
108 3-30  Asco  8g/f             4798

DASHIKI 3 ch f £900
82  3-13  Newb  7gd              1210

DATAHILL 4 b f £0
0   5-7   Sout  12af  [72]        588

DAUNTED 7 b g £11461
52a 4-14  Sout  14af      59      185
56a 3-10  Sout  14af      58      321
63a 1-10  SOUT  11af      58      330*
33a 10-12 Wolv  12af      62      484
49a 8-10  Sout  16af      62      491
59a 1-8   SOUT  11af [60]        574*
59a 1-5   SOUT  12af [60]        723*
63a 1-5   SOUT  12af [60]        745* P
64a 1-4   SOUT  14af [60]        854*

DAVALA 2 b c £0
38  11-11 Yarm  6g/f             1727
35  11-13 Sali  6fm              2287
30  12-13 Warw  7.1g/s           4996

DAVE 3 b g £3059
66  1-12  FOLK  6gd       55     3380+
24  16-17 Wind  6gd       63     4126
46  10-16 Brig  7sft  [63]       4144
42  15-16 Good  5g/f      62     4528
7a  13-13 Wolv  9.5ap     61     5292

DAVID JUNIOR 2 ch c £8143
87  3-12  Thir  7g/f             4591
92  1-5   ASCO  7g/f             4776*

DAVIDS CHOICE 2 b g £0
4   12-12 Muss  7.1g/s           5142

DAVIDS GIRL 2 b f £643
5a  12-12 Ling  8ap  [53]          78
21a 7-16  Sout  8af  [49]         164
23a 5-9   Wolv  9.4af [42]        238
21a 5-5   Ling  8ap  [35]        1416
29  6-8   Nott  8.2sft    45     1740
33  6-18  Sali  7fm       40     2292
44  5-17  Leic  7gd  [38]        2704
24  8-11  Yarm  7g/f [38]        2852
11  8-10  Yarm  8g/f      38     3712
33  6-14  Newm  7gd  [38]        4195
37  6-15  Yarm  7g/s [40]        4587
41  3-17  Kemp  7g/f [40]        4794
42  2-20  Yarm  7g/f [40]        5120

DAVIDS MARK 4 b g £5712
50a 10-14 Ling  6ap       57      897
53  3-15  Folk  6g/s      55     1267
51  4-18  Bath  5.7g/f    54     1788
48a 4-13  Wolv  5af       53     2201
48  4-18  Ling  6gd       51     2396
58  1-16  WIND  5fm       50     3640*
57  2-18  Pont  5g/s      52     3974
43  10-15 Chep  5.1gd     54     4489
37a 11-13 Wolv  5.1ap     55     5156
57a 3-12  Ling  6ap       55     5241

DAVIDS SYMPHONY 2 ch c £0
28  11-11 Sali  6g/s             3110
```

```
48  16-18 Leic  7g/f             3342
37  8-11  Wind  8.3fm            3798
39  17-17 Warw  7.1gd            4269

DAVORIN 3 br c £5717
81  1-12  NEWM  7g/s             1152*
79  6-7   Thir  8g/f  [83]       1770
67a 10-13 Ling  7ap       83     4318 VIS
77  6-12  Epso  8.5gd     80     4909
55  8-13  Bath  8sft      78     5172

DAVY CROCKETT 2 b g £2961
61  7-10  Newc  5g/f             2158
15  16-20 Newc  8sft             2682
66  5-15  Pont  8gd              3239
69  6-12  Carl  5.9fm            3544
43  11-14 Muss  8gd       69     4519
74  1-11  NEWC  7fm  [67]        4863*
44  15-21 Donc  6hvy             5202

DAWN AIR 3 b f £850
57  3-8   Thir  12g/s            1472
41  10-13 Thir  12g/f            1768
0   18-18 Hayd  14gd      57     2905 P
30  15-20 Beve  16.2gd    52     3312

DAWN DUEL 3 b f £0
45  9-14  Sout  6gd              1281
6   8-8   Muss  7.1gd            1554

DAWN INVASION 5 b h £3049
105 3-8   Leop  10g/s [100]       994

DAWN PIPER 4 b g £7059
83a 1-12  LING  8ap              401*
84a 7-14  Ling  7ap       85      518
89a 2-8   Ling  7ap  [83]        879 VIS
78  13-20 Newm  7g/s      84     1151 vis
82  2-10  Warw  7.1sft [82]      1525 vis
62  9-10  Beve  8.5g/f   83      1833 vis
72  4-7   Brig  7g/f      82     2045 vis

DAWN SURPRISE 3 b f £32601
94  2-10  Sali  9.9g/f           1718
92  1-11  SALI  8fm              2419* T
93  5-9   Newm  7fm       90     3006 t
96  1-9   KEMP  8g/f  [89]       3689* t
100 1-7   THIR  8g/s [91]        4208* t
97  2-10  Newm  8g/f [93]        4890 t

DAWTON 6 br h £0
47  10-11 Newb  11g/f     78     3256

DAY CARE 3 gr c £2000
63  2-10  Good  9.9gd            4877

DAY FLIGHT 3 b c £71000
89  1-12  SALI  12g/s            1501*
117 1-4   YORK  10.4g/s          1706*
117 4-15  Chan  12g/s            2308
109 4-8   Newb  11g/f [114]      4639

DAY OF RECKONING 3 b f £4195
66  3-15  Wind  10fm             3292
80  1-11  WIND  10gd             4125*

DAY ONE 2 ch c £2358
69a 7-12  Ling  8ap              102
77  3-12  Newm  12g/f            3783
58  5-11  Good  14gd             5029
70  2-10  Muss  12g/s            5145

DAY OR NIGHT 2 gr c £27401
106 3-    Sain  10g/s             9 bl
105 2-8   Long  10.5g/s         1434

DAY TO REMEMBER 3 gr c £12374
71  5-17  Kemp  7gd              1136
94  1-9   WIND  8.3g/f [80]      3979*
86  3-8   Good  8sft      85     4265
95  1-9   WIND  10g/s     85     4943*

DAYANO 3 b c £245655
112 2-15  Capa  12gd             2142
117 2-7   Duss  12sft            3497

DAYBREAKING 2 br c £0
66a 7-14  Ling  7ap              4971
63  5-12  Bath  8sft             5170
```

DAYDREAM DANCER 3 gr f £6616
59	5-12	Warw	7.1gd	1129
43a	12-14	Ling	10ap	53	2064
33	12-14	Wind	10gd	53	2617
45	10-11	Ling	11.5g/f	53	2842
52	3-14	Chep	8.1g/s	50	3090 BL
37	8-14	Chep	8.1gd	49	3733 bl
54	**1-11**	**BRIG**	**9.9g/f**	**47**	**3982* bl**
62	**1-10**	**BRIG**	**9.9b/f**	**49**	**4763* bl**
52a	4-12	Wolv	12.2ap	54	5339 bl

DAYGAR 2 b c £0
58 11-18 Leic 7g/f 3342

DAYTIME GIRL 3 gr f £6905
79 3-14 Newm 10g/f 76 1192
2 5-6 Pont 12sft 76 1429
78 1-8 CHES 10.3gd [76] 2283*
63 6-8 Ches 12.3g/s 78 2746

DAZE 3 b f £6812
76 3-6 Newm 10gd 1892
77 1-5 CHES 12.3sft 4075*
73 7-15 Newb 11g/f 75 4643
73 4-11 Newm 14g/f 74 4919

DAZZLING BAY 4 b g £9619
47 6-7 Thir 6sft [105] 1227
49 13-14 York 6g/s 103 1703
102 3-10 York 6g/f 100 2357
102 5-29 Asco 6fm 100 2581
104 2-8 Hayd 6gd [102] 2949 bl
65 3-22 Good 6m 102 3622
80 14-19 Ripo 6g/s 101 3937 bl
97 3-10 Beve 6gd [99] 4718 bl
58 14-14 Ripo 6gd 99 4786 bl
84 12-13 Donc 5sft 98 5218 e

DE BULLIONS 2 b g £0
28 11-14 Hayd 6fm 4385

DEAL IN FACTS 5 ch m £0
3a 9-10 Wolv 7af [35] 394
0 16-16 Sout 6af [35] 447

DEANGATE 3 ch g £0
0 P-8 Pont 12g/f 2608
0 12-13 Carl 6.9fm 4504 T

DEAR SIR 4 ch g £0
34 9-11 Ling 16gd 49 3200

DEBBIE 5 b m £0
39a 7-12 Wolv 9.4af 45 427
32a 9-16 Sout 11af [45] 445
40a 4-9 Wolv 9.4af [40] 525

DEBS BROUGHTON 2 b f £1258
46 12-13 Nott 5.1gd 1987
44 15-19 Newb 6g/f 2310
59 2-8 Wind 6g/f 2449
46 7-12 Wind 6gd 56 3825
59 3-20 Leic 6g/f 56 4451
47 5-16 Yarm 8g/s 56 4632

DECELERATE 3 ch c £2128
52a 1-14 LING 12ap [58] 103*
11a 15-16 Sout 14af 58 206
54a 8-13 Ling 10ap [55] 912
0 8-8 Ling 10ap [55] 1026

DECO LADY 3 ch f £0
30a 5-10 Wolv 7af [50] 8 vis
37a 6-13 Wolv 8.5af [50] 39
19a 8-12 Wolv 8.5af [50] 47

DECORATION 2 b c £0
53 11-11 Newb 7g/f 3959

DEE DEE GIRL 2 b f £0
18a 15-15 Ling 7ap [58] 52
10a 11-12 Ling 8ap [53] 675

DEE EN AY 3 ch g £0
31 12-12 York 7g/s 1688
43 10-16 Ripo 8gd 2987
60 5-11 Thir 8g/f 3572
48 6-10 Hayd 8.1gd 3739

DEE PEE TEE CEE 10 b g £463

50 7-16 Beve 8.5g/s [46] 3850
41 3-16 Carl 11.9g/f 46 4348
21 11-15 Yarm 10.1g/s [45] 5122

DEEDAY BAY 2 b f £6734
87 1-8 DONC 6gd 2750*
82 4-11 Sali 6g/s 3110
87 2-6 Wind 6g/s [87] 4217

DEEKAZZ 5 b m £0
31 11-20 Catt 12g/f 39 3354
25 15-19 Beve 9.9g/f 39 3505
38 6-11 Ling 10fm 35 3748 vis

DEEP PURPLE 3 b g £6797
90 1-13 KEMP 10gd 3186*
87 4-14 Sand 10g/s 85 4097
84 6-15 Newb 11g/f 85 4643

DEEPER IN DEBT 5 ch g £3290
74a 2-11 Ling 8ap 71 12
74a 2-12 Ling 8ap 72 517
74a 4-11 Ling 8ap 73 714
75a 3-12 Ling 8ap 73 932
70a 3-12 Ling 8ap [73] 1042
62 5-9 Epso 8.5hvy [70] 1298
51 10-15 Brig 8fm 69 1691
52 7-9 Good 8gd 68 2540
32 18-20 Kemp 9g/f 65 2857
48 13-16 Kemp 9gd 62 3187

DEEWAAR 4 b g £0
46 7-17 Bath 10.2sft 49 1541
34 11-15 Sand 10g/f 47 2099
40 18-18 Bath 10.2gd [45] 5023

DEFANA 3 b g £4495
39a 5-8 Ling 8ap [54] 326
53 3-11 Pont 12g/f 54 2790
43 3-8 Warw 10.9gd [54] 3055
16 11-14 Leic 8g/f [52] 3344
46 6-13 Redc 14.1qd 50 4249
55 1-14 REDC 10fm 48 4560*
51 7-15 Wind 10g/f [53] 4834 P
28a 8-11 Wolv 12.2ap 49 5009

DEFERLANT 7 ch g £0
51 10-13 Kemp 12g/f 70 1916 vis
7 15-15 Newb 13.3g/f 60 2311 vis
31 12-17 Bath 11.7gd 50 3145 P

DEFINING 5 b g £81716
82 11-17 Newb 12g/f 95 1759
99 3-9 Newm 12g/f [95] 2246
98 7-19 Newc 16.1g/s 95 2771
101 4-19 York 13.9g/s 95 4023
109 1-20 HAYD 14fm 98 4383*
113 1-5 ASCO 16.2g/f[105] 4815*
104 6-11 Newm 16sft [107] 5138

DEFINITE GUEST 6 gr g £6900
83 3-13 Epso 8.5g/f 82 2207
73 13-15 York 8.9g/f 82 2404
76 9-9 Sand 10g/s 82 2896
54 15-18 Newb 8g/f 80 3265
81 5-21 Good 8fm 80 3565
70 10-16 Redc 8g/f 81 3768

DEFINITELY ROYAL 2 b f £0
34a 7-8 Ling 6ap 5081
52a 9-13 Wolv 8.6ap 5288

DEFINITELY SPECIAL 5 b m £0
44a 7-15 Ling 7ap [40] 216
38a 9-15 Ling 7ap [40] 263
37a 8-13 Ling 6ap [40] 340
31a 7-15 Ling 7ap [40] 411
3a 9-13 Sout 6af 40 500
0 10-10 Ling 5ap [40] 832
35a 8-12 Ling 7ap [35] 1074 P
22a 6-10 Ling 7ap [35] 1181 p
14 4-7 Chep 7.1sft [35] 1335 p
0 7-8 Brig 8gd [35] 1548 p

DEGREE OF HONOR 2 ch f £0
13 10-11 Ayr 7.2g/s 4653
24a 11-12 Wolv 7.1ap 5324

DEIGN TO DANCE 3 b f £5235

65a 5-10 Ling 7ap [75] 911
39 19-20 Nott 6.1gd 73 1239
37 8-14 Sali 7g/f [70] 1720 P
60 5-16 Ling 7g/f [64] 1982
67a 1-12 LING 8ap [62] 2394*
45 10-14 Chep 8.1g/s 65 3090
60 3-12 Wind 8.3fm 61 3291
62 2-11 Wind 8.3fm 60 3799
57 5-12 Kemp 9sft 60 4032
52 5-13 Pont 8g/s [62] 5153
67a 3-13 Ling 10ap 65 5299

DEJEEJE 3 ch c £0
0 9-9 Thir 6fm 4380
2 7-7 Redc 7fm 4561

DEL MAR SUNSET 4 b g £4633
46a 12-13 Wolv 8.5af 89 44
75a 7-12 Sout 8af 86 141
81a 3-10 Wolv 9.4af 83 278
81a 4-12 Wolv 9.4af 82 382
58a 5-12 Wolv 8.5af 80 688
73a 8-11 Ling 8ap [78] 800
83a 1-7 WOLV 8.5af 75 942* P
7 12-12 Folk 9.7sft 68 1273 p
48 12-16 Bath 8gd 65 5022

DELAWARE TRAIL 5 b g £0
0 8-8 Sout 8af [45] 1200
2 9-11 Pont 8sft 45 1425 P

DELCIENNE 2 b f £5596
53a 2-11 Ling 8ap [50] 77
17a 11-15 Sout 7af [50] 87
18 13-13 Nott 8.2gd 52 1242 T
7 11-14 Warw 8.1sft 47 1529
45 3-13 Beve 8.5g/f [45] 1947
43 9-14 Redc 10fm 44 2299
46 2-13 Bath 8fm 42 2667
51 1-9 BRIG 8fm [42] 2834*
42 5-15 Beve 8.5g/s 48 3182
45 7-18 Carl 7.9fm 46 3547
51 1-12 BRIG 8gd [45] 4904*
41 8-19 Yarm 8g/s [49] 5119
35a 8-12 Wolv 8.6ap [50] 5329

DELEGATE 11 ch g £3348
44 13-14 Wind 5g/f 67 2266
35 7-11 Bath 5.7fm [67] 2412
77 1-8 BATH 5.7fm [63] 2669*

DELFINIA 3 b f £280
6 15-16 Sand 10g/s 2131
46 4-8 Chep 12.1gd 2368
24 6-8 Chep 12.1g/f 2623

DELFOS 3 ch c £83944
114 1-4 SAIN 10g/s 1696*
116 2-9 Mais 10sft 3316
114 2-9 Deau 10hvy 4158
116 1-9 LONG 10g/s 4730*

DELIGHTFUL GIFT 4 b f £0
37 6-15 Beve 7.5g/f [48] 1944
0 14-15 Sout 8af 45 2338
37 8-16 Beve 7.5gd 45 2891
10 17-17 Pont 8g/f 45 4626

DELIGHTFULLY 3 b f £4293
34 7-15 Folk 6g/s 1078
73a 2-6 Wolv 8.5af 1377
75 4-11 Bath 8fm [69] 1904
64a 6-15 Ling 12ap [69] 2393
70 3-7 Warw 10.9fm 67 2576
61a 1-8 LING 12ap [67] 2739* BL

DELLA SALUTE 2 gr f £0
74 6-10 Newm 6g/f 3063
67 8-9 Epso 7fm 3539

DELLAGIO 3 b c £3573
73a 8-9 Ling 5ap 85 914
34 19-19 Newm 6g/s 82 1154
18 15-17 Asco 6sft 75 1417
11 16-17 Yarm 7g/f [68] 1729
52 4-8 Brig 5.3g/f 60 1942
49 8-9 Sand 5g/f 57 2387
47 8-16 Ling 7gd 53 3024
59 1-12 CARL 5.9g/f 50 3655*

| 1 | 14-14 | Yarm | 7gd | 56 | 3995 |
| 44 | 10-18 | Bath | 5.7g/f | 56 | 4412 |

DELPHIE QUEEN 3 ch f £43493

85	4-11	Newb	6gd	81	1734
91	3-13	Hayd	6g/f	81	1881
93	1-12	NEWM	7g/f	83	2249*
102	2-20	York	6g/f	90	2407
106	1-6	SALI	7g/s	[95]	3113*
94	6-12	Asco	7g/f	[102]	4811
91	6-15	Newm	6gd	[102]	5088

DELSARTE 4 b c £9067

106	9-13	Nad	12g/f	[112]	990
107	2-8	Newb	13.3g/f		1757 T
101	5-9	Newm	12g/f	[111]	3233 t
108	6-6	Ches	13.4sft	107	4104 t
106	4-7	Donc	12fm	[106]	4494 VIS

DELTA FORCE 4 b g £8928

41a	3-9	Sout	11af	[41]	204
50a	1-10	WOLV	12af	[41]	250*
50a	1-10	SOUT	16af	[51]	307*
53a	2-9	Sout	16af	51	331
62a	1-9	SOUT	12af	58	456*
57a	4-12	Sout	11af	63	534
56a	4-13	Sout	14af	63	590
45a	5-7	Sout	12af	[63]	594
51	3-13	Brig	11.9g/f	49	1373
50	2-8	Bath	17.2fm	49	2035
48	6-10	Carl	14.1fm	50	2444

DELTA LADY 3 b f £0

0	16-16	Redc	8sft	46	1147
0	6-7	Sout	8af	[45]	1591
17	9-10	Beve	9.9g/f	[45]	1946
41	5-12	Thir	7g/f	[43]	2215
11	14-17	Leic	7gd	[42]	2704
32	8-16	Thir	8af	42	3414
0	12-12	Newc	8sft	[40]	4284
32	9-15	Carl	7.9fm	[40]	4507
32	6-17	Pont	7g/f	40	4626

DELTA STAR 4 ch f £0

| 40 | 12-17 | Hayd | 8.1g/s | | 4768 |
| 15a | 12-13 | Wolv | 9.5ap | | 5290 |

DELUSION 3 b f £447

52	6-13	Ripo	6g/f	65	2011
49	3-12	Thir	7g/f	[65]	2215
18	11-15	Ayr	8gd	[56]	2504
1	15-15	Leic	7g/f	[53]	3515
25	7-11	Carl	6.9g/f	[53]	3651

DEMOCRATIC DEFICIT 2 b c £75364

112	1-7	CURR	6g/f		2819*
112	2-5	Curr	7g/f		4154
103	4-7	Curr	7g/f		4734
109	5-6	Long	7g/f		4955

DEMOLITION FRANK 2 b c £0

| 52 | 11-14 | Carl | 6.9fm | | 4503 |
| 17 | 10-10 | Catt | 7sft | | 5317 |

DEMOLITION MOLLY 2 b f £4804

69a	4-8	Sout	5af	77	169
59a	9-14	Sout	5af	73	485 P
56a	6-11	Sout	5af	68	609 T
45a	8-10	Ling	5ap	64	712 t
72	2-8	Nott	5.1fm	70	1002 tp
74a	1-8	SOUT	5af	62	1031* t p
45	15-15	Ches	5.1g/s	70	1572 tp
10	19-19	York	5gd	70	4989 tp
32a	13-13	Wolv	6ap	70	5181 tp

DEMON DANCER 7 gr g £10282

| 116 | 2-7 | Deau | 10hvy | | 4016 |

DEN PERRY 2 ch c £695

51	6-7	Beve	5g/f		2167
17	10-13	York	6g/f		2358
19	7-7	Pont	6g/f		2792
48	7-8	Ches	5.1g/f		3081
52	8-11	Ches	7fm		3633
36	7-7	Ripo	6g/s		3935
28	5-5	Ches	6.1sft		4105 P
52	8-8	Ripo	5gd		4307

DENEBOLA 3 br f £39908

106	3-8	Long	8g/s		1432
114	4-11	Long	8g/s		4434
115	2-7	Long	7sft		5070

DENISE BEST 6 ch m £0

18	11-13	Warw	12.6gd	51	3056
42	5-15	Chep	10.2g/s	50	4299 p
32a	5-12	Ling	8ap	[40]	4659 p

DENNICK 2 b g £295

| 64 | 4-7 | Hami | 6g/f | | 2473 |

DENOUNCE 3 b c £2140

| 88 | 2-17 | Newm | 8gd | | 1166 |
| 77 | 8-24 | Newm | 8fm | | 1495 |

DENS JOY 7 b m £0

61a	8-19	Wolv	9.4af	64	38 p
0	19-19	Wind	10sft	[52]	1650
31	16-19	Newb	10gd	52	1736
23	10-18	Wind	11.6g/f	50	1960
41	11-16	Yarm	10.1fm	50	2146
26	8-9	Newb	8g/f	47	2529

DENVER 2 b c £9256

71a	2-14	Sout	8af		226
82a	1-10	WOLV	7af		276* BL
59a	7-10	Ling	10ap	77	568
82a	2-10	Sout	7af	77	794 bl
87a	1-7	SOUT	8af	80	855* bl

DEO GRATIAS 4 b c £0

| 25 | 17-19 | Bath | 17.2gd | 49 | 3147 |

DEPORTIVO 3   £0

| 88 | 14-14 | Sha | 5g/f | | 210 |

DEPRESSED 2 ch f £1409

53a	7-12	Ling	6ap		4178
61	7-17	Yarm	6gd		4610
68a	3-12	Wolv	6ap		4921
68a	4-12	Wolv	5.1ap		4981
68a	2-13	Wolv	5.1ap	[64]	5207

DEPUTY OF WOOD 2 b f £0

| 56 | 8-10 | York | 5g/s | | 1709 |

DERAASAAT 3 ch f £450

62	8-9	Ches	11.4gd	[95]	1568
84	6-7	Good	9.9g/f	[93]	1844
82	12-12	Sand	9g/f	89	2385

DERWENT 5 b g £911

45	16-20	Donc	10.3g/s	84	1519
66	9-9	Thir	12gd	80	1969
51	8-10	Beve	9.9g/s	75	2323 bl
70	4-10	Pont	10g/f	70	2794 bl
61	6-6	Beve	9.9gd	[69]	3313 bl
55	6-6	Pont	10gd	67	3678 bl
37	9-13	Nott	10gd	64	3992 bl
64	3-13	Newc	10.1g/f	62	4406 VIS
53	13-15	Nott	10g/f	62	4849 vis

DESCARTES 2 b c £6734

| 90 | 1-15 | NEWB | 8hvy | | 5221* |

DESERT AIR 5 ch g £0

| 59 | 13-16 | Wind | 11.6gd | 69 | 3829 |

DESERT ARC 6 b g £6442

33	12-13	Muss	7.1g/f	57	1122
64	1-19	REDC	6g/f	55	2125*
67	1-13	HAMI	6g/f	62	2315*
58	6-11	Ayr	6gd	63	2542
39	11-13	Ayr	7.2g/s	65	2568
18	13-13	Sali	6g/f	65	3109
53	10-20	Ripo	6gd	64	4785

DESERT BATTLE 3 ch g £0

31	15-18	Nott	8.2sft	67	1470
0	19-20	Wind	11.6sft	64	1648
0	16-17	Hayd	8.1gd	60	2243 BL
24a	12-12	Sout	7af	[55]	2496 bl

DESERT BEAU 2 b g £0

| 49a | 7-11 | Wolv | 7af | 64 | 29 |
| 37a | 6-12 | Ling | 8ap | [57] | 78 VIS |

DESERT BUZZ 2 b c £0

59	7-12	Beve	5sft		1631
68	6-13	Nott	5.1gd		1987
57	8-14	Redc	6fm		2297
67	5-12	Carl	5gd		2933
49	9-18	Donc	6g/s		3376
48	10-12	Thir	5g/s		3832
46	8-14	Thir	7g/s		4206
52	8-16	Beve	7.5g/f	56	4597 P
54	6-18	Newc	6g/f	53	5013 p

DESERT CHIEF 2 b c £1402

| 79 | 2-14 | Newc | 6fm | | 4865 |
| 77 | 6-23 | Newm | 6gd | | 5084 |

DESERT CITY 5 b g £0

| 0 | 20-20 | Hayd | 11.9g/s | 65 | 4771 |

DESERT CLASSIC 2 b f £0

| 65 | 9-14 | Newm | 7g/f | | 3752 |
| 49 | 14-16 | Sali | 7gd | | 4330 |

DESERT COMMANDER 2 b c £5184

79	4-16	Sali	7g/s		3111
74	6-10	Donc	7g/f		3594
89	1-7	YARM	6gd		3869* T

DESERT CORAL 3 ch f £0

| 0 | 13-13 | Sout | 8af | | 2383 |

DESERT CRISTAL 3 ch f £18755

77	2-8	Epso	8.5hvy		1297
80	6-11	Asco	8sft		1419
80	3-11	Asco	8gd	[80]	3128
77	1-10	LING	7gd	[79]	3446*
82	3-6	Wind	8.3g/f	78	3978
82	2-4	Yarm	7sft	[78]	4148
81	3-15	Kemp	8gd	78	4362
72	9-13	Sand	8.1gd	78	4607
90	1-12	GOOD	8gd	[78]	4872+
90	3-13	Bath	8sft	84	5172

DESERT DAISY 3 gr f £0

57	9-15	Bath	8g/s	65	1099
27	13-15	Ripo	12.3g/f	62	1785
19	9-10	Leic	8gd	[59]	2133
19	12-16	Chep	7.1gd	[59]	2369 VIS
51	6-17	Bath	5.7gd	[47]	5020
46	6-19	Bath	5.7sft	47	5176
6	18-18	Yarm	6g/s	47	5354

DESERT DANCE 4 b g £0

| 39a | 11-12 | Ling | 8ap | [65] | 1042 |

DESERT DEER 6 ch h £0

| 70 | 14-15 | Newb | 8g/f | [114] | 1758 |

DESERT DEMON 2 b c £899

| 81 | 5-12 | Newm | 6g/f | | 3280 |
| 75 | 3-8 | Sali | 6sft | | 4577 |

DESERT DESTINY 4 b g £16993

93	7-11	Hayd	7.1gd	[107]	2184 vis
110	2-8	Newm	7g/f	[105]	2765 T
96	5-8	Newb	7g/f	[110]	3253 t
107	2-5	Warw	7.1gd	[110]	4270 t
105	4-8	Epso	7g/f	[110]	4472 t

DESERT DIPLOMAT 3 br g £0

| 0 | 7-8 | Wind | 8.3g/s | 68 | 1257 |
| 1 | 14-14 | Nott | 8.2g/f | 66 | 2634 |

DESERT DREAMER 3 b g £1309

92	5-15	Ches	7.6gd	93	1583
90	8-18	Good	9g/f	93	1813
89	6-17	Epso	7g/f	92	2212
84	7-7	Ches	7g/s	90	2749
80	11-17	Good	7fm	88	3550
0	W-15	Kemp	8g/f	85	4362
79	12-21	Donc	7fm	85	4482
72	12-16	Kemp	6fm	82	4713

DESERT FANTASY 5 b g £6828

| 110 | 2-12 | Curr | 6g/f | | 4152 tbl |

DESERT FERN 2 b f £277

| 49a | 4-11 | Sout | 6af | | 2336 |
| 11a | 14-14 | Sout | 7af | | 2492 |

DESERT FURY 7 b g £0

| 39a | 8-12 | Wolv | 8.5af | 52 | 1379 |
| 25a | 10-15 | Sout | 6af | 48 | 1750 |

DESERT [continued]

41	6-20	Yarm	8fm	44	2149
40a	5-16	Sout	8af	43	3487
17	12-15	Newc	6hvy	41	4211
30a	6-12	Ling	8ap	[40]	4659
32	4-13	Ayr	8sft	[40]	5275 T

DESERT GLORY 2 gr f £0

63	11-19	Leic	7gd		5045

DESERT HAWK 3 b c £2491

65	13-24	Newm	8fm		1495
70	11-15	Newb	8gd		1763
68	5-10	Good	8gd		2378
72	4-16	Kemp	9g/f	69	3039
65	7-8	Asco	10g/f	69	3391
43	8-9	Newb	9gd		3922
59	6-12	Good	9.9sft	68	4268
71	2-13	Bath	8gd		4546
12	10-13	Chep	8.1hvy		4709
71	2-15	Bath	8gd	66	4827
32	9-14	Pont	8g/f	[66]	4937

DESERT HEAT 5 b h £4901

22a	9-15	Sout	12af	[70]	89
57a	4-10	Wolv	12af	[60]	154 P
0	13-13	Wolv	9.4af	60	287 p
51a	2-9	Wolv	9.4af	[57]	633 VIS
66a	1-9	WOLV	9.4af	57	647* VIS
66a	2-10	Wolv	8.5af	61	753 BL
42a	8-9	Wolv	8.5af	64	809 vis
2	14-14	Newc	10.1sft	72	964 vis
52a	4-7	Wolv	8af	[64]	1341 vis
58	2-10	Ayr	8g/s	[66]	1446 bl

DESERT IMAGE 2 b c £7311

52a	8-11	Wolv	7af	68	29
72a	1-15	LING	7ap	68	337*
76a	2-11	Ling	10ap	73	497
63a	6-6	Wolv	9.4af	75	702
67	10-18	Leic	10g/s	75	1017
56	8-19	Warw	10.9gd	70	1124
71	3-14	Bath	10.2gd	68	1403
77	3-13	Bath	10.2g/f	[69]	1791
73	2-4	Bath	11.7fm	[73]	2413
69	4-6	Warw	10.9fm	73	2780
55	9-10	Ling	11.5gd	72	3334
62	7-12	Bath	11.7g/f	70	3845
57	7-16	Ches	10.3g/f	68	4515

DESERT IMP 2 b f £6419

64	9-10	Newb	6gd		3917
82	3-15	Kemp	6g/f		4357
78	3-17	Yarm	6gd		4610
82	1-14	REDC	6g/s	[78]	5106*

DESERT ISLAND DISC 7 b m £26917

30	16-18	Bath	10.2g/s	75	1098
77	4-13	Wind	10gd	[73]	1381
77	4-10	Sali	12g/f	76	1721
70	8-15	Kemp	10fm	75	2067
34	3-5	Sali	12fm	73	2422
61	8-11	Good	12gd	73	2538
68	6-12	Kemp	9g/f	71	2860
75	1-5	BRIG	11.9gd	[71]	2956+
70	5-8	Brig	11.9g/f	73	3299
81	1-7	KEMP	12g/f	73	3519*
78	1-14	BRIG	11.9fm	72	3674+
75	6-14	Sand	10g/s	75	4097
76	3-12	Epso	12g/f	75	4292
66	8-9	Kemp	12g/f	75	4360
64	11-17	Wind	10g/f	74	5050
76	3-8	Brig	9.9sft	[74]	5095
41	9-13	Newb	16sft	74	5194
46a	11-16	Ling	12ap	[59]	5296

DESERT LEADER 3 b c £1078

65	8-9	Hayd	8.1g/f		1882
60	7-14	Hayd	8.1g/s		2231
69a	2-12	Sout	6af		2722
61	7-10	Hayd	8.1g/s	69	3138
39	17-17	York	7g/f	67	4398
0	17-18	Ayr	7.2sft	67	4622

DESERT LIGHT 2 b c £5074

2a	10-10	Wolv	5af	30	69 VIS
35a	8-10	Sout	5af	[23]	139
0	10-10	Sout	8af	23	189 e
46a	6-11	Sout	7af	[23]	207 e
0	10-11	Wolv	8.5af	[35]	279 e
59a	1-9	LING	6ap	[35]	327* vis
35a	3-12	Sout	6af	[35]	377 vis
46a	7-11	Sout	6af	54	872 vis
45	7-8	Nott	5.1fm	53	1002 vis
57a	2-8	Sout	5af	53	1031 vis
60	2-10	Hami	5g/s	53	1605 vis
53a	5-13	Wolv	5.1ap	55	5156 vis

DESERT LIGHTNING 2 ch c £652

79a	3-14	Ling	7ap		4971

DESERT LORD 4 b c £19500

82	6-10	Newm	6g/f	84	3584
89	1-20	NEWM	7g/f	82	3782*

DESERT LOVER 2 b c £0

70	6-8	Newm	6g/f		1934

DESERT MOONBEAM 2 b f £0

48	6-11	Sali	6g/f		3863
25	14-15	Chep	7.1gd		4483
51	10-11	Sali	7gd		4853

DESERT MOVE 2 b f £3653

80	1-14	THIR	7g/s		4204*

DESERT OPAL 4 ch c £646

91	9-24	Donc	8gd	95	951
90	8-27	Newb	8gd	95	1231
87	5-14	Kemp	8hvy	94	1512
81	12-18	Good	8g/f	92	1812 VIS
66	6-7	Wind	8.3fm	90	2787

DESERT PHOENIX 2 ch f £0

53	6-10	Ripo	5gd		2983
29	14-18	Donc	6g/s		3376

DESERT QUEST 4 b g £33675

77	7-12	Hami	12.1gd	89	1746 vis
94	2-11	Epso	10.1g/f	89	2208 BL
96	4-12	Wind	11.6fm	92	2759 bl
80	11-21	York	10.4gd	92	3118 bl
99	1-10	ASCO	12gd	92	3777* bl
97	5-6	Ches	13.4sft	94	4104 bl
91	10-18	Newb	10gd	94	4681 bl

DESERT QUILL 4 ch f £836

48a	2-7	Wolv	14.8af	[50]	2200
51	5-6	Muss	16g/f	57	2807
32	7-8	Hayd	11.9gd	57	2881
39	8-15	Chep	16.2gd	[52]	3400
43	4-8	Catt	15.8g/f	[47]	3666

DESERT REIGN 3 ch c £9305

71a	5-15	Ling	7ap	[67]	875
74	1-16	EPSO	8.5gd	65	3219*
73	4-14	Kemp	10g/f	71	3690
76	2-12	Epso	8.5gd	71	4909
75	3-14	Newb	8hvy	72	5227

DESERT ROYALTY 4 b f £23522

84	2-13	Wind	10gd	[82]	1381
95	1-10	SALI	12g/f	82	1721+
97	2-7	Hayd	11.9g/f	[82]	1921
95	4-13	York	11.9g/s	92	3076
47	9-9	Newm	12g/f	92	3278
92	7-10	Asco	12gd	92	3777
97	3-9	York	11.9g/s	[90]	4058
84	9-10	Donc	14.6fm	[92]	4460

DESERT STAR 4 b c £3300

104	3-15	Donc	8fm	98	4531
67	13-13	Newm	8g/f	[99]	4887

DESERT TOMMY 3 b g £0

24a	11-14	Ling	10ap		367
30a	13-15	Ling	12ap		521 H Bl

DESIGN 3 ch g £379

68	4-12	Nott	10hvy		5190

DESIGNER CITY 2 b f £0

47a	7-12	Wolv	5af	[57]	32
0	10-10	Pont	6hvy	[57]	1070
27	12-16	Hayd	6g/f	[52]	2182
30	10-14	Donc	6g/f	[50]	2428
29	8-10	Redc	6gd	[50]	2559
1	11-12	Catt	6g/f	[45]	2849
27	4-9	Ripo	5g/f	39	3645
21	9-11	Beve	5g/s	[35]	4237
21	9-10	Ripo	6gd	[35]	4788
8a	11-12	Wolv	6ap	[35]	5157

DESIREE 3 b f £0

44	13-15	Nott	8.2g/s		4649
21	14-18	Wind	10g/s		4944

DESIRES DESTINY 5 b m £618

36a	7-13	Sout	8af	[48]	199
35a	6-14	Sout	8af	[45]	354
34a	7-16	Sout	11af	[40]	445
29a	6-12	Wolv	8.5af	[35]	584
31a	3-8	Sout	8af	[35]	1200
41	9-15	Beve	9.9sft	45	1307
35a	2-7	Sout	8af	[35]	1593
19	8-10	Beve	9.9g/f	[45]	1946

DESPERATION 2 b g £1681

44a	8-15	Sout	5af		4089
69	5-8	Newc	7sft		4283
76a	2-13	Wolv	8.6ap		4979
79	3-8	Muss	9g/s	[75]	5140

DESTINATE 2 b c £19294

64	7-8	Newm	5g/f		1190
99	1-8	NEWM	6g/f		1934*
93	9-12	Newm	7g/f		3060
101	4-10	Good	7fm		3532
97	4-10	Asco	7gd	[95]	3774
100	2-3	Sand	8.1g/s	[100]	4066
101	2-6	Good	8g/f	[100]	4524

DESTINATION DUBAI 3 b c £22393

88	1-8	HAYD	10.5g/f		1489* VIS
95	3-6	Good	12g/f	91	2021 vis
92	8-17	Asco	12g/f	92	2519 vis
92	7-13	York	11.9g/s	92	3076 T
61	13-13	Donc	10.3fm	[90]	4463 t
96	1-13	ASCO	10g/f	[90]	4772* vis t

DETONATE 2 b c £1676

77	6-8	Newb	5.2gd		1205
78	4-6	Asco	5sft		1422
73	7-8	Good	5g/f		1816
66	6-10	Sali	6gd		2697
77	3-8	Ches	5.1g/f	76	3082
54	11-13	Newm	5g/f	75	3943

DETROIT DANCER 2 b c £0

16	15-17	Donc	6g/f		2424
51	5-15	Beve	5g/s		3178
24	15-18	Newc	6g/s		3699

DEUXIEME 3 b f £6723

79	3-12	Newb	7g/f		2352
62	3-11	Folk	7g/s		3048
65	5-10	Newb	7gd		3921
68	2-13	Bath	5.7g/f	[72]	4413
71	2-10	Ripo	6g/f	[72]	4790
60a	1-12	WOLV	6ap	[67]	5162*

DEVANT 4 b f £3067

8	11-14	Kemp	8hvy	85	1512
79	4-14	Donc	8gd	[83]	1877
75	7-9	Leic	8fm	80	2108
80	2-13	Donc	8gd	[79]	2753
74	14-20	Newm	8fm	79	3001
81	3-5	Hayd	10.5g/s	78	3904
70	5-9	Good	8g/f	77	4183

DEVILS BITE 3 ch c £0

0	P-9	Ling	7ap	[77]	764
4a	P-9	Wolv	9.4af	[77]	1340

DEVILS ISLAND 2 b c £0

49	5-7	Chep	6.1hvy		4705
51	8-14	Newc	6fm		4865
58a	11-14	Ling	7af		4971

DEVINE COMMAND 3 b g £420

53a	9-11	Sout	8ap		322
20a	14-14	Ling	10ap		473
54a	2-12	Ling	7ap		536
39a	5-6	Ling	8ap	[56]	651

DEVINE LIGHT 4 b f £0

31	8-8	Ayr	10g/f	65	1895
23	9-10	Muss	9g/f	[60]	2811

```
20  6-7    Carl  11.9g/f [60]   3226 P
 3  11-12  Carl  6.9fm    56    3548 p
13  8-8    Hami  9.2sft  [50]   4694 p
 9  12-12  Muss  8gd     [50]   4809
10  13-13  Ayr   10sft   [45]   5276
```

DEVIOUS AYERS 2 b g £685
```
61a 3-10   Ling  6ap            260
68a 4-6    Wolv  8.5af          1377
56  8-11   Kemp  8hvy           1514
35  14-17  Newm  12g/f   63     3618
48  6-6    Hami  9.2g/s  61     4137
34a 12-14  Ling  10ap   [62]    4448
31a 9-11   Wolv  8.6ap  [58]    5356
```

DEVIOUS PADDY 3 b c £0
```
28a 5-10   Sout  8af    [76]    143
 0  12-13  Wolv  8.5af  [68]    699 T
41a 7-8    Sout  11af   [60]    857 t
```

DEVISE 5 b g £28478
```
79  1-16   BATH  5.7g/s [72]    1103*
72  6-10   Wind  6gd    [78]    1383
51  27-30  Newm  7gd     78     1481
80  1-14   KEMP  5g/f    76     1914*
76  5-6    Bath  5.7fm   81     2416
81  5-12   Sali  5gd     80     2698
82  4-16   Newm  5g/f    80     3033
80  7-22   Good  5fm     80     3537
86  2-20   Hayd  5fm     79     3792
88  3-6    Sand  5g/s    82     4098
90  2-11   Bath  5g/s   [82]    4201
91  2-16   Hayd  5fm     86     4382
82  8-9    Good  6g/f    88     4537
```

DEVITO 3 ch g £1708
```
58  2-8    Leic  11.8g/f        1961
45  5-7    Newb  12g/f          2879
35  13-20  Beve  16.2gd  53     3312
```

DEVON FLAME 5 b g £14769
```
72  2-16   Good  6gd     66     2023
79  1-14   WIND  5g/f    68     2266+
76  2-6    Bath  5.7fm   71     2416
78  2-10   Kemp  6g/f    75     2861
78  4-11   Asco  6.5gd   75     3069
65  10-16  Newb  6g/f    76     3269
52  19-26  Good  6fm     75     3569
79  2-15   Bath  5.7g/f  73     3966
52  11-12  Good  6sft    73     4184
74  9-16   Leic  5gd     77     4700
```

DEVON MAID 4 ch f £0
```
14a 15-15  Ling  7ap            263
```

DEVOTE 6 b g £0
```
17  9-10   Bath  10.2gd         1402 bl
29  6-9    Wind  11.6fm         3294 bl
22  9-15   Chep  18sft   39     4056
```

DEWIN COCH 2 b g £0
```
43  14-17  Warw  7.1gd          4269
64  7-11   Chep  7.1hvy         4704
40  6-6    Brig  6gd            4900
```

DEXILEOS 5 b g £640
```
42  9-18   Bath  10.2g/s 65     1098
25  10-12  Folk  9.7sft   60    1273
 0  10-11  Warw  8.1hvy   57    1536
32  12-18  Nott  8.2g/s   52    1778 T
38  7-9    Yarm  7fm      47    2150 t
32  12-17  Newm  7g/f     42    2768 t
51  7-9    Epso  7gd     [40]   3215 t
42  3-12   Brig  6g/f     40    3301 t
59  6-10   Wind  6g/f    [40]   3977 t
17  8-16   Folk  6g/f    [45]   4370 t
41  9-16   Chep  7.1hvy  [45]   4707 t
45a 3-11   Wolv  7.1ap   [45]   5210 t
```

DHABYAN 4 ch c £0
```
42  8-8    Donc  10.3gd  [98]   2234
```

DHAKHIRAH 3 b f £0
```
65a 6-11   Ling  10ap     70    12
```

DHAULAR DHAR 2 b c £6778
```
87  2-12   Newm  7gd            4194
89  1-7    CHES  7g/f           4511*
84  9-13   Newb  7sft   [90]    5195
```

DHEFAAF 2 b c £0
```
54  7-10   Leic  5g/f           1826
```

DHEHDAAH 3 b c £648
```
58  7-10   Leic  10g/f   65     1965
62  3-6    Beve  12.1g/s 63     2322
59  5-10   Bath  11.7g/f 61     2978 BL
```

DIAGON ALLEY 4 ro g £0
```
25a 8-9    Wolv  9.4af  [35]    821
 0  6-6    Wolv  9.4af  [30]    1800
```

DIAL SQUARE 2 b g £7368
```
23a 11-13  Wolv  6af             3
31a 9-11   Wolv  7af            396
47a 1-11   LING  8ap    [40]    535* BL
47a 3-15   Ling  7ap     45     846 bl
45a 2-15   Ling  7ap    [45]    969 bl
43a 3-12   Ling  8ap    [45]    1073 bl
53a 1-6    LING  8ap    [45]    1246*
59a 1-5    LING  8ap    [51]    1416*
52a 1-4    LING  10ap   [51]    1454*
39  10-16  Ling  7gd     54     3024
25  17-20  Yarm  8gd     52     3996
16  17-19  Thir  12g/f   52     4594
39a 10-12  Wolv  8.6ap  [54]    5329
38a 9-13   Wolv  8.6ap   54     5365
```

DIAMOND CIRCLE 2 br f £0
```
63  5-14   Yarm  7sft            5251
```

DIAMOND DAN 2 b g £0
```
40  16-23  Newm  6gd             5084
```

DIAMOND DAZZLER 6 br g £0
```
 0  8-8    Sout  11af            420 bl
```

DIAMOND GEORGE 3 b g £0
```
52a 5-8    Wolv  6af    61       422
33a 6-9    Wolv  7af    57       510
41  11-17  Warw  7.1sft 60      1526
```

DIAMOND GREEN FR 3 b c £167987
```
119 2-7    Long  8g/s            1855
122 2-11   Asco  8g/f            2469
115 2-6    Deau  8sft            3168
119 2-11   Asco  8g/s            4434
92  8-11   Asco  8g/f            4801
114 8-5    Lone  8g/s            5308
```

DIAMOND HERITAGE 2 ch c £0
```
35  12-15  Beve  5g/s            3178
49  10-12  Hayd  6sft            4770
51  5-9    Nott  6.1hvy          5185
```

DIAMOND HOMBRE 2 gr c £367
```
62  4-10   Newm  5fm             2089
73  6-8    Sali  6gd             3451
67a 7-10   Ling  5ap             3743
```

DIAMOND JOSH 2 ch g £664
```
74  3-11   Wind  5g/f            2450
 0  W-15   Folk  6g/f            4369
67  6-11   Newm  6sft            5265
```

DIAMOND KATIE 2 b f £8571
```
64  8-15   Kemp  6g/f            4357
78  7-26   Newb  6.5g/f          4679
81  3-13   Newm  6g/f            4918
```

DIAMOND LODGE 3 ch f £43638
```
77  4-17   Newm  8gd             1166
79  1-18   WIND  8.3g/f          1810*
84  2-13   Sand  8.1g/s  [79]   2126
86  1-8    WIND  8.3g/s  [80]   2620*
93  1-13   NEWM  8g/f     81    3277*
96  1-12   GOOD  9fm      87    3535*
90  5-9    Kemp  8g/f    [87]   3689
97  2-10   Kemp  8fm      92    4389
```

DIAMOND MAX 5 b g £545
```
74a 7-13   Wolv  8.5af   85      44
64  20-32  Newm  9g/f            4916
83  2-20   Donc  7sft    81     5367
```

DIAMOND ORCHID 4 gr f £9481
```
45a 3-14   Sout  8af     [45]    354
48a 2-13   Sout  12af    [45]    575 P
42a 4-11   Wolv  12af    [45]    666 p
48a 2-14   Ling  12ap    [45]    827 p
54  2-17   Bath  10.2sft 47     1541
56  1-18   WIND  11.6g/f 49     1960* vis
45a 5-14   Ling  10ap    46     2589 vis
58  1-9    YARM  14.1g/f 53     2856* vis
32  12-13  Sali  14.1gd  56     3454 vis
49a 2-13   Ling  16ap    45     3822 vis
51  12-15  Ches  15.9g/f 57     4512 vis
48a 4-11   Wolv  12.2ap  47     5009 p
```

DIAMOND RACKET 4 b g £0
```
 0  15-16  Sout  5af     [40]    374 bl
23a 6-10   Wolv  5af     [35]    781 bl
 0  11-12  Sout  5af     [30]    904 bl
 0  9-9    Sout  5af     [30]    981 bl
```

DIAMOND RIBBY 3 br f £0
```
27a 9-10   Ling  8ap             831
```

DIAMOND RING 5 b m £2400
```
34  5-12   Chep  5.1sft  [45]   1336
26  14-20  Beve  5g/f    [45]   1948
42  3-11   Bath  5g/f    [40]   2412
16  15-19  Leic  5gd     40     2702
44  3-13   Bath  5gd     [40]   3143
52  6-11   Bath  5gd     [40]   3372
49  2-20   Redc  6g/f    45     3767
43  4-11   Nott  5.1gd   47     4038
42  9-20   Chep  6.1g/s  47     4368
41  8-16   Warw  5g/s    [45]   4995
```

DIAMOND SHANNON 3 b f £4024
```
20  7-8    Donc  6gd             953
44  7-8    Thir  5sft           1228
45  5-17   Nott  6.1g/f  50     1606
61a 1-16   SOUT  7af     49     2335*
59a 2-13   Sout  8af     56     2497
28a 14-15  Sout  7af     [59]   2999
28  19-20  Nott  6.1g/s  58     4646
41a 8-11   Wolv  7.1ap   [58]   5178
43a 6-12   Wolv  5.1ap   [58]   5362
```

DIAMOND TANGO 3 b f £0
```
112 5-13   Long  12sft          4567
```

DIAMOND WAY 3 ch c £2961
```
68a 1-12   LING  8ap     59     402* VIS
```

DIAMONDS AND DUST 2 b c £9885
```
82  4-12   Newm  6g/f            3280
77  3-13   Hayd  6gd            3736
77  4-14   Folk  7gd            4115
84  1-17   YORK  7f      77     4396*
78  7-12   Asco  7g/f    82     4810
91  6-29   Newm  6gd            5087
```

DIAMONDS WILL DO 7 b m £0
```
46  6-12   Chep  12.1g/s 56     3085
```

DIAPHANOUS 5 b m £0
```
46a 4-12   Wolv  5af     [37]    242 bl
23a 8-13   Wolv  5af     [45]    312 bl
26a 7-9    Ling  5ap     [45]    413 bl
3a  9-10   Ling  5ap     [40]    832 T
18  17-17  Bath  5g/f    37     2981 bl
 9  14-15  Wind  5gd     37     3165 bl
23  7-9    Kemp  5g/f    [35]   3687 bl
13a 13-15  Sout  5af     37     4043 bl
 9  13-18  Chep  8.1gd   [35]   4485
49  7-10   Wind  6gd     [30]   4835
40  6-11   Good  6gd     [30]   5030
```

DIATONIC 2 b g £728
```
52  9-9    Donc  5gd             929
57a 8-10   Ling  5ap            2017
43  8-13   York  6g/f           2358
59a 2-7    Sout  7af            2721
47  7-14   Muss  8gd     62     4519
```

DICK THE TAXI 10 b g £1597
```
74a 3-9    Wolv  12af    74      467
70  3-14   Ches  12.3gd  67     2285
54  9-15   Ripo  12.3g/f 67     2526
53  4-9    Ches  10.3g/s [67]   2745
```

DICKIE DEADEYE 6 b g £14312
```
58a 5-14   Ling  10ap    60      101
41a 9-14   Ling  10ap    60     230
55  6-19   Donc  10.3gd  58     924
```

55	5-14	Folk	9.7g/s	57	1083
60	2-9	Pont	10hvy	56	1254
59	2-9	Pont	10sft	56	1430
62	3-19	Newb	10gd	56	1736
75	1-12	CHEP	12.1g/s	57	3085*
66	1-8	DONC	12g/s	57	3222*
72	3-12	Hayd	11.9gd	69	3734
62	4-10	Wind	10g/f	[70]	3980
58	9-14	York	11.9gd	70	4327
69	3-18	Sali	9.9gd	69	4850
61	8-11	Wind	11.6g/s	[69]	4942

DICTION 2 br f £7456

36	7-11	Thir	6g/f		1968
43	5-8	Hayd	6g/f		2183
68a	1-7	SOUT	7af		2721*
70a	1-11	SOUT	6af	60	3393*
48	5-6	Muss	7.1g/f	67	3560
74a	2-13	Sout	7af	67	4040

DIDNT TELL MY WIFE 4 ch g £8594

66a	1-11	LING	8ap	60	12*
49	6-13	Warw	7.1hvy	[64]	1537
61a	6-11	Ling	8ap	64	2018
53a	9-12	Ling	8ap	[63]	2394
65	4-17	Hayd	8.1gd	63	2947
66	3-20	Newm	8g/f	63	3232
68	1-9	NEWB	9gd	63	3922*
66	3-12	Sali	8g/s	69	4077
46	15-19	York	7.9g/f	67	4399
62	6-17	Warw	8.1g/s	67	4668
67	3-15	Nott	8.2hvy	65	5191
47	8-17	Newb	9sft	65	5198

DIDOE 5 br m £8732

18	15-17	Warw	8.1fm	49	2572
37	7-17	Warw	8.1g/f	47	2909
39	9-16	Brig	9.9g/f	45	3175
53	1-8	BATH	10.2g/f	[45]	3370*
53	2-11	Ling	10fm	47	3748
54	1-14	BATH	8g/f	47	3963*
32	8-11	Brig	8g/s	53	4141
30	17-20	Chep	7.1gd	51	4488
40	10-15	Beve	8.5g/f	51	4598

DIEGO CAO 3 b g £11299

89	1-16	SAND	10gd	78	4609*
86	4-9	Wind	10g/s	84	4943
92	2-17	Wind	10g/f	84	5050
72a	8-10	Ling	12ap	88	5239

DIEQUEST 3 ch c £0

60	8-9	Wind	8.3g/f		3979
60	8-11	Wind	10gd		4125
30	13-18	Wind	10g/s		4944

DIFFERENT PLANET 3 b c £730

80	4-15	Newb	8g/f		1763
70	4-12	Leic	8fm		2106
71	5-14	Wind	8.3g/s		2622

DIGGER 4 ch g £6387

70a	2-12	Wolv	16.2af	65	7 t
59a	5-11	Wolv	16.2af	65	48 t
75a	2-16	Sout	11af	70	97 t
74a	3-10	Sout	12af	70	138 t
55a	6-12	Sout	14af	72	173 p
75a	1-9	SOUT	11af	71	391*
64a	4-7	Sout	12af	74	504
62a	9-15	Ling	12ap	74	549 p
72a	2-7	Wolv	12af	73	642
44a	5-10	Sout	16af	73	743
17	17-19	Donc	10.3gd	64	924

DIGITAL 7 ch g £28774

91a	10-15	Ling	7ap	93	887
93	3-13	Kemp	7sft	93	945
86	4-13	Newc	7hvy	92	1035
78	16-27	Newb	8gd	91	1231
87	3-14	Kemp	8hvy	90	1512
86	6-18	Ches	7.6gd	90	1598
87	8-16	Good	7g/f	88	1817
81	8-13	Kemp	7gd	87	2172
82	5-8	Sand	7.1g/f	85	2389
90	2-13	Ayr	7.2g/s	83	2568
91	2-18	Newc	7sft	83	2684
96	2-15	York	7gd	87	3117
78	7-21	Asco	7g/f	87	3441

92	8-12	Good	7fm	[90]	3555
88	8-16	Newb	7g/f	90	3954
90	2-8	Ches	7sft	90	4073
93	2-8	Good	7g/s	88	4231
83	12-16	Good	7g/f	90	4523
88	5-15	Newm	7g/f	88	4891
79	7-16	Newm	7sft	87	5101
84	6-20	Newm	7g/s	85	5286
85	4-10	Catt	7sft	85	5320

DIKTATIT 2 b f £0

52	13-19	Wind	5g/f		1805
56	5-10	Hayd	5gd		3755
45	7-9	Bath	5g/f		3847

DIKTATORIAL 2 br c £42064

81	7-8	Newm	7g/f		3585
98	1-14	SAND	7.1g/s		4069*
104	1-9	NEWM	7gd		4881*

DIL 8 b g £291

31a	9-16	Sout	6af	54	94
39a	7-16	Sout	6af	51	166
30a	12-16	Sout	7af	51	208
45a	3-10	Wolv	6af	48	246
31a	7-9	Sout	6af	[45]	487 vis
7a	8-9	Sout	7af	[45]	661

DILIGENT LAD 4 b g £0

2	9-9	Hami	12.1gd	[57]	1507
0	13-13	Ripo	12.3g/f	55	2008

DILIZA 5 b m £0

40a	4-11	Ling	8ap	[49]	343
42a	8-13	Ling	10ap	[47]	429
34a	6-11	Ling	8ap	[45]	535

DILYS 4 b f £0

45a	4-15	Ling	7ap	[48]	216
30a	8-15	Ling	7ap	[45]	411

DINE N DASH 3 ch g £0

35	11-11	Sali	7gd		3884
35	6-9	Good	6sft		4262
39	11-13	Bath	5.7g/f		4413
2a	9-13	Wolv	8.6ap	[45]	5232

DINGLEY LASS 4 ch f £0

44a	6-8	Ling	10ap		3787
40	10-14	Bath	13.1g/s	48	4203
38	12-14	Warw	16.2g/f	45	4423

DINNER DATE 2 ch c £0

59	9-13	Donc	7hvy		5199

DISABUSE 3 ch g £4485

38a	6-15	Sout	8af	50	84
54a	2-12	Sout	7af	[48]	416
54a	1-10	SOUT	8af	48	463*
49a	3-11	Sout	11af	54	746
56a	4-15	Sout	12af	54	867
54a	4-11	Wolv	12af	55	937
51	5-10	Newc	10.1g/f	50	2162
51	4-12	Nott	8.2g/s	50	2931 BL
51	5-12	Nott	14.1gd	49	3105
38a	8-14	Sout	12af	55	3486 bl
0	13-15	Sout	8af	52	4132 bl
23	16-16	York	11.9gd	49	4990 P
41a	8-13	Wolv	8.6ap	[48]	5212 VIS

DISCO DIVA 3 ch f £1638

45a	7-8	Ling	7ap	69	933
46	12-17	Sali	6g/f	68	1722
51	10-15	Ling	7g/f	66	1983
10	15-15	Leic	6g/f	62	2398
0	18-18	Hayd	6gd	57	3737
56	2-17	Leic	7gd	52	5056
55a	2-12	Wolv	8.6ap	[53]	5329

DISCOMANIA 2 b c £373

64	12-15	Newb	7g/f		2876
83	4-8	Epso	7sft		3214
78	6-9	Epso	7fm		3539
52	12-13	Newm	8gd	75	4193

DISCUSS 2 b f £2525

87	2-13	Newm	6g/f		4918

DISENGAGE 2 gr c £0

76a	7-15	Ling	7ap	77	177

DISGUISE 2 b c £3406

82	5-15	Wind	6gd		3163
82	2-8	Newm	6g/f		3473
75	4-11	Bath	5.2g/f		4543
79	2-15	Nott	5.1gd	[78]	4859 T

DISHDASHA 2 b c £418

18	14-14	Donc	6g/f		1874
50	7-13	York	6g/f		2358
54	3-8	Redc	7g/s		2563
12a	10-10	Sout	7af	62	3483
40	14-16	Leic	7fm	[55]	3811
44	12-18	Catt	7g/f	54	4673

DISPARITY 3 b f £1125

43	14-14	Kemp	10g/s		2678
62	4-11	Leic	10g/f		3208 T
64a	2-8	Ling	10ap		3787 t
11a	7-9	Ling	12ap	[65]	4449
47a	15-16	Ling	12ap	65	4973 t
25a	15-16	Ling	12ap	[60]	5296 t

DISPOL CHARM 2 br f £0

45	5-13	Ripo	5gd		4303
41	8-9	Catt	6g/f		4670

DISPOL EVITA 4 ch f £2174

55a	2-12	Ling	8ap	[47]	150
37a	11-13	Ling	10ap	53	215
52a	9-11	Ling	12ap	53	624
50a	4-7	Ling	10ap	50	736
55a	2-14	Ling	12ap	50	801
38a	7-8	Ling	12ap	53	3026
32a	4-7	Ling	10ap	52	3287
35	9-14	Brig	11.9fm	48	3674
18	9-12	Sali	12g/f	48	3868
0	U-14	Pont	10g/f	45	4624

DISPOL FOXTROT 6 ch m £2968

66	2-15	Hami	9.2gd	65	1388
64	3-15	Hami	8.3g/s	65	1602

DISPOL IN MIND 2 b f £4647

58	2-6	Catt	5g/f		3014
67	3-8	Ling	5gd		3445
69	1-11	BATH	5g/f		3962*

DISPOL ISLE 2 gr f £6963

67	4-18	York	7gd		2360
63	4-12	Carl	5gd		2933
67	4-15	Nott	5.1gd		3988
66	4-12	Carl	5g/f	[65]	4343
68	3-10	Ayr	6g/s	65	4655
68	5-17	Catt	7gd	65	4963
60	6-14	Ayr	6sft	65	5035
84	3-21	Donc	6hvy		5202

DISPOL KATIE 3 ch f £5301

76	14-20	Thir	5g/s	85	1476
77	6-15	Ripo	6g/f	83	1782
83	3-9	Nott	5.1gd	81	3106
82	5-8	Hami	5g/f	81	3591
23	18-18	Beve	5g/s	80	3852
83	2-14	York	5g/s	80	4027
77	9-20	Donc	5dm	81	4496
72	11-15	Ayr	5g/s	81	4654

DISPOL PETO 4 gr g £1814

44a	11-13	Sout	7af	62	556
48a	5-6	Sout	7af	[62]	593
61a	2-9	Wolv	7af	59	629 p
19a	8-9	Wolv	7af	59	684 bl
55a	5-10	Wolv	7af	[59]	1319 p
49	9-14	Muss	7.1gd	57	1794 p
56a	2-12	Sout	7af	57	2337 p

DISPOL VELETA 3 b f £14155

52a	3-13	Sout	6af		319
44a	7-13	Sout	6af		444
65a	1-10	SOUT	8af	53	662*
57a	4-6	Wolv	9.4af	57	702
70	1-18	NOTT	8.2fm	64	1007*
67	3-11	Ripo	8gd	67	1176
44	13-18	Thir	8g/f	68	1769
59	10-15	Ripo	10g/f	67	1976
75a	1-8	SOUT	8af	67	2495*
55	12-13	Newc	8g/s	68	2773

```
56   9-10  Hayd  8.1g/s  67   3138
49a  11-11 Sout  8af     74   4044
70   2-20  York  7.9gd   65   4321

DISPOL VERITY 4 b f £0
0    12-13 Wolv  5af     49   2201
25   11-20 Nott  6.1g/f  45   2630
11a  11-13 Sout  8af     42   3094
28   10-17 Ripo  6g/s    40   3262
22   12-17 Pont  8g/f    40   4626
16   6-13  Ayr   8sft    [35]  5275

DISSIDENT 6 b h £14100
55a  1-8   LING  10ap    [73]  1026* VIS
64   8-20  Warw  10.9gd  70   1128 vis
76   2-12  Sout  11gd    70   1286 vis
69   2-11  Leic  10g/s   65   1357 vis
80   1-19  NEWM  12g/f   70   1484* vis
63   4-13  Kemp  14.4hvy 76   1516 vis
61   5-9   Donc  12g/f   77   2078 vis
81   6-13  Epso  12fm    76   2255 vis T
73   5-6   Epso  10.1g/f [84]  2874
44   12-12 Epso  12gd    83   4292 vis

DISTANT CONNECTION 3 b c £29361
65   8-11  Newm  10gd    [75]  1148
60   10-17 Warw  7.1sft  75   1526
59   8-15  Ches  7.6gd   75   1583
66   6-12  Good  7g/f    72   1847
79   1-12  SAND  7.1g/f  70   2098*
84   2-20  Newb  7g/f    76   2314
81   1-6   RIPO  8g/f    74   2525*
85   5-11  Sand  7.1g/s  81   2918
88   3-15  York  7gd     81   3117
91   2-11  York  7g/f    82   3433
76   10-17 Good  7fm     82   3550
95a  1-14  LING  7ap     85   4180+
95a  3-13  Ling  7ap     91   4318

DISTANT COUNTRY 5 b g £6307
75   6-18  Catt  7gd     75   998
65   6-17  Thir  8g/s    75   1214
64   12-16 Thir  7g/s    73   1474 p
74   2-13  Ripo  8g/f    71   2010 p
74   5-12  Newc  6g/f    71   2160 p
73   2-8   Donc  8g/f    71   2425 p
70   5-25  Asco  9g/f    71   3443 p
54   13-16 Redc  8g/f    71   3768 p
73   3-16  Redc  7g/f    71   3809 p
69   8-21  Donc  7fm     72   4482 p

DISTANT COUSIN 7 b g £2209
49a  7-7   Ling  12ap    [74]  1009 vis
59   5-11  Donc  12g/f   64   1875 vis
63   3-6   Ripo  12.3g/f 64   1980 vis
25   15-17 Nott  14.1g/f 61   2156 vis
6    8-8   Donc  14.6gd  60   2754 vis
58   4-5   Newm  12g/f   58   3587 vis
58   3-9   Redc  14.1fm  56   4559 vis
18   8-8   Redc  14.1fm  56   4932 vis
1    17-20 York  13.9gd  54   5004 BL

DISTANT KING 11 b g £0
1    16-18 Thir  6fm     43   3609

DISTANT PROSPECT 7 b g £25570
95   4-17  Ches  18.7gd  90   1569
96   2-14  Hayd  16.2gd  90   2239
86   12-19 Newc  16.1g/s 94   2771
78   12-17 Asco  16.2gd  93   3125
96   3-19  Good  21fm    90   3531
97   8-34  Newm  18sft   92   5135
99   2-24  Donc  12sft   92   5372

DISTANT TIMES 3 b c £9291
74   5-22  Donc  7gd     74   955
81   1-6   WARW  6.1sft  [73]  1088*
78   3-14  Ripo  6g/s    79   1360
63   13-18 Newm  6g/s    79   1933
52   11-12 Ripo  6g/f    78   2482 VIS
74   5-12  Hayd  6sft    76   3273 vis
79   1-10  BEVE  5g/f    [74]  3503+
35   17-18 Beve  5g/s    76   3852
72   6-14  York  5g/s    76   4027
46   11-20 Ripo  6gd     75   4278

DISTINCTION 5 b g £37650
83   14-17 Newb  12gd    [107] 1230


90   5-8   Newb  13.3g/f [107] 1757
114  1-14  YORK  13.9gd  105  3119*
116  1-7   DONC  12fm    [111] 4494*
109  6-24  Flem  16g/s   108  5323

DISTINCTIVE MIND 2 b g £0
42   12-14 Hayd  6fm          4385
48   8-11  Beve  5g/f         4599
61   9-15  Nott  5.1gd        4859

DISTINCTLY GAME 2 b c £82667
81   2-6   Hami  5gd          1503
81   2-16  Ripo  6g/f         1780
79a  2-11  Wolv  6af          2051
82   1-18  YORK  5g/f         2360*
80   4-12  Hayd  5gd     81   3756
96   2-13  York  6gd     80   4004
104  2-22  Donc  6fm     [81]  4458

DISTINCTLYSPLENDID 3 b g £0
24a  8-13  Wolv  8.5af   [36]  46
35a  10-16 Sout  7af     [36]  66
49a  9-15  Ling  12ap    [34]  118
30a  11-12 Ling  10ap    [40]  267 BL

DISTINCTLYTHEBEST 4 b c £0
5    9-9   Newc  9g/s         3697 T
14   8-8   Redc  9g/f         3805
26   8-8   Catt  7g/f         4440

DIUM MAC 3 b g £0
50   7-9   Thir  7g/f         3413
5    5-5   Pont  8gd     [70]  3683

DIVA DANCER 4 ch f £0
0    15-16 Sout  8af     [40]  442
1a   10-12 Sout  14af    [30]  640
14   10-15 Nott  10gd    [35]  1991 BL
40   8-9   Redc  16fm    [30]  2298 bl
8    11-14 Carl  17.2gd  33    2937 bl

DIVANI 2 b f £0
21   19-19 Wind  5g/f         1805

DIVERTED 3 b f £0
0    9-9   Wolv  8.5af        751
49a  13-15 Ling  7ap          875
29   8-9   Folk  9.7sft       980
27   10-13 Folk  7g/s         1270
16   12-13 Bath  8fm     40   2667
31   5-10  Yarm  8g/f    36   3712
18   10-10 Yarm  10.1gd  [36]  3874

DIVINA 3 b f £1282
0    11-13 Sout  8af          553
8a   8-12  Wolv  9.4af        686
28a  11-13 Ling  12ap         873
0    8-9   Leic  6g/s         1015
19a  4-6   Ling  8ap     [30]  1292 VIS
45a  3-5   Sout  8af     [30]  1440 vis
34a  2-7   Sout  8af     [30]  1591 vis
37a  2-8   Ling  10ap    [35]  1713 vis
22   8-10  Beve  8.5g/f  [40]  1943 vis
14a  10-13 Sout  8af     38   3094 vis

DIVINE DIVA 2 b f £276
62   11-12 Newb  6g/f         3251
72   4-13  Chep  6.1gd        3399

DIVINE GIFT 3 b c £10429
104  1-7   DONC  8gd     [87]  949*
92   4-7   Kemp  8g/s    [104] 1113
60   4-5   Ayr   8sft    [102] 5038
93   7-9   Donc  7sft    [102] 5214

DIVINE PROPORTIONS 2 b f £269050
107  1-7   CHAN  5gd          3008*
112  1-8   MAIS  5.5gd        3498*
118  1-9   DEAU  6sft         4159*
118  1-10  LONG  8g/f         4954*

DIVINE SPIRIT 3 b g £11244
68   12-15 Ches  5.1g/s  83   1572
68   12-14 Thir  5g/f    83   1766
54   17-18 Newm  6g/f    82   1933
85   3-11  Redc  5g/f    80   2121
75   6-16  Leic  5g/f    80   2400
89   1-12  AYR   5g/s    79   2566*
82   7-11  Newm  5g/f    86   2734


87   3-10  Ches  5.1g/f  85   3080
85   6-10  Sand  5g/f    85   3356
76   13-21 Good  5fm     85   3567 p
84   3-8   Sand  5g/s    84   3889

DIVINELY DECADENT 2 b rf £5216
88   1-17  YARM  6gd          4610*
88   9-14  Newm  7g/f         4914

DIWAN 6 b g £0
0    11-12 Warw  12.6g/s      4991
19a  9-12  Wolv  8.6ap        5230

DIXIE DANCING 5 ch m £1908
59a  5-12  Ling  7ap     60   1024
2a   14-15 Sout  8af     58   2500
58a  4-12  Ling  8ap     [56]  3286
63a  2-14  Ling  7ap     55   3429
57   3-13  Good  6gd     55   3952

DIXIE QUEEN 2 b f £469
61   5-12  Beve  5sft         1631
70   7-12  Hami  5gd          2178
52   9-11  Warw  7.1gd        3053
61   3-11  Newc  7gd          3429
36   10-13 York  7.9gd   [65]  4325
44a  9-11  Wolv  8.6ap   [62]  4978 BL

DIXIEANNA 2 ch f £1528
82   2-14  Wind  5gd          4121

DIZZY FUTURE 2 b g £0
68   7-12  Wind  8.3g/f       4829
14   29-29 Newm  6gd          5087

DIZZY IN THE HEAD 5 b g £23680
0    19-19 Redc  6sft    69   1145
62   1-11  REDC  6sft    [67]  1662* e
56   6-10  Newc  5g/f    [65]  2161 e
67   3-13  Hami  6g/f    65   2315 bl
76   1-19  BEVE  6gd     62   2512+ bl
80   2-7   Warw  6.1fm   [67]  2598 bl
83   1-9   WARW  5.5fm   73   2779* bl
55   14-15 Beve  5sft    86   2942 bl
38   9-9   Ches  5.1g/f  [80]  3100 bl
40   12-13 Catt  5g/f    79   3350 bl
83   1-8   HAMI  6g/s    [77]  3880* bl
77   7-11  Muss  7.1g/s  78   5144 bl

DIZZY LIZZY 2 g rf £0
22   13-13 Epso  5g/f          2870
18   5-5   Chep  5.1g/s        3086
0    9-11  Chep  8.1g/s        4296

DOCDUCKOUT 4 b g £0
0    P-12  Wolv  6af     57   385

DOCKLANDS BLUE 2 ch f £2879
40a  6-13  Wolv  5af             3
62a  3-12  Wolv  5af            32
49a  7-10  Ling  5af           258
60a  2-5   Ling  5ap           289
42a  8-11  Wolv  6af     [60]   481
52a  7-9   Ling  5ap     [57]   572
56a  3-8   Ling  6ap     [55]   691
50a  6-15  Ling  7ap     54    815
55a  4-15  Ling  7ap     54    901
53a  3-8   Ling  7ap     54    933
46   8-14  Warw  7.1sft  54   1085
41   8-20  Yarm  6g/f    52   1730 BL

DOCKLANDS DUDE 2 ch g £0
60   6-9   Donc  5gd          929
29   8-10  Bath  5g/s         1097

DOCKLANDS GRACE 2 g rf £418
41a  5-7   Wolv  5af          1652
58   5-8   Ling  5gd          3445
51   3-7   Folk  5gd          3907

DOCTOR DENNIS 6 b g £6034
49a  4-16  Sout  6af     49    92 vis
47a  4-15  Sout  6af     49   168 vis
42a  6-16  Sout  7af     49   208 vis
45a  5-13  Ling  6ap     47   740 vis
54a  1-13  LING  6ap     47   767* bl
40a  6-12  Ling  6ap     51   844 bl
44   8-10  Brig  7g/f    49   1941 vis
54   1-16  BRIG  6fm     47   2262* vis
```

```
6    14-17  Wind  6fm    52   2975 vis
52   6-17   Brig  7g/f   52   3176 vis
13   14-19  Yarm  6g/s   51   4636 vis
18   10-15  Brig  6gd   [50]  4905 vis
32a  10-12  Wolv  7.1ap [50]  5233 vis
```

DOCTOR DINO 2 ch c £23169
```
95   3-7    Deau  8hvy         4156
103  2-4    Long  9hvy         5164
```

DOCTOR HILARY 2 b c £9908
```
77   4-11   Nott  6.1sft       1739
83   1-7    AYR   6g/f         1893*
99   2-7    Kemp  6fm          2071
84   3-10   Ches  5.1g/s       2744 VIS
95   2-8    Ayr   6gd    90    3303
87   5-6    Wind  6fm   [93]   3800
```

DOCTOR JOHN 7 ch g £6563
```
25a  4-9    Ling  12ap  [35]   414
42a  2-9    Sout  16af   35    612 P
42a  1-8    WOLV  16.2af 35    690* p
46   6-12   Newc  16.1sft 45   965
44a  2-7    Wolv  16.2af [45]  1263 p
45a  2-7    Sout  14af  [45]   1407
39   8-13   Nott  14.1gd [45]  1990 p
45a  2-6    Sout  16af   43    3397
47   4-10   Thir  16sft  43    3834 p
19   12-19  Catt  15.8g/f 45   4675
52   2-20   Catt  15.8gd 45    4965
```

DOCTORATE 3 b c £15182
```
64   9-17   Donc  8gd           919
83   1-13   FOLK  7g/s         1270*
87   2-8    Beve  7.5g/f 80    2166
81   5-10   Newb  8g/f   84    2877
85a  3-14   Ling  7ap    83    4180
76   9-15   Hayd  8.1g/f 83    4352
91   1-25   NEWB  7gd    81    4683*
83   8-15   Newm  7g/f   86    4891
91   4-11   Muss  7.1g/s 86    5144
```

DOCTORED 3 ch g £21957
```
66a  8-9    Ling  8ap   [54]   756 P
28a  15-15  Ling  7ap    54    815 p
64a  4-11   Ling  8ap   [50]   841 bl
52a  6-9    Ling  10ap  [50]   899 bl
64   1-7    FOLK  7g/s   57    1081* p
67a  1-5    SOUT  8af   [54]   1440* p
33   10-11  Folk  6sft   61    1578 p
61   1-16   BATH  8fm   [60]   2032* p
68   1-13   BATH  10.2gd [60]  3144* bl
74   1-11   LING  10gd  [60]   3201* bl
76   1-8    NEWM  10g/f [71]   3471* bl
81   3-6    Nott  10g/f  77    3578 bl
68   10-14  Kemp  10g/f  77    3690 bl
66   6-9    Sand  10g/f  77    3862 bl
75   8-10   Nott  10gd   77    3990 bl
72a  4-14   Ling  10ap  [75]   4742 bl
75   7-15   Nott  10gd   75    4860 bl
37   10-11  Newm  14g/f  75    4919 bl
```

DOCTORS CAVE 2 b c £8249
```
62   7-7    Kemp  6fm           2071
59   8-12   Newb  6g/f          2348
77   7-14   Newm  7g/f          2766
65   7-8    Beve  7.5gd         3311
90   1-10   GOOD  6g/f          3511*
71   8-9    Deau  6sft          4159
84   9-9    Newb  6g/f   [89]   4680
45   11-14  Newm  6sft   88     5098
```

DOCTRINE 3 b f £2750
```
101  4-9    Kemp  8g/s   [99]   1110
88   8-19   Asco  8g/f   99     2491
91   5-10   Chep  10.2g/s [96]  3089
59   9-9    Newb  12fm   [93]   3629
```

DOITFORREEL 2 b f £5284
```
37   12-14  Newb  6fm           3626
57   8-15   Nott  5.1gd         3988
70   3-11   Bath  5g/f          4409
68   1-9    PONT  6g/s   [68]   5154*
90   5-8    Newm  6sft   [68]   5267
72   3-16   Nott  5.1hvy 68     5343
```

DOITNOW 3 b g £12705
```
84   1-9    RIPO  6g/f          2485*
```

```
91   2-15   Hayd  6gd    81    2950
93   2-16   Newb  6g/f   87    3269
87   6-10   Asco  6gd    89    3778
91   6-12   Newm  7gd    89    4225
78   11-13  Asco  6.5g/f 88    4773
```

DOLCE PICCATA 3 ch f £794
```
53   15-19  Newm  6g/s   92    1154
50   5-7    Kemp  6hvy   [89]   1513
85   4-12   Wind  5g/f   85    1809
76   5-10   Leic  6gd    [84]   2137
76   7-12   Ripo  6gd    82    2482
60   8-8    Kemp  6g/s   [82]   2677
63   9-10   Sand  5g/f   77    3356 bl
69   11-21  Good  5fm    77    3567 bl
61   7-8    Sand  5g/s   74    3889 bl
69   6-16   Good  5g/f   70    4528 bl
49a  9-12   Ling  6ap    68    4976 bl
```

DOLLAR LAW 8 ch g £0
```
0    14-15  Nott  8.2hvy 60    5191 t
```

DOLLY PEEL 2 b f £0
```
0    17-18  Pont  5g/s         3968
```

DOLLY WOTNOT 2 b f £628
```
40a  5-13   Wolv  9.4af  [67]   37
65   5-10   Beve  12.1g/s 67   1165
21   16-20  Wind  11.6sft 67   1648
64   5-8    Brig  9.9g/f 64    2046
62   3-8    Hami  11.1g/f [62]  2319
```

DOLMA 3 b f £30201
```
105  2-7    Mais  7sft          1156
111  3-9    Chan  8g/s          2306
116  3-12   Deau  6.5g/s        3838
```

DOLPHINELLE 7 b g £663
```
42a  5-16   Ling  7ap    [49]   180 vis
47a  3-15   Ling  7ap    [49]   216 vis
45a  5-12   Ling  10ap   [49]   267 vis
54a  4-12   Ling  8ap    [47]   571 vis
50a  3-12   Ling  8ap    [47]   675 vis
```

DOLZAGO 4 b g £6129
```
71a  1-7    LING  13ap   [48]   546* BL
66a  2-12   Ling  13ap   60     762 bl
72a  3-12   Ling  13ap   64     877 bl
0    13-13  Kemp  14.4hvy 69   1516 bl
42   9-11   Newb  13.3fm 65    2651 bl
29   8-8    Epso  12g/f  65    2869 bl
```

DOMART 4 gr c £0
```
46   10-11  Newb  13.3fm 73    2651
```

DOMENICO 6 b g £515
```
63   12-14  Asco  16.2g/f 74   1928
67   3-11   Newm  12g/f  71    2244
11   26-29  Asco  20g/f  70    2471
62a  6-11   Ling  16ap   65    3450
40   14-17  Pont  17.1g/s 63   3970
48   12-17  Newm  14.8gd 63    4196
```

DOMINER 2 b c £0
```
38   6-6    Bath  5g/f          1786
35   6-7    Bath  5.7fm         1900
40   6-7    Bath  5g/f          2976
35   8-8    Good  6g/f   [40]   4540 P
```

DOMIRATI 4 b g £5245
```
55   17-19  Kemp  6fm    79    2070
79   4-11   Ches  5.1gd  78    2286
83   2-12   Sali  5gd    78    2698
77   7-16   Newm  5g/f   79    3033
84   2-17   Sand  5g/f   79    3341
43   14-14  Newb  5.2fm  82    3628
82   4-6    Sand  5gd    [82]   4498
83   5-18   Pont  5g/s   82    5149
```

DON ARGENTO 3 gr g £435
```
48   9-12   Warw  7.1gd         1125
40   12-19  Brig  9.9g/f 45    1940
3    14-14  Chep  7.1gd  45    2199
0    U-13   Warw  8.1gd  40    3058
43   3-16   Brig  9.9g/f 40    3175
16   10-12  Brig  9.9g/f 40    3300
2    11-11  Brig  9.9g/f 40    3982
```

DON FAYRUZ 12 b g £0

```
6a   12-13  Ling  10ap   [54]   429
```

DON FERNANDO 5 b h £3653
```
73   7-11   Warw  15sft  80    1087
77   5-14   Asco  16.2g/f 78   1928
70   10-29  Asco  20g/f  76    2471
100  6-12   Asco  22.2fm [76]  2583
85   2-12   Newm  16.1g/f 80   3032
```

DON PASQUALE 2 b r c £0
```
71a  5-10   Ling  7ap          5264
```

DON PELE 2 b c £19235
```
32   15-19  Kemp  6g/f          1911
94   2-18   Chep  6.1gd         2194
94   1-18   WIND  6g/f          2618*
106  1-8    NEWB  6g/f          3254*
45   22-22  Donc  6fm    [84]   4458
```

DONALD 4 b g £561
```
56   3-8    Bath  17.2fm 56    2035
4    14-19  Newb  13.3g/f 56   2311
55   6-10   Sali  14.1gd 55    2699
32   13-19  Bath  17.2gd 52    3147
```

DONASTRELA 2 b f £8939
```
57a  9-12   Ling  8ap           19
52a  6-10   Ling  8ap          1021
39   11-18  Wind  8.3g/s        1258
29   11-14  Ling  11.5g/f 53   2014
62   1-14   BATH  10.2fm 50    2664* VIS
58   4-13   Bath  10.2gd [57]  3144 vis
69   1-11   BATH  10.2g/f 57   3373* vis
69   3-16   Thir  12g/f  63    3573 vis
67   3-12   Bath  11.7g/f 63   3845 vis
70   5-13   Kemp  14.4fm 65    4395 vis
69   4-14   Catt  12g/f  66    4672 vis
51   7-14   Epso  12gd   66    4910 vis
```

DONEGAL SHORE 5 b h £1274
```
38a  4-10   Sout  6af    [66]   308 t
50a  2-8    Sout  7af    [66]   373 VIS
46a  2-9    Sout  7af    [51]   639 vis t
38a  4-10   Wolv  8.5af  51     754 vis t
48a  3-12   Wolv  8.5af  48    1379 vis t
38a  7-16   Sout  8af    48    2805 vis t
26   6-19   Nott  6.1gd  [46]  3104 vis t
36a  7-16   Sout  8af    46    3159 vis t
40   4-17   Thir  8g/s   43    3830 vis t
31a  8-15   Sout  5af    43    4043 vis t
```

DONNA VITA 3 b f £2500
```
83   4-5    Ling  11.5sft [90]  1619
79   8-9    Sand  8.1g/s [90]   2917
79   9-14   Newb  10g/f  85    3961
42   13-13  Yarm  10.1gd 43    4613
```

DONNAS DOUBLE 9 ch g £5899
```
51   5-12   Hami  9.2g/s 56    2832 p
50   6-9    Hami  9.2gd  56    3132 p
55   3-8    Hami  9.2fm  56    3250 p
46   4-15   Newc  7gd    [54]   3426 p
47   3-6    Hami  12.1g/f 50   3588 p
52   4-17   Hami  9.2g/s 50    4008 VIS
46   6-12   Newc  8sft   [50]   4284 p
63   2-17   Ayr   9.1g/s [49]   4620 p
32   16-19  Beve  9.9g/f 49    4720 p
63   2-6    Muss  12gd   [52]   4805 p
38   8-18   Pont  12g/f  52    4938 p
```

DONT CALL ME BABE 2 b g £0
```
7    13-15  Brig  7sft          5192
```

DONT CALL ME DEREK 2 b g £19078
```
66a  4-9    Ling  5ap            76
53a  5-26   Ling  5ap           289
60a  6-9    Ling  5ap           572 BL e
61a  8-12   Ling  6ap    66     880
56   7-12   Good  9fm    62    3625
54   7-8    Folk  7g/f   62    3724
68   2-10   Hayd  8.1g/s 61    3906
71a  1-11   SOUT  8af    58    4044*
68   3-14   Yarm  8g/s   [66]  4252
71   2-17   Nott  8.2gd  65    4862
79   1-20   CATT  12gd   65    4966*
83a  1-12   WOLV  12.2ap 71    4983*
83   1-19   BATH  11.7gd 74    5024*
```

DONT LET GO 2 b f £0

38a 10-10 Ling 5ap 176
2a 8-11 Ling 6ap 233
21 14-14 Wind 8.3g/s 2622
22 8-9 Folk 7fm 2716

DONT MATTER 4 b f £0
0 8-8 Wind 11.6g/f 59 2796

DONT SIOUX ME 6 b g £0
54a 10-10 Ling 12ap 90 570 t
55 5-6 Wind 11.6fm [83] 2972
75 10-15 Nott 10gd 80 4860

DONT TELL MUM 2 b f £33739
87 1-8 BATH 5fm 2033*
91 6-17 Asco 5g/f 2490
90 2-24 Newb 5.2g/f 3266

DONT TELL ROSEY 4 b g £0
58a 7-14 Ling 6ap 74 1025

DONT TELL SIMON 3 ch g £0
17 10-12 Ripo 9g/f 1784
23 7-8 Redc 10g/f 2124
0 11-13 Pont 8g/s 3973

DONT TELL TRIGGER 2 b f £6612
60 10-10 Sali 5g/f 1716
62 6-9 Hayd 6g/f 1920
68 1-7 CHEP 6.1gd 2115*
37 11-14 Leic 6g/f 66 3212
65 7-11 Newm 7fm 68 3407
73 1-12 NEWM 7g/f [65] 3750*
79 8-16 Curr 6g/f [65] 4153
55 7-12 Bath 8g/f 69 4410

DONT WORRY BOUT ME 7 b g £0
11a 8-15 Ling 12ap [40] 707 vis

DONYANA 2 b f £11793
78 5-14 Newm 7g/f 3944
91 1-16 SALI 7gd 4329*
91 4-13 Newm 8fm 86 4725

DOOHULLA 3 ch f £0
96 5-20 York 6g/f 89 2407
91 7-19 Newm 6fm 89 3002

DOOIE DANCER 2 b c £0
69 7-20 Yarm 8sft 5252

DORA CORBINO 4 b f £2216
42a 5-7 Wolv 9.4af [48] 561
41a 3-5 Sout 11af [45] 772
35a 2-5 Wolv 12af [45] 823
0 9-12 Wolv 12af [40] 891
18a 6-8 Wolv 12af [40] 1265
28 3-9 Warw 15g/s [40] 1329
35 2-8 Brig 11.9gd [40] 1547
42a 2-8 Sout 14af [40] 1840
41 3-13 Beve 12.1g/f [40] 1945
59 4-8 Warw 18fm [39] 2781
20a 7-10 Sout 14af [40] 3158

DORCHESTER 6 b g £344
75a 3-16 Ling 7ap 74 20
67a 6-12 Wolv 7af 74 704
75 5-19 Leic 6g/s 74 1354
57 7-16 Nott 6.1sft [74] 1743

DORINGO 3 b c £962
51 8-12 Warw 7.1gd 1125
58 12-16 Wind 10gd 1384
39 11-13 Wind 10g/f 2453
49 8-16 Bath 8gd 52 4828
57 2-12 Brig 8sft 50 5094

DORIS SOUTER 4 b f £4650
78a 2-14 Ling 10ap 73 736
66a 9-9 Ling 10ap 73 876
68a 5-7 Ling 12ap [72] 1009
64 9-10 Sali 12g/f 70 1721
73 3-7 Ling 10ap 70 2015
58 10-14 Wind 10g/f 70 2265
68 3-10 Wind 10fm 68 2761
71 2-8 Wind 10fm 68 2973

DORISIMA 3 ch f £0
28 8-10 Ripo 6gd 4790 e

49 9-9 Newc 10.1g/f 5015

DORMY TWO 4 b f £418
37 13-15 Beve 9.9sft 55 1307 p
46 3-10 Muss 16gd 50 1551 p
44 6-8 Muss 16gd 48 1793 p

DORN DANCER 2 b f £5343
47 9-13 Redc 6g/f 1818
85 1-9 CHES 5.1gd 2281*
62 5-6 Beve 5gd 2513
74 8-10 York 5gd 84 3115
21 21-21 Donc 6.5fm 81 4457
80 6-10 Ayr 6g/s 81 4655
58 15-17 Catt 7gd 79 4963
50 9-10 Catt 6sft 79 5318

DORN HILL 2 b f £0
49 5-6 Bath 5g/f 1786
40 13-18 Leic 5fm 2109

DOROTHYS FRIEND 4 b g £65710
71 10-14 Hayd 16.2gd 79 2239
90 1-9 NEWM 14.8fm 78 2596*
92 1-17 ASCO 16.2gd 85 3125*
88 8-15 Good 14g/f 88 3510
101 1-10 ASCO 16.2gd 88 3776*
90 10-19 York 13.9g/s 95 4023

DORSET 3 b f £0
35 16-17 Newm 8gd 1166
24 14-16 Bath 10.2g/f 1790
23 6-8 Chep 12.1gd 2368

DORUBAKO 3 b c £1500
94 4-9 Ches 5.1g/f 3100

DOUBLE ASPECT 3 b c £7619
91 4-17 Newb 10gd 1737
84 1-13 SALI 9.9gd 2700*
89 5-7 Newm 10g/f 88 3474
88 4-9 Pont 12g/s 86 3969

DOUBLE BLADE 9 b g £0
34 6-10 Redc 11g/f [45] 1819
25 8-11 Muss 16gd 40 3557

DOUBLE DAGGER LADY 3 b f £877
64 6-10 Wind 10g/f 1959
63 4-13 Wind 10g/f 2453
63 5-14 Wind 8.3fm 2974
51 6-10 Yarm 7g/s 62 4251
62a 3-12 Wolv 7.1ap [60] 5325

DOUBLE DEPUTY 3 b c £13796
85 1-10 GOOD 9.9gd 4877* T
89 1-19 DONC 10.3sft 80 5201+ t

DOUBLE GREEN 3 b f £7711
104 3-6 Long 15gd 4565

DOUBLE HONOUR 6 gr g £0
99 8-12 Asco 22.2fm[102] 2583

DOUBLE KUDOS 2 gr c £846
81 2-14 Yarm 7gd 3489
71 7-15 Folk 7gd 4114
68 7-10 Redc 9fm 4558

DOUBLE M 7 ch h £27815
60a 4-15 Ling 7ap [49] 366 vis
58a 1-9 LING 5ap 51 435* vis
58a 3-13 Ling 6ap 57 448 vis
51a 7-14 Ling 7ap 54 499 vis
59a 2-13 Ling 6ap [56] 544 vis
58a 4-10 Ling 6ap [56] 765 vis
61a 2-12 Ling 6ap 56 880 vis
66a 1-13 LING 6ap 56 902* vis
44a 11-14 Ling 6ap 64 1025 vis
46 6-19 Warw 6ap 49 1127 vis
43 5-18 Bath 5.7g/f 47 1788 vis
47 5-18 Good 5gd 47 1867 vis
54 3-16 Good 6gd 47 2023 vis
59 2-12 Folk 6g/s 53 2269 vis
63 1-18 LING 6gd 53 2396* vis
63 3-14 Ling 6gd 58 2585 vis
58 6-12 Sali 5gd 58 2698 vis
58a 6-11 Ling 6ap 61 3333 vis
71 1-22 GOOD 5fm 58 3537* vis

72 2-16 Wind 5fm 65 3640 vis
61 9-13 Newb 5.2g/f 66 3960 vis
59 7-17 Wind 6gd 66 4126 vis
59 9-15 Sali 5gd 66 4335 vis
72 3-13 Bath 5.7gd 65 4548 vis
63 7-15 Good 5gd 65 4751 vis

DOUBLE OBSESSION 4 b c £42894
55 13-19 York 11.9sft 94 1668
84 7-9 Thir 12g/f 92 1969
87 1-14 Hayd 16.2gd 90 2239
101 1-29 ASCO 20g/f 86 2471* vis
97 5-17 Asco 16.2gd 95 3125 vis
110 4-9 Good 16fm [95] 3552 vis
102 2-10 Asco 16.2gd 95 3776 vis
108 4-9 Deau 15sft [95] 4161 vis

DOUBLE RANSOM 4 b g £15235
53a 2-14 Ling 10ap 50 236 bl
54a 2-12 Ling 8ap 53 406 bl
53a 3-14 Ling 10ap 53 498 bl
61a 1-10 LING 8ap 52 770* bl
59a 4-11 Ling 8ap 58 820 bl
57 2-16 Newc 10.1sft 55 1278 bl
63 1-14 HAMI 8.3gd 56 1504* bl
55 6-14 Nott 10g/s 59 1776 bl
64 2-12 Hami 9.2g/s 58 2832 bl
70 1-17 HAYD 8.1gd 61 3759+ bl
65 6-17 Hami 9.2g/s 65 4008 bl
63 5-11 Yarm 10.1g/s 65 5353 bl

DOUBLE SPEY 5 b g £0
38 6-11 Hayd 10.5g/s 41 2226

DOUBLE TURN 4 ch g £0
66 5-9 Hayd 11.9g/f 1885
47 10-13 Hayd 11.9g/s 2230
55 6-7 Hami 11.1g/f [70] 2478

DOUBLE VODKA 3 b g £26417
47 12-18 Nott 8.2sft 67 1470
60 6-18 Thir 8g/f 64 1769
66 2-9 Beve 8.5g/f 62 2168
66 4-13 Newc 8g/s 63 2773
66 7-13 Redc 11g/s 63 2960
70 1-9 DONC 10g/f 63 3378*
77 1-6 RIPO 10g/f 64 3647*
77 1-10 PONT 8g/s 67 3972*
33 11-11 Redc 10fm 73 4931
76 3-7 Pont 8g/f 73 4935
58 11-14 Ayr 10sft 73 5037

DOUGHTY 2 b g £0
31 9-9 Ches 5.1gd 2281
28 10-10 Bath 5.7fm 2666
28 19-20 Wind 6fm 2970
31 11-13 Bath 5.7g/f 3368 T

DOVE COTTAGE 2 b c £8933
58 6-10 Leic 5g/f 1826
62 5-7 Warw 5fm 2573
60 3-7 Bath 5g/f 2890
69 1-8 CHEP 6.1gd 60 3729*
72 2-12 York 7g/s 65 4064
68 5-14 Donc 7fm 68 4535
72 4-17 Good 8gd 67 4871

DOVEDALE 4 b f £284
57 7-17 Hayd 8.1g/s 4768
71 4-18 Bath 10.2gd 5023
56a 5-13 Wolv 9.5ap 5290

DOVEDON HERO 4 ch g £10239
57 17-20 Newm 12gd 80 1172
64 11-19 Newm 12g/f 79 1484
82 2-8 Newm 12gd 77 1889 bl
71 8-11 Donc 12gd 78 2233 bl
78 4-11 Sand 14g/f 78 2391 bl
75 6-7 Newm 12g/f 76 2737 bl
49 12-15 Newm 12g/f 75 3066 bl
74 2-7 Newm 14.8g/f 72 3475 bl
69 7-11 Newm 16.1g/f 72 3779 bl
73 3-9 Kemp 12g/f 70 4360 bl
72 4-8 Redc 14.1fm 70 4932 bl
73a 2-12 Wolv 12.2ap 70 4983 bl
69a 4-12 Wolv 13.9ap 70 5160 bl
76a 2-16 Ling 12ap 70 5261 bl

DOVEDON LASS 3 b f £0
| 17 | 8-10 | Yarm | 10.1g/f | | 1724 |

DOVER STREET 2 ch c £430
57	5-17	Donc	6g/f		2424
62	8-18	Wind	6gd		2618
49	10-18	Donc	6g/s		3376
41	9-14	Muss	8gd	62	4519
68	4-15	Pont	10g/f	[59]	4933
59	9-19	Pont	8g/s	65	5147

DOWAGER 3 b f £13829
96	5-11	Ling	7sft	[99]	1620
91	4-9	Cork	6fm	[99]	2457
83	6-8	Hayd	6gd	[97]	2949
103	3-11	Newb	6g/f	[96]	3268
89	11-12	Good	7fm	[100]	3564
73	7-12	Pont	6g/s	[100]	3971
80	8-8	Newm	6gd	[100]	4226
70	10-11	Ches	6.1g/f	[96]	4510 BL
100	1-8	YARM	6g/s	[96]	4588*
84	10-15	Newm	6gd		5088

DOWER HOUSE 8 ch g £5134
83a	1-13	LING	10ap	77	26*
78a	10-13	Ling	10ap	82	134
82a	4-14	Ling	10ap	81	452
78a	6-13	Ling	10ap	81	519
75a	5-8	Sout	11af	80	595
81a	4-14	Ling	10ap	80	625 t
71a	10-14	Ling	10ap	80	758 t
79a	5-12	Ling	8ap	79	888
56	16-20	Newb	10gd	79	1235 t
59	12-19	Hayd	10.5g/s	76	4766
62	10-14	Ayr	10sft	74	5037 t

DOWN TO THE WOODS 6 ch g £0
43a	9-13	Wolv	9.4af	50	1223
0	14-18	Nott	14.1sft	45	1469
35a	8-14	Ling	10ap	[45]	1712 P

DOWNLAND 8 b g £12518
47	8-16	Newc	6sft	52	1277
56	2-11	Redc	6sft	[50]	1662
58	1-18	AYR	7.2g/f	50	1897*
50	6-15	Pont	6g/f	56	2280
57	5-14	Thir	7fm	56	2466
66a	1-16	SOUT	8af	55	2805*
75a	1-13	SOUT	7af	61	3155*
70a	3-10	Sout	8af	67	3395
57	13-16	Redc	7g/f	69	3809
75a	2-8	Sout	7af	[69]	4093
65	6-17	York	7g/f	66	4398
61	5-18	Ayr	7.2sft	66	4622
35	17-19	Newc	7g/f	64	5014

DOYEN 4 b c £571200
118	2-11	Epso	12g/f	[121]	2209
125	1-6	ASCO	12fm	[121]	2579+
130	1-11	ASCO	12g/f	[124]	3442*
0	7-8	Leop	10g/f	[124]	4571
110	7-11	Newm	10sft	[127]	5136

DR CERULLO 2 b c £7990
62a	9-14	Sout	7af	75	158
75a	1-9	WOLV	9.4af	[75]	238*
76a	3-9	Ling	10ap	75	365
78a	3-6	Ling	10ap	75	403
64	10-14	Bath	10.2gd	75	1403
77	2-9	Ripo	12.3gd	72	2984
72	4-12	Hayd	11.9gd	74	3734
77	4-13	Warw	12.6gd	73	4274
77	3-16	Good	12gd	[73]	4745
42	8-13	Newb	16sft	73	5194

DR COOL 7 b g £0
1	14-14	Wind	11.6fm	69	3638
31	15-17	Kemp	12sft	66	4033
38	7-7	Good	14sft	60	4267
28	9-9	Redc	14.1fm	55	4559
1	20-20	York	13.9gd	52	5004

DR FOX 3 b g £0
48a	11-11	Ling	7ap	[61]	1008
35	11-13	Nott	8.2gd	55	1242
39	7-10	Newc	5sft	[51]	1682
37	7-14	Leic	6g/f	[47]	1963 P
22	16-17	Ling	7gd	44	2397 p

| 21 | 13-17 | Leic | 7gd | [40] | 2704 p |

DR JULIAN 3 b g £0
9a	8-12	Sout	12af	[43]	194 p
0	12-14	Sout	8af	[45]	354 vis
41a	5-7	Sout	14af	[45]	376 p
3a	8-12	Sout	14af	[40]	443 p
9a	9-12	Wolv	12af	40	469 p

DR RAJ 5 ch g £0
| 0 | 9-9 | Sout | 11af | | 505 t |
| 2a | 11-11 | Wolv | 9.4af | | 580 t P |

DR SHARP 4 ch g £23677
66	8-17	Ripo	16g/s	71	1361
81	1-11	BEVE	16.2sft	70	1629*
85	2-8	Donc	14.6gd	76	2754
83	1-8	HAYD	14gd	76	2887*
74	9-17	Asco	16.2gd	80	3125
79	6-9	Hayd	14gd	80	3760
86	1-12	CHES	15.9sft	79	4106*
71	14-20	Hayd	14fm	82	4383
77	4-11	Newm	16sft	81	5271
90	2-7	Donc	16.5sft	80	5374

DR SYNN 3 br c £6969
61	8-17	Kemp	7gd		1136
65	6-13	Nott	6.1sft		1464
68	3-17	Sali	6g/f	65	1722
66	6-20	Newb	7fm	65	2650
68	5-9	Wind	6gd	65	2797
59	9-11	Newm	7g/f	67	3283
67	2-12	Kemp	6sft	[66]	4029
53	8-9	Ling	7gd	66	4110
68	3-16	Sali	7sft	66	4582
67	4-20	Ripo	6gd	66	4785
41	18-20	Wind	6g/s	66	4946
74	1-11	GOOD	6gd	[66]	5030*
35	17-20	Yarm	7sft	70	5256

DR THONG 3 ch c £20782
82	4-19	Newb	8gd		1236
81	1-20	DONC	7g/s		1518*
81	2-12	Good	7g/f	78	1847
82	4-13	Newm	7fm	79	2590
87	1-12	LEIC	8g/f	79	2922*
66	11-13	Beve	7.5g/s	83	3179
84	4-12	Sand	7.1g/f	83	3860
87	2-8	Good	8sft	82	4265
77	7-18	Kemp	8g/f	83	4714
78	5-10	Epso	7gd	[83]	4912

DR ZALO 2 ch c £852
| 80 | 3-8 | Good | 6g/s | | 4540 |
| 65 | 5-12 | Wind | 6g/s | | 4945 |

DRAGON FLYER 5 b m £24510
88a	4-10	Ling	5ap	[95]	883
101	2-8	Cork	5g/s	[95]	1159
89	7-14	Bath	5gd	[104]	1400
90	8-20	York	5g/f	101	1683
50	11-12	Epso	5g/f	[98]	2206
101	11-19	Asco	5g/f	[98]	2468
94	3-9	Ches	5.1g/f	[98]	3100
94	4-10	Ayr	5g/f	[98]	3304
92	3-7	Newm	5fm	[98]	3409
95	11-13	Good	5fm	[98]	3551
94	4-7	Nott	5.1gd	[95]	3989
102	1-12	LEIC	5g/f	[93]	4454*
67	11-11	Hami	5sft	[98]	4693
91	7-15	Newm	5g/f	[98]	4879
102	3-12	Epso	5g/f	98	4908
93	9-10	Newm	5gd	98	5090

DRAGON PRINCE 4 b g £0
3	10-10	Pont	10g/f	68	2794
30	12-12	Catt	7g/f	[68]	3017
29	16-14	Carl	6.9g/f	68	3229

DRALION 2 ch c £0
68	5-6	Yarm	6g/f		2851
59	5-6	Yarm	5.6g/f		3361
32	15-18	Wind	6gd		3824

DRAMATIC QUEST 7 b g £0
63	7-10	Newm	10fm	70	3404 p
42	12-14	Wind	11.6fm	70	3638 p
56	10-14	York	11.9gd	70	4327 p

| 58 | 11-16 | York | 11.9gd | 65 | 4990 p |

DRAMATIC REVIEW 2 b c £0
17	10-15	Beve	5g/s		1161
65	5-7	Hami	6gd		1744
28a	7-11	Wolv	6af		2051
55	6-10	Newc	8hvy		4213 VIS
34	10-16	Yarm	8g/s	64	4632 P

DRAMATICUS 2 b c £4297
72	3-6	Warw	5hvy		1531
89	1-12	HAYD	6sft		4770*
102	7-9	Newm	6g/f		4888
32	8-8	Donc	6sft	[100]	5217

DRAX 2 b c £903
68	3-11	Thir	7fm		2462
62	8-10	Catt	7g/f		2845
68	12-15	Newm	7fm		3005
75	4-20	Redc	7fm	71	4337

DREAM ALIVE 3 b c £941
54	8-12	Hayd	10.5gd		3740 T
74	3-9	Wind	8.3g/f		3979 t
72	4-11	Beve	9.9sft		4261 t
31	14-16	Yarm	11.5g/s	70	4589 t

DREAM ALONG 2 b c £0
| 30 | 15-15 | Newm | 8gd | | 4883 |
| 0 | 12-16 | Bath | 8sft | | 5170 |

DREAM EASY 3 b g £866
26a	8-13	Sout	8af		2383
70	5-13	Newm	8fm		2595
69	4-9	Newm	7g/f		3282
61	5-11	Newm	8gd	[70]	3923
61	3-14	Carl	9.3g/f	[70]	4347
3	16-17	Newc	10.1g/f	67	5016 BL
15	17-18	Newm	8sft	63	5272

DREAM FALCON 4 b g £0
| 14 | 16-19 | Warw | 10.9sft | 50 | 1090 |

DREAM MAGIC 6 b g £8422
79	4-20	Newb	10gd	78	1235
33	8-10	Hayd	10.5g/s	78	1346
78	5-19	Newb	10gd	77	1736
57	13-15	Sand	10g/f	77	2099
18	12-12	Kemp	10gd	75	3185
77	3-10	Good	9.9gd	73	3949
77	2-10	Wind	10g/f	[73]	3980
78	3-14	Sand	10g/s	75	4097
80	3-11	Epso	10.1gd	75	4293
83	3-16	Sand	10gd	77	4609
58	14-19	Hayd	10.5g/s	77	4766
49	10-11	Redc	10fm	79	4931
73	9-10	Yarm	10.1sft	[77]	5255 VIS

DREAM OF DUBAI 3 b f £0
16a	8-8	Ling	7ap		713
5	16-16	Ling	7g/f	[62]	1982
50	8-14	Wind	10gd	60	2617
38	12-14	Chep	8.1g/s	60	3090
38a	10-14	Ling	7ap	55	3746
13a	12-12	Ling	10ap	55	4113 P
0	15-16	Chep	7.1hvy	[48]	4707 BL

DREAM PLAY 3 b f £7764
| 109 | 3-7 | Sand | 12g/s | | 3013 |

DREAM SCENE 3 b f £547
| 72 | 3-9 | Redc | 9fm | | 4336 |

DREAM TONIC 2 b c £5486
63	6-12	Newb	6g/f		2348
43	9-15	Newb	8hvy		5221
87	1-9	MUSS	8g/s		5331*

DREAM VALLEY 3 b f £0
64	6-11	Wind	10gd		4125
55a	6-9	Ling	12ap		4315
44	5-6	Chep	12.1gd	[60]	4486 H

DREAMERS LASS 2 b f £1263
62	2-6	Bath	5g/f		1786
53	9-13	Nott	5.1gd		1987
58	6-12	Bath	5.7gd		3141
37	9-10	Brig	6g/s	[60]	4139
27	12-12	Bath	5.7gd	56	4545

DREAMING OF YOU 3 b f £4128

76	1-14	WARW	8.1sft		1527*
43	15-20	Asco	8g/f	75	1927
69	7-10	Wind	10fm	73	2761

DREAMING WATERS 3 ch f £0

38a	14-14	Ling	10ap	63	1618
35	12-14	Wind	8.3g/f	60	1956
55	5-9	Warw	6.1fm	[55]	2778

DREAMS FORGOTTEN 4 b f £431

58	4-13	Pont	10g/f	57	2038
31	11-11	Yarm	10.1gd	[57]	3875
0	17-19	Chep	8.1g/s	[57]	4366
1	16-18	Pont	12g/f	55	4938

DREAMS UNITED 3 b r f £0

| 9a | 11-11 | Ling | 8ap | [45] | 535 |

DREEMON 2 ch g £655

68	7-15	Wind	6g/f		2263
72	3-13	Epso	7g/f		2870
72	8-15	Ling	7gd		3285
63a	9-14	Ling	7ap	74	4177
36	10-12	Bath	8g/f	70	4410
63	9-17	Ling	7g/f	72	4894

DRESS PEARL 2 b f £616

16a	7-11	Wolv	6af	[54]	73
0	10-11	Sout	7af	[47]	207
17a	7-9	Sout	6af	[40]	981
20a	3-7	Wolv	6af	[35]	1312 P
34a	2-9	Wolv	6af	[35]	1803 BL

DRIZZLE 2 ch c £316

30a	9-13	Wolv	8.5af		111
56a	3-10	Sout	8af		162
40a	12-12	Ling	8ap	60	798

DROOPYS JOEL 2 b g £0

34a	9-9	Ling	5ap		931
20	10-10	Hayd	5sft		1107
31	7-8	Hami	5gd		2177

DRUID 2 b g £0

53a	5-12	Wolv	8.5af		28
25a	9-12	Ling	8ap	52	402
40a	6-15	Sout	7af	[52]	462

DRUM DANCE 2 b c £3192

88	2-18	Leic	5fm		2109
82	2-6	Sand	5gd		2364
72	4-8	Sali	6sft		4577
21	14-14	Newm	6sft	80	5098

DRURY LANE 4 b c £294

42a	10-11	Sout	7af	75	585
28a	9-12	Wolv	6af	[75]	646 bl
21a	11-13	Sout	7af	[60]	858 bl
38	18-20	Newc	6sft	65	1393 bl
23	15-16	Redc	6g/f	60	1824 bl
55	4-18	Thir	6g/f	58	2214 bl
42	12-14	Thir	7fm	56	2466 bl
11	14-17	Redc	6gd	56	2561 bl
56	4-14	Ling	6gd	53	3289 bl
28	14-14	Catt	6g/f	53	3352 bl
43	11-11	Thir	6g/f	53	3574 bl
45	8-20	Hayd	6fm	51	3796 bl
2	19-20	Newc	6g/f	49	4408 bl

DRY ICE 2 b c £3851

79	5-15	Wind	6g/f		2263
83	1-9	WARW	7.1fm		2776*
74	5-8	Beve	7.5gd		3311
83	6-14	Donc	7fm	84	4535
72	8-14	Newb	7sft	82	5193

DRY WIT 3 b f £0

49	9-12	Newm	7g/f	65	2249
50	6-8	Wind	8.3gd	62	3162
29	11-13	Yarm	10.1gd	59	3492
37	10-14	Sali	9.9g/f	57	3867
46	6-14	Bath	8g/f	53	4411

DU PRE 3 b f £6390

62	7-10	Sali	7gd		2659
75	2-9	Brig	8gd	[74]	2953
76	1-12	WIND	8.3fm	69	3291*
75	3-10	Newb	10fm	74	3630

| 51 | 10-10 | Wind | 10g/f | [74] | 3980 |

DUAL PURPOSE 9 b g £268

68	9-14	Ling	11.5gd		3335
50	6-10	Ling	14fm		3742
58	4-8	Chep	7.1sft		4055
45	9-15	Chep	8.1g/s	59	4300
39	12-16	Chep	10.2g/s	59	4365
28a	8-12	Wolv	8.6ap	[55]	5230 BL

DUB DASH 3 b g £2254

| 23a | 11-15 | Ling | 12ap | | 118 |
| 75a | 1-14 | SOUT | 12af | | 194* |

DUBAI DREAMER 2 gr c £1580

| 82a | 2-10 | Ling | 7ap | | 5264 |

DUBAI DREAMS 3 b g £2857

18a	10-14	Sout	8af	57	60 vis
60a	1-10	SOUT	12af	54	138* vis
57a	4-5	Sout	14af	59	201 vis
22a	11-15	Sout	12af	58	257 vis
54a	4-6	Sout	12af		388
58a	2-10	Sout	8af	56	463 bl
54a	5-12	Wolv	9.4af	56	513 vis
35a	8-12	Sout	11af	56	534
40	7-9	Beve	12.1gd	53	2892
35	10-18	Pont	8gd	50	3242
45a	6-15	Sout	8af	53	4132 bl
34	7-14	Pont	10g/f	45	4624 T
40a	6-12	Wolv	7.1ap	[50]	5233

DUBAI ESCAPADE 2 b f £0

| 64 | 5-11 | Nott | 5.1g/f | | 2151 |

DUBAI LIGHTNING 4 b r g £0

| 30 | 6-11 | Ayr | 9.1sft | [80] | 5067 P |

DUBAI SEVEN STARS 6 ch m £0

| 78 | 14-34 | Newm | 18sft | 70 | 5135 |

DUBAI SUCCESS 4 b c £66184

116	1-17	NEWB	12gd	[110]	1230*
114	4-7	Newm	12fm	[110]	1493
113	8-11	Epso	12g/f	[113]	2209
115	2-7	Curr	14gd	[113]	2817
114	2-4	Newb	13.3g/f	[112]	3958
115	4-13	Curr	14gd	[112]	4733
98	8-9	San	12sft	[112]	5168

DUBAI SURPRISE 2 b f £68953

80	3-13	Newb	7g/f		3252
82	1-7	REDC	7g/f		3770*
105	1-12	GOOD	7sft	[84]	4264*
92	8-9	Asco	8g/f	[100]	4798
88	2-8	Sain	8Very	[100]	5315

DUBAI VENTURE 2 ch c £0

| 80 | 6-14 | Newb | 7g/f | | 3752 |

DUBAIAN GIFT 5 b g £0

92	10-11	Newb	5.2gd	106	1207
86	12-13	Newm	5g/f	[105]	1479
95	7-11	Good	5g/f	103	1845
83	8-12	Epso	5g/f	[103]	2206
76	19-19	Asco	5g/f	[101]	2468

DUBAIAN MIST 2 b f £870

55a	5-10	Ling	8ap		232
43a	12-15	Ling	7ap		472
53	5-16	Ling	6g/f	53	1985
56	2-16	Catt	5g/f	52	4676

DUBAWI 2 b c £146891

104	1-5	GOOD	6gd		2221*
107	1-12	NEWM	7g/f		3060*
121	1-7	CURR	7gd		4734*

DUBOIS 3 b c £11076

88	1-10	GOOD	8g/f		1815* VIS
52	10-11	Sand	10g/s	82	2127 vis t
96	1-11	ASCO	8gd	[82]	3128* vis t
63	12-13	Newm	8g/f	90	3277 vis t

DUBONAI 4 ch c £3733

42	11-12	Newc	12.4sft	54	1680
35	8-18	Wind	11.6g/f	51	1960 t
51	3-14	Leic	12gd		2402
37	9-17	Warw	8.1fm	49	2440
41a	9-16	Sout	8af	53	3487

58a	1-15	SOUT	8af	50	4132*
47	9-14	Carl	6.9g/f	54	4345
51a	4-13	Wolv	8.6ap	54	4982

DUBROVSKY 4 ch g £1085

86	4-17	Sand	8.1g/s	85	1351
79	8-13	Donc	8gd	[85]	2753
81	6-9	Kemp	8g/f	[84]	3689 T
66	7-8	Newm	10g/f	[82]	3945

DUCAL DIVA 2 b f £1339

64	7-13	Thir	6g/s		2689
67	2-6	Muss	5g/f		3525
44a	6-15	Sout	5af		4089
46	7-10	Redc	5fm	[66]	4338
51	7-10	Muss	5gd	60	4804
57a	4-12	Wolv	5.1ap	[60]	4922
47a	8-13	Wolv	5.1ap	[54]	5207 P

DUCK ROW 9 ch g £8392

112	2-17	York	7.9g/s	108	1686
97	9-11	Epso	8.5fm	[108]	2252
100	5-8	Curr	8g/f	[108]	2820
96	10-13	Newb	10g/f	[106]	3957
98	6-8	Wind	10g/s	[104]	4220
84	4-8	Nott	8.2hvy	[102]	5346

DUCS DREAM 5 b g £5376

29a	10-16	Sout	11af	61	97
32a	16-16	Ling	12ap	59	218
57a	7-11	Ling	12ap	[56]	816
51	7-13	Catt	13.8gd	56	997
59	1-10	YARM	11.5fm	53	2147*
44	8-15	Newb	13.3g/f	56	2311
27	9-10	Newm	12g/f	58	2530
55	5-11	Yarm	11.5gd	54	3367
42	10-15	Wind	11.6fm	54	3481
53	3-18	Warw	10.9g/s	51	4669
54	3-14	Epso	12gd	51	4910
48	5-18	Pont	12g/f	51	4938

DUE DILIGENCE 5 ch g £0

| 14 | 12-13 | Muss | 7.1g/s | 50 | 1463 |
| 0 | 14-14 | Redc | 7g/f | [45] | 2102 |

DUE TO ME 4 gr f £2225

44a	5-12	Ling	7ap	[40]	566 e
43a	2-11	Ling	8ap	[40]	786 bl e
35a	5-9	Ling	8ap	[40]	1185 e
46a	1-5	LING	8ap	[40]	1245* P
44	4-17	Kemp	7hvy	[45]	1642 p
38a	6-14	Ling	10ap	[45]	1712 p
45	3-16	Brig	7fm	45	2258 p
45	4-11	Brig	7fm	45	2334 p
44	7-17	Brig	7g/f	45	3176 p
31	8-12	Sali	8g/s	44	4077 p
33	7-15	Folk	9.7g/f	[45]	4373 p

DUELLING BANJOS 5 ch g £5411

40a	8-10	Sout	8af	65	387
65	4-18	Wind	8.3gd	65	1385
41	11-12	Redc	8g/f	[65]	1823
36	11-13	Newb	8fm	63	2647
63	7-14	Wind	8.3g/f	63	4832
73	1-17	LEIC	10gd	61	5062*
58	7-19	Pont	10g/s	67	5148

DUGGANS DILEMMA 3 b g £0

| 1a | 8-8 | Sout | 11af | 52 | 614 |
| 17a | 6-7 | Wolv | 5af | [48] | 703 VIS |

DUKE OF MODENA 7 ch g £0

| 70 | 9-10 | Ayr | 8sft | 86 | 4685 |
| 47 | 13-14 | Hami | 8.3g/s | 84 | 4820 |

DUKE OF VENICE 3 b c £51801

109	1-4	DONC	8g/s	[106]	1520* T
105	2-6	Newm	10g/f	[109]	1931 t
109	1-10	ASCO	16.2g/f	[109]	2557* t
107	5-8	Good	12g/f	[114]	3507 t
92	10-10	York	15.9gd	[114]	4000 t

DUKES VIEW 3 b g £0

0	10-11	Warw	12.6sft	68	1528
40	13-16	Wind	11.6g/s	66	2621
66	5-5	Brig	9.9fm	66	2837 BL

```
60  5-9    Brig   9.9gd    63     2955 bl
13  18-19  Chep   12.1gd   62     3398 bl
43  6-7    Brig   11.9g/f  [58]   3715
36  10-19  Brig   9.9sft   55     4145
47  6-11   Yarm   11.5g/s  [53]   4584
2   12-12  Brig   11.9fm   53     4764 bl
```

DULCE DE LECHE 3 b g £0
```
58a 7-9    Ling   5ap             492 BL e
45a 6-12   Ling   7ap             536 bl e
53a 4-10   Sout   6af      60     592 bl e
50a 12-15  Ling   7ap      [57]   671 bl e
23a 10-13  Sout   6af      54     797
0   7-7    Folk   7g/s     50     1081 bl e
```

DULCIMER 3 ch f £0
```
41  13-13  Newb   7gd             1210
50  10-17  Sali   6g/s            1497
47  12-12  Good   7g/f            1846
38  11-14  Sali   7fm             2291
```

DUMARAN 6 b g £13812
```
89a 9-14   Ling   10ap     92     758
82  14-24  Donc   8gd      92     951
96  2-17   Kemp   10g/s    90     1111
95  3-14   York   10.4g/s  92     1704
90  5-13   Epso   8.5g/f   92     2207 vis
71  9-15   York   7.9g/s   92     4061
91  6-18   Newb   10gd     90     4681
0   32-32  Newm   9g/f     90     4916
```

DUMFRIES 3 ch g £2363
```
80  5-10   Wind   11.6gd   81     1382
82  3-9    Ches   12.3gd   81     1582
77  6-13   Hayd   11.9gd   80     2238
77  5-10   Wind   10fm     78     2785 VIS
```

DUMNONI 2 b f £18840
```
83a 1-10   WOLV   7af      [73]   36*
82a 10-15  Ling   7ap      [81]   885
81  6-17   Leic   7g/s     81     1020
79  3-8    Wind   8.3g/s   79     1257
37  11-13  Good   9g/f     79     2024
77  4-12   Newm   7g/f     78     2249
84  1-13   NEWM   7fm      77     2590*
84  3-20   Chep   7.1g/s   80     3088
83  2-7    Kemp   7g/f     80     3522
83  2-8    Newm   8g/f     80     3947
6   9-10   Epso   7gd      [80]   4912
```

DUNASKIN 4 b g £65005
```
67  15-24  Donc   8gd      87     928
74  8-20   Donc   10.3g/s  85     1519
72  7-19   York   11.9sft  85     1668
80  5-11   Ripo   10g/f    82     2483
85  6-13   York   11.9g/s  81     3076
79  3-10   Ripo   12.3g/s  81     3261
88  1-6    NEWC   10.1gd   [80]   3430*
94  1-20   HAYD   10.5fm   83     3794*
104 1-11   YORK   10.4g/s  88     4021*
83  11-19  York   7.9gd    98     4987
```

DUNCANBIL 2 b f £826
```
47a 6-14   Sout   7af      56     158
20a 11-12  Wolv   7af      53     2049
0   15-15  Sout   7af      50     2384
47  2-7    Catt   13.8g/f  [45]   3019
5   P-20   Beve   16.2gd   45     3312
```

DUNDONALD 5 ch g £830
```
0   6-9    Wolv   9.4af    [45]   633 vis t
0   8-11   Wolv   12af     [45]   689 BL t
34a 8-13   Wolv   8.5af    [40]   699 bl t
39a 3-12   Wolv   8.5af    [35]   777 bl t
25a 4-13   Wolv   8.5af    [35]   826 bl t
16a 7-7    Wolv   9.4af    [40]   862 bl t
19a 6-6    Wolv   8.5af    [35]   957 bl t
37  5-14   Sout   12g/s    [35]   1047 bl t
20  8-8    Yarm   11.5g/f  35     1135 bl t
32a 3-5    Wolv   8.5af    [35]   1264 bl t
28  3-7    Chep   7.1sft   [35]   1335 t
32a 10-14  Wolv   9.4af    [35]   1561 bl t
0   9-9    Sout   11af     [35]   1838 bl t
28  6-12   Brig   8gd      [35]   4904 t
```

DUNDRY 3 b g £6828
```
75  3-13   Sali   9.9gd           2700
80  3-13   Kemp   10gd            3186
```

```
79  2-9    Nott   10g/s    [78]   4034
81  2-5    Good   11sft    [77]   4188 P
84a 1-9    LING   12ap     [79]   4449* p
56  12-12  Wind   11.6g/f  85     4833 p
```

DUNE RAIDER 3 b c £3533
```
80  7-17   Newb   10gd            1737
49  11-16  Donc   10.3gd          2751
78  1-6    CHEP   12.1gd          4486*
84  6-15   Leic   11.8gd   82     5043
35  21-24  Donc   12sft    83     5372
```

DUNEDIN RASCAL 6 b g £0
```
39a 15-16  Ling   7ap      72     22 bl
68a 4-13   Wolv   6af      70     113 bl
49a 7-10   Ling   6ap      [70]   133 bl
53a 9-10   Ling   5ap      68     231 bl
22a 15-16  Ling   7ap      66     323 bl
23a 8-13   Ling   6ap      [66]   400 bl
44a 10-14  Ling   7ap      [62]   450 bl
18a 11-13  Ling   6ap      [57]   544 bl
```

DUNHILL STAR 4 b c £4807
```
100 2-8    Donc   12gd     [108]  950
```

DUNLEA 8 b g £0
```
2   16-16  Brig   7gd      [35]   4901 vis
```

DUNLEA DANCER 3 b g £5957
```
55  3-12   Beve   9.9sft   56     1306
52  4-8    Beve   12.1g/f  56     2164
59  2-7    Ayr    13.1g/s  53     2546
69  1-5    HAMI   12.1g/s  57     2827*
59  6-18   Hayd   14gd     63     2905
```

DUNLOWS MINSTREL 2 ch c £0
```
25  10-10  Wind   8.3g/f          4831
```

DUNMAGLASS 2 ch c £0
```
66  10-15  Newb   7g/f            2876
73  7-15   Ling   7gd             3285
```

DUNMIDOE 4 b f £0
```
18  8-10   Warw   8.1g/s   [40]   1328
0   8-8    Wolv   7af      [35]   1565
```

DUNN DEAL 4 b g £5635
```
61a 3-11   Sout   5af      58     859
41a 10-14  Ling   6ap      59     1025
64  1-19   WARW   5gd      59     1127*
66a 2-12   Sout   5af      63     1442
65  7-17   Nott   5.1g/s   65     1774
64  5-11   Hayd   5g/f     65     1886
45  14-16  Ayr    5g/f     65     2029
62  6-18   Hayd   5gd      64     2951
63  6-15   Wind   5gd      63     3165
60  5-12   Nott   5.1g/f   [62]   3577
```

DUO LEONI 3 ch f £4629
```
53a 7-16   Ling   7ap      60     20
54a 2-12   Wolv   7af      60     129
21a 13-15  Sout   6af      60     168
52a 6-10   Ling   7ap      [60]   765
61a 1-10   WOLV   7af      58     864*
```

DUROOB 2 b c £4224
```
59a 8-10   Ling   6ap             3817
79  3-17   Chep   6.1sft          4052
77  3-11   Chep   7.1hvy          4704
82  1-12   REDC   8g/s     [72]   5107*
```

DUSK DANCER 4 b g £273
```
58a 4-16   Ling   7ap             290
59a 12-14  Ling   10ap     65     434
0   11-13  Wolv   8.5af    [61]   699 BL
```

DUSKY WARBLER 5 br g £17600
```
108 2-6    Nott   14.1fm   [107]  1005
108 2-13   Asco   16.2sft  [107]  1418
84  8-8    Bade   16gd     [107]  1993
61  12-13  Asco   20g/f    [107]  2518
```

DUSTINI 2 ch c £1332
```
48  3-4    Folk   5g/s            1077
45  5-5    Brig   5.3g/f          1367
71  3-14   Bath   5sft            1538 BL
56  10-11  Yarm   6g/f            1727 P
33a 7-7    Ling   7ap             2839 bl
```

DUSTY CARPET 6 ch g £0

```
59a 13-16  Ling   12ap     76     293
69a 12-16  Ling   12ap     75     404
64a 7-16   Ling   12ap     71     493
52a 11-11  Ling   16ap     70     605
1   18-19  Wind   10sft    [65]   1650
34  12-14  Sali   9.9g/f   60     3867
32  11-15  Chep   8.1g/s   55     4300
```

DUSTY DANE 2 b c £1380
```
61  5-7    Folk   5sft            1574 T
60  6-8    Beve   7.5gd           2511 t
73  5-10   Sali   6gd             2697
74  3-8    Brig   7gd             2952
43a 9-10   Sout   7af      72     3483
60  6-11   Ches   7sft     [71]   4072
76  4-11   Chep   8.1g/s   [67]   4363
```

DUSTY DAZZLER 3 ch f £10431
```
96a 2-13   Ling   6ap      94     235
87a 1-7    LING   6ap      [95]   431+
87a 6-10   Ling   5ap      [95]   883
74  12-14  Bath   6g/f     [87]   1400
81  5-13   Yarm   6g/f     85     1726
```

DUSTY WUGG 5 b m £187
```
38a 5-9    Sout   6af      [46]   533 p
39a 3-10   Sout   6af      [45]   851 p
29a 7-10   Sout   6af      [45]   907 p
45  5-18   Catt   7gd      [45]   996 p
11  7-17   Pont   6hvy     [40]   1065 p
```

DUTCH GOLD 4 ch c £20750
```
93  10-17  Newb   12gd            1230
96  5-10   York   13.9g/s  [111]  1705 BL
110 2-11   Epso   8.5fm    [110]  2252 bl
101 5-7    Sand   10g/s    [110]  2898 bl
94  3-10   Asco   8gd      [110]  3124 bl
```

DUTCH KEY CARD 3 b g £3435
```
46a 5-10   Sout   5af      63     4094
69a 1-11   WOLV   5.1ap    [61]   5363*
```

DUTY PAID 3 b f £309
```
87a 5-11   Ling   8ap      89     80
```

DUXFORD 3 ch g £1172
```
50  8-10   Wind   6g/f            4835
73a 2-12   Ling   8ap             4975
```

DVINSKY 3 b c £0
```
68  10-10  Ches   5.1g/f   90     3080 T
71  14-17  Good   7fm      88     3550 BL
61a 6-10   Wolv   7.1ap    [85]   4920
47a 4-12   Wolv   5.1ap    [78]   5362 t
```

E BRIDE 2 gr f £730
```
51  5-8    Pont   6g/f            2603
57  4-13   Nott   6.1g/f          4843
65  4-14   Redc   7sft            5301
```

E MINOR 4 b f £0
```
54a 5-11   Wolv   16.2af   66     48
52a 5-9    Wolv   12af     62     424
39a 7-11   Wolv   12af     58     557
45a 6-12   Wolv   12af     56     634
38a 6-7    Wolv   16.2af   50     866
15a 7-8    Wolv   12af     47     1342
```

EACHY PEACHY 5 ch m £0
```
28  5-12   Brig   11.9fm   35     4764
```

EAGER ANGEL 5 b m £6488
```
27a 11-16  Sout   7af      [37]   61
29a 6-10   Sout   6af      37     91 p
40a 3-15   Sout   6af      [35]   167 p
42a 7-12   Wolv   5af      [41]   242 p
44a 2-13   Sout   7af      [45]   356 p
45a 4-8    Sout   8af      45     489 p
38a 9-13   Sout   7gd      45     556 p
48a 1-11   WOLV   7af      [45]   579* p
50a 5-10   Sout   6af      51     657 p
59a 1-7    SOUT   7af      51     680+ p
41a 10-10  Wolv   8.5af    52     753 p
49a 3-8    Sout   7gd      57     1195 p
49  9-15   Sout   7gd      57     1282 p
27  13-15  Redc   7sft     54     1660 p
10a 9-9    Wolv   [56]            2801 p
23a 11-13  Wolv   8.6ap    54     5365
```

EAGLE FEATHERS 3 b f £0
37 7-12 Ripo 9g/f 1784

EAGLE RISE 4 b c £35211
113 2-14 Colo 8gd 3664
113 1-7 COLO 8sft 4839*

EARL OF LINKS 2 ch c £6485
80 3-5 Kemp 5g/s 1114
80 1-6 WARW 5hvy 1531*
70 6-6 Ling 6gd 80 3022
48 24-24 Newb 5.2g/f 3266
66 4-9 Ches 7sft 74 4074
38 6-6 Chep 5.1g/s 74 4298

EARLSFIELD RAIDER 4 ch g £1435
62a 1-5 WOLV 12af [58] 583* e

EARLSTON 4 ch g £0
49a 4-7 Sout 7af [64] 589 e T
34a 7-9 Wolv 8.5af [64] 664 t
0 P-9 Wolv 7af 64 684 BL t

EARLY MARCH 2 br c £82049
115 1-6 LONG 7gd 4564*
117 2-6 Long 7g/f 4955

EASIBET DOT NET 3 gr g £13205
62a 2-11 Wolv 12af [58] 6 p
62a 1-12 WOLV 12af 57 75* p
51a 5-8 Wolv 14.8af 63 277 p
52a 4-6 Wolv 12af [62] 752 VIS
16 9-15 Newc 12.4hvy 61 1034 p
63 2-10 Muss 12gd 58 1796 p
60 3-7 Ayr 10g/f 58 2030 BL
50 9-11 Thir 12g/f 61 2217 bl
59 5-7 Beve 9.9gd 61 2654 p
64 3-10 Hayd 10.5g/s 60 3139 p
69 1-6 HAMI 12.1g/f 60 3588* p
43 3-5 Hami 12.1sft 67 4012 p
72 4-9 Muss 12g/f 66 4553 p
74 3-17 Newc 10.1g/f 69 5016 p
74 2-13 Muss 12g/s 69 5333 p

EASILY AVERTED 2 b c £0
49a 12-13 Wolv 6af 74 1
67a 6-10 Ling 5ap 71 217
53a 5-9 Ling 5ap [70] 405
57a 5-9 Ling 5ap [66] 492 T
38a 10-10 Ling 5ap 63 712 t
40a 9-11 Ling 6ap 63 735
43 15-17 Kemp 5sft 71 944
46 10-10 Brig 5.3fm 65 1694 P
39 6-10 Brig 7g/f [59] 1938 p
0 15-15 Ling 7.6fm 53 3788
14 7-7 Brig 5.3sft [48] 4169 t

EAST CAPE 6 b g £3940
43a 5-16 Sout 11af 44 97
33a 8-15 Sout 12af 42 257
34a 5-10 Sout 12af 40 321
32a 3-10 Sout 11af [40] 375
21a 7-12 Sout 11af 40 534
46a 1-7 SOUT 14af [35] 724*
0 8-9 Sout 14af [45] 849
17a 11-16 Sout 14af 45 1033
13 11-16 Newc 10.1sft 45 1278
43 6-12 Newc 12.4sft 40 1680
46 3-10 Redc 14.1g/s 43 2562
37 5-9 Beve 12.1gd 43 2892
43 2-13 Beve 12.1g/f 42 3502
46 4-12 Beve 12.1sft 42 4259
54 7-9 Redc 14.1fm 45 4559
44 9-12 Redc 14.1g/s 45 5108
46 3-13 Ayr 10sft [45] 5276

EAST FLARES 4 gr g £0
25a 10-12 Wolv 9.4af 67 382
41a 11-14 Ling 10ap 60 622

EAST RIDING 4 b f £573
47 5-13 Muss 7.1g/f [50] 1119
11a 6-7 Wolv 5af [50] 1320
43 6-13 Muss 7.1g/s 49 1463
43 3-11 Warw 8.1hvy 45 1536
29 10-16 Redc 10g/f 45 1821
32 11-13 Pont 10g/f 45 2038
31 8-11 Thir 10g/f 40 2217

2 5-5 Warw 12.6fm [37] 2441
35 5-5 Carl 9.3gd 37 2674
33 7-10 Muss 9g/f [37] 2811
43 10-12 Catt 6g/f [37] 2849 P

EASTBOROUGH 4 b g £7409
75a 6-12 Ling 8ap [80] 234
57a 14-16 Ling 12ap 78 293
64a 3-13 Ling 10ap [75] 429
68a 1-9 WOLV 9.4af [67] 480*
62a 7-14 Ling 10ap 67 674
69a 3-11 Ling 8ap 67 714
67a 4-9 Wolv 8.5af 66 809
65 3-9 Folk 9.7sft [62] 978
58 4-18 Bath 10.2g/s 62 1098
60 6-18 Wind 8.3gd 60 1385
55 6-16 Brig 11.9fm 60 1693
63 2-12 Newb 10g/f 58 2354
63 3-10 Newb 11g/f 60 2875
65 2-13 Bath 10.2gd [60] 3144
66a 8-16 Ling 12ap 65 5261

EASTER OGIL 8 ch g £4917
62a 6-14 Ling 13ap 63 147
65a 4-14 Ling 10ap 63 174
65a 2-16 Ling 12ap 62 218
63a 2-14 Ling 13ap 63 264
65a 5-8 Ling 10ap [63] 294
61a 9-16 Ling 12ap 64 404
68a 3-14 Ling 10ap 64 434
66a 3-16 Ling 12ap 64 493
66a 2-11 Ling 13ap [64] 515
62a 4-12 Ling 8ap 64 607
38a 12-14 Ling 10ap 64 622
94a 9-11 Ling 10ap [64] 693
41a 12-13 Ling 10ap 63 726
0 11-11 Wolv 8.5af 63 806
58 8-9 Folk 9.7sft [56] 978
60 2-14 Folk 9.7g/s 56 1083
98 6-12 Kemp 10gd [56] 1139
53 5-12 Folk 9.7sft 57 1273
48 11-14 Hami 12.1gd 55 1746
57 8-9 Sand 10g/s [55] 2128
60a 6-13 Wolv 8.6ap 59 5183
59a 6-13 Wolv 9.5ap 58 5292

EASTERN BLUE 4 ch f £1625
50a 2-11 Sout 6af 48 91 p
50a 2-16 Sout 6af 48 166 p
0 W-13 Ling 6ap [50] 400 p
34a 6-13 Sout 6af 50 500 p
45a 5-13 Ling 6ap [50] 544
47a 3-13 Ling 6ap 48 767 p

EASTERN BREEZE 5 b g £29039
98a 6-14 Ling 10ap [96] 82
100a4-16 Ling 12ap 95 293 e
105a1-13 LING 10ap 95 433*
103a2-11 Ling 10ap [102] 693
101a7-14 Ling 10ap [102] 884
98 5-6 Newm 9gd [102] 1168
84 13-21 York 10.4gd 102 3118 e
106 1-9 NEWM 12g/f [102] 3233+ e
4 P-9 Good 12fm [105] 3563 e

EASTERN DAGGER 4 b g £0
4 14-14 Pont 8hvy [60] 1253
0 10-12 Sout 7af [56] 2337
49 7-7 Pont 10g/f [48] 2605
59 6-8 Newc 10.1sft [48] 2687
17 16-16 Beve 7.5gd 48 2891

EASTERN HOPE 5 b g £4059
57 12-14 Nott 10fm [69] 1006
49 7-13 Redc 7sft [67] 1142
65 3-12 Redc 8g/f [63] 1823 bl
31 11-12 Sand 8.1g/s 63 2129 bl
57 9-15 Beve 7.5g/s 63 2324 bl
64 3-16 Redc 8g/s 60 2958
28 16-20 Newm 8g/f 60 3232
60 1-12 NEWC 8sft [59] 4284*
52 7-17 Yarm 8g/s [59] 5348

EASTERN MAGENTA 4 b g £0
41 14-14 Nott 10fm [70] 1006

EASTERN MANDARIN 2 b g £0
63 5-10 Newc 8hvy 4213

61 5-8 Hami 8.3g/s 4816

EASTERN PEARL 3 ch f £0
57 10-13 Thir 5sft 76 1229
38 8-9 Hayd 5g/s 73 1344
53a 10-11 Sout 5af 69 2380

EASTERN SCARLET 4 b g £0
24 11-17 Thir 8g/s 41 3830
41a 5-11 Wolv 7.1ap [45] 5210 p
39a 4-13 Wolv 8.6ap [45] 5232 VIS

EASTWELL MAGIC 2 b f £0
46a 13-13 Ling 7ap 3329
38 13-14 Kemp 8g/f 4356

EASTWELL VIOLET 4 b f £0
0 10-10 Sout 14af 44 3158

EASY BREEZE 3 b g £0
3a 10-10 Wolv 7af 4
17a 13-14 Ling 6ap 23
1a 8-11 Wolv 8.5af 128

EASY FEELING 2 b f £16808
78 3-9 Hayd 6g/f 1920
80 3-7 Leic 5gd 2132
67 4-8 Hayd 5gd 2241
89 1-9 GOOD 6fm 77 3623*
83 5-16 Curr 6g/f [77] 4153
72 12-21 Donc 6.5fm 85 4457

EASY MOVER 2 ch f £6630
51 5-8 Newm 6g/f 3473
66 5-9 Brig 6g/f 3981
81 1-11 THIR 7fm 4381*
77 2-4 Sand 7.1gd [76] 4606
69 9-12 Asco 7g/f 77 4810
61 12-19 Pont 8g/s 75 5147

EAU PURE 7 b m £0
36a 4-9 Ling 13ap [40] 1456

EBINZAYD 8 b g £0
69 9-10 Carl 14.1fm 77 2444
74 7-9 Redc 16sft 75 2963
66 5-6 Newc 14.4sft 73 4287
69 5-8 Ayr 17.5g/s 71 4657

EBORACUM 3 b f £20616
43 8-8 Beve 7.5g/f 65 2166
34a 9-12 Sout 7af [62] 2496
66 2-12 Hayd 8.1gd 60 2904
66 2-5 Donc 10.3g/s 63 3377
57 11-16 Thir 12g/f 63 3573
51 4-10 Redc 10g/f 63 3772 BL
73 1-6 HAMI 9.2g/s 62 4137* bl
81 1-20 YORK 7.9gd 68 4321* bl
83 1-11 AYR 8sft 75 4621* bl

EBORACUM LADY 4 b f £0
47 6-15 Warw 10.9g/f 50 2910
45a 5-13 Sout 8af 50 3094
32 10-13 Yarm 10.1gd 48 3492

EBORARRY 2 b c £356
60 4-4 Beve 7.5sft 2938
54 10-11 Beve 7.5gd 3500
55 10-11 Beve 7.5g/s 3851

EBTIKAAR 2 b c £0
77 8-14 Newm 7g/f 3752

ECCENTRIC 3 ch g £12095
69a 4-11 Ling 8ap 696
73a 1-9 LING 7ap 764*
79a 1-8 LING 7ap 71 933*
63 11-16 Kemp 6g/s 76 1116
78a 4-11 Ling 6ap 76 2841
75a 2-11 Ling 6ap 75 3198
81a 2-11 Ling 7ap [75] 3331
59 13-17 Good 7fm 74 3550
89a 2-13 Ling 7ap 80 4318
83a 6-12 Wolv 7.1ap 84 5159

ECCENTRICITY 2 ch f £0
76 6-10 Yarm 7fm 2863

ECHELON 2 b f £4891
108 1-13 NEWM 6gd 4223*

98 7-9 Asco 8g/f 4798

ECHO OF LIGHT 2 b c £551
79 4-21 Newm 8sft 5097 T

ECHOES IN ETERNITY 4 b f £70113
105 4-8 Newm 9fm [109] 1491 T
100 4-5 Curr 8g/f [109] 1997 t
103 5-6 Good 9.9fm [107] 3621 t
105 1-10 DONC 14.6fm[106] 4460* t
0 11-11 Long 10.5g/f[106] 4948

ECOLOGICALLY RIGHT 2 b f £4752
59 7-16 Thir 6g/s 4205
72 6-9 Beve 7.5g/f 4600
79 1-13 NOTT 6.1g/f 4843*
75 6-8 Donc 6sft [75] 5217

ECOMIUM 3 b c £12511
95 1-11 NEWM 10gd 1148*
111 2-14 Curr 10sft 4959

EDDIES JEWEL 3 b g £949
11a 9-10 Wolv 7af [36] 8 VIS
36 2-15 Nott 10gd [35] 1991
34 5-11 Ripo 8gd 35 2986
48 4-9 Beve 7.5gd 35 3310
36 5-13 Beve 12.1g/f 35 3502
3 11-11 Beve 12.1g/s [39] 3856
24 6-18 Beve 9.9g/s 37 4243
37 4-15 Carl 9.3fm [40] 4505

EDEN STAR 2 b f £0
17 10-10 Wind 5fm 3476
0 18-18 Wind 5gd 3824
37a 11-12 Ling 6ap 4178
30 11-11 Bath 5g/f 4409

EDGE FUND 2 b c £3977
74 3-5 Nott 5.1fm 1001
81 3-9 Wind 5g/s 1256
80 3-12 Ling 5gd 1981
81 2-6 Chep 6.1gd 2367
82 3-10 Leic 6gd 2703
64 22-24 Newb 5.2g/f 3266 P
82 3-7 Kemp 6g/f 79 3686
61 9-11 Bath 5g/f [79] 3962

EDGE OF BLUE 2 b c £629
73 6-8 Asco 5gd 3438
73 3-6 Sand 5g/f 3857
54 10-14 Wind 5gd 4121
67 5-7 Epso 6gd [68] 4466

EDGE OF ITALY 2 ch f £0
48a 10-12 Ling 6ap 4179
64 6-11 Bath 5.7gd 4543
59a 6-12 Wolv 6ap 4921

EDGED IN GOLD 2 ch f £0
47 6-8 Chep 5.1g/s 3896
44 9-11 Bath 6ap 4200

EDGEHILL 3 b c £2098
64 4-14 Thir 7sft 2692
67 2-8 Asco 10g/f 60 3391
60 8-14 Redc 10fm 64 4342

EDITH BANKES 2 ch f £0
16 10-11 Bath 8gd 4544
49 7-14 Wind 8.3g/f 5049

EDMO YEWKAY 4 b g £0
48 12-13 Catt 13.8gd 66 997
52 11-13 Hayd 14sft 65 1109 bl

EFFECTIVE 3 ch g £8257
57a 8-13 Wolv 6af 68 45
36a 10-13 Ling 6ap 65 471
60a 3-15 Sout 6af 62 550
49a 14-14 Ling 7ap 62 604
55a 5-13 Sout 7af [60] 858
43a 9-15 Ling 7ap [60] 935 VIS
65a 1-14 LING 6ap 58 1025* vis
57a 5-13 Wolv 6af 62 1221 vis
68 2-18 Wind 6g/f [62] 1806
57 8-17 Wind 6gd 64 2451
70 1-12 CATT 7g/f [63] 3017*
54 6-7 York 6g/f [67] 3436

EFFIE GRAY 5 b m £0
19a 12-13 Sout 12af [45] 575
38a 7-13 Wolv 8.5af [45] 699
43a 4-9 Wolv 8.5af [45] 811 BL

EFIDIUM 6 b g £25205
68 2-12 Thir 7g/s 65 1215
45 9-20 Ripo 8g/s 65 1366
63 4-13 Muss 7.1gd 65 1553
68 2-12 Redc 8g/f [64] 1823
65 3-18 Thir 8g/f 64 1972
72 1-16 YORK 7g/f 64 2057*
66 5-12 Donc 7gd 70 2235
73 3-6 Redc 7g/s [69] 2564
71 5-10 Carl 6.9gd 69 2935
68 4-10 Hayd 7.1g/s 69 3137
75 1-8 THIR 8fm 68 3608*
75 2-16 Redc 8g/f 71 3768
67 9-13 Redc 7fm [74] 4341
40 21-21 Donc 7fm 74 4482

EFIMAC 4 b f £437
12 11-14 Donc 6g/s [45] 1522
35 10-14 Redc 7g/f [43] 2102
40 7-19 Beve 5g/s 43 2326 BL
31 4-8 Ripo 6g/f [40] 2480 bl
25 10-19 Beve 5gd 40 2657 VIS
44 7-12 Carl 6.9fm 38 3548
33 12-16 Beve 8.5g/s [38] 3850
44 3-15 Thir 8fm [40] 4379

EFISTORM 3 b c £0
68 11-12 Leic 8g/f [88] 4454
51 10-12 Hayd 6sft 88 4779

EFORETTA 2 ch f £0
47 8-15 Nott 6.1g/s 4644
29 10-11 Wind 6g/s 4941
39a 12-14 Ling 7ap 5257

EFRHINA 4 ch f £3282
56 10-17 Wind 10fm 65 3477
65 7-11 Wind 10fm [63] 3802
67 3-14 Sali 9.9g/f 63 3867
54 10-17 Kemp 12sft 63 4033
69 2-11 Folk 9.7gd [64] 4120
51 8-12 Good 9.9sft 63 4268
49a 10-12 Ling 8ap 68 4743 P
66 3-15 Bath 10.2gd [68] 4826
63a 4-12 Wolv 12.2ap 64 4924
58a 3-12 Wolv 12.2ap 64 4983
59a 8-13 Wolv 9.5ap 60 5292
57a 6-12 Wolv 12.2ap 60 5328

EGERTON 3 b c £98592
119 2-4 Bade 12sft 4428

EGO TRIP 3 b c £12811
7 8-11 Newc 8sft 54 1395
57 1-14 NEWC 8gd 50 1872*
58 3-14 Redc 10fm 53 2299
20 9-14 Catt 12g/f 54 3192
51 4-5 Carl 11.9g/f 54 3653
62 1-19 THIR 12g/f 52 4594* BL
71 2-20 Catt 12gd 58 4966 bl
72 1-11 CATT 13.8sft [65] 5129* bl
60 6-13 Muss 12g/s 65 5333 bl

EGYPTIAN LADY 2 ch f £0
44 11-14 Ches 7sft 4102
57 8-12 Carl 5g/f 4343
68 5-11 Thir 7fm 4381

EHAB 5 b g £0
47a 6-9 Ling 8ap 57 763

El El 9 b g £0
26 7-11 Newm 12g/f 46 2244

EIDSFOSS 2 b g £0
39 5-8 Brig 5.3fm 4759
57 9-13 Wind 6g/f 5048

EIGHT 8 ch g £0
29 12-19 Chep 12.1gd 47 3398
33 13-19 Beve 9.9g/f 47 3505
43 4-9 Yarm 14.1g/f 47 3703
33 9-17 Catt 12sft 45 3929
26 13-17 Yarm 8g/s [45] 5348

EIGHT ELLINGTON 3 b g £302
33 11-15 Folk 6g/f [59] 1078
53 4-20 Chep 6.1gd 59 2372
56 6-10 Newb 5.2fm [58] 2649
57 7-9 Warw 6.1g/f [58] 2906
8 18-19 Chep 6.1sft 58 4054
45a 6-12 Wolv 6ap [55] 5162

EIGHT WOODS 6 ch g £360
60a 3-6 Sout 12af [65] 392
11a 4-9 Wolv 9.4af [60] 633

EIJAAZ 3 b c £421
54 8-16 Newm 7fm 2092
36 7-8 Warw 7.1fm 2575
64 4-9 Brig 8gd 2953
56 11-15 Nott 8.2g/s [67] 4649
62a 10-16 Ling 12ap 65 4973

EISTEDDFOD 3 ch g £59713
75 1-13 FOLK 5sft 1575*
80 3-8 Good 6gd 75 2375
87 3-7 Ches 7g/s 75 2749
89 1-7 WIND 6fm [80] 3293*
95 1-7 SALI 7g/s [84] 4082*
100 1-26 AYR 6g/s 87 4652+
105 1-12 HAYD 6sft 93 4779*

EIZAWINA DOCKLANDS 3 b g £0
27 22-24 Newm 8fm 1495
71 7-17 Newb 8g/f 1762 T
33 12-13 Newm 8g/f 1935 t
10 12-15 Ayr 8gd 2504 t
51 8-10 Newm 8g/f 2732 t
40 7-11 Leic 10g/f [50] 2924 t

EJAY 4 b f £899
36a 6-15 Sout 6af [45] 172
13a 9-12 Sout 7af [40] 416
36a 6-13 Wolv 6af [40] 582
8a 9-10 Wolv 6af [40] 667
47a 2-16 Sout 5af [40] 720
27a 10-16 Sout 5ap 46 1046
28 15-20 Ripo 5gd 46 1179
19 9-12 Chep 5.1sft [40] 1336
45 2-10 Kemp 5hvy [40] 1644
20a 7-10 Sout 6af [45] 1837

EKATERINA 2 b f £0
20 9-9 Catt 6g/f 4670
14 14-17 Redc 7g/s 5105
55 6-8 Ayr 8sft 5273

EL CHAPARRAL 4 b g £6264
63 7-17 Kemp 7gd 1136
63 6-17 Sali 6g/s [74] 1497
57 10-17 Nott 5.1g/s 70 1774
50 12-16 Ling 7g/f 66 2063 P
69 2-14 Wind 8.3g/f 62 2799
54 11-16 Kemp 7gd 63 3184
70 2-17 Wind 10fm 63 3477
52 10-13 Wind 8.3gd [68] 3828
74 1-10 WIND 10g/f [68] 3980*
43 11-11 Brig 8g/s 74 4141
63 9-13 Wind 8.3g/s 73 4221
54a 9-14 Ling 10ap [72] 4448

EL COTO 4 b c £33200
80 17-24 Donc 8gd 96 951
104 1-27 NEWB 8gd 94 1231*
103 5-9 Hayd 7.1g/f [101] 1486
104 5-17 York 7.9g/s 102 1686
97 9-20 Asco 7g/f 102 1926
83 8-11 Hayd 7.1gd [102] 2184
97 13-31 Asco 8g/f 102 2489
103 4-19 Newm 7g/f 100 3061 BL
29 20-21 Asco 7g/f 100 3441 bl
102 4-21 Good 8fm 100 3565
82 8-15 York 7.9g/s 100 4061
99 9-32 Newm 9g/f 100 4916 bl

EL GIZA 6 ch g £0
31a 7-11 Ling 8ap [45] 535

EL HAMRA 6 gr g £0
44a 5-7 Wolv 7af 54 860
44 9-9 Folk 9.7sft [40] 978
0 14-15 Folk 16.4g/s 36 3049

EL MAGNIFICO 3 b g £0
44a	6-12	Ling	8ap	56	402
46a	7-11	Ling	10ap	51	497 P
42	8-14	Ling	11.5g/f	48	2014
38	11-15	Leic	11.8gd	48	2134 VIS
5a	8-12	Ling	12ap	[42]	3819 BL

EL PALMAR 3 b g £4887
67	3-6	Newc	5sft		1392
53	3-10	Newc	5sft	[68]	1682
9	17-19	York	6g/f	68	2055
73	1-12	THIR	7g/f	[68]	2215*
63a	2-8	Sout	6af	[65]	2379
53	9-13	Ayr	7.2g/s	72	2568

EL PEDRO 4 b g £653
28a	10-14	Sout	8af	50	165
40a	5-10	Wolv	12af	[47]	250
44a	4-8	Wolv	12af	[45]	347
45a	3-13	Sout	12af	[45]	575
34a	4-7	Ling	10ap	[45]	1182
16a	7-7	Sout	14af	[45]	1407
39a	2-9	Sout	11af	[40]	1838
37	4-13	Beve	12.1g/f	[40]	1945

EL POTRO 2 b c £0
39	7-13	Ripo	5gd	4303
26	12-12	Hayd	6sft	4770

EL REY DEL MAMBO 2 b c £674
72a	3-12	Ling	6ap	4896

EL REY ROYALE 2 b g £4430
78	1-15	PONT	6gd		3239*
59	6-7	Ripo	6g/s		3935
49	15-19	Pont	8g/s	75	5147

ELA DARGENT 5 b m £0
25a	8-9	Wolv	12af	59	424 t

ELA FIGURA 4 ch f £970
47	6-15	Brig	5.3g/f	56	1371
41	12-16	Bath	5.7sft	56	1540
33	8-16	Brig	6fm	50	2262
50	3-10	Brig	5.3fm	50	2331 P
50	6-8	Sand	5gd	[50]	2361
53	5-6	Folk	5fm	[49]	2717 p
43	8-15	Wind	5gd	49	3165 p
35	13-17	Sand	5gd	49	3341 p
42	14-22	Good	5fm	48	3537
47	5-11	Sand	5sft	46	4070 p
49	3-9	Thir	5g/s	46	4210 p
32	12-19	Bath	5.7sft	46	5176 p

ELA JAY 5 b m £0
43a	5-10	Sout	16af	45	491

ELA PAPAROUNA 3 b f £5572
64	3-14	Sout	6gd	[76]	1281
66	8-20	Newb	7g/f	73	1761
69	6-17	Kemp	7gd	71	2174
74	3-10	Sali	7gd	[70]	2659
75	2-13	Leic	7g/f	70	3346
74	3-9	Newm	8g/f	72	3780
68	3-10	Sali	8sft	[72]	4578

ELA RE 5 ch g £0
43a	4-10	Sout	12af	47	421
31a	7-13	Sout	14af	45	590
44a	4-16	Sout	12af	43	2340
49a	4-14	Sout	12af	43	3486
40a	6-12	Wolv	9.5ap	[45]	5234

ELECTION SEEKER 2 b c £0
70	8-12	Good	7fm		3568
51	14-18	Newm	7gd		3927
63	9-15	Good	8g/s		4233
70	7-13	Sali	7sft		4576
39	15-17	Good	8gd	65	4871

ELECTRAS DREAM 3 ch f £0
9	16-19	Newm	7fm	2092
41a	11-14	Ling	10ap	2740
37	9-11	Leic	10g/f	3208
56	6-9	Leic	7gd	5041

ELECTRIQUE 4 b g £0
66	8-9	Sand	9g/s	[80]	3892

42 18-19 Kemp 10fm 75 4392
42	18-19	Kemp	10fm	75	4392
61a	9-14	Ling	10ap	[72]	4742
63a	11-12	Ling	8ap	70	5079 BL
41a	9-12	Ling	8ap	70	5238 bl

ELECTROCUTIONIST 3 b c £80546
118	2-9	San	12sft	5168

ELEGANT FASHION 5 ch m £359827
117	3-14	Sha	10g/f	212
111	2-14	Sha	10g/f	1438

ELEGANT GRACIE 3 ch f £2138
50a	7-14	Ling	10ap		53
32a	12-13	Ling	10ap		148
62a	3-9	Ling	10ap		269
67a	2-15	Ling	12ap	[61]	521
34a	6-11	Ling	12ap	[67]	672
57a	2-8	Sout	11af	[67]	857
39a	4-9	Sout	11af	[65]	985

ELGIN MARBLES 2 b c £8939
86	1-14	BATH	5gd		1401*
29	6-7	Donc	6g/s		3221
46a	12-12	Ling	7ap	84	3820
86	2-10	Newm	6fm	80	4727
87	2-12	Newm	6gd	80	4882
75	5-14	Newm	6sft	84	5098
80a	5-9	Ling	6ap	[83]	5237

ELHEBA 4 b g £0
42a	8-10	Ling	12ap	[55]	24 bl

ELIDORE 4 b f £2573
64	13-19	Leic	6g/s	78	1354
66	5-7	Chep	7.1gd	[74]	3402
52	14-20	Hayd	6fm	69	3796 VIS
71	2-15	Chep	8.1sft	64	4057
66	4-15	Chep	8.1g/s	69	4300
68	5-17	Warw	8.1g/s	68	4668
68	6-17	Leic	10gd	66	5062
22	14-17	Newb	9sft	66	5198
63	5-8	Nott	8.2hvy	[63]	5346
66a	4-13	Wolv	8.6ap	63	5364

ELISHA 2 ch f £8198
75	4-15	Wind	5gd		1380
71	5-10	Thir	5g/f		1764
71	1-11	GOOD	5gd		2020*
53	10-10	Ches	5.1g/s		2744
68	6-12	Ling	5gd	73	3284
58	6-9	Good	7fm	69	3624
71	2-14	Epso	6g/f	67	4471
74	2-9	Brig	6fm	68	4758

ELITISTA 2 gr f £0
44a	5-13	Wolv	8.5af	[58]	43
5	12-14	Warw	8.1sft	52	1529

ELIZABETHAN AGE 2 b f £4771
82	2-7	Newm	7g/f	3616
88	2-16	Sali	7gd	4330
78	12-14	Newm	7gd	4914

ELIZABETHS CHOICE 2 b f £0
52	8-10	Newm	7fm	2594
42	10-13	Kemp	6gd	3183

ELLA FALLS 8 b m £0
17a	7-12	Wolv	16.2af	36	156

ELLAMYTE 3 b f £0
26a	8-9	Wolv	7af	53	31 vis
7a	12-13	Ling	6ap	48	448 vis
22a	7-9	Wolv	9.4af	[45]	522
24a	9-10	Ling	5ap	[40]	653 T
14a	5-8	Wolv	7ap	[35]	1676
16	15-18	Nott	8.2gd	[45]	1992

ELLAS WISH 3 ch f £0
3a	13-15	Ling	12ap	[60]	118 BL

ELLE NINO 2 b f £0
72a	7-14	Ling	7ap	5258

ELLE ROYAL 5 br m £0
29a	11-14	Ling	10ap	[45]	828
12a	12-13	Ling	13ap	[40]	1076
11a	6-6	Sout	11af	[35]	1409 BL

ELLEN MOONEY 4 ch f £2112
71a	2-9	Sout	8af	69	163 p
71a	2-7	Sout	8af	70	332 p
71a	3-8	Sout	8af	70	489 p
65a	4-8	Sout	8af	70	597
47a	10-10	Ling	12ap	70	936
30	9-14	Hayd	8.1g/s	64	1348
35	13-15	Hami	8.3g/s	61	1602 BL
44	8-9	Ayr	7.2fm	[57]	1910 bl

ELLENARE 2 ch f £0
33	9-9	Pont	5sft	1424
10a	9-11	Wolv	6af	2051

ELLENS ACADEMY 9 b g £35372
79a	4-11	Sout	6af	80	386
74a	6-13	Wolv	6af	79	482
79a	3-10	Sout	6af	[79]	532
73a	4-10	Sout	7af	79	611
81	2-30	Newm	6g/f	78	1481
79	4-19	Thir	6g/f	80	1767
77	4-8	Donc	6g/f	[80]	2074
87	2-18	Newc	6g/s	79	2770
90	2-10	York	6gd	83	3116
89	3-15	York	6gd	86	3434
87	5-11	Hayd	6gd	[86]	3758
84	6-13	York	6gd	86	4322
45	21-26	Ayr	6g/s	86	4652
89	2-14	Ripo	6gd	84	4786
74	13-14	Newm	6sft	[86]	5100

ELLENS LAD 9 b g £2079
45a	11-12	Wolv	5af	[78]	70 bl
73a	1-11	WOLV	6af	[70]	153* bl
67a	7-11	Sout	6af	73	418 bl
58a	5-13	Sout	6af	72	551 bl
51a	9-13	Wolv	6af	70	687 bl
58	11-17	Kemp	5sft	72	944

ELLENS PRINCESS 2 b f £398
75	5-13	Good	7fm		3554
69	4-12	Folk	7gd		3908
65	7-15	Kemp	6gd		4357
29	12-13	Leic	6gd	72	4697
43	16-16	Good	7gd	65	5031

ELLERSLIE TOM 2 br g £0
60	9-11	York	7.9gd	5003
36	5-5	Nott	8.2hvy	5186

ELLIEBOW 2 br f £0
57	11-12	Redc	6g/f	2119
21	15-20	Hayd	6gd	2882
1	9-9	Ripo	6gd	4277

ELLINA 3 b f £5456
59	10-18	Wind	8.3g/s		1258
68	4-20	Wind	10sft		1651
66	6-12	Sand	10gd	67	2366
55	4-5	Brig	11.9g/f	66	2642
61	7-11	Ling	11.5g/f	66	2842
69	1-10	LING	11.5gd	63	3334*
51	10-17	Newm	12ap	67	3618
29	13-16	Yarm	11.5g/s	65	4589
65	3-20	Catt	12gd	63	4966
56a	5-16	Ling	12ap	[60]	5296

ELLIOTS CHOICE 3 b c £3739
71	4-13	Thir	5sft	71	1229
68	4-9	Hayd	5g/s	71	1344
52	11-13	Hami	5g/f	70	2320
65	7-12	Thir	5g/s	68	2690
68	4-13	Wind	5fm	68	2784
59	3-9	Beve	5sft	[66]	2945
62	6-11	Ripo	6gd	66	2985
32a	8-8	Sout	6af	66	3092
31	11-11	York	7g/f	66	3433
50	12-15	Thir	5g/s	63	3833
39	15-18	Beve	5g/s	63	3852
59	2-4	Ripo	5g/s	[63]	3936 VIS
25	4-5	Yarm	6sft	[60]	4150 BL
42	14-19	Beve	5g/s	60	4240 bl
53	5-20	Ripo	6gd	60	4278 bl
37	14-19	Leic	7g/f	56	4452 bl
48	8-19	Ling	5g/f	53	4739
40	6-13	Warw	7.1g/s	[50]	4994
29a	11-12	Wolv	7.1ap	[48]	5233

ELLIOTS WORLD 2 b c £26505
101 1-8 YORK 7g/s 3078*
106 1-7 YORK 7gd 4003*
100 6-10 Donc 7fm 4493
104 4-8 Asco 8g/f 4797
60 7-8 Donc 8sft [100] 5216

ELLIS CAVE 2 gr g £311
51 7-16 Ripo 6g/f 1780
30 12-13 Donc 6gd 2236
55a 4-10 Sout 7af 2802 VIS
51a 7-9 Sout 6af 3157
15a 10-11 Sout 6af 55 3393 vis

ELLOVAMUL 4 b f £5897
54 4-8 Hami 9.2g/f 52 2475
45 8-13 Yarm 11.5fm 52 2868
54 4-7 Muss 12gd 52 2966
47 8-11 Yarm 11.5gd 50 3367
57 1-13 YARM 10.1gd 50 3492+
43a 8-14 Ling 10ap 53 3605
31 7-8 Brig 11.9sft 53 4143
43 11-19 Leic 10g/f 51 4456
45 10-19 Beve 9.9g/f 51 4720
11 13-18 Pont 12g/f 50 4938
55 1-15 YARM 10.1g/s [46] 5122* bl
42a 7-13 Wolv 9.5ap [50] 5338

ELLWAY HEIGHTS 7 b g £2978
53 2-10 Hami 13g/f 51 2479
56 2-10 Muss 12g/f 53 2813
55 2-12 Muss 16gd 51 2964
53 5-7 Hami 13gd 53 3134
52 3-7 Muss 13gd 53 3530
50 8-17 Kemp 12sft 53 4033
52 6-15 Ches 15.9g/f 51 4512
24 7-11 Beve 12.1g/f [51] 4716
15 12-18 Pont 12g/f 51 4938

ELLWAY PROSPECT 4 ch f £0
53a 4-13 Wolv 16.5ap 52 5366

ELMS SCHOOLBOY 2 ch c £0
50 9-9 Sand 5gd 4497
52 11-15 Nott 5.1gd 4859
31a 11-13 Wolv 6ap 5182
59 8-10 Newm 6sft 5266

ELMUSTANSER 3 b c £14924
88 2-16 Sand 10g/s 2131 T
87 1-7 NEWM 10g/f 2534* t
98 2-6 Newm 10g/f 95 3749 t
100 2-13 Kemp 12g/f [95] 4715 t
8 16-19 Newm 12gd 98 5085 t

ELOQUENT KNIGHT 2 b c £0
63 8-18 Newm 8fm 4722
58 7-15 Newb 8hvy 5221

ELRAFA MUJAHID 2 b f £2091
72a 3-11 Ling 8ap 3786
74 7-18 Nott 8.2g/s 4035
69a 1-14 LING 7ap 4658*

ELSHADI 3 b c £34450
71 13-14 Epso 12fm [96] 2254 VIS
105 2-5 Asco 12g/f [96] 2554 bl
96 6-7 Newb 10g/f [104] 3264 bl
102 2-6 Wolv 10g/f [100] 3754 bl

ELSIE HART 2 b f £5409
75 1-6 NEWC 5sft 1274*
92 3-6 York 6sft 1669
72 14-15 Asco 5g/f 2472

ELSIE WAGG 2 b f £1057
66 3-11 Good 5gd 2020
74 4-7 Leic 5gd 2132
67 5-11 Ripo 5g/s 3258
65 6-9 Ches 6.1fm 71 3632
15 7-8 Good 6g/f 70 4536

ELSINORA 3 b f £5540
49a 11-12 Ling 8ap 60 798
50 9-10 Brig 7g/f 57 1941
35 10-14 Wind 10gd 53 2617 VIS
47 2-8 Carl 7.9gd [50] 2932 P
36 6-14 Leic 8g/f [45] 3344 p
46 3-15 Leic 7g/f [43] 3515 BL

36 5-9 Brig 7sft [42] 4164
46 2-16 Folk 6g/f [45] 4370 bl
44 4-15 Yarm 7g/s [45] 4587 bl
49 2-17 Kemp 7g/f [45] 4794 bl
47 1-16 BRIG 7gd [45] 4901* vis
48 3-17 Warw 8.1g/s [45] 4992 vis
49 1-20 YARM 7g/f [45] 5120* vis
39a 7-12 Wolv 7.1ap [49] 5233 vis

ELSUNDUS 6 b g £0
15 6-6 Hami 8.3g/f [85] 3205

ELTIHAAB 3 b f £1120
46 9-11 Hayd 8.1gd 2885
60 3-9 Thir 7fm 3610
52 4-8 Yarm 6gd 3873 T

ELTIZAAM 2 b c £711
76 6-12 Newm 7g/f 3470
71a 5-11 Ling 8ap 3786
80 6-11 Epso 7gd 4289
78 3-9 Warw 7.1g/s 76 4666
76 5-17 Ling 7g/f 75 4894
69 11-14 Catt 7sft 74 5126

ELUSIVE DOUBLE 2 ch c £29414
106 1-7 LEOP 7g/f 3494*
106 3-5 Curr 7g/f 4154
97 6-7 Curr 7gd 4734

ELUSIVE DREAM 2 b c £45597
57a 7-10 Wolv 7af 36
62a 8-12 Ling 10ap 120
74a 1-10 SOUT 12af 61 2998*
86 1-10 FOLK 7g/s 67 3051*
87 1-7 BRIG 11.9g/f [61] 3173+
79 1-10 HAMI 13fm 67 3249*
89 3-13 York 13.9g/s 81 4062
96 1-8 AYR 13.1sft 81 4690*
92 2-14 Asco 12g/f 85 4814

ELUSIVE KITTY 2 b f £2153
69a 5-6 Ling 6ap 79
66a 5-11 Ling 7ap 70 261
64a 6-9 Ling 10ap 69 365
0 R-9 Thir 7fm [69] 3610 t
69 3-11 Wind 8.3fm 69 3799 t
58 3-10 Hami 9.2g/s [69] 4135 t
59 5-10 Sali 8sft [68] 4578
67 3-8 Brig 8fm [68] 4762 t
65 5-7 Epso 10.1gd [66] 4911 t
49 6-13 Bath 10.2sft [66] 5173
25a 12-12 Wolv 12.2ap 62 5339 BL

ELVINA 2 b f £5369
48a 4-8 Sout 5af 197
64 1-9 KEMP 5g/f 3687*
24 15-19 Wind 6g/f 57 5053

ELVINA HILLS 2 ch f £0
12 9-9 Warw 5sft 1084
61 7-12 Warw 5sft 1524
66 5-8 Good 6gd 2537
61 6-13 Epso 7gd 2870
62a 10-13 Ling 7ap 3329

ELVINGTON BOY 7 ch g £0
2 U-20 Thir 5g/f 74 1765

ELZEES 3 b c £0
54a 9-12 Ling 8ap 428
23 8-10 Good 9.9gd 4877

EMARADIA 2 ch f £10636
53a 3-13 Wolv 6af 54 1
54a 4-13 Ling 6ap [54] 25
51a 5-10 Wolv 5af 54 69
45a 4-10 Sout 5af [54] 139
47a 2-12 Sout 6af [52] 200
50a 2-9 Wolv 5af [52] 247 bl
50a 3-9 Ling 5ap [48] 405 bl
56a 1-11 WOLV 6af [48] 466* bl
57a 2-9 Wolv 7af 54 510 bl
48a 8-12 Wolv 7af [54] 560 bl
61a 1-7 WOLV 5af [54] 703* bl
61a 2-13 Sout 6af 60 797 bl
62a 2-9 Wolv 5af [60] 835 bl
51a 6-11 Wolv 5af 60 958 bl
39 6-7 Brig 6fm 54 3693

44 8-11 Bath 5g/f 54 3849
57a 3-11 Sout 6af [60] 4041
28 9-12 Brig 5.3g/s 47 4140
45 4-17 Kemp 7g/f [45] 4794
40a 9-12 Wolv 7.1ap 57 5112
57a 3-11 Wolv 7.1ap [57] 5178 bl
37a 7-12 Wolv 7.1ap [53] 5358 vis

EMARATIS IMAGE 6 b g £0
0 12-13 Ling 10ap [45] 412
35a 6-15 Ling 7ap [40] 708
41a 4-13 Ling 6ap [40] 788
32a 6-10 Ling 5ap [40] 832
27a 4-12 Sout 6af [40] 982
33a 6-7 Wolv 5af [40] 1562

EMBASSY LORD 2 b g £1053
57a 7-13 Wolv 6af 60 1 bl
78 4-15 Ches 5.1g/s 67 1572 bl
71 8-9 Hayd 6g/f [80] 1918 bl
68 9-16 Leic 5g/f 80 2400 bl

EMBASSY SWEETS 2 b f £413
48a 10-11 Ling 6ap 135
56a 11-12 Ling 8ap 175
56 4-8 Epso 8.5hvy 1297
0 11-11 Bath 13.1g/f 57 4415
34a 13-16 Ling 12ap [55] 4899

EMBER DAYS 4 grf £10245
54a 5-11 Ling 8ap 57 12
49a 5-13 Ling 10ap 54 104
55a 2-13 Ling 10ap 52 178
54a 2-13 Ling 10ap 52 215
54a 5-14 Ling 10ap 55 339
28 17-20 Warw 10.9gd 64 1128 BL
60 3-13 Bath 8sft 62 1542 P
55 10-12 Bath 8g/f 61 1792 p
64 2-15 Kemp 9gd 59 2170 p
64 3-9 Yarm 10.1fm 59 2866 p
66 1-7 BATH 10.2g/f 59 2979* p
67 3-14 Folk 9.7g/s 65 3052 p
62 2-17 Newm 10g/f 65 3238 p
62 4-11 Bath 10.2g/f 65 3373 p
15 17-17 Wind 10fm 67 3477 p

EMBOSSED 2 b c £22805
75 6-15 Wind 6gd 3163
101 1-15 SAND 7.1g/f 3337*
94 6-10 Asco 7gd 3774
106 2-8 Sand 7.1g/s [98] 4096
106 2-5 Donc 7fm [100] 4461
105 2-9 Newm 8sft [100] 5099
82 10-13 Newb 7sft [100] 5195

EMERALD BAY 2 b c £420
71 4-7 Ayr 6g/f 3761

EMERALD DANCER 2 b f £0
34 13-15 Sali 6gd 4851

EMERALD DESTINY 2 b g £0
62 5-6 Hayd 8.1sft 4783
40 14-15 Pont 10g/f 4933
10 12-12 Newc 7g/f 5011

EMERALD FIRE 4 b f £1112
43a 11-12 Ling 6ap [77] 106 VIS
68a 5-14 Ling 6ap 73 149 vis
63a 6-14 Ling 6ap 70 407 vis
62a 10-13 Ling 7ap 69 474
49 11-13 Sali 6g/s 66 3109
54 8-17 Wind 6gd 63 4126
53 5-16 Sali 7sft 60 4582
65 2-18 Leic 6gd 57 5039

EMERALD LODGE 2 b c £10424
67 3-5 Yarm 5.2gd 3993
67 5-11 Hayd 5g/f 4349
86a 1-12 LING 6ap 4896* VIS
89a 1-8 LING 6ap [79] 5081* vis

EMERALD PENANG 2 b c £4622
41 5-5 Leic 5g/s 1014
77 4-7 Yarm 6fm 2144
78 1-13 EPSO 7g/f 2870*
66 7-9 Good 7fm 78 3624
58 10-13 Newm 8gd 77 4193
54 10-13 Wind 8.3g/f 75 5051

EMERAUDE DU CAP 2 b f £523
35	17-18	Wind	6gd		2618	
48	10-17	Nott	6.1gd		2927	
53	3-10	Beve	5g/f		3504	
37	8-9	Yarm	6sft	51	4146	

EMILE ZOLA 2 b c £6022
| 87 | 1-12 | GOOD | 8g/f | | 4522* | |
| 70 | 5-5 | Epso | 8.5gd | | 4906 | |

EMILYS DAWN 2 b f £0
55a	6-11	Ling	6ap		51	
13a	13-15	Sout	7af	[57]	184	
48a	7-15	Ling	7ap	55	295	
2a	11-11	Ling	8ap	[51]	496	

EMINENCE GIFT 2 b f £0
| 23 | 12-12 | Hami | 6gd | | 2178 | |
| 12 | 14-17 | Donc | 6g/f | | 2424 | |

EMINENT AURA 3 ch f £0
| 0 | 9-9 | Sout | 7af | | 871 | VIS |

EMMAS VENTURE 2 b f £1361
59	5-9	Donc	5gd		929	
57	2-10	Thir	5sft		1224	
41	6-7	Newc	5sft		1394	
46	4-11	Beve	5g/f		1831	
30	8-11	Thir	6gd		1968	
41a	4-10	Sout	5af	[49]	4129	

EMMERVALE 5 b m £0
52	5-20	Yarm	6g/f	50	1730	vis
31	9-16	Brig	6fm	50	2262	vis
0	11-13	Yarm	6g/f	50	2347	vis
30a	9-14	Ling	7ap	45	3746	vis

EMPANGENI 2 b g £0
55	11-13	Warw	7.1g/s		4664	
66	5-13	Brig	8sft		5091	
59a	10-12	Ling	8ap		5293	

EMPEROR CAT 3 b g £1201
58a	2-10	Sout	6af	58	592	
56a	3-9	Sout	7af	[58]	661	
4a	12-13	Sout	6af	56	797	
15a	8-10	Sout	6af	[54]	851	VIS
15	13-16	Bath	8fm	[54]	2032	bl
32	11-17	Leic	7gd	[50]	2704	bl
37a	6-13	Sout	7af	48	3155	
35	6-14	Folk	6gd	45	4116	
0	16-16	Chep	7.1hvy	[45]	4707	

EMPERORS WELL 5 ch g £7800
47	12-19	Beve	9.9g/f	57	3505	bl
57	3-19	Brig	9.9sft	55	4145	bl
65	1-15	BEVE	8.5g/f	55	4598*	bl
70	1-19	BEVE	9.9g/f	61	4720+	bl

EMPIRES GHODHA 2 b c £11623
79	5-10	Sali	5g/f		1716	
86	3-8	Good	5g/f		1816	
84	2-8	Wind	5g/f		1955	
84	3-18	Leic	5fm		2109	BL
90	1-7	BATH	5fm		2415*	bl
89	5-9	Asco	5g/f		2516	bl
84	3-5	Sand	5g/s		2895	bl
89	4-10	York	5gd	88	3115	bl
84	6-9	Good	6fm	88	3623	
79	8-13	Newm	5g/f	87	3943	bl
84	8-18	Wind	5g/f	84	4830	bl
72	6-14	Newm	6sft	82	5098	bl

EMPIRICAL POWER 3 b c £323
| 88 | 6-16 | Newm | 7sft | 95 | 5101 | |

EMPRESS EUGENIE 3 b f £330
76	4-18	Wind	8.3g/s		1258	
47	6-6	Pont	10sft		1428	
35	5-7	Newc	10.1gd		1871	

EMPRESS JOSEPHINE 3 b f £4926
50a	2-12	Wolv	6af	[55]	33	vis
51a	4-15	Sout	5af	54	187	vis
59a	1-11	WOLV	6g/f	53	507*	vis
60a	2-12	Wolv	5af	56	641	vis
45a	5-10	Wolv	5af	56	749	vis
59a	3-12	Sout	5af	60	1442	vis

| 41 | 14-15 | Ling | 5g/f | 56 | 2062 | vis |
| 28 | 11-12 | Ling | 5g/f | 53 | 2743 | vis |

EMSAM BALLOU 3 ch f £2208
68a	3-15	Ling	7ap		814	
68a	3-12	Ling	8ap		881	
63	3-9	Kemp	6sft		946	
36	9-10	Yarm	7g/s	66	4251	
10	18-18	Leic	6ap	64	5039	
35a	13-14	Ling	7ap	[60]	5263	

EMTILAAK 3 b g £8574
81a	2-11	Ling	7ap	[79]	1008	
72	3-9	Ripo	8gd	[79]	1178	
79	1-7	PONT	6g/f	[78]	2042*	
44	9-9	Folk	6g/f	78	2271	
59a	9-11	Ling	6ap	78	2841	
76	4-9	Epso	6fm	76	3543	
76a	4-11	Ling	6ap	76	3744	

ENAMOURED 2 b f £0
| 64 | 5-11 | Donc | 8sft | | 5205 | |
| 53 | 7-15 | Nott | 8.2hvy | | 5344 | |

ENBORNE AGAIN 2 ch c £0
57	7-10	Redc	6gd		4244	
23	14-18	Ayr	6g/s		4617	
44	11-14	Newc	6fm		4865	

ENCANTO 2 ch f £25531
54	11-19	Wind	5g/f		1805	
53	6-18	Chep	6.1gd		2194	
74	2-7	Bath	5fm		2415	
89	2-13	Curr	6.3gd		2815	
75	2-6	Epso	6g/s		3041	
85	1-10	NOTT	6.1g/f		3418*	
84	4-11	Newm	6g/f	83	3614	
80	5-12	Wind	6gd	83	3825	
66	3-10	Nott	6.1gd	[82]	4858	

ENCHANTED 5 b m £24462
99	1-15	RIPO	6g/f	88	1782*	
97	1-7	ASCO	7g/f	[88]	1925*	
92	7-11	Newm	7fm	95	2090	
0	7-9	Cork	6fm	[95]	2457	
95	7-12	Good	7fm	[94]	3564	
85	7-8	Newm	6gd	[94]	4226	
99	4-15	Donc	7fm	[92]	4479	
75	8-11	Hami	5sft	[92]	4693	
27	15-15	Newm	6gd	[94]	5088	

ENCHANTED OCEAN 5 b m £0
40	13-17	Leic	10g/s		1019	
50	11-11	Sali	12fm	60	2293	
13	8-8	Newb	12g/f	55	3270	
34	7-12	Sali	12g/f	53	3868	
30	12-14	Bath	13.1g/s	49	4203	

ENCHANTED PRINCESS 4 b f £7643
0	15-18	Wind	8.3g/s	72	1059	
65	5-13	Bath	8sft	70	1542	VIS
77	1-20	ASCO	8g/f	67	1927*	BL
78	6-7	Pont	8g/f	[74]	2278	bl
42	7-10	Newm	8g/f	74	2767	bl

ENCHANTMENT 3 b f £41483
69	5-11	Sali	6g/s	81	1498	
81	2-15	Ripo	6g/f	79	1782	
92	1-8	BATH	5fm	[79]	1901+	
99	1-11	REDC	5g/f	85	2121+	
97	2-6	Sand	5g/f	[85]	2390	
93	4-10	Ches	5.1g/f	92	3080	
103	1-14	YORK	5g/s	92	4027+	
101	4-11	Beve	5g/s	[92]	4238	
87	4-9	Donc	6gd	[101]	4481	
93	4-11	Hami	5sft	[100]	4693	

ENCOMPASS 3 b f £858
55	9-12	Sand	10g/f		2193	
68	3-9	Pont	12g/f		2992	
67	6-14	Ling	11.5gd		3335	

ENCORA BAY 3 b f £660
61	6-11	Sali	7gd		3884	
67	3-14	Warw	7.1gd		4275	
47	10-15	Ling	7gd		4445	

ENCORE ROYALE 4 b f £0
| 38a | 7-12 | Wolv | 8.5af | 50 | 1379 | |

ENCOUNTER 8 br g £2985
46	5-8	Folk	9.7sft	50	1579	
29a	6-12	Wolv	9.4af	47	2054	
0	12-12	Wolv	7af	47	2204	BL
23	11-14	Leic	8g/f	47	2402	
26	11-19	Beve	9.9g/s	49	1164	
37	7-15	Hami	9.2gd	46	1388	
48	3-19	Redc	8sft	45	1661	
43	5-14	Carl	7.9fm	47	1954	
44	6-10	Newc	8g/f	47	2159	
40	8-14	Leic	8g/f	47	2402	
44	8-16	Redc	8g/s	46	2958	
46	2-8	Hami	9.2fm	46	3250	
47	5-9	Hami	9.2g/f	45	3593	
39	9-17	Hayd	8.1gd	45	3759	
36	8-17	Hami	9.2g/s	45	4008	
40	5-9	Redc	10gd	45	4248	
47	3-17	Pont	8g/f	45	4626	
34	5-13	Brig	8gd	[45]	4902	
47	2-16	Warw	8.1g/s	[45]	4993	
19	14-19	Yarm	8g/s	[45]	5119	
44	3-13	Ayr	8sft	[45]	5275	

ENCOURAGEMENT 2 b f £2026
43	8-11	Nott	5.1g/f		2151	
79	3-14	Newb	6fm		3626	
43	10-11	Bath	5g/s		4200	
74	4-9	Sand	5g/f	[75]	4497	
77	3-13	Newm	6fm	[75]	4726	
73	7-13	Good	6g/f	[75]	4918	

END OF AN ERROR 5 b m £0
| 7 | 9-12 | Muss | 16gd | 31 | 2964 | |

ENDLESS SUMMER 6 b g £18435
80	3-22	Donc	6gd	78	921	
74	5-10	Wind	6gd	[80]	1383	
72	5-10	Thir	7g/f	[80]	1970	T
68	10-20	York	6g/f	80	2059	
75	4-8	Sand	5gd	[78]	2361	
72	6-9	Warw	5.5fm	74	2779	
71	9-12	Newm	5g/f	73	3279	
79	2-12	Ches	5.1sft	73	4107	
87	1-16	LEIC	5gd	76	4700+	
93	1-19	GOOD	6gd	82	4747*	
81	7-19	Sali	6gd	82	4855	

ENFORCER 2 b c £8815
82	4-13	Wind	6fm		3478	
77	5-18	Wind	6gd		3824	
83	2-18	Ling	6gd		4108	
71	8-17	York	7gd	78	4396	
88	1-16	GOOD	7gd	78	5031*	
61	10-14	Newb	7sft	83	5193	

ENFORD PRINCESS 3 b f £3513
85	4-11	Sali	6g/s	90	1498	
77	9-13	Newm	8g/f	88	3277	
84	3-5	Sali	8gd	85	3885	
83	4-8	Good	7sft	84	4263	
82	7-14	Sali	7gd	84	4331	
83	4-13	Sand	8.1gd	82	4607	
77	6-12	Good	8gd	[82]	4872	
77	7-11	Good	8gd	80	5027	

ENGLISH FELLOW 2 b c £1149
79	3-11	Nott	6.1sft		1739	
76	4-13	Carl	5fm		1950	
76	4-14	Redc	6fm		2297	
13	14-14	Leic	6g/f	79	3212	
59	7-14	Hayd	6gd	[76]	3735	
13	17-17	York	7g/f	70	4396	
35	16-19	Pont	8g/s	65	5147	

ENGLISH ROCKET 3 b g £0
| 39 | 9-9 | Wind | 10g/s | 73 | 4943 | |
| 3 | 13-15 | Nott | 8.2hvy | 70 | 5191 | |

ENHANCER 6 b g £851
72	7-16	Sand	10g/s		2131	
71	7-14	Ling	11.5gd		3335	
75	3-10	Yarm	11.5gd		3997	
73	5-13	Good	16g/f	73	4527	
79	6-19	Newm	12gd	70	5085	

ENJOY THE BUZZ 4 b c £12327
| 30a | 9-13 | Wolv | 5af | 45 | 110 | |

36a	4-11	Wolv	6af	[42]	296
36a	4-13	Wolv	5af	[45]	312
18a	11-13	Wolv	6af	40	384
42a	2-16	Sout	6af	[40]	447
41a	3-12	Wolv	7af	[40]	528
47a	1-13	WOLV	6af	[40]	582+
47a	2-10	Wolv	6af	40	667
40a	4-15	Sout	6af	[45]	773
47a	2-10	Wolv	6af	[45]	822
12	17-18	Ling	6gd	45	2396
53	1-14	LING	5g/f	43	2585*
23a	9-16	Sout	6af	45	2806
53	2-17	Bath	5g/f	47	2981
54	1-5	FOLK	5g/s	47	3050*
47	7-14	Ling	6gd	51	3289
54	3-16	Ling	6gd	50	3602
55	2-15	Ling	6fm	50	3790
50	5-13	Warw	6.1gd	52	4272
51	5-20	Chep	6.1g/s	52	4368
31	9-19	Yarm	5g/f	51	4636
50	6-19	Ling	5g/f	51	4739

ENNA 5 ch m £2688

41	4-12	Sout	7gd	[51]	1284
42	6-13	Leic	10fm	[51]	2107
31a	9-16	Sout	7af	51	2335
41	8-17	Warw	8.1g/f	51	2909
47	4-17	Chep	8.1g/s	51	3087
36	12-17	Brig	7g/f	48	3176
45a	4-13	Ling	10ap	[45]	3288
48	2-15	Ling	7.6fm	45	3788
35	9-14	Bath	8g/f	45	3963
34	6-15	Chep	8.1sft	45	4057
30	7-9	Brig	7sft	[45]	4164
45	4-13	Warw	10.9g/f	45	4419
38a	3-12	Ling	8ap	[40]	4659
51	1-18	KEMP	10g/f	[45]	4791*

ENRAPTURE 3 b f £6881

78	1-10	NEWB	7gd		3921*
82	3-8	Good	7sft	79	4263
57	18-25	Newb	7gd	79	4683

ENSEMBLE 4 b g £2506

0	19-20	Catt	15.8gd	40	4965
55	1-6	YARM	14.1sft	[40]	5249*
32a	9-13	Wolv	16.5ap	50	5366

ENTAILMENT 2 b g £7319

56	8-18	Pont	5g/s		3968
80	1-16	THIR	6gd		4205*
66	8-14	Donc	7sft	76	5213

ENTERTAIN 2 b f £0

67	12-16	Kemp	7g/f		3035
39	13-15	Folk	7gd		3381

ENTERTAINING 2 b f £1462

42	6-8	Pont	6g/f		2603
70	5-12	Folk	7gd		3908
73	2-13	Nott	6.1g/f		4843
65	5-13	Wind	6g/f	[70]	5048

ENTUSIASMO 3 ch f £3873

77	2-5	San	12g/f		2301

ENVIRONMENT AUDIT 5 ch g £0

53a	7-9	Sout	11af	75	391	
32a	10-12	Sout	11af	69	534	
56	7-9	Folk	12sft	70	979	
53	12-19	Newm	12g/f	65	1484	VIS
50	11-12	Wind	10g/f	[65]	2800	vis
39	7-8	Ling	11.5g/s	[60]	4181	vis

ENVIRONMENTALIST 5 b h £0

24	11-13	Muss	7.1g/f	[58]	1119	t
21	11-15	Hami	6gd	50	1508	t
15	13-18	Ayr	7.2g/f	45	1897	t
25	8-10	Muss	9g/f	[40]	2811	BL t
17	9-11	Muss	8g/f	[40]	3558	t
2	12-12	Ayr	9.1g/f	30	3766	bl t

EPALO 5 b h £581709

120	11-13	KRAN	9gd		1859*
112	2-7	Colo	11gd		3663
113	3-13	Arli	10fm		4014

EPAMINONDAS 3 ch c £1685

49	7-17	Asco	6sft	75	1417

42	17-20	Newb	7g/f	73	2314
44	12-13	Newm	7fm	70	2590
66	2-11	Leic	10g/f	[66]	2924
60	8-10	Asco	8gd	[66]	3067
68	4-8	Asco	10g/f	66	3391
48	7-11	Wind	10gd	[65]	4124

EPHESUS 4 b c £15815

86a	3-10	Wolv	8.5af	[85]	511	vis
60a	7-10	Sout	7af	85	611	vis
59a	7-12	Wolv	8.5af	85	688	vis
47a	9-10	Wolv	12af	82	810	p
61	9-15	Warw	8.1sft	79	1530	vis
79	6-19	Sali	7g/f	79	1723	vis
83	1-18	GOOD	8g/f	76	1849*	vis
76	4-7	Good	7gd	78	2223	vis
81	2-8	Sand	7.1g/f	78	2389	vis
82	2-9	Good	8gd	78	2540	vis
68	18-20	Newm	8fm	81	3001	vis
68a	10-12	Ling	8ap	[81]	3199	vis
68	12-19	Good	8g/f	80	3512	vis
78	3-12	Leic	8fm	78	3813	vis
52	6-7	Ripo	8gd	[78]	4304	vis
66	3-11	Leic	10gd	[76]	4701	vis

EPIPHANY 2 br f £7120

88	2-8	Asco	6g/f		3386	
78	1-7	AYR	6g/f		3761*	
78	7-13	Leic	6gd	84	4697	
80	8-17	Catt	7gd	82	4963	T

EPITOMISE 2 b f £320

70	6-11	Ling	5gd		2395	
69	4-8	Catt	5g/f		2847	
46	10-10	Wind	6fm		3290	
27	6-7	Kemp	6g/f	69	3686	
50	10-14	Warw	6.1g/f	65	4420	T

EQDAAM 2 b c £7483

85	3-14	Newm	7g/f		2766
85	3-10	Donc	7gd		3594
86	1-19	LEIC	7gd		5055*

EQUUS 3 b g £0

25a	8-12	Wolv	12af	65	2203
0	10-13	Sout	14af	62	2494

ERMINE GREY 2 gr g £3903

80a	1-11	WOLV	7af	75	29*	vis
68a	6-10	Wolv	7af	81	112	vis
76	8-18	Leic	10g/s	75	1017	bl
63	7-16	Leic	8g/s	73	1359	bl
74	3-17	Hayd	8.1gd	70	2243	vis
83a	4-8	Sout	7af	81	2723	vis
73	4-6	Newm	8g/f	71	3472	vis

ERRACHT 5 gr m £3774

55a	3-12	Wolv	5af	54	124
27a	8-8	Wolv	5af	54	274
32a	7-12	Wolv	5af	54	641
41a	5-11	Wolv	5af	54	748
68	1-15	BRIG	5.3g/f	60	1371+
54	6-20	Thir	5g/f	65	1765
48	16-18	Good	5g/f	65	1867
56	11-15	Ling	5g/f	64	2062
42	7-13	Bath	5gd	[63]	3143
49a	5-10	Ling	5ap	51	3332
52	8-16	Wind	5fm	61	3640
48	10-13	Brig	5.3g/f	60	3984
8	16-16	Pont	5fm	60	4754

ERROL 5 ch g £0

0	9-10	Sout	16af	[30]	984

ERSAAL 3 ch g £2117

53a	3-11	Wolv	12af	55	72	
37a	9-14	Sout	8af	54	160	
17a	11-15	Sout	11af	54	196	
17a	10-15	Sout	12af	52	257	BL
18a	10-14	Ling	10ap	48	757	
36a	3-12	Wolv	12af	[45]	891	bl
13a	11-11	Ling	10ap	[45]	970	bl
43a	1-8	WOLV	12af	[40]	1265*	T
45a	3-5	Ling	12ap	[40]	1411	t
0	10-10	Kemp	12hvy	[45]	1645	t P
7	15-16	Folk	12fm	42	2718	t

ERSHAAD 3 b c £26381

110	3-8	Chan	9g/s		2307
110	2-6	Chan	9gd		3657

ERTE 3 ch g £1335

18	13-16	Leic	8g/s	64	1359
43	6-10	Leic	8gd	[62]	2133
42	6-7	Brig	9.9fm	[62]	2332
45	3-8	Redc	10gd	[58]	2548
57a	2-15	Ling	12ap	48	2741
19	11-12	Brig	9.9g/f	51	3300
42	7-10	Beve	12.1g/f	51	3499

ERUPT 11 b g £1128

22a	5-8	Wolv	9.4af	[35]	1561
26	7-10	Redc	11g/f	[45]	1819
37a	3-13	Sout	8af	30	2497
40	9-13	Muss	8gd	[40]	2967
35	8-16	Beve	8.5g/s	[40]	3850
33	4-12	Hami	8.3g/s	[40]	4007
43	3-12	Newc	8sft	[40]	4284
19	9-15	Carl	9.3fm	[45]	4505

ESATTO 4 b g £0

60a	5-13	Wolv	6af	67	45	
52	15-17	Wind	6g/f	75	2451	
46	9-9	Epso	6g/f	72	2871	t

ESCALADE 6 b g £1698

25a	12-14	Ling	10ap	50	236	
23a	9-13	Wolv	9.4af	48	281	
57	4-14	Nott	10g/s	57	1777	p
32	12-16	Redc	10g/f	57	1821	p
52	5-11	Thir	12g/f	57	2217	VIS
48	4-15	Ayr	10.9g/s	55	2545	p
58	3-16	Folk	12fm	55	2718	p
54	4-10	Newb	11g/f	52	2875	p
49	3-9	Beve	12.1gd	52	2892	p
46	5-12	Chep	12.1g/s	55	3085	p
35	6-7	Kemp	12g/f	47	3519	p
39	8-11	Ling	10fm	47	3748	vis

ESCAYOLA 4 b g £22101

78	8-12	Good	14g/f	88	1861	vis
92	2-7	York	13.9g/f	87	2355	vis
82	11-19	Newc	16.1g/s	87	2771	bl
61	16-17	Asco	16.2gd	87	3125	bl
93	2-13	Good	16g/f	85	4527	vis
98	1-16	ASCO	16.2g/f	88	4803*	vis
97	5-34	Newm	18sft	90	5135	vis

ESHAADEH 3 b f £0

45	5-7	Redc	7fm		4561	T
41	8-9	Leic	7gd		5041	t

ESHER COMMON 6 b g £0

0	19-19	Donc	10.3gd	65	924	t

ESKDALE 2 b g £3507

47	8-16	Ripo	6g/f		1780
35	9-10	Pont	5gd		3457
73	3-14	Ches	7sft		4102
69	2-14	Muss	7.1g/f		4171
69	6-8	Newc	7sft	[73]	4283
64	4-6	Muss	8g/f	[67]	4552

ESKIMOS NEST 2 b f £0

66	8-14	Yarm	7gd		4611

ESPADA 7 b g £4080

53a	9-11	Ling	8ap	[81]	145	
59a	2-15	Ling	7ap	[74]	216	
62a	8-16	Ling	7ap	69	323	
58a	7-14	Ling	7ap	[65]	450	
39	7-13	Wind	8.3g/s	[77]	1058	
34	15-18	Wind	8.3gd	65	1385	
44	4-10	Brig	7g/f	[58]	1938	
46	4-16	Bath	8fm	[58]	2032	BL
54	1-17	LING	7gd	48	2397*	bl
52	5-8	Wind	8.3g/f	54	2448	bl
41	9-17	Warw	8.1g/f	52	2909	bl
54	4-13	Kemp	7g/f	52	3034	bl
50	6-9	Epso	7gd	[52]	3215	bl
27	10-11	Kemp	7gd	52	3685	bl
27	13-15	Thir	8fm	[50]	4379	bl
42	10-20	Chep	7.1gd	50	4488	bl

ESPERANCE 3 ch g £1020

49a	7-10	Ling	13ap	61	11
50a	7-13	Ling	10ap	60	104

50a 9-13 Ling 10ap 57 178 P
7a 11-14 Ling 13ap 55 264
22a 11-12 Ling 10ap 51 542
3 13-17 Bath 10.2sft 48 1541
48 5-14 Wind 8.3g/f 45 2799
38 5-8 Epso 10.1g/s 45 3044
38 8-12 Kemp 8g/f 44 3524
40 5-11 Yarm 8g/f 44 3706
53a 5-13 Ling 10ap [48] 4112
48 2-14 Bath 8g/f 45 4411
44 4-14 Redc 10fm 45 4560
47 5-17 Yarm 8g/s [46] 5348 p

ESPERANTO 3 b c £24310
106 2d-8 Long 10.5g/s 1434
108 4-5 Long 10.5g/s 1853

ESQUIRE 2 b c £6240
76 6-13 Kemp 8g/f 4355
92 1-16 NEWB 7g/f 4677*

ESRAR 2 b c £0
58 9-13 Warw 7.1g/s 4664

ESSAY BABY 4 b f £0
41a 4-13 Ling 10ap [45] 412
48a 4-14 Ling 12ap 45 768
20a 13-14 Ling 12ap [45] 827
17a 13-13 Ling 13ap 45 896

ESSEX STAR 3 b f £887
36 10-20 Yarm 6g/f 53 1730
49a 3-16 Sout 7af 50 2335
49a 3-13 Sout 8af 49 3094
39 5-14 Folk 6gd 48 4116

ESTABLISHMENT 7 b g £332
62 11-18 Kemp 16g/s 79 1112
69 8-19 Newm 12g/f 77 1484
73 8-14 Asco 16.2g/f 77 1928
39 10-13 Chep 8gd 75 2198
58 14-29 Asco 20g/f 70 2471
63 8-13 Asco 16.2g/f 67 3387
65 4-7 Good 14sft 65 4267
59 12-13 Good 16g/f 63 4527

ESTEBAN 4 b g £0
4 12-14 Pont 8hvy [57] 1253
53 4-9 Thir 7g/f [54] 2216
22 11-11 Ripo 8gd 52 2986

ESTEPONA 3 ch g £322
71 4-11 Beve 8.5sft 1304
36 10-15 Thir 7g/s 1473
27 12-12 Ripo 8g/f 1978
59 8-17 Hayd 10.5fm 65 4388
52 11-20 Hayd 11.9g/s 63 4771

ESTIHLAL 3 b f £12839
0 7-10 Pont 6hvy 1070
63 4-17 Sali 6g/f 60 1722
69 1-13 CARL 5.9fm [60] 1949*
70 2-8 Good 6gd 64 2375
65 4-11 Sali 6gd 64 2661
79 1-19 LEIC 6g/f 64 2925*
76 4-14 Thir 6g/f 72 3416
78 3-7 Brig 6fm 73 3693
68 5-13 Good 8g/f 73 3952

ESTILO 4 b g £0
0 10-11 Folk 12g/f 30 2273

ESTIMATE 3 b f £6180
55a 4-7 Ling 10ap 64 16 vis
34a 7-10 Wolv 12af [60] 359
23a 9-9 Wolv 12af 60 424 vis
27a 8-8 Sout 8af 55 489 vis
53 1-10 YARM 10.1g/f [62] 1724* vis
41 12-13 Pont 10g/f 62 2038 vis
42 7-8 Kemp 9g/s 57 2680 vis
56 2-14 Pont 8g/f 52 2993 vis
57 2-13 Yarm 10.1gd 52 3492 vis
27a 11-14 Ling 10ap 45 3605 vis
46 4-12 Newb 10gd 53 3916 vis
25 8-10 Beve 9.9sft 53 4260 vis

ESTIMATION 3 b f £5858
66a 3-7 Ling 10ap 68 16
62a 6-14 Sout 8af 68 93

56a 5-9 Sout 8af 67 163
73a 1-11 SOUT 8af 66 255*
69a 3-7 Sout 8af 69 332
58a 6-8 Sout 8af 69 489
66a 3-7 Sout 7af 68 680
57a 5-5 Wolv 8.5af 68 861
53a 12-12 Ling 7ap 67 1024
59 8-14 Yarm 8g/f 68 1131
61a 7-12 Ling 8ap 66 1613
52a 10-11 Ling 8ap 64 2018
49a 7-15 Sout 8af 61 2500

ESTOILLE 3 b f £3340
16 7-7 Pont 8g/f 2042
13 13-14 Donc 5gd 2237
22 8-9 Beve 5sft 2945 T
40 7-9 Thir 7fm 3610 t
29a 6-11 Sout 5af 30 4094 t
23 8-9 Thir 5g/s 30 4217 t
46a 4-13 Wolv 5.1ap [45] 5231 t
52 1-18 YARM 6g/s 40 5354* t

ESTRELLA LEVANTE 3 ch g £209
49a 5-11 Ling 8ap [52] 145 BL e
46a 7-10 Ling 10ap [52] 540 e
49a 5-12 Ling 8ap [52] 571
46a 3-6 Ling 8ap [49] 651
40a 10-11 Ling 8ap 49 732 bl e
40a 6-10 Ling 8ap 49 770 bl e
34a 8-15 Ling 7ap [45] 969 bl e
21 10-10 Brig 8gd 53 2954
22 11-11 Ling 10fm 48 3748
30a 12-13 Ling 10ap [38] 4112 p
65 7-15 Ling 7gd [45] 4445 bl
28a 8-12 Ling 8ap [40] 4659 bl

ESTUARY 9 ch g £0
31a 11-13 Ling 13ap 53 896
6 14-14 Sout 12g/s [45] 1047
0 12-13 Sout 14af 50 2494 BL

ETAAR 2 b c £1304
84 4-11 Newm 7g/f 3234
76 4-11 Beve 7.5g/s 3851
71 4-15 Nott 6.1g/s 4644

ETCHING 4 b f £3748
62 1-10 BATH 11.7gd 58 1399*
34 9-12 Thir 16gd 60 1637
23 16-17 Nott 14.1g/f 60 2156
62 5-9 Redc 14.1fm 60 4559
0 18-20 Bath 17.2gd 60 4824

ETENDARD INDIEN 3 b c £25704
113 1-6 LONG 15gd 4565*

ETERNAL BEAUTY 4 b f £0
8a 6-7 Wolv 5af 348

ETERNAL BLOOM 6 b m £2198
46a 1-12 SOUT 6af [35] 377*
38a 2-10 Wolv 7af [35] 394
13a 13-16 Sout 6af [35] 447
5a 13-14 Sout 6af 45 501 VIS
1a 12-15 Sout 6af [45] 773
41a 3-8 Sout 6af [45] 1201
35a 3-9 Wolv 7af [45] 1266
17a 8-8 Sout 6af [45] 1588
30 9-16 Nott 6.1gd [40] 1989

ETERNAL DANCER 3 b g £0
4a 12-12 Wolv 9.4af 686
0 9-10 Sout 8af [45] 850 BL

ETERNAL SUNSHINE 2 b f £360
0 8-8 Hayd 6g/f 2183
3 10-10 Thir 6fm 2461
33 8-9 Leic 5g/f 2921
34a 3-6 Sout 5af 3093 VIS
0 10-10 Sout 5af [39] 4129 BL

ETERNALLY 2 ch c £3373
4 7-8 Muss 5g/f 1091
63a 3-12 Sout 5af 1439 P
55a 5-11 Sout 5af 1752 p
49 3-6 Brig 6fm 2330 p
54a 1-6 SOUT 5af 3093* p
29 8-8 Donc 5g/f 53 3374 p
29a 9-12 Wolv 5.1ap [57] 4981 VIS

ETESAAL 4 b c £0
86 15-16 Newm 9sft [106] 5139

ETLAALA 2 ch c £66422
94 1-10 NEWB 7g/f 3955*
117 1-10 DONC 7fm 4493*
88 8-9 Newm 7sft [100] 5137

ETMAAM 3 b c £27344
82 1-16 NEWC 7sft 966*
62 5-11 Ripo 8gd 77 1176
87 1-13 BATH 10.2g/f [75] 1791*
90 2-9 Donc 10.3g/f 80 2079
91 1-8 YORK 10.4g/f 84 2406*
98 3-17 Asco 12g/f 91 2519
74 15-16 Good 12fm 94 3534
63 17-21 York 11.9gd 94 3999
86 6-10 York 11.9g/f 92 4324 BL
63 6-8 Nott 10hvy 90 5187

ETOILE RUSSE 2 b c £0
64 7-13 York 6g/f 3431

ETON 8 ch g £9587
71 3-19 Donc 10.3gd 70 924
38 10-17 Pont 12hvy 70 1064
54 5-8 Muss 12gd [70] 1552
75 1-6 YORK 10.4g/f [67] 2356*
75 2-6 Newc 12.4sft [73] 2686
74 3-5 Brig 11.9gd [73] 2956
70 5-15 Epso 10.1gd [73] 3216
59 2-14 Catt 12g/f [73] 3668
20 9-11 Wind 10gd [69] 4124
66 4-14 York 10.4g/f 68 4402
48 15-19 Leic 10g/f 68 4456

ETTRICK WATER 5 ch g £32975
87 5-12 Hayd 8.1g/f 86 1883 vis
99 1-13 KEMP 7gd 86 2172* vis
99 1-11 NEWM 7gd 92 2532+ vis
78 10-21 Asco 7g/f 95 3441 vis
103 1-16 GOOD 7g/f 94 4523+ vis
100 6-15 Asco 7g/f 99 4800 vis
98 4-16 Newm 7sft 100 5101 vis
101a 7-14 Ling 7ap 100 5262 vis

EUGENIE 2 ch f £0
32a 1-8 Ling 6ap 49
0 13-13 Ling 6ap 364
19a 13-15 Sout 7af [45] 462

EUIPPE 3 b f £4032
52 11-15 Ripo 10g/f 64 1976
62 5-9 Yarm 14.1g/f 62 2345
72 1-18 HAYD 14gd 60 2905*
68 4-10 Hayd 16.2sft 70 3275
45 7-9 Yarm 14.1g/f 69 3703

EUKLEIA 2 ch f £0
66 6-13 Thir 6g/s 2689
60 8-10 Nott 6.1g/f 3418
45a 5-15 Sout 5af 4089
25 17-19 Carl 5.9g/f 65 4344

EUNICE CHOICE 3 b g £0
10a 15-15 Ling 7ap 670
0 9-9 Sout 6af 2493

EUROBOUND 3 b f £0
58 5-10 Bath 11.7g/f [74] 4414

EUROLINK ARTEMIS 6 b m £3112
4a 11-11 Wolv 12af [52] 6 bl e
37a 9-13 Wolv 9.4af 52 38 p
32a 8-14 Sout 8af 47 160 p
0 13-13 Wolv 8.5af [43] 300 p
41a 4-11 Ling 10ap [40] 970 p
27a 10-14 Ling 10ap [40] 1072 p
44a 1-6 WOLV 9.4af [40] 1262* p
49 1-7 CHEP 10.2sft [40] 1332* p
40a 3-10 Wolv 9.4af [45] 1564 p
0 P-16 Sout 12af 41 2340 p
20a 11-12 Wolv 9.5ap [45] 5234 p

EUROLINK ZANTE 7 b g £0
46a 11-11 Ling 8ap [49] 145 P
45a 7-12 Ling 8ap [45] 571 BL
41a 6-12 Ling 8ap [45] 649 bl

41a 7-14 Ling 10ap [45] 705 bl
23 11-13 Warw 10.9g/f 50 4419

EVA JEAN 3 b f £0
38 14-18 Wind 8.3g/f 1810
59 5-13 Nott 8.2g/f 4847
22 16-17 Redc 10sft 60 5307

EVA PERON 4 b f £0
33a 10-15 Ling 7ap [59] 935
36 8-17 Beve 8.5g/s [55] 1160
33 6-10 Bath 10.2gd [49] 1402
32 8-12 Brig 9.9fm 45 1695
39 7-16 Bath 8fm [45] 2032 P

EVA SONEVA SO FAST 2 ch c £6958
53 10-16 Sali 7gd 3882
82 5-12 Newm 7gd 4194
84 2-12 Good 8g/f 4522
84 1-10 WIND 8.3g/f [80] 4831*

EVALUATOR 2 b c £13873
70a 6-12 Ling 8ap 19
74 4-17 Kemp 7gd 1136
75 3-18 Nott 8.2sft 70 1470
44 11-16 Beve 8.5sft 72 1628
62 6-20 Newb 7g/f 72 2314
80 1-20 NEWB 7fm 70 2650*
82 2-12 Leic 8g/f 75 2922
89 2-9 Sali 8g/s 78 3112
81 8-19 Good 8g/f 83 3512
90 2-14 Wind 8.3gd [83] 4122
91 2-17 Asco 8g/f 85 4777

EVANESCE 2 b f £9621
71a 2-9 Ling 5ap 931
70a 2-5 Ling 5ap 1041
69 4-9 Yarm 5.2g/f 1133
74 2-5 Ripo 5g/s 1362
73 2-12 Hami 6gd 2178
79 1-13 SALI 6fm 2287*
76 2-6 Carl 5fm 2442
50 8-10 Sali 6gd 2697
70 11-24 Newb 5.2g/f 3266
58 4-6 Yarm 5.2gd 3488
46 10-12 Wind 6gd 74 3825
39 12-14 Catt 5g/f 71 4437
46 13-17 Catt 7gd 67 4963

EVANGELIST 3 b f £1671
13a 12-16 Sout 6af 40 166
40a 3-8 Sout 7af [40] 373
16a 9-13 Wolv 6af [40] 483
46a 1-10 WOLV 6af [40] 667* VIS
17a 7-10 Wolv 6af [45] 822 vis t
32a 6-10 Sout 6af [45] 907 t p
0 14-15 Ling 7ap [45] 969 bl t

EVASIVE QUALITY 2 b f £0
63 10-12 Newb 6af 3251

EVEN EASIER 3 gr f £561
48a 8-10 Ling 7ap 62 432
49a 7-12 Ling 8ap 55 603 p
48a 5-11 Ling 8ap [53] 696 p
55 7-15 Bath 8g/s 60 1099 p
58 6-19 Brig 9.9g/f 55 1940
55 4-18 Sali 7fm 55 2292 BL
52 4-8 Brig 8g/f 55 2432 bl
53 5-8 Sali 8gd 55 2701 bl
53 7-16 Brig 9.9g/f 53 3175 bl
47 5-6 Brig 8g/f 55 3718 bl
7 12-14 Good 8sft 50 4189 bl

EVEN HOTTER 3 b f £0
33 12-17 Bath 5g/f 1787
50 5-10 Newb 6gd 2309
2 11-11 Sali 6gd 54 2661

EVENING FRAGRANCE 2 gr g £0
8a 11-11 Ling 6ap 51
0 11-11 Sout 8af 159 BL
0 15-15 Sout 7af 184 bl
0 11-11 Wolv 8.5af [19] 279 bl

EVER CHEERFUL 2 b g £5441
64a 4-15 Ling 7ap [67] 52
78a 6-13 Ling 7ap [66] 119
68a 2-6 Wolv 7af [73] 283

75a 1-13 LING 6ap [67] 364* P
57a 10-10 Ling 7ap 75 432 p
60a 5-15 Ling 7ap [73] 671 p
63a 2-7 Ling 5ap [73] 737 p
55a 6-9 Wolv 5af [70] 835 p
52a 8-12 Ling 6ap 66 4976 p
58 9-17 Bath 5.7gd [66] 5020 p

EVEREST 7 ch g £38272
82 7-24 Donc 8gd 85 928
72 13-19 Newm 10g/f 85 1478
70 10-19 Ripo 10g/f 83 1781
66 9-13 Ches 10.3gd 80 2284
75 14-17 Carl 7.9gd 78 2672
89 1-20 NEWM 8fm 76 3001*
90 1-18 NEWB 8g/f 80 3265*
75 7-10 Pont 8gd 85 3460
88 4-10 Ayr 8gd 85 4685
25 31-32 Newm 9g/f 85 4916

EVERY NOTE COUNTS 4 b g £0
0 21-22 Donc 12gd 75 918
40 15-19 Beve 9.9g/s 70 1164
39 14-16 Redc 10g/f 67 1821
53 6-8 Wind 8.3g/f 62 2448
56 6-11 Newc 10.1g/s 62 2726
44 6-18 Newc 8g/f [60] 5017

EVIYRN 8 b g £0
9 12-12 Sout 16gd 35 1285 vis

EVOLVING TACTICS 4 b c £0
102 9-11 Nad 9g/f 991
65 27-31 Asco 8g/f 110 2489 VIS

EVOQUE 3 b f £0
58 10-10 Newm 8g/f 1191

EX MILL LADY 2 br f £5398
48a 5-14 Ling 6ap 146
59 4-13 Folk 5sft 1575
67 2-8 Donc 5gd 2075
64 2-6 Folk 5fm [59] 2717
60 1-6 LING 5gd [59] 3023*

EXALTED 11 b g £0
45 5-12 Newc 14.4sft 55 1396
52 5-8 Ayr 13.1fm 54 1905
41 8-9 Hami 13gd 54 2176
49 6-7 Hami 13gd 51 2708

EXCEED AND EXCEL 4 b c £0
90 19-20 Newm 6g/f 3062 T

EXCELLENTO 4 ch c £0
28 17-17 York 7.9g/s 102 1686
95 9-14 Sand 8.1g/f 102 2096

EXCELSIUS 3 ch c £25420
109 1- SAIN 8sft 108*
79 9-10 Donc 8gd [106] 922
101 3-4 Wind 8.3sft [106] 1649
94 9-9 Wind 8.3fm [103] 2757
71 11-15 York 7.9g/s 99 4061
99 4-8 Hayd 8.1fm [96] 4386 BL
101 2-10 Hayd 8.1g/s 96 4767 bl

EXCESSIVEPLEASURE 4 br g £55865
103 3-9 Nad 8af 988 tbl

EXCLUSIVE DANIELLE 3 ch f £3455
70 5-8 Ripo 10g/s 1365
77 1-6 CATT 12g/f 4441*

EXCUSEZ MOI 2 b c £1568
81a 2-9 Ling 6ap 5237

EXECUTE 7 ch h £96747
115 2-8 Long 10gd 1061
118 1-8 LONG 10.5hvy 1558*
113 11-19 Long 12g/f 4956

EXIT SMILING 2 ch c £5216
77 2-6 Hami 5gd 1386
23 3-7 Hami 6gd 1744
67 17-24 Newb 5.2g/f 3266
54 5-9 Good 7fm 74 3624
42 13-14 Muss 8gd 72 4519
71 1-17 REDC 7g/s [67] 5105*
59 10-14 Donc 7sft 72 5213

EXIT TO HEAVEN 3 ch f £1286
58a 2-10 Wolv 12af [57] 154
62a 2-14 Sout 12af [60] 194
55a 5-10 Wolv 12af 60 243
39a 7-10 Sout 12af 58 321
39a 6-10 Wolv 12af [58] 359
46a 7-9 Wolv 12af 58 424 P
2a 9-9 Sout 16af 53 612

EXPECTED BONUS 5 b g £524
46 10-15 Kemp 9gd 55 2170 bl
51 4-7 Beve 9.9gd 52 2654
4 17-18 Pont 10g/f 51 2988
36 9-13 Bath 8g/f 47 3526 bl
43 6-20 Yarm 8gd 44 3996
25 15-15 Folk 9.7g/f [45] 4373

EXPECTEDTOFLI 6 b m £0
0 10-11 Wolv 6af [35] 1261 t
0 15-15 Sout 8af 30 2725 t

EXPEDITIOUS 2 b c £0
44 22-23 Newm 7g/f 4885 t
61a 6-10 Ling 7ap 5259 BL t

EXPLICIT 3 ch c £0
44a 12-14 Ling 10ap 2740
0 10-10 Pont 10gd 3243
40 9-9 Wind 8.3g/f 3979
0 8-9 Sout 7af 4131
20a 11-12 Ling 8ap [40] 4659

EXPLODE 7 b g £2689
44 4-11 Warw 8.1hvy 52 1536
38 9-19 Redc 8sft 52 1661
56 2-17 Hayd 8.1gd 49 3759
55 2-15 Redc 9g/s 52 5111
17 10-16 Nott 8.2hvy 52 5347

EXPLOSIVE FOX 3 gr c £0
55a 11-14 Ling 13ap [67] 4892
1 7-8 Bath 17.2sft 65 5175

EXPONENTIAL 2 b g £3916
28 13-13 Beve 5ap 2889 BL e
81 1-15 NOTT 5.1gd 3988* bl e

EXPRESS LILY 5 b m £0
0 10-12 Catt 12sft 5319

EXTEMPORISE 4 ch c £3748
38a 8-11 Wolv 5af 48 643
38a 3-10 Wolv 6af [45] 822 T
39a 5-10 Wolv 7af 45 864 t
43 1-10 WARW 8.1g/s [40] 1328*
54 1-17 KEMP 7hvy [45] 1642*
49a 6-15 Sout 7af 52 2384
36 15-20 Chep 7.1gd 52 4488
53a 2-13 Wolv 8.6ap [50] 5212

EXTERIOR 3 ch c £28415
91a 1-8 LING 10ap 3787*
97 1-5 GOOD 9sft 83 4185*
92 4-11 Good 9g/f 91 4525
104 1-8 NOTT 10hvy 91 5187+

EXTINGUISHER 5 ch g £0
1 18-19 Newc 6sft 70 967
43 9-11 Ripo 6g/f 66 1977
56 9-20 York 6g/f 66 2059
55 8-15 Beve 7.5g/s 62 2324
42 5-10 Ayr 9.1gd 59 2571 VIS
47 14-18 Catt 7g/f 57 2848 vis
20a 11-14 Sout 6af 55 4130

EXTRA COVER 3 b g £6831
73a 2-10 Ling 8ap 1021
77 2-14 Wind 10g/s 1259
72 2-10 Folk 9.7sft [75] 1580
66a 3-13 Sout 8af [74] 2383 BL
77a 1-6 SOUT 6af [69] 3095* bl
64a 6-9 Sout 6af 75 3485 bl
50 6-8 Pont 6gd [75] 3684 bl
37a 13-13 Ling 7ap 72 4318
61 7-15 Kemp 8ap 69 4713 bl
65a 4-12 Ling 8ap [67] 4974 bl
62a 6-12 Wolv 7.1ap [63] 5325 bl

EXTRA MARK 2 b c £2638

78	2-5	Hami	5g/s		1601
78a	2-11	Sout	5af		1752
80	4-8	Sand	5gd		2188
38	20-20	Ling	7gd	75	4444
7	14-14	Hami	6sft	72	4692

EXTREME BEAUTY 2 ch f £11990

66	6-13	Ling	6g/f		2061
75	1-16	PONT	6g/f		2275*
88	7-17	Asco	6g/f		2553
90	3-10	Newm	6fm		3003
84	10-11	Newm	7g/f	[93]	3781

EXTREMELY RARE 3 b f £4663

69	2-11	Catt	6gd		999
51	7-14	Sout	6gd		1281
65	1-8	REDC	6sft		1659*
55	10-18	Donc	7gd	69	2755
67	7-15	Redc	5g/s	68	2961
54	9-11	Ripo	6gd	68	2985
64	6-7	Sand	5g/s	66	4099
65	6-20	Wind	6g/f	64	4946
43	12-19	Wind	6g/f	64	5053

EYES DONT LIE 6 b g £0

6	9-9	Muss	12g/f	[35]	1121
14	8-10	Muss	12g/s	[35]	5145 p

EYES ONLY 3 b f £5616

84	1-17	NEWM	8gd		4228*

EZZ ELKHEIL 5 b g £2902

78a	2-12	Ling	16ap	74	478
76a	4-10	Ling	12ap	76	570
78a	3-14	Ling	12ap	75	731
70a	10-12	Ling	13ap	75	877
57	12-20	Epso	12hvy	74	1295
61	7-13	Kemp	12g/f	72	1916
64	7-13	Ches	10.3gd	70	2284

FAAYEJ 4 b g £8341

87	1-15	SAND	10g/f	78	2099*
85	4-8	Sand	10gd	83	2363
84	5-14	Sand	10g/s	83	4097
85	3-8	Ayr	13.1sft	83	4690 P

FABRANESE 4 b f £0

31a	12-15	Ling	12ap		2393

FABRIAN 5 b g £0

54a	5-12	Wolv	7af	55	74 e
56a	4-11	Ling	8ap	[53]	145 e
30a	10-14	Ling	10ap	53	230 e
46a	8-12	Ling	8ap	53	406

FABULOSO 3 b f £0

21a	5-8	Sout	8af	[45]	1841
44	6-11	Yarm	7g/f	41	3711
20	10-12	Kemp	9sft	41	4032
45	6-7	Epso	8.5g/f	[45]	4474
44	5-17	Kemp	7g/f	[45]	4794
18	14-17	Warw	8.1g/s	[40]	4992

FACE THE LIMELIGHT 5 b g £0

39	14-19	Beve	9.9g/s	66	1164
38	6-8	Redc	10gd	[65]	2548
29	7-11	Catt	12g/f	[62]	3190

FACT AND FICTION 2 b c £0

0	7-7	Nott	6.1g/f		2629

FACTUAL LAD 6 b g £5814

52	13-19	Newb	10gd	68	1736
42	10-12	Bath	10.2fm	68	2036
74	1-11	BRIG	9.9fm	67	2260*
63	7-10	Sand	10gd	72	3336
61	10-15	Brig	8fm	72	3694
66	9-11	Epso	10.1gd	71	4293
75	3-15	Nott	10g/f	70	4849
49a	8-11	Wolv	12.2ap	62	5180
64a	2-13	Wolv	9.5ap	[60]	5338

FACTUAL LADY 3 b f £0

4	11-12	Redc	6fm		4557

FADAEL 2 b f £1163

47	7-11	Warw	5g/f		2911
71	6-14	Yarm	7gd		3489

65	3-11	Wind	8.3fm		3798
65	3-7	Muss	7.1gd	[72]	4518
56	8-11	Pont	8fm	65	4753
63a	5-13	Wolv	8.6ap	[64]	4979

FADEELA 2 ch f £4818

74a	2-14	Sout	7af	[67]	98 e
77a	1-10	WOLV	7af	67	112* e
59a	11-15	Ling	7ap	74	177 e
91	5-9	Kemp	8g/s	[69]	1110
67	8-20	Newm	7g/f	69	1186
54	13-20	Newb	7g/f	70	1761
58	7-11	Newm	6fm	67	2093

FAILED TO HIT 10 b g £376

31a	6-10	Wolv	12af		250 bl
50a	3-12	Wolv	12af	52	469 vis
36a	4-8	Wolv	16.2af	52	563 vis
32a	6-9	Ling	13ap	[51]	787 vis

FAINT HEART 2 b f £7711

102	3-6	Chan	8gd		4728

FAIR ALONG 2 b c £267

62	7-9	Wind	5g/s		1256
41	8-11	Yarm	6g/f		1728
65	7-13	Nott	5.1gd		1987
74	4-10	Wind	8.3fm		3803
55	9-13	Newm	8gd	72	4193
52	9-13	Wind	8.3g/f	72	5051

FAIR COMPTON 3 b f £4298

65	4-14	Brig	6fm		1690
59	6-10	Brig	6g/f	[65]	2048
50	5-9	Chep	5.1gd	65	2195
56	4-19	Leic	6g/f	62	2925
66	5-10	Ling	7gd	[60]	3446
53	5-7	Ling	6fm	[60]	3789
64	1-10	LING	6gd	57	4109*
49	9-18	Leic	6gd	58	5039

FAIR MIX 6 b h £82103

116	3-8	Long	10.5hvy		1558
118	2-7	Chan	12g/s		2459
118	1-10	MAIS	10gd		4837*
107	4-9	San	12sft		5168

FAIR OPTIONS 3 gr c £551

10	17-17	Sali	6g/s		1497
54	7-14	Brig	6fm		1690
66	3-19	Donc	6g/f		1876
36	16-16	Brig	7fm	65	2258

FAIR SHAKE 4 b g £6519

46	7-19	Newc	6sft	67	967
41	10-13	Newc	7hvy	67	1035
65	3-20	Newc	6sft	65	1393 P
61	5-13	Ayr	7.2g/s	66	2568 p
52	15-18	Newc	6g/s	66	2770 p
70	2-15	Newc	6gd	65	3424 VIS
67	6-19	York	6gd	68	4005 vis
73	2-18	Redc	6fm	67	4339 vis
31	14-18	Ayr	7.2sft	69	4622 vis
62	8-11	Hami	6gd	69	4818 p
44	15-19	Newc	7g/f	68	5014 p

FAIR SPIN 4 ch g £1454

59	7-11	Ayr	6gd	65	2542
64	3-17	Hayd	8.1gd	63	2947
60	7-18	Pont	8gd	63	3242
51	9-12	Redc	8gd	62	4246
62	5-17	Ayr	7.2sft	60	5063
45	9-15	Nott	8.2hvy	60	5191
63	3-17	Redc	10sft	58	5307

FAIRGAME MAN 6 ch g £4103

46	7-20	Ripo	5gd	50	1179
40	8-15	Muss	5gd	49	1555
44	2-20	Beve	5g/f	[45]	1948 p
34	7-19	Beve	5gd	45	2657 p
36	5-14	Newc	5g/s	45	2775 p
50	1-20	BEVE	5g/s	43	3180* p
45	8-18	Carl	5g/f	49	3228 p
40	9-18	Pont	5gd	47	3463 p
36	8-18	Beve	5g/s	46	3852 p
40	8-18	Pont	5g/s	46	3974 p
48	2-16	Warw	5g/s	[45]	4995 p

FAIRLAND 5 b g £238

44a	3-14	Ling	10ap	[45]	1712
50	4-19	Brig	9.9g/f	45	1940
38	10-12	Warw	10.9fm	49	2436
47a	6-14	Ling	10ap	49	2589
0	18-18	Warw	10.9g/s	47	4669
33	14-18	Kemp	10g/f	[46]	4791
23	10-15	Yarm	10.1g/s	[46]	5122

FAIRLIE 3 b f £3898

66	5-7	Carl	9.3fm	67	1953
55	7-7	Hami	8.3g/f	[65]	2474
42	7-9	Beve	8.5sft	62	2940
64	1-14	BEVE	7.5g/s	[59]	3177*
60	3-9	Newc	10.1g/s	[59]	3702
35	8-8	Ripo	10g/s	59	3938

FAIRLY GLORIOUS 3 b g £0

39a	8-11	Wolv	6af		466
35a	11-11	Wolv	6af		481
4a	9-12	Wolv	9.4af		686

FAIRMILE 2 b c £1526

84	3-9	Folk	7g/s		3047
82	3-18	Newm	7gd		3927
74	6-11	Sali	7gd		4853
83	4-14	Newb	7sft	79	5193

FAIRMORNING 4 b g £1113

40a	4-15	Sout	16af	41	67
40a	3-10	Wolv	12af	[40]	250
42a	2-10	Wolv	12af	40	315
24a	6-10	Wolv	16.2af	40	358
25a	5-7	Sout	14af	[40]	724
41a	2-8	Wolv	12af	[40]	1265

FAIRY MONARCH 5 b g £1814

46	2-13	Ripo	12.3g/f	46	2008 p
31	8-15	Ayr	10.9g/s	48	2545 p
52	2-20	Catt	12g/f	46	2850 p
29	15-19	Thir	12g/f	49	4594 p
45	8-19	Beve	9.9g/f	49	4720 p
46	6-20	Kemp	12g/f	[47]	4796 p

FAIRY WIND 6 b h £207

33a	10-11	Wolv	12af	49	72
28a	12-13	Ling	13ap	48	342
30a	9-13	Sout	12af	[45]	575
34a	3-7	Wolv	16.2af	[45]	1802
26	8-11	Newm	12g/f	50	2244

FAIT LE JOJO 7 b g £0

0	12-12	Kemp	14.4g/f	85	3688
68	11-17	Nott	14.1g/s	85	4647

FAITES VOS JEUX 2 b f £0

36a	9-12	Wolv	6af	[58]	42
0	13-14	Beve	7.5sft	[50]	4256
12	15-19	Thir	6g/f	45	4595
39	5-10	Catt	6gd	[40]	4964
23a	10-12	Wolv	6ap	[45]	5162

FAITH HEALER 3 br f £3339

15	18-18	Nott	8.2sft	65	1470
23	18-20	Asco	8g/f	60	1927 P
20	14-15	Leic	11.8gd	55	2134 p
53	4-10	Yarm	8g/f	55	2344 BL
44	6-14	Wind	10gd	52	2617 bl
61a	1-13	SOUT	8af	50	3094* bl
47	10-11	Newm	8g/f	55	3283 bl
26	6-6	Brig	8g/f	55	3718 bl
0	17-19	Kemp	8g/f	[50]	4795 bl
47a	6-11	Wolv	7.1ap	[57]	5178 bl

FAITHFUL FLASH 2 b f £0

41	6-6	Yarm	7g/f		2343
39	8-14	Beve	7.5sft		2939
50	4-8	Brig	6g/f		3172
51	6-11	Thir	7g/f		3570 BL
48	5-9	Yarm	6sft	51	4146

FAITHFUL WARRIOR 6 ch g £0

68	20-22	Newm	8sft	91	5103

FAITHFULL GIRL 2 b f £0

36a	9-10	Ling	5ap		1071
51a	9-10	Ling	5ap		2017
7	8-8	Brig	6g/f		2043

FAITHISFLYING 2 ch c £0

FALBRAV etc. — racing form listing

```
25  13-15  Warw   5g/s          1325
42  6-11   Yarm   6g/f          1728
52  11-13  Nott   5.1gd         1987
37  6-6    Leic   5fm           2110
30  6-9    Nott   6.1hvy [50]   5185

FALBRAV  5 b h  £816000
128 1-14   SHA    10g/f         212*

FALCON GOER  2 b f  £0
49  8-13   Redc   6g/f          1818
25  13-16  Thir   6g/s          4205
47  8-10   Newc   6g/f          4403

FALL IN LINE  4 gr g  £20721
78a 1-12   WOLV  12af    60     484*
86a 1-7    SOUT  12af    66     504+
88a 1-11   LING  13ap   [60]    515*
89a 1-12   SOUT  11af    66     534*
84a 1-15   SOUT  10ap    66     549+
84a 1-13   LING  10ap   [86]    569*

FALLUJAH  2 ch f  £0
3   14-14  Yarm   7sft          5251

FAME  4 ch g  £0
71  6-13   Bath   11.7sft  80   5174

FAMILIAR AFFAIR  3 b g  £6698
79  7-12   Hayd  8.1gd    82    3738
34  10-10  Pont  8g/s     80    3972
79  1-7    RIPO  8gd     [78]   4304*
75  3-8    Hami  9.2sft  [78]   4694
35  11-14  Pont  8g/f    [78]   4937

FAMOUS GROUSE  4 b g  £1495
72  17-19  Newm 10g/f    100    1478
102 4-6    Epso  10.1gd [98]    4290
96  6-8    Donc  10.3fm   98    4530
71  14-17  Newm 12g/f     98    4889

FANCY FOXTROT  3 b c  £7305
92a 1-10   LING  8ap    [82]   1021+
80  10-20  Newm 8fm      92     1496
72  14-18  Good  9g/f    90     1813
91  3-17   Epso  9g/f    87     2212
87  9-19   Newm 6fm      89     3002
83a 7-12   Ling  8ap    [90]    3199
84  9-17   Good  7fm     89     3550
59  16-16  Newb 9g/f     87    3954 BL
82a 6-13   Ling  7ap     84    4897 P

FANLING LADY  3 gr f  £0
41  8-12   Ripo  8g/f    [74]   1978
55  7-9    Ripo  10g/s    73    3260
32  10-10  Redc  10g/f    72    3772

FANNYS FANCY  4 b f  £5621
87  7-11   Newb  5.2gd    91    1207
76  10-20  York  5g/s     91    1683
79  15-29  Asco  6fm      90    2581
92  3-8    Newm 6g/f      88  3235 T
87  5-10   Asco  6gd      88    3773
88  5-14   Sali  7gd      88    4331 t
92  5-15   Newb 6gd     [87]    5088

FANTAISISTE  2 b f  £7253
52  11-15  Folk   7gd           3381
71  3-8    Brig   7g/f          3716
79a 2-12   Ling   6ap           4179
87a 1-11   LING   6ap     75    4972*

FANTASIAS FOREST  2 b f  £0
42  11-14  Folk   7fm           2714
44  18-19  Leic   7gd           5040
0   14-15  Brig   7sft          5192

FANTASMIC RIVER  3 ch f  £0
14a 10-14  Sout   8af           170

FANTASTIC LOVE  4 b g  £11000
100 8-15   Good  9.9g/f  102  3506 T
103 7-19   York  13.9g/s 102  4023 t
105 3-15   Donc  14.6fm  101  4491 t
107 2-5    Newm 12g/f  [103]  4886 t

FANTASTIC LUCK  2 b c  £0
10  16-18  Newm 8fm            4722
15  14-14  Leic   8gd          5059
61  10-20  Yarm  8sft          5252

FANTASTIC NIGHT  2 ch f  £0
40  16-19  Leic   7gd          5045
32  10-10  Newm 6sft          5266

FANTASTIC STAR  2 b f  £0
36  9-11   Warw   5gd          1123
31  12-13  Redc   6g/f         1818
33a 9-12   Sout   7af          3394

FANTASTIC VIEW  3 ch c  £2000
97  5-5    Newm 8g/f   [113]   1188
112 4-9    Donc  8fm    [113]  4495

FANTASTICO  4 b f  £863
62  4-10   Hayd  14g/f    64   1923
45  9-9    Hami  13gd     62   2176
59  3-10   Newc  16.1g/s  60   3701 p
38  12-17  Pont  17.1g/s  59   3970 p
54  6-7    Newc  16.1g/f  58  4405 p

FANTASY BELIEVER  6 b g  £74703
2   12-13  Newc  7hvy    94    1035
82  17-20  Newm 7g/s     94    1151
58  29-30  Newm 6g/f     92    1481
72  14-20  Asco  7g/f    90    1926
82  9-17   Epso  6fm     86    2256
87  4-18   Newc  6g/s    83    2770
96  1-11   NEWB 6g/f     83   2878+
55  10-11  Asco  6.5gd   87    3069
97  1-15   NEWC 6g/f     91  3424*
97  2-28   Good  6fm     89    3622
88  10-19  York  6gd     95    4005
77  20-22  Donc  5.6fm   94    4459
103 2-24   Ayr   6sft    95    4686
95  6-14   Ripo  6gd     98    4786
103 3-20   York  6gd     98    5001

FANTASY CRUSADER  5 ch g  £16574
32  16-19  Yarm  7g/f    49    1132
42  3-12   Brig   9.9fm   47   1695
51  3-19   Brig   9.9g/f  47   1940 p
39  10-16  Yarm  10.1fm  47   2146 p
50  3-11   Brig   9.9fm   48   2260 p
53a 2-14   Ling  10ap    48   2589 p
40  9-12   Ling  10g/f   50   2844 p
17  17-20  Newm 8g/f     50   3232 p
45  3-9    Brig   9.9fm   48   3695 p
58  1-11   LING  10fm    48  3748* p
56  3-20   Yarm  8gd     52   3996 p
62  1-12   GOOD 9g/f     52  4539* p
20a 10-13  Wolv  8.6ap   55   4982 p
61a 1-12   LING  8ap    [55]  5077* p
51a 10-16  Ling  12ap   [58]  5296 p

FANTASY DEFENDER  2 b g  £0
56  9-10   Hayd   5sft         1107
35  8-10   Beve   5sft         1632
41  8-13   Donc   6gd          2236
54  11-17  Ling   7g/f         2584
58  9-18   Newc   6g/s         3699
59  5-7    Yarm   6gd          3994
36  13-20  Redc   7fm     60   4337

FANTASY RIDE  2 b c  £10204
73  7-16   Newm 7g/f           3582
96  1-9    YARM 8sft          4147*
93  5-9    Pont   8g/s   [94]  5150
96  2-9    Newm 10g/s  [94]   5281

FANTORINI  2 b c  £529
62  8-10   Donc   7g/f         3594
82  4-8    Sand   8.1gd        4608

FAR FOR LULU  3 ch f  £0
16a 14-15  Sout   7af    [40]   462
0   12-12  Ling   7ap    [35]   536

FAR NOTE  5 ch g  £11893
68a 1-16   SOUT  6af    63    92* bl
42a 7-9    Sout   7af    65   193 bl
47a 6-11   Sout   5af    65   386 bl
68a 2-11   Sout   5af    65   418 bl
60a 9-16   Sout   5g/f   65   461 bl
43a 9-15   Sout   6af    68   550 bl
71a 4-10   Sout   6af    67   660 bl
62a 6-13   Sout   6af    67   741 bl
74a 1-11   SOUT  5af    67   859* bl
48  12-20  Newc  6sft   66   1393 bl

81a 1-12   SOUT  5af    70   1442* bl
64  4-20   Thir   6gd    66   1638 bl
62  4-13   Pont   5g/f  [65]  2279 bl
54  7-19   Beve   6gd    65   2512 bl
68  4-12   Thir   5g/s   64   2690 bl
60  8-18   Donc   6gd    63   2752 bl
5   10-10  Hayd  7.1g/s  65   3137 bl

FARAWAY ECHO  3 gr f  £4282
33  15-18  Nott   8.2fm   61   1007
36a 6-7    Wolv   7af     57   1376
51  3-8    Nott   8.2sft  52   1740 VIS
28  8-10   Chep   8.1g/f  50   2624
49  5-16   Thir   8g/f    49   3414 vis
55  1-5    HAMI  12.1sft  47  4012*
37a 5-8    Sout  12af     47   4128

FARAWAY LOOK  6 br g  £0
53a 4-14   Sout   8af     61   195
54a 4-13   Wolv   9.4af   60   281
47a 5-10   Sout   8af     58   387
6a  10-11  Sout  12af     58   458

FAREWELL GIFT  3 b c  £14435
79  4-10   Newm 6g/f   [92]  1191
80  3-17   Sali   6g/s  [87]  1497
77  2-8    Kemp  7g/f  [80]  1912
84  3-9    Kemp  6gd   [80]  2173
82  2-10   Newb  6g/f  [80]  2309
85  3-8    Kemp  6g/s  [80]  2677
81  3-7    Kemp  7g/f   82   3522
79  3-8    Newm 6g/f  [81]  3784
82  1-12   KEMP  6sft  [80] 4029* VIS
77  7-25   Newb  7gd    80  4683 vis

FARNBOROUGH  3 b c  £0
61a 5-11   Ling   8ap          841
62a 7-11   Ling   7ap         1008
43  9-14   Sali   7g/f        1720
50  7-9    Ling   7g/f  [59]  1984
13  13-13  Beve   9.9gd   55   3309
27  17-18  Carl   7.9fm   55   3547
44  4-15   Bath   8g/s    50   4202
35  5-12   Chep  10.2hvy  47   4708
31a 9-12   Wolv   7.1ap [48]  5233

FARNE ISLE  5 ch m  £1215
65  4-13   Hayd  11.9g/s       2230
69  3-4    Ripo  12.3g/f       2484
45  7-16   Ripo  8gd           2987
47  13-13  York  11.9g/f  70   3437

FARRIERS CHARM  3 b f  £7754
67a 1-7    WOLV  7af     59  1376*
51  12-20  Newb  7g/f    63   1761
58  7-11   Wind   8.3fm   63   3799
67  1-12   KEMP  9sft    63  4032*
64  5-11   Wind   8.3g/s  66   4222
56  10-18  Sali   9.9gd   66   4850
53a 10-13  Wolv   8.6ap   68   5364

FARTHING  2 b f  £2902
77  2-6    Yarm   5.2gd        3488
67  4-6    Sand   5g/f         3857
75  2-11   Bath   5g/f         4409
72  3-10   Muss   5gd   [74]   4804

FASCINATION STREET  3 b f  £6580
70  2-9    Thir   7fm    [69]  3610
62  3-7    Brig   7g/f   [65]  3985
66  2-10   Warw   8.1g/f [65]  4421
70  1-9    CATT  7g/f   [65] 4674*
61  6-17   Nott   8.2gd   65   4862

FASHION HOUSE  2 b f  £1480
68  5-17   Yarm   6gd          4610
75  2-14   Redc   6g/s         5106

FAST AND FURIOUS FR  3 b g  £7764
107 3-9    Long  11sft         1158

FAST CINDY  4 b f  £0
31a 10-11  Wolv  16.2af   60    48
8a  11-12  Wolv  16.2af   57   156
0   8-8    Wolv  14.8af   55   277

FAST GATE  5 gr h  £0
91a 8-15   Ling   7ap     92  887 BL T
```

FAST HEART 3 b c £1500

100	8-13	Newm	5g/f	[99]	1479 t
78	14-20	York	5g/s	99	1683 t
98	4-9	Hayd	6g/f	[99]	1918 t
75	13-20	York	6g/f	97	2407 t

FAST LANE 5 ch g £0

13	13-16	Newc	7sft		966
0	17-17	Beve	8.5g/s	[40]	1160 P

FASYLITATOR 2 b c £1241

73	6-7	Catt	7g/f		3665
75	3-17	Wind	6g/f		3975
68	6-10	Brig	6g/s		4139
68	10-20	Ling	7gd	72	4444
73a	4-11	Ling	6ap	69	4972
69	6-14	Newb	7sft	69	5193

FATAYAAT 3 b f £0

54	10-11	Bath	8fm		2031

FATEHALKHAIR 12 ch g £0

19	11-17	Pont	12hvy	62	1064

FATHER SEAMUS 6 b g £0

0	13-13	Ling	10ap	[20]	3288 P

FATTAAN 4 b g £0

9	13-15	Chep	16.2gd	[63]	3400

FAVOUR 4 b f £2811

73	2-10	Donc	6g/f	71	1878
62	9-16	York	7g/f	71	2057
70	6-11	Pont	6g/f	73	2791
64	7-11	Donc	7g/s	71	3223
46	12-13	Newc	7gd	69	3428
67	3-9	Pont	6g/f	67	4627
51	11-15	Newc	5fm	67	4870
61	7-18	Leic	6gd	66	5039

FAVOURABLE 3 b f £0

24	17-18	Wind	8.3g/f		1810
29	11-15	Bath	10.2gd		4826
38	16-18	Bath	10.2gd		5023

FAVOURABLE TERMS 4 b f £200200

117	1-10	Asco	8g/f	[108]	2487*
93	6-7	Newm	8fm	[108]	3004
118	1-6	GOOD	9.9fm	[112]	3621*

FAVOURING 2 ch c £2268

42	4-8	Muss	5g/f		1091
41	11-12	Beve	5sft		1631
64	8-12	Carl	5.9fm		3544
69	2-9	Catt	6sft	64	3931
64	4-7	Sand	5sft	64	4065
51	7-10	Ayr	6g/f	64	4655
56	6-18	Pont	6g/f	62	4934 VIS

FAVOURITA 2 b f £18583

76	1-8	BRIG	7g/f		3716*
95	4-12	Good	7sft		4264
96	5-8	Donc	8fm		4476
102	2-14	Newm	7g/f	[99]	4914
104	3-8	Newm	7sft	[100]	5133

FAVOURITE NATION 3 ch c £975

92	6-15	Asco	7g/f		2486

FAYR FIRENZE 2 b c £1553

60a	5-12	Wolv	5af	[52]	32 bl
45a	6-11	Wolv	6af	[52]	73 bl
44a	9-15	Ling	7ap	49	846 bl
28a	4-8	Wolv	7af	[49]	892 bl
35a	6-12	Ling	6ap	[45]	1075 VIS
45a	2-7	Wolv	6af	[45]	1312 vis
38	5-6	Warw	7.1g/s	[45]	1330 vis
46a	2-7	Ling	6ap	[45]	1453 vis
46	2-7	Brig	7gd	[45]	1549 vis
48	4-9	Ling	7g/f	[45]	1984

FAYR JAG 5 b g £145000

73	13-15	York	6sft	[110]	1667
117	1-14	ASCO	6fm	[109]	2580*
101	13-20	Newm	6g/f	[109]	3062
103	10-12	York	5g/s	[113]	4060
99	9-8	Bade	8sft	[113]	4426

FAYRWAY RHYTHM 6 b g £0

1a	10-14	Sout	14af	40	185

0	9-10	Sout	16af	[39]	307 vis

FAYRZ PLEASE 2 ch g £315

61a	3-8	Sout	5af		197
57a	4-13	Sout	6af		444
58a	4-11	Sout	5af	62	609
34a	12-15	Sout	6af	[60]	795
27	12-13	Donc	7gd	[58]	925
31	13-15	Newc	5fm	55	4870
4	9-10	Catt	6gd	[55]	4964

FEAAT 3 b f £9306

79	3-10	Sali	9.9g/f		1718
81	1-8	REDC	10g/f		2124*
95	6-9	Asco	12g/f		2517
88	6-9	Newm	12g/f	[94]	3278
95	4-7	Good	14fm	[90]	3619

FEARBY CROSS 7 b g £4551

61a	9-16	Ling	7ap	67	22
60a	10-16	Ling	7ap	67	55
66a	6-15	Ling	7ap	66	698
64a	7-14	Ling	7ap	66	1010
67	4-14	Ling	7sft	67	1625
63	5-7	Good	7gd	66	2223
52	8-12	Kemp	7g/s	65	2679
63	8-17	Newm	7g/f	65	2768
63	5-10	Newm	6g/f	64	3584
41	4-9	Newm	6gd	62	3924
64	6-12	Newm	6gd	61	4229
70	1-16	SALI	7sft	61	4582* bl
65	5-20	Leic	7gd	66	5046
58	8-20	Yarm	7sft	66	5256 bl

FEARLESS SPIRIT 2 ch f £0

69	5-18	Nott	8.2g/f		4842

FEARN ROYAL 5 b m £10184

102	2-12	Tipp	7.5hvy		4961

FEAST OF ROMANCE 6 b g £9443

47a	3-12	Wolv	8.5af	[51]	47
48a	6-15	Ling	7ap	[51]	216 p
46a	3-11	Ling	8ap	[50]	343 p
45a	3-11	Wolv	7af	50	378 p
55a	1-11	WOLV	7af	[49]	440* p
58a	3-12	Wolv	7af	[48]	512 p
60a	2-9	Sout	7af	[54]	555 bl
54a	6-12	Ling	8ap	[53]	571 p
62a	2-7	Sout	7af	[53]	589 bl
61a	1-9	SOUT	7af	[56]	661* bl
50a	5-13	Wolv	8.5af	[58]	699 bl
44a	12-14	Ling	7ap	58	1010 p
49	3-19	Yarm	7g/f	48	1132
1	12-15	Folk	6g/s	48	1267
46	6-9	Yarm	7fm	47	2150 bl
42	4-13	Yarm	6g/f	47	2347 bl
24a	15-15	Sout	7af	[56]	2999
49	2-16	Yarm	7gd	45	4616 bl
46a	11-14	Ling	7ap	54	5300 bl

FEATHER BOA 3 b f £0

65a	8-12	Ling	8ap	67	17

FEED THE METER 4 b f £5225

18	16-19	Donc	6g/f		1876
53	2-10	Beve	9.9gd	50	2510
58	1-8	WIND	11.6g/f	52	2796*
48	11-11	Asco	12gd	57	3070
34	10-17	Newm	10g/f	55	3238

FEEL THE NEED 2 ch c £0

0	9-10	Thir	5fm		3606

FEELING BLUE 5 b m £0

16a	10-11	Wolv	5af	47	508
0	16-16	Sout	5af	[45]	720

FELICITY 4 b f £36427

79	7-8	Newm	9fm	[97]	1491
102	3-9	Cork	10.2g/f	[97]	1857
95	4-7	Hayd	11.9g/f	[97]	1921
108	1-10	CHEP	10.2g/s	[94]	3089+
2	11-13	Deau	10sft	[94]	4160

FELICITY GER 3 ch f £22535

111	1-11	HOPP	6.5gd		3839*

FELIDAE 3 ch c £0

43a	5-13	Wolv	8.5af		39
0	14-15	Sout	11af	46	196
12a	9-10	Wolv	12af	[45]	315
23a	11-13	Wolv	8.5af	40	559 BL T

FELIX HOLT 3 b g £0

1a	8-12	Wolv	12af	[32]	114 bl

FELLBECK FRED 2 gr c £0

29	8-8	Hayd	5gd		2241
39	13-13	Thir	6g/s		2689
40	7-9	Leic	5gd		2921
34a	4-6	Sout	5af		3093

FELLOW SHIP 3 b g £0

59a	10-11	Ling	8ap	[73]	273

FEMINIST 2 b f £847

42	5-6	Sali	5g/s		1499
76	3-8	Kemp	5gd		2171
48	7-7	Bath	5fm		2415
34	9-11	Bath	5.7g/f	[74]	3848

FEN GAME 2 b c £0

78	6-11	Nott	8.2g/s		4648
69	9-23	Newm	7g/f		4885

FEN GYPSY 6 b g £17693

59a	5-12	Ling	8ap	62	607
61a	4-13	Ling	10ap	60	726
13a	10-10	Ling	8ap	60	769
56a	7-12	Ling	8ap	[59]	878 bl
52a	9-13	Ling	10ap	[59]	912 bl
60	2-13	Wind	8.3g/s	[60]	1058
62	1-12	SOUT	7gd	[60]	1284*
63	2-11	Warw	8.1hvy	60	1536
59	4-12	Sand	8.1g/s	60	2129
59	5-16	Chep	7.1gd	[60]	2369
65	1-13	KEMP	9g/f	59	3034*
70	2-15	Ches	7.6g/f	65	3102
60	4-16	Kemp	7gd	59	3184
72	1-8	WIND	8.3fm	65	3641*
71	4-11	Kemp	8g/f	71	3685
68	4-13	Kemp	7sft	70	4030
72	3-15	Chep	8.1g/s	70	4300
37	18-19	York	7.9g/f	70	4399
23	16-16	Bath	8gd	70	5022

FEN SHUI 2 b f £5265

97	1-15	KEMP	7g/f		4710*
68	8-8	Newm	7sft		5133

FENDER 3 b c £0

51	7-13	Nott	10gd		4861 BL
45	7-11	Good	14gd		5029 bl

FENRIR 2 ch c £4532

62	7-11	Beve	7.5g/f		3500
85	1-12	AYR	7.2hvy		4083*
73	5-8	Redc	7gd	[86]	4247
85	3-4	Ayr	8g/s	[83]	4619
27	8-8	Muss	8gd	83	4807
52	7-7	Leic	10gd	[83]	5044

FENWICKS PRIDE 6 b g £464

57	3-17	Nott	6.1sft	54	1606
46	8-16	Redc	6g/f	55	1824 vis
49	7-18	Pont	5g/s	55	3974
37	14-14	Carl	6.9g/f	53	4345
20	11-13	Muss	5g/f	[50]	5146 vis

FERN HOUSE 2 b c £0

53	12-12	Carl	5g/f		4343

FERNERY 4 b f £431

76	4-10	Hayd	10.5sft	[83]	1104
73	7-13	Wind	10gd	[82]	1381

FERRARA FLAME 2 b f £1060

36	8-11	Bath	5.7g/f		3848
44a	9-14	Sout	6af		4127
37	7-17	Ling	6g/f		4316
63	2-14	Wind	8.3g/f		5049
32a	11-13	Wolv	8.6ap	[58]	5355

FESTIVE AFFAIR 5 b g £367

23a	15-16	Sout	6af	53	166
49a	3-9	Sout	5af	[51]	335

2a 11-13 Sout 6af 49 500
15a 4-7 Sout 6af [47] 1032

FESTIVE CHIMES 3 b f £532
40 7-7 Newc 6g/s 2728
55 3-7 Catt 7g/f 3194
35a 7-9 Sout 6af 3396
45 8-19 Chep 6.1sft 45 4054
36 6-13 Carl 6.9fm [52] 4504
43 9-16 Catt 7g/f 50 4676 P

FESTIVE STYLE 3 b f £13966
113a3-8 Nad 8af 599

FEU DUTY 3 b f £3770
56 6-9 Muss 5g/s 62 1457
72 1-7 CARL 5fm 60 1951*
25 9-10 Hayd 5g/s 66 2227
47 12-13 Hami 5g/f 68 2320
44 18-18 Carl 5g/f 67 3228 BL e
41 13-15 Muss 5g/f 65 3561
8 18-18 Redc 6fm 63 4339

FFIFFIFFER 6 b h £2954
52a 4-13 Ling 13ap 55 896
61a 1-11 WOLV 12af 55 937*
34a 10-16 Sout 14af 61 1033
0 8-9 Folk 15.4sft 59 1271

FFIZZAMO GO 3 b g £258
18 6-7 Newm 12fm 3405 BL
32 4-6 Redc 14.1g/f 3771 bl
18 6-10 Bath 11.7g/s 4199 bl

FIAMMA ROYALE 5 b m £0
18a 15-16 Sout 5af 53 183 P
46a 4-12 Wolv 6af 49 385
39a 12-13 Ling 6ap 48 740
11a 12-13 Ling 6ap 48 767
30 13-16 Bath 5.7sft 50 1540
46 6-17 Bath 5g/f 45 2981
51 7-11 Bath 6g/f [44] 3372

FICTIONAL 3 b c £12571
90 1-16 LEIC 5g/f 79 2400*
77 6-9 Wind 5g/f 85 2797

FIDDLE ME BLUE 3 ch f £6922
77 5-13 Thir 5sft 77 1229
68 9-12 Wind 5g/f 77 1809
55 14-18 Wind 6g/f 75 2268
66 9-21 Good 5fm 72 3567
78 1-11 BATH 5g/f 70 3849*
78 3-6 Sand 5gd [77] 4498
74 6-12 Yarm 5.2g/s 77 4585 VIS
80 11-15 Newm 6gd [76] 5088 vis
80 2-11 Muss 5g/s 76 5332

FIDDLERS CREEK 5 b g £4519
59a 6-9 Sout 11af 75 391
58a 10-15 Ling 12ap 72 549 VIS
40 7-14 Newc 10.1sft 60 964 p
47 7-10 Muss 14g/f 57 1118 T
51 1-11 AYR 9.1sft [54] 5067* t
57 4-13 Muss 12g/s 52 5333 p

FIDDLERS FORD 3 b g £8397
75a 3-14 Ling 10ap 367
75a 2-14 Ling 10ap 473
78a 2-14 Ling 10ap [72] 759
73a 6-10 Ling 10ap 817
75a 4-13 Ling 12ap [72] 873
2 7-8 Newc 12.4hvy[72] 1038
77a 4-14 Ling 10ap 72 2392
52 10-16 Wind 11.6g/s 72 2621
78 1-8 WARW 18fm [72] 2781*

FIDDLES MUSIC 3 b f £5572
24a 9-9 Ling 8ap 1022
49 1-6 YARM 10.1g/f 1134*
45 4-14 Bath 10.2fm 45 2664
39 5-9 Brig 8fm [45] 2834
21 6-10 Folk 12g/s 45 3051
41 5-7 Brig 11.9g/f [43] 3715
33a 7-12 Ling 10ap 40 4113
48 1-9 BRIG 8sft 40 4165*
40 6-13 Folk 9.7g/f [46] 4372
30 7-10 Brig 9.9fm 46 4763

FIEFDOM 2 br c £7845
64 5-11 Nott 5.1gd 1237
95 4-11 York 6g/s 1687
86 1-17 DONC 6g/f 2424*
99 2-9 Asco 6gd 89 3127
83 4-7 Thir 7g/f 3412
98 3-5 Epso 8.5gd [98] 4906
87 7-9 Pont 8g/s [95] 5150

FIELD SPARK 4 b g £8846
48 6-17 Nott 14.1gd 55 1238 p
60 1-16 LEIC 11.8g/f 54 1830*
62 5-6 Ripo 12.3g/f 60 1980 p
62 2-11 Thir 12g/f 58 2217 p
60 3-9 Thir 12fm 59 2465 p
40 13-19 Carl 11.9gd 59 2673 p
59 2-8 Donc 12g/s 57 3222 p
31 12-12 Beve 12.1sft 58 4259 p
45 8-16 Yarm 11.5g/s 58 4589 p
53 4-18 Pont 12g/f 55 4938 p
59a 2-11 Wolv 12.2ap 55 5117 p
56a 3-12 Wolv 12.2ap 55 5328 p

FIENNES 5 b g £303
36a 5-13 Wolv 6af [42] 30 p
38a 6-15 Sout 6af [42] 167 vis
43a 3-15 Sout 6af [42] 253 vis
15a 9-10 Wolv 5af [42] 286 vis
37a 7-9 Sout 6af [45] 335 vis
7a 13-14 Ling 6ap [45] 652 vis

FIEPES SHUFFLE 4 b c £14789
112 2-13 Hamb 6hvy 3009

FIERY ANGEL 3 ch f £0
13 10-10 Sali 6g/s 4081

FIFE AND DRUM 6 b g £0
0 U-13 Ling 10ap 59 104 p
47a 9-14 Ling 10ap 59 236 p
46a 9-14 Ling 13ap 57 264 p
47a 7-12 Ling 8ap 54 406 bl
10a 14-14 Ling 10ap 52 498 p
40 6-12 Brig 9.9fm 49 1695 p
34 17-19 Brig 9.9g/f 48 1940 p
32 12-16 Yarm 10.1fm 48 2146 p
24 13-17 Warw 8.1g/f 45 2909 p

FIFTH COLUMN 3 b g £0
68 7-12 Leic 8fm 2106
14 11-11 Beve 8.5gd 2656
36 9-9 Nott 8.2g/f 3581
55 5-9 Thir 8g/f [60] 4593
2 P-8 Ayr 10sft [53] 5034

FIGAROS QUEST 2 b c £0
70 6-11 Sand 8.1g/s 3890
45 11-14 Kemp 8g/f 4356
45a 8-12 Wolv 8.6ap 5115

FIGGYS BREW 2 ch f £0
61 13-19 Leic 7gd 5045

FIGHT THE FEELING 5 ch g £3535
58a 1-11 WOLV 12af 52 72* VIS
32a 6-6 Wolv 9.4af 57 249 vis
52a 4-11 Wolv 12af 55 380 vis
56a 2-9 Sout 12af 55 456 vis
58a 2-11 Wolv 12af 57 557 vis
41a 8-12 Wolv 12af 57 634 BL
26a 14-14 Ling 12ap 56 801
50a 5-11 Wolv 12af 55 937 vis
31 11-16 Leic 11.8g/f 51 1830
39 6-17 Nott 14.1g/f 47 2156
38 10-10 Sali 14.1gd 45 2699
42 5-8 Donc 14.6gd 45 2754
25 9-13 Warw 12.6g/s [45] 4665 vis

FIGHT YOUR CORNER .5 b h £1755
90 8-12 Hami 12.1gd 109 1746 T
101 3-7 Sali 14.1gd[107] 4333 t

FIGHTING TOM CAT 2 ch c £4833
45 11-12 Newm 6g/f 3280 T
70 6-7 Yarm 6gd 3869 t
84 1-8 YARM 6g/s 4250* t

FIGURA 6 b m £431
49a 14-14 Ling 10ap 64 434

60a 3-14 Ling 10ap 60 520
63a 5-11 Ling 12ap 60 624
57a 6-7 Ling 10ap 59 736
57a 6-9 Ling 10ap 58 876
56a 6-13 Ling 10ap [58] 912
46a 5-14 Ling 10ap 56 1618
35 16-19 Brig 9.9g/f 49 1940
41 8-16 Yarm 10.1fm 49 2146
2 8-8 Brig 8g/f 45 2432 VIS
11 8-8 Epso 8.5g/f [41] 2873 T
43a 5-13 Ling 10ap [54] 3288
0 14-14 Ling 10ap 52 3605

FILEY BUOY 2 b g £0
22 13-20 Newc 6sft 2682
35 7-7 Catt 7g/s 3189
17 13-14 Thir 7g/s 4206
43 7-17 Redc 7g/s 5105 VIS

FILLIEMOU 3 gr f £1689
57 9-20 Newb 7g/f 65 1761
38 10-10 Good 9.9gd 62 2225
49 8-18 Donc 7gd 59 2755
54 5-14 Chep 8.1g/s 57 3090
57 2-12 Wind 8.3fm 54 3291
55 4-6 Brig 8g/f 56 3718
54 4-11 Wind 8.3fm 56 3799
32 18-20 Chep 7.1gd 54 4488
35a 12-13 Wolv 8.6ap [53] 5184
26 15-18 Newm 8sft 53 5272 VIS

FILM MAKER 4 br f £157542
119 2-4 Lone 11g/s 5309 bl

FINAL DIVIDEND 7 b g £3674
45a 4-10 Ling 13ap 48 11
47a 3-14 Ling 16ap 46 107 P
19 11-15 Ripo 12.3g/f 46 2526
43 5-13 Yarm 11.5fm 45 2868
36 6-18 Pont 12g/s 45 2988
42 5-19 Chep 12.1gd 44 3398
55 1-7 BRIG 11.9g/f [44] 3715*
41 6-17 Catt 12sft 49 3929

FINAL LAP 7 b g £185
0 10-10 Wolv 12af 22 243
0 11-11 Wolv 12af [30] 689
26a 3-13 Wolv 8.5af [30] 826
0 7-8 Wolv 12af [30] 1265

FINAL OVERTURE 2 b f £0
3 7-8 Pont 6g/f 2603

FINAL PROMISE 2 b c £460
57 10-14 Sali 7sft 4575
66 8-11 Sali 7gd 4853
73 4-14 Newb 6sft 5197

FINAL VIEW 4 b g £0
0 9-12 Wolv 12af 114 BL

FINANCIAL FUTURE 4 b g £0
62 17-19 Newm 12g/f 98 1484
56 15-17 Newb 12g/f 96 1759
28 12-13 Epso 12fm 90 2255
70 8-11 Newb 11g/f 85 3256
72 7-8 Ches 12.3fm 75 3637
67 7-17 Thir 12fm 70 4377 BL
11 14-14 Catt 12g/f 69 4672 bl

FINANCIAL TIMES 2 b c £1622
84 2-12 Newb 6g/f 2348

FINDERS KEEPERS 3 b g £14241
77a 2-15 Ling 7ap [87] 875
77a 3-11 Ling 7ap [84] 1008
78 1-13 MUSS 7.1g/f [80] 1119*
49 8-17 Asco 6sft 80 1417
67 8-15 Ling 7g/f 77 1983
45 8-8 Brig 7fm [74] 2259
82a 1-11 LING 6ap 72 3744*
51a 12-13 Ling 7ap 79 4318
33 8-8 Hami 5g/s [72] 4822

FINE FRENZY 4 b f £0
37 7-17 Beve 8.5g/s [47] 1160
33a 4-4 Wolv 7af [45] 1378
8 11-13 Leic 7g/f [45] 1827 p

FINE LADY 2 ch f £2622
51	6-11	Chep	8.1g/s		4296
72	2-15	Chep	7.1gd		4483
67	3-8	Hami	8.3g/s		4816
73	2-9	Catt	7sft	[69]	5131

FINE PALETTE 4 ch c £14125
84	1-9	LING	10sft		1623*
89	1-14	LEIC	10g/f		1828*
89	5-9	Newm	12g/f	[87]	2246
88	5-9	Sand	10g/s	87	2896
93	3-9	Asco	10g/f	86	3439
61	19-20	Hayd	10.5fm	88	3794

FINE SILVER 3 gr c £54907
84	4-14	York	7sft	83	1665
81	10-14	Newm	8g/f	83	1930
95	1-4	AYR	8g/f	[83]	2026*
94	4-27	Asco	8g/f	88	2521
97	2-13	Newm	8g/f	91	3277
100	2-16	Good	9.9fm	93	3553
103	3-32	Newm	9g/f	96	4916
103	2-8	Nott	8.2hvy	[98]	5346

FINGER OF FATE 4 br c £1198
33a	9-10	Sout	12af	63	421
0	12-12	Wolv	8.5af	63	479
0	7-8	Sout	16af	63	554
0	14-14	Ling	10ap	56	622 BL
20a	12-13	Sout	6af	50	741 bl
0	12-12	Ling	6ap	45	844 bl
42a	2-10	Sout	5af	[40]	1408 bl
36a	6-12	Sout	5af	40	1442 bl
33a	4-6	Wolv	6af	[40]	1671
29a	6-10	Sout	6af	[40]	1837 bl
27	13-20	Beve	5g/f	[45]	1948 bl
38	8-10	Muss	5g/s	42	2968 bl
41a	3-10	Sout	5af	[38]	3156 bl
0	14-15	Newc	7gd	[42]	3426 bl
49	3-10	Leic	7fm	[42]	3812 bl
36	6-13	Brig	5.3g/f	42	3984 bl
31	10-15	Redc	6fm	45	4562 bl
12	12-13	Muss	7.1gd	45	4806 bl

FINIANS GOLD 2 b c £0
| 10a | 9-10 | Wolv | 5af | 59 | 69 |

FINISHED ARTICLE 7 b g £4001
78	13-27	Newb	8gd	90	1231
94	5-18	Good	8g/f	90	1812
92	3-14	Sand	8.1g/f	90	2096
79	16-31	Asco	8g/f	90	2489
88	10-15	Sand	8.1g/s	89	2915
63	19-21	Good	8fm	89	3565
79	9-10	Sand	8.1g/s	87	4067
90	4-22	Newm	8sft	85	5103
81	8-13	Newm	8g/s	85	5284

FINNEGANS RAINBOW 2 ch c £0
| 40 | 11-14 | Leic | 8gd | | 5059 |

FINNFOREST 4 ch g £0
| 4a | 12-14 | Ling | 16ap | 53 | 4319 |

FINNINGLEY CONNOR 3 b g £0
0	14-15	Sout	6af	[65]	167
21a	10-13	Sout	5af	[50]	858
0	16-17	Beve	8.5g/s	[50]	1160
15	11-12	Sout	7gd	[50]	1284

FIORE DI BOSCO 3 b f £1385
71	5-11	Hami	6gd	82	1745
51	10-11	Ripo	6g/f	80	1977
72	4-8	Leic	7g/f	76	2403
73	4-9	Pont	6g/f	73	2609
52	6-6	Carl	5.9gd	[73]	2934

FIRE AT WILL 2 b c £0
42	7-9	Chep	5.1g/f		2625
52	7-8	Bath	5gd		2977
29	8-8	Wind	5g/s		4218 VIS
31	7-11	Bath	8gd		4544

FIRE CAT 4 ch g £0
48a	7-16	Sout	6af	[48]	65
32a	12-16	Sout	5af	49	183
0	11-11	Wolv	7af	[45]	396 P
0	7-8	Sout	6af	[45]	1201
15	10-12	Chep	5.1sft	[45]	1336 p

15	9-11	Folk	6sft	40	1578
25	13-18	Good	5g/f	35	1867
28	6-6	Folk	5fm	[35]	2717

FIRE DOME 11 ch g £0
| 22a | 16-16 | Ling | 7ap | 60 | 20 |
| 5a | 13-13 | Ling | 7ap | 52 | 761 T |

FIRE DRAGON 3 b g £539
| 78 | 5-8 | Ches | 12.3g/s | 82 | 2746 bl |
| 78 | 4-9 | Sand | 14g/s | 80 | 3893 P |

FIRE FINCH 3 ch f £450
60	6-11	Bath	8g/s		1101
81	6-7	Newb	10gd		1733
58	8-11	Bath	8fm		2031
2	6-6	Newb	12g/f	69	2353
12	14-14	Catt	12g/f	69	3192

FIRE UP THE BAND 5 b h £19703
88a	7-10	Ling	5ap	[106]	883
100	7-17	Donc	6gd	[106]	952
100	3-7	Kemp	6gd	[105]	1137
81	4-7	Thir	6sft	[105]	1227 VIS
82	21-29	Asco	6fm	102	2581
105	1-9	CHES	5.1g/f	[99]	3100*
83	12-13	Good	5fm	[99]	3551
99	11-12	York	5g/s	[99]	4060
60	21-24	Ayr	6sft	99	4686 vis

FIREBELLY 3 b f £519
79a	5-9	Ling	8ap	[95]	756 VIS
67	7-7	Leic	7fm	95	3814
0	10-10	Newm	6gd	90	4884 vis

FIREBIRD 3 b f £878
| 66 | 3-10 | Sali | 6gd | | 3452 |

FIREBIRD RISING 3 b f £759
40	5-7	Pont	6g/f		2042
39	9-14	Donc	6gd		2237
59	3-5	Carl	6.9fm	67	2446
58	6-11	Carl	6.9gd	64	2936
50	9-17	Ripo	6g/s	61	3262
44	4-11	Carl	6.9g/f	[58]	3651
46	7-15	Catt	7sft	58	3933
28	7-14	Beve	7.5sft	[53]	4256
45	3-13	Carl	6.9fm	[50]	4504
26	14-16	Catt	6g/f	47	4676

FIREBREAK 4 £127000
116	5-14	Sha	8g/f		211
118	4-15	Newb	8gd		1758 T
116	2-8	Donc	7fm	[115]	4477 t
119	1-12	NEWM	7sft	[116]	5134* t

FIRENZE 3 ch f £3283
| 43 | 9-10 | Newb | 5.2fm | | 2649 |
| 71a | 1-9 | SOUT | 6af | | 3396* |

FIRESONG 2 b c £0
| 76 | 6-19 | Leic | 7gd | | 5055 |

FIREWIRE 6 b g £5447
| 69 | 1-14 | WIND | 8.3g/f | 59 | 2799* |
| 32 | 16-16 | Kemp | 9g/f | 65 | 3039 |

FIREWORK 6 b g £3596
45a	11-12	Ling	6ap	66	628 p
38a	11-14	Ling	6ap	[63]	819 p
24a	12-13	Ling	6ap	58	902
48	6-11	Folk	6sft	63	1578 p
61	5-16	Good	6gd	61	2023 p
47	9-17	Wind	6gd	60	2451 p
64	1-6	FOLK	6fm	[60]	2715* p
37	9-10	Epso	6g/s	64	3045 p
49	12-17	Wind	6gd	62	3643 p
56	4-11	Epso	6gd	[59]	4294
63	4-19	Nott	6.1g/f	[57]	4845 p

FIROZI 5 b m £0
| 50 | 5-16 | Carl | 7.9g/f | 49 | 3650 |

FIRST ACORN 2 b f £0
| 33a | 10-14 | Sout | 8af | [42] | 88 p |
| 2a | 9-11 | Sout | 7af | [42] | 207 p |

FIRST CANDLELIGHT 3 b f £0
| 70 | 9-11 | Asco | 8sft | | 1419 |
| 55 | 17-17 | Epso | 7g/f | 85 | 2212 |

| 79 | 7-9 | Newm | 7fm | 82 | 3006 |
| 40 | 12-12 | Sand | 7.1g/f | 78 | 3860 |

FIRST CENTURION 3 b c £6352
87	1-12	KEMP	8hvy		1511*
81	8-14	Asco	10g/f	87	1924
59	11-13	Hayd	11.9gd	85	2238
82	4-6	Newm	10g/f	83	3749
73	5-9	Ayr	13.1sft	80	5068
55a	9-10	Ling	12ap	78	5239

FIRST CHARTER 5 b h £100492
37	9-9	Ches	13.4gd	[109]	1596
114	1-7	NEWM	12g/f	[109]	2762*
118	2-9	Good	12fm	[109]	3563
117	1-10	YORK	15.9gd	[112]	4000*
116	3-13	Curr	14gd	[112]	4733

FIRST CLASS GIRL 5 b m £0
| 10a | 4-9 | Sout | 12af | | 353 |
| 14 | 10-13 | Leic | 10fm | | 2107 |

FIRST CLASS LADY 4 ch f £0
| 35a | 5-11 | Ling | 8ap | [45] | 535 |
| 0 | 12-15 | Ling | 12ap | [40] | 707 |

FIRST COUNSEL 3 b c £935
| 79 | 5-9 | Hayd | 8.1g/f | | 1882 |
| 79 | 3-14 | Hayd | 8.1g/s | | 2231 |

FIRST DAWN 3 ch f £0
61	7-9	Asco	7g/f		1929
58	11-17	Kemp	7gd	70	2174
47	8-8	Sali	8gd	66	2701
2	16-19	Chep	8.1g/s	[60]	4366

FIRST DYNASTY 4 br c £4045
80a	1-9	WOLV	9.4af	[79]	1340+
65	7-15	Warw	8.1sft	79	1530
72	6-10	Beve	8.5g/f	77	3501
74	3-13	Nott	10gd	74	3992
62	7-13	Bath	11.7sft	72	5174 p

FIRST EAGLE 5 b g £555
| 0 | 12-13 | Wolv | 9.4af | 50 | 281 vis |
| 41 | 3-14 | Pont | 10g/f | 40 | 4624 vis |

FIRST ECLIPSE 3 b f £0
| 39 | 9-12 | Catt | 5g/f | 53 | 3193 |
| 30 | 11-12 | Donc | 5g/f | 50 | 3599 |

FIRST FOUGHT 2 b g £0
| 35 | 18-20 | Yarm | 8sft | | 5252 |

FIRST MAITE 10 b g £2958
64a	7-11	Sout	8af	71	186
75a	2-11	Sout	8af	70	255
54a	6-10	Sout	8af	71	318 bl
68a	6-8	Wolv	8.5af	[71]	360
54a	6-10	Sout	8af	[70]	502 t
44a	4-7	Sout	12af	[67]	679
50	3-8	Nott	10g/f	50	2157
53	2-17	Warw	8.1fm	50	2572
65a	3-15	Sout	8af	65	2725
42	5-18	Pont	10g/f	50	2988

FIRST OF MAY 3 b f £908
54a	3-15	Ling	7ap		472
63a	4-12	Ling	8ap		623
42a	6-7	Ling	8ap	53	910

FIRST ORDER 3 b g £4865
105	2-12	Newm	5g/f	100	3279
69	22-24	Asco	5gd	100	3466
75	6-7	Nott	5.1gd	[101]	3989
77	2-12	Sand	5gd	[100]	4605

FIRST PRESSURE 3 b g £0
| 45a | 6-15 | Sout | 16af | 58 | 67 |
| 44a | 13-14 | Ling | 16ap | 58 | 107 P |

FIRST RHAPSODY 2 b f £332
17	12-15	York	6g/f		2056
30	11-16	Pont	6g/f		2275
65a	4-12	Wolv	6ap		4921

FIRST ROW 2 b c £0
| 80 | 5-15 | Sand | 7.1g/f | | 3337 |

FIRST RULE 2 ch c £650

FISBY and related entries

49 7-8   Kemp 5hvy   1510
70 4-11 Wind 5g/f   2450
70 4-7   Ling 5g/f   2738
60 8-12 Ling 5gd   72   3284
61 8-10 Newm 6fm   72   4727

FISBY 3 ch g £2716
42a 5-9   Ling 8ap   3195
67   5-17 Wind 8.3fm   3480
39   14-15 Newb 6gd   65   3920
45   10-16 Sali 8gd   64   4334
38   10-12 Brig 8fm   [60]   4761
64a 1-12 WOLV 8.6ap [55]   5329*

FISHERS DREAM 2 b g £598
54a 2-11 Wolv 6af   [44]   73 vis
33a 6-12 Sout 5af   [54]   200 vis
49a 4-9   Sout 5af   [54]   256 vis
29a 7-10 Sout 6af   [48]   308 vis

FISHLAKE FLYER 3 b f £1053
49   4-9   Redc 5sft [71]   1146 VIS
66   3-8   Donc 5g/f [66]   2075
59   4-9   Leic 5g/f [64]   3347

FISIO THERAPY 4 b g £765
76   9-27 Newb 8gd   83   1231
81   4-10 Hayd 10.5g/s 82   1346
0   P-12 Ches 10.3gd 81   1586

FISSION 2 ch f £4806
78a 3-8   Sout 5af   79   169 bl
0   W-7   Sout 6af   79   333 bl
52a 6-11 Wolv 6af   [79]   466 bl
69a 3-12 Wolv 7af   [75]   560 bl
67a 1-15 LING 7af   [72]   671* bl
45a 9-14 Ling 7ap   [72]   804 bl
73   2-17 Ling 6g/f   70   4740
69   10-11 Newm 6sft   [71]   5270

FIT TO FLY 3 b c £4360
67a 2-8   Wolv 6af   [81]   750
68a 5-15 Ling 7ap   [72]   814
69a 1-11 SOUT 6af   [72]   869*
76   5-13 Sand 8.1gd 75   2365
68a 6-8   Sout 7af   67   2723
64   9-10 Nott 10g/s [75]   2930
65   5-10 Asco 8gd   [75]   3067
0   12-14 Hayd 10.5gd 70   3741
57a 8-11 Sout 8af   66   4044
60   7-15 Bath 8gd   65   4827
22a 11-11 Wolv 12.2ap 62   5117
47a 9-12 Wolv 7.1ap [58]   5325 P

FITTING GUEST 3 ch c £8319
67   6-14 Wind 10g/s   1259
72   2-11 Beve 9.9g/f 65   1834
72   2-15 Ripo 10g/f   65   1976
76   1-5   LEIC 10g/f   [69] 2401*
65   14-27 Asco 8g/f   74   2521

FITZ THE BILL 3 b f £550
2a   14-15 Sout 6af   41   168
32a 8-10 Ling 8ap   [35] 410
19a 8-14 Ling 12ap   [35] 968
35a 3-6   Ling 10ap   [30] 1455 BL
46   3-10 Yarm 10.1g/f [30] 1724 bl
33   7-13 Leic 10fm   [42] 2107 bl
22   11-11 Yarm 10.1gd [42] 3362 bl
13   9-12 Yarm 16gd   42   3493 T

FITZWARREN 3 b g £1235
33   14-19 York 6g/f   69   2055 vis
71   3-15 Redc 5g/s   67   2961 vis
42   10-10 Hayd 5g/s   67   3135 vis
52   9-12 Donc 5g/f   68   3599 vis
60   3-8   Pont 6gd   [68] 3684
58   6-8   Redc 6g/f   67   3808
29   17-18 Redc 6fm   63   4339 vis
55   6-16 Pont 5fm   59   4754
23   18-19 Nott 6.1g/f [59] 4845 vis
39   12-14 Redc 7g/s   62   5109

FIVE DYNASTIES 3 b c £87838
89   3-4   Ling 11.5sft   1622
111 8-15 Chan 12g/s   2308
112 1-5   ASCO 12g/f   2554*
101 8-10 Curr 12g/f   2822

FIVE GOLD 3 b g £0
43   11-14 Chep 7.1gd   67   2199
42   7-8   Leic 7g/f   65   2403
40   17-19 Leic 7g/f   62   4452
41   10-13 Warw 7.1g/s [55] 4667
40   9-13 Ayr   10sft   [50] 5276

FIVE YEARS ON 2 b g £1460
69a 2-9   Ling 5ap   76
52a 4-4   Sout 5af   222
60   4-6   Muss 8gd   [73] 4520
67   4-15 Bath 8gd   64   4827
69a 5-12 Wolv 7.1ap   67   5008

FIVEOCLOCK EXPRESS 4 gr g £7562
0   8-8   Wolv 7af   [90] 838 vis
92a 4-15 Ling 7ap   90   887 P
82   2-16 Thir 7g/s   78   1474 p
48   13-14 Ling 7sft   81   1624 vis
70   7-10 Thir 7g/f   [81] 1970 vis
72   5-7   Newm 8fm   [81] 2091
92a 2-12 Ling 8ap   [90] 3199 p
61   16-25 Asco 9g/f   78   3443 p
64   10-12 Newm 6g/f   76   3942 p
67   9-10 Leic 8gd   [71] 4702 p
58   11-20 Leic 7gd   69   5046 p

FIXATEUR 2 b c £5141
89   4-4   Long 9hvy   5164

FIZZY LADY 3 b f £6235
71a 4-12 Ling 8ap   428
63a 4-11 Wolv 6af   [67] 481
54a 1-9   SOUT 7af   [64] 613* T
48   7-7   Folk 7g/f   [67] 2272 t
43   11-14 Chep 8.1g/s 64   3090 t
13   12-15 Leic 7g/f   [60] 3515 t
42   7-15 Bath 8g/s   55   4202 t
27   14-20 Chep 7.1g/s 55   4367 t
53   2-18 Chep 8.1gd   [52] 4485 t
39   4-12 Chep 10.2hvy 50   4708 t
41   10-18 Kemp 10g/f   [50] 4791 t
57   1-16 NOTT 10gd   50   4857*
42   7-9   Good 11gd   [52] 5026

FIZZY LIZZY 4 b f £3220
19   12-19 Redc 6g/f   39   2125
11a 11-16 Sout 6af   36   2806
26   8-17 Ripo 6g/s   34   3262
43   1-10 CARL 5.9fm   [32] 3545*
34a 9-11 Sout 6af   [33] 4041 P

FIZZY POP 5 b m £0
41   6-9   Thir 7fm   3610
7   8-10 Hami 9.2g/s   4135

FLAG LIEUTENANT 2 b c £1840
84   2-19 Leic 7gd   5055

FLAG POINT 2 b c £851
80   3-8   Sali 7gd   2695
65   7-14 Ling 7.6g/f   3601
68   9-14 Folk 7gd   4115
72   11-17 Good 8gd   75   4871
66   11-20 Yarm 8g/s   71   5349

FLAMAND 2 ch f £0
68   5-16 Pont 6g/f   2275

FLAMBE 5 b g £311
50a 4-16 Sout 8af   60   86
58a 4-10 Sout 8af   58   318 BL

FLAMBOYANT LAD 3 ch c £34233
83   3-11 Donc 10.3gd   930
78   3-8   Newm 10fm   3007
78   3-9   Nott 10g/s   [80] 4034
84   2-13 Leic 10g/f   [79] 4453
89   1-5   PONT 10g/f   [79] 4630*
91   1-17 NEWM 10g/f   80   4917*
94   1-19 NEWM 12gd   84   5085*

FLAME OF ZARA 5 ch m £0
54   7-12 Newc 16.1sft 54   965
54   4-17 Nott 14.1gd 52   1238
46   7-11 Ayr   15sft   53   5032

FLAME PRINCESS 4 ch f £182
51a 3-7   Ling 6ap   [40] 706

17a 11-13 Ling 6ap   [40] 788
31a 8-10 Ling 8ap   [45] 831
32a 14-15 Ling 7ap   40   846

FLAME QUEEN 3 b f £633
57   9-13 Newm 7fm   74   2590
45   11-12 Hayd 8.1gd   71   2904
55   9-12 Wind 8.3fm   69   3291
65   4-11 Yarm 7g/f   66   3711
40   8-14 Yarm 8g/s   [64] 4252
60   4-13 Leic 10g/f   [64] 4453
46   12-13 Yarm 10.1gd 62   4613
56   7-26 Redc 8fm   60   4926
71   8-8   Leic 8gd   [57] 5057

FLAMENCA 4 b f £0
0   9-10 Wolv 12af   40   243

FLAMENCO BRIDE 4 b f £1266
64   7-14 Sali 12g/s   69   3114
67   7-13 Asco 16.2g/f 69   3387
72   3-12 Kemp 14.4g/f 67   3688
57   11-19 Sali 14.1gd 70   4856

FLAMING SPIRT 5 b m £1387
49a 4-14 Ling 10ap   50   3605
51   4-16 Wind 11.6gd 50   3829
53   2-12 Newb 10gd   50   3916
1   17-19 Brig 9.9sft 50   4145

FLAMINGO PALACE 3 ch g £0
0   7-7   Newm 12g/f   1936

FLAMJICA 3 ch f £2134
70   4-11 Newm 8g/f   2248
74   2-13 Newm 8fm   [70] 2595

FLAPDOODLE 6 b m £638
54   5-14 Ling 5g/f   56   2585
44   12-17 Bath 5g/f   54   2981
35   11-15 Chep 5.1gd   51   3403
28   14-16 Wind 5fm   48   3640
46   3-8   Folk 5gd   43   4118 VIS
4   11-15 Brig 6gd   [45] 4905 bl
45   5-16 Warw 5g/s   [45] 4995 bl
28a 8-13 Ling 5.1ap   [45] 5231 bl

FLARAN 4 b g £1116
35   15-17 Sand 5g/f   61   3341
54   5-13 Brig 5.3g/f 59   3984
46   11-17 Wind 6gd   59   4126
61   3-15 Good 5gd   57   4751
60   3-19 Wind 6g/f   58   5053

FLASH RAM 3 b c £9595
64   6-8   Nott 5.1fm   71   1002
68   4-11 Redc 7g/f   [70] 1822
66   2-8   Ripo 6gd   [66] 2527 VIS
71   2-14 Thir 7sft   [66] 2692 bl
62   6-12 Catt 6g/f   [64] 2849 bl
70   1-10 CARL 6.9g/f [64] 3230* bl
63   6-18 Hayd 6gd   67   3737 bl
63   3-14 Muss 7.1g/f 65   4175
20   19-19 York 7.9g/f 64   4399

FLASHING BLADE 4 b f £6180
73   15-17 Donc 6gd   [85] 952
60   7-14 Thir 5gd   [85] 1216
72   13-14 Bath 5gd   [78] 1400
47   12-15 Ripo 6gd   78   1782 T
63   9-11 Newm 6fm   74   2093 t P
69   1-13 NOTT 8.2g/f [70] 2633* t
58   7-12 Nott 8.2g/s 70   2931 t
64   6-11 Donc 7g/s   68   3223 t
67   5-13 Thir 7g/f   66   3571 t
50   7-12 Pont 6g/s   [64] 3971 t
69   2-8   Thir 8fm   64   4378 t

FLAUNT N FLIRT 2 b f £1112
38   9-10 Good 6gd   4876
67a 10-14 Ling 7ap   5258
70a 2-12 Wolv 7.1ap   5324

FLAUNTING IT 2 ch f £383
66   5-15 Folk 7gd   3381
54   8-11 Sali 7gd   3883
63   4-5   Good 6sft   4234
49   6-14 Yarm 7g/s   63   4583

FLAXBY 2 b g £351
23	14-20	Newc	6sft		2682
34	8-10	Catt	6g/f		4436
63	4-14	Newc	6fm		4865
69	8-21	Donc	6hvy		5202

FLEET ANCHOR 3 b c £1530
45	9-9	Warw	6.1g/f		2906
52	7-17	Ripo	6g/s	60	3262
42	9-20	Thir	6g/f	57	3575
58	2-18	Chep	7.1g/s	54	3900
49	5-19	Chep	6.1sft	54	4054
60	3-13	Bath	8gd	52	4546
37	5-13	Chep	8.1hvy	52	4709
52	10-11	Good	8gd	55	5027
47	11-18	Newm	8sft	55	5272

FLEETFOOT MAC 3 b g £6186
68	1-6	CHEP	12.1sft	[59]	1331*
66	1-20	WIND	11.6sft	59	1648*
46	8-11	Sand	14g/s	65	2130
30	14-14	Ches	12.3gd	65	2285
68a	3-11	Sout	12af	63	2804
68	4-12	Wind	11.6gd	65	3161
59	9-13	Beve	12.1g/f	66	3502
35	13-16	Warw	16.2gd	66	4276 VIS

FLEETING MOON 4 ch f £5066
49a	2-9	Ling	12ap		324
65a	2-7	Ling	13ap		546
63a	1-5	SOUT	11af	[55]	772*
63a	3-12	Ling	16ap	62	813
69	2-10	Bath	13.1g/f	63	1789
60a	4-8	Ling	12ap	63	3026

FLEETWOOD BAY 4 b g £2251
57	16-17	Leic	7g/s	77	1020
52	14-20	Wind	6g/s	75	1255
60	6-15	Warw	8.1sft	72	1530
74	3-13	Ling	7.6g/f	69	2587
66	6-10	Epso	7g/f	69	2872
65	9-20	Chep	7.1g/s	69	3088
68	2-12	Kemp	8g/f	67	3524 T
64	6-11	Kemp	8g/f	67	3685 t
54	7-12	Sali	8g/s	66	4077 t
54	10-13	Warw	6.1gd	66	4272

FLETCHER 10 b g £1463
23a	12-13	Ling	13ap	45	896
43	5-13	Brig	11.9g/f	45	1373
47a	1-9	LING	16ap	[45]	1414*
40	7-13	Nott	14.1gd	[45]	1990
26	12-18	Newm	12fm	45	2088
19	10-14	Bath	18.2fm	40	2417 p
37	4-10	Carl	14.1fm	38	3549 p

FLIGHT COMMANDER 4 b g £0
55	5-10	Hami	9.2g/s		4135
59	7-13	Newc	10.1g/f	66	4406
23	16-20	Hayd	11.9g/s	64	4771
21	11-11	Ayr	15sft	62	5032
44	12-13	Muss	12g/s	58	5333 VIS

FLIGHT OF ESTEEM 4 b g £8699
97a	2-16	Ling	12ap	91	293
97a	2-16	Ling	12ap	92	475

FLIGHTY FELLOW 4 ch g £18813
80	15-24	Donc	8gd	92	951 bl
72	6-12	Pont	8hvy	92	1066
98	1-10	BEVE	8.5g/f	90	1833+
80	18-31	Asco	8g/f	94	2489
90	6-14	Hayd	8.1gd	94	2903 bl
97	2-7	York	7.9g/s	94	3077
92	4-10	Pont	8gd	94	3460
76	16-20	Hayd	10.5fm	94	3794 bl
99	4-15	Donc	8fm	92	4531 bl
96	3-14	Asco	8g/f	94	4813 bl
79	10-19	York	7.9gd	94	4987 bl

FLING 3 b f £16519
73	1-9	SOUT	10gd		1283*
82	5-7	Ling	10g/f	80	2015
86	2-10	Newm	10fm	80	2592
85	2-9	Newm	12gd	81	3926
85	4-7	Hayd	10.5sft	83	4781
96	5-12	Yarm	14.1sft	[83]	5254
86	3-6	Muss	16g/s	[83]	5334

82	4-7	Donc	16.5sft	87	5374

FLINT RIVER 5 b g £21959
84a	1-9	WOLV	7af	74	31*
58a	14-15	Ling	7ap	81	81
83a	2-12	Wolv	6af	81	361
73a	7-13	Wolv	6af	82	482
76a	8-12	Wolv	8.5af	82	632
76a	12-15	Ling	7ap	80	887
86a	1-9	WOLV	7af	78	940*
76	2-7	Muss	7.1g/f	[74]	1094
76	4-18	Ches	7.6gd	74	1598
64	10-16	Good	7g/f	74	1817
66	9-13	Kemp	7gd	73	2172
75	2-15	Brig	8fm	71	3694
75	2-11	Brig	8g/s	73	4141
75	5-13	Epso	8.5gd	74	4469
75a	8-12	Wolv	7.1ap	83	5159

FLIP FLOP AND FLY 3 b g £8953
30	14-15	Newb	8gd	90	1206
23	11-11	Sali	6g/s	85	1498 BL
89	1-15	LING	7g/f	79	1983*
82	7-17	Epso	7g/f	84	2212
82	6-9	Sali	8g/s	85	3112
87	2-9	Sand	7.1g/f	84	3338
85	5-12	Sand	7.1g/f	85	3860
78	8-10	Kemp	8fm	85	4389

FLIPANDO 3 b g £33638
75	4-17	Asco	6sft	76	1417
86	2-13	Hayd	6g/f	75	1881
84	2-10	Donc	7g/f	77	2427
90	1-15	HAYD	6gd	79	2950*
89	5-11	Newm	6g/f	86	3941
92	3-12	Newm	7gd	86	4225
94	1-8	MUSS	8gd	86	4516+

FLOOSIE 2 b f £0
29	9-9	Sand	6g/f		3355 T
13	10-14	Leic	6g/f		3517 t

FLOPPIE DISK 3 b f £0
15a	13-13	Wolv	5af	63	110

FLORENZAR 6 b m £0
13a	10-12	Wolv	9.4af	54	464
28a	9-12	Ling	10ap	49	542

FLORIAN 6 b g £0
31a	12-12	Ling	8ap	[63]	2394
52	8-14	Wind	8.3g/f	63	2799 P
43	13-16	Kemp	7gd	61	3184 p
55	6-8	Brig	8fm	[59]	3676
40	6-9	Brig	7sft	[57]	4164
29	18-18	Bath	5.7g/f	55	4412
36	8-19	Yarm	6g/s	55	4636

FLORIDA HEART 3 ch f £548
73	4-20	Asco	8g/f	76	1927
69	6-8	Kemp	9g/s	76	2680

FLOSSYTOO 2 b f £4719
57	10-15	Donc	5gd		920
72	1-8	HAYD	5g/s		1343*
67	9-10	Thir	5g/f		1764
28	12-12	Beve	5g/f		2165
52	9-12	Hayd	5gd	74	3756

FLOTTA 5 ch g £13417
87a	4-12	Ling	13ap	84	877
86	5-20	Newm	12gd	86	1172
85	7-17	Newb	12g/f	86	1759
86	4-12	Muss	14fm	85	2085
85	4-7	York	13.9g/f	83	2355
86	3-7	Newm	12g/f	82	2737
64	7-7	Sand	14g/s	82	2899
86	1-6	PONT	12gd	80	3681*
80	6-12	Epso	12gd	83	4292
82	5-15	Newb	11g/f	82	4643
72	10-14	Asco	12g/f	83	4814
47	10-19	Newm	12gd	81	5085
78	6-13	Donc	12sft	81	5215

FLOWER SEEKER 2 b f £0
38	16-17	Warw	7.1gd		4269
30	9-11	Chep	7.1hvy		4704
12	12-14	Sali	8gd		4852

FLOWERDRUM 4 b f £17022
64	8-13	Newc	7hvy	77	1035
86	1-14	YARM	8g/f	76	1131*
85	4-12	Hayd	8.1g/f	83	1883
92	1-13	SALI	8gd	83	2662*
76	14-21	Good	8fm	87	3565
95	5-12	Bath	8g/f	[86]	3965
53	10-12	Yarm	10.1sft	86	4149
88	5-13	Asco	8g/f	88	4802

FLUR NA H ALBA 5 b g £8178
86	1-12	AYR	7.2fm	79	1909* p
49	12-13	Ayr	7.2g/s	83	2568 p
81	3-7	Ayr	7.2gd	[83]	3326 p
81	4-11	Hayd	6g/f	[82]	4350 p
48	13-18	Ayr	7.2sft	81	4689 p
83a	3-12	Wolv	7.1ap	80	5159 p

FLUSHING MEADOWS 3 b c £390
80	5-8	Yarm	6g/s		4588 T

FLY KICKER 7 ch g £0
12	7-14	Carl	17.2gd	30	2937 p
33	6-9	Ayr	15gd	27	3327 p

FLY ME TO DUNOON 2 b f £0
29	8-8	Muss	7.1g/f		3559
41	6-8	Yarm	6g/s		4250 VIS
48a	10-11	Ling	8ap		4738 vis

FLY MORE 7 ch g £0
43	12-15	Sali	6gd	76	3888
57	13-19	Beve	5g/s	74	4240

FLY SO HIGH 3 b f £0
34a	10-16	Ling	7ap		670
38a	7-9	Ling	7ap		764
10	8-8	Donc	6gd		953 VIS
0	11-11	Leic	10g/f		2924

FLY TO DUBAI 2 b c £0
44	11-19	Kemp	6g/f		1911
60	6-11	Ayr	6g/s		2569
12a	13-13	Ling	7ap		3330

FLYING ADORED 3 b f £14316
72	3-13	Folk	7g/s	[74]	1270
53	10-12	Leic	8g/f	72	2922
79	1-9	GOOD	8gd	69	3950+
84	1-8	GOOD	8sft	74	4265*
80	5-13	Sand	8.1gd	80	4607
86	3-9	Wind	10g/s	80	4943
27	16-19	Donc	10.3sft	80	5201

FLYING BANTAM 3 b g £16966
72	2-14	Thir	6gd	[71]	1639
72	2-6	Redc	6g/f	[71]	2104
71	2-14	Donc	6g/f	[70]	2428
67	4-12	Catt	6g/f	[70]	2849 P
51	7-10	Hami	6gd	70	3203
73	2-8	Pont	6gd	[68]	3684
68	4-8	Nott	5.1gd	[70]	4039
56	7-20	Ripo	6gd	70	4278
70	4-15	Redc	6fm	69	4562
82	1-10	RIPO	6g/f	[68]	4790*
74a	3-13	Wolv	6ap	73	5114
82a	1-12	WOLV	6ap	73	5291*
87	2-16	Redc	6sft	79	5304

FLYING DANCER 2 b f £1108
72	3-13	Wind	6fm		3639
72a	4-12	Ling	6ap		4178
44	17-21	Donc	6fm		4490
60	9-15	Hayd	6sft	70	4765

FLYING EDGE 4 b g £1554
32a	12-13	Wolv	6af	56	384
56a	2-11	Sout	7af	51	585
34a	7-9	Wolv	7af	51	629
57	1-5	Hami	6gd	61	1508
44	14-19	Redc	7g/f	60	1820
56	6-20	York	6g/f	59	2409
56	5-16	Carl	5.9fm	57	2445
42	16-18	Catt	7g/f	57	2848
48	10-10	Carl	6.9gd	57	2935
51	8-13	Thir	7g/f	55	3571
54	4-20	Hayd	6fm	53	3796
41	8-14	Hami	6g/s	52	4818
39	11-19	Ayr	6sft	54	5069

45a	4-12	Wolv	7.1ap	[50]	5229

FLYING EXPRESS 4 ch c £5724

86	6-20	Newm	7g/s	87	1151
76	12-17	Sand	8.1g/s	86	1351
87	2-11	Donc	7g/f	84	2076
68	8-9	Ches	7gd	85	2282
85	3-8	Sand	7.1g/f	85	2389
54	11-12	Ches	7.6fm	85	3634
74a	9-14	Ling	7ap	83	4180
43	23-24	Newb	5g/f	82	4642

FLYING FAISAL 6 b h £2791

18a	8-11	Wolv	6af	[44]	296
28a	9-13	Ling	6ap	[45]	340
25a	10-16	Sout	6af	[40]	447 bl
41a	6-12	Wolv	6af	[35]	524
22a	8-13	Ling	6ap	[35]	541
29a	4-10	Wolv	6af	[40]	667
10a	15-15	Ling	7ap	[40]	708
23a	8-11	Wolv	6af	[40]	778 p
29a	3-12	Sout	5af	[35]	904
37a	10-12	Wolv	5af	[35]	960
24a	4-11	Wolv	6af	[35]	1261 bl
30	6-12	Chep	5.1sft	[45]	1336 bl
49	1-7	BRIG	6af	[45]	1368* bl
23	8-10	Brig	5.3gd	[45]	1544 bl
37	10-18	Wind	6af	[47]	1806 bl
31	9-10	Brig	7g/f	[47]	1938 bl
22	13-16	Nott	6.1gd	[47]	1988 bl
1	18-20	Nott	6.1g/f	44	2630

FLYING HEART 2 ch f £0

53	7-10	Good	6gd	4876
53	8-13	Wind	6g/f	5048
47	8-14	Newb	6sft	5197

FLYING HIGHEST 2 b f £0

14	7-7	Chep	6.1hvy	4705

FLYING PASS 2 b g £4616

31	8-8	Kemp	5hvy		1510
74	3-19	Kemp	6g/f		1911
67	8-15	Wind	6g/f		2263
73	2-13	Epso	7g/f		2870
79a	2-13	Ling	7ap		3330
71	5-7	Newm	7g/f	75	3753
66	6-12	Sali	6g/s	74	4079 VIS
72	4-12	Bath	8g/f	72	4410
79	2-16	Nott	10g/f	72	4848
62	7-13	Wind	8.3g/s	70	4940

FLYING PATRIARCH 2 gr c £0

49a	11-12	Ling	10ap		120 bl
46	13-16	Wind	10gd		1384
21	8-10	Good	14gd	47	2376 bl

FLYING RED 3 b f £0

3	8-8	Hami	11.1gd	1390

FLYING RIDGE 2 ch f £3590

51	14-19	Newb	6gd	2310
69	5-13	Hayd	6gd	3736
76	5-7	Ches	6.1g/f	4050
80	1-12	CARL	5g/f	4343*

FLYING SPIRIT 5 b g £17231

71	1-16	BRIG	11.9fm	58	1693*
80	1-5	BRIG	11.9fm	[66]	2329*
82	1-8	EPSO	12gd	69	3217*
60	9-15	Bath	11.7g/f	76	3964
81	2-12	Epso	12gd	76	4292

FLYING SPUD 3 ch g £3856

49a	5-7	Wolv	6af		863
49a	4-8	Wolv	7af	[47]	1222
43	5-14	Warw	8.1sft	47	1529
54	1-8	NOTT	8.2sft	47	1740*
30	7-9	Good	11g/f	50	2019
22a	7-12	Wolv	8.5af	50	2205
23	15-17	Warw	8.1g/f	50	2909
53	2-15	Beve	8.5g/s	48	3182
40	9-16	Beve	8.5g/s	[50]	3850
47	11-15	Carl	7.9g/f	48	4346
44	5-19	Yarm	8g/s	[48]	5119
39a	5-12	Wolv	9.5ap	[45]	5209

FLYING TACKLE 6 ch g £4865

39a	10-14	Ling	6ap	51	328 p

24	7-8	Newc	6sft	[51]	963 p
50	7-10	Newc	5g/f	[49]	2161
47	3-15	Pont	6g/f	49	2280 p
47	2-19	Beve	5gd	48	2657 p
55	1-17	BATH	5g/f	48	2981* p
32	15-20	Beve	5g/s	48	3180 p
44	9-18	Carl	5g/f	48	3228 p
10	17-18	Pont	5gd	51	3463 p
34	11-20	Newc	6g/f	50	4408 p
55	2-15	Carl	5fm	[50]	4508 p
44	11-19	Ling	5g/f	53	4739 p

FLYING TARA 2 b f £0

4	7-7	Leic	6g/f	1964

FLYING TREATY 7 br h £0

55a	11-12	Wolv	6af	88	361
73a	8-16	Sout	7af	88	419
54a	9-10	Wolv	8.5af	[84]	511
49a	6-7	Wolv	12af	79	642
63	8-18	Catt	7gd	66	998
56	7-13	Muss	7.1g/f	63	1122
70a	5-12	Ling	8ap	[73]	2840
47	6-10	Brig	8gd	60	2954 BL
29	8-12	Wind	10fm	58	3295 P

FLYING WITH EAGLES 3 ch g £0

40	13-14	Brig	6fm		1690
37	14-15	Leic	6g/f		1829
34	13-14	Yarm	7fm		2148
32a	6-12	Sout	7af		2339
5	17-20	Beve	16.2gd	42	3312

FLYOFF 7 b g £0

22a	9-11	Ling	12ap	[46]	2588 vis
32	10-10	Leic	11.8g/f	[45]	3211 vis

FOCUS GROUP 3 b c £3552

82	1-9	REDC	9fm	4336*

FOGGIELOAN 3 b f £0

0	9-13	Wolv	8.5af	[48]	39

FOKINE 3 b c £59200

104a	2-15	Ling	7ap	[114]	885
111	2-10	Newb	7gd	[114]	1234
111	1-8	NEWM	7g/f	[114]	1932*
112	2-15	Asco	7g/f	[113]	2486

FOLD WALK 2 ch f £633

0	7-10	Thir	5sft		1224
47	4-8	Beve	5sft		1303
0	U-11	Beve	5g/f		1831
0	11-12	Newc	6gd		1869
43	5-7	Beve	5gd		3308
44a	3-14	Sout	6af	[46]	4127
30	11-14	Thir	7g/s	[46]	4206
14	13-16	Beve	7.5g/f	46	4597

FOLEY MILLENNIUM 6 ch g £19944

21	8-8	Folk	5g/s	[50]	1269
51	1-10	KEMP	5hvy	[45]	1644*
62	1-11	BATH	5.7fm	[49]	2412*
65	1-17	WARW	5fm	59	2599*
67	1-18	HAYD	5gd	62	2951*
27	12-13	Bath	5gd	[66]	3143
70	2-9	Ayr	5gd	66	3307
74	1-12	NOTT	5.1g/f	[66]	3577*
68	4-7	Ling	6fm	[73]	3789
76	2-8	Nott	5.1gd	[73]	4039
58	8-12	Newm	5gd	73	4197
73	5-12	Yarm	5.2g/s	74	4585
70	5-14	Redc	5fm	[73]	4930
57	15-18	Pont	5g/s	71	5149

FOLEY PRINCE 3 b g £7692

68a	7-14	Ling	7ap	[67]	804
60a	3-15	Ling	7ap	[67]	935
50a	7-9	Wolv	7af	67	940
74	1-18	WIND	8.3sft	65	1647*
75	2-14	Wind	8.3g/f	69	1956
75	2-13	Sand	8.1gd	70	2365
75	3-14	Nott	8.2g/f	72	2634
69	6-12	Leic	8g/f	72	2922

FOLGA 2 b f £4765

62	3-6	Muss	5g/f	3525
44	9-12	Thir	5g/s	3832
75	1-8	MUSS	5gd	4517*

73	5-18	Wind	5g/f	70	4830

FOLIO 4 b g £0

88	6-20	Newm	7g/f	87	3782

FOLLOW MY LEAD 2 b f £0

49	9-11	Wind	5g/f	2450
44	7-8	Newb	5.2fm	2646
60	7-13	Kemp	6g/f	4358

FOLLOW THE GAME 2 b c £0

47a	10-10	Ling	7ap	5264

FOLLOWING FLOW 2 b c £7377

72	9-15	Newm	7fm		3005
83a	3-13	Ling	7ap		3329
86	1-7	CATT	7g/f		3665*
86	2-9	Ches	7sft	80	4074
29	15-17	Donc	8fm	83	4480
80	10-14	Catt	7sft	83	5126

FOMALHAUT 5 b h £0

100	8-10	Deau	8sft	4017

FONG SHUI 2 ch c £3928

50	4-11	Yarm	6g/f		1728
78a	7-13	Ling	7ap		3329
83	1-14	FOLK	7gd		4115*
82	4-9	Warw	7.1g/s	81	4666
57	19-29	Newm	6gd		5087 VIS

FONGS THONG 3 ch c £33350

114	1-8	NEWB	7g/f		3253+
114	1-9	GOOD	8fm	[108]	3620*
105	5-8	Donc	7fm	[108]	4477
100	7-11	Asco	8g/f	[108]	4801 T

FONGTASTIC 2 ch c £4269

86	3-12	Newm	6g/f	3280
91	1-16	NEWM	7g/f	3582*

FONTHILL ROAD 4 ch g £26816

66	6-11	Hami	6g/f	72	2477
76	1-4	HAMI	6g/s	[70]	2831*
74	3-10	Hayd	7.1g/s	70	3137
76	2-20	Hayd	6g/s	70	3796
81	2-6	Hayd	6g/s	70	3903
84	1-19	YORK	6gd	73	4005+
86	1-12	NEWM	6gd	78	4229*
78	6-26	Ayr	6g/s	81	4652
78	8-19	Sali	6gd	82	4855

FOODBROKER FOUNDER 4 ch g £1500

93	7-10	Good	9.9g/f	[103]	1862
96	5-16	Asco	10g/f	100	2556
98	6-9	Sand	5g/s	98	2896
83	15-15	Good	9.9g/f	97	3506
79	6-7	Wind	11.6g/s	[94]	4219
77	8-11	Epso	10.1gd	[92]	4467
80	12-13	Good	10g/f	[90]	4772

FOOLISH GROOM 2 ch g £4229

70	3-12	Hayd	8.1sft		1108
77	4-9	Hayd	8.1g/f		1882
72	5-14	Hayd	8.1g/s		2231
55	6-11	Redc	9g/s	71	2565 P
69	3-10	Hayd	8.1g/s	69	3138 Tp
67	5-9	Donc	8.1g/s	69	3378 t p
51	9-12	Ches	7.6fm	68	3634 t p
79	2-17	Hayd	8.1g/s	[66]	4768
65	3-14	Pont	8g/f	[68]	4937
0	P-12	Wolv	8.6ap	68	5116

FOOLISH THOUGHT 3 b g £1330

57a	7-11	Ling	8ap	63	12
62a	4-16	Ling	7ap	63	20
48a	16-16	Ling	7ap	62	144
51a	6-15	Ling	7ap	[60]	366 VIS
54a	5-14	Ling	7ap	[58]	450
38a	4-9	Wolv	9.4af	[58]	480 P
53a	1-12	WOLV	6af	[56]	524* p
41a	5-9	Wolv	7af	[54]	825
33a	14-15	Ling	7ap	52	913 p
12a	11-12	Ling	7ap	[49]	1074 T p
1	20-20	Nott	6.1gd	47	2928 p

FOOLS ENTIRE 2 ch g £7018

62a	1-13	LING	6ap	[65]	25*
64a	3-9	Ling	6ap	63	105

68a	2-15	Ling	7ap	64	177	
69a	2-11	Ling	7ap	[64]	220	P
69a	2-10	Ling	7ap	68	337	
53a	9-10	Ling	7ap	70	432	
71a	3-12	Ling	7ap	69	545	VIS
71	6-7	Donc	8gd	[69]	949	
46	13-18	Nott	8.2fm	69	1007	
29	14-17	Yarm	7g/f	[66]	1729	
0	18-19	York	6g/f	63	2055	
55a	7-11	Ling	7ap	[67]	3331	
52a	9-11	Ling	6ap	63	3744	
57a	3-13	Sout	6af	56	4091	e
60	4-5	Good	7sft	[59]	4186	e
57	5-14	Yarm	8g/s	[58]	4252	e
41	12-19	Leic	7g/f	58	4452	e
75	8-11	Newm	6sft	[55]	5270	e
20	17-18	Yarm	6g/s	55	5354	e

FOOT FAULT 2 b f £0

61a	4-11	Ling	6ap		51
43a	6-8	Sout	6af	61	223
23a	15-15	Ling	7ap	60	295
57a	4-10	Ling	10ap	[57]	843
55a	4-9	Ling	10ap	[57]	899
41a	4-6	Ling	10ap	[57]	972

FOOTBALL CRAZY 5 b g £0

59	13-20	Epso	12hvy	83	1295	bl
70	10-18	Nott	14.1g/s	80	1772	

FOOTSTEPSINTHESAND 2 b c £38865

100	1-20	NAAS	6g/s		5163*
108	1-6	LEOP	7sft		5248*

FOR LIFE 2 b c £1060

88	3-12	York	6gd		3122
78	18-22	Donc	6fm		4458

FOR NOWT 2 b c £0

44	6-7	Redc	5gd		2547
38	12-20	Hayd	6gd		2882
47	9-11	Newc	7gd		3429
35	10-15	Redc	6gd		3769
7	13-15	Catt	7sft		3930

FORA SMILE 3 ch c £0

39a	7-11	Wolv	6af		466	
44a	10-12	Wolv	7af		560	
49a	10-15	Ling	7ap		671	
18a	7-9	Wolv	8.5af		751	
34a	11-11	Ling	6ap	[45]	898	
40	5-7	Folk	7g/s	45	1081	
23a	7-8	Ling	10ap	[45]	1183	VIS

FORBEARING 7 b g £1365

59	3-10	Leic	11.8g/f	[73]	3211	
56	2-8	Bath	10.2g/f	[73]	3370	vis
33	6-11	Beve	12.1g/f	[62]	4716	

FORCE NINE 2 br c £0

72	5-10	Yarm	8g/s		4631

FORCE OF NATURE 4 b f £1479

55	10-10	Sali	9.9g/f		1718
85	2-6	York	11.9g/f		2058
60	4-4	Ripo	12.3g/f	[85]	2484

FOREHAND 2 b f £0

49	13-14	Yarm	7sft		5250

FOREIGN AFFAIRS 6 ch h £57245

112	3-7	Mais	15.5sft	[102]	987
101	5-8	Colo	12sft	[102]	1556
113	1-7	COLO	11gd	[102]	3663*
111	1-7	LEOP	12g/f	[102]	4019*
107	2-9	Taby	12gd	[102]	4574
107	2-6	Donc	12sft	[109]	5369

FOREST AIR 4 br f £2343

31	9-15	Hami	9.2gd	49	1388	
49	1-10	AYR	8g/s	[49]	1446*	
38	8-19	Redc	8sft	49	1661	
36	7-8	Hami	9.2g/f	47	2475	
49	5-13	Muss	8gd	[46]	2967	
50	2-8	Ayr	10gd	[46]	3151	P
42	6-13	Ayr	10gd	46	3325	p
33	7-12	Ayr	9.1g/f	46	3766	p

FOREST DELIGHT 2 ch f £0

63	7-14	Wind	5gd		4121	
54	8-10	Ling	5g/f		4893	
49	11-12	Bath	5sft		5169	

FOREST HEATH 7 gr g £0

24a	10-12	Ling	10ap	49	542	p
1a	14-14	Ling	12ap	[45]	827	p

FOREST MAGIC 4 b c £3025

95	4-8	Donc	12gd		950
97	9-17	Newb	12gd	[100]	1230
94	5-9	Ches	13.4gd	[100]	1596
79	7-8	Newb	13.3g/f	[100]	1757

FOREST QUEEN 7 b m £0

0	11-13	Wolv	8.5af	[30]	826
8a	10-10	Wolv	8.5af	[30]	1801
0	13-13	Hami	5gd	20	2181
0	9-9	Sout	8af	20	2996

FOREST RAIL 4 b f £0

46	12-12	Leic	5g/s		4454
7	8-8	Yarm	6g/s		4588

FOREST TUNE 6 b g £774

40	14-19	Donc	10.3gd	62	924	bl
30	10-14	Folk	9.7g/s	61	1083	
49	8-16	Brig	11.9fm	59	1693	
54	6-16	Leic	11.8g/f	59	1830	
48	9-11	Brig	9.9fm	52	2260	
54a	11-14	Ling	10ap	62	2392	
51	6-9	Ches	10.3g/s	[50]	2745	
44	4-17	Newm	10g/f	50	3238	
47	5-10	Newm	10fm	50	3404	
49	3-13	Folk	9.7g/f	48	3726	bl

FOREST VIKING 2 b g £397

43	5-6	Pont	6g/f		2039	
52	8-17	Donc	6g/f		2424	
39	11-13	York	6g/f		3431	
34	22-24	Redc	6fm	[58]	4928	
24	19-21	Donc	6hvy		5202	

FORESTIER 4 ch c £97166

109	2-6	Long	15.5g/s		1431
118	1-6	LONG	15.5gd		2000*
118	1-4	MAIS	15gd		3317*

FOREVER MY LORD 5 b g £296

49a	4-9	Ling	13ap	56	18
50a	3-10	Sout	14af	54	90
37a	14-14	Ling	16ap	54	107
36a	8-12	Ling	10ap	50	542
24a	10-14	Ling	12ap	47	711
43a	9-12	Ling	13ap	47	762
38	6-8	Ayr	13.1fm	49	1905

FOREVER PHOENIX 3 b f £73028

61a	1-8	WOLV	8.5af	[74]	248*
63a	5-16	Sout	7af	70	419
54a	6-13	Ling	6ap	68	471
74a	1-10	SOUT	6af	65	657*
84a	1-11	LING	6ap	70	760*
86a	2-14	Ling	6ap	80	874
90a	1-7	LING	5ap	83	1011+
80	3-9	Thir	5g/s	[83]	1217
96	1-12	LING	5g/s	81	1615*
96	2-9	Nott	6.1g/s	[81]	1773
2	R-12	Epso	5g/f	[92]	2206
64	9-10	York	6g/f	92	2357
97	2-10	Ayr	5g/f	[92]	3304
97	3-24	Asco	5gd	92	3466
78	7-10	Asco	6gd	92	3773
96	3-7	Nott	5.1gd	[93]	3989
96	6-11	Beve	5g/s	[93]	4238
102	1-16	HAYD	5g/s	92	4382*
103	6-22	Donc	5.6fm	99	4459
86	6-11	Hami	5sft	[98]	4693
103	3-10	Newm	6gd	98	4884
102	5-10	Newm	5gd	99	5090

FORFEITER 2 ch c £4501

68	2-8	Muss	5g/f		1091	
65	6-9	Muss	5g/s		1458	
75	2-11	Thir	7fm		2462	BL
77	2-5	Muss	7.1g/f		2612	bl
80	3-14	Catt	7sft	76	5126	
38	19-20	Donc	7sft	76	5373	VIS

FORGE LANE 3 b c £850

45a	9-15	Ling	7ap		670	
53a	9-12	Ling	8ap		734	
55	9-17	Ling	7g/s		1617	
62	12-15	Newb	8g/f		1763	
46a	10-15	Ling	12ap	55	2741	
58	4-16	Brig	9.9g/f	55	3175	
56	2-12	Brig	9.9g/f	55	3300	P
41	9-9	Brig	9.9fm	55	3695	BL
33	8-11	Brig	9.9g/f	55	3982	bl
35a	8-12	Ling	10ap	52	4113	bl
0	17-18	Warw	10.9g/s	53	4669	p

FORGED 3 b c £7898

16	20-20	Bath	10.2gd		1398
84	3-8	Chep	12.1gd		2113
81	2-16	Donc	10.3gd		2751
97	1-6	THIR	12g/f	79	3415*

FORGERY 2 ch c £553

82	3-20	Yarm	8sft		5252

FORMALISE 4 b g £387

44	13-14	Kemp	5g/f	68	1914	
60	7-12	Sali	6fm	65	2289	
46	5-9	Chep	6.1g/f	62	2626	
39	9-10	Kemp	6g/f	62	2861	
53	5-13	Sali	6g/s	58	3109	
44	13-17	Wind	6fm	57	3643	
47	9-15	Bath	5.7g/f	55	3966	
55	4-15	Sali	5gd	52	4335	p
34	12-13	Bath	5.7gd	54	4548	p
40	14-19	Ling	5g/f	54	4739	p

FORMERIC 7 ch g £612

2a	15-15	Sout	6af	40	168	
0	10-13	Sout	8af	40	228	vis
3a	8-12	Sout	8af	[33]	309	vis
0	9-13	Sout	7af	[35]	356	vis
41	3-16	Newc	6sft	35	1277	vis
0	16-17	Kemp	7hvy	[40]	1642	vis
8	11-14	Newc	6g/s	[39]	2730	vis
0	14-16	Hami	6g/s	39	4009	

FORMIDABLE WILL 2 b c £0

7	11-11	Wind	6g/s		4941
49a	11-12	Wolv	7.1ap		5179

FORPETESAKE 2 ch g £0

28	9-10	Newc	5g/f		2158	VIS
33	6-10	Thir	6fm		2461	
54	6-14	Beve	7.5sft		2939	
61	8-11	Beve	7.5g/f		3500	
60	6-8	Redc	7gd		4247	
43	8-8	Hami	8.3g/s	[58]	4816	
20	15-15	Pont	10g/f	[58]	4933	

FORREST GUMP 4 ch g £1253

23	10-12	Newc	8g/f		4407	bl
54	2-10	Ripo	6gd		4788	
44	9-19	Redc	6g/s	[52]	5110	

FORT 3 ch g £42279

80	3-7	Nott	8.2sft	[90]	1741
83	11-18	Epso	10.1fm	87	2250
93	3-11	Asco	12gd	87	3070
89	2-10	Asco	12fm	87	3444
80	10-16	Good	12fm	87	3534
91	5-13	Donc	10.3fm	[88]	4463
102	1-14	ASCO	12g/f	88	4814*
92	6-17	Newm	12g/f	93	4889

FORT CHURCHILL 3 b g £7789

76	5-10	Yarm	11.5g/f		1725	
72	3-10	Yarm	11.5fm	69	2147	
67	4-8	Newm	10g/f	[72]	2673	
75	2-17	Catt	12sft	71	3929	BL
69	7-13	Warw	12.6gd	72	4274	bl
79	1-10	SALI	12sft	[71]	4579+	bl
67	9-19	Hayd	10.5g/s	77	4766	bl
80	2-11	Newm	14g/f	76	4919	bl
44	7-9	Ayr	13.1sft	78	5068	bl

FORT DIGNITY 3 b c £4000

110	4-10	Newb	7gd		1234
73	4-4	York	10.4g/f	[108]	1706

FORT MCHENRY 4 b g £2877

62	8-15	Folk	6sft	74	976

61	8-11	Hami 6g/f		72	2477
62	1-6	**YARM** 6g/f	[70]		3710* p
49a	12-14	Ling 7ap		76	3821 p

FORTHRIGHT 3 b g £10093

93a	1-7	**LING** 10ap		88	325*
68a	8-14	Nad 8af			598
67	5-5	Sand 10g/s	[92]		1316
92	6-27	Asco 8g/f		90	2521
53	13-13	Newm 8g/f		90	3277 p
75	7-9	Asco 10g/f		89	3439 p
47	9-10	Pont 8g/s		87	3972 p
85a	6-13	Ling 7ap		85	4318 p
82	9-17	Asco 8g/f		83	4777 BL
68	6-14	Pont 8g/f	[81]		4937 bl

FORTNUM 2 b c £1226

58	5-8	Kemp 5hvy			1510
67	3-4	Ling 5g/s			1614
60	9-15	Wind 6g/f			2263
63	5-11	Newb 7fm		65	3627
58	3-12	Sali 6g/s		63	4079
56	10-17	Ling 7g/f		61	4894

FORTUNA MEA 4 b f £0

0	6-7	Chep 10.2sft	[40]		1332
0	9-9	Wolv 14.8af		45	1654

FORTUNATE DAVE 5 b g £0

35a	11-13	Ling 13ap	[60]		602

FORTUNATE ISLE 2 ch c £2655

82	2-23	Newm 7g/f			4885

FORTUNE POINT 6 ch g £6768

63a	4-13	Ling 10ap	[63]		429
49a	10-13	Wolv 8.5af		59	559
58a	2-6	Sout 8af	[59]		586
61a	1-14	**LING** 10ap		54	718*
63a	3-14	Ling 12ap		60	768
63a	2-13	Ling 10ap	[60]		912
0	19-20	Wind 11.6g/s		62	1056
49	12-14	Nott 10g/s		60	1777
61a	4-12	Ling 8ap	[61]		2394
45	10-13	Newb 8fm		60	2647
60a	6-14	Sout 8af	[61]		3392
63	2-9	Brig 9.9fm		56	3695 vis
48	9-16	Chep 10.2g/s		59	4365 vis

FORTUNES FAVOURITE 3 ch f £3479

53a	4-15	Sout 12af			89
32a	5-14	Sout 12af			194
3a	9-9	Sout 16af		48	336
30a	3-7	Sout 14af	[45]		638
36a	4-9	Sout 12af	[45]		774
14a	12-16	Sout 14af		40	1033
50	1-8	**RIPO** 10g/s	[42]		1363*
41	7-12	Newc 12.4sft		45	1680
0	10-10	Redc 11g/f	[45]		1819

FORTUNES PRINCESS 3 b f £12832

78	2-7	Newm 10g/f			2534
81	2-6	Pont 10g/f			2793
76	1-10	**PONT** 10gd			3243*
79	2-8	Leic 10g/f		77	3514
73	9-19	Kemp 10fm		77	4392

FORTY FORTE 7 b g £2272

56a	2-11	Wolv 8.5af	[59]		128 p
14a	11-13	Sout 8af		57	228 p
20a	11-13	Wolv 9.4af		55	287 p
32a	8-8	Wolv 8.5af	[55]		362 p
29a	9-13	Wolv 8.5af	[50]		699
48a	3-9	Sout 11af	[48]		985
31	9-19	Warw 10.9sft		48	1090
20a	6-7	Wolv 8.5af		45	1341 T p
53a	1-7	**WOLV** 8.5af	[45]		1672* t p
26a	9-13	Wolv 8.5af	[52]		2052 t p

FORWARD MOVE 2 ch c £5946

91	2-14	Kemp 8g/f			4356
101	1-18	**NEWM** 8fm			4722*

FORZEEN 2 ch c £17643

71a	3-11	Sout 5af			1752
76	4-7	Bath 5fm			2415
76	2-7	Warw 5fm			2573
78a	3-7	Ling 5ap			2839
87	1-12	**LING** 5gd		74	3284*

81	4-8	Donc 5g/f		80	3374
79	7-10	Thir 5fm		83	3607
53	21-22	Donc 6fm	[74]		4458
90	1-18	**WIND** 5g/f		80	4830*
75	8-11	Epso 5g/f		86	4907
86a	1-13	**WOLV** 6ap	[80]		4980*

FORZENUFF 2 b c £420

43a	9-9	Ling 6ap		70	105
64a	3-10	Ling 5ap		65	217
62a	5-10	Ling 5ap		65	371
48a	7-10	Ling 6ap		65	494
53a	6-8	Ling 6ap		62	673
55a	8-12	Ling 8ap		59	798
52	10-14	Ling 5g/f		63	2585
33	12-12	Ling 5g/f		59	2743
37	12-16	Ling 7gd		55	3024 T
1	19-19	Yarm 6g/s		51	4636

FOSSGATE 3 ch g £3347

73	2-9	Ripo 8gd			1178
13	16-16	Beve 8.5sft		74	1628
74	3-9	Beve 8.5g/f		71	2168
65	6-8	Nott 10g/f		71	2631
72	4-9	Carl 9.3fm	[70]		3546 P
68	4-13	Pont 8g/s	[70]		3973 VIS
64	4-7	Ripo 8gd	[70]		4304 p
63	8-14	Redc 7g/s		68	5109 p

FOUR AMIGOS 3 b c £11667

74	5-16	Kemp 6g/s		77	1116
88	1-13	**THIR** 5sft		77	1229*
73	9-14	Ripo 6g/s		87	1360
68	6-12	Ayr 5g/s		85	2566
84	3-15	Hayd 6gd		83	2950
69	7-10	Ches 5.1g/f		83	3080
75	9-12	Hayd 6sft		82	3273
64	11-14	York 5g/s		80	4027
73	4-7	Good 5sft		78	4236
72	9-15	Sand 5gd		76	4604
51	7-8	Hami 5g/s	[75]		4822

FOUR JAYS 3 b g £0

65a	13-14	Ling 10ap		72	122
55a	5-12	Ling 8ap	[70]		150 p
55a	8-15	Ling 7ap	[64]		216 p
55a	5-15	Ling 7ap		60	266 p
53a	9-16	Ling 7ap		60	323 p
46a	9-15	Ling 7ap	[58]		366 p

FOUR KINGS 3 b c £1469

64a	5-9	Ling 5ap			1023
52	8-14	Sout 6gd			1281
64	3-7	Pont 6g/f			2042 T
64	3-7	Hami 8.3g/f	[63]		2474 t
51	9-10	Newm 8g/f	[63]		2732 t
10	6-6	Muss 9g/f		63	3529 t
20	16-17	Newc 7g/s		63	3700
0	17-17	Catt 12sft		60	3929 t

FOUR PENCE 3 b c £2094

57	4-5	Warw 12.6fm			2441
75	2-7	Newb 12g/f	[65]		2879
32a	6-10	Ling 12ap	[68]		4314

FOUR PLEASURE 2 ch f £0

23	16-17	Yarm 6gd			4610
38	23-23	Newm 7g/f			4885

FOURSQUARE 3 b g £8683

93	1-9	**HAYD** 5g/s		84	1344+
92	5-15	Ches 5.1g/s		92	1572
78	10-15	Hayd 5g/f		92	1917
92	4-16	Leic 5g/f		90	2400
62	12-15	Hayd 6gd		89	2950
91	3-10	Ayr 5gd		88	3150

FOURSWAINBY 3 b g £442

48	6-9	Ripo 8gd			1178
46	3-6	Newc 8sft		48	1679

FOURTH DIMENSION 5 b g £417

80	10-13	York 11.9g/s		86	3076
52	4-6	Pont 12gd	[83]		3458
82	7-15	Good 14g/f		83	3510
79	7-12	York 13.9g/f		81	4400
59	15-20	York 10.4gd		80	4986

FOX 2 b c £16617

96	2-5	Good 6gd			2221
97	1-10	**NEWM** 7fm			2594*
101	4-12	Newm 7g/f			3060
102	3-10	Good 7fm			3532
95	6-8	Sand 7.1g/s	[100]		4096

FOX COVERT 3 b g £5492

57	7-11	Catt 6gd	[71]		999
35	14-14	Ripo 6g/s		69	1360 P
0	11-11	Newc 7sft		64	1678
61	2-13	Carl 5.9fm	[59]		1949 VIS
59	3-19	York 6g/f		59	2055 vis
41	5-6	Redc 6gd		59	2551 vis
55	8-12	Catt 6g/f	[58]		2849
56	4-10	Hami 6g/f		57	3203 vis
29	14-18	Pont 6gd		56	3463
32	10-20	Ripo 6gd		55	4278 vis
54	3-14	Newc 5g/f	[55]		4404 vis
62	1-19	**THIR** 6g/f		53	4595* vis
42	13-19	Ling 5g/f		55	4739 vis

FOX HOLLOW 2 b c £2332

45a	13-13	Ling 7ap	[35]		119
6a	7-8	Ling 8ap	[35]		326
23a	9-14	Ling 6ap	[35]		495
51a	3-9	Sout 7af	[30]		613
51a	2-9	Wolv 8.5af	[48]		865
0	6-7	Folk 7g/s		40	1081
55a	2-7	Wolv 9.4af		51	1324
51a	3-6	Sout 11af	[51]		1754
26	9-15	Wind 11.6g/f	[38]		2267
0	12-15	Sout 12af		51	2503
26a	8-14	Ling 10ap		50	3449
21	10-10	Yarm 10.1gd	[35]		4612

FOXHAVEN 2 ch c £10598

83	3-16	Sali 7gd			3882
89	2-13	Kemp 8g/f			4355
95	2-11	Good 8gd			4746
100	1-3	**LEIC** 7g/f	[88]		5061*
88	6-13	Newb 7sft	[88]		5195

FOXIES FUTURE 2 b f £1235

47a	5-13	Sout 6af	[67]		63 P
55a	7-14	Sout 7af		65	158
56a	4-8	Sout 7af		65	223
49a	3-7	Sout 6af		60	333
22	16-19	Ayr 6sft		56	5069

FOXILLA 3 ch f £7621

24a	9-14	Ling 10ap	[63]		759
46a	7-10	Ling 10ap	[57]		843
55	3-14	Wind 10g/f		52	2452
60	1-14	**WIND** 10gd		52	2617*
59	4-8	Wind 11.6g/f		61	2796
61	3-8	Asco 10g/f		58	3391
66	2-10	Newb 10fm		58	3630

FOXY GWYNNE 2 b f £1766

38a	10-12	Ling 6ap			4178
73	3-12	Warw 7.1g/f			4417
70	2-10	Catt 7sft			5127

FOXY TRIX 5 b m £0

0	7-8	Wolv 12af			644

FRAAMBUOYANT 2 b f £0

24a	11-14	Sout 7af			2492
25	10-11	Newc 7fm			4863
7a	9-11	Wolv 7.1ap			5113
43	6-10	Catt 7sft			5317 VIS

FRAAMTASTIC 7 b m £5016

33a	2-14	Sout 7af	[30]		573
28a	4-12	Sout 11af	[30]		640 p
37a	1-16	**SOUT** 8af	[35]		719* p
31a	6-10	Sout 8af		41	792 p
31a	15-15	Ling 7ap		40	846 BL
50a	1-13	**WOLV** 8.5af	[40]		894* p
47a	1-8	**SOUT** 8af	[45]		1200* p
40	2-7	Chep 7.1sft	[40]		1335 p

FRABROFEN 3 b f £924

63	5-6	Newc 5gd			1392
9a	10-12	Wolv 6ap			5157
29	9-13	Catt 5sft			5321

FRAGRANT STAR 3 gr f £0

77	8-8	Newb 7gd	[81]		1233

73	7-10	Newm	10fm	81	2592
19	10-10	Newm	8g/f	78	2767
59	10-11	Asco	8gd	[74]	3128
56	9-11	Yarm	7g/f	72	3711

FRALOGA 2 b f £20123

111	3-10	Long	8g/f		4954

FRAMBO 2 b f £1102

41a	5-14	Sout	8af	[57]	95
20a	9-9	Sout	11af	54	608
36a	7-10	Sout	11af	54	658 P
44a	5-9	Ling	10ap	[49]	899 p
20	10-14	Sout	10g/s	45	1051 BL
0	6-8	Pont	12hvy	[45]	1250 p
40a	4-8	Ling	12ap	[45]	2065 T p
41a	4-15	Ling	12ap	42	2741 t
36	4-10	Beve	12.1g/f	40	3499 t p
35	3-14	Nott	16g/f	40	3580 bl
34	3-7	Chep	12.1sft	36	4053 bl t
22	6-8	Chep	16.2g/s	35	4302 bl t

FRAMBROISE 2 ch f £0

30	13-17	Yarm	6gd		4610 VIS

FRANCIS FLUTE 6 b g £1359

44	7-14	Hami	8.3gd	50	1504
53	2-18	Ayr	7.2g/f	47	1897
52	4-10	Newc	8g/f	51	2159
60	7-12	Ayr	8g/s	[51]	2543
30	9-14	Ayr	7.2gd	[51]	3324
18	9-9	Hami	9.2g/f	49	3593
44	10-17	Ayr	7.2sft	49	5063

FRANELA 2 b f £0

65	10-14	Kemp	7g/f		4711
36	8-10	Catt	7sft		5127

FRANGIPANI 3 b f £533

58	3-4	Brig	8fm		2261
27	12-17	Wind	11.6fm	[70]	2788
34	14-15	Wind	11.6fm	65	3481 T
35	7-10	Hayd	8.1gd	[65]	3739

FRANK SONATA 3 b c £56085

87	6-15	Newb	8gd	90	1206
99	1-13	YORK	10.4sft	88	1664*
106	3-11	Newb	11g/f	92	1756
108	1-13	HAYD	11.9gd	93	2238+
109	1-7	HAYD	11.9sft	[101]	3274*
101	9-9	Donc	14.6fm	[105]	4532
89	7-8	Long	12hvy	[105]	5165
104	2-8	Newb	12hvy	[105]	5224

FRANKIES WINGS 2 b c £0

39a	10-16	Sout	8af		192
67	7-17	Leic	10g/s		1019
60	6-10	Kemp	11.1gd		1140
11	8-9	Yarm	14.1g/f	60	2345
31	8-10	Folk	12g/s	60	3051 BL
44	11-11	Ling	10gd	[60]	3201 bl

FRANKLINS GARDENS 4 b c £19700

109	4-11	Sand	10g/s	[108]	1350
105	4-6	Hayd	10.5fm	[108]	3793
99	7-9	Deau	12.5hv√	108]	4312
101	8-7	Donc	12fm	[108]	4494
103	6-9	Asco	12g/f	[105]	4812
113	2-10	Newm	16sft	[105]	5138
106	6-8	Long	15.5hv√	105]	5245

FRANKS QUEST 4 b g £8436

16a	7-8	Sout	7af	[58]	373
47a	2-8	Sout	11af	[55]	574
55a	3-8	Wolv	8.5af	[55]	630
55a	3-14	Ling	10ap	54	718
46a	6-11	Ling	8ap	54	820
44	10-17	Beve	8.5g/s	[50]	1160
50a	4-10	Wolv	8.5af	53	1322
38	7-11	Pont	8sft	50	1425
55a	2-8	Wolv	9.4af	50	1657
58a	1-13	WOLV	8.5af	[53]	2052*
65a	1-13	SOUT	8af	53	2497*
27a	11-15	Sout	8af	53	2500
21	12-13	Kemp	7g/f	55	3034
62a	3-14	Ling	7ap	60	5300

FRANKSALOT 4 ch g £9619

21	16-16	Ling	7g/f	65	2063

73	1-11	BRIG	7g/f	64	2644*
71	4-10	Epso	7g/f	69	2872
61	5-10	Brig	8gd	70	2954
70	4-6	Brig	7fm	[69]	3696
79a	1-14	LING	7ap	69	3821*
71	5-14	Epso	8.5gd	70	4295
75	3-13	Epso	8.5gd	70	4469
55	12-18	Kemp	8g/f	70	4714
77a	6-12	Ling	8ap	76	5238

FRANKSKIPS 4 b g £850

38a	13-14	Ling	10ap	69	174
56a	11-16	Ling	7ap	66	323
57a	5-12	Wolv	8.5af	62	479
46a	12-13	Ling	7ap	60	565
55a	7-12	Ling	8ap	60	607
57a	3-9	Ling	8ap	56	763
59a	3-15	Ling	7ap	55	913
47a	8-12	Ling	8ap	55	1013

FRANSISCAN 2 ch g £0

31	7-7	Hami	6gd		1744
39	8-12	Newc	6gd		1869
41	6-8	Redc	7g/s		2563 VIS
46	10-10	Newc	8hvy		4213 vis
44	5-16	Beve	7.5g/f	45	4597 P

FRANTIC 2 ch f £418

34	10-11	Nott	5.1g/f		2151
65	4-8	Pont	6g/f		2603
63	4-9	Nott	5.1gd		2926

FRASCATI 3 b f £32178

71a	2-12	Wolv	5af	70	35
64a	5-12	Wolv	5af	73	109
77a	1-16	SOUT	5af	72	205*
66a	8-11	Sout	5af	78	418
58a	14-16	Sout	5af	78	461
62a	8-11	Sout	5af	77	655
71a	4-11	Wolv	5af	75	958
74	1-5	MUSS	5g/f	67	1096*
7	17-19	Beve	5sft	71	1627
73	2-8	Hami	5gd	[71]	1749
74	3-10	Thir	5g/f	70	1973
70	8-15	Muss	5fm	70	2084
81	1-10	DONC	5gd	70	2429*
82	1-11	CHES	5.1g/s	75	2747*
80	2-10	Muss	5g/s	78	2968
67	8-9	Nott	5.1gd	78	3106
63	7-12	Ches	5.1sft	77	4107
67	4-13	Ches	5.1g/f	76	4514
83	3-11	Hami	5sft	[76]	4693
74	10-12	Epso	5g/f	82	4908
77	9-13	Muss	5g/s	80	5143

FRATERNITY 7 b g £0

28a	6-12	Wolv	9.4af	[38]	302
15a	7-10	Sout	11af	[40]	375
8a	9-12	Wolv	12af	[35]	523 VIS

FREAK OCCURENCE 2 b c £8030

85a	1-11	LING	8ap	77	54* VIS
86a	4-10	Ling	8ap	84	132
90a	2-10	Ling	8ap	[84]	232
49a	9-11	Sout	8af	84	252
80	7-15	Newb	8gd	85	1206
84	3-13	Kemp	9hvy	82	1515
85	4-14	York	7.9g/s	82	1707
83	6-18	Hayd	8.1g/f	82	1919
84	3-13	Sand	8.1g/s	[81]	2126
66	14-18	Epso	10.1fm	81	2250
77	6-14	Wind	8.3gd	[81]	4122
72	8-13	Wind	8.3g/s	81	4221 vis
58a	12-14	Ling	7ap	80	4446 vis
62	16-25	Newb	7gd	77	4683 vis
61	9-11	Good	8gd	74	5027
70	7-16	Redc	6sft	70	5304

FREDDIE FRECCLES 2 ch c £0

37a	11-14	Sout	8af		88
41a	6-7	Ling	8ap	70	341
49	13-17	Beve	8.5g/f	65	4721

FREDERICK JAMES 10 b g £0

0	13-14	Ling	7sft	40	1625
24	11-16	Nott	6.1gd	[35]	1989
23	12-12	Sali	7fm	[31]	2288
0	15-15	Chep	8.1sft	31	4057

FREDS FIRST 2 b g £0

19a	10-10	Wolv	7af		36
35a	5-13	Wolv	8.5af		2052
0	8-8	Chep	12.1g/f		2623
2a	10-11	Sout	12af	[35]	3154

FREE LIFT 2 ch f £7605

91	1-12	NEWB	6g/f		3251*
67	10-11	Sali	6gd		4332

FREE OPTION 8 ch g £4489

66a	14-14	Ling	10ap	74	122
62a	1-16	LING	7ap	[73]	180* BL
55a	3-16	Ling	7ap	[73]	214 bl
73a	7-11	Ling	8ap	[73]	273
71a	5-12	Ling	8ap	73	369
42a	12-13	Wolv	8.5af	73	439
55a	3-9	Ling	8ap	[71]	717 bl
64a	3-10	Ling	10ap	[71]	738 bl
64a	1-8	LING	7ap	[65]	1247*
65a	5-11	Ling	8ap	65	2018

FREE STYLE 4 ch f £2997

28a	6-13	Wolv	9.4af	50	287
41a	3-8	Sout	11af	[47]	420
13a	12-13	Sout	14af	45	590
43a	1-15	LING	12ap	[40]	707+
33a	4-10	Wolv	12af	[40]	780
45a	5-14	Ling	12ap	[45]	827
42a	5-13	Ling	13ap	45	896
52	2-13	Brig	11.9g/f	48	1373
1	12-17	Bath	11.7sft	48	1543
44	4-7	Leic	11.8g/f	50	1967
48	5-11	Folk	12g/f	48	2273
28	8-9	Yarm	14.1g/d	48	2856
0	12-13	Warw	12.6gd	48	3056

FREE TRIP 3 ch c £26311

88	1-22	DONC	7gd	78	955*
83	6-20	Newm	7g/f	85	1186
45	13-15	Ches	7.6gd	85	1583
88	2-15	Ling	7g/f	83	1983
83	5-17	Epso	7g/f	83	2212
90	5-27	Asco	8g/f	85	2521
89	5-17	Good	7fm	89	3550
93	2-12	Sand	7.1g/f	88	3800
99	1-7	SAND	8.1gd	89	4499*
94	7-15	Asco	7g/f	94	4800

FREE WHEELIN 4 b g £870

56	14-20	Kemp	6gd	80	1138
59	3-8	Hayd	6g/s	[75]	1345
30	13-16	Nott	6.1sft	[72]	1743
23a	11-14	Sout	6af	[65]	2502
60	7-11	Sand	5sft	63	4070
44	13-17	Wind	6gd	63	4126

FREE WILL 7 ch g £0

22	16-20	Catt	12g/f	55	2850

FREEDOM NOW 6 b g £0

70	9-17	Ripo	16g/s	76	1361
44	12-18	York	13.9g/s	75	1689
59	6-9	Ripo	16g/f	72	2009
66	7-10	Carl	14.1fm	69	2444
54	7-10	Thir	16fm	68	3611

FREELOADER 4 b g £9302

72	7-20	Newb	10gd	74	1235
74	4-9	Hayd	10.5g/s	74	2185
72	3-5	Leic	10g/f	[73]	2401
71	8-16	Kemp	9g/f	72	3039
81	1-16	KEMP	9gd	72	3187*
80	4-19	Good	8g/f	77	3512
77	5-13	Wind	8.3g/s	78	4217
81	4-16	Sand	10gd	78	4609
82	3-20	York	8.9gd	78	4999

FREMEN 4 ch c £0

87	12-24	Donc	8gd	93	951
91	7-15	Newm	7g/f	93	4891
70	19-22	Newm	8sft	92	5103

FRENCH GIGOLO 4 ch g £0

56a	4-9	Ling	8ap	[59]	3195
50a	6-13	Ling	10ap	[59]	4112

FRENCH GOLD 2 b f £0

48	11-16	Bath	8gd		5019
54	8-11	Bath	8sft		5171

FRENCH HORN 7 b g £3272

52a	1-11	LING	8ap	[50]	343* p
51a	4-10	Wolv	8.5af	[50]	398
41a	3-11	Wolv	9.4af	[50]	580 p
49a	5-12	Ling	8ap	[50]	675 p
48a	3-14	Ling	10ap	48	757 p
0	P-10	Ling	8ap	48	766 bl

FRENCH KISSES 2 b f £0

27	15-16	Pont	6g/f		2275
41	12-18	Donc	6g/s		3376
23	10-12	Beve	8.5sft		4257

FRENCH RISK 4 b g £0

0	8-8	Wolv	12af	48	1342
14	15-16	Yarm	10.1fm	45	2146

FRENCH SCHOOL 2 b f £400

0	15-15	Folk	7gd	3381
65a	4-10	Ling	7ap	4442

FRENCHMANS LODGE 4 b g £852

15a	11-12	Wolv	7af	52	956
13	13-13	Folk	7g/s	[45]	1270
26	7-10	Brig	5.3gd	[45]	1544 BL
23	7-10	Kemp	5hvy	[45]	1644 bl
52	2-14	Leic	6g/f	[35]	1963 bl
31	5-19	Redc	6gd	35	2125 bl
39	6-11	Bath	5.7fm	[40]	2412 bl
44a	6-15	Sout	5af	[39]	2803 bl

FRESH CONNECTION 3 b f £0

56a	7-12	Ling	8ap		428
7a	14-14	Ling	6ap		495
45a	7-9	Ling	8ap		1022
39	5-6	Yarm	10.1g/f		1134 P
23a	4-5	Ling	8ap	[35]	1416

FRIAR TUCK 9 ch g £5593

24	15-16	Newc	6sft	52	1277
37	7-10	Hami	6gd	52	1391
40	8-13	Muss	7.1g/s	52	1463
56	1-15	HAMI	6gd	50	1508*
54	4-14	Ayr	6g/f	55	1898
54	6-10	Ayr	7.2g/f	55	2027
59	4-12	Newc	6g/f	55	2160
45	9-11	Hami	6g/f	55	2477
47	8-11	Ayr	6gd	55	2542
37	7-8	Hami	6gd	55	2713
43	4-4	Hami	6g/s	[53]	2831
52	9-15	Newc	6gd	51	3424
46	7-20	Hayd	6fm	51	3796

FRIDA 2 b f £0

7	11-14	Leic	6g/f	3517

FRIDAYS TAKINGS 4 ch g £0

0	13-14	Sout	8af	70	99 bl
46a	9-13	Wolv	8.5af	67	251 bl
30a	9-10	Sout	8af	64	318 bl
44a	8-11	Sout	8af	59	457 VIS
0	15-16	Warw	8.1g/s	[40]	4993 bl
0	12-12	Wolv	8.6ap	[50]	5337 bl

FRIENDS HOPE 3 ch f £4036

22	9-12	Catt	12gd	56	1000
55	1-11	SOUT	10gd	52	1280*
58	5-5	Brig	9.9g/f	58	1372
55	2-5	Carl	6.9fm	56	2446

FRIMLEYS MATTERRY 4 b g £4774

36a	6-7	Sout	7af	[53]	636
0	7-7	Sout	8af	[53]	721
45	6-13	Muss	7.1g/f	[45]	1119
36	6-11	Redc	6sft	[45]	1662
39	6-19	Redc	6g/f	45	2125
64	5-10	Redc	6gd	[42]	2559
0	16-16	Redc	8g/s	50	2958
50	3-18	Thir	6fm	50	3609
56	1-20	REDC	6g/f	49	3767*
40	6-16	Hami	6g/s	53	4009
52	6-12	Redc	6gd	[53]	4425
41	8-20	Newc	6g/f	53	4408

FRISBY RIDGE 2 b f £431

0	12-15	Beve	5g/s	1161

FRITH 2 b c £5639

46	5-8	Beve	5sft		1303
13	10-12	Newc	6gd		1869 BL
42	5-11	Thir	6g/f		1968
43	5-13	Beve	5g/s		2321
48	4-8	Muss	5gd		2611 bl
37	9-14	Beve	7.5sft		2939
54	3-15	Redc	6g/f	[43]	3769 bl

FRITH 2 b c £5639

89	2-15	Newm	7fm		3005
84	3-16	Newm	7g/f		3582
100	5-8	Asco	8g/f		4797
60	8-8	Donc	8sft	[100]	5216

FRIXOS 4 ch g £0

27a	6-13	Ling	10ap	[70]	3025 bl
44	6-15	Chep	16.2gd	[53]	3400 bl
43	10-19	Chep	12.1gd	50	3727 bl
15	12-18	Chep	8.1gd	[47]	4485 bl

FRIZZANTE 5 b m £196000

110	2-8	Newm	6g/f	[99]	1187
116	1-13	NEWM	5g/f	[105]	1479*
113	3-19	Asco	5g/f	[111]	2468
117	1-20	NEWM	5g/f	[111]	3062+
100	10-12	Deau	6.5g/s	[111]	3838
90	17-19	Hayd	6fm	[115]	4384

FROGS GIFT 2 gr f £0

9	14-16	Ripo	6g/f	1780
51	6-9	Carl	5.9gd	2671
47	8-12	Thir	6g/f	3411

FROM THE NORTH 3 ch f £0

0	14-14	Thir	6gd		1639
61	5-8	Donc	5g/f		2075 VIS
41	13-15	Redc	5g/s	54	2961 vis
45	4-12	Carl	5.9g/f	52	3655 vis
18	10-13	Carl	6.9fm	[50]	4504 vis
44	7-19	Thir	6g/f	50	4595 P

FROMSONG 5 b g £7583

75a	12-16	Sout	5af	90	171
105	2-7	Nott	5.1fm	[90]	1004
94	4-11	Newb	5.2gd	95	1207
106	4-13	Newm	5g/f	[95]	1479
89	4-5	Wind	5g/s	[95]	1957
99	4-10	Kemp	5fm	[95]	2068
79	7-8	Sali	6mm	[99]	2421
95	8-12	Sand	5g/s	[97]	2913
95	7-8	Asco	5gd	97	3123
83	6-12	Leic	5gd	[95]	4454
82	10-10	Newm	5gd	90	5090

FRONT STAGE 2 b c £794

64	8-10	Newb	7g/f	3955
88	3-14	Kemp	8g/f	4356

FRONTIER 7 b g £11086

70	2-14	Leic	10g/f	66	1828
76	1-13	CHES	10.3gd	69	2284* t
82	2-8	Chep	10.2g/f	72	2628 t
77	3-12	Wind	11.6fm	72	2759 t

FRUHLINGSSTURM 4 b c £18182

107	5-7	Newm	12g/f		2762
115	1-6	EPSO	10.1g/s	[111]	3043*
102	7-7	Ayr	10g/f	[112]	3306
115	3-8	Wind	10g/s	[112]	4220
106	4-16	Newm	9sft	[112]	5139

FRUIT OF GLORY 5 b m £43104

94	4-7	Kemp	6gd		1137
93	3-13	Epso	5sft	90	1293
89	7-30	Newm	6g/f	90	1481
92	4-16	Good	7g/f	90	1817
92	2-5	Wind	6g/f	[90]	1957
98	1-9	NOTT	5.1gd	89	3106+
95	4-8	Newm	6g/f	92	3235
96	2-10	Asco	6gd	94	3773
99	2-12	Pont	6g/s	[94]	3971
93	5-6	Sand	5g/s	95	4098
97	3-11	Ches	6.1g/f	[95]	4510
87	7-10	Newm	6gd	94	4884
97	3-10	Newm	5gd	92	5090
91a	8-14	Ling	7ap	92	5262

FU FIGHTER 3 b g £1808

71	8-17	Newb	10gd	1737

FU FIGHTER 3 b g £1808

73	5-11	Sand	14g/s	72	2130
67	4-10	Good	14gd	72	2376
70	3-8	Warw	18fm	[71]	2781
50	11-15	Chep	18sft	70	4056
51	9-12	Good	16g/s	68	4235
62	2-11	Yarm	11.5g/s	[68]	4584

FU MANCHU 2 b c £4339

64	9-12	Newm	7g/f	3470
87	1-18	NEWM	7gd	3927*

FUBOS 2 b g £0

9a	15-16	Sout	8af	[75]	192
59a	5-16	Ling	7ap	[61]	290 VIS
48a	6-10	Ling	8ap	61	455 vis
1	17-17	Yarm	7g/f	[66]	1729 vis

FUEL CELL 3 b c £6095

76	8-19	Newb	8gd		1236
65	11-17	Newb	8g/f		1762
69	3-8	Ling	9g/f		2013
68	3-14	Sali	8fm	65	2423
56	8-14	Wind	8.3fm	65	2971
75	1-7	FOLK	9.7gd	[65]	3385*
73	3-9	Sand	10g/f	70	3862 BL
70	5-13	Ling	10g/s	70	4182 bl
65	10-19	Kemp	10fm	70	4392 bl
75	3-17	Leic	10gd	69	5062 bl

FULL EGALITE 8 gr g £0

30a	4-12	Ling	12ap	[30]	1180 bl
20a	6-7	Ling	12ap	[30]	1243 bl

FULL ENGLISH 4 b f £0

0	10-13	Wolv	8.5af	39
0	14-15	Sout	12af	89

FULL OF ZEST 2 ch f £1090

82	2-13	Donc	7hvy	5199

FULL PITCH 8 ch g £3262

25a	9-10	Sout	6af		532
42a	12-13	Wolv	6af	70	687
43	6-8	Hayd	6g/s	[60]	1345
67	1-17	WARW	5hvy	[55]	1532*
53	13-17	Nott	5.1g/s	70	1774
20a	12-13	Wolv	6af	68	2053
61	8-18	Hayd	5gd	68	2951
42	12-13	Warw	6.1gd	65	4272
38a	10-12	Wolv	6ap	[58]	5155

FULL SPATE 9 ch g £8488

67	6-16	Bath	5.7g/s	[69]	1103
67	7-19	Leic	6g/s	68	1354
53	5-10	Warw	6.1hvy	68	1533
71	4-16	Nott	6.1sft	[68]	1743
62	6-16	Redc	6g/f	67	1824
70	4-16	Good	6gd	69	2023
69	6-12	Newc	6g/f	68	2160
70	3-17	Wind	6g/f	68	2451
69	2-9	Chep	6.1g/f	68	2626
68	7-18	Donc	6gd	68	2752
61	9-14	Leic	6gd	68	3213
62	11-19	Chep	7.1gd	68	3401
70	2-17	Wind	6fm	66	3643
72	1-20	HAYD	6fm	68	3796*
53	6-7	Folk	6g/s	[66]	3910
65	9-19	York	6gd	71	4005
61	8-13	Warw	6.1gd	69	4272
60	12-20	Wind	6g/s	69	4946
57a	9-13	Wolv	6ap	69	5010
70	4-19	Wind	6g/f	69	5053

FULLANDBY 2 b c £422

72a	2-11	Wolv	7.1ap	5228

FULLY FLEDGED 4 b f £0

9	10-10	Bath	11.7gd	49	1399

FULVIO 3 b g £0

35a	16-16	Ling	7ap	72	22
64a	4-14	Ling	6ap	70	121 vis
47a	9-10	Ling	8ap	[70]	133 vis
56a	10-16	Ling	7ap	68	181
51a	10-15	Ling	7ap	66	266
42a	11-12	Ling	8ap	[63]	2394
8	13-13	Kemp	7g/f	60	3034
34	7-7	Brig	8g/f	60	3174 vis
50a	5-12	Ling	8ap	[58]	3286 vis

8a 14-14 Ling 7ap 56 3821
21 11-15 Sali 6gd 53 3888 vis
22 9-9 Brig 7sft [49] 4164 vis
42a 4-12 Wolv 7.1ap [50] 5233

FUN TO RIDE 3 ch f £9402
95 1-10 NEWM 6g/f 1191*
94 2-14 Ches 6.1g/s 90 1570
36 20-20 York 6g/f 93 2407
84 14-19 Newm 6fm 93 3002
90 11-22 Donc 5.6fm 92 4459

FUNFAIR 5 b g £12550
109 2-15 Donc 8fm 103 4531
108 3-13 Newm 8g/f [104] 4887
102 6-11 Newm 8g/s [106] 5283

FUNFAIR WANE 5 b g £71594
62 10-11 Newm 7g/f 95 2532
91 7-15 Newc 5g/s 95 2727
93 4-7 Newm 5fm [93] 3409
77 19-24 Asco 5gd 93 3466
1 27-28 Good 5fm 93 3622
88 6-16 Hayd 5fm 90 4382
87 12-22 Donc 5.6fm 90 4459
103 1-24 AYR 6sft 90 4686*
74 6-9 Hami 6g/s [98] 4817

FURL AWAY 2 b g £0
62 10-12 Newm 7g/f 3470

FURNITURE FACTORS 4 b g £0
14 7-9 Pont 10sft 60 1430
0 10-12 Wolv 9.4af 50 2054 P

FURTHER OUTLOOK 10 gr g £23124
88 1-17 KEMP 5sft 75 944*
74a 3-14 Ling 6ap 73 1025
75 10-20 Kemp 6gd 87 1138
62 11-14 Ches 5.1gd 86 1594
66 11-11 Good 5g/f 84 1845
80 4-10 Sand 5gd 82 2189
87 2-14 Wind 5g/f 82 2266
87 3-12 Sali 5gd 84 2698
24 15-16 Wind 6fm 84 2758
84 7-12 Newm 5g/f 84 3279
79 10-14 Newb 5.2fm 84 3628
77 6-16 Wind 6gd 84 3827
83 5-13 Newb 5.2g/f 83 3960
91 1-8 KEMP 5sft [83] 4031*
82 5-11 Bath 5g/s [81] 4201
77 12-14 Epso 5gd 90 4291
70 3-12 Sand 5gd [87] 4605
86 5-11 Hayd 5sft 82 4780
89 2-15 Catt 5sft 82 5125 P
84 4-13 Muss 5g/s 82 5143 P
79 7-13 Donc 5sft 85 5218 p

FUSILLADE 4 ch g £0
23 14-14 Thir 7sft 2692
0 19-20 Catt 12g/f 40 3354

FUSS 3 b f £0
49 6-8 Newb 10hvy 5226

FUTOO 3 b g £11910
60 6-16 Beve 8.5sft 63 1628
58 5-14 Newc 8gd 61 1872
65 1-17 HAYD 8.1gd 59 2243*
65 3-8 Ayr 7.2gd [61] 2506
55 7-13 Beve 7.5g/s 61 3147
70 1-13 BEVE 9.9gd 61 3309*
70 3-6 Ripo 10g/f 66 3647
70 4-12 Beve 9.9g/s 66 3854
72 2-12 Ripo 10gd 66 4282
54 8-13 Newc 10.1g/f 66 4406
58 8-17 Newc 10.1g/f 70 5016

FUTURE DEAL 3 b f £4005
69 4-10 Newb 7gd 3921
61 3-11 Wind 6g/f 4836
61a 1-12 WOLV 6ap 5157*

FUTURE TO FUTURE 4 gr g £0
23 14-17 Kemp 12sft 54 4033
0 14-16 Ling 16ap 49 4319

FUTURISTIC 4 b g £844
60a 2-13 Wolv 8.5af 57 559

46a 9-10 Wolv 8.5af 57 753 VIS
15 16-20 Ripo 8g/s 54 1366

FYODOR 3 b c £556
64 13-14 Thir 5g/f 85 1766
77 6-10 Leic 6gd [84] 2137
77 7-16 Leic 5g/f 82 2400
52 20-20 Donc 5fm 79 4496
70 7-19 Good 6gd 74 4747
70 4-14 Redc 5fm [71] 4930
45 12-15 Ayr 5sft 69 5036
13 19-20 Yarm 7sft 67 5256

GABANA 3 br f £3104
57 12-22 Donc 7gd 71 955
68 6-15 Bath 8g/s 69 1099
55 9-14 Wind 8.3g/f 67 1956
68 3-10 Yarm 8g/f 65 2344
69 2-8 Sali 8gd 65 2701
71 3-13 Warw 8.1gd 65 3058
71 3-14 Yarm 8gd 65 3363

GABANNA 2 b c £710
72 6-12 Wind 8.3g/f 4829
74 3-10 Nott 10hvy 5188

GABLESEA 10 b g £0
0 16-16 Hayd 10.5sft 24 3276

GABOR 4 b g £0
53a 11-13 Ling 10ap 61 178 bl e
46a 13-16 Ling 12ap 61 218 bl e
31 14-16 Brig 11.9fm 58 1693
16 9-11 Folk 12g/f 54 2273 bl
38 5-5 Brig 11.9g/f [50] 3983 bl

GAELIC PRINCESS 4 b f £285
47a 11-13 Wolv 6af 87 618
80a 14-15 Ling 7ap 85 887
81 6-15 Ripo 6g/f 87 1782
42 19-19 Kemp 6fm 85 2070
74 9-12 Sali 6fm 82 2289
77 12-29 Asco 6fm 85 2581
63 15-25 Asco 7g/f 79 3443
61 5-15 Sali 6gd 77 3888

GAELIC PROBE 10 b g £0
20a 6-9 Wolv 14.8af [34] 301 P

GAELIC ROULETTE 4 b f £1245
67 3-5 Leic 11.8g/f 70 2923
69 8-11 Sand 14g/f 70 3340
37 10-12 Sali 12g/f 70 3868

GAFF 2 b c £8958
101 2-6 Leop 7sft 5248

GAIETY GIRL 3 b f £0
50 9-11 Beve 9.9g/f 65 1834
57 6-12 Pont 10g/f 64 2277
48 5-7 Ayr 13.1g/s 64 2546
43 8-12 Hayd 8.1gd 60 2904
29 10-12 Carl 6.9fm 57 3548 BL
0 20-20 Newc 6g/f 53 4408
49 8-9 Newc 10.1g/f [46] 5015

GALA SUNDAY 4 b g £0
32 7-7 Thir 8sft [95] 1225
26 19-19 Newm 10g/f 90 1478
63 12-14 York 10.4g/s 87 1704
62 7-10 Beve 9.9g/s 80 2323
31 12-13 Redc 10gd 77 2560
49 6-7 Redc 9g/s [72] 2962
48 7-9 Carl 9.3fm [70] 3546
54 6-9 Redc 8g/f [68] 3806 BL
42 16-19 York 7.9g/f 65 4399
45 12-15 Redc 7.5g/f 60 4719
1 25-26 Redc 8fm 55 4926

GALANDORA 4 b f £7788
40 5-9 Folk 12sft 45 979 t
37 6-10 Folk 12g/s 45 1082 t
51 1-12 SOUT 16gd 45 1285*
0 11-11 Beve 16.2sft 49 1629
54 1-8 MUSS 16gd 47 1793*
55 2-14 York 13.9g/f 53 2060
46 8-11 Sand 14g/f 53 2391
53 3-15 Folk 16.4g/s 52 3049
54 3-19 Bath 17.2gd 52 3147

49 7-12 Yarm 16gd 52 3493
50 7-14 Warw 16.2g/f 50 4423
48a 5-14 Ling 16ap [50] 4663
48a 7-14 Ling 16ap 48 5082

GALAXY FALLON 6 b m £0
37a 6-8 Sout 11af [30] 857
12a 9-12 Sout 7af [30] 909
26 6-15 Nott 10gd [30] 1991

GALEOTA 2 b c £53684
81 4-10 Sali 5g/f 1716
95 1-15 WIND 6gd 3163*
102 5-11 York 6g/s [85] 4022
103 5-8 Kemp 6fm [100] 4390 P
112 1-4 DONC 6fm [100] 4529*
114 1-9 NEWB 6g/f [100] 4680*

GALEY RIVER 5 ch g £2350
45a 8-11 Ling 8ap 47 669
37a 10-13 Ling 7ap 47 739 e
39a 5-10 Ling 8ap 45 770
40a 7-14 Ling 10ap [45] 828
40a 5-11 Ling 10ap [40] 970
43a 1-14 LING 10ap [40] 1072*
35a 6-9 Ling 10ap [45] 1289
44a 2-10 Wolv 9.4af [45] 1564
37a 3-5 Wolv 9.4af [45] 1674
38a 5-14 Ling 10ap [45] 1712 p
37 7-15 Kemp 9gd 41 2170
42 4-12 Newb 10g/f 41 2354
37 5-10 Newb 11g/f 40 2875
12 11-17 Newm 10g/f 40 3238
41 6-12 Newm 10g/f 38 3785
40a 4-13 Ling 10ap 41 3823 p
26 5-12 Newm 10gd 38 3916

GALLANT BOY 4 ch g £3552
79a 5-14 Ling 12ap 80 83 t
74a 11-13 Ling 10ap 79 134 t
77a 5-16 Ling 12ap 77 218 t
0 10-10 Wolv 9.4af 77 278 t
73a 8-16 Ling 12ap 77 293 t
69a 13-16 Ling 12ap 76 404 t
75a 4-15 Ling 12ap 73 549 t
64a 9-10 Ling 12ap 73 570 vis t
45a 13-14 Ling 12ap 71 731 t
70 5-13 Ches 10.3gd 74 2284 vis t
67 7-11 Warw 12.6fm 72 2601 vis t
64 6-8 Wind 10fm 69 2973 vis t
69 4-7 Kemp 14.4g/f 69 3037 t
70 8-15 Ches 10.3gd 69 3099 vis t
56 5-7 Newm 14.8g/f 69 3281 vis t
67 4-17 Wind 10fm 66 3477 vis t
69 4-8 Ches 12.3fm 66 3637 vis t
64 4-15 Bath 11.7g/f 65 3964 vis t
64 4-13 Folk 12gd 65 4119 vis t
56 13-15 Ches 15.9g/f 64 4512 vis t
59 9-11 Wind 11.6g/s [63] 4942 vis t
58a 8-16 Ling 12ap 59 4973 vis t
48 12-19 Bath 11.7gd 63 5024 vis t
42 8-10 Newm 12sft [63] 5102 BL t

GALLANTIAN 2 gr c £0
54a 10-14 Ling 7ap 5076
33 8-15 Brig 7sft 5192
71 7-14 Yarm 7sft 5250

GALLAS 3 b c £1084
23 15-16 Beve 8.5sft 64 1628 VIS
53 9-12 York 7.9g/f [61] 2410
46 8-11 Beve 8.5gd [61] 2656
56 2-14 Beve 7.5g/s [57] 3177 vis
36 9-12 Newm 8fm 55 3410 vis
39 14-18 Carl 7.9fm 53 3547 vis
23 16-16 Beve 8.5g/s [49] 3850 vis

GALLEGO 2 br c £0
6 12-12 Hayd 6gd 2902
33a 11-13 Ling 7ap 3330 BL
17 10-10 Hayd 5g/s 3901 VIS

GALLEON BEACH 7 b g £300
66 4-7 Beve 16.2sft 70 2941
55 8-9 Beve 16.2g/s 66 3181
44 14-19 Good 21fm 60 3531

GALLERY BREEZE 4 b f £5536

64a	2-16	Ling	7ap	61	55	
52a	10-15	Ling	7ap	64	151	
73	1-18	DONC	7gd	64	2755*	
54	11-17	Newb	7g/f	70	3257	
65a	9-13	Ling	7ap	70	3791	
42	9-11	Brig	8g/s	69	4141	
54	9-16	Sali	7sft	67	4582	P
58a	5-12	Ling	8ap	[65]	4974	bl
68a	2-12	Wolv	7.1ap	[65]	5006	bl

GALLERY GOD 8 ch g £0

69	15-17	Kemp	10g/s	100	1111
70	9-13	Epso	12fm	98	2255
77	10-12	Asco	22.2fm	[95]	2583
68	9-10	Asco	12g/f	90	3444
61	7-9	Good	12sft	83	4183
70	9-13	Epso	10.1g/f	80	4473

GALLEY LAW 3 ch g £2771

0	11-11	Wolv	9.4af		115
27a	7-14	Sout	12af	[25]	194
37a	3-12	Wolv	12af	[30]	523
39a	2-10	Wolv	12af	[30]	581
41a	1-12	SOUT	11af	[30]	640*
41a	2-10	Sout	8af	[30]	719
43a	2-10	Wolv	12af	[40]	780
31a	4-9	Sout	12af	[45]	1204

GALLOWAY MAC 4 ch c £3176

48a	3-8	Sout	8af		355
62a	3-11	Sout	7af		488
25a	12-13	Sout	6af		659
56a	1-7	SOUT	8af		721*
60a	2-13	Sout	7af	[60]	858
62	4-9	Folk	9.7sft	[60]	978
57	6-14	Folk	9.7g/s	60	1083
36a	9-14	Sout	8af	60	1198
56a	5-12	Ling	8ap	[57]	5077

GALVANISE 3 b c £5503

76	6-17	Donc	8gd		919	
90	1-8	RIPO	10g/f		2523*	
75	7-11	Newm	10g/f	87	3029	
89	3-14	Ripo	10gd	85	4305	
85	7-13	Donc	10.3fm	[85]	4463	T

GAMBLE OF THE DAY 2 ch c £0

83	6-13	Donc	7hvy		5200

GAMBLING SPIRIT 2 ch f £0

58	11-18	Nott	8.2g/f		4842

GAME DAME 3 ch f £4176

81	4-11	Newb	10g/f		2349
81	1-11	CHEP	8.1g/f	[78]	2627*
73	5-6	Ripo	10g/f	78	3647

GAME FLORA 2 b f £6708

0	12-13	Sout	6af	[53]	63
55	1-11	PONT	6sft	[50]	1426*
53	4-17	Nott	6.1sft	57	1606
38	9-13	Ripo	6g/f	58	2011
51	5-14	Catt	6g/f	56	3018
15	16-18	Pont	5gd	54	3463
45	6-12	Carl	5.9g/f	54	3655
0	12-14	Sout	6af	49	4130
49	2-14	Beve	7.5sft	[51]	4256
11a	12-12	Wolv	9.5ap	[45]	5209

GAME GURU 4 b g £11846

62a	3D-12	Wolv	7af	59	74	bl
61a	3-16	Sout	6af	59	166	bl
46a	10-16	Sout	7af	59	208	bl
63a	1-13	SOUT	8af	59	228*	
40a	7-8	Sout	8af	65	393	
65a	1-4	SOUT	8af	[65]	417*	
63a	3-10	Sout	8af	[64]	502	
66a	1-13	SOUT	7af	64	556*	bl
63a	4-6	Sout	7af	[62]	593	bl
60a	6-9	Wolv	8.5af	66	809	bl
67a	1-8	SOUT	11af	[66]	857*	P
55	9-20	Warw	10.9gd	62	1128	bl
57	5-12	Sout	11gd	62	1286	bl
53a	5-6	Sout	11af	[70]	1754	p

GAME LAD 2 b c £9036

66a	3-6	Sout	5af		3484
82	4-18	Newc	6g/s		3699

59	9-16	Thir	6g/s		4205	
76	3-17	York	7g/f	73	4396	
66	7-18	Pont	6g/f	73	4934	
80	2-14	Catt	7sft	73	5126	
80	1-14	REDC	7sft	[76]	5301*	
87	4-20	Donc	7sft	83	5373	

GAMESETNMATCH 3 b g £1108

40	6-8	Epso	8.5g/f	[70]	2873	
38a	10-11	Ling	6ap	67	3333	bl
50	4-11	Epso	7fm	[67]	3541	p
54	3-11	Epso	6gd	[57]	4294	p

GAMUT 5 b h £247338

115	2-17	Newb	12gd	[117]	1230	t
120	1-7	NEWM	12fm	[117]	1493*	t
122	1-10	SAIN	12g/s	[117]	3012*	
122	4-11	Asco	12g/f	[117]	3442	t
116	5-4	Bade	12sft	[117]	4428	

GANYMEDE 3 gr c £9221

85	2-17	Leic	10g/s		1019	
53	3-6	Thir	12g/s	[80]	1213	
83	2-14	Asco	10g/f	80	1924	
82	2-8	Good	11gd	[81]	2222	
80	2-6	Ling	10g/f	[81]	2843	VIS
76	8-11	Newm	10g/f	80	3236	
75	4-12	Newm	12g/f	[77]	3783	
79	3-6	Catt	12g/f	[75]	4441	
71	6-16	Good	12gd	[75]	4745	

GARANCE 2 b f £0

60	11-15	Newb	7g/f		2876
73	7-7	Newm	7g/f		3616
38	8-11	Chep	8.1g/s		4296
1	14-14	Sali	8gd		4852

GARDASEE 2 gr g £0

40a	7-11	Sout	6af		2336
51	7-20	Newc	6sft		2682
52a	6-11	Sout	7af		2995

GARDEN SOCIETY 7 ch g £0

24	8-8	Newm	6fm	[75]	2591
60	7-8	Newm	8fm	70	3583
57	11-19	York	7.9g/f	66	4399
56	7-17	Nott	8.2gd	63	4862
63	5-17	Leic	10gd	60	5062
53	8-10	Donc	10.3sft	60	5206

GARGOYLE GIRL 7 b m £3784

8a	10-11	Wolv	12af	55	557	p
49	5-10	Muss	14g/f	52	1118	p
59	1-10	MUSS	16gd	52	1551*	
48	10-12	Newc	12.4sft	58	1680	
59	6-12	Muss	14fm	60	2085	
5	11-13	Newc	16.1sft	58	2685	
52	4-6	Muss	16g/f	58	4555	
48	6-20	York	13.9gd	56	5004	
53	6-6	Muss	16g/s	[55]	5334	

GARHOUD 2 b c £0

56	9-11	Newm	8gd		3925

GARNETT 3 b c £2078

61	4-17	Wind	11.6fm		2788
76	3-7	Newm	12fm		3405
73	3-10	Ling	14fm		3742
69	9-13	Kemp	14.4fm	75	4395
66a	3-9	Ling	12ap	[75]	4449
60	5-7	Nott	16g/f	70	4846

GARNOCK BELLE 3 b f £0

0	11-13	Wolv	6af	[45]	397
3a	12-12	Sout	8af	35	656
24a	5-13	Wolv	8.5af	[35]	826
1a	12-13	Wolv	8.5af	[30]	894

GARNOCK VENTURE 2 b c £6499

27a	9-10	Wolv	7af	60	112	
51a	4-14	Sout	7af	53	158	BL
50a	3-10	Sout	7af	53	203	bl
28a	4-6	Sout	6af	50	316	bl
25a	11-15	Sout	7af	[49]	462	bl
52a	7-12	Wolv	7af	[47]	560	bl
56a	1-9	SOUT	7af	[47]	871*	bl
36a	8-12	Wolv	6af	55	1374	bl
58	3-9	Muss	5g/s	55	1457	bl
51	7-10	Hami	5g/s	55	1605	bl

49	7-19	York	6g/f	55	2055	bl
74a	1-8	SOUT	6af	[54]	2379*	bl
23	11-13	Newc	6sft	55	2683	bl
44	7-13	Muss	7.1g/f	55	2812	bl
52a	5-8	Sout	6af	62	3092	bl
39	5-11	Carl	6.9g/f	[52]	3651	bl
14	12-14	Beve	7.5sft	[49]	4256	bl

GARRIGON 2 b c £1971

45a	8-12	Wolv	6af	[66]	42	
64a	2-11	Ling	7ap	60	261	
55a	5-10	Ling	7ap	62	432	
53a	7-12	Ling	7ap	62	545	
59a	4-12	Ling	8ap	62	603	P
45a	15-15	Ling	7ap	[60]	671	BL
61a	4-12	Ling	7ap	60	729	
61a	6-14	Ling	7ap	[60]	804	
62a	2-10	Ling	10ap	[60]	843	

GARRYURRA 3 gr f £0

72	5-9	Sali	9.9g/f		1719
16	10-10	Chep	12.1gd	74	2114

GARSTON STAR 3 ch g £9488

55	3-5	Brig	9.9g/f	53	1372
61	1-9	GOOD	11g/f	52	2019*
60	2-7	Brig	11.9fm	57	2333
60	2-7	Epso	12g/s	55	3040
51	12-12	Sand	14g/f	60	3359
52	5-5	Carl	11.9g/f	57	3653
67	1-11	GOOD	11gd	55	3948*
9a	6-8	Sout	12af	55	4092
46	6-9	Good	16gd	62	4875

GASPARINI 3 ch c £1693

18	12-14	Thir	6g/s		1216
50	10-20	York	7g/s		1518
33	12-19	York	6g/f	64	2055
54	4-11	Redc	9g/s	59	2565
59	3-11	Carl	6.9gd	57	2936
48	9-13	Beve	7.5g/s	59	3179
56	3-9	Thir	7g/f	[59]	3413
37	12-20	Thir	7g/f	55	3575

GATEMAN 7 b g £144018

115	2-10	Donc	8gd		922	
118	1-6	NEWM	9gd	[112]	1168*	
116	2-10	Sand	8.1g/s	[112]	1349	
109	11-15	Newb	8g/f	[115]	1758	
113	3-11	Epso	8.5fm	[113]	2252	
117	1-9	WIND	8.3fm	[113]	2757+	
116	2-10	Asco	8gd	[113]	3124	
117	2-7	Ayr	10g/f	[113]	3306	
117	2-8	Wind	10g/s	[114]	4220	
116	2-12	Long	10g/f	[114]	4950	

GATWICK 3 b c £135352

91	1-17	DONC	8gd		919*
94	3-15	Newb	8gd	83	1206
99	1-18	GOOD	9g/f	87	1813*
107	1-18	HAYD	8.1g/f	95	1919+
104	10-14	Epso	12fm	[104]	2254
103	6-13	Asco	10g/f	[104]	2520
99	8-16	Good	9.9fm	104	3553
106	5-9	Deau	10hvy	[104]	4158
112	1-11	BEVE	9.9g/s	102	4239+
109	5-18	Newb	10gd	107	4681
109	7-32	Newm	10g/f	107	4916
97	11-16	Newm	9sft	[108]	5139

GAUDALPIN 2 b f £2867

67a	3-10	Ling	5ap		1071
70	4-8	Newm	5gd		1170
66	7-11	Ling	5gd		2395
68	4-17	Nott	6.1gd		2927
25	13-14	Leic	6g/f	67	3212
55	7-19	Nott	6.1g/s	65	4645
65	2-11	Catt	5gd	[61]	4962
66a	2-13	Wolv	6ap	[64]	5182
42a	10-13	Wolv	5.1ap	[64]	5207

GAVIOLI 2 b c £2544

45	5-7	Leic	6g/f		1964	
13	18-18	Chep	6.1gd		2194	
68	4-6	Chep	6.1gd		2367	T
68	2-7	Nott	6.1g/f		2629	t
42	10-11	Sali	6g/f		3110	t
50	9-14	Leic	6g/f	70	3212	t

67	3-8	Chep	6.1gd	65	3729 t
52	5-6	Chep	6.1g/s	65	3897 t

GAVROCHE 3 b c £27115

73a	1-9	WOLV	9.4af	63	441*
69a	2-6	Wolv	8.5af	69	470
73a	3-6	Wolv	9.4af	71	702
49a	5-10	Sout	12af	71	796 VIS
77	2-8	Brig	9.9g/f	[71]	1369
74	2-13	Kemp	9hvy	71	1515
74	5-14	York	11.9g/s	73	1708
84	1-9	DONC	10.3g/f	73	2079*
87	1-8	GOOD	9.9gd	78	2377*
84	4-10	Wind	10fm	84	2785
94	1-6	CHES	10.3g/f	84	3084*
82	9-16	Good	9.9fm	89	3553
25	8-8	Folk	9.7g/s	[89]	3912
87	8-11	Beve	9.9g/s	89	4239

GAY ROMANCE 3 ch f £694

60	8-10	Sali	7gd		2659
51	10-14	Wind	8.3fm		2974
63	6-14	Newb	9fm		3631
60	5-12	Ripo	10gd	62	4282
67	3-17	Nott	8.2gd	62	4862
56	10-18	Newm	8sft	64	5272

GAYLE STORM 3 b f £0

48a	8-15	Ling	7ap	63	337
38a	8-10	Ling	8ap	58	455
43a	8-12	Ling	8ap	52	603
49a	5-12	Sout	8af	52	656

GDANSK 7 b g £0

59	9-15	Pont	6hvy	73	1251
0	U-8	Hayd	6g/s	[73]	1345
44	8-14	Donc	6g/s	[70]	1522

GEE BEE EM 2 b f £5794

74	2-6	Good	6gd		2373
79	1-10	BATH	5.7fm		2666*
71	4-4	Kemp	6g/f		2859
79	4-4	Bath	5g/f		3369
67	9-10	Kemp	6g/f	76	3521
41a	11-11	Ling	6ap	75	4972

GEESPOT 5 b m £190

0	12-12	Wolv	6af	[44]	297
38a	4-15	Ling	7ap	[40]	411
34a	12-13	Ling	7ap	45	474
41a	7-12	Ling	8ap	[45]	538 P
28a	9-12	Ling	8ap	[40]	710 p
38a	3-10	Ling	8ap	[40]	831
35a	12-15	Ling	7ap	40	846
37a	7-15	Ling	7ap	[40]	969

GEISHA LADY 2 b f £3138

65	6-8	Sand	5gd		2188
71	3-12	Bath	5.7gd		3141
73	2-13	Chep	6.1gd		3399
75	4-8	Chep	6.1gd	76	3729
71	2-17	Warw	7.1gd	[74]	4271
29	17-19	Pont	8g/s	71	5147

GELLER 3 b g £859

68	5-11	Chep	10.2gd	[83]	2196
69	4-4	Sali	9.9fm	[83]	2290
57	8-10	Newb	8g/f	72	2877
58	8-16	Epso	8.5gd	68	3219
56	5-8	Newm	7g/f	65	3612

GEM BIEN 5 b g £550

51a	15-15	Ling	7ap	82	81
49	17-17	Thir	8g/s	82	1475
37	8-8	Newb	8g/f	[80]	2313
53	3-16	Beve	8.5g/s	[76]	3850
2a	8-8	Sout	7af	[73]	4093

GEMI BED 8 b g £3268

40a	3-14	Ling	13ap	41	264 bl
46a	6-13	Ling	13ap	[45]	602 bl
52a	1-8	LING	16ap	45	733* bl
49a	5-12	Ling	16ap	50	813 bl
45	4-9	Folk	12sft	49	979 bl

GEMINI GIRL 3 b f £0

49	7-14	Bath	5gd	56	1404
44	9-9	Thir	5g/f	54	2219
32	8-9	Muss	5g/f	50	2614

37	12-15	Redc	5g/s	46	2961
32	7-7	Ayr	7.2gd	46	3153
14	15-16	Thir	8g/f	42	3414
11	18-18	Carl	7.9fm	40	3547
4	8-9	Ripo	5g/f	36	3645 VIS

GEMINI LADY 4 b f £431

0	15-19	Redc	8sft	45	1661
47	2-18	Nott	8.2gd	[45]	1992
16	12-14	Leic	8g/f	46	2402
13	13-17	Hayd	8.1gd	46	2947
26	9-17	Carl	7.9fm	[45]	4506
48	4-16	Catt	9g/f	45	4676 BL
23	13-19	Kemp	8g/f	[47]	4795 bl
35a	8-11	Wolv	7.1ap	[45]	5210 bl

GEMMA 3 b f £0

37a	7-14	Ling	12ap	[40]	103
0	11-13	Ling	10ap	[40]	412
14a	13-14	Ling	13ap	[35]	537 P

GEMS BOND 4 b g £0

38	21-25	Asco	7g/f	80	3443
51	9-12	Chep	8.1g/s	77	3898
74	5-15	Sand	7.1gd	75	4500
55	14-15	Nott	10gd	73	4860
38a	11-12	Ling	8ap	72	5238

GENERAL FEELING 3 b g £12163

67	3-13	Folk	5sft		1575
68	3-17	Bath	5g/f		1787
40	11-20	Chep	6.1gd	67	2372
68	4-9	Wind	6gd		2619
78	1-18	GALW	7g/f	65	3656*
79	1-6	BRIG	8g/f	71	3718*
68	4-8	Good	8sft	76	4265
64	14-25	Newb	7gd	76	4683

GENERAL FLUMPA 3 b g £3626

62	6-12	Warw	7.1gd		1129
57a	3-9	Wolv	9.4af		1340
64	3-20	Wind	11.6sft	64	1648
63a	5-12	Wolv	12af	65	2203
64	2-6	Warw	10.9fm	65	2780
57	6-15	Nott	10gd	65	3108
65	3-11	Yarm	10.1gd	[64]	3875
66	4-13	Ling	10af	65	4182

GENERAL GB 7 b g £12653

68a	1-9	WOLV	8.5af	[65]	811*
70a	2-9	Sout	12af	65	856
55a	7-10	Ling	12ap	65	936
71	5-14	Nott	10fm	[73]	1006
75	2-20	Epso	12hvy	69	1295
57	10-14	Hami	12.1gd	69	1389
50	12-17	Newb	12g/f	72	1759
8	19-19	Carl	11.9gd	70	2673 bl
61	5-7	Epso	12g/s	70	3040
66a	3-14	Sout	8af	[65]	3392
71	2-12	Newc	9hvy	65	4215
61	10-20	Hayd	11.9g/s	66	4771
50	14-17	Leic	10gd	66	5062
50	6-17	Newb	9sft	66	5198

GENERAL HAIGH 2 b g £293

54a	6-8	Ling	5ap		3600
54	4-7	Folk	5gd		3907
75	4-18	Ling	6gd		4108
47a	9-11	Ling	6ap	72	4972

GENERAL JUMBO 2 b c £2072

86	2-16	Newb	8hvy		5220

GENERAL MAX 2 b c £842

71	3-6	Ayr	6gd		2028
62	7-7	Thir	7g/f		3412
50	12-18	Ripo	6g/s		3939
48	13-17	York	7g/f	64	4396

GENERAL NUISANCE 2 ch g £2698

69	2-9	Donc	5gd		929
55	6-10	Bath	5g/s		1097
65	4-11	Kemp	5hvy		1640
52	5-6	Leic	5fm		2110
60	4-6	Yarm	7g/f		2343 P
59	3-5	Brig	6fm		2833 p
60	2-8	Brig	6g/f		3172 p
53	3-8	Yarm	6gd		3491 BL

50	7-8	Chep	6.1gd	60	3729 p
54	3-5	Yarm	6gd	[59]	3871 bl
40	9-9	Yarm	6sft	55	4146 p

GENERAL SMITH 5 b g £0

4	13-14	Pont	8hvy	[59]	1253
40	10-13	Muss	7.1gd	58	1553
23	16-18	Thir	8g/f	55	1972
0	18-18	Thir	6g/f	55	2214
0	10-10	Beve	5g/f	[50]	3503

GENEROUS GESTURE 3 b f £7180

76a	1-15	SOUT	6af	[73]	795*
67a	5-8	Ling	7ap	75	933
72	6-20	Nott	6.1gd	74	1239
83a	1-8	SOUT	6af	74	1441* VIS
49	11-20	Newb	7g/f	75	1761 vis
67	6-8	Brig	7fm	75	2259 vis
81a	5-8	Sout	7af	80	2723 vis
55	6-7	Leic	6g/f	[73]	3518 vis
45	8-8	Folk	7gd	[70]	4117
60	9-20	Nott	6.1g/s	66	4646
39	13-19	Wind	6g/f	61	5053
48	9-18	Yarm	6g/s	58	5354

GENEROUS MEASURE 2 b c £0

10	12-15	Brig	7sft		5192

GENEROUS OPTION 2 ch f £8200

77	5-8	Donc	6gd		2750
88	1-16	NOTT	6.1gd		3103*
89	3-8	Ayr	6g/f	86	3303
85	4-10	Ripo	6gd	85	4306
85	4-10	Ayr	6g/s	84	4655
46	10-14	Newm	6sft	83	5098

GENEROUS SHARE 3 ch f £0

0	11-13	Wolv	8.5af	[50]	46
15a	6-8	Sout	7af	[47]	320

GENEROUS SPIRIT 3 ch c £0

68	8-14	Folk	7g/s		1080
58	9-17	Sali	6g/s		1497
56	7-13	Folk	5sft		1575
61	6-14	Brig	6fm		1690
52	7-12	Folk	6gd	62	3380

GENGHIS 5 br g £8730

86	2-7	Newm	12g/f	80	2737
79	5-8	Hayd	14gd	80	2887
83	2-11	Newb	11g/f	80	3256
77	8-21	York	11.9gd	81	3999
83	3-8	Hayd	11.9g/f	80	4353
86	3-17	Nott	14.1g/s	80	4647
84	2-14	Asco	12g/f	80	4775

GENNIE BOND 2 b f £2837

68	4-7	Newm	6g/f		2733
78	3-8	Asco	6gd		3071
81	2-10	Wind	6fm		3290
49	11-11	Newm	6g/f	79	3614
53	16-21	Donc	6.5fm	79	4457
51	22-26	Newb	6.5g/f		4679

GENTLE RAINDROP 3 b f £0

69	9-15	Newb	6g/f		1763
67	5-9	Asco	7g/f		1929
54	10-12	Newb	7g/f		2352
38	13-14	Chep	8.1g/s	65	3090
45	10-11	Wind	8.3fm	62	3799
58	7-10	Sali	6g/s	[62]	4081 BL
52	12-18	Bath	10.2gd	[58]	5023
4a	10-12	Wolv	8.6ap	58	5116 bl

GENTLE RESPONSE 4 b f £1503

8a	13-13	Ling	6ap	[45]	340
21a	9-9	Ling	5ap	[45]	413
31a	6-11	Ling	6ap	35	728 BL
42a	3-13	Ling	6ap	[35]	788 bl
46a	1-15	LING	7ap	[35]	830* bl
33a	9-15	Ling	7ap	[45]	969 bl
36a	5-9	Ling	7ap	[45]	1248 bl
36a	6-8	Ling	7ap	[45]	1413 bl
0	12-15	Brig	6gd	[45]	4905 VIS

GENTLE WARNING 4 b f £0

25	8-8	Sand	8.1g/f		3858
0	11-11	Beve	9.9sft		4261
5	13-13	Leic	10g/f		4453 BL

GENTLEMAN GEORGE 2 b g £0
14a	9-10	Sout	7af	50	203
0	8-8	Ling	8ap	[45]	326
20a	9-9	Ling	5ap	[45]	405

GENTLEMANS DEAL 3 b c £7772
77	4-20	Newm	8g/f		3237
81	1-8	CHEP	7.1sft		4055*
88a	1-13	WOLV	9.5ap	75	5161*

GENUINE JAY GEE 2 b c £0
44a	8-10	Ling	6ap	260

GENUINELY 3 b f £950
31a	11-15	Ling	7ap		670
21	16-18	Wind	8.3g/s		1258
39a	6-15	Ling	12ap	40	2741
41	3-11	Yarm	11.5gd	39	3367 VIS
28	7-14	Nott	16g/f	39	3580 vis
37	3-8	Chep	16.2g/s	40	4302 vis

GEOGRAPHY 4 ch g £0
1a	P-10	Ling	10ap	[53]	540	p
0	8-9	Wolv	9.4af	[53]	633	p
49a	6-14	Ling	10ap	53	718	p
41a	11-14	Ling	12ap	53	768	p
13	12-13	Brig	11.9g/f	45	1373	p
0	16-19	Brig	9.9gd	[40]	4903	p

GEOJIMALI 2 ch c £0
52	5-7	Ayr	6gd		3148
61	6-7	Ayr	7.2g/f		3302
50	5-7	Ayr	6g/f		3761

GEORDIE DANCER 2 b c £0
55	11-12	Carl	5g/f		4343
60	5-6	Muss	8g/f		4552
58	7-10	Newc	7fm		4864

GEORDIELAND 3 gr c £7764
111	3-8	Long	12hvy	5165

GEORGE STUBBS 5 b g £14652
70a	5-16	Ling	7ap	70	22 bl
67a	6-15	Ling	7ap	70	50 bl
46a	7-11	Ling	6ap	[69]	130 bl
65a	6-16	Sout	7af	[69]	161 P
70a	3-15	Sout	11af	67	196
71a	2-8	Sout	12af	67	225
57a	7-8	Ling	16ap	71	288
39a	6-7	Sout	12af	70	504
66a	2-7	Sout	12af	[65]	594
67a	3-7	Sout	14af	65	681
52a	6-10	Wolv	12af	65	810
56a	4-9	Sout	12af	65	856
56	7-14	Donc	18gd	65	926
65	3-11	Warw	15sft	62	1087
66	1-17	RIPO	16g/s	62	1361*
65	3-10	Hami	13gd	65	1506
64	5-18	York	13.9g/s	65	1689
58	5-9	Ripo	16g/f	63	2009
57	5-9	Ayr	13.1g/s	63	2567
45	11-12	Newm	16.1g/f	62	3032

GEORGE THE BEST 3 b g £804
50	13-14	Ripo	6g/s	82	1360
72	6-10	Hayd	8g/f	78	1488
68	4-11	Hami	6gd	75	1745
63	14-18	Newc	6g/s	73	2770
60	6-15	Hayd	6gd	70	2950
31	13-13	Beve	7.5g/s	68	3179
46	11-12	Hayd	6sft	68	3273
4	20-20	Ripo	6gd	64	4278
63	5-15	Ayr	5sft	62	5036
46	6-13	Catt	5sft	[62]	5321

GEORGIE BELLE 2 ch f £1033
64	3-5	Leic	5g/s	1014
58	3-15	Beve	5g/s	1161
38a	13-14	Ling	7ap	5257

GEORGINA 2 ch f £0
75	8-10	Yarm	7fm	2863
31	14-15	Folk	7gd	3381
59	7-8	Brig	7g/f	3716

GERI ROULETTE 5 b m £300
44a	3-11	Wolv	12af	[51]	6

0	7-12	Wolv	12af	51	75

GERMANICUS 2 b c £0
20a	12-13	Wolv	8.6ap	5355

GERONIMO 6 b g £5401
45a	7-13	Wolv	6af	55	45	
58a	2-12	Wolv	7af	55	68	p
38a	9-15	Sout	6af	57	168	p
60a	2-10	Wolv	6af	57	345	p
43a	8-13	Wolv	6af	57	384	p
60a	3-9	Wolv	7af	59	629	p
64a	1-10	WOLV	8.5af	58	753*	p
35a	9-11	Wolv	8.5af	64	806	p
53a	4-7	Wolv	7af	62	860	

GET STUCK IN 8 b g £0
1	16-19	Newc	6sft	73	967
39	14-16	Muss	5sft	69	1120
19	12-13	Newc	5sft	69	1276

GET TO THE POINT 2 ch c £2150
56a	5-8	Ling	6ap	[65]	49	
42a	9-14	Sout	8af	[63]	226	e
10a	8-8	Sout	7af	[59]	389	VIS
77	2-14	Sout	6gd	[63]	1281	
80	2-14	Brig	6fm	[72]	1690	
68	5-15	Leic	6g/f	[72]	1829	
56	9-10	Brig	6g/f	[72]	2048	
37	9-11	Nott	6.1g/f	72	2155	
51	7-8	Brig	7g/f	66	2434	
59	5-13	Wind	5fm	62	2784 BL	
53	7-14	Yarm	7gd	60	3995 bl	

GHAILL FORCE 2 b g £435
66	2-19	Kemp	8g/f	4792

GHANTOOT 3 ch c £4970
42	11-11	Ripo	8gd		1177
58	8-13	Nott	6.1sft		1464
66	7-10	Beve	7.5g/f		1832
30	11-12	Ripo	8g/f		1978
67	3-11	Redc	9g/s	62	2565 VIS
77	1-9	BRIG	9.9gd	66	2955* vis
68	3-17	Newm	10g/f	72	3238 vis
54	13-19	Donc	10.3sft	73	5201 vis

GHASIBA 2 gr f £1592
69	6-8	Asco	6g/f		3386
75	2-12	Folk	7gd		3908
87	7-8	York	6g/s		4059
60	15-21	Donc	6.5fm	82	4457
78	9-9	Asco	8g/f	[82]	4798

GHURRA 2 b f £5379
84	1-7	YARM	6g/f		3709*
84	7-11	Sali	6gd		4332
85	4-14	Newm	6sft	87	5098

GIANTS ROCK 2 ch c £1150
78	3-5	Asco	7g/f	4776
0	R-14	Bath	8gd	5018

GIBRALTAR BAY 2 b f £268
53	12-14	Yarm	7gd	3489
59	4-11	Wind	8.3fm	3798
47	15-18	Nott	8.2g/s	4035

GIDAM GIDAM 2 b c £698
74	6-8	York	7gd	4326
68	6-10	Yarm	8g/s	4631
67	3-11	Bath	10.2gd	4825

GIFT HORSE 4 ch g £6047
69	11-16	Good	7g/f	82	1817
89	2-13	Kemp	7gd	80	2172
90	3-12	Kemp	7g/s	84	2679
89	8-20	Newm	8fm	87	3001
86	4-10	Hayd	8.1g/s	86	4767
31	30-32	Newm	9g/f	86	4916

GIFT VOUCHER 3 ch c £5950
60	11-17	Newb	10gd		1737
78	3-9	Kemp	12g/f		2862
44	8-10	Pont	10gd		3243
84	2-5	Newm	12g/f	80	3587 T
83	1-10	YARM	11.5gd	[80]	3997* t

GIFTED FLAME 5 b g £11137
48	9-19	Beve	9.9g/s	66	1164
56	10-14	Hami	8.3gd	65	1748
66	4-13	Carl	7.9fm	63	2447
56	7-11	Ripo	8gd	63	2986
57	7-20	Newm	8g/f	63	3232 p
66	3-10	Beve	8.5g/f	61	3501
72	1-16	CARL	7.9g/f	61	3650*
66	4-12	Ayr	9.1g/f	68	3766
72	3-14	Beve	7.5g/s	67	4241
69	6-15	Carl	7.9g/f	67	4346
63	8-16	Thir	8g/f	67	4592
76	1-15	BEVE	7.5g/f	67	4719*
51	15-26	Redc	8fm	72	4926

GIFTED GAMBLE 2 b c £28575
61	7-10	Hayd	5sft		1107
71	3-6	Hami	5gd		1386
79	3-11	Hayd	5g/f		1880 BL
77	3-9	Ches	5.1gd		2281 bl
85	2-13	Carl	5gd		2670 bl
87	2-3	Hami	5fm		3247 bl
80	1-8	LING	5gd		3445* bl
80	5-9	Good	5af	82	3623 bl
74	9-13	Muss	5g/f	80	4551
91	2-14	Hami	6sft	80	4692
86	11-24	Redc	6fm	[80]	4928 P
94	3-29	Newm	6gd		5087
99	4-8	Donc	6sft	[84]	5217

GIFTED LASS 2 b f £0
0	14-14	Redc	6g/s	5106
14a	10-11	Wolv	7.1ap	5228

GIFTED MUSICIAN 2 b c £518
73	4-15	Newb	8hvy	5221

GIG HARBOR 4 b c £30315
88a	2-14	Ling	12ap	84	83
84a	6-13	Ling	10ap	85	134
94a	1-16	LING	12ap	85	293*
51a	11-16	Ling	12ap	89	475
97a	1-10	LING	12ap	89	570*
96a	5-14	Ling	10ap	95	758
96a	6-12	Ling	13ap	95	877
62	11-12	Wind	11.6fm	82	2759
83	4-16	Kemp	9g/f	80	3039
64	13-18	Newb	8g/f	80	3265
72	8-10	Good	9.9gd	79	3949

GIKO 10 b g £3552
24a	11-14	Ling	13ap	[40]	537
35a	3-15	Ling	12ap	[35]	707 bl
21a	12-14	Ling	12ap	[35]	827 bl
32a	6-14	Ling	12ap	[35]	968 bl
20a	7-12	Ling	12ap	[35]	1180 bl
43	2-11	Sali	12fm	38	2293
38	3-10	Warw	12.6g/f	40	2912
21	11-19	Bath	17.2gd	38	3147
26	8-10	Sali	14.1gd	37	3887
34	10-15	Folk	12g/f	[35]	4374
74	2-7	Sali	8sft	[35]	4581
26	16-20	Kemp	12g/f	[47]	4796

GILDAS FORTUNA 2 b f £370
72	4-14	Redc	6g/s	5106

GILDED COVE 3 b c £6981
45a	10-11	Wolv	5af	69	155
56a	7-10	Sout	6af	69	390
52a	7-15	Sout	6af	67	550
60a	3-12	Sout	6af	[67]	610
65a	3-13	Sout	6af	65	741
65a	5-13	Wolv	6af	65	807
64a	1-8	WOLV	6af	[64]	941*
55a	1-8	WOLV	5af	[64]	1218*
55a	4-13	Wolv	6af	64	2053
58a	4-14	Sout	6af	[63]	2502

GILLYS GENERAL 4 ch g £1446
49a	4-7	Sout	7af	[46]	636
25a	10-14	Ling	7ap	[45]	783 BL
46a	1-9	WOLV	7af	[40]	1266*
39a	6-12	Ling	7af	[49]	2204
27	11-16	Chep	7.1gd	[49]	2369
18a	12-15	Sout	7af	48	2501 P
19	10-11	Epso	7fm	[44]	3541

GIMASHA 2 b f £1990

GIN N FONIC 4 ch g £0 (preceded by)

71	4-12	Nott	6.1g/f		4844
77	2-13	Wind	6g/f		5047
48	12-12	Bath	5sft		5169

GIN N FONIC 4 ch g £0

43	7-7	Chep	7.1gd	[70]	3402

GINGER COOKIE 2 ch f £0

40	15-20	York	6g/f		4401

GINGER ICE 3 ch g £185

7a	15-15	Ling	7ap	[55]	117
37a	7-11	Ling	8ap	[47]	145 P
46a	6-12	Ling	10ap	[38]	272
44a	3-6	Ling	10ap	[40]	409 p
42a	5-13	Ling	10ap	[40]	539 VIS
0	10-10	Ling	16ap	[40]	650 vis

GINGIEFLY 2 b c £806

64	10-15	Leic	7g/f		4455
78	3-12	Wind	8.3g/f		4829

GINGKO 6 b g £4531

61a	6-12	Ling	12ap	65	56
62a	6-16	Sout	11af	65	97
72a	1-8	LING	10ap	[62]	294*
71a	5-14	Ling	10ap	70	434
63a	10-14	Ling	10ap	70	674
73a	3-16	Ling	12ap	68	5261
66	3-11	Yarm	10.1g/s	63	5353

GINNER MORRIS 8 b g £0

0	9-9	Sout	11af	[27]	204
4a	6-11	Sout	8af	[30]	372 bl

GIOCOSO 4 b c £7966

79	6-7	Good	7gd	85	2223
67	9-12	Kemp	9g/f	82	2860
65	9-12	Kemp	10gd	80	3185
83	1-12	LEIC	8fm	76	3813*
80	4-12	Chep	8.1g/s	82	3898
84	5-14	Wind	8.3gd	[83]	4122
67	4-8	Chep	7.1g/s	[82]	4301
71	9-18	Kemp	8g/f	80	4714
76	6-13	Bath	8sft	78	5172

GIRL WARRIOR 3 ch f £533

66	6-12	Good	7g/f		1846
66	4-11	Bath	8fm		2031
51	12-12	Sand	10gd	69	2366

GIRLSWEEKEND 2 b f £0

22a	10-12	Ling	6ap		4896
61a	7-14	Ling	7ap		5257

GIRONDE 3 b c £5393

79	4-11	Newm	10gd		1148
84	3-16	Wind	10gd		1384
78	12-17	Asco	12g/f	87	2519
91	3-12	Wind	11.6gd	85	3161
93	1-5	CATT	12sft	[88]	3934* VIS

GITCHE MANITO 2 b c £2365

75	3-11	Sali	7gd		3883
52	11-11	Newm	7gd		4190
80	5-8	Kemp	7fm		4393
80	2-6	Brig	7fm	[76]	4760

GIUNCHIGLIO 5 ch g £9523

62a	3-6	Ling	10ap	62	1027
68	1-17	KEMP	10g/f	62	1913*
44	12-15	Kemp	9gd	64	2170
66	3-9	Ches	10.3g/s	[64]	2745
68	6-15	Ches	10.3g/f	64	3099
60	10-16	Kemp	9gd	64	3187
58	4-6	Leic	10fm	64	3815
71	1-9	CHES	12.3sft	64	4076*
62	6-16	Ches	10.3g/f	70	4515
47	13-18	Ayr	10.9sft	70	4623
60a	4-12	Wolv	12.2ap	67	4983
24	16-19	Pont	10g/s	65	5148

GIUST IN TEMP 4 b c £391

10a	6-12	Wolv	12af	[37]	114
28a	5-14	Sout	8af	33	165
0	13-15	Sout	11af	33	196
42a	4-9	Wolv	9.4af	[30]	314
34a	2-9	Wolv	9.4af	[30]	399
19a	9-11	Wolv	9.4af	40	465

25a	6-9	Wolv	9.4af	[40]	522
39	9-11	Pont	10g/f	[36]	2991
50	4-8	Bath	10.2g/f	[36]	3370
34	8-13	Folk	9.7g/f	40	3726
32	10-16	Beve	8.5g/s	[40]	3850

GIVE HIM CREDIT 4 b g £0

28a	5-9	Sout	6af	[68]	1194
6	12-12	Redc	8g/f	[65]	1823 bl
53	8-12	Catt	7g/f	[60]	3017 P
24	11-14	Catt	6g/f	[60]	3191 p
25	6-15	Newc	7gd	[52]	3426 p

GIVEMETHEMOONLIGHT 4 ch f £12795

41a	3-13	Wolv	8.5af	[48]	46
48a	2-11	Ling	8ap	[46]	145
39a	4-9	Sout	11af	[46]	224
60a	2-8	Wolv	8.5af	[46]	248
53a	2-15	Ling	7ap	[44]	263
49a	2-13	Wolv	9.4af	44	287
48a	5-13	Ling	10ap	[51]	338
52a	2-12	Wolv	9.4af	47	427 VIS
55a	1-9	WOLV	8.5af	[48]	437* vis
64a	3-9	Wolv	9.4af	[48]	480 vis
49a	5-14	Ling	10ap	54	498 vis
52a	3-13	Wolv	8.5af	50	559 vis
34a	6-9	Wolv	9.4af	54	620 vis
58a	1-9	WOLV	9.4af	50	629* vis
61a	2-9	Wolv	7af	56	647 vis
59a	3-12	Wolv	7af	56	704 vis
55a	6-10	Wolv	8.5af	56	753 vis
62a	3-9	Wolv	8.5af	60	809 P

GIVEN A CHANCE 2 b g £1551

0	11-12	Wolv	8.5af	[52]	28
20a	11-14	Sout	8af	[47]	95
19a	4-12	Sout	8af	[40]	309
18a	5-9	Sout	8af	35	486
5a	8-14	Sout	7af	[30]	573
0	5-8	Pont	12hvy	[40]	1250
45	3-11	Warw	8.1hvy	40	1534
34	4-16	Nott	10hvy	40	1611
46	2-13	Beve	8.5g/f	[45]	1947
45	6-9	Beve	8.5g/f	43	2168
20	8-10	Pont	10g/f	46	2794
35	6-13	Warw	8.1gd	46	3058
46	3-15	Beve	8.5g/s	46	3182

GIVEN A CHOICE 2 b c £373

81	4-14	Newm	7g/f		3752
76	7-11	Nott	8.2g/s		4648
75	5-15	Newm	8gd		4883

GIVERAND 4 b f £0

18a	7-12	Wolv	6af	[44]	33
29	10-14	Ling	7sft	45	1625
21	10-13	Bath	5gd	[42]	3143
27	13-15	Wind	5gd	42	3165

GJOVIC 3 br c £3785

81a	2-10	Ling	10ap	[75]	886
78	5-9	Hayd	8.1sft	80	1105
16	14-14	York	7.9g/s	78	1804 BL
78	4-10	Hayd	10.5g/f	[75]	1922
77	3-10	Good	8gd	75	2225
75	3-6	Newb	12g/f	75	2353
61	8-16	Wind	11.6g/s	75	2621
59	6-12	Good	11gd	72	4749

GLAD BIG 2 b c £459

76	3-17	Ling	6gd		4443
66	8-12	Hayd	6sft		4770

GLAD LION 3 b c £9155

93	2-8	Duss	8.5sft		5075

GLADS IMAGE 2 ch f £0

40	18-18	Nott	8.2g/f		4842
48	6-13	Warw	7.1g/s		4996

GLADYS AYLWARD 4 b f £0

29a	5-9	Sout	11af	[54]	505
0	7-10	Sout	12af	[54]	552 P

GLANWORTH 3 ch c £0

0	10-10	Yarm	11.5g/f		1725
0	6-7	Newm	12g/f		1936
0	11-11	Newm	8af		2248
0	11-13	Sout	8af	30	2497 BL

GLARAMARA 3 b c £11268

86a	11-15	Ling	7ap	[94]	885 BL
98	2-7	Newm	7g/s	[94]	1150
85	10-14	Newm	8g/f	[96]	1480
101	3-15	Ches	7.6gd	96	1583
93	8-20	York	6g/f	98	2407
70	13-15	Asco	7g/f	[98]	2486
99	4-6	Ches	7g/f	[97]	3098
98	4-10	Asco	6gd	97	3778
96	4-5	Ches	7.6g/f	[97]	4047
86	8-13	Ches	7.6sft	97	4103
71	17-24	Ayr	6sft	95	4686

GLASSON LODGE 2 b f £1815

55a	4-7	Sout	5af		1029
75	5-9	Wind	5g/s		1256
64	6-13	Carl	5fm		1950
58	3-7	Chep	6.1gd		2115
48	4-8	Wind	6g/f		2449 VIS
59	2-9	Chep	5.1g/f		2625
57	2-8	Bath	5g/f		2977
46	6-8	Brig	6g/f		3172
44	6-8	Chep	6.1gd	55	3729
49	4-5	Yarm	6gd	[55]	3871 vis

GLAZED FROST 2 gr f £17183

94	2-7	Deau	8hvy		4156

GLEBE GARDEN 3 b f £6674

82	5-11	Asco	8sft	[89]	1419
69	5-7	Nott	8.2sft	[89]	1741
70	6-8	Ling	7g/f	83	2742
59	11-11	Asco	8gd	[81]	3128
66	8-10	Sand	8.1g/f	[75]	3339
76	1-11	YARM	7g/f	70	3711*
79	2-10	Yarm	7g/s	74	4251
63	10-14	Epso	7g/f	74	4465
62a	11-13	Ling	7ap	78	4897

GLEN IDA 2 ch c £6844

88	3-14	Sand	7.1g/s		4069
86	2-8	Hayd	8.1g/f		4351
91	1-12	NEWC	8fm		4866*

GLEN INNES 3 b f £24038

87	1-8	NEWC	8hvy		1039*
88	2-11	Asco	8sft		1419
101	2-6	Nott	10.4sft	[91]	1666
84	7-8	Epso	8.5g/f	[101]	2211
96	4-14	Donc	10.3sft	[101]	5370

GLEN VALE WALK 7 ch g £538

44	6-11	Hayd	10.5g/f	47	1884 bl
48	3-11	Leic	11.8fm	45	2112 bl
47	5-12	Warw	10.9fm	47	2436 bl

GLENCAIRN STAR 3 b c £0

26	11-16	Newc	7sft		966
0	11-11	Ayr	8sft	64	4621
0	16-18	Newc	8g/f	[60]	5017

GLENCALVIE 3 ch c £7895

46	21-24	Newm	8fm		1495
55	5-16	Ripo	8gd		2987
65	15-20	Newm	8g/f		3237
59	4-13	Ling	7g/f	59	3604
75	1-14	YARM	7g/f	68	3995* VIS
72	1-17	LING	6g/f	68	4740* vis
52a	13-13	Ling	7ap	74	4897 vis

GLENCOE SOLAS 4 ch f £11764

60	6-16	Nott	6.1sft	68	1465
63	4-11	Folk	6sft	66	1578
70	2-8	Bath	5.7fm	65	2034 BL
69	2-11	Newm	6fm	65	2093 bl
74	1-13	DONC	6gd	66	2232*
68	5-17	Wind	6gd	72	2451
74	3-9	Chep	6.1g/f	72	2626
76	2-10	Epso	6g/s	72	3045
58	6-21	Bath	5.7gd	72	3146
58	12-15	Newc	6g/f		3424

GLENDALE 3 ch g £1463

67a	1-6	LING	8g/f	[68]	651*
59	11-18	Leic	10g/s	68	1017
42	13-14	Newm	10g/f	65	1192
37	9-16	Beve	8.5sft	62	1628
52	7-9	Beve	8.5g/f	59	2168 P

47a	5-8	Sout	8af	62	2495	p
10	9-9	Brig	9.9gd	52	2955	vis
39	12-18	Kemp	10g/f	[50]	4791	
45a	8-14	Ling	7ap	[57]	5294	
55a	5-13	Wolv	9.5ap	57	5361	

GLENROCK 6 ch g £0

50a	7-12	Wolv	7af	53	74
27a	9-16	Sout	7af	50	202

GLENVIEWS POLLY 4 b f £0

27a	6-10	Wolv	7af	[42]	298	
1a	8-13	Sout	7af	[45]	356	
0	11-11	Wolv	7af	[35]	440	vis

GLESNI 4 gr f £0

29a	10-14	Ling	12ap	14
33a	7-9	Ling	10ap	476

GLIDE 3 ch g £1195

72	3-19	Warw	10.9gd	70	1124	
5	12-14	York	11.9g/s	71	1708	
73	3-10	Good	14gd	70	2376	VIS

GLIDING BY 2 ch f £0

50a	10-12	Ling	8ap		100
55	9-13	Kemp	10g/f		3038
18	13-15	Wind	10fm		3292
2	7-8	Brig	11.9fm	52	3692

GLIMMER OF LIGHT 4 b g £0

69	6-20	Donc	10.3g/s	78	1519	
48	13-14	Wind	10g/f	76	2265	
70	7-8	Newm	10g/f	73	2735	
48	9-10	Sand	10g/f	70	3336	
22	16-16	Chep	10.2g/s	69	4365	BL

GLOBAL ACHIEVER 3 b c £9380

63a	3-6	Wolv	8.5af		468	
73a	2-7	Sout	7af		531	
69a	2-7	Wolv	7af		617	
74a	1-8	WOLV	6af	[67]	750+	
26	16-16	Kemp	6g/s	72	1116	
37	8-9	Muss	5g/s	70	1457	BL
25	15-17	Yarm	7g/f	[65]	1729	
55a	7-13	Wolv	6af	69	2053	
40	9-15	Redc	6fm	60	4562	
16	14-14	Catt	6gd	55	4967	T
56a	12-12	Wolv	7.1ap	67	5008	t
73a	1-12	WOLV	5.1ap	64	5326*	

GLOBAL BANKER 2 b c £0

31	17-20	Wind	6fm		2970
55a	5-8	Ling	5ap		3600 T

GLOBE BEAUTY 6 b m £0

13a	6-6	Ling	10ap	409
18a	7-7	Sout	7af	589

GLOBE TREKKER 2 gr f £1089

31	11-13	Hayd	6gd		3736
79	4-13	York	7.9gd		4325
71	4-12	Newc	8fm		4866
51	7-9	Ayr	8sft	[71]	5033

GLOCCA MORRA 6 b g £3048

105	3-13	Naas	5g/f	2327

GLORIA NIMBUS 2 b f £0

7	7-8	Hayd	5g/s		1343
0	9-9	Hayd	6g/f		1920
61	6-9	Ches	5.1gd		2281
17	9-12	Bath	5.7gd		3141
26	9-10	Catt	5gd	[50]	4968

GLORIOUS STEP 2 b f £9815

85	3-10	Yarm	7fm		2863
87	1-10	WIND	8.3fm		3803*
71	8-8	Deau	7hvy		4157
95	1-11	PONT	8fm	85	4753*

GLORY GIRL 4 ch f £0

27a	6-8	Sout	6af	[45]	1588
39	6-17	Nott	6.1sft	45	1606

GLORY QUEST 6 b g £25709

61a	5-9	Wolv	8.5af	72	2
75a	2-10	Wolv	14.8af	72	34
78a	2-10	Sout	14af	75	90
74a	3-8	Sout	16af	75	140

67a	5-12	Sout	14af	77	173	
70a	5-8	Sout	12af	77	225	p
75a	2-8	Wolv	14.8af	73	277	p
73a	2-6	Sout	12af	71	388	p
67a	7-9	Wolv	12af	71	467	p
72a	3-7	Sout	16af	73	529	
68a	5-7	Sout	14af	71	681	
71a	2-10	Wolv	12af	67	810	vis
70a	2-8	Wolv	16.2af	68	837	vis
77a	1-6	SOUT	12af	68	870*	vis
19	13-22	Donc	12gd	69	918	vis
71	3-18	Nott	14.1g/s	65	1772	
74	4-9	Thir	12g/f	67	1969	
78	1-4	HAYD	14g/s	67	2229*	
39	20-29	Asco	20g/f	75	2471	
29	3-10	Sali	14.1gd	75	2699	
83	1-8	DONC	14.6gd	73	2754*	
28	29-34	Newm	18sft	77	5135	

GLOVED HAND 2 b f £5005

90	1-11	NOTT	5.1g/f		2151*
72	14-17	Asco	5g/f		2490
82	10-13	Muss	5g/f	89	4551
69	6-6	Beve	5g/f	[89]	4717

GO BANANAS 3 b g £1070

84	6-9	Sand	7.1g/f	87	3338
84	4-7	Leic	7fm	86	3814
71a	9-13	Ling	7ap	84	4318
64	17-24	Newb	7g/f	82	4642

GO BETWEEN 3 b f £8652

83	2-20	Warw	7g/f	78	1761
69	7-12	Newm	7g/f	81	2249
73	6-8	Newb	6fm	80	2648
75	6-13	Leic	7g/f	79	3346
89	1-8	MUSS	7.1g/f	79	3528*
59	7-8	Newm	7gd	85	3928
70	13-14	Sali	7gd	85	4331

GO CLASSIC 3 b f £0

47a	14-14	Ling	13ap	69	147
62a	7-12	Ling	16ap	65	813
4	13-14	Kemp	14.4sft	64	948
23	14-16	Leic	11.8g/f	62	1830

GO FOR GOLD 3 b c £29150

81	3-4	York	10.4g/s	1706
113	2-8	Good	12g/f	3507
114	3-7	York	11.9gd	4001
111	7-9	Donc	14.6fm	4532

GO FREE 3 gr g £868

56a	2-12	Sout	7af		2339
56a	5-10	Sout	8af	[56]	2997
28	9-14	Leic	8g/f	[54]	3344
55a	5-11	Sout	6af	[54]	4041
23	10-13	Warw	7.1g/s	[49]	4994
34	13-17	Leic	7gd	49	5056

GO GARUDA 3 b c £866

69	3-11	Hayd	8.1gd	2885
55	12-17	Wind	8.3fm	3480

GO GO GIRL 3 ch f £3692

43a	9-14	Ling	6ap	[63]	23
71	1-16	BATH	5.7sft	63	1540*
66	7-20	Wind	6g/s	69	4946

GO GREEN 3 ch f £6633

41a	8-13	Sout	8af		553	
44	8-12	Hayd	8.1sft		1108	
59	13-20	Bath	10.2gd		1398	
48	7-8	Ches	10.3gd		1597	
45	5-16	Bath	8fm	[59]	2032	
38	7-14	Nott	8.2g/f	49	2634	
48	2-17	Chep	8.1g/s	46	3087	T
56	1-11	CHEP	10.2gd	[46]	3730*	t
53	4-11	Brig	9.9g/f	54	3982	t
59	3-15	Nott	10g/s	54	4037	t
60	2-19	Brig	9.9sft	54	4145	t
41	6-15	Chep	10.2g/s	54	4299	t
35	13-14	Chep	10.2gd	54	4487	t
53	3-10	Sali	12sft	[55]	4574	t
57	2-11	Leic	10gd	[54]	4701	t
31	13-20	Catt	12gd	54	4966	t
46	6-15	Leic	11.8gd	[54]	5060	t
52	4-7	Yarm	11.5g/s	[50]	5351	t

GO MO 2 br c £4348

48	12-12	Newb	6g/f		2348
71	6-18	Wind	6gd		3824
67a	6-12	Ling	6ap		4178
67	8-17	Ling	7g/f	71	4894
62	8-13	Wind	8.3g/s	71	4940
74	2-20	Newb	6hvy	68	5225
77	2-10	Catt	6sft	70	5318

GO PADERO 3 ch c £15596

92	1-11	MUSS	7.1g/s	83	5144*
88	4-13	Newm	8g/s	85	5284
92	1-10	CATT	7sft	85	5320*

GO SOLO 3 b c £3007

63	14-22	Donc	8gd	78	955
77	3-16	Leic	7g/f	77	1825
80	3-13	Sand	8.1gd	77	2365
48	5-9	Hayd	10.5gd	[77]	2901
73	3-7	Epso	8.5fm	77	3542
69	9-14	Epso	8g/f	76	4295
36	15-20	Ayr	10g/s	75	4656
47	8-14	Pont	8g/f	[74]	4937

GO SUPERSONIC 3 b f £694

68	4-8	Sand	8.1g/s		4101
63	4-9	Bath	10.2gd		4547

GO TECH 4 b g £39048

53	20-24	Donc	8gd	85	928
69	9-13	Newc	7hvy	83	1035
79	6-16	Thir	7g/s	80	1474
72	8-19	Redc	7g/f	79	1820
68	6-10	Hayd	8.1gd	78	2242
81	2-11	Ripo	10g/f	76	2483
63	4-8	Newc	10.1sft	[76]	2687
71	6-8	Nott	10g/s	76	2929
64	7-10	York	7.9g/s	76	3074
76	4-15	Donc	10.3g/f	73	3598
82	2-16	Sand	10gd	74	4609
84	1-8	PONT	10fm	74	4755*
90	1-11	REDC	10fm	78	4931*
95	1-20	YORK	10.4gd	84	4986*
51	18-24	Donc	12sft	90	5372

GO YELLOW 3 b g £6543

61	13-20	Newm	7g/f	75	1186
51	11-14	Ches	6.1g/s	73	1570
68	5-19	York	6g/f	70	2055
68	2-20	Chep	6.1gd	68	2372
73	4-20	Newb	7fm	68	2650
64	6-10	Leic	7g/f	[69]	2920
68	1-5	YARM	7gd	[69]	3366*
66	4-7	Leic	6g/f	69	3518
57	10-12	Sand	7.1g/f	69	3860
66	2-8	Folk	7g/f	67	4117
60a	11-12	Wolv	7.1ap	67	5008
66	6-14	Redc	7g/s	67	5109

GOBLIN 3 b g £13694

54	4-12	Folk	6sft	64	975
67a	1-13	SOUT	8af	[62]	1193*
62	5-14	Bath	10.2gd	62	1403
72	1-11	BEVE	9.9g/f	62	1834*
74	3-18	Newm	12fm	71	2088
67	5-14	Wind	10g/f	70	2452
77	1-7	WARW	10.9fm	70	2576*
73	3-6	Warw	10.9fm	75	2780

GODSEND 2 b f £7658

79	2-19	Wind	5g/f		1805
76	1-11	WARW	5g/f		2911*
79	2-8	Chep	6.1gd	74	3729
75	3-14	Warw	6.1g/f	74	4420
73	8-16	Newm	7g/f	76	4913

GOGETTER GIRL 2 b f £2576

72	6-15	Donc	5gd		920	
67	2-9	Warw	5sft		1084	
76	4-8	Newm	5g/s		1149	
53	10-12	Warw	5sft		1524	
72	4-10	Leic	5g/f		1826	
63	6-15	York	5g/f		2056	
44a	11-12	Ling	6ap	[68]	4179	
54	9-14	Redc	5fm	66	4556	P
49	11-19	Nott	6.1g/s	66	4645	p
48	20-24	Redc	6fm	[66]	4928	p

50	11-13	Brig	8sft	[60]	5091 p
56a	6-13	Wolv	8.6ap	[55]	5355 p

GOJO 3 b f £1420

68	4-20	Nott	6.1gd	67	1239
72	2-16	Nott	6.1sft	67	1465
54	9-16	Bath	5.7sft	67	1540
46	15-18	Wind	6g/f	70	2268
55	12-20	Nott	6.1g/s	68	4646
36	19-20	Wind	6g/s	63	4946
0	F-12	Ling	6ap	63	4976 P

GOLANO 3 gr g £1317

68a	10-14	Ling	12ap	75	83
81a	2-14	Ling	10ap	74	2392
65	10-12	Wind	11.6fm	80	2759
74	8-14	Sand	10g/s	80	4097
77	6-8	Hayd	11.9g/f	79	4353
58	13-19	Hayd	10.5g/s	76	4766 VIS

GOLBAND 2 b f £0

54	5-6	Hami	6g/f		2316

GOLD CARD 3 b g £6160

48a	2-9	Sout	8af	[71]	983
65	2-6	Hami	11.1g/s	[70]	1604
62	5-15	Ripo	12.3g/f	66	1785
55	5-8	Newc	12.4g/f	[63]	2163
64	2-5	Hami	12.1g/s	61	2827 VIS
62	1-8	AYR	10gd	[60]	3151* vis

GOLD GUEST 4 ch g £6270

45a	4-13	Wolv	8.5af	54	40 VIS
52a	4-12	Wolv	7af	54	68 vis
60a	1-14	LING	10ap	52	230*
67a	1-14	LING	10ap	60	339*
66a	7-14	Ling	10ap	66	434
67	7-19	Chep	7.1gd	66	3401
65	4-11	Good	11gd	65	3948
58	5-14	York	10.4g/f	62	4402
61	6-19	Bath	11.7gd	62	5024
63	2-11	Catt	12sft	[62]	5128

GOLD GUN 2 b c £0

36	14-15	Newm	8gd		4883
51	16-21	Newm	8sft		5097

GOLD HISTORY 3 b c £45065

100	2-7	Donc	8gd	[97]	949
103	1-7	NEWM	9g/f	[100]	1189*
101	3-5	Sand	10g/s	[98]	1316
95	5-5	Asco	12g/f	[103]	2554
75	16-18	Newb	8g/f	103	3265
86	10-16	Good	9.9fm	100	3553
89	6-11	York	10.4g/s	97	4021
96	5-11	Beve	9.9g/s	94	4239
98	1-11	GOOD	9g/f	92	4525*
93	8-13	Asco	10g/f	[94]	4772

GOLD MAJESTY 2 b f £0

7	11-11	Sali	5gd		2658
45	8-13	Kemp	6gd		3183
39	9-13	Bath	5.7g/f		3368
28	13-14	Sali	7sft		4575
49	8-16	Bath	5.7gd	[45]	4823

GOLD MASK 3 b c £7202

69	6-12	Newm	7g/s		1152
84	2-10	Good	8g/f		1815
79	1-10	GOOD	8gd	[78]	2378* VIS
65	15-27	Asco	8g/f	83	2521 BL

GOLD MEDALLIST 4 ch g £46917

86	6-8	Newb	13.3g/f	[102]	1757
80	7-8	Sand	16.4g/s	[102]	2914
103	4-10	Asco	16.2gd	100	3776
113	1-9	DEAU	15sft	[100]	4161*
114	5-8	Long	15.5sft	[100]	4569
113	5-11	Newm	16sft	[112]	5138

GOLD QUAY 2 b f £2543

73	2-13	York	6g/f		2358
79	4-6	Wind	5fm		2786
64	6-8	Ches	5.1g/f		3081

GOLD QUEEN 2 b f £6491

79	3-11	Newb	6gd		3915
80	1-12	BEVE	7.5g/s		4242*

GOLD RELIC 3 b f £0

48	12-14	Wind	8.3fm		2974
39	9-9	Bath	10.2gd		4547

GOLD RING 4 ch g £54515

82	7-20	Newm	12gd	85	1172
90	2-14	Hami	12.1gd	85	1389
90	3-19	York	11.9sft	87	1668
87	6-12	Good	14g/f	87	1861
83	5-7	York	13.9g/f	86	2355
92	3-13	York	11.9g/s	85	3076
93	1-11	NEWB	11g/f	85	3256*
85	6-8	Newm	12g/f	[91]	3617
100	2-19	York	13.9g/s	91	4023
97	4-7	Hami	13g/s	97	4819
48	13-19	Newm	12gd	97	5085

GOLD TYPE 5 b h £4577

106	3-11	Hopp	6.5gd		3839

GOLDBRICKER 4 b g £1449

31a	6-8	Sout	8af	51	393
45a	5-13	Wolv	8.5af	46	559
54a	1-9	WOLV	9.4af	[46]	665*

GOLDEN ANTHEM 2 ch f £5323

79	1-11	KEMP	5hvy		1640*
68	16-17	Asco	6g/f		2553
90	3-9	Newm	6g/f		2763
92	6-9	Sand	7.1g/f		3357
92	6-9	Ayr	6sft	[90]	4684
73	14-14	Newm	7g/f	[92]	4914
77	7-11	Newm	6sft	[90]	5270

GOLDEN APPLAUSE 2 b f £0

60	7-13	Chep	6.1gd		3399

GOLDEN ASHA 2 ch f £648

75	3-11	Beve	5g/f		4599
75	7-10	Ling	5g/f		4893

GOLDEN BANKES 3 ch f £0

42	12-15	Ling	7gd		4445
32	7-10	Catt	6gd		4964

GOLDEN BOOT 5 ch g £2884

64	6-14	Hami	12.1gd	67	1389 p
55	8-18	Nott	14.1sft	67	1469 p
55	9-10	Hami	13gd	67	1506 p
68	1-6	BRIG	11.9g/f	[63]	2047* vis

GOLDEN BOUNTY 5 b h £0

52	10-10	Wind	6gd	[80]	1383
58	6-9	Chep	6.1g/f	75	2626
51	10-10	Kemp	6g/f	75	2861
26	14-15	Sali	6gd	68	3888
53	10-15	Good	5gd	61	4751

GOLDEN CHALICE 4 ch g £12814

79a	12-15	Ling	7ap	90	81
73a	5-8	Wolv	8.5af	[88]	360
47a	6-7	Ling	6ap	[85]	431 VIS
79	12-27	Newb	8g/f	90	1231
84	9-16	Thir	7g/s	88	1474
95	1-14	LING	7sft	86	1624*
45	19-20	Asco	7g/f	91	1926
69	17-19	Newm	7g/f	91	3061
68	12-16	Newm	7sft	90	5101

GOLDEN CHANCE 7 b g £3017

39	8-15	Ripo	12.3g/f	49	2526
56	1-13	YARM	11.5fm	48	2868*

GOLDEN DIXIE 5 ch g £2210

60	10-11	Newb	8g/f	82	2878
84	2-10	Hayd	6g/s	80	3136
77	5-11	Newm	6fm	80	3408
82	5-19	York	6gd	82	4005
75	8-19	Kemp	6fm	81	4394
35	24-26	Ayr	6g/s	81	4652
72	9-19	Sali	6gd	78	4855
67a	9-14	Ling	7ap	[75]	5080

GOLDEN DRIFT 2 ch f £1735

51a	11-13	Ling	7ap		119
44	12-18	Wind	8.3g/f		1810
51	5-11	Newm	8g/f		2248
49	7-16	Wind	11.6g/s	60	2621
63	2-11	Ling	10gd	[58]	3201

52	5-11	Yarm	10.1gd	[60]	3875
46	11-14	Redc	10fm	60	4342
63	3-12	Beve	12.1g/f	59	4601
53	6-8	Redc	14.1fm	59	4932

GOLDEN DUAL 3 b g £846

62a	5-9	Ling	10ap	[73]	269
52a	7-13	Ling	10ap	[73]	338
40a	10-14	Ling	10ap	[65]	430
56a	6-16	Ling	12ap	58	493
16a	13-13	Sout	14af	57	590
39a	7-14	Ling	12ap	55	711
49a	9-14	Ling	12ap	55	768
58a	2-13	Ling	13ap	53	896 VIS
20	9-19	Folk	12sft	60	979 vis
14	16-17	Nott	14.1gd	55	1238 vis
16a	7-12	Ling	12ap	[56]	3819 bl

GOLDEN DYNASTY 2 ch c £0

61	8-8	Sali	7gd		2695
63	9-11	Newb	7g/f		3959
50	6-9	Chep	8.1g/s		4297
66	7-10	Kemp	8g/f		4712

GOLDEN EMPIRE 3 br c £9040

73a	2-12	Wolv	9.4af		939
77	2-9	Muss	12g/f	[78]	1121 vis
53	4-4	Hayd	11.9g/s	[77]	1347 vis
70	1-8	HAMI	11.1gd	[77]	1390*
42	14-16	Wind	11.6g/s	73	2621
61	8-10	Ling	11.5gd	72	3334

GOLDEN FEATHER 2 ch c £545

88	3-13	Donc	7hvy		5200

GOLDEN FIELDS 3 b f £446

0	9-12	Wolv	16.2af	45	7 vis
1	10-10	Thir	16sft	44	3834
39	7-13	Warw	10.9g/f	45	4419 bl
10	8-11	Beve	12.1g/f	[45]	4716 bl
43	3-11	Redc	10sft	[40]	5303 bl

GOLDEN FURY 2 ch c £4393

68	4-17	Donc	6g/f		2424
85	3-14	Newm	7g/f		3752
88	4-5	Sali	8gd		4328
88	2-8	Sand	8.1gd	[87]	4608
78	3-12	Newc	8fm	[85]	4866

GOLDEN GATE 2 b c £0

44	16-20	Yarm	8sft		5252
28	13-15	Nott	8.2hvy		5344

GOLDEN GRACE 3 b c £1865

70	9-14	Newm	10g/f	90	1192
94	4-13	York	10.4sft	88	1664
89	4-14	Asco	10g/f	88	1924
57	17-17	Asco	12gd	88	2519
53	12-12	Hayd	8.1gd	88	3738
63	13-17	Wind	10g/f	85	5050

GOLDEN ISLAND 3 ch f £24315

74	3-12	Good	9g/f		1864
78	2-12	Sand	10g/f		2193
90	1-6	CHES	10.3g/s	[85]	2748*
83	5-6	Asco	10gd	85	3072
90	1-9	NEWM	8g/f	83	3780*
85	9-12	Bath	8g/f	[83]	3965
89	3-14	Sali	7gd	85	4331
96	2-13	Asco	8g/f	85	4802

GOLDEN KEY 3 b c £0

70	9-17	Newb	10gd		1737
32	10-11	Chep	10.2gd		2196

GOLDEN LEGACY 2 b f £44485

79	2-14	Redc	6fm		2297
87	8-17	Asco	6g/f		2553
82	1-8	CATT	10gd		3348*
97	1-9	CHES	6.1fm	85	3632*
87	3-7	Ches	6.1g/f	[96]	4050
104	1-9	AYR	6sft	[96]	4684*
110	4-7	Newm	8g/f		4880

GOLDEN LEGEND 7 b g £0

4a	7-8	Wolv	7af	[30]	1656
12a	7-10	Ling	12ap	[30]	1714

GOLDEN NUN 4 b f £84705

86 11-17 Donc 6gd [99] 952 p
101 2-6 Curr 7sft [99] 1436
99 3-11 Ling 7sft [96] 1620 p
97 1-9 NOTT 6.1g/s [100] 1773* bl
102 3-11 Hayd 6gd [100] 2240 bl
102 1-9 CORK 6fm [100] 2457*
103 7-9 York 6g/s [101] 3075 bl
102 5-12 Good 7fm [101] 3564 bl
103 7-12 Deau 6.5g/s [101] 3838 bl
104 5-8 Bade 6sft [101] 4426 bl
103 4-8 Donc 7fm [104] 4477 bl
86 10-12 Asco 6g/f [104] 4799 bl
59 11-12 Newm 7sft [104] 5134 bl

GOLDEN OLDIE 6 b g £0
0 10-10 Ling 8ap 831 BL

GOLDEN QUEEN 3 b f £376
21a 14-14 Ling 10ap 4448
43 3-10 Yarm 10.1gd 4612
11 14-15 Bath 10.2gd 4826

GOLDEN QUEST 3 ch c £14091
76a 1-8 WOLV 12af 808*
87a 1-6 LING 12ap 79 915*
74 7-11 Ripo 12.3gd 82 1174
86 1-11 SAND 14g/s 78 2130*
86 5-17 Asco 12g/f 82 2519

GOLDEN SAHARA 3 b c £17510
43 14-14 Newm 8g/f [96] 1480 VIS
96 3-6 Sali 7g/s [96] 3113 vis t
102 1-12 GOOD 7fm [95] 3555* t
101 3-16 Good 7g/f 98 4523 t
85 14-15 Newm 7g/f 99 4891 t

GOLDEN SHELL 5 ch m £0
0 10-12 Ayr 7.2sft [35] 5274

GOLDEN SPECTRUM 5 ch g £1981
57 3-15 Hami 6gd 57 1508
57 5-9 Ayr 7.2fm [58] 1910
35 10-16 Carl 5.9fm 58 2445
28 15-18 Pont 8gd 57 3242
60 3-18 Catt 7g/f 55 3670 VIS
47 12-20 Redc 6g/f 55 3767 vis
28 14-15 Catt 7sft 55 3933 vis
41 12-14 Carl 6.9g/f 53 4345 vis
55 3-15 Beve 8.5g/f 51 4598
31 17-26 Redc 8fm 4926
30 10-15 Redc 9g/s 51 5111

GOLDEN SQUARE 2 ch g £0
59 9-12 Hayd 6sft 4770
58 6-13 York 6gd 4988

GOLDEN SQUAW 2 ch f £0
50 6-10 Beve 7.5gd 2652
41 11-18 Donc 6g/s 3376
33 14-14 Thir 7g/s 4207
28 9-10 Beve 7.5g/f [47] 4602 BL

GOLDEN STRAVINSKY 2 b c £24648
95 1-8 CAPA 5.5gd 2303*

GOLDEVA 5 gr m £54625
100 1-17 DONC 6gd [91] 952*
102 5-15 York 6sft [100] 1667
47 11-11 Newc 6g/s [102] 2769
100 5-9 York 6g/s [101] 3075 T
95 4-5 Ches 6.1fm [100] 3636 t
106 1-12 PONT 6g/s [97] 3971+
95 5-11 Ches 6.1g/f [105] 4510
87 9-14 Newm 6sft [104] 5100
95 6-12 Donc 6sft [103] 5371

GOLDHILL PRINCE 2 b c £14976
54 8-9 Donc 5gd 929
61 4-10 Bath 5g/s 1097 P
55 9-14 Bath 5g/s 1401 p
70a 2-8 Wolv 5af 1653 p
69 1-11 RIPO 6gd 1779* p
69 1-4 AYR 6fm 1906* p
69 1-8 HAMI 5gd 2177* p
69 1-6 BRIG 6fm 2330* p
62 3-4 Brig 7g/f 2640 p
51a 6-11 Sout 6af 70 3393 p
57 5-11 Thir 5gd 3570 p
64 3-7 Yarm 6gd [65] 3994 p

60 9-19 Ling 6g/f [63] 4895 p

GOLFAGENT 6 b g £0
37a 4-10 Sout 16af [40] 984 t
11 6-9 Warw 15g/s [40] 1329 t

GOLNESSA 3 b f £0
0 11-12 Sout 8af 848
18 12-12 Warw 7.1gd 1125
26 6-7 Nott 8.2hvy 1610

GONDOLIN 4 b g £0
74 8-8 Newb 13.3gd 84 3918
17 10-12 Ches 15.9sft 82 4106 VIS

GONE FISHING 2 ch f £3042
64 7-13 Ling 6g/f 2061
84 2-10 Redc 7g/s 2959
83 3-11 Beve 7.5g/s 3851
75a 3-8 Ling 7ap [80] 4447

GONE LOCO 3 b f £0
18 9-10 Chep 8.1g/f 50 2624

GONE TOO FAR 6 b g £3380
55 1-9 AYR 15gd 46 3327* vis

GONENDUNNETT 4 b g £11349
70a 1-12 WOLV 5af 63 35* vis
50a 10-13 Wolv 5af 70 110 vis
70a 3-11 Wolv 5af 69 155 vis
54a 10-10 Ling 5ap 69 329 vis
57a 8-10 Wolv 5af 69 349 vis
49a 10-11 Sout 5af 67 655 vis
51a 8-11 Wolv 5af 67 748 p
0 15-15 Folk 6g/s 54 1267 vis
32 10-13 Yarm 6g/f 50 1726
51a 6-13 Wolv 6af 64 2053 p
44 6-16 Brig 6fm 2262 vis
59 1-13 YARM 5g/f 50 2347* vis
42 7-12 Ling 5g/f 57 2743 vis
61 3-14 Yarm 6g/f 57 2855 vis
62 1-11 BRIG 5.3gd 57 2957* vis
54 8-15 Newc 6gd 60 3424 vis
56 5-9 Brig 5.3fm 60 3673 vis
35 11-13 Brig 5.3g/f 59 3984 vis
62 2-12 Brig 5.3g/s 59 4140 vis
41 11-12 Yarm 5.2g/s 60 4585 vis
16 15-16 Pont 5fm 60 4754 p
45 11-19 Nott 6.1g/f [60] 4845 p

GONFILIA 4 b f £83300
106 2-11 Ling 7sft 1620 t
107 1-8 GOOD 8g/f [100] 1863* t
105 1-8 EPSO 8.5g/f [102] 2211* t
80 9-10 Asco 8g/f [102] 2487 t
106 4-12 Good 7fm [103] 3564 t
106 2-15 Donc 7fm [102] 4479 t
110 1-10 REDC 7fm [102] 4929+ t

GOOD ARTICLE 3 b c £0
48 12-14 Wind 10g/s 1259 e
0 B-9 Folk 9.7sft 1581 e
6 16-16 Sand 10g/s 2131 e
0 13-15 Ayr 8gd [35] 2504 T

GOOD FORM 3 b g £0
24a 14-15 Ling 7ap [41] 216
14a 5-8 Wolv 9.4af [36] 299
16a 6-10 Wolv 7af [35] 394
0 12-13 Ling 6ap [30] 541 BL

GOOD INVESTMENT 2 b g £653
73 3-15 Pont 6gd 3239
71 5-14 Thir 7g/s 3831
57 9-12 Ayr 7.2hvy 4083
46a 11-11 Wolv 8.6ap [69] 4978

GOOD LOSER 4 b g £0
26 15-17 Beve 8.5g/s [60] 1160 t
0 9-10 Yarm 10.1g/f [60] 1724 t

GOOD TIME BOBBY 7 b g £1022
50 3-6 Pont 8g/f 2037
0 7-7 Wolv 14.8af 2200
46 4-10 Carl 6.9g/f 3230
36 12-17 Catt 5g/f 51 3667
36 15-20 Redc 6g/f 51 3767
14 16-18 Pont 5g/s 46 3974

14 13-17 Carl 7.9fm [45] 4506

GOOD TIMING 6 gr g £421
44a 2-9 Wolv 9.4af [45] 314
9a 15-16 Sout 11af [45] 445
34a 7-11 Wolv 9.4af [45] 580
17 13-15 Beve 7.5g/f [45] 1944
3 13-15 Ayr 10.9g/s 40 2545

GOOD VIBRATIONS 2 b f £1006
54a 2-12 Ling 8ap [42] 78
51a 3-15 Ling 7ap 52 295
39a 5-9 Wolv 7af 53 510
50a 6-15 Ling 7ap [51] 671
47a 7-11 Ling 6ap 51 728 P

GOOD WEE GIRL 2 b f £10147
59 7-10 Bath 5.7fm 2666
37 14-17 Nott 6.1gd 2927
73 2-6 Brig 6g/f 3171
80 1-14 LEIC 6g/f 3517*
70 5-8 Chep 6.1gd 74 3729
74 1-11 CHES 7sft [74] 4072*
67 8-13 Newm 8gd 80 4193
68 9-20 Ling 7gd 71 4444
33 11-20 Yarm 8g/s 71 4635
38a 9-12 Wolv 7.1ap [68] 5158

GOODBYE BEN 2 b c £0
60 9-19 Newm 7g/s 5285

GOODBYE MR BOND 3 b g £43898
33a 9-14 Sout 8af 58 99
56a 4-14 Sout 8af 56 160
48a 5-13 Wolv 9.4af 56 281
44a 6-10 Sout 8af 55 387 VIS
42a 3-10 Wolv 8.5af 53 754
51 4-16 Newc 8hvy 51 1036
55 3-20 Ripo 8g/s 51 1366
54 4-19 Redc 8sft 52 1661
60 1-10 NEWC 8g/f 52 2159*
66 1-11 HAMI 8.3g/f 58 2317*
79 1-8 REDC 8gd 61 2550*
76 1-17 CARL 7.9gd 67 2672*
77 3-9 Asco 8gd 73 3465
77 2-9 Carl 9.3fm [71] 3546
73 6-13 Ripo 8fm 71 4279
81 1-15 HAYD 8.1g/f 71 4352+
73 7-20 York 8.9gd 77 4999
85 6-22 Newm 8sft 77 5103

GOODBYE MRS CHIPS 5 ch m £0
26 6-8 Ayr 7.2g/s [45] 1448 t

GOODENOUGH MOVER 7 ch g £45932
65a 8-16 Ling 7ap 68 22
69a 2-14 Ling 6ap 65 1025
74 1-19 SALI 7g/f 67 1723*
72 2-16 Ling 7g/f 69 2063
75 2-14 Chep 7.1gd 69 2199
84 1-11 CHEP 7.1gd 70 2370*
85 1-13 NEWB 7ap 77 2880*
83 5-20 Chep 7.1g/s 82 3088
85 2-7 Chep 7.1gd [80] 3402
67 7-7 Sali 7g/s [82] 4082
53 15-15 Sand 7.1gd 82 4500
92 1-19 SALI 6gd 80 4855+
95a 1-14 LING 7ap 86 5262+

GOODENOUGH STAR 4 b f £0
4a 9-10 Sout 11af 40 330

GOODRICKE 2 b c £9429
83 2-8 Wind 5g/s 1053
88 1-5 LEIC 5g/s 1353*
99 1-7 NOTT 6.1sft 1738*
89 9-13 Asco 6g/f 2467

GOODWOOD FINESSE 3 b f £6868
74 1-8 GOOD 9gd 2536*
67 5-12 Newb 10g/f 75 3255
71 6-7 Good 14sft 75 4267
75 3-12 Good 11gd 74 4749
74 6-7 Newm 12sft 74 5268

GOODWOOD PRINCE 3 b g £0
0 14-14 Ling 6ap 70 121
57a 8-14 Ling 6ap 68 149
60a 6-10 Ling 5ap 65 231

59a	5-10	Ling	5ap	64	329	
46a	12-14	Ling	6ap	64	407	
38	17-19	Leic	6g/s	68	1354	
42	18-18	Good	5g/f	62	1867	VIS
44	12-14	Kemp	5g/f	62	1914	
33	10-16	Brig	6fm	55	2262	
42	8-11	Brig	7g/f	52	2644	
38a	11-12	Ling	6ap	55	5241	vis
37a	10-13	Wolv	6ap	[55]	5359	vis

GOODWOOD PROMISE 4 b g £0

0	14-14	Sout	8af	40	160	
13a	12-15	Sout	5af	[40]	172	
20a	15-15	Sout	5af	[33]	253	BL

GOODWOOD SPIRIT 2 b c £9289

82	2-4	Kemp	6g/f		2859
79	2-13	Bath	5.7g/f		3368
81	3-9	Good	6gd		3951
82	1-6	EPSO	7g/f	[79]	4470*
80	5-12	Asco	7g/f	81	4810

GOOSE CHASE 2 b g £0

68	10-23	Newm	7g/f		4885
51	6-15	Brig	7sft		5192
67	9-14	Yarm	7sft		5250

GORDYS JOY 4 b f £418

39a	3-7	Wolv	14.8af	[35]	2200
3	14-14	Bath	18.2fm	40	2417
6	12-15	Chep	16.2gd	[40]	3400

GORELLA 2 ch f £7711

101	3-8	Deau	7hvy	4157
106	7-10	Long	8g/f	4954

GORTUMBLO 2 b c £8647

90	1-8	GOOD	5g/f		1816*
89	3-8	Epso	6fm		2251
42	10-10	Sali	6gd		2697
53	8-9	Good	6fm	90	3623
54	7-7	Ches	7g/f	86	4509
46	9-9	Brig	6fm	80	4758 BL

GOSLAR 3 ch f £9188

80	3-9	Sali	9.9g/f		1719
91	1-8	CHEP	12.1gd		2368*
91	4-9	Newm	12g/f	[87]	3278
95	4-9	York	11.9g/s	[90]	4058
98	4-12	Yarm	14.1sft	[90]	5254

GOT ONE TOO 7 ch g £2561

77	2-14	Asco	16.2g/f	72	1928
64	12-29	Asco	20g/f	73	2471

GOT TO BE CASH 5 ch m £7754

37a	4-7	Wolv	9.4af	[45]	893
46	2-15	Beve	9.9sft	40	1307
57	1-8	FOLK	9.7sft	45	1579*
35	10-12	Brig	9.9fm	51	1695
52	5-13	Pont	10g/f	52	2038
28	11-11	Folk	9.7fm	52	2719
52	7-16	Hayd	10.5sft	52	3276
56	1-14	CHEP	10.2g/s	59	3895*
49	4-13	Nott	10gd	56	3992
25	11-12	Newc	9hvy	54	4215
36	10-18	Warw	10.9g/s	54	4669

GOTYA 4 b f £0

0	8-8	Wolv	12af	644

GOUACHE 2 bl f £4436

88	3-10	Curr	6sft	5072

GOVERNMENT 3 b c £286

25	15-15	Newb	8g/f		1763
46	4-8	Ripo	10g/f		2523 BL
50	5-8	Catt	7g/f		4440
27	7-8	Catt	6gd	[45]	4969

GRACE DARLING 3 b f £0

0	5-6	Chep	12.1sft	1331

GRACEFUL AIR 3 b f £5326

51a	4-7	Wolv	6af	[64]	863
18	5-10	Pont	6hvy	[64]	1070
64	2-8	Muss	7.1gd	[62]	1554
64	2-14	Ayr	8g/f	[62]	1896

59	4-8	Beve	7.5g/f	[62]	2169	
46	7-8	Thir	8fm	62	2464	
58	5-8	Ayr	7.2gd	[62]	2506	
61	4-14	Pont	8g/f	59	2993	p
66	4-4	Hami	9.2g/f	[59]	3204	
54	5-8	Muss	7.1g/f	57	3528	
44	11-14	Muss	7.1g/f	55	4175	VIS
52	10-15	Carl	7.9g/f	55	4346	
56	3-6	Muss	8gd	[52]	4520	
56	2-16	Bath	8gd	52	4828	p
42	9-15	Redc	9g/s	53	5111	p

GRACEFUL FLIGHT 2 gr f £0

6	16-16	Thir	6g/s	4205
8	10-12	Redc	6fm	4557

GRACIA 5 gr m £365

21	11-18	Wind	8.3g/s	67	1059
59	7-14	Yarm	8g/f	67	1131
60	4-9	Epso	8.5hvy	[66]	1298

GRACIES GIFT 2 b c £790

58	4-4	Newc	5gd	1868
57	4-9	Muss	5fm	2083

GRACILIS 7 b g £0

32a	7-10	Sout	16af	80	743
50	15-17	Ches	18.7gd	80	1569
40	8-8	Donc	14.6sft	75	5204

GRACIOUS AIR 5 b m £2065

1a	14-16	Sout	11af	40	97	P
26a	10-13	Ling	10ap	[40]	539	VIS
39a	1-8	SOUT	8af	[35]	635*	vis
30a	5-16	Sout	8af	[35]	719	vis
44a	3-10	Sout	8af	45	792	vis
45a	3-9	Wolv	9.4af	[45]	821	BL
0	10-10	Sout	8af	[45]	850	bl

GRADY 5 ch g £0

21	6-10	Chep	8.1sft	[40]	1334
33	6-13	Ripo	12.3g/f	40	2008
19	12-14	Ches	12.3gd	38	2285
28	6-15	Ayr	10.9g/s	38	2545
9	12-13	Yarm	11.5fm	35	2868
23	7-12	Chep	12.1g/s	35	3085
14	13-14	Catt	12g/f	[30]	3668

GRAFT 5 b g £4712

35	11-14	Newc	10.1sft	65	964
60	6-19	Beve	9.9g/s	60	1164
65	2-14	Nott	10g/s	60	1776 BL
39	14-18	Newm	12fm	62	2088
42	10-15	Ripo	12.3g/f	62	2526 bl
66	1-20	KEMP	9g/f	60	2857* bl
49	13-25	Asco	7g/f	63	3443 bl

GRAHAM ISLAND 3 b c £7438

88	1-5	NEWB	11gd		1211*
66	6-6	Ches	12.3gd	[84]	1584
85	6-7	Good	11g/f	[84]	1814
48	8-9	Ayr	13.1g/s	85	2567
85	5-12	Wind	11.6g/f	83	4833
83a	4-10	Ling	12ap	83	5239

GRALMANO 9 b g £0

71a	7-7	Ling	12ap	88	695
67	12-17	Ches	18.7gd	85	1569
79	6-7	York	13.9g/f	83	2355
73	13-29	Asco	20g/f	83	2471

GRAMADA 2 b f £0

46	10-13	Wind	6fm	3639

GRAMPIAN 5 b h £20208

103	2-4	Ripo	12.3g/s	[102]	1364
86	6-12	Hami	12.1gd	102	1746
106	2-8	Donc	10.3gd	[100]	2234
107	3-15	Hayd	11.9gd	102	2948
65	18-19	York	13.9g/s	102	4023
103	2-7	Sali	14.1gd	[102]	4333
100	5-14	Asco	12g/f	102	4814

GRAN CLICQUOT 9 gr m £5354

35a	8-10	Ling	8ap	45	770
37a	8-14	Ling	10ap	[45]	828
42a	2-12	Ling	8ap	[40]	1451
46	7-19	Brig	9.9g/f	45	1940
52	1-16	GOOD	9gd	45	2220*

22	13-17	Warw	8.1fm	48	2572
51	2-20	Kemp	9g/f	48	2857
42	7-11	Kemp	8g/f	48	3685
35	8-15	Folk	9.7g/f	[48]	4373
28	12-19	Kemp	8g/f	[47]	4795

GRAN DANA 4 b g £6201

79	2-9	Leic	11.8g/s		1016
79	1-9	MUSS	12g/f		1121*
75	9-14	Hami	12.1gd	82	1389
64	10-18	York	13.9g/s	80	1689
64	8-8	Hami	12.1g/f	77	2318
36	17-19	Carl	11.9gd	73	2673
48	13-13	Newc	10.1g/f	70	4406
39	10-11	Ayr	15sft	66	5032

GRANARY GIRL 2 b f £0

56	8-14	Bath	5gd	1401
47	8-18	Chep	6.1gd	2194

GRANATO 3 b c £1538

59	11-19	Newm	6g/s	87	1154
54	8-11	Hami	6gd	87	1745
88	4-13	Newm	8g/f	85	2247
86	4-9	Sand	7.1g/f	85	3338

GRAND APOLLO 3 ch f £2132

71	2-11	Bath	8fm		2031
67	5-11	Sali	8fm		2419
68a	6-12	Ling	8ap	70	4743
67a	5-12	Wolv	8.6ap	68	5116
41a	13-13	Ling	10ap	66	5299

GRAND BUT ONE 3 ch c £14896

77	6-17	Newm	8gd		1166
89	2-17	Newb	8g/f		1762
87	2-12	Ripo	8g/f		1978
74	3-13	Newm	8fm	[87]	2595
87	1-16	RIPO	8g/f	[87]	2987*
84	6-14	Asco	8g/f	87	4813
85	1-14	PONT	8g/f	[87]	4937*

GRAND FOLLY 3 ch f £0

64a	4-15	Ling	12ap	[65]	118

GRAND FROMAGE 6 ch g £838

33	13-14	Asco	16.2g/f	70	1928
49	5-13	Chep	18gd	67	2198
57	3-6	Ches	15.9g/f	60	3101

GRAND GIRL 2 b f £0

59	7-7	Kemp	7g/f	4359
18	11-13	Sali	7sft	4576
52	8-11	Chep	7.1hvy	4704
35a	5-11	Wolv	7.1ap	5113

GRAND HOMBRE 4 br c £167597

104	4-12	Nad	10af		992 t vis

GRAND IDEAS 5 br g £1193

75a	2-14	Ling	7ap	5240

GRAND LASS 4 b f £2732

28a	6-9	Sout	11af	[55]	204	
50a	3-13	Wolv	9.4af	52	281	BL
51a	4-6	Sout	12af	[50]	392	vis
50a	1-11	WOLV	9.4af	[50]	580*	P
0	W-9	Wolv	9.4af	[50]	633	p
46a	2-9	Wolv	8.5af	[50]	664	p
50a	5-10	Wolv	8.5af	50	753	p
43a	4-7	Wolv	9.4af	[49]	862	p
56	3-14	Sout	12g/s	[53]	1047	p
27	13-19	Warw	10.9sft	53	1090	p
39	8-12	Sout	11gd	53	1286	p
36a	4-5	Wolv	12af	[49]	1375	

GRAND MARQUE 2 ch c £19906

76	5-10	Newm	7fm		2594
88	1-15	NEWB	7g/f		2876*
101	1-8	NEWB	7g/f		3267*
103	2-3	Sali	8g/f	[100]	3865
103	5-10	Donc	7fm	[96]	4493
94	7-8	Asco	8g/f	[96]	4797

GRAND MUSIC 4 b c £0

0	12-12	Newm	12g/f		3783
30a	10-14	Ling	13ap		4898 BL

GRAND OPTION 2 ch c £8174

55a	7-10	Ling	5ap			882
84	3-7	Kemp	5sft			943
84	2-5	Kemp	5g/s			1114
68	3-11	Nott	5.1gd			1237
88	2-10	Sali				1716
55	5-11	Good	5gd			2020
57	20-24	Newb	5.2g/f			3266 BL
72	7-10	Kemp	6g/f		76	3521
64	4-17	Warw	7.1gd	[71]		4269
68	6-9	Warw	7.1g/s		69	4666 bl
60	16-20	Ling	7g/f		69	4741 bl
75	1-12	**PONT**	6g/s	[63]		5152*

GRAND PASSION 3 b g £81623

103a2-14		Ling	10ap	[103]		82
106a2-13		Ling	10ap		100	433
106a1-11		**LING**	10ap	[104]		693+
100a 9-14		Ling	10ap			884
68	9-10	Ches	10.3gd[103]			1585
96	4-5	Good	8g/f	[103]		2022
107	2-10	Leop	10g/f	[103]		2456
109	1-8	**CURR**	8g/f	[103]		2820*
108	3-5	Leop	8g/f	[103]		4020
100	6-13	Newm	8g/f	[106]		4887

GRAND PLACE 2 b g £6334

57	12-18	Wind	6gd			2618
73	4-8	Kemp	6g/f			2858
55	23-24	Newb	5.2g/f			3266
76	1-7	**FOLK**	5gd	[73]		3907*
45	15-16	Newm	6gd		73	4224
82	4-21	Donc	6fm	[71]		4490
67	4-19	Nott	6.1g/s		71	4645
74	5-11	Epso	6g/f		74	4907

GRAND PRAIRIE 8 b g £0

58a	5-11	Ling	13ap	[65]		515

GRAND RAPIDE 3 ch f £3416

41	6-16	Hayd	6g/f			2182
40	10-14	Thir	7sft			2692
53	9-17	Wind	8.3fm			3480
49	4-18	Chep	7.1g/s		51	3900
58	1-15	**BATH**	8g/s		48	4202*
43	13-19	Beve	9.9g/f		54	4720
28a	12-13	Wolv	9.5ap		54	4925
37	8-17	Yarm	8g/s	[54]		5348

GRAND REWARD 3 b c £32285

106	2-5	Curr	7gd		1559
108	5-8	Curr	7gd		1995
40	15-15	Asco	7gd		2486
104	3-12	Curr	6g/f		4152
110	3-12	Curr	6g/f		4732 tBL
107	2-17	Curr	6sft		5073 tbl

GRAND SHOW 2 b c £441

61	4-10	Pont	6fm		4752
74	5-11	Newm	6sft		5265

GRAND VIEW 8 ch g £1990

26a	6-13	Ling	6ap	[35]		541 P
0	11-14	Sout	7af	[35]		573 p
39	4-17	Pont	6hvy	[35]		1065 p
40	2-10	Warw	6.1g/s	[40]		1327 p
38a	1-6	**LING**	8ap	[30]		1415* p
14	7-9	Ayr	6g/s	[40]		1447 p
32	7-16	Nott	6.1gd	[40]		1989 p
30	11-17	Ling	7gd		38	2397 p
0	19-19	Nott	6.1gd	[36]		3104 p
22	7-18	Thir	6fm		36	3609 p

GRAND WELCOME 2 b g £1901

50	12-14	Bath	5gd			1401
65	7-11	Nott	6.1sft			1739
48	13-17	Ling	7gd			2584
68	2-6	Brig	7sft			4163 BL
72	2-11	Newc	7fm	[71]		4863 bl
50	12-19	Redc	8sft		66	5302 bl

GRAND WIZARD 3 b c £2566

71a	1-9	**LING**	10ap			269*
68a	4-10	Ling	12ap		72	936
56	17-17	Sali	14.1g/s		71	1502
48	10-10	Yarm	11.5fm		67	2147 T
0	9-9	Ches	12.3sft		65	4076
55	6-11	Leic	10gd	[60]		4701

GRANDALEA 3 b f £4352

67	5-8	Wind	8.3g/s	[78]		2620
75	3-8	Wind	8.3gd		75	3162
79a	1-11	**LING**	7ap	[75]		3331*
77	6-14	Epso	8.5gd		78	4295

GRANDE ROCHE 2 b c £0

57	14-21	Donc	6sft		5368

GRANDE TERRE 3 b f £0

0	P-12	Hayd	8.1sft			1108
49	7-8	Hayd	10.5g/f			1489
34	14-14	Ayr	8g/f	[65]		1896
25	12-12	Kemp	9sft		60	4032
41	12-19	Thir	12g/f		55	4594
0	12-13	Newc	16.1fm		50	4868

GRANDMA LILY 5 b m £4443

77a	1-12	**SOUT**	6af		67	85*
72a	5-16	Sout	6af		72	171
55a	9-11	Sout	6af		72	198
73a	3-9	Sout	5af		72	415
56a	13-16	Sout	5af		72	461
45a	10-15	Sout	6af		73	550
60a	8-10	Sout	6af		71	657
46	17-18	Catt	7gd		67	998
39	17-20	Ripo	5gd		63	1179
62	3-16	Nott	6.1sft		60	1465
30	14-16	Thir	8g/f		61	4592
61	3-19	Nott	6.1g/f	[60]		4845
58	4-20	Yarm	7sft		59	5256
66a	4-12	Wolv	7.1ap	[67]		5340

GRANDMA RYTA 2 b r f £0

38	9-11	Beve	5g/f		4599
35	9-11	Catt	5gd		4962

GRANDMAS GIRL 2 b f £260

56	10-15	Wind	6gd			3163
70	4-8	Brig	7g/f			3716
69	5-12	Warw	7.1g/f			4417
68	8-13	Newm	8fm		70	4725
51	10-13	Wind	8.3g/s		67	4940

GRANDOS 2 b c £0

56	11-14	Hayd	6gd		3735
71	5-14	Ches	7sft		4102
60	8-16	Thir	6g/s		4205

GRANITA 2 b f £0

36	10-11	Sali	6g/f		3863

GRANSTON 3 b g £19874

76	3-22	Donc	7gd		72	955
78	1-11	**RIPO**	8gd		73	1176*
75	6-20	Newm	8fm		78	1496
72	6-11	Pont	8fm		78	2040
66	7-10	Donc	7g/f		77	2427
78	2-8	Newm	7gd		75	3612
78	5-12	Newm	7gd		75	4225
78	3-21	Donc	7fm		74	4482
83	1-17	**ASCO**	8g/f		75	4777*

GRANT 4 b c £0

58a	5-12	Wolv	7af		64	704 P
62a	6-10	Ling	5ap		64	755 p

GRANUAILE OMALLEY 3 b f £0

5a	12-13	Sout	6af	[50]		254
0	13-13	Sout	7af	[45]		356

GRASP 2 b c £349

65	4-12	Bath	8sft		5170 T
38	14-16	Yarm	10.1g/s		5352 t

GRASS WIDOW 2 b f £0

25	9-9	Catt	7sft		5316

GRASSLANDIK 8 b g £0

7a	16-16	Sout	5ap	45	1046 vis

GRAVARDLAX 3 ch c £279

82	7-7	Kemp	8g/s			1113
80	4-20	Bath	10.2gd	[89]		1398
63	8-11	Newb	11g/f		85	1756 BL
78	10-17	Asco	8g/f		82	4777

GRAZE ON 2 b c £13947

76	2-10	Pont	5gd		3457
82	1-18	**PONT**	5g/s		3968*

84	2-10	Beve	5sft		82	4258
85	5-13	Muss	5g/f		84	4551
62	10-15	York	6gd		83	4985
57	11-21	Donc	6hvy			5202

GREAT AS GOLD 4 b g £8603

56a	3-15	Sout	16af		55	67 p
66	1-13	**PONT**	21.6hvy		55	1252* p
66	2-11	Beve	16.2sft		60	1629 p

GREAT BELIEF 2 b c £939

75	3-11	Wind	5gd		3160
65	6-10	Wind	5fm		3476
77	4-13	Wind	6g/f		5047

GREAT BLASKET 3 b f £0

43	8-12	Wind	8.3fm	54	3291
0	9-9	Brig	8sft	52	4165
38	8-15	Bath	8g/s	52	4202
22	11-14	Redc	10fm	48	4560

GREAT BLOOD 2 ch f £10282

92	2-7	Chan	5gd		3008

GREAT EXHIBITION 3 b c £3162

21	9-12	Kemp	8hvy			1511 T
77	3-16	Newm	7fm	[85]		2092 t
75	2-15	Ling	7gd	[80]		4445 t
72	2-11	Good	6gd	[77]		5030 t

GREAT FOX 3 b c £1359

45	14-19	Sali	6gd		79	4855 T
85	6-11	Newm	6sft	[73]		5270
74	3-11	Muss	5g/s		73	5332

GREAT GENERAL 2 ch c £0

22	7-8	Yarm	6g/s		4250
57	10-13	Warw	7.1g/s		4664

GREAT GIDDING 3 b g £854

57	7-10	Nott	14.1sft			1742
50	3-8	Leic	11.8g/f			1961
53	8-11	Folk	9.7g/f			2274
22	15-18	Hayd	14gd		59	2905
30	5-9	Wind	11.6fm	[55]		3294
7	14-14	Nott	16g/f		55	3580 BL

GREAT NEWS FR 3 b f £13312

104	1-	**MAIS**	7fV		58*

GREAT OPINIONS 2 b f £1475

39	9-11	Nott	5.1g/f			2151
86	2-10	Yarm	7fm			2863
60	10-13	Kemp	7g/f			3520
58	11-12	Folk	7gd	[75]		3908 BL

GREAT SCOTT 3 b g £4038

71	9-12	Kemp	7g/s		87	2679
76	10-11	Sand	7.1g/s		87	2918
75	5-6	Sand	10g/f		84	3358
84	3-15	Donc	10.3g/f		80	3598
77	4-6	Ripo	10g/f		80	3647
78	7-10	Ches	10.3sft		82	4071
56	13-15	Sand	7.1gd		80	4500 BL
41	12-14	Hami	8.3g/s		77	4820
63	5-14	Pont	8g/f	[77]		4937
49	7-8	Ayr	10sft	[74]		5034 P

GREAT VIEW 5 b g £11335

42a	8-13	Ling	10ap		48	805
54a	1-13	**LING**	13ap		45	896* vis
57	2-19	Warw	9.9sft		53	1090 vis
65	1-13	**BRIG**	11.9g/f		55	1373* vis
66	2-17	Bath	11.7sft		61	1543 vis
63	4-16	Leic	11.8g/f		65	1830 vis
51	10-18	Newm	12fm		64	2088 vis
70	2-10	Warw	12.6g/f		62	2912 vis
67	3-7	Brig	11.9g/f	[65]		3173 vis
51	7-7	Kemp	12g/f		65	3519 vis
71	2-13	Warw	12.6gd		64	4274 vis
64	4-16	Yarm	11.5g/s		67	4589 vis
42	9-14	Epso	12gd		66	4910 bl

GREATCOAT 2 ch c £0

60	8-13	Donc	7hvy		5199

GREATEST BY PHAR 3 b c £0

41a	9-11	Ling	8ap		496
28a	12-13	Ling	10ap		601

GREEK STAR 3 b g £427					
53	4-8	Leic	11.8g/f		1961
46	9-10	Sand	10g/f		2386
18	15-17	Newm	12g/f	48	3618
18	6-12	Brig	11.9fm	45	4764

GREEK SUN 3 b c £44693					
114	2-7	Arli	10fm		4015

GREEN CONVERSION 3 ch g £0					
2	P-8	Catt	15.8g/f		3666

GREEN FALCON 3 b c £1218					
47a	13-15	Ling	7ap		472
60a	3-12	Ling	7ap		566
70a	3-11	Ling	8ap		697
50	8-17	Yarm	7g/f	[66]	1729
56	7-9	Donc	10.3g/f	63	2079
37	13-13	Sand	8.1gd	60	2365 VIS
39	11-20	Yarm	8gd	55	3996 T
43	7-12	Good	9.9sft	53	4268

GREEN GINGER 8 ch g £0					
0	14-16	Warw	8.1g/s	[45]	4993

GREEN MANALISHI 3 b c £28979					
81a	4-8	Ling	5ap	77	818
82a	2-9	Ling	5ap	76	914
86	2-15	Ches	5.1g/s	78	1572
92	1-12	WIND	5g/f	81	1809*
77	9-17	Muss	5fm	88	2082
93	3-16	Leic	5g/f	88	2400
95	1-9	NEWM	5fm	89	2593*
88	5-16	Wind	6fm	91	2758
91	5-10	Ches	5.1g/f	91	3080
74	20-24	Asco	5gd	91	3466
82	10-21	Good	5fm	90	3567
82	10-14	Epso	5gd	89	4291
85	12-15	Newm	5g/f	[87]	4879

GREEN MASTER 4 bl g £0					
0	8-12	Wolv	12.2ap	[40]	5208

GREEN N GOLD 4 b f £4460					
57	1-13	PONT	18hvy	49	1069*
4	10-13	Pont	21.6hvy	57	1252
59	4-9	Newc	16.1gd	57	1870
15	8-9	Redc	14.1g/f	57	2105
33	8-9	Pont	18g/f	57	2607
28	8-12	Muss	16gd	55	2964
39	10-17	Pont	17.1g/s	53	3970

GREEN OCEAN 4 gr f £0					
38	15-15	Beve	9.9sft	58	1307
17	14-17	Wind	11.6fm	[50]	2788

GREEN PIRATE 2 b c £0					
41	11-13	Newm	7fm		4724

GREEN RIDGE 2 b f £1543					
68a	6-13	Wolv	6af	71	1
63	2-8	Redc	6sft	[70]	1659
59	4-10	Newb	5.2fm	[68]	2649
47	11-11	Newm	5g/f	68	2734
51	11-18	Hayd	5gd	65	2951
0	12-13	Chep	8.1hvy	60	4709
22a	11-14	Ling	7ap	[62]	5080

GREEN SWALLOW 3 b f £7711					
110	3-6	Long	9.3hvy		1557
109	7-7	Long	10gd		2001

GREENBOROUGH 6 b g £0					
22a	7-12	Wolv	12af	[30]	523 P
3a	7-12	Wolv	9.4af	[30]	668 p

GREENSLADES 5 ch h £28426					
93	4-20	Newm	7g/s	89	1151
93	4-30	Newm	6g/f	90	1481
99	2-20	Asco	7g/f	91	1926
86	13-29	Asco	6fm	95	2581
99	3-19	Newm	7g/f	95	3061
66	14-21	Asco	7g/f	95	3441
90	6-10	Asco	8gd	96	3775
95	6-16	Newb	7g/f	95	3954
89	10-15	Asco	7g/f	93	4800
94	5-15	Newm	7g/f	93	4891
97a	3-14	Ling	7ap	90	5262

GREENWICH MEANTIME 4 b g £6495					
74	8-11	Nott	16fm	80	1003
81	3-17	Ripo	16g/s	79	1361
36	16-18	York	13.9g/s	80	1689
53	9-10	Sand	14g/f	77	2192
77	3-10	Carl	14.1fm	77	2444
53	14-19	Carl	11.9gd	77	2673
70	7-9	Beve	16.2g/s	75	3181
66	5-10	Thir	16fm	72	3611
63	6-6	Beve	16.2g/s	70	3853
44	7-7	Thir	16g/s	65	4209
59	4-7	Newc	16.1g/f	60	4405
64	3-14	Catt	12g/f	60	4672
71a	1-12	WOLV	12.2ap	58	5328*

GREENWOOD 6 ch g £3180					
40a	10-11	Sout	6af	78	386
77a	3-14	Ling	7ap	75	518
72a	11-14	Ling	7ap	75	604
63a	8-12	Ling	8ap	[75]	878
68a	6-12	Ling	8ap	[73]	1042
77	6-16	Good	7g/f	77	1817
85	2-7	Brig	7g/f	77	2045
64a	7-12	Ling	8ap	73	5238

GREGORIAN 7 b g £0					
16	14-18	Wind	11.6g/f	51	1960

GRELE 3 gr f £0					
49	7-14	Thir	7sft		2692
60	5-7	Ches	7.6g/f		3079
46	6-18	Carl	7.9fm	47	3547
55	4-14	Carl	9.3g/f	[45]	4347
16	11-15	Carl	7.9fm	[45]	4507
20	12-16	Nott	10gd	45	4857

GRETNA 3 ch f £3702					
82	1-10	FOLK	9.7sft		977*
71	8-13	Kemp	9gd	82	1141
30	14-14	Asco	10g/f	82	1924
38	8-8	Kemp	9g/s	79	2680
59	14-14	Newb	10g/f	77	3961 BL

GREY ADMIRAL 3 gr g £0					
65	9-13	Sali	9.9gd		2700
29	10-12	Chep	12.1g/s	68	3085

GREY BOY 3 gr g £0					
58	8-17	Ling	7g/f		1617
70	5-10	Beve	7.5g/f		1832

GREY CLOUDS 4 gr f £16762					
71	4-19	Beve	9.9g/s	67	1164
70	2-9	Nott	10sft	67	1467
62	8-19	Ripo	10g/f	69	1781
78	1-13	PONT	10g/f	69	2038*
82	2-10	Beve	9.9g/s	75	2323
84	3-10	Newm	10fm	78	2592
81	2-8	Ches	10.3g/f	[79]	3083
82	2-4	York	10.4g/f	79	3435
58	5-7	Hami	9.2g/s	79	3879
64	10-13	Yarm	10.1gd	79	4613
58	8-8	Pont	10fm	79	4755

GREY COSSACK 7 gr g £9074					
74	9-17	Leic	7g/s	77	1020
82	1-19	REDC	6sft	75	1145*
58	12-19	Beve	5sft	80	1627
41	12-14	Ayr	6g/f	80	1898
74	5-7	Hayd	6g/s	79	2187
22	18-20	York	6g/f	78	2409
54	11-11	Hami	6g/f	78	2477
70	11-18	Newc	6g/s	75	2770
65	5-10	Hayd	6g/s	73	3136
30	10-11	Donc	6g/f	[73]	3375
43	16-19	Newc	7g/f	68	5014

GREY FORTUNE 5 gr m £267					
39	12-14	Thir	8gd		1636
50	4-10	Newc	7hvy		4216
34	7-10	Ripo	6gd		4790

GREY GURKHA 3 gr c £0					
42	6-10	Newc	5sft		1682
37	9-16	Hayd	6g/f		2182
30	6-9	Beve	5sft		2945

GREY LILAS 3 gr f £311533					
113	1-8	LONG	8g/s		1432*
114	2-13	Long	8g/s		1854
116	3-17	Chan	12.5g/s		2460
116	1-7	DEAU	10Very		4309*
118	1-11	LONG	8g/s		4434*
117	2-10	Long	10g/f		4953

GREY ORCHID 3 gr f £0					
2	14-14	Thir	8gd		1636
22	6-7	Pont	6g/f		2042
11	15-19	Beve	5g/s	49	2326
7	13-13	Muss	7.1g/f	45	2812
0	16-18	Beve	9.9g/s	40	4243

GREY PEARL 4 gr f £21215					
70a	5-16	Ling	7ap	73	181
73a	3-11	Wolv	7af	71	241
61a	4-8	Wolv	7af	71	280
71a	5-11	Wolv	7af	72	363
78a	1-13	LING	7ap	71	474*
85a	1-14	LING	7ap	77	518*
84a	3-11	Ling	7ap	[82]	627
79a	6-8	Ling	7ap	[82]	879
92a	4-8	Ling	7ap	[81]	1043
76	6-14	Yarm	8g/f	83	1131 t
68	4-8	Newm	6fm	[81]	2591
93	1-6	NEWM	6g/f	[81]	2736*
90	9-12	Good	7fm	[86]	3564
52	11-11	Ches	6.1g/f	[86]	4510
82	8-10	Beve	5g/f	[86]	4718 t P

GREY SAMURAI 4 gr g £0					
29	6-6	York	11.9g/f		2058
18	12-13	Hayd	11.9g/s		2230
29	8-8	Redc	10gd		2548
5	11-15	Warw	10.9g/f	35	2910 P
9	8-12	Nott	14.1g/f	30	3420

GREY SWALLOW 3 gr c £554603					
116	1-8	LEOP	8sft		1301*
117	4-14	Newm	10g/f		1480
117	3-8	Curr	8g/f		1995
123	1-10	CURR	12g/f		2822*
120	4-8	Leop	10g/f		4571
94	18-19	Long	12g/f		4956

GREYFIELD 8 b g £0					
55	5-18	Newm	12fm	55	2088
55	7-11	Chep	10.2gd	55	2371
32	6-8	Newb	12g/f	53	3270
45	7-13	Sali	14.1gd	50	3454
36	11-19	Chep	12.1gd	45	3727

GREZIE 2 gr f £545					
60	4-9	Donc	5gd		929
59a	4-10	Ling	5ap		1071
60	3-5	Leic	5g/s		1353
19	12-14	Yarm	7g/s	60	4583

GRIGOROVITCH 2 b c £0					
43	8-10	Good	6g/f		3511

GRIST MIST 3 gr f £0					
53	8-14	Wind	10g/s		1055
54	14-20	Bath	10.2gd		1398
0	17-20	Wind	11.6sft	59	1648 T
40	6-9	Good	11g/f	55	2019 t
22	15-16	Good	9g/f	55	2220 t

GRIZEBECK 2 b g £0					
24	8-8	Hayd	8.1g/f		4351

GRIZEDALE 5 ch g £325					
95	5-19	Newm	7g/f	94	3061 t
16	21-21	Asco	7g/f	94	3441 t
39	8-8	Good	7g/s	93	4231 t
71	15-16	Good	7g/f	90	4523 t
75	13-15	Asco	7g/f	90	4800 t
76	13-18	York	7gd	85	5000 t
83	6-12	Newb	6sft	82	5196 t

GROOM TESSE 3 ch c £425662					
116	1-15	CAPA	12gd		2142* bl

GROOMS AFFECTION 4 b c £10244					
87	1-8	SAND	10gd	79	2363*
86	6-12	Wind	11.6fm	84	2759
79	7-10	Asco	12g/f	84	3444
75	7-8	Newb	13.3gd	83	3918
30	16-17	Newm	14.8gd	82	4196 T

GROOMSMAN 2 b g £436
| 75 | 4-14 | Leic | 8gd | | 5058 |
| 56 | 11-16 | Newb | 8hvy | | 5220 |

GROSVENOR SQUARE 2 b c £5681
| 82 | 6-14 | Hayd | 6fm | | 4385 |
| **98** | 1-13 | **NEWM** | 7fm | | 4724* |

GROUND PATROL 2 b g £1816
49a	8-11	Ling	7ap		213
76a	3-12	Ling	8ap		428
71a	4-11	Ling	8ap		496
69a	3-10	Ling	10ap	70	676
63	6-14	Wind	10g/s	[70]	1055
50	8-10	Good	11g/f	68	1865
34a	7-8	Sout	8af	70	2495 VIS
69	4-8	Brig	8fm	[62]	4762 T
68a	6-14	Ling	10ap	66	5083 t
66a	4-13	Ling	10ap	65	5299 t

GROUND RULES 2 b c £1956
| 73 | 2-7 | Sand | 7.1g/s | | 2897 |
| 67 | 9-12 | Good | 7fm | | 3568 |

GROUNDCOVER 2 b c £0
| 62 | 10-12 | Good | 8g/f | | 4522 |
| 63 | 7-14 | Leic | 8gd | | 5058 |

GROUNDSWELL 7 b g £0
| 0 | 11-12 | Wolv | 16.2af | 42 | 7 |

GROUP CAPTAIN 2 b c £6153
64	5-10	Hayd	6g/s		2228
76	4-12	Sand	7.1g/f		2388
85	2-11	Warw	7.1gd		3053
88	2-8	Asco	7gd		3467
74	8-10	Asco	7gd	[80]	3774
81	2-14	Folk	7gd	[88]	4115
79	3-11	Chep	8.1g/s	[88]	4363
56	12-14	Newb	7sft	80	5193

GROUVILLE 3 b g £3339
81a	1-12	LING	8ap		428*
58a	9-9	Ling	8ap		756
16	16-18	Leic	10g/s	72	1017 BL

GROWLER 3 ch g £6802
0	15-16	Leic	8g/s	61	1359
59	3-8	Brig	7g/f	56	2434
27	11-16	Epso	8.5gd	57	3219
57	2-12	Brig	7fm	55	3677 VIS
74	1-9	**GOOD**	6sft	[56]	4262* vis
56	16-17	Ling	6g/f	70	4740 vis
56	7-10	Newc	7fm	[70]	4869 vis

GRUB STREET 8 b g £3106
24a	3-14	Sout	8af	[35]	573
31a	4-16	Sout	8af	[30]	719
34a	1-10	**SOUT**	8af	30	792*
28a	7-16	Sout	11af	[35]	852

GRUFF 5 ch g £0
7a	10-11	Sout	5af	[35]	578
0	13-14	Sout	6af	[35]	637
0	12-12	Sout	5af	[30]	904
3	12-17	Pont	6hvy	[30]	1065
31	8-16	Nott	6.1gd	[30]	1989
7a	13-15	Sout	7af	32	2384
3	12-19	Nott	6.1gd	[32]	3104

GRUMPYINTMORNING 5 b g £0
55	12-14	Folk	7g/s	[53]	1080
29	11-14	Ling	7sft	53	1625
0	P-17	Warw	8.1fm	53	2572
24	11-15	Warw	10.9g/f	53	2910 BL

GRYSKIRK 2 b c £5511
33	4-4	Folk	5g/s		1077
70	6-8	Newm	5g/f		1190
58	3-11	Yarm	6g/f		1728
68	7-12	Sand	7.1g/f		2388
70	8-13	Newm	6g/f	68	3065
54	7-9	Brig	7g/f	68	3297
65a	3-12	Ling	7ap	64	3820
50a	10-13	Sout	7af	64	4040 e
66	5-20	Ling	7ap	64	4444
34	10-20	Yarm	8g/s	64	4635
81a	1-11	LING	8ap	[62]	5235*

GUADALOUP 2 ch f £0
| 46 | 13-20 | York | 6g/f | | 4401 |

GUADIARO 2 b c £0
| 63 | 7-11 | Hayd | 5g/f | | 4349 |
| 50 | 16-21 | Donc | 6sft | | 5368 |

GUARD 3 b c £0
21a	8-10	Wolv	7af	[44]	8
8	11-12	Brig	7fm	37	3677 t
1a	13-13	Ling	10ap	41	3823 t

GUARDIAN SPIRIT 5 b m £0
| 18 | 17-18 | Nott | 8.2g/s | 53 | 1778 |
| 11a | 13-14 | Ling | 7ap | 45 | 3746 |

GUILDED FLYER 5 b g £13403
74	8-20	Newb	10gd	81	1235
89	1-12	**CHES**	10.3gd	80	1586*
73	9-11	Epso	10.1g/f	87	2208
91	3-12	Kemp	9gd	87	2860
74	8-12	Kemp	10gd	87	3185

GUILDENSTERN 2 b c £401
58	9-13	Chep	6.1gd		3399
75	4-11	Wind	6g/s		4941
70	5-10	Newm	6sft		5266

GUINEA A MINUTE 2 ch f £2271
62	9-19	Newb	6g/f		2310
66	3-6	Epso	6g/s		3041
59	6-10	Wind	6fm		3290
61	6-7	Newm	6g/f	67	3753
64a	5-13	Sout	7af	63	4040
67	3-12	Sali	8sft	61	4580
69	3-12	Ayr	8sft	62	5065
48	18-20	Yarm	8g/s	64	5349

GULCHINA 2 b f £376
| 78 | 4-19 | Newm | 7g/s | | 5279 |

GULF 5 ch g £4449
64	18-18	Kemp	16g/s	99	1112
106	3-8	Newb	13.3g/f	[97]	1757
99	5-8	Donc	16.4g/g	[105]	2914
94	5-7	Sali	14.1gd	[105]	4333 T

GUN SALUTE 3 b g £5645
44a	8-16	Ling	7ap	[53]	123
57a	1-13	**LING**	6ap	[52]	219* P
36a	12-15	Ling	7ap	56	266 p
36a	8-13	Ling	6ap	55	471 p
55a	1-13	**LING**	6ap	[53]	544* p
48a	8-13	Ling	6ap	53	740 p
52a	4-14	Ling	6ap	53	874 p
51a	6-15	Ling	7ap	53	913 p
1	14-15	Folk	6g/s	50	1267 p
44	6-10	Brig	7g/f	47	1941
22	11-16	Brig	6fm	46	2262 p
28	11-18	Ling	6gd	46	2396 BL

GUNNERBERGKAMP 2 b g £0
36	10-11	Thir	7g/f		3570
26	11-15	Redc	6g/f		3769
4	14-15	Catt	7sft		3930

GUNNHILDR 3 ch f £0
| 0 | 11-12 | Wolv | 7af | 60 | 129 vis |
| 3 | 20-20 | Yarm | 6g/f | 54 | 1730 |

GUNS BLAZING 5 b g £8124
28	15-15	Brig	5.3g/f	61	1371 vis
49	8-17	Warw	5hvy	[61]	1532
66	1-17	**NOTT**	5.1g/s	58	1774* bl
68	3-18	Good	5g/f	65	1867 bl
57	6-10	Brig	5.3g/f	62	2044 bl
59	10-17	Warw	5fm	66	2599 bl
73	1-12	**LING**	5g/f	66	2743+ bl
52	8-11	Brig	5.3gd	73	2957 bl
69	7-17	Sand	5g/f	72	3341 bl
66	12-22	Good	5fm	72	3537 bl

GURRUN 2 b c £0
64	14-15	Newm	7fm		3005
65	9-11	Newm	7g/f		3234
63	11-18	Newm	7gd		3927
20	15-15	Folk	7gd		4114
49	6-9	Brig	6fm	67	4758

GUSTAVO 3 b c £1902
60	11-12	Newm	7g/s		1152
51	8-20	Donc	7g/s		1518
59	9-12	York	7g/s		1688
34	9-11	Hayd	8.1gd		2886
59a	2-15	Sout	8af	54	4132 BL
59	2-18	Warw	10.9g/s	54	4669 bl

GUYANA 2 b c £546
57	15-15	Newb	7g/f		2876
69	9-15	Sand	7.1g/f		3337
70a	3-10	Ling	6ap		3818
32	16-17	Ling	7g/f	71	4894
2	17-20	Newb	6hvy	65	5225

GWAZI 3 b g £362
22a	9-14	Sout	8af		170 t
37a	9-13	Sout	8af		199 t
21a	11-16	Sout	11af	[45]	445 t P
37a	3-9	Wolv	9.4af	[40]	633 vis t
27	14-17	Beve	8.5g/s	[40]	1160 t
5a	6-6	Wolv	7af	[40]	1804 t

GWEN JOHN 3 ch f £856
74	5-10	Good	8gd		2224
72	3-8	Good	9gd		2536
56	11-12	Newb	10g/f	74	3255
44	8-9	Carl	9.3fm	[72]	3546 BL
8	12-13	Bath	10.2sft	[70]	5173

GWYNETH 2 b f £0
| 80 | 5-8 | Kemp | 7g/s | | 2676 |
| 69 | 9-13 | Good | 7fm | | 3554 |

GYPSY FAIR 2 b f £0
| 46 | 7-8 | Thir | 5g/s | | 1212 |
| 38 | 9-10 | Muss | 5gd | | 1550 |

GYPSY JOHNNY 2 gr c £4622
| 84 | 1-4 | BEVE | 7.5sft | | 2938* |
| 49 | 11-11 | Ayr | 8sft | 85 | 4688 VIS |

GYPSY ROYAL 2 b f £0
46	11-20	Wind	6fm		2970
52	9-12	Warw	7.1g/f		4418
38	11-16	Bath	5.7gd		4823

H HARRISON 4 b g £13445
30	18-18	Catt	7gd	82	998
76	6-13	Muss	7.1g/f	82	1122
72	4-10	Warw	7.1sft	[80]	1525
79	5-18	Ches	7.6gd	80	1598
73	4-10	Thir	7g/f	[78]	1970
86	1-9	**CHES**	7gd	76	2282+
39	16-20	York	6g/f	83	2409
32	23-28	Asco	7g/f	83	2558
83	3-10	Epso	7g/f	83	2872
70	5-8	Pont	6gd	81	3461
66	8-12	Ches	7.6fm	81	3634
58	11-13	Ches	7.6sft	79	4103
73a	6-14	Ling	7ap	79	4180
82	5-11	Yarm	8gd	79	4615
77	8-13	Muss	7.1gd	78	4806
80	3-10	Epso	7gd	[78]	4912 p
67a	6-12	Wolv	7.1ap	74	5289 p
62	10-20	Donc	7sft	77	5367

HAADEF 3 b c £17980
92	3-17	Newb	10gd		1737
94	1-16	**SAND**	10g/s		2131*
100	4-5	Asco	12g/f		2554
42	15-15	Hayd	11.9gd	99	2948
61	14-15	Leic	11.8gd	98	5043 BL
103	2-8	Nott	10hvy	98	5187 bl

HAAFHD 3 ch c £430124
121	1-5	**NEWM**	8g/f	[115]	1188*
126	1-14	**NEWM**	8g/f	[120]	1480+
119	4-11	Asco	8g/f	[124]	2469
101	9-11	Good	8fm	[122]	3533
125	1-11	**NEWM**	10sft	[122]	5136*

HAATMEY 2 b c £7057
75	3-9	Folk	7g/f		3721
67	4-12	Ayr	7.2hvy		4083
82	2-10	Redc	9fm		4558
86	1-11	**BATH**	10.2gd	[76]	4825*
87	4-7	Leic	10gd	[87]	5044

HABANERO 3 b c £16594
23	15-18	Leic	10g/s	72	1017
20	9-9	Sand	10g/s	71	1318
54	5-18	Wind	8.3sft	68	1647
71	3-14	Wind	8.3g/f	66	1956
73	1-13	**SAND**	8.1gd	66	2365*
75	3-18	Leic	10gd	69	2706
79	3-10	Sand	8.1g/f	[72]	3339
80	1-7	**EPSO**	8.5fm	72	3542*
74	6-8	Newm	8g/f	79	3947
66	9-13	Epso	8.5gd	79	4469
43	17-17	Asco	8g/f	78	4777
73a	6-13	Ling	10ap	76	5299

HABIBTI SARA 4 ch f £0
| 8a | 12-12 | Wolv | 12af | [35] | 523 |

HABITUAL 3 b g £1495
40a	10-10	Ling	7ap		911
32a	10-10	Ling	8ap		1021
53	4-20	Beve	16.2gd	50	3312
46	5-14	Yarm	11.5g/f	50	3714
61a	1-14	**LING**	16ap	[49]	4663*
41	8-13	Newc	16.1fm	60	4868
40a	9-11	Wolv	12.2ap	60	5117

HABITUAL DANCER 3 b g £8591
59	6-13	Donc	7gd		925
64	1-14	**SOUT**	10g/s	52	1051*
63	2-6	Pont	12sft	59	1429
58	3-5	Hami	12.1g/s	59	2827
33	11-18	Hayd	14gd	59	2905
59	5-17	Pont	17.1g/s	58	3970
41	8-9	Ripo	16gd	58	4308
66	1-11	**AYR**	15sft	57	5032*

HABSHAN 4 ch g £7175
53	9-19	Yarm	8g/f		1130
70	4-9	Newm	8gd	70	1891
71	3-10	Newb	8g/f	69	2350
68	5-12	Nott	8.2g/s	68	2931
72	1-8	**NEWM**	8g/f	67	3583*
66	7-16	Nott	8.2g/s	69	4036
74	3-16	Sali	8gd	69	4334

HACHITA 2 ch f £9115
87	1-13	**KEMP**	7g/f		3520*
86	3-4	Sand	7.1g/f		3859
91	2-4	Ches	7.6g/f	[83]	4513

HADATH 6 br g £305
66a	5-12	Ling	8ap	66	17 P
67a	3-15	Ling	7ap	66	50 p
46a	10-11	Ling	8ap	68	131
43a	4-16	Ling	7ap	[68]	180 p
30a	8-16	Ling	7ap	[67]	214 p

HADRIAN 2 b c £6447
57	6-7	Newc	6g/s		2774
89	2-9	Epso	7fm		3539
91	1-12	**THIR**	7g/f		4591*
74	12-14	Catt	7sft	83	5126

HAENERTSBURG 2 b f £0
58	9-20	York	6g/f		4401
46	7-18	Ayr	6g/s		4617
42	8-13	Newc	6g/f		5012

HAGLEY PARK 4 b f £3142
12a	12-13	Wolv	5af	50	110
17a	12-15	Sout	5af	48	187
44a	2-10	Wolv	5af	[46]	286
43a	2-10	Wolv	5af	[45]	527
26a	6-8	Wolv	5af	[45]	619
39a	5-16	Sout	5af	[45]	720
52a	4-7	Ling	5ap	[45]	737 VIS
41a	3-12	Wolv	5af	[45]	889 vis
21a	11-12	Wolv	5af	[45]	960 vis
32a	3-8	Sout	5af	[45]	1199
50a	1-7	**WOLV**	5af	[40]	1562*
14a	11-13	Wolv	5af	49	2201
43a	7-15	Sout	5af	[48]	2803
45	9-17	Bath	5g/f	48	2981 vis
44	9-13	Wind	6fm	45	3479
40	5-11	Bath	5g/f	45	3849
0	14-14	Ling	7ap	[47]	4660
41a	5-13	Wolv	5.1ap	[45]	5231

HAIBAN 2 b c £3672
68	4-6	Hami	8.3g/s		3878
77	2-14	Ches	7sft		4102
74	3-7	Hami	8.3sft		4691

HAIL THE CHIEF 7 b h £8634
97a	1-8	**WOLV**	8.5af	[100]	360*
87a	4-10	Wolv	8.5af	[100]	511
97a	10-11	Ling	10ap	[96]	693
68	3-8	Muss	8g/s	[76]	1461
49	14-18	Ches	7.6gd	76	1598
68	6-12	Good	9fm	73	3625
56	8-10	Wind	10g/f	[73]	3980
66	8-14	Epso	8.5gd	70	4295
58	11-15	Epso	7g/f	70	4475
64	10-14	Wind	8.3g/f	67	4832

HAITHEM 6 b g £1700
17a	9-11	Sout	8af	36	255 e
16a	6-12	Sout	8af	[36]	309 e
0	13-14	Sout	8af	[40]	354 e
28a	10-10	Wolv	8.5af	[40]	398 e
9a	7-12	Wolv	12af	30	469 e
40a	3-9	Wolv	9.4af	[30]	525 e
19a	10-11	Wolv	9.4af	[30]	580 e
10a	6-8	Sout	8af	[40]	635 e t
0	8-12	Wolv	9.4af	[40]	668 e
39a	5-12	Ling	8ap	[40]	710 t
44a	6-10	Ling	8ap	45	766 t
45a	1-11	**LING**	8ap	[35]	786* t
30a	8-8	Ling	10ap	45	900 t
36a	7-10	Ling	8ap	45	917 t
0	10-13	Wolv	8.6ap	[45]	5232 t

HAJEER 5 b g £720
0	10-10	Wolv	14.8af	53	34
24a	11-15	Sout	16af	53	67
38a	12-14	Ling	16af	51	107
25a	7-16	Sout	16af	48	206
10a	7-8	Wolv	14.8af	44	277 p
29a	5-9	Sout	16af	45	336
37a	2-4	Wolv	14.8af	[40]	426

HALABALOO 2 b f £1288
68a	3-8	Ling	6ap		49
81	5-17	Newm	7gd		1171
33	11-11	Asco	8sft		1419
73	3-12	Good	7g/f	[78]	1846
57	6-11	Newm	8gd	[75]	3923
60	6-8	Sand	8.1g/s	[73]	4101 BL

HALCYON EXPRESS 2 b c £325
| 47 | 8-12 | Wind | 6g/s | | 4945 |
| 80 | 4-14 | Muss | 7.1g/s | | 5330 T |

HALCYON MAGIC 5 b g £4973
0	10-15	Sout	8af	39	84 bl
50	2-15	Folk	6g/s	49	1267 bl
39	9-17	Nott	6.1sft	50	1606 bl
24	15-20	Yarm	8fm	50	2149 bl
48	2-9	Newm	8g/f	48	2529 bl
33	14-17	Newm	7g/f	48	2768 bl
47	6-13	Kemp	7g/f	48	3034 bl
36	12-20	Newm	8g/f	48	3232 bl
52	1-16	**YARM**	7gd	46	4616* bl
47	5-16	Chep	7.1hvy	[46]	4707 bl

HALF A HANDFUL 3 b c £2849
2a	10-10	Ling	6ap		973
31	12-15	Folk	6g/s		1078
45	11-14	Sout	6gd		1281
65	6-15	Leic	6g/f		1829
69	3-9	Wind	6gd	65	2619
68	3-12	Catt	6g/f	[65]	2849
69	2-7	Ayr	7.2gd	65	3153
65	3-12	Folk	6gd	65	3380 VIS
26	11-11	Leic	8g/f	66	3516 vis

HALF INCH 4 b f £271
46a	11-13	Ling	10ap	[59]	912
61	4-14	Folk	9.7g/s	59	1083 p
49	12-15	Beve	9.9sft	60	1307 p
44	7-7	Epso	12g/s	58	3040 p

HALICARDIA 3 br f £27300
103	3-9	Kemp	8g/s	[97]	1110
106	1-7	**GOOD**	9.9g/f	[97]	1844*
104	2-6	Newb	10g/f	[106]	2351

HALLA SAN 2 b c £1418
43	8-10	Thir	5fm		3606
45	13-18	Pont	5g/s		3968
70	5-16	Thir	6g/s		4205
73	4-12	Thir	7g/f		4591
77	3-12	Newm	8gd	70	5089

HALLAHOISE HYDRO 3 ch g £0
| 25 | 12-20 | Ripo | 6gd | 57 | 4278 |
| 0 | 18-19 | Thir | 6g/f | 53 | 4595 |

HALLAND 6 ch g £0
82	8-8	Newm	12g/f	[82]	3617
79	10-13	Yarm	16g/s	82	4634
84	12-34	Newm	18sft	82	5135

HALLE BOP 2 b f £6967
| 84 | 2-10 | Newb | 6gd | | 3917 |
| **93** | 1-15 | **KEMP** | 6g/f | | 4357+ |

HALLHOO 2 gr c £17975
82	3-8	Asco	6g/f		3438
88	1-11	**NEWB**	6g/f		3959*
90	2-11	Hayd	8.1fm	81	4387
95	2-11	Ayr	8sft	85	4688
46	8-9	Newm	8sft	[89]	5099

HALLINGS OVERTURE 5 b g £1720
64a	6-13	Ling	10ap	65	726
57a	7-8	Ling	10ap	63	900
76	2-17	Kemp	7gd	[60]	1136
6	16-16	Sali	8gd	70	4334

HALLOWED DREAM 2 b f £1937
45	7-10	Yarm	8g/f		3713
59	9-10	Newm	7gd		4191
64	8-13	Leic	8gd		4450
87	2-15	Newm	8fm		4723
82	6-9	Newm	8sft	[80]	5099

HALLUCINATE 2 b c £4900
59	11-12	Ling	6g/f		1981
51	4-6	Wind	6fm		2783
74	2-18	Leic	7g/f		3342
73	3-6	Folk	7g/f	69	3723
74	4-12	York	7g/s	71	4064
87	3-13	York	7.9gd	[70]	4325

HALMAHERA 9 b g £39615
96	10-17	Donc	6gd	[102]	952
93	2-7	Thir	6sft	[101]	1227 bl
86	4-8	Beve	5sft	[102]	1626 bl
87	6-14	York	5g/s	102	1703 bl
89	6-10	York	6gd	100	2357 bl
81	20-29	Asco	6fm	100	2581
97	5-15	Newc	5g/s	98	2727
101	6-28	Good	6fm	98	3622
86	9-19	Ripo	6g/f	99	3937
107	1-22	**DONC**	5.6fm	98	4459+
94	9-15	Newm	6sft	[101]	4879
95	7-14	Newm	6sft	[101]	5100
89	9-12	Donc	6sft	[100]	5371

HAMAASY 3 b g £0
66	5-9	Ripo	6sft	[61]	2485
42	7-10	Beve	5sft	[61]	2944
56	7-12	Donc	5g/f	61	3599
32	15-15	Thir	5g/s	60	3833

HAMAIRI 3 ch c £54070
102	2-	Leop	7sft		1299
106	2-6	Leop	6sft		2455
111	2-5	Leop	8g/f		4020
111	1-12	**TIPP**	7.5hvy		4961*

HAMBLEDEN 7 b g £12729
97	6-10	Ches	10.3gd	[101]	1585
93	9-14	Good	12g/f	[101]	1843
102	4-13	Asco	12fm	100	2582
101	4-15	Hayd	11.9gd	99	2948
81	13-15	Good	14g/f	98	3510
99	6-10	Asco	12gd	98	3777
100	3-6	Ches	13.4sft	96	4104

HAMBURG SPRINGER 2 b g £0
35	12-14	Donc	6gd		1874
20	5-5	Pont	5g/f		2789
38	8-12	Beve	5g/f		4596

67	15-15	Ripo	5gd	45	4784
19	16-16	York	7.9gd	[45]	4997

HAMMER OF THE GODS 4 ch g £1197

41	3-6	Yarm	7g/f	48	3708 t
47	3-5	Yarm	6sft	[45]	4150 VIS
31	11-16	Yarm	7gd	45	4616 t

HANA DEE 3 b f £942

54a	10-15	Ling	7ap	[72]	875
52	14-15	Bath	8g/s	70	1099
62	6-20	Newb	7g/f	67	1761
18	13-14	Newm	8g/f	65	1930
46	11-14	Redc	7fm	62	2295
57	4-7	Ayr	7.2gd	59	3153
55	5-11	Sali	8gd	57	3455
53	3-12	Pont	8gd	56	3679
39	9-12	Bath	8g/f	56	3846
23	12-15	Bath	8g/s	52	4202
46	4-10	Brig	9.9fm	49	4763
49a	5-9	Ling	8ap	[47]	5242
42a	7-11	Wolv	8.6ap	[47]	5356

HANABAD 4 ch c £1608

101	4-10	Curr	6g/f		1996

HANAMI 4 b f £7839

105	3-5	Curr	8g/f	[110]	1997
92	6-6	Curr	10gd	[110]	2816
2	12-13	Deau	10sft	[110]	4160

HANAZAKARI 3 b c £0

42	9-10	Yarm	11.5gd	3997
33a	5-10	Ling	12ap	4314

HAND CHIME 6 ch g £2307

88a	3-10	Ling	7ap	87	262
68a	9-12	Wolv	6af	87	361
66a	13-16	Sout	7af	87	419
89a	5-11	Ling	7ap	[85]	627
65	9-13	Kemp	7sft	78	945
53	9-13	Redc	7sft	[75]	1142
70	2-6	Yarm	7gd	72	3708
52	7-15	Sali	8gd	72	3888
52	10-10	Brig	7sft	69	4168
61	6-20	Leic	7gd	65	5046
46	11-20	Yarm	7sft	63	5256

HANDRIA 6 b m £6429

100	3-	Toul	10.5g/s	57 bl	

HANDSOME CROSS 3 b c £1801

70	5-10	Warw	7.1sft	[85]	1525
83	5-15	Ling	7gd	84	1983
69	6-9	Kemp	6gd	[84]	2173
53	12-13	Newb	7g/f	81	2880
80	3-21	Good	5fm	80	3567
77	8-15	Sand	5gd	80	4604
74	7-15	Catt	5sft	79	5125

HANDSOME LADY 2 ch f £4475

78	1-6	AYR	5g/s		1445*
68	6-10	Thir	5g/f		1764
68	10-12	Beve	5g/f		2165
71	5-10	Ches	5.1g/s		2744
71	6-12	Hayd	5gd	77	3756 VIS
76	4-12	Muss	5gd	74	4172
61	11-12	Ayr	5g/s	[75]	4651
64	3-6	Muss	5g/s	[75]	5141

HANNAHS DREAM 2 b f £2331

58	6-10	Catt	6g/f	4436
76	2-9	Beve	7.5g/f	4600
72	3-12	Newc	7g/f	5011

HANNAHS TRIBE 2 b f £0

57	9-12	Carl	5.9fm	3544
40	9-14	Thir	7g/s	3831
61	9-14	Muss	7.1g/s	5330

HANSEATIC LEAGUE 2 b c £8528

83	2-12	Ripo	5g/f		1974
86	2-8	Hayd	5gd		2241
61	6-18	Pont	5g/s		3968
88	1-11	WIND	6g/s	[82]	4941*

HANSOMELLE 2 b f £16625

56	4-10	Carl	5g/f	3227
76	1-5	HAMI	6g/f	3589*

80	2-19	Carl	5.9g/f	72	4344
76	4-14	Hami	6sft	75	4692
84	1-17	CATT	7gd	75	4963*
83	3-14	Donc	7sft	77	5213

HANZANO 6 b h £2795

99	3-10	Taby	8g/f	[95]	4573
86a	14-14	Ling	7ap	100	5262

HAPPY AS LARRY 2 b c £4238

86a	1-14	LING	7ap	5076* T

HAPPY BANKER 2 gr c £0

47	14-16	Sali	7g/s	3111

HAPPY CAMPER 4 b g £222

0	11-13	Ling	6ap		400
36a	11-13	Ling	6ap	60	902
47a	6-12	Ling	7ap	[55]	1074
47a	5-8	Ling	7ap	[50]	1247
45	3-17	Kemp	7hvy	[45]	1642
25	8-13	Leic	7g/f	[45]	1827
14a	12-14	Ling	10ap	43	2589
33	5-16	Warw	8.1g/s	[45]	4993

HAPPY CRUSADER 2 b c £4747

100	6-	Sain	10g/s		9
102	2-4	Donc	8g/s	[104]	1520
102	4-7	Good	11g/f	[104]	1814
97	8-13	Asco	10g/f	[104]	2520

HAPPY EVENT 2 b c £7670

88	1-15	WIND	6g/f		2263*
60	7-10	Sali	6gd		2697
61	19-24	Newb	5.2g/f		3266
87	1-8	BATH	5.7g/s	[83]	4198*
80	4-6	Leic	7gd	[86]	4699

HARAMBEE 4 b f £0

0	P-19	York	11.9sft	80	1668
0	U-10	Beve	9.9g/s	80	2323
26	11-11	Ripo	10g/f	80	2483
38	8-8	Hayd	11.9gd	73	2881

HARBOUR HOUSE 4 b g £4291

44a	2-16	Ling	7ap	[39]	214
34a	7-15	Ling	7ap	43	266
41a	7-13	Ling	6ap	[45]	340
46a	2-12	Ling	8ap	[45]	648
37a	8-13	Ling	7ap	45	739
40a	6-12	Ling	8ap	[45]	1073
38a	3-9	Ling	6ap	[45]	1248
49	1-10	BRIG	5.3gd	[45]	1544*
45	3-10	Kemp	5hvy	[45]	1644
8	15-16	Brig	6fm	46	2262
47	2-11	Brig	5.3gd	45	2957
40	6-16	Wind	5fm	46	3640
44	6-15	Ling	6fm	46	3790
40	5-10	Brig	7sft	45	4168
38	9-19	Bath	5.7sft	45	5176

HARBOUR LEGEND 2 b f £0

26	13-16	Pont	6g/f		2275
34	6-7	Catt	7g/f		3189
24	11-12	Ayr	7.2hvy		4083 BL

HARBOUR PRINCESS 3 b f £205

33a	9-13	Sout	6af		319
40a	6-9	Ling	5ap		405
26a	6-8	Sout	5af		742
8a	6-6	Sout	8af	[40]	1203
30a	3-5	Ling	7ap	[40]	1288
24	4-8	Brig	8gd	[35]	1548
8a	8-8	Ling	10ap	[35]	1713 VIS

HARCOURT 4 b c £0

37	12-16	Epso	10.1hvy	88	1296
52	14-17	Newb	12g/f	86	1759

HARD BUCK 4 b c £388463

116	2-13	Nad	12g/f	990
125	2-11	Asco	12g/f	3442

HARD TO CATCH 6 b g £15994

62a	7-14	Ling	6ap	70	407
56a	7-14	Ling	6ap	[69]	516
67a	2-13	Ling	7ap	65	565
68a	4-14	Ling	7ap	65	604
72a	1-12	LING	6ap	65	628*

63a	9-12	Ling	6ap	70	880
72a	4-14	Ling	6ap	70	897 bl
71a	5-14	Ling	7ap	70	1010
68	5-16	Bath	5.7g/s	[70]	1103
25	16-16	Nott	6.1sft	[69]	1743
49	10-14	Kemp	5g/f	66	1914 bl
74	1-10	BRIG	5.3g/f	66	2044* bl
80	1-12	FOLK	5g/f	66	2269* bl
80	3-7	Warw	6.1fm	[77]	2598 bl
76	3-4	Brig	5.3fm	77	2838 bl
26	10-10	Hayd	6g/s	79	3136 bl
75	6-26	Good	6fm	80	3569 bl
78	3-12	Newm	6g/f	77	3751 bl
70a	7-14	Ling	7ap	77	4180
64	12-19	Kemp	6fm	77	4394 bl
36a	14-14	Ling	7ap	75	4446 bl

HARD TOP 2 b c £0

75	5-21	Newm	8sft	5097

HARELDA 4 ch f £3328

78a	1-7	SOUT	12af		588*
6a	6-6	Sout	12af	81	870
57	18-20	Newm	12gd	81	1172

HARFORD BRIDGE 3 ch g £0

0	10-10	Wolv	8.5af	839

HARIBINI 4 b f £0

26a	12-14	Ling	10ap	48	1618
0	16-17	Kemp	10g/f	45	1913

HARIK 10 ch g £1056

63a	6-8	Ling	16ap	76	288
48	2-14	Bath	18.2fm	42	2417 bl t
36	7-15	Folk	16.4g/s	43	3049 bl t

HARIPUR 4 b c £0

91a	7-10	Ling	7ap	97	262
64a	10-13	Ling	10ap	97	519

HARLESTONE LINN 2 ch g £0

57	12-23	Newm	7g/f	4885
63	7-11	Bath	8sft	5171

HARLOT 3 b f £295

49a	8-14	Ling	10ap	59	101
57a	3-13	Ling	10ap	56	215 P
42a	12-14	Ling	10ap	56	339 p
54a	10-11	Ling	12ap	56	624

HAROLDINI 2 b g £2184

67	7-14	Bath	5gd		1401
72	4-11	Yarm	6g/f		1727
72	2-6	Leic	5fm		2110
60	6-14	Leic	6g/f	70	3212
77a	2-11	Sout	6af	70	3393
62	7-12	Newm	7g/f	[70]	3750
27	17-19	Nott	6.1g/s	65	4645
36a	9-12	Wolv	6ap	[73]	5177 P

HARRINGTON BATES 3 ch g £267

69	4-8	Donc	5g/f		2075
66	6-9	Ripo	6g/f		2485
49	8-14	Thir	7sft		2692
64	5-12	Catt		64	3193

HARRISON POINT 4 br c £18243

79a	1-15	LING	7ap	73	698*
80a	1-12	LING	8ap	76	888*
84	2-9	Newm	8gd	81	1891
86	2-7	Good	7gd	81	2223
84	10-20	Newm	8fm	84	3001
92a	1-13	LING	7ap	83	3791*
76	13-21	Donc	7fm	84	4482
85	6-18	York	7gd	84	5000

HARRISONS FLYER 3 b g £17203

56	7-12	Catt	6g/f		2849
70	2-10	Beve	5sft		2944
36	12-13	Beve	7.5g/s	67	3179
67	2-9	Leic	5g/f	[67]	3347 BL
34	15-20	Thir	6g/f	65	3575 bl
63	2-9	Thir	6fm	[67]	4380
0	U-14	Newc	5g/f	[67]	4404 VIS
53	12-17	Beve	5g/f	66	4603
48	12-19	York	5gd	64	4989 P
75	1-8	BRIG	5.3sft	66	5096* p
75a	1-13	WOLV	5.1ap	66	5156* p

81 1-11 MUSS 5g/s 72 5332*

HARRY CAME HOME 3 b g £0
38a	10-13	Ling	12ap		873	
34	10-10	Kemp	11.1gd		1140	
37	12-12	Sali	12g/s		1501	
53	11-11	Bath	8fm		1904	
0	16-18	Sali	7fm	35	2292	
0	11-12	Ling	12ap	[30]	3819	
2	11-12	Sali	8g/s	30	4077	BL
21	14-19	Chep	8.1g/s	[30]	4366	bl
29	13-15	Wind	10g/f	[30]	4834	bl

HARRY LAD 3 ch g £0
54a	5-12	Wolv	9.4af		686
42a	5-8	Wolv	12af		808
3	6-6	Thir	12g/s		1213

HARRY POTTER 5 b g £15336
0	11-12	Wolv	9.4af	70	513	
57a	14-15	Ling	7ap	65	698	
70a	3-12	Ling	8ap	[61]	878	VIS
23	11-16	Newc	8hvy	70	1036	vis
72	1-17	THIR	8g/s	67	1214*	vis
70	8-16	Thir	7g/s	71	1474	vis
71	6-12	Hayd	8.1g/f	71	1883	vis
54	9-10	Hayd	8.1gd	71	2242	BL
64	5-14	Ayr	9.1gd	69	2571	bl
82	1-12	AYR	8gd	69	3328*	vis
81	1-9	NOTT	8.2g/f	[69]	3423*	vis
80	5-8	Thir	8fm	80	3608	vis
56	13-14	Wind	8.3gd	[80]	4122	vis
80	3-8	York	8.9g/f	[79]	4397	vis
71	8-10	Ayr	8sft	79	4685	vis
59	14-20	York	8.9gd	77	4999	vis

HARRY THE HOOVER 3 b g £0
0	9-11	Wolv	8.5af	[78]	128
57a	12-12	Ling	8ap	70	5079

HARRY TU 3 b g £0
30a	8-10	Wolv	7af		4	
15a	13-14	Ling	10ap		53	
1a	9-12	Sout	8af		460	
0	9-12	Ling	10ap	[35]	654	e T

HARRY UP 3 ch c £8401
86	2-6	Leic	6g/s	[93]	1018
92	3-5	Hayd	5sft	92	1106
80	9-15	Ches	5.1g/s	90	1572
87	3-7	Nott	6.1g/s	[90]	1771
93	4-11	Redc	5g/f	89	2121
61	16-20	York	6g/f	89	2407
64	21-21	Good	5fm	87	3567

HARRYCAT 3 b g £2647
66	7-17	Newm	8gd		4228
56	5-6	Muss	8gd		4520
66	6-10	Pont	8g/f		4939
81	2-10	Newm	12sft		5102
73	3-8	Redc	10sft	[70]	5306

HARRYS HOUSE 2 gr c £4425
66	4-10	Pont	5g/s		3457
57	7-18	Pont	5g/s		3968
70	4-8	Newc	7sft		4283
71	3-14	Carl	6.9fm	[68]	4503
79	1-11	CATT	5gd	[67]	4962*
54	8-10	Catt	6sft	77	5318

HARRYS SIMMIE 2 ch f £0
46	10-10	Catt	7g/f		2845
20	13-14	Hayd	6gd		3735
35a	10-13	Wolv	8.6ap		4979

HARTSHEAD 4 b g £25739
0	14-14	Sout	12af	[65]	194	
69	2-20	Thir	6gd	63	1638	
41	8-9	Ripo	6g/f	[68]	2007	
63	6-16	Carl	5.9fm	68	2445	
75	1-10	REDC	6gd	[68]	2559*	
79	1-6	CARL	5.9gd	[68]	2934+	
70	4-11	Donc	6g/f	[72]	3375	
82	1-11	THIR	6g/f	72	3574*	
82	1-13	REDC	7fm	[75]	4341+	
83	2-13	Muss	7.1gd	78	4806	
84	3-18	York	7gd	79	5000	

HARVEST WARRIOR 2 br c £15344

79	2-6	Warw	5hvy		1531	
84	2-9	Ches	5.1gd		2281	
94	1-12	HAYD	6gd		2902*	
71	5-7	Donc	6g/s		3221	
101	2-15	Hayd	6sft	95	4765	
85	12-24	Redc	6fm	[95]	4928	
103	2-8	Donc	6sft	[97]	5217	

HASAIYDA 3 b f £10773
83	1-8	LING	9g/f		2013*
76	4-6	Asco	10gd	75	3072
83	1-9	SAND	10g/f	75	3862*
59	8-11	Epso	12gd	80	4468
71	12-16	Sand	10gd	80	4609

HASAYIS 3 b f £4232
70	1-8	WARW	8.1sft		1086*
48	10-17	Yarm	7g/f	[70]	1729
70	4-13	Leic	7g/f	68	3346
63	7-14	Bath	8g/f	68	3963

HASHID 4 b g £550
52	6-9	Leic	11.8g/s		1016	
68	3-11	Chep	10.2gd	[77]	2196	bl
41	8-9	Newm	14.8fm	70	2596	VIS
34	12-14	Sali	12g/s	70	3114	
62	6-19	Chep	12.1gd	65	3398	
64	5-14	Bath	13.1g/g	62	4203	

HASHIMA 2 b f £1199
76	3-12	Folk	7gd		3909
67a	4-14	Ling	7ap		5257

HASHIMIYA 2 b f £0
68	6-19	Leic	7gd		5040

HASTY PRINCE 6 ch g £0
0	S-13	Kemp	12g/f	[88]	4715

HAT TRICK MAN 3 gr c £370
64	6-15	Wind	10fm		3292
48	8-9	Sand	10g/f	72	3862
51	3-7	Yarm	11.5g/s	[70]	5351

HATCH 3 ch c £14833
69a	2-12	Wolv	7af	[79]	560	
74a	2-8	Ling	7ap	[74]	713	
83a	1-15	LING	7ap	[74]	814*	
79	3-6	Leic	6g/s	[79]	1018	
90	1-7	MUSS	7.1g/f	[79]	1094*	
91	3-8	Muss	7.1g/s	88	1460	
75	13-18	Good	9g/f	90	1813	
89	4-5	Sand	7.1gd	[90]	2362	
67a	11-12	Ling	8ap	[88]	3199	
78	10-11	Newm	6g/f	88	3941	T

HATCH A PLAN 3 b g £6969
44a	9-12	Ling	6ap		1044	
0	U-16	Leic	8g/s	66	1359	
58	7-12	Pont	10g/f	66	2277	
73	1-12	WIND	10g/f	[62]	2800*	
75	2-6	Ches	10.3g/f	68	3084	
78	2-8	Newm	10g/f	[72]	3471	
74	4-7	Leic	11.8fm	[74]	3816	
49	10-11	Sali	12g/s	74	4080	
64	11-16	Sand	10gd	72	4609	
68	5-11	Wind	11.6g/s	[70]	4942	P

HATHLEN 3 b c £3770
1	8-8	Newc	12.4hvy	[77]	1038
77	6-11	Ripo	12.3gd	77	1174
2	6-6	Pont	12sft	76	1429
74	5-13	Thir	12g/f	[76]	1768
75	6-11	Sand	14g/s	73	2130
80	1-10	GOOD	14gd	73	2376+
77	5-12	Sand	14g/f	76	3359
65	6-7	Thir	16g/s	76	4209
76	7-13	Yarm	16g/s	75	4634
64	6-6	Muss	16gd	73	4808

HATHRAH 3 gr f £52903
117	1-9	KEMP	8g/s	[103]	1110*
117	3-16	Newm	8fm	[111]	1492

HAULAGE MAN 6 ch g £2710
37	10-11	Hami	6g/f	58	2477	
61	2-14	Newc	6g/s	[58]	2730	
48	11-16	Redc	8g/s	59	2958	
69	2-7	York	6g/f	[57]	3436	p

53	9-20	Hayd	6fm	60	3796	p
52	8-15	Redc	6fm	58	4562	p
39	12-19	Ayr	6sft	57	5069	p

HAUNT THE ZOO 9 b m £582
0	5-5	Brig	8gd	[35]	1546
42a	8-15	Sout	8af	59	2338
58a	3-15	Sout	8af	59	2500
52a	8-15	Sout	8af	57	2725
29a	12-16	Sout	8af	55	3159

HAUNTING MEMORIES 2 b c £16653
84	4-5	Newm	6g/f		3586
99	1-9	YORK	6g/s		4026*
99	2-6	Leic	7gd		4699
97	3-9	Pont	7gd	[97]	5150

HAVANA ROSE 4 b f £0
0	16-16	Sout	8af	[30]	719	P
20a	8-10	Wolv	5af	[30]	781	p

HAVANTADOUBT 4 ch f £0
44	7-12	Folk	9.7sft	65	1273	
29	14-17	Kemp	10g/f	60	1913	
7	13-14	Folk	9.7g/s	55	3052	p
41	5-15	Folk	9.7g/f	[50]	4373	T
33	9-18	Warw	10.9g/s	48	4669	t
8	18-20	Kemp	12g/f	[45]	4796	t

HAVE FAITH 3 b f £1632
85	3-6	Ripo	8g/f	85	2525
77	6-10	Newb	8g/f	85	2877
64	6-6	Donc	8g/f	84	3597
30	7-8	Nott	10hvy	81	5187

HAVE SOME FUN 3 ch g £1692
38a	6-14	Sout	8af		170	
64a	3-12	Ling	8ap		401	
60a	2-9	Ling	10ap		476	
31	12-13	Newb	8fm	59	2647	
22	11-11	Bath	8gd	55	3142	
35a	13-13	Ling	7ap	59	3791	
18a	13-14	Ling	7ap	59	3821	BL

HAVETOAVIT 3 b g £9067
48	5-8	Thir	12g/s	[61]	1472
61	3-15	Ripo	12.3g/f	60	1785
66	2-8	Beve	12.1g/f	60	2164
63	4-7	Ripo	12.3g/f	65	2528
53	11-13	Redc	11g/s	63	2960
55	4-6	Thir	12g/f	60	3415
70	1-10	REDC	10g/f	58	3772*
70	2-14	Redc	10fm	65	4342
16	14-16	Ches	10.3g/f	65	4515
45	11-17	Newc	10.1g/f	65	5016

HAVOC 5 b g £0
0	9-10	Sout	8af	[50]	868

HAWAAJES 3 b g £6961
70	11-24	Newm	8fm		1495
75	3-10	Beve	7.5g/f		1832
77	1-16	HAYD	6g/f		2182*
76	4-7	Newm	6g/f	75	2764
31	12-12	Hayd	6sft	75	3273

HAWADETH 9 ch g £0
82	5-18	Kemp	16g/s	80	1112	p
62	17-29	Asco	20g/f	79	2471	p

HAWK 6 b g £0
40a	14-14	Ling	6ap	72	292	
30a	7-13	Ling	6ap	[69]	400	
8a	10-13	Wolv	6af	[65]	483	
0	11-12	Wolv	5af	60	641	P
2	11-11	Bath	5.7fm	[63]	2412	

HAWK ARROW 2 ch c £0
67	7-14	Leic	8gd		5059

HAWKES BAY 2 b c £872
56	10-13	Newm	6fm		4726
73	3-14	Leic	8gd		5059

HAWKIT 2 b g £10827
72a	2-13	Wolv	8.5af	[73]	43
73a	3-16	Sout	8af	[72]	192
70a	3-14	Sout	8af	[72]	226
69a	5-8	Wolv	8.5af	72	645

72a 2-9 Wolv 8.5af [72] 751
70a 1-10 WOLV 8.5af [69] 839*
61a 7-8 Ling 8ap [71] 934
67 1-8 HAMI 9.2gd [74] 1505*
81 2-14 Wind 10g/f 74 2452
71 7-10 Newm 8g/f [74] 2732
70 10-14 Newb 7af 78 3961
71 5-13 Ches 7.6sft 78 4103 T

HAWKS TOR 2 b c £0
56 6-7 Ayr 7.2g/s 2570

HAWRIDGE KING 2 b g £864
71 3-7 Leic 6g/f 1964
70 5-9 Warw 7.1fm 2776
58 6-11 Wind 8.3fm 3798
70a 5-14 Ling 7ap 70 4177
68 5-12 Sali 8sft 68 4580

HAWRIDGE PRINCE 4 b g £24434
85 1-19 NEWB 10gd 76 1736*
92 1-5 SALI 9.9gd 80 2694+
99 2-12 Kemp 10gd 90 3185
98 4-10 Asco 12gd 95 3777
108 2-7 Wind 11.6g/s [95] 4219
80 16-18 Newb 10gd 95 4681

HAWRIDGE SENSATION 2 ch g £0
51 7-10 Wind 8.3g/f 4831

HAWRIDGE STAR 2 b c £1128
81 6-8 Sali 7gd 2695
83 2-14 Sali 7sft 4575
51 12-16 Bath 8gd 5019

HAYDN 3 b c £393
79a 5-10 Sout 6af [85] 532
46 14-16 Kemp 6g/s 80 1116
0 17-17 Asco 6sft 77 1417
65 5-8 Good 6gd 73 2375
44 13-14 Yarm 7gd 70 2855
54 6-8 Newm 10g/f [65] 3471
0 12-12 Newm 10g/f 64 3785
0 14-14 Yarm 8g/s [62] 4252 VIS

HAYRAAN 2 b c £0
59 7-13 Newc 7g/f 5012
62 7-14 Yarm 7sft 5251

HAYSTACKS 8 b g £207
35 3-9 Ayr 13.1g/s [35] 1449 p
37 7-8 Muss 16gd 40 1793 p

HAZARISTA 3 b f £91619
110 1-9 CORK 10.2g/f 1857*
109 3-7 Curr 12g/f 3321
107 3-8 York 11.9g/s 4024

HAZE BABYBEAR 4 b f £0
26a 9-14 Sout 6af [56] 2502
18a 14-16 Sout 5af 54 2806
19a 6-10 Sout 5af [52] 3156 BL

HAZEWIND 3 gr g £25218
34a 11-14 Ling 6ap 449 T
67a 4-15 Ling 7ap [51] 670
57a 2-12 Ling 7ap 51 729 t
64a 1-10 LING 7ap [64] 765* t
56 7-13 Kemp 9gd 62 1141 t
6 17-17 Warw 7.1sft 60 1526
52 7-16 Leic 7g/f 58 1825 t
58 9-16 Ling 7g/f [58] 1982 VIS
59 2-10 Good 9.9gd 56 2225 vis t
62 5-11 Chep 10.2gd 56 2371 vis t
65 1-13 WARW 8.1gd 57 3058* t
70 1-11 NEWM 7g/f 65 3283* vis t
66 6-6 Newm 8g/f 65 3472 vis t
71 4-12 Newm 7gd 65 4225 vis t
74 1-17 YORK 7g/f 65 4398* vis t
69 6-7 Sali 8sft [65] 4581 vis t
74a 4-12 Wolv 8.6ap 70 4923 vis t
73a 4-12 Wolv 7.1ap 70 5008 vis t
73a 3-13 Wolv 9.5ap 70 5161 vis t
74a 3-12 Wolv 7.1ap [69] 5340 vis t

HAZYVIEW 3 b c £75221
88 2-18 Leic 10g/s 67 1017
88 1-14 NEWM 10g/f 73 1192*
92 1-9 SAND 10g/s 79 1318*

111 1-5 NEWM 10g/f [84] 1482*
106 2-4 Ling 11.5sft [84] 1622
114 1-6 NEWM 10g/f [103] 1931*
110 8-14 Epso 12fm [110] 2254
115 3-9 Mais 10sft [110] 3316
102 6-7 Arli 10fm [110] 4015

HE JAA 3 gr f £0
74 7-19 Newb 8gd 1236
2 P-9 Newm 10fm 1494

HE WHO DARES 5 b g £5929
59a 2-16 Ling 7ap 55 144
58a 2-14 Ling 10ap 57 339
54a 12-14 Ling 7ap 57 604
59a 3-13 Ling 10ap 57 726
57a 4-9 Ling 8ap 57 763
65 3-14 Pont 8hvy [60] 1253
64 1-14 LING 7sft 60 1625*
67 2-11 Bath 10.2fm 63 1899

HEAD BOY 3 ch g £2655
58a 4-15 Ling 7ap 59 337
31a 10-12 Ling 8ap 59 402
32a 12-12 Ling 8ap 58 603
53 5-15 Wind 6g/s 58 1054
50 6-16 Leic 8g/s 57 1359
41 5-9 Folk 7sft 57 1577
59 4-9 Epso 7gd 53 3218
60 2-13 Ling 7g/f 55 3604
57 8-15 Ling 7.6fm 59 3788
44 9-16 Brig 7sft [59] 4144
41 8-19 Chep 8.1g/s [59] 4366
57 6-13 Warw 7.1g/s [55] 4667
56a 3-12 Wolv 7.1ap [53] 5358

HEAD OF STATE 2 br g £5402
55a 1-5 WOLV 5af 40 237*
44a 8-10 Ling 5ap 54 371
26a 12-14 Sout 5af 52 485
61a 1-11 SOUT 6af 50 591* VIS
36a 8-8 Ling 6ap 56 673 vis
61a 3-11 Sout 6af 60 872 vis
36 10-15 Wind 6g/s 60 1054 vis
48a 9-11 Sout 5af 60 2380 vis
27 5-5 Ayr 6gd [57] 2541 vis

HEAD TO KERRY 4 b g £3530
19 17-18 Nott 14.1g/s 67 1772
58 8-10 Kemp 16fm 65 2073
53 9-11 Sand 14g/f 62 2391
58 3-11 Newb 13.3fm 58 2651
58 5-12 Warw 15g/f 58 2908
56 3-8 Newb 12g/f 57 3270 T
56 4-19 Chep 12.1gd 57 3398
57 2-7 Kemp 12g/f 55 3519 t
52 4-12 Kemp 14.4g/f 55 3688 t
55 5-17 Kemp 12sft 54 4033
56 4-12 Good 9.9sft 54 4268
41 9-16 Ches 10.3g/f 55 4515 P
48a 6-11 Wolv 12.2ap 55 5180

HEADLAND 5 b g £12439
52a 4-15 Sout 6af [71] 172 bl
65a 1-16 SOUT 6af [71] 227* bl
43a 4-8 Sout 7af [68] 320 bl
59a 2-8 Wolv 8.5af [68] 362 bl
48a 7-9 Sout 6af [60] 459 bl
52a 7-11 Wolv 7af 59 562 bl
57a 3-7 Sout 7af 59 589 bl
24a 11-12 Wolv 6af [57] 646 bl
43a 3-10 Wolv 7af [53] 890 bl
41a 9-15 Sout 7af 51 2501 bl e
25a 6-9 Sout 7af [49] 2801 bl e
53 2-20 Nott 6.1gd 49 2928 bl e
56a 2-9 Sout 6af 51 3485 bl e
59 1-13 THIR 7g/f 51 3571* bl e
50 5-15 Catt 7sft 55 3933 bl e
50a 5-13 Sout 6af 55 4091 bl e
63a 1-14 SOUT 6af 55 4130* bl e
46 11-18 Catt 7g/f 58 4438 bl e
59 5-19 Nott 6.1g/f [58] 4845 bl e
34 17-17 Ayr 7.2sft 57 5063 bl e

HEALEY 6 ch g £0
37 8-18 Pont 10g/f 48 2988
28 12-18 Pont 8gd 48 3242

38 7-19 Brig 9.9sft 45 4145

HEART OF ETERNITY 2 b f £324
49 14-15 Wind 5gd 1380
45 4-4 Ling 5g/s 1614
22 12-17 Wind 6g/f 3975

HEART SPRINGS 4 b f £1556
40 7-9 Hayd 11.9g/f 1885
48 8-13 Wind 10g/f 2453
39 10-12 Warw 15g/f 45 2908
45a 4-11 Ling 16ap 45 3450
41a 5-13 Ling 16ap 42 3822
46 2-15 Chep 18sft 40 4056
32 14-14 Warw 16.2g/f 45 4423
40 9-15 Good 16gd 45 5025

HEART STOPPING 2 b f £0
75 7-19 Newm 7g/s 5279

HEARTBEAT 3 b f £662
55a 4-14 Ling 6ap 449
37a 8-12 Ling 7ap [59] 566
2a 7-8 Wolv 8.5af 55 645 VIS
50 4-14 Sout 10g/s 52 1051
44 4-17 Beve 8.5g/s [52] 1160
47 5-15 Ripo 10g/f 47 1976
39 9-15 Leic 11.8gd 47 2134
28 7-11 Yarm 11.5g/f 45 2346 BL
43 3-13 Bath 8fm 41 2667 bl T

HEARTBREAKER 4 b g £0
7a 8-10 Sout 14af 39 3096

HEARTHSTEAD DREAM 3 ch g £17852
2 18-18 Thir 8g/f 72 1769
54 2D-4 Carl 11.9fm [69] 1952
61 2-10 Leic 8gd [69] 2133
66 1-8 HAMI 11.1g/f [65] 2319* BL
67 5-7 Hami 8.3g/f [62] 2474 bl
71 1-6 NEWC 12.4sft [63] 2686* bl
71 2-8 Hami 11.1g/f 68 3207 bl
74 1-10 RIPO 12.3g/f 68 3649* bl
71 3-3 Ripo 12.3g/s 71 3940 bl
71 3-9 Ripo 16gd 71 4308
73 4-12 Beve 12.1g/f 70 4601
74 3-20 York 13.9gd 69 5004
63 8-12 Redc 14.1g/s 69 5108 bl

HEARTHSTEAD WINGS 2 b c £60275
96 1-16 RIPO 6g/f 1780*
99 4-11 Asco 7fm 2578
96 6-12 Newm 7g/f 3060
105 1-6 GOOD 8g/f [99] 4524*
105 3-10 San 8sft [99] 5167

HEARTS DESIRE 3 b f £1656
73 6-10 Good 8gd 2224
72 2-7 Ches 7.6g/f [77] 3079
53 6-9 Redc 9fm [70] 4336
55 10-26 Redc 8fm 68 4926

HEARTSONFIRE 2 b f £3949
68 4-14 Leic 6g/f 3517
31 14-15 Nott 5.1gd 3988
67 7-15 Leic 7g/f 4455
48 4-10 Nott 6.1gd [67] 4858
68a 1-13 WOLV 6ap [63] 5182*

HEAT OF THE NIGHT 2 b f £2212
78 4-16 Kemp 7g/f 3035
61 9-13 Kemp 7g/f 3520
77 2-12 Warw 7.1g/f 4418
77 5-13 Redc 7fm [75] 4927

HEATHERS GIRL 5 ch m £6074
5a 11-12 Wolv 7af [46] 512
57a 1-9 WOLV 9.4af [40] 633*
37a 6-10 Wolv 8.5af 58 754
49a 2-7 Wolv 9.4af [58] 862
55 4-7 Warw 10.9g/s [45] 1326
53a 2-6 Sout 11af [54] 1754
54a 2-16 Sout 12af 50 2340
55a 4-9 Sout 12af [52] 2724
55a 2-8 Sout 12af 52 4128
39a 7-11 Wolv 12.2ap 50 5180

HEATHWOOD 2 b c £0
62a 9-14 Ling 7ap 4971

HEATHYARDS JOY 3 ch f £2034
29a 7-15 Sout 7af 462
19a 12-12 Wolv 7af 560
33a 4-6 Wolv 7af [30] 779
21a 4-5 Sout 8af [30] 986
34 2-6 Warw 7.1g/s [30] 1330
29 5-7 Brig 7gd [35] 1549
24 5-9 Kemp 6hvy [35] 1641
27a 6-9 Wolv 6af [35] 1803
33 8-15 Beve 7.5g/f [35] 1944
46 3-14 Beve 7.5g/s 32 3177
37 2-16 Thir 8g/f 3414

HEATHYARDS PRIDE 3 b c £10661
43a 4-14 Sout 12af 194
54a 1-8 WOLV 9.4af 299*
0 19-19 Warw 10.9sft 53 1090
47 4-14 Carl 7.9fm 50 1954
47 5-13 Bath 11.7gd 50 3145
57 1-13 WARW 10.9g/f 49 4419*
61 1-10 PONT 12g/f 52 4938*
67a 1-11 WOLV 12.2ap 58 5117*

HEATHYARDSBLESSING 6 b g £1091
46a 6-16 Sout 7af [50] 61
46a 2-15 Sout 6af [46] 167
57a 3-16 Sout 6af [46] 227
37a 8-13 Ling 6ap 46 451
28a 6-13 Wolv 6af [46] 483
41a 5-12 Wolv 6af [45] 524 P
6a 12-12 Wolv 6af [45] 646 p
48a 3-11 Sout 6af [45] 775
33a 5-10 Sout 6af [45] 907
44a 5-12 Wolv 6af [45] 960

HEAVENS WALK 3 ch c £833
50 5-9 Kemp 5g/f 3687
36 8-12 Kemp 6sft 4029
51 4-9 Good 5sft 4262
61a 3-12 Wolv 6ap [50] 5157

HEBENUS 5 b g £464
45 2-8 Ayr 7.2g/s [45] 1448
42 7-13 Hami 6g/f 45 2315
30 14-16 Carl 7.9g/f 45 3650
39 4-10 Ayr 6sft [45] 5278

HEDINGHAM KNIGHT 2 b c £0
60 6-10 Newm 5fm 2089
58 9-9 Newm 6g/f 2531

HEFIN 6 ch g £2331
65a 1-14 LING 16ap 59 107*
23a 10-12 Wolv 13.9ap 64 5160

HEIDELBURG 3 b f £1305
62a 6-16 Ling 7ap 63 22
66a 2-13 Wolv 6af 63 41
65a 3-11 Ling 8ap 65 136
60a 10-16 Ling 7ap 65 144
45a 9-11 Wolv 7ap 64 241 BL
56a 10-16 Ling 7ap 64 270

HEIDIS DASH 2 b f £375
66 8-10 Sali 5g/f 1716
60 4-6 Sand 5g/f 2097

HEIR TO BE 5 b g £224
71 5-11 Warw 15sft 74 1087
47 14-18 Newb 16gd 74 1232
69 6-17 Ripo 16g/s 72 1361

HEISSE 4 b c £0
93 5-8 Donc 12gd 950
68 14-18 Kemp 16g/s 97 1112
46 17-20 Epso 12hvy 95 1295 VIS
83 8-15 Donc 14.6fm 93 4491
77 11-17 Newm 12g/f 91 4889

HEKTIKOS 3 ch g £0
15a 8-9 Ling 13ap 62 18
0 11-11 Ling 12ap [57] 672
26a 11-12 Ling 8ap 50 1013
0 5-5 Ling 8ap [40] 1245

HELDERBERG 4 b f £0
30 19-20 Asco 8g/f 70 1927
64 5-15 Redc 9g/f 67 2120

48 6-6 Beve 8.5gd [66] 2514

HELEN HOUSE 2 b f £762
59 7-11 Newm 6sft 5265
75 3-17 Yarm 6g/s 5350

HELEN SHARP 2 ch f £0
57 11-16 Newm 7g/s 5280

HELIBEL 2 gr f £0
72a 4-10 Ling 5ap [73] 13
0 W-14 Warw 7.1gd [72] 4275

HELIOS QUERCUS 2 br c £126303
110 1-7 LONG 8g/s 4729*
95 1-8 SAIN 8Very 5315*

HELIXALOT 3 ch g £0
0 14-14 Ling 13ap 4898

HELLBENT 4 b g £211
38a 8-13 Sout 8af [50] 199
37a 8-10 Wolv 6af 48 379
3a 12-13 Wolv 6af [45] 582 BL
32a 11-15 Ling 7ap [40] 708
34a 9-13 Ling 6ap [40] 788
30a 5-12 Ling 8ap [35] 971
36a 6-14 Ling 10ap [35] 1072
35a 3-12 Ling 12ap [35] 1180
0 4-7 Chep 10.2sft [40] 1332
20a 6-8 Wolv 9.4af [35] 1561
29a 5-10 Ling 12ap [35] 1714

HELLO HOLLY 6 b m £0
34a 6-10 Ling 13ap 45 11
40a 6-14 Ling 16ap 41 107

HELLO ITS ME 3 ch g £13289
89 2-14 Newm 10g/f 83 1192
75 11-13 York 10.4sft 85 1664
88 2-14 Hayd 8.1gd 85 2903
90 5-8 Nott 8.2g/f 87 3421
88 4-10 Newm 10g/f 86 3615
90 3-11 Beve 9.9g/s 85 4239
83 5-8 Donc 12fm 87 4534
78 12-17 Newm 10g/f 87 4917

HELLO ROBERTO 2 b f £13816
78a 2-8 Sout 5af 77 169
75a 4-10 Ling 5ap 77 217
63a 7-7 Ling 7ap 79 368
77a 2-10 Ling 6ap 77 494
50a 8-10 Sout 6af [77] 532
76a 2-8 Ling 6ap 75 673
77a 5-8 Ling 5ap 75 818
70 3-8 Newc 5g/s 65 2731
64 9-15 Redc 5g/s 66 2961
76 1-10 CHES 5.1g/f 66 3080*
67 10-18 Carl 7ap 72 3228
51 20-21 Good 5fm 72 3567
56a 10-11 Ling 6ap 72 3744
54a 4-11 Sout 5af 69 4094
58 7-13 Ches 5.1g/f 71 4514
55 7-12 Sand 5gd [71] 4605
57 10-12 Redc 5sft [69] 5305

HELLO SID 3 ch c £0
2a 9-9 Ling 5ap 621 BL

HELLO TIGER 3 gr g £0
0 8-9 Sout 8af 983
0 19-19 Yarm 7g/s 1130
0 10-10 Sout 8af 2997
0 5-5 Yarm 7gd 3366 P

HELM 3 b c £292
53 10-15 Leic 10g/s 1358
70a 4-14 Ling 13ap 4898
57 6-11 Good 14gd 5029

HENESEYS LEG 4 b f £17145
71 1-15 WARW 8.1sft 60 1530*
75 1-7 LING 10g/f 65 2015*
79 1-5 CARL 9.3gd 70 2674*
70a 5-7 Ling 10ap 73 3287
79 3-8 Ripo 10g/s 77 3938
56 16-17 Thir 12fm 77 4377

HENNDEY 3 b g £2290

76 2-16 Newc 7sft 966
78 2-13 Folk 7g/s 1270

HENRIK 2 b c £36571
98 1-7 GOOD 6g/f 1848*
105 2-12 Newm 7g/f 3060
114 3-8 Donc 8sft 5216

HENRY AFRIKA 5 b g £0
72a 5-13 Wolv 9.4af 76 127 P
71a 7-13 Wolv 8.5af 73 439 p
0 12-12 Wolv 7af 72 704 p

HENRY HALL 8 b h £4697
93 3-7 Nott 5.1fm [93] 1004
75 10-13 Beve 5g/s [93] 1162
96 3-20 York 5g/s 93 1683
91 9-20 Epso 5fm 93 2253
95 3-13 York 5g/f 94 2359
64 10-11 Sand 5g/s 94 2894
92 8-12 Newm 5g/f 93 3279
77 15-20 Hayd 5fm 93 3792
87 7-14 Epso 5gd 91 4291
69 10-11 Hayd 5sft 89 4780
80 8-12 Epso 5g/f 86 4908
59 12-13 Muss 5g/s 83 5143

HENRY ISLAND 11 ch g £2104
59 5-9 Folk 15.4sft 69 1271
63 7-8 Bath 17.2fm 68 2035
60 4-7 Warw 16.2gd 65 3057
60 7-11 Sand 14g/f 61 3340
52 10-12 Sand 16.4g/f 60 3861
62 2-16 Warw 16.2gd 57 4276
54 10-15 Ches 15.9g/f 58 4512
55 4-20 Bath 17.2gd 57 4824
34 13-15 Good 16gd 55 5025

HENRY TUN 5 b g £4125
68a 3-12 Wolv 5af [56] 70 bl
52a 5-13 Wolv 5af 56 110 bl
49a 8-16 Sout 5af 58 183 bl
39a 13-16 Sout 5af 58 205 vis
47a 3-10 Wolv 5af [55] 286 vis
38a 5-9 Ling 5ap [52] 413 bl
30a 7-11 Wolv 5af 50 508 vis
56a 2-12 Sout 5af [47] 587 bl
57a 1-11 SOUT 5af [51] 775* bl
53a 3-9 Sout 5af [51] 793 bl
33a 7-12 Sout 5af 51 853 bl
53a 2-16 Sout 5ap 51 1046 p
29 7-12 Chep 5.1sft [40] 1336 p
38 7-18 Good 5g/f 40 1867 p
39 6-20 Beve 5g/f [40] 1948 p
40 8-11 Bath 5.7fm [41] 2412 p
30a 13-15 Sout 5af [52] 2803 p

HER OWN KIND 2 b f £5780
83 2-13 Redc 7fm 4927
90 1-11 DONC 8sft 5205*

HERE TO ME 3 ch f £9674
70 5-20 Newb 7g/f 72 1761
69 3-16 Ling 7g/f [70] 1982
71 4-17 Kemp 7gd 70 2174
64 4-6 Bath 8fm 69 2414
76 2-20 Newb 7fm 68 2650
75 1-9 WARW 6.1g/f [68] 2906*
74 3-9 Epso 7gd 72 3218
72a 5-11 Ling 6ap 72 3744
71 6-8 Good 7sft 72 4263
74 2-17 Warw 8.1g/s 70 4668
66a 8-12 Wolv 7.1ap 70 5008

HERENCIA 2 b c £868
53 11-13 Thir 6g/s 2689
45 7-8 Yarm 7g/f 3491
50 8-12 Thir 5g/s 3832
55 4-14 Thir 7g/f 4206
56 2-20 Leic 7g/f 52 4451 p
55 6-19 Redc 8sft 54 5302 p

HERES HARRY 4 b c £0
1 18-18 Wind 6g/f 1806
0 8-8 Sand 5gd 2361

HERES THE PLAN 2 b f £5005
80 1-10 NEWM 6gd 1887*

HERETIC and surrounding entries (race form index)

```
78  7-9   Newm  6g/f          2763
80  6-11  Newm  7fm    81     3407
70  10-13 Newc  7g/s   80     3698
76a 4-8   Wolv  8.6ap  [79]   5007

HERETIC  6 b g  £10003
109 1-7   THIR  8sft   [105]  1225*
73  4-4   Asco  8sft   [105]  1420
56  19-19 Newm  10g/f  105    3061
79  10-11 York  7g/s   [103]  4063 VIS

HERIOT  3 b g  £0
3   10-12 Kemp  8hvy          1511
23  9-10  Good  8gd           2378 BL
25  8-8   Warw  7.1fm         2575 VIS
62  7-10  Sali  8gd           3452 bl

HERMITAGE COURT  3 ch g  £6099
86  1-20  NEWM  8g/f          3237*
86  4-14  Newb  10g/f  84     3961
83  6-13  Epso  8.5gd  84     4469
77  12-17 Asco  8g/f   84     4777

HERNANDITA  6 b m  £536
65  4-13  Pont  17.1g/f 64    2276
52  15-29 Asco  20g/f  64     2471
59  6-12  Warw  15g/f  61     2908

HERNANDOS BOY  3 b g  £1153
51  5-8   Pont  10hvy         1067
41  9-12  Beve  9.9sft  62    1306
51  7-11  Redc  10sft   62    1663
44  12-13 Redc  11g/s   59    2960
59  2-10  Ripo  12.3g/f 55    3649

HERNE BAY  4 b g  £3790
64a 1-12  SOUT  16af   56     1753*
32  14-17 Nott  14.1g/f 62    2156
52  5-6   Ches  15.9g/f 60    3101 p

HERODOTUS  6 b g  £0
0   13-13 Epso  12fm   87     2255
2   12-12 Wind  11.6fm 82     2759
9   13-14 Sali  12g/s  75     3114 t
4   7-7   Sali  14.1gd [55]   4333 t
32a 12-13 Wolv  9.5ap  55     5361

HERONS WING  3 ch c  £0
57a 8-14  Ling  10ap          473

HES A DIAMOND  2 ch c  £4231
67  5-13  Sali  6fm           2287
80  1-8   BRIG  7gd           2952*
80  3-9   Brig  7gd           3297
68  8-11  Newb  7fm    77     3627
62  16-20 Ling  7gd    75     4444
24  15-20 Yarm  8g/s   75     4635

HES A ROCKET  2 b c  £8592
23a 12-13 Ling  6ap    [50]   25
20a 8-11  Wolv  6af    [50]   73
40a 3-12  Sout  6af    [40]   200 VIS
10a 6-9   Ling  6ap    [40]   327 vis
32  5-9   Leic  6g/s   [40]   1015 vis
56  1-8   FOLK  5g/s   [40]   1268* BL
61  1-9   MUSS  5g/s   46     1457* bl
68  3-10  Hami  5g/s   62     1605 bl
60  6-13  Hayd  5g/f   63     1881 bl
50  7-10  Hayd  5g/s   63     2227 bl
56  10-15 Redc  5g/s   62     2961 bl
55  6-15  Muss  5g/f   60     3561 bl
37  9-9   Wind  5fm    58     3804 bl
57  2-16  Catt  5sft   [58]   3932 P
56  7-10  Hami  5g/s   [58]   4010 p
28  16-17 Beve  5g/f   55     4603 bl
48  9-19  Ling  5g/f   55     4739 bl
34  15-17 Bath  5.7gd  [52]   5020 bl

HES A STAR  2 ch c  £0
52  9-18  Chep  6.1gd         2194
62  4-5   Brig  5.3g/f        2430
67  7-18  Wind  6gd           2618
62  6-11  Newb  7fm    62     3627
62  6-20  Ling  7g/f   61     4741
61  9-17  Good  8gd    61     4871

HEVERSHAM  3 b c  £9582
65a 4-9   Wolv  7af           381
90a 1-12  LING  8ap           623*

85a 2-5   Ling  8ap    79     694
74  7-9   Kemp  9sft   [82]   947
75  7-7   Thir  8g/f   [80]   1770
62  9-11  Pont  8g/f   78     2040
72  4-8   Brig  7fm    [74]   2259
78  2-8   Yarm  8g/f   [73]   2854
70  5-7   Pont  10g/f  [73]   2994
52  7-9   Donc  8g/s   73     3378
8   17-17 Newc  7g/s   71     3700
63  7-20  York  7.9gd  67     4321
63  7-19  York  7.9g/f 67     4399
68  2-16  Thir  8g/f   65     4592
69  2-17  Beve  8sft   65     4721
32  23-26 Redc  8fm    66     4926
54  12-18 Newm  8sft   66     5272

HEY PRESTO  4 b g  £10351
62  14-19 Kemp  6fm    74     2070
64  10-12 Sali  6fm    72     2289
61  9-12  Sali  5gd    69     2698
69  5-10  Kemp  6g/f   69     2861
68  6-14  Leic  6g/f   69     3213
75  1-25  ASCO  7g/f   69     3443*
55  19-20 Newm  7g/f   73     3782
15  13-13 Kemp  7sft   73     4030
60  18-21 Donc  7fm    72     4482
63  9-16  Good  7gd    71     4873

HEYBROOK BOY  2 ch c  £1366
50  8-20  Newc  6sft          2682
74  4-15  Pont  6gd           3239
79  2-8   Muss  7.1g/f        3559

HEYWARD PLACE  4 b f  £0
0   12-12 Sout  7af           416
0   18-19 Yarm  8g/f          1130 T
0   10-10 Folk  9.7sft        1580 t

HEZAAM  3 b c  £28258
65  12-20 Newm  7g/f   78     1186
76  5-18  Thir  8g/f   77     1769
69  8-10  Good  9.9gd  75     2225
86  1-16  SAND  10g/s  74     2919*
86  1-3   RIPO  12.3g/s 79    3940*
84  2-9   Good  12sft  80     4183
75  4-7   Hayd  14sft  84     4778
57  9-13  Bath  11.7sft 82    5174

HI DARL  3 ch f  £0
31  10-12 Hayd  8.1gd  56     2904
27  13-13 Leic  7g/f   54     3346
18  13-18 Chep  7.1g/s 50     3900
32  8-15  Carl  5fm    [45]   4508
30  16-17 Kemp  7g/f   [45]   4794
8   16-20 Yarm  6g/s   [40]   5121
38  5-10  Ayr   6sft   [35]   5278

HIAMOVI  2 b c  £1266
41  11-11 Nott  5.1gd         1237
52a 5-10  Sout  7af           2802
63a 2-14  Sout  6af           4127
52  12-19 Ling  6ap    [64]   4895
27a 10-12 Wolv  6ap    [60]   5177

HIATS  2 b c  £0
38  13-15 Donc  5gd           920
47  6-6   Redc  5sft          1143
22  10-10 Newc  5g/f          2158

HIAWATHA  4 b g  £13594
1a  12-13 Wolv  9.4af  71     127
67a 1-9   WOLV  9.4af  [66]   239*
58a 4-9   Sout  11af   66     391
78a 1-6   WOLV  9.4af  [66]   423*
76a 3-13  Ling  10ap   76     519
76a 7-14  Ling  10ap   76     625
72a 7-11  Ling  8ap    [76]   800
74  1-7   AYR   10g/f         2030*
71  7-14  Wind  10g/f  75     2265
52  5-9   Ches  10.3g/s [75]  2745
0   7-7   Hami  9.2g/s  72    3879
2   20-20 Wolv  12g/f   72    4656

HIBERNATE  10 ch g  £0
10  12-13 Beve  12.1g/f [45]  1945
31  6-8   Muss  12g/f  40     2616
39  4-10  Muss  12g/f  40     2813
22  10-11 Catt  12g/f  [39]   3190

28  13-20 Catt  12g/f  39     3354
30  5-7   Muss  13g/f  37     3530

HICCUPS  4 b g  £15097
83  2-9   Thir  5g/s   [80]   1217 p
50  13-17 Donc  6g/s   81     1523 p
82  3-19  Thir  6g/f   81     1767 p
82  1-8   DONC  6g/f   [80]   2074* p
62  10-17 Redc  6gd    82     2561 p
77  6-17  Pont  6g/f   81     2990 p
73  3-11  Donc  6g/f   [80]   3375 p
79  3-19  Ripo  6g/s   79     3937
71  9-16  Muss  5g/f   78     4174

HICKERTHRIFTCASTLE  5 ch g  £0
0   12-15 Wind  11.6g/f       2267

HIDDEN CHANCE  2 ch f  £5712
70  7-16  Kemp  7g/f          3035
71  1-15  FOLK  7gd           3381*
51  11-13 Newm  6g/f   72     4193
69  8-20  Ling  7gd    70     4444
73  4-16  Nott  10g/f  67     4848
54  11-19 Pont  8g/s   67     5147

HIDDEN DRAGON  5 b g  £10645
104a2-15 Ling  7ap    97     887
106a2-8  Ling  7ap    [100]  1043
93  11-20 Asco  7g/f   100    1926
77  10-11 Donc  7g/f   98     2076
91  6-19  Ripo  6g/s   96     3937
92  4-12  Leic  5g/f   [94]   4454
90  7-24  Ayr   6sft   94     4686
81  9-14  Ripo  6gd    90     4786 P

HIDDEN HOPE  3 ch f  £60338
80  2-18  Wind  8.3g/s        1258
106 1-9   CHES  11.4gd [75]   1568*
104 5-9   Asco  12g/f  [106]  2517
107 4-8   Hayd  11.9gd[106]   2946
107 2-12  Deau  12.5g/s[106]  3837
104 3-8   Asco  12g/f  [109]  4774

HIDDEN JEWEL  2 ch c  £10780
17  18-18 Leic  5fm           2109
48a 6-11  Sout  6af           2336
47a 6-10  Sout  7af           2802
61  9-11  Thir  7fm    [48]   4381
93  2-21  Donc  6hvy          5202
79  3-14  Nott  6.1hvy [82]   5342

HIDDEN STAR  2 br c  £551
72  3-6   Wind  6fm           2783
68  6-15  Pont  6gd           3239

HIDDENSEE  2 b c  £0
34  13-14 Leic  8gd           5058

HIGGYS PRINCE  2 b c  £0
37  10-15 Warw  5g/s          1325
53  7-8   Kemp  7gd           2171

HIGH ACCOLADE  4 b c  £113448
118 4-11  Epso  12g/f  [116]  2209
115 2-6   Asco  12fm   [116]  2579
116 3-8   Asco  12g/f  [116]  3030
116 8-11  Asco  12g/f  [116]  3442
113 2-7   Colo  12gd   [116]  4018 vis
109 4-8   Donc  18fm   [115]  4478 vis T
116 1-9   ASCO  12g/f  [114]  4812* vis t

HIGH ACTION  4 ch g  £21455
75  15-20 Newm  12gd   95     1172
52  15-20 Donc  10.3g/s 90    1519
81  8-17  Asco  16.2gd  85    3125 T
93  1-7   NEWM  14.8g/f 82    3475* t
89  1-3   CHES  18.7fm  85    3635* t
91  8-20  Hayd  14fm    90    4383 t
87  5-15  Donc  14.6fm  90    4491 t

HIGH CANE  4 ch f  £552
9a  12-13 Ling  10ap   [67]   715
67  3-16  Newc  7sft   [65]   966
3   17-17 Thir  8g/s   63     1214
0   20-20 Newc  6sft   60     1393
30  12-15 Redc  7sft   56     1660
0   15-15 Sout  8af    52     2338

HIGH CARD  2 b g  £2072
```

65a 8-14 Ling 7ap 4970
65a 6-12 Wolv 8.6ap 5115
83 2-15 Newb 8hvy 5221

HIGH CHART 2 b f £4971
77 1-15 WIND 5gd 1380*
77 4-6 York 6sft 1669
78 4-8 Wind 5g/f 1955
81 12-17 Asco 5g/f 2490
65 3-6 Yarm 5.2gd 3488
71 8-11 Newm 6g/f 82 3614
64 6-12 Wind 6gd 76 3825 T
63 14-20 Ling 7gd 73 4444
41 25-26 Newb 6.5g/f 4679
47 15-18 Wind 5g/f 67 4830 t
43 10-14 Wind 8.3g/f [62] 5049 t

HIGH CHARTER 3 b g £0
49 9-12 Nott 10hvy 5190

HIGH CLASS PET 4 b f £0
28 12-16 Ripo 8gd 2987
23 6-9 Newc 9g/s 3697

HIGH DAWN 2 b c £0
69 6-8 Wind 5g/s 1053

HIGH DIVA 4 b f £0
16a 10-13 Wolv 8.5af [48] 46
38a 6-12 Ling 10ap [45] 267 P
34a 6-13 Ling 10ap [45] 412 p
39a 4-11 Sout 12af 45 458
3a 6-7 Sout 16af 40 529
23a 5-12 Wolv 9.4af [40] 668
2a U-12 Ling 8ap [40] 710
38a 5-11 Ling 8ap [35] 786

HIGH DRAMA 7 b g £4732
43 1-14 BATH 18.2fm 34 2417*
40 2-15 Folk 16.4g/s 38 3049
42 4-17 Pont 17.1g/f 40 3970

HIGH DYKE 2 b c £0
62 7-10 Leic 6gd 2703
62 5-11 Warw 5g/f 2911
67 6-18 Leic 7g/f 3342
72 5-17 Warw 7.1gd 4271
70 7-9 Warw 7.1g/s 72 4666

HIGH ESTEEM 7 b g £0
13a 14-16 Sout 6af 60 92
45a 4-7 Sout 6af [58] 317 P
24a 8-9 Sout 6af [56] 487 p
31a 9-13 Sout 6af [53] 3482 VIS
18 14-16 Catt 5sft [47] 3932 BL

HIGH FINANCE 4 b f £309
58 5-7 Muss 7.1g/f [79] 1094
82 6-7 Asco 7g/f [79] 1925
53a 14-14 Ling 7ap 77 4180

HIGH FLASH 3 ch c £6426
107 3-6 Chan 9gd 3657

HIGH FREQUENCY 3 ch c £0
68 10-17 Newm 8gd 1166
68 6-10 Good 8g/f 1815
66 7-17 Chep 8.1gd 2117

HIGH HOPE 5 ch h £439
73a 11-14 Ling 12ap 80 83
80a 3-16 Ling 12ap 78 218 BL e
75a 7-16 Ling 12ap 78 293 bl e
68 5-7 Good 14sft 71 4267 P

HIGH JINKS 8 b g £0
28a 5-15 Sout 16af 39 67
26a 7-13 Ling 16ap 37 137
2a 11-16 Sout 16af 37 206 P

HIGH MINDED 2 b c £0
66 7-12 Ripo 5g/f 1974
35 6-8 Ayr 5gd 2505

HIGH PETERGATE 2 b f £0
65 5-12 Ripo 5g/f 1974
61 4-10 Redc 5fm 4338
42 10-18 Ayr 6g/s 4617
36 16-18 Pont 6g/f 62 4934

HIGH POINT 5 b g £34858
82a 1-14 LING 12ap 76 83*
58a 15-16 Ling 12ap 80 293
79a 7-16 Ling 12ap 80 404
62a 7-16 Ling 12ap 79 475
82a 2-11 Ling 16ap 77 605
84 3-18 Kemp 16g/s 79 1112
83 3-18 York 13.9g/s 80 1689
83 3-10 Kemp 16fm 80 2073
80 6-12 Newm 16.1g/f 80 3032
65 12-13 Asco 16.2g/f 79 3387
77 5-17 Newm 14.8gd 77 4196
85 1-13 YARM 16g/s 75 4634+
88 3-34 Newm 18sft 78 5135

HIGH POLICY 7 ch g £535
57a 5-12 Wolv 16.2af 66 7 p
46a 6-14 Sout 14af 65 185 p
65a 4-8 Sout 16af 64 554 p
65a 3-13 Sout 14af 64 2494

HIGH REACH 4 b g £22052
88 3-20 Kemp 6gd 89 1138
91 6-30 Newm 6gd 89 1481
94 3-29 Asco 6fm 89 2581
88 7-11 Newb 6g/f 91 2878
98 3-28 Good 6fm 91 3622
98 9-11 Newb 5.2g/f [94] 4678
88 10-15 Newm 6g/f [94] 4879
92a 10-14 Ling 7ap 94 5262

HIGH RESERVE 3 b f £6435
70 3-17 Newm 8gd 4228
78 1-7 SALI 8sft [70] 4581*

HIGH RHYTHM 2 b f £0
59 6-13 Wind 6g/f 5048

HIGH RIDGE 5 ch g £24374
11 9-10 Warw 6.1hvy 58 1533 p
64 1-18 BATH 5.7g/f 55 1788* p
62 5-14 Chep 7.1gd 60 2199 p
74 1-6 BATH 5.7fm 60 2416* p
71 2-17 Wind 6g/f 66 2451 p
70 3-9 Warw 5.5fm 68 2779 p
65 4-12 Bath 5.7gd 69 3146 p
74 1-7 PONT 6gd [69] 3244* p
72 2-7 Leic 6g/f [69] 3518 p
72 2-26 Good 6fm 68 3569 p
71 4-17 Wind 6fm 69 3643 p
62 10-19 Good 6gd 71 4747 p
63 11-20 Wind 6g/s 70 4946 p
46 14-19 Wind 6gd 70 5053 p

HIGH SCHOOL 3 b f £2554
70 2-9 Folk 9.7sft 980
68 6-8 Folk 12sft 1272
71 4-11 Beve 9.9g/f 1835
74 2-14 Wind 10gd 68 2617
57 6-8 Brig 11.9g/f 72 3299

HIGH TREASON 2 ch c £0
66 12-14 Newm 7g/f 2766
79 8-11 Donc 8fm 4462
45 21-23 Newm 7g/f 4885
52 11-11 York 7.9gd 5003

HIGH VIEW 3 ch c £0
28 7-12 Kemp 8hvy 1511
42 16-17 Newb 10gd 1737
55 9-18 Wind 10g/f 1959
30 13-14 Hayd 8.1g/s 2231
0 10-10 Folk 12g/s 58 3051
26 11-14 Good 8sft 54 4189
0 13-13 Warw 12.6g/s [49] 4665

HIGH VOLTAGE 3 ch g £25847
99 1-14 RIPO 6g/s 91 1360* t
99 3-9 Hayd 6g/f [99] 1918 t
100 6-20 York 6gd 99 2407 t
88 7-9 Newm 5fm 98 2593 t
83 17-19 Newm 6fm 96 3002 t
85 8-10 Asco 6gd 94 3778
101 1-14 CHES 6.1g/f 92 4048* t
64 21-22 Donc 5.6fm 96 4459 t
51 12-12 Hayd 6sft 96 4779 t

HIGHBURY LASS 2 ch f £0

0 12-12 Ripo 5g/f 1974
28 6-7 Redc 7fm 2294
19 10-15 Catt 7sft 3930

HIGHER LOVE 2 b f £1715
67 6-13 Leic 8g/f 4450
72 2-8 Hayd 8.1sft 4782

HIGHEST 5 b h £0
83 7-10 York 13.9g/s 1705
112 7-13 Asco 20g/f [115] 2518 T

HIGHEST REGARD 2 b c £0
52a 7-11 Wolv 7.1ap 5228
70 7-17 Yarm 6g/s 5350

HIGHEST RETURN 2 b c £425
74 4-7 Ayr 7.2g/f 3302
49 11-12 Good 7fm 3568

HIGHFLUTING 3 b f £0
7a 13-14 Ling 10ap 759
27 9-9 Sali 9.9g/f 1719
0 16-16 Bath 10.2g/f 1790
0 7-7 Brig 11.9g/f 1939

HIGHLAND CASCADE 2 ch f £8238
77 1-11 YARM 6g/f 1727*
80 3-5 Yarm 6g/f 2341
76 2-6 Wind 6fm 2783
75 8-21 Donc 6.5fm 78 4457
79 3-13 Leic 6g/f 75 4697
72 8-29 Newm 6gd 5087

HIGHLAND DIVA 2 ch f £823
80 4-16 Sali 7gd 4330

HIGHLAND GAMES 4 b g £12019
87 2-5 Muss 14g/s 85 1459
49 13-18 York 13.9g/s 85 1689
92 2-9 Thir 12g/f 85 1969
91 4-9 Newm 12g/f [87] 2246
88 5-13 Asco 12fm 87 2582
93 3-8 Newm 12g/f [87] 3617
91 3-10 Asco 16.2gd 87 3776
72 13-15 Donc 14.6fm 90 4491
0 P-16 Asco 16.2g/f 89 4803

HIGHLAND LASS 3 b f £0
45 8-13 Wind 6fm 2756
39 10-10 Ling 6g/s 3446
50 6-10 Newb 7gd 3921
45 10-17 Wind 6gd 58 4126
22 13-14 Catt 6gd 55 4967

HIGHLAND REEL 7 ch g £14267
93 1-18 GOOD 8g/f 85 1812*
78 11-14 Sand 8.1g/f 87 2096
52 26-31 Asco 12g/f 87 2489
84 4-13 Sali 8gd 87 2662
79 9-18 Newb 8g/f 86 3265
89 3-19 Good 8g/f 85 3512
86 3-9 Kemp 8g/f [85] 3689
61 4-9 Good 9sft [87] 4266

HIGHLAND WARRIOR 5 b h £16278
64 3-19 Newc 6sft 62 967
68 3-13 Muss 7.1g/f 63 1122
66 2-13 Newc 5sft 63 1276
68 3-20 Thir 5g/s 63 1476
62 4-12 Hami 6g/s [65] 1600
76 1-14 AYR 6g/f 66 1898*
75 6-15 Muss 5fm 73 2084
73 7-12 Newc 6gd 73 2160
66 8-13 Hami 5gd 73 2320
71 4-11 Ayr 6gd 73 2542
74 6-18 Newc 6g/s 73 2770
70 6-13 Hayd 6gd 73 2884
74 3-9 Ayr 6g/f 72 3307
35 15-15 Newc 6gd 72 3424
75 2-7 Ayr 6hvy 71 4087
67 6-15 Ayr 5g/s 71 4654
70 4-19 Ayr 6gd 70 5069
73 2-12 Redc 5sft [69] 5305
63 6-11 Muss 5g/s 69 5332

HIGHLIGHT GIRL 3 ch f £0
47 14-20 Wind 10sft 1651
38 9-11 Chep 8.1g/f 2627

HILARIOUS 4 b f £275
37 5-14 Warw 8.1hvy 51 1535
47a 4-12 Wolv 7af 49 2049
44 5-14 Leic 8g/f 47 2402
33a 6-13 Sout 8af 45 3094
42 4-12 Wind 10ap 44 3295
33a 9-14 Ling 10ap 44 3605 P
27 6-14 Chep 10.2g/s 43 3895 p
30 8-10 Brig 7sft 43 4168 BL
32 12-15 Folk 12g/f [40] 4374 bl
16 13-19 Brig 9.9gd [40] 4903

HILBRE ISLAND 4 b c £6025
110 3-6 Nott 14.1fm[111] 1005
77 16-17 Newb 12gd [111] 1230
0 P-13 Asco 16.2sft[110] 1418 BL
111 5-9 Sand 16.4g/f[110] 2095
92 9-9 Good 16fm [110] 3552

HILITES 3 ch f £4416
83 3-7 Kemp 6hvy [83] 1513
50 11-11 Newb 6gd 83 1734
81 3-10 Leic 6gd [82] 2137
68 10-16 Leic 5g/f 82 2400
81 6-9 Newm 7fm 80 3006
75 3-7 Chep 7.1gd [79] 3402
62 9-12 Good 9fm 79 3535
69 4-7 Epso 8.5fm 79 3542
66 9-15 Newb 6gd 76 3920
70 8-14 Epso 7gd 74 4465 P
54 14-26 Ayr 6g/s 74 4652 p
62a 6-12 Wolv 6ap 71 5291 p

HILL FAIRY 2 ch f £378
74 6-12 Hami 6gd 2178
72 4-7 Nott 8.2gd 3991
55 5-8 Hayd 8.1sft 4782

HILLABILLA 2 b f £0
21 15-17 Chep 6.1sft 4052
46 16-16 Sali 7gd 4330

HILLS OF ARAN 2 b c £11000
102 4-8 Donc 8sft 5216

HILLS OF GOLD 5 b g £16156
66 4-13 Redc 7sft [66] 1142
75 1-20 RIPO 8g/s 66 1366+
66 7-18 Newc 7sft 71 2684
75 3-10 York 7.9g/s 71 3074
77 2-9 Donc 8g/s 71 3225
76 2-6 Beve 9.9gd [71] 3313
78 1-16 CHES 7g/f 74 4051*
77 4-10 Hami 8.3g/s 74 4136
77 6-15 Hayd 8.1g/f 78 4352
78 6-18 Ayr 7.2sft 77 4689
38 19-20 York 8.9gd 76 4999
57 12-16 Catt 7sft 75 5130

HILLS SPITFIRE 3 b c £894
84 3-11 Pont 10g/f 2991

HILLSIDE HEATHER 2 ch f £8219
70 4-7 Redc 5gd 2547
70 3-5 Pont 5g/f 2789
72 2-10 Ripo 5gd 2983
60 7-11 Ripo 5g/s 3258
71 2-10 Beve 5gd 3504
71 4-9 Redc 6g/f 69 3807
65 5-10 Ches 5.1g/f 69 4049
45 7-10 Beve 5sft 67 4258 P
57 6-14 Redc 5fm 64 4556 p
76 1-10 MUSS 5g/f [61] 4804* p

HILLTIME 4 b g £588
53 9-20 Thir 6gd 65 1638
27 13-18 Thir 6g/f 62 2214
44 8-14 Newc 5g/s 58 2775
45 10-16 Redc 8g/s 53 2958
51 3-10 Nott 8.2g/f 51 3579
36 15-16 Redc 7g/f 50 3809

HILLTOP FANTASY 2 b f £0
54a 4-11 Ling 7ap 213

HILLTOP RHAPSODY 3 b f £4622
33 15-17 Newm 8gd 1166
47 9-16 Donc 10.3gd 2751

71 1-14 WIND 8.3fm 2974*
46 14-17 Hayd 10.5fm 69 4388
72 4-14 Wind 8.3g/f 69 4832

HILLY BE 3 b f £0
3 8-8 Warw 8.1sft 1086

HINCHLEY WOOD 5 b g £360
46a 6-12 Ling 7ap 566
0 10-12 Wolv 9.4af [40] 668
37a 7-15 Ling 7ap [40] 708
0 10-14 Ling 10ap [40] 784
32a 5-15 Ling 7ap [35] 830
39a 5-9 Ling 6ap [35] 1012
49a 4-12 Ling 7ap [35] 1074 BL
36a 2-6 Ling 6ap [35] 1184 bl
34a 6-9 Ling 6ap [45] 1248 bl

HINODE 3 ch c £416
52 14-17 Newm 8gd 1166
58 17-24 Newm 8fm 1495
66a 3-11 Sout 8af 3091
54 5-5 Brig 11.9sft 63 4166
60 4-11 Yarm 11.5g/s [60] 4584
33 18-19 Sali 14.1gd 60 4856
44 7-15 Leic 11.8gd [57] 5060

HIP HOP HARRY 3 b c £10446
74a 3-14 Ling 10ap 72 122
76a 1-13 LING 10ap 72 178*
49a 8-9 Sout 11af 76 391
84a 2-15 Ling 12ap 75 549
86a 1-11 LING 10ap 77 716* VIS
89a 2-14 Ling 12ap 83 731 vis
33 18-19 Newm 12g/f 86 1484
46 14-14 Leic 10g/f 82 1828 vis
54 5-6 Pont 12gd 80 3681

HIRAYNA 5 b m £1358
39 3-4 Redc 11gd 2549
50 8-14 Warw 7.1g/f 2907
62 4-7 Ches 7.6g/f 3079
49 4-14 Bath 8g/f 50 3963
34 8-19 Brig 9.9sft 50 4145
41 11-19 Beve 9.9g/f 48 4720
2 16-19 Kemp 8g/f [48] 4795

HIS MAJESTY 2 ch c £1129
5a 10-10 Ling 5ap 882
45 3-4 Folk 5gd 3382
63 2-5 Yarm 6gd 3871
55 6-9 Yarm 6sft 62 4146
44 13-20 Leic 7g/f 60 4451

HISPANIOLA 5 ch m £0
12a 10-12 Wolv 7af 60 129
1a 10-12 Wolv 12af 55 244

HISTORIC PLACE 4 b g £3374
74 2-13 Hayd 11.9g/s 2230
72 4-13 Sali 9.9gd 2700
87 8-9 Newm 12g/f 3233
81 3-8 Ayr 17.5g/s 80 4657
77 15-34 Newm 18sft 80 5135
66 6-7 Donc 16.5sft 79 5374

HITS ONLY CASH 2 b c £516
51 6-6 Carl 5g/f 3652
59 7-10 Hayd 5gd 3755
65 5-18 Ayr 6g/s 4617
62 7-12 Hayd 6sft 4770
62 4-8 Yarm 5.2sft 63 5253
64 5-16 Nott 5.1hvy 63 5343

HITS ONLY MONEY 4 br g £0
81 8-10 Warw 7.1gd [98] 1126
81 15-18 Good 8g/f 97 1812
75 9-11 Donc 7g/f 95 2076
69 14-18 Newc 7sft 92 2684
63 7-8 Pont 6gd 90 3461
70 7-11 Hayd 6gd [90] 3758

HOBART JUNCTION 9 ch g £0
0 19-19 Chep 12.1gd 37 3727

HOH BLEU DEE 3 b g £8982
69 10-12 Good 7g/f 88 1847
79 6-13 Sand 8.1g/s [84] 2126
66 15-16 Sand 10g/s 82 2919

76 2-10 Asco 8gd [82] 3067
76 1-7 SALI 8gd [75] 3453* BL
65 9-15 Brig 8fm 75 3694
58 4-14 Newm 7gd [75] 4195 bl
49 8-10 Sali 12sft [73] 4579

HOH HEDSOR 2 ch f £0
55 12-19 Leic 7gd 5040
50 12-16 Newb 8hvy 5220

HOH HOH HOH 2 ch c £4401
95 1-7 BATH 5.7fm 1900*

HOH MY DARLING 2 br f £402
61 7-10 Newm 7gd 4191
65 4-10 Wind 8.3g/f 4831
58 7-12 Redc 8g/s 5107

HOH NELSON 3 b c £920
71 3-11 Ripo 8gd 1177
37 9-9 Wind 11.6g/f 70 1807
57 8-10 Leic 11.8gd [70] 2707
62 6-15 Chep 18sft 65 4056
64 2-20 Good 16g/s 62 4235

HOH VISS 3 b g £0
68a 5-15 Ling 12ap [72] 118
58a 10-16 Ling 12ap 70 218

HOHS BACK 4 b g £1136
44a 7-14 Sout 8af 66 99 p
45a 7-13 Wolv 8.5af 64 251 p
33a 9-10 Sout 8af 62 387 p
37a 9-12 Wolv 8.5af 59 564 p
22a 12-15 Sout 8af 55 1028 p
63 2-17 Thir 8g/s 60 1214 p
20a 9-10 Wolv 8.5af 51 1322 p
58 6-13 Muss 7.1gd 63 1553 p
28a 10-15 Sout 8af 51 1755 p
40 7-10 Newc 8g/f 63 2159 p
38a 5-15 Sout 8af 48 2338 p
13a 10-13 Sout 8af 48 2497 p
44 11-11 Warw 8.1fm 60 2600 p
32 13-16 Beve 7.5gd 60 2655 p
30 14-15 Ches 7.6g/f 57 3102 p
45 7-13 Muss 8g/f 54 3526 p
43 7-12 Newc 9hvy 51 4215 p
39 8-15 Thir 8fm [49] 4379 p
42 5-17 Carl 7.9fm [45] 4506 p

HOLBECK GHYLL 2 ch c £1441
83 3-18 Chep 6.1gd 2194
66 8-9 Asco 5g/f 2516
75 3-13 Carl 5gd 2670

HOLD THE LINE 2 b g £1463
43a 7-13 Wolv 8.5af [70] 43
68a 5-12 Ling 10ap [67] 120
62a 6-8 Ling 10ap [67] 626 P
68a 1-12 SOUT 8af [65] 848* p
53a 6-14 Sout 8af 65 1198 p

HOLD UP 3 ch f £0
52 7-7 Newm 10g/f 2534
30 10-17 Wind 11.6fm 2788
62 7-8 Newm 10fm 3007
50 7-12 Wind 8.3fm 60 3291
50 8-11 Yarm 7g/f 57 3711
45 9-16 Bath 8gd 53 4828
19 15-19 Yarm 8g/s [50] 5119

HOLDERNESS GIRL 11 b m £0
0 6-6 Pont 8g/f [30] 2037
0 13-13 Sout 8af 25 2497

HOLIDAY CAMP 2 b c £920
79 3-14 Newb 6sft 5197

HOLIDAY COCKTAIL 2 b g £0
32 9-12 Beve 5g/f 4596

HOLLINGWOOD SOUL 2 ch f £0
35 7-11 Beve 5g/f 1831
25 9-11 Thir 6g/f 1968
18 9-13 Beve 5g/s 2321
36 10-14 Beve 7.5sft 2939
16 12-13 Catt 7g/f 3349

HOLLOW JO 4 b g £424

48	15-15	Sout	7gd		72	1282
64	9-19	Leic	6g/s		72	1354
64	4-14	Kemp	5g/f		69	1914
45	9-12	Leic	6fm		68	2111

HOLLY ROSE 5 b m £1842

23	10-15	Folk	6g/s	55	1267 p
53	2-12	Brig	9.9fm	52	1695 p
52	4-11	Bath	10.2fm	52	1899 p
22	13-13	Pont	10g/f	54	2038 p
54	4-12	Warw	10.9fm	52	2436 p
53	4-12	Ling	10g/f	52	2844 p
55	2-14	Folk	9.7g/s	52	3052 p
35	16-19	Beve	9.9g/f	53	3505 VIS
4a	13-14	Ling	10ap	50	3605
1	11-19	Brig	9.9sft	53	4145 p

HOLLY SPRINGS 2 b f £3236

84	2-15	Kemp	6g/f		4357
84	11-26	Newb	6.5g/f		4679
82	2-13	Wind	6g/f		5048

HOLLY WALK 3 ch f £3325

10	11-16	Redc	8sft	50	1147
65	2-4	Beve	12.1sft	[50]	1308 BL
38	5-10	Nott	14.1hvy	48	1612 bl
43	5-13	Beve	12.1g/f	46	1836 bl
50	4-14	Redc	10fm	46	2299 VIS
49a	3-15	Sout	12af	46	2503 P
53a	2-11	Sout	12af	46	2804 p
3	13-14	Catt	12g/f	50	3192 p
30a	3-8	Sout	12af	50	4092 p

HOLLYWOOD CRITIC 3 b g £583

41	8-15	Ayr	8gd		2504
41	8-9	Hayd	10.5gd		2901
45	5-8	Hami	8.3fm		3246
62	3-6	Hami	11.1sft	[47]	4011

HOLLYWOOD HENRY 4 b g £3822

58	1-17	WARW	8.1fm	54	2440* P
29	6-6	Epso	8.5g/s	56	3042 p
47	5-12	Kemp	8gd	56	3524 p
56a	4-12	Ling	8ap	[55]	5077 p
50a	4-13	Wolv	9.5ap	[55]	5338 p

HOLY ORDERS 7 b h £28935

102	4-12	Asco	22.2fm		2583 bl
111	1-11	FAIR	14g/s	[110]	4162* bl
111	5-8	Long	20g/f	[110]	4951 bl
92	4-6	Muss	16g/s		5334 bl

HOME AFFAIRS 2 b c £5255

83	5-11	Newm	7g/f		3234
93	1-14	YARM	7gd		4611*
86	9-9	Newm	7sft	[88]	5137

HOME BY SOCKS 5 ch m £0

11	10-12	Sout	7gd		1284
42	12-16	Donc	10.3gd	[40]	2751

HOME COMING 6 b r g £0

28a	6-10	Sout	6af	[35]	352 VIS
3a	8-10	Wolv	7af	[35]	394

HOME FRONT 3 b g £0

6	11-11	Beve	5g/s		4237

HOMEBRED STAR 3 ch c £0

57	7-14	Wind	8.3g/s		2622
36	7-11	Folk	7g/s		3048
34	10-10	Chep	7.1gd		3732

HOMERIC TROJAN 4 ch c £0

45a	6-12	Sout	8af	[56]	460
0	11-11	Sout	11af	50	746
37	12-12	Newc	16.1sft	46	965
8a	6-9	Sout	12af	[45]	1204
0	6-7	Wolv	16.2af	[45]	1263

HOMEWARD 3 ch f £0

55	5-10	Chep	7.1gd		3732
45	13-17	Newm	8gd		4228

HOMME DANGEREUX 2 b c £591

66a	3-10	Sout	6af		2382
49	8-9	Sand	5g/f		3355
52a	5-6	Sand	5af		3484
22	8-8	Sand	7.1g/s	60	4100

HONEST INJUN 3 b c £8571

77a	1-9	WOLV	7af		381*
77	4-8	Wind	8.3g/s	79	1257
76	4-13	Kemp	9hvy	78	1515
59	12-18	Thir	8g/f	77	1769
74	5-10	York	7.9g/s	76	3074
74	4-9	Donc	8g/s	74	3378
68	5-10	Pont	8g/s	74	3972
74	2-14	Newm	7gd	[74]	4195
77	2-10	Leic	8gd	[72]	4702
76	5-12	Muss	8gd	[72]	4809

HONEY RYDER 2 b f £3307

80	2-12	Thir	6g/f		3411
82	2-5	Yarm	5.2gd		3993
75	14-26	Newb	6.5g/f		4679
76	4-10	Good	8gd	[83]	4876

HONEYMOONING 3 b f £961

60	7-20	Wind	10sft		1651
71	4-7	Newm	12g/f		1936
66	3-8	Beve	12.1gd		2515
57	8-10	Nott	10g/s	[68]	2930

HONEYS GIFT 5 b m £0

29a	7-14	Ling	10ap	[40]	784

HONEYSTREET 4 b f £0

26	13-14	Ches	12.3gd	55	2285
33	13-20	Kemp	9g/f	52	2857

HONOR ROUGE 5 ch m £0

64	6-13	Kemp	12g/f	74	1916
0	13-14	Brig	11.9fm	70	3674

HONORINE 4 b f £12125

67	6-7	Newm	8fm	[80]	2091
62	10-12	Good	9fm	80	3535
76	5-15	Kemp	8g/f	78	4362
85	1-5	NOTT	10gd	75	4860*
93	7-10	Newm	10gd	[80]	5086
81	8-14	Donc	10.3sft	[80]	5370

HONOUR HIGH 2 gr g £0

65	7-12	Good	8g/f		4522
55	7-14	Sali	8gd		4852
54	5-13	Warw	7.1g/s		4996

HOOPS AND BLADES 3 gr c £0

18	16-17	Donc	8gd		919
45	8-11	Newm	8g/f		2248 T
56	16-20	Newm	8g/f		3237 t
48	9-12	Hayd	10.5gd		3740
7	12-15	Chep	18sft	49	4056 t

HOPE SOUND 4 b g £419

57	7-13	Newc	16.1sft	62	2685 p
61	4-6	Catt	15.8g/f	60	3015 p

HOPELESSLY DEVOTED 2 b f £3377

40	10-20	Hayd	6gd		2882
48	6-7	Beve	5gd		3308
62	1-10	HAYD	5g/s		3901*
36a	10-14	Sout	6af	[58]	4127
51	5-19	Carl	5.9g/f	58	4344
55	4-14	Redc	5fm	56	4556

HORIZONTAL 4 ch g £0

51a	6-14	Ling	6ap		449
56a	6-9	Ling	5ap		1023
53	8-15	Sout	7gd	60	1282
3	12-14	Warw	8.1hvy	57	1535
55	5-9	Yarm	7fm	55	2150 T
11a	13-14	Ling	10ap	53	2589

HORMUZ 8 b g £0

0	19-19	Redc	8sft	48	1661
33	11-14	Muss	7.1g/f	45	2615
30	11-15	Ches	7.6g/f	42	3102
9	10-15	Carl	9.3fm	[40]	4505

HORNER 3 b c £9163

61	11-15	Newb	8gd	83	1206
82	4-9	Wind	11.6g/f	80	1807
85	2-8	Chep	12.1gd	[80]	2113
86	1-5	WARW	12.6fm	[80]	2441*
49	10-10	Sali	12gd	85	2660
72	3-6	Pont	12gd	[82]	3458 BL
85	2-11	Epso	12gd	81	4468

HORNINGSHEATH 2 b f £0

31	20-23	Newm	6gd		5084
61	10-14	Yarm	7sft		5250

HORNPIPE 2 b c £5301

45	6-6	Sand	5gd		2364
88	1-7	NOTT	6.1g/f		2629*

HORS LA LOI 8 ch g £0

63	10-14	Leic	10g/f	74	1828

HOT LIPS PAGE 3 b f £4173

71	5-10	Newb	7g/f	70	2312
77	1-10	CHEP	8.1g/f	69	2624*
73	4-12	Wind	8.3fm	75	3291
52	8-9	Newm	8g/f	74	3780
35	10-11	Wind	8.3g/s	73	4222

HOUDINI BAY 2 b f £720

3	8-8	Hayd	5g/s		1343
35a	8-8	Wolv	5af		1653
40	2-4	Ayr	6fm		1906

HOUSE MARTIN 2 b f £271

76	4-16	Newm	7g/f		3582
72	10-16	Sali	7gd		4330

HOUSE OF BLUES 3 b g £409

60	15-20	Bath	10.2gd		1398
18a	9-12	Wolv	12af	60	2203
47	5-11	Leic	10g/f	[57]	2924
55	3-8	Catt	15.8g/f	[57]	3666

HOUT BAY 7 ch g £27155

54a	1-9	SOUT	5af	51	415*
56a	3-13	Ling	6ap	57	451
42a	6-15	Sout	6af	56	550
62	2-18	Beve	5g/s	56	3852
54	4-12	Ches	5.1sft	56	4107
64	1-12	NEWM	5gd	56	4197+
71	1-19	BEVE	5g/s	62	4240*
69	3-26	Ayr	5g/s	67	4618
79	1-15	AYR	5g/s	67	4654*
75	6-18	Pont	5g/s	75	5149
71	7-12	Redc	5sft	[75]	5305

HOV 4 gr g £1099

30a	11-12	Wolv	9.4af	84	382
45a	8-8	Sout	11af	80	595
62	8-16	Newc	8hvy	75	1036
72	2-13	Redc	7sft	[72]	1142
68	6-20	Newc	6sft	72	1393 P
57	8-15	Warw	8.1sft	72	1530 p
47	10-12	Redc	8g/f	[70]	1823

HOVMAN 5 ch g £5823

105	2-10	Taby	8g/f		4573

HOWARDS DREAM 6 b g £1500

0	10-10	Muss	14g/f	40	1118 t
26	4-7	Ayr	10g/s	[35]	1450 t
0	18-18	Ayr	7.2g/f	30	1897 t
2	6-6	Hami	11.1gd	[30]	2180 t
20	7-10	Hami	13g/f	30	2479 t
23	7-10	Muss	12g/f	28	2813 t
25	7-7	Hami	13gd	25	3134 t
0	5-6	Hami	12.1g/f	25	3588 t
66	4-6	Ayr	10.9sft	[30]	4687 t
7	8-9	Ayr	13.1sft	[30]	5277 t

HOWARDS PRINCESS 2 gr f £3454

69	5-7	Hayd	6gd		2883
72	2-11	Ripo	5g/s		3258
73	2-4	Hami	5g/s		4134
66	4-8	Muss	5gd	[73]	4517
60	9-15	Ripo	5gd	69	4784

HOWARDS ROCKET 3 ch c £0

12	7-7	Hami	9.2gd		1747
48	8-11	Hayd	8.1gd		2885
44	6-8	Hami	8.3fm		3246
31	9-12	Ayr	9.1g/f	47	3766
9	11-15	Ayr	7.2hvy	45	4088

HOWS THAT 2 ch f £3622

45	13-15	Pont	6gd		3239
57	11-16	Newm	7g/f		3582
48	7-18	Ripo	6g/s		3939

54	10-14	Folk	7gd		4115
58	2-9	Ripo	6gd		4277
64	1-18	**NEWC**	6g/f	53	5013*

HOWS THINGS 3 b g £3138

69a	2-14	Sout	8af	65	93
70a	2-11	Sout	8af	67	186
68a	3-6	Wolv	9.4af	70	249
62a	6-7	Wolv	8.5af	70	700
16	14-17	Hayd	8.1gd	63	2947
45	7-9	Newb	9gd	60	3922
39	10-15	Chep	8.1g/s	57	4300
73a	2-12	Wolv	7.1ap	[67]	5340

HSI WANG MU 3 ch f £1038

69a	2-12	Wolv	9.4af	[50]	686
44a	5-10	Wolv	8.5af	[68]	839
49	9-18	Leic	10g/s	50	1017
45	5-11	Sout	10gd	49	1280
57	9-11	Bath	8fm	[47]	2031
30	11-14	Bath	10.2fm	46	2664
22a	13-13	Wolv	8.6ap	62	5365

HUBOOB 2 b c £0

| 56 | 11-11 | Good | 8gd | | 4746 |

HUGGIN MAC 3 b f £0

| 66 | 6-12 | York | 7g/s | | 1688 |
| 47 | 7-8 | Beve | 7.5g/f | | 2169 |

HUGH THE MAN £610

| 69a | 2-8 | Wolv | 9.4af | 67 | 157 |
| 0 | 13-13 | Wolv | 8.5af | 69 | 251 P |

HUGO THE BOSS 2 ch g £0

35a	13-14	Ling	7ap		5078
46a	8-10	Ling	7ap		5259
39a	10-12	Ling	8ap		5295

HUGS DESTINY 3 b g £852

| 73 | 5-12 | York | 7.9g/f | | 2410 |
| 76a | 2-14 | Ling | 10ap | | 2740 |

HULA BALLEW 4 ch f £7254

28	9-16	Newc	8hvy	61	1036
58	5-20	Ripo	8g/s	59	1366
23	13-14	Hami	8.3gd	58	1504
13	9-10	Newc	8gd	54	2508
48	5-9	Ayr	7.2gd	54	2508
52	5-9	Pont	8g/f	54	2604 P
39	9-18	Donc	7gd	51	2755 p
66	1-14	**PONT**	8g/f	51	2993* p
56	5-18	Pont	8gd	57	3242 p
58	5-13	Yarm	10.1gd	60	3492 p
66	2-15	Carl	7.9g/f	59	4346 p
64	3-16	Thir	8g/f	62	4592 p
49	11-17	Newc	8fm	62	4867 p

HUM 3 ch f £0

| 26 | 14-14 | Newc | 8g/f | 56 | 2993 |
| 2 | 14-16 | Epso | 8.5gd | 56 | 3219 P |

HUMDINGER 3 b f £0

10a	10-10	Sout	14af	63	90
1a	13-14	Sout	14af	62	185 e
1a	6-12	Wolv	12af	60	244
0	14-15	Sout	12af	60	257
0	11-11	Wolv	12af	50	380 VIS
0	10-10	Sout	8af	47	791
16a	8-9	Ling	12ap	40	842
2	12-13	Nott	10gd	40	3992

HUMID CLIMATE 4 ch g £0

0	8-8	Ches	7sft	82	4073
29	7-7	Pont	8g/f	[78]	4629
66	13-15	Nott	10gd	78	4860
24	18-19	Pont	10g/s	74	5148

HUMILITY 3 b f £0

| 41 | 11-17 | Bath | 5g/f | | 1787 |

HUMOUROUS 2 b c £5161

78	5-16	Leic	7fm		3811 T
96	1-14	**KEMP**	8g/f		4356* t
57	9-9	Pont	8g/s	[92]	5150 t

HUNIPOT 2 ch f £0

| 45 | 7-8 | Beve | 5sft | | 1303 |
| 29 | 9-10 | Beve | 5sft | | 1632 |

8	11-13	Beve	5g/s		2321
14	8-8	Catt	5g/f		2847
25	6-6	Catt	5g/f		3014 BL
2	13-15	Redc	6g/f		3769

HUNTERS VALLEY 3 b f £3686

62	8-13	Kemp	8fm	[80]	2072
67	2-14	Sali	7fm	[78]	2291
68	4-11	Sali	8fm	[78]	2419
36	8-10	Newm	8g/f	70	2767
65	4-9	Wind	8.3g/f	[66]	3979
68	4-20	York	7.9gd	66	4321
64a	3-12	Ling	8ap	[65]	4975
23	15-16	Bath	8gd	65	5022

HUNTING LODGE 3 ch c £0

| 73 | 14-16 | Newm | 8g/f | 96 | 3059 |

HUNTING PINK 2 b f £1465

49a	4-11	Ling	8ap	[48]	77
39a	4-16	Sout	8af	[49]	164
49a	2-15	Sout	7af	[49]	462
44a	3-8	Sout	8af	49	490
49a	4-8	Sout	8af	[48]	577
46a	3-5	Sout	7af	[48]	682 BL

HURRICANE ALAN 4 b c £145495

106	3-6	Newm	9gd	[110]	1168
117	1-10	**SAND**	8.1g/s	[110]	1349+
116	5-15	Newb	8g/f	[116]	1758
103	10-16	Asco	8g/f	[114]	2470
116	3-10	Asco	8gd	[114]	3124
107	7-11	Good	8fm	[114]	3533
117	3-12	Sali	8gd	[114]	3886
115	3-7	Good	8gd	[114]	4232
117	2-11	Long	8g/f	[114]	4949
112	3-7	San	8gd	[114]	5074

HURRICANE COAST 4 b g £28026

59a	1-16	**SOUT**	7af	[55]	61*
64a	2-16	Sout	6af	62	92
55a	3-11	Wolv	8.5af	[55]	128
61a	4-11	Sout	6af	62	198
63a	4-16	Sout	6af	[62]	227
63a	1-10	**SOUT**	6af	[61]	308*
69a	1-7	**SOUT**	6af	[61]	317*
80a	1-13	**LING**	6ap	[61]	400+ BL
80a	3-7	Ling	6ap	[61]	431 bl
72a	1-10	**LING**	5ap	65	453* bl
76a	3-16	Sout	5af	71	461 bl
84a	2-13	Wolv	6af	81	482 bl
68a	12-14	Ling	7ap	75	518 bl
70a	9-13	Wolv	6af	82	618 bl
84a	4-10	Ling	5ap	81	692 bl
85a	1-13	**WOLV**	6af	80	807* bl
58a	9-10	Wolv	6af	80	834 bl
75	1-16	**SOUT**	7gd	66	1282* bl
73	6-19	Leic	6g/s	73	1354 bl
56	6-14	Kemp	8hvy	73	1512 bl
76	4-20	Chep	7.1g/s	73	3088 bl

HURRICANE FLOYD 6 ch g £1903

84	11-20	Newm	7g/s	89	1151
42	8-14	Kemp	8hvy	88	1512
71	10-11	Newm	7fm	86	2090
66	14-28	Asco	7g/f	83	2558
73	4-7	Yarm	8g/f	80	2853
72	2-11	Epso	6gd	[77]	4294
19	14-18	Ayr	7.2sft	74	4689 BL
46a	10-10	Wolv	7.1ap	[74]	4920 bl

HURSLEY 2 b f £0

| 7 | 14-14 | Ling | 7.6g/f | | 3601 |
| 59 | 10-12 | Folk | 7gd | | 3908 |

HUSKY 6 b g £1849

38a	5-10	Wolv	12af	[45]	315 p
48a	1-7	**LING**	10ap	[45]	1182* p
45a	3-5	Ling	10ap	[45]	1412 p
18a	13-14	Ling	10ap	[45]	1712 p
40	5-9	Brig	9.9fm	45	3695 p
50	4-11	Ling	10fm	45	3748 p

HUXLEY 5 b g £4882

33	12-12	Pont	8hvy	85	1066
56	20-27	Newb	8gd	83	1231
51	9-18	Asco	8sft	80	1423 T
39	18-19	Newb	10gd	77	1736

71	4-20	Newm	8g/f	70	3232
53	8-9	Nott	8.2g/f	[70]	3423 t
83	1-16	**THIR**	8g/f	70	4592* t
57	16-20	York	8.9gd	78	4999 t

HYMN OF LOVE 4 ch f £0

| 52 | 5-5 | Curr | 8g/f | | 1997 bl |

HYMN OF VICTORY 2 b c £2570

60	9-13	Carl	8fm		1950
70	5-10	Newc	5g/f		2158
63	2-11	Ayr	6g/s		2569
54	6-9	Pont	6g/f	74	2989
66	2-7	Muss	5g/f	[72]	4549
46	12-15	Ripo	5gd	66	4784
53	4-12	Pont	6g/f	[61]	5152

HYMNS AND ARIAS 3 b f £0

0	9-9	Wolv	8.5af	[47]	664
42a	4-8	Sout	11af	[47]	857
2	14-14	Wolv	10g/s	47	1051
29	10-11	Sout	10gd	45	1280
0	7-7	Sout	8af	[45]	1591
16	10-12	Thir	7g/f	[43]	2215 P

HYPNOTIC 2 ch c £24095

76a	4-7	Ling	8ap		3196
97a	1-13	**LING**	7ap	88	3330*
98a	1-12	**LING**	7ap	88	3820*
99a	3-8	Ling	7ap	[96]	4176
102	1-11	**CRAO**	8.3g/s	[96]	4429*
86	7-7	Ling	8ap	[96]	4729

I GOT RHYTHM 6 g r m £0

| 19 | 9-12 | Sout | 16gd | 45 | 1285 |
| 7 | 8-12 | Newc | 14.4sft | 45 | 1396 |

I HAD A DREAM 3 b f £6600

| 104 | 2-10 | Newm | 10gd | [92] | 5086 |
| 84 | 7-14 | Donc | 10.3sft | [92] | 5370 |

I SEE NO SHIPS 4 b f £0

| 1 | 7-8 | Ripo | 6g/f | | 2527 |
| 0 | 17-17 | Bath | 11.7gd | 38 | 3145 |

I T CONSULTANT 5 b g £0

| 0 | 12-12 | Wolv | 6af | [45] | 33 bl |
| 0 | 13-13 | Newc | 5sft | 49 | 1276 |

I WISH 5 ch m £9442

65a	1-15	**LING**	7ap	62	50*
53a	4-10	Ling	6ap	[65]	133
58a	6-15	Ling	7ap	64	266
57a	9-13	Ling	7ap	63	474
60a	5-10	Ling	7ap	62	799
58a	8-12	Ling	7ap	61	1024
57	4-16	Bath	5.7sft	58	1540
60	1-18	**WIND**	6g/f	[56]	1806*
57	5-15	Ling	5g/f	56	2062
50	5-6	Good	7gd	56	2539
60	3-8	Newb	6fm	56	2648
47	13-13	Wind	6fm	57	3479
59	2-10	Brig	7fm	57	3672
61	2-10	Ling	6gd	57	4109
49	6-19	Wind	6gd	57	5053
60a	4-14	Ling	7ap	[59]	5263

I WISH I KNEW 2 b r c £0

40a	10-12	Wolv	5af		32
68a	9-13	Ling	7ap		119
23a	6-6	Wolv	7af	[63]	779
40	11-14	Warw	7.1sft	55	1085
35	11-16	Ling	6g/f	50	1985
38	7-18	Sali	7fm	45	2292 VIS
20	11-12	Brig	6g/f	45	2435 vis

I WONT DANCE 3 b c £426

75	8-11	Newb	6gd	82	1734
72	7-8	Brig	7fm	[80]	2259
69	7-9	Sali	8g/s	78	3112
75	4-9	Ling	7gd	75	3447
63a	8-13	Ling	7ap	73	4318

IAM FOREVERBLOWING 2 ch f £630

55	5-9	Warw	5g/f		1084
50	4-6	Sali	5g/s		1499
36	5-7	Bath	5.7fm		1900
4a	10-11	Wolv	6af		2051
46	15-15	Asco	5g/f		2472

20 11-11 Sali 6g/f   [45] 3863
11 9-10 Ches 5.1g/f   45   4049

IAMBACK 3 b f £5162
14a 6-8   Wolv 8.5af   [44] 248 P
48a 2-8   Wolv 9.4af   [44] 299 p
45a 6-11 Wolv 7af   [47] 396 bl
52a 1-6   WOLV 8.5af   [47] 526* p
35a 6-12 Wolv 9.4af   50   747 e
31a 7-9   Wolv 8.5af   [50] 811 e
33a 4-12 Sout 8af   [48] 905 p
39a 3-6   Wolv 8.5af   [48] 957 p
0   8-10 Chep 8.1sft [45] 1334 p
50a 1-10 WOLV 9.4af   [45] 1564*
50a 1-5   WOLV 9.4af   [45] 1674*
40a 9-14 Ling 10ap   [45] 1712
9a 9-12 Wolv 9.4af   55   2054
35 15-17 Leic 7gd   53   5056 p
23a 12-13 Wolv 8.6ap   53   5183 p

IANINA 4 b f £0
79 7-8   Good 8g/f   1863

IBERUS 6 b g £1903
33 25-27 Newb 8gd   85   1231
33 18-20 Donc 10.3g/s 80   1519 BL
68 7-19 Redc 7g/f   74   1820 p
67 5-6   Redc 7g/s   [72] 2564
70 4-12 Beve 8.5gd   69   2890
70 2-8   Hayd 10.5g/f 69   4354
65 7-14 Asco 12g/f   68   4775
58 10-17 Leic 10gd   67   5062
67 4-15 Nott 8.2hvy   67   5191

ICANNSHIFT 3 b g £8549
53a 12-14 Ling 10ap   70   174
45a 13-15 Ling 7ap   66   266
57a 10-16 Ling 7ap   66   323
53a 9-13 Ling 10ap   [60] 429
53a 6-14 Ling 10ap   [57] 477
43 8-14 Folk 9.7g/s   54   1083
52 2-12 Folk 9.7sft   50   1273
55 1-11 LEIC 10g/s   50   1357*
58 3-17 Bath 10.2sft 51   1541
36 12-17 Kemp 10g/f   55   1913
58 3-15 Sand 10g/f   54   2099
53 6-15 Kemp 9gd   54   2170
58 3-12 Newb 10g/f   54   2354
35a 11-14 Ling 10ap   55   2589
56 3-8   Epso 10.1g/s 55   3044
46 10-16 Brig 9.9g/f   55   3175
53 4-9   Epso 10.1fm   53   3538
59 2-13 Warw 10.9g/f 53   4419
51 6-12 Good 9g/f   53   4539
56 5-18 Good 8gd   55   4750

ICARUS DREAM 3 ch g £0
59 11-17 Wind 10fm   70   3477
49 9-11 Good 11gd   68   3948 P
41 10-12 Good 16g/s   65   4235

ICE AND FIRE 5 b g £0
3a 10-11 Sout 11af   52   746 bl

ICE DRAGON 3 b f £0
52 7-14 Yarm 7fm   2148
46 8-16 Brig 7sft   [63] 4144

ICE PALACE 4 ch f £28212
96 3-10 Beve 8.5g/f   94   1833
101 2-7   Pont 8g/f   [94] 2278
100 1-6   NEWC 10.1g/s [96] 2772*
100 4-12 Yarm 10.1sft 96   4149
82 17-32 Newm 9g/f   96   4916

ICE PLANET 3 b c £830
11 15-16 Newc 7sft   966
71 3-8   Thir 5sft   1228
56 5-15 Thir 7g/s   1473
50 14-17 Ripo 6g/s   69   3262
65 5-11 Donc 6g/s   69   3379

ICE RUBY 2 b f £0
32 9-12 Ripo 5gd   1173
38 9-15 Warw 5g/s   1325
32a 7-8   Wolv 5af   1653

ICECAP 3 b f £6085
53a 5-15 Ling 7ap   55   50

39a 9-16 Ling 7ap   [55] 123
44a 8-14 Ling 10ap   54   230
49a 2-12 Ling 10ap   [51] 267
0   16-16 Sout 8af   51   3159
56 1-10 BRIG 7fm   49   3672*
33 13-14 Bath 8g/f   53   3963
23 15-20 Chep 7.1g/s   53   4367
48 7-15 Epso 7g/f   53   4475

ICED DIAMOND 5 b g £4962
60a 1-11 WOLV 7af   52   558*
25a 9-9   Wolv 7af   58   629
49 7-10 Newb 8g/f   58   2350
53 7-17 Newm 7g/f   55   2768
52 7-15 Ches 7.6g/f   54   3102
47 9-16 Kemp 7gd   54   3184
52 4-12 Yarm 7gd   52   3490
53 4-12 Ches 7.6fm   52   3634 T
42 7-16 Ches 7g/f   52   4051
54 2-14 Carl 6.9g/f   50   4345 t
49 6-20 Chep 7.1gd   50   4488 t
56a 5-14 Ling 7ap   57   5300

ICEMAN 2 b c £104322
84 2-14 Bath 5sft   1538
97 1-13 NEWB 6g/f   1760*
112 1-13 ASCO 6g/f   2467*
117 2-10 Donc 7fm   [100] 4493
111 3-9   Newm 6g/f   [100] 4888
114 4-9   Newm 7sft   [100] 5137

ICENASLICE 3 b f £9131
46 9-10 Hami 5g/s   55   1605
69 1-9   THIR 5g/f   51   2219*
51a 4-11 Sout 5af   51   2380
69 1-8   NEWC 5g/s   62   2731*
53 8-12 Catt 5g/f   66   3193
72 4-21 Good 5fm   66   3567
66 9-14 York 5g/s   70   4027
64 4-8   Hami 5g/s   [70] 4822

ICENI WARRIOR 2 b g £0
69a 5-9   Ling 5ap   931

ICEY RUN 4 b g £0
48 7-10 Ling 14fm   3742
41a 14-16 Ling 16ap   [45] 4663

ICING 2 br f £5474
55 6-16 Nott 6.1gd   3103
69a 4-10 Ling 6ap   3817
80a 1-8   LING 7ap   4447*
67 11-16 Newm 7g/f   75   4913

IDAHO QUEST 7 b g £7711
107 3-6   Long 15.5g/s   1431

IDEALIST 2 b c £65414
108 2-10 San   8sft   5167

IDEALISTIC 3 b f £7714
55 10-16 Wind 10gd   1384
84 2-10 Hayd 10.5g/f   1922
88 2-8   Chep 12.1gd   2368
82 2-14 Ling 11.5gd [82] 3335
77 1-7   BATH 11.7g/f [82] 3967*

IDLE JOURNEY 3 b c £0
46 4-19 Kemp 8g/f   [48] 4795
32 8-15 Yarm 10.1g/s [48] 5122

IDLE POWER 6 b g £28741
62 8-20 Wind 6g/s   74   1255
61 10-18 Ches 7.6gd   71   1598 p
78 1-16 GOOD 6gd   70   2023+ p
82 1-7   BRIG 9g/f   73   2045+ p
63 14-17 Epso 6fm   77   2256 p
79 2-7   Good 7gd   [77] 2374 p
83 3-11 Asco 6.5gd   77   3069 p
73 8-16 Newb 6g/f   79   3269 p
64 9-26 Good 6fm   77   3569 p
75 2-5   Good 7sft   [78] 4186 p
85a 1-14 LING 7ap   75   4446+ p
85 1-16 GOOD 7gd   77   4873* p
70a 11-12 Wolv 7.1ap   82   5159 p
64a 9-12 Ling 6ap   82   5297 p

IF BY CHANCE 5 ch g £8637
64a 5-13 Wolv 6af   70   113 bl

48a 10-10 Wolv 6af   68   349
72 2-19 Newc 6sft   64   967 bl
64 4-19 Redc 6sft   68   1145 bl
68 4-20 Newc 6sft   68   1393 bl
75 1-20 THIR 6gd   68   1638* bl
61 8-14 Kemp 5g/f   74   1914 bl
49 15-15 Muss 5fm   74   2084 bl
53a 8-13 Wolv 6ap   69   5181
74 4-12 Redc 5sft   [73] 5305 bl

IF PARADISE 3 b c £27385
106 1-5   HAYD 5sft   100 1106+
70 9-11 Newb 6gd   [105] 1732
90 6-12 Epso 8g/f   [105] 2206
97 13-19 Asco 5g/f   [105] 2468
100 9-13 Good 5fm   [102] 3551
74 9-9   Donc 5fm   [100] 4481
98 2-10 Beve 5g/f   [98] 4718
104 2-10 Newm 5gd   98   5090
87 8-12 Newb 6sft   98   5196

IFFRAAJ 3 b c £747
93 4-20 Newm 7g/f   86   1186

IFFY 3 b g £6425
60a 4-12 Ling 7ap   60   545
56 7-12 Leic 8g/f   60   2922
62 4-16 Epso 8.5gd   58   3219
66 1-8   ASCO 10g/f   58   3391*
68 3-14 Kemp 10g/f   63   3690
53a 8-13 Wolv 8.6ap   [63] 5336

IFIT 2 b f £508
55 12-18 Leic 7g/f   3342
59 8-14 Newb 6fm   3626
61 9-11 Epso 7gd   4289
57 10-13 Leic 8g/f   4450
53 3-17 Redc 7g/s   [58] 5105

IFTERADH 3 b c £5961
91a 1-10 LING 7ap   911*
94 2-20 Newm 7g/f   83   1186

IFTIKHAR 5 b g £320
52 9-11 Hayd 10.5g/f 63   1884
6   16-17 Hayd 8.1gd   60   2947
28 14-16 Hayd 10.5sft 57   3276
54 4-12 Newm 10g/f   52   3785
47 7-14 York 10.4g/f 52   4402
39 10-13 Nott 10gd   [52] 4861
0   14-15 Redc 9g/s   52   5111 BL
33 12-13 Ayr   10sft   [52] 5276

IGNITION 2 ch f £1176
58 5-12 Thir 6g/f   3411
67 4-14 Ches 7sft   4102
63 3-17 Warw 7.1gd   4269
63 4-14 Carl 6.9fm   [67] 4503
54 10-18 Catt 7g/f   65   4673
54 10-17 Catt 7gd   60   4963

IKAN 4 br f £1451
76a 10-10 Ling 5ap   [89] 883
90 3-13 Beve 5gd   [89] 1162
83 9-14 Bath 5gd   [89] 1400
63 16-20 York 5g/s   88   1683

IKHTYAR 4 b c £72935
106 3-4   Asco 8sft   [117] 1420
115 6-15 Newb 8g/f   [117] 1758
118 2-9   Sand 10g/s   [113] 2128
119 3-10 Asco 10g/f   [113] 2488
114 6-12 Sand 10g/f   [116] 2916
115 3-7   Ayr   10g/f   [116] 3306 VIS

IKTIBAS 3 b c £4936
86 1-9   THIR 8g/f   4593* T
93 5-6   Newm 10sft   5269 t

IKTITAF 3 b c £9967
58 8-19 Yarm 7g/f   1130
82 3-20 Bath 10.2gd   1398
84 1-8   CHES 10.3gd   1597*
85 7-14 Asco 10g/f   87   1924
74 13-17 Newm 10g/f   85   4917
88 3-19 Donc 10.3sft 83   5201

IL BIMBO DE ORO 5 ch h £5915
100 3-7   San   15gd   1998

IL CAVALIERE 9 b g £0

52	5-11	Beve	16.2sft	63	1629
49	8-13	Pont	17.1g/f	62	2276

IL COLOSSEO 2 b g £4825

80	3-8	Redc	7gd		4247
68	4-9	Ayr	7.2sft		5064
87a	1-12	WOLV	7.1ap		5324*

IL PRANZO 2 b c £3404

49a	8-10	Ling	5ap		1071
71	6-11	Wind	5gd		3160
70	3-6	Yarm	5.2gd		3361
72	5-12	Chep	5.1gd	[72]	3728
66	7-11	Bath	5.7gd	[71]	4543
69	4-19	Bath	5gd	70	5021
76a	1-13	WOLV	5.1ap	[68]	5207*
75	3-8	Yarm	5.2sft	75	5253

ILE FACILE 3 b c £11038

61a	2-13	Sout	6af		319	
59a	4-11	Wolv	7af		396	
71a	2-15	Ling	7ap		472	
70a	4-7	Sout	7af	[70]	531	
68a	1-7	LING	6ap	[70]	706*	
51a	9-9	Ling	8ap	[67]	1040	
73	2-12	Pont	10g/f	67	2277	T
65	7-18	Leic	10gd	69	2706	t
54	4-9	Hayd	10.5gd	[69]	2901	
76	1-14	CATT	12g/f	68	3192*	t
74	4-10	Ling	11.5gd	75	3334	t
61	5-6	Nott	11g/f	72	3578	t

ILE MICHEL 7 b g £1355

30a	8-12	Wolv	8.5af	86	688
52	16-16	Good	7g/f	85	1817
79	4-8	Chep	10.2gd	[82]	2197
69	3-6	York	10.4g/f	[82]	2356
36	8-8	Wind	8.3g/s	[78]	2620
52	15-18	Kemp	8gd	76	4714
63a	5-10	Wolv	7.1ap	[72]	4920
78a	6-12	Wolv	7.1ap	[67]	5006
56a	9-12	Wolv	7.1ap	[67]	5340

ILL DO IT TODAY 3 b g £0

61	6-12	Nott	10hvy		5190
60	7-8	Redc	10sft		5306

ILL FLY 4 ch g £0

55	8-15	Leic	10g/s		1358

ILLEANA 3 ch f £3364

65	4-9	Folk	9.7sft		980
59	7-14	Bath	10.2gd	64	1403
23	14-20	Wind	11.6sft	61	1648
58	1-8	NEWC	12.4g/f	[58]	2163*
51	9-11	Ling	11.5g/f	58	2842
58a	3-8	Ling	12ap	58	3026
20	11-14	Nott	16g/f	55	3580
26	8-9	Good	16gd	53	4875

ILLICIUM 5 b m £0

47	6-9	Muss	12g/f		1121
36	9-11	Beve	8.5sft		1304
48	7-9	Hami	12.1gd		1507
0	P-14	York	13.9g/f	40	2060

ILLUSIONIST 6 b g £0

12a	9-9	Sout	7af	[40]	555 vis
6a	5-9	Wolv	9.4af	[35]	633 vis
11a	5-5	Sout	12af	[35]	723 vis

ILLUSIVE 7 b g £3653

34a	12-13	Ling	6ap	67	471
26a	15-15	Sout	6af	64	550
60a	3-12	Ling	6ap	60	628 bl
55a	5-10	Ling	7ap	60	765 bl
48a	11-12	Ling	6ap	[60]	880 bl
50a	7-13	Ling	6ap	60	902 bl
62a	2-15	Ling	7ap	[60]	935 bl
62a	2-14	Ling	6ap	58	1010 bl
50a	6-14	Ling	6ap	58	1025 bl
61	2-18	Bath	5.7g/f	55	1788 bl
54a	9-12	Ling	6ap	[60]	2016 bl
39	13-19	Beve	5gd	59	2512 bl
61	4-14	Yarm	6g/f	58	2855 bl
40	14-17	Pont	6gd	58	2990 bl
56a	5-11	Ling	6ap	58	3333 bl

ILLUSTRIOUS DUKE 6 b g £423

16a	13-13	Ling	6ap	49	451
37a	10-11	Wolv	7af	48	562
0	10-12	Wolv	9.4af	45	747
15a	11-13	Wolv	8.5af	[40]	894
30a	6-12	Wolv	7af	40	956 BL
23a	11-15	Sout	8af	40	1028 bl
40a	2-7	Sout	7af	[40]	1202 bl
31a	7-11	Wolv	6af	40	1337 bl

ILLUSTRIOUS MISS 3 b f £64774

96	1-13	NEWB	7gd		1210*
114	1-11	LING	7sft		1620+
114	3-15	Curr	8g/f		2005
96	5-7	Newm	8fm	[112]	3004

ILOVETURTLE 3 b g £206

9a	12-16	Sout	16af	45	206
3a	12-15	Sout	12af	45	257
6	14-22	Donc	12gd	57	918
41a	3-7	Sout	14af	[40]	1407
49	5-11	Newm	12g/f	54	2244
0	U-20	Catt	12g/f	50	3354
47	6-13	Beve	12.1g/f	50	3502
40	6-10	Thir	16sft	46	3834

ILTRAVITORE 3 ch c £0

55	7-8	Kemp	7g/f		1912
54	8-14	Sali	7fm		2291
65	5-12	Kemp	6sft		4029
42	14-15	Sali	5gd	65	4335
48	14-17	Ling	6g/f	60	4740
41	11-17	Bath	5.7gd	[57]	5020

ILWADOD 2 b c £8285

39a	6-13	Wolv	9.4af		37
56	1-16	NOTT	10hvy	45	1611+
61	2-6	Newc	8sft	51	1679
61	2-15	Leic	11.8gd	56	2134
64	2-9	Yarm	14.1g/f	56	2345
66	2-7	Ripo	12.3g/f	60	2528 VIS
57	7-18	Hayd	14gd	62	2905 vis

IM A DARK HORSE 3 b g £0

44	11-13	Thir	12g/f		1768
47	5-7	Carl	9.3fm		2443
1	7-7	Catt	13.8g/f		3019

IM AIMEE 2 ch f £11981

77a	2-10	Ling	5ap		882
61	6-10	Hayd	5sft		1107
72	3-8	Thir	5g/s		1212
74	7-9	Ches	5.1gd		1567
69	4-11	Hayd	5g/f		1880
65	7-12	Ling	5g/f		1981
76	2-8	Ches	5.1g/f	74	3082
79	2-9	Hayd	5sft	73	3271
79	2-8	Donc	5g/f	73	3374
79	2-9	Ches	6.1fm	76	3632
78	3-6	Hayd	6g/s	76	3902
64	7-10	Ches	5.1g/f	77	4049
70	4-6	Chep	5.1g/s	76	4298
68	4-11	Bath	5g/f	[76]	4409
69	5-12	Bath	5.7gd	73	4545

IM DANCING 3 b f £1169

25a	7-13	Sout	8af	[60]	1193 e
63	2-11	Redc	10sft	59	1663

IM SO LUCKY 2 b c £6383

56	7-11	Ayr	6g/s		2569
86	1-11	WARW	7.1gd		3053*
90	2-8	Muss	8gd	85	4807
91	4-14	Donc	8sft	87	5203

IM SPARTACUS 2 b c £18255

46a	8-10	Ling	5ap		882
73	2-10	Bath	5g/s		1097
72	1-5	BRIG	5.3g/f		1367*
64	6-7	Nott	6.1sft		1738
74	5-7	Kemp	6fm		2071
56	9-10	Sali	5gd		2697
74	6-13	Newm	7g/f	70	3065
77	5-8	Asco	7gd		3467
71	4-6	Folk	5g/f	68	3723
78	1-8	SAND	7.1g/s	69	4100*
79	5-11	Hayd	8.1fm	75	4387

75	4-12	Asco	7g/f	75	4810 P
79	2-13	Wind	8.3g/f	74	5051 p
76	5-14	Donc	8sft	74	5203 p

IMOYA 5 b m £4140

101	3-9	Nava	10g/s	[97]	1435

IMPARTIAL 2 b c £440

74a	3-11	Ling	8ap		21

IMPELLER 5 ch g £65291

79	10-27	Newb	8gd	87	1231
88	7-18	Good	8g/f	87	1812
90	2-14	Sand	8.1g/f	87	2096
84	6-13	Epso	8.5g/f	87	2207
88	9-31	Asco	8g/f	87	2489
89	5-18	Newb	8g/f	87	3265
93	2-15	Good	9.9g/f	86	3506
93	2-21	Good	8fm	87	3565
102	1-11	EPSO	10.1gd	[90]	4467*
95	3-13	Asco	10g/f	[92]	4772
91	11-32	Newm	9g/f	95	4916
101	2-13	Newm	8g/s	92	5284

IMPERATIVE 4 ch c £1301

62a	4-15	Ling	12ap	[75]	521
16a	6-8	Wolv	12af	[70]	644
58a	3-5	Wolv	12af	[70]	701 T
56a	3-8	Wolv	12af	[68]	808 t

IMPERATRICE 2 b f £0

5a	15-15	Sout	5af		4089
39	6-17	Ling	6g/f		4316
28	6-8	Brig	5.3fm		4759
28	17-19	Wolv	6af		4895 P

IMPERIAL BRIEF 2 br g £6399

100	2-3	Leop	9hvy		5314

IMPERIAL DANCER 5 b h £185984

116	1-	CAPA	10g/s		59*
116	7-14	Sha	12g/f		209
118	3-17	Newb	12gd	[117]	1230
107	6-16	Kran	12g/f	[117]	1859
108	9-11	Epso	12g/f	[117]	2209
111	7-12	Sand	10g/s	[117]	2916
116	3-8	Muni	10gd	[117]	3662
112	7-9	York	10.4gd	[114]	4002
114	3-4	York	8.9gd	[110]	4323
116	6-8	Leop	10g/f	[110]	4571
112	2-8	Newb	11g/f	[110]	4639
110	14-19	Long	12g/f	[110]	4956
110	3D-9	San	12sft	[110]	5168

IMPERIAL DRAGON 4 b g £276

53a	9-12	Ling	8ap		881
62	4-16	Newc	7sft		966
55	10-17	Kemp	7gd		1136

IMPERIAL DYNASTY 2 b c £0

60	9-13	Thir	6g/s		2689
65	5-13	Pont	6gd		3682
49	10-12	Ayr	7.2hvy		4083
52	11-20	Redc	7fm	63	4337

IMPERIAL ECHO 3 b g £16916

68	7-8	Muss	7.1g/s	85	1460
73	9-18	Newm	6g/f	83	1933
79	4-12	Ripo	6g/f	80	2482
62	9-9	Pont	6gd	80	2609 VIS
78	2-5	Hami	6gd	[78]	3131
81	2-12	Newc	5gd	78	3427 vis
63	17-21	Good	5fm	80	3567 vis
81	3-8	Redc	6g/f	80	3808 vis
79	4-14	York	5g/s	80	4027
88	1-20	RIPO	6g/s	80	4278*
81	3-12	Hayd	6sft	84	4779
90	4-16	Redc	6sft	84	5304
83	5-11	Muss	5g/s	84	5332

IMPERIAL MISS 2 b f £0

54	11-13	Ling	6g/f		2061
70	6-10	Pont	6g/f		2610
70	8-16	Kemp	7g/f		3035
65	6-15	Folk	7gd		3381
58	11-13	Kemp	7gd		3520
48	17-20	Ling	7gd	66	4444

IMPERIAL PRINCESS 3 b f £0

11a 13-14 Ling 6ap [40] 495

IMPERIAL ROYALE 3 ch g £0
63	5-13	Hayd	11.9g/s	[60]	2230	
31	9-10	Leic	11.8gd	[65]	2707	
57	6-10	Nott	10g/s	[62]	2930	
25	10-14	Catt	12g/f	62	3192	
52	8-13	Nott	10g/f	59	3419	P
28	13-17	Catt	12sft	55	3929	p
40	10-14	York	10.4g/f	54	4402	p
37	12-16	Bath	8gd	51	4828	p
47a	7-13	Wolv	9.5ap	51	4925	p

IMPERIAL SOUND 2 b c £12246
94	1-6	BEVE	5gd		2513*
98	2-5	Beve	5gd		2888
89	10-24	Newb	5.2g/f		3266
97	1-4	RIPO	6gd	[93]	3644*
78	17-22	Donc	6fm		4458
93	6-13	Muss	5g/f	93	4551

IMPERIAL STRIDE 3 b c £2500
105	4-5	Newm	8g/f	[113]	1188
103	7-16	Newm	9sft	[113]	5139
97	9-11	Newm	8g/s	[109]	5283

IMPERIAL WIZARD 3 ch g £0
37a	10-14	Ling	6ap		449
25	8-9	Kemp	5g/f		3687
31	10-12	Kemp	6sft		4029
53	9-13	Bath	5.7g/f		4413
32	14-17	Kemp	7g/f	[45]	4794

IMPERIALISTIC 3 b f £24772
87	4-22	Donc	7gd	85	955	
95	1-9	HAYD	8.1sft	84	1105*	p
96	1-7	BEVE	7.5sft	90	1305+	p
72	8-8	Epso	8.5g/f	[94]	2211	p
90	5-5	Sand	8.1g/s	[94]	4095	p
96	5-13	Ripo	8gd	93	4279	
95	3-10	Hayd	8.1g/s	93	4767	p
91	6-14	Donc	10.3sft	[91]	5370	

IMPERIOLI 2 b c £0
41	13-16	Leic	7fm		3811
43	6-7	Hami	8.3sft		4691
34	18-21	Newm	8sft		5097

IMPERIUM 2 b g £11835
76a	4-11	Ling	6ap	[79]	135	
79a	6-15	Ling	7ap	79	177	
57a	4-9	Ling	7ap	[77]	764	T
50a	7-11	Ling	6ap	[75]	898	t
73a	2-9	Ling	5ap	[75]	1023	
57	11-16	Bath	5.7g/s	[72]	1103	
54	12-14	Bath	5gd	68	1404	
58	5-10	Bath	5.7sft	[68]	1539	
72	1-10	BRIG	5.3fm	65	1694*	
76	1-8	BRIG	5.3g/f	69	1942*	
70	3-9	Chep	5.1gd	75	2195	
55	12-16	Leic	5g/f	74	2400	
67	7-12	Kemp	5g/f	73	3036	
51a	10-11	Ling	6ap	72	3198	
66	6-9	Epso	6fm	71	3543	
51	19-21	Good	5gd	71	3567	
69	2-5	Brig	5.3g/f	[71]	3720	
60	7-13	Brig	5.3g/f	68	3984	
68	3-7	Good	5sft	68	4236	
48	14-16	Good	5g/f	67	4528	

IMPERSONATOR 4 b g £3042
74	10-17	Sand	8.1g/s	80	1351	
75	4-4	Ling	7.6g/s	[78]	1616	BL
80	3-8	Hayd	8.1fm	76	3797	
78	3-13	Wind	8.3g/s	76	4221	
75	7-16	Sand	10gd	76	4609	
70	3-3	Newm	10sft	76	5104	

IMPISH JUDE 6 b m £293
43	4-18	Nott	14.1sft	49	1469

IMPRESSIVE FLIGHT 5 b m £396
68	8-9	Ripo	6g/f	92	3646
73	12-19	Ripo	6g/s	90	3937
75	11-16	Muss	5g/f	87	4174
84	6-9	Good	6g/f	83	4537
76	5-9	Pont	6g/s	83	4627
81	7-14	Ripo	6gd	82	4786

71 8-10 Newm 6gd 82 4884 BL

IMPROVISE 2 b f £2896
66	6-9	Newm	6g/f		2245
72a	2-10	Ling	7ap		4442
78	2-13	Newm	6fm		4726

IMPULSIVE BID 3 b f £1597
63	4-7	Sout	6g/s	[66]	1050
52	12-20	Nott	6.1gd	64	1239
62	2-11	Newc	7sft	62	1678
29	15-18	Donc	7gd	63	2755
60	5-11	Carl	6.9gd	63	2936
56	9-13	Beve	9.9gd	62	3309
0	11-12	Pont	8gd	60	3679
50	9-17	Hayd	10.5fm	56	4388

IMSHY 3 ch f £0
64	13-15	Newm	6gd	5088

IMTALKINGGIBBERISH 3 b c £2772
68	7-12	Newm	7g/s		1152
72	5-12	York	7g/s		1688
85	8-15	Asco	7g/f		2486
79	2-8	Newm	6gd	[85]	3784
54	5-11	Wind	6g/f	[79]	4836
51	4-11	Good	6gd	[75]	5030
62a	2-12	Wolv	6ap	[75]	5157

IMTIHAN 5 ch h £0
43	7-19	Warw	10.9sft	51	1090	
10	11-13	Chep	18gd	49	2198	T

IMTIYAZ 5 ro h £10712
110	2-5	Good	8g/f	[109]	2022	t
108	2-6	Epso	10.1g/d	[109]	3043	t
99	4-6	Newm	10g/f	[108]	3754	t

IMTOUCHINGWOOD 3 b f £0
11	17-18	Wind	10g/f	1959

IN DEEP 3 b f £1780
60	8-14	Donc	10.3gd	77	923
58	15-18	Epso	10.1fm	75	2250
63	6-16	Wind	11.6g/s	70	2621
50	8-12	Newb	10g/f	65	3255
68	2-10	Nott	10gd	62	3990

IN DREAMS 2 b c £0
68	8-8	Good	5g/f	1816
36	15-20	Wind	6fm	2970
63	8-12	Good	8g/f	4522
71	5-11	Wind	6g/s	4941
57a	8-14	Ling	7ap	5076

IN EVERY STREET 3 b r f £0
45a	7-9	Ling	8ap	3197
49	6-7	Nott	10g/f	3422

IN EXCELSIS 2 b c £1000
89	5-11	Asco	7fm	2578
98	5-7	Curr	7gd	4734

IN LUCK 5 b m £0
7a	9-10	Sout	14af	52	90
16a	7-11	Wolv	12af	47	380

IN RHUBARB 2 b c £0
41	6-6	Yarm	5.2gd		3361	T
56	8-10	Muss	5gd		4804	
42	7-10	Catt	5gd		4968	

IN SPIRIT 5 b g £0
41a	11-13	Ling	10ap	60	104
24a	13-14	Ling	10ap	56	236
0	9-11	Wolv	12af	53	380

IN THE FAN 2 b g £9201
94	2-10	Newm	7fm		2594
94	1-8	EPSO	7gd		3214*
95	3-8	Newm	7g/f		3585
96	2-7	Nott	8.2gd	[93]	3991

IN THE KNOW 2 b c £0
61	11-21	Donc	6sft	5368

IN THE LEAD 2 b f £0
61	7-16	Newb	7g/f	4677

IN THE PINK 4 gr f £10224

35 8-13 Warw 7.1hvy [67] 1537
27	17-20	Asco	8g/f	65	1927	
69	1-6	GOOD	7gd	62	2539*	
76	2-18	Donc	7gd	67	2755	
66	10-12	Yarm	7fm	67	2864	
75	2-9	Sali	7gd	72	3456	
60	7-9	Newm	8g/f	72	3780	
66	4-10	Yarm	7g/s	72	4251	
73	5-24	Newb	7g/f	70	4642	
68	3-10	Newc	7fm	[71]	4869	

IN THE RIBBONS 2 ch f £3049
93	3-3	Leop	9hvy	5314

IN THE SHADOWS 2 b f £0
42	7-8	Bath	5.7g/s	4198
52	12-14	Kemp	7g/f	4711
33a	13-14	Ling	7ap	4970

IN THE STARS 6 ch g £0
44a	8-14	Ling	10ap	52	498	VIS

IN TUNE 4 b g £0
21	14-18	Bath	10.2g/s	55	1098	
3	16-17	Bath	10.2sft	50	1541	BL
6a	13-15	Sout	6af	50	1750	bl
33	8-16	Chep	7.1gd	[40]	2369	T
19	10-17	Chep	8.1g/s	40	3087	t
1a	11-13	Ling	10ap	[42]	3288	t

INAGH 2 b f £550
38	6-6	Warw	5fm	2437
63	3-7	Chep	6.1hvy	4705
0	3-13	Wolv	8.6ap	4979

INCA WOOD 2 b f £3271
74	2-9	Yarm	8sft		4147
78	2-5	Epso	8.5gd		4464
54	10-11	Good	8gd		4746
79	4-9	Ayr	8sft	[74]	5033

INCH BY INCH 5 b m £13820
47	7-15	Leic	6g/f	58	2398	bl
50a	4-10	Ling	5ap	48	3332	bl
44	18-22	Good	5fm	56	3537	bl
65	1-15	CHEP	5.1gd	53	4489*	bl
68	1-15	GOOD	5gd	60	4751*	bl
76	1-19	NOTT	6.1g/f	[60]	4845*	bl
62a	1-13	WOLV	6ap	[55]	5359*	bl

INCHCAPE ROCK 2 ch c £1090
62	8-10	Sali	5g/f		1717
46a	9-13	Ling	7ap		3330
41	12-17	Chep	6.1sft		4052
74	2-9	Chep	8.1g/s		4297
39	10-11	Bath	10.2gd	[78]	4825

INCHCONNEL 3 b g £0
4	11-11	Donc	10.3gd	[67]	930	BL
20	8-8	Newm	12g/s	[60]	1153	bl
2	15-16	Nott	10hvy	55	1611	

INCHCOONAN 6 b m £1052
46a	4-7	Sout	8af	62	332	
36a	4-9	Sout	7af	[60]	555	
46a	2-11	Wolv	6af	[55]	778	p
36a	2-9	Wolv	7af	[55]	825	p

INCHDURA 6 ch g £0
58	11-18	Newc	7sft	72	2684
59	14-15	York	7gd	72	3117
65	6-17	Newc	7g/s	67	3700
61	9-16	Thir	8g/f	66	4592
33	12-17	Newc	10.1g/f	64	5016
63a	5-13	Wolv	9.5ap	61	5292

INCHENI 3 b f £34875
102	2-13	Newm	7gd	[75]	1169
86	14-16	Newm	8fm	[103]	1492
100	3-8	Good	8g/f	[103]	1863
103	1-6	NEWB	10g/f	[101]	2351*
93	4-10	Chep	10.2g/d	[102]	3089
92	6-10	Sali	9.9g/f	[100]	3866

INCHING 3 b f £2828
49a	6-14	Ling	6ap	[60]	23	
54a	4-11	Sout	6af	57	91	VIS
49a	6-16	Sout	5af	55	183	vis
50a	2-12	Wolv	5af	[53]	242	

41a	6-13	Sout	6af	[53]	254
50a	4-7	Wolv	5af	[51]	348
48a	4-13	Ling	6ap	49	740
25a	9-12	Ling	6ap	49	844 p
38a	8-11	Wolv	5af	49	958
23	14-20	Yarm	6g/f	48	1730 t
14	17-20	Beve	5g/f	[45]	1948 t
51	2-15	Ling	5g/f	45	2062
38	6-12	Folk	5g/f	47	2269
36	7-10	Brig	5.3fm	47	2331
54	2-14	Ling	5g/f	46	2585
19	9-9	Muss	5g/f	46	2614
29	9-12	Ling	5g/f	49	2743

INCHINNAN 7 b m £0

56a	5-14	Ling	10ap	58	520
36	10-15	Hami	9.2gd	57	1388
53	5-12	Ling	12.4sft	54	1680

INCHLOSS 3 b g £20677

37	11-13	Donc	7gd		925
68	4-12	Hayd	8.1sft		1108
76	1-13	NOTT	6.1sft		1464*
82	2-14	York	7.9g/s	73	1707
51	10-11	Pont	8g/f	77	2040
58	10-10	Donc	7gd	77	2427
69	6-9	Leic	8gd	77	2705
80	1-10	NOTT	8.2gd	[74]	3107*
84	2-8	Nott	8.2g/f	77	3421
87	2-12	Hayd	8.1gd	79	3738
86	4-11	Beve	9.9g/s	81	4239
71	12-13	Donc	10.3fm	[84]	4463
67	16-17	Newm	10g/f	83	4917

INCHNADAMPH 4 b g £10909

43	6-11	Beve	9.9sft	50	1633
60	2-11	Hayd	10.5g/s	47	2226 T
60	2-15	Ayr	10.9g/s	50	2545 t
62	1-7	HAMI	13gd	50	2708* t
66	1-7	HAMI	13gd	58	3134* t
65	5-13	York	11.9g/f	63	3437 t
48	8-20	York	13.8ap	62	5004 t
67	2-10	Catt	13.8sft	61	5322 t

INCHPAST 2 ch c £20981

69a	5-11	Ling	8ap		21
48a	13-14	Sout	7af		98
23	14-18	Wind	8.3sft	65	1647
26	15-16	Wind	11.6g/s	60	2621
57	4-14	Catt	12g/f	55	3192 BL
65	1-11	YARM	11.5gd	55	3367* bl
65	2-17	Newm	12g/f	62	3618 bl
70	1-11	BEVE	12.1g/s	[64]	3856* bl
78	1-8	CATT	13.8g/f	67	4439* bl
82	1-9	REDC	14.1fm	73	4559* bl

INCISE 3 ch f £1648

91	6-14	Bath	5gd	[93]	1400
89	7-15	Ches	5.1g/s	93	1572
65	10-12	Epso	5g/f	[90]	2206
85	4-6	Sand	5g/f	[90]	2390
84	4-11	Newm	5g/f	85	2734 T
77	8-21	Good	5fm	83	3567
79	5-9	Wind	5g/f	81	3976

INCISOR 3 b g £8946

49	5-16	Nott	10gd	51	1240
56	1-5	BRIG	9.9g/f	50	1372*
62a	1-14	LING	10ap	52	2064*
71a	1-12	WOLV	8.5af	58	2205*
38	13-14	Wind	10g/f	69	2452

INCLINE 4 b g £2620

82a	2-15	Ling	7ap	77	81
84a	2-16	Ling	7ap	80	181
85a	6-11	Ling	7ap	[82]	627

INCROYABLE 3 gr f £5291

63	2-13	Newc	10.1g/f	59	4406
67	1-13	NOTT	10g/s	[59]	4650*
27	12-14	Epso	12gd	66	4910

INCURSION 3 b c £4585

84	1-20	WIND	10sft	[82]	1651*
75	10-14	Asco	10g/f	84	1924
83	3-8	Nott	10g/f	83	2631
84	7-12	Wind	11.6gd	84	3161
78	7-11	Sali	12g/s	83	4080

INDALO GREY 8 b g £0

63a	5-12	Wolv	13.9ap	67	5160

INDEPENDENT SPIRIT 2 ch g £0

18	9-9	Nott	5.1gd		2926
40	10-13	Thir	6g/f		4590
29a	12-12	Wolv	5.1ap		4922
9a	10-11	Wolv	7.1ap		5113

INDESATCHEL 2 b c £53538

107	3-8	Curr	6.3gd		3319
106	2-16	Curr	6g/f		4153
106	3-11	Curr	6g/f		4431
111	2-6	Curr	6g/s		4736

INDI ANO STAR 3 b c £0

56	6-16	Newc	7sft		966
63	6-12	Hayd	8.1sft		1108
56	6-11	Newc	8sft		1279
55	8-14	Ayr	8g/f	[62]	1896
50	5-9	Thir	7g/f	[60]	2216
36	5-7	Ayr	9.1gd	55	2509 VIS
30	9-11	Redc	10sft	[52]	5303

INDIAN BAZAAR 8 ch g £2069

32	17-18	Good	5g/f	50	1867
32	10-12	Folk	5g/f	50	2269
55	2-18	Ling	6gd	50	2396
35	12-14	Ling	5g/f	51	2585
41	12-17	Warw	5fm	51	2599
51	2-12	Ling	5g/f	51	2743
0	16-17	Wind	6fm	53	2975
43	6-13	Bath	5gd	[53]	3143
31	13-15	Chep	5.1gd	53	3403
46	9-16	Ling	6g/f	51	3602
18	10-15	Sali	6gd	49	3888 p
25	11-15	Bath	5.7g/f	49	3966 bl
45	9-18	Bath	5.7g/f	45	4412
47	8-15	Chep	5.1gd	45	4489
25	14-15	Good	5gd	48	4751

INDIAN BLAZE 9 ch g £5027

29a	12-13	Ling	10ap	55	104
50a	8-14	Ling	10ap	52	174
54a	6-11	Ling	13ap	[48]	515
48a	2-14	Ling	10ap	45	757
53a	1-10	LING	8ap	45	766*
54a	2-13	Ling	10ap	51	805
32a	10-11	Ling	8ap	53	820
55a	3-12	Ling	8ap	52	845
43a	6-10	Ling	8ap	52	917
45a	7-12	Ling	8ap	52	1013
52	6-16	Kemp	9ap	50	3187
38a	10-13	Ling	10ap	50	3823
12	15-19	Kemp	8g/f	[49]	4795

INDIAN CALL 3 ch g £0

41	11-14	Donc	10.3gd	66	923
13	18-18	Leic	10g/s	66	1017
44	11-12	Warw	7.1gd	[60]	1125
22a	12-13	Wolv	8.6ap	55	5365

INDIAN CHASE 7 b g £5026

47a	2-7	Ling	16ap		1291 VIS
62	6-10	Nott	14.1sft		1742 vis
52	12-16	Sand	10g/s		2131 vis
0	9-9	Pont	18g/f	55	2607 vis
38	8-14	Sali	12g/s	45	3114
50	4-15	Chep	16.2gd	[40]	3400
21a	8-13	Ling	16ap	40	3822
51	1-15	CHEP	18sft	40	4056*
47a	2-14	Ling	16ap	[45]	4663
42a	10-14	Ling	16ap	46	5082

INDIAN CREEK 5 £0

115	9-14	Sha	12g/f		209

INDIAN DOVE 2 b f £0

57a	6-11	Ling	8ap		4738
53	10-13	Brig	8sft		5091

INDIAN EDGE 3 ch g £1154

57a	9-11	Ling	7ap	[62]	1008
66	5-13	Nott	6.1sft	[65]	1464
74	2-11	Nott	6.1sft	[65]	1607
55	11-16	Ling	7g/f	[65]	1982
33	12-13	Wind	6fm	[63]	2756
43	9-19	Chep	6.1sft	62	4054

36	11-19	Chep	8.1g/s	[58]	4366
35a	8-12	Wolv	6ap	[51]	5162

INDIAN HAVEN 4 ch c £2500

109	5-10	Sand	8.1g/s	[117]	1349
110	9-15	Newb	8g/f	[114]	1758
105	6-10	Long	7g/s	[114]	2139

INDIAN LILY 3 ch f £0

51	5-15	Folk	6g/s		1078
41	9-13	Folk	7g/s		1270
50	6-13	Folk	5sft		1575
46	7-13	Warw	6.1fm	55	2439
42	7-19	Leic	6g/f	53	2925
34	7-12	Folk	6g/s	50	3911 T
33	10-16	Yarm	7gd	47	4616
31	15-18	Kemp	10g/f	[45]	4791

INDIAN MAIDEN 3 br f £3883

58a	7-13	Wind	6af	73	41
39a	11-14	Ling	6ap	[70]	516
32	4-9	Wind	6fm	[72]	2760
31	11-12	Bath	5.7gd	70	3146
56	11-20	Hayd	6fm	66	3796
72	1-18	LEIC	6gd	62	5039*

INDIAN MUSIC 7 b g £3504

44a	6-9	Wolv	8.5af	[35]	664 p
42a	1-12	SOUT	6af	[40]	982*
42	5-17	Pont	6hvy	[40]	1065
37a	4-8	Sout	6af	[45]	1201
29a	4-6	Sout	6af	[45]	1405
38a	3-7	Sout	7af	[45]	1590
37a	3-6	Wolv	6af	[40]	1671
52a	2-11	Wolv	6af	[38]	2202
39a	4-15	Sout	7af	44	2501
38a	6-16	Sout	6af	44	2720
49a	2-16	Sout	6af	42	2806
33a	7-15	Sout	6af	40	3000
24	12-14	Catt	6g/f	[46]	3191
59a	6-11	Sout	6af	[45]	4041
43	5-15	Newc	6hvy	42	4211
39	10-11	Hami	6af	45	4818
0	10-10	Ayr	6sft	[45]	5278

INDIAN OAK 3 b f £0

25a	8-10	Ling	5ap		548
30a	7-9	Ling	5ap	[35]	621
0	13-13	Ling	7ap	35	739
13a	14-14	Ling	7ap	[35]	804

INDIAN PACE 3 ch c £7384

92	3-	Leop	7sft		1299

INDIAN PEARL 2 b f £0

34	8-8	Bath	5fm		2033

INDIAN PIPE DREAM 2 br c £0

63	9-13	Kemp	8g/f		4355
69	6-14	Sali	8gd		4852

INDIAN SHORES 5 b m £0

37a	9-10	Wolv	6af	58	282
33a	9-12	Wolv	5af	53	385
34a	6-11	Wolv	5af	48	508 P
32a	8-11	Wolv	7af	[45]	579 p
26a	9-16	Sout	5af	[40]	720 p
14a	12-13	Ling	6ap	[40]	788 p
10	18-18	Donc	7g/f	53	2080
26	16-20	Hayd	6fm	48	3796
40	10-19	Ayr	6sft	45	5069

INDIAN SMOKE 2 b g £0

40	16-18	Leic	5fm		2109

INDIAN SOLITAIRE 5 b g £550

72	3-22	Donc	12gd	71	918 VIS
56	9-19	York	11.9sft	73	1668 vis
70	6-11	Ripo	10g/f	73	2483 vis
67	7-7	Beve	9.9gd	73	2654 vis
37	9-10	Newm	12sft	[72]	5102 p

INDIAN SPARK 10 ch g £3104

92	4-7	Nott	5.1fm	[98]	1004
77	7-7	Kemp	6gd	[96]	1137
90	4-14	York	6g/s	95	1703
93	4-15	Hayd	5g/f	93	1917
70	6-12	Hayd	6g/s	[92]	2186
86	11-29	Asco	6fm	92	2581

80 11-15 Newc 5g/s 91 2727
33 10-10 York 6gd 90 3116
74 9-15 York 6g/f 87 3434
62 6-9 Ripo 6g/f 83 3646
70 8-19 York 6gd 78 4005
30 23-26 Ayr 6g/s 75 4652
59 7-14 Redc 5fm [71] 4930
67 9-16 Redc 6sft 68 5304

INDIAN STEPPES 5 b m £2119
73 6-9 Nott 6.1g/s [70] 1773
64 6-18 Donc 7g/f 70 2080
64 4-13 Donc 6gd 68 2232
65 3-9 Wind 6fm [67] 2760
71 7-8 Newm 6g/f 66 3235
57 6-11 Newm 6fm 66 3408
71 3-18 Leic 6gd 66 5039

INDIAN TRAIL 4 ch g £8756
76 9-13 Newb 7g/f 83 2880
93 1-16 NEWB 6g/f 83 3269*

INDIAN WARRIOR 8 b g £1686
45a 1-9 WOLV 7af [40] 310* bl
35a 9-15 Ling 7ap [40] 411 bl
24a 10-11 Wolv 7af [45] 579 bl
42a 4-14 Ling 6ap [45] 709 bl
13a 8-10 Wolv 6af [45] 822 bl
34a 5-8 Sout 6af [45] 1201 bl
42a 5-8 Ling 7ap [45] 1413
0 15-17 Kemp 7hvy [45] 1642
18 14-18 Nott 8.2gd [45] 1992 bl
38 3-20 Yarm 6g/s [40] 5121 bl

INDIAN WELCOME 4 ch g £0
52a 13-13 Ling 10ap 75 26 bl
64a 8-12 Ling 8ap 74 932 bl

INDIAN WELL 2 b g £0
58 14-17 Warw 7.1gd 4271

INDIANA BLUES 3 ch f £8846
71 4-12 Good 7g/f [93] 1846
28 11-16 Hayd 6g/f [89] 2182
56 7-10 Newb 5.2fm [83] 2649 BL
69 3-9 Brig 8gd [75] 2953
65 5-9 Sali 7gd 68 3456
66 3-19 Chep 6.1sft 66 4054
65 4-13 Warw 6.1gd 65 4272
67 3-13 Bath 5.7g/f [65] 4413
67 2-9 Catt 7g/f [63] 4674
68 1-11 WIND 6g/f [63] 4836*
65a 3-11 Wolv 7.1ap [63] 5357

INDIANNIE STAR 2 b f £15659
86 2-6 Newb 5.2gd 1735
81 1-12 LING 5g/f 1981*
84 6-8 Sand 5g/f 2094
79 13-17 Asco 5g/f 2490
83 5-7 Chan 5gd 3008
84 1-5 CHEP 5.1g/s 3086*
84 3-8 Newb 6g/f 3254
93 5-11 Newm 7g/f [87] 3781

INDIANS LANDING 3 b c £758
18 10-11 Leic 10gd 4701
71 3-12 Nott 10hvy 5190
64 5-8 Redc 10sft 5306

INDIBAR 3 b g £0
23 8-8 Redc 10g/f 2124

INDIBRAUN 2 b c £5977
76 5-9 Newc 5sft 962
84 1-14 DONC 6g/f 1874*
81 4-6 Pont 6g/f 2039
57 4-5 Muss 7.1g/f 2612
58a 8-10 Sout 7af 82 3483
76 3-11 Ches 7sft [77] 4072
68 4-14 Muss 7.1g/f [77] 4171
46 12-19 Nott 6.1g/s 72 4645 P
46a 6-13 Wolv 6ap [70] 4980

INDIENA 2 ch f £11778
72 4-10 Newm 6g/f 3064
78 5-12 Newb 5g/f 3251
81 2-5 Hayd 6fm 3795
77 4-7 Ches 6.1g/f [79] 4050
80 2-21 Donc 6.5fm 74 4457

79 3-12 Nott 6.1g/f [77] 4844

INDIVIDUAL TALENTS 4 ch f £0
63 8-20 Epso 12hvy 69 1295
40 16-18 Nott 14.1g/s 68 1772
0 8-8 Newm 12gd 68 1889

INDONESIA 2 ch c £0
41 8-12 Beve 8.5sft 4257
64 8-10 Redc 9fm 4558
73 5-16 York 7.9gd 4997

INDRANI 3 b f £1654
18a 13-13 Wolv 6af 50 436
34a 6-9 Sout 7af [45] 613
42a 4-13 Sout 6af 45 797
32a 8-11 Sout 6af 45 872
34a 7-8 Sout 5af 45 1031
23a 4-7 Wolv 6af [45] 1312
23a 7-7 Ling 6ap [45] 1453 P
43 2-9 Kemp 6hvy [45] 1641
0 8-9 Wolv 6af [40] 1803
38 5-19 Leic 6g/f 43 2925
15 9-10 Hami 6g/f 43 3203
35 8-14 Yarm 6gd 42 3870
24 9-12 Folk 6g/s 42 3911
41 2-5 Yarm 6sft [38] 4150 p
6 13-15 Yarm 7g/s [40] 4587

INDRAPURA STAR 3 b g £0
0 13-13 Wolv 8.5af [47] 46
0 6-7 Sout 8af [40] 721
0 7-8 Ling 10ap [35] 829

INESCAPABLE 3 b c £3390
46 9-10 Sali 6gd 3452
32 8-10 Ling 6g/f 3603
54 4-5 Good 7gd 3953
6 19-20 Chep 7.1g/s 53 4367
56 1-18 LEIC 7gd [49] 4698*
35 8-13 Brig 8gd [53] 4902
37 14-17 Leic 7gd 53 5056

INFIDELITY 3 b f £1247
60a 6-10 Ling 10ap 70 568
56a 8-10 Ling 10ap 67 676
46 10-14 Donc 10.3gd 70 923
33 8-9 Ches 12.3gd 65 1582
60 6-11 Beve 9.9g/f 62 1834
52 10-13 Pont 10g/f 62 2038
58 6-8 Hami 9.2g/f 58 2475 P
58 3-7 Ayr 9.1gd 58 2509 P
53 5-8 Hayd 11.9gd 57 2881 VIS
29 16-19 Leic 10g/f 57 4456
61 4-16 Ches 10.3g/f 57 4515 p
31a 9-13 Wolv 9.5ap 52 4925
55a 4-13 Wolv 8.6ap [52] 5336

INGLETON 2 b c £22131
66 7-15 Nott 5.1gd 3988
74 4-20 York 6g/f 4401
88 1-18 AYR 6g/s 4617*
94 1-15 YORK 6gd 77 4985*
96 1-14 NEWM 6sft 84 5098*

INGLEWOOD 4 ch g £0
8a 7-9 Wolv 14.8af [35] 301

INGRANDIRE 5 b h £0
87 9-13 Asco 20g/f 2518

INHABITANT 2 ch c £26127
105 1-8 DEAU 7sft 3169*
102 2-7 Deau 6gd 3658

INISTRAHULL ISLAND 3 b g £1327
49a 10-16 Ling 7ap 56 22
56a 4-15 Ling 7ap 56 50
60a 2-15 Ling 7ap [57] 117
62a 3-16 Ling 7ap 59 144
59a 3-13 Ling 6ap 59 471 VIS
57a 6-14 Ling 7ap 59 499
47a 11-12 Ling 8ap 58 607
0 6-8 Ripo 6g/f [56] 2480 BL
1 15-19 Thir 8g/s [56] 2688

INK IN GOLD 3 b g £214
60 10-17 Chep 8.1gd 2117
56 5-10 Newc 7hvy 4216

29 9-11 Ripo 12.3gd 4281
1 11-13 Chep 8.1hvy 55 4709
23 11-13 Warw 7.1g/s [50] 4994
41a 4-12 Wolv 9.5ap [45] 5209
40a 3-13 Wolv 8.6ap [45] 5232

INKA DANCER 2 ch f £1709
73 3-11 Bath 5.7gd 4543
66 4-16 Bath 5.7gd 4823
73 3-13 Wind 6g/f 5047

INMOM 3 b f £1042
59 3-7 Nott 8.2hvy 1610
15 11-11 Donc 12g/f 61 1875
53a 4-15 Sout 8af 60 2338
56 6-18 Leic 10gd 58 2706
51 6-12 Beve 9.9gd 58 2893
24a 14-16 Sout 8af 55 3487 T
6 18-18 Beve 9.9g/s 54 4243
58 6-8 Redc 10sft [52] 5306

INN FOR THE DANCER 2 b g £0
52a 8-13 Wolv 8.6ap 5288

INNCLASSIC 3 b f £4585
2 10-11 Newb 6g/f 1732
48 17-18 Wind 6g/f 75 2268
53a 3-8 Sout 6af [75] 2379 BL
67 1-9 WARW 6.1fm [67] 2778+ bl
56a 2-10 Sout 5af [65] 3156 bl
56 8-11 Bath 5g/f [65] 3372 bl
46 9-11 Bath 5g/f 63 3849 bl
31 15-18 Leic 6gd 60 5039 bl
55a 7-13 Wolv 5.1ap 59 5156 bl
36a 9-12 Wolv 5.1ap 55 5326 bl

INNOCENT REBEL 3 ch c £907
66 8-10 Good 8g/f 1815
73a 4-13 Ling 10ap 2066
66 3-11 Folk 9.7gd 4120
56 10-19 Sali 14.1gd 68 4856

INNOCENT SPLENDOUR 2 b f £5102
81 2-13 Kemp 7g/f 3520
84 1-15 FOLK 7gd 4114*
82 7-17 Good 8gd 80 4871

INNPURSUIT 2 b c £0
65a 7-13 Wolv 8.6ap 5288

INNSTYLE 3 b f £4006
40 6-12 Ling 6g/f [67] 2586
37 10-13 Wind 5fm 64 2784
54 7-20 Ling 6g/f 60 4317
64 3-18 Bath 5.7g/f 60 4412
55 8-13 Bath 5.7gd 57 4548
52 15-17 Ling 6g/f 64 4740
70 1-17 BATH 5.7gd [61] 5020+
43a 9-13 Wolv 6ap 67 5114
39a 10-11 Wolv 7.1ap [63] 5357

INSIGNIA 2 b c £0
66 5-10 Leic 5g/f 1826
62 5-7 Folk 5g/f 3722
55a 8-12 Ling 6ap 4178

INSIGNIFICANCE 4 b c £0
39a 7-10 Wolv 8.5af 46 753
31a 9-10 Ling 8ap 45 766 BL

INSINUATION 2 b f £189
79 6-7 Kemp 7g/f 4359

INSPECTOR BLUE 6 ch g £0
22 10-14 Yarm 11.5g/f 35 3714

INSTANT RECALL 3 ch c £13695
77a 3-15 Ling 7ap 875
82a 1-11 LING 7gd 1008*
70 10-20 Newm 7g/f 80 1186
76 4-14 Ches 6.1g/s 78 1570
81 5-11 Newb 6g/f 78 1734
82 4-9 Kemp 6gd [78] 2173
76 5-7 Newm 6g/f 78 2764 BL
90a 1-11 LING 6ap 78 2841* bl
83 2-10 Kemp 6gd [78] 3188 bl
75 4-11 Donc 6g/s 78 3379 bl
72 7-15 Newb 6gd 80 3920 bl
72a 11-14 Ling 7ap 84 4446 bl

INSTINCT 3 b g £7386
60a	5-15	Ling	7ap		670
62a	7-15	Ling	7ap		814
64	3-12	Folk	6sft	62	975
42	9-15	Wind	6g/s	62	1054
53	10-17	Sali	6g/f	62	1722
32	12-14	Chep	7.1gd	61	2199
53	3-11	Epso	7fm	[59]	3541
60	3-6	Brig	5g/f	59	3718
60	2-19	Chep	6.1sft	56	4054
64	1-6	YARM	6g/s	[58]	4586*
48	14-20	Wind	6g/s	60	4946

INSTRUCTOR 3 ch c £3748
84a	2-10	Ling	7ap	[78]	911
87a	1-9	Brig	8ap	[78]	1022*
57	16-18	Good	9g/f	79	1813
68	8-12	Sand	8.1g/s	77	2129
65	10-16	Good	7gd	75	4873

INSUBORDINATE 3 ch c £4349
27	16-18	Nott	8.2fm	59	1007
62	1-11	NEWC	7sft	56	1678*
52	8-17	Ayr	7.2sft	61	5063

INTAVAC BOY 3 ch g £2493
63	6-14	Thir	6gd		1639
46	6-15	Nott	5.1g/f		2152
51	4-9	Beve	5sft		2945
45	11-18	Hayd	6gd	60	3737
63	2-17	Newc	8fm	57	4867
67	2-13	Pont	8g/s	[57]	5153

INTELLIBET ONE 3 b f £879
44a	7-12	Wolv	5af	60	109
39a	12-12	Wolv	5af	60	124
15	15-18	Thir	6g/f	60	2214
48	11-17	Warw	5fm	57	2599
57	3-18	Hayd	5gd	54	2951
42	4-17	Wind	6fm	54	2975
53	7-15	Wind	5gd	56	3165
41	9-14	Catt	6g/f	56	3352
39	21-22	Good	5fm	55	3537
40	10-16	Wind	5fm	54	3640

INTENDANT 3 b c £64085
118	1-8	MUNI	10gd		3662*

INTENDED 2 b f £0
71	11-16	Sali	7gd	4329

INTENSITY 7 b g £1336
17a	9-10	Wolv	14.8af	63	34
39a	9-10	Sout	12af	60	138
56a	3-14	Ling	12ap	55	711
9a	9-11	Sout	11af	55	746
18	16-19	Donc	10.3gd	60	924
59	2-17	Nott	14.1gd	55	1238
37	11-13	Brig	11.9g/f	58	1373

INTER VISION 4 b c £4412
69	11-16	Muss	8g/f	88	1120
16	14-15	Pont	6hvy	88	1251
83	5-19	Thir	6g/f	86	1767
52	11-17	Redc	6gd	84	2561
66	7-10	Hayd	6g/s	82	3136
84	4-11	Thir	6g/f	79	3574
87	2-9	Ripo	6g/f	79	3646
72	10-16	Redc	7g/f	79	3809
81	7-20	Donc	5fm	82	4496
76	10-14	Ripo	6gd	81	4786 P

INTERCEPTOR 4 ch c £0
77	11-19	Newm	10g/f	88	1478

INTERIM PAYMENT 2 b f £0
74	5-13	Leic	8g/f	4450

INTERNATIONALGUEST 5 b g £4259
71a	11-16	Ling	12ap	81	293 vis
83a	2-16	Ling	12ap	78	404 vis
22a	14-16	Ling	12ap	81	475 vis
69a	8-11	Ling	8ap	80	547 vis
76a	7-10	Ling	12ap	80	570 bl
84a	2-11	Ling	10ap	78	716 vis
60	16-24	Donc	8gd	81	928 bl
60	10-20	Wind	11.6g/s	78	1056 bl
59	5-8	Newc	10.1sft	[75]	2687 bl

69	5-8	Wind	10fm	73	2973 vis
66	5-6	Beve	9.9gd	[71]	3313 bl
58	14-16	Wind	11.6gd	70	3829 P
51	8-9	Yarm	10.1g/s	[67]	4254 bl
48a	13-14	Ling	10ap	[75]	4742 bl
45	12-19	Pont	10g/s	66	5148 p

INTERSTICE 6 b h £413
18a	10-11	Wolv	12af	[58]	6
0	11-12	Wolv	12af	58	75
32a	9-15	Sout	12af	54	257
50a	3-10	Sout	11af	51	330
37a	6-9	Sout	12af	51	456 P
34a	5-9	Wolv	9.4af	50	647 p

INTERWOVEN 2 b c £0
31	10-10	Redc	6gd	4244
61	16-19	Leic	7gd	5055

INTIKRAFT 2 ch c £0
33a	9-13	Wolv	6af	[68]	3 vis
48a	7-9	Ling	6ap	60	105 BL

INTITNICE 2 b c £0
33a	11-12	Wolv	5af	[52]	32 bl
22a	9-16	Sout	8af	[45]	164
53a	9-11	Ling	7ap	[45]	213
0	12-13	Wolv	8.5af	[39]	300
20a	11-14	Ling	6ap	[40]	495 bl
0	11-11	Sali	8gd	48	3455 p
3	17-18	Chep	7.1g/s	40	3900

INTO THE BREEZE 4 b g £0
47	20-20	Asco	7g/f	95	1926

INTO THE DARK 3 ch c £44224
101	1-16	DONC	10.3gd		2751* VIS
109	1-11	NEWM	10g/f	90	3236+ vis t
116	1-11	YORK	11.9gd	100	4324* vis t
117	1-6	AYR	10.9sft	[114]	4687+ vis t

INTO THE SHADOWS 4 ch f £13628
66	3-11	Newc	8sft		1279
72	3-9	Hami	12.1gd		1507
71	4-7	Hami	9.2gd		1747
75	1-9	NEWC	10.1g/f	[72]	5015*
78	1-7	NEWM	12sft	72	5268*

INTOXICATING 2 b c £4774
90	1-10	LEIC	6gd		2703*
88	3-11	Sali	6g/s		3110

INTREPID JACK 2 b c £0
51	13-16	Newb	8hvy	5220

INTRICATE WEB 7 b g £33721
75a	3-13	Wolv	9.4af	72	127
80a	1-12	WOLV	9.4af	72	382*
83a	1-12	WOLV	9.4af	76	513+
85a	2-8	Sout	11af	79	595
84a	4-10	Wolv	12af	85	810
70	6-10	Hayd	10.5sft	[78]	1104
51	7-10	Hayd	10.5g/s	76	1346
81	1-19	RIPO	10g/f	74	1781+
80	3-12	Hayd	8.1g/f	77	1883
76	3-10	Hayd	8.1gd	78	2242
70	12-15	York	8.9g/f	78	2404
86	1-13	REDC	10gd	78	2560*
73	10-14	Hayd	8.1gd	83	2903
72	12-15	Donc	10.3g/f	83	3598
67	15-20	Hayd	10.5fm	81	3794
69	5-7	Pont	8g/f	[80]	4629
74	6-19	Hayd	10.5g/s	80	4766
74	9-20	York	10.4gd	75	4986

INTRIGUED 2 gr f £16352
78	3-12	Beve	7.5g/s	4242
91	1-5	EPSO	8.5gd	4464*
109	4-10	Long	8g/f	4954

INTRIGUING GLIMPSE 2 b f £11749
66a	1-9	LING	5ap		76*
70a	1-10	LING	5ap	66	217*
73a	3-8	Ling	6ap	71	268
71	3-10	Folk	6sft	71	1576
77	2-12	Wind	5g/f	71	1809
77	2-8	Brig	5.3g/f	71	1942
82	2-9	Sand	5g/f	74	2387
70	7-9	Epso	6fm	78	3543

INTRODUCTION 2 b g £0
25a	11-13	Ling	6ap		25
46a	7-15	Ling	7ap		52
41a	11-14	Ling	6ap		146
23a	9-12	Ling	8ap	47	845
0	13-15	Wind	11.6g/f	[45]	2267
31	10-20	Beve	16.2gd	40	3312
10	5-7	Chep	12.1sft	35	4053
0	9-10	Bath	11.7g/s	[35]	4199 VIS

INVADER 7 b h £4377
86a	4-10	Ling	10ap	[86]	179
86a	3-12	Ling	8ap	[86]	234 bl
67a	7-8	Wolv	7af	85	285 bl
78a	8-14	Ling	10ap	82	452 bl
73a	6-10	Wolv	8.5af	[82]	511 bl
53a	10-12	Wolv	8.5af	78	632 bl
59	9-12	Sand	8.1g/s	80	2129 bl t
66	8-13	Ling	7.6g/f	78	2587 bl t
79a	1-12	LING	8ap	[74]	2840* bl t
58	10-12	Kemp	10gd	78	3185 bl t
47	6-6	Yarm	7g/f	75	3708 t
67	6-5	Kemp	8g/f	72	4362 bl t
64	8-13	Epso	8.5gd	72	4469 bl t
56	14-14	Wind	8.3g/f	69	4832 bl t

INVASIAN 3 ch c £28538
88	1-14	HAYD	8.1g/s		2231*
91	2-6	Ripo	8g/f	86	2525
81	8-13	Newm	8g/f	88	3277
67	15-17	Good	7fm	87	3550
102	1-8	FOLK	9.7g/s	[86]	3912*
101	2-11	Beve	9.9g/s	95	4239

INVER GOLD 7 b h £0
8a	7-8	Wolv	12af	[74]	347

INVERTIEL 2 br c £1643
69	4-6	Hami	6g/f		3202
81	2-5	Hami	6g/f		3589
0	12-12	Ayr	7.2hvy		4083
34	10-14	Hami	6sft	80	4692
60	7-12	Newc	7g/f	[75]	5011
56	6-12	Muss	7.1g/s	[75]	5142 VIS

INVESTMENT AFFAIR 4 b g £0
41	10-16	Ches	10.3g/f	60	4515

INVITATION 6 b g £3866
45	11-22	Donc	12gd	76	918
64	6-20	Wind	11.6g/s	74	1056
73	4-17	Sali	14.1g/s	70	1502
76	2-19	Wind	10sft	[70]	1650
67	8-19	Newb	10gd	70	1736
75	2-10	Sand	14g/f	72	2192
2	28-29	Asco	20g/f	73	2471

INVITING 3 b f £0
61	14-20	Newm	8g/f	3237

INVOGUE 4 b f £0
20a	6-11	Sout	12af	[40]	3154
10a	10-14	Sout	8af	[40]	3392

IO CALLISTO 3 br f £0
0	9-9	Beve	5sft	2945

IONIAN SPRING 9 b g £16662
94	1-20	NEWB	10gd	85	1235*
88	9-19	Newm	10g/f	90	1478
97	1-9	HAYD	10.5g/s	90	2185*
89	9-21	York	10.4gd	95	3118
76	18-20	Hayd	10.5fm	95	3794
89	5-11	York	10.4g/s	93	4021
74	7-8	York	8.9g/f	[91]	4397

IPHIGENIA 2 b f £6523
45a	7-12	Wolv	6af	[63]	42
13a	14-14	Sout	7af	[63]	98
70	7-11	Bath	8fm	[50]	1904
63	5-11	Bath	8fm	[50]	2031
46	7-11	Brig	7fm	52	2334
71	2-9	Folk	7fm	[50]	2716
63	4-13	Warw	8.1gd	65	3058
62	5-16	Epso	8.5gd	65	3219
71	3-19	Chep	7.1gd	64	3401
76	1-8	FOLK	7g/f	65	3724*
73	2-15	Catt	7sft	71	3933

| 52 | 6-8 | Folk | 7gd | [73] | 4117 |
| 70 | 6-14 | Epso | 7gd | 72 | 4465 |

IPLEDGEALLEGIANCE 7 b g £2768

40a	5-11	Wolv	12af	[50]	6
45a	6-11	Wolv	12af	50	72
22a	8-10	Wolv	12af	[48]	250
42a	2-9	Sout	12af	[46]	353
34a	5-8	Sout	11af	[46]	420
36a	3-5	Sout	12af	[45]	446
32a	6-9	Sout	11af	[45]	505
17a	5-10	Wolv	12af	[35]	581
9a	8-10	Wolv	12af	[35]	780
42a	7-14	Ling	12ap	[35]	827
0	10-15	Sout	12af	30	867
23a	5-9	Sout	11af	[35]	985
42a	5-8	Ling	10ap	[35]	1026
22	8-9	Ayr	13.1g/s	[35]	1449
30	5-15	Nott	10gd	[35]	1991
30	5-10	Hami	13g/f	30	2479 BL
38	2-10	Redc	14.1g/s	30	2562 bl
24	11-20	Catt	12g/f	35	2850 bl
38	3-12	Muss	16gd	35	2964 bl
33a	2-10	Sout	14af	30	3158 bl
29	7-9	Ayr	15gd	30	3327 bl
18	7-7	Muss	13g/f	30	3530 bl

IPSA LOQUITUR 4 b f £282

57	10-17	Leic	10g/s		1019
61	4-11	Leic	12g/s	60	1357
0	P-16	Leic	11.8g/f	58	1830

IQTE SAAB 3 b c £13128

106	1-7	NEWM	7g/s		1150*
95	6-8	Newm	7g/f	[104]	1932
95	9-11	Newb	6g/f	[104]	3268
104	5-8	Epso	7g/f	[102]	4472
104	3-10	Redc	7fm	[100]	4929

IRANOO 7 b g £0

| 26 | 7-8 | Muss | 12gd | | 1552 t |

IRELANDS EYE 9 b g £208

| 33a | 3-7 | Sout | 14af | [30] | 357 |
| 9a | 4-6 | Wolv | 16.2af | [30] | 395 |

IRIE RASTA 5 ch g £0

| 9 | 15-16 | Nott | 10hvy | 66 | 5345 |

IRISH BALLAD 2 b c £329

0	8-9	Yarm	8sft		4147
53	10-11	Nott	8.2g/s		4648
67a	4-12	Wolv	8.6ap		5115

IRISH BLADE 2 b c £7478

56a	9-12	Ling	8ap		100
71	4-14	Wind	10g/s		1259
76	3-12	Sali	12g/s		1501
71	10-10	Wind	10fm	79	2785
67	7-12	Hayd	11.9gd	75	3734
61	11-14	Newb	10g/f	70	3961
72	3-10	Good	16g/s	68	4235
72	2-15	Ches	15.9g/f	68	4512
80	1-19	SALI	14.1gd	69	4856*
76	5-15	Good	16gd	78	5025
60	6-13	Newb	16sft	77	5194

IRISH CHAPEL 8 b g £0

| 27 | 8-9 | Leic | 8g/f | | 1966 |
| 0 | 9-10 | Sout | 11af | | 2499 |

IRISH PLAYWRIGHT 4 b g £528

48	8-10	Chep	7.1gd		3732
53a	13-14	Ling	13ap		4892
65a	3-13	Wolv	9.5ap		5290 BL

IRON TEMPTRESS 3 ch f £0

20	13-13	Thir	7g/f	65	3571
39a	10-11	Sout	8af	60	4044
47	6-8	Catt	13.8g/f	56	4439
30	10-12	Beve	12.1g/f	56	4601 BL
19	8-11	Catt	13.8g/f	[53]	4671

IRON WARRIOR 4 b g £0

| 4 | 15-18 | Pont | 12g/f | 55 | 4938 |

IRONY 5 gr g £733

| 81 | 7-13 | Kemp | 7sft | 89 | 945 |
| 85 | 9-17 | Sand | 8.1g/s | 89 | 1351 |

87	4-10	Beve	8.5g/f	87	1833
77	13-13	Epso	8.5g/f	86	2207
70	10-13	Sali	8gd	85	2662

IROQUOIS PRINCESS 2 ch f £0

22	8-9	Pont	6g/s		5154
20a	9-11	Wolv	7.1ap		5228
41	9-14	Nott	6.1hvy		5342

IRREVERSIBLE 2 b f £0

| 73a | 6-14 | Ling | 7ap | | 5258 |

IRUSAN 4 br g £4170

55	6-20	Donc	7g/s		1518
61	8-19	Donc	6g/f		1876
29	13-16	Hayd	6g/f		2182
62a	4-12	Sout	6af	[57]	2722
50a	6-15	Sout	7af	[63]	2999
53a	5-9	Sout	6af	61	3485
33	8-15	Ayr	7.2hvy	58	4088
59a	2-13	Wolv	8.6ap	54	5005 BL
65a	1-12	WOLV	7.1ap	55	5112* bl

ISAAC 5 b g £17036

57a	1-12	WOLV	12af	[45]	891*
53a	2-16	Sout	14af	51	1033
63	1-12	SOUT	11gd	55	1286*
65	1-18	NOTT	14.1sft	55	1469*
40	10-11	Pont	12g/f	64	2041
71	2-9	Hami	13gd	63	2176
66	4-8	Hami	12.1g/f	62	2318
67	4-10	Leic	11.8gd	[65]	2707
71	1-12	NOTT	14.1gd	64	3105*
64	6-8	Epso	12gd	70	3217
31	16-17	Catt	12sft	69	3929
60	8-13	Warw	12.6gd	68	4274
68	4-15	Ches	15.9g/f	66	4512
72	2-9	Good	16gd	65	4875
54	7-20	York	13.9gd	67	5004
70	4-10	Pont	18g/s	66	5151

ISAZ 4 b c £0

73	5-14	Folk	7g/s	[75]	1080
70	5-17	Sali	6g/f	[74]	1497
65	5-19	Donc	6g/f	[73]	1876
7	8-9	Wind	6fm	[72]	2760
39	12-17	Wind	6fm	70	2975

ISIDORE BONHEUR 3 b c £7750

98	4-7	Newm	9g/f		1189 BL
100	4-5	Newm	10g/f	[98]	1482 bl
99	4-6	Ches	12.3gd	[98]	1584 bl
75	4-4	Newm	14.8g/f	[98]	3027
88	12-15	Donc	8fm	98	4531
80	14-17	Newm	10g/f	93	4917

ISITLOVEYOURAFTER 2 b f £0

12	9-10	Hayd	6g/s		2228
38	5-8	Ayr	5gd		2505
52	6-8	Muss	7.1g/f		3559
11	14-14	Redc	5fm	50	4556

ISKANDER 3 b g £1569

84	6-14	Ripo	6g/s	93	1360 bl
83	9-14	York	7sft	90	1665 bl
74	14-17	Epso	9g/f	87	2212
59	10-12	Ripo	6g/f	84	2482
59	9-15	Hayd	6gd	81	2950 bl
74	6-12	Hayd	6sft	77	3273 bl
77	4-12	Hayd	8.1gd	73	3738 bl
59	10-15	Kemp	8g/f	73	4362 bl
54	5-8	Hami	9.2sft	[72]	4694 bl
64	10-12	Muss	8gd	[72]	4809 bl
69	4-14	Pont	8g/f	[71]	4937 bl
39a	13-13	Wolv	9.5ap	69	5161 bl

ISLAND HOUSE 8 ch h £8963

105	3-12	Kemp	10gd	[113]	1139
103	7-11	Sand	10g/s	[113]	1350
102	5-10	Good	9.9g/f	[111]	1862
108	3-7	Newm	12g/f	[109]	2762
103	3-9	Newm	12g/f	[106]	3233

ISLAND LIGHT USA 4 ch g £0

18	20-20	Newm	12gd	90	1172
44	17-20	Donc	10.3g/s	85	1519
48	16-19	Ripo	10g/f	80	1781
20	9-9	Hayd	10.5g/s	76	2185

ISLAND RAPTURE 4 b f £4751

72	11-17	Sand	8.1g/s	79	1351
68	8-9	Newm	8gd	77	1891
73	4-5	Sand	9g/f	74	2191
50	10-10	Newm	10fm	74	2592
70a	3-12	Ling	8ap	[71]	2840
72	2-7	Brig	8g/f	71	3174
67	6-14	Bath	8g/f	71	3963
61	11-14	Epso	8.5gd	71	4295
70a	2-12	Ling	8ap	69	4743
74a	3-12	Wolv	8.6ap	69	4923
71a	5-12	Ling	8ap	69	5238

ISLAND SOUND 7 b g £4170

0	6-6	Newm	10g/f	[102]	3754
103	3-6	Epso	10.1gd	[98]	4290
100	3-5	Newb	9gd	[99]	4682

ISLAND SPELL 3 b f £1840

64	3-6	Ches	7gd	[76]	1587
49	5-12	Thir	7g/f	[75]	1971
61	3-7	Newc	6g/s	[70]	2728
41	15-15	Redc	5g/s	68	2961
52	10-12	Catt	5gd	68	3193
55	9-14	Thir	6g/f	64	3416 P

ISLAND STAR 3 b g £0

44a	6-13	Ling	6ap	[57]	219
30a	12-15	Ling	7ap	[52]	263
24a	8-11	Ling	8ap	[52]	343
17a	10-13	Ling	6ap	[48]	400 VIS
37a	14-14	Ling	7ap	[45]	450
38a	4-6	Ling	10ap	[40]	1455
7	6-8	Brig	11.9gd	[40]	1547

ISLAND SWING 2 ch f £12195

49	15-19	Wind	5g/f		1805
71	1-8	HAYD	6g/f		2183*
86	1-13	YORK	6g/f		2358*
86	4-10	Kemp	6g/f	83	3521
52	11-12	Wind	6gd	82	3825
74	8-13	Warw	6.1gd	81	4273
83	3-4	Yarm	6g/s	[78]	4633
75	4-19	Ling	6g/f	[81]	4895
85	1-9	NOTT	6.1hvy	[78]	5185*
13	15-20	Newb	6hvy	85	5225

ISLANDS FAREWELL 4 b g £4557

49	7-11	Muss	9g/f		1095
0	17-19	Redc	8sft	50	1661
54	2-8	Hami	8.3fm		3246
50	5-13	Muss	8g/f	53	3526
10a	11-15	Sout	8af	51	4132
50	3-14	Good	8sft	51	4189
51	2-14	Pont	10g/f	49	4624
53	2-12	Brig	11.9fm	49	4764

ISLE DREAM 2 ch f £0

0	10-10	Redc	5fm		4338
12	7-10	Pont	6fm		4752
25a	13-13	Wolv	5.1ap		5207

ISLE OF LIGHT 2 b f £0

| 0 | 13-14 | Leic | 5g/f | | 3517 |
| 18a | 8-10 | Sout | 5af | | 4129 |

ISLEOFHOPEANTEARS 5 b g £0

| 61 | 10-18 | Bath | 10.2gd | | 5023 |

ISLERO NOIR 3 b c £7764

| 112 | 3-9 | Deau | 10hvy | | 4158 |

ISMAHAAN 5 ch m £0

| 67 | 6-11 | Wind | 10fm | | 3802 |
| 49 | 5-11 | Ripo | 12.3gd | | 4281 |

ISSY BLUE 2 b f £0

61	9-15	Folk	7gd		3381
56	8-13	Hayd	6gd		3736
45	11-16	Sali	7gd		3882

IT MUST BE SPEECH 2 b c £856

0	9-9	Wolv	9.4af	[63]	238
58a	5-8	Sout	11af	58	614
63a	2-15	Sout	12af	58	867
31a	5-7	Sout	12af	[65]	1030
25	16-17	Beve	8.5g/f	60	4721
23	15-20	Catt	12gd	57	4966

ITALIAN COUNSEL 7 b g £0
10a 12-13 Ling 10ap [30] 539
32a 4-10 Ling 12ap [30] 1714

ITALIAN MIST 5 b g £13925
51a 1-12 WOLV 6af [39] 297* e
47a 3-13 Wolv 6af 50 384 e
45a 5-13 Ling 6ap 50 451 e
58a 1-14 SOUT 6af 49 501* e
56a 2-11 Wolv 7af 54 558 e
54a 9-16 Ling 7ap 54 600 e
67a 1-12 SOUT 5af 54 853* e
49 3-17 Kemp 5sft 45 944 e
68a 1-13 WOLV 6af 63 1221* e
24 7-15 Folk 6g/s 53 1267 e
66a 4-12 Sout 6af 68 1442 e
41a 10-13 Wolv 6af 68 2053 e
33 13-19 Bath 5.7sft 49 5176 e

ITALIAN TOUCH 2 b g £0
55 7-14 Warw 6.1g/f 4422
50 9-15 Nott 6.1g/s 4644
62 8-15 Nott 5.1gd 4859
38 7-9 Catt 7sft 5131

ITHACA 3 ch f £11663
90 3-7 Newm 7g/s [102] 1150
78 6-9 Ches 11.4gd[102] 1568
90 5-7 Newb 10gd [102] 1733
100 3-9 Sand 8.1g/s [94] 2917
97 4-12 Bath 8g/f [100] 3965
100 3-15 Donc 7fm [100] 4479
90 5-10 Redc 7fm [98] 4929

ITS A BLESSING 3 b f £0
12a 12-14 Ling 10ap 367

ITS A MYSTERY 5 b m £0
21 11-14 Yarm 11.5g/f 39 3714 T

ITS BLUE CHIP 2 b g £8212
50a 7-11 Ling 7ap 213 e
58a 3-11 Wolv 9.4af 438 e
59a 9-13 Ling 10ap 601 e
67 1-12 WIND 11.6g/s 58 1260* e
51 4-7 Donc 14.6g/s 64 1521 e
54 6-20 Wind 11.6sft 64 1648 e
61a 4-12 Wolv 12af 62 2203 e
68a 1-11 SOUT 12af 60 2804* e
50 10-12 Wind 11.6gd 65 3161 e
38 13-17 Newm 12ap/f 65 3618
47 7-11 Beve 12.1g/s [64] 3856
34 13-20 York 13.9gd 59 5004 e
41a 7-12 Wolv 12.2ap 55 5339

ITS DEFINITE 5 b g £0
36 25-34 Newm 18sft 75 5135 p

ITS ECCO BOY 5 ch g £3268
34a 13-16 Ling 7ap 55 20
57a 3-12 Wolv 7af 55 74
46a 6-16 Ling 7ap [54] 123
54a 4-16 Ling 7ap 54 144
44a 8-15 Ling 7ap 53 266
58a 4-14 Ling 6ap 53 328
51a 4-10 Wolv 7af 51 379
57a 1-13 SOUT 6af 52 500*
18a 7-9 Wolv 7af 57 684
40a 9-13 Sout 6af 57 741
52a 7-10 Ling 7ap [57] 765
50 12-14 Wind 5g/f 64 2266
51 7-8 Newm 12af [60] 2591
46 13-17 Newm 7g/f 60 2768
13 14-14 Leic 6g/f 58 3213
31a 10-13 Sout 6af [55] 3482
53a 6-12 Ling 8ap [53] 4974
38a 12-12 Ling 8ap [53] 5077
38a 6-12 Wolv 7.1ap [49] 5229

ITS MY SON 3 b g £0
0 9-9 Wind 10fm 3642

ITS PEGGY SPEECH 2 b f £0
44 17-21 Donc 6sft 5368

ITS THE LIMIT 5 b g £1979
91 4-10 Asco 12g/f 92 3444
84 13-20 Hayd 14fm 92 4383
96 4-16 Asco 16.2g/f 91 4803

15 32-34 Newm 18sft 92 5135

ITSA MONKEY 2 b g £720
45a 9-10 Ling 5ap 882
24 6-6 Brig 6fm 2330
44a 2-6 Sout 5af 3093
32 12-12 Catt 7g/f 55 3351
42 8-11 Thir 7g/f 3570 P
37a 12-13 Sout 7af 49 4040
62 7-12 Beve 8.5sft [43] 4257 BL
22 14-14 Carl 6.9fm [49] 4503 bl
26 11-16 Beve 7.5g/f 49 4597 bl

ITSONLYAGAME 4 b c £1709
51a 1-6 LING 10ap [60] 409*
51a 8-14 Ling 10ap [60] 477
24a 9-11 Ling 13ap [55] 515
48a 5-14 Ling 10ap 50 757
25a 7-9 Ling 12ap 48 842 VIS
50a 2-6 Ling 10ap [45] 972
1 13-17 Bath 11.7sft 50 1543 vis

IVANA ILLYICH 2 ch f £2222
65 5-12 Warw 5sft 1524
60 9-19 Wind 5g/f 1805
74 4-13 Ling 6g/f 2061
58 8-14 Leic 6g/f 72 3212
73 3-12 Wind 6gd 70 3825
74 3-8 Sand 7.1g/s 73 4100
73 7-20 Ling 7g/f 72 4444
72 10-20 Ling 7g/f 72 4741

IVORY COAST 2 b f £7054
26a 7-13 Wolv 8.5af 111
56a 4-10 Ling 8ap 232
57a 4-9 Ling 10ap 57 365
60a 1-11 LING 10ap 56 497*
64 2-7 Carl 9.3fm 59 1953
44 8-14 Wind 10g/f 61 2452
52 7-14 Wind 10gd 60 2617
17 11-13 Bath 10.2gd [59] 3144
53 5-7 Yarm 10.1g/f [59] 3704
34 9-10 Yarm 10.1gd [59] 3874
54 1-7 BRIG 9.9sft [57] 4142* BL
37 9-11 Leic 10gd [57] 4701 bl

IVORY LACE 2 b f £15064
51a 8-10 Ling 5ap 66 217
56a 5-10 Ling 5ap 60 371
55a 2-9 Ling 5ap [60] 405
34a 11-14 Sout 5af 55 485
57a 1-10 LING 5ap [55] 548*
56a 3-10 Ling 6ap [52] 606
70 1-9 BATH 5g/s 60 1102*
71 1-14 BATH 5gd 65 1404*
71 4-10 Brig 5.3fm 70 1694
79 1-9 CHEP 5.1gd 70 2195*
70 5-8 Sand 5g/s 77 3889
67 13-15 Sand 5gd 77 4604
64 12-19 Good 6gd 77 4747
68a 4-12 Ling 6ap 68 4976

IVORY VENTURE 3 b f £1449
17a 13-15 Sout 5af 57 187
0 13-13 Ling 6ap [45] 271
14a 13-14 Ling 6ap 54 328
22a 8-9 Ling 5ap [50] 413
26a 9-12 Ling 7ap [45] 536
16a 12-12 Ling 8ap [45] 571 BL
41a 1-10 LING 5ap [35] 653* bl
7a 13-15 Ling 7ap [35] 708 bl

IVORY WOLF 2 ch c £0
42 8-9 Brig 5.3fm 2257
43 7-7 Warw 5fm 2573
8 10-10 Folk 7g/s 3046 P

IVOWEN 4 b f £15678
106 3-6 Curr 10gd 2816

IVY HOUSE LAD 4 b g £0
0 5-6 Ling 10ap 972

IVY LEAGUE STAR 3 b f £3886
65 5-7 Newm 12g/f 1936
16a 10-12 Wolv 12af 65 2203
72 1-20 HAYD 11.9g/s 62 4771*
68a 5-12 Wolv 12.2ap 70 4924

71 5-12 Redc 14.1g/s 69 5108

IVY MOON 3 b f £1104
14a 8-12 Wolv 7af 52 129
44a 3-10 Wolv 8.5af [47] 398
39a 6-11 Wolv 7af 45 562
36a 7-12 Ling 8ap [45] 648
47 3-18 Wind 6g/f [50] 1806
39 5-9 Ling 7g/f [50] 1984
46 3-16 Chep 7.1gd [45] 2369
45 4-17 Warw 8.1g/f 45 2909
33 8-11 Brig 7g/f [44] 3298
31 5-8 Chep 8.1gd 43 3731
16 11-14 Bath 8g/f 45 4411

IZMAIL 5 b g £7898
46 13-13 Epso 5sft 74 1293
53 19-20 Thir 5g/s 72 1476
63 10-15 Muss 5fm 69 2084
64 7-17 Warw 5fm 66 2599
40 10-11 Brig 5.3gd 66 2957
72 1-18 CARL 5g/f 66 3228*
18 18-18 Pont 5gd 70 3463
37 10-12 Ches 5.1sft 70 4107
52 14-18 Bath 5.7g/f 69 4412
54 12-15 Chep 5.1gd 69 4489
58 5-13 Ches 5.1g/f 69 4514
32 18-19 York 5gd 67 4989 vis
54a 10-13 Wolv 5.1ap 65 5341 BL
26a 12-12 Wolv 5.1ap [65] 5362

IZZA 3 br f £0
0 14-14 Sout 6af [30] 637

IZZET MUZZY 6 ch g £0
44a 9-11 Sout 5af 65 418

J R STEVENSON 7 ch g £8726
77a 3-13 Ling 10ap 76 26
75a 5-13 Ling 10ap 76 134
81a 1-14 LING 10ap 75 265*
81a 2-12 Ling 8ap 79 369
68a 12-14 Ling 10ap 80 452
71 4-18 Asco 8sft 77 1423
74 6-19 Newb 10gd 76 1736
64 5-6 Hami 8.3g/s [75] 2828
68 8-9 Asco 8gd 72 3465
63 6-16 Bath 8gd 69 5022
68 1-17 YARM 8g/s [67] 5348+

JAAMID 2 b c £1718
81 4-7 Catt 7g/f 3665
51 10-16 Thir 6g/s 4205
84 2-11 Bath 8sft 5171

JABAAR 6 gr g £26062
45 21-24 Donc 8gd 89 928
88 3-20 Donc 10.3g/s 87 1519
90 5-14 York 10.4g/s 87 1704
84 6-8 Ayr 10g/f 87 1895 VIS
85 2-9 Ches 10.3g/s[86] 2745
90 5-21 York 10.4gd 86 3118 vis
73 10-21 York 11.9gd 85 3999
80 8-14 Ripo 10gd 83 4305 BL
89 2-18 Newb 10gd 83 4681
56 18-20 York 10.4gd 84 4986
69 11-13 Donc 12sft 84 5215
63 11-24 Donc 12sft 81 5372 vis

JABRAAN 2 b c £0
74 8-19 Leic 7gd 5055

JACARANDA 4 ch g £6212
63 11-17 Leic 7g/s 72 1020
69 5-12 Thir 7g/s 70 1215
26 10-11 Chep 7.1gd 69 2370
59 9-20 Kemp 9g/f 67 2857
73 2-8 Epso 10.1g/s 67 3044
70 4-6 Beve 9.9gd [68] 3313
72 1-10 NEWM 10fm 68 3404*
72 3-6 Leic 10fm 71 3815
61 6-15 Bath 11.7g/f 71 3964
65 10-16 Sand 10gd 71 4609
70 5-14 Asco 12g/f 71 4775
53 10-11 Wind 11.6g/s [70] 4942

JACK DAWSON 7 b g £13572
80 1-12 MUSS 14fm 71 2085*

72 8-11 Newm 16.1g/f 76 3779

JACK DURRANCE 4 b g £0
22	17-18	Bath	10.2g/s		74	1098	
2	10-10	Bath	10.2gd	[65]		1402	VIS
45	4-15	Wind	11.6g/f	[55]		2267	
22	9-10	Warw	12.6g/f		45	2912	
34	10-19	Bath	17.2gd		42	3147	
12	10-12	Nott	14.1g/f		39	3420	

JACK OF TRUMPS 3 b c £19931
85a	5-10	Ling	10ap	[62]		179	
66a	1-13	LING	10ap	[80]		338*	
66a	11-14	Ling	10ap		78	452	
61	7-14	Folk	9.7g/s		67	1083	
65	4-10	Newm	12g/f		64	2530	
77	1-14	SALI	12g/s		64	3114*	
76	1-13	YORK	11.9g/f		70	3437*	
77	1-9	GOOD	12sft		73	4183*	
71	9-9	Muss	12g/f		78	4553	

JACK SULLIVAN 3 ch c £86172
103a2-14	Nad	8af			598	
101	4-9	Nad	9af	[90]	989	
93	4-6	Sand	7.1g/f		2190	
93	9-28	Asco	7g/f	100	2558	T
96	5-9	Good	8fm	[98]	3620	BL t

JACK THE GIANT 2 b c £0
| 64 | 8-20 | Wind | 6fm | | 2970 |
| 67 | 9-11 | Newm | 7gd | | 4190 |

JACKADANDY 2 b g £1464
70	4-8	York	7g/s		3078
69	3-6	Hami	8.3g/s		3878
41	13-14	Thir	8fm		4376

JACKIE KIELY 3 ch g £15203
47a	7-16	Ling	7ap			290	
60a	6-14	Ling	10ap			473	
60a	2-10	Ling	10ap		59	676	
47a	8-10	Ling	10ap	[59]		843	
49	5-12	Wind	11.6g/s		58	1260	
47	5-11	Warw	12.6sft		56	1528	
50	4-14	Ling	11.5g/f		52	2014	
55	2-7	Brig	9.9fm	[50]		2312	
57a	1-15	SOUT	12af		50	2503*	
18	14-14	Bath	10.2fm		56	2664	
64	1-16	BRIG	9.9g/f		55	3175*	T
60	1-17	NEWM	10g/f		61	3238*	t
54	9-20	Catt	12g/f		61	3354	t
36	10-11	Yarm	11.5gd		61	3367	t
68	3-12	Newm	10g/f		65	3785	t
49	7-9	Sand	10g/f		65	3862	t
67	4-14	Epso	8.5gd		65	4295	t
54	10-19	Leic	10g/f		65	4456	t
67	3-12	Good	9g/f		65	4539	t
66	5-12	Epso	8.5gd		65	4909	t
50a	10-15	Wolv	9.5ap		65	5161	t

JACKS CHECK 3 b g £0
| 41 | 14-17 | Hayd | 8.1g/s | | 4768 |
| 37 | 10-10 | Pont | 8g/f | | 4939 |

JACKS DELIGHT 4 b g £0
11a	7-9	Sout	7af		661	
0	14-14	Leic	6g/f		1963	
11a	10-11	Wolv	6af		2202	VIS

JACOB 3 b g £0
46a	5-15	Sout	6af	[63]	795
37a	4-12	Sout	8af	[60]	848
0	8-8	Wolv	7af	[60]	892

JACOBIN 3 b c £0
| 51 | 10-10 | Sand | 10g/f | | 2386 |
| 3 | 10-12 | Newm | 12g/f | | 3783 |

JADAN 3 b g £12240
56	9-13	Thir	5sft		74	1229	
46	14-15	Ches	5.1g/s		72	1572	
72	3-10	Carl	5gd		70	2675	
70	6-8	Newc	5g/s		70	2731	
71	6-15	Redc	5g/s		70	2961	
77	1-10	HAYD	5g/s		70	3135*	
77	5-10	Sand	5g/f		75	3356	
66	10-15	Thir	5g/s		75	3833	
49	9-14	Ches	6.1g/f		75	4048	
80	1-8	HAMI	5g/s	[74]		4822*	

76 6-15 Catt 5sft 78 5125

JADE STAR 4 b f £4731
41a	4-9	Sout	12af		48	456	
53a	1-9	WOLV	9.4af		48	620*	
20a	11-14	Ling	10ap		52	757	
56a	2-7	Wolv	9.4af		52	961	
50a	6-13	Wolv	9.4af		53	1223	p
55	4-15	Beve	9.9sft		53	1307	
50	4-13	Yarm	11.5fm		51	2868	
1	14-14	Folk	9.7g/s		51	3052	p
50	3-11	Yarm	10.1gd	[50]		3362	
19a	15-16	Sout	8af		53	3487	
16	17-18	Kemp	10g/f	[49]		4791	p

JADEERON 5 b g £4790
57a	2-13	Ling	13ap		53	342	g
63a	2-9	Wolv	12af		54	467	p
65a	2-12	Wolv	12af		58	634	p
66a	3-12	Ling	13ap		62	762	p
64	4-11	Nott	16fm		64	1003	p
63	4-10	Muss	14g/f		65	1118	p
61	7-17	Ripo	16g/s		65	1361	p
43	10-11	Donc	12g/f		64	1875	p
61a	6-12	Wolv	12.2ap		64	4924	p
66a	6-16	Ling	12ap		64	4973	p
60a	3-12	Wolv	13.9ap		60	5160	p

JAGGED 3 b g £11872
53a	6-16	Ling	7ap		59	20	
60a	3-12	Wolv	7af	[61]		71	
41a	10-16	Ling	7ap	[60]		123	
41a	13-14	Ling	6ap		60	897	
21	8-10	Warw	6.1hvy		57	1533	
45	8-18	Bath	5.7g/f		54	1788	
58a	2-16	Sout	6af		51	2720	VIS
59	3-14	Ling	6gd		55	3289	BL
55	6-16	Ling	6g/f		55	3602	bl
58	3-17	Wind	6fm		55	3643	vis
64a	1-15	SOUT	5af		55	4043+	vis
67a	2-14	Sout	6af		61	4130	vis
63	2-18	Bath	5.7g/f		58	4412	vis
64	4-13	Bath	5.7gd		58	4548	vis
71a	1-13	WOLV	5.1ap		63	5341*	vis

JAGGER 4 gr c £8000
88	13-19	Newc	16.1g/s		97	2771
103	3-15	Good	14g/f		97	3510
97	8-19	York	13.9g/s		97	4023
107	4-4	Kemp	12fm	[101]	4391
83	11-13	Curr	14gd	[101]	4733

JAHANGIR 5 b g £422
42a	3-12	Ling	8ap	[45]		648
45a	3-15	Ling	7ap	[45]		708
26a	9-13	Ling	6ap		45	767
43a	10-14	Ling	6ap	[45]		819
38a	7-10	Ling	8ap	[45]		831

JAHIA 5 br m £0
26	11-12	Pont	8hvy	75	1066
40	7-8	Brig	9.9g/f	70	3719
40	9-9	Newb	9gd	70	3922
45	9-16	Sali	8gd	63	4334

JAILBIRD 3 b f £0
| 25 | 8-8 | Bath | 5.7fm | 58 | 1903 | |
| 20 | 13-13 | Warw | 6.1fm | 55 | 2439 | VIS |

JAIR OHMSFORD 5 b g £9975
67a	1-13	WOLV	9.4af		57	281*
59a	4-11	Wolv	9.4af		64	465
74a	1-7	SOUT	12af	[64]		594*
77a	1-6	SOUT	12af		70	683*
67	4-17	Pont	12hvy		66	1064
67	3-14	Nott	10g/s		66	1777

JAKARMI 2 b g £22748
61a	2-12	Wolv	8.5af			28
55a	6-13	Wolv	8.5af			111
51a	5-10	Sout	8af	[62]		162
35a	7-11	Wolv	8.5af	[60]		279
57a	1-8	WOLV	8.5af	[55]		383*
55a	6-12	Wolv	7af	[56]		560
62a	1-8	WOLV	8.5af	[56]		630*
64a	3-10	Wolv	8.5af		60	753
67	2-18	Nott	8.2fm		62	1007
67a	2-13	Sout	8af	[64]		1193

68	2-14	Bath	10.2gd		64	1403
70	3-18	Wind	8.3sft		65	1647
74a	2-12	Wolv	12af		70	2203
76	1-18	LEIC	10gd		65	2706*
78	1-10	NOTT	10g/s	[72]		2930*
39	14-15	Nott	10gd		76	3108
70	7-12	Sand	10gd		76	4502
66	5-12	Good	11gd		73	4749
58	11-12	Wind	11.6g/f		73	4833

JAKE BLACK 4 b g £12758
33a	7-13	Sout	12af	[45]		575	
45a	1-12	WOLV	8.5af	[40]		777*	
51a	1-7	WOLV	9.4af	[45]		893*	VIS
0	5-5	Sout	8af	[45]		908	vis
50	3-16	Newc	10.1sft		50	1278	
63	1-9	PONT	10sft		50	1430+	
50	5-17	Bath	10.2sft		50	1541	
30	15-16	Redc	10g/f		59	1821	
54	4-8	Newc	12.4g/f	[59]		2163	
56	4-9	Redc	10gd		58	4248	
66	1-14	YORK	10.4g/f		58	4402*	
26	12-16	Ches	10.3g/f		58	4515	
45	8-13	Nott	10g/s	[58]		4650	
44	10-17	Newc	10.1g/f		63	5016	

JAKE THE SNAKE 2 ch c £3147
| 83a | 1-12 | LING | 8ap | | 175* |

JAKEAL 5 b g £1238
47a	10-15	Ling	7ap		54	913	
51	4-17	Thir	8g/s		57	1214	
27	11-20	Ripo	8g/s		55	1366	
49	11-16	Beve	7.5gd		53	2655	
54	2-16	Beve	7.5gd		53	2891	P
11	13-16	Nott	8.2hvy		53	5347	

JALAMID 2 b c £4953
| 82 | 1-12 | SAND | 7.1g/f | | 2388* | T |
| 82 | 11-12 | Newm | 7g/f | | 3060 | t |

JALISSA 2 b f £400
| 73a | 4-8 | Ling | 7ap | | 4447 |

JALONS STAR 6 b g £0
36	10-10	Sand	10g/f	59	3336
41	7-9	Epso	10.1fm	60	3538
14	13-14	Wind	11.6fm	57	3638

JALOUHAR 3 b g £4614
61a	1-14	SOUT	6af	[60]		65*	p
51a	5-16	Sout	6af		60	166	p
35a	5-7	Sout	6af	[59]		317	p
55a	4-9	Sout	6af	[57]		533	p
44a	6-7	Sout	7af	[57]		589	p
52a	5-11	Ling	6ap		55	728	
48a	8-10	Ling	6af	[55]		765	
31a	5-10	Sout	6af	[52]		851	
26a	12-12	Wolv	5af	[49]		960	vis
49	2-7	Brig	6g/f	[46]		1368	p
24	9-16	Nott	6.1gd	[49]		1988	p
23	6-6	Nott	8.2g/f	[47]		2154	
66	7-12	Hayd	6g/s	[47]		2186	
44	2-8	Ripo	6g/f	[46]		2480	
62	10-11	Warw	7.1fm	[46]		2777	
33	7-8	Hayd	6gd	[46]		2949	
80	6-6	Ches	7g/f	[46]		3098	
44	7-11	Donc	6g/f	[46]		3375	
48	8-8	Donc	6g/f	[46]		3596	
47	11-11	Hayd	6gd	[46]		3758	

JALOUSIE DREAM 3 b f £573
61	7-8	Ripo	10g/s			1365
44	5-12	Ripo	6g/f			1784
42	3-8	Ripo	10g/f			2523
2	12-14	Catt	12g/f		47	3192
34	8-8	Catt	13.8g/f		45	4439

JAMAARON 2 ch c £5412
79	3-10	Folk	7g/s			3046
52	7-9	Folk	7g/f			3721
83	1-15	GOOD	8g/s			4233*
52	14-17	Good	8gd		77	4871

JAMAICAN FLIGHT 11 b h £1961
49a	3-9	Sout	16af	52	336
49a	4-10	Sout	16af	50	491
31a	4-6	Sout	12af	48	870

```
39  4-13  Pont  18hvy    52    1069
35  4-13  Pont  21.6hvy  51    1252
33a 5-12  Pont  16af     45    1753
48  5-5   Pont  18g/f   [45]   4628
0   18-20 Catt  15.8gd   45    4965

JAMES CAIRD 4 ch g £25281
73  6-9   Newm  10gd    [82]   1890
87  2-15  Redc  10g/f    82    2101
88  2-15  York  8.9g/f   84    2404
91  2-12  Kemp  9g/f     84    2860
85  7-18  Newb  8g/f     87    3265
76  11-20 Hayd  10.5fm   86    3794
91  3-13  Donc  10.3fm  [84]   4463
93  2-8   Pont  10fm     87    4755

JAMESTOWN 6 b g £731
48a 6-11  Ling  8ap     [50]   145
48a 3-13  Sout  8af      48    221
46a 5-10  Sout  8af      47    318
4a  9-9   Sout  11af     47    391
11a 10-11 Sout  8af      46    457
51a 7-10  Sout  8af     [46]   502
37a 9-13  Wolv  8.5af    45    559
0   8-8   Sout  11af    [45]   722
39  13-19 Yarm  7g/f     50    1132
32a 4-6   Wolv  9.4af   [40]   1262
31  11-17 Warw  8.1fm    47    2440
44  4-5   Hami  9.2g/f  [45]   3206
27a 8-11  Sout  8af     [38]   4090
10  13-16 Warw  8.1g/s  [45]   4993

JAN BRUEGHEL 4 ch g £371
68a 4-9   Wolv  7af      66    27
54a 7-16  Sout  7af     [66]   161
40a 3-8   Sout  7af     [65]   320
42a 4-11  Wolv  7af     [63]   440
25a 8-12  Wolv  7af     [63]   512

JANE JUBILEE 2 b f £15988
52  3-3   Redc  5sft            1658
72  5-12  Redc  6g/f            2119
77  2-7   Hami  6g/f            2473
88  2-10  Catt  6g/f            2845
93  1-12  CATT  7g/f     77    3351*
96  1-6   MUSS  7.1g/f   84    3560*
89  5-7   York  7gd     [95]   4003
67  10-12 Good  7sft    [95]   4264
82  11-14 Newm  7g/f    [93]   4914
68  13-29 Newm  6gd             5087

JANES VALENTINE 3 b f £0
29a 9-13  Ling  6ap     [52]   271
31a 4-6   Ling  10ap    [47]   409
35a 8-12  Ling  7ap     [45]   536
37a 4-15  Ling  7ap     [45]   708
0   15-15 Ling  7ap     [40]   969
15a 8-8   Ling  7ap     [40]   1413
0   17-17 Kemp  7hvy    [35]   1642
1a  6-7   Ling  6ap     [35]   1715 VIS

JANGO MALFOY 2 ch c £0
66a 7-12  Ling  10ap            120
60a 5-11  Ling  7ap             220
50a 8-11  Ling  7ap      61     261 BL T
45a 9-15  Ling  7ap      61     337
35a 11-12 Ling  8ap      57     603
17a 10-13 Sout  8af     [57]    1193
31  8-14  Folk  12gd     52    3383 t
11  12-14 Nott  16g/f    52    3580 t

JAOLINS 2 b f £3417
46a 6-13  Ling  6ap             25
38a 10-15 Ling  7ap             52
56a 1-10  LING  6ap     [52]   606*
59a 2-15  Ling  7ap     [52]   671
45a 10-12 Ling  7ap      52    729
22a 10-11 Sout  6af      56    872
55a 5-15  Ling  7ap      56    901
43  9-14  Warw  7.1sft    54   1085
36  7-10  Bath  5.7sft  [52]   1539
32  12-16 Ling  8af      48    1985
30  14-18 Sali  7fm      44    2292
44  7-17  Leic  7gd     [40]   2704
32a 6-11  Sout  8af     [52]   3091
47a 5-14  Sout  8af     [49]   3392
26  9-13  Folk  9.7g/f  [40]   4372

38  4-17  Warw  8.1g/s  [40]   4992

JARRAAF 3 ch c £0
47a 4-14  Sout  8af     [62]   170
40a 4-8   Wolv  8.5af   [62]   248
55a 5-10  Sout  8af      58    678
64a 5-12  Wolv  9.4af   [56]   939

JARVO 3 b g £3424
66  2-9   Sout  10gd    [66]   1283
47a 5-6   Wolv  8.5af   [66]   1377
65  4-8   Warw  7.1fm   [66]   2575 T
44  12-12 Leic  8g/f     66    2922
44  10-16 Epso  8.5gd    62    3219 t
66  2-12  Bath  8g/f     60    3846
64  3-14  Newm  7gd     [62]   4195
32  14-14 Good  8g/f     62    4542
62a 4-12  Wolv  8.6ap    60    5116

JASMICK 6 ch m £1568
66  5-5   Newm  12g/f    76    3587
56  7-12  Kemp  14.4g/f  76    3688
70  9-12  Sand  16.4g/f  74    3861
63  6-9   Pont  12g/s    72    3969
69  7-14  Bath  13.1g/s  70    4203
75  2-7   Good  14sft    67    4267

JASMINE HILL 2 ch f £0
37  10-11 Ripo  5g/s            3258
49  6-10  Beve  5g/f            3504
47  7-12  Thir  5g/s            3832
31  8-10  Redc  5fm             4338

JASMINE PEARL 2 b f £1255
53a 5-10  Sout  7af      68    203
47a 3-8   Sout  7af     [62]   389
39a 6-11  Ling  6ap      53    735
38a 11-15 Ling  7ap      49    815
32  8-12  Folk  6sft     53    975
42a 4-7   Ling  6ap     [45]   1453
12  16-16 Ling  6g/f     49    1985
48  2-6   Folk  6fm     [45]   2715
40  5-12  Brig  6g/f     48    3301
40  6-12  Folk  6gd      48    3380
37  6-12  Brig  7fm      46    3677
12  13-14 Folk  6gd      44    4116
20  9-19  Kemp  6g/f    [40]   4793

JATH 3 b f £7184
83  15-16 Newm  8fm             1492
62  6-6   Newm  10g/f   [85]   1931
70  10-13 Sand  8.1g/s  [85]   2126
80  6-12  Sand  7.1g/f   82    3860
83  1-4   YARM  7sft    [80]   4148*
79  8-17  Asco  8g/f     80    4777
72  12-18 York  7gd      80    5000
51  10-10 Catt  7sft     78    5320

JAVA DANCER 3 b g £0
52  7-11  Hayd  8.1gd           2885
49  6-11  Thir  8g/f            3572
43a 6-10  Sout  8af             4042

JAVA DAWN 4 b f £371
23  10-17 Bath  11.7sft  48    1543
0   10-11 Ling  12ap    [45]   2588
56a 3-8   Ling  12ap    [42]   2739
35  6-15  Folk  16.4g/s  42    3049
38  7-19  Chep  12.1gd   40    3727

JAVA GOLD 3 ch f £0
23  12-13 Bath  5.7g/f          3844
25  14-17 Bath  5.7gd           5020
23a 10-12 Wolv  5.1ap           5362

JAVELIN 8 ch g £0
42  6-10  Warw  12.6g/f  51    2912
47  5-10  Sali  14.1gd   49    3887 P
38  9-14  Bath  13.1g/s  45    4203 BL

JAWWALA 5 b m £0
0   R-17  Pont  17.1g/s  59    3970
5   16-16 Warw  16.2gd   59    4276 p

JAY 2 ch f £4064
42  9-10  Newm  6gd             1887
40  9-9   Newm  6g/f            2245
60  2-4   Brig  7g/f            2640 BL
40  9-12  Catt  7g/f     55    3351 bl

52  2-8   Yarm  6gd             3491
54  8-12  Newm  7g/f    [52]   3750 bl
62  1-5   YARM  6g/f    [53]   3871* bl
29  17-20 Redc  7fm      61    4337 P
55  9-20  Leic  7g/f     60    4451

JAY GEES CHOICE 4 b g £18583
89  6-24  Donc  8gd      93    951
59  23-27 Newb  8gd      91    1231
7   12-14 Kemp  8hvy     89    1512
87  3-11  Donc  7g/f     86    2076
81  9-13  Epso  8.5g/f   86    2207
84  4-8   Donc  8g/f     84    2425
62  11-12 Kemp  7g/s     84    2679
85  5-16  Newb  7g/f     83    3954
45  6-8   Chep  7.1g/s  [83]   4301
89  1-7   PONT  8g/f    [82]   4629*
88  3-12  Good  8gd     [85]   4872
81  4-10  Epso  7gd     [85]   4912
93a 1-12  WOLV  7.1ap    84    5159*

JAYANJAY 4 b g £35462
77a 2-14  Ling  6ap      73    149
60a 13-14 Ling  6ap      76    292
74a 4-13  Wolv  6af      76    482
78  3-10  Brig  5.3g/f   78    2044
78  4-17  Epso  6fm      77    2256
78  3-9   Epso  6g/f     77    2871
82  1-10  EPSO  6g/s     77    3045+
80  5-17  Sand  5g/f     80    3341
85  2-9   Brig  5.3fm    80    3673
86  2-16  Wind  6gd      80    3827
66  5-8   Kemp  5sft    [82]   4031
78  8-14  Epso  5g/f     82    4291
93  1-12  EPSO  5g/f     81    4908*
73a 6-12  Ling  6ap      82    5297

JAYCEE STAR 3 ch f £0
0   11-13 Ling  6ap             364
5a  14-14 Ling  6ap             449
6a  15-15 Ling  7ap             472

JAYER GILLES 4 br g £2828
79  2-8   Chep  12.1g/f         2623
79  2-9   Pont  12g/f           2992
55  5-12  Newm  12g/f           3783
2   12-13 Newb  16sft    78    5194

JAZIL 9 b g £0
27a 6-6   Sout  11af            1754 t
22  11-11 Newm  12g/f    60    2244 t
34  9-10  Leic  11.8g/f [50]   3211 t
40  9-15  Chep  16.2gd  [50]   3400 vis t
2   14-14 Yarm  14.1g/s [45]   5123 vis t

JAZRAWY 2 b c £4988
71  4-9   Ripo  6g/f            2522
70  4-14  Ling  7.6g/f          3601
79a 1-12  WOLV  8.6ap           5115*

JAZZ MESSENGER 4 b g £723
96  6-17  Sand  8.1g/s   95    1351
49  15-17 York  7.9g/s   95    1686
92  9-16  Newb  7g/f     95    3954
71  10-15 York  7.9g/s   95    4061
88  6-11  Epso  10.1gd  [93]   4467

JAZZ PRINCESS 2 b f £52080
113 1-9   CURR  7sft            4958*

JAZZ SCENE 3 b c £17706
84  9-10  Newb  7gd     [88]   1234
86  8-27  Asco  8g/f     88    2521
97  2-7   Ches  8g/f     87    2749
99  2-11  Sand  7.1g/s   92    2918
99  4-7   Curr  8gd     [92]   3318
97  5-10  Kemp  8fm      95    4389
99  2-10  Ayr   8sft     93    4685
92  4-10  Newm  8g/f    [93]   4890
98  2-5   Ayr   8sft    [93]   5038 VIS
79  15-22 Newm  8sft     93    5103 vis

JAZZY MILLENNIUM 7 ch g £7473
40  8-13  Sout  6g/s     55    1052 bl
53  3-16  Brig  6fm      53    2262 bl
54  6-11  Brig  7gd      53    2644 bl
54  3-11  Brig  5.3gd    53    2957 bl
56  3-17  Brig  7g/f     53    3176 bl
```

47 7-15 Chep 5.1gd 54 3403 bl
56 4-16 Ling 6g/f 53 3602 bl
59 1-15 LING 53 3790* vis
61 2-10 Brig 7sft 56 4168 vis
63 2-15 Epso 7g/f 58 4475 bl
43 12-19 Nott 6.1g/f [59] 4845 bl
61a 5-14 Ling 7ap [59] 5263 bl

JE SUIS BELLE 2 ch f £9951
62 7-20 Wind 6fm 2970
66 3-18 Pont 5g/s 3968
81 2-5 Good 6sft 4234
75 1-10 AYR 6g/s 69 4655*
57 13-16 Newm 7g/f 71 4913

JEDBURGH 3 b c £14508
84 9-15 Newm 8gd 93 1206
98 3-20 Newm 8g/f 93 1496
99 3-12 Good 7g/f 97 1847
100 2-6 Sali 7g/s [97] 3113
94 8-17 Good 7fm 97 3550
100 2-5 Ches 7.6g/f [96] 4047
97 5-16 Good 7g/f 99 4523
87 13-15 Newm 7g/f 97 4891

JEDEYDD 7 b g £3361
52 10-14 Muss 7.1gd 61 1794 t
53 8-16 York 7g/f 61 2057 t
57 4-15 Beve 7.5g/s 57 2324 t
57 13-16 Beve 7.5gd 56 2655 t
56 6-17 Newm 7g/f 56 2768 t
50 4-13 Muss 8gd [55] 2967 t p
38 10-14 Carl 6.9g/f 55 3229 t
48 7-12 Yarm 7gd 53 3490 t
46 10-13 Thir 7g/f 53 3571 BL t
58 1-13 HAYD 6gd [53] 3757* bl t
41 9-20 Newc 6g/f 55 4408 bl t

JEEPSTAR 4 b g £29744
30 16-20 Epso 12hvy 77 1295
48 10-12 Ches 12.3gd 77 1599
55 6-9 Donc 12g/f 75 2078
74 2-13 Ayr 10gd 70 3325
77 2-10 Newm 10g/f 71 3615
81 1-9 PONT 12g/s 74 3969*
73 8-12 York 13.9g/f 77 4400
84 1-9 MUSS 12g/f 77 4553*
85 2-8 Donc 14.6sft 80 5204
81 4-24 Donc 12sft 80 5372

JEFFSLOTTERY 2 b g £414
46 11-14 Thir 7g/s 4207
49 6-8 Hami 8.3g/s 4816
47 7-10 Catt 7sft 5127
71 2-8 Ayr 8sft [45] 5273 BL

JELANI 5 b h £16900
78 15-17 Newb 12gd 1230
106 6-7 Newm 12fm 1493
108 3-10 York 13.9g/s[106] 1705

JELLY BABY 3 b f £5807
22 14-14 Wind 10g/s 1259
67a 1-11 LING 12ap 2588* BL
67a 1-15 LING 12ap 55 2741* bl
18 9-9 Ripo 12.3gd 65 2984 bl

JEMS LAW 5 b m £0
0 10-13 Wind 8.3g/s 1058 VIS
0 13-13 Leic 10fm 2107 vis

JENAVIVE 4 b f £0
32a 9-13 Ling 13ap 49 896

JENNA STANNIS 2 ch f £0
67 11-14 Newm 7g/f 3944
74 8-16 Sali 7gd 4329
60 10-18 Nott 8.2g/f 4842

JENNVERSE 2 b f £0
57 6-12 Bath 5sft 5169

JEROME 3 b c £0
65 8-16 Beve 8.5sft 75 1628

JERRYS GIRL 2 ch f £5216
76 3-13 Carl 5fm 1950
18 6-7 Hami 6gd 2473
62 4-7 Ayr 6gd 3323

---

71 1-6 MUSS 5g/f 3525*
52 8-9 Redc 6g/f 72 3807

JESSE SAMUEL 3 ch g £0
18 14-14 Warw 7.1sft 50 1085
40 4-6 Warw 7.1g/s [45] 1330
0 8-9 Folk 7sft 45 1577

JESSIAUME 2 gr f £366
70 4-11 Newm 6sft 5265

JESSICAS STYLE 2 b f £0
38 13-14 Redc 6fm 2297
43a 7-15 Sout 5af 4089
35 9-10 Redc 6gd 4244

JESSIE 4 ch f £3207
13a 10-14 Sout 8af 47 62
19a 10-14 Sout 8af 44 195
36a 5-9 Sout 7af [41] 303
14a 6-13 Sout 7af [45] 356
33a 5-8 Sout 8af 40 489 T
41a 2-8 Sout 8af 40 597 t
41a 2-7 Sout 7af 40 680 t
41a 2-11 Sout 7af [40] 771 t
37a 4-8 Sout 7af [40] 847 t
35 7-15 Redc 7sft 1660 t
37a 5-16 Sout 7af 40 2335 VIS
41 4-18 Donc 7gd 43 2755 vis
41 3-11 Ripo 8gd 43 2986 vis
15 12-17 Carl 7.9fm [45] 4506 vis

JESSINCA 7 b m £1408
49a 4-13 Wolv 9.4af 46 38
27a 6-14 Sout 9af 46 62
19a 9-15 Sout 8af 45 84
22a 8-13 Wolv 9.4af 43 281
25a 10-11 Wolv 7af 40 378 vis
5a 6-8 Sout 8af 40 597
7a 10-16 Sout 7af 35 2335
40 3-11 Folk 9.7fm 40 2719
43 2-12 Ling 10g/f 40 2844
30 9-14 Folk 9.7g/s 39 3052
32 5-11 Bath 10.2g/f 39 3373
7 11-19 Brig 9.9sft 38 4145

JEUNE LOUP 2 b g £0
59 8-13 York 6gd 3120
77 4-12 Newc 7gd 3425
71 7-9 York 6g/s 4026

JEWEL IN THE SAND 2 b f £68675
76 1-6 SAND 6g/f 2097*
109 1-17 ASCO 6g/f 2553*
106 1-10 NEWM 6fm 3003*
95 11-12 Curr 7g/f 4432
89 7-7 Newm 6g/f [100] 4880

JEWEL OF INDIA 5 ch g £0
75a 7-11 Ling 8ap 85 547
79a 11-14 Ling 10ap 83 625
66 6-7 Wind 8.3gd [80] 3826

JEZADIL 6 b m £210
0 13-14 Ling 12ap [40] 968
11a 13-13 Ling 13ap [40] 1076 p
6 3-7 Chep 10.2sft [35] 1332
12 9-9 Ayr 13.1g/s [35] 1449 p
18 6-6 Beve 12.1gd [27] 2653

JIDIYA 5 b g £2772
51 8-13 Thir 12g/f 1768
44 9-11 Thir 8g/f 3572
73 2-6 Ripo 10g/f 3648
47 8-13 Folk 12gd 70 4119
66 3-8 Hayd 10.5g/f 70 4354
66 3-5 Pont 10g/f [68] 4630
55 14-16 York 11.9gd 66 4990

JILLY WHY 3 b f £12422
14a 8-8 Wolv 6af [63] 750
53 4-12 Redc 6gd [60] 4245
72 1-9 THIR 6fm [57] 4380*
77 1-13 CHES 5.1g/f 67 4514*
68 7-16 Redc 6fm 73 4562
53 9-12 Hayd 6sft 72 4779
74 2-8 Hami 5g/s [72] 4822
71a 4-13 Wolv 6ap 72 5114
65 11-18 Pont 5g/s 72 5149

62a 5-12 Wolv 6ap 70 5291
59a 6-12 Wolv 5.1ap 70 5326

JIM LAD 4 b g £0
0 5-7 Chep 10.2sft [40] 1332 vis

JIMMY BYRNE 4 ch g £17178
32 15-16 Sout 7g/s 70 1049
68 4-9 Pont 10hvy 68 1254
71 1-6 NEWC 10.1sft [68] 1397*
60 7-16 Redc 10g/f 72 1821
65 5-7 Ripo 10g/f [72] 1979
61 6-15 Ripo 12.3g/f 68 2526 P
58 1-9 HAYD 10.5gd [67] 2901*
79 1-10 HAYD 10.5g/s 70 3139*
81 3-16 Hayd 10.5sft 76 3276
77 6-14 Ripo 10gd 78 4305
49 13-20 Ayr 10g/s 78 4656

JIMMY GEE 2 b g £0
18a 12-15 Sout 7af [49] 87
19a 7-14 Sout 8af [49] 95

JIMMY HAY 3 b g £0
26 14-14 Warw 7.1g/f 2907
6a 12-14 Ling 10ap 4661
2 15-15 Wind 10g/f 4834
0 12-12 Warw 12.6g/s 4991

JIMMY RYAN 3 b c £18967
80 7-11 Newb 6gd 84 1734
55 7-11 Nott 6.1g/f 83 2155
94 1-11 NEWM 5g/f 81 2734*
95 2-8 Asco 5gd 86 3123
100 1-21 GOOD 5fm 88 3567*

JINKSONTHEHOUSE 3 b f £7495
55 4-10 Bath 5.7sft [60] 1539
26 16-17 Sali 6g/f 60 1722
59 1-7 BATH 5fm [57] 1902*
47 7-12 Chep 6.1gd 60 2118
44 4-11 Bath 5.7fm [60] 2412
38 11-19 Leic 5gd 58 2702
55 1-6 MUSS 5g/f [58] 2808*
58 4-11 Bath 5g/f [56] 3372
58 2-9 Wind 5fm 56 3804
54 4-11 Bath 5g/f 56 3849
17 11-11 Nott 5.1gd 56 4038

JOANS JEWEL 3 ch f £0
48a 5-8 Ling 6ap 691
50a 5-10 Ling 5ap 802
50a 6-10 Ling 7ap 911
11 15-20 Yarm 6g/f 54 1730
40 7-16 Ling 6g/f 51 1985
0 14-14 Folk 6gd 48 4116
33 13-17 Kemp 7g/f [45] 4794 P
15 11-20 Yarm 7g/s [40] 5120 p

JOCKS BOY 2 b g £0
17a 13-15 Sout 7af 87
40a 5-10 Sout 5af 139

JOE CHARLIE 3 ch g £0
9a 11-10 Sout 6af 53 591 BL

JOE JO STAR 2 b g £0
58 6-11 Nott 5.1gd 1237
52 6-10 Beve 5sft 1632
56 9-12 Carl 5g/f 4343
23 16-19 Redc 6.1g/s 57 4645

JOE NINETY 2 ch g £946
58a 5-10 Ling 5ap 882
69a 6-9 Ling 5ap 931
45 7-7 Folk 5sft 1574
50 10-18 Chep 6.1gd 2194
51 3-7 Redc 7fm 2294
42 8-8 Wind 6g/f 2449 BL
34 11-13 Sali 7g/f [47] 3864
46 4-9 Yarm 6sft 47 4146
32 11-17 Ling 8g/f [47] 4316 P

JOELY GREEN 7 b g £1089
58a 5-10 Wolv 16.2af 59 358 bl
38a 10-13 Ling 13ap [57] 602 bl
43a 6-14 Ling 12ap 55 711
54a 6-12 Ling 13ap 55 762
51a 6-12 Ling 16ap 53 813

29 10-13 Brig 11.9g/f 45 1373
50 2-8 Muss 16gd 45 1793 bl
3 12-13 Pont 17.1g/f 48 2276 bl
45 8-14 Bath 18.2fm 48 2417 bl
31 11-12 Warw 19.1fm 45 2577 bl
0 15-15 Folk 16.4g/s 40 3049 bl
46 4-7 Brig 11.9g/f [39] 3715
32a 10-14 Ling 16ap [45] 4663 p

JOEY PERHAPS 3 b g £3020
16 17-18 Nott 8.2sft 64 1470
0 12-13 Carl 5.9fm [60] 1949
17 12-14 Bath 10.2fm 55 2664
43 6-15 Beve 8.5g/s 50 3182
57 3-13 Beve 9.9gd 50 3309
53 2-6 Muss 9g/f 48 3529
59 3-16 Carl 7.9g/f 55 3650
52a 6-13 Ling 10ap 55 3823

JOEY THE SCHNOZE 6 ch g £0
21a 7-7 Ling 13ap 546
0 8-9 Pont 12g/f 2992

JOHANNIAN 6 b h £11060
56 13-15 Warw 8.1sft 84 1530
47 13-14 Donc 8g/f [79] 1877
75 3-9 Muss 8fm [74] 2087
67 5-7 Wind 8.3g/f [74] 2264
61 9-11 Ripo 10g/f 74 2483
74 2-12 Nott 8.2g/s 71 2931
69 9-16 Kemp 9gd 72 3187
73 4-8 Wind 8.3fm 71 3641
62 6-12 Chep 8.1g/s 71 3898
69 3-11 Brig 8g/s 69 4141
72 2-15 Chep 8.1g/s 69 4300
76 1-14 GOOD 8g/f 69 4542*
76 2-11 Yarm 8gd 69 4615
23 11-14 Newb 8hvy 71 5227

JOHN FORBES 2 b c £6825
74 9-11 Asco 7fm 2578
86 1-7 NEWC 6g/s 2774*
85 10-12 Newm 7g/f 3060
73 8-8 Asco 7gd 3467
61 9-11 Ayr 8sft 87 4688
59 11-15 York 6gd 82 4985 BL
41 12-14 Donc 8sft 75 5203 bl
57 7-10 Catt 6sft 70 5318
74 5-20 Donc 7sft 70 5373

JOHN OGROATS 6 b g £1477
36 7-9 Thir 5g/s [81] 1217
65 16-20 Thir 5g/s 76 1476
52 11-20 Thir 7g/f 72 1765
10 14-14 Ayr 6g/f 72 1898 P
51 8-10 Ayr 7.2g/f 67 2027
42 10-13 Pont 5g/f [62] 2279
38 11-16 Carl 5.9fm 62 2445
36 16-19 Beve 5gd 62 2512 VIS
31 18-20 Beve 5g/s 55 3180 p
29a 12-15 Sout 5af 51 4043 BL e
30 12-15 Carl 5fm [47] 4508
23 13-16 Warw 5g/s [45] 4995 bl
47 1-10 AYR 6sft [45] 5278*

JOHN ROBIE 2 ch c £1962
68 6-8 Ling 5gd 3445
82 3-20 York 5g/f 4401
79a 4-9 Ling 6ap 5237

JOHNNY ALLJAYS 3 b g £0
0 11-11 Newc 8sft 50 1395
32 9-13 Beve 8.5g/f [45] 1947
33 10-18 Sali 7fm 42 2292 BL
31 8-12 Brig 8g/f 42 2435 bl
28 8-13 Bath 8fm 39 2667 bl
42 4-9 Brig 8fm [38] 2834 P
32 4-12 Brig 7fm 36 3677 p
30 10-12 Brig 8g/f 34 3986 p

JOHNNY CHI 2 ch c £0
9 19-19 Newm 7g/s 5285

JOHNNY JUMPUP 2 ch c £24644
90 1-14 BATH 5sft 1538*
96 1-11 SALI 6g/s 3110*
94 7-8 Sand 7.1g/s 4096
102 1-4 CHES 7.6g/f [93] 4513*

102 2-13 Newb 7sft [96] 5195

JOHNNY PARKES 3 b g £5031
89 1-8 NOTT 5.1fm 75 1002*
71 11-15 Ches 5.1g/s 83 1572
88 3-14 Thir 5g/f 83 1766
78 7-11 Redc 5g/f 83 2121

JOHNNY ROOK 3 ch g £0
66a 7-13 Ling 10ap 2066

JOHNS CHAMP 4 b g £0
0 8-8 Newc 10.1sft [50] 2687

JOHNSTONS DIAMOND 6 b g £16057
62a 8-10 Sout 6af 77 390
42a 12-15 Sout 6af 75 550
82a 1-13 WOLV 6af 72 687+
67a 7-10 Wolv 6af 78 834
91 4-13 Beve 6g/s [85] 1162
86 6-14 Ches 5.1gd 89 1594
90 2-11 Ripo 6gd 88 1977
77 8-10 York 6g/f 90 2357
67 22-29 Asco 6fm 88 2581
75 9-11 Hami 6fm 89 3248
65 18-19 York 6gd 87 4005
59 14-16 Hayd 5fm 84 4382 BL
53 12-13 Ches 5.1g/f 80 4514
91 3-26 Ayr 6g/s 84 4652
85 6-11 Hayd 5sft 85 4780
94 3-9 Hami 6g/s [85] 4817
86 8-18 York 7gd 89 5000
95 3-16 Redc 6sft 88 5304

JOINT ASPIRATION 2 ch f £13896
86 1-11 SALI 7gd 3883*
96 1-7 KEMP 7g/f 4359*
102 6-9 Asco 8g/f 4798

JOINT DESTINY 2 b f £1899
38a 7-13 Ling 8gap [56] 25
27a 5-9 Wolv 9.4af 53 441
39a 8-13 Ling 7ap 49 761
46a 2-5 Ling 8ap [45] 1416
49a 1-8 LING 10ap [45] 1713*
40 7-10 Yarm 11.5fm 52 2147
51 5-8 Hami 9.2g/f 49 2475
36 8-13 Yarm 10.1gd 49 3492
37 6-6 Epso 8.5fm 49 3540

JOLIE 2 b f £0
29 9-12 Nott 6.1g/f 4844

JOLIZERO 2 br c £7499
60a 7-14 Sout 7af 98
64 4-13 Nott 8.2g/f 2633
47 9-15 Nott 10gd 58 3108
60 3-17 Newm 12g/f 57 3618
64 2-11 Beve 12.1g/s [59] 3856
57 5-10 Yarm 14.1g/s 62 4255
51 9-18 Ayr 10.9sft 62 4623
53a 6-16 Ling 12ap [60] 4899
83 1-8 NEWB 10hvy [58] 5226*

JOMACOMI 3 b c £4163
80a 1-5 WOLV 12af 701*
82 3-10 Wind 11.6gd 80 1382
78 6-14 York 11.9g/s 81 1708
76 7-13 Hayd 11.9gd 80 2238
73 6-9 Ripo 12.3gd 78 2984

JOMUS 2 b g £5999
39a 13-15 Ling 7ap [65] 52
55a 5-10 Ling 8ap 60 132
56a 5-12 Ling 7ap 57 545
61a 2-12 Sout 8af 56 656
67a 1-12 LING 8ap 60 798*
69a 2-7 Sout 8af 63 855
51 9-15 Ling 7g/f 65 1983
54 10-13 Sand 8.1gd 63 2365
47 10-14 Wind 8.3fm 61 2971
60 4-12 Ling 7.6gd [59] 3448
17 7-7 Epso 8.5fm 59 3542
53 3-19 Chep 8.1g/s [58] 4366
50 5-13 Nott 10g/s [58] 4650
57a 10-14 Ling 10ap 66 5083
57a 6-13 Wolv 8.6ap [61] 5336

JONALTON 4 b g £0

0 10-16 Sout 16af 31 206

JONANAUD 5 b g £0
65a 6-14 Ling 13ap 4898
68 7-18 Bath 10.2gd 5023

JONNY EBENEEZER 4 b g £92175
57a 12-16 Ling 7ap 70 22
55a 2-16 Sout 7af [70] 61 P
45a 7-7 Wolv 7af 63 860
42 13-15 Folk 6sft 77 976 p
0 18-19 Redc 6sft 75 1145 p
54 2-12 Sout 7gd [75] 1284
28 9-13 Warw 7.1hvy [68] 1537 p
52 2-13 Leic 7g/f [63] 1827
60 1-10 BRIG 7g/f [63] 1938*
53 9-16 Brig 7fm 58 2258
55a 3-15 Sout 7af 53 2501
61a 1-15 SOUT 6af 51 3000* bl
27 7-19 Nott 6.1gd [56] 3104 bl
68 2-15 Wind 5gd 62 3165 bl
67 2-16 Kemp 7gd 62 3184 bl
68 1-17 SAND 5sft 56 3341+ bl
81 1-11 NEWM 6fm 63 3408* bl
64a 4-9 Sout 6af 66 3485 bl
83 1-10 NEWM 6af 71 3584+ bl
94 1-16 WIND 6gd 79 3827* bl
56 17-19 Ripo 6g/s 83 3937 bl
92 8-22 Donc 5.6fm 90 4459 bl
46 23-24 Ayr 6sft 90 4686 bl
101 1-11 HAYD 5sft 89 4780+ bl e
98 3-15 Newm 7g/f 95 4891 bl e
106 1-20 YORK 6gd 96 5001* bl e
96 6-14 Newm 7sft [96] 5100 bl e

JONNY FOXS 2 ch c £0
60a 6-10 Ling 5ap 2017
37 8-13 Beve 5g/f 2321
45 6-9 Leic 5g/f 2921 BL
46 13-14 Wind 5gd 4121
1 8-8 Brig 5.3fm [48] 4759 bl

JONNYEM 3 b g £322
0 13-14 Carl 9.3g/f 4347
58 4-9 Thir 8g/f 4593
46 9-9 Catt 9g/f 4674
3 18-20 Catt 12gd 52 4966

JONQUIL 2 ch c £11141
75 4-15 Newb 7fm 2876
96 1-12 GOOD 7fm 3568*
95 8-10 Donc 7fm 4493

JOOLS 6 b g £8683
52a 7-11 Ling 8ap 72 714
50a 11-12 Ling 8ap 70 932
84 1-13 WIND 8.3g/s [78] 1057*
82 5-17 Sand 8.1g/s 81 1351
80 3-4 Ling 7.6g/s [81] 1616
56 8-9 Newm 10gd [80] 1890
59 14-15 Sand 10g/f 80 2099
80 4-8 Wind 8.3g/s [78] 2620
70 4-7 Wind 8.3fm 78 2787
78 6-16 Kemp 9g/f 77 3039
80 5-13 Asco 7gd 77 3068
57 9-9 Asco 8gd 76 3465
0 U-8 Wind 8.3fm 76 3641
72 6-15 Brig 8fm 76 3694
38 7-7 Wind 8.3gd [75] 3826
65 10-14 Epso 8.5gd 74 4295

JORDANS ELECT 4 ch g £10196
60 5-15 Hami 9.2gd 66 1388
73 1-14 HAMI 8.3gd 65 1748*
46 12-18 Thir 8g/f 69 1972
77 1-8 HAMI 9.2gd 69 2179+
76 4-11 Hami 8.3g/f 75 2317
49 8-8 Donc 8g/f 73 2425
65 4-6 Hami 8.3g/s [73] 2828
76 3-9 Hami 9g/f 73 3593

JORDANS SPARK 3 ch c £3494
50 5-8 Hami 11.1gd 1390
31 7-8 Ripo 10g/f 2523
12 12-12 Hayd 10.5gd 3740
28 6-6 Hami 11.1sft [49] 4011
57 1-8 HAMI 9.2g/s [49] 4133* P
56 6-13 Newc 10.1g/f 57 4406 p

| 9 | 14-18 | Newc | 8g/f | [57] | 5017 p |
| 49a | 6-11 | Wolv | 8.6ap | [57] | 5356 BL |

JOROBADEN 4 gr g £11771

68a	2-13	Ling	10ap		715
87	1-17	LEIC	10g/s		1019*
82	6-20	Newm	12gd	83	1172
91	1-13	KEMP	14.4hvy	83	1516*
75	8-18	York	13.9g/s	87	1689
87	6-14	Hayd	16.2gd	90	2239
67	18-19	Newc	16.1g/s	89	2771
75	15-20	Hayd	14fm	87	4383

JOSEAR 2 b c £266

52	4-7	Folk	5sft		1574
52	8-8	Kemp	5gd		2171
39	10-11	Wind	5g/f		2450

JOSEPH HENRY 2 b c £13632

85	1-7	MUSS	5g/f		1117*
103	1-6	NOTT	5.1sft		1466+
97	4-11	York	6gd	[100]	4998
103	4-11	Newm	6sft	[100]	5132
101	3-8	Donc	6sft	[100]	5217
93	5-11	Newm	6g/f	[100]	5270

JOSEPHUS 3 ch c £0

| 80 | 11-11 | Newm | 8g/s | [104] | 5283 |

JOSH 2 b c £24670

97	1-12	HAYD	6sft		3272*
95	3-6	Wind	6fm		3800
94	7-22	Donc	6fm		4458
99	1-4	YARM	6g/s		4633*
105	6-9	Newm	6g/f		4888

JOSHAR 2 b f £1505

2	8-10	Thir	5sft		1224
47	3-7	Newc	5sft		1394
41	8-11	Thir	5gd		1634
48a	3-7	Sout	6af		1751
52	3-12	Newc	6g/f		1869
43	4-11	Thir	6g/f		1968
0	13-13	York	6g/f		2358

JOSHUAS BOY 4 ch c £233

43	3-9	Ayr	6g/s	[45]	1447 BL
35	8-18	Ayr	7.2g/f	45	1897 P
37	9-20	Redc	6g/f	42	3767 p

JOSHUAS GOLD 3 b c £6896

60a	2-15	Ling	7ap	56	815
67	3-8	Muss	7.1gd	[58]	1554
51	6-14	Newc	8gd	58	1872
9	13-14	Nott	8.2g/f	56	2634
41	9-16	Ling	7gd	54	3024
56	8-11	York	7g/f	51	3433
59	1-18	CARL	7.9fm	51	3547*
60	4-18	Catt	7g/f	57	3670 VIS
59	2-14	Muss	7.1g/f	55	4175 vis
58	3-14	Carl	6.9g/f	55	4345 vis
40	13-19	Leic	7g/f	58	4452 vis
57	5-13	Muss	8g/f	[57]	4554
53	7-17	Beve	8.5g/f	57	4721 vis
33	15-17	Newc	8fm	57	4867 vis

JOSTLE 2 b c £0

| 50 | 11-10 | Newm | 7fm | | 4724 T |

JOURSANVAULT 3 gr c £16620

108	2-5	Sain	8gd		1060
108	2-5	Chan	8g/s		2639

JOUVERT 3 ch c £0

33a	6-11	Wolv	8.5af	[49]	128
16a	11-16	Ling	7ap	[45]	214

JOY AND PAIN 3 b g £4979

38a	14-15	Ling	7ap		472
60a	8-13	Ling	10ap		601
59a	6-12	Ling	8ap		623
53a	7-12	Ling	7ap	58	729
60a	1-15	LING	7ap	55	815*
43	6-12	Folk	6sft	58	975
70	2-14	Sali	7g/f	[58]	1720
67	3-15	Ling	7g/f	65	1983
49	8-14	Sali	8fm	67	2423
24	17-19	Wind	6g/f	66	5053
32	16-20	Yarm	7sft	63	5256

JOYCE 2 b c £7604

90	4-4	Curr	5g/f		1994
100	2-4	Leop	6g/f		2454

JOYCES CHOICE 5 b g £4105

53	2-20	Ripo	5gd	52	1179
24	9-10	Hami	5g/f	54	1391
0	R-15	Muss	5gd	54	1555 P
50	5-10	Newc	5g/f	[53]	2161
48	4-10	Hami	5g/f	[52]	2476
34	10-14	Newc	5g/s	50	2775
39	12-20	Beve	5g/s	48	3180
37	10-19	Donc	5g/s	48	3220 BL
50	2-8	Muss	5g/f	[45]	3527 p
43	6-17	Catt	5g/f	45	3667 p
49	1-16	WARW	5g/s	[45]	4995* VIS

JOYEAUX 2 b f £0

53a	8-10	Ling	7ap		4442
69	6-14	Hayd	6sft		4769
56a	4-12	Wolv	6ap		5177

JUANTORENA 2 ch c £11415

96	2-8	Newm	6g/f		1934
95	2-10	Newc	5g/f		2158
101	4-15	Asco	5g/f		2472
77	3-7	Yarm	6gd	[95]	3869
80	4-14	Wind	5gd	[92]	4121
88	2-11	Hayd	5g/f	[92]	4349
85	1-11	BEVE	5g/f	[83]	4599*

JUBILEE COIN 2 ch f £0

27	10-10	Newb	6gd		4637
24	10-10	Good	6gd		4876

JUBILEE STREET 5 b g £15874

39a	9-10	Wolv	7g/f	[51]	1319
52	4-14	Donc	6g/s	[49]	1522
55	3-18	Ayr	7.2g/f	52	1897
61	1-18	DONC	7g/f	52	2080*
52	10-17	Newm	7g/f	58	2768
51	7-12	Beve	8.5gd	58	2890
56	6-13	Thir	7g/f	56	3571
63	1-18	CATT	7g/f	55	3670*
63	2-14	Beve	7.5g/s	57	4241
65	1-18	CATT	7g/f	58	4438*
59	8-15	Beve	7.5g/f	62	4719
59	7-19	Newc	7g/f	62	5014
39	16-16	Catt	7sft	62	5130

JUBILEE TIME 3 b c £0

0	W-13	Wolv	8.5af		39
0	W-9	Ling	10ap		269

JUBILEE TREAT 4 b f £450

31	13-14	Yarm	8g/f	78	1131
75	7-7	Ling	10g/f	76	2015
0	6-6	Newc	10.1g/s	[74]	2772

JUDDA 3 b c £0

24	15-19	Donc	6g/f		1876
38	11-16	Newm	7fm		2092
2a	12-12	Sout	7af		2339
19	11-12	Nott	10hvy		5190 T P

JUDGE DAMUSS 2 ch c £0

0	18-18	Ripo	6g/s		3939
0	12-12	Redc	8g/s		5107

JULES LEE 2 ch g £0

24	13-13	Sali	7g/f		3864
0	13-14	Wind	8.3g/f		5049 P

JUMBOS FLYER 7 ch g £0

| 8 | 10-10 | Carl | 5.9fm | | 3545 |

JUMEIRAH SCARER 2 b g £2652

62a	3-11	Ling	7ap		220
71a	2-11	Ling	8ap		322
77a	2-12	Ling	8ap		428

JUMMANA 3 ch f £0

| 82a | 11-15 | Ling | 7ap | 92 | 81 |

JUN FAN 2 br c £0

67	5-7	Redc	5g/f		2100
69	6-14	Redc	6fm		2297

JUNGLE LION 5 ch g £5359

47a	7-13	Sout	8af	[55]	188 t
1a	12-13	Wolv	8.5af	52	251 t
44a	6-8	Wolv	8.5af	[47]	362 t
47a	2-8	Sout	11af	[47]	420 e
18a	10-13	Sout	14af	47	590 t
57a	1-9	SOUT	12af	[45]	774* t
10a	13-15	Sout	12af	56	867 t
51a	1-16	SOUT	14af	45	1033* t
50a	6-11	Sout	12af	53	1197 t
41	8-17	Nott	14.1gd	50	1238 t
38a	6-12	Sout	16af	52	1753 t

JUNIPER BANKS 3 ch g £427

44	6-14	Newc	5g/f	[67]	4404
52	6-10	Ripo	6gd	[62]	4790
44	10-15	Ayr	5sft	57	5036
34	12-19	Redc	6g/s	[57]	5110
59a	3-13	Wolv	5.1ap	57	5156
11a	12-12	Wolv	5.1ap	57	5326
44a	6-11	Wolv	5.1ap	[57]	5363

JUST A FLUKE 3 b c £9355

78	4-17	Leic	10g/s		1019
59	7-10	Pont	10sft	77	1427 T
77	2-7	Carl	9.3fm	[77]	2443
70	3-8	Newc	10.1sft	[77]	2687
52	13-15	Epso	10.1gd	[77]	3216
78	5-9	Carl	9.3fm	[75]	3546
68	2-10	Hami	9.2g/s	[74]	4135
68	1-6	MUSS	8gd	[72]	4520*
66	4-14	Hami	8.3g/s	71	4820

JUST A GLIMMER 3 b f £11780

47a	11-11	Ling	8ap	82	80
78a	3-8	Wolv	7af	79	285
66a	7-16	Sout	7af	78	419
85a	1-12	WOLV	7af	76	840*
86a	2-9	Wolv	7af	82	940
80	7-10	Warw	7.1gd	[84]	1126
83	1-10	WARW	7.1sft	[80]	1525+
63	13-16	Good	7g/f	84	1817
52	15-16	Good	7gd	82	4873
65a	12-12	Wolv	7.1ap	63	5159

JUST A TRY 2 ch c £0

42	8-8	Newb	7g/f		3267
70	6-16	Sali	7g/f		3882
70	7-11	Chep	8.1g/s		4363

JUST BEWARE 2 b f £0

3	13-13	Ling	6g/f		2061
35	8-8	Kemp	7g/s		4092
47a	10-14	Ling	7ap		5257

JUST BONNIE 2 b c £0

0	6-6	Chep	6.1qd		2367
29	9-10	Wind	5fm		3476
0	17-17	Wind	6g/f		3975
13	15-16	Nott	6.1g/s	[35]	4644

JUST CLIFF 2 b c £0

23a	11-12	Ling	6ap		4896
66	4-13	Warw	7.1g/s		4996
66a	4-11	Wolv	7.1g/s		5228

JUST DANCE ME 3 gr f £1720

71	2-4	Hami	9.2gd		2709
36	6-11	Wind	8.3g/f		5052

JUST DASHING 5 b g £0

0	12-13	Sali	9.9gd		2700
31	9-10	Ling	6g/f		3603
12	16-18	Wind	10g/s		4944

JUST DO IT 2 b c £1870

63a	6-11	Ling	8ap		3786
73	2-14	Sali	8g/s		4078
56	5-9	Chep	8.1g/s		4297
56	14-18	Catt	7g/f	75	4673
56	9-13	Wind	8.3g/s	66	4940

JUST ELIZABETH 2 b f £0

32	13-14	Hayd	6sft		4769
13	8-9	Catt	7sft		5131
14	21-21	Donc	6sft		5368

JUST FILLY 2 ch f £0

| 59a | 8-12 | Ling | 8ap | | 19 |

JUST FLY 3 b g £12716
```
81a  5-15  Ling  7ap        81    81
72a  7-14  Ling  6ap        80    149
77a  5-11  Ling  8ap       [79]   273
83a  2-14  Ling  6ap        79    292
88a  2-16  Sout  7af        80    419
88a  2-14  Ling  7ap        85    518
0   17-18  Asco  8sft       80    1423
81   3-16  Good  7g/f       78    1817
46  12-13  Kemp  7g/f       78    2172
67  13-20  Chep  7.1g/s     78    3088
67   8-17  Newb  7g/f       78    3257
24  12-13  Kemp  7sft       75    4030
64  13-24  Newb  7g/f       72    4642
79   2-18  Kemp  8g/f       72    4714
77   2-14  Wind  8.3g/f     70    4832
78a  5-12  Ling  6ap        82    5297
```

JUST JAMES 5 b g £0
```
72  15-15  York  6sft      [113]  1667
86  13-16  Asco  8g/f      [113]  2470
99  11-13  Newb  7g/f      [113]  3957
```

JUST ONE LOOK 3 b f £807
```
70a  7-12  Ling  7ap        73    1024
67   8-20  Nott  6.1gd      71    1239
53   7-10  Hayd  6g/f       69    1488
47  15-17  Kemp  7gd        68    2174
13a  8-8   Sout  8af        65    2495
57   6-14  Chep  8.1g/s     61    3090
32  10-15  Chep  8.1sft     58    4057
55   5-20  Chep  7.1g/s     55    4367
41   7-12  Brig  8sft       53    5094
56a  3-13  Wolv  8.6ap     [53]   5184
52a  3-11  Wolv  8.6ap     [51]   5356
```

JUST ONE SMILE 3 b f £1765
```
64a  2-16  Ling  7ap        62    22
0   16-16  Newc  6sft       63    1277
63   3-15  Redc  7sft       62    1660
52   6-10  Donc  6g/f       62    1878
41  10-10  Ayr   7.2g/f     62    2027
45   5-17  Redc  6gd        60    2561
47  10-11  Pont  6g/f       57    2791 BL
44  11-14  Leic  6g/f       55    3213 bl
```

JUST RED 6 ch h £0
```
12a 10-10  Wolv  12af             359
```

JUST TIM 3 ch c £10914
```
79a  4-10  Ling  10ap      [78]   886
78   1-11  BATH  8g/s      [78]   1101*
77   4-8   Sand  8.1g/s     78    1315
69  12-14  Newm  8g/f       76    1930
78   1-7   CHEP  8.1gd     [74]   2116*
78   5-10  Newb  8g/f       80    2350
64   7-8   Wind  8.3g/s    [80]   2620
64  14-19  Good  8g/f       78    3512 T
```

JUST WAZ 2 ch c £4527
```
70   8-11  Beve  7.5g/s           3851
72   1-8   NEWC  7sft             4283*
53   5-8   Muss  8gd        70    4807
39  10-14  Donc  8sft       68    5203
```

JUST WIZ 7 b g £3708
```
74a  3-10  Wolv  8.5af      71    5 bl
71a  2-6   Wolv  9.4af      70    249 bl
70a  6-15  Ling  12ap       70    549 bl
51a  3-5   Wolv  12af      [70]   616 bl
50a 10-11  Ling  10ap       68    716 bl
65a  2-9   Wolv  8.5af     [68]   811 bl
47a  3-7   Wolv  9.4af     [62]   862 bl
0   11-13  Wind  8.3g/s    [40]   1058 bl
41a  2-4   Wolv  12af      [58]   1323 bl
42a  5-7   Wolv  8.5af     [58]   1341 bl
```

JUSTALORD 5 b g £32412
```
82a  6-13  Ling  6ap        82    235 p
73a  8-9   Sout  5af        82    415 p
88a  2-16  Sout  5af        82    461 p
92a  1-10  LING  5ap        85    567+ p
94a  2-10  Ling  5ap        88    692 p
95a  3-10  Ling  5ap       [89]   883 p
49  13-17  Kemp  5sft       69    944 p
66   6-17  Warw  5fm        67    2599 p
75   1-13  CATT  5g/f       67    3350* BL
65   7-12  Nott  5.1g/f    [67]   3577 bl
```

82 1-16 MUSS 5g/f 72 4174* bl

JUSTAQUESTION 2 b f £47818
```
72   7-15  Donc  5gd              920
78   1-11  WARW  5gd              1123*
93   1-6   YORK  6sft             1669*
82  12-17  Asco  6g/f             2553
85   3-11  Warw  7.1gd            3053
89   2-9   Good  7fm        82    3624
95   1-10  ASCO  8gd       [82]   3774*
93   5-12  Good  7sft      [93]   4264
77   9-26  Newb  6.5g/f           4679
91   6-8   Newm  7sft      [93]   5133
93   4-8   Newm  8g/s      [93]   5282
```

JUSTE POUR LAMOUR 4 ch g £8281
```
65   8-13  Ripo  8g/f       76    2010
76   4-11  Newm  7fm        76    2090
60   7-8   Sand  10gd       74    2363
50   9-10  Leic  7g/f      [74]   2920 BL
63  10-20  Newm  8g/f       72    3232
70   4-11  Newm  6fm        72    3408
68   7-10  Newm  6g/f       70    3584
56   7-12  Newm  6g/f       70    3751
76   1-12  BRIG  8g/f       67    3986*
64   5-11  Brig  8g/s       67    4141
79   2-13  Epso  8.5gd      72    4469
74   6-24  Newb  7g/f       72    4642
78   4-12  Muss  8g/f      [74]   4809
```

JUSTENJOY YOURSELF 2 b f £368
```
27   6-6   Folk  5sft             974
45   8-15  York  5g/f             2056
37a  6-7   Sout  5af              2498
44   4-9   Leic  5g/f             2921
35   8-9   Catt  6sft       42    3931
47   3-9   Yarm  6sft       42    4146
8   15-16  Beve  7.5g/f     46    4597
```

JUSTICE JONES 3 b g £0
```
8a   9-10  Wolv  8.5af            839
45  10-12  Warw  7.1gd            1125
53  17-20  Bath  10.2gd           1398
47  16-20  Wind  10sft            1651
24  10-11  Brig  9.9fm      50    2260
14  10-11  Yarm  7g/f      [47]   2852
0   16-19  Nott  6.1gd     [43]   3104 BL
```

JUWWI 10 ch g £736
```
63a 10-14  Ling  6ap        72    292
69a  4-10  Ling  5ap        72    329
54a 11-14  Ling  6ap        70    407
51a  9-9   Ling  5ap       [69]   492
43a  4-12  Wolv  6af              646
59a  4-9   Sout  5af       [63]   793 p
24  14-15  Folk  6sft       65    976 p
43a  6-8   Wolv  5af       [60]   1218
48   2-11  Bath  5.7fm     [62]   2412
54   6-11  Good  6gd        62    2535
32   6-14  Newc  6g/s      [58]   2730
24a 14-15  Sout  5af       [55]   2803
22  11-13  Bath  5gd       [50]   3143
25  17-19  Donc  5g/s       50    3220
```

KABEER 6 ch g £853
```
74   4-14  Yarm  7fm              2148
67   3-8   Warw  7.1fm            2575
52  11-14  Warw  7.1g/f           2907
60   8-8   Newm  8g/f       70    3583
61a  5-14  Ling  7ap        66    3821
64   6-14  Wind  8.3g/f     63    4832
50  12-17  Leic  10gd       62    5062
61a  6-14  Ling  7ap       [59]   5263 T
```

KABIS AMIGOS 2 ch c £0
```
61   9-14  Leic  5gd              5058 T
57   9-16  Newb  8hvy             5220 t
```

KABIS BOOIE 3 ch c £671
```
66   3-13  Leic  10g/f            4453
12   9-9   Good  11gd      [70]   5026
```

KABREET 2 b c £12547
```
74a  1-11  LING  6ap       [77]   51*
64a  9-15  Ling  7ap        74    177
81a  1-8   LING  6ap        73    268*
82a  3-7   Ling  7ap        78    368
87a  1-10  LING  6ap        78    494*
```

```
68   9-11  Newb  6gd        85    1734
61  15-18  Newm  6g/f       82    1933
49   8-11  Donc  6g/s       78    3379
47   8-8   Sand  5g/s       74    3889 VIS
```

KAFIL 10 b g £0
```
0   13-13  Ling  6ap       [35]   541 vis
18a  7-10  Ling  7ap       [35]   1181 bl
0    7-7   Ling  6ap       [30]   1715 bl
```

KAGGAMAGIC 2 ch g £0
```
70   5-14  Redc  6fm              2297
58   4-20  Newc  6sft             2682
66   7-11  Warw  7.1gd            3053
32  15-19  Carl  5.9g/f     69    4344
56   7-14  Newc  6fm       [65]   4865
```

KAGOSHIMA 8 b g £1330
```
26a  7-15  Sout  16af       46    67 vis
33a  6-8   Sout  16af       43    140 vis
19a  8-16  Sout  16af       43    206 vis
42a  2-10  Sout  16af      [39]   307 vis
40a  2-7   Sout  14af      [40]   357 vis
39a  3-12  Sout  14af      [40]   443 vis
34a  3-9   Sout  16af      [40]   576 vis
11a  6-8   Wolv  16.2af     40    690 vis
```

KAHIRA 2 ch f £1756
```
60   8-10  Yarm  8g/s             4631
80   2-19  Leic  7gd              5040
```

KAHYASI PRINCESS 4 b f £0
```
65   5-5   Muss  14g/s      84    1459
```

KAID 9 b g £0
```
6a   7-10  Wolv  12af      [35]   581
```

KAIETEUR 5 b h £2500
```
96   6-9   Sand  10g/s    [117]   2128
103  8-10  Asco  10g/f    [117]   2488
99   5-7   Newb  10g/f    [114]   3264 BL
108  4-6   Donc  10.3fm   [111]   4492
```

KAJUL 3 b f £0
```
46  10-11  Sali  7gd              3884
38a 10-11  Ling  8ap              4977
```

KALAMAN 4 b c £138740
```
112  2-6   Newm  9gd      [119]   1168
112  1-5   GOOD  8g/f     [116]   2022+
117  3-12  Sand  10g/s    [116]   2916
119  1-7   AYR   10g/f    [116]   3306+
113  6-9   York  10.4gd   [116]   4002
```

KALAMANSI 3 b f £0
```
57   6-12  Ripo  9g/f             1783
26  16-18  Wind  10g/f            1959
32  12-16  Newm  7fm              2092
36   8-8   Hami  9.2g/f     53    2475
40   8-14  Yarm  11.5g/f    50    3714
```

KALANI STAR 4 b c £0
```
62a  7-12  Wolv  7.1ap     [70]   5340
```

KALANISHA 4 ch g £425
```
56   7-15  Leic  10g/s            1358
27   6-10  Kemp  12hvy     [45]   1645
14a 11-16  Sout  12af       42    2340
34a  3-10  Sout  14af       36    3096 BL
28a  5-14  Ling  10ap      [35]   4662 bl
```

KALATUNA 3 ch f £10282
```
108  2-7   Chan  12g/s            2304
```

KALI 2 gr f £8887
```
76a  2-12  Ling  8ap              100
67   3-9   Folk  9.7sft           980
71   3-18  Wind  8.3g/f           1810
78   2-17  Kemp  7gd        72    2174
74   1-8   WARW  7.1fm     [76]   2575+
75   6-25  Newb  7gd        76    4683
79a  4-13  Ling  7ap        76    4897
72   6-11  Donc  7sft       75    5219
80a  2-13  Wolv  8.6ap      74    5364
```

KALIKA 2 b f £0
```
28a  6-11  Wolv  6af              2051
27  12-16  Pont  6g/f             2275
33a  8-14  Sout  7af              2492
1   13-13  Redc  7fm       [35]   4927
```

KALIMENTA 3 ch f £0
56	6-11	Ling	10gd	[65]	3201
52	7-11	Bath	10.2g/f	65	3373
32	11-12	Kemp	9sft	65	4032
16	15-16	Chep	10.2g/s	62	4365

KALISHKA 3 b c £0
70	6-11	Beve	8.5sft		1304
62	5-14	Ayr	8g/f	[63]	1896
38	14-18	Pont	8gd	63	3242
48	11-13	Nott	10g/f	60	3419
52	8-17	Beve	8.5g/f	58	4721 BL
29	13-18	Leic	10gd	[55]	5042

KALLISTAS PRIDE 3 b f £4699
0	11-13	Wolv	8.5af		39
17	9-13	Leic	7g/f		1827
63	2-8	Sand	5gd		2361
42	9-19	Leic	5gd	58	2702
62	1-13	SALI	6g/s	58	3109*
52	12-13	Wind	6fm	61	3479
56	6-12	Nott	5.1g/f	[61]	3577
47	11-11	Sand	5sft	60	4070 VIS
59	5-8	Folk	5gd	60	4118 VIS
43	12-15	Sali	5gd	59	4335 vis
36	13-19	Nott	6.1g/f	[58]	4845 vis
45a	7-12	Wolv	6ap	[56]	5155 vis

KALMINI 2 b f £9165
74	7-13	Newb	7g/f		3252
78	2-13	Good	7fm		3554
77	1-12	FOLK	7gd		3909*
73	5-9	Newc	8sft	80	4285
75	4-4	Sand	7.1gd	[76]	4606
69	12-17	Good	8gd	75	4871 VIS

KALOU 5 br g £1241
50a	3-14	Sout	8af	48	165
50a	3-13	Ling	10ap	48	805
39	7-17	Newm	10g/f	48	3238
48	3-10	Newm	10fm	48	3404
45	9-16	Wind	11.6gd	48	3829
39	7-18	Warw	10.9g/s	47	4669

KALUANA COURT 8 b m £0
15	13-20	Bath	17.2gd	68	4824
1	19-20	York	13.9gd	66	5004
0	33-34	Newm	18sft	68	5135
0	7-7	Newm	12sft	64	5268

KALUSH 3 b g £0
3	17-17	Donc	8gd	[66]	919
14	9-9	Sout	10gd	[64]	1283
8	6-6	Donc	10.3g/f	[61]	2426
2	8-9	Pont	8gd	[58]	3462

KAMAKIRI 2 b c £13437
75	7-16	Sali	7g/s		3111
101	1-6	ASCO	7g/f		3390*
103	1-4	SAND	7.1g/f		3859*

KAMALA 4 b f £0
0	9-10	Wolv	12af		154
1a	P-12	Wolv	12af	50	244 VIS
0	6-6	Sout	12af	[50]	392

KAMANDA LAUGH 3 ch g £31827
77a	1-10	LING	6ap		973*
80	2-17	Warw	7.1sft	73	1526
86	1-12	DONC	7g/f	77	1879*
90	1-9	LEIC	8gd	80	2705*
93	1-22	NEWM	8sft	83	5103*
89	5-13	Newm	8g/s	87	5284

KAMAS WHEEL 5 ch m £0
24	8-13	Redc	8gd	38	2552
22	7-14	Yarm	8gd	35	3363
32	6-16	Carl	7.9g/f	32	3650
26	7-15	Chep	8.1sft	31	4057

KAMENKA 3 ch f £2049
61	4-7	Newc	6g/s	[73]	2728
70	4-12	Donc	5g/f	70	3599
68	4-15	Thir	5g/s	70	3833
23	17-20	Ripo	6gd	69	4278
19	11-15	Hami	6sft	67	4696
44	3-8	Catt	6gd	[65]	4969
57	3-19	Redc	6g/s	[65]	5110 VIS

| 27a | 6-12 | Wolv | 6ap | [62] | 5157 vis |

KAMES PARK 2 b g £7688
80	4-8	Hayd	8.1g/f		4351
81	2-7	Hami	8.3sft		4691
84	1-9	AYR	7.2sft		5064*

KANAD 2 b c £4785
81	3-11	Yarm	6g/f		1727 T
77	2-13	Nott	5.1gd		1987 t
55	7-17	Donc	6g/f		2424 t
77	2-17	Ling	6gd	[77]	4443 t
69	5-13	Newm	6fm	[77]	4726 t
80	1-10	CATT	7sft	[75]	5127* BL t

KANDIDATE 2 b c £4207
59	15-15	Newm	7fm		3005
94	3-8	Newb	7g/f		3267
81	7-10	Asco	7gd		3774
98	6-8	Asco	8g/f	[90]	4797
80a	2-11	Ling	8ap	[95]	5235

KANGARILLA ROAD 5 b g £1124
26	18-20	Donc	5gd	75	927
59	7-20	Thir	5g/f	70	1765
70	2-16	Ayr	5g/f	66	2029
52	13-15	Muss	5fm	66	2084
47	14-19	Beve	5gd	66	2512
53	14-17	Catt	5g/f	66	2846

KANGRINA 2 b f £3413
69a	5-11	Ling	8ap		4744
74a	4-11	Wolv	8.6ap		4978
79a	1-13	WOLV	8.6ap		5288*

KANZ WOOD 7 ch g £643
20a	14-14	Sout	8af	65	93
59a	8-11	Ling	8ap	65	136
50a	7-11	Wolv	7af	62	241
19a	15-15	Ling	7ap	[59]	366
47a	5-10	Ling	8ap	55	769
37a	9-11	Ling	8ap	55	820
22	5-10	Chep	8.1sft	[45]	1334
35	5-17	Kemp	7hvy	[45]	1642
45a	3-7	Wolv	8.5af	[50]	1672
49a	4-13	Wolv	8.5af	[45]	2052
46a	3-12	Wolv	7af	[45]	2204 VIS
37a	6-13	Sout	8af	45	2497 vis
34a	10-15	Sout	7af	45	2501 vis

KAPAJE 2 b f £550
30	18-19	Newb	6g/f		2310
69	5-13	Chep	6.1gd		3399
70	3-15	Folk	7gd		4114
48	8-19	Kemp	8g/f	[70]	4792

KAPAROLO 5 ch g £0
| 33 | 7-11 | Beve | 16.2sft | 68 | 1629 |
| 44 | 14-15 | Good | 16gd | 66 | 5025 |

KAPPELMANN 2 gr c £6338
| 101 | 2-8 | Deau | 7sft | | 3169 |

KARAKUM 5 b g £273
39	4-10	Warw	12.6g/f	44	2912
27	10-17	Bath	11.7gd	42	3145
5	9-12	Brig	11.9fm	40	4764

KARAMEA 3 gr f £6389
84	3-10	Newb	10gd		1209
70	1-8	THIR	12g/s	[82]	1472*
60	5-5	Leic	11.8g/f	82	2923
30	11-11	Sali	12g/s	80	4080
36	8-8	Hayd	11.9g/f	77	4353

KARAOKE 4 b g £12916
27a	14-14	Ling	10ap	65	520
62a	7-13	Ling	10ap	65	726
73a	1-14	LING	10ap	65	803*
33	15-18	Bath	10.2g/s	74	1098
61	11-20	Newb	10gd	72	1235
65	5-12	Sand	8.1g/s	70	1352
46	5-5	Nott	10sft	68	1609
67	4-17	Kemp	10g/f	65	1913
69	2-12	Bath	10.2fm	65	2036
69	2-15	Kemp	10fm	65	2067
43	8-8	Sand	10gd	67	2363
38	8-8	Nott	10g/s	67	2929
65	9-16	Kemp	9g/f	67	3039

68	3-12	Kemp	10gd	67	3185
69	1-12	WIND	10fm	65	3295*
66	7-10	Newm	10g/f	63	3615
63	5-14	Brig	11.9fm	68	3674

KARAOKE KING 6 ch h £0
46a	6-11	Wolv	7af	57	378
48a	15-16	Ling	7ap	55	600
46a	11-13	Ling	6ap	54	740
46a	9-10	Ling	7ap	[54]	765
0	P-14	Ling	7sft	62	1625

KARASHINKO 3 b g £0
| 2 | 13-13 | Newm | 8g/f | | 1935 |
| 0 | 15-14 | Donc | 5gd | | 2237 |

KARATHAENA 4 b f £0
52a	8-15	Ling	7ap	[78]	814
13a	12-12	Ling	8ap	[78]	878
41	8-18	Wind	8.3g/s	68	1059
46	14-15	Beve	9.9sft	65	1307
47	10-13	Bath	8sft	60	1542 VIS
52	8-20	Hayd	11.9g/s	55	4771
32	10-18	Pont	12g/f	55	4938

KAREEB 7 b g £930
79a	6-11	Ling	8ap	[78]	800
62	14-17	Leic	7g/s	78	1020
39	19-20	Wind	6g/s	78	1255
75	4-16	York	7g/f	76	2057
39	21-28	Asco	7g/f	76	2558
76	6-15	York	7gd	75	3117
65	14-20	Newm	7g/f	73	3782
61	6-13	Kemp	7sft	71	4030
70	4-17	York	7g/f	69	4398
65	11-24	Newb	7g/f	69	4642

KARELIAN 3 gr g £1051
| 75 | 3-14 | Ayr | 10sft | 73 | 5037 BL |
| 64 | 6-11 | Muss | 16g/s | 72 | 5335 |

KARENS CAPER 2 b f £5633
| 72a | 2-14 | Ling | 7ap | | 5076 |
| 85a | 1-12 | LING | 8ap | | 5293* |

KARITA 2 ch f £0
| 0 | 9-10 | Thir | 5sft | | 1224 |

KARLU 2 ch c £3059
| 72 | 9-15 | Ling | 7gd | | 3285 |
| 81 | 1-11 | CHEP | 7.1hvy | | 4704* |

KARMA CHAMELIAN 3 b f £0
37	12-13	Kemp	8fm		2072
47	5-8	Warw	7.1fm		2575
43	7-9	Warw	6.1fm	[44]	2778

KARMINSKEY PARK 5 b m £10685
59	6-13	Newc	5sft	62	1276
64	2-17	Warw	5hvy	[62]	1532
54	6-19	Beve	5sft	62	1627
63	5-13	Newc	5gd	62	1873
60	3-13	Pont	5g/f	[62]	2279
66	2-19	Beve	5gd	62	2512
69	1-6	HAMI	5gd	61	2712*
65	7-8	Hami	5g/s	72	2830
59	7-9	Nott	5.1gd	65	3106
56	7-17	Pont	5gd	65	3241
48	9-15	Hami	5gd	64	3680
52	8-10	Hami	5g/s	[62]	4010
52	5-12	Redc	6gd	[60]	4245
48	10-18	Leic	6gd	58	5039
43a	6-13	Wolv	6ap	[55]	5359

KARYON 4 b f £0
38	5-13	Ripo	12.3g/f	40	2008
1a	9-10	Sout	14af	38	3158
0	10-10	Carl	14.1fm	35	3549

KASHIMO 5 b h £713
58a	5-14	Ling	12ap	58	731
59a	3-14	Ling	12ap	58	801
59	4-8	Yarm	11.5g/f	58	1135

KASHMAR FLIGHT 2 b f £0
60	8-12	Warw	5sft		1524
48	7-13	Redc	6g/f		1818
55	6-11	Thir	7fm		2462
63	5-10	Catt	7g/f		2845

41 11-11 Pont 8fm 59 4753

KASHTANKA 2 ch c £0
0 17-18 Newc 6g/s 3699
55 6-14 Thir 7g/s 4207
52 6-11 Thir 7fm 4375

KASKA 3 b f £0
71 7-17 Newm 8gd 1166
80 6-17 Newb 10gd 1737

KASTHARI 5 gr g £60000
115 1-8 DONC 18fm [112] 4478*
90 11-11 Newm 16sft [116] 5138

KASUS 6 br g £5282
97 2-8 Bade 14sft 4425

KATALI 6 ch m £0
6a 13-15 Sout 6af [35] 172
0 11-13 Ling 6ap [30] 541

KATANA 2 b f £0
50 14-18 Nott 8.2g/s 4035
46 12-15 Good 8g/s 4233
64a 5-11 Ling 8ap 4738
66 5-15 York 7.9gd [62] 5002

KATAVI 3 b f £0
66a 5-14 Ling 7ap 5240

KATAYEB 3 b f £0
21 8-9 Sand 10gd 4501

KATHOLOGY 6 b g £1083
56a 13-15 Sout 5af 77 64
69 17-20 Epso 5fm 84 2253
81 6-9 Sali 5fm 83 2420
78 7-12 Sali 5gd 83 2698
63 8-11 Sand 5g/s 82 2894
81 3-17 Sand 5g/f 79 3341
79 5-14 Newb 5.2fm 79 3628
66 7-11 Muss 5gd 78 5332

KATHRYN JANEWAY 2 b f £0
62 12-19 Leic 7gd 5045
55 6-11 Donc 8sft 5205

KATHYS JOB 2 b f £0
63 9-15 Donc 5gd 920

KATIE BOO 2 br f £22053
65 3-8 Muss 5gd 1795
70 2-15 York 5g/f 2056
76 1-6 CARL 5fm 2442*
80 3-6 Hami 6gd 2711
77 5-8 Ches 5.1g/f 79 3082
84 2-7 York 5g/f 79 3432
84 2-10 Thir 5fm 78 3607
89 1-7 CHES 6.1g/f [81] 4050*

KATIE KAI 3 b f £259
2 5-5 Ayr 8sft 5038

KATIE KILLANE 2 ch f £0
31 7-9 Nott 5.1gd 2926
0 12-14 Leic 6g/f 3517
43 13-15 Nott 5.1gd 4859
16a 12-12 Wolv 5.1ap 4981 P

KATIE MERNAGH 4 b f £0
30 5-6 Yarm 14.1sft 5249 BL

KATIES BATH TIME 3 b f £0
0 11-11 Sout 6af 45 591
2 12-12 Catt 5gd [40] 995

KATIES BISCUIT 2 b f £0
44 6-9 Catt 6g/f 4670
60 10-13 Redc 7fm 4927
62 6-14 Redc 7sft 5301

KATIES ROLE 2 b f £1199
44a 3-14 Sout 8af [57] 95
55a 3-7 Wolv 5af [52] 284
43a 4-15 Sout 7af [53] 462
50a 4-12 Wolv 7af [50] 560
44a 3-9 Wolv 8.5af [50] 865
36 7-11 Donc 10.3gd [57] 930
2 13-14 Sout 10g/s 55 1051

KATIYPOUR 7 ch g £12636
67a 7-14 Ling 10ap 69 803
73a 3-8 Ling 10ap 69 900
77a 1-12 LING 8ap 69 932+
78a 2-12 Ling 8ap [75] 1042
40 8-9 Epso 8.5hvy [72] 1298
77 1-15 BRIG 8fm 72 1691*
72 4-7 Wind 8.3g/f [75] 2264
55 12-15 Epso 10.1gd [75] 3216
78 3-9 Epso 10.1fm 75 3538
77 4-15 Brig 8fm 75 3694
75 5-9 Sand 9g/s [75] 3892
73 7-11 Epso 10.1gd 75 4293
68 7-13 Epso 10.1g/f 75 4473
74a 3-14 Ling 10ap [75] 4742

KATY JEM 2 b f £0
26 15-16 Newm 7g/s 5280

KATY OHARA 5 b m £470
17a 9-14 Sout 6af 45 501
45a 2-13 Wolv 6af [45] 582
20a 6-10 Wolv 6af [45] 822
36 10-16 Catt 7g/f 45 4676

KATZ PYJAMAS 2 b f £0
28a 9-10 Sout 5af [42] 139
1 19-19 Chep 6.1sft 47 4054
0 13-14 Bath 8g/f 45 4411

KAURI FOREST 3 ch c £5174
75 3-17 Kemp 7gd 1136
85 2-20 Newm 8g/f 3237
82 2-6 Donc 7g/f 3595 T
70a 3-11 Ling 8ap [83] 4977 t
73a 4-14 Ling 7ap [77] 5240 t

KAVI 4 ch g £0
58a 7-14 Ling 10ap 61 520
57a 8-14 Ling 10ap 61 622 bl
28a 11-14 Ling 12ap 60 711

KAWAASER 2 br c £856
84 3-20 Naas 6g/s 5163

KAY TWO 2 ch c £34948
102 2-4 Curr 5g/f 1994
106 1-9 TIPP 5hvy 4960*
107 3-11 Newm 5sft 5132

KAYF ARAMIS 2 b c £0
28 12-12 Sand 7.1g/f 2388

KAYMICH PERFECTO 4 b g £0
43 14-17 Nott 8.2gd 63 4862
25 13-17 Newc 10.1g/f 60 5016

KEBREYA 4 ch g £0
0 10-12 Wolv 16.2af 65 7 VIS

KEDROSS 3 ch f £0
33a 7-9 Sout 7af [63] 613
40a 7-12 Wolv 6af 55 1374
0 14-15 Sout 8af 51 1755
27 5-8 Leic 11.8g/f [58] 1961
32a 7-12 Wolv 7af 46 2049
38 15-18 Sali 7fm 55 2292 BL

KEELUNG 3 b c £11896
65a 4-12 Ling 8ap 734
81a 2-12 Ling 8ap 881
86 2-11 Donc 10.3gd 930
91 1-5 NEWC 10.1sft [85] 1275*
88 3-8 Sali 9.9g/s 85 1500
90 2-11 Sand 10g/s 85 2127
58 16-17 Asco 12g/f 88 2519
81 7-10 York 11.9gd 88 4324
80 14-18 Newb 10gd 88 4681
68 17-17 Newm 10g/f 86 4917 P

KEEP BACCKINHIT 2 b f £12938
73 3-7 Newm 6g/f 2733
0 10-12 Bath 5.7gd 3141
78 3-10 Wind 6fm 3290
83 1-9 GOOD 7fm 75 3624*
72 5-8 Sand 7.1g/s 80 4100
53 17-21 Donc 6.5fm 80 4457
81 4-10 Newm 6fm 78 4727
82 6-16 Good 7gd 78 5031

KEEP ME WARM 2 ch g £1392
70 4-12 Bath 5sft 5169
74a 2-13 Wolv 6ap 5287

KEEP ON MOVIN 2 b f £7075
73a 3-11 Ling 8ap 75 54
71a 1-12 LING 10ap [74] 116*
86 5-18 Leic 10g/s 73 1017
54 8-10 Beve 12.1g/s 73 1165
74 2-5 Leic 11.8g/f 72 2923
64 7-8 Epso 12gd 75 3217
67 4-12 Sali 12g/f 73 3868
44 13-13 Kemp 14.4fm 71 4395

KEEP THE PEACE 6 br g £0
2 17-19 Chep 12.1gd 50 3398 t P

KEEPASHARPLOOKOUT 2 b c £903
66 4-6 Redc 5sft 1143
57 4-6 Hami 5gd 1503
23 10-10 Newc 6sft 1677
55 4-13 Beve 5g/s 2321

KEEPERS KNIGHT 3 b c £5272
67a 1-9 LING 10ap 60 365*
69a 3-11 Ling 10ap 61 497
65a 5-10 Ling 10ap 68 676 BL
5a 7-10 Sout 12af 68 796
25 15-19 Warw 10.9gd 66 1124
55 9-14 Wind 8.3fm 65 2971
65 3-7 Folk 9.7gd 62 3384
53 5-5 Folk 9.7g/s 62 3914
66 4-9 Good 11gd [62] 5026
61 5-10 Donc 10.3sft 62 5206
58 8-16 Nott 10hvy 62 5345 T

KEEPERS LODGE 3 ch f £9307
64 4-6 Ches 7gd [72] 1587
37 16-20 Asco 8g/f 72 1927
49 7-8 Donc 8g/f 69 2425
72 1-12 HAYD 8.1gd 66 2904*
66 8-12 Hayd 6sft 70 3273
70 3-6 Donc 8g/f 70 3597
74 5-10 Ches 10.3sft 70 4071
74 2-10 Beve 9.9sft 70 4260
37 15-17 Hayd 10.5fm 70 4388

KEHAAR 3 ch c £60445
92 1-12 NEWB 7g/f 2352+
97 1-16 NEWM 8g/f 86 3059+
82 11-12 Good 7fm [93] 3555
105 1-15 ASCO 7g/f 93 4800*

KELBROOK 5 b g £418
66 5-14 Thir 8gd 1636
23 8-9 Hayd 11.9g/f 1885
42 4-7 Ayr 10gd 65 2507

KELSEAS KOLBY 4 b g £6589
45 13-17 Leic 7g/s 57 1020
30 13-15 Thir 7gd 55 1635 vis
57 1-13 LEIC 7g/f [53] 1827* vis
49 4-9 Leic 8g/f [53] 1966 vis
58 3-9 Brig 8g/f [55] 2431 vis
58 4-15 Thir 8g/s [55] 2688 vis
58 4-16 Carl 7.9g/f 55 3650 vis
56 2-10 Leic 7fm [55] 3812 vis
61 2-20 Yarm 8gd 55 3996 vis
60a 5-12 Ling 8ap [57] 4320 vis
60 3-14 Good 8g/f 57 4542
0 18-18 Sali 9.9gd 57 4850

KELTIC FLUTE 5 b g £0
0 11-13 Wolv 8.5af [43] 300 VIS
32a 4-10 Wolv 7af [35] 394 vis
0 10-12 Wolv 8.5af [35] 584 vis
17a 6-12 Wolv 7af [35] 663 vis
28a 7-15 Ling 7ap [30] 830 vis
8a 6-7 Sout 6af [30] 1032 vis
7a 7-7 Sout 7af [30] 1202 vis

KELTIC RAINBOW 2 b f £326
58a 3-13 Wolv 8.5af [58] 43
39a 4-9 Wolv 9.4af 58 351
46 6-9 Sout 10gd [57] 1283
23a 9-12 Wolv 8.5af 55 2205 VIS
9 9-9 Wind 11.6fm [50] 3294 P
30 4-7 Chep 12.1sft 45 4053

32	5-9	Brig	8sft	45	4165	
15	9-12	Chep	12.1g/s	[40]	4364	
25	12-18	Leic	10gd	[35]	5042	vis

KELTOS 6 gr h £32282

107	2-4	Deau	8hvy		4311
106	4-12	Long	7g/s		4731
113	2-12	Newm	7sft		5134

KELUCIA 3 ch f £7204

86	5-7	Donc	8gd	[104]	949
98	11-16	Newm	8fm	[100]	1492
96	5-8	Kemp	8fm	[100]	2069
97	6-11	Asco	8g/f	[100]	2555
91	6-9	Sand	8.1g/s	[98]	2917
97	6-7	Ayr	10g/f	[97]	3306
91	6-9	Good	8fm	[97]	3620
73	7-8	Muss	8gd	93	4516
65	16-19	York	7.9gd	90	4987

KEMPSEY 2 ch c £900

60	10-12	Ling	5g/f		1981	
68	6-11	Wind	5g/f		2450	
74a	4-7	Ling	5ap		2839	
68	4-12	Ling	5gd	71	3284	
65	4-6	Good	5sft	67	4187	P
34	6-8	Good	6g/f	65	4536	p
51	13-18	Wind	5g/f	63	4830	p
61	8-11	Wind	6g/s	[63]	4941	
59a	6-11	Ling	8ap	[59]	5235	

KENMORE 2 b c £2500

71	4-13	Newm	6fm		4726
91	2-23	Newm	6gd		5084

KENNINGTON 4 ch c £6276

57a	1-12	SOUT	7af		416*	
23a	13-13	Sout	7af	59	556	
56a	4-13	Sout	6af	59	741	VIS
24a	9-13	Sout	7af	[56]	858	vis
54	3-13	Sout	6g/s	55	1052	vis
55a	4-13	Wolv	6af	54	1221	vis
44a	9-15	Sout	6af	55	1750	vis
47	7-18	Donc	7g/f	54	2080	vis
54	2-13	Yarm	6g/f	52	2347	vis
48a	7-16	Sout	6af	54	2720	vis
33	7-17	Wind	6fm	53	2975	vis
52	4-19	Donc	5g/s	53	3220	BL
24	12-14	Thir	5g/f	52	3417	bl
57a	2-15	Sout	5af	51	4043	vis
42	4-9	Yarm	5.2g/s	51	4253	vis
37	5-19	Yarm	6g/s	50	4636	

KENNY THE TRUTH 4 b g £3543

2a	12-15	Sout	6af	40	168	T
35a	3-12	Sout	8af	[40]	309	t
38a	2-16	Sout	8af	[40]	442	t
28a	3-8	Sout	8af	[40]	635	t
40a	3-10	Sout	8af	40	678	t
37a	4-12	Wolv	8.5af	[40]	777	t
37a	5-9	Wolv	9.4af	[40]	821	t
53a	1-10	SOUT	8af	[40]	850*	t
36a	4-5	Sout	8af	[40]	908	t
44	3-10	Chep	8.1sft	[45]	1334	t
45a	3-15	Sout	8af	50	1755	t
32	9-18	Nott	8.2gd	[45]	1992	t
0	P-16	Sout	12af	49	2340	t
46a	6-16	Sout	8af	49	2805	t
43a	5-16	Sout	8af	48	3159	t
26	12-16	Hayd	10.5sft	42	3276	t

KENS DREAM 5 b g £6582

66	10-13	Wind	10gd	[80]	1381
82	3-9	Newm	10gd	[77]	1890
80	4-14	Wind	10g/f	79	2265
86	1-8	NEWM	10g/f	79	2735*
82	4-11	Newb	11g/f	82	3256
83	6-10	Newm	10g/f	82	3615

KENSINGTON GB 3 b c £5751

56	6-13	Folk	7g/s	[77]	1270
68	3-11	Nott	6.1sft	[72]	1607
68	2-19	Donc	6g/f	[67]	1876
51	6-20	Chep	6.1gd	66	2372
67	1-10	RIPO	6gd	[64]	4788*
55a	6-12	Ling	6ap	64	4976
56a	5-13	Wolv	6ap	[62]	5327

KENTMERE 3 b c £2982

68	6-12	Leic	8fm	[71]	2106	T
79a	1-14	LING	10ap	[67]	2740+	BL

KENTUCKY BANKES 2 b c £0

23a	11-11	Sout	5af		1752	
33	6-7	Chep	6.1gd		2115	
24	8-8	Brig	6g/f		3172	BL

KENTUCKY BLUE 4 b g £1529

85	3-10	Hayd	10.5g/s	85	1346
52	12-19	York	11.9sft	85	1668
49	13-14	Ripo	10gd	82	4305

KENTUCKY BULLET 7 b g £1420

49a	2-11	Wolv	12af	45	72	
45a	5-12	Wolv	12af	49	244	
49a	3-9	Sout	11af	48	331	
15a	7-11	Sout	12af	50	458	
36a	6-15	Sout	12af	49	867	
47a	3-11	Wolv	12af	47	937	
20a	6-8	Wolv	12af	47	1342	
33a	9-16	Sout	12af	45	2340	
27a	5-11	Sout	12af	[42]	3154	
28a	5-14	Sout	12af	37	3486	P

KENTUCKY EXPRESS 3 b c £2490

47	7-12	Thir	7g/f		1971
73	2-16	Hayd	6g/f		2182
68	3-9	Ripo	6g/f		2485

KENTUCKY KING 4 b g £7145

61a	6-10	Sout	6af	[89]	532	
60a	6-12	Wolv	8.5af	85	688	
77a	8-14	Ling	10ap	80	758	
84a	1-11	LING	8ap	[80]	800*	
75a	7-12	Ling	8ap	81	888	
86	3-13	Wind	8.3g/s	[85]	1057	
69	12-20	Newb	10gd	85	1235	
56	12-15	Warw	8.1sft	83	1530	
52	11-14	Donc	8g/f	[81]	1877	
83	3-15	Epso	10.1gd	[79]	3216	
83a	5-13	Ling	7ap	81	3791	
84	2-7	Wind	8.3gd	[80]	3826	
0	R-15	Bath	11.7g/f	80	3964	
84	4-16	Nott	8.2g/s	80	4036	
0	R-11	Wind	10gd	[83]	4124	

KENWYN 2 b c £0

61	9-10	Sali	5g/f		1717
30	15-15	Wind	6gd		3163

KEON 2 b c £0

79	7-13	Donc	7hvy		5200

KERASHAN 2 b c £2261

82	4-8	Kemp	7fm		4393
85	2-10	Kemp	8g/f		4712
51	15-20	Yarm	8sft		5252

KERESFORTH 2 b c £4369

22a	10-12	Sout	5af		1439	
52	7-11	Thir	5gd		1634	
63	2-11	Beve	6g/f		1831	BL
66	1-6	FOLK	5g/f		2270*	bl
51	9-12	Ling	5gd	65	3284	
65	2-4	Folk	5gd		3382	bl
47	8-8	Yarm	6gd		3491	bl

KERGOLAY 2 b c £0

60a	6-11	Wolv	8.6ap		4978
50a	10-11	Ling	8ap		5236

KERNEL DOWERY 4 b g £7568

40	8-18	Bath	10.2g/s	60	1098	p
53	8-11	Leic	10g/s	58	1357	p
59	2-19	Brig	9.9g/f	54	1940	e
61	1-16	YARM	10.1fm	54	2146*	e
67	1-7	BRIG	9.9g/f	[58]	2433*	e
61	7-9	Yarm	10.1fm	64	2866	e
53	7-9	Brig	9.9fm	64	3695	e
56	4-5	Brig	9.9sft	63	4167	p
61	5-19	Leic	10g/f	62	4456	e
47	13-18	Sali	9.9gd	62	4850	e
61a	4-11	Wolv	12.2ap	60	5117	e
32a	14-16	Ling	12ap	[59]	5296	e

KERNY 2 b c £0

26a	9-11	Sout	5af		1752

49	6-10	Thir	5fm		3606
56	11-15	Nott	5.1gd		3988
27	10-14	Catt	5g/f	51	4437

KERRISTINA 3 b f £0

24	13-14	Warw	8.1sft		1527	
29	11-11	Bath	8fm		2031	
54	10-11	Sali	8fm		2419	
39a	7-8	Ling	12ap		2739	VIS
0	12-12	Brig	9.9g/f	30	3300	vis
18	10-11	Chep	10.2gd	[30]	3730	

KERRYS BLADE 2 ch c £2136

2	11-11	Yarm	6g/f		1728
60	5-20	Hayd	6gd		2882
53	6-11	Hami	6g/s		4006
69	2-14	Muss	8gd	63	4519
47	6-20	Yarm	8g/s	63	4635
60a	8-13	Wolv	8.6ap	[66]	4979

KESHYA 3 b f £2421

65	3-15	Bath	8g/s	63	1099
65	4-14	Bath	10.2gd	63	1403
67a	2-5	Wolv	8.5af	63	1655
64	4-14	Chep	8.1g/s	63	3090

KESTREL CROSS 2 b g £51389

95	1-13	CURR	6.3gd		2815*

KEW THE MUSIC 4 b g £3658

59	7-15	Folk	6sft	67	976	
55	10-19	Leic	6g/s	65	1354	
49	10-19	Sali	7g/f	62	1723	
24	11-12	Yarm	7gd	59	3490	
36	16-17	Hayd	8.1gd	59	3759	
51	4-13	Brig	5.3g/f	52	3984	VIS
0	15-15	Newc	6hvy	52	4211	VIS
48	8-20	Chep	6.1g/s	52	4368	vis
59	1-19	YARM	6g/s	49	4636*	vis
44	10-16	Pont	5fm	55	4754	vis
45	9-19	Wind	6g/f	56	5053	vis
49a	8-12	Ling	6ap	56	5241	vis

KEY FACTOR 3 b f £267

56	4-6	Redc	6g/f		2104
49	10-11	Beve	7.5g/s		2325
0	11-11	Thir	7fm		2463
0	14-14	Sout	6af	55	4130

KEY IN 3 ch f £588

54	12-17	Newm	8gd		1166
46	6-9	Bath	10.2gd		4547
64a	3-14	Ling	13ap		4892
32	6-11	Catt	13.8sft	[60]	5129

KEY OF GOLD 3 b g £314

65a	8-8	Sout	7af	79	2723
46	11-13	Hayd	6gd	75	2884
58	4-8	Pont	6gd	[70]	3684
0	16-16	Ches	7g/f	65	4051
6	11-12	Newb	6gd	[60]	4245

KEY OF SOLOMON 2 ch c £2384

71	6-14	Bath	8gd		5018	T
82	3-11	Bath	8sft		5171	t
82	2-9	Muss	8g/s		5331	

KEY PARTNERS 3 b g £9689

76	1-12	WARW	7.1gd		1129*
50	7-8	Brig	9.9g/f	[70]	1369
85	2-14	York	7sft	70	1665
62	8-16	Leic	7g/f	70	1825
54	11-12	Hayd	8.1gd	82	3738

KEY SECRET 2 ch f £19903

68a	1-8	WOLV	5af		1653*
76	1-6	LEIC	5fm		2110*
84	1-10	YORK	5gd	73	3115*
82	4-10	Thir	5fm	81	3607
79	4-13	Newm	5g/f	81	3943
95	1-6	WIND	5gd	80	4123*
95	6-9	Chan	5.5gd	[80]	4563
80	7-12	Ayr	5g/s	[93]	4651

KEY TO PLEASURE 4 b g £27465

114	2-11	Hopp	6.5gd		3839
114	2-8	Bade	6sft		4426

KEYAKI 3 b f £9991

(continued)

63	6-17	Kemp	7gd		1136
55	6-17	Ling	7g/s		1617
78	1-6	YARM	7g/f		2342*
82	1-8	LING	7g/f	75	2742*
78	4-6	Donc	8g/f	80	3597
80	4-4	Yarm	7sft	[80]	4148
74	9-25	Newb	7gd	79	4683
71	8-11	Donc	7sft	78	5219

KEYALZAO 2 b f £0

17	15-20	Newc	6sft		2682
36	8-15	Redc	6g/f		3769
47	9-12	Thir	7g/f		4591
37	12-13	Redc	7fm		4927

KEYNES 2 ch c £1788

58a	3-10	Sout	7af	2802
65a	11-13	Ling	7ap	3329
75	2-14	Ling	7.6g/f	3601 VIS

KHABFAIR 3 b c £33244

92	4-11	Newb	6g/f	91	2878
98	1-5	ASCO	6g/f	91	3388+
100	3-10	Asco	6gd	94	3778
97	6-11	Newm	6g/f	95	3941
88	8-13	York	6gd	95	4322
102	1-13	ASCO	6.5g/f	95	4773+
107a	2-14	Ling	7ap	99	5262

KHAFAYIF 3 b f £640

55	15-17	Newm	7gd		1171
65	3-8	Beve	7.5g/f		2169
49	10-10	Sali	7g/f		2659
49	5-5	Good	7gd	[63]	3953

KHALIDIA 3 b c £5306

73	1-14	DONC	6g/f		2428*
79	2-7	Newm	6g/f	71	2764

KHANJAR 4 ch g £10640

78	2-11	Muss	9g/f	[82]	1095 VIS
67	4-8	Muss	8g/s	[77]	1461 vis
54	13-14	Leic	10g/f	75	1828 vis
76a	1-8	SOUT	7af	[70]	4093*
83	2-7	Ripo	8gd	[73]	4304
68	8-18	Ayr	7.2sft	78	4689
81	2-20	York	8.9g/f	76	4999

KHARISH 2 b c £9437

87	4-9	Asco	7gd		3126
85	3-12	Newm	7g/f		3470
82	2-11	Sand	8.1g/s		3890
91	1-13	KEMP	8g/f	[83]	4355*
92	4-17	Donc	8fm	88	4480

KHELEYF 3 b c £49950

114	1-15	ASCO	7g/f	[108]	2486*
100	14-20	Newm	6g/f	[108]	3062
111	3-8	Good	7g/f	[112]	3508
107	6-10	Deau	8sft	[112]	4017
106	5-11	Good	7gd	[111]	4874

KHUZDAR 4 ch g £1116

54a	4-10	Ling	12ap	[39]	24
1a	15-16	Sout	11af	47	97
20a	7-10	Sout	16af	[43]	307
42a	3-9	Ling	16ap	[40]	454
42a	2-12	Wolv	12af	40	469
8a	11-12	Wolv	12af	[40]	523 P
38a	5-14	Ling	13ap	[40]	537 P

KIAMA 2 b f £0

64	8-18	Nott	8.2g/f	4842
66	6-15	Newb	8hvy	5221

KIBRYAA 3 ch c £7154

73	6-13	Newm	8g/f	78	2247
84	2-13	Newc	8g/s	76	2773
80	2-13	Beve	7.5g/s	78	3179
80	4-10	Sand	8.1g/f	[78]	3339 P
83	5-12	Hayd	8.1gd	80	3738 p
71	7-8	Newm	8g/f	80	3947 p

KICKEN KRIS 4 b c £335196

118	1-13	ARLI	10fm	4014*

KIDZPLAY 8 b g £9327

10	16-22	Donc	12gd	65	918
67	3-14	Hami	12.1gd	63	1389

64	4-9	Newc	10.1sft	[64]	1681
68	2-6	Hami	11.1gd	[64]	2180
71	1-7	AYR	10gd	64	2507*
66	5-11	Newc	10.1g/s	69	2726
61	3-8	Ayr	10gd	[69]	3151
33	4-5	Hami	12.1sft	69	4012
66	5-8	Hami	13g/s	69	4138
62	6-18	Ayr	10.9sft	65	4623 P
53	8-11	Muss	16g/s	63	5335

KIKIS GIRLS 3 b f £0

0	7-7	Nott	10g/f	3422
0	15-15	Nott	8.2g/s	4649

KILCULLEN LASS 3 ch f £0

41a	10-12	Ling	8ap	[50]	734
39	10-15	Bath	8g/s	47	1099

KILDARE CHILLER 10 ch g £0

35	6-14	Sout	12g/s	1047

KILINDINI 3 gr g £415

61	6-10	Folk	9.7sft		1580
2	U-11	Folk	9.7g/f		2274
67	5-15	Wind	10fm		3292
69	4-5	Sand	10g/s		3894
38	9-11	Bath	13.1g/f	68	4415

KILKENNY KITTEN 2 b f £0

51	6-9	Newc	5sft	962 T
50a	7-7	Sout	5af	1029 t
16	13-15	York	5g/f	2056 t

KILLALA 4 b g £2497

66	3-14	Muss	7.1gd	65	1794
58	5-9	Muss	7.1fm	65	2086
59	5-8	Muss	7.1g/f	64	2809
60	2-15	Newc	7gd	[62]	3426
60	2-11	Muss	8g/f	[62]	3558
48	4-10	Leic	7fm	[58]	3812
0	16-16	Ches	10.3g/f	55	4515
1a	13-13	Wolv	8.6ap	54	4982

KILLENA BOY 2 b g £279

35a	8-10	Ling	6ap	3818
39	8-17	Wind	6g/f	3975
68	5-10	Beve	7.5g/f	4602
35	26-29	Newm	6gd	5087

KILLERBY NICKO 3 ch g £421

44a	6-15	Sout	6af		795
56	7-12	Catt	5gd	[59]	995
44	6-13	Carl	5.9fm	[57]	1949
36	9-19	York	6g/f	57	2055
46a	5-13	Sout	8af	52	2497
2	U-13	Newc	6sft	52	2683 BL
44	3-13	Muss	7.1g/f	50	2812 bl
40	9-16	Beve	7.5gd	50	2891 bl
44	5-17	Ripo	6g/s	46	3262 bl

KILLING JOKE 3 b c £2065

75a	1-12	WOLV	16.2af	63	156*
0	11-13	Pont	18hvy	74	1069
57	15-17	Ripo	16g/s	73	1361

KILLING ME SOFTLY 2 b g £2729

29a	11-15	Sout	7af		184
52a	1-11	WOLV	8.5af		279*
49a	2-8	Wolv	8.5af	[53]	383
31a	8-10	Sout	11af	51	658
52	4-18	Warw	10.9g/s	51	4669
38	12-15	Leic	11.8gd	[51]	5060
17a	10-11	Wolv	8.6ap	[48]	5356

KILLINGTON 2 ch c £1257

75	2-6	Sand	5g/f	3857
45a	9-12	Ling	6ap	4178 T
23	19-19	Ling	6g/f	4895

KILLMOREY 3 ch g £5213

59	16-24	Newm	8fm		1495
62	10-13	Kemp	8fm		2072
66	2-9	Pont	8gd		3462
61	6-14	Newb	10g/f	62	3961
75	1-4	NEWC	12.4sft	62	4288+

KILLOCH PLACE 3 b g £464

27	12-18	Leic	10g/s	55	1017
0	17-19	Warw	10.9gd	51	1124 BL

8	7-11	Newc	8sft	47	1395 VIS
37	10-14	Redc	7fm	42	2295 vis
39	3-8	Ripo	6g/f	[42]	2480 vis
33	4-13	Muss	7.1g/f	40	2812 vis
29	8-15	Beve	8.5g/s	40	3182 vis
28	9-15	Yarm	7g/s	[40]	4587 vis

KILMEENA LAD 7 b g £990

69a	7-16	Ling	7ap	72	22
29a	12-14	Ling	6ap	70	121
56a	11-16	Ling	7ap	69	181
73a	2-16	Ling	7ap	67	323
60a	5-14	Ling	6ap	67	407

KILMEENA STAR 5 b h £3666

51a	6-10	Ling	6ap	[39]	133
16a	10-13	Ling	6ap	[40]	340
20a	9-12	Wolv	7af	[40]	528 P
28a	12-15	Ling	7ap	[40]	708 p
35a	4-15	Ling	7ap	[35]	830 p
50a	1-12	LING	6ap	35	844* BL
55a	2-9	Ling	6ap	[48]	1012 bl
21	8-10	Kemp	5hvy	[42]	1644 bl
44a	7-12	Ling	6ap	[54]	2016 bl
15	10-11	Bath	5.7fm	[37]	2412 bl

KILMINCHY LADY 2 b f £0

24a	10-13	Wolv	8.5af		111
42a	6-10	Ling	8ap		229
37	5-6	Brig	9.9fm		2835
0	13-14	Leic	8g/f	[45]	3344
0	10-11	Yarm	8g/f	40	3706

KILMOVEE 2 gr f £0

59	5-16	Ripo	6g/f		1780
60	9-12	Redc	6g/f		2119
69	5-7	Redc	5gd		2547
68	5-8	Catt	5g/f		2847
50	11-19	Carl	5.9g/f	69	4344
52	11-14	Redc	5fm	67	4556
56	8-14	Hayd	7g/s	[67]	4769

KIMBERLEY HALL 2 ch f £0

46	7-7	Redc	5g/f	2100
28	9-13	Ripo	5gd	4303
0	13-13	Thir	6g/f	4590
23	11-12	Nott	6.1g/f	4844

KIMOE WARRIOR 6 ch g £0

28a	5-8	Wolv	12af	[35]	1265 bl
2a	13-15	Sout	8af	30	2725 p

KINBRACE 3 b f £0

62	6-12	Sand	7.1g/f	61	2098
57	5-14	Wind	8.3fm	60	2971
60	5-13	Bath	8gd	59	4546
28a	9-9	Ling	8ap	[57]	5242

KIND 3 b f £46209

84	3-17	Newm	7gd		1171
88	1-8	KEMP	7g/f	[80]	1912*
86	1-9	KEMP	6gd	[82]	2173+
90	1-8	KEMP	6g/s	[82]	2677*
93	1-8	NEWM	6g/f	86	3235*
103	1-11	HAMI	5sft	[89]	4693*

KIND EMPEROR 7 br g £1858

41	9-12	Yarm	7gd	64	3490
62	4-11	Yarm	10.1gd	[62]	3875
62	7-9	Yarm	10.1g/s	[62]	4254
65	2-16	Yarm	11.5g/s	62	4589
66	6-15	Nott	10g/f	64	4849
59	6-11	Yarm	10.1g/s	62	5353

KINDA CUTE 2 b f £0

28a	10-12	Ling	8ap	[40]	78

KINDJHAL 4 b c £10282

109	2-8	Long	12sft	1698

KINDLELIGHT DEBUT 4 b f £1720

54	13-13	Ling	7.6g/f	79	2587
36	17-17	Newb	7g/f	77	3257
76	3-9	Sali	7gd	74	3456
12	9-9	Newm	8g/f	74	3780
66	7-15	Kemp	8g/f	74	4362
64	16-21	Donc	7fm	74	4482
48	21-24	Newb	7g/f	72	4642
68a	3-12	Ling	8ap	68	4743

KINDLELIGHT DREAM 2 b f £0

```
63  10-10  Redc  7fm    [70]   4929
69a  6-12  Ling  8ap      68   5079
51a 11-12  Wolv  7.1ap  [67]   5340
```

KINDLELIGHT DREAM 2 b f £0
```
22   8-9   Warw  5sft           1084
59a  6-10  Ling  7ap            4442
0    R-14  Ling  7ap            4658
```

KINDLING 2 br f £5813
```
60   5-12  Redc  6fm            4557
78   4-13  Redc  7fm            4927
85   1-8   MUSS  9g/s           5140*
```

KINDNESS 4 ch f £4852
```
46a  6-12  Ling  8ap     52     1045
15   7-14  Warw  8.1hvy  52     1535
44   9-20  Yarm  8fm     50     2149
51   2-9   Pont  8g/f    48     2604
50   8-11  Folk  9.7fm   48     2719
45   8-16  Brig  9.9g/f  48     3175
53   2-6   Epso  8.5fm   48     3540
36  11-14  Bath  8g/f    50     3963
31  14-15  Folk  9.7g/f [50]    4373
49   7-16  Bath  8gd     50     4828
51   6-11  Wind  8.3g/f [49]    5054
49a  4-13  Wolv  8.6ap  [49]    5212
```

KINFAYRE BOY 2 b g £0
```
0    8-8   Redc  7g/s           2563
```

KING AFTER 2 b g £3892
```
78a  1-9   LING  5ap           931*
75   6-8   Newm  5g/s           1149
80   6-9   Ches  5.1gd          1567
57   5-7   Kemp  6g/f     84    3686
71   5-11  Ches  7sft   [80]    4072
66   8-16  Newm  6gd      75    4224
58  12-14  Epso  6g/f     71    4471
48  14-18  Wind  5g/f     67    4830
```

KING AT LAST 5 b b £0
```
56a  8-12  Ling  8ap            4975
66a  7-14  Ling  7ap            5240
```

KING CARNIVAL 3 ch c £0
```
67  12-12  Good  7g/f     95    1847
89   7-14  Sand  8.1g/f   92    2096
78   7-8   Sand  7.1g/f   90    2389
63  15-16  Newb  7g/f     87    3954
```

KING DAVID 4 b g £0
```
49a 11-16  Ling  7ap      57      22
19a 15-16  Sout  7af     [56]    161
```

KING EGBERT 3 b c £833
```
58   4-9   Wind  5fm      60    3804
51   7-9   Wind  5g/f     60    3976
61   3-16  Good  5g/f     56    4528
54   8-15  Good  5gd      56    4751
52a  6-13  Wolv  5.1ap    55    5156
52   5-18  Yarm  6g/s     55    5354
```

KING EIDER 5 b g £0
```
62  13-13  Yarm  16g/s    85    4634
82   9-17  Newm  12g/f    83    4889
52  24-34  Newm  18sft    86    5135
```

KING FLYER 8 b g £5975
```
62a  8-12  Ling  16ap     66    813
81   2-11  Nott  16fm     78    1003
81   3-18  Newb  16gd     80    1232
57  11-12  Good  14g/f    80    1861
85   2-13  Chep  18gd     80    2198
61  19-29  Asco  20g/f    81    2471
75   9-12  Newm  16.1g/f  80    3032
56   7-7   Newm  14.8g/f  77    3475 bl
79   5-13  Yarm  16g/s    75    4634
58a  3-16  Ling  12ap    [60]   4899 e
58a  6-16  Ling  12ap    [58]   5296
```

KING FOREVER 2 b c £0
```
79   6-15  Newm  7fm            3005
```

KING GABRIEL 2 b g £0
```
54  11-16  Newb  7g/f           4677
75   6-11  Bath  8sft           5171
```

KING HALLING 5 b h £266

KING HARSON 5 b g £16073
```
56   8-18  Newm  12fm     65    2088
49   6-6   Ches  15.9g/f  62    3101 P
37  14-19  Chep  12.1gd   60    3398
51   4-8   Hayd  10.5g/f  55    4354 BL
43a  5-11  Wolv  12.2ap   54    5009 p
```

KING HARSON 5 b g £16073
```
76  11-16  Thir  7g/s     82    1474 vis
83   2-10  Thir  7g/f    [82]   1970 vis
51  11-11  Donc  7g/f     82    2076 vis
26  26-28  Asco  7g/f     82    2558 vis
80   6-18  Catt  7g/f     80    2848 vis
60  11-13  Newc  9gd      79    3428 vis
87   1-8   CHES  7sft     77    4073+ vis
60   5-5   Good  7sft    [77]   4186 vis
0   18-18  Ayr   7.2sft   85    4689 vis
70  17-18  York  7gd      85    5000 vis
87   2-10  Catt  7sft     82    5320 vis
```

KING HENRIK 2 b c £285
```
65   4-11  Thir  7fm             2462
65   6-10  Catt  7g/f            2845
53   7-7   Ayr   7.2g/f          3302
28  18-18  Catt  7g/f     61     4673
```

KING JOCK 3 b c £0
```
73  16-27  Asco  8g/f     92    2521
```

KING MARJU 2 b c £11865
```
71   6-12  Good  7fm             3568
87   2-14  Warw  6.1g/f          4422
92   1-13  NEWM  6fm            4726*
94   2-16  Good  9gd      85    5031
98   3-13  Newb  7sft    [85]   5195
```

KING NICHOLAS 5 b g £7892
```
28a  7-10  Sout  8af      56    791 t
61a  1-10  SOUT  6af     [51]   851+ t P
47  10-18  Catt  7gd     [50]   996 t p
48   4-16  Newc  6sft     50    1277 t p
56   1-17  NOTT  6.1sft   50    1606* t p
17   9-19  Nott  6.1gd   [53]   3104 BL
39   6-13  Hayd  6g/f    [53]   3757 t p
52a  8-11  Sout  6af     [57]   4041 t p
54   6-14  Beve  7.5g/s   52    4241 t p
64a  1-13  WOLV  8.6ap    55    5183* t p
59a  4-13  Wolv  8.6ap    57    5365 t p
```

KING OF BLUES 2 ch c £8230
```
49  10-17  Donc  6g/f            2424
66   8-14  Folk  7fm             2714
76a  4-13  Ling  7ap            3330 T
80   1-11  NEWB  7fm      71    3627* t
47   7-8   Sand  7.1g/s   75    4100 t
82   3-13  Newm  8fm      75    4725 t
```

KING OF BOXMEER 5 b g £5634
```
104  3-8   Bade  16gd          1993 bl
```

KING OF CASHEL 3 b c £1464
```
88   3-5   Sand  7.1gd   [88]   2362
80   9-11  Sand  7.1g/s   86    2918
```

KING OF DIAMONDS 3 b c £11278
```
64a  2-11  Ling  6ap             898
66a  6-11  Ling  7ap            1008
79a  2-12  Ling  6ap            1044
53  12-13  Ling  7.6g/f   77    2587
72   7-10  Sand  8.1g/f  [74]   3339
77   1-8   NEWM  8g/f     70    3947*
68  10-12  Newm  7gd      77    4225
81   4-13  Epso  8.5gd    77    4469
65  11-11  Yarm  8gd      77    4615
84a  2-10  Ling  12ap     76    5239
82a  2-13  Ling  10ap     76    5299
```

KING OF DREAMS 3 b c £19616
```
88   1-11  DONC  10.3gd         930*
68  11-14  Newm  10g/f    89    1192
99   1-7   NEWM  10g/f    89    3474*
96   5-20  Hayd  10.5fm   94    3794
0    F-21  York  11.9gd   94    3999
```

KING OF FIRE 2 b g £0
```
46   9-19  Kemp  6g/f            1911
```

KING OF KNIGHT 3 gr g £1900
```
72   4-19  Yarm  8g/f            1130
61   5-16  Leic  8g/s     70    1359
```

KING OF LOVE 2 b c £5772
```
52   9-17  Yarm  7g/f    [69]   1729
56   7-10  Newm  12g/f    67    2530
53   9-11  Yarm  10.1gd  [62]   3875
61   4-14  Yarm  8g/s    [60]   4252
61a  2-16  Ling  12ap    [59]   4899
61a  4-16  Ling  12ap    [60]   5296
```

KING OF LOVE 2 b c £5772
```
79   1-9   CARL  5.9gd          2671*
```

KING OF MEZE 3 b g £0
```
49a  6-12  Ling  8ap             623
35a  6-8   Ling  6ap             691
37a 11-15  Sout  6af             795
0    9-15  Sout  12af     40    2503
27   9-16  Warw  8.1g/s  [40]   4993 T
```

KING OF MUSIC 2 ch c £830
```
35a  8-13  Wolv  6af               3
55   8-14  Yarm  7fm     [72]   2148
50   7-7   Yarm  7gd      68    3872
55   6-14  Yarm  8g/s    [60]   4252
58a  2-9   Ling  8ap     [52]   5242
```

KING OF TORY 2 b c £2559
```
92   2-6   Leop  6gd             2300
```

KING PRIAM 8 b g £1271
```
30a  7-15  Sout  12af     34    257 bl
25a  8-14  Sout  12af    [34]   305 bl
32a  4-10  Sout  12af     35    321 bl
49a  1-9   SOUT  12af    [35]   353* bl
30a  4-4   Sout  8af     [35]   417 bl
37a  5-16  Sout  11af    [45]   445 bl
21a  9-10  Sout  16af     45    491 p
33a  6-10  Sout  12af    [45]   552 vis
34a  6-13  Sout  12af    [40]   575 bl
29a  4-7   Sout  14af    [40]   638 bl
33a  5-7   Sout  12af    [40]   679 bl
2a   6-7   Sout  14af     40    724 bl
33a  5-16  Sout  11af    [35]   852 bl
22a  4-4   Sout  14af    [35]   854 bl
0   20-22  Donc  12gd     35    918 bl
6a   7-9   Sout  12af    [35]   1204 bl
21a  6-7   Sout  14af    [30]   1407 bl
22a  6-9   Sout  12af    [30]   2381 p
```

KING REVO 3 b g £10387
```
81a  4-12  Ling  12ap     79     56
88   1-14  HAMI  12.1gd   79    1389*
23  15-19  York  11.9sft  85    1668
```

KING SPINNER 7 b g £0
```
0   12-12  Nott  14.1gd   55    3105
```

KING SUMMERLAND 7 b g £327
```
46   5-6   Hami  8.3sft  [50]   4695
45   4-11  Ayr   9.1sft  [50]   5067
```

KING TOP 3 b g £270
```
19   4-4   Redc  11gd            2549
```

KING ZAFEEN 2 b c £439
```
56  13-14  Newm  7g/f            3752
71   4-14  Thir  8fm            4376 T
64   9-10  Yarm  8g/s           4631 t
43  16-19  Redc  8sft     67    5302
```

KINGDOM OF DREAMS 2 b c £0
```
68   7-13  Donc  7hvy            5199
```

KINGHAM 4 ch g £0
```
50a 11-12  Ling  8ap      78    369
45a  7-7   Ling  6ap     [73]   431
```

KINGKOHLER 5 b g £0
```
72a  6-7   Ling  12ap    [75]   1009
```

KINGS ACCOUNT 2 ch c £12598
```
78   2-14  Thir  7g/s            3831
83   2-12  Ayr   7.2hvy          4083
82   2-11  Chep  8.1g/s          4363
83   1-10  BEVE  7.5g/f  [82]   4602*
91   1-12  AYR   8sft     82    5065*
```

KINGS BALLET 5 b g £830
```
51a  7-12  Wolv  5af      56    124
45a  9-16  Sout  5af      54    183
43a  8-14  Ling  6ap      52   328 P
43a  8-11  Wolv  5af      50   507 p
```

48a 2-11 Wolv 5af 47 643 p
36a 9-11 Sout 5af 47 859 p
46a 4-12 Wolv 5af [47] 960 p
43 11-19 Warw 5gd 56 1127 p
51 11-13 Epso 5sft 56 1293 p
40 13-17 Warw 5hvy [54] 1532 p
25 16-18 Wind 6g/f [52] 1806 VIS

KINGS CAPRICE 3 ch c £19905
72 7-11 Sali 6g/s 88 1498
87 3-5 Wind 6g/f [87] 1957
70 4-10 Newb 6g/f [87] 2309
87 1-13 WIND 6fm [85] 2756*
87 7-11 Sand 7.1g/s 85 2918
86 4-7 Wind 6fm [85] 3293
87 4-11 Hayd 6g/s [85] 3758
91 1-13 KEMP 7sft 85 4030*
76 5-8 Good 7g/s 89 4231
66 16-24 Ayr 6sft 89 4686
94 2-16 Newm 7sft 88 5101
87 7-12 Newb 6sft 88 5196

KINGS COLLEGE BOY 4 b g £15427
39 17-20 Thir 6gd 63 1638
39 8-14 Ayr 6g/f 61 1898
60 3-13 Hami 5g/s 58 2320 bl
60 2-12 Ripo 5g/f 58 2524 bl
61 3-8 Hami 5g/s 60 2830 bl
52 8-15 Beve 5sft 60 2942 VIS
63 3-14 Catt 6g/f 60 3352 bl
53 7-12 Newc 5sft 60 3427 bl
67 3-15 Pont 5gd 60 3680 bl
51 9-10 Hami 5g/s [61] 4010 bl
71 1-12 CHES 5.1sft 61 4107* bl
62 9-19 Beve 5g/s 68 4240 bl
71 2-13 Ches 5.1g/f 68 4514 bl
69 4-26 Ayr 5g/s 68 4618 bl
60 12-15 Ayr 5g/s 68 4654 bl
71 4-19 York 5gd 68 4989 vis
65 8-12 Redc 5sft [68] 5305 vis

KINGS COUNTY 6 b g £10790
99 3-27 Newb 7.9g/s 95 1231
81 11-17 York 7.9g/s 95 1686
98 3-11 Newm 7fm 95 2090
42 29-31 Asco 9g/s 95 2489
75 14-18 Newb 8g/f 95 3265
97 2-11 Good 9g/f 93 4525
85 12-32 Newm 9g/f 93 4916

KINGS EMPIRE 3 b g £875
81 4-8 Nott 10g/f 83 2631
80 4-6 Ches 10.3g/f 83 3084
10 19-19 Hayd 10.5g/s 82 4766 T
54 14-19 Donc 10.3sft 80 5201 t

KINGS ENVOY 5 b g £1090
72 4-11 Muss 9g/f [50] 1095
74 3-7 Muss 9g/s [60] 1462
61 5-10 Muss 12gd 65 1796
51 9-10 Newc 10.1g/f 64 2162
35 10-12 Newc 9hvy 60 4215
15 15-18 Ayr 10.9sft 59 4623

KINGS GAIT 2 b c £5818
58 6-12 Ripo 5gd 1173
79 1-9 PONT 5sft 1424*
86 4-7 Nott 6.1sft 1738

KINGS KAMA 2 b c £1507
76 4-7 Yarm 6gd 3869
76 4-13 Warw 7.1g/f 4416
76a 3-14 Ling 7ap 5076

KINGS MAJESTY 2 b c £6439
57 7-13 Newm 7fm 4724
81a 2-14 Ling 7ap 5078
86a 1-10 LING 7ap 5264*

KINGS MINSTREL 3 b c £0
28 14-15 Newb 8g/f 1763
52 7-13 Newb 8g/f 1935
3 10-10 Good 9.9gd 4877
46 7-11 Wind 8.3g/f 5054

KINGS MOUNTAIN 4 b g £0
23 18-20 Warw 10.9gd 60 1128
12 10-10 Redc 14.1g/s 50 2562

KINGS POINT 3 b c £10325
101a5-9 Ling 8ap [107] 1040
81 10-10 Newb 7gd [107] 1234
87 5-5 Good 8g/f [104] 2022
97 3-8 Sali 6fm [99] 2421
90 11-28 Asco 7g/f 99 2558
105 4-8 Newm 7g/f [99] 2765
87 13-19 Newm 7g/f 100 3061
105 3-9 Good 8fm [98] 3620
101 7-8 Epso 7g/f [103] 4472
96 8-14 Newm 7g/f [103] 4638
99 7-11 Good 7gd [100] 4874 BL

KINGS QUAY 2 b c £21296
100 1-8 SAND 5gd 2188*
76 12-13 Asco 6fm 2467
99 2-4 Newm 6fm 3406
104 1-5 NEWB 7gd [91] 3919*
91 6-9 Newm 7gd [100] 4881

KINGS ROCK 3 ch g £8789
63a 2-13 Sout 8af [69] 553
48a 6-12 Wolv 9.4af [65] 686
51a 9-10 Ling 10ap 63 817
59 7-18 Nott 8.2fm 63 1007
46 6-11 Newc 7sft 61 1678
58 3-10 Leic 8gd [58] 2133
9 10-13 Warw 8.1gd 58 3058
53 1-14 LEIC 8g/f [55] 3344* BL
59 2-10 Yarm 8g/f 55 3712 bl
58 1-14 BEVE 7.5sft [55] 4256* bl
37 18-19 Leic 7g/f 61 4452 bl
42 12-16 Sali 7sft 60 4582 bl
0 14-14 Pont 8g/f [58] 4937 bl

KINGS SQUARE 4 b g £0
18 12-14 York 11.9gd 40 4327

KINGS THOUGHT 5 b h £6616
88 6-8 Donc 12gd [98] 950
92 8-17 Kemp 10g/s 98 1111
96 4-16 Epso 10.1hvy 96 1296
98 6-19 Newm 10g/f 95 1478
107 4-10 Ches 10.3gd [95] 1585
99 4-8 Donc 10.3gd [98] 2234
96 3-8 Pont 9g/f 96 2606

KINGS TOPIC 4 ch g £3721
47a 2-7 Ling 10ap [45] 1182
50a 1-9 LING 10ap [45] 1289*
55a 1-5 LING 10ap [45] 1412*
44 7-12 Brig 9.9fm 55 1695

KINGS WELCOME 6 b g £0
37 6-11 Catt 12sft [92] 5128
0 10-10 Yarm 10.1sft [85] 5255

KINGSCROSS 6 ch g £19825
72 4-15 Folk 6sft 73 976
76 2-19 Leic 6g/s 72 1354
82 1-17 DONC 6g/s 73 1523*
60 15-19 Kemp 6fm 79 2070
67 5-10 Epso 6g/s 78 3045
44 19-19 Ripo 6g/s 77 3937
84 2-12 Good 6sft 75 4184
85 2-11 Hayd 6g/f [75] 4350
77 6-19 Good 6gd 80 4747
84 4-19 Sali 6gd 80 4855
84 4-18 York 7gd 80 5000
44 20-20 Newm 7g/s 80 5286

KINGSDON 7 b g £11437
8a 10-12 Wolv 12af [35] 523 vis t
39a 1-12 LING 10ap [35] 654* vis t
9a 9-14 Ling 10ap [40] 784 vis t
39a 4-14 Ling 10ap [40] 1072 vis t
39 4-16 Newc 10.1sft 40 1278 vis t
47 1-7 AYR 10g/s [40] 1450* vis t
55a 1-14 LING 10ap [45] 1712* vis t
60a 1-14 LING 10ap 52 2589* vis t
62 1-11 NEWC 10.1g/s 57 2726* vis t
60 3-5 Beve 9.9sft 63 2943 vis t

KINGSGATE BAY 2 b g £5506
57 7-13 Sali 6fm 2287
64a 5-7 Ling 5ap 2839
64 5-6 Sand 5g/f 3857
77 1-19 CARL 5.9g/f 66 4344*

KINGSHOLM 2 ch c £848
78 6-15 Sand 7.1g/f 3337
78 3-11 Sand 8.1g/s 3890
65 7-14 Thir 8fm 4376

KINGSMAITE 2 b g £12822
68a 2-15 Sout 7af [66] 184
78a 1-14 SOUT 8af [66] 226*
77a 2-11 Sout 8af 74 252
69 11-22 Donc 7gd 77 955
63 4-7 Beve 7.5sft 74 1305
44 9-12 Donc 7g/f 70 1879
61 5-11 Nott 6.1g/f 66 2155
72 1-6 REDC 6gd 63 2551* BL
72a 3-8 Sout 7af [75] 4093 bl
49 16-18 Redc 6fm 68 4339 bl
66 5-17 Beve 8.5g/f 67 4721 bl
44 14-19 Newc 7g/f 66 5014 bl
79a 2-22 Wolv 6ap 72 5291 bl

KINGSTON TOWN 3 ch g £3716
65a 2-10 Wolv 7af 8 P
70a 1-15 SOUT 8af [62] 96* p
67a 9-14 Ling 10ap 70 434 p
55a 7-11 Wolv 9.4af 70 465 p
62a 4-12 Sout 8af 67 530 p
47a 7-8 Sout 11af 67 595 p
49 6-9 Epso 10.1fm 63 3538 bl
51 7-7 Yarm 10.1g/f [63] 3704 bl
62a 2-11 Sout 8af [63] 4090 p
50 5-12 Newc 8sft [57] 4284 p
41a 10-14 Ling 10ap [62] 4448 p

KINGSWORD 3 bl c £3799
96 5-8 Donc 10.3gd 2234
100 2-7 Pont 10g/f [93] 2605
69 14-16 Good 9.9fm 97 3553

KINISKA 3 b f £0
57 9-10 Good 8gd 2224
0 11-11 Ling 8ap [60] 4977

KINKOZAN 3 ch c £0
57 6-11 Hayd 8.1gd 2885
3a 12-14 Ling 10ap 54 3449

KINNAIRD 3 ch f £43858
112 4-15 Curr 8g/f [99] 2005
99 5-11 Asco 8g/f [107] 2555
107 2-10 Chep 10.2g/s[110] 3089
110 2-18 Deau 10g/s [110] 3836
113 2-13 Curr 10gd [110] 4735 t

KINRANDE 2 b c £1470
71 3-10 Wind 8.3g/f 4831
76a 3-12 Ling 8ap 5293

KINSMAN 6 b g £3859
47a 9-15 Ling 7ap 54 50 p
55a 6-15 Ling 7ap [53] 117 p
49a 9-16 Ling 7ap 53 144 p
28a 15-15 Ling 7ap 51 266
58a 2-14 Ling 7ap 51 344 bl
60a 1-16 LING 7ap 52 600* bl
61a 5-11 Ling 8ap 58 669 bl
52a 4-15 Ling [58] 935 bl
49 6-11 Brig 7fm 53 2334 bl
47 10-17 Ling 7gd 53 2397 bl
25 11-11 Brig 7g/f 51 2644 bl
38 11-15 Ling 7.6fm 51 3788 bl
51a 5-14 Ling 7ap [55] 5294 bl

KINTORE 3 ch c £267
30 6-7 Hami 9.2gd 1747
34 4-7 Ayr 9.1gd 50 2509
0 10-11 Muss 9gd 47 2969

KIPSIGIS 3 b g £722
58 7-9 Nott 10g/s 4034
62 4-9 Sand 10gd 4501
66a 4-14 Ling 13ap 4892

KIRAT 6 b g £317
38a 11-15 Ling 12ap 521
50a 4-11 Ling 12ap 672

KIRKBYS TREASURE 5 ro g £33556
40a 5-13 Wolv 8.5af 55 40

62 1-13 MUSS 7.1g/f 55 1122*
63 2-14 Muss 7.1gd 58 1794
68 1-9 MUSS 7.1fm 62 2086*
70 3-16 Carl 5.9fm 66 2445
67 9-17 Carl 7.9gd 66 2672
77 1-8 MUSS 10g/f 67 2809*
79 2-10 Carl 6.9gd 73 2935
47 13-13 Newc 7gd 74 3428
77 2-10 Muss 7.1g/f 74 3562
79 2-12 Newm 6g/f 76 3942
68 6-13 Ches 7.6sft 76 4103
52 17-26 Ayr 6g/s 75 4652
79 3-13 Muss 7.1gd 75 4806
79 5-11 Muss 7.1g/s 76 5144
80 3-10 Catt 7sft 75 5320
80 2-20 Donc 7sft 75 5367

KIRKHAM ABBEY 4 b g £11093
51 7-8 Ayr 10g/f 65 1895 vis
67 3-11 Leic 10gd 65 2135 vis
69 2-7 Brig 9.9g/f [65] 2433 vis
60 6-12 Wind 10g/f [65] 2800 vis
62 5-8 Hami 9.2fm 65 3250 vis
73 1-9 BRIG 9.9fm 63 3695*
57 11-13 Epso 10.1g/f 69 4473
77 1-15 NOTT 10g/f 69 4849*

KIRKHAMMERTON 2 ch c £0
36 14-18 Wind 6gd 3824
50 8-10 Brig 6g/s 4139
36 7-8 Good 6g/f 4540
21 14-15 Nott 6.1g/s 4644

KIROV KING 4 b c £0
62 9-20 Wind 11.6g/s 78 1056
33 7-13 Kemp 14.4hvy 75 1516
57 7-11 Donc 12g/f 70 1875
46 15-15 Sand 10g/f 70 2099
37 6-7 Brig 11.9g/f [65] 3173
38 10-12 Good 9.9sft 62 4268

KISS THE RAIN 3 b f £589
48a 3-12 Wolv 5af 50 109
51a 3-16 Sout 5af 49 183 vis
43a 4-8 Wolv 5af 51 274 vis
35a 6-12 Wolv 6af 50 385 vis
22a 12-16 Sout 6af 49 2806
35 16-18 Catt 7g/f 57 4438
37 8-14 Catt 6gd 54 4967 vis

KISSES FOR ME 3 b f £4408
100 5-9 Newm 10fm 1494
34 7-7 Epso 12g/f 2210
101 3-11 Curr 9g/f 3322
67 8-9 York 11.9g/s 4058

KISSING A FOOL 2 b g £3010
50 5-6 Folk 5sft 974
59 1-7 NEWC 5sft 1394*
36 11-11 Thir 5gd 1634
41a 5-7 Sout 6af 1751

KISSING LIGHTS 2 b f £18845
69 5-13 Ling 6g/f 2061
90 1-6 WARW 5fm 2437*
79 6-9 Newm 6g/f 2763
100 3-6 Asco 6g/f 3440
73 8-8 York 6g/s [100] 4059
97 3-11 Donc 5fm [100] 4533

KISWAHILI 2 ch f £5766
88 2-8 Epso 7gd 3214
94 1-8 HAMI 8.3g/s 4816*

KITCAT 3 b f £20995
98 3-11 Colo 8sft 4840
102 2-8 San 8sft 5166

KITCHEN SINK 2 ch c £0
52 10-13 Wind 6g/f 5048
57 10-12 Bath 5sft 5169

KITLEY 3 b c £0
45 13-14 Wind 10g/s [65] 1259
10 16-18 Wind 8.3sft 65 1647
62 6-16 Ling 9g/f [63] 1982
20 14-14 Sali 8fm 62 2423
49a 10-14 Ling 10ap [60] 2740

KITTENS JOY 3 ch c £357542
122 1-7 ARLI 10fm 4015*
124 2-3 Lone 12g/s 5311

KITTYLEE 4 b f £0
23a 12-12 Ling 10ap [25] 267
0 12-14 Sout 12af [25] 305
2a 6-7 Sout 14af [30] 357 P

KNEAD THE DOUGH 3 b g £1198
67a 2-7 Ling 6ap 706
61 6-13 Bath 5.7g/f 4413
54 7-13 Warw 7.1g/s 4667
57 2-8 Catt 6gd [55] 4969
1 19-19 Wind 6g/f 55 5053
47a 5-12 Wolv 6ap [55] 5162 P

KNICKYKNACKIENOO 2 b g £8248
36a 12-16 Sout 8af [56] 192
51a 4-9 Sout 7af [51] 871
55 2-14 Warw 7.1sft 51 1085
0 W-14 Warw 8.1sft 53 1529
56 2-9 Folk 7sft 53 1577
7 12-13 Good 9g/f 56 2024
58 3-18 Sali 7fm 55 2292
64 1-8 SALI 8gd 55 2701*
53 7-14 Wind 8.3fm 59 2971
61 2-11 Sali 8gd 59 3455
51 5-11 Leic 8g/f 59 3516
62a 3-12 Ling 8ap [59] 4320
39 11-14 Good 8g/f 59 4542

KNIGHT OF HEARTS 3 gr g £712
26a 5-7 Wolv 12af 959
38a 5-9 Wolv 9.4af 1340
47 11-12 Leic 8fm 2106
23a 11-16 Sout 8af 45 3159
61 4-6 Hami 11.1sft [42] 4011
2 8-8 Chep 16.2g/s 46 4302
46a 2-12 Wolv 9.5ap [45] 5209

KNIGHT OF SILVER 7 gr g £0
40 8-19 Bath 17.2gd 45 3147

KNIGHT ON THE TILES 2 ch g £0
71a 7-13 Ling 7ap 79 15 bl
61a 6-15 Ling 7ap [77] 52 bl
47a 10-10 Ling 5ap 70 217
50a 11-15 Ling 7ap 69 337 bl
41a 9-12 Wolv 7af [65] 560
0 9-9 Wind 6gd 75 2619 bl
0 14-14 Beve 7.5g/s [72] 3177 bl
30 8-9 Ling 7gd 62 3447 bl
26 12-15 Ling 6fm 55 3790 bl

KNIGHT TO REMEMBER 2 ch g £370
5a 8-10 Wolv 5af 51 69
21a 7-10 Sout 8af 47 189
49a 3-15 Sout 7af [45] 462
50a 4-9 Sout 7af [48] 613 P
0 9-9 Wolv 8.5af [48] 865
28 9-10 Newc 5sft [48] 1682
43 5-15 Beve 7.5g/f [45] 1944
37 9-12 Thir 7g/f [45] 2215
40a 5-9 Sout 6af [43] 2493
9 7-8 Carl 7.9gd [40] 2932
17 13-16 Thir 8g/f 38 3414

KNIGHTSBRIDGE HILL 2 b c £279
67 5-9 Folk 7g/f 3721
68 6-14 Sali 8g/s 4078
75 4-15 Chep 7.1gd 4483
6 17-17 Good 8gd 77 4871

KNOCK BRIDGE 2 b f £9891
61 4-13 Redc 6g/f 1818
63 2-9 Muss 5fm 2083
61 8-11 Wind 5g/f 2450
67 3-9 Chep 5.1hvy 65 4706
37 15-19 Bath 5gd 65 5021
74 1-14 CATT 7sft 65 5126*
58 12-20 Donc 7sft 69 5373

KNOCKDOO 11 ch g £362
3a 10-12 Wolv 12af 35 469
17a 3-8 Wolv 16.2af 30 563

KNOCKTOPHER ABBEY 7 ch g £0
19a 12-13 Ling 13ap [68] 602

47 7-9 Good 9sft [60] 4266 bl
25 11-14 Epso 12gd 56 4910 bl

KNOT IN DOUBT 3 b g £0
48 9-10 Beve 7.5g/f 1832
2 12-12 Thir 7g/f 2215

KNOT IN WOOD 2 b c £845
21 10-10 Catt 6gd 4436
33 6-10 Pont 6fm 4752
68 3-13 York 6gd 4988

KNOWN MANEUVER 5 b g £0
31a 10-15 Sout 16af 59 67
24a 10-12 Sout 14af 53 173
37a 4-13 Sout 12af [45] 575
39a 4-6 Sout 12af 45 683 BL
0 9-9 Sout 14af [40] 849

KODIAC 3 b c £4033
80 1-15 WIND 10g/f 4445*
82 7-17 Asco 8g/f 82 4777
58 17-20 Newm 7g/s 82 5286

KOLYMA 2 ch f £0
40 8-8 Sali 6gd 3451
68 5-12 Folk 7gd 3909
55 12-13 Leic 8g/f 4450

KOMAC 2 b c £5781
69 6-8 York 5sft 1670
73 2-10 Newm 5fm 2089
69 4-13 Carl 5gd 2670
59 6-9 Nott 5.1gd 2926
75a 1-15 SOUT 5af [69] 4089*
78 7-9 Donc 5fm [72] 4481
0 P-24 Redc 6fm [72] 4928

KOMATI RIVER 4 b g £0
42a 6-14 Ling 13ap 52 259
15a 8-11 Sout 12af 51 458
1 16-17 Bath 11.7sft 48 1543
16 12-13 Kemp 12g/f 45 1916

KOMENA 5 b m £598
50a 2-13 Wolv 6af [45] 30
38a 4-12 Wolv 7af 50 129
25a 10-16 Ling 7ap [49] 214
37a 5-13 Ling 6ap [47] 400
19a 9-13 Ling 6ap 47 448
24a 8-12 Wolv 6af [45] 524
17 8-13 Yarm 6g/f 47 2347
30 10-20 Nott 6.1g/f 45 2630 BL
42 5-20 Nott 6.1gd 43 2928
14 16-17 Brig 7g/f 42 3176
22 8-12 Folk 6g/s 40 3911
17 14-15 Folk 7g/f [40] 4371

KOMOTO 3 b g £3213
74a 1-9 LING 8ap 3197*
44 9-11 Leic 7g/f 70 3516
51 10-12 Bath 11.7g/f 67 3845
59 4-5 Brig 11.9sft 63 4166 VIS
0 17-20 Bath 17.2gd 60 4824 BL

KOMREYEV STAR 2 b c £0
49 9-13 Thir 6g/f 4590
37 13-14 Newc 6fm 4865
51 8-14 Nott 6.1hvy 5342

KONG 2 b c £1312
77 4-6 Hayd 8.1sft 4783
79 3-14 Leic 8gd 5058

KONIGSTIGER 2 b c £130880
109 1-10 SAN 8sft 5167*

KONKER 9 ch g £571
53 3-6 Newc 10.1sft [67] 1397

KOODOO 3 gr c £0
61 8-14 Thir 8gd 1636
42 6-12 Thir 7g/f [62] 1971
47 8-14 Redc 10fm 55 2299
22 8-11 Muss 9gd 52 2969*
32 13-18 Carl 7.9fm 46 3547
44 5-6 Hami 9.2g/s 43 4137
36 8-13 Ayr 10sft [45] 5276

KOOL 5 b g £28341

99	3-10	Warw	7.1gd		1126
101	7-11	Leic	7gd		1356
91	5-14	Ling	7sft	95	1624
93	5-20	Asco	7g/f	92	1926
95	3-13	Kemp	7gd	90	2172
90	5-11	Newm	7g/f	90	2532
92	4-11	Warw	7.1fm	[89]	2777
86	9-20	Newm	7g/f	89	3782
93	2-16	Newb	7g/f	89	3954
91	3-8	Good	7g/s	90	4231
86	6-16	Good	7g/f	89	4523
95	2-15	Asco	7g/f	89	4800

KOOL ACCLAIM 3 b f £4467

65	2-10	Ling	6gd		3603
74	1-8	YARM	6gd		3873*
67	12-15	Sand	5gd	76	4604

KOOL OVATION 2 b c £1455

52	9-13	York	6gd	3431
67	3-10	Hayd	5gd	3755
72	3-14	Newc	6fm	4865

KOSTAR 3 ch g £7743

74	4-13	Wind	6fm		2756
77	1-10	SALI	6gd		3452*
63	11-15	Newb	6gd	77	3920
72	4-15	Kemp	6g/f	76	4713
82a	2-12	Wolv	5.1ap	74	5326

KRASIVIS BOY 2 b c £1795

39a	9-11	Ling	8ap		3786
77	2-15	Good	8g/s		4233
73a	4-11	Ling	8ap		4738
43	12-13	Wind	8.3g/f	70	5051

KRATAIOS 4 b c £0

108	12-15	Newb	8g/f	1758

KRISTAL FOREST 4 b g £0

9a	12-15	Sout	16af	40	67

KRISTALCHEN 2 b f £355

57	7-11	Ches	7fm	3633
67	9-18	Nott	8.2g/s	4035
65	7-13	Leic	8g/f	4450
62	4-10	Nott	10hvy	5188

KRISTALS DREAM 3 b f £1798

75	3-8	Brig	9.9g/f	[75]	1369	
75	5-13	Bath	10.2g/f	[74]	1791	
49	7-8	Ches	10.3gd	[74]	2283	
78	2-8	Wind	11.6g/f	74	2796	
68	5-6	Thir	12g/f	76	3415	
2	12-12	Sali	12g/f	76	3868	T

KRISTENSEN 5 ch g £14912

83	5-17	Ripo	16g/s	83	1361	p
83	9-17	Ches	18.7gd	83	1569	p
78	6-14	Asco	16.2g/f	81	1928	p
85	2-12	Muss	14fm	79	2085	p
85	5-19	Newc	16.1g/s	81	2771	p
70	10-17	Asco	16.2gd	82	3125	p
79	7-19	Good	21fm	80	3531	p
80	3-21	York	11.9gd	77	3999	p
66	8-8	Ayr	17.5g/s	77	4657	p
78	2-6	Muss	16gd	75	4808	p
82	10-34	Newm	18sft	77	5135	p
77	3-11	Muss	16g/s	76	5335	p

KRISTIANSAND 4 b g £378

33	8-9	Hami	9.2gd	65	3132
60	6-8	Hami	9.2fm	65	3250
66	4-9	Hami	9.2g/f	64	3593
49	10-17	Hami	9.2g/s	64	4008

KRISTIKHAB 2 ch c £1616

48	7-9	Newc	5sft		962	
38	5-5	Hami	5g/s		1601	
73	4-6	Ayr	6g/f		2028	
75	2-8	Hami	5gd		2177	
0	10-10	Sout	6af		2382	
15	12-13	Curr	6.3gd		2815	
54	7-10	Carl	5g/f		3227	
44	5-5	Hami	6g/f	[65]	3589	
44	8-10	Hayd	5g/s	[62]	3901	P
0	19-19	Carl	5.9g/f	56	4344	
49	8-14	Hami	6sft	53	4692	
11	15-16	Nott	5.1hvy	53	5343	

KRISTINEAU 6 ch m £0

47	5-14	York	13.9g/f	48	2060	t
36	7-13	Pont	17.1g/f	47	2276	t
39	6-10	Hami	13g/f	47	2479	t
20	9-14	Carl	17.2gd	43	2937	t P
0	18-18	Pont	10g/f	43	2988	t

KRISTINOR 2 ch c £0

76	6-16	Newm	7g/f	3582
35	9-14	Sali	8gd	4852

KRISTOFFERSEN 3 ch c £0

66a	12-14	Ling	13ap	75	147	
69a	9-14	Ling	12ap	74	731	
49a	8-11	Ling	12ap	[71]	816	BL

KRUGERRAND 5 ch g £25570

76a	9-11	Ling	10ap	82	716	
68	13-24	Donc	8gd	82	928	
68	10-13	Wind	8.3g/s	[80]	1057	
26	13-18	Asco	8sft	79	1423	
87	1-15	YORK	8.9g/f	77	2404*	
86	3-7	Wind	8.3fm	84	2787	
76	6-12	Kemp	10gd	84	3185	
78	11-15	Good	9.9g/f	84	3506	
86	5-15	Donc	10.3g/f	84	3598	
94	1-14	WIND	8.3gd	[85]	4122+	
88	5-11	Good	9g/f	89	4525	
46	27-32	Newm	9g/f	89	4916	
64	13-13	Newm	8g/s	89	5284	

KRULLIND 2 b g £0

29	21-23	Newm	8gd	5084
71	6-19	Newm	7g/s	5285
71	6-17	Yarm	6g/s	5350

KRUMPET 2 b f £0

64	7-15	Folk	7gd	3381
60	9-12	Folk	7gd	3908

KRYNICA 2 br f £5814

82	1-10	PONT	6g/f		2610*
81	4-7	Donc	6g/s		3221
19	14-14	Yarm	7g/s	81	4583

KRYSSA 3 ch f £21441

52a	4-8	Ling	6ap		691	
62a	1-10	LING	5ap		802*	
61a	3-15	Ling	7ap	60	901	
64	3-9	Bath	5g/s	60	1102	
62	5-17	Sali	6g/f	60	1722	
67	1-17	KEMP	7ap	59	2174*	
70	3-20	Newb	7fm	64	2650	
77	1-14	CHEP	8.1g/s	66	3090*	
73	3-6	Epso	8.5fm	72	3540	
76	1-11	WIND	8.3fm	72	3799*	
58	11-13	Sand	8.1gd	75	4607	
67a	6-14	Ling	10ap	[75]	4742	

KSCHESSINKA 3 br f £7348

83	1-10	NEWB	6g/f		2309*
83	3-7	Newm	6g/s	78	2764
66	6-7	Wind	6fm	[81]	3293

KUDBEME 2 b f £0

43	12-18	York	5g/f	2360
53	6-13	Newc	6g/f	5012

KUMAKAWA 5 ch g £1051

20a	14-16	Sout	7af	[42]	61	bl
31a	13-15	Ling	7ap	[45]	366	bl
45a	5-10	Sout	8af	[45]	502	bl
30a	8-11	Ling	8ap	[45]	535	bl
55a	3-8	Sout	8af	[45]	577	bl
42a	7-10	Ling	10ap	[45]	738	bl
29a	8-14	Ling	10ap	45	757	bl
50a	2-10	Sout	8af	[45]	791	bl
31a	6-12	Ling	8ap	49	845	bl
38a	7-15	Sout	8af	49	1028	bl
0	9-13	Wind	8.3g/s	[40]	1058	bl
0	8-8	Brig	8gd	[40]	1548	bl
29	5-12	Brig	8gd	[40]	4904	
27a	10-13	Wolv	9.5ap	[47]	5338	

KUMALA OCEAN 2 ch f £1192

57a	2-12	Sout	7af	3394
64	5-8	Muss	7.1g/f	3559
55	9-15	Folk	7gd	4114

67	2-14	Carl	6.9fm	[62]	4503
60	8-18	Catt	7g/f	64	4673

KUMARI 2 b f £0

44a	8-12	Wolv	5af	[50]	32
23a	7-8	Sout	6af	48	223
29a	11-13	Wolv	6af	45	436

KUNDA 3 b f £14300

98	2-8	Epso	8.5g/f	[96]	2211
96	3-11	Warw	7.1fm	[96]	2574
89	7-9	Sand	8.1g/s	[96]	2917
89	7-7	Asco	8g/f	[96]	3389
84	10-12	Bath	8g/f	[94]	3965

KURINGAI 2 b c £850

47a	8-8	Ling	6ap	72	268
24a	10-10	Ling	6ap	67	494
64a	4-8	Ling	6ap	67	673
73	3-8	Nott	5.1fm	72	1002
64	8-16	Kemp	6g/s	72	1116
28	17-17	Sali	6g/f	71	1722
44	10-10	Brig	6g/f	[69]	2048
43	10-12	Folk	6gd	65	3380
35	10-12	Nott	5.1g/f	[65]	3577

KURM 3 b c £7711

105	3-4	Sain	10g/s	1696

KUSSHARRO 3 ch c £0

28	9-10	Ripo	6gd	4790

KUSTER 8 b g £7399

49	14-19	York	11.9sft	91	1668	bl
92	6-10	York	11.9g/f	91	2405	bl
95	1-4	WIND	8g/f	[90]	2798*	bl
89	6-14	York	13.9gd	90	3119	bl

KUSTOM KIT FOR HER 3 b f £1441

9a	12-14	Sout	8af	[53]	170	BL
28a	10-13	Sout	6af	[53]	254	bl
43a	6-12	Sout	7af	[50]	416	
41a	8-13	Sout	6af	[50]	444	
1a	10-13	Sout	6af	45	500	bl
0	13-13	Sout	12af	[45]	575	
45a	2-5	Wolv	12af	[45]	583	
18a	3-9	Wolv	9.4af	[45]	665	
45a	2-7	Sout	8af	[45]	721	T
43a	2-5	Sout	11af	[45]	772	t
3a	4-8	Ling	10ap	[45]	829	t
0	8-12	Sout	8af	[45]	848	
37a	8-14	Sout	8af	[45]	3392	t
3a	10-11	Sout	8af	[42]	4090	t

KWAHERI 6 b m £0

15	9-10	Sali	14.1gd	45	3887

KWAI BABY 3 gr f £0

13	7-7	Good	9.9g/f		4541
3	9-10	Good	9.9gd	[35]	4877
12	9-11	Wind	8.3g/f	[35]	5054
1	8-8	Bath	17.2sft	35	5175

KWAME 2 b f £9305

76	2-12	Ling	5g/f		1981	
77	1-11	LING	5gd		2395*	
83	2-5	Chep	5.1g/s		3086	
50	13-13	Good	5g/f		3509	
80	2-7	Sand	5sft	75	4065	
75	5-16	Newm	6gd	78	4224	
79	3-14	Epso	5g/f	78	4471	VIS
69	9-13	Leic	6g/f	78	4697	vis
62a	5-8	Ling	6ap	[77]	5081	vis

KYALAMI 4 b g £235

9a	6-16	Sout	16af	25	206
1a	8-12	Wolv	12af	25	244
39a	3-10	Sout	16af	[24]	307
19a	4-7	Sout	14af	[30]	357 e

KYBER 3 ch g £1851

39	5-7	Catt	13.8g/f		3019
57	4-9	Pont	12gd		3462
61	3-9	Newc	9g/s		3697
59	3-5	Catt	12sft		3934
37	10-13	Newc	16.1fm	62	4868
28	6-13	Ayr	10sft	[60]	5066
61	4-10	Muss	12g/s	[60]	5145
49	5-10	Catt	13.8sft	55	5322

KYKUIT 2 b f £24648
103 1-8 CAPA 7.5gd 4430*

KYLE OF LOCHALSH 3 gr g £426
46a 9-14 Ling 10ap 59 101
45a 10-14 Ling 10ap 58 236
56a 3-12 Ling 8ap 55 406 P
29a 11-14 Ling 10ap 55 498 p
43 10-11 Leic 10gd 57 2135
30 12-14 Wind 10g/f 57 2265
47 5-10 Muss 9g/f [52] 2811 BL
47 5-11 Yarm 10.1gd [49] 3362
26 12-13 Folk 9.7g/f 46 3726
38 6-13 Ayr 10sft [45] 5276

KYLKENNY 8 b g £3411
84a 4-8 Sout 12af 85 225
77a 3-9 Sout 12af 84 856 t
56 11-20 Wind 11.6g/s 76 1056
58 13-20 Newb 10gd 75 1235 t
72 6-8 Nott 10g/f 75 2157 t
76 5-10 York 11.9g/f 73 2405 t
75 3-8 Newm 10g/f 72 2735 t
79 4-14 Sali 12g/s 72 3114 t
71 4-10 Newm 10fm 72 3404 t
70 4-14 Sali 9.9g/f 70 3867 t
23 14-14 York 11.9gd 70 4327 t
62 10-14 Asco 12g/f 70 4775 t
62 8-17 Leic 10gd 67 5062 t

KYTHIA 3 b f £2006
75 4-13 Bath 10.2g/f [72] 1791
76 3-12 Sand 10gd 72 2366
74 2-5 Brig 11.9gd [73] 2956
48 7-8 Brig 11.9g/f 73 3299
71 6-13 Warw 12.6gd 72 4274
55 9-12 Beve 12.1g/f 70 4601
49 14-18 Sali 9.9gd 67 4850

LA BELLA GRANDE 2 ch f £0
51 12-16 Newm 7g/s 5280

LA BELLA ROSA 2 b f £0
3 10-10 Beve 5sft 1632
1 8-11 Ripo 6g/f 1779 VIS
1 17-17 Donc 6g/f 2424

LA CALERA 3 ch f £888
35 5-11 Epso 7fm 3541 VIS
43 3-11 Carl 6.9g/f [65] 3651 vis
44 3-9 Brig 8sft 49 4165 vis
4 12-16 Folk 6g/f [47] 4370 bl
40 9-18 Leic 7gd [45] 4698
48 5-15 Wind 10g/f [45] 4834 P
35 11-17 Warw 8.1g/s [45] 4992 bl
43 4-20 Yarm 7g/s [45] 5120 bl

LA CONCHA 3 b g £0
56a 8-12 Ling 8ap 428
43a 9-15 Ling 12ap 521
37a 11-13 Ling 10ap 601
61 8-14 Wind 10g/s 1259
3 8-10 Nott 14.1hvy 55 1612
27 8-11 Yarm 11.5g/f 52 2346 VIS

LA CORUJERA 3 b f £0
17a 10-16 Sout 6af [62] 65

LA CORUNA 3 b f £723
60 4-7 Kemp 6hvy 1513

LA CUCARACHA 3 b f £10350
102 2-14 Bath 5gd 1400
94 6-11 Newb 6gd [99] 1732
94 3-9 Wind 6g/f [99] 1958

LA CYGNE BLANCHE 2 gr f £0
23 11-13 Nott 6.1g/f 4843
36a 14-14 Ling 7ap 5076
50a 6-13 Wolv 6ap 5182

LA DANSEUSE 2 b f £0
52a 6-10 Ling 8ap [53] 232
51a 5-9 Ling 10ap 51 365

LA FONTEYNE 2 b f £1469
0 13-13 Ling 6ap 25
57 5-8 Redc 6sft 1659

0 17-17 Hayd 8.1gd 58 2243
49a 2-9 Sout 6af [55] 2493
17 12-17 Leic 7gd [55] 2704
44a 5-6 Sout 6af [50] 3095
0 16-18 Hayd 6gd 48 3737
47 3-10 Newc 7hvy [44] 4216
0 19-20 Yarm 7g/s [45] 5120
26 4-12 Ayr 7.2sft [45] 5274

LA HERMANA 3 ch f £0
79 7-10 Sali 9.9g/f 3866

LA INA 3 b f £30986
103 2-15 Duss 8sft 1702

LA LANDONNE 2 b f £4005
70a 5-12 Ling 8ap 19
59a 1-14 LING 6ap 146*
61 4-6 Warw 6.1sft [70] 1088
70 3-10 Chep 8.1g/f 68 2624
60 6-19 Leic 6g/f 68 2925
53a 6-11 Ling 7ap [68] 3331
37 11-13 Ling 7g/f 66 3604
1 11-14 Yarm 8g/s [63] 4252 VIS
63a 2-13 Wolv 6.8ap 58 5183

LA MAGO 4 b f £0
0 14-14 Carl 9.3g/f 4347

LA MAITRESSE 2 b f £3049
86 3-6 Leop 6g/s 3314

LA MUETTE 4 b f £0
3a 7-7 Sout 16af 80 529
20 10-15 Newc 12.4hvy 75 1034
63 8-8 Kemp 8ap [75] 1115
38 16-20 Warw 10.9gd 70 1128

LA MUSIQUE 2 b c £0
2 18-18 Newm 8fm 4722
12a 12-12 Ling 8ap 5295

LA PEREGRINA 3 b f £1266
58a 2-12 Ling 7ap 566
62a 5-12 Ling 8ap 623

LA PERSIANA 3 gr f £38243
66 5-19 Yarm 8g/f 1130
79 2-18 Thir 8g/f 72 1769
85 1-6 DONC 10.3g/f [75] 2426*
91 1-10 WIND 10fm 70 2785*
100 1-4 YORK 10.4g/f 87 3435*
104 2-12 Yarm 10.1sft 96 4149
99 3-11 Yarm 10.1gd[100] 4614

LA PETITE CHINOISE 3 ch f £6670
54a 6-15 Ling 7ap [69] 670
66a 8-15 Ling 7ap 69 901 BL
71 4-5 Ayr 9.1g/f [66] 2025
72 2-7 Hami 11.1g/f [66] 2478
75 2-11 Ling 11.5g/f 66 2842
70 5-14 Catt 12g/f 70 3192
79 1-8 LING 11.5fm 70 3747*

LA PROFESSORESSA 3 b f £665
62 6-11 Bath 8fm [66] 2031
55 12-12 Sand 7.1g/f 66 2098
42 11-14 Wind 10g/f 62 2452
58 5-14 Kemp 10g/f 59 3690
58 3-12 Kemp 9sft 58 4032
29 13-16 Chep 10.2g/s 58 4365

LA PROVIDENCE 2 b f £0
0 9-10 Sout 5af 4129 BL e
0 14-14 Muss 7.1g/f 4171 bl e
5a 11-12 Wolv 7.1ap 5158 bl e

LA PUCE 3 b f £11424
73a 4-6 Sout 8af 70 506
47a 8-10 Ling 10ap 68 568
74a 1-8 WOLV 8.5af 66 645*
74a 1-8 WOLV 8.5af 68 809*
62a 4-5 Wolv 8.5af 71 861
58 6-10 Yarm 8g/f 66 2344
52 8-13 Leic 7g/f 64 3346
47 7-8 Newm 7g/f 62 3612 T
52 8-8 Folk 7g/f 62 3724
61a 2-11 Wolv 7.1ap [71] 5178
65 1-18 NEWM 8sft 56 5272*

LA ROSE 3 b f £0
0 9-10 Wolv 12af [38] 250
14a 6-8 Wolv 12af [35] 347 vis

LA SYLPHIDE GB 7 ch m £31250
84 2-10 Hayd 10.5g/s 77 1346
82 5-19 York 11.9sft 82 1668
77 6-9 Hayd 10.5g/s 82 2185
51 10-11 Ripo 10g/f 80 2483
85 2-14 Ripo 10gd 78 4305
90 1-7 HAYD 10.5sft 82 4781*
103 3-10 Newm 10gd [85] 5086
87 4-6 Donc 12sft [90] 5369

LA VIE EST BELLE 3 b f £6993
74a 6-9 Ling 5ap 76 914
54 10-14 Ches 6.1g/s 76 1570
68 4-12 Chep 6.1gd 73 2118
18 9-11 Sali 6gd 70 2661
47 11-11 Wind 8.3fm 68 3799
49 6-10 Ling 6gd 65 4109
67 1-7 GOOD 5sft 60 4236*
59 8-16 Good 5g/f 64 4528
66 4-20 Nott 6.1g/s 64 4626
55a 5-12 Ling 6ap 63 4976
67 2-17 Bath 5.7gd [63] 5020

LA VIGNA 3 ch g £0
27a 8-15 Ling 7ap [35] 830 P
21a 10-12 Wolv 5af [30] 889 p
22a 7-10 Ling 6ap [30] 973 p

LA VIOLA 2 b f £0
61 6-14 Redc 6g/s 5106
71 5-14 Muss 7.1g/s 5330

LAABBIJ 3 ch c £1490
79 6-19 Newb 8gd 1236
61 10-20 Wind 10sft 1651
71 5-10 Leic 10g/f 76 1965
74 3-9 Wind 10fm [75] 3642 BL
73 2-7 Chep 12.1g/s [75] 3899 bl

LAAWARIS 3 b c £0
68 8-9 Sand 10g/s 85 1318
37 12-13 Kemp 9hvy 82 1515
61 9-10 Good 11g/f 80 1865

LABELLED WITH LOVE 4 ch g £1699
55 2-13 Leic 10fm 2107
43 5-7 Brig 9.9fm 2332
48 6-13 Newb 8fm 52 2647
15a 9-9 Ling 8ap [50] 3197
34a 5-14 Ling 7ap [48] 4660 T
44 2-12 Brig 8gd [45] 4904 t
44a 2-13 Wolv 8.6ap [45] 5232 t

LABRETT 6 b g £9061
78a 1-12 LING 8ap 71 17* p
54a 7-13 Wolv 9.4af 76 127 p
72a 6-11 Sout 8af 76 186 p
85a 1-11 LING 8ap [75] 273+ t
82a 3-12 Ling 8ap 83 369 t
76a 9-14 Ling 10ap 83 452 t
79a 5-11 Ling 8ap 83 547 p
83a 2-12 Ling 8ap 81 888 t p
83a 3-9 Wolv 7af 82 940 t p
71a 7-8 Wolv 8.5af 82 1219 t p

LACONIA 2 b f £3657
70a 5-10 Ling 5ap [61] 13
37a 9-12 Wolv 5af [61] 32
52a 4-10 Ling 5ap [65] 802
60 5-12 Catt 5gd [65] 995
73 2-9 Bath 5g/s 65 1102
59 6-8 Thir 5sft [69] 1228
74 2-14 Bath 5gd 69 1404
56 6-17 Bath 5g/f [73] 1787
53 2-15 Nott 5.1g/f [72] 2152
44 8-14 Donc 5gd [72] 2237
58 8-13 Wind 5fm 68 2784
26a 11-12 Wolv 5.1ap 64 5326

LACONICOS 2 ch c £2043
79 2-5 Leic 5g/s 1014
76 3-13 Nott 5.1gd 1987
80 2-14 Folk 7fm 2714
62 10-12 Catt 7g/f 78 3351 VIS

LADEENA 2 b f £1502
80 2-16 Newm 7g/s   5280

LADIES DAY 3 b f £0
32a 9-14 Ling 12ap [70] 14

LADIES KNIGHT 3 b g £3852
51a 9-12 Wolv 5af [56]   70
0   16-16 Sout 5af   54   183
57a 1-15 SOUT 5af [54] 253*
44a 6-9   Sout 5af [56] 335
58a 3-9   Ling 5ap   55   435
58a 2-13 Ling 6ap   55   471
46a 5-11 Wolv 5af   55   508
46a 8-12 Ling 6ap   56   628
52a 6-13 Ling 6ap   55   740
54a 3-12 Sout 5af   55   853
52a 7-14 Ling 6ap   55   897
51a 5-16 Sout 5af   53   1046
42a 8-11 Wolv 6af   53   1337

LADRUCA 2 b f £3562
43   8-10 Newm 6gd   1887
46   7-20 Hayd 6gd   2882
60   5-12 Newm 7g/f   3750
61   1-13 SALI 7g/f   3864*
23   19-20 Redc 7fm   60   4337

LADY ALRUNA 4 ch f £0
5a   7-13 Wolv 6af [53]   30 VIS
14a 8-10 Wolv 7af [40] 298

LADY ANN SUMMERS 2 ch f £1164
84   10-17 Asco 5g/f   2490
70   3-8   Kemp 5g/f   2858
77   4-8   Asco 6gd   3071
58   10-13 Newm 5g/f   76 3943 BL
52a 14-14 Ling 7ap   73 4177 P

LADY ARNICA 5 b m £0
0   7-7   Sout 14af [45] 638 VIS
0   8-8   Ling 16ap   45   733 vis

LADY AT LEISURE 4 ch f £1260
42a 6-10 Ling 10ap [50] 540
29a 11-12 Ling 8ap   [45] 648
28a 10-14 Ling 10ap [45] 705
41a 1-7   LING 10ap [35] 1244*
7   10-13 Kemp 10hvy [40] 1643

LADY BAHIA 3 b f £5803
28a 7-9   Wolv 9.4af   64   351
34a 6-6   Ling 10ap   64   403
67a 1-10 SOUT 6af   54   592*
47a 7-11 Sout 5af   60   609
73a 1-9   WOLV 5af   [64]   835*

LADY BLADE 3 b f £0
51   7-10 Yarm 8g/f   64 2344
58a 4-14 Ling 10ap   [61] 2740
39   8-13 Pont 12gd   60 3240
58   5-10 Newb 10fm   57 3630
46   9-12 Kemp 9sft   59 4032 BL
43a 9-12 Ling 8ap   [60] 4320 bl
22a 13-13 Wolv 8.6ap [55] 5184

LADY CHEF 2 ch f £5231
45   8-15 Warw 5g/s   1325
55   5-18 Chep 6.1gd   2194
74   1-17 LING 7g/f   2584*
78   3-9   Good 7fm   74   3624
54   8-12 Bath 8g/f   76   4410
56   11-13 Wind 8.3g/s 75   4940

LADY DAN 2 b f £2802
62   4-10 Beve 5sft   1632
69   3-15 York 5g/f   2056
75   2-18 York 5g/f   2360
33   9-10 Beve 7.5gd   2652
70   6-10 York 5gd   73   3115
59   7-9   Redc 6g/f   70   3807
69   3-12 Carl 5g/f [68] 4343
0   P-16 Ripo 5g/f [65] 4787

LADY DORIS WATTS 2 b f £439
65   8-13 Newm 6g/f   4918
68   2-13 Warw 7.1g/s   4996
60   7-14 Redc 6g/s   5106

52   6-10 Catt 6sft   64   5318

LADY DOUBLE U 4 b f £0
0   11-11 Sout 7af   488
48a 7-7   Wolv 7af   617
35   9-11 Pont 6sft   1426
18   15-20 Beve 5g/f [45] 1948
37   7-19 Redc 6g/f   45 2125

LADY DULCET 4 b f £0
0   10-10 Chep 8.1sft [40] 1334

LADY EDGE 2 ch f £0
13   11-11 Catt 5gd   4962

LADY ELLENDUNE 2 b f £0
26a 6-11 Ling 6ap [42] 233 bl
0   13-13 Wolv 6af [40] 397

LADY ERICA 2 b f £1180
65a 2-7   Sout 5af   1029
64   5-8   Thir 5g/s   1212
67a 4-8   Wolv 5af   1653
57a 3-10 Ling 5ap   2017
41   9-9   Chep 5.1hvy 59 4706
17   10-10 Catt 5gd [57] 4968 VIS

LADY FILLY 2 ch f £18652
83   1-7   KEMP 5sft   943*
91   1-8   THIR 5g/s   1212*
93   1-6   SALI 5g/s   1499*
90   7-17 Asco 5g/s   2490
64   5-5   Sand 5g/s   2895
76   5-8   Donc 6sft [94] 5217

LADY FRANPALM 4 b f £0
34   15-17 Kemp 7gd [54] 1136
43   7-13 Folk 7g/s [54] 1270
49   9-10 Ling 7gd [52] 3446
0   13-13 Sout 6af   47   4091
24   10-11 Good 6gd [40] 5030

LADY GEORGINA 3 gr f £12488
71   3-16 Leic 8g/s   71 1359
52   6-8   Nott 8.2g/s [71] 1775
78   1-16 LING 8g/f [70] 1982*
81   2-12 Newm 7g/f   75   2249
78   1-7   GOOD 7gd [75] 2374*
81   5-12 Yarm 7fm   78   2864

LADY HECCLES 5 b m £0
0   10-10 Ling 8ap   785

LADY HEN 2 b f £0
61   8-10 Newm 6g/f   3063
60   6-14 Leic 6g/f   3517
40   8-13 Nott 6.1g/f   4843

LADY HOPEFUL 2 b f £2399
63   5-10 Muss 5gd   1550
64   4-8   Muss 5gd   1795
66a 2-14 Sout 7af   2492
62   2-7   Muss 7.1g/f   2810
47   7-9   Ches 5.1g/f   3097
42   5-6   Hami 6fm   66   3245 VIS
60   5-16 Ripo 5gd [62] 4787
40   14-17 Catt 7gd   61   4963
58   4-9   Pont 6g/s [59] 5154 BL
27   14-16 Nott 5.1hvy 59 5343 bl

LADY INDIANA 2 b f £0
0   9-11 Ripo 6g/f   1779
6   16-17 Donc 6g/f   2424
5   7-8   Redc 7g/s   2563
16   11-12 Beve 8.5sft   4257

LADY JEANNIE 7 b m £0
32   7-7   Wind 8.3g/f [48] 2264
29   10-11 Folk 9.7fm   48 2719
30   11-14 Folk 9.7g/s 43 3052
33a 8-11 Ling 16ap   40 3450

LADY JUSTICE 4 b f £277
28   13-16 Nott 6.1sft 70 1465
49   4-15 Nott 5.1g/f [65] 2152
22   14-15 Leic 6g/f   60 2398 BL
46a 8-10 Ling 5ap   55 3332
35   6-6   Folk 5g/f [50] 3725

LADY KARR 3 b f £4089

50   7-9   Redc 9fm   4336
67   3-9   Newc 10.1g/f   5015
71   1-12 CATT 12sft   5319*

LADY KORRIANDA 2 ch f £645
60a 2-14 Ling 6ap   146
33   9-11 Good 6gd [60] 5030
36a 9-14 Ling 7ap [57] 5294

LADY LAKOTA 2 b f £0
28   14-17 Yarm 6gd   4610

LADY LAKSHMI 4 ch f £840
40a 3-8   Wolv 12af [40] 1265
41a 2-9   Ling 13ap [40] 1456
42a 3-14 Ling 10ap [40] 4661 T

LADY LE QUESNE 2 ch f £10102
69   6-19 Newb 6g/f   2310
86   2-8   Newb 5.2fm   2646
85   1-6   EPSO 6g/s   3041*
84   1-4   BATH 5g/f   3369*
75   13-26 Newb 6.5g/f   4679
81   7-16 Newm 7g/f   80 4913

LADY LEXIE 3 b f £0
49   6-13 Newm 8g/f   1935

LADY LIESEL 4 b f £209
21a 10-11 Ling 8ap [45] 535
0   14-14 Ling 6ap [40] 652
42a 3-12 Ling 8ap [40] 710
33a 7-7   Ling 8ap   40   910
24a 11-15 Ling 7ap [40] 969
32a 4-5   Ling 8ap [40] 1245
25a 7-12 Ling 8ap [40] 1451
28   12-15 Folk 9.7g/f [45] 4373
21a 9-14 Ling 10ap [35] 4662
22   12-13 Brig 8gd [45] 4902

LADY LONDRA 2 b f £0
73   7-13 Wind 6fm   3478
60   9-18 Wind 6gd   3824

LADY LUCINDA 3 b f £0
20   10-11 Beve 9.9sft   4261
5   12-13 Leic 10g/f   4453

LADY LUISA 2 b f £201
63   11-15 Ling 7gd   3285
72   6-8   Asco 7gd   3467
48   8-17 Warw 7.1gd   4269
35   11-11 Chep 8.1g/s   4363
53   14-20 Ling 7g/f   60 4741

LADY MCNAIR 4 b f £2554
75   4-20 Wind 11.6g/s 78 1056
67   11-19 Newb 10gd   76 1736
79   2-7   Ling 10g/f 74 2015
77   4-15 Sand 10g/f 74 2099

LADY MISHA 2 b f £7583
61   5-11 Warw 5gd   1123
67   5-11 Nott 6.1sft   1739
58   10-12 Redc 6g/f   2119
63   3-10 Beve 7.5gd   2652
70   1-13 NEWC 7g/s 62 3698*
73   2-9   Newc 8sft   69 4285
73   5-12 Ayr   8sft   73 5065
40   11-14 Donc 8sft   73 5203

LADY MO 2 b f £17379
26a 10-13 Ling 6ap [55] 25
21a 5-9   Ling 6ap [50] 327
52a 3-12 Ling 8ap   49   402
53a 5-6   Sout 8af   51   506
57a 1-9   SOUT 8af [51] 596*
64a 1-5   SOUT 7af [51] 682*
37a 12-14 Ling 7ap   62   804
75a 1-8   WOLV 7af [60] 1222*
76a 2-11 Wolv 8.5af 70 1339
62   3-14 Sali 7g/f [65] 1720
45   13-17 Kemp 7gd   63 2174
61   6-10 Asco 8gd [60] 3067
69   1-9   EPSO 7g/s [60] 3215*
67   2-12 Ling 7.6gd [66] 3448
59   2-11 Epso 7fm [66] 3541
67   3-10 Brig 7fm   3672
56   5-10 Yarm 7g/s   66 4251

67 5-15 Epso 7g/f 66 4475

LADY MYTTON 4 ch f £367
67	5-7	Thir	8sft	[87]	1225
4	16-18	Ayr	7.2sft	84	4689

LADY NATILDA 3 ch f £685
28a	8-12	Sout	6af	53	85 BL
21a	7-12	Wolv	7af	53	129
47a	4-10	Wolv	6af	48	349
46a	3-12	Wolv	6af	48	385
13a	11-14	Sout	6af	47	501
42a	6-11	Wolv	7af	47	558 P

LADY NETBETSPORTS 5 b m £1813
50	7-10	Beve	9.9gd	63	2510
66	3-7	Hami	13gd	63	2708
34	7-8	Donc	14.6gd	61	2754
65	2-7	Beve	16.2sft	61	2941
35	8-8	Hayd	14g/s	62	3140
9	10-10	Hayd	16.2sft	62	3275

LADY OF GDANSK 4 ch f £0
0	14-14	Sout	8af	45	195

LADY OF THE LINKS 3 b f £0
46	4-6	Newc	5sft	[56]	1392
32	8-10	Folk	6sft	56	1576
37	5-6	Newc	8sft	55	1679 VIS
5	16-19	York	6g/f	49	2055 vis
6	8-12	Ayr	7.2sft	[45]	5274 T

LADY ORIANDE 3 b f £0
22a	6-10	Ling	6ap		973
32	8-15	Folk	6g/s		1078

LADY PEACHES 3 ch f £830
73	7-9	Newm	10fm		1494
68	3-20	Wind	10sft		1651
62	8-10	Newm	10fm	67	2592
68	4-11	Ling	11.5g/f	67	2842
42	5-7	Brig	11.9g/f	[65]	3173

LADY PEKAN 4 b f £10422
60a	1-12	WOLV	5af	53	124* BL
58a	4-11	Wolv	5af	57	155 bl
66a	1-8	WOLV	5af	57	274* bl
59a	6-10	Wolv	6af	63	349 bl
61a	3-10	Ling	5ap	63	453 bl
60a	5-10	Sout	5af	63	660 bl
49a	6-11	Wolv	5af	63	748 bl
58a	7-10	Ling	5ap	62	755 bl
49a	7-11	Wolv	5af	60	958 bl
61	2-5	Muss	5g/f	60	1096 P
66	2-13	Epso	5sft	60	1293 bl
47	9-15	Brig	5.3g/f	60	1371 bl
37	9-12	Ling	5g/s	62	1615 bl
62	3-13	Newc	5gd	61	1873 bl
58	5-10	Brig	5.3g/f	61	2044 bl
66	3-15	Ling	5g/f	61	2062 bl
55	9-14	Wind	5g/f	62	2266 bl
51	8-10	Donc	5g/f	62	2429 bl
46	13-17	Warw	5fm	62	2599 bl
34	17-19	Leic	5g/f	62	2702 bl
53a	8-13	Wolv	5.1ap	58	5156 bl

LADY PILOT 2 b f £0
84	9-9	Sand	7.1g/f		3357
49	12-15	Kemp	6g/f		4357
63	6-17	Yarm	6gd		4610
69	7-17	Ling	7g/f	70	4894

LADY PISTE 2 b f £7836
49a	7-10	Wolv	7af	67	112 T
48a	4-11	Ling	6ap	[63]	233 t
36a	12-15	Ling	7ap	55	295 BL
51a	4-14	Ling	6ap	[52]	495 vis t
54a	2-10	Ling	6ap	[52]	548 vis t
52a	5-10	Ling	6ap	[51]	606 vis t
51a	3-15	Ling	7ap	[55]	671 vis t
55a	1-14	LING	7ap	[53]	804* vis t
41a	7-15	Ling	7ap	[54]	935 vis t
55	1-14	LING	7g/f	[61]	1984* vis t
58	4-10	Newm	8g/f	[61]	2732

LADY PREDOMINANT 2 b f £2023
54a	2-13	Ling	6ap	[55]	25
41a	12-15	Ling	7ap	55	177
42a	4-10	Ling	10ap	[52]	291
37a	4-8	Ling	8ap	[52]	326
24a	11-12	Ling	8ap	[45]	649
40a	6-9	Ling	7ap	[45]	764
38a	11-15	Ling	7ap	45	901
49a	1-5	SOUT	8af	[45]	986*
28	12-13	Nott	8.2gd	50	1242
5a	5-5	Wolv	8.5af	47	1655 T
0	13-13	Bath	8fm	47	2667
7	14-15	Bath	8g/s	45	4202
0	16-19	Kemp	8af	[45]	4793
26a	10-12	Wolv	9.5ap	[45]	5209

LADY PROTECTOR 4 b f £12271
37a	8-12	Wolv	5af	[42]	242
38a	4-9	Sout	5af	[40]	335
51a	1-16	SOUT	5af	[40]	374+
44a	7-11	Wolv	5af	48	507
50a	3-12	Sout	5af	[48]	587
37a	9-11	Wolv	5af	48	643
39a	10-12	Sout	5af	48	1442
40	7-15	Muss	5gd	48	1555
54	1-13	NEWC	5gd	45	1873+
59	1-15	LING	5g/f	52	2062*
59	3-10	Donc	5fm	55	2429
60	3-22	Good	5fm	55	3537
56	3-11	Bath	5g/f	57	3849
36	8-11	Nott	5.1gd	57	4038
49	7-15	Newc	5fm	57	4870

LADY REDERA 3 b f £0
33	16-18	Nott	8.2g/s	60	1778
21	13-14	Sali	8fm	55	2423
12	11-11	Bath	10.2g/f	48	3373 BL

LADY STRATAGEM 5 gr m £592
27	7-10	Redc	14.1g/s	47	2562
32	10-18	Pont	10g/f	45	2988
42	3-13	Beve	12.1g/f	42	3502
24	9-10	Catt	13.8g/f	42	3669
13	14-16	Carl	11.9g/f	40	4348
0	13-15	Carl	9.3fm	[40]	4505

LADY STRIPES 3 gr f £0
42a	8-12	Ling	7ap	62	545
54a	6-10	Ling	10ap	60	676
30a	7-7	Wolv	6af	[58]	863
49a	7-14	Ling	10ap	52	2064

LADY SUESANNE 2 b f £0
50	8-11	Yarm	6g/f		1727
25a	12-14	Sout	7af		2492
31	11-11	Thir	7fm		4375
42	12-17	Yarm	6gd		4610

LADY SUNSET 3 b f £0
48	10-12	Catt	5gd	[65]	995 BL
23	8-9	Redc	5sft	[62]	1146
10	17-18	Thir	8g/f	60	1769
7	11-13	Carl	5.9fm	[55]	1949 P

LADY TAVERNER 3 b f £0
37	15-18	Wind	8.3g/f		1810
62	10-13	Kemp	10g/f		3038
54	5-7	Asco	8gd		3469
47	9-15	Epso	7g/f	57	4475
47	8-12	Brig	8fm	[54]	4761

LADY TILLY 7 b m £0
5	9-12	Ayr	7.2sft	[30]	5274 t

LADY VEE 2 b f £0
39	8-11	Hami	6g/s		4006
56	5-10	Catt	6g/f		4436
43	10-19	Kemp	8g/f		4792
30	16-18	Newc	6g/f	55	5013

LADY WEST 4 b f £0
2	14-14	Wind	8.3g/f	38	2799

LADY XANTHIA 3 ch f £0
15a	8-10	Wolv	7af	[40]	890
27a	4-7	Ling	10ap	[35]	1244
27a	8-9	Ling	13ap	[35]	1456

LADYS VIEW 3 b f £0
68	11-13	Yarm	10.1gd	84	4613
80	6-11	Good	8gd	82	5027

LADYSTGEORGE 4 b f £0

17a 6-12 Sout 6af 35 85
0 11-11 Wolv 6af [34] 296

LADYWELL BLAISE 6 b m £235
27a	6-16	Ling	7ap	[41]	214
41a	4-12	Ling	10ap	[41]	267
19a	7-11	Ling	8ap	[45]	343
43a	3-10	Ling	8ap	[45]	410
41a	6-12	Ling	8ap	[45]	538

LAFFAH 9 b g £0
0	12-13	Chep	18gd	58	2198 bl

LAFI 5 ch g £50800
88	7-19	Thir	6g/f	92	1767
95	3-17	Epso	6fm	91	2256
103	1-29	ASCO	6fm	91	2581*

LAGGAN BAY 4 b g £2756
77	7-17	Sali	14.1g/s	77	1502
75	6-11	Newb	12g/f	75	1759
72	7-21	York	11.9gd	75	3999
69	7-17	Newm	14.8gd	75	4196
67	19-34	Newm	18sft	72	5135 vis
76	2-11	Newm	16sft	70	5271 bl

LAGGAN MINSTREL 5 b g £0
31a	7-9	Wolv	7af	55	31 P
39a	14-16	Ling	7ap	54	55 T
28a	8-15	Sout	6af	[48]	167
0	12-12	Sout	8af	45	530
10	12-13	Leic	7g/f	[52]	1827 p

LAGO DI COMO 7 b g £1460
52a	1-7	SOUT	11af	[45]	1589* t
41a	9-13	Ling	12g/f	60	1986 t

LAGO DORTA 4 ch c £4600
95	6-10	Donc	8gd	[109]	922
101	4-6	Newm	9gd	[109]	1168
80	7-10	Ches	10.3gd	[106]	1585
87	8-10	Good	9.9g/f	[104]	1862
103	6-31	Asco	8g/f	100	2489
100	6-18	Newb	8gd	100	3265
83	12-12	Sali	8gd	[100]	3886
93	11-14	Newb	7g/f	[99]	4638
69	22-22	Newm	8sft	97	5103

LAGOSTA 4 ch g £0
0	13-13	Thir	12g/f	[46]	1768

LAHOB 4 ch c £213
38	8-10	Newm	12g/f	64	2530
54	6-7	Newm	14.8g/f	61	3281
24	7-12	Newm	12g/f	[58]	3783
40	10-11	Yarm	14.1gd	55	3998
35	7-13	Warw	12.6g/s	[50]	4665
44a	3-12	Wolv	9.5ap	[45]	5234

LAIRD DARA MAC 4 b c £0
0	7-9	Sout	12af	[40]	774

LAKAAM 3 b f £733
6a	14-14	Ling	10ap		759
60a	8-13	Ling	12ap		873
59	3-9	Leic	11.8g/s		1016

LAKE CAREZZA 2 b c £0
63	5-13	York	6gd		4988
67	9-17	Yarm	6g/s		5350

LAKE CHARLOTTE 3 b f £5965
70	3-9	York	7gd		3121
63	2-5	Yarm	7gd		3366
70	3-8	Yarm	6gd		3873
66	1-11	BEVE	5g/s	[70]	4237*
57	6-9	Pont	6g/f	70	4627 T

LAKE CHINI 2 b c £1463
54a	11-14	Ling	7ap		4970
75	7-19	Leic	7gd		5055
80	2-11	Newm	6sft		5265

LAKE DIVA 3 ch f £3627
59	3-12	Newc	8gd		4407
55	4-8	Hami	9.2g/s	[61]	4821
36	10-13	Pont	8g/s	[91]	5153
61a	1-11	WOLV	8.6ap	[57]	5356*

LAKE EYRE 4 b f £612

0 10-12 Wolv 6af [39] 33
41a 3-11 Sout 6af 37 91
34a 9-12 Wolv 6af [39] 242
47a 3-13 Sout 6af [39] 254
50a 5-13 Sout 6af [45] 319
30a 9-13 Wolv 6af 45 384
31a 8-9 Sout 6af [47] 459
29a 5-8 Sout 6af [45] 1588
30a 5-10 Sout 6af [45] 1837

LAKE GARDA 3 b c £28481

82	5-5	Hayd	5sft	85	1106
84	3-9	Hayd	5g/s	85	1344
93	1-14	CHES	6.1g/s	85	1570*
95	1-7	NOTT	6.1g/s	[91]	1771*
53	22-22	Donc	5.6fm	93	4459

LAKE O GOLD 5 ch m £0

37	8-20	Catt	15.8gd	47	4965

LAKE OF DREAMS 5 b g £0

52	11-15	Leic	10g/s		1358
35	12-13	Wind	10g/f		2453
29a	5-10	Sout	14af	40	3096

LAKE VERDI 5 ch g £1352

39	14-18	Wind	6g/f	[60]	1806 t
57a	4-12	Ling	6ap	[60]	2016 t
53	3-5	Folk	5g/s	54	3050 t
52	9-11	Bath	5g/f	[53]	3372 t
51	7-16	Ling	6g/f	52	3602 t
51	2-6	Yarm	6g/f	[52]	3710 t
23	6-9	Newm	6gd	50	3924 t
6	10-16	Folk	6g/f	[46]	4370 t

LAKE WAKATIPU 2 b f £1115

59	7-14	Leic	6g/f		3517
51	4-11	Hami	6g/s		4006
53	3-7	Ches	7g/f		4511
37	6-8	Hayd	8.1sft	[57]	4782
55	6-9	Ayr	7.2sft	[57]	5064

LAKELANDS LADY 3 ch f £0

40a	10-11	Sout	6af	77	255
37a	13-15	Sout	6af	72	550
54a	7-11	Sout	5af	67	655
42a	11-11	Sout	5af	64	859 P
29	17-20	Redc	6g/f	54	3767
42	9-18	Pont	5g/s	49	3974
23	14-16	Warw	6g/s	[45]	4995
37	4-20	Yarm	6g/s	[45]	5121
45a	4-12	Wolv	7.1ap	[54]	5358

LAKESDALE 2 b f £6302

35	11-11	Good	5gd		2020
63	2-7	Chep	6.1gd		2115
60	2-6	Yarm	7g/f		2343
50	9-17	Nott	6.1gd		2927
62	4-9	Brig	7g/f	63	3297
50	9-11	Newm	7fm	68	3407
64	2-12	Newm	7g/f	[60]	3750
49	3-15	Catt	7sft	[60]	3930
67a	6-12	Ling	6ap	[59]	4179
60	1-17	LING	5af	[59]	4316*
39	10-14	Yarm	7g/s	58	4583
19	13-16	Yarm	8g/s	58	4632
51	8-18	Newc	6g/f	56	5013

LAKESIDE GUY 2 b c £2598

33a	10-11	Ling	7ap		220
7a	15-16	Ling	7ap		290
21a	8-8	Ling	6ap		691
70a	4-5	Ling	5ap		725
20a	8-8	Sout	5af	57	1031 T
60	3-6	Folk	5fm	[55]	2717
55	5-12	Kemp	5g/f	58	3036
56	6-9	Leic	5g/f	[56]	3347
57	2-6	Folk	5g/f	[56]	3725
27	11-14	Folk	6gd	55	4116
54a	3-12	Wolv	6ap	[54]	5162
53a	4-11	Wolv	5g/f	[55]	5363

LAKOTA BRAVE 9 ch g £11367

87a	1-10	WOLV	8.5af	80	5*
92a	2-13	Wolv	8.5af	86	44
88a	2-12	Ling	8ap	[90]	234
75a	5-10	Wolv	9.4af	90	278
87a	2-8	Wolv	8.5af	[90]	360
88a	4-13	Ling	10ap	88	433
72a	7-10	Wolv	8.5af	[88]	511
43a	13-13	Ling	10ap	88	519
23a	10-12	Wolv	8.5af	86	688
75a	6-8	Wolv	7af	[83]	838 t
68	4-7	Sali	8sft	[70]	4581
56	10-16	Bath	8gd	69	5022
68	2-17	Yarm	8g/s	[66]	5348

LALTRO MONDO 2 b c £13317

102	2-4	Curr	5g/f		1994
106	3-7	Curr	6g/f		2819

LAMA ALBARQ 2 ch c £0

45	14-20	Wind	6fm		2970
55	6-7	Folk	6g/f		3722
57a	10-14	Ling	7ap		4970

LAMBRIGGAN LAD 2 b g £0

26	9-11	Bath	8gd		4544
53a	9-14	Ling	7ap		5078
30	8-10	Nott	10hvy		5188

LAMH EILE 2 b f £11168

80	1-11	AYR	6g/s		2569*
91	1-7	CATT	7g/f		3189*
89	3-10	Asco	7gd		3774
73	13-21	Donc	6.5fm	88	4457

LAMPOS 4 b g £2536

40a	3-10	Wolv	12af	[45]	315
52a	1-12	SOUT	14af	[45]	443*
57a	2-10	Sout	16af	51	491
44a	5-8	Sout	16af	51	554
37a	7-16	Sout	14af	55	1033
47	7-12	Sout	16gd	54	1285 vis
0	11-12	Newc	14.4sft	54	1396 vis
37a	8-11	Wolv	12.2ap	54	5117 p
47a	7-13	Wolv	16.5ap	51	5366

LANAS TURN 2 b f £283

7	14-15	York	5g/f		2056
41a	5-14	Sout	7af		2492
34	8-10	Beve	7.5gd		2652
32	16-17	Nott	6.1gd		2927
52	4-11	Thir	7g/f		3570
43	6-14	Thir	7g/s	[52]	4206 BL
45	9-16	Beve	7.5g/f	52	4597 bl

LAND ARMY 3 b f £0

39	13-18	Wind	8.3g/f		1810

LAND N STARS 4 b g £21006

0	9-13	Kemp	14.4hvy	75	1516
85	1-14	ASCO	16.2g/f	72	1928*
78	5-29	Asco	20g/f	79	2471
82	4-12	Newm	16.1g/f	79	3032
88	1-13	GOOD	16g/f	79	4527*
92	3-13	Yarm	16g/s	85	4634
89	6-34	Newm	18sft	82	5135
78	5-11	Newm	16sft	85	5271

LAND OF FANTASY 5 ch g £4757

61a	1-12	LING	16ap	56	478*
62a	2-8	Sout	16af	59	554
61a	3-8	Ling	16ap	59	733

LAND OF NOD 2 b f £281

62a	7-12	Ling	8ap		19
55	4-9	Warw	8.1sft		1089
51	7-12	Newb	10g/f	63	3255
44	14-16	Thir	12g/f	62	3573 BL
50	5-16	Brig	7sft	[60]	4144 VIS
40	6-19	Chep	8.1g/s	[60]	4366 vis
1	16-18	Good	8gd	53	4750 vis

LANDESCENT 3 b g £3912

53a	2-10	Ling	12ap	[52]	24 vis
49a	6-14	Ling	12ap	[55]	103 vis
43a	6-13	Ling	16ap	55	137 vis
35a	9-12	Wolv	10ap	[53]	272 vis
44a	7-13	Ling	12ap	53	342
27a	4-4	Wolv	14.8af	[50]	426
47a	5-13	Ling	13ap	[46]	602
49a	1-14	LING	10ap	[45]	705*
51a	1-14	LING	10ap	[45]	828*
33a	5-7	Wolv	9.4af	50	961
41	6-11	Bath	10.2fm	50	1899

LANDING STRIP 3 b g £1017

77a	3-13	Wolv	6af	77	41
77a	4-15	Sout	5af	77	64
70a	8-16	Sout	5af	77	171
4	20-20	Kemp	6gd	77	1138
0	20-20	Wind	6g/s	77	1255
54	5-8	Bath	5.7fm	[74]	2669
13	11-11	Brig	5.3gd	72	2957
22	25-26	Good	6fm	72	3569
20	11-12	Brig	5.3g/s	66	4140
35a	7-12	Wolv	6ap	66	4984

LANDINIUM 5 b m £12803

98	4-12	Kemp	10gd	[104]	1139
95	4-6	York	10.4g/s	[100]	1684
94	1-5	SAN	12g/f	[100]	2301*

LANDOFHEARTSDESIRE 4 b f £0

0	14-14	Sout	8af	48	62 vis
19a	6-9	Sout	7af	[43]	304 vis
4a	7-13	Sout	7af	[45]	356 vis
15	16-18	Nott	8.2gd	[45]	1992 vis

LANDUCCI 3 b c £6953

69a	2-8	Wolv	8.5af		1220
50	7-18	Wind	8.3sft	68	1647
59	6-14	Wind	8.3g/f	66	1956
67	1-16	BRIG	7sft	[63]	4144* T
67	3-14	Epso	7gd	65	4465 t
67	4-17	Ling	6g/f	65	4740 t
54	10-19	Newc	7g/f	65	5014 t
71a	2-12	Wolv	7.1ap	[65]	5325 t

LANE MARSHAL 2 gr c £0

48	6-6	Newc	5sft		1274
51	5-9	Pont	5sft		1424
13	15-16	Ripo	5g/f		1780
30	7-7	Beve	5g/f		2167
47	7-14	Beve	7.5sft		2939 BL
42	6-6	Leic	5g/f		3209 bl
46	5-15	Catt	7sft		3930 bl
26a	11-14	Sout	6af		4127 bl
37	5-9	Ripo	6gd		4277 bl

LANGE BLEU 5 ch g £0

23	8-9	Hami	12.1gd		1507 e
0	11-11	Muss	9g/f		4550

LANGFORD 4 ch g £17933

81	2-14	Donc	8g/f	[79]	1877
87	1-23	RIPO	8g/f	87	2010*
84	12-31	Asco	8g/f	87	2489
79	15-20	Newm	8fm	85	3001
90	1-6	HAMI	8.3g/f	[85]	3205+
89	4-8	Hayd	8.1fm	86	3797
63	11-11	Good	9g/f	86	4525
83	11-18	Newb	10gd	86	4681
84	5-14	Asco	8g/f	86	4813
69	19-32	Newm	9g/f	86	4916

LANGSTON BOY 2 b c £3512

55	4-5	Leic	5g/s		1014
70	2-5	Leic	5g/s		1353
70	3-12	Beve	5sft		1631
71	9-13	Newm	7g/f	73	3065
80a	2-14	Ling	7ap	70	4177
69	4-7	Ches	7g/f	73	4509
56	3-12	Newm	8gd	73	5089

LANOS 5 ch g £0

55a	4-14	Ling	13ap	60	264 t
47a	5-6	Sout	12af	60	388 t
51a	5-14	Ling	12ap	59	711 t
58	5-14	Kemp	14.4sft	59	948 t

LAPADAR 4 b f £0

37a	8-11	Wolv	16.2af	65	48 p
44a	5-10	Sout	14af	65	90 p
0	9-10	Wolv	14.8af	[60]	125 BL
17a	6-9	Sout	16af	54	336 bl
23a	4-5	Sout	12af	[50]	446 p

LAPDANCING 3 ch f £0

31	9-11	Muss	9g/f		1095
10	8-8	Hami	9.2gd		1505

LARA BAY 4 b f £0

43	11-16	Redc	10g/f	64	1821
36a	12-13	Ling	12g/f	64	1986

53 9-10 Wind 10fm 60 2761 T

LARA FALANA 6 b m £10079
54a	7-10	Ling	7ap	60	799	
61a	2-9	Ling	10ap	60	876	
57a	5-13	Ling	10ap	[60]	912	
69	4-7	Ling	10g/f	66	2015	
70	2-11	Brig	9.9fm	66	2260	
63a	6-14	Ling	10ap	61	2392	
67	4-11	Folk	9.7fm	68	2719	
69a	1-7	LING	10ap	61	3287*	
56	8-12	Good	9fm	68	3535	

LARAD 3 br g £5452
43a	3-12	Ling	8ap	[45]	538	BL
62a	5-8	Ling	10ap	[45]	626	bl
0	9-9	Ling	8ap	[53]	717	bl
30a	7-12	Ling	8ap	50	845	bl
42a	5-10	Ling	8ap	50	917	bl
41a	5-12	Ling	8ap	[45]	1073	bl
49a	1-8	LING	10ap	[45]	1183*	bl
49a	3-6	Ling	8ap	[45]	1246	bl
51a	3-7	Wolv	9.4af	51	1324	bl
44	4-14	Warw	8.1sft	47	1529	bl
28	6-9	Folk	7sft	47	1577	bl
49	1-10	BEVE	9.9g/f	[45]	1946*	bl
43	7-11	Hayd	10.5g/s	50	2226	bl
50	6-14	Redc	10fm	48	2299	bl
43	7-14	Bath	10.2fm	48	2664	bl
31	6-12	Newb	10gd	48	3916	bl
40	5-10	Brig	9.9fm	46	4763	bl
34	9-16	Nott	10gd	46	4857	bl
38	4-15	Yarm	10.1g/s	[45]	5122	bl
49a	1-12	WOLV	9.5ap	[40]	5209*	bl

LARAS GIRL 2 b f £1013
37	9-16	Pont	6g/f		2275
35	4-4	Brig	7g/f		2640
35	8-9	Ling	6gd		3020
20	10-13	Catt	7g/f		3349
48	3-13	Sali	7g/f	[40]	3864
55	3-14	Thir	7g/s	[51]	4206
18	11-16	Yarm	8g/s	51	4632

LARGO 4 ch f £365
77	10-19	Newm	12g/f	91	1484
89	5-10	Sali	10g/f	90	1721

LARGS 4 ch f £2617
39a	8-11	Wolv	7af	48	562
45a	3-13	Sout	6af	[46]	659
56a	3-13	Sout	7af	[45]	858
46a	2-10	Sout	6af	[45]	907
30	6-15	Folk	6g/s	48	1267
48a	3-15	Sout	6af	48	1750
52a	2-12	Wolv	7af	47	2049

LARK IN THE PARK 4 ch f £0
14a	12-12	Ling	8ap	49	1045	
8	11-14	Hayd	8.1g/s	47	1348	
24	9-9	Pont	8g/f	44	2604	
41	5-14	Pont	8g/f	42	2993	T
32	10-14	Bath	8g/f	40	3963	
4	11-15	Carl	9.3fm	[40]	4505	t

LARKING ABOUT 4 ch f £1257
19	11-11	Beve	9.9sft	65	1633	
39	9-11	Bath	10.2fm	62	1899	
35	13-18	Newm	12fm	57	2088	
52	6-11	Sand	14g/f	52	3340	
50	7-11	Yarm	14.1gd	52	3998	BL
55	2-10	Yarm	16sft	52	4151	bl
0	13-13	Redc	14.1fm	51	4340	bl

LARKWING 3 b c £27218
90	2-14	Wind	10g/s		1055
79	3-8	Ches	10.3gd		1597
82	1-7	NEWM	12g/f	[85]	1936*
90	2-16	Good	12fm	84	3534
87	5-10	York	11.9gd	88	4324
0	S-13	Kemp	12g/f	[88]	4715
86	7-17	Newm	12g/f	88	4889

LARKYS LOB 4 b g £11137
0	12-15	Sout	8af	50	84	e
50a	2-10	Wolv	6af	45	245	
46a	2-12	Wolv	6af	[48]	297	
50a	1-9	SOUT	7af	[48]	304*	

47a	4-11	Wolv	7af	54	378
45a	5-11	Wolv	7af	48	558
44a	3-9	Sout	7af	[47]	639
45a	2-12	Wolv	6af	[47]	646
43a	4-9	Sout	7af	[47]	661
36a	6-9	Wolv	7af	47	684
49a	3-11	Wolv	6af	[45]	778
61a	1-6	SOUT	6af	[45]	1405+
53a	2-8	Sout	6af	[45]	1588
55a	2-15	Sout	6af	51	1750
66a	1-13	WOLV	5af	53	2201+
46a	6-14	Sout	6af	[63]	2502
50	2-20	Beve	5g/s	45	3180
45	3-19	Donc	5g/s	45	3220
63a	5-13	Wolv	6ap	63	5010
29	9-13	Muss	5g/s	[47]	5146
61a	8-13	Wolv	5.1ap	65	5341

LAS RAMBLAS 7 b g £0
26	13-15	Carl	5fm	[48]	4508	t p
35	19-26	Ayr	5g/s	48	4618	t p
11	8-9	Hami	6g/s	[45]	4817	bl e
12	9-10	Ayr	6sft	[45]	5278	t p

LASANGA 5 ch g £1272
54	14-14	Wind	8.3gd	[80]	4122
45	17-19	Kemp	10fm	77	4392
71	2-11	Wind	8.3g/f	[75]	5054
62a	6-12	Wolv	7.1ap	[70]	5340

LASKA 3 br f £866
65	4-15	Leic	6g/f		1829
58	4-7	Pont	6g/f		2042
64	11-11	Warw	7.1fm		2574

LASSER LIGHT 4 b g £0
47	10-13	Sali	9.9gd		2700
54	7-13	Wind	8.3gd		3828
55	5-5	Good	11sft		4188
6	11-12	Brig	11.9fm	55	4764
33a	12-13	Wolv	8.6ap	[50]	5212

LAST APPOINTMENT 4 b c £883
81	5-16	Good	7g/f	80	1817
70	7-7	Good	7gd	79	2223
82a	3-13	Ling	7ap	78	3791
59a	13-14	Ling	7ap	79	4180

LAST CHAPTER 2 b g £0
37	16-19	Newm	7g/s		5285

LAST LOVE 3 b f £7186
99	1-	LEOP	7sft	1299*

LAST PIONEER 2 b g £761
60	9-12	York	6gd		3122
50	9-14	Thir	7g/s		4204
69	4-8	Hami	8.3g/s		4816
67	4-12	Ayr	8sft	65	5065

LAST REBEL 5 b g £0
40a	6-8	Ling	7ap	[79]	1247
0	15-15	Wind	11.6g/f	[70]	2267

LASTING DELIGHT 2 b f £2317
67a	1-13	WOLV	8.5af		111*
37a	8-10	Sout	8af	70	190
0	W-7	Ling	10ap	68	325
53a	10-11	Ling	10ap	68	497

LASTING IMAGE 2 br f £0
24	15-17	Yarm	6gd	4610

LASTOFTHEWHALLEYS 6 b m £0
0	9-9	Wolv	7af	[35]	825

LATALOMNE 10 ch g £4164
78	1-15	RIPO	12.3g/f	70	2526*
76	4-7	Hami	13gd	76	2708
56	11-15	Bath	11.7g/f	76	3964
48	12-12	York	13.9g/f	76	4400

LATE ARRIVAL 7 b g £742
10	17-20	Ripo	8g/s	50	1366	
40	9-14	Hami	8.3gd	47	1748	
30	7-14	Carl	7.9fm	45	1954	
38	10-13	Carl	7.9fm	44	2447	vis
36a	2-9	Sout	8af	36	2996	vis
31a	6-16	Sout	8af	36	3159	bl

35	7-19	Beve	9.9g/f	40	3505	bl
42	4-17	Catt	12sft	40	3929	
23	9-14	Pont	10g/f	40	4624	

LATE OPPOSITION 3 b c £12384
77	4-18	Leic	10g/s	62	1017	
71	2-12	Wind	11.6g/s	63	1260	
67	2-10	Wind	11.6gd	63	1382	
68	2-20	Wind	11.6sft	67	1648	
39	11-11	Beve	9.9g/f	67	1834	
62	9-18	Leic	10gd	69	2706	
68	3-15	Nott	10gd	68	3108	VIS
75	1-6	HAMI	11.1sft	[68]	4011*	vis
75	2-6	Newc	14.4sft	68	4287	vis
72	2-8	Ayr	17.5g/s	70	4657	vis
1	11-11	Newm	14g/f	71	4919	vis

LATEEN SAILS 4 ch c £1625
90	7-9	Sand	10g/s	[114]	2128	T
48	15-16	Asco	8g/f	[114]	2470	t
103	5-6	Hayd	10.5fm	[110]	3793	t

LATERAL THINKER 2 b f £9944
72a	2-10	Ling	5ap		1071
64	2-15	Warw	5g/s		1325
73	3-15	Wind	5gd		1380
40a	4-7	Wolv	5af		1652
73	1-6	LING	6gd	67	3022*
59	16-24	Newb	5.2g/f		3266
72	5-10	Kemp	5ap	70	3521
71a	2-12	Ling	7ap	69	3820
63a	6-14	Ling	7ap	71	4177
54	8-14	Yarm	7g/s	70	4583
66	6-19	Ling	6g/f	[68]	4895
62	4-14	Wind	8.3g/f	[65]	5049
67a	1-12	WOLV	7.1ap	[68]	5158*

LATICE 3 ch f £226901
114	1-6	LONG	9.3hvy		1557*
119	1-17	CHAN	12.5g/s		2460*
110	8-13	Long	12sft		4567
116	7-19	Long	12g/f		4956

LATIF 3 b c £525
59	16-19	Newb	8gd		1236
83	4-9	Asco	7g/f		1929 T

LATIN EXPRESS 2 b c £0
38	9-11	Bath	5.7gd	4543
51	14-23	Newm	6g/f	5084

LATIN QUEEN 4 b f £0
37	5-5	Sali	12fm	55	2422
39	8-15	Warw	10.9g/f	50	2910
43	5-12	Wind	10fm	45	3295
47	5-19	Chep	12.1gd	45	3727
9	9-12	Newb	10gd	45	3916

LATIN REVIEW 3 ch f £0
48	19-20	York	6g/f	96	2407

LATINO MAGIC 4 ch c £53667
105	2-7	Curr	10g/s	1560
105	3-6	Leop	7g/f	2455
108	3-8	Curr	8g/f	2820
110	1-8	LEOP	10g/f	3496*
106	4-5	Leop	8g/f	4020

LAUGH N CRY 3 b f £0
46	10-12	Sand	10g/f	2193
61	5-8	Good	9gd	2536

LAURA LEA 4 b g £0
0	P-9	Wolv	9.4af	665
47	12-20	Donc	5g/f	1518

LAUREL DAWN 5 gr g £8123
58a	4-12	Wolv	5af	58	124
64a	5-10	SOUT	5af	58	187*
0	10-10	Ling	5ap	63	231
59a	3-8	Wolv	5af	63	274
56a	7-9	Sout	5af	62	415
39a	11-13	Wolv	6af	61	1221
38	10-15	Muss	5gd	52	1555
46	7-13	Pont	5g/f	[49]	2279
59	1-19	BEVE	5gd	49	2657*
48	5-17	Catt	5g/f	49	2846
63	2-18	Hayd	5gd	59	2951
56	5-12	Bath	5.7gd	61	3146

55	8-17	Pont	5gd	61	3241	
60	6-18	Pont	5gd	61	3463	
58	7-11	Thir	6g/f	61	3574	
38	14-18	Beve	5g/s	60	3852	
55	8-12	Newm	6g/f	60	3942	
43	8-12	Ches	5.1sft	58	4107	
52	8-19	Beve	5g/s	56	4240	
53	3-19	Yarm	6g/s	55	4636	
52	3-14	Catt	6gd	54	4967	

LAUREN LOUISE 2 b f £0

40	11-11	York	6g/s	1687	T
34a	9-14	Sout	7af	2492	t
26	11-13	York	7.9gd	4325	t

LAURENS GIRL 3 b f £317

34a	9-10	Ling	8ap	1021
61	6-11	Folk	9.7g/f	2274
47	4-11	Leic	10g/f	2924

LAURO 4 b f £13491

72a	3-8	Wolv	8.5af	71	1219	
76	2-15	Hami	8.3g/s	73	1602	
78	4-10	Beve	9.9g/s	77	2323	
72	4-12	Ayr	8g/s	[77]	2543	
69	8-15	Hayd	8.1g/f	74	4352	
75	1-8	HAMI	9.2sft	[72]	4694*	
29	12-14	Ayr	10sft	74	5037	
73a	5-13	Wolv	8.6ap	72	5364	

LAUROLLIE 2 b f £0

19	10-11	Ches	7fm	3633
38	12-14	Folk	7gd	4115
47	10-11	Chep	8.1g/s	4363
41	9-12	Wind	6g/s	4945

LAVISH TIMES 3 ch c £937

46a	7-9	Ling	5ap	[52]	405	bl
40a	5-8	Wolv	5af	[47]	619	bl
57a	3-7	Wolv	5af	[45]	703	bl
44	11-12	Catt	5gd	[51]	995	bl
45a	6-8	Sout	5af	51	1031	bl
52	3-14	Bath	5gd	51	1404	bl
47	6-8	Hami	5gd	51	1509	bl
46	8-10	Hami	5g/s	51	1605	bl
44	6-7	Carl	5fm	50	1951	bl
45	5-6	Muss	5g/f	[48]	2808	bl
6a	7-10	Sout	5af	[45]	3156	P
6	11-12	Carl	5.9g/f	43	3655	

LAW BREAKER 5 ch g £12180

84a	5-13	Wolv	6af	85	41
88a	2-12	Ling	6ap	[85]	106
92a	1-13	LING	6ap	85	235+
68a	5-7	Ling	6ap	[90]	431
92a	5-10	Ling	5ap	90	567
90	2-22	Donc	6gd	85	921
90	9-17	Donc	6gd	[85]	952
70	16-19	York	6gd	89	4005
63	12-13	York	6gd	87	4322
83	8-16	Leic	5gd	85	4700
40	16-19	Sali	6gd	85	4855
58a	11-12	Ling	6ap	89	5297

LAW MAKER 3 b g £2955

22a	14-15	Ling	7ap	[40]	263	
28a	11-13	Sout	6af	[40]	319	
23a	9-16	Sout	5af	[35]	374	
24a	10-13	Sout	6af	[35]	444	bl
7a	13-13	Ling	6ap	35	767	bl
39a	6-13	Ling	6ap	[35]	788	bl
34a	9-14	Ling	6ap	35	897	bl
38a	4-12	Ling	6ap	[40]	1075	VIS
40a	2-8	Ling	5ap	[40]	1290	vis
44	3-20	Beve	5gd	[40]	1948	vis
43	7-15	Nott	5.1g/f	[40]	2152	vis
61	4-14	Donc	5gd	[43]	2237	vis
48	3-12	Folk	5g/f	43	2269	vis
43	6-14	Ling	5g/f	46	2585	vis
50	2-17	Warw	5fm	46	2599	vis
41	10-17	Sand	5g/f	48	3341	vis
20	15-18	Pont	6gd	48	3463	vis

LAWAAHEB 3 b c £0

60	8-9	Kemp	12gd	70	2175	
54	14-18	Leic	10gd	69	2706	
28a	13-14	Ling	10ap	[67]	4448	
17	7-7	Epso	10.1gd	[63]	4911	P

LAWGIVER 3 b c £0

17	8-9	Sout	10gd		1283	
2	15-15	Nott	10gd	[35]	1991	P

LAWOOD 4 gr g £5228

67a	4-11	Ling	8ap		697	BL
61a	8-12	Wolv	7af	70	840	bl
78	1-14	NOTT	10fm	[72]	1006*	
78	2-7	Thir	12sft	[75]	1226	
79	4-11	Hayd	10.5g/f	75	1884	
52	12-13	Ches	10.3gd	75	2284	
53	9-10	York	11.9g/f	75	2405	

LAWRENCE OF ARABIA 4 b g £0

56	8-16	Kemp	9gd	58	3187
59	6-13	York	11.9g/f	58	3437
57	6-11	Yarm	14.1gd	58	3998
0	9-10	Yarm	16sft	58	4151
55	8-9	Redc	14.1fm	58	4559
0	14-15	Leic	11.8gd	[56]	5060

LAY DOWN SALLY 5 ch m £594

45a	2-15	Sout	6af	[47]	172	
41a	8-16	Sout	6af	[47]	227	
27a	6-10	Sout	6af	[45]	308	bl
34a	7-14	Ling	6ap	[45]	652	

LAYED BACK ROCKY 2 ch c £1565

37	6-6	Leic	6g/f		3513
63	9-14	Ches	7sft		4102
63	2-7	Ches	7g/f		4511
60	6-6	Hayd	8.1sft	[62]	4783
63	6-14	Nott	6.1hvy	[60]	5342

LAYMAN 2 ch c £94123

116	1-7	DEAU	6gd		3658*
115	2-9	Deau	6sft		4159
116	3-6	Long	7g/f		4955

LAZIO 3 b c £26761

113	2-9	Colo	8gd	1860

LAZZAZ 5 b g £10902

55a	13-14	Ling	13ap	65	147	
44a	9-14	Ling	13ap	62	259	
60a	4-10	Sout	11af	62	330	
57a	3-10	Sout	12af	60	421	
60a	5-9	Wolv	12af	62	467	
57a	3-12	Wolv	12af	60	484	
66a	3-11	Ling	13ap	[58]	515	
57a	3-13	Sout	14af	57	590	
45a	7-12	Wolv	12af	57	634	
60a	2-14	Ling	12ap	57	711	
34	8-16	Leic	11.8g/f	49	1830	
44	5-15	Ripo	12.3g/f	47	2526	
47	6-16	Folk	12fm	47	2718	
47	4-20	Catt	12g/f	46	2850	P
49	3-18	Pont	10g/f	45	2988	
44	4-17	Bath	11.7gd	45	3145	
50	2-19	Chep	12.1gd	47	3398	
43	6-19	Beve	9.9g/f	47	3505	
47	5-10	Catt	13.8g/f	47	3669	
45	5-19	Brig	9.9sft	45	4145	
54	1-14	WARW	16.2g/f	45	4423*	
57	1-13	WARW	12.6g/s	[50]	4665*	
33	9-18	Pont	12g/f	54	4938	
55a	6-14	Ling	16ap	54	5082	
42a	8-12	Wolv	12.2ap	53	5328	
22a	12-13	Wolv	16.5ap	53	5366	

LE CARRE 6 gr g £31944

116	1-7	MAIS	15.5sft		987*
116	3-8	Long	20g/f		4951

LE CHIFFRE 2 br c £545

70	3-13	Newc	7g/f	5012

LE CORVEE 2 b c £7328

98	1-10	DONC	7g/f		3594*
95	3-7	Nott	8.2gd		3991
95	4-5	Donc	7fm		4461
92a	2-8	Wolv	8.6ap	[94]	5007

LE MERIDIEN 6 ch m £6035

55	5-10	Donc	5g/f	55	2429	
20	17-19	Beve	5gd	55	2657	
42	7-14	Newc	5g/s	53	2775	vis
43	7-11	Warw	5.5gd	51	3054	vis
51	6-20	Beve	5g/s	51	3180	vis
46	5-19	Donc	5g/s	51	3220	p
56	1-14	THIR	6g/f	48	3416*	p
43	8-18	Pont	5gd	49	3463	p
56	3-15	Ling	6fm	51	3790	
43	10-12	Pont	5g/s	[51]	3971	p

LE ROYAL 4 b g £2817

103	2-7	Colo	15sft	4838

LE TISS 3 b c £13621

82	4-9	Kemp	9sft	[82]	947
46	9-11	Newb	11g/f	81	1756
82	2-9	Kemp	12gd	78	2175
91	1-5	SALI	14.1fm	79	2418*
92	4-17	Asco	12g/f	86	2519
79	12-16	Good	12fm	89	3534
3	13-13	York	13.9g/s	89	4062

LE VIE DEI COLORI 4 b c £49099

118	3-11	Good	8fm	3533
114	8-11	Long	8g/s	4434
116	3-7	Long	7sft	5070

LEAGUE OF NATIONS 2 b c £1185

65	8-13	Newb	6g/f	1760
36a	5-11	Wolv	6af	2051
80	2-6	Warw	7.1fm	2597

LEAHSTAR 4 ch f £0

0	16-16	Sout	16af	29	206

LEAPING BRAVE 3 b g £2726

77	4-17	Warw	7.1sft	77	1526
73	2-7	Chep	8.1gd	[76]	2116
73	4-11	Chep	7.1gd	76	2370
63	9-12	Leic	8g/f	76	2922
68	8-9	Sand	7.1g/f	74	3338
55	9-14	Chep	8.1gd	70	3733

LEARN THE LINGO 8 b g £0

0	11-12	Wolv	9.4af	939	t P

LEARNED LAD 5 ch g £954

62a	5-11	Ling	8ap	65	136	
57a	10-13	Ling	10ap	65	178	
67a	2-13	Ling	10ap	[62]	569	
67a	5-14	Ling	10ap	68	622	
62a	9-14	Ling	10ap	68	674	
14a	11-12	Ling	8ap	66	1613	
39	12-15	Sand	10g/f	56	2099	
29	12-16	Good	9gd	56	2220	BL
26	15-16	Kemp	9g/f	53	3039	
28	15-16	Kemp	9gd	53	3187	
7	18-19	Good	8g/f	48	3512	
6	14-18	Good	8gd	48	4750	

LEBENSTANZ 4 b f £0

67a	6-12	Ling	8ap		881
69	6-9	Sali	9.9g/f		1719
54	6-13	Wind	10g/f		2453
56	6-13	Pont	12gd	67	3240
51	9-10	Newc	16.1g/s	65	3701
56	8-11	Yarm	14.1gd	61	3998

LEG SPINNER 3 b g £17184

73	3-19	Yarm	8g/f		1130
70	3-7	Carl	9.3fm		2443
80	1-6	BATH	11.7fm		2668*
76	7-9	Good	14fm	78	3556
84	1-7	LEIC	11.8fm	[77]	3816*
87	1-13	KEMP	14.4fm	79	4395*

LEGACY 4 b g £0

54	7-8	Nott	8.2hvy	[103]	5346

LEGAL APPROACH 5 b h £833

95	4-4	Ripo	12.3g/s		1364
78	10-12	Hami	12.1gd	109	1746

LEGAL BELLE 2 ch f £381

70	4-17	Yarm	6g/s	5350

LEGAL SET 7 gr g £19198

33a	11-14	Ling	6ap	66	121
42a	8-13	Ling	6ap	[64]	271
59a	4-11	Ling	6ap	60	728
43a	10-10	Ling	7ap	[60]	765
50a	5-14	Ling	6ap	[59]	819

45a 12-14 Ling 6ap 56 897
53a 2-12 Ling 7ap [53] 1074
25 12-15 Hami 6gd 55 1508
19 15-18 Ayr 7.2g/f 52 1897
42 9-9 Ayr 7.2fm [52] 1910
37 10-12 Newc 6g/f 49 2160 t
37 9-13 Hami 5g/f 49 2320 t
49 4-11 Hami 6gd 45 2477 t
52 2-11 Ayr 6gd 45 2542 t
58 1-8 HAMI 6gd 45 2713* t
63 4-18 Donc 6gd 57 2752 t
51 7-13 Hayd 6gd 56 2884 t
63 2-17 Pont 6g/f 59 2990 t
60 4-10 York 6gd 58 3116 t
49 10-11 Hami 6fm 58 3248 t
46 11-15 Newc 6gd 60 3424 t
65 2-8 Pont 6gd 60 3461 t
52 12-16 Redc 7g/f 63 3809 t
61 4-8 Hami 6g/s [63] 3880 t
58 5-7 Ayr 6hvy 63 4087 t
51 7-12 Redc 6gd [60] 4245 t
56 8-18 Redc 6gd 60 4339 t
62 2-18 Catt 7g/f 58 4438 t
61 4-13 Muss 8g/f [57] 4554 t
56 9-15 Beve 7.5g/f 60 4719 t
24 11-12 Pont 10fm [60] 4757 t
50 5-18 Newc 8g/f [60] 5017 t
65 2-16 Catt 7sft 60 5130 t
56a 5-12 Wolv 6ap [60] 5155 t
59a 7-14 Ling 7ap [60] 5263 t
52a 8-14 Ling 7ap 56 5300 t

LEGALIS 5 ch g £5043
47a 4-13 Wolv 6af [71] 30
53a 10-13 Wolv 6af 69 113
49a 9-11 Wolv 6af [65] 153 P
56a 3-7 Sout 6af [60] 317 BL
58a 2-9 Sout 6af [58] 459 bl
20a 13-13 Ling 6ap 58 471 bl
56a 3-9 Sout 6af [57] 533 bl
58a 1-7 SOUT 7af [57] 589* bl
57a 3-10 Wolv 7af 60 685 bl
37a 6-9 Wolv 7af [56] 825 bl
49a 4-10 Sout 6af [56] 851 bl
52a 2-10 Wolv 7af [55] 890 bl

LEGALITY 3 b f £0
47a 6-14 Ling 10ap 54 236
21a 14-14 Ling 10ap [51] 477
46 6-13 Yarm 10.1gd 51 3492
23 8-13 Nott 10gd 50 3992

LEGALLY FAST 2 b c £0
46 10-11 Newm 8gd 3925
59 9-14 Bath 8gd 5018

LEGEND OF DANCE 2 b f £0
57 12-12 Folk 7gd 3908
54 13-13 Leic 8g/f 4450
49a 8-11 Ling 8ap 4738

LEGION OF HONOUR 5 b h £0
40 11-16 Bath 8fm [60] 2032
0 14-14 Sout 12af 50 3486
9 13-13 Warw 10.9g/f 45 4419

LEICESTER SQUARE 3 ch c £6600
110 2-8 Kemp 8fm [107] 2069 T
100 7-13 Asco 10g/f [107] 2520 t

LEIGHTON 4 b g £2974
64 9-10 Hayd 10.5sft [81] 1104
78 5-19 Ripo 10g/f 80 1781 P
78 4-7 Ayr 10g/f 80 2030
39 7-8 Newc 10.1sft [80] 2687 p
76 2-5 Hami 9.2g/f [78] 3206
68 8-17 Wind 10fm 75 3477
76 3-7 Leic 11.8fm [74] 3816
58 11-13 Warw 12.6gd 74 4274
42 9-9 Kemp 12g/f 74 4360

LEIGHTON BUZZARD 2 b g £0
58 7-15 Nott 6.1g/s 4644
60 10-16 Nott 5.1gd 4859

LEITRIM HOUSE 3 ch c £74099
110a1-9 LING 8ap 1040+
115 1-5 CURR 7gd 1559*

114 4-8 Curr 8g/f 1995
95 7-15 Asco 7g/f [114] 2486

LEITRIM ROCK 4 b g £0
23 15-20 Warw 10.9gd 55 1128
35 8-16 Bath 8fm [52] 2032
45 4-7 Brig 9.9fm [49] 2332
35 6-17 Chep 8.1g/s 44 3087
29 8-11 Yarm 8g/f 42 3706

LEKKA DING 2 b f £0
50a 9-14 Ling 7ap 5076
73 8-13 Donc 7hvy 5200

LEMARATE 7 b g £393
33a 3-9 Wolv 7af [40] 310
37a 3-10 Sout 6af [40] 352 bl
19a 8-16 Sout 8af [40] 442 bl
10a 12-12 Wolv 7af [40] 528
20a 5-8 Sout 8af [40] 635

LENNEL 6 b g £13431
65 5-20 Warw 10.9gd 68 1128
67 7-20 Epso 12hvy 68 1295 bl
62 4-15 Hami 9.2gd 67 1388 bl
51 11-14 Nott 10g/s 66 1776
60 7-7 Ayr 10g/f 66 2030 bl
67 4-14 Ches 12.3gd 64 2285 p
55 13-15 Ches 10.3g/f 64 3099 bl
61 6-10 Hayd 10.5g/s 64 3139 bl
67 4-16 Hayd 10.5sft 64 3276 bl
75 1-13 AYR 10gd 64 3325+ bl
72 3-8 Ches 12.3fm 68 3637 bl
73 2-14 Brig 11.9fm 68 3674 bl
72 3-14 Hayd 10.5gd 68 3741 bl
71 3-9 Ches 12.3sft 71 4076 bl
67 7-12 Epso 12gd 71 4292 bl
69 5-20 Ayr 10g/s 71 4656 bl
64 6-8 Ayr 13.1sft 69 4690 bl
69 2-14 Epso 12gd 67 4910 bl

LENWADE 3 gr f £5344
16 11-14 Sout 10g/s 53 1051
35 10-16 Nott 10gd 51 1240
40a 3-4 Ling 10ap [45] 1454
15a 7-8 Ling 10ap [40] 1713 BL
0 15-15 Beve 8.5g/s 38 3182
27 7-11 Yarm 8g/f 35 3706
31 4-10 Yarm 8g/f 35 3712
33 5-10 Yarm 10.1gd [35] 3874
41 2-11 Brig 9.9g/f 33 3982
41 2-13 Folk 9.7g/f [35] 4372
50 1-10 YARM 10.1gd [40] 4612*
50 3-10 Brig 9.9fm 46 4763
46 2-19 Brig 9.9gd 40 4903
50 2-15 Yarm 10.1g/s [45] 5122

LEOBALLERO 4 ch g £6731
77 5-9 Newm 8gd 78 1891
83 3-11 Newm 7g/f 77 2532 t
80 5-11 Leic 7g/f 80 3210 t
83 4-14 Wind 8.3gd [79] 4122 t
66 15-19 Kemp 10fm 79 4392 t
90 2-15 Newm 7g/f 79 4891 t
64 21-22 Newm 8sft 88 5103 t

LEONALTO 2 ch c £776
59 7-8 Wind 5g/s 1053
67 5-5 Kemp 5g/s 1114
55 3-5 Brig 5.3g/f 1367 BL
54 6-9 Ches 5.1g/f 3097 bl
42 5-7 Leic 5g/f 63 3343 bl
32 8-9 Bath 5g/f [59] 3847 bl

LEONOR DE SOTO 3 b f £0
36a 11-11 Ling 8ap 59 131
53a 6-13 Sout 8af [59] 188
48a 6-13 Ling 10ap 55 215

LEONORA TRUCE 4 b f £0
2a 7-8 Wolv 9.4af 49 157
30a 8-13 Wolv 8.5af [44] 300
17a 11-16 Sout 6af [40] 447
11a 8-12 Wolv 7af [35] 663 bl

LEOPARD CREEK 3 ch f £2400
42 9-11 Catt 6gd 999
24 12-16 Nott 6.1sft 62 1465

57 2-7 Carl 5fm 55 1951 P
39 10-19 Redc 6g/f 55 2125 p
59 2-19 Beve 5g/s 54 2326 p
36 8-10 Carl 5gd 57 2675 p
36 16-20 Beve 5g/s 55 3180 p
0 15-15 Newc 7gd [53] 3426 VIS
40 7-12 Carl 5.9g/f 50 3655
39a 5-15 Sout 5af 47 4043

LEOPARD SPOT 6 b g £0
45 7-9 Hayd 14gd 50 3760
36 8-17 Pont 17.1g/s 48 3970
34 7-8 Hami 13g/s 48 4138 T P

LEOPHIN DANCER 5 b g £2409
39a 8-14 Ling 12ap [38] 103
30a 6-14 Sout 12af [38] 305
23a 7-10 Wolv 12af [40] 315
39a 1-12 LING 12ap [35] 1180*
41a 2-7 Ling 12ap [35] 1287
40a 2-5 Ling 12ap [40] 1411
40a 3-9 Ling 13ap [40] 1456
28 4-8 Brig 11.9gd [40] 1547

LEOS LUCKY STAR 2 b c £12711
92 1-6 AYR 6g/f 2028*
100 1-7 PONT 6g/f 2792*
90 8-8 Sand 7.1g/s 4096
83 10-10 Donc 7fm 4493

LEPORELLO 4 b c £3850
117 3-10 Ches 10.3gd[114] 1585
105 7-11 Epso 8.5fm [114] 2252

LERIDA 2 ch g £0
46 6-6 Hami 5gd 1386

LES ARCS 4 b g £7992
37 10-12 Pont 8hvy 85 1066
51 12-20 Donc 10.3g/s 80 1519
75 2-7 Beve 9.9gd 70 2654 P
80 1-6 HAMI 8.3g/s [70] 2828*
78 3-12 Beve 8.5gd 76 2890
78 6-15 Donc 10.3g/f 77 3598
55 16-21 York 11.9gd 77 3999
51 6-7 Pont 8g/f [76] 4628
47 10-14 Hami 8.3g/s 74 4820
79 3-11 Muss 7.1g/s 72 5144 T

LESCAPADE 2 ch c £2562
84 3-15 Newm 7fm 3005
75 5-5 Ches 7.6g/f 4046
84 4-15 Leic 7g/f 4455
84 3-10 Kemp 8g/f [85] 4712

LESLINGTAYLOR 2 b g £4738
62 5-18 Pont 5g/s 3968
74 3-10 Redc 6gd 4244
80 1-9 CATT 6g/f 4670*
76 5-14 Catt 7sft 75 5126
67 11-20 Donc 7sft 73 5373

LET IT BE 3 ch f £8578
44 2-8 Ripo 10g/s 1363
31 5-16 Nott 10hvy 45 1611
30 7-13 Beve 12.1g/f [45] 1945
43 5-14 Redc 10fm 40 2299
47 1-11 PONT 12g/f 40 2790*
56 1-20 CATT 12g/f 46 3354*
50 5-16 Thir 12g/f 46 3573
55 2-13 Redc 14.1gd 51 4249
44 10-19 Thir 12g/f 51 4594
54 5-13 Newc 16.1fm 51 4868

LET ME TRY AGAIN 4 b g £2500
100 8-17 Newb 12gd [107] 1230
88 4-13 Asco 16.2sft[105] 1418

LET SLIP 2 b f £0
61 12-19 Newm 7g/s 5279

LET THE LION ROAR 3 b c £227009
111 1-5 NEWB 10gd 1208*
111 3-10 York 10.4g/f[108] 1685
119 3-14 Epso 12fm [110] 2254 VIS
115 5-10 Curr 12g/f [110] 2822 BL
116 2-7 York 11.9gd[118] 4001 vis
102 8-9 Donc 14.6fm[118] 4532 vis

LETANG BLEU 6 gr g £0
| 11a | 8-9 | Ling | 13ap | | 787 t p |

LETS GET IT ON 3 b f £4856
62	15-22	Donc	7gd	78	955
66	8-13	Thir	5sft	77	1229
69	5-14	Ripo	6g/s	77	1360
82	2-11	Hami	6gd	75	1745
70	7-13	Hayd	6g/f	75	1881
72	8-9	Pont	6g/f	79	2609
76	5-15	Hayd	6gd	77	2950
61	3-5	Hami	6gd	[76]	3131
52	15-16	Leic	5gd	74	4700
66	6-12	Redc	5sft	[71]	5305

LETS PARTY 4 b f £0
22	11-11	Beve	8.5sft	[52]	1304 t
0	11-11	Pont	8sft	52	1425 BL t
15	7-7	Ches	7.6g/f	[45]	3079 t

LETS PRETEND 3 b f £282
| 63 | 4-10 | Bath | 11.7g/f | | 4414 |

LETS ROLL 3 b g £44238
70	2-11	Ripo	8gd	69	1176
68	6-9	Sand	10g/s	69	1318
77	2-14	Newm	8g/f	70	1930
76	2-12	Sand	9g/f	71	2385
78	3-13	Newc	8g/s	72	2773
83	1-13	REDC	11g/s	73	2960*
87	1-10	RIPO	12.3g/s	76	3261+
81	5-13	York	13.9g/s	83	4062
88	2-8	Ayr	13.1sft	83	4690
87	4-15	Leic	11.8gd	84	5043

LEVANTINE 6 b g £2786
55a	3-16	Sout	7af	[41]	61 P
38a	3-16	Sout	4af	41	86 p
40a	3-11	Wolv	7af	[45]	579 BL
30a	5-11	Wolv	4af	[45]	778 bl
36a	6-12	Sout	8af	[40]	905 p
49a	1-12	LING	8ap	[40]	4659*
48	2-19	Kemp	8g/f	[48]	4795
43	4-13	Brig	8gd	[48]	4902
30a	7-13	Wolv	8.6ap	[45]	5232

LEVELLED 9 b g £2577
0	16-16	Sout	6af	50	92
25a	8-11	Wolv	5af	45	508
8a	9-12	Wolv	6af	40	641
21a	7-10	Wolv	6af	[40]	667
19a	10-13	Ling	6ap	[35]	788
35a	4-10	Ling	6ap	[35]	832 BL
23a	5-12	Sout	5af	[35]	904 bl
23a	5-9	Sout	5af	[35]	981 bl
31a	7-8	Sout	6af	[35]	1199
35a	2-7	Wolv	5af	[35]	1309
32a	3-10	Sout	5af	[35]	1408
24a	3-7	Wolv	6af	[35]	1566
44a	1-12	WOLV	5af	[35]	1799*
24a	11-16	Sout	6af	47	2720
37	6-14	Newc	5g/s	47	2775
42a	5-15	Sout	6af	45	3000
33	14-20	Beve	5g/s	45	3180
38	6-19	Donc	5g/s	45	3220
44	4-20	Redc	6g/f	41	3767
15a	14-15	Sout	5af	42	4043
5	15-16	Warw	5g/s	[45]	4995

LEVITATOR 3 b c £11023
70	9-16	Wind	10gd		1384
72	2-5	Warw	12.6fm		2441
72	2-7	Kemp	14.4g/f	70	3037
68	7-12	Sand	14gd	70	3359
77	1-9	SAND	14g/s	68	3893*
70	4-10	Yarm	14.1g/s	74	4255

LEWIS ISLAND 5 b g £270
49	14-20	Ayr	10g/s	80	4656
62	13-20	York	10.4gd	75	4986
74a	4-16	Ling	12ap	70	5261

LEXICON 4 ch f £0
| 0 | 17-17 | Ayr | 9.1g/s | | 4620 |

LEYAALY 5 ch m £2344
| 0 | 6-7 | Sout | 12af | [30] | 588 |
| 16a | 9-12 | Ling | 12ap | [30] | 1180 |

0	7-8	Chep	10.2sft	[30]	1333 T P
36a	1-8	WOLV	9.4af	[30]	1561*
40a	2-16	Sout	7af	38	2335 p
39a	4-13	Sout	8af	38	2497 p
0	20-20	Kemp	9g/f	38	2857 p

LIABILITY 2 b f £0
36	11-14	Thir	7g/s		3831
58	6-13	York	7.9gd		4325
44	6-11	Newc	7fm		4863

LIAKOURA 2 b c £13124
92	1-16	SALI	7g/s		3111*
85	8-8	Newm	7g/f		3585
101	1-5	SALI	8gd		4328* P

LIAMELISS 2 ch f £0
50	6-6	Leic	6g/f		2399
59	15-16	Kemp	7g/f		3035
55	10-14	Yarm	7gd		3489
25	13-15	Folk	6g/f		4369

LIBERA 3 b f £0
| 55 | 9-10 | Sali | 7gd | | 2659 |

LIBERTY FLAG 3 b f £6848
| 69 | 2-14 | Wind | 8.3fm | | 2974 |
| 73 | 1-8 | SAND | 8.1g/f | | 3858* |

LIBERTY ROYAL 4 b g £4954
75a	7-13	Ling	10ap	78	26
69a	13-13	Ling	10ap	76	134
60a	11-16	Ling	12ap	74	218
69a	6-12	Ling	8ap	71	517
37	10-18	Wind	8.3g/s	69	1059
58	6-9	Epso	8.5hvy	[66]	1298
67	3-16	Good	9gd	64	2220 P
57	8-20	Kemp	9g/f	64	2857 p
66	3-8	Brig	8fm	[64]	3676 p
63	4-12	Brig	8g/f	62	3986 p
70	1-16	SALI	8gd	62	4334* p
53	9-17	Warw	8.1g/s	65	4668 p
63a	9-12	Ling	8ap	68	5079 p

LIBERTY RUN 2 ch c £792
| 47 | 17-21 | Newm | 8sft | | 5097 |
| 80a | 3-10 | Ling | 7ap | | 5259 |

LIBERTY SEEKER 5 ch g £1040
37	8-9	Pont	10hvy	64	1254
45	8-11	Donc	12g/f	60	1875 P
61	2-9	Ayr	15gd	55	3327

LIBRE 4 b g £5033
62	9-19	Donc	10.3gd	70	924 t p
59	5-14	Newc	10.1sft	70	964 t p
59	4-9	Pont	10sft	67	1430 bl
52	10-11	Hayd	10.5g/f	64	1884 p
47	7-14	Redc	7g/f	[61]	2102 p
24a	9-13	Sout	8af	55	2497 bl
63	1-16	BEVE	7.5gd	55	2655* bl t
33	9-12	Hami	9.2g/s	59	2832 bl t
40	14-14	Carl	6.9g/f	60	3229 bl t
45	10-17	Newc	7g/f	59	3700 bl t

LIBRETTIST 2 b c £18048
105	1-11	NEWM	7g/f		3234*
114	1-5	DONC	7fm		4461*
112	5-9	Newm	7sft	[100]	5137

LIEUDAY 5 b g £437
24a	5-9	Wolv	7af	[45]	1266 p
25	14-18	Nott	8.2g/s	48	1778 p
57	3-9	Thir	9g/f	[46]	2216 p
43	10-14	Muss	7.1g/f	49	2615 p

LIFE IS BEAUTIFUL 5 b m £7031
46	6-15	Beve	9.9sft	46	1307
50	1-13	BEVE	12.1g/f	[60]	1945*
40	5-10	Beve	9.9gd	50	2510
51	1-6	BEVE	12.1gd	[50]	2653*
45	6-9	Beve	12.1gd	56	2892
51	2-6	Redc	14.1g/f	[53]	3771
43	4-16	Carl	11.9g/f	50	4348
53	2-19	Beve	9.9g/f	48	4720

LIFTED WAY 5 b h £11358
| 56a | 9-12 | Ling | 8ap | 74 | 932 |
| 80 | 1-12 | SAND | 8.1g/s | 72 | 1352* |

80a	1-12	LING	8ap	74	1613*
61	14-14	Sand	8.1g/f	80	2096
75	6-12	Kemp	7g/s	80	2679
81	5-9	Asco	8gd	79	3465
76	4-8	Sand	7.1g/s	78	3891
68	10-10	Sand	8.1g/s	78	4067
51	14-15	Sand	7.1gd	76	4500

LIGHT BRIGADE 5 b g £0
40a	6-16	Sout	14af	49	1033
40a	7-11	Sout	12af	46	1197
26a	10-13	Ling	12g/f	45	1986
50a	5-11	Ling	12ap	[41]	2588 vis
4	16-17	Warw	8.1g/f	40	2909

LIGHT OF DUBAI 2 b f £630
| 80 | 4-7 | Kemp | 7g/f | | 4359 |

LIGHT OF MORN 3 gr f £8276
75	2-8	Folk	12sft		1272
84	3-6	York	11.9g/f		2058
89	1-14	LING	11.5gd		3335*
94	4-9	Newb	12fm		3629
94	6-10	Donc	14.6fm	[92]	4460
97	4-5	Newm	12g/f	[93]	4886

LIGHT THE DAWN 4 ch f £0
17	14-14	Warw	8.1sft		1527
40	7-16	Hayd	6g/f		2182
14	11-13	Nott	8.2g/f		2633
48	5-17	Leic	7gd	47	5056

LIGHT WIND 3 ch f £13747
70	5-12	Sali	12g/s		1501
80	1-8	CHEP	12.1g/f		2623*
88	1-6	WIND	11.6fm	[79]	2972+
88	5-9	Newb	12fm	[86]	3629
87	6-7	Hayd	10.5sft	86	4781
87	3-6	Good	12gd	86	5028
96	6-12	Yarm	14.1sft	[85]	5254

LIGHTED WAY 2 b f £2384
41	12-13	Wind	6fm		3639
67	6-17	Chep	6.1sft		4052
61	6-11	Bath	5g/s		4200
75	2-11	Bath	5.7gd	[64]	4543
66	2-9	Chep	5.1hvy	63	4706

LIGHTENING FIRE 2 b g £0
59	9-15	Pont	6gd		3239
50	7-8	Muss	7.1g/f		3559
48	12-14	Thir	8fm		4376
50	11-16	York	7.9gd		4997

LIGHTHORNE LAD 2 ch c £0
37	9-10	Newm	5fm		2089
38	11-11	Wind	5g/f		2450
20	13-17	Wind	6g/f		3975

LIGHTNING PROSPECT 2 ch f £0
| 21 | 12-13 | Ripo | 5gd | | 4303 |

LIGHTNING STAR 9 b g £0
| 28 | 7-9 | Wind | 11.6fm | | 3294 bl |

LIGNE DEAU 3 ch c £4388
46	7-11	Pont	6sft		1426
52	5-20	Chep	6.1gd	59	2372
62	3-12	Ling	6g/f	[57]	2586
51	6-11	Donc	6g/s	62	3379
52	6-10	Chep	7.1gd	[59]	3732
31	11-19	Chep	6.1sft	57	4054 VIS
35	6-13	Chep	8.1hvy	53	4709
66	1-19	REDC	6g/s	[53]	5110* BL

LILIAN 4 b f £0
0	6-8	Wolv	9.4af	[46]	299 T P
16a	5-8	Sout	8af	[46]	355 vis
6a	6-9	Wolv	9.4af	[40]	665 e
3a	9-13	Ling	10ap	[37]	3025
30	8-10	Leic	11.8g/f	[46]	3211 vis
13	11-12	Nott	14.1g/f	42	3420 vis
33	6-11	Yarm	8g/f	38	3706 BL

LILLAS FOREST 2 b g £0
| 42 | 11-12 | Thir | 7g/f | | 4591 |
| 63 | 8-11 | York | 7.9gd | | 5003 |

LILLEBROR 6 b h £1055

LILLI MARLANE 4 b f £5781 *(continued)*

46	12-13	Hayd	14sft	65	1109	
47	7-7	Warw	16.2gd	62	3057	
58	3-11	Sand	14g/f	56	3340	
47	11-12	Sand	16.4g/f	57	3861	

LILLI MARLANE 4 b f £5781

70	2-18	Asco	8sft	72	1423	
59	6-15	Hami	8.3g/s	72	1602	
65	9-15	Kemp	10fm	72	2067	BL
54	9-12	Newb	10g/f	70	2354	
75	1-11	FOLK	9.7fm	68	2719*	
58	7-8	Nott	10g/s	72	2929	
45	14-15	Epso	10.1gd	[72]	3216	
66	5-6	Newm	10g/f	72	3749	
46a	11-12	Ling	8ap	69	4743	
73a	4-12	Ling	8ap	69	5079	
42a	8-12	Ling	8ap	69	5238	

LILLIANNA 3 ch f £1163

61	4-7	Nott	8.2sft		1468
47	10-18	Wind	8.3g/f		1810
62	3-11	Beve	8.5gd		2656
47	10-11	Ling	10gd	[65]	3201
55	7-12	Ripo	10gd	62	4282
35	7-11	Yarm	11.5g/s	[60]	4584

LILLS STAR LAD 6 ch g £0

| 0 | 10-10 | Sout | 7af | [30] | 1839 |
| 2 | 13-15 | Nott | 10gd | [30] | 1991 |

LILTING PROSE 2 ch f £0

| 65 | 5-10 | Wind | 6fm | | 3290 |
| 60 | 11-13 | Newm | 6g/f | | 4918 |

LILY LENAT 2 b f £739

37	10-11	Good	5gd		2020
73	4-8	Kemp	5gd		2171
74	3-11	Ling	5gd		2395
55	9-9	Asco	6gd	73	3127
62	13-17	Ling	7g/f	72	4894	P
75a	5-11	Ling	6ap	72	4972	p

LILY OF THE GUILD 4 ch f £2246

54a	2-16	Ling	7ap	54	270	
46a	10-13	Ling	7ap	54	474	
48a	10-13	Ling	7ap	54	565	
56a	2-13	Ling	7ap	52	761	
56a	4-15	Ling	7ap	54	913	
54	4-8	Bath	5.7fm	54	2034	
52	5-17	Ling	7gd	53	2397	
47	8-13	Sali	6g/s	52	3109	
38	13-19	Chep	7.1gd	51	3401	
2	13-16	Folk	6g/f	[50]	4370	
51a	2-12	Wolv	7.1ap	[48]	5233	P

LIMERICK BOY 6 b h £1125

| 86 | 6-9 | Ches | 13.4gd | | 1596 |

LIMIT 2 b f £2142

67	3-8	Hayd	8.1sft		4782
0	9-9	Ayr	8sft		5033
73a	2-11	Ling	8ap		5236
61a	6-12	Wolv	7.1ap		5324

LIMIT DOWN 2 b g £367

65a	8-10	Ling	5ap		13	
46a	10-14	Sout	7af	64	158	
56a	5-11	Ling	7ap	[64]	213	
32a	6-9	Wolv	9.4af	57	351	
52a	5-13	Wolv	6af	55	436	VIS
53a	3-14	Ling	6ap	[55]	495	vis
37a	6-10	Ling	5ap	[53]	548	

LIMITED MAGICIAN 3 b f £0

| 0 | 13-13 | Sout | 6af | | 444 |
| 0 | 9-9 | Sout | 6af | | 1194 |

LIMONIA 2 b f £0

54	5-6	Warw	5hvy		1531
67	6-19	Wind	5g/f		1805
58	7-11	Nott	5.1g/f		2151
70	6-14	Wind	5gd		4121
55	7-9	Chep	5.1hvy	65	4706

LIN IN GOLD 2 b g £0

| 66 | 5-5 | Brig | 8g/f | 81 | 1370 |

LINBY LAD 4 ch g £0

| 58a | 14-14 | Ling | 10ap | 70 | 803 |

| 18a | 13-13 | Ling | 10ap | [60] | 912 | BL |

LINCOLN DANCER 6 b g £8068

51a	16-16	Sout	5af	85	171	
62a	10-16	Sout	7af	78	419	
20a	10-10	Sout	7af	73	611	VIS
79	4-18	Catt	7gd	77	998	
81	3-19	Redc	6sft	76	1145	
80	4-15	Pont	6hvy	76	1251	
86	1-10	WIND	6gd	[78]	1383*	
56	12-17	Donc	6g/s	84	1523	

LINCOLNEUROCRUISER 2 b c £7562

63	5-12	Ripo	5gd		1173
78	2-9	Pont	5sft		1424
80	3-7	Nott	6.1sft		1738
85	1-14	REDC	6fm		2297*
91	2-6	Hami	6gd		2711
53	12-14	Leic	6g/f	88	3212

LINDA GREEN 3 b f £3259

| 63 | 1-12 | CATT | 5gd | [58] | 995* |
| 57 | 4-9 | Muss | 5g/s | 60 | 1457 |

LINDAS COLIN 2 b c £1892

39	12-13	Newm	7fm		4724
80a	2-11	Wolv	8.6ap		4978
78a	2-13	Wolv	8.6ap		5288

LINDENS LADY 4 b f £434

49	10-15	Ripo	6g/f	72	1782	
55	6-9	Ripo	6g/f	[72]	2007	
40	11-15	Pont	6g/f	67	2280	
56	5-8	Thir	8fm	67	2464	
46	6-6	Redc	7g/s	[63]	2564	
48	5-7	Pont	6gd	[60]	3244	BL e
23	12-12	Newc	5gd	57	3427	bl e
52	5-18	Catt	7g/f	53	3670	
51	4-14	Carl	6.9g/f	51	4345	
49	3-16	Yarm	7gd	50	4616	
46	8-16	Catt	7g/f	50	4676	
18a	11-13	Wolv	6ap	[49]	5211	bl

LINDHOLM 4 b c £3994

| 110 | 3- | Sain | 8sft | | 108 |

LINE AHEAD 2 b f £0

| 44 | 16-18 | Nott | 8.2g/s | | 4035 |

LINE DRAWING 3 b c £5376

82	2-8	Ches	10.3gd		1597
78	4-10	Sand	10g/f		2386
70	3-5	Warw	10.9fm		2602
76	3-11	Wind	10gd	[74]	4125
79	2-11	Ripo	12.3gd	[74]	4281

LINENS FLAME 5 ch g £9269

69	1-14	KEMP	14.4sft	54	948*
72	1-9	FOLK	15.4sft	64	1271*
71	2-13	Kemp	14.4hvy	71	1516
31	10-10	Kemp	16fm	75	2073
63	8-10	Sand	14g/f	75	2192
27	16-16	Good	12gd	[73]	4745
75	4-13	Newb	16sft	71	5194
43	10-11	Newm	16sft	71	5271

LINNET 2 b f £0

| 72 | 6-16 | Newm | 7g/s | | 5280 |

LINNGARI 2 ch c £14267

83	3-4	Yarm	7g/f		3707
98a	1-8	LING	7ap		4176*
100	1-4	SAND	7.1gd	[93]	4606*

LINNING WINE 7 b g £12697

81a	13-14	Ling	12ap	93	83
87a	8-13	Ling	10ap	90	134
89a	2-10	Ling	10ap	[90]	179
94a	1-12	LING	8ap	[88]	234*
82a	13-13	Ling	10ap	94	433
96a	2-11	Ling	8ap	93	547
85	4-24	Donc	8gd	83	928
67	8-12	Ches	10.3gd	83	1586
74	6-14	Donc	8g/f	[82]	1877
80	4-8	Newb	8g/f	[82]	2313
75	5-7	Wind	8.3gd	[81]	3826
80	5-10	Sand	8.1g/s	81	4067
59	5-9	Good	9sft	[80]	4266
53a	8-10	Wolv	7.1ap	[94]	4920

| 82a | 1-14 | LING | 7ap | [93] | 5080* |

LINZIS LAD 2 ch g £0

| 37 | 10-11 | Thir | 7fm | | 4375 |
| 66 | 8-14 | Muss | 7.1g/s | | 5330 |

LION HUNTER 5 b h £868

82a	13-14	Ling	10ap	88	625
88a	6-11	Ling	10ap	85	716
88	10-12	Kemp	10gd	[84]	1139
89	3-13	Wind	10gd	[84]	1381
85	8-17	Newb	12g/f	87	1759

LIONS DOMANE 6 b g £0

40a	11-16	Sout	7af	[47]	161
8a	13-15	Sout	6af	[47]	167
13a	9-12	Wolv	6af	[44]	297
40a	5-12	Wolv	6af	[40]	528
22a	6-10	Wolv	6af	[40]	667
15a	8-9	Wolv	7af	[40]	825
0	P-18	Catt	7gd	[57]	996
2a	8-9	Wolv	6af	[40]	1266
27	11-13	Muss	7.1gd	55	1553
0	10-10	Ayr	8g/s	[52]	2544
40	8-13	Muss	8gd	[47]	2967
0	14-14	Ayr	7.2gd	[44]	3324
23	8-9	Ayr	7.2g/f	[44]	3764

LIQUID FORM 4 br g £0

40	10-10	Warw	7.1sft	[85]	1525
79	7-9	Hayd	10.5g/s	85	2185
73	7-12	Kemp	10gd	83	3185
69	6-6	Newm	10g/f	80	3749
72	8-19	Kemp	10fm	75	4392
71	5-13	Yarm	10.1gd	73	4613
62	12-15	Nott	10gd	73	4860

LIQUID LOVER 2 b c £0

57	10-12	Newb	6g/f		2348
30	11-13	Epso	7g/f		2870
56	13-15	Ling	7gd		3285
58	12-15	Leic	7g/f		4455

LIQUIDATE 3 b g £3445

70	1-12	CATT	12gd	62	1000*
25	10-11	Ripo	12.3gd	67	1174
43	10-11	Sand	14g/s	66	2130

LIQUIDO 5 br h £1408

| 103 | 3-7 | Colo | 15sft | | 4838 |

LIRAGE 2 b f £0

| 35 | 12-14 | Hayd | 6sft | | 4769 |

LISA MONA LISA 2 b f £11734

66	1-9	DONC	5gd		929*
69	4-8	Thir	5g/s		1212
73	1-6	YARM	7g/f		2343*
69	10-13	Newm	7g/f	72	3065
62a	4-11	Sout	6af	72	3393
75	1-6	FOLK	7g/f	70	3723*
34	7-9	Ches	7sft	74	4074
59	6-14	Muss	8gd	73	4519

LISEBERG 2 b c £0

| 0 | 14-14 | Thir | 7g/s | | 4206 |

LISS ARD 2 b c £3015

| 100 | 3- | Leop | 9gd | | 10 |

LISSAHANELODGE 5 br g £1899

45a	1-14	LING	12ap	[40]	968*	
47a	2-13	Ling	13ap	[40]	1076	
40	7-13	Brig	11.9g/f	46	1373	
39	6-18	Wind	11.6g/f	46	1960	
42	6-15	Newb	13.3g/f	43	2311	
32	6-9	Yarm	14.1g/f	42	2856	P

LISTEN TO ME 2 g r g £0

44	5-5	Leic	5g/s		1353
30	12-14	Bath	5sft		1538
50	5-13	Sali	7g/f		3864
23	14-17	Ling	6g/f		4316

LISTEN TO REASON 3 b c £3455

65	1-7	CATT	7g/f		3194*
36	11-11	Kemp	6g/f	65	3685
53	8-14	Yarm	7gd	65	3995
50	12-14	Muss	7.1g/f	65	4175

LITERATIM 4 b c £13522				
69	4-20	Donc 7g/s		1518
84	1-6	DONC 7g/f		3595*
90	2-10	Sand 8.1g/s	84	4067
85	8-13	Donc 10.3fm	[86]	4463
91	3-19	York 7.9gd	86	4987

LITERATURE 2 b f £5954			
82	1-12	WARW 7.1g/f	4417*

LITHOS 2 ch c £4486				
78	2-11	Wind 8.3fm		3798
69	6-15	Good 8g/s		4233
79	5-8	Hayd 8.1g/f		4351
84	1-6	MUSS 8g/f	[77]	4552*

LITTLE BISCUIT 2 br f £8603				
69a	1-4	WOLV 5af		938*
69	1-10	THIR 5sft		1224*
69	2-11	Thir 5gd		1634
56	5-9	Muss 5fm		2083
56	4-13	York 5g/f		2358
64	2-8	Muss 5g/f		2611
60	6-8	Ches 5.1g/f	63	3082
58	4-9	Hayd 5sft	65	3271
37	12-19	Bath 5gd	60	5021
53	8-16	Nott 5.1hvy	58	5343

LITTLE BOB 3 ch g £6187				
70	4-11	Ripo 8gd		1177
69	4-14	Thir 8gd		1636
75	2-5	Ayr 9.1g/f	[70]	2025
81	3-16	Donc 10.3gd	[69]	2751
2	7-7	Ripo 9g/s	[75]	3263
75	1-9	NEWC 9g/s	[75]	3697*
52	12-15	Hayd 8.1g/f	75	4352
66	7-20	Ayr 10g/s	73	4656
63	9-14	Ayr 10sft	72	5037

LITTLE BUD 9 br m £0			
38a	7-14	Ling 12ap	14

LITTLE DALHAM 2 b c £10592				
76	4-10	Catt 7g/f		2845
83	2-11	Sali 6g/s		3110
84	1-13	YORK 6g/f		3431*
72	6-8	Sand 7.1g/s	82	4100
63	4-20	Newb 6hvy	82	5225

LITTLE EDWARD 6 gr g £3232				
97a	5-10	Ling 5ap	[99]	883
92	8-11	Newb 5.2gd	97	1207
93	5-11	Good 5g/f	97	1845
91	8-10	Kemp 5fm	[97]	2068
55	16-17	Epso 6fm	94	2256
86	5-8	Sali 6fm	[94]	2421
46	11-11	Sand 5g/s	92	2894
52	23-24	Asco 5gd	92	3466
72	13-14	Newb 5.2fm	90	3628
85	5-16	Wind 6gd	88	3827
58	6-8	Kemp 5sft	[83]	4031
81	4-19	Kemp 6fm	82	4394
74	6-6	Sand 5gd	[82]	4498
62	19-24	Newb 7g/f	82	4642

LITTLE ENGLANDER 4 b g £4721				
49	5-9	Pont 10sft	62	1430
41	9-16	Leic 11.8g/f	59	1830
44	8-11	Leic 10gd	55	2135
61	5-13	Nott 8.2g/f	[52]	2633
62	1-12	NOTT 8.2g/s	55	2931*
52	7-12	Kemp 8g/f	58	3524
43	10-14	Good 8g/f	58	4542
55	4-17	Nott 8.2gd	57	4862
57	4-20	Leic 7gd	57	5046
54	5-15	Nott 8.2hvy	57	5191

LITTLE EYE 2 b g £8898				
63a	4-13	Wolv 6af	65	1
70a	2-10	Wolv 7af	63	112
70a	2-10	Ling 8ap	63	132
68a	3-11	Ling 7ap	68	261
61a	4-8	Wolv 7af	[68]	276
69a	4-11	Ling 10ap	68	497
46a	9-10	Ling 10ap	68	568
70a	3-15	Ling 7ap	[66]	670
56	9-11	Redc 7g/f	[66]	1822
59a	6-12	Ling 8ap	[63]	2394

61	4-14	Wind 8.3fm	62	2971 VIS
55	7-16	Epso 8.5gd	62	3219 vis
68	2-7	Folk 9.7gd	61	3384 vis
71	1-14	KEMP 10g/f	62	3690* vis

LITTLE FLUTE 2 b c £2004				
28a	9-12	Wolv 8.5af	[52]	28
52a	2-5	Wolv 5af	48	237
49a	4-10	Ling 5ap	52	371
44a	7-14	Sout 5af	50	485
30a	7-10	Sout 6af	48	592
40a	7-8	Ling 6ap	48	673
34a	10-13	Ling 7ap	45	761
52a	1-7	WOLV 6af	[45]	1312*
39	6-12	Brig 6g/f	46	2435
34	6-16	Folk 6g/f	[46]	4370
47	4-16	Warw 5g/s	[45]	4995
33	5-20	Yarm 6g/s	[45]	5121

LITTLE FOX 9 br m £0				
35	6-6	Wind 11.6fm	[45]	2972
25	7-7	Brig 11.9g/f	[45]	3715
10a	11-13	Ling 16ap	49	3822

LITTLE GANNET 3 ro f £0			
38a	13-14	Ling 10ap	2740
43	14-14	Ling 11.5gd	3335

LITTLE GOOD BAY 4 b c £0				
93a	11-14	Ling 7ap	98	5262 vis

LITTLE INDY 2 ch c £0				
36	11-11	Wind 5gd		3160
54	11-12	Newm 7g/f		3470
63	10-13	Warw 7.1g/f		4416
54	6-11	Chep 7.1hvy		4703
40a	9-13	Wolv 6ap	[60]	5182

LITTLE JIM 3 b c £202513			
117a1-14	NAD 8af		598*
117	3-9	Nad 9af	989

LITTLE JIMBOB 3 b g £14195				
78	1-7	CARL 9.3fm	[70]	2443*
80	2-9	Leic 8gd	75	2705
68	4-9	Beve 8.5sft	77	2940
80	3-8	Nott 8.2g/f	75	3421
75	5-14	Epso 7gd	75	4465
80	2-7	Pont 8g/f	75	4935
80	4-19	Pont 10g/s	75	5148
66a	8-13	Ling 10ap	75	5299

LITTLE LONDON 3 b g £0				
0	P-8	Good 8sft	79	4265

LITTLE MISS GRACIE 2 gr f £9905				
87	3-8	Kemp 7g/s		2676
83	3-10	Redc 7g/s		2959
80	2-10	Wind 8.3fm		3803
86	1-8	PONT 8fm	[85]	4756*
90	4-9	Pont 8g/s	[85]	5150

LITTLE MISS LILI 3 b f £0			
0	8-8	Brig 8fm	4762
0	13-13	Nott 10gd	4861

LITTLE MISS TRICKY 5 br m £0				
0	8-12	Ling 10ap	[35]	654

LITTLE RICHARD 4 b g £2279				
0	9-12	Wolv 12af	44	75 vis
22a	8-10	Wolv 12af	[40]	315
0	9-12	Sout 14af	[35]	443 p
40a	4-14	Ling 13ap	[30]	537 p
22a	3-10	Wolv 12af	[30]	581 p
40a	1-10	LING 16ap	[30]	650* p
40a	4-15	Ling 12ap	[30]	707 p
40a	8-14	Ling 12ap	[40]	827 p
40a	2-14	Ling 12ap	[40]	968 p
40a	3-13	Ling 13ap	[40]	1076 p
32a	5-9	Ling 16ap	[40]	1414 p
19a	4-5	Wolv 14.8af	[40]	1563 p
17	10-14	Yarm 14.1g/s	[40]	5123 p

LITTLE RIDGE 3 b g £7744				
27	10-10	Leic 6gd	[83]	2137
33	10-11	Hayd 6g/f	[82]	4350
56a	12-13	Ling 7ap	77	4897
81	1-12	REDC 5sft	[72]	5305*

77a	3-12	Wolv 5.1ap	78	5326

LITTLE SKY 6 gr m £0				
0	12-12	Wolv 16.2af	46	7
18a	7-7	Ling 12ap	[45]	1243
2	17-18	Newm 12fm	45	2088
12	9-9	Yarm 14.1g/f	40	2856 e

LITTLE TASK 6 b g £5281				
39	3-10	Beve 8.5g/f	[30]	1943
38	1-15	NOTT 10gd	[30]	1991*
37	4-15	Ripo 12.3g/f	37	2526
44	1-8	MUSS 12g/f	36	2616*
27	14-20	Catt 12g/f	44	2850
39	4-9	Beve 12.1gd	44	2892
34	6-8	Hami 11.1g/f	39	3207
17	11-13	Beve 12.1g/f	35	3502
32a	9-12	Wolv 9.5ap	[45]	5234

LITTLE TOBIAS 5 ch g £4528				
45	6-12	Sout 16gd	51	1285
2	13-18	Nott 14.1sft	51	1469
57	1-10	CARL 14.1fm	50	3549*
53	3-7	Newc 16.1g/f	55	4405
53	3-19	Catt 15.8g/f	54	4675
13	14-14	Pont 17.1g/f	53	4936
56	4-11	Ayr 15sft	53	5032

LITTLE VENICE 4 b f £18180				
54	16-20	Kemp 6gd	78	1138
78	5-19	Sali 7g/f	76	1723
80	3-10	Newb 7g/f	76	2312
90	1-10	NEWM 8g/f	76	2767*
85	11-20	Newm 8fm	86	3001
57	9-10	Pont 8gd	86	3460
76	7-14	Wind 8.3gd	[84]	4122
92	1-11	YARM 8gd	82	4615*

LITTLE WALTHAM 2 ch f £0			
0	14-14	Leic 6g/f	3517
2a	10-11	Ling 8ap	3786
0	8-8	Yarm 6g/s	4250

LITTLE WARNING 2 b f £0			
52	7-11	Bath 5g/f	3962
63	7-11	Bath 5g/f	4409
65	5-16	Nott 5.1gd	4859
24	17-21	Donc 6hvy	5202

LITTLE WIZZY 2 b f £5945				
60	3-9	Donc 5gd		929
44	7-10	Bath 5g/s		1097
75	1-12	WARW 5sft		1524*
73	3-5	Wind 5sft		1646
38	6-6	Wind 5g/f		1808
0	19-19	Bath 5gd	72	5021
2	18-20	Newb 6hvy	66	5225

LITTLESTAR 3 b c £1160				
42	14-17	Leic 10g/s		1019
0	10-12	Wind 11.6g/s	60	1260
23	13-20	Wind 11.6sft	56	1648 BL
26	12-14	Ling 11.5g/f	52	2014 bl
57	2-9	Brig 9.9gd	48	2955
30	11-14	York 10.4g/f	54	4402

LITTLETON LIBERTY 3 b f £0				
6a	8-9	Ling 7ap		764 BL
0	7-7	Wolv 5af	[35]	1309 P

LITTLETON TELCHAR 4 ch c £4407				
78	1-13	WIND 10g/f		2453*
58	7-8	Wind 10fm	78	2973
5	9-9	Good 12sft	76	4183

LITTLETON VALAR 3 ch g £0				
1a	13-14	Sout 8af	40	165 p
0	8-9	Wolv 9.4af	[40]	314 BL
42	4-8	Ripo 10g/s	[30]	1363
25a	4-9	Sout 11af	[30]	1838 bl e
25	7-15	Nott 10gd	[30]	1991

LITTLETON ZEPHIR 5 b m £2183				
34a	7-11	Wolv 7af	47	378
46a	2-12	Wolv 9.4af	47	464 bl
23a	8-12	Wolv 8.5af	46	479 bl
0	12-12	Wolv 9.4af	46	747 bl
46a	1-12	LING 8ap	[45]	1451*
38a	5-7	Sout 7af	[45]	1590

44a	7-15	Sout	8af	48	2725
41	8-14	Folk	9.7g/s	48	3052
38	11-19	Beve	9.9g/f	47	3505

LITZINSKY 6 b g £0

51a	7-11	Ling	16ap	59	605
34	9-11	Nott	16fm	55	1003

LIVADIYA 8 b m £49647

108	2-5	Curr	8g/f	[87]	1997
111	2-6	Curr	10.5g/f	[87]	2004

LIVE IN HOPE 2 b f £0

25	13-13	Redc	6g/f	1818
31	10-16	Pont	6g/f	2275
21	14-15	Pont	6gd	3239

LIVE WIRE LUCY 3 b f £0

52	8-8	Sali	6fm		2421
44	11-11	Donc	7g/s	93	3223
71	9-10	Newb	10fm	85	3630
61	9-10	Nott	10gd	80	3990
44	12-12	Sand	10gd	73	4502
18	14-15	Bath	8gd	65	4827

LIVELY FELIX 7 b g £0

38a	4-16	Sout	6af	[40]	447	
17a	10-12	Wolv	7af	[40]	528	
9a	6-8	Sout	7af	[40]	847	
24a	7-10	Wolv	7af	[40]	890	vis
18a	10-12	Ling	7ap	[35]	1074	BL

LIVIA 3 b f £435

47a	10-15	Ling	7ap		472	
57a	6-13	Ling	10ap		601	
46a	10-11	Ling	8ap		696	
55a	4-15	Ling	7ap	54	815	
11	12-12	Folk	6sft	53	975	
50	6-14	Warw	7.1sft	54	1085	
0	9-9	Folk	7sft	50	1577	BL
19	12-14	Sali	7g/f	[50]	1720	P
35	7-13	Bath	8fm	45	2667	e
10	14-16	Nott	10gd	45	4857	VIS
49	2-17	Warw	8.1g/s	[45]	4992	vis
42a	4-12	Wolv	8.6ap	[50]	5230	vis
31a	11-12	Wolv	8.6ap	[50]	5329	vis

LIVVIES LADY 2 b f £0

37a	11-14	Ling	7ap	5078
17a	14-14	Ling	7ap	5257

LIWAS LAKE 2 ch f £750

67	3-6	Sand	5g/f	2097	
35	7-9	Wind	5g/f	2795	T
38	11-12	Thir	5g/s	3832	

LIZARAZU 5 b h £0

58	9-10	Nott	8.2gd	[75]	3107
63	8-11	Kemp	7g/f	72	3685
44	11-12	Leic	8fm	72	3813
42	12-13	Wind	8.3g/s	69	4221
50	10-20	Yarm	7sft	63	5256

LIZHAR 2 b f £1200

73a	3-6	Sout	6af	73	182	
56a	5-5	Wolv	5af	72	237	
63a	4-8	Wolv	6af	72	422	
62a	6-14	Sout	5af	69	485	
57a	4-9	Ling	5ap	[69]	492	
25a	7-9	Sout	6af	[69]	533	
48a	4-10	Ling	5ap	[69]	548	
57a	2-7	Wolv	5af	[60]	703	BL
46a	8-9	Wolv	5af	[57]	835	bl
57a	4-11	Sout	6af	57	872	
37a	6-9	Ling	6ap	[57]	1012	
45	8-9	Bath	5g/s	54	1102	
18	14-19	Leic	6g/f	50	2925	

LLAMADAS 2 b g £3217

72	3-10	Muss	5gd		1550	
59	9-18	York	5g/f		2360	
65	3-11	Ayr	6g/s		2569	
59a	4-11	Sout	7af		2995	P
53	10-12	Newc	7gd		3425	p
68	3-12	Muss	5g/f	64	4172	BL
68	6-12	Carl	5g/f	[64]	4343	bl
64	6-8	Muss	5gd	[67]	4517	bl
46	15-18	Carl	7g/f	67	4673	bl
66a	2-12	Wolv	5.1ap	[64]	4922	VIS

54a	7-13	Wolv	6ap	[64]	5182	vis

LOADED GUN 4 ch g £2668

0	12-12	Sout	8af	[62]	460
55	2-8	Ayr	10hvy	52	4084
56	4-14	York	11.9gd	54	4327
51	7-18	Ayr	10.9sft	54	4623
60	3-13	Ayr	10sft	[53]	5066
51	4-17	Newb	9sft	53	5198
31a	13-13	Wolv	9.5ap	55	5361

LOADERFUN 2 br c £10326

78	4-18	Leic	5fm		2109
90	2-15	Wind	6gd		3163
100	1-8	SALI	6g/f		4577*
82	2-2	Ripo	6gd	[100]	4789

LOBENGULA 2 b g £0

49	10-13	York	6gd	4988
69	5-14	Redc	7sft	5301

LOBOS 4 ch g £2331

67a	1-11	LING	8ap	62	131*

LOCAL POET 3 b c £6567

73	1-8	DONC	6gd	[98]	953*	
92	5-7	Newm	7g/s	[98]	1150	
90	8-15	Ches	5.1g/s	95	1572	
90	5-9	Hayd	6g/f	[92]	1918	
63	17-20	York	6g/f	92	2407	T
75	18-19	Newm	6fm	89	3002	t
72	14-20	Hayd	6fm	86	3792	t

LOCATOR 2 b c £0

62a	5-11	Ling	6ap	51
51	10-14	Thir	8gd	1636
39	17-17	Newb	8g/f	1762

LOCH INCH 7 ch g £3186

42	14-18	Good	5g/f	57	1867	bl
42	9-10	Brig	5.3g/f	57	2044	bl
29	12-12	Folk	5g/f	53	2269	bl
52	4-17	Warw	5fm	51	2599	bl
26	9-11	Brig	5.3gd	51	2957	bl
55	4-15	Wind	5gd	51	3165	bl
53	2-15	Chep	5.1gd	51	3403	bl
57	3-11	Thir	6g/f	52	3574	bl
58	3-16	Wind	5fm	52	3640	bl
0	P-15	Bath	5.7g/f	52	3966	bl

LOCH LAIRD 9 b g £3791

45a	7-14	Ling	6ap	51	328	
26a	8-13	Ling	6ap	49	448	
51a	1-15	LING	7ap	47	846*	
47a	9-15	Ling	7ap	53	913	
45	5-11	Folk	6sft	54	1578	
45	10-16	Brig	7fm	52	2258	
39	13-17	Ling	7gd	52	2397	
50	4-17	Brig	7g/f	49	3176	
44	4-12	Sali	8g/s	48	4077	
49	3-10	Brig	7sft	48	4168	
32	10-20	Chep	7.1g/s	47	4367	P
33a	7-14	Ling	7ap	[49]	4660	

LOCH QUEST 2 ch c £0

81	5-12	Good	8g/f	4522
66	8-11	Good	8gd	4746
60	8-14	Bath	8gd	5018

LOCHBUIE 3 b c £37251

74	4-14	Donc	10.3gd	72	923	
84	1-11	RIPO	12.3gd	72	1174*	
91	1-9	CHES	12.3gd	78	1582*	
97	3-10	Sali	12gd	86	2660	
100	1-9	GOOD	14fm	90	3556*	
100	4-13	York	13.9g/s	97	4062	
102	4-20	Hayd	14fm	97	4383	
97	3-7	Newm	14g/f	[98]	4878	

LOCHRIDGE 5 ch m £17874

104	2-10	Kemp	5fm	[106]	2068
92	14-19	Asco	5g/f	[106]	2468
76	13-14	Asco	6fm	[106]	2580
104	3-9	York	6g/s	[103]	3075
105	2-8	Donc	6g/f	[102]	3596
88	4-12	Pont	6g/s	[101]	3971
94	14-19	Hayd	6fm	[101]	4384

LOCK AND KEY 2 b f £16637

100	2-7	Leop	7g/f		3494
108	2-11	Curr	6g/f		4431

LOCKSTOCK 5 b g £6906

55a	4-9	Wolv	7af	63	31	
68a	1-14	SOUT	8af	60	93*	bl
64a	4-11	Sout	8af	65	186	bl
54a	7-12	Sout	8af	65	530	bl
24a	13-13	Ling	10ap	65	726	P
75	1-13	BATH	8sft	65	1542*	p
65	8-18	Good	8g/f	72	1849	p
62	7-11	Chep	7.1gd	72	2370	p
63	9-15	Sand	7.1gd	71	4500	
72	5-14	Wind	8.3g/f	70	4832	p
69	4-16	Bath	8gd	70	5022	p

LOCOMBE HILL 7 b g £16005

44a	8-14	Sout	8af	64	62	
30a	12-16	Sout	6af	64	94	
41a	11-15	Ling	7ap	[60]	366	
60a	2-4	Sout	8af	[60]	417	
4	10-14	Pont	8hvy	[64]	1253	
11	9-9	Muss	7.1fm	62	2086	
60	5-13	Hami	6g/f	60	2315	
0	15-16	Beve	7.5gd	60	2655	
62	4-13	Hayd	6gd	60	2884	VIS
57	4-10	Hayd	6g/s	60	3136	
41	11-14	Carl	6.9g/f	60	3229	vis
68	1-15	AYR	7.2hvy	59	4088*	
67	5-14	Beve	7.5g/s	64	4241	
69	3-17	York	6g/f	64	4398	
73	1-18	AYR	7.2sft	64	4622*	
73	2-11	Hami	6g/s	64	4818	
74	2-17	Ayr	7.2sft	69	5063	
38	9-14	Newb	8hvy	70	5227	

LODGER 4 ch c £1008

65	12-13	York	11.9g/s	92	3076
88	6-10	Asco	12g/f	92	3444
90	4-8	Newm	12g/f	[91]	3617
87	9-20	Hayd	14fm	89	4383
85	10-16	Asco	16.2g/f	88	4803

LODGICIAN 2 b c £1868

66	4-7	Newc	6g/s		2774
72	3-8	York	7g/s		3078
54	9-11	Beve	7.5g/f		3500
66	4-14	Muss	8gd	70	4519
56	11-18	Catt	7g/f	68	4673
46	11-18	Pont	6g/f		4934

LOGGER RHYTHM 4 b g £425

59	7-11	Bath	8g/s		1101
51	12-15	Leic	10g/s		1358
52	4-8	Thir	12g/s		1472
30	13-16	Leic	11.8g/f	60	1830
11	15-15	Chep	8.1g/s	56	4300

LOGISTICAL 4 b c £0

0	13-13	Warw	7.1hvy	[67]	1537	
56	10-16	Ling	7g/f	65	2063	
51	5-11	Chep	7.1gd	62	2370	
50	11-17	Newm	7g/f	59	2768	
18	15-16	Kemp	7gd	56	3184	T
38	9-20	Chep	7.1g/s	52	4367	
37	14-20	Chep	7.1gd	52	4488	
29a	9-14	Ling	7ap	[47]	4660	

LOHENGRIN 4 ch c £120000

117	3-14	Sha	8g/f		211

LOITOKITOK 2 b g £0

39a	8-11	Ling	8ap	3786
46	10-14	Kemp	8g/f	4356
67	8-10	Kemp	8g/f	4712

LOJO 2 ch f £4395

38	7-12	Newc	6gd	1869
51	3-8	Hayd	6g/f	2183
65	2-10	Thir	6fm	2461
69	1-4	BRIG	7g/f	2640*

LOLA LOLA 3 b f £0

4	10-10	Good	8gd		2378
28a	8-13	Sout	8af	45	3094
3	18-18	Chep	7.1g/s	43	3900

LOLA SAPOLA 2 b f £5204

37	7-8	Newm	6g/f	3473

```
68  9-14   Newm  7g/f          3944
61  9-9    Newm  7gd           4192
79  1-6    BRIG  7fm          4760*
78  4-19   Pont  8g/s    75    5147
75  7-20   Yarm  8g/s    75    5349

LOLAS DESTINY 3 b f  £0
38a 5-11   Wolv  9.4af  [52]   438
48a 6-13   Sout  8af    [52]   553
0   8-9    Sout  8af    [52]   596

LOMAPAMAR 3 b f  £5554
73  3-5    Good  11sft  [78]   4188
54  12-12  Good  11gd    78    4749
0   13-14  Ling  13ap   [78]   4898
72  1-12   NOTT  10hvy  [70]   5190*

LOMMEL 3 b c  £0
31  15-15  Newb  8gd     93    1206
26  8-8    Muss  7.1g/s  89    1460

LONDONER 5 ch g  £10918
62a 6-13   Ling  10ap    65    178
61a 7-8    Ling  10ap   [65]   294
54a 10-12  Ling  8ap     62    607
54a 8-13   Ling  10ap    59    726
50a 11-14  Ling  12ap    59    801
54a 3-12   Ling  8ap     53    1013
58  2-10   Brig  7g/f    53    1941
57  2-9    Yarm  7fm     53    2150
63  1-11   BRIG  7fm     55    2334*
53  7-17   Warw  8.1fm   61    2440
56  5-17   Warw  8.1fm   60    2572
62  3-11   Brig  7g/f    60    2644
58  5-12   Ling  7.6gd  [60]   3448
66  2-8    Brig  8fm    [60]   3676
38  12-15  Brig  8fm     60    3694
42  7-11   Brig  8g/s    60    4141
69a 1-12   LING  8ap    [60]   4320*
58  6-14   Good  8ap     60    4542

LONE PIPER 8 b g  £196
32a 6-12   Wolv  5af     45    109
16a 12-13  Wolv  5af    [45]   312
30a 8-9    Sout  5af     45    335
12a 9-10   Wolv  5af    [40]   527 BL
36a 6-16   Sout  5af    [35]   720
47a 4-11   Sout  5af    [35]   775
35a 3-10   Wolv  5af    [35]   781
21a 6-12   Sout  5af    [35]   904
42a 6-12   Wolv  5af    [35]   960
0   11-12  Chep  5.1sft [45]   1336 P
31  6-7    Brig  6gd    [40]   1368 P
13  14-16  Nott  6.1gd  [40]   1988

LONER 6 b g  £856
1   15-16  Redc  8g/f    52    2958
55  2-13   Muss  8g/f    50    3526 p
40  9-18   Catt  7g/f    50    3670 p

LONG ROAD 3 b c  £13950
85  2-15   Newb  8g/f          1763
90  2-13   Newm  8g/f          1935
88  2-4    Newc  8g/s          2729
88  1-8    NEWM  10fm   [85]   3007*

LONG WEEKEND 6 b h  £3990
22a 7-13   Wolv  6af    [45]   397 e
38a 6-13   Ling  6af     45    451 vis
35a 6-12   Wolv  7af    [40]   528 e
50a 2-13   Ling  6ap     40    767 vis
45a 1-10   LING  5ap    [40]   788* vis
48a 1-10   LING  5ap    [40]   832* vis
53a 4-12   Ling  6ap     54    844 vis
41a 6-13   Ling  6ap     48    902 vis
7   11-15  Folk  6g/s    48    1267 vis
41  6-18   Bath  5.7g/f  46    1788 vis
37  9-16   Good  6gd     45    2023 vis
12  12-15  Pont  6g/f    45    2280 vis
35  9-18   Ling  6gd     45    2396
34  21-26  Good  6fm     43    3569
43a 4-13   Wolv  6ap    [50]   5211
51a 3-12   Wolv  7.1ap  [50]   5233

LOOK AGAIN 3 ch g  £4273
91  1-9    NOTT  10g/s         4034*
89  4-13   Donc  10.3fm [85]   4463

LOOK AT THE STARS 2 b c  £3588
65  9-15   Wind  6gd           3163
86  1-13   HAYD  6gd          3736*
74  14-16  Curr  6g/f          4153

LOOK EAST 4 b g  £0
0   10-12  Wolv  12af   [35]   114 p

LOOK HERES CAROL 4 ch f  £24133
85  3-17   Donc  6g/s    83    1523
91  3-9    Nott  6.1g/s [83]   1773
80  6-11   Hayd  6gd    [87]   2240
91  3-11   Warw  7.1fm  [87]   2777
97  1-15   YORK  7gd     87    3117*
90  7-20   Newm  7g/f    91    3782
94  5-11   York  7g/s   [91]   4063
96  2-14   Sali  7gd     91    4331
96  7-15   Donc  7fm    [91]   4479
68  10-12  Asco  7g/f   [92]   4811

LOOK HONEY 4 b c  £7711
112 3-10   Long  10g/s         2635 bl

LOOK NO MORE 2 ch g  £0
46a 7-11   Ling  8ap    [47]   77
29a 8-11   Wolv  8.5af  [47]   279

LOOKING DOWN 3 ch f  £1362
73a 3-11   Ling  8ap     72    80
40a 13-15  Ling  7ap    [72]   216
10  13-13  Redc  7sft   [70]   1142
11  12-14  Redc  7g/f   [67]   2102

LOOKING FOR LOVE 5 b m  £0
59a 7-16   Ling  7ap     62    55 p

LOOKING GREAT 2 b c  £0
59  7-8    Kemp  5g/f          2858
37  14-15  Wind  6gd           3163
67  9-10   Wind  8.3fm         3803
50  13-15  Good  8fm           4233

LOOKOUTHEREICOME 3 b f  £0
45a 8-11   Ling  8ap           496
25a 12-12  Ling  8ap           734
44  9-17   Wind  11.6fm        2788
26  10-11  Wind  10fm          3802
23  8-10   Warw  8.1g/f [45]   4421

LOOKS COULD KILL 2 b c  £15508
92  2-12   Good  7fm           3568
91  1-6    HAMI  8.3g/s       3878*
91  4-11   Hayd  8.1fm   86    4387
90  3-11   Ayr   8sft    86    4688
94  2-14   Newb  7sft    85    5193

LOOKS THE BUSINESS 3 b g  £1444
71a 2-13   Ling  10ap   [68]   601 t
62a 4-12   Wolv  9.4af  [68]   686 t
75a 5-10   Ling  10ap   [69]   886 t
57  9-14   Wind  10g/s  [69]   1055 t
38  14-16  Beve  7.5g/s  69    1163 t
59  8-16   Bath  10.2g/f [65]  1790

LORD ADMIRAL 3 b c  £4140
86  3-     Leop  10sft         1302

LORD ARTHUR 3 b g  £257
26a 11-12  Sout  6af           2722
54a 4-6    Sout  6af           3095
35a 9-9    Sout  6af     56    3485
46  9-15   Newc  6hvy    53    4211
29  15-15  Carl  7.9g/f  53    4346 BL

LORD BASKERVILLE 3 b c  £3649
44a 13-15  Ling  7ap     67    337
19a 12-14  Ling  6ap    [60]   495
58  6-12   Catt  5gd    [60]   995
36  12-16  Newc  6sft    60    1277
58  3-8    Hami  5gd    [57]   1509
40  7-13   Carl  5.9fm  [57]   1949
43  8-8    Newc  5g/s    57    2731
33  13-14  Newc  5g/s    57    2775
45  13-17  Catt  5g/f    57    2846
57  2-14   Catt  6g/f    53    3018
56  2-10   Hami  6g/f    53    3203
53  4-17   Ripo  6g/s    54    3262
48  8-18   Carl  7.9fm   54    3547
49  4-14   Beve  7.5sft [53]   4256

LORD CHALFONT 2 ch g  £0
29  12-15  Warw  5g/s          1325 BL
20a 9-12   Sout  5af           1439 bl
34a 7-10   Sout  6af           2382
0   9-10   Sout  7af           2802
30  9-11   Ches  7fm           3633 P
17  9-11   Wind  8.3fm         3798 bl
34  9-12   Beve  8.5sft        4257 bl
0   16-16  Yarm  8g/f     30   4632 bl

LORD CHAMBERLAIN 11 b g  £11078
49a 2-10   Wolv  8.5af  [49]   311 bl
56a 1-10   WOLV  7af     49   379* bl
46a 4-11   Sout  8af     49    457 bl
54a 4-13   Wolv  8.5af   53    559 bl
51a 11-16  Ling  7ap     53    600 bl
58a 2-10   Wolv  7ap     56    685 bl
59a 2-10   Wolv  8.5af   56    754 bl
42a 9-10   Sout  8af     57    792 bl
59  3-16   Bath  8fm    [53]   2032 bl
52  4-20   Yarm  8fm     53    2149 bl
56  4-16   Chep  7.1gd  [55]   2369 bl
48  8-17   Ling  7gd     53    2397 bl
55  3-14   Muss  7.1g/f  51    2615 bl
36  11-15  Thir  8g/s   [51]   2688 bl
53  2-17   Warw  8.1g/f  51    2909 bl
41  7-17   Chep  8.1g/s  51    3087 bl
55  1-14   CHEP  8.1gd   50   3733* bl
57  4-15   Ling  7.6fm   55    3788 bl
24  11-15  Chep  8.1sft  55    4057 bl
57  2-20   Chep  7.1g/s  55    4367 bl
54  5-12   Good  9g/f    55    4539 bl
46  9-16   Yarm  7gd     55    4616 bl

LORD CONYERS 5 b m  £557
26  7-14   Sout  12g/s         1047
11  12-16  Newc  10.1sft 40    1278
39  4-11   Pont  8sft    40    1425
28  4-6    Pont  8g/f   [40]   2037 P

LORD DARNLEY 3 b c  £10282
115 2-6    Long  12g/s         2824

LORD DU SUD 3 gr c  £58416
118 1-6    LONG  12sft        1852*
113 6-15   Chan  12g/s         2308
117 4-8    Long  12sft         4566
117 2-7    Long  15g/f         4947

LORD DUNDEE 6 ch h  £0
34  9-9    Ayr   13.1g/s 85    2567
0   9-9    Hayd  11.9gd  78    2900 T
44  4-7    Carl  11.9g/f [65]  3226 t

LORD ELROND 2 b c  £0
62  8-8    Wind  5g/f          1955

LORD EUROLINK 10 b g  £0
42  16-16  Sand  10gd    72    4609
8   19-19  Pont  10g/s   70    5148

LORD GIZZMO 7 ch g  £0
9a  11-12  Wolv  12af    45    484
27a 6-11   Wolv  12af    45    557
7a  12-17  Wolv  12af    40    634

LORD GREYSTOKE 2 b c  £0
32a 10-11  Wolv  7af     64    29
29a 13-15  Ling  7ap     61    177
10a 9-9    Ling  10ap    56    365
2   17-18  Wind  8.3sft  60    1647
22  13-19  Chep  8.1g/s [55]   4366
0   12-13  Warw  12.6g/s [48]  4665
31  11-16  Nott  10gd    45    4857 BL

LORD JOHN 2 b c  £2822
69  8-13   Donc  5gd           954
56  4-15   Beve  5g/s          1161
59  7-8    Muss  5gd           1795
60  4-14   Leic  6g/f    65    3212
37a 9-11   Sout  6af     62    3393
53  7-13   Newc  7g/s    64    3698
56  4-9    Catt  6sft    62    3931
40  10-19  Carl  5.9g/f  55    4344
```

LORD KINTYRE (continued)

60	2-14	Catt	5g/f	53	4437 BL
58	3-14	Redc	5fm	53	4556 bl

LORD KINTYRE 9 b g £0
66	8-11	Bath	5g/s	[83]	4201

LORD LAHAR 5 b g £4113
46	6-6	Ayr	10g/f		1894
29	8-11	Leic	11.8fm	45	2112
7	12-12	Yarm	16gd	40	3493
28	13-19	Chep	12.1gd	40	3727
49	5-16	Beve	8.5g/s	[37]	3850
31	7-15	Chep	10.2g/s	45	4299
49	4-11	Bath	13.1g/f	45	4415
0	17-19	Catt	15.8g/f	47	4675
53a	2-11	Wolv	12.2ap	45	5009
38	6-14	Yarm	14.1g/s	[49]	5123
58a	1-11	**WOLV**	12.2ap	49	5180*
11a	10-12	Wolv	12.2ap	54	5328

LORD LAMB 12 gr g £889
54	3-9	Redc	16fm	[70]	2298
52	4-6	Newc	12.4sft	[65]	2686
59	8-9	Redc	16sft	60	2963
33	5-11	Catt	12g/f	[60]	3190
51	3-15	Chep	16.2gd	[55]	3400

LORD LINKS 3 ch g £10078
84	4-12	Good	7g/f	86	1847
81	9-27	Asco	8g/f	85	2521
75	7-11	Asco	8gd	[84]	3128
56	17-17	Good	7fm	82	3550
67	7-9	Good	8gd	78	3950
79	4-14	Epso	7gd	78	4465
75	8-25	Newb	7gd	78	4683
81	3-12	Epso	8.5gd	77	4909
86	1-11	**GOOD**	8gd	77	5027*

LORD MAYFAIR 2 b c £1330
76	2-11	Hami	6g/s		4006
73	5-12	Thir	7g/f		4591
68	6-12	Hayd	6sft		4770

LORD MAYOR 3 b c £47685
95	3-13	York	10.4sft	88	1664
102	1-18	**EPSO**	10.1fm	88	2250*
106	5-13	Asco	10g/f	[96]	2520
98	5-7	Hayd	11.9sft	[103]	3274
98	6-9	Deau	10hvy	[103]	4158

LORD MELBOURNE 5 b g £4051
44a	2-11	Wolv	6af	[44]	296
48a	1-15	**LING**	7ap	[45]	411*
47a	4-13	Ling	6ap	51	451
51a	3-11	Wolv	7af	50	562
45a	13-16	Ling	7ap	50	600
42a	5-15	Ling		[50]	708
53a	1-11	**WOLV**	6af	[50]	778*
37a	6-9	Wolv	8.5af	[50]	811
41a	8-15	Sout	7af	50	2501

LORD MERLIN 4 b g £0
0	12-13	Wolv	6af	[78]	30
0	15-15	Sout	6af	[70]	167

LORD NELLSSON 8 b g £269
52	4-6	Bath	11.7fm		2668
51	7-10	Leic	11.8g/f		3211
65	10-14	Ling	11.5gd		3335
60	5-15	Chep	18sft	59	4056
48	8-11	Bath	13.1g/f	58	4415
47	7-20	Bath	17.2gd	56	4824

LORD NORMACOTE 2 b g £0
45	7-11	Yarm	6g/f		1728
60	8-8	Brig	7gd		2952
65	4-9	Folk	7g/f		3721
44	13-13	Newm	8gd	68	4193
44	16-20	Leic	7gd	63	4451
45	7-16	Yarm	8g/s	63	4632 BL

LORD OF ADVENTURE 2 b c £0
50	8-15	Folk	6g/f		4369

LORD OF DREAMS 2 ch c £2140
44	11-13	Chep	6.1gd		3399
74	5-16	Good	8g/s		4233
63	13-21	Donc	6fm		4490
77a	3-11	Ling	8ap	[68]	4738

LORD OF DREAMS (continued)

70	4-13	Wind	8.3g/s	70	4940
73	2-19	Pont	8g/s	67	5147

LORD OF METHLEY 4 gr g £3608
36a	6-14	Sout	8af	50	60 vis
39	11-17	Beve	8.5g/s	[50]	1160 vis
37	8-11	Pont	8sft	50	1425 bl
36	7-13	Ripo	12.3g/f	48	2008
49	1-12	**HAMI**	8.3g/s	[46]	4007* bl

LORD OF THE EAST 5 b g £16764
54	10-16	Sout	7g/s	65	1049
68	3-12	Thir	6g/s	65	1215
70	2-12	Hami	6g/s	[65]	1600
34	14-20	York	6g/f	67	2059
77	1-14	**THIR**	7fm	67	2466*
78	3-18	Donc	6gd	71	2752
78	2-9	Epso	6g/s	71	2871
76	3-10	Epso	6g/s	74	3045
73	2-9	Epso	7gd	[73]	3215
82	1-11	**DONC**	6g/f	[75]	3375*
67	10-15	York	6g/f	82	3434
52	17-26	Good	6fm	74	3569
58	20-21	Donc	7fm	78	4482

LORD OF THE FENS 4 b g £0
19	17-19	Donc	6g/f		1876
0	17-17	Chep	8.1gd		2117
22	6-8	Ripo	6g/f		2527

LORD OF THE SEA 2 b c £2307
74a	5-15	Ling	7ap	73	177
65a	3-12	Ling	8ap	[73]	514
71a	3-10	Ling	10ap	71	568
74a	4-12	Ling	8ap	70	798
0	10-10	Ling	10ap	[70]	886
52	7-10	Good	11g/f	70	1865
59	9-10	Good	9.9gd	67	2225
67	4-10	Good	8gd	[67]	2378
38	13-13	Newm	7fm	64	2590
46	6-8	Good	8sft	61	4265
38	12-14	Good	8g/f	59	4542
59a	7-11	Ling	8ap	[59]	4977
57a	8-14	Ling	7ap	[59]	5263 BL

LORD WISHINGWELL 3 b g £1020
0	8-8	Ripo	10g/s		1363 P
33	3-9	Kemp	6hvy	[40]	1641 VIS
40	3-19	Redc	6g/f	38	2125 vis
5	10-13	Newc	6sft	37	2683 vis
55	4-9	Thir	7g/f	[34]	3413 vis
37	6-9	Kemp	5g/f	[37]	3687 vis
22	7-14	Folk	6gd	37	4116
1	14-15	Carl	7.9fm	[35]	4507 vis
29	8-16	Brig	7gd	[30]	4901
4	17-19	Redc	6g/s	[30]	5110 p

LORD ZINC 3 b g £0
8	17-17	Bath	5g/f		1787

LORIANA 3 b f £79789
100	3-11	San	11gd		1999

LORIEN HILL 3 b f £7522
68	6-18	Wind	8.3g/s	[71]	1258
66	5-18	Nott	8.2g/s	69	1778
73	1-8	**BEVE**	7.5g/f	[67]	2169*
71	7-10	Newb	7g/f	73	2312
73	2-8	Ling	7g/f	69	2742
66	8-11	Newm	7g/f	73	3283
77	3-12	Sand	7.1g/f	73	3860
67	7-9	Ling	7gd	73	4110
70	5-18	Kemp	8g/f	73	4714

LORNA DUNE 2 b f £3176
62	3-10	Newc	6sft		1677
61	6-16	Pont	6g/f		2275
63	8-13	Carl	5gd		2670
50	6-10	Carl	5g/f		3227
59a	7-13	Sout	7af	62	4040
62	4-20	Leic	7g/f	60	4451
65	1-16	**YARM**	8g/s	60	4632*
62	12-16	Nott	10g/f	66	4848 VIS
60	5-14	Wind	8.3g/f	[66]	5049 vis

LOS ORGANOS 2 b r f £1036
72	3-15	Newb	8hvy		5221
87	8-8	Newm	8g/s		5282

LOST SOLDIER THREE 3 b g £45470
77	6-15	Newb	8g/f		1763
89	1-11	**CHEP**	10.2gd		2196*
90	5-10	Wind	10fm	90	2785
95	4-11	Newm	10g/f	88	3236
94	2-8	Newb	13.3gd	87	3918
104	1-13	**YORK**	13.9g/s	87	4062*
105	1-15	**DONC**	14.6fm	97	4491*
97	4-7	Newm	14g/f	[104]	4878

LOST SPIRIT 8 b g £0
4a	14-14	Ling	10ap	[45]	1712
0	11-11	Leic	11.8fm	40	2112

LOTTIE 3 b f £815
44	7-9	York	7gd		3121
10	5-5	Yarm	7gd		3365
46	4-6	Donc	7g/f		3595
0	17-19	Thir	6g/f	45	4595
4	14-18	Leic	7gd	[45]	4698

LOTTIE DUNDASS 2 ch f £1317
72	5-10	Pont	6g/f		2610
75	2-10	Folk	7g/s		3046
64	7-12	Warw	7.1g/f		4418
73	4-11	Pont	8fm	73	4753

LOUGHLORIEN 5 b g £3990
44	8-11	Hayd	5g/f	54	1886
38	8-15	Pont	5gd	53	2280
37	11-19	Beve	5gd	53	2512 vis
37	9-19	Beve	5gd	50	2657
36	9-20	Nott	6.1gd	46	2928 vis
53	3-14	Catt	6g/f	[44]	3191
53	3-9	Catt	5gd	[44]	3353
51	4-17	Catt	5g/f	50	3667 vis
48	7-20	Redc	6g/f	50	3767
55	1-15	**CARL**	5fm	[49]	4508*
57	2-14	Catt	6gd	54	4967
50	3-13	Catt	5sft	[56]	5321

LOUIS GEORGIO 5 b g £0
31	12-15	Brig	5.3g/f	55	1371
10a	12-15	Sout	6af	50	1750
21	12-16	Nott	6.1gd	[45]	1988

LOUIS PRIMA 3 gr c £0
0	8-8	Muss	5g/f	[38]	3527 bl
27	8-12	Carl	5.9g/f	38	3655
27	11-14	Newc	5g/f	[35]	4404
0	15-15	Hami	6sft	30	4696

LOUISE PARIS 2 b f £0
2a	11-11	Ling	8ap		3786

LOUISE RAYNER 2 b f £4909
43	5-6	Yarm	7g/f		2343
59	4-10	Beve	7.5gd		2652
55	9-18	Leic	7g/f		3342
43a	9-12	Ling	7ap	58	3820
75	1-10	**NOTT**	10hvy	[56]	5188*

LOUISIADE 3 b g £3545
44	11-13	Thir	5sft	72	1229
63	3-11	Hami	6gd	68	1745
34	8-11	Nott	6.1g/f	67	2155
49	10-11	Ripo	6gd	65	2985
60	3-12	Newm	8fm	63	3410
61	3-11	Leic	8g/f	63	3516
49	7-9	Thir	8sft	62	3835
49	10-13	Muss	8g/f	[60]	4554

LOUPHOLE 2 ch g £17853
75	3-7	Ling	5g/f		2738
74	4-8	Ling	6gd		3021
82	1-6	**BRIG**	5.3g/f		3296*
77	7-11	Nott	5.1gd	82	3987
74	7-14	Epso	6g/f	82	4471
83	3-18	Wind	5g/f	78	4830
87	1-11	**EPSO**	5g/f	77	4907*
73	10-29	Newm	6gd		5087

LOUVAIN 2 b f £4754
96	3-11	Crao	8.3g/s		4429

LOVE AFFAIR 2 b f £12345
77	2-13	Good	7fm		3554
66	7-9	Newm	7g/f		4192
65	8-21	Donc	6fm		4490

77 2-16 Newm 7g/f 71 4913

LOVE ALWAYS 2 b f £2445
82 4-16 Sali 7gd   4329
85 2-14 Kemp 7g/f   4711

LOVE AND BUBBLES 3 b f £35986
110 2-10 Sain 10.5sft   1850
112 1-7   CHAN 9g/s   2814*

LOVE AND HONOUR 2 b f £0
0   20-20 Yarm 8sft   5252

LOVE AND LAUGHTER 2 b f £4841
68 6-12 Hayd 6sft   3272
77 1-11 CHES 7fm   3633*
41 14-14 Donc 7fm   75 4535

LOVE ANGEL 2 b c £1231
86 4-6   Newm 6g/f   3031
82 3-7   Ayr   6gd   3323

LOVE ATTACK 2 b f £0
26a 6-11 Wolv 7.1ap   5113
49a 6-11 Wolv 7.1ap   5228
49 18-21 Donc 6sft   5368

LOVE BEAUTY 2 b c £2186
68 4-6   Hami 6g/f   2316
70 11-15 Newm 7fm   3005
84 2-6   Hayd 8.1sft   4783
64 5-9   Muss 8g/s [79] 5331

LOVE FROM RUSSIA 2 b c £0
20 15-16 Thir 6g/s   4205
49 11-11 Donc 8fm   4462
48 7-9   Catt 6g/f   4670
32 11-13 York 6gd   4988

LOVE IN SEATTLE 4 b c £5382
12 13-14 Newc 10.1sft 80 964
80 1-8   MUSS 8g/s [78] 1461*
49 12-14 Donc 8g/f [80] 1877
58 7-9   Muss 8fm   [79] 2087
64 10-11 Hami 8.3g/f 78 2317
61 14-20 York 10.4gd 75 4986

LOVE IN THE MIST USA 2 b f £0
47a 7-13 Wolv 6af   [67] 126
49a 10-15 Ling 7af   62 295

LOVE ME TENDER 2 b f £0
53 7-7   Redc 7g/f   3770
70 5-10 Newm 7gd   4191
55 8-11 Newm 6sft   5265

LOVE OF LIFE 3 b f £904
1   10-10 Folk 9.7sft   977
0   14-14 Folk 7g/s   1080
41 6-8   Yarm 8g/f   2854
34 7-11 Brig 7g/f [38] 3298
45 2-11 Carl 6.9g/f [38] 3651
26 11-13 Brig 8gd   [49] 4902
0   R-11 Wolv 7.1ap [47] 5357 VIS

LOVE PALACE 2 b c £10195
76 2-4   Beve 7.5sft   2938
85 2-6   Hami 8.3g/s   3878
87 4-8   York 7gd   4326
95 1-7   HAMI 8.3sft [85] 4691*
93 5-9   Newm 8sft [95] 5099

LOVE THIRTY 2 b f £12045
74 6-7   Yarm 6g/f   3709
78 2-8   Yarm 6g/s   4250
95 5-26 Newb 6.5g/f   4679
89 1-10 GOOD 8g/f [94] 4876*

LOVE TRIANGLE 3 ch g £1578
83 3-12 Sand 7.1g/f 79 2098
69 7-8   Kemp 6g/s [80] 2677
68 11-11 Sand 7.1g/s 80 2918
68 9-9   Sali 8g/s 79 3112
76 4-7   Sali 8gd   [76] 3453
72 5-9   Sand 10g/f 75 3862
66a 7-14 Ling 10ap [74] 4742

LOVE YOU ALWAYS 4 ch g £300
21 8-9   Pont 10hvy [95] 1068
90 6-6   Donc 10.3fm [92] 4492

---

59 8-11 Leic 10gd [92] 4701

LOVEISDANGEROUS 3 b f £0
51a 5-8   Sout 5af   55 1031
43 10-10 Hami 5g/s 53 1605
35 8-13 Ripo 6g/f 50 2011

LOVELLIAN 3 b f £0
34a 9-11 Wolv 9.4af [52] 115
27a 8-9   Ling 10ap [47] 269

LOVELORN 2 b g £554
59a 3-11 Sout 6af   2336
58 10-12 Carl 5.9fm   3544
38 13-15 Nott 5.1gd   3988

LOVES DESIGN 7 b g £0
0   8-8   Wolv 12af [52] 347
37a 6-10 Wolv 8.5af [52] 398 p
32a 8-11 Wolv 9.4af 50 465
20a 10-12 Wolv 7af   [48] 512 p
40a 5-11 Wolv 9.4af [45] 580
46a 5-9   Wolv 8.5af [45] 664
49 4-13 Leic 7g/f [45] 1827

LOVES TRAVELLING 4 b g £24341
84 2-11 Donc 12gd 74 2233
87 1-19 CARL 11.9gd 80 2673*
95 2-13 York 11.9g/s 83 3076
87 10-20 Hayd 14fm 90 4383
45 14-14 Asco 12g/f 90 4814

LOVEYOULONGTIME 3 gr f £0
39 8-10 Newb 6g/f   2309
47 8-10 Newb 5.2fm   2649
37 4-6   Ling 5gd   3023

LOW CLOUD 4 b g £6233
73 6-12 Ches 10.3gd 77 1586
59 11-19 Ripo 10g/f 76 1781
75 3-12 Donc 7gd   75 2235 vis
76 5-13 Carl 7.9fm 75 2447 vis
77 1-6   BEVE 8.5gd [75] 2514* vis
73 4-8   Muss 7.1g/f 76 2809 vis
53 5-6   Epso 8.5g/s 76 3042 vis
78 4-15 Ches 10.3g/f 76 3099
60 12-12 Good 9fm   76 3625
51 10-10 Hami 8.3g/s 75 4136 vis
24 17-20 Ayr   10g/s 73 4656

LOWESTOFT PLAYBOY 2 ch g £421
42 8-10 Newm 5fm   2089
79 6-9   Newm 6g/f   2531
67 5-8   Kemp 5g/f   2858
62 7-8   Ling 5gd   3445
56 21-24 Redc 6fm   [67] 4928
65a 4-8   Ling 6ap   [62] 5081
68a 5-13 Wolv 5.1ap [68] 5207
47 20-20 Yarm 8g/s 65 5349

LOYAL LOVE 2 b f £8206
61 6-13 Kemp 6g/f   4358
96 1-13 NEWM 6g/f   4918*

LOYAL TYCOON 6 br g £14518
58 17-22 Donc 6gd   86 921
77 7-15 Pont 6hvy 83 1251
82 2-17 Donc 6g/s 80 1523
82 5-19 Kemp 6fm   81 2070
49 15-17 Epso 6fm   81 2256
74 8-28 Asco 7g/f 80 2558
93 1-9   EPSO 6g/f 79 2871+
71 8-11 Asco 6.5gd 82 3069
89 5-11 Hami 6fm   90 3248
89 5-15 York 6g/f 89 3434
57 22-26 Good 6fm   91 3569
87 2-10 Wind   [87] 3977

LOYALTY LODGE 2 ch c £0
47 10-11 York 6g/s   1687
63 6-9   Ripo 6gd   2522
35 10-10 Redc 7g/s   2959
32 14-20 Redc 7fm   59 4337

LUALUA 3 ch g £5957
75 4-10 Hayd 6g/f 76 1488
81 2-14 Thir 5g/f 75 1766
80 3-11 Nott 6.1g/f 77 2155
54 14-16 Leic 5g/f 77 2400

---

71 4-12 Ayr   5g/s 77 2566
70 3-10 Hayd 5g/s 76 3135
65 14-21 Good 5fm   75 3567
53 13-15 Thir 5g/s 73 3833 VIS
63 6-14 Redc 5fm   [72] 4930

LUAS LINE 2 b f £16549
102 2-8   Curr 7g/f   3843
87 7-12 Good 7sft   4264

LUBECK 2 b c £4193
83 5-12 York 6gd   3122
84 1-8   NEWM 6g/f   3473*
67 9-13 York 6gd   84 4004

LUBINAS 5 b g £0
37 7-18 Nott 14.1sft 46 1469
43a 5-9   Wolv 14.8af 46 1654

LUCAYAN BELLE 3 b f £0
0   7-8   Ripo 10g/s   1363 VIS

LUCAYAN DANCER 4 b g £10283
62 6-16 Sout 7g/s 65 1049
49 5-14 Pont 8hvy [63] 1253
54 5-5   Beve 9.9sft 60 2943
39 16-19 Good 8g/f 58 3512
62 1-19 BRIG 9.9sft 55 4145*
56 4-18 Ayr   10.9sft 57 4623
66 1-12 PONT 10fm [57] 4757*
68 2-17 Newc 10.1g/f 61 5016
65 3-10 Donc 10.3sft 61 5206
66 4-17 Redc 10sft 62 5307

LUCAYAN LEGEND 3 b c £16740
48 6-12 Kemp 8hvy   1511
81 3-10 Good 8g/f   1815
91 1-12 RIPO 8g/f   1978*
97 2-27 Asco 8g/f 89 2521
65 15-16 Good 9.9fm 94 3553

LUCAYAN MONARCH 5 ch g £8116
17a 12-14 Sout 8af   65 60
40a 9-12 Sout 8af   62 141 p
42a 6-14 Sout 8af   62 195 p
54a 4-13 Sout 8af   58 221 p
48a 2-10 Wolv 7af   [55] 298 p
56a 1-8   SOUT 7af   [55] 320* p
57a 1-8   SOUT 7af   [53] 373* p
56a 2-11 Wolv 7af   [56] 440 p
55a 5-12 Wolv 7af   [56] 512 p
0   13-13 Wolv 8.5af 55 559 BL
55a 8-16 Ling 7ap   54 600 p
58a 2-11 Ling 8ap   54 732 p
54a 3-13 Ling 7ap   54 739 p
58a 2-10 Ling 8ap   54 769 p
56a 3-7   Ling 8ap   55 910 p
48a 6-15 Ling 7ap   [55] 935 p
53a 5-12 Ling 7ap   [54] 1074 p
59a 2-8   Ling 7ap   [52] 1247 p

LUCEBALL 4 b f £0
40a 9-13 Ling 6ap   46 740 bl
23a 11-11 Ling 6ap   46 760 bl

LUCEFER 6 b g £6385
40a 9-12 Ling 8ap   50 1013 t
40 8-19 Yarm 7g/f 47 1132
48 3-8   Folk 9.7sft 46 1579
39 4-12 Brig 9.9fm 46 1695
45 4-18 Nott 8.2gd [45] 1992
39 8-15 Kemp 9gd   45 2170
46 3-12 Brig 8g/f 44 3986
53 1-11 BRIG 8g/s 44 4141*
39 8-15 Chep 8.1g/s 51 4300
48 5-16 Yarm 7gd   52 4616
49 9-18 Good 8gd   52 4750
35 12-19 Yarm 8g/s [50] 5119
47a 5-13 Wolv 8.6ap [48] 5212

LUCHI 3 ch f £0
51a 6-13 Ling 6ap   364
23a 10-11 Ling 6ap   543

LUCID DREAMS 5 b g £7206
55a 5-14 Ling 7ap   52 344
43a 7-11 Wolv 7af   51 558
56a 4-16 Ling 7ap   51 600
57a 1-11 LING 8ap   52 732*

58a	2-10	Ling	8ap	58	770	
56a	3-11	Ling	8ap	54	820	P
60a	1-7	LING	8ap	58	910*	p
58a	5-12	Ling	8ap	61	1013	p

LUCIFEROUS 2 ch f £0

69	5-8	Sali	6gd		3451
64	6-18	Ling	6gd		4108

LUCIUS VERRUS 3 b c £4953

50a	3-13	Ling	6ap		219	
52a	4-13	Sout	6af		254	
56a	3-7	Wolv	5af	[50]	348	
44a	14-16	Ling	7ap	50	600	
55a	1-7	WOLV	5af	[48]	1320*	
23	16-17	Warw	5hvy	[54]	1532	
50a	5-15	Sout	6af	54	1750	VIS
52a	2-13	Wolv	5af	52	2201	vis
35a	9-16	Sout	6af	52	2720	vis
43a	5-16	Sout	6af	52	2806	vis
46a	6-15	Sout	6af	50	3000	vis
29	15-20	Hayd	6fm	49	3796	vis
53a	3-14	Sout	6af	49	4130	BL e

LUCKY 3 b f £38025

107	1-6	CURR	7sft		1436*

LUCKY AGAIN 3 b r g £0

49	17-19	Newb	8gd		1236
45	4-9	Folk	9.7sft		1581
55	7-11	Folk	9.7g/f		2274
33	5-5	Brig	11.9g/f	62	2642

LUCKY ARCHER 11 b g £0

45	7-11	Leic	10gd	54	2135
31	11-17	Warw	8.1fm	50	2572
31	11-17	Warw	8.1g/f	48	2909
32	7-8	Bath	10.2g/f	[45]	3370
38	6-14	Pont	10g/f	45	4624

LUCKY ARTHUR 3 ch f £2203

63	8-9	Ling	10sft		1623
59	5-16	Bath	10.2g/f		1790
61	8-18	Wind	10g/s		1959
62	3-7	Hami	11.1g/f	[60]	2478
61	2-10	Bath	11.7g/f	59	2978
54	3-12	Chep	12.1g/s	59	3085
39	15-16	Thir	12g/f	60	3573
53	8-20	Catt	12gd	56	4966
46	10-13	Hams	12g/s	54	5333 VIS

LUCKY EMERALD 2 b f £4483

67	2-9	Nott	5.1gd		2926
62	7-11	Wind	5gd		3160
74	1-12	CHEP	5.1gd		3728*
0	14-14	Warw	6.1g/f	72	4420
69	5-19	Bath	5gd	72	5021 T
53a	9-9	Ling	6ap	[70]	5237 t

LUCKY JUDGE 7 b g £20016

45	4-15	Newc	12.4hvy	60	1034
38	12-14	Hami	12.1gd	59	1389
64	1-12	THIR	16gd	55	1637*
48a	5-13	Sout	14af	50	2494
75	1-13	NEWC	16.1sft	60	2685*
77	1-9	REDC	16sft	68	2963*
60	6-12	Ches	15.9sft	73	4106
73	5-7	Thir	16g/s	73	4209

LUCKY LARGO 4 b g £2053

39	10-14	Newc	10.1sft	68	964 bl
48	5-17	Beve	8.5g/s	[65]	1160 bl
33	14-15	Hami	9.2gd	58	1388
40	8-14	Hami	8.3gd	58	1504 bl
60	4-7	Muss	8fm	[53]	2081 bl
42	7-15	Ayr	8gd	[53]	2504 bl
59	2-10	Ayr	9.1gd	53	2571 bl
55	6-10	Muss	12g/f	58	2813 bl
51	7-7	Ayr	10.9gd	57	3149 bl
42	10-13	Ayr	10gd	57	3325 bl
30	8-11	Muss	8g/f	[55]	3558 bl
21	14-17	Hami	9.2g/s	52	4008 bl
37	8-8	Ayr	10hvy	52	4084 bl
31	8-17	Carl	7.9fm	[48]	4506 bl
41	11-18	Ayr	10.9sft	48	4623 bl

LUCKY LEO 4 b g £9246

61	9-11	Leic	10g/s	68	1357

71	1-9	DONC	12g/f	64	2078*
76	1-10	NEWB	11g/f	68	2875*
56	9-15	Newm	12g/f	68	3066

LUCKY OWNERS 4 b c £640000

120	1-14	SHA	8g/f		211*

LUCKY PIPIT 3 b f £18328

96	5-13	Newm	7gd	[103]	1169
103	2-11	Warw	7.1fm	[102]	2574
102	1-5	YARM	7gd	[102]	3365*
93	8-12	Good	7fm	[102]	3564
0	14-15	Donc	7fm	[100]	4479
97	4-12	Asco	7g/f	[100]	4811
80	8-10	Redc	7fm	[98]	4929

LUCKY PISCEAN 3 b g £0

55	5-16	Newc	7sft		966
53	8-11	Beve	8.5sft		1304
12	19-20	Donc	7g/s		1518
15	15-18	Beve	9.9g/s	54	4243
22	11-13	Newc	16.1fm	52	4868

LUCKY RED PEPPER 2 b c £4475

80	1-18	LEIC	7g/f		3342*

LUCKY ROMANCE 5 b m £0

37a	5-9	Wolv	9.4af	[45]	314
24a	9-10	Wolv	8.5af	[45]	398 BL

LUCKY SPIN 3 b f £35237

84	2-13	Newb	7gd		1210
97	1-17	LING	7g/s		1617*
101	1-6	LEIC	7gd	[90]	2136*
107	1-11	WARW	7.1fm	[97]	2574+
85	12-12	Good	7fm	[104]	3564
98	3-14	Newb	7g/f	[102]	4638

LUCKY STORY 3 b c £68200

116	2-12	Sali	8gd	[118]	3886
115	7-11	Long	8g/s	[118]	4434
122	2-11	Asco	8g/f	[118]	4801
4	9-11	Newm	10sft	[123]	5136

LUCKY STRIKE 6 br g £78160

114	1-10	BADE	6gd		2140*
116	1-13	HAMB	6hvy		3009*
113	3-8	Bade	6sft		4426

LUCKY VALENTINE 4 b f £1619

48	2-10	Brig	5.3fm	44	2331 p
44	4-12	Brig	5.3g/f	47	2645 bl
52	3-17	Bath	5g/f	46	2981 bl
54a	3-10	Ling	5ap	49	3332 p
39	6-7	Brig	6g/f	51	3717 bl

LUCRETIUS 5 b g £0

45a	9-12	Ling	8ap	[47]	401
15a	13-14	Ling	8ap	[45]	709
1a	14-14	Ling	7ap	[45]	783 P
40a	4-9	Ling	8ap	[40]	1185
32	4-10	Warw	6.1g/s	[40]	1327

LUCY PARKES 2 ch f £377

45	8-8	Thir	5g/s		1212
54	4-10	Hayd	5gd		3755
45	11-18	Pont	5g/s		3968
27	10-12	Beve	5g/f	[51]	4596
30	14-15	Ripo	5gd	51	4784

LUGANA POINT 2 b c £0

40	7-12	Beve	5g/f		4596
30a	9-13	Wolv	6ap		5287

LUIS MELENDEZ 2 ch c £7123

84	4-13	Kemp	8g/f		4355
84	3-8	Sand	8.1gd		4608
84	1-14	LEIC	8gd		5058*

LUJAIN ROSE 2 b f £0

63	9-18	Nott	8.2g/f		4842

LUKE AFTER ME 4 b g £2826

37a	7-8	Sout	8af	[48]	577
56	2-18	Catt	7gd	[53]	996
53	13-13	Muss	7.1g/f	[51]	1119
33	10-13	Muss	7.1g/s	51	1463
55	2-15	Thir	7gd	51	1635
36	12-18	Ayr	7.2g/f	54	1897
59	4-9	Ayr	7.2fm	[54]	1910

56	3-9	Thir	7g/f	[55]	2218
42	11-14	Thir	7fm	54	2466
51	9-14	Muss	7.1g/f	54	2615
24	9-10	Leic	7fm	[52]	3812

LUKE SHARP 3 g r g £0

15	15-16	Hayd	6g/f		2182
22	8-13	Muss	7.1g/f	35	2812
0	8-9	Sout	6af	[33]	3396 bl

LUMBACK 5 b g £0

19	9-10	Carl	6.9g/f		3230 T

LUNA BLU 2 b f £0

31	14-15	Folk	7gd		4114

LUNAR EXIT 3 g r g £636

89	6-8	York	10.4g/f	97	2406
33	11-11	Newm	10g/f	94	3029
86	6-13	Kemp	12g/f	[92]	4715
52	16-17	Newm	12g/f	92	4889 BL

LUNAR LEADER 3 b f £0

23a	9-12	Wolv	7af	65	129 p
57	10-14	Nott	10fm	[70]	1006 p
19	12-12	Sout	11gd	65	1286 p
4	19-20	Epso	12hvy	65	1295 p
26	12-14	Hami	8.3gd	60	1504 t p
2	10-10	Newm	12g/f	55	2530
0	17-17	Warw	8.1g/f	45	2909 VIS
1	U-8	Epso	10.1g/s	45	3044

LUNAR LORD 8 b g £2380

53	7-9	Donc	10.3gd	58	924
21	8-10	Bath	10.2gd	[57]	1402 P
44	7-17	Nott	14.1g/f	53	2156
49	8-11	Chep	10.2gd	53	2371
51	4-8	Epso	12g/f	50	2869
50	2-12	Nott	14.1gd	44	3105
51	2-12	Nott	14.1g/f	49	3420
47	8-19	Chep	12.1gd	50	3727
42	6-13	Warw	12.6g/s	[49]	4665
37	12-20	Kemp	12g/f	[46]	4796

LUNAR SKY 2 b f £302

73	7-10	Yarm	7fm		2863
72	6-14	Newm	7g/f		3944
72	4-10	Redc	9fm		4558
65	14-16	Nott	10g/f	72	4848

LUNAR SOVEREIGN 5 br h £0

102	11-13	Nad	12g/f		990 t
95	10-10	Asco	10g/f	[110]	2488 T
10	11-11	Asco	12g/f	[110]	3442 t

LUNDYS LANE 3 b c £620

88a	10-14	Ling	10ap	[107]	82
73a	7-10	Wolv	9.4af	100	278
89a	4-8	Wolv	8.5af	[100]	360 BL
81	8-10	Donc	8gd	[107]	922 bl
42	27-27	Newb	8gd	105	1231
46	21-21	York	10.4gd	100	3118
95	7-15	Donc	8fm	94	4531
91	10-32	Newm	9g/f	94	4916

LUNDYS LIABILITY 3 £670391

120	1-9	NAD	9af		989*

LUNE DOR 3 b f £220986

112	1-7	SAIN	12g/s		3013*
114	1-12	DEAU	12.5g/s		3837*
118	1-14	CAPA	10g/s		5244*

LUPINE HOWL 3 b c £0

43	9-10	Hayd	6g/f	62	1488
41	12-16	Leic	7g/f	58	1825
34	9-13	Carl	5.9fm	[58]	1949 P
24	13-14	Redc	7fm	48	2295
24	6-7	Ripo	10gd	[44]	2982 p
42	10-15	Leic	7g/f	[44]	3515 p

LUTEUR DES PICTONS 5 ch g £0

31a	12-15	Ling	12ap		521

LUXI RIVER 4 b g £256

47a	5-10	Wolv	12af	[66]	359
52a	5-6	Sout	12af	[66]	392
41a	4-9	Sout	11af	[59]	505
50a	4-7	Sout	12af	[55]	588

LUXOR 7 ch g £0
25	11-11	Hayd	10.5g/f	40	1884 p
10	8-10	Ayr	9.1gd	40	2571
53	7-15	Ches	10.3g/f	37	3099
26	11-13	Ayr	10gd	47	3325
16	10-13	Nott	10gd	43	3992
0	8-8	Hayd	10.5g/f	45	4354
6	15-16	Ches	10.3g/f	45	4515

LYCA BALLERINA 3 b f £7494
72	5-20	Newm	7g/f	73	1186
74	3-14	Warw	8.1sft	[73]	1527
72	4-20	Newm	7g/f	73	1761
73	1-11	BEVE	7.5g/s	[71]	2325*
66	10-13	Newc	8g/s	75	2773
75	3-10	Leic	7g/f	[73]	2920

LYDGATE 4 b c £1500
106	9-19	Asco	5g/f		2468 T
110	4-7	Good	6g/f	[106]	4526 t
102	8-10	Newm	5gd	106	5090 t

LYDIAS LOOK 7 b m £4030
25a	12-13	Ling	6ap	45	451
35a	5-10	Ling	5ap	[40]	653
41a	5-11	Ling	6ap	40	760
37a	4-9	Ling	6ap	[45]	1248
41	5-20	Beve	5g/f	[45]	1948
52	1-19	BEVE	5g/s	45	2326*
41	6-19	Beve	5gd	51	2657
39	13-20	Beve	5g/s	50	3180
23	9-11	Nott	5.1gd	48	4038

LYES GREEN 3 ch c £0
47	4-7	Chep	12.1g/s		3899
54a	12-14	Ling	13ap		4892

LYFORD LASS 3 b f £4268
70	2-8	Newc	8hvy		1039
71	1-11	NEWC	8sft		1279*
55	8-15	Hami	8.3g/s	72	1602
2	14-14	Ayr	10sft	70	5037
54	12-17	Redc	10sft	68	5307

LYGETON LAD 5 b g £23330
73a	10-13	Wolv	8.5af	95	44 t
101a	1-15	LING	7ap	95	81* t
99a	7-13	Ling	6ap	100	235 t
106a	1-10	LING	7ap	100	262* t
104a	5-13	Ling	10ap	105	433 t
103a	5-10	Ling	12ap	104	570
97a	6-11	Ling	10ap	[103]	693 t
103a	5-15	Ling	7ap	102	887 t
104a	1-8	LING	7ap	[102]	1043* t
52	7-9	Epso	8.5hvy	[74]	1298 t
64	8-14	Ling	7sft	74	1625 t
64	7-9	Newm	8gd	72	1891 t
66	8-25	Asco	7g/f	68	3443 t
60	4-6	Yarm	7g/f	68	3708 t
60	6-7	Yarm	7gd	68	3872 t
105a	5-14	Ling	7ap	102	5262 t

LYNS RESOLUTION 4 b g £384
10	14-18	Chep	8.1gd		4485
67	4-13	Nott	8.2g/f		4847

LYONELS GLORY 3 b c £16172
113	3-6	Long	12g/s		2824
102	6-8	Good	12g/f		3507
110	3-9	Long	10g/s		4730

LYRIC DANCES 2 ch f £0
37	11-17	Chep	6.1sft		4052

LYRICAL GIRL 2 b f £5296
51a	3-11	Ling	8ap	[64]	77
53a	1-16	SOUT	8af	[57]	164*
60a	1-10	LING	10ap	[55]	291*
42a	5-6	Ling	10ap	59	403
27	10-11	Bath	10.2g/f	59	3373
50	6-15	Leic	7g/f	[59]	3515
31	14-14	Chep	8.1gd	59	3733
3	12-12	Chep	12.1g/s	[54]	4364

LYRICAL LADY 2 b f £0
56a	4-14	Ling	6ap		146
32a	6-8	Sout	5af	[65]	197
26	15-17	Bath	5g/f	[57]	1787
13	10-12	Chep	6.1gd	52	2118 BL

0	19-20	Chep	6.1gd	53	2372 P
20	10-18	Chep	8.1gd	[45]	4485 p
16	8-12	Brig	8gd	[40]	4904

LYRICAL WAY 4 b g £3581
55a	2-13	Ling	10ap	51	104 bl
60a	2-14	Ling	10ap	54	174 bl
62a	1-14	LING	10ap	62	236* vis
64a	4-14	Ling	10ap	62	434 vis
36a	12-14	Ling	10ap	62	520 vis
63a	5-8	Ling	10ap	62	900 vis
56	7-17	Kemp	10g/f	62	1913 bl
55	6-11	Leic	10gd	60	2135 bl
61	4-5	Brig	11.9fm	[60]	2329 bl

LYSANDERS QUEST 6 br g £1719
36	15-19	Brig	9.9g/f	40	1940
33	8-10	Ling	14fm	[37]	3742
65a	5-9	Ling	12ap	[40]	4315
47	1-15	FOLK	12g/f	[40]	4374*
39	9-20	Kemp	12g/f	[40]	4796

LYSANDRA 2 b f £2208
74	2-12	Warw	7.1g/f		4417
77	4-16	Newm	7g/s		5280

LYTHAM 3 b g £1096
67a	2-13	Wolv	8.6ap	[65]	5336

M FOR MAGIC 5 ch g £1175
33	5-20	Thir	9g/f	41	3575
46	2-15	Newc	8hvy	40	4211
51	4-7	Redc	7fm	[45]	4561
48	5-10	Ripo	6gd	[45]	4788
25	14-19	Redc	6g/s	[45]	5110 bl

MA YAHAB 3 ch c £4040
73	3-11	Beve	9.9g/f	71	1834
76	3-10	Newc	10.1g/f	72	2162
41	7-7	Ripo	12.3g/f	72	2528
75	4-14	Hayd	10.5gd	72	3741
75	4-9	Redc	9fm	[72]	4336
78a	2-14	Ling	10ap	[72]	4742

MAAM 2 ch f £0
44a	8-12	Ling	8ap		5295

MABEL RILEY 3 b f £0
9a	11-12	Sout	6af	49	85
0	15-16	Sout	6af	49	94
17a	7-9	Sout	8af	46	163 P
39a	5-13	Wolv	8.5af	[41]	300 p
40a	7-8	Wolv	8.5af	[45]	362 VIS
12	9-12	Sout	7gd	[45]	1284

MABELLA 2 b f £276
47	8-13	Sali	6fm		2287
72	5-9	Wind	5g/f		2795
51	7-13	Kemp	6gd		3183
62	4-11	Bath	5.7g/f		3848
57	10-13	Warw	6.1gd	66	4273
62	12-20	Ling	7g/f	63	4741

MAC 4 ch g £0
70	15-16	Asco	16.2g/f	90	4803 BL
0	17-19	Newm	12gd	85	5085

MAC COIS NA TINE 2 b c £1692
66	7-8	York	5sft		1670
74	2-7	Ayr	6g/f		1893
71	3-8	Beve	7.5gd		2511
76	7-13	Newm	7g/f	72	3065

MAC LOVE 3 b g £75082
72	5-6	Leic	6g/s	[106]	1018
89	4-6	Asco	6sft	[105]	1421
104	2-11	Newb	6gd	[102]	1732
107	2-8	Sali	6fm	[102]	2421
108	6-19	Newm	6fm	105	3002
98	6-11	Newb	6g/f	[105]	3268
108	1-8	DONC	6g/f	[103]	3596*
98	13-19	Hayd	6fm	[104]	4384
111	1-8	EPSO	7g/f	[104]	4472*
94	9-12	Asco	6g/f	[103]	4799
113	1-11	GOOD	7gd	[106]	4874*

MAC REGAL 3 b c £8206
79	3-5	Newb	10gd		1208
86	2-4	York	10.4g/s		1706

MAC THE KNIFE 3 b c £0
43	17-19	Newm	6g/s	86	1154
34	10-11	Sali	6g/s	83	1498
18	8-9	Ling	7g/f	[79]	1984
28	8-12	Sali	7fm	[70]	2288
20	8-9	Brig	8fm	[60]	2834
23	13-18	Leic	7gd	[50]	4698

MACABRE 2 b c £2300
90	2-5	Asco	7g/f		4776

MACARONI GOLD 3 b g £6620
56a	3-10	Ling	13ap	57	11
66a	1-15	SOUT	16af	57	67*
68a	1-10	SOUT	14af	63	90*
67a	2-14	Ling	16ap	63	107
56a	9-12	Ling	16ap	66	478
68a	4-7	Sout	14af	66	681 BL
65a	4-12	Ling	14af	65	813 bl
51a	5-8	Wolv	16.2af	65	837 bl
56	7-10	Muss	16g/f	64	1093
63	3-18	Nott	14.1sft	60	1469
55a	3-12	Sout	16af	64	1753
60	6-16	Kemp	16g/f	58	4361
58	6-11	Redc	14.1g/s	58	5108

MACAULAY 2 ch c £790
81a	3-10	Ling	7ap		5264

MACCHIATO GB 3 br f £0
38	7-10	Beve	12.1g/s	56	1165
53	5-11	Ling	11.5g/f	56	2842
13	13-13	Bath	10.2gd	[54]	3144
27a	9-14	Ling	10ap	52	3449
38	9-14	Yarm	11.5g/f	49	3714
19a	8-16	Sout	14af	44	4045 BL
35	9-15	Folk	12g/f	[40]	4374 bl

MACHINIST 4 br g £20356
61	7-14	Ayr	6g/f	82	1898
59	17-28	Asco	7g/f	80	2558
71	9-13	Donc	8gd	[77]	2753
89	1-9	AYR	6g/f	75	3307+
87	2-15	York	6g/f	82	3434
82	4-19	Ripo	6g/s	83	3937
83	5-12	Good	6sft	82	4184
75	7-26	Ayr	6g/s	82	4652

MACLEAN 3 b g £20556
76	2-19	Yarm	8g/f		1130
80	1-7	MUSS	9g/s		1462*
82	3-14	Newm	8g/f	76	1930
68	6-11	Sand	10g/s	77	2127
79	4D-6	Newm	8g/f	77	3472 VIS
72	6-8	Wind	8.3fm	77	3641 vis
85	1-10	CHES	10.3sft	76	4071* P
65	11-11	Epso	10.1gd	80	4293 p

MACPURSIE 3 br f £0
41a	5-7	Sout	7af		636
23a	4-7	Sout	8af		721

MACS ELAN 4 b g £2357
34	16-20	Donc	7g/s		1518
50	5-8	Chep	7.1sft		4055
25a	7-14	Ling	10ap	[35]	4662
49	6-18	Wind	10g/s	[35]	4944
63	2-11	Wind	8.3g/f	[35]	5052
64	2-12	Catt	12gd	[46]	5319

MACS TALISMAN 4 ch c £7402
25	17-18	Wind	10af	[67]	1806
47a	10-12	Ling	6ap	[67]	2016
40	12-17	Wind	6af	60	2451
56a	2-9	Sout	7af	[55]	2801
53	3-13	Muss	8gd	[55]	2967
25	15-20	Newm	9af	56	3232
34	11-13	Warw	6.1gd	52	4272
1	W-18	Good	8gd	47	4750 t P
63a	1-14	LING	7ap	[56]	5294* t p
71a	1-13	WOLV	8.6ap	62	5365* t p

MAD 3 br f £0
47a	8-9	Ling	12ap		4315
0	10-10	Sali	8sft		4578
48a	9-12	Ling	8ap		4975
64a	6-14	Ling	7ap		5240

MAD CAREW 4 ch g £4839
75a	2-14	Ling	10ap	70		122 bl e
73a	5-16	Ling	12ap	72		493 bl e
80a	1-14	LING	10ap	72		674* bl e
63a	13-14	Ling	10ap	79		758 bl e
67a	4-11	Ling	12ap	[79]		816 bl e
34	11-16	Epso	10.1hvy	79		1296 bl e
77	5-18	Good	8g/f	76		1849
76	5-8	Sand	10gd	76		2363
71	4-9	Good	8gd	76		2540 bl e
61	10-12	Good	9fm	74		3625 bl e
72	5-16	Good	12gd	[73]		4745 bl
74	4-8	Brig	9.9sft	[73]		5095 bl

MAD MARTY WILDCARD 2 ch c £0
26	13-13	Wind	6g/f		5047
27	13-14	Newb	6sft		5197

MAD MAURICE 3 ch g £0
32	17-20	Donc	7g/s		1518
44	12-17	Ling	7g/s		1617 P
42	10-10	Hayd	10.5g/f		1922 p
17	13-14	Yarm	11.5g/f	45	3714 p
26	13-15	Folk	12g/f	[45]	4374 BL

MAD MICK MEESON 3 b g £0
54a	7-15	Ling	7ap	[58]	117 T
33a	10-16	Sout	6af	55	166 t
46a	4-13	Ling	6ap	[55]	219 t
46a	8-15	Ling	7ap	[50]	263 VIS

MADAAR 5 b g £0
12a	12-15	Sout	8af	37	2725
44	8-11	Pont	10g/f	[46]	2991

MADAEH 3 b f £1500
92	4-7	Good	9.9g/f	[94]	1844
56	14-19	Asco	8g/f	93	2491

MADALYAR 5 b g £0
0	12-12	Wolv	8.5af	79	688

MADAM CAVERSFIELD 2 b f £2560
60	5-8	Bath	5fm		2033
62	7-9	Newm	6g/f		2245
72	3-12	Sand	7.1g/f		2388
65	4-13	Epso	7g/f		2870
73	4-11	Newm	7fm	70	3407
66	6-8	Brig	7g/f	[71]	3716
72	2-11	Chep	8.1g/s	[71]	4296
50	9-11	Bath	8sft	[70]	5171

MADAME FATALE 2 br f £0
34	15-16	York	7.9gd		4997
41a	10-13	Wolv	8.6ap		5288

MADAME GUILLOTINE 2 b f £0
13	13-14	Redc	6g/s		5106
0	13-13	Wolv	6ap		5287

MADAME MARIE 4 b f £816
21	11-14	Folk	9.7g/s	54	1083
54	7-17	Ling	7g/s	[50]	1617
53	2-18	Nott	8.2g/s	50	1778
23	15-17	Warw	8.1fm	50	2440
46	6-20	Kemp	9g/f	50	2857
46	7-14	Folk	9.7g/s	50	3052
41a	7-14	Ling	10ap	49	3605
56a	8-15	Ling	12ap	[48]	4111
39a	8-14	Ling	16ap	51	4319
36	4-12	Brig	11.9fm	48	4764

MADAME ROUX 6 b m £0
8a	6-7	Wolv	6af	[30]	1566
4a	5-7	Ling	6ap	[30]	1715

MADAME TOPFLIGHT 2 b f £10453
56	8-9	Ches	5.1gd		2281
77	2-7	Muss	5g/s		2965
84	1-7	AYR	6gd		3323*
76	5-9	Ches	6.1fm	80	3632
92	2-9	Deau	5hvy	[80]	4155
48	8-9	Ayr	6sft	[93]	4684
60	9-11	York	6gd	[93]	4998

MADAMOISELLE JONES 4 b f £8479
48	10-20	Donc	10.3g/s	66	1519
63	4-8	Nott	8.2g/s	[64]	1775

83	5-7	Asco	7g/f	[64]	1925
70	1-9	LEIC	8fm	64	2108*
60	6-9	Good	8gd	68	2540
66	4-6	Epso	8.5g/s	67	3042
60	6-6	Wind	8.3g/f	67	3978
48	11-13	Wind	8.3g/s	66	4221
40	10-13	Epso	8.5gd	66	4469

MADDIES A JEM 3 b f £17925
53a	11-11	Ling	8ap	68	136
75	1-15	FOLK	6sft	66	976*
79	1-8	FOLK	5g/s	[72]	1269*
74	3-16	Nott	6.1sft	[75]	1743
71	5-11	Newm	6fm	75	2093
67	6-13	Donc	6gd	75	2232
77	4-13	Wind	6fm	73	3479
78	2-13	Good	6gd	73	3952
77	1-8	NOTT	5.1gd	[73]	4039*
64	6-9	Yarm	5.2g/s	75	4253
74	2-9	Pont	6g/f	75	4627

MADGE 2 b f £0
70	6-13	Redc	7fm		4927

MADHAHIR 3 b c £4055
64a	2-11	Wolv	16.2af	61	48 p
25a	9-12	Wolv	16.2af	62	156 p
12a	8-9	Sout	16af	62	336 VIS
53a	11-12	Ling	16ap	60	813 e
65	1-9	FOLK	12sft	58	979*
65	3-8	Yarm	11.5g/f	63	1135
38	10-18	Nott	14.1sft	62	1469
26	8-11	Beve	16.2sft	62	1629
41	10-16	Leic	11.8g/f	60	1830
48	6-8	Newc	12.4g/f	[57]	2163

MADHAVI 2 gr f £1170
72	7-10	Newm	6g/f		3063
82	3-12	Newb	6g/f		3251
74	5-8	Good	6fm		3536
49	9-12	Wind	6gd	75	3825
56	20-26	Newb	6.5g/f		4679 BL
65	17-29	Newm	6gd		5087 bl

MADIBA 4 b g £9082
41a	8-14	Ling	13ap	57	259 BL
60a	1-10	SOUT	11af	[57]	306* bl
48a	6-10	Sout	12af	60	421 bl
0	11-11	Ling	13ap	[58]	515 bl
61a	2-13	Sout	14af	55	590
58a	2-8	Wolv	16.2af	55	690
61a	2-10	Wolv	16.2af	60	812
37	12-18	Newb	16gd	60	1232
61	2-12	Thir	16gd	55	1637
65a	2-12	Sout	16af	60	1753
56	9-14	Asco	16.2g/f	60	1928
40	11-17	Nott	14.1g/f	60	2156
57	8-12	Newm	16.1g/f	59	3032
2	P-11	Ling	16gd	59	3200
0	5-10	Yarm	16sft	56	4151
57	2-7	Newc	16.1g/f	54	4405
46	6-20	Catt	15.8gd	54	4965
61	2-15	Good	16gd	54	5025
66a	6-16	Ling	12ap	63	5261

MADID 3 br c £23302
97	1-17	NEWB	8g/f		1762*
114	1-6	SAND	7.1g/f		2190*
108	9-11	Asco	8g/f		2469

MADRA RUA 3 b g £0
13	9-11	Hami	6gd	63	1745
45	7-7	Carl	5fm	60	1951 P
33	11-15	Ayr	5sft	55	5036

MADRASEE 6 b m £2595
69a	2-10	Ling	5ap	67	329
37a	12-14	Ling	6ap	[68]	516
57a	9-10	Ling	5ap	68	755
67a	4-12	Ling	6ap	65	880
65a	5-14	Ling	6ap	65	1025
75	7-13	Epso	5sft	78	1293
70	5-12	Ling	5g/s	77	1615
55	13-17	Wind	6g/f	76	2451
54	8-9	Epso	6gd	73	2871
59	18-22	Good	5fm	70	3537
56	6-13	Good	6gd	67	3952
62	7-12	Good	6sft	65	4184

61	6-15	Good	5gd	62	4751
65	2-8	Brig	5.3sft	60	5096

MAEVEEN 4 b f £0
30a	4-14	Ling	10ap	[35]	4662 e

MAFAHEEM 2 b c £5489
87	1-13	YORK	6gd		4988*

MAFRUZ 5 ch g £0
22	9-11	Newc	10.1g/s	58	2726
6	11-13	Muss	8gd	[55]	2967

MAGANDA 3 b f £4442
84	1-8	RIPO	10g/s		1365*
83	6-11	Newb	11g/f	84	1756
51	13-13	Newm	8g/f	83	2247
50	18-20	York	8.9gd	80	4999

MAGARI 3 b f £813
50	4-9	Thir	7fm		3610
51	8-13	Wind	8.3gd		3828
7a	12-15	Sout	8af	53	4132
39	5-13	Carl	6.9fm	[53]	4504
53	3-16	Bath	8gd	50	4828
48	4-19	Yarm	8g/s	[50]	5119

MAGDELAINE 2 b f £0
3	18-18	Nott	8.2g/s		4035
19a	12-13	Wolv	8.6ap		4979
31a	12-12	Wolv	7.1ap		5179

MAGENTA RISING 4 ch f £0
0	9-9	Sout	12af	60	456 VIS
0	17-17	Thir	8g/s	54	3830

MAGGIE JORDAN 2 b f £4745
89	1-10	NEWM	6sft		5266*

MAGGIE MAQUETTE 3 ch f £0
10a	11-12	Wolv	7af		71
33a	8-13	Ling	6ap		219
54a	5-14	Ling	6ap		449
49a	6-10	Ling	5ap	[55]	802
28a	12-16	Sout	5ap	52	1046

MAGGIE TULLIVER 2 b f £3621
44	12-20	Wind	6fm		2970
75	7-16	Sali	7gd		4329
51	15-19	Leic	7gd		5040
76a	1-13	WOLV	8.6ap		5355*

MAGGIES CHOICE 2 b f £0
30a	8-12	Wolv	8.5af	[56]	28
13a	11-12	Ling	8ap	[53]	78

MAGGIES PET 6 b m £5172
46a	3-14	Sout	8af	46	60 T
34a	6-16	Sout	8af	46	86 t
37a	7-12	Ling	8ap	[46]	150 t
43a	2-13	Wolv	8.5af	[44]	300 t
46a	5-12	Wolv	9.4af	45	427 t
47a	2-8	Sout	8af	45	489 t
45a	2-9	Wolv	9.4af	[45]	522 t
41a	4-12	Ling	8ap	[45]	648 t
40a	5-13	Sout	8af	[45]	776 t
52a	1-12	WOLV	8.5af	45	1379* t
40a	6-12	Wolv	7af	50	2049 t

MAGHANIM 4 b c £11496
97	5-7	Good	7g/f	[102]	1811
103	3-6	Nott	8.2g/f	[98]	2154
101	2-28	Asco	7g/f	96	2558
90	10-19	Newm	7g/f	98	3061
94	9-12	Good	7fm	[98]	3555
77	10-11	Good	9g/f	97	4525

MAGIC AMIGO 3 ch g £8279
74a	2-6	Wolv	7af	[75]	1321
73	1-10	FOLK	9.7sft	[73]	1580*
52	13-14	Asco	10g/f	74	1924
77	2-8	Ches	10.3gd	[71]	2283
78	3-6	Donc	10.3g/f	[71]	2426
43a	8-10	Sout	12af	74	2998
76	4-13	Beve	9.9gd	75	3309
72	3-8	Newm	10g/f	75	3471
72	6-7	Wind	10fm	75	3801
78	2-5	Folk	9.7g/s	75	3914
68	6-9	Yarm	10.1g/s	[75]	4254

41a 14-14 Ling 10ap [74] 4742

MAGIC AMOUR 6 ch g £6449
61	2-16	York	7g/f	60	2057	
56	6-10	Newb	8g/f	61	2350	
49	7-7	Yarm	7g/f	60	2853	
59	4-11	Leic	7g/f	58	3210	
36	18-25	Asco	7g/f	57	3443	
36	16-16	Redc	7g/f	55	3809	
61	1-13	WARW	6.1gd	53	4272*	VIS
34	15-15	Epso	7g/f	59	4475	vis
51	7-20	Ripo	6gd	57	4785	BL

MAGIC BOX 6 b g £0
| 5a | 15-16 | Sout | 8af | 48 | 3159 p |

MAGIC CHARM 6 b m £274
8a	10-14	Sout	12af	[39]	305
26a	10-14	Ling	13ap	[35]	537
6a	8-10	Wolv	12af	[35]	581
38	4-8	Ayr	13.1fm	40	1905
8	15-18	Newm	12fm	40	2088
32	6-11	Thir	12g/f	38	2217
1	13-15	Ripo	12.3g/f	35	2526
26	8-10	Muss	12g/f	35	2813
26	6-12	Nott	14.1g/f	30	3420

MAGIC COMBINATION 11 b g £15599
75	2-12	Newc	16.1g/f	70	965	
71	5-10	Carl	14.1fm	71	2444	
75	2-9	Pont	18g/f	71	2607	
80	2-9	Redc	16sft	72	2963	
85	1-8	HAYD	14g/s	72	3140+	
87	1-9	HAYD	14gd	75	3760*	
69	11-12	York	13.9g/f	85	4400	

MAGIC EAGLE 7 b g £0
27a	5-11	Wolv	6af	[45]	296	
28a	7-16	Sout	6af	[40]	447	
0	10-10	Wolv	6af	[40]	667	
19a	8-12	Sout	5af	[35]	904	VIS
36	12-18	Catt	7gd	[35]	996	
0	7-10	Sout	7af	[35]	1839	

MAGIC FLO 2 ch f £0
56	9-17	Yarm	6gd	4610
61a	6-14	Ling	7ap	4971
59	10-16	Newm	7g/s	5280

MAGIC GENIE 2 b f £0
53	5-13	York	6g/f	2358
45	8-20	Hayd	6g/f	2882
36	7-7	Beve	5gd	3308

MAGIC GLADE 4 b g £26263
60a	10-12	Ling	6ap	[85]	106	
74a	7-16	Sout	5af	80	171	
53a	8-11	Sout	6af	76	386	
83a	1-10	SOUT	5af	73	660*	
83a	2-7	Ling	5ap	77	1011	
90	1-16	MUSS	5g/f	78	1120*	
87	3-17	Muss	5fm	87	2082	
76	15-20	Epso	5fm	87	2253	
71	13-13	York	5g/f	87	2359	
90	3-12	Leic	5g/f	[86]	4454	

MAGIC GREY 8 br h £0
| 54a | 5-16 | Sout | 6af | 227 |

MAGIC MAMMAS TOO 3 b g £3038
55a	3-14	Sout	8af	53	93	
63a	2-14	Sout	8af	[53]	170	
53a	2-13	Sout	8af	[53]	199	
47a	6-13	Sout	8af	53	221	
64a	2-7	Sout	8af	[53]	334	
49a	5-12	Sout	7af	[53]	416	
53a	3-10	Sout	8af	53	677	
50a	4-10	Sout	8af	53	792 p	
38	9-13	Muss	7.1g/s	52	1463	VIS
50	5-15	Thir	8g/s	[50]	2688 p	
30	16-16	Carl	7.9g/f	48	3650	

MAGIC MERLIN 3 b c £4846
83	3-11	Bath	8fm	1904
83	1-17	CHEP	8.1gd	2117*
81	4-9	Leic	8fm	2705

MAGIC MUSIC 5 b m £0
| 58 | 9-17 | Donc | 6g/s | 73 | 1523 |

| 43 | 10-13 | Donc | 6gd | 71 | 2232 |
| 40 | 13-14 | Thir | 6g/f | 69 | 3416 |

MAGIC RED 4 ch g £6764
51a	1-10	SOUT	14af	40	3096*
58a	1-10	SOUT	14af	47	3158*
55a	4-13	Ling	16ap	53	3822
58a	2-16	Sout	14af	53	4045

MAGIC SPIN 4 b f £0
59	6-10	Sali	6g/s	4081
62	5-14	Warw	7.1gd	4275
60a	6-12	Ling	8ap	4975

MAGIC STING 3 ch c £16350
67	5-14	Wind	10g/s	1055	
52a	5-8	Wolv	8.5af	1220	
63	6-10	Wind	11.6gd	65	1382	
68	1-11	REDC	10sft	63	1663*	
73	1-6	HAMI	11.1gd	[66]	2180*	
58	12-18	Leic	10gd	69	2706	
71	3-6	Ches	10.3g/f	68	3084	
73	3-12	Beve	9.9g/s	68	3854	
75	2-13	Ling	10g/s	68	4182	
81	1-16	CHEP	10.2g/s	68	4365*	
74	2-8	Hami	9.2sft	[75]	4694	
74	5-9	Wind	10g/s	75	4943	

MAGIC STONE 4 br g £0
| 24a | 14-15 | Ling | 7ap | [45] | 366 |
| 50a | 4-10 | Ling | 8ap | [40] | 785 |

MAGIC TREE 2 ch f £0
| 65 | 13-16 | Kemp | 7g/f | 3035 |

MAGIC VERSE 3 ch f £1939
52	18-24	Newm	8fm	1495	
47	15-18	Wind	10g/f	1959	
52a	4-13	Sout	8af	2383	
52a	4-16	Sout	8af	53	2805	
53a	4-13	Sout	8af	53	3094	
41	5-8	Brig	9.9g/f	52	3719	
39	4-9	Brig	8sft	49	4165	
55	1-13	BRIG	8gd	[46]	4902*	
39	8-12	Brig	8gd	54	5094	
35	10-17	Yarm	8g/s	[53]	5348	

MAGIC WARRIOR 3 b g £0
53a	8-11	Ling	8ap	60	12
54a	5-14	Ling	10ap	58	230
56a	4-12	Ling	8ap	55	406
52a	4-14	Ling	10ap	55	498
52a	6-14	Ling	10ap	54	622
41a	9-14	Ling	10ap	52	2589
26	13-14	Chep	8.1gd	52	3733
36	10-19	Kemp	8g/f	[50]	4795

MAGICAL GIFT 2 b f £0
| 68a | 4-12 | Ling | 8ap | 100 |
| 50a | 6-11 | Ling | 7ap | 213 |

MAGICAL MIMI 3 b f £317
36	11-11	Ripo	8gd	79	1176
31	17-20	Newm	8fm	76	1496
53	8-14	Nott	8.2g/f	72	2153
70	4-9	Pont	8g/f	69	2604
61	5-6	Carl	9.3g/f	69	3231
48	13-13	Nott	10g/f	68	3419
48	5-6	Donc	8g/f	67	3597
32	15-16	Thir	8g/f	64	4592

MAGICAL QUEST 4 b c £3591
69	8-14	Ling	11.5gd	3335
87	1-10	LING	14fm	3742*
75	11-13	Good	16g/f	85	4527

MAGICAL ROMANCE 2 b f £121586
76	4-9	Wind	5g/s	2795
86	1-13	KEMP	6gd	3183*
68	6-6	Asco	6g/f	3440
98	1-13	LEIC	6gd	83	4697*
114	1-7	NEWM	6g/f	[83]	4880*

MAGICO 2 ch c £1206
25a	14-15	Ling	7ap	60	177	
38a	7-12	Ling	8ap	53	402	VIS
32a	7-14	Ling	6ap	[49]	495	vis
3a	14-15	Sout	7af	45	2501	
44	3-9	Brig	8fm	[48]	2834	BL

48	2-14	Leic	8g/f	[44]	3344	bl
24	9-14	Bath	8g/f	50	4411	bl
13	15-16	Brig	7gd	[48]	4901	

MAGISTRETTI 4 b c £121982
114	6-11	Epso	12g/f	[121]	2209	
111	4-8	Newm	12g/f	[121]	3030	
103	4-7	Newb	10g/f	[121]	3264	
115	2-13	Arli	10fm	[121]	4014	bl

MAGNETIC POLE 3 b c £10152
86	2-20	Bath	10.2gd	1398	
86	3-12	Ripo	9g/f	1783	
61	8-10	Ripo	12.3g/s	85	3261	
80	2-6	Catt	12g/f	[83]	4441	
75	2-5	Pont	10g/f	[83]	4630	BL
92	1-8	BRIG	11.9sft	[77]	5092+	

MAHARAAT 3 b c £1108
79	5-17	Newm	8gd	1166	T
75	5-9	Ling	10sft	1623	t
83	2-11	Folk	9.7g/f	2274	VIS

MAHARIB 4 b c £2957
| 105 | 3-11 | Fair | 14g/s | 4162 |

MAHLSTICK 6 b g £181
27a	6-12	Ling	8ap	[35]	971	
31a	3-10	Ling	7ap	[35]	1181	
27a	4-5	Ling	7ap	[35]	1288	T
18a	4-6	Ling	6ap	[35]	1415	t
0	20-20	Chep	6.1gd	44	2372	
15	9-12	Brig	8gd	[40]	4904	

MAHMJRA 2 b c £0
57	10-11	York	7.9gd	5003
63	8-13	Brig	8sft	5091
41a	11-12	Ling	8ap	5293

MAHMOOM 3 ch c £25984
63	17-20	Newm	7g/f	92	1186	
74	14-20	Newm	8fm	90	1496	
72	6-7	Nott	6.1g/s	[87]	1771	
78	8-12	Ripo	6g/f	84	2482	VIS
93	1-7	NEWM	6g/f	81	2764*	vis
98	2-19	Newm	6fm	89	3002	
91	6-17	Good	7fm	92	3550	
100	2-11	Newm	6g/f	92	3941	

MAID FOR LIFE 3 b f £0
47a	4-13	Wolv	8.5af	39
37	8-8	Brig	9.9g/f	56	3719
42	6-10	Beve	9.9sft	56	4260
8	16-16	Bath	8gd	54	4828

MAID THE CUT 2 ch f £261
24a	13-16	Sout	8af	192	
48a	4-13	Sout	8af	553	
22a	8-10	Sout	7af	53	794	
20	12-18	Chep	7.1g/s	51	3900	
38	5-15	Bath	8g/s	45	4202	
40	6-18	Kemp	10g/f	[45]	4791	
37	5-12	Warw	12.6g/s	[45]	4991	

MAID TO TREASURE 3 b f £1319
78	4-16	Sand	10g/s	2131
72	6-14	Kemp	10g/s	2678
62	3-8	Newm	10hvy	[76]	5226
0	12-12	Catt	12sft	[75]	5319

MAIDANNI 2 b c £5681
82	4-18	Newm	8fm	4722
85	1-16	YORK	7.9gd	4997*
72	8-14	Donc	8sft	84	5203

MAIDS CAUSEWAY 2 ch f £129226
90	2-19	Newb	6g/f	2310	
98	1-8	KEMP	7g/s	2676*	
103	2-9	Sand	7.1g/f	3357	
105	1-11	NEWM	7g/f	[98]	3781*	
110	3-8	Donc	8fm	[100]	4476	
110	2-9	Asco	8g/f	[100]	4798	
110	1-8	NEWM	7sft	[100]	5133*	

MAIDSTONE MIDAS 3 b c £3000
44	15-16	Wind	10gd	1384
11	4-4	Ling	11.5sft	1622
69a	5-13	Ling	10ap	2066
56	6-7	Warw	10.9fm	64	2576

MAJESTIC DESERT 3 b f £221874
113	1-8	NEWB	7gd	[111]	1233*
107	9-16	Newm	8fm	[111]	1492
108	7-15	Curr	8g/f	[111]	2005
114	2-11	Asco	8g/f	[111]	2555
113	2-	Leop	7g/y	[111]	3011
114	2-8	Deau	8gd	[111]	3659
111	4-10	Deau	8sft	[111]	4017
106	4-5	Newm	8g/f	[113]	4915
111	2-7	San	8gd	[113]	5074

MAJESTIC MISSILE 3 b c £4250
114	5-19	Asco	5g/f	[116]	2468
103	8-13	Good	5fm	[116]	3551
104	6-11	Newb	5.2g/f	[112]	4678

MAJESTIC MOVEMENT 2 ch c £860
75	5-11	Sand	8.1g/s		3890
59	10-14	Ches	7sft		4102
70	3-15	Pont	10g/f		4933
70	5-19	Redc	8sft	68	5302

MAJESTIC STAR 3 b f £0
| 37 | 7-8 | Newb | 10hvy | | 5226 |

MAJESTIC VISION 2 ch c £1935
70a	4-13	Wolv	9.4af		37
58	9-14	Wind	10g/s		1259
68	6-12	Nott	14.1gd	67	3105
71	2-10	Catt	13.8g/f	67	3669
70	5-16	Kemp	16g/f	67	4361
70	3-19	Sali	14.1gd	67	4856
55	10-12	Redc	14.1g/s	68	5108

MAJESTICAL 2 b c £1895
65a	3-5	Ling	5ap		1041
60	4-5	Brig	5.3g/f		1367
56	12-12	Ling	5g/f		1981
47	10-12	Ling	5gd	62	3284
59	4-6	Brig	6fm	[58]	3671
75	2-9	Bath	5g/f	[58]	3847
58	4-12	Bath	5.7gd	60	4545
62	7-18	Wind	5g/f	60	4830
50	6-19	Bath	5gd	59	5021

MAJHOOL 4 b g £2607
64a	8-16	Ling	7ap	72	20
53a	8-9	Ling	5ap	[72]	492
56a	4-8	Ling	7ap	[70]	730
51a	5-15	Ling	7ap	[67]	935
52	1-11	BRIG	7g/f	[60]	3298*
0	11-11	Epso	7fm	[60]	3541
25	18-18	Catt	7g/f	57	4438

MAJIK 4 ch g £5018
61a	3-16	Sout	6af	60	92
71a	1-15	SOUT	6af	60	168*
71a	3-9	Sout	7af	67	193
47a	7-11	Sout	6af	69	386
71a	3-16	Sout	7af	69	419
69a	4-13	Sout	7af	69	556 P
12	15-19	Redc	6sft	60	1145
62	4-20	Wind	6g/s	60	1255 p
47	10-20	Newc	6sft	57	1393 VIS
56	4-16	Sali	7sft	59	4582
51	5-19	Wind	6g/f	58	5053
61	3-19	Bath	5.7sft	58	5176

MAJLIS 6 b g £3163
63a	2-10	Sout	12af	58	138
31a	8-12	Sout	14af	58	173
69a	1-14	LING	13ap	61	264* bl
69a	9-16	Ling	12ap	71	493 bl
50a	12-14	Ling	12ap	69	731 bl
70a	5-12	Ling	13ap	68	877
45	9-10	Muss	14g/f	68	1118
53	10-16	Brig	11.9fm	65	1693 bl

MAJOR BLADE 6 b g £0
44	14-19	Newb	10gd	61	1736
16	15-17	Kemp	10g/f	58	1913
23	10-12	Wind	10fm	54	3295

MAJOR EFFORT 3 b c £429
| 81 | 4-7 | Thir | 8g/f | [80] | 1770 |
| 61 | 12-13 | Sand | 8.1g/s | [80] | 2126 |

MAJOR FAUX PAS 2 b g £3101

| 87a | 1-12 | WOLV | 7.1ap | | 5179* |

MAJOR PROJECT 3 ch g £0
| 0 | 9-10 | Sout | 8af | 35 | 662 |
| 0 | 12-13 | Beve | 8.5g/f | [30] | 1947 |

MAJORCA 3 b c £20448
79	3-10	Newm	6g/f		1191
83	2-15	Leic	6g/f		1829
70	4-16	Hayd	6g/f	[78]	2182
83	1-11	THIR	7fm	[78]	2463*
93	1-13	NEWC	8g/s	82	2773*
62	15-16	Newm	8g/f	87	3059

MAJORS CAST 3 b c £16026
75	3-14	Warw	7.1g/f		2907
85	1-5	GOOD	7gd		3953*
89	3-4	Yarm	7sft	[85]	4148
96a	1-13	LING	7ap	85	4318*
93	3-13	Asco	6.5g/f	91	4773

MAKARIM 7 ch g £1070
50a	6-10	Wolv	12af	60	243 VIS
59a	3-14	Ling	13ap	60	259 p
45a	10-13	Ling	13ap	57	342 p
36a	11-12	Ling	16ap	57	478 p
56a	3-8	Wolv	16.2af	54	690 p
45a	5-10	Wolv	16.2af	58	812 p
42a	8-13	Ling	13ap	55	896 p
45	4-12	Warw	15g/f	43	2908 p
22	14-19	Bath	17.2gd	43	3147 p
34	5-9	Yarm	14.1g/f	41	3703 p

MAKE IT HAPPEN NOW 2 b f £316
53	7-14	Bath	5sft		1538
55	4-6	Bath	5g/f		1786
30	17-17	Asco	5g/f		2490
37	9-11	Sali	6g/f	[50]	3863
20a	13-15	Sout	5af	[50]	4089
17	11-12	Bath	8g/f	45	4410

MAKE IT SNAPPY 2 b f £810
60	8-10	Newm	7gd		4191
22	17-19	Leic	7gd		5045
68a	3-14	Ling	7ap		5257

MAKE MY HAY 4 b g £4086
47a	2-9	Sout	11af	[30]	224 BL
44a	3-6	Sout	11af	[45]	306 bl
53a	6-7	Ling	13ap	[45]	546
52	1-10	KEMP	12hvy	[40]	1645*
51	2-18	Wind	11.6g/f	46	1960
50	5-16	Folk	12fm	49	2718
51	5-13	Warw	12.6gd	49	3056
37	5-8	Newb	12g/f	49	3270
42	6-13	Folk	12gd	47	4119
48	2-20	Kemp	12g/f	[45]	4796
48	4-12	Brig	11.9sft	46	5093

MAKE US FLUSH 2 b f £12159
50	4-8	Hayd	5g/s		1343
52	7-9	Hayd	6g/f		1920
69	4-12	Hami	6gd		2178
63	9-10	Pont	6gd		2610
70	1-20	HAYD	6gd		2882*
77	1-9	HAYD	5sft	70	3271*
65	7-9	Ches	6.1fm	73	3632
75	2-12	Hayd	5gd	73	3756
77	1-6	HAYD	6g/s	73	3902*
66	7-10	Ripo	6gd	76	4306
24	12-14	Hami	6sft	74	4692
74	6-15	Hayd	6sft	74	4765
24a	11-13	Wolv	6ap	[72]	4980

MAKEPEACE 2 b c £322
55	11-15	Wind	6g/f		2263
69	4-7	Ayr	7.2g/s		2570
65	7-14	Ches	7sft		4102
44	18-20	Ling	7gd	66	4444

MAKES PERFECT 2 b f £0
| 57 | 8-13 | Bath | 5.7g/f | | 3368 |
| 41 | 6-6 | Brig | 6fm | | 3671 |

MAKFOOL 3 b c £45328
83a	12-15	Ling	7ap	[96]	885
94	3-7	Donc	8gd	[96]	949
94	4-7	Newm	7g/s	[95]	1150
69	9-15	Ches	7.6gd	92	1583
96	2-18	Hayd	8.1g/f	90	1919
101	1-17	EPSO	7g/f	93	2212*
65	21-27	Asco	8g/f	98	2521
92	8-19	Newm	7g/f	98	3061
83	12-12	Good	7fm	[97]	3555

MAKHLAB 4 b c £13547
95	5-10	Donc	8gd	[108]	922
107	5-11	Leic	7g/s	[108]	1356
105	4-9	Hayd	7.1g/f	[108]	1486
109	2-11	Hayd	7.1gd	[105]	2184
106	2-6	Ches	7g/f	[108]	3098 BL
85	13-13	Newb	7g/f	[108]	3957 bl

MAKSAD 4 b c £0
| 77 | 15-20 | Asco | 7g/f | 95 | 1926 |

MAKTAVISH 4 b c £31748
73a	10-15	Sout	5af	84	64 p
73a	7-11	Wolv	5af	82	155 p
86a	1-11	SOUT	5af	80	655* p
84	1-20	DONC	5gd	76	927* p
86	2-16	Muss	5g/f	81	1120 p
86	1-9	THIR	5g/s	[81]	1217* p
86	3-14	Ches	5.1gd	85	1594 p
50	14-15	Hayd	5g/f	85	1917 p
77	14-20	Epso	5fm	85	2253 p
75	8-11	Ches	5.1g/s	83	2747 p
83	4-10	Ayr	5gd	81	3150 p
82	6-20	Hayd	5fm	81	3792 p
67	12-16	Muss	5gd	80	4174 p
68	9-16	Hayd	5fm	79	4382 p
59	14-15	Ayr	5g/s	78	4654 p

MAKTU 2 ch c £545
59	5-11	Wind	8.3fm		3798
71	3-9	Chep	8.1g/s		4297
61	4-19	Kemp	8g/f		4792

MAKTUB 5 b h £134242
13	8-13	Asco	16.2sft		1418
91	6-10	York	13.9g/s		1705
115	2-7	San	12gd		2636
101	11-12	Sand	10g/s	[110]	2916
115	2-11	Cope	12gd	[110]	3660
116	2-11	Veli	12fm	[110]	4570

MAKULU 4 b g £1872
35	15-20	Wind	11.6g/s	77	1056
15	18-18	Newb	16gd	76	1232 bl
75	2-6	York	10.4g/f	[75]	2356 P
48	7-9	Ches	10.3g/s	[74]	2745 p

MAKUTI 2 b f £16080
| 93 | 3-10 | Curr | 6.3gd | | 4737 |

MAKYBE DIVA 7 b m £1176471
| 120 | 1-24 | FLEM | 16g/s | 112 | 5323* |

MALAAH 8 gr g £0
37a	8-12	Ling	8ap	[45]	649 bl
0	14-14	Ling	6ap	[45]	709 bl
38a	4-14	Ling	7ap	[45]	783 bl
28a	8-10	Sout	6af	[40]	907 bl
25a	10-15	Ling	7ap	[40]	969 bl

MALAHIDE EXPRESS 3 gr g £8074
53a	6-16	Sout	6af	65	92 bl
65a	3-13	Wolv	5af	65	110 bl
61a	5-11	Sout	6af	64	198 bl
54a	9-16	Sout	5af	64	205 bl
49a	7-15	Sout	5af	[64]	253 bl
59a	4-9	Sout	5af	60	415 bl
49a	5-15	Sout	6af	62	550 bl
42a	9-11	Wolv	5af	[60]	748 bl
74a	2-9	Sout	5af	[60]	793 bl
50	8-13	Muss	7.1g/f	57	1122
55	5-13	Newc	5sft	57	1276
54	5-15	Muss	5gd	55	1555
56	4-11	Hayd	5g/f	55	1886
59	1-13	HAMI	5g/f	55	2320*
53	9-17	Catt	5gd	58	2846
48	9-18	Hayd	5gd	58	2951
59	3-17	Beve	5g/f	57	4603
34a	13-13	Wolv	5.1ap	60	5156

MALAIKA 2 b f £1425
| 65 | 5-8 | Ripo | 5gd | | 4307 |
| 67 | 4-15 | Nott | 5.1gd | | 4859 |

68 3-12 Bath 5sft 5169

MALAK AL MOULOUK 4 ch g £1378
64 4-12 Wind 10g/f [65] 2800
67 2-12 Wind 10fm 65 3295
61 11-16 Wind 11.6gd 67 3829
47 11-16 Sali 8gd 67 4334

MALAPROPISM 4 ch g £34329
81 6-11 Good 5g/f 88 1845
70 15-17 Muss 5fm 87 2082
75 12-17 Epso 6fm 86 2256
75 7-11 Sand 5g/s 84 2894
83 6-10 Ayr 5gd 82 3150
79 12-24 Asco 5gd 84 3466
83 4-14 Newb 5.2fm 82 3628
77 9-20 Hayd 5fm 81 3792
80 6-13 Newb 5.2g/f 81 3960
75 6-11 Bath 5g/s [80] 4201
84 1-20 **DONC** 5fm 78 4496*
76 7-12 Yarm 5.2g/s 81 4585
81 6-12 Epso 5gd 82 4908
91 1-15 **CATT** 5sft 82 5125*
98 1-13 **MUSS** 5g/s 88 5143+
84 10-13 Donc 5sft 95 5218
69a 10-12 Ling 6ap 94 5297

MALARKEY 7 b g £18244
40a 5-10 Ling 12ap 916 p
69 1-11 **NOTT** 16fm 65 1003*
73 2-11 Warw 15sft 66 1087
77 1-18 **NEWB** 16gd 70 1232*
76 5-10 Kemp 16gd 75 2073
80 3-13 Chep 18gd 76 2198
19 25-29 Asco 20g/f 77 2471

MALCHEEK 2 br c £444
78 4-8 York 6g/f 2408

MALIBU 3 b g £6914
76 4-13 Kemp 9gd 76 1141
75 6-18 Epso 10.1fm 76 2250
71 5-8 Nott 10g/f 75 2631
68 11-16 Sand 10g/s 75 2919
79 1-7 **BRIG** 8g/f 73 3174*
66 5-7 Epso 8.5fm 78 3542
68 7-9 Sand 9g/s [78] 3892
65 12-14 Epso 7gd 78 4465 VIS
60 15-17 Asco 8g/f 76 4777

MALINAS 3 b c £86620
109 2-18 Hamb 12hvy 3010
108 3-7 Colo 12gd 4018

MALINSA BLUE 2 b f £12585
63 6-11 Nott 6.1sft 1739
71 2-13 Donc 6gd 2236
75 2-12 Hayd 6gd 2902
83 6-16 Curr 6g/f 4153
80 2-11 Thir 7fm [77] 4381
82 1-14 **DONC** 7fm 75 4535*
70 12-16 Newm 7g/f 80 4913

MALLARD 6 b g £2746
67 3-10 Newc 8g/f 64 2159
52 12-16 Beve 7.5gd 64 2655
78a 2-12 Ling 8ap [74] 2840
63 6-17 Hayd 8.1gd 63 2947
57 8-15 Ches 7.6g/f 62 3102
57 7-17 Newc 7g/f 60 3700
65a 11-14 Ling 7ap 77 4180
76a 4-14 Ling 7ap 76 4446
72a 3-10 Wolv 7.1ap [75] 4920

MALLIA 11 b g £3923
48 4-11 Redc 6sft [45] 1662
48a 1-11 **WOLV** 6af [46] 2202*
39a 6-15 Sout 7af 46 2501
46a 3-16 Sout 6af 46 2720
48a 2-15 Sout 6af 45 3000
48a 4-13 Sout 6af [46] 3482
9 8-13 Hayd 6gd [44] 3757
17 12-16 Hami 6g/s 42 4009

MALMAND 4 ch g £1474
47a 5-12 Wolv 8.5af [42] 47 vis
0 12-12 Wolv 12af [42] 114 vis
30a 7-14 Sout 8af 44 160 BL

9a 8-12 Wolv 9.4af [40] 302 vis
45a 1-9 **WOLV** 9.4af [40] 314* vis
24a 10-13 Ling 10ap [40] 412 vis
40a 4-11 Wolv 9.4af [46] 580 vis
29a 7-9 Wolv 9.4af [45] 821 vis

MALUTI 3 ch g £4957
45 8-14 Bath 5gd 53 1404
46 6-16 Ling 6g/f 50 1985
50 3-12 Brig 6g/f 48 2435
56 1-12 **BRIG** 5.3g/f 48 2645*
55 4-15 Redc 5g/s 53 2961
57 2-7 Bath 5g/f 53 3371
20 13-13 Brig 5.3g/f 54 3984
53 7-16 Good 5g/f 55 4528
53a 5-12 Wolv 5.1ap 55 5326

MALVERN LIGHT 3 b f £4791
97 4-13 Newm 7gd 1169
91 8-11 Ling 7sft [99] 1620
58 8-11 Hayd 6gd [97] 2240
101 3-9 Newm 7fm 96 3006

MAMBAZO 2 b c £956
32 8-8 Newm 6g/f 3473
0 17-17 Chep 6.1sft 4052
49 12-14 Yarm 7gd 4611
60 9-12 Wind 8.3g/f 4829
64a 2-12 Wolv 6ap [54] 5177

MAMBINA 2 ch f £16122
53a 7-12 Ling 8ap 100
49a 8-12 Ling 8ap 734
67 4-19 Warw 10.9gd 65 1124
56 4-10 Pont 10sft 66 1427
61 5-20 Wind 11.6sft 66 1648
36 8-8 Brig 9.9g/f 65 2046
61 4-13 Nott 10.5gd 62 3419
57 8-14 Hayd 10.5gd 62 3741
63 2-4 Beve 9.9g/s [62] 3855
62 2-6 Hami 11.1sft [60] 4011
62 3-16 Chep 10.2g/s 59 4365
64 2-13 Nott 10g/s [59] 4650
56 4-12 Pont 10fm [59] 4757
77 1-7 **EPSO** 10.1gd [63] 4911*
75 1-17 **NEWC** 10.1g/f 66 5016*
70 6-19 Pont 10g/s 72 5148
67 6-19 Donc 10.3sft 72 5201
70 3-16 Nott 10hvy 68 5345

MAMBOS MELODY 2 b f £0
43 14-19 Leic 7gd 5045

MAMCAZMA 6 gr g £5700
88 7-9 Newm 12g/f [95] 2246
83 15-19 Newc 16.1g/s 95 2771
91 4-14 York 13.9gd 92 3119
87 11-15 Good 14g/f 90 3510
61 11-11 Newm 16.1g/f 89 3779
72 11-17 Newm 14.8gd 86 4196
70 10-17 Nott 14.1g/s 85 4647
88 2-16 Asco 16.2g/f 80 4803
35 11-11 Newm 16sft 81 5271

MAMOOL 5 b h £37461
112 3-7 Deau 10hvy [115] 4016
118 1-4 **KEMP** 12fm [118] 4391* t
110 15-19 Long 12g/f [118] 4956
116 7-24 Flem 16g/s 115 5323

MAMORE GAP 6 b h £0
63a 8-12 Ling 8ap 73 369
60a 13-14 Ling 10ap 70 674
64 9-14 Nott 10fm [73] 1006
67 5-20 Newm 8g/f 70 3232
54 8-14 Sali 9.9g/f 68 3867
59 5-11 Wind 10gd [67] 4124
63 5-15 Chep 8.1g/s 67 4300
60 11-14 Wind 8.3g/f 64 4832

MAN AT ARMS 3 b c £4977
68 4-16 Bath 10.2g/f [69] 1790
80 1-7 **BRIG** 11.9fm 69 2333*
75 4-11 Good 12gd 74 2538
57 8-9 Ripo 12.3gd 78 2984 VIS
48 12-12 Wind 11.6gd 78 3161
79 4-12 Sand 14g/f 78 3359
77 6-9 Good 14fm 75 3556

69 10-13 Kemp 14.4fm 76 4395
45 9-11 Epso 12gd 76 4468 P
54 7-11 Newm 14g/f 72 4919 p

MAN CRAZY 2 b f £705
49a 10-11 Ling 7ap 70 261
57a 8-11 Ling 6ap 65 760
58a 6-15 Ling 7ap 60 901
37 17-20 Nott 6.1gd 68 1239
46 14-17 Kemp 7gd 65 2174
38 7-10 Redc 6gd [60] 2559
54 4-13 Sali 6g/s 55 3109 bl
46 10-14 Ling 6gd 55 3289 bl
45 7-13 Bath 5.7g/f [54] 3844 bl
52 4-12 Sand 5gd [50] 4605 bl
42 9-17 Leic 7gd 50 5056
68 11-11 Newm 6sft [48] 5270
45 4-18 Yarm 6g/s 48 5354

MAN O WORLD 2 b c £21808
101 1-4 LEOP 6g/f 2454*

MAN OF LETTERS 3 b c £14143
80 4-17 Donc 8gd 919
77 3-9 Warw 8.1sft 1089
78 2-7 Beve 7.5sft 73 1305
77 2-8 Muss 7.1g/s 73 1460
75 1-8 **MUSS** 7.1gd [76] 1554*
78 2-10 Leic 10g/f 76 1965
70 5-11 Sand 10g/s 76 2127
77 3-9 Beve 8.5sft 78 2940
70 9-11 Newm 10g/f 78 3236

MAN THE GATE 4 b g £6837
59a 3-13 Ling 10ap 58 104
44a 12-13 Ling 10ap 58 178
48a 8-14 Ling 10ap 58 236
60 2-9 Folk 12sft 55 979
59 5-11 Leic 10g/s 59 1357
51 11-17 Sali 14.1g/s 58 1502
58 3-16 Leic 11.8g/f 56 1830
49 6-18 Newm 12fm 56 2088
61 2-10 Newb 11g/f 55 2875
61 1-7 **EPSO** 12g/s 55 3040*
56 5-8 Epso 12gd 57 3217
57 8-16 Wind 11.6gd 59 3829
52 8-11 Good 11gd 59 3948
39 7-13 Folk 12gd 64 4119

MANA DARGENT 7 b g £13532
79 11-17 Ripo 16g/s 89 1361
94 5-17 Ches 18.7gd 89 1569
68 11-18 York 13.9g/s 89 1689
69 18-29 Asco 20g/f 88 2471
73 11-17 Asco 16.2gd 86 3125
91 1-13 **ASCO** 16.2g/f 84 3387*
92 5-19 Good 21fm 87 3531
90 7-16 Asco 16.2g/f 88 4803
27 30-34 Newm 18sft 88 5135

MANAAR 4 b g £7568
83 8-20 Newm 7g/s 86 1151
84 5-11 Donc 7g/f 85 2076
78 7-28 Asco 7g/f 83 2558
88 2-13 Asco 7gd 81 3068
0 B-7 Ayr 7.2gd [83] 3326
84 2-10 Epso 7gd [83] 4912
56 18-18 York 7gd 83 5000 BL

MANASHIN 4 b f £0
3a 7-8 Sout 8af 355
0 4-5 Wolv 12af [35] 823

MANDAHAR 5 b g £0
55a 9-11 Ling 8ap 697
48a 15-15 Ling 7ap 814
34 7-9 Kemp 6sft 946
19 16-17 Kemp 7gd 1136
19a 12-14 Ling 10ap [45] 1712
0 10-10 Sout 11af [40] 2499 VIS

MANDARIN SPIRIT 4 b g £6820
53 11-13 Yarm 6g/f 77 1726
59 5-7 Brig 7g/f 75 2045 bl
61 5-7 Folk 7g/f [72] 2272 bl
55 10-12 Newm 6gd 69 4229
64 5-18 Catt 6g/f 64 4438 bl
71 1-15 EPSO 7g/f 64 4475* bl

67a 4-13 Wolv 6ap 66 5010 bl
69 3-20 Yarm 7sft 66 5256 bl

MANDATUM 3 b g £9913
77 2-4 Ripo 12.3g/f 2484
78 2-10 Pont 10gd 3243
83 1-12 NEWM 12g/f 3783*
81 4-8 Donc 14.6sft 79 5204

MANDINKA 4 b g £0
2 13-13 Redc 8gd 32 2552
26 4-18 Beve 9.9g/s 32 4243
29 8-13 Warw 10.9g/f 35 4419
26 10-12 Pont 10fm [35] 4757

MANDOBI 3 ch c £46563
80 4-7 Nott 6.1g/s [93] 1771
98 2-17 Epso 7g/f 92 2212
106 1-27 ASCO 8g/f 95 2521*
105 2-9 Good 8fm [102] 3620

MANDOOB 6 b g £6665
59a 7-12 Ling 12ap 64 56
55a 10-14 Ling 13ap 62 147
56a 4-12 Wolv 12af 60 484 P
65a 1-5 WOLV 12af [59] 616* p
68a 1-12 WOLV 12af 59 634* p
34a 10-10 Wolv 12af 71 810 p
50 12-14 Kemp 14.4sft 73 948
62a 2-5 Wolv 12af [71] 1375 p
51 12-16 Brig 11.9fm 69 1693 p
64a 4-11 Ling 12ap [65] 2588 VIS
65a 4-8 Ling 12ap [60] 2739 vis
50a 6-13 Ling 16ap 55 3822 t

MANDRAKE EL MAGO 5 b h £22981
103 2-12 Jage 8.6aw 1697
104 3-9 Taby 12gd 4574

MANDYS COLLECTION 5 ch m £0
14a 15-16 Sout 5ap 45 1046
0 U-9 Ling 6ap [45] 1248
18a 5-6 Wolv 6af [40] 1671
14a 9-12 Wolv 5af [40] 1799 P

MANEKI NEKO 2 b c £2215
74 4-8 Newm 6g/f 3473
79 2-9 Brig 6g/f 3981
76 2-6 Muss 8g/f 4552
57 15-16 Good 7gd 75 5031

MANGO MISCHIEF 3 ch f £39924
92 1-4 Sali 9.9fm [85] 2290*
94 2-10 Wind 10fm 85 2761
94 4-10 Sali 9.9g/f [92] 3866
98 2-11 Epso 10.1gd [92] 4467
83 10-13 Asco 10g/f [90] 4772
102 1-14 DONC 10.3sft [90] 5370*

MANGROVE CAY 2 b c £314
67 8-15 Folk 7gd 4114
69 4-7 Muss 7.1gd 4518
69a 5-12 Wolv 6ap 4921
68a 5-13 Wolv 6ap [67] 5182 VIS

MANGUS 10 b g £234
37a 3-13 Wolv 5af [40] 312 BL e
31a 7-10 Ling 5ap [40] 653 bl e
26a 6-10 Wolv 5af 40 749 bl e
25a 8-12 Wolv 5af [35] 889 bl e
10a 7-8 Ling 5ap [35] 1290 bl e
33 5-10 Brig 5.3gd [35] 1544 bl

MANHATTAN JACK 3 ch g £1255
41 8-12 Ripo 9g/f 1784
73 5-8 Ripo 10g/f 2012
72 2-8 Hami 11.1g/f 2319
64 9-13 Redc 11g/s 69 2960

MANIATIS 7 b g £10702
63a 6-9 Sout 12af 95 856
74 1-14 SOUT 12g/s [90] 1047* vis
77a 1-5 WOLV 12af [75] 1375* vis
58 10-19 York 11.9sft 76 1668 vis
76a 2-10 Sout 11af [73] 2048 vis
76a 1-9 SOUT 12af [73] 2724* vis
75 3-4 Wind 10g/f [70] 2798 vis

MANIC 2 br f £4774

55 8-8 Ling 5gd 3445
76a 1-12 WOLV 6ap 4921*
62 3-9 Nott 6.1hvy [70] 5185
61 9-20 Yarm 8g/s 64 5349

MANIKATO 10 b g £0
17a 7-9 Wolv 7af [30] 310
22a 7-9 Wolv 9.4af [30] 399
14a 9-12 Wolv 8.5af [30] 777 T P
24 11-12 Warw 10.9fm 25 2436
31 9-11 Chep 10.2gd [26] 3730

MANNORA 4 b f £0
56 4-20 Yarm 6g/f 53 1730
27 12-16 Brig 6fm 53 2262
27 13-18 Ling 6gd 53 2396
37 9-20 Nott 6.1g/f 51 2630
37 11-14 Ling 6gd 50 3289
37a 9-10 Ling 5ap 50 3332

MANNY 4 b f £0
0 8-8 Wolv 12af [35] 1265
0 12-12 Newc 14.4sft 35 1396 P
6a 5-5 Wolv 9.4af [35] 1674 p

MANNYMAN 3 b f £0
59 8-14 Warw 7.1gd 4275
34 7-15 Yarm 7g/s 4587
2a 13-14 Ling 7ap 5080

MANORSHIELD MINX 2 b f £0
58 9-14 Newb 6fm 3626
59 9-14 Chep 8.1gd 4484
59 10-13 Sali 7sft 4576
35 12-19 Kemp 8g/f 4792

MANORSON 5 ch g £5746
83 10-17 Newb 12g/f 95 1759
53 11-13 Epso 12fm 90 2255 T
94 2-17 Newm 12g/f 85 4889 t
93 4-19 Newm 12gd 89 5085 t

MANRIQUE 2 ch c £0
35 20-21 Donc 6sft 5368

MANSFIELD PARK 3 b f £11046
108 3-9 Donc 8fm [100] 4495
107 3-13 Asco 8g/f 100 4802
109 1-8 LEIC 8gd [102] 5057+

MANSIYA 2 ch f £1006
71 2-9 Folk 7g/f 3721
68 6-18 Nott 8.2g/f 4842

MANTEL MINI 5 b m £231
24a 9-10 Ling 8ap 785 BL
40 6-6 Epso 10.1g/s 3043 P
29a 12-12 Ling 8ap 3286 p
25 10-10 Ling 6g/f [30] 3603 VIS

MANTILLA 7 b m £0
33a 7-13 Ling 13ap [30] 1076 vis

MANTLES PRIDE 9 b r g £0
0 9-10 Chep 8.1sft [45] 1334

MANTLES PRINCE 10 ch g £0
0 6-10 Wolv 16.2af 60 812

MANY THANKS 4 b f £0
19a 5-8 Wolv 12af [70] 644
10a 6-7 Sout 12af [70] 679 P

MANYANA 3 b c £17765
72 5-5 Newb 10gd 1208
108 1-7 GOOD 11g/f [100] 1814* T
107 11-15 Chan 12g/s [100] 2308
94 8-8 Good 12g/f [106] 3507 t

MAPLE SYRPLE 3 b f £0
89 8-11 Warw 7.1fm 2574 T

MARAAHEL 3 b c £66376
111 2-11 Newb 11g/f 93 1756
107 2-17 Asco 12g/f 100 2939
117 1-8 GOOD 12g/f [103] 3507*
118 4-9 Donc 14.6fm[112] 4532

MARAAKEB 3 br c £5564
67 6-16 Donc 10.3gd 2751
84 1-9 SAND 10gd 4501*

MARABAR 5 b m £8317
54a 5-12 Wolv 5af [74] 70
29a 11-11 Wolv 7af 70 363
29a 6-9 Sout 7af [65] 555
35a 5-9 Sout 7af [58] 639
38a 7-12 Ling 6ap 52 844 BL
28a 10-11 Wolv 5af 49 958 p
50 1-17 PONT 6hvy [70] 1065* bl
39 7-12 Sout 7gd [65] 1284 bl
9 17-17 Warw 5hvy [60] 1532 bl
64 3-19 Beve 5sft 60 1627 bl
57a 1-6 WOLV 7af [45] 1804* bl
51a 2-10 Sout 6af [45] 1837 bl
56a 2-12 Wolv 7af 50 2204 bl
46a 6-16 Sout 7af 50 2335 bl
49 6-8 Thir 8fm 61 2464 bl
48 11-11 Pont 6g/f 59 2791 bl
58 4-9 Thir 5g/s 56 4210
34 14-18 Leic 6gd 56 5039
34a 8-12 Wolv 7.1ap [54] 5358 bl e

MARAJUANA 2 b f £4316
82 1-11 WIND 5g/f 2450*
0 W-9 Newm 6g/f 2763

MARAKASH 4 b g £732
41a 7-13 Wolv 8.5af [60] 39
30a 12-14 Ling 10ap 52 101 P
51a 2-12 Ling 8ap [51] 675 T p
0 8-9 Ling 8ap [51] 717 tp
39a 6-10 Ling 8ap [48] 831 t p

MARAUD 10 ch g £195
36a 5-10 Sout 16af [25] 307
17a 3-6 Wolv 16.2af [30] 395

MARAVEDI 4 ch f £0
24a 12-13 Wolv 9.4af 47 1223
23a 8-12 Ling 8ap [45] 1451 VIS
0 8-8 Sout 14af [40] 1840 vis
4 9-9 Ayr 13.1sft [35] 5277

MARBLE ARCH 8 b g £0
36 10-11 Muss 16g/s 84 5335

MARBURYANNA 4 ch f £0
0 17-17 Hayd 8.1g/s 4768
33a 11-12 Wolv 7.1ap 5006

MARBUSH 3 ro c £8137
85 3-17 Newm 8gd 1166
88 2-12 Ripo 9g/f 1783
85 1-7 MUSS 8fm 2081*
83 5-11 Asco 8gd [85] 3128
85 3-8 Newm 10g/f [83] 3945 T

MARBYE 4 b f £83979
100 5-10 Asco 8g/f 2487 T
116 1-8 DEAU 8gd 3659*

MARCELA ZABALA 2 b f £5474
32a 7-8 Sout 5ap 1048
58 1-6 LEIC 5g/f 3209*
0 8-8 Ling 6ap [55] 3745
59 1-9 YARM 6sft 54 4146*
42 10-19 Nott 6.1g/s 58 4645
0 21-21 Donc 6hvy [55] 5202

MARCHETTA 2 b f £1007
68 6-12 Folk 7gd 3909
78 5-7 Kemp 7g/f 4359
73 3-13 Warw 7.1g/s 4664

MARCHING SONG 2 b c £13677
78 5-8 Newb 5.2gd 1205
81 3-10 Leic 5g/f 1826
84 2-11 Wind 5g/f 2450
95 4-13 Newm 7g/f 83 3065
85 2-8 Sali 6gd 3451
88 1-7 FOLK 6g/f [85] 3722*
93 2-16 Newm 6gd 86 4224
76 5-6 Sali 6gd [91] 4854

MARCUS EILE 2 b c £1078
85a 3-10 Ling 8ap [86] 229
68a 4-6 Ling 10ap 83 403
69a 4-6 Wolv 8.5af 83 470
2a 8-8 Wolv 8.5af 77 645

39 19-20 Donc 7sft 80 5367

MARDONICDECLARE 3 b g £0
2 9-9 Pont 8gd 3462

MAREDSOUS 4 b f £7711
105 3-8 Long 12sft 1698

MAREN 3 b c £0
80 7-15 Sand 7.1gd 83 4500 T
0 18-18 Kemp 8g/f 82 4714 t
62 12-12 Epso 8.5gd 82 4909 t

MARENGO 9 b g £0
0 13-14 Sout 8af 37 160
2a 11-14 Sout 12af [34] 305
0 7-7 Sout 14af [35] 357
13a 6-12 Sout 11af [30] 640
9a 7-8 Sout 11af [30] 722
12a 7-12 Wolv 9.4af [30] 782 P
13 6-9 Pont 10sft 30 1430
28 4-5 Brig 8gd [30] 1546
17a 7-7 Sout 8af [30] 1593
2 13-13 Nott 10gd 25 3992
24a 9-11 Sout 8af [20] 4090
29 11-11 Epso 6gd [30] 4294

MARGALITA 3 b f £0
45a 9-12 Ling 8ap 234
70a 6-11 Ling 6ap 75 760
40 17-20 Wind 6g/s 75 1255 T
14 20-20 Asco 8g/f 72 1927 BL t
63 6-10 Sand 5gd 69 2189 t
53 10-17 Wind 6g/f 68 2451 t
42 9-10 Epso 7g/f 65 2872 t
22 16-17 Sand 5gd 63 3341 t
51 11-15 Good 5gd 60 4751 bl t
33a 10-14 Ling 7ap [55] 5294 bl t
41a 8-13 Wolv 6ap [55] 5359 bl t

MARGARETS DREAM 3 b f £477
49 3-18 Yarm 6g/s 47 5354

MARGARETS WISH 3 gr f £1477
10a 16-16 Sout 7af [38] 61
1a 11-16 Sout 8af [40] 442
44a 4-10 Ling 10ap [30] 540
7a 7-12 Ling 10ap [30] 654
0 12-13 Wolv 8.5af [30] 826
43 1-8 CHEP 10.2sft [35] 1333*
26 8-13 Kemp 10hvy [40] 1643
8 10-11 Hayd 10.5g/s 43 2226
30 10-11 Chep 10.2gd 43 2371
0 15-17 Chep 8.1g/s 42 3087
31 6-11 Bath 10.2g/f 42 3373 BL
18 8-14 Chep 10.2g/s 40 3895 bl

MARGERY DAW 3 b f £1726
64a 2-13 Ling 10ap 148
61a 5-13 Ling 10ap 64 215
64a 2-9 Ling 10ap [64] 269
56a 5-12 Ling 8ap [64] 401
65 8-10 Ches 10.3gd [64] 1585
50a 8-14 Ling 10ap 64 1618
50 11-16 Brig 11.9fm 64 1693
22 6-7 Leic 11.8g/f 60 1967
51 3-6 Brig 11.9g/f [60] 2047
23 16-18 Newm 12fm 60 2088
17 7-7 Brig 9.9fm [55] 2332
39 5-9 Brig 8g/f [50] 2431
1 19-19 Brig 9.9sft 46 4145
30 10-15 Folk 9.7g/f [45] 4373
33a 8-14 Ling 10ap [45] 4661
12 15-19 Brig 9.9gd [40] 4903 bl

MARGOLD 3 ch f £468
25a 6-12 Wolv 12af 55 75
5a 7-7 Sout 8af [55] 334
0 11-12 Sout 14af [45] 443
49 3-13 Ripo 12.3g/f 50 2008
7 18-20 Catt 12g/f 48 2850
28 17-20 Catt 12g/f 47 3354

MARHABA MILLION 2 gr c £0
54 8-15 Sali 8gd 4851

MARHOON 2 ch c £6164
67 4-12 Wind 6g/s 4945
78 2-15 Brig 7sft 5192 T

80a 1-12 LING 8ap 5295* t

MARIA BONITA 3 b f £2533
52 4-9 Sout 10gd 1283
59 12-13 Bath 10.2g/f [70] 1791
65 4-7 Bath 10.2g/f 65 2979 BL
54 8-10 Newm 10fm 65 3404 bl
53a 4-13 Ling 10ap [63] 4112 bl
50 3-11 Yarm 11.5g/s [63] 4584 bl
65 3-9 Good 11gd [60] 5026
60a 3-12 Wolv 12.2ap 61 5339

MARIA DELFINA 2 ch f £664
60a 3-12 Ling 8ap 5295

MARIA MARIA 2 ch f £383
12a 14-15 Sout 7af 184
0 11-11 Wolv 9.4af 438 P
1a 7-9 Sout 8af 983
49 4-7 Nott 8.2hvy 1610
1 10-11 Yarm 11.5g/f 48 2346
0 11-11 Sout 8af [45] 3091

MARIANIS 2 b f £369
65 4-6 Good 6g/f 1866
59 10-19 Newb 6g/f 2310
66 5-9 Folk 7g/s 3047

MARIANS GIFT 2 ch f £0
29 11-15 York 5g/f 2056

MARIANS MAID 2 b f £0
48 13-18 Wind 6gd 2618
54 6-9 Ling 6gd 3020
48 13-14 Yarm 7gd 3489

MARIAS MAGIC 3 b f £3689
86 1-18 BATH 10.2gd 5023*
60 9-11 Yarm 10.1g/s 75 5353

MARIDAY 3 b r g £0
34 6-7 Good 9.9g/f 4541
55a 9-14 Ling 13ap 4898
46 6-8 Brig 11.9sft 5092

MARINAITE 3 b f £8761
68a 2-12 Sout 8af 460
79a 1-7 SOUT 7af 531*
72 5-16 Sout 7g/s 75 1049
75 2-20 Nott 6.1gd 73 1239
77a 2-8 Sout 6af 75 1441
56 14-17 Nott 5.1g/s 74 1774
76 3-14 Nott 8.2g/f 73 2153
58 12-13 Redc 7fm [73] 4341
98 3-8 Leic 8gd [73] 5057
53 14-16 Catt 7sft 73 5130
51 13-16 Redc 6sft 73 5304

MARINE CITY 3 b f £6698
78 1-8 FOLK 12sft 1272*
74 6-9 Ches 12.3gd 77 1582
60 6-6 Redc 11g/f 75 2103
72 3-4 Newc 12.4sft 74 4288
77 4-13 Yarm 16g/s 72 4634 P
77 3-7 Nott 16g/f 72 4846 p
60 5-13 Newb 16sft 71 5194 p

MARINNETTE 3 ch f £0
93 5-7 Curr 12g/f 3321
32 14-14 Donc 10.3sft 5370

MARINO MOU 4 b c £541
0 7-7 Wolv 9.4af 509
0 7-7 Wolv 9.4af 561
6a 6-7 Sout 12af 1030 BL
44 3-9 Folk 15.4sft 30 1271
0 10-10 Muss 16gd 45 1551
22 9-9 Newc 16.1gd 45 1870

MARITA 2 ch f £287
40a 3-11 Wolv 8.5af [51] 279
36a 5-8 Wolv 8.5af [45] 383
28a 7-8 Sout 8af 45 490 VIS

MARITIMA 2 b f £0
0 U-19 Leic 7gd 5045

MARITIME BLUES 4 b g £9731
59 11-14 Nott 10fm [68] 1006
63 7-19 Beve 9.9g/s 65 1164

58 7-11 Leic 10g/s 62 1357
66 1-11 DONC 12g/f 58 1875*
43 9-11 Pont 12g/f 63 2041
57 6-9 Thir 12fm 65 2465
64 3-8 Donc 12g/s 64 3222
45 12-13 York 11.9g/f 64 3437
41 11-12 Newm 10g/f 62 3785
65 1-8 AYR 10hvy 60 4084+
49 7-9 Redc 10gd 63 4248
64 5-13 Newc 10.1g/f 63 4406
53 8-18 Ayr 10.9sft 63 4623
48a 8-12 Wolv 12.2ap 61 4983
66 2-17 Redc 10sft 60 5307

MARK YOUR CARD 2 ch f £0
45 8-18 Ripo 6g/s 3939
31 13-14 Thir 7g/s 4204
3 12-13 York 7.9gd 4325
29 11-13 Thir 6g/f 4590

MARK YOUR WAY 4 b g £0
34 11-14 Sali 9.9g/f 55 3867
4 13-15 Chep 10.2g/s 52 4299
30 10-13 Warw 10.9g/f 52 4419

MARKER 4 ch g £21525
85 6-13 Kemp 7sft 92 945
79 8-20 Kemp 6gd 90 1138
79 13-30 Newm 6g/f 88 1481
82 4-14 Ling 7sft 85 1624
79 9-19 Kemp 6fm 83 2070
79 4-12 Kemp 7g/s 80 2679
71 10-13 Newb 7g/f 80 2880
73 10-20 Chep 7.1g/s 79 3088 vis
75 4-6 Hayd 6g/s 76 3903
83 1-12 GOOD 6sft 73 4184*
64 10-16 Redc 6sft 78 5304

MARKET AVENUE 5 b m £3836
51 6-16 Redc 10g/f 62 1821
40 7-10 Pont 10g/f 62 2794
59 5-9 Hami 9.2gd 62 3132
57 7-12 Ayr 8gd 61 3328
54 5-12 Ayr 9.1g/f 58 3766
64 1-13 NEWC 10.1g/f 58 4406*
42 11-16 Ches 10.3g/f 64 4515
61 9-15 Nott 10g/f 63 4849
64 6-17 Newc 10.1g/f 63 5016 P
56a 6-13 Wolv 9.5ap 62 5361 p

MARKET LEADER 3 b f £2598
69 3-6 Thir 12g/f 72 3415
72 3-7 Good 14sft 71 4267
60 3-6 Chep 12.1gd [71] 4486 BL
55 3-11 Good 14gd [67] 5029

MARKET TREND 2 b f £7200
76 2-7 Epso 6gd 4466
85 1-11 AYR 7.2g/s 4653*
83 7-17 Catt 7gd 82 4963
59 10-12 Newm 8gd 82 5089

MARKO JADEO 6 b g £0
19 10-10 Newb 8g/f [91] 4890

MARKSGOLD 2 b c £570
44a 10-14 Ling 6ap 146
61 3-12 Warw 7.1gd 1125
64a 6-6 Wolv 7af 1321
46 6-10 Bath 5.7sft [60] 1539
30 10-14 Sali 7g/f [60] 1720
37a 5-8 Ling 12ap [57] 2065
41 9-17 Leic 7gd [55] 2704

MARLENES GIRL 2 b f £0
6 15-15 Beve 5g/s 3178
55 6-10 Hayd 5gd 3755
12 16-18 Pont 5g/s 3968

MARMADUKE 7 ch g £834
54a 6-15 Sout 12af 61 257
65a 2-10 Wolv 16.2af 61 358
65a 5-12 Ling 16ap 63 478
64a 4-14 Ling 12ap 63 801

MARNE 2 b g £0
29a 4-4 Wolv 5af 938

MARNIE 7 ch m £6292

45a	9-11	Ling	8ap	49	732
54a	1-12	LING	8ap	47	845*
50a	3-10	Ling	8ap	53	917
40a	9-12	Ling	8ap	51	1045
53	2-16	Bath	8fm	[51]	2032
54	2-6	Bath	8fm	51	2414
51	5-8	Bath	8fm	52	2665
48	5-11	Bath	8gd	51	3142
39	5-6	Epso	8.5fm	49	3540
39	8-14	Bath	8g/f	48	3963
39	6-19	Kemp	8g/f	[47]	4795

MAROMITO 7 b g £9855

29a	11-12	Sout	5af	[55]	587
30a	10-13	Sout	6af	50	741
40a	3-7	Wolv	7af	45	860
49a	1-8	LING	5ap	[40]	1290+
48a	1-10	SOUT	5af	[40]	1408*
49	10-18	Good	5g/f	55	1867
23a	9-13	Wolv	5af	47	2201
58	3-13	Catt	5g/f	55	3350
51	8-17	Catt	5g/f	55	3667
66	1-15	SALI	5gd	55	4335*
57	4-15	Chep	5.1gd	55	4489
55	9-15	Good	5gd	63	4751

MARON 7 b g £391

30a	5-13	Ling	6ap	[35]	541 bl
38a	2-10	Wolv	5af	[35]	781 bl
23a	4-6	Ling	6ap	[40]	1184 bl

MARREL 6 b g £0

48	5-11	Ling	16gd	39	3200 vis
41	6-19	Chep	12.1gd	42	3727

MARSAD 10 ch g £13074

77	18-30	Newm	6g/f	90	1481
86	3-14	York	6g/f	88	1703
85	8-19	Kemp	6fm	88	2070
91	2-10	York	6g/f	86	2357
44	11-16	Wind	6fm	89	2758
66	20-28	Good	6fm	88	3622
77	8-16	Wind	6gd	86	3827
90	2-13	York	6gd	85	4322
83	8-14	Ripo	6gd	87	4786
74	14-20	York	6gd	86	5001
84	4-12	Newb	6sft	84	5196

MARSH ORCHID 3 b g £2059

74	5-12	Newm	7g/s		1152
76	2-9	Nott	8.2g/f		3581
69	2-8	Redc	9g/f		3805
23	9-9	Yarm	10.1g/s	[75]	4254

MARSHAL BOND 6 b g £0

0	9-9	Wolv	9.4af	[45]	522 bl

MARSHALL 4 b c £10282

115	2-10	Mais	10gd	4837

MARSHALLSPARK 5 b g £13538

63	7-8	Hami	5gd	[70]	1749
25	15-20	York	6g/f	67	2059
49	9-15	Pont	6gd	64	2280
62	5-8	Hami	6gd	61	2713
70	1-14	LEIC	6g/f	60	3213+
37	8-8	Pont	6gd	66	3461
75	1-8	AYR	6g/f	65	3763*
72	6-20	Donc	5fm	71	4496
76	2-19	Good	6gd	71	4747

MARSHMAN 4 ch g £18572

90a	4-15	Ling	7ap	89	81
67	17-24	Donc	8gd	89	928
93	3-20	Newm	7g/s	89	1151
82	7-14	Ling	7sft	90	1624
85	8-11	Newm	7fm	90	2090
47	18-21	Asco	7g/f	89	3441
81	12-20	Newm	7g/f	86	3782
79	10-16	Newb	7g/f	84	3954
83	3-8	Ches	7sft	84	4073
77	3-8	Chep	7.1g/s	[82]	4301 BL
83	5-18	Ayr	7.2sft	90	4689
94	1-18	YORK	7gd	79	5000*
83	5-16	Newm	7sft	85	5101
91a	6-14	Ling	7ap	89	5262

MARTALINE 5 gr h £22641

115	5-7	Newm	12fm	1493
116	2-9	Deau	12.5hvy	4312

MARTHA REILLY 8 ch m £0

26a	6-9	Sout	16af	[35]	576
11a	9-10	Ling	16ap	[35]	650

MARTILLO 4 b c £77885

116	5-11	Nad	9g/f	991
108	9-16	Asco	8g/f	2470
115	1-6	HOPP	8gd	3166*

MARTIN HOUSE 5 b g £0

31	18-18	Catt	7g/f	60	2848
46	9-16	Hayd	10.5sft	55	3276

MARTON MERE 8 ch g £0

26	8-11	Catt	12g/f	[36]	3190
0	14-14	Catt	12g/f	[32]	3668

MARY CARLETON 3 ch f £0

30	13-16	Newm	7fm		2092
39	6-6	Yarm	7g/f		2342
23	13-14	Thir	7sft		2692
4	10-11	Brig	9.9g/f	40	3982
0	10-12	Wolv	12.2ap	[40]	5208

MARY GRAY 2 gr f £0

57	5-8	Catt	6g/f		3348
67	11-13	Good	7fm		3554
31	12-13	Newc	7g/f		5012
58	9-19	Redc	8sft	64	5302

MARY READ 2 ch f £37904

73	3-8	Pont	5hvy		1249
81	1-9	MUSS	5g/s		1458*
85	3-12	Beve	5g/f		2165
95	1-6	WIND	5fm		2786*
100	2-13	Good	5g/f		3509
86	9-12	Newb	5.2g/f	[100]	3956
100	2-12	Ayr	5g/s	[100]	4651
89	7-29	Newm	6gd		5087

MARYSIENKA 3 b f £1114

30	11-11	Donc	6g/s	76	3379
49	5-8	Pont	6gd	[73]	3684
66	9-15	Thir	5g/s	73	3833
68	3-9	Wind	5g/f	68	3976
48	4-14	Newc	5g/f	[68]	4404
62	11-15	Sand	5gd	68	4604 P
27a	12-13	Wolv	6ap	68	5114

MAS O MENOS 2 b g £2134

62	2-3	Redc	5sft		1658
4a	11-11	Wolv	6af		2051
0	20-20	Hayd	6gd		2882
68	2-9	Catt	6g/f		4670
40	13-15	Ripo	5gd	65	4784
3	17-18	Newc	6g/f	62	5013

MASA 2 b f £5801

92	1-13	LING	6g/f	2061*
87	9-17	Asco	6g/f	2553
77	7-10	Newm	6fm	3003

MASAFI 2 b c £29670

31a	10-13	Wolv	6af		3
60a	2-12	Ling	8ap	52	845
67a	1-16	SOUT	8af	53	3159*
70	1-6	CARL	9.3g/f	59	3231+
76	1-12	BRIG	9.9g/f	59	3300*
86	1-7	FOLK	9.7gd	59	3384*
73a	1-10	SOUT	8af	59	3395*
96	1-6	MUSS	9g/f	75	3529+
88	1-9	CARL	9.3fm	[69]	3546+
79	5-15	Brig	8fm	79	3694
90	7-8	Pont	10fm	92	4755

MASJOOR 4 ch g £1139

58a	7-14	Ling	12ap	60	801
63a	2-7	Sout	12af	[59]	1030
23	11-18	Nott	14.1sft	59	1469

MASKED 3 b c £7673

71	8-16	Wind	10gd		1384
71	7-9	Ling	10sft		1623
71	4-17	Chep	8.1gd		2117
77	1-7	HAMI	11.1g/f	[70]	2478*
71	5-9	Ripo	12.3gd	71	2984

77	2-8	Newb	12g/f	71	3270
82	2-12	Kemp	14.4g/f	75	3688
72	11-13	Kemp	14.4fm	79	4395
59	9-11	Newm	14g/f	79	4919

MASQUERADER 2 ch c £0

64	7-8	York	7g/s	3078

MASSEY 7 br g £19310

75a	12-15	Sout	5af	95	64
76a	14-16	Sout	5af	95	171
67a	12-13	Ling	6ap	93	235
96a	1-12	WOLV	6af	90	361+
68a	12-13	Wolv	6af	95	482
87a	1-10	SOUT	8af	[95]	532*
48	7-14	Hami	6gd	57	3129
36	12-14	Catt	6g/f	55	3352
24	15-18	Catt	7g/f	52	3670
13	12-15	Ayr	7.2hvy	50	4088
35	7-15	Carl	5fm	[47]	4508 vis
86a	13-14	Ling	7ap	95	5262

MASSIF CENTRALE 3 ch c £23187

72	7-12	Sali	12g/s		1501
98	2-17	Newb	10gd		1737
103	11-14	Epso	12fm		2254
90	1-7	NEWB	12g/f	[100]	2879*
96	7-8	Good	12g/f	[100]	3507
90	5-7	Newm	14g/f	[98]	4878
105	1-15	LEIC	11.8gd	96	5043+
0	6-8	Newb	12hvy	[101]	5224

MASTER COBBLER 2 b c £3339

83	4-8	Newb	5.2fm		2646
83	2-7	Ayr	6gd		3323
79	2-11	Bath	10.2gd		4825
69	4-8	Muss	9g/s	[84]	5140

MASTER JOSEPH 2 b c £2961

49	4-7	Bath	5.7fm		1900
61	7-12	Newb	6g/f		2348
64	8-17	Ling	7g/f		2584
53	11-13	Newc	7g/s	64	3698
65	2-13	Newm	8gd	60	4193
61	5-20	Redc	7fm	60	4337

MASTER MAHOGANY 3 b g £5252

36a	9-10	Ling	6ap		606
61	4-8	Warw	8.1sft		1086
68	9-20	Bath	10.2gd		1398
70	8-13	Bath	10.2g/f	[69]	1791
55	6-13	Good	9g/f	69	2024
43	5-6	Newb	12g/f	66	2353
64	4-18	Leic	10gd	64	2706
49	6-13	Bath	10.2gd	[64]	3144
30	10-15	Sali	8gd	62	3455
63	3-12	Bath	8g/f	60	3846
38	10-19	Chep	8.1g/s	[60]	4366
67	1-13	BATH	8gd	59	4546*
58	6-15	Bath	8gd	61	4827

MASTER MARVEL 3 ch c £20731

89	2-17	Donc	8gd		919
84	1-11	MUSS	9g/f		1095*
90	1-20	NEWM	8fm	82	1496*
86	8-18	Epso	10.1fm	89	2250
61	19-27	Asco	8g/f	89	2521
81	6-7	Sand	8.1gd	89	4499
85	9-17	Newm	10g/f	86	4917

MASTER NIMBUS 4 b g £0

23	10-17	Carl	7.9fm	[49]	4506

MASTER OF THE RACE 2 ch c £1538

91	2-19	Newm	7g/s	5285

MASTER RAT 3 b g £0

3	11-14	Warw	7.1gd	4275
28	12-12	Sand	5gd	4605
8	17-17	Bath	5.7gd	5020

MASTER RATTLE 4 b g £1299

41a	15-16	Ling	7ap	56	270
42a	10-15	Ling	7ap	[53]	366
15a	11-13	Ling	6ap	50	448
35a	11-11	Wolv	7af	47	562
41a	5-14	Ling	6ap	[45]	709
48a	2-13	Ling	7ap	45	739
24a	11-14	Ling	7ap	[45]	783

42a	8-15	Ling	7ap	47	913 BL
0	9-9	Wolv	7af	[45]	1266 bl
41	2-16	Nott	6.1gd	[40]	1989

MASTER ROBBIE 5 b g £15064

67	12-13	Kemp	7sft	94	945
80	19-20	Newm	7g/s	94	1151
70	24-30	Newm	6g/f	92	1481
87	8-20	Asco	7g/f	90	1926
95	1-11	NEWM	7fm	88	2090*
86	6-9	Ches	7gd	91	2282
66	19-28	Asco	7g/f	92	2558
84	9-19	Newm	7g/f	91	3061
66	12-21	Asco	7g/f	91	3441
80	15-20	Newm	7g/f	89	3782 VIS
71	14-16	Newb	7g/f	88	3954
81	8-16	Good	7g/f	86	4523
81	7-16	Good	7g/f	84	4873
87	4-16	Newm	7g/f	84	4891
73	15-18	York	7gd	84	5000

MASTER ROLE 4 ch c £1020

62a	2-7	Wolv	9.4af	561
2a	6-8	Wolv	12af	808

MASTER T 5 b g £0

30a	12-14	Ling	10ap	[60]	477
49a	7-13	Ling	13ap	[55]	602

MASTER THEO 2 b c £6769

71a	5-12	Ling	10ap		116
78	7-24	Newm	8fm	[77]	1495
77	3-12	Leic	8fm	[77]	2106
72	3-11	Beve	7.5g/s	[77]	2325
71	3-4	Newc	8g/s	[77]	2729
78	3-9	Good	8gd	74	3950
68	8-13	Redc	7fm	[74]	4341
76	3-10	Leic	8gd	[73]	4702
69a	4-11	Ling	8ap	[73]	4977
80	2-11	Good	8gd	73	5027

MASTER WELLS 3 b g £15579

82	1-6	PONT	10sft		1428*
69	8-14	York	11.9g/s	85	1708
76	8-13	Hayd	11.9gd	82	2238
83	2-8	Ches	12.3g/s	79	2746
75	7-9	Ripo	12.3gd	80	2984
71	11-12	Sand	14g/f	78	3359
80	2-12	Ches	15.9sft	75	4106
84	1-7	THIR	16g/s	75	4209*
79	4-8	Ayr	17.5g/s	79	4657
43	8-9	Ayr	13.1sft	81	5068
63	7-7	Donc	16.5sft	80	5374

MASTERMAN READY 3 b g £7866

61	8-12	Sand	10g/f		2193
68	7-13	Sali	9.9gd		2700
69	6-14	Sali	12g/s	70	3114
61	8-13	Sali	14.1gd	67	3454
69	1-11	YARM	14.1gd	64	3998*
64	3-10	Yarm	14.1g/s	66	4255
67	6-9	Redc	14.1fm	66	4559
75	1-9	GOOD	16gd	66	4875*

MASTMAN 2 ch c £10150

80	2-15	Newb	7g/f		2876
80	5-8	Newb	7g/f		3267
82	4-9	Epso	7fm		3539 T
91	1-5	CHES	7.6g/f	[80]	4046* t
89	3-5	Newb	8g/f	[85]	4640 t

MATCH BALL 2 b f £0

19	11-11	Ripo	5g/s	3258

MATERIAL WITNESS 7 b g £84920

70	13-20	Kemp	6gd	88	1138
72	11-14	Ling	7sft	86	1624
88	2-16	Good	7g/f	83	1817
61	8-8	Donc	6g/f	[84]	2074
92	1-7	GOOD	7gd	84	2223*
96	1-11	WARW	7.1fm	[89]	2777+
102	1-19	NEWM	7g/f	94	3061*
105	2-12	Good	7fm	[99]	3555
93	9-28	Good	6fm	94	3622
104	4-11	York	7g/s	[100]	4063
107	1-8	GOOD	7g/f	100	4231*
103	6-8	Epso	7g/f	[105]	4472
99	7-14	Newb	7g/f	[105]	4638

80	15-15	Asco	7g/f	105	4800

MATHMAGICIAN 5 ch g £206

26a	4-8	Sout	8af	[35]	635 P
31a	5-10	Sout	8af	35	677 bl
37a	4-11	Sout	7af	[35]	771 bl
21a	8-10	Sout	8af	35	792 p
34a	4-16	Sout	11af	[35]	852 bl
7a	6-9	Sout	11af	[35]	906 bl
28a	6-10	Sout	16af	[35]	984 p
21	10-12	Sout	11gd	30	1286 bl
23a	3-10	Sout	8af	[35]	1406 bl
21a	5-7	Sout	8af	[35]	1593 bl

MATOURAKA 3 b f £0

7	16-17	Newb	9sft	69	5198

MATRIARCHAL 3 ch f £0

12a	10-15	Sout	8af	[38]	96
4a	13-14	Sout	8af	[38]	170
0	13-14	Redc	7g/f	[34]	2102
16	5-8	Ripo	8gd	[34]	2480
5a	8-9	Sout	7af	[30]	2801
11	11-14	Thir	9g/f	30	3417
0	9-13	Hayd	6gd	[30]	3757

MATRIMONY 3 b c £0

0	P-7	Newc	10.1gd	1871 T

MATSUNOSUKE 2 b c £0

2	F-10	Pont	6fm	4752
59	10-23	Newm	6g/f	5084

MATTY TUN 5 b g £13351

77	9-13	Beve	5g/s	[87]	1162
104	5-13	Newm	5g/s	[87]	1479
93	5-20	York	5g/s	94	1683
88	7-15	Hayd	5g/f	93	1917
24	29-29	Asco	6fm	92	2581
83	10-15	Newc	5g/s	92	2727
85	5-11	Sand	5g/s	90	2894
80	10-20	Hayd	5fm	87	3792
78	10-20	Donc	5fm	83	4496
76	10-20	Pont	5g/s	81	5149
92	1-13	DONC	5sft	81	5218*

MAUNBY RAVER 2 ch g £5649

69a	1-13	WOLV	6af	55	1*
66a	2-13	Sout	6af	[55]	63
66a	1-9	LING	6ap	62	105*
62a	5-14	Sout	7af	67	158
53a	7-15	Ling	7ap	66	337
62	4-6	Ripo	6g/f	[65]	1975
37	13-14	Catt	6g/f	63	3018 VIS

MAUNBY ROCKER 3 ch g £0

24a	12-14	Sout	8af	60	160
35a	14-14	Ling	10ap	57	339
40a	9-10	Sout	8af	[54]	502
40a	6-6	Sout	7af	[48]	593
32a	5-9	Sout	12af	[45]	774

MAUREEN ANN 3 b f £0

28a	11-14	Ling	12ap	[48]	103 h
52	9-16	Beve	7.5gd	55	2655
45	10-16	Beve	7.5gd	55	2891
43	10-17	Hayd	8.1gd	51	3759
28	14-16	Yarm	7gd	48	4616
45	7-16	Catt	7g/f	48	4676

MAUREENS LOUGH 2 b f £8069

52	3-10	Thir	5sft		1224
32	6-6	Ayr	5g/s		1445
59	1-7	REDC	7fm		2294*
46	5-8	Redc	7g/s		2563
59	4-14	Beve	7.5sft		2939
51	4-13	Catt	7g/f		3349
56	1-11	THIR	7g/f		3570*
45	9-12	Newm	7g/f	[57]	3750
52	5-14	Thir	7g/s	[55]	4206
15	16-19	Carl	5.9g/f	55	4344
31	15-17	York	7g/f	53	4396
55	2-16	Beve	7.5g/f	50	4597
32	6-8	Muss	8gd	53	4807

MAURO 2 b f £1573

51	4-15	Leic	5g/s	1353
70	2-6	Nott	5.1sft	1466
70	4-19	Wind	5g/f	1805

44	6-6	Epso	6g/s	3041
39	11-11	Nott	5.1gd	65	3987

MAWHOOB 5 gr g £0

10a	10-10	Sout	11af	[47]	142 vis
1a	14-14	Sout	14af	47	185 vis
0	9-9	Sout	12af	[45]	353 vis

MAXAMILLION 2 b c £5031

71	5-11	Chep	7.1hvy		4704
67	4-13	Brig	8sft		5091
88	1-15	BRIG	7sft		5192*
81	6-20	Donc	7sft	81	5373

MAXILLA 3 b f £5905

54a	4-14	Ling	10ap	[72]	14
66a	1-13	LING	10ap	[63]	148*
72	4-9	Nott	10sft	72	1467
61	8-19	Wind	10sft	[72]	1650
59	5-10	Beve	9.9g/s	71	2323
66	6-14	Folk	7g/s	69	3052
76	2-12	Hayd	11.9gd	69	3734
75	4-12	York	13.9g/f	74	4400

MAXIMINUS 3 b g £0

38a	11-14	Ling	10ap		53
70	4-10	Folk	9.7sft		1580
58a	9-15	Ling	12ap	[59]	2393
58	6-19	Wind	11.6fm	[56]	2788
33	13-15	Wind	11.6fm	55	3481
43a	8-14	Ling	16ap	[50]	4663

MAXIS PRINCESS 2 b f £0

50a	9-9	Ling	5ap	[60]	76 T
52	6-14	Bath	5gd	56	1404
41	9-10	Brig	5.3fm	54	1694
19	11-13	Wind	5fm	52	2784 P

MAXWELL 3 b c £5325

107	2-	Sain	8sft	108

MAY MORNING 2 b f £1528

69	4-11	Bath	5g/s	4200
81	2-12	Redc	6fm	4557

MAYADEEN 2 b c £4949

85	3-11	Newb	7g/f	3959
80	1-14	BATH	8gd	5018*

MAYBE SOMEDAY 3 ch g £3163

74a	3-7	Ling	10ap	73	325
63a	4-9	Wolv	9.4af	74	441
69a	6-12	Ling	7ap	73	545
68a	3-8	Ling	10ap	[71]	626
64a	3-11	Ling	8ap	[67]	696 P
47a	10-10	Ling	10ap	67	817 p
60a	2-9	Sout	7af	[67]	871 BL
9	15-17	Hayd	8.1gd	60	2243 p
0	9-12	Sout	7af	[60]	2337 bl
31	7-11	Yarm	7g/f	[55]	2852 bl
1	14-15	Leic	7g/f	[55]	3515 bl

MAYFAIR MAUNDY 4 ch f £0

0	4-4	Brig	7gd	[35]	1545
0	10-10	Kemp	5hvy	[35]	1644

MAYNOOTH PRINCE 2 b g £0

47	7-11	Newc	7fm	4863
16	11-12	Redc	8g/s	5107

MAYS DREAM 2 b f £0

37	8-11	Ayr	7.2g/s	4653

MAYSTOCK 3 ch f £9159

72a	1-10	LING	13ap	62	11* vis
70a	4-14	Ling	12ap	68	83 vis
67a	7-14	Ling	13ap	69	147 vis
79a	1-13	LING	13ap	68	342* vis
71a	10-14	Ling	12ap	78	731 vis
77a	3-9	Ling	10ap	77	876
52	8-10	Bath	11.7gd	77	1399
63	10-10	Sali	12g/f	77	1721 vis
74	3-13	Epso	10.1g/f	72	4473
61	11-16	Good	12gd	[73]	4745
69	7-17	Wind	10g/f	72	5050 vis
33	11-13	Bath	11.7sft	72	5174 vis

MAYZIN 3 b g £12128

54a	5-16	Ling	7ap	[45]	214 P

54a	4-15	Ling	7ap	[51]	263 p
57a	3-14	Ling	7ap	51	344 p
61a	2-15	Ling	7ap	[51]	366 p
52a	4-13	Ling	6ap	54	448 p
67a	**1-12**	**LING**	**7ap**	**[54]**	**566* p**
67a	2-16	Ling	7ap	60	600 p
65a	3-15	Ling	7ap	62	698 p
66a	3-12	Ling	6ap	62	880 p
69a	**1-14**	**LING**	**6ap**	**62**	**897* p**
69a	4-14	Ling	6ap	69	1025 p
45	10-18	Bath	5.7g/f	55	1788 p
49	8-16	Ling	7g/f	53	2063 p
49	7-10	Sand	5gd	53	2189 p
24	14-18	Ling	6gd	51	2396 p
14	14-16	Ling	6ap	49	3602 p
46	7-17	Wind	6fm	49	3643 p
40	10-15	Ling	7.6fm	47	3788 p
51	3-11	Sand	5sft	46	4070
38	5-16	Folk	6g/f	[47]	4370

MAZEPA 4 b c £2504
86	6-7	Kemp	6gd	[96]	1137
98	3-9	Newm	6fm	95	1490
73	8-14	York	6g/s	95	1703
2	5-5	Wind	6g/f	[95]	1953
76	15-15	Newm	7g/f	93	4891
58	12-12	Newb	6sft	90	5196

MAZRAM 5 b m £0
21	15-16	Beve	8.5g/s		3850
23	8-13	Carl	6.9fm		4504 BL
11	13-16	Brig	7gd		4901 bl

MAZUNA 3 b f £60189
71	1-11	LING	11.5g/f	59	2842*
71	2-12	Newb	10g/f	67	3255
73	3-5	Asco	12gd	68	3468
72	2-14	Newb	10g/f	68	3961
102	2-10	Donc	14.6fm	[69]	4460
108	**1-8**	**ASCO**	**12g/f**	**[97]**	**4774+**
106	6-14	Capa	10g/s	[97]	5244

MBOSI 3 b g £5420
87	3-4	Ayr	8g/f	[86]	2026
85	3-6	Epso	8.5g/s	84	3042
51	8-9	Donc	8g/s	84	3225
89	2-6	Newm	10.1gd	[83]	3430
68	14-15	Donc	10.3g/f	84	3598
64	3-4	Ayr	10g/f	[84]	3762
53	13-13	Wind	8.3g/s	82	4221 BL
32	13-13	Epso	8.5gd	78	4469 bl

MCCRACKEN 8 b g £0
34	6-13	Pont	21.6hvy	58	1252 t

MCELDOWNEY 2 b c £11236
75	3-6	Hami	6fm		2316
77	2-8	Beve	7.5gd		2511
80	2-9	Warw	7.1fm		2776
82	2-6	Hami	6fm	79	3245
82	3-10	Good	6g/f		3511
0	10-10	Asco	7gd	[77]	3774
67	7-11	Thir	7fm	[82]	4381 BL
78	2-7	Muss	7.1gd	[77]	4518
64	5-14	Hami	6sft	76	4692
80	**1-9**	**CATT**	**7sft**	**[76]**	**5316***

MCQUEEN 3 ch g £21461
61a	3-13	Wolv	8.5af	61	40
75a	**1-14**	**SOUT**	**8af**	**61**	**99***
57a	7-14	Sout	8af	74	195
63a	15-16	Ling	12ap	74	493
46	6-12	Folk	9.7sft	60	1273
49	8-14	Nott	10g/s	55	1776
20	12-18	Wind	11.6g/f	52	1960
60a	6-15	Sout	8af	70	2500
21a	9-10	Sout	12af	68	2998
59	2-13	Nott	10gd	50	3992
63	**1-14**	**GOOD**	**8sft**	**50**	**4189***
72	**1-15**	**CHEP**	**10.2g/s**	**58**	**4299***
53	8-16	Ches	10.3g/f	66	4515
66	5-19	Hayd	10.5g/s	66	4766
77	**1-17**	**NEWB**	**9sft**	**65**	**5198***
80	**1-17**	**REDC**	**10sft**	**71**	**5307***
81	2-16	Nott	10hvy	77	5345

MEADAAF 3 b c £7983
79	1-8	BRIG	9.9g/f	[71]	1369*

80	2-15	Ripo	12.3g/f	75	1785
84	3-12	Pont	10g/f	79	2277
84	6-13	Redc	11g/s	80	2960
85	3-8	Newb	13.3gd	80	3918

MEADOW HAWK 4 ch g £0
34	10-10	Nott	14.1sft		1742

MEATH 3 b c £41100
108	2-	Leop	8sft		1301
112	**1-5**	**CURR**	**10g/f**		**2006***
61	14-14	Epso	10fm		2254

MECCAS MATE 3 g r f £4414
44	5-10	Beve	5sft		2944
54	6-9	York	7gd		3121
55	5-12	Newm	6g/f	55	3942
62	**1-9**	**THIR**	**5g/s**	**55**	**4210+**
55	3-15	Hami	6sft	57	4696

MEDAGLIA DORO 5 br h £670391
122	2-12	Nad	10af		992 t

MEDALLA 4 g r c £1373
71	3-13	Pont	8g/s		3973
61	5-11	Beve	9.9sft		4261
55	7-12	Newc	8sft		4407
61	7-17	Newc	10.1g/f	70	5016

MEDALLIST 5 b g £0
66	6-12	Sand	8.1g/s	72	1352
57	6-9	Newc	10.1sft	[69]	1681 bl e

MEDIA PUZZLE 7 ch h £0
111	12-24	Flem	16g/s	112	5323 bl

MEDICA BOBA 3 b f £500
59	7-11	Sali	8fm		2419
56	8-14	Wind	8.3fm		2974
48	13-17	Wind	8.3fm		3480
43	11-13	Wind	8.3gd		3828
47	11-14	Chep	10.2gd	59	4487
58	3-9	Good	16gd	55	4875
33a	13-14	Ling	16ap	54	5082

MEDICINAL 3 g r c £37486
109	3-4	Leop	10g/s		1700
109	**1-10**	**LEOP**	**10g/f**		**2456* BL**
101	4-8	Leop	10g/f		3496 bl
111	3-6	Curr	10g/f		3840 bl

MEDITATION 2 ch f £4238
58	9-10	Yarm	7fm		2863
67a	7-13	Ling	7ap		3330
63a	7-14	Ling	7ap		4970
77a	**1-14**	**LING**	**7ap**		**5078***
29	20-20	Donc	7sft	71	5373

MEDUSA 4 b f £0
45	9-16	Nott	6.1sft	70	1465
47	10-10	Newb	7g/f	66	2312
41	10-11	Brig	7g/f	60	2644

MEELUP 3 ch g £6066
39a	12-16	Ling	7ap	[64]	180 P
53a	8-16	Ling	7ap	60	270 p
41a	11-14	Ling	7ap	57	499 p
54a	2-8	Ling	7ap	[53]	730 p
57a	2-9	Ling	8ap	53	763 p
61a	**1-11**	**LING**	**8ap**	**55**	**820* p**
56a	7-13	Ling	10ap	[59]	912 p
35a	12-12	Ling	10ap	[59]	1042 p
45	13-18	Wind	8.3gd	60	1385 p
63	2-14	Hami	8.3gd	57	1748 p
37	10-12	Sand	8.1g/s	59	2129 p
35	16-19	Chep	7.1gd	58	3401 p
40	12-17	Hayd	8.1g/s	56	3759 p
44	8-20	Chep	7.1g/s	54	4367 p
1	15-18	Good	8gd	51	4750 p
40a	11-13	Wolv	8.6ap	56	5183 p

MEGABOND 3 b g £1810
58a	5-11	Sout	6af	62	872
36a	10-12	Sout	7af	[62]	2496
53a	4-8	Sout	6af	59	3092
41	11-20	Thir	6g/f	57	3575
39	10-20	Newc	6g/f	54	4408
65	**1-13**	**CARL**	**6.9fm**	**[54]**	**4504* P**
37	11-12	Brig	8fm	[60]	4761 p

55a	5-11	Wolv	7.1ap	[60]	5178 p
53a	9-14	Ling	7ap	[60]	5263 VIS

MEGANS MAGIC 4 b f £6327
49	6-16	Newc	8hvy	60	1036
71	**1-15**	**BEVE**	**9.9sft**	**60**	**1307***
71	2-20	Ripo	8g/s	65	1366
55	7-15	Hami	8.3g/s	69	1602
54	7-7	Ripo	10g/f	[69]	1979
69	3-11	Ripo	10g/f	68	2483
61	6-9	Ripo	10g/s	68	3260
70	4-13	Ayr	10gd	68	3325
64	4-10	Beve	9.9sft	68	4260 e
54	9-13	Newc	10.1g/f	68	4406 BL e
67	5-16	Thir	8g/f	67	4592 bl e

MEGEC BLIS 3 b f £5265
83	3-6	Curr	7sft		1436

MEGELL 2 ch f £3762
53	6-8	Pont	5hvy		1249
66	2-11	Yarm	6g/f		1728
46	11-13	Carl	5gd		2670
69	5-6	Folk	7g/f	68	3723
65	**1-7**	**YARM**	**6gd**	**[67]**	**3994***
33	14-19	Nott	6.1g/s	65	4645

MEHMAAS 7 b g £2958
29a	7-11	Wolv	8.5af	[51]	128 vis
27	10-14	Hami	8.3gd	55	1504
0	18-19	Redc	8sft	55	1661 vis
15	18-18	Thir	8g/f	51	1972 vis
21	16-16	York	7g/f	51	2057 vis
48	4-8	Redc	8gd	46	2550 vis
18	13-16	Redc	8g/s	44	2958 vis
0	8-9	Sout	8af	43	2996 vis
58	**1-15**	**NEWC**	**7gd**	**[43]**	**3426* vis**
41	13-17	Newc	7g/s	56	3700 vis
48	11-16	Redc	7g/f	56	3809 vis
29	5-12	Hami	8.3g/s	[56]	4007 vis
40	7-12	Newc	8sft	[53]	4284 vis

MEISSEN 3 ch f £7255
77	2-10	Sand	10g/f		2386
77	2-9	Kemp	12g/f	[75]	2862
77a	**1-14**	**LING**	**13ap**	**[76]**	**4898***

MEKURIA 3 b f £453
65	9-13	Hayd	11.9gd	83	2238
42	18-19	Carl	11.9gd	80	2673
76	4-8	Nott	10g/s	75	2929

MELAINA 2 b f £9585
50a	6-12	Wolv	5af	[52]	32
56a	**1-11**	**WOLV**	**6af**	**[52]**	**73* P**
52a	2-6	Sout	6af	53	316 p
42a	7-13	Wolv	6af	53	436 p
37a	6-10	Sout	6af	53	592 p
57a	**1-12**	**WOLV**	**6af**	**53**	**1374* p**
67	**1-10**	**FOLK**	**6sft**	**62**	**1576* p**
53	9-17	Sali	6g/f	61	1722 p
56	5-12	Chep	6.1gd	66	2118 p
31	15-19	Leic	6g/f	65	2925 p

MELALCHRIST 2 b g £12268
80	**1-12**	**BEVE**	**5sft**		**1631***
82	2-7	Redc	5g/f		2100
87	2-6	Beve	5gd		2513
99	**1-5**	**BEVE**	**5gd**		**2888***
87	3-5	Hami	6g/f	[94]	3589
75	10-13	York	6gd	94	4004
59	10-21	Donc	6hvy	[94]	5202

MELANDRE 2 b f £6713
58	6-7	Thir	5g/s		1471
53	9-10	York	5g/s		1709
67	4-15	York	5g/f		2056
67	5-18	York	5g/f		2360
0	W-10	Thir	5fm	[64]	3606
74	**1-14**	**CATT**	**5gd**	**64**	**4437***
76	2-15	Ripo	5gd	69	4784
58	9-11	Epso	5g/f	73	4907

MELFORD RED 4 b g £0
2a	15-16	Sout	8af	43	2805

MELINDAS GIRL 3 b f £0
32	9-14	Warw	8.1sft	52	1529
35	6-10	Brig	9.9fm	49	4763

20 9-12 Brig 8sft 47 5094 VIS

MELODIAN 9 b h £10827
36a 5-12 Sout 11af 51 534 bl
56 4-14 Newc 10.1sft 60 964 bl
60 5-19 Beve 9.9g/s 59 1164 bl
67 1-9 PONT 10hvy 59 1254* bl
64 2-11 Beve 9.9sft 62 1633 bl
65 3-9 Newc 10.1sft [62] 1681 bl
66 2-9 Newc 10.1g/s [62] 3702 bl
70 1-14 HAYD 10.5gd 62 3741* bl
58 6-12 Newc 9hvy 65 4215 bl
61 9-12 Beve 12.1sft 65 4259 bl
49 10-13 Newc 10.1g/f 65 4406 bl
51 15-16 York 11.9gd 64 4990 bl
55 10-17 Redc 10sft 60 5307 bl

MELODY KING 3 b g £2867
28 15-15 Wind 6g/s 69 1054 bl
63 3-8 Bath 5.7fm 67 1903 bl
69 2-9 Chep 5.1gd 66 2195 bl
66 5-11 Ches 5.1gd 66 2286 bl
66 4-8 Bath 5.7fm [68] 2669 bl
65 3-12 Kemp 5g/f 67 3036 bl
67 6-10 Ches 5.1g/f 67 3080 bl
64 5-7 Bath 5g/f 67 3371 bl
2 U-12 Nott 5.1g/f [67] 3577 bl
40 8-13 Bath 5.7g/f [65] 3844 bl
64 6-14 Ches 6.1g/f 65 4048 bl
55 9-16 Good 5g/f 61 4528 vis
57 4-18 Leic 7gd [58] 4698 bl
38 12-17 Bath 5.7gd [55] 5020 bl
40 10-18 Yarm 6g/s 53 5354 bl

MELODY QUE 2 b f £0
66 6-12 Beve 7.5g/s 4242

MELOGRANO 3 ch g £1877
36a 6-12 Wolv 16.2af 46 7
36a 7-11 Wolv 16.2af 46 48
38a 2-7 Sout 11af [45] 1589
34a 8-16 Sout 12af 44 2340
26 12-15 Ayr 10.9g/s 54 2545
35 12-18 Pont 10g/f 50 2988
50a 1-12 WOLV 12.2ap [40] 5208*

MELROSE AVENUE 2 b c £6773
75 5-12 Sand 7.1g/f 2388
86 1-7 SAND 7.1g/s 2897*
93 5-5 Curr 6g/f 4154
91 4-4 Ayr 8g/s 4619

MELS MOMENT 2 b c £0
22 14-14 Sali 7sft 4575
74 6-15 Newm 8gd 4883
2a U-14 Ling 7ap 5078
73a 4-12 Wolv 7.1ap 5179
72a 6-13 Wolv 8.6ap [74] 5288

MELVINO 2 b c £1414
66 4-7 Hami 6gd 1744
66 7-18 Leic 5fm 2109
78 3-7 Hami 6g/f 2473
59 4-6 Hami 6fm 78 3245 VIS
53 10-10 Ripo 6gd 76 4306 vis
47 18-21 Donc 6fm [76] 4490

MEMBERSHIP 4 ch c £0
79 8-9 Donc 7sft 5214

MEMORY MAN 3 b g £780
25 11-12 Ling 6g/f 2586
68 4-14 Warw 7.1g/f 2907
70a 3-9 Ling 8ap 3197
19 7-7 Kemp 7g/f 67 3522
24 9-13 Carl 6.9fm [65] 4504

MENAI STRAIGHTS 3 ch g £5828
55a 6-12 Wolv 9.4af [66] 939
33 15-16 Beve 7.5g/s 65 1163
60 6-14 Ayr 8g/f [63] 1896
58 3-7 Muss 8fm [62] 2081
59 5-14 Redc 7fm 60 2295 P
64 1-11 CARL 6.9gd 59 2936*
67 3-7 Ayr 7.2gd 64 3153
50 9-14 Carl 6.9g/f 64 3229
59 6-10 Newc 7fm [63] 4869
62 6-19 Newc 7g/f 63 5014

61 7-14 Redc 7g/s 63 5109
59a 2-14 Ling 7ap 56 5300

MENEEF 3 b c £2911
64 3-5 Yarm 7gd 3366
76 2-15 Nott 8.2g/s 4649
76 3-10 Pont 8g/f [76] 4939

MENELAUS 3 b c £0
54 6-10 Yarm 11.5gd 3997

MENHOUBAH 3 b f £293059
107a2-8 Nad 8af 599 p
89 7-9 Nad 9af [100] 989
101 2-9 Ches 11.4gd 1568 p
105 1-11 SAN 11gd [100] 1999* p
97 13-17 Chan 12.5g/s[100] 2460
101 6-6 Good 9.9fm [106] 3621 p
59 8-8 York 11.9g/s[106] 4024 p
106 8-10 Long 10g/f [106] 4953

MENNA 2 b f £0
63 5-9 Ches 5.1gd 2281
62 7-7 Hayd 6gd 2883

MENOKEE 3 b c £6600
105 2-6 Newm 10sft [95] 5269

MEPHISTO 5 b g £184528
78 10-20 Newm 12gd 88 1172
89 5-17 Newb 12gd 86 1759
95 1-10 YORK 11.9g/f 86 2405*
101 1-15 NEWM 12g/f 88 3066*
104 1-15 GOOD 14g/f 92 3510*
110 1-19 YORK 13.9g/s 99 4023*

MERCARI 2 ch f £0
57 9-9 Ripo 6g/f 2522
35 12-16 Nott 6.1gd 3103
57 8-12 Redc 6fm 4557
63 6-15 Nott 5.1gd 4859
64 4-18 Newc 6g/f 61 5013

MERCHANT 2 ch c £56400
73 5-10 Folk 7g/s 3046
79 3-18 Donc 6g/s 3376
80 2-12 Carl 5.9fm 3544
87 1-11 HAMI 6g/s [78] 4006+
101 1-12 YORK 7g/s 84 4064*
98 1-13 NEWM 8gd 84 4193*
92 1-5 NEWB 8g/f [99] 4640*
104 4-10 San 8sft [99] 5167
79 7-8 Sain 8Very [99] 5315

MERCURIOUS 3 ch f £9612
42a 3-14 Sout 14af 41 185
40a 4-10 Wolv 12af 41 243
38a 4-13 Ling 13ap [40] 1076
46a 1-7 WOLV 16.2af [40] 1263*
25 5-9 Warw 15g/s [40] 1329
10a 4-7 Wolv 16.2af [45] 1802
49a 2-10 Sout 14af 42 3096
54a 1-6 SOUT 16af 45 3397*
47 2-10 Thir 16sft 41 3834
31a 5-16 Sout 14af 51 4045
53 1-20 CATT 15.8gd 45 4965*

MERDIFF 4 b g £13698
69a 1-13 WOLV 8.5af [64] 39* T
40 12-16 Sout 7g/s 62 1049
50 7-15 Redc 9g/f 60 2120
42a 10-15 Sout 8af 64 2500
65a 2-15 Sout 7af [62] 2999
65 1-15 CHES 7.6g/f 55 3102*
66a 2-13 Sout 7af 62 3155
38 10-12 Ches 7.6fm 59 3634
61a 4-14 Ling 7ap 63 3821
61 2-16 Ches 7g/f 59 4051
8 15-18 Ayr 7.2sft 61 4622
31 16-17 Nott 8.2gd 60 4862
71a 1-13 WOLV 6ap [63] 5327*

MERGER 2 gr c £16055
110 2-5 Curr 8g/s 5071

MERLINS CITY 4 b f £0
0 19-19 Redc 6g/s 5110
17 10-11 Redc 10sft 5303

MERLINS DANCER 4 b g £18009
60 10-17 Donc 6g/s 75 1523
73 5-16 Nott 6.1sft [75] 1743
83 1-9 RIPO 6g/f [72] 2007*
69 8-12 Ripo 5g/f 80 2524
65 11-17 Pont 5gd 80 3241
81 7-24 Asco 5gd 80 3466
83 4-22 Good 5fm 79 3537
89 1-26 GOOD 6fm 80 3569*
83 13-22 Donc 5.6fm 87 4459

MERLINS PROFIT 4 b g £918
33 5-8 Ayr 7.2g/s [45] 1448
42 4-10 Redc 11g/f [40] 1819
46 2-10 Beve 9.9g/f [40] 1946
32 7-15 Ayr 10.9g/s 44 2545
0 U-12 Hami 8.3g/s [43] 4007
40 4-8 Hami 9.2g/s [43] 4133
39 3-15 Carl 9.3fm [40] 4505
35 6-19 Brig 9.9gd [40] 4903
24 8-11 Ayr 9.1sft [40] 5067 BL

MERMAIDS CRY 2 b f £1100
51 2-11 Thir 6g/f 1968
24 7-7 Leic 5gd 2132
7a 11-11 Sout 6af 2336
24 9-9 Leic 5g/f 2921

MERRYMADCAP 2 b c £0
47 13-15 Wind 6g/f 2263
72 5-9 Sali 7gd 2696
70 6-10 Folk 7g/s 3046
66 6-9 Folk 7g/f 3721
2 8-9 Chep 8.1g/s 4297
71 6-13 Sali 7sft [63] 4576
55 15-20 Ling 7g/f 63 4741
58 11-19 Ling 6g/f [65] 4895 BL

MERRYMAKER 4 b g £15308
58 4-16 Brig 11.9fm 59 1693
53 6-11 Donc 12g/f 59 1875 bl
56 4-10 Yarm 11.5fm 55 2147
62 1-7 AYR 13.1g/s 55 2546*
62 2-9 Hayd 11.9gd 60 2900
69 1-8 NEWB 12g/f 62 3270*
49 11-13 York 11.9g/f 67 3437
50 8-12 Hayd 11.9gd 67 3734
73 3-12 Beve 12.1sft 65 4259
72 5-9 Muss 12g/f 70 4553
65 5-8 Ayr 13.1g/f 70 4690
78a 1-12 WOLV 12.2ap 69 4924*
69 5-13 Bath 11.7sft 71 5174

MERSEY SOUND 6 b g £0
26 17-18 Newb 16gd 70 1232
58 13-17 Sali 14.1g/s 67 1502

MERWAHA 3 b f £1693
78 4-10 Good 8gd 2224
69 3-7 Asco 8gd 3469
66 4-8 Sand 8.1g/f 3858 BL

MESAYAN 3 ch c £433
44 9-11 Newm 8g/f 2248 T
66 4-11 Hayd 8.1gd 2885 t

MESHAHEER 5 b h £14124
92 9-9 Hayd 7.1g/f [106] 1486 t
107 2-14 Newb 7g/f [105] 4638 t
108 1-9 DONC 7sft [105] 5214* t

MESMERISED 4 b f £0
9a 13-13 Wolv 5af [45] 312
18a 9-13 Wolv 6af [45] 397
1a 14-16 Sout 6af [40] 447
0 13-13 Wolv 6af [35] 483
0 6-7 Wolv 5af [30] 1309 p
8a 7-8 Wolv 7af [30] 1676 p
3 10-10 Thir 6g/f 35 1973
8 12-13 Leic 10fm [35] 2107 p

MESSE DE MINUIT 2 ch c £3636
79a 1-12 LING 8ap 102*
50 9-11 Ripo 12.3gd 77 1174
76 3-6 Beve 9.9gd [75] 3313
68 6-12 Bath 11.7g/f 75 3845

METEORITE SUN 6 b g £645

52	8-14	Newc	10.1sft	75	964
72	3-9	Pont	10hvy	70	1254

METHODICAL 2 b f £285

61	4-18	Donc	6g/s		3376
51	9-18	Ling	6gd		4108
66	5-10	Newb	6g/f		4637
2	19-20	Newb	6hvy	67	5225

METICULOUS 6 gr g £0

15a	7-8	Sout	7af	[30]	320
3a	7-11	Sout	8af	[30]	372
3a	9-11	Sout	12af	30	458
0	10-10	Sout	12af	[30]	552
0	12-14	Sout	7af	[30]	573 BL
5a	8-10	Sout	8af	30	677
14a	8-9	Sout	5af	[30]	981
19	8-12	Sout	7gd	[30]	1284
6	13-14	Donc	6g/s	[30]	1522
13a	10-16	Sout	7af	[30]	1839

METOLICA 2 b f £0

1a	11-12	Sout	5af	1439
15	11-16	Ripo	6g/f	1780
36	11-11	Beve	7.5g/s	3851

MEXICAN 5 b h £1069

4	19-19	Beve	9.9g/s	49	1164 p
22	7-8	Ayr	7.2g/s	[45]	1448 p
30a	3-8	Sout	8af	[40]	1841 vis
33a	5-10	Sout	12af	37	2998 p
40a	2-16	Sout	8af	37	3159 vis
12	7-13	Ayr	8sft	[40]	5275 t

MEXICAN PETE 4 b g £8884

32	15-20	Epso	12hvy	76	1295
80	3-12	Ches	12.3gd	74	1599
70	8-18	Nott	14.1g/s	75	1772
80	2-9	Donc	12g/f	74	2078
71	7-11	Donc	12gd	77	2233
77	4-6	Kemp	12g/s	77	2681
82	4-11	Asco	12gd	77	3070
82	3-6	Leic	11.8g/f	77	3345
82	2-6	Pont	12gd	78	3681
76	6-7	Leic	11.8fm	[78]	3816
76	9-17	Thir	12fm	79	4377

MEZEREON 4 b f £0

49a	7-14	Ling	10ap	[58]	477
50a	7-13	Wolv	9.4af	55	1223

MEZUZAH 4 b g £0

60	8-12	Pont	8hvy	86	1066
74	5-10	Hayd	8.1gd	83	2242
66	9-13	Sali	8gd	80	2662
52	16-20	York	10.4gd	77	4986
60	10-16	Catt	7sft	74	5130
55	13-17	Redc	10sft	70	5307

MI ODDS 7 b g £18647

81a	1-16	SOUT	11af	73	97*
86a	2-13	Wolv	9.4af	79	127
89a	1-8	SOUT	12af	83	225+
92a	2-10	Wolv	9.4af	89	278
100a	1-10	WOLV	8.5af	[90]	511*
98a	5-12	Wolv	8.5af	99	836
59a	14-14	Ling	10ap	[99]	884
61	10-19	Donc	10.3gd	70	924
57	8-11	Hayd	10.5g/f	67	1884
3	10-10	Hayd	10.5g/s	67	3139
29	11-16	Yarm	11.5g/s	62	4589

MICHABO 3 b g £10554

68	4-8	Ling	9g/f		2013
72	3-13	Wind	10g/f		2453
80	2-13	Sali	9.9gd		2700
70	6-13	Kemp	10gd	[80]	3186
80	2-9	Wind	10fm	[78]	3642
80	1-5	SAND	10g/s	[78]	3894*
80	3-9	Good	12sft	77	4183
57	11-12	Good	11gd	80	4749

MICHAELS DREAM 5 b g £1394

23a	6-12	Sout	14af	[40]	443 vis
40	3-16	Redc	10g/f	40	1821 vis
42	3-11	Donc	12g/f	40	1875
4	11-11	Pont	12g/f	40	2041 bl
46	4-18	Newm	12fm	45	2088 bl

1	12-15	Ripo	12.3g/f	44	2526 bl
38	10-12	Beve	12.1sft	42	4259

MICHAELS PRIDE 2 b f £0

42	10-15	Nott	8.2hvy	5344

MICHELLE MA BELLE 4 b f £5761

69a	8-10	Ling	7ap	76	799
76a	2-12	Ling	7ap	75	1024
76	2-6	Folk	7g/s	[75]	1079
67	8-19	Sali	7g/f	75	1723
45	14-20	Asco	8g/f	75	1927
68	7-11	Yarm	7gd	73	3364 BL
78	1-17	WIND	6fm	70	3643* bl
34	13-16	Wind	6gd	76	3827 bl
46	12-12	Good	6sft	75	4184 bl
47	16-19	Good	6gd	74	4747 bl

MICKEHAHA 7 b c £0

56	8-8	Epso	7gd	3214

MICKEY BOGGITT 2 b c £0

0	11-12	Ripo	5g/f	1974
21	7-7	Redc	7fm	2294

MICKEY PEARCE 2 b c £0

34	16-20	Wind	6fm	2970
43	10-13	Chep	6.1gd	3399
45	13-16	Sali	7gd	3882
54	8-11	Ches	7sft	4072

MICKLEDO 2 b c £0

58	11-12	Hayd	7g/s	3272
52	9-18	Pont	5g/s	3968

MICKLEDOR 4 ch f £7903

39	8-14	Leic	6g/f	[47]	1963 vis
27	13-19	Redc	6g/f	47	2125 bl
45	3-19	Beve	5g/s	45	2326 P
41	1-20	Muss	7.1g/f	43	2615 p
53	1-20	NOTT	6.1gd	43	2928* p
55	1-14	HAMI	6gd	50	3129* p
34	13-14	Catt	6g/f	54	3352 p
50	8-20	Redc	6g/f	54	3767 p
56	3-15	Newc	6hvy	53	4211 p
46	6-20	Newc	6g/f	53	4408 p
52	5-16	Catt	7g/f	52	4676 p
52	6-11	Hami	6g/s	52	4818 p

MICKLEGATE 3 b f £552

49	4-5	Carl	6.9fm	63	2446
60	4-11	Carl	6.9gd	61	2936
23	12-14	Beve	7.5g/s	[60]	3177
0	P-13	Carl	6.9fm	[58]	4504

MIDAS WAY 4 ch g £10900

100	2-6	Ches	13.4sft	95	4104
87	7-15	Donc	14.6fm	95	4491
98	3-16	Asco	16.2g/f	93	4803
85	23-34	Newm	18sft	95	5135

MIDCAP 2 b f £916

50	12-12	Newb	6g/f		3251
73	6-13	Good	7fm		3554
65	8-12	Folk	7gd		3909
72	3-12	Warw	7.1g/f	[73]	4418
70	6-17	Ling	7g/f	70	4894

MIDDLE EARTH 2 ch c £3273

77	2-10	Wind	5fm		3476
68	8-8	Kemp	6sft		4028
76a	2-8	Ling	6ap		5081 T

MIDDLE EASTERN 2 b c £277

58	5-7	Newc	6g/s		2774
68	4-14	Hayd	6gd		3735
56	10-12	Carl	5g/s		4343
31	9-10	Ayr	6g/s	68	4655

MIDDLEHAM PARK 3 b g £830

23a	6-10	Sout	8af	[65]	143
29a	14-16	Sout	7af	57	208
54a	2-10	Sout	8af	52	677
39	7-9	Thir	7g/f	[60]	2218
37	9-13	Redc	8gd	54	2552
44	10-20	Catt	12g/f	51	3354
54a	4-12	Wolv	8.6ap	[54]	5337

MIDDLEHAM ROSE 3 b f £408

29a	6-9	Wolv	9.4af	[35]	399
14a	6-9	Sout	8af	35	486
30a	2-6	Wolv	12af	[35]	1673
1	14-14	Redc	10fm	33	2299
5a	5-8	Sout	12af	33	4092

MIDDLEMARCH 4 ch c £0

86	7-10	Donc	8gd	[109]	922
99	4-7	Curr	10g/s	[109]	1560 p
72	13-14	York	10.4g/s	105	1704
102	5-15	York	8.9g/f	100	2404 P
2	8-8	Curr	8g/f	[100]	2820 p

MIDDLEMISS 4 b f £368

0	7-7	Chep	10.2sft	[40]	1332
18a	10-12	Ling	8ap	[40]	1451
34	2-4	Brig	7gd	[35]	1545 p

MIDDLETHORPE 7 b g £3572

66	1-22	DONC	12gd	62	918* bl
62	5-13	Catt	13.8gd	62	997 bl
67	6-13	Hayd	14sft	67	1109 bl
58	7-14	York	11.9gd	65	4327 bl
58	10-16	York	11.9gd	65	4990 bl

MIDDLETON GREY 5 gr g £14327

54a	6-9	Wolv	8.5af	85	2
79a	4-11	Sout	8af	82	255
73a	7-12	Wolv	9.4af	82	382
83a	3-13	Wolv	8af	79	807 bl
88a	2-12	Wolv	7af	80	840 bl
53	12-17	Leic	7g/s	64	1020 bl
67	3-14	Chep	7.1gd	62	2199 bl
63	5-17	Newm	7g/f	63	2768 bl
68	2-10	Hayd	7.1g/s	63	3137 bl
75	1-12	NEWM	6g/f	64	3942* bl
56	14-20	Newm	7g/s	71	5286 bl

MIDGES PRIDE 4 b g £0

0	10-10	Sout	8af	49	678

MIDMAAR 2 b c £0

62a	8-10	Ling	5ap		176
37a	11-11	Ling	7ap		220
58a	8-10	Ling	8ap		232
2a	10-10	Sout	12af	63	2998
19a	9-10	Sout	8af	60	3395
26a	12-13	Ling	10ap	55	3823
21a	10-15	Sout	8af	52	4132

MIDNIGHT ARROW 6 b m £0

17	15-15	Ches	7.6g/f	50	3102
37	8-12	Carl	6.9fm	45	3548

MIDNIGHT BALLARD 3 b c £5189

69	6-10	Newm	6g/f	[84]	1191
70	4-14	Thir	6gd	[82]	1639
80	2-16	Leic	7g/f	77	1825
46	15-15	Ling	7g/f	77	1983
80	1-9	FOLK	7fm	[80]	2716+
72	8-11	Leic	7g/f	80	3210
28	19-19	Kemp	6fm	79	4394 BL
63a	9-13	Thir	7ap	74	4897 bl
38a	11-13	Wolv	6ap	73	5114 bl

MIDNIGHT IN MOSCOW 2 b c £238

22	6-6	Pont	6g/f	2039
42	14-18	Ripo	6g/s	3939
37	9-9	York	6g/s	4026

MIDNIGHT LACE 2 ch f £731

9	9-9	Wind	5g/f		2795
45	16-16	Nott	6.1gd		3103
65	3-13	Nott	6.1g/f		4843
8	12-20	Newb	6hvy	63	5225

MIDNIGHT MAMBO 3 b f £489

26a	10-13	Ling	5ap		219
48a	5-15	Ling	7ap		263
52a	5-7	Wolv	7af		617
43a	5-14	Ling	10ap	[45]	828
23a	7-7	Wolv	9.4af	[45]	893 BL
22	12-20	Yarm	8gd	40	3996
1	14-15	Chep	10.2g/s	40	4299
45	2-15	Folk	9.7g/f	[40]	4373

MIDNIGHT PARKES 5 br g £15989

33	20-20	Thir	6gd	68	1638
61	4-15	Pont	6g/f	66	2280

54	8-19	Beve	5gd	66	2512
67	3-17	Redc	6gd	64	2561
68	5-9	Warw	5.5fm	65	2779
53	9-13	Hayd	6gd	65	2884
69	3-17	Pont	6g/f	65	2990 p
73	1-17	PONT	5g/f	67	3241* p
47	12-15	Pont	5gd	72	3680 p
64	9-18	Redc	6fm	70	4339 p
73	3-20	Donc	5fm	70	4496
56	13-17	Beve	5g/f	69	4603
65	7-16	Pont	5fm	70	4754
71	3-19	Ayr	6sft	69	5069

MIDNIGHT PRINCE 3 b c £0

49	6-10	Catt	7g/f	53	3016
51	5-18	Carl	7.9fm	51	3547
20	8-12	Beve	9.9g/s	49	3854

MIDNIGHT PROMISE 3 b g £0

16a	7-11	Sout	7af		488
25a	13-15	Ling	7ap		670

MIDNIGHT TYCOON 2 b c £6744

81	1-5	HAMI	5g/s		1601*
92	3-7	Beve	5g/f		2167
82	4-6	Hami	6gd		2711
27	9-9	Hayd	5sft	88	3271

MIDSHIPMAN 6 b h £7036

56a	7-8	Wolv	8.5af	[92]	360
0	16-16	Ling	12ap	86	475
25a	9-9	Sout	12af	86	856
63	7-20	Wind	11.6g/s	75	1056 VIS
41	17-18	Kemp	16g/s	75	1112 vis
58	3-9	Pont	10sft	65	1430 BL
52	10-14	Nott	12g/s	62	1776
45	9-10	Yarm	11.5fm	60	2147 vis T
59a	2-15	Sout	8af	55	2500 vis t
64a	2-16	Sout	8af	55	2805 vis t
61a	2-10	Sout	12af	55	2998 vis t
58a	4-10	Sout	8af	60	3395 vis t
27	10-15	Wind	10.2g/s	55	4299 vis t
54	6-18	Good	8gd	53	4750 vis t
57a	5-11	Wolv	12.2ap	57	5117 vis t
65a	1-13	WOLV	9.5ap	56	5361* vis t

MIDSHIPMAN EASY 3 ch g £1771

73	3-14	Wind	10g/s		1259
78	2-20	Wind	10sft		1651
62	11-16	Sand	10g/s	[77]	2131
45	7-8	Ches	12.3g/s	75	2746
28	6-8	Donc	12g/s	74	3222
51	14-14	Kemp	10g/f	70	3690 e
35	10-12	Brig	11.9sft	65	5093

MIGHTY EMPIRE 2 b c £10699

73	7-10	Donc	6g/f		2077
12	14-15	Beve	5g/s		3178
71	4-18	Leic	3g/f		3342
80	1-7	NEWM	7g/f	66	3753*
84	2-17	Donc	8fm	76	4480
78	7-13	Newm	8fm	80	4725

MIGHTY MAX 6 b g £0

2a	10-10	Wolv	16.2af	40	358 t

MIGHTY PIP 8 b g £0

23	12-18	Warw	10.9g/s	49	4669
42	5-19	Brig	9.9gd	[45]	4903

MIGRATION 8 b g £0

40	9-18	Nott	14.1sft	60	1469
2a	10-12	Sout	16af	55	1753
32	10-13	Warw	12.6gd	50	3056
0	17-17	Newm	10g/f	50	3238

MIJDAAF 3 b c £1788

78	6-10	Sand	10g/f		2386
86	2-11	Pont	10g/f		2991

MIKADO 2 b c £68264

112	1-	LEOP	9gd		10*
108	4-7	Curr	14gd		2817
109	4-8	Good	12g/f		3507
113	3-19	York	13.9g/s	106	4023
117	5-9	Donc	14.6fm		4532
112	1-14	CURR	10sft	[106]	4959*

MIKAO 3 b g £9657

MIKASA 4 b g £412

84	5-24	Newm	8fm		1495
76	3-12	York	7.9g/f		2410
80	2-8	Newm	10fm		3007
72	4-12	Hayd	10.5gd	[80]	3740
68a	2-9	Ling	12ap	[80]	4315
69	1-18	WIND	10g/s	[78]	4944*

6a	10-11	Sout	7af	[51]	488
35a	7-10	Ling	12ap	[45]	916
30	8-14	Sout	12g/s	[45]	1047
41	3-8	Muss	12gd	[40]	1552
21	8-10	Redc	11g/f	[40]	1819
4a	10-13	Wolv	8.5af	[40]	2052 P
30	5-15	Ayr	10.9g/s	40	2545
12	10-14	Carl	17.2gd	36	2937
12	11-11	Catt	12g/f	[30]	3190
20	9-9	Ayr	15gd	30	3327
38	6-8	Catt	15.8g/f	[25]	3666 BL

MIKES MATE 2 b g £0

1a	16-16	Sout	8af		192
0	14-15	Thir	7g/s		1473
0	12-12	Ripo	9g/f		1784
0	13-13	Hayd	11.9g/s		2230

MILITARY TWO STEP 3 b g £0

41	14-18	Nott	8.2fm	67	1007
45	13-18	Nott	8.2sft	65	1470
8	9-11	Newc	7sft	62	1678 p
35	9-11	Thir	7g/f	[58]	2218 p
20	11-16	Brig	7gd	[50]	4901
13	14-20	Yarm	7g/s	[45]	5120 p

MILK AND SULTANA 4 b f £12716

0	13-14	Hayd	8.1g/s	58	1348
58	6-11	Chep	10.2gd	53	2371
43	9-11	Warw	12.6fm	53	2601
42	8-13	Warw	12.6gd	51	3056
56	2-17	Bath	11.7gd	51	3145
33	11-19	Chep	12.1gd	49	3398
57	2-15	Wind	11.6fm	53	3481
52	4-9	Ches	12.3sft	51	4076
62	1-8	HAYD	10.5g/f	52	4354*
67	1-16	CHES	10.3g/f	59	4515*
61	4-13	Nott	10g/s	[59]	4650
37	15-18	Sali	9.9gd	62	4850
66a	3-12	Wolv	12.2ap	66	4924
57	7-19	Bath	11.7gd	60	5024
40a	8-12	Wolv	13.9ap	64	5160

MILK IT MICK 3 b c £16464

109a	2-9	Ling	8ap	[118]	1040
106	5-10	Newb	7gd	[118]	1234
106	8-14	Newm	8g/f	[114]	1480
109	3-8	Donc	10g/f	[108]	3596
96	3-5	Ches	7.6g/f	[107]	4047
115	2-9	Donc	8fm	[107]	4495

MILL BY THE STREAM 2 b c £0

33	14-19	Kemp	6g/f		1911
58	10-18	York	5g/f		2360
40	12-13	York	8g/f		3431
56	6-10	Yarm	8g/f		3713
0	18-18	Pont	6g/f	56	4934
24	9-9	Pont	6g/s	[52]	5154 VIS

MILL EMERALD 7 b m £0

0	12-12	Sout	14af	[40]	443

MILL END CHATEAU 2 ch g £0

53	9-12	Ripo	5g/f		1974
0	12-13	York	5g/f		2358

MILL END TEASER 3 b f £0

9a	10-10	Wolv	5af	[45]	527

MILLAFONIC 4 b c £0

97	6-15	Redc	10g/f	95	2101
87	8-14	Asco	10g/f	95	2556
92	8-9	Sand	10g/s	95	2896 VIS
1	12-14	Newb	10hvy	93	5223

MILLAGROS 4 b f £8732

56	11-15	Hami	8.3g/s	80	1602
76	4-8	Ayr	10g/f	78	1895
71	4-9	Muss	8fm	[76]	2087
56	6-10	Ayr	9.1gd	75	2571
65	3-5	Hami	9.2g/f	[74]	3206

74	3-9	Carl	9.3fm	[72]	3546 VIS
76	1-5	AYR	8hvy	[70]	4086* P
76	3-8	Thir	8fm	74	4378 p
76	3-12	Muss	8gd	[74]	4809 p
75	4-14	Ayr	10sft	73	5037 p
67a	9-13	Wolv	8.6ap	72	5364 p

MILLBAG 3 b c £17400

107	1-6	ASCO	6sft	[100]	1421*
78	7-9	Hayd	6g/f	[107]	1918
103	5-6	Curr	10g/f	[107]	2818

MILLEMIX 3 bl c £74345

111	1-8	LONG	10.5g/s		1434*
119	2-5	Long	10.5g/s		1853

MILLENARY 7 b h £192500

103	3-13	Asco	16.2sft	[117]	1418
119	1-10	YORK	13.9g/s	[117]	1705+ bl
116	3-10	York	15.9gd	[118]	4000 bl
119	1-8	DONC	18fm	[117]	4478* bl
120	1-11	NEWM	16sft	[119]	5138* bl

MILLENIO 4 ch c £866

70a	2-12	Ling	8ap	[64]	2394
2a	15-15	Sout	8af	64	2500

MILLENNIUM FORCE 6 b g £35520

96	8-9	Hayd	7.1g/f	[111]	1486
54	16-17	York	7.9g/s	110	1686
107	4-11	Hayd	7.1gd	[107]	2184
111	2-6	Long	7g/s	[107]	2826
102	3-6	Ches	7gd	[107]	3098
108	3-9	Curr	7gd	[107]	3320
100	8-13	Newb	7g/f	[108]	3957
76	8-8	Hayd	8.1fm	[106]	4386
107	3D-12	Long	7g/s	[106]	4731
104	9-15	Asco	7g/f	106	4800
95	5-12	Tipp	7.5hvy	[106]	4961
104	2-9	Donc	7sft	[104]	5214
108	2-12	Donc	6sft	[103]	5371

MILLENNIUM HALL 5 b g £13160

33	13-15	Hami	9.2gd	57	1388
53	6-14	Hami	8.3gd	57	1504
55	3-12	Newc	12.4sft	54	1680
59	3-9	Hami	13gd	54	2176
64	1-8	HAMI	12.1g/f	53	2318*
68	1-10	HAMI	13g/f	60	2479*
49	12-19	Carl	11.9gd	59	2673
55	6-9	Hayd	11.9gd	68	2900
53	6-7	Hami	13gd	62	3134
34	13-17	Hami	9.2g/s	62	4008
52	6-8	Hami	13g/s	62	4138
61	7-12	Muss	14g/f	62	4170
27	6-6	Muss	16g/f	59	4555

MILLER HILL 2 b g £718

31	12-12	Beve	5sft		1631
57a	2-7	Sout	6af		1751
24	8-11	Beve	5g/f		1831

MILLFIELDS DREAMS 5 b g £3926

62	1-20	CHEP	6.1gd	47	2372*
2	11-11	Good	6gd	54	2535
52	12-20	Chep	7.1g/s	60	3088
55	11-16	Newb	6g/f	59	3269
38	7-7	York	6g/f	[59]	3436
53	6-13	Bath	5.7g/f	[57]	3844
49	10-20	Chep	6.1g/s	55	4368
40	8-18	Chep	8.1gd	[55]	4485
48	7-19	Ling	5g/f	[52]	4739
41	5-13	Warw	7.1g/s	[50]	4994 P

MILLIETOM 2 b g £0

3a	10-11	Wolv	6af		73 P
0	16-16	Sout	8af		164 BL
8a	9-11	Sout	5af	[30]	578 bl

MILLINSKY 3 ch f £4561

56	7-14	Donc	5gd		2237
73	3-10	Newb	5.2fm		2649
61	2-9	Kemp	5g/f		3687
57	3-15	Sali	5gd	56	4335
63	2-11	Wind	6g/f	[56]	4836

MILLION PERCENT 4 b g £4529

43a	8-9	Wolv	7af	83	27
62	11-17	Donc	6g/s	83	1523

MILLIONHEIR (cont.)
79 6-19 Thir 6g/f 82 1767
82 2-8 Donc 6g/f [80] 2074
79 2-8 Newm 6fm [81] 2591
68 6-16 Wind 6fm 80 2758 VIS
64 6-10 Hayd 6g/s 79 3136
62 9-26 Ayr 6g/s 77 4652

MILLIONAIA 3 b f £80493
117 2-17 Chan 12.5g/s 2460

MILLKOM ELEGANCE 5 b m £464
39 8-20 Catt 12g/f 45 2850 bl
44 3-17 Thir 8g/f 45 3830 bl
27 11-17 Pont 8g/f 45 4626 bl

MILLQUISTA DOR 2 b f £0
0 17-19 Kemp 8g/f 4792
49a 7-12 Wolv 8.6ap 5115

MILLSTREET 5 ch g £11500
95 8-9 Good 12fm [110] 3563 t
114 5-9 York 10.4gd[110] 4002 t
0 8-8 Leop 10g/f [110] 4571 t

MILLVILLE 4 ch g £25935
72a 1-14 LING 10ap 430*
75a 9-11 Ling 7ap [80] 627
86a 1-14 LING 12ap 77 731*
89a 1-12 Ling 13ap 82 877*
79 8-20 Newm 12gd 87 1172
86 5-8 Newm 12g/f [85] 3617
87 4-21 York 11.9gd 85 3999
89 5-20 Hayd 14fm 85 4383
64 13-17 Newm 12g/f 85 4889
92 2-13 Donc 12sft 85 5215
72 10-24 Donc 12sft 87 5372

MILLY GOLIGHTLY 3 b f £0
40 11-14 Thir 8gd 1636
35 6-7 Newc 10.1gd 1871
47 8-11 Thir 7fm 2463

MILLY WATERS 3 b f £1013
81 5-8 Leic 5g/f [85] 5057
90a 5-12 Ling 8ap [83] 5298

MILLYBAA 4 b f £3500
84 4-9 Nott 6.1g/s [100] 1773
95 7-8 Chan 6g/f [100] 2305
30 12-12 Pont 6g/s [97] 3971
90 4-8 Newm 6gd [97] 4226
86 8-12 Curr 6g/s [97] 4732
90 8-15 Newm 5g/f [93] 4879
70 9-17 Curr 6sft [93] 5073 BL
52 10-12 Donc 6sft [90] 5371

MILLYS LASS 6 b m £0
25a 7-13 Wolv 5af [40] 312 BL

MIMAS GIRL 5 b m £402
24a 5-12 Sout 6af [35] 377 t
26a 9-16 Sout 6af [35] 447 t
36a 5-6 Wolv 8.5af [30] 526 t
32a 3-14 Sout 6af [30] 637 bl
20a 7-10 Sout 8af 30 678 bl
5a 9-16 Sout 8af [30] 719 t P
7a 13-15 Ling 7ap [35] 830 bl t
36a 3-12 Sout 7af [35] 909 t p
17a 6-7 Sout 7af [35] 1202 t p

MIMI MOUSE 2 br f £16273
61 6-8 Thir 5g/s 1212
64 4-14 Donc 6g/f 1874
76 3-18 York 5g/f 2360
82 1-5 PONT 5g/f 2789*
93 1-7 YORK 5g/f 83 3432*
76 14-22 Donc 6fm [79] 4458
74 8-12 Ayr 5g/f [88] 4651

MIMIC 4 b f £4217
56 13-20 Thir 6gd 72 1638
38 8-8 Bath 5.7fm [70] 2669
46 10-11 Newm 6fm 68 3408
41 9-12 Newm 6g/f 63 3751
72 1-15 SALI 6gd 63 3888*
50 5-11 Nott 5.1gd 58 4038
41 11-15 Redc 6fm 68 4562
47 11-19 Wind 6g/f 67 5053
72a 3-13 Wolv 6ap 67 5181

MINA ALSALAAM 2 b f £0
0 15-16 Nott 6.1gd 3103
28 13-14 Newb 6fm 3626

MIND ALERT 3 b g £4715
57 11-13 Hayd 6g/f 72 1881
71 2-9 Pont 6g/f 70 2609
20 15-15 Hayd 6gd 70 2950
51 8-8 Newm 7g/f 67 3612
33 9-15 Hami 6sft 64 4696 BL
51 9-15 Newc 5fm 64 4870 bl
61 5-14 Redc 7g/s 60 5109
70a 1-14 LING 7ap 57 5300*
56a 5-13 Wolv 8.6ap 57 5365

MIND PLAY 3 b f £0
31a 6-9 Sout 8af [40] 596 bl
24a 9-10 Sout 11af 40 658 bl

MIND THE TIME 2 b g £0
2a 14-14 Sout 8af 226
25a 9-13 Sout 6af 444
7a 6-6 Wolv 6af 631
24a 4-12 Sout 5af [35] 904
15 9-9 Leic 5g/f [35] 3347

MINDFUL 2 b c £0
54 11-13 Donc 5gd 954
49a 6-8 Sout 5ap 1048
24a 10-11 Sout 6af 2336
19 13-13 Ripo 5gd 4303

MINDSET 3 b f £0
59 8-11 Sali 7gd 3884

MINE 6 b h £117315
102 2-7 Thir 8sft [99] 1225
102 3-17 York 7.9g/s 99 1686 vis
110 1-20 ASCO 7g/f 99 1926+ vis
112 1-31 ASCO 8g/f 105 2489* vis
112 5-15 Sand 8.1g/s 108 2915 vis
106 2-5 Newm 8g/f [108] 3613 vis
94 7-11 York 7g/s [108] 4063 vis
112 5-15 Donc 8fm 108 4531 vis
112 3-15 Asco 7g/f 108 4800 vis

MINE BEHIND 4 b c £26444
80 1-20 WIND 6g/s 72 1255*
71 6-10 Hami 6gd 72 1391
86 2-19 Thir 6g/f 78 1767
84 2-14 Ayr 6g/f 78 1898
75 8-17 Muss 5fm 82 2082 P
80 7-17 Epso 6fm 82 2256
25 12-16 Wind 6fm 81 2758
86 1-12 BATH 5.7gd 79 3146*
58 12-15 York 6g/f 84 3434
15 16-16 Wind 6gd 83 3827
79 7-19 Kemp 6fm 82 4394
92 1-12 YARM 5.2g/s 82 4585*
91 4-16 Leic 5gd 88 4700
77 12-20 York 6g/f 88 5001
94 4-18 Pont 5g/s 88 5149

MINEKO 2 b f £0
74 8-19 Newm 7g/s 5279

MINERAL STAR 2 b c £819
52 9-13 Newm 7fm 4724
79 3-15 York 7.9gd 5002

MING THE MERCILESS 4 b g £0
45a 5-7 Sout 8af [63] 334
26a 6-8 Sout 11af [63] 420

MING VASE 2 b c £1775
66 6-12 Beve 5sft 1631
64a 2-10 Sout 7af 2802
54a 5-11 Sout 7af 2995
58 6-6 Hayd 6g/s 64 3902
51 8-9 Newc 8sft 62 4285
59 5-18 Pont 6g/s 60 4934
65 3-9 Pont 6g/s [57] 5154

MINGUN 4 b c £3353
109 3-14 Curr 10sft 4959
104 8-11 Newm 10sft 5136

MINIMUM BID 3 b f £2098

MINIMUM BID (cont.)
54 9-15 Ling 5g/f 56 2062
38 13-14 Ling 5g/f 56 2585
55 2-12 Kemp 5g/f 54 3036
50 9-14 Ling 6gd 55 3289
61a 2-10 Ling 5ap 55 3332
47 10-20 Ling 6g/f 57 4317
46 10-15 Epso 7g/f 57 4475

MINIRINA 4 b f £0
2a 8-8 Sout 5af [45] 742
9a 4-7 Wolv 5af [45] 1320
35a 4-7 Wolv 5af [40] 1562
19a 7-12 Wolv 5af [35] 1799
10 8-13 Hami 5gd 35 2181

MINIVET 9 b g £7447
20a 7-9 Sout 16af 58 336
52 5-8 Muss 12g/f 55 2616 bl
52 4-8 Hami 13g/s 52 4138
64 1-9 MUSS 14gd 51 4521*
48 9-13 Muss 12g/s 57 5333

MINK MITTEN 2 b f £0
57 10-16 Newm 7g/f 3582 T
44 8-12 Newc 7g/f 5011 t

MINNESINGER 2 b f £0
48 7-11 Donc 8sft 5205

MINNESOTA 2 ch c £10439
80 2-10 Bath 5.7fm 2666
82 1-15 LING 7gd 3285*
87 3-3 Sali 8g/f [83] 3865
81 3-4 Sand 7.1gd [85] 4606

MINORITY REPORT 4 b g £2301
75 3-17 Chep 8.1gd 2117
51 8-13 Nott 8.2g/f 2633
80 2-5 Sand 8.1g/f 3360
57 12-15 Bath 11.7g/f 78 3964

MINSTREL HALL 5 b m £0
50 4-8 Muss 12gd 1552
57 5-8 Ayr 10gd [50] 3151
45 7-13 Ayr 10gd 50 3325

MINSTRELS DOUBLE 3 ch g £0
40 5-10 Carl 6.9g/f 3230
25 10-11 Ripo 12.3gd 4281

MINTLAW 2 b f £5902
76 2-7 Ayr 6g/f 3761
73 5-9 Ayr 8sft 5033
85 1-14 MUSS 7.1g/s 5330*

MIRABILIS 2 b f £0
98 9-10 Long 8g/f 4954

MIRACLE BABY 2 b f £0
58 7-14 Nott 6.1hvy 5342

MIRAGE PRINCE 2 ch g £423
56 6-15 Beve 5g/s 1161
46 10-14 Donc 6g/f 1874
70 6-9 Warw 7.1fm 2776
71 5-11 Beve 7.5g/f 3500
77 4-5 Ches 7.6g/f 4046
61 13-17 Warw 7.1gd [73] 4271

MIRASOL PRINCESS 3 ch f £5944
65 8-10 Wind 6gd [81] 1383
74 7-12 Wind 5g/f 78 1809
66 4-8 Bath 5fm [78] 1901
70 6-9 Sand 5g/f 76 2387
70 6-12 Kemp 5g/f 73 3036
67a 6-11 Ling 6ap 73 3198
71 4-7 Bath 5g/f 71 3371
42 15-16 Wind 5fm 69 3640
76 1-9 WIND 5fm 69 3804*
56 7-7 Good 5sft 73 4236
76 3-15 Sand 5gd 73 4604
56 9-14 Redc 5fm [74] 4930

MIRJAN 8 b g £105432
85 3-10 Muss 16g/f 85 1093
97 1-9 NEWC 16.1g/s 86 2771* bl
98 7-34 Newm 18sft 93 5135 bl

MIS CHICAF 3 b f £10752
68 2-9 Thir 6g/s [71] 1477

80 1-10 DONC 6g/f 70 1878*
93 1-19 YORK 6g/f 76 2055*
52 18-20 York 6g/f 90 2407

MISARO 3 b g £1857
64 8-19 Beve 5sft 79 1627
70 5-8 Beve 7.5g/f 76 2166
72 6-7 Ches 7g/s 73 2749
75 2-16 Hami 6g/s 70 4009
67 4-20 Ripo 6gd 73 4278
56 13-15 Ayr 5g/s 73 4654

MISBEHAVIOUR 5 b g £0
22a 13-15 Ling 7ap [45] 411 p
34a 7-12 Ling 8ap [40] 710
20a 8-14 Ling 10ap [40] 784 p

MISCHIEF 8 ch g £0
1 14-15 Ripo 12.3g/f 37 2526
0 P-9 Yarm 14.1g/f 36 3703

MISHAP 2 b f £0
0 14-14 Yarm 8g/s 5118

MISKINA 3 b f £3990
41 13-15 Bath 8g/s 59 1099
59a 3-11 Wolv 8.5af 57 1339
33 7-8 Hami 9.2g/s 57 1603
61a 1-12 WOLV 7af 55 2049*
28 5-5 Ayr 8hvy 58 4085 T
2 15-18 Newc 8g/f [58] 5017
61a 4-12 Wolv 7.1ap [58] 5325

MISS ADELAIDE 3 b f £2383
69a 4-12 Ling 8ap 881
65 4-8 Newc 8hvy [80] 1039
69 2-6 Ayr 10g/f [77] 1894
52 7-10 Chep 8.1g/f 69 2624

MISS BEAR 2 b f £0
54 10-11 Thir 7fm 4381
49 9-16 York 7.9gd 4997

MISS CASSIA 2 b f £6895
76 3-8 Newm 5gd 1170
76 2-11 Ling 5gd 2395
0 S-12 Bath 5.7gd 3141
64 3-6 Brig 5.3g/f 3296
76 1-6 GOOD 5sft 70 4187*
70 17-26 Hami 6.5g/f 4679
75 6-18 Wind 5g/f 73 4830

MISS CELERITY 4 b f £0
11a 11-12 Ling 8ap [30] 401
6a 10-13 Ling 6ap [30] 541
41a 4-9 Ling 8ap [30] 717
10a 10-11 Ling 8ap [30] 786
0 13-13 Wind 8.3g/s [35] 1058
0 10-10 Ling 7ap [35] 1181
0 11-11 Sout 8af [30] 4090

MISS CEYLON 4 b f £0
4a 10-10 Sout 6af [45] 1837
41 11-12 Thir 5g/s 35 2690
0 19-19 Donc 5g/s 41 3220
28 7-10 Beve 5g/f [39] 3503 BL
20 16-18 Beve 5g/s 39 3852 bl
26 13-14 Redc 5fm [35] 4930
5 11-13 Catt 5sft [35] 5321

MISS CHAMPERS 3 b f £11361
52a 8-13 Wolv 9.4af 66 38
47a 5-12 Wolv 7af 62 129
68a 1-9 SOUT 8af 59 163*
69a 1-13 SOUT 8af [59] 188*
64a 3-16 Sout 7af 65 202
60a 5-13 Sout 8af 65 221
69a 2-13 Wolv 8.5af 66 251
59a 9-13 Wolv 8.5af 67 439
61a 1-10 SOUT 8af [67] 502*
73a 1-8 SOUT 8af 66 597*
65a 4-9 Wolv 9.4af 72 620
62a 9-10 Ling 7ap 71 799

MISS CHANCELOT 3 b f £0
1 12-12 Catt 6g/f 2849
22 8-9 Thir 7fm 3610
4 8-10 Catt 6gd 4964
7a 11-12 Wolv 6ap 5162

MISS CHILDREY 3 ch f £5182
108 3-9 Leop 7g/s 1701
86 7-9 Donc 8fm 4495 t
55 12-12 Asco 7g/f 4811

MISS COTSWOLD LADY 2 b f £1881
42 5-7 Leic 5gd 2132
64 4-6 Warw 5fm 2437
75 2-7 Newm 6g/f 2733
46 8-10 Ripo 5gd 2983
60 8-14 Warw 6.1g/f 73 4420
42 20-20 Ling 7g/f 70 4741
29a 11-12 Wolv 5.1ap [65] 4922 VIS

MISS CUISINA 2 b f £0
39 16-17 Ling 7g/f 2584
20a 8-10 Sout 7af 2802
46 9-11 Ches 7sft 4072

MISS DANBYS 9 b m £0
1a 6-9 Sout 11af 1838

MISS DANGEROUS 9 b m £0
12a 11-11 Wolv 5af 45 958

MISS DE BOIS 7 ch m £0
14 12-14 Catt 12g/f 3668
7 8-11 Wind 10gd 4124
0 17-18 Chep 8.1gd 4485

MISS DEFYING 2 b f £0
0 11-11 Nott 8.2g/s 4648

MISS DINAMITE 2 b f £0
0 18-19 Kemp 8g/f 4792

MISS ELOISE 3 b f £4986
55 6-11 Warw 8.1hvy 58 1534
60 2-17 Hayd 8.1gd 56 2243
54 6-9 Pont 8g/f 57 2604
51 9-13 Newc 8g/s 57 2773
66 1-12 BEVE 9.9gd 57 2893*
53 8-15 Nott 10gd 63 3108
49 11-13 Beve 9.9gd 63 3309
29 9-12 Beve 9.9g/s 61 3854 BL
44 13-17 Hayd 10.5fm 58 4388

MISS EMMA 4 b f £25704
116 1-11 MAIS 6sft 5313*

MISS FAYE 4 b f £184
7 7-7 Chep 7.1sft [40] 1335 P
10 3-4 Brig 7gd [35] 1545 p
25 10-16 Nott 6.1gd [30] 1989 p

MISS FLEURIE 4 b f £1303
35a 9-11 Sout 6af 869
19 12-16 Newc 7sft 966
15a 7-8 Sout 8af [45] 1200
31a 2-6 Sout 12af [35] 1592
32 6-7 Muss 12gd 32 2966
20 7-13 Pont 12gd 32 3240
0 18-20 Catt 12g/f 32 3354
47 2-11 Redc 10sft [30] 5303

MISS FRANCE 3 ch f £7711
107 3-6 Sain 10.5g/s 1157

MISS GEORGE 6 b m £28497
87a 1-8 LING 7ap [83] 879*
77 9-22 Donc 6gd 89 921
91a 7-8 Ling 7ap [85] 1043
82 3-10 Wind 6gd [83] 1383
87 9-11 Ling 7sft [83] 1620
83 6-9 Wind 6g/f [82] 1958
66 8-16 Wind 6fm 82 2758
71 12-16 Newm 5g/f 82 3033
85 3-13 Wind 6fm 80 3479
53 11-16 Wind 6gd 81 3827
72 3-8 Kemp 5sft [81] 4031
74a 10-14 Ling 7ap 85 4180
60 15-19 Kemp 6fm 79 4394
84a 3-14 Ling 7ap 83 4446
88a 2-12 Wolv 7.1ap 83 5159
99a 1-12 LING 8ap [83] 5298*

MISS GLORY BE 5 b m £2704
63a 3-13 Wolv 9.4af 60 38 p
34a 11-14 Sout 8af 59 93 p

37a 9-14 Sout 8af 58 165 p
50a 6-13 Wolv 8.5af 56 251 p
40a 11-14 Ling 10ap 54 339 p
51a 3-12 Wolv 8.5af 51 564 p
21a 5-8 Sout 8af 51 597 p
55a 2-16 Sout 8af 49 3487 p
55a 3-14 Ling 10ap 49 3605 p
55a 3-13 Ling 10ap 52 3823 p
42a 7-15 Sout 8af 52 4132 p
36 6-15 Folk 9.7g/f [45] 4373 p
47 3-15 Yarm 10.1g/s [45] 5122 p

MISS GOOD TIME 2 gr f £0
49 9-9 Yarm 5.2g/f 1133
59 6-10 Muss 5gd 1550
55 9-11 Nott 6.1sft 1739
40 6-20 Hayd 6gd 2882
38 6-7 Ripo 6g/s 3259
47 5-15 Redc 6g/f 3769 BL
43 6-16 Beve 7.5g/f 45 4597 bl

MISS GRACE 4 ch f £823
52 19 Wind 8.3gd 60 1385
69a 4-14 Ling 10ap 70 1618
36 11-20 Asco 8g/f 57 1927
58 3-15 Kemp 9gd 54 2170

MISS HERMIONE 2 ch f £0
7a 12-12 Ling 6ap 4896
37 10-14 Yarm 8g/s 5118
69 5-17 Yarm 6g/s 5350

MISS HOOFBEATS 3 b f £0
22 14-16 Nott 10gd 51 1240
0 8-8 Sout 12af 47 1444
2a 15-15 Ling 12ap 42 2741
0 10-10 Newm 10fm 42 3404

MISS INKHA 3 b f £1677
53 16-17 Newm 7gd 1171
61 12-24 Newm 8fm 1495
60 6-10 Good 8gd 2378
59 6-8 Sali 8gd 63 2701
63 2-5 Brig 9.9sft 61 4167
52 11-17 Hayd 10.5fm 61 4388
64 3-20 Hayd 11.9g/s 61 4771
62 5-19 Bath 11.9g/f 62 5024

MISS ISSY 3 b f £2522
56a 4-11 Ling 8ap 57 12
51a 8-15 Ling 7ap [55] 117 VIS
58a 1-15 LING 7ap 53 151* vis
48a 9-15 Ling 7ap 58 266 vis
58a 3-15 Ling 7ap [58] 366 vis

MISS IVANHOE 4 b f £750
98 9-20 Newm 7g/s 102 1151
96 6-11 Ling 7sft [102] 1620
78 15-19 York 7.9gd 100 4987

MISS JELLYBEAN 2 b f £0
47 9-15 York 5g/f 2056
28 7-7 Muss 5g/f 4549
35 7-7 Catt 5sft 5124

MISS JUDGED 2 b f £0
6a 10-13 Sout 6af [40] 63 T
46a 8-13 Wolv 6af [33] 126
19a 9-12 Sout 6af [50] 200 e t
26a 13-15 Ling 7ap 50 295 t
19a 7-8 Wolv 8.5af [45] 383 BL e
46a 6-13 Sout 6af [45] 444 bl e
15a 9-13 Wolv 6af [45] 582 bl e
24a 9-11 Sout 5af 45 609 bl e

MISS JUDGEMENT 2 b f £9461
58a 6-9 Ling 5ap [49] 76
25a 5-10 Ling 6ap [58] 973
55 3-16 Ling 6g/f 52 1985
61 2-13 Warw 6.1fm 53 2439
70 1-20 NOTT 6.1g/f 53 2630*
61 3-19 Leic 6g/f 65 2925
48a 3-11 Ling 6ap 65 3198
49 10-13 Leic 7g/f 64 3346
67 1-7 LING 6fm [62] 3789*
30 17-20 Ling 6g/f 64 4317
48 13-18 Bath 5.7g/f 64 4412
38 18-20 Nott 6.1g/s 64 4646

52 7-17 Bath 5.7gd [62] 5020

MISS JULIE JAY 2 b f £0
46a 10-15 Ling 7ap 58 177

MISS KOEN 5 b m £3480
24a 6-8 Wolv 8.5af [60] 630
45a 3-9 Ling 13ap [53] 787 T
56a 1-11 LING 12ap [53] 816* t
53a 8-9 Ling 10ap 53 876 t
55 3-9 Folk 12sft 55 979 t
40 8-10 Folk 12g/s 55 1082 t
37 11-17 Nott 14.1gd 53 1238 t
35 10-10 Bath 13.1g/f 51 1789 t

MISS LADYBIRD 3 b f £0
48 8-10 Hayd 8.1g/s 63 3906

MISS LANGKAWI 3 gr f £1590
60 10-13 Kemp 9ap 74 1141
66 9-10 Wind 11.6gd 74 1382
74 3-7 Newm 12sft 71 5268
48 12-14 Donc 10.3sft [71] 5370

MISS LAUGEVAL 2 b f £12464
81 4-12 Newb 6g/f 3251
79 1-13 GOOD 7fm 3554*
63 11-12 Good 7sft [82] 4264
83 10-14 Newm 7g/f [77] 4914
83 2-5 Nott 8.2hvy [81] 5186

MISS LEHMAN 6 ch m £0
28 6-10 Beve 8.5g/f [40] 1943

MISS LIBRATE 6 b m £0
42 8-10 Bath 8g/s 1100
4a 8-8 Wolv 8.5af 1220

MISS LYVENNET 3 ch f £0
17 17-18 Catt 7gd [60] 996

MISS MADAME 3 b f £11036
62a 3-7 Wolv 7af 62 1376
56 3-8 Brig 5.3g/f 61 1942
41 6-9 Chep 5.1gd 61 2195
68 1-12 LING 7.6gd [58] 3448*
69 2-6 Brig 8g/f 65 3718
73 1-7 YARM 7gd 65 3872*
65 6-8 Thir 8fm 69 4378
20 16-18 Kemp 8g/f 69 4714

MISS MALONE 2 b f £1732
65 7-19 Newb 6g/f 2310
78 7-13 Curr 6.3gd 2815
77 2-13 Kemp 6gd 3183
76 4-8 Asco 7fm 80 3624
55 14-21 Donc 6.5fm 75 4457
64 5-9 Chep 5.1hvy 71 4706
60 7-19 Ling 6g/f [71] 4895

MISS MAMBO 3 b f £49441
110 3-13 Long 8g/s 1854
112 2-9 Chan 8g/s 2306
78 5-5 Newm 8g/f 4915

MISS MEGGY 2 b f £23127
90 1-10 THIR 5g/f 1764*
92 1-12 BEVE 5g/f 2165*
86 9-17 Asco 5g/f 2490
84 6-10 Newm 6fm 3003
85 5-10 Beve 5sft 90 4258
90 6-21 Donc 6.5fm 90 4457
99 4-9 Ayr 6sft [88] 4684 VIS

MISS MERENDA 3 b f £264
55 15-24 Newm 8fm 1495
56 7-10 Yarm 11.5g/f 1725
43 9-11 Folk 9.7g/f 2274
58a 4-13 Wolv 9.5ap 5290

MISS MILLIETANT 2 b f £0
9a 10-11 Ling 6ap 51
17a 13-14 Ling 10ap 473
29a 6-15 Ling 7ap [30] 830 VIS
22a 8-12 Sout 7af [30] 909

MISS MONICA 3 ch f £955
59 6-14 Warw 8.1sft 1527
71 4-12 Good 9g/f 1864

69 3-6 Brig 9.9fm 2835
44 14-15 Hayd 8.1g/f 69 4352
56 11-17 Leic 10gd 67 5062

MISS MONZA 3 b f £857
56 8-10 Sali 6gd 3452
37 10-10 Newb 7gd 3921
65 3-10 Sali 6g/s 4081
28 12-13 Bath 5.7g/f [68] 4413
42 8-11 Wind 6g/f [62] 4836

MISS MYTTON 3 ch f £0
3 15-16 Ches 7g/f 67 4051

MISS NOTERIETY 4 b f £0
0 11-12 Sout 7af [25] 2337
0 7-8 Ripo 8g/f [25] 2480 T P
0 10-10 Sout 5af [23] 3156 BL t

MISS OCEAN MONARCH 4 ch f £420
8a 11-12 Sout 7af [30] 909
6a 8-10 Sout 8af [30] 1406
8a 8-8 Wolv 9.4af [30] 1561
15a 9-10 Wolv 8.5af [30] 1801
42 2-10 Beve 8.5g/f [40] 1943
24 9-11 Redc 8fm 40 2296
25 8-10 Beve 9.9gd 40 2510
20 7-7 Muss 12gd 39 2966 BL e
2 13-13 Beve 12.1g/f 35 3502 bl e

MISS PARTICULAR 2 b f £0
62 11-23 Newm 7g/f 4885

MISS PATRICIA 2 b f £1320
57 7-12 Bath 5.7gd 3141
62 7-14 Newb 6fm 3626
77 4-10 Newb 6gd 3917
79 3-14 Yarm 7g/s 74 4583

MISS PEACHES 6 b m £2523
47a 2-11 Ling 8ap [45] 408
40a 8-12 Ling 8ap [45] 538
50a 1-12 LING 8ap [45] 648*
42a 3-10 Ling 8ap 47 770
42a 5-12 Ling 8ap 47 845
47a 4-12 Ling 8ap 47 1045
46 6-19 Yarm 7g/f 47 1132
44 5-20 Yarm 8fm 46 2149
35 10-12 Ling 10g/f 46 2844

MISS PEBBLES 3 ch f £10282
30a 7-7 Ling 10ap 71 16
69a 5-13 Ling 10ap 71 178 P
70a 6-14 Ling 10ap 71 265 p
72 1-9 FOLK 9.7sft [70] 978*
68 4-12 Folk 9.7sft 70 1273
59 7-19 Wind 10sft [68] 1650
62 7-18 Good 8g/f 68 1849
63 5-20 Asco 8g/f 67 1927 VIS
79 1-10 WIND 10fm 65 2761* vis
70 2-12 Wind 10g/f [65] 2800 vis
73 5-8 Ripo 10g/s 74 3938 vis
51 13-14 Sand 10g/s 74 4097 vis
50 13-16 Good 12gd [73] 4745

MISS POLARIS 3 b f £6803
61 6-15 Nott 8.2g/s 4649
80 1-10 PONT 8g/f 4939*
79a 2-13 Wolv 9.5ap 74 5161

MISS POPPETS 4 ch f £0
56a 9-11 Ling 6ap 67 760
55a 11-12 Ling 7ap 67 1024

MISS PORCIA 3 ch f £3932
60 1-9 THIR 7g/f [59] 2218*
61 2-8 Ayr 7.2gd [59] 2506
41 7-8 Sali 8gd 59 2701

MISS PRIM 3 ch f £0
17 8-8 Catt 6gd 4969
19a 8-12 Wolv 6ap 5157

MISS PROCURER 3 b f £632
59 5-9 York 7g/f 3121
42 11-12 Newm 8fm 69 3410 T
57 4-15 Leic 7g/f [69] 3515
46 5-10 Hayd 8.1gd [64] 3739 t
35 3-7 Brig 9.9sft [57] 4142

MISS ROSIE 2 b f £749
75 4-10 Donc 6g/f 2077
68 4-11 Beve 7.5g/f 3500
66 7-14 Thir 7g/s 3831

MISS SHANGRI LA 3 b f £0
51 11-13 Newb 7gd 1210
46 9-13 Wind 10g/f 2453
21 6-6 Brig 9.9fm 2835
32 10-11 Ling 10fm 49 3748

MISS SHARAPOVA 2 b f £805
76 4-13 Good 7fm 3554

MISS ST ALBANS 3 b f £0
36 12-14 Nott 10gd 1241
0 7-9 Folk 9.7sft 1581
16 15-16 Newm 7fm 2092
30 10-11 Folk 9.7g/f 2274
0 20-20 Yarm 7g/s [40] 5120

MISS SUDBROOK 2 ch f £0
17 11-11 Bath 6g/f 3848
67 4-11 Chep 7.1hvy 4704
19a 10-12 Wolv 6ap 4921

MISS THE BOAT 2 b f £3300
85 2-16 Sali 7gd 4329

MISS TILLY 3 b f £0
40 14-17 Sali 6g/s 1497
0 17-18 Sali 7fm 46 2292

MISS TOLERANCE 2 ch f £812
64 12-15 Kemp 6g/f 4710
79 3-13 Wind 6g/f 5048
68a 7-9 Ling 6ap 5237

MISS TRENDSETTER 2 b f £0
10 18-20 Hayd 6gd 2882
27 8-13 Catt 7g/f 3349
3 15-15 Catt 7sft 3930 P

MISS TRIAL 2 b f £2004
69 6-8 Kemp 6sft 4028
74 3-14 Warw 6.1g/f 4422
71 3-6 Brig 7fm 4760
74 3-14 Redc 6g/s [71] 5106

MISS TRINITY 4 b f £0
44a 14-15 Ling 7ap [64] 814
38a 10-12 Sout 5af 64 853
5a 9-9 Ling 6ap [57] 1012 p
27 19-19 Yarm 7g/f 52 1132

MISS TRUANT 2 b f £0
64 6-9 Yarm 5.2g/f 1133
72 6-15 Wind 5gd 1380

MISS WIZZ 4 b f £4683
3a 9-12 Sout 8af [37] 309
13a 4-14 Sout 7af [35] 573 p
37a 1-14 SOUT 8af [35] 637* p
19 6-8 Newc 6sft [40] 963 p
28a 4-10 Sout 5af [40] 1408 p
40 4-10 Newc 5g/f [37] 2161 p
35 5-19 Beve 5g/s 37 2326 p
46 1-14 NEWC 6g/s [37] 2730* p
39 8-18 Catt 7g/f 45 3670 p
37 11-20 Redc 6g/f 45 3767 p
0 13-14 Sout 6af 43 4130 p
35 11-16 Catt 7g/f 45 4676 p
26 8-10 Ayr 6sft [45] 5278 p

MISS WONG ONE 3 b f £302
56a 3-15 Sout 6af 55 168
3a 10-10 Sout 6af 56 657

MISS WOODPIGEON 8 b m £529
31 3-9 Wind 11.6fm 3294
31 7-11 Chep 10.2gd [40] 3730

MISSATACAMA 2 b f £326
71a 4-14 Ling 7ap 5078
68a 5-12 Ling 8ap 5293

MISSED A BEAT 2 b f £3500
43 8-19 Kemp 6g/f 1911
65 4-13 Sali 6fm 2287

47	14-18	Leic	7g/f		3342
78	1-17	LING	6gd	[62]	4443*
79	5-15	Hayd	6sft	76	4765
2	20-20	Newb	6hvy	75	5225

MISSED TURN 2 b f £279

47a	5-12	Sout	5af		1439
55	4-11	Thir	5gd		1634
47a	4-7	Sout	6af		1751
28	6-7	Leic	5g/f	56	3343
36	9-9	Brig	5g/f	[49]	3981
38	12-17	Catt	7gd	47	4963

MISSELLA 2 g r f £337

50	16-19	Leic	7g/f	5040
67	4-11	Donc	8sft	5205

MISSIE 4 ch f £0

38	9-12	Thir	7g/f	[50]	1971
1	12-13	Hami	5g/f	50	2181

MISSIE BAILEYS 2 ch f £3445

71	6-10	Newb	6gd		3917
70a	5-8	Ling	7ap		4447
70	8-14	Kemp	7g/f		4711
68	1-14	WIND	8.3g/f	[70]	5049*

MISSIN MARGOT 2 b f £0

50	5-9	Catt	6g/f	4670
47a	7-12	Wolv	6ap	4921
42	6-10	Catt	6g/f	4968

MISSION AFFIRMED 3 ch g £9980

35a	9-13	Sout	5af		659
67a	1-10	SOUT	7af	55	794+
54a	5-7	Sout	8af	63	855
70a	1-14	SOUT	8af	63	1198+
32	12-16	Beve	8.5sft	68	1628
62a	4-8	Sout	8af	68	2495
54	10-10	Hayd	8.1g/s	69	3138
53	5-6	Muss	9g/f	63	3529
69a	2-11	Sout	8af	65	4044
63	3-18	Catt	7g/f	60	4438
52	8-17	Nott	8.2gd	61	4862

MISSION MAN 3 b c £6734

72	4-13	Donc	7gd	[84]	925
80	2-12	Newm	7g/s	[82]	1152
84	1-11	NOTT	6.1sft	[82]	1607*
82	4-15	Ling	7gd	[82]	1983
77	7-7	Newm	6g/f		2764
82	4-11	Asco	8gd	[80]	3128
80	5-10	Sand	8.1g/f	[80]	3339
70	7-10	Pont	8g/s	79	3972
65	11-12	Newm	7gd		4225

MISSION TO MARS 4 b g £12908

75a	2-12	Ling	12ap	70	526
87a	1-16	LING	12ap	72	493*
97a	1-7	LING	12ap	85	695*
98a	3-10	Wolv	12af	95	810

MISSPERON 2 b f £9926

60	5-13	Redc	6g/f		1818
77	3-12	Redc	6g/f		2119
80	1-8	PONT	6g/f		2603*
79	3-10	York	5gd	77	3115
76	4-9	Ches	6.1fm	77	3632
59	12-21	Donc	6fm	[76]	4490
80	2-10	Ayr	6g/s	76	4655 P

MISSUS LINKS 2 b f £5363

72a	1-11	LING	6ap		135*
70	5-20	Nott	6.1gd	70	1239
74	2-11	Newb	6gd	70	1734
74	5-12	Sand	7.1g/f	71	2098
44	13-15	Leic	6g/f	71	2398
62	6-11	Sali	6gd	71	2661
73	4-20	Wind	6g/s	70	4946
64	8-18	Leic	6gd	70	5039

MISSY CINOFAZ 2 ch f £326

40	13-14	Yarm	7g/f	4611
66a	4-14	Ling	7ap	4971

MIST OPPORTUNITY 2 b g £0

8	10-12	Ripo	5g/f	1974
38	11-11	Thir	7fm	2462
54	8-11	Newc	7gd	3429

29	12-14	Thir	7g/s	4206

MISTBLACK 4 b f £0

0	8-10	Sout	5af	3156

MISTER ARJAY 3 b c £158

42a	8-13	Wolv	9.4af	78	127 bl e
62	9-17	Thir	8g/s	78	1475
59	6-10	Beve	9.9g/s	76	2323
55a	11-12	Wolv	12.2ap	70	4983
64	11-17	Redc	10sft	70	5307

MISTER AZIZ 2 b c £0

45	10-19	Kemp	6g/f		1911
49a	8-11	Sout	7af		2995
65	5-9	Sand	5g/f		3355
48	11-14	Warw	6.1g/f	65	4420

MISTER BELL 2 g r c £640

55	3-5	Hami	5g/s		1601
54	6-7	Bath	5fm		2415
40	12-13	Chep	6.1gd		3399
44	8-12	Bath	5.7gd	60	4545
27	14-19	Bath	5gd	54	5021

MISTER BENJI 4 b g £2107

57a	1-16	SOUT	8af	51	86* p
48a	7-16	Sout	7af	56	208 p
30a	9-12	Wolv	8.5af	56	479 p
56a	5-13	Sout	7af	56	556 p
50a	7-12	Wolv	8.6ap	[55]	5337

MISTER BUZZ 2 b c £296

49	11-14	Redc	6fm		2297
38	11-20	Newc	6sft		2682
63	8-12	York	6gd		3122
62	4-8	Catt	6g/f		3348
61	4-10	Redc	6gd	[60]	4244
36	13-19	Carl	5.9g/f	60	4344
45	13-20	Redc	8sft	57	5302

MISTER CHALK 3 g r c £0

0	18-18	Wind	10g/s	4944

MISTER CLINTON 6 ch g £9386

52a	7-13	Ling	10ap	56	178
29a	13-14	Ling	10ap	56	230
49a	11-14	Ling	7ap	53	344
42a	10-12	Ling	8ap	53	406 P
39a	11-14	Ling	10ap	[50]	477
33a	11-11	Ling	8ap	50	669 T p
42a	6-13	Ling	10ap	46	761 bl
54	3-11	Brig	7fm	53	2334
54	4-11	Brig	7g/f	53	2644
44	8-12	Ling	10g/f	53	2844
66	1-10	BRIG	8gd	53	2954*
62	2-17	Brig	7g/f	58	3176
48	10-12	Ling	7.6gd	[59]	3448
66	1-8	BRIG	8fm	[59]	3676*
54	6-16	Brig	7sft	[62]	4144
53	8-15	Epso	7g/f	62	4475
59	9-14	Wind	8.3g/f	61	4832
51	9-17	Nott	8.2gd	61	4862

MISTER COMPLETELY 3 b g £7653

65a	2-8	Ling	6ap	[52]	691
50a	6-12	Ling	7ap	52	729
50a	5-15	Ling	7ap	52	815
31	7-12	Folk	6sft	51	975
36	10-16	Ling	6g/f	49	1985
42a	9-14	Ling	10ap	49	2064
16	17-17	Ling	7gd	47	2397
40a	7-11	Ling	12ap	[47]	2588
48	1-13	BATH	8fm	42	2667*
26a	6-9	Sout	8af	50	2996
19	10-14	Nott	16g/f	46	3580
55a	1-12	LING	10ap	49	4113*
10	14-19	Brig	9.9sft	51	4145
43	5-18	Kemp	10g/f	[47]	4791
49	3-16	Nott	10gd	47	4857
47	3-6	Yarm	14.1sft	[47]	5249

MISTER ELEGANT 2 b c £447

33	18-18	Wind	10gd	2618
70	4-15	Sali	8gd	4851
61	6-14	Yarm	8g/s	5118

MISTER GENEPI 2 b c £15667

78	5-16	Sali	7g/s	3111

88	2-10	Donc	7g/f		3594
84	2-18	Newm	7gd		3927
87	1-17	Epso	7gd	[86]	4289
99	7-10	Donc	7fm	[86]	4493
102	3-9	Newm	7gd	[95]	4881
96	1-15	YORK	7.9gd	[100]	5002*

MISTER GRAHAM 9 b g £0

23	9-14	Sout	12g/s		1047 p
45a	4-7	Ling	16ap		1291
16a	6-6	Ling	10ap		1455 p

MISTER LINKS 4 b c £8209

94	3-7	Hayd	6g/f	[109]	1487
92	1-4	LEIC	7g/f	[104]	1962*

MISTER MAL 7 b g £10228

54a	5-16	Sout	7af	58	208 bl e
54a	3-10	Wolv	6af	58	245 bl e
27a	10-12	Wolv	7af	56	704 bl e
49	6-18	Catt	7gd	[55]	996 bl e
56	1-16	NEWC	6sft	50	1277* bl e
32	9-18	Thir	6g/f	54	2214 bl
40	7-14	Catt	6g/f	[54]	3191 bl e
54	3-18	Pont	5g/s	53	3974
65a	1-13	SOUT	8af	55	4091*
62	2-19	Beve	5g/s	54	4240
57	7-26	Ayr	5g/s	58	4618

MISTER MARMADUKE 3 b g £2671

78	4-10	Muss	7.1g/f	80	3562
83	3-14	Ches	6.1g/f	78	4048
78	5-14	Muss	8gd	78	4174
28	8-8	Muss	8gd	79	4516
76	9-13	Muss	7.1gd	78	4806
16a	13-13	Wolv	6ap	76	5114

MISTER MERLIN 3 ch g £0

0	19-19	Thir	12g/f	45	4594
0	20-20	Kemp	12g/f	[45]	4796

MISTER MINTY 2 b c £0

13	13-13	Hayd	6gd	3736

MISTER MONET 3 b c £111100

102	2-16	Newm	8g/f	92	3059
110	1-4	HAMI	9.2g/f	[92]	3204*
113	1-9	ASCO	10g/f	98	3439*
121	1-6	HAYD	10.5fm	[106]	3793*
122	1-9	DEAU	10hvy	[106]	4158*
0	P-11	Newm	10sft	[117]	5136

MISTER MUJA 3 g r g £3877

65	7-11	Sali	7gd		3884 T
66	6-14	Warw	7.1gd		4275 t
78a	1-14	LING	7ap		5240* t

MISTER PUTT 6 b g £1081

62	2-9	Folk	15.4sft	60	1271 bl
31	15-15	Good	16gd	60	5025 bl

MISTER REGENT 3 b c £567

70	3-14	Thir	6g/s		1216
52	8-14	Thir	6g/f		1639
26	12-12	Thir	7g/f		1971
46	10-10	Catt	7g/f	64	3016 BL
29	14-14	Muss	7.1g/f	60	4175 bl
51	8-20	Chep	7.1gd	55	4488 bl

MISTER RIGHT 3 ch g £636

63	3-11	Wind	8.3g/f		5054
46	10-11	Yarm	10.1g/s	63	5353

MISTER RUSHBY 4 b g £0

12a	12-16	Sout	6af	[40]	447
0	9-9	Sout	12af	[35]	1204
4a	9-10	Sout	8af	[30]	1406

MISTER SACHA 3 b c £41179

112	1-7	LONG	9.3sft	1851*
113	3-4	Deau	8hvy	4311
115	3-11	Long	8g/f	4949

MISTER SAIF 2 ch c £7651

89a	2-6	Ling	6ap	[85]	79
89a	2-13	Ling	7ap	[84]	119
82	7-20	Newm	7g/f	87	1186
0	U-20	Newm	8fm	86	1496
86	5-14	York	7sft	86	1665

74	9-13	Sand	8.1g/s	[85]	2126
90	4-17	Epso	7g/f	85	2212
90	2-5	Sand	7.1g/f	[85]	2362
40	11-11	Asco	6.5gd	87	3069
72	12-17	Good	7fm	87	3550

MISTER SWEETS 5 ch g £3484

63	6-20	Thir	6gd	73	1638
61	10-20	York	6g/f	71	2409
76	1-17	NEWM	7g/f	68	2768*
77	5-15	York	7gd	73	3117
42	14-15	York	6g/f	73	3434
61	12-19	York	6gd	72	4005
59a	6-8	Sout	7af	[72]	4093
43	19-20	Ripo	6gd	70	4785
35	22-26	Redc	8fm	68	4926 T
58	9-19	Newc	7g/f	66	5014 t
8	20-20	Yarm	7sft	64	5256 t

MISTER TRICKSTER 3 b c £4256

74	6-18	Leic	10g/s	63	1017
27	13-19	Warw	10.9gd	63	1124
36	11-20	Wind	11.6sft	61	1648
66	1-14	CHEP	7.1gd	58	2199*
51	11-20	Newb	7fm	62	2650
46	8-11	Leic	8g/f	62	3516
16	13-15	Chep	8.1sft	61	4057
58	3-12	Brig	8fm	[60]	4761

MISTER TROUBRIDGE 2 ch c £0

55	13-13	Sali	7sft	4576
57	9-11	Sali	7gd	4853
31	9-15	Brig	7sft	5192

MISTERNANDO 4 b c £42335

0	9-13	Asco	16.2sft	[101]	1418
107	2-17	Ches	18.7gd	101	1569
110	6-9	Sand	16.4g/f	[105]	2095
111	8-13	Asco	20g/f	[105]	2518
108	3-8	Sand	16.4g/s	[109]	2914 VIS
111	3-9	Good	16fm	[108]	3552 vis

MISTERS SISTER 2 b f £0

35	14-16	York	7.9gd	4997
31	7-9	Nott	10hvy	5189
53	13-16	Yarm	10.1g/s	5352 BL

MISTRAL SKY 4 b g £21391

61a	9-16	Ling	7ap	70	20 vis
62a	11-16	Ling	7ap	70	55 vis
71a	1-14	LING	6ap	68	121* vis
51a	9-11	Ling	6ap	[68]	130 vis
77a	2-14	Ling	7ap	72	604 vis
70a	11-15	Ling	7ap	74	698 vis
43a	13-13	Wolv	6af	73	807 vis
71	2-17	Leic	7g/s	66	1020 vis
51	11-19	Sali	7g/f	68	1723 vis
44	4-4	Leic	7g/f	[67]	1962 vis
69	3-16	Ling	7g/f	67	2063 P
65	3-11	Chep	7.1gd	67	2370 p
69	5-13	Ling	7.6g/f	66	2587 p
74	4-10	Leic	7g/f	[66]	2920 bl
64	7-16	Kemp	7gd	66	3184 vis
74	1-7	LEIC	6g/f	[64]	3518* vis
73	2-9	Yarm	6g/f	70	3705 vis
77	2-7	Ling	6fm	[72]	3789 vis
80	1-9	NEWM	6ap	72	3924+ vis
78a	2-13	Wolv	6ap	72	5181 vis
25a	12-12	Wolv	6ap	74	5291 vis

MISTRESS HOLLIE 2 b f £0

27a	7-12	Wolv	8.5af		28 p
35a	8-11	Ling	8ap	[35]	696 p

MISTRESS TWISTER 3 b f £10325

69	3-11	Thir	7fm		2463
64	3-10	Redc	6gd		2559
64	8-10	Catt	7g/f	70	3016
74	3-12	Carl	6.9fm	67	3548
59	11-20	York	7.9gd	68	4321
79	1-26	REDC	8fm	67	4926*

MISTY BAY 2 b f £0

10	9-10	Ripo	5gd	2983

MISTY HEIGHTS 3 b f £13834

102	3-	Leop	7sft	1300
109	2-9	Leop	7g/s	1701

108	8-15	Curr	8g/f	2005

MISTY MAN 5 ch g £2817

29a	4-9	Sout	11af	[30]	204
35a	3-14	Sout	12af	[30]	305 BL
31a	5-9	Wolv	9.4af	[30]	399 bl
40a	1-12	WOLV	12af	35	469* bl
20a	4-7	Sout	11af	[45]	1589 bl
34	5-13	Kemp	10hvy	[40]	1643 bl
29a	5-9	Sout	11af	[45]	1838 bl
37a	8-12	Wolv	9.5ap	[45]	5234 bl

MISTY MILLER 2 b c £0

62	5-6	Redc	5sft	1143
52	8-10	Newc	5g/f	2158
67	6-8	York	6g/f	2408

MISTY PRINCESS 2 gr f £0

51	11-15	Donc	5gd	920
65	5-8	Newm	5gd	1170
64	6-12	Warw	5sft	1524
51	14-19	Wind	5g/f	1805
22a	9-10	Sout	6af	2382
26	13-16	Nott	6.1gd	3103
60a	8-10	Ling	5ap	3743

MITCHAM 8 br g £0

68	18-20	Kemp	6gd	95	1138

MITCHELLAND 2 b f £6985

74	4-15	Donc	5gd		920
77	1-4	NEWC	5hvy		1037*
74	9-9	Ches	5.1gd		1567
59	6-8	Thir	5g/f		2213
79	6-7	Hayd	6gd		2883
77	3-9	Hayd	5sft	74	3271
72	5-13	Newc	7g/s	74	3698
57	5-5	Hami	6g/s	[74]	3877
64	5-9	Catt	6sft	74	3931 VIS
56	13-15	Hayd	6sft	67	4765 vis
61a	5-12	Wolv	5.1ap	[65]	4922
65a	2-12	Wolv	7.1ap	[60]	5158

MITH HILL 3 b c £11275

59	7-12	Hayd	10.5gd		3740
74	1-4	BEVE	9.9g/s		3855*
78a	1-16	LING	12ap	68	4973*
83a	1-16	LING	12ap	70	5261*
39	17-24	Donc	12sft	78	5372

MITRAILLETTE 2 ch f £4154

65	6-8	Donc	6gd		2750
76	5-10	Nott	6.1g/f		3418
72	4-12	Folk	7gd		3909
84	1-20	LING	7gd	73	4444*

MITRASH 4 b c £0

31	8-11	Ripo	12.3gd	4281

MITSUKI 5 b m £0

30	9-10	York	6gd	66	3116
62	5-14	Thir	6g/f	63	3416
60	8-11	Thir	6g/f	63	3574
41	9-9	Thir	5g/s	61	4210

MITY DANCER 4 br f £4751

104	3-11	Cope	12gd	3660

MITZI CASPAR 3 ch f £3657

9a	7-12	Sout	8af		848
14	15-17	Donc	8gd		919
23	15-18	Wind	8.3g/s		1258
7	24-24	Newm	8fm		1495
34a	3-9	Wolv	6af	[30]	1803
35a	2-10	Sout	7af	[30]	1842
54a	1-12	SOUT	8af	[37]	2339*
37a	9-16	Sout	8af	54	2805
6	13-14	Yarm	6gd	52	3870
0	14-15	Sout	8af	52	4132
13	12-15	Yarm	7g/s	[45]	4587 BL

MIX IT UP 3 gr f £0

31	10-10	Bath	8g/s	1100

MIZHAR 8 b g £4059

21a	11-11	Wolv	7af	59	378 vis
39a	5-13	Wolv	6af	[55]	483
52a	2-12	Wolv	7af	[55]	512
36a	5-9	Sout	7af	[55]	555
30a	8-12	Wolv	6af	[50]	646 p
5	11-17	Pont	6hvy	[55]	1065
59a	1-4	WOLV	7af	[48]	1378* p
53a	3-8	Wolv	7af	[52]	1656 p
53a	2-7	Wolv	8.5af	[52]	1672 p
0	P-16	Nott	6.1gd	[52]	1988 p

MIZZ TEE 2 b f £7715

86	2-10	York	5g/s	1709
81	1-12	RIPO	5g/f	1974*
86	5-12	Beve	5g/f	2165

MKUZI 5 ch h £41415

114	1-7	CURR	14gd	2817*
109	3-7	Leop	12g/f	4019
111	2-11	Fair	14g/s	4162
99	8-11	Newm	16sft	5138

MOANING MYRTLE 3 br f £0

60a	4-9	Ling	12ap	4449
0	11-14	Ling	13ap	4898

MOAYED 5 b g £50772

74a	1-12	LING	8ap	[80]	571* bl t
83a	2-14	Ling	10ap	80	625 bl t
82a	6-14	Ling	10ap	82	758 bl t
88a	3-15	Ling	7ap	82	887 bl t
80	3-13	Newc	7hvy	80	1035 bl t
89	1-30	NEWM	6g/f	80	1481* bl t
74	10-17	Muss	5fm	87	2082 bl t
85	4-8	Sand	7.1g/f	86	2389 bl t
61	14-16	Newm	7sft	85	5101 bl t
96a	1-12	LING	6ap	84	5297+ bl t

MOBANE FLYER 4 b g £8895

60	12-15	York	7gd	70	3117
52	10-13	Newc	7gd	67	3428
54	6-16	Beve	8.5g/s	[63]	3850
64	3-12	Newc	9hvy	60	4215
62	3-14	York	10.4g/f	60	4402
66	1-13	MUSS	8g/f	[60]	4554*
64	3-17	Newc	8fm	63	4867
70	2-15	Nott	8.2hvy	63	5191
70	2-10	Donc	10.3sft	63	5206
63	6-16	Nott	10hvy	64	5345

MOBARHEN 2 b c £2378

75	5-10	Donc	7g/f		3594
69	5-14	Sali	8g/s		4078
78	2-14	Thir	8fm		4376
78	3-20	Yarm	8g/s	73	4635
55	9-12	Newm	8gd	76	5089

MOBO BACO 7 ch g £5819

43	4-10	Bath	10.2gd	[60]	1402
56	4-13	Bath	8sft	60	1542
52	9-12	Bath	8g/f	57	1792
38	9-16	Bath	8fm	[57]	2032
35	7-16	Chep	7.1gd	[54]	2369
45	7-17	Warw	8.1fm	52	2572
58	1-17	WARW	8.1g/f	52	2909*
52	5-17	Chep	8.1g/s	58	3087
49	9-25	Asco	7g/f	55	3443
54	6-15	Ling	7.6fm	54	3788
29	9-14	Good	8sft	54	4189
55	4-20	Chep	7.1g/s	54	4367
54	3-18	Chep	8.1gd	[52]	4485
58	2-18	Good	8gd	52	4750
59a	2-12	Wolv	8.6ap	[53]	5337

MOCCA 3 b f £10344

79	4-14	Newm	10g/f	76	1192
84	5-11	Newb	11g/f	76	1756
86	1-12	SAND	10gd	75	2366*
86	6-9	Newb	12fm	[87]	3629
92	2-13	Donc	10.3fm	[87]	4463
88	6-13	Asco	10gd	[88]	4772
92	5-14	Donc	10.3sft	[88]	5370

MOCHACCINO 2 b f £0

11a	14-15	Sout	5af	4089
33	8-13	Ripo	5gd	4303
20	12-13	Nott	6.1g/f	4843
29a	11-13	Wolv	5.1ap	5207 VIS

MODEL FIGURE 3 b f £0

56	10-13	Ling	7g/f	71	3604

MODEM 7 b g £0

21a	10-13	Sout	12af	[40]	575	e
0	B-14	Ling	10ap	[40]	784	vis

MODESTA 3 b f £26399

81	4-10	Newb	10gd		1209
85	1-10	**YARM**	11.5g/f		1725+
92	2-13	Hayd	11.9gd	83	2238
87	8-9	Asco	12g/f	[78]	2517
82	6-13	York	13.9g/s	88	4062
99	5-10	Donc	14.6fm	[88]	4460
104	1-12	**YARM**	14.1sft	[95]	5254*

MODESTY BLAISE 4 br f £1463

69a	1-11	**WOLV**	7af		396*
58a	7-8	Sout	8af	70	489
46a	5-8	Sout	7af	[68]	744
42a	12-12	Wolv	12.2ap	66	4983

MODRAJ 2 b f £864

64	9-12	Newb	6g/f	3251
80	3-10	Newb	6gd	3917

MODULOR 12 gr g £0

0	10-11	Beve	12.1g/f	4716
2	10-11	Catt	12sft	5128

MOFEYDA 3 b f £0

48a	6-14	Ling	12ap	14

MOKABRA 3 b c £5937

93	6-11	Newm	7gd	107	1167
105	3-5	Curr	7gd	[107]	1559
102	8-9	Colo	8gd	[107]	1860
83	17-27	Asco	8g/f	104	2521 VIS

MOKARABA 2 ch f £5178

78	4-7	Newm	7g/f		3616
81	4-18	Nott	8.2g/s		4035
79	2-14	Chep	8.1gd		4484
87	2-14	Donc	8sft	80	5203

MOLCON 3 b g £18583

72	5-19	Newm	6g/s	78	1154
86	1-17	**ASCO**	6sft	77	1417*
78	5-7	Ling	6sft	81	1621
86	3-18	Newm	6g/f	81	1933
77	4-10	Donc	7g/f	83	2427
84	4-11	Newm	7g/f	83	2532
62	10-12	Kemp	7g/s	83	2679
89	1-9	**LING**	7gd	81	3447*
82	8-20	Newm	7g/f	84	3782
72	7-13	Kemp	7sft	84	4030
5	17-18	Kemp	8g/f	84	4714
60	10-11	Donc	7sft	82	5219

MOLEHILL 3 b f £429

52	7-13	Hayd	11.9g/s		2230
56	5-8	Pont	12g/f		2608
54	4-9	Pont	12g/f		2992
49	7-17	Pont	17.1g/s	59	3970
49	8-12	Good	16g/s	56	4235

MOLEM 2 br c £543

77	6-8	Kemp	7fm	4393
66	4-5	Nott	8.2hvy	5186

MOLINIA 3 b f £2861

27	11-18	Wind	8.3sft	65	1647	
0	P-14	Nott	8.2g/f	62	2153	
56	4-20	Newb	7g/f	62	2314	
41	11-14	Newm	8.2g/f	60	2634	
56	4-11	Newm	7g/f	56	3283	
47	7-13	Ling	7g/f	55	3604	
53	3-14	Yarm	7gd	53	3995	T
1	14-15	Yarm	7g/s	[51]	4587	t
58a	1-12	**WOLV**	7.1ap	[50]	5233*	t

MOLLY DANCER 2 b f £421

45	9-13	Kemp	6gd		3183
44	9-12	Thir	6g/f		3411
69	3-9	Brig	6g/f		3981
53	5-6	Chep	5.1g/s	71	4298
44	6-11	Beve	5g/f	[67]	4599

MOLLY MARIE 2 b f £5679

81	2-7	Leic	5gd		2132
78	4-8	Donc	6gd		2750
66	6-11	Ripo	5g/s		3258
78	2-13	Hayd	6gd	[78]	3736

72	7-12	York	7g/s	77	4064
67	10-21	Donc	6.5fm	77	4457
64	9-21	Donc	6fm	[77]	4490
75	2-14	Hayd	6sft	[77]	4769

MOLLY MOON 3 gr f £0

60	14-14	Thir	5g/f	89	1766
71	8-10	Ches	5.1g/f	86	3080
56	7-7	Wind	6fm	[82]	3293

MOLLYS SECRET 6 b m £4492

52a	1-9	**WOLV**	12af	45	424*	p
27a	8-12	Wolv	12af	51	484	p
32a	9-12	Wolv	12af	50	634	p
30a	12-13	Ling	10ap	48	805	p
47	3-12	Ling	10g/f	45	2844	p
40	7-20	Catt	12g/f	45	3354	p
50	3-19	Chep	12.1gd	44	3727	p
45	6-19	Brig	9.9sft	47	4145	BL
48	3-13	Warw	10.9g/f	47	4419	bl

MOLLZAM 2 b c £0

57	9-9	Sali	7gd	2696
59	12-16	Sali	7g/s	3111

MOLOTOV 4 b g £8649

47	1-20	BEVE	5g/f	[45]	1948*
17a	10-13	Wolv	5af	51	2201
1	17-20	Nott	6.1g/f	46	2630
47	4-18	Pont	5gd	45	3463
53	1-12	**BRIG**	5.3g/s	45	4140*
50	3-16	Folk	6g/f	[50]	4370
52	3-15	Carl	5fm	[50]	4508
39	4-19	Yarm	6g/s	50	4636
62	1-13	**MUSS**	5g/s	[50]	5146*

MOMBASSA 4 b g £0

91	8-22	Newm	8sft	92	5103

MOMENTS I TREASURE 3 ch f £0

56a	6-11	Ling	8ap		841
45	9-10	Beve	12.1g/s	67	1165

MOMENTS OF JOY 4 b f £0

94	7-7	Newm	12fm	[105]	1493

MOMMKIN 3 b f £424

74	5-10	Good	11g/f	77	1865	
69	5-8	Ches	10.3gd	[76]	2283	
67	5-6	Sali	9.9gd	[74]	2663	
48	4-7	Folk	9.7gd	71	3384	
55	9-12	Bath	11.7g/f	68	3845	VIS

MOMTIC 3 ch c £16158

81	3-13	Kemp	9gd	80	1141
82	3-8	Sand	8.1g/s	80	1315
77	9-18	Good	9g/f	80	1813
80	4-11	Sand	10g/s	80	2127
82	4-6	Ripo	8g/f	80	2525
90	1-16	**KEMP**	9g/f	80	3039*
91	2-6	Newm	8g/f	85	3472
87	5-8	Folk	9.7g/s	[86]	3912

MON PETIT DIAMANT 3 b f £0

0	13-15	Sout	12af	[40]	89

MON PLAISIR 2 br f £0

31a	12-14	Ling	7ap	5078
48	10-14	Yarm	7sft	5251

MON SECRET 5 b g £6540

60a	2-12	Wolv	7af	55	74
64a	1-9	**SOUT**	7af	58	193*
54a	3-8	Wolv	7af	61	280
54a	4-8	Sout	8af	61	393
51a	7-13	Sout	7af	[60]	858
23	12-13	Muss	7.1gd	57	1553
51	6-14	Muss	7.1gd	55	1794
15	14-15	Beve	7.5g/s	53	2324
47	6-13	Muss	8g/f	51	3526
56	1-14	**CARL**	6.9g/f	51	4345*
43	11-15	Beve	8.5g/f	55	4598
53a	9-13	Wolv	8.6ap	59	5183
50a	6-13	Wolv	9.5ap	[57]	5338

MONA LISA 2 ch f £10000

107	4-9	Asco	8g/f	4798

MONAD 2 b f £0

28	10-11	Sali	7gd	3883
49	11-17	Warw	7.1gd	4269
57	8-13	Sali	7sft	4576
60a	8-11	Ling	8ap	4744

MONASH GIRL 3 b f £0

24	6-9	Brig	8fm		2834
53	11-17	Wind	8.3fm	[30]	3480
9	11-12	Brig	8sft	30	5094

MONASH LAD 2 ch c £2943

46	12-18	Leic	5fm		2109
81	5-9	Newm	6gd		2531
79	3-8	Ling	6gd		3021
76	3-6	Hami	6g/f		3202
73	4-8	Ayr	6g/f	79	3303
76	3-10	Catt	6sft	74	5318

MONASHEE MISS 2 ch f £631

45	4-4	Nott	5.1sft	1608
25a	8-10	Sout	6af	2382
43a	3-7	Sout	7af	2721
3a	10-11	Sout	7af	2995
0	P-12	Sout	7af	3394

MONASHEE PRINCE 2 ch c £5884

80	2-9	Yarm	5.2g/f		1133
83	1-6	**HAMI**	5gd		1386*
87	5-9	Ches	5.1gd		1567
87	3-8	Wind	5g/f		1955
74	4-7	Redc	5g/f		2100
62	12-13	Newm	5g/f	85	3943
59	13-16	Newm	6gd	81	4224
55	9-14	Hami	6sft	78	4692

MONASHEE ROSE 2 br f £11256

52	7-9	Sand	5g/f		3355
82	1-6	**CARL**	5g/f		3652*
78	1-12	**MUSS**	5g/f	72	4172*
79	2-12	Bath	5.7gd	75	4545
67	10-15	Ripo	5gd	77	4784
74	10-18	Wind	5g/f	77	4830
82	6-9	Tipp	5hvy	[77]	4960

MONDURU 7 b g £4468

21a	8-13	Ling	10ap	[35]	412	bl
38a	1-12	**WOLV**	8.5af	[35]	584*	bl e
39a	2-12	Ling	10ap	[35]	654	bl
48a	2-14	Ling	10ap	[45]	828	bl e
47a	3-6	Ling	10ap	[47]	972	bl e
52a	2-13	Wolv	9.4af	47	1223	bl e
52a	1-6	**LING**	10ap	[50]	1455*	bl e

MONICAS REVENGE 2 b f £0

48	9-14	Warw	6.1g/f	4422
46	8-11	Chep	7.1hvy	4703
45a	8-11	Wolv	8.6ap	4978

MONKEY MADGE 2 br f £935

70	2-13	Thir	6g/f	4590
39	7-9	Pont	6g/s	5154

MONKEY OR ME 2 b g £828

22a	11-13	Wolv	6af		126
30a	10-15	Sout	7af		184
34a	8-9	Wolv	7af		381
0	12-16	Sout	8af	[30]	719
32a	4-12	Sout	7af	[30]	909
32a	2-6	Sout	8af	[30]	1203
32	3-6	Warw	7.1g/s	[30]	1330
31a	3-10	Sout	7af	[35]	1842
34	4-13	Beve	8.5g/f	[35]	1947
6	12-18	Beve	9.9g/s	33	4243
1	15-15	Carl	7.9fm	[35]	4507

MONOLITH 6 b g £1484

81	3-9	Ayr	13.1g/s	82	2567
75	16-34	Newm	18sft	80	5135

MONSAL DALE 5 ch g £0

13a	8-11	Wolv	12af	45	937	
17a	7-10	Sout	16af	[45]	984	
23	14-17	Nott	14.1gd	50	1238	P
34a	6-7	Ling	16ap	[40]	1291	p

MONSIEUR BOND 4 ch c £105902

105	5-17	Donc	6gd	[110]	952
117	1-13	**CURR**	7sft	[110]	1062*
117	1-15	**YORK**	6sft	[114]	1667*

83	12-14	Asco	6fm	[117]		2580
110	6-20	Newm	6g/f	[117]		3062
104	9-12	Deau	6.5g/s	[117]		3838
113	5-19	Hayd	6fm	[115]		4384 BL
115	4-7	Long	7sft	[115]		5070 bl

MONSIEUR MIRASOL 2 b c £6673

72	3-7	Muss	5g/f		1117
75	3-9	Muss	5g/s		1458
71	5-13	Carl	5fm		1950
81	1-20	NEWC	6sft		2682*
54	8-9	Pont	6g/f	77	2989
80	2-6	Hayd	6g/s	77	3902
76	4-10	Beve	5sft	79	4258
73	7-17	York	7g/f	79	4396
73	5-10	Newm	6fm	75	4727
76	15-24	Redc	6fm	[79]	4928 BL
9	14-20	Newb	6hvy	73	5225

MONSOON RAIN 2 b c £8556

87	2-14	Newm	7g/f	3752
107	1-11	DONC	8fm	4462*

MONT SAINT MICHEL 2 b c £0

44	14-14	Yarm	7gd	4611
67	6-14	Leic	8gd	5058

MONTANA 3 b c £259

49a	8-14	Ling	6ap	[68]		23
35a	13-15	Ling	7ap	[60]		117
56	10-15	Wind	5gd		65	3165
65	4-7	Brig	6g/f	[60]		3985
1	18-19	Yarm	6g/s		55	4636

MONTARA 5 b h £1488

49a	1-12	WOLV	9.5ap	[45]	5234* P
54a	5-13	Wolv	9.5ap	[45]	5338 p

MONTE MAJOR 2 b g £8049

28a	10-12	Ling	8ap			102
52a	6-11	Sout	8af			159
61a	3-16	Ling	7ap			290
59a	4-10	Ling	7ap		63	432
64a	2-6	Sout	8af	[61]		503
81a	1-15	LING	9ap	[61]		875*
75	2-7	Sout	6g/s	[70]		1050
0	9-9	Thir	6g/s	[72]		1477

MONTE MAYOR LAD 3 b g £813

61a	3-14	Ling	6ap	[62]		23 BL
66a	3-13	Wolv	6af		62	45 bl
59a	4-12	Wolv	7af	[62]		71 bl
27	14-16	Nott	6.1sft	[70]		1743
55	7-12	Leic	6fm		64	2111 bl
45a	10-15	Sout	8af		64	2338 P

MONTE VERDE 3 b f £0

36a	10-12	Wolv	5af	[50]	70 p
31a	15-16	Ling	7ap	[48]	180 p

MONTECITO 2 b f £1865

71	8-10	Newb	6gd		3917
74	8-16	Sali	7gd		4330
80	3-6	Sali	6gd		4854
23	22-23	Newm	6gd	[82]	5084

MONTGOMERY 3 b g £0

51	6-7	Bath	11.7g/f		3967
50	6-9	Good	9sft		4266
37	5-7	Good	9.9g/f		4541
43	8-15	Wind	10g/f	[48]	4834

MONTGOMERYS ARCH 2 b c £86749

92	1-10	FOLK	7g/s		3046*
109	1-8	GOOD	6fm		3566*
111	4-6	Long	7g/f		4955
115	3-9	Newm	7sft	[100]	5137

MONTJEU BABY 2 b f £0

44	11-16	Nott	6.1gd	3103
53	14-16	Sali	7gd	4329
43	12-15	Chep	7.1gd	4483

65	6-16	Bath	8gd	5019

MONTMARTRE 4 b r f £0

0	13-14	York	13.9gd	92	3119
67	8-8	Thir	8fm	92	3608

MONTOSARI 5 ch g £4209

47a	1-14	LING	13ap	[40]		537*
44a	6-14	Ling	10ap	[45]		705
47a	3-14	Ling	12ap	[45]		827
53a	1-7	LING	12ap	[45]		1243+
54a	2-5	Ling	10ap	[45]		1412
20	13-18	Wind	11.6g/f		54	1960
56a	3-14	Ling	16ap		54	4319
38	10-20	Kemp	12g/f	[46]		4796
40a	12-14	Ling	16ap		55	5082

MONTURANI 4 b f £109286

102	2-	Toul	10.5g/s		57
106	3-8	Kemp	8g/s	[104]	1115
101	6-5	Sain	10.5g/s	[104]	2143
110	2-10	Asco	8g/f	[104]	2487
110	4-7	Newm	8fm	[104]	3004
113	4-8	Deau	8gd	[104]	3659
108	5-13	Deau	10sft	[104]	4160
114	1-13	CURR	10gd	[104]	4735*
89	11-14	Capa	10g/s	[104]	5244

MOON BIRD 2 b f £0

20	13-13	Wind	6fm	3478

MOON DAZZLE 3 b f £26233

96	1-13	NEWM	8g/f		1935*
106	4-11	Asco	8g/f		2555
92	5-9	Sand	8.1g/s	[106]	2917
97	5-7	Asco	8g/f	[106]	3389
98	2-12	Bath	8g/f	[104]	3965
97	6-13	Asco	8g/f	104	4802

MOON EMPEROR 7 b g £1126

84a	11-16	Ling	12ap	89	404
71a	6-16	Ling	12ap	87	475
75	9-18	Kemp	16g/s	87	1112 VIS
79	4-18	York	13.9g/s	89	1689 vis
75	6-10	Sand	14g/f	76	2192
70	6-11	Sand	14g/f	75	2391
69	8-11	Ling	16gd	74	3200
61	13-16	Kemp	16ap	74	4361
58	7-15	Good	16gd	67	5025

MOON FOREST 2 b r c £8424

78	2-17	Warw	7.1gd		4269
75	4-18	Ayr	6g/s		4617
78	1-13	WARW	7.1g/s		4996*
86	1-14	NEWB	7sft	76	5193*

MOON LEGEND 3 ch f £6448

51	7-16	Newm	7fm		2092
70	3-12	Yarm	7fm	65	2864
52	9-13	Leic	7g/f	66	3346
71	1-9	THIR	7fm	[66]	3610*
60	9-17	Ling	6g/f	66	4740
65a	6-12	Wolv	7.1ap	66	5008

MOON MISCHIEF 2 b f £518

58	7-10	Newm	6gd		1887
69a	3-7	Sout	5af		2498
62	8-10	Ches	5.1g/s		2744
14	9-9	Pont	6g/f	69	2989

MOON ROYALE 6 ch m £0

17a	8-10	Sout	6af	[30]	352
8a	8-9	Sout	7af	[30]	639 vis
0	8-8	Sout	11af	[30]	857
23	14-16	Beve	8.5g/s	[34]	3850

MOON SHOT 7 gr g £5010

70a	3-10	Sout	11af	[64]	142
74a	1-6	WOLV	12af	[61]	752*
74a	2-6	Sout	12af	72	870
71a	4-7	Ling	12ap	[71]	1009
25	15-19	Wind	10sft	[71]	1650

MOON SPINNER 7 b m £0

32	10-10	Bath	11.7g/f	4414
52	8-13	Nott	8.2g/f	4847
35a	9-10	Wolv	7.1ap	4920
53	12-12	Yarm	14.1sft	5254

MOON UNIT 3 b f £34805

107	1-8	CORK	5g/s	1159*
105	2-6	Curr	5g/f	2818

MOONFLEET 3 b f £208

16	8-8	Beve	7.5gd		3311
56	3-6	Brig	6gd		4900
62	8-15	York	7.9gd		5002
12	19-19	Redc	8sft	59	5302

MOONGLADE 3 ch f £0

9a	11-15	Sout	8af		96	t
10a	8-10	Sout	8af		143	t
11a	10-14	Sout	6af	[30]		637 t
9a	13-13	Ling	6ap	[30]		788 t P
17	8-10	Warw	6.1g/s	[30]		1327 t
34	5-16	Nott	6.1gd	[30]		1989 BL
18	15-17	Ling	7gd		35	2397 bl
26	6-12	Brig	5.3g/f		33	2645 bl
0	12-12	Brig	6g/f		31	3301 bl

MOONJAZ 7 ch h £10859

84	1-13	DIEL	11.5	[92]	1437*

MOONLIGHT APPEAL 2 ch f £0

0	13-13	York	6gd	4988

MOONLIGHT MAN 3 ch c £24144

105	2-11	Newm	7gd	105	1167
98	2-6	Asco	6sft	[105]	1421
91	7-8	Newm	7g/f	[105]	1932
93	15-19	Newm	6fm	103	3002
106	2-8	Newb	7g/f	[103]	3253
104	4-12	Good	7fm	[100]	3555
104	2-7	Leic	7fm	100	3814
104	6-9	Donc	8fm	[100]	4495
84	9-10	Newm	7fm	[100]	4929

MOONLIGHT SONG 7 b m £232

44	3-8	Ayr	7.2g/s	[45]	1448
25	10-15	Redc	7sft	45	1660
18a	8-10	Wolv	8.5af	[40]	1801
0	15-16	Sout	7af	34	2335
16	14-18	Donc	7gd	44	2755
21	13-16	Beve	7.5gd	44	2891 BL
1a	13-13	Sout	7af	30	3155

MOONLIGHT TANGO 3 b r f £520

73	5-20	Bath	10.2gd		1398
76	5-10	Sali	9.9g/f	[76]	1718
77	4-10	Chep	12.1gd	72	2114

MOONMAIDEN 2 ch f £0

68	10-14	Newm	7g/f		3944
53	5-11	Chep	8.1g/s		4296
77	5-11	Nott	8.2g/s		4648
68	7-13	Redc	7fm	[77]	4927

MOONSHAFT 3 b r c £857

5	17-17	Leic	10g/s		1019
65	7-11	Newm	10gd		1148
62	4-6	Pont	10sft		1428
13	8-8	Beve	12.1g/f	69	2164
57	4-10	Hami	9.2g/s	[67]	4135
68a	5-12	Wolv	8.6ap	67	4923
36a	13-14	Ling	7ap	[66]	5240 VIS

MOONSHINE BEACH 6 b g £28014

61	4-11	Warw	15sft	63	1087
34	7-13	Pont	21.6hvy	63	1252
59	6-18	Nott	14.1g/s	60	1772 P
58	3-9	Ripo	16g/f	58	2009 p
58	6-13	Chep	18gd	58	2198 p
56	5-14	Bath	18.2fm	55	2417 p
56	4-12	Warw	19.1fm	53	2577
67	P-12	Warw	15g/f	54	2908
73	1-7	WARW	16.2gd	54	3057*
65	1-19	BATH	17.2gd	59	3147*
44	13-13	Asco	16.2g/f	66	3387
67	3-10	Thir	16fm	63	3611
75	1-6	BEVE	16.2g/s	65	3853*
77	1-16	WARW	16.2gd	69	4276*
57	13-13	Good	16g/f	71	4527
71	3-20	Bath	17.2gd	70	4824
79	1-14	PONT	17.1g/f	70	4936*
82	1-10	PONT	18g/s	73	5151*

MOONSHINE BILL 5 ch g £500

54	3-19	Warw	10.9sft	52	1090

45 7-9 Pont 10hvy 52 1254

MOONSIDE 2 gr f £0
33 12-16 Bath 5.7gd 4823
41 15-19 Leic 7gd 5045
41 14-19 Newm 7g/s 5279 VIS

MOONSTRUCK 2 ch c £0
58a 7-11 Ling 8ap 4738

MOORS MYTH 3 b c £4339
79 3-12 Newm 7g/s 1152
52 6-15 Thir 7g/s 1473
71 5-14 Warw 7.1g/f [80] 2907
64 6-9 Wind 8.3g/f [76] 3979
75 1-7 REDC 7fm [73] 4561+
62a 7-13 Ling 7ap 73 4897

MOOSE MALLOY 7 ch g £0
5a 5-6 Ling 8ap [30] 1292 p

MORAG 3 b f £1489
68 4-16 Leic 8g/s 70 1359
64 10-13 Bath 10.2g/f [70] 1791
59 8-14 Wind 8.3g/f 70 1956
58 11-16 Brig 7fm 67 2258
60 6-10 Hayd 8.1g/s 64 3138
60 6-14 Yarm 8gd 64 3363 P
63 2-14 Yarm 7gd 61 3995
46 7-16 Brig 7sft [61] 4144
51 7-19 Leic 7gd 60 4452
39 11-12 Good 9g/f 60 4539
38 15-20 Leic 7gd 58 5046
24a 10-11 Wolv 7.1ap [58] 5178

MORAHIB 6 ch h £838
67 2-7 Yarm 10.1g/f [88] 3704
0 10-11 Wind 10gd [80] 4124

MORBIDEZZA 4 b f £4577
103 3-11 Dort 9.3gd 2637

MORGAN LEWIS 3 b g £7518
62 7-10 Sand 5g/f 63 3356
73 1-18 HAYD 6gd 63 3737*
72 3-15 Newb 6gd 69 3920
75 2-7 Sand 5g/s 68 4099
72 3-8 Hami 5g/s [69] 4822

MORITAT 4 b c £1453
17a 13-14 Sout 6af [60] 2502
48 6-15 Chep 5.1gd 53 3403
55 3-15 Muss 5g/f 53 3561
55 5-15 Ling 6fm 53 3790
48 6-17 Wind 6gd 53 4126 t
56 3-20 Chep 6.1g/s 53 4368 t
35 14-15 Chep 5.1gd 51 4489 t
30 10-14 Catt 6gd 54 4967

MORNIN RESERVES 5 b g £0
71 13-13 Newm 5g/f [108] 1479
91 15-19 Asco 5g/f [107] 2468
79 11-12 Sand 5g/s [105] 2913

MORNING AFTER 4 b f £271
64 8-14 Donc 8g/f [78] 1877
67a 6-12 Ling 8ap [74] 2840
68 6-11 Yarm 7gd 72 3364
67a 4-12 Ling 8ap 68 4743

MORNING HAWK 3 b f £0
38a 7-10 Ling 8ap 52 455
47a 4-8 Sout 11af 46 614
34a 5-7 Wolv 9.4af [45] 893
37a 6-8 Ling 10ap [45] 1183
34 9-20 Beve 16.2gd 42 3312
38 4-14 Nott 16g/f 42 3580 BL
40 9-11 Yarm 14.1gd 38 3998 bl
30 4-8 Chep 16.2g/s 40 4302 bl
18 11-19 Brig 9.9gd [35] 4903 bl

MORNING MAJOR 2 b g £0
39 10-20 Newc 6sft 2682
56 8-12 Newc 7gd 3425
49 10-14 Thir 7g/s 4204

MORNING SUN 3 b f £0
0 15-15 Sout 11af 40 196
0 9-9 Wolv 9.4af [40] 314 BL e

MORNING WORLD 2 b c £0
32 10-12 Ripo 5gd 1173
29 10-10 Muss 5gd 1550
46 6-11 Hayd 5g/f 1880

MOROZOV 5 b h £0
0 P-13 Asco 16.2sft 1418
0 P-10 York 13.9g/s 1705

MORRIS DANCING 5 b g £206
6a 9-10 Sout 11af [40] 375 p
29a 7-12 Wolv 9.4af 40 464 p
6a 9-10 Wolv 12af [30] 581 p
0 14-16 Sout 8af [30] 719 p
31a 5-14 Ling 10ap [30] 784
25a 11-14 Ling 12ap [30] 827
5a 8-10 Sout 8af [30] 1406 p
20a 7-8 Wolv 9.4af [30] 1561
32a 3-9 Sout 11af [30] 1838 VIS
18a 5-9 Sout 12af [30] 2381 vis
5 10-10 Warw 12.6g/f 30 2912 vis

MORSE 3 b c £48391
59 16-22 Donc 7gd 81 955
83 2-16 Kemp 6g/s 79 1116
87 2-10 Wind 6gd [82] 1383
85 3-10 Hayd 6g/f 82 1488
92 1-7 LING 6sft 83 1621*
93 2-7 Nott 6.1g/s [88] 1771
82 8-18 Newm 6g/f 91 1933
4a 11-11 Ling 6ap 83 2841
90 6-11 Asco 6.5gd 90 3069
58 14-16 Newb 6g/f 89 3269
33 13-14 Ches 6.1g/f 87 4048
58 15-15 Hayd 8.1g/f 85 4352
80 1-13 WARW 7.1g/s [83] 4667*
72 8-12 Hayd 6sft 83 4779
83a 2-10 Wolv 7.1ap [78] 4920
79 5-11 Donc 7sft 81 5219

MORSON BOY 4 b g £0
28 12-12 Hami 12.1gd 99 1746
79 12-14 Hayd 16.2gd 99 2239
90 7-14 York 13.9gd 97 3119
60 15-15 Good 14g/f 92 3510
90 7-10 Asco 16.2gd 92 3776

MORVERN 4 ch g £0
52a 4-9 Ling 12ap [51] 324 vis
0 14-16 Sout 14af 51 1033 vis
40 5-9 Redc 14.1g/f 48 2105
21 6-7 Ayr 13.1g/s 45 2546

MOSCOW BALLET 3 b c £47721
100 6-10 York 10.4g/s 1685
103 6-8 Chan 9g/s 2307
113 1-13 ASCO 10g/f 2520*
105 7-10 Curr 12g/f 2822
110 3-7 Arli 10fm 4015

MOSCOW BLUE 3 ch c £0
59 6-8 Epso 8.5hvy 1297
73 7-9 Hayd 8.1g/f 1882

MOSCOW MARY 2 b f £0
10a 8-9 Wolv 6af [65] 247
11a 8-8 Wolv 5af [55] 1218
26a 10-12 Wolv 6af 50 1374
25 12-13 Warw 6.1fm 55 2439
13 10-10 Brig 7fm 50 3672
25 7-16 Folk 6g/f [45] 4370
24 13-17 Warw 8.1g/s [40] 4992

MOSCOW MUSIC 2 ch c £53694
91 2-8 Newb 5.2gd 1205
75 1-4 LING 5g/s 1614*
98 2-8 Sand 5g/f 2094
88 6-7 Newm 6g/f 3028
96 2-5 York 5g/s [100] 4025
99 3-22 Donc 6fm [100] 4458
98 5-9 Newm 7gd [100] 4881

MOSCOW TIMES 2 b c £4314
67a 10-13 Ling 7ap 119
66 6-17 Sali 6g/f 71 1722
72 5-20 Newb 7fm 70 2650
72 7-10 Asco 8gd [70] 3067
76 1-11 SALI 8gd 70 3455*

74 3-11 Kemp 8g/f 72 3685
57 11-15 Kemp 8g/f 72 4362
70a 5-13 Ling 7ap 72 4897

MOSHKIL 2 b c £0
63 10-12 Sand 7.1g/f 2388
46 11-14 Sali 8g/s 4078
69 6-11 Bath 8gd 4544

MOSS VALE 3 b c £84396
96 4-19 Newm 6g/s 100 1154
111 1-15 CHES 5.1g/s 100 1572*
115 1-9 HAYD 6g/f [106] 1918+
114 1-8 SALI 6fm [112] 2421+
87 20-20 Newm 6g/f [112] 3062
107 9-12 York 6g/f [112] 4060
111 2-12 Curr 6g/s [112] 4732
111 2-14 Newm 6sft [110] 5100

MOSSMANN GORGE 2 b c £2128
50 11-13 Carl 5fm 1950
56 6-13 Thir 6g/f 4590
62 5-14 Newc 6fm 4865
66 2-12 Muss 7.1g/s [62] 5142

MOST DEFINITELY 4 b g £18031
64 2-10 Carl 14.1fm 62 2444
3 12-13 Newc 16.1sft 62 2685 bl
63 6-9 Redc 16sft 62 2963
65 2-10 Thir 16fm 60 3611
66 3-9 Muss 14gd 62 4521
68 2-9 Redc 14.1fm 62 4559
69 2-8 Redc 14.1fm 64 4932
77 1-12 REDC 14.1g/s 65 5108*
79 2-11 Muss 16g/f 62 5335

MOST SAUCY 7 br m £5425
71a 5-13 Ling 10ap 72 26
70a 5-12 Ling 12ap 72 56
67a 5-10 Sout 12af 71 138
67a 8-14 Ling 13ap 71 147
63a 9-16 Ling 12ap 68 218
54 6-12 Sout 11gd 65 1286
55 6-10 Bath 11.7gd 65 1399
59 5-16 Brig 11.9fm 62 1693
48 7-16 Leic 11.8g/f 62 1830
61 3-7 Leic 11.8g/f 61 1967
59 4-11 Sali 12fm 59 2293
58 5-11 Warw 12.6fm 59 2601
53 7-11 Newb 13.3fm 59 2651
57 4-8 Epso 12gd 57 3217
58a 3-11 Ling 16ap 55 3450
56 3-7 Kemp 12g/f 55 3519
39 10-14 Brig 11.9fm 54 3674
58a 1-14 LING 16ap 53 4319*
30 9-20 Bath 17.2gd 56 4824
52a 9-14 Ling 16ap 55 5082

MOSTANAD 2 b g £0
45 10-13 York 6gd 3120

MOSTARSIL 6 ch g £7436
54 12-18 Kemp 16g/s 71 1112 p
71 6-17 Sali 14.1g/s 70 1502 p
72 3-14 Asco 16.2g/f 68 1928 p
69 4-10 Sand 14g/f 68 2192 p
73 1-11 SAND 14g/f 68 2391* p
70 6-19 Carl 11.9gd 71 2673 p
20 7-7 Kemp 14.4g/f 70 3037 p
61 6-14 Brig 11.9fm 68 3674 p

MOSTASHAAR 2 b c £0
74 7-16 Leic 7fm 3811
80 5-19 Leic 7gd 5055

MOTARASSED 2 b c £6843
81 3-6 Yarm 6g/s 2851
94 1-8 SALI 6gd 3451*
74 5-5 Donc 7fm [88] 4461

MOTH BALL 2 b c £40604
86 2-8 Asco 6g/f 3438
85 3-18 Wind 6gd 3824
87 1-9 GOOD 6gd 3951*
76 7-13 Warw 6.1gd 83 4273
88 3-13 Muss 5g/f 83 4551
97 1-9 BRIG 6fm 84 4758*
106 4-24 Redc 6fm [83] 4928

110 1-11 YORK 6gd [92] 4998*

MOTHECOMBE DREAM 2 b c £0
47 12-16 Leic 7fm 3811
47 10-10 Kemp 8g/f 4712
60 7-12 Bath 8sft 5170

MOTIVATOR 2 b c £124804
111 1-11 NEWM 8gd 3925*
121 1-8 DONC 8sft 5216*

MOTIVE 3 ch c £9180
65 5-11 Kemp 8hvy 1514
86 1-18 WIND 10g/f 1959*
91 2-8 York 10.4g/f 86 2406
73 8-11 Newm 10g/f 90 3029
90 8-17 Newm 10g/f 90 4917
86 9-15 Leic 11.8gd 90 5043

MOTORWAY 3 b c £4368
75 6-20 Bath 10.2gd 1398
79 1-15 WIND 10fm 3292*
81 5-7 Wind 10fm 83 3801

MOTU 3 b g £598
70 7-16 Kemp 6g/s 77 1116
37 11-17 Asco 6sft 75 1417
71 8-14 Newm 8g/f 72 1930
59 7-20 Newb 7g/f 71 2314
63 7-10 Nott 8.2gd [70] 3107
58 9-14 Beve 7.5g/s 67 4241
65 3-17 Warw 8.1g/s 64 4668 BL
55 6-13 Pont 8g/s [63] 5153 bl

MOUFTARI 3 b c £2286
69 5-11 Ripo 8gd 1177
79 4-8 Ches 10.3gd 1597
75 5-10 Hayd 10.5g/f [84] 1922
78 2-6 Bath 10.2g/f [84] 2980
75a 3-15 Ling 12ap [80] 4111
59 5-13 Nott 10gd [80] 4861 BL

MOUNT ARAFAT 2 b g £0
0 9-9 Bath 8.1g/s 4297
27 8-11 Bath 8gd 4544
2 11-11 Bath 10.2gd 4825 T

MOUNT BENGER 4 ch g £6288
64 6-14 Nott 10fm [65] 1006
37 11-11 Chep 10.2gd 65 2371
58 4-8 Epso 10.1g/s 62 3044 P
67 1-16 HAYD 10.5sft 60 3276* p
59 9-17 Kemp 12sft 64 4033 p
62 3-9 Redc 10gd 62 4248 p
50 10-18 Ayr 10.9sft 62 4623 p
66 2-19 Bath 11.7gd 61 5024 VIS

MOUNT BUTLER 2 b c £0
52 7-8 York 6g/f 2408
51 13-15 York 7.9gd 5002
51 6-9 Nott 10hvy 5189

MOUNT COTTAGE 3 b f £435
43 6-9 Pont 8gd 3462
49 4-6 Brig 8.1g/s 3905
48 6-11 Beve 9.9sft 4261
4 14-15 Yarm 10.1g/s [48] 5122

MOUNT EPHRAM 2 b g £4761
56 4-4 Newc 5hvy 1037
59 5-10 Newc 6sft 1677
53 6-12 Newc 6gd 1869
53 4-8 Redc 7g/s 2563
73 1-7 MUSS 7.1g/f 2810* P
74 4-7 Catt 7g/f 3189 BL
67 2-13 Catt 7g/f 3349 bl
37 7-8 Muss 8gd 72 4807
54 8-12 Muss 7.1g/s [70] 5142 bl
34 17-19 Redc 8sft 62 5302

MOUNT HILLABY 4 b f £15964
62a 1-11 WOLV 7af 51 378*
21a 9-10 Sout 8af 51 463
55 7-17 Hayd 8.1gd 59 3759
65 2-16 Nott 8.2g/s 57 4036
34 9-12 Newc 9hvy 57 4215
66 1-19 YORK 7.9g/f 60 4399+
56 10-15 Beve 7.5g/f 63 4719
63 5-19 Newc 7g/f 63 5014

70a 1-13 WOLV 8.6ap 62 5364*

MOUNT KELLET 2 ch g £0
9 16-18 Ayr 6g/s 4617
51a 7-12 Wolv 5.1ap 4922
43a 7-12 Wolv 7.1ap 5158

MOUNT LOGAN 8 b h £0
11a 11-13 Sout 8af 199
20a 11-13 Ling 10ap 338

MOUNT PEKAN 4 b c £673
17 17-19 Beve 9.9g/s 49 1164
50 3-14 Hami 8.3gd 46 1748
28 7-8 Hami 9.2gd 47 2179
37 6-8 Redc 8gd 46 2550
0 17-17 Hayd 8.1gd 44 2947
41 5-14 Ayr 7.2gd [41] 3324
19 8-15 Newc 7gd [41] 3426
35 8-17 Newc 7g/s 41 3700
22 7-12 Hami 8.3g/s [39] 4007

MOUNT ROYALE 6 ch g £10436
25a 8-10 Sout 8af 58 318
42a 7-10 Sout 8af 58 387 vis
49a 6-9 Sout 6af [54] 459 vis
53a 3-13 Sout 7af 52 556 vis t
61a 1-11 SOUT 7af 52 585* vis t
65a 1-9 WOLV 7af 58 684* vis t
49a 8-10 Wolv 7af 63 704 vis t
39a 7-10 Wolv 7af 62 864 vis t
45 6-13 Sout 6g/s 53 1052 vis t
65a 2-8 Sout 7af 61 1195 vis t
65a 2-10 Wolv 7af [61] 1319 vis t
57 2-13 Muss 7.1g/s 51 1463 vis t
54 3-15 Thir 7gd 53 1635 vis t
30a 12-13 Wolv 6ap [64] 5327 vis t

MOUNT SUPERIOR 8 b g £1278
42a 1-10 SOUT 8af [40] 352* bl
37a 5-13 Wolv 6af [45] 582 bl
26a 10-12 Ling 8ap [40] 710 bl
12a 7-12 Sout 6af [40] 982 bl

MOUNT VETTORE 3 br g £8305
83a 1-11 WOLV 6af 481*
85 2-22 Donc 7gd 76 955
75 8-9 Hayd 8.1sft 82 1105
69 11-20 Newm 8fm 82 1496
71 8-11 Pont 8g/f 80 2040
68 9-12 Pont 10g/f 78 2277
51 9-9 Beve 8.5sft 75 2940
68 6-11 Newm 7g/f 72 3283
66 6-16 Redc 8g/f 69 3768
70 3-19 Leic 7g/f 67 4452
77 2-26 Redc 8fm 67 4926

MOUNTAIN BREEZE 2 b f £0
1 12-12 Beve 7.5g/s 4242
40a 10-11 Wolv 8.6ap 4978
24 9-12 Pont 6g/s 5152

MOUNTAIN MEADOW 3 ch g £4444
86 2-14 Nott 10gd 1241
85 1-8 BEVE 12.1gd 2515*

MOUNTCHARGE 2 b g £335
82a 3-10 Ling 8ap 79 132
21 19-20 Newm 8fm 80 1496
62 10-13 Newm 7fm 80 2590
67 5-7 Yarm 8g/f 77 2853
50 10-10 Nott 10gd 74 3990
41 13-17 Warw 8.1g/s 70 4668

MOUSEMAN 3 b g £0
46 5-8 Brig 5.3g/f 60 1942
35 9-9 Warw 6.1fm [59] 2778 bl
7 12-12 Catt 5g/f 55 3193

MOVIE KING 5 ch g £2045
53 7-12 Ches 12.3gd 71 1599
42 15-19 Ripo 10g/f 68 1781
67 2-11 Leic 10gd 65 2135 P
41 13-13 Ches 10.3gd 65 2284 p
15 13-13 Redc 10gd 65 2560 p
57 6-10 Sand 10g/f 63 3336
63 3-6 Pont 10gd 62 3678
47 13-16 Thir 8g/f 60 4594

MOYNE PLEASURE 5 b g £2475
0 13-15 Sout 12af 46 257
2a 8-10 Wolv 16.2af 45 358
11a 8-12 Wolv 12af [40] 523
0 11-16 Sout 8af [35] 719 P
20a 6-10 Wolv 12af [35] 780
26a 8-16 Sout 11af [35] 852
38 8-12 Newc 16.1sft 40 965 p
31a 2-6 Sout 11af [30] 1409 p
4 7-8 Brig 11.9gd [40] 1547 p
33a 2-8 Wolv 9.4af [30] 1561 p
24a 3-6 Sout 12af [30] 1592 p
43a 1-6 WOLV 9.4af [35] 1800* p
42 4-10 Beve 8.5g/f [40] 1943 p
42 6-10 Newc 10.1g/f 42 2162 p
36a 7-16 Sout 12af 45 2340 p
26a 8-13 Sout 8af 45 2497 p
28 7-8 Muss 12g/f 38 2616 p
0 R-11 Newc 10.1g/s 38 2726 p

MOZAFIN 2 b c £11480
66 6-10 Newc 5g/f 2158
85 2-17 Donc 6g/f 2424
77 4-12 Hayd 6sft 3272
82 3-7 Catt 7g/f [88] 3665
83 2-8 Sand 7.1g/s 78 4100
61 8-8 Newc 7sft [81] 4283
90 2-12 Thir 7g/f [79] 4591 VIS
87 1-6 HAYD 8.1sft [82] 4783* vis

MPENZI 2 b f £0
67 7-23 Newm 7g/f 4885
46 14-16 Newb 8hvy 5220

MR AITCH 2 b c £1945
82 2-12 Wind 8.3g/f 4829
75a 4-12 Ling 8ap 5293

MR BELVEDERE 3 b g £1284
53 11-18 Nott 8.2fm 70 1007
59 9-16 Leic 7g/f 68 1825
27 10-10 Leic 8gd [65] 2133 bl
52 3-12 Sali 7fm [65] 2288 P
54 2-9 Brig 8g/f [61] 2431
18 10-11 Leic 8g/f 56 3516
53a 4-12 Ling 10ap 51 4113
23 8-10 Brig 9.9fm 51 4763
7 15-17 Newb 9sft 50 5198

MR BOUNTIFUL 5 b g £3317
58a 1-16 LING 7ap 55 22*
63a 2-15 Ling 7ap 61 50
55a 3-16 Ling 7ap [63] 123
60a 8-16 Ling 7ap 63 144
53a 11-16 Ling 7ap 62 270
55a 8-14 Ling 7ap 60 499 p
41 9-15 Thir 7gd 55 1635
53 4-18 Ayr 7.2g/f 54 1897 p
50 8-14 Thir 7fm 53 2466 p
46 10-18 Catt 7g/f 51 2848 p
44 6-14 Catt 6g/f 50 3352 T p
55 4-10 Carl 5.9fm [50] 3545 tp
31 13-18 Catt 7g/f 48 3670 BL t
55a 4-13 Wolv 6ap [55] 5359 t

MR DINGLAWI 3 b g £0
14a 12-12 Ling 7ap 566
28a 10-12 Ling 8ap 675 BL
73a 5-13 Ling 12ap 873
16 7-8 Brig 11.9sft [70] 5092 T

MR DINOS 5 b h £34598
110 4-10 York 13.9g/f[122] 1705
122 2-9 Sand 16.4g/f[122] 2095
112 6-13 Asco 20g/f [120] 2518

MR DIP 4 b g £1038
36a 7-10 Ling 8ap [65] 785
14a 6-12 Sout 8af [57] 848
38 10-15 Warw 8.1sft 58 1530
47 7-8 Chep 10.2g/f 53 2628
50 5-15 Warw 10.9g/f 53 2910
53 2-12 Chep 12.1g/s 50 3085
51 6-16 Hayd 10.5sft 50 3276
33 15-19 Chep 12.1gd 48 3727

MR ED 6 ch g £45220
77 2-11 Sand 14g/f 74 2391

77	2-7	Sand	14g/s	75	2899 p
83	1-12	**KEMP**	14.4g/f	74	3688* p
88	2-17	Nott	14.1g/s	80	4647 p
90	2-34	Newm	18sft	80	5135 p

MR FLEMING 5 b g £206

40a	3-8	Ling	10ap	[45]	829 bl
27a	11-14	Ling	10ap	[45]	1712 bl
0	15-17	Newm	10g/f	40	3238 bl

MR FORTYWINKS 10 ch g £519

46	12-17	Ripo	6ap	56	1361
49	5-10	Muss	16gd	55	1551
43	8-14	York	13.9g/f	50	2060
34	6-12	Muss	16gd	47	2964
49	3-11	Muss	16g/f	45	3557

MR HULLABALOU 3 b g £3983

40a	10-11	Ling	6ap		898
19	15-15	Folk	6g/s		1078
77	4-17	Sali	6g/s		1497
70	5-8	Kemp	7g/f	[79]	1912
64	7-9	Kemp	6gd	[77]	2173
61	9-13	Ling	7.6g/f	73	2587
59	8-9	Wind	6g/f	70	2797
61	7-9	Epso	7gd	65	3218
75	1-10	LING	6g/f	[61]	3603*

MR INDEPENDENT 3 b g £0

55	9-18	Nott	8.2sft	65	1470
51	8-10	Leic	10g/f	63	1965
0	13-13	Good	9g/f	63	2024 VIS

MR JACK DANIELLS 3 b g £11718

76	3-17	Warw	7.1sft	71	1526
76	6-14	Newm	8g/f	73	1930
78	3-13	Newm	8g/f	73	2247
48	8-9	Leic	8gd	75	2705
74	4-10	Newb	8g/f	75	2877
80	1-10	**SAND**	8.1g/f	[74]	3339*
75	4-9	Sand	10g/f	75	3862
61	13-14	Newb	10g/f	75	3961
79	3-15	Hayd	8.1g/f	75	4352
33	25-25	Newb	7gd	75	4683 BL

MR KALANDI 2 gr c £553

71	3-14	Donc	6g/f		1874
44	7-13	Donc	6gd		2236
51	14-14	Newm	7g/f		3752
55	6-14	Warw	6.1g/f	63	4420
56	8-9	Warw	7.1g/s	59	4666

MR LAMBROS 2 ch c £5706

82a	3-6	Ling	6ap		79
79a	1-16	**LING**	7ap		290*
88a	2-11	Ling	7ap	[80]	627
84	7-13	Asco	6.5g/f	85	4773
68	7-10	Epso	7gd	[85]	4912
58	11-12	Newb	6sft	84	5196

MR LEAR 5 b g £0

47	9-12	Ches	12.3gd	72	1599
43	8-9	Donc	12g/f	70	2078
60	9-16	Nott	10hvy	68	5345

MR LEHMAN 7 ch g £0

0	10-12	Sout	8af	460
23a	7-9	Sout	11af	505

MR LEWIN 3 ch g £0

51	7-8	Ayr	7.2gd	[60]	2506
41	9-10	Hayd	8.1g/s	57	3906
52a	5-13	Wolv	9.5ap	54	4937
23	10-12	Brig	8sft	53	5094
35a	8-12	Wolv	7.1ap	[50]	5229

MR LOVERMAN 4 ch g £0

0	12-12	Ling	8ap	[45]	1451
22a	8-13	Wolv	8.5af	[40]	2052
0	12-12	Sout	7af	[40]	2337

MR MALARKEY 4 b g £8962

81	4-19	Leic	6g/s	79	1354 bl
73	10-30	Newm	6g/f	80	1481 bl
78	4-13	Yarm	6g/f	79	1726 bl
63	6-8	Donc	6g/f	[78]	2074 bl
80	3-20	York	6g/f	76	2409 bl
73	3-10	Kemp	6g/f	77	2861 bl
73	8-16	Newm	5g/f	77	3033 bl

74	6-15	Newc	6gd	78	3424 bl
86	1-9	**YARM**	6g/f	77	3705* bl T
39	7-8	Kemp	5sft	[82]	4031 bl t
80	6-19	Kemp	6fm	82	4394 bl
52	12-12	Yarm	5.2g/s	82	4585 bl

MR MARUCCI 2 b c £0

65	5-14	Thir	7g/s	4207
45	9-11	Thir	7fm	4375
66a	5-11	Wolv	8.6ap	4978

MR MAXIM 2 ch g £0

51	9-17	Donc	6g/f		2424
59	5-9	Carl	5.9gd		2671
62	8-10	Redc	7g/s		2959
54	9-14	Muss	7.1g/f		4171
59	4-16	Beve	7g/f	57	4597
61	7-15	Pont	10g/f	[57]	4933

MR MAYFAIR 2 ch g £0

64	7-13	Warw	7.1g/s	4664
56a	7-12	Ling	8ap	5295

MR MIDASMAN 3 b c £2430

68	6-14	Donc	10.3gd	72	923
64	9-16	Beve	7.5g/s	71	1163
51	11-18	Nott	8.2sft	69	1470
27	13-16	Beve	8.5sft	66	1628
33	10-12	Donc	7g/f	63	1879
54	4-12	Pont	8gd	60	3679
54a	6-11	Sout	8af	57	4044
59	3-17	Hayd	10.5fm	55	4388
61	3-16	Ches	10.3g/f	55	4515
56a	3-9	Wolv	9.5ap	[56]	5360

MR MIDAZ 5 ch g £0

47	5-16	Hayd	10.5sft	45	3276
43	5-10	Carl	14.1fm	45	3549
34	5-16	Carl	11.9g/f	45	4348

MR MISCHIEF 3 b g £14072

84a	1-10	**WOLV**	14.8af	78	34*
83a	1-10	**SOUT**	11af	[84]	142*
88a	3-16	Ling	12ap	85	404
42a	12-16	Ling	12ap	86	475
93a	1-10	**WOLV**	12af	85	810*
45	12-17	Catt	12sft	70	3929

MR MISTRAL 5 b g £7758

76	2-14	Yarm	7fm	2148
91	1-4	**NEWC**	8g/s	2729*
9	25-25	Asco	7g/f	87	3443

MR MOON 3 b g £0

31a	6-7	Sout	7af		1196
32	6-8	Muss	8gd	35	1798
15	12-14	Carl	7.9fm	35	1954
33	10-14	Redc	10fm	35	2299
26	7-7	Ayr	13.1g/s	35	2546
29	6-16	Thir	8g/f	32	3414 VIS
13	10-11	Carl	6.9g/f	[29]	3651 BL
19	5-18	Beve	9.9g/s	29	4243
24	9-14	Redc	10fm	30	4560
25	15-18	Leic	10gd	[30]	5042

MR PERRY 8 br g £0

0	9-11	Wolv	12af	[30]	689
32a	5-12	Wolv	8.5af	[30]	777
3a	10-12	Sout	8af	[30]	905

MR PERTEMPS 5 b g £4427

43a	7-16	Sout	6af	56	92
57a	3-10	Wolv	6af	55	345
61a	1-12	**WOLV**	6af	55	385* P
64a	2-13	Sout	6af	61	551 p
51a	5-12	Sout	5af	[60]	587 p
44	14-20	Chep	6.1g/s	54	4368 p
53a	8-13	Wolv	6ap	63	5010 p
48	6-13	Muss	5g/s	[52]	5146

MR SMITHERS JONES 4 br g £2626

51a	2-6	Sout	11af	[50]	306
58a	1-7	**SOUT**	14af	[50]	376*
55a	3-9	Sout	12af	55	456
44a	3-4	Sout	14af	[56]	854

MR SPLIFFY 4 b g £2657

51a	8-13	Wolv	5af	[54]	70
37a	8-15	Sout	6af	[52]	172

46a	4-15	Sout	5af	[49]	253 vis
31a	7-10	Wolv	5af	[49]	286 vis
39a	5-9	Sout	5af	[47]	335 vis
50a	1-9	**LING**	5ap	[47]	413+ vis
11a	12-13	Ling	6ap	[53]	544 vis
45a	7-7	Ling	5ap	[53]	737 vis
52a	5-11	Sout	5af	[51]	775 vis
24	18-20	Wind	6g/s	59	1255
43	11-14	Wind	5g/f	55	2266
38	11-12	Ripo	5g/f	55	2524
34	11-19	Beve	5gd	57	2657
44	10-17	Catt	5g/f	50	2846
26	11-13	Catt	5g/f	46	3350
36	8-14	Thir	5g/f	46	3417
44	10-11	Thir	5g/f	46	3574
46	2-17	Catt	5g/f	43	3667

MR STROWGER 2 b c £521

7a	11-11	Ling	7ap		213
44	6-14	Warw	8.1sft	50	1529
44	3-9	Good	11g/f	47	2019
1	15-15	Bath	8g/s	45	4202
3	11-12	Chep	10.2hvy	45	4708

MR STYLISH 7 b g £0

0	9-9	Wolv	7af	53	27 vis t
48a	4-16	Sout	7af	[53]	66 vis t
53a	4-12	Wolv	7af	53	74 vis t
58a	4-16	Sout	7af	[50]	161 vis t
38a	9-16	Sout	7af	50	208 vis t
33a	7-10	Wolv	6af	50	245 vis t
28a	6-8	Sout	7af	[47]	373 vis t
35a	6-11	Wolv	7af	[45]	579 vis t

MR TAMBOURINE MAN 3 b c £16085

75	6-14	Newm	10g/f	83	1192
71	7-8	Sali	9.9g/s	83	1500
62	7-11	Sand	10g/s	80	2127
83	1-14	**WIND**	10g/f	75	2452*
83	3-6	Epso	10.1g/f	[81]	2874
87	1-5	**PONT**	10gd	83	3459*
85	4-9	Kemp	12g/f	84	4360
89	2-9	Muss	12g/f	84	4553
71	7-12	Good	11gd	84	4749
74	10-12	Wind	11.6g/f	85	4833

MR UPPITY 5 b g £1473

15a	13-16	Sout	5af	[40]	720
20a	7-12	Sout	6af	[35]	904 e
41a	2-12	Sout	6af	[35]	982 e
34a	4-9	Wolv	7af	[40]	1266 e
27a	5-6	Sout	6af	[40]	1405 e
42a	3-10	Sout	6af	[40]	1837 e
35	6-16	Nott	6.1gd	[40]	1988 e
24	5-13	Yarm	6g/f	40	2347 e
37a	4-16	Sout	6af	39	2720 e
42	2-12	Brig	6g/f	38	3301 e
30	8-15	Folk	7g/f	[40]	4371 e
31	5-19	Kemp	6g/f	[40]	4793 e

MR VELOCITY 4 b g £26136

72	3-12	Sand	8.1g/s	70	1352
73	2-8	Nott	8.2g/s	[70]	1775
76	1-6	**REDC**	7g/s	[70]	2564*
66	11-15	York	7gd	72	3117
65	6-12	Leic	8fm	72	3813
76	3-14	Epso	8.5gd	71	4295
81	1-13	**EPSO**	8.5gd	71	4469*
82	1-12	**MUSS**	8gd	[75]	4809+
86	2-14	Newb	8hvy	76	5227
75	6-20	Donc	7sft	79	5367

MR WHIZZ 7 ch g £5860

33a	9-10	Ling	10ap	[40]	370
39a	1-16	**SOUT**	8af	[35]	442* BL e
36a	4-12	Wolv	8.5af	40	479 bl e
43a	4-13	Sout	8af	[45]	776 bl e
37a	3-5	Sout	8af	[45]	908 bl e
31	2-7	Chep	10.2sft	[40]	1332 p
38	2-13	Kemp	10hvy	[40]	1643 p
13	11-12	Bath	10.2fm	40	2036 p
33	5-15	Folk	16.4g/s	36	3049
44	1-8	**BRIG**	11.9fm	34	3692* p
22	11-17	Pont	17.1g/s	40	3970 p
56	4-12	Chep	12.1g/s	[40]	4364 p
31	7-19	Brig	9.9gd	[40]	4903 p

MR WOLF 3 b c £11081
65	2-12	Catt	5gd	[62]	995
68	2-9	Redc	5sft	[62]	1146
76	1-6	NEWC	5sft	[70]	1392*
80	1-9	THIR	6g/s	[70]	1477*
76	6-14	Thir	5g/f	79	1766
74	6-12	Ripo	6g/f	79	2482
37	13-13	Hayd	6gd	78	2884
57	9-10	Ches	5.1g/f	78	3080
62	13-19	York	6gd	74	4005
75	5-12	Newm	5gd	74	4197
78	2-15	Ayr	5g/s	73	4654
66	6-8	Hami	5g/s	[73]	4822

MRS BOZ 3 b f £0
20a	12-14	Ling	10ap		53
13a	4-7	Ling	6ap	[35]	1715
18	9-9	Folk	7fm	[29]	2716
3	12-12	Brig	7fm	29	3677

MRS BROWN 3 b f £532
62a	3-5	Wolv	7af		425
49a	5-13	Sout	8af		553
49a	6-7	Wolv	7af		617
25	10-14	Folk	12gd	55	3383
53a	5-14	Ling	10ap	55	3605
45a	8-13	Ling	10ap	55	3823
56a	4-13	Wolv	8.6ap	54	5005
47	5-12	Brig	8sft	54	5094
33	14-18	Newm	8sft	51	5272

MRS CEE 3 b f £0
| 8a | 7-8 | Sout | 7af | [76] | 389 BL |

MRS CHIPPY 2 ch f £0
| 24 | 16-19 | Newm | 7g/s | | 5279 |

MRS CUBE 5 ch m £3125
47a	1-12	WOLV	9.4af	[35]	782*
44a	1-13	WOLV	8.5af	[35]	826*
42a	3-10	Sout	8af	[45]	850
40a	3-7	Wolv	9.4af	[45]	893
43a	4-14	Ling	10ap	[45]	1712
42	10-19	Brig	9.9g/f	45	1940
21	14-16	Yarm	10.1fm	45	2146

MRS GEE 2 b f £634
| 64a | 2-11 | Sout | 8af | [63] | 159 |
| 25a | 10-11 | Sout | 8af | 65 | 252 |

MRS KEPPLE 2 b f £320
44	4-5	Hami	5g/s		1601
46	8-10	Leic	5g/f		1826
46	7-10	Beve	7.5gd		2652

MRS MOH 3 b f £30747
61	11-14	Ripo	6g/s	83	1360
28	14-14	York	7sft	81	1665
70	5-10	Donc	7g/f	77	2427
87	1-7	CHES	7g/s	74	2749*
86	3-11	York	7g/f	80	3433
90	1-12	HAYD	8.1gd	80	3738+
90	2-8	Muss	8gd	84	4516
88	2-6	Hami	8.3sft	[86]	4695
0	U-19	York	7.9gd	86	4987
85	4-11	Donc	7sft	86	5219

MRS PANKHURST 3 b f £519
73	5-14	Donc	10.3gd	73	923
2	9-10	Pont	10sft	73	1427
72	5-10	Good	9.9gd	73	2225
59	6-10	Newm	8g/f	73	2767
67	8-13	Sand	8.1gd	71	4607
71	4-11	Good	8gd	69	5027
69	5-19	Pont	10g/s	69	5148
49a	12-13	Ling	10ap	67	5299

MRS PHILIP 5 b m £0
46	7-10	Bath	11.7g/f		4414
48	8-15	Bath	10.2gd		4826
28	11-18	Wind	10g/s		4944
59	9-18	Bath	10.2gd		5023

MRS SHILLING 3 b f £3728
70	3-11	Sali	7gd		3884
65	4-15	Ling	7gd		4445
70	2-15	Beve	7.5g/f	65	4719
70	4-10	Pont	8g/f	[67]	4939
71a	3-12	Wolv	8.6ap	67	5116

MRS SPENCE 3 b f £0
7	13-13	Thir	5sft	68	1229
49	6-9	Hayd	5g/s	68	1344
29	14-15	Redc	7sft	63	1660
16	19-19	Nott	6.1g/f	[58]	4845
0	15-15	Ayr	5sft	52	5036 BL

MRS ST GEORGE 3 b f £0
| 69 | 8-10 | Asco | 6gd | 85 | 3773 |

MRS WILLY NILLY 2 ch f £0
11	15-15	Warw	5g/s		1325
37	12-12	Warw	5sft		1524
0	16-16	Nott	6.1gd		3103 P

MS POLLY GARTER 2 b f £353
63	4-14	Bath	5sft		1538
53	12-19	Wind	5g/s		1805
44	6-8	Bath	5fm		2033
33	11-12	Ling	5gd	59	3284
40	8-8	Chep	5.1g/s	[52]	3896
9	18-19	Bath	5gd	45	5021

MS THREE 2 b f £0
22	12-13	Hayd	6gd		3736
25a	6-10	Sout	5af		4129
50	5-11	Beve	5g/f		4599
64	6-10	Muss	5gd		4804
46	10-18	Newc	6g/f	55	5013
26a	12-13	Wolv	5.1ap	[55]	5207

MT DESERT 2 b c £0
| 63 | 6-15 | Sali | 8gd | | 4851 |
| 68 | 6-14 | Leic | 8gd | | 5059 |

MTILLY 3 b rf £0
| 54 | 8-10 | Pont | 8g/f | | 4939 |
| 18 | 10-12 | Nott | 10hvy | | 5190 |

MUBTAKER 7 ch h £62000
123	1-4	NEWB	13.3g/ff	[130]	3958*
114	7-4	Bade	12sft	[130]	4428
115	4-10	Wood	12gd	[130]	5247

MUDAWIN 3 b g £16091
42	12-17	Donc	8gd		919
97	1-19	NEWB	8gd		1236*
75	13-20	Newm	8fm	90	1496
100	1-14	ASCO	10g/f	90	1924*
82	14-17	Asco	12g/f	98	2519

MUDDY 2 ch g £0
61	5-8	Yarm	6g/s		4250
54	8-14	Warw	6.1g/f		4422
67	11-14	Yarm	7gd		4611
22	8-9	Nott	6.1hvy	[65]	5185

MUESTRA 2 ch f £374
24	11-15	Warw	5g/s		1325
33	10-14	Bath	5sft		1538
40	8-11	Kemp	5hvy		1640
40	7-8	Bath	5fm		2033
40	5-8	Wind	6g/f		2449
56a	3-12	Sout	7af		3394
29	9-13	Sali	7g/f	[54]	3864
26	10-17	Redc	7g/s	[45]	5105

MUFREH 5 b r g £12664
80a	2-9	Wolv	7af	77	31
88a	1-16	SOUT	7af	78	419+
74a	5-10	Sout	7af	86	611
90a	2-10	Wolv	6af	85	834
61	4-16	Sout	7g/s	60	1049
47	12-15	Sout	7gd	60	1282

MUGEBA 2 b f £5499
42a	9-14	Ling	6ap		146
60a	2-10	Ling	6ap		260
52a	5-9	Wolv	7af		381
54a	5-5	Ling	8ap	64	804
52	1-11	YARM	7g/f	[59]	2852*
60	2-12	Folk	6gd	59	3380 T
63	2-11	Yarm	7g/f	60	3711 t
51	7-14	Yarm	6g/f	60	3870 BL t
58	6-20	Yarm	7sft	61	5256

MUHAREB 5 ch g £1119
| 93 | 5-10 | Asco | 12g/f | 94 | 3444 |

76	9-10	Asco	12gd	94	3777
39	11-11	Epso	10.1gd	[92]	4467
92	5-13	Asco	10g/f	[90]	4772
38	17-17	Newm	12g/f	90	4889
0	19-19	Newm	12gd	90	5085

MUHAYMIN 3 ch c £521
69	8-14	Newm	10g/f	85	1192
84	9-14	Newm	8g/f	85	1930
82	4-8	Good	9.9gd	83	2377
73	7-9	Leic	8gd	82	2705

MUJAGEM 8 b rm £0
| 0 | 8-9 | Sout | 7af | [45] | 304 bl |

MUJALINA 6 b g £0
| 31 | 27-34 | Newm | 18sft | | 5135 |

MUJAWER 3 b g £0
68	5-9	Newm	7g/f		3282
55	12-14	Newb	9fm		3631
50	11-14	Warw	7.1gd		4275 BL

MUJAZAF 2 b c £858
| 76 | 3-8 | Pont | 8fm | | 4756 |

MUJKARI 8 ch g £0
| 23a | 12-13 | Wolv | 9.5ap | [46] | 5338 bl |

MUKAFEH 3 b c £4811
103	7-10	Newb	7gd		1234
106	2-6	Newm	8gd	[100]	1888
102	5-15	Asco	7g/f	[105]	2486

MUKTASB 2 b c £880
| 74a | 2-8 | Ling | 6ap | | 49 |

MULAN PRINCESS 4 b f £0
| 28a | 13-14 | Ling | 6ap | [52] | 516 |

MULBERRY LAD 2 b c £2405
69	5-7	Ling	5g/f		2738
70	2-7	Bath	5g/f		2976
67	4-6	Brig	5.3g/f		3296
67	2-6	Brig	6fm	[68]	3671 BL
46	7-9	Brig	6fm	68	4758 bl T
67a	6-11	Ling	6ap	65	4972 bl
56a	6-12	Wolv	6ap	[64]	5177 bl

MULBERRY WINE 2 b f £0
75	6-8	Kemp	7g/s		2676
75	4-9	Folk	7g/s		3047
73	5-13	Kemp	7g/f		3520
42	8-12	Sali	6g/s	77	4079
64	12-20	Ling	7gd	72	4444
25	16-17	Good	8gd	66	4871

MULSANNE 6 b g £0
| 11 | 12-13 | Warw | 10.9g/f | 30 | 4419 |

MULTAHAB 4 b c £2660
49a	5-12	Wolv	5af	[55]	242
58a	2-9	Ling	5ap	53	435
67a	4-9	Ling	5ap	[56]	572
62a	2-10	Ling	5ap	[60]	802
68a	4-9	Ling	5ap	[60]	1023
47	12-17	Nott	5.1g/s	63	1774
40	11-14	Donc	5gd	[58]	2237 BL
47	10-14	Yarm	6g/f	53	2855 t
30	8-12	Newm	6g/f	50	3751 t
35	9-13	Brig	5.3g/f	45	3984 t
38	9-11	Sand	5sft	45	4070 t
33	6-12	Brig	5.3g/s	45	4140 t
47a	9-13	Wolv	5.1ap	55	5156 t
44a	10-12	Ling	6ap	55	5241 t

MULTICOLOUR 4 ch f £0
| 3 | 15-17 | Bath | 10.2sft | | 1541 |

MULTIPLE CHOICE 3 ch c £1160
67a	7-7	Ling	5ap	83	1011
38	16-19	Newm	6g/s	79	1154
5	9-9	Hayd	5g/s	75	1344
38	10-10	Carl	5gd	70	2675
67a	2-18	Sout	8af	[65]	3091 e t
63a	4-14	Sout	8af	[65]	3392 e t
37	6-11	Carl	6.9g/f	[64]	3651 e t
64a	4-11	Sout	8af	64	4044 e t
46	13-20	Chep	6.1g/s	55	4368 e t
52a	7-12	Ling	6ap	64	4976 BL C

53a 10-14 Ling 7ap [64] 5080 bl e

MUMBLING 5 ch g £0
63a 9-14 Ling 13ap 69 147
37 15-16 Good 12gd [69] 4745

MUNAAHEJ 3 b c £0
8 15-18 Leic 7gd 4698

MUNAAWASHAT 3 b f £19948
71 3-8 Brig 9.9g/f 68 2046
76 1-7 HAMI 8.3g/f [68] 2474*
74 2-6 Hami 8.3g/s [71] 2828
44 8-8 Newm 10g/f [71] 3471
77 1-6 WIND 8.3g/f 71 3978*
82 1-11 WIND 8.3g/s 73 4222*
69 8-8 Thir 8fm 80 4378

MUNAAWESH 3 b c £6147
46a 9-11 Ling 8ap 841
70 3-7 Sout 6g/s [70] 1050
25a 9-13 Sout 8af [65] 1193
50 14-15 Sout 7gd 69 1282
51 9-11 Warw 8.1hvy 66 1534
40 13-14 Ayr 8g/f [64] 1896
38a 9-15 Sout 8af 56 2338
46 13-18 Leic 10gd 59 2706
34a 7-11 Sout 12af 53 2804
64 4-13 Redc 11g/s 55 2960 BL
57 2-11 Muss 9gd 56 2969 bl
52 8-13 Beve 9.9gd 56 3309 bl
56 4-6 Muss 56 3529 bl
57 2-10 Redc 10g/f 56 3772 bl
58 2-11 Yarm 14.1gd 56 3998 bl
49 9-14 Redc 10fm 56 4342 bl
56 4-8 Catt 13.8g/f 56 4439 bl
56 5-19 Thir 12g/f 54 4594 bl
41 10-20 Catt 15.8gd 54 4965 bl

MUNADDAM 2 ch c £7654
88 2-7 Yarm 6g/f 3709
88 2-14 Hayd 6fm 4385
92 1-16 BATH 5.7gd 4823*

MUNFARID 4 ch c £527
54a 3-10 Wolv 12af [75] 359 T
33a 7-11 Ling 13ap [62] 515 t
62a 4-12 Ling 13ap 60 762 t
27a 11-15 Sout 12af 60 867 t
54 9-14 Kemp 14.4sft 69 948 t
0 11-11 Warw 15sft 66 1087 t
0 11-16 Sout 14af 54 4045 t

MUNGO JERRY 3 b c £1534
71 3-8 Hayd 10.5g/f 1489
72 6-10 Hayd 10.5g/f 1922
74 3-10 Leic 11.8gd [70] 2707

MUNSEF 2 b c £645
57 12-23 Newm 6gd 5084
71 3-14 Yarm 7sft 5251

MUQARRAR 4 ch c £1470
52a 6-12 Wolv 7af 54 74 e
50a 6-10 Wolv 7af 52 379 e
39a 6-11 Sout 8af 52 457 BL e
2a 16-16 Sout 8af 49 2805 bl e
3 16-19 Yarm 8g/s [45] 5119 t
50 1-13 AYR 8sft [40] 5275* VIS

MUQBIL 4 ch c £44170
102 8-11 Sand 10g/s [113] 1350
116 1-8 DONC 10.3gd[113] 2234+
116 1-7 NEWB 10g/f [113] 3264*
117 2-6 Hayd 10.5fm[114] 3793
100 4-7 Good 9.9g/f [114] 4538
104 5-9 Asco 12g/f [114] 4812

MUQTADI 6 b g £3039
0 8-8 Wolv 8.5af [51] 360
55a 3-13 Ling 6ap [51] 400
54a 9-14 Ling 7ap [51] 450
34a 6-13 Ling 6ap [51] 544
50a 10-16 Ling 7ap 51 600
48a 4-12 Ling 8ap [49] 675
54a 1-9 LING 8ap [49] 717*
53a 5-10 Ling 10ap [49] 738
42a 8-11 Ling 8ap 52 820
10a 10-10 Wolv 7af [50] 890

47a 4-8 Ling 10ap [50] 1026
41 5-13 Wind 8.3g/s [50] 1058
44 4-15 Folk 6g/s 47 1267
9 9-17 Kemp 7hvy [45] 1642
45 6-16 Bath 8fm [45] 2032
38 9-11 Warw 8.1fm 44 2600
28 10-17 Warw 8.1g/f 44 2909
2 13-17 Chep 8.1g/s 44 3087

MURAABET 2 b c £1102
86 3-21 Newm 8sft 5097
72 6-14 Yarm 7sft 5250

MURAQEB 4 ch g £0
22a 13-14 Ling 10ap 430
30a 13-14 Ling 10ap 52 718
41a 10-14 Ling 12ap 52 768
24a 5-9 Sout 14af [45] 849
17 11-11 Nott 16fm 50 1003 bl
14 11-12 Sout 16gd 50 1285
21 10-16 Warw 8.1g/s [45] 4993 bl
49 6-10 Donc 10.3sft 40 5206

MURASHAH 4 ch c £0
0 13-13 Donc 8gd [80] 2753 t

MURBAAT 3 b c £1896
78 3-12 Ripo 8g/f 1978
82 2-8 Ripo 10g/f 2523

MURDINGA 5 br g £0
60a 12-14 Ling 10ap 68 803 BL

MURZIM 5 b g £0
24a 12-12 Ling 13ap 59 762

MUSAHIM 2 b c £741
80 7-13 Newm 6gd 4223
80 3-10 Newc 6gd 4403

MUSANID 4 ch c £9999
111 3-10 Newm 10g/f [100] 1483
84 6-6 Asco 12fm [107] 2579
105 3-7 Newb 10g/f [107] 3264
88 3-4 Newm 12g/f [107] 3946

MUSARDIERE 2 b f £0
58 7-12 Redc 6fm 4557
60 5-12 Nott 6.1g/f 4844
57 11-13 Redc 7fm 4927

MUSEEB 2 b c £2360
85 4-14 Hayd 6fm 4385
86 2-16 Newb 7g/f 4677

MUSHAJER 2 gr c £1221
87 3-13 Newb 6g/f 1760
85 4-8 Sali 7gd 2695

MUSIC MAID 6 b m £6279
40 13-20 Asco 8gd 62 1927
68 1-10 NEWB 7g/f 62 2312*
51 10-13 Asco 7gd 65 3068
54 7-9 Sali 7gd 65 3456
70 8-14 Sali 7gd 64 4331
58 11-15 Sand 7.1gd 64 4500
55 11-18 Kemp 8g/f 64 4714

MUSIC MIX 2 gr c £3024
73a 4-12 Ling 8ap 102
46a 6-15 Sout 7af 184
52a 6-14 Sout 8af 226
23 12-18 Wind 8.3sft 63 1647
50 11-18 Leic 10gd 59 2706 e
67a 1-13 LING 10ap 55 3823*
55 4-12 Folk 12g/s 55 3913
52 4-15 Nott 10g/s 55 4037
56 8-12 Ripo 10gd 55 4282
55 9-20 Catt 12gd 62 4966 VIS

MUSIC TEACHER 2 ch f £0
38 12-13 Kemp 6g/f 4358

MUSICAL DAY 2 ch f £8268
66 11-13 Newb 7g/f 3252
70 7-14 Yarm 7gd 3489
55 10-12 Folk 7gd 3909
79 2-12 Beve 7.5g/s 4242
75 12-26 Newb 6.5g/f 4679
83 4-16 Newm 7g/f 78 4913

77a 3-11 Wolv 8.6ap [78] 4978
75a 1-11 LING 8ap [75] 5236* BL

MUSICAL FAIR 4 b f £10045
35 21-22 Donc 6gd 78 921
44 14-17 Donc 6g/s 77 1523
65 8-13 Yarm 6g/f 77 1726
77 2-13 Newc 5gd 74 1873
81 1-10 THIR 5g/f 73 1973*
79 5-14 Wind 5g/f 78 2266
75 6-12 Ripo 5g/f 78 2524
33 10-10 Ayr 5gd 77 3150 VIS
58 11-18 Beve 5gd 76 3852
77 3-16 Muss 5g/f 75 4174
68 12-20 Donc 5fm 75 4496
77 3-12 Yarm 5.2g/s 75 4585
75a 5-13 Wolv 6ap 75 5181
45a 12-13 Wolv 5.1ap 74 5341

MUSICAL GIFT 3 ch c £3657
12a 13-14 Ling 12ap 14
66a 1-7 WOLV 9.4af [70] 509*
70a 4-13 Ling 7ap 70 565
70a 4-7 Wolv 8.5af 70 700
70a 5-12 Ling 8ap 69 932 P
44 7-18 Wind 8.3g/s 69 1059 p
56a 7-12 Wolv 7.1ap 69 5289

MUSICAL LYRICS 3 b f £0
29 8-8 Hami 9.2g/s 67 1603

MUSICAL SCORE 5 b m £2113
85 3-5 San 12g/f 2301

MUSICAL TOP 4 ch f £450
58 3-8 Carl 6.9g/f [60] 3654
44 9-10 Brig 7sft 59 4168
35 16-18 Bath 5.7g/f 57 4412
57 4-16 Bath 8gd 55 4828
56a 5-13 Wolv 8.6ap 55 5005

MUSICANNA 3 b f £5415
76 2-11 Newm 8g/f 2248
78 1-17 HAYD 8.1g/s 4768* T

MUSICO 2 ch c £3176
75 4-18 Chep 6.1gd 2194
75 6-18 Wind 6gd 2618
70 4-20 Wind 6fm 2970
79 2-11 Newb 7fm 72 3627
75 3-6 Chep 6.1g/s 72 3897
54 16-21 Donc 6gd [74] 4490
38 12-13 Wind 8.3g/s 73 4940

MUSIOTAL 3 ch c £5015
0 13-13 Muss 7.1g/f 1119
48 5-8 Hami 5gd 48 1509
46 5-10 Hami 5g/s 48 1605
25 10-19 York 6g/f 48 2055
55 2-13 Newc 6sft 46 2683
58 1-7 AYR 7.2gd 52 3153*
47 8-18 Hayd 6gd 55 3737
55 4-5 Ayr 8hvy 55 4085
48 8-15 Ayr 5sft 54 5036
40 14-17 Ayr 7.2sft 54 5063

MUSKATSTURM 5 b g £0
72 8-11 Warw 15sft 80 1087
63 10-20 Epso 12hvy 75 1295
58 7-7 Newm 14.8g/f 70 3281
7 10-10 Yarm 14.1g/s 66 4255

MUSKETIER 2 gr c £35986
109 2-7 Long 8g/s 4729
113 1-4 LONG 9hvy 5164*

MUSLIN 3 ch f £1396
38 11-14 Nott 10gd 1241
50 3-9 Folk 9.7sft 1581
57a 8-15 Ling 12ap 2393
25 13-18 Hayd 14gd 55 2905
55 2-11 Yarm 11.5gd 52 3367
53 5-13 Redc 14.1fm 54 4340
55 6-19 Thir 12g/f 54 4594
48a 11-14 Ling 16ap 53 5082

MUST BE MAGIC 7 b g £0
62a 4-13 Ling 10ap [63] 569 vis
60a 5-14 Ling 10ap 63 674 vis

51a 10-13 Ling 10ap [60] 912 vis
50 9-9 Newm 8gd 61 1891 vis
31 14-15 Kemp 9gd 59 2170 vis
41 13-16 Kemp 9g/f 58 3039 vis
17 16-17 Kemp 12sft 56 4033 vis
0 16-18 Warw 10.9g/s 53 4669 vis

MUST BE SO 2 b f £2328
49a 3-12 Ling 8ap [60] 78
49a 1-11 LING 8ap [50] 233*
45a 5-15 Ling 7ap 50 295
26a 8-12 Ling 8ap 48 402
34a 13-15 Ling 7ap [48] 671
17a 11-11 Ling 8ap 48 735
32a 6-7 Ling 8ap [45] 1453
23 8-9 Kemp 6hvy [40] 1641
32 4-10 Brig 5.3fm 37 2331 T
17 10-12 Brig 5.3g/f 35 2645 t
20 13-13 Ling 7g/f 32 3604 t
21 5-7 Brig 6g/f 32 3717 t
40 12-16 Good 5g/f 30 4528 t

MUSTAJED 3 b c £218
89 6-7 Good 7g/f 1811
93 8-8 Kemp 8fm 2069 VIS

MUSTAKHLAS 3 ch c £0
60 11-17 Newm 8gd 1166

MUSTANG ALI 2 ch c £1757
65a 3-15 Ling 7ap [65] 52
79 6-14 Nott 10gd [66] 1241
64 7-9 Wind 11.6g/f 73 1807
70 3-9 Kemp 12gd 68 2175
60 5-10 Good 14gd 68 2376
65 5-12 Wind 10g/f [68] 2800
70 3-10 Bath 11.7g/f 68 2978
67 5-10 Ling 11.5gd 69 3334
58 6-8 Ling 11.5fm 66 3747
64 6-14 Chep 10.2gd 65 4487
46 13-19 Bath 11.7gd 63 5024
41 8-12 Brig 11.9sft 63 5093

MUTABARI 10 ch g £0
4a 7-7 Wolv 8.5af [45] 1341
19a 9-12 Ling 8ap [45] 1451
12a 10-10 Wolv 9.4af [40] 1564
20 10-18 Donc 7g/f 35 2080
22 14-16 Brig 7fm 35 2258
27 9-12 Sali 7fm [35] 2288
23 8-11 Epso 7fm [30] 3541
0 P-14 Good 8sft 26 4189

MUTAFANEN 3 gr c £28502
101 1-14 DONC 10.3gd 84 923*
101 3-4 Epso 10.1hvy[100] 1294
103 3-18 Good 9g/f 97 1813
108 3-13 Asco 10g/f [99] 2520
69 20-21 York 10.4gd 99 3118
106 4-16 Good 9.9fm 103 3553
105 4-20 Hayd 10.5fm 103 3794 VIS
98 10-11 Beve 9.9g/s 103 4239 vis
83 6-7 Newm 14g/f [103] 4878

MUTAHAYYA 3 b c £7350
104 2-7 Kemp 8g/s [104] 1113
95 5-7 Good 11g/f [105] 1814
85 12-13 Asco 10g/f [105] 2520
90 14-16 Newm 9sft [102] 5139

MUTAJAMMEL 2 b c £7297
83 4-12 Newm 7gd 4194
91 1-8 SAND 8.1gd 4608*

MUTAKARRIM 7 ch h £4878
111 3-12 Curr 12g/f 107 2821 bl

MUTAMAASEK 2 ch c £486
77 5-12 Newm 7g/f 3470
60 7-11 Newm 8gd 3925
84 4-11 Nott 8.2g/s 4648
65 5-15 Pont 10g/f [84] 4933

MUTAMARED 4 ch c £6730
87 1-12 THIR 7g/f 1971*
88 3-24 Newb 9g/f 82 4642
79 8-20 Newm 7g/s 83 5286

MUTANABI 2 b c £1746

72a 2-10 Ling 6ap 3818
76a 3-14 Ling 7ap 4970

MUTARAFAA 4 b g £8156
31a 7-12 Wolv 8.5af [44] 47 e
46a 2-14 Sout 8af 44 62 e
48a 2-15 Sout 8af 44 84 e
49a 2-14 Sout 8af 46 160 e
58a 1-13 SOUT 8af 46 221* e
59a 1-13 WOLV 8.5af 53 251* e
43a 4-5 Wolv 8.5af 58 346 e
52a 3-8 Sout 8af 58 393 e
56a 2-9 Wolv 8.5af [58] 437 e
54a 4-12 Wolv 8.5af 55 564 e
51a 7-14 Ling 10ap 54 622
51a 7-11 Ling 8ap 53 732 vis
33a 8-10 Ling 8ap 53 769 vis
53a 2-10 Sout 8af [51] 868 vis
39a 13-15 Ling 7ap 51 913 vis
36a 9-15 Sout 8af 53 1028 e
0 16-16 Nott 8.2hvy 51 5347 vis

MUTASALLIL 4 b c £32125
90 1-8 RIPO 10g/f 2012* T
101 1-7 PONT 10g/f [87] 2605* t
102 2-7 Asco 10gd [98] 3464 t
98 7-20 Hayd 10.5fm 100 3794 t
108 1-8 DONC 12fm 100 4534+ t

MUTASSEM 3 b c £963
65a 8-12 Ling 8ap 881
70 7-14 Folk 7g/s 1080
51 13-20 Newb 7fm 69 2620
2 11-11 Newm 8gd [69] 3923
36 9-9 Ling 7gd 4110
43 13-20 Ling 6g/f 58 4317
61 2-19 Yarm 6g/s 52 4636
41a 8-12 Wolv 8.6ap 58 5116
44a 7-14 Ling 7ap [55] 5294
49 8-18 Yarm 6g/s 58 5354

MUTAWAFFER 3 b c £649
95 7-10 York 10.4g/s [99] 1685
102 4-9 Donc 7sft [99] 5214

MUTAWAQED 6 ch g £54244
43 11-14 York 6g/s 86 1703 t
86 4-19 Kemp 6fm 85 2070 t
89 2-17 Epso 6fm 84 2256 t
85 8-18 Newc 6g/s 86 2770 t
94 1-15 YORK 6g/f 85 3434+ t
79 16-28 Good 6fm 90 3622 t
92 2-6 Sand 6g/s 89 4098 t
91 9-22 Donc 5.6fm 90 4459 t
92 4-24 Ayr 6sft 90 4686 t
47 19-20 York 6gd 88 5001 t

MUTAWASSEL 3 b c £10200
97 4-5 Sand 10g/s [90] 1316
100 3-3 Ches 10.3gd [95] 1595
60 16-16 Good 9.9fm 100 3553 BL

MUTAYAM 4 b g £3455
33 6-8 Hami 6gd 39 2713 t
37 8-8 Hami 5g/s 39 2830 t
44 6-10 Muss 5g/s 39 2968 t
17 14-15 Muss 5g/f 43 3561 t
59 1-14 NEWC 5g/f [45] 4404* t
32 21-26 Ayr 5g/s 48 4618 t
47 7-9 Hami 5g/f [50] 4817 t

MUY BIEN 2 ch c £12113
73a 1-13 SOUT 6af [75] 63* VIS
75a 5-11 Ling 6ap [75] 135 vis
77a 2-14 Sout 7af 74 158 vis
79a 2-7 Sout 6af 75 333 vis
78a 2-8 Wolv 6af 75 422 vis
16a 10-10 Sout 6af [78] 532 vis
72a 3-9 Wolv 5af [77] 835 BL

81 1-15 WIND 6g/s 69 1054* bl
78 2-6 Warw 6.1sft [69] 1088 bl
82 3-17 Asco 6sft 76 1417 bl
59 9-11 Donc 7sft 78 5219

MUYASSIR 8 b g £2982
48a 9-14 Ling 10ap 56 265
51a 8-14 Ling 10ap 56 339
55a 1-12 LING 8ap 53 406*
52 12-12 Kemp 8g/f [63] 1915
44 8-10 Newb 8g/f 63 2350
44 8-9 Good 8gd 63 2540
34 10-11 Bath 8gd 60 3142
44a 9-12 Ling 8ap [54] 5077
52a 7-13 Wolv 8.6ap [54] 5184

MUZIO SCEVOLA 3 ch c £1896
78a 2-13 Ling 12ap 873
60 5-9 Leic 11.8g/s 1016
60 5-5 Newb 11gd 1211
0 6-7 Donc 14.6g/s 68 1521
61 3-6 Muss 8g/f 65 2807
40 11-14 Pont 17.1g/f 62 4936

MY ACE 6 b m £0
45 6-11 Muss 9g/f 1095 bl t

MY BAYARD 5 ch g £5420
65a 6-12 Wolv 8.5af 69 632
70a 2-8 Sout 7af [69] 744
50a 5-11 Wolv 8.5af 69 806
0 19-22 Donc 12gd 58 918
73a 1-10 WOLV 7af [65] 1319*
41 15-19 Redc 7g/f 59 1820
59 4-8 Hami 6gd 57 2713
67 3-6 Carl 5.9gd [56] 2934 BL
57 7-18 Carl 5g/f 60 3228 bl
59 3-16 Hami 6g/s 60 4009

MY COUNTRY CLUB 7 b h £0
43 6-12 Sout 7gd [53] 1284
36 6-13 Leic 7g/f [53] 1827
29a 7-13 Wolv 8.5af [53] 2052
0 18-19 Nott 6.1gd [47] 3104 BL
37 6-11 Chep 10.2gd [43] 3730

MY DREAM 2 b f £309
45 4-4 Bath 5fm 2411

MY DUBAI 2 ch f £751
80 3-19 Newm 7g/s 5279 T

MY GACHO 2 b c £6018
0 17-18 Wind 6gd 3824
79 3-17 Warw 7.1gd 4271
83 3-21 Donc 6fm 4490
26 12-14 Newm 6sft 80 5098

MY GALLIANO 8 b g £869
41 13-19 Wind 10sft [68] 1650
68 3-5 Sali 9.9gd 68 2694
60 6-8 Epso 10.1g/s 68 3044
61 5-9 Epso 10.1fm 66 3538

MY GIRL PEARL 3 b f £8057
20a 9-12 Wolv 7af [48] 71 BL
7a 12-13 Ling 7ap 45 739 bl
40a 2-8 Wolv 7af [40] 1565
48a 4-6 Wolv 7af [40] 1804
47 2-12 Sali 7fm [50] 2288
31 9-20 Chep 6.1gd 50 2372
44 6-20 Nott 6.1gd 47 2928
46 5-17 Brig 7g/f 45 3176
51 1-12 BRIG 6.1g/s 45 3301*
45 7-15 Ling 6fm 48 3790
45 3-12 Folk 6g/s 48 3911
45 6-20 Chep 6.1g/s 47 4368
52 1-20 CHEP 7.1gd 47 4488*
50 4-16 Yarm 7gd 52 4616
39 8-16 Chep 7.1hvy [50] 4707

MY HOPE 3 b f £573
23 10-11 Kemp 8hvy 1514
70 8-15 Newb 8g/f 1763
59 9-14 Nott 8.2g/f 70 2634
55 8-14 Chep 8.1g/s 67 3090
63 3-11 Bath 10.2g/f 64 3373
22 10-12 Pont 8gd 63 3679

MY LAST BEAN 7 gr g £0
48	6-18	Warw	10.9g/s	55	4669
0	18-18	Pont	12g/f	53	4938

MY LEGAL EAGLE 10 b g £15130
41a	1-5	WOLV	14.8af	[40]	1563*
47a	4-9	Wolv	14.8af	46	1654
45a	2-7	Wolv	16.2af	[45]	1802
49	1-14	YORK	13.9g/f	45	2060*
54	1-17	NOTT	14.1g/f	45	2156*
60	1-15	NEWB	13.3g/f	52	2311*
63	2-8	Hayd	14gd	58	2887

MY LILLI 4 b f £4024
52a	3-13	Ling	10ap	[48]	338
52a	4-12	Ling	10ap	52	542
52a	7-11	Ling	12ap	50	624
50a	6-14	Ling	12ap	50	768
52a	4-12	Ling	8ap	49	845
57a	1-12	LING	8ap	49	1045*
54a	3-14	Ling	10ap	54	1618
45	8-20	Yarm	8fm	49	2149
0	14-14	Ling	10ap	54	2589

MY LINE 7 b g £0
0	10-13	Pont	18hvy	61	1069 bl

MY LITTLE SOPHIA 4 b f £0
23a	5-6	Wolv	7af		779
40	11-14	Warw	8.1sft		1527
2	7-7	Hayd	11.9g/f		1921
3a	15-15	Sout	7af	43	2501 P

MY MAITE 4 b g £3942
56a	3-12	Ling	8ap	54	17 t
46a	6-13	Ling	10ap	53	104 t
59a	2-14	Ling	10ap	52	498 vis t
57a	4-14	Ling	10ap	57	622 t
48a	10-13	Ling	10ap	57	726 bl t
53a	9-9	Ling	10ap	56	903 vis t
48	1-18	NOTT	8.2gd	[45]	1992* bl t
46	6-11	Brig	9.9fm	47	2260 bl t
31	11-14	Wind	8.3g/f	47	2799 vis t
50	4-16	Kemp	9gd	46	3187 t p
41	5-12	Kemp	8gd	46	3524 t p
36	11-13	Folk	9.7g/f	46	3726 t p
52	3-11	Ling	10fm	46	3748 t p
45	3-15	Folk	9.7g/f	[46]	4373 t p
47	3-18	Kemp	10gd	[46]	4791 vis t
54a	4-13	Wolv	9.5ap	53	5361 vis t

MY MATE HENRY 4 ch g £0
11a	11-15	Sout	12af	[45]	89

MY MICHELLE 3 b f £0
35	14-15	Wind	6g/s	74	1054
66	8-11	Bath	8fm	[72]	1904
61	4-9	Nott	8.2g/f	[68]	3581
59	5-9	Nott	10g/s	[64]	4034
58	4-10	Warw	8.1g/f	[62]	4421
51	6-13	Nott	10gd	[57]	4861
36a	11-13	Wolv	9.5ap	55	5361

MY PARIS 2 b g £38131
60a	7-16	Sout	8af		192
68a	3-9	Wolv	7af		381
68a	2-7	Sout	7af		1196
68	2-15	Thir	7g/s	[64]	1473
73	2-12	Ripo	9g/f	[73]	1784
68	5-11	Pont	8g/f	73	2040
83	2-6	Donc	10.3g/f	[73]	2426
85	2-7	Pont	10g/f	[78]	2994
80	1-7	RIPO	9g/s	[80]	3263*
92	1-7	LEIC	7fm	80	3814*
98	1-12	NEWM	7gd	87	4225*

MY PENSION 3 b g £4853
58	7-11	Kemp	8hvy		1514
70	4-17	Ling	7g/s		1617
67	3-4	Ayr	7.2fm		1907
42	11-17	Hayd	8.1gd	68	2243
33	11-14	Yarm	8gd	[65]	4252
67	6-7	Epso	10.1gd	[60]	4911
64a	3-13	Wolv	8.6ap	60	5183
67a	1-9	LING	8ap	[60]	5242*
67a	2-11	Wolv	8.6ap	[60]	5356

MY PORTFOLIO 2 b g £468

71 4-14 Sali 8g/s 4078
72 7-13 Kemp 8g/f 4355
54 11-14 Leic 8gd 5058

MY PRINCESS 2 b f £5819
76	3-15	Wind	6g/f		2263
48	5-7	Hami	6g/f		2473
82	3-5	Newm	6g/f		3586
80	1-7	BRIG	7fm		3691*
69	7-13	York	6gd	78	4004
76	5-13	Newm	8gd	78	4193
78	5-17	Donc	8fm	75	4480
81	3-17	Catt	7gd	75	4963
65	14-14	Catt	7sft	78	5126

MY PUTRA 2 b c £2999
86	3-9	York	6g/s		4026
87	2-18	Newm	8fm		4722

MY RASCAL 2 b c £0
71	7-12	Good	7fm		3568
46	10-14	Thir	7g/s		3831
64	9-13	Warw	7.1g/f		4416
58a	7-14	Ling	7ap		5076

MY RENEE 4 b f £14048
104	3-6	Leop	14g/f		2138
107	2-8	Asco	12g/f		4774

MY RISK 5 b h £95679
116	1-12	SAIN	8sft		993*
116	1-10	CHAN	8g/s		2458*
117	3-10	Deau	8sft		4017

MY SHARP GREY 5 gr m £0
41a	8-13	Ling	10ap	[54]	569

MY SUNSHINE 3 b f £0
63	10-16	Sand	10g/s		2131
58	7-12	York	7.9g/f		2410
46	8-12	Bath	8g/f	62	3846
44a	8-12	Ling	8ap	[59]	4320
30	11-13	Bath	8gd	54	4546
11	14-16	Bath	8gd	50	4828 BL

MY TRUE LOVE 5 b g £276
64	5-8	Warw	18fm		2781
51	9-9	Newm	12g/f		3233
58	4-10	Ling	14fm		3742
49	10-14	Warw	16.2g/f	55	4423

MY WILD ROVER 4 b g £0
11a	8-9	Ling	6ap		1012 T p
0	7-7	Wolv	5af		1320 t p
0	10-10	Newc	5sft		1682 t
0	16-16	Nott	6.1gd	[30]	1989 VIS

MYANNABANANA 2 ch c £5335
60a	1-12	WOLV	8.5af	[52]	28*
67a	1-14	SOUT	8af	[60]	95* VIS
67a	3-10	Sout	8af	67	190 vis
61a	5-11	Sout	8af	67	252 vis
62a	5-7	Ling	10ap	66	325 vis
61a	3-9	Wolv	9.4af	65	441 vis
49a	4-9	Sout	11af	63	608 vis
65a	4-8	Wolv	8.5af	63	645 BL
0	7-7	Sout	8af	62	855 bl
49	5-14	Sout	10g/s	55	1051 P
14	12-16	Redc	8sft	55	1147 p
39	8-16	Nott	10gd	52	1240 p
43	7-8	Muss	9g/f	[46]	4173 vis
37	9-12	Ripo	10gd	46	4282 vis
36	7-14	Redc	10fm	45	4560 vis
19	9-11	Catt	13.8g/f	[45]	4671 vis
37	7-16	Nott	10gd	40	4857 vis
27	11-13	Ayr	10sft	[40]	5276 bl

MYND 3 b g £12826
60a	4-14	Ling	6ap	[56]	23
68a	1-7	WOLV	5af	[58]	348*
67a	1-11	WOLV	5af	59	508*
66a	2-11	Wolv	5af	66	748
58a	11-14	Ling	6ap	66	897
66	2-19	Warw	5gd	62	1127
68	1-20	RIPO	5gd	62	1179*
62	9-20	Thir	5g/s	67	1476
50	9-19	Beve	5sft	66	1627
53	6-13	Pont	5g/f	[65]	2279
58	4-14	Newc	5g/s	64	2775

42 14-18 Hayd 5gd 63 2951
59 6-10 Hami 5g/s [62] 4010
48 12-19 Beve 5g/s 61 4240
38 17-20 Ripo 6gd 59 4785 P
63 9-12 Redc 5sft [57] 5305

MYRTUS 5 ch g £360
23a	3-4	Wolv	12af		1323
26a	7-12	Sout	16af	45	1753
32a	5-6	Sout	16af	40	3397

MYSTERINCH 4 b g £6145
93	3-7	Thir	8sft		1225
96	7-19	Newm	10g/f	94	1478
88	8-13	Epso	8.5g/f	92	2207
96	2-11	Warw	7.1fm	[91]	2777
85	7-14	Hayd	8.1gd	91	2903
74	7-7	York	7.9g/s	91	3077
77	17-20	Newm	7g/f	90	3782
83	4-7	Thir	8g/s	[87]	4208

MYSTERIUM 9 gr g £3191
40a	3-12	Wolv	16.2af	40	7 vis
23a	3-10	Wolv	14.8af	40	34 vis
39a	3-10	Wolv	14.8af	[40]	125 vis
40a	3-13	Ling	16ap	40	137 vis
37a	3-4	Wolv	14.8af	[40]	426 vis
36a	4-9	Ling	16ap	[40]	454 vis
43a	1-6	WOLV	16.2af	[40]	824* vis
16a	5-7	Wolv	16.2af	[45]	1263 vis
30a	6-9	Ling	16af	[45]	1414 vis

MYSTERLOVER 4 b g £0
23a	12-14	Ling	10ap		430
53a	7-15	Ling	12ap		521
51a	7-12	Ling	13ap	56	762 T
38a	12-12	Ling	16ap	51	813 t

MYSTERY LOT 2 b f £3095
69a	6-13	Ling	7ap		3330
34	2-16	Sali	7g/f		3882
77	2-11	Chep	7.1hvy		4703
76	3-13	Wind	8.3g/f	74	5051

MYSTERY MAID 2 b f £0
45	11-14	Bath	6gd		1401
45	6-6	Good	6g/f		1866
50	12-19	Newb	6g/f		2310
15	13-13	Kemp	6gd		3183
37	14-14	Kemp	7g/f	[45]	4711

MYSTERY MOUNTAIN 4 b g £0
0	9-9	Sout	6af	[60]	533
29a	5-9	Sout	7af	[53]	661
35a	4-11	Wolv	6af	[47]	778

MYSTERY PIPS 4 b f £1320
33	11-15	Muss	5gd	52	1555 vis
39	10-13	Newc	5g/f	51	1873 vis
33	7-10	Thir	5g/f	51	1973 vis
32	11-19	Beve	5g/s	49	2326 vis
47	4-9	Muss	5gd	47	2614 vis
24	15-18	Hayd	5gd	46	2951 vis
42	8-20	Beve	5g/f	45	3180 vis
43	4-14	Thir	5g/s	45	3417 vis
45	3-17	Catt	5g/f	43	3667 vis
42	14-26	Ayr	5g/s	45	4618 vis
34	12-16	Warw	5g/s	[45]	4995 vis
19a	12-13	Wolv	5.1ap	[45]	5231 vis

MYSTERY SOLVED 4 b f £0
29	11-14	Sout	12g/s	[50]	1047
0	15-15	Sout	8af	45	1755

MYSTIC LAD 3 gr g £1266
76a	2-12	Ling	8ap		623
34	19-19	Newb	8gd		1236

MYSTIC MAN 6 b g £11325
45a	9-10	Sout	7af	89	611
66a	11-12	Wolv	8.5af	87	836
74	15-27	Newb	8gd	87	1231
62	13-17	Thir	8g/s	85	1475
90	1-14	DONC	8g/f	[82]	1877*
91	3-13	Ripo	8g/f	88	2010
80	10-28	Asco	7g/f	88	2558
91	4-18	Newc	7sft	88	2684
91	3-13	York	6gd	87	4322
88	7-9	Good	6g/f	88	4537

```
69  12-26  Ayr   6g/s        87   4652
78  9-19   York  7.9gd       88   4987

MYSTIC MOON 2 br f £0
30a 13-14  Ling  6ap               146
48a 9-15   Ling  7ap               472
36a 9-12   Ling  7ap               566
59  6-9    Folk  9.7sft            980
44  8-13   Nott  8.2gd      55    1242
53  4-11   Sout  10gd       55    1280
2   14-16  Nott  10hvy      55    1611
45a 11-14  Ling  10ap       54    2064
42  4-11   Yarm  10.1gd    [51]   3362
37  7-10   Yarm  10.1gd    [48]   3874
36  8-15   Nott  10g/s      48    4037
0   8-9    Brig  8sft       45    4165
43  8-9    Bath  10.2gd    [40]   4547

MYSTIC PROMISE 2 gr g £205
0   12-12  Ling  10ap      [30]   120 BL
14a 11-11  Wolv  6af       [30]   466 bl
2a  9-11   Sout  6af        30    591 bl
23a 8-12   Sout  8af        30    656 VIS
0   5-7    Sout  8af       [30]   721 vis
32a 9-9    Ling  10ap      [30]   899 vis T
32a 3-6    Sout  8af       [30]   1203 t
30a 4-8    Wolv  7af       [30]   1314 t
15a 5-6    Sout  7af       [35]   1410 t
23a 6-6    Wolv  9.4af     [35]   1675 t
8a  10-13  Sout  8af       [32]   2383 t

MYSTICAL GIRL 3 ch f £36309
75  3-15   Bath  8g/s       73    1099
79  3-16   Beve  8.5sft     73    1628
90  1-18   THIR  8g/f       75    1769*
89  2-10   Good  11g/f      80    1865
94  1-13   SAND  8.1g/s    [85]   2126*
96  3-18   Epso  10.1fm     90    2250
62  12-19  Asco  8g/f       94    2491
86  6-11   Newm  10g/f      94    3029
90  8-21   Good  8fm        94    3565
93  5-12   Yarm  10.1sft    92    4149
101 1-10   KEMP  8fm        91    4389*

MYSTICAL LAND 2 b c £61330
80  2-10   Hayd  5sft             1107
91  1-5    DONC  5g/s             1517*
107 2-9    Asco  6g/f             2516
106 3-7    Newm  6g/f             3028
107 2-8    Good  6fm              3566
90  5-9    Deau  6sft             4159
110 2-9    Newb  6g/f     [100]   4680 VIS

MYTHICAL CHARM 5 b m £3181
47a 6-12   Wolv  9.4af     50     427
20a 13-13  Ling  10ap      [48]   569
40a 7-12   Ling  8ap       [45]   649
37a 9-14   Ling  10ap      [45]   705
35a 6-11   Ling  10ap      [45]   970
42a 3-7    Ling  10ap      [40]   1182
32a 3-5    Ling  8ap       [40]   1711
44  7-20   Asco  8g/f       50    1927 t
43  11-15  Kemp  9gd        53    2170 t
47  7-14   Wind  8.3g/f     51    2799 t
41  3-17   Wind  6fm        51    2975 t
51  5-13   Kemp  7g/f       51    3034 t
40  15-19  Good  8g/f       49    3512 t
38  7-13   Good  8g/f       49    3952 t
52  2-14   Good  8sft       48    4189 t
59  2-14   Good  8g/f       48    4542 t
42  9-19   Kemp  8g/f      [55]   4795 t
14  12-17  Newb  9sft       55    5198 t

MYTHICAL KING 7 b g £0
47  8-12   Newc  12.4sft    53    1680
51  6-14   Nott  10g/s      53    1777
12a 11-11  Wolv  12.2ap     52    5180

MYTORI 2 ch f £0
22  15-16  Leic  7fm              3811
29  6-7    Nott  8.2gd            3991
17  6-7    Chep  6.1hvy           4705

MYTTONS BELL 2 b f £7003
79  2-9    Hayd  6g/f             1920
61a 3-11   Wolv  6af              2051
59  10-12  Hayd  6sft             3272
70  3-9    Ches  6.1fm     70     3632

63  7-13   Hayd  6gd       [70]   3736
56  5-14   Muss  7.1g/f    [69]   4171
11  15-18  Ayr   6g/s       [65]   4617
56  3-12   Muss  7.1g/s    [65]   5142
67  1-10   CATT  7sft      [58]   5317*
54  10-16  Nott  5.1hvy     65    5343

MYTTONS DREAM 2 br f £3953
37  6-8    Hayd  5g/s             1343
66  6-7    Ches  5.1g/s           1573
63  1-11   BEVE  5g/f             1831*
55  9-10   Ches  5.1g/s           2744
56  4-9    Pont  6g/f       66    2989
50  12-13  Newc  7g/s       60    3698
44  12-20  Leic  7g/f       58    4451

NAADDEY 3 b c £1045
0   7-7    Newm  9g/f       [92]   1189
75  6-6    Newm  8gd        [92]   1888 vis
92  4-8    Nott  8.2g/f     88    3421

NAAHY 4 ch c £47288
104 1-7    GOOD  7g/f      [103]   1811*
109 1-6    LEOP  7g/f      [103]   2455*
101 7-8    Newm  7g/f      [106]   2765
109 4-9    Curr  7gd       [106]   3320
108 4-8    Good  7g/f      [106]   3508
100 6-11   Hopp  6.5gd     [106]   3839
69  7-7    Good  8g/s      [109]   4232
99  7-8    Donc  7fm       [107]   4477
109 5-15   Asco  7g/f       107    4800

NABTAT SAIF 3 b f £0
51  11-14  Wind  10gd       70    2617
52  10-17  Newb  10g/f      67    3257 T
39  14-17  Wind  10fm       63    3477

NADESZHDA 4 ch f £3455
80a 1-8    LING  12ap       66    3026*

NADIR 3 b c £0
63  9-17   Newm  8gd              4228
55  6-12   Newc  8g/f             4407
35  10-18  Wind  10g/s     [65]   4944

NAFFERTON GIRL 3 b f £0
51  4-15   Folk  6g/s             1078
2a  7-7    Wolv  9.4af      50    1324
43a 8-14   Ling  10ap       50    2064
41  10-14  Bath  10.2fm     50    2664

NAFFERTON HEIGHTS 3 b c £0
52  10-16  Newc  7sft             966
47  5-12   Beve  9.9sft     52    1306
45  8-13   Beve  12.1g/f    49    1836
24  9-14   Redc  14.1g/f    47    2123
5   18-20  Beve  16.2gd     46    3312
39  6-10   Beve  12.1g/f    46    3499 BL
0   12-12  Pont  8gd        42    3679

NAHEEF 5 b h £18150
110 5-6    Curr  10.5g/f[113]  2004 TBL
0   8-8    Newm  12g/f [111]   3030 vis t
111 1-7    WIND  11.6g/s[109]  4219* vis t
103 5-8    Good  9.9gd [109]   4748 vis t
4   10-11  Newm  10sft         5136 vis t

NAIVETY 2 ch f £1692
81  2-9    Newm  7gd             4192
70  7-9    Beve  7.5g/f          4600

NAJAABA 3 b f £20264
48a 4-12   Sout  6af        57    85
49a 3-12   Wolv  7af        57    129
62a 1-14   SOUT  8af       [56]   170*
70a 1-7    SOUT  8af        56    332*
76a 1-8    SOUT  8af        62    393*
71a 1-12   WOLV  9.4af      62    427*
76a 1-8    SOUT  8af        71    489*
74a 5-7    Ling  10ap       75    736
80a 1-5    WOLV  8.5af      75    861*
87  5-8    Kemp  8g/s       [78]   1115
83  6-8    Newm  9fm        [82]   1491
74  5-15   Hami  8.3g/s     82    1602
67  10-12  Good  8gd        [82]   4872
88a 7-12   Ling  8ap        [80]   5298

NAJEEBON 5 ch h £6698
82  11-30  Newm  6g/f       89    1481

62  15-19  Thir  6g/f       87    1767
65  16-19  Kemp  6fm        85    2070
83  3-12   Sali  6fm        83    2289
56  6-8    Newm  6fm        [82]   2591
82  3-11   Newb  6g/f       80    2878
76  7-11   Asco  6.5gd      80    3069
65  12-16  Newb  6g/f       80    3269
67  9-12   Newm  6gd        78    4229
80  2-19   Kemp  6fm        76    4394
79  3-19   Good  6gd        78    4747
69  10-19  Sali  6gd        78    4855

NAKWA 5 b g £13760
46a 3-12   Wolv  12af       43    244
57a 1-10   WOLV  12af       [45]   315*
57a 2-10   Sout  12af       51    421
56a 2-12   Wolv  12af       54    484
47a 5-13   Sout  14af       56    590
51  3-15   Newc  12.4hvy    56    1034
61  2-13   Hayd  14sft      55    1109
65  2-10   Hami  13gd       60    1506
73  1-10   HAYD  14g/f      63    1923*
74  2-4    Hayd  14g/s      74    2229
71  6-8    Hayd  14gd       72    2887
64  10-12  Newm  16.1g/f    72    3032
56  10-10  Hami  13fm       70    3249
18  16-18  Ayr   10.9sft    65    4623
63  22-34  Newm  18sft      65    5135

NAMASTE 3 b f £0
55a 7-15   Ling  12ap             118

NAMAT 3 b f £4645
73  2-9    Redc  9mf              4336
76  1-15   BATH  10.2gd           4826*

NAMED AT DINNER 3 ch g £0
40  11-12  Beve  9.9sft     75    1306
39  16-18  Thir  8g/f       73    1769
0   19-19  York  7.9gd      68    2055
30  20-20  York  7.9gd      62    4321
46  15-18  Catt  7g/f       62    4438
38  7-13   Carl  6.9fm     [55]   4504
39  10-18  Leic  7gd       [50]   4698 BL
40  8-16   Nott  10gd       50    4857 VIS

NAMKING 2 b c £0
61  7-10   Muss  5gd              1550
60  8-8    Muss  5gd              1795
48a 6-9    Sout  6af              3157

NAMROC 3 b c £9265
85  1-13   NEWM  8fm              2595*
88  4-9    Sali  8g/s       85    3112
89  2-7    Pont  8g/f      [85]    4629
92  4-17   Newm  10g/f      87    4917
78  7-14   Newb  10hvy      87    5223

NAMROUD 5 b g £1110
55  20-22  Donc  6gd        90    921
80  6-13   Newc  7hvy       88    1035
80  10-12  Hayd  8.1g/f     86    1883
30  25-28  Asco  7g/f       85    2558 BL
71  7-8    Muss  7.1g/f     82    2809 bl
68  7-8    Hayd  8.1fm      80    3797
73  4-13   Ches  7.6sft     77    4103
64  9-18   Ayr   7.2sft     75    4689
74  6-11   Muss  7.1g/s     72    5144
63  9-20   Yarm  7sft       72    5256

NAN JAN 2 b f £1462
59  8-8    Donc  6gd              2750
58  7-7    Epso  6gd              4466
81  2-12   Nott  6.1g/f           4844 T

NANABANANA 2 b f £15400
102 2-12   Good  7sft             4264
98  2-8    Newm  6sft             5267

NANNA 2 b f £15426
8a  7-9    Wolv  6af              247
35a 5-8    Sout  7af              389
51a 2-11   Wolv  6af              466
30a 9-10   Sout  6af        51    592
47a 3-8    Wolv  6af       [50]    750
44a 7-16   Sout  5ap        50    1046
48a 2-7    Wolv  5af       [48]    1320
68  1-17   BATH  5g/f      [48]    1787*
```

51 6-8 Bath 5.7fm 54 2034
56a 2-11 Sout 5af 51 2380
67 1-15 REDC 5g/s 58 2961*
72 1-12 CATT 5g/f 64 3193*
65 6-12 Donc 5g/f 69 3599
64 7-15 Thir 5g/s 69 3833
69 3-14 Redc 5fm [68] 4930
44a 8-12 Wolv 5.1ap 59 5326

NANTON 2 gr c £0
66 7-10 Sali 5g/f 1717
71a 6-12 Ling 8ap 5293

NANTUCKET SOUND 2 b c £3926
72a 4-12 Ling 8ap 175
58 9-16 Leic 8g/s 70 1359
71 4-18 Wind 8.3sft 67 1647
71 1-12 BATH 10.2fm 67 2036*
58 8-8 Nott 10g/f 70 2631
61 8-12 Wind 11.6gd 70 3161

NAPAPIJRI 2 gr f £305
69 5-9 Newm 7gd 4192
33 7-8 Hayd 8.1sft 4782
69 4-14 Bath 8gd 5018

NAPPER TANDY 4 ch c £6399
112 2-8 Leop 10g/s 994 bl
112 4-6 Curr 10.5g/f 2004 bl

NARCISO 4 ch g £0
47 10-14 Hayd 8.1g/s 2231
52 8-11 Beve 7.5g/s 2325
33a 9-12 Sout 6af 2722
14 10-10 Carl 6.9g/f 3230
47 6-13 Redc 14.1fm 49 4340
26 13-14 York 10.4g/f 49 4402
36 6-19 Catt 15.8g/f 49 4675

NARRATIVE 6 b h £1373
82 8-9 Ches 13.4gd[108] 1596
102 4-6 Nott 8.2g/f [106] 2154
96 6-8 Pont 8g/f 100 2606
74 18-21 York 10.4gd 100 3118

NASHAAB 6 b g £29312
74a 9-13 Wolv 8.5af 89 44
76a 5-12 Ling 8ap [86] 234 vis
72a 12-13 Ling 10ap 83 433
71a 7-12 Ling 8ap 78 517 BL
79 7-22 Donc 6gd 88 921
75 9-20 Kemp 6gd 87 1138
90 2-18 Ches 7.6gd 87 1598
94 3-18 Good 8g/f 88 1812
94 1-12 CHES 7.6fm 88 3634*
85 5-8 Ches 7sft 90 4073
86 7-16 Good 7g/f 90 4523
83 8-14 Asco 8g/f 90 4813
80 14-32 Newm 9g/f 90 4916 vis
98 1-19 YORK 7.9gd 90 4987+ vis
86 14-22 Newm 8sft 95 5103 vis

NASSAU STREET 3 gr g £397
29a 10-15 Ling 12ap 118
33a 3-12 Wolv 9.4af [40] 668 VIS
22a 8-12 Wolv 12af [40] 891 vis
0 11-14 Chep 10.2g/s 37 3895
35 3-15 Folk 12ap [40] 4371

NASSEEM DUBAI 2 ch c £1972
76 7-12 Carl 5.9fm 3544
69 6-14 Ches 7sft 4102
80 2-14 Thir 7g/s 4204
72 5-14 Thir 8fm [80] 4376
80 3-11 Ayr 7.2g/s [76] 4653
78a 7-11 Ling 6ap 78 4972
71 7-14 Ayr 6sft 78 5035

NASSIRIA 3 b f £2032
74 6-24 Newm 8fm 1495
0 6-6 York 10.4sft 1666
50 11-11 Newb 10g/f 2349
18 12-13 Pont 12gd 69 3240
53 7-13 Yarm 10.1gd 65 3492
68 3-8 Brig 9.9g/f 65 3719 P
63a 3-10 Ling 12ap [64] 4314 p

NATALIE JANE 2 ch f £7955
67 7-18 Nott 8.2g/f 4842

77 3-16 Bath 8gd 5019
84 1-9 NOTT 10hvy 5189*
88 3-9 Newm 10g/s 5281

NATALIYA 3 b f £7000
107 3-8 Newb 7gd 1233
109 7-16 Newm 8fm [104] 1492
75 9-9 Sand 8.1g/s [110] 2917
99 4-7 Asco 8g/f [108] 3389
31 11-12 Pont 6g/s [105] 3971
0 P-15 Donc 7fm [102] 4479 VIS

NATHAN BRITTLES 4 ch g £5688
80 1-18 CATT 7gd 72 998*

NATHAN DETROIT 3 b c £0
37a 12-14 Ling 6ap 23
38a 11-16 Ling 7ap [60] 123 BL
39 15-17 Wind 6fm 56 3643
0 13-15 Bath 5.7g/f 51 3966 P

NATIONAL CURRENCY 4 b c £176000
121 2-14 Sha 5g/f 210

NATIONAL TRUST 2 b c £0
57 11-19 Newm 7g/s 5285

NATIVE TITLE 6 b g £26178
83 4-14 Ches 5.1gd 81 1594
77 8-20 York 6g/f 83 2059
93 1-17 EPSO 6fm 82 2256*
75 18-29 Asco 6fm 91 2581
73 16-18 Newc 6g/s 88 2770
89 3-10 York 6gd 87 3116
69 19-28 Good 6fm 87 3622
70 10-26 Ayr 6g/s 86 4652
79 8-13 Donc 5sft 86 5218

NATIVE TURK 3 b c £1034
42 14-19 Yarm 8g/f 1130
19 11-11 Folk 7g/s 3048 BL
71a 2-10 Sout 8af 4042
57 5-7 Epso 8.5g/f [69] 4474

NATMSKY 5 b g £0
0 19-20 Catt 12g/f 35 2850
17 9-11 Catt 12g/f [30] 3190
0 15-15 Thir 8fm [30] 4379

NATURAL GRACE 3 ch f £0
0 14-16 Sout 6af 65

NAUGHTY GIRL 3 b f £4533
32a 10-13 Ling 6ap [74] 271
53a 11-14 Ling 7ap [70] 450
28a 8-13 Sout 6af 62 551
0 8-8 Sout 8af 62 597 VIS
41 15-16 Bath 5.7sft 70 1540
25 15-18 Wind 6g/f [65] 1806 vis
46 9-12 Folk 5g/f 60 2269 BL
28 9-11 Bath 5.7fm [60] 2412
45 5-8 Yarm 8g/f [55] 2854 T
48 4-8 Wind 8.3gd 50 3162 vis t
37 4-14 Ayr 7.2gd [50] 3324 vis t
0 12-14 Yarm 8gd 50 3363 vis t
51 2-8 Chep 8.1gd 44 3731 vis t
28 12-14 Bath 8g/f 46 3963 vis t
50 1-14 BATH 8g/f 46 4411* vis t
36 10-17 Pont 8g/f 52 4626 vis t
41 8-17 Leic 7gd 48 5056 vis t

NAUTICAL 6 gr g £9511
32 14-20 Warw 10.9gd 62 1128
50 9-17 Bath 10.2sft 55 1541
52a 4-14 Ling 10ap 52 2589
46 6-12 Ling 10ap 52 2844
48 4-11 Bath 8gd 50 3142
50 3-7 Brig 8g/f 50 3174
40 11-12 Kemp 8g/f 50 3524
58 2-8 Wind 8.3fm 50 3641
48 7-12 Newm 6g/f 52 3942
61 1-20 CHEP 7.1g/s 52 4367*
70a 1-13 WOLV 8.6ap 55 4982*
56a 8-12 Ling 8ap [55] 5077
71a 2-12 Wolv 7.1ap 65 5112

NAUTICAL STAR 9 b g £0
32 5-9 Ayr 13.1g/s [35] 1449

NAVAL ATTACHE 2 b g £0
53 10-16 York 7.9gd 4997
37 17-20 Yarm 8sft 5252

NAVAL FORCE 2 b c £860
62 9-20 Wind 6fm 2970
79a 4-13 Ling 7ap 3329 T
81 3-12 Carl 5.9fm 3544 t
47 16-16 Newm 6gd 79 4224 t
52 13-14 Newb 7sft 77 5193 t

NAVIGATION 2 ch c £0
50 11-20 York 6g/f 4401
60 6-14 Newc 6fm 4865
64a 7-13 Wolv 5.1ap 5207

NAWAAEM 2 b f £0
77 5-19 Newm 7g/s 5279

NAWAMEES 6 b h £8432
84a 4-11 Ling 16ap 82 605
88a 2-7 Ling 12ap 82 695
91 2-12 Wind 11.6fm 84 2759 P
88 10-15 Good 14g/f 90 3510 p
69 12-14 Asco 12g/f 88 4814 p

NAWOW 3 b g £3360
79a 6-14 Ling 12ap 80 83
67a 15-16 Ling 12ap 79 404
78 3-11 Nott 16fm 76 1003
74 5-18 Newb 16gd 77 1232
73 6-18 York 13.9g/s 76 1689
70 10-15 Newb 11g/f 74 4643
77 2-16 Good 12gd [74] 4745
60 7-19 Sali 14.1gd 69 4856
74 4-11 Wind 11.6g/s [75] 4942

NAYYIR 6 ch g £212231
117 3-11 Nad 9g/f [117] 991
98 16-20 Newm 6g/f 3062
122 2-11 Good 8fm 3533
120 2-7 Good 8g/s [120] 4232
114 4-11 Asco 8g/f [120] 4801
107 6-7 Long 7sft [120] 5070

NAZAAHA 2 gr f £476
76 4-14 Newb 6fm 3626

NAZZWAH 3 ch f £0
66 6-12 Newb 7g/f 2352
39 6-8 Good 9gd 2536
32 9-9 Brig 8gd 2953

NDOLA 5 b g £1671
46a 1-12 WOLV 9.4af [35] 302*
19a 12-16 Sout 11af [45] 445
27a 12-14 Ling 10ap [45] 828
40a 3-14 Ling 10ap [40] 1072

NE OUBLIE 2 b c £645
49 6-8 Hayd 5gd 2241
71 4-8 Ling 5gd 3445
69 3-12 Thir 5g/s 3832
50 10-12 Muss 5g/f 67 4172

NEAP TIDE 3 br g £0
35 11-20 Bath 10.2gd 75 1403
29 19-20 Newb 7g/f 75 2314

NEARLY A FOOL 6 b g £19251
61a 1-14 LING 7ap 53 344* vis
63a 1-13 LING 6ap 55 448* vis
44a 12-14 Ling 7ap 61 499 vis
63a 2-10 Ling 7ap [60] 765 vis
67a 1-13 SOUT 7af [60] 858* vis
58a 8-14 Ling 7ap 62 1010 vis
73 1-16 SOUT 7g/s 65 1049* vis
72 3-9 Nott 8.2g/f [71] 3423 vis
67 4-10 Nott 8.2g/f 71 3579 vis
55a 8-14 Ling 7ap 66 3821 vis
58 5-8 Folk 7gd [71] 4117 vis
56 11-15 Beve 7.5g/f 69 4719 vis
62 5-16 Bath 8gd 67 5022 vis
72a 1-14 LING 7ap [60] 5263* vis
69a 2-14 Ling 7ap [60] 5294 vis

NEATH 3 b f £856
64 5-11 Wind 10gd 4125
69 3-9 Sand 10gd 4501

45	7-13	Bath	10.2sft		5173

NEBRASKA CITY 3 b g £0

39a	10-12	Ling	6ap	[69]	1044
46	6-8	Bath	5.7fm	64	1903
28	13-14	Wind	8.3fm	59	2971
53	4-12	Folk	6gd	55	3380 T
65	6-10	Ling	7gd	[55]	3446 t
28	13-16	Ling	6g/f	54	3602
13	13-15	Sali	6gd	52	3888 vis

NEBRASKA TORNADO 4 br f £50599

101	5-5	Long	9.3gd		2002
115	4-16	Asco	8g/f		2470
113	3-8	Deau	8gd		3659
116	3-5	Newm	8g/f		4915

NECKAR VALLEY 5 b g £0

50	12-20	Ayr	10g/s	77	4656

NECKLACE 3 b f £59399

97	12-16	Newm	8fm		1492
108	6-15	Curr	8g/f		2005
107	4-7	Epso	12g/f		2210
116	3-11	Arli	9.5fm		4013

NEE LEMON LEFT 2 b f £2398

68	2-7	Muss	5g/f		1117
21	6-6	Hami	5gd		1503
68	3-5	Ripo	5g/f		2481
44	7-8	Catt	5g/f		2847
53	6-7	Muss	5g/s		2965 P
39	4-4	Hami	5g/s	[63]	4134
9	12-12	Muss	5g/f	63	4172 BL

NEEDLES AND PINS 3 b f £2250

85	4-5	Ripo	6gd	[105]	1175
73	7-9	Nott	6.1g/s	[102]	1773
83	5-11	Hayd	6gd	[97]	2240
92	7-10	Ayr	5g/f	[92]	3304
73	12-14	York	5g/s	90	4027

NEEDWOOD BUCOLIC 6 br g £0

42	10-10	Newc	5g/f		2161
31	9-16	Chep	7.1gd		2369
37	7-10	Hami	5g/f		2476
12a	13-16	Sout	6af	41	2806
27	9-14	Hami	6gd	40	3129
18	13-14	Ayr	7.2gd	[37]	3324
27	7-9	Ayr	7.2g/f	[33]	3764 BL

NEEDWOOD MYSTIC 9 b m £1030

67	2-5	Brig	11.9fm	[67]	2329

NEEDWOOD SPIRIT 9 b g £0

6	15-16	Carl	11.9g/f	35	4348
5	16-19	Catt	15.8g/f	35	4675

NEFERURA 2 b f £0

44	11-17	Yarm	6gd		4610
61	9-13	Redc	7fm		4927
52	13-20	Yarm	8sft		5252

NEGAS 2 b g £0

50	17-18	York	5g/f		2360
43	10-10	Carl	5g/f		3227
54	11-12	Newc	7gd		3425
23	17-18	Ripo	6g/s		3939

NEGWA 3 b f £0

46	5-11	Donc	10.3gd	[74]	930
43	8-8	Brig	9.9g/f	[74]	1369
6	10-11	Newm	8gd	[70]	3923

NELLA FANTASIA 2 ch f £0

62	6-11	Nott	5.1g/f		2151
73	6-10	Leic	6gd		2703

NELLIE GWYN 2 b f £0

46	15-21	Donc	6sft		5368

NELSONS LUCK 3 b c £0

26	15-15	Ling	7gd		4445

NEMO FUGAT 5 b g £3047

1	17-19	Newc	6sft	70	967
23	13-14	Ayr	6g/f	66	1898
62	5-10	Newc	8g/f	62	2159
60	6-11	Hami	8.3g/f	62	2317
38	7-10	Ayr	9.1gd	59	2571

64	2-14	Catt	6g/f	58	3352 VIS
62	5-11	Thir	6g/f	58	3574 vis
63	2-8	Carl	6.9g/f	[60]	3654 vis
30	15-15	Catt	7sft	60	3933 vis
41	13-16	Brig	7sft	[62]	4144 vis
62	3-19	York	7.9g/f	60	4399 vis
53	8-13	Muss	8g/f	[60]	4554 vis

NEON BLUE 3 b g £18811

67	5-9	Thir	6g/s	[68]	1477
72	1-19	DONC	6g/f	[68]	1876*
61	7-8	Beve	7.5g/f	68	2166
68	3-12	Ripo	6gd	68	2482
68	3-11	Ripo	6gd	68	2985
71	3-12	Hayd	6sft	68	3273
78	1-11	YORK	7g/f	68	3433*
63	6-16	Ches	7g/f	72	4051
69	7-13	Redc	7fm	[72]	4341
53	8-11	Ayr	8sft	72	4621
55	11-14	Redc	7g/s	70	5109

NEPAL 2 ch f £844

59	6-12	Redc	6fm		4557
68	2-10	Newc	7fm		4864
58	5-13	Newc	7g/f		5012

NEPHETRITI WAY 3 b f £368

78	7-11	Asco	8sft	[87]	1419
78	5-6	Leic	7gd	[87]	2136
73	5-5	Sand	7.1gd	[87]	2362
63	5-7	Brig	8g/f	78	3174

NEPRO 2 b c £7839

91	3-13	Curr	6.3gd		2815

NEPTUNE 8 b g £1321

36a	5-9	Ling	16ap	[40]	454
0	11-15	Ling	12ap	[35]	707
31a	9-10	Ling	12ap	[35]	916
38a	2-12	Ling	12ap	[35]	1180
33a	4-7	Ling	12ap	[35]	1287
30	5-10	Kemp	12hvy	[30]	1645
60a	3-11	Ling	12ap	[35]	2588
58a	5-8	Ling	12ap	[45]	2739
37	3-17	Bath	11.7gd	35	3145

NEQAAWI 3 br f £3494

55	5-8	Beve	7.5g/f		2169 T
68	1-5	CARL	6.9fm	59	2446* t
42	11-11	Carl	6.9gd	66	2936 t

NEROS RETURN 3 b c £1264

90	6-7	Kemp	8g/s		1113
100	8-10	Newb	7gd		1234
84	6-9	Hayd	6g/f	[105]	1918
75	15-20	York	6g/f	100	2407
95	7-9	Sand	10g/s	95	2896
80	5-5	Asco	6g/f	93	3388 BL
86	7-10	Asco	6gd	93	3778

NESNAAS 3 ch g £0

40	11-12	Donc	7g/f	72	1879
44	15-20	Newb	7fm	68	2650

NESSEN DORMA 2 b g £16035

58a	5-11	Wolv	7af	70	29
72a	1-10	SOUT	8af	[66]	162*
75a	1-11	SOUT	8af	69	252*
73a	4-7	Ling	10ap	76	325
75a	5-11	Ling	10ap	75	497
76	5-11	Ripo	12.3gd	75	1174
82	2-5	Leic	11.8g/s	74	1355
82	1-7	DONC	14.6g/s	74	1521*
87	3-14	York	11.9g/s	79	1708
85	3-11	Sand	14g/s	80	2130
86	8-10	Asco	16.2g/f	[81]	2557 VIS
71	9-9	Beve	16.2g/s	83	3181
76	7-8	Ayr	13.1sft	83	4690

NEUTRAL NIGHT 3 b f £3539

25a	6-13	Wolv	8.5af	[45]	46 vis
43a	7-12	Wolv	7af	[45]	71 vis
36a	3-12	Wolv	6af	[44]	297 vis
14a	10-10	Ling	8ap	[45]	410 vis
33a	7-12	Wolv	7af	[45]	524 vis
36a	5-11	Wolv	7af	[45]	579 vis
40a	3-11	Sout	7af	[40]	771 vis
40a	2-8	Sout	7af	[40]	847 vis

33a	4-13	Wolv	8.5af	[40]	894 vis
41a	3-12	Sout	6af	[40]	982 vis
40a	3-7	Sout	7af	[40]	1202 BL
47a	1-8	WOLV	7af	[40]	1565* vis
47a	2-6	Wolv	6af	[40]	1671 vis
51a	2-6	Wolv	7af	[45]	1804 vis
33a	8-16	Sout	7af	45	2335 vis

NEUTRINO 2 b c £551

69	12-19	Leic	7gd		5055
81	4-13	Donc	7hvy		5199
71a	4-12	Wolv	7.1ap		5324

NEVADA DESERT 4 b g £13090

74	4-19	Ripo	10g/f	71	1781
72	5-13	Ripo	8g/f	71	2010
77	2-9	Ripo	10g/s	71	3260
71	7-13	York	11.9g/f	71	3437
78	1-10	HAMI	8.3g/s	71	4136+ P
72	8-13	Ripo	8gd	71	4279 p
23	18-20	Ayr	10g/s	73	4656 p
56	8-14	Hami	8.3g/s	72	4820 p
62	6-10	Catt	7sft	71	5320 p

NEVEN 4 b g £596

62a	2-14	Sout	8af	61	99

NEVER AWAY 2 b f £0

62	9-10	Newm	6g/f		3064
61	10-12	Newm	6gd		3280
63	13-14	Newm	7g/f		3944
52	11-13	Kemp	6gd		4358
38	11-14	Yarm	7g/s	59	4583

NEVER CRIED WOLF 3 b g £0

62a	6-12	Ling	8ap		428
39a	10-11	Ling	8ap		496
59a	7-15	Ling	7ap		671
42a	6-9	Ling	8ap		717 P
25a	12-12	Ling	8ap	52	845 p

NEVER FORGET BOWIE 8 b g £0

0	8-8	Hami	9.2g/s	[40]	4133
36	11-19	Redc	6g/s	[40]	5110
21	5-12	Ayr	7.2sft	[40]	5274

NEVER PROMISE 6 b m £0

33	6-15	Carl	9.3fm	[40]	4505 vis
11	8-13	Ayr	8sft	[40]	5275 vis

NEVER WILL 3 b c £9904

72	2-13	Muss	7.1g/f		1119
90	2-24	Newm	8fm		1495
87	1-7	HAMI	9.2gd		1747*
80	12-18	Good	9g/f	94	1813
50	23-27	Asco	8g/f	88	2521

NEVER WITHOUT ME 3 ch g £18648

48a	2-15	Sout	6af	44	168 VIS
50a	2-8	Wolv	5af	47	274
39a	6-10	Wolv	6af	47	345
39a	4-14	Sout	6af	50	501 vis
41a	5-12	Wolv	5af	48	641 vis
49a	2-12	Sout	5af	46	853
57a	1-16	SOUT	5ap	48	1046*
47	8-20	Ripo	5gd	55	1179
54a	3-6	Sout	6af	[54]	1443
48	4-10	Warw	6.1hvy	52	1533
64a	1-14	SOUT	6af	[54]	2502*
68a	1-16	SOUT	6af	60	2720*
65	2-14	Leic	6g/f	56	3213
58	4-8	Pont	6gd	61	3461
69	2-15	Pont	5gd	61	3680
67	2-9	Yarm	5.2g/s	62	4253
70	6-16	Leic	5gd	65	4700
52	12-20	Ripo	6gd	65	4785

NEVERLETME GO 2 b f £435

73	4-4	Nott	5.1g/f		3576
71	5-15	Kemp	6g/f		4357

NEVINSTOWN 3 b c £0

3a	10-14	Sout	8af	53	99 BL T
34a	8-12	Ling	8ap	[45]	648 VIS

NEW DAY DAWNING 3 ch f £0

0	13-13	Nott	6.1sft	[48]	1464
56	6-8	Donc	5g/f	[48]	2075
8	16-19	Beve	5g/s	48	2326

0	20-20	Redc	6g/f	47	3767

NEW FOUNDATION 3 b f £0
28a	12-13	Wolv	6af	57	45 t

NEW LARGUE 2 b f £0
103	8-10	Long	8g/f	4954

NEW MEXICAN 3 ch g £1475
99	4-7	Donc	8gd	[103]	949 P
100	5-7	Newm	9g/f	[102]	1189

NEW MORNING 3 b f £41738
82	2-10	Yarm	11.5g/f		1725
73	**1-8**	**LEIC**	11.8g/f		1961*
106	4-9	Asco	12g/f		2517
106	5-8	Hayd	11.9gd	[104]	2946
110	**1-10**	**SALI**	9.9g/f	[104]	3866+
103	6-13	Curr	10gd	[104]	4735

NEW OPTIONS 6 b g £709
44a	11-12	Wolv	5af	69	35
65a	4-16	Sout	5af	67	205
64a	5-10	Wolv	6af	67	349 bl
64a	4-9	Sout	6af	[66]	487
42a	8-12	Sout	6af	[64]	610 bl
41a	5-12	Wolv	6af	[64]	646 bl
53a	10-11	Ling	6ap	60	728
58a	3-13	Ling	6ap	57	902
8	9-17	Pont	6hvy	[57]	1065 p
56a	3-8	Ling	7ap	[56]	1247 p
30	17-20	Newc	6sft	56	1393 p
12	14-14	Nott	10g/s	52	1776
35a	7-12	Wolv	7af	50	2204 bl
44a	5-16	Sout	6af	48	2720 bl

NEW ORDER 3 b f £13424
71	3-12	York	7g/s		1688
76	**1-11**	**HAYD**	8.1gd		2886+
83	**1-8**	**GOOD**	7sft	71	4263*
80	6-17	Asco	8g/f		4777
23	17-19	Donc	10.3sft	78	5201

NEW PROSPECTIVE 5 b g £0
41a	11-15	Sout	5af	[45]	253
0	12-13	Sout	7af	[45]	356

NEW REALM 2 b c £0
50	14-19	Newm	7g/s	5285

NEW SEEKER 4 b c £10850
105	2-4	Asco	8sft	[103]	1420
101	4-28	Asco	7g/f	103	2558
104	8-10	Asco	8gd	[103]	3124
96	4-20	Curr	7g/f	103	3441 BL
98	10-12	Curr	6g/f	[103]	4152

NEW SOUTH WALES 4 b c £11990
114	3-9	Sand	16.4g/f	[105]	2095 t
73	10-13	Asco	20g/f	[105]	2518 t

NEW WISH 4 b g £0
61	5-10	Nott	8.2g/f	66	3579
58	9-16	Redc	7g/f	64	3809
45	12-17	York	7g/f	61	4398
17	11-18	Newc	8g/f	[57]	5017

NEW YORK 2 b f £417
56a	4-13	Wolv	8.5af		111
34	13-17	Yarm	7g/f	[70]	1729
56	10-16	Ling	7g/f	[68]	1982 T
54	3-8	Catt	7g/f	[65]	4440 t
52	5-12	Brig	8fm	[60]	4761 t
44	8-19	Redc	6g/s	[55]	5110 BL

NEW YORK CITY 3 b c £0
33	8-9	Nott	10g/s	4034

NEWCLOSE 3 b g £716
6a	12-16	Sout	7af	46	202
42a	3-13	Wolv	8.5af	[41]	300 T
37a	3-13	Sout	7af	[45]	356 t
38a	3-16	Sout	11af	[40]	445 t
36a	4-12	Wolv	12af	[40]	523 t
21	7-10	Warw	8.1g/s	[40]	1328 t

NEWCORP LAD 4 b g £7361
24	15-17	Thir	8g/s	73	1214
48	4-6	Newc	10.1sft	[71]	1397
55	9-12	Redc	8g/f	[69]	1823

53	8-13	Ches	10.3gd	66	2284
53	7-12	Hami	9.2g/s	62	2832
59	4-9	Hami	9.2gd	60	3132
60	4-18	Pont	8gd	60	3242
64	2-10	Nott	8.2g/f	59	3579
62	4-17	Hayd	8.1gd	59	3759
48	14-15	Carl	7.9g/f	59	4346 VIS
62	3-13	Muss	8g/f	[59]	4554
72	**1-17**	**NEWC**	8fm	59	4867* p
71	4-26	Redc	8fm	65	4926 p
38	7-18	Newc	8g/f	[69]	5017 p

NEWCORR 5 b g £550
27a	10-10	Ling	8ap	40	917
0	14-14	Ling	12ap	[40]	968
27a	6-9	Ling	8ap	[35]	1185
35a	3-6	Ling	8ap	[35]	1292
35	2-5	Brig	8gd	[35]	1546
33a	4-4	Ling	7ap	[35]	1710
33	7-11	Epso	7fm	[32]	3541 P
11	7-14	Chep	10.2g/s	32	3895 p

NEWNHAM 3 ch g £3412
74	2-13	Wind	8.3gd		3828
70	4-11	Wind	10gd		4125
76	2-6	Chep	12.1gd		4486
62	3-10	Muss	12g/s	[80]	5145

NEWS SKY 3 b c £4588
66	15-19	Newb	8gd		1236
76	2-11	Hayd	8.1gd		2885
76	2-15	Wind	10fm		3292
67	3-6	Ripo	10g/f	[80]	3648
75	3-7	Epso	10.1gd	[79]	4911
66	8-18	Bath	10.2gd	[75]	5023 P

NEWSROUND 2 ch c £8151
100	2-13	Newm	6gd		4223
101	**1-10**	**NEWB**	6g/f		4637*
78	7-11	York	6gd	[96]	4998

NEWTON 3 b c £21808
109	**1-7**	**CURR**	7sft		1063*
101	4-5	Curr	7gd		1559
115	6-7	Long	8g/s		1855 bl
105	6-8	Curr	8g/f		1995 bl
42	11-11	Asco	8g/f		2469 VIS

NEWTONIAN 4 ch g £734
66a	3-14	Sout	12af		194
68a	3-6	Sout	12af	70	388
42a	8-15	Ling	12ap	[69]	521
40	4-11	Catt	12sft	[69]	5128

NEWTOWN CHIEF 3 b c £0
22	15-16	Ling	7gd	54	3024
1	13-14	Folk	12gd	49	3383
19a	11-14	Ling	10ap	49	3449 P
0	11-11	Yarm	8g/f	43	3706 BL

NEXT FLIGHT 4 b g £8388
46a	3-9	Sout	11af	[44]	224
35a	6-16	Sout	11af	[45]	445
45a	2-7	Sout	14af	[45]	638
41a	3-8	Sout	11af	[45]	722
45a	2-9	Sout	14af	[40]	849
69	3-9	Muss	12g/f	[45]	1121
55	**1-12**	**NEWC**	14.4sft	48	1396*
51	4-12	Newc	12.4sft	52	1680
53	3-9	Redc	14.1g/f	52	2105
54a	2-13	Sout	14af	45	2494
53	3-13	Newc	16.1sft	50	2685
48	4-12	Muss	16gd	50	2964
33a	6-10	Sout	14af	50	3158
41	8-10	Catt	13.8g/f	48	3669

NEXT TIME 2 b f £930
73	4-13	Donc	5gd		954
64	5-7	Muss	5g/f		1117
25	10-10	York	5g/s		1709
56	7-8	Epso	6fm		2251
62	4-11	Warw	5g/f		2911
45	4-7	Leic	5g/f	63	3343
35	8-10	Ches	5.1g/f	59	4049
27	11-14	Catt	5g/f	55	4437

NEXT TIME AROUND 2 b c £10886
89	**1-15**	**DONC**	5gd	920*

89	3-8	Newm	5g/s		1149
95	5-8	Sand	5g/f		2094
83	12-15	Asco	5g/s		2472
94	4-12	Ayr	5g/s	[97]	4651
35	11-11	York	6gd	[98]	4998

NIAGARA 7 b g £0
22	12-17	Pont	12hvy	69	1064
64	6-9	Yarm	10.1fm	66	2866
7	16-17	Newm	10g/f	64	3238

NIBBLES 2 b g £0
0	13-14	Sout	6af	4127

NICE TUNE 2 b f £3525
83	3-16	Sali	7gd	4329
95	4-6	Good	8g/f	4524
72	7-19	Leic	7gd	5045
87	5-7	Newb	7hvy	5222

NICHOLAS NICKELBY 3 gr g £4331
37a	6-10	Wolv	7af		4
62a	2-12	Wolv	7af		71
65a	2-11	Wolv	9.4af		115
37	7-13	Warw	7.1hvy	[62]	1537
65	6-11	Redc	7g/f	[60]	1822
61	2-9	Leic	8g/f	[60]	1966
1	10-10	York	11.9g/f	60	2405
1	13-15	Thir	8gd	[60]	2688
47a	4-9	Sout	7af	[62]	2801 P
33	3-19	Nott	6.1gd	[58]	3104 p
55	4-12	Newm	6g/f	54	3942 p
55	4-11	Beve	5g/s	[53]	4237
52	2-13	Carl	6.9fm	[53]	4504 p
54	5-10	Ripo	6gd	[52]	4790 p
39	11-16	Bath	8gd	52	4828 p

NICIARA 7 b g £0
13a	8-10	Sout	16af	[32]	307
11a	9-9	Sout	16af	[30]	576

NICK THE SILVER 3 gr c £0
35	14-18	Leic	10g/s	70	1017
57	6-9	Wind	11.6g/f	65	1807
36	10-15	Newb	13.3g/f	62	2311
2	R-14	Sali	12g/s	60	3114
42	11-13	Sali	14.1gd	60	3454
31	12-17	Newm	12g/f	57	3618

NICKEL SUNGIRL 3 b f £0
8a	8-13	Wolv	6af	[45]	30
3a	11-12	Sout	8af	[40]	309

NIETZSCHE 3 b c £3074
61	9-11	Newm	10gd		1148
86	2-16	Wind	10gd		1384
74	5-18	Wind	10g/f		1959
70	2-8	Newb	10hvy	[85]	5226

NIFTY ROY 4 b g £0
0	16-16	Redc	10g/f	45	1821
0	13-14	Carl	7.9m	45	1954
5a	13-15	Sout	6af	35	3000
9	11-14	Hami	6gd	35	3129

NIGHT AIR 3 b g £10269
69	**1-15**	**THIR**	7g/s		1473*
72	5-16	Leic	7g/f	74	1825
80	2-13	Redc	7fm	[74]	4341
81	2-25	Newb	7gd	76	4683

NIGHT CAP 4 ch g £1207
58a	3-14	Ling	6ap	[47]	133
48a	6-14	Ling	6ap	51	328
33a	7-9	Ling	5ap	49	435
11a	11-13	Ling	6ap	47	767 BL
46a	2-12	Ling	6ap	[45]	1075
28a	7-9	Ling	6ap	[45]	1248
46	3-18	Ling	6gd	43	2396
21	17-17	Wind	6fm	43	3643
45	4-15	Ling	6fm	43	3790
27	8-15	Brig	6gd	[45]	4905

NIGHT CLUB QUEEN 2 ch f £0
32	13-14	Wind	6fm	3639
46	9-11	Newb	6g/f	3915
29	14-15	Kemp	6g/f	4357

NIGHT DANCE 12 ch g £0

4 18-20 Newm 8g/f 25 3232

NIGHT DRIVER 5 b g £0

25	13-13	Bath	8sft	66	1542
46	14-18	Good	8g/f	59	1849
0	12-12	Sand	8.1g/s	55	2129
37	11-12	Ling	10g/f	48	2844 e
8	13-13	Folk	9.7g/f	45	3726 P
1a	10-12	Ling	12ap [62]		3819 bl e

NIGHT FROLIC 3 b f £7576

69	1-11	KEMP	8hvy		1514*
68	3-7	Carl	9.3fm	66	1953
55	6-12	Sand	10gd	66	2366
59	6-11	Wind	8.3fm	63	3799
29	9-14	Yarm	8g/s [61]		4252
56	4-13	Chep	8.1hvy	59	4709
60	2-18	Newc	8g/f [58]		5017
59	5-18	Newm	8sft	58	5272

NIGHT GUEST 2 b c £0

73	8-14	Sand	7.1g/s		4069
52	12-13	Kemp	8g/f		4355
11	15-15	Sali	8gd		4851

NIGHT HOUR 2 b c £6182

80	4-14	Kemp	8g/f		4356
90	1-14	SALI	8gd		4852*
81	7-9	Newm	8sft [88]		5099

NIGHT KISS 3 ch f £0

54a	12-12	Ling	8ap	60	17
7	13-14	Kemp	8hvy	64	1512
52	9-19	Sali	7g/f	64	1723
45	10-20	Asco	8g/f	62	1927

NIGHT MAIL 4 b g £0

32a	6-9	Sout	11af	40	331
22	8-15	Carl	9.3fm [40]		4505

NIGHT MARKET 6 ch g £3189

0	11-15	Sout	8af	45	1755
54	1-17	WARW	8.1fm	47	2572*
3	9-10	Pont	10g/f	52	2794
51	7-16	Carl	7.9g/f	52	3650
1	18-19	Brig	9.9sft	51	4145 P
41	6-17	Carl	7.9fm [50]		4506

NIGHT OF JOY 2 b f £16206

64	4-6	Leic	5g/f		2399
82	4-10	Yarm	7fm		2863
86	1-14	NOTT	8.2g/s		4035*
92	1-9	NEWC	8sft	80	4285*
80	9-11	Hayd	8.1fm	87	4387
78	7-14	Donc	8sft	88	5203

NIGHT OUT 2 b f £0

58	9-11	Ripo	5g/s		3258
62	6-13	Wind	6fm		3639
51	10-11	Bath	5g/f		3962

NIGHT PROSPECTOR 4 b c £63800

75	11-20	York	5g/s	92	1683
107	1-12	EPSO	5g/f [89]		2206*
87	10-12	Sand	5g/s [105]		2913
71	12-12	York	5g/s [105]		4060
79	8-9	Donc	5fm [102]		4481 BL

NIGHT SIGHT 7 b g £17313

51	9-11	Donc	12g/f	67	1875
73	2-11	Pont	12g/f	67	2041
71	3-11	Donc	12gd	68	2233
63	4-8	Donc	14.6gd	70	2754
43	4-8	Donc	12g/s	69	3222
74	1-6	PONT	10gd	67	3678*
66	5-14	York	11.9gd	69	4327
74	1-17	THIR	12fm	69	4377*
71	4-14	Asco	12g/f	71	4775
72	5-11	Redc	10fm	70	4931
76	2-16	York	11.9gd	70	4990

NIGHT STORM 3 b f £5162

61a	5-14	Ling	10ap [72]		367
67a	3-11	Ling	8ap [65]		496
66a	3-12	Ling	8ap	66	603
67a	3-8	Ling	7ap [66]		713
66a	6-12	Ling	8ap	66	798
19	15-17	Ling	7g/s [70]		1617

68a 1-11 WOLV 7.1ap [65] 5357*

NIGHT WARRIOR 3 b g £1274

67a	9-13	Ling	10ap	75	26
35a	11-16	Sout	11af	70	97
49a	7-15	Sout	11af	67	196
68a	4-16	Ling	12ap	67	218
63a	10-14	Ling	10ap	67	434
66a	4-9	Wolv	12af	67	467
68a	4-16	Ling	12ap	66	493
67a	2-7	Sout	12af	66	504
56a	7-15	Ling	12ap	65	549

NIGHT WOLF 4 gr g £1036

68a	6-12	Ling	8ap	69	932
0	15-16	Newc	8hvy	69	1036
55	8-15	Brig	8hvy	69	1691
67	3-9	Muss	7.1fm	66	2086
19	8-8	Redc	8gd	66	2550
10	13-13	Newb	7g/f	66	2880
12	16-16	Kemp	7g/f	65	3184
44	8-9	Yarm	6g/f	62	3705
37	5-6	Yarm	6g/f [62]		3710
23	14-16	Ches	7g/f	57	4051
34	11-15	Thir	8fm [52]		4379

NIGHT WORKER 3 b c £0

55	6-15	Wind	6g/s	65	1054
25	10-17	Asco	6sft	63	1417
36	9-18	Wind	8.3sft	60	1647
34	13-20	Newb	7g/f	57	2314
30	9-17	Wind	6fm	53	2975
50	6-16	Ling	7gd	53	3024
58	5-9	Leic	5g/f [50]		3347
17	14-16	Ling	6fm	50	3790
22	10-18	Chep	7.1g/s	50	3900
32	9-15	Bath	8g/s	46	4202
45	7-16	Chep	7.1hvy [45]		4707

NIGHTFALL 2 b c £6734

86	1-8	ASCO	6g/f		3438* T
83	6-6	Wind	6fm		3800 t
71a	11-14	Ling	7ap	86	4177 t

NIGHTS CROSS 3 b c £33323

101	4-5	Hayd	5sft	104	1106
108	3-11	Newb	6gd [104]		1732
111	8-19	Asco	6fm [105]		2468
101	10-14	Asco	6fm [105]		2580
97	7-11	Newb	6gd [107]		3268
97	17-24	Asco	5gd	107	3466
97	3-5	Ches	6.1fm [105]		3636
104	3-10	Curr	6gd [105]		3842 BL
105	3-11	Newm	6g/f	99	3941 VIS
89	8-14	York	5g/s	99	4027 vis
77	10-11	Deau	6hvy [99]		4313 vis
109	1-15	NEWM	5g/f [101]		4879* vis
64	14-17	Curr	6sft [101]		5073 bl

NIGHTSPOT 3 ch g £11099

83	6-13	York	10.4sft	82	1664
83	3-7	Pont	10g/f [80]		2994
85	2-6	Nott	10g/f	80	3578
85	1-14	NEWB	10g/f	81	3961*
62	6-9	Good	12sft	83	4183
47	11-11	Epso	12gd	83	4468

NIKIFOROS 3 b c £537

48	8-9	Asco	7g/f		1929
68	6-15	Newm	8fm		2595
41	8-11	Hayd	8.1gd		2886 P
60a	4-11	Ling	7ap [67]		3331
63	4-10	Chep	7.1gd [65]		3732
55	7-19	Chep	6.1sft	64	4054 T
46	12-20	Ling	6g/f	61	4317

NIMBUS TWOTHOUSAND 3 b f £0

34a	8-11	Wolv	12af [48]		6 bl
38a	6-15	Sout	8af [44]		96 bl
41a	5-15	Sout	8af	45	1028 bl

NIMELLO 7 b g £18991

79a	2-16	Sout	7af [78]		161
89a	1-10	WOLV	9.4af	78	278+
78a	9-13	Ling	10ap	85	433
68a	9-12	Wolv	8.5af	85	836
91a	1-8	WOLV	8.5af	84	1219*
51	8-18	Asco	8sft	77	1423

83	1-6	EPSO	8.5g/s	75	3042*
61	13-16	Nott	8.2g/s	78	4036
11	13-14	Newb	8hvy	78	5227

NINA FONTENAIL 3 gr f £1164

57	9-10	Kemp	11.1gd		1140
3	12-17	Bath	10.2sft	50	1541
43	14-17	Chep	8.1gd [45]		2117
34	5-8	Chep	12.1gd [45]		2368
63	4-7	Bath	11.7g/f [40]		3967
45a	2-12	Ling	10ap	40	4113
42	5-17	Warw	8.1g/s [45]		4992

NINAH 3 b f £0

29	16-17	Warw	7.1sft	71	1526
24	11-12	Chep	6.1gd	68	2118
31	10-11	Chep	8.1g/f [64]		2627
34	17-18	Bath	5.7g/f	58	4412
43	10-16	Bath	8gd	53	4828
24	15-19	Bath	5.7sft	48	5176
29a	8-11	Wolv	8.6ap [45]		5356

NINAHS INTUITION 2 b c £387

60	4-15	Warw	5g/s		1325
71	4-6	Warw	5hvy		1531
58	8-8	Kemp	5g/f		2858

NINE RED 3 b f £1660

54	10-20	Newb	7g/f	64	1761
56	9-12	Sand	7.1g/f	61	2098
35	9-14	Sali	8fm	58	2423
56a	2-8	Sout	7af	58	2723
19	15-16	Brig	7sft [59]		4144
56	9-14	Warw	7.1gd [59]		4275

NINJA STORM 2 b c £267

72	4-11	Wind	5gd		3160
74	5-10	Wind	5fm		3476
68a	6-10	Ling	5ap		3743
65	7-7	Sand	5sft	75	4065

NIOBES WAY 3 b f £2319

70	7-13	Kemp	10g/f		3038
61	4-7	Asco	8gd		3469
69	3-5	Sand	10g/s		3894
69	2-11	Good	14gd [66]		5029
44	6-8	Bath	17.2sft	66	5175

NIP NIP 2 b f £0

46	9-11	Sali	7gd		3883
30	8-8	Bath	5.7g/s		4198

NIPPING 2 b f £7711

97	3-7	Chan	6gd		4957

NIPPY NIPPER 3 b f £0

0	18-18	Leic	7gd		4698
9a	10-12	Wolv	8.6ap		5230 T
9	14-17	Yarm	8g/s		5348 t

NISR 7 b g £1788

80	2-12	Newm	6gd	73	4229

NISTAKI 3 ch c £2897

75	4-13	Folk	7g/s		1270
68	6-12	York	7.9g/f		2410
63	4-11	Beve	8.5gd		2656
75	2-8	Redc	6g/f	70	3808

NITE OWL FIZZ 5 b g £426

28a	9-13	Wolv	8.5af [55]		46
52a	5-11	Wolv	8.5af [55]		128
45a	4-10	Wolv	8.5af [55]		311
49a	2-10	Wolv	8.5af [55]		398
38a	7-12	Wolv	8.5af	50	479
49a	4-8	Wolv	8.5af [48]		630

NITEOWL DREAM 4 ch f £0

39	4-15	Beve	5.7g/f [58]		1944
8a	13-16	Sout	7af	55	2335
19	13-14	Leic	8g/f	55	2402
21a	12-15	Sout	8af [48]		2803

NITEOWL EXPRESS 3 b f £0

37a	8-15	Sout	6af		795
40a	6-7	Wolv	6af		863
26a	5-6	Sout	8af [40]		1203
37a	4-9	Wolv	6af [40]		1803 BL
5	10-19	Nott	6.1gd [36]		3104

13	9-15	Newc	7gd	[36]	3426

NITEOWL LAD 2 ch c £1110
42	7-10	Beve	5sft		1632
0	19-20	Newc	6sft		2682
67	2-10	Carl	5g/f		3227
65	5-10	Pont	5gd		3457

NIVERNAIS 5 b g £5698
59	13-20	Wind	6g/s	81	1255
75	7-16	Good	6gd	80	2023
69	9-10	Sand	5gd	80	2189
70	8-9	Sali	5fm	77	2420
73	6-11	Newb	6g/f	75	2878
63	7-17	Newb	7g/f	73	3257 t
70	6-14	Newb	5.2fm	71	3628
69	3-15	Sali	6gd	71	3888
79	1-17	WIND	6gd	70	4126*
75	5-19	Kemp	6fm	75	4394

NO CHANCE TO DANCE 4 b c £949
13	14-14	Nott	10g/s	55	1777
43	10-20	Yarm	8fm	50	2149 T
45	4-14	Leic	8g/f	48	2402 t
51	3-12	Hami	9.2g/s	46	2832 t
44	6-20	Newm	8g/f	48	3232 t
44	6-13	Folk	9.7g/f	47	3726 t
37	7-17	Hami	9gd	45	4008 t
24	9-15	Yarm	10.1g/s	[45]	5122 t

NO COMMISSION 2 b g £9157
18	9-9	Newc	5sft		962
50	5-6	Hami	5gd		1503
69	4-7	Ayr	6g/f		1893
58	7-10	Hayd	6g/s		2228
64a	5-10	Sout	6af		2382
81	4-5	Hami	6g/s		2829
63	8-12	Carl	5gd		2933
77	2-7	Ayr	6gd		3148
75	1-6	HAMI	6fm	70	3245*
57	11-12	Catt	7g/f	76	3351
66	5-9	Ches	7sft	75	4074
58	9-19	Carl	5.9g/f	73	4344
19	13-14	Hami	6sft	71	4692

NO DILEMMA 3 ch g £0
25	13-14	Wind	10g/s		1055

NO FRONTIER 5 ch m £0
55a	9-11	Ling	8ap	71	80 T

NO GROUSE 4 b g £2883
59a	11-16	Sout	7af	76	419
70a	5-12	Wolv	8.5af	73	632
61a	9-12	Wolv	7af	71	840
73	7-18	Catt	7gd	75	998
75	3-7	Muss	7.1g/f	[75]	1094
58	12-16	York	7g/f	73	2057
0	15-15	Pont	6g/f	72	2280
70	12-17	Carl	7.9gd	72	2672 P
71	7-18	Catt	7g/f	72	2848 p
59	7-12	Catt	7g/f	[70]	3017 p
62	5-12	Ches	7.6fm	68	3634 p
55	14-16	Redc	7g/f	68	3809 p
64	5-17	York	5af	64	4398 p
65	4-15	Beve	7.5g/f	63	4719 p
68	2-19	Newc	7g/f	63	5014 p
59	5-16	Catt	7sft	63	5130 p

NO REFUGE 4 ch c £11633
96	3-8	Bade	14sft	[94]	4425
106	1-7	COLO	15sft	[94]	4838* BL
99	18-34	Newm	18sft	107	5135 BL

NO TIME 3 b c £29240
63a	14-15	Sout	5af	90	64
78a	8-13	Ling	6ap	85	235
82a	6-14	Ling	6ap	83	292
70a	6-12	Wolv	6af	83	361
80a	6-14	Ling	7ap	80	518
84a	2-10	Ling	5ap	78	567
91a	1-10	LING	5ap	80	692*
105a	1-10	LING	5ap	[85]	883+
82	11-20	Donc	5gd	98	927
80	10-16	Muss	5gd	95	1120
53	19-19	Thir	6g/f	92	1767
62	12-12	Epso	5g/f	87	4908

NOAHS ARK 3 b f £7679
102	2-11	Curr	9g/f		3322

NOBBLER 2 br c £0
69	7-14	Chep	8.1gd		4484
56	11-15	York	7.9gd		5002
72	6-16	Yarm	10.1g/s		5352

NOBLE CALLING 7 b h £2511
45a	10-14	Ling	10ap	[60]	477
52	3-8	Bath	17.2fm	52	2035
43	7-12	Newb	10g/f	52	2354
57	3-14	Bath	18.2fm	52	2417
59	2-12	Warw	15g/f	52	2908

NOBLE CYRANO 9 ch g £0
18a	6-10	Sout	11af	35	330
12a	7-8	Sout	11af	[35]	420

NOBLE DESERT 2 b f £0
41a	8-10	Ling	6ap		258
56	7-12	York	7g/s		1688
37	5-8	Yarm	6gd		3873
19a	10-14	Sout	6af	49	4130
14	12-15	Carl	7.9fm	[45]	4507
16	7-12	Brig	8gd	[40]	4904
27	12-17	Warw	8.1g/s	[40]	4992

NOBLE DUTY 2 b c £4854
86	2-5	Newb	8g/f		4640
83	3-11	York	7.9gd		5003

NOBLE LOCKS 5 ch g £2301
58a	5-11	Wolv	7af	65	241
74a	1-10	WOLV	6af	65	246*
36a	8-10	Wolv	6af	73	345
37a	14-15	Sout	6af	72	550
40a	11-12	Wolv	7af	70	704
25a	12-13	Wolv	6af	68	1221
60a	4-11	Wolv	6af	66	1337
15a	13-13	Wolv	6af	65	2053

NOBLE MIND 3 b g £1889
79	2-14	Wind	8.3g/s		2622
66	7-14	Warw	7.1g/f		2907
50	9-15	Wind	10fm		3292
56a	3-10	Sout	8af	[68]	4042
44a	11-13	Wolv	8.6ap	[64]	5336

NOBLE MOUNT 3 b g £442
60a	5-13	Ling	6ap		364
62a	7-11	Wolv	6af		481
38	11-13	Folk	5sft		1575
45	3-13	Hami	5gd	55	2181
30a	7-8	Sout	6af	59	3092
31a	12-14	Ling	7ap	[55]	5294

NOBLE PENNY 5 b m £1105
34	10-19	Redc	8sft	50	1661
46	6-18	Nott	8.2g/s	50	1778
51	2-18	Donc	7g/f	48	2080
34	10-12	Donc	7gd	49	2235
42	4-13	Redc	8gd	49	2552
43	6-11	Ripo	8gd	49	2986 P
48	5-17	Newc	7g/s	46	3700

NOBLE PHILOSOPHER 4 ch g £0
0	7-7	Sout	11af	[45]	1589

NOBLE PURSUIT 6 b g £3167
44a	4-14	Sout	8af	58	62
57a	4-14	Sout	8af	56	165
27a	7-9	Sout	11af	[56]	204 p
60a	2-10	Sout	8af	55	502
56a	2-8	Sout	8af	[57]	577
33a	7-9	Sout	7af	[57]	639
37a	7-12	Wolv	9.4af	55	747
60a	3-9	Wolv	8.5af	[53]	811
40a	5-9	Ling	12ap	53	842
37a	5-10	Sout	8af	[53]	868
36a	7-12	Sout	8af	[53]	905
48	10-14	Thir	7fm	53	2466
57	2-15	Thir	8g/s	[53]	2688
45	4-16	Beve	7.5gd	49	2891
32	13-18	Pont	10g/f	50	2988
51	3-15	Newc	7gd	[50]	3426
38	12-16	Carl	7.9g/f	50	3650
40	9-17	Thir	8g/s	50	3830
32	8-12	Newc	8sft	[49]	4284

NOBRATINETTA 5 b m £425
3	13-13	Hayd	14sft	77	1109
78	4-12	Thir	16gd	76	1637
52	15-18	Nott	14.1g/s	75	1772 P

NOCATEE 2 b g £4163
28a	9-14	Sout	8af	[57]	95
41a	10-14	Sout	8af	[49]	226
43a	3-9	Wolv	9.4af	[45]	314 VIS
51a	3-9	Sout	11af	45	608
42a	4-10	Sout	11af	45	658 P
53	3-10	Nott	14.1hvy	49	1612
59	1-14	REDC	14.1g/f	52	2123* p

NOD N A WINK 6 b g £0
0	11-11	Ling	8ap		343

NODINA 2 br c £0
40	12-14	Warw	6.1g/f		4422
72	5-10	Ling	5g/f		4893
53	10-13	Wind	6g/f		5047

NODS NEPHEW 7 b g £2036
51a	2-10	Sout	8af	48	792
25a	7-10	Sout	8af	[52]	868
57	2-17	Beve	8.5g/s	[58]	1160
58	2-7	Warw	10.9g/s	[58]	1326

NODS STAR 3 ch f £592
54	5-11	Newc	8sft		1279
46	9-20	Donc	7g/s		1518
31	9-12	Ripo	8g/f		1978
27a	7-15	Sout	12af	47	2503
36	7-12	Beve	9.9gd	45	2893
46	3-13	Redc	14.1gd	42	4249
37	7-20	Catt	15.8gd	45	4965

NOFAS MAGIC 4 b f £576
53	3-8	Newc	12.4hvy		1038
71	8-13	Wind	10gd	[80]	1381

NOK TWICE 3 b g £642
66	3-18	Galw	7g/f	62	3656

NOMINATE 3 b g £0
1a	11-12	Wolv	12af	60	244 T

NONNO CARLO 4 ch c £60915
112	3-7	Capa	10g/s		1858

NOODLES 2 b c £1776
57	8-10	Hayd	6g/s		2228
74	2-9	Carl	5.9gd		2671 VIS
65	8-15	Pont	6gd		3239 vis
29	10-10	Thir	5fm	73	3607
34	16-18	Ripo	6g/s	[69]	3939 BL

NOORA 3 ch f £9354
76	2-6	Ches	7gd		1587
56	10-12	Good	7g/f		1846
72	2-9	Wind	7gd	[80]	3121
69	4-11	Sali	7gd	[75]	3884
72	3-8	Sand	8.1g/s	[72]	4101
75a	1-11	LING	8ap	[69]	4977*

NOORAIN 2 ch f £2280
78	3-9	Wind	5g/f		2795
69	4-12	Bath	5.7gd		3141
80	2-7	Thir	7g/f		3412
38	7-7	Newm	7g/f	80	3753

NOPEKAN 4 b g £0
0	13-13	Asco	12fm	94	2582
48	7-9	Hayd	10.5gd	[89]	2901
65	8-8	Ches	12.3fm	80	3637
50	7-13	Nott	10gd	73	3992 P

NOPLEAZINU 4 ch f £0
0	5-6	Yarm	6g/s		4586
50	10-13	Nott	8.2g/f		4847
51a	6-13	Wolv	9.5ap		5290

NORCROFT 2 b c £6067
80	2-4	Folk	5g/s		1077
77	1-11	NOTT	5.1gd		1237*
53	6-6	Asco	5sft		1422
51	7-7	Nott	6.1sft		1738
71	8-9	Asco	6gd	85	3127
74	7-11	Newm	6g/f	80	3614

NORDHOCK 2 g r f £3273 and surrounding entries:

75	4-8	Sand	7.1g/s	77	4100 BL
63	11-14	Epso	6g/f	75	4471 bl
36	12-13	Newm	8fm	73	4725 bl
69a	3-12	Wolv	7.1ap	[69]	5158
0	9-9	Newm	10g/s	[69]	5281

NORDHOCK 2 g r f £3273

56	6-7	Newm	6g/f		2733
63	1-8	YARM	6fm		2865*
52	6-9	Brig	7g/f	63	3297
61	3-7	Newm	7g/f	60	3753

NORDIC DANCER 2 b f £0

31a	11-15	Ling	7ap	[60]	52

NORDWIND 3 b c £34170

82	3-9	Hayd	8.1g/f		1882
75	4-14	Hayd	8.1g/s		2231
82a	1-9	LING	8ap		3195*
83	1-6	NOTT	10g/f	75	3578*
82	2-9	Sand	10g/f	77	3862
86	1-11	EPSO	12gd	79	4468*
97	1-12	GOOD	11gd	83	4749*
77	12-15	Leic	11.8gd	93	5043

NORMA SPEAKMAN 4 ch f £0

13	11-11	Thir	12g/f	48	2217
33	6-10	Beve	9.9gd	45	2510
0	20-20	Catt	12g/f	43	2850
25	10-14	Catt	12g/f	[40]	3668

NORSE DANCER 4 b c £343620

113	4-10	Sand	8.1g/s	[117]	1349
120	3-15	Newb	8g/f	[117]	1758
62	14-16	Asco	8g/f	[117]	2470
116	4-12	Sand	10g/s	[117]	2916 BL
113	4-11	Good	8fm	[116]	3533 bl
117	1-12	SALI	8gd	[115]	3886+
123	2-9	York	10.4gd	[116]	4002
122	2-8	Leop	10g/f	[116]	4571
79	10-11	Asco	8g/f	[121]	4801
113	4-11	Newm	14g/f	[121]	5136

NORTH BY NORTHEAST 5 ch g £0

11a	11-11	Sout	8af	62	255 p

NORTH LANDING 4 b g £0

14a	7-7	Sout	7af	[45]	1590
16	9-9	Newc	10.1g/s	[40]	3702

NORTH LIGHT 3 b c £1088680

119	1-10	YORK	10.4g/s		1685*
123	1-14	EPSO	12fm	[115]	2254+
122	2-10	Curr	12g/f	[115]	2822
121	5-19	Long	12g/f	[115]	4956

NORTH POINT 6 b g £259

29	13-16	Brig	11.9fm	55	1693 P
45	8-8	Bath	17.2fm	51	2035 BL
46	4-7	Brig	11.9fm	48	2836 bl

NORTH SEA 3 b f £0

24	7-10	Folk	9.7sft		977
62	7-13	Newm	8fm		2595

NORTH SHORE 2 b c £0

70	6-15	Newb	7g/f		2876
89	5-11	Donc	8fm		4462
52	9-11	Wind	6g/s		4941

NORTHANGER ABBEY 2 ch c £0

44	16-16	Sali	7g/s		3111
63	13-15	Sand	7.1g/f		3337
65	5-11	Bath	10.2gd		4825
44	12-15	Pont	10g/f		4933

NORTHERN DESERT 5 b g £0

53	10-10	Hayd	8.1g/s	96	4767
34	18-19	York	7.9gd	90	4987
64	12-20	Donc	7sft	82	5367

NORTHERN GAMES 5 b g £15227

34	13-18	Thir	8g/f	59	1972
39	13-14	Thir	7fm	57	2466
64	1-14	CATT	6g/f	63	3352* bl
49	4-8	Carl	6.9g/f	[59]	3654 bl
65	2-13	Warw	6.1gd	59	4272 bl
60	4-18	Catt	7g/f	59	4438 bl
69	2-18	Ayr	7.2sft	61	4622 bl
80	1-19	AYR	6sft	65	5069* bl
84	1-16	CATT	7sft	71	5130* bl
52	15-16	Redc	6sft	79	5304 bl

NORTHERN NYMPH 4 b g £6104

76a	4-12	Sout	14af	77	173
78a	2-10	Sout	16af	76	743
76a	3-8	Wolv	16.2af	80	837
47	10-14	Donc	18gd	77	926
73	8-13	Hayd	14sft	75	1109 T
62	5-18	Nott	14.1sft	70	1469
6	6-11	Beve	16.2sft	68	1629
68	2-10	Hayd	14g/f	66	1923
68	3-4	Hayd	14g/s	68	2229
69	4-8	Hayd	14gd	66	2887
57	7-8	Hayd	14g/s	66	3140
66	5-15	Ches	15.9g/f	65	4512
61	5-20	Bath	17.2gd	64	4824
68	2-20	York	13.9gd	62	5004

NORTHERN REVOQUE 2 b f £0

12	5-5	Donc	5g/s		1517
13	13-16	Ripo	6g/f		1780
21	13-17	Donc	6g/f		2424
9a	5-6	Sout	5af		3093
10	7-7	Ripo	6g/s		3259 BL
35	7-13	Catt	7g/f		3349 bl
43	4-15	Catt	7sft		3930
47	7-11	Ches	7sft		4072 P
2	16-17	Redc	7g/s	[45]	5105
42	7-8	Ayr	8sft	[45]	5273

NORTHERN SECRET 2 b f £796

69	7-15	Newm	7fm		3005
72	3-12	Folk	7gd		3908
50	7-14	Thir	7g/s		4204
58	15-17	Ling	7g/f	70	4894

NORTHERN SPIRIT 3 b g £3841

40	9-16	Nott	10gd	55	1240
42	6-10	Nott	14.1hvy	53	1612
33	9-15	Ripo	12.3g/f	50	1785
51	3-14	Redc	14.1g/f	46	2123 P
37	11-20	Beve	16.2gd	48	3312 p
53	1-10	BEVE	12.1g/f	48	3499* BL

NORTHERN SPLENDOUR 2 ch c £1013£

91	3-9	Newm	6g/f		2531
93	1-10	REDC	6g/s		2959*
103	1-7	NOTT	8.2gd		3991*

NORTHERN SUMMIT 3 b g £0

0	12-12	Catt	12gd	40	1000
12a	6-8	Sout	12af	40	1444
0	6-6	Wolv	12af	[35]	1673

NORTHERN SVENGALI 8 b g £0

3	16-16	Ayr	5g/f	40	2029 t
5	13-13	Hami	5g/f	36	2320 t P
34	8-10	Hami	5g/s	[36]	2476 tp
45	5-8	Hami	5g/s	36	2830 tp
44	5-10	Muss	5g/s	36	2968 tp
37	6-14	Hami	6gd	44	3129 tp

NORTHSIDE LODGE 5 b g £12931

83a	4-13	Ling	10ap	83	134
87a	2-14	Ling	10ap	83	452
87a	2-13	Ling	10ap	85	519
83a	12-14	Ling	10ap	87	625
92a	3-14	Ling	10ap	87	758
0	10-14	Epso	10.1hvy	83	1296
42	10-12	Ches	10.3gd	80	1586
79	3-14	Leic	10g/f	77	1828
75	5-15	Kemp	10fm	77	2067
79	2-11	Good	12gd	76	2538
56	11-15	Newm	12g/f	78	3066
55	7-10	Ripo	12.3g/s	76	3261
55	11-14	Brig	11.9fm	75	3674
71	5-17	Thir	12fm	70	4377
56	9-19	Pont	10g/s	69	5148

NORTON 7 ch g £16380

53	21-24	Donc	8gd	98	951
95	5-27	Newb	8gd	96	1231
85	7-16	Epso	10.1hvy	96	1296
88	4-14	Kemp	8hvy	93	1512
93	7-31	Asco	8g/f	90	2489
77	8-13	Sali	8gd	90	2662 VIS
92	3-8	Sand	7.1g/s	90	3891
99	1-10	SAND	8.1g/s	90	4067*
31	14-14	Asco	8g/f	94	4813
82	11-13	Newm	8g/f	94	5284

NORTON ROSE 2 ch f £0

1	18-20	Newc	6sft		2682

NORWEGIAN 3 b c £3730

61a	5-6	Wolv	8.5af		468
69a	1-6	SOUT	8af		503*
64a	4-10	Ling	10ap	65	676
69a	3-12	Ling	8ap	65	798 VIS
32	15-18	Thir	8g/f	65	1769 vis

NOSSENKO 2 b f £1163

33a	9-10	Ling	6ap		258
59a	2-14	Ling	6ap		449

NOSTRADAMUS 5 b h £0

67	10-10	Asco	16.2gd	93	3776

NOT AMUSED 4 ch g £0

0	13-13	Bath	11.7sft	77	5174

NOTA BENE 2 b c £19204

86	2-11	Sali	6g/f		3863
88	1-13	WIND	6g/s		5047*
99	1-11	NEWM	6sft	[84]	5270*

NOTABILITY 2 b c £5572

59	8-11	Newm	8gd		3925
85	2-14	Yarm	7gd		4611
90	1-16	BATH	8gd		5019*

NOTABLE GUEST 3 b c £7806

71	5-14	Wind	10g/s		1259
94	3-11	Newm	10g/f	84	3236
86	1-8	HAMI	9.2g/f	[87]	3592*

NOTHING DAUNTED 7 ch g £0

9	12-14	Newc	6g/s	[55]	2730

NOTHING MATTERS 2 b f £0

38a	5-12	Ling	8ap	[43]	78
31a	6-8	Ling	8ap	[40]	326
25a	9-11	Ling	8ap	[40]	408
21a	10-15	Sout	7af	[40]	462

NOTJUSTAPRETTYFACE 2 b f £10722

88	1-8	KEMP	5g/f		2858*
96	4-12	Newb	5.2g/f		3956
99	4-8	York	5g/s		4059
62	10-12	Ayr	5g/s	[100]	4651

NOTNOWCATO 2 b c £2840

79	2-13	Warw	7.1g/f		4416
84	3-11	Sali	7gd		4853

NOUL 4 ch g £4848

54a	2-12	Wolv	8.5af	[72]	47
73a	1-11	SOUT	8af	69	186* bl
52a	9-12	Wolv	9.4af	73	382 bl
73a	2-6	Wolv	9.4af	[73]	423 bl
62a	5-6	Sout	12af	72	683 bl
59	5-19	Donc	10.3gd	60	924 bl
29	5-15	Newc	12.4hvy	59	1034 P
28	15-15	Hami	9.2gd	58	1388 p

NOUNOU 3 b c £11066

55	7-16	Newc	7g/f		966
62a	5-6	Wolv	7af		1321
60	7-16	Bath	10.2g/f		1790
62	8-14	Chep	7.1gd	65	2199
67	1-5	FOLK	9.7g/s	60	3914*
60	5-13	Folk	12gd	63	4119
70	1-14	EPSO	12gd	63	4910*
66	5-12	Brig	11.9sft	68	5093

NOUVEAU RICHE 3 ch f £10398

81	2-10	Good	8gd		2224
79	3-11	Sali	8fm		2419
79	1-17	WIND	8.3fm		3480*
81	2-5	Sali	8gd		3885
80	3-13	Sand	8.1gd	77	4607
78	5-7	Hayd	10.5sft	77	4781

NOVA TOR 2 b f £21654

68a	1-7	SOUT	5af		1029*
73	1-11	THIR	5gd		1634*

65 11-12 Beve 5g/f 2165
78 4-10 Ches 5.1g/s 2744
86 1-8 CHES 5.1g/f 77 3082*
69 5-8 Ayr 6g/f 81 3303
83 4-7 York 5g/f 83 3432
64 8-9 Ches 6.1fm 80 3632
88 1-13 NEWM 5g/f 79 3943+
89 3-7 Sand 5sft 85 4065
77 11-13 Muss 5g/f 87 4551
93 6-10 Curr 6.3gd [87] 4737 p
68 10-12 Newm 6gd 87 4882 P

NOVELINA 2 b f £557
61a 3-13 Wolv 8.6ap 5355

NOW AND AGAIN 5 b g £1249
48a 3-7 Sout 8af 334
50a 4-12 Sout 7af 416
46a 3-7 Wolv 9.4af 509
43a 3-12 Wolv 7.1ap [48] 5229

NOW LOOK AWAY 2 b f £0
34 8-8 Hayd 10.5g/f 1489

NOW LOOK HERE 7 b g £0
75a 6-15 Sout 5af 79 64
61a 13-16 Sout 5af 77 171 bl
66a 11-16 Sout 5af 77 205

NOWADAY 2 b c £0
41 7-7 Newc 6g/s 2774
66 6-8 Beve 7.5gd 3311
70 6-11 Beve 7.5g/s 3851
55 8-14 Thir 7g/s 4207

NOWELL HOUSE 7 ch g £287
63a 6-13 Wolv 9.4af 77 127
63a 5-8 Sout 16af 77 140
69a 3-8 Wolv 14.8af 75 277
50a 6-6 Sout 12af 70 388
81 6-19 York 11.9sft 82 1668

NUFOOS 2 b f £26524
85 3-10 York 5g/s 1709
89 1-7 LEIC 6g/f 1964*
83 11-17 Asco 6gd 2553
74 8-10 Newm 6fm 3003
97 1-10 BEVE 5sft 85 4258*
101 3-9 Ayr 6sft [94] 4684
100 2-11 York 6gd [98] 4998

NUIT SOMBRE 3 b g £770
31a 13-13 Wolv 8.5af 84 44 bl
72 13-17 Sand 8.1g/s 83 1351
72 5-15 Warw 8.1sft 81 1530
72 4-10 Hayd 8.1gd 79 2242
61 6-8 Donc 8g/f 76 2425

NUKHBAH 3 b f £978
78 3-18 Wind 8.3g/s 1258
67 4-14 Warw 8.1sft [70] 1527
71 5-5 Ayr 9.1g/f [70] 2025
16 13-14 Wind 10gd 66 2617
8 14-14 Chep 8.1g/s 65 3090

NUMERO DUE 2 b c £707
63 6-15 Pont 10g/f 4933
68 3-5 Nott 8.2hvy 5186

NUMITAS 4 b c £0
92 8-17 Ches 18.7gd 91 1569
45 23-29 Asco 20g/f 89 2471

NUMPTY 3 b g £0
22a 5-6 Sout 6af 49 316 t
36a 5-11 Sout 6af 45 591 t
49a 11-13 Ling 10ap [40] 715 t
22 12-16 Nott 10gd 40 1240 t
0 10-11 Newc 8sft 40 1395 t
18a 6-10 Sout 7af [40] 1842 t

NUNKI 3 ch g £9646
79 3-15 Leic 10g/s 1358
89 1-10 HAYD 10.5g/f 1922*
77 7-8 York 10.4g/f 87 2406
89 9-11 Epso 10.1gd [87] 4467
89 4-15 Nott 10gd 85 4860 VIS
86 3-8 Nott 10hvy 85 5187 vis

NUTS FOR YOU 2 b f £4568
54a 9-11 Ling 8ap 21
62a 2-10 Sout 8af 162
72 1-14 CHEP 10.2gd 61 4487*
48a 11-12 Wolv 12.2ap 69 4924

NUTTY TIMES 2 ch f £1563
64a 2-4 Wolv 5af 938
59a 3-7 Sout 5af 1029
60 3-10 Bath 5g/s 1097
48 13-15 Wind 5gd 1380
0 7-7 Sout 6af 1751
44 8-8 Bath 5g/f 2977

NUZOOA 3 b f £19815
95 1-11 NEWB 10g/f 2349*
90 5-9 Newm 12g/f [92] 3278
81 7-11 Epso 10.1gd [92] 4467 BL
99 1-6 GOOD 12gd 90 5028*

NUZZLE 3 b f £5731
40a 6-7 Ling 10ap 62 16
58a 3-11 Wolv 9.4af [58] 115 vis
51a 1-13 SOUT 8af [58] 199* vis
27a 7-7 Sout 8af 58 332 vis
7a 12-12 Wolv 9.4af 58 427 vis
28a 10-14 Ling 10ap 53 498
45 5-10 Bath 11.7gd 50 1399
29a 11-14 Ling 10ap 50 1618
53 2-11 Hayd 10.5g/f 47 1884
34 6-12 Bath 10.2fm 47 2036
23 10-12 Newb 10g/f 46 2354
45 3-6 Bath 8fm 46 2414 vis
47 7-8 Bath 8fm 45 2665 vis
47 3-14 Pont 8g/f 45 2993 vis
48 11-15 Ches 10.3g/f 45 3099
26 9-11 Bath 10.2g/f 44 3373
37 9-18 Kemp 10g/f [45] 4791
38a 5-13 Wolv 8.6ap [45] 5232 vis

NYRAMBA 3 b f £23250
109 2-8 Newb 7gd [109] 1233
109 5-13 Long 8g/s [109] 1854
109 5-9 Chan 8g/s [109] 2306
106 2-12 Good 7fm [107] 3564
83 5-12 Pont 8g/s [107] 3971
98 5-15 Donc 7fm [106] 4479

NYSAEAN 5 b h £87003
109 5-10 Sain 10g/s [114] 833
112 4-8 Long 10gd [114] 1061
107 5-12 Kemp 10g/f [115] 1139
115 2-11 Sand 10g/s [112] 1350
116 1-7 CURR 10g/s [112] 1560*
113 3-6 Curr 10.5g/f[112] 2004
107 4-9 Sand 10g/s [114] 2128
103 5-8 Wind 10g/s [114] 4220
113 3-4 Long 12sft [114] 4568
97 6-8 Newb 11g/f [112] 4639

OAKLEY ABSOLUTE 2 ch c £0
19 11-11 Chep 7.1hvy 4703
61 7-15 Sali 8gd 4851
57 10-16 Newb 8hvy 5220

OAKLEY RAMBO 5 br g £4673
81 5-17 Leic 7g/s 80 1020
67 14-17 Sand 8.1g/s 79 1351
65 6-18 Asco 8sft 79 1423
82 2-14 Ling 7sft 77 1624
58 14-16 Good 7g/f 80 1817
64 6-7 Chep 8.1gd [80] 2116
65 7-7 Good 7gd [80] 2374
63 7-12 Chep 8.1g/s 76 3898
60 8-13 Kemp 7sft 76 4030
48a 12-12 Wolv 7.1ap [66] 5006

OASES 4 ch g £2688
53a 11-12 Ling 8ap 57 17
51a 10-15 Ling 7ap 59 50
26a 8-9 Wolv 7af 58 940 e
61 2-15 Folk 6sft 58 976
39 8-10 Hami 6gd 60 1391
34 6-10 Warw 6.1hvy 60 1533
39 7-11 Folk 6sft 60 1578
37 18-19 Redc 7g/f 58 1820
38 13-18 Donc 6gd 55 2752
56 3-16 Newm 7gd 54 3184 vis

57 5-19 Chep 7.1gd 54 3401 vis
51 6-18 Catt 7g/f 54 3670 vis
39 10-15 Catt 7sft 54 3933 vis
56 4-14 Beve 7.5g/s 52 4241 P
49 9-20 Leic 7gd 51 5046 p
43a 5-12 Wolv 7.1ap [51] 5358 p

OASIS STAR 3 b f £43942
88 1-20 NEWM 7g/f 75 1186*
88 1-15 CHES 7.6gd 81 1583+
88 5-18 Hayd 8.1g/f 86 1919
91 1-5 SAND 7.1gd [86] 2362*
94 2-9 Newm 7fm 87 3006
87 7-8 Nott 8.2g/f 89 3421
94 5-14 Newb 7g/f [89] 4638
89 5-13 Asco 6.5g/f 89 4773
80 9-16 Newm 7sft 92 5101

OASIS WAY 2 b f £0
70 5-15 Folk 7gd 4114
73 5-14 Chep 8.1gd 4484
65 16-26 Newb 6.5g/f 4679
65 6-13 Wind 8.3g/s 72 4940
68 7-14 Newb 7sft 70 5193

OATCAKE 2 ch f £688
74 3-21 Donc 6sft 5368

OBAY 3 ch c £11080
70 4-14 Wind 10g/s 1055
80 1-6 THIR 12g/s 1213*
86 4-10 Good 11g/f 85 1865
88 2-6 Newb 12g/f 84 2353
79 3-6 Wind 11.6fm [84] 2972 BL
85 2-4 Hami 12.1g/s 84 3881
26 13-17 Nott 14.1g/s 85 4647

OBE BOLD 3 b f £13700
54a 4-4 Wolv 5af [65] 1338
51a 3-8 Sout 6af 65 1441
46 11-13 Newc 5gd 60 1873
54 2-6 Ripo 6gd [60] 1975
59 8-10 Leic 6gd [57] 2137
42 8-10 Hayd 5g/s 57 2227
69a 1-9 SOUT 6af [54] 2493*
54 5-10 Carl 5gd 61 2675
55 4-5 Hami 6gd [57] 3131
61 3-12 Catt 5g/f 57 3193
51 8-12 Donc 5gd 59 3599
69 1-8 REDC 6g/f 59 3808*
63 7-14 Ches 6.1g/f 66 4048
31 14-20 Ripo 6gd 68 4278
64 4-9 Pont 6g/f 67 4627
15 12-15 Hami 6sft 67 4696 t
47a 8-13 Wolv 6ap [64] 5327

OBE GOLD 2 b c £200423
71 3-10 Beve 5sft 1632
91 1-10 SALI 5g/f 1716*
79 4-8 Epso 6fm 2251
92 2D-9 San 6gd 2823
85 4-8 Newb 7g/f 3267
1 U-8 Good 6fm 3566 VIS
93 3-5 Hami 6g/s [97] 3877
98 3-4 Donc 6fm [89] 4529
104 1-12 NEWM 6gd 90 4882* vis
105 1-24 REDC 6fm [89] 4928* vis
105 2-29 Newm 6gd 5087 vis
103 5-9 Mais 6sft [89] 5312 vis

OBE ONE 4 b g £7197
62 9-16 Muss 5g/f 77 1120
64 16-30 Newm 6g/f 75 1481
54 11-19 Thir 6g/f 72 1767
57 6-11 Ripo 6gd 69 1977
74 4-15 Muss 5fm 69 2084
62 8-11 Ches 5.1gd 69 2286
71 2-13 York 5g/f 69 2359
64 3-19 Beve 5gd 69 2512
53 8-17 Redc 6gd 69 2561
50 11-14 Newc 5g/s 68 2775
67 6-12 York 5g/s 68 3073
64 7-10 Ayr 5gd 68 3150
67 4-17 Pont 5gd 68 3241
46 18-26 Good 6fm 68 3569
67 4-16 Muss 5g/f 66 4174
70 4-18 Redc 6fm 66 4339

65	5-17	Beve	5g/f	67	4603
49	11-26	Ayr	6g/s	66	4652
66	5-16	Pont	5fm	67	4754
58a	7-13	Wolv	6ap	65	5010 BL

OBEZYANA 2 ch c £1332
| 0 | 21-21 | Newm | 8sft | | 5097 |
| 77a | 2-12 | Ling | 8ap | | 5293 |

OBLIQUE 2 b f £475
45a	12-14	Ling	7ap		5076
66a	11-14	Ling	7ap		5258
60	4-14	Nott	6.1hvy		5342

OBOE 2 ch f £0
44a	5-8	Wolv	7af		276
35a	9-14	Ling	6ap		449
26a	8-14	Ling	6ap		495
2a	6-6	Ling	8ap	[40]	1246

OBRIGADO 4 b g £11713
53	10-14	Donc	8g/f	[80]	1877
84	2-11	Newm	7fm	80	2090
25	27-28	Asco	7g/f	82	2558
84	1-7	AYR	7.2gd	[81]	3326*
74	9-16	Redc	8g/f	82	3768 VIS
85a	2-14	Ling	7ap	82	4180
72a	10-14	Ling	7ap	82	4446

OBSERVATION 3 ch f £0
17	8-10	Folk	9.7sft		977
37	12-18	Wind	8.3g/s		1258
0	15-15	Bath	10.2gd		4826
0	10-12	Warw	12.6g/s		4991

OBSERVER 2 b c £4610
83	1-4	FOLK	5g/s		1077*
80	3-6	Chep	6.1gd		2367 VIS
75	7-9	Asco	6gd	86	3127

OCEAN AVENUE 5 b g £17270
86	1-13	KEMP	12g/f	76	1916*
79	8-13	Asco	12fm	84	2582
67	6-12	Kemp	14.4g/f	83	3688
90	1-9	KEMP	12g/f	82	4360*
83	7-13	Kemp	12g/f	[88]	4715

OCEAN GIFT 2 b c £494
67	6-10	Good	5g/f		3511
80	4-10	Newb	7g/f		3955
84	8-9	Newb	6g/f		4680
72	8-21	Newm	8sft	[88]	5097

OCEAN OF STORMS 9 b h £3700
73	10-13	Epso	8.5g/f	80	2207 T
55	12-13	Asco	12fm	78	2582 t
74	4-6	Epso	10.1g/f	[78]	2874 t
73	5-11	Newb	11g/f	78	3256 t
82	2-12	Good	9fm	76	3625 t
73	7-10	Good	9.9gd	79	3949 t

OCEAN ROCK 3 b c £0
70a	7-13	Ling	12ap		873
48	15-17	Newb	10gd		1737
41	13-16	Sand	10g/s		2131
1	14-14	Folk	12gd	55	3383
14	11-13	Warw	12.6g/s	[50]	4665

OCEAN TIDE 7 b g £5757
61a	3-10	Sout	16af	75	743 vis
76	3-14	Donc	18gd	73	926 vis
74	4-10	Muss	16g/f	75	1093 vis
70	4-11	Beve	16.2sft	77	1629 vis
55	8-13	Chep	18gd	73	2198 vis
73	3-9	Pont	18g/f	72	2607 BL
69	5-6	Catt	15.8g/f	70	3015 bl
73	2-9	Beve	16.2g/s	70	3181 vis
51	5-10	Hayd	16.2sft	68	3275

OCEANCOOKIE 2 b f £670
65	5-20	York	6g/f		4401
62a	5-14	Ling	4ap		4658
70	6-21	Donc	6hvy		5202

OCEANICO DOT COM 2 br f £19634
59	7-9	Ches	5.1gd		2281
40	12-17	Nott	6.1gd		2927
70	2-12	Thir	5g/s		3832
72	1-13	RIPO	5gd	[67]	4303*

76	3-14	Catt	5g/f	73	4437
77	1-13	MUSS	5g/f	67	4551*
70	6-15	Ripo	5gd	74	4784
63	8-15	York	6gd	74	4985

OCHIL HILLS DANCER 2 b f £364
62	7-15	York	5g/f		2056
68	5-12	Hami	6gd		2178
61	7-12	Carl	5gd		2933
46	4-4	Donc	5g/s		3224
39	5-6	Hami	5g/f	66	3590
60	6-12	Muss	5g/f	62	4172 T
27	14-14	Catt	5g/f	61	4437 t
20	11-14	Hami	6sft	59	4692 t

OCOTILLO 4 b g £0
| 0 | 12-13 | Ayr | 10sft | | 5066 |

OCTENNIAL 5 gr g £0
| 23 | 11-20 | Nott | 6.1gd | 50 | 2928 |
| 0 | 13-19 | Nott | 6.1gd | [50] | 3104 |

OCTOBER MIST 10 gr g £3741
| 75 | 1-8 | NEWC | 12.4hvy | | 1038* |

ODABELLA 4 b f £1115
71	3-14	Yarm	8g/f	69	1131
49	9-15	Hami	8.3g/s	69	1602
64	8-13	Pont	10g/f	68	2038
55	4-7	Ayr	13.1g/s	67	2546 T

ODDSMAKER 3 b g £25750
79	3-9	Hayd	8.1sft	72	1105
82	2-10	Pont	10sft	73	1427
72	5-9	Ches	12.3gd	73	1582
88	1-14	YORK	7.9g/s	77	1707*
55	20-27	Asco	8g/f	83	2521
90	1-13	DONC	8gd	[83]	2753*
84	5-14	Hayd	8.1gd	86	2903
91	3-13	Newm	8g/f	87	3277
82	7-11	York	7g/f	88	3433
62	13-16	Good	9.9fm	88	3553
85	10-13	Donc	10.3fm	[88]	4463
85	6-10	Ayr	8sft	86	4685

ODIHAM 3 b g £15345
88	1-11	SAND	10g/s	78	2127*
84	9-17	Asco	12g/f	85	2519
89	4-16	Good	12fm	85	3534
61	10-10	York	11.9gd	87	4324
89	5-15	Leic	11.8gd	87	5043
90	4-13	Donc	12sft	87	5215

OEUF A LA NEIGE 4 b g £13341
64	5-14	Thir	6gd	[70]	1639
60	8-11	Redc	7g/f	[67]	1822
51	6-11	Thir	6g/f	63	2214
68	1-20	THIR	6g/f	61	3575*
49	5-8	Carl	6.9g/f	[61]	3654
24	7-7	Folk	6g/s	[66]	3910
75	1-13	BATH	5.7gd	64	4548*
77	1-20	WIND	6g/s	68	4946*
76	5-19	York	5gd	74	4989
63	8-19	Wind	6g/f	74	5053
43	16-16	Redc	6sft	73	5304

OFARABY 3 b g £20805
78a	6-13	Ling	10ap	80	26
80a	4-13	Wolv	9.4af	80	127
85a	3-11	Ling	10ap	79	716
89	1-14	NEWC	10.1sft	79	964*
87	6-20	Epso	12hvy	86	1295
83	4-12	Ches	10.3gd	86	1586
92	2-9	Hayd	10.5g/s	86	2185
88	5-12	Kemp	10gd	90	3185
78	13-20	Hayd	10.5fm	90	3794
95	3-9	Newm	10gd	88	4227
95	1-10	YARM	10.1sft	[88]	5255*

OFF BEAT 2 ch g £3914
80a	1-15	LING	7ap	73	177* bl
58a	9-11	Ling	7ap	77	261 bl
77a	6-7	Ling	7ap	77	368 bl
77a	3-12	Ling	7ap	75	729 bl
50	13-15	Wind	6g/s	75	1054 bl
42	7-8	Bath	5.7fm	72	1903 bl
36	18-20	Newb	7g/f	68	2314 bl
33	17-20	Newb	7fm	65	2650 bl

43	12-16	Sali	8gd	65	4334
59	8-14	Chep	10.2gd	65	4487
54	6-12	Brig	8fm	[60]	4761
69a	7-14	Ling	10ap	69	5083
48	8-13	Muss	12g/s	56	5333

OFF COLOUR 2 b c £489
56	4-7	Sand	7.1g/s		2897
66	10-15	Sand	7.1g/f		3337
71	6-14	Kemp	8g/f		4356

OFF HIRE 8 b g £1250
48a	2-11	Wolv	5af	48	508 vis
47a	3-12	Wolv	5af	48	641 vis
45a	4-12	Sout	5af	48	853 vis
41a	8-16	Sout	5ap	48	1046 vis
21	9-13	Yarm	6g/f	52	2347 vis
41	5-19	Beve	5g/s	49	2657 vis
38	11-20	Beve	5g/s	46	3180 vis

OFFICERS PINK 4 ch f £0
2	10-10	Donc	6g/f	70	1878 t
44	8-13	Donc	6g/f	70	2232
60	10-13	Wind	6fm	68	3479 t

OGILVY 3 ch c £1848
67	14-19	Newb	8g/f		1236
63	8-8	Newm	10fm		3007
78	2-14	Newb	9fm		3631

OH BOY 4 b c £8964
0	17-18	Wind	8.3g/s	68	1059
44	14-19	Sali	7g/f	65	1723
52	5-12	Sand	8.1g/s	60	2129
68	1-10	NEWB	8g/f	60	2350*
76	1-13	NEWB	8fm	64	2647*
60	17-20	Newm	8fm	72	3001
39	16-17	Newb	7g/f	72	3257
42	10-13	Kemp	7sft	71	4030
24	15-16	Sali	8gd	70	4334
55	7-7	Sali	8sft	[67]	4581

OH DARA 2 b f £6114
88	1-8	CATT	5g/f		2847*
87	3-8	Ches	5.1g/f		3081
83	7-12	Newb	5.2g/f	[90]	3956
84	5-12	Muss	5g/f	88	4172

OH FRIGATE 2 b g £0
| 40a | 10-11 | Ling | 8ap | | 77 |

OH GOLLY GOSH 3 ch g £6797
79	2-9	Warw	8.1sft		1089
75	2-11	Newc	8sft	[76]	1279
74	9-24	Newm	8fm	[76]	1495 P
75	4-18	Thir	8g/f	76	1769 p
73	2-4	Ayr	7.2fm	[74]	1907 p
29	18-18	Epso	10.1fm	74	2250 p
65	5-9	Nott	8.2g/f	[71]	3581 VIS
62	3-8	Redc	9g/f	[69]	3805 p
65a	1-9	SOUT	7af	[66]	4131* vis
55	9-17	York	7g/f	66	4398 vis
60a	10-12	Wolv	7.1ap	66	5008 p

OH SO HARDY 3 b f £851
39	14-16	Wind	10gd		1384
57	4-7	Brig	11.9g/f		1939
55	3-8	Chep	12.1gd		2368

OH SO ROSIE 3 b f £9859
51a	9-11	Ling	8ap	60	136 p
64	4-17	Leic	7g/s	60	1020
62	3-18	Wind	8.3g/s	60	1059
54	3-14	Hayd	8.1g/s	60	1348
46	9-14	Ling	7sft	60	1625 p
60	3-9	Leic	8fm	58	2108
2	2-11	Redc	8fm	58	2296
49	5-6	Bath	8fm	58	2414
41	11-20	Kemp	9g/f	57	2857
27	13-14	Pont	8g/f	57	2993
61	1-14	YARM	8gd	53	3363* p
50	9-16	Carl	7.9g/f	55	3650 p
31	12-14	Chep	8.1gd	55	3733 p
58	4-20	Yarm	8gd	55	3996 p
57	2-12	Sali	8g/s	55	4077 p
57	5-14	Good	8g/f	58	4542 p
55a	2-12	Ling	8ap	[54]	5077 p
53	7-20	Yarm	7sft	57	5256 p

29a 9-12 Wolv 8.6ap [54] 5337 p

OK PAL 4 b g £18389
2a U-10 Ling 5ap 92 692
90a 3-10 Wolv 6af 90 834
55 13-13 Beve 5g/s [90] 1162
73 7-10 Wind 6gd [85] 1383
68 6-12 Ling 5g/s 85 1615
67 12-12 Sali 5gd 80 2698 BL
65 6-8 Nott 5.1gd [75] 4039 bl
84 1-12 SAND 5gd [72] 4605*
85 2-16 Leic 5gd 78 4700
86 3-19 Sali 6gd 81 4855
92 1-18 PONT 5g/s 82 5149+

OKOBOJI 2 ch c £0
65a 5-12 Ling 8ap 100
68a 9-12 Ling 8ap 175

OKTIS MORILIOUS 2 b g £10415
40a 9-11 Sout 8af 159
30a 8-15 Sout 7af 462
18a 9-11 Wolv 9.4af 580
42a 4-10 Ling 8ap [45] 831
47a 1-11 LING 10ap [45] 970*
47a 2-8 Ling 10ap [45] 1183
45 3-6 Chep 12.1sft [45] 1331
41a 4-8 Ling 10ap [45] 1713
50 2-9 Good 11g/f 45 2019
34 6-7 Brig 11.9fm 44 2333
53 2-14 Bath 10.2g/f 44 2664
55 5-7 Bath 10.2g/f 48 2979
55 1-8 WARW 10.9gd [48] 3055+
34 9-12 Brig 9.9g/f 55 3300
54 4-12 Bath 11.7g/f 54 3845
23 11-15 Nott 10g/s 54 4037
58 1-10 BATH 11.7g/s [53] 4199*
45 8-10 Yarm 10.1gd [55] 4612
57 4-13 Newc 16.1fm 55 4868
54 6-14 Pont 17.1g/f 55 4936

OL LUCY BROON 3 b f £0
0 9-9 Muss 5g/s 56 1457
22 14-18 Hayd 6gd 54 3737
16 15-15 Carl 5fm [49] 4508 VIS
49 7-15 Ayr 5sft 45 5036
41a 5-13 Wolv 6ap [49] 5211

OLASO 5 br h £28169
119 1-8 COLO 12sft 1556*

OLD BAILEY 4 gr g £6582
46 6-16 Newc 6sft 49 1277 bl
42 9-20 Newc 6sft 49 1393 bl
43 5-13 Muss 7.1gd 47 1553 bl
31 9-18 Ayr 7.2g/f 45 1897 bl
61a 1-12 WOLV 7af 54 2204* vis
26 9-16 Carl 5.9fm 46 2445 vis
33a 11-12 Sout 7af [59] 2496 bl
43a 9-15 Sout 7af [59] 2999 vis
39 5-14 Hami 6gd 3129 P
46 5-14 Catt 6g/f [45] 3191 bl
15 13-18 Thir 6fm 43 3609 p
55a 3-11 Sout 8af [58] 4090 vis
50 1-15 NEWC 6hvy 41 4211* vis

OLD HARRY 4 b g £0
22 15-16 Ling 7g/f 52 2063
33 10-15 Chep 5.1gd 47 3403 T
12 13-15 Ling 6fm 42 3790 t
22 8-19 Kemp 6g/f [40] 4793

OLDENWAY 4 b g £18655
33a 9-13 Wolv 9.4af 70 127
49a 10-11 Sout 8af 67 186
62a 10-14 Ling 10ap 65 625
59a 9-14 Ling 10ap 63 803
73 2-19 Donc 10.3gd 70 924
74 2-14 Nott 10fm [70] 1006
72 4-10 Muss 12gd 72 1796
76 2-8 Ayr 10g/f 72 1895
80 1-10 BEVE 9.9g/s 72 2323+
77 4-13 Redc 10gd 72 2560
77 7-15 Hayd 11.9gd 70 2948
81 1-5 HAMI 9.2g/f [76] 3206*

OLDSTEAD FLYER 2 b c £0
26 10-11 Hayd 5g/f 1880

49a 6-10 Sout 6af 2382
33 14-14 Newm 7g/f 2766
7a 9-11 Sout 7af 2995

OLIGARCH 2 b c £15185
85 2-10 Brig 6g/s 4139
83 10-22 Donc 6fm 4458
85 3-10 Yarm 8g/s 4631
78 1-13 BRIG 8sft [86] 5091*
83 7-20 Donc 7sft 85 5373

OLIMP 8 ch g £0
11a 8-8 Wolv 16.2af 49 563

OLIVANDER 3 b c £1911
66 8-12 York 7g/s [80] 1688
74 3-8 Brig 7fm [75] 2259 BL
71 9-12 Sand 9g/f 75 2385 bl
73 2-8 Brig 8fm [74] 4762 bl T

OLIVIA ROSE 5 b m £25681
57 7-15 Beve 9.9sft 60 1307
66 1-9 NOTT 10sft 60 1467*
67 3-5 Nott 10sft 65 1609
67 1-16 REDC 10g/f 65 1821*
75 2-13 Pont 10g/f 70 2038
76 3-10 Beve 9.9g/s 73 2323
81 1-11 RIPO 10gd 73 2483*
79 4-10 Wind 10fm 79 2761
88 1-9 RIPO 10g/s 79 3260*
86 3-6 Newc 10.1gd [83] 3430
71 10-10 Newm 10g/f 83 3615
83 9-11 Yarm 10.1gd [83] 4614
77 11-15 Nott 10gd 83 4860

OLIVIA TWIST 2 ch f £0
53 9-9 Folk 7g/s 3047

OLLIJAY 3 b g £0
11 6-6 Donc 7g/f 3595
18 6-8 Chep 7.1sft 4055
53 10-14 Warw 7.1gd 4275
36 12-17 Leic 7gd 50 5056
27a 7-9 Wolv 9.5ap [47] 5360

OLYMPIAS 3 b f £991
64 4-9 Folk 9.7sft 980
13 8-8 Folk 12sft 1272
54 7-12 Good 9g/f 1864
51 6-10 Good 14gd 60 2376
51 4-13 Pont 12gd 58 3240
2 14-15 Chep 18sft 56 4056
54 3-11 Bath 13.1g/f 52 4415 BL
0 16-20 Bath 17.2gd 53 4824 bl

OLYMPIC 2 b c £1941
85 2-20 Naas 6g/s 5163

OMAHA CITY 10 b g £14572
47a 10-12 Ling 8ap [75] 1042
65 10-18 Good 8g/f 72 1812
75a 2-11 Ling 8ap 70 2018
76 1-9 GOOD 8gd 69 2540*
72 12-20 Newm 8fm 74 3001
67 10-19 Good 8g/f 73 3512
67 13-21 Good 8fm 74 3565
62 10-15 Sand 7.1gd 71 4500
66 10-24 Newb 7g/f 70 4642
78 1-14 WIND 8.3g/f 69 4832*
77a 2-12 Ling 8ap [69] 4974
79a 1-12 LING 8ap 70 5079*

OMAN GULF 3 b c £720
84 10-10 York 10.4g/s 1685
82 4-4 Ayr 8g/f [87] 2026
64 18-22 Newm 8sft 83 5103
67 8-20 Donc 7sft 78 5367

OMAN SEA 3 b f £518
61 5-5 Ches 7.6g/f 4047

OMASHERIFF 2 ch c £17340
101 4-22 Donc 6fm 4458 bl

OMETSZ 3 br f £0
111 5-7 Long 10gd 2001

OMIKRON 3 b c £44789
102 3-18 Hamb 12hvy 3010

ON ACTION 2 b c £648
66 3-9 Catt 6g/f 4670
59 5-10 Pont 6fm 4752

ON CLOUD NINE 3 ro f £4509
77 2-10 Folk 9.7sft 977
60 6-8 Chep 12.1gd 2113
67 7-14 Kemp 10g/s 2678
41 12-14 Folk 9.7g/s 66 3052
68 4-16 Thir 12g/f 64 3573
63 3-11 Beve 12.1g/s [64] 3856
63 1-12 CHEP 12.1g/s [62] 4364*
48 5-6 Muss 12gd [62] 4805
34a 9-12 Wolv 12.2ap 59 5339

ON EVERY STREET 3 b g £5506
72 4-6 Newm 10gd 1892 VIS
64 3-8 Good 11gd 2222 vis
76 1-5 WARW 10.9fm [72] 2602* vis T
40 4-4 Ayr 10g/f [77] 3762 vis
75 6-8 York 8.9g/f [77] 4397 BL
33 7-8 Hami 9.2sft [77] 4694 bl
1 19-19 Donc 10.3sft 75 5201
33 15-17 Redc 10sft 70 5307

ON GUARD 6 b g £237
47a 3-14 Ling 10ap [45] 705 vis
43a 6-14 Ling 12ap [45] 827 vis
9 18-19 Warw 10.9sft 55 1090 vis
25 10-17 Bath 10.2sft 52 1541 vis
36a 4-5 Wolv 9.4af [40] 1674
12 15-18 Wind 11.6g/f 48 1960

ON THE BRIGHT SIDE 2 b f £545
73 3-12 Carl 5gd 2933

ON THE LEVEL 5 ch m £0
21a 9-13 Wolv 5af [45] 312
6a 10-10 Ling 5ap [40] 653 BL
0 12-13 Yarm 6g/f 43 2347

ON THE TRAIL 6 ch g £26203
31a 9-12 Wolv 7af 56 68
15a 14-16 Sout 6af 56 94
30a 10-15 Sout 6af 53 168
18a 8-13 Sout 6af 50 500
0 11-12 Wolv 6af [50] 524 BL
20a 11-16 Sout 6af [45] 720 bl
13a 10-15 Sout 6af [45] 773
47a 1-10 WOLV 6af [45] 822+
45a 3-10 Sout 6af [45] 907
55a 1-7 SOUT 6af [45] 1032*
55a 2-5 Wolv 6af [50] 1310
58a 1-6 SOUT 6af [50] 1443*
43a 3-11 Wolv 6af [56] 2202
39a 4-12 Sout 7af [56] 2337
49 3-20 Beve 5g/s 45 3180
55a 3-13 Sout 6af [56] 3482
55 1-15 PONT 5gd 46 3680*
53 1-18 PONT 5g/s 48 3974*
56 4-19 Beve 5g/s 54 4240
52 5-20 Newc 6g/f 54 4408
58 2-15 Redc 6fm 54 4562
36 7-19 Yarm 6g/s 54 4636
63 1-14 CATT 6gd 54 4967*
59 2-19 Ayr 6sft 54 5069
56a 4-12 Wolv 7.1ap 56 5112
57a 3-13 Wolv 6af [55] 5359

ON THE WATERFRONT 3 ch c £3500
61a 5-11 Ling 8ap 322
61a 5-14 Ling 10ap 473
72a 4-15 Ling 7ap 814
68 2-5 Brig 8g/f 66 1370
52 10-18 Thir 8g/f 67 1769
68 4-17 Hayd 8.1gd 66 2243
66 2-7 Hami 8.3g/f [66] 2474
63 5-9 Good 8gd 66 3950

ON THE WATERLINE 2 b f £9624
66 2-11 Nott 5.1gd 1237
75 3-7 Ches 5.1g/s 1573
44 9-10 Leic 5g/f 1826
74 4-8 Good 6fm 3536
80 2-11 Nott 5.1gd 75 3987
56 11-16 Newm 6gd 76 4224
21 20-21 Donc 6.5fm 76 4457
82 1-12 WIND 6g/s [72] 4945* VIS

ON THE WING 3 b f £0

59a	6-8	Ling	6ap	[72]	5081 vis
56	7-14	Newm	6sft	79	5098 vis
28	12-14	Pont	8g/f	[78]	4937

ONCE 4 gr g £560

75	3-10	Hayd	14g/f	75	1923
36	22-29	Asco	20g/f	75	2471
60	10-13	Asco	16.2g/f	73	3387
65	7-11	Good	11gd	71	3948 BL
12	10-11	Bath	13.1g/f	68	4415 bl
56	12-15	Nott	10g/f	65	4849 bl
56a	7-12	Wolv	13.9ap	62	5160

ONCE AROUND 2 b c £0

13a	7-9	Wolv	9.4af		238
60a	7-14	Ling	10ap		367
35a	12-12	Ling	8ap		514
38	11-12	Sali	12g/s		1501
29a	7-8	Ling	12ap	[51]	2065

ONDA NOVA 3 b f £15845

111	1-7	MAIS	7sft		1156*

ONE ALONE 2 b f £367

20a	8-10	Sout	7af	55	203
8a	8-9	Wolv	9.4af	49	351
42	12-15	Ling	7g/f	45	1983
28	11-18	Donc	7gd	45	2755
35	10-14	Wind	8.3g/f	45	2799
33a	4-13	Ling	10ap	[45]	3025 VIS
44a	3-12	Ling	12ap	[39]	3819 BL

ONE COOL CAT 3 b c £58037

44	13-14	Newm	8g/f		1480
105	5-7	Curr	8gd		3318
119	1-10	CURR	6g/f		3842*
118	3-12	York	5g/s		4060
110	6-19	Hayd	6fm		4384

ONE FOR ME 6 b r m £0

39	17-19	Good	21fm	39	3531

ONE GOOD THING 2 b c £0

61	10-18	Wind	6gd		3824
71	5-14	Leic	8gd		5059
59	12-20	Yarm	8sft		5252

ONE GREAT IDEA 2 b g £2803

79	2-10	Hayd	6gd		3755
83	5-14	Hayd	6fm		4385
84	2-11	Beve	5g/f		4599

ONE LAST TIME 4 b g £1126

38	14-16	Sout	7g/s	72	1049
21	19-20	Ripo	8g/s	69	1366
38	9-14	Hami	8.3gd	63	1504
63	2-16	Redc	6g/f	59	1824
44	14-17	Warw	5fm	61	2599
34	13-18	Pont	5gd	60	3463

ONE MORE ROUND 6 b h £10184

109	2-9	Curr	7gd	[106]	3320

ONE N ONLY 3 b f £1526

49	4-13	Muss	7.1g/f	[57]	1119
50	5-6	Hami	5g/f	[55]	1387
47	4-8	Hami	9.2gd	[55]	1505
61	3-14	Ayr	8g/f	[55]	1896

ONE OF DISTINCTION 3 b f £0

23	8-9	Wind	10fm		3642

ONE OF EACH 2 ch f £0

57	5-6	Wolv	5g/f		3525
62	5-12	Thir	5g/s		3832
27a	11-15	Sout	5af		4089

ONE OF THEM 5 ch g £0

17	16-19	Wind	10sft	[62]	1650 BL
30a	11-13	Ling	12g/f	57	1986 bl

ONE OFF 4 b g £774

94	7-11	Fair	14g/s	[87]	4162
70	4-5	Pont	18g/f	[90]	4628

ONE PUTRA 2 b c £8122

77	5-10	Good	6g/f		3511
94	1-18	WIND	6gd		3824*
93	3-5	Ches	6.1sft		4105
94	6-9	Newb	6g/f	[91]	4680

ONE SO MARVELLOUS 3 ch f £8089

66	9-20	Newm	8g/f		3237
1	9-9	Nott	10g/s		4034
81	1-13	LEIC	10g/f		4453*
82	2-15	Nott	10gd	75	4860

ONE TO WIN 2 b f £1600

78a	2-8	Ling	7ap		4447

ONE UPMANSHIP 3 ch g £6767

51	11-17	Sali	6g/f	69	1722 p
57	8-10	Brig	6g/f	[68]	2048 e
44	11-20	Newb	7g/f	66	2314
55	6-16	Chep	7.1gd	[66]	2369 bl
67	3-9	Warw	6.1fm	[61]	2778
64	2-7	Catt	7g/f	[64]	3194
61	6-12	Ling	7.6gd	[64]	3448
64	1-10	HAYD	8.1gd	[64]	3739*
66a	2-13	Ling	10ap	[65]	4112
67	3-9	Good	9sft	[65]	4266
57a	7-14	Ling	10ap	[65]	4448
43a	13-13	Wolv	8.6ap	[65]	5336

ONE WAY TICKET 4 ch c £15819

16	16-18	Wind	8.3gd	65	1385 p
22	12-13	Warw	7.1hvy	[65]	1537 p
45	13-19	Redc	6g/f	60	1820 p
62	3-19	Kemp	6fm	57	2070 p
68	2-12	Leic	6fm	57	2111 p
42	9-13	Hami	6g/f	57	2315 p
64	3-6	Bath	5.7fm	62	2416 p
72	1-9	CHEP	6.1g/f	62	2626* p
38a	8-16	Sout	6af	59	2806 p
54	7-12	Bath	5.7gd	69	3146 p
63	8-14	Leic	6g/f	69	3213 p
69	4-15	Chep	5.1gd	69	3403 p
73	1-13	BRIG	5.3g/f	69	3984* p
69	5-12	Brig	5.3g/s	69	4140 p
55	11-15	Sali	5gd	69	4335 p
72	2-15	Good	5gd	68	4751 p

ONEFORTHEBOYS 4 b g £830

49a	8-10	Ling	6ap	[36]	133
6a	7-12	Sout	8af	[36]	309
37a	9-12	Ling	8ap	[40]	538
38a	6-6	Sout	8af	[40]	586
38a	2-10	Ling	6ap	[35]	653
52a	4-7	Ling	6ap	[35]	706
35a	8-13	Ling	6ap	[40]	788
42a	9-14	Ling	6ap	[45]	819
37a	3-10	Ling	6ap	[40]	973
42a	7-12	Ling	7ap	[40]	1074
17a	6-8	Ling	6ap	[40]	1290
32a	3-5	Ling	6ap	[40]	1452
0	17-17	Wind	6fm	39	2975
0	15-19	Nott	6.1gd	[39]	3104

ONEIRO WAY 2 b c £0

69	9-14	Sand	7.1g/s		4069
27	10-14	Sali	8gd		4852

ONESHOTTWOLIONS 2 b c £0

53	12-12	Newm	7g/f		3470

ONIZ TIPTOES 3 ch g £1051

0	14-14	Donc	6g/f		2428
36	6-8	Pont	12g/f		2608 P
39	4-7	Ripo	10gd	[35]	2982 BL
39	2-10	Beve	12.1g/f	35	3499 VIS
0	10-12	Folk	12g/s	39	3913 vis

ONLINE INVESTOR 5 b g £3220

12	12-15	Pont	6hvy	70	1251
44	13-16	Thir	7g/s	67	1474
61	5-17	Donc	6g/s	67	1523
73	2-20	Thir	5g/f	65	1765
41	11-12	Ayr	7.2fm	69	1909
73	5-15	Muss	5fm	69	2084
63	5-13	Pont	5g/f	[69]	2279
57	12-13	York	5g/f	69	2359
41	14-14	Newc	5g/s	67	2775
51	17-18	Carl	5g/f	64	3228 VIS
59	11-22	Good	5fm	64	3537
51	10-26	Good	6fm	64	3569
64	2-10	Hami	5g/s	[62]	4010
63	4-12	Brig	5.3g/s	62	4140
62	4-17	Beve	5g/f	62	4603
54	8-16	Pont	5fm	62	4754
57	6-19	Ayr	6sft	61	5069

ONLY FOR GOLD 9 b g £0

24a	5-10	Wolv	5af	[35]	781
27a	7-12	Sout	7af	[30]	909

ONLY FOR SUE 4 ch g £5557

54a	1-12	WOLV	12af	45	244*
18a	8-11	Wolv	12af	53	380
28a	9-12	Wolv	12af	53	484 P
54	3-17	Nott	14.1gd	51	1238 BL
61	1-17	BATH	11.7sft	53	1543* bl
49	8-17	Nott	14.1g/f	60	2156 bl

ONLY IF I LAUGH 2 ch g £3110

59a	4-13	Sout	6af	[76]	63 bl
75a	3-9	Ling	5ap	70	914
67a	4-8	Sout	5af	70	1031
11	8-8	Folk	5g/s	[75]	1268 h bl
57	2-7	Bath	5fm	[70]	1902 bl
54a	3-9	Sout	6af	[68]	2493
44	9-12	Ayr	5g/s	63	2566
60	5-19	Leic	5gd	63	2702
48	3-6	Muss	5g/f	[59]	2808
33	12-12	Donc	5g/f	60	3599 bl
66a	4-12	Wolv	5.1ap	67	5326

ONLY ONE LEGEND 5 b g £4111

60a	6-12	Wolv	5af	74	35
56a	8-12	Wolv	5af	73	109 bl
71a	3-14	Ling	6ap	72	149 bl
66a	9-14	Ling	6ap	72	292 bl
60a	12-16	Sout	5af	72	461 p
39a	11-15	Sout	6af	70	550 p
36a	10-12	Sout	6af	[70]	728 bl
47a	7-14	Ling	6ap	[65]	819 bl
58	3-8	Newc	6sft	[60]	963 p
45	9-15	Hami	6gd	58	1508 p
40	3-16	Nott	6.1gd	[55]	1988 bl
62a	1-12	SOUT	6af	[60]	2337* bl
40a	5-9	Sout	7af	[60]	2801 bl
37a	13-15	Sout	7af	[60]	2999 bl
39	8-14	Catt	6g/f	[52]	3191 bl
12	18-18	Catt	7g/f	48	3670 bl

ONLY WORDS 7 ch g £0

28	6-7	Beve	16.2sft	34	2941

ONLYTIME WILL TELL 6 ch g £25469

70a	8-12	Ling	8ap	79	888
56	20-24	Donc	8gd	95	951
73	5-12	Hayd	6g/s	[93]	2186
94	4-9	Ches	7gd	93	2282
94	2-5	Asco	6g/f	91	3388
82	7-8	Thir	8fm	91	3608
95	1-10	WIND	6gd	[91]	3977*
93	4-13	York	6gd	91	4322
89	6-24	Ayr	6sft	91	4686
99	1-17	NEWB	6sft	90	5196+
91	8-12	Donc	6sft	[95]	5371

ONTOS 8 b g £0

0	12-13	Pont	18hvy	10	1069

ONWARD TO GLORY 4 b c £3812

65	9-14	Sali	12g/s	73	3114
65	11-11	Sand	14g/f	70	3340
61	4-10	Yarm	11.5gd	[68]	3937
63	6-20	Hayd	11.9g/s	65	4771
54	10-19	Bath	11.7gd	63	5024
68	1-10	CATT	13.8sft	60	5322*

ONYA 3 ch f £0

9a	10-10	Ling	12ap	[44]	24
33a	16-16	Ling	7ap	[39]	290 T

ONYERGO 2 b c £2403

71	3-8	Newc	7sft		4283
75	3-9	Ayr	7.2sft		5064
76	3-9	Muss	8g/s		5331

ONYX 3 b g £0

32	6-8	Donc	6gd		953
42	8-11	Nott	6.1sft		1607
44a	7-12	Wolv	6ap		5162

OOPS 5 b g £6982

24	8-10	Redc	14.1g/s	45	2562
47	1-7	**BEVE**	16.2sft	41	2941*
23	6-10	Hayd	16.2sft	45	3275
47	2-12	Yarm	16gd	43	3493
49	3-10	Thir	16sft	44	3834
50	2-9	Ripo	16gd	45	4308
49	4-14	Warw	16.2g/f	45	4423
41	3-19	Catt	15.8g/f	48	4675
35	9-20	Catt	15.8gd	46	4965

OOS AND AHS 4 b f £0

0	8-9	Sout	12af		353

OPEN BOOK 3 br f £471

37	10-12	Sali	12g/s		1501
37	11-16	Bath	10.2g/f		1790
50	10-18	Wind	10g/f		1959
38	8-8	Good	11gd		2222
49	3-15	Folk	12g/f	[49]	4374
44a	7-14	Ling	16ap	[49]	4663
50	3-20	Kemp	12g/f	[48]	4796

OPEN HANDED 3 b g £2625

17a	11-13	Wolv	8.5af	57	40 t
27a	10-16	Sout	7af	51	202 t
37a	6-11	Wolv	7af	[45]	440 t
26a	10-13	Wolv	8.5af	[40]	699 t
47	11-18	Catt	7gd	[35]	996 t
59	1-7	**BEVE**	8.5g/s	[35]	1160* t
25	13-20	Ripo	8g/s	59	1366 t
51	5-18	Donc	7g/f	57	2080 t
50	5-16	Beve	7.5gd	55	2891 t
38	7-9	Donc	8g/s	53	3225 t
25	8-14	Good	8sft	49	4189 t
13	10-11	Ayr	9.1sft	[47]	5067

OPEN MIND 3 b f £762

51	4-8	Hami	5gd	52	1509
47	3-13	Carl	5.9fm	[52]	1949
54	7-8	Donc	5g/f	[52]	2075
42	6-13	Warw	6.1fm	50	2439
20	13-20	Ripo	6gd	48	4278
12	16-19	Thir	6g/f	48	4595

OPEN VERDICT 2 b c £260

49	16-18	York	5g/f		2360
59	4-9	Ches	5.1g/f		3097
24	14-16	Bath	5.7gd		4823 T

OPENING CEREMONY 5 br m £33304

56	6-7	Ripo	10g/f	[68]	1979
72	2-7	Ayr	10gd	68	2507
66	4-11	Newc	10.1g/s	68	2726 P
70	2-7	Redc	9g/s	[70]	2962
79	1-15	**CHES**	10.3g/f	70	3099*
69	5-10	Hayd	10.5g/s	70	3139
78	1-15	**DONC**	10.3g/f	72	3598*
67	5-6	Leic	10fm	75	3815
76	2-9	Yarm	10.1g/s	[75]	4254
75	4-20	Ayr	10g/s	75	4656
63a	8-14	Ling	10ap	[75]	4742

OPERA BABE 3 b f £0

0	7-7	Donc	14.6g/s	72	1521
23	11-12	Sali	12g/f	72	3868

OPERA COMIQUE 3 b f £450

85	6-9	Newm	10fm		1494 T
85	8-10	Donc	14.6fm		4460 t
76	10-12	Yarm	14.1sft		5254 t

OPERA STAR 2 b f £538

38a	10-11	Ling	7ap		213
55a	5-11	Wolv	8ap		496
61	10-20	Bath	12g/f		1398
63	3-6	Bath	11.7fm	[63]	2668
55	6-8	Warw	18fm	[63]	2781
9a	8-8	Sout	12af	62	4128

OPERASHAAN 4 b g £0

47a	8-13	Ling	10ap	[56]	338

OPHISTROLIE 2 b c £0

24	10-15	Newb	8hvy		5221

OPTIMAITE 7 b g £0

61a	6-13	Ling	12g/f	71	1986 t

OPTIMAL 3 gr f £4056

26	10-13	Bath	10.2gd	[62]	3144
57	6-10	Ling	11.5gd	62	3334
70	1-8	**BRIG**	9.9g/f	61	3719* BL
2	14-14	Redc	10fm	64	4342 bl

OPTIMUM 2 br c £0

54	14-15	Leic	7g/f		4455
67	5-8	Pont	8fm		4756
59a	10-14	Ling	7ap		4971

OPTIMUM NIGHT 5 b g £207

35	10-11	Muss	9g/f		1095
29	3-7	Ayr	10g/s	[40]	1450
26a	8-10	Wolv	9.4af	[40]	1564
19a	4-10	Sout	7af	[35]	1839 P
30	5-10	Beve	8.5g/f	[35]	1943 p
14	9-15	Ayr	10.9g/s	30	2545 p

OPTIMUS 2 ch c £1703

74a	5-12	Ling	6ap		4179
79a	2-14	Ling	7ap		4970
80a	4-10	Ling	7ap		5264

ORAKE PRINCE 4 b g £0

29a	11-12	Ling	10ap	[46]	272

ORANGE TOUCH 4 b c £30454

97	6-10	Newm	10g/f	[101]	1483
115	1-4	**NEWM**	12g/f	[101]	3946*
118	1-5	**GOOD**	14g/s	[112]	4230*
101	8-13	Curr	14gd	[112]	4733

ORANGINO 6 b g £2008

31	10-12	Hami	6g/s	[40]	1600
47	2-19	Redc	6g/f	39	2125
28	7-13	Redc	8gd	40	2552
45	2-14	Hami	6gd	40	3129
29	8-20	Thir	6g/f	43	3575
0	15-16	Hami	6g/s	43	4009
24	21-26	Redc	8fm	45	4926

ORANMORE CASTLE 2 b c £2045

89	2-10	Newb	6g/f		4637
70	6-10	Newm	6sft		5266

ORATION 3 b g £0

2	13-13	Kemp	10gd		3186

ORATORIO 2 b c £331203

100	1-7	**CURR**	6g/f		2003*
94	7-13	Asco	6g/f		2467
112	1-8	**CURR**	6.3gd		3319*
117	2-6	Curr	6g/f		3841
117	1-5	**CURR**	7g/f		4154*
119	1-6	**LONG**	7g/f		4955*
116	2-9	Newm	7sft		5137

ORCADIAN 3 b g £33650

104	3-8	Kemp	8fm	[103]	2069
88	7-8	Newb	7g/f	[103]	3253
94	6-10	Redc	7fm	[101]	4929
106	6-16	Newm	9sft	[99]	5139
114	1-8	**NEWB**	12hvy	[99]	5224*

ORCHESTRATION 3 ch c £574

58a	4-11	Ling	6ap		543
36a	4-16	Wolv	6af	[67]	631
37	12-17	Yarm	7g/f	[69]	1729
52	9-13	Wind	5fm	64	2784
0	17-18	Hayd	6gd	59	3737 BL
51a	6-13	Wolv	8.6ap	54	5005
41a	7-12	Wolv	8.6ap	[51]	5329

ORGANIZER 4 b c £7764

91	3-12	Jage	8.6aw		1697

ORIENTAL MOON 4 ch f £0

16a	6-9	Sout	8af	40	163 P
30a	5-9	Wolv	9.4af	[36]	239 p
17a	8-12	Ling	12ap	[35]	1180 VIS

ORIENTAL WARRIOR 3 b c £375

109	5-9	Donc	8fm		4495

ORIENTOR 6 b h £46458

110	2-17	Donc	6gd	[104]	952
110	4-13	Curr	7sft	[104]	1062
79	5-7	Thir	6sft	[109]	1227
93	9-15	York	6sft	[109]	1667

OPTIMUM (continued right column)

103	5-10	Curr	6g/f	[109]	1996
102	3-6	Curr	5g/f	[109]	2818
114	1-12	**SAND**	5g/s	[105]	2913*
114	5-12	York	5g/f	[115]	4060
108	7-19	Hayd	6fm	[115]	4384
109	6-15	Long	5g/f	[115]	4952

ORIGINAL SIN 4 b g £0

27a	10-10	Ling	10ap	[52]	370
43a	12-14	Ling	7ap	[46]	450
20a	11-12	Ling	8ap	[45]	538

ORINOCOVSKY 5 ch g £7849

62a	1-8	**SOUT**	11af	[64]	420*
42a	7-12	Wolv	12af	64	484
59a	3-10	Sout	12af	[64]	552
45a	10-11	Ling	16ap	62	605
52a	2-5	Sout	12af	[58]	745
55a	3-9	Ling	12ap	55	842
57a	2-4	Sout	14af	[55]	854
16	17-19	Warw	10.9sft	55	1090
62a	1-4	**WOLV**	12af	[55]	1323*
62a	3-5	Wolv	12ap	55	1375
34	12-14	Brig	11.9fm	59	3674

ORION EXPRESS 3 b c £738

63	6-11	Catt	6gd		999
64	6-16	Beve	7.5g/s	66	1163
61	7-16	Beve	8.5sft	65	1628
44	10-11	Beve	9.9g/f	63	1834
62	4-14	Redc	7fm	62	2295
52	6-13	Redc	8gd	62	2552
60	4-10	Hayd	8.1g/s	62	3138
60	6-13	Beve	9.9gd	62	3309
57	6-9	Newc	10.1g/s	[60]	3702
47	13-20	York	7.9gd	58	4321
41a	10-13	Wolv	9.5ap	55	5361

ORIONS BELT 4 ch g £370

13a	14-15	Ling	7ap	[55]	935
49a	3-9	Ling	6ap	[55]	1012
38a	7-8	Ling	7ap	[49]	1247

ORLAR 2 b f £810

70	5-12	Warw	7.1g/f		4418
23	8-8	Hayd	8.1sft		4782
75a	3-14	Ling	7ap		5258

ORO STREET 8 b g £181

49a	5-11	Wolv	12af	65	557
40a	3-5	Sout	12af	[61]	723

ORO VERDE 2 ch c £3512

75a	7-11	Ling	6ap	[91]	135
87a	2-10	Ling	5ap	[91]	176
72	9-11	Sali	6g/s	91	1498
87	6-7	Ling	6sft	91	1621
89	3-6	Sand	5g/f	[86]	2390
73	8-9	Newm	5fm	87	2593
52	16-16	Newm	7sft	86	5101

ORPEN ANNIE 2 b f £1898

42	18-19	Wind	5g/f		1805
67	3-8	Pont	6g/f		2603
62	6-9	Folk	7g/s		3047
43a	8-11	Sout	6af	66	3393
61	4-12	Newm	7g/f	[65]	3750
57	8-20	Leic	7g/f	59	4451
61	2-16	Yarm	8g/s	59	4632

ORPEN WIDE 2 b c £2228

0	18-18	Donc	6g/f		3376
71	3-13	Thir	6g/f		4590
83	3-6	Leic	7gd		4699
50	10-15	Newm	8gd		4883 T
42	8-14	Newm	6sft	71	5098
68	2-9	Nott	6.1hvy	[71]	5185
53	5-10	Catt	6sft	64	5318

ORPENBERRY 3 b f £0

19	13-13	Hayd	6g/f	72	1881
4	11-11	Nott	6.1g/f	68	2155
44	8-12	Pont	8gd	62	3679
42	14-18	Catt	7g/f	57	4438
30	12-18	Leic	7gd	[50]	4698

ORPENDONNA 2 b f £980

38	11-18	Ayr	6g/s		4617
78	3-18	Nott	8.2g/f		4842

65 6-15 York 7.9gd 5002

ORPHAN 2 b c £579
38	10-11	Ayr	6g/s		2569
76	5-12	Hayd	6sft		3272
70	4-10	Muss	5gd		4804
60	4-11	Catt	5gd		4962

OSCAR PEPPER 7 b g £7437
60	5-12	Hayd	8.1g/f	64	1485	
43	10-18	Thir	8g/f	63	1972	
57	6-15	Redc	9g/f	63	2120	
65	3-8	Hami	9.2gd	63	2179	vis
63	4-11	Ripo	10g/f	63	2483	vis
56	5-13	Redc	10gd	63	2560	vis
69	2-16	Redc	8g/s	63	2958	vis
60	4-8	Hami	9.2fm	63	3250	vis
72	1-19	BEVE	9.9g/f	64	3505*	vis
65	4-6	Pont	10gd	69	3678	vis
71	3-9	Redc	8g/f	[67]	3806	vis
54	12-19	York	7.9g/f	67	4399	vis

OSIDY 2 b c £7711
108	3-6	Long	7gd	4564

OSLA 3 ch f £0
26	8-16	Nott	6.1gd		1988	
7a	10-12	Sout	7af		2339	
38	8-17	Leic	7gd		2704	
30	10-11	Leic	10g/f		2924	
3	6-8	Warw	10.9gd		3055	
0	14-14	Leic	8g/f	[30]	3344	BL

OSO NEET 6 b g £0
31a	7-8	Ling	7ap	[30]	1413
8	9-13	Kemp	10hvy	[30]	1643

OSORNO 3 ch g £0
39a	10-14	Ling	10ap	53

OSTERHASE 5 b g £73468
114	1-13	NAAS	5g/f	[94]	2327*	bl
114	1-6	CURR	5g/f	[94]	2818*	bl
109	3-8	Curr	5g/f	[94]	4433	bl
114	4-15	Long	5g/f	[94]	4952	bl

OTAGO 3 b c £10605
62	3-6	Redc	6g/f		2104
44	12-14	Yarm	7fm		2148
59	4-6	Folk	5fm		2717
54	5-11	Ripo	6gd	57	2985
41	11-13	Kemp	7g/f	57	3034
53	4-13	Muss	8g/f	55	3526
61	2-15	Bath	8g/s	53	4202
62	1-15	CARL	7.9g/f	53	4346*
33	13-14	Good	8g/f	58	4542
66	1-12	BRIG	8fm	[58]	4761*
39	12-13	Pont	8g/s	[64]	5153
61a	5-13	Wolv	8.6ap	[64]	5336

OTYLIA 4 ch f £258
40a	5-13	Sout	6af	[52]	659	
46a	4-8	Wolv	6af	[52]	750	
27a	8-14	Sout	6af	47	4130	
0	15-16	Folk	6g/f	[48]	4370	
28	7-15	Brig	6gd	[45]	4905	VIS
24	14-19	Bath	5.7sft	45	5176	vis

OUDE 2 b c £21388
96	1-12	NEWM	7g/f	3470*
105	2-7	York	7gd	4003
107	3-10	Donc	7fm	4493

OUIJA BOARD 3 b f £917722
115	1-9	NEWM	10fm	[93]	1494*
122	1-7	EPSO	12g/f	[110]	2210+
114	1-7	CURR	12g/f	[110]	3321*
121	3-19	Long	12g/f	[110]	4956
123	1-4	LONE	11g/s	[110]	5309*

OULTON BROAD 8 b g £0
29a	7-14	Sout	12af	[37]	305	P
29a	5-9	Sout	16af	35	612	p
29a	6-10	Ling	16ap	[35]	650	p
0	6-7	Wolv	16.2af	[30]	1802	p

OUNINPOHJA 3 b g £8912
78	4-16	Donc	10.3gd	2751
75	3-16	Ripo	12gd	2987
69	2-10	Carl	6.9g/f	3230
75	5-19	Kemp	10fm	72	4392
75	1-13	AYR	10sft	[72]	5066*

OUR CHELSEA BLUE 5 ch m £417
52a	6-13	Wolv	6af	60	41	
55a	6-12	Wolv	5af	59	124	
43a	11-16	Sout	5af	58	183	
47a	7-10	Wolv	6af	56	349	
48a	3-11	Wolv	5af	53	508	
38a	6-12	Wolv	5af	53	641	
15a	13-13	Ling	6ap	51	902	t
36a	9-16	Sout	5ap	48	1046	t
25a	8-9	Ling	6ap	[45]	1248	t

OUR CHOICE 2 b c £266
47	8-8	Newm	5g/s		1149
68	4-6	Hami	5gd		1386
68	7-8	Newm	6g/f		1934
60a	6-12	Ling	7ap	65	3820
55	7-13	Newm	8gd	62	4193
67	6-12	Redc	8g/s	[59]	5107

OUR DESTINY 5 b g £16735
15a	9-16	Sout	8af	40	86	vis
45a	2-9	Wolv	9.4af	[37]	239	vis
33a	3-9	Wolv	8.5af	[45]	437	vis
50a	2-11	Wolv	9.4af	45	465	vis
41a	4-11	Wolv	12af	52	557	vis
13a	7-9	Wolv	9.4af	52	647	vis
50a	1-12	SOUT	8af	[50]	905*	vis
54a	1-6	WOLV	8.5af	[50]	957*	
46a	6-15	Sout	8af	56	1028	vis
60a	1-7	WOLV	8.5af	[52]	1341*	
62	2-10	Bath	10.2gd	[47]	1402	
50	4-17	Bath	10.2sft	49	1541	
48	3-6	Brig	11.9fm	[62]	1692	
58	1-19	BRIG	9.9g/f	51	1940*	
51	9-16	Yarm	10.1fm	57	2146	
57	4-9	Brig	9.9g/f	[55]	2643	
61	1-12	LING	10g/f	55	2844*	
47	7-13	Warw	12.6gd	55	3056	
58	5-17	Wind	10fm	58	3477	
50	6-8	Brig	8fm	[58]	3676	
51	6-9	Brig	9.9fm	58	3695	
49	8-16	Chep	10.2g/s	56	4365	
48	4-18	Chep	8.1gd	[56]	4485	
42	8-18	Warw	10.9g/s	53	4669	
53a	5-12	Wolv	12.2ap	55	5328	
57a	3-13	Wolv	9.5ap	55	5361	

OUR EMMY LOU 3 ch f £4574
65	2-14	Catt	12g/f	59	3192	
60	4-8	Brig	11.9g/f	59	3299	
49	5-11	Beve	12.1g/s	[62]	3856	
31a	6-8	Sout	12af	61	4128	BL
68	1-11	YARM	11.5g/s	[60]	4584*	
58	5-12	Pont	10fm	[60]	4757	
45a	9-16	Ling	12ap	[58]	4899	

OUR FRED 7 ch g £0
64a	6-10	Ling	5ap	70	329	bl
59a	7-10	Ling	5ap	68	453	bl
35	13-19	Leic	5gd	57	2702	bl

OUR FUGITIVE 2 gr c £9202
68	4-6	Nott	5.1sft		1466
52	8-11	Warw	5g/f		2911
76	3-10	Wind	5fm		3476
76	2-12	Chep	5.1gd		3728
87	1-6	CHEP	5.1g/s	75	4298*
91	2-14	Newm	6sft	81	5098

OUR GAMBLE 3 b f £217
24	6-7	Kemp	6hvy	[90]	1513
61	11-12	Good	7g/f	86	1847
43	9-9	Kemp	6gd	[82]	2173
19	10-11	Sali	6gd	75	2661
62	5-6	Brig	7fm	[70]	3696
50	8-12	Sand	5gd	[65]	4605

OUR GLENARD 4 b g £1301
42a	5-15	Sout	8af	47	84
45a	2-10	Sout	11af	45	330
46a	2-13	Ling	10ap	[45]	412
20a	11-13	Sout	12af	[45]	575
23a	5-8	Sout	11af	[45]	722
41a	6-13	Ling	13ap	45	896
43a	4-9	Ling	10ap	[45]	1289
1	10-11	Beve	9.9sft	45	1633
36a	7-14	Ling	10af	[45]	1712
43	4-10	Beve	9.9g/f	[45]	1946

OUR IMPERIAL BAY 5 b g £2496
60a	10-12	Ling	16ap	66	813	bl
47	10-14	Kemp	14.4sft	64	948	bl
50a	1-9	SOUT	11af	[58]	985*	P
33a	8-11	Sout	12af	55	1197	vis
51a	3-7	Ling	16ap	[55]	1291	vis
28	12-17	Warw	8.1fm	51	2572	p
65a	3-9	Sout	12af	[48]	2724	p
37a	6-10	Sout	14af	55	3096	p
45a	3-10	Sout	14af	55	3158	p
49	7-15	Chep	16.2gd	[52]	3400	p
29	8-12	Chep	12.1g/s	[45]	4364	vis
41	5-11	Beve	12.1g/f	[40]	4716	p

OUR JAFFA 3 br f £12659
77	4-14	Nott	10gd		1241	
84	1-11	BATH	8fm		1904*	
85	1-14	NOTT	8.2g/f	77	2153*	
85	2-10	Newm	8g/f	83	2767	
84a	5-13	Ling	7ap	83	4318	
80	7-13	Sand	8.1gd	83	4607	
76	6-10	Newm	8g/f	[83]	4890	

OUR KES 2 b f £403
29	8-8	Thir	8g/f		2213
65	8-13	Kemp	8g/f		4355
55	11-15	Newm	8fm		4723
72	4-12	Wind	8.3g/f		4829
40	13-16	York	7.9gd	[65]	4997
52a	9-11	Ling	8ap	[62]	5235

OUR KID 3 ch g £0
54	7-12	Beve	9.9sft	64	1306	
39	11-15	Ripo	12.3g/f	62	1785	BL
0	6-7	Wolv	12af	[62]	2050	bl

OUR LITTLE ROSIE 3 b f £3487
52a	7-11	Ling	8ap		322	
38a	8-12	Ling	8ap		514	
62a	5-13	Ling	10ap		601	
59a	1-7	WOLV	12af	[58]	959*	
0	19-19	Warw	10.9gd	60	1124	
1a	P-12	Wolv	12af	60	2203	
0	14-14	Hayd	10.5gd	60	3741	
14a	15-16	Ling	12ap	[56]	4899	

OUR LITTLE SECRET 2 ch f £582
48	5-7	Muss	5g/f		4549
58a	3-12	Wolv	5.1ap		4922
64a	3-13	Wolv	5.1ap		5207

OUR LOUIS 2 b f £3161
18	6-10	Thir	5sft		1224	
39	8-8	Beve	5sft		1303	
43	5-11	Beve	5g/f		1831	
60	4-5	Ripo	5g/f		2481	P
60	1-8	MUSS	5g/f		2611*	
45	5-5	Beve	5gd		2888	
47	7-8	Donc	5g/f	56	3374	
45	8-10	Thir	5fm	54	3607	
19	10-10	Beve	5sft	54	4258	
46	7-14	Catt	5g/f	54	4437	
46	7-14	Redc	5fm	54	4556	

OUR NIGEL 2 gr c £0
47	8-8	Sand	5gd	2188
39	7-7	Bath	5g/f	2976
31	7-8	Wind	5g/s	4218
13	15-16	Bath	5.7gd	4823

OUR OLD BOY 4 b r g £0
24a	8-16	Sout	5af	[35]	374
11a	8-11	Sout	5af	[35]	578
0	12-12	Wolv	7af	[35]	663

OUR PADDY 4 b g £0
0	13-13	Wolv	8.5af	55	40

OUR PLACE 5 b g £0
0	10-10	Wolv	16.2af	48	812

OUR SION 4 b g £0
2	9-9	Kemp	6sft	946

35 14-14 Brig 6fm 1690
0 15-16 Nott 6.1gd [35] 1989

OUR TEDDY 4 ch g £3475
91a 4-11 Ling 8ap 93 547
39 24-24 Donc 8gd 93 951 VIS
64 17-18 Good 8g/f 90 1812
87 5-14 Sand 8.1g/f 87 2096 BL
90 4-15 York 8.9g/f 87 2404 bl
87 4-7 Pont 10g/f [87] 2605 bl
52 14-15 Sand 8.1g/s 87 2915 bl
61 9-9 Kemp 8g/f [85] 3689 bl

OUR WILDEST DREAMS 2 b f £0
40 10-12 Newc 8fm 4866

OUT AFTER DARK 3 b g £15318
62 5-17 Asco 6sft 76 1417
80 1-8 PONT 8g/f [75] 3684*
88 1-7 SAND 5g/s 76 4099*
85 3-11 Hayd 6g/f [81] 4350
85 2-15 Sand 5gd 81 4604
85 6-13 Asco 6.5g/f 81 4773

OUT FOR A STROLL 5 b g £0
0 16-18 Asco 8sft 77 1423
65 10-14 Ling 7sft 77 1624
74 7-13 Newc 7gd 75 3428
66 10-16 Nott 8.2g/s 73 4036
65 7-20 Leic 7gd 70 5046

OUT OF MY WAY 2 ch f £0
30a 8-12 Ling 8ap [35] 78
10a 14-15 Ling 7ap 31 295
31a 14-15 Ling 7ap [35] 671
22a 8-12 Ling 8ap [30] 971
22a 4-4 Ling 10ap [30] 1454
11 11-11 Ling 11.5g/f 27 2842

OUT OF TUNE 4 ch g £0
33a 9-12 Ling 7ap [45] 1074
0 9-9 Muss 5gd [40] 1797

OUTEAST 4 b f £0
42 4-16 Catt 5sft [44] 3932

OUTER HEBRIDES 3 b g £3950
66 14-20 Newm 7g/f 83 1186 vis
63 15-20 Newm 8fm 81 1496 vis
81 4-12 Donc 7g/f 77 1879
81a 2-13 Ling 7ap 76 4897 T
84 2-20 Yarm 7sft 76 5256 t

OUTRAGEOUS FLIRT 2 b f £1753
31 7-8 Thir 5g/f 2213
13 12-13 Carl 5gd 2670
48 7-10 Ripo 5gd 2983
41 3-9 Ripo 6gd 4277
50 3-16 Beve 7.5g/f 45 4597
66 2-9 Catt 7sft [47] 5316

OUTSIDE INVESTOR 4 b g £0
32a 12-12 Ling 8ap [75] 3199
35 16-17 Wind 10fm 75 3477
19 12-13 Folk 12gd 70 4119

OUTWARD 4 b g £0
9 13-14 Thir 8gd 1636
29 17-18 Thir 8g/f 62 1972
1 15-15 Ripo 12.3g/f 58 2526
30 15-18 Pont 10g/f 50 2988
2 10-11 Muss 16g/f 45 3557

OVAMBO 6 b g £3460
97 4-7 Wind 11.6g/s 4219
97 6-14 Asco 12g/f 100 4814
101 4-17 Newm 12g/f 100 4889

OVER RATING 3 ch f £652
61a 2-13 Wolv 8.5af [68] 39
41a 6-11 Wolv 9.4af [64] 115
47a 7-13 Wolv 9.4af 60 281
7a 10-10 Sout 12af 60 321
38a 6-9 Ling 10ap [56] 476 P

OVER THE LIMIT 2 b f £0
61 9-21 Donc 6sft 5368

OVER THE RAINBOW 3 b c £6939
82a 1-10 LING 10ap [89] 886*

OVER THE YEARS 2 b g £281
83 10-18 Epso 10.1fm 87 2250
65 15-17 Asco 12g/f 85 2519
76 10-16 Sand 10g/s 82 2919 BL
81 6-11 Epso 10.1gd 82 4293
75 7-9 Wind 10g/s 80 4943 P
51 10-13 Bath 11.7sft 78 5174 T

OVER THE YEARS 2 b g £281
27a 13-14 Sout 8af 88
18 5-6 Thir 12g/s 1213
33 4-10 Nott 14.1hvy 40 1612
5 16-20 Beve 16.2gd 37 3312
23 11-13 Redc 14.1gd 35 4249 BL

OVER TIPSY 2 b c £0
48 9-17 Chep 6.1sft 4052
51 10-17 Ling 6gd 4443
47 13-16 Newb 7g/f 4677
39 9-12 Bath 8sft 5170

OVER TO YOU BERT 5 b g £7064
15a 8-8 Sout 8af [49] 577
40a 6-14 Ling 6ap [49] 652
34a 5-9 Wolv 8.5af [45] 811
47a 1-10 LING 8ap [45] 831*
45 4-13 Wind 8.3g/s [45] 1058
11 7-10 Chep 8.1sft [45] 1334
23 13-18 Nott 8.2gd [45] 1992
20 14-16 Chep 7.1gd [42] 2369
41 3-17 Warw 8.1g/f 40 2909
37 3-17 Chep 8.1g/s 40 3087
48 1-11 BATH 8gd 39 3142*
45 8-19 Chep 7.1gd 45 3401
40 4-9 Brig 9.9fm 45 3695
19 7-12 Newb 10gd 44 3916
44 6-18 Chep 8.1gd [45] 4485

OVERDRAWN 3 b g £0
79 7-8 Sand 8.1g/s 96 1315
87 9-20 Newm 8fm 94 1496
88 10-18 Hayd 8.1g/f 92 1919
78 13-17 Epso 7g/f 90 2212
75 8-10 Donc 7g/f 87 2427 BL
73 17-21 Donc 7fm 84 4482
61 16-21 Asco 8g/f 80 4777
9 11-11 Good 8gd 75 5027 bl
64a 5-11 Wolv 7.1ap [70] 5357 bl

OVERJOY WAY 2 b f £0
59 7-12 Warw 7.1g/f 4417
62 8-12 Wind 8.3g/f 4829
62a 5-14 Ling 7ap 5076

OVERRIDE 3 b c £2975
66a 6-14 Ling 6ap 73 149
45a 9-10 Ling 7ap 71 262
73a 1-8 LING 7ap [68] 730*
72 5-10 Leic 7g/f [75] 2920

OVERSTRAND 5 b g £0
72 5-10 Muss 16g/f 78 1093

OVERTOP WAY 2 b c £0
58 15-17 Warw 7.1gd 4271
63a 7-13 Wolv 8.6ap 4979

OVIGO 4 b g £4756
69a 3-13 Wolv 8.5af 67 44
63a 3-14 Sout 8af 67 99
41a 7-8 Sout 12af 67 225
71a 1-5 WOLV 8.5af 65 346*
64a 4-16 Sout 7af 65 419
68a 6-13 Wolv 8.5af 69 439
64a 3-12 Wolv 9.4af 69 464
0 P-12 Wolv 8.5af 69 632

OWED 2 b c £0
8 10-11 Hami 6g/s 4006 T
52 10-14 Hayd 6fm 4385 t
65 4-13 Thir 6g/f 4590

OWN LINE 5 b g £0
23 13-20 Catt 15.8gd 45 4965

OXFORD STREET PETE 2 b g £745
70 3-11 Ches 7fm 3633
30 13-14 Ches 7sft 4102
44 7-7 Ches 7g/f 4511

PAARL ROCK 9 ch g £0
0 8-10 Wolv 16.2af 48 812
0 10-12 Wolv 12af [45] 891 vis
0 7-7 Wolv 16.2af [40] 1263 vis

PABLO 5 b h £10115
80 19-24 Donc 8gd 105 951
102 1-10 WARW 7.1gd [103] 1126+ p
92 10-10 Sand 8.1g/s [103] 1349 p
89 9-17 York 7.9g/s 103 1686 p
73 13-15 Sand 8.1g/s 100 2915

PACIFIC OCEAN 4 b c £3297
51a 3-10 Sout 8af [46] 143 T
49a 4-13 Sout 8af [46] 199 t
63a 2-7 Wolv 9.4af [48] 509 t
61a 3-7 Wolv 9.4af [48] 561 t
54a 3-8 Wolv 12af [60] 644 t
51 6-10 Bath 8g/s [60] 1100 t
27 8-12 Folk 9.7sft 55 1273 t
52 4-17 Warw 8.1fm 52 2440 t
49 3-15 Warw 10.9g/f 53 2910 t
52 6-17 Wind 10fm 53 3477 t
52 7-11 Ling 10fm 53 3748 t
23 13-14 Sali 9.9g/f 52 3867 P
57a 3-15 Sout 8af 55 4132 t

PACIFIC PIRATE 2 b c £0
74 10-13 Newm 6gd 4223
66 6-13 Newm 6fm 4726
50 9-12 Newc 7g/f 5011

PACIFIC RUN 3 b c £0
33 12-18 Wind 10g/s 4944
0 8-8 Brig 11.9sft 5092

PACIFIC STAR 2 b c £0
39 10-11 Yarm 6g/f 1728
71 6-12 Sand 7.1g/f 2388
73 5-14 Folk 7fm 2714
68 6-8 Brig 7gd 2952

PACKIN EM IN 6 b h £2054
33a 3-10 Wolv 7af [35] 394
38a 2-13 Ling 6ap [35] 541
11a 9-14 Sout 6af [35] 637
46a 1-15 LING 7ap [35] 969*
0 12-12 Ling 6ap [35] 1075
2 11-17 Kemp 7hvy [45] 1642
0 9-10 Wind 6g/f [45] 3977 bl

PADDY BOY 3 br g £207
44a 3-6 Wolv 8.5af 526
56a 7-10 Ling 10ap 886
41 11-13 Sali 9.9gd 2700
19 8-9 Wind 11.6fm [48] 3294
38a 7-14 Sout 12af 48 3486

PADDY MUL 7 ch h £6735
36a 2-14 Sout 12af [35] 305 t
41a 1-7 SOUT 14af [35] 357* t
28a 4-9 Sout 16af [40] 576 t
34a 3-7 Sout 14af [40] 724 t
38a 4-9 Sout 14af [40] 849 t
42 5-12 Newc 16.1sft 40 965 t
62 3-6 Newc 12.4sft [40] 2686 t
43 3-20 Catt 12g/f 40 2850 t
54 1-12 MUSS 16gd 49 2964* t
38a 4-10 Sout 14af 49 3158 t
45 4-10 Hami 13fm 48 3249 t
0 P-10 Thir 16fm 48 3611 t

PADDY OLIVER 2 b g £0
39 11-13 Warw 7.1g/s 4996

PADDYS TERN 2 b c £0
27 12-13 Wind 6fm 3478

PADDYWACK 6 b g £29515
64a 6-13 Wolv 6af 72 113 bl
77a 1-11 WOLV 5af 70 155+ bl
57a 10-11 Sout 6af 75 198 bl
31a 9-10 Wolv 6af 75 245 bl
50 15-20 Newc 6sft 73 1393 bl
67 4-19 Beve 5sft 70 1627 bl
40 16-19 Thir 6g/f 67 1767 bl
66 3-20 York 6g/f 64 2059 bl
62 5-20 York 6g/f 64 2409 bl
64 3-12 Ripo 5g/f 64 2524 bl

```
23  13-17  Redc  6gd          64   2561 bl
72   1-12  THIR  5g/s         64   2690* bl
75   1-15  BEVE  5sft         68   2942* bl
58   7-10  York  6gd          73   3116 bl
74   3-17  Pont  5gd          73   3241 bl
56   6-11  Donc  6g/f  [73]        3375 bl
76   3-18  Beve  5g/s         73   3852 bl
73   3-8   Nott  5.1gd [73]        4039 bl
69   8-20  Donc  5fm          72   4496 bl
73   4-15  Ayr   5g/s         72   4654 bl
75   5-16  Leic  5gd          72   4700 bl
72   5-12  Redc  5sft  [72]        5305 bl
```

PADRAO 2 b c £0
```
72  11-13  Newm  6gd               4223
```

PAGAN CEREMONY 3 ch g £0
```
24  11-11  Ripo  12.3gd            4281
42  10-10  Sali  12sft             4579
43a 14-14  Ling  13ap              4892
```

PAGAN DANCE 5 b g £26948
```
94a 3-7   Ling  12ap     90    695 p
94  4-20  Epso  12hvy    90   1295 p
94  2-19  Newm  12g/f    90   1484 p
97  2-13  Asco  12fm     92   2582 p
96  6-19  Newc  16.1g/s  92   2771 p
73  13-17 Asco  16.2gd   94   3125 p
88  11-19 York  13.9g/s  94   4023 p
98  2-8   Donc  12fm     92   4534 p
92  4-14  Asco  12g/f    92   4814 p
```

PAGAN MAGIC 3 b c £8116
```
80  3-9   Ling  10sft           1623
70  11-18 Good  9g/f     75     1813
79  1-9   KEMP  12gd     74     2175*
61  13-16 Sand  10g/s    76     2919
78  5-11  Sali  12g/s    76     4080
76  4-11  Epso  12gd     75     4468
69  7-16  Good  12gd [75]       4745
79a 3-10  Ling  12ap     74     5239
```

PAGAN PRINCE 7 br g £6975
```
68  8-10  Sand  8.1g/s   73   4067
80  1-13  WIND  8.3g/s   72   4221*
79  4-15  Kemp  8g/f     78   4362
74  6-18  Kemp  8g/f     78   4714
80  4-20  York  8.9gd    77   4999
77  5-13  Bath  8sft     77   5172
```

PAGAN QUEST 2 b c £0
```
64  7-10  Newb  6g/f          4637
38  18-23 Newm  6gd           5084
```

PAGAN SKY 5 ch g £8318
```
69  14-19 Newm  10g/f   86   1478
75  15-15 Redc  10g/f   86   2101
85  6-19  Kemp  10fm    84   4392
86  4-18  Newm  10gd    84   4681
85  5-17  Newm  12g/f   83   4889
89  3-14  Newb  10hvy   83   5223
71  9-24  Donc  12sft   85   5372
```

PAGAN STORM 4 ch g £536
```
54a 15-15 Ling  7ap     71     698
38a 11-15 Ling  7ap [67]       935 bl
39  7-7   Muss  7.1g/f [70]   1094 bl
58  8-15  Hami  6gd    67     1508 bl
58  5-20  Thir  6gd    67     1638
51  10-16 Redc  6g/f   65     1824
48  10-12 Ayr   7.2fm  65     1909
20  14-18 Thir  6g/f   60     2214
58  3-17  Newm  7g/f   55     2768 T
53  8-13  Kemp  7g/f   56     3034 t
34  15-20 Yarm  8gd    55     3996 t
45  11-20 Chep  7.1gd  54     4488
23  9-18  Newc  8g/f [52]     5017
39a 6-11  Wolv  7.1ap [45]    5210
```

PAGAN SWORD 2 ch c £0
```
61  8-19  Newm  7g/s           5285
```

PAGEANT 7 br m £0
```
0   10-13 Wolv  8.5af [34]    300
26a 6-9   Wolv  7af   [35]    310
7a  5-11  Sout  8af   [35]    372
31a 4-11  Ling  8ap   [35]    408
18a 11-12 Ling  8ap   [35]    571
```

```
4a  9-12  Wolv  8.5af [35]    584 BL
23a 5-12  Wolv  7af   [35]    663 bl
18a 7-16  Sout  8af   [30]    719 bl
```

PAINT THE LILY 3 b f £419
```
40  12-12 Sand  10g/f          2193
55  11-14 Kemp  10g/s          2678
55  4-6   Ches  10.3g/s        2748
32  10-13 Pont  12gd    58     3240
26  13-19 Catt  15.8g/f 54     4675
```

PAINTBOX 3 b f £2294
```
56  6-7   Asco  8gd            3469
64  3-13  Wind  8.3gd          3828
66  2-7   Epso  8.5g/f         4474
62  6-15  Bath  10.2gd [69]    4826
49a 12-14 Ling  10ap    68     5083
```

PAINTBRUSH 3 b f £0
```
40a 8-12  Ling  8ap  [47]     150
35a 5-13  Ling  10ap [45]     412
32a 4-14  Ling  10ap [40]     784
```

PAINTED MOON 3 ch f £0
```
0   9-9   Newm  7g/f           3282
```

PAIRING 6 ch g £0
```
56a 14-14 Ling  7ap    78      518
```

PALABELLE 3 b f £0
```
48  9-18  Wind  8.3g/f        1810
61  7-11  Bath  8fm           2031
50  7-11  Chep  8.1g/f        2627
54  5-11  Hayd  8.1gd         2886
46  9-11  Ling  10gd  [60]    3201
```

PALACE THEATRE 3 b g £888
```
55  8-19  Redc  6sft   77     1145
77  3-20  Thir  6gd    75     1638
```

PALACE WALK 2 b c £0
```
53  9-15  Sali  8gd           4851
65  6-11  York  7.9gd         5003
47  15-16 Newb  8hvy          5220
```

PALANZO 6 b g £0
```
70  5-20  Thir  5g/s   68     1476
58  7-20  Thir  6gd    68     1638
46  10-15 Pont  6g/f   67     2280
```

PALATINATE 2 br c £5400
```
78  4-8   Sali  6gd           3451
82  3-11  Newm  7gd           4190
86  1-13  SALI  7sft          4576*
85  4-11  Sali  7gd   [80]    4853
```

PALAWAN 7 br g £1231
```
84a 2-16  Sout  5af   79      205
77a 11-16 Sout  5af   84      461
76a 7-10  Ling  5ap   83      567
78a 6-10  Ling  5ap   82      692
79  10-13 Epso  5sft  85     1293
26  13-14 Ches  5.1gd 84     1594
45  15-15 Hayd  5g/f  82     1917
31  20-20 Epso  5fm   82     2253 BL
39  11-11 Bath  5g/s [74]    4201
55  18-20 Donc  7sft  70     4496
50  12-15 Good  5gd   63     4751 P
```

PALVIC MOON 3 ch f £558
```
45  5-11  Pont  6sft  [60]   1426
60  3-8   Redc  6sft  [56]   1659
33a 6-6   Sout  6af  [60]    3095
43  12-17 Ripo  6g/s   60    3262
3   17-18 Pont  5g/s   55    3974 BL
20  17-17 Leic  7gd    50    5056 P
```

PAMIR 2 b g £4267
```
58  9-13  Newm  6fm           4726
73  3-12  Wind  6g/s          4945
77a 1-13  WOLV  6ap           5287*
```

PANCAKE ROLE 4 b g £0
```
26  6-7   Warw  12.6fm   35   2782
8   14-16 Brig  9.9g/f   32   3175
0   11-11 Yarm  11.5gd   32   3367
0   11-12 Newb  10gd     30   3916
```

PANCAKEHILL 4 ch f £0
```
54a 5-15  Ling  7ap  [56]    117
```

```
11a 14-16 Sout  7af    55    202
52a 7-14  Ling  7ap    53    344
36a 11-12 Ling  8ap    53    406 p
28a 9-11  Sout  8af    51    457 p
21a 10-12 Ling  8ap  [47]    571 bl
38a 6-12  Ling  8ap  [45]    648 T
27a 7-14  Ling  6ap  [45]    709 bl
25a 14-14 Ling  10ap [45]    828
0   10-10 Sout  8af  [45]    868
```

PANFIELD BELLE 3 b f £0
```
18  6-6   Ling  5gd           3023
```

PANGLOSS 3 ch g £1790
```
71  3-12  Wind  11.6g/s 72   1260
65  7-10  Good  9.9gd   70   2225
70  5-10  Sali  12gd    69   2660 p
52  9-17  Newm  12g/f   67   3618 BL
63  4-11  Sali  12g/s   65   4080 p
63  5-12  Good  16g/s   64   4235 bl
58  6-10  Sali  12sft  [62]  4579 bl
60  6-9   Good  11gd   [60]  5026 bl
```

PANGO 4 ch g £40711
```
63a 9-11  Ling  8ap    71     12
77  2-18  Good  8ap    71    1849
75  2-7   Wind  8.3g/f [72]  2264
80  1-10  EPSO  7g/f   72    2872*
86  1-20  CHEP  7.1g/s 77    3088*
89  1-19  GOOD  8g/f   81    3512*
87  2-13  Ches  7.6sft 85    4103
86  4-16  Good  7g/f   86    4523
72  10-14 Asco  8g/f   86    4813
81  8-19  York  7.9gd  86    4987
```

PANJANDRUM 5 b g £8739
```
66a 1-10  LING  5ap    65    231*
60a 8-10  Ling  5ap    68    329
61a 3-9   Ling  5ap  [68]    492
60a 5-14  Ling  6ap  [67]    516
65a 1-12  SOUT  6af  [65]    610*
60a 7-13  Wolv  6af    71    687
51a 6-7   Ling  5ap  [66]    737
58a 8-9   Sout  5af  [66]    793
26a 12-12 Ling  6ap    63    880
54  4-15  Brig  5.3g/f 56    1371
24  15-17 Warw  5hvy [56]    1532
52  8-18  Good  5sft   55    1867
68a 1-12  WOLV  5.1ap [61]   5362*
```

PANSHIR 3 ch g £7452
```
80  5-17  Donc  8gd            919
49  7-10  Bath  8g/s          1100
74  3-20  Donc  7g/s  [73]    1518
68  11-14 Newm  8g/f   73     1930
84  1-20  NEWB  7g/f   72     2314+
84  2-11  Newm  7g/f   79     3283
73  6-7   Kemp  7g/f   81     3522
```

PANTS 4 b f £2114
```
58a 1-15  LING  7ap  [52]    117*
49a 13-16 Ling  7ap   59     144
44a 8-15  Ling  7ap  [57]    366
51a 7-13  Ling  7ap   55     474
7a  14-14 Ling  7ap   55     499
```

PANZER 3 b g £0
```
70  6-17  Leic  10g/s         1019
```

PAOLINI 7 ch h £446927
```
118 1-11  NAD   9g/f          991*
115 6-11  Long  8g/s          4434
```

PAPALITY 2 b f £0
```
76  5-10  Newm  6g/f          3063
69  8-15  Newm  7g/f          4710
```

PAPARAAZI 2 b c £211
```
63  5-10  Beve  7.5g/f        4602
46  9-10  Newc  7fm           4864
70a 3-11  Wolv  7.1ap         5228
```

PAPEETE 3 b f £4434
```
54  4-10  Leic  8gd  [73]    2133
47  4-9   Brig  8g/f  [70]   2431 BL
50  7-10  Ling  11.5gd 60    3334
40  13-14 Kemp  10g/f  56    3690
62  1-8   BRIG  11.9sft [72] 4143*
53  11-16 Kemp  16g/f  58    4361
```

62a 2-12 Wolv 12.2ap 56 5339

PAPER TALK 2 br c £2966
89 3-6 Newm 6g/f 3031
91 2-8 York 7gd 4326

PAPINEAU 4 ch c £212999
116 1-14 **GOOD** 12g/f [103] 1843* T
118 1-9 **SAND** 16.4g/f[111] 2095+ t
123 1-13 **ASCO** 20g/f [111] 2518* t

PAPPY 3 b f £480
16a 4-8 Sout 8af [52] 355
28 11-12 Wind 8.3fm 50 3291
48 3-18 Chep 7.1g/s 48 3900
23 18-20 Chep 6.1g/s 46 4368
37 11-17 Kemp 7g/f [45] 4794
33 8-17 Warw 8.1g/s [40] 4992

PAR INDIANA 2 b f £1670
57a 4-10 Wolv 7af 36
59a 3-9 Wolv 9.4af 240
69 3-11 Muss 9g/f 1095
60 3-6 Hami 11.1g/s [60] 1604
38 6-8 Hami 11.1g/f [60] 2319
43 6-8 Hami 9.2g/s [57] 4821

PAR JEU 2 b f £0
69 10-16 Kemp 7g/f 3035

PARACHUTE 5 ch g £0
28 12-13 Bath 11.7sft 79 5174

PARADISE BREEZE 3 b f £0
30 11-13 Wind 6fm 2756
22 9-11 Folk 7g/s 3048
47 5-10 Ling 6g/f 3603

PARADISE GARDEN 7 b g £211
22 9-12 Sout 11gd 35 1286
26a 5-6 Sout 11af [35] 1409
27a 4-7 Sout 8af [35] 1593 vis
33 3-15 Nott 10gd [30] 1991
25 8-11 Hayd 10.5g/s 27 2226

PARADISE ISLE 3 b f £42657
79 10-14 Thir 5g/f 90 1766
91 4-9 Newm 5fm 88 2593
94 2-9 Nott 5.1gd 88 3106
109 1-10 **ASCO** 6gd 91 3778*
80 7-11 Ches 6.1g/f [100] 4510
109 1-10 **NEWM** 6gd 100 4884*
98 3-15 Newm 6gd [105] 5088

PARADISE MILL 2 b f £1290
77 2-14 Yarm 7sft 5250

PARADISE VALLEY 3 b g £7463
44a 4-11 Wolv 12af [54] 6 t
50a 5-14 Ling 12ap [54] 103 t
47a 2-10 Wolv 14.8af [54] 125 t
36a 5-12 Wolv 16.2af 50 156 t
52a 1-8 **WOLV** 12af [45] 347* t
5a 6-6 Wolv 12af [53] 752
48a 8-14 Ling 12ap 53 768 t
53a 5-13 Ling 10ap 53 805 t
17a 7-7 Wolv 16.2af 52 866 t
53a 2-8 Ling 10ap [52] 1026 t
26 14-19 Warw 10.9sft 52 1090 t
39 5-17 Bath 11.7sft 47 1543 t
45 4-6 Brig 11.9fm [47] 1692 t
45 3-13 Nott 14.1gd [45] 1990 t
56 1-15 **WIND** 11.6g/f [45] 2267* t

PARAGON OF VIRTUE 6 ch g £5194
81a 1-14 **LING** 10ap 74 122*
75a 7-16 Ling 12ap 79 218
81a 3-14 Ling 10ap 79 452
78a 4-13 Ling 10ap 79 519
79a 7-11 Ling 10ap 79 716
78a 3-12 Ling 8ap 77 888
73a 6-6 Ling 10ap 77 1027
72a 5-12 Ling 8ap 75 1613

PARALLEL LINES 3 ch g £230
26a 9-10 Ling 8ap 56 455
21a 8-11 Sout 6af 48 591
16a 12-14 Ling 6ap [45] 709 bl
43a 4-13 Ling 6ap 45 767 bl

20a 8-10 Ling 5ap [40] 832 VIS
35 10-14 Warw 7.1sft 49 1085 vis
44a 3-7 Ling 6ap [45] 1453
37 6-7 Bath 5fm [46] 1902 bl
34 9-16 Ling 6g/f 46 1985 bl
37 8-9 Thir 5g/f 46 2219 bl

PARASOL 5 br h £8452
114 2-10 Ches 10.3gd[114] 1585 vis
77 9-10 Good 9.9g/f [114] 1862 vis
90 10-11 Epso 8.5fm [114] 2852 vis
92 4-5 Newb 9gd [111] 4682 vis

PARCHMENT 2 ch c £263
45 4-4 Newc 5hvy 4214

PARDISHAR 6 b g £0
71 11-13 Wind 10gd [85] 1381

PARDON MOI 2 ch f £1864
49a 5-15 Sout 7af [49] 87
36a 4-12 Sout 6af [49] 200
50a 3-6 Wolv 6af [49] 283
25a 4-9 Ling 6ap [49] 327
47a 4-13 Wolv 6af 49 436
44a 7-10 Ling 6ap [47] 606
24 7-8 Folk 5g/s [45] 1268
32a 4-8 Sout 6af [45] 1588 P
50 1-7 **KEMP** 6hvy [45] 1641*
30 13-20 Yarm 6g/f 51 1730
50 4-16 Ling 6g/f 48 1985
39 7-12 Brig 6g/f 48 2435
9 18-19 Leic 6g/f 48 2925
19 6-6 Yarm 6g/f [47] 3710
34 9-14 Yarm 6gd 47 3870
16 10-14 Folk 6gd 43 4116
0 14-19 Kemp 6g/f [40] 4793
0 18-20 Yarm 7g/s [40] 5120

PARIS BELL 2 b c £20521
68 3-6 Redc 5sft 1143
55 5-10 Beve 5sft 1632
65 8-13 Carl 5fm 1950
56 7-12 Catt 7g/f 67 3351
64 4-6 Hayd 6g/s 64 3902
53 8-14 Redc 5fm 64 4556
72 1-14 **AYR** 6sft 62 5035*
79 1-20 **NEWB** 6hvy 65 5225*
83 1-10 **CATT** 6sft 75 5318*

PARIS DREAMER 3 b f £0
9a 8-12 Wolv 6af [42] 297
27a 7-9 Wolv 9.4af [40] 525
17a 8-9 Sout 11af 40 608

PARIS HEIGHTS 2 gr g £390
43 10-11 Thir 7fm 2462
72 6-10 Redc 7g/s 2959
64 4-8 Redc 7gd 4247
44 17-18 Catt 7g/f 68 4673
35 17-18 Pont 6gd 63 4934
43 8-12 Redc 8g/s [63] 5107 VIS

PARIS LATINO 5 b g £0
30a 10-10 Ling 5ap 802
41a 12-12 Ling 8ap 881 T

PARIS TAPIS 2 gr f £4275
24 7-10 Thir 6fm 2461
52a 4-12 Sout 7af 3394
59 2-15 Redc 6g/f 3769
59 2-10 Hayd 5g/s 3901
65a 1-10 **SOUT** 5af [58] 4129*
50a 7-12 Wolv 5.1ap [60] 4981
57 6-8 Yarm 5.2sft 60 5253

PARISI PRINCESS 3 ch f £0
27 9-11 Beve 9.9sft 4261
29 7-11 Catt 13.8g/f 4671
37 9-13 Nott 10gd 4861

PARISIAN PLAYBOY 4 gr g £9373
20a 9-12 Wolv 7af 51 956
32 17-19 Yarm 7g/f 50 1132
29 7-11 Warw 8.1hvy 48 1536
37 7-18 Nott 8.2gd [45] 1992
49 1-16 **REDC** 8g/s 42 2958*
49 2-12 Ayr 9gd 45 3328
54 1-17 **NEWC** 7g/s 45 3700*

30 14-17 Hayd 8.1gd 51 3759
31 11-12 Redc 8gd 49 4246
43 11-17 Ayr 7.2sft 49 5063

PARK APPROACH 2 gr f £2902
78 4-11 Newb 6gd 3915
76 3-14 Wind 5gd 4121
78 2-9 Sand 5gd 4497

PARK AVE PRINCESS 2 b f £3189
49a 6-11 Wolv 7af 63 29
49a 9-10 Ling 8ap 58 132
52a 2-15 Ling 7ap 52 295
59a 2-12 Ling 8ap 54 402
58a 5-12 Ling 7ap 58 729
61a 3-15 Ling 7ap 58 815
63a 2-15 Ling 7ap 59 901
35a 9-11 Sout 5af 62 4094
41 18-20 York 7.9gd 62 4321
29 12-15 Redc 6fm 58 4562

PARK LAW 2 b f £7699
90 2-8 Kemp 7g/s 2676
85 1-16 **KEMP** 7g/f 3035*
93 5-9 Sand 7.1g/f 3357
85 6-6 Good 8g/f [89] 4524

PARK ROMANCE 2 b f £11611
92 2-6 Good 6g/f 1866
92 1-9 **NEWM** 6g/f 2245*
95 5-17 Asco 6g/f 2553
98 3-11 Newm 7g/f [90] 3781

PARK STAR 3 b f £2146
54a 5-12 Wolv 5af 65 35
53a 6-14 Ling 6ap 63 121
54a 12-16 Ling 7ap 61 144
33a 15-16 Sout 5af 58 205 vis
50a 7-10 Ling 5ap 58 231
40a 6-12 Sout 5af [56] 587
57a 3-10 Sout 6af 56 657
55a 2-13 Ling 6ap 53 740
42a 10-11 Ling 6ap 55 760
50 10-20 Ripo 5gd 60 1179
0 U-19 Leic 6g/s 58 1354
52 4-16 Nott 6.1sft 58 1465
56 4-15 Redc 7sft 56 1660
10 17-18 Donc 5gd 55 2755
37a 9-13 Wolv 6ap [55] 5359

PARKER 6 b g £633
47a 16-16 Ling 7ap 66 270 bl
67a 4-16 Ling 7ap 66 323 bl
64a 3-12 Wolv 7af 65 840
58a 6-10 Wolv 7af 65 864
51a 11-14 Ling 7ap 63 1010 bl
56a 6-10 Wolv 8af [61] 1319
33 12-13 Bath 8sft 62 1542
48a 5-13 Wolv 6af 59 2053 bl
39 10-14 Chep 7.1gd 59 2199 bl
25 16-18 Catt 7g/f 55 3670 bl
34 16-20 Chep 7.1gd 51 4488 T

PARKSIDE PURSUIT 6 b g £17469
59 9-17 Nott 5.1g/s 68 1774
72 1-18 **GOOD** 5g/f 68 1867*
73 1-16 **AYR** 5g/f 65 2029*
67 9-15 Muss 5fm 71 2084
70 4-12 Sali 6fm 71 2289
77 1-7 **WARW** 6.1fm [70] 2598+
74 3-8 Bath 5.7fm [70] 2669
77 1-4 **BRIG** 5.3fm 73 2838*
33 15-17 Pont 5gd 76 3241
57 14-26 Good 6fm 75 3569
57 11-16 Leic 5gd 70 4700
63 7-19 York 5gd 70 4989
30 3-8 Brig 5.3sft 70 5096
44a 11-13 Wolv 6ap 68 5181
62a 5-13 Wolv 5.1ap 63 5341

PARKVIEW LOVE 3 b c £7012
96a 8-9 Ling 8ap [104] 1040
103 3-11 Newm 7gd 104 1167
90 12-14 York 7sft 104 1665
91 12-18 Hayd 8.1g/f 103 1919
95 8-17 Epso 9g/f 100 2212
74 18-27 Asco 8g/f 97 2521
70 14-17 Good 7fm 94 3550

```
91  4-10  Good   9.9gd         90   3949
85  5-8   Muss   8gd           88   4516
91  3-8   Pont   10fm          86   4755
82  11-17 Newm   10g/f         86   4917
62  11-11 Donc   7sft          85   5219 BL
```

PARLIAMENT ACT 3 b c £0
```
27  13-19 Donc   6g/f               1876 T
42  8-15  Nott   5.1g/f             2152 t
40  8-9   Warw   6.1fm              2778 t
```

PARLIAMENT SQUARE 3 b c £2017
```
83  3-11  Newm   10gd               1148
58  5-9   Sand   10gd               4501
69a 2-14  Ling   13ap               4892
```

PARNASSIAN 4 ch g £23039
```
36  7-14  Pont   8hvy   [58]        1253
54  8-18  Wind   8.3gd   58         1385
56  3-15  Warw   8.1sft  56         1530
58  3-14  Ling   7sft    55         1625
62  1-18  NOTT   8.2g/s  56         1778*
57  3-9   Newm   8gd     56         1891
49  8-16  Good   9gd     59         2220
57  5-13  Newb   8fm     59         2647
65  1-17  HAYD   8.1gd   58         2947*
78  1-9   DONC   8g/s    61         3225*
68  5-12  Good   9fm     71         3625
66  4-12  Leic   8fm     71         3813
74  3-10  Sand   8.1g/s  71         4067
68  7-14  Epso   8.5gd   70         4295
70  3-7   Sali   8sft    [70]       4581
79  1-16  BATH   8gd     70         5022*
58  3-14  Newb   8hvy    74         5227
```

PARSLEYS RETURN 2 b c £0
```
27  7-7   Yarm   6fm                2144
21  5-5   Yarm   6g/f               2341
22  10-10 Newm   7fm                2594
```

PART TIME LOVE 2 b c £2541
```
65  6-7   Good   6g/f               1848
63  1-5   YARM   6fm                2145*
```

PARTNERS IN JAZZ 3 gr c £14364
```
86  5-18  Newm   6g/f    88         1933
51  10-11 Hayd   6gd     [88]       3758
69  13-19 Ripo   6g/s    86         3937
83  5-14  York   5g/s    86         4027
92  1-13  YORK   6gd     84         4322*
83  4-12  Hayd   6sft    89         4779
80  10-20 York   6gd     88         5001
```

PARTY BOSS 2 gr c £0
```
55  8-8   Kemp   7fm                4393
```

PARTY PLOY 5 b g £25939
```
37a 6-10  Wolv   14.8af  67         34
0   18-18 Nott   14.1sft 63         1469
57  7-18  Nott   14.1g/s 60         1772
59  2-9   Redc   14.1g/f 57         2105
67  1-9   HAMI   13gd    57         2176*
67  1-9   THIR   12fm    60         2465*
63  7-19  Carl   11.9gd  65         2673
71  1-7   AYR    10.9gd  63         3149*
76  2-10  Ripo   12.3g/s 68         3261
75  1-6   LEIC   11.8g/f 68         3345*
62  7-14  Brig   11.9fm  70         3674
65  4-9   Yarm   10.1g/s [70]       4254
72  4-17  Thir   12fm    70         4377
61a 5-12  Wolv   12.2ap  69         4983
```

PARTY PRINCESS 3 b f £7614
```
39  12-15 Wind   6g/s    63         1054
40  7-11  Newc   7sft    60         1678
66  1-13  RIPO   6g/f    57         2011*
62  4-18  Wind   6g/f    64         2268
48  10-11 Newm   5g/f    64         2734
33  13-19 Leic   6g/f    63         2925
17  12-14 Yarm   6gd     62         3870
8   19-20 Ripo   6gd     60         4278
33  17-20 Nott   6.1g/s  58         4646
68a 1-12  LING   6ap     57         5241*
```

PAS DE SURPRISE 6 b g £1350
```
57a 3-12  Wolv   8.5af   58         479
38a 12-13 Wolv   8.5af   58         559
55a 5-11  Ling   8ap     55         732
54a 5-9   Ling   8ap     55         763
51a 4-7   Ling   8ap     53         910
35a 10-12 Wolv   8.5af   52         1379
45  10-16 York   7g/f    55         2057
55  5-15  Kemp   9gd     55         2170
51  4-20  Kemp   9g/f    53         2857
57  4-15  Ches   7.6g/f  53         3102
56  5-16  Kemp   9gd     53         3187
55  4-12  Ayr    8gd     53         3328
42  13-19 Good   8g/f    53         3512
42  7-14  Chep   8.1gd   52         3733
36  12-15 Beve   8.5g/f  50         4598
45  10-17 Ayr    9.1g/s  [50]       4620
37a 6-13  Wolv   8.6ap   [45]       5232
26a 11-13 Wolv   9.5ap   [45]       5338 p
```

PASCALI 4 b f £0
```
48  7-18  Bath   5.7g/f  55         1788
```

PASO DOBLE 5 b g £2641
```
36a 11-12 Ling   12ap    65         56
59a 5-9   Sout   11af    62         331
45a 8-12  Wolv   9.4af   62         464
64a 2-12  Wolv   9.4af   62         479
54a 6-13  Wolv   8.5af   [61]       699
62a 2-12  Wolv   9.4af   61         747
0   13-13 Ling   12g/f   61         1986
55  5-16  Good   9gd     57         2220
58  4-12  Sali   7fm     [57]       2288
66a 2-15  Sout   8af     61         2725 P
36  14-20 Kemp   9g/f    57         2857 p
43  9-10  Newm   10fm    57         3404
33  10-14 Wind   11.6fm  55         3638
```

PASS GO 2 b c £448
```
73a 3-10  Ling   5ap                176
41  8-13  Muss   7.1g/f             1119
4   13-13 Folk   5sft               1575
32  7-9   Chep   5.1gd   60         2195 T
36  10-12 Brig   6g/f    55         2435 BL t
3a  14-14 Ling   10ap    55         3449 t
```

PASS THE PORT 3 ch g £3455
```
58  5-12  Kemp   8hvy               1511
79a 1-13  SOUT   8af                2383*
72  6-11  Asco   8gd     [80]       3128
54  9-13  Bath   8sft    78         5172
```

PASSANDO 4 b f £0
```
34a 11-14 Ling   10ap               430
```

PASSING GLANCE 4   £49000
```
99  11-14 Sha    8g/f               211
118 1-11  EPSO   8.5fm  [115]       2252*
97  10-11 Good   8fm    [118]       3533
116 4-12  Sali   8gd    [118]       3886
106 5-7   Good   8g/s   [118]       4232
```

PASSION FRUIT 3 b f £1474
```
37  17-20 York   7.9gd   57         4321
42  12-16 Catt   7g/f    55         4676
46  7-14  Pont   8g/f    [50]       4937
41  6-12  Brig   8sft    50         5094
46  1-12  AYR    7.2sft  [47]       5274* BL
```

PASSIONATELY ROYAL 2 b c £0
```
42  8-11  Catt   5gd                4962
38  10-14 Nott   6.1hvy             5342
```

PASTORAL PURSUITS 3 b c £88028
```
116 2-6   Sand   7.1g/f [110]       2190
111 1-11  NEWB   8gd    [110]       3268*
117 1-8   DONC   7fm    [110]       4477+
113 5-7   Long   7sft   [110]       5070
```

PATANDON GIRL 4 b f £0
```
40a 9-14  Ling   6ap     51         328
32a 11-13 Ling   6ap     48         451
```

PATAPAN 2 b c £5915
```
86  3-8   Capa   5.5gd              2303
```

PATAU 2 ch c £0
```
45  14-16 Newm   7g/f               3582
```

PATAVELLIAN 6 b g £40172
```
112 3-12  Long   5g/s   [95]        1856 bl
107 10-20 Newm   6g/f   [115]       3062 bl
119 3-19  Hayd   6fm    [114]       4384 bl
108 7-15  Long   5g/f   [114]       4952 bl
115 3-11  Mais   6sft   [114]       5313 bl
```

PATIENTES VIRTIS 4 ch f £0
```
28a 6-13  Wolv   6af    [51]        30 vis
26a 9-15  Sout   6af    [49]        167 vis
```

PATRICIA RAY 2 b f £0
```
33a 11-16 Sout   8af                192
```

PATRICIAN DEALER 2 br g £0
```
41  9-11  Chep   7.1hvy             4703
24a 11-12 Wolv   8.6ap              5115
```

PATRIXPRIAL 3 gr c £5392
```
73  5-8   Ches   10.3gd             1597
51  5-7   Newm   12fm               3405
77  1-10  YARM   14.1g/s 70         4255*
78  8-13  Yarm   16g/s   78         4634
73  4-9   Ayr    13.1sft 76         5068
65  6-11  Newm   16sft   75         5271
```

PATRIXTOO 3 gr c £1292
```
66  7-14  Wind   10g/s              1055
68  5-15  Leic   10g/s              1358
35  11-13 Newm   7fm     60         2590
61  2-11  Yarm   10.1gd  [57]       3875
62  4-17  Hayd   10.5fm  60         4388
55  8-12  Beve   12.1g/f 60         4601
69  5-10  Newm   12sft   [58]       5102
```

PATRONAGE 2 b c £671
```
80  5-18  Newm   7gd                3927
81  5-11  Epso   7gd                4289
87  3-18  Newm   8fm                4722
```

PATRONOFCONFUCIUS 2 b g £0
```
59  9-9   Asco   7gd                3126
35  12-14 Sali   7sft               4575
```

PATS MIRACLE 3 ch f £0
```
18a 9-11  Sout   6af     44         91
0   12-13 Sout   8af     38         228
2a  8-9   Ling   12ap    [35]       414 BL
```

PATS NEMESIS 2 b f £0
```
51a 9-10  Ling   5ap                176
0   10-10 Ling   6ap                260
24  13-15 Folk   6g/s               1078
11  12-13 Folk   7g/s               1270
0   14-16 Sout   7af     35         2335
```

PATTERDALE 3 b g £6865
```
79  2-11  Sali   7gd    [86]        3884
79  1-7   BRIG   6g/f   [86]        3985*
73  7-14  Epso   7gd     76         4465
74  2-14  Pont   8g/f   [74]        4937
73  6-17  Wind   10g/f   74         5050
63  6-14  Newb   8hvy    73         5227
```

PATTERN MAN 2 b c £0
```
36a 9-13  Wolv   8.5af              43
44  8-10  Nott   14.1sft            1742
5   P-20  Beve   16.2gd  50         3312
0   16-16 Sout   14af    50         4045
```

PATTERNMAKER 2 b g £0
```
61  6-12  Wind   6g/s               4945
```

PATTERSON 3 br f £0
```
35  8-11  Wind   10fm               3802
34a 12-15 Ling   12gd               4111
0   6-6   Chep   12.1gd             4486
```

PATXARAN 2 b f £1196
```
41  8-16  Pont   6g/f               2275
60  5-6   Hami   6g/f               3202
67  4-7   Redc   7g/f               3770
63  6-9   Newc   8sft    70         4285
67  3-11  Pont   8fm     66         4753
70  6-16  Nott   10g/f   66         4848
28  18-19 Redc   8sft    66         5302
```

PAULA 4 b f £0
```
0   11-11 Newc   8sft               1279
30  6-8   Thir   12g/s              1472 P
60  6-11  Beve   9.9g/f             1835
1   15-15 Redc   9g/f    53         2120 VIS
```

PAULA JO 2 b f £0

33	6-6	Beve	5gd		2513
55	8-13	Beve	5gd		2889
37	11-13	York	6gd		3120
39	14-18	Pont	5g/s		3968
21	13-14	Redc	5fm	45	4556 P

PAULA LANE 3 b f £0

44a	9-12	Sout	14af	72	173
47a	8-9	Wolv	12af	72	467
28a	5-7	Sout	16af	70	529
32	12-19	Warw	10.9sft	55	1090
27	6-9	Folk	15.4sft	52	1271

PAULINES PRINCE 2 b c £4340

52	6-7	Warw	5fm		2573
71a	1-10	SOUT	7af		2802*
72a	4-10	Sout	7af	72	3483
59	9-18	Pont	6g/f	70	4934
65	8-14	Catt	7sft	65	5126

PAVILION 2 b f £0

22	14-15	Kemp	7g/f		4710

PAWAN 4 ch g £17188

54	5-8	Newc	6sft	[62]	963
46a	2-7	Sout	6af	[62]	1032
64	2-19	Redc	6sft	58	1145
42a	8-13	Wolv	6af	55	1221
59	3-13	Newc	5sft	58	1276
61	5-20	Newc	6sft	61	1393
71	3-11	Redc	7g/f	[61]	1822
26	11-14	Ayr	6g/f	61	1898
65	2-9	Muss	7.1fm	61	2086
80	10-11	Hayd	7.1gd	[61]	2184
70	1-4	WARW	7.1fm	[63]	2438*
62	6-11	Warw	8.1fm	69	2600
71	6-17	Carl	7.9gd	68	2672
64	3-8	Muss	7.1fm	66	2809
59	11-18	Catt	7g/f	66	2848
74	1-7	REDC	9g/s	[66]	2962*
54	9-10	York	7.9g/s	72	3074
71	5-6	Newc	10.1gd	[73]	3430
57	13-15	Donc	10.3g/f	72	3598
52	14-16	Redc	8g/f	70	3768
53	13-17	Ayr	7.2sft	67	5063
43a	8-12	Wolv	7.1ap	59	5112
45a	10-13	Wolv	8.6ap	59	5183
23a	11-12	Wolv	8.6ap	[54]	5337

PAWN BROKER 7 ch g £22290

98a	10-14	Ling	10ap	[99]	884
109	1-5	NEWM	8g/f	[105]	3613*
102	4-8	Wind	10g/s	[109]	4220
96	6-7	Good	9.9g/f	[109]	4538
68	26-32	Newm	9g/f	109	4916
102	8-16	Newm	9sft	[108]	5139

PAWN IN LIFE 5 b g £2915

53a	5-12	Wolv	7af	60	68
62a	1-16	SOUT	7af	58	202*
47a	9-11	Wolv	7af	62	363
48a	10-13	Sout	7af	62	556
47a	9-11	Sout	7af	62	585 bl
64a	2-9	Wolv	7af	61	684
52a	7-12	Wolv	7af	60	704
46a	8-13	Sout	6af	60	741 P

PAX 7 ch g £6435

75	6-20	Donc	5gd	82	927
71	6-9	Thir	5g/s	[81]	1217
75	8-20	Thir	5g/s	80	1476
87	1-20	YORK	6g/f	78	2059*
80	8-17	Epso	6fm	83	2256
73	9-17	Pont	6g/f	83	2990
78	8-11	Hami	6fm	83	3248
80	10-24	Asco	5gd	83	3466
65	16-26	Good	6fm	83	3569
69	7-11	Hayd	6g/f	[80]	4350
73	8-15	Ayr	5g/s	79	4654
59	13-15	Catt	5sft	78	5125

PAY ATTENTION 3 b f £5351

52	4-16	Redc	8sft	52	1147
42	8-11	Sout	10gd	52	1280
57	2-16	Nott	10hvy	51	1611
30	7-7	Carl	9.3fm	57	1953
64	2-13	Beve	9.9gd	53	3309
66	1-9	NEWC	10.1g/s	[60]	3702*
58	4-11	Beve	12.1g/s	[60]	3856
51	5-10	Beve	9.9sft	63	4260

PAY THE SILVER 6 gr g £2448

57	11-20	Warw	10.9gd	73	1128 p
69	4-15	Warw	8.1sft	71	1530 p
49	11-15	Brig	8fm	71	1691 p
57a	2-13	Ling	12g/f	54	1986 p
56	10-16	Good	9gd	69	2220 p
71	3-5	Brig	11.9fm	[69]	2329 p
65	3-8	Epso	12gd	65	3217 p
48a	9-11	Ling	16ap	59	3450 p
0	P-14	Brig	11.9fm	64	3674 p

PAY TIME 5 ch m £0

22	6-8	Redc	6sft	[45]	1659
0	20-20	Beve	5g/f	[40]	1948
14	9-13	Hami	5gd	40	2181
47	5-9	Thir	7fm	[34]	3610
42	6-10	Ripo	6gd	[35]	4788
18	15-19	Redc	6g/s	[40]	5110
32	8-13	Catt	5sft	[40]	5321

PAYOLA 3 b f £4462

70	1-6	RIPO	10g/f		3648*
81	6-9	York	11.9g/s	[66]	4058
65	5-11	Epso	12gd	72	4468
64	6-8	Brig	9.9sft	[70]	5095

PAYS DAMOUR 7 b g £5796

41a	9-12	Sout	5af	63	853
40	11-12	Thir	7g/s	65	1215
69	1-14	DONC	5g/s	[62]	1522*
52	12-16	Redc	6g/f	68	1824
61a	3-12	Sout	7af	[57]	2337
34a	7-14	Sout	6af	[57]	2502
39	5-14	Newc	6g/s	[66]	2730
57	13-18	Catt	7g/f	66	2848
59	3-7	York	6g/f	[62]	3436
51	8-26	Good	6fm	64	3569 T
50	2-13	Hayd	6gd	[60]	3757 t
11	10-10	Hami	5g/s	[57]	4010 t
1	7-7	Ayr	6hvy	57	4087
44	9-11	Hami	6g/s	52	4818
47	8-19	Ayr	6sft	51	5069

PEACE LILY 2 b f £0

69	5-13	Wind	6g/f		5047
64	9-16	Newm	7g/s		5280

PEACE OFFERING 4 b c £3048

103	3-8	Cork	5g/s	[102]	1159 p

PEACE TREATY 2 b f £0

12a	8-8	Sout	6af	49	223
8a	10-14	Sout	8af	[45]	354
2a	8-8	Sout	8af	30	490
23a	8-11	Wolv	9.4af	[30]	580 T
16a	7-10	Sout	8af	30	662 bl t
2	11-13	Beve	8.5g/f	[35]	1947
31	6-9	Thir	5g/f	35	2219
28	10-17	Leic	7gd	[30]	2704

PEACEFUL FRONTIER 2 b f £0

23	13-15	Beve	5g/s		3178
0	B-10	Beve	5g/s		3504
0	14-15	Redc	6g/f		3769

PEAK OF PERFECTION 3 b g £21467

80	5-14	Nott	10gd		1241
76a	3-6	Wolv	8.5af	[73]	1377
73	5-9	Kemp	12gd	73	2175
76a	1-11	LING	12ap	[73]	2393*
90	1-8	CHES	12.3g/s	73	2746*
88	1-12	SAND	14g/f	82	3359*
95	2-13	York	13.9g/s	85	4062
90	8-16	Asco	16.2g/f	90	4803
90	6-8	Donc	14.6sft	90	5204

PEAK PARK 4 br g £3664

46	7-10	Kemp	16fm	48	2073
34	7-9	Pont	18g/f	46	2607 VIS
48	2-9	Yarm	14.1g/f	46	2856 vis
25	10-15	Folk	16.4g/s	45	3049 vis
36	3-10	Yarm	16sft	46	4151 vis
49a	2-14	Ling	16ap	46	4319 vis
53a	2-14	Ling	16ap	45	5082 vis
53a	3-13	Wolv	16.5ap	50	5366 vis

PEAK TO CREEK 3 b c £15400

110	3-5	Newm	8g/f	[111]	1188
117	2-8	Newm	7g/f	[111]	1932
111	3-6	Sand	7.1g/f	[115]	2190

PEARL FARM 3 b f £597

27	9-12	Kemp	6sft		4029
69a	3-14	Ling	7ap		5240

PEARL GREY 3 gr f £8350

96	4-11	Ches	6.1g/f	[108]	4510 T
101	2-12	Asco	7g/f	[104]	4811 t
62	14-15	Newm	6gd	[100]	5088 t

PEARL ISLAND 3 b c £0

33	13-13	Warw	7.1g/s		4667
28	16-17	Hayd	8.1g/s		4768

PEARL OF LOVE 3 b c £0

102	7-8	Chan	9g/s		2307
102	10-11	Asco	8g/f	[114]	2469

PEARL OF YORK 3 b f £5063

46	10-14	Nott	10gd		1241
48	13-19	Brig	9.9g/f	55	1940
59	2-14	Redc	10fm	52	2299
46a	5-15	Sout	12af	52	2503
66	1-11	MUSS	9gd	55	2969*
55	3-6	Carl	9.3g/f	61	3231
61	5-9	Newc	10.1g/s	[63]	3702

PEARL PRIDE 3 ch f £0

13	10-11	Redc	10sft	70	1663
46	12-15	Ripo	10g/f	70	1976
56	8-9	Beve	7.5gd	68	3310
7	10-11	Beve	12.1g/s	[63]	3856

PEARLS A SINGER 2 ch f £0

47	11-14	Ling	7.6g/f		3601
74	5-18	Nott	8.2g/s		4035
71	5-9	Beve	7.5g/f		4600
53	13-17	Good	8gd	71	4871

PEARNICKITY 3 b f £0

51	13-18	Wind	10g/f		1959
4	8-8	Chep	12.1gd		2368
27	9-11	Wind	10fm		3802
0	8-10	Bath	11.7g/s		4199

PEARSON GLEN 4 ch g £0

39a	6-11	Wolv	12af	[58]	6
34	16-26	Redc	8fm	54	4926

PEARTREE HOUSE 10 b g £0

0	11-14	Sout	8af	[45]	354
16a	8-10	Sout	8af	40	463
17a	7-12	Wolv	8.5af	[35]	584
21a	7-8	Wolv	7af	[30]	1314
39	6-11	Pont	8sft	48	1425
28a	6-8	Wolv	7af	[30]	1565
38	6-18	Nott	8.2gd	[45]	1992
7	19-20	Yarm	8fm	45	2149
17a	11-15	Sout	7af	27	2384
34	8-20	Yarm	8gd	40	3996
10	16-17	Pont	8g/f	40	4626

PEBBLE MILL 2 b c £0

45	10-14	Newc	6fm		4865
39	12-14	Leic	8gd		5059

PEDLAR OF DREAMS 2 b f £830

69	3-11	Ripo	5g/s		3258
63	5-8	Muss	5gd		4517
31	9-13	Nott	6.1g/f		4843

PEDLERS PROFILES 4 br g £0

37a	8-9	Ling	10ap		476
25a	9-11	Ling	8ap	[40]	535
17a	12-15	Ling	7ap	[35]	830 BL

PEDRILLO 3 b g £12469

92	3-10	Kemp	8fm	87	4389
103	1-6	HAMI	8.3sft	[87]	4695*
64	22-32	Newm	9g/f	92	4916

PEDRO JACK 7 b g £1857

53	11-15	Folk	6sft	75	976
56a	1-5	WOLV	6af	[83]	1310*
40	9-14	Donc	6g/s	[72]	1522
49	9-13	Yarm	6g/f	72	1726

50 12-20 York 6g/f   67   2059
55 3-6   Folk 6fm   [62] 2715
37a 12-13 Sout 6af   [70] 3482

PEE JAYS DREAM 2 ch g £0
54a 6-11 Sout 5af   1752
55 10-13 Thir 6g/s   2689
55 7-10 Newc 6g/f   4403
42 12-18 Pont 6g/f   59   4934

PEEPTOE 2 ch f £3072
78 3-11 Sali 5gd   2658
77 2-16 Nott 6.1gd   3103
70 5-10 Brig 6g/s   4139
71 4-8   Good 6g/f   75   4536
60 7-15 Nott 5.1gd   [72] 4859

PEERESS 3 ch f £34833
82 1-11 BATH 8fm   2031*
93 1-8   THIR 8fm   82   2464*
101 1-9   NEWM 7fm   88   3006*
100 3-17 Good 7fm   94   3550
93a 4-12 Ling 8ap   [96] 5298

PEGGY LOU 3 b f £0
0   8-10 Wolv 14.8af [47] 125

PELLA 3 ch f £12860
53 7-9   Folk 9.7sft   980
59 8-10 Kemp 11.1gd   1140
60 6-20 Wind 10sft   1651
64 2-14 Nott 8.2g/f   58   2153
58 5-10 Chep 8.1g/f   61   2624
62 3-12 Hayd 8.1gd   61   2904
66 2-16 Kemp 9gd   60   3187
66 3-13 Nott 10g/f   63   3419
57 8-11 Wind 8.3fm   63   3799
69 1-14 YARM 8g/s   [61] 4252*
58 7-16 Sali 8gd   67   4334
69 1-17 BEVE 8.5g/f   63   4721*
60 4-13 Pont 8g/s   [65] 5153
65a 5-13 Ling 10ap   65   5299

PENALTY CLAUSE 4 b g £0
41a 5-7   Sout 14af   [45] 376 p

PENALTY KICK 2 b c £3949
52 11-11 Newm 7g/f   3234
75 6-14 Sand 7.1g/s   4069
66 8-14 Kemp 8g/f   4356 BL
83 1-16 NOTT 10g/f   68   4848*
71 5-13 Wind 8.3g/s   74   4940

PENANG SAPPHIRE 2 b g £4193
63a 6-10 Ling 6ap   3817
25 16-17 Chep 6.1sft   4052
41 15-17 Ling 6gd   4443
63 1-16 NOTT 5.1hvy   54   5343+

PENDING 3 b g £1163
68 3-13 Nott 8.2g/f   2633
67 8-10 Nott 8.2gd   [75] 3107
66 6-12 Kemp 8g/f   72   3524 P
47 8-11 Newm 8gd   [70] 3923
65 3-5   Brig 9.9sft   70   4167 p
28 15-16 Yarm 11.5g/s 69   4589 p

PENEL 3 b g £1155
43a 6-8   Ling 7ap   [64] 713
54 8-18 Nott 8.2fm   60 1007 BL
64 2-13 Warw 7.1g/s   [58] 4667
58 5-10 Wind 6g/f   [62] 4835
0   13-13 Wolv 8.6ap   62   5183 bl

PENINSULAR 2 ch c £0
71 7-8   Newb 5.2gd   1205

PENKENNA PRINCESS 2 b f £35997
47 8-9   Good 6gd   3951
91 1-13 KEMP 6g/f   4358*
90 3-10 Newm 6fm   84   4727
104 1-14 NEWM 7g/f   [84] 4914*
106 2-8   Newm 7sft   [100] 5133

PENNESTAMP 2 b c £1187
56 12-15 Donc 6gd   920
53 6-13 Sali 6fm   2287
61 6-11 Sali 6g/s   3110
69 4-9   Sand 5g/f   3355

---

65 4-7   Kemp 6g/f   68   3686
68 3-6   Wind 5gd   66   4123
50 9-19 Nott 6.1g/s   65   4645
64 5-19 Ling 6g/f   [65] 4895
46 8-14 Wind 8.3g/f   [62] 5049

PENNY CROSS 4 b f £1085
62 11-13 Kemp 7sft   88   945
65 14-17 Thir 8g/s   88   1475
78 11-18 Good 8g/f   86   1812
72 7-11 Donc 7g/f   84   2076
78 3-5   Carl 9.3gd   80   2674

PENNY ISLAND 2 b c £765
71 7-18 Leic 7g/f   3342
75 6-16 Leic 7fm   3811
78 3-15 Good 8g/s   4233
75 5-13 Newm 8fm   74   4725
71 10-16 Good 7gd   72   5031

PENNY PICTURES 5 b g £6881
88 3-29 Asco 20g/f   87   2471
88 5-10 Asco 16.2gd   87   3776
73 20-34 Newm 18sft   87   5135

PENNY PIE 3 b f £0
53a 9-15 Ling 7ap   63   151
43a 13-14 Ling 10ap   60   339 VIS

PENNY STALL 3 b f £1703
42 9-10 Leic 10g/f   62   1965
60 4-18 Hayd 14gd   62   2905
65 2-10 Hayd 16.2sft 62   3275
63 6-17 Pont 17.1g/s 63   3970
64 4-19 Sali 14.1gd   63   4856

PENNY VALENTINE 3 ch f £0
10a 10-12 Sout 6af   38   85
24a 9-12 Ling 8ap   [35] 571
9a 6-12 Ling 10ap   [35] 654
0   15-15 Ling 12ap   [35] 707

PENNY WEDDING 2 b f £0
54 9-18 Newm 8fm   4722
54 6-16 York 7.9gd   4997

PENRITH 3 b c £21822
91 1-11 PONT 8g/f   85   2040+
77 3-4   Sali 9.9fm   [90] 2290
69 11-12 Kemp 9g/f   89   2860
92 3-9   Ayr   8gd   88   3305
85 5-10 Pont 8gd   88   3460
53 20-20 Hayd 10.5fm   88   3794
91 2-10 Hami 8.3g/s   86   4136
89 3-8   Muss 8gd   86   4516
89 4-19 York 7.9gd   86   4987
79 13-22 Newm 8sft   86   5103

PENSION FUND 10 b g £389
43 5-11 Beve 9.9sft   49   1633
50 5-11 Hayd 10.5g/s 49   2226
43 6-17 Warw 8.1fm   49   2572
48 4-18 Pont 10g/f   49   2988

PENTECOST 5 ch g £92699
95 10-24 Donc 8gd   100 951
92 6-17 York 7.9g/s   98   1686
62 25-31 Asco 8g/f   96   2489
103 1-15 SAND 8.1g/s   94   2915*
108 4-10 Asco 8gd   [94] 3124
94 9-21 Good 8fm   98   3565
110 1-10 ASCO 8gd   100 3775*
102 9-12 Sali 8gd   [100] 3886
105 9-15 Donc 8fm   106 4531
112 1-5   NEWB 9gd   [106] 4682*
77 8-13 Newm 8g/f   [110] 4887

PENWELL HILL 4 b g £8223
59a 6-12 Sout 8af   69   141
60a 5-15 Sout 11af   68   196
72a 1-10 SOUT 8af   66   318*
59a 7-12 Wolv 9.4af   69   513
76a 2-12 Sout 8af   69   530
76a 2-12 Wolv 8.5af   73   632
7   16-17 Thir 8g/s   57   1214
38 6-10 Pont 10g/f   54   2794
35 14-18 Pont 10g/f   54   2988
36 11-18 Pont 8gd   54   3242
51 3-13 Muss 8g/f   51   3526

---

52 1-17 CARL 7.9fm   [50] 4506*
22 11-15 Redc 9g/s   51   5111

PENZANCE 3 ch c £6371
68 6-13 Kemp 9hvy   78   1515
75 4-8   Ches 10.3gd [78] 2283
82 1-8   NOTT 10g/f   78   2631*
78 10-11 Asco 12gd   82   3070
70 13-19 Kemp 10fm   80   4392
72 14-15 Newb 11g/f   80   4643

PEOPLETON BROOK 2 b c £0
68 5-7   Bath 5fm   2415
60a 6-7   Ling 5ap   2839
60 18-24 Newb 5.2g/f   3266
34 15-19 Nott 6.1g/s   67   4645
21 17-17 Ling 7gd   63   4894
0   0-12 Pont 6g/s   [63] 5152 BL

PEPE 3 b f £6440
37a 6-11 Wolv 9.4af   438 p
28a 6-9   Sout 11af   51   608 p
53a 3-7   Sout 12af   [48] 1030
19 12-19 Warw 10.9gd   49   1124
56a 1-8   SOUT 12af   49   1444*
42a 4-7   Wolv 12af   [57] 2050
0   11-15 Sout 12af   55   2503
5a 8-8   Sout 12af   54   4092 p
57 1-11 CATT 13.8g/f [54] 4671* p

PEPPER ROAD 5 ch g £6997
1   20-20 Ripo 8g/s   52   1366
18 14-15 Thir 7gd   50   1635
57 1-13 CARL 7.9fm   48   2447*
55 2-14 Carl 6.9g/f   51   3229
59 2-16 Carl 7.9g/f   53   3650
56 2-20 Chep 7.1gd   53   4488
46 10-17 Newc 8fm   54   4667 P
53a 6-12 Ling 8ap   [54] 5077
35a 9-12 Wolv 7.1ap   [54] 5358

PEPPERCORN FR 7 b h £22535
102 1-8   DUSS 8.5sft   5075*

PEPPERMINT TEA 2 b f £1605
60 10-18 Wind 6gd   2618
31 11-12 Hayd 6gd   2902
79 2-17 Yarm 6gd   4610

PEPPERSHOT 3 b g £0
11a 12-12 Ling 12ap   60   56
41a 9-13 Ling 16ap   56   137

PEPPERSTORM 3 br c £57746
112 1-14 COLO 8gd   3664*
115 1-16 BADE 8sft   4424*

PEQUENITA 4 b f £0
62 6-19 Wind 10sft   [69] 1650 bl
57 5-17 Newb 9sft   69   5198 bl

PERCHERON 2 ch g £630
29 9-11 Hami 8g/s   4006
53 9-14 Thir 7g/s   4207
73 3-8   Muss 9gd   4517

PERCUSSIONIST 3 b c £124702
86 1-8   NEWM 12g/s   1153*
118 1-4   LING 11.5sft [88] 1622*
119 4-14 Epso 12fm   [113] 2254
0   10-10 Curr 12g/f [113] 2822
114 2-6   Ayr   10.9sft [118] 4687
112 3-7   Long 12sft [118] 4947
109 6-9   San   12sft [118] 5168
109 5-8   Long 15.5hvy [118] 5245 bl

PERCY DOUGLAS 3 b c £522
58a 3-9   Wolv 5af   56   275 vis
24a 11-11 Wolv 5af   56   508 vis
22a 10-12 Wolv 5af   56   641 p
29 9-13 Sout 6g/s   53   1052 p
45 11-17 Warw 5hvy   [50] 1532 vis
32 13-16 Ayr   5g/f   50   2029 vis
50 8-12 Ayr   8g/s   [45] 2543
48 6-7   Pont 10g/f   [45] 2605
47 11-13 Donc 10g/f   [45] 2753
11 18-18 Hayd 5gd   45   2951 vis
35 7-19 Donc 10gd   43   3220 T
59 5-10 Beve 5g/f   [40] 3503 t

22	11-15	Pont	5gd	40	3680 t
18	19-20	Redc	6g/f	45	3767 t
54	6-8	Hami	6g/s	[45]	3880 t
66	7-7	Nott	5.1gd	[40]	3989 t
28	9-12	Redc	6gd	[40]	4245 t

PERCY VERANCE 6 ch g £0

35	5-10	Redc	11g/f		1819
36	4-14	Carl	17.2gd	40	2937

PEREGIAN 6 b g £184

46a	5-6	Wolv	8.5af	[49]	957
52a	3-12	Ling	7ap	[49]	1074
29	11-13	Muss	7.1g/s	49	1463
22	15-17	Brig	7g/f	48	3176

PERELANDRA 4 ch f £3985

70	**1-8**	**LING**	**11.5g/s**	**[75]**	**4181***
71	10-17	Thir	12fm	75	4377
74	4-8	Ayr	13.1sft	72	4690
52	4-6	Muss	12gd	[71]	4805

PERERIN 3 b c £2277

37	13-14	Sout	6gd		1281
50	**1-7**	**BRIG**	**7gd**	**[45]**	**1549***
40	9-18	Sali	7fm	48	2292
38	8-11	Brig	7fm	48	2334 BL
41	8-15	Leic	7g/f	[46]	3515 bl
48	3-10	Yarm	8g/f	46	3712 bl
24	8-14	Bath	8g/f	46	4411 bl
31	6-13	Brig	8gd	[45]	4902
16	11-16	Warw	8.1g/s	[45]	4993 VIS
29	8-20	Yarm	7g/s	[40]	5120 vis
48	3-17	Yarm	8g/s	[40]	5348 vis

PERESTROIKA 6 ch g £703

0	10-10	Sout	16af	65	743
31	12-22	Donc	12gd	65	918
56	4-11	Donc	12g/f	60	1875
54	8-12	Muss	14fm	60	2085
54	4-8	Hayd	14g/s	55	3140
26	10-10	Catt	13.8g/f	52	3669

PEREZ 2 b c £0

37	10-17	Wind	6g/f		3975
53	13-13	Newm	6gd		4223
79	6-15	Leic	7g/f		4455
65	8-11	Bath	5.7gd		4543

PERFECT BALANCE 3 b g £3766

27	17-18	Nott	8.2fm	60	1007
63	**1-16**	**REDC**	**8sft**	**55**	**1147***
57	6-16	Nott	10gd	61	1240
39	5-8	Hami	9.2g/s	60	1603
60	4-11	Redc	10sft	60	1663
1a	11-12	Wolv	12af	60	2203
38	7-11	Redc	9g/s	57	2565
0	17-18	Hayd	14gd	57	2905

PERFECT CHOICE 2 gr c £5460

68	7-13	Newb	6g/f		1760
89	**1-12**	**NEWB**	**6g/f**		**2348***
77	8-11	Asco	7fm		2578
91	6-8	Newm	6g/f		3585

PERFECT HINDSIGHT 3 b g £0

51	7-15	Wind	6g/s	62	1054
15	15-16	Leic	7g/f	60	1825
56	8-9	Warw	6.1g/f	[55]	2906
15	16-16	Ling	6g/f	55	3602 BL

PERFECT LOVE 3 b f £0

65a	8-11	Ling	8ap	80	80
62a	12-16	Ling	12ap	77	218 BL
3	12-12	Carl	6.9fm	75	3548
58	12-16	Ches	7g/f	75	4051
36	13-13	Redc	7fm	[70]	4341
46	15-17	York	7g/f	70	4398
26	14-15	Newc	5fm	62	4870

PERFECT NIGHT 3 b f £4354

72a	**1-10**	**WOLV**	**11af**	**[67]**	**4***
74a	**1-11**	**SOUT**	**6af**	**67**	**91***
57a	6-10	Wolv	7af	[72]	152

PERFECT PORTRAIT 4 ch g £786

75	3-6	Folk	7g/s	[74]	1079
69	7-15	Sout	7gd	74	1282
73	7-16	Good	7g/f	73	1817 VIS

60	4-4	Redc	7g/f	[72]	2122 vis

PERFECT PUNCH 5 b g £2382

70	2-14	Nott	10g/s	62	1777
58	7-8	Nott	10g/f	67	2157
55	7-10	Leic	11.8gd	[67]	2707
56	7-16	Yarm	11.5g/s	66	4589
70	2-19	Sali	14.1gd	65	4856
20	16-20	York	13.9gd	68	5004

PERFECT SETTING 4 b g £127

63	6-11	Ches	5.1gd	66	2286
42	10-12	Ling	5g/f	63	2743
35	9-13	Bath	5gd	[60]	3143

PERFECT SOLUTION 2 ch f £0

49	11-13	Newm	6fm		4726
65a	8-9	Ling	6ap		5237

PERFECT STORM 5 b h £2120

87	7-8	Donc	12gd	[92]	950
59	17-17	Newb	12gd	[92]	1230
87	5-19	Newm	12g/f	92	1484
96	4-12	Hami	12.1gd	91	1746
86	7-12	Wind	11.6fm	93	2759
33	14-19	Newm	12gd	91	5085
76	10-14	Newb	10hvy	90	5223
84	7-13	Newm	8g/s	87	5284

PERFECT TONE 2 ch f £0

70	5-11	York	7.9gd		5003

PERFECTPERFORMANCE 2 ch c £8639

102	**1-8**	**SALI**	**7gd**		**2695***
102	2-8	Newm	7g/f		3585
112	**1-3**	**SALI**	**8g/f**		**3865***
112	**1-8**	**ASCO**	**8g/f**	**[100]**	**4797***
94	7-9	Newm	7sft	[100]	5137

PERFIDIOUS 6 b g £4359

71a	3-8	Ling	10ap	[70]	294
74a	2-16	Ling	12ap	70	493
71a	5-15	Ling	12ap	70	549
74a	3-14	Ling	10ap	72	625
33	15-15	Epso	10.1gd	[73]	3216

PERFORMING ART 2 b c £0

56	10-11	Donc	8fm		4462

PERGOLACHA 2 b f £884

78a	2-12	Ling	8ap		19

PERIANTH 2 ch c £760

61	4-5	Wind	5sft		1646
63	9-12	Ling	5g/f		1981
56	10-15	Wind	6g/f		2263
39a	10-12	Ling	7ap	65	3820
62	3-12	Bath	5.7gd	61	4545
63	8-19	Ling	6g/f	[62]	4895
50	10-18	Pont	6g/f	62	4934

PERIDA 4 b f £0

42	9-16	Folk	12fm	48	2718
12	19-19	Bath	17.2gd	45	3147
40	9-11	Yarm	11.5gd	45	3367

PERLE DOR 3 b f £12968

74	**1-11**	**REDC**	**7g/f**	**[70]**	**1822***
78	**1-10**	**YARM**	**8g/f**	**70**	**2344***
88	**1-6**	**DONC**	**8g/f**	**74**	**3597***
77	5-8	Thir	8fm	80	4378

PERRYWINKLE 2 b f £0

0	18-18	Newc	6g/s		3699

PERRYWINKLE BOY 3 b c £415

56	4-5	Pont	8gd		3683
18	8-13	Pont	8g/s		3973
0	10-10	Newc	7hvy		4216
0	P-13	Ayr	10sft	[40]	5066 T
14	7-12	Ayr	7.2sft	[40]	5274 t

PERSARIO 5 b m £9760

90	**1-20**	**KEMP**	**6gd**	**78**	**1138***
74	17-30	Newm	6g/f	86	1481

PERSEPHONE HEIGHTS 3 br f £0

3a	9-9	Ling	13ap	52	18

PERSIAN CARPET 2 b f £2709

56	7-17	Ling	7g/f		2584
66	4-9	Warw	7.1fm		2776
70	2-15	Pont	6gd		3239
67	2-14	Hayd	6gd	[70]	3735
46	6-15	Folk	6g/f	[70]	4369
39	23-26	Newb	6.5g/f		4679
41	20-29	Newm	6gd		5087

PERSIAN DAGGER 3 b c £711

53	12-14	Wind	10g/s		1055
66	7-14	Wind	10g/s		1259
73	6-9	Ling	10sft		1623
56	5-7	Brig	11.9fm	65	2333
68	3-12	Warw	15g/f	64	2908

PERSIAN GENIE 3 br f £1076

66	8-14	Kemp	10g/s		2678
67	8-13	Kemp	10gd		3038
64	7-13	Kemp	10gd		3186
51	8-10	Newb	10fm	63	3630
50	11-17	Kemp	12sft	62	4033
57	2-10	Sali	12g/f	[60]	4579
45	6-18	Pont	12g/f	55	4938

PERSIAN KHANOOM 2 b f £0

65a	6-11	Ling	8ap		5236

PERSIAN KING 7 ch g £1066

61	12-20	Wind	11.6g/s	84	1056
47	14-20	Epso	12hvy	81	1295
65	9-13	Kemp	12g/f	78	1916
61	7-10	Sand	14g/f	70	2192
60	6-11	Newb	13.3fm	65	2651
65	3-8	Epso	12g/f	65	2869
59	4-8	Ling	11.5fm	61	3747

PERSIAN LASS 4 ch f £625

93a	5-14	Ling	10ap	[94]	82

PERSIAN LIGHTNING 5 b g £27560

106	4-10	Newm	10g/f	[102]	1483
105	4-14	Good	12g/f	[102]	1843
110	**1-11**	**EPSO**	**10.1g/f**	**102**	**2208***
107	4-14	Sout	12g/f	107	2556
102	6-9	Good	12fm	[107]	3563

PERSIAN MAJESTY 4 b c £22024

103	6-11	Sand	10g/s		1350
116	3-14	Good	12g/f	[108]	1843
114	3-6	Asco	12fm	[113]	2579
110	5-8	Newm	12g/f	[113]	3030
104	4-9	Good	12fm	[113]	3563
96	9-9	Asco	12g/f	[113]	4812 BL

PERSIAN PUNCH 11 ch g £0

0	P-13	Asco	16.2sft	[118]	1418

PERSIAN ROCK 2 b c £10943

87	2-13	Donc	5gd		954
90	**1-13**	**WIND**	**6fm**		**3478***
91	**1-6**	**CHEP**	**6.1g/s**	**82**	**3897***
82	12-22	Donc	6fm		4458
82	8-12	Asco	7g/f	88	4810

PERSONIFY 2 ch c £5359

88	**1-6**	**YARM**	**6g/f**		**2851***
87	4-4	Ches	7.6g/f		4513
50	9-14	Newm	6sft	86	5098 VIS

PERTEMPS BIANCA 3 b f £0

5a	6-11	Sout	11af	[45]	191 BL
23a	6-11	Ling	8ap	[45]	343 bl
0	12-12	Wolv	12af	40	469 bl
0	7-7	Sout	7af	40	680 bl

PERTEMPS CONECTION 3 b f £0

0	13-14	Sout	12af		194

PERTEMPS MAGUS 4 b f £5295

58	3-18	Donc	7gd	57	2755
67	**1-15**	**CATT**	**7sft**	**57**	**3933***
56	6-15	Ayr	7.2hvy	63	4088
61	3-10	Yarm	7g/s	59	4251
55	6-18	Ayr	7.2sft	63	4622 P
56a	6-14	Ling	7ap	[62]	5080 VIS
59a	4-14	Ling	7ap	58	5300 vis

PERTEMPS RED 3 ch c £0

3a	13-13	Ling	12ap		873

9　12-12　Warw　7.1gd　　　　1129

PERTEMPS SIA 4 b c £395
3　13-14　Bath　18.2fm　37　2417
36　5-19　Bath　17.2gd　37　3147
37　3-12　Nott　14.1g/f　36　3420

PERTEMPS WIZARD 4 br g £0
0　9-10　Sout　8af　47　677

PERTINO 8 b g £0
33　9-11　Leic　11.8fm　53　2112 p

PERUVIA 4 b f £0
57　7-9　Nott　10sft　76　1467
54a　5-10　Sout　11af　[75]　2499 VIS
33　11-12　Hami　9.2g/s　70　2832 vis t

PERUVIAN BREEZE 3 b g £3619
59　5-13　Kemp　9gd　60　1141
45　6-8　Hami　11.1gd　[59]　1390
63a　1-8　LING　12ap　[59]　2065*
46　7-7　Brig　11.9fm　60　2333
1a　9-11　Sout　12af　65　2804
47　2-9　Wind　11.6fm　[58]　3294

PERUVIAN CHIEF 7 b g £7490
96a　8-10　Ling　5ap　　　883 vis
98　2-11　Newb　5.2gd　95　1207 vis
95　9-13　Newm　5g/f　[97]　1479 vis
84　9-11　Good　5g/f　96　1845 vis
95　7-10　Kemp　5fm　[96]　2068 vis
0　U-28　Good　6fm　95　3622 vis
75　12-16　Hayd　5fm　95　4382 vis
94　10-22　Donc　5.6fm　95　4459
96　3-9　Good　6g/f　92　4537
75　12-14　Ripo　6gd　92　4786 bl

PERUVIAN PRINCE 2 b c £2765
89　2-8　Kemp　7fm　　　4393

PERUVIAN STYLE 3 b g £21508
85a　1-8　LING　5ap　76　818*
85a　1-9　LING　5ap　78　914*
53　10-19　Newm　6g/s　81　1154
76　5-10　Hayd　6g/f　78　1488
58　10-11　Newb　6gd　76　1734
53　7-10　Hayd　5g/s　73　3135
69　6-7　Bath　6fm　73　3371 BL
69　5-9　Epso　6fm　70　3543
76　2-7　Brig　6fm　70　3693
60　7-9　Wind　5fm　69　3804
77　1-14　EPSO　7gd　70　4465*
34　18-19　Good　6gd　74　4747

PESQUERA 2 b f £802
53　10-17　Yarm　6gd　　　4610
77　3-11　Wind　6g/s　　　4941

PETANA 4 gr f £4027
33　5-9　Ayr　6g/s　[45]　1447 bl
27　12-20　Beve　5g/f　[45]　1948 bl
31　4-13　Hami　5gd　42　2181 bl
37　8-19　Beve　5g/f　40　2326 bl
52　1-9　MUSS　5g/f　38　2614* P
41a　7-10　Ling　5ap　49　3332 p
37　10-17　Catt　5g/f　49　3667 p
33　10-15　Carl　5fm　[49]　4508 p

PETARDIAS MAGIC 2 ch c £26100
87a　1-6　LING　6ap　[82]　79*
87a　4-9　Ling　8ap　[84]　756
85　1-16　KEMP　6g/s　77　1116*
86　3-19　Newm　6g/s　84　1154
75　7-14　Ripo　6g/s　85　1360
93　2-7　Ling　6sft　85　1621
67　14-14　Newm　6sft　[88]　5100
73　11-13　Donc　5sft　85　5218

PETER PAUL RUBENS 3 ch c £64359
44　9-11　Kemp　8hvy　　　1514
74　4-12　York　7g/s　　　1688
100　1-9　ASCO　7g/f　　　1929*
87　5-28　Asco　7g/f　90　2558
106　1-9　SAND　7.1g/f　90　3338*
109　1-17　GOOD　7fm　96　3550*
109　1-5　CHES　7.6g/f　[105]　4047+
109　2-8　Epso　7g/f　[105]　4472

PETER ROUGHLEY 2 b g £834
41　7-7　Hami　8.3sft　　　4691
58　4-10　Catt　7sft　　　5127
64　2-10　Catt　7sft　　　5317

PETERS CHOICE 2 ch g £6868
90a　1-12　WOLV　5af　[67]　32+
90a　1-10　WOLV　5af　74　69*
53　13-16　Muss　5g/f　79　1120
48　12-13　Thir　5sft　79　1229
67　5-9　Muss　5g/f　72　1457 P
54　12-16　Ayr　5g/f　69　2029
48　7-12　Ayr　5g/s　66　2566
68　2-18　Carl　5g/f　63　3228 BL
59　8-15　Muss　5g/f　66　3561 bl

PETERS DELITE 2 b c £1482
61　9-12　Hayd　6gd　　　2902
70　3-10　Thir　5fm　　　3606
71　3-4　Newc　5hvy　　　4214
55　9-14　Warw　6.1g/f　69　4420

PETERS IMP 9 b g £4734
55　1-11　CATT　12g/f　[25]　3190*
51　5-11　Muss　16g/f　51　3557
50　3-14　Catt　12g/f　[51]　3668
46　4-6　Redc　16g/f　48　3810
29　8-19　Catt　15.8g/f　45　4675
43　3-11　Catt　12sft　[45]　5128

PETERS PLOY 4 ch g £0
1a　12-12　Sout　6af　　　2722
12　10-11　Leic　10g/f　　　3208
0　14-15　Ling　12ap　　　4111
0　8-10　Ling　12ap　　　4314

PETIT CALVA 3 b f £15036
100　3-7　Mais　7sft　　　1156
107　2-8　Long　8g/s　　　1432

PETIT PARIS 3 £223463
118　2-9　Nad　9af　　　989 t

PETITE COLLEEN 2 b f £342
54a　5-13　Wolv　8.5af　[72]　111
26　16-19　Warw　10.9gd　68　1124
66　4-14　Wind　10g/f　65　2452
48　15-18　Leic　10gd　65　2706
63　6-12　Wind　11.6gd　62　3161 P
43　12-15　Wind　11.6fm　62　3481 p
50　5-15　Chep　8.1sft　60　4057
40　11-16　Chep　10.2g/s　59　4365
53a　4-11　Wolv　8.6ap　[57]　5356 VIS

PETITE ELLE 2 b f £721
54a　3-4　Wolv　5af　　　938
47　4-5　Yarm　6fm　　　2145 VIS
37a　4-7　Sout　7af　　　2721
56　3-8　Yarm　6fm　　　2865

PETITE GIRL 2 gr f £0
24　10-12　Nott　6.1g/f　　　4844

PETITE MAC 4 b f £0
25　15-18　Pont　5g/s　53　3974
37　7-9　Thir　5g/s　53　4210

PETITE NOIRE 2 b f £0
10　9-10　Bath　5g/s　　　1097
28a　6-7　Sout　7af　　　2721 T
28a　5-8　Ling　6ap　　　3745 t

PETITE ROSE 3 b f £9568
91　1-15　FOLK　6g/s　　　1078+
93　2-5　Ripo　6gd　　　1175
62　7-9　Nott　6.1g/s　[95]　1773

PETITE SPECTRE 2 ch f £0
34　17-23　Newm　6gd　　　5084
69a　8-14　Ling　7ap　　　5258

PETONGSKI 6 b g £0
13　19-20　Ripo　5gd　50　1179 bl e
40　8-13　Newc　5sft　50　1276 bl e
33　7-11　Redc　6sft　[47]　1662

PETRION 3 b f £434
45　12-15　Leic　6g/f　　　1829
44　19-16　Newm　7fm　　　2092
45a　3-12　Sout　7af　　　2339

28　6-7　Muss　8g/f　46　2613
8　16-20　Yarm　7g/s　[45]　5120

PETROLERO 4 gr g £0
49a　4-10　Sout　8af　[41]　143 t
14a　10-13　Sout　8af　[44]　199 t
21　9-14　Hayd　10.5gd　44　3741

PETROLINA 3 b f £0
8　11-11　Nott　6.1sft　　　1607
17a　13-15　Ling　12ap　　　2393
56a　4-10　Sout　8af　　　2997
47a　8-16　Sout　8af　55　3487
28　9-14　Newm　7gd　[53]　4195 T

PETROSA 4 ch f £1357
69　4-12　Good　9fm　70　3535
72　5-14　Sali　9.9g/f　70　3867
67　8-15　Newb　11g/f　70　4643
74　3-14　Wind　8.3g/f　69　4832
45　5-18　Wind　10g/s　[69]　4944

PETRULA 5 ch g £4526
81　2-12　Ches　10.3gd　77　1586 bl
77　6-19　Ripo　10g/f　81　1781 bl
73　14-17　Thir　12fm　81　4377
38　16-20　Ayr　10g/s　80　4656 bl
79　7-20　York　10.4gd　77　4986 bl

PETTICOAT HILL 2 b f £0
41a　13-14　Ling　7ap　　　5076

PEVENSEY 2 b c £9652
63　6-10　Hayd　6g/s　　　2228
16　11-13　Pont　6gd　　　3682
85　1-15　NEWM　8gd　　　4883* BL
88　3-7　Leic　10gd　[87]　5044 bl

PEYTO PRINCESS 5 b m £0
52a　10-16　Ling　7ap　61　20
62a　4-16　Ling　7ap　61　55
53a　5-14　Ling　6ap　60　121
54a　6-15　Ling　7ap　59　151

PHANTOM FLAME 3 b g £466
16a　10-13　Wolv　8.5af　55　40
38a　5-11　Wolv　7af　49　378
41a　2-9　Wolv　9.4af　[45]　525
13a　11-11　Wolv　7af　[45]　579
21a　8-10　Sout　8af　40　678

PHANTOM SONG 2 gr c £0
23　14-14　Hayd　6gd　　　3735
29　15-18　Pont　5g/s　　　3968

PHANTOM STOCK 3 b g £10277
41a　8-11　Wolv　12af　50　72
43a　6-10　Sout　12af　49　138
62a　1-8　WOLV　14.8af　49　277*
61a　2-9　Sout　16af　55　336
65a　1-10　WOLV　16.2af　55　358*
65a　4-11　Ling　13ap　[65]　515
66a　2-8　Ling　16ap　63　733
68a　1-12　LING　16ap　64　813*
36a　7-8　Wolv　16.2af　64　837
67　4-14　Donc　18gd　67　926

PHANTOM WIND 3 b f £46178
101　6-8　Newb　7gd　　　1233
97　5-11　Newb　6gd　[98]　3268
111　1-12　GOOD　7fm　[98]　3564*
111　3-6　Leop　8g/f　[98]　4572

PHARAOH HATSHEPSUT 6 b m £0
8a　10-12　Wolv　7af　40　956
21　10-10　Muss　16g/f　40　1093
19　11-15　Hami　9.2gd　35　1388
19　11-15　Redc　7sft　35　1660 VIS
1　10-10　Ayr　9.1gd　35　2571
35　6-10　Muss　9g/f　[32]　2811
21　10-14　Ayr　7.2gd　[32]　3324
32　9-12　Carl　6.9fm　32　3548 BL
33　6-8　Ayr　8g/f　26　3763 bl
25　10-16　Catt　5sft　[26]　3932 bl

PHARLY REEF 12 b g £0
24　4-8　Chep　10.2sft　[30]　1333

PHAROAHS GOLD 5 b g £7947

67a	1-13	WOLV	8.5af	60	40*	e
41a	8-14	Sout	8af	65	99	e
54a	9-11	Sout	8af	65	186	e
32a	11-13	Wolv	8.5af	62	251	e
64a	2-10	Sout	8af	61	318	e
42a	10-13	Wolv	8.5af	63	439	e
60a	5-9	Wolv	7af	62	940	e
51	7-17	Leic	7g/s	52	1020	vis
52a	3-14	Sout	8af	60	1198	e
48a	7-10	Wolv	8.5af	60	1322	e
53	1-15	**HAMI**	9.2gd	50	1388*	vis
11	9-14	Warw	8.1hvy	55	1535	vis
52	7-14	Hami	8.3gd	54	1748	vis
54a	9-14	Ling	10ap	60	2392	
45	4-10	Ayr	9.1gd	53	2571	
23	16-17	Newm	7g/f	52	2768	vis
33	11-15	Catt	7sft	51	3933	
1	17-17	Hami	9.2g/s	51	4008	vis
40	8-12	Redc	8gd	49	4246	vis
43	13-15	Carl	7.9g/f	49	4346	P
39	10-16	Chep	7.1hvy	[48]	4707	p
16a	11-13	Wolv	8.6ap	55	4982	BL e

PHECKLESS 4 ch g £1284

66a	6-16	Ling	7ap	70	181
68a	4-16	Ling	7ap	69	270
45a	15-16	Sout	7af	69	419
66a	3-14	Ling	7ap	[69]	450
62a	4-14	Ling	6ap	[67]	516
51a	10-10	Ling	5ap	66	755
56a	9-12	Ling	8ap	[66]	878
54a	8-13	Ling	6ap	66	902
60	3-15	Folk	6sft	57	976
42	12-18	Wind	6g/f	[58]	1806
41	13-20	Leic	7gd	57	5046
40a	11-14	Ling	7ap	[60]	5294

PHI 2 b c £1608

72	7-14	Yarm	7gd	4611
81	2-10	Wind	8.3g/f	4831
74	5-14	Leic	8gd	5058

PHI PHI 2 b f £0

62	7-11	Wind	5g/f	2450

PHILHARMONIC 3 b g £2025

101	4-15	Newc	5g/s	101	2727
97	10-19	Newm	6fm	101	3002
65	20-24	Ayr	6s/t	100	4686
87	5-9	Hami	6g/s	[98]	4817
74	16-20	York	6gd	95	5001

PHILLY DEE 2 b f £1344

47a	3-11	Wolv	6af	[47]	73	
49a	2-10	Sout	6af	[47]	139	
31a	5-12	Sout	6af	[47]	200	
48a	3-9	Sout	6af	[47]	256	
32a	3-9	Ling	5ap	[47]	413	bl
16a	10-14	Ling	6ap	[47]	495	bl
15a	10-10	Ling	5ap	[47]	548	bl
0	9-10	Sout	6af	[45]	851	
0	8-8	Ling	5ap	[40]	1290	bl
43	10-17	Bath	5g/f	[49]	1787	
21a	7-9	Sout	6af	[40]	2493	
9	7-7	Brig	6g/f	[42]	3985	bl

PHILOSOPHIC 10 b g £0

18a	7-9	Ling	16ap	[40]	454
10a	14-14	Ling	13ap	[35]	537 P
2a	13-13	Ling	13ap	[35]	602 p

PHLAUNT 2 b f £1447

67	4-8	Good	6gd		2537
46	9-11	Warw	5g/f		2911
66	3-14	Hayd	6gd		3735
52	3-6	Brig	7sft	[70]	4163
38a	8-14	Ling	7ap	[68]	4658

PHLUKE 2 b g £7037

75a	3-14	Sout	7af	75	158
71a	2-10	Ling	6ap	[73]	258
70a	5-15	Ling	7ap	73	337
71a	3-7	Sout	7af	[72]	531
56a	7-15	Ling	7ap	[70]	670
58	5-12	Folk	6sft	70	975
72	1-16	**BEVE**	7.5g/s	67	1163*
74	2-16	Leic	8g/s	70	1359
68	7-17	Warw	7.1sft	73	1526

66	4-13	Good	9g/f	73	2024
67	8-12	Leic	8g/f	72	2922
60	6-11	Leic	8g/f	70	3516
48	13-17	York	7g/f	68	4398
53	10-17	Nott	8.2gd	65	4862

PHOEBE WOODSTOCK 2 ch f £810

78	3-15	Kemp	7g/f	4710

PHOENIX EYE 3 b c £0

33	8-8	Ches	10.3gd		1597
50	8-10	Hayd	10.5g/f		1922
55	9-11	Beve	7.5g/s		2325
30a	12-12	Wolv	7.1ap	[50]	5233

PHOENIX NIGHTS 4 b g £1681

25a	10-13	Wolv	9.4af	52	287	
38a	5-6	Wolv	9.4af	[47]	423	
25a	10-10	Wolv	8.5af	[45]	511	
0	9-9	Sout	12af	[45]	774	BL
69	6-8	Ches	10.3g/f	[52]	3083	
6	4-4	Newm	12g/f	[52]	3946	
53	4-8	Muss	9g/f	[52]	4173	
34	6-7	Thir	8g/s	[52]	4208	
49	9-11	Muss	9g/f	[52]	4550	
52	6-6	Hami	8.3sft	[52]	4695	

PHOENIX REACH 4 b c £5250

113	6-10	Asco	10g/f	[115]	2488
114	6-10	Sain	12g/s	[115]	3012
110	10-11	Asco	12g/f	[115]	3442 VIS

PHONE TAPPING 3 b g £0

40	10-11	Newm	8g/f		2248
53	6-11	Beve	8.5gd		2656
53	6-16	Ripo	8gd		2987
32	10-14	Hayd	10.5gd	55	3741
56	7-17	Redc	10sft	55	5307

PHOTOFIT 4 b g £0

71	6-14	Folk	7g/s		1080
4	14-18	Asco	8sft	72	1423

PHRED 4 ch g £1926

44	6-18	Wind	8.3g/s	66	1059	
65	4-12	Hayd	8.1g/f	65	1485	
61	6-14	Ling	7sft	64	1625	
61	5-12	Bath	8g/f	63	1792	
64	4-14	Chep	7.1gd	62	2199	
62	2-8	Wind	8.3g/f	61	2448	
47	9-13	Newb	8fm	61	2647	
65	10-20	Kemp	9ap	60	2857	
50	5-9	Newb	9gd	60	3922	
0	19-19	Chep	8.1g/s	[58]	4366	
41	9-12	Good	9g/f	55	4539	T
20a	9-13	Wolv	8.6ap	54	4982	t

PHRENOLOGIST 3 gr g £2588

67a	1-14	**LING**	6ap		23*
56a	3-11	Ling	6ap	[69]	130
52a	13-16	Ling	7ap	67	323
2	9-9	Ling	7g/f	[65]	1984
21a	11-12	Wolv	6ap	65	4984
35a	12-13	Wolv	6ap	65	5010 BL

PHYSICAL 2 b c £0

49	9-14	Newb	6sft	5197
70	8-17	Yarm	6g/s	5350

PIANO STAR 4 b g £0

92	8-12	Kemp	10gd	[103]	1139
65	10-10	Ches	10.3gd	[100]	1585 VIS

PIANOFORTE 2 b c £2079

79	6-12	Newm	6g/f	3280
92	2-16	Leic	7fm	3811
74	4-9	Yarm	8sft	4147

PIC UP STICKS 5 gr h £52602

98	1-9	**NAD**	6.5g/f	90	790*
99	3-11	Newb	5.2gd	96	1207
97	6-29	Asco	6fm	96	2581
95	8-24	Asco	5gd	96	3466
81	17-28	Good	6fm	96	3622
86	16-22	Donc	5.6fm	95	4459
102	1-14	**RIPO**	6gd	93	4786*
90	9-20	York	6gd	97	5001
94	7-13	Muss	5g/s	95	5143
97	5-12	Newb	6sft	97	5196

PICATRIP 3 b f £0

10a	15-15	Ling	7ap	[40]	216

PICCLED 6 b g £13582

82a	8-10	Wolv	6af	96	834
80	3-20	Donc	6gd	76	927
44	16-16	Muss	5g/f	78	1120
1	19-19	Beve	5sft	78	1627
62	10-11	Ches	5.1gd	77	2286
86	1-13	**YORK**	5g/f	77	2359*
23	15-15	Newc	5g/s	83	2727
83	5-16	Newm	5g/f	83	3033
30	24-24	Asco	5gd	83	3466
0	R-20	Hayd	5fm	83	3792
69	16-20	Donc	5fm	83	4496
85	3-15	Ayr	5g/s	83	4654

PICCLEYES 2 b g £6552

63a	5-13	Wolv	6af	65	1	
64a	3-13	Wolv	8.5af	[63]	111	
59	8-16	Ling	7g/f	[65]	1982	
40	12-20	Newb	7g/f	63	2314	
46	8-20	Chep	6.1gd	63	2372	bl
66	1-12	**LING**	6g/f	[59]	2586*	bl
35	11-17	Wind	6fm	63	2975	bl
47	9-9	Epso	7gd	[63]	3215	bl
62	3-12	Donc	6gd	60	3599	bl
55	6-9	Wind	5fm	61	3804	bl
40	8-10	Wind	6g/f	[61]	3977	bl
62	3-17	Ling	6g/f	60	4740	bl
69	2-19	Nott	6.1g/f	[60]	4845	bl

PICCOLO PRINCE 3 ch g £14593

40a	8-12	Wolv	6af	58	385
60a	2-11	**SOUT**	5af	53	485*
62a	2-11	Sout	6af	58	609
66a	1-13	**SOUT**	5af	60	797*
67a	2-11	Sout	6af	64	
71	1-7	**SOUT**	6g/s	[65]	1050*
68	2-9	Hayd	5g/s	68	1344
49	9-14	Ches	6.1g/s	68	1570
71	2-13	Ripo	6ap	68	2011
13	12-12	Ripo	6gd	69	2482
23	14-15	Hayd	6gd	68	2950
65	5-12	Donc	5g/f	67	3599
47	8-20	Ripo	6gd	67	4278
56	5-15	Hami	6sft	66	4696

PICCOLOMINI 2 b c £650

81	3-14	Muss	7.1g/s	5330

PICK A BERRY 2 b f £0

32a	9-14	Ling	7ap		220
40a	15-15	Ling	7ap		875
0	9-10	Pont	6hvy		1070
55	6-9	Warw	6.1g/f		2906
49	9-12	Ling	7.6gd	[57]	3448
19	7-8	Yarm	6g/s	[55]	3873

PICK OF THE CROP 2 ch c £2716

61a	5-13	Wolv	6af	[73]	3
67a	1-13	**SOUT**	6af	[73]	444*
74a	2-6	Wolv	7af	71	615
68a	8-12	Ling	7ap	74	729
56	11-13	Kemp	9gd	74	1141
42	22-25	Newb	7gd	72	4683
41	18-20	Leic	7gd	69	5046

PICKAPEPPA 2 ch f £0

48	9-14	Ling	6gd	4443
80	5-14	Kemp	5g/f	4711

PICKLE 3 b f £28729

57a	3-14	Ling	6ap		449
32a	7-11	Ling	6ap		543
22	4-10	Pont	6hvy		1070
63	1-9	**FOLK**	7sft	55	1577*
56	7-20	Yarm	6gd	61	1730
64	3-17	Kemp	7gd	62	2174
53	3-13	Newm	7fm	63	2590
59	6-14	Wind	8.3fm	63	2971
73	1-9	**EPSO**	7gd	63	3218*
79	1-13	**LEIC**	7g/f	63	3346*
81	1-12	**NEWM**	8fm	69	3410*
80	2-7	Epso	8.5fm	74	3542
62	12-13	Sand	8.1gd	80	4607
82	4-12	Epso	8.5gd	80	4909

PICO ALTO 3 b f £0

1	16-18	Chep	8.1gd		4485	
19	12-13	Warw	7.1g/s		4667	
14a	11-12	Ling	8ap		4974	T
1a	11-12	Wolv	8.6ap		5230	

PICOT DE SAY 2 b g £2100

59	11-18	Wind	6gd		2618
54	7-9	Brig	6g/f		3981
53	11-13	Kemp	8g/f		4355
64	3-14	Wind	8.3g/f		5049
66	2-19	Redc	8sft	60	5302
63	5-20	Yarm	8g/s	60	5349

PICTAVIA 2 ch f £48830

102	2-6	Naas	6g/f		2328
107	2-12	Curr	7g/f		4432

PIDDIES PRIDE 2 b f £13260

58	5-7	Thir	5g/s		1471	
53	6-14	Donc	6g/f		1874	
63	6-8	Good	6gd		2537	VIS
57	4-20	Hayd	6gd		2882	vis
68	1-8	BRIG	6g/f		3172*	
72	1-4	FOLK	5gd		3382*	
79	3-10	Kemp	6g/f	69	3521	
76	2-11	Newm	6g/f	70	3614	
72	11-11	Newm	7g/f	[70]	3781	
73	4-13	York	6gd	74	4004	
55	12-14	Warw	6.1g/f	73	4420	
62	5-8	Good	6g/f	73	4536	
29a	9-13	Wolv	6ap	[69]	4980	
65	7-21	Donc	6hvy	[70]	5202	
67	2-8	Yarm	5.2sft	66	5253	
49	12-16	Nott	5.1hvy	66	5343	

PIE CORNER 2 ch c £0

33	11-14	Bath	5sft		1538
56	10-10	Sali	5g/f		1717
30	13-14	Folk	7fm		2714
7	13-13	Bath	5.7g/f		3368

PIETER BRUEGHEL 5 b g £27735

67	8-11	Donc	7g/f	86	2076	
79	4-10	York	6g/s	82	2357	
80	9-18	Newc	6g/s	82	2770	
69	10-17	Pont	6gd	80	2990	
89	1-10	YORK	6gd	80	3116*	
89	3-11	Hami	6fm	86	3248	
89	3-11	Hayd	6gd	[86]	3758	
89	2-19	Ripo	6g/s	86	3937	
64	16-26	Ayr	6gd	86	4652	
75	11-14	Ripo	6gd	86	4786	

PIKE BISHOP 2 b c £8814

91	1-8	WIND	5g/f		1955*
108	1-5	RIPO	5g/f		2481*

PILCA 4 ch g £0

28	11-13	Nott	10gd		4861

PILGRIM PRINCESS 5 b m £469

36a	6-16	Sout	6af	47	94	
46a	3-10	Wolv	6af	45	282	
32a	5-13	Wolv	6af	[45]	397	
45a	4-11	Wolv	7af	45	562	
40a	6-10	Sout	6af	45	657	
0	10-10	Wolv	7af	45	685	
17a	9-10	Wolv	7af	45	864	
42	7-16	Newc	6sft	45	1277	
36a	4-10	Sout	6af	[45]	1837	P
32	5-10	Carl	5.9fm	[40]	3545	

PILGRIMS PROGRESS 4 b g £435

74	4-9	Hayd	14gd	73	3760	
52	8-8	Hami	13g/s	73	4138	
65	5-6	Muss	16gd	72	4808	
54	8-11	Ayr	15sft	70	5032	
44	8-10	Catt	13.8sft	65	5322	P

PILLARS OF WISDOM 2 ch c £874

73	7-8	Kemp	7fm		4393
77	3-13	Newm	7fm		4724

PINAFORE 2 ch f £1427

69	3-18	Ling	6gd		4108
66a	2-14	Ling	7ap		4658
64	2-6	Brig	6gd		4900

61a	4-13	Wolv	5.1ap	[65]	5207	

PINCHBECK 5 b g £14103

53	16-19	Leic	6g/s	76	1354	
77	4-17	Donc	6g/s	76	1523	
83	1-13	YARM	6g/f	76	1726*	p
40	17-18	Donc	6gd	80	2752	p
90	1-10	HAYD	6g/f	80	3136*	p
85	4-15	Newc	6gd	87	3424	p
68	6-11	Hayd	6gd	[87]	3758	p
72	10-13	York	6gd	86	4322	p

PINCHING 3 ch f £4656

80	4-13	Newb	7gd		1210	
68	3-7	Nott	8.2sft		1468	
74	2-18	Wind	8.3g/f		1810	VIS
74	3-7	Redc	9g/s	[75]	2962	vis
62	13-20	Newm	8g/f	[75]	3237	vis
71	10-11	Pont	8g/f	[73]	4939	vis

PINE BAY 3 b f £4160

68	6-9	Asco	6gd		1929	
68	7-10	Good	8gd		2224	
32a	14-14	Ling	10ap		2740	
35	23-25	Newb	7gd	64	4683	
68	1-10	WIND	6g/f	[63]	4835*	

PINK BAY 2 b f £1326

60	4-15	Folk	6g/f		4369
70a	2-12	Wolv	6ap		4921

PINK SAPPHIRE 3 ch f £3169

34	15-16	Kemp	6g/s	72	1116	
75	2-20	Asco	6gd	69	1927	
75	4-12	Sand	7.1g/f	73	2098	
69	6-6	Asco	10gd	73	3072	
72	4-9	Sali	7gd	72	3456	
54	12-18	Leic	6gd	70	5039	BL

PINK SUPREME 3 ch f £0

14	13-13	Donc	7gd		925	
48	11-15	Leic	6gd		1829	T
56	10-18	Wind	6g/f	70	2268	t
44	7-8	Ling	7g/f	65	2742	t
37	11-19	Leic	6gd	60	2925	t
38	6-14	Beve	7.5g/s	[58]	3177	
45	10-17	Wind	6fm	51	3643	
47	4-12	Folk	6g/s	51	3911	
24	9-14	Folk	6gd	49	4116	
0	16-16	Folk	6g/f	[48]	4370	

PINS N NEEDLES 3 gr f £0

51a	10-11	Ling	7ap		1008	
60a	6-13	Ling	10ap		2066	
20	13-15	Bath	10.2gd		4826	
31a	10-12	Wolv	12.2ap	58	5339	

PINTLE 4 b f £19381

63	4-6	Bath	5.7fm	67	2416	
75	1-12	YARM	7gd	65	2864*	
79	1-11	LEIC	7g/f	67	3210*	
74	6-19	Good	8g/f	74	3512	
75	4-15	Sand	7.1gd	74	4500	
82	1-10	NEWC	7fm	[73]	4869*	

PIPER 4 ch g £0

23	14-17	Newc	7g/s	36	3700

PIPER GENERAL 2 br g £0

53	7-13	Warw	7.1g/s		4996

PIPER LILY 2 b f £5497

69	5-7	Ches	5.1g/s		1573
82	1-8	HAYD	6gd		2241*
72	6-6	Wind	5fm		2786
72	8-8	Ches	5.1g/f	86	3082
54	12-15	York	6gd		4985
62	8-8	Yarm	5.2sft	73	5253

PIPERS ASH 2 b f £4085

72	6-14	Newb	6fm		3626
89	1-6	SAND	5g/f		3857*

PIPS PEARL 2 b f £0

4	18-19	Kemp	6g/f		1911	
24	18-20	Wind	6fm		2970	
41	8-11	Sali	6g/s		3110	
42	10-10	Wind	8.3fm		3803	
40	5-17	Ling	6g/f		4316	VIS

2	17-17	Redc	7g/s	[45]	5105	vis t

PIPS SONG 8 ch g £2968

0	13-13	Wolv	6af	52	41	
0	10-10	Wolv	7af	[50]	152	
43a	10-16	Sout	6af	[48]	227	
22a	7-11	Wolv	6af	[45]	296	
19a	8-13	Wolv	6af	[45]	397	
47a	1-13	WOLV	6af	[40]	483*	
24a	9-12	Wolv	6af	[40]	524	
32a	9-11	Wolv	7af	46	558	
57a	3-14	Ling	6ap	[48]	819	
18a	10-12	Ling	6ap	48	844	
34a	5-5	Wolv	6af	[50]	1310	
0	11-11	Wolv	6af	[45]	1337	
37a	6-11	Wolv	6af	[47]	2202	

PIPSSALIO 6 b g £1205

39a	3-16	Sout	16af	42	206	bl t
28a	6-8	Sout	16af	45	554	bl
45a	2-11	Wolv	12af	[45]	666	t
37	6-18	Nott	14.1sft	45	1469	t
48	2-10	Kemp	12hvy	45	1645	t
3a	13-16	Sout	12af	42	2340	t
35	11-15	Good	16gd	45	5025	t

PIQUET 5 br m £7256

48a	1-12	LING	10ap	[39]	272*	
44a	3-13	Ling	10ap	[45]	412	
51a	1-12	LING	8ap	[45]	538*	
49a	6-13	Ling	7ap	51	565	
52a	6-11	Ling	8ap	50	669	
43a	9-14	Ling	10ap	50	718	
47a	7-10	Ling	8ap	50	766	
38	14-19	Brig	9.9g/f	45	1940	
40	6-6	Brig	11.9g/f	[45]	2047	
47a	3-13	Ling	10ap	[47]	3025	
33	12-17	Wind	10fm	42	3477	
55a	1-14	LING	10ap	46	3605*	
0	8-8	Brig	9.9g/f	49	3719	
42a	7-13	Ling	10ap	50	3823	
27	13-15	Folk	9.7g/f	[45]	4373	
38	8-18	Kemp	10ap	[45]	4791	

PIRAN 2 b g £0

56	8-15	Chep	7.1gd		4483	
57	9-16	Newb	7g/f		4677	
69	5-12	Wind	8.3g/f		4829	
53	12-13	Brig	8sft	[70]	5091	

PIRI PIRI 4 b f £4997

64	6-14	Leic	10g/f	66	1828
70	2-10	Yarm	11.5fm	65	2147
70	3-8	Hami	12.1g/f	65	2318
62	8-8	Newm	10g/f	68	2735
70	3-5	Newm	10g/f	67	3587
72	2-12	Newm	10g/f	67	3785
69	7-19	Kemp	10fm	69	4392
55	9-16	Yarm	11.5g/s	69	4589
60	10-15	Nott	12g/f	67	4849

PIRLIE HILL 4 b f £5804

48	3-10	Hami	6gd	45	1391	
40	4-9	Ayr	6g/s	[45]	1447	
7a	9-10	Sout	6af	[45]	1837	
61	2-6	Ayr	6fm	[45]	1908	
46	5-16	Ayr	5g/f	45	2029	
45	8-12	Newc	6g/f	50	2160	
55	1-13	HAMI	5gd	50	2181*	
51	6-13	Hami	5gd		2320	
50	7-9	Muss	5gd	55	2614	
49	4-6	Hami	5gd	55	2712	
50	4-10	Muss	5g/s	53	2968	
48	11-18	Carl	5gd	53	3228	
47	6-12	Newc	5g/f	53	3427	
47	5-15	Muss	5g/f	51	3561	
33	13-20	Hayd	6fm	49	3796	
0	16-16	Hami	6g/s	47	4009	
32	5-11	Carl	5fm	[47]	4508	

PIROETTA 2 b f £0

53	10-12	Warw	7.1g/f		4417

PIROUETTES 3 b f £316

46a	4-16	Ling	7ap	[58]	123	
47a	3-14	Sout	8af	[55]	170	
53a	4-13	Ling	10ap	55	215	
0	8-8	Wolv	8.5af	[50]	248	P

51a 9-14 Ling 7ap 55 344
8 20-20 Newm 8g/f 53 3232
39 11-16 Ling 6g/f 49 3602 BL
34a 9-13 Ling 10ap 45 3823 T
37a 4-14 Ling 7ap [45] 4660
35 9-19 Yarr 8g/s [45] 5119

PISTE BLEU 4 b f £3536
0 15-15 Sout 12af 58 867
7 13-17 Pont 12hvy 55 1064
31 9-10 Muss 12gd 53 1796
55 1-13 **RIPO** 12.3g/f 53 2008*
50 6-11 Leic 11.8fm 51 2112
30 4-6 Beve 12.1gd [54] 2653
27 13-17 Bath 11.7gd 52 3145
24 16-18 Kemp 10g/f [48] 4791

PITCAIRN ISLAND 2 ch f £0
38 10-13 Donc 7hvy 5199
55 12-21 Donc 6sft 5368

PITCH UP 2 b c £11181
74 7-8 Sand 5gd 2188
78 3-6 Sand 5gd 2364
68 6-20 Wind 6fm 2970
89 1-9 **SAND** 5gd 3355*
99a 1-10 **LING** 5ap [81] 3743*
86 5-13 Newm 5g/f 90 3943
89 7-11 Donc 5fm [87] 4533 BL
84 9-29 Newm 6gd 5087
88 11-11 Newm 5sft [87] 5132

PITTON MILL 4 b g £0
44a 11-15 Ling 12ap 2393
2 15-17 Wind 11.6fm 2788

PITTSBURGH 2 ch c £914
82 4-5 Newb 8g/f 4640
68 7-16 Bath 8gd 5019

PIVOTAL FLAME 2 b c £42788
101 1-11 **YORK** 6g/s 1687*
98 5-12 Newm 7g/f 3060
101 4-8 Sand 7.1g/s 4096
102 1-6 **LEIC** 7gd [100] 4699*
104 6-24 Redc 6fm [100] 4928
95 1-21 **DONC** 6hvy 5202*

PIVOTAL POINT 4 b g £169000
48 10-14 York 6g/s 91 1703
0 10-16 Wind 6fm 90 2758
102 1-8 **ASCO** 5gd 88 3123*
104 2-24 Sand 5gd 96 3466
105 1-28 **GOOD** 6fm 90 3622*
115 1-9 **LONG** 5g/s [91] 4435*
108 5-11 Newb 5.2g/f [13] 4678
119 1-12 **ASCO** 6g/f [100] 4799*

PIVOTALS PRINCESS 2 ch f £3048
66 3-4 Donc 5g/s 3224
72 3-16 Ripo 5gd 4787
78 2-13 York 6gd 4988

PIZAZZ 3 ch c £13463
73 5-10 Newm 6gd 1191
75 2-12 Kemp 8hvy 1511
80 5-15 Newb 8g/f [79] 1763
87 2-12 Sand 7.1g/f 79 2098
86 2-12 Newb 7g/f [79] 2352
43 24-27 Asco 8g/f 82 2521
88 3-9 Ling 7gd 82 3447
94 1-7 **KEMP** 7g/f 82 3522* BL
68 16-16 Good 7g/f 92 4523 bl
88 13-14 Newb 7g/f [92] 4638 bl

PLACE COWBOY 3 b c £6597
77 1-11 CATT 6gd 999*
71 5-10 Brig 5g/f [75] 2048
80 2-13 Newm 7fm 74 2590
82 4-11 Sand 7.1g/s 76 2918
74 6-9 Epso 5g/f 77 3218

PLACE ROUGE 4 b f £4286
106 4- Toul 10.5g/s 57

PLAIN CHANT 7 b g £0
26 8-12 Warw 19.1fm 35 2577

PLANET 2 b c £1314

---

44 14-16 Newb 7g/f 4677
63a 8-14 Ling 7ap 4971
73a 2-12 Wolv 8.6ap 5115

PLANET TOMATO 2 b c £2534
88 3-8 Newb 5.2gd 1205
80 2-8 Kemp 5hvy 1510

PLANTERS PUNCH 3 b c £9045
60 9-17 Kemp 7gd 1136
60 16-20 Bath 10.2gd 1398
60 7-15 Ripo 10g/f 62 1976
70 1-11 **LEIC** 10gd 62 2135*
53 9-16 Wind 11.6g/s 69 2621 VIS
63 7-12 Wind 10g/f [69] 2800 vis
52 9-17 Newm 10g/f 68 3238 vis
73 3-13 Ling 10g/s 67 4182
74 2-15 Nott 10g/f 68 4849
77 2-17 Leic 10gd 69 5062
76 2-19 Pont 10g/s 69 5148

PLATEAU 5 b g £20900
81 6-22 Donc 6gd 85 921
54 28-30 Newm 6g/f 84 1481
88 2-20 Epso 5fm 82 2253
62 21-24 Asco 5gd 84 3466
60 20-26 Good 6fm 84 3569
84 3-14 Epso 5gd 82 4291
76 9-15 Ayr 5g/s 83 4654

PLATINUM BOY 3 b g £209
19a 14-14 Ling 10ap 55 236 p
0 10-11 Wolv 12af 51 380 bl
3a 9-10 Sout 12af [48] 552 vis
0 10-11 Wolv 12af [45] 666 p
27a 11-14 Ling 10ap [45] 705 p
33a 3-14 Ling 10ap [40] 784 p
25a 7-12 Ling 8ap [35] 971 p
35a 7-14 Ling 10ap [35] 1072 p
17a 5-5 Ling 10ap [35] 1412 p
12 11-15 Nott 10gd [35] 1991 p

PLATINUM CHARMER 3 b g £11307
41a 4-11 Sout 11af [65] 191
64a 2-6 Sout 12af [65] 392
52a 1-5 **SOUT** 12af [65] 446* p
56a 10-14 Ling 12ap 61 801
62a 2-7 Wolv 16.2af 60 866
56 1-8 **MUSS** 12gd [58] 1552* p
57a 4-6 Sout 11af [65] 1754 p
55 2-10 Redc 11g/f [55] 1819 p
58 4-4 Carl 11.9fm [55] 1952 p
33 8-8 Newc 12.4g/f [56] 2163 p
60 3-8 Muss 12g/f 55 2616 p
61 2-13 Yarm 11.5fm 55 2868 p
48 5-7 Carl 11.9g/f [57] 3226 p
56 1-14 **CATT** 12g/f [55] 3668* p
51 7-17 Catt 12sft 60 3929 p
51 6-11 Ayr 15sft 53 5032 p
36 5-11 Catt 13.8sft [53] 5129 p

PLATINUM CHIEF 2 b g £205
0 15-16 Sout 8af [53] 164 bl
48a 4-11 Sout 7af [53] 207
43a 5-11 Wolv 8.5af [47] 279
40a 6-8 Wolv 8.5af [47] 383
31a 6-8 Sout 8af 47 490
47a 5-9 Sout 7af [45] 613
27a 9-13 Sout 8af [45] 776
33a 5-5 Wolv 9.4af [45] 1311
29a 3-6 Sout 7af [45] 1410 bl
9a 4-7 Sout 8af [40] 1591 bl
38a 4-6 Wolv 9.4af [40] 1675 P
16 10-13 Beve 8.5g/f [45] 1947

PLATINUM PIRATE 2 b g £17430
33a 9-13 Wolv 9.4af [55] 37 BL
12a 8-9 Wolv 9.4af [48] 238
57a 2-10 Ling 10ap [40] 291 bl
48a 9-11 Ling 10ap 56 497 bl
57a 2-9 Ling 10ap [55] 899 bl
64 1-12 **REDC** 10sft 55 1144* VIS
61 3-11 Sout 10gd 61 1280 vis
52 6-12 Beve 9.9sft 61 1306 vis
62 5-11 Redc 10sft 64 1663 vis
62 4-8 Hami 11.1g/f [63] 2319 vis
59a 7-13 Ling 10ap [61] 4112 vis

65a 1-14 **LING** 10ap [61] 4448* vis
68 1-11 **LEIC** 10gd [65] 4701* vis
61 3-8 Ayr 10sft [65] 5034 bl
52 10-16 Nott 10hvy 64 5345 bl

PLATTOCRAT 4 b g £0
17a 5-9 Sout 8af 983
25a 7-11 Wolv 6af 2202
22 7-10 Ayr 8g/s 2544
1a 12-13 Sout 6af 35 4091
42 7-8 Catt 7g/f [30] 4440

PLAUSABELLE 3 b f £2651
23 7-16 Redc 8sft 51 1147
52 2-11 Pont 8sft 49 1425 BL
43 9-12 Newc 12.4sft 52 1680 bl
41 12-16 Thir 12g/f 52 3573
46 3-18 Beve 9.9g/s 48 4243 bl
53 2-14 Redc 10fm 48 4560 bl

PLAY BOUZOUKI 3 b f £904
63 3-9 Nott 8.2g/f 3581
68 4-17 Newm 8gd 4228
57 7-15 Bath 10.2gd 4826
67a 6-12 Wolv 8.6ap 69 5116

PLAY MASTER 3 b g £11777
75a 2-9 Wolv 7af 381
80a 1-6 **WOLV** 8.5af 468*
80a 2-8 Wolv 8.5af 73 645
52 9-14 Donc 10.3gd 74 923
73 1-8 **WIND** 8.3g/s 71 1257*
33 11-14 York 7.9g/s 74 1707
73a 3-8 Sout 8af 73 2495
15 24-25 Asco 7g/f 73 3443
73 5-15 Hayd 8.1g/f 73 4352

PLAY THAT TUNE 4 ch f £4842
86 7-17 York 7.9g/s 96 1686
88 5-5 Sand 5g/f 95 2191
77 4-6 Hami 8.3gd [93] 2710
92 3-7 York 7.9g/s 89 3077
93 3-11 Donc 7g/s 89 3223
78 9-11 York 7g/s [90] 4063

PLAY THE MELODY 3 b g £4319
70 3-10 Folk 9.7sft 1580
76 1-11 **FOLK** 9.7gd 4120*

PLAY UP POMPEY 2 b c £0
55 10-17 Ling 7g/f 2584
62 8-8 Ling 8g/f 3021
68a 9-13 Ling 7ap 3329
49 13-15 Folk 7gd 4114
56 10-15 Good 8g/s 4233
59 8-8 Sali 6sft [58] 4577

PLAYFUL ACT 2 b f £165255
87 2-14 Newm 7g/f 3944
90 1-9 **NEWM** 7gd 4192*
109 1-8 **DONC** 8fm [90] 4476*
112 1-9 **ASCO** 8g/f [90] 4798*

PLAYFUL DANE 7 b g £20782
61 1-16 **REDC** 6g/f 55 1824*
47 5-18 Thir 5g/f 58 2214
46 9-11 Ayr 6gd 58 2542
72 1-14 **THIR** 5g/f 57 3417+
72 3-18 Redc 6fm 67 4339
83 1-15 **NEWC** 5fm 68 4870*
82 2-14 Redc 5g/f [68] 4930
82 1-19 **YORK** 5gd 74 4989*

PLAYFUL SPIRIT 4 b f £3349
47a 1-15 **SOUT** 6af [46] 167* vis
33a 7-10 Wolv 6af 46 282 vis
31a 6-13 Wolv 6af [45] 397 vis
54a 3-9 Sout 6af [45] 459 vis
41a 3-13 Sout 6af 45 500 vis
35a 7-12 Sout 5af [49] 587 vis
38a 7-10 Sout 6af 49 657 vis
46a 3-16 Sout 5ap 45 1046 vis
37 7-10 Donc 6g/f 47 1878 vis
46 8-15 Ling 5g/f 46 2062 vis
13 11-13 Donc 6g/f 46 2232 vis
14a 15-16 Sout 6af 46 2720 vis
37 9-16 Warw 5g/s [45] 4995 vis
15 13-20 Yarm 6g/s [45] 5121 vis

PLAYTIME BLUE 3 b g £12300
51a 8-10 Ling 5ap 61 231
63a 2-9 Wolv 5af 59 275
60a 2-10 Wolv 6af 59 349
61a 3-14 Ling 6ap 61 407
54a 6-10 Ling 5ap 61 453
71a 1-11 WOLV 5af 60 643*
73a 2-13 Wolv 6af 66 687
72a 1-10 WOLV 5af 66 749*
58 4-17 Kemp 5sft 63 944
63 3-19 Warw 5gd 63 1127
48 10-17 Warw 5hvy [62] 1532
53 6-14 Kemp 5g/f 62 1914
51 7-12 Folk 5g/f 61 2269
60 5-9 Sali 5fm 61 2420
63 3-15 Wind 5gd 59 3165
60 3-18 Carl 5gd 59 3228
57 9-22 Good 5fm 60 3537
49 7-15 Pont 5gd 60 3680
41 10-15 Bath 5.7g/f 59 3966
49a 9-13 Wolv 5af 71 5181
59a 9-13 Wolv 5.1ap 69 5341

PLEA BARGAIN 2 b c £5086
79 3-15 Sali 8gd 4851
83 1-14 YARM 7sft 5251*

PLEASANT 3 b f £1414
64 4-9 Wind 10fm 3642
73 2-11 Wind 10gd 4125
28 12-15 Bath 10.2gd 4826
33 8-18 Wind 10g/s 4944

PLEASANTLY PERFECT 6 b h £2011173
124 1-12 NAD 10af 992* t bl

PLEASURE SEEKER 3 b f £0
57 7-17 Sali 6g/s 1497
65 9-11 Bath 8fm 1904
10 9-10 Yarm 8g/f 60 2344
25 10-14 Newm 7gd [57] 4195
37 6-12 Chep 10.2hvy 52 4708

PLEASURE TIME 11 ch g £1435
30a 5-10 Wolv 5af [45] 527 vis
35a 7-16 Sout 5af [45] 720 vis
12a 10-13 Ling 6ap 45 767 vis
38a 1-9 SOUT 5af [40] 981* vis
31a 6-8 Sout 5af [45] 1199 vis
7 16-16 Brig 6fm 48 2262 vis
37a 7-13 Wolv 5.1ap [45] 5231 vis

PLENTY CRIED WOLF 2 b g £1110
33 17-18 Donc 6g/s 3376
35 14-18 Newc 6g/s 3699
77 4-11 Thir 7fm 4381
64 7-14 Carl 6.9fm [71] 4503
74 3-11 Newc 7fm [68] 4863
65a 6-13 Wolv 8.6ap [68] 4979
66 3-9 Catt 7sft [69] 5316

PLOVERS LANE 3 b g £0
49 14-17 Newb 10gd 1737
55 8-8 Chep 12.1gd 2113 P

PLUM 4 br f £3523
75 1-10 BRIG 7sft 67 4168+
62 7-16 Catt 7sft 70 5130

PLUMMET 3 b f £2756
74 4-18 Wind 10g/f 1959
80 2-13 Kemp 10gd 3186
76 3-11 Wind 10fm 3802

PLUMPIE MAC 3 b f £0
41 6-8 Thir 7sft 49 2693
33 11-14 Beve 7.5g/s [49] 3177
19 16-18 Carl 7.9fm 44 3547

PLUNGINGTON TAVERN 2 b c £0
34 9-11 Ayr 7.2g/s 4653

PLUTOCRAT GB 8 b g £2064
70 2-10 Muss 16g/f 70 1093
26 10-10 Muss 12gd 71 1796 VIS

POACHERS PARADISE 3 ch g £0
26a 12-13 Wolv 6af 49 436
23a 8-13 Sout 6af 47 797

39 6-14 Sout 10g/s 45 1051
11 10-16 Redc 8sft 45 1147

POCKETWOOD 2 b c £0
60 11-12 Sand 7.1g/f 2388

POETICAL 3 ch f £4824
87 12-15 Donc 7fm 4479
101 3-12 Tipp 7.5hvy 4961

POETRY N PASSION 3 b f £0
50 7-8 Sand 8.1g/s 4101
45 7-19 Redc 6g/s 5110
47a 10-14 Ling 7ap 5240
43 5-7 Yarm 11.5g/s 5351

POINT CALIMERE 3 b g £3775
55a 7-9 Ling 5ap [85] 1023
66 4-14 Sout 6gd [82] 1281
67 5-9 Hayd 5g/s 82 1344
44 16-19 Sali 7gd 78 1723
70a 1-12 SOUT 6af [70] 2722* BL

POINT MAN 4 b g £185
1a 8-11 Wolv 6af [30] 1261 BL
31 3-5 Brig 8gd [30] 1546
18a 4-8 Wolv 7af [30] 1676

POINT OF DISPUTE 9 b g £3039
82 5-13 Newb 7g/f 80 2880 vis
83 2-17 Newb 7g/f 80 3257 vis
71 8-8 Sand 7.1g/s 82 3891 vis
77a 4-14 Ling 7ap 79 4180 vis
69a 9-14 Ling 7ap 78 4446 vis
81a 3-12 Wolv 7.1ap [76] 5006 vis

POINTED 3 br f £547
36 15-20 Donc 7g/f 1518
43 10-11 Beve 9.9g/f 1835
49 3-8 Redc 10gd 2124
0 13-16 Sout 14af 45 4045

POISE 3 b f £4290
87 1-9 WIND 10fm 3642*

POKER 3 ch g £2933
57a 1-12 SOUT 8af 45 656*
0 14-16 Redc 8sft 55 1147
11 18-20 Chep 7.1g/s 55 4367
7a 13-13 Wolv 9.5ap 53 4925

POKER PLAYER 2 ch g £0
78 5-23 Newm 6gd 5084

POLANSKI MILL 5 b g £0
4 P-14 Kemp 14.4sft 62 948
34 11-15 Newb 13.3g/f 62 2311
49 9-19 Bath 17.2gd 55 3147
21 10-12 Yarm 16gd 52 3493
22a 10-13 Ling 16ap 50 3822 T P

POLAR BEAR 4 ch g £50236
92 3-14 Ling 7sft 88 1624
61 24-31 Asco 8g/f 90 2489
110 1-18 NEWC 7sft 90 2684+
111 1-11 YORK 7g/s [103] 4063*
111 7-11 Long 8g/f [103] 4949
112 3-12 Newm 7sft [108] 5134

POLAR BEN 5 b g £42200
115 2-11 Leic 7g/s [112] 1356
115 2-9 Hayd 7.1g/f [112] 1486
98 8-8 Newm 7g/f [112] 2765
113 1-13 NEWM 8g/f [111] 4887+
92 9-12 Newm 7sft [111] 5134

POLAR DANCER 2 b f £3049
60a 6-11 Ling 8ap 21
68a 3-12 Ling 10ap 120
0 18-20 Wind 11.6sft 65 1648
56 3-11 Ling 10gd [59] 3201
33 11-17 Newm 12g/f 59 3618
0 11-12 Folk 12g/s 55 3913
57 3-7 Good 9.9g/f [53] 4541
57 3-10 Good 9.9gd [55] 4877
44 8-9 Good 11gd [63] 5026

POLAR DAWN 3 b f £8254
78 2-13 Sali 6fm 2287
67 6-13 Chep 6.1gd 3399

70 4-16 Sali 7gd 3882
73 1-17 WARW 7.1gd [70] 4271*
66 10-29 Newm 6gd 5087

POLAR FORCE 3 ch g £1202
44a 8-16 Sout 6af 63 94
59a 3-14 Ling 6ap 63 121
60a 4-14 Ling 6ap 62 407
49a 9-12 Ling 6ap 61 628
52a 7-14 Ling 6ap 59 874
63a 3-14 Ling 6ap 59 897
37 16-20 Ripo 5gd 60 1179
42 3-7 Brig 6g/f [60] 1368
0 10-13 Yarm 6g/f 55 2347

POLAR GALAXY 3 br f £0
30 9-9 Thir [54] 2216
37 5-7 Muss 8g/f 50 2613
32 12-18 Carl 7.9fm 45 3547
41 4-13 Hayd 6gd [45] 3757
21a 10-11 Sout 6af [41] 4041 P

POLAR HAZE 6 ch g £6481
54a 1-15 SOUT 6af [46] 172* vis
42a 9-15 Sout 5af 53 187 vis
64a 2-16 Sout 6af [46] 227 vis
46a 4-13 Ling 6ap [53] 340 vis
47a 2-13 Wolv 6af [53] 483 vis
38a 6-14 Sout 6af 53 501 vis
56a 1-9 SOUT 6af [53] 533* vis
54a 5-12 Sout 6af [58] 610 vis
40a 7-12 Wolv 6af [58] 646 vis
56a 4-6 Wolv 6af [56] 941 vis
16a 5-7 Sout 6af [56] 1032 bl
38a 5-6 Sout 6af [55] 1443 bl
32 8-10 Brig 7g/f [40] 1938 vis
38 4-16 Nott 6.1gd [40] 1989 bl
0 13-13 Yarm 6g/f 37 2347 vis
44 2-20 Yarm 6g/s [40] 5121 vis

POLAR IMPACT 5 br h £4045
56 12-16 Good 7g/f 72 1817
70 5-11 Good 6gd 70 2535
77 1-9 WIND 6fm [69] 2760*
75 4-17 Sand 5gd 75 3341
71 5-17 Wind 6gd 75 4126
62 9-12 Good 6sft 75 4184

POLAR JEM 4 b f £60809
75 3-9 Nott 10sft 74 1467
68 4-19 Wind 10sft [74] 1650
79 1-7 RIPO 10g/f [73] 1979*
88 1-15 KEMP 10fm 79 2067*
89 1-5 SAND 9g/f 76 2191*
96 1-10 NEWM 10fm 86 2592*
96 6-21 York 10.4gd 94 3118
96 3-7 Newm 10g/f 92 3474
100 2-9 Newb 12fm [92] 3629
104 1-11 YARM 10.1gd [98] 4614+
91 6-8 Asco 8g/f [98] 4774

POLAR KINGDOM 5 b g £17655
63a 10-11 Ling 8ap 72 12
54a 7-11 Sout 8af 72 255
74a 3-11 Sout 8af 70 386
85a 1-15 SOUT 8af 72 505*
88a 1-10 SOUT 7af 78 611+
65a 10-13 Wolv 6af 78 618
63 12-20 Kemp 6gd 78 1138
77 3-30 Newm 6g/s 74 1481
69 12-18 Newc 6g/s 75 2770

POLAR MAGIC 3 ch c £14280
81 1-14 THIR 7sft 2692*
77 2-9 Ling 7gd 70 4110
84a 1-13 LING 7ap 73 4897*

POLAR PASSION 2 b f £0
50 5-7 Ches 7g/f 4511
43 11-14 Hayd 6sft 4769

POLAR SUN 3 b g £836
57 6-16 Newm 7fm 2092
70 3-9 Newm 10gd 3282
58 6-12 Kemp 6sft 4029

POLAR TRYST 5 ch m £3673
74 1-11 BATH 13.1g/f 62 4415*

46 12-14 Asco 12g/f 72 4775

POLAR WAY 5 ch g £55926
78 14-14 Asco 6fm [111] 2580
105 3-8 Newb 7g/f [110] 3253
115 2-21 Asco 7g/f 110 3441
97 9-13 Newb 7g/f [114] 3957
112 1-5 **WARW** 7.1gd [114] 4270*
108 3-11 Good 7gd [114] 4874
108 4-12 Newm 7sft [114] 5134

POLE STAR 6 b g £0
89 10-11 Newm 16sft [115] 5138

POLESWORTH 2 b f £0
43a 5-12 Sout 7af 3394
43 10-11 Ches 7sft 4072
50 10-12 Warw 7.1g/f 4418

POLICY MAKER 4 b c £142648
123 1-7 **CHAN** 12g/s 2459*
117 2-10 Sain 12g/s 3012
119 1-4 **LONG** 12sft 4568*
80 19-19 Long 12g/f 4956

POLISH BARON 7 b g £0
4a 6-9 Sout 12af [70] 353

POLISH EAGLE 2 b c £1290
64 11-21 Newm 8sft 5097
75 2-14 Yarm 7sft 5251

POLISH EMPEROR 3 ch g £18387
78a 1-12 **WOLV** 5af 70 109* bl
66a 10-16 Sout 5af 77 171 bl
78a 4-14 Ling 6ap 76 292 bl
83a 2-10 Sout 5af 76 660 bl
84a 2-10 Ling 5ap 77 755 bl
67 5-17 Kemp 5sft 73 944 bl
29 16-16 Bath 5.7g/s [72] 1103 bl
69 3-15 Brig 5.3g/f 70 1371 bl
81 1-20 **THIR** 5g/f 70 1765* e
64 13-17 Epso 6fm 78 2256 e
72 8-14 Wind 5g/f 78 2266 e
73 10-22 Good 5fm 77 3537 e
75 6-12 Newm 5gd 75 4197 e
48 10-12 Yarm 5.2g/s 74 4585 e
82 1-14 **REDC** 5fm [73] 4930* e
75a 7-13 Wolv 5.1ap 77 5341 e

POLISH INDEX 2 b c £0
2 17-18 Newm 8fm 4722

POLISH RHAPSODY 3 b f £0
37a 11-12 Ling 8ap 514
49a 11-15 Ling 7ap 814
4 6-8 Pont 10hvy [48] 1067
16a 9-9 Ling 10ap [45] 1289

POLISH ROSE 3 ch f £0
59 8-15 Ling 7gd 4445
53 5-8 Brig 8fm 4762
34 8-8 Newb 10hvy 5226

POLISH SPIRIT 9 b g £4358
41 14-16 Kemp 9gd 65 3187
52 7-10 Nott 8.2g/f 65 3579
61 6-14 Sali 9.9g/f 60 3867
65 1-12 **GOOD** 9.9sft 60 4268*
0 19-19 Bath 11.7gd 63 5024

POLISH SUMMER 6 b h £936095
118 2-14 Sha 12g/f 209
118 1-10 **SAIN** 10g/s 833*
117 1-13 **NAD** 12g/f 990*
113 5-8 Long 10.5hvy 1558
112 7-10 Sain 12g/s 3012
112 4-4 Long 12sft 4568

POLKA PRINCESS 4 b f £209
7a 12-13 Wolv 9.4af 52 287
18a 13-16 Sout 11af [45] 445
36a 7-14 Ling 13ap [40] 537 P
36a 3-10 Ling 16ap [40] 650 p
0 13-15 Ling 12ap [40] 707
33a 10-14 Ling 12ap [40] 827 p
17a 9-14 Ling 12ap [35] 968 p
0 12-12 Ling 12ap [35] 1180 BL
1a 5-5 Wolv 14.8af [30] 1563 p

POLLITO 2 b g £968
79 5-13 Wind 6fm 3478
65 6-9 Brig 6g/f 3981
82 4-11 Epso 7gd 4289
79a 3-11 Ling 8ap [77] 4744

POLLY ALEXANDER 2 ch f £33250
73 5-7 Kemp 5sft 943
69 1-9 **WARW** 5sft 1084*
83 1-5 **RIPO** 5g/s 1362*
89 3-6 Newb 5.2gd 1735
89 2-7 Capa 5.5gd 2302
93 1-10 **SALI** 6gd 2697*
71 9-10 Newm 6fm 3003
70 14-29 Newm 6gd 5087

POLLY PERKINS 2 b f £32755
76 1-8 **MUSS** 5gd 1795*
98 1-8 **SAND** 5g/f 2094*
82 11-17 Asco 5g/f 2490
77 8-9 Newm 6gd 2763
106 1-5 **SAND** 5g/s 2895*

POLONIUS 3 b g £386
84 6-6 Sali 7g/s [91] 3113

POLYFIRST 3 b f £7711
104 3-7 Deau 10Very 4309

POLYGONAL 4 b g £10318
90 6-15 York 8.9g/f 89 2404
62 19-21 York 10.4gd 89 3118
88 5-9 Asco 10g/f 87 3439
99 1-6 **NEWM** 10g/f 85 3749*
87 8-8 Donc 10.3fm 94 4530

POMFRET LAD 6 b g £0
41 19-20 Donc 5gd 100 927
41 14-14 Ches 5.1gd 100 1594
47 12-14 York 6g/s 100 1703
92 14-22 Donc 5.6fm 96 4459
56 22-24 Ayr 6sft 96 4686
83 12-15 Newm 7g/f 92 4891
59 17-20 York 6gd 87 5001
45 18-18 Pont 5g/s 83 5149 bl

POMPEY BLUE 2 b f £3021
69a 1-13 **WOLV** 6af [71] 3*
70a 5-9 Ling 6ap 71 105
39a 5-7 Sout 6af 71 333
59a 5-10 Ling 6ap 70 494
57a 7-10 Ling 5ap 68 712
49 7-8 Good 6gd 66 2375
52 9-14 Ling 5g/f 62 2585
19 12-13 Wind 5fm 58 2784
45 8-19 Donc 5g/s 54 3220

POMPEY CHIMES 4 b g £418
49 4-9 Kemp 6sft 946
45 13-14 Folk 7g/s 1080
34 15-18 Bath 5.7g/f 55 1788

PON MY SOUL 2 b g £3161
59 1-14 **BEVE** 7.5sft 2939*
68 6-12 Newm 7g/f 3750
45 8-20 Yarm 8g/s 65 4635
63 6-14 Wind 8.3g/f [60] 5049

PONDERON 4 ch g £1800
84 8-18 Kemp 16g/s 91 1112
92 6-17 Ches 18.7gd 89 1569
69 11-14 Hayd 16.2gd 88 2239

PONENTE 2 b f £425
71 6-11 Newb 6gd 3915
56 9-12 Warw 7.1g/f 4417
61 3-9 Catt 7sft 5131

PONGEE 4 b f £148807
92 3-10 Sali 12g/f 87 1721
103 1-7 **HAYD** 11.9g/f [87] 1921*
110 1-8 **HAYD** 11.9gd [96] 2946*
109 2-7 Good 14fm [107] 3619
109 2-8 York 11.9g/s[107] 4024

PONT ALLAIRE 3 b f £3739
80 1-7 **NOTT** 8.2sft 1468*
69 7-7 Newb 10gd [79] 1733

69 5-10 Newm 8g/f 79 2767

PONT NEUF 4 b f £9922
24a 13-14 Ling 10ap 61 520
59a 8-11 Ling 12ap 58 624 T
49a 4-5 Wolv 12af [55] 701 t
64 2-17 Wind 11.6fm [55] 2788 t
56 5-7 Muss 12gd 55 2966 t
64 1-9 **WIND** 11.6gd [65] 3164* t
68 1-15 **WIND** 11.6fm 60 3481+ t
62 7-14 Wind 11.6fm 65 3638 t
69 2-16 Wind 11.6gd 65 3829
68 3-17 Catt 12sft 65 3929 t
61 9-16 York 11.9gd 67 4990 t
24 15-20 York 13.9gd 67 5004 t
39a 9-11 Wolv 12.2ap 56 5180 t
9a 11-12 Wolv 12.2ap 55 5328 t

POOKAS DAUGHTER 3 b f £366
4a 13-13 Wolv 9.4af 58 38
0 12-12 Wolv 7af 54 129
30a 5-7 Sout 8af 49 332
31a 7-11 Wolv 7af [45] 440
0 10-10 Sout 8af 45 463 BL
25a 7-13 Ling 6ap [35] 541
9a 8-12 Wolv 8.5af [35] 584 P
28a 2-12 Wolv 7af [35] 663 p
1a 14-15 Ling 7ap [30] 830 p
0 12-12 Sout 7af [30] 909 p

POP UP AGAIN 4 ch f £0
68 8-12 Ayr 7.2fm 75 1909
26 9-10 Newb 7af 75 2350
59 12-18 Newc 7sft 73 2684
45 15-17 Pont 6g/f 71 2990
55 12-17 Ayr 7.2sft 68 5063

POPES HILL 3 b c £2238
75 4-9 Hayd 11.9g/f 1885
68 4-8 Chep 12.1g/f 2623
73 6-9 Kemp 12g/f 2862
74 3-10 Ling 11.5gd 73 3334
74 4-12 Sand 16.4g/f 72 3861
74 4-7 Thir 16g/s 72 4209
70 6-13 Good 16g/f 71 4527 BL

POPPYFIELDS 2 b f £0
39 17-17 Warw 7.1gd 4271

POPPYLINE 4 b f £1079
51a 9-12 Ling 7ap 58 1024
45 11-18 Good 8g/f 55 1849
0 U-14 Carl 7.9fm 55 1954
55 3-20 Yarm 8fm 53 2149
47 6-14 Leic 8g/f 53 2402
57 3-10 Brig 8gd 53 2954
47 10-17 Brig 7g/f 53 3176
40 7-8 Brig 8fm [51] 3676 BL
40 6-12 Folk 6g/s 51 3911 bl
57 5-7 Brig 6g/f [48] 3985 bl
42 4-16 Folk 6g/f [47] 4370 bl

POPPYS FOOTPRINT 3 ch f £8376
44 21-22 Donc 7gd 85 955
72 11-20 Newm 7g/f 83 1186
62 10-14 Ripo 6g/s 80 1360
72 5-14 York 7.9g/s 75 1707
81 3-12 Donc 7g/f 75 1879
79 4-8 Beve 7.5g/f 77 2166
58 9-10 Donc 7g/f 76 2427
0 P-12 Hayd 8.1gd 75 2904
83 1-8 **THIR** 8fm 75 4378*
53 10-11 Ayr 8sft 79 4621

PORLEZZA 5 ch m £16268
117 2-8 Chan 5g/s 2305
105 8-20 Newm 6g/f 3062

PORT DARGENT 2 b f £0
60 10-14 Muss 7.1g/s 5330

PORT MORENO 3 b c £0
19a 8-10 Sout 11af [48] 142 vis
27a 5-9 Sout 16af [45] 576 vis
12a 9-11 Wolv 12af [45] 666 BL
15 18-19 Bath 17.2gd 40 3147 vis

PORT N STARBOARD 3 ch g £740
60 4-8 Good 11gd 2222

68	5-6	Ling	10g/f		2843	
67	4-9	Nott	10g/s		4034	
60	4-5	Good	11sft		4188	
0	12-12	Wolv	12.2ap	68	4924	
54a	11-14	Ling	10ap	65	5083	VIS

PORT NATAL 6 b g £472

33a	7-10	Wolv	7af	40	379	bl
44a	2-13	Wolv	6af	[40]	397	bl
0	U-13	Wolv	8.5af		699	
20a	7-15	Sout	6af	[45]	773	bl

PORT SODRICK 3 b g £1052

55a	6-9	Ling	8ap		3197
64	6-9	Nott	8.2g/f		3581
65a	4-8	Ling	10ap		3787
45	5-10	Yarm	10.1gd	[62]	4612
42	9-15	Wind	10g/f	[60]	4834
36	7-12	Warw	12.6g/s	[55]	4991
60	2-8	Bath	17.2sft	50	5175

PORT ST CHARLES 6 b g £5350

78a	1-13	WOLV	6af	74	113*	
74a	5-11	Sout	6af	77	386	
56a	11-13	Wolv	6af	77	482	
44a	9-12	Sout	6af	[76]	610	
50a	12-13	Wolv	6af	74	807	
51a	4-6	Wolv	8.5af	[72]	957	
68	4-16	Bath	5.7g/s	[70]	1103	
35	15-20	Wind	6g/f	68	1255	
43	8-18	Wind	6g/f	[66]	1806	
64	4-10	Brig	5.3g/f	66	2044	
62	3-10	Sand	5gd	63	2189	
58	7-14	Wind	5g/f	63	2266	
60	7-9	Sali	5fm	63	2420	
39	14-19	Leic	5gd	62	2702	
47	4-14	Catt	6g/f	[60]	3191	
54	7-18	Pont	5gd	58	3463	
53	6-9	Brig	5.3fm	58	3673	BL
36	12-18	Bewe	5g/s	56	3852	bl
62a	2-11	Sout	6af	[60]	4041	
46	7-13	Warw	6.1gd	54	4272	

PORTHCAWL 3 b f £13820

78	1-8	SAND	8.1g/s		4101*
84	1-13	SAND	8.1gd	75	4607*
70	10-13	Asco	8g/f	79	4802

PORTICHOL PRINCESS 4 b f £0

| 0 | 6-8 | Ling | 10ap | | 829 t |

PORTMANTEAU 3 b f £13619

29	13-18	Wind	8.3g/s		1258
90	1-11	BEVE	9.9g/f		1835*
71	8-12	Kemp	9g/f	85	2860
94	1-10	NEWB	10fm	85	3630*
95	2-7	Wind	10fm	88	3801

PORTMEIRION 3 b f £0

| 53 | 10-15 | Nott | 8.2g/s | | 4649 |

PORTRAIT OF A LADY 3 ch f £25128

74	3-8	Folk	12sft	[69]	1272
74	1-13	THIR	12g/f	[74]	1768*
82	3-10	Chep	12.1gd	74	2114
84	1-6	NEWB	12g/f	74	2353*
89	1-5	LEIC	11.8g/f	81	2923*
94	3-9	Newm	12g/f	[87]	3278
0	6-7	Good	14fm	[93]	3619

PORTRAYAL 2 b f £23081

106	3-8	Mais	5.5gd		3498
106	2-6	Chan	8gd		4728
108	5-10	Long	8g/f		4954

POSH SHEELAGH 2 b f £0

| 0 | 14-15 | Sout | 7af | | 87 |
| 31a | 9-9 | Wolv | 7af | | 381 |

POSTERITAS 3 b f £26040

80	3-10	Good	8gd		2224
80	2-11	Sali	8fm		2419
86	1-6	PONT	10g/f		2793*
98	5-11	Newm	10g/f	84	3236
92	1-12	YARM	10.1sft	82	4149*
86	6-13	Donc	10.3fm	[88]	4463
62	11-13	Kemp	12g/f	[88]	4715

POSTGRADUATE 2 b c £5096

| 71a | 5-14 | Ling | 7ap | | 4970 |
| 87a | 1-9 | LING | 6ap | | 5237* |

POTENT HEIR 2 b c £4813

| 95 | 1-10 | NEWC | 6g/f | | 4403* |

POTSDAM 6 ch g £472

| 44a | 7-13 | Wolv | 8.5af | 47 | 559 t |
| 46a | 2-11 | Wolv | 7af | [45] | 579 t |

POUILLY FUME 3 b f £0

| 21 | 18-20 | Wind | 10sft | | 1651 |

POULE DE LUXE 3 b f £5590

| 73 | 1-17 | KEMP | 7gd | | 1136* |
| 47 | 13-16 | Sali | 7sft | 69 | 4582 |

POWER AND DEMAND 7 b g £0

| 10a | 4-5 | Wolv | 8.5af | [35] | 1264 |
| 1a | 8-8 | Wolv | 7af | [35] | 1314 T |

POWER BIRD 3 b f £852

56a	8-12	Ling	6ap	[78]	106	
42a	10-12	Sout	8af	78	141	
40a	10-12	Ling	8ap	[72]	150	
54a	8-13	Ling	10ap	65	215	
55a	2-14	Ling	7ap	[62]	450	
54a	11-13	Ling	7ap	60	565	
54a	9-12	Ling	8ap	60	607	
45	13-16	Ling	7g/f	62	2063	
26a	8-12	Sout	7af	[56]	2337	VIS
36	5-6	Folk	6fm	[52]	2715	BL
32	12-17	Warw	8.1g/f	52	2909	bl

POWER NAP 3 b f £0

45	6-6	Ches	10.3g/s		2748 t	
39	9-9	York	7gd	[48]	3121 t	
33	13-16	Thir	12g/f	47	3573 t	
13	9-10	Redc	10g/f	40	3772	VIS
0	16-18	Leic	7gd	[40]	4698	BL

POWER TO BURN 2 b g £421

36a	8-9	Ling	6ap	60	105 T	
54a	3-13	Wolv	6af	55	436	VIS
46a	5-10	Sout	6af	54	592	vis
35	9-15	Folk	6g/s	[52]	1078	vis
8	17-19	Chep	6.1sft	52	4054	vis

POWERFUL PARRISH 3 b f £1420

51	11-13	Kemp	8fm		2072	
78	2-11	Chep	8.1g/f		2627	
66	4-6	Bath	10.2g/f	[78]	2980	
56	12-12	Newb	10g/f	78	3255	
64	7-10	Newb	10fm	74	3630	T
44	8-10	Bath	11.7g/f	[72]	4414	

POWERSCOURT 4 b c £431049

120	1-6	CURR	10.5g/f		2004*	
120	2-10	Asco	10gd		2488	
116	5-12	Sand	10g/s		2916	
117	2-8	Muni	10gd		3662	
121	4-13	Arli	10fm		4014	vis
121	3-8	Leop	10g/s		4571	BL
120	3-3	Lone	12g/s		5311	vis

PRAGUE 6 b g £0

| 15a | 14-14 | Ling | 10ap | [62] | 430 |

PRAIRIE FALCON 10 b g £1487

84	3-20	Newm	12gd	82	1172
72	7-8	Newm	12gd	84	1889
79	9-14	Hayd	16.2gd	84	2239
0	P-9	Newm	14.8fm	81	2596

PRAIRIE LAW 4 b g £558

34	6-17	Newm	10g/f	42	3238
42	4-13	Folk	9.7g/f	42	3726
44	3-12	Newb	10gd	42	3916
41	9-14	Warw	16.2g/f	45	4423
31	13-19	Thir	12g/f	45	4594

PRAIRIE OYSTER 3 b f £0

| 17 | 11-12 | Good | 9g/f | | 1864 |

PRAIRIE SUN 3 b f £4874

43a	4-7	Sout	12af		1030
56	4-10	Beve	12.1g/s	56	1165
40	5-7	Donc	14.6g/s	57	1521
59	1-13	BEVE	12.1g/f	55	1836*
42	7-8	Newc	12.4g/f	[59]	2163

0	10-15	Sout	12af	47	2503	
41	10-12	Beve	9.9gd	57	2893	VIS
51	6-20	Catt	12g/f	55	3354	P
51	10-16	Thir	12g/f	55	3573	p
51	6-10	Catt	13.8g/f	52	3669	
57	3-8	Catt	13.8g/f	48	4439	

PRAIRIE WOLF 8 ch g £3861

0	15-16	Epso	10.1hvy	86	1296	
53	14-20	Donc	10.3g/s	85	1519	
72	9-14	Leic	10g/f	80	1828	
70	10-15	Kemp	10fm	78	2067	
52	5-7	Ayr	10gd	76	2507	
80	1-6	BEVE	9.9gd	[74]	3313*	
75	9-15	Good	9.9g/f	78	3506	
67	9-10	Good	9gd	77	3949	
53	13-13	Epso	10.1g/f	75	4473	
70	7-8	Brig	9.9sft	[73]	5095	

PRAKARA 2 ch f £0

| 29 | 15-19 | Newm | 7g/s | | 5279 |

PRALIN STAR 2 ch c £264

2	15-15	Ling	7gd		3285
58	4-6	Brig	7sft		4163
50	12-12	Good	8g/f		4522

PRAYERFUL 5 b m £0

| 49 | 5-7 | Warw | 10.9g/s | [40] | 1326 T |

PRE EMINANCE 3 b c £0

| 70 | 6-13 | Kemp | 8fm | | 2072 |

PRECIOUS FREEDOM 3 b g £0

0	16-16	Sout	7af	[48]	66	p
0	10-10	Sout	6af	[43]	308	VIS
0	15-16	Sout	6af	[40]	447	BL
13a	7-11	Sout	5af	[35]	578	bl

PRECIOUS MYSTERY 4 ch f £6151

60	4-14	Wind	11.6fm	57	3638	
65	2-8	Brig	11.9sft	57	4143	
54a	12-16	Ling	12ap	60	4973	
70	1-12	BRIG	11.9sft	60	5093*	
59	6-10	Catt	13.8sft	67	5322	

PRECIOUS SAMMI 2 b c £0

59	8-9	Folk	7ap		3047
67a	5-14	Ling	7ap		4971
35	11-14	Yarm	8g/s		5118
48a	9-10	Ling	7ap	[60]	5264

PRELUDE 3 b f £3864

53	5-6	Ches	7gd		1587
65	8-10	Good	8gd		2224
45	8-11	Chep	8.1g/f		2999
57	6-6	Ches	10.3g/f	63	3084
62	6-16	Thir	12g/f	60	3573
58	6-7	Ayr	10.9g/f	60	3765
63	1-12	RIPO	10gd	56	4282*
63	5-12	Beve	12.1g/f	61	4601
52	10-20	Catt	12g/f	61	4966

PREMIER CHEVAL 4 ch g £0

| 27a | 13-14 | Ling | 10ap | 54 | 101 |
| 16a | 14-14 | Ling | 10ap | 51 | 230 |

PREMIER DREAM 3 ch c £5179

58	6-8	Warw	8.1sft		1086
68	6-11	Ripo	8gd		1177
73	3-11	Beve	8.5sft		1304
72	1-11	WARW	8.1hvy	67	1534*
0	14-14	Newc	8gd	70	1872
65	4-11	Ripo	8gd	70	2986
2	11-12	Chep	8.1g/s	69	3898
27	14-14	Chep	10.2gd	69	4487

PREMIER FANTASY 2 b c £4979

65 6-16 Thir 6g/s 4205
94 1-11 HAYD 5g/f 4349*

PREMIER PROSPECT 3 b f £1456
60 2-18 Galw 7g/f 56 3656

PREMIER ROUGE 3 b g £3185
69 4-11 Beve 7.5g/s 2325
66 4-11 Hayd 8.1gd 2886
62 3-4 Beve 9.9g/s 3855
70 2-14 Yarm 8g/s [65] 4252
66 3-13 Chep 8.1hvy 67 4709
56 8-16 Bath 8gd 67 5022

PREMIER TIMES 2 ch c £3250
62 5-7 Muss 5g/s 2965
62 1-7 RIPO 6g/s 3259*
33 6-6 Muss 7.1g/f 59 3560
48 7-15 Redc 6g/f [59] 3769
32 8-15 Catt 7sft [59] 3930

PRENUP 2 ch f £13757
59a 8-11 Ling 6ap 135
57 4-20 Wind 11.6sft 58 1648
69 1-8 BRIG 9.9g/f 58 2046*
78 1-6 BEVE 12.1g/s 62 2322*
74 2-10 Newm 12g/f 67 2530
81 2-13 Redc 11g/s 73 2960
53 8-12 Sali 12g/f 76 3868
76 6-17 Thir 12fm 76 4377

PRESENT N CORRECT 11 ch g £0
9a 9-10 Wolv 7af [30] 298 bl
11a 8-9 Wolv 7af [30] 310 bl
9a 10-12 Wolv 6af [30] 524 bl

PRESENT ORIENTED 3 ch c £0
87 5-17 Newm 10gd 1737
48 8-11 Chep 10.2gd [82] 2196

PRESIDENTS LADY 6 b m £0
5a 12-12 Wolv 8.5af [42] 47
0 13-15 Sout 8af 42 84
0 13-13 Sout 8af [30] 199

PRESKANI 2 b g £0
0 16-16 Leic 7fm 3811
27a 12-15 Sout 5af 4089
27 13-15 Nott 6.1g/s 4644
37a 9-12 Wolv 6ap 4921 P

PRESS EXPRESS 2 ch c £3621
69 7-18 Newm 7gd 3927
79 6-12 Newm 7gd 4194
79 1-15 CHEP 7.1gd 4483*
78 8-17 Good 8gd 79 4871
23 13-14 Newm 6sft 78 5098
67 7-14 Donc 7sft 75 5213

PRESTO SHINKO 3 b c £19659
82a 1-11 LING 6ap [78] 898*
72 6-14 Ches 6.1g/s 78 1570
79 3-7 Ling 6sft 78 1621
82 2-11 Nott 6.1g/f 77 2155
85 1-8 GOOD 6gd 77 2375*
85 3-7 Wind 6fm [83] 3293
81 4-16 Wolv 8gd 83 3827
63 12-19 Sali 6gd 83 4855

PRESTO VENTO 4 b f £0
75 7-9 Newm 6fm 90 1490
79 11-11 Ling 7sft [90] 1620

PRESTON HALL 3 b c £0
61a 7-13 Ling 10ap 601
52a 8-10 Ling 10ap 886
41 6-11 Folk 7g/s 3048
44 5-7 Folk 9.7gd [50] 3385
0 12-12 Folk 12g/s 49 3913

PRESUMPTIVE 4 b c £12384
63 5-17 Ling 7g/s 1617
82 3-13 Sali 8gd 77 2662
75 13-20 Newm 8fm 78 3001
85 1-8 SAND 7.1g/s 77 3891+
0 17-18 Ayr 7.2sft 82 4689 BL
76 10-18 York 7gd 82 5000

PRETTY KOOL 4 b f £3446

39 10-13 Nott 8.2g/f 2633
50 5-16 Ling 6g/f 49 3602
52a 3-14 Ling 7ap 49 3746
53 1-12 FOLK 6g/s 48 3911*
44 7-20 Chep 7.1g/s 53 4367
19 13-19 Yarm 6g/s 52 4636

PRETTY STAR 4 b c £3555
93 2-9 Pont 12g/s 88 3969
67 15-21 York 11.9gd 88 3999

PRETTY WOMAN 2 ch f £0
29 11-11 Beve 5g/f 4599
40 10-10 Ling 5g/f 4893

PREVEZA 4 br f £0
2a 13-13 Ling 6ap 219

PRIDE 4 b f £112007
115 1-11 CHAN 10sft [80] 1699*
110 3-5 Sain 10.5g/s [80] 2143
112 5-10 Sain 12g/s [80] 3012
114 2-13 Deau 10sft [80] 4160
114 3-13 Long 12sft [80] 4567
108 13-19 Long 12g/f [80] 4956
119 1-8 LONG 12hvy [80] 5165*

PRIDE OF KINLOCH 3 ch f £3130
9a 12-12 Sout 8af 62 141
11a 15-16 Sout 7af 60 202
37a 7-12 Wolv 6af 54 385
15a 6-11 Sout 7af [50] 488
47 9-12 Thir 7g/s 65 1215
60 4-20 Ripo 8g/s 60 1366
0 13-14 Warw 8.1hvy 59 1535
59 3-19 Redc 7g/f 57 1820
52 7-16 York 7g/f 57 2057
50 9-20 York 6g/f 58 2409
7 17-17 Redc 6gd 57 2561
56 3-17 Ripo 6gd 55 3262
59 2-20 Thir 6g/f 55 3575
57 6-20 Redc 6g/f 58 3767
22 15-15 Redc 6fm 57 4562
5 15-16 Nott 8.2hvy 55 5347

PRIDE OF LONDON 2 b f £0
22 17-17 Nott 6.1gd 2927
64 8-14 Yarm 7gd 3489
41 12-16 Sali 7gd 3882

PRIDE OF POONA 2 b f £0
26a 8-8 Ling 6ap 5081
49a 8-14 Ling 7ap 5257

PRIDEWAY 7 b m £0
8a 8-8 Wolv 9.4af 65 157 bl

PRIDEWOOD DOVE 5 b m £0
0 11-11 Chep 10.2gd 2196
0 P-8 Warw 18fm 2781

PRIDEYEV 4 ch g £0
0 9-10 Wolv 16.2af 57 812

PRIMA STELLA 4 gr f £7184
50a 10-12 Wolv 5af 70 35
68a 2-12 Wolv 5af [70] 70
48a 11-14 Ling 6ap 68 149
68a 4-10 Wolv 6af 67 282
78a 1-11 SOUT 6af 67 386*
67a 10-14 Ling 7ap 73 518
75a 2-10 Sout 7ap 73 611
63a 6-13 Wolv 6af 73 687
70a 6-10 Ling 7ap 73 799
52a 12-14 Ling 6ap 71 874
37 7-8 Newb 6fm 62 2648
37 8-17 Wind 6fm 58 2975

PRIMARILY 2 b c £1477
27 11-12 Beve 5g/f 4596
69 5-12 Hayd 6sft 4770
68 2-9 Pont 6g/s 5154
66 2-9 Catt 7sft [68] 5317

PRIMATECH 3 b f £214
23 8-18 Chep 7.1g/s 48 3900
43 4-15 Carl 7.9fm [45] 4507 P
37 9-17 Warw 8.1g/s [45] 4992 p
39 3-20 Yarm 7g/s [40] 5120 p

PRIME CONTENDER 2 b c £0
55 7-14 Newb 6sft 5197
77 5-21 Donc 6sft 5368

PRIME OFFER 8 b g £9878
3a 13-13 Sout 7af [55] 858
60a 2-10 Ling 8ap 55 917
51a 4-12 Ling 8ap 52 1013
65 1-20 YARM 8fm 53 2149*
62 2-11 Brig 7fm 59 2334
67 1-9 NEWM 8g/f 61 2529*
67 5-16 Redc 8g/s 65 2958
64 4-8 Brig 8fm [65] 3676
67 2-16 Brig 7sft [64] 4144
39 18-26 Redc 8fm 65 4926

PRIME POWERED 3 b g £5555
90 5-14 Newm 10g/f 89 1192
89 5-18 Epso 10.1fm 89 2250
83 8-16 Good 12fm 88 3534 P
89 2-10 Good 9.9gd 85 3949
83 8-11 Epso 10.1gd 87 4293 p
86 4-12 Good 11gd 85 4749 p
1 14-14 Newb 10hvy 85 5223 BL

PRIME RECREATION 6 b g £9384
48a 14-16 Sout 5af 71 205
64a 6-9 Sout 5af 68 415
43a 16-16 Sout 5af 68 461
54a 6-10 Sout 5af 64 660
44a 8-10 Wolv 5af 64 749 P
58 9-17 Kemp 5sft 68 944
38 15-19 Warw 5gd 65 1127
65 3-17 Nott 5.1g/s 61 1774
48 9-14 Kemp 5g/f 62 1914
41 12-19 Leic 5gd 62 2702
69 4-12 Newm 5g/f 61 3279
35 11-12 Nott 5.1g/f [66] 3577
24 12-12 Newm 5gd 64 4197
73 1-9 YARM 5.2g/s 65 4253*
61 8-12 Yarm 5.2g/s 71 4585
72 3-12 Redc 5sft [70] 5305

PRIMED UP 2 b g £0
24 12-12 Good 7fm 3568

PRIMESHADE PROMISE 3 ch f £535
47 13-14 Wind 8.3fm 2974
37 11-15 Wind 10fm 3292
57 3-10 Chep 7.1gd 3732
24 8-13 Chep 8.1hvy 57 4709
72 7-8 Leic 8gd [53] 5057

PRIMO WAY 3 b c £7142
81 1-14 SOUT 6gd [80] 1281*
84 3-11 Newb 6gd 80 1734
68 6-11 Nott 6.1g/f 81 2155
87 3-11 Donc 7g/f 81 2427
70 11-13 Newb 7g/f 82 2880
86 3-25 Newb 7gd 82 4683
73 14-18 York 7g/f 83 5000
80a 7-12 Wolv 7.1ap 82 5159 P

PRIMUS INTER PARES 3 b c £8857
104 1-14 HAYD 8.1gd 95 2903*
74 16-16 Newm 9g/f 100 3059

PRINCE AARON 3 b g £53025
56a 2-13 Ling 6ap [47] 219
63a 1-14 LING 6ap 54 328*
70a 1-13 LING 6ap 58 451*
60a 6-14 Ling 6ap [68] 516
72a 2-12 Ling 6ap 68 628
86a 1-14 LING 6ap 71 874*
72 3-9 Ripo 6g/f [72] 2007
90 1-19 KEMP 6fm 72 2070+
81 5-17 Epso 6fm 81 2256
96 1-11 ASCO 6.5gd 81 3069*
100 1-8 NEWM 6gd [89] 4226*
24 24-24 Ayr 6sft 96 4686

PRINCE ALBERT 6 ch g £215
0 8-13 Wind 8.3g/s 1058 T
4 11-12 Folk 9.7sft 40 1273 t
37 3-13 Kemp 10hvy [35] 1643

PRINCE CHARMING 2 b c £39954
90 1-5 KEMP 5g/s 1114*

102	1-6	ASCO	5sft		1422*
83	8-8	Sand	5g/f		2094
91	6-9	Deau	5hvy		4155
107	1-12	AYR	5g/s	[98]	4651*
102	8-9	Newm	6g/f	[98]	4888
104	5-11	Newm	6sft	[100]	5132
105	4-9	Mais	6sft	[100]	5312

PRINCE CYRANO 5 b g £3506

43	22-22	Donc	6gd	90	921
62	15-20	Kemp	6g/f	86	1138
74	14-30	Newm	6g/f	83	1481
73	6-14	Ling	7sft	79	1624
46	11-11	Newm	7fm	76	2090
71	3-11	Newm	6fm	72	3408
70	5-12	Newm	6g/f	71	3751
77	2-11	Sand	5sft	71	4070
54	9-12	Newm	5gd	71	4197
52	13-16	Leic	5gd	72	4700
62	8-19	York	5gd	70	4989

PRINCE DAYJUR 5 b g £5499

43	18-19	Thir	6g/f	79	1767
81	1-10	KEMP	6g/f	74	2861+ VIS
68	11-16	Newm	5g/f	77	3033 vis
65	7-9	Ayr	6g/f	77	3307 vis

PRINCE DOMINO 4 b g £0

34a	16-16	Ling	7ap	[49]	180 BL e

PRINCE DU SOLEIL 7 b g £0

0	13-13	Ling	16ap	42	137
36a	6-12	Ling	8ap	[40]	710
37a	6-11	Ling	8ap	[40]	786 P
34a	8-14	Ling	10ap	[35]	1072 H
22	8-9	Yarm	7fm	35	2150

PRINCE HECTOR 5 ch g £3838

63	10-20	Wind	6g/s	79	1255
82	2-13	Yarm	6g/f	78	1726
75	6-11	Donc	7g/f	80	2076
80	2-8	Newb	8g/f	[80]	2313
82	4-11	Yarm	5gd	80	3364

PRINCE HOLING 4 ch g £397

58	5-9	Pont	10hvy	[89]	1068
57	7-9	Ayr	13.1g/s	89	2567
38	8-9	Hayd	11.9gd	84	2900 t
0	8-8	Donc	12g/s	75	3222
63	7-10	Catt	13.8g/f	65	3669 t

PRINCE IVOR 3 b g £0

0	14-15	Ling	12ap	[40]	118
27a	12-15	Ling	7ap	[40]	216
30a	9-13	Ling	10ap	[40]	539
10a	7-8	Ling	10ap	[35]	1026 BL
24a	8-14	Ling	10ap	[35]	4662 vis T
0	19-19	Brig	9.9gd	[35]	4903 vis t

PRINCE KIRK 4 b c £42148

122	1-5	LONG	9.3gd		2002* BL

PRINCE MINATA 9 b g £209

27a	8-11	Wolv	12af	48	557
26a	13-13	Ling	10ap	45	805
37a	3-12	Sout	8af	[40]	905
24a	10-15	Sout	8af	40	1028
41	4-14	Sout	12g/s	[40]	1047
19a	11-12	Wolv	8.5af	40	1379
32a	6-12	Ling	8ap	[40]	1451

PRINCE NAMID 2 b c £4187

66	4-12	Ripo	5gd		1173
77	3-9	Pont	5sft		1424
75	1-3	REDC	5sft		1658*

PRINCE NASSEEM 7 b h £0

0	7-10	Wolv	16.2af	40	812

PRINCE NUREYEV 4 b g £6600

89	9-17	Kemp	10g/s	97	1111
77	9-14	York	10.4g/s	95	1704
80	9-13	Asco	12fm	92	2582
93	2-9	Sand	10g/s	87	2896

PRINCE OF ARAGON 8 b g £0

35a	7-15	Sout	7af	43	2501
2a	13-16	Sout	8af	39	2805

PRINCE OF BLUES 5 b g £7544

36a	11-13	Wolv	6af	80	41
62a	11-15	Sout	5af	80	64
70a	6-12	Ling	6ap	[80]	106 P
57a	9-11	Wolv	5af	73	155 p
33a	9-10	Wolv	6af	70	246
62a	2-10	Ling	5ap	64	453 p
12a	10-10	Sout	5af	65	660 p
25a	13-13	Wolv	6af	65	687
26a	10-10	Wolv	5af	65	749 bl
59a	4-7	Ling	5ap	61	1011 p
51	10-19	Warw	5gd	58	1127 p
65	4-13	Epso	5sft	58	1293 p
67	5-7	Hayd	6g/f	[58]	1487 p
60	13-20	York	5g/s	62	1683 p
54	8-15	Hayd	5g/f	64	1917 p
60	3-7	Hayd	6g/s	62	2187 p
64	3-11	Ches	5.1gd	62	2286 p
56	5-11	Ayr	6gd	60	2542 p
57	7-11	Ches	5.1g/s	60	2747 p
64	7-8	Ches	10.3g/f	[59]	3083
63	3-7	Leic	6g/f	[59]	3518 bl
34	23-26	Good	6fm	59	3569 bl
60	3-6	Hayd	6g/s	59	3903 bl
56	3-12	Ches	5.1sft	57	4107 bl
49	16-16	Hayd	5fm	56	4382 bl
47	10-13	Ches	5.1g/f	56	4514 bl
53	12-16	Leic	5gd	56	4700 p

PRINCE OF GOLD 4 b c £11001

64	8-14	Nott	10fm	[72]	1006
54a	5-14	Sout	8af	65	1198
63	7-20	Ripo	8g/s	69	1366
44	7-8	Nott	8.2g/s	[67]	1775
61	6-16	York	7g/f	64	2057
52	7-10	Hayd	8.1gd	63	2242
70	1-15	BEVE	7.5g/s	63	2324* P
53	10-11	Warw	8.1fm	67	2600 p
55	10-17	Hayd	8.1gd	67	2947 p
54	14-15	Ches	10.3g/f	66	3099 p
54	8-10	Beve	8.5g/f	66	3501 p
48	10-12	Leic	8fm	64	3813 BL
47	13-14	Beve	7.5g/s	64	4241 p
63	5-15	Beve	7.5g/f	62	4719 p
65	3-20	Ripo	6gd	62	4785 p
71	2-19	York	5gd	63	4989 p
52	9-16	Catt	7sft	65	5130 p
69a	1-12	WOLV	6ap	[57]	5155* p
70a	2-13	Wolv	6ap	[63]	5327 p

PRINCE OF PERLES 3 b g £426

20a	10-12	Sout	8af	35	656 VIS
9a	14-15	Ling	7ap	[35]	708 vis
35a	3-13	Sout	6af	35	797 bl
27a	9-15	Ling	7ap	[35]	830 bl

PRINCE OF THE WOOD 3 ch g £2124

39a	4-12	Wolv	16.2af	46	7
46a	2-9	Ling	16ap	[45]	1414
48a	1-7	WOLV	16.2af	[45]	1802*
51	4-14	York	13.9g/f	51	2060 P
44	7-13	Chep	18gd	46	2198 p
51	5-13	Pont	17.1g/f	51	2276 p
37	9-9	Redc	16sft	49	2963 p
49	4-9	Ayr	15gd	45	3327 BL

PRINCE OF THEBES 3 b c £11337

97	1-9	ASCO	8gd	87	3465*
91	3-8	Folk	9.7g/s	[90]	3912

PRINCE PROSPECT 7 b g £2773

20a	8-9	Sout	11af	[48]	204
23a	7-13	Wolv	9.4af	46	287
49a	1-9	WOLV	9.4af	[45]	525*
51a	2-11	Wolv	9.4af	[45]	580
51a	2-11	Wolv	12af	[47]	689
14a	9-11	Wolv	12af	50	937
43a	8-13	Wolv	9.4af	49	1223
33	7-11	Ayr	9.1sft	[40]	5067

PRINCE PYRAMUS 6 b g £0

45	10-19	Beve	5sft	45	1627
5	18-20	Beve	5g/f	[45]	1948

PRINCE RENESIS 3 b g £0

38	8-10	Bath	5.7sft		1539
48	10-11	Thir	7fm		2463
49	9-12	Catt	6g/f		2849
18	6-7	Brig	9.9sft		4142
0	16-16	Nott	10gd	48	4857
41a	5-12	Wolv	8.6ap	[45]	5230

PRINCE SAMOS 2 b c £2317

80	4-8	Asco	6g/f		3438
69	7-18	Wind	6gd		3824
80	5-8	Kemp	6sft		4028
82a	3-12	Ling	6ap		4179
80	3-14	Newm	6sft	80	5098

PRINCE SLAYER 8 b g £0

41a	9-13	Ling	10ap	[65]	569

PRINCE TUM TUM 4 b c £3715

91	10-17	York	7.9g/s	105	1686
98	6-8	Newm	7g/f	[103]	2765
97	4-8	Newb	7g/f	[101]	3253
103	3-5	Warw	7.1gd	[97]	4270

PRINCE VALENTINE 2 b g £905

67a	8-12	Ling	8ap		102
70a	7-12	Ling	8ap		175
29a	10-14	Ling	10ap		473
41a	7-12	Ling	7ap	[65]	536
61	3-8	Warw	8.1sft	[57]	1086
58	5-11	Warw	8.1hvy	60	1534
56	4-11	Brig	9.9fm	58	2260 BL
7	7-7	Brig	9.9g/f	[58]	2433 bl
47	4-12	Brig	9.9g/f	55	3300
34a	9-12	Ling	10ap	52	4113
1	16-19	Brig	9.9sft	52	4145 P
21	14-19	Kemp	8ap	[49]	4795 bl

PRINCE VECTOR 2 b c £0

70	11-19	Leic	7gd		5055

PRINCE VETTORI 2 b c £0

63	9-10	Newb	7g/f		3955
59	8-11	Chep	8.1g/s		4363
69a	6-11	Ling	8ap		4744

PRINCEABLE LADY 2 b f £0

67	7-10	Pont	6g/f		2610
44	10-16	Nott	6.1gd		3103
11	12-12	Thir	6g/f		3411
47	9-10	Hayd	5gd		3755

PRINCELET 2 b c £277

73	4-20	Yarm	8sft		5252

PRINCELY VALE 2 b c £12337

53	7-15	Warw	5g/s		1325
55	4-7	Chep	6.1gd		2115
71	1-10	THIR	6fm		2461* P
65	1-8	REDC	7g/s		2563* p
76	1-5	BRIG	6fm		2833* p
70	3-14	Leic	6g/f	74	3212 p
67	4-6	Muss	7.1g/f	74	3560 p
69	5-6	Hayd	6g/s	72	3902 p
74	2-6	Chep	5.1g/s	69	4298 p

PRINCELYWALLYWOGAN 2 b c £0

70	6-14	Folk	7gd		4115

PRINCESS ALINA 3 b f £0

53a	8-14	Ling	10ap		367
61a	8-11	Ling	10ap	67	497

PRINCESS BANKES 3 b f £370

29a	11-11	Ling	8ap	[68]	841
36a	6-8	Wolv	8.5af	[60]	1220
36	11-20	Yarm	6g/f	55	1730
26a	10-12	Wolv	7af	50	2049
47	7-9	Folk	7fm	[45]	2716
41	4-13	Folk	9.7g/f	[45]	4372
41	3-12	Brig	11.9fm	45	4764
40	15-18	Bath	10.2gd	[45]	5023
32	7-15	Yarm	10.1g/s	[45]	5122

PRINCESS ERICA 4 b f £441

10	15-16	Nott	6.1sft	58	1465
11	12-14	Donc	6g/s	[58]	1522 P
15a	11-15	Sout	6af	48	1750 p
44	4-10	Donc	6g/f	48	1878 p
18	10-16	Nott	6.1gd	[45]	1988 p
35	9-19	Redc	6g/f	45	2125 p

PRINCESS GALADRIEL 3 b f £14933
54 2-10 Folk 6sft 50 1576
63 1-20 **YARM** 6g/f 50 1730*
59 3-13 Ripo 6g/f 57 2011
64 2-10 Yarm 8g/f 58 2344
46 7-11 Folk 9.7fm 61 2719
57 6-11 Ling 11.5g/f 61 2842
56 3-8 Folk 7g/f 59 3724
53 6-9 Ling 7gd 58 4110
63 1-10 **YARM** 7g/s 56 4251*
64 3-17 Beve 8.5g/f 61 4721
44 10-15 Nott 8.2hvy 61 5191
69 2-18 Newm 8sft 61 5272
37a 12-13 Wolv 8.6ap [61] 5336

PRINCESS GRACE 4 b f £0
29a 6-14 Sout 8af 39 160

PRINCESS ISMENE 3 b f £5027
59a 1-8 **LING** 8ap [54] 326* bl
51a 5-12 Ling 8ap 60 402 bl
54a 2-9 Sout 7af [59] 613 bl
58a 2-5 Sout 7af [59] 682 bl
52a 4-14 Ling 7ap [57] 804 bl
58a 3-10 Ling 10ap [55] 843 bl
51 3-6 Yarm 10.1g/f [55] 1134 bl
38a 4-13 Sout 8af [55] 1193 bl
30 13-16 Nott 10gd 55 1240 bl
35 5-8 Nott 8.2sft 55 1740 bl
43 4-9 Good 11g/f 47 2019 bl
29 6-11 Yarm 11.5g/f 45 2346 bl
0 R-10 Leic 7fm [45] 3812 bl
19 9-10 Beve 9.9sft 45 4260
0 R-18 Chep 8.1gd [45] 4485
0 R-9 Wolv 9.5ap [48] 5360 VIS

PRINCESS KAI 2 b f £7009
52a 3-13 Ling 6ap [60] 25 BL
61a 1-5 **LING** 5ap [55] 289* bl
50a 9-10 Ling 5ap 61 371 bl
35a 8-10 Ling 6ap 61 494 bl
51a 3-10 Ling 5ap [61] 548 bl
59 4-9 Bath 5g/s 56 1102 bl
58 2-9 Muss 5g/s 55 1457 bl
58 2-10 Brig 5.3fm 55 1694 bl
58 6-15 Ling 5g/f 57 2062 bl
38 13-18 Wind 6g/f 57 2268 bl

PRINCESS KIOTTO 3 b f £9298
58 5-9 Ripo 8gd 1178
53a 2-8 Sout 12af 53 1444
55 3-18 Hayd 14gd 55 2905
71 1-20 BEVE 16.2gd 55 3312*
73 1-13 **NEWC** 16.1fm 62 4868*
73 2-10 Pont 18g/s 66 5151

PRINCESS LINKS 2 b f £0
0 15-15 Newb 8hvy 5221

PRINCESS MAGDALENA 4 ch f £0
43 11-13 Bath 8sft 57 1542
34 7-15 Wind 11.6g/f [55] 2267
34 9-11 Folk 9.7fm 52 2719
42 7-9 Wind 11.6gd [50] 3164

PRINCIPAL WITNESS 3 b c £1565
68 13-19 Newb 8gd 1236
82 4-17 Newb 8g/f 1762
80 2-12 Leic 8fm 2106
39 26-27 Asco 8g/f 82 2521
65a 5-14 Ling 10ap [82] 2740
64 13-16 Newm 8g/f 80 3059

PRINCIPESSA 3 b f £6604
76 5-18 Wind 8.3g/s 1258
60 11-20 Bath 10.2gd 1398
65 9-13 Bath 10.2g/f [69] 1791
61 10-12 Sand 10gd 67 2366
72 2-18 Leic 10gd 65 2706
72 2-12 Beve 9.9gd 65 2893
54 9-12 Newb 10g/f 70 3255
73 2-12 Bath 11.7g/f 68 3845
60 4-5 Ches 12.3sft [68] 4075
74 3-9 Bath 10.2gd [70] 4547
74 2-15 Bath 10.2gd [70] 4826
34 16-20 Catt 12gd 70 4966
19a 10-10 Ling 12ap 72 5239

PRINS WILLEM 5 b g £7470
90 2-20 Newm 12gd 86 1172
92 3-19 Newm 12g/f 88 1484
90 4-14 Hayd 16.2gd 90 2239
89 4-14 York 13.9gd 90 3119
83 9-21 York 11.9gd 89 3999
71 12-17 Newm 12g/f 87 4889 VIS'
86 3-10 Newm 12sft [85] 5102

PRINTSMITH 7 br m £3627
42a 1-12 **SOUT** 8af [32] 309*
47a 4-14 Sout 8af [35] 354
38a 4-11 Wolv 7af [45] 579
44a 3-13 Sout 8af [45] 776
46a 2-10 Sout 8af [45] 850
50a 1-5 **SOUT** 8af [45] 908*
1a 12-14 Sout 8af 50 1198
33 5-14 Hayd 8.1g/s 45 1348
28 11-19 Redc 8sft 45 1661
27a 9-15 Sout 8af 48 1755
41 4-16 Warw 8.1g/s [45] 4993

PRIORS DALE 3 b c £2279
74a 2-12 Ling 8ap 72 17
70a 7-14 Ling 10ap 72 122
66a 2-14 Ling 10ap [72] 430
57a 6-12 Ling 10ap [72] 514
60a 6-11 Ling 8ap [70] 697
68 4-18 Good 8g/f 66 1849
34 14-16 Sali 8gd 66 4334
31 14-16 Bath 8gd 65 5022 T

PRITHEE 2 b f £0
69 7-16 Newm 7g/s 5280

PRIVATE BENJAMIN 4 gr g £8650
42a 9-13 Ling 13ap [56] 602
64a 1-11 **LING** 12ap [56] 672*
56a 7-14 Ling 12ap 58 731
54a 6-10 Ling 12ap 60 936
53 3-16 Brig 11.9fm 49 1693
47 9-19 Brig 9.9g/f 49 1940
54 1-11 **SALI** 12fm 49 2293*
29 9-11 Good 12gd 54 2538
47 5-7 Brig 11.9fm 50 2836
38 10-14 Sali 12g/s 49 3114
37 12-16 Wind 11.6gd 46 3829
44 5-11 Good 11gd 46 3948
57a 3-14 Ling 16ap 53 5082

PRIVATE CHARTER 4 b c £22053
86a 13-14 Ling 10ap [110] 884
110 2-10 Newm 10g/f [110] 1483
92 10-14 Good 12g/f [110] 1843
104 6-6 Curr 10.5g/f[110] 2004
94 7-7 Donc 12fm [105] 4494
108 1-5 **NEWM** 12g/f [102] 4886* P

PRIVATE JESSICA 3 ch f £260
56 10-13 Newb 7gd 1210
50 9-13 Nott 6.1sft 1464
49 4-5 Yarm 7gd 3366
0 15-15 Sout 8af 55 4132
1 17-18 Good 8gd 50 4750

PRIVATE SEAL 8 b g £3362
44a 8-12 Ling 10ap [41] 272 t
46a 6-10 Ling 10ap [40] 370 t
37a 3-13 Ling 10ap [40] 539 t p
39a 2-15 Ling 12ap [40] 707 t
42a 2-14 Ling 10ap [40] 784 t p
34a 9-14 Ling 12ap [40] 827 t
44a 2-10 Ling 12ap [40] 916 t
8a 12-14 Ling 12ap [40] 968 t
41a 5-9 Ling 10ap [45] 1289 t
41 11-19 Brig 9.9g/f 45 1940 t
29 8-8 Nott 10g/f 41 2157 t
32 9-12 Warw 10.9fm 41 2436 t
51 3-9 Brig 9.9g/f [41] 2643 t
51a 2-13 Ling 10ap 45 3288 t
41 6-10 Newm 10fm 45 3404 t
56 3-7 Yarm −10.1g/f [43] 3704 t
46 4-19 Brig 9.9sft 45 4145 t
31 9-15 Folk 9.7g/f [45] 4373 t

PRIVY SEAL 3 b c £199843
110 1-7 **KEMP** 8g/s [105] 1113*

108 2-5 Sand 10g/s [110] 1316
102 2-6 Ches 12.3gd[110] 1584
108 3-15 Capa 12gd [110] 2142 vis
101 9-13 Asco 10g/f [109] 2520 VIS
110 4-4 Long 10g/s [109] 2825
107 2-8 Good 9.9gd [107] 4748

PRIZE FIGHTER 2 b g £5720
81 2-17 Ling 7g/f 2584
84a 1-11 **SOUT** 7af 2995*
91a 2-10 Sout 7af 85 3483

PRIZE RING 5 ch g £1720
49 6-20 Catt 12g/f 52 2850
57 2-8 Hayd 14g/s 50 3140
49 6-10 Carl 14.1fm 52 3549
37 9-9 Hayd 14gd 52 3760

PRIZEMAN 6 b g £3080
61 24-27 Newb 8gd 95 1231
97 2-10 Hayd 8.1gd 92 2242

PRO TEMPORE 2 b f £4823
65 4-5 Pont 5g/f 2789
68 1-10 **CARL** 5g/f 3227*
68 6-10 Thir 5fm 70 3607
65 6-11 Nott 5.1gd 67 3987
66 3-19 Carl 5.9g/f 65 4344
54 9-18 Catt 7g/f 64 4673
55 8-18 Pont 6g/f 64 4934
56 6-17 Redc 7g/s [64] 5105

PROCLAMATION 2 gr c £7163
96 1-21 **NEWM** 8sft 5097*

PROCRASTINATE 2 ch g £2834
64 3-4 Newc 5hvy 1037
53 7-7 Muss 5g/f 1117
59 6-10 Newc 6sft 1677
55 5-12 Newc 6gd 1869
55 3-8 Hami 5gd 2177
40 7-13 Beve 6g/s 2321 P
45 5-10 Thir 6fm 2461
58 2-7 Beve 5gd 3308
42 11-20 Leic 7g/f 54 4451
70 3-7 Muss 5g/f [54] 4549
44 10-10 Muss 5g/f [68] 4804

PROCREATE 4 b g £0
2 17-18 Ayr 7.2g/f 46 1897
29 8-10 Muss 7.1g/f 42 3562
34 6-10 Ayr 6sft [45] 5278

PROFILER 8 b g £0
0 8-10 Wolv 14.8af 40 34

PROFITS REALITY 2 br c £7459
57 7-10 Newc 6sft 1677
79 5-10 Donc 6g/f 2077
76 5-18 Newc 6g/s 3699
85 4-5 Hami 6g/s 3877
68 3-11 Hami 6g/s 4006
86 1-7 **MUSS** 7.1gd [77] 4518*
89 3-14 Hami 6sft 81 4692
83 8-9 Pont 8g/s [84] 5150

PROMENADE 3 b f £0
71 5-7 Nott 6.1g/s [89] 1771
69 10-11 Redc 5g/f 86 2121
67 9-9 Newm 5fm 83 2593

PROMOTE 7 gr g £0
6a 10-14 Ling 13ap 50 264
0 14-14 Ling 10ap [45] 705
41 6-13 Nott 14.1gd 40 1990
41 6-12 Warw 19.1fm 40 2577
21 10-11 Ling 16gd 40 3200
8 11-12 Yarm 16gd 40 3493 t

PROMOTED DEPUTY 2 b f £5200
75a 1-10 **LING** 7ap 4442*

PROMOTER 4 ch g £15054
72 10-18 Newb 16gd 88 1232
74 9-18 York 13.9g/s 88 1689
92 2-29 Asco 20g/f 85 2471
83 9-19 Newc 16.1g/s 85 2771
91 4-17 Asco 16.2gd 88 3125
52 18-19 Good 21fm 89 3531

58a 4-8 Wolv 8.5af ... continued

58a	4-8	Wolv	8.5af		1220	
54	7-20	Donc	7g/s		1518	
24a	10-12	Wolv	7af	53	2204	
0	P-15	Warw	10.9g/f	50	2910	BL
47	4-9	Ayr	7.2g/f	[50]	3764	VIS
18	18-20	Yarm	8gd	[48]	3996	bl

PURPLE DOOR 2 b f £0

54	6-11	Bath	5.7g/f		3848
44	10-14	Muss	7.1g/f		4171
59	6-17	Ling	6gd		4443
36	23-29	Newm	6gd		5087

PURPLE RAIN 3 b f £0

43	7-8	Warw	8.1sft		1086
49	10-11	Ripo	8gd		1177
56	6-7	Nott	8.2sft		1468
36a	5-12	Wolv	8.5af	53	2205
20	10-15	Ayr	8gd	[50]	2504

PURR 3 b g £0

51	12-17	Newb	10gd		1737	
51	6-8	Good	11gd		2222	
16	13-14	Bath	10.2fm	54	2664	VIS
0	15-17	Pont	17.1g/s	49	3970	
47	8-11	Folk	9.7gd	[49]	4120	
30	9-12	Good	9.9sft	45	4268	
29	14-15	Folk	12g/f	[49]	4374	
35	4-6	Yarm	14.1sft	[49]	5249	

PUSHKIN 6 b h £3924

83	20-20	Hayd	14fm	105	4383
96	2-5	Pont	18g/f	[100]	4628
95	5-7	Hami	13g/s	96	4819
0	34-34	Newm	18sft		5135

PUSSY CAT 2 b f £0

44	8-11	Sali	6g/f		3863
31	6-6	Wind	6g/s		4217
59	13-16	Sali	7gd		4330
43	5-6	Brig	7fm	[50]	4760
32	10-12	Bath	8sft	[50]	5170

PUTRA KUANTAN 4 b c £18689

95	6-17	Kemp	10g/s	93	1111	
101	3-19	Newm	10g/f	92	1478	
103	1-14	SAND	8.1g/f	94	2096*	
93	15-31	Asco	8g/f	101	2489	
88	6-7	York	7.9g/s	100	3077	
94	11-21	Good	8fm	100	3565	
89	13-32	Newm	9g/f	98	4916	
91	12-22	Newm	8sft	97	5103	

PUTRA PEKAN 6 b h £52040

112	1-4	ASCO	8sft	[106]	1420+	bl
112	1-4	WIND	8.3sft	[108]	1649*	bl
103	7-10	Chan	8g/s	[108]	2458	bl
86	7-8	Hayd	8.1fm	[110]	4386	bl
112	2-7	Colo	8sft	[110]	4839	bl
94	3-8	Duss	8.5sft	[110]	5075	
101	8-11	Newm	8g/s	[109]	5283	bl

PUTRA SANDHURST 6 b h £10332

106	1-4	RIPO	12.3g/s	[104]	1364*
100	9-10	Newm	10g/f	[104]	1483
98	7-13	Epso	12fm	104	2255
102	7-9	Newm	10g/f	[102]	3233
80	8-9	Asco	10g/f	102	3439

PUTRA SAS 3 b c £18568

96	2-4	Sand	8.1g/s	[90]	1317
103	2-3	Ches	10.3gd	[90]	1595
103	6-13	Capa	12gd	[90]	2142

PUYA 2 b f £3064

83	2-11	Wind	6g/s		4941
82	2-10	Newm	6sft		5266

PYRRHIC 4 b g £1221

47a	5-12	Ling	10ap	[31]	272	bl
54a	3-10	Ling	10ap	[40]	370	bl
24a	7-13	Ling	10ap	[40]	412	bl
61a	2-13	Ling	10ap	[48]	429	bl
39a	10-15	Ling	12ap	[50]	521	bl
48a	6-12	Ling	10ap	50	542	bl
45a	5-14	Ling	10ap	[45]	705	bl
31a	13-14	Ling	12ap	45	768	bl
62a	6-14	Ling	10ap	[45]	828	bl
26a	8-11	Ling	10ap	[45]	970	bl
35a	6-8	Ling	10ap	[45]	1026	bl
16a	6-7	Ling	10ap	[40]	1182	bl

QABAS 4 b g £0

71	5-17	Kemp	10g/f	69	1913
66	8-11	Brig	9.9fm	69	2260
62	6-8	Sand	10gd	69	2363

QADAR 2 b c £6450

97	2-7	Good	6g/f		1848	T
95	3-5	Good	6gd		2221	t
86a	1-14	LING	7ap		4971*	t

QASIRAH 3 b f £7500

81	10-13	Newm	7gd	[102]	1169	
82	5-9	Ches	11.4gd	[100]	1568	BL
96	3-8	Epso	8.5g/f	[98]	2211	bl
89	6-19	Asco	8g/f	95	2491	bl
81	11-16	Newm	8g/f	95	3059	bl
73	10-10	Kemp	8fm		4389	bl

QAWAAFIL 2 b f £2976

62	5-6	Leic	6g/f		2399
60	8-17	Yarm	6gd		4610
48	7-13	Nott	6.1g/f		4843
75	1-9	CATT	7sft	[64]	5131*
38	15-20	Donc	7sft	71	5373

QOBTAAN 4 b g £7548

36a	5-16	Sout	8af	47	86
47a	3-14	Sout	8af	45	160
36a	4-13	Sout	8af	45	228
57a	1-10	Wolv	8.5af	[45]	300*
58a	1-10	SOUT	8af	51	387*
43a	7-11	Sout	8af	57	457
20a	10-14	Sout	8af	56	1198
41a	9-12	Wolv	8.5af	55	1379
46a	7-16	Sout	8af	53	3487
12	17-17	Hayd	8.1gd	53	3759
53a	4-13	Wolv	8.6ap	[51]	5184
60a	1-12	WOLV	8.6ap	[51]	5337*

QUALITAIR WINGS 4 b g £7411

61a	6-12	Ling	8ap	62	17	
74	3-16	Thir	7g/s	72	1474	
60	11-12	Hayd	8.1g/f	73	1883	
57	17-17	Carl	7.9gd	73	2672	
70	8-18	Catt	7g/f	73	2848	
75	2-6	Epso	8.5g/s	71	3042	
59	9-9	Beve	7.5gd	72	3310	BL
75	2-8	Newm	8g/f	72	3583	
67	8-16	Redc	8g/f	72	3768	
67	6-10	Hami	8.3g/s	72	4136	
74	3-12	Redc	8gd	72	4246	
63	8-20	Ayr	10g/s	72	4656	
66	5-14	Hami	8.3g/s	72	4820	
60	8-16	Catt	7sft	70	5130	

QUANTICA 5 b g £0

57	6-19	Redc	6sft	66	1145
56	15-20	Thir	5g/s	66	1476
43	15-20	Thir	6gd	64	1638
21	15-20	York	6g/f	62	2409
24	15-18	Donc	6gd	58	2752
30	16-20	Newc	6g/f	55	4408
41	6-19	Yarm	6g/s	55	4636

QUANTUM LEAP 6 b g £12230

61a	4-12	Ling	8ap	60	17	
66a	1-14	LING	10ap	60	101*	
67a	5-14	Ling	10ap	66	122	
63a	3-13	Ling	10ap	63	178	
58a	11-14	Ling	10ap	63	434	
59a	6-14	Ling	10ap	62	520	
62a	3-11	Ling	8ap	62	547	
55a	8-12	Ling	8ap	61	607	
65a	3-14	Ling	7ap	62	1010	vis
60	8-12	Bath	8g/f	65	1792	
70	3-18	Good	7g/f	65	1849	vis
75	1-16	LING	7gd	66	2063*	vis
69	6-13	Kemp	7gd	72	2172	vis
67	6-7	Good	7gd	[72]	2374	vis
75	4-13	Ling	7.6g/f	71	2587	vis
74	2-10	Epso	7g/f	71	2872	vis
72	4-10	Epso	6g/s	71	3045	vis
29	22-25	Asco	7g/f	72	3443	vis
49	20-24	Newb	7g/f	72	4642	vis
68	6-16	Good	7gd	70	4873	vis

QUARRY ISLAND 2 b f £4134

8a	10-13	Wolv	9.4af	[45]	37	VIS
41a	4-12	Ling	8ap	[40]	78	
33a	7-11	Sout	7af	[40]	207	
36a	5-10	Ling	10ap	[40]	291	
47a	2-9	Sout	8af	[40]	596	vis
24a	9-12	Sout	8af	40	656	vis
0	7-9	Sout	7af	[45]	871	
36a	7-9	Ling	10ap	[45]	899	BL
38	2-6	Chep	12.1sft	[40]	1331	
42	8-17	Bath	10.2sft	35	1541	
52	1-4	CARL	11.9fm	[40]	1952*	

QUARRYMOUNT 3 b g £22301

43	12-14	Brig	6fm		1690	
62	2-16	Epso	8.5gd	55	3219	
69a	1-14	LING	10ap	59	3449*	
67	2-7	Ayr	10.9g/f	63	3765	
78	1-5	BRIG	11.9sft	63	4166*	
77	2-4	Newc	12.4sft	69	4288	
79	2-12	Wind	11.6g/f	70	4833	
84	1-11	NEWM	14g/f	70	4919*	
85	2-11	Wind	11.6g/s	[70]	4942	
82	5-8	Donc	14.6sft	81	5204	

QUARTER TO 5 g r m £0

0	15-15	Ling	7ap	[35]	830

QUARTINO 3 b c £1287

46	10-11	Newm	10g/f	89	3029	
67	9-11	Sali	12g/s	85	4080	
65	8-12	Good	11gd	83	4749	BL
3	7-7	Nott	12g/s	83	4846	bl
78	2-8	Brig	9.9sft	[70]	5095	

QUATRE SAISONS 2 ch c £0

60	7-10	Newm	6sft		5266

QUAY WALLOPER 3 b g £0

55	7-12	Ripo	9g/f		1783	
18	12-14	Redc	14.1g/f	50	2123	
0	8-15	Sout	12af	46	2503	
9	14-18	Hayd	14gd	40	2905	VIS
27	12-20	Catt	12g/f	35	3354	vis
0	17-18	Beve	9.9g/s	26	4243	

QUDRAAT 3 b c £6269

70	5-12	Sand	10g/f		2193
71	8-9	Kemp	12g/f		2862
81	1-11	RIPO	12.3gd		4281*
89	2-12	Good	11gd	80	4749
87	7-15	Leic	11.8gd	88	5043
58	12-13	Donc	12sft	87	5215

QUDRAH 4 b f £1500

84a	7-14	Ling	10ap	85	758	BL
34a	8-9	Sout	12af	84	856	bl
83a	5-9	Ling	10ap	84	876	
100	4-6	Nott	14.1fm	[81]	1005	
49	8-9	Newm	12g/f	[85]	3278	
1	5-6	Pont	12gd	[85]	3458	
1	12-12	Yarm	10.1sft	40	4149	
3	16-17	Nott	14.1g/s	78	4647	

QUEDEX 8 b g £28485

68	1-10	KEMP	16fm	60	2073*	
67	5-13	Chep	18gd	65	2198	
73	2-13	Newc	16.1sft	64	2685	
74	1-7	SAND	14g/s	64	2899*	
77	1-10	HAYD	16.2sft	70	3275*	
67	9-19	Good	21fm	76	3531	
50a	10-12	Wolv	12.2ap	64	4924	
87	4-34	Newm	18sft	74	5135	

QUEEN ASTRID 4 b f £8690

106	2-9	Nava	10g/s		1435

QUEEN CHARLOTTE 5 ch m £1660

69	2-6	Muss	8g/f	68	1092
56	11-19	Redc	7g/f	68	1820
53	9-13	Ripo	8g/f	68	2010
53	7-9	Newm	8g/f	66	2529
63	5-19	York	7.9g/f	64	4399
63	6-16	Thir	8g/f	64	4592
50	11-19	Newc	7g/f	62	5014

QUEEN EXCALIBUR 5 ch m £226

39a 8-16 Ling 7ap [47] 290 p
0 9-10 Wolv 8.5af [47] 311 p
32a 7-10 Ling 8ap [45] 410 bl
14a 9-11 Ling 8ap [40] 786 p
35 7-22 Donc 12gd 45 918
40 6-20 Warw 10.9gd 45 1128
52 3-7 Warw 10.9g/s [45] 1326
5a 5-6 Sout 12af [35] 1592

QUEEN LOUISA 3 b f £0
12a 10-11 Wolv 6af 153 t
0 10-11 Wolv 6af 778
13 11-11 Redc 10sft 5303

QUEEN LUCIA 3 b f £2780
64 4-9 Ripo 8gd 1178
59 4-7 Muss 9g/s 1462
20 4-4 Ayr 7.2fm 1907
51 5-14 Wind 10gd 58 2617
56 4-12 Beve 9.9gd 58 2893
35a 7-14 Ling 10ap 55 3449
56 2-12 Kemp 9sft 53 4032
51 3-15 Bath 8g/s 53 4202
50a 7-13 Wolv 8.6ap 55 5005

QUEEN NEFITARI 2 b f £0
61 10-15 York 7.9gd 5002

QUEEN OF BULGARIA 3 b f £0
37a 9-10 Wolv 5af 61 749
24 7-9 Leic 6g/s [61] 1015
34 10-16 Nott 6.1sft 60 1465
0 13-14 Leic 6ap [56] 1963
33 9-13 Warw 6.1fm 50 2439
20 11-12 Folk 6gd 45 3380
0 13-15 Brig 6gd [45] 4905
3 19-20 Yarm 6g/s [40] 5121

QUEEN OF ICENI 2 b f £1752
42 19-23 Newm 7g/f 4885
80 2-19 Leic 7gd 5045
68 10-19 Newm 7g/s 5279

QUEEN OF NIGHT 3 b f £8136
55a 1-13 WOLV 6af [78] 30*
51a 5-11 Wolv 6af [78] 153
7a 7-7 Sout 6af [76] 317
23a 4-9 Sout 6af [74] 1194
1 18-19 Beve 5sft 70 1627
41a 4-8 Wolv 7af [70] 1656
0 R-8 Ripo 6g/f [60] 2480
4 10-14 Newc 6g/s [60] 2730
56a 1-15 SOUT 5af [60] 2803*
58a 1-10 SOUT 5af [55] 3156*
59 2-9 Catt 5g/f [55] 3353
44 12-15 Muss 5g/f 60 3561
56 5-15 Pont 5gd 60 3680
37 6-11 Nott 5.1gd 56 4038
48 6-9 Thir 5g/s 56 4210

QUEEN OF POLAND 2 b c £38294
87 1-10 YARM 7fm 2863*
105 1-9 SAND 7.1g/f 3357*
107 2-8 Donc 8fm 4476
107 6-10 Long 8gd 4954

QUEEN TOMYRA 2 b f £443
51 13-15 Newm 8fm 4723
56 11-19 Leic 7gd 5040
72a 3-12 Wolv 7.1ap 5179

QUEENS DANCER 2 b f £1966
29 15-15 Newm 8fm 4723
67 5-15 Newb 8hvy 5221
70 2-15 Nott 8.2hvy 5344

QUEENS ECHO 3 b f £1069
67 2-10 Newc 7hvy 4216
53 5-12 Newc 8g/f 4407
18 8-13 Ayr 10sft [57] 5066
38a 9-10 Wolv 8.6ap [55] 5329

QUEENS FANTASY 2 ch f £4965
40a 7-14 Sout 8af 88
19a 10-11 Wolv 9.4af 438
56 4-9 Leic 11.8g/s 1016
2 16-16 Nott 10gd 55 1240 BL
60 2-5 Brig 9.9g/f 55 1372 VIS
65a 1-12 WOLV 12af 56 2203* vis

56a 6-13 Sout 14af 63 2494 vis
58 6-13 Nott 10g/f 62 3419 vis

QUEENS GLORY 2 b f £1511
48 6-11 Kemp 5hvy 1640
72 2-5 Brig 6g/f 1937
66 6-9 Brig 5.3fm 2257
50 5-5 Brig 5.3g/f 2430
70 5-6 Ling 6gd 72 3022
60 7-14 Leic 6g/f 72 3212
10a 11-11 Sout 6af 70 3393
26a 6-8 Ling 6ap [66] 3745 VIS
38 6-6 Chep 6.1g/s 66 3897
46 3-8 Brig 5.3fm [57] 4759

QUEENS HAND 2 b f £0
33 11-17 Redc 7g/s 5105
41a 7-13 Wolv 6ap 5287

QUEENS RHAPSODY 4 b g £10288
88a 2-7 Ling 6ap [90] 431
85a 9-14 Ling 7ap 90 518
89a 2-13 Wolv 6af 87 618
94a 4-8 Wolv 7af [87] 838
90a 7-15 Ling 7ap 90 887
95 4-10 Warw 7.1gd [85] 1126
67 10-17 Thir 8g/s 85 1475
74 9-18 Ches 7.6gd 85 1598
80 7-21 Donc 7fm 82 4482
82 5-26 Ayr 6g/s 82 4652
84 3-20 Newm 7g/s 80 5286
84 3-20 Donc 7sft 80 5367

QUEENS SQUARE 3 b f £0
23 9-9 Redc 5sft [50] 1146
14a 7-8 Sout 6af 50 1441
36 7-13 Beve 8.5g/f [45] 1947
5 17-19 Redc 6g/f 45 2125

QUEENSBERRY 4 b g £2666
38a 7-11 Wolv 12af [55] 6 vis
38a 4-10 Wolv 14.8af [52] 125
53a 1-14 SOUT 8af 49 160*
46a 2-9 Sout 11af [49] 204
0 13-14 Ling 16ap 51 4319 BL
3a 10-11 Wolv 12.2ap 50 5009

QUEENSLANDER 3 b f £0
28 11-11 Muss 9g/f 1095

QUEENSTOWN 2 b g £2454
88a 2-14 Sout 8af [88] 88 bl
87a 2-11 Ling 7ap [85] 213 bl
37 10-10 Asco 8gd [88] 3067 bl
72a 3-12 Ling 8ap [84] 3286 bl
57 5-7 Sali 8gd [80] 3453 bl
52 7-12 Pont 8gd 69 3679 bl
45 11-14 Yarm 7gd 64 3995 bl
59 4-13 Warw 7.1g/s [60] 4667 H bl

QUERIDO 2 b c £4051
85 4-12 York 10g/f 3122
93 1-9 FOLK 7g/f 3721*

QUEST ON AIR 5 b g £462
43a 2-7 Ling 12ap [45] 1243
36 11-13 Nott 14.1gd [45] 1990
36 6-10 Yarm 11.5fm 44 2147

QUEUE UP 2 b c £562
76 3-17 Donc 6g/f 2424
15 12-13 Pont 6gd 3682
44 11-15 Nott 6.1g/s 4644

QUICK 4 b g £0
1 P-12 Warw 19.1fm 59 2577 vis
54 9-12 Warw 15g/f 59 2908 vis

QUICK GRAND 2 b r f £0
42 6-7 Ayr 6gd 3323
54 6-6 Muss 5g/f 3525
35 6-7 Ayr 6g/f 3761

QUICKFIRE 2 b f £7605
85 2-12 Newb 6g/f 3251
92 1-14 KEMP 7g/f 4711*

QUICKS THE WORD 4 b g £3303
46 8-19 Newc 6sft 70 967

24 12-19 Redc 6sft 67 1145
61 4-17 Warw 5hvy [63] 1532 bl
44 9-11 Hayd 5g/f 63 1886 bl
30 12-16 Carl 5.9fm 60 2445 bl
46 7-15 Thir 8g/s [60] 2688
58 2-13 Muss 8gd [54] 2967
58 2-20 Newm 8g/f 54 3232
53 6-17 Hayd 8.1gd 55 3759
59 2-15 Ayr 7.2hvy 54 4088

QUICKSTYX 3 b f £5076
68a 1-12 LING 8ap 514*
71 4-18 Nott 8.2fm 69 1007
68 5-16 Beve 7.5g/s 69 1163
67 4-12 Ripo 10gd 68 4282
69 4-14 Chep 10.2gd 68 4487
68 6-12 Beve 12.1g/f 68 4601
62 7-13 Newc 16.1fm 67 4868
65 6-20 Catt 12gd 67 4966
12 6-6 Good 12gd 65 5028 VIS

QUIDDITCH 3 b f £0
15a 7-10 Sout 8af 143

QUIDNET 2 ch f £0
4a 9-9 Sout 5af [46] 256 P

QUIET READING 6 b g £4213
33a 12-14 Sout 8af 69 195 vis
68a 3-13 Wolv 8.5af 67 251 vis
68a 3-10 Sout 8af 67 318 vis
68a 4-13 Wolv 8.5af 67 439 vis
58a 6-12 Wolv 8.5af 67 479 vis
57a 3-11 Wolv 8.5af 66 806 vis
69a 2-14 Sout 8af 65 1198 vis
67a 2-10 Wolv 8.5af 65 1322 vis
8 8-14 Warw 8.1hvy 48 1535 vis
54a 11-11 Ling 8ap 67 2018 vis
65a 4-15 Sout 8af 67 2500 vis
50a 9-15 Sout 8af 67 2725 vis

QUIET STORM 4 b f £4168
100 7-10 Newm 10g/f [94] 1483
81 16-18 Good 8g/f 98 1812
91 3-7 Pont 8g/f [96] 2278
91 6-12 Good 7fm [93] 3555

QUIET TIMES 4 ch g £18832
79a 2-13 Wolv 6af 75 45 bl
69a 9-16 Sout 5af 77 171 bl
87a 1-10 SOUT 6af 77 390* bl
86a 4-16 Sout 5af 83 461 bl
69a 9-13 Wolv 6af 86 482 bl
74a 4-10 Sout 6af [85] 532 bl
92a 1-10 WOLV 6af 83 834* bl
62 5-19 Redc 6sft 67 1145 bl
64 5-16 Newc 6sft 67 1277 bl
37 8-12 Hami 6g/s [65] 1600 bl
37 18-20 Thir 6gd 65 1638 bl
91a 2-12 Ling 6ap 88 5297 bl

QUIFF 3 b f £256851
100 1-10 SALI 9.9g/f 1718*
106 3-9 Asco 12g/f [84] 2517
119 1-8 YORK 11.9g/s[105] 4024*
118 2-9 Donc 14.6fm[119] 4532

QUILANGA 3 b f £25704
112 1-18 DEAU 10g/s 3836*

QUINCANNON 2 b g £0
63a 4-12 Wolv 6af 42
54a 6-13 Sout 6af 319

QUINN 4 ch g £0
0 10-10 Sout 16af [45] 984
19 10-13 Beve 12.1g/f [40] 1945

QUINTILLION 3 gr f £0
14a 8-10 Ling 6ap 973
31 12-19 Donc 6g/f 1876
0 7-7 Muss 8g/f 44 2613
4 10-10 Catt 6gd [40] 4964

QUINTOTO 4 b g £0
55 6-8 Muss 9g/f [69] 4173
7 14-14 York 10.4g/f 65 4402
56 9-19 Leic 10g/f 65 4456
23 15-17 Warw 8.1g/s 63 4668

48a 12-13 Wolv 9.5ap 57 5292
16a 13-13 Wolv 9.5ap [57] 5338 P

QUIRKIE 2 b f £0
46a 8-10 Wolv 7af 36

QUITO 6 b r £89335
99a 2-15 Sout 5af 95 64 bl
93a 6-15 Ling 7ap 95 81 bl
98a 4-16 Sout 5af 98 171 bl
98a 5-13 Ling 6ap 98 235 bl
109a1-13 WOLV 6af 98 618+ bl
87a 10-12 Wolv 8.5af 105 836 bl
106a6-15 Ling 7ap 105 887 bl
105 2-24 Donc 8gd 101 951 bl
96a 5-8 Ling 7ap [105] 1043 bl
104 5-10 Warw 7.1gd [103] 1126 bl
102 6-9 Hayd 7.1g/f [103] 1486 bl
110 1-14 YORK 6g/s 103 1703* bl
109 10-15 Newb 8g/f [103] 1758 bl
101 6-11 Hayd 7.1gd [111] 2184 bl
106 5-11 Newc 6g/s [110] 2769 bl
109 1-8 HAYD 6gd [110] 2949* bl
104 6-13 Newb 7g/f [108] 3957 bl
107 5-24 Ayr 6sft 106 4686 bl
105 3-14 Newm 6sft [105] 5100 bl
110 3-9 Donc 7sft [105] 5214 bl
105 5-11 Newm 8g/s [104] 5283 bl
112 1-12 DONC 6sft [104] 5371+ bl

QUIZZENE 2 gr c £3465
71 5-20 Yarm 8sft 5252
83 1-16 YARM 10.1g/s 5352*

RAAKAAN 3 b c £4238
78 3-14 Wind 8.3g/s 2622
82 1-11 LEIC 10g/f 3208*

RABBIT 3 b f £0
36 12-13 Wind 8.3gd 3828
51 9-13 Nott 8.2g/f 4847
44 5-11 Good 6gd 5030

RABITATIT 3 b f £5738
65 2-15 Bath 8g/s 62 1099
64 4-7 Carl 9.3fm 63 1953
41 9-9 Beve 8.5g/f 63 2168
67 2-8 Hami 9.2g/f 62 2475
73 5-6 Hami 8.3gd [62] 2710
61 5-14 Folk 9.7g/s 63 3052
53 6-7 Sali 8gd [62] 3453
62 2-4 Sand 10g/s 62 4068
58 7-14 Chep 10.2gd 62 4487
58 4-8 Hami 9.2sft [60] 4694 P
12 12-12 Pont 10fm [60] 4757

RACCOON 4 b g £43534
67 4-20 Thir 5g/f 74 1765
88 1-15 HAYD 5g/f 74 1917* VIS
91 1-17 MUSS 5fm 84 2082+ vis
69 16-20 Epso 5fm 81 2253 vis
90 8-28 Good 6fm 90 3622 vis
91 7-20 Hayd 5fm 90 3792 vis
76 19-22 Donc 5.6fm 89 4459 vis
73 11-24 Ayr 6sft 89 4686 T

RACE THE ACE 3 b g £16787
74 4-15 Leic 10g/s 1358
64 5-6 Newm 10gd 1892
74 2-8 Pont 12g/f 2608
72 3-12 Nott 14.1gd 68 3105
76 3-12 Sand 16.4g/f 70 3861
84 1-12 GOOD 16g/s 70 4235*
85 2-7 Nott 16g/f 77 4846
93 1-11 NEWM 16sft 79 5271*

RACHELS VERDICT 3 b f £5863
57 4-12 Ling 6g/f 2586
66 5-8 Newm 6g/f 3784
72 1-10 SALI 6g/s 4081*

RACING NIGHT 4 b g £0
57a 11-12 Ling 8ap 79 888
63 9-12 Sand 8.1g/s 75 1352

RADIANT BRIDE 3 ch f £4582
27a 10-14 Ling 12ap [45] 103
45a 2-12 Wolv 16.2af 45 156
26a 5-11 Sout 11af [45] 191

24a 11-14 Ling 13ap 45 259
32a 11-13 Ling 13ap 45 342 p
34a 2-9 Ling 16ap [40] 454 p
37a 6-14 Ling 13ap [35] 537 p
43a 1-9 SOUT 16af [35] 576* BL
48a 2-5 Sout 12af [45] 723 bl
42a 8-12 Ling 13ap 45 762 bl
49a 1-9 LING 13ap [45] 787* bl
37a 4-6 Wolv 16.2af [45] 824 bl

RADISH 3 b f £3562
63 12-20 Newm 8g/f 3237
77 1-13 BATH 10.2sft 5173*

RADLETT LADY 3 ch f £0
51a 8-12 Ling 6ap 1044
39 10-13 Folk 5sft 1575
20 14-19 Donc 6g/f 1876
39 9-13 Wind 6fm 2756
36 11-16 Warw 5g/s [45] 4995

RADMORE SPIRIT 4 b f £0
0 8-9 Wolv 9.4af 665
33 10-15 Nott 5.1g/f 2152
13a 10-11 Wolv 5.1ap 5363

RAETIHI 3 b f £365
29 11-19 Donc 6g/f 1876
35 4-4 Ripo 5g/s 3936
27 10-14 Newc 5g/f 4404
16a 9-12 Wolv 6ap [40] 5157

RAFFELBERGER 3 b g £45775
116 1-8 BADE 6sft 4426*

RAFFERTY 5 ch g £1268
85 7-20 Newm 8fm 82 3001 bl
83 5-11 Yarm 7gd 82 3364 bl
84 3-8 Wind 8.3fm 81 3641
77 4-7 Wind 8.3gd [81] 3826
81 7-11 Yarm 8gd 81 4615 bl
72 9-14 Asco 8g/f 79 4813 bl

RAFFISH 2 ch g £3764
50 8-9 Folk 7g/f 3721
79 4-17 Warw 7.1qd 4271
78a 1-11 LING 8ap 4744*
30 28-29 Newm 6gd 5087

RAFTERS MUSIC 8 b g £2385
69a 4-13 Wolv 6af 72 45
74a 3-13 Wolv 6af 72 113
72a 2-11 Wolv 6af [74] 153
68a 6-16 Sout 5af 73 205
72a 3-10 Wolv 6af 72 349
55a 8-13 Wolv 6af 71 807
64a 2-6 Wolv 6af [69] 941
25 16-16 Sout 7g/s 66 1049
47 5-14 Donc 6g/s [63] 1522
62 5-17 Nott 5.1g/s 60 1774
35a 4-11 Wolv 6af [66] 2202

RAGAMUFFIN 6 ch g £0
68 7-17 Donc 6g/s 77 1523
52 13-19 Thir 6g/f 73 1767
60 5-9 Ripo 6g/f [70] 2007
51 11-12 Newc 6g/f 70 2160

RAGASAH 6 b m £0
40a 7-13 Ling 10ap 3288
33a 4-12 Ling 8ap [40] 4659

RAGAZZI 3 ch g £469
42 10-14 Thir 6g/s 1216
38 5-14 Donc 6g/f 2428
2 17-17 Leic 7gd 2704
68a 3-9 Sout 6af 3396
44a 5-10 Sout 8af [65] 4042
1 11-13 Carl 6.9fm [60] 4504

RAGGED GLORY 2 br c £2804
80 4-8 Good 5g/f 1816
58 6-11 Good 5gd 2020
78 2-15 Ling 7gd 3285
44 13-14 Sali 8g/s [77] 4078
80a 2-11 Ling 8ap [76] 4744 VIS
72a 6-8 Wolv 8.6ap [77] 5007 vis

RAGGED JACK 2 b g £5642

0 U-8 Ling 6ap 49
76a 4-10 Ling 5ap 176
65 2-12 Ling 6g/f [77] 2586
73 3-9 Warw 6.1g/f [72] 2906
66 1-4 HAMI 5gd [72] 3133* BL
61a 5-11 Ling 7ap [72] 3331
68a 6-11 Ling 6ap 70 3744
57 6-10 Wind 10g/f [70] 3980
32 12-14 Newm 7gd [70] 4195 P

RAHEED 3 b g £315
65a 6-9 Ling 8ap 1022
38 10-12 Beve 9.9sft 66 1306
0 15-15 Ripo 6g/f 65 1976
52 8-19 Leic 7g/f 62 4452
37 4-6 Yarm 6g/s [62] 4586 VIS

RAHEEL 3 ch g £4276
58a 2-14 Ling 12ap [54] 103 t
40a 8-13 Ling 16ap 54 137 t
48a 6-14 Ling 10ap 53 230 t
38a 7-14 Ling 13ap 53 259 t
47a 5-13 Ling 13ap 53 342 t
53a 4-9 Ling 10ap [46] 476 t
48a 7-11 Ling 8ap 49 669 t
51a 6-14 Ling 12ap 49 731 t
59a 1-14 LING 10ap 49 757* t
56a 4-13 Ling 10ap 55 805 t
60a 3-13 Ling 10ap [57] 912 t
56a 7-12 Ling 8ap [60] 2394 t
43 8-8 Wind 8.3g/f 57 2448 t
0 12-12 Newb 10gd 55 3916 t
49a 7-12 Ling 8ap [60] 4320 t
43a 11-16 Ling 12ap [58] 4899 t
54a 11-16 Ling 12ap 58 4973 BL t
11 12-15 Yarm 10.1g/s [50] 5122 t

RAHJEL SULTAN 6 b g £3761
40a 3-5 Wolv 12af [40] 583 T
31a 6-13 Wolv 8.5af [40] 894 t P
63 1-10 BATH 8g/s [40] 1100* t
41 6-14 Pont 8hvy [62] 1253 t
1 26-26 Redc 8fm 59 4926 t

RAHWAAN 5 b g £9755
88 1-14 DONC 18gd 83 926*
33 17-17 Ches 18.7gd 87 1569

RAIN STOPS PLAY 2 b c £7124
83 3-8 Kemp 7fm 4393
63 8-16 Newb 7g/f 4677
84 2-16 Bath 8gd 5019
85 1-11 BATH 8sft 5171*

RAINBOW COLOURS 3 gr f £0
60 7-11 Beve 9.9g/f 1835
40 9-13 Nott 8.2g/f 2633 T

RAINBOW IRIS 2 b f £3352
58 4-10 Beve 5g/f 3504
49 5-11 Hami 6g/s 4006
73 2-16 Thir 6g/s 4205
56 14-21 Donc 6fm [70] 4490
57 6-14 Hami 6sft 70 4692
69 5-15 York 6g/f 66 4985
48a 8-13 Wolv 6ap [68] 5182
63 4-10 Catt 6sft 68 5318

RAINBOW QUEEN 4 b f £1583
83 3-4 York 10.4g/f 95 3435
2 11-11 York 10.4g/s 92 4021
50 11-11 Yarm 10.1gd [88] 4614

RAINBOW RISING 2 b c £11737
81 4-12 Carl 5.9fm 3544
93 1-12 Ripo 6g/s 3935
84 9-22 Donc 6fm 4458

RAINBOW SKY 2 b f £0
41 20-23 Newm 7g/f 4885

RAINBOW TREASURE 2 ch f £0
64 7-8 York 6g/f 4326
63 6-11 Ayr 7.2g/s 4653
15 12-14 Redc 6g/s 5106

RAINBOW WORLD 4 b c £1690
4a 11-12 Wolv 8.5af 81 688
68a 3-11 Ling 12ap [77] 816

55a 8-10 Ling 12ap 70 936
16 18-20 Wind 11.6g/s 75 1056
62 3-15 Wind 11.6g/f [65] 2267 P
30 10-11 Good 12gd 65 2538 p
60 3-8 Wind 10fm 59 2973 p
58 7-16 Kemp 9gd 59 3187 p
50 7-12 Wind 10fm 58 3295 p
49 9-17 Wind 10fm 57 3477 T p

RAINSBOROUGH HILL 3 b c £0
40 8-10 Folk 9.7sft 1580
26 17-19 Chep 12.1gd 48 3727

RAINSTORM 9 b g £1228
35a 6-12 Wolv 8.5af 45 1379
44 5-11 Bath 10.2fm 45 1899
41 6-16 Good 9gd 44 2220
39 7-14 Ches 12.3gd 44 2285
38 7-20 Kemp 9g/f 42 2857
27 11-18 Pont 10g/f 42 2988
11 23-25 Asco 7g/f 40 3443
43 2-19 Beve 9.9g/f 40 3505
38 8-16 Carl 7.9g/f 40 3650
34 5-14 Chep 8.1gd 40 3733

RAISE A TUNE 2 ch c £3455
62 9-12 Good 8g/f 4522
80a 1-11 LING 8ap 4738*

RAISON DETRE 2 b c £0
56 12-19 Newm 7g/s 5285

RAJAM 6 b g £10212
57 8-22 Donc 12gd 74 918
73 6-13 Catt 13.8gd 74 997
16 7-13 Pont 18hvy 72 1069
76 1-10 MUSS 12gd 69 1796* VIS
75 3-8 Ayr 13.1fm 75 1905 vis
73 7-12 Muss 14fm 75 2085 vis
75 6-14 Ches 12.3gd 74 2285 vis
76 5-19 Carl 11.9gd 73 2673 vis
77 2-8 Epso 12gd 73 3217 vis
80 2-13 York 11.9g/f 75 3437 vis
69 4-6 Pont 12gd 78 3681 vis
62 8-15 Bath 11.7g/f 77 3964 vis
42 9-12 Ches 15.9sft 77 4106
58 9-12 Epso 12gd 75 4292 vis

RAJAYOGA 3 ch c £0
15a 11-13 Sout 8af [62] 1193
54 7-14 Wind 8.3g/f 62 1956
58 4-11 Ling 10gd [60] 3201
57 7-12 Newm 10g/f 59 3785
46 7-11 Yarm 10.1g/s 57 5353

RAJWA 2 ch c £8198
88 2-10 Good 6g/f 3511 T
97 2-9 York 6g/s 4026 t
102 2-4 Donc 6fm 4529 t

RAKTI 4 b c £668000
123 2-14 Sha 10g/f 212
125 1-10 ASCO 10g/f [121] 2488+
110 8-12 Sand 10g/s [121] 2916
119 5-8 Leop 10g/f [121] 4571
124 1-11 ASCO 8g/f [122] 4801+

RAMBO BLUE 4 b g £0
14 12-13 Nott 10gd 4861
69 6-18 Bath 10.2gd 5023
51a 10-13 Wolv 9.5ap 5290

RAMPAGE 3 ch f £3751
80 1-7 NEWC 6g/s 2728*

RAMSGILL 2 b c £0
51a 8-13 Wolv 8.6ap 5355

RANCHO CUCAMONGA 2 ch f £5422
58 7-18 York 5g/f 2360
63 7-13 Carl 5gd 2670
77 1-17 NOTT 6.1gd 2927*
23 8-8 Ayr 6g/f 74 3303
40 7-9 Good 6fm 74 3623
69 5-11 Nott 5.1gd 70 3987
67 5-14 Catt 5g/f 68 4437
15 18-19 Nott 6.1g/s 68 4645
67 2-18 Pont 6g/f 64 4934 VIS

RANDALLS TOUCH 2 b c £0
0 11-11 Hayd 5g/f 4349
0 12-12 Wolv 6ap 4921
14a 8-11 Wolv 7.1ap 5113

RANDOM QUEST 6 b g £14300
84 7-18 Newb 16gd 90 1232
90 7-17 Ches 18.7gd 88 1569
82 8-14 Hayd 16.2gd 86 2239
89 2-17 Asco 16.2gd 84 3125
62 9-11 Newm 16.1g/f 86 3779

RANGOON 3 ch c £7398
75 2-9 Kemp 6sft 946
79 2-14 Folk 7g/s 1080
63 5-13 Folk 7g/s [78] 1270
77 2-5 Good 7gd [78] 3953
73 1-10 WARW 8.1g/f [77] 4421*

RANI TWO 5 b m £4100
52 11-13 Ches 10.3gd 74 2284
62 9-10 Newm 10fm 74 2592
69 6-10 Wind 10fm 72 2761
73 5-15 Ches 10.3g/f 71 3099
47 4-4 York 10.4g/f 71 3435
68 4-8 Ripo 10g/s 68 3938
61 10-11 Epso 10.1gd 68 4293
71 2-19 Leic 10g/f 68 4456
70 2-18 Sali 9.9gd 69 4850
49 11-19 Pont 10g/s 69 5148

RANNY 4 b f £2776
53a 4-11 Ling 8ap 50 669
51a 2-10 Ling 7ap 50 799
55a 2-15 Ling 7ap 50 913
34 15-19 Yarm 7g/f 51 1132
46 6-20 Yarm 6g/f 49 1730
49 4-17 Newm 7g/f 48 2768
49 4-14 Yarm 8gd 48 3363
52a 5-14 Ling 7ap 51 3746
42 6-12 Brig 8g/f 46 3986

RANSACKER 2 b c £554
55 5-8 Brig 6g/f 2043
64 3-13 Donc 6gd 2236

RANVILLE 6 ch g £404
81 9-12 Wind 11.6fm 92 2759
78 10-14 York 13.9gd 90 3119
86 5-9 Pont 12g/s 86 3969
79 8-17 Newm 14.8gd 86 4196

RAPHAEL 5 b m £22217
66 11-18 Catt 7gd 76 998
81 1-16 THIR 7g/s 75 1474*
63 11-18 Ches 7.6gd 78 1598
81 3-8 Thir 8fm 79 2464
52 15-18 Newc 7sft 79 2684
80 4-18 Catt 7g/f 79 2848
76 8-15 York 7gd 77 3117
82 2-11 Donc 7g/s 77 3223
87 2-13 Newc 7gd 79 3428
84 2-8 Thir 8fm 80 3608
30 16-16 Redc 8g/f 80 3768

RAPID FLOW 2 b c £0
64 8-11 Newb 7g/f 3959
78 8-13 Newm 6gd 4223

RAPID RIVER 2 b f £0
59 8-20 York 6g/f 4401

RAPID ROMANCE 2 b f £275
64 5-16 Nott 6.1gd 3103
63 6-10 Nott 6.1g/f 3418
62 4-7 Chep 6.1hvy 4705

RAPSCALLION 4 b g £0
96a 7-14 Ling 10ap [85] 82 BL

RARE COINCIDENCE 2 ch g £8890
54a 3-15 Sout 7af [54] 87 P
56a 2-16 Sout 8af [54] 164 p
37a 8-11 Sout 7af [54] 207 p
62a 1-8 SOUT 8af 56 490* p
71a 1-12 WOLV 8.5af 62 564+ p
71a 3-7 Sout 8af 68 855 p
30a 6-7 Wolv 8.5af 70 942 p
56a 8-14 Sout 8af 70 1198 p
54 4-8 Hami 9.2g/s 69 1603 p
67 4-14 Newc 8gd 67 1872 p
59 4-8 Hami 9.2gd 67 2179 p
41a 11-15 Sout 8af 69 2338 p
0 9-9 Hami 9.2gd 67 3132 p
63 3-10 Hayd 8.1g/s 65 3906 p
62 4-14 Muss 7.1g/f 65 4175 p
49 10-18 Ayr 7.2sft 63 4622 T
50 9-17 Ayr 7.2sft 60 5063 p

RARE PRESENCE 5 b g £0
8 11-15 Wind 11.6g/f [50] 2267 vis t

RAREFIED 3 b c £6241
63 8-17 Leic 10g/s 1019
82 1-10 WIND 11.6gd 75 1382*
48 7-9 Ches 12.3gd 81 1582
78 7-10 Sali 12gd 82 2660
46 8-10 Pont 8g/s 80 3972
70 7-12 Redc 8gd 76 4246
66 9-12 Muss 8gd [74] 4809
76 4-11 Redc 10fm 74 4931
60 10-19 Pont 10g/s 73 5148

RAS TAILTEANN 3 b c £0
39a 7-13 Wolv 8.5af 60 40

RASA SAYANG 2 b c £2626
49 9-11 Nott 5.1gd 1237
70 2-13 Beve 5gd 2889
72 2-8 Catt 6g/f 3348
60 6-9 Redc 6g/f 68 3807

RASHIDA 2 b f £772
73 3-5 Hayd 6fm 3795
62 8-12 Warw 7.1g/f 4418

RASID 5 b g £15007
59a 3-10 Ling 12ap [79] 24
64a 12-14 Ling 10ap 70 122
66a 5-14 Ling 10ap 65 174
66a 3-14 Ling 10ap 63 265
71a 1-14 LING 10ap 63 434*
0 P-16 Ling 12ap 67 493
72a 2-7 Ling 12ap [67] 1009
78 3-7 Thir 12sft [75] 1226
78 1-6 NEWC 10.1sft [75] 1397*
62 13-19 Newm 12g/f 79 1484
62 13-15 Kemp 10fm 75 2067
74a 5-14 Ling 10ap 71 2392
76 3-8 Newm 10g/f 73 2735
80 1-8 NOTT 10g/s 73 2929*
59 12-14 Ripo 10gd 78 4305
73 11-15 Newb 11g/f 78 4643
46 20-20 York 10.4gd 77 4986
72a 12-16 Ling 12ap 74 5261
61 11-16 Nott 10hvy 75 5345

RASSEEM 2 b f £2344
80 2-4 Nott 5.1g/f 3576
60 7-11 Bath 5g/s 4200
80 3-12 Redc 6fm 4557
60 6-12 Nott 6.1g/f [76] 4844

RATHMULLAN 4 ch g £2433
32a 11-15 Ling 7ap [38] 216
10a 12-13 Ling 6ap [40] 340 p
29a 8-12 Sout 8af [35] 905
40a 3-7 Sout 6af [35] 1032 bl
37 4-7 Brig 6g/f [40] 1368 bl
37a 3-8 Wolv 7af [40] 1565 bl
42a 1-6 WOLV 6af [40] 1671* bl
42a 3-4 Ling 7ap [40] 1710 bl
40a 5-10 Wolv 8.5af [40] 1801 bl
22 9-18 Donc 7g/f 40 2080 bl
14a 13-16 Sout 6af 40 2720 bl
40 10-11 Brig 7g/f [36] 3298 bl
29 4-7 Brig 6g/f 36 3717 bl
21a 10-12 Ling 8ap [40] 4659 bl
43 3-12 Brig 8gd [35] 4904

RATIO 6 ch g £0
104 10-19 Hayd 6fm 4384 t
88 11-12 Asco 6g/f 4799 t

RATUKIDUL 2 b f £5174
76 1-12 FOLK 7gd 3908*
80 5-11 Pont 8fm 80 4753

80 9-16 Good 7gd   80   5031

RAVE REVIEWS 3 b f £20700
102 3-9   Newm 10fm [81]   1494
105 1-7   NEWB 10gd [81]   1733*
84 9-9   Asco 12g/f [105]   2517
86 9-12 Deau 12.5g/s[105]   3837

RAVEL 3 b c £0
28 12-15 Thir 7g/s   1473
42 13-15 Leic 6g/f   1829
43 11-14 Redc 10fm   47   2299

RAVEN 2 b f £0
39 9-14 Wind 8.3g/f   5049
71 6-21 Donc 6sft   5368

RAVENGLASS 5 b h £0
80 8-8   Donc 12gd   [83]   950
78 6-18 Newb 16gd   83   1232
79 5-8   Newm 12gd   81   1889
0   P-13 Chep 18gd   79   2198

RAWAABET 2 b c £0
67 8-9   Sali 7gd   2696
65 11-15 Sand 7.1g/f   3337

RAWALPINDI 3 ch g £854
47 8-13 Folk 7g/s   1270
48 10-16 Newm 7fm   2092
51 9-13 Newm 8fm   2595
58a 2-8   Sout 12af   52   4092
50 5-11 Bath 13.1g/f 56   4415
41 9-14 Pont 17.1g/f 55   4936

RAWDON 3 b c £0
69 9-17 Newm 8gd   1166
79 5-10 Sand 10g/f   2386 VIS

RAWYAAN 5 b h £0
106 8-13 Nad 12g/f [108]   990 bl
85 7-9   Ches 13.4gd[112]   1596 bl
90 13-14 Good 12g/f [112]   1843 bl

RAYBERS MAGIC 3 b f £0
1   8-8   Ripo 10g/f   2523
0   8-8   Carl 7.9gd   2932
0   13-14 Beve 7.5g/s   3177
22 7-8   Hami 9.2g/f   3592

RAYMONDS PRIDE 3 b g £10934
61a 8-11 Wolv 5af   71   155 bl
33a 9-13 Sout 6af   68   551 bl
39a 11-11 Sout 5af   65   655 bl
61 5-19 Newc 6sft 71   967 bl
77 1-13 NEWC 5sft 69   1276* bl
83 1-20 NEWC Redc 75 1393* bl
84 4-20 Thir 5g/s 82   1476 bl
74 5-19 Beve 5sft 82   1627 bl
59 13-14 Ripo 6gd   82   4786 bl
68 9-10 Catt 7sft 80   5320 bl

RAYSHAN 4 b g £0
74 14-17 Ches 18.7gd 104   1569
82 7-10 York 11.9g/f 95   2405
80 16-19 Newc 16.1g/s 90   2771 BL
45 19-19 York 13.9g/s 90   4023

RAYSOOT 3 b c £5362
51 8-14 Thir 6g/s   1216
60a 2-12 Wolv 8.5af   53   2205
59 5-14 Nott 8.2g/f 60   2634
37 9-9   Epso 7gd   58   3218
69 1-12 BATH 8g/f   56   3846* T

RAYWARE BOY 8 b g £0
0   9-9   Ling 13ap   787 vis

RAZA CAB 2 b g £5341
82 3-10 Newm 7fm   2594
94a 1-13 LING 7ap   3329*
94 6-7   York 7gd   [90]   4003
98a 2-8   Ling 7ap   [90]   4176
92 9-17 Donc 8fm   95   4480

RAZE 2 ch f £0
65 8-9   Newm 7gd   4192

RAZKALLA 6 b g £56615
112 4-13 Nad 12g/f [112]   990

101 5-5   Newm 12g/f [113]   4886
111 9-24 Flem 16g/s 111   5323

REACHING OUT 2 b c £0
0   10-10 Sout 7af   2802
62 15-19 Leic 7gd   5055

READ FEDERICA 2 ch f £4882
83 1-19 NEWM 7g/s   5279*

READY TEDDY GO 2 b g £0
49a 7-10 Ling 7ap   5259

REAL COOL CAT 2 gr f £422
61 4-13 York 6gd   4988
69 10-13 Donc 7hvy   5200

REAL ESTATE 10 b g £0
24 10-15 Wind 11.6g/f [52]   2267
45 7-12 Warw 15g/f   48   2908
37 8-15 Folk 16.4g/s 48   3049
24 12-19 Bath 17.2gd 43   3147

REAL QUALITY 2 b r g £4607
91 2-18 Ayr 6g/s   4617
90 1-13 NEWC 7g/f   5012*

REAL TING 8 br g £0
0   9-11 Wolv 6af   [30]   1261

REALISM 3 b g £23923
58a 3-13 Wolv 8.5af   39
50a 5-15 Sout 8af   96
3a 10-11 Wolv 9.4af   115
47a 4-10 Sout 8af   55   463
63a 4-7   Wolv 7af   [53]   617
66a 1-10 SOUT 8af   53   678*
45a 8-10 Wolv 8.5af 53   753
45 5-18 Wind 8.3g/s 65   1059
52a 7-14 Sout 8af   65   1198
64 3-12 Hayd 8.1g/f 62   1485
59 6-12 Bath 8g/f   61   1792
67 1-8   NOTT 10g/f   60   2157*
69 2-11 Chep 10.2gd 60   2371
75 1-8   CHEP 10.2g/f 63   2628*
79 1-10 PONT 10g/f   69   2794*
50 7-8   Newb 12g/f   74   3270
84 1-8   LEIC 10g/f   74   3514*
70 5-6   Pont 10gd   79   3678
77 6-13 Epso 10.1g/f 83   4473
90 8-15 Nott 10gd   82   4860

REAP 6 b g £1584
52a 7-13 Ling 10ap   [65]   569
69 3-16 Newc 8hvy   67   1036
57 8-12 Hayd 8.1g/f 67   1485
63 6-12 Redc 8g/f   [67]   1823
27 17-17 Leic 10gd   65   5062
64 4-11 Yarm 10.1g/s 62   5353

REBATE 4 b g £1642
71a 8-11 Ling 10ap   72   716
71a 5-9   Ling 10ap   70   903
28 12-14 Folk 9.7g/s 70   1083
49 12-12 Sand 8.1g/s 67   1352
53 12-18 Good 8g/f   64   1849
71a 3-11 Ling 8ap   69   2018
58 3-7   Brig 9.9g/f [62]   2433
62 6-8   Chep 10.2g/f 62   2628
62 3-7   Bath 10.2g/f 60   2979
56 5-10 Sand 10g/f   60   3336
55 9-19 Good 8g/f   60   3512 T
60 5-12 Newm 10g/f   58   3785 t
55 6-11 Good 11gd   58   3948 t
60a 5-14 Ling 10ap   [65]   4448 t
54 7-11 Leic 10gd   [58]   4701 t

REBEL LEADER 7 br g £0
77 12-18 Newb 8g/f   90   3265

REBEL RAIDER 5 b g £3762
59a 1-13 WOLV 8.6ap 50   5005*
49a 9-13 Wolv 8.6ap [55]   5184
58a 2-12 Wolv 12.2ap 55   5328

REBEL REBEL 2 b c £12495
71 7-12 Newm 6g/f   3280
65 8-12 Newm 10gd   3470
72 5-11 Newm 8gd   3925

71 4-20 Ling 7gd   68   4444
85 1-20 YARM 8g/s 68   4635*
90 1-20 LING 7g/f 74   4741*
91 2-12 Asco 7g/f 84   4810

REBEL ROUSER 3 b g £0
46 5-9   Warw 8.1sft   1089
38a 5-7   Wolv 9.4af 47   1324
9a 7-8   Sout 12af   47   1444

REBELLE 4 b g £0
42a 8-8   Sout 16af   63   140

REBUTTAL 2 b c £56258
89 2-18 Wind 6gd   3824
99 1-8   KEMP 6sft   4028*
109 3-9   Newb 6g/f   4680
118 2-9   Newm 6g/f   4888

RECADERO 7 b h £0
30a 10-15 Sout 6af   167
54a 8-12 Ling 8ap   234

RECALL 3 b f £0
0   13-15 Sout 8af   96
39a 11-13 Ling 10ap   148

RECKLESS FRED 5 ch g £0
49a 7-14 Ling 6ap   449
41a 10-12 Ling 8ap   514
9a 10-10 Ling 10ap   738

RECKLESS MOMENT 2 b f £0
10a 12-12 Wolv 5af   [49]   32
0   16-17 Warw 8.1g/s [45]   4992

RECOGNISE 3 ch g £3827
81 2-9   Hami 12.1gd   1507
55 4-6   Hami 11.1g/s   1604
80 2-8   Beve 12.1gd   2515
73 2-8   Warw 18fm   [80]   2781

RECOUNT 4 b g £3126
48 9-16 Epso 10.1hvy 77   1296
64 11-12 Muss 14fm   77   2085
57 6-7   Folk 5g/f   [75]   2272
69 5-9   Good 8gd   75   2540
50a 12-12 Ling 8ap   [72]   2840
62 11-16 Kemp 9gd   70   3187
80 2-10 Sand 10g/f   70   3336
75 3-17 Wind 10fm   68   3477
66 4-7   Kemp 12g/f   68   3519
71 3-9   Yarm 10.1g/s [75]   4254
71 9-16 Sand 10gd   75   4609

RECTANGLE 4 ch g £1516
19 20-20 Donc 5gd   83   927
10 8-9   Thir 5g/s [80]   1217
66 11-13 York 5g/f   77   2359
42 13-15 Beve 5sft   72   2942
70 2-7   Pont 6gd   [68]   3244
52 11-18 Pont 5gd   67   3463
61 7-15 Muss 5g/f   67   3561
40 11-13 Ches 5.1g/f 66   4514
49 18-26 Ayr   5g/s   66   4618

RECYCLING RITA 4 ch f £0
0   16-16 Ling 7ap   214

RED ACER 2 ch g £0
27a 6-16 Sout 8af   [49]   164
2a 13-14 Sout 8af   [49]   226
10a 9-10 Ling 10ap   [35]   291
0   9-12 Wolv 9.4af [35]   782
0   14-15 Wind 11.6g/f [25]   2267

RED ADMIRAL 2 b c £5099
46 14-14 Sand 7.1g/s   4069
93 1-10 YARM 8g/s   4631*

RED AFFLECK 2 b c £7719
77 3-9   Yarm 5.2g/f   1133
85 2-11 Newm 7gd   4190
85 1-13 WARW 7.1g/s   4664*
68 7-12 Newm 8gd   83   5089
87 4-14 Donc 7sft   83   5213
79 8-20 Donc 7sft   82   5373

RED APACHE 2 b c £0
55 13-15 Leic 7g/f   4455

58	13-17	Yarm	6g/s		5350

RED BIRR 3 b g £6071

72	9-22	Donc	7gd	77	955
76	4-11	Beve	9.9gf	75	1834
84	1-6	SALI	9.9gd	[75]	2663*
80	7-16	Sand	10g/s	82	2919
70	8-9	Good	14fm	82	3556

RED BLOOM 3 b f £73656

114	4-16	Newm	8fm	[113]	1492
113	3-11	Asco	8g/f	[113]	2555
114	1-4	YORK	8.9gd	[113]	4323*
110	4-13	Curr	10gd	[113]	4735

RED CHAIRMAN 2 br c £359

74	9-14	Newm	7g/f		2766
81	5-15	Newm	7fm		3005
84	4-4	Newm	6fm		3406
76	6-11	Newm	6g/f	82	3614

RED CONTACT 2 b c £0

63a	9-12	Ling	8ap		102
58a	7-11	Ling	7ap		220
74a	4-10	Ling	8ap		229
45	14-16	Ling	7g/f	[68]	1982

RED CRYSTAL 6 b m £0

0	6-6	Sout	11af		306 P

RED DAMSON 3 b g £6856

82	2-10	Ling	14fm	[80]	3742
84a	1-15	LING	12ap	[80]	4111*
92	2-13	Kemp	14.4fm	85	4395

RED DELIRIUM 7 b g £846

13a	12-14	Sout	8af	54	62 bl
37a	6-12	Wolv	7af	54	68 bl
48a	8-16	Sout	7af	[50]	161 bl
9a	13-16	Sout	7af	50	202 bl
42a	4-10	Wolv	12af	[48]	250 bl t
29a	6-10	Wolv	8.5af	[45]	311 bl t
38a	4-16	Sout	11af	[45]	445 bl
43a	5-8	Sout	11af	[40]	574 bl
53a	2-13	Sout	8af	[40]	776 bl
33a	5-10	Sout	8af	[50]	850 bl
39a	5-12	Sout	8af	[50]	905 bl
49a	2-9	Sout	11af	[50]	985 bl
47a	5-11	Sout	12af	49	1197 bl
18	12-15	Hami	9.2gd	40	1388 bl

RED DUCHESS 2 ch f £0

73	9-16	Sali	7gd		4329
58	9-15	Newm	8fm		4723

RED FEATHER 3 b f £37872

106	3-	Leop	7g/y		3011
108	1-7	CURR	8gd		3318* t
102	4-6	Leop	8g/f		4572 t
72	9-13	Newm	8g/f		4887 T

RED FINESSE 2 b f £0

60	8-13	Wind	6fm		3639
58	9-23	Newm	6gd		5084

RED FLYER 5 br g £1481

47a	1-7	SOUT	7af	[40]	1202*

RED FOREST 5 b g £22473

48a	3-11	Sout	12af	47	1197 t
63a	1-8	WOLV	12af	47	1342* t
45	6-17	Bath	11.7sft	53	1543 t
60	1-11	PONT	12g/f	48	2041* t
66	1-11	THIR	12g/f	54	2217* t
53	5-12	Newb	10g/f	58	2354 t
62	9-19	Carl	11.9gd	65	2673 t
65a	3-10	Sout	12af	63	2998 t
63	3-10	Hami	13fm	63	3249 t
64	3-10	Catt	13.8g/f	61	3669 t
72	1-12	MUSS	14g/f	61	4170* t
61	6-12	Beve	12.1sft	61	4259 t
77	1-8	REDC	14.1fm	67	4932* t
67	7-8	Donc	14.6sft	72	5204 t

RED FORT 4 b g £47839

96	1-10	HAYD	10.5g/s	88	1346*
103	3-17	Newb	12g/f	94	1759
113	1-14	ASCO	10g/f	97	2556+
111	4-21	York	10.4gd	105	3118

112	2-6	Donc	10.3fm	[113]	4492

RED GALAXY 4 b f £0

63	15-17	Leic	7g/s	80	1020 t
0	P-18	Asco	8sft	75	1423 t
22	17-18	Leic	6gd	70	5039
17a	13-13	Wolv	8.6ap	63	5364 e

RED HOT RUBY 3 ch f £1112

22	14-16	Hayd	6g/f		2182
49	3-10	Beve	5sft		2944
40	3-4	Hami	5gd		3133
35	11-19	Thir	6g/f	46	4595

RED LANCER 3 ch g £64211

58a	6-13	Wolv	8.5af	60	559
75a	1-9	SOUT	11af	60	608*
82a	1-6	WOLV	9.4af	68	702+
82a	2-10	Sout	12af	74	796
89	2-9	Kemp	9sft	[80]	947
88	2-9	Hayd	8.1sft	80	1105
95	2-15	Newb	8gd	80	1206
96	2-9	Sand	10g/s	84	1318
109	1-6	CHES	12.3gd	[88]	1584*
109	3-7	Good	11g/f	[110]	1814
91	6-10	Asco	16.2g/f	[110]	2557
100	14-19	Newc	16.1g/s	110	2771
97	6-7	Hayd	11.9sft	[108]	3274
101	7-16	Good	12fm	105	3534
104	6-7	York	11.9gd	[105]	4001

RED LANTERN 3 ch g £0

41a	11-14	Ling	7ap		5240

RED LEICESTER 4 b f £4369

47	3-14	Donc	6g/s	[50]	1522
31	12-20	Yarm	6g/f	50	1730
35	5-14	Leic	6gd	[48]	1963 VIS
58	1-15	NOTT	5.1g/f	[48]	2152* vis
41a	6-13	Wolv	5af	54	2201 vis
41	19-19	Beve	5gd	56	2512 vis
47	5-11	Warw	5.5gd	51	3054 vis
28	16-19	Donc	5g/s	51	3220 vis
16	10-11	Nott	5.1gd	47	4038 vis
42	6-16	Warw	5g/s	[45]	4995 vis
49a	3-13	Wolv	5.1ap	[45]	5231 vis

RED MARTEENEY 2 ch c £0

36	11-17	Wind	6g/f		3975
58	6-14	Warw	6.1g/f		4422
57	13-19	Ling	6g/f		4895

RED MELODICA 4 b f £0

37a	8-12	Wolv	7af	55	2049
0	16-16	Sout	7af	50	2335

RED MO 3 b c £6338

95	2-6	Mais	7sft		1155

RED MONARCH 3 ch g £8119

40a	9-15	Sout	6af		795
48	10-14	Thir	6gd		1639
56	7-17	Bath	5g/f		1787
54	6-12	Ripo	8g/f		1978
58	2-12	Brig	8g/f	52	2435
64	1-17	RIPO	6g/s	55	3262*
66	1-10	HAMI	5g/s	[61]	4010*
25	10-12	Redc	6gd	[63]	4245

RED MOOR 3 gr g £4248

40a	8-11	Wolv	9.4af	[45]	115
46a	6-13	Sout	8af	[45]	199 P
44a	5-9	Sout	11af	[45]	224 p
46a	2-8	Sout	11af	[45]	722
33a	6-7	Wolv	9.4af	[45]	893
51a	1-11	SOUT	12af	45	1197*
50a	2-9	Wolv	12af	[45]	1313
50a	3-9	Wolv	14.8af	48	1654
28a	10-16	Sout	12af	48	2340

RED MOUNTAIN 3 b c £0

28	9-9	Hayd	10.5gd		2901
27	7-9	Newc	9g/s		3697
0	11-12	Catt	12sft		5319

RED OPERA 2 ch c £0

57	7-8	Pont	8fm		4756
47	9-12	Newc	8fm		4866
44a	12-14	Ling	7ap		4970

58a	8-14	Ling	7ap		5078

RED PEONY 2 b f £13573

94	1-9	EPSO	7fm		3539*
96	3-12	Good	7sft		4264
92	6-8	Donc	8fm		4476
95	2-3	Leic	7gd	[99]	5061

RED RACKETEER 2 b c £323

77	4-14	Yarm	7sft		5250

RED RACKHAM 4 b g £0

63a	7-14	Ling	13ap		4892
38a	16-16	Ling	12ap	63	5261

RED RIOT 2 b c £836

73	5-11	Beve	7.5g/s		3851
71	3-5	Epso	8.5gd		4464
47	9-11	Bath	10.2gd		4825

RED RIVER REBEL 6 b g £3062

32	12-16	Leic	11.8g/f	58	1830
52	4-11	Pont	12g/f	58	2041
48	8-11	Warw	12.6fm	55	2601
61	2-9	Beve	12.1gd	55	2892
57	2-13	Warw	12.6gd	51	3056
54	4-13	Beve	12.1g/f	55	3502

RED RIVER ROCK 2 b c £813

85	3-14	Folk	7gd		4115
69	9-11	Nott	8.2g/s		4648
57	9-16	Bath	8gd		5019
79a	4-13	Wolv	8.6ap	[75]	5288

RED ROCKY 2 b f £2155

46a	6-14	Ling	6ap		146
41a	5-8	Sout	5af		197
60a	5-10	Ling	6ap	[52]	258
3a	7-9	Ling	6ap	[52]	327
17	10-13	Carl	5.9fm	[55]	1949
37	5-10	Leic	8gd	[55]	2133
36	8-13	Warw	6.1fm	48	2439 P
50	2-17	Leic	7gd	[48]	2704 p
11	16-19	Leic	6g/f	46	2925 p
44	3-14	Leic	8g/f	[46]	3344 p
45	5-15	Leic	7g/f	[46]	3515 p
47	3-18	Leic	7gd	[45]	4698 p
45	3-18	Leic	10gd	[45]	5042 p
33a	8-12	Wolv	9.5ap	[45]	5209 p

RED ROMEO 3 ch g £26237

74	2-14	Ripo	6g/s	74	1360
84	4-13	Hayd	6gd	75	1881
78	4-8	Good	6gd	75	2375
91	1-9	PONT	6g/f	75	2609*
87	1-9	WIND	6g/f	78	2797*
93	1-10	KEMP	6gd	[84]	3188*
93	2-11	Donc	6g/s	90	3379
97	3-8	Newm	6g/f	[92]	4226

RED RUDY 2 ch c £562

72	6-13	Wind	6fm		3478
69	3-14	Thir	7g/s		4204
64	7-10	Beve	7.5g/f		4602
42	7-20	Newb	6hvy	68	5225

RED SAHARA 3 ch f £8561

81	1-20	NEWB	7g/f	70	1761*
76	6-9	Leic	8fm	78	2108
66	6-12	Newm	7gd	78	2249
83	2-8	Wind	8.3gd	77	3162
75	4-5	Sali	8gd	80	3885
36	11-11	Wind	8.3g/s	78	4222
76	8-11	Yarm	8gd	77	4615
12	10-10	Newc	7fm	[75]	4869 BL

RED SAIL 3 ch f £1792

74	3-11	Newm	8g/f		2248
70	3-14	Newb	9fm		3631
9	9-9	Sand	10gd		4501
64	5-9	Newc	10.1g/f	[76]	5015

RED SCORPION 4 ch g £4955

69a	3-14	Wolv	16.2af	69	48
68a	5-14	Ling	16ap	69	107
75a	1-8	LING	16ap	67	288*
74a	6-12	Ling	16ap	75	478
70a	5-11	Ling	16ap	73	605
66	8-12	Thir	16gd	72	1637

62 2-9 Redc 16fm [69] 2298
68 3-9 Newm 14.8fm 65 2596
53 8-8 Hayd 14gd 65 2887
64 6-13 Asco 16.2g/f 64 3387
67 5-11 Newm 16.1g/f 64 3779
56 12-16 Kemp 16g/f 63 4361

RED SILK 3 b f £0
2a 14-14 Ling 10ap 367
5 14-14 Wind 10g/s 1055

RED SKELTON 3 ch c £880
2 10-10 Pont 10sft 77 1427
61 8-8 Good 9.9gd 77 2377 T
32 10-10 Leic 11.8gd [70] 2707 BL t
39 10-11 Yarm 10.1gd [67] 3362 bl t
58a 3-14 Ling 10ap [75] 4448
47 8-14 Catt 12g/f 60 4672
48 12-20 Hayd 11.9g/s 60 4771
34 11-20 Catt 15.8gd 52 4965
27a 16-16 Ling 12ap [60] 5296
27a 11-12 Wolv 12.2ap 60 5339

RED SOVEREIGN 3 b f £4865
26 12-17 Asco 6sft 76 1417
41 15-17 Sali 6g/f 72 1722
78 1-12 KEMP 5g/f 68 3036+
73 7-15 Sand 5gd 75 4604
93 5-15 Newm 5g/f [74] 4879
58 8-17 Bath 5.7gd [81] 5020
42a 7-12 Wolv 5.1ap [79] 5362

RED SPELL 2 ch c £17440
80a 1-11 LING 8ap 21*
61 12-13 Wind 8.3g/s [79] 1057
80 5-15 Newb 8gd 79 1206
85 1-14 NEWM 8g/f 77 1930*
85 2-13 Newm 8g/f 79 2247
76 6-13 Sali 8gd 81 2662
85 3-10 Newb 8g/f 81 2877

RED STORM 5 ch m £1635
0 13-13 Wolv 9.4af 51 281
21a 6-11 Wolv 12af 48 380
50a 1-9 WOLV 9.4af [45] 522* VIS
36a 5-9 Wolv 9.4af 51 620 vis
28a 14-14 Ling 10ap 50 718
23a 6-7 Wolv 9.4af 50 961 BL T

RED SUN 7 b g £6579
59 1-9 NEWC 16.1gd 48 1870* t
66 2-9 Ripo 16g/f 54 2009 t
59 6-13 Pont 17.1g/f 60 2276 t
37 10-13 Newc 16.1sft 60 2685 t
52 6-10 Sali 14.1gd 60 3887 t
59 3-15 Ches 15.9g/f 56 4512 t
6 12-20 Bath 17.2gd 56 4824 t

RED TOP 3 b f £14220
84 2-17 Newm 7g/f 1171
85 3-11 Asco 8sft 1419
84 2-9 Asco 7g/f [87] 1929
83 7-19 Asco 8g/f 84 2491
76 2-10 Sali 7gd [84] 2659
84 1-7 CHES 7.6g/f [82] 3079+

RED TUNE 3 ch c £10282
108 2-7 Long 9.3sft 1851

RED WINE 5 b g £0
81a 5-10 Wolv 12af 94 810
88 7-18 Kemp 16g/s 94 1112

REDBANK 2 b c £1613
63a 3-10 Wolv 7af [71] 36 T
62a 3-15 Sout 7af [67] 184 BL
60a 7-11 Ling 7ap 65 261 bl
57a 2-8 Ling 8ap [65] 326 bl
42a 9-12 Ling 7ap 63 545
48a 8-15 Ling 7ap [60] 670
56a 7-12 Ling 8ap [60] 734

REDI 3 b c £4911
65a 7-12 Ling 8ap [69] 1042
71 4-15 Ripo 10g/f 67 1976
58 6-14 Sali 8fm 68 2423
71 3-14 Wind 11.6fm 67 3638
73 1-7 CHEP 12.1g/s [67] 3899*
62 9-17 Nott 14.1g/s 71 4647

76a 2-16 Ling 12ap 70 4973

REDMARLEY 3 b g £0
43 6-12 Ripo 9g/f 1784
12 7-8 Beve 12.1g/f 59 2164

REDOUBTABLE 13 b h £9264
20a 6-12 Sout 6af [35] 377
48a 1-13 LING 6ap [35] 541*
27a 4-14 Sout 6af [45] 637
48a 1-14 LING 7ap [45] 783*
38 13-15 Ling 7ap 49 846
24 9-16 Newc 6sft 45 1277
52 1-9 AYR 6g/s [45] 1447*
38 7-17 Nott 6.1sft 47 1606 bl
33 11-18 Ayr 7.2g/f 50 1897
51 2-20 Nott 6.1g/f 48 2630
55 1-16 BEVE 7.5gd 48 2891*
53 6-15 Ches 7.6g/f 54 3102
44 8-14 Carl 6.9g/f 54 3229
52 4-18 Thir 6fm 53 3609
39 11-18 Catt 7g/f 53 3670
32 11-16 Hami 6g/s 51 4009
51 4-15 Newc 6hvy 51 4211
31 13-20 Newc 6g/f 50 4408
29 9-13 Warw 7.1g/s [49] 4994

REDRIGHTRETURNING 2 br f £1219
82 3-6 Leop 6gd 2300

REDSPIN 4 ch c £4112
66a 3-8 Ling 16ap 75 288
63 12-19 Donc 10.3gd 75 924
36 15-18 Newb 16gd 73 1232 P
68 4-29 Asco 20g/f 68 2471
71 4-10 Sali 14.1gd 68 2699
65 4-7 Sand 14g/s 68 2899
47 12-12 Newm 16.1g/f 67 3032
49 12-19 Good 21fm 65 3531
32 8-9 Yarm 14.1g/f 65 3703
64 3-12 Muss 14g/f 60 4170
57 8-15 Ches 15.9g/f 60 4512
44 10-15 Good 16gd 59 5025

REDSWAN 9 ch g £1076
60 2-19 Chep 8.1g/s [59] 4366 t

REDWOOD ROCKS 3 b g £11896
40 20-22 Donc 7gd 80 955
83 1-8 MUSS 7.1g/s 78 1460*
52 13-14 York 7sft 82 1665
78 6-8 Muss 8gd 82 4516
49 11-13 Muss 7.1gd 81 4806

REDWOOD STAR 4 b f £4088
58 4-18 Good 5g/f 57 1867 e
46 12-15 Ling 5g/f 57 2062 e
42 10-15 Leic 6g/f 56 2398 e
55 3-12 Brig 5.3g/f 54 2645 e
45 17-22 Good 5fm 54 3537 e
56 4-9 Brig 5.3fm 54 3673 e
57 2-13 Brig 5.3g/f 54 3984 e
56 3-12 Brig 5.3g/s 54 4140 e
61 2-15 Chep 5.1gd 54 4489 e

REEDSMAN 2 ch c £734
44a 8-11 Ling 8ap [49] 77 bl
23a 10-15 Sout 7af [49] 87 bl
54a 2-14 Ling 6ap [45] 495
2 13-16 Redc 8sft 53 1147 P
14 12-14 Newc 8gd 50 1872
16 15-19 Redc 6g/f 46 2125 VIS
0 11-11 Pont 12g/f 42 2790

REEFSCAPE 3 gr c £52430
112 7-15 Chan 12g/s 2308
109 2-6 Long 15gd 4565
120 1-7 LONG 15g/f 4947*

REEM ONE 3 b f £10891
79 1-8 HAMI 9.2g/s 4821*
79 2-14 Ayr 10sft 73 5037
79 2-7 Newm 12sft 75 5268

REEM TWO 3 b f £2591
55 6-7 Ches 7.6g/f 3079
58 3-8 Hami 9.2g/f 3592
66 2-5 Ches 12.3sft 4075
40 7-14 Carl 9.3g/f [55] 4347

REFERENCE 2 b c £0
42 18-18 Leic 7g/f 3342
17 16-18 Wind 6gd 3824
3 12-14 Bath 8gd 5018

REFLEX BLUE 7 b g £2534
48a 1-8 WOLV 16.2af 40 563* vis
44a 4-9 Sout 16af 46 612 vis

REFUSE TO BEND 4 b c £418990
107 8-11 Nad 9g/f 991
111 8-15 Newb 8g/f 1758 T
123 1-16 ASCO 8g/f [115] 2470* t
123 1-12 SAND 10g/s 2916+ t
85 11-11 Good 8fm [121] 3533 t
117 3-11 Asco 10sft [121] 4801 t
112 5-11 Newm 10sft [121] 5136 t

REGAL ALI 5 ch g £0
0 12-12 Wolv 9.4af [30] 939

REGAL ATTIRE 2 ch c £0
76 6-6 Asco 7g/f 3390

REGAL DREAM 2 b c £1526
50 7-10 Wind 5fm 3476
80 3-7 Epso 6gd 4466
73 3-16 Bath 5.7gd 4823

REGAL FANTASY 4 b f £3374
19 12-12 Warw 10.9fm 40 2436
27 10-20 Catt 12g/f 36 2850
40 1-11 MUSS 16g/f 32 3557*
37 5-10 Thir 16sft 36 3834

REGAL FLIGHT 3 b c £0
49 6-9 Thir 7g/f [57] 2216
21 14-14 Wind 10g/f 53 2452
57 6-9 Brig 8gd [50] 2953
38 9-13 Ling 7g/f 50 3604
35 16-20 Chep 6.1g/s 50 4368

REGAL GALLERY 5 b m £10355
54a 4-14 Ling 10ap 52 101
60a 1-13 LING 10ap 53 215*
63a 1-14 LING 10ap [58] 477*
70a 1-11 LING 12ap 61 624*
68a 3-7 Ling 10ap 66 736
67a 4-14 Ling 10ap 66 803
73a 2-8 Ling 12ap 65 3026
74a 4-16 Ling 12ap 70 4973
65a 6-12 Wolv 13.9ap 70 5160
66a 13-16 Ling 12ap 70 5261

REGAL LUSTRE 2 b f £1384
53 3-4 Newc 5gd 1868
55 5-11 Ayr 6g/s 2569
56 2-5 Hami 5gd 3130
49 6-12 Catt 7g/f 61 3351
24 6-6 Hami 6g/f 57 3590

REGAL PERFORMER 3 b g £3031
55 10-14 Wind 10g/s 1259
44 19-20 Bath 10.2gd 1398
59 2-14 Ling 11.5g/f 54 2014
61 2-7 Warw 10.9fm 57 2576
51 3-5 Brig 11.9g/f 57 2642
56 4-10 Folk 12g/s 58 3051
53 5-14 Folk 12gd 55 3383
26 6-8 Brig 11.9fm 52 3692
4 6-7 Chep 12.1sft 49 4053 BL

REGAL REPOSE 4 b f £0
19a 7-7 Ling 16ap [50] 1291
0 7-9 Sout 11af [50] 1838
0 6-7 Wolv 14.8af [50] 2200
0 14-15 Chep 16.2gd [45] 3400

REGAL SETTING 3 br g £27396
71 6-9 Kemp 12g/f 77 4360
90 1-17 NOTT 14.1g/s 77 4647+
94 1-7 HAYD 14sft 82 4778+

REGAL SONG 8 b g £1495
8a 13-13 Ling 6ap 58 448 bl
46a 10-13 Ling 6ap 53 740 bl
38 17-17 Kemp 5sft 70 944 bl
45 8-8 Hami 5gd [68] 1749 bl

30	19-19	Beve	5g/s	64	4240 bl
38	20-26	Ayr	5g/s	60	4618 bl
15	13-13	Muss	5g/s	[51]	5146
57a	1-13	**WOLV**	6ap	[49]	5211* bl

REGAL VINTAGE 4 ch g £0

34	8-15	Newc	12.4hvy	69	1034 vis
42	5-13	Pont	21.6hvy	65	1252 vis

REGENCY MALAYA 3 b f £1066

17a	8-14	Sout	8af	[45]	354 BL t
20a	5-9	Sout	11af	35	608 bl t
40a	2-10	Ling	8ap	[35]	831 bl t
19a	7-13	Wolv	8.5af	[40]	894 bl t
37a	7-12	Ling	8ap	[40]	1073 bl t
46a	3-8	Ling	10ap	[40]	1183 bl t
42a	2-6	Ling	8ap	[40]	1246 bl t
36a	5-6	Wolv	9.4af	[45]	1675 bl t
38a	6-8	Ling	10ap	[45]	1713 bl t

REGENCY RED 6 ch g £3504

46	4-13	Redc	14.1fm	45	4340
51	11-15	Ches	15.9g/f	46	4512
53	1-11	**BEVE**	12.1g/f	[46]	4716*
40	15-20	Kemp	12g/f	[46]	4796
27	12-20	Catt	15.8gd	48	4965
45	4-14	Yarm	14.1g/s	[46]	5123

REGENTS SECRET 4 br c £7959

64	4-6	Muss	8g/f	67	1092
60	7-13	Muss	7.1gd	66	1553
61	7-9	Ayr	7.2fm	[65]	1910
65	2-13	Redc	8gd	63	2552
59	4-12	Hami	9.2g/s	63	2832
45	11-12	Ayr	8gd	61	3328
60	3-10	Muss	7.1g/f	61	3562
63	3-17	Hayd	8.1gd	59	3759
36	12-17	Hami	10fm	59	4008
56	6-19	York	7.9g/f	59	4399
49	11-13	Muss	8gd	[59]	4554
63	3-26	Redc	8fm	56	4926 p
61	3-18	Newc	8g/f	[56]	5017 p
67a	1-13	**WOLV**	9.5ap	58	5292*

REGINA 2 b f £8501

79	3-4	Nott	5.1g/f		3576
92	1-5	**YARM**	5.2gd		3993*
85	6-11	Sali	6gd		4332
94	1-7	**CATT**	5sft	[88]	5124*

REGINA SAURA 6 ch m £15821

102	2-15	Napl	10ap		3170 bl

REGIS FLIGHT 2 b c £0

66	8-13	Thir	6g/s		2689
64	6-13	York	6gd		3120

REGISTRAR 2 ch c £1744

68	5-13	Newm	7fm		4724
77	2-14	Leic	8gd		5059
67a	7-12	Ling	8ap		5293

REGULATED 3 b g £6692

64a	2-11	Sout	7af	[73]	488
4a	11-12	Wolv	9.4af	[67]	686
65a	1-9	**LING**	10ap	[65]	899*
44a	5-13	Sout	8af	[65]	1193
39	5-10	Yarm	10.1g/f	[69]	1724
63	1-13	**LEIC**	10fm	[65]	2107*
42	6-15	Wind	11.6g/f	[65]	2267
0	9-9	Brig	9.9g/f	[67]	2643
36a	5-13	Ling	12ap	[65]	3025
0	12-12	Ling	12ap	[63]	3819
0	7-10	Bath	11.7g/s	[62]	4199 BL
38	10-12	Good	9g/f	57	4539
44	11-15	Wind	10g/f	[54]	4834

REHEARSAL 3 b c £9716

89	2-19	Newb	8gd		1236
97	1-24	**NEWM**	8fm		1495*
97	5-6	Newm	10g/f	[94]	1931
90	6-16	Newm	8g/f	96	3059
72	8-10	York	11.9gd	95	4324

REHIA 3 b f £4451

54a	7-10	Ling	5ap	60	371
34a	6-14	Ling	6ap	[57]	495
44a	5-10	Ling	5ap	[57]	548
52a	4-10	Ling	6ap	[54]	606

49a	4-7	Wolv	5af	[49]	703
45	11-14	Bath	5gd	57	1404
55	3-10	Brig	5.3fm	53	1694
38	5-7	Bath	5fm	[53]	1902
31	10-10	Brig	5.3fm	53	2331
55	3-7	Bath	5g/f	52	3371
57	1-9	**RIPO**	5g/f	52	3645*
34	17-19	Ling	5g/f	53	4739
19a	10-13	Wolv	6ap	[49]	5211

REIDIES CHOICE 3 b g £5945

51	12-14	Ripo	8g/s	77	1360
79	2-12	Donc	7g/f	72	1879
64	7-11	Pont	8g/f	72	2040
76	4-6	Redc	7g/s	[74]	2564
76	2-10	Catt	9g/f	73	3016
62	9-11	York	7g/f	74	3433
77	3-13	Redc	7fm	[73]	4341
52	5-13	Warw	7.1g/s	[73]	4667
78	2-10	Newc	7fm	[73]	4869

REIGN OF FIRE 3 b f £0

25	14-18	Wind	8.3g/s		1258
50	13-13	Bath	10.2g/f	[64]	1791
30a	11-12	Ling	8ap	[60]	4320
0	12-14	Pont	10g/f	53	4624
14	13-16	Nott	10gd	48	4857 VIS

REJOYCE 3 ch f £0

0	8-8	Wolv	8.5af		383

REJUVENATE 3 ch c £0

81a	9-13	Ling	10ap	85	134

RELATIVE HERO 3 ch g £1633

8a	12-13	Sout	8af	56	221 P
7	9-9	Leic	8g/f	[62]	1966
36	8-13	Leic	10fm	[62]	2107 p
52	2-10	Leic	11.8g/f	[57]	3211 p
52	3-11	Chep	10.2gd	[51]	3730 VIS
44	6-11	Beve	12.1g/s	[51]	3856 vis
29	4-10	Bath	11.7g/s	[50]	4199 vis

RELAXED 3 b f £5486

86	1-17	NEWM	7gd		1171*
93	8-11	Asco	8g/f	[82]	2555

RELAXED GESTURE 3 ch c £16549

110	2-4	Leop	10g/s		1700

RELEASED 2 b f £0

56	11-13	Leic	8g/f		4450

RELLIM 4 b f £582

56a	2-13	Wolv	5af	50	110
51a	6-11	Wolv	5af	54	155 P
52a	5-16	Sout	5af	54	183
46a	6-9	Wolv	5af	52	275
40a	5-9	Ling	5ap	50	435
34a	8-12	Sout	5af	[48]	587
17a	11-12	Wolv	5af	[45]	889
1	16-16	Warw	5g/s	[45]	4995
3a	13-13	Wolv	5.1ap	[45]	5231

REMAADD 3 gr c £16283

102	1-17	**NEWB**	10gd		1737*
110	3-8	Good	12g/f	[100]	3507
108	2-4	Newm	12g/f	[107]	3946

REMEMBRANCE 3 b g £929

71a	3-14	Ling	12ap	66	14 t
67a	6-15	Ling	12ap	[63]	118 t P
31a	6-14	Sout	12af	[65]	194 BL t
50a	2-12	Ling	10ap	[63]	272 t
24a	12-13	Ling	10ap	[57]	569 t

REMINISCENT 4 b g £3036

66a	3-12	Ling	12ap	63	56 vis
66a	5-14	Ling	13ap	63	147 vis
69a	2-5	Sout	14af	62	201 vis
67a	2-14	Ling	13ap	65	259 bl
65a	4-7	Sout	14gd	67	529 bl
60	2-16	Leic	11.8g/f	55	1830 vis
65a	4-13	Ling	12ap	65	1986 vis
56	5-11	Sali	12fm	58	2293 vis
50	8-11	Newb	13.3fm	57	2651 vis
16	14-17	Bath	11.7gd	55	3145 vis

REMONSTRATE 3 b g £0

66	6-10	Beve	7.5g/f		1832
49	9-14	Hayd	8.1g/s		2231

RENDEZVOUS POINT 2 ch f £3094

79a	1-12	**LING**	8ap		19*
76	8-9	Newm	10fm		1494
68	8-9	Donc	10.3g/f	77	2079

RENDORO 2 ch c £0

41a	12-12	Ling	8ap		100

RENE BARBIER 3 b g £5863

37	10-13	Nott	6.1sft		1464
57	4-11	Nott	6.1sft		1607
69	1-14	**DONC**	5gd		2237*
64	5-9	Pont	6g/f	69	2609
61	6-10	Carl	5gd	69	2675
52	8-11	Ripo	6gd	65	2985 VIS
49	12-18	Catt	7g/f	62	4438
51	9-19	Nott	6.1g/f	[59]	4845
47	9-14	Redc	7g/s	56	5109

RENOS MAGIC 3 b f £0

40	8-8	Thir	5sft		1228

RENS MAGIC 6 gr g £0

9	12-14	Yarm	14.1g/s	[35]	5123

REPEAT 3 ch g £4190

55a	1-16	**SOUT**	7af	[50]	66*
53a	4-11	Wolv	8.5af	[52]	128
40a	12-16	Sout	7af	[55]	161
48a	6-16	Ling	7ap	[55]	180
51a	4-9	Wolv	9.4af	[53]	239
59a	1-10	**WOLV**	7af	[51]	298*
43a	2-4	Wolv	7af	[51]	350
35a	10-10	Wolv	7af	58	379 P
50a	4-10	Sout	8af	[56]	502 p
48a	4-6	Sout	8af	[53]	586 p
28a	8-9	Wolv	8.5af	[47]	811 p
32a	7-9	Wolv	7af	[47]	825 p
28	10-19	Leic	5gd	45	2702
42	6-17	Warw	8.1g/f	45	2909
3	14-19	Nott	6.1gd	[42]	3104
38	11-11	Brig	7g/f	[40]	3298

REPENT AT LEISURE 4 b g £0

44	8-10	Yarm	11.5gd		3997
11	8-10	Yarm	14.1g/s	48	4255
37	11-15	Folk	12g/f	[48]	4374

REPERTORY 11 b g £525

99	9-11	Newb	5.2gd	108	1207
90	11-13	Newm	5g/f	[108]	1479
88	10-11	Good	5g/s	108	1845
86	7-12	Epso	5g/f	[105]	2206
87	6-8	Sali	6fm	[102]	2421
75	9-11	Sand	5g/s	95	2894

REPETOIRE 3 ch f £0

7a	14-14	Ling	12ap		14
0	15-15	Sout	8af	[49]	96
3a	10-12	Wolv	9.4af	[40]	302 BL e
0	6-6	Wolv	16.2af	[30]	395

REPULSE BAY 6 b g £416

29	6-6	Muss	8g/f	57	1092
44	8-10	Hami	13gd	55	1506
51	3-8	Muss	16gd	51	1793
41	7-10	Hayd	14g/f	51	1923
55	5-11	Donc	12gd	50	2233
3	14-15	Ayr	10.9g/s	51	2545
29	9-10	Muss	12g/f	50	2813
21	12-13	Ayr	10gd	49	3325 BL
38	7-11	Muss	16g/f	49	3557
36	7-8	Ayr	10hvy	46	4084
44	8-12	Muss	14g/f	46	4170
1	17-18	Ayr	10.9sft	45	4623

REQQA 2 b c £7486

82	6-12	York	6gd		3122
98	1-13	**PONT**	6gd		3682*
99	4-6	Ripo	6gd		4280
63	4-4	Donc	6fm		4529

RESCIND 4 b f £0

27a	10-12	Wolv	9.5ap	[45]	5234

RESERVOIR 3 b g £9611

84	2-7	Hami	9.2gd	[77]		1747
84	1-8	GOOD	11gd	[80]		2222*
79	7-10	Wind	10fm		82	2785
78	5-9	Newm	12gd		80	3926
41	11-13	York	13.9g/s		80	4062
82	2-8	Hayd	11.9g/f		77	4353

RESIDENTIAL 3 ch c £345
73	4-10	Ling	7gd			3446
68	6-17	Newm	8gd			4228
51	4-18	Wind	10g/s	[64]		4944

RESISTANCE HEROINE 2 b f £668
51	7-16	Nott	6.1gd			3103
51	12-15	Folk	7gd			3381
75	3-7	Redc	7g/f			3770
39	7-11	Chep	8.1g/s	[78]		4296
79	4-20	Ling	7g/f		73	4741

RESONANCE 2 b f £2343
73a	4-12	Ling	8ap			19
68a	3-12	Ling	10ap			116
58a	2-11	Ling	12ap	[70]		672
25a	8-14	Ling	10ap	[70]		759
66	3-10	Ling	12g/s		64	1082
52	7-10	Sali	14.1gd		64	3887

RESONATE 5 b h £11462
56a	9-12	Ling	8ap		59	17
53a	6-11	Ling	8ap		57	136
74	4-19	Sali	7g/f		71	1723
69	10-16	Kemp	7ap		72	3039
80	1-13	EPSO	10.1g/f		72	4473*
65a	2-12	Wolv	12.2ap		64	4924

RESPLENDENT CEE 5 ch h £0
73	18-19	Ripo	6g/s		100	3937

RESPLENDENT KING 3 b g £4109
71a	3-15	Ling	7ap		71	337
70a	3-10	Ling	8ap		72	455
66a	5-12	Ling	8ap		70	603
56a	5-8	Ling	7ap	[69]		713 BL
64	3-8	Epso	8.5hvy	[67]		1297
77	2-8	Ling	9g/f	[65]		2013
70	3-7	Brig	11.9fm		70	2333
73	3-9	Brig	9.9gd		70	2955 P
25	13-16	Epso	8.5gd		70	3219 bl

RESPLENDENT ONE 3 b c £3268
100	6-8	Kemp	8fm			2069
54	27-27	Asco	8g/f		98	2521
99	4-16	Newm	8g/f		98	3059
98	4-9	Good	8fm	[97]		3620
79	8-10	Hayd	8.1g/s		97	4767

RESPLENDENT PRINCE 2 ch c £0
70a	8-13	Ling	7ap			3330

RESSOURCE 5 b g £0
37a	5-13	Ling	13ap	[40]		1076 bl e

RESTART 2 b g £4919
48a	7-10	Sout	8af		68	190
37	10-14	Newc	8gd		63	1872
44	8-18	Hayd	14gd		60	2905
62	1-13	REDC	14.1gd		55	4249*
56	8-13	Redc	14.1fm		61	4340
65	2-13	Newc	16.1fm		58	4868
34	12-14	Pont	17.1g/f		58	4936

RESTORATION 2 gr c £1455
75	2-14	Redc	7sft			5301

RETAIL THERAPY 3 b f £1054
53a	6-9	Ling	10ap	[33]		269
50a	2-10	Wolv	12af	[35]		359
31a	6-9	Wolv	12af		35	424
28	12-17	Nott	14.1gd		48	1238
18	15-15	Folk	12g/f	[45]		4374 BL

RETIREMENT 4 b g £8481
77a	2-13	Ling	10ap		72	26
83	1-18	ASCO	8sft		75	1423*
80	3-18	Ches	7.6gd		78	1598
61	10-13	Donc	8gd	[82]		2753
44	10-10	York	7.9g/s		82	3074
76	7-10	Sand	8.1g/s		80	4067
69	11-13	Ripo	8gd		78	4279

60	11-20	Donc	7sft		76	5367

REVEILLEZ 5 gr g £554
88	6-18	Kemp	16g/s		93	1112
93	5-12	Good	14g/f		92	1861

REVELINO 5 b g £0
65	6-9	Ches	12.3sft		75	4076

REVENIR 3 ch g £7356
69	7-12	Newb	7g/f			2352
77	2-11	Hayd	8.1gd			2886
71a	2-9	Ling	8ap			3195
66	2-8	Catt	7g/f	[74]		4440
71	4-7	Epso	10.1gd	[72]		4911
76a	1-14	LING	10ap		68	5083*
52	10-10	Donc	10.3sft		76	5206

REVERIE SOLITAIRE 3 b f £17993
106	3-7	Chan	12g/s			2304
106	2-10	Deau	12.5Ver			4310

REVERSIONARY 3 b c £5287
54	8-12	Catt	5gd	[56]		995
36	10-13	Nott	8.2gd		55	1242
42	5-11	Newc	7sft		53	1678 BL
29	10-13	Ripo	6g/f		50	2011 bl
9	15-19	York	6g/f		50	2055
37	7-13	Newc	6sft		45	2683 bl
53	1-8	CARL	7.9gd	[43]		2932* bl
32	9-15	Beve	8.5g/s		51	3182 bl
50a	3-16	Sout	8af		49	3487 bl
55	2-11	Ayr	9.1sft	[48]		5067 bl
53	2-13	Ayr	10sft	[50]		5276 bl

REVIEN 2 b g £1004
62	3-10	Catt	5gd			4968
62a	3-12	Wolv	6ap			5177

REVIEWER 6 b g £0
21a	15-15	Ling	12ap		74	549
62	7-18	Newm	12fm		70	2088
41	12-15	Newb	13.3g/f		70	2311
63	5-6	Kemp	12g/s		65	2681 bl
66	5-14	Sali	12g/s		63	3114

REVIVALIST 2 b f £0
49	9-14	Folk	7fm			2714

REWAYAAT 3 b f £0
55	9-10	Thir	5g/f		80	1973

REX ROMELIO 4 ch g £744
33a	10-11	Wolv	7af		65	241
0	10-10	Sout	8af		60	387
49a	2-9	Sout	11af	[50]		505 VIS
1a	12-12	Ling	10ap		50	542 vis

REZZAGO 3 b c £2310
66a	1-10	WOLV	7af			8*

RHAPSODY IN SILVER 2 gr c £0
55	9-10	Folk	7g/s			3046

RHETORIC 5 b g £1456
11a	8-10	Sout	16af	[40]		984
38a	4-8	Wolv	12af	[35]		1265
36a	1-6	SOUT	11af	[35]		1409*
1	12-13	Kemp	10hvy	[40]		1643
19a	6-8	Sout	14af	[40]		1840

RHETORICAL 3 b g £0
44	5-10	Redc	10g/f		57	3772
36	12-13	Ling	10g/s		57	4182 BL
44	6-9	Muss	14gd		55	4521
28	10-19	Catt	15.8g/f		50	4675
40	11-20	Kemp	12g/f	[49]		4796

RHINEFIELD BOY 3 ch g £0
9	8-9	Muss	5gd			1797
11	11-13	Hami	5gd		48	2181

RHOSLAN 2 b c £0
63	10-11	Newm	7g/f			3234
38	13-14	Ling	7.6g/f			3601
62	10-15	Folk	7gd			4114

RHUM 4 ch g £0
0	P-13	Pont	8g/s			3973
51	5-6	Newc	10.1sft			4286

15	10-13	Ayr	10sft			5066

RIBBONS AND BOWS 4 gr f £3383
48	13-20	Wind	11.6g/s		80	1056
73	6-10	Sali	12g/f		75	1721
52a	8-13	Ling	12g/f		70	1986 BL
52	4-5	Sali	12fm		65	2422
1	13-13	Pont	12gd		62	3240
32a	9-13	Ling	16ap		55	3822
51	4-15	Chep	12g/s		51	4299
50	5-18	Warw	10.9g/s		51	4669
44	5-14	Yarm	15gd		50	5123 VIS
65a	1-13	WOLV	9.5ap	[48]		5338* vis
46a	8-13	Wolv	9.5ap		54	5361 vis

RIBBONS OF GOLD 2 b f £0
52	6-9	Warw	5sft			1084
23	10-11	Bath	5.7g/f			3848

RICH ALBI 2 b c £285
71	6-12	Ripo	5g/f			1974
52	14-18	York	7gd			2360
71	4-13	Thir	6g/s			2689 VIS
37	12-13	York	6gd		73	4004 BL
11	18-19	Pont	8g/s		70	5147

RICH CHIC 3 b f £516
28	12-14	Hayd	8.1g/s			2231
51	4-4	Newc	8g/s			2729
44	8-16	Ripo	8gd			2987

RICH DANCER 3 b f £0
26a	6-10	Wolv	7af	[55]		8

RICHEMAUR 4 b f £971
81	4-14	Yarm	8g/f		80	1131
65	16-17	Sand	8.1g/s		79	1351
52	12-15	Hami	8.3g/s		77	1602 BL
73	4-11	Donc	12gd		75	2233
3	11-11	Good	12gd		73	2538
56	9-10	Newb	11g/f		70	2875

RICHIE BOY 3 b c £8575
60	9-12	Newb	7g/f			2352
61	6-17	Wind	8.3fm			3480
56a	10-13	Ling	10ap	[64]		4112
38	12-15	Chep	8.1g/s		63	4300 P
57	1-12	WARW	12.6g/s	[58]		4991*
48	8-18	Leic	10gd	[58]		5042
67	1-15	NOTT	8.2hvy		58	5191*
66	1-11	REDC	10sft	[63]		5303*

RICHIE RICH 8 b g £0
30a	10-11	Ling	6ap	[55]		130
40a	11-15	Ling	7ap		55	151

RICHMOND LODGE 4 br g £0
0	14-14	Sali	9.9g/f		56	3867
22	5-5	Brig	9.9sft		54	4167

RICHTEE 3 ch f £16122
64	1-14	REDC	10fm		55	2299*
67	2-11	Redc	9g/s		61	2565
71	5-13	Redc	11g/s		65	2960
76	1-16	THIR	12g/f		67	3573*
73	3-7	Ayr	10.9g/f		70	3765
72	1-4	HAMI	12.1g/s		70	3881*
65	4-4	Newc	12.4sft		72	4288
58	6-7	Nott	16g/f		72	4846

RICKY MARTAN 3 ch c £0
2a	10-10	Ling	8ap		70	455
48a	9-12	Ling	8ap		63	603 BL
35a	8-11	Ling	6ap		57	735 bl
43a	9-15	Ling	7ap		52	815 bl
6	10-10	Bath	5.7sft	[58]		1539 VIS
46	6-8	Brig	7g/f		53	2434
39	11-18	Carl	7.9m		49	3547
37a	6-14	Ling	10ap	[45]		4661
35	13-20	Kemp	12g/f	[45]		4796
0	9-12	Wolv	12.2ap	[40]		5208

RIDAPOUR 5 b g £0
13	12-14	Donc	18gd		60	926

RIDDER 2 b f £12919
73	4-19	Kemp	6g/f			1911
72	5-10	Bath	5.7fm			2666
62	7-11	Sali	6g/s			3110

81	2-10	Kemp	6g/f	71	3521
83	2-12	Sali	6g/s	76	4079
85	1-20	**YORK**	6g/f	[81]	4401*

RIDE SAFARI 2 b g £413

72	6-12	Ling	5g/f		1981
73	3-5	Brig	5.3g/f		2430
78	4-14	Folk	7fm		2714

RIDGE BOY 3 b c £14756

74	5-10	Good	8g/f		1815
68	6-17	Chep	8.1gd		2117
51	7-13	Wind	6fm		2756
72	1-14	**WIND**	8.3fm	67	2971*
62	12-16	Kemp	9gd	73	3187
68	3-10	Wind	10g/f	[70]	3980
76	2-16	Sali	8gd	70	4334
80	1-12	**EPSO**	8.5gd	72	4909*
39	10-14	Newb	8hvy	76	5227

RIDGEBACK 4 ch g £0

57	16-22	Donc	6gd	80	921

RIDICULE 4 b g £0

59a	8-16	Sout	5af	68	205 bl
27a	10-13	Sout	6af	66	551 bl
61	8-16	Bath	5.7g/s	[66]	1103 bl
50	12-19	Leic	6g/s	63	1354 vis
32	7-10	Warw	6.1hvy	59	1533 vis
40	11-18	Bath	5.7g/f	55	1788 vis T
39	7-8	Sand	5gd	[51]	2361 vis t
4	17-20	Nott	6.1gd	47	2928 vis t
32	11-13	Bath	5.7g/f	[44]	3844 bl t

RIFLEMAN 4 ch g £0

64	15-18	Catt	7gd	80	998
44	17-19	Ripo	10g/f	78	1781
47	8-8	Hami	9.2gd	75	2179 P
42	7-7	Redc	9g/s	[72]	2962 p

RIGHT ANSWER 2 b f £16193

73	4-11	Ling	5gd		2395
87	1-11	**SALI**	5gd		2658*
97	2-6	Wind	5fm		2786
100	2-10	York	5gd	95	3115
95	5-6	Asco	6g/f		3440
97	3-12	Newb	5.2g/f	[98]	3956
67	20-22	Donc	6fm	[95]	4458
86	10-11	Newm	5gft	[97]	5132

RIGHT APPROACH 5 b h £446927

118	1-11	**NAD**	9g/f	[116]	991* t

RIGHT TO ROAM 2 b c £256

48	4-5	Yarm	6g/f		2341
60	7-17	Ling	6gd		4443 BL
56a	5-12	Ling	6ap		4896

RIGHTFUL RULER 2 b c £586

82	4-11	Bath	8gd		4544
80	4-16	Bath	8gd		5019
55	14-20	Yarm	8sft		5252

RIGHTPRICE PREMIER 2 b f £5412

46	3-8	Muss	5gd		1091
67	2-8	Hayd	5g/s		1343
68a	1-7	**WOLV**	5gf		1652*
56	5-6	Carl	5fm		2442

RIGHTY HO 10 b g £5968

42	1-9	**AYR**	13.1g/s	[40]	1449*
44	3-10	Redc	11g/f	[45]	1819
45	3-10	Beve	9.9g/f	[45]	1946
40	7-20	Catt	12g/f	45	2850
30	6-11	Catt	12g/f	[44]	3190
50	1-6	**REDC**	14.1g/f	[43]	3771*
28	10-13	Beve	14.1fm	50	4340
45	3-11	Beve	12.1g/f	[48]	4716

RIGONZA 3 ch g £1971

58	11-16	Beve	7.5g/s	74	1163
48	8-10	Pont	10sft	72	1427
64	5-11	Redc	9g/s	70	2565
52	13-13	Redc	11g/s	68	2960 VIS
59	3-7	Ripo	9g/s	[65]	3263
60	4-9	Newc	9g/s	[62]	3697
62	2-5	Catt	12sft	[62]	3934

RILEY BOYS 3 ch g £19387

66a	1-8	**WOLV**	7af	[64]	892*
67	2-16	Beve	7.5g/s	64	1163
73	1-18	**NOTT**	8.2sft	66	1470*
75	2-16	Beve	8.5sft	69	1628
77	1-19	**BEVE**	8.5g/f	71	2168*
77	2-8	Leic	7g/f	74	2403
75	2-6	Beve	8.5gd	[74]	2514
85	2-9	Beve	8.5sft	74	2940
84	2-10	Nott	8.2gd	[79]	3107 P
73	6-10	Nott	8g/s	81	3972

RILEYS DREAM 5 b m £6643

8	8-17	Pont	6hvy	[52]	1065
40	5-12	Sout	7gd	[49]	1284
31	10-16	Bath	5.7sft	45	1540
33	9-18	Wind	6g/f	[45]	1806
45	1-14	**LEIC**	6g/f	[45]	1963*
17	13-16	Chep	7.1gd	[43]	2369
15	12-20	Nott	6.1gd	43	2928
48	5-11	Brig	7g/f	[40]	3298 P
50	1-7	**BRIG**	6g/f	43	3717* p
48	2-9	Brig	7sft	[48]	4164 p
27	17-20	Chep	6.1g/s	48	4368 p

RILEYS ROCKET 5 b m £0

0	11-12	Wolv	9.4af	[35]	782
0	10-10	Beve	9.9g/f	[40]	1946
22	11-11	Leic	10gd	40	2135
8a	12-15	Sout	7af	32	2384

RILL 2 ch f £490

75	4-18	Nott	8.2g/f		4842

RING OF DESTINY 5 b g £0

75	14-20	Newm	12gd	94	1172
65	11-19	York	11.9sft	92	1668
81	8-13	Epso	12fm	89	2255

RINGAROOMA 2 b f £1117

69	5-10	Newm	6g/f		3064
57	9-14	Yarm	7gd		3489
70	4-15	Folk	7gd		4114
68	2-10	Catt	6g/f	[69]	4436
20	13-13	Leic	6gd	69	4697

RINGMOOR DOWN 5 b m £79737

91	6-11	Newb	5.2gd	93	1207
105	1-14	**BATH**	5gd	[93]	1400+
103	3-10	Curr	6g/f	[93]	1996
112	4-19	Asco	5g/f	[103]	2468
105	2-12	Sand	5g/s	[106]	2913
103	4-9	York	6g/s	[106]	3075
111	1-13	GOOD	5fm	[106]	3551+
111	1-8	**CURR**	5g/f	[108]	4433*
94	7-12	Asco	5g/f	[108]	4799
105	8-15	Long	5g/f	[108]	4952
110	2-15	Newm	6gd	[108]	5088

RINGSIDE JACK 8 b g £638

49	3-13	Pont	18hvy	52	1069
51	7-13	Hayd	14sft	52	1109
9	9-11	Beve	16.2sft	50	1629

RINGSIDER 3 ch g £20428

56	11-15	Ches	7.6gd	82	1583
37	17-18	Epso	10.1fm	80	2250
82	2-19	Good	8g/f	77	3512
89	1-10	**GOOD**	9fm	77	3625*
81	9-11	Beve	9.9g/s	84	4239
94	1-12	**WIND**	11.6g/f	83	4833*

RINJANI 3 b c £0

87	9-10	Wind	10fm	92	2785 T
65	7-8	Folk	9.7g/s	[90]	3912 t

RINNEEN 3 b f £664

49	9-14	Bath	10.2gd	57	1403
37	9-20	Wind	11.6sft	54	1648
48	5-14	Ling	11.5g/f	51	2014 VIS
48	3-10	Folk	12g/s	49	3051 vis
50	4-14	Folk	12gd	46	3383 vis
34	5-8	Chep	16.2g/s	46	4302 vis

RIO BRANCO 3 b f £3455

74a	1-5	**WOLV**	7af		425*

RIO DE JANEIRO 3 b c £0

88	7-7	York	11.9gd		4001 VIS

RIO DE JUMEIRAH 3 b f £13125

85	3-5	Ling	11.5sft	[78]	1619
77	6-14	Asco	10g/f	78	1924
44	11-11	Sand	10g/s	78	2127
77	5-9	Leic	8gd	75	2705
88	1-5	**DONC**	10.3g/s	75	3377*
90	2-6	Ripo	10g/f	82	3647

RIO RIVA 2 b c £1084

85	2-12	Hayd	6sft		4770

RIPCORD 6 b g £0

22a	5-9	Ling	12ap	[35]	414
27a	6-10	Ling	12ap	[35]	1104
31	8-16	Folk	12fm	30	2718

RIPPLE EFFECT 3 ch f £11799

60a	12-16	Ling	7ap	73	20 t
67a	1-10	**LING**	6ap	[70]	133* t
59a	15-16	Ling	7ap	76	181 t
60a	2-13	Ling	6ap	[70]	271 t
62a	2-13	Ling	6ap	[67]	400 t
73a	1-14	**LING**	7ap	[67]	450* t
74a	2-13	Ling	7ap	71	474
45a	10-14	Ling	6ap	[73]	516
58a	5-8	Ling	7ap	[72]	730
81a	1-10	**LING**	7ap	72	799* t
79a	5-12	Ling	6ap	79	880 t
61a	6-9	Wolv	7af	79	940 t
52	7-14	Donc	6g/s	[75]	1522

RIQUEWIHR 4 ch f £1193

64	4-10	Ling	6gd	60	4109
65	3-20	Nott	6.1g/s	60	4646
63	4-18	Leic	6gd	62	5039

RISE 2 b f £11084

45a	12-13	Ling	7ap	86	15 bl
79a	4-13	Ling	7ap	[84]	119 bl
69a	7-10	Ling	5ap	[81]	176 bl
68a	7-8	Ling	6ap	79	268 bl
47a	9-10	Ling	6ap	76	494 bl
36	16-20	Wind	6g/s	70	1255 bl
56	6-10	Folk	6sft	64	1576 bl
54	7-15	Ling	7g/f	60	1983 bl
48	7-18	Wind	6g/f	57	2268 bl
68	1-11	**SALI**	6gd	53	2661* bl
68	2-19	Leic	6g/f	64	2925 bl
61	7-12	Hayd	6sft	65	3273 bl
74	1-14	**YARM**	6gd	64	3870* bl
74	2-20	Ling	6g/f	70	4317 bl
75	8-11	Ches	6.1g/f	[70]	4510 bl

RISING SHADOW 3 b g £3128

79	6-7	Newm	6g/f	82	2764
90	2-12	Hayd	6sft	82	3273
85	4-11	York	7g/f	84	3433
74	6-7	Leic	7fm	84	3814
51	10-14	Ches	6.1g/f	84	4048
61	15-26	Ayr	6g/s	82	4652

RISK FREE 7 ch g £0

51	10-15	Ches	7.6g/f	59	3102 bl
41	6-9	Catt	6g/f	[59]	3353 vis
54	7-10	Muss	7.1g/f	59	3562 vis
34	13-15	Catt	7sft	56	3933 vis
32	13-16	Ches	7g/f	56	4051 vis
57a	8-12	Wolv	7.1ap	[65]	5006 bl

RISK SEEKER 4 b c £45964

115	2-7	Mais	15.5sft		987
119	1-13	**ASCO**	16.2sft		1418*
113	4-9	Sand	16.4g/f		2095
112	4-4	Mais	15gd		3317

RISKA KING 3 b g £11573

44	8-11	Sout	8af	75	255
43a	7-10	Sout	8af	73	318
43a	7-8	Sout	7af	[69]	744
58	12-18	Ches	7.6gd	74	1598
34	19-19	Redc	7g/f	73	1820
53	8-9	Muss	7.1fm	70	2086
67	4-6	Beve	8.5gd	[66]	2514
68	3-6	Hami	8.3g/s	[66]	2828
71	3-10	Carl	6.9gd	66	2935
64	6-9	Beve	7.5gd	67	3310
76	1-14	**BEVE**	7.5g/s	67	4241*
75	5-15	Carl	7.9g/f	73	4346

75 4-10 Leic 8gd [72] 4702
74a 1-12 WOLV 8.6ap 65 4923*
65a 7-12 Ling 8ap 68 5079

RISKAVERSE 5 b m £83799
115 2-11 Arli 9.5fm 4013

RISKY WAY 8 b g £0
0 8-9 Sout 12af [45] 774 p

RIVA ROYALE 4 b f £483
93 8-11 Leic 7g/s [84] 1356
83 10-11 Ling 7sft [84] 1620
38 14-15 Ripo 6g/f 84 1782
84 4-10 Newb 7g/f 82 2312
68 6-6 Good 7gd 82 2539
63 9-11 Yarm 7gd 80 3364 P

RIVAL 5 b g £0
0 10-11 Wolv 12af [45] 689
0 9-9 Wolv 8.5af [40] 811

RIVELLI 4 b f £0
0 12-12 Wolv 12af 58 75 bl
43a 10-12 Wolv 5af 55 124 bl
2a 10-12 Wolv 16.2af 50 156
18a 13-16 Sout 7af 45 208 bl
0 11-12 Wolv 8.5af [40] 777

RIVENDELL 8 b m £0
24a 6-12 Wolv 6af [20] 297 t
4a 9-14 Sout 14af [30] 573 t
0 8-9 Wolv 8.5af [30] 664 t

RIVER ALHAARTH 2 b c £5668
74 5-13 Warw 7.1g/f 4416
80 1-14 LEIC 8gd 5059*

RIVER BISCUIT 2 ch c £0
73 8-15 Newm 7fm 3005
73 5-6 Asco 7g/f 3390
30 14-14 Sali 8g/s 4078
75 5-16 Good 7gd 70 5031

RIVER CANYON 8 b g £0
6a 9-9 Sout 6af [50] 639

RIVER CARD 2 ch f £0
62 7-10 Yarm 8g/s 4631
40 10-12 Muss 7.1g/s 5142

RIVER DANCER 5 b g £575540
117 1-14 SHA 10g/f 1438*

RIVER DAYS 5 b m £1879
41a 12-12 Wolv 5af 68 35 bl t
17a 12-13 Wolv 6af 68 41 bl t
46a 9-14 Ling 6ap [65] 516 bl t
51a 2-8 Wolv 5af 619 bl t
38a 10-11 Wolv 5af 56 748 bl t
22a 6-11 Wolv 6af [56] 778 VIS
40a 5-12 Ling 6ap 49 844 vis t
46a 2-11 Wolv 5af 45 958 vis t
43a 4-8 Wolv 5af [46] 1218 vis t

RIVER FALCON 4 b g £29219
77 5-20 Donc 5gd 80 927
76 7-16 Muss 5g/f 79 1120
87 1-20 YORK 5g/s 78 1683*
71 11-17 Muss 5fm 84 2082
74 7-10 York 6g/f 84 2357
88 3-18 Newc 6g/s 84 2770
61 11-15 York 6g/f 83 3434
92 1-11 HAYD 6gd [84] 3758*
71 11-16 Hayd 5fm 90 4382
64 18-24 Ayr 6sft 90 4686
90 4-11 Hayd 5sft 88 4780
84 5-20 York 6gd 87 5001
75 10-13 Muss 5g/s 85 5143
58 14-16 Redc 6sft 83 5304

RIVER GYPSY 3 b c £1744
78 2-12 Sali 12g/s 1501

RIVER LARK 4 b f £1295
48a 2-15 Sout 5af [47] 253
47a 6-9 Sout 5af [47] 487
50a 4-11 Sout 5af 47 655
48a 4-11 Sout 5af 48 859
44a 6-16 Sout 5ap 48 1046

43 8-19 Warw 5gd 48 1127
37 6-14 Donc 6g/s [45] 1522
35 5-10 Kemp 5hvy [45] 1644
17 13-19 Beve 5g/s 43 2326 p
43a 3-15 Sout 5af [41] 2803 BL
0 17-19 Nott 6.1gd [41] 3104 bl

RIVER LIFFEY 2 b c £2888
63 8-18 Newc 6g/s 3699
85 2-11 Ches 7sft 4072
86 2-12 Beve 8.5sft 4257

RIVER LINE 3 b g £273
52 4-8 Redc 10g/f 2124
32 7-11 Muss 9gd 50 2969
36 12-13 Beve 9.9gd 47 3309
40 10-10 Newc 16.1g/s 47 3701
35 9-13 Redc 14.1fm 47 4340

RIVER NUREY 3 gr c £5444
76 3-14 Yarm 7fm [72] 2148
75 2-8 Warw 7.1fm [72] 2575
69 5-9 Brig 8gd [72] 2953
73 2-11 Thir 8g/f [70] 3572
68 2-6 Hayd 8.1g/s [70] 3905
61 4-12 Newc 8g/f [68] 4407

RIVER OF BABYLON 3 b f £7573
70 2-12 Warw 7.1gd 1129
54 6-17 Yarm 7g/f [64] 1729
68 5-17 Newm 8gd [64] 4228
70 1-8 CATT 7g/f [64] 4440*
74a 1-12 LING 8ap 70 4743*

RIVER OF DIAMONDS 3 b g £4284
65 8-17 Newm 8gd 4228
42 7-18 Wind 10g/s 4944
73 2-8 Brig 11.9sft 5092
54 1-7 YARM 11.5g/s [60] 5351*

RIVER OF FIRE 6 ch g £3199
0 7-9 Warw 15g/s [35] 1329 vis
29a 3-5 Wolv 14.8af [30] 1563
0 9-12 Sout 16af 30 1753 vis
31 4-15 Nott 10gd [30] 1991 vis
23 8-10 Yarm 11.5fm 30 2147 vis
26 9-14 Bath 18.2fm 30 2417 vis
25 11-16 Folk 12fm 30 2718 vis
40 1-15 FOLK 16.4g/s 30 3049* vis
37 5-9 Ayr 15gd 38 3327 vis
36 6-12 Yarm 16gd 38 3493 vis

RIVER ROYALE 2 b c £2610
87 3-13 Newm 6gd 4223
89 3-23 Newm 6gd 5084
87 3-19 Newm 7g/s 5285

RIVER TREAT 3 ch c £7953
82 1-12 WARW 7.1gd [85] 1125*
68 6-8 Muss 7.1g/s 85 1460
81 5-12 Ripo 6g/f 83 2482
66 9-9 Wind 8gd 82 2797
78 4-7 Kemp 7g/f 80 3522
80 2-13 Yarm 10.1gd 78 4613
52 9-11 Redc 10fm 80 4931

RIVERBRIDE 2 br f £6338
97 2-11 Crao 8.3g/s 4429

RIVERWELD 2 ch g £836
42 6-11 Ripo 6g/f 1779
50 4-7 Redc 7fm 2294
58 2-8 Redc 7g/s 2563
56 5-14 Beve 7.5sft 2939
30 12-16 Beve 7.5g/f 57 4597
22 12-17 Redc 7g/s [55] 5105

RIVIERA RED 4 b g £0
0 11-12 Newm 12g/f 3783
55a 8-14 Ling 13ap 4898

RIYADH 6 ch g £7512
63 9-14 Donc 18gd 85 926 vis
69 8-10 Muss 16gd 83 1093 vis
62 9-18 Newb 16gd 78 1232 vis
63 10-17 Ripo 16g/s 72 1361 vis
75 3-12 Thir 16gd 70 1637 vis
63 9-12 Muss 14fm 70 2085 bl
70 3-13 Pont 17.1g/f 70 2276 vis

66 7-29 Asco 20g/f 68 2471 vis
45 7-7 Beve 16.2sft 65 2941 vis
68 2-13 Asco 16.2g/f 62 3387 vis
43 16-19 Good 21fm 62 3531 vis
69 2-10 Newc 16.1g/s 66 3701
0 6-10 Yarm 16sft 69 4151
68 7-16 Kemp 16g/f 68 4361
70 4-13 Good 16g/f 66 4527
58 6-20 Bath 17.2gd 66 4824
70 4-14 Pont 17.1g/f 66 4936
70 3-10 Pont 18g/s 64 5151

RIYMA 2 b f £0
45 10-10 Yarm 7fm 2863
64 9-12 Beve 7.5g/s 4242

RO ERIDANI 4 b f £0
27a 7-11 Ling 8ap [45] 408
15a 11-13 Ling 10ap [40] 539
0 12-12 Ling 10ap [35] 654 BL

ROAD RAGE 2 b f £5587
80 3-11 Newm 7g/f 3234
83 1-7 NEWM 7g/f 3616*
37 8-8 Donc 8fm 4476

ROAD TO HEAVEN 2 ch c £978
59 3-7 Sand 7.1g/s 2897
68 8-15 Sand 7.1g/f 3337
59 11-15 Leic 7g/f 4455
49 13-19 Pont 8g/s 65 5147 T

ROAMING VAGABOND 3 ch g £0
31 6-6 Hami 11.1g/s 1604
0 18-18 Wind 11.6g/f 55 1960
24 7-9 Brig 8fm [52] 2834

ROAN RAIDER 3 gr g £3488
13a 13-16 Sout 6af [44] 65 vis t
44a 7-13 Sout 6af [42] 254 vis t
37a 11-16 Ling 7ap [42] 290 BL t
26a 11-13 Sout 6af [45] 659 bl t
30 18-19 Yarm 7g/f 49 1132 vis
47 3-15 Muss 5gd 45 1555 vis
32 4-9 Muss 5gd [47] 1797 vis
30 10-14 Leic 6g/f [47] 1963 vis
36 5-16 Nott 6.1gd [47] 1988 vis
64 3-14 Donc 5gd [45] 2237 vis
55 5-14 Donc 6g/f [49] 2428 P
26 12-20 Nott 6.1g/f 49 2630 p
62 2-9 Beve 5sft [53] 2945 vis
39 12-15 Wind 5gd 53 3165 vis
58 2-19 Donc 5g/s 53 3220 vis
46 5-9 Thir 6fm [57] 4380 vis
47 9-16 Pont 5fm 57 4754 vis
45 8-15 Newc 5fm 57 4870 vis
39 7-14 Catt 6gd 54 4967 vis

ROAR BLIZZARD 5 b h £0
40a 11-12 Ling 8ap [59] 234 t

ROB ROY 2 b c £8629
97 1-23 NEWM 7g/f 4885*

ROBBIE CAN CAN 5 b g £7137
61a 1-11 WOLV 12af 51 557*
59a 3-12 Wolv 12af 58 634
64a 1-14 LING 12ap 57 711*
65 2-22 Donc 12gd 62 918

ROBBO 10 b g £0
56 8-10 Pont 18g/s 5151

ROBESON 2 br c £0
52 9-10 Newm 7fm 2594
77 5-18 Newm 8fm 4722

ROBIN SHARP 5 ch h £1244
24a 10-13 Sout 8af [55] 188 p
2a 8-8 Wolv 7af 52 280 VIS
49a 2-11 Sout 8af 48 457 vis T
40a 6-12 Sout 8af 48 530 vis t
26a 11-13 Ling 7ap 48 761 vis t
45a 5-15 Ling 7ap 48 846 vis
0 12-12 Wolv 7af 45 956 vis
9a 7-9 Wolv 7af [45] 1266 vis
38a 4-12 Ling 8ap [45] 1451 p
0 12-17 Kemp 7hvy [35] 1642 p
42a 2-5 Ling 8ap [40] 1711 p

ROBINZAL 2 b g £1701

62	9-10	Donc	7g/f			3594
76	3-14	Thir	7g/s			3831
73	2-14	Thir	7g/s			4207
70	6-11	Thir	7fm	[75]		4381
64	7-12	Ayr	8sft		69	5065

ROBMANTRA 2 b c £1188

37	6-6	Warw	7.1fm			2597
34	5-6	Wind	6fm			2783
81	3-5	Chep	5.1g/s			3086
56	6-6	Wind	5gd		73	4123
20	15-15	Chep	7.1gd	[70]		4483 P
60	4-9	Chep	5.1hvy		63	4706 p
45	8-19	Bath	5gd		59	5021 p
57	7-16	Nott	5.1hvy		58	5343 p

ROBURY 2 b g £0

47	7-9	Pont	5sft		1424
30	9-10	Donc	6g/f		2077
27	11-12	Carl	5gd		2933

ROBWILLCALL 4 b f £4358

9	14-15	Muss	5gd	52		1555
21	5-9	Muss	5gd	[49]		1797
51	1-10	HAMI	5g/f	[45]		2476* p
49	5-9	Muss	5g/f	50		2614 p
49	5-8	Hami	5g/f	50		3591
38	10-18	Pont	5g/s	49		3974
46	5-15	Carl	5fm	[47]		4508 p
40	15-26	Ayr	5sft	47		4618
37	13-19	Ayr	6sft	46		5069 p
39	7-13	Muss	5sft	[46]		5146 p
48	2-13	Catt	5sft	[45]		5321 p

ROCAMADOUR 2 b c £10232

91	5-5	Newb	7gd		3919
89	1-12	BEVE	8.5sft		4257*
92	2-4	Ayr	8g/s	[88]	4619
101	2-5	Epso	8.5gd	[87]	4906

ROCINANTE 4 b g £7152

0	9-9	Wolv	9.4af	54	647
41a	8-9	Ling	8ap	54	763
22a	8-10	Sout	8af	[51]	868
51a	3-12	Wolv	7af	49	956
27	11-19	Warw	10.9sft	49	1090
51	1-11	PONT	8sft	46	1425*
56	1-19	REDC	8sft	51	1661*
20a	8-12	Wolv	9.4af	53	2054
12	14-14	Leic	8g/f	53	2402
47a	6-16	Sout	8af	51	3487
4	13-15	Redc	9g/s	53	5111
24	9-16	Nott	8.2hvy	51	5347

ROCK CHICK 2 ch f £0

59	9-13	Ling	6g/f		2061

ROCK CONCERT 5 b m £7686

57a	2-13	Wolv	8.5af	54		40 vis
60a	1-15	SOUT	8af	55		84*
56a	3-9	Sout	8af	58		163
59a	2-13	Wolv	8af	[58]		188 vis
64a	1-13	WOLV	9.4af	56		287*
62a	2-5	Wolv	8.5af	62		346
59a	3-11	Wolv	9.4af	62		465
52a	8-13	Wolv	8.6ap	62		5365

ROCK DOVE 2 b f £5974

75	1-15	NOTT	5.1gd	4859*

ROCK FEVER 2 ch f £0

66	8-10	Pont	6g/f		2610
64	10-13	Newm	6g/f		4918
34	7-15	Brig	7sft		5192
52	14-17	Yarm	6g/s		5350

ROCK HAVEN 2 b c £0

34	10-13	Pont	6gd	3682

ROCK LOBSTER 3 b c £4740

47	7-12	Redc	10sft	73		1144
31	5-5	Leic	11.8g/s	71		1355
58	6-11	Redc	10sft	65		1663
70a	3-12	Wolv	12af	68		2203
55a	6-11	Sout	12af	67		2804
66	1-13	NOTT	10g/f	60		3419*
66	4-9	Newc	10.1g/s	[64]		3702
65	6-10	Nott	10gd	64		3990

ROCKBURST 2 b f £9590

59	5-8	Pont	5hvy			1249
72	2-14	Donc	6g/f			1874
77	1-12	HAMI	6gd			2178*
81	3-7	Hayd	6gd			2883
59	8-12	York	7g/s		78	4064
86	1-10	NOTT	6.1gd	[75]		4858*
61	15-29	Newm	6gd			5087

ROCKERFELLA LAD 4 b g £0

49	10-19	Beve	9.9g/s	68	1164
23	18-20	Ripo	8g/s	65	1366

ROCKET 3 ch g £1289

43	9-12	Warw	7.1gd		1129
50a	4-8	Ling	7ap		1247
62	3-10	Bath	5.7sft		1539
26	11-14	Sali	7g/f		1720
62	3-10	Wind	6g/f	[57]	3977

ROCKET FORCE 4 ch c £0

78	11-12	Kemp	10gd	[104]		1139
84	10-10	Newm	10g/f	[102]		1483
36	11-Epso	10.1g/f		97		2208 VIS

ROCKETS N ROLLERS 4 b c £34654

95a	3-8	Wolv	7af	[108]		838
103	3-10	Donc	8gd	[104]		922
107	3-13	Curr	7sft	[104]		1062
101	2-10	Warw	7.1gd	[104]		1126
109	3-11	Leic	7g/s	[104]		1356
109	1-9	HAYD	7.1g/f	[102]		1486*
106	4-4	Wind	8.3sft	[106]		1649
106	5-10	Long	7g/s	[106]		2139
99	4-6	Leop	7g/s	[106]		2455
91	8-11	York	7g/f	[104]		4063
62	10-11	Good	7gd	[102]		4874

ROCKLEY BAY 2 b c £872

65a	4-8	Ling	6ap			49
61	8-17	Sali	6g/s			1497
38	15-20	Newb	7g/f		65	2314
37	7-9	Wind	6gd		62	2619
16	9-13	Warw	8.1gd		58	3058 BL
53	2-14	Folk	6gd		55	4116 T
26	19-20	Chep	6.1g/s		55	4368 t
41a	7-12	Ling	8ap	[57]		4974 t

ROCKPILER 2 b g £414

3	4-4	Ripo	6g/f		3644
2	14-14	Thir	8fm		4376

ROCKY RAMBO 3 b g £0

0	8-8	Thir	12g/s		1472
0	12-13	Sout	8af		2383 BL

ROCKY REPPIN 4 b g £434

55	13-14	Nott	10fm	[60]		1006 BL
24	13-17	Thir	8g/s		57	1214 bl
29	15-18	Nott	8.2g/s		54	1778 bl
13	17-18	Donc	7g/f		51	2080
47a	3-15	Sout	7af		46	2384
43a	4-16	Sout	8af		46	3159
32a	10-16	Sout	8af		45	3487
30	8-16	Warw	8.1g/s	[45]		4993
32	11-19	Yarm	8g/f	[40]		5119

ROCKYS GIRL 2 b f £0

38	11-13	Kemp	6gd		3183
54a	7-10	Ling	7ap		4442
15	15-15	Kemp	7g/f		4710
31	13-14	Yarm	7sft		5251
42	15-17	Yarm	6g/s		5350

RODIAK 5 b g £0

0	10-12	Sout	14af	[45]	443
0	13-13	Ling	10ap	[40]	539 bl

ROEHAMPTON 3 b c £5375

95	6-7	Newm	9g/f			1189
80	5-6	Ches	12.3gd	[97]		1584 T
98	3-8	Donc	10.3fm		97	4530 VIS
68	13-14	Asco	12g/f		97	4814 vis
9	8-8	Nott	10hvy		96	5187 BL

ROJABAA 5 b g £0

50	6-16	Yarm	10.1fm	53	2146
49	5-8	Redc	10gd	[53]	2548
49	5-9	Brig	9.9g/f	[53]	2643 p
49	5-8	Bath	10.2g/f	[51]	3370
38	11-18	Kemp	10g/f	[48]	4791

ROKO 2 b g £5342

53a	7-11	Sout	5af			1752
42	9-13	York	6g/f			2358
40	11-20	Hayd	6gd			2882
58	4-15	Beve	5g/s			3178
62	3-7	Beve	5gd			3308 BL
58	3-10	Hayd	5g/s			3901
59a	1-14	SOUT	6af	[59]		4127* bl
45	12-17	York	7g/f		59	4396 VIS
47	8-9	Chep	5.1hvy		59	4706 vis
27	13-16	Nott	5.1hvy		54	5343 vis

ROLEX FREE 6 ch g £6660

55a	12-15	Ling	12ap		80	549 p
23a	6-10	Sout	16af		70	743 p
26	8-8	Wind	10fm		67	2973
34a	8-13	Ling	10ap	[60]		3288 bl t
51	3-8	Bath	10.2g/f	[60]		3370 VIS
62a	1-14	SOUT	12af		53	3486* vis
52	4-8	Brig	11.9fm		54	3692 vis
67a	1-12	LING	12ap	[57]		3819* vis
0	11-12	Ches	15.9sft		51	4106 vis
50	4-8	Ling	11.5g/s	[51]		4181 vis
60	3-12	Chep	12.1g/s	[51]		4364 vis
0	20-20	Bath	17.2gd		51	4824 vis

ROLLERBIRD 2 b f £1328

66a	2-12	Ling	8ap		5295

ROLLSWOOD 4 ch g £0

66a	5-13	Ling	10ap			715 P
65	6-12	Hayd	10.5gd			3740
63a	6-15	Ling	12ap			4111 p
55	8-18	Sali	9.9gd		62	4850
63a	7-16	Ling	12ap		62	4973 T p

ROMA VALLEY 2 gr f £0

45	13-14	Kemp	7g/f		4711
37	19-19	Leic	7gd		5040

ROMAN ARMY 2 b c £0

64	5-15	Nott	8.2hvy		5344

ROMAN EMPIRE 3 b g £7125

31a	11-16	Sout	6af		59	94
52a	9-15	Ling	7ap	[59]		117
22a	7-9	Ling	8ap	[56]		717 BL
50a	4-14	Ling	6ap	[52]		819 VIS
61a	1-15	SOUT	6af		50	1750+ bl
59a	3-12	Sout	7af	[57]		2496 bl
60a	3-14	Sout	7af	[57]		2502 bl
52a	5-13	Sout	7af		58	3155 bl
49	4-15	Catt	7sft		51	3933 bl
33	10-16	Hami	6g/s		51	4009 bl
56	1-20	NEWC	6g/f		49	4408*
49a	8-12	Wolv	6ap	[58]		5155 bl

ROMAN FORUM 3 b c £0

74	6-8	Ripo	10g/f		2012
74	5-9	Kemp	12g/f		2862

ROMAN KING 9 b g £0

26	10-14	Sout	12g/s	[70]	1047

ROMAN LOVE 3 ch f £0

40a	4-9	Sout	7af	4131

ROMAN MAZE 3 ch g £8151

70a	1-12	WOLV	7af			71*
64a	4-10	Wolv	7.1gd	[68]		152
52	12-14	Muss	7.1gd		67	1794
66	5-10	Ayr	7.2g/f		67	2027
55	7-13	Ling	7.6g/f		65	2587
63	7-15	York	7gd		63	3117
58	7-11	Leic	7g/f		63	3210
62	4-13	Thir	7gd		63	3571
66	2-12	Ches	7.6fm		60	3634
57	4-16	Brig	7sft	[61]		4144
67	2-17	York	7g/f		61	4398
33	12-18	Ayr	7.2sft		61	4622
70a	3-13	Wolv	6ap	[65]		5327

ROMAN MISTRESS 4 ch f £5433

54	11-20	Thir	6gd	68	1638

ROMAN QUINTET *(continued)*

Fig	Pos	Crse	Dist/Gng	OR	Race
67	4-13	Newc	5gd	66	1873
57	6-10	Thir	5g/f	66	1973
64	3-13	Donc	6gd	65	2232
62	8-12	Thir	5g/s	65	2690 bl
64	5-9	Nott	5.1gd	65	3106 bl
60	7-14	Thir	6g/f	64	3416 bl
63	4-8	Hami	5g/f	62	3591
69	1-11	**NOTT**	5.1gd	61	4038* bl
59	10-19	Beve	5g/s	60	4240 bl
41	22-26	Ayr	5g/s	66	4618 bl
57	9-19	York	5gd	66	4989 bl

ROMAN QUINTET 3 ch c £6771

Fig	Pos	Crse	Dist/Gng	OR	Race
60a	4-12	Wolv	5af	68	35
50a	8-14	Ling	6ap	66	121 T
63a	2-10	Ling	5ap	63	231 t
39a	9-10	Sout	5af	63	660 t
50a	10-14	Ling	6ap	62	874 t p
38	14-17	Kemp	5sft	62	944
62	3-13	Newb	5.2g/f	60	3960
69	2-13	Bath	5.7gd	60	4548
70	2-20	Wind	6g/s	62	4946
68	2-19	Wind	6g/f	62	5053 p
68a	2-14	Ling	7ap	[60]	5263

ROMAN THE PARK 3 b f £5323

Fig	Pos	Crse	Dist/Gng	OR	Race
36a	3-5	Sout	8af	[40]	986
41a	1-6	Sout	8af	[40]	1203*
39a	2-6	Sout	7af	[45]	1410
34a	3-7	Sout	8af	[45]	1591
46	1-13	**BEVE**	8.5g/f	[40]	1947*
46	3-7	Muss	8g/f	42	2613
38	4-11	Muss	9gd	44	2969
48	3-18	Carl	7.9fm	42	3547
46	2-15	Carl	7.9fm	[45]	4507
36	10-17	Warw	8.1g/s	[45]	4992

ROMANOVA 2 b f £458

Fig	Pos	Crse	Dist/Gng	OR	Race
66	8-11	Newb	6gd		3915
72	4-12	Warw	7.1g/f		4417
54	13-19	Leic	7gd		5040

ROMANTIC DRAMA 2 b f £0

Fig	Pos	Crse	Dist/Gng	OR	Race
36a	7-10	Sout	7af	65	203 bl
0	13-13	Warw	6.1gd	61	4272
0	13-13	Bath	8gd	55	4546
0	13-13	Warw	7.1g/s	[49]	4994 T

ROMANTIC GIFT 2 b f £0

Fig	Pos	Crse	Dist/Gng	OR	Race
58	10-19	Wind	5g/f		1805
63	8-13	Ling	6g/f		2061
63	8-15	Folk	7gd		3381
66	12-14	Newm	7g/f		3944
10	13-14	Ayr	6sft	64	5035

ROMANY NIGHTS 4 b g £12781

Fig	Pos	Crse	Dist/Gng	OR	Race
69a	5-13	Wolv	6af	75	687
52a	11-13	Wolv	6af	74	807
72a	4-9	Wolv	7af	72	940 vis
78	3-19	Leic	6g/s	75	1354 vis
71	4-11	Ripo	6g/f	76	1977 vis
81	2-20	York	6g/f	76	2059 vis
78	2-7	Hayd	6g/s	76	2187 BL
81	2-11	Ches	5.1gd	78	2286 bl
80	4-12	Sali	5gd	78	2698 bl
77	6-11	Ches	5.1g/s	78	2747 bl
51	16-17	Pont	6g/f	78	2990 bl
84	2-12	Bath	5.7gd	78	3146 bl
74	7-13	Catt	5g/f	77	3350 bl
76	5-26	Good	6fm	78	3569 bl
78	3-9	Ripo	6g/f	81	3646 bl
43	12-12	Donc	6sft	[79]	5371 bl

ROMANY PRINCE 5 b g £28688

Fig	Pos	Crse	Dist/Gng	OR	Race
103	3-12	Good	14g/f	100	1861
105	3-12	Asco	22.2fm	[100]	2583
110	1-8	**SAND**	16.4g/s	[100]	2914*
109	5-9	Good	16fm	[110]	3552
109	5-10	York	15.9gd	[109]	4000
104	7-8	Donc	18fm	[108]	4478

ROMARIC 3 b g £836

Fig	Pos	Crse	Dist/Gng	OR	Race
94	4-5	Warw	7.1gd	[85]	4270
41	10-14	Pont	8g/f	[84]	4937 vis
53	15-20	Donc	7sft	80	5367 vis

ROME 4 br g £2003

Fig	Pos	Crse	Dist/Gng	OR	Race
62a	9-14	Ling	16ap	72	107

Fig	Pos	Crse	Dist/Gng	OR	Race
60a	3-11	Ling	12ap	[70]	672
0	12-13	Kemp	14.4hvy	69	1516
68	3-10	Sand	14g/f	65	2192
63	5-11	Sand	14g/f	66	2391
61	5-8	Epso	12g/f	65	2869 P
65	4-11	Sand	14g/f	64	3340
53	14-16	Kemp	16g/f	64	4361
54	11-14	Asco	12g/f	62	4775

ROMEOS DAY 3 ch g £5738

Fig	Pos	Crse	Dist/Gng	OR	Race
29	11-16	Nott	10hvy	54	1611
54	2-10	Yarm	10.1g/f	[54]	1724
51	4-15	Ripo	12.3g/f	52	1785
52	3-14	Ling	11.5g/f	52	2014
25	11-14	Redc	14.1g/f	52	2123
45	7-20	Beve	16.2gd	50	3312
38	8-14	Nott	16g/f	50	3580 VIS
0	8-12	Folk	12g/s	45	3913
19	5-10	Bath	11.7g/s	[42]	4199 vis
45	4-10	Yarm	10.1gd	[40]	4612 vis
39	10-15	Wind	10g/f	[40]	4834 vis
47	1-19	**BRIG**	9.9gd	[40]	4903* vis
54a	1-11	**WOLV**	12.2ap	45	5009*

ROMIL STAR 7 b g £12039

Fig	Pos	Crse	Dist/Gng	OR	Race
45	7-17	Nott	14.1gd	54	1238
43	8-12	Sout	16gd	54	1285 VIS
47	2-10	Muss	16gd	50	1551 BL
58a	1-9	**SOUT**	11af	[65]	1838* vis
52	4-6	Brig	11.9g/f	[50]	2047 bl
67a	1-7	**WOLV**	14.8af	[65]	2200* vis
60a	1-9	**SOUT**	12af	[65]	2381* vis
64a	3-10	Sout	11af	[65]	2499 vis
52	5-6	Newc	12.4sft	[50]	2686 vis
67a	2-9	Sout	12af	[65]	2724 vis
56	1-17	**CATT**	12sft	50	3929* vis
46	11-12	Muss	14g/f	54	4170 vis
50	6-14	York	11.9gd	54	4327 vis

RONDELET 3 b g £13891

Fig	Pos	Crse	Dist/Gng	OR	Race
76	2-8	Wind	8.3g/s	76	1257
65	9-14	York	7.9g/s	77	1707
79	2-17	Chep	8.1gd	[76]	2117
80	3-12	Sand	9g/f	76	2385
82	2-6	Ches	10.3g/s	[76]	2748
84	1-15	**EPSO**	10.1gd	[76]	3216*
81	7-15	Donc	10.1gd	81	3598
81	4-11	Epso	10.1gd	81	4293
79	5-12	Sand	10gd	81	4502
52	5-20	York	8.9gd	80	4999

RONNIE FROM DONNY 3 b c £2400

Fig	Pos	Crse	Dist/Gng	OR	Race
62a	9-13	Wolv	6af	74	113
60a	10-16	Sout	5af	70	205 P
74a	1-11	**WOLV**	7af	70	241*
62a	4-8	Wolv	7af	73	285
2a	11-11	Sout	6af	73	386
50a	7-7	Wolv	8.5af	72	700
1	U-19	Newc	6sft	70	967
71	5-18	Catt	7gd	70	998
58	5-13	Redc	7sft	[70]	1142
48	11-16	Newc	6sft	70	1277
52	11-16	Redc	6g/f	67	1824
65	5-16	York	7g/f	67	2057
66	5-15	Beve	7.5g/s	66	2324
65	5-18	Catt	7g/f	65	2848
1	17-17	Pont	6g/f	65	2990
47	10-14	Catt	6g/f	63	3352
49	14-18	Redc	6fm	61	4339
7a	12-12	Wolv	6ap	66	4984
59a	10-12	Wolv	7.1ap	[66]	5006

RONNIES LAD 2 b g £5100

Fig	Pos	Crse	Dist/Gng	OR	Race
48a	5-8	Sout	5ap		1048
33a	8-12	Sout	5af		1439
63	1-12	**NEWC**	6gd		1869*
62	2-6	Brig	6fm		2330 P
63	2-5	Brig	6fm		2833 p
49	8-9	Brig	7g/f	65	3297 p
50	4-9	Brig	6g	63	4758

ROOD BOY 2 b c £806

Fig	Pos	Crse	Dist/Gng	OR	Race
61a	4-13	Wolv	8.5af		43
57a	3-8	Sout	6af	61	223
56a	4-10	Sout	7af	60	794
70	5-11	Bath	8g/s	[57]	1101
50	5-8	Wind	8.3g/s	57	1257

Fig	Pos	Crse	Dist/Gng	OR	Race
54	12-17	Chep	8.1gd	[55]	2117
45	5-11	Wind	8.3g/f	[55]	5052
32	10-17	Newb	9sft	55	5198

ROODEYE 2 b f £9778

Fig	Pos	Crse	Dist/Gng	OR	Race
86	2-8	Bath	5fm		2033
94	1-9	**WIND**	5g/f		2795*
90	5-13	Good	5g/f		3509
89	6-12	Newb	5.2g/f	[94]	3956
96	3-11	Sali	6gd	[94]	4332
84	4-4	Yarm	6g/s	[96]	4633
79	13-24	Redc	6fm	[96]	4928

ROOFTOP PROTEST 7 b g £5236

Fig	Pos	Crse	Dist/Gng	OR	Race
77	1-15	**CHES**	15.9g/f	63	4512* T

ROOKS BRIDGE 2 ch g £0

Fig	Pos	Crse	Dist/Gng	OR	Race
29	14-14	Warw	6.1g/f		4422
13a	13-14	Ling	7ap		4658
30a	7-11	Wolv	7.1ap		5113
47a	9-13	Wolv	5.1ap		5207

ROPPONGI DANCER 4 b f £182

Fig	Pos	Crse	Dist/Gng	OR	Race
11a	7-10	Wolv	14.8af	[30]	125 t
2a	9-16	Sout	16af	25	206 VIS
21a	5-9	Wolv	14.8af	[25]	301 BL t
17a	3-9	Sout	12af	[30]	353 bl t
9a	8-9	Ling	16ap	[30]	454 bl t
10a	5-8	Wolv	16.2af	30	563 bl t
30	7-13	Yarm	11.5fm	30	2868 bl

ROSABLANCA 2 b f £0

Fig	Pos	Crse	Dist/Gng	OR	Race
51a	14-14	Ling	7ap		5258

ROSACARA 3 b f £2174

Fig	Pos	Crse	Dist/Gng	OR	Race
67	2-9	Ayr	7.2gd	63	2508 T
70	2-14	Wind	8.3fm	66	2971 t
2	15-16	Epso	8.5gd	66	3219 t
50	7-9	Catt	7gd	[68]	4674 t

ROSAPENNA 2 b f £0

Fig	Pos	Crse	Dist/Gng	OR	Race
66	5-7	Newm	6g/f		2733
26	14-16	Nott	6.1gd		3103
67a	5-10	Ling	6ap		3817
72	6-15	Kemp	7g/f	[64]	4710
34	11-12	Newm	8gd	70	5089

ROSE BIEN 2 b f £0

Fig	Pos	Crse	Dist/Gng	OR	Race
45	9-14	Yarm	8g/s		5118

ROSE OF YORK 4 b f £313

Fig	Pos	Crse	Dist/Gng	OR	Race
57	4-10	Ripo	6gd		4790
37	10-19	Redc	6g/f	[53]	5110

ROSE TEA 5 ro m £0

Fig	Pos	Crse	Dist/Gng	OR	Race
0	8-9	Warw	15g/s	[40]	1329 BL

ROSEANNA 3 b f £5500

Fig	Pos	Crse	Dist/Gng	OR	Race
100	3-13	Newm	7gd		1169

ROSECLIFF 2 b c £637

Fig	Pos	Crse	Dist/Gng	OR	Race
75	4-11	Newm	6g/f		3925
78	4-16	Yarm	10.1g/s		5352

ROSEIN 2 b f £3393

Fig	Pos	Crse	Dist/Gng	OR	Race
76a	1-11	**SOUT**	5af		1752*
76	7-12	Beve	5g/f		2165
75	6-10	Ripo	6gd	78	4306

ROSENCRANS 3 b c £59916

Fig	Pos	Crse	Dist/Gng	OR	Race
102a	3-14	Nad	8af		598 TVIS
106a	1-15	**LING**	7ap		885* VIS
104a	4-9	Ling	8ap		1040 vis t
56	6-6	Sand	7.1g/f	[100]	2190 vis t

ROSES OF SPRING 6 gr m £2294

Fig	Pos	Crse	Dist/Gng	OR	Race
66	7-12	Ling	5g/s	85	1615 p
82	3-11	Good	5g/f	83	1845 p
59	17-17	Muss	5fm	83	2082 p
55	10-10	Donc	5g/f	82	2429 p
75	10-12	Newm	5g/f	80	3279 p
79	6-22	Good	5fm	78	3537 p
69	7-9	Brig	5.3fm	78	3673 p
35	11-13	Good	6gd	77	3952 p

ROSIE MAC 3 ch f £1564

Fig	Pos	Crse	Dist/Gng	OR	Race
54	6-11	Thir	7fm		2463
64	3-14	Thir	7sft		2692
60	4-9	York	7gd		3121
47	6-9	Thir	7g/f	[62]	3413

```
51   6-6    Ripo   10g/f   59   3647
49   10-20  York   7.9qd   57   4321
65   4-9    Newc   10.1g/f [54]  5015

ROSIE MALONEY  2 b f  £0
0    12-12  Wolv   8.5af         28
18   11-12  Warw   7.1qd         1129

ROSIE MUIR  2 b r f  £0
18   10-11  Bath   5.7gd         4543
54   7-13   Wind   6g/f          5048

ROSIELLA  2 b f  £4424
24   12-13  Ling   6g/f          2061
69   5-18   Wind   6gd           2618
73   1-11   BATH   5.7g/f        3848*
73   3-8    Bath   5.7g/s [71]   4198
74   4-14   Catt   5g/f    73    4437
64   6-19   Nott   6.1g/s  73    4645
46   16-18  Wind   5g/f    72    4830

ROSIES RESULT  4 ch g  £3708
36   10-13  Newc   5sft   54    1276
35   10-13  Hami   5g/f   50    2320
40   10-20  Beve   5g/s   45    3180
52   1-19   DONC   5g/s   45    3220*
39   9-14   Thir   5g/f   51    3417
36   11-17  Catt   5g/f   50    3667
45   6-18   Pont   5g/s   50    3974
4    13-15  Newc   6hvy   50    4211
32   11-15  Carl   5fm   [48]   4508

ROSINGS  3 ch f  £0
46   14-14  Wind   8.3fm         2974
33   9-9    Redc   9fm           4336

ROSKILDE  4 b g  £0
77   8-10   Pont   8gd   100    3460
77   14-15  Donc   8gd   98     4531

ROSS IS BOSS  2 gr g  £0
3    10-10  Newc   6g/f          4403
0    23-24  Redc   6fm           4928

ROSS MOOR  2 b c  £0
32   14-18  Newm   8fm           4722

ROSSALL POINT  3 b g  £1643
69   4-11   Chep   10.2gd        2196
59   5-17   Wind   11.6fm        2788
53   8-15   Wind   10fm          3292
63   4-11   Yarm   14.1gd  62    3998
42   12-16  Warw   16.2gd  62    4276
67   3-15   Good   16gd    61    5025
61   3-8    Bath   17.2sft 61    5175

ROSSBEIGH  2 b c  £0
66   10-11  Newm   7gd           4190

ROSSELLI  8 b g  £0
15   13-15  Hami   6gd    46    1508
46   7-8    Beve   5sft  [46]   1626
15   11-12  Hayd   6g/s  [46]   2186
13   10-12  Ayr    8g/s  [46]   2543
72   8-11   Warw   7.1fm [46]   2777
0    8-8    Hayd   6gd   [46]   2949
0    F-7    Ayr    7.2gd [46]   3326

ROSSIN GOLD  2 b g  £0
47a  6-13   Wolv   6ap           5287 BL

ROSTI  3 b g  £3547
38a  5-14   Sout   8af    50     60
44a  4-16   Sout   7af    47     202
46a  1-9    SOUT   7af   [45]    303*
50a  1-14   SOUT   8af   [45]    354*
42a  3-11   Ling   8ap   [45]    408
33a  8-12   Sout   8af    46     530
40a  6-13   Sout   8af   [45]    776
18   8-8    Ayr    7.2g/s [45]   1448

ROTTECK  4 br c  £22535
116  2-10   Bade   11gd          2141
118  3-7    Duss   12sft         3497

ROTUMA  5 b g  £20074
38   9-14   Newc   10.1sft 66    964 bl
64   5-9    Pont   10hvy   65    1254 bl
54   8-15   Hami   9.2gd   65    1388 bl
67   3-11   Hayd   10.5g/f 62    1884 bl

69   1-10   NEWC   10.1g/f 62    2162* bl
64   6-13   Ches   10.3gd  68    2284 bl
76   1-7    BEVE   9.9gd   65    2654* bl
76   2-8    Nott   10g/s   72    2929 bl
70   5-9    Ripo   10g/s   73    3260 bl
78   1-6    LEIC   10fm    73    3815* bl
69   9-14   Ripo   10gd    75    4305 bl
61   9-20   Ayr    10sft   75    4656 bl
72   7-14   Ayr    10sft   75    5037 bl
73   8-17   Redc   10sft   73    5307

ROUGE BLANC  4 b f  £0
0    9-10   Muss   6gd     54    1551 P
3    7-9    Ripo   16g/f   54    2009 T
19   13-14  York   13.9g/f 54    2060 BL t

ROUGE ET NOIR  6 b g  £769
30   14-16  Ripo   8gd           2987
42   7-8    Hami   8.3fm         3246
49   4-6    Ripo   10gd          3648
52   3-13   Redc   14.1fm  50    4340 T
33   9-19   Catt   15.8g/f 51    4675 t

ROUSING THUNDER  7 b g  £0
0    10-10  Sout   16af  [41]    307 p
0    16-16  Sout   11af  [45]    445 t p

ROUTE BARREE  5 ch g  £0
38a  7-10   Ling   12ap  [46]    24

ROUTE SIXTY SIX  7 b m  £2170
33a  8-13   Sout   8af    45    221
18a  8-13   Wolv   9.4af  42    287
24   6-14   Warw   8.1hvy 45    1535 p
51   2-5    Carl   9.3gd  43    2674
2    16-18  Donc   7gd    43    2755
42   8-17   Hayd   8.1gd  47    3759
45   6-8    Ripo   10g/s  45    3938

ROVELLA  3 b f  £0
38   7-8    Folk   12sft         1272
18   12-16  Nott   10hvy   40    1611
19a  7-10   Wolv   8.5af  [40]   1801
27   8-13   Beve   12.1g/f [40]  1945

ROVING VIXEN  2 b f  £580
45a  9-13   Wolv   6af           126
26a  11-14  Sout   8af           226
28a  13-14  Ling   7ap           804
47   8-12   Warw   7.1gd         1129
36a  4-8    Wolv   7af   [40]    1565 P
0    13-13  Kemp   10hvy [40]    1643 p
38a  3-10   Wolv   8.5af [40]    1801 BL
45a  3-13   Wolv   8.5af [35]    2052 bl
42   4-13   Bath   8fm    41    2667 bl
30   7-8    Yarm   8g/f  [41]   2854 bl
0    9-11   Yarm   8g/f   40    3706 bl
31   5-16   Brig   7gd    40    4901
37   6-17   Warw   8.1g/s [40]  4992 bl
36   5-20   Yarm   7g/s  [40]   5120

ROWAN LODGE  2 ch c  £13723
41   14-15  Wind   6g/f          2263
76   3-13   Thir   6g/s          2689
84   1-6    BRIG   6g/f          3171*
82   2-6    Folk   7g/f   77     3723
85   1-9    CATT   6sft   77     3931*
71   9-16   Newm   6gd    81     4224
87   2-7    Ches   7g/f   79     4509
65   9-10   Newm   6fm    84     4727
83   4-15   York   6gd    84     4985

ROWAN PURSUIT  2 b f  £6655
64a  3-13   Ling   7ap    53    15 bl
62a  1-12   LING   8ap   [63]   78* bl
67a  1-15   LING   7ap    63   295* bl
69a  3-10   Ling   7ap    70    432 bl
67a  5-13   Ling   7ap    70    474 bl
50a  7-11   Ling   8ap   [69]   696 bl
43   11-12  Bath   8g/f   64    3846 bl
0    16-16  Brig   7sft   70    4144

ROWAN TREE  2 b c  £0
94   8-12   Newm   7g/f          3060
97   7-10   Good   7fm           3532

ROWAN WARNING  2 b c  £0
42   5-7    Nott   6.1g/f        2629

ROXANNE MILL  5 b m  £13351
55a  7-12   Wolv   5af    70     35
73   3-8    Folk   5g/s  [75]   1269
77   2-12   Ling   5g/s   74    1615
65   6-8    Hami   5gd   [74]   1749
81   3-15   Muss   5fm    75    2084
78   2-9    Sali   5fm    75    2420
76   3-9    Muss   5g/f   75    2614
65   5-12   Ling   5g/f   76    2743 P
72   6-9    Nott   5.1gd  75    3106 p
67   1-9    CATT   5g/f  [74]   3353* p
77   2-8    Hami   5g/f   73    3591 p
36   9-16   Catt   5sft  [74]   3932 p
75   2-8    Folk   5gd    73    4118 p
54   16-16  Muss   5g/f   73    4174 p

ROY MCAVOY  5 b g  £0
53a  14-16  Ling   7ap    65    144
25a  10-11  Wolv   8.5af  60    806
27a  14-14  Ling   6ap    55    897
41a  10-12  Ling   8ap    55    1013 P
25a  4-5    Ling   10ap  [45]   1412
16   10-13  Leic   7g/f  [40]   1827

ROYAL ABIGAIL  2 b f  £0
41   15-17  Nott   6.1gd         2927
52   13-16  Newm   7g/f          3582

ROYAL ACCOLADE  2 b f  £0
59   9-12   Warw   5sft          1524
46   16-19  Wind   5g/f          1805 T
46   7-7    Ling   5g/f          2738 BL

ROYAL ADVOCATE  4 b g  £270
64a  4-11   Ling   8ap    63    2018
60a  5-12   Ling   8ap   [63]   2394
42   6-17   Wind   6fm    60    2975

ROYAL ALCHEMIST  2 b f  £10965
89   1-11   NOTT   6.1sft        1739*
93   2-9    Newm   6g/f          2763
91   7-11   Newm   7g/f          3781
83   8-12   Good   7sft  [94]    4264
94   5-9    Newb   6g/f  [94]    4680
74   13-14  Newm   7g/f  [94]    4914

ROYAL APPROACH  3 b f  £0
60   5-8    Hayd   10.5g/f       1489
1a   11-11  Sout   12af   63    2804
40   9-13   Nott   10g/s [60]    4650

ROYAL ATALZA  7 gr g  £3309
62a  1-8    WOLV   12af         644* P
0    8-10   Sout   16af   51    743 bl

ROYAL AWAKENING  2 b c  £266
18a  12-12  Wolv   6af           42
36a  8-10   Ling   6ap           600
45   11-15  Redc   5g/s   55    2961
50   4-7    Catt   7g/f  [55]   3194
43   5-12   Carl   5.9g/f  51   3655
48   7-8    Redc   6g/f   51    3808
56   4-8    Catt   7g/f  [49]   4440

ROYAL AXMINSTER  8 b g  £4253
13a  5-10   Wolv   14.8af  41    34
11a  7-10   Sout   11af    40    330
32a  5-7    Ling   12ap   [35]  1287
45   2-18   Newm   12fm    40    2088
33   7-15   Ripo   12.3g/f 41    2526
0    U-10   Newb   11g/f   40    2875
48   1-19   CHEP   12.1gd  40   3727*

ROYAL BATHWICK  4 b f  £2748
74   3-8    Leic   10g/f   73    3514
76   3-12   Sali   12g/f   73    3868
72   4-9    Good   12sft   75    4183
65   6-11   Wind   11.6g/s [73]  4942
58   8-13   Bath   11.7sft 70    5174

ROYAL CASTLE  10 b g  £0
41   6-9    Newc   16.1gd  46    1870
47   6-9    Redc   16fm   [44]   2298

ROYAL CAVALIER  6 b g  £18040
69a  6-8    Sout   12af    87    225
69a  12-16  Ling   12ap    85    293
102  1-8    DONC   12gd   [97]   950+
96   4-9    Ches   13.4gd [98]   1596
```

101	5-15	Hayd	11.9gd	98	2948
89	9-14	York	13.9gd	98	3119
69	17-19	York	13.9g/s	97	4023

ROYAL CHALLENGE 3 b c £15343

82	2-10	Newb	5.2fm		2649
81	1-10	**BEVE**	5sft		2944*
83	1-10	**SAND**	5g/f	75	3356+
70	6-21	Good	5fm	76	3567
81	3-11	Bath	5g/s	[80]	4201
82	2-6	Sand	5gd	[79]	4498
68	8-15	Kemp	6g/f	79	4713

ROYAL COPENHAGEN 2 b f £10282

102	2-8	Deau	7hvy		4157

ROYAL COZYFIRE 2 b g £2562

46	5-7	Chep	6.1gd		2115
67	1-9	**CHEP**	5.1g/f		2625*

ROYAL DIGNITARY 4 br g £0

82a	15-15	Ling	7ap	96	887 vis

ROYAL DISTANT 3 ch f £2100

75	6-9	Hayd	8.1sft	79	1105
64	7-7	Beve	7.5sft	79	1305
71	7-14	York	11.9g/s	76	1708
43	9-9	Donc	10.3g/f	74	2079
62	8-12	Pont	10g/f	72	2277
44	9-11	Redc	9g/s	70	2565
57	8-12	Beve	9.9gd	68	2893
70	2-5	Pont	10gd	65	3459
66	7-16	Thir	12g/f	65	3573
55	14-20	York	7.9gd	67	4321
64	7-12	Beve	12.1g/f	65	4601
47	9-20	York	13.9gd	63	5004
56	9-17	Redc	10sft	60	5307

ROYAL EXPOSURE 7 b g £0

15a	4-6	Wolv	9.4af	[30]	1800

ROYAL FANTASY 4 ch f £56514

111	2-4	Mais	15gd		3317
115	2-13	Long	12sft		4567

ROYAL FASHION 3 b f £576

57a	2-10	Ling	6ap	[65]	133
56a	9-16	Ling	7ap	65	181
58a	6-16	Ling	7ap	62	270
51a	6-13	Ling	10ap	[60]	569
33a	9-12	Ling	8ap	[58]	675

ROYAL FLIGHT 3 b c £0

42	13-17	Kemp	7gd		1136
48	14-15	Nott	8.2g/s		4649
12	13-16	Bath	8gd	50	4828

ROYAL FLYNN 2 b g £282

25	6-6	Ayr	6g/f		2028
70	4-8	Beve	7.5gd		2511
62	10-15	Pont	6gd		3239
60	5-14	Muss	7.1g/f	[70]	4171
57	5-14	Muss	8gd	65	4519

ROYAL GAME 2 b c £0

54a	10-11	Ling	8ap		4744

ROYAL GRAND 4 ch c £623

68a	3-10	Sout	6af	72	390
29a	11-13	Sout	7af	71	551
36a	8-8	Sout	7af	[69]	744 VIS
52	13-18	Catt	7gd	66	998

ROYAL INDULGENCE 4 b g £3922

49	1-12	**AYR**	9.1g/f	43	3766*
46	4-15	Folk	9.7g/f	[48]	4373
47	4-14	Pont	10g/f	48	4624

ROYAL ISLAND 2 b c £15708

88	1-10	**BEVE**	5sft		1632*
88	1-4	**NEWC**	5gd		1868*
101	2-8	Epso	6fm		2251
92	9-15	Asco	5g/f		2472
73	11-13	Good	5g/f		3509
1	10-11	York	6g/s	[100]	4022

ROYAL JELLY 2 b f £5265

65	11-15	Kemp	7gd		4710
71	8-19	Leic	7gd		5045
80a	1-14	**LING**	7ap		5257*

ROYAL JET 2 b c £2586

83	3-12	Good	8g/f		4522
76	6-18	Newm	8fm		4722
85	2-15	Pont	10g/f		4933 VIS
66	5-10	Nott	10hvy	[83]	5188 vis

ROYAL LOGIC 3 b f £0

18	10-10	Newb	6g/f		2309
37	7-8	Good	9gd		2536
35	6-8	Brig	8fm		4762
12	14-16	Brig	7gd	[45]	4901

ROYAL LUSTRE 3 b c £2970

69	11-20	Newm	8g/f		3237
74	3-5	Pont	8gd		3683
60	9-11	Wind	10gd		4125
65	2-7	Good	9.9g/f	[67]	4541
59	5-10	Good	9.9gd	[67]	4877

ROYAL MELBOURNE 4 ch g £3409

56	1-12	**NEWC**	12.4sft	51	1680+
44	6-6	Ripo	12.3g/f	55	1980
32	10-15	Ayr	10.9g/s	54	2545
2	9-9	Beve	12.1gd	54	2892

ROYAL MILLENNIUM 6 b g £118012

114	1-11	**NEWC**	6g/s	[110]	2769*
101	12-12	Deau	6.5g/s	[110]	3838
114	4-19	Hayd	6fm	[111]	4384
116	1-12	**CURR**	6g/s	[111]	4732*
115	3-15	Long	5g/f	[111]	4952
117	1-14	**NEWM**	6sft	[111]	5100*

ROYAL MISTRESS 2 b f £4754

97	3-8	Deau	7sft		3169

ROYAL MOUGINS 2 br c £665

18	12-12	Newm	6g/f		3280
71	5-13	Warw	7.1g/s		4664
70	5-15	Sali	8gd		4851
73	3-19	Pont	8g/s	68	5147
79	5-13	Donc	7hvy	[68]	5199

ROYAL NITE OWL 3 b g £462

14a	8-10	Wolv	8.5af		839
29	11-12	Hayd	8.1sft		1108
28a	4-6	Sout	7af	[45]	1410
39	4-19	Redc	6g/f	40	2125
38	3-12	Carl	5.9g/f	40	3655
17	11-20	Yarm	6g/s	[40]	5121

ROYAL ORISSA 2 b c £14250

70	4-12	Newb	6g/f		2348
83	5-8	Sali	7gd		2695
86	3-15	Wind	6gd		3163
75	8-10	Kemp	6g/f	78	3521
83	2-21	Donc	6fm	[78]	4490 t
80	5-12	Newm	6gd	80	4882 t
87	2-20	Donc	7sft	79	5373 t

ROYAL OVATION 4 b g £0

5a	15-15	Sout	6af	[30]	172
0	10-10	Wolv	8.5af	[30]	311

ROYAL PARDON 2 b f £745

55	7-14	Redc	6fm		2297
50	8-16	Nott	6.1gd		3103
58	4-7	Folk	6g/f		3722
59	4-19	Carl	5.9g/f	58	4344
63	5-20	Ling	7g/f	57	4741

ROYAL PAVILLION 3 b c £4196

70a	3-13	Ling	6ap		364
74a	1-6	**WOLV**	6af		631*
66	4-15	Wind	6g/s	70	1054
58	10-16	Kemp	6g/s	70	1116

ROYAL PRINCE 3 gr c £28722

76	4-14	Folk	7g/s		1080
83	1-14	**YARM**	7fm	[77]	2148+
95	1-8	**LEIC**	7gd	78	2403*
88	3-7	Leic	7fm	89	3814
95	3-7	Sand	8.1gd	89	4499
89	4-14	Asco	8g/f	89	4813 T
99	1-10	**NEWM**	8g/f	[89]	4890*

ROYAL PRODIGY 4 ch g £4973

65a	1-12	**WOLV**	12af	[63]	114*

67a	1-14	**LING**	13ap	63	259*
58a	9-13	Ling	13ap	69	342
62a	4-13	Ling	13ap	[66]	602
63a	2-5	Wolv	12af	[66]	616
0	19-20	Bath	17.2gd	59	4824

ROYAL RACER 6 b g £7196

52	1-14	**FOLK**	9.7g/s	47	1083*
51	3-12	Folk	9.7sft	50	1273
43	6-8	Folk	9.7sft	50	1579
46	7-17	Ling	7gd	50	2397
42	9-20	Newm	8g/f	49	3232 VIS
54	1-13	**FOLK**	9.7g/f	48	3726* BL
51	6-19	Beve	9.9g/f	52	4720 bl
0	15-15	Redc	9g/s	52	5111 bl

ROYAL REBEL 8 b g £36810

73	5-13	Asco	16.2sft		1418
110	7-9	Sand	16.4g/f	[112]	2095
113	4-13	Asco	20g/f	[112]	2518
102	4-8	Sand	16.4g/s	[110]	2914
112	2-9	Good	16fm	[110]	3552 vis
105	7-10	York	15.9gd	[110]	4000 vis

ROYAL SAILOR 2 b c £0

50	11-18	Newm	8fm		4722
69	7-15	York	7.9gd		5002
63a	7-10	Ling	7ap		5264
41	11-15	Nott	8.2hvy		5344

ROYAL SAPPHIRE 2 b c £0

76	9-13	Donc	7hvy		5200

ROYAL SHEPLEY 3 b f £0

0	13-13	Sout	6af		659
0	15-15	Sout	6af		795
0	10-10	Sout	6af		851

ROYAL STARLET 3 b f £0

53	8-10	Good	8gd		2378
39	8-10	Bath	11.7g/f	53	2978
48	4-14	Yarm	11.5g/f	49	3714
38	5-12	Folk	12g/s	49	3913
21	9-11	Brig	9.9g/f	48	3982 VIS
3	12-12	Good	16g/s	45	4235
35	8-11	Yarm	11.5g/s	[45]	4584

ROYAL STORM 5 b h £40964

86	15-20	Newm	7g/s	95	1151
102	1-9	**NEWM**	6fm	95	1490*
101	4-29	Asco	6fm	98	2581
99	6-19	Newm	7g/f	99	3061
85	9-21	Asco	7g/f	99	3441
91	14-28	Good	6fm	99	3622
101	2-20	Newm	7g/f	97	3782
91	8-8	Epso	7g/f	[99]	4472
94	9-16	Good	7g/f	99	4523
109	1-14	**NEWB**	7g/f	[99]	4638*
86	14-15	Asco	7g/f	104	4800
98	9-11	Good	7g/f	[105]	4874
109	4-12	Donc	6sft	[105]	5371

ROYAL SUPREMACY 3 ch f £0

0	16-16	Bath	5.7sft	56	1540
14	18-18	Bath	5.7g/f	52	1788
13	11-11	Bath	5g/f	47	3849 T

ROYAL TIGRESS 3 b f £25729

97	3-10	Curr	8hvy		895
107	1-	**LEOP**	7sft		1300*
96	7-11	Asco	8g/f		2555
64	7-8	York	11.9g/s		4024 VIS

ROYAL TRIGGER 4 b g £0

0	20-20	Wind	11.6g/s	74	1056
2	19-19	Newb	10gd	70	1736 T
42	11-11	Newb	13.3fm	70	2651 t
33	15-19	Bath	17.2gd	53	3147 BLt
34	16-19	Chep	12.1gd	53	3727 blt
2	14-14	Bath	13.1g/s	49	4203 bl t

ROYAL UPSTART 3 b g £610

3	12-14	Sout	10g/s	46	1051
38a	3-5	Wolv	9.4af	[45]	1311 BL
41a	2-6	Wolv	9.4af	[40]	1675 bl
29	6-14	Redc	14.1g/f	40	2123 bl
29	5-11	Yarm	11.5g/f	40	2346 bl
0	7-11	Pont	12g/f	35	2790 bl
17	8-10	Beve	12.1g/f	30	3499

ROYAL WARRANT 3 b c £44926
84a	3-7	Ling	8ap	80	341
73a	6-10	Ling	7ap	80	432
87a	1-5	LING	8ap	79	694*
86a	3-9	Ling	8ap	[79]	756
88	4-18	Good	9g/f	83	1813
91	2-18	Epso	10.1fm	84	2250
95	2-10	Wind	10fm	88	2785
97	2-11	Newm	10g/f	88	3029
91	6-16	Good	9.9fm	93	3553

ROYAL WEDDING 2 b c £0
74	7-7	Yarm	6g/f		3709
69	8-9	York	6g/s		4026
68	8-12	Thir	7g/f		4591

ROYAL WINDMILL 5 b g £1484
45	8-18	Catt	7gd	[50]	996 p
34	13-17	Beve	8.5g/s	[48]	1160 p
43	5-10	Ayr	8g/s	[47]	1446 p
56	2-10	Ayr	8g/s	[45]	2544 p
44	7-14	Muss	7.1g/f	45	2615 p
49	6-15	Thir	8g/s	[45]	2688 p
48	6-13	Muss	8gd	[46]	2967 p
49	3-20	Redc	6g/f	45	3767
23	14-15	Carl	5fm	[47]	4508

ROYAL ZEPHYR 3 b f £0
| 44 | 10-13 | Bath | 8gd | 64 | 4546 |

ROYALE PEARL 4 gr f £1477
34a	10-12	Ling	8ap	[45]	649
15a	13-14	Ling	10ap	[45]	705
36a	4-14	Ling	12ap	[40]	968
44a	1-9	LING	12ap	[40]	1456*
43	4-13	Nott	14.1gd	[45]	1990
37a	5-8	Ling	12ap	42	3026
42	5-12	Yarm	16gd	[40]	3493
0	13-13	Ling	16ap	40	3822

ROYALTEA 3 ch f £261
41a	6-7	Wolv	7af		284
50a	6-9	Wolv	7af		381
57a	4-6	Wolv	8.5af		468
12a	7-10	Wolv	8.5af	[51]	839
24a	7-12	Wolv	9.4af	51	2054
39	8-14	Carl	9.3g/f	[47]	4347
38	10-17	Kemp	7g/f	[45]	4794

ROZANEE 3 ch f £333
61a	3-14	Ling	10ap		53
64a	6-11	Ling	12ap	62	624
33	13-20	Warw	10.9gd	62	1128
0	12-12	Good	9.9sft	60	4268

RUBAIYAT 3 b g £3377
2	12-12	Kemp	8hvy		1511
26	17-20	Yarm	8fm	55	2149
54a	4-15	Sout	12af	52	2503
56a	3-15	Ling	12ap	52	2741
57a	2-14	Ling	10ap	50	3449
53a	5-12	Ling	10ap	53	4113
67	3-10	Warw	8.1g/f	[53]	4421
62a	3-13	Wolv	9.5ap	55	4925
73a	2-11	Ling	8ap	[55]	4977

RUBIES 2 ch f £3083
74	2-11	Bath	5g/s		4200
69	6-9	Sand	5gd		4497
73	2-16	Bath	5.7gd		4823
78	4-19	Leic	7gd	[77]	5045

RUBY ANNIVERSARY 3 b f £0
0	12-12	Wolv	7af	[43]	71
0	12-13	Sout	8af	[38]	199
0	8-9	Sout	11af	[38]	224

RUBY MUJA 2 b f £3741
37	10-11	Sali	5gd		2658
61	8-11	Wind	5gd		3160
63	3-9	Bath	5gd		3847
65	1-8	WIND	5g/s	[55]	4218*
36	15-19	Ling	6g/f	[62]	4895

RUBY MURRAY 2 b f £0
49	13-18	Wind	6gd		3824
62	9-15	Kemp	6g/f		4357
42	13-13	Newm	6g/f		4918

RUBY REBEL 2 ch f £0
0	15-15	Beve	5g/s		1161
4	10-11	Beve	5g/f		1831
1	10-11	Thir	6g/f		1968 BL
3	9-10	Thir	6fm		2461 bl

RUBY ROCKET 3 b f £58518
102	5-8	Newb	7gd	[105]	1233
107	2-11	Hayd	6gd	[105]	2240
106	3-11	Newc	6g/s	[105]	2769
108	2-9	York	6g/s	[105]	3075
105	3-7	Leop	6gd	[105]	3495
105	2-7	Good	6g/f	[105]	4526
95	7-12	Curr	6g/s	[105]	4732
111	1-15	NEWM	6gd	[105]	5088*
106	3-12	Donc	6sft	[105]	5371

RUBY WINE 2 b f £1736
| 85 | 2-11 | Newb | 6gd | | 3915 |

RUBYANNE 2 b f £3354
67	6-8	Wind	5g/f		1955
85	1-6	YARM	5.2gd		3361*
82	8-12	Newb	5.2g/f		3956

RUBYS DREAM 2 b f £2438
72	4-12	Warw	5sft		1524
71	2-11	Kemp	5hvy		1640
78	3-19	Wind	5g/f		1805
67	4-13	Nott	5.1gd		1987
73	3-9	Brig	5.3fm		2257
65	5-12	Bath	5.7gd		3141
68	4-11	Ripo	6g/f		3258
55	8-14	Leic	6g/f		3517
62	12-18	Wind	5gd	69	4830
38	13-19	Bath	5gd	64	5021
19a	12-13	Wolv	6ap	[64]	5182

RUDAKI 2 ch c £794
63	13-14	Newm	7g/f		2766
64	4-8	Yarm	6g/s		4250
67	3-10	Newc	7fm		4864
41	24-29	Newm	6gd		5087

RUDOOD 4 b g £0
| 78a | 5-12 | Ling | 8ap | 78 | 517 |
| 39 | 9-9 | Muss | 8fm | [78] | 2087 |

RUE DE PARIS 4 br g £0
29	11-17	Ripo	6g/s	42	3262
40	5-10	Leic	7fm	[40]	3812
32a	7-13	Sout	6af	40	4091
12	15-15	Folk	7g/f	[40]	4371 P

RUE DE VERTBOIS 2 ch f £0
| 0 | 11-11 | Ling | 6ap | [49] | 233 |

RUE LA FAYETTE 4 b f £6338
| 107 | 2-13 | Chan | 5g/s | | 2638 |

RUGGTAH 3 gr f £564
25	10-12	Good	9g/f		1864
64	3-10	Bath	11.7g/f		4414
61a	5-14	Ling	13ap		4898
28	10-11	Good	14gd	[65]	5029

RULE OF LAW 2 b c £684087
115	2-10	York	10.4g/f	[§110]	1685 T
119	2-14	Epso	12fm	[114]	2254 t
116	4-10	Curr	12g/f	[114]	2822 t
121	1-7	YORK	11.9gd	[118]	4001* t
121	1-9	DONC	14.6fm	[120]	4532* t

RULES FOR JOKERS 3 b g £0
| 9 | 22-22 | Donc | 7gd | 82 | 955 |
| 34a | 6-8 | Wolv | 7af | [80] | 1222 |

RUM CREEK 2 ch c £0
46	15-16	Sali	5gd		3111
72	8-13	Wind	6fm		3478
53	11-14	Sali	7sft		4575
0	16-16	Bath	5.7gd		4823

RUM DESTINY 5 b g £0
22	12-18	Thir	6g/f	53	2214 vis
2	18-19	Sand	5gd	50	2657 vis
0	20-20	Beve	5g/s	47	3180 vis
33	13-19	Donc	5g/s	47	3220 vis

| 26 | 13-17 | Catt | 5g/f | 42 | 3667 bl |

RUM SHOT 3 b c £24850
102	4-11	Newb	6gd	[97]	1732
64	9-9	Hayd	6g/f	[97]	1918
106	1-5	CHES	6.1fm	[100]	3636*
111	3-13	Newb	7g/f	[100]	3957
95	6-11	Deau	6hvy	[100]	4313
83	14-14	Newb	7g/f	[108]	4638

RUMAN 2 b g £0
| 48 | 11-12 | Hayd | 6sft | | 4770 |
| 55 | 7-13 | York | 6gd | | 4988 |

RUMBALARA 2 b f £5407
72	7-13	Good	7fm		3554
86	2-11	Epso	6gd		4289
81	1-11	BATH	8gd		4544*

RUMBLING BRIDGE 3 ch g £1918
40	9-11	Sali	8gd	61	3455
44	9-14	Sali	9.9g/f	59	3867
60	2-5	Brig	11.9sft	56	4166
56	3-12	Brig	11.9sft	53	5093

RUMOUR 4 b f £2919
| 85a | 1-10 | SOUT | 8af | | 2997* |

RUMOUR MILL 2 b c £0
50a	10-10	Ling	8ap	68	132
38a	5-9	Wolv	9.4af	62	351 P
2	15-16	Nott	10gd	55	1240
48	10-16	Bath	10g/f	[50]	1790
4a	11-12	Wolv	8.5af	50	2205
2	17-17	Wind	11.6fm	[45]	2788
38	8-14	Leic	8g/f	[40]	3344 BL
32	8-11	Chep	10.2gd	[40]	3730 bl
14	10-14	Good	8sft	40	4189
11	12-13	Folk	9.7g/f	[40]	4372
0	12-14	Bath	8g/f	40	4411 bl
9	15-18	Chep	8.1gd	[40]	4485

RUN ON 6 b h £0
11	15-17	Nott	6.1sft	54	1606
38	12-18	Bath	5.7g/f	53	1788
23	13-16	Brig	6fm	50	2262
19	16-18	Ling	6gd	50	2396
44	5-13	Bath	5gd	[46]	3143
48	5-5	Brig	5.3g/f	[46]	3720
0	15-16	Brig	6gd	[45]	4905 bl
26a	10-13	Wolv	5.1ap	[45]	5231

RUSKY DUSKY 2 b c £3901
44	11-13	Newb	6g/f		1760
79	3-10	Bath	5.7fm		2666
79	2-20	Wind	6fm		2970
57	5-11	Sali	6g/f	[79]	3863
75	5-7	Sand	5sft	79	4065
79	6-21	Donc	6fm	[75]	4490 VIS
61	6-16	Bath	5.7gd	[77]	4823 vis
74	4-10	Ling	6g/f	[77]	4893 BL

RUSSALKA 2 b f £2543
65a	2-13	Wolv	8.5af	[63]	111
60a	2-9	Wolv	9.4af	[66]	240
50a	10-14	Ling	10ap	[65]	367 P
45	15-15	Bath	8g/s	63	1099
40a	5-11	Wolv	8.5af	60	1339
0	8-11	Warw	12.6sft	57	1528
55	2-5	Brig	9.9fm	52	2837
54	6-16	Brig	9.9g/f	53	3175
36	7-12	Brig	9.9g/f	53	3300
38	6-10	Yarm	10.1gd	[51]	3874
6	13-15	Nott	10g/s	51	4037 VIS
28	10-14	Redc	10fm	50	4560 vis
46	5-18	Leic	7gd	[50]	4698
29	11-19	Kemp	8g/f	[47]	4795

RUSSIAN APPLAUSE 4 b g £330
53	9-13	Wind	8.3gd		3828
5	11-11	Folk	9.7gd		4120
69	4-14	Warw	7.1gd		4275
59	5-11	Wind	8.3g/f	[65]	5054

RUSSIAN BLUE 2 b c £103588
110	1-4	CURR	5g/f		1994*
109	2-7	Curr	6g/f		2819
115	3-6	Curr	6gd		3841
112	3-9	Deau	6sft		4159

109 3-7 Curr 7gd 4734
108 5-9 Newm 6g/f 4888

RUSSIAN CAFE 3 b f £1702
61 3-11 Good 6gd 5030 T
59 2-19 Redc 6g/s 5110 t

RUSSIAN COMRADE 8 b g £0
2 P-12 Chep 8.1g/s 67 3898

RUSSIAN CONSORT 2 ch c £4978
85a 2-13 Ling 7ap 3329
88a 1-11 LING 8ap 3786*
81 11-13 Newb 7sft [88] 5195

RUSSIAN DANCE 3 b r f £0
34 8-8 Pont 8g/f 98 2606

RUSSIAN GENERAL 2 b c £4105
75 1-6 BATH 5g/f 1786*

RUSSIAN HILL 4 ch f £26550
112 2-11 Chan 10sft 1699
114 2-11 Long 10.5g/f 4948

RUSSIAN ICON 3 b f £0
0 12-13 Ling 10ap 3288
23 10-10 Ling 14fm 3742

RUSSIAN REVOLUTION 2 b f £6322
85 3-15 Newm 8fm 4723 T
85 1-9 AYR 8sft 5033* t

RUSSIAN RHYTHM 4 ch f £116000
120 1-15 NEWB 8g/f [117] 1758+

RUSSIAN RIO 2 b g £0
42a 9-15 Sout 5af 4089
70 5-12 Carl 5g/f 4343
48 5-12 Beve 5g/f 4596

RUSSIAN ROCKET 2 b g £12016
51 7-11 Kemp 5hvy 1640
77 5-12 Ling 5g/f 1981
82 2-9 Brig 5.3fm 2257
81a 1-7 LING 5ap 2839*
82 2-12 Ling 5gd 77 3284
77a 5-10 Ling 5ap [80] 3743
58 17-24 Redc 6fm [79] 4928
85 1-8 YARM 5.2sft 79 5253*

RUSSIAN RUBY 3 b f £0
77 5-9 Newm 8g/f 84 3780

RUSSIAN SERVANA 2 b f £832
33 9-10 Bath 5.7fm 2666
57 2-9 Leic 5g/f 2921
50 5-10 Beve 5g/f 3504
31 5-5 Yarm 6gd [52] 3871

RUSSIAN SYMPHONY 3 ch c £1406
59 10-14 Folk 7g/s 1080
60 6-16 Sali 7sft 69 4582 BL
66 7-17 Ling 6gd 69 4740 bl
44 8-10 Ripo 6gd [65] 4788 bl
72a 2-12 Wolv 7.1ap 67 5008 bl

RUSSIAN VALOUR 3 b c £450
72 10-11 Newm 7gd 113 1167
21 6-6 Asco 6sft [113] 1421
87 7-12 Leic 7gd [108] 4454 BL
70 7-8 Yarm 6g/s [108] 4588 bl

RUSSIANNIGHTINGALE 2 b g £0
0 12-13 York 6gd 4988
10 9-9 Catt 7sft 5131

RUST EN VREDE 5 b g £4470
57a 1-13 SOUT 8af [45] 776*
67a 1-15 SOUT 8af 53 1028*

RUSTIC CHARM 4 b f £0
1 P-11 Leic 10gd [67] 4701

RUSTLER 2 b c £0
60a 7-13 Wolv 8.6ap 5355

RUSTY BOY 3 b f £0
35 7-7 Catt 7g/f 3194
0 7-7 Carl 11.9g/f 3226
0 9-9 Ripo 9g/f 38 3645

RUTLAND CHANTRY 10 b g £0
42 5-19 Warw 10.9sft 47 1090
37 10-17 Nott 14.1gd 47 1238

RUTTERS REBEL 3 b g £5854
64 5-7 Thir 12sft [74] 1226
8 9-9 Ches 12.3gd 72 1582
70 4-6 Redc 11g/f 72 2103
67 7-8 Hami 12.1g/f 72 2318
76 2-10 Leic 11.8gd [70] 2707
72 4-9 Ripo 12.3gd 72 2984
47 9-10 Ripo 12.3g/s 72 3261
74 1-7 AYR 10.9g/f 70 3765*
67 11-17 Thir 12fm 72 4377
72 6-9 Muss 12g/f 71 4553
61 9-12 Wind 11.6g/f 71 4833

RYANS BLISS 4 b f £3032
34a 8-12 Ling 8ap [55] 675
29a 8-10 Ling 8ap [50] 785
45a 2-11 Ling 10ap [40] 970
37a 5-14 Ling 10ap [40] 1072
45a 3-9 Ling 10ap [45] 1289
49a 2-14 Ling 10ap [45] 1712
38 8-12 Warw 10.9fm 44 2436
31 9-15 Warw 10.9g/f 44 2910
30a 10-14 Ling 10ap 44 3605
44 5-11 Ling 10fm 41 3748
57 6-11 Folk 9.7gd [40] 4120
61a 1-14 LING 10ap [45] 4661*
56a 3-12 Ling 8ap [57] 5077

RYANS FUTURE 3 b c £9677
77a 4-14 Ling 10ap 75 122
83a 1-14 LING 10ap 75 174*
81a 5-14 Ling 10ap 80 265
80a 5-14 Ling 10ap 80 452
70a 8-13 Ling 10ap 80 519
66 9-15 Epso 10.1gd [79] 3216
62 5-5 Kemp 8g/f [79] 3523
78 2-9 Sand 9g/s [74] 3892
74 7-14 Sand 10g/s 75 4097
74 4-13 Epso 10.1g/f 75 4473
77 5-15 Nott 10gd 75 4860
75 8-20 York 10.4gd 75 4986
83 1-16 NOTT 10hvy 73 5345*

RYANS LIL OL GAL 2 b f £0
16 14-15 Warw 5g/s 1325
0 12-12 Sout 5af 1439
0 11-11 Ripo 6g/f 1779

RYANS QUEST 5 b m £826
47a 8-9 Ling 5ap [48] 1023
28 15-15 Ling 5g/f 45 2062
30 8-12 Brig 5.3g/f 42 2645
54 3-9 Kemp 5g/f [39] 3687

RYDAL 3 ch c £10845
80a 13-15 Ling 7ap [89] 885 bl
84 4-8 Muss 7.1g/s 89 1460
69 11-20 York 6g/f 87 2407 bl
77 6-9 Newm 5fm 83 2593 bl
84 2-10 Hayd 6g/s 80 3135 bl
82 4-12 Hayd 6sft 80 3273 bl
78 7-21 Good 5fm 84 3567 bl
88 1-8 SAND 5g/s 83 3889* VIS
88 4-7 Sand 5g/s 87 4099 vis
82 8-13 Asco 6.5g/f 87 4773 bl
81 8-13 Muss 5g/s 86 5143 vis

RYE 3 b f £1463
57a 1-10 LING 8ap 785*
66a 6-6 Ling 12ap 70 915
60 7-10 Folk 12g/s 70 1082
0 4-6 Chep 12.1sft [65] 1331

RYEDANE 2 b c £1168
24 9-10 Newc 6sft 1677
71 3-7 Redc 5g/f 2100
63 9-13 Carl 5gd 2670
55 5-9 Pont 5g/f 70 2989
68 3-8 Donc 5g/f 66 3374
56 7-12 Hayd 5gd 65 3756
46 12-19 Carl 5.9g/f 65 4344

RYMERS RASCAL 12 b g £7766
49 3-11 Pont 8sft 49 1425

52 2-18 Thir 8g/f 49 1972
46 8-13 Carl 7.9fm 51 2447
45 8-15 Thir 8g/s [51] 2688
52 2-17 Hayd 8.1gd 49 2947
27 15-17 Hayd 8.1gd 49 3759
43 6-17 Thir 8g/s 49 3830
52 1-15 THIR 8fm [48] 4379*
53 2-17 Pont 8g/f 48 4626
54 3-11 Ayr 9.1sft [49] 5067

RYONO 5 ch h £25704
120 1-6 DEAU 8sft 3168*

SAADA ONE 3 b f £0
54a 4-14 Ling 10ap 53

SAADIGG 2 b c £4609
77a 3-13 Ling 7ap 3330
72a 4-11 Ling 8ap 3786
89 1-8 HAYD 8.1g/f 4351*
73 6-7 Leic 10gd [87] 5044

SAAMEQ 3 b g £1025
49 6-11 Donc 10.3gd 930
4 7-8 Pont 10hvy 1067
3 7-7 Ayr 9.1gd 45 2509
46 3-10 Muss 12g/f 42 2813
51 4-8 Hami 11.1g/f 43 3207
51 4-7 Ayr 10.9g/f 49 3765

SABALARA 4 b f £0
56 8-16 Sout 7g/s 63 1049
40 7-14 Hayd 8.1g/s 61 1348
0 15-15 Redc 7sft 58 1660
38 13-20 Yarm 8fm 55 2149 e

SABANA 5 b g £5964
25a 11-13 Wolv 5af 47 110
26a 4-12 Wolv 6af [44] 297
35a 3-13 Wolv 6af [45] 397
41a 5-13 Ling 6ap 45 448 bl
28a 9-11 Wolv 7af [45] 579 bl
54a 1-12 WOLV 6af [45] 646* bl
41a 3-15 Sout 6af [52] 773 bl
11a 11-12 Ling 6ap 50 844 bl
42a 6-13 Wolv 6af 48 1221 bl
0 13-15 Folk 6g/s 47 1267 bl
33 8-11 Redc 6sft [45] 1662
38 11-18 Wind 6g/f [45] 1806 bl
8 14-20 Nott 6.1gd 43 2928
50 1-19 NOTT 6.1gd [41] 3104* P
46 6-14 Ling 6gd 48 3289 p
30 9-18 Thir 6fm 47 3609 p

SABANDER BAY 3 b f £0
51 8-10 Sali 6g/s 4081
37 8-10 Sali 8sft 4578

SABBAAG 3 ch c £4537
74a 2-5 Wolv 7af 425
78a 1-7 SOUT 8af 460*
23a 10-10 Ling 10ap 76 568 T

SABBEEH 3 b c £5997
95 9-14 Newb 7g/f [110] 4638 T
99 1-5 AYR 8sft [110] 5038* t

SABBIOSA 2 b f £0
49 7-7 Newm 6g/f 2733
58 10-15 Folk 7gd 3381
64 8-12 Folk 7gd 3908
61 7-15 Good 8g/s 4233

SABLE N SILK 2 b f £3010
49a 6-12 Wolv 6af 42
59a 1-13 WOLV 6af 126*
43a 11-11 Ling 7ap 68 261
21a 7-9 Wolv 7af 61 510
2a 6-6 Wolv 6af 57 615 BL

SABO PRINCE 2 ch c £0
30 7-11 Ripo 6g/f 1779
39 5-5 Brig 6g/f 1937
37 9-9 Brig 5.3fm 2257
39 8-9 Chep 5.1g/f 2625

SABRELINE 4 ch f £0
41a 5-11 Wolv 12af 45 72
46a 5-10 Wolv 12af [45] 154

5a	14-16	Sout	16af	48	206
0	9-9	Wolv	9.4af	[45]	525 BL

SABRINA BROWN 2 br f £10223

53a	7-11	Ling	6ap		51
54a	6-11	Ling	7ap		220
61	2-11	Sali	6gd	55	2661
68	2-14	Chep	8.1g/s	60	3090
38	14-17	Newb	7g/f	60	3257
62	6-10	Hayd	8.1g/s	64	3906
75	1-19	CHEP	6.1sft	63	4054+ T
76	2-8	Good	7sft	71	4263 t
57	14-16	Good	7gd	72	4873

SACCHARINE 3 b f £515

26	10-10	Newm	8g/f		2732
43	3-6	Folk	5g/f		3725
36	6-7	Brig	5g/f	[44]	3985
25a	7-9	Sout	7af	[44]	4131

SACHIN 2 b c £4468

58a	10-11	Ling	8ap	72	54 BL
53a	7-11	Ling	6ap	67	735
43a	6-8	Ling	7ap	65	933
25	9-9	Ling	7gd	67	3447
62	4-7	Epso	8.5g/f	[62]	4474
69	1-15	BATH	6gd	64	4827*
65	3-13	Pont	8g/s	[65]	5153
60	8-18	Newm	8sft	65	5272
56a	7-13	Wolv	8.6ap	[65]	5336

SACHO 6 br g £5634

94	3-10	Bade	6gd		2140

SACHSENWALZER 6 ch g £0

40	9-11	Leic	10gd	53	2135

SACRANUN 2 ch c £1088

87	3-12	Hayd	6sft		3272
78	7-14	Hayd	6fm		4385
75	4-12	Hayd	6sft		4770

SACRED NUTS 2 b c £17553

62	5-13	Donc	6gd		2236
84	1-7	HAMI	6g/f		2473*
95	1-9	ASCO	6gd	83	3127*
88	3-8	Asco	7gd		3467
90	5-11	Newm	6g/f	93	3614
102	4-11	York	6g/s	[93]	4022

SACSAYHUAMAN 5 b m £0

0	7-7	Sout	12af	[57]	594

SADDLERS QUEST 7 b g £0

40	13-16	Hayd	10.5sft	63	3276
41	9-14	Wind	11.6fm	60	3638
30	8-9	Ches	12.3sft	55	4076 P
19	13-16	Carl	11.9g/f	50	4348

SADIE JANE 3 b f £0

0	10-10	Wolv	7af		8

SADIE THOMPSON 2 b f £5954

72	8-13	Newb	7g/f		3252
79	1-12	WARW	7.1g/f		4418*

SADIES STAR 2 b f £0

57	8-11	Thir	7fm		4381
55	5-10	Newc	7fm		4864
21a	12-13	Wolv	8.6ap		5288

SADLERS PRIDE 4 b c £3604

69	2-8	Hami	11.1gd		1390
70	2-10	Nott	14.1sft	[72]	1742
62	4-4	Hayd	14g/s	72	2229
40	12-13	Beve	12.1g/f	70	3502
2	15-15	Chep	18sft	65	4056
52	8-14	York	11.9gd	63	4327 T
56	5-14	Catt	12g/f	60	4672

SADLERS ROCK 6 b g £0

59a	9-15	Ling	12ap		4111
69	7-7	Wind	11.6g/s		4219

SADLERS SWING 8 b g £414

40a	2-12	Wolv	8.5af	[40]	777
39a	4-9	Wolv	9.4af	[40]	821
15	9-10	Warw	8.1g/s	[40]	1328

SAFA PARK 3 ch c £0

50	8-8	Ling	9g/f		2013
67	9-13	Kemp	10gd		3186 T

SAFARI SUNSET 2 b c £13389

92	1-18	LEIC	5fm		2109*
102	3-15	Asco	5g/f		2472
81	4-5	Chep	5.1g/s		3086
97	3-13	Good	5g/f		3509
91	8-8	Kemp	6fm	[99]	4390
88	9-11	Donc	5g/f	[99]	4533

SAFENDONSEABISCUIT 2 b c £8245

70	5-7	Good	6g/f		1848
82	3-10	Donc	6g/f		2077
79	3-14	Folk	7fm		2714
71	4-8	Brig	7gd		2952
75	2-14	Leic	6g/f	77	3212
49	10-11	Newm	6g/f	78	3614 BL
48	12-13	Warw	6.1gd	73	4273
73	3-9	Brig	6fm	70	4758
83	1-18	PONT	6g/f	70	4934*
65	18-29	Newm	6gd		5087

SAFFA GARDEN 2 b f £0

59	8-12	Ripo	5g/f		1974
61	10-10	Newm	5g/f		3064
50	11-11	Sali	6gd		4332

SAFFRON FOX 3 ch f £3310

86	4-9	Hayd	8.1sft	87	1105
80	7-9	Sand	10g/s	87	1318
82	4-13	Sand	8.1g/s	[83]	2126
83	2-11	Asco	8gd	[81]	3128
49	10-10	Newb	10fm	79	3630
63	7-8	Ripo	10g/s	79	3938
75	5-7	Pont	8g/f	79	4935 P
19	18-19	Donc	10.3sft	76	5201 p

SAFFRON RIVER 2 b c £0

32a	10-12	Wolv	6af		42
58a	4-6	Sout	6af	59	182
41a	5-12	Wolv	6ap	[56]	5157

SAFIRAH 3 b f £5258

68	3-6	Ling	10g/f		2843
68	5-13	Kemp	10gd		3186
72	5-11	Wind	10fm		3802
61	10-19	Hayd	10.5g/s	72	4766
75	2-18	Bath	10.2gd	[69]	5023
73	1-8	REDC	10sft	[69]	5306*

SAFRANINE 6 b m £499

45a	9-13	Wolv	6af	60	45 p
45a	10-15	Sout	5af	57	187 p
30a	11-14	Ling	6ap	52	328 p
36a	10-11	Wolv	5af	48	507 p
19a	12-16	Sout	5af	[45]	720 p
50	9-15	Ripo	6g/f	70	1782
59	9-10	Thir	7g/f	[70]	1970
55	10-11	Newm	6fm	67	2093
51	9-10	Donc	5g/f	63	2429 p
15	16-17	Redc	6gd	63	2561 p
50	8-17	Warw	5fm	63	2599 p
62	6-6	Hami	8.3gd	[63]	2710
59	9-9	Warw	5.5fm	60	2779 p
39	17-17	Catt	5g/f	60	2846 p
31	14-14	Thir	6g/f	61	3416
59	6-8	Donc	6g/f	[61]	3596

SAFSOOF 2 b c £6071

85	2-8	Kemp	5gd		2171
87	10-15	Asco	5g/f		2472
97a	1-6	SOUT	5af		3484*
92	3-6	Beve	5g/f	[93]	4717

SAHAAT 5 b g £5951

78a	8-10	Ling	10ap	[97]	179
0	12-12	Ling	8ap	[97]	234
80a	7-12	Wolv	8.5af	89	836
30	22-24	Donc	8gd	84	928
43	14-20	Wind	11.6g/s	78	1056
52	14-18	Nott	14.1g/s	74	1772
74	5-8	Chep	10.2g/f	73	2628
39	10-12	Nott	8.2g/s	72	2931 BL
74a	2-14	Sout	8af	[70]	3392
69	5-16	Wind	11.6gd	70	3829
64	8-16	Nott	8.2g/s	70	4036
67	4-11	Wind	10gd	[69]	4124

43	6-12	Chep	12.1g/s	[68]	4364
66	7-15	Nott	10g/f	65	4849
68	4-17	Newc	10.1g/f	64	5016
74	1-19	PONT	10g/s	64	5148*

SAHARA MIST 2 b f £0

27	14-15	Donc	5gd		920
51a	6-7	Sout	5af		1029
48	5-6	Nott	5.1sft		1466
35	12-15	Nott	5.1gd		3988 VIS
47	10-11	Pont	8fm	45	4753

SAHARA PRINCE 4 b c £9854

86	1-6	HAYD	6g/s	74	3903+

SAHARA SCIROCCO 3 b g £0

2a	14-14	Ling	7ap	[61]	5080
0	11-12	Wolv	8.6ap	61	5116

SAHARA SILK 3 b f £8830

26a	10-11	Sout	5af	68	418 vis
0	14-14	Sout	5af	65	485 vis
49a	6-11	Sout	6af	60	591 vis
69a	1-11	SOUT	5af	60	609* vis
67a	3-8	Ling	6ap	66	673 vis
64a	4-10	Ling	5ap	67	712 vis
70a	1-11	SOUT	5af	66	872* vis
70a	2-4	Wolv	5af	[68]	1338 vis
0	8-8	Sout	5af	68	1441 vis
70a	3-11	Sout	5af	68	2380 vis
0	12-12	Ayr	5g/s	62	2566 vis
50	9-11	Newm	5g/f	62	2734 vis
51	7-14	Catt	6g/f	58	3018 vis

SAHARA STORM 3 b f £0

63a	10-12	Ling	7ap	74	1024
62	10-17	Kemp	7gd	72	2174

SAHARAN SONG 3 ch f £0

62	12-19	Newb	8gd		1236
33	9-12	Ripo	9g/f		1784
45	9-14	Wind	10gd	62	2617
3	12-13	Nott	10g/s	[59]	4650
26a	12-13	Wolv	8.6ap	55	5005

SAHEM 7 b g £22711

75	5-14	Donc	18gd	80	926
74	7-14	Hami	12.1gd	78	1389
78	4-10	Hami	13gd	78	1506
72	7-18	York	13.9g/s	76	1689
81	1-10	CARL	14.1fm	73	2444*
81	2-9	Ayr	13.1g/s	79	2567
53	17-17	Asco	16.2gd	82	3125
79	3-6	Pont	12gd	80	3681
81	3-9	Pont	12g/s	78	3969
87	1-8	HAMI	13g/s	78	4138*
76	12-20	Hayd	14fm	84	4383
87	3-9	Muss	12g/f	83	4553
75	6-7	Hami	13g/s	83	4819

SAHOOL 3 b f £87450

103	2-9	Newm	10fm	[86]	1494
103	2-7	Newb	10gd	[86]	1733
109	2-9	Asco	12g/f	[103]	2517
108	2-8	Hayd	11.9gd	[107]	2946
101	1-9	NEWB	12fm	[107]	3629*
89	5-8	York	11.9g/s	[107]	4024

SAIDA LENASERA 3 b f £0

59	9-14	York	11.9g/s	76	1708
67	6-9	Donc	10.3g/f	72	2079
64	6-10	Newm	12g/f	69	2530
29	10-12	Beve	9.9g/s	64	3854
64	5-14	Chep	10.2gd	63	4487
63	5-20	Catt	12gd	63	4966
54a	7-16	Ling	12ap	[60]	5296

SAIF SAREEA 4 b g £0

39	11-13	Hami	6g/f	48	2315
24	8-8	Hami	6gd	52	2713
2	14-16	Redc	8g/s	48	2958

SAILING THROUGH 4 b g £0

81	13-13	Asco	10g/f	[92]	4772

SAILMAKER 3 ch g £3440

77	2-11	Bath	8g/s		1101
67	3-12	Kemp	8hvy		1511
78	7-13	Bath	10.2g/f	[75]	1791

78	3-8	Good	9.9gd	75	2377 T
72	4-6	Sali	9.9gd	[75]	2663 t

SAILORMAN 3 b g £0

63a	9-13	Ling	10ap	2066

SAINT CLEMENTS 2 b c £0

51	9-14	Donc	6g/f	1874
41	10-13	Donc	6gd	2236
31	4-4	Newc	8hvy	4212

SAINT ETIENNE 3 b f £4855

76a	1-15	LING	7ap		670*
91	5-8	Newm	7g/f		1932
90	10-12	Good	7fm	[90]	3564

SAINT LAZARE 3 b c £0

23	16-17	Leic	10g/s	1019

SAINT ZITA 3 b f £0

48a	7-12	Ling	8ap	623
23a	10-14	Ling	10ap	759
1	7-8	Warw	10.9gd	3055 BL

SAINTLY PLACE 3 ch g £778

36	12-13	Sali	6g/s	63	3109
39	13-15	Newb	6gd	60	3920
27	15-19	Chep	6.1sft	60	4054
45	5-14	Bath	8gd	50	4411
56	2-15	Yarm	7g/s	[50]	4587
31	8-13	Warw	7.1g/s	[50]	4994
30a	9-12	Wolv	7.1ap	[48]	5229

SAINTLY SCHOLAR 3 b f £0

50a	10-15	Ling	7ap	814
55a	9-15	Ling	7ap	875
65a	5-11	Ling	7ap	1008

SAINTLY THOUGHTS 9 b g £0

0	15-18	Nott	14.1sft	50	1469 p

SAKE 2 b g £0

33	12-12	Newc	8fm	4866 T
47	12-16	York	7.9gd	4997

SALAGAMA 4 br f £2273

78	4-15	Hami	8.3g/s	85	1602
86	3-5	Sand	8g/f	85	2191
39	9-10	Newm	8g/f	83	2767
18	20-20	Newm	8fm	83	3001 BL

SALAMANCA 2 ch f £152141

97	1-10	NEWB	6gd		3917*
96	1-26	NEWB	6.5g/f		4679*
95	6-14	Newm	7g/f	[94]	4914

SALAMBA 3 ch c £0

58	5-7	Muss	9g/s		1462
66	10-12	Sand	14g/f	72	3359
60	8-9	Hayd	14gd	70	3760
60	5-20	York	13.9gd	66	5004
61	7-12	Redc	14.1g/s	66	5108
66	7-10	Pont	18g/s	65	5151

SALDENTIGERIN 3 b f £24648

112	2-9	Colo	12sft	4841

SALEEN 4 b f £0

23a	10-12	Ling	8ap	401

SALERNO 4 ch g £0

41a	11-12	Wolv	5af	55	124
41a	7-11	Wolv	6af	[53]	153 p
43a	7-9	Wolv	5af	50	275 p
22a	8-10	Wolv	5af	[50]	286 p
16a	9-9	Sout	5af	[50]	335 bl

SALFORD CITY 3 b c £68160

117	1-10	NEWB	7gd		1234+
116	6-14	Newm	8g/f	[115]	1480
114	5-14	Epso	12fm	[115]	2254
109	9-12	Sand	10g/s	[115]	2916

SALFORD FLYER 8 b g £813

39a	12-12	Ling	13ap	70	877
36a	6-10	Ling	12ap	[70]	916 BL
50	7-18	Bath	10.2g/s	60	1098 bl
47	3-10	Bath	10.2gd	[54]	1402 bl
49	3-17	Bath	11.7sft	54	1543 bl
12	16-18	Wind	11.6g/f	49	1960 bl

SALFORD ROCKET 4 b g £0

5a	8-9	Wolv	9.4af		1340
28	9-10	Folk	9.7sft		1580
29	6-7	Brig	11.9g/f		1939
0	9-10	Hami	12g/f	30	2479
12a	6-16	Sout	14af	30	4045
2	9-10	Yarm	14.1g/s	29	4255

SALINJA 2 b c £3824

81	3-8	Newm	8g/f	3473
81	3-13	Sali	7sft	4576
84	2-15	Newm	8gd	4883

SALINOR 4 ch g £7440

79	1-18	WIND	8.3gd	70	1385*
82	1-12	KEMP	8g/f	[75]	1915*
70	16-17	Carl	7.9gd	80	2672
82	6-11	Yarm	8gd	80	4615
58	12-12	Good	8gd	[79]	4872

SALISBURY PLAIN 3 b c £0

50	10-13	Kemp	9hvy	82	1515
50	18-18	Good	9g/f	80	1813

SALLY TRAFFIC 4 b f £0

0	15-16	Sout	7af	[35]	66 p
18a	7-12	Sout	6af	[30]	377

SALON PRIVE 3 b g £2504

66a	2-14	Ling	6ap	[68]	23
42a	9-13	Ling	6ap	65	902
21	15-15	Brig	8fm	63	1691 BL
68a	2-11	Ling	6ap	63	3333
47	6-12	Newm	6g/f	60	3751
58	2-20	Chep	6.1g/s	53	4368
25	11-19	Yarm	6g/s	55	4636

SALONIKA SKY 3 ch f £0

0	12-13	Wolv	6af	[45]	397
16a	6-11	Sout	5af	[35]	578
7a	12-14	Sout	5af	[35]	637 BL
23	6-6	Muss	5g/f	[40]	2808 bl
8	14-14	Catt	6g/f	[35]	3191

SALSA BRAVA 2 b f £48180

84	1-19	WIND	5g/f		1805*
100	3-17	Asco	6fm		2553
105	2-10	Newm	6fm		3003
105	2-8	York	6g/s	[100]	4059
99	4-9	Newb	6g/f	[100]	4680

SALSALINO 4 ch c £750

103	6-17	Newb	12gd	[107]	1230
68	3-10	York	13.9g/s	[107]	1705
81	12-14	Good	12g/f	[107]	1843
85	15-19	York	13.9g/s	103	4023
79	15-15	Donc	14.6fm	100	4491

SALSELON 5 b h £115639

96	9-10	Sand	8.1g/s		1349
121	2-15	Newb	8g/f	[113]	1758 BL
119	3-16	Asco	8g/f	[118]	2470 bl
108	7-10	Asco	8gd	[118]	3124 bl
113	5-10	Deau	8sft	[118]	4017
115	2-4	York	8.9gd	[118]	4323 VIS
107	3-7	Good	9.9g/f	[118]	4538 bl
111	2-13	Newm	8g/f	[116]	4887 bl
112	6-11	Newm	10sft	[116]	5136 bl

SALTANGO 5 b h £2655

67a	8-14	Ling	10ap	72	2392
77	3-19	Carl	11.9gd	72	2673
74	5-11	Sand	14g/f	73	3340

SALUT SAINT CLOUD 2 b c £10679

50a	4-15	Sout	7af	[45]	87 vis
41a	5-16	Sout	8af	[50]	164 vis
32	6-16	Redc	8sft	50	1147 vis
41	8-12	Thir	7g/f	[48]	2215
48a	5-15	Sout	7af	48	2384 vis
54	1-8	REDC	10gd	[46]	2548*
54	3-7	Brig	11.9fm	52	2836
60a	3-14	Sout	12af	53	3486
53	3-7	Brig	11.9g/f	[53]	3715
63a	1-16	SOUT	14af	53	4045* p
19a	4-8	Sout	12af	53	4092 p
72	1-8	CHEP	16.2g/s	53	4302* p
58	8-14	Warw	16.2g/f	59	4423 p

SALUT THOMAS 2 ch c £52570

87	3-7	Chan	5gd	3008 bl
99	3-7	Deau	6gd	3658 bl
109	3-9	Chan	5.5gd	4563 bl
111	2-9	Mais	6sft	5312 bl

SALVIATI 7 b g £10271

35	20-20	York	5g/s	90	1683
61	12-15	Hayd	5g/f	89	1917
65	16-17	Muss	5fm	87	2082
65	23-29	Asco	6fm	87	2581
72	12-15	Newc	5g/s	84	2727
63	15-16	Newm	5g/f	80	3033
59	8-12	Bath	5.7gd	80	3146 P
63	12-17	Pont	5gd	80	3241 p
79	4-13	Catt	5g/f	77	3350 p
78	5-22	Good	5fm	75	3537 p
86	1-14	NEWB	5.2fm	77	3628+ p
64	18-20	Hayd	5fm	83	3792 p
77	10-13	Newb	5.2g/f	83	3960 p
50	10-11	Bath	5g/s	[82]	4201 p
55	9-12	Yarm	5.2g/s	80	4585

SAM THE SORCERER 3 b g £1914

41	9-11	Nott	6.1sft		1607
48a	1-9	WOLV	6af	[45]	1803*
3a	9-10	Sout	7af	[51]	1842
47	3-13	Newc	6sft	45	2683
33	11-15	Newc	6hvy	45	4211
12	16-18	Yarm	6g/s	45	5354

SAMALAN 2 b g £0

18	9-12	Newm	5gd	1869
38	11-13	Beve	5gd	2889

SAMANDO 4 ch f £57570

110	3-10	Sain	10g/s	833
114	3-11	Chan	10sft	1699
115	1-11	LONG	10.5g/f	4948*

SAMAR QAND 4 b f £684

27a	6-12	Wolv	8.5af	[49]	47 p
27a	5-12	Wolv	12af	[49]	114 p
34a	3-11	Sout	11af	[41]	191 p
36a	5-12	Wolv	9.4af	[38]	302 p
30a	3-12	Sout	11af	[35]	640
36a	3-16	Sout	11af	[35]	852 T
12a	4-9	Sout	11af	[35]	906 t
3	13-14	Sout	12g/s	[35]	1047 t

SAMARA SOUND 3 b c £0

7a	10-10	Sout	6af	45	592
60a	6-12	Ling	6ap	[40]	1044
37	13-14	Bath	5gd	55	1404

SAMARIA 3 b f £2281

19	13-17	Wind	11.6fm		2788
75	4-11	Wind	10fm		3802
75	2-10	Yarm	11.5gd		3997
65	4-11	Ripo	12.3gd	[74]	4281
69a	3-14	Ling	13ap	[72]	4898 VIS
84	7-12	Yarm	14.1sft	[70]	5254

SAMBA BEAT 5 ch m £0

7a	11-13	Sout	8af	[45]	776
0	9-10	Sout	8af	45	791
0	9-9	Sout	11af	[35]	906 bl
0	8-10	Sout	7af	[35]	1839

SAMBARINA 2 b f £586

73	3-12	Hayd	6gd	2902
67	5-14	Leic	6g/f	3517

SAMMAGEFROMTENESSE 7 b g £366

36a	2-14	Ling	10ap	[35]	4662 p

SAMMYS SHUFFLE 8 b g £0

51a	6-14	Ling	10ap	58	101 bl
56a	7-14	Ling	10ap	57	174 bl
50a	5-14	Ling	10ap	56	236 bl
45a	9-14	Ling	10ap	53	622 bl
50a	4-14	Ling	10ap	50	718 bl
48a	7-13	Ling	10ap	50	805 bl
36	9-13	Brig	11.9g/f	48	1373 bl
20	11-12	Brig	9.9fm	48	1695 bl
47	4-16	Yarm	10.1fm	47	2146 bl
36a	8-14	Ling	10.1fm	46	2589 bl
44	5-9	Yarm	10.1fm	45	2866 bl

SAMOLIS 2 b g £0

0	10-10	Sout	8af	35	190 BL

SAMS SECRET 2 b f £4919

75	2-20	York	6g/f		4401
76	3-5	Pont	5g/f		4625
75	2-10	Nott	6.1gd		4858
53	12-14	Donc	7sft	72	5213

SAMSON QUEST 2 b c £0

75a	5-13	Ling	7ap		3330
62	9-14	Sali	7sft		4575

SAMUEL CHARLES 6 b g £22749

61a	1-12	**LING**	8ap	55	1013*
64a	2-8	Wolv	8.5af	60	1219
64	3-15	Brig	8fm	63	1691
70	1-12	**REDC**	8g/f	[63]	1823*
74	2-12	Ayr	7.2fm	70	1909
74	2-4	Redc	7g/f	[72]	2122
76	3-7	Good	7gd	[72]	2374
73	3-12	Ayr	8g/s	[72]	2543
71	4-13	Ayr	7.2g/s	72	2568
77	2-10	Leic	7g/f	[71]	2920
17	11-11	Yarm	7gd	71	3364
78	1-6	**BRIG**	7fm	[70]	3696*
74	6-13	Redc	7fm	[75]	4341
57	10-13	Muss	7.1gd	75	4806
76a	1-10	**WOLV**	7.1ap	[75]	4920*
77a	4-12	Wolv	7.1ap	[75]	5006
80a	3-12	Wolv	7.1ap	75	5289

SAN ANTONIO 4 b g £0

53	8-10	Warw	7.1sft	[82]	1525
58	6-6	Sand	10g/f	79	3358
23	12-12	Leic	8fm	73	3813

SAN DENG 2 gr c £642

49	8-8	Asco	6g/f		3438
65	3-7	Folk	6g/f		3722
40	13-17	Chep	6.1sft		4052
44	14-17	Ling	6gd	[63]	4443
49a	8-11	Ling	6ap	60	4972

SAN DIMAS 7 gr g £0

18	9-11	Muss	16g/f	35	3557 vis

SAN HERNANDO 4 b g £7238

69	6-14	Kemp	14.4sft	73	948
73	4-18	Newb	16gd	73	1232
66	10-17	Sali	14.1g/s	72	1502
68	7-14	Asco	16.2g/f	71	1928
73	4-15	Newb	13.3g/f	69	2311
63	9-10	Sali	14.1gd	71	2699
73	4-11	Ling	16gd	70	3200
71	2-13	Sali	14.1gd	70	3454
69	8-12	Sand	16.4g/f	70	3861
69	8-16	Kemp	16g/f	68	4361
41	19-19	Sali	14.1gd	68	4856
75	1-15	**GOOD**	16gd	65	5025*
75	3-11	Newm	16sft	68	5271

SAN LORENZO 3 ch f £2265

59	8-12	Good	7g/f		1846
66	3-16	Hayd	6g/f		2182
67	2-9	Ripo	6g/f		2485

SAN MARCO 6 b g £0

14a	11-13	Sout	14af	45	590 p
14a	7-11	Wolv	12af	[45]	666 bl

SANBONAH 3 b f £0

21	14-14	Newm	8g/f	72	1930

SANCHI 2 b c £1087

93	3-11	Donc	8fm		4462

SAND AND STARS 3 ch f £16132

67	3-6	Redc	11g/f	69	2103
69	5-12	Sand	10gd	69	2366
75	2-8	Thir	12g/s	68	2691
84	1-9	**RIPO**	12.3gd	70	2984*
85	2-13	Pont	12gd	76	3240
72	8-13	York	13.9g/s	81	4062
83	3-11	Epso	12gd	81	4468
84	2-6	Good	12gd	82	5028

SAND IRON 2 b f £283

67a	6-8	Ling	7ap		4447

SAND N SEA 3 b f £0

37	16-19	Asco	8g/f	87	2491

SAND REPEAL 2 b g £2009

68	7-12	Newm	7g/f		3470
76	3-9	Yarm	8sft		4147
77	2-10	Nott	10hvy		5188

SANDENISTA 3 b f £0

67a	7-11	Ling	8ap	72	80

SANDGATE CYGNET 3 ch f £5306

56a	6-13	Wolv	5af	61	110
59a	4-16	Sout	5af	59	183 p
65a	1-9	**WOLV**	5af	58	275* p
66a	1-10	**WOLV**	6af	58	282* p

SANDOKAN 3 b g £0

51	7-11	Folk	9.7gd		4120
13	11-11	Wind	8.3g/f		5052
58	7-12	Nott	10hvy		5190
17	8-12	Catt	12sft		5319

SANDORRA 6 b m £3358

38a	3-9	Sout	7af	[43]	304
47a	1-13	**SOUT**	7af	[45]	356+
35a	6-10	Sout	8af	46	463
15a	11-12	Wolv	8.5af	46	564
18a	10-13	Sout	8af	[45]	776
50a	1-7	**SOUT**	7af	[45]	1590*
46	6-15	Redc	7sft	51	1660
5a	12-16	Sout	7af	47	2335
32a	8-13	Sout	7af	47	3155
41	5-15	Ayr	7.2hvy	46	4088

SANDRONE 3 b f £0

11a	14-15	Ling	7ap	[53]	117 BL

SANDY BAY 5 b g £1154

0	12-12	Wolv	12af	[45]	891
37	8-11	Muss	9g/f	[40]	1095 P
32	8-14	Ayr	7.2gd	[37]	3324
28	11-14	Catt	12g/f	[35]	3668
39	4-5	Hami	9.2g/s	[35]	3876
36	12-13	Newc	10.1g/f	30	4406
52	3-6	Muss	12gd	[30]	4805
60	5-10	Muss	12g/s	[30]	5145

SANDYS LEGEND 2 ch c £1114

46	11-15	Newm	8gd		4883
66a	5-12	Wolv	8.6ap		5115
67a	2-13	Wolv	8.6ap		5355 VIS

SANGIOVESE 4 b g £23672

79a	1-14	**SOUT**	8af	63	195+
69a	10-14	Ling	10ap	69	452
74a	3-10	Sout	7af	78	611
74a	3-12	Wolv	8.5af	78	688
66	5-13	Kemp	7sft	68	945
70	2-12	Hayd	8.1g/f	66	1485
69	3-12	Bath	8g/f	66	1792
76	1-12	**NEWB**	10g/f	67	2354*
77	1-6	**KEMP**	12g/s	73	2681*
74	7-15	Newm	12g/f	78	3066
74	5-15	Bath	11.7g/f	76	3964
64	14-19	Kemp	10fm	76	4392
76	5-17	Wind	10g/f	75	5050
85	1-14	**NEWB**	8hvy	74	5227*

SANT JORDI 2 b c £15250

78a	3-7	Ling	6ap		3196
87	1-17	**WIND**	8g/f		3975*
94	2-11	Sali	7gd	[80]	4853
101	3-5	Curr	8g/s	[80]	5071

SANTA CATALINA 4 br f £323

45a	3-13	Sout	8af	[35]	199 t
20a	7-14	Sout	8af	[45]	354 t
31a	10-12	Ling	8ap	[45]	648 t
41a	5-10	Sout	8af	45	792
33a	4-10	Sout	8af	[45]	850
4a	10-11	Wolv	12af	40	937
18a	13-14	Ling	10ap	[40]	1072 p

SANTA CATERINA 3 b f £3379

77	4-10	Sali	9.9g/f		1718

SANTA FE 2 b c £8811

80	5-7	Yarm	6g/f		3709
93	1-15	**LEIC**	7g/f		4455*
100	4-9	Newm	7gd	[91]	4881

SANTANDO 4 b c £5335

97a	5-16	Ling	12ap	98	293 vis
99a	3-13	Ling	10ap	97	433 vis
70	14-15	Hayd	11.9gd	97	2948 vis
86	8-14	York	13.9gd	94	3119 vis
95	4-15	Good	14g/f	90	3510 vis
80	9-10	Asco	16.2gd	90	3776 vis
83	12-19	York	13.9g/s	90	4023 vis
79	10-15	Donc	14.6fm	90	4491 vis
81	8-13	Donc	12sft	88	5215

SANTIBURI LAD 7 b g £10132

54	3-11	Beve	9.9sft	54	1633
64	2-6	Ripo	12.3g/f	54	1980
69	1-11	**HAYD**	10.5g/s	54	2226*
67	1-5	**BEVE**	9.9sft	57	2943*
72	2-10	Hayd	10.5g/s	66	3139
48	17-19	Beve	9.9g/f	68	3505
63	8-19	York	7.9g/f	68	4399
63	7-19	Hayd	10.5g/s	67	4766
20	14-17	Newc	10.1g/f	65	5016

SAOIRE 2 ch f £28730

105	3-12	Curr	7g/f		4432
105	2-9	Curr	7sft		4958

SAORSIE 6 b g £0

23a	7-13	Ling	16ap	40	3822

SAPOSCAT 4 b g £0

27	8-8	Bath	10.2g/f		3370 T

SAPPHIRE DREAM 2 b f £13010

77	2-8	Pont	5hvy		1249
86	2-9	Ches	5.1gd		1567
86	1-9	**HAYD**	6g/f		1920*
84	6-12	Beve	5g/f		2165
52	17-17	Asco	6g/f		2553
83	4-5	Hayd	6fm	[84]	3795
82	4-10	Ches	5.1g/f	83	4049
62	11-21	Donc	6g/f	[80]	4490

SAPPHIRE PRINCESS 2 b f £2940

35	4-6	Folk	5g/f		2270
54	5-9	Chep	5.1g/f		2625
52	5-8	Bath	6g/f		2977
41	6-8	Yarm	6gd		3491
57a	1-8	**LING**	6ap	[51]	3745*
55	5-9	Bath	5g/f	[50]	3847
38	7-7	Yarm	6gd	[54]	3994
11	19-20	Leic	7g/f	47	4451

SAPPHIRE SKY 3 b f £0

13a	12-12	Ling	6ap		1044
3	12-13	Folk	5sft		1575
0	15-15	Nott	5.1g/f		2152

SARAH BROWN 2 b f £0

28	7-7	Bath	5.7fm		1900
48	10-14	Folk	5fm		2714 VIS
50	10-14	Sali	8g/s		4078 P
0	10-11	Chep	8.1g/s		4296 p

SARATAN 7 b g £10282

110	2-10	Long	7g/s		2139 bl

SARATOGA SPLENDOUR 3 b f £0

40	6-8	Newc	8hvy		1039
19	10-13	Ripo	6g/f	49	2011
5	9-11	Muss	9gd	45	2969

SAREM 2 b c £664

71	7-11	Newb	7g/f		3959
79	4-23	Newm	7g/f		4885

SARENNE 3 b f £0

46 6-10 Hami 9.2g/s 4135
45 6-14 Carl 9.3g/f 4347
53 5-8 Brig 11.9sft 5092

SARGENTS DREAM 3 b f £0
1a	14-14	Ling	6ap		23
0	10-10	Wolv	12af		154
7a	13-16	Ling	7ap		214
0	10-12	Sout	6af	[30]	377

SARIBA 5 b m £1456
1a	7-8	Wolv	16.2af	40	690
35a	6-13	Ling	13ap	[35]	1076
45a	1-7	LING	16ap	[35]	1291*
38	5-8	Bath	17.2fm	40	2035
40	6-14	Bath	18.2fm	40	2417

SARISTAR 3 b f £16771
86	1-19	NEWM	6g/s	80	1154*
41	18-18	Newm	6g/f	84	1933
72	7-9	Ling	7gd	84	3447 T
83	5-8	Good	7sft	83	4263
89	1-9	PONT	6g/f	82	4627*
73	13-13	Asco	6.5g/f	88	4773
89	6-10	Newm	6g/d	89	4884
65	9-12	Newb	6sft	88	5196

SARN 4 b g £2498
18a	11-14	Sout	8af	43	160
18a	9-13	Wolv	8.5af	[40]	894
22a	4-10	Sout	8af	[35]	1406
6	15-15	Thir	7gd	50	1635 p
39	7-14	York	13.9g/f	45	2060
49	4-11	Hayd	10.5g/s	45	2226
36	8-14	Ches	12.3g/f	41	2285
44	3-15	Ripo	12.3g/f	41	2526
47	2-7	Hami	13gd	40	2708
41	7-8	Hayd	14gd	44	2887
46	4-6	Ches	15.9g/f	43	3101
30	7-19	Chep	12.1gd	43	3398
44	4-11	Muss	16g/f	41	3557

SAROS 3 b c £9054
0	15-16	Redc	8sft	53	1147
56a	1-6	SOUT	7af	[45]	1410*
55a	1-7	SOUT	8af	[51]	1591*
45a	6-15	Sout	8af	55	1755
6a	14-15	Sout	7af	55	2384
59	2-13	Muss	7.1g/f	53	2812
48	7-10	Catt	7g/f	53	3016
62	3-13	Thir	7g/f	57	3571
35	7-8	Carl	6g/f	[57]	3654
65	1-14	MUSS	7.1g/f	58	4175*
56	9-18	Catt	7g/f	64	4438
23a	11-12	Wolv	7.1ap	61	5112
59a	3-13	Wolv	8.6ap	[58]	5336

SARRAAF 8 ch g £11877
66a	4-12	Wolv	7af	68	840
74	2-18	Catt	7gd	68	998
65	3-6	Muss	8g/f	68	1092
76	2-13	Muss	7.1g/f	71	1122
64	5-17	Thir	8g/s	71	1214
56	7-8	Muss	8g/s	[72]	1461
71	5-14	Hami	8.3gd	71	1748
70	3-16	York	7g/f	70	2057
72	3-8	Donc	8g/f	71	2425
70	3-13	Ayr	7.2g/s	70	2568
72	5-18	Newc	7sft	70	2684
58	9-9	Ayr	8g/f	69	3305
54	5-11	Muss	8g/f	[69]	3558
65	2-9	Ayr	7.2g/f	[65]	3764
50	9-17	Hami	9.2g/s	64	4008
64	3-8	Muss	9g/f	[64]	4173
65	4-19	York	7.9g/f	64	4399
63	6-11	Muss	8g/f	[64]	4550
52	9-17	Ayr	9.1g/s	[64]	4620
63	4-17	Newc	8fm	63	4867
44	11-16	Catt	7sft	61	5130
58a	9-13	Wolv	9.5ap	59	5292
50a	6-13	Wolv	8.6ap	57	5365

SARRE 4 b f £7711
| 109 | 3-12 | Sain | 8sft | | 993 |

SARTAENA 2 b f £0
| 43 | 8-12 | Chep | 5.1gd | | 3728 |
| 42 | 7-8 | Chep | 5.1g/s | | 3896 |

22 7-8 Brig 5.3fm 4759 BL

SASHAY 5 b m £1715
58a	4-11	Wolv	16.2af	61	48
57a	3-12	Wolv	16.2af	60	156
52a	4-8	Wolv	14.8af	59	277
34a	5-8	Wolv	16.2af	57	690
58a	2-12	Ling	16ap	56	813
11	10-12	Sout	16gd	45	1285
49	3-10	Bath	13.1g/f	45	1789
41	6-8	Bath	17.2fm	45	2035
30	11-16	Warw	16.2gd	45	4276

SASPYS LAD 7 b g £0
57	6-7	Thir	12sft	[70]	1226
42	5-6	Hami	11.1gd	[65]	2180
47	15-16	Wind	11.6gd	60	3829

SASTRE 2 b f £313
23	17-18	Leic	5fm		2109
65	4-6	Epso	6g/s		3041
21a	12-13	Ling	7ap		3330
29	9-12	Sali	6g/s	65	4079 P

SATANS SISTER 3 ch f £0
| 22 | 10-10 | Good | 8gd | | 2224 |

SATCHEM 2 b r c £48029
86	2-7	Leic	6g/f		1964
89	1-5	YARM	6g/f		2341*
104	1-13	NEWM	7g/f	87	3065*
115	1-8	KEMP	6fm	[95]	4390*
110	4-9	Newm	6g/f		4888

SATIN FINISH 2 b f £8676
83	4-10	Newm	6g/f		3063
81	1-11	RIPO	5g/s		3258*
96	4-6	Asco	6g/f		3440
66	10-12	Newb	5.2g/f	[98]	3956
72	6-6	Ripo	6gd	[97]	4280

SATIN KISS 2 b f £12259
90	1-6	LEIC	6g/f		2399*
68	10-10	Newm	6fm		3003
95	1-5	HAYD	6fm	[90]	3795*
95	4-11	Sali	6gd	[88]	4332

SATIN ROSE 2 b f £0
57	5-14	Donc	6g/f		1874
47a	6-14	Sout	7af		2492
36	13-14	Thir	7g/s		4207
56	6-10	Beve	7.5g/f	[54]	4602
32	15-18	Newc	6g/f	54	5013

SATSU 3 ch f £0
50	9-18	Nott	8.2fm	60	1007
26	8-12	Redc	10sft	58	1144
26	6-11	Newc	8sft	55	1395
18a	12-12	Wolv	7af	52	2049

SATTAM 5 b g £4265
82	2-15	Sand	7.1gd	77	4500 vis
78	3-18	Kemp	8g/f	79	4714 vis
74	8-12	Good	8gd	[79]	4872 vis

SATURDAYS CHILD 2 ch f £0
| 0 | 11-11 | Bath | 5.7gd | | 4543 |

SAUCEPOT 2 ch f £1421
63	9-11	Ling	5gd		2395
65	6-9	Wind	5g/f		2795
68	2-8	Ling	5gd		3445
35	11-12	Hayd	5gd	65	3756
65	3-11	Bath	5g/f	[63]	3962
65	6-11	Bath	5g/f	[63]	4409
43	9-12	Bath	5.7gd	63	4545

SAUCY 3 b f £506
49	6-10	Folk	9.7sft		977
40	6-9	Warw	8.1sft		1089
32	9-14	Ling	11.5g/f	50	2014 BL
49a	5-14	Ling	10ap	50	2064 bl
48	3-14	Bath	10.2fm	48	2664 bl
35	5-11	Muss	9gd	42	2969
0	13-14	Chep	10.2g/s	46	3895 bl

SAUCY PICKLE 2 b f £0
| 43a | 8-11 | Ling | 7ap | | 220 |
| 41a | 10-12 | Ling | 8ap | | 428 |

17a 10-12 Ling 7ap 536

SAVANNAH BAY 5 ch g £1500
13	7-13	Asco	16.2sft	[111]	1418
102	4-8	Newb	13.3g/f	[111]	1757 bl
107	8-9	Sand	16.4g/f	[111]	2095 bl
100	7-12	Asco	22.2fm	[106]	2583 bl

SAVANNAH RIVER 3 b f £3122
0	8-10	Pont	6hvy		1070 T
48	3-16	Nott	10gd	45	1240 t
46	2-11	Warw	12.6sft	46	1528 t
37	5-14	Redc	14.1g/f	45	2123 t
38	4-6	Beve	12.1g/s	45	2322 t
50	3-14	Catt	12g/f	42	3192 t
40	6-20	Beve	16.2gd	42	3312 t
0	16-17	Newm	12g/f	45	3618 t
43	4-13	Redc	14.1gd	43	4249 t
10	10-12	Ripo	10gd	45	4282 t

SAVANNAH SUE 3 b f £0
9	7-8	Redc	6sft		1659
12a	9-12	Sout	7af		2339
21a	10-12	Sout	6af		2722
27	14-15	Redc	5g/s	30	2961

SAVERNAKE BRAVE 2 b c £2166
9a	10-10	Sout	7af	52	203
46a	5-6	Wolv	7af	[48]	283 BL
50a	2-12	Wolv	6af	48	1374 bl
39	8-10	Brig	5.3fm	48	1694 bl
42	4-12	Brig	6g/f	46	2435
38	7-12	Brig	5.3g/f	46	2645
21	10-12	Brig	6g/f	43	3301
37a	7-15	Sout	5af	47	4043
47	1-15	FOLK	7g/f	[40]	4371*
34	12-17	Kemp	7g/f	[45]	4794
42a	4-11	Wolv	7.1ap	[45]	5210

SAVILES DELIGHT 4 b g £20596
37a	9-16	Sout	6af	56	92
56a	4-16	Ling	7ap	[52]	214 p
60a	3-14	Ling	6ap	54	328 p
62a	2-13	Wolv	6af	54	384 p
59a	4-11	Wolv	5af	59	507 bl
67	3-20	Wind	6g/s	64	1255
72	1-10	WARW	6.1hvy	64	1533*
74	2-17	Nott	5.1g/s	68	1774
68	7-19	Kemp	6fm	70	2070
77	1-13	HAYD	6gd	70	2884*
82	1-10	HAYD	7.1g/s	74	3137*
79	4-7	Chep	7.1gd	[74]	3402
67	3-5	Good	7sft	[77]	4186
63	13-19	Kemp	6fm	77	4394
71a	4-13	Wolv	5.1ap	67	5341 bl

SAVIOURS SPIRIT 2 ch g £7998
70a	3-10	Ling	6ap	[77]	258
71a	2-13	Ling	6ap	[72]	364
75a	2-11	Ling	6ap	[70]	543
74a	1-8	LING	6ap	[70]	691*
68	9-14	Epso	7g/f	72	4465
65	10-25	Newb	7gd	72	4683
74a	2-12	Ling	6ap	70	4976
66a	5-13	Wolv	6ap	72	5114

SAVOIE 2 ch f £0
| 59 | 13-19 | Newm | 7g/s | | 5279 |

SAVOY CHAPEL 2 b r c £0
54a	9-12	Ling	6ap		4179
57	12-13	Warw	7.1g/f		4416
45	13-13	Warw	7.1g/s		4664
46	8-10	Wind	8.3g/f		4831

SAWAH 3 gr g £0
10a	14-14	Ling	10ap		53
0	12-15	Sout	8af		96
2a	10-10	Sout	8af		143
27a	6-10	Wolv	6af	20	245
25a	5-12	Wolv	6af	[30]	297
9a	10-12	Sout	7af	[30]	909

SAWWAAH 7 b g £23961
6	24-24	Donc	8gd	82	928
57	8-8	Muss	8g/s	[80]	1461
84	1-19	REDC	7g/f	78	1820*
85	3-10	Thir	7g/f	[78]	1970

81 4-13 Epso 8.5g/f 82 2207
64 16-28 Asco 7g/f 84 2558
68 13-18 Newc 7sft 84 2684
75 8-10 Epso 7g/f 82 2872
83 3-25 Asco 7g/f 80 3443
65 15-21 Good 8fm 80 3565
85 2-8 Hayd 8.1fm 81 3797
88 1-16 NEWB 7g/f 81 3954+
0 13-13 Ches 7.6sft 84 4103
87 4-21 Donc 7fm 84 4482
6 10-10 Epso 7gd [85] 4912

SAXE COBURG 7 b g £6986
51a 5-12 Wolv 8.5af 54 1379
68 1-17 BATH 10.2sft 54 1541+
57 9-14 Nott 10g/s 64 1776
65 3-11 Bath 10.2fm 64 1899
59 3-17 Nott 14.1g/f 62 2156
54 10-11 Sali 12fm 62 2293
60 3-7 Warw 12.6fm 60 2782
52 5-10 Warw 12.6g/f 60 2912
60 3-7 Kemp 14.4g/f 60 3037
53 4-8 Newb 12g/f 58 3270
38 9-11 Beve 12.1g/s [56] 3856
58 4-17 Kemp 12sft 56 4033
53 6-14 Bath 13.1g/s 53 4203
38 13-19 Sali 14.1gd 55 4856
0 P-16 Ling 12ap [55] 4899

SAXON LIL 2 b f £0
39 13-17 Warw 7.1gd 4269

SAY WHAT YOU SEE 4 b c £9580
51a 9-12 Wolv 9.4af 72 513
69a 4-14 Ling 10ap 68 674
74a 2-14 Ling 10ap 68 803
78a 1-8 LING 10ap 72 900*
69 5-18 Bath 10.2g/s 73 1098
72 4-14 Leic 10g/f 71 1828
77 2-8 Nott 10g/f 71 2157
75 2-8 Sand 10gd 71 2363 vis
52 9-13 Redc 10gd 72 2560 vis
72 4-12 Kemp 10gd 72 3185 vis
62 8-12 Good 9fm 71 3625 vis

SAYADAW 4 b c £2500
110 4-17 Newb 12gd 1230 T

SAYRIANNA 3 br f £0
29 13-14 Wind 8.3g/f 2622
51 11-13 Kemp 10g/f 3038
42 4-7 Folk 9.7gd 3385
26 7-12 Folk 12g/s 49 3913

SAYWAAN 2 ch f £5694
89 1-19 LEIC 7gd 5045*

SCABIUN 6 £18539
111 4-17 San 8gd 5074

SCALE THE HEIGHTS 2 b g £0
67 9-15 Newb 7g/f 2876
61 8-11 Warw 7.1gd 3053
46 7-9 Chep 8.1g/s 4297
33 13-14 Chep 8.1gd 4484

SCALLOWAY 4 b g £0
25 16-17 Warw 8.1g/s 68 4668
51a 14-16 Ling 12ap 65 5261

SCANDINAVIA 2 b c £22000
108 2-8 Asco 8g/f 4797
87 8-4 Lone 8.5Fast 5310

SCARBOROUGH FLYER 2 b c £0
0 12-12 Pont 6g/s 5152
12a 10-13 Wolv 6ap 5287

SCARLET EMPRESS 2 b f £0
16a 13-13 Ling 7ap 78 15 bl
49 15-15 Newb 7g/f 76 3920
32 9-9 Pont 6g/f 71 4627

SCARLET INVADER 2 b c £1430
78 4-10 Leic 7g/f 2703
68 8-18 Leic 7g/f 3342
79 2-11 Sali 7gd 3883
66 6-12 Sali 8sft 80 4580
31 12-12 Newm 8gd 80 5089

SCARLETT BREEZE 3 b f £413
3 17-20 Yarm 6g/f 53 1730
33 13-16 Ling 6g/f 51 1985
21 12-12 Brig 6g/f 48 2435
58 5-10 Newb 5.2fm [48] 2649
43 8-12 Kemp 5g/f 47 3036
52 4-9 Kemp 6g/f [46] 3687
26a 11-15 Sout 5af 46 4043
38 4-14 Folk 6gd 46 4116
55 7-13 Bath 5.7g/f [45] 4413
0 14-15 Brig 6gd [45] 4905
9 15-20 Yarm 6g/s [45] 5121

SCARLETT ROSE 2 b f £2169
67a 7-13 Ling 7ap 119
56 6-14 Sout 6gd [71] 1281
50 10-12 Newm 7g/f 68 2249
68 3-13 Leic 7g/f 65 3346
67 3-8 Newm 7g/f 65 3612
57 7-8 Good 7sft 65 4263
44 15-19 Leic 7g/f 64 4452
48a 13-14 Ling 7ap 62 5300

SCARP 2 b c £0
66 9-18 Newm 7gd 3927
61 11-12 Newm 9g/f 4194
67 7-18 Newm 8fm 4722

SCARPIA 4 ch g £0
58 9-14 Warw 7.1g/f [39] 2907
18 17-19 Chep 7.1gd 45 3401
38a 5-13 Ling 10ap 40 3823

SCARRABUS 3 b c £1696
73 4-10 Kemp 11.1gd [67] 1140
52 10-14 York 11.9g/s 75 1708
66 6-10 Good 9.9gd 70 2225
55 3-7 Folk 9.7gd [69] 3385
66 4-17 Newm 12g/f 65 3618
67a 3-9 Ling 12ap [66] 4315
58a 5-9 Ling 12ap [66] 4449
39 7-9 Good 16gd 65 4875

SCARROTTOO 6 ch g £9845
53a 8-14 Ling 7ap 54 344
47a 3-13 Ling 6ap [52] 544 BL e
47a 5-11 Wolv 7af 52 562 BL e
36a 16-16 Ling 7ap 52 600
28a 11-13 Ling 7ap 50 739
50a 5-13 Ling 7ap 50 761
51 5-15 Folk 6sft 54 976
57 1-19 YARM 7g/f 51 1132*
55 4-15 Thir 7gd 51 1635
45 12-16 Brig 7fm 55 2258
58 3-17 Ling 7ap 55 2397
60 1-11 EPSO 7fm [55] 3541*
55 5-15 Ling 7.6fm 55 3788
35 14-20 Yarm 8gd 55 3996
59 3-15 Epso 7gd 55 4475
0 16-16 Yarm 7gd 55 4616
39a 9-13 Wolv 8.6ap [48] 5212 bl e
39a 5-12 Wolv 7.1ap [48] 5233

SCARY NIGHT 4 b g £3670
4a 12-13 Sout 6af 75 551
24a 11-12 Sout 6af [75] 610 p
65a 1-9 SOUT 5af [68] 793* p
55a 6-12 Sout 5af 68 853 p
18a 7-9 Sout 6af [63] 1194 p
31a 10-11 Wolv 8af 58 1337 p
48a 6-15 Sout 5af 54 1750 p
0 13-13 Wolv 5af 51 2201 p
54a 2-15 Sout 5af [51] 2803 p
25 18-19 Donc 5g/s 51 3220 p
33a 10-15 Sout 5af 51 4043 p
29a 9-13 Wolv 6ap [50] 5211 p

SCENIC FLIGHT 3 b f £0
31 13-14 Warw 7.1sft 55 1085
25a 8-8 Ling 7ap [50] 1247 T
27 9-9 Kemp 6hvy [45] 1641 BL

SCENIC LADY 8 b m £0
53 5-11 Folk 9.7fm 59 2719
41 7-8 Epso 12g/f 59 2869

SCENT 2 b f £438

72 5-11 Newb 6gd 3915
60 12-16 Sali 7gd 4330
67 3-11 Chep 7.1hvy 4703
65 5-19 Pont 8g/s 66 5147

SCHAPIRO 3 b g £6840
33 11-13 Kemp 9hvy 77 1515
80 3-9 Wind 11.6g/f 75 1807
79 4-9 Kemp 12gd 77 2175 BL
88 1-18 PONT 12g/f [78] 2608* bl

SCHINKEN OTTO 3 ch c £0
21 14-17 Hayd 8.1gd 53 2243
38 6-13 Muss 7.1g/f 48 2812
37 7-15 Beve 8.5g/s 46 3182
51 5-14 Carl 9.3g/f [45] 4347
34 12-19 Thir 6g/f 45 4595

SCHOLARSHIP 3 b g £417
23 20-20 Newb 7fm 67 2650
70a 3-9 Ling 8ap [67] 3195

SCHOONER 3 b g £330
55a 5-14 Ling 12ap 14
70a 3-15 Ling 12ap 118

SCIENCE ACADEMY 2 ch f £6928
47a 9-11 Ling 6ap 51
43 10-20 Wind 11.6sft 60 1648
40 5-7 Leic 11.8g/f 58 1967
60 6-10 Bath 11.7g/f 54 2978
59 2-14 Folk 12gd 51 3383
64 1-14 YARM 11.5g/f 54 3714*
72 1-12 FOLK 12g/s 60 3913*
52 6-8 Brig 11.9sft 67 4143
63a 7-13 Ling 10ap 67 5299

SCIENTIST 3 ch c £5911
61 10-12 Newm 7g/s 1152
22 13-14 Thir 8gd [80] 1639
75 3-20 Newb 7g/f 75 2314
55 9-10 Newb 8g/f 74 2877
48 6-7 Epso 8.5fm 72 3542
55 12-17 Nott 8.2gd 69 4862
76 1-14 REDC 7g/s 66 5109*
24 8-8 Nott 8.2hvy [69] 5346

SCISSORS 2 ch f £0
59 10-10 Pont 6g/s 2610
63 8-10 Folk 7g/s 3046

SCOOBY DOOBY DO 3 b f £0
43 5-9 Redc 5sft 1146
49 6-7 Newc 6g/s [60] 2728
40 15-17 Ripo 6g/s 60 3262
32 6-9 Ripo 5g/f 55 3645 P
5 18-20 Ripo 6gd 50 4278 p
0 17-18 Leic 7gd [49] 4698 p

SCORCH 3 b c £986
45a 4-5 Wolv 7af 425
42a 9-12 Ling 8ap [53] 514
51 2-6 Yarm 10.1g/f [51] 1134

SCORCHIO 3 b g £739
35a 6-7 Wolv 9.4af 46 1324
44a 2-4 Ling 10ap [45] 1454
28a 5-6 Wolv 12af [45] 1673
48 4-7 Warw 10.9fm 45 2576
40 6-11 Pont 12g/f 45 2790

SCORPIO SALLY 2 b f £0
26 14-16 Pont 6g/s 2275
65 5-5 Hami 6g/s 2829
58 6-12 Newc 7gd 3425
65 5-12 Beve 7.5g/s 4242
54 5-7 Muss 7.1gd [63] 4518
43 16-16 Nott 10g/f 63 4848

SCOTLAND THE BRAVE 4 ch f £13238
9 14-15 Hami 8.3g/s 69 1602
68 13-10 Ayr 7.2g/f 67 2027
80 5-7 Pont 8g/f [67] 2278
48 8-8 Thir 8fm 67 2464
59 4-12 Catt 7g/f [66] 3017
72 1-11 DONC 7g/s 66 3223* P
66 4-9 Newm 8g/f 70 3780 p
70 2-5 Ayr 8hvy [70] 4086 p
57 9-18 Ayr 7.2sft 70 4622

66	7-17	Ayr	7.2sft	69	5063 p

SCOTT 3 gr g £10508

52	7-11	Beve	7.5g/s		2325
26	10-11	Beve	8.5gd		2656
53	6-6	Ling	10g/f		2843
1	12-14	Folk	12gd	55	3383
52	3-14	Yarm	11.5g/f	50	3714
64a	1-8	SOUT	12af	50	4092*
56a	4-16	Ling	12ap	[60]	4899
68	1-16	YORK	11.9gd	60	4990*
67	2-12	Brig	11.9sft	58	5093
67	3-10	Catt	13.8sft	64	5322

SCOTTISH EXILE 2 b f £14052

70a	2-12	Wolv	5af	[60]	32
64a	3-9	Ling	5ap	[60]	76
71a	1-8	SOUT	5af	[64]	197* VIS
3a	6-7	Sout	6af	70	333 vis
63a	4-14	Sout	5af	68	485 vis
65	4-8	Nott	5.1fm	68	1002 vis
58a	3-4	Wolv	5af	[66]	1338 vis
69	1-8	HAMI	5gd	68	1509* vis
55	10-12	Wind	5g/f	68	1809 vis
39	8-9	Chep	5.1gd	68	2195 vis
70	2-9	Muss	5g/f	68	2614 vis
73	1-13	WIND	5fm	68	2784* vis
51	11-12	Catt	5g/f	71	3193 vis
74	3-8	Hami	5g/f	71	3591 vis
50	4-5	Brig	5.3g/f	[71]	3720 vis
42	7-9	Newm	6gd	71	3924 vis
46	10-14	Redc	5fm	[70]	4930 vis

SCOTTISH RIVER 4 b g £22376

31a	9-13	Wolv	8.5af	65	40
58a	7-11	Ling	8ap	62	136
60a	3-14	Ling	10ap	59	230
61a	3-13	Wolv	9.4af	59	287
52a	10-14	Ling	10ap	59	339
64a	1-11	WOLV	9.4af	58	465*
62a	5-13	Ling	10ap	[62]	569
74a	1-13	WOLV	8.5af	[62]	699*
74a	1-12	WOLV	9.4af	68	747*
58a	7-9	Wolv	8.5af	68	809
63a	5-7	Wolv	8.5af	73	942
66	6-16	Epso	10.1hvy	73	1296
80	1-19	WIND	10sft	[72]	1650*
76	4-12	Kemp	8g/f	[77]	1915
64	6-8	Chep	10.2gd	[77]	2197
64	6-8	Wind	8.3g/s	[77]	2620
86	1-8	EPSO	10.1g/s	75	3044*
85	2-15	Epso	10.1gd	[75]	3216
86	4-6	Newc	10.1gd	[82]	3430
64	17-20	Hayd	10.5fm	82	3794
81	4-12	Epso	12gd	81	4292
70	10-13	Epso	10.1g/f	81	4473
78	6-14	Asco	12g/f	80	4775

SCOTTS VIEW 5 b g £260971

113	3-13	Nad	12g/f	[112]	990
117	1-12	KEMP	10gd	[115]	1139*
114	3-14	Sha	10g/f	[115]	1438
115	3-10	Bade	11gd	[115]	2141
114	7-11	Epso	12g/f	[115]	2209
115	5-10	Asco	10g/f	[115]	2488
104	5-7	Ayr	10g/f	[115]	3306
113	4-8	Muni	10gd	[115]	3662

SCOTTYS FUTURE 6 b g £4634

80a	7-14	Ling	10ap	83	452
59a	1-10	LING	10ap	[81]	540*
45a	11-12	Wolv	8.5af	80	632
66a	1-10	LING	10ap	[78]	738*
74a	8-9	Ling	10ap	75	903
60	6-11	Wind	10gd	[72]	4124
75	5-8	York	8.9g/f	[72]	4397
78	4-11	Muss	9g/f	[72]	4550
67	8-17	Ayr	9.1g/s	[72]	4620

SCRAMBLE 5 ch g £303

52a	3-14	Sout	8af	52	62 b le
48a	4-15	Sout	8af	52	84 bl t
40a	6-9	Sout	7af	51	193 b le
46a	4-13	Wolv	8.5af	50	251 t p
48	6-15	Thir	7gd	52	1635 t
23	14-18	Thir	8g/f	52	1972 t
37	11-13	Muss	8g/f	50	3526 t p

33	6-11	Muss	8g/f	[50]	3558 t p

SCRAPPY DOO 3 b g £0

0	14-15	Sout	8af	[26]	96

SCREENPLAY 3 ch g £0

57	10-14	Newm	10g/f	75	1192

SCREWDRIVER 2 b c £21889

88	2-13	Newb	6g/f	1760
100	1-8	EPSO	6fm	2251*

SCRIPTED 2 b g £610

70a	4-12	Ling	6ap	4896
75	4-12	Newc	7g/f	5011

SCRIPTORIUM 3 b c £2379

65a	6-10	Ling	10ap		886
55	10-14	Wind	10g/s		1055
63	2-15	Redc	9g/f	58	2120
57	4-7	Brig	9.9g/f	[61]	2433
65	2-13	Nott	10g/f	61	3419
53	8-11	Yarm	10.1gd	[62]	3875
46	10-15	Bath	8gd	62	4827
56	7-9	Leic	7gd	[61]	5041 VIS

SCRIPTWRITER 2 b c £1106

64	5-9	Ayr	7.2sft	5064
83	2-20	Yarm	8sft	5252

SCROOBY BABY 2 b f £2052

73	2-12	Bath	5.7gd		3141
60	7-10	Nott	6.1g/f		3418
83a	2-10	Ling	6ap		3817
67	4-9	Brig	6g/f		3981
59a	12-14	Ling	7ap	75	4177
54	15-21	Donc	6fm	[72]	4490

SCRUNCH 3 b f £952

49	6-9	Kemp	6sft		946
57	9-12	Good	7g/f		1846
72	4-10	Sali	7gd		2659
57a	3-6	Sout	6af	[68]	3095

SCURRA 4 b g £5922

2a	14-16	Sout	8af	53	86
21	6-15	Newc	12.4hvy	53	1034
12	13-16	Newc	10.1sft	51	1278
50	3-10	Ayr	8g/s	[51]	1446
58	1-15	AYR	10.9g/s	47	2545*
54	2-11	Newc	10.1g/s	52	2726
55	4-7	Hami	13gd	55	3134
52	6-14	Hayd	10.5gd	55	3741
46	5-8	Ayr	10hvy	54	4084
61	2-16	Carl	11.9g/f	53	4348
46	4-11	Catt	13.8sft	[58]	5129
50	7-13	Muss	12g/s	57	5333

SEA COVE 4 b f £0

45a	4-11	Sout	12af	35	1197
43	5-8	Muss	16gd	45	1793
44a	5-16	Sout	12af	44	2340
38	5-8	Thir	12g/s	43	2691
31a	4-10	Sout	14af	41	3096

SEA FERN 3 b g £0

50	5-6	Newc	5sft		1392
40	11-16	Ayr	5g/f	53	2029
39	7-12	Catt	5g/f	50	3193
34	10-15	Muss	5g/f	47	3561
43	6-19	Thir	6g/f	45	4595
8	10-10	Ripo	6gd	[45]	4790

SEA HOLLY 3 b g £2960

70a	2-15	Sout	12af	[74]	89
73a	1-15	LING	12ap	[74]	118*
77a	4-14	Ling	13ap	73	147
0	8-8	Sout	12af	74	225

SEA HUNTER 2 b c £10307

61	7-11	Nott	5.1gd		1237
84	1-6	HAMI	5gd		1503*
64	4-6	Wind	5g/f		1808
95	2-13	Newm	7g/f	81	3065
88	3-11	Newm	7fm	84	3407
84	5-12	York	7g/s	87	4064
83	10-17	Donc	8fm	87	4480
90	4-12	Newm	8gd	84	5089

SEA JADE 5 b m £822

34	4-10	Warw	8.1g/s	[40]	1328
43	2-8	Brig	8gd	[40]	1548
40a	2-4	Ling	7ap	[40]	1710
26	8-8	Bath	5.7fm	45	2034

SEA LARK 2 b g £0

51a	9-12	Wolv	7.1ap	5324

SEA MAP 2 ch c £0

34	9-9	Warw	7.1fm	2776
60	10-18	Leic	7g/f	3342
0	U-11	Wind	8.3fm	3798
54	10-16	Bath	8gd	5019
60	6-15	Nott	8.2hvy	5344

SEA MARK 8 ro g £647

62	3-16	Sout	7g/s	60	1049
59	5-14	Muss	7.1gd	61	1794
42	11-13	Ripo	8g/f	61	2010

SEA NYMPH 3 b f £7348

71	5-20	Newm	8g/f		3237
75	2-17	Wind	8.3fm		3480
79	1-13	WIND	8.3gd		3828*
79	2-11	Wind	8.3g/s	76	4222
37	13-13	Sand	8.1gd	78	4607

SEA OF GOLD 3 b f £1503

58	14-17	Newm	7gd		1171
65	6-18	Wind	8.3g/f		1810
72	2-6	Brig	9.9fm		2835
67	6-12	Wind	8.3fm	72	3291
61a	4-14	Ling	10ap	[70]	4448
17	15-15	Bath	8gd	68	4827
35a	11-12	Ling	8ap	[68]	4975 VIS

SEA OF HAPPINESS 4 b g £0

0	13-13	Beve	12.1g/f	[45]	1945
22	9-9	Redc	16fm	[41]	2298
10	15-20	Catt	12g/f	40	2850

SEA PLUME 4 b f £0

44a	10-10	Ling	13ap	75	11
63a	11-14	Ling	16ap	75	107
46a	7-12	Sout	14af	70	173
70	5-8	Folk	12sft	[75]	1272
65	10-12	Muss	14fm	74	2085
69	8-10	Sali	14.1gd	70	2699
65	9-11	Sand	14g/f	67	3340 BL

SEA STORM 6 b g £21147

66	16-18	Catt	7gd	84	998
78	5-13	Muss	7.1g/f	83	1122 p
68	8-17	Thir	8g/s	81	1475 p
81	3-12	Ayr	7.2fm	79	1909
77	7-10	Ayr	7.2g/f	79	2027
84	1-9	MUSS	8fm	[79]	2087* p
78	10-15	York	8.9g/f	83	2404 p
73	7-8	Pont	8g/f	82	2606 p
76	6-9	Ayr	8gd	83	3305
85	5-13	Newc	7gd	81	3428 p
77	6-8	Thir	8fm	79	3608 p
79	4-16	Redc	7g/f	78	3809 p
76	3-13	Ches	7.6sft	78	4103 p
65	19-21	Donc	7fm	78	4482 p
84	2-18	Ayr	7.2sft	76	4689
87	1-13	MUSS	7.1gd	79	4806* p
79	8-11	Muss	7.1g/s	81	5144

SEA TERN 4 b f £0

0	9-10	Sout	7af	[35]	1839
2	14-15	Nott	10gd	[35]	1991

SEA THE WORLD 3 b g £4863

57a	3-12	Wolv	5af	63	35
26a	11-12	Wolv	5af	62	109 -
41a	11-15	Sout	5af	60	187
53a	7-16	Sout	5af	60	205 VIS
54a	5-9	Sout	5af	58	415 vis
57a	1-12	SOUT	5af	[56]	587* vis
64a	3-11	Sout	5af	62	655 vis
65a	2-11	Sout	5af	-61	859 vis
53a	6-7	Ling	5ap	63	1011 vis
56a	9-12	Sout	5af	63	1442 vis
24	11-11	Folk	6sft	53	1578 vis

SEA YA MAITE 10 b g £1182

0	14-14	Sout	12af	[30]	305

10a	5-9	Sout	12af	[30]	353 t
31a	2-11	Sout	8af	[30]	372 t
42a	3-9	Sout	11af	[35]	505 t
31a	5-9	Wolv	9.4af	[35]	525 t
36a	4-8	Sout	11af	[40]	574 t
27a	5-7	Sout	14af	[35]	638 t
20a	10-16	Sout	11af	[35]	852 t
44a	2-12	Sout	8af	[35]	905 t
28a	4-8	Sout	8af	[40]	1200 t
27	7-10	Beve	8.5g/f	[40]	1943 t
26a	8-16	Sout	8af	40	2805 t
11a	7-9	Sout	8af	40	2996 t

SEAFIELD TOWERS 4 ch g £2168

48	15-16	Muss	5g/f	78	1120 p
64	10-19	Thir	8g/f	78	1767 p
78	3-15	Hayd	5g/f	77	1917 p
61	14-17	Muss	5fm	77	2082 p
70	12-20	Epso	5fm	78	2253 p
41	12-17	Redc	6gd	75	2561 p
54	9-10	Ayr	5gd	73	3150 p
69	7-11	Hami	6g/f	73	3248 p
60	8-9	Ayr	5gd	73	3307 p
43	13-15	York	6g/f	70	3434 p

SEAGOLD 3 b f £0

38	16-16	Wind	10gd		1384
58	10-11	Bath	8fm		1904
13a	14-15	Ling	12ap		2393
2a	14-14	Ling	10ap	[45]	4661 bl

SEAL OF OFFICE 5 ch g £0

1	17-18	Wind	8.3gd	67	1385
0	P-17	Kemp	10g/f	63	1913

SEAMLESS 2 b c £0

71	5-12	Hayd	6gd	2902
68a	5-13	Wolv	6ap	5287

SEAMUS SHINDIG 2 b g £6358

90	1-5	PONT	5g/f	4625*
88	4-21	Donc	6hvy	5202

SEANS MEMORY 3 b g £1024

1a	9-14	Sout	12af		194
37a	8-10	Wolv	12af		359
52a	2-7	Sout	12af		588 P
49a	6-8	Ling	16ap	55	733
0	P-16	Sout	14af	50	1033 p

SEARCH MISSION 3 b f £1716

84	2-12	Yarm	7fm	79	2864
33	9-9	Sali	7gd	80	3456

SEASON TICKET 2 b f £0

29	15-15	Nott	5.1gd	3988
53	8-18	Ling	6gd	4108
29	17-20	York	6g/f	4401
31	10-10	Newc	7fm	4864

SEASONS ESTATES 2 b f £4967

60	4-9	Warw	5sft		1084
49	10-14	Bath	5gd		1401
61	4-11	Sali	7gd		3883
66	3-20	Ling	7gd	62	4444
69	1-17	LING	7g/f	62	4894*

SEATTLE ART 10 b g £0

1	12-12	Newb	10g/f	35	2354

SEATTLE PRINCE 6 gr g £0

0	8-10	Yarm	16sft	51	4151
9	17-20	Catt	15.8gd	51	4965

SEATTLE ROBBER 2 b g £0

64	14-19	Leic	7gd	5055

SECAM 5 gr g £422

10a	13-14	Ling	12ap	52	711 BL
44a	3-15	Sout	8af	47	1028
39	9-13	Sali	6g/s	45	3109
36	11-12	Ling	7.6gd	[44]	3448
28a	11-16	Sout	8af	44	3487 bl

SECLUDED 4 b g £3507

67	5-14	Wind	10g/f		2265
60	8-12	Wind	10g/f	[69]	2800
40	14-20	Newm	8g/f	67	3232
71	1-5	BRIG	9.9sft	64	4167* BL

SECRET DIVA 2 ch f £0

36	9-11	Good	5gd	2020

70	5-16	Ches	10.3g/f	68	4515 bl
28	15-19	Pont	10g/s	68	5148 bl

SECOND GENERATION 6 ch g £179

9a	14-15	Sout	6af	[37]	172
20a	5-11	Sout	5af	[35]	578
21a	5-8	Ling	5ap	[30]	1290
30a	3-6	Ling	6af	[30]	1415
24a	4-7	Wolv	6af	[30]	1566
13a	5-6	Wolv	9.4af	[30]	1800

SECOND MINISTER 4 ch g £1530

51a	3-16	Sout	6af	[50]	65 BL
58a	2-11	Ling	6ap	[50]	130 bl
60a	3-10	Ling	5ap	[60]	802 bl T
44a	8-11	Sout	6af	[60]	869 bl t
29a	6-6	Wolv	6af	[60]	941 bl t
0	18-18	Ling	6gd	50	2396 bl t
2	10-11	Good	6gd	50	2535 bl
17a	11-11	Ling	6ap	55	3333 bl
33a	13-13	Sout	6af	[55]	3482 bl

SECOND OF MAY 3 ch f £608

63a	2-14	Sout	8af	62	60
52	8-9	Brig	9.9fm	65	3695

SECOND PAIGE 7 b g £621

35a	4-10	Ling	16ap	[40]	650 bl

SECOND REEF 2 b c £595

66a	3-15	Sout	5af	4089
54	19-24	Redc	6fm	4928

SECOND USER 3 b c £0

24a	11-12	Ling	8ap	428
24a	13-13	Ling	10ap	601
20	20-20	Wind	10sft	1651
15	18-18	Wind	10g/f	1959

SECOND VENTURE 5 b g £212

37a	4-13	Wolv	8.5af	[37]	46 p
31a	8-10	Wolv	8.5af	[40]	398 p
35a	3-16	Sout	8af	[40]	442 BL T
28a	8-12	Wolv	7af	[40]	528 bl t

SECOND WARNING 3 ch c £0

63	5-8	Epso	8.5hvy		1297
55a	8-12	Ling	8ap	[62]	2394
61	5-13	Wind	8.3gd	[60]	3828
60	6-9	Nott	10g/s	[60]	4034

SECOND WIND 9 ch g £0

0	9-9	Hami	6g/s	[40]	4817 t P
0	12-13	Ayr	8sft	[40]	5275 t

SECRET AFFAIR 2 b c £0

58a	8-12	Ling	6ap	4179
77	8-15	Leic	7g/f	4455
55	10-11	Bath	8sft	5171

SECRET BLOOM 2 b g £2032

0	15-15	Sout	7af	[43]	87
52a	4-6	Wolv	7af	[38]	283 VIS
44a	4-8	Wolv	8.5af	[47]	383 vis
26a	11-12	Wolv	7af	[47]	560 vis
37a	5-10	Sout	11af	47	658 vis
48a	4-9	Wolv	8.5af	[45]	865 vis
44a	2-5	Sout	8af	[45]	986 vis
41a	4-6	Sout	8af	[45]	1203 BL
48a	1-5	WOLV	9.4af	[45]	1311* vis
45a	3-6	Wolv	9.4af	[45]	1675 vis
34a	7-12	Wolv	9.5ap	[45]	5209 vis

SECRET CAVERN 2 b c £362

72	6-13	Hayd	6gd	3736
55	7-11	Thir	7fm	4375
72	4-15	Brig	7sft	5192

SECRET CHARM 3 b f £18019

113	5-16	Newm	8fm		1492
111	5-15	Curr	8g/f		2005
81	11-11	Asco	8af	[112]	2555
112	1-9	DONC	8fm	[110]	4495*
99	5-13	Newm	8g/f	[110]	4887

SECRET CONNECTION 4 b f £0

0	7-9	Wolv	9.4af	665

27	12-13	Sali	6fm		2287
34	10-12	Chep	5.1gd		3728
34	7-13	Sali	7g/f		3864
31	9-17	Ling	6g/f		4316
30a	11-11	Ling	8ap	[40]	4738

SECRET FLAME 3 b f £7388

80	3-17	Newb	8g/f		1762
81	3-11	Newb	10g/f		2349
80	1-2	HAMI	9.2gd	[78]	2709*
65	9-10	Sand	8.1g/f	[78]	3339
72	6-12	Sand	10gd	76	4502
68a	5-14	Ling	10ap	[74]	4742

SECRET FORMULA 4 b f £1151

68	20-20	Newm	7g/s	82	1151
32	18-19	Sali	7g/f	79	1723

SECRET HISTORY 2 b f £8004

77	2-10	Pont	7g/s		2610
77	3-5	Hami	6g/s		2829
73	5-8	Asco	6g/f		3386
77	1-14	THIR	7g/s	[76]	4207*
65	7-14	Donc	7fm	75	4535
80	2-13	Wind	8.3g/s	71	4940
83	3-14	Newb	7sft	75	5193

SECRET JEWEL 4 b f £1806

69	6-16	Sand	10g/s		2131
49	8-17	Wind	11.6fm	[72]	2788
35	5-8	Donc	12g/s	71	3222
19	17-17	Kemp	12sft		4033
54	12-18	Sali	9.9gd	67	4850 P
57	2-15	Leic	11.8gd	[65]	5060 BL
46	2-6	Yarm	14.1sft	[60]	5249 bl

SECRET MELODY 3 b f £32306

104	1-11	COLO	8sft	4840*
104	3-8	San	8sft	5166

SECRET OF SECRETS 3 b g £0

0	13-14	Newc	5g/f	4404
0	10-10	Ripo	6gd	4788

SECRET PACT 2 br c £14541

67	4-9	Muss	5g/s		1458
74	2-10	Newc	6sft		1677
83	3-8	Epso	7gd		3214
58	7-9	Catt	6sft	75	3931
80	1-14	CARL	6.9fm	[75]	4503*
85	1-18	CATT	7g/f	75	4673*
89	2-17	Good	8g/f	79	4871
90	3-14	Donc	8sft	84	5203

SECRET PLACE 2 ch g £19859

57a	2-14	Ling	8ap		100
75a	2-12	Ling	8ap		175
76a	1-7	WOLV	7af		284*
86a	1-10	LING	7ap	77	432*
85a	3-5	Ling	8ap	84	694
78	9-20	Newm	7g/f	84	1186
93	1-12	GOOD	7g/f	82	1847*
61	16-17	Epso	7g/f	90	2212
50	13-13	Asco	7g/f	90	3068

SECRETARY GENERAL 3 b c £20584

83	7-20	Newm	8fm	88	1496
90	2-7	Nott	8.2sft	[88]	1741
90	8-18	Hayd	8.1g/f	92	1919
89	5-13	Newm	8g/f	90	2247
76	9-16	Newm	8g/f	88	3059
97	1-8	NOTT	8.2g/f	88	3421*
97	2-8	Folk	9.7g/s	[91]	3912
96	2-10	York	11.9gd	91	4324
84	8-13	Kemp	12g/f	[94]	4715
81	11-15	Leic	11.8gd	94	5043

SEDGE 4 b g £3294

60	1-14	REDC	7g/f		2102*
37	12-16	Redc	8g/s	60	2958
29	16-18	Pont	8gd	60	3242
46	7-10	Beve	8.5g/f	57	3501
53	7-15	Beve	8.5g/f	54	4598
53	4-15	Redc	9g/s	52	5111

SEEJAY 3 b f £421

21a	12-14	Ling	12ap		14
47a	9-14	Ling	10ap		53
50a	3-12	Ling	8ap	48	1045

3	17-17	Bath	10.2sft	49	1541
36	8-18	Nott	8.2gd	[45]	1992
34	9-11	Chep	10.2gd	42	2371

SEEKING A WAY 3 b f £3862

68	2-6	Bath	11.7fm		2668
65	3-7	Nott	10g/f		3422
56	7-9	Sand	14g/s	70	3893
61	6-11	Bath	13.1g/f	68	4415
75a	2-14	Ling	13ap	[66]	4898
64	3-8	Brig	11.9sft	[70]	5092

SEEKING AN ALIBI 2 ch c £0

58	10-14	Leic	8gd		5058
65a	8-12	Ling	8ap		5293 T

SEEKING THE DIA 3 b c £0

102	12-20	Newm	6g/f		3062

SEEL OF APPROVAL 5 b g £4576

109	2-9	Newm	6fm	103	1490

SEEYAAJ 4 b g £0

79	5-7	Leic	11.8fm	[80]	3816
75	9-15	Newb	11g/f	79	4643
36	10-13	Newb	16sft	77	5194

SEGUIDILLA 3 b f £0

22	14-15	Folk	6g/s	[84]	1078
37	6-6	Newc	5sft	[82]	1392

SEKWANA 5 b m £0

26a	13-14	Ling	10ap	[60]	477 p
0	10-11	Ling	13ap	[48]	515 p
17	11-11	Brig	7fm	45	2334 bl t

SELEBELA 3 ch f £38096

56	7-18	Nott	8.2sft	60	1470
74	1-7	LEIC	11.8g/f	58	1967*
85	1-15	LEIC	11.8gd	63	2134+
101	1-5	SALI	12fm	82	2422*
100	2-10	Sali	12gd	87	2660
96	2-9	Newm	12g/f	[93]	3278
97	3-9	Newb	12fm	[95]	3629
98	2-9	York	11.9g/s	[95]	4058
74	10-10	Donc	14.6fm	[95]	4460

SELECTIVE 5 b g £3476

87	4-7	Thir	8sft	[104]	1225
90	13-20	Asco	7g/f	100	1926
44	24-28	Asco	7g/f	97	2558
92a	4-12	Ling	8ap	[94]	3199
49	10-10	Asco	8gd	93	3775
82	4-8	Good	7g/s	91	4231
88	6-8	Pont	10fm	88	4755
90	5-19	York	7.9gd	88	4987
92	5-22	Newm	8sft	88	5103 P

SELF BELIEF 3 b f £0

60	11-14	Thir	5g/f	67	1766
17	12-14	Newc	5g/f	[67]	4404
3	15-15	Newc	5fm	62	4870

SELF DEFENSE 7 b g £18725

101	8-19	Newc	16.1g/s	100	2771
99	6-17	Asco	16.2gd	100	3125
104	5-15	Good	14g/f	100	3510
105	5-19	York	13.9g/s	100	4023
114	2-9	Asco	12g/f	[102]	4812
96	3-8	Newb	12hvy	[112]	5224

SELF RAZIN 2 b f £0

40a	11-12	Ling	8ap		100

SELF RESPECT 2 b c £0

70	7-16	Yarm	10.1g/s		5352

SELIKA 2 ch c £411

54	12-13	Newm	6gd		4223
69	9-14	Yarm	7gd		4611
76	4-16	York	7.9gd		4997 BL
68	8-19	Pont	8g/s	73	5147 bl

SELKIRK GRACE 4 b g £270

68	5-11	Leic	10gd		4701
55	4-12	Catt	12sft		5319

SELKIRK STORM 2 b c £5802

79	1-10	NEWC	6sft		1677*
79	2-8	Thir	5g/f		2213

69	5-6	Hami	6gd		2711
65	7-7	York	5g/f	86	3432
61	11-13	York	6gd	81	4004
56	14-17	York	7g/f	77	4396
59	10-15	Hayd	6sft	72	4765
72	3-14	Ayr	6sft	65	5035
48	14-21	Donc	6hvy	[81]	5202

SEMELLE DE VENT 2 b f £4963

65a	6-12	Ling	10ap		116
35a	3-7	Wolv	12af	[63]	959
59	3-10	Beve	12.1g/s	58	1165
0	20-20	Wind	11.6sft	58	1648
47a	9-15	Ling	12ap	55	2741 BL
59a	2-14	Ling	10ap	52	3605 VIS
35	7-11	Brig	9.9g/f	55	3982 vis
59a	3-13	Wolv	8.6ap	55	5005 vis
61a	1-9	WOLV	9.5ap	[55]	5360* vis

SEMENOVSKII 3 b g £6087

41a	13-13	Wolv	6af	74	45
64a	3-14	Ling	6ap	[70]	516
71	6-16	Newm	5g/f	72	3033
48	11-11	Newm	6fm	71	3408
75	1-12	NEWM	6g/f	69	3751*
56	15-19	York	6gd	73	4005 VIS
53	16-19	Kemp	6fm	73	4394 vis
51	15-19	Good	6gd	72	4747
51	13-16	Catt	7sft	70	5130
67	5-20	Yarm	7sft	68	5256

SEMPER PARATUS 4 b g £6556

60a	1-12	WOLV	7af	52	74* bl
58a	4-16	Sout	6af	60	94 bl
50a	8-15	Ling	7ap	59	151 bl
53a	4-9	Sout	6af	[59]	459 bl
46a	8-11	Sout	7af	58	585 bl
23	12-17	Thir	8g/s	56	1214 bl
57	2-17	Nott	6.1sft	53	1606 bl
23a	12-15	Sout	8af	56	2338
55a	3-16	Sout	6af	53	2806 bl
39	14-17	Wind	6fm	54	3643 bl
35	11-16	Ches	7g/f	52	4051 bl
41	12-20	Chep	6.1g/s	49	4368 bl
55	1-16	CHEP	7.1hvy	[47]	4707* bl

SENDEED 2 b c £0

62	14-15	Sand	7.1g/f		3337 T
47	16-18	Newm	7gd		3927 t

SENDINTANK 4 ch g £69726

69a	1-11	WOLV	12af	50	380*
67a	1-10	SOUT	12af	56	421*
68a	1-11	SOUT	12af	55	458*
67a	1-9	WOLV	12af	56	467*
66	3-17	Pont	12hvy	60	1064
72	1-10	YARM	16sft	62	4151*
81	1-17	NEWM	14.8gd	67	4196+
83	1-6	NEWC	14.4sft	68	4287*
81	1-8	HAYD	11.9g/f	68	4353*
89	3-20	Hayd	14fm	82	4383
99	1-11	MUSS	16g/s	85	5335*
102	1-7	DONC	16.5sft	91	5374*

SENESCHAL 3 b c £13869

75	10-15	Newb	8gd	94	1206
72	8-8	Sali	9.9g/s	92	1500
68	12-16	Good	9.9fm	87	3553
16	10-16	Ches	10.3sft	80	4071
70	9-12	Newm	7gd	75	4225
54	14-14	Epso	7gd	70	4465
70	5-25	Newb	7gd	67	4683
79	1-19	NEWC	7g/f	67	5014*
74	6-17	Ayr	7.2sft	73	5063
78	2-14	Redc	7g/s	73	5109
67	6-16	Catt	7sft	73	5130
71	1-11	DONC	7sft	72	5219*

SENEX 4 b c £265066

110	3-8	Colo	12sft		1556
119	1-7	SAN	12gd		2636*
118	1-11	VELI	12fm		4570*

SENIOR MINISTER 6 b g £2541

48	8-11	Bath	10.2fm	63	1899
58	1-9	BRIG	8g/f	[62]	2431*
64	10-16	Beve	7.5gd	68	2655
45	8-10	Brig	8gd	62	2954

4	12-12	Wind	10fm	60	3295
5	12-12	Kemp	8g/f	60	3524
9	15-19	Chep	8.1g/s	[60]	4366
1	19-19	Leic	7g/f	60	4452
2a	12-13	Wolv	8.6ap	55	4982

SENIOR WHIM 2 b c £0

20	8-9	Nott	10hvy		5189

SENNA 4 b g £0

6a	12-12	Ling	8ap	52	406

SENNEN COVE 4 ch g £4688

4a	11-13	Sout	8af	36	221 t
32a	10-13	Sout	6af	[35]	319 t
12a	7-10	Wolv	7af	[35]	394 t
29a	6-12	Sout	7af	[35]	909
32a	3-7	Ling	10ap	[30]	1244 t
0	6-6	Ling	8ap	[30]	1292 bl t
40	6-10	Ayr	8g/s	[40]	1446
46	1-10	BEVE	8.5g/f	[40]	1943* t
48	1-14	MUSS	7.1g/f	42	2615* t
33	9-20	Yarm	8gd	44	3996 t
35	7-17	Carl	7.9fm	[45]	4506 t

SENOR BENNY 5 b r h £7700

106	3-17	Curr	6sft		5073

SENOR BOND 3 ch g £563

59a	6-7	Sout	8af	73	855
70	3-6	Warw	6.1sft	[72]	1088
53	12-16	Beve	7.5g/s	72	1163
64	6-9	Pont	6g/f	68	2609
47a	10-15	Sout	7af	[65]	2999
44a	10-13	Sout	6af	60	4091

SENOR EDUARDO 7 gr g £5554

53	9-16	Newc	7sft	[54]	966
45	11-19	Yarm	7g/f	54	1132
54	3-15	Thir	8g/s	[51]	2688
49	5-17	Warw	8.1g/f	51	2909
57	1-11	YARM	10.1gd	[48]	3362*
53	6-7	Yarm	10.1g/f	[54]	3704
55	2-8	Hami	9.2g/s	54	4133
55	3-14	York	11.9gd	54	4327
36	15-15	Beve	8.5g/f	54	4598
58	3-19	Beve	9.9g/f	54	4720
44	7-18	Pont	12g/f	55	4938
20	12-15	Redc	9g/s	55	5111

SENOR MIRO 5 b g £604

47a	3-11	Ling	8ap	[50]	145
54a	3-16	Ling	7ap	[50]	180
0	P-4	Wolv	7af	[54]	350

SENOR SET 3 b g £1063

69a	2-13	Sout	8af		2383

SENOR TORAN 3 b g £942

42a	10-11	Ling	8ap	[52]	145
51a	3-10	Ling	10ap	[46]	540
58a	4-10	Ling	10ap	[45]	738
48a	3-8	Ling	10ap	[47]	1026
25	16-19	Beve	9.9g/s	56	1164
48a	2-6	Ling	10ap	[47]	1455
30	5-6	Brig	11.9fm	[53]	1692 P

SENTIERO ROSSO 2 b c £9410

70	4-10	Newc	5g/f		2158
78	2-18	Pont	5g/s		3968
78	1-4	NEWC	5hvy		4214*
101	3-6	Ripo	6gd		4280
73	9-12	Ayr	5g/s	[96]	4651
88	9-24	Redc	6fm	[96]	4928
74	8-11	York	6gd	[96]	4998
66	13-14	Donc	7sft		5213

SENTRY 3 b c £16841

74a	1-14	LING	12ap	[87]	14*
87	1-20	NEWM	12gd	82	1172*
88	4-14	Hami	12.1gd	85	1389
90	3-17	Sali	14.1g/s	85	1502
87	3-14	Hayd	16.2gd	86	2239
48	21-29	Asco	20g/f	86	2471
82	7-17	Asco	16.2gd	86	3125

SENZA SCRUPOLI 3 ch g £463

0	12-14	Sout	12af	[73]	194
47	3-8	Ripo	10g/s	[70]	1363 bl

SEPARATED 2 b f £0
56a 10-12 Ling 8ap 175
48a 5-9 Wolv 9.4af 240

SERAPH 4 ch g £4383
39a 3-12 Wolv 9.4af [36] 302 p
43a 1-10 SOUT 11af [40] 375* p
31a 8-13 Sout 12af [45] 575 p
31a 3-10 Wolv 12af [40] 780 p
43a 3-15 Sout 12af 40 867 p
41a 2-9 Sout 12af [45] 1204 p
41a 1-5 LING 12ap [40] 1411* p
0 9-9 Ling 13ap [40] 1456 p
41a 3-8 Sout 14af [40] 1840 p
31 9-13 Ripo 12.3g/f 40 2008 p
15a 11-14 Sout 12af 40 3486 p

SERBELLONI 4 b g £0
59 5-10 Wind 10g/f [70] 3980

SERENE PEARL 2 b f £320
6 11-12 Ripo 5gd 1173
62 8-10 Thir 5g/f 1764
22 6-6 Carl 5fm 2442
53 6-8 Catt 5g/f 2847 T
56a 4-6 Sout 5af 3484 t
34a 13-13 Sout 7af 57 4040 t
27 10-11 Catt 5gd [53] 4962 t

SERENGETI SKY 3 br c £271
4 8-8 Pont 10hvy 1067
38 4-4 Beve 12.1sft 1308
0 6-9 Folk 9.7sft 1581

SERGEANT CECIL 5 ch g £53246
3 20-20 Epso 12hvy 88 1295
87 3-11 Good 12gd 85 2538
78 5-7 Sand 14g/s 86 2899
96 1-11 ASCO 12gd 86 3070+
96 2-15 Good 14g/f 89 3510
99 2-20 Hayd 14fm 93 4383
98 2-15 Donc 14.6fm 93 4491
96 3-14 Asco 12g/f 93 4814

SERGEANT LEWIS 2 gr c £0
44 6-6 Brig 7fm 4760
33 18-19 Ling 6g/f 4895

SERGEANT SHINKO 2 ch g £0
0 11-11 Newc 7fm 4863
39a 11-13 Wolv 8.6ap 4979 BL
17 9-10 Nott 10hvy 5188 bl

SERGEANT SLIPPER 6 ch g £5621
42a 5-15 Sout 6af 46 187 vis
0 13-13 Sout 6af 45 500 vis
40a 3-10 Wolv 5af [45] 527 vis
14a 10-13 Wolv 5af [45] 582 vis
42a 3-11 Wolv 5af 45 643 vis
48a 1-16 SOUT 5af [45] 720+ vis
54a 2-15 Sout 6af [45] 773 vis
66a 7-8 Wolv 7af [47] 838 vis
59a 1-9 SOUT 5af [51] 1194* vis
55 5-11 Redc 6sft [46] 1662 vis
10 14-16 Brig 6fm 46 2262 vis
16 14-20 Nott 6.1g/f 44 2630 vis

SERGEANT SMALL 2 b g £0
23 17-18 Ling 6gd 4108
0 20-20 York 6g/f 4401

SERGEANTS INN 7 b g £0
0 7-7 Sout 14af [30] 724

SERIEUX 5 b h £9709
79a 10-11 Ling 8ap 92 547
87 11-24 Donc 8gd 92 951
60 14-17 Kemp 10g/s 90 1111
93 2-27 Newb 8g/f 88 1231
34 18-18 Newb 8g/f 90 3265
31 21-21 Good 8fm 90 3565
76 8-9 Kemp 8g/f [88] 3689
64 12-14 Wind 8.3gd [84] 4122 P
76 9-21 Donc 7fm 80 4482 p
84 4-24 Newb 8g/f 80 4642 p
43 12-14 Asco 8g/f 80 4813 p
79 5-13 Good 8gd [80] 4872 p

SERRAMANNA 3 ch f £1520
74 6-10 Newb 10gd 1209
52 5-5 Donc 10.3g/s 76 3377
76 3-10 Nott 10gd 73 3990
72 3-11 Ripo 12.3gd [73] 4281
64 8-17 Nott 14.1g/s 72 4647

SERRAVAL 6 ch m £2087
59 2-13 Folk 9.7g/f 55 3726
59 3-11 Good 11gd 59 3948
50 5-8 Brig 11.9sft 57 4143
60 3-12 Good 9.9sft 57 4268

SERRE CHEVALIER 3 b g £7337
80 2-13 Kemp 8fm 2072
81 1-5 SAND 8.1g/f 3360*
74 8-15 Sand 7.1gd 79 4500
59 15-20 Newm 9g/s 78 5286

SES SELINE 3 b f £738
33 4-4 Donc 8g/s 1520
37 5-7 Nott 8.2hvy 1610
13 8-8 Leic 11.8g/f 1961
8 13-13 Redc 14.1gd 40 4249 P
10 16-18 Leic 10gd [40] 5042 BL

SESSAY 3 b g £4336
57 4-15 Thir 7g/s [69] 1473
71 3-14 Ches 6.1g/s 69 1570
67 5-11 Redc 7g/f [69] 1822
51 18-21 Good 5fm 69 3567
59 6-20 Ripo 6gd 68 4278
64 8-17 York 7g/f 68 4398
65 6-26 Ayr 5g/s 65 4618
71 1-10 CATT 6gd [65] 4964*
62 9-15 Ayr 5sft 71 5036

SESTINA 3 ch f £0
40a 13-16 Ling 7ap 65 22

SET ALIGHT 3 b f £690
56 9-13 Newb 7gd 1210
48 4-6 Yarm 7g/f 2342
50 3-9 Folk 7fm 2716
39a 8-13 Sout 6af 53 4091
25 8-10 Yarm 7g/s 50 4251

SETTLEMENT CRAIC 3 b c £11797
84a 1-13 LING 12ap 873*
89 4-11 Ripo 12.3gd 85 1174
89 3-11 Sand 10g/s 85 2127
81 11-17 Asco 12g/f 86 2519
93 1-12 WIND 11.6gd 85 3161*
77 13-16 Good 12fm 91 3534
35 15-15 Leic 11.8g/f 90 5043

SEVEN MAGICIANS 2 b f £405
82 4-14 Newm 7g/f 4711

SEVEN NO TRUMPS 7 ch g £7190
83 2-17 Kemp 5sft 80 944
77 5-20 Kemp 6gd 82 1138
61 12-20 Wind 6g/s 82 1255
74 11-20 Thir 5g/s 80 1476
47 11-12 Ling 5g/s 80 1615 p
76 3-14 Kemp 6fm 77 1914
77 6-19 Kemp 6fm 77 2070 p
67 10-14 Wind 5g/f 77 2266
77 4-9 Sali 5fm 77 2420 p
68 8-12 Sali 5gd 75 2698 p
57 8-12 Ling 5g/f 76 2743 p
79 2-12 York 5g/s 75 3073 p
72 8-17 Sand 5g/f 77 3341 p
61 10-18 Beve 5g/s 76 3852 p
77 4-13 Newb 5.2g/f 76 3960 p
69 7-11 Bath 5g/s [75] 4201 p
0 P-13 Wolv 5.1ap 74 5341

SEVEN SHIRT 3 b g £0
44 8-15 Chep 8.1sft 60 4057
17 14-15 Chep 8.1g/s 60 4300
49 7-7 Epso 8.5g/f [60] 4474
46 6-16 Chep 7.1hvy [60] 4707
0 17-17 Warw 8.1g/s [45] 4992

SEVEN YEAR ITCH 3 b c £3518
71a 2-14 Ling 10ap 53
82 2-9 Ling 10sft 1623
89 2-8 Ripo 10g/f 2012 BL

SEVERELY 2 b f £0
57 7-10 Wind 6fm 3290

SEVILLANO 3 b g £16023
108 1-6 LEIC 6g/s [99] 1018+
95 1-6 HAMI 5gd [106] 1387+
93 7-11 Newb 6gd [106] 1732

SEWMORE CHARACTER 3 b c £3963
76a 2-11 Ling 8ap 72 131
73a 4-12 Ling 8ap 74 369
54a 6-14 Ling 10ap [74] 430
74a 2-11 Ling 8ap [72] 697
60a 5-10 Ling 8ap [70] 1021
48 15-16 Nott 8.2g/s 68 4036
32 14-14 Beve 7.5g/s 64 4241
69a 2-14 Ling 10ap [66] 4448
66a 9-16 Ling 12ap 68 4973
46a 15-16 Ling 12ap 67 5261

SEWMUCH CHARACTER 5 b g £5857
55 4-8 Hayd 6g/s [72] 1345
26 15-16 Nott 5.1sft [70] 1743
63 6-12 Donc 7gd 67 2235
61 4-9 Chep 6.1g/f 65 2626
64 2-17 Wind 6fm 63 2975
37 7-7 Pont 6gd [63] 3244
71 1-7 FOLK 6g/s [62] 3910*
29 17-17 Wind 6gd 49 4126
72 6-13 Bath 5.7gd 69 4548
70a 3-13 Wolv 6ap 68 5010
46a 10-12 Wolv 7.1ap 68 5289

SEWSO CHARACTER 3 b c £11928
98 4-15 Ches 7.6gd 96 1583
92 10-18 Good 9g/f 96 1813
96 3-8 York 10.4g/f 95 2406
94 4-14 Hayd 8.1gd 95 2903
95 4-13 Newm 9g/s 95 3277
93 7-12 Good 7fm [94] 3555 BL
92 4-8 Folk 9.7g/s [92] 3912
91 6-11 Beve 9.9g/s 90 4239
79 7-7 Sand 8.1gd 88 4499
90 2-19 Hayd 10.5g/s 85 4766
78 4-8 Nott 10hvy 87 5187

SEYAADI 2 b c £1617
81 5-14 Newm 7g/f 2766
82 2-8 York 7g/s 3078
80a 5-13 Ling 7ap 3329

SEYED 4 b g £216
49 3-15 Beve 7.5g/f 1944

SFORZANDO 3 b f £3630
70 1-17 YARM 7g/f [65] 1729*
67 5-12 Newm 7g/f 69 2249
65 7-20 Newb 7fm 68 2650
53 7-8 Wind 8.3gd 67 3162

SGT PEPPER 2 b c £1978
94 9- Sain 10g/s 9
90 8-8 Newm 7g/f [100] 1932
84 11-15 Asco 7g/f [98] 2486
92 4-6 Sali 7g/s [95] 3113
91 6-10 Kemp 8fm 92 4389
91 5-5 Newb 9gd [89] 4682
75 15-17 Newm 10g/f 89 4917

SHAABAN 3 b c £0
59 13-17 Newb 8g/f 1762
69 7-13 Kemp 8fm 2072
66 7-10 Good 8gd 2378
52 5-6 Ches 10.3g/s 2748
29 9-11 Newm 8gd [69] 3923

SHAAMITS ALL OVER 4 br f £206
52a 6-14 Ling 10ap 53
46a 10-13 Ling 10ap 148
38a 11-14 Ling 10ap 50 265
9a 7-9 Ling 12ap [50] 324 P
11a 14-14 Ling 10ap [40] 1072
29a 3-7 Sout 8af [35] 1593 BL
36 6-16 Brig 7gd [30] 4901
34 8-11 Wind 8.3g/f [30] 5052

SHADES OF GREEN 2 b f £0
57 10-15 Newm 8fm 4723

62a 6-14 Ling 7ap 5257

SHADOWFAX 3 b g £1928

49a	6-16	Sout	6af		65	
58a	2-13	Sout	6af	[67]	254	
56a	4-13	Sout	6af	[60]	319	BL
36a	11-12	Wolv	6af	60	385	bl
36a	8-13	Sout	6af	[58]	659	P
34a	7-10	Wolv	8.5af	56	754	e
63a	2-11	Sout	6af	[52]	869	bl
0	8-8	Wolv	7af	[58]	1656	VIS

SHADY DEAL 8 b g £843

0	11-11	Sout	5af	[30]	775
11a	9-10	Wolv	5af	[30]	781
30	13-19	Warw	5gd	52	1127
22	8-15	Folk	6g/s	52	1267
47	3-11	Redc	6sft	[49]	1662
32	14-18	Bath	5.7g/f	49	1788
34	7-16	Nott	6.1gd	[47]	1988
47	3-20	Nott	6.1gd	45	2928
33	15-17	Bath	5g/f	45	2981
13	8-19	Nott	6.1gd	[45]	3104

SHADY REFLECTION 3 b f £18150

88	1-11	ASCO	8sft	[75]	1419*
91	5-7	Good	9.9g/f	[91]	1844

SHAHAMA 3 gr c £0

64	12-15	Sand	7.1g/f		3337
45	12-14	Sali	8g/s		4078

SHAHEER 2 b c £1096

70	6-13	Newb	6g/f		1760
76	2-19	Kemp	6g/f		1911
48	12-18	Chep	6.1gd		2194
74	6-20	Ling	7gd	73	4444
65	13-16	Nott	10g/f	71	4848

SHAHM 4 b g £2072

54a	1-16	SOUT	7af	47	208*
28a	8-14	Sout	6af	53	501
44a	7-11	Ling	8ap	53	820

SHAHZAN HOUSE 5 b h £27142

94	3-16	Epso	10.1hvy	94	1296	
99	2-14	York	10.4g/s	94	1704	
98	3-11	Epso	10.1g/f	96	2208	P
100	3-9	Sand	10g/s	96	2896	p
103	3-20	Hayd	10.5fm	96	3794	p
100	3-11	York	10.4g/s	97	4021	p
90	6-14	Newb	10hvy	97	5223	p

SHALAMAK 2 b f £0

0	12-13	Wolv	8.5af	[57]	43

SHALATI PRINCESS 3 b f £206

49a	7-11	Ling	8ap		496
25a	11-12	Ling	8ap		623
35a	6-10	Ling	8ap		785
46a	7-10	Ling	7ap	[45]	911
44a	4-8	Ling	10ap	[45]	1183
51	9-12	Sali	12g/s	[45]	1501
42a	3-8	Ling	10ap	[45]	1713
41a	7-15	Ling	12ap	43	2741
47a	5-8	Ling	10ap	[41]	3787

SHALAYA 3 b f £0

87	5-14	Asco	10g/f	87	1924
81	11-12	Sand	9g/f	87	2385

SHALBEBLUE 7 b g £0

35	11-18	Newm	12fm	50	2088 bl
41	9-14	Ches	12.3gd	50	2285 bl
23	8-8	Muss	12g/f	45	2616 bl
36	8-19	Beve	9.9g/f	42	3505 bl
18	11-17	Catt	12sft	42	3929 bl

SHALIMAR 2 b f £5915

88	3-7	Capa	5.5gd		2302

SHAMAN 7 b g £0

52a	5-12	Ling	10ap	52	542
37a	12-14	Ling	12ap	50	768
44	4-8	Folk	9.7sft	45	1579

SHAMARA 4 b f £13364

86	2-19	Ripo	10g/f	81	1781
89	2-5	Sand	9g/f	83	2191

91	4-6	Newc	10.1g/s	[85]	2772
84	7-10	Chep	10.2g/s	[90]	3089
102	2-11	Yarm	10.1gd	[90]	4614
94	6-10	Newm	10gd	[92]	5086

SHAMARDAL 2 b c £198819

103	1-7	AYR	6gd	3148*
114	1-10	GOOD	7fm	3532*
122	1-9	NEWM	7sft	5137*

SHAMBAR 5 gr g £2582

83	3-16	Sand	10g/s	2131
66	5-13	Wind	10g/f	2453
99	3-6	Epso	10.1g/s	3043

SHAMDIAN 4 b g £0

75	9-20	Newb	10gd	85	1235
59a	9-14	Ling	7ap	[83]	5240 t

SHAMELESS 7 ch g £0

0	9-9	Sout	12af	2381 t
37	8-11	Beve	9.9sft	4261 t
0	9-11	Beve	12.1g/f	4716 t
2	9-11	Catt	12sft	5128 t

SHAMOAN 2 ch c £2559

85	2-7	Curr	6g/f	2003

SHAMONE 2 ch c £0

13a	10-10	Sout	5af	[38]	139 P
27a	8-9	Sout	5af	[28]	256 p

SHAMROCK BAY 2 b f £447

20	9-10	Nott	6.1g/f	3418
72	4-9	Beve	7.5g/f	4600
63	8-19	Leic	5g/f	5040

SHAMROCK CITY 7 b g £226

85	6-8	Donc	10.3gd	[93]	2234
35	31-31	Asco	8g/f	93	2489
52	12-12	Kemp	9g/f	88	2860

SHAMROCK TEA 2 b c £4125

22a	8-13	Sout	6af	[65]	63
42	12-13	Hayd	6g/f	60	1881
54	5-9	Thir	5g/f	55	2219
62	1-13	NEWC	6sft	52	2683*
58	4-11	Ripo	6gd	59	2985
37	13-18	Hayd	6gd	59	3737
33	14-19	Nott	6.1g/f	[59]	4845
9	20-20	Leic	7gd	57	5046

SHAMWARI FIRE 3 ch g £4833

48a	4-10	Wolv	7af	[52]	4
0	13-14	Sout	8af	52	62
28a	14-16	Sout	7af	[47]	161
24a	4-8	Wolv	9.4af	[45]	299
33a	6-15	Ling	7ap	[45]	411
11a	13-15	Ling	7ap	[45]	969
43	7-18	Nott	8.2g/s	48	1778
54	1-15	BEVE	7.5g/f	[46]	1944*
50	6-15	Beve	7.5g/s	51	2324
42	8-17	Warw	8.1fm	51	2440
34	10-17	Warw	8.1fm	50	2572
46	3-16	Beve	7.5gd	50	2891
51	3-18	Pont	8gd	50	3242
43	8-13	Muss	8g/f	49	3526
29	13-17	Thir	8g/s	49	3830
49	1-15	FOLK	9.7g/f	[47]	4373*
50	3-17	Carl	7.9fm	[49]	4506
49	6-10	Yarm	10.1gd	[49]	4612
44	9-19	Beve	9.9g/f	49	4720
48	3-13	Brig	8gd	[49]	4902

SHANGHAI LILY 2 b f £16294

101	1-11	NEWB	6gd	3915*
104	1-4	NEWB	7g/f	4641*

SHANGHAI SURPRISE 3 b c £0

15a	5-5	Sout	8af	[46]	1440
2	8-8	Nott	8.2sft	52	1740 bl
52	8-8	Donc	5g/f	[45]	2075 bl
39	7-9	Thir	5g/f	45	2219 P
0	9-10	Sout	5af	[40]	3156 bl

SHANKLY BOND 2 ch c £0

55	8-14	Thir	7g/s	4204
70	9-14	Hayd	6fm	4385
72	6-12	Thir	7g/f	4591

SHANNKARAS QUEST 3 b c £0

24a	12-12	Ling	8ap	623
15a	11-11	Ling	8ap	696
0	12-12	Kemp	6sft	4029

SHANNON SPRINGS 2 b c £6178

95	2-12	Newm	7g/f	3470
101	3-7	York	7gd	4003
97	2-11	Donc	8fm	4462
93	7-10	San	8sft	5167

SHANNONS DREAM 8 gr m £0

0	7-8	Chep	12.1g/f	[18]	2623
26	4-5	Brig	11.9g/f	[18]	3983

SHANTY STAR 4 gr c £3300

0	9-10	York	13.9g/f	[105]	1705
1	P-9	Sand	16.4g/f	[105]	2095
106	3-5	Newm	12g/f	[105]	4886
91	9-11	Newm	16sft	[104]	5138

SHAPE UP 4 b g £11930

33a	3-8	Wolv	12af	53	1342 bl
54	2-8	Folk	9.7sft	50	1579 bl
46	4-18	Wind	11.6g/f	50	1960 bl
61	1-18	NEWM	12fm	50	2088* bl
65	1-14	CHES	12.3gd	53	2285* bl
66	1-13	MUSS	12g/s	58	5333* bl

SHAPIRA 3 ch f £80989

107	1-15	DUSS	8sft	1702*

SHARAAB 3 b c £1998

71	6-11	Newm	10gd		1148
64	8-11	Beve	9.9g/f	75	1834 t
64	5-16	Newm	7fm	[74]	2092 t
76	2-12	York	7.9g/f	[70]	2410 t
26	9-10	Pont	10gd	[73]	3243 t
65	7-14	Kemp	10g/f	70	3690 t
26	16-16	Thir	8g/f	68	4592 t

SHARABAD 6 b g £0

40	5-6	Ayr	10g/f		1894
44	7-11	Pont	10g/f		2991
0	10-11	Muss	8g/f		3558
29	10-16	Carl	11.9g/f	45	4348

SHARABY 2 b f £2262

76	3-16	Kemp	7g/f		3035
65	12-13	Good	7fm		3554
54	11-12	Beve	7.5g/s		4242
82	2-19	Newm	7g/s	[70]	5279

SHARADI 3 b c £13491

51	7-8	Good	11gd	[77]	2222
62	10-13	Redc	11g/s	70	2960
54	8-17	Newm	12g/f	60	3618
67	2-9	Sand	14g/s	59	3893
71	2-12	Good	16g/s	65	4235
74	2-12	Muss	14gd	66	4521
77	1-6	MUSS	16g/f	66	4555*
71	3-11	Newm	14g/f	71	4919
83	1-8	BATH	17.2sft	70	5175*

SHARAIJI BLOSSOM 2 b f £7263

75	3-9	Beve	7.5g/f	4600
84	1-18	NOTT	8.2g/f	4842*

SHARDDA 4 b f £591

63	3-8	Newc	8hvy	[65]	1039
0	15-15	Hami	8.3g/s	65	1602
16	12-12	Newc	9hvy	63	4215
0	11-12	Newc	8g/f	[60]	4407 T
16	10-18	Newc	8sft	[55]	5017
40	5-11	Redc	10sft	[50]	5303 t

SHAREB 2 b c £0

58	11-23	Newm	6gd	5084

SHARED DREAMS 2 b f £751

78	3-16	Newm	7g/s	5280

SHARES 4 b g £2210

61	2-14	Newc	10.1sft	56	964
52	4-13	Ayr	10sft	[60]	5066

SHARMY 8 b g £0

89	11-13	Asco	10g/f	[94]	4772
53	11-19	Newm	12gd	90	5085

SHAROURA 7 ch m £14699
47a	5-11	Sout	6af	52	91
56	5-10	Thir	5g/f	62	1973
48	8-15	Leic	6g/f	60	2398
68	1-11	PONT	6g/f	59	2791*
50	13-17	Pont	6g/f	66	2990
65	3-14	Hami	6gd	64	3129
64	4-9	Ayr	6g/f	64	3307
70	2-14	Thir	6af	64	3416
70	4-12	Carl	6.9fm	64	3548
54	8-16	Ches	7g/f	66	4051
56	12-18	Redc	6fm	65	4339
68	3-18	Ayr	7.2sft	64	4622
53	11-18	Leic	6gd	64	5039
49a	12-14	Ling	7ap	58	5300 p

SHARP AS A TACK 2 b f £9538
53	8-10	Wind	6fm		3290
80	2-10	Nott	6.1g/f		3418
85	1-16	SALI	7gd		3882*
47	12-12	Good	7sft	[83]	4264
89	2-4	Newb	6g/f	[83]	4641 BL
78	6-7	Newb	7hvy	[88]	5222 bl

SHARP DIVERSION 2 ch f £0
51	6-10	Redc	5fm		4338

SHARP HAT 9 b g £5488
73a	1-12	WOLV	5af	[66]	70*
71a	3-11	Wolv	6af	[69]	153
55a	5-10	Wolv	6af	72	246
52a	5-10	Wolv	5af	[72]	286
71a	2-7	Sout	6af	[71]	317
0	13-13	Sout	6af	70	551
44a	7-12	Sout	6af	[70]	610
62a	5-13	Sout	6af	66	741
56a	5-9	Sout	6af	[66]	793
44a	8-12	Sout	5af	64	853
34a	12-14	Ling	6ap	62	1025 bl
53	7-19	Beve	5sft	64	1627
53	7-11	Hami	6g/f	62	2477
65	7-18	Newc	6g/s	59	2770
61	3-17	Catt	5g/f	59	2846
57	7-18	Hayd	5gd	62	2951
67	2-13	Catt	5g/f	60	3350
61	4-10	Hami	5g/s	[63]	4010
64	5-26	Ayr	5g/s	63	4618
41	16-20	Ripo	6gd	63	4785
45	14-19	York	5gd	62	4989
49	9-19	Ayr	6sft	62	5069
60a	4-13	Wolv	5.1ap	59	5156

SHARP N FROSTY 2 b g £959
65	4-11	Nott	5.1gd		1237
45	7-7	Ches	5.1g/s		1573
64	4-6	Warw	7.1fm		2597
62	4-12	Ling	7g/f	67	3351
0	U-9	Newc	8sft	63	4285
37	9-20	Yarm	8g/s	63	4635
62	5-9	Nott	10hvy	[57]	5189

SHARP NEEDLE 3 b f £12984
77	9-17	Newm	7gd		1171
71	2-7	Muss	9g/s		1462
67	5-18	Wind	8.3g/f		1810
75	1-8	HAMI	9.2g/f	68	2475*
78	1-9	REDC	8g/f	[70]	3806*
74	4-8	Thir	8fm	73	4378
85a	1-12	LING	8ap	73	5238+

SHARP REPLY 2 b c £273
87	4-13	Donc	7hvy		5200

SHARP RIGGING 4 b g £0
43	16-17	Leic	10gd	69	5062

SHARP SECRET 6 b m £4115
55	5-9	Leic	8fm	55	2108
60	1-9	PONT	8g/f	55	2604*
50	8-14	Pont	8g/f	57	2993
50	7-8	Thir	8fm	57	4378
26a	7-13	Wolv	8.6ap	53	4982

SHARP SPICE 8 b m £0
21a	6-12	Ling	12ap	[35]	1180 vis

SHARPINCH 5 b g £0
17a	14-15	Ling	7ap	70	50

0	16-16	Ling	7ap	65	323

SHARPLAW DESTINY 3 b f £0
44a	5-7	Wolv	7af	55	1376
45a	10-14	Ling	10ap	53	2064
37	12-18	Sali	7fm	50	2292 BL
10	9-9	Brig	8fm	[47]	2834

SHARPLAW STAR 2 b f £19726
92	1-7	LEIC	5gd		2132*
99	3-17	Asco	5g/f		2490
97	1-6	BEVE	5g/f		4717*
84a	3-5	Ling	5ap	[100]	5260

SHARPLAW VENTURE 4 b f £2024
79	3-6	Hami	8.3gd	[95]	2710
73a	8-12	Ling	8ap	[90]	3199
80	7-9	Kemp	8g/f	[88]	3689

SHARVIE 7 b g £0
15a	7-10	Ling	16ap	[40]	650 p
6a	5-6	Wolv	16.2af	[35]	824 VIS

SHASTYE 3 b f £5279
62	7-18	Wind	10g/f		1959
56	3-7	Newb	12g/f		2879
71	4-10	Pont	10gd		3243
76a	1-14	LING	13ap	[73]	4892*
78	9-12	Yarm	14.1sft	[73]	5254

SHATIN HERO 3 ch c £1251
63a	2-10	Wolv	8.5af	57	5 p
51a	8-12	Wolv	7af	55	74 p
52a	5-14	Sout	8af	59	160 p
59a	3-13	Sout	8af	[59]	188 p

SHATIN LEADER 2 b f £823
0	P-9	Muss	5fm		2083
44	6-8	Muss	5g/f		2611
61	3-10	Carl	5g/f		3227
57	4-6	Carl	5g/f		3652
41	11-12	Muss	5g/f	61	4172
5	18-18	Ayr	6g/s	[59]	4617
3	18-18	Newc	5g/f	52	5013

SHATIN SPECIAL 3 ch f £3023
9a	7-10	Wolv	12af	49	243 p
38a	2-10	Wolv	12af	[49]	250 p
35a	5-10	Sout	11af	40	330 p
45a	2-5	Sout	12af	[40]	446 p
0	F-12	Sout	11af	45	534 p
36a	4-5	Sout	12af	[45]	616 p
48a	1-11	WOLV	12af	[45]	666* p
20a	6-11	Sout	11af	46	746 p
23a	6-9	Sout	12af	[45]	774 p
31	6-10	Yarm	10.1g/f	[51]	1724 p
29	9-18	Wind	11.6g/f	47	1960 p
35	8-13	Ripo	12.3g/f	47	2008 p
42a	3-16	Sout	12af	40	2340 p
20a	8-9	Sout	12af	[40]	2724 p

SHATIN STAR 2 b c £0
39	13-13	Newm	7fm		4724

SHAYADI 7 b g £514
75	5-12	Ches	10.3gd	79	1586 t P

SHAYMEES GIRL 2 b f £2522
14a	12-13	Wolv	6af		126
28a	5-6	Wolv	6af		631
57a	3-15	Sout	6af		795
58a	3-7	Wolv	6af		863
26	8-8	Hami	5gd	57	1509
45	3-10	Catt	6gd	[52]	4964
47a	10-13	Wolv	5.1ap	56	5156
55a	2-11	Wolv	5.1ap	[52]	5363

SHAZANA 3 gr f £0
68	6-13	Newb	7gd		1210
57	7-12	Sand	10g/f		2193
59a	6-14	Ling	10ap		2740

SHEAPYS LASS 3 b f £0
24a	11-11	Sout	5af	60	418
9a	11-13	Sout	6af	[60]	444 VIS
0	12-13	Sout	8af	[50]	553
14a	14-16	Sout	5af	[45]	720

SHEARWATER 6 b m £0

0	10-10	Wolv	14.8af	[22]	125

SHEBAAN 3 b f £0
47	17-17	Newm	7gd	[58]	1171
5	13-14	Newc	8gd	55	1872
6	8-9	Wind	6gd	50	2619
12	11-11	Yarm	7g/f	45	3711
19	11-14	Newm	7gd	[42]	4195
0	17-20	Yarm	7g/s	[40]	5120

SHEBOYGAN 2 ch f £8106
86	3-13	Kemp	6g/f		4358
86	1-13	REDC	7fm		4927*
92	3-7	Newb	7hvy	[84]	5222

SHEER FOCUS 6 b g £0
16	18-19	Beve	9.9g/f	48	4720 P
18	13-16	Brig	8gd	[47]	4902 p
7a	12-12	Wolv	9.5ap	[45]	5234

SHEER TENBY 7 b h £0
81	19-29	Asco	6fm	99	2581 BL T

SHEKAN STAR 2 b f £0
30	15-18	Donc	6g/s		3376
48	12-18	Newc	6g/s		3699
46	10-18	Ripo	6g/s		3939
51	8-14	Redc	6g/s		5106

SHERBOURNE 2 b f £0
27	10-11	Kemp	5hvy		1640
48	10-13	Nott	5.1gd		1987
46	6-6	Yarm	5.2gd		3488
52	12-14	Newm	7gd		3752
34	10-10	Newm	7gd		4191
29	15-20	Leic	7g/f	47	4451
7	14-16	Yarm	8g/s	47	4632
54a	7-8	Wolv	8.6ap	[45]	5007

SHERIFFS DEPUTY 4 b g £689
68	8-12	Hayd	8.1g/f	72	1883
48	8-12	Nott	8.2g/s	70	2931
68	3-11	Bath	8gd	68	3142
27	15-16	Hayd	10.5sft	68	3276
55	9-12	Leic	8fm	66	3813

SHERSHA 5 b m £8958
103	2-7	Leop	5g/f	[87]	3495

SHERWOOD FOREST 4 ch g £1459
21	8-10	Ayr	8g/s	[44]	2544 vis
56	3-10	Muss	9g/f	[44]	2811 vis
40	6-7	Ayr	10.9gd	44	3149 vis
36	8-8	Hami	11.1g/f	44	3207 vis
44	5-13	Ayr	10gd	44	3325 vis
47	2-11	Muss	16g/f	42	3557 vis
44	6-12	Muss	14g/f	44	4170 vis
16	13-14	York	11.9gd	45	4327 vis
31	8-16	Carl	11.9g/f	45	4348 vis

SHERZABAD 7 b g £0
9	10-11	Leic	11.8fm	44	2112

SHES A DIAMOND 7 b m £0
0	14-16	Sout	8af	[40]	442

SHES A FOX 3 b f £0
46	7-10	Sali	8sft		4578
47	11-13	Nott	8.2g/f		4847

SHES MY DREAM 2 ch f £0
32a	10-10	Ling	5ap		1071
52	8-9	Yarm	5.2g/f		1133
47a	10-10	Ling	5ap		2017
12	7-7	Chep	6.1gd		2115

SHES MY OUTSIDER 2 b f £4434
68	11-16	Kemp	7g/f		3035
79	3-13	Kemp	7g/f		3520
84	1-14	CHEP	8.1gd		4484*
84	7-8	Newm	7sft	[82]	5133

SHES OUR LASS 3 b f £22609
45a	12-15	Ling	7ap	57	815
44	10-13	Donc	7gd	[60]	925
61	1-14	WARW	7.1sft	54	1085*
62	3-13	Nott	8.2gd	60	1242
64	1-9	AYR	7.2fm	[60]	1910*
76	1-8	AYR	7.2gd	[63]	2506*
75	1-11	LEIC	8g/f	69	3516*

80 1-9 **THIR** 8sft 74 3835*
85 2-5 Ayr 8hvy 80 4085
71 7-11 Ayr 8sft 80 4621

SHESHALAN 3 ch c £438
65 4-8 Newb 10hvy 5226

SHIBUMI 3 ch f £0
56 5-14 Donc 5gd 2237
49 5-12 Ling 6g/f 2586
55 4-16 Ling 7gd 53 3024
57 4-18 Carl 7.9fm 52 3547

SHIELALIGH 3 ch f £1022
71a 8-8 Ling 5ap 84 818
65 7-19 Newm 6g/s 83 1154 T
68 3-8 Bath 5fm [80] 1901 t
34 10-11 Nott 6.1g/f 77 2155 t
56 6-9 Wind 6gd 72 2619 t P
44 6-16 Catt 5sft [70] 3932 p
67 5-9 Thir 5g/s 67 4210 p
61 5-17 Bath 5.7gd [66] 5020 p

SHIFTING PLACE 2 ch f £50159
89 1-9 **SAN** 6g/f 2823*
108 2-8 Mais 5.5gd 3498

SHIFTY 4 b g £2752
51a 4-14 Sout 8af 54 60 bl
56a 2-16 Sout 8af 54 86 bl
50a 3-8 Wolv 9.4af 55 157 bl
53a 4-16 Sout 6af 55 166 bl
54a 2-16 Sout 7af 54 202 bl
38a 6-11 Sout 8af 54 255 bl
45a 5-10 Sout 12af 54 421
36a 12-14 Ling 10ap 54 718
0 13-16 Newc 8hvy 52 1036 bl
34 9-14 Pont 8hvy [51] 1253 VIS
50 4-13 Muss 7.1g/s 51 1463 vis
41 8-13 Muss 7.1gd 51 1553
50 5-19 Redc 8sft 49 1661
50 2-14 Carl 7.9fm 48 1954
49a 4-15 Sout 7af 48 2384
52 4-16 Beve 7.5gd 49 2655 vis
42 9-10 Carl 6.9gd 49 2935 vis
37 9-11 Ripo 8gd 49 2986
21 13-13 Muss 8g/f 47 3526

SHIFTY NIGHT 3 b f £3722
24 15-15 Leic 6g/f 1829
36 10-14 Donc 5gd 2237
35a 4-16 Sout 6af 42 2806
51a 1-8 **SOUT** 6af 42 3092*
39 10-14 Thir 6g/f 49 3416
48 6-13 Ling 7g/f 47 3604
33 10-14 Yarm 6gd 47 3870
34 9-14 Yarm 7gd 47 3995
46a 4-13 Sout 6af 49 4091 P
29 12-18 Yarm 6g/s 45 5354

SHINGLE STREET 2 b c £1311
53 7-14 Donc 6g/f 1874
38 9-13 Donc 6gd 2236
60 8-13 York 7.9gd 4325
75 2-13 Brig 8sft 5091
52 5-15 Brig 7g/f 5192

SHINKO FEMME 3 b f £6461
50 10-12 York 7g/s [62] 1688
0 13-13 Carl 5.9fm [60] 1949
28 13-19 York 6g/f 60 2055
38 5-15 Ayr 8gd [55] 2504
56 1-10 **MUSS** 7.1g/f 48 2812*
46 9-10 Catt 7g/f 54 3016
43 9-15 Leic 7g/f [53] 3515
53 1-10 **LEIC** 7fm [53] 3812*
44 3-14 Beve 7.5sft [53] 4256
38 8-15 Yarm 7g/s [51] 4587

SHINY THING 2 br f £0
74 5-15 Kemp 7g/f 4710
56 8-16 Bath 8gd 5019

SHIRLEY NOT 8 gr g £0
1 20-20 Ripo 5gd 46 1179
11 12-12 Sout 7gd [46] 1284

SHIRLEY OAKS 6 b m £7156
24a 12-15 Ling 7ap [40] 411

36a 5-14 Ling 6ap [40] 652
29a 10-15 Ling 7ap [40] 708
44a 2-13 Ling 6ap [40] 788
42a 3-15 Ling 7ap [40] 969
49a 1-12 **LING** 6ap [40] 1075*
34 6-17 Kemp 7hvy [45] 1642
49a 3-6 Wolv 7af [45] 1804
54 1-12 **SALI** 7fm [43] 2288*
53 2-17 Ling 7gd 49 2397
40 9-17 Warw 8.1fm 51 2572
40 11-17 Brig 7g/f 51 3176
51 6-9 Sali 7gd 49 3456
49 7-15 Ling 7.6fm 50 3788

SHIROCCO 3 b c £427817
116 1-18 **HAMB** 12hvy 3010*
118 3-4 Bade 12sft 4428
119 11-9 **SAN** 12sft 5168*

SHISH 2 b f £358
39a 6-8 Wolv 5af 1653
25a 6-7 Sout 6af 1751
56a 4-10 Ling 5ap 2017
44 3-6 Folk 5g/f 2270
38 7-8 Wind 6g/f 2449

SHIVAREE 2 ch f £10389
84 3-6 Good 6g/f 1866
84 1-5 **HAMI** 6g/s 2829*
88 4-10 Newm 6fm 3003
88 7-9 Sand 7.1g/f 3357
83 3-7 Ripo 6g/s [92] 3935
80 10-13 Newm 8fm 87 4725
73 13-14 Catt 7sft 83 5126

SHOHRAH 2 ch f £10395
97 1-8 **ASCO** 6g/f 3386*
103 5-9 Asco 8g/f 4798

SHOLAY 5 b g £260
41a 8-13 Ling 13ap 602
40a 7-12 Ling 8ap 675
0 9-9 Ling 12ap 52 842
19 12-12 Brig 9.9fm 50 1695
37 4-12 Chep 12.1g/s 45 3085
20 10-11 Good 11gd 45 3948

SHOLTO 6 b g £1272
53 7-17 Warw 5hvy [62] 1532 bl
66 2-13 Pont 5g/f [59] 2279 bl
36 15-17 Warw 5fm 64 2599 bl
33a 11-13 Wolv 6ap [63] 5327 bl

SHONGWENI 3 gr g £1352
76 4-10 Yarm 11.5g/f 1725
61a 3-15 Ling 12ap 2393
67 3-17 Wind 11.6fm 2788
64 8-12 Sand 14g/f 67 3359 BL
60 5-10 Newc 16.1g/s 65 3701

SHOOTING LODGE 3 b f £0
72 5-16 Sand 10g/s 2131

SHORT CHANGE 5 b g £3066
47 8-13 Brig 11.9g/f 54 1373
47 4-17 Bath 11.7sft 54 1543
46 5-11 Brig 9.9fm 47 2260
52 1-12 **WARW** 10.9fm 47 2436*

SHORT CHORUS 3 ch f £6880
31 8-8 Nott 5.1fm 53 1002
42 4-8 Folk 5g/s [50] 1268 P
30a 9-12 Wolv 6af 1374 p
55 1-10 **HAMI** 5g/s 47 1605* p
56 2-15 Redc 5g/s 50 2961 p
52 4-12 Catt 5g/f 50 3193 p
55 2-12 Donc 5g/f 52 3599 p
59 4-8 Sand 5g/s 54 3889 p
40 13-16 Good 5g/f 58 4528 p
59 3-15 Ayr 5sft 55 5036 p

SHORT PAUSE 5 b h £72348
113 3-8 Long 10gd 1061
114 1-8 **LONG** 12sft 1698*
115 3-7 Chan 12g/s 2459
115 4-10 Sain 12g/s 3012
115 2-4 Long 12sft 4568

SHORTBREAD 2 ch c £0

65 13-19 Leic 7gd 5055
61 8-16 Newb 8hvy 5220

SHOSOLOSA 2 br f £10570
57 11-19 Newb 6g/f 2310
75 2-8 Good 6gd 2537
74 2-17 Nott 6.1gd 2927
71 3-11 Bath 5.7g/f [72] 3848
73 10-26 Newb 6.5g/f 4679
74 5-16 Newm 9g/f 70 4913
36 16-20 Donc 7sft 70 5373

SHOT TO FAME 5 b g £63093
77 5-12 Pont 8hvy 94 1066
73 18-27 Newb 8gd 92 1231
111 1-14 **KEMP** 8hvy 89 1512*
108 1-6 **NOTT** 8.2g/f [101] 2154*
111 2-9 Wind 8.3fm [101] 2757
114 1-10 **ASCO** 8gd [107] 3124+
112 5-12 Sali 8gd [111] 3886
102 5-8 Hayd 8.1fm [111] 4386
71 12-13 Newm 8g/f [111] 4887

SHOTACROSS THE BOW 6 b g £0
66a 4-10 Wolv 8.5af 66 5
14a 11-14 Sout 8af 65 99

SHOTLEY DANCER 5 ch m £10940
37a 4-10 Sout 8af 40 677
6a 10-11 Sout 7af [40] 771
27 12-17 Beve 8.5g/s [40] 1160
35a 4-16 Sout 7af 37 2335
38 3-13 Redc 8gd 37 2552
17a 5-9 Sout 8af 36 2996
37 3-13 Pont 12gd 36 3240
44 1-13 **BEVE** 12.1g/f 34 3502*
41 4-10 Ripo 12.3g/f 40 3649
52 2-6 Beve 16.2g/s 42 3853
51 1-10 **BEVE** 9.9sft 46 4260*
24 11-19 Catt 15.8g/f 49 4675

SHOW ME HEAVEN 7 b m £0
3a 12-13 Ling 10ap 338

SHOW ME THE LOLLY 3 b f £0
16a 7-10 Wolv 7af 8
0 10-10 Sout 12af 54 138

SHOW NO FEAR 3 b c £5681
72 1-13 **KEMP** 9gd 67 1141*
53 8-13 Kemp 9hvy 71 1515
55 11-18 Thir 8g/f 71 1769
64 6-10 Leic 10g/f 70 1965

SHOWTIME ANNIE 3 b f £9085
20a 6-9 Wolv 8.5af [65] 751
63a 1-7 **WOLV** 6af [59] 863*
37 16-20 Nott 6.1gd 64 1239
56a 4-7 Wolv 7af 60 1376
66 1-14 **AYR** 8g/f [58] 1896*
59 5-16 Ches 7g/f 63 4051
56 8-14 Muss 7.1g/f 63 4175
49 9-19 Leic 7g/f 61 4452
71 2-11 Ayr 8sft 61 4621
53 12-17 Newc 8fm 68 4867
45 16-17 Ayr 7.2sft 66 5063

SHOWTIME FAYE 2 b f £0
29 9-11 Newc 7fm 4863
34 8-9 Ayr 7.2sft 5064
26a 8-11 Wolv 7.1ap 5228

SHREDDED 4 b c £8679
67 9-19 Wind 10sft [75] 1650
81 2-19 Newb 10gd 75 1736
83 1-10 **SAND** 14g/f 76 2192*
72 8-12 Wind 11.6fm 80 2759
76 6-8 Newb 13.3gd 79 3918 T
80 3-9 Ayr 13.1sft 78 5068 t
45 14-24 Donc 12sft 78 5372 t

SHRINE MOUNTAIN 2 b c £1026
68 9-12 Newm 6g/f 3280
92 2-4 Yarm 7g/f 3707
91 7-7 York 7gd 4003
29 16-17 Donc 8fm 90 4480

SHRINK 3 b f £6049
71a 2-5 Ling 5ap 725

70a	1-9	LING	5ap	[68]	1023*
65	4-9	Thir	6g/s	[70]	1477
63	4-10	Brig	6g/f	[69]	2048
41	16-18	Wind	6g/f	67	2268 BL
41	9-12	Nott	5.1g/f	[65]	3577
59	3-14	Yarm	6gd	62	3870 T

SHUCHBAA 2 b f £550

44	3-11	Thir	6g/f		1968
0	11-13	York	6g/f		2358
18	12-14	Beve	7.5sft		2939
24	7-9	Ripo	6gd	[40]	4277

SHUHEB 3 ch f £1500

62	5-8	Ling	10g/f	2013
96	4-6	Newb	10g/f	2351

SHUJUNE AL HAWAA 2 ch f £850

76	5-8	Good	5g/f		1816
65	6-12	Hayd	6gd		2902
70	3-7	Ayr	7.2g/f		3302
51	9-11	Newb	7fm	70	3627
37	11-11	Ches		[68]	4072
53	18-20	Ling	7g/f	64	4741
67	6-17	Good	8gd	64	4871 VIS
43	10-12	Ayr	8sft	63	5065 vis

SHUSH 6 b g £0

38	15-19	Sali	14.1gd	61	4856
48	7-12	Brig	11.9sft	58	5093

SHYSHIYRA 3 b f £0

32	10-11	Pont	10g/f	2991

SI SI AMIGA 3 b f £4750

89	4-9	Ches	11.4gd		1568
94	4-6	Newm	10g/f	[92]	1931
95	5-6	Newb	10g/f	[92]	2351
85	8-8	Hayd	11.9gd	[94]	2946
25	12-13	York	13.9g/s	92	4062

SI SI SI 2 b f £0

52	7-7	Catt	7g/f	3665

SIAN THOMAS 3 ch f £820

60	3-7	Epso	8.5g/f	4474
49	12-15	Nott	8.2g/s	4649
63	5-15	Bath	10.2gd	4826

SIDESHOW 2 ch f £429

65	11-18	Nott	8.2g/s	4035
57	4-8	Hayd	8.1sft	4782 VIS

SIEGFRIEDS NIGHT 2 ch g £17888

37a	7-8	Sout	5af	52	169
52a	3-4	Sout	5af	[52]	222
44a	5-9	Sout	5af	[48]	256
51a	1-6	SOUT	6af	45	316*
45a	4-14	Sout	5af	50	485
47a	3-10	Sout	6af	50	592
54a	2-10	Sout	11af	50	658
50a	3-10	Sout	12af	55	796
63	3-14	Donc	10.3gd	55	923
60	3-12	Catt	12gd	55	1000
47	6-12	Wind	11.6g/s	57	1260
60	2-7	Donc	14.6g/s	55	1521
68	1-15	RIPO	12.3g/f	58	1785*
68	3-15	Leic	11.8gd	66	2134
69	3-9	Yarm	14.1g/f	66	2345
63	5-7	Ripo	12.3g/f	65	2528
67a	5-11	Sout	12af	64	2804
65	3-9	Ripo	12.3gd	64	2984
56	7-14	Catt	12g/f	65	3192
57	7-17	Newm	12g/f	62	3618
65	2-9	Yarm	14.1g/f	62	3703
58	5-8	Catt	13.8g/f	65	4439
42	9-13	Newc	16.1fm	64	4868

SIENA GOLD 2 b r f £93823

95	1-8	NEWM	5gd		1170*
98	1-6	NEWB	5.2gd		1735*
87	8-17	Asco	5g/f		2490
92	1-24	NEWB	5.2g/f		3266*
87	8-13	Good	5g/f		3509
91	4-9	Deau	5hvy		4155
89	7-9	Chan	5.5gd		4563
97	3-8	Newm	6sft	[93]	5267

SIENA STAR 5 b g £1039

74a	7-14	Ling	12ap	77	83
80a	2-8	Ling	10ap	75	900

SIENNA SUNSET 5 ch m £12672

25	10-14	Hayd	8.1g/s	60	1348
48	6-9	Nott	10sft	60	1467
47	6-11	Folk	9.7fm	57	2719
59	2-11	Bath	10.2g/f	55	3373
47	4-8	Brig	9.9g/f	55	3719
62	1-8	RIPO	10g/s	55	3938*
60	3-10	Beve	9.9sft	58	4260
44	12-19	Leic	10g/f	58	4456
43	7-13	Nott	10g/s	[58]	4650
20	11-17	Newb	9sft	58	5198
56a	3-13	Wolv	9.5ap	[56]	5338

SIERA SPIRIT 3 b f £2443

57a	4-13	Ling	6ap		364
56a	3-11	Ling	6ap		543
55a	8-15	Ling	7ap		875
61	2-12	Folk	6sft	55	975
57	3-14	Warw	7.1sft	55	1085

SIERRA 3 ch f £0

67	5-6	Pont	10g/f		2793
45	6-10	Pont	10gd		3243
51	6-12	Pont	8gd	65	3679
60	5-20	York	7.9gd	62	4321
44	12-14	Chep	10.2gd	62	4487

SIERRA NEVADA 3 ch f £0

0	16-16	Sout	6af	65

SIERRA VISTA 4 ch f £21627

56	14-20	Donc	5gd	79	927
78	3-16	Muss	5g/f	77	1120 P
72	10-20	Thir	5g/s	78	1476 p
67	9-20	York	5g/s	78	1683 p
75	5-15	Ripo	6g/f	78	1782 p
84	1-18	NEWC	6g/s	76	2770*
76	6-10	York	6gd	81	3116
68	9-13	Newc	7gd	81	3428
56	15-19	Ripo	6g/s	80	3937
72	5-11	Hayd	6g/f	[79]	4350
70	8-26	Ayr	6g/s	79	4652
68	9-15	Catt	5sft	77	5125

SIGHTS ON GOLD 5 ch h £54322

107	1-6	EPSO	10.1gd	[114]	4290* t
115	1-8	NEWB	11g/f	[114]	4639* t
105	7-12	Long	10g/f	[114]	4950
115	2-16	Newm	9sft	[114]	5139 t

SIGN OF LUCK 2 ch f £405

69	9-14	Kemp	7g/f	4711
75a	4-14	Ling	7ap	5258

SIGN OF PROMISE 2 b f £0

0	12-14	Yarm	8g/s	5118

SIGN WRITER 2 b c £2572

77	6-6	Newm	6g/f		3031
87	2-12	Newm	6g/f		3280
70a	4-8	Ling	5ap		3600
72	3-8	Yarm	6g/s	[83]	4250
60	8-13	Wind	8.3g/f	77	5051

SIGNOR PANETTIERE 3 b c £2213

60	8-17	Sali	6g/f	67	1722
72	2-8	Bath	5.7fm	67	1903
67	6-11	Newm	5g/f	70	2734
65	7-13	Wind	5fm	70	2784
67	2-11	Bath	5g/f	[69]	3372

SIGNORA PANETTIERA 3 ch f £0

54	6-10	Beve	12.1g/s	58	1165
0	8-8	Pont	12hvy	[58]	1250
26a	6-8	Ling	12ap	[58]	2065
1	11-11	Yarm	11.5g/f	55	2346
31	9-10	Bath	11.7g/f	50	2978
42	7-10	Sali	12sft	[40]	4579
37	4-11	Catt	13.8g/f	[40]	4671
30	6-6	Yarm	14.1sft	[40]	5249

SILBER MOND 2 g r c £0

60	11-20	Yarm	8sft	5252
62	10-16	Yarm	10.1g/s	5352

SILCAS GIFT 3 b f £30000

109	1-13	NEWM	7gd	[103]	1169*
108	8-16	Newm	8fm		1492
88	5-9	Nott	6.1g/s	[109]	1773
88	9-15	Asco	7g/f	[109]	2486
99	9-9	York	6g/s	[107]	3075

SILENCE IS GOLDEN 5 ch m £84800

103	1-17	KEMP	10g/s	95	1111*
104	2-8	Newm	9fm	[99]	1491
94	9-5	Sain	10.5g/s	[99]	2143
106	2-7	Sand	10g/f	[100]	2898
117	2-6	Good	9.9fm	[101]	3621

SILENCIO 3 b g £0

72	7-16	Wind	10gd		1384
56	13-20	Wind	10sft		1651
55	14-18	Wind	10g/f		1959
65	7-11	Chep	10.2gd		2196
52	5-7	Warw	12.6fm	60	2782
48	7-10	Bath	11.7g/f	60	2978

SILENT ANGEL 4 b f £0

5a	11-11	Sout	5af	[30]	578 VIS
0	10-10	Wolv	5af	[30]	781 P

SILENT HAWK 3 b c £8554

89	4-24	Newm	8fm		1495 T
91	1-6	NEWM	10gd		1892* t
85	12-18	Epso	10.1fm	90	2250 VIS
86	4-11	Newm	10g/f	89	3029 vis t
75	10-14	Sand	10g/s	87	4097 t
80	11-13	Donc	10.3fm	[87]	4463 t
86	5-10	Yarm	10.1sft	[85]	5255 vis t

SILENT JO 2 b c £4599

92	3-12	Good	7fm	3568
91	2-15	Leic	7gd	4455
93	3-3	Leic	7gd	5061

SILENT SPRING 2 b f £0

64	8-10	Newm	6g/f	3064

SILENT STORM 4 ch c £6469

62a	3-12	Sout	6af		2722
70	3-5	Sand	8.1g/f		3360
50	13-17	Hayd	8.1gd	67	3759
50a	10-14	Ling	7ap	67	3821 VIS
70a	2-13	Sout	6af	64	4091
69a	3-12	Wolv	6ap	67	4984
76a	1-13	WOLV	6ap	67	5010*

SILENT WITNESS 4 b g £456000

124	1-14	SHA	5g/f	210*

SILISTRA 4 g r g £0

35a	13-13	Ling	10ap	[65]	148 p
33a	14-14	Ling	10ap	65	174 H bl
29a	13-15	Ling	7ap	[55]	263 h bl
36a	8-11	Ling	12ap	[50]	672 vis
0	14-14	Ling	10ap	50	757 vis
0	11-11	Folk	12g/f	50	2273
30	14-17	Brig	7g/f	46	3176 p
39	5-13	Folk	9.7g/f	40	3726 p
35	7-12	Brig	8g/f	39	3986 p
32	6-15	Folk	9g/f	[40]	4371 p

SILK AND SCARLET 2 b f £78424

106	1-6	LEOP	6g/s	3314*
108	1-8	CURR	7g/f	3843*
100	7-12	Curr	7g/f	4432

SILK CRAVAT 3 ch g £0

53	8-13	Newm	8fm	2595

SILK FAN 3 b f £18118

101	1-11	SAND	7.1g/s	92	2918*
98	6-12	Good	7fm	[95]	3564
95	4-5	Sand	8.1g/s	[95]	4095
98	4-14	Sali	7gd	95	4331
97	4-11	Yarm	10.1gd	[95]	4614
89	4-8	Leic	8gd	[95]	5057

SILKEN BRIEF 4 b f £540

76a	3-11	Ling	8ap	[78]	273 t
75a	6-14	Ling	10ap	77	452 t
0	11-11	Ling	8ap	75	714 t

SILKEN JOHN 3 ch g £0

38	13-16	Bath	10.2g/f	1790

57 5-10 Sali 12sft 4579
0 11-11 Good 14gd 5029

SILLOTH SPIRIT 4 b g £433
0 12-12 Newc 8g/f 4407
31 4-5 Pont 10g/f 4630
29 13-13 Nott 8.2g/f 4847

SILSONG 2 ch f £0
58 5-11 Sali 7gd 3883
41 15-17 Warw 7.1qd 4269
66 8-11 Nott 8.2g/s 4648
62 11-16 Nott 10g/f 65 4848

SILVALINE 5 gr g £29981
62a 6-14 Ling 10ap 66 674
60a 11-14 Ling 10ap 66 803
67a 4-8 Ling 10ap 65 900
76 5-20 Newb 10gd 75 1235
68 5-16 Epso 10.1hvy 75 1296
50 14-19 Ripo 10g/f 74 1781
71 6-15 Kemp 10fm 74 2067
61 8-10 Hayd 8.1gd 73 2242
72a 1-14 LING 10ap 63 2392*
84 1-9 SAND 10g/s 74 2896*
75 8-11 Asco 12gd 79 3070
83 3-10 Newm 10g/f 80 3615
71 10-20 Hayd 10.5fm 80 3794
86 2-14 Sand 10g/s 80 4097
84 6-9 Newm 10gd 82 4227
60a 10-14 Ling 10ap [72] 4742

SILVER BARK 2 b f £0
57 8-13 Newm 6fm 4726
65 5-10 Good 6gd 4876

SILVER CACHE 3 b f £0
47a 10-11 Ling 8ap 322
33a 9-11 Wolv 9.4af 438
58a 5-11 Ling 8ap 697
55 4-5 Brig 9.9g/f 54 1372

SILVER CHIME 4 gr f £7120
56a 9-14 Ling 6ap 68 874
37 11-16 Nott 6.1sft 69 1465
68 4-16 Redc 6g/f 67 1824
72 1-11 NEWM 6fm 67 2093*
62 5-15 Leic 6g/f 70 2398
41 6-9 Wind 6fm [70] 2760
64 6-9 Epso 6g/f 70 2871
29 11-12 Newm 6g/f 68 3751
60 9-12 Newm 6g/f 67 3942
57 11-18 Redc 6fm 65 4339
46 14-15 Epso 7g/f 65 4475
56 10-20 Nott 6.1g/s 63 4646 BL
5a 12-12 Wolv 6ap [60] 5155

SILVER CITY 4 ro g £1913
83 2-6 Epso 10.1g/f [80] 2874
67 7-11 Newb 11g/f 81 3256
69 10-10 Good 9.9gd 81 3949
64 12-13 Epso 10.1g/f 79 4473
66 10-16 Good 12gd [73] 4745
70 4-15 Leic 11.8gd [70] 5060

SILVER COURT 2 b c £0
0 6-6 Leic 7gd 4699
14 14-16 Bath 8gd 5019
5 9-9 Nott 10hvy 5189

SILVER CREEK 2 gr c £0
28 11-11 Bath 5g/f 3962
53 12-15 Folk 7g/f 4114
51 16-17 Warw 7.1gd 4271
30a 10-14 Ling 7ap 4658

SILVER CRYSTAL 3 b f £0
51a 4-15 Sout 8af [45] 96
43a 5-11 Wolv 9.4af [45] 115
27a 7-14 Sout 8af [50] 170 P
0 9-9 Sout 11af 47 331 VIS
0 8-8 Sout 8af 47 393 vis
0 8-8 Ling 10ap [45] 829

SILVER DREAMER 2 b f £0
0 11-11 Chep 8.1g/s 4296
47 11-12 Warw 7.1g/f 4417

SILVER EMPEROR 3 gr g £0

42a 7-7 Wolv 7af 284 BL
39a 7-12 Sout 8af 460 bl

SILVER GILT 4 b g £11587
96 3-4 Ripo 12.3g/s[102] 1364
104 3-8 Donc 10.3gd[102] 2234
109 2-8 Sand 16.4g/s[100] 2914
108 6-9 Good 16fm [110] 3552
97 5-10 York 15.9gd[109] 4000
94 8-8 Donc 18fm [108] 4478

SILVER HIGHLIGHT 2 gr f £2175
69 9-13 Newb 7g/f 3252
84 2-10 Yarm 8g/f 3713
80 2-11 Bath 8gd 4544

SILVER ISLAND 2 ch c £0
27a 11-12 Ling 8ap 102
43a 7-13 Sout 8af 2383
39a 7-12 Sout 6af 2722
0 12-14 Chep 10.2g/s 45 3895
43 6-17 Kemp 7g/f [45] 4794
4 15-20 Yarm 7g/s [40] 5120 T

SILVER LOUIE 4 gr f £0
18a 12-14 Ling 10ap 51 757
0 11-12 Ling 8ap [45] 1073
3 R-15 Kemp 9gd 45 2170

SILVER MASCOT 4 gr g £8723
31a 8-16 Sout 6af 45 166
33a 4-13 Wolv 6af [45] 397
24a 7-13 Ling 6ap 45 448
42a 2-12 Wolv 7af [40] 528
52a 2-9 Sout 7af [40] 661
28a 5-11 Sout 7af [45] 771
56a 1-9 WOLV 7af [45] 825*
53a 4-12 Wolv 7af 53 956
55a 2-9 Sout 6af [52] 1194
56 3-12 Sout 7gd [48] 1284
39 10-18 Ayr 7.2g/f 55 1897
28 11-18 Thir 6g/f 53 2214
58 1-16 CARL 5.9fm 50 2445*
61 2-8 Hami 6gd 56 2713
37a 12-15 Sout 7af [60] 2999
35 10-13 Catt 5g/f 58 3350
25 12-12 Newm 6g/f 57 3942
0 26-26 Ayr 5g/s 57 4618

SILVER MISTRESS 5 gr m £0
14 7-10 Kemp 12hvy [45] 1645

SILVER PHANTOM 2 b c £0
13 11-15 Beve 5g/s 1161

SILVER PRELUDE 3 gr c £11085
54 7-7 Nott 6.1g/s [90] 1771
79 8-11 Redc 5g/f 87 2121
67 11-16 Leic 5g/f 84 2400
85 3-11 Newm 5g/f 80 2734
86 1-16 NEWM 5g/f 80 3033+
65 8-10 Hayd 5g/s 86 3135
70 16-21 Good 5fm 84 3567
67 9-9 Wind 5g/f 83 3976
68 17-20 Donc 5fm 82 4496
76 10-15 Sand 5g/f 82 4604
83 14-15 Newm 5g/f [80] 4879

SILVER PROPHET 4 gr g £5350
63a 8-12 Ling 12ap 69 56
58a 7-10 Sout 12af 66 138
44 18-20 Newb 10gd 79 1235 t
70 5-19 Wind 10sft [75] 1650
70 5-13 Kemp 12g/f 73 1916
69 5-15 Newb 13.3g/f 70 2311
69 7-10 Sali 14.1gd 69 2699
27 16-19 Chep 12.1gd 66 3398 P
71 1-17 KEMP 12sft 65 4033*
67 5-13 Warw 12.6gd 67 4274
61 6-19 Sali 14.1gd 66 4856
72 3-13 Bath 11.7sft 65 5174

SILVER REIGN 3 gr g £0
51 5-9 Kemp 6sft 946
42 6-15 Folk 6g/s 1078
0 9-9 Good 6sft 4262
20 18-19 Bath 5.7sft 48 5176

SILVER RHYTHM 3 ch f £535

52 3-5 Newc 10.1sft 1275
48 5-6 Hami 11.1g/s 1604
51 7-7 Hami 11.1g/f [52] 2478
51 8-16 Thir 12g/f 50 3573
5a 7-8 Sout 12af 49 4092
36 5-11 Catt 12sft [46] 5128

SILVER SASH 3 gr f £3759
76 6-11 Newb 10g/f 2349
78 3-14 Kemp 10g/s 2678
77 1-7 CATT 13.8g/f 3019*
85 5-9 York 11.9g/s [79] 4058
75 8-13 Kemp 14.4fm 80 4395

SILVER SEEKER 4 gr g £1171
86a 5-8 Wolv 7af [96] 838 P
0 13-13 Newc 7hvy 89 1035 p
53 10-10 Thir 7g/f [84] 1970 p
59 2-14 Redc 7g/f [84] 2102
39 8-8 Muss 7.1g/f 60 2809
50 6-14 Carl 6.9g/f 56 3229
35 9-10 Muss 7.1g/f 54 3562
36 7-16 Hami 6g/s 51 4009
25 15-20 Newc 6g/f 48 4408
42 11-12 Muss 8gd [45] 4809

SILVER SONG 2 gr c £0
44 12-14 Kemp 8g/f 4356
51 11-15 Sali 8g/f 4851
61 11-16 Yarm 10.1g/s 5352

SILVER SWING 2 gr c £0
38a 9-12 Ling 6ap 4896
31 10-12 Wind 6g/s 4945
44 6-9 Pont 6g/s 5154

SILVER VISAGE 2 b c £0
69 5-9 Yarm 5.2g/f 1133
63 5-11 Yarm 6g/f 1727
67 5-17 Ling 7g/f 2584
10 16-20 Yarm 8g/s 63 4635 BL
71a 5-11 Ling 8ap [60] 5236 P

SILVER WRAITH 2 b c £23570
81 4-7 Beve 6g/f 1848
85 2-8 Brig 6g/f 2043
91 1-9 BRIG 5.3fm 2257*
93 1-4 BATH 5fm 2411*
101 3-13 Newm 7g/f 88 3065
97 1-11 NEWM 7fm 90 3407*
101 3-8 Good 6fm 3566
97 5-8 Sand 7.1g/s [100] 4096

SILVERHAY 3 b g £14330
69 4-16 Beve 8.5sft 68 1628
68 2-6 Redc 11g/f 68 2103
64 4-7 Hami 11.1g/f [69] 2478
70 1-10 HAYD 8.1g/s 66 3138*
75 1-12 PONT 8gd 68 3679*
69 4-10 Pont 8g/s 73 3972
74 3-11 Ayr 8sft 72 4621

SILVERLEAF 2 b c £0
78 6-14 Newm 7g/f 2766
73 5-12 Good 7fm 3568
75 5-14 Sand 7.1g/s 4069
68 7-14 Kemp 8g/f 4356
4 20-20 Yarm 8g/s 72 4635

SILVERSKAYA 3 b f £51408
111 1-7 CHAN 12g/s 2304*
112 1-10 DEAU 12.5Ver 4310*
111 6-13 Long 12g/f 4567
111 8-19 Long 12sft 4956

SILVERSTEIN 3 b c £904
84 3-15 Newb 8g/f 1763

SILVERTOWN 9 b g £599
35 12-14 Newc 10.1sft 68 964
65 7-10 Newc 10.1g/f 68 2162
38 16-19 Carl 11.9gd 68 2673
0 17-17 Newc 10.1g/f 66 5016
69 4-12 Redc 14.1g/s 66 5108

SIMIANNA 5 b m £54886
84 5-13 Beve 5g/s [89] 1162
91 5-14 Bath 5gd [88] 1400
92 2-14 Ches 5.1gd 88 1594 p

SIMLET 9 b g £0 (continued from previous)

81	8-15	Ripo	6g/f	90	1782
86	6-17	Muss	5fm	90	2082 p
63	7-11	Hayd	6gd	[90]	2240 p
96	2-9	Cork	6fm	[90]	2457
89	7-29	Asco	6fm	90	2581
98	7-11	Newc	6g/s	[96]	2769 p
94	4-11	Hami	6fm	93	3248 p
90	6-15	York	6g/f	92	3434
97	5-28	Good	6fm	93	3622 p
92	7-10	Curr	6g/f	[93]	3842 p
89	3-12	Pont	6g/s	[94]	3971 p
102	2-11	Beve	5g/s	[94]	4238 p
103	1-11	CHES	6.1g/f	[97]	4510+ p
93	5-11	Hami	5sft	[97]	4693 p
92	8-12	Asco	6g/f	[97]	4799 p
90	7-10	Redc	7fm	[97]	4929 p

SIMLET 9 b g £0

44	5-20	Catt	15.8gd	45	4965

SIMON THE POACHER 4 br g £0

0	7-10	Wolv	12af	[42]	154
0	10-14	Wolv	12af	[42]	194

SIMONAS 5 gr h £129870

120	2-10	Wood	12gd	5247

SIMONDA 3 ch f £4955

79	2-9	Wind	8.3g/f	3979
80	1-10	BATH	11.7g/f	4414*

SIMONOVSKI 3 b c £1479

61a	7-15	Ling	7ap		875
64	8-14	Bath	10.2gd	70	1403
57	3-11	Leic	10g/f	[67]	2924
61	2-15	Chep	16.2gd	[63]	3400
48	15-16	Kemp	16g/f	60	4361
34	17-19	Sali	14.1gd	59	4856

SIMONS SEAT 5 ch g £0

63	6-11	Nott	16fm	67	1003
51	6-9	Newm	14.8fm	65	2596
25	6-12	Newm	12g/f	[62]	3783
0	10-10	Yarm	16sft	60	4151
62a	8-14	Ling	13ap	[58]	4892
57a	6-13	Wolv	16.5ap	58	5366

SIMPLE EXCHANGE 3 b c £13173

112	4-13	Asco	10g/f	2520
112	4-7	Arli	10fm	4015

SIMPLE IDEALS 9 b g £291

30a	4-10	Sout	14af	27	90
20a	11-12	Sout	14af	27	173
39	5-13	Newc	16.1sft	32	2685
50	4-9	Redc	16sft	32	2963
7a	8-10	Sout	14af	27	3158
35	6-10	Newc	16.1g/s	35	3701
26	7-10	Thir	16sft	35	3834
27	5-9	Ripo	16gd	35	4308

SIMPLEX 2 b c £38534

112	2-	Sain	10g/s	9
112	2-8	Long	12hvy	5165

SIMPLIFY 2 b c £6281

80	4-8	Newb	5.2gd		1205
75	5-7	Yarm	6fm		2144
78	3-6	Warw	7.1fm		2597
80	2-6	Ling	6gd	75	3022 BL
69	5-14	Leic	6g/f	75	3212 bl
72	7-11	Newb	7fm	77	3627 bl
80	1-13	WARW	6.1gd	73	4273* bl
70	8-14	Epso	6g/f	79	4471 bl
64	13-16	Good	7gd	77	5031 bl

SIMPLY HONEST 9 ch g £0

50	11-14	Asco	16.2g/f	58	1928

SIMPLY RED 3 ch g £0

51	9-13	Donc	7gd	[30]	925
0	8-9	Warw	8.1sft	[40]	1089 VIS
0	7-7	Wolv	6af	[40]	1312 vis
0	12-14	Leic	6g/f	[40]	1963

SIMPLY ST LUCIA 2 b f £5138

69a	1-14	SOUT	7gd	2492*
80	3-3	Sand	8.1g/s	4066
65	3-4	Newc	8hvy	4212

74	6-11	Hayd	8.1fm	75	4387

SIMPLY THE GUEST 4 b g £7105

31a	7-14	Sout	8af	34	93 t
38a	2-12	Sout	8af	[34]	309 t
47a	2-14	Sout	8af	[35]	354 t
55a	1-11	SOUT	8af	45	457* t
64a	1-12	SOUT	8af	53	530* t
56a	4-13	Sout	7af	[60]	858 t
21a	11-14	Sout	8af	60	1198 t
28	13-15	Redc	6fm	59	4562 t
34	16-20	Leic	7gd	54	5046 t

SIMPSONS MOUNT 3 ch g £12377

49a	6-9	Ling	5ap		621 e
52a	5-11	Ling	5ap		898
71a	3-9	Ling	5ap		1023
63	7-17	Sali	6g/f	69	1722
62	5-17	Bath	6g/f	[69]	1787
49	10-16	Good	6gd	66	2023
68	1-9	FOLK	7g/f	62	2271*
66	5-9	Sand	5g/f	68	2387
42	16-16	Good	5g/f	66	4528
60	10-17	Ling	6g/f	66	4740
73a	1-12	LING	6ap	65	4976*

SINAMAY 3 b f £0

0	10-13	Pont	8g/s	3973

SINGHALESE 2 ch f £20212

79	4-10	Donc	7g/f		3594
83	3-10	Nott	8.2g/s		4035
76	3-10	Newm	7gd		4191
94	1-17	DONC	8fm	79	4480*

SINGHALONGTASVEER 2 b g £500

0	10-11	Ripo	6g/f		1779
49	5-7	Redc	7fm		2294
50	3-7	Ripo	6g/s		3259
51	7-11	Thir	7g/f		3570
43	9-14	Thir	7g/s	[51]	4206
68	5-14	Carl	6.9fm	[49]	4503
53	9-18	Newc	6g/f	59	5013
40	9-17	Redc	7g/s	[59]	5105

SINGITTA 3 b f £0

47	11-14	Wind	10g/s	1259
22	7-8	Chep	12.1gd	2368
23	9-13	Bath	10.2sft	5173

SINGLE TRACK MIND 6 b g £1316

3a	10-10	Wolv	7af	[35]	394
45a	2-15	Ling	7ap	[30]	708
41a	5-10	Ling	8ap	[40]	831
45a	4-15	Ling	7ap	40	846
40a	5-15	Ling	7ap	[45]	969
39a	9-14	Ling	7ap	45	1010
45a	2-12	Ling	8ap	[45]	1073
45a	3-8	Ling	7ap	[45]	1413
34a	5-12	Ling	8ap	[45]	1451 P
16	8-17	Kemp	7hvy	[45]	1642
34	7-7	Brig	7g/f	45	2045
42	6-17	Ling	7gd	44	2397 p
42	4-9	Newm	8g/f	44	2529 p
35	7-12	Ling	10g/f	42	2844
21	7-8	Epso	8.5g/f	[42]	2873 p
0	13-17	Wolv	8.6ap	[45]	5232 p

SINGLET 3 ch c £0

65	7-16	Donc	10.3gd	2751
68	8-13	Kemp	10gd	3186

SINGLETARY 4 b c £488045

123	1-5	LONE	8g/s	5308*

SINGULARITY 4 b g £0

0	11-12	Wolv	12af	[45]	891
8a	11-12	Ling	8ap	[40]	1451
30a	11-12	Ling	8ap	[37]	3286 p
0	R-12	Ling	8ap	[40]	4659 bl

SINISTRA 3 br f £0

56	10-17	Newb	10gd	1737

SINJAREE 5 b g £1463

35a	8-14	Sout	8af	52	165
19a	10-15	Sout	11af	52	196 VIS
0	10-10	Sout	8af	50	318 vis
44a	5-12	Wolv	9.4af	45	747

47a	1-9	WOLV	9.4af	[45]	821*
3a	7-7	Wolv	9.4af	46	961
41	6-9	Pont	10hvy	45	1254
9	12-17	Newm	10g/f	42	3238
38	7-14	Hayd	10.5gd	40	3741
32	14-16	Nott	8.2g/s	39	4036
31	7-16	Warw	8.1g/s	[40]	4993
44a	4-12	Wolv	9.5ap	[45]	5234
51	6-17	Yarm	8g/s	[40]	5348

SINK OR SWIM 6 b m £0

25a	10-11	Ling	12ap		816
21a	11-12	Ling	8ap		878
31a	5-6	Ling	10ap		1455
0	8-10	Kemp	12hvy	[30]	1645

SION HILL 3 b g £0

56	13-17	Pont	5gd	78	3241
22	10-10	Sand	5g/f	78	3356 VIS
63	11-13	Redc	7fm	[75]	4341
59	10-17	Beve	8.5g/f	68	4721
48	9-13	Pont	8g/s	[64]	5153
58a	7-12	Wolv	7.1ap	[60]	5325

SIR ALFRED 5 b g £279

7	8-8	Epso	12gd	58	3217
51	4-13	Sali	14.1gd	55	3454
51	10-16	Wolv	11.6gd	55	3829
43a	11-13	Wolv	8.6ap	[52]	5184 vis

SIR ANTHONY 2 b c £9998

85	1-13	THIR	6g/s		2689*
84	3-7	Donc	6g/s		3221
90	2-13	Newc	7g/s	85	3698
86	6-12	York	7g/s	90	4064
89	2-8	Redc	7gd	[90]	4247
93	3-17	Donc	8fm	87	4480

SIR BLUEBIRD 2 ch c £0

53	11-14	Wind	5gd		4121
81	9-13	Newm	6gd		4223
66	6-10	Newb	6g/f		4637
37a	10-11	Ling	6ap	68	4972

SIR BOND 3 ch g £416

30	9-11	Donc	10.3gd		930
30	4-6	Thir	12g/s		1213
28	5-7	Ayr	10g/s	[40]	1450

SIR DESMOND 5 gr g £16769

53a	11-13	Wolv	6af	80	45 p
79a	3-12	Ling	6ap	[80]	106 p
76a	4-14	Ling	6ap	78	149 p
79a	3-14	Ling	6ap	77	292 p
65a	8-13	Wolv	6af	77	482 p
55	18-18	Newc	6g/s	80	2770 p
83	3-8	Asco	6g/f	80	3123 p
79	5-12	Newm	6g/f	77	3279 p
74	6-12	Newm	6g/f	77	3942 p
79	4-12	Good	6sft	77	4184 p
40	20-26	Ayr	6g/s	77	4652 p
74	4-15	Catt	5sft	76	5125 p
85	1-16	REDC	6sft	76	5304+ p

SIR DON 5 b g £6887

61	9-18	Catt	7gd	67	998 vis
46	10-12	Thir	7g/s	66	1215 vis
4	17-17	Donc	6g/s	64	1523 vis
0	20-20	York	6g/f	62	2409 vis
69	1-11	HAMI	6g/f	61	2477* vis
30	16-18	Donc	6gd	66	2752 vis
63	3-12	Catt	7g/f	[66]	3017 vis
60	5-9	Ayr	6g/f	66	3307 vis
54	8-14	Catt	6g/f	66	3352 BL
40	24-26	Good	6fm	66	3569 vis
39	14-17	Wind	6gd	63	4126 vis
39	14-16	Brig	7sft	[63]	4144 vis
48	9-13	Ches	5.1g/f	61	4514 vis
4	16-18	Ayr	7.2sft	61	4622

SIR EDWARD BURROW 6 b g £419

4	8-11	Catt	13.8sft	[35]	5129
46	2-9	Ayr	13.1sft	[30]	5277

SIR EDWIN LANDSEER 4 gr c £0

46	20-28	Asco	7g/f	82	2558
54	13-16	Newb	6g/f	79	3269
62	20-22	Good	5fm	75	3537

64	11-14	Newb	5.2fm	75	3628
67	7-13	Newb	5.2g/f	69	3960

SIR ERNEST 3 b g £4351

69	7-8	Hami	5gd	75	1509
78	6-15	Ches	5.1g/s	75	1572
54	11-11	Redc	5g/f	75	2121
78	2-10	Hayd	5g/s	75	2227
38	11-12	Ayr	5g/s	76	2566
65	4-9	Warw	6.1fm	[76]	2778
79	2-10	Ches	5.1g/f	76	3080
10	17-17	Pont	5gd	72	3241
33	14-14	York	5g/s	76	4027
46	14-14	Epso	5gd	74	4291 P
59	6-13	Ches	5.1g/f	71	4514

SIR FRANCIS 6 b g £0

61a	9-12	Ling	8ap	72	517
67a	10-14	Ling	7ap	69	604
67a	8-15	Ling	7ap	68	698
57a	10-14	Ling	7ap	67	1010
58	5-13	Warw	7.1hvy	[65]	1537

SIR FRANK GIBSON 2 b c £1246

27a	13-14	Sout	7af	56	158
34a	7-10	Wolv	8.5af	[50]	398
44a	4-9	Sout	8af	45	486
48a	2-8	Sout	11af	45	614
45a	3-10	Sout	11af	45	658
0	8-10	Sout	12af	46	796
38a	5-8	Ling	10ap	[45]	1713
17a	5-7	Wolv	12af	[45]	2050
56	5-9	Wind	11.6gd	[50]	3164
27a	9-13	Ling	10ap	[40]	3288 P

SIR GALAHAD 3 ch g £417

43a	7-15	Sout	6af		795
46a	7-11	Sout	6af		869
42	5-12	Redc	10sft	55	1144
51	3-11	Newc	8sft	53	1395
36	4-6	Newc	8sft	52	1679

SIR GEORGE TURNER 5 ch g £2327

81	10-11	Sand	10g/s		1350
70	14-14	York	10.4g/s	104	1704
98	8-15	Redc	10g/f	100	2101
41	10-11	Epso	10.1g/f	100	2208
61	13-14	Asco	10g/f	98	2556 VIS
94	7-15	Good	9.9g/f	95	3506
92	8-10	Asco	12gd	95	3777
86	11-16	Good	7g/f	92	4523
93	3-10	Ayr	8sft	89	4685

SIR HAYDN 4 ch g £1096

73	3-14	Nott	10fm	[71]	1006
69	6-11	Leic	10g/s	71	1357
78	10-19	Wind	10sft	[70]	1650
67	6-8	Newm	12gd	70	1889
59	7-7	Newm	12g/f	67	2737 VIS
65	5-8	Nott	10g/s	65	2929 vis
64	3-12	Wind	10fm	64	3295 bl
50	11-15	Wind	11.6fm	64	3481 vis
51	11-14	Sand	10g/s	64	4097 bl
80	7-7	Good	9.9g/f	[62]	4538
62	8-15	Nott	10g/f	62	4849 vis

SIR JASPER 2 b g £5906

53a	6-13	Wolv	6af		126 VIS
58a	1-11	SOUT	7af	[65]	207* vis
73a	1-8	SOUT	7af	[59]	389* vis
49a	9-13	Wolv	6af	61	436 vis
51a	3-6	Wolv	8.5af	61	470 vis
49a	4-6	Wolv	7af	62	615 vis
2a	10-10	Sout	7af	59	794 vis

SIR LAUGHALOT 3 b c £5917

70a	2-16	Ling	7ap	68	20
42a	16-16	Ling	7ap	70	181
68a	2-16	Ling	7ap	[70]	290
66a	7-16	Ling	7ap	70	323
72a	3-14	Ling	7ap	68	604
72a	2-11	Ling	8ap	69	714
72a	4-12	Ling	8ap	70	932
72	2-12	Sand	8.1g/s	70	1352
62	15-15	Newb	11g/f	70	4643

SIR LOIN 3 ch g £4499

15	10-10	Hayd	5g/s	60	2227

53	7-8	Newc	5g/s	60	2731
57	5-15	Redc	5g/s	55	2961
60	2-12	Catt	5g/f	55	3193
47	6-20	Thir	6g/f	57	3575
51	8-15	Thir	5g/s	57	3833
64	2-11	Beve	5g/s	[55]	4237
66	2-16	Good	5g/f	60	4528 VIS
66	2-15	Ayr	5sft	60	5036 vis

SIR MONTY 2 ch c £382

68	5-14	Ling	7.6g/f		3601
65	6-11	Sali	7gd		3883
76	4-15	Good	8g/s		4233
52	9-12	Sali	8sft	73	4580

SIR NIGHT 4 b g £284

47	4-16	Redc	10g/f	53	1821
45	7-11	Hayd	10.5g/f	53	1884
26	8-9	Thir	12fm	52	2465

SIR NINJA 6 b g £844

48a	4-12	Ling	10ap	[80]	272
63	2-14	Sout	12g/s	[75]	1047
63	8-13	Sout	11gd	65	1286
57	7-14	Nott	10g/s	61	1776

SIR SANDROVITCH 8 b g £0

31	14-19	Beve	5sft	60	1627
31	14-20	Thir	5g/f	58	1765 p
45	6-19	Beve	5gd	54	2512 p
45	7-19	Leic	5gd	54	2702 p

SIRAJ 4 b g £3232

63a	2-14	Ling	6ap	61	121 BL
60a	5-10	Ling	5ap	64	231 bl
49a	8-10	Wolv	7af	[64]	1319
63a	1-11	SOUT	6af	[62]	4041*
35	10-12	Newm	5gd	68	4197
57	9-20	Wind	6g/s	62	4946
44a	7-12	Wolv	7.1ap	59	5112 T
61a	4-12	Wolv	6ap	[59]	5155
51a	9-14	Ling	7ap	56	5300

SIRCE 2 b f £0

32	17-19	Newb	6g/f		2310
26	6-6	Wind	6fm		2783
22	8-12	Bath	5.7gd		3141
9	12-12	Bath	8g/f	45	4410
59	4-14	Yarm	8g/s	[45]	5118

SISTER GEE 2 b f £1806

53a	4-14	Sout	7af		2492
59a	3-9	Sout	6af		3157
61a	2-6	Sout	5af		3484
34	13-19	Nott	6.1g/s	61	4645

SISTER MOONSHINE 3 ch f £0

73	10-11	Hami	5sft		4693 BL

SISTER SOPHIA 4 b f £607

20	14-14	Yarm	8g/f	68	1131
37	14-16	Kemp	7gd	65	3184
63	3-12	Yarm	7gd	62	3490
54	6-9	Newm	8g/f	62	3780
36	7-10	Yarm	7g/s	61	4251
7	17-17	Warw	8.1g/s	59	4668
48a	7-12	Ling	8ap	[55]	5077 T

SIX PACK 6 ch g £888

44a	2-13	Wolv	8.5af	[40]	894
46a	2-9	Ling	10ap	[45]	1289
36a	4-10	Wolv	9.4af	[45]	1564
32a	10-14	Ling	10ap	[45]	1712

SIX PERFECTIONS 4 bl f £211800

117	2-5	Long	9.3gd		2002
110	6-16	Asco	8g/f		2470
117	2-10	Deau	8sft		4017
117	3-5	Lone	8g/s		5308

SIXTILSIX 3 ch c £438

32	8-11	Folk	7g/s		3048
31	12-15	Wind	10fm	[40]	3292
44a	3-12	Ling	10ap	40	4113
0	11-14	Pont	10g/f	45	4624
37a	6-12	Wolv	9.5ap	[45]	5209

SKATER BOY 2 b g £0

3a	12-12	Ling	8ap		175

19	8-9	Brig	9.9g/f		2643

SKELLIGS ROCK 4 b c £0

69	5-20	Wind	11.6g/s	78	1056
26	8-13	Kemp	14.4hvy	77	1516

SKELTHWAITE 2 b g £216

26a	12-12	Ling	8ap		19
35a	12-15	Ling	7ap		52
19a	13-14	Sout	8af		95
41	9-14	Beve	7.5g/s		3177
0	9-9	Sout	7af	[35]	4131
34	3-13	Folk	9.7g/f	[35]	4372
11	11-11	Yarm	11.5g/s	[35]	4584
0	U-14	Ling	10ap	[35]	4662

SKI JUMP 4 gr g £6944

87	1-8	CHEP	10.2gd	[82]	2197* bl
81	6-6	Kemp	12g/s	85	2681 bl
80	9-20	Hayd	10.5fm	85	3794 VIS
82	6-21	York	11.9gd	83	3999 vis
83	7-20	Hayd	14fm	81	4383 vis
81	7-9	Muss	12g/f	81	4553 vis
63	12-17	Nott	14.1g/s	81	4647 vis
83	4-20	York	10.4gd	79	4986 vis
77	4-11	Muss	16g/s	78	5335 vis

SKIBEREEN 4 b g £3160

50a	5-9	Ling	10ap	[74]	476
54a	6-15	Ling	12ap	[70]	521 bl t
73	4-14	Nott	10fm	[72]	1006
70	5-11	Muss	9g/f	[72]	1095
40a	8-8	Wolv	8.5af	65	1219 P
72	3-8	Nott	8.2g/s	[70]	1775
68	5-18	Thir	8g/f	69	1972
51	10-13	Ches	10.3gd	69	2284
55	12-16	Nott	8.2g/s	67	4036
36	17-19	York	7.9g/f	65	4399
53	2-10	Yarm	10.1gd	[65]	4612
64	2-13	Nott	10gd	[57]	4861
34	8-14	Epso	12gd	57	4910

SKIDDAW JONES 4 b g £1122

21	11-14	Hami	8.3gd	54	1504
49	5-7	Ayr	10g/f	52	2030
41	8-10	Newc	10.1g/f	52	2162
36	6-8	Hami	9.2gd	52	2179
47	2-12	Ayr	9.1g/f	47	3766
38	6-8	Ayr	10hvy	47	4084
15	14-17	Carl	7.9fm	[47]	4506

SKIDDAW WOLF 2 ch f £2743

56	8-18	York	5g/f		2360
65	3-9	Carl	5.9gd		2671
61	6-12	Carl	5gd		2933
64	5-8	Donc	5g/f	63	3374
64	4-15	Ripo	5gd	63	4784
66	2-12	Pont	5g/s	[63]	5152
53	9-16	Nott	5.1hvy	63	5343

SKIDMARK 2 b c £22424

77a	3-13	Ling	7ap		119
82a	1-10	LING	8ap		229*
84a	2-7	Ling	8ap	79	341
91a	1-10	LING	10ap	79	568*
99a	1-3	LING	10ap	[86]	727*
106a	3-9	Ling	8ap	[92]	1040
100	4-4	Epso	10.1hvy	[102]	1294
85	9-10	York	10.4g/s	[102]	1685
102	6-8	Good	9.9gd	[97]	4748

SKIDROW 2 b c £7529

62	7-9	Warw	7.1fm		2776
90	1-12	NEWC	7gd		3425*
92	2-5	Ches	7.6g/f	[88]	4046
92	2-4	Newc	8hvy	[88]	4212
91	3-9	Newm	8sft	[89]	5099

SKIP OF COLOUR 4 b g £4585

61a	4-12	Ling	8ap	[83]	401
34a	5-7	Wolv	9.4af	[75]	509
75a	1-13	SOUT	6af	[65]	659*
77a	2-13	Sout	6af	71	741
64a	10-12	Ling	6ap	74	880
65	6-17	Redc	6gd	75	2561
73	5-11	Ches	5.1g/s	73	2747
29	22-26	Ayr	6g/s	71	4652

SKIPPIT JOHN 2 b g £1376
72	2-10	Beve	5sft		1632
65	6-8	Muss	5gd		1795
56	6-17	Donc	6g/f		2424
64	8-13	Newc	7g/s	72	3698
48	9-9	Catt	6sft	72	3931
55a	7-14	Sout	6af	[65]	4127

SKY COVE 2 b g £0
| 0 | 9-9 | Wolv | 9.4af | | 240 |
| 0 | 13-16 | Sout | 8af | [40] | 442 |

SKY CRUSADER 2 b c £5422
87	1-14	FOLK	7fm		2714*
85	6-9	Asco	7gd		3126
80a	5-12	Ling	7ap	84	3820
84	3-12	Asco	7g/f	83	4810

SKY DOME 10 ch g £2423
65a	1-14	SOUT	8af		62* vis
63a	3-15	Muss	8af	63	84 vis
53	5-19	Yarm	7g/f	53	1132 bl

SKY GALAXY 3 ch f £0
74	7-12	Donc	7g/f	82	1879
58	10-14	Nott	8.2g/f	79	2153
57	6-7	Brig	8g/f	75	3174 VIS

SKY QUEST GB 6 b g £20384
88	1-6	SAND	10g/f	82	3358* t p
93	1-10	GOOD	9.9gd	84	3949* t p
86	12-18	Newb	10gd	91	4681 t p

SKYES FOLLY 4 b g £6509
76	7-12	Thir	16gd	80	1637
33	14-14	Asco	16.2g/f	78	1928
54	13-14	Hayd	16.2gd	75	2239
73	3-7	Newm	14.8g/f	72	3475
74	3-6	Redc	16g/f	72	3810 BL
74	3-12	York	13.9g/f	72	4400 bl
76	4-17	Nott	14.1g/s	72	4647 bl
67	4-20	York	13.9gd	70	5004 bl
78a	2-12	Wolv	13.9ap	69	5160 bl

SKYHARBOR 3 b g £3801
0	15-15	Ches	7.6gd	88	1583
66	5-8	Newm	6fm	[85]	2591
55	11-15	Hayd	6gd	80	2950
70	5-21	Good	5fm	75	3567
79	2-9	Wind	5g/f	73	3976
78	3-7	Sand	5g/s	73	4099
77	4-15	Sand	5gd	76	4604 VIS
60	13-15	Kemp	6g/f	76	4713 vis
68	9-19	Good	6gd	76	4747 vis
61a	7-12	Wolv	5.1ap	74	5326

SKYLARK 7 ch m £0
28a	7-12	Sout	7af	[58]	2337
49	12-18	Catt	7g/f	57	2848
11a	14-16	Sout	8af	52	3159

SKYLARKER 5 b g £16608
78a	4-11	Ling	8ap	[79]	273
83a	2-12	Wolv	9.4af	78	382
83a	3-12	Wolv	9.4af	79	513
82a	3-12	Wolv	8.5af	79	632
64a	12-14	Ling	10ap	79	758 VIS
58	11-12	Sand	8.1g/s	75	1352
41	14-19	Wind	10sft	[72]	1650
72	4-12	Bath	10.2fm	70	2036
77	4-11	Chep	10.2gd	70	2371
78	1-10	WARW	12.6g/f	69	2912*
76	5-14	Wind	11.6m	74	3638
73	5-12	Epso	12gd	74	4292
84	1-14	ASCO	12g/f	74	4775*
84	2-13	Bath	11.7sft	77	5174

SKYSCAPE 2 b f £610
| 70 | 3-14 | Bath | 8gd | | 5018 |

SKYWARDS 2 b c £11374
71	5-8	York	5sft		1670
91	1-10	NEWM	5fm		2089*
104	3-9	Asco	5gd		2516
91	7-13	Good	5g/f		3509
87	10-10	Donc	6fm	[100]	4533 T

SLALOM 4 b g £4478
| 76a | 1-12 | WOLV | 9.4af | | 939* e |

33	19-20	Newb	10gd	76	1235
67a	7-12	Ling	8ap	[75]	2840 e
74	5-10	Nott	8.2gd	[74]	3107 P
67	8-20	Newm	8g/f	74	3232 p
70	5-5	Hayd	10.5g/s	72	3904 p
47	13-19	Pont	10g/s	70	5148
77a	2-12	Ling	8ap	68	5238

SLATE GREY 2 gr c £0
2	13-13	Donc	6gd		2236
48	11-17	Donc	6g/f		2424
48	8-10	Carl	5g/f		3227
58	8-10	Hayd	5g/f		3755
34	12-18	Ayr	6g/s	[57]	4617 VIS
0	20-21	Donc	6hvy		5202 vis

SLAVONIC 3 ch c £974
78	5-9	Kemp	9sft	[79]	947
71	4-11	Bath	8g/s	[79]	1101 BL
75	4-8	Brig	9.9g/f	[72]	1369 VIS
73	6-13	Bath	10.2g/f	[72]	1791 bl
73	4-10	Good	9.9gd	73	2225 bl
63	7-10	Pont	8g/f	[73]	4939 bl
59	9-19	Donc	10.3sft	70	5201
55	11-13	Muss	12g/s	67	5333 P

SLEEPING INDIAN 3 b c £21534
| 86 | 1-11 | WIND | 8.3g/f | | 5054* |
| 110 | 1-11 | NEWM | 8g/s | | 5283+ |

SLIP CATCH 2 b f £0
| 36 | 14-18 | Ling | 6gd | | 4108 |
| 63 | 6-12 | Warw | 7.1g/f | | 4417 |

SLIP DANCE 2 br f £94398
100	1-9	NEWM	6g/f		2763*
103	2-11	Newm	7g/f		3781
101	6-12	Curr	7g/f		4432
108	1-10	CURR	6.3gd		4737*
109	5-7	Newm	6g/f		4880

SLITE 2 gr f £1096
23	12-13	Bath	5.7g/f		3368
52	2-13	Sali	7g/f		3864
36	5-8	Wind	5g/s		4218
55	5-20	Leic	7g/f	54	4451
58	5-14	Yarm	8g/s	[54]	5118

SMALL STAKES 2 b c £0
| 68 | 7-9 | Sand | 5gd | | 4497 |
| 57a | 5-12 | Wolv | 6ap | | 5177 |

SMALL TIME BLUES 2 b f £0
| 0 | 10-10 | Nott | 6.1gd | | 4858 |

SMART BOY PRINCE 2 b g £7173
59a	8-14	Sout	7af	[55]	98
55a	4-10	Sout	8af	[50]	162
61a	6-16	Sout	8af	[50]	192
47a	6-8	Wolv	7af	[55]	276
58a	1-15	SOUT	7af	[55]	462*
68a	1-9	SOUT	8af	61	486*
63a	7-12	Ling	8ap	66	798
54a	5-9	Sout	7af	[66]	871
47	9-19	Warw	10.9gd	65	1124
54a	3-13	Sout	8af	[65]	1193
27	8-9	Brig	8g/f	[60]	2431
15	11-12	Ripo	10gd	58	4282
41	6-8	Hayd	10.5g/f	58	4354
19	13-18	Good	8gd	53	4750
57	2-16	Nott	10gd	53	4857
56	2-18	Leic	10gd	[54]	5042

SMART DANNY 3 gr g £0
22a	13-15	Sout	6af		795
46	5-8	Nott	5.1fm	52	1002
40a	5-12	Wolv	6af	49	1374
37	7-20	Beve	5g/f	[45]	1948
21	8-13	Newc	6sft	43	2683
46	8-15	Redc	5g/s	41	2961
40	5-10	Hami	6g/f	41	3203
27	12-18	Hayd	6gd	44	3737

SMART DAWN 2 ch f £0
0	19-19	Kemp	6g/f		1911
62	13-15	Kemp	6g/f		4710
22	14-15	Sali	8gd		4851

SMART HOSTESS 5 gr m £2324

66	15-20	Donc	5gd	93	927
80	9-13	York	6gd	93	4322
74	9-11	Hami	5sft	[91]	4693
94	3-14	Ripo	6gd	91	4786
63	18-20	York	6gd	92	5001
77	13-13	Donc	5sft	92	5218

SMART JOHN 4 b g £16020
55	4-5	Nott	10sft	60	1609
69	1-11	HAYD	10.5g/f	60	1884*
65	4-8	Chep	10.2g/f	63	2628
72	2-10	Pont	10g/f	63	2794
73	1-9	HAYD	11.9gd	63	2900*
71	3-8	Hayd	14g/s	70	3140
67	5-12	Hayd	11.9gd	70	3734
70	4-9	Newm	12gd	70	3926
77	1-13	WARW	12.6gd	69	4274*
75	3-17	Thir	12fm	72	4377
66	9-14	Asco	12g/f	72	4775
67	6-16	York	11.9gd	70	4990

SMART MINISTER 4 gr g £3809
21a	12-12	Wolv	8.5af	51	1379
7	13-19	Redc	8sft	51	1661
41	7-15	Beve	7.5g/f	[49]	1944
68	1-8	RIPO	6g/f	[46]	2527*
52	15-18	Catt	7g/f	64	2848
43	6-7	Pont	6gd	[64]	3244

SMART SCOT 5 ch g £6051
34a	1-11	SOUT	8af	[30]	372* p
37a	1-14	SOUT	7af	[35]	573* p
45a	1-11	SOUT	7af	[40]	771* p
54a	1-8	SOUT	7af	[45]	847* p
53a	2-5	Sout	8af	[45]	908 p
0	14-14	Sout	8af	54	1198 p
53a	5-13	Wolv	8.6ap	[52]	5184
16a	11-12	Wolv	7.1ap	[52]	5358

SMART STARPRINCESS 2 b f £12090
59a	4-12	Wolv	5af	[61]	32 bl
62a	4-10	Wolv	5af	61	69 bl
65a	1-4	SOUT	5af	[58]	222* bl
61a	1-9	SOUT	5af	[58]	256* bl
66a	1-10	LING	5ap	58	371* bl
67a	1-9	LING	5ap	[58]	405* VIS
69a	2-14	Sout	5af	63	485 vis
63a	3-11	Sout	5af	67	609 vis
62a	5-10	Ling	5ap	67	712 vis
23	17-19	Leic	6g/f	61	2925
40	12-14	Leic	6g/f	60	3213
39	10-12	Donc	5g/f	57	3599 bl
58	4-8	Brig	5.3sft	54	5096 P
16	12-13	Muss	5g/s	[54]	5146 P

SMARTER CHARTER 11 br g £597
29a	5-12	Ling	12ap	[35]	1180
26a	7-7	Ling	12ap	[35]	1287
37	2-7	Ayr	10g/s	[35]	1450
27	7-13	Kemp	10hvy	[35]	1643
40	6-14	York	13.9g/f	30	2060
45	5-11	Leic	11.8fm	30	2112
17	11-15	Ayr	10.9g/s	40	2545
42	4-8	Muss	13g/f	40	2616
35	5-9	Yarm	14.1g/f	40	2856
29	6-7	Epso	12g/s	38	3040
32	4-7	Muss	13g/f	37	3530
33a	3-14	Ling	10ap	[35]	4662
32	7-14	Yarm	14.1g/s	[35]	5123
35	5-9	Ayr	13.1sft	[35]	5277

SMEORACH 3 ch f £0
32	7-10	Ayr	8g/s		1446
5	8-8	Hami	11.1g/f		2319
19	7-8	Catt	15.8g/f		3666

SMIDDY HILL 2 b f £14752
70	3-12	Ripo	5g/s		1173
66	2-6	Ayr	5g/s		1445
79	4-10	York	5g/s		1709
85	1-15	YORK	5g/f		2056*
69	4-8	Thir	5g/f		2213
79	5-12	Ling	5gd		3284
85	1-6	YARM	5.2gd		3488*
71	9-12	Muss	5g/f	82	4172
87	2-13	Muss	5g/f	82	4551
87	3-11	Epso	5g/f	84	4907

49 6-6 Muss 5g/s [84] 5141

SMILING STARDUSTER 2 b c £0
35 13-14 Thir 7g/s 3831
25a 12-14 Sout 6af 4127
33 7-7 Muss 7.1gd 4518

SMIRFYS DANCE HALL 4 b f £432
55 4-11 Thir 8g/f 3572
43 9-14 Catt 12g/f 57 4672
34a 11-13 Wolv 8.6ap 53 5005

SMIRFYS NIGHT 5 b g £338
24 17-17 Nott 5.1g/s 63 1774
42 11-13 Pont 5g/f [58] 2279
13 19-20 Beve 5g/s 55 3180
50 5-20 Hayd 6fm 50 3796
50 4-18 Pont 5g/s 49 3974
43 12-14 Redc 5fm [49] 4930

SMIRFYS PARTY 6 ch g £586
20 14-15 Hami 6gd 56 1508
14 13-15 Pont 6g/f 54 2280
43 8-13 Hayd 6gd 51 2884 vis
51 3-20 Hayd 6fm 48 3796 vis
45 5-18 Pont 5g/s 49 3974 vis
37 9-17 Wind 6gd 49 4126 vis
53 8-14 Redc 5fm [48] 4930 vis

SMIRFYS SYSTEMS 5 b g £1720
35 7-7 Thir 6sft [80] 1227
2 17-18 Ches 7.6gd 80 1598
73 5-8 Donc 6g/f [78] 2074
56 8-10 Hayd 6g/s 76 3136
32 9-11 Donc 6g/f [76] 3375
78 2-11 Thir 6g/f 72 3574
60 10-18 Ayr 7.2sft 73 4689
60a 8-12 Wolv 6ap 73 5291

SMITH N ALLAN OILS 4 b g £11053
57a 3-16 Ling 7ap 55 55 p
50a 11-15 Ling 7ap [56] 117 p
56a 1-12 LING 8ap [56] 150* p
40a 7-16 Sout 7af 56 202 p
60a 1-15 LING 7ap 55 266* p
67a 1-16 LING 7ap 61 323* p
58a 10-14 Ling 7ap 65 499 p
46 9-13 Muss 7.1gd 60 1553 p
54 7-14 Muss 7.1gd 59 1794 p
53 8-18 Thir 8g/f 59 1972 p
51 10-15 Beve 7.5g/s 57 2324 p
48 11-13 Carl 7.9fm 57 2447 p
55 7-14 Thir 7fm 57 2466 p
57 5-16 Beve 7.5gd 55 2655 p
61 2-18 Catt 7g/f 54 2848 p
55 2-12 Catt 7g/f [54] 3017 p
53 4-14 Carl 6.9g/f 54 3229 p
52 6-12 Yarm 7gd 54 3490 p
49 7-18 Catt 7g/f 54 3670 p
73a 5-12 Wolv 7.1ap [65] 5006 p

SMOKIN BEAU 7 b g £67841
101 6-17 Donc 6gd [98] 952
101 2-7 Kemp 6gd [98] 1137
101 7-13 Newm 5g/f [98] 1479
77 10-14 Ches 5.1gd 98 1594
88 17-19 Asco 5g/f [97] 2468 BL
97 4-16 Wind 6fm 97 2758 bl
89 14-24 Asco 5gd 96 3466 bl
86 15-28 Good 6fm 96 3622
103 1-20 HAYD 5fm 93 3792*
112 1-19 RIPO 6g/s 98 3937+
112 1-6 SAND 5g/s 108 4098*

SMOKIN JOE 2 b c £5564
70a 2-6 -Sout 6af 67 182
68a 2-10 Ling 5ap 67 217
75a 1-10 LING 6ap [69] 258*
69a 6-8 Ling 6ap 75 268
67a 4-10 Ling 6ap 74 494
41a 10-11 Sout 5af 72 609
-60a 5-11 Ling 6ap 70 735
14 14-17 Asco 6sft 68 1417
19 18-18 Leic 10gd 63 2706
25 12-12 Folk 6gd 60 3380 VIS
53a 8-11 Ling 6gd 62 3744 vis
41 14-20 Ling 6g/f 57 4317 vis
37 16-19 Ling 5g/f 53 4739 BL

52a 5-12 Wolv 7.1ap 58 5112 bl
56a 3-14 Ling 7ap [55] 5294 bl

SMOKINCANON 2 ch c £1699
76 3-6 Folk 5sft 974
82a 1-10 LING 5ap 1071*
63 6-7 Thir 5g/s 1471
65a 5-10 Ling 5ap 2017

SMOOTHIE 5 gr g £6907
64a 1-11 WOLV 12af [60] 6*
50a 9-11 Wolv 12af 64 72
60a 4-15 Sout 11af 64 196
55 7-15 Wind 11.6fm 63 3481
56 6-12 Hayd 11.9gd 63 3734
3 13-13 Folk 12gd 58 4119
62 1-19 LEIC 10g/f 58 4456* p
52 9-18 Sali 9.9gd 60 4850 p
62a 3-16 Ling 12ap [60] 5296 p

SMOOTHLY DOES IT 3 b g £6745
54 11-14 Bath 10.2gd 67 1403
72 2-18 Wind 8.3sft 64 1647
48 9-13 Good 9g/f 67 2024
63 6-14 Wind 10g/f 67 2452
54 9-14 Wind 8.3g/f 66 2799
62 4-14 Chep 8.1gd 64 3733
55 8-12 Brig 8g/f 63 3986
69 1-15 CHEP 8.1g/s 62 4300*
71 2-13 Chep 8.1hvy 66 4709
68 6-9 Wind 10g/s 69 4943
57 9-16 Bath 8gd 69 5022

SNAP 3 ch c £13384
71 2-13 Nott 6.1sft 1464
74 1-14 THIR 6gd 1639*
76 3-8 Beve 7.5g/f 73 2166
79 1-8 THIR 7sft 73 2693*
85 3-13 Newc 7gd 78 3428

SNINFIA 4 b f £289
38 10-18 Bath 10.2g/s 65 1098
45 7-10 Bath 11.7gd 60 1399
51 7-13 Bath 8sft 60 1542
51 4-17 Nott 14.1g/f 55 2156
49 7-19 Bath 17.2gd 53 3147
34 9-13 Sali 14.1gd 50 3454
33 8-10 Carl 14.1fm 50 3549
0 14-16 Sout 14af 46 4045
0 10-11 Bath 11.7g/s [46] 4199 P

SNOOKERED AGAIN 2 b g £4189
60 5-11 Thir 6gd 1634
75a 1-11 SOUT 6af 2336*
50 7-9 Pont 6g/f 72 2989
76a 3-10 York 7af 74 3483
44 10-12 York 7g/s 68 4064
58 8-20 Redc 7fm 64 4337

SNOW BUNTING 6 ch g £10321
52 8-17 Leic 7g/s 54 1020
39 14-19 Yarm 7g/f 53 1132
55 3-14 Ayr 6g/f 50 1898
23 15-16 Ayr 5g/f 50 2029
64 2-12 Newc 6g/f 55 2160
48 8-12 Donc 7gd 54 2235
53 5-17 Redc 6gd 59 2561
64 3-15 Newc 6gd 58 3424
64 3-10 Newm 6g/f 58 3584
62 4-12 Newm 6g/f 62 3751
60 7-18 Redc 6fm 61 4339
57 6-15 Redc 6fm 60 4562
66 1-20 LEIC 7gd 59 5046*

SNOW CHANCE 3 ch f £0
13 13-14 Redc 10fm 37 2299
22a 8-11 Sout 8af [34] 3091
0 13-14 Nott 16g/f 34 3580

SNOW GOOSE 3 b f £61244
80 11-13 Newm 7gd [105] 1169
95 4-11 Warw 7.1fm [103] 2574
103 2-9 Sand 8.1g/s [100] 2917
103 3-7 Asco 8gd [103] 3389
101 3-10 Sali 9.9g/f [103] 3866
103 2-11 Colo 8sft [103] 4840
106 1-8 SAN 8sft [103] 5166*

SNOW JOKE 3 b f £434
48 7-12 Warw 7.1gd 1125
69 4-8 Kemp 7g/f [57] 1912
54 8-17 Kemp 7gd 60 2174
0 14-14 Wind 10gd 57 2617
0 11-13 Warw 8.1gd 53 3058
33 10-12 Wind 8.3fm 53 3291
63 5-11 Sali 7gd [49] 3884
14 17-20 Chep 7.1g/s 53 4367

SNOW LYNX 2 ch f £0
25 16-16 Newm 7g/s 5280

SNOW RIDGE 3 b c £66000
122 2-14 Newm 8g/f [113] 1480
110 7-14 Epso 12fm [120] 2254

SNOW TEMPEST 2 b c £0
69 7-9 Sali 7gd 2696
62 9-16 Sali 7g/s 3111
56 14-15 Ling 7gd 3285
68 6-8 Sand 8.1gd 4608

SNOW WOLF 3 ch g £6460
67 7-14 Kemp 5g/f 79 1914
81 1-6 REDC 6g/f [76] 2104*
84 2-9 Folk 6g/f 82 2271
63 9-12 Ripo 6g/f 78 2482
53 9-10 Kemp 6gd [81] 3188
80 4-9 Wind 5g/f 79 3976
62 14-15 Sand 5g/f 79 4604
54 14-15 Catt 5sft 78 5125
56a 9-12 Wolv 5.1ap 76 5326

SNOWDRIFT 2 b f £210
0 13-13 Nott 6.1g/f 4843
58a 5-5 Ling 5ap 5260 BL

SNOWED UNDER 3 gr g £4060
71 5-11 Beve 8.5sft 1304
64 5-12 Ripo 9g/f 1783
56 5-6 Beve 12.1g/s 65 2322
42 12-15 Nott 10gd 60 3108
52 7-13 Nott 10g/f 58 3419
60 1-18 BEVE 9.9g/s 55 4243*
52 6-19 Leic 10g/f 58 4456
60 3-12 Pont 10fm [58] 4757
46 9-10 Donc 10.3sft 58 5206

SNOWS RIDE 3 gr c £7035
84a 1-11 WOLV 16.2af 72 48*
93a 1-8 SOUT 16af 83 140*
30 14-14 Donc 16gd 82 926
48 16-18 Kemp 16g/s 81 1112
36 15-18 York 13.9g/s 79 1689
55 9-10 Kemp 16fm 75 2073 BL
63 7-11 Sand 14g/f 69 2391
41 6-6 Nott 16g/f [65] 2632
64 4-16 Warw 16.2gd 60 4276
41 14-19 Sali 14.1gd 60 4856
59 4-15 Good 16gd 58 5025
66 2-11 Catt 13.8sft [58] 5129

SNUKI 4 b c £0
58a 10-11 Ling 8ap 68 136
43a 13-14 Ling 10ap 65 265 bl
52a 9-14 Ling 10ap 62 520
42a 10-14 Ling 10ap 59 622
45a 9-13 Ling 10ap 53 726 bl e

SO DETERMINED 3 b g £1236
41 12-12 Newb 7g/f 2352
62 2-4 Brig 9.9fm 3675
54a 11-15 Ling 12ap [60] 4111

SO ELEGANT 2 b f £0
41 10-13 Warw 7.1g/s 4996
49a 5-11 Wolv 7.1ap 5228

SO INDEPENDENT 2 b f £0
37 8-8 Catt 6g/f 3348
26 11-12 Carl 5.9fm 3544

SO SOBER 5 b g £1872
15a 14-16 Sout 5af 46 183
35a 8-9 Wolv 5af 44 275
48a 1-13 WOLV 5af [45] 312*
47a 5-11 Wolv 5af 47 507
41a 4-12 Wolv 5af 46 641

41a	8-11	Ling	6ap	46	728
29a	8-11	Sout	5af	[45]	775
34a	4-12	Wolv	5af	[45]	889
41	3-10	Brig	5.3gd	[45]	1544
34	8-20	Beve	5g/f	[45]	1948
27	12-19	Donc	5g/s	40	3220
29	9-15	Chep	5.1gd	40	3403
46	5-16	Catt	5sft	[37]	3932
31a	6-15	Sout	5af	40	4043

SO SURE 4 b g £0

42a	4-11	Sout	11af	52	746
42a	6-14	Ling	10ap	52	757
34	9-13	Bath	10.2gd	[60]	3144 bl

SO VITAL 3 b c £4705

71a	2-15	Ling	12ap		118
73a	1-15	LING	12ap		521*
3a	7-7	Sout	14af	73	681
73a	3-10	Ling	12ap	73	936
52	14-19	Newm	12g/f	73	1484 P
41	11-13	Kemp	12g/f	70	1916 p
3	13-13	Pont	17.1g/f	63	2276

SO WILL I 3 ch c £31450

111	3-10	Newb	7gd		1234
107	1-11	NEWB	6gd	[109]	1732*
100	4-11	Newc	6g/s	[109]	2769
108	4-11	Newb	6g/f	[109]	3268
105	7-8	Good	7g/f	[108]	3508
105	5-13	Newb	6g/f	[108]	3957
112	3-7	Good	6g/f	[106]	4526
106	4-11	Good	6g/f	[106]	4874 P

SOAKED 10 b g £12619

51a	7-16	Sout	5af	57	183 bl
50a	2-9	Sout	5af	[55]	335 bl
39a	6-9	Ling	5ap	53	435 bl
45a	7-13	Ling	6ap	53	451 bl
40a	9-11	Wolv	5af	51	507 bl
45a	4-8	Wolv	5af	[49]	619 bl
25a	7-11	Wolv	5af	[47]	778 bl
50a	2-12	Wolv	5af	[45]	889 bl
53a	3-12	Wolv	5af	[45]	960 bl
46a	4-16	Sout	5ap	47	1046 bl
29	15-19	Beve	5sft	60	1627 bl
60	4-16	Ayr	5g/f	59	2029 bl
61	1-10	NEWC	5g/f	[59]	2161* bl
51	2-10	Hami	5g/f	[59]	2476 bl
62	1-14	NEWC	5g/f	57	2775* bl
63	5-18	Carl	5g/f	63	3228 bl
66	2-14	Thir	5g/f	63	3417 bl
49	3-8	Muss	5g/f	[63]	3527 bl
26	14-15	Pont	5g/f	63	3680 bl
50	3-16	Catt	5sft	[62]	3932 bl
34	18-19	Beve	5g/f	61	4240 bl
52	9-17	Beve	5g/f	59	4603 bl

SOAP WATCHER 3 b g £1703

73	1-6	COPE	8gd	[60]	3661*

SOAR 2 b f £98816

96	1-8	KEMP	5gd		2171*
103	2-17	Asco	5g/f		2490
109	1-6	ASCO	5g/f		3440*
115	1-8	YORK	6g/s	[100]	4059*
99	6-7	Newm	6g/f	[100]	4880

SOBA JONES 7 b g £13466

76a	1-10	WOLV	6af	66	349*
77a	2-11	Sout	5af	72	386
68a	4-11	Sout	5af	72	418
77a	3-13	Wolv	6af	75	482
77a	2-10	Sout	6af	[75]	532
70a	5-13	Wolv	6af	76	618
55	6-19	Newc	6sft	72	967 6
74	5-18	Donc	6gd	70	2752
59	4-6	Carl	5.9gd	[70]	2934
74	2-17	Pont	5gd	69	3241
63	5-11	Donc	6g/f	[69]	3375
59	9-18	Beve	6g/s	72	3852
68	5-8	Nott	5.1gd	[72]	4039

SOCIAL CONTRACT 6 b g £476

52a	6-16	Ling	7ap	54	144
45a	13-14	Ling	7ap	52	344
44a	7-13	Sout	7af	50	556
43a	7-11	Sout	5af	50	585 vis

41a	6-12	Ling	8ap	[47]	675 vis
36a	8-15	Ling	7ap	[47]	708
40a	6-8	Ling	7ap	[47]	730
43a	2-14	Ling	7ap	[45]	783 vis
38a	10-15	Ling	7ap	45	846 vis
31a	12-15	Ling	7ap	[45]	935 vis
30a	7-12	Wolv	7af	45	956 vis
29	8-10	Epso	6g/s	48	3045
44	8-17	Brig	7g/f	48	3176
45	8-9	Epso	7gd	[48]	3215
28	8-9	Brig	7sft	[44]	4164 vis
48	6-11	Epso	6gd	[45]	4294 vis

SOCIETY MUSIC 2 b f £11714

82	1-8	PONT	5hvy		1249*
77	3-6	Pont	6g/f		2039
81	1-5	MUSS	7.1g/f		2612*
78	3-7	Catt	6g/f		3189
77	6-13	Newc	7g/s	80	3698
73	7-16	Newm	6gd	78	4224
75	5-17	York	7g/f	74	4396
76	8-20	Ling	7g/f	74	4741 BL
57	9-14	Ayr	6sft	74	5035 bl

SOCIETY PET 5 b m £0

38	9-10	Sali	6g/s	[40]	4081
0	19-19	Kemp	6g/f	[40]	4793

SOCIETY TIMES 11 b g £750

36	7-11	Muss	8g/f	[16]	3558 T
16	10-12	Ayr	9.1g/f	24	3766 t
22	7-8	Hami	9.2g/s	[24]	4133 t
38	8-8	Muss	9g/f	[24]	4173 t
44	5-6	Ayr	10.9sft	[30]	4687 t

SOFISTICATION 3 b f £3838

38a	9-16	Ling	7ap		290
68a	1-15	LING	7ap		472*

SOFT FOCUS 2 b f £0

61a	7-11	Ling	8ap		4744
50a	7-11	Wolv	8.6ap		4978
37a	11-11	Ling	8ap		5235
30	12-14	Nott	6.1hvy		5342

SOFT MIST 4 gr f £0

40a	6-7	Sout	8af	61	332
30a	11-11	Wolv	9.4af	57	465
25	14-20	Ripo	8g/s	60	1366
34	8-11	Beve	9.9sft	57	1633
33	11-18	Thir	8g/f	54	1972
0	17-17	Warw	8.1fm	51	2440

SOIGNEE 2 b f £10282

103	2-9	Deau	8sft	5243

SOKOKE 3 ch g £1348

62	2-6	Ling	5gd		3023
64	3-9	Leic	5g/f		3347
0	8-9	Good	6sft		4262
58	8-13	Bath	5.7g/f		4413
25a	7-12	Wolv	6ap	[58]	5157

SOL ROJO 2 b g £0

49	12-13	Wind	6g/f	5048
58a	9-12	Wolv	7.1ap	5179
68a	7-11	Ling	8ap	5236
74a	5-13	Wolv	8.6ap	5288

SOLAR FALCON 2 ch f £0

39	10-12	Wind	8.3g/f	4829
1	15-16	Bath	8gd	5019

SOLAR POWER 3 b f £26552

85	2-14	Yarm	8g/f	80	1131
82	4-11	Asco	8sft	[83]	1419
89	4-14	Newm	8g/f	84	1930
87	4-9	Newm	7fm	84	3006
84	3-8	Newm	7gd	84	3928
89	1-11	HAYD	6g/f	[83]	4350*
93	2-12	Hayd	6sft	84	4779
91	2-10	Newm	6gd	84	4884

SOLAR PRINCE 3 b g £0

18	17-17	Catt	5g/f	55	3667
0	14-15	Hami	6sft	48	4696

SOLARIAS QUEST 2 b g £2859

84	3-14	Chep	8.1gd	4484

84	3-6	Hayd	8.1sft	4783
84	2-9	Nott	10hvy	5189

SOLDERA 4 b f £22126

103	3-10	Asco	8g/f	[103]	2487
104	4-6	Curr	10gd	[103]	2816
103	9-13	Deau	10sft	[103]	4160
106	4-13	Asco	8g/f	101	4802
93	12-16	Newm	9sft	[103]	5139

SOLDIER HOLLOW 4 b c £10282

113	2-10	Long	10g/s	2635

SOLDIERS TALE 3 ch c £6590

99	2-10	Newm	6g/f	1191
101	1-12	YORK	7g/s	1688*

SOLE AGENT 2 b g £656

57	11-12	Good	8g/f	4522
70	3-13	Brig	8sft	5091
31	10-15	Brig	7sft	5192

SOLEIL DHIVER 2 b f £0

26a	8-15	Sout	7af	[45]	87
25a	7-12	Wolv	9.4af	[40]	302
20a	5-8	Sout	8af	35	490
29	9-15	Beve	7.5g/f	[40]	1944

SOLENT 2 b c £5858

95	1-14	NEWM	7g/f	2766*
89	9-10	Good	7fm	3532
96	3-5	Sali	8gd	4328

SOLINIKI 3 b g £0

45	17-17	Leic	7g/s	80	1020
56	7-11	Donc	6g/s	79	3379
35	24-25	Newb	7gd	76	4683
49a	8-13	Wolv	6ap	70	5114 BL

SOLIPSIST 3 ch c £0

58	14-17	Newb	8g/f	1762
44	10-14	Sali	7fm	2291

SOLLER BAY 7 b g £1611

77	2-18	Wind	8.3g/s	75	1059
22	16-18	Ches	7.6gd	75	1598
51	8-8	Hayd	8.1fm	75	3797
70	4-5	Ayr	8hvy	[73]	4086
49	12-12	Redc	8gd	72	4246
50	11-17	Ayr	9.1g/s	[69]	4620
23	11-11	Wind	11.6g/s	[67]	4942

SOLMORIN 6 b m £0

28a	5-6	Ling	10ap	409

SOLO FLIGHT 7 gr g £12906

89	2-9	Newm	10gd	[85]	1890
81	6-11	Donc	12gd	85	2233
45	15-15	Donc	10.3g/f	85	3598
88	2-8	Newm	10gd	[85]	3945
73	9-9	Newm	10gd	85	4227
91	1-6	NEWB	11g/f	85	4643*
92	3-17	Newm	12g/f	87	4889
79	7-19	Newm	12gd	88	5085

SOLO SOLE 2 b c £432

47a	11-11	Ling	8ap		21
60a	9-11	Ling	6ap		135
71a	3-11	Ling	7ap		213
16	14-14	Bath	10.2gd	72	1403
28	13-18	Wind	8.3sft	69	1647
49	10-14	Nott	8.2g/f	65	2634

SOLOR 3 b c £3621

76a	4-9	Ling	8ap		1022
91	1-20	BATH	10.2gd		1398*
1	11-14	Newb	10hvy	89	5223

SOLSKJAER 4 b c £73968

106	2-8	Curr	8g/f	2820
110	2-8	Leop	10g/f	3496
113	1-6	CURR	10g/f	3840*
104	8-9	York	10.4gd	4002

SOLVED 3 b f £0

45	8-8	Bath	5fm	[79]	1901

SOMAYDA 9 b g £550

29	11-16	Good	9gd	47	2220
18	11-12	Newb	10g/f	47	2354

```
21  15-20  Kemp   9g/f     40    2857
41  3-13   Sali   6g/s     40    3109 P
12  15-19  Chep   12.1gd   40    3398 p
41  6-14   Wind   11.6fm   40    3638
29  5-14   Good   8sft     39    4189 p

SOME NIGHT 2 b f £0
66  5-6    Good   6g/f           1866
31  11-11  Bath   5g/s           4200
27  10-14  Redc   6g/s           5106

SOMEONES ANGEL 3 gr f £0
3   10-11  Pont   6g/s           1426

SOMERSET WEST 4 b g £7262
53a 6-9    Ling   5ap   [58]     492
28a 8-13   Ling   6ap   [58]     544
34a 13-14  Ling   6ap   [52]     819
54a 1-12   LING   7ap   [50]    1074*
67  1-14   LING   7sft   63     1625*
51  9-9    Yarm   7fm    66     2150
56  7-11   Good   6gd    66     2535
73  1-19   LEIC   5gd    66     2702*
68  7-13   Sali   6g/s   72     3109
50  9-12   Bath   5.7gd  72     3146

SOMETHING 2 b c £1866
86  2-17   Wind   6gd            3975
73  6-6    Sali   6gd            4854

SOMETHING EXCITING 2 ch f £25373
75  4-13   Newb   7g/f           3252
68  10-13  Good   7fm            3554
65  13-16  Sali   7gd            4329
83  1-12   SALI   8sft   71     4580*
94  1-17   GOOD   8gd    78     4871*
110 1-9    NEWM   8sft  [87]    5099*
99  2-8    Newm   8g/s [100]    5282

SOMETHINGABOUTHER 3 b f £1091
28a 5-12   Wolv   6af   [48]      33
23a 10-12  Wolv   5af    44      109
35a 9-13   Sout   6af   [40]     254
30a 4-6    Wolv   6af   [40]     313
28a 5-7    Wolv   6af   [40]     348
10a 8-8    Wolv   5af   [40]     619
37a 3-10   Ling   5ap   [40]     653
33a 7-7    Ling   6ap   [35]     706
34a 5-10   Ling   5ap   [40]     832
33  13-17  Bath   5ap   [48]    1787
44  2-13   Hami   5gd    45     2181
26  9-10   Brig   5.3fm  45     2331
0   19-19  Beve   5gd    45     2657
32  14-17  Bath   5ap    43     2981

SOMEWHERE MY LOVE 3 br f £4716
69a 1-11   LING   8ap            496*
60a 11-12  Ling   7ap    68      729
62a 10-12  Ling   8ap    68      798
67a 3-5    Wolv   8.5af  66     1655
32  16-18  Leic   6gd    64     5039

SOMEWIN 4 b f £0
31  11-15  Chep   16.2gd        3400 P

SOMNUS 4 b g £227708
111 7-15   York   6sft  [117]   1667
119 2-11   Newc   6g/s  [117]   2769
111 5-20   Newm   6g/f  [117]   3062
120 1-12   DEAU   6.5g/s [117]  3838*
121 2-19   Hayd   6fm   [118]   4384
121 1-7    LONG   7sft  [118]   5070*

SON AND HEIR 3 b c £0
27a 12-12  Ling   8ap           4975

SON OF REMBRANDT 3 b g £733
48a 9-13   Ling   6ap   [66]     364
32a 13-14  Sout   5af    62      485 BL
67a 5-5    Ling   5ap   [56]     725
54a 3-9    Sout   5af   [56]     871
26  6-9    Leic   6g/s  [64]    1015
50a 3-8    Wolv   7af   [53]    1222
44  11-14  Brig   6fm   [60]    1690
4a  12-12  Wolv   8.5af  52     2205
0   18-18  Sali   7fm    55     2292

SON OF THUNDER 3 ch g £6791
56  6-8    Muss   7.1gd         1554

56  1-8    MUSS   8gd    50     1798*
35  6-7    Ayr    9.1gd  55     2509
58  2-7    Muss   8g/f   53     2613
35  8-13   Warw   8.1gd  57     3058
65  1-13   MUSS   8g/f   55     3526*
52  9-14   Muss   7.1g/f 61     4175
42a 10-13  Wolv   8.6ap [61]    5336

SONDERBORG 2 b f £3586
46a 6-10   Sout   7af    62      203
51a 6-15   Ling   7ap    57      295 p
50a 4-12   Ling   8ap    54      402 p
44a 5-12   Ling   7ap   [52]     536 p
44a 3-10   Sout   8af    49      662 p
46a 2-6    Wolv   7af   [49]     779 p
52a 2-14   Ling   7ap   [49]     804 BL e
54a 2-15   Ling   7ap    51      846 bl e
46a 10-15  Ling   7ap    51      901 bl e
45  11-11  Leic   10g/s  59     1357
59  2-8    Muss   8gd    55     1798 e
37  6-9    Thir   7g/f  [58]    2218 bl e
9a  14-16  Sout   8af    52     2805
0   16-16  Brig   9.9g/f 55     3175
36  9-11   Wind   8.3fm  52     3799 bl
46  6-12   Kemp   9sft   52     4032 bl
48a 6-12   Ling   10ap   50     4113 bl
51a 6-9    Ling   12ap  [49]    4449 bl e
48  3-19   Kemp   8g/f  [49]    4795 bl
29  13-19  Yarm   8g/s  [49]    5119 bl

SONEARSOFAR 4 b g £0
34  11-11  Beve   7.5g/s        2325
30  6-10   Carl   6.9g/f        3230
43  7-13   Pont   8g/s          3973
15  13-18  Beve   9.9g/s   44   4243
1a  11-11  Wolv   7.1ap  [45]   5210

SONG KOI 3 b f £1063
37  10-11  Catt   6gd            999
50  2-14   Newc   5g/f  [60]    4404
35  18-19  Ling   5g/f   55     4739
43a 4-12   Wolv   6ap   [50]    5162

SONG OF THE SEA 3 ch f £450
66  8-16   Sand   10g/s         2131
65  9-14   Kemp   10g/s         2678
47  4-7    Newb   12g/f         2879 T
48  12-12  Sand   16.4g/f  62   3861 t
2   13-15  Chep   18sft    62   4056
25a 7-10   Ling   12ap   [58]   4314

SONG OF VALA 3 ch g £1246
66  9-9    Kemp   9sft   [81]    947
79  5-8    Chep   12.1gd [80]   2113
69  7-8    Nott   10g/f   78    2631
74  6-10   Sand   8.1g/f [75]   3339 T
75  3-8    Newm   8g/f    75    3947
68a 4-12   Ling   8ap    [74]   4975 t

SONG SPARROW 2 b f £0
51a 12-14  Ling   7ap           4971
56a 14-16  Ling   7ap           5078

SONGERIE 2 b f £28770
89  1-11   CHEP   7.1hvy        4703*
0   9-9    Curr   7sft          4958
105 1-3    DEAU   8sft          5243*

SONGGARIA 2 b f £2031
49  2-6    Folk   5g/f          2270
56  3-8    Wind   6g/f          2449
30  7-8    Muss   5g/f          2611
53  2-14   Beve   7.5sft        2939

SONGLARK 4 br c £11278
101 5-10   Newm   10g/f [107]   1483 VIS
107 2-14   Good   12g/f [107]   1843 vis t
111 4-6    Asco   12fm  [105]   2579 vis t

SONGTHRUSH 2 gr f £4882
87  1-16   NEWM   7g/s          5280*

SONIC ANTHEM 2 b g £0
7   17-18  Ayr    6g/s          4617

SONNE DE LOUP 2 ch f £0
0   12-13  Wolv   6af             3
39a 9-15   Ling   7ap            52
3a  R-10   Sout   8af   [42]     162

SONNTAG BLUE 2 b c £0
51  11-13  Wind   6fm           3478
59  10-14  Hayd   6gd           3735
41a 9-10   Ling   6ap           3817
48  10-15  Nott   6.1g/s        4644

SONO 7 b g £417
51  9-10   Muss   16g/f   75    1093
71  5-12   Thir   16gd    73    1637 p
69  4-9    Ripo   16g/f   70    2009 p

SONOMA 4 ch f £4631
70  5-11   Nott   16fm    72    1003
61  8-18   Newb   16gd    72    1232
36  6-13   Kemp   14.4hvy 70    1516
58  9-18   Nott   14.1g/s 68    1772
42  12-17  Nott   14.1g/f 66    2156
67  1-6    NOTT   16g/f  [60]   2632*
65  4-10   Nott   14.1gd  62    3105
64  4-10   Thir   16fm    62    3611
47  4-10   Yarm   16sft   62    4151
56  3-6    Muss   16g/f   61    4555

SOOYOU SIR 2 b g £0
49  10-12  Thir   7g/f          4591
42  13-15  Pont   10g/f         4933
32  8-9    Catt   7sft          5316

SOPHOMORE 10 b g £199
27a 9-13   Wolv   8.5af [42]    300
32a 6-8    Sout   11af  [40]    574
31a 3-12   Wolv   9.4af [35]    782
0   14-16  Sout   11af  [30]    852

SOPHRANO 3 b g £3431
58a 2-15   Sout   8af   [68]     96
50a 13-13  Ling   10ap   65     178 VIS
60  5-6    Nott   8.2g/f [63]   2154
59  3-4    Warw   7.1fm  [63]   2438
49  9-11   Hayd   6gd   [60]    3758
61  3-8    Hami   6g/s  [60]    3880
43  3-12   Hami   8.3g/s [56]   4007
32  7-8    Chep   7.1g/s [55]   4301
43  4-13   Carl   6.9fm [55]    4504
22  12-13  Warw   7.1g/s [50]   4994

SORBIESHARRY 4 gr g £8326
43a 4-11   Wolv   12af   46      72
49a 2-14   Sout   8af    44     165
47a 2-13   Sout   8af    44     228
29a 5-13   Wolv   9.4af   49    287 p
49a 2-10   Sout   8af    48     387 p
45a 3-10   Sout   8af    48     463 p
37a 5-11   Wolv   9.4af   48    465 p
51a 1-13   WOLV   8.5af   48    559* p
38a 5-11   Sout   11af   49     746 p
32a 10-10  Sout   8af    49     792 p
54a 1-7    WOLV   9.4af   48    961* p
50a 4-15   Sout   8af    54    1028 p
40a 11-13  Wolv   9.4af   50   1223 p
40a 5-15   Sout   8af    50   1755 p
35a 8-15   Sout   8af    49   4132 p
33a 11-13  Wolv   8.6ap [48]   5212 p

SORCERESS 2 b f £0
41  9-12   Redc   6fm           4557
40  11-13  Wind   6g/f          5047

SORRENTO KING 7 ch g £0
5a  7-8    Sout   14af  [30]    1840 t

SOTERIO 4 b c £13380
102 1-8    BADE   14sft        4425*

SOTONIAN 11 br g £2523
28a 5-16   Sout   5af   [40]    374
41a 3-11   Wolv   5af    40     507
37a 3-10   Wolv   5af   [40]    667
24a 7-11   Wolv   5af    40     748
41a 5-13   Ling   6ap   [40]    788
36a 3-10   Ling   5ap   [40]    832
35a 3-6    Ling   6ap   [40]   1184
26a 4-5    Ling   6ap   [40]   1452
22a 5-12   Wolv   5af   [40]   1799
43  1-16   NOTT   6.1gd [40]   1989*
14a 11-15  Sout   6af    38    3000
0   18-19  Kemp   6g/f  [40]   4793
3   20-20  Yarm   6g/s  [40]   5121
```

SOUL DANCE 3 b f £1280
65 2-10 Wind 6g/f 4835 T
0 W-11 Wolv 5.1ap 5363 t

SOUL PROVIDER 3 ch f £2285
60a 5-11 Wolv 6af [64] 481
47a 3-6 Wolv 6af [63] 631
50a 4-15 Sout 6af [58] 795
59a 3-11 Ling 8ap [56] 841
53 2-9 Leic 6g/s [56] 1015
53 4-12 Warw 7.1gd [52] 1125
40 9-13 Bath 8fm 52 2667
35 5-11 Yarm 7g/f [52] 2852
28 8-14 Beve 7.5g/s [50] 3177
24a 12-14 Ling 7ap 52 3746 BL
35 7-14 Newm 7gd [44] 4195 P
14a 12-14 Ling 7ap [45] 4660 p

SOULACROIX 3 b c £14082
90 2-5 Asco 12gd 84 3468
95 1-8 NEWB 13.3gd 85 3918*
81 7-13 York 13.9g/s 88 4062
95 3-19 Newm 12gd 90 5085
77 10-13 Donc 12sft 90 5215

SOUMILLON 2 br f £0
1a 12-12 Wolv 8.6ap 5115

SOUND AND VISION 2 b c £0
65 5-7 Ayr 6g/f 1893
59 6-13 Donc 6gd 2236
65 5-8 Beve 7.5gd 2511
59 6-20 Newc 6sft 2682
60 5-13 Thir 6g/f [66] 4590 BL
41 14-18 Pont 6g/f 63 4934 bl

SOUND BLASTER 3 ch g £0
70 5-8 Brig 9.9g/f [75] 1369
70 4-13 Sand 8.1gd 74 2365

SOUND BREEZE 2 ch c £365
78 4-10 Newm 6sft 5266

SOUND OF FLEET 3 ch c £10051
76 4-16 Wind 10gd 1384
77 6-17 Newb 8gd 1762
83 1-10 LEIC 10g/f 77 1965*
82 5-8 York 10.4g/f 84 2406
78 10-14 Wind 10fm 82 2785
85 2-10 Hami 13fm 80 3249
48 10-13 York 13.9g/s 85 4062
73 12-13 Kemp 14.4fm 84 4395
20 15-17 Nott 14.1g/s 82 4647

SOUND THAT ALARM 2 b c £1039
75 2-9 Ches 5.1g/f 3097
67 6-9 Sand 5g/f 3355

SOUND THE DRUM 2 b c £2858
82 3-11 Sali 6g/f 3863
85 2-15 Nott 6.1g/s 4644

SOUNDS LUCKY 8 b g £3626
53a 10-14 Ling 6ap 68 407 bl
54a 5-13 Ling 6ap 66 471 bl
40a 12-12 Ling 6ap 64 628 bl
64a 1-7 LING 5ap [60] 737* bl
58a 2-14 Ling 6ap [60] 819 bl
54a 6-14 Ling 6ap 60 874 bl
51a 8-14 Ling 6ap 57 897 bl
46a 4-9 Ling 6ap [57] 1012 bl
24a 12-12 Sout 5af 54 1442 bl
0 16-16 Sout 6af 53 2720 bl
9 15-20 Nott 6.1gd 45 2928 bl
2a 13-13 Wolv 6ap [50] 5211 bl

SOUTH FACE 3 ch g £1730
86 2-13 Donc 7gd 925

SOUTH OTHE BORDER 2 b c £0
64 9-12 Sand 7.1g/f 2388
63 11-14 Newm 7g/f 3752
63 10-14 Sand 7.1g/s 4069
12 13-14 Sali 8gd 4852

SOUTHAMPTON JOE 4 ch g £0
14 12-17 Chep 8.1g/s 51 3087
37 6-8 Bath 10.2g/f [48] 3370 VIS

SOUTHBURGH 3 b g £0
38 20-20 Newm 8g/f 3237

SOUTHERN AFRICA 2 b c £18810
94 1-8 NEWB 5.2fm 2646*
88 2-5 Sand 5g/s 2895
97 1-8 ASCO 7gd 3467*

SOUTHERN BAZAAR 3 ch c £4579
84 2-4 Brig 8fm 2261
79 1-8 BRIG 8fm 4762* T

SOUTHERN STAR 4 gr g £288
52 4-8 Newc 12.4hvy 1038

SOUTHERN TIDE 2 b c £0
47 17-18 Leic 7g/f 3342
57 11-18 Wind 6gd 3824
21 10-11 Chep 7.1hvy 4704
37 13-15 Newm 8gd 4883

SOVEREIGN DREAMER 4 b c £0
10 18-19 York 11.9sft 82 1668
75 6-9 Thir 12g/f 80 1969 t
46 11-11 Donc 12gd 78 2233 t
61 7-9 Newm 14.8fm 76 2596 t
64 7-8 Ling 11.5fm 73 3747
52 11-14 Catt 12g/f 70 4672 t
51 11-20 York 13.9gd 68 5004 t

SOVEREIGN GIRL 3 b f £0
21 15-16 Bath 10.2g/f 1790
25 6-8 Leic 11.8g/f 1961

SOVEREIGN SPIRIT 2 b c £0
60 11-14 Sand 7.1g/s 4069
57 7-15 Chep 7.1gd 4483
62 6-8 Pont 8fm 4756

SOVEREIGN STATE 7 b g £4773
49 1-20 CATT 12g/f 41 2850* p
51 4-13 Warw 12.6gd 47 3056 p
45 5-20 Catt 12g/f 47 3354 p
53 2-7 Muss 13g/f 47 3530 p
38 8-10 Thir 16sft 50 3834 p
52 2-13 Redc 14.1fm 49 4340 p
46 8-19 Thir 12g/f 50 4594 p

SOVEREIGNTY 2 b c £1871
87 2-6 Yarm 6g/f 2851
84 4-15 Wind 6gd 3163

SOVIET SCEPTRE 2 ch c £4109
60a 6-12 Ling 8ap 100
70 3-13 Nott 6.1sft 1464
35 10-19 Donc 6g/f [73] 1876
60 4-10 Hayd 8.1gd [70] 3739 T
62 6-14 Yarm 7gd 68 3995 t
38 8-14 Newm 7gd [68] 4195 t
26 9-10 Yarm 10.1gd [62] 4612
65 1-15 WIND 10g/f [60] 4834*
61 5-9 Good 11gd [66] 5026
38a 12-13 Wolv 9.5ap 66 5161

SOVIET SONG 4 b f £534453
109 2-8 Kemp 8g/s [114] 1115
111 3-10 Sand 8.1g/s [114] 1349
120 1-5 CURR 8g/f [114] 1997*
119 2-6 Asco 8g/f [114] 2470
122 1-7 NEWM 8fm [114] 3004+
120 1-11 GOOD 8fm [115] 3533*
123 1-6 LEOP 8g/f [115] 4572*
100 6-11 Asco 8g/f [120] 4801

SOVIET SPIRIT 3 ch f £421
60 5-7 Nott 8.2sft 1468
20 19-20 Wind 10sft 1651
60 5-11 Beve 7.5g/s 2325
20 3-8 Yarm 8g/f [63] 2854
56 5-12 Wind 8.3fm 59 3291
5 13-15 Leic 7g/f [59] 3515
42 4-10 Yarm 10.1gd [55] 3874
9 7-9 Brig 8sft 53 4165
36 7-10 Yarm 10.1gd [51] 4612
15a 10-12 Ling 8ap [48] 4974 BL

SOVIET TREAT 3 b f £0
60 5-12 Ripo 8g/f [95] 1978

SOVIETTA 3 b f £4504
62 4-7 Nott 10g/f 3422
68 3-7 Bath 11.7g/f 3967
43 9-10 Bath 11.7g/f 4414
62 1-15 LEIC 11.8gd [65] 5060*

SOWERBY 2 b c £361
62 9-11 York 6g/s 1687
53 6-13 York 6g/f 2358
63 4-13 Beve 5gd 2889
59 10-10 York 5gd 72 3115
21 9-10 Beve 5sft 64 4258

SOYUZ 4 ch g £16820
85 2-13 Wind 8.3g/s [82] 1057
84 3-17 Sand 8.1g/s 82 1351
90 1-4 LING 7.6g/s [82] 1616*
85 5-13 Kemp 7gd 87 2172
81 9-18 Newc 7sft 87 2684
55 19-20 Chep 7.1g/s 85 3088
82 7-18 York 8gd 83 5000
83a 5-12 Wolv 7.1ap 82 5159
92 1-20 DONC 7sft 81 5367*

SPA LANE 10 ch g £0
35a 8-15 Sout 16af 56 67
23a 6-10 Wolv 14.8af [55] 125

SPACE COWBOY 4 b c £0
51 14-17 Wind 10g/f 78 5050

SPACE MAKER 2 b c £4484
80 4-15 Wind 6g/f 2263
26 8-8 Ayr 5gd 2505
85 1-12 BEVE 5g/f 4596*

SPACE SHUTTLE 2 b c £37301
81 3-5 Donc 5g/s 1517
80 2-11 Hayd 5gd 1880
81 1-13 DONC 6gd 2236* BL
85 3-6 Beve 5gd 2513 bl
87 3-11 Newm 6g/f 85 3614 bl
92 3-9 Redc 6g/f 86 3807
105 1-13 YORK 6gd 86 4004*
105 1-6 RIPO 6g/f [93] 4280*
61 12-21 Donc 6hvy [85] 5202

SPACED 2 b c £20413
44 12-19 Kemp 6g/f 1911
69 6-17 Ling 7g/f 2584
91 1-9 FOLK 7g/f 3047*
85 3-12 York 7g/s 81 4064
91 1-11 HAYD 8.1fm 81 4387*

SPAINKRIS 5 b g £0
10a 9-9 Wolv 12af 70 467

SPANISH ACE 3 b g £8214
71a 14-15 Ling 7ap [103] 885
90 8-11 Newm 7gd 106 1167
70 18-18 Hayd 8.1g/f 98 1919
84 10-17 Epso 7g/f 92 2212 VIS
93 5-19 Newm 6fm 88 3002 vis
86 5-16 Newb 6g/f 88 3269 vis
73 15-21 Good 5fm 87 3567 vis
76 4-8 Kemp 5sft [85] 4031 vis
93 1-11 BATH 5g/s [85] 4201+ H Bl
77 18-22 Donc 5.6fm 89 4459 h bl

SPANISH DON 6 b g £113342
73 14-27 Newb 8gd 86 1231
74 13-18 Good 8g/f 86 1812
81 5-8 Newb 8g/f [84] 2313
92 1-12 KEMP 9g/f 83 2860*
100 1-12 KEMP 10gd 88 3185*
98 5-15 Good 9.9g/f 95 3506
92 9-18 Newb 10gd 95 4681
106 1-32 NEWM 9g/f 94 4916*
107 1-6 NEWM 10sft [100] 5269*

SPANISH GOLD 3 b f £0
60a 13-16 Ling 7ap 75 181
8a 12-12 Wolv 9.4af 72 382

SPANISH LAW 2 b g £0
51 7-7 Ayr 7.2g/s 2570

SPANISH RIDGE 2 b c £437
81 5-11 Newb 7g/f 3959

74	4-13	Newm	7fm		4724
43	18-19	Leic	7gd		5055

SPANISH STAR 6 b g £5536

7a	12-16	Sout	8af	45		86
50a	4-10	Sout	11af	[45]		142
47a	1-15	SOUT	11af	41		196*
45a	4-9	Sout	11af	46		331
18a	6-11	Sout	12af	46		458
56a	1-10	SOUT	12af	[45]		552*
50a	3-8	Sout	11af	[45]		574
51a	3-5	Sout	12af	[54]		745
27a	8-15	Sout	12af	51		867
0	9-9	Sout	11af	[49]		985 vis
5a	11-11	Sout	12af	49		1197 vis
19a	7-11	Sout	12af	[47]		3154
20a	10-14	Sout	12af	43		3486
32a	4-12	Wolv	12.2ap	[40]		5208

SPARK UP 3 b f £5860

64a	2-9	Wolv	8.5af	64	2 bl
44a	6-12	Wolv	7af	64	129 bl
51a	6-8	Wolv	7af	64	280 bl
50a	7-11	Wolv	7af	64	363 bl
49a	7-10	Wolv	8af	62	463 bl
43a	6-9	Wolv	7af	59	629 bl
58a	2-5	Wolv	8.5af	57	861
48a	4-7	Wolv	8.5af	57	942 VIS
52a	4-8	Wolv	8.5af	55	1219 bl
61a	1-10	WOLV	8.5af	55	1322+ bl
45	8-9	Nott	10sft	67	1467
60	6-20	Asco	8g/f	65	1927 bl
32	16-18	Donc	7g/f	63	2080 bl
52	7-18	Donc	7gd	60	2755 bl
57	6-14	Pont	8g/f	59	2993

SPARKFORD 2 b c £0

45	12-15	Newm	8gd	4883

SPARKLING CLEAR 2 b f £0

35a	6-13	Sout	6af	[50]		63 VIS
18a	9-11	Sout	6af	47		872
16	10-12	Folk	6sft	45		975 vis
0	6-7	Wolv	6af	[45]		1312
0	7-7	Brig	7gd	[40]		1549 vis

SPARKLING JEWEL 4 b f £1257

67	8-11	Newm	6fm	77		2093
72	6-12	Sali	6fm	77		2289
75	2-8	Bath	5.7fm	[74]		2669 BL
63	8-10	Kemp	6g/f	74		2861

SPARKLING WATER 5 b h £0

54	11-18	Newb	16gd	75	1232

SPARKWELL 2 b c £0

79	5-16	Newb	7g/f	4677

SPARTAN ODYSSEY 3 b g £0

0	7-8	Wolv	7af	892

SPARTAN PRINCIPLE 4 b f £0

34a	8-12	Wolv	9.4af	939

SPARTAN SPEAR 3 b g £0

36	11-13	Nott	6.1sft		1464
14	11-11	Redc	7g/f	[68]	1822
0	9-9	Donc	8g/s	63	3378 P

SPEAGLE 2 ch c £0

47	12-14	Redc	6fm		2297
66	5-7	Ayr	7.2g/s		2570
75	6-8	Epso	7gd		3214
34	12-14	Muss	8gd	63	4519

SPEAR 2 b c £5577

85	2-16	Newm	7g/f	3582
69	3-12	Ayr	7.2hvy	4083
84	1-10	REDC	9fm	4558*

SPEAR THISTLE 2 ch c £7705

92	4-11	Donc	8fm	4462
79	4-11	Good	8gd	4746
87	1-16	NEWB	8hvy	5220*

SPEARIOUS 3 b g £0

66	4-17	Bath	5g/f	[70]	1787 T

SPECIAL BRANCH 4 ch g £0

0	16-17	Pont	17.1g/s	48	3970

0	16-16	Carl	11.9g/f	45	4348

SPECIAL DELIVERY 4 b f £5500

103	3-8	Newm	9fm	1491

SPECIAL GOLD 2 b c £421

76	5-10	Hayd	5sft	1107
69	4-7	Thir	5g/s	1471

SPECIAL KALDOUN 5 b h £48890

114	3-6	Deau	8sft	3168
118	1-7	DEAU	10hvy	4016*
114	3-10	Mais	10gd	4837
114	3-12	Long	10g/f	4950

SPECIALISE 2 b f £0

19	11-13	Catt	7g/f	3349
0	P-11	Thir	7g/f	3570
47	10-14	Carl	6.9fm	4503

SPECTACULAR HOPE 4 b f £0

1a	8-8	Wolv	16.2af	46	690

SPECTAIT 2 b g £1531

78	2-11	Chep	7.1hvy	4704
13a	11-12	Wolv	6ap	4921
69a	3-12	Wolv	8.6ap	5115

SPECTESTED 3 ch g £2201

52	7-19	Warw	10.9gd	65	1124
3	9-10	Nott	14.1hvy	61	1612
52a	2-7	Wolv	12af	[56]	2050 P
41	5-6	Warw	10.9fm	50	2780
52	9-12	Wind	11.6gd	46	3161 p
60	4-10	Nott	10gd	46	3990 p
57	2-8	Chep	16.2g/s	55	4302 p

SPECTOR 4 gr c £0

59	7-19	Yarm	8g/f	1130
39	13-17	Ling	7g/s	1617
0	16-17	Chep	8.1gd	2117

SPECTROMETER 7 ch g £0

51	14-14	Hami	12.1gd	85	1389
40	19-19	Newc	16.1g/s	82	2771
37	21-19	York	11.9gd	80	3999

SPECTRUM OF LIGHT 2 b f £0

53	12-12	Redc	6g/f	2119
57	5-5	Ripo	6g/f	2481

SPECTRUM STAR 4 b g £0

18	9-13	Ayr	10sft	[40]	5066
29	7-9	Ayr	13.1sft	[35]	5277

SPEED COP 4 ch f £13115

92a	2-10	Ling	5ap	[100]	883
95	3-14	Bath	5gd	[100]	1400
77	9-12	Epso	5g/f	[99]	2206
73	18-19	Asco	5g/f	[99]	2468
95	4-10	Asco	6gd	95	3773
90	6-6	Sand	5g/s	95	4098
89	9-14	Epso	5g/f	94	4291 VIS
70	8-12	Leic	5g/f	[94]	4454 vis

SPEED DIAL HARRY 2 b c £9245

68a	5-10	Ling	5ap		1071
72	2-6	Redc	5sft		1143
67	3-6	Ayr	5g/s		1445
75a	1-7	SOUT	6af		1751* VIS
78	3-7	Yarm	6fm		2144 BL
81	2-10	Ches	5.1g/s		2744 vis
81	1-5	HAMI	5gd		3130* vis
52	7-8	Ayr	6g/f	85	3303 vis
70	4-5	Hami	6g/f	[83]	3589

SPEED OF SOUND 2 ch f £4076

60	3-6	Sali	5g/s	1499
74	3-6	Wind	6g/f	1808
69	4-11	Nott	5.1g/f	2151

SPEED ON 11 b g £0

36	8-17	Nott	6.1sft	46	1606
34a	7-13	Wolv	5af	52	2201

SPEED RACER 3 b f £1378

37	14-14	Redc	7fm	62	2295
57	5-7	Newc	6g/s	[57]	2728
22	14-14	Catt	6g/f	57	3018
53	3-9	Pont	8gd	[55]	3462

48	6-10	Newc	7hvy	[51]	4216
47	3-7	Redc	7fm	[49]	4561
57	7-13	Nott	8.2g/f	[45]	4847
39	7-17	Warw	8.1g/s	[45]	4992

SPEEDBIRD 3 ch f £1117

70	12-17	Newm	7gd		1171
74	2-17	Yarm	7g/f	[70]	1729
57	7-14	Nott	8.2g/f	72	2153

SPEEDFIT FREE 6 b g £948

55a	5-16	Sout	7af	[58]	61 bl
51a	4-11	Wolv	6af	[56]	153 bl
55a	2-10	Sout	6af	[55]	308 bl
50a	5-12	Wolv	6af	55	385 bl
40a	6-12	Wolv	6af	[53]	646 bl
54a	2-10	Sout	6af	[51]	851 vis
52	4-8	Newc	6sft	[58]	963 bl
50	9-18	Catt	7gd	[58]	996 bl
7	10-17	Pont	6hvy	[58]	1065 bl
50a	3-5	Wolv	6af	[52]	1310 bl
47a	7-12	Sout	5af	52	1442 vis
14	14-14	Hami	8.3gd	52	1504
47a	4-15	Sout	6af	50	1750 vis
38	9-12	Ayr	7.2fm	48	1909 vis
36	9-10	Ayr	7.2g/f	48	2027 vis
44	6-12	Leic	6fm	47	2111 p
43	10-12	Hayd	6g/s	[47]	2186 vis
39	7-7	Warw	6.1fm	[46]	2598 p
1	20-20	Nott	6.1g/f	46	2630 p
59	11-11	Warw	7.1fm	[46]	2777
3a	14-15	Sout	6af	43	3000 vis
6	13-14	Hami	6gd	43	3129 vis
2	19-19	Ayr	6sft	40	5069 vis

SPEEDIE ROSSINI 2 b g £0

45	12-14	Ling	7.6g/f	3601
48	9-9	Folk	7g/f	3721
41	14-14	Folk	7gd	4115
45	12-18	Newm	8fm	4722 BL

SPEEDY JAMES 8 ch g £874

26a	8-16	Sout	6af	[40]	447
2a	14-14	Sout	6af	40	501 vis
59	2-8	Newc	6sft	[40]	963
0	16-17	Pont	6hvy	[40]	1065

SPEEDY SPIRIT 2 ch f £0

39	9-10	Newb	6g/f	4637
1	16-16	Bath	8gd	5019
30	11-14	Newb	6sft	5197

SPEIGHTSTOWN 2 gr c £6211

74	7-14	Sand	7.1g/s		4069
85	3-11	Nott	8.2g/s		4648
84	1-12	WIND	8.3g/f		4829*
75	7-13	Wind	8.3g/f	82	5051

SPENCE APPEAL 2 b c £0

57	9-13	York	6gd	3120
49	8-10	Yarm	8g/f	3713
67	11-13	Donc	7hvy	5200

SPERRIN VALLEY 2 ch f £0

14a	12-14	Ling	7ap	4658

SPES BONA 3 b c £372

47	10-13	Newm	8fm		2595
55	4-16	Ripo	8gd		2987
13	13-13	Wind	8.3gd		3828
38	15-17	Beve	8.5g/f	59	4721
54	7-11	Wolv	12.2ap	54	5009

SPIDERS WEB 4 gr g £576

8a	14-16	Ling	7ap		290
0	12-12	Ling	8ap		401
28a	9-11	Ling	12ap		672
50a	10-13	Ling	10ap		715
0	B-14	Ling	10ap	[30]	784 BL
31a	2-13	Wolv	8.5af	[30]	826 bl
16a	13-16	Sout	11af	[35]	906 bl
12a	11-12	Ling	8ap	[35]	971 bl
23a	7-7	Ling	10ap	[35]	1244 bl
0	10-10	Sout	8af	[35]	1406 bl
3	11-12	Wind	10fm	29	3295 bl

SPILL A LITTLE 2 b c £0

51	6-7	Sand	7.1g/s	2897
81	5-11	Bath	8gd	4544

65 9-11 Good 8gd 4746

SPIN KING 3 b c £2756
67	7-14	Newm	10g/f	82	1192
78	4-20	Newm	8fm	80	1496
64	11-16	Leic	7g/f	80	1825
75	3-8	Leic	7g/f	78	2403
77	4-12	Leic	8g/f	76	2922
70	7-11	Newm	7g/f	75	3283
60	6-8	Newm	7g/f	74	3612 VIS
26	13-14	Newm	7gd	[72]	4195

SPINDOR 4 ch g £6845
45a	12-15	Ling	7ap	61	151 bl
61a	2-11	Wolv	7af	59	378 bl
50a	5-9	Sout	6af	[58]	459 bl
60a	3-11	Wolv	7af	59	558 bl
50a	4-10	Wolv	7af	59	685 bl
62a	2-14	Ling	6ap	58	897 bl
63a	1-14	LING	7ap	58	1010* bl
53a	7-13	Wolv	6af	61	1221 bl
62a	3-10	Wolv	7af	[61]	1319 bl
64	3-14	Hami	8.3gd	61	1504 bl
50	6-15	Brig	8fm	61	1691 bl
51	12-12	Bath	8g/f	62	1792 bl
56a	9-11	Ling	8ap	61	2018 bl
58a	4-15	Sout	7af	[60]	2999 bl

SPINETAIL RUFOUS 6 b g £3007
27a	11-14	Ling	7ap	[48]	4660 bl t
53	1-19	KEMP	6gd	[40]	4793+ bl
58	1-15	BRIG	6gd	[48]	4905* bl
52	7-8	Brig	5.3sft	55	5096 bl
53	7-19	Bath	5.7sft	55	5176 bl

SPINNAKERS GIRL 2 b f £1846
63	9-12	Hami	6gd		2178
71	3-5	Muss	7.1g/f		2612
66	2-11	Newc	7gd		3429
71	4-13	Newc	7g/s	70	3698
62a	8-13	Sout	7af	70	4040
32	11-12	Muss	7.1g/s	[69]	5142
60	4-8	Ayr	8sft	[64]	5273
41	8-10	Catt	7sft	[64]	5317 BL

SPINNING COIN 2 b f £0
20	19-19	Newb	6g/f		2310
71	6-16	Kemp	7g/f		3035
70	7-13	Kemp	7g/f		3520
56	8-15	Good	8g/s		4233
41	9-12	Bath	8g/f	67	4410

SPINNING DOVE 4 ch f £1787
67a	3-16	Ling	7ap	62	323
68a	2-12	Ling	8ap	[65]	514
0	R-11	Ling	8ap	[67]	697
63a	5-12	Ling	8ap	[67]	1042
0	R-15	Beve	7.5g/f	[65]	1944

SPINNING JENNI 4 b f £0
0	13-13	Ling	6ap	[54]	544

SPIRIT OF CHESTER 2 b f £19223
82	4-6	Newb	5.2gd	1735
101	2-17	Asco	6gd	2553
67	9-13	Curr	6.3gd	2815
101	3-8	York	6g/s	4059

SPIRIT OF FRANCE 2 b c £12843
72	2-6	Newc	5sft		1274
90	2-8	Sand	5gd		2188
97	1-9	RIPO	6g/f		2522*
96	2-9	Pont	6g/f	89	2989
96	5-10	Asco	7gd	[95]	3774
95	3-5	Newm	8fm	94	4725

SPIRITS AWAKENING 5 b g £11174
48	10-18	Wind	8.3gd	58	1385
53	6-18	Good	8g/f	58	1849
56	3-12	Sand	8.1g/s	56	2129
62	2-10	Newb	8g/f	56	2350
60	4-25	Asco		58	3443
64	2-8	Sand	7.1g/s	58	3891
56	6-10	Sand	8.1g/s	58	4067
53	9-14	Good	8g/f	60	4542
67	1-17	NOTT	8.2gd	58	4862*
51	8-15	Nott	8.2hvy	62	5191
39	14-20	Yarm	8g/f	62	5256

SPITFIRE BOB 5 b g £0
42a	10-11	Wolv	9.4af	66	465
40	12-14	Catt	12g/f	61	4672

SPITTING IMAGE 3 ch f £9714
48a	7-12	Wolv	16.2af	64	7
56	8-13	Catt	13.8gd	62	997
61	3-10	Muss	14g/f	62	1118
55	7-10	Hami	13gd	62	1506
56	3-4	Carl	11.9fm	[61]	1952
61	4-9	Redc	14.1g/f	61	2105
63	1-9	REDC	16fm	[60]	2298*
64	2-6	Nott	16g/f	[58]	2632
64	3-9	Redc	16sft	58	2963
64	1-6	REDC	16g/f	59	3810*
48	6-9	Ripo	16gd	61	4308
47	7-8	Redc	14.1fm	61	4932

SPLENDID TOUCH 3 b f £0
46a	8-15	Ling	12ap	[38]	118
3a	10-10	Sout	11af	[40]	375
0	8-8	Ling	11.5g/s	[35]	4181

SPLIFF 3 b c £12898
97	1-11	SALI	6g/s	87	1498*
87	7-18	Newm	6g/f	95	1933
87	12-19	Newm	6fm	94	3002
87	11-12	Newm	5g/f	93	3279 BL
75	11-11	Newm	5g/f	91	3941
91	5-9	Good	6g/f	89	4537
46	11-12	Hayd	6sft	89	4779

SPLODGER MAC 5 b g £10330
16	14-16	Beve	7.5gd	43	2891
29	10-11	Ripo	8gd	43	2986
57	1-10	BEVE	8.5g/f	38	3501*
56	2-16	Redc	7g/f	53	3809
51	6-16	Nott	8.2g/s	53	4036
42	10-12	Redc	8gd	55	4246
56	2-15	Thir	8fm	[53]	4379
56	4-15	Beve	8.5g/f	53	4598
29	19-26	Redc	8fm	53	4926

SPORTING GESTURE 7 ch g £6266
59	8-19	York	11.9sft	75	1668
78	5-9	Thir	12g/f	74	1969
79	4-10	York	11.9gd	75	2405
79	4-10	Carl	11.9gd	75	2673
72	4-10	Ripo	12.3g/s	75	3261
79	3-13	York	11.9g/f	74	3437
78	6-8	Ches	12.3fm	77	3637
0	U-21	York	11.9gd	75	3999
79	2-17	Thir	12fm	75	4377
76	5-17	Nott	14.1g/s	76	4647

SPORTSMAN 5 b g £292
30a	4-8	Wolv	16.2af	40	690 bl
29a	4-12	Sout	16af	40	1753 bl
25	11-13	Ripo	12.3g/f	35	2008 bl

SPORTULA 2 b f £0
54a	12-12	Ling	10ap	116

SPOT IN TIME 4 b f £0
0	7-8	Wolv	12af		808
67	8-9	Sali	9.9g/f		1719
56	8-16	Donc	10.3gd		2751
17	7-10	Carl	6.9g/f		3230
3	8-8	Brig	11.9sft	55	4143

SPOTLIGHT 3 ch f £9100
104	4-8	Newb	7gd	[101]	1233
83	16-16	Newm	8fm	[101]	1492
108	2-7	Good	9.9g/f	[101]	1844

SPREE 2 gr f £4947
13	6-6	Sali	5g/s		1499
89	1-6	SAND	5gd		2364*
45	9-9	Asco	5gd		2516
63	12-13	Good	5g/f		3509
27	7-10	Nott	6.1gd	[92]	4858

SPREE VISION 8 b g £2568
38	6-16	Newc	10.1sft	52	1278
54	8-14	Hami	12.1gd	52	1389
53	4-9	Hayd	11.9gd	53	2900 vis
55	2-7	Ayr	10.9gd	50	3149 vis
58	2-7	Carl	11.9g/f	[50]	3226 vis
41	4-6	Hami	12.1g/f	51	3588
0	5-5	Hami	12.1sft	49	4012 vis
49	6-17	Ayr	9.1g/s	[47]	4620 vis
46	4-13	Ayr	10sft	[47]	5276 vis

SPRING ADIEU 3 b f £691
62	4-8	Good	9gd		2536
55	9-12	Beve	9.9gd	66	2893
53	11-14	Kemp	10g/f	64	3690
60	4-8	Brig	11.9sft	62	4143
52	7-11	Bath	13.1g/f	60	4415 BL

SPRING BREEZE 3 ch g £6902
39	6-12	Redc	10sft	56	1144
49	9-13	Beve	12.1g/f	53	1836 P
57	2-14	Redc	14.1g/f	51	2123 p
60	3-20	Beve	16.2gd	55	3312 p
57	2-14	Nott	16g/f	55	3580 BL
50	5-13	Redc	14.1gd	52	4249 bl
56	2-6	Muss	16g/f	52	4555 VIS
62	1-19	CATT	15.8g/f	52	4675* vis
56	6-13	Newc	16.1fm	60	4868 vis
60	3-11	Ayr	15sft	59	5032 vis

SPRING DANCER 3 b f £432
50a	13-15	Ling	7gd	67	901
47	8-15	Wind	10ap	63	1054
18	13-14	Sali	7g/f	[58]	1720
43	5-9	Good	11g/f	53	2019
40a	3-12	Wolv	8.5af	53	2205
51	6-12	Carl	6.9fm	50	3548 T
31	12-17	Thir	8g/s	49	3830 t
46	6-16	Catt	7g/f	47	4676 t
36a	7-11	Wolv	7.1ap	[45]	5210 t

SPRING GIFT 7 b m £0
0	8-9	Sout	11af	[45]	505

SPRING GODDESS 3 b f £5780
84	3-14	Asco	10g/f	82	1924
78	9-18	Epso	10.1fm	82	2250
82	4-8	York	10.4g/f	82	2406
85	3-6	Asco	10gd	81	3072
85	3-12	Good	9fm	81	3535

SPRING JIM 3 b g £9890
72	4-7	Folk	7g/f	[72]	2272
79	1-14	NOTT	8.2g/f	70	2634*
84	2-16	Kemp	9g/f	75	3039
81	4-6	Nott	10g/f	79	3578
85	2-12	Sand	10gd	79	4502

SPRING PURSUIT 7 b g £321
0	10-12	Wolv	12af	46	75
49	4-14	Bath	13.1g/s	46	4203

SPRING SURPRISE 3 b f £450
83	6-9	Kemp	8g/s	1110

SPRING TIME GIRL 2 b f £0
37	10-11	Beve	5g/f	4599

SPRING WHISPER 2 b f £0
55a	10-12	Ling	10ap		120 VIS
32a	8-10	Sout	8af		162
46a	7-9	Ling	10ap	55	365 vis
2a	13-14	Ling	7ap	[49]	4660 BL
9	17-20	Kemp	12g/f	[45]	4796
0	18-19	Brig	9.9gd	[40]	4903 vis

SPRINGALONG 3 ch g £291
63a	4-9	Ling	10ap	[75]	269
53a	7-14	Ling	10ap	[75]	430
67a	4-13	Ling	10ap	[67]	715
67a	5-14	Ling	10ap	67	803
34	13-18	Bath	10.2g/s	67	1098
46	10-18	Nott	10ap	63	1778
58	7-11	Brig	9.9fm	60	2260
29a	8-11	Ling	12ap	[62]	2588
45	6-11	Yarm	10.1gd	[56]	3362

SPRINGTIME ROMANCE 3 b r f £6562
70	3-14	Wind	10g/s		1055
64	6-8	Newm	12g/s		1153
79	1-12	GOOD	9g/f		1864*
74	6-8	Good	9.9gd	80	2377
77	4-8	Kemp	10gd	80	2680
22	8-8	Wind	8.3gd	80	3162 VIS

SPURADICH 4 b c £60162

SPY GUN *(continued)*

62	10-10	Beve	8.5g/f	93	1833
94	3-7	Pont	10g/f	[93]	2605
79	6-9	Asco	10g/f	91	3439
99	1-18	**NEWB**	10gd	90	4681*

SPY GUN 3 ch g £3607

26a	9-14	Sout	8af	60	60
62a	1-14	Sout	8af	55	165*
59a	4-16	Sout	7af	61	208
56a	3-5	Wolv	8.5af	60	346
51a	5-8	Sout	8af	60	393
37a	8-12	Wolv	8.5af	58	564
38a	8-9	Wolv	7af	56	629
39a	5-10	Wolv	8.5af	56	754
43a	7-10	Sout	8af	56	792
51a	4-10	Wolv	7af	54	864
26	15-19	Warw	10.9sft	52	1090
46	6-15	Sout	7gd	50	1282
54a	2-15	Sout	8af	52	1755
30	13-16	York	7g/f	50	2057
20	13-13	Newb	8fm	50	2647

SPY KING 2 ch c £12234

81	2-6	Hami	6g/f		3202
93	1-18	**NEWC**	6g/s		3699*
96	1-5	**HAMI**	6g/s		3877*
92	3-16	Newm	6gd	90	4224

SPY MASTER 6 b g £569

28a	3-11	Sout	5af	[35]	578 bl t
36a	2-14	Sout	6af	[35]	637 bl t
32a	5-15	Sout	6af	[40]	773 bl t
16a	7-10	Sout	6af	[40]	851 bl t
22a	6-9	Sout	5af	[35]	981 t P
23a	5-11	Wolv	6af	[35]	1261 bl t
11a	10-16	Sout	6af	31	2806 t p
9	11-19	Nott	6.1gd	[31]	3104 bl t
29a	8-13	Sout	6af	[31]	3482 t p
22	23-26	Ayr	5g/s	35	4618 t p

SQUARE DANCER 8 b g £0

0	8-9	Ayr	6g/s	[40]	1447 t
2	12-12	Hami	6g/s	[40]	1600 t
11	16-18	Ayr	7.2g/f	35	1897 t

SQUAW DANCE 2 ch f £16749

49	6-17	Wind	6g/f		3975
73	3-14	Hayd	6sft		4769
84	2-9	Ayr	8sft		5033
103	1-8	**NEWM**	8g/s	[81]	5282*

SQUEAKY 6 ch m £0

46a	10-14	Ling	10ap	60	101
44a	13-14	Ling	7ap	[56]	450 P

SQUIRTLE TURTLE 4 ch g £3142

69a	1-9	**SOUT**	11af	65	331* bl
24a	9-11	Wolv	12af	69	557 bl
17	13-13	Kemp	12g/f	68	1916 bl T
62	4-11	Newm	12g/f	67	2244 bl
45	5-5	Brig	11.9fm	[67]	2329 bl
56	4-6	Nott	16g/f	[60]	2632

SRI DIAMOND 4 b g £1360

21	10-14	Kemp	8hvy	80	1512
76	8-18	Good	8g/f	78	1812
67	6-12	Sand	8.1g/s	76	2129
77	2-13	Newb	8fm	92	2647

SRI LIPIS 2 ch c £1016

80	4-10	Newm	7fm		2594
83	4-15	Newm	7fm		3005

ST ANDREWS 4 b c £59502

78	2-4	Leic	7g/f		1962
89	6-28	Asco	7g/f	93	2558
100	2-15	Sand	8.1g/s	92	2915
86	5-21	Asco	7g/f	92	3441
88	7-10	Asco	8gd	95	3775
109	1-10	**HAYD**	8.1g/s	94	4767*
84	18-32	Newm	7g/f	99	4916
104	1-8	**NOTT**	8.2hvy	[104]	5346*

ST ANDREWS STORM 2 b c £9505

94	1-9	**NEWM**	6g/f		2531*
101	4-7	Newm	6g/f		3028
88	4-8	Newb	6g/f		3254
85	8-13	Newb	7sft	[100]	5195

ST AUSTELL 4 b g £0

33	8-9	Newm	6gd	73	3924
36	11-12	Newm	5gd	70	4197
52	11-18	Bath	5.7g/f	65	4412
26	16-19	Nott	6.1g/f	[58]	4845
52a	5-13	Wolv	6ap	[54]	5359

ST BARCHAN 3 ch g £8785

72	4-6	Ling	10g/f		2843
73	2-9	Newc	9g/s		3697
75	3-11	Beve	9.9sft		4261
77	1-9	**GOOD**	11gd	[72]	5026*

ST CASSIEN 3 b g £0

23a	16-16	Sout	6af	[40]	227
31a	10-12	Ling	10ap	[35]	267

ST FRANCIS WOOD 3 ch f £4694

72	13-13	Newm	7gd		1169
76a	2-13	Ling	10ap		2066
81	1-4	**BRIG**	8fm	[90]	2261*
22	18-19	Asco	8g/f	90	2491

ST GEORGES GIRL 3 b f £0

0	17-18	Wind	8.3g/s		1258
21	7-9	Kemp	6hvy	[30]	1641
0	8-8	Sout	6af	[25]	2379
2	11-11	Yarm	7g/f	[25]	2852

ST IVIAN 3 b g £4919

59a	5-16	Sout	5af	63	205 vis
70a	1-10	**WOLV**	6af	63	245* vis
63a	4-10	Wolv	6af	68	345 vis
63a	6-11	Sout	6af	68	418 vis
36a	11-13	Ling	6ap	67	471 vis
69a	2-15	Sout	6af	66	550 vis
51a	7-10	Sout	5af	68	660 vis
60a	7-13	Sout	6af	66	741 p
68a	2-10	Wolv	7af	66	864 vis
55	9-16	Sout	7g/s	64	1049 vis
24	19-19	Warw	5gd	64	1127 vis
43a	9-13	Wolv	6af	67	2053 p
39	14-14	Thir	7fm	60	2466 vis
45	8-19	Leic	5gd	60	2702 p
53a	7-13	Sout	7af	66	3155 p
51a	7-9	Sout	6af	64	3485 vis
46	10-16	Ling	6g/f	55	3602 vis
58a	3-12	Wolv	5.1ap	[61]	5362

ST JEROME 4 ch g £0

0	17-18	Nott	14.1sft	58	1469
0	15-16	Leic	11.8g/f	57	1830
0	17-17	Nott	14.1g/f	55	2156

ST JUDE 4 b c £0

48	7-11	Thir	8g/f		3572
47	7-11	Beve	9.9sft		4261
15	12-16	Warw	8.1g/s	[45]	4993

ST PANCRAS 4 b c £11409

87	14-20	Newm	7g/s	95	1151
90	8-19	Newm	10g/f	90	1478
74	8-14	York	10.4g/s	88	1704
88	2-7	Newm	8fm	[84]	2091
71	8-11	Epso	10.1g/f	84	2208 BL
85	1-8	**BATH**	8fm	78	2665*
86	5-20	Newm	8fm	80	3001
85	3-11	Leic	7g/f	80	3210
88	2-7	Sali	7g/s	[80]	4082
72	8-9	Newm	10gd	82	4227
72	7-20	Donc	7sft	82	5367

ST PETERSBURG 4 ch g £34622

94	2-24	Donc	8gd	82	928
94	1-12	**PONT**	8hvy	86	1066*
62	21-27	Newb	8gd	93	1231
100	2-14	Kemp	8hvy	93	1512
102	1-7	**YORK**	7.9g/s	93	3077+
105	3-15	York	7.9g/s	97	4061
94	6-8	Hayd	8.1fm	[101]	4386

ST SAVARIN 2 ch g £22387

66a	8-11	Ling	8ap	74	54 BL
65a	5-10	Sout	8af	72	190
73a	1-11	**LING**	7ap	68	261*
76a	2-7	Ling	7ap	71	368
62a	5-10	Ling	8ap	72	455
70a	3-10	Ling	6ap	72	494

ST SAVARIN *(continued)*

79a	1-12	LING	7ap	72	545*
60	7-15	Ches	7.6gd	77	1583
52	13-15	Ling	7g/f	74	1983
74	3-13	Beve	7.5g/s	72	3179
76	3-9	Beve	7.5gd	72	3310
78	1-10	**MUSS**	7.1g/f	73	3562*
70a	10-13	Ling	7ap	76	3791
54a	11-13	Ling	7ap	76	4318
64	11-14	Epso	7gd	76	4465
73	5-10	Leic	8gd	[74]	4702
78	2-11	Redc	10fm	73	4931
74a	5-13	Wolv	9.5ap	73	5161

ST TROPEZ 3 b f £0

50	9-18	Wind	8.3g/s		1258
43	13-20	Wind	10sft		1651
35	9-13	Muss	7.1g/f	50	2812
0	18-19	Kemp	8g/f	[48]	4795 bl

STAFF NURSE 4 b f £2020

0	12-15	Newc	12.4hvy	45	1034
21a	9-11	Sout	12af	40	1197
34a	4-8	Sout	14af	[40]	1840
0	8-13	Sout	14af	40	2494
27	5-13	Pont	12gd	35	3240
37a	3-16	Sout	14af	32	4045
32a	3-8	Sout	14af	32	4128
37	2-11	Beve	12.1g/f	[35]	4716
36	4-9	Ayr	13.1sft	[35]	5277

STAFFORD KING 7 b h £0

27	14-19	Chep	12.1gd	40	3727
6	9-14	Chep	10.2g/s	40	3895
18	10-15	Chep	18sft	36	4056

STAGBURY HILL 2 ch c £7251

97	1-9	**NEWM**	6g/f		2531*
99	6-10	Good	7fm		3532
94	3-5	Ches	7.6g/f		4046
102	6-8	Kemp	6fm	[100]	4390

STAGE DIRECTION 7 b g £0

0	12-12	Chep	12.1g/s	43	3085

STAGE LEFT 3 ch f £1516

70	2-12	Nott	10hvy		5190

STAGE RIGHT 3 b c £12053

58a	4-15	Ling	7ap		472
59	6-14	Wind	8.3g/s		2622
88	1-9	**KEMP**	12g/f		2862*
86	5-6	Good	12fm	85	3534
85	4-8	Newb	13.3gd	85	3918
85	6-11	Sali	12g/s	85	4080
94	3-5	Good	14g/s	[85]	4230

STAGE SCHOOL 2 b f £1523

75	2-17	Yarm	6g/s		5350

STAGE SECRET 3 ch c £0

62	7-9	Wind	10fm		3642

STAGE TWO 3 b c £790

29a	12-13	Ling	12ap		873
0	6-7	Wolv	12af		959
59	4-9	Muss	12g/f		1121
0	7-11	Warw	12.6sft	45	1528
0	9-10	Kemp	12hvy	[45]	1645
47	2-13	Beve	12.1g/f	[40]	1945
27	8-14	Redc	14.1g/f	40	2123 VIS

STAGECOACH RUBY 3 b f £1720

30a	10-10	Ling	10ap	46	676 c
29a	9-12	Ling	8ap	[45]	1073 e
39a	5-8	Ling	10ap	[45]	1183 e
36a	4-6	Ling	8ap	[40]	1246
38a	3-5	Ling	8ap	[40]	1416
40	3-7	Brig	7gd	[40]	1549
31	7-10	Brig	7fm	39	3672
3	7-7	Brig	6g/f	39	3717
33	5-15	Folk	7g/f	[40]	4371
40a	1-14	**LING**	10ap	[35]	4662*
41	8-17	Kemp	7g/f	[45]	4794

STAGNITE 4 ch g £4764

0	17-20	Chep	6.1gd	59	2372
54	6-14	Yarm	6g/f	55	2855
60	2-14	Ling	6gd	54	3289 P
62	1-15	**CHEP**	5.1gd	54	3403* p

STALLONE (cont.)

60	8-22	Good	5fm	62	3537 p
48	8-9	Brig	5.3fm	59	3673 p
54	6-15	Sali	5gd	58	4335 p
54	5-18	Bath	5.7g/f	58	4412 p
40	11-13	Bath	5.7gd	57	4548 p
42	11-16	Pont	5fm	57	4754 p
36a	11-13	Wolv	6ap	[55]	5359 p

STAKHANOV 2 b g £0

50	15-18	Newm	7gd	3927

STAKHANOVITE 4 b c £0

55	9-11	Bath	8g/s	1101

STALLONE 7 ch g £3715

43	13-20	Donc	10.3g/s	73	1519
76	3-19	Ripo	10g/f	72	1781
72	4-7	Ripo	10g/f	[72]	1979
78	3-10	York	11.9g/f	73	2405
62	6-10	Ripo	12.3g/s	73	3261
71	8-13	York	11.9g/f	72	3437
68	8-17	Thir	12fm	70	4377
65	6-14	Catt	12g/f	70	4672
66	6-14	Redc	10fm	66	4931 t
71	3-16	York	11.9gd	66	4990
66	5-13	Muss	12g/s	66	5333

STAMFORD BLUE 2 b c £5548

45a	9-13	Ling	6ap	[53]	25 p
0	13-16	Sout	8af	[49]	164
49a	3-11	Ling	6ap	[45]	233 BL
33a	5-9	Wolv	6af	[45]	247 bl
50a	2-9	Ling	6ap	[50]	327 bl
54a	4-9	Ling	5ap	[50]	405 bl
43a	6-10	Ling	6ap	53	494 bl
61a	2-10	Ling	6ap	[53]	606 bl
47a	8-15	Ling	7ap	[53]	671 bl
52a	6-10	Ling	6ap	58	712 bl
36a	11-14	Ling	7ap	[58]	804 bl
66	**1-9**	**LEIC**	6g/s	[56]	1015* bl
72	2-15	Wind	6g/s	62	1054 bl
50a	9-12	Ling	6ap	58	5241

STANBURY 2 ch c £1342

81	2-9	Newc	5sft	962

STANCE 5 b g £8800

72	9-29	Asco	20g/f	77	2471
82	2-19	Good	21fm	75	3531 P
62	14-16	Asco	16.2g/f	79	4803 p
33	26-34	Newm	18sft	79	5135 p

STANCOMB WILLS 2 b c £2842

58	13-18	Newm	7gd		3927
71	7-11	Newm	7gd		4190
77	2-10	Beve	7.5g/f		4602
83	2-12	Ayr	8sft	75	5065

STAND BY 6 b m £0

0	11-15	Sout	8af	50	84 vis

STANHOPE FORBES 2 b c £994

50a	6-11	Ling	8ap	[69]	77
38a	11-14	Sout	7af	58	158 P
53a	2-11	Ling	6ap	[53]	233
52a	5-8	Ling	6ap	55	268 p
43a	3-9	Ling	6ap	[55]	327
39a	5-14	Ling	6ap	[53]	495

STANLEY ARTHUR 2 b g £0

27	13-19	Ayr	6g/s	4617
34	13-13	Newc	7g/f	5012

STANLEY CRANE 3 br g £1732

57	12-14	Asco	10g/f	78	1924 t
63	5-14	Yarm	7fm	[75]	2148 t
52	4-7	Carl	9.3fm	[70]	2443 t
59a	5-9	Ling	8ap	[66]	3197 t
53	4-11	Leic	8g/f	69	3516 t
49	3-10	Redc	10g/f	57	3772 t
27	10-15	Nott	10g/s	55	4037 t

STANS GIRL 2 b f £1926

48	8-11	Warw	5gd		1123
60	3-8	Hayd	5g/s		1343
56	2-11	Ripo	6g/f		1779
0	12-12	Wind	6g/s	[60]	4945
14	9-9	Nott	6.1hvy	[56]	5185

STAR APPLAUSE 3 b f £424

0	14-15	Sout	5af	46	187
18a	11-13	Wolv	5af	[45]	312
4a	10-13	Wolv	6af	[45]	397 VIS
41	6-9	Muss	5g/f	34	2614
16	16-18	Hayd	5gd	42	2951
11	13-14	Thir	5g/f	40	3417
2	15-15	Muss	5g/f	40	3561
40	4-8	Ayr	6g/f	35	3763

STAR DUSTER 2 gr f £7681

38	9-12	Chep	5.1gd		3728
69	2-15	Nott	5.1gd		3988
57	10-11	Bath	5g/f		4409
71	2-18	Wind	5g/f	65	4830
70	2-11	Epso	5g/f	65	4907
72	2-19	Bath	5gd	67	5021

STAR FERN 2 br g £0

61a	4-11	Ling	7ap		220
67a	5-12	Ling	8ap		428
48a	5-9	Ling	7ap		764
44a	13-14	Ling	7g/f	59	1010
46	11-17	Ling	7g/s	[57]	1617
32	15-16	Ling	7g/f	[55]	1982
20	12-19	Yarm	6g/s	52	4636
47a	4-12	Wolv	6ap	[47]	5157

STAR LAD 3 ch g £4720

0	11-12	Wolv	6af	[57]	33 bl
53a	6-12	Wolv	5af	[57]	70 bl
44a	8-12	Wolv	5af	52	124 bl
50a	6-16	Sout	6af	[49]	227 bl
47a	3-10	Wolv	7af	[47]	298 bl
48a	**1-4**	**WOLV**	7af	[47]	350* vis
28a	9-11	Wolv	7af	[47]	440 vis
27a	7-13	Wolv	6af	[45]	582 vis
49a	**1-15**	**SOUT**	6af	[45]	773* bl
41a	4-10	Wolv	5af	[45]	822 bl
47a	5-8	Wolv	5af	[46]	1218 bl
36	10-17	Nott	6.1sft	48	1606 bl
43a	3-13	Wolv	5af	47	2201 bl
17	15-18	Ling	6gd	46	2396 bl
30a	8-16	Sout	6af	45	2720 bl

STAR MAGNITUDE 3 ch c £3233

49	11-19	Yarm	8g/f		1130
77	2-20	Donc	7g/s		1518
75	2-10	Beve	7.5g/f		1832
73	5-18	Bath	10.2gd	[75]	5023

STAR MEMBER 5 b g £28862

52	5-13	Kemp	14.4hvy	77	1516
88	**1-18**	**YORK**	13.9g/s	77	1689*
88	4-14	Asco	16.2g/f	86	1928
98	**1-7**	**YORK**	13.9g/f	85	2355*
99	2-14	York	13.9gd	92	3119
98	6-19	York	13.9g/s	97	4023
91	6-15	Donc	14.6fm	97	4491
8	15-19	Newm	12gd	96	5085

STAR OF KILDARE 2 b f £0

42	15-18	York	5g/f	2360
48	10-13	Beve	5gd	2889
25	8-10	Beve	5g/s	3504
30	12-12	Thir	5g/s	3832
23a	7-10	Sout	5af	4129

STAR OF LIGHT 2 b g £3835

75a	**1-15**	**LING**	7ap	[73]	52*
78	3-17	Newb	7g/f	76	3257
81	4-12	Sand	10gd	77	4502

STAR OF NORMANDIE 4 b f £21146

80a	2-13	Wolv	9.4af	74	38
83a	**1-11**	**LING**	8ap	75	80*
85a	**1-13**	**LING**	10ap	81	134*
81a	2-11	Ling	8ap	[83]	273
77a	8-13	Ling	10ap	83	433
40a	12-13	Ling	10ap	83	519
77	9-15	Nott	10gd	79	4860
82	9-10	Newm	10gd	[78]	5086
87a	8-12	Ling	8ap	[82]	5298
97	2-14	Donc	10.3sft	[78]	5370

STAR OVATION 7 ch g £0

36	14-18	Catt	7g/f	54	3670

STAR PUPIL 3 ch c £9649

78	4-12	Newm	7g/s		1152
85	2-11	Sali	6g/s	80	1498
72	7-7	Ling	6sft	80	1621 VIS
70	14-18	Hayd	8.1g/f	83	1919
72	5-7	Wind	8.3fm	82	2787
75	5-7	Sali	7g/s	[79]	4082
62	5-8	Chep	7.1g/s	[76]	4301
76	4-25	Newb	7gd	73	4683 vis
76	**1-9**	**LEIC**	7gd	[73]	5041* BL

STAR SENSATION 4 b f £1391

84	6-27	Newb	8gd	86	1231
86	5-10	Beve	8.5g/f	86	1833
55	6-8	Newb	8g/f	[85]	2313 e
44	13-13	Sali	8gd	84	2662
56	10-11	Yarm	7gd	82	3364
76	4-11	Brig	8g/s	78	4141
73	9-11	Yarm	8gd	77	4615
65	11-16	Good	7gd	75	4873

STAR SEVENTEEN 6 ch m £0

31a	5-5	Sout	12af		745
28a	9-11	Ling	12ap	[60]	816
0	15-16	Sout	14af	50	1033

STAR SIDE 2 b c £0

67	6-15	Folk	7gd	4114

STAR VALLEY 4 b c £33415

107	3-10	Chan	8g/s	2458
116	1-11	DEAU	6hvy	4313*

STAR WELCOME 3 ch f £209

29a	7-7	Sout	7af	636
54a	3-10	Ling	8ap	785

STAR WONDER 4 b f £0

6a	9-12	Wolv	7af	[35]	663 bl

STARBECK 6 b m £3638

88	9-11	Leic	7g/s	[84]	1356
95	7-11	Ling	7sft	[84]	1620
90	5-8	Good	8gd	[88]	1863
85	4-7	Asco	7g/f	[88]	1925
71	10-10	Asco	8g/f	[88]	2487
66	12-14	Hayd	8.1gd	86	2903
86	5-11	Asco	6.5gd	86	3069
80	4-11	Donc	7g/s	82	3223
80	8-10	Newm	6g/f	83	3584
77	11-20	Newm	7g/f	81	3782
79	4-8	Newm	7gd	81	3928
81	13-15	Donc	7fm	[79]	4479
63a	8-12	Ling	8ap	66	4743
79	9-12	Asco	7g/f	[79]	4811
76	8-16	Newm	7sft	77	5101

STARBRIGHT 3 b g £0

0	12-14	Carl	9.3g/f	4347

STARCHY 2 b f £6175

88	1-14	NOTT	6.1hvy	5342*

STARCROSS VENTURE 2 b f £323

56a	3-14	Ling	6ap	146
40a	8-13	Sout	6af	319
43a	8-14	Ling	6ap	449

STARGEM 3 b f £5182

70	2-13	Wind	6fm		2756
68a	2-9	Sout	6af	[75]	3396
49	9-9	Yarm	6g/f	73	3705
64	2-9	Good	6sft	[66]	4262
58	2-6	Yarm	6g/s	[64]	4586

STARJESTIC 3 b f £0

2	13-13	Bath	10.2sft	5173

STARLIGHT RIVER 2 b f £710

21	8-9	Nott	5.1gd		2926
57	7-8	Good	6fm		3536
66	3-8	Chep	5.1g/s		3896
40	9-14	Catt	5g/f	64	4437
64	4-17	Ling	7g/f	62	4894
55a	8-11	Ling	8ap	[62]	5235

STARMIX 3 br c £429

53a	9-13	Ling	12ap	873
42	9-9	Ling	10sft	1623

73 4-10 Good 8g/f 1815
41 11-12 Wind 11.6gd 69 3161
56 7-11 Sali 8gd 68 3455 BL
47 8-10 Yarm 10.1gd [65] 3874

STARRY LODGE 4 b c £39681
99 1-13 EPSO 12fm 92 2255*
102 3-21 York 10.4gd 95 3118
98 5-10 Asco 12gd 96 3777
102 5-7 Donc 12fm [96] 4494

STARRY MARY 5 b m £1911
38a 9-12 Ling 12ap 51 56
43a 7-14 Ling 16ap 51 107
39a 6-14 Ling 13ap 47 264
58 2-10 Folk 12g/s 53 1082
57 2-12 Sout 16gd 55 1285
0 16-18 Nott 14.1sft 55 1469
48 5-6 Nott 16g/f [55] 2632
42 10-16 Chep 10.2g/s 52 4365

STARS AT MIDNIGHT 4 b f £0
12 16-16 Yarm 10.1fm 49 2146
0 14-15 Chep 8.1sft 48 4057
38 6-20 Chep 7.1g/s 46 4367

START OF AUTHORITY 3 ch g £0
3 15-15 Wind 10fm 3292
62 5-6 Hayd 8.1g/s 3905
26 9-10 Warw 8.1g/f 4421

STARTLED 5 ch m £0
0 11-13 Sout 7af [45] 356

STATE CITY 5 ch h £728
97 4-7 Good 7g/f [110] 1811 T

STATE DILEMMA 3 b c £20547
86 5-20 Newm 8fm 89 1496
97 1-14 YORK 7sft 89 1665*
83 12-27 Asco 8g/f 94 2521
83 8-16 Newm 8g/f 94 3059
53 14-15 York 7.9g/s 93 4061
94 4-10 Kemp 8fm 91 4389
78 7-10 Newm 8g/f [90] 4890

STATE OF BALANCE 5 ch m £3740
60a 4-13 Ling 10ap 148
54a 7-13 Ling 10ap 62 215
58a 8-14 Ling 10ap 62 520
38a 4-9 Wolv 9.4af [62] 1340
61a 1-14 LING 10ap 59 1618*
53a 6-12 Ling 8ap [60] 4320
46a 8-16 Ling 12ap [60] 4899

STATEROOM 6 ch g £1283
72a 5-14 Ling 10ap 71 625 bl
73 3-7 Ripo 10g/f [72] 1979 bl
67 11-16 Kemp 9g/f 72 3039 bl

STATOYORK 11 b g £0
35a 4-10 Wolv 5af [45] 527
7a 11-13 Wolv 6af [45] 582 e

STAVROS 4 b c £0
46 9-14 Thir 6g/s [46] 1216
17 13-15 Muss 5gd 46 1555
45 5-10 Newc 5sft [46] 1682
2 19-20 Beve 5g/f [45] 1948

STEAL THE THUNDER 2 br c £518
0 8-8 Muss 5g/f 1091
65 5-6 Hami 5gd 1386
44 5-11 Ripo 6g/f 1779
50 8-9 Muss 5fm 2083
0 12-13 Beve 5g/f 2321 BL
53 7-8 Ripo 5gd 4307
62 5-6 Muss 5g/s [54] 5141
46 6-9 Catt 7sft [54] 5316

STEALING BEAUTY 4 b f £724
77 4-8 Newm 12gd 76 1889
60 7-10 Chep 12.1gd 76 2114
67 5-5 Brig 11.9gd [75] 2956

STEDFAST MCSTAUNCH 2 gr g £6125
69 4-8 Kemp 5hvy 1510
84 2-7 Nott 6.1sft 1738
83 3-8 Brig 6g/f 2043

83 1-11 THIR 7fm 2462*

STEEL BLUE 3 b c £26239
74a 8-15 Sout 5af 82 64 p
60a 9-12 Ling 6ap [82] 106 p
87 1-22 DONC 6gd 82 921*
59 17-20 Kemp 6gd 86 1138
61 25-30 Newm 6g/f 86 1481 VIS
93 1-11 RIPO 6g/f 85 1977*
95 2-12 Hayd 6g/s [85] 2186
81 5-10 York 6g/f 91 2357
97 3-15 Newc 5g/s 95 2727

STEEL PRINCESS 3 b f £25704
112 1-10 SAIN 10.5sft 1850*

STEELY DAN 5 b g £19703
36a 9-13 Ling 6ap 57 471
49a 9-13 Ling 7ap 53 565
50a 12-16 Ling 7ap 53 600
55a 2-11 Ling 8ap 50 669
56a 2-14 Ling 10ap 50 718
59a 1-13 LING 7ap 50 739*
59a 3-10 Ling 8ap 57 766
66a 1-13 LING 10ap 57 805*
76a 1-9 LING 10ap 64 903*
75a 2-10 Ling 12ap 70 936
80a 1-7 LING 12ap [64] 1009*
85a 1-12 LING 8ap [75] 1042*
68 6-8 Yarm 11.5g/f 70 1135
54 10-12 Sand 8.1g/s 67 1352
67 4-12 Redc 8g/f [67] 1823
61 10-12 Kemp 8g/f [67] 1915
58 9-16 Ling 7g/f 65 2063

STEENBERG 5 ch g £39640
108 2-13 Curr 7sft [109] 1062
117 1-7 HAYD 6g/f [110] 1487*
113 2-15 York 10ap [110] 1667
102 9-14 Asco 6fm [113] 2580
93 18-20 Newm 6g/f [113] 3062
78 12-12 Asco 6g/f [111] 4799

STELLA MARAIS 3 b f £0
33 6-6 Bath 8fm 67 2414

STELLITE 4 ch g £2046
29 7-16 Newc 10.1sft 45 1278
48 1-8 AYR 7.2g/s [45] 1448*
40 7-19 Redc 8sft 47 1661
38 10-17 Newc 7g/s 47 3700
35 7-15 Ayr 7.2hvy 46 4088
46 2-10 Ayr 6sft [45] 5278

STEP DANZER 3 b f £133768
102 2-11 San 11gd 1999

STEPASTRAY 7 gr g £0
39 5-16 Redc 10g/f 48 1821
21 13-15 Redc 9g/f 46 2120
36 9-20 Catt 12g/f 44 2850
34 7-18 Pont 10g/f 44 2988
43 5-5 Hami 9.2g/f [41] 3206
36 9-14 Catt 12g/f [41] 3668
37 11-16 Beve 8.5g/s [41] 3850 vis
24 8-9 Redc 10gd 40 4248
32 7-15 Carl 9.3fm [40] 4505 vis

STEPHANIES MIND 2 b f £1542
61 8-19 Wind 5g/f 1805
75 3-13 Ling 6g/f 2061
81 4-19 Newb 6g/f 2310
57 4-5 Yarm 5.2gd [78] 3993
45 8-11 Bath 5g/s [78] 4200 P

STEPHANO 3 ch g £10952
58 7-13 Donc 7gd 925
56 5-11 Beve 8.5gd [75] 2656
44 10-10 Hayd 8.1g/s 62 3906
72 1-14 REDC 10fm 59 4342*
73 1-17 HAYD 10.5fm 62 4388*
72 2-14 Chep 10.2gd 65 4487
56 13-17 Leic 10gd 69 5062

STEPPENWOLF 3 gr c £0
46a 6-11 Ling 8ap [47] 696
61a 7-13 Ling 10ap [47] 715
31a 7-11 Ling 10ap [45] 970 P
12 13-13 Brig 11.9g/f 45 1373 p

28 7-16 Nott 10hvy 45 1611
41 12-16 Bath 10.2g/f [40] 1790
56a 8-14 Ling 10ap [37] 2740
27 9-11 Bath 8gd 37 3142
14 5-6 Redc 14.1g/f [37] 3771
15 6-6 Redc 16g/f 37 3810

STERLING GUARANTEE 6 b g £754
55a 2-10 Ling 10ap [69] 370
54a 4-14 Ling 12ap 53 711
52a 7-14 Ling 12ap 53 768
47a 4-9 Ling 12ap 53 842 VIS

STERLING SUPPORTER 2 b f £0
4 12-12 Redc 6fm 4557

STETCHWORTH PRINCE 2 b c £12360
97 1-6 NEWM 6g/f 3031*
97 4-8 Good 6fm 3566
90 6-11 York 6g/s 4022

STEVEDORE 3 ch c £9233
51 14-18 Thir 8g/f 79 1769
71 7-13 Sand 8.1g/s [77] 2126
63 7-13 Newm 7fm 77 2590
56a 4-11 Sout 8af [74] 3091 BL
72 1-15 LEIC 7g/f [70] 3515*
71 5-12 Bath 8g/f 70 3846
77 1-9 LING 7gd 69 4110*
63 5-8 Good 8sft 73 4265
63 13-25 Newb 7gd 73 4683
71 5-16 Good 7gd 72 4873
62a 6-11 Wolv 7.1ap [70] 5357

STEVES CHAMP 4 b c £6600
82 8-9 Ches 5.1g/f 3100 T
113 2-15 Newm 5g/f 4879 bl

STEVMARIE STAR 2 b f £0
51 9-14 Hayd 6sft 4769
48 6-10 Catt 7sft 5127
0 12-13 Wolv 6ap 5287

STILETTO LADY 3 b f £261
61a 4-5 Wolv 8.5af 63 1655
25 14-14 Wind 8.3g/f 61 1956
30 12-17 Hayd 8.1gd 59 2243
0 11-11 Muss 9gd 55 2969 BL

STING LIKE A BEE 5 b g £9179
56a 1-12 WOLV 9.4af 49 464*
37a 7-12 Wolv 8.5af 55 564
58a 2-11 Sout 11af 55 746
40a 4-11 Wolv 8.5af 55 806
50 4-19 Donc 10.3gd 50 924
42 6-15 Hami 9.2gd 50 1388
46 6-7 Ayr 10g/f 49 2030
57 1-10 AYR 9.1gd 48 2571*
53 5-7 Ayr 10.9gd 55 3149

STOCKING ISLAND 3 ch f £2967
71 13-17 Newm 10g/f 1171
81 2-8 Ripo 10g/s 1365
73 3-9 Hayd 11.9g/f 1885
69 8-11 Newb 10g/f [79] 2349
72 7-12 Nott 14.1gd 73 3105
66 3-5 Ches 12.3sft [71] 4075
0 P-9 Ling 12ap [70] 4449

STOIC LEADER 4 b g £30531
52a 4-10 Wolv 5af 58 749
41a 8-13 Sout 7af [55] 858
67a 1-7 WOLV 7af 55 860*
71a 1-15 LING 7ap 61 913*
62 4-19 Newc 6sft 71 967
39 13-16 Sout 7g/s 68 1049
80 1-12 HAYD 8.1g/f 66 1485*
80 1-13 MUSS 7.1gd 72 1553*
79 1-14 HAMI 6g/s [66] 1600*
76 9-16 Good 7g/f 80 1817
22 18-18 Good 8g/f 80 1849
81 2-12 Ayr 8g/s [79] 2543
84 4-17 Carl 7.9gd 79 2672
85 2-8 Muss 7.1g/f 79 2809
78 6-10 Carl 6.9gd 79 2935
70 5-8 Ches 10.3g/f [79] 3083
84 2-6 Ayr 8gd [83] 3152
78 5-9 Ayr 8g/f 83 3305

77	6-8	Ches	7sft	81	4073
82	4-15	Hayd	8.1g/f	80	4352
75	11-21	Donc	7fm	80	4482
76	4-7	Pont	8g/f	[78]	4629
73	4-6	Hami	8.3sft	[78]	4695
77	7-13	Muss	7.1gd	77	4806

STOKESIES WISH 4 ch f £6786

45	12-19	Warw	5gd	66	1127
47	11-20	Wind	6g/s	66	1255
40	15-16	Good	6gd	64	2023
68	2-11	Good	6gd	61	2535
49	12-18	Donc	6gd	64	2752
51	5-17	Wind	6fm	64	2975
66	4-14	Leic	6g/f	64	3213
55	8-14	Thir	6g/f	63	3416
63	6-13	Wind	6fm	64	3479
65	3-7	Ling	6fm	[62]	3789
65	3-10	Ling	6gd	60	4109
39	11-16	Brig	7sft	[60]	4144
54	7-15	Chep	5.1gd	60	4489
71	1-20	NOTT	6.1g/s	60	4646*
67	5-20	Wind	6g/s	65	4946

STOLEN 2 b c £0

47	12-17	Warw	7.1gd		4269
61	12-14	Chep	8.1gd		4484
41a	9-13	Wind	8.6ap		4979
55	8-12	Bath	8sft		5170

STOLEN HOURS 4 b c £10358

18	18-20	Epso	12hvy	75	1295
16	11-16	Sali	14.1g/s	73	1502
58	8-13	Kemp	12g/f	70	1916
50	9-14	Wind	10g/f	60	2265
61	2-11	Newb	13.3fm	58	2651
71	2-8	Epso	12g/f	58	2869
55	3-7	Epso	12g/s	60	3040
70	1-5	NEWM	12gd	63	3587*
67	3-9	Newm	12gd	65	3926
61	7-16	Chep	10.2g/s	65	4365

STOLEN SONG 4 b g £4605

58a	4-14	Ling	10ap	58	339 p
65a	1-10	SOUT	16af	58	491* e
35a	6-7	Sout	12af	[64]	594 e
21	16-18	Newb	16gd	62	1232
42	11-12	Nott	14.1gd	59	3105
51	6-12	Wind	10fm	55	3295
59	3-15	Wind	11.6fm	55	3481
59	2-14	Wind	11.6fm	54	3638
53	6-16	Wind	11.6gd	55	3829

STONE CREST 6 b m £0

18	11-18	Donc	7g/f	30	2080
0	12-13	Sout	8af	30	2497
1	14-15	Thir	8g/s	[30]	2688

STONEACRE 4 ch f £0

3	11-11	Catt	6gd	999

STONOR LADY 2 b f £3224

55a	2-15	Ling	7ap		52
47a	12-13	Ling	7ap		119
48a	6-11	Sout	8af	56	252
37a	10-12	Ling	8ap	56	603
41a	11-15	Ling	7ap	[56]	671 VIS
38a	10-15	Ling	7ap	48	815 e
49a	1-9	WOLV	8.5af	[48]	865* e
24	8-14	Sout	10g/s	48	1051
16	9-10	Yarm	8g/f	46	3712

STOOP TO CONQUER 4 b g £19362

69	8-17	Sali	14.1g/s	70	1502
63	10-14	Asco	16.2g/f	68	1928
77	1-13	PONT	17.1g/f	66	2276*
72	4-9	Pont	18g/f	73	2607
81	1-7	GOOD	14sft	72	4267*
71	9-13	Good	16g/f	77	4527
86	1-10	NEWB	16sft	76	5194*

STOP MAKING SENSE 2 b f £10282

109	2-6	Long	7gd	4564

STOP THE NONSENSE 3 b c £0

73a	5-9	Ling	8ap		1022
5	14-14	Nott	10gd	[65]	1241
0	18-18	Nott	8.2g/s	60	1778 T

43	8-9	Thir	7g/f	[53]	2216 BL t

STOPWATCH 9 b g £0

0	11-12	Ling	10ap	[35]	654 p
10a	9-15	Ling	12ap	[35]	707 p
30a	5-8	Ling	16ap	35	733 p
0	13-15	Folk	16.4g/s	25	3049 p

STORM CHASE 2 b c £0

27a	12-12	Ling	6ap	4178
49	7-11	Beve	5g/f	4599

STORM CLEAR 5 b h £0

42a	10-13	Ling	10ap	51	805

STORM CLOUDS 3 gr g £0

37	9-15	Thir	7g/s		1473
27	13-15	Ripo	10g/f	52	1976

STORM FURY 2 b g £838

57	13-16	Sali	7g/s		3111
69	3-6	Leic	6g/f		3513
66	7-10	Newb	7g/f		3955
61	9-13	Warw	6.1gd	70	4273
57	10-14	Epso	6g/f	68	4471 BL
56	11-17	Ling	7g/f	64	4894

STORM SHOWER 5 b g £0

27a	7-13	Wolv	8.5af	[41]	46 vis
16a	8-15	Sout	8af	41	84 vis
37a	4-9	Sout	7af	[39]	303 vis

STORM SILK 2 b c £7607

79	4-9	Good	6gd	3951
107	1-8	KEMP	7fm	4393*

STORMONT 4 gr c £0

80	7-9	Wind	6g/f		1958
103	12-19	Asco	5g/f		2468
102	7-12	Sand	5g/s	[104]	2913 VIS
97	8-8	Newb	7g/f	[104]	3253
16	26-28	Good	6fm	104	3622 vis

STORMVILLE 7 b g £1248

1	13-19	Newc	6sft	62	967
6	11-15	Newc	7gd	[57]	3426
57	2-17	Newc	7g/s	50	3700
28	9-15	Ayr	7.2hvy	54	4088
42	13-14	Carl	6.9g/f	54	4345

STORMY DAY 4 b f £3572

55	6-10	Bath	11.7g/f		4414
66a	1-16	LING	12ap	[60]	5296* e

STORMY NATURE 3 b f £6494

76	3-16	Kemp	6g/s	76	1116
41	9-17	Asco	6sft	76	1417
61	10-13	Hayd	6g/f	75	1881
67	8-12	Newm	6gd	73	4229
62	11-20	Nott	6.1g/s	70	4646
74a	1-12	WOLV	7.1ap	66	5008*
75a	2-12	Wolv	7.1ap	70	5289

STORY OF ONE 2 b g £3767

67	2-8	Beve	5sft		1303
44	9-12	Beve	5sft		1631
69a	1-10	LING	5ap		2017*
60	3-5	Yarm	6fm		2145
37	5-6	Brig	6fm		2330
51	5-9	Leic	5g/f		2921

STORYVILLE 2 b r c £0

47	13-17	Ling	6ap	4443

STRAFFAN 2 b f £6554

58	6-11	Warw	5gd		1123
55	3-8	Beve	5sft		1303
65a	3-8	Wolv	5af		1653
63	2-12	Newc	6gd		1869
39	5-8	Hami	5gd		2177
37	4-6	Brig	6fm		2330
59	1-8	BATH	5g/f		2977*
62	2-6	Leic	5g/f		3209
63	2-7	Leic	5g/f	59	3343
25	12-12	Hayd	5gd	60	3756

STRANGELY BROWN 3 b g £18333

43a	7-12	Wolv	9.4af		686
48	8-11	Catt	6gd		999
52	3-16	Nott	10hvy	55	1611

50	9-15	Ripo	10g/f	55	1976
0	14-15	Sout	12af	55	2503
69	2-20	Beve	16.2gd	55	3312
69	1-14	NOTT	16g/f	55	3580*
77	1-12	SAND	16.4g/f	65	3861*
74	1-8	AYR	17.5g/s	71	4657*
77	3-6	Muss	16gd	76	4808
68	5-11	Newm	14g/f	76	4919
67	4-8	Bath	17.2sft	75	5175

STRATEGY 4 br f £0

58	12-20	Asco	8g/f	80	1927
78	6-10	Newm	10fm	80	2592
73	8-10	Wind	10fm	78	2761 VIS

STRATHCLYDE 5 b g £0

30a	10-10	Ling	5ap	79	567
20	17-17	Sand	5g/f	79	3341
18	12-12	Newm	6g/f	75	3751
58	7-8	Nott	5.1gd	[69]	4039

STRATHSPEY 5 ch m £0

72a	5-16	Ling	12ap	69	4973
55	5-8	Brig	9.9sft	[69]	5095
52	4-17	Yarm	8g/s	[66]	5348

STRATHTAY 2 ch f £8937

73	3-12	Ripo			1974
69	8-12	Hami	6gd		2178
62	5-9	Ripo	6g/f		2522
55	6-9	Catt	6sft	69	3931
53	8-14	Muss	7.1g/f	[66]	4171 P
42	13-18	Catt	7g/f		4673
60	2-18	Newc	6g/f	55	5013 VIS
64	1-12	MUSS	7.1g/s	[55]	5142* vis
63	4-19	Redc	8sft	59	5302 vis

STRAVMOUR 7 ch h £7405

44a	4-16	Sout	11af	43	97
46a	3-5	Sout	14af	43	201
45a	1-15	SOUT	14af	43	257*
27a	7-10	Sout	12af	46	421
28a	5-7	Sout	12af	46	504
45a	3-9	Sout	12af	[45]	774
37a	3-6	Wolv	16.2af	[45]	824
48a	1-9	SOUT	14af	[45]	849*
46a	1-10	SOUT	14af	[45]	984*
55a	1-9	SOUT	12af	[45]	1204*

STRAVONIAN 4 b g £0

32	7-9	Muss	12g/f	1121
47	7-10	Hami	9.2g/s	4135
46	5-13	Ayr	10sft	5066
42	6-10	Muss	12g/s	5145

STRAW BEAR 3 ch c £23087

82	2-10	Sand	8.1g/f	[77]	3339
80	3-9	Sand	9g/s	[77]	3892
77	5-10	Hami	8.3g/s	77	4136
89	1-20	AYR	10g/s	77	4656*
99	1-19	HAYD	10.5g/s	83	4766*
95	3-15	Nott	10gd	89	4860

STRAWBERRY DALE 2 b f £9224

84	1-12	CARL	5gd		2933*
92	1-7	THIR	7g/f		3412*
85	9-11	Newm	7g/f		3781
83	9-21	Donc	6.5fm	90	4447

STRAWBERRY FAIR 3 b f £287

75	4-11	Chep	8.1g/f		2627
61	7-14	Wind	8.3fm		2974 T
52	10-10	Sand	8.1g/f	[73]	3339 t
58	6-9	Catt	7g/f	[70]	4674 t

STRAWBERRY PATCH 5 b g £10386

0	11-11	Ayr	6gd	64	2542 p
42	10-10	Muss	5g/s	60	2968 p
55	5-12	Newc	5g/f	55	3427 p
40	11-15	Muss	5g/f	55	3561 p
57	2-8	Ayr	6g/f	52	3763 p
61	1-13	NEWB	5.2g/f	53	3960* p
57	7-12	Newm	5gd	58	4197 p
56	6-18	Redc	6fm	58	4339 p
62	2-26	Ayr	5g/s	57	4618 p
32	13-16	Pont	5fm	57	4754 p
22	17-19	Ayr	6sft	60	5069 p

STREAM OF GOLD 3 b c £22455

73	5-8	Newm	10fm		3007
87	1-13	PONT	8g/s		3973*
91	4-7	Sand	8.1gd	89	4499
103	1-16	NEWM	7sft	87	5101*

STREET BALLAD 2 b f £852

64	4-13	Pont	6gd		3682
65	7-12	Beve	7.5g/s		4242
66	3-10	Catt	6g/f		4436
62	7-11	Pont	8fm	67	4753
55	11-17	Catt	7gd	64	4963
48	7-12	Muss	7.1g/s	[62]	5142

STREET CRED 2 ch c £5421

82	1-20	WIND	6fm		2970*
72	8-8	Newb	6g/f		3254
74	9-10	Asco	7gd		3774
14	12-12	Sali	6g/s	83	4079

STREET DANCER 2 b g £0

36	15-18	Ripo	6g/s		3939
54	11-11	Thir	7fm		4381
50	8-13	Thir	6g/f		4590
64	5-14	Nott	6.1hvy		5342

STREET GAMES 5 b g £0

21	5-14	Chep	10.2g/s	35	3895
27a	6-14	Ling	10ap	[35]	4662

STREET LIFE 5 ch g £13399

67a	6-14	Ling	10gd	67	174
69a	2-9	Sout	11af	67	391
54a	5-12	Wolv	9.4af	67	464
77	2-20	Newb	10gd	71	1235
77	3-11	Leic	10g/s	75	1357
78	3-19	Wind	10sft	[74]	1650
75	4-15	Kemp	10fm	74	2067
76	3-8	Sand	10gd	73	2363
74	5-8	Newm	10g/f	73	2735
77	4-15	Newm	12g/f	73	3066
75	4-19	Kemp	10fm	72	4392
74	4-17	Wind	10g/f	72	5050
80	1-11	YARM	10.1g/s	71	5353*

STRENSALL 6 b g £8731

60a	2-12	Wolv	5af	56	124
50a	7-15	Sout	5af	58	187
44	17-20	Thir	5g/f	77	1765
83	2-15	Muss	5fm	76	2084
70	7-13	York	5g/f	77	2359
71	7-12	Ripo	5g/f	77	2524
82	3-12	Thir	5g/s	77	2690
76	4-8	Hami	5g/s	76	2830
69	7-10	Muss	5g/s	78	2968
78	5-13	Catt	5g/f	77	3350
59	11-12	Newc	5gd	77	3427
80	5-7	Nott	5.1gd	[76]	3989
73	5-12	Ches	5.1sft	76	4107
79	2-16	Muss	5g/f	76	4174
61	8-13	Ches	5.1g/f	77	4514
74	9-10	Beve	5g/f	[76]	4718
62	11-12	Redc	5sft	[75]	5305
52	10-11	Muss	5g/s	75	5332

STRETFORD END 2 b c £1435

0	F-7	Ayr	6gd		3148
89	2-18	Newc	6g/s		3699
73	4-16	Thir	6g/s		4205

STRETTON 6 br g £15690

69	7-12	Ches	10.3gd	81	1586
78	6-10	Beve	8.5g/f	80	1833
78	9-15	Redc	10g/f	79	2101
75	9-15	York	8.9g/f	78	2404
83	3-13	Redc	10gd	78	2560
81	4-9	Sand	10g/s	80	2896
74	8-10	Newm	10g/f	78	3615
83	1-14	RIPO	10gd	80	4305*
75	7-13	Yarm	10.1gd	80	4613
85	3-20	York	10.4gd	80	4986

STRIDER 3 ch c £8804

79a	2-9	Wolv	9.4af		1340
78	4-9	Donc	10.3g/f	78	2079
77	4-9	Ripo	10g/s	77	3260
81	1-9	SAND	9g/s	[76]	3892*
36	14-14	Ripo	10gd	78	4305 VIS

STRIDES OF FIRE 3 b c £0

17	16-17	Sali	6g/s		1497
28	10-11	Nott	6.1sft		1607 BL

STRIKE 3 b c £8856

82	2-5	Newb	11gd		1211
74	6-12	Sali	12g/s		1501
81	1-9	HAYD	11.9g/f		1885*
90	5-10	Asco	16.2g/f	[82]	2557 VIS

STRIKE GOLD 2 b c £557

56	13-14	Sand	7.1g/s		4069
76	3-15	Chep	7.1gd		4483
53	7-11	Chep	7.1hvy		4703

STRIKE LUCKY 3 ch g £1439

42a	10-15	Ling	7ap		263
55a	1-6	WOLV	9af		313*
15a	15-16	Sout	6af	53	2806
47	8-14	Ling	6gd	51	3289 P
14a	12-13	Wolv	6ap	[49]	5211

STRIKING AMBITION 4 b c £41266

95a	9-10	Ling	5ap	[105]	883
88	13-17	Donc	6gd	[113]	952
105	3-11	Deau	6hvy	[113]	4313
117	1-17	CURR	6sft	[113]	5073*
117	2-11	Mais	6sft	[113]	5313

STRIKING ENDEAVOUR 2 b c £3455

79	1-7	FOLK	5sft		1574*
73	6-7	Yarm	6fm		2144
33	20-21	Donc	6fm	[81]	4490
10	14-14	Ayr	6sft	76	5035

STRONG HAND 3 b f £9838

88a	1-13	WOLV	9.4af	74	38+
90a	1-13	WOLV	9.4af	82	127+
59a	8-10	Wolv	9.4af	88	278
80	6-24	Donc	8gd	82	928 T
74	3-12	Pont	8hvy	80	1066
67	9-11	Donc	7g/s	78	3223
64	9-13	Ches	7.6sft	76	4103
64	12-13	Ripo	8gd	74	4279
68	6-20	Ayr	10g/s	72	4656
77	2-14	Hami	8.3g/s	72	4820
71	4-16	Catt	7sft	72	5130

STUNNING MAGIC 4 b g £0

38a	8-8	Ling	10ap	[33]	294
2a	9-9	Ling	12ap	[35]	414 BL

STUNNING SPARK 2 b f £0

28	9-10	Wind	8.3g/f		4831
8	12-14	Wind	8.3g/f		5049

STYLISH DANCER 3 b f £0

53	11-18	Wind	10g/f		1959
52	5-8	Good	11gd		2222
14	7-9	Pont	12g/f		2992
37a	6-14	Ling	10ap	49	3449
0	15-15	Ling	12ap	[47]	4111
5	9-12	Chep	10.2hvy	45	4708

STYLISH PRINCE 4 b g £0

0	8-8	Sout	11af	[45]	574

STYLISH SUNRISE 3 b g £798

39a	8-8	Ling	8ap	[70]	934
37	4-10	Yarm	10.1g/f	[70]	1724
51	3-13	Leic	10fm	[65]	2107 T
52	5-8	Hami	11.1g/f	[65]	2319 t
37	7-7	Warw	12.6fm	56	2782 t
51a	3-13	Ling	10ap	[56]	3288 t
1	14-15	Nott	10g/s	53	4037 t
48a	5-14	Ling	16ap	50	4319 VIS

SUALDA 5 b g £34129

60	5-14	Ches	12.3gd	59	2285
63	2-15	Ripo	12.3g/f	59	2526
69	1-9	BEVE	12.1gd	62	2892*
73	2-7	Hami	13gd	68	3134
70	3-8	Hami	11.1gd	68	3207
79	1-8	CHES	12.3fm	70	3637*
79	4-11	Newm	16.1g/f	75	3779
81	1-21	YORK	11.9gd	74	3999*
64	10-12	York	13.9g/f	78	4400

SUAVE QUARTET 2 b c £869

77a	2-12	Ling	8ap		102
20	5-5	Brig	8g/f	[78]	2641 BL

SUBADAR MAJOR 7 b g £0

0	9-9	Ripo	16gd	30	4308
2	15-15	Ches	15.9g/f	30	4512
0	18-19	Sand	15.8g/f	30	4675

SUBLIMITY 4 b c £24520

114	1-10	DONC	8gd	[102]	922* t
107	7-10	Sand	8.1g/s	[110]	1349 t
107	4-10	Good	9.9g/f	[110]	1862 t
87	11-11	Epso	8.5fm	[110]	2252 t
107	3-5	Newm	8g/f	[110]	3613 t
90	11-12	Sali	8gd	[108]	3886 t

SUBMISSIVE 3 ch c £3367

62	8-12	Newm	7g/s		1152
80a	1-6	WOLV	9.4af		1377*
64	10-13	Wind	8.3g/s	75	4221

SUBPOENA 2 b c £5210

96	1-8	YORK	7gd		4326*
84	7-9	Newm	7gd		4881

SUBTLE AFFAIR 2 b f £533

75	7-11	Donc	8fm		4462
75	3-16	Yarm	10.1g/s		5352

SUBTLE BREEZE 3 ch f £621

69	3-15	Ling	7gd		4445
58	7-15	Nott	8.2g/s		4649
59a	6-11	Ling	8ap		4977

SUBTLE MOVE 3 b f £0

16a	11-16	Sout	6af	[49]	65 vis
0	12-14	Sout	8af	49	99 vis
1a	14-14	Sout	8af	40	165 vis
0	15-16	Ling	7ap	[40]	214
24a	11-13	Sout	6af	[35]	254
4a	14-16	Sout	5af	[30]	374

SUBYAN DREAMS 2 b f £3398

75	5-8	Asco	6gd		3071
75	3-14	Leic	6g/f		3517
95	3-5	Newb	7gd		3919
77	9-12	Good	7sft	[95]	4264
75	5-14	Sali	8gd	[95]	4852

SUCCESSION 2 ch f £19016

43	9-14	Leic	6g/s		3517
52	10-18	Newc	6g/s		3699
59	10-18	Newm	7gd		3927
61	6-12	Beve	8.5sft		4257
77	1-14	MUSS	8gd	63	4519*
80	1-14	YARM	7g/s	69	4583*
88	1-8	MUSS	8gd	76	4807+
91	3-17	Good	8gd	83	4871

SUCCESSOR 4 ch c £0

37	11-14	Hayd	8.1g/s		2231
58	6-13	Nott	8.2g/f		2633

SUCHWOT 3 b g £1295

44	10-18	Nott	8.2fm	59	1007
54	6-19	Warw	10.9gd	56	1124
60	2-11	Warw	8.1hvy	56	1534
5	9-13	Chep	8.1hvy	58	4709
3	19-20	Catt	12gd	56	4966

SUDDEN 9 ch g £0

0	6-6	Ling	10ap		972

SUDDEN DISMISSAL 2 b c £9885

83	4-18	Wind	6gd		3824
93	1-18	LING	6gd		4108*
96	7-8	Kemp	6fm	[87]	4390
95	1-11	SALI	7gd	[95]	4853*
87	7-11	Newb	7sft		5195

SUDDEN FLIGHT 6 b g £8018

2a	12-12	Sout	14af	80	173
75a	9-16	Ling	12ap	80	293
66a	13-16	Ling	12ap	75	493
64a	8-15	Ling	12ap	75	549
71a	3-6	Sout	12af	70	870
17	11-12	Ches	12.3gd	68	1599
60	11-19	Wind	10sft	[68]	1650

70	4-10	Kemp	16fm	65	2073
70	3-8	Hayd	14gd	67	2887
73	1-6	**CHES**	15.9g/f	67	3101*
72	6-11	Ling	16gd	72	3200
64	5-7	Kemp	12g/f	70	3519
40	8-12	Kemp	14.4g/f	70	3688
70	3-17	Kemp	12sft	67	4033
63	9-20	Hayd	11.9g/s	67	4771

SUDDEN IMPULSE 3 b f £0

66	6-11	Sali	8fm		2419
52a	7-14	Ling	10ap		2740

SUDRA 6 b g £2899

46a	8-16	Sout	7af	55	208
42a	7-13	Sout	8af	55	228 p
45a	3-10	Wolv	8.5af	[53]	311 p
49a	3-8	Wolv	8.5af	[53]	362 BL
43a	4-8	Sout	7af	[53]	373 bl
51a	4-12	Wolv	7af	[49]	512 bl
50a	3-9	Sout	7af	[49]	555 bl
56a	1-9	**SOUT**	7af	[47]	639+ bl
48a	4-9	Wolv	8.5af	[47]	664 bl
53a	3-16	Sout	8af	53	2805
38a	9-15	Sout	8af	53	4132 bl

SUERTE 3 b f £0

49a	4-11	Wolv	9.4af	[62]	115
24a	13-13	Ling	10ap	57	215
38a	10-12	Wolv	9.4af	57	427
35	13-18	Nott	8.2g/s	57	1778
0	12-12	Wolv	9.4af	49	2054 P
32	8-11	Folk	9.7fm	49	2719
0	13-13	Sout	8af	43	3094

SUEZ 2 b f £71237

98	1-8	**GOOD**	6fm		3536*
111	1-11	**SALI**	6gd		4332*
113	2-7	Newm	6g/f	[100]	4880

SUGAR CUBE TREAT 7 b m £0

23a	9-9	Wolv	7af	41	31
13a	10-11	Sout	6af	41	91
0	9-9	Sout	8af	35	163
11a	10-12	Wolv	6af	[35]	297
0	13-15	Sout	6af	[30]	773
0	14-17	Pont	6hvy	[30]	1065
45	5-8	Hayd	6g/s	[30]	1345 P
27	8-16	Nott	6.1sft	30	1465 p
43	9-13	Pont	5g/f	[31]	2279
3	6-6	Hami	5gd	31	2712
3	12-12	Ches	7.6fm	31	3634
0	U-13	Hayd	6gd	[31]	3757

SUGAR SNAP 4 b f £0

3a	11-11	Sout	12af	40	458
0	14-14	Sout	6af	[35]	2502

SUGARBABE 2 b f £0

17a	10-14	Sout	8af	[48]	95

SUGGESTIVE 6 b g £61444

98	4-10	Donc	8gd	[109]	922 vis
92	5-8	Newm	6g/f	[107]	1187 BL
109	2-7	Good	7g/f	[107]	1811 bl
110	1-11	**HAYD**	7.1gd	[107]	2184* bl
107	4-6	Long	7g/s	[107]	2826 bl
89	10-10	Asco	8gd	[109]	3124 bl
113	2-8	Good	7g/f	[109]	3508 bl
113	2-13	Newb	7g/f	[111]	3957 bl
104	6-8	Donc	7fm	[111]	4477 bl
102	6-14	Newb	7g/f	[111]	4638 bl
98	8-11	Good	7gd	[110]	4874 bl

SUGITANI 2 b c £0

63	8-8	York	7gd		4326 T
52	16-23	Newm	7g/f		4885 t

SUITCASE MURPHY 2 b g £441

35a	4-5	Wolv	5af	50	237
31a	10-13	Wolv	6af	47	436
35	6-15	Carl	5fm	[45]	4508
47	3-19	Thir	6g/f	45	4595
18	10-19	Kemp	6af	[45]	4793
0	15-17	Warw	8.1g/s	[45]	4992

SUIVEZ MOI 2 ch c £0

61	12-17	Yarm	6g/s		5350

SUJOSISE 3 b c £0

23	12-14	Thir	6gd		1639
22	9-10	Carl	6gd	49	2675
32	11-14	Catt	6g/f	47	3018 VIS
24	13-17	Ripo	6g/s	42	3262

SUKUMA 2 ch f £0

51	8-9	Hayd	6g/f		1920
41a	7-14	Sout	7af		2492
52	11-14	Newb	6fm		3626

SULAMANI 5 b h £778410

116	4-10	Asco	10g/f	[125]	2488
125	2-8	Newm	12g/f	[125]	3030 T
125	3-11	Asco	12g/f	[125]	3442 t
126	1-9	**YORK**	10.4gd	[124]	4002* t
125	1-10	**WOOD**	12gd	[124]	5247*

SUMMER BOUNTY 8 b g £10061

39	12-20	Warw	10.9gd	64	1128
72	1-14	**WARW**	8.1hvy	62	1535*
79	1-14	**NOTT**	10g/s	68	1777*
67	11-15	Kemp	10fm	76	2067
80	3-13	Ches	10.3gd	76	2284
76	2-8	Newc	10.1sft	[76]	2687
76	10-15	Ches	10.3g/f	76	3099
75	5-8	Leic	10g/f	76	3514

SUMMER CHARM 2 b f £0

43	11-18	Ling	6gd		4108
55	12-17	Warw	7.1gd		4271
39	11-14	Warw	6.1g/f		4422
23a	11-14	Ling	7ap		4658

SUMMER CHERRY 7 b g £872

3	15-16	Brig	11.9fm	45	1693 t
46	2-11	Folk	12g/f	41	2273 t
44	5-10	Newm	12g/f	41	2530 t
43	7-16	Folk	12fm	45	2718 t
39	7-7	Brig	11.9fm	40	2836 t
22	13-16	Brig	9.9g/f	40	3175 t

SUMMER JOY 3 b f £0

0	9-9	Warw	8.1sft		1089
5	14-14	Sali	7fm		2291

SUMMER RECLUSE 5 gr g £398

67a	8-12	Ling	8ap	77	517
82a	7-11	Ling	7ap	[77]	627 P
79a	5-11	Ling	8ap	[77]	800 p
77a	4-12	Ling	8ap	77	888 p

SUMMER SERENADE 3 b f £2216

72	2-13	Wind	10g/f		2453
78	3-13	Kemp	10g/f		3038

SUMMER SHADES 6 b m £12995

53a	6-10	Wolv	8.5af	64	1322
65	5-12	Kemp	8g/f	[70]	1915
74	2-9	Leic	8fm	69	2108
67	4-11	Redc	8fm	69	2296
68	4-8	Thir	8fm	72	2464
69	3-10	Newm	8g/f	70	2767
62	5-7	Redc	9g/s	[69]	2962
54	6-9	Nott	8.2g/f	[67]	3423
74	1-10	**NOTT**	8.2g/f	67	3579*
75	2-9	Newm	8g/f	70	3780
70	5-6	Wind	8.3g/f	72	3978
77	2-12	Muss	8gd	[71]	4809
39a	11-12	Wolv	8.6ap	63	4923
46a	11-13	Wolv	8.6ap	63	5364

SUMMER SILKS 2 ch f £0

42	8-15	Beve	5g/s		3178
59	4-11	Newc	7gd		3429
35	12-14	Thir	7g/s		3831
34	15-20	Redc	7fm	62	4337
38	17-17	Catt	7g/f		4963

SUMMER SPECIAL 4 b g £1514

48	5-13	Sout	6g/s	55	1052
40	5-16	Newc	10.1sft	51	1278
48	3-15	Hami	9.2gd	51	1388
35	12-12	Newc	12.4sft	50	1680
42	5-18	Wind	11.6g/f	48	1960
25	11-14	Ches	12.3gd	47	2285
46	3-15	Ayr	8gd	[47]	2504 p
46	3-10	Ayr	8g/s	[47]	2544 p
41	7-13	Muss	8gd	[44]	2967

SUMMER STOCK 6 b g £0

23a	11-13	Ling	10ap	[52]	429 t
38a	7-12	Wolv	9.5ap	[45]	5234 t P

SUMMER SUNSET 3 ch f £0

9	19-19	Asco	8g/f	95	2491 BL

SUMMER WINE 5 b m £0

40	9-9	Nott	10sft	75	1467

SUMMERISE 3 b f £632

45a	7-12	Ling	8ap	50	1045
49	6-11	Sout	10gd	55	1280
52	3-14	Warw	8.1sft	53	1529
33	8-16	Nott	10hvy	53	1611
75	6-8	Leic	8gd	[51]	5057

SUMMITVILLE 4 b f £15000

101	3-6	York	10.4g/f	[111]	1684
105	6-8	Hayd	11.9gd	[107]	2946
98	3-7	Good	14fm	[104]	3619
102	4-8	Asco	12g/f	[102]	4774

SUMORA 2 b f £18712

97a	1-8	**LING**	5ap		3600*
105	1-12	**NEWB**	5.2g/f		3956*
88	6-11	Donc	5fm		4533
94	8-11	Newm	5sft	[100]	5132

SUN AND SHOWERS 2 b c £0

65	9-20	Yarm	8sft		5252

SUN BIRD 6 ch g £875

89	5-12	Hami	12.1gd	103	1746

SUN HILL 4 b g £11387

59a	1-13	**SOUT**	14af	52	590*
68a	1-10	**WOLV**	16.2af	57	812*
78a	1-8	**WOLV**	16.2af	66	837*
29	13-14	Donc	18gd	79	926
0	10-11	Warw	15sft	80	1087
70	5-17	Sali	14.1g/s	72	1502
58	12-18	Nott	14.1g/s	70	1772
41	14-20	Hayd	11.9g/s	67	4771
45	12-15	Good	16gd	65	5025
2	13-13	Newb	16sft	65	5194

SUN KING USA 2 b r c £92179

117	3-4	Lone	8.5Fast		5310

SUN KISSED 2 ch c £6913

93	1-5	**NEWM**	6g/f		3586*
97	2-5	Sali	8gd		4328
42	9-9	Newm	8sft	[93]	5099

SUN ON THE SEA 4 ch f £750

84	6-6	York	10.4g/s	[107]	1684

SUNCLIFF 2 b g £0

0	13-13	Wolv	8.6ap		5288 BL

SUNDANCE 2 ch c £12236

96	1-11	**WIND**	5gd		3160*
93a	2-10	Ling	5ap		3743
101	1-8	**RIPO**	5gd		4307*
89	6-12	Ayr	5g/s	[98]	4651
41	10-11	York	6gd	[97]	4998

SUNDAY CITY 3 ch c £2856

77	3-13	Thir	12g/f		1768
65	3-8	Pont	12g/f		2608 VIS
66	5-6	Bath	10.2g/f		2980 vis
69	5-11	Yarm	14.1gd	69	3998
70	2-11	Bath	13.1g/f	69	4415
6	13-13	Newc	16.1fm	69	4868

SUNDAY DOUBT 3 b r c £7711

110	3-6	Long	7g/s		2826

SUNDAY SYMPHONY 2 b r c £13888

85	2-11	Newm	8gd		3925
91	1-14	**THIR**	8gd		4376*
91	1-7	**LEIC**	10gd	[83]	5044* t
55	9-11	Newm	10g/s	[89]	5281

SUNDRIED TOMATO 4 b g £629

83a 9-15 Sout 5af 92 64
77a 11-16 Sout 5af 90 171
66a 11-13 Ling 6ap 88 235
70a 8-10 Ling 7ap 85 262
64a 10-12 Wolv 6af 85 361
72a 6-16 Sout 7af 82 419
77a 4-13 Wolv 6af 79 482
71a 6-13 Wolv 6af 78 618
58a 10-13 Wolv 6af 78 687
72a 6-13 Wolv 6af 75 807
61 9-16 Bath 5.7g/s [73] 1103
58 8-16 Sali 7sft 70 4582
66 5-11 Hami 6g/s 68 4818
62 10-20 Wind 6g/s 68 4946
48 10-19 Wind 6g/f 66 5053

SUNDROP 3 b f £93655
118 2-16 Newm 8fm 1492
74 6-7 Epso 12g/f [117] 2210
107 1-10 **NEWM** 10gd [115] 5086*

SUNGIO 5 b g £9620
34a 12-14 Ling 10ap 60 230
51a 5-14 Ling 13ap 57 264
42a 1-9 **LING** 16ap [53] 452
49a 3-13 Ling 13ap [53] 602
52a 1-11 **WOLV** 12af [53] 689*
53a 2-9 Ling 13ap [52] 787 bl
44a 3-7 Wolv 16.2af 52 866 bl
53a 3-13 Ling 13ap 52 896 bl
49a 5-7 Ling 16ap [52] 1291 bl
41 8-15 Good 16gd 45 5025
59a 1-13 **WOLV** 16.5ap 52 5366* bl

SUNISA 3 b f £6831
74a 2-9 Ling 8ap [82] 1022
80a 1-8 **WOLV** 8.5af [72] 1220*
83 3-9 Donc 10.3g/f 76 2079
76 8-12 Sand 9g/f 78 2385
82 2-8 Kemp 9g/s 78 2680
0 19-19 Kemp 10fm 82 4392
80 5-19 Donc 10.3sft 82 5201

SUNLEY SENSE 8 b g £1075
81 3-14 Wind 5g/f 79 2266
64 9-12 Ripo 5g/f 79 2524
69 10-12 Sali 5g/f 79 2698
51 12-12 York 5g/s 77 3073
59 6-10 Beve 5g/f [74] 3503 vis

SUNNY GLENN 5 ch h £0
56a 14-14 Ling 10ap [85] 82
97 11-11 Epso 12g/f [78] 2209
79 6-11 Good 12gd 83 2538
79 7-7 Newm 12g/f [83] 2762
44 16-19 Hayd 10.5g/s 80 4766

SUNNY LADY 2 ch f £9972
65a 6-12 Ling 8ap 102
45a 9-16 Sout 8af 192
75 2-10 Kemp 11.1gd 1140
73 2-13 Thir 12g/f [73] 1768
77 2-7 Brig 11.9g/f [73] 1939
78 2-10 Good 14gd 74 2376
81 1-5 **BRIG** 11.9g/f 75 2642+
73 4-5 Brig 11.9gd [80] 2956
80 4-12 Wind 11.6g/f 77 4833
74a 6-10 Ling 12ap 77 5239

SUNNY NATURE 2 b f £0
0 19-19 Newm 7g/s 5279

SUNNY TIMES 2 b f £428
65 5-8 Ling 6gd 3021
46 7-10 Beve 5g/f 3504
39 10-15 Folk 6g/f 4369
55 5-19 Kemp 8g/f [51] 4792
68 2-14 Yarm 8g/s [57] 5118
61 8-20 Yarm 8g/s 63 5349

SUNNYSIDE ROYALE 5 b g £1651
22 13-17 Nott 14.1gd 45 1238 t
50a 1-7 **SOUT** 14af [45] 1407* t
41a 3-7 Sout 11af [45] 1589 t
15a 8-12 Sout 16af 49 1753 t

SUNRIDGE FAIRY 5 b m £0
13a 14-15 Sout 8af 51 1028

29 6-10 Beve 9.9g/f [35] 1946

SUNSET BLUES 4 ch g £207
27a 5-9 Wolv 8.5af 751 BL e
50a 10-12 Ling 8ap 881 bl e
2a 10-12 Wolv 9.4af 939 bl e
41a 3-9 Ling 8ap [40] 1185 bl e
0 8-8 Sout 8af [40] 1841 bl e

SUNSET DREAMER 3 ch f £0
53a 6-11 Ling 8ap 322
44a 11-15 Ling 7ap 472
45 11-17 Kemp 7gd 1136
34a 14-14 Ling 10ap 52 2064
37 13-18 Kemp 10g/f [49] 4791
0 18-19 Yarm 8g/s [47] 5119

SUNSET KING 3 b c £0
17a 15-16 Ling 7ap [59] 123
20a 12-12 Ling 8ap 52 1013

SUNSET MIRAGE 3 br f £8975
76 2-15 Leic 10g/s 1358
62 6-10 Yarm 11.5g/f 1725
74 1-7 **CARL** 9.3fm 68 1953*
55 11-13 Sand 8.1gd 71 2365
63 6-10 Chep 8.1g/f 70 2624
57 10-14 Folk 9.7g/s 69 3052
70 4-13 Yarm 10.1gd 68 3492 VIS
73 2-8 Brig 9.9g/f 68 3719 vis
70 3-5 Folk 9.7g/s 68 3914 vis
74 2-6 Hami 9.2g/s 68 4137 BL

SUNSET STRIP 2 b c £3469
80 2-6 Ayr 6g/f 2028
85 2-9 Folk 7g/s 3047
79 3-8 Sali 6gd 3451
70 6-18 Newc 6g/s [78] 3699

SUNSHINE ON ME 3 ch f £0
61 9-14 Newb 9fm 3631
59a 5-15 Ling 12ap 4111
56a 9-14 Ling 13ap 4892
42a 12-16 Ling 12ap [60] 5296

SUNSTRACH 5 b h £49281
110 3- Capa 10g/s 59
109 3-11 Sand 10g/s 1350
111 4-5 Long 9.3gd 2002
108 3-9 Sand 10g/s [112] 2128
107 3-7 Sand 10g/s [112] 2898

SUPAMACH 3 b f £1449
72a 3-13 Ling 10ap 2066
69 4-12 York 7.9g/f 2410
66 4-14 Wind 8.3fm 2974
44 10-12 Newm 8fm 66 3410
11 16-17 Hayd 10.5fm 65 4388
0 9-10 Sali 8sft [63] 4578
50a 9-12 Wolv 8.6ap 68 5116 P

SUPER BOBBINA 3 b f £40880
114 3-14 Capa 10g/s 5244

SUPER BOSTON 4 b g £0
16 12-15 Nott 8.2g/f 2633
44 6-6 Newc 10.1sft 4286

SUPER BRAND 4 b f £11173
93 2-9 Nad 6.5g/f 90 790

SUPER CANYON 6 ch g £1559
64a 4-13 Wolv 6af 68 687 vis t
69a 2-7 Wolv 7af 68 860
12a 14-14 Ling 7ap 66 1010 vis t
31 13-18 Donc 7g/f 56 2080
1 19-20 Nott 6.1g/f 54 2630 vis t
49a 9-13 Sout 7af 65 3155 t

SUPER DOMINION 7 ch g £4747
34a 5-10 Wolv 9.4af [40] 1564
46a 1-10 **WOLV** 8.5af [40] 1801* p
42a 4-12 Wolv 9.4af 40 2054 p
18a 9-12 Sout 7af 45 2204 p
49a 1-15 **SOUT** 8af 47 2725* p
27a 10-16 Sout 8af 47 3159 p
23a 12-16 Sout 8af 47 3487 p
38 8-17 Thir 8g/s 47 3830 p
48a 5-11 Sout 8af [46] 4090 p

48 4-17 Pont 8g/f 47 4626 p

SUPER FELLOW 10 b g £9727
38 3-12 Yarm 16gd 35 3493
47 1-10 **THIR** 16sft 36 3834*
49 1-17 **PONT** 17.1g/s 42 3970*
34 5-19 Catt 15.8g/f 45 4675
55 5-14 Pont 17.1g/f 45 4936

SUPER KING 3 b f £1709
61 9-12 Leic 8fm 2106
42 12-12 York 7.9g/f [68] 2410
50a 7-10 Sout 8af [65] 2997
55 8-13 Beve 7.5g/s 65 3179
58 5-13 Beve 9.9gd 59 3309
67 2-12 Beve 9.9g/s 59 3854
67 3-6 Newc 10.1sft [61] 4286
0 19-20 Hayd 11.9g/s 66 4771
49 9-17 Newc 10.1g/f 65 5016

SUPER LINA 3 gr f £10282
108 2-6 Sain 10.5g/s 1157
112 4-7 Long 10gd 2001

SUPER SONG 4 b g £0
33a 12-12 Ling 8ap 77 888
43 9-18 Wind 8.3g/s 73 1059 T
47 10-17 Thir 8g/s 73 1214 t
47 10-12 Leic 6fm 70 2111 t
41 16-17 Wind 6g/f 65 2451 t
16 13-17 Wind 6fm 58 2975 t
55 6-16 Kemp 7gd 58 3184 t
19 22-22 Good 5fm 53 3537 t
19 19-20 Chep 7.1gd 51 4488 t
21 13-16 Chep 7.1hvy [48] 4707 VIS

SUPERCHIEF 8 b g £2095
55a 8-11 Ling 8ap 65 131 bl t
65a 2-15 Ling 7ap 62 266 bl t
44a 14-16 Ling 7ap 62 323 bl t
71a 6-14 Ling 7ap [65] 450 bl t
62a 4-13 Ling 6ap 65 471 bl t
68a 3-14 Ling 7ap 65 499 bl t
67a 5-14 Ling 7ap 65 604 bl t
62a 5-12 Ling 6ap 65 628 bl t
69a 2-15 Ling 7ap 64 698 bl t
58a 5-11 Ling 8ap 64 714 bl t
39a 10-12 Ling 8ap 65 1613 bl t
4 11-16 Folk 6g/f [45] 4370 t
19a 12-14 Ling 7ap [64] 5080 bl t
55a 10-14 Ling 7ap 62 5300 bl t

SUPERCLEAN 4 ch f £0
15a 9-12 Ling 8ap [30] 971
15a 10-12 Ling 12ap [30] 1180
21 6-8 Chep 10.2sft [30] 1333 VIS
2a 9-10 Ling 12ap [30] 1714 vis

SUPERFLING 3 ch g £277
54 9-11 Sali 7gd 3884
63 4-13 Bath 5.7g/f 4413
47 9-10 Wind 6g/f 4835
39a 12-14 Ling 7ap [60] 5263

SUPERPRIDETWO 4 b g £0
9a 9-10 Ling 7ap [35] 1181 vis

SUPERSTITIOUS 2 b c £0
64 7-12 York 6gd 3122
37 10-10 Good 6g/f 3511
70 6-10 Newb 7g/f 3955
0 21-21 Donc 6fm [70] 4490
27 18-20 Donc 7sft 67 5373

SUPREMACY 5 ch g £5533
0 10-13 Asco 16.2sft [104] 1418
105 4-9 Newm 12g/f [104] 3233
107 7-9 Good 16fm [104] 3552
97 4-5 Good 14g/s [105] 4230
94 9-15 Donc 14.6fm 105 4491
107 3-5 Asco 16.2g/f [103] 4815

SUPREME SALUTATION 7 ch g £14053
49a 6-14 Sout 8af 68 99
40a 8-9 Sout 7af 66 193
43a 12-13 Sout 7af 63 556
64a 1-10 **SOUT** 8af [60] 868*
64a 1-15 **LING** 7ap [60] 935*
56 11-18 Wind 8.3gd 58 1385

82 1-11 WARW 8.1hvy 68 1536*
75a 4-12 Ling 8ap 73 1613
85 1-14 **NOTT** 10g/s 78 1776*
67 11-14 Wind 8.3gd [83] 4122
84 4-13 Wind 8.3g/s 83 4221
56 15-16 Sand 10gd 83 4609
61 14-18 Kemp 8g/f 83 4714

SURDOUE 3 b g £1892
14a 9-9 Wolv 8.5af 81 2
33a 12-16 Sout 11af 75 97
16a 13-14 Sout 8af 72 195
62a 5-15 Sout 12af 65 257
41a 8-10 Sout 12af 63 321 P
61a 2-12 Sout 11af 63 534
51a 4-7 Sout 12af [63] 594
66a 2-6 Sout 12af 63 683
40a 8-12 Wolv 9.4af 61 747
4 11-14 Pont 8hvy [56] 1253
1 18-18 Wind 8.3gd 56 1385
58a 13-16 Ling 12ap 65 4973
59a 10-13 Wolv 9.5ap 60 5292

SURE FUTURE 8 b g £219
37 3-10 Kemp 12hvy [45] 1645

SURF THE NET 3 b f £4053
94 3-6 Leic 7gd 2136
49 15-19 Asco 8g/f 92 2491
74 10-11 Donc 7g/s 92 3223
78 3-5 Yarm 7gd [92] 3365
88 4-6 Wind 8.3g/f 87 3978
76 9-10 Kemp 8fm 85 4389 P
59 19-25 Newb 7gd 82 4683 VIS
72 11-20 Newm 7g/s 79 5286 vis

SURREPTITIOUS 3 ch f £6087
68 1-9 **NEWM** 7g/f 3282*
62 3-11 Newm 8gd [68] 3923
48 8-8 Good 7sft 68 4263

SURREY DOWNS GIRL 2 ch f £0
0 7-7 Sout 5af 2498

SURVEYOR 4 ch g £197368
112 2-16 Kran 10gd 1859 bl

SURWAKI 2 b c £3051
86 3-15 Sand 7.1g/f 3337
88 2-14 Sand 7.1g/s 4069
86 9-10 Donc 7fm 4493

SUSIEDIL 3 b f £0
52 10-16 Leic 8g/s 65 1359
31 10-18 Wind 8.3sft 63 1647
51 6-14 Nott 8.2g/f 60 2153
41 6-8 Brig 8g/f 57 2432
39 13-17 B:ig 7g/f 52 3176 VIS
24 15-16 Catt 7g/f 49 4676
30 7-13 Brig 8gd [45] 4902
0 12-13 Wolv 8.6ap [45] 5232

SUSPICIOUS MINDS 3 b f £0
62a 7-12 Ling 8ap 881
59 14-24 Newm 8fm 1495
30 11-13 Newm 8g/f 1935
50 13-14 Kemp 10g/s 2678

SUSSEX STYLE 2 b g £0
30a 9-10 Ling 6ap 260
48a 10-13 Ling 6ap 364
43a 9-12 Ling 8ap 623
51a 6-11 Ling 6ap 898
58a 7-12 Ling 6ap [53] 1044
35 6-8 Brig 5.3g/f 53 1942
28 15-16 Ling 6g/f 53 1985
36 8-9 Folk 6g/f 50 2271 T
44 5-12 Brig 6g/f 50 2435 t

SUSTAINABLE STYLE 3 gr f £0
37 8-11 Wind 8.3g/f 5054
4 16-17 Yarm 8g/s 5348

SUTTERS FORT 3 br c £0
66a 10-14 Nad 8af 598 t

SUTURIA 2 b f £0
58a 12-14 Ling 7ap 5258

SUVARI 3 b f £0
59a 6-15 Ling 7ap 875
41 13-19 Yarm 8g/f 1130

SVENSON 3 ch c £0
0 12-13 Sout 6af 319
25a 10-11 Wolv 8ap 396
0 11-11 Pont 10g/f 2991
13 11-16 Thir 8g/f 30 3414
38 9-12 Newc 8g/f [30] 4407
2 13-15 Carl 7.9fm [30] 4507
43 6-10 Catt 6gd [30] 4964
30 13-19 Redc 6g/s [30] 5110

SWAGGER STICK 3 gr c £14792
95 1-18 **LEIC** 10g/s 71 1017*
92 1-5 **LEIC** 11.8g/s 80 1355*
10 W-11 Newb 11g/f 90 1756
92 6-17 Asco 12g/f 90 2519
89 8-15 Hayd 11.9gd 90 2948
79 10-11 Newm 10g/f 90 3236
88 6-10 Ches 10.3sft 89 4071
86 9-13 Donc 10.3fm [88] 4463
87 7-18 Newb 10gd 88 4681 BL
83 5-19 Newm 12gd 86 5085 bl

SWAHILI DANCER 3 b c £0
47 5-8 Redc 10g/f 2124

SWAIN DAVIS 4 b f £0
0 13-13 Sout 14af 63 2494

SWAINSON 3 br c £7214
77a 3-14 Ling 10ap 759
77 4-9 Ling 10sft 1623
83a 1-13 **LING** 10ap 2066*
87 2-8 Good 9.9gd 79 2377
64 16-16 Sand 10g/s 84 2919
51 5-5 Asco 12gd 84 3468
69 14-16 Good 12fm 84 3534

SWAINSWORLD 3 b g £6532
68 4-12 Thir 7g/f 1971
72 4-11 Thir 7fm 2463
75 1-11 **BEVE** 8.5gd 2656*
58 8-9 Beve 8.5sft 78 2940

SWALLOW FALLS 2 b f £0
32 8-9 Ches 5.1g/f 3097
63 5-11 Ches 7fm 3633
53 10-14 Hayd 6sft 4769

SWALLOW SENORA 2 b f £0
66 11-19 Newm 7g/s 5279

SWAN NEBULA 2 b f £32933
83 3-8 Donc 6gd 2750 T
77 5-13 Newb 7g/f 3252 t
86 1-14 **NEWB** 6fm 3626* t
91 1-21 **DONC** 6.5fm 82 4457* t
76 7-9 Ayr 6sft [82] 4684 t

SWEDISH SHAVE 6 ch h £20564
106 2-12 Deau 6sft 3167
110 2-11 Deau 6hvy 4313

SWEENEY TODD 2 ch g £0
56 6-7 Brig 7fm 3691
45 8-13 Sali 7g/f 3864

SWEEP THE BOARD 3 b c £0
53 13-14 Newb 9fm 3631
60 6-13 Wind 8.3gd 3828
34 11-12 Beve 12.1g/f 62 4601

SWEET AROMA 4 b f £0
13a 10-15 Sout 12af [26] 89

SWEET AT HEART 3 b f £0
12a 9-13 Sout 8af 2383
35 7-11 Ripo 12.3gd 4281
36 5-6 Catt 12g/f 4441

SWEET AZ 4 b f £0

45 13-17 Chep 8.1gd [39] 2117
0 13-20 Chep 6.1gd 39 2372
35 8-13 Bath 10.2gd [37] 3144 P

SWEET CANDO 2 b f £3389
57a 4-10 Wolv 7af 65 112
51 6-11 Hami 6gd 64 1745
55 9-14 Newb 7fm 62 2295
68 2-12 Ayr 5g/s 59 2566 P
40 7-10 Carl 5gd 59 2675 p
61 5-8 Newc 5g/s 59 2731 p
34 8-10 Hami 6g/f 64 3203 p
54 11-13 Newb 5.2g/f 62 3960 p
61 3-12 Newm 5gd 58 4197 p
51 10-26 Ayr 5g/s 59 4618 p
32 8-15 Hami 6sft 59 4696 p
55 6-15 Ayr 5sft 58 5036 p

SWEET COINCIDENCE 2 b f £4312
69 3-8 Good 6gd 2537
55 8-17 Nott 6.1gd 2927
81 1-13 **CHEP** 6.1gd 3399*

SWEET CORAL 3 b f £0
21a 7-12 Sout 6af 43 85
37a 7-12 Sout 7af [40] 416
36a 4-16 Sout 8af [40] 442 P
27a 8-10 Sout 8af [40] 502
16a 8-10 Wolv 6af [40] 667 BL
16a 7-11 Sout 7af [40] 771 bl

SWEET FURY 2 b c £0
0 12-13 Wolv 9.4af [68] 37

SWEET INDULGENCE 3 ch c £2231
86 7-14 Newm 8g/f 84 1930
71 10-16 Newm 8g/f 84 3059
81 5-13 Newm 8g/f 84 3277
83 3-5 Kemp 8g/f [83] 3523
79 4-8 Newm 8g/f 81 3947
80 7-11 Beve 9.9g/s 79 4239

SWEET LORRAINE 2 b f £1664
69 2-15 Folk 7gd 3381
65 7-12 Folk 7gd 3908

SWEET MARGUERITE 2 b f £588
62 5-9 Hayd 6g/f 1920
65 4-16 Pont 6g/f 2275
54 4-8 Ayr 5gd 2505
63 6-17 Nott 6.1gd 2927
29 18-20 Redc 7fm 63 4337
44 8-18 Ayr 6g/s [60] 4617
52 7-16 Ripo 6gd [55] 4787
54 7-18 Newc 6gd 55 5013

SWEET NAMIBIA 2 ch f £1010
65a 3-13 Wolv 6ap 5182
65a 3-13 Wolv 6ap 5287

SWEET PICKLE 3 b f £1319
69 2-10 Brig 6g/f [70] 2048
68 4-7 Warw 6.1fm [70] 2598
57 6-7 Ling 6fm [69] 3789
26 20-20 Ling 6g/f 66 4317
58 8-13 Warw 7.1g/f [63] 4667
55 6-19 Nott 6.1g/f [58] 4845

SWEET POTATO 2 b f £0
55 5-10 Redc 6gd 4244
64 8-13 Redc 7fm 4927
46 8-17 Redc 7g/s 5105

SWEET REFLECTION 4 b f £0
36a 9-14 Ling 10ap [45] 828 T
28a 9-14 Ling 10ap [40] 1072 t
2a 5-5 Ling 12ap [40] 1411
12 13-16 Good 9gd 40 2220 t

SWEET REPLY 3 ch f £5395
58 16-20 Newm 7af 80 1186
74 5-7 Thir 8g/f [78] 1770
73 1-8 **BRIG** 7fm [75] 2259*
87 9-11 Warw 7.1fm [75] 2574
61 10-13 Beve 7.5g/s 75 3179
70 5-9 Ling 7gd 73 4110
56 13-14 Epso 7gd 71 4465
55 10-14 Redc 7g/s 68 5109 P
48a 11-13 Ling 10ap 65 5299

SWEET REPOSE 3 b f £0
| 40 | 7-9 | Ripo | 8gd | | 1178 |
| 57 | 8-11 | Beve | 9.9g/f | | 1835 |

SWEET ROYALE 2 b f £4388
68	2-8	Muss	5gd		1795
80	1-8	**AYR**	5gd		2505*
23	5-5	Hami	5gd		3130
44	11-12	Newb	5.2g/f	[84]	3956

SWEET SIOUX 2 ch f £0
| 34a | 10-12 | Wolv | 7.1ap | | 5324 |

SWEET STREAM 4 b f £156426
107	3-12	Deau	12.5g/s		3837
117	1-13	LONG	12sft		4567*
105	3-9	San	12sft		5168

SWEET TALKING GIRL 3 b f £0
3a	9-10	Wolv	7af		4
11	9-10	Warw	6.1g/s	[40]	1327
0	16-16	Nott	6.1sft	40	1465
0	18-20	Thir	6gd	33	3575 T P
0	12-12	Folk	6g/s	30	3911 t p
0	12-12	Brig	5.3g/s	25	4140 t p

SWEETEST REVENGE 2 ch f £2555
80a	2-11	Ling	6ap	[78]	135
75a	5-10	Ling	5ap	78	217
76a	4-8	Ling	6ap	78	268
59	11-18	Wind	6g/f	75	2268
74a	6-11	Ling	6ap	77	2841
64	9-12	Kemp	6g/f	72	3036
63a	3-11	Ling	7ap	[74]	3331
74a	3-11	Ling	6ap	72	3744
62	7-15	Bath	5.7g/f	67	3966 P

SWEETSTOCK 5 b m £0
| 0 | 13-15 | Sout | 16af | 35 | 67 |

SWEETWATER 4 b f £0
61a	6-12	Wolv	12.2ap	70	4983
42	7-10	Newm	12sft	[70]	5102
54a	8-13	Wolv	16.5ap	60	5366

SWELL LAD 2 b c £1852
62	11-11	Asco	7fm		2578
56	15-15	Sand	7.1g/f		3337
74	6-11	Newb	7g/f		3959
72	2-12	Bath	8g/f	70	4410 BL
66	9-13	Newm	8fm	72	4725
24	13-13	Wind	8.3g/s	69	4940 bl

SWELLMOVA 5 b g £4568
62	2-17	Kemp	10g/f	58	1913
69	1-10	**NEWM**	12g/f	59	2530*
63	6-15	Newm	12g/f	66	3066

SWIFT ALCHEMIST 3 b f £5948
57a	8-10	Wolv	8.5af	73	5
62	8-12	Sand	8.1g/s	70	1352
50	10-12	Hayd	8.1g/f	67	1485
61	3-13	Warw	7.1hvy	[67]	1537
47a	10-12	Ling	8ap	[62]	2394
42	12-16	Kemp	7gd	59	3184
50	11-15	Donc	10.3g/f	56	3598
53	7-16	Wind	11.6gd	55	3829 P
53	7-17	Kemp	12sft	55	4033 p
58	1-9	**REDC**	10gd	52	4248* p
8	18-19	Leic	10g/f	56	4456 p
26	14-19	Bath	11.7gd	56	5024 p

SWIFT DAME 2 b f £0
47	15-16	Sali	7gd		4330
61a	5-10	Ling	7ap		4442
0	12-12	Nott	6.1g/f		4844
56	7-12	Bath	5sft	[63]	5169

SWIFT OSCAR 2 b c £0
| 68 | 6-13 | York | 6g/f | | 3431 |
| 61 | 7-16 | Sali | 7gd | | 3882 |

SWIFT SAILING 3 b c £2093
27	13-14	York	7.9g/s	80	1707
61	11-15	Ling	7g/f	77	1983 BL
54	10-20	Newb	7g/f	73	2314
69	2-8	Nott	10g/f	69	2631
70	4-5	Brig	9.9fm	69	2837

SWIFT SAILOR 3 gr c £5417
| 79 | 3-18 | Bath | 10.2gd | | 5023 |
| **83** | 1-10 | **MUSS** | 12g/s | | 5145* |

SWIFT TANGO 4 b g £95337
87a	1-14	LING	10ap	82	452+
92	2-12	Nad	10g/f	90	789
95	3-24	Donc	8gd	88	928
63	4-9	Pont	10hvy	[90]	1068 vis
101	1-17	NEWB	12g/f	90	1759*
102	2-13	Epso	12fm	96	2255
103	3-13	Asco	12fm	98	2582
102	6-15	Hayd	11.9gd	100	2948
99	4-9	Asco	10g/f	100	3439
104	3-10	Asco	12gd	100	3777
108	1-6	**CHES**	13.4sft	100	4104*
106	2-5	Good	14g/s	[100]	4230
112	3-7	Donc	12fm	[102]	4494
112	2-5	Asco	16.2g/f	[106]	4815

SWINBROOK 3 ch g £5470
64	9-10	Newm	6g/f		1191
69	12-18	Newm	6g/f	83	1933
85	2-9	Kemp	6gd	[80]	2173
75	1-6	**FOLK**	5fm	[80]	2717*
60	14-19	Good	6gd	80	4747
44	15-19	Sali	6gd	80	4855

SWING WEST 10 b h £0
| 27a | 4-7 | Wolv | 16.2af | 30 | 866 bl |
| 22a | 9-16 | Sout | 14af | 30 | 1033 P |

SWING WING 5 b g £71818
108	5-6	Long	15.5g/s	[109]	1431
71	16-17	Ches	18.7gd	108	1569
110	1-7	**SAN**	15gd	[108]	1998*
114	2-19	Newc	16.1g/s	105	2771
111	4-10	York	15.9gd	[110]	4000
112	4-9	Deau	12.5hv	[110]	4312

SWINTON 3 gr c £0
| 53 | 7-10 | Newc | 7hvy | | 4216 |
| 39 | 8-12 | Newc | 8g/f | | 4407 |

SWORDS 2 b c £262
44	13-18	Newm	8fm		4722
65	8-15	Newm	8gd		4883
74	5-7	Leic	10gd		5044
61	15-20	Yarm	8g/s	72	5349

SWORDS AT DAWN 3 ch f £0
| 0 | 10-10 | Hami | 9.2g/s | | 4135 |

SWORN TO SECRECY 3 ch f £0
42a	8-11	Ling	6ap	[69]	898
62	9-20	Nott	6.1gd	67	1239
37a	7-11	Wolv	8.5af	64	1339
50	10-14	Wind	8.3g/f	64	1956
58	11-12	Sand	7.1g/f	64	2098 BL
56	6-18	Wind	6g/f	61	2268 bl
46	11-12	Kemp	5g/f	59	3036
17	11-15	Leic	7g/f	[57]	3515 bl
34	7-10	Leic	7fm	[54]	3812

SWYNFORD PLEASURE 8 b m £2237
55	2-11	Donc	12g/f	53	1875
45	5-11	Pont	12g/f	53	2041
51	4-11	Thir	12g/f	55	2217
53	3-8	Hayd	11.9gd	51	2881

SWYNFORD WELCOME 7 b m £0
| 46a | 4-12 | Wolv | 8.5af | [40] | 47 |
| 46a | 7-16 | Sout | 7af | [40] | 61 |

SYBILL 4 b f £0
| 8a | 5-8 | Wolv | 7af | | 892 |
| 2a | 7-7 | Sout | 7af | | 1196 |

SYDNEY STAR 3 b f £8210
80	1-6	**CHES**	7gd		1587*
73	9-13	Newm	8g/f	86	2247
81	7-20	Newm	7g/s	84	5286

SYDNEYROUGHDIAMOND 2 b g £0
65	9-12	Hayd	6sft		3272
65	5-12	Ayr	7.2hvy		4083
73	8-14	Hayd	6fm		4385
64	8-15	Hayd	6sft	75	4765
32	10-14	Ayr	6sft	70	5035

SYLVA ROYAL 3 gr f £2677
70a	4-11	Ling	7ap		1008
0	W-7	Asco	8gd		3469
54	4-10	Ling	6g/f		3603
37	6-8	Yarm	6gd		3873
30a	9-14	Sout	6af	52	4130
54a	1-14	**LING**	7ap	[49]	4660*
48	4-12	Brig	8sft	54	5094
54a	3-9	Ling	8ap	[54]	5242

SYLVAN TWISTER 5 br g £183
32a	5-7	Ling	10ap	[35]	1182
25a	5-7	Ling	10ap	[35]	1244
36a	5-9	Ling	13ap	[35]	1456
33a	3-10	Ling	12ap	[30]	1714

SYLVATICUS 3 b c £0
| 0 | 8-8 | Kemp | 7g/f | | 1912 |
| 11 | 17-17 | Wind | 8.3fm | | 3480 |

SYNDACO 5 b h £3258
| 77 | 3-13 | Diel | 11.5 | | 1437 |

SYSTEMATIC 5 b h £72904
98	3-8	Donc	12gd	[111]	950
117	2-7	Newm	10g/f	109	1493
117	1-9	CHES	13.4gd	[109]	1596*
106	10-11	Epso	12g/f	[113]	2209
110	5-6	Asco	12fm	[113]	2579
106	6-8	Newm	12g/f	[113]	3030

SZEROKI BOR 5 b h £0
| 31a | 8-8 | Wolv | 16.2af | 67 | 837 |

T E LAWRENCE 4 b c £34194
| 107 | 1-15 | NAPL | 5g/f | [83] | 3170* |

T K O GYM 4 b g £0
45a	7-15	Sout	12af	[42]	89
31a	7-9	Sout	7af	[42]	303 VIS
12a	5-5	Wolv	8.5af	45	346

TAAKEED 2 b c £0
| 55 | 13-19 | Newm | 7g/s | | 5285 |

TAAQAAH 3 ch g £4637
79	2-11	Thir	7fm		2463
85	2-10	Newb	8g/f	78	2877
33	10-10	Kemp	6gd	[81]	3188
65	2-10	Chep	7.1gd	[80]	3732

TABARKA 3 b f £0
| 35a | 5-8 | Sout | 5af | [60] | 742 |
| 22a | 11-13 | Sout | 6af | 60 | 797 |

TABLEAU 3 ch c £13681
82	3-13	Donc	7gd		925
86	8-12	**LEIC**	8fm		2106*
90	1-6	**NEWM**	8g/f	84	3472*
22	9-10	Ches	10.3sft	86	4071
84	7-13	Ripo	8gd	86	4279

TABOOR 6 b g £11339
60a	9-10	Ling	5ap	69	329 h bl
59a	8-14	Ling	6ap	69	407 h bl
57a	8-10	Ling	5ap	67	453 h bl
63a	5-11	Sout	5af	64	655 h bl
45a	11-11	Wolv	5af	64	748 h bl
54	7-19	Warw	5gd	57	1127 h bl
53	5-15	Brig	5.3g/f	57	1371 h bl
41	12-17	Warw	5hvy	[57]	1532 h bl
57	2-10	Sand	5gd	53	2189 h bl
46	9-9	Sali	5fm	56	2420 h bl
51	6-11	Brig	5.3gd	56	2957 h bl
42	11-17	Sand	5g/f	55	3341 h bl
59	1-9	**BRIG**	5.3fm	53	3673* h bl
47	8-13	Brig	5.3g/f	56	3984 h bl
61	2-12	Newm	5gd	56	4197 h bl
51	9-13	Bath	5.7gd	59	4548 h bl
59	5-8	Brig	5.3sft	59	5096 h bl
65a	2-12	Ling	6ap	61	5241 h bl

TACA DOLI 5 br m £0
| 0 | 13-14 | Ling | 10ap | 52 | 757 |

TADAWUL 3 b f £5330
65	10-20	Newm	8g/f		3237
70	1-7	**EPSO**	8.5g/f		4474*
67	6-10	Leic	8gd	[75]	4702

64 8-8 Brig 9.9sft [72] 5095

TADRIS 3 b f £0
89a 8-14 Ling 10ap [103] 82

TADZIO 4 bl g £0
0 15-15 Sout 12af 89
0 11-11 Wolv 8.5af 128 VIS

TAFAAHUM 3 b c £223
29 18-20 Newm 8fm 88 1496
42 6-6 Ripo 8g/f 88 2525

TAFFRAIL 6 b g £750
100 5-6 Nott 14.1fm [86] 1005 p
43 7-7 Leic 11.8fm [80] 3816

TAG TEAM 3 ch c £15198
71a 1-9 LING 5ap 572*
81a 1-11 LING 6ap 67 735*
82a 3-8 Ling 5ap 77 818
43 14-19 Newm 6g/s 77 1154
71 5-12 Wind 5g/f 72 1809
78 1-8 BATH 5.7fm 72 1903*
76 3-9 Folk 6g/f 76 2271
84a 2-11 Ling 6ap 77 2841
62 12-15 Catt 5sft 76 5125

TAGULA BAY 2 b f £1897
71 2-12 Beve 5sft 1631
62 3-13 Redc 6g/f 1818
66 5-15 York 5g/f 2056

TAGULA BLUE 4 b g £6104
0 U-16 Newc 8hvy 80 1036 t
49 9-10 Warw 7.1sft [80] 1525 VIS
0 P-13 Ripo 8g/f 78 2010 t
54 3-9 Hayd 10.5gd [78] 2901 BL t
68 6-18 Pont 8gd 70 3242
58 5-9 Nott 8.2g/f [69] 3423
67 4-12 Newc 9hvy 67 4215
50 13-19 York 7.9g/f 67 4399 t
71 1-17 WARW 8.1g/s 64 4668* t
73 3-16 Bath 8gd 70 5022 t
69 5-16 Nott 10hvy 70 5345 t

TAGULA SUNRISE 2 ch f £47306
81 2-13 Carl 5fm 1950
86 2-12 Beve 5g/f 2165
86 2-5 Pont 5g/f 2789
75 15-24 Newb 5.2g/f 3266
81 3-18 Newc 6g/s [85] 3699
76 2-10 Redc 5fm [82] 4338
79 1-2 DONC 6fm [81] 4490*
88 1-15 HAYD 6sft 77 4765*

TAHIRAH 4 b f £9900
74 11-12 Sali 6fm 89 2289
78 7-11 Newm 7g/f 89 2532
77 8-21 Asco 7g/f 86 3441
17 20-20 Newm 7g/f 85 3782
89 8-12 Bath 8g/f [85] 3965
95 8-15 Donc 7fm [83] 4479
99 3-12 Asco 7g/f [85] 4811
45 12-12 Newm 7sft [85] 5134
95a 2-12 Ling 8ap [92] 5298

TAHLAL 2 b c £0
62 5-10 Carl 5g/f 3227
46 11-16 Thir 6g/s 4205
63 8-17 Warw 7.1gd 4271
62 4-10 Newc 7fm [63] 4864
34a 11-11 Ling 8ap [61] 5236 P

TAHREEB 3 ch c £56286
106 4-11 Newm 7gd 108 1167
108 2-5 Newm 10g/f [108] 1482
112 1-8 KEMP 8fm [108] 2069*
111 1-11 DORT 9.3gd [108] 2637*
113 4-15 Sand 8.1g/s 108 2915
112 3-14 Colo 8gd [108] 3664

TAHRIR 2 gr f £4792
90 2-7 Kemp 7g/f 4359
87 3-4 Newb 7g/f 4641

TAHTHEEB 3 b f £17406
78 1-14 NEWB 9fm 3631*
105 2-10 Sali 9.9g/f 3866

100 4-10 Newm 10gd [100] 5086

TAILI 3 b f £0
0 8-7 Muss 8fm 2081
0 6-6 Catt 12g/f [30] 4441
0 9-10 Muss 12g/s [30] 5145 BL

TAIPAN TOMMY 2 ch c £0
55 6-7 Folk 5sft 1574
37 6-7 Leic 6g/f 1964
52 8-10 Leic 6gd 2703
60 6-8 Kemp 5g/f 2858
48 6-6 Brig 6g/f 3171

TAIYO 3 b f £2908
51a 7-15 Ling 7ap 55 50
41a 15-16 Ling 7ap 54 144
52a 6-14 Ling 7ap 52 344
50a 5-12 Ling 8ap 52 406
51a 4-7 Wolv 9.4af [50] 561
46a 4-9 Wolv 9.4af 50 647
18a 9-10 Wolv 8.5af 50 754 VIS
32a 11-12 Ling 8ap 47 1045
0 P-18 Nott 8.2gd [45] 1992
8 18-20 Yarm 8fm 45 2149
49 1-11 YARM 8g/f 42 3706*
48 5-20 Yarm 8gd 46 3996
41 6-16 Yarm 7g/f 46 4616
32a 8-14 Ling 7ap [49] 4660

TAJ INDIA 2 b c £0
74 5-8 Asco 6g/f 3438
70 8-13 Warw 7.1g/f 4416

TAJAATHUB 2 ch f £439
78 4-19 Leic 7gd 5040

TAKE A BOW 3 b c £66706
92 1-14 WIND 8.3g/s 2622*
97 1-9 SALI 8g/s 84 3112*
91 4-17 Good 7fm 90 3550
104 1-12 SAND 7.1g/f 90 3860+
102 2-15 York 7.9g/s 93 4061
105 2-7 Sand 8.1gd 98 4499
108 2-32 Newm 8g/s 98 4916
108 3-11 Newm 8g/s [102] 5283

TAKE GOOD TIME 4 ch g £0
46 4-10 Newc 5sft 1682

TAKE IT THERE 2 ch f £0
69 9-16 Kemp 7g/f 3035
68 10-13 Newb 7g/f 3252

TAKEMETOYOURHEART 2 ch f £0
23a 12-12 Ling 6ap 4179
0 11-12 Wind 8.3g/f 4829

TAKES TUTU 5 b g £8759
78 9-10 Warw 7.1gd [83] 1126
53 15-17 Thir 8g/s 80 1475 vis
70 7-19 Ripo 10g/f 76 1781
78 2-9 Muss 8fm [73] 2087 bl
76 2-8 Hami 9.2gd 73 2179 bl
77 5-11 Hami 8.3g/f 77 2317 P
79 5-17 Carl 7.9gd 74 2672 p
57 17-18 Catt 7g/f 74 2848 bl
81 2-11 Leic 7g/f 74 3210 bl
44 20-25 Asco 7g/f 76 3443 bl
43 20-21 Good 8fm 74 3565 bl
79 3-15 Brig 8fm 76 3694 bl
58 5-8 Muss 9g/f [76] 4173 vis
70 7-13 Epso 8.5gd 76 4469 vis
79a 4-14 Ling 7ap [76] 5080 vis

TAKHLEED 2 b c £457
76a 5-8 Ling 7ap 4176
76 5-5 Newb 8g/f 4640

TAKHMIN 2 b c £2312
52 9-14 Redc 6fm 2297
80 2-13 Thir 6g/s 2689
86 3-6 Asco 7gd 3390
81 6-11 Ayr 8sft 84 4688

TAKRICE 3 b f £6207
106 2- Leop 7sft 1300

TAKS GIRL 2 ch f £0

0 13-13 Beve 5g/s 2321
19 7-7 Redc 5gd 2547
0 19-20 Hayd 6gd 2882
24 9-13 Catt 7g/f 3349

TALBOT AVENUE 6 b g £29509
66 8-14 Ches 5.1gd 82 1594
79 5-15 Hayd 5g/f 80 1917
77 5-20 York 6g/f 80 2059
80 8-20 Epso 5fm 80 2253
87 2-11 Sand 5g/s 80 2894
104 2-9 Ches 5.1g/f [80] 3100
85 7-15 York 6g/f 92 3434
102 2-5 Ches 6.1fm [92] 3636
109 8-12 York 5g/s [90] 4060
104 2-12 Leic 5g/f [99] 4454
104 2-9 Donc 5fm [99] 4481
101 7-11 Newb 5.2g/f [101] 4678
106 2-20 York 6gd 100 5001

TALCEN GWYN 2 b c £16516
73 4-9 Brig 5.3fm 2257
81 1-5 BRIG 5.3g/f 2430*
81 4-8 Ches 5.1g/f 81 3082
70 7-12 Ling 5gd 80 3284
80 4-9 Good 6fm 79 3623
76 5-6 Good 5sft 79 4187
68 9-14 Epso 5g/f 78 4471
79 4-13 Muss 5g/f 78 4551
85 1-15 RIPO 5gd 76 4784*
62 10-11 Epso 5g/f 82 4907
64 4-6 Muss 5g/s [81] 5141
71 7-8 Yarm 5.2sft 81 5253

TALE OF DUBAI 2 ch f £0
45 14-15 Newm 8fm 4723

TALE OF THE TIGER 3 ch c £0
1a 12-13 Ling 6ap 364 VIS
5a 5-6 Sout 8af 503 vis

TALK TO MOJO 7 ch g £0
15 18-22 Donc 12gd 80 918

TALLDARKNANDSOME 5 b g £0
65 12-20 York 10.4gd 76 4986 bl
42 15-24 Donc 12sft 76 5372 bl

TALLY 4 ch g £16333
36a 8-8 Wolv 7af 72 285
50a 13-14 Ling 6ap 70 407
18a 12-12 Sout 6af [67] 610
29 12-18 Bath 10.2g/s 58 1098
38 6-11 Warw 8.1hvy 56 1536
42 11-14 Muss 7.1gd 54 1794
56 3-16 Ayr 5gd 54 2029
60 1-12 NEWC 6g/f 50 2160*
59 2-18 Thir 6g/f 56 2214
0 19-20 Newb 5g/f 57 2409
39 12-19 Beve 5gd 57 2512
62 2-12 Thir 5g/f 57 2690
63 4-11 Ches 5.1g/s 56 2747
60 4-15 Beve 5sft 59 2942
69 3-12 York 5g/s 59 3073
49 16-18 Carl 5g/f 59 3228
61 7-15 Newc 6gd 66 3424
69a 1-9 SOUT 6af 59 3485*
68 4-12 Nott 5.1g/f [66] 3577
42 10-16 Wind 6gd 67 3827
58 11-19 York 6gd 67 4005
58a 6-13 Sout 6af 64 4091
60 8-17 Beve 5g/f 65 4603
47 13-20 Ripo 6gd 64 4785
28a 10-12 Wolv 6ap 64 4984
29 17-19 York 5gd 61 4989

TALWANDI 3 b c £4334
58 6-15 Leic 10g/s 1358
80 3-10 Yarm 11.5g/f 1725
83 1-7 BRIG 11.9g/f 1939*

TAMALAIN 2 b f £426
78 5-16 Sali 7gd 4330
83 1-5 Newm 8fm 4723

TAMARELLA 3 b f £0
10a 11-11 Sout 6af 59 91
15a 13-14 Ling 6ap 59 121

41a 9-13 Ling 6ap 54 451
45a 7-13 Ling 6ap 49 740
34a 8-13 Ling 6ap 49 767
17 5-5 Muss 5g/f 59 1096
30 12-13 Newc 5gd 56 1873
52 7-15 Ling 5g/f 52 2062 VIS
31 11-15 Leic 6g/f 51 2398 vis
38 8-20 Nott 6.1g/f 49 2630 vis
48 5-17 Bath 5g/f 47 2981 BL
12 9-9 Brig 5.3fm 47 3673 bl
0 14-16 Folk 6g/f [46] 4370
6 17-20 Yarm 6g/s [45] 5121 bl
22a 11-13 Wolv 5.1ap [45] 5231 vis

TAMARILLO 3 gr f £0
98 5-11 San 11gd [90] 1999
67 9-10 Asco 16.2g/f [99] 2557
62 10-10 Chep 10.2g/s [99] 3089

TAMARINA 2 ch f £0
15a 12-14 Sout 8af 95
44a 8-11 Sout 8af 159
52a 4-9 Wolv 9.4af [50] 240
34a 7-11 Wolv 9.4af [55] 438 P
0 15-15 Sout 7af [55] 462 BL
14a 14-15 Ling 12ap [55] 521 p
0 10-10 Beve 9.9gd 50 2510
6 12-14 Leic 8g/f [45] 3344 p
35 5-11 Chep 10.2gd [38] 3730 bl
17 5-7 Brig 9.9sft [38] 4142 bl
18 11-18 Chep 8.1gd [35] 4485 bl

TAMATAVE 2 b c £2201
64 6-11 Newm 8gd 3925 T
82 4-12 Good 8g/f 4522 t
88 2-12 Newc 8fm 4866 t
77 4-11 Bath 8sft [85] 5171 t

TAMINOULA 3 b f £0
71 7-12 Good 9fm 80 3535
43 7-8 Good 8sft 80 4265
75 6-13 Sand 8.1gd 77 4607
65 13-17 Asco 8g/f 77 4777
63 12-17 Wind 10g/f 74 5050
68a 8-13 Wolv 9.5ap 74 5161 BL

TAMORA 2 ch f £420
63 6-8 Asco 6gd 3071
26 14-14 Newb 6fm 3626
67 8-9 Beve 7.5g/f 4600
65a 3-13 Wolv 8.6ap [65] 4979
41 14-19 Pont 8g/s 65 5147

TANAFFUS 4 ch g £0
26a 12-14 Ling 6ap [70] 449
0 10-10 Sout 8af 60 677
20a 12-13 Sout 7af [60] 858
7 13-13 Sout 6g/s 52 1052
0 17-17 Ripo 6g/s 47 3262 BL

TANAJI 5 b m £0
56a 14-14 Ling 10ap 78 452

TANCRED ARMS 8 b m £312
33 13-18 Catt 7gd [45] 996
34 4-8 Ayr 7.2g/s [45] 1448
17 9-9 Ayr 7.2gd 40 2508
0 12-15 Newc 7gd [38] 3426
44 4-17 Newc 7g/s 35 3700 vis
28 8-17 Pont 8g/f 40 4626 vis

TANCRED IMP 3 b f £1169
16 8-16 Redc 8sft 45 1147
29 5-11 Newc 8sft 45 1395
42 3-8 Hami 9.2gd [45] 1505
21 12-15 Ripo 12.3g/f 45 1785
9 10-10 Beve 12.1g/f 41 3499
45 3-12 Ripo 10gd 40 4282
26 9-13 Warw 10.9g/f 40 4419

TANCRED MISS 5 b m £3409
42a 1-15 SOUT 7af 35 2384*
23 8-9 Ayr 7.2gd 44 2508
39a 3-9 Sout 8af 40 2996
32 11-17 Newc 7g/s 42 3700
11 9-12 Newc 8sft [40] 4284

TANCRED TIMES 9 ch m £14037
32a 11-16 Sout 5ap 52 1046

59 4-10 Hami 6gd 57 1391
54 4-15 Hami 6gd 57 1508
52 8-13 Newc 5gd 56 1873
55 3-11 Hami 6g/f 55 2477
58 3-6 Hami 5gd 55 2712
51 1-14 CATT 6g/f [55] 3191+
64 4-14 Catt 6g/f 61 3352
60 1-7 YORK 6g/f [55] 3436*
64 3-9 Yarm 6g/f 61 3705
66 2-17 Wind 6gd 61 4126
59 8-20 Nott 6.1g/s 64 4646

TANDAVA 6 ch g £4365
72 1-10 MUSS 14g/f 70 1118*
58 10-10 Hami 13gd 73 1506
72 5-12 Muss 14fm 72 2085 P
73 4-9 Hami 13gd 72 2176 p
62 9-13 Newc 16.1sft 70 2685 p
66 5-10 Hami 13fm 70 3249 p

TANGA DANCER 3 ch f £0
31a 11-13 Wolv 9.4af 50 38
15a 12-14 Sout 8af 47 165

TANGIBLE 2 b f £0
59 7-13 Brig 8sft 5091
63a 5-14 Ling 7ap 5257
40a 10-13 Wolv 8.6ap 5355

TANGO STEP 3 b c £0
32a 7-12 Wolv 7af 54 68

TANIA DI SCEPTRE 4 b f £0
0 13-13 Wolv 16.5ap 51 5366 P

TANK 3 ch g £0
28 7-10 Good 9.9gd 4877

TANMEYA 3 gr f £0
51 12-14 Kemp 10g/s 2678

TANNE BLIXEN 3 b f £0
0 9-9 Sout 6af 3396
31 12-14 Warw 7.1gd 4275
6 11-11 Wind 6g/f 4836
29a 9-12 Wolv 6ap 5162

TANNING 2 b f £1153
61 6-12 Chep 5.1gd 3728
66 2-11 Bath 5g/f 3962
66 3-15 Folk 6g/f 4369
54 14-17 Ling 7g/f 65 4894

TANNOOR 3 b c £6674
80 3-10 Kemp 11.1gd [80] 1140
79 1-6 AYR 10g/f [77] 1894*
75 5-12 Pont 10g/f 80 2277
61 10-12 Kemp 9g/f 78 2860
44 6-7 Folk 9.7gd 77 3384
69 4-11 Newm 8gd [75] 3923 P

TANTE ROSE 4 b f £176900
104 1-11 HAYD 6gd [107] 2240+
116 1-9 YORK 6g/s [107] 3075*
120 1-19 HAYD 6fm [111] 4384+

TANTIEN 2 b f £591
46 5-8 Hayd 5g/s 1343
56 4-10 Newc 6sft 1677
68 9-12 Beve 5g/f 2165
54 5-7 Pont 6g/f 2792
26 20-20 Redc 7fm 65 4337
12 13-14 Yarm 7g/s 60 4583

TANTRIC 5 br g £2927
45a 9-12 Wolv 7af 66 704
19a 10-10 Wolv 7af 63 864
56 3-14 Redc 7g/f [60] 2102
53 8-10 Carl 6.9gd 58 2935
49 9-12 Catt 7g/f [58] 3017
61 3-7 Pont 6gd [58] 3244
59 3-18 Pont 5gd 55 3463
58 4-18 Beve 6g/f 58 3852
59 3-10 Hami 5g/s [58] 4010

TANZANI 2 b f £364
72 4-6 Yarm 6g/f 2851
79 7-8 Newb 6g/f 3254

TANZANITE 2 b f £1036

35 11-11 Newb 6gd 3915
38 6-10 Nott 6.1gd 4858
76 3-16 Newb 8hvy 5220

TAP 6 b g £6076
17a 14-16 Sout 7af [53] 66
7a 11-13 Sout 8af [51] 188
58 1-13 MUSS 7.1g/s 50 1463* P
60 1-15 THIR 7gd 54 1635* p
58 5-12 Catt 7g/f [58] 3017 p
44 11-14 Beve 7.5g/s 58 4241 p

TAP DANCE CITY 7 b h £0
97 17-19 Long 12g/f 4956

TAP DANCER 6 b g £0
26a 9-12 Ling 8ap [40] 4659
21 9-19 Brig 9.9gd [35] 4903

TAPA 2 b f £0
64 6-10 Good 6gd 4876
41 21-29 Newm 6gd 5087

TAPAU 6 b m £0
54 5-8 Folk 5g/s [73] 1269
43 9-10 Donc 6g/f 71 1878
46 10-18 Thir 6g/f 69 2214
44 14-17 Wind 6g/f 66 2451
37 13-18 Donc 7gd 62 2755 P
58 8-12 Yarm 7fm 62 2864 p
21 20-20 Chep 7.1g/s 59 3088 p

TAPLEON 3 br f £0
34 6-9 Redc 5sft 1146
0 9-9 Ayr 6g/s [40] 1447
3a 10-10 Sout 7af [40] 1842

TAPPIT 5 b g £1938
27 15-15 Folk 6sft 69 976
31 15-16 Bath 5.7g/s [69] 1103
46 11-15 Brig 5.3g/f 64 1371 P
23 11-13 Warw 7.1hvy [64] 1537 p
56 3-14 Leic 6g/f [57] 1963 p
46 9-10 Newc 5g/f [57] 2161 BL
39 5-11 Bath 5.7fm [54] 2412 p
39 16-17 Bath 5g/f 52 2981
38 12-16 Ling 6g/f 49 3602
5 15-15 Ling 6fm 46 3790
28 6-15 Sali 6gd 46 3888
37 13-15 Chep 5.1gd 45 4489 bl
29 5-15 Brig 6gd [45] 4905
49 1-20 YARM 6g/s [45] 5121*
52 5-19 Bath 5.7sft 51 5176
39a 6-13 Wolv 6ap [48] 5211

TARA TARA 2 b f £4362
84 1-9 NEWC 5sft 962*
78 8-9 Ches 5.1gd 1567
69 15-17 Asco 5g/f 2490
59 10-11 Nott 5.1gd 80 3987

TARABUT 2 b f £0
58 8-12 Warw 7.1g/f 4417
64 7-19 Leic 7gd 5040

TARAGAN 2 b f £0
53 7-14 Hayd 6sft 4769
19 9-10 Catt 7sft 5317

TARAKALA 2 ch f £33965
103 2- Leop 9gd 10
103 1-9 YORK 11.9g/s 4058* bl
100 4-10 Donc 14.6fm 4460 bl

TARANAI 2 ch f £0
45a 9-13 Ling 7ap 57 15
54a 6-9 Ling 6ap 57 105
53a 4-15 Ling 7ap 55 295
23a 11-11 Ling 10ap 54 497
41a 12-12 Ling 7ap 51 729
40a 7-9 Ling 8ap 51 763
33 12-14 Warw 7.1sft 48 1085 BL
42 4-7 Brig 7gd [45] 1549
32 6-9 Kemp 6hvy [45] 1641

TARANAKI 5 b h £21602
75a 1-11 LING 6ap [70] 130*
70a 8-14 Ling 6ap 75 292
78 4-13 Kemp 7sft 79 945

86	1-17	LEIC	7g/s	79	1020*
80	4-20	Kemp	6gd	83	1138
75	8-14	Ling	7sft	83	1624
91	1-16	GOOD	7g/f	82	1817*
88	5-11	Newm	7fm	88	2090
83	8-13	Asco	7gd	88	3068
55	15-21	Asco	7gd	88	3441
52a	12-13	Ling	7ap	75	3791
89	3-16	Newb	9g/f	86	3954
73	6-8	Good	7g/s	87	4231
71a	5-14	Ling	7ap	75	4446
16	19-19	Sali	6gd	85	4855
87	4-16	Good	7gd	85	4873
73	10-16	Newm	7sft	84	5101

TARANDOT 3 b f £4895

88	2-11	Beve	9.9g/f		1835
87	1-6	YORK	11.9g/f		2058*
84	7-10	Asco	16.2g/f	[87]	2557
48	9-11	Newm	10g/f	87	3029

TARAS TREASURE 2 b f £5386

72	2-13	Redc	6g/f		1818
71	6-12	Redc	6g/f		2119
74	4-10	Pont	6g/f		2610
75	3-10	Catt	7g/f		2845
67	5-9	Redc	6g/f	73	3807
74	1-13	THIR	6g/f	[71]	4590*
68	5-14	Donc	7sft	72	5213

TARAWAN 8 ch g £0

35	14-18	Ayr	10.9sft	70	4623 vis
0	17-18	Sali	9.9gd	67	4850 vis

TARDIS 3 ch f £0

39	7-8	Brig	9.9g/f	64	2046
15	8-10	Yarm	8g/f	64	2344
34	8-11	Leic	10g/f	[61]	2924
21	11-14	Yarm	8gd	55	3363
41	6-10	Yarm	8g/f	49	3712
19	10-15	Yarm	7g/s	[45]	4587
30	7-20	Yarm	7g/s	[40]	5120 VIS

TARFAH 3 b f £33087

85	1-7	ASCO	8gd		3469+
97	1-7	WIND	8.3gd	[82]	3826*
90	2-10	Ches	10.3sft	85	4071
100	1-13	ASCO	8g/f	90	4802*

TARJMAN 4 b c £800

99	7-9	Wind	8.3fm	[111]	2757
101	5-5	Newm	8g/f	[111]	3613

TARKEEZ 3 b c £0

36a	8-10	Sout	8af	[70]	4042

TARKWA 4 gr f £1435

0	8-12	Wolv	12af	44	75
36a	6-9	Wolv	9.4af	[45]	314
0	13-13	Ling	10ap	[45]	412
43a	1-5	LING	8ap	[40]	1711*
22	7-10	Beve	9.9g/f	[45]	1946
37	7-16	Good	9gd	44	2220
36	5-8	Brig	8g/f	40	2432

TAROT CARD 3 b f £0

76	9-9	Donc	8fm	[104]	4495

TARRAMAN 2 b c £1666

85	2-11	York	7.9gd		5003

TARTAN SPECIAL 2 b c £419

63	4-7	Ayr	6gd		3148
73	6-9	York	6g/s		4026
59	5-14	Warw	6.1g/f		4422

TARTATARTUFATA 2 b f £1609

0	13-15	Beve	5g/s		1161
64	4-9	Pont	5sft		1424
56a	9-10	Ling	5ap		3743
54	8-11	Nott	5.1gd	60	3987
66a	2-15	Sout	5af	[60]	4089
30	8-10	Beve	5sft	65	4258
21	18-21	Donc	6hvy		5202

TARTIRUGA 3 b g £957

40	13-14	Sali	7fm		2291
0	13-13	Sali	9.9gd		2700
7	11-12	Chep	12.1g/s	47	3085

66	8-17	Wind	8.3fm	[45]	3480
33	5-18	Chep	7.1g/s	45	3900
51	6-10	Warw	8.1g/f	[45]	4421
48	2-12	Chep	10.2hvy	45	4708
46	4-19	Brig	9.9gd	[49]	4903

TARTOUCHE 3 b f £35189

92	1-14	KEMP	10g/s		2678*
94	1-6	ASCO	10gd	87	3072*
96	1-13	DONC	10.3fm	[89]	4463*
96	2-7	Hayd	10.5sft	91	4781

TARUSKIN 3 b g £9313

90	3-20	Newm	7g/f	82	1186
88	1-5	BRIG	8g/f	84	1370*
83	3-11	Sali	6g/s	87	1498
77	11-17	Epso	7g/f	86	2212
70	12-16	Newm	8g/f	85	3059
69	11-12	Good	8gd	[84]	4872

TASDEED 2 ch c £3543

97	1-13	DONC	7hvy		5200*

TASHKIL 3 b c £372

54	14-15	Asco	6g/f	[106]	2486
84	5-8	Donc	6g/f	[103]	3596
91	7-8	Ches	7sft	98	4073 T

TASHREEFAT 3 b f £2687

70	3-7	Newm	10g/f		2534
70	4-13	Kemp	10gd		3186
65	2-10	Bath	11.7g/f		4414
54	4-11	Good	14gd	[68]	5029 T

TASHYRA 2 b f £0

68	4-13	Bath	5.7g/f		3368
64	4-8	Chep	5.1g/s		3896
52	11-15	Kemp	6g/f		4357
36	11-12	Bath	5.7gd	64	4545

TASKS MUPPET 2 ch f £323

66	5-13	Bath	5.7g/f		3368
62	5-8	Chep	5.1g/s		3896
51	5-15	Folk	6g/f		4369
35	10-12	Bath	5.7gd	61	4545
58	4-16	Nott	5.1hvy	57	5343

TASNEEF 5 b g £0

44	8-11	Pont	12g/f	63	2041
51	6-11	Warw	12.6fm	60	2601
51	6-10	Newb	11g/f	60	2875
48	8-15	Wind	11.6fm	57	3481 bl
49	4-13	Warw	12.6g/s	[50]	4665 bl
50	4-20	Kemp	12g/f	[49]	4796
38	5-15	Yarm	10.1g/s	[48]	5122

TASS HEEL 5 b g £0

14	13-14	Epso	12gd	54	4910

TATA NAKA 3 ch f £12686

53a	5-14	Ling	10ap		53
39a	7-11	Wolv	9.4af		115
32a	9-14	Ling	10ap	50	757
22	18-20	Donc	7g/s	[46]	1518
18	5-5	Yarm	7g/f	[45]	1731
28	11-11	Newm	6fm	40	2093 VIS
22a	10-16	Sout	8af	40	2805 T P
46	2-11	Yarm	10.1gd	[37]	3362
46	2-14	Yarm	11.5g/f	43	3714
45	3-8	Brig	11.9sft	43	4143
44	4-15	Folk	12g/f	[45]	4374
71	1-13	YARM	10.1gd	45	4613*
37	7-12	Pont	10fm	[45]	4757
74	10-10	Newm	10gd	[68]	5086
55	8-11	Yarm	10.1g/s	68	5353

TATWEER 3 b g £4358

54a	5-14	Ling	6ap		23 vis
50a	5-16	Sout	6af	[60]	65 vis
50a	5-16	Sout	6af	58	94 vis
34a	13-15	Ling	7ap	55	151 vis
27a	11-13	Ling	6ap	[52]	219 vis
37a	10-12	Wolv	5af	[52]	242 vis
45	5-15	Folk	6g/s	49	1267 vis
59	1-10	NEWC	5sft	[47]	1682* vis
27	12-13	Pont	6g/f	[60]	2279 vis
43	9-14	Newc	5g/s	58	2775 vis
27	10-10	Epso	6g/s	56	3045 vis
34	8-10	Nott	8.2g/f	53	3579 vis

16	18-19	Chep	12.1gd	53	3727 vis
53	2-12	Hami	8.3g/s	[48]	4007 vis
44a	5-15	Sout	8af	48	4132 BL e

TAVALU 2 b c £0

54	6-7	Ches	7g/f		4511
24	11-14	Sali	8gd		4852

TAWNY WAY 4 b f £27990

76	5-10	Hayd	10.5sft	[84]	1104
85	1-13	WIND	10gd	[82]	1381*
92	2-10	Sali	12g/f	83	1721
75	6-9	Ayr	13.1g/s	86	2567
87	7-9	Newm	12g/f	[86]	3278
93	1-8	NEWM	12g/f	[86]	3617*
93	1-9	NEWM	12g/f	87	3926*
74	11-14	Asco	12g/f	91	4814
70	9-19	Newm	12gd	91	5085

TAWOOS 5 b m £0

43	13-14	Donc	10.3sft		5370 BL

TAWQEET 2 ch c £6390

60	14-21	Newm	8sft		5097
78	1-15	NOTT	8.2hvy		5344*

TAXMAN 2 ch c £279

58	12-14	Yarm	7sft		5250
65a	4-13	Wolv	8.6ap		5355

TAYIF 7 gr g £13675

36a	9-16	Sout	7af	[58]	66
57a	3-13	Ling	6ap	[52]	271 t
60a	2-14	Ling	6ap	52	328 t
64a	1-13	LING	6ap	[52]	340+ t
67a	1-14	LING	6ap	61	407* t
68a	2-13	Ling	6ap	65	448 t
60a	6-12	Ling	6ap	66	628 t
66a	7-15	Ling	7ap	66	698 t
68a	2-13	Ling	7ap	65	902 t
35a	14-14	Ling	6ap	65	1025 t
57	5-20	Wind	6g/s	62	1255 t
66	3-11	Folk	6sft	59	1578 t
73	1-18	THIR	6g/f	59	2214* t
53a	7-13	Wolv	6ap	[65]	5327 t

TBM CAN 5 b g £0

60	6-10	Muss	14g/f	65	1118
61	5-10	Hami	13gd	65	1506
57	5-10	Muss	12gd	62	1796

TCHERINA 2 b f £7568

59	7-9	Ripo	6g/f		2522
60	7-8	Donc	6gd		2750
78	2-7	Catt	7g/f		3665
78	3-12	Beve	8.5sft	[73]	4257
68	11-17	Donc	8fm	73	4480
76	1-8	HAYD	8.1sft	[73]	4782*

TE ANAU 7 b m £0

9a	7-8	Sout	8af	[30]	635
23a	6-10	Sout	8af	30	677
24a	6-7	Ling	10ap	[30]	1244
0	8-9	Sout	11af	[30]	1838

TE QUIERO GB 5 gr g £12850

87a	5-13	Wolv	8.5af	93	44 t
95a	2-12	Sout	8af	92	141 t
94a	3-8	Sout	12af	94	225 t
54a	9-10	Wolv	9.4af	94	278 t
77a	9-16	Sout	7af	93	419 t
68a	8-16	Ling	12ap	92	475 t
55a	11-13	Ling	10ap	90	519 t
96a	2-12	Wolv	8.5af	88	688 e t
103a	2-12	Wolv	8.5af	93	836 e t
75	7-13	Wind	8.3g/s	[82]	1057 t P
76	7-12	Jage	8.6aw	[82]	1697 t
68	7-9	Newm	10gd	[80]	1890 t
68	7-13	Newb	8fm	75	2647 t
47	12-13	Asco	7gd	72	3068 e t
52	11-12	Newm	6g/f	68	3942 t
95a	12-14	Ling	7ap	100	5262 e t

TEA FOR TEXAS 7 ch m £0

0	11-11	Wolv	6af	[30]	1261

TEAM MATE 6 b g £209

69a	8-10	Ling	12ap	78	570
77	5-7	Newm	12g/f	78	2737

73 5-15 Newm 12g/f 76 3066

TEAM PLAYER 3 b c £0
65 8-12 York 7.9g/f 2410

TEAM TACTICS 3 b f £0
31 10-10 Ling 11.5gd 59 3334
35a 11-14 Ling 7ap 55 3746

TECHNICIAN 9 ch g £0
11a 5-6 Ling 6ap [40] 1184 bl

TEDBURROW 12 b g £2943
74 5-8 Beve 5sft [95] 1626
79 3-12 Hayd 6g/s [90] 2186
92 4-8 Donc 6g/f [88] 3596

TEDSDALE MAC 5 ch g £19819
44 8-18 Donc 7g/f 52 2080 p
51 4-16 Carl 5.9fm 50 2445
56 2-16 Beve 7.5gd 50 2655
49 5-12 Beve 8.5gd 50 2890
61 2-10 York 7.9g/s 53 3074
59 3-9 Ripo 10g/s 57 3260
62 2-10 Beve 8.5g/f 57 3501
62 2-15 Donc 10.3g/f 57 3598
60 5-12 Beve 12.1sft 59 4259
60 2-19 York 7.9g/f 59 4399
45 10-14 Catt 12g/f 60 4672
45 11-26 Redc 8fm 59 4926
66 1-18 NEWC 8g/f [57] 5017*
52 8-19 Pont 10g/s 63 5148
64 4-10 Donc 10.3sft 63 5206

TEDSTALE 6 ch g £6763
76 16-20 Newm 7g/s 85 1151
65 12-17 Thir 8g/f 84 1475
75 5-14 Donc 8g/f [82] 1877 bl
66 15-15 York 8.9g/f 80 2404 bl
86 3-17 Carl 7.9gd 80 2672 bl
77 6-12 Beve 8.5gd 80 2890 bl
81 4-6 Hami 8.3g/f [81] 3205 bl
76 5-10 Beve 8.5g/f 80 3501
79 3-16 Redc 8g/f 78 3768 bl
72 9-16 Nott 8.2g/s 78 4036 bl
79 4-14 Ripo 10gd 78 4305 bl
63 8-11 Muss 9g/f [77] 4550 bl
62 12-20 York 8.9gd 77 4999 bl

TEDZAR 3 b g £0
21a 10-12 Wolv 8.5af [35] 47 bl
25a 8-11 Ling 8ap [35] 408

TEE JAY KASSIDY 4 b g £3359
38a 1-12 SOUT 7af [35] 909*
36a 2-5 Wolv 8.5af [40] 1264
13 5-7 Chep 7.1sft [40] 1335
41a 2-7 Sout 7af [40] 1590
0 13-17 Kemp 7hvy [40] 1642
22a 4-8 Sout 8af [40] 1841
41 2-16 Brig 7fm 35 2258
34 5-11 Brig 7fm 35 2334
36 7-11 Brig 7g/f 40 2644

TEEBA 2 ch f £544
80 4-23 Newm 6gd 5084

TEEHEE 5 b g £1530
63a 5-10 Wolv 7af [70] 152 bl
45a 7-8 Wolv 7af 70 280 bl
56a 4-9 Wolv 7af 68 629 bl
49a 6-8 Sout 7af 66 1195 bl
18a 11-13 Wolv 6af 64 2053 bl
44a 7-15 Sout 8af 64 2338 bl
63a 2-12 Sout 7af [61] 2496 bl
62a 3-15 Sout 7af [60] 2999 bl
59a 4-13 Sout 7af 60 3155 bl
32 12-19 Chep 8.1g/s [58] 4366 bl

TEFI 5 ch g £371
13a 11-15 Sout 6af [43] 172 bl
0 9-9 Sout 7af [41] 304 bl
37a 3-4 Wolv 7af [45] 350 bl t
33a 5-8 Sout 7af [45] 373 bl t

TELEFONICA 3 b f £1267
67 4-13 Newm 8g/f 1935
52 11-12 Newm 7g/f 77 2249
72a 2-10 Sout 8af [74] 2997

TELEGRAM SAM 2 b c £0
51 9-13 York 6gd 4988
52 11-14 Redc 7sft 5301

TELEMACHUS 4 b g £23319
73 6-10 Hayd 10.5g/s 88 1346
90 1-20 DONC 10.3g/s 86 1519*
69 10-14 Donc 10.4g/s 89 1704
86 10-15 Redc 10g/f 90 2101
76 8-13 Redc 10gd 89 2560
83 8-13 York 11.9g/f 87 3076
75 14-15 Good 9.9g/f 86 3506 BL
70 14-20 Hayd 10.5fm 83 3794 bl
89 1-14 SAND 10g/s 80 4097* bl
85 5-14 Ripo 10gd 85 4305 bl
83 8-18 Newb 10gd 85 4681 bl

TELEPATHIC 3 b g £1377
30a 13-14 Ling 6ap 69 149
27a 10-10 Wolv 6af 66 345
46a 7-10 Wolv 5af 62 749
35a 7-8 Wolv 5af [56] 1218
61 6-15 Hami 6gd 66 1508
48 7-12 Hami 6g/s [66] 1600 BL
42 10-11 Hayd 5g/f 64 1886
57 9-12 Hayd 6g/s [62] 2186
55 4-4 Warw 7.1fm [59] 2438
63 6-12 Ayr 8g/s [59] 2543
68 9-11 Warw 7.1fm [57] 2777
92 5-6 Ches 7g/f [57] 3098
57 6-6 Ayr 8gd [57] 3152
58 5-6 Hami 8.3g/f [57] 3205
43 4-7 Ayr 7.2gd [57] 3326 T
6 11-11 Donc 6g/f [57] 3375 t
58 7-8 Donc 6g/f [57] 3596
56 8-11 Hayd 6gd [55] 3758
56 5-8 Hami 6g/s [55] 3880
38 13-18 Pont 5g/s [57] 3974
39 8-13 Muss 5g/s [52] 5146

TELL THE TREES 3 br f £2863
56 7-8 Ling 9g/f 2013
52 5-14 Bath 10.2fm 53 2664
51 5-20 Beve 16.2gd 52 3312
62 1-8 CATT 15.8g/f [48] 3666*

TEMPER TANTRUM 5 b g £6457
57a 8-15 Ling 7ap 62 50 p
65a 2-15 Ling 7ap 61 151 p
63a 3-16 Ling 7ap 63 270 p
62a 5-16 Ling 7ap 63 323 p
60a 5-14 Ling 7ap 62 499 p
69a 2-14 Ling 6ap [62] 516 p
58a 13-15 Ling 7ap 63 698 p
62 4-10 Brig 7g/f 60 1941 p
38 12-12 Kemp 7g/s 60 2679 p
60 5-10 Epso 7g/f 60 2872 p
57 4-7 Brig 8g/f 58 3174 p
51 6-10 Brig 7sft 57 4168 p
56 5-20 Chep 7.1gd 56 4488 p
47 8-16 Yarm 7gd 55 4616 p
57a 3-13 Wolv 8.6ap 54 4982 p
64a 1-13 WOLV 8.6ap [54] 5184* p
61a 3-13 Wolv 8.6ap 58 5365 p

TEMPESTAD 2 b f £1503
79 3-19 Leic 7gd 5040
90 5-8 Newm 8g/s 5282

TEMPLE BELLE XPRES 2 b f £0
37 12-15 Nott 6.1g/s 4644
25 10-13 Nott 6.1g/f 4843

TEMPLE OF ARTEMIS 4 b c £0
18a 13-16 Sout 16af 60 206

TEMPLE PLACE 3 b c £10450
100 3-7 Newm 9g/f [91] 1189
100 3-6 Ches 12.3gd[100] 1584

TEMPLET 4 b c £10465
71 2-8 Newc 12.4hvy 1038
63 3-8 Hami 11.1gd 1390
48 4-6 Hami 11.1gd [70] 2180
68 5-16 Donc 10.3gd [68] 2751 VIS
68 3-7 Wolv 10.9gd 65 3149 BL
25 13-13 Ayr 10gd 65 3325 bl

38 10-12 Hayd 11.9gd 64 3734
69 2-5 Hami 9.2g/s [64] 3876 bl
70 1-10 HAMI 9.2g/s [60] 4135* bl
69 4-15 Carl 7.9g/f 66 4346
59 11-19 Hayd 10.5g/s 72 4766 bl
70a 4-12 Wolv 7.1ap 70 5289 bl

TEMPSFORD 4 b c £14100
58a 5-9 Sout 12af 89 856
38 17-18 York 13.9g/s 88 1689
90 5-16 Asco 16.2g/f 86 4803
15 31-34 Newm 18sft 86 5135
98 1-13 DONC 12sft 86 5215*
65 13-24 Donc 12sft 92 5372

TEMPTATION ISLAND 5 b m £0
12a 10-10 Wolv 8.5af 45 754
0 13-13 Sout 8af [45] 776

TEN CARAT 4 ch c £1564
95 3-12 Newm 16.1g/f 91 3032
75 13-19 Good 21fm 95 3531
87 9-17 Newm 14.8gd 95 4196

TEN CENTS 2 b f £1209
57 4-6 Wind 6g/s 4217
78 4-13 Kemp 6g/f 4358
70 4-17 Yarm 6gd 4610

TEN PAST SIX 12 ch g £0
0 13-14 Sout 12af [23] 305 bl e

TENDER 3 b f £4425
42a 7-16 Ling 7ap [60] 123
56 3-5 Muss 5g/f 58 1096
45 5-18 Wind 6g/f [57] 1806
76 7-7 Asco 7g/f [57] 1925
44 8-10 Brig 5.3g/f 57 2044
50 5-16 Brig 6fm 55 2262
46 8-18 Ling 6gd 55 2396 P
48 7-20 Nott 6.1g/f 53 2630 p
2 15-17 Wind 6fm 51 2975 VIS
48 4-11 Warw 5.5gd 51 3054 p
56a 1-10 LING 5ap 49 3332* p
34 13-16 Wind 5fm 52 3640 p
45 7-11 Bath 5g/f 52 3849 p
47 3-11 Nott 5.1gd 48 4038 p
43 6-8 Folk 5gd 48 4118 p
54 6-12 Sand 5gd [48] 4605 p

TENDER FALCON 4 br g £35828
69 5-15 Sand 10g/f 67 2099
75 1-10 LEIC 11.8gd [67] 2707*
65 9-11 Asco 12gd 69 3070
76 2-6 Leic 11.8g/f 69 3345
83 1-15 BATH 11.7g/f 71 3964*
84 1-12 EPSO 12gd 76 4292*
84 3-14 Asco 12g/f 82 4775
72 8-24 Donc 12sft 82 5372

TENDERLIT 2 b f £33379
98 1-7 CAPA 5.5g/f 2302*
87 3-9 San 6g/f 2823

TENNYS GOLD 3 b f £5519
69 4-18 Wind 8.3g/f 1810
69 3-10 Good 8gd [70] 2378
55 5-9 Bath 10.2gd [70] 4547
64 4-17 Hayd 8.1g/s [70] 4768
66 3-9 Leic 7gd [66] 5041
68a 1-12 WOLV 7.1ap [60] 5325*
63a 7-13 Wolv 8.6ap 66 5364

TENTATIVE 3 ch f £215
76 11-14 Bath 5gd [92] 1400
75 6-6 Newm 6g/f [90] 2736

TEORBAN 5 b g £4062
46a 6-8 Wolv 16.2af 70 837
60 1-15 CHEP 16.2gd [58] 3400*
59 7-12 Sand 16.4g/f 58 3861
52 7-16 Warw 16.2gd 57 4276
53 9-15 Ches 15.9g/f 55 4512
62 2-20 Bath 17.2gd 55 4824

TEQUILA SHEILA 2 ch f £9910
56 7-16 Pont 6g/f 2275
83 1-6 HAMI 6gd 2711*
46 6-6 Hami 6fm 80 3245

87	1-12	WIND	6gd		78	3825*
61	6-7	Ches	6.1g/f	[78]		4050
70	7-14	Hami	6sft		84	4692
86	4-17	Catt	7gd		81	4963

TERDAD 11 ch g £0

23a	10-10	Sout	16af	48	491 p

TERENURE GIRL 3 br f £0

0	6-6	Yarm	6g/s		4586
26	10-10	Wind	6g/f		4835
30a	14-14	Ling	7ap		5240

TERESA 4 b f £5964

81	2-18	Kemp	16g/s	76	1112
77	6-29	Asco	20g/f	78	2471
76	7-12	Newm	16.1g/f	77	3032
60	11-19	Good	21fm	75	3531
58	7-12	Ches	15.9sft	73	4106
3	17-17	Nott	14.1g/s	71	4647
75	2-13	Newb	16sft	70	5194
45	9-11	Newm	16sft	70	5271

TERMINATE 2 ch g £0

52	11-11	Beve	7.5g/f		3500
53a	7-11	Ling	8ap		3786
70	5-9	Yarm	8sft		4147
18	14-20	Yarm	8g/f	67	4635

TERMONFECKIN 6 b g £0

28	10-11	Nott	16fm	58	1003
20	15-17	Nott	14.1gd	55	1238
34	7-7	Warw	10.9g/s	[55]	1326

TERN INTERN 5 b g £0

11a	10-12	Wolv	8.5af	[35]	777
25a	11-15	Ling	7ap	[35]	830
0	11-12	Sout	8af	[30]	905
0	15-15	Sout	8af	30	1028 bl

TERRAQUIN 4 b c £977

53a	10-12	Ling	8ap	79	369
77a	4-12	Ling	8ap	76	517
42	13-13	Kemp	7sft	79	945
41	19-20	Kemp	6gd	78	1138
66	5-18	Asco	8sft	76	1423
38	13-13	Kemp	7gd	74	2172
72	5-7	Good	7gd	[74]	2374 P
68	5-12	Kemp	7g/s	70	2679 p
67	7-13	Newb	7gd	70	2880 p
69	7-16	Kemp	9g/f	69	3039 p
13	19-19	Good	8g/f	67	3512 p
39	9-12	Sali	8g/s	65	4077
65	3-8	Folk	7gd	[65]	4117
58	6-16	Sali	8gd	63	4334 p
37	14-16	Sali	7sft	61	4582 VIS

TESARY 2 b f £8740

66	6-10	York	5g/s		1709
76	2-13	Ling	6g/f		2061
77	1-7	LING	5g/f		2738*
73	4-6	Ling	6gd	73	3022
74	3-12	Ling	5gd	75	3284
75	3-13	Warw	6.1gd	75	4273
31	13-14	Epso	6g/f	75	4471
80	2-19	Nott	6.1g/f	75	4645

TETCHY 4 b f £0

38	12-14	Warw	8.1sft		1527
22	14-14	Hayd	8.1g/s		2231

TETCOTT 3 ch f £1899

67	5-10	Sali	7gd		2659
71	10-10	Newb	7gd		3921
64	4-10	Sali	6g/s		4081
57	3-13	Warw	7.1g/s	[72]	4667
53a	10-13	Ling	10ap	68	5299

TETOU 3 ch f £2331

67a	1-14	LING	10ap		53*
54a	9-14	Ling	10ap	70	1618
56	11-14	Leic	10g/f	69	1828

TETRA SING 2 b f £0

58	7-8	Newc	7sft	4283
68	9-9	Beve	7.5g/f	4600
35	11-12	Newc	8fm	4866

TEWITFIELD LASS 2 b f £0

14	13-14	Beve	7.5sft		2939
39	5-13	Catt	7g/f		3349
30	9-11	Thir	7g/f		3570
13	11-15	Catt	7sft		3930

TEXAS GOLD 5 ch g £51605

94a	1-12	LING	6ap	[85]	106*
90a	3-13	Ling	6ap	88	235
91	2-11	Good	5g/f	87	1845
91	4-20	Epso	5fm	87	2253
48	26-29	Asco	6fm	90	2581
87	6-8	Asco	5gd	89	3123
89	6-12	Newm	5g/f	88	3279
85	12-28	Good	6fm	89	3622
90	2-14	Epso	5gd	87	4291
95	2-22	Donc	5.6fm	87	4459
100	1-9	GOOD	6g/f	89	4537*
109	4-11	Newb	5.2g/f	[89]	4678
100	4-15	Newm	5g/f	[106]	4879
53	11-12	Donc	6sft	[104]	5371

TEXT 3 b g £1491

42	7-13	Warw	8.1gd	63	3058
77	2-10	Ling	7gd	[60]	3446
74	3-5	Good	7gd	[65]	3953
44	5-9	Good	6sft	[65]	4262
66	6-15	Ling	7gd	[65]	4445
53	9-15	Bath	8gd	65	4827 VIS
49a	10-12	Wolv	8.6ap	68	4923 P

TEYAAR 7 b g £1116

55a	11-16	Ling	7ap	65	20
31a	10-14	Ling	6ap	64	121
61a	3-10	Ling	5ap	62	231 VIS
29a	14-14	Ling	6ap	63	407 bl
53a	9-10	Ling	5ap	63	453 bl
35a	6-13	Sout	6af	62	551 bl
52a	7-12	Ling	6ap	60	628
19a	13-13	Sout	6ap	58	741
53a	5-13	Ling	6ap	55	902
10	12-13	Sout	6g/s	53	1052
49a	2-8	Wolv	5af	[53]	1218
50a	4-5	Wolv	6af	[53]	1310

THAAYER 8 b g £0

42a	8-16	Sout	7af	[40]	61
4a	13-13	Sout	8af	38	221

THADEA 3 b f £0

45	12-18	Nott	8.2fm	63	1007
42	13-17	Warw	7.1sft	63	1526
0	P-16	Leic	7g/f	60	1825

THAI EXPRESS 3 b f £426

68	3-6	Cope	8gd	3661

THAI HI 3 b f £0

32a	9-16	Ling	7ap		214
16a	12-13	Ling	8ap	[56]	271

THAJJA 3 b c £13780

105	1-4	SAND	8.1g/s		1317*
89	8-9	Donc	8fm	[98]	4495
102	2-14	Asco	8g/f	98	4813
83	17-22	Newm	8sft	100	5103

THAKAFAAT 2 b f £5499

78	5-7	Newm	7g/f		3616
83	1-10	NEWM	7gd		4191*
73	6-12	Newm	8gd	87	5089

THAMINAH 3 b f £750

95	5-12	Asco	7g/f	[87]	4811
73	12-15	Newm	8gd	[89]	5088

THARAA 2 b f £1243

17a	14-16	Sout	8af		192
69	2-11	Ripo	8gd		1177
51	7-7	Nott	8.2sft		1468
68	5-17	Kemp	7gd	69	2174
39a	9-11	Ling	7ap	[69]	3331

THARUA 2 b f £1542

76	3-23	Newm	7g/f	4885
67	3-14	Yarm	8g/s	5118

THATS ALL JAZZ 6 b m £0

0	8-8	Sout	7af	[45]	373
28a	10-15	Ling	7ap	[45]	411

34a	7-13	Ling	10ap	[40]	539
0	B-14	Ling	10ap	[40]	784
34a	10-14	Ling	10ap	[40]	828

THATS RACING 4 ch g £414

28a	2-9	Sout	11af	[35]	906
36	6-17	Pont	12hvy	35	1064
4	12-13	Pont	21.6hvy	35	1252
0	9-16	Sout	14af	33	4045
16	9-9	Redc	10gd	31	4248

THE ABBESS 2 gr f £6338

87	1-15	NOTT	6.1g/s	4644*

THE BARONESS 4 b f £0

44a	8-11	Ling	6ap	57	3333
42a	9-15	Sout	5af	55	4043
23	19-19	Ling	5g/f	51	4739

THE BEDUTH NAVI 4 b g £3006

38a	2-12	Wolv	12af	[40]	523
38a	12-16	Ling	16ap	[35]	650
51a	1-5	WOLV	12af	[35]	823*
46a	2-16	Sout	11af	[35]	852
48a	3-16	Sout	14af	47	1033
45	4-12	Sout	16gd	47	1285
0	8-9	Wolv	14.8af	47	1654

THE BEST YET 5 ch h £2935

77a	2-10	Ling	7ap	72	262
77a	4-14	Ling	7ap	76	518
68a	8-12	Ling	8ap	[75]	1042
40	12-12	Sali	6fm	70	2289

THE BLOCK MONSTER 5 b m £0

2a	9-10	Sout	6af		308
0	10-10	Sout	8af	[45]	502
0	12-12	Wolv	8.5af	[35]	584 BL

THE BONUS KING 4 b g £6358

75a	4-12	Wolv	8.5af	85	688
84a	5-8	Ling	7gd	[83]	879
85	2-12	Pont	8hvy	84	1066
68	8-10	Hayd	10.5sft	[84]	1104
53	13-13	Wind	10gd	[84]	1381
63	11-15	Warw	8.1sft	84	1530
77	7-10	Beve	8.5g/f	80	1833
83	2-10	Ayr	7.2g/f	80	2027
72	4-7	Chep	8.1gd	[77]	2116
55	10-13	Ayr	7.2g/s	80	2568
60	11-11	Leic	7g/f	78	3210
64a	5-8	Sout	7af	[74]	4093
69	7-10	Leic	8gd	[75]	4702
65a	6-12	Wind	8.6ap	67	4923

THE BUTTERFLY BOY 3 ch c £409

41	10-12	Warw	7.1gd		1129
41a	3-7	Wolv	5af		1320
8	14-20	Chep	6.1gd	60	2372
12	12-12	Kemp	5g/f	55	3036

THE CATS WHISKERS 4 b f £450

89	9-15	Donc	7fm	4479
92	6-15	Newm	5g/f	4879

THE CHEQUERED LADY 2 b f £0

46	12-12	Folk	7gd	3909

THE COIRES 2 b c £5499

70	8-11	Newm	7g/f		3234
78	7-14	Newm	7g/f		3752
91	1-12	NEWM	7gd		4194*
89	6-17	Donc	8fm	87	4480
70	11-12	Asco	7g/f	86	4810

THE COMPOSER 2 b c £6213

83	4-10	Kemp	8g/f	4712
86	1-15	SALI	8g/f	4851*

THE COPT 5 b g £0

0	14-15	Sout	8af	43	2725 T
0	15-15	Sout	6af	38	3000 t

THE COUNT 5 b g £0

23	5-13	Ayr	8sft	[40]	5275

THE CROOKED RING 2 b g £25080

76	5-8	Newm	5g/f	1190
83	2-14	Bath	5gd	1401
78	3-7	Ches	5.1g/s	1571

```
82   2-11   Nott   6.1sft           1739
75   1-7    WARW 5fm              2573* VIS
88   3-4    Kemp   6g/f             2859
74   4-8    Ches   5.1g/f           3081
86   1-8    AYR    6g/f      77     3303*
96   1-10   KEMP   6g/f      84     3521*
95   2-7    Kemp   6g/f      87     3686
104  3-13   York   6gd       91     4004
81   6-11   York   6gd      [94]    4998
87   5-21   Donc   6hvy     [81]    5202

THE DUKE OF DIXIE  2 b c  £1734
86   3-8    York   6g/f             2408
84   3-12   Newm   7gd              4194
51   6-11   Bath   10.2gd           4825

THE FAIRY FLAG  6 ch m  £289
55   4-11   Beve   9.9sft    59     1633 p
49   11-14  Nott   10g/s     59     1777 p
39   12-18  Ayr    10.9sft   57     4623 p
44   7-10   Catt   13.8sft   55     5322 p

THE FISIO  3 b g  £12892
43a  12-14  Ling   6ap       72     149
72a  1-10   LING   6ap       66     329*
74a  1-9    SOUT   5af       72     415*
71a  5-10   Ling   5ap       76     453
67a  6-11   Sout   5af       74     655
79a  3-10   Ling   5ap       73     755
68a  8-14   Ling   6ap       75     874
68   7-17   Kemp   5sft      75     944
73   2-16   Bath   5.7g/s   [70]    1103 vis
53   14-20  Ripo   5gd       70     1179 vis
69   4-8    Folk   5g/s     [72]    1269 vis
77   1-8    HAMI   5gd      [70]    1749* vis
63   8-10   Sand   5gd       73     2189 vis
56   2-9    Wind   6fm      [73]    2760 vis
56   14-17  Sand   5g/f      75     3341 vis
0    9-10   Beve   5g/f     [75]    3503 vis
53   9-12   Ches   5.1sft    74     4107 vis
39   16-16  Leic   5gd       72     4700 vis

THE FOOTBALLRESULT  3 b f  £0
11a  11-12  Ling   7ap      [63]    536
30a  10-12  Ling   8ap      [53]    623
34   5-14   Sali   7g/f     [58]    1720
21   11-12  Sali   7fm      [54]    2288
37   9-14   Bath   10.2fm    45     2664

THE FOXS HEAD  3 b f  £0
45   5-8    Hami   9.2gd            1505
20   7-8    Hami   11.1g/f          2319

THE FUN MERCHANT  3 b g  £8731
62   7-12   Warw   7.1gd            1129
69   1-15   AYR    8gd      [63]    2504*
69   1-10   NEWM   8g/f     [63]    2732*
70   2-12   Newm   8fm       65     3410
53   7-11   Leic   8g/f      65     3516
66   5-15   Bath   8gd       68     4827
61a  9-14   Ling   10ap      67     5083
64a  7-13   Wolv   9.5ap     67     5161
69   3-18   Newm   8sft      66     5272 P

THE GAIKWAR  4 b c  £9689
56a  12-13  Ling   10ap      77     26
30a  11-13  Wolv   9.4af     75     127
70a  4-16   Ling   7ap       70     181 bl
56a  8-11   Wolv   7af       69     241 bl
67a  4-15   Ling   7ap       69     266 bl
64a  6-16   Ling   7ap       67     323 bl
61a  4-14   Ling   7ap      [66]    450 bl
61a  2-12   Ling   8ap      [65]    571 bl
64a  5-15   Ling   7ap       63     698 bl
60a  8-14   Ling   10ap      63     803 bl
71a  1-12   LING   8ap      [62]    878* bl
69   2-9    Epso   8.5hvy   [68]    1298 bl
0    U-14   Warw   8.1hvy    68     1535 bl
58   11-12  Bath   8g/f      68     1792 bl
40   17-20  Kemp   9g/f      65     2857 bl
44   17-20  Chep   7.1g/s    65     3088 bl
67   4-19   Chep   7.1gd     61     3401 bl
61   3-12   Kemp   8g/f      61     3524 bl
62   2-11   Kemp   8g/f      61     3685 bl
61   3-12   Chep   8.1g/s    61     3898 bl
52   6-12   Sali   8g/s      62     4077 bl

THE GAMBLER  3 ch g  £1272
```

```
0    16-16  Sout   8af       57     86 e
42   9-13   Muss   7.1g/f    55     1122 p
0    14-16  Newc   10.1sft   55     1278 p
36   11-20  Newc   6sft      52     1393 p
51   2-13   Muss   7.1gd     50     1553 p
39a  8-15   Sout   6af       48     1750 p
15   16-17  Warw   8.1fm     51     2572 p
32   12-14  Muss   7.1g/f    51     2615 p
22   12-18  Thir   6fm       48     3609 p
45   6-15   Newc   6hvy      45     4211 p
41   5-15   Thir   8fm      [45]    4379 p

THE GAY FOX  9 gr g  £1335
10a  10-16  Sout   8af       42     86 bl t
51a  5-11   Ling   6ap      [42]    130 bl t
18a  11-15  Sout   6af      [40]    167 bl t
34a  10-15  Ling   7ap      [44]    216 bl t
34a  5-10   Wolv   6af       42     245 bl t
40a  2-15   Ling   7ap      [40]    411 bl t
41a  4-13   Wolv   6af      [45]    582 bl t
45a  2-14   Ling   6ap      [45]    652 bl t
44a  3-14   Ling   6ap      [45]    709 bl t
35a  8-8    Ling   7ap      [45]    730 bl t
26a  9-14   Ling   7ap      [45]    783 t p
39a  3-9    Wolv   7af      [45]    825 bl t
37a  11-15  Ling   7ap       45     846 bl t
42a  8-15   Ling   7ap      [45]    935 bl t
38a  6-15   Ling   7ap      [40]    969 t p

THE GEEZER  2 ch c  £332
64a  4-12   Ling   8ap              5295

THE GREAT GATSBY  4 b c  £56901
114  3-7    San    12gd             2636
89   7-8    Newm   12g/f [119]      3030
104  4-4    Newb   13.3g/f[112]     3958 BL
95   8-9    Deau   15sft [112]      4161 bl

THE JOB  2 ch c  £3112
62a  1-11   LING   8ap      [65]    77*
53a  4-10   Sout   8af       62     189
51a  6-15   Ling   7ap       62     337
59a  2-8    Ling   7ap       59     933
57   5-18   Nott   8.2fm     59     1007
8    15-18  Wind   8.3sft    57     1647
61a  5-12   Wolv   7.1ap    [59]    5325

THE JOBBER  3 b g  £4337
79   4-8    Kemp   6g/s     [82]    2677
75   10-16  Newm   5g/f      82     3033
72   6-10   Kemp   6gd      [82]    3188
85a  2-11   Ling   6ap       78     3744
82   2-15   Newb   6gd       78     3920
19   14-14  Ches   6.1g/f    78     4048
71   5-15   Kemp   6g/f      78     4713

THE KEEP  2 ch f  £0
62   7-8    Ling   6gd              3021
54   10-14  Newb   6fm              3626
58   9-17   Warw   7.1gd            4271
53   4-14   Warw   6.1g/f           4422
26   11-13  Leic   6gd       58     4697
51a  8-8    Wolv   8.6ap    [54]    5007

THE KELT  7 b g  £3066
45   1-14   CARL   17.2gd    35     2937* t
3a   9-10   Sout   14af      41     3096 t

THE KHAMSIN  5 b h  £0
100  7-9    Asco   12g/f            4812

THE KIDDYKID  4 b g  £50638
104  3-17   Donc   6gd      [106]   952
81   7-8    Newm   6g/f     [104]   1187
112  1-10   CURR   6g/f     [104]   1996*
111  4-11   Newc   6g/s     [111]   2769
101  6-12   Sand   5g/s     [111]   2913
103  8-11   Newb   6g/f     [110]   3268
109  2-10   Curr   6g/f     [110]   3842
99   7-11   Deau   6hvy     [110]   4313

THE KING OF ROCK  2 b c  £1578
32a  8-14   Sout   8af      [63]    95
36a  12-14  Sout   7af       57     158
38a  8-13   Wolv   6af       50     436 BL
56   5-19   Warw   10.9gd    57     1124
54   4-12   Beve   9.9sft    47     1306
43   8-15   Ripo   12.3g/f   56     1785
```

```
49a  2-15   Sout   12af      45     2503
54   4-10   Bath   11.7g/f   56     2978
48   6-14   Folk   12gd      55     3383
50   5-15   Nott   10g/s     54     4037

THE KINGS BISHOP  3 b g  £915
63a  4-12   Ling   8ap              514
50a  13-15  Ling   7ap              814
78   3-14   Folk   7g/s             1080

THE LADY WOULD  5 ch m  £0
16a  10-12  Sout   5af      [35]    904
26a  8-12   Ling   6ap      [35]    1075
16a  7-11   Wolv   6af      [35]    1261 BL

THE LAST CAST  5 ch g  £9628
82   1-17   SALI   14.1g/s  74     1502*
82   11-34  Newm   18sft     76     5135

THE LAST MOHICAN  5 b g  £3348
24a  4-9    Wolv   14.8af   [31]    301 P
33a  2-6    Wolv   16.2af   [30]    395 p
41a  3-14   Ling   13ap     [35]    537 p
35a  2-8    Wolv   16.2af    35     563 p
19a  4-10   Wolv   12af     [35]    581 p
44a  4-9    Ling   13ap     [35]    787 p
29a  7-14   Ling   12af     [40]    968 p
26a  8-13   Ling   13ap     [40]    1076 p
35a  3-7    Ling   12ap     [30]    1287 p
34a  2-5    Wolv   14.8af   [30]    1563 p
38a  1-6    SOUT   12af     [30]    1592* p
2a   10-10  Ling   12ap     [30]    1714 p
10a  8-9    Sout   12af     [38]    2381
12a  7-16   Sout   14af     [35]    4045

THE LAVERTON LAD  2 ch g  £0
0    14-16  Sout   8af      [41]    164
3a   11-12  Wolv   9.4af    [35]    302

THE LEATHER WEDGE  4 b c  £1756
50a  2-15   Sout   5af       47     187
39a  9-9    Wolv   5af       49     275
47a  6-10   Wolv   5af      [49]    286
24a  11-11  Wolv   5af       48     507
42a  4-16   Sout   5af      [45]    720
17a  10-11  Sout   5af      [45]    775
32a  5-12   Wolv   5af      [45]    889
55a  2-12   Wolv   5af      [45]    960
44a  5-12   Sout   5af       47     1442
46a  5-15   Sout   5af      [45]    2803 p
29   9-9    Catt   5g/f     [40]    3353 BL
47a  3-15   Sout   5af      [45]    4043 p
27a  9-13   Wolv   5.1ap    [45]    5231
45   4-13   Catt   5sft     [40]    5321

THE LOOSE SCREW  5 b g  £421
0    14-14  Sout   8af       48     60
28   10-19  Warw   10.9sft   49     1090
22   9-16   Newc   10.1sft   45     1278
19   13-16  Redc   10g/f     45     1821
11   12-14  York   13.9g/f   45     2060
23   12-17  Hayd   8.1gd     40     2947 P
52   5-9    Newc   9g/s     [35]    3697 p
69   5-17   Hayd   8.1g/s   [35]    4768 p
32   6-16   Warw   8.1g/s   [45]    4993 p
43   2-12   Ayr    7.2sft   [40]    5274 p

THE LORD  4 b g  £1601
78   3-5    Asco   6g/f      87     3388
82   7-14   Newb   5.2fm     84     3628
70   6-6    Hayd   6g/s      84     3903
65   13-13  Newb   5.2g/f    82     3960 P
75   6-12   Ches   5.1sft    81     4107

THE MOG  5 b g  £0
3a   7-10   Sout   8af      [45]    850 bl t

THE NIBBLER  3 b g  £0
55   4-8    Yarm   8g/f             2854
41a  6-9    Ling   8ap              3195
48a  7-8    Ling   10ap             3787
37   6-9    Thir   8g/f     [52]    4593
3    12-12  Brig   8sft      49     5094

THE NUMBER  3 gr g  £2958
68   3-11   Thir   8g/f             3572
69   3-5    Ayr    8hvy      65     4085
61   5-14   Muss   7.1g/f    65     4175
67   2-6    Muss   8gd      [64]    4520
```

THE OLD SOLDIER and other entries (horse racing form guide)

60	6-17	Newc	8fm	64	4867
54a	7-12	Wolv	8.6ap	63	5116 P

THE OLD SOLDIER 6 b g £1739

44	7-13	Sout	6g/s	55	1052
27	13-16	Newc	6sft	53	1277
55	2-14	Muss	7.1g/f	50	2615
35	12-20	Newc	6g/f	51	4408
54	2-13	Warw	7.1g/s	[50]	4994
48	5-13	Muss	5g/s	[50]	5146
54a	2-12	Wolv	7.1ap	[50]	5229

THE PALLETMAN 4 ch g £0

26a	9-9	Ling	8ap	3195

THE PEN 2 ch f £9452

51	7-12	Thir	6g/f		3411
65	1-15	REDC	6g/f		3769*
62	2-20	Redc	7fm	56	4337
68	1-19	REDC	8sft	58	5302*

THE PERSUADER 4 b g £0

44	13-13	Catt	13.8gd	80	997
40	19-20	Newm	12gd	78	1172
29	10-11	Beve	16.2sft	74	1629
41	13-15	Newb	13.3g/f	71	2311

THE PHEASANT FLYER 2 ch g £9910

79	3-10	Brig	6g/s		4139
86	1-14	WARW	6.1g/f		4422*
92	1-10	NEWM	6fm	81	4727*
67	12-13	Newb	7sft	[88]	5195

THE PLAINSMAN 2 b g £187

26	6-7	Pont	6g/f	2792

THE PLAYER 5 b g £0

61	12-14	Epso	8.5gd	72	4295

THE PRINCE 10 b g £42170

75	1-8	YARM	8g/f	[85]	2854*
71	1-5	HAMI	9.2g/s	[84]	3876*
73	1-9	GOOD	9sft	[84]	4266*
77	1-11	MUSS	9g/f	[79]	4550+
75	1-17	AYR	9.1g/s	[79]	4620*
94	1-20	YORK	8.9gd	79	4999*
94	3-13	Newm	8g/s	88	5284

THE QUIET WOMAN 2 b f £0

68	14-24	Newb	5.2g/f		3266

THE RECRUITER 4 gr g £0

11a	8-10	Sout	11af	[40]	375 vis

THE RING 4 b g £3994

65	7-11	Nott	16fm	70	1003
73	2-17	Ripo	16g/s	69	1361
72	3-11	Beve	16.2sft	72	1629
6	13-13	Newc	16.1sft	71	2685
71	5-12	Newm	16.1g/f	70	3032
57	9-10	Hami	13fm	70	3249
58	5-7	Newm	14.8g/f	68	3475
62	5-9	Muss	14gd	65	4521 VIS

THE RIP 3 ch c £644

25	7-7	Carl	9.3fm	[72]	2443
59	3-9	Thir	8g/f	[70]	4593
41	12-20	Catt	12gd	57	4966

THE ROUNDSILLS 10 ch g £241

25	11-16	Hayd	10.5sft	40	3276
14	6-6	Pont	12gd	35	3681

THE SPOOK 4 b g £0

0	10-10	Muss	9g/f	[39]	2811
23	15-16	Carl	7.9g/f	39	3650
0	9-9	Ayr	7.2g/f	[39]	3764
44	5-11	Ayr	9.1sft	[35]	5067
34	7-11	Redc	10sft	[40]	5303

THE STAFFORD 2 b g £0

0	10-10	Ling	8ap	232

THE STICK 3 b f £0

61a	7-15	Ling	7ap	63	901
27	10-12	Catt	12gd	63	1000
2	11-11	Warw	8.1hvy	60	1534
53	7-14	Ayr	8g/f	[57]	1896
42	12-14	Redc	10fm	55	2299
35	14-20	Chep	8.1g/s	52	3090

THE TATLING 6 £231937

109	7-14	Sha	5g/f		210
113	2-12	Long	5g/s	[113]	1856
110	3-10	Kemp	5fm	[112]	2068
108	4-8	Chan	5g/f	[112]	2305
120	1-19	ASCO	5g/f	[112]	2468*
99	9-12	Sand	5g/s	[115]	2913
118	3-13	Good	5fm	[115]	3551
118	2-12	York	5g/s	[115]	4060
117	2-9	Long	5g/s	[115]	4435
120	1-11	NEWB	5.2g/f	[116]	4678*
111	3-12	Asco	6g/f	[116]	4799
119	2-15	Long	6g/f	[116]	4952

THE TERMINATOR 2 b c £391

27	7-7	Ches	5.1g/s		1571
0	10-10	Hayd	6g/s		2228
0	20-20	Newc	6sft		2682
24	7-7	Ayr	6g/f		3761 P
38	9-13	Ripo	5gd		4303
56	4-7	Ches	7g/f	[35]	4511
54	7-8	Muss	9g/s	[50]	5140

THE TRADER 5 £79200

111	6-14	Sha	5g/f		210 bl
115	1-12	LONG	5g/s	[109]	1856* bl
113	3-8	Chan	5g/s	[109]	2305 bl
105	10-19	Asco	5g/f	[113]	2468 bl
115	1-12	DEAU	6sft	[113]	3167* bl
114	5-12	Deau	6.5g/s	[113]	3838 bl
89	19-19	Hayd	6fm	[114]	4384 bl
89	14-15	Long	5g/f	[114]	4952 bl

THE VARLET 4 b g £4157

33	10-10	Sand	14g/f	72	2192
72	3-10	Newm	12g/f	70	2530
54	6-8	Epso	12g/f	70	2869
71	1-13	SALI	14.1gd	68	3454* P
45	10-11	Newm	16.1g/f	70	3779 p
20	13-14	Bath	13.1g/s	69	4203 p
49	16-16	Kemp	16g/f	69	4361 t

THE VIOLIN PLAYER 3 b g £4617

55	9-9	Hayd	8.1sft	80	1105
72	8-13	Thir	8g/f	80	1769
67	8-13	Newm	8g/f	78	2247
70	10-10	Nott	10g/s	[74]	2930
67	5-8	Ling	11.5fm	72	3747
56	7-11	Epso	12gd	68	4468
72a	2-14	Ling	10ap	66	5083
76a	1-13	LING	10ap	66	5299*

THE WARLEY WARRIOR 3 b g £0

47	6-11	Pont	6sft		1426 bl
24	11-14	Thir	6gd		1639 bl
0	13-13	Ripo	6g/f	51	2011 bl

THE WAY WE WERE 3 ch c £1132

0	6-8	Wind	8.3g/s	77	1257
62	5-13	Good	9g/f	75	2024
53	12-13	Sand	8.1gd	72	2365
73	2D-11	Sali	8gd	69	3455
28	13-15	Bath	8gd	69	4827

THE WHISTLING TEAL 8 b g £36400

102	7-17	Newb	12gd	[107]	1230
112	2-9	Ches	13.4gd	[107]	1596
114	1-8	NEWB	13.3g/f	[107]	1757*
108	5-7	Curr	14gd	[107]	2817
94	4-8	Newb	12hvy	[112]	5224

THE WIZARD MUL 4 br g £610

1	14-19	Newc	6sft	64	967
38	10-20	Ripo	8g/s	62	1366
46	12-17	Newc	7g/s	60	3700
41	8-16	Hami	6g/s	57	4009
48	8-14	Carl	6.9g/f	54	4345
33	14-20	Newc	6g/f	54	4408 BL
53	3-15	Redc	9g/s	51	5111
44	5-13	Ayr	10sft	[50]	5276

THEAS DANCE 2 b f £766

79	5-10	Yarm	7fm		2863
17	8-8	Asco	6gd		3071
74	3-5	Good	6sft		4234
48	9-14	Yarm	7g/s	65	4583

THEATRE 5 b g £4868

72	15-17	Sali	14.1g/s	83	1502
1	S-12	Good	14g/f	80	1861
86	2-10	Kemp	16fm	80	2073
86	2-9	Newm	14.8fm	81	2596
85	3-7	Sand	14g/s	83	2899
57	15-17	Asco	16.2gd	82	3125
62	13-17	Newm	14.8gd	80	4196
75	7-13	Good	16g/f	77	4527
72	12-16	Asco	16.2g/f	75	4803
80	13-34	Newm	18sft	77	5135

THEATRE BELLE 3 b f £0

53	8-11	Ripo	8gd		1177
16	13-15	Thir	7g/s		1473
0	13-15	Sout	12af	54	2503
43	6-8	Thir	12g/s	54	2691
47	5-11	Pont	12g/f	51	2790 VIS
17	11-13	Redc	14.1fm	49	4340
31	7-19	Catt	15.8g/f	47	4675

THEATRE LADY 6 b m £10639

39a	1-13	LING	10ap	[30]	539*
44a	2-12	Ling	8ap	[40]	710
39a	8-10	Ling	8ap	45	766
42a	3-11	Ling	8ap	[40]	786
44a	6-13	Ling	10ap	40	805
42a	3-11	Ling	10ap	[45]	970
36a	8-12	Ling	8ap	45	1045
49	4-19	Warw	10.9sft	50	1090
39a	3-12	Ling	8ap	[40]	1451
49	5-19	Brig	9.9g/f	46	1940
36	6-14	Carl	7.9fm	46	1954
44	6-12	Warw	10.9fm	45	2436
19	11-13	Yarm	11.5fm	44	2868 vis
49	1-17	BATH	11.7gd	41	3145*
49	5-16	Brig	9.9g/f	47	3175
53	1-19	CHEP	12.1gd	46	3398*
44	10-19	Beve	9.9g/f	52	3505
40	6-9	Yarm	14.1g/f	49	3703
53	1-20	KEMP	12g/f	[47]	4796*

THEATRE OF DREAMS 2 b c £7557

73	5-13	Donc	5gd		954
79	4-7	Ches	5.1g/s		1573
79	1-9	MUSS	5fm		2083*
85	10-13	Good	5g/f		3509
72	6-8	Ripo	5gd	[89]	4307
50	12-12	Ayr	5g/s	[86]	4651

THEATRE TIME 4 b g £0

67	6-6	Leic	10fm	79	3815
66	7-8	Hayd	11.9g/f	77	4353

THEATRE TINKA 4 b g £5406

70a	1-11	SOUT	11af	[62]	191* p
58a	5-9	Sout	11af	70	391 p
55a	5-12	Wolv	12af	68	484 p
52a	5-10	Sout	12af	[68]	552 p
58a	2-7	Sout	12af	[62]	679 p
62	4-13	Catt	13.8gd	60	997 p
29	11-12	Sout	11gd	57	1286 p
46a	5-5	Wolv	12af	[59]	1375 p
60	2-11	Warw	12.6fm	56	2601 p
52	8-12	Warw	15g/f	56	2908 p
59	4-10	Catt	13.8g/f	57	3669 p
59	3-19	Thir	12g/f	55	4594 p
20	16-19	Bath	11.7gd	56	5024 p

THEFLYINGSCOTTIE 2 gr g £0

43	10-13	Bath	5.7g/f	3368
0	12-12	Chep	5.1gd	3728

THEME PARK 4 b g £0

31a	7-7	Sout	14af	[60]	376
0	7-7	Sout	12af	[53]	588 t

THEME SONG 5 b g £34893

98	1-12	CURR	12g/f	85	2821* p
81	11-14	York	13.9gd	95	3119 P

THEMESOFGREEN 3 ch g £0

40	9-15	Nott	5.1g/f		2152
53	7-10	Newb	6g/f		2309
38	8-12	Ling	6gd		2586
45	5-13	Muss	7.1g/f	54	2812

THEORIST 3 b g £0

17a	12-13	Wolv	8.5af	60	40 P

THESAURUS 4 gr g £0
| 46a | 5-14 | Sout | 8af | | 62 | 62 |

THEVENIS 2 ch c £0
58a	5-14	Sout	8af	[59]		88
49a	7-14	Sout	8af	[60]		226
0	9-10	Sout	12af		60	796

THEWHIRLINGDERVISH 6 ch g £21586
82	3-13	Hayd	14sft		78	1109
79	4-17	Ripo	16g/s		78	1361
52	10-12	Thir	16gd		79	1637
81	3-7	York	13.9g/f		78	2355
84	1-9	PONT	18g/f		77	2607*
86	3-17	Asco	16.2gd		82	3125
84	2-3	Ches	18.7fm		83	3635
85	6-11	Newm	16.1g/f		83	3779
80	9-13	Yarm	16g/s		82	4634
76	11-16	Asco	16.2g/f		80	4803

THIHN 9 ch g £12441
83	10-24	Donc	8gd		90	928
97	1-20	NEWM	7g/s		90	1151*
86	11-27	Newb	8gd		95	1231
50	28-32	Newm	9g/f		94	4916

THINGMEBOB 4 b f £2250
| 86 | 5-6 | York | 10.4g/s | [104] | | 1684 |
| 94 | 5-7 | Hayd | 11.9g/f | [104] | | 1921 |

THINK IT OVER 5 ch m £0
8a	13-16	Ling	7ap			290
14a	9-13	Ling	6ap			400
2a	12-12	Ling	8ap			675

THINK QUICK 3 b f £1671
0	10-10	Wolv	12af	[40]		250 t
16a	14-16	Sout	11af	[40]		445
35a	5-12	Wolv	12af	[35]		523
33a	6-11	Wolv	9.4af	[35]		580
22a	6-11	Wolv	12af	[35]		666
35a	3-11	Wolv	12af	[35]		689
39a	4-5	Sout	12af	[35]		745
19a	7-10	Wolv	12af	[35]		780
22a	3-5	Wolv	12af	[35]		823
14a	12-16	Sout	11af	[35]		852
5a	7-9	Sout	11af	[35]		906
13a	6-9	Sout	11af	[30]		985
42a	2-11	Sout	12af	[20]		3154
27	7-12	Nott	14.1g/f		35	3420
39	4-14	Catt	12g/f	[32]		3668
0	12-16	Sout	14af		35	4045

THIRD EMPIRE 3 b g £2848
62	3-12	Redc	10sft		62	1144
10	9-11	Redc	10sft		62	1663
62	5-13	Newc	8g/s		60	2773
66	2-6	Carl	9.3g/f		60	3231
59	4-5	Pont	10gd		67	3459
42	8-12	Newc	9hvy		64	4215

THIRTEEN TRICKS 3 b f £5323
0	13-13	Kemp	9hvy		75	1515
74	3-8	Kemp	9g/s		75	2680
74	4-12	Newb	10g/f		75	3255
72	1-4	BRIG	9.9fm	[74]		3675*
53	11-13	Ling	10g/s		74	4182

THIS IS MY SONG 2 b f £846
| 70 | 7-11 | Newb | 6gd | | | 3915 |
| 81 | 3-9 | Newm | 7gd | | | 4192 |

THIS WAY THAT WAY 3 b g £0
| 27a | 10-13 | Sand | 8af | | | 553 |

THISTLE 3 ch c £8493
17	9-13	Pont	8g/s			3973
76	2-17	Newm	8gd			4228
78	2-12	Newc	8g/f			4407
80	2-13	Nott	8.2g/f	[76]		4847
76	1-11	WIND	8.3g/f	[76]		5052*

THOMAS LAWRENCE 3 ch g £844
49	6-10	Ling	6g/f	[93]		3603
76	3-12	Kemp	6sft	[88]		4029
0	7-9	Thir	6fm	[80]		4380 BL

THORNABY GREEN 3 b g £6924
| 62 | 4-7 | Carl | 5fm | | 63 | 1951 |

62	4-14	Catt	6g/f		61	3018
67	1-10	HAMI	6g/f		61	3203*
54	11-13	Thir	7g/f		64	3571
64	5-18	Hayd	6gd		64	3737
58	4-16	Hami	6g/s		64	4009
58	7-14	Muss	7.1g/f		64	4175
63	2-15	Hami	6sft		62	4696
17	18-19	Ayr	6sft		63	5069

THORNBER COURT 2 b f £1789
48	7-8	Catt	6g/f			3348
40	4-9	Ripo	6gd			4277
54	8-8	Muss	5gd			4517
70	2-16	Ripo	5gd	[56]		4787
64	3-11	Catt	5gd	[66]		4962
54	5-7	Catt	5sft	[64]		5124

THORNTOUN PICCOLO 2 ch f £0
| 53 | 8-12 | Ayr | 7.2hvy | | | 4083 |
| 70 | 5-11 | Ayr | 7.2g/s | | | 4653 |

THORNY MANDATE 2 b c £0
| 19 | 11-11 | Sali | 7gd | | | 3883 |
| 59 | 12-13 | Sali | 7sft | | | 4576 |

THREAT 7 br g £183
1a	12-13	Wolv	8.5af	[43]		46
11a	9-11	Wolv	6af	[40]		296
34a	4-10	Sout	6af	[40]		352
25a	7-16	Sout	5af	[40]		374
6a	10-11	Wolv	7af	[40]		440 p
34a	3-13	Ling	6ap	[35]		541
37	4-12	Chep	5.1sft	[45]		1336
36	4-10	Brig	5.3gd	[45]		1544
34	6-10	Kemp	5hvy	[45]		1644
44	7-18	Wind	6g/f	[45]		1806
43	5-10	Brig	7g/f	[45]		1938
38	4-16	Nott	6.1gd	[45]		1988 bl

THREE ACES 2 ch f £0
47	9-11	Sali	5gd			2658
62	5-9	Nott	5.1gd			2926
20	6-6	Brig	5.3g/f			3296
33	19-20	Ling	7gd		65	4444 BL
55	7-20	Ling	7g/f		58	4741 bl
37	11-12	Ayr	8sft		56	5065 bl
51	7-19	Rcdc	8sft		53	5302 bl

THREE BOARS 2 ch c £0
30	7-7	Yarm	6gd			3869
51	10-18	Newm	8fm			4722
56	9-15	Pont	10g/f			4933

THREE DAYS IN MAY 4 b f £0
| 10a | 10-10 | Warw | 17af | | 60 | 74 |

THREE DEGREES 2 gr f £2065
| 75 | 3-15 | Nott | 6.1g/s | | | 4644 |
| 80 | 2-13 | Newc | 7g/f | | | 5012 |

THREE DEUCES 2 gr f £326
73	5-14	Wind	5gd			4121
64a	4-14	Ling	7ap			5076
72a	6-9	Ling	6ap			5237

THREE EAGLES 7 ch g £0
| 30 | 6-7 | Warw | 16.2gd | | 31 | 3057 bl |

THREE GRACES 4 ch g £3300
| 109 | 3-11 | Hayd | 7.1gd | [109] | | 2184 vis T |

THREE PENNIES 2 b f £4533
42	10-13	Redc	6g/f			1818
77	1-10	BEVE	7.5gd			2652*
77	3-4	Beve	7.5sft			2938
28	11-11	Newb	7fm		74	3627
52	12-14	Donc	7fm		72	4535
47	10-13	Leic	6gd		67	4697
77a	5-8	Wolv	8.6ap	[64]		5007

THREE SECRETS 3 b f £11425
62	7-10	Newm	6g/f			1191
81	1-14	WARW	7.1g/f	[85]		2907*
85	2-5	Yarm	7gd	[85]		3365
97	3-5	Sand	8.1g/s	[85]		4095
74	11-13	Asco	8g/f		92	4802

THREE SHIPS 3 ch c £0
| 69 | 10-15 | Newb | 8g/f | | | 1763 |

| 60 | 5-11 | Thir | 7fm | | | 2463 |
| 64a | 9-12 | Wolv | 7.1ap | | 69 | 5008 |

THREE STRIKES 2 b f £0
| 47 | 10-18 | Leic | 5fm | | | 2109 |
| 62 | 5-12 | Bath | 5sft | | | 5169 |

THREE VALLEYS 3 ch c £11000
| 113 | 2-5 | Newm | 8g/f | [118] | | 1188 |
| 84 | 11-14 | Newm | 8g/f | [117] | | 1480 |

THREE WELSHMEN 3 b g £4967
19a	14-15	Ling	7ap	[65]		670
6a	8-9	Wolv	8.5af	[60]		865
53	5-13	Nott	8.2gd		54	1242 BL
60	1-14	WARW	8.1sft		52	1529* bl
52	3-9	Folk	7sft		59	1577 bl
29	13-15	Leic	11.8gd		57	2134
46	7-14	Sali	8fm		57	2423 bl
16	8-9	Brig	9.9gd		55	2955 bl
62	2-13	Warw	8.1gd		55	3058 P

THREE WRENS 2 b f £1923
| 67 | 3-12 | Redc | 8g/s | | | 5107 |
| 67 | 1-8 | AYR | 8sft | | | 5273* |

THREEZEDZZ 6 ch g £23039
47	12-19	Sali	7g/f		65	1723
60	7-14	Chep	7.1gd		62	2199
25	9-11	Good	6gd		60	2535
67	1-19	CHEP	7.1gd		58	3401* T
52	11-17	Wind	6fm		61	3643 t
71	1-6	YARM	7g/f		61	3708* t
60a	7-14	Ling	7ap		67	3821 t
85	1-12	CHEP	8.1g/s		67	3898* t
82	3-16	Nott	8.2g/s		76	4036 t
76	3-15	Chep	8.1sft		76	4057 t
83	1-8	CHEP	7.1g/s	[78]		4301* t
75	14-21	Donc	7fm		84	4482 t
28	20-20	York	8.9gd		81	4999 t
50	15-17	Wind	10g/f		81	5050 t
49	13-13	Bath	8sft		80	5172 t

THROUGH THE SLIPS 3 ch f £417
46	7-11	Leic	10g/f			3208
42	8-9	Nott	8.2g/f			3581
47a	3 9	Sout	7af			4131
0	16-16	Catt	7g/f		51	4676

THROW THE DICE 2 b c £6071
88	2-12	Hayd	6sft			3272
83	1-14	HAYD	6gd			3735*
91	4-15	Hayd	6sft		87	4765

THROWMEUPSOMETHING 3 b g £0
| 0 | 10-10 | Muss | 12g/s | | | 5145 |

THUMAMAH 5 b m £0
35a	9-9	Ling	8ap		53	763
13a	11-11	Ling	8ap		53	820
0	14-14	Hayd	8.1g/s		54	1348 t
31	6-9	Leic	8g/f	[49]		1966 t
5a	11-16	Sout	7af		36	2335 VIS
0	15-17	Thir	8g/s		43	3830 t

THUNDER CALLING 2 b f £365
| 72 | 4-10 | Newm | 6gd | | | 1887 |

THUNDERCLAP 5 b g £3849
56a	1-10	SOUT	8af		49	791*
56a	2-11	Wolv	8.5af		49	806
42a	8-10	Ling	8ap		55	917
23a	10-10	Wolv	8.5af		55	1322
0	16-19	Redc	8g/s		55	1661 P
41	9-15	Catt	7sft		55	3933

THUNDERING SURF 7 b g £0
| 64 | 13-17 | Newm | 12g/f | | 93 | 1759 |
| 66 | 9-9 | Newm | 12g/f | [90] | | 2246 |

THUNDERWING 2 b c £12966
79	3-7	Thir	7g/f			3412
86	1-14	THIR	7g/s			3831*
98	1-4	NEWC	8hvy			4212*
100	1-4	AYR	8g/s	[91]		4619*

THURLESTONE ROCK 4 ch g £7490
| 70 | 11-19 | Kemp | 6fm | | 78 | 2070 |
| 75 | 5-12 | Sali | 6fm | | 77 | 2289 |

TI–TIME

28	17-17	Wind	6g/f	77	2451
80	1-19	**KEMP**	6fm	75	4394*
66	11-19	Good	6gd	78	4747

THWAAB 12 b g £0

0	9-10	Ayr	8g/s	[43]	2544
25	13-16	Carl	7.9g/f	38	3650 vis
40	8-9	Redc	8g/f	[38]	3806 vis
12	10-12	Brig	8gd	[40]	4904 vis

THYOLO 3 ch c £9796

96	2-20	Newm	8fm	90	1496
82	10-13	York	10.4sft	90	1664
102	3-27	Asco	8g/f	95	2521
77	11-15	Sand	8.1g/s	99	2915
89	7-9	Good	8fm	[99]	3620
87	15-18	Newb	10gd	97	4681
95	8-15	Leic	11.8gd	97	5043

TI ADORA 2 b f £0

67	9-15	Kemp	7g/f	4710
53	14-19	Leic	7gd	5040
60	8-16	Yarm	10.1g/s	5352

TIAMO 2 ch c £0

59	12-18	Newm	7gd	3927
75	6-12	Good	8g/f	4522
65	7-11	York	7.9gd	5003

TIBER TIGER 4 b g £7889

67	4-18	Wind	8.3g/s	75	1059 vis
84	1-9	**NEWM**	8gd	74	1891* bl
67	7-7	Newm	8fm	[80]	2091 bl
82	2-11	Warw	8.1fm	80	2600 bl
78	13-17	Carl	7.9gd	80	2672 bl
43	19-20	Newm	8fm	80	3001 bl
71	5-8	Newm	8g/f	78	3583 bl
75	5-16	Redc	8g/f	76	3768 bl
76	5-16	Redc	7g/f	76	3809
65	6-11	Brig	8g/s	75	4141
62	13-14	Epso	8.5gd	75	4295 bl
67	10-11	Yarm	8gd	72	4615 bl
58	13-14	Wind	8.3g/f	70	4832 P
47	11-11	Yarm	10.1g/s	67	5353

TICERO 3 ch c £296

39	13-17	Donc	8gd		919
23	14-14	Ches	6.1g/s	80	1570
4	8-8	Leic	7g/f	77	2403
37a	11-11	Ling	8ap	72	3198 BL
62	4-19	Leic	7g/f	65	4452 bl
44	12-15	Bath	8gd	63	4827 bl
13a	12-12	Ling	8ap	[63]	4974 bl

TICKI TORI 2 b f £1468

75	3-16	York	7.9gd	4997
76	3-14	Yarm	7sft	5250

TICKLE 5 b m £217

48a	6-11	Ling	6ap	[50]	130 VIS
34a	7-13	Ling	6ap	[50]	271 vis t
34a	4-9	Ling	5ap	[48]	413 vis t
51a	8-14	Ling	6ap	[47]	516 vis t
39a	3-14	Ling	6ap	[50]	652 vis t
27	6-17	Pont	6hvy	[57]	1065 vis t
50	6-8	Folk	5g/s	[54]	1269 BL t
25	13-18	Wind	6g/f	[54]	1806 t
25a	10-15	Sout	5af	[45]	2803 t

TICKLEPENNY LOCK 2 b c £0

20a	10-12	Sout	6af	[40]	200
25a	12-15	Sout	7af	[35]	462
2a	9-9	Sout	8af	35	486
9a	10-10	Sout	11af	30	658

TICTACTOE 2 b f £2331

51a	3-13	Sout	6af	[58]	63
40a	6-14	Sout	6af	[58]	95
59a	1-9	**WOLV**	6af	[54]	247*
30a	6-8	Sout	7af	[57]	389
25	6-8	Folk	5g/s	[57]	1268
37	9-10	Brig	7fm	54	3672
32	7-13	Warw	7.1g/s	[50]	4994 VIS

TIDAL 5 b r m £26739

52	6-17	Bath	10.2sft	55	1541
67	1-10	**CHEP**	12.1gd	55	2114+
84	1-11	**CHEP**	10.2gd	61	2371*
61	7-11	Good	12gd	65	2538
87	3-10	Chep	10.2g/s	[74]	3089
75	4-15	Epso	10.1gd	[74]	3216
81	7-9	Newb	12fm	[84]	3629
90	1-19	**KEMP**	10fm	83	4392*
80	10-11	Yarm	10.1gd	[88]	4614

TIDAL FURY 2 b c £281

56	12-15	Pont	6gd	3239
71	4-14	Thir	9g/s	4207

TIDES 3 b f £0

43	8-9	Newm	7g/f	3282
46	6-8	Newm	6g/f	3784
10	8-8	Yarm	6gd	3873

TIDY 4 b c £19039

56a	11-13	Wolv	6af	78	687
83	1-13	**NEWC**	7hvy	74	1035+
78	5-15	Pont	6hvy	80	1251
82	U-19	Leic	6g/s	80	1354
64	8-13	Ayr	7.2g/s	80	2568
84	3-18	Newc	7sft	80	2684
76	7-10	Carl	6.9gd	80	2935
62	15-15	York	7gd	80	3117
84	4-13	Newc	7gd	78	3428
81	4-14	Newb	8hvy	78	5227
77	5-20	Newm	7g/s	77	5286
47	16-20	Donc	7sft	76	5367

TIEGS 2 ch f £0

2	12-12	Warw	7.1g/f	4417

TIFFIN BROWN 2 b r g £0

56	10-12	York	6gd	3122

TIFFIN DEANO 2 b c £263

57	5-15	Beve	5g/s		1161
62	8-9	Muss	5g/s		1458
55	10-12	Hayd	6gd		2902
33	13-14	Donc	7fm	62	4535
61	4-10	Catt	5gd	[56]	4968

TIGER BOND 2 b r c £0

43	10-15	Beve	5g/s	3178
57	5-10	Redc	5fm	4338

TIGER DAWN 2 b g £2660

40	13-16	Bath	8gd	5019 BL
70a	1-11	**WOLV**	7.1ap	5113*

TIGER FROG 5 b g £4801

68	1-8	**HAMI**	11.1g/f	55	3207* bl
63	5-6	Leic	11.8g/f	60	3345 bl
65	3-10	Ripo	12.3g/f	62	3649 bl

TIGER HUNTER 2 b g £380

2	8-8	Yarm	6fm	2865
34	10-17	Ling	6g/f	4316
18	15-19	Kemp	8g/f	4792
54a	3-11	Wolv	7.1ap	5113

TIGER TIGER 3 b c £28586

76a	1-11	**LING**	8ap		697*
73a	3-8	Ling	8ap	[72]	934
85	1-9	**EPSO**	8.5hvy	[72]	1298*
89	2-8	Sali	9.9g/s	83	1500
85	7-18	Good	9g/f	85	1813
83	7-18	Epso	10.1fm	85	2250
87	4-10	Sali	12gd	84	2660
85	2-6	Cope	8gd	83	3661
94	1-14	**NEWB**	10hvy	83	5223*
95	4-10	Yarm	10.1sft	[83]	5255

TIGER TOPS 5 ch g £0

64a	5-13	Ling	7ap	65	565
28a	9-11	Ling	8ap	65	714

TIGGERS TOUCH 2 b f £454

68	4-11	Sali	6g/f		3863
69	9-16	Sali	7gd		4330
69	6-14	Sali	7sft		4575
59	7-13	Wind	6g/f	[73]	5047

TIGHT CIRCLE 2 b f £3164

38	7-11	Good	5gd	2020
72	5-11	Ling	5gd	2395
70	6-10	Ches	5.1g/s	2744
80	1-13	**BATH**	5.7g/f	3368*

TIGHT SQUEEZE 6 b r m £15584

81a	1-16	**LING**	12ap	76	218*
77a	6-16	Ling	12ap	79	293
79a	5-16	Ling	12ap	78	404
82a	3-16	Ling	12ap	78	475
74a	7-13	Ling	10ap	79	519
78a	8-14	Ling	10ap	79	625
86a	1-7	**LING**	10ap	78	736*
78a	8-12	Ling	13ap	81	877
89a	1-6	**LING**	10ap	80	1027*
76	7-10	Sali	12g/f	80	1721
73	8-14	Leic	10g/f	80	1828
78	6-7	Ling	10g/f	78	2015
79	3-7	Beve	9.9gd	76	2654

TIGRESS 4 b f £1760

0	11-11	Wolv	5af	63	155 bl
55a	6-10	Wolv	6af	61	282 bl
50a	5-13	Wolv	6af	59	384 bl
58a	2-11	Wolv	6af	56	507 bl
49a	6-11	Wolv	5af	56	643 bl
60a	2-10	Wolv	5af	56	749 bl
53a	7-9	Sout	5af	[56]	793 bl
48a	9-11	Wolv	5af	60	958 bl

TIKITANO 3 b f £0

10	18-19	Donc	6g/f		1876
18	14-16	Newm	7fm		2092
0	13-13	Wind	5ap	55	2784
14a	10-10	Ling	5ap	52	3332

TILL THERE WAS YOU 3 b f £0

18a	12 12	Ling	8ap		428
14	10-11	Folk	7g/s		3048
42	11-11	Bath	5g/f		3372
9	12-16	Brig	7gd		4901

TILLA 4 b f £3496

67	5-10	Sand	14g/f	67	2192
63	6-9	Pont	18g/f	67	2607
63	10-11	Sand	14g/f	66	3340
69	2-9	Hayd	14gd	66	3760
74	2-10	Sali	14.1gd	66	3887
69	6-17	Newm	14.8gd	70	4196
71	5-12	York	13.9g/f	69	4400
57	9-19	Sali	14.1gd	69	4856

TILLERMAN 8 b h £10750

115	5-16	Asco	8g/f	[117]	2470
111	6-11	Good	8fm	[117]	3533
91	8-8	Donc	7fm	[115]	4477

TILLINGBORN DANCER 2 b c £0

59	10-13	Carl	5fm	1950
15	11-11	Ayr	6g/s	2569
58	9-10	Catt	7g/f	2845
41	10-11	Newc	7gd	3429
52	9-18	Ripo	6g/s	3939

TILT 2 b c £0

62	8-14	Leic	8gd	5058

TIMBER ICE 4 b f £0

61	10-13	York	11.9g/f	75	3437
62	5-10	Yarm	11.5gd	[72]	3997
52	5-13	Leic	10g/f	[65]	4453

TIMBER SCORPION 2 b c £0

73	5-10	Redc	9fm	4558
49	7-11	Bath	10.2gd	4825

TIMBUKTU 2 b c £414

17a	10-11	Sout	8af		159
37a	6-9	Wolv	9.4af		240
10a	7-9	Wolv	9.4af	[45]	314
21	9-14	Sout	10g/s	40	1051
38	7-16	Nott	10gd	40	1240
41	2-9	Ayr	13.1g/s	[40]	1449
0	8-8	Brig	11.9gd	[40]	1547
15	12-18	Hayd	14gd	44	2905

TIME FLYER 4 b c £0

43a	7-12	Ling	7ap	[45]	566
47a	10-11	Ling	8ap	[40]	697
16a	10-14	Ling	12ap	[40]	968
25a	12-14	Ling	10ap	[40]	1072
17	16-19	Yarm	8g/f	[40]	1130
29	6-10	Warw	6.1g/s	[35]	1327 BL

TIME FOR MEE 2 ch f £0

32	9-16	Ripo	5gd		4787
0	11-12	Pont	6g/s		5152

TIME FOR YOU 2 b f £4053

32	10-10	Newm	6gd			1887
70	4-17	Ling	7g/f			2584
70	1-9	LING	6gd			3020*
47	11-11	Newm	7fm		71	3407
67	4-6	Chep	6.1g/s		69	3897
57a	8-14	Ling	7ap		66	4177
23	27-29	Newm	5gd			5087

TIME MARCHES ON 6 b g £3605

26a	4-12	Wolv	9.4af	[40]		668
2a	9-10	Wolv	12af	[40]		780
51	1-14	PONT	10g/f		40	4624* T
38	8-12	Pont	10fm	[40]		4757 t

TIME N TIME AGAIN 5 b g £21359

65a	4-13	Wolv	5af		67	110
70a	2-11	Wolv	5af		67	155
62a	5-10	Wolv	6af		68	345
72a	1-11	SOUT	5af		68	418* P
69a	8-16	Sout	5af		74	461 p
80a	1-13	SOUT	6af		73	551* p
79a	3-13	Wolv	6af		79	618 p
84a	3-10	Sout	5af		78	660 p
83a	3-13	Wolv	6af		78	687 p
84a	1-13	WOLV	6af		79	807* p
75a	5-10	Wolv	6af		81	834 p
75	16-17	Donc	6gd	[74]		952 p
65	7-18	Ches	7.6gd		74	1598
66	6-16	Nott	6.1sft	[74]		1743 p
67	3-11	Ripo	6gd		70	1977 p
55	7-9	Ripo	6g/f	[70]		2007 p
73	3-11	Ches	5.1g/s		68	2747
73	2-13	Hayd	6gd		68	2884 p
72	2-6	Carl	5.9gd	[70]		2934 p
68	3-10	Hayd	6g/s		70	3136 p
57	6-8	Pont	6gd		69	3461 p

TIME TO REGRET 4 b g £9905

32a	6-10	Wolv	9.4af	[45]		1564
53	2-15	Beve	7.5g/f	[53]		1944
52	4-14	Redc	7g/f	[53]		2102
40	13-13	Carl	7.9fm		52	2447
54	1-18	PONT	8gd		50	3242*
50	7-9	Beve	7.5gd		56	3310
41	10-13	Muss	8af		53	3526
46	12-15	Carl	7.9g/f		52	4346
55	2-15	Beve	8.5g/f		50	4598
50	5-19	Beve	9.9g/f		50	4720
64	1-15	REDC	9g/s		51	5111+
48a	6-13	Wolv	8.6af	[51]		5212
53	4-16	Nott	8.2hvy		59	5347

TIME TO RELAX 3 b f £6897

64a	2-15	Sout	6af	[64]		795
54a	4-11	Sout	6af	[64]		869
68	1-15	BATH	8g/s		64	1099*
53	8-12	Beve	9.9sft		66	1306
68	2-8	Hami	9.2g/s		66	1603
68	3-14	Newc	8gd		66	1872

TIME TO REMEMBER 6 b g £3380

46	14-16	Thir	7g/s		69	1474
50	14-20	Thir	6gd		67	1638
34	16-20	Thir	5g/f		64	1765
56	6-9	Ayr	7.2fm	[60]		1910
5	17-18	Thir	6g/f		58	2214
38	14-18	Donc	6gd		57	2752
48	7-14	Carl	6.9g/f		57	3229
61	2-22	Good	5fm		55	3537
41	15-26	Good	6fm		57	3569
40	12-18	Catt	7g/f		55	3670
49	10-16	Thir	8g/f		57	4592
28	12-14	Catt	6gd		55	4967
48a	6-12	Wolv	8.6af	[52]		5337

TIME TO SUCCEED 2 b g £0

0	12-12	Beve	8.5sft		4257
15	19-20	York	6g/f		4401

TIME TRAVELLER 2 b g £0

6a	10-10	Ling	6ap		3817
0	17-17	Ling	6ap		4316 BL

TIMELY TWIST 2 b f £0

3a	7-11	Ling	6ap	[47]	233
26a	7-10	Ling	10ap	[47]	291

TIMES REVIEW 3 b c £7392

83	2-10	Hayd	6g/f		79	1488
78	5-12	Donc	7g/f		81	1879
86	1-10	LEIC	6gd	[81]		2137*
62	14-20	York	6g/f		85	2407
65	8-15	Hayd	6gd		84	2950
60	7-9	Ripo	6g/f		83	3646
30	11-14	Ches	6.1g/f		81	4048

TIMES THE MASTER 3 b g £0

0	13-13	Sout	6af	40	797

TIMMY 2 b c £0

56	8-12	Beve	5sft	1631
19	12-16	Ripo	6g/f	1780
16	10-13	Beve	5g/s	2321
35	11-14	Beve	7.5sft	2939
44	5-7	Ripo	5gd	3259 BL
0	15-15	Redc	6g/f	3769 bl
0	14-14	Sout	6af	4127

TINIAN 5 b g £3081

60a	5-16	Sout	7af	[65]		161
58a	3-9	Wolv	9.4af	[62]		239
52a	7-12	Ling	10ap	[62]		272
41a	5-11	Ling	8ap	[57]		343 P
50a	3-4	Sout	8af	[54]		417
19a	10-12	Wolv	8.5af		49	479
50a	3-6	Sout	8af	[45]		586
0	12-13	Sout	8af	[45]		776
57	4-18	Catt	7gd	[56]		996
46	9-17	Beve	8.5g/s	[54]		1160
50	4-10	Ayr	8g/s	[52]		1446 p
30a	5-8	Wolv	7af	[45]		1656 BL
35a	4-7	Wolv	8.5af	[45]		1672 bl
50	3-9	Leic	8g/f	[50]		1966
55	2-16	Yarm	10.1fm		50	2146
42	4-10	Ayr	8g/s	[53]		2544
21	8-11	Newc	10.1g/s		53	2726
30a	3-11	Sout	12af	[45]		3154

TINKERS FIRST 2 b f £0

14	9-9	Bath	5g/f		3847
15	15-17	Ling	6g/f		4316
23a	10-10	Ling	7ap		4442 P

TINTA 4 b f £0

0	12-12	Sout	16af	55	1753

TINTAWN GOLD 4 b f £1479

36a	11-14	Ling	10ap		53	718
39	9-16	Good	9gd		50	2220
50	4-16	Folk	12fm		48	2718
51	2-15	Warw	10.9g/f		48	2910
40	10-13	Folk	9.7g/f		48	3726
48	2-15	Folk	12g/f	[47]		4374 P
0	19-20	Kemp	12g/f	[47]		4796 p

TINY TIM 6 b g £3409

32a	4-13	Ling	6ap	[35]	541
39a	4-11	Ling	8ap	[35]	786
37a	2-15	Ling	7ap	[35]	830
35a	3-12	Ling	8ap	[35]	971
27a	5-10	Ling	7ap	[35]	1181
36a	2-6	Ling	8ap	[35]	1292
35a	2-6	Ling	6ap	[35]	1415
43	1-4	BRIG	7gd	[35]	1545*
23a	5-7	Wolv	6af	[35]	1566 BL
40a	2-7	Ling	6ap	[35]	1715
36a	2-10	Sout	7af	[35]	1839
22	11-15	Folk	7g/f	[40]	4371

TIOGA GOLD 5 b g £0

16a	5-7	Sout	11af	[40]		1589 P
0	9-9	Redc	14.1g/f		35	2105
0	10-16	Sout	14af		30	4045
2	11-11	Catt	13.8sft	[30]		5129

TIP THE DIP 4 ch c £3270

89	2-15	Newb	11g/f		84	4643
79	10-17	Newm	12g/f		85	4889
89	3-10	Yarm	10.1sft	[85]		5255 T
0	23-24	Donc	12sft		85	5372 t

TIP TOES 2 b f £250

29	10-10	Leic	5g/f		1826

48	6-8	Bath	5g/f		2977
28	7-8	Brig	6g/f		3172
44	4-7	Ripo	6g/s		3259
42	5-8	Yarm	6gd		3491
34	12-12	Newm	7g/f	[45]	3750
35	6-15	Catt	7sft	[49]	3930
40	4-16	Yarm	8g/s	45	4632
52	8-14	Yarm	8g/s	[45]	5118

TIPSY LADY 3 b f £0

37	15-17	Sali	6g/s			1497
60	7-12	Good	7g/f			1846
56	9-11	Sali	8fm			2419
62	8-14	Newb	9fm			3631
63	5-8	Sand	8.1g/f			3858
64	5-8	Sand	8.1g/s	[62]		4101
32	15-16	Sali	7sft		62	4582

TIPSY LILLIE 2 ch f £5453

53	5-11	Kemp	5hvy			1640
29	7-8	Brig	5g/f			2043
29	11-13	Donc	6gd			2236
33a	8-11	Sout	6af			2336
58	1-9	LEIC	5g/f			2921*
56	4-6	Leic	5g/f			3209
59	1-8	YARM	6gd			3491*
60	4-7	Yarm	6gd	[59]		3994
62	4-9	Nott	6.1hvy	[59]		5185

TIT FOR TAT 2 b f £281

38	14-18	Leic	5fm			2109
56	5-11	Thir	7fm			2462
63	4-14	Thir	7g/s			4204
4	19-20	Yarm	8g/s		61	4635
42	12-18	Newc	6g/f		56	5013 BL

TITIAN FLAME 4 ch f £0

23	19-20	Kemp	9g/f		58	2857
32a	9-14	Sout	8af	[55]		3392

TITIAN LASS 4 ch f £2480

7a	11-14	Sout	8af		48	60 bl
37a	9-16	Ling	7ap		45	270 bl
29a	4-13	Wolv	9.4af		45	287
46a	1-10	LING	8ap	[45]		410* bl
43a	5-13	Ling	7ap		46	739 bl
48a	2-12	Ling	8af		46	1013 bl
45a	5-12	Ling	8ap		46	1045 bl
20	16-20	Yarm	8fm		48	2149 bl

TITIAN TIME 2 b f £49138

81	2-11	Newb	7g/f		3959
87	3-7	Kemp	7g/f		4359
91	1-15	NEWM	8fm		4723*
112	2-10	Long	8g/f		4954

TITO GOFIRST 2 b c £0

58	9-10	Newm	6sft		5266

TITUS ROCK 2 b f £0

13	12-12	Carl	5gd		2933

TITUS SALT 2 ch g £4629

71a	2-10	Wolv	7af			36
78a	1-15	SOUT	7af	[71]		184* BL
78a	3-10	Sout	7af		76	794 bl
61	13-22	Donc	7gd		75	955 bl

TIVISKI 2 b f £10231

78	3-13	Donc	5gd			954
67	4-4	Muss	5gd			1117
82	1-7	CHES	5.1g/s			1573*
77	8-12	Beve	5g/f			2165
62	4-7	Pont	6gd			2792
71	5-8	Ches	5.1g/f			3081
37	9-9	Ches	6.1fm		77	3632
73	9-16	Curr	7g/f	[77]		4153
64	9-17	York	7g/f		73	4396
54	14-15	Hayd	8sft		70	4765

TIYOUN 6 b g £8791

82	2-13	Catt	13.8gd		73	997
69	6-10	Hami	13gd		75	1506
88	1-9	RIPO	16g/f		74	2009*
76	7-7	York	13.9g/f		82	2355
91	2-6	Catt	15.8g/f		81	3015
72	10-19	Good	21fm		85	3531

TIZ MOLLY 3 ch f £0

3	P-7	Folk	9.7gd		3385

TIZ WIZ 3 b f £465

12	9-16	Redc	8sft	46	1147
43	2-9	Ayr	6g/s	[45]	1447
10	10-12	Carl	5.9g/f	43	3655
14	10-14	Beve	7.5sft	[41]	4256
0	13-13	Ayr	8sft	[40]	5275

TIZDUBAI 3 b f £750

88	6-8	Epso	8.5g/f		2211 T
86	7-7	Newm	8fm		3004 t

TIZI OUZOU 3 ch f £1087

49	6-9	Sand	10gd		4501
55	2-15	Wind	10g/f		4834

TIZZY MAY 3 ch c £7726

86a	11-14	Ling	10ap	[96]	82
78	13-17	Kemp	10g/s	96	1111
105	2-19	Newm	10g/f	95	1478
101	5-14	Good	12g/f	[98]	1843
69	10-13	Epso	12fm	98	2255
106	4-7	Newm	12g/f	[98]	2762
0	8-8	Sand	16.4g/s	[98]	2914
97	7-9	Good	12fm	[100]	3563
93	5-6	Newm	10g/f	[100]	3754
88	5-7	Wind	11.6g/s	[97]	4219
84	9-13	Kemp	12g/f	[95]	4715
78	9-14	Newb	10hvy	90	5223

TIZZYS LAW 3 b f £9868

73	1-8	THIR	5sft		1228*
61	6-9	Thir	6g/s	[70]	1477
62	4-13	Ripo	6g/f	69	2011
64	5-10	Hayd	6g/s	69	2227
62	8-11	Newm	5g/f	67	2734
52	11-15	Thir	5g/s	64	3833
68	1-8	FOLK	5gd	60	4118+
62	5-7	Good	5sft	67	4236
66	5-16	Good	5g/f	65	4528

TO WIT TO WOO 3 b g £1254

53a	4-12	Wolv	12af	56	75
62a	2-12	Wolv	9.4af	56	513
14a	8-9	Wolv	9.4af	58	647
32	9-14	Folk	9.7g/s	58	1083 P
40	5-11	Warw	8.1hvy	53	1536 p

TOBEROE COMMOTION 6 b g £0

5a	11-12	Wolv	12af	46	469
1	14-16	Bath	8fm	[45]	2032 BL

TOBYS DREAM 2 b c £3835

35	10-10	Leic	6gd		2703
85	1-12	CARL	5.9fm		3544*
67	8-13	York	6gd	82	4004
76	6-14	Epso	6gd	82	4471
45	11-12	Newm	6gd	79	4882

TOCCATA ARIA 6 b m £6962

51	1-15	WARW	10.9g/f	45	2910*
56	1-14	FOLK	9.7g/s	51	3052*
30	9-13	Pont	12gd	53	3240
38	7-8	Chep	8.1gd	53	3731

TODDEANO 8 b g £0

8a	9-10	Wolv	7af		890 P
0	13-13	Leic	7g/f		1827 t

TODLEA 3 b g £11243

1a	13-13	Wolv	9.4af	79	127
69a	11-14	Ling	10ap	75	174
62a	6-8	Ling	10ap	[70]	294 t
75	4-12	Sand	8.1g/s	75	1352
76	4-19	Newb	10gd	73	1736
76	3-15	Kemp	10fm	72	2067
69	6-14	Wind	10g/f	72	2265
74	3-20	Kemp	9g/f	71	2857
77	2-7	Bath	10.2g/f	71	2979
77	3-16	Kemp	9gd	71	3187
79	1-12	KEMP	8g/f	73	3524*
51	13-15	Brig	8fm	76	3694
76	3-7	Ripo	8gd	[78]	4304
76	3-11	Muss	9g/f	[76]	4550
55	13-18	Kemp	8g/f	76	4714

TOFFEE VODKA 2 b f £6459

66	6-13	Kemp	6gd		3183

76	3-8	Good	6fm		3536
75a	1-12	LING	6ap		4178*
68	7-21	Donc	6fm	[77]	4490
69	9-16	Newm	7g/f	73	4913

TOHAMA 2 b f £0

75	6-7	Newm	7g/f		3616
65	8-12	Beve	7.5g/s		4242
74	5-14	Sali	7sft		4575
72	10-17	Good	8gd	74	4871

TOILE 3 ch f £239

49	6-7	Sali	14.1gd		4333

TOJONESKI 5 b g £4059

2a	10-15	Ling	12ap	[40]	707 VIS
30a	7-11	Ling	8ap	[40]	786
35a	3-15	Ling	7ap	[35]	830 p
32a	4-12	Ling	8ap	[35]	971 p
40a	2-6	Wolv	9.4af	[35]	1262 p
41	2-10	Warw	8.1g/s	[35]	1328 p
47	2-17	Kemp	7hvy	[40]	1642 p
46	3-18	Nott	8.2gd	[45]	1992 p
47	3-17	Warw	8.1fm	45	2440 p
49	4-14	Muss	7.1g/f	45	2615 p
60	2-8	Epso	8.5g/f	[47]	2873 p
45	7-17	Hayd	8.1gd	46	2947 p
58	3-11	Muss	8g/f	[46]	3558 p
42	9-15	Ling	7.6fm	45	3788 p
38	7-10	Brig	7sft	45	4168 p

TOKEWANNA 4 b f £4260

7a	11-12	Wolv	7af	54	2204
8	18-18	Donc	7gd	54	2755
52	3-7	Ches	7.6g/f	[50]	3079 T
45	7-8	Muss	7.1g/f	52	3528
49a	4-14	Ling	7ap	47	3746 t
48	5-14	Bath	8g/f	50	3963 t
49	4-17	Carl	7.9fm	[49]	4506 t
50	3-16	Catt	7g/f	47	4676 t
45	5-19	Kemp	8g/f	[48]	4795 t
37	10-19	Yarm	8g/s	[48]	5119 t
50a	1-11	WOLV	7.1ap	[45]	5210* t
54a	1-13	WOLV	8.6ap	[45]	5232* t
27a	10-13	Wolv	8.6ap	53	5365 t

TOLAGA BAY 6 ch m £0

0	4-4	Wolv	12af		1323

TOLDO 2 gr g £14977

43	7-8	Hayd	5gd		2241
40	9-9	Carl	5.9gd		2671
43	9-12	Carl	5gd		2933
48	4-5	Hami	5gd		3130 BL
3	12-12	Carl	5.9fm		3544 bl
55	2-15	Catt	7sft	[45]	3930
72	1-14	MUSS	7.1g/f	[53]	4171*
67	1-10	NEWC	8hvy	[53]	4213*
77	1-19	PONT	8g/s	67	5147*
56	11-14	Donc	7sft	73	5213

TOLEDO SUN 3 b g £4078

45a	10-13	Ling	10ap	59	104
50a	7-14	Ling	10ap	57	230
53a	3-8	Sout	11af	55	595
44	5-8	Yarm	11.5g/f	45	1135
57a	1-9	WOLV	14.8af	51	1654*
46	2-13	Nott	14.1gd	[45]	1990

TOM BELL 4 b g £5031

51	2-17	Pont	12hvy	45	1064
37	9-17	Nott	14.1gd	47	1238
49	4-11	Leic	11.8fm	47	2112
47	4-10	Hami	13g/f	48	2479
50	2-14	Carl	17.2gd	47	2937
45	4-15	Folk	16.4g/s	47	3049
39	12-19	Chep	12.1gd	49	3727 vis
62	1-12	BRIG	11.9fm	49	4764*

TOM FOREST 2 b c £4450

77	6-10	Donc	6g/f		2077
88	2-9	Ripo	6g/f		2522
80	2-7	Pont	6g/f		2792
71	5-7	Ayr	7.2g/f		3302
57	11-12	York	7g/s	82	4064
53	11-14	Newb	7sft	77	5193

TOM FROM BOUNTY 4 ch g £0

26	10-20	Yarm	6g/s	[45]	5121

TOM TUN 9 b g £17317

0	7-7	Hayd	6g/f	[97]	1487 bl
95	2-14	York	6g/s	93	1703 bl
66	8-12	Hayd	6gd	[94]	2186 bl
101	4-8	Hayd	6gd	[93]	2949 bl
101	2-11	Hami	6fm	96	3248 bl
70	16-19	Ripo	6g/s	97	3937 bl
104	3-19	York	6gd	97	4005 bl
100	5-13	York	6gd	99	4322 bl
87	10-24	Ayr	6sft	99	4686 bl
93	8-20	York	6gd	97	5001 bl
96	3-13	Donc	5sft	94	5218 bl
95	7-12	Donc	6sft	[94]	5371 bl

TOMASINO 6 br g £4384

56	4-6	York	10.4g/f	[93]	2356
21	6-6	Newc	12.4sft	[83]	2686
57	7-8	Ayr	10gd	[76]	3151 T
73	1-7	CARL	11.9g/f	[76]	3226* t
65	9-13	York	11.9g/f	75	3437 t
74	3-7	Thir	16g/s	70	4209 t
0	8-8	Ayr	13.1sft	70	4690 t

TOMBOLA 2 b c £424

76	4-9	Sali	7gd		2696
61	12-16	Newm	7g/f		3582
59	13-13	Warw	7.1g/f		4416

TOMINA 4 b g £3064

76	2-18	Newb	16gd	75	1232
26	11-13	Newb	16sft	75	5194

TOMMY CARSON 8 b g £3419

27a	5-13	Ling	16ap	38	137
43a	3-8	Sout	16af	40	554
21	10-13	Yarm	11.5fm	40	2868
43a	1-13	LING	16ap	38	3822*
50	6-15	Good	16gd	40	5025

TOMMY SMITH 6 ch g £4134

7	9-9	Thir	5g/s	[77]	1217 bl
55	20-20	Thir	5g/s	75	1476 bl
60	8-20	Thir	5g/f	72	1765 bl
48	11-11	Hayd	5g/f	72	1886 bl
75	1-13	PONT	5g/f	[67]	2279* t
67	8-13	York	7af	74	2359 bl
18	16-17	Pont	5gd	72	3241 bl
0	8-10	Beve	5g/f	[71]	3503 bl
49	15-19	Beve	5g/s	71	4240 bl
44	11-17	Newb	5g/f	68	4603 bl

TOMOBEL 2 b f £1244

43	10-15	York	5gd		2056
64	9-12	Folk	7gd		3909
55	5-17	Warw	7.1gd		4269
66	2-20	Yarm	6g/s	60	4635

TOMOKIM 2 b c £0

0	10-10	Ling	6ap		258
0	11-11	Ling	8ap	[30]	786 VIS

TOMOOHAT 2 b f £7072

92	1-23	NEWM	6gd		5084+

TOMSK 4 b g £387

33a	6-10	Wolv	8.5af	[40]	1801
24	3-14	Chep	10.2g/s	35	3895
10a	10-14	Ling	10ap	[35]	4662

TOMTHEVIC 6 ch g £0

31	14-14	Kemp	5g/f	60	1914
36	11-12	Folk	5g/f	59	2269
50	8-14	Ling	5g/f	57	2585 P
50	7-17	Bath	5g/f	53	2981
51	4-9	Catt	5g/f	[50]	3353
39	11-19	Beve	5g/s	49	4240
52	5-15	Sali	5gd	49	4335
41	11-15	Chep	5.1gd	46	4489
10	16-19	Yarm	6g/s	46	4636
21	10-13	Muss	5g/s	[48]	5146

TON CHEE 5 b g £0

4a	6-10	Wolv	16.2af	[30]	824
0	7-7	Wolv	16.2af	[30]	1802
13	6-14	Carl	17.2gd	20	2937
0	10-12	Muss	16gd	20	2964

TONG ICE 5 gr g £0
5a 8-9 Ling 8ap [40] 1185 P
0 6-6 Ling 6ap [30] 1415 bl
24a 5-5 Ling 6ap [30] 1452

TONI ALCALA 4 b g £25113
38a 9-11 Wolv 16.2af 66 48
66a 3-6 Wolv 12af [64] 752
55a 5-7 Wolv 16.2af 64 866
66 4-12 Newc 16.1sft 63 965
29 7-15 Newc 12.4hvy 63 1034
63 2-10 Muss 14g/f 63 1118
56 3-13 Pont 21.6hvy 63 1252
73 1-5 MUSS 14g/s 64 1459*
67 6-12 Thir 16gd 68 1637
68 1-8 AYR 13.1fm 66 1905*
70 3-12 Muss 14fm 68 2085
68 5-9 Hami 13gd 68 2176
71 2-13 Pont 17.1g/f 68 2276
67 4-10 Carl 14.1fm 67 2444
66 5-9 Pont 16gd 68 2607
76 1-6 MUSS 16g/f 68 2807*
77 1-10 NEWC 16.1g/s 73 3701*
76 5-6 Redc 16g/f 79 3810
66 5-12 Ches 15.9sft 77 4106
67 6-6 Newc 14.4sft 75 4287
62 7-8 Ayr 17.5g/s 72 4657
68 4-6 Muss 16gd 68 4808
30 13-14 Pont 17.1g/f 68 4936
0 10-10 Pont 18g/s 66 5151

TONIGHT 2 b g £721
24 3-4 Ayr 6fm 1906
55 4-8 Hayd 6g/f 2183
57 3-6 Yarm 7g/f 2343
43 6-13 Catt 7g/f 3349
46 7-10 Newc 8hvy [60] 4213
50 10-20 Leic 7g/f 57 4451 BL
33 8-16 Yarm 8g/s 57 4632

TONTO 2 gr g £832
52a 7-10 Ling 6ap [76] 260
52a 7-13 Ling 6ap [70] 364 p
48a 4-11 Sout 7af [65] 488
60a 3-13 Sout 8af [65] 553
47a 7-12 Sout 8af 60 656
0 F-13 Wyth 8ap 60 756 p
77a 6-9 Ling 8ap [58] 843 p
39a 10-10 Ling 10ap 3058 p

TONY JAMES 2 b c £89460
102 1-6 PONT 6g/f 2039*
104 4-13 Asco 6g/f 2467
100 5-7 Newm 6g/f 3028
110 1-11 YORK 6g/s [100] 4022*
107 6-6 Long 7g/f [100] 4955
83 9-9 Mais 6sft [100] 5312

TONY THE TAP 2 b g £29201
68a 4-10 Ling 6ap 258
83a 1-5 LING 5ap 725*
85 2-16 Leic 5g/f 75 2400
84 2-9 Newm 5fm 79 2593
86 2-11 Newm 5g/f 79 2734
80 5-9 Epso 7gd 80 3218
87 2-11 Newm 8gd 80 3408
87 1-9 EPSO 6fm 80 3543*
70 9-10 Newm 6g/f 80 3584
78 7-19 York 6gd 83 4005
86 5-12 Newm 6gd 82 4229
86 2-12 Yarm 5.2g/s 82 4585
72 12-13 Asco 6.5g/f 82 4773

TONY TIE 8 b g £17504
60 6-14 Newc 10.1sft 72 964
80 2-19 Beve 9.9g/s 71 1164
75 2-8 Muss 8g/s [75] 1461
75 5-8 Ayr 10g/f 76 1895
57 15-15 Kemp 10fm 75 2067
76 2-11 Hami 8.3g/f 73 2317
86 1-12 AYR 8g/s [73] 2543*
76 6-18 Newc 7sft 79 2684
86 1-6 AYR 8gd [83] 3152*
73 11-16 Redc 8g/f 84 3768
62 6-7 Hami 9.2g/s 84 3879
70 9-10 Hami 8.3g/s 84 4136
82 5-10 Ayr 8sft 82 4685

67 7-14 Hami 8.3g/s 80 4820
55 17-20 York 8.9gd 77 4999
64 10-11 Muss 7.1g/s 75 5144

TOO KEEN 3 ch f £0
30a 5-12 Sout 7af 2339
30 11-14 Thir 7sft 2692
20a 8-10 Sout 8af 2997

TOP ACHIEVER 3 ch g £860
61 7-12 Hayd 8.1sft 1108
69 7-11 Beve 8.5sft 1304
44 11-18 Nott 8.2g/s 62 1778
45 6-15 Ayr 8gd [59] 2504 BL
59 2-12 Folk 12g/s 55 3913

TOP DIRHAM 6 ch g £14239
73 2-16 Newc 8hvy 70 1036
73 3-17 Thir 8g/s 71 1214
76 2-10 Newc 8g/f 71 2159
65 11-15 York 8.9g/f 71 2404
73 8-17 Carl 7.9gd 71 2672
77 1-9 AYR 8g/f 70 3305*
77 6-13 Newc 7gd 71 3428
75 6-12 Muss 8gd [72] 4809

TOP FORM 2 b f £6253
58 8-9 Newm 6g/f 2245
58 5-6 Brig 6g/f 3171
81 1-12 THIR 6g/f 3411*
73 5-14 Warw 6.1g/f 80 4420
58 21-26 Newb 6.5g/f 4679
52 11-11 Epso 5g/f 77 4907

TOP GEAR 2 b f £1780
86 2-14 Sali 8gd 4852

TOP LINE DANCER 3 b c £260
69 4-11 Catt 6gd 999
38 12-13 Redc 7sft [70] 1142
64 8-14 Redc 7fm 68 2295
14 9-9 Thir 8g/f [65] 4593 T

TOP MARK 2 b c £0
22 11-15 Newb 8hvy 5221

TOP OF THE CLASS 6 b m £1410
45a 5-13 Wolv 9.4af 48 38 vis
27a 7-15 Sout 8af 46 84 vis
18a 10-13 Wolv 9.4af 44 281 vis
33a 6-11 Wolv 9.4af 45 465 vis
45a 3-11 Wolv 12af 45 557 vis
47a 3-9 Wolv 9.4af 45 620 vis
50a 4-11 Ling 12ap 45 624 vis
29a 8-14 Ling 12ap 46 711 vis
45a 7-7 Ling 10ap 46 736 vis
28a 14-14 Ling 12ap 46 768 vis
44a 3-14 Ling 10ap [45] 828 vis
43a 5-15 Sout 12af 45 867 vis
23a 7-12 Wolv 12af [45] 891 vis
59 4-20 Warw 10.9gd 58 1128 vis
45 7-12 Sout 11gd 58 1286 vis
42 7-11 Bath 10.2fm 56 1899 vis
29a 7-13 Ling 12g/f 40 1986 vis
31 8-10 Chep 12.1gd 54 2114 vis

TOP PLACE 3 b f £0
28a 7-10 Ling 5ap 548 P
31a 8-14 Ling 6ap 652 p
40a 9-11 Ling 6ap 898 p
35a 5-12 Ling 6ap [45] 1075 p
31 5-10 Warw 6.1g/s [40] 1327 p
0 10-10 Brig 5.3gd [40] 1544 p
37 6-8 Warw 7.1fm [35] 2575
34 8-11 Good 6gd [35] 5030

TOP PURSUIT 2 b g £0
59 7-8 Brig 7gd 2952

TOP ROMANCE 3 ch f £2500
86 8-13 Newm 7gd 1169
94 4-8 Epso 8.5g/f [102] 2211
75 8-10 Sali 9.9g/f [100] 3866

TOP SEED 2 b c £29224
103 4- Sain 10g/s 9
109 2-5 Newb 10gd [108] 1208
109 4-10 York 10.4g/s[108] 1685
93 13-15 Chan 12g/s [108] 2308

94 3-10 Asco 16.2g/f[108] 2557
92 2-4 Newm 14.8g/f[108] 3027
79 16-19 York 13.9g/s 105 4023
94 8-14 Asco 12g/f 102 4814
0 P-8 Newb 12hvy [98] 5224
0 P-6 Donc 12sft [98] 5369 T

TOP SON 4 b c £0
15a 13-14 Ling 12ap 103
1a 11-14 Sout 14af 25 185

TOP SPEC 3 b g £21435
87 8-13 York 10.4sft 87 1664
71 11-14 Asco 10g/f 85 1924
74 5-8 Chep 10.2gd [83] 2197
69 12-16 Sand 10g/s 80 2919
76 2-7 Sali 8gd [77] 3453
73 7-14 Newb 10g/f 76 3961
80 1-4 SAND 10g/s [76] 4068*
82 2-19 Kemp 10fm 76 4392
84 1-12 SAND 10gd 76 4502*
88 9-13 Asco 10g/f [80] 4772
80 4-10 Newm 12sft [82] 5102
76 2-10 Donc 10.3sft 82 5201

TOP STYLE 6 ch g £2231
5a 7-12 Sout 11af [30] 640
32a 2-10 Ling 7ap [30] 1181
40a 2-7 Ling 10ap [30] 1244
52 1-13 AYR 10sft [40] 5276*

TOP TENOR 4 b c £0
0 12-12 Ling 16ap 73 478
56a 11-15 Ling 12ap 72 549
56a 6-11 Ling 12ap [70] 816 BL
43a 4-10 Ling 12ap [65] 916 bl

TOP THE CHARTS 2 b c £6238
80 4-11 Newm 7gd 4190
82 4-16 Newb 7g/f 4677
86 3-14 Sali 8gd 4852
92 2-14 Donc 7sft 83 5213

TOP TREES 5 b g £6858
34a 11-11 Wolv 12af 51 72
38 9-11 Sali 12fm 46 2293
43 6-19 Bath 17.2gd 45 3147
56 1-11 SAND 14g/f 45 3340*
56 5-12 Sand 16.4g/f 53 3861
46 8-14 Bath 13.1g/s 52 4203
46 5-13 Warw 12.6g/s [50] 4665

TOPARUDI 3 b g £5420
48 9-11 Ripo 8gd 71 1176
74 1-16 LEIC 8g/s 69 1359*
47 11-13 Newm 8g/f 73 2247
75 3-10 Asco 8gd [73] 3067

TOPATOO 2 ch f £730
76 3-10 Newm 6sft 5266

TOPKAMP 4 b f £17710
104 2-10 Bade 6gd [104] 2140
93 3-9 Cork 6fm [104] 2457
89 3-6 Newm 6g/f [104] 2736
100 6-9 York 6g/s [102] 3075

TOPKAT 3 b g £8334
66 8-13 Sali 9.9gd 2700
69 2-7 Folk 9.7gd 3385
73 5-14 Newb 9fm 3631
83 1-11 SALI 12g/s 70 4080+
74 7-13 Kemp 14.4fm 77 4395

TOPPLE 3 b f £0
37 9-10 Good 9g/f 1864

TOPPLING 5 b g £0
31a 15-16 Ling 7ap 57 20
37a 9-13 Wolv 6af 57 41
21a 12-14 Ling 6ap 52 328
46 8-12 Leic 6fm 58 2111
36 8-18 Thir 6g/f 58 2214
44 8-11 Good 6gd 55 2535
58 4-20 Nott 6.1g/f 55 2630
38 13-14 Ling 6gd 55 3289
37 11-14 Catt 5g/f 55 3352 P
47 9-13 Thir 7g/f 53 3571 p
14 14-15 Ling 7.6fm 50 3788 p

30	11-20	Chep	7.1g/s	48	4367 BL

TOPTON 9 b g £9104

72a	1-11	LING	8ap	66	136* bl
66a	4-8	Ling	10ap	[69]	294 bl
66a	3-12	Sout	8af	69	530 bl
74a	1-11	LING	8ap	69	714+ bl
47	13-13	Wind	8.3g/s	[80]	1057 bl
0	15-18	Asco	8sft	80	1423 bl
65	9-14	Donc	8g/f	[78]	1877 bl
76	4-7	Newm	8fm	[76]	2091 bl
77	6-13	Donc	8gd	[76]	2753 bl
81	2-7	Yarm	8g/f	76	2853 bl
80	6-20	Newm	8fm	76	3001 bl
80	5-9	Beve	8g/s	79	3225 bl
77	4-8	Newm	8g/f	77	3583 bl
68	7-12	Leic	8fm	76	3813 bl
72	5-12	Chep	8.1g/s	76	3898 bl
52	13-20	Yarm	7sft	74	5256 bl

TOQUE 2 ch f £0

61	9-19	Leic	7gd		5040
42a	9-12	Ling	8ap		5295

TORCELLO 6 b g £1665

90	5-8	Pont	10fm	89	4755
89	4-14	Newb	10hvy	87	5223

TORCHLIGHT 4 b f £0

45	11-18	Wind	8.3g/f		1810
6	13-13	Nott	8.2g/f		2633 BL T

TORINMOOR 3 ch c £9634

87	5-8	Sali	9.9g/s	93	1500
94	3-10	Wind	10fm	91	2785
93	3-11	Newm	10g/f	91	3029
92	5-21	York	11.9gd	91	3999
96	4-9	Newm	10gd	90	4227

TORNADO BAY 3 b f £0

40	11-12	Ripo	9g/f		1783
0	7-7	Wolv	12af		2050

TORO BRAVO 3 b g £414

22a	13-16	Sout	11af	67	97
7a	8-11	Sout	11af	[64]	191 BL
38a	8-12	Ling	10ap	[60]	267 bl
46a	5-8	Wolv	8.5af	[60]	362 bl
52a	3-6	Wolv	9.4af	[55]	423 bl

TORONTO HEIGHTS 3 ch g £9149

74a	2-11	Wolv	6af	[76]	481
76a	1-11	LING	6ap	[76]	543*
82a	1-8	LING	6ap	73	673*
72a	9-12	Ling	7ap	79	729
42	19-20	Newm	7g/f	79	1186
73a	7-11	Ling	6ap	79	3744
59	12-12	Newm	6gd	75	4229

TORQUEMADA 3 ch c £5825

62a	3-11	Ling	6ap		898
44	11-15	Wind	6g/s	68	1054
0	16-17	Asco	6sft	65	1417
45	8-20	Newb	7g/f	60	2314
64a	3-11	Ling	6ap	57	2841
56a	7-11	Ling	6ap	60	3333
31	9-15	Sali	6gd	59	3888
66	1-19	LEIC	7g/f	55	4452*
61	5-17	Ling	6g/f	60	4740
65a	3-14	Ling	7ap	[60]	5263

TORRENS 2 b c £4887

81	4-14	Sand	7.1g/s		4069
77	1-9	CHEP	8.1g/s		4297*
64	7-12	Sali	8sft	79	4580
65	10-19	Pont	8g/s	75	5147
76	3-19	Redc	8sft	71	5302
42	14-20	Donc	7sft	71	5373 T

TORRENT 9 ch g £12039

45a	2-13	Wolv	5af	[45]	312 bl
35a	6-13	Ling	6ap	45	448 bl
40a	3-14	Sout	6af	45	501 bl
48a	1-10	WOLV	5af	[45]	527+ bl
39a	5-11	Wolv	5af	45	643 bl
45a	3-16	Sout	5af	[45]	720 bl
18a	8-15	Sout	6af	[45]	773 bl
40a	7-11	Sout	5af	45	859 bl
54a	1-12	WOLV	5af	[45]	889+ bl

42a	9-12	Wolv	5af	[45]	960 bl
40	9-20	Ripo	5gd	49	1179 bl
34	9-15	Muss	5gd	47	1555 bl
56	1-12	RIPO	5gd	45	2524* bl
53	2-19	Leic	5gd	52	2702 bl
52	7-20	Beve	5g/s	54	3180 bl
39	8-18	Thir	6fm	54	3609 bl
51	7-17	Catt	5g/f	54	3667 bl
58	2-17	Beve	5gd	53	4603 bl
29	20-20	Ripo	6gd	57	4785 bl
37	7-13	Catt	5sft	[56]	5321 bl

TORRESTRELLA 3 b f £140838

117	1-13	LONG	8g/s		1854*

TORRID KENTAVR 7 b g £6469

47	7-16	Newc	8hvy	60	1036
70	1-14	PONT	8hvy	[59]	1253*
72	2-12	Beve	8.5gd	65	2890

TORTUETTE 3 b f £0

3a	9-9	Wolv	9.4af	45	351
11a	10-11	Ling	8ap	[45]	408 VIS
0	9-9	Sout	8af	[35]	596 P

TORZAL 3 b r g £0

0	13-16	Sout	8af	40	86
4a	14-20	Sout	8af	[35]	170
0	15-15	Leic	11.8gd	[45]	5060

TOSHI 2 b c £0

57	7-10	Good	6g/f		3511
64	8-14	Ches	7sft		4102

TOSS THE CABER 2 ch c £0

53	7-7	Ayr	6g/f		1893
16	8-8	York	6g/f		2408

TOTAL FORCE 3 b c £0

59	11-17	Chep	8.1gd		2117
31	16-20	Newb	7fm	62	2650

TOTAL TURTLE 5 b g £750

92	6-8	Donc	12fm	103	4534
75	5-5	Asco	16.2g/f	[100]	4815

TOTALLY SCOTTISH 8 b g £866

47	3-12	Sout	16gd	45	1285
51	3-20	Catt	15.8gd	45	4965

TOTALLY YOURS 3 b f £4346

84	9-13	Newm	7gd	[93]	1169
91	4-6	Leic	7gd	[90]	2136
30	17-19	Asco	8g/f	89	2491
85	5-11	Donc	7g/s	89	3223
63	11-12	Good	9fm	87	3535
70	8-11	Hayd	6g/f	[85]	4350
70	9-15	Kemp	6g/f	82	4713
88	2-19	Sali	8g/f	82	4855
60	10-12	Newb	6sft	83	5196
70	9-11	Newm	8sft	[83]	5270 P

TOUCH OF EBONY 5 b g £640

12	15-17	Carl	7.9fm	[48]	4506
27	10-14	Epso	12gd	45	4910
49	2-14	Yarm	14.1g/s	[45]	5123 p
39	3-9	Ayr	13.1sft	[46]	5277

TOUCH OF LAND 4 b c £85669

117	1-10	BADE	11gd		2141*
115	3-11	Veli	12fm		4570
121	1-12	LONG	10g/f		4950*

TOUCH OF SILK 2 ch f £1500

69	5-19	Wind	5g/f		1805
73	2-6	Sand	5g/f		2097
74	15-17	Asco	6g/f		2553
46	11-14	Hayd	6fm	[73]	4385

TOUCH OF SPICE 2 ch g £0

0	16-17	Wind	6g/f		3975
36a	9-14	Ling	7ap		4658
7	16-19	Kemp	6gd		4792

TOUCH OF SPIRIT 5 b m £0

0	9-11	Sout	8af	[35]	372

TOUGH LOVE 5 ch g £0

42	22-24	Donc	8gd	93	951
81	16-19	Newc	7hvy	91	1035

87	7-20	Newm	7g/s	89	1151
61	16-17	Thir	8g/s	88	1475
31	10-10	Pont	8gd	86	3460
81	5-8	Hayd	8.1fm	84	3797
67	10-13	Ches	7.6sft	81	4103
69	15-21	Donc	7fm	78	4482

TOUPIE 2 ch f £25704

108	1-9	CHAN	5.5gd		4563*

TOURMALET 3 b f £666

74a	2-11	Ling	8ap	72	136

TOURNEDOS 2 b c £74094

95	1-8	NEWB	5.2gd		1205*
95	2-7	Beve	5g/f		2167
106	2-15	Asco	5g/f		2472
86	8-24	Newb	5.2g/f		3266
106	1-13	GOOD	5g/f		3509*
78	7-9	Deau	6sft		4159
105	3-7	Bade	6gd		4427
105	2-11	Donc	5fm	[100]	4533
101	5-10	Curr	6.3gd	[100]	4737
104	2-9	Tipp	5hvy	[100]	4960
103	6-11	Newm	5sft	[100]	5132

TOUT LES SOUS 3 ch g £0

19	7-8	Leic	11.8g/f		1961
0	9-9	Kemp	12g/f		2862

TOUT SEUL 4 b c £21400

115	1-1	LEIC	7g/s	[113]	1356*
58	15-15	Newb	8g/f	[113]	1758
69	11-11	Hayd	7.1gd	[110]	2184
0	6-9	Curr	7gd	[110]	3320
91	10-12	Sali	8gd	[107]	3886
106	4-13	Newm	8g/f	[105]	4887
109	4-11	Newm	8g/s	[105]	5283

TOWN END TOM 2 b c £0

61	5-10	Newm	5fm		2089
22	6-7	Nott	6.1g/f		2629
60	6-11	Warw	5g/f		2911
36	16-20	Redc	7fm	60	4337
26	16-19	Bath	5gd	58	5021 BL

TOWN HOUSE 2 g rf £4206

57	5-5	Nott	5.1fm		1001
56	7-11	Warw	5gd		1123
74	2-7	Ches	5.1g/s		1571
74	1-13	NOTT	5.1gd		1987*
66	7-10	Ches	5.1g/s		2744
58	7-9	Hayd	5sft	73	3271
39	9-10	Thir	5fm	73	3607
22a	10-12	Wolv	5.1ap	[70]	4981

TRACKATTACK 2 ch c £529

76	3-9	Ling	6gd		3020
64a	5-9	Sout	6af		3157
64	7-13	Bath	5.7g/f		3368
51	10-11	Newb	7fm	75	3627
30	12-17	Ling	6g/f	[70]	4316 BL

TRACTOR BOY 2 b c £5278

51	12-14	Wind	5gd		4121
90	1-13	WIND	6g/f		5048*

TRADE FAIR 4 b c £41840

69	14-15	York	6sft	[120]	1667
106	3-8	Newm	7g/f	[120]	2765
116	1-9	CURR	7gd	[120]	3320*
106	6-8	Good	7g/f	[117]	3508

TRAFALGAR SQUARE 2 b c £0

56	8-13	Newm	7fm		4724

TRAGEDIAN 2 ch c £920

83	3-19	Leic	7gd		5055

TRAGIC DANCER 8 b g £0

32	8-9	Folk	12sft	47	979

TRAIANOS 2 b c £0

69	5-12	Newm	6g/f		2348
75	6-11	Newm	7g/f		3234
77	5-16	Newm	7g/f		3582
77	7-11	Hayd	8.1fm	79	4387

TRANCE 3 ch g £22156

75a	1-10	SOUT	8af	[75]	143*

59	9-16	Redc	10g/f	75	1821	
77	4-10	Newc	10.1g/f	75	2162	
86	**1-11**	**DONC**	12gd	75	2233*	
88	**1-9**	**AYR**	13.1g/s	82	2567*	
16	9-9	Pont	12g/s	87	3969	
83	11-20	Hayd	14fm	87	4383	
79	7-17	Nott	14.1g/s	86	4647	
90	3-7	Hayd	14sft	84	4778	
91	9-34	Newm	18sft	87	5135	
77	5-7	Donc	16.5sft	85	5374	

TRANQUIL SKY 3 b f £5959

53	18-20	Newm	7g/f	88	1186	
61	16-20	Newm	8fm	86	1496	
87	5-18	Good	9g/f	83	1813	
88	2-11	Pont	8g/f	83	2040	
81	7-13	Newm	8g/f	87	2247	
73	4-10	Asco	8gd	[85]	3067	
80	7-10	Kemp	8fm	83	4389	
82	5-13	Muss	7.1gd	80	4806	
79	5-11	Good	8gd	80	5027	

TRANQUILIZER 2 b f £1745

63	6-10	Wind	8.3fm		3803	T
0	U-15	Good	8g/s		4233	t
52	7-19	Kemp	8g/f		4792	t
72	2-14	Bath	8gd		5018	t
69a	3-13	Wolv	8.6ap	[69]	5288	t

TRANSACTION 2 ch c £31137

80a	3-9	Ling	5ap		931	
84	2-10	Leic	6gd		2703	
91	**1-12**	**YORK**	6gd		3122*	
93	**1-11**	**NEWM**	6g/f	85	3614*	
82	6-13	York	6gd	90	4004	
86	8-22	Donc	6fm		4458	
56	15-15	Hayd	6sft	89	4765	

TRANSCENDANTALE 6 b m £3020

45	2-8	Yarm	11.5g/f	40	1135	
46	3-15	Beve	9.9sft	40	1307	
49	5-9	Nott	10sft	45	1467	
64	6-7	Hayd	11.9g/f	[47]	1921	
38	9-13	Pont	10g/f	47	2038	
75	7-7	Pont	8g/f	[47]	2278	
41	4-10	Beve	9.9gd	47	2510	
30	8-9	Pont	8g/f	47	2604	
43	4-8	Hayd	11.9gd	47	2881	
37	5-8	Wind	8.3gd	42	3162	
20	9-12	Hayd	11.9gd	42	3734	
34	7-15	Thir	8fm	[40]	4379	
11	15-17	Pont	8g/f	40	4626	

TRANSGRESS 2 b c £896

78	3-15	Newb	7g/f		2876	
65	8-16	Sali	7g/s		3111	
56	6-9	Good	6gd		3951	
68	5-6	Epso	7g/f	[69]	4470	

TRANSIT 5 b g £0

47	5-8	Newc	12.4hvy	[65]	1038	p

TRANSKEI 3 b f £264

26	13-16	Ripo	8gd		2987	
4	4-5	Catt	12sft		3934	
2	10-14	Carl	9.3g/f		4347	
0	12-12	Ayr	7.2sft	[35]	5274	

TRANSVESTITE 2 b c £1629

76	5-8	Kemp	5gd		2171	
80	4-18	Wind	6gd		2618	
72	3-9	Nott	5.1gd		2926	
59	6-7	Ches	7g/f	75	4509	
71	11-20	Ling	7g/f	72	4741	VIS
76a	3-11	Ling	6ap	70	4972	vis

TRAPPETO 2 b c £0

65	11-17	Warw	7.1gd		4271	

TRAVEL TARDIA 5 br h £1460

36a	11-14	Ling	10ap	54	236	
2a	13-13	Ling	10ap	[51]	429	
23a	8-11	Ling	8ap	[40]	786	
37a	4-9	Wolv	7af	[40]	825	
53a	**1-10**	**WOLV**	7af	[35]	890*	T
12a	7-9	Sout	11af	[35]	985	t
32	15-18	Catt	7gd	[30]	996	t

TRAVEL TIP 2 ch c £429

69	4-8	Pont	8fm		4756	
0	P-14	Leic	8gd		5058	

TRAVELLERS JOY 4 b f £205

23a	9-12	Ling	6ap	[45]	1075	
23	8-12	Chep	5.1sft	[40]	1336	
39a	3-7	Wolv	5af	[40]	1562	
16a	8-12	Wolv	5af	[40]	1799	
36	5-16	Nott	6.1gd	[40]	1989	
14	9-20	Chep	6.1gd	35	2372	
30	6-19	Leic	5gd	33	2702	
30	8-11	Warw	5.5gd	32	3054	

TRAVELLERS TALE 4 b g £2803

60a	4-6	Wolv	9.4af	71	249	
59a	13-14	Ling	10ap	70	434	
65	7-14	Nott	10fm	[71]	1006	
65	6-18	Bath	10.2g/s	71	1098	
54	12-19	Newb	10gd	68	1736	
62	7-11	Sali	12fm	66	2293	
54	6-10	Leic	11.8gd	[64]	2707	
53	7-7	Bath	10.2g/f	61	2979	
51	6-15	Wind	11.6fm	59	3481	
57	2-11	Good	11gd	55	3948	
59	2-17	Kemp	12sft	55	4033	
41	11-14	Bath	13.1g/s	52	4203	
57a	3-11	Wolv	12.2ap	54	5180	
54a	4-12	Wolv	12.2ap	54	5328	

TRAVELLING BAND 6 b g £1728

65a	13-14	Ling	10ap	78	452	
58	13-14	Hayd	8.1gd	80	2903	
70	6-15	Epso	10.1gd	[77]	3216	
64	9-14	Sand	10g/s	75	4097	
71	2-9	Good	9sft	[72]	4266	VIS
50	12-17	Ayr	9.1g/s	[72]	4620	vis
43	13-16	Bath	8gd	70	5022	BL

TRAVELLING TIMES 4 ch g £2074

44a	4-12	Wolv	6af	[52]	33	vis
49a	3-16	Sout	7af	[52]	66	vis
52a	2-16	Sout	6af	50	94	vis
35a	7-15	Sout	6af	52	168	vis
22a	11-16	Sout	7af	52	202	vis
37a	5-10	Sout	6af	[51]	308	vis
30a	6-7	Sout	6af	[51]	317	vis
22	11-16	Nott	6.1gd	[49]	1988	bl
5	15-16	Carl	5.9fm	45	2445	bl
38	4-19	Beve	5gd	45	2657	bl
13	12-14	Hami	6gd	41	3129	vis
58a	2-13	Sout	6af	[40]	3482	vis
32a	6-14	Sout	6af	47	4130	vis
39a	6-13	Wolv	5.1ap	[45]	5231	vis

TRAYTONIC 3 b c £21105

97	5-14	Thir	5g/f	98	1766	
79	14-18	Newm	6g/f	97	1933	
104	**1-12**	**HAYD**	6g/s	[95]	2186*	
108	3-20	York	6g/f	100	2407	
102	8-19	Newm	6fm	101	3002	
103	7-11	Newm	6g/f	101	3941	
104	4-15	Asco	7g/f	101	4800	
101	6-9	Donc	7sft	[101]	5214	

TRE COLLINE 5 b g £10901

29	12-19	Newc	6sft	75	967	
40	11-13	Redc	7sft	[72]	1142	
45	16-20	Newc	6sft	69	1393	
56	9-19	Redc	7g/f	65	1820	
37	15-16	York	7g/f	65	2057	VIS
75a	**1-15**	**SOUT**	8af	60	2338*	
55a	5-12	Sout	7af	[60]	2496	
83a	**1-15**	**SOUT**	8af	66	2500*	
73a	4-12	Ling	8ap	[75]	2840	
70	6-10	Nott	8.2gd	[73]	3107	
82a	**1-12**	**LING**	8ap	[75]	3286*	
38	7-15	Newc	7gd	[70]	3426	
78a	6-13	Ling	7ap	79	3791	
70a	8-14	Ling	7ap	78	4180	
71a	4-10	Wolv	7.1ap	[76]	4920	

TREASON TRIAL 3 b g £10652

0	11-11	Hayd	8.1gd		2885	
56	6-16	Epso	8.5gd	62	3219	
47	4-14	Leic	8g/f	[62]	3344	
54	3-10	Hayd	8.1gd	[57]	3739	
56	**1-10**	**YARM**	10.1gd	[57]	3874*	
59	3-4	Sand	10g/s	[57]	4068	
54	3-5	Brig	11.9sft	57	4166	
61	4-16	Kemp	16g/f	57	4361	
66	**1-20**	**YORK**	13.9gd	58	5004*	

TREASURE CAY 2 ch c £16510

78a	**1-10**	**LING**	5ap		176*	e
76a	5-9	Ling	5ap	77	914	
75	3-9	Thir	6g/s	[75]	1477	
83	5-13	Hayd	6g/f	75	1881	BL T
78	3-9	Sand	5g/f	75	2387	t
83	**1-10**	**CARL**	5gd	75	2675*	e t
57	9-10	Hayd	5g/s	79	3135	e t
83	3-10	Sand	5g/f	79	3356	e t
84	2-21	Good	5fm	79	3567	e t
70	6-8	Sand	5g/s	82	3889	e t

TREASURE HOUSE 3 b c £750

95a	8-15	Ling	7ap	[96]	885	
50	12-15	Newb	8gd	94	1206	
64	5-6	Asco	6sft	[91]	1421	
77	8-12	Good	7g/f	88	1847	
69	14-19	Kemp	6fm	85	4394	
59	14-16	Leic	5gd	80	4700	
65	13-18	Pont	5g/s	75	5149	

TREASURE THE LADY 3 b f £0

81	9-13	Asco	8g/f	96	4802	T

TREASURE TRAIL 4 b g £3643

55a	8-14	Ling	13ap	65	264	
53a	5-8	Ling	16ap	65	288	
0	10-13	Kemp	14.4hvy	73	1516	
59	11-18	Nott	14.1g/s	70	1772	
69	**1-8**	**BATH**	17.2fm	65	2035*	
67	6-10	Kemp	16fm	70	2073	

TREASURY 2 b f £0

43	17-18	Nott	8.2g/f		4842	

TREAT ME WILD 2 ch f £7518

71	**1-10**	**BATH**	5g/s		1097*	
71	6-11	Warw	7.1gd		3053	
65	5-9	Brig	7g/f	71	3297	
77	**1-7**	**KEMP**	6g/f	68	3686*	
67	4-12	Sali	6g/s	73	4079	
55	9-14	Donc	7fm	73	4535	
58	16-29	Newm	6gd		5087	

TREBELLO 3 b c £0

38	8-8	Hami	9.2g/s		4821	

TREBLE SEVEN 2 b f £0

69	6-14	Yarm	7gd		4611	
45	12-13	Newm	6g/f		4918	

TREE CHOPPER 3 ch f £0

0	7-7	Newb	10g/f		3264	

TREE ROOFER 5 b g £836

19a	12-13	Ling	7ap	48	761	
44a	9-10	Ling	5ap	[48]	802	
45a	8-14	Ling	6ap	[45]	819	
49a	2-12	Ling	6ap	45	844	

TREE TOPS 3 b f £2728

73	5-13	Newb	7gd		1210	
73	2-7	Nott	8.2sft		1468	
75	3-11	Beve	9.9g/f		1835	
74	3-12	Newb	10g/f	72	3255	
69	6-10	Newb	10fm	72	3630	
44	11-12	Sand	10gd	72	4502	
16	15-18	Wind	10g/s	[69]	4944	
13	11-13	Bath	10.2sft	[65]	5173	

TREETOPS HOTEL 4 ch g £5406

40a	14-15	Ling	7ap	62	266	
60a	2-14	Ling	10ap	58	520	p
44	9-15	Brig	8fm	60	1691	
46	11-16	Ling	7g/f	57	2063	
48	9-17	Ling	7gd	54	2397	
57	2-17	Warw	8.1fm	54	2440	
58	4-7	Brig	11.9g/f	[55]	3173	
60	2-25	Asco	7g/f	55	3443	p
30	11-11	Good	11gd	58	3948	p
45	12-17	Wind	6gd	58	4126	T p
61a	4-12	Ling	8ap	[60]	4320	VIS

TREFFLICH 3 ch c £9598

105 2-7 Curr 8gd 3318

TREGARRON 2 b r c £9574
43a	11-13	Wolv	6af		62	1
83	1-10	**NEWB**	5.2fm	[62]		2649*
73	4-10	Sand	5g/f		70	3356
74	2-9	Epso	6fm		70	3543
66	7-7	Sand	5g/s		72	4099
76	3-20	Ripo	6gd		71	4278
42	15-15	Sand	5gd		73	4604
60	10-15	Kemp	6g/f		73	4713
50	16-20	Newm	7g/s		71	5286

TREGENNA 3 b f £774
49	4-5	Yarm	7gd		3365
16	5-6	Donc	7g/f		3595
44	14-17	Newm	6g/f		4228
0	18-18	Kemp	10g/f	[47]	4791

TREMAR 2 b c £37620
79	4-7	Kemp	5sft		943
82	3-8	Wind	5g/s		1053
97	2-8	Kemp	6sft		4028
94a	1-12	**LING**	6ap		4179*
104	4-8	Kemp	6fm	[90]	4390
109	1-7	**CHAN**	6gd	[90]	4957*
100	6-9	Newm	7sft		5137

TREMPJANE 2 b f £5188
80	1-6	**GOOD**	6gd		2373*
74	5-6	Wind	5fm		2786
82	5-6	Newm	6g/f		3031
65	8-9	Good	7fm	80	3624
11	8-8	Good	6g/f	80	4536

TRENCH COAT 3 ch c £1175
74a	2-15	Ling	7ap	[73]	814
41	7-8	Muss	7.1gd	[72]	1554
60	10-16	Leic	7g/f	70	1825
19a	13-15	Sout	8af	67	2500

TRESOR SECRET 4 b g £1490
59	16-19	Newm	10g/f	85	1478
73	5-9	Newm	10gd	[80]	1890
35	7-7	Chep	8.1gd	[75]	2116 BL
67a	2-11	Ling	12ap	[72]	2588
65a	2-8	Ling	12ap	[65]	2739

TREVIAN 3 ch g £3262
45a	14-15	Ling	7ap	70	337
69a	1-10	**LING**	8ap	65	455*
64a	6-11	Ling	10ap	65	497
63a	6-12	Ling	8ap	68	603
68a	5-12	Ling	8ap	67	798 BL
62	8-14	Good	8g/f	67	4542

TREW CLASS 3 ch f £11926
55	7-14	Warw	8.1sft		1527
39	17-20	Wind	10sft		1651
79	1-10	**SAND**	10g/f		2386*
80	1-7	**PONT**	10g/f	[76]	2994*
78	3-5	Donc	10.3g/s	77	3377
71	8-13	Yarm	10.1gd	77	4613
78	6-12	Wind	11.6g/f	77	4833

TREW FLIGHT 2 b c £0
4	19-21	Newm	8sft	5097
63	5-9	Catt	7sft	5316

TREW STYLE 2 ch c £385
57	15-21	Newm	8sft	5097
79	4-19	Newm	8g/f	5285

TRIAGE 3 b f £0
23	8-9	Kemp	6sft	946

TRIBUTE 3 b g £0
69	10-15	Ches	5.1g/s	80	1572
76	7-14	Thir	5g/f	79	1766
71	5-9	Folk	6g/f	79	2271
75	5-11	Newm	5g/f	77	2734 VIS
74	5-14	Ches	6.1g/f	75	4048
34	24-24	Newb	7g/f	73	4642
44	11-11	Muss	5g/s	71	5332

TRICK CYCLIST 3 b c £7633
88a	2-8	Ling	5ap	80	818
85a	4-9	Ling	5ap	81	914
71	7-20	Wind	6g/s	81	1255

66	6-8	Bath	5fm	[78]		1901
66	7-9	Wind	6g/f		76	2797
76	2-10	Beve	5g/f	[72]		3503
77	1-5	**BRIG**	5.3g/f	[72]		3720*
69	3-13	Bath	5.7g/f	[72]		3844
73	5-7	Sand	5g/s		73	4099
62	15-20	Donc	5fm		72	4496
71	4-17	Bath	5.7gd	[71]		5020
55	8-11	Muss	5g/s		71	5332

TRICK OF LIGHT 2 b f £0
0	W-16	Sali	7gd	4329

TRICKSHOT 2 ch f £1190
62	2-7	Hami	6gd	1744
24	16-16	Pont	6g/f	2275
51	7-11	Newc	7gd	3429

TRICKSTEP 3 b c £5398
72	1-8	**AYR**	10sft	[47]	5034*
53a	5-12	Wolv	12.2ap	58	5339 BL

TRICKY VENTURE 4 gr g £1505
77	2-11	Beve	9.9sft	[65]	4261
61	4-11	Leic	10gd	[73]	4701

TRIFTI 3 b g £1078
69a	4-10	Ling	8ap		1021
26	11-11	Newm	10gd		1148
34	10-12	Ling	6g/f		2586
58a	8-11	Ling	6ap	65	2841
59a	4-9	Ling	8ap	[62]	3197
59	2-8	Folk	7g/f	58	3724
29	9-9	Good	8gd	58	3950
34	12-12	Brig	8fm	[56]	4761

TRIGGER MEAD 4 b f £0
8a	11-14	Ling	10ap	[50]	4661

TRIGGERS DOUBLE 3 ch c £0
0	15-15	Ling	12ap	2393

TRIGONY 2 b g £0
0	12-12	Newc	7gd	3425
49	12-14	Thir	7g/s	4204
69	6-10	Redc	9fm	4558

TRILEMMA 3 b f £18035
0	9-9	Newc	10.1sft	[63]	1681 BL
46	11-15	Nott	10gd	63	3108
58	6-17	Newm	12g/f	62	3618
69	1-9	**RIPO**	16gd	61	4308*
78	1-7	**NEWC**	16.1g/f	67	4405*
85	1-7	**NOTT**	16g/f	72	4846*
50	7-13	Newb	16sft	79	5194

TRIM IMAGE 2 b r f £4128
71	3-7	Redc	5gd		2547
73	3-7	Muss	5g/s		2965
76	1-8	**CHEP**	5.1g/s		3896*
50	12-13	Muss	5g/f	74	4551

TRINAREE 3 b f £0
25	12-14	Donc	5gd		2237
26	12-14	Donc	6g/f		2428
2	15-17	Leic	7gd		2704
2	16-16	Thir	8g/f	38	3414

TRINCULO 6 b g £14516
93a	1-15	**SOUT**	5af	88	64* p
91a	6-16	Sout	5af	92	171 p
81a	10-13	Ling	6ap	92	235 p
75a	7-12	Wolv	6af	92	361 p
84a	10-16	Sout	5af	90	461 e
78a	8-10	Ling	5ap	89	567 p
2a	U-10	Ling	5ap	88	692 e
92	2-20	Donc	5gd	86	927 p
87	5-7	Nott	5.1fm	[86]	1004 p
63	11-13	Beve	5g/s	[89]	1162 p
62	11-11	Newb	5.2gd	89	1207 bl
37	6-7	Hayd	6g/f	[86]	1487 p
61	15-20	York	5g/s	85	1683 p
59	9-9	Yarm	5.2g/s	80	4253 p
67	10-16	Hayd	5fm	80	4382 p
72	5-15	Ayr	5g/s	75	4654 ble
87	1-13	**CATT**	5sft	[75]	5321*

TRINITY 8 b h £0
46	8-20	Newc	6sft	53	1393

33	10-15	Thir	7gd	51	1635
37	10-12	Newc	5gd	48	3427
21	19-20	Hayd	6fm	48	3796

TRINITY FAIR 3 b f £0
39	11-12	York	7.9g/f	2410
54	13-13	Kemp	10g/f	3038
38	10-11	Thir	8g/f	3572
36	10-10	Yarm	11.5gd	3997

TRINITY JOY 3 b f £10282
106	2-7	Deau	10Very	4309

TRIPHENIA 6 b g £0
38	9-9	Donc	12g/f	75	2078

TRIPLE JUMP 3 ch g £9470
80	2-16	Ripo	8gd		2987
76	1-11	**THIR**	8g/f		3572*
80	3-10	Ches	10.3sft	75	4071
40	15-19	Hayd	10.5g/s	75	4766

TRIPLE ZERO 2 b f £3786
37	8-8	Good	6gd	2537
62	14-16	Kemp	7g/f	3035
72	1-14	**LING**	7.6g/f	3601*

TRIPTI 3 b f £1923
43a	8-11	Ling	6ap	[57]	130
39a	6-13	Ling	6ap	[53]	271
47a	2-13	Ling	6ap	[53]	340
33a	10-13	Ling	6ap	48	451
20a	10-14	Ling	6ap	[45]	709
48a	2-11	Ling	6ap	45	728
29a	8-12	Ling	6ap	47	844
27a	13-14	Ling	6ap	47	874
18a	10-12	Ling	6ap	[45]	1075
28	13-15	Brig	5.3g/f	54	1371
33	12-16	Wind	5fm	49	3640
45	4-8	Folk	5gd	44	4118
45	5-11	Epso	6gd	[45]	4294

TRISHAY 3 gr f £0
36a	10-12	Ling	7ap	59	545
27a	7-8	Ling	10ap	[56]	626

TRITONVILLE LODGE 2 b g £0
64	7-16	Newb	8hvy	5220

TRIVIAL PURSUIT 3 b c £0
26	9-11	Yarm	7g/f	2852

TROFANA FALCON 3 b g £0
26a	8-15	Sout	8af	96
17a	11-14	Sout	8af	170
39	11-13	Hayd	11.9g/s	2230
0	16-16	Donc	10.3gd	2751

TROIS ETOILES 3 ch f £610
59	5-16	Hayd	6g/f		2182
56	9-20	Newb	7fm	61	2650
59	5-12	Leic	8g/f	60	2922
53	5-11	Ling	10gd	[58]	3201
57	3-8	Chep	8.1gd	57	3731
52	6-13	Bath	8gd	55	4546
32a	10-13	Wolv	9.5ap	54	4925 VIS
47a	6-12	Wolv	8.6ap	[54]	5329

TROJAN FLIGHT 3 ch g £19835
69	4-14	Thir	6g/s		1216
68	5-16	Beve	8.5sft	69	1628
60	4-11	Newc	7sft	69	1678
59	6-8	Beve	7.5g/f	66	2166 P
52	8-14	Nott	8.2g/f	63	2634
37	6-6	Carl	9.3g/f	60	3231
55	4-20	Thir	9gd	60	3575
66	3-18	Hayd	6gd	60	3737
65	2-15	Thir	5g/s	59	3833
71	1-18	**BEVE**	5g/s	59	3852+
71	2-20	Ripo	6gd	64	4278
72	1-18	**REDC**	6fm	64	4339*
61	9-26	Ayr	5g/s	67	4618
61	4-15	Hami	6sft	67	4696
73	2-16	Pont	5fm	67	4754
71	4-15	Ayr	5sft	69	5036
63	7-19	Ayr	6sft	69	5069

TROJAN WOLF 9 ch g £0
24a	7-8	Sout	11af	[40]	574

33a 4-7 Sout 14af [35] 724
0 16-16 Sout 11af [35] 852
9a 5-9 Sout 11af [35] 906

TROMP 3 ch c £1056
60 5-14 Sali 7fm 2291
56 6-9 Folk 7fm 2716
73a 2-13 Wolv 9.5ap 5290

TROMPE LOEIL 2 b f £1095
69a 2-12 Ling 10ap [60] 116
60a 4-11 Sout 8af [71] 159
38a 8-14 Sout 8af [71] 226
26a 8-9 Ling 10ap 66 365
53a 7-10 Ling 10ap 63 676
55a 6-10 Ling 10ap [60] 843
56a 9-15 Ling 7ap 60 901 P
45 8-15 Bath 8g/s 52 1099 p
0 13-14 Warw 8.1sft 50 1529 p

TROODOS JET 3 b g £5425
67 4-9 Ripo 6g/f [65] 2485
62 4-9 Warw 6.1g/f [65] 2906
66a 4-9 Sout 6af [65] 3396
62 1-4 RIPO 9g/f [64] 3936*
9 12-12 Redc 6gd [64] 4245
6 13-15 Hami 6sft 64 4696
24 14-15 Ayr 5sft 59 5036

TROPICAL CORAL 3 ch f £857
61a 11-13 Ling 10ap 76 26
73a 4-11 Ling 8ap 74 136
62a 5-14 Sout 8af 73 195
74a 2-14 Ling 10ap 71 265
66a 6-12 Wolv 9.4af 72 382

TROPICAL LADY 4 b f £81914
111 1- LEOP 7g/y 3011*
111 1-11 CURR 9g/f 3322*
109 2-6 Curr 10g/f 3840
102 5-5 Leop 8g/f 4020
107 5-13 Curr 10gd 4735

TROPICAL SON 4 b g £2915
25a 8-14 Sout 8af 41 195 vis
34a 7-13 Sout 8af 41 221 vis
42a 2-12 Wolv 9.4af [38] 302 vis
38a 5-14 Sout 8af [40] 354 vis
48a 1-14 LING 10ap [40] 412* vis
19a 9-12 Wolv 9.4af 45 464 vis
60a 2-13 Ling 13ap [46] 602 vis
37a 5-7 Wolv 12af 46 642 vis
48a 7-14 Ling 10ap 53 718 vis
50a 5-14 Ling 12ap 49 768 vis
32a 9-12 Wolv 12.2ap 47 5328 BL e

TROPICAL STAR 4 ch g £111731
108 2-9 Nad 8af 988 tv

TROPICAL STORM 3 ch g £5794
75 3-8 Kemp 7g/f 1912
46 9-14 Thir 7sft [70] 2692
73 4-8 Newm 6g/f [70] 3784
76 2-7 Folk 6g/s [70] 3910
73 1-10 NEWC 7hvy [73] 4216*

TROTTERS BOTTOM 2 b g £0
75a 6-10 Ling 5ap [87] 176
73a 7-9 Ling 5ap 82 914
67 5-9 Kemp 6gd [79] 2173

TROUBADOUR 3 b c £8800
111 2-8 Hayd 8.1fm 4386
69 11-13 Newm 8g/f 4887

TROUBLE MOUNTAIN 6 br g £16589
65a 7-16 Sout 11af 69 97
74a 2-15 Sout 11af 69 196
69a 3-15 Sout 12af 69 257
72a 3-9 Sout 11af 72 391
75 3-19 Beve 9.9g/s 70 1164
72 3-12 Sout 11gd 70 1286
72 5-12 Ches 12.3gd 69 1599 bl
67 2-16 Redc 10g/f 67 1821 bl
70 4-6 Ripo 12.3g/f 67 1980 bl
69 3-13 Ches 10.3gd 70 2284 bl
59 7-11 Ripo 10ap 70 2483 bl
73 2-14 Hayd 10.5gd 68 3741
75 1-5 HAYD 10.5g/s 68 3904*

75 4-13 Ripo 8gd 71 4279
78 2-20 Ayr 10g/s 71 4656
74 3-19 Hayd 10.5g/s 71 4766
76 5-14 Ayr 10sft 75 5037

TROUBLE NEXT DOOR 6 b g £829
53a 3-9 Ling 12ap [35] 324
38a 2-9 Ling 12ap [35] 414

TROUBLEINPARADISE 3 b f £0
13 17-18 Leic 10g/s 61 1017
0 18-19 Warw 10.9gd 58 1124 BL
14a 13-15 Ling 12ap 54 2741

TROUBLESOME GERRI 2 b f £632
54 6-14 Bath 5sft 1538
61 3-6 Bath 5g/f 1786
12 5-6 Chep 6.1gd 2367

TROUSERS 4 b g £9713
74a 3-16 Ling 7ap 72 22
67a 6-11 Ling 8ap 74 131
63a 7-12 Ling 8ap 72 932
64 1-16 NEWC 8hvy 55 1036*
64 3-12 Nott 8.2g/s 62 2931
64 4-9 Donc 8g/s 62 3225

TRUCKLE 2 b c £410
64 8-11 Nott 6.1sft 1739
68 6-14 Thir 8fm 4376
73 4-15 York 7.9gd 5002

TRUE 3 ch f £3247
67 7-18 Wind 8.3g/s 1258
62 11-20 Newb 7g/f 73 1761
63 2-12 Thir 7g/f [70] 2215
47 12-18 Donc 7gd 65 2755
65 3-10 Catt 7g/f 63 3016
64 4-13 Beve 7g/s 63 3179
44 12-13 Leic 7g/f 63 3346
53 6-13 Pont 8g/s [63] 3973
61 8-14 Beve 7.5g/s 61 4241
62 2-9 Thir 8g/f [58] 4593
39 14-17 Beve 8.5g/f 58 4721
62 5-10 Pont 8g/f [56] 4939
50 9-18 Newm 8sft 56 5272

TRUE COMPANION 4 b g £11458
62a 3-14 Ling 10ap 59 101
65a 3-14 Ling 10ap 60 174
60a 8-14 Ling 10ap 63 434
68a 1-14 LING 10ap 62 520*
68a 3-14 Ling 10ap 66 674
38a 8-11 Ling 8ap 66 714
70a 3-9 Ling 10ap 66 903
71 1-20 WARW 10.9gd 65 1128*
76 4-12 Ches 12.3gd 71 1599
76 2-15 Sand 10g/f 71 2099
58a 13-14 Ling 10ap 74 2392

TRUE HOLLY 4 b f £0
34a 9-11 Ling 6ap 40 728
36a 7-13 Ling 6ap [40] 788 VIS
34a 5-8 Sout 7af [35] 847

TRUE LOVER 7 b g £6600
110 3-11 Newm 16sft 5138

TRUE MAGIC 3 b f £14410
62 5-8 Thir 5sft [65] 1228
58 6-19 Donc 6g/f [65] 1876
71 2-11 Redc 5g/f 62 2121
73 2-10 Carl 5gd 66 2675
70 1-9 LEIC 5g/f [69] 3347*
77 1-15 THIR 5g/s 69 3833*
68 8-16 Muss 5g/f 74 4174
66 13-20 Donc 5fm 74 4496
71 7-18 Pont 5g/s 72 5149

TRUE NIGHT 7 b g £43286
45 13-13 Muss 7.1g/f 80 1122
64 14-19 Leic 6g/s 79 1354
71 10-16 Thir 7g/s 77 1474
56 12-19 Thir 6g/f 76 1767
75 4-12 Ayr 7.2fm 74 1909
84 2-19 Kemp 6fm 74 2070
80 3-9 Ches 7gd 77 2282
81 3-28 Asco 7g/f 77 2558
76 11-17 Carl 7.9gd 77 2672

88 3-20 Newm 8fm 78 3001
88 1-13 ASCO 7gd 78 3068*
90 1-13 NEWC 7gd 81 3428*
88 3-12 Ches 7.6fm 83 3634
69 12-16 Redc 8g/f 83 3768
60 12-13 Ches 7.6sft 83 4103
79 2-8 York 8.9g/f [83] 4397
64 12-18 Ayr 7.2sft 83 4689
49 8-10 Epso 7gd [82] 4912

TRUE PATRIOT 3 b g £0
22 17-17 Newb 10gd 1737
9 8-9 Good 11g/f 53 2019 BL

TRUE TO YOURSELF 3 b g £1834
35 10-12 Hayd 8.1sft 1108
42a 2-5 Wolv 9.4af [45] 1311
45a 1-6 WOLV 12af [40] 1673*
43 8-15 Leic 11.8gd 47 2134
30a 6-15 Sout 12af 43 2503

TRUENO 5 b g £27084
85 1-9 NEWM 10gd [80] 1890*
85 2-8 Chep 10.2gd [83] 2197
56 11-13 Redc 10gd 84 2560
84 5-10 Newm 10g/f 84 3615
81 5-8 Newm 10g/f [82] 3945
74 7-9 Kemp 12g/f 82 4360
84 6-20 York 10.4gd 81 4986

TRULLITTI 3 b f £4714
77 3-8 Ripo 10g/s 1365
68 5-10 Nott 10g/s [75] 2930
0 P-12 Hayd 11.9gd 73 3734
82 1-5 GOOD 11sft [73] 4188* BL
60 11-12 Yarm 14.1sft [84] 5254 bl

TRUMAN 3 b c £2056
62 7-19 Donc 6g/f 1876
72 3-10 Newb 6g/f 2309
56 5-9 Folk 7fm [72] 2716
62 11-25 Newm 7gd 70 4683
72a 2-12 Wolv 8.6ap 67 5116

TRUST RULE 4 b c £3222
81 12-17 Kemp 10g/s 98 1111
91 6-19 Newm 12g/f 98 1484
96 5-13 Epso 12fm 97 2255
81 10-13 Asco 12fm 95 2582
90 11-15 Hayd 11.9gd 94 2948
74 14-19 York 13.9g/s 91 4023
77 16-20 Hayd 14fm 90 4383
91 4-15 Donc 14.6fm 90 4491 T P
84 7-14 Asco 12g/f 90 4814 tp

TRUSTED INSTINCT 4 b c £0
39a 14-15 Ling 12ap 77 549
26a 10-11 Ling 8ap 72 714
0 16-18 Wind 8.3g/s 72 1059 T
2 18-18 Newm 12fm 67 2088 t
12 9-9 Brig 8g/f [62] 2431
5 5-5 Yarm 6sft [57] 4150
0 17-17 Carl 7.9fm [50] 4506 P

TRUSTED MOLE 6 b g £7492
48 5-16 Ling 11.8g/f 52 1830
58 1-11 LEIC 11.8fm 52 2112*
50 6-9 Hami 13gd 52 2176
59 2-12 Warw 10.9fm 55 2436
60 1-7 WARW 12.6fm 56 2782*
45 8-10 Warw 12.6g/f 56 2912
23 10-10 Ripo 12.3g/f 58 3649
48 7-14 Catt 12g/f 55 4672
40a 7-11 Wolv 12.2ap 54 5117

TRY THE AIR 2 ch f £0
13a 8-10 Sout 8af 59 189
18a 11-12 Ling 8ap 54 402

TRYLKO 2 ch f £1490
84 2-8 Donc 8gd 2750

TRYSTING GROVE 3 b f £2541
54 9-11 Ripo 8gd 1177
36 8-15 Thir 7g/s 1473
45 9-11 Thir 7fm 2463
45 5-14 Beve 7.5g/s 3177
22 15-18 Carl 7.9fm 43 3547
52 1-7 CHEP 12.1sft 40 4053*

TSARBUCK 3 b c £4472

28	15-19	Yarm	8g/f		1130
35	7-8	Epso	8.5hvy		1297
25	8-12	Kemp	8hvy		1511
56a	1-10	SOUT	7af	[45]	1842*
46	5-13	Beve	8.5g/f	[51]	1947
62a	2-15	Sout	7af	55	2384
51	5-8	Thir	7sft	49	2693
60a	2-8	Sout	6af	58	3092
58a	3-13	Sout	7af	58	3155
62a	3-9	Sout	6af	59	3485 VIS
20	12-14	Folk	6gd	49	4116 vis
39	9-19	Thir	6gd	47	4595
37	6-20	Yarm	7g/s	[45]	5120 P
59a	4-12	Ling	6ap	59	5241 p
46a	10-12	Wolv	7.1ap	[59]	5325 p

TSAROXY 2 b c £5567

81	3-7	Newc	6g/s		2774
72	3-7	Ayr	6gd		3148
81	1-10	REDC	6gd		4244*
82	5-14	Ayr	6sft	78	5035
46	10-10	Catt	6sft	78	5318 BL

TSHUKUDU 3 ch f £1132

4a	7-7	Wolv	7af	46	1376
5a	12-15	Ling	12ap	42	2741
36a	9-12	Ling	8ap	[38]	3286
23	10-14	Leic	8g/f	[38]	3344
36	3-10	Yarm	10.1gd	[38]	3874
3a	11-12	Ling	10ap	36	4113
40	2-7	Brig	9.9sft	[36]	4142
28	7-13	Folk	9.7g/f	[35]	4372
0	11-14	Ling		[35]	4662
14	14-19	Brig	9.9gd	[35]	4903

TUCKER 2 b c £4755

67	8-23	Newm	6gd		5084
86	1-11	NEWM	6sft		5265*

TUDOR BELL 3 b c £22577

67	8-17	Donc	8gd		919
76	2-8	Pont	10hvy		1067
82	3-14	Nott	10gd	[75]	1241
77	1-6	HAMI	11.1g/s	[75]	1604*
82	1-9	WIND	11.6g/f	75	1807*
81	6-8	Hami	12.1g/f	78	2318
88	2-5	Sali	14.1fm	78	2418
87	1-10	SALI	14.1gd	78	2699*
83	3-6	Catt	15.8g/f	83	3015
68	11-13	Yarm	16g/s	83	4634
73	4-7	Nott	16g/f	81	4846
73	5-6	Muss	16g/s	[79]	5334

TUMBAGA 3 b c £0

58	13-17	Newm	8gd		1166
50	13-17	Newb	10gd		1737
71	5-13	Kemp	8fm		2072 T

TUMBLEBRUTUS 3 b c £0

90	9-14	Newm	8g/f		1480

TUMBLEWEED GALORE 2 b g £3670

48	7-7	Sand	7.1g/s		2897
76	3-18	Leic	7g/f		3342
76	3-11	Beve	7.5g/f		3500
83	3-11	Newm	8gd	[73]	3925
72	6-13	Newm	8gd	78	4193
82	2-20	Ling	7g/f	73	4741
82a	3-8	Wolv	8.6ap	[76]	5007 BL
77	5-14	Newb	7sft	76	5193

TUNGSTEN STRIKE 3 ch g £35775

46	11-16	Wind	11.6g/s	68	2621
79	1-7	KEMP	14.4g/f	66	3037*
88	1-11	LING	16gd	71	3200*
87	3-9	Good	14fm	81	3556
91	2-11	Newm	16.1g/f	83	3779
104	1-7	NEWM	14g/f	[86]	4878*
44	28-34	Newm	18sft	93	5135

TUNING FORK 4 b c £11000

43	12-12	Kemp	10gd	[100]	1139
97	7-14	Good	12g/f	[98]	1843
94	10-10	Bade	11gd	[98]	2141
47	14-14	Asco	10g/f	95	2556 T
27	15-15	Sand	8.1g/s	92	2915 t

91	3-21	Good	8fm	89	3565
77	12-16	Newb	7g/f	89	3954
61	8-8	Wind	10g/s	[89]	4220
69	9-11	Good	9g/f	88	4525
58	11-14	Asco	8g/f	86	4813 P

TURBO 5 b g £6547

75a	14-14	Ling	10ap	94	758 p
82	10-17	Kemp	10g/s	94	1111 p
95	4-17	Newb	12g/f	93	1759 p
72	13-15	Hayd	11.9gd	93	2948 p
75	12-21	York	11.9gd	93	3999 p
76	7-8	Donc	12fm	91	4534 p
84	13-18	Newb	10gd	91	4681 p
93	2-14	Newb	10hvy	89	5223 p
67	12-24	Donc	12sft	90	5372 p

TURF PRINCESS 2 b f £5257

59a	2-14	Sout	8af	[59]	95
54a	6-10	Sout	8af	61	190
63a	1-6	WOLV	7af	[61]	283*
60a	2-8	Sout	7af	[62]	389
57a	4-9	Wolv	7af	62	510
57a	5-12	Wolv	7af	[62]	560
55	3-11	Newc	7sft	57	1678
48	7-12	Thir	7g/f	[56]	2215
47	4-14	Beve	7.5g/s	[56]	3177
45a	9-11	Sout	8af	57	4044
6	14-15	Newc	6hvy	53	4211
23	17-20	Newc	6g/f	50	4408

TURFTANZER 4 b g £0

54a	5-10	Sout	11af	[41]	142
11a	9-11	Sout	11af	[40]	191 T
31a	5-14	Sout	12af	[36]	305 t
21a	7-12	Sout	14af	[35]	443 t
39a	4-8	Sout	11af	[35]	722 t
17a	6-10	Sout	8af	[40]	850 t
2	16-17	Pont	12hvy	35	1064 t
0	8-9	Pont	10sft	35	1430 t
14	9-10	Redc	11g/f	[35]	1819 t
15	12-13	Ripo	12.3g/f	35	2008 t
40	4-8	Redc	10gd	[30]	2548 t
28	5-6	Beve	12.1gd	[30]	2653 t
22	7-10	Ripo	12.3g/f	30	3649 t
14	10-12	Newc	8sft	[30]	4284 t
34	5-14	Pont	10g/f	30	4624 t
27	9-12	Pont	10fm	[30]	4757 t
38	6-11	Redc	10sft	[30]	5303 t

TURIBIUS 5 b g £5735

72a	6-10	Ling	5ap	79	567
85a	1-10	LING	5ap	77	755*
77a	3-7	Ling	5ap	81	1011
70	8-11	Good	5g/f	79	1845
43	18-19	Kemp	6fm	79	2070
73	9-16	Newm	5g/f	78	3033
63	12-17	Sand	5g/f	77	3341
22	26-26	Good	6fm	78	3569
58	10-16	Leic	5gd	73	4700 vis
71	4-19	Good	6gd	73	4747 vis

TURKANA GIRL 2 ch f £0

51	6-13	Nott	6.1g/f		4843

TURKISH DELIGHT 2 b f £1113

58a	3-13	Wolv	6af	[70]	126
58a	8-15	Ling	7ap	68	177
41a	5-8	Sout	6af	57	1441
60	6-19	York	6g/f	65	2055
45	12-18	Wind	6g/f	62	2268
42	8-19	Leic	6g/f	59	2925
60	3-10	Hami	6g/f	57	3203
48	10-18	Hayd	6g/f	59	3737
0	14-14	Yarm	6gd	59	3870
39	15-20	Ling	6g/f	57	4317 P
35	13-19	Thir	6g/f	55	4595
40	15-19	Ling	5g/f	55	4739

TURKS AND CAICOS 2 b g £3762

59a	4-12	Wolv	8.5af		28
38a	7-10	Sout	8af		162
59a	2-8	Sout	8af	[58]	355
56a	2-6	Wolv	8.5af	[58]	526
59a	1-10	SOUT	11af	54	658*
51	7-8	Hami	11.1g/f	58	3207
52a	6-13	Wolv	9.5ap	55	4925

48a	6-12	Wolv	12.2ap	55	5339

TURKS WOOD 2 b c £0

79	4-12	Ling	5g/f		1981
67	5-14	Hayd	6gd		3735
74	5-7	Yarm	6gd		3869
67	10-11	Hayd	8.1fm	75	4387
52	8-11	Ayr	8sft	72	4688 BL
34	8-12	Pont	6g/s	[68]	5152

TURKU 5 b g £0

42a	9-16	Sout	7af	[53]	61 vis

TURN AROUND 3 b g £6008

56a	8-13	Wolv	6af	74	41
51a	10-14	Ling	6ap	69	149
54a	7-10	Wolv	6af	66	345
0	14-18	Wind	8.3g/s	63	1059
51a	2-7	Wolv	8.5af	[58]	1341
53a	1-8	WOLV	7af	[52]	1656*
46a	5-12	Wolv	7af	52	2204
68a	1-15	SOUT	7af	51	2501*
27a	14-16	Sout	6af	57	2720

TURN N BURN 3 b c £2563

53	7-8	Newm	12g/s		1153
77	3-10	Pont	10gd	[73]	3243
75	2-7	Bath	11.7g/f	[78]	3967
61a	4-10	Ling	12ap	[78]	4314

TURN OF PHRASE 5 b g £4810

41a	8-11	Ling	16ap	56	605 bl
53	8-13	Beve	12.1g/f	59	3502 bl
62	2-12	Muss	14g/f	54	4170 VIS
63	1-16	CARL	11.9g/f	54	4348* vis
63	4-9	Muss	14gd	60	4521 vis

TURN ON THE STYLE 2 ch g £4676

52	9-13	Hayd	6g/f		3736
59	7-10	Catt	6g/f		4436
75	2-10	Muss	5gd		4804
71	1-10	CATT	5gd		4968*

TURNAROUND 2 gr c £11352

80	3-8	Hayd	5gd		2241
83	2-7	Newc	6g/s		2774
82	1-10	THIR	5fm		3606*
37	13-19	York	6gd	81	4004
83	2-14	Donc	7fm	78	4535
68	8-12	Newm	6gd	81	4882

TURNBERRY 2 b c £3335

55a	7-10	Ling	8ap	65	132 BL
58a	4-11	Ling	7ap	59	261 bl
61a	4-7	Ling	7ap	59	368 bl
57a	3-9	Wolv	7af	59	510 bl
45a	6-12	Sout	8af	57	656 bl
58	2-14	Warw	8.1sft	55	1529 VIS
61	2-18	Sali	7fm	55	2292 vis
49	5-8	Brig	7g/f	55	2434 vis

TURNER 3 gr g £1672

65	6-9	Hayd	11.9g/f	[73]	1885
73	3-8	Ches	10.3gd	[73]	2283
68	3-6	Ches	10.3g/s	[72]	2748
67	8-8	Asco	10g/f	72	3391
62	10-14	Redc	10fm	72	4342
0	17-17	Hayd	10.5fm	70	4388 VIS

TURNKEY 2 br c £10165

89	2-8	Newm	5g/f		1190
102	1-8	KEMP	5hvy		1510*
99	5-13	Asco	6g/f		2467
102	4-8	Curr	6.3gd		3319
87	7-11	York	6g/s	[100]	4022

TURNOVER 2 ch f £0

55	5-11	Chep	7.1hvy		4703
25	13-14	Leic	5gd		5059

TURNSTILE 3 gr c £7838

76	4-5	Newb	11gd		1211
78	2-7	Newm	12g/f		1936
53	9-11	Sand	14g/s	74	2130
78	3-14	Sali	12g/s	72	3114
79	2-12	Newm	12g/f	[72]	3783
66	8-11	Sali	12g/s	77	4080
75	6-13	Kemp	14.4fm	75	4395
75	1-11	GOOD	14gd	[73]	5029*

TURTLE BAY 2 ch f £0
54a 8-8 Ling 7ap 4176

TURTLE DANCER 6 b g £1152
67 2-9 Newc 10.1sft [66] 1681
0 11-13 Sout 14af 66 2494

TURTLE MAGIC 2 b f £2036
49a 8-9 Ling 5ap 931
70 2-15 Beve 5g/s 1161
56 3-15 Warw 5g/s 1325
66 6-14 Bath 5gd 1401
26a 6-7 Wolv 5af 1652
55 4-12 Newc 6gd 1869
42 9-20 Hayd 6gd 2882
57 3-6 Leic 5g/f 3209 BL
34a 4-8 Ling 6ap [54] 3745 P
53 6-11 Bath 5g/f [53] 3962 p
49 4-8 Wind 5g/s [53] 4218 p
32 11-15 Folk 6g/f [51] 4369 VIS

TURTLE PATRIARCH 3 b c £2809
35 10-15 Folk 6g/s 1078
2 16-16 Epso 8.5gd 62 3219
49 8-11 Sali 8gd 62 3455
57 4-5 Folk 9.7g/s 58 3914
62 2-13 Folk 12gd 58 4119
59 6-17 Hayd 10.5fm 60 4388
38a 12-16 Ling 12ap [59] 4899
75 2-8 Redc 10sft [58] 5306

TURTLE VALLEY 8 b g £6348
60a 5-12 Ling 13ap 60 762
55a 9-12 Ling 16ap 60 813
73 3-14 Kemp 14.4sft 70 948
77 1-11 WARW 15sft 69 1087*
72 9-13 Hayd 14sft 75 1109
65 12-17 Sali 14.1g/s 73 1502

TUSCAN DREAM 8 b g £2250
28a 12-15 Sout 5af [41] 253
19a 11-16 Sout 5af [40] 374
13a 9-11 Wolv 5af 40 508
14a 7-10 Wolv 5af [40] 527
22a 7-10 Wolv 5af [35] 781
30a 2-12 Sout 5af [30] 904
30a 2 9 Sout 5af [30] 981
32a 5-8 Sout 5af [35] 1199
40a 1-7 WOLV 5af [35] 1309*
33a 5-10 Sout 5af [40] 1408
36a 5-7 Wolv 5af [40] 1562
2a 11-12 Wolv 5af [40] 1799

TUSCAN FLYER 6 b g £2013
32 9-12 Hami 6g/s [64] 1600
43 13-16 Redc 6g/f 64 1824
65 3-9 Yarm 7fm 62 2150
47 12-20 York 6g/f 62 2409
60 4-19 Leic 5gd 62 2702 bl
44 11-15 Beve 5sft 61 2942 bl
61 4-18 Carl 5g/f 60 3228 bl
50 7-8 Ayr 5g/f 61 3763 bl
45 7-9 Yarm 5.2g/s 60 4253 bl
46 11-17 Beve 5g/f 58 4603 bl
63 3-16 Pont 5fm 58 4754 bl

TUSCAN TREATY 3 b f £0
34a 14-16 Ling 7ap 60 22
37a 12-15 Ling 7ap [56] 117
30a 14-14 Ling 7ap 51† 344
49 8-13 Bath 8sft 60 1542
24 4-5 Yarm 7g/f [57] 1731
38 7-16 Brig 6fm 53 2262 VIS
43 6-15 Leic 6g/f 53 2398 vis
26 13-20 Nott 6.1g/f 50 2630 -
28 13-20 Newm 8g/f 47 3232 vis
30 4-15 Brig 6gd [45] 4905 vis

TUSCARORA 5 b m £13271
46 7-16 Nott 6.1sft 57 1465
39 9-20 Asco 8g/f 54 1927
49 5-17 Warw 8.1fm 52 2440
58 2-10 Brig 8gd 52 2954
56 6-20 Chep 7.1g/s 52 3088
61 1-8 WIND 8.3gd 52 3162*
44 9-17 Newb 7g/f 58 3257
60 5-12 Good 9fm 56 3535

64 1-8 CHEP 8.1gd 56 3731*
60 3-16 Ches 7g/f 59 4051
61 3-11 Wind 8.3g/s 61 4222
59 4-16 Sali 8gd 61 4334
50 8-19 Nott 6.1g/f [60] 4845

TUVALU 2 ch c £556
67 8-12 Sand 7.1g/f 2388
69 5-13 Epso 7g/f 2870
64 6-17 Warw 7.1gd 4269
69 4-13 Wind 8.3g/f 68 5051

TWEED 7 ch g £0
15 10-12 Chep 12.1g/s [50] 4364

TWELVE BAR BLUES 3 ch f £0
54 11-16 Wind 10gd 1384
68 7-9 Sali 9.9g/f 1719
54 5-7 Brig 11.9g/f 1939
59 10-14 Chep 10.2gd 67 4487

TWENTYTWOSILVER 4 gr g £0
36a 10-13 Ling 10ap [70] 429

TWICE NIGHTLY 2 b g £1642
76 3-7 Thir 5g/s 1471
74 3-16 Ripo 6g/f 1780
70 6-13 Carl 5gd 2670
63 5-12 Catt 7g/f 73 3351
60 9-13 Newc 7g/s 69 3698
59 7-14 Muss 7.1g/f [66] 4171
49 8-19 Nott 6.1g/s 63 4645

TWICE UPON A TIME 5 ch m £2056
73 4-8 Hami 5gd [73] 1749
71 4-15 Ripo 6g/f 73 1782
56 14-15 Muss 5fm 72 2084
25 15-17 Redc 6gd 71 2561
61 8-9 Warw 5.5fm 69 2779
67 4-9 Nott 5.1gd 67 3106
39 14-17 Pont 5gd 67 3241
48 8-12 Nott 5.1g/f [65] 3577
59 6-16 Muss 5g/f 63 4174
57 7-17 Beve 5g/f 61 4603

TWILIGHT BLUES 5 ch h £8600
93 5-9 Wind 6g/f [114] 1958
98 11-14 Asco 6fm [114] 2580
99 5-12 Sand 5g/s [105] 2913 P
106 2-10 Redc 7fm [103] 4929
94 8-14 Newm 6sft [103] 5100

TWILIGHT YEARS 3 b g £0
49 9-10 Hayd 10.5g/f 1922
45 7-8 Beve 12.1gd 2515
44 4-7 Catt 13.8g/f 3019
37 6-14 Nott 16g/f 45 3580
31 10-13 Redc 14.1gd 43 4249

TWO MILES WEST 3 b c £19599
100 2-10 Asco 16.2g/f 2557
106 2-12 Leop 14g/s 3315
112 6-13 Curr 14gd 4733 t

TWO OF A KIND 3 ch g £3266
54a 5-10 Ling 13ap 64 11
39a 5-10 Wolv 14.8af [61] 125
57a 1-9 LING 12ap [56] 324*

TWO OF CLUBS 2 b g £4703
63a 4-11 Wolv 7af 70 29
60a 3-11 Wolv 7af [66] 396
66a 3-6 Sout 8af 62 506
64a 1-6 WOLV 7af [61] 779* P
39 5-14 Beve 7.5sft [68] 4256 p
71a 1-11 WOLV 7.1ap [62] 5178* p

TWO STEP KID 3 ch c £72025
89 6-7 Newm 7g/s 1150
92 4-14 Thir 5g/f 88 1766
102 1-20 YORK 6g/f 88 2407*
103 3-19 Newm 6fm 95 3002
101 4-11 York 5fm 97 3434
100 4-28 Good 6fm 95 3622
101 4-9 Good 6g/f 98 4537

TWO STEPS TO GO 4 b g £0
0 11-11 Sout 11af [40] 191
32a 4-14 Sout 12af [36] 305 vis

29a 4-10 Sout 11af [40] 375 bl
30a 5-9 Wolv 9.4af [35] 480 bl

TWOFAN 3 b c £7971
70 2-5 Newc 10.1sft 1275
84 2-8 Hayd 10.5g/f 1489
74 1-10 NOTT 14.1sft 1742*
74 6-7 Sand 14g/s 82 2899
80 4-7 Newm 14.8g/f 80 3475
80 5-9 Good 14fm 80 3556

TWYLA THARP 2 b f £1348
66 10-18 Nott 8.2g/s 4035
82 2-11 Donc 8sft 5205

TYBALT 2 b c £1538
71 2-9 Ling 6gd 3020
63 5-18 Donc 6g/s 3376
51 8-13 Pont 6gd 3682
48 12-20 Redc 7fm 66 4337
69 3-20 Ling 7g/f 62 4741 VIS
50 17-20 Yarm 8g/s 64 5349 vis

TYCHEROS 2 b g £0
50 11-13 Wind 6g/f 5048

TYCHY 5 ch m £35300
92 5-30 Newm 6g/f 90 1481
95 3-20 Epso 5fm 90 2253
44 27-29 Asco 6fm 90 2581
88 11-24 Asco 5gd 92 3466
103 5-13 Good 5fm [92] 3551
99 1-10 ASCO 6gd 92 3773*
70 8-12 Pont 6g/s [97] 3971
97 4-14 Epso 5gd 97 4291
93 15-19 Hayd 6fm [98] 4384
74 9-11 Ches 6.1g/f [97] 4510
90 7-15 Newm 6gd [95] 5088

TYCOON 3 b c £138387
120 3-10 Curr 12g/f 2822
119 6-11 Asco 12g/f 3442
0 9-9 York 10.4gd 4002
119 3-9 Donc 14.6fm 4532 T

TYCOON HALL 4 ch c £0
45 16-17 Kemp 10g/s 90 1111

TYNE 3 b c £434
75 7-13 Thir 5sft 85 1229
79 6-11 Redc 5g/f 83 2121
77 4-6 Redc 6gd 80 2551
61 9-10 Muss 5g/s 77 2968

TYNEHAM 4 b c £1488
57a 1-12 WOLV 8.6ap [59] 5230* P
30 11-17 Yarm 8g/s [59] 5348 p

TYPE ONE 5 b g £6147
78a 1-13 LING 6ap [78] 271*
72a 11-14 Ling 6ap 84 292
82a 1-9 LING 5ap [78] 492+
26a 13-13 Wolv 6af 82 618
65a 7-10 Ling 5ap 80 692
49 18-22 Donc 6gd 78 921
26 17-19 Redc 6sft 78 1145
67 2-14 Donc 6g/s [75] 1522 P
41 14-16 Redc 6g/f 72 1824
37 7-7 Hayd 6g/s 70 2187 vis
49 4-14 Newc 6g/s [67] 2730

TYPHOON GINGER 9 ch m £0
46 9-9 Donc 7sft [60] 5214

TYPHOON TILLY 6 b g £7896
77 3-14 Ling 12ap 75 83
75a 6-16 Ling 12ap 75 404
77a 4-12 Ling 16ap 75 478
78a 3-11 Ling 16ap 75 605
69a 6-7 Ling 12ap 75 695
73 4-14 Kemp 14.4sft 73 948
55 10-18 Ling 16g/s 71 1112
70 3-10 Sali 14.1gd 69 3887
73 2-14 Bath 13.1g/s 68 4203
75 1-16 KEMP 16g/f 68 4361*
76 6-13 Yarm 16g/s 73 4634
65 7-11 Muss 16g/s 73 5335

TYRONE SAM 2 b g £0

```
57  7-10   Pont  5gd              3457
33  9-10   Redc  5fm              4338
41  14-14  Muss  7.1g/s           5330
```

TYRRELLSPASS 7 b g £0
```
5a  10-12  Wolv  7af     [35]     663 t
22  5-8    Chep  10.2sft [30]    1333 t
```

TYSON RETURNS 2 b g £0
```
50  11-11  Nott  6.1sft          1739
36a 9-14   Sout  6af             2336
```

TYTHEKNOT 3 b g £8900
```
73  2-12   Hayd  8.1sft          1108
66  3-10   Pont  10sft   75      1427
75  6-13   Newc  8g/s    75      2773
71  4-10   Nott  10g/s   [74]    2930
76  3-5    Pont  10gd    72      3459
70  1-6    NEWC  10.1sft [74]    4286*
74  5-11   Ayr   8sft    74      4621 P
21  13-14  Ayr   10sft   73      5037 p
45  15-19  Donc  10.3sft 73      5201
```

TYTHERLEY 3 b f £0
```
0   P-18   Wind  8.3g/f          1810
```

TYUP POMPEY 3 ch g £535
```
52  4-7    Good  9.9g/f          4541
46  14-18  Bath  10.2gd          5023
56  5-8    Newb  10hvy  [60]     5226
```

TYZACK 3 b g £0
```
60  5-6    Warw  6.1sft [71]     1088
59  7-11   Redc  7g/f   [69]     1822
41  8-9    Donc  8g/s    65      3378
42  10-14  Yarm  7gd     60      3995
39  8-14   Pont  10g/f   55      4624
```

UGLY SISTER 2 gr f £0
```
30  9-11   Yarm  6g/f            1728
34a 7-10   Sout  7af             2802
43  6-6    Brig  7sft            4163
0   20-20  Leic  7g/f    52      4451
```

UHOOMAGOO 6 b g £52885
```
78a 1-8    SOUT  7af     [67]    744+ bl
78  7-27   Newb  8gd     82      1231 bl
77  7-17   Thir  8g/s    82      1475 bl
78  7-12   Hayd  8.1g/f  81      1883 bl
90  1-11   DONC  7g/f    80      2076+ bl
98  1-13   EPSO  8.5g/f  85      2207* bl
85  11-31  Asco  8g/f    87      2489 bl
82  13-28  Asco  7g/f    94      2558 bl
96  3-21   Asco  7g/f    92      3441 bl
89  7-21   Good  8fm     92      3565 bl
80  14-16  Good  7g/f    94      4523 bl
83  12-15  Asco  7g/f    94      4800 bl
85a 9-14   Ling  7ap     85      5262 bl
```

UHURU PEAK 3 ch c £3163
```
44a 3-8    Sout  5af             742
39a 10-11  Sout  6af             869
64  5-11   Catt  6gd             999
35  11-19  York  6g/f    62      2055
53  7-14   Redc  7fm     57      2295
56  3-14   Catt  6g/f    54      3018
56  2-17   Ripo  6g/s    54      3262
33  13-20  Thir  6g/f    55      3575
43  6-9    Thir  8sft    55      3835
47  8-19   Thir  6g/f    53      4595 BL
60  3-14   Redc  7g/s    50      5109 bl
```

UIG 3 ch f £5186
```
66  8-20   Bath  10.2gd          1398
60  8-10   Sali  9.9g/f          1718
78  3-18   Wind  10g/f           1959
77  2-11   Wind  10fm    [77]    3802
63  9-9    York  11.9g/s [77]    4058
74  4-11   Wind  8.3g/s  75      4222
75  2-9    Bath  10.2gd  [74]    4547
67  7-7    Hayd  10.5sft 74      4781
71  2-7    Epso  10.1gd  [72]    4911
```

ULFAH 3 b f £53805
```
104 1-7    LEOP  6g/f            3495*
109 1-12   CURR  6g/f            4152*
```

ULSHAW 6 ch g £0
```
7a  11-11  Wolv  16.2af   54     48
```

```
4   11-13  Pont  21.6hvy  57     1252
42  10-12  Warw  19.1fm   55     2577
22  16-19  Bath  17.2gd   45     3147
34  10-15  Chep  16.2gd   [45]   3400
```

ULTIMATA 4 ch f £4967
```
45  9-9    Newm  10gd   [82]     1890
85  2-8    Wind  8.3g/s [80]     2620
85  2-6    Wind  8.3g/f  80      3978
67  9-12   Yarm  10.1sft 80      4149
62  15-20  York  8.9gd   81      4999
86  1-3    NEWM  10sft   81      5104*
80  6-10   Yarm  10.1sft [82]    5255
```

ULTRA MARINE 4 b c £0
```
31  7-8    Redc  10gd   [54]     2548 bl
13  17-20  Catt  12g/f   50      2850 bl
0   13-13  Warw  12.6gd  50      3056
```

ULUNDI 9 b g £0
```
97a 10-13  Ling  10ap   105      433
88  11-14  Good  12g/f  [107]    1843
94  12-15  Redc  10g/f  102      2101
71  12-14  Asco  10g/f  95       2556
```

ULYSEES 4 b g £10768
```
61a 6-10   Wolv  8.5af   71      5
27a 13-14  Sout  8af     68      93
28a 9-10   Wolv  7af    [63]     152
76  1-10   HAMI  6gd     64      1391*
63  7-15   Hami  6gd     70      1508
75  3-12   Newc  6g/f    70      2160
78  1-11   AYR   6gd     70      2542*
71  8-18   Newc  7sft    76      2684
58  5-6    Carl  5.9gd  [74]     2934
55  14-15  Newc  6gd     74      3424
52  7-8    Hami  6g/s   [73]     3880
71  4-7    Ayr   6hvy    73      4087 P
62  7-18   Ayr   7.2sft  71      4689
38  11-11  Hami  6g/s    70      4818 VIS
65  5-19   Ayr   6sft    68      5069
60  8-10   Catt  7sft    66      5320
```

UMNIYA 2 b f £52236
```
73  3-12   Warw  5sft            1524
88  2-6    York  6sft            1669
81  1-13   REDC  6g/f            1818*
92  3-7    Kemp  6fm             2071
97  3-6    Naas  6g/f            2328
97  4-17   Asco  6g/f            2553
80  5-9    Newm  6g/f            2763
88  6-8    York  6g/s   [91]     4059
92  6-12   Good  7sft   [91]     4264 VIS
99  4-12   Curr  7g/f   [91]     4432 BL
94  3-26   Newb  6.5g/f          4679 vis
96  5-14   Newm  7g/f  [100]     4914 vis
97  6-10   San   8sft  [100]     5167 vis
72  8-8    Sain  8Very [100]     5315 vis
```

UN AUTRE ESPERE 5 b g £1477
```
0   12-12  Wolv  9.4af  [35]     782
23a 6-13   Wolv  8.5af  [35]     826
17a 10-13  Wolv  8.5af  [30]     894
32a 9-12   Wolv  9.4af  [30]     939 bl
12a 8-10   Ling  7ap    [30]    1181 bl
29a 5-8    Wolv  7af    [30]    1314 bl
37  1-7    CHEP  7.1sft [30]    1335* bl
17a 5-10   Sout  8af    [30]    1406 bl
1   14-17  Bath  11.7sft 45     1543 bl
```

UNBRIDLEDS DREAM 3 gr c £0
```
54  19-24  Newm  8fm             1495
```

UNCLE BATTY 4 b g £0
```
50  4-13   Leic  10fm            2107
43  5-8    Chep  12.1g/f         2623
```

UNCLE BERNON 4 ch g £0
```
64a 7-12   Ling  6ap    [78]     106
56a 14-16  Ling  7ap     72      181
```

UNCLE BULGARIA 2 b c £532
```
60a 3-11   Sout  7af             2995
62  7-14   Folk  7gd             4115
62  10-13  Kemp  7gd             4355
61  5-20   Yarm  8g/s    65      4635
63  6-20   Yarm  8g/s    61      5349
```

UNCLE JOHN 2 b c £3085

```
41a 11-11  Ling  8ap     69      54
55a 5-10   Sout  8af     68      189
51  7-13   Good  9g/f    67      2024
53  7-8    Good  9.9gd   65      2377
62  4-9    Brig  9.9gd   60      2955
63  2-7    Brig  11.9g/f [60]    3173
58  4-5    Asco  12gd    61      3468
49  9-13   Ling  10g/s   60      4182
51  9-14   Chep  10.2gd  58      4487
0   12-12  Chep  10.2hvy 55      4708
64a 3-11   Wolv  12.2ap  60      5117 BL
65a 2-16   Ling  12ap    [60]    5296 bl
```

UNDER MY SKIN 3 ch f £0
```
56  12-13  Kemp  10g/f           3038 T
53  7-10   Newb  7gd             3921 t
```

UNDER MY SPELL 3 b f £6601
```
48  17-22  Donc  7gd     75      955
67  10-20  Nott  6.1gd   72      1239
70  2-16   Nott  6.1sft  [70]    1743
71  2-12   Chep  6.1gd   70      2118
66  5-18   Wind  6g/f    70      2268
80  1-15   LEIC  6g/f    70      2398*
52  10-15  Hayd  6gd     70      2950
48  9-19   Ayr   6gd     76      3307
72  8-13   Wind  6fm     70      3479
2   10-12  Chep  8.1g/s  74      3898
```

UNDERGRADUATE 2 b c £0
```
75  5-11   Bath  8sft            5171
```

UNDERTHEMISTLETOE 2 b f £420
```
54  6-13   Redc  5gd             1818
55  3-5    Hami  5gd             3130
38  10-13  York  5gd             3431
40  6-11   Catt  5gd     [55]    4962
```

UNDETERRED 8 ch g £12107
```
43  11-19  Redc  6sft    77      1145
70  5-14   Ayr   6g/f    77      1898
63  7-11   Ripo  6g/f    77      1977
67  10-17  Epso  6fm     73      2256 vis
72  4-20   York  6g/f    73      2409 vis
70  4-17   Redc  6gd     72      2561 vis
73  4-17   Pont  6g/s    71      2990 vis
78  1-8    PONT  6gd     70      3461*
60  12-26  Good  6fm     74      3569
58  13-19  Good  6g/f    75      4747
```

UNFURLED 2 ch c £2204
```
78  6-10   Kemp  6g/f            4712
88  2-21   Newm  8sft            5097
```

UNICORN REWARD 4 b c £814
```
29  23-24  Donc  8gd     84      928
67  4-12   Pont  8hvy    80      1066
47  12-13  Ripo  8f      78      2010
```

UNINTENTIONAL 2 b f £836
```
56a 5-10   Wolv  9.4af  [57]     36
58a 2-9    Wolv  9.4af  [35]     238
40a 6-6    Wolv  8.5af  [60]     468
29a 8-11   Wolv  8.5af   58     1339
39  6-16   Nott  10hvy   55     1611
1   14-14  Ling  11.5g/f 52     2014
0   P-7    Chep  12.1g/s [52]   3899 VIS
10  10-12  Chep  10.2hvy 52     4708
25a 10-12  Wolv  7.1ap  [48]    5229 BL
```

UNION JACK JACKSON 2 b c £946
```
64  4-11   Ayr   6g/s            2569
65  7-12   Hayd  6gd             2902
67  7-18   Newc  6g/s            3699
67a 6-13   Sout  7af     71      4040
64  4-20   Yarm  8g/s    65      4635
65  4-20   Yarm  8g/s    62      5349
```

UNITED NATIONS 3 ch c £9841
```
95  1-17   NEWM  8gd             1166*
92  3-4    Sand  8.1g/s          1317
93  4-8    Muss  8gd     94      4516 VIS
62  8-10   Newm  8g/f   [92]     4890 vis
```

UNITED SPIRIT 2 b f £6993
```
56a 4-13   Wolv  6af             126
56  7-17   Kemp  7gd     60      2174
49  6-8    Ayr   7.2gd  [58]     2506
58  3-16   Ling  7gd     55      3024 P
```

66 1-16 LING 6g/f 55 3602* BL
70a 1-14 LING 7ap 61 3746* bl
65 4-9 Ling 7gd 65 4110 bl
64 5-20 Ling 6g/f 65 4317
45 14-20 Nott 6.1g/s 64 4646 bl

UNITED UNION 3 b g £0
48 4-9 Leic 6g/s [65] 1015
42 9-9 Bath 5g/s 65 1102 BL

UNLEADED 3 ch f £2187
10a 7-14 Sout 14af 30 185
33a 2-9 Wolv 14.8af [30] 301
36a 1-6 WOLV 16.2af [35] 395*
40a 2-9 Sout 16af [40] 576
31a 5-10 Ling 16ap [40] 650
33 8-14 Kemp 14.4sft 40 948
18a 4-7 Wolv 16.2af [40] 1263
6a 5-7 Wolv 16.2af [35] 1802

UNLIMITED 2 b c £5705
73a 2-8 Sout 5ap 1048
75a 1-12 SOUT 5af 1439*
75 2-4 Newc 5gd 1868
68 5-8 Thir 5g/f 2213
56a 7-10 Sout 7af 79 3483
61 3-4 Ripo 6g/f [77] 3644
69 5-13 Warw 6.1gd 72 4273
16 10-10 Ayr 6g/s 69 4655

UNO MENTE 5 b m £633
56 10-15 Beve 9.9sft 62 1307
37 10-15 Hami 8.3g/s 60 1602
44 8-16 Redc 10g/f 58 1821
46 6-11 Redc 8fm 55 2296
55 3-9 Pont 8gd 53 2604
47 7-14 Pont 8g/f 53 2993
45 9-18 Pont 8gd 53 3242
44 9-19 Beve 9.9g/f 51 3505
41 11-16 Nott 8.2g/s 51 4036 VIS
15 19-19 Beve 9.9g/f 48 4720 vis

UNPRECEDENTED 3 br g £369
20a 11-12 Sout 8af 57 656
56 12-12 Newm 7g/s [50] 1152
56 4-12 Ripo 8g/f [50] 1784 VIS
55 7-12 Ripo 8g/f [50] 1978 vis
25 7-9 Thir 8g/f [40] 4593 vis
12 11-11 Wind 8.3g/f [48] 5054 vis

UNREAL 2 b f £9446
72 6-6 Newb 5.2gd 1735
86 2-10 Newm 6g/f 3063
72 6-8 Good 6fm 3536
81 2-13 Warw 6.1gd 80 4273
81 1-9 SAND 5gd [80] 4497*

UNSCRUPULOUS 5 ch g £24238
80 3-7 Newm 8fm [80] 2091
97 1-28 ASCO 7g/f 80 2558*

UNSHAKABLE 5 b g £30592
88 8-24 Donc 8gd 92 951
74 11-17 Kemp 10g/s 90 1111
95 1-17 SAND 8.1g/s 88 1351*
100 3-15 Sand 8.1g/s 94 2915
89 10-21 Good 8fm 94 3565
91 5-10 Asco 8gd 94 3775
97 4-15 York 7.9g/s 93 4061
97 5-32 Newm 9g/f 93 4916
95 7-22 Newm 8sft 94 5103
74 12-13 Newm 8g/s 93 5284

UNSHAKEN 10 b h £0
0 13-13 Hami 6g/f 57 2315
0 12-12 Ayr 8g/s .. [57] 2543

UNSHOODA 3 ch f £0
97 7-8 Newb 7gd [95] 1233
49 9-11 Hayd 6gd [95] 2240

UNSUITED 4 b f £12138
18a 14-16 Ling 7ap [60] 123
36a 11-15 Ling 7ap [53] 263
27a 10-13 Ling 10ap [53] 338
38a 3-9 Wolv 9.4af [40] 522
37a 2-12 Wolv 9.4af [40] 668
32a 6-9 Wolv 9.4af [40] 821
32 4-10 Chep 8.1sft [45] 1334

55 1-13 KEMP 10hvy [40] 1643*
66 1-15 KEMP 9gd 50 2170*
71 1-8 KEMP 9g/s 61 2680*
70 3-11 Newb 11g/f 69 3256
67 8-16 Sand 10gd 68 4609
33 16-18 Sali 9.9gd 68 4850

UNTIDY DAUGHTER 5 b m £862
56 5-15 Beve 9.9sft 55 1307 BL
40 7-10 Muss 12gd 52 1796 bl
54 3-13 Pont 10g/f 52 2038 p
42 7-11 Newc 10.1g/s 52 2726 p

UP TEMPO 6 b g £20966
63a 2-10 Wolv 7af 59 379 p
62a 1-9 SOUT 6af [59] 459* p
63a 3-9 Wolv 7af 61 684 bl
73a 1-13 SOUT 6af 61 741* bl
75 1-19 NEWC 6sft 65 967+ bl
73 1-13 REDC 7sft [71] 1142* bl
80 4-12 Thir 7g/s 77 1215 bl
76 2-8 Hayd 6g/s [77] 1345 bl
67 10-19 Redc 7g/f 77 1820 bl
66 11-16 York 7g/f 77 2057 bl
76 5-9 Ches 7gd 76 2282 bl
68 8-20 York 6g/f 76 2409 bl
81a 1-12 WOLV 7.1ap 72 5289* bl

UP THE AISLE 7 b g £0
5 11-13 Leic 10g/f 4453
17 5-5 Pont 10g/f 4630

UPTHEDALE 3 b g £668
41 7-14 Warw 7.1sft 48 1085
33a 4-5 Wolv 9.4af [45] 1311
35 3-8 Hami 9.2g/s 40 1603
1 U-11 Redc 10sft 40 1663
36 5-13 Beve 12.1g/f [40] 1945
12 10-14 Redc 14.1g/f 39 2123
51 6-8 Beve 12.1gd [35] 2515

URABANDE 2 b f £1116
2 12-12 Ripo 5gd 1173
65a 2-12 Sout 5af 1439
20a 10-11 Sout 5af 1752
33 6-13 Beve 5g/s 2321
44 4-10 Thir 6fm 2461
2 7-8 Yarm 6fm 2865

URBAN CALM 3 b f £3546
65 4-8 Thir 5sft 1228
63 2-13 Folk 5sft 1575
63 2-14 Donc 5gd 2237
25 9-10 Redc 6gd [63] 2559
45 4-5 Folk 5g/s 63 3050

URBAN ROSE 3 b f £1214
64 7-20 Nott 6.1gd 67 1239
37 14-17 Warw 7.1sft 65 1526
64 3-12 Chep 6.1gd 64 2118
53 8-18 Wind 6g/f 64 2268
56 4-14 Yarm 6gd 63 3870 t
32 9-13 Good 6gd 63 3952 t
63 4-16 Good 5gd 60 4528 t p
44 13-15 Good 5gd 58 4751 t p

UREDALE 2 b c £2618
60 5-6 Newc 5sft 1274
51a 8-11 Sout 5af 1752
63 6-7 Redc 5g/f 2100
61 5-7 Catt 7g/f 3189
65 1-13 CATT 7g/f 3349*
38 13-13 Newc 7g/s 68 3698
30 14-14 Muss 8gd 66 4519

UROWELLS 4 b g £0
83 8-9 Newm 12g/f [92] 2246
80 9-13 York 11.9g/s 92 3076
77 7-9 Pont 12g/s 88 3969
64 11-20 Ayr 10g/s 83 4656 VIS
52 9-14 Hami 8.3g/s 78 4820 vis

URSA MAJOR 10 b g £0
39 12-14 Leic 10g/f 52 1828
46 7-16 Yarm 10.1fm 50 2146
20 6-7 Kemp 14.4g/f 48 3037
37 8-17 Newm 10g/f 48 3238
41 7-13 Folk 9.7g/f 45 3726

USHINDI 2 b f £2692
35 13-13 Newb 7g/f 3252
60 12-18 Nott 8.2g/s 4035
71 4-12 Warw 7.1g/f 4418
76 2D-17 Catt 7gd 69 4963

USTAD 2 br c £0
68 8-11 Newm 7gd 4190
67 7-8 Sand 8.1gd 4608

UTAH FLATS 3 ch g £0
0 7-7 Sout 7af 531 P
28a 10-10 Sout 6af 659 BL

VADEMECUM 3 br g £0
67 6-7 Beve 7.5sft 82 1305
14 10-11 Hami 6gd 80 1745
45 11-11 York 7g/f 77 3433
66 10-13 Redc 7fm [73] 4341
24 10-15 Hami 6sft 70 4696
48 13-19 Newc 7g/f 65 5014
40a 11-12 Wolv 7.1ap [60] 5325

VAGUE STAR 2 b c £1762
37 13-14 Warw 6.1g/f 4422
74 3-15 Nott 5.1gd 4859
72a 3-8 Ling 6ap 5081
60a 8-10 Ling 7ap [74] 5264

VAL DE FLEURIE 9 b m £0
52 6-9 Folk 12sft 58 979

VAL DE MAAL 4 ch c £1218
63a 3-11 Wolv 6af 68 1337
33 14-14 Ling 7sft 73 1624
62 4-9 Ripo 6g/f [71] 2007
69 7-9 Ches 7gd 69 2282
68 4-17 Wind 6gd 69 4126
66 6-13 Warw 6.1gd 69 4272
55 11-20 Ripo 6gd 67 4785
30a 9-12 Wolv 6ap 65 4984
55a 6-13 Wolv 6ap [63] 5327 P

VAL DISERE 2 ch c £0
26a 12-13 Wolv 6ap 4980

VALANCE 4 br g £17348
80 3-8 Newm 12gd 76 1889
79 5-10 Sali 14.1gd 76 2699
84 1-12 NEWM 16.1g/f 75 3032*
82 4-13 Asco 16.2g/f 80 3387
75 8-19 Good 21fm 80 3531
80 2-12 York 13.9g/f 79 4400
69 13-16 Asco 16.2g/f 81 4803

VALAZAR 4 b g £1603
46a 9-12 Wolv 5af 64 109
0 11-11 Wolv 6af [62] 153
28a 14-16 Sout 6af [59] 227
34a 10-12 Sout 5af [54] 587
18a 9-11 Sout 5af [50] 775
27a 7-12 Wolv 5af [45] 889 BL
41a 2-8 Sout 5af [40] 1199
44a 3-6 Sout 6af [45] 1405
41 2-16 Nott 6.1gd [45] 1988
45 3-19 Leic 5gd 45 2702
47a 4-15 Sout 5af [45] 2803
15 16-17 Catt 5g/f 46 3667

VALDASHO 5 b m £0
16a 9-10 Ling 10ap [30] 738

VALDESCO 6 ch g £0
64 11-19 Carl 11.9gd 70 2673
62 7-10 Hayd 10.5g/s 67 3139 P
43 13-17 Pont 17.1g/s 64 3970 bl

VALE DE LOBO 2 b f £3929
56a 5-7 Ling 6ap 3196
79a 1-12 SOUT 7af 3394*
75 3-13 Newm 8gd 72 4193

VALENTIA 3 b f £0
40a 8-10 Ling 5ap 802

VALENTIN 2 ch f £15438
95 1-8 ASCO 6gd 3071*
101 2-6 Asco 6gd 3440
85 8-11 Newm 7g/f 3781

83 8-11 Sali 6gd [100] 4332

VALENTINA GUEST 3 b f £3049
102 3-12 Leop 14g/s 3315

VALERIAN 3 b g £2300
72a 1-11 WOLV 9.4af 115*

VALET 2 b c £0
0 19-19 Leic 7gd 5055
29 9-9 Muss 8g/s 5331

VALEUREUX 6 ch g £2508
52 3-10 Pont 10g/f 52 2794
57 2-18 Pont 10g/f 52 2988
44 4-7 Epso 12g/s 52 3040
49 8-20 Catt 12g/f 55 3354

VALIANT ACT 2 b f £220
60 6-11 Chep 7.1hvy 4704
68 3-13 Warw 7.1g/s 4996

VALIANT AIR 3 b g £1879
33a 4-7 Wolv 12af [57] 959
53 5-9 Muss 12g/f [55] 1121 VIS
50 2-8 Pont 12hvy [55] 1250
38a 4-8 Sout 12af 45 1444
3 10-10 Nott 14.1hvy 45 1612
31 7-14 Redc 14.1g/f 42 2123
38 4-11 Pont 12g/f 40 2790 BL
40 5-16 Nott 10gd 40 4857 bl
33 11-18 Leic 10gd [40] 5042 bl
15 7-11 Catt 12sft [40] 5128
35a 3-12 Wolv 12.2ap [40] 5208 bl

VALIANT EFFORT 5 b g £0
34 16-17 Newb 12g/f 75 1759

VALIANT ROMEO 4 b c £6696
51 5-20 Ripo 5gd 54 1179
55 2-15 Muss 5gd 53 1555
57 2-11 Hayd 5g/f 54 1886 vis
49 4-19 Beve 5gd 56 2512 vis
45 11-17 Catt 5g/f 55 2846 vis
55 5-20 Beve 5g/s 54 3180 vis
58 2-15 Muss 5gd 53 3561
10 15-15 Pont 5gd 53 3680
51 3-9 Yarm 5.2g/s 55 4253 P
56 3-19 Ling 5g/s 54 4739 p
55 3-13 Muss 5g/s [54] 5146 vis
31a 12-13 Wolv 6ap [53] 5359 vis

VALIOS 2 b c £0
59 11-15 Wind 6g/f 3163
52 7-7 Folk 6g/f 3722

VALIXIR 3 b c £190944
116 3-5 Ling 10.5g/s 1853
118 3-15 Chan 12g/s 2308
121 1-9 MAIS 10sft 3316*
121 1-8 LONG 12sft 4566*
113 10-19 Long 12g/f 4956

VALJARV 3 b f £10240
84a 9-15 Ling 7ap [96] 885
93 7-13 Newm 7gd [95] 1169
92 13-16 Newm 8fm [95] 1492
82 10-18 Newm 6g/f 95 1933
91 7-11 Warw 7.1fm [93] 2574
89 4-6 Newm 6g/f [93] 3178 BL
97 4-19 Newm 6fm 90 3002 bl
95 2-8 Newm 6g/f 90 3235 bl
77 9-10 Asco 6gd 92 3778 VIS
90 9-11 Newm 6g/f 92 3941
93 5-10 Newm 6gd 91 4884 bl
80 13-20 York 6gd 91 5001
93 4-15 Newm 6gd [91] 5088
89 4-11 Newm 6sft [90] 5270
80a 12-12 Ling 8ap [90] 5298

VALLEE ENCHANTEE 3 b f £694292
116 1-14 SHA 12g/f 209*
112 4-8 Long 10.5hvy 1558
115 3-11 Epso 12g/f 2209
117 5-11 Asco 12g/f 3442
118 6-19 Long 12g/f 4956

VALLERA 3 b f £0
113 4-13 Long 12sft 4567

VALUABLE GIFT 6 ch g £0
2a 15-16 Sout 6af 53 92 P
34a 8-11 Wolv 6af [49] 153 e
28a 8-10 Sout 6af [45] 308 bl e
21a 8-9 Sout 6af [45] 533 bl e
10a 8-12 Sout 6af [40] 982 bl e
0 13-17 Pont 6hvy [40] 1065 t p
26 8-19 Redc 6g/f 30 2125 p

VALUE PLUS 2 b f £1466
79 2-5 Hami 5g/s 2829 P
0 B-12 Bath 5.7gd 3141

VAMOSE 3 ro g £748
62 4-5 Brig 8g/f 72 1370
60 8-10 Yarm 11.5g/f [69] 1725
52 4-7 Ripo 9g/s [66] 3263

VAMP 3 b f £6976
64 7-13 Newb 7gd 1210
79 2-11 Bath 8fm 1904
76 3-11 Folk 9.7g/f 2274
75 1-6 BATH 10.2g/f [73] 2980*
75 5-8 Asco 10g/f 77 3391
71 11-19 Kemp 10fm 77 4392
74 4-13 Yarm 10.1gd 75 4613
80 3-12 Wind 11.6g/f 75 4833
72 2-3 Newm 10sft 75 5104

VAMPIRE QUEEN 2 b f £2947
53a 6-10 Wolv 7af 36
51a 10-14 Sout 7af 98
41a 7-15 Sout 7af 184
55a 1-13 WOLV 6af 49 436*
51a 4-11 Sout 6af 56 591
33a 7-13 Sout 6af 55 797
48a 8-15 Ling 7ap 55 815

VANBRUGH 3 ch g £4109
49a 8-16 Sout 11af 65 97 vis t
66a 2-14 Sout 14af 60 185 vis t
66a 2-16 Sout 16af 60 206 vis t
46a 6-8 Wolv 14.8af 65 277 vis t
78a 1-9 SOUT 16af 65 336* vis t
61a 9-11 Ling 16ap 77 605 vis t
34a 6-7 Sout 14af 77 681 vis t
36 11-12 Thir 16gd 64 1637 t
40 13-18 Nott 14.1g/s 60 1772 vis t
27 10-10 Hayd 14g/f 55 1923 vis t
26 13-17 Nott 14.1g/f 51 2156 vis t
37 9-13 Pont 17.1g/f 51 2276 t
37 7-14 Bath 18.2fm 45 2417 t
0 9-13 Sout 14af 65 2494 vis t
21 8-12 Yarm 16gd 41 3493 t p
0 7-10 Yarm 16sft 37 4151 vis t
30 7-10 Yarm 14.1g/s 37 4255 vis t
47 6-14 Warw 16.2g/f 35 4423 vis t
12 11-14 Yarm 14.1g/s [40] 5123 vis t
10a 12-12 Wolv 13.9ap 65 5160 vis
27a 11-13 Wolv 16.5ap 55 5366 vis t

VANCOUVER GOLD 2 b f £538
75 3-11 Thir 7fm 4381
63 5-11 Newc 7fm 4863

VANDENBERGHE 4 b g £8360
47a 3-12 Wolv 12af 49 75
30a 5-16 Sout 16af 49 206
54a 1-8 WOLV 9.4af 48 1657*
40 5-12 Brig 9.9fm 48 1695
49a 3-12 Wolv 9.4af 52 2054
49 4-11 Folk 12g/f 48 2273
51 3-12 Warw 10.9fm 48 2436
49 5-12 Ling 10g/f 49 2844
44 6-17 Bath 11.7gd 48 3145
49 3-19 Chep 12.1gd 48 3398
47 3-10 Carl 14.1fm 46 3549
54a 3-13 Ling 16ap 51 3822
52a 4-14 Ling 16ap 53 4319
42 7-15 Folk 12g/f [47] 4374
41 7-20 Kemp 12g/f [46] 4796
58a 1-14 LING 16ap 50 5082*

VANDERLIN 5 ch g £40530
109a3-8 Ling 7ap [107] 1043
109 3-5 Good 8g/f [105] 2022
107 5-11 Epso 8.5fm [105] 2252

108 3-9 Wind 8.3fm [107] 2757
109 1-6 CHES 7g/f [107] 3098*
103 8-8 Good 7g/f [109] 3508
106 3-11 York 7g/s [109] 4063
106 3-8 Epso 7g/f [107] 4472
108 2-11 Good 7gd [105] 4874
98 7-12 Newm 7sft [105] 5134

VANGELIS 5 gr h £42148
117 1-8 LONG 10gd 1061*

VANILLA MOON 4 b f £816
46a 5-9 Ling 12ap [48] 324 vis
43a 2-6 Ling 10ap [48] 409 vis
56a 4-7 Ling 13ap [48] 546 vis
48 3-18 Wind 11.6g/f 48 1960 vis
37 6-8 Wind 11.6g/f 48 2796 vis
47 4-11 Yarm 11.5gd 46 3367 vis
39 6-14 Yarm 11.5g/f 44 3714 vis
44a 4-14 Ling 16ap [45] 4663 vis

VANISHED 4 b f £0
25a 12-12 Sout 5af [60] 587 p
40a 8-10 Sout 5af 60 660 BL
12a 9-9 Sout 5af [55] 793 bl

VANTAGE 3 b g £8843
81a 2-10 Ling 10ap 77 817
81a 2-10 Ling 10ap [80] 886
77 3-8 Newm 12g/s [80] 1153
80 1-4 BEVE 12.1sft [80] 1308*
83 4-5 Leic 11.8g/s 85 1355
81 5-9 Wind 11.6g/f 80 1807
72 13-18 Epso 10.1fm 79 2250 BL
74 4-5 Good 9sft 78 4185 P
73 6-13 Yarm 10.1gd 77 4613 bl
69 7-12 Wind 11.6g/f 75 4833 bl

VAR 5 b h £108879
116 1-7 GOOD 6g/f 4526* BL
114 2-11 Newb 5.2g/f 4678 bl
121 1-15 LONG 10gd 4952* bl

VARENKA 2 b f £16422
74 5-7 Catt 7g/f 3665
98 1-11 BEVE 7.5g/s 3851*
98 2-8 Capa 7.5gd 4430

VARIETY CLUB 3 b g £0
9 16-16 Chep 7.1gd 2369
8 14-17 Chep 8.1g/s 55 3087 VIS
0 10-10 Yarm 8g/f 52 3712 BL

VARNAY 3 b f £0
78 11-14 York 7sft 89 1665 vis

VARUNI 3 b f £5503
67a 1-8 LING 10ap 626*
61a 7-10 Ling 10ap 66 817
66 2-10 Beve 12.1g/s 64 1165
25 15-20 Wind 11.6sft 64 1648
59 9-12 Sand 10gd 62 2366
56 5-10 Folk 12g/s 60 3051
53 4-10 Sali 12sft [57] 4579

VAS Y CARLA 3 ch f £1280
59 12-14 Yarm 8g/f 84 1131
67 2-8 Beve 7.5g/f [80] 2169
40 10-10 Chep 8.1g/f 75 2624

VASYWAIT 5 b h £7711
100 3-12 Deau 6sft 3167

VATORI 2 ch c £7711
108 3-7 Long 8g/s 4729

VAUDEVIRE 3 b g £465
10a 6-8 Wolv 7af 892
0 9-9 Sout 8af 983
20a 3-7 Wolv 6af [30] 1309 BL
0 7-7 Wolv 6af [30] 1566 bl
19 4-5 Ayr 6gd [23] 2541 bl
42 4-6 Muss 5g/f [23] 2808 bl
11 7-9 Ripo 5g/f 39 3645 bl

VAUGHAN 3 b c £1058
76 8-11 Good 9g/f 92 4525
91 4-13 Kemp 12g/f [90] 4715
88 8-17 Newm 12g/f 90 4889

VEGAS QUEEN 2 br f £5915
92 3-8 Capa 7.5gd 4430

VELOCITAS 3 b g £2000
60 4-8 Donc 6gd 953
48 10-14 Sout 6gd 1281
54 12-16 Ling 7g/f [58] 1982
37 9-17 Hayd 8.1gd 57 2243
59 5-10 Warw 8.1g/f [54] 4421
62a 2-13 Wolv 9.5ap 54 4925
62a 2-9 Wolv 9.5ap [57] 5360 VIS

VELOCITYS IMAGE 4 b f £0
7a 7-7 Wolv 5af [40] 348
8a 7-14 Sout 7af [35] 573

VELVET HEIGHTS 2 b c £5512
73 10-14 Newm 7g/f 2766
72 7-15 Sand 7.1g/f 3337
86 1-11 SAND 8.1g/s 3890*
77 7-9 Newc 8sft 87 4285
68 11-13 Newm 8fm 85 4725

VELVET JONES 11 gr g £0
17 7-8 Chep 7.1sft 4055

VELVET RHYTHM 3 b f £0
0 9-9 Sout 11af 224
0 8-8 Sout 7af 320
5a 8-11 Sout 7af 488
0 12-12 Sout 11af [30] 640

VELVET TOUCH 2 b f £2300
42a 8-14 Ling 6ap 146
56a 2-8 Sout 6ap 197
58a 2-4 Sout 6af 222
56a 2-13 Wolv 6af 54 436
46a 6-11 Ling 6ap [57] 543
32 9-12 Folk 6sft 60 975
38a 6-8 Sout 6af 55 1441
58 5-13 Folk 5sft [57] 1575
26a 11-11 Sout 5af 54 2380 VIS
33a 8-9 Sout 6af [54] 2493
0 12-12 Wolv 6ap [46] 5162
28 14-18 Yarm 6g/s 52 5354

VELVET WATERS 3 b f £12796
64 3-16 Bath 10.2g/f [59] 1790
56 6-8 Brig 9.9g/f 59 2046
60 4-9 Yarm 14.1g/f 59 2345
60 1-10 BATH 11.7g/f 57 2978*
63 2-10 Ling 11.5gd 59 3334
66 2-16 Thir 12g/f 59 3573
73 1-12 BATH 11.7g/f 61 3845*
74 3-11 Sali 12g/s 67 4080
75 3-13 Kemp 14.4fm 70 4395
64 9-16 Good 12gd [71] 4745

VELVETEEN RABBIT 2 b f £2420
66 9-10 Newm 6g/f 3063
68 3-15 Folk 7gd 3381
75 2-12 Folk 7gd 3909
59 7-14 Yarm 7g/s 74 4583
65 8-12 Ayr 8sft 72 5065

VENABLES 3 ch c £1875
102a5-15 Ling 7ap [106] 885
47 11-11 Newm 7gd 106 1167 T
2 11-11 Newb 6gd [104] 1732 t

VENDORS MISTAKE 2 b f £800
51a 7-10 Ling 8ap 232
46a 8-15 Ling 7ap 54 295
43a 6-13 Wolv 6af 51 436
51 3-20 Yarm 6g/f 48 1730
48 3-9 Thir 5g/f 48 2219
41 6-10 Brig 5.3fm 48 2331
39 6-18 Yarm 6g/s 47 5354

VENEER 2 b c £0
51 4-6 Folk 5sft 974
55 8-10 Hayd 5sft 1107
39 15-18 Chep 6.1gd 2194
57 5-12 Muss 7.1g/s [55] 5142

VENERDI TREDICI 3 b f £0
14 11-11 Redc 9g/s 55 2565
26 12-13 Muss 7.1g/f 52 2812
11 7-7 Brig 9.9sft [48] 4142

VENETIAN KING 2 b g £1700
74 5-8 York 6g/f 2408
78 2-7 Ayr 7.2g/f 3302

VENETIAN ROMANCE 3 ch f £430
34a 5-8 Wolv 7af [56] 1222
26 10-14 Warw 8.1sft 55 1529 BL e
27 18-19 Brig 9.9g/f 50 1940 P
18 10-14 Sali 8fm 45 2423 p
37 7-14 Chep 8.1g/s 40 3090
28 7-14 Folk 12gd 40 3383
38 3-12 Folk 12g/s 37 3913
21 12-13 Redc 14.1gd 37 4249
34 9-18 Leic 10gd [35] 5042 VIS
31 8-14 Yarm 14.1g/s [35] 5123

VENEZIANA 3 ch f £0
21 15-15 Wind 11.6fm 63 3481
28 8-10 Hayd 8.1gd [63] 3739

VENGEANCE 4 b c £21301
88 7-17 Kemp 10g/s 91 1111
95 3-20 Epso 12hvy 90 1295
101 1-12 WIND 11.6fm 90 2759*
100 5-13 York 11.9g/s 98 3076
96 5-7 Asco 10gd [98] 3464

VENGEROV 3 b c £4041
74a 1-13 SOUT 8af [71] 553*
42a 6-8 Wolv 8.5af 73 645
64 3-4 Bath 11.7fm [72] 2413
54 10-10 Nott 10g/s [70] 2930

VERASI 2 b g £432
36a 8-13 Wolv 9.4af 37
69 4-11 Kemp 8hvy 1514
58 10-15 Leic 11.8gd 67 2134
54 7-7 Warw 10.9fm 66 2576 BL
56a 7-14 Ling 13ap [64] 4898
38 9-11 Good 14gd [60] 5029 bl

VERBIER 2 b f £5805
66 6-15 Kemp 6g/f 4357
79 1-9 BEVE 7.5g/f 4600*
79 5-17 Good 8gd 75 4871

VERITABLE 2 br f £358
73 4-10 Sali 5g/f 1717
44 11-13 Wind 6fm 3639
54 10-15 Kemp 6g/f 4357

VERKHOTINA 3 b f £5087
48 6-12 Warw 7.1gd [75] 1125
85 1-12 CHEP 6.1gd 72 2118*
66 9-18 Wind 6g/f 78 2268
80 3-8 Ling 7g/f 80 2742
64 8-11 Asco 8gd [80] 3128

VERMILION CREEK 4 b f £4777
43a 7-13 Wolv 9.4af 47 38
34a 10-14 Sout 8af 47 93
19a 11-14 Sout 8af 42 165
31a 6-9 Wolv 9.4af [39] 239
29a 5-9 Wolv 7af [40] 310
33a 8-16 Sout 11af [35] 445 P
31a 6-12 Wolv 12af [30] 523 p
21a 6-12 Wolv 9.4af [30] 668 p
39 6-17 Beve 8.5g/s [50] 1160
54 2-14 Hayd 8.1g/s 48 1348
40 9-14 Leic 8g/f 53 2402
50 6-12 Nott 8.2g/s 53 2931
36 11-17 Hayd 8.1gd 51 3759
56 1-17 PONT 8g/f 49 4626* p

VERMILLIANN 3 b f £0
78 10-14 Bath 5gd [98] 1400
44 9-9 Nott 6.1g/s [93] 1773
51 16-16 Leic 5g/f 88 2400

VERSTONE 2 b f £0
28 8-9 Newc 5sft 962
28a 8-8 Sout 5ap 1048
32 8-8 Pont 5hvy 1249

VERTEDANZ 4 b f £0
21 18-19 Chep 7.1gd 49 3401
9 20-20 Yarm 8gd 44 3996
19 12-15 Folk 7g/f [40] 4371

VERY EXCLUSIVE 4 b g £0
0 13-14 Ling 13ap 47 259

VERY WISE 2 b c £3595
84 1-20 YARM 8sft 5252*

VESPONE 4 ch c £145505
117 2-8 Long 10.5hvy 1558
115 2-7 Capa 10g/s 1858
101 8-11 Epso 8.5fm [118] 2252 VIS
114 2-7 Newb 10g/f [118] 3264 vis t
98 12-13 Arli 10fm [118] 4014 vis
98 5-7 Good 9.9g/f [112] 4538 t

VESTA FLAME 2 b f £381
25a 8-13 Wolv 8.5af 111
0 8-9 Wolv 9.4af 240
33a 3-9 Wolv 9.4af [35] 399
33a 3-12 Wolv 8.5af [35] 584
2 11-12 Catt 12gd 35 1000

VETTORIOUS 2 ch c £0
56 12-13 Donc 7hvy 5200

VIABLE 2 b g £0
56 9-11 Beve 7.5g/s 3851

VIAGRAH 3 b g £0
4a 10-12 Wolv 9.4af 686

VIBE 3 gr g £327
0 U-9 Ripo 8gd 1178
53 7-11 Newc 8sft 1279
42 13-20 Donc 7g/s 1518
73 4-10 Beve 7.5g/f 1832
47 11-12 Pont 10g/f 74 2277
67 6-7 Beve 9.9gd 72 2654

VICARIO 3 gr g £6600
62 5-10 Folk 9.7sft 1580
63 1-14 LING 11.5g/f 50 2014*
61 3-8 Beve 12.1g/f 56 2164
65 3-7 Ripo 12.3g/f 60 2528
66 2-10 Folk 12g/s 61 3051
57 6-14 Catt 12g/f 61 3192
55 5-9 Sand 14g/s 63 3893
54 4-9 Ripo 16gd 61 4308
63 3-13 Newc 16.1fm 60 4868

VICARS DESTINY 6 b m £10306
68 2-14 Donc 18gd 65 926
68 2-13 Pont 18hvy 67 1069
55 13-17 Ripo 16g/s 68 1361
56 8-10 Hayd 14g/f 69 1923 p
53 10-13 Pont 17.1g/f 68 2276
63 6-6 Catt 15.8g/f 65 3015
66 4-9 Beve 16.2g/s 65 3181
68 3-6 Beve 16.2g/s 63 3853
66 3-17 Pont 17.1g/s 63 3970
68 2-7 Thir 16g/s 61 4209
75 3-5 Pont 18g/f [64] 4628
68 3-14 Pont 17.1g/f 64 4936
60 9-10 Pont 18g/s 64 5151

VICAT COLE 3 ch c £0
24 23-24 Newm 8fm 1495
70a 5-15 Ling 12ap 2393
72 7-9 Kemp 12g/f 2862
37 8-9 Epso 10.1fm 70 3538

VICIOUS KNIGHT 6 b g £2262
87 14-15 York 8.9g/f 100 2404
78 21-31 Asco 8g/f 100 2489
82 12-19 Newm 7g/f 98 3061
71 13-21 Asco 7g/f 98 3441
84 10-12 Good 7fm [95] 3555
93 5-15 York 7.9g/s 90 4061
86 3-7 Thir 8g/s [90] 4208
70 13-19 York 7.9gd 88 4987
72 7-14 Newb 8hvy 85 5227

VICIOUS PRINCE 5 b g £274
72 4-7 Thir 12sft [75] 1226
68 8-9 Hayd 10.5g/s 74 2185
70 8-19 Carl 11.9gd 72 2673
72 5-9 Redc 16sft 70 2963

VICIOUS WARRIOR 4 b g £16940

VICTOR (cont.)

```
49a 11-13 Wolv  8.5af   78      44
88  2-17  Thir  8g/s    83    1475
79  8-10  Beve  8.5g/f  86    1833
89  5-15  Redc  10g/f   85    2101
90  3-15  York  8.9g/f  86    2404
87  7-21  York  10.4gd  86    3118
91  2-9   Ayr   8g/f    86    3305
90  2-10  Pont  8gd     86    3460
91  3-13  Ripo  8gd     86    4279
75  15-32 Newm  9g/f    86    4916
82  6-19  York  7.9gd   86    4987
```

VICTIMISED 2 b g £0
```
19  9-15  Beve  5g/s          1161
46  14-17 Ling  7g/f          2584
52  5-8   Brig  6g/f          3172
```

VICTOR BUCKWELL 2 br c £0
```
17  11-11 Ayr   7.2g/s        4653
48  9-13  Newc  7g/f          5012
54  8-15  Newb  8hvy          5221
```

VICTORIA PEEK 2 b f £638
```
69  4-7   Ches  5.1g/s        1571
47  8-8   Epso  6fm           2251
22  7-8   Ayr   5gd           2505
```

VICTORIAN DANCER 3 b f £0
```
0   10-11 Newc  7sft    59    1678
```

VICTORIANA 3 b f £422
```
41  6-11  Nott  6.1sft        1607
59  4-12  Kemp  6sft          4029
48  5-11  Beve  5g/s          4237
25  15-19 Nott  6.1g/f [57]   4845
0   11-11 Good  6gd    [54]   5030
```

VICTORY DESIGN 2 b c £0
```
80  6-13  Newm  6gd           4223
```

VICTORY FLIP 3 b f £747
```
55a 3-10  Wolv  7af    [55]      8 p
51a 6-12  Wolv  7af    [55]     71 p
49a 4-9   Sout  8af    54      163 p
43a 6-12  Wolv  5af    [52]    242 p
37a 8-13  Sout  8af    [52]    254 p
7a  13-13 Wolv  6af    49      384 p
35a 6-12  Wolv  8.5af  45      564 p
41a 5-7   Sout  7af    45      680 p
36a 3-10  Sout  8af    40      791
```

VICTORY HYMN 2 b f £0
```
43  7-8   Good  6gd           2537
56  5-7   Muss  7.1g/f        2810
51  13-13 Kemp  7g/f          3520
```

VICTORY LAP 2 ch f £306
```
68a 3-16  Sout  8af            192
64  8-12  Sali  12g/s         1501
64  6-13  Thir  12g/f         1768
61  5-8   Beve  12.1g/f 67    2164
59  7-8   Warw  18fm   [65]   2781
```

VICTORY MOON 5 b h £335195
```
115 3-12  Nad   10af           992
```

VICTORY QUEST 3 b g £11982
```
67a 2-12  Sout  14af   63     173 vis
72a 1-5   SOUT  14af   63     201* vis
73a 2-15  Sout  14af   72     257 vis
43a 16-16 Ling  12ap   73     404 vis
0   7-7   Sout  12af   73     504 vis
79a 1-7   SOUT  14af   73     681* vis
84a 1-10  SOUT  16af   79     743* vis
73a 4-8   Wolv  16.2af 85     837 vis
```

VICTORY VEE 3 ch g £301
```
59a 3-12  Wolv  7af    59      68
0   9-10  Wolv  7af    58     685
32a 6-11  Wolv  8.5af  57     806
0   11-11 Wolv  12af   55     937
31a 10-10 Wolv  7af    [52]  1319
```

VICTORY VENTURE 4 b g £0
```
21  14-14 Wind  10g/f  77    2265
44  9-11  Newb  11g/f  74    3256
47  13-17 Wind  10fm   69    3477
42  16-16 Wind  11.6gd 65    3829
```

VIENNAS BOY 3 b c £11622
```
77  4-6   Leic  6g/f   [92]  1018
88  4-7   Ling  6sft   89    1621
80  6-18  Newm  6g/f   86    1933
81  4-10  Leic  6gd    [84]  2137
84  6-14  Wind  5af    84    2266
62  13-16 Leic  5g/f   83    2400
74  5-8   Kemp  6g/s   [82]  2677
85  2-9   Wind  6g/f   82    2797
74  5-10  Kemp  6gd    [83]  3188
83  4-5   Kemp  6g/f   [83]  3523
81  4-7   Sali  7g/s   [82]  4082
78  1-14  NEWM  7gd    [82]  4195*
49  19-20 Newm  7g/s   79    5286
```

VIEW THE FACTS 5 br m £0
```
13a 8-10  Wolv  5af    [45]   527 e
0   10-12 Ling  10ap   [35]   654 e T
```

VIEWFORTH 6 b g £3514
```
78  4-16  Muss  5g/f   78    1120 bl
77  4-13  Newc  5sft   78    1276 bl
69  12-30 Newm  6g/f   77    1481 bl
69  9-19  Thir  6g/f   75    1767 bl
68  7-20  York  6g/f   73    2059
48  14-20 York  6g/f   71    2409 bl
49  12-14 Newc  5g/s   69    2775
68  4-18  Hayd  5gd    67    2951 bl
68  3-10  Muss  5g/s   67    2968 bl
64  8-10  Ayr   5gd    67    3150 bl
57  15-18 Carl  5g/f   67    3228 bl
57  8-12  Newc  5gd    66    3427 bl
49  12-20 Hayd  6fm    64    3796 bl
49  8-12  Redc  6gd    [62]  4245 VIS
26  24-26 Ayr   5g/s   59    4618 bl
58  3-11  Hami  6g/s   52    4818 bl
```

VIGOROUS 4 b f £1568
```
20  15-17 Donc  6g/s   73    1523
71  5-8   Hami  5gd    [73]  1749
49  8-10  Thir  5g/f   70    1973
52  16-17 Catt  5gd    68    2846
59  6-15  Pont  5gd    67    3680
66  2-20  Ripo  6gd    63    4785
58  5-15  Newc  5fm    63    4870
```

VIJAY 4 ch c £2221
```
38a 9-12  Wolv  7af    60      74 BL
42a 10-11 Wolv  5af    58     643 bl
55a 3-11  Wolv  5af    58     748 P
34a 10-13 Wolv  6af    55     807 p
56  6-20  Ripo  5gd    60    1179
14  15-15 Hami  6gd    59    1508 bl
50  2-9   Muss  5gd    [57]  1797 VIS
47  9-16  Ayr   5g/f   57    2029
53  7-13  Hami  5g/f   54    2320 vis
36  6-10  Hami  5gd    [54]  2476 p
0   14-14 Hami  6gd    52    3129 p
27  8-9   Catt  5g/f   [49]  3353 bl
45  2-10  Carl  5.9fm  [49]  3545
37  6-9   Ayr   7.2g/f [45]  3764
```

VIKING SPIRIT 2 b c £14156
```
70  8-15  Wind  6gd          3163
75  2-13  York  6g/f         3431
82  2-17  Chep  6.1sft       4052
85  1-14  WARW  6.1g/f 73    4420*
95  1-19  NOTT  6.1g/s 79    4645*
82  7-12  Newm  6gd    93    4882
```

VILLA CHIGI 2 ch c £0
```
47  10-12 Newc  7g/f         5011
```

VILLAROSI 2 b f £0
```
73  5-16  Newm  7g/s         5280
```

VILLARRICA 2 ch f £982
```
76  4-14  Sali  5g/f         4575
79  3-13  Redc  7fm          4927
```

VIN DU PAYS 3 b g £2065
```
73a 1-12  WOLV  16.2af 66       7*
50a 6-10  Sout  14f    77      90
0   9-11  Warw  15sft  59    1087
18  11-11 Newb  11g/f  55    3256
19  10-10 Sali  14.1gd 50    3887
12  10-13 Folk  12gd   45    4119
5   14-16 Warw  16.2gd 45    4276
```

```
56a 10-12 Wolv  12.2ap 70    4983
10a 11-12 Wolv  13.9ap 60    5160
```

VINANDO 3 ch c £22554
```
83  1-14  WIND  10g/s        1259*
68  7-11  Newb  11g/f  84    1756
99  1-5   ASCO  12gd   84    3468+ T
94  5-13  Kemp  12g/f  [94]  4715 t
103 1-17  NEWM  12g/f  94    4889* t
```

VINCENT 8 b g £7568
```
42a 1-14  SOUT  14af   33     185*
48a 1-16  SOUT  16af   39     206*
42a 4-9   Sout  16af   46     336
48a 3-10  Wolv  16.2af 46     358
49a 1-4   WOLV  14.8af [46]   426*
39a 6-10  Sout  16af   49     491
46a 3-9   Sout  16af   46     612
```

VINDICATION GB 4 ch g £225
```
85  12-20 Asco  14g/f  93    1926 t
91  6-11  Newm  7fm    92    2090 t
87  6-11  Warw  7g/f   91    2532 t
82  7-11  Warw  7.1fm  [89]  2777 t
82  10-16 Good  7g/f   88    4523 t
81  9-15  Newm  7g/f   87    4891 t
73a 9-12  Wolv  7.1ap  82    5159 t
24  20-20 Donc  7sft   83    5367
```

VINNIE ROE 6 b h £432080
```
115 2-6   Leop  14g/f        2138
113 2-7   Leop  12g/f        4019 bl
121 1-13  CURR  14gd         4733* bl
123 2-24  Flem  16g/s  117   5323 bl
```

VINO VENUS 2 b f £0
```
47  8-9   Brig  6g/f         3981
38  5-6   Brig  6gd          4900
```

VINTAGE PREMIUM 7 b g £21472
```
96a  7-11 Ling  10ap   [104]  693
94a  6-12 Wolv  8.5af  100    836
100a 8-14 Ling  10ap   [98]   884
104  1-14 YORK  10.4g/s 98   1704*
108  2-12 Hami  12.1gd 101   1746
```

VINTAGE STYLE 4 ch g £0
```
48a 5-9   Wolv  7af    62      27 bl
43a 8-16  Sout  6af    58      92 bl
26  15-20 Nott  6.1g/f 54    2630
1   19-20 Nott  6.1gd  54    2928 VIS
```

VIOLA DA BRACCIO 3 ch f £0
```
42  10-14 Warw  8.1sft       1527
65  5-13  Newm  8g/f         1993
56  5-7   Hami  11.1g/f [65] 2478
47a 6-10  Sout  8af    [63]  2997
```

VIOLET AVENUE 3 ch f £458
```
44  10-14 Ayr   8g/f   [62]  1896
55  6-14  Nott  8.2g/f 59    2634
59  4-12  Hayd  8.1gd  59    2904
55  7-12  Ling  7.6gd  [58]  3448
53  5-14  Yarm  7gd    57    3995
40  7-14  Yarm  8g/s   55    4252
24  13-18 Warw  10.9g/s 53   4669 BL
```

VIOLET PARK 3 b f £15466
```
67  2-11  Folk  7g/s         3048
66  2-9   Newm  7g/f         3282
71  3-17  Wind  8.3fm        3480
75  1-10  CHEP  7.1gd        3732*
77  1-8   NEWM  7gd          3928*
66  12-25 Newb  7gd    75    4683
```

VIP 2 ch c £323
```
69  4-14  Yarm  7sft         5251
```

VIRGINIA WATERS 2 b f £14189
```
102 3-9   Curr  7sft         4958
101 2-10  Curr  6sft         5072 t
```

VIRGINS TEARS 2 b f £0
```
53  7-16  York  7.9gd        4997
32  10-14 Newb  6sft         5197
```

VISION OF DREAMS 3 b f £0
```
8a  12-12 Wolv  5af    [74]    70 H bl
```

VISION VICTORY 2 b c £335

62	4-6	Newc	5sft		1274
43	10-12	Beve	5sft		1631
51	10-14	Redc	6fm		2297
41	11-14	Donc	7fm	60	4535
38	13-19	Redc	8sft	55	5302

VISIONIST 2 b c £34358

91	1-13	YORK	6gd		3120*
94	4-8	Newm	7g/f		3585
103	3-16	Curr	6g/f		4153
105	3-8	Kemp	6fm		4390

VISORAMA 4 gr f £44441

111	2-5	Sain	10.5g/s		2143
113	3-10	Sain	12g/s		3012
110	7-13	Long	12sft		4567

VITA SPERICOLATA 7 b m £5401

75	8-13	Beve	5g/s	[86]		1162
65	9-14	Ches	5.1gd	86		1594
84	3-8	Beve	5sft	[86]		1626
83	5-17	Muss	5fm	85		2082 vis
42	17-17	Epso	6fm	84		2256 vis
56	12-15	Beve	5sft	83		2942 bl
98	8-9	York	6g/s	[83]		3075
82	5-7	Newm	5fm	[81]		3409
85	5-5	Ches	6.1fm	[81]		3636
78	6-12	Pont	6g/s	[81]		3971
84	9-11	Beve	5g/s	[81]		4238 vis

VITELUCY 5 b m £206

38a	5-11	Wolv	12af	[45]		666
33a	5-12	Wolv	12af	[45]		891
43a	3-10	Sout	16af	[45]		984
9a	5-6	Wolv	12af	[40]		1313 P
7a	5-12	Wolv	12.2ap	[40]		5208 vis

VITTORIOSO 2 b g £2065

37a	7-13	Wolv	6af			3 P
61a	5-12	Wolv	6af			42 p
45a	8-15	Sout	7af			184 p
52a	5-7	Wolv	7af	[57]		284 BL
56a	3-10	Ling	5ap		54	371 bl
58a	3-9	Ling	5ap	[53]		621 bl
56a	2-8	Sout	5af	[54]		742 bl
53a	7-10	Ling	5ap	[54]		802 VIS
40	8-9	Leic	5g/f	[54]		3347 bl
41	5-6	Folk	5g/f	[51]		3725 bl
37	10-19	Thir	6g/f		45	4595
49	7-18	Leic	7gd	[45]		4698
46	6-15	Wind	10g/f	[40]		4834
48	5-18	Leic	10gd	[45]		5042

VIVA ATLAS ESPANA 4 b f £0

0	16-16	Ling	7ap	[52]		290
2	8-8	Folk	9.7sft		45	1579

VIVRE SA VIE 3 ch f £1742

45a	4-11	Wolv	9.4af			438
49a	3-6	Sout	8af			503
56a	2-8	Wolv	12af			644
37a	5-5	Wolv	12af			701
7	7-11	Catt	13.8sft	[60]		5129

VIZULIZE 5 b m £215

48a	12-14	Ling	7ap		53	344
48a	6-12	Ling	8ap		53	406
41a	5-11	Sout	7af	[50]		488
39a	9-13	Ling	7ap		48	739
34a	9-10	Ling	8ap		48	770 VIS
41a	4-15	Ling	7ap	[45]		969
34a	10-12	Ling	8ap		45	1045
4	11-12	Brig	8gd	[45]		4904
46	3-16	Warw	8.1g/s		40	4993

VLASTA WEINER 4 b g £420

19a	7-12	Wolv	6af	[38]		297 bl
41a	2-9	Wolv	7af	[40]		310 bl
31a	5-11	Ling	8ap	[40]		408 bl
10a	10-16	Sout	8af	[40]		442 bl
41a	4-12	Wolv	7af	[40]		528 bl
36a	6-10	Sout	8af		40	678 bl
40a	4-12	Ling	8ap	[40]		710 bl
29a	6-10	Ling	8ap		40	769 bl
23	12-16	Nott	6.1gd	[40]		1989 bl
0	16-20	Chep	6.1gd		35	2372 bl

VOCATIVE 2 gr f £0

64	7-12	Newc	8fm		4866

VOICE MAIL 5 b g £13869

64	7-9	Folk	9.7sft	[70]		978
0	9-9	Epso	8.5hvy	[68]		1298
72	1-12	BATH	8g/f		68	1792+
81	1-11	BATH	10.2fm		73	1899*
76	3-12	Bath	10.2fm		73	2036
69	11-13	Epso	8.5g/f		78	2207
83	2-8	Bath	8fm		78	2665
74	7-12	Kemp	9g/f		78	2860
80	3-8	Ches	10.3g/f	[79]		3083
80	4-12	Good	9fm		78	3625
72	8-15	Brig	8fm		78	3694
77	3-15	Bath	11.7g/f		77	3964
68	12-19	Kemp	10fm		77	4392
66a	8-12	Ling	8ap		70	5079 vis

VOICE OF AN ANGEL 2 b f £0

54a	5-7	Sout	5af		1029
37	8-10	Muss	5gd		1550
62a	5-8	Wolv	5af		1653
0	12-12	Newc	6gd		1869
46	5-8	Muss	5g/f		2611

VOILE 3 b f £0

93	7-12	Asco	7g/f	[105]		4811
87	8-15	Newm	6gd	[100]		5088
84a	9-12	Ling	8ap	[95]		5298

VOIR DIRE 2 b c £707

61	13-15	Newb	7g/f			2876
68	7-8	Newb	7g/f			3267
61	8-14	Sali	8g/s			4078
43	8-14	Sali	8gd			4852
67	3-9	Nott	10hvy	[63]		5189

VOIX DU NORD 2 b c £178283

115	1-	SAIN	10g/s		9*
115	1-9	LONG	11sft		1158*
120	1-5	LONG	10.5g/s		1853*

VOLATICUS 3 b c £2374

63	2-8	Donc	6gd			953
0	14-14	Thir	6g/s			1216
59	4-19	York	6g/f		60	2055
61	4-8	Newc	5g/s		58	2731 VIS
37	12-14	Catt	6g/f		58	3018 vis

VOLITIO 2 b c £0

19	16-16	Sali	7gd			3882
46	13-14	Folk	7gd			4115
62	11-14	Chep	8.1gd			4484
64	7-14	Bath	8gd			5018
56	10-20	Yarm	8g/s		60	5349

VON WESSEX 2 b g £8135

72	6-13	Donc	5gd			954
39a	5-5	Ling	5ap			1041
76	1-9	YARM	5.2g/f			1133*
47	6-8	Beve	5sft			1303
63	3-11	Thir	6gd			1634
66	3-6	Leic	5fm			2110
65	1-13	BEVE	5g/s			2321*
58	4-7	Beve	5gd			3308
50	6-10	Hayd	5g/s	[63]		3901 T
37	6-8	Wind	5g/s	[61]		4218
62	2-8	Brig	5.3fm	[58]		4759 P

VONADAISY 3 b f £4290

73	1-14	WARW	7.1gd	[70]		4275*
43	21-25	Newb	7gd		70	4683
68a	5-12	Ling	8ap		70	4743 BL
52a	9-12	Wolv	8.6ap		68	4923 bl
55a	4-11	Wolv	7.1ap	[68]		5178

VONDOVA 2 b f £12806

66	3-6	Warw	5fm			2437
65	7-8	Kemp	7g/s			2676
86	1-10	NEWM	6g/f			3064*
87	8-9	Sand	7.1g/f			3357
88	2-7	Ches	6.1g/f	[83]		4050
76	9-11	Sali	6gd	[84]		4332

VOOM 2 b f £361

58	8-10	Bath	5.7fm		2666
51	4-8	Yarm	6fm		2865
55	3-8	Bath	5g/f		2977

VORTEX 5 b h £127280

77a	1-13	WOLV	8.5af	73		439* e t
79a	1-12	LING	8ap	75		517* e t
86a	1-12	WOLV	8.5af	78		632* e t
91a	1-7	WOLV	8.5af	83		700* e t
100a	1-12	WOLV	8.5af	89		836+ e t
93a	12-14	Ling	10ap	[97]		884 e t
80	17-27	Newb	8gd	97		1231 t
104	1-12	JAGE	8.6aw	[97]		1697* t
103	3-20	Asco	7g/f	97		1926 e t
98	10-31	Asco	8g/f	98		2489 e t
107	2-18	Newb	8g/f	98		3265 e t
99	4-21	Asco	7g/f	98		3441 e t
107	2-10	Asco	8gd	103		3775 e t
106	1-10	TABY	8g/f	[103]		4573*
103	4-10	Redc	7fm	[105]		4929 e t

VRISAKI 2 b c £1967

55a	7-14	Ling	6ap			146
62a	2-7	Wolv	7af			284
17a	8-9	Wolv	7af		60	510
43	4-9	Folk	7sft		55	1577
28	9-14	Newc	8gd		53	1872 P
48	9-14	Ling	11.5g/f		53	2014
49	3-11	Yarm	11.5g/f		49	2346
45	6-14	Bath	10.2fm		49	2664
51	3-13	Yarm	11.5fm		49	2868
13	11-14	Folk	12gd		48	3383
0	17-17	Newm	12g/f		46	3618
17	14-14	Yarm	11.5g/f		46	3714

VRUBEL 5 ch g £425

45a	2-12	Wolv	9.5ap	[45]		5234 VIS

WAAEDAH 3 ch f £0

43	19-20	Newb	7g/f	78	1761

WAATHEB 2 b c £0

57	11-12	Newb	6g/f		2348
73	7-23	Newm	6gd		5084
70a	8-11	Ling	8ap		5236

WAFANI 5 b g £0

15	11-13	Leic	10fm		2107 bl

WAGGLEDANCE 2 b g £1798

57	5-7	Beve	5g/s			2167
46	9-15	Beve	5g/s			3178
46	8-10	Pont	5gd			3457
65	7-10	Carl	5g/s			4343
66	2-12	Newb	5g/s	[56]		4596 P
48	9-10	Muss	5gd	[66]		4804 p

WAHCHI 5 ch g £0

26	7-9	Pont	10hvy	[90]		1068
30	19-19	Newm	12g/f	85		1484
8	16-19	York	11.9sft	78		1668
58	10-10	Newc	10.1g/f	72		2162
59	6-13	Redc	10gd	67		2560

WAHOO SAM 4 ch g £18227

5	12-12	Thir	7g/s	70		1215 BL
42	8-10	Newc	8g/f	65		2159
64	3-13	Carl	7.9fm	59		2447
67	1-12	HAMI	9.2g/s	59		2832*
71	1-9	HAMI	9.2gd	64		3132*
61	8-13	Ayr	10gd	67		3325
75	1-9	HAMI	9.2g/f	67		3593+
74	2-7	Hami	9.2g/s	70		3879
48	11-17	Hami	9.2g/s	70		4008

WAINWRIGHT 3 b g £6231

58a	5-12	Wolv	7af	[60]		71 p
60a	3-16	Sout	8af		60	94
61a	3-15	Sout	5af		60	187
64a	1-13	SOUT	8af	[60]		254*
67a	1-10	WOLV	6af		62	345*
56a	9-14	Ling	6ap		68	407
35	9-19	Newc	6sft		63	967
48	11-17	Nott	5.1g/s		62	1774
30	11-19	Ripo	8gd		60	1977
52	6-14	Redc	7g/f	[60]		2102 p

WAIT FOR SPRING 3 b f £1660

74	5-13	Kemp	10g/f			3038
72	2-5	Sand	10g/s			3894
37	16-17	Newm	8gd			4228
46	9-15	Bath	10.2gd	[69]		4826

WAIT FOR THE WILL 8 ch g £15419
68	16-20	Newm	12gd	90	1172 bl
58	16-19	Newm	12g/f	89	1484 bl
61	10-12	Good	14g/f	86	1861
89	1-11	**GOOD**	12gd	82	2538* bl
94	1-7	**NEWM**	12g/f	85	2737* bl
95	2-8	Newm	12g/f	[90]	3617 bl
90	5-5	Good	14g/s	[90]	4230 bl
76	10-13	Kemp	12g/f	[90]	4715 bl

WAKE 4 b c £6296
85a	1-12	**LING**	8ap		881*
59	6-6	Newm	9gd	[90]	1168
72	10-10	Good	9.9g/f	[90]	1862
88	6-13	Newm	8g/s	90	5284

WAKE UP HENRY 2 ch c £1151
59a	10-12	Ling	8ap		19
55a	6-14	Sout	8af		88
46	8-11	Warw	8.1hvy	60	1534
56	3-10	Leic	10g/f	58	1965
50	4-7	Brig	11.9fm	58	2333
0	13-14	Pont	10g/f	55	4624 VIS

WALK IN THE PARK 2 b c £20123
91	3-8	Sain	8Very		5315

WALKAMIA 3 gr f £111323
107	1-	TOUL	10.5g/s		57*
115	3-10	Long	10g/s		4953
113	2-14	Capa	10g/s		5244

WALKER BAY 5 ch m £0
23a	11-11	Ling	6ap	[48]	130 BL
33a	8-16	Ling	7ap	[48]	180
6a	12-16	Ling	7ap	[44]	214 bl
42a	5-10	Ling	10ap	[40]	370
35a	9-14	Ling	13ap	[40]	537

WALKONTHEWILDSIDE 2 b c £6842
64	5-5	Newm	6g/f		3586
82	4-16	Leic	7fm		3811
87	1-13	**WARW**	7.1g/f		4416* VIS
53	9-9	Newm	7gd	[83]	4881

WALL STREET RUNNER 3 ch f £0
17	20-20	Nott	6.1g/s	62	4646
57a	8-14	Ling	7ap	[62]	5080
59a	7-13	Wolv	8.6ap	62	5183
49a	10-14	Ling	7ap	[59]	5263
52a	8-12	Wolv	7.1ap	[59]	5325

WALTZING BEAU 2 ch g £2359
49a	8-10	Ling	8ap		229
59a	2-11	Wolv	9.4af		438
57a	9-14	Ling	10ap		473
44	12-15	Leic	11.8gd	59	2134
27	9-10	Good	14gd	59	2376 VIS
49	8-14	Bath	10.2fm	55	2664 vis
48	2-8	Warw	10.9gd	[53]	3055
47	3-13	Brig	9.9g/f	47	3300
43	6-11	Brig	9.9g/f	46	3982
48a	6-14	Ling	16ap	55	4319
7	8-12	Brig	11.9fm	45	4764

WALTZING WIZARD 4 b g £2734
51a	5-16	Ling	7ap	52	144
52a	2-16	Sout	7af	50	208
53a	3-10	Wolv	7af	52	379
42a	5-10	Sout	8af	52	463
48a	4-11	Wolv	7af	50	558
45a	5-9	Wolv	7af	49	684
56	5-10	Hami	6gd	55	1391
52	5-13	Muss	7.1g/s	55	1463
48	7-15	Thir	7gd	55	1635
52	5-18	Ayr	7.2g/f	53	1897
55	4-10	Ayr	7.2g/f	53	2027
46	9-13	Carl	7.9fm	52	2447
51	6-14	Muss	7.1g/f	52	2615
55	3-18	Catt	7g/f	51	2848
55	4-10	Carl	6.9gd	51	2935
27	15-14	Carl	6.9g/f	51	3229
47	6-8	Carl	6.9g/f	[51]	3654
42	11-14	Carl	6.9g/f	51	4345

WANCHAI LAD 3 b c £2105
90	3-15	Ches	5.1g/s	88	1572
85	7-20	York	6g/f	88	2407

87	5-9	Newm	5fm	86	2593
66	9-11	Ches	5.1g/s	86	2747
79	11-20	Donc	5fm	85	4496
44	15-15	Ayr	5g/s	85	4654
64	11-18	Ayr	7.2sft	82	4689

WANDERING ACT 2 b c £0
56	7-7	Brig	7fm		3691
46	7-9	Yarm	8sft		4147

WANNA SHOUT 6 b m £7189
47a	2-12	Ling	8ap	[45]	538
50a	1-12	**LING**	8ap	[45]	649*
54a	2-14	Ling	10ap	[45]	705
58a	1-10	**LING**	8ap	50	917*
60a	2-12	Ling	8ap	57	1045
47a	7-14	Ling	10ap	58	1618
51	5-12	Bath	10.2fm	58	2036
48	8-13	Newb	8fm	56	2647
48a	6-8	Ling	12ap	58	3026
57a	3-7	Ling	10ap	55	3287
51a	6-14	Ling	7ap	54	3746

WANSDYKE LASS 2 b f £0
66	5-15	Newb	7g/f		2876

WANT 3 ch c £0
71	10-24	Newm	8fm		1495
68	10-17	Newb	8g/f		1762

WAR AT SEA 2 b c £0
77	5-11	Newm	7gd		4190

WAR OWL 6 gr g £15382
52a	4-13	Ling	10ap	53	178
58a	2-8	Sout	8af	53	393
52a	8-14	Ling	10ap	57	674
66a	1-13	**LING**	10ap	57	726+
71	1-18	**BATH**	10.2g/s	60	1098*
68	3-20	Warw	10.9gd	66	1128
71	5-10	Hayd	10.5g/s	74	1346
55	12-19	Wind	10sft	[72]	1650
75	1-14	**WIND**	10g/f	70	2265*
74	9-15	Ches	10.3g/f	73	3099
73	8-15	Donc	10.3g/f	73	3598
55	4-7	Hami	9.2g/s	73	3879
59	14-16	Sand	10gd	73	4609

WAR PENNANT 2 b g £0
55	6-10	Wind	8.3g/f		4831
38a	9-12	Wolv	8.6ap		5115

WARAQA 5 b m £0
7a	14-14	Ling	6ap	52	328

WARBRECK 3 ch c £0
0	15-15	Thir	7g/s		1473
51	7-11	Hayd	8.1gd		2886
59	8-17	Hayd	8.1g/s		4768 BL
67a	5-12	Ling	8ap		4975 bl

WARDEN COMPLEX 3 b g £18974
75a	3-10	Ling	7ap		911
81	2-15	Folk	6g/s		1078
87	1-16	**LEIC**	7g/f	75	1825*
90	1-10	**DONC**	7g/f	83	2427*
84	7-13	Asco	7gd	86	3068
84	5-9	Sand	7.1g/f	86	3338
87a	2-14	Ling	7ap	85	4446

WARDEN WARREN 5 b g £18247
48a	16-16	Ling	7ap	70	55 bl
52a	12-13	Wolv	6af	70	113 p
56a	7-10	Wolv	7af	[67]	152 p
69a	2-9	Sout	7af	64	193 bl
73a	1-8	**WOLV**	7af	66	280* bl
73a	3-11	Wolv	7af	72	363 bl
74a	4-11	Sout	7af	72	585 bl
50a	6-10	Sout	7af	72	611 bl
75a	1-12	**WOLV**	7af	71	704* bl
65a	7-12	Wolv	7af	74	840 bl
41a	9-9	Wolv	7af	74	940 p
80a	1-8	**SOUT**	7af	73	1195* p
0	18-18	Ches	7.6gd	72	1598 p
44	12-13	Yarm	6g/f	72	1726 p
68	4-18	Donc	7g/f	69	2080 p
79	1-4	**REDC**	7g/f	[69]	2122* p
60	9-12	Donc	7gd	74	2235 p
52	9-11	Newm	7g/f	73	2532 p

77	2-7	Yarm	7gd	73	3872 p
56	12-20	Yarm	7sft	74	5256 bl
40	18-20	Donc	7sft	73	5367 p

WARES HOME 2 b c £3151
31a	7-13	Sout	6af	[80]	63
60a	6-10	Ling	8ap	70	132
56a	7-10	Ling	7ap	67	432
44a	6-6	Sout	8af	62	506
0	8-8	Wind	8.3g/s	70	1257
67	3-6	Ripo	6g/f	[67]	1975 VIS
57	4-12	Thir	7g/f	[67]	2215 vis
48	3-5	Ayr	6gd	[65]	2541 vis
52	3-11	Yarm	7g/f	[60]	2852
55	2-14	Catt	6g/f	[55]	3191
44	3-14	Ayr	7.2gd	[55]	3324
0	11-11	Muss	8g/f	[55]	3558 P
49	3-6	Yarm	6g/f	[55]	3710
42	7-15	Newc	6hvy	46	4211

WARIF 2 ch c £0
63a	11-12	Ling	10ap		116
34	5-6	Beve	9.9sft		1630
29	7-10	Yarm	10.1g/f		1724
25a	8-8	Ling	12ap	[53]	2065 BL
21a	11-12	Wolv	9.5ap	[45]	5209

WARLINGHAM 5 b g £11183
19a	8-12	Wolv	6af	[63]	33 e
33a	12-16	Ling	7ap	[57]	123
55a	2-16	Ling	7ap	[54]	180
54a	1-16	**LING**	7ap	[54]	214*
41a	14-16	Ling	7ap	55	270
37a	10-13	Wolv	6af	54	384
55a	8-14	Ling	7ap	[54]	450
61a	1-12	**WOLV**	7af	[52]	512*
62a	1-11	**WOLV**	7af	58	562*
46a	5-9	Wolv	7af	61	629
31a	7-10	Wolv	7af	61	685
60	1-5	**YARM**	7g/f	[57]	1731*
50	10-10	Brig	7af	58	1941
57	5-16	Brig	7fm	58	2258
52	7-17	Wind	6g/f	58	2451
58	5-11	Brig	6g/f	57	2644
53	8-14	Yarm	6g/f	56	2855
41	8-12	Yarm	7gd	56	3490
50	9-17	Wind	6fm	56	3643
5	17-19	Yarm	6g/s	54	4636
12a	12-12	Wolv	7.1ap	60	5112
53a	7-12	Ling	6ap	58	5241
55a	7-14	Ling	7ap	58	5300

WARNINGCAMP 3 b g £990
76	4-12	Sand	10g/f		2193
69	6-13	Sali	9.9gd		2700
75	3-11	Leic	10g/f		3208
53	16-16	Nott	8.2g/s	80	4036

WARRAD 3 b c £5847
86	4-4	Sand	8.1g/s		1317
91a	3-12	Ling	8ap	[88]	3199
90	5-16	Good	9.9fm	88	3553
89	3-5	Good	9sft	88	4185

WARREN PLACE 4 ch g £0
16a	13-16	Sout	8af	43	3487
14	18-20	Redc	6g/f	40	3767
41	8-11	Beve	5g/s	[35]	4237
37	9-14	Newc	6g/f	[35]	4404

WARRSAN 5 b h £751612
118	3-14	Sha	12g/f		209
111	5-13	Nad	12g/f	[119]	990
120	3-7	Newm	12fm	[117]	1493
122	1-11	**EPSO**	12g/f	[117]	2209+
122	2-12	Sand	10g/s	[118]	2916
114	9-11	Asco	12g/f	[120]	3442
122	1-4	**BADE**	12sft	[120]	4428*
114	9-19	Long	12g/f	[120]	4956

WASALAT 2 b f £4125
74	4-9	Hayd	6g/s		1920
78	2-10	Hayd	6g/s		2228
81	3-9	Ripo	6g/f		2522
82	2-9	Brig	7g/f	80	3297
37	9-9	Epso	7fm		3539
69	6-9	Ches	7sft	79	4074

WASHBROOK 3 b g £606
22	16-18	Nott	8.2sft	64	1470	
44	11-14	Wind	8.3g/f	61	1956	
59	3-14	Redc	7fm	58	2295	
51	8-18	Catt	7g/f	58	4438	
23	17-17	Newc	8fm	57	4867	
36	15-17	Ayr	7.2sft	55	5063	T

WASHINGTON PINK 5 b g £0
2	15-17	Pont	12hvy	50	1064	
25	13-19	Beve	9.9g/s	50	1164	
38	4-12	Newc	14.4sft	45	1396	
22	8-8	Muss	12gd	[45]	1552	
18	10-14	York	13.9g/f	40	2060	
0	11-12	Muss	16gd	38	2964	P

WASTED TALENT 3 b f £9210
60a	5-7	Ling	10ap	73	16	p
62a	3-15	Sout	12af	[68]	89	p
44a	1-9	SOUT	11af	[60]	224*	p
74	1-10	BATH	11.7gd	70	1399*	p
81	2-10	Chep	12.1gd	72	2114	VIS
68	11-29	Asco	20g/f	75	2471	
57	10-12	Epso	12gd	76	4292	vis
72	4-16	Good	12gd	[75]	4745	vis

WATAMU 3 b c £17123
25	13-15	Newb	8gd	81	1206	
52	9-13	Kemp	9hvy	80	1515	
90	1-10	GOOD	11g/f	78	1865*	
90	2-6	Good	12g/f	83	2021	
87	6-10	Sali	12gd	86	2660	
88	3-16	Good	9.9fm	83	3553	VIS
85	5-10	Good	9.9gd	85	3949	vis

WATCHFUL WITNESS 4 ch c £922
69	3-10	Nott	14.1sft		1742	
57	4-6	York	11.9g/f		2058	
2	16-17	Wind	11.6fm		2788	
36a	11-11	Ling	16ap	55	3450	VIS

WATCHING 7 ch g £16960
86	3-18	Catt	7gd	83	998	
63	22-30	Newm	6g/f	83	1481	
87	2-20	York	5g/s	83	1683	
86	5-20	Epso	5fm	83	2253	
85	5-13	York	5g/f	85	2359	
73	7-16	Wind	6fm	85	2758	
70	10-15	Beve	5sft	84	2942	
65	11-12	York	5g/s	84	3073	
74	13-20	Newm	7g/f	80	3782	
88	2-19	York	6gd	78	4005	
85	3-12	Good	6sft	78	4184	
88	3-18	Ayr	7.2sft	82	4689	
77	11-18	York	7gd	83	5000	

WATCHMYEYES 2 ch g £8918
70	6-13	Bath	5.7g/f		3368	
69	4-11	Ches	7fm		3633	
78	4-17	Chep	6.1sft		4052	
81	2-20	Ling	7gd	73	4444	
79a	2-11	Ling	8ap	[77]	4738	
84a	1-11	WOLV	8.6ap	[77]	4978*	
88a	1-8	WOLV	8.6ap	[77]	5007*	P

WATER OF LIFE 4 b f £304
46a	5-10	Ling	12ap	[49]	24	
49a	3-14	Ling	12ap	[49]	103	
49a	7-13	Ling	10ap	[51]	429	
15a	12-14	Ling	10ap	51	498	

WATER PISTOL 2 b g £0
73	8-14	Folk	7gd		4115	
55	9-11	Chep	8.1g/s		4363	
76	6-11	Good	8gd		4746	
54	9-14	Newb	7sft	72	5193	

WATER TAXI 3 ch c £1858
76	4-12	Sali	12g/s		1501	
77	3-7	Newm	12g/f		1936	
71	3-5	Warw	12.6fm		2441	

WATERFRONT DANCER 2 b g £0
24	15-15	Nott	5.1gd		4859	
45	9-10	Ling	5g/f		4893	
25a	11-12	Wolv	5.1ap		4981	
41	13-13	Wind	6g/f		5048	

WATERLINE BLUE 3 b g £0

| 48 | 5-13 | Leic | 7g/f | [76] | 1827 | T |
| 31a | 11-12 | Ling | 6ap | [76] | 2016 | t |

WATERLINE DANCER 3 b f £0
40a	10-16	Sout	7af	[48]	161	vis t
41a	8-10	Ling	10ap	[45]	540	t
32a	8-12	Ling	8ap	[45]	571	vis t
29a	9-15	Ling	7ap	[40]	708	vis t
24a	7-12	Wolv	8.5af	[40]	777	t
35a	4-10	Wolv	7af	[35]	890	t
0	14-17	Kemp	7hvy	[40]	1642	vis t

WATERLINE LOVER 2 ch f £645
56	6-8	Newm	5gd		1170	
64	10-15	Wind	5gd		1380	
46	11-12	Warw	5sft		1524	
60	4-5	Good	6gd		2221	
57	7-18	Donc	6g/s		3376	
55	6-8	Chep	6.1gd	59	3729	
60	4-6	Wind	5gd	56	4123	
22	17-19	Bath	5gd	57	5021	VIS

WATERLINE SPIRIT 3 b g £0
0	15-16	Sout	8af	48	86	
0	16-17	Bath	11.7gd	43	3145	
2	11-11	Muss	16g/f	40	3557	

WATERLOO CORNER 2 b g £0
| 11 | 9-10 | Catt | 7sft | | 5127 | |

WATERPARK 6 b m £9891
27	13-17	Nott	6.1sft	48	1606	
59	1-15	REDC	7sft	48	1660*	
0	13-15	Sout	8af	54	1755	
63	2-8	Thir	8fm	56	2464	

WATERSHIP CRYSTAL 3 b f £0
| 60 | 10-11 | Newb | 10g/f | | 2349 | |

WATERSHIP DOWN 7 b g £0
| 38 | 9-13 | Nott | 14.1gd | [45] | 1990 | |
| 2 | 16-16 | Folk | 12fm | 40 | 2718 | |

WATERSIDE 4 ch g £28086
77a	9-15	Ling	7ap	82	81	
83a	4-13	Ling	6ap	81	235	
53	10-15	Folk	6sft	71	976	
54	12-16	Bath	5.7g/s	[71]	1103	
70	12-16	Warw	6.1hvy	68	1533	
38	11-16	Nott	6.1sft	[68]	1743	
68a	3-12	Ling	6ap	[82]	2016	
76	1-7	FOLK	7g/f	[68]	2272*	
78	1-8	SAND	7.1g/f	74	2389*	
86	2-12	Kemp	7g/s	80	2679	
74	4-9	Epso	6g/f	78	2871	
75	6-12	Ches	7.6fm	82	3634	
70	16-20	Newm	7g/f	82	3782	
80	3-7	Sali	7g/s	[80]	4082	
83	1-5	GOOD	7sft	[80]	4186*	
68	12-15	Sand	7.1gd	82	4500	
64	13-16	Good	7gd	80	4873	

WATHAB 3 b c £4572
| 98 | 4-7 | Curr | 7sft | | 1063 | |
| 101 | 3-7 | Curr | 8gd | | 3318 | t |

WAVERLEY ROAD 6 ch g £2093
44a	1-13	LING	16ap	41	137*	
37a	7-14	Ling	13ap	45	264	
26a	13-14	Ling	12ap	45	801	
36a	4-9	Ling	16ap	[45]	1414	

WAVERTREE DREAM 2 b g £0
| 66a | 10-13 | Ling | 7ap | 86 | 15 | |

WAVERTREE GIRL 3 b f £1408
65a	3-9	Ling	7ap	[90]	764	
42a	8-11	Ling	8ap	[82]	841	
67	5-7	Beve	7.5sft	80	1305	
69	7-20	Newb	7g/f	75	1761	
56	4-6	Ayr	6fm	[72]	1908	
69	3-11	Sali	6gd	67	2661	BL
25a	10-11	Ling	7ap	[68]	3331	bl
52	11-14	Yarm	6gd	67	3870	bl

WAVERTREE SPIRIT 3 ch g £0
| 55 | 6-6 | Newm | 10gd | | 1892 | |

WAVERTREE WARRIOR 2 br c £3627

57	9-12	Newb	6g/f		2348	
75	3-13	York	6gd		3120	
81	2-7	Yarm	6gd		3869	
44	10-10	Curr	6.3gd		4737	
84	3-16	Good	7gd	77	5031	
49	9-14	Donc	8sft	77	5203	P

WAVET 3 b f £868
48a	8-14	Ling	10ap		53	
43a	9-13	Ling	10ap	55	215	
14a	12-14	Ling	13ap	50	259	
43a	7-14	Ling	10ap	47	2589	
50a	2-13	Sout	8af	46	3094	

WAY OUT 3 b f £0
| 19 | 11-11 | Chep | 8.1g/f | | 2627 | |
| 0 | 10-11 | Hayd | 8.1gd | | 2886 | |

WAYWARD MELODY 4 b f £0
| 24a | 4-5 | Ling | 12ap | [40] | 1411 | BL e |

WAYWARD SHOT 2 b g £553
63	5-13	Beve	5gd		2889	
48	7-10	Thir	5fm		3606	
49	12-18	Pont	5g/s		3968	
59	5-18	Catt	7g/f	58	4673	
63	4-14	Catt	7sft	58	5126	

WAZIR 2 b c £6862
| 92a | 2-7 | Ling | 6ap | | 3196 | |
| 84 | 1-8 | GOOD | 6g/f | | 4540* | |

WAZIRI 2 b c £6290
73a	4-11	Ling	8ap		21	
79	1-10	GOOD	9.9gd	74	2225*	
69	7-15	Epso	10.1gd	[77]	3216	
59	9-9	Good	14fm	73	3556	
72	3-9	Newb	9gd	75	3922	
54	10-13	Ling	10g/s	74	4182	
45	7-13	Chep	8.1hvy	70	4709	
49	15-17	Leic	10gd	68	5062	VIS

WEAKEST LINK 3 b g £839
62a	2-11	Wolv	7af		396	
59a	3-13	Sout	6af		444	
49a	3-7	Sout	7af	[63]	636	
54a	7-15	Ling	7ap	60	815	
24	15-18	Hayd	6gd	58	3737	
38	14-15	Beve	8.5g/f	55	4598	
44	4-10	Catt	6gd	[51]	4964	

WEAVER OF DREAMS 4 b g £0
| 0 | 11-15 | Newc | 12.4hvy | 48 | 1034 | |

WEAVER SPELL 3 b g £0
0	5-7	Wolv	6af	[40]	1312	
19a	6-6	Sout	7af	[40]	1410	
35	4-8	Nott	8.2sft	35	1740	
0	9-11	Pont	12g/f	35	2790	
1	10-11	Catt	13.8g/f	[35]	4671	VIS
11	17-18	Leic	10gd	[35]	5042	vis

WEB RACER 2 b f £0
53	5-6	Ayr	6g/f		2028	
46	9-11	Thir	7fm		2462	
36a	8-12	Sout	7af		3394	BL

WEBBINGTON LASS 3 b f £0
0	8-8	Ling	10ap	[45]	1183	
10	11-18	Chep	7.1g/s	40	3900	VIS
12	14-19	Chep	6.1sft	40	4054	vis

WEBBSWOOD LAD 3 b c £1923
| 68a | 3-11 | Ling | 8ap | | 322 | |
| 74a | 2-11 | Ling | 8ap | | 496 | |

WEDDING CAKE 3 ch f £4609
45	8-14	Wind	8.3g/s		2622	
71	3-6	Bath	10.2g/f		2980	
73	4-14	Ling	11.5gd		3335	
70a	1-10	LING	12ap	[73]	4314+	
53	10-12	Good	11gd	73	4749	

WEDDING PARTY 2 ch f £35254
72	3-13	Kemp	6gd		3183	
81a	1-10	LING	6ap		3818*	
84a	4-14	Ling	7ap	80	4177	
89	1-16	NEWM	7g/f	79	4913*	
95	2-7	Newb	7hvy	[83]	5222	

WEDLOCK 2 b c £451
69	4-10	Hayd	6g/s		2228
63	8-9	Ripo	6g/f		2522
45	12-13	Thir	6g/s		2689

WEDOWANNAGIVEUTHAT 3 b f £0
58	7-11	Ripo	8gd		1177
36	14-20	Donc	7g/s		1518
44	6-8	Beve	7.5g/f		2169
9	12-12	Beve	9.9gd	55	2893
12a	12-13	Sout	8af	55	3094
31	12-16	Thir	8g/f	49	3414

WEE DINNS 3 b f £12366
72	7-10	Newb	10gd		1209
68	5-18	Nott	8.2sft	69	1470
77	2-8	Brig	9.9g/f	67	2046
80	2-12	Sand	10gd	70	2366
85	1-12	**NEWB**	10g/f	75	3255*
89	2-12	Good	9fm	82	3535
83	6-10	Good	9.9gd	85	3949
84	6-12	Yarm	10.1sft	85	4149

WEECANDOO 6 b m £1200
51	7-7	Sand	10g/s	[90]	2898
65	9-9	Asco	10g/f	90	3439
87	5-8	Donc	10.3fm	84	4530
89	7-11	Yarm	10.1gd	[84]	4614
92	8-10	Newm	10gd	[82]	5086
85	6-6	Newm	10sft	[82]	5269

WEET A HEAD 2 b c £4278
83a	3-14	Sout	8af	[85]	88
70a	5-6	Wolv	9.4af	81	702
81	3-10	Hayd	10.5sft	[84]	1104
71	5-10	Pont	10sft	82	1427
81	6-13	York	10.4sft	80	1664
80	3-14	Donc	8g/f	[80]	1877
75	4-11	Pont	8g/f	77	2040
63	6-8	Ches	10.3gd	[79]	2283
67	8-12	Hayd	8.1gd	77	3738
68	8-10	Leic	8gd	[75]	4702
73	3-15	Leic	11.8gd	[72]	5060

WEET AN HAUL 2 b g £3561
56a	1-14	**SOUT**	7af	44	158*
50a	2-10	Sout	7af	50	203
18a	11-11	Sout	8af	55	252
42	7-13	Ripo	6g/f	55	2011
25a	8-12	Wolv	8.5af	55	2205
52	3-16	Thir	8g/f	49	3414 VIS
21a	12-12	Wolv	8.6ap	[52]	5329 vis

WEET AN STORE 2 gr c £0
| 0 | 13-13 | Wolv | 8.5af | | 43 T |
| 9 | 8-8 | Beve | 12.1gd | | 2515 t |

WEET FOR ME 8 b g £2017
0	18-18	York	13.9g/s	85	1689
3	9-9	Ripo	16g/f	80	2009
75	2-6	Ches	15.9g/f	75	3101
54	6-7	Newm	14.8g/f	74	3475
74	5-9	Hayd	14gd	74	3760
71	6-12	York	13.9g/f	72	4400
11	14-17	Nott	14.1g/s	72	4647
45	12-12	Redc	14.1g/s	69	5108

WEET N MEASURES 2 b c £0
| 59 | 5-10 | Hayd | 5g/s | | 3901 |
| 56a | 5-14 | Sout | 6af | | 4127 |

WEET WATCHERS 3 b g £6213
40a	11-11	Wolv	7af	74	241
59a	1-9	**SOUT**	7af	[71]	555*
71a	6-11	Sout	7af	77	585
53a	4-8	Sout	7af	[70]	744
56	3-17	Beve	8.5g/s	[67]	1160
41	16-19	Redc	7g/f	60	1820
55	5-14	Redc	7g/f	[56]	2102
64	1-8	**RIPO**	8g/f	[55]	2480*
0	P-16	Beve	7.5gd	55	2655
48	13-18	Catt	7g/f	62	4438
13a	13-13	Wolv	6ap	[64]	5327

WEET YER TERN 2 b c £2167
| 72 | 4-5 | Nott | 5.1fm | | 1001 |
| 67 | 2-5 | Brig | 5.3g/f | | 1367 |

| 67a | 4-10 | Sout | 6af | | 2382 |

WEIRS ANNIE 3 b f £0
40	7-11	Nott	6.1sft		1607
17	16-17	Bath	5g/f		1787
9	13-15	Nott	5.1g/f		2152

WEKIWA SPRINGS 7 gr g £0
| 11a | 6-9 | Wolv | 8.5af | | 437 T |

WELCOME ARCHIE 4 ch g £0
24	9-10	Ayr	8g/s		1446
26	9-11	Redc	6sft		1662
31	10-15	Beve	7.5g/f		1944
5	12-13	Muss	8gd		2967

WELCOME BACK 6 ch g £180
| 0 | 12-12 | Wolv | 16.2af | 33 | 156 |
| 30a | 3-9 | Wolv | 14.8af | [33] | 301 |

WELCOME DREAM 2 ch f £0
| 45 | 7-15 | Beve | 5g/s | | 1161 |
| 3a | 11-11 | Sout | 7af | | 2995 |

WELCOME SIGNAL 4 ch g £3073
58a	12-14	Ling	10ap	67	2392
64	5-9	Newm	8g/f	67	2529
55	5-17	Newm	10g/f	65	3238 P
55	8-12	Newm	10g/f	65	3785 p
63	3-16	Brig	7sft	[63]	4144 p
70	2-19	Leic	7g/f	63	4452 p
74	2-16	Bath	8gd	67	5022 p

WELCOME STRANGER 4 b g £33329
70	8-13	Wind	8.3g/s	[78]	1057
72	9-18	Good	8g/f	78	1812
68	9-15	Sand	10g/f	77	2099
81	2-13	Ling	7.6g/f	75	2587
86	1-7	**YARM**	8g/f	76	2853*
89	2-9	Asco	8gd	81	3465
95	1-5	**KEMP**	8g/f	[81]	3523*
97	2-9	Kemp	8g/f	[81]	3689
94	8-15	Donc	8fm	92	4531
102	1-14	**ASCO**	8g/f	92	4813*
79	14-19	York	7.9gd	98	4987

WELKINOS BOY 3 ch g £1423
43	13-16	Donc	10.3gd		2751
66	5-9	Pont	12g/f		2992
58	6-11	Leic	10g/f		3208
64	3-11	Yarm	14.1gd	62	3998
65	3-6	Newc	14.4sft	63	4287
40	12-20	York	13.9gd	62	5004

WELL CONNECTED 4 b g £0
| 3 | 11-14 | Carl | 9.3g/f | [45] | 4347 |
| 18 | 11-17 | Carl | 7.9fm | [45] | 4506 |

WELL ESTABLISHED 2 b c £0
| 74 | 6-21 | Newm | 8sft | | 5097 |

WELL KNIT 3 b f £0
69a	7-9	Ling	8ap		756
61a	15-15	Ling	7ap		885
56	7-7	Donc	8gd		949
50	7-7	Newm	7g/s		1150
15	13-16	Nott	10hvy	55	1611
21	13-14	Ling	11.5g/f	50	2014

WELL KNOWN 3 b f £5551
85	1-9	**SALI**	9.9g/f		1719*
72	8-9	Newb	12g/f	[92]	3629
65	9-10	Sali	9.9g/f	[92]	3866

WELL MADE 7 br h £10563
| 113 | 2-8 | Colo | 12sft | | 1556 |

WELL MEET AGAIN 4 ch g £444
53	3-14	Carl	7.9fm	53	1954
37	12-15	Beve	7.5g/s	53	2324
54	4-17	Warw	8.1fm	53	2572
49	5-10	Pont	10g/f	53	2794

WELLINGTON HALL 5 b g £15840
46a	8-13	Ling	10ap	57	104 bl
64	1-8	**YARM**	11.5g/f	53	1135*
52	9-16	Brig	11.9fm	63	1693
70	1-12	**NEWM**	10g/f	62	3785*
71	3-13	Warw	12.6gd	65	4274
62	5-16	Yarm	11.5g/s	67	4589

| **79** | 1-10 | **DONC** | 10.3sft | 66 | 5206* |

WELSH AND WYLDE 4 b g £0
| 20a | 10-11 | Sout | 12af | 52 | 1197 |
| 0 | 6-6 | Sout | 16af | 49 | 3397 p |

WELSH BORDER 5 ch g £0
| 0 | 10-10 | Ling | 10ap | [82] | 179 |

WELSH DREAM 7 b g £0
| 28 | 6-6 | Muss | 16g/f | 49 | 2807 |
| 42 | 6-11 | Muss | 16g/f | 46 | 3557 |

WELSH EMPEROR 5 b g £32288
99	1-7	**THIR**	6sft	[109]	1227+ bl
108	4-15	York	6sft	[109]	1668 bl
104	6-11	Newc	6g/s	[109]	2769 bl
105	5-13	Hamb	6hvy	[109]	3009 bl
109	2-11	York	7g/s	[107]	4063 bl
107	8-19	Hayd	6fm	[107]	4384 bl
109	1-9	**HAMI**	6g/s	[107]	4817+ bl
95	8-11	Mais	6sft	[107]	5313 bl

WELSH EMPRESS 3 b f £421
42	7-13	Nott	8.2gd	52	1242
51	3-8	Muss	8gd	50	1798
0	10-10	Yarm	8g/f	52	2344
34	10-15	Bath	8g/s	50	4202
26	12-20	Chep	7.1g/s	50	4367
31	15-17	Kemp	7g/f	[45]	4794

WELSH GALAXY 2 b f £0
29a	10-13	Ling	7ap		3330
3	17-18	Nott	8.2g/s		4035
0	13-13	York	7.9gd		4325
58	10-14	Chep	8.5gd		4484
31	10-10	Newm	6fm	53	4727

WELSH MAIN 7 br g £0
| 65 | 9-12 | Nott | 14.1gd | 70 | 3105 |

WELSH WHISPER 5 b m £1643
21a	7-10	Wolv	8.5af		311
5a	7-9	Wolv	8.5af		437
32a	4-12	Wolv	8.5af	[30]	584
11a	8-12	Wolv	9.4af	[35]	782
22a	7-13	Wolv	8.5af	[35]	826
30a	5-10	Wolv	7af	[35]	890
17a	6-11	Wolv	6af	[35]	1261
29a	6-8	Wolv	7af	[35]	1314
42a	1-7	**WOLV**	6af	[30]	1566*
36a	3-8	Wolv	7af	[30]	1676
30	9-14	Leic	6g/f	[45]	1963
21a	9-11	Wolv	6af	[44]	2202

WELSH WIND 7 b g £5313
54a	4-13	Ling	10ap	56	104 t
58a	2-14	Ling	10ap	56	230 t
56a	3-14	Ling	10ap	56	339 t
58a	2-14	Ling	10ap	[56]	477 t
23a	12-12	Wolv	8.5af	56	564 t
57a	3-14	Ling	10ap	56	622 t
62a	1-9	**LING**	8ap	56	763* t P
58a	9-14	Ling	12ap	62	801 t p
61a	4-13	Ling	10ap	[60]	912 t p
51	9-14	Nott	10g/s	59	1777 t p

WEMBURY POINT 2 gr c £0
38	9-10	Good	6g/f		3511
59	10-11	Newb	6g/f		3959
61	11-13	Warw	7.1g/f		4416
65	6-14	Carl	6.9fm		4503
60	13-20	Ling	7g/f	62	4741
61	9-13	Brig	8sft	[56]	5091
70a	5-11	Ling	8ap	[56]	5235 VIS

WENDYS GIRL 3 b f £8525
46a	7-9	Wolv	5af	[64]	835
33a	8-8	Ling	7ap	64	933
55	5-7	Sout	8g/f	[60]	1050
51a	2-8	Wolv	7af	[57]	1222
0	P-12	Wolv	6af	55	1374
54	4-10	Hami	5g/s	55	1605
33	7-13	Hami	5gd	53	2181
63	1-13	**WARW**	6.1fm	50	2439+ bl
8	12-13	Newc	5sft	56	2683 bl
66	1-14	**CATT**	6g/f	56	3018* bl
61	6-12	Catt	5g/f	62	3193 bl
40	5-8	Muss	5g/f	[63]	3527 bl

```
59   5-15   Thir   5g/s      62   3833 bl
62a  3-11   Sout   5af       62   4094 bl
59   3-7    Brig   5.3sft   [61]  4169 bl

WENTBRIDGE BOY 3 gr g  £0
2a   13-13  Sout   6af             254

WERE STONYBROKE 5 b g  £0
16   19-20  Newm  8g/f      57   3232

WESSEX 4 ch c  £0
60   15-16  Thir   7g/s      89   1474
74   6-10   Thir   7g/f     [83]  1970
72   8-11   Hami   8.3g/f    80   2317
67   7-13   Ayr    7.2g/s    76   2568
70   5-12   Ayr    8gd       72   3328
43   9-9    Carl   9.3fm    [72]  3546
59   11-16  Thir   8g/f      68   4592
57   8-20   Ripo   6gd       65   4785 VIS

WEST COUNTRY 3 br c  £327
42   18-22  Donc   7gd       79   955
58   8-10   Hayd   6g/f      77   1488
53   4-4    Bath   11.7fm   [70]  2413

WEST END WONDER 5 b g  £309
31   15-16  Donc   10.3gd          2751
36   4-4    Brig   9.9fm           3675
47   7-10   Yarm   11.5gd          3997

WEST HIGHLAND WAY 3 b g  £3409
79   1-4    AYR    7.2fm    [80]  1907*
79   5-6    Ripo   8g/f      80   2525
56   9-11   Ayr    8sft      78   4621
71a  5-12   Wolv   7.1ap     75   5289

WESTBOROUGH 3 ch g  £9293
53   2-10   Newc   6sft     [56]  1682
54   5-7    Carl   5fm       55   1951
26a  8-12   Sout   7af      [53]  2339
51   5-13   Newc   6sft      53   2683
60   2-4    Hami   5gd      [51]  3133
50   7-9    Leic   5g/f     [55]  3347
23a  8-11   Sout   5af       48   4094
49   6-11   Beve   5g/s     [54]  4237
43   7-14   Newc   5g/f     [52]  4404 VIS
55   2-19   Thir   6g/f      52   4595 T
46   9-11   Wind   6g/f     [52]  4836 t
64   1-8    CATT   8gd      [52]  4969* t
69   1-15   AYR    5sft      58   5036* t

WESTBROOK BLUE 2 b c  £5256
84   3-15   Donc   5gd             920
76a  1-8    SOUT   5ap            1048*
83   3-4    Bath   5g/f            3369
76a  4-10   Ling   5ap      [81]  3743
76   6-10   Ches   5.1g/f   80   4049

WESTCOURT DREAM 4 ch f  £4246
44   3-11   Redc   8fm       46   2296
55   1-10   BEVE   9.9gd     46   2510*
21   8-8    Thir   12g/s     45   2691
49   6-14   York   10.4g/f   52   4402
32   14-19  Thir   12g/f     52   4594
39   8-15   Redc   9g/s      49   5111

WESTER LODGE 2 ch c  £1090
76   9-15   Leic   7g/f            4455
82   2-12   Newc   7g/f            5011
61   8-14   Yarm   7sft            5251

WESTERN 3 ch g  £3157
76a  1-14   LING   13ap      68   147*
77a  2-8    Ling   16ap      71   288
70a  14-16  Ling   12ap      78   404
23a  9-10   Sout   16af      76   743
42   11-14  Sali   12g/f     74   3114
36   11-12  Kemp   14.4g/f   74   3688
50   12-17  Kemp   12sft     70   4033
43   12-19  Sali   14.1gd    60   4856
0    18-19  Bath   11.7gd    56   5024 p
65a  10-16  Ling   12ap      65   5261 p

WESTERN BLUEBIRD 6 b g  £1236
29   6-10   Muss   16gd      51   1551
44   4-8    Muss   16gd      45   1793 BL
13   11-14  York   13.9g/f   45   2060 bl
46   2-6    Muss   16g/f     42   2807 bl
16   7-12   Muss   16gd      42   2964 bl

WESTERN COMMAND 8 b g  £1146
3a   10-12  Sout   8af      [20]  309
0    8-10   Sout   11af      30   330
19a  4-11   Sout   8af      [30]  372
18a  5-9    Sout   12af      30   456
23a  6-12   Wolv   9.4af     30   464
16a  6-10   Wolv   12af     [30]  581
4a   8-12   Sout   11af     [30]  640 p
20a  5-12   Wolv   9.4af    [30]  782 p
15a  11-16  Sout   11af     [30]  852 p
0    9-15   Sout   12af      30   867
29a  5-10   Sout   16af     [30]  984
45a  5-16   Sout   14af      30   1033 p
39a  3-9    Sout   12af     [45]  1204 p
30a  3-6    Wolv   12af     [45]  1313 p
19a  5-8    Wolv   12af      40   1342 p
19a  9-10   Wolv   9.4af    [40]  1564 p
27a  5-8    Sout   14af     [35]  1840
35a  2-9    Sout   12af     [35]  2381 p
27a  6-9    Sout   12af     [35]  2724 p
11a  7-10   Sout   14af      35   3096
4a   8-11   Sout   12af     [35]  3154 p
25a  6-14   Sout   12af      25   3486 p

WESTERN RIDGE 7 b g  £0
35   8-17   Bath   11.7sft   53   1543
1    P-12   Warw   15g/f     50   2908

WESTERN ROOTS 2 ch g  £6373
82a  4-6    Ling   6ap             79
1a   15-15  Ling   7ap       80   177
81a  2-10   Ling   7ap       80   432
81a  4-5    Ling   8ap       81   694
71a  8-10   Ling   10ap      80   817
74   7-9    Hayd   8.1sft    79   1105
71   6-12   Donc   7g/f      77   1879
78   1-10   LEIC   8gd      [74]  2133*
71   5-12   Ayr    8g/s     [78]  2543
65   5-10   Newm   8g/f     [78]  2732
20   9-9    Nott   8.2g/f   [75]  3423
37a  11-14  Ling   10ap     [72]  4448
17a  12-12  Wolv   8.6ap    69   4923
70a  2-14   Ling   7ap      [67]  5080
32   16-18  Newm   8sft      65   5272

WESTERNER 5 b h  £281698
122  1-6    LONG   15.5g/s         1431*
121  2-6    Long   15.5gd          2000
121  2-13   Asco   20g/f           2518
122  1-8    LONG   15.5sft         4569*
122  1-8    LONG   20g/f           4951*
122  1-8    LONG   15.5hvy         5245*

WESTERNMOST 6 b g  £0
14   12-14  Carl   17.2gd   40   2937

WESTFIELD BOY 2 b c  £0
2    20-21  Newm   8sft            5097
58   12-16  Yarm   10.1g/s         5352

WESTLAKE BOND 2 b f  £1376
64   5-14   Redc   6g/s            5106
75   2-21   Donc   6sft            5368

WESTLAND 2 gr c  £6790
85   2-14   Newb   6sft            5197
90   1-17   YARM   6g/s            5350*

WESTMEAD ETOILE 4 b f  £670
31a  9-10   Ling   8ap      [45]  410
38a  3-8    Sout   8af       40   597 VIS
27a  10-12  Ling   8ap      [40]  1073 vis
12a  7-8    Wolv   7af      [40]  1565 vis
8    10-17  Kemp   7hvy     [45]  1642 BL
26a  3-10   Sout   7af      [35]  1839 vis T

WESTMEAD TANGO 3 b f  £0
13a  9-13   Wolv   6af      [53]  30 vis
30a  14-15  Ling   7ap       52   151
31a  6-13   Ling   6ap      [49]  400
32a  6-9    Ling   5ap      [49]  413 vis
19a  11-14  Ling   6ap      [45]  709
27a  7-12   Ling   6ap      [40]  1075

WESTMORELAND ROAD 4 b c  £10623
111  2-7    Newm   12g/f   [112]  2762
107  2-9    Newm   12g/f   [112]  3233
100  4-7    Sali   14.1gd  [108]  4333

                     1926
```

```
78   7-8    Newb   11g/f   [106]  4639

WET LIPS 6 ch g  £0
57   13-21  York   11.9gd    76   3999 bl t

WETHAAB 7 b g  £0
0    8-9    Sout   11af     [35]  906 t p
0    8-9    Sout   11af     [35]  985 t p
7a   5-6    Wolv   9.4af    [30]  1262 vis t
0    6-6    Wolv   12af     [30]  1313 t p
0    9-9    Warw   15g/s    [30]  1329 t p

WHALEEF 6 br g  £1740
77   2-11   Wind   10gd     [82]  4124 T P

WHAT A DANCER 6 b g  £21085
75a  7-15   Ling   7ap       78   81
85a  1-16   LING   7ap       77   181+
87a  4-11   Ling   7ap      [83]  627
86a  3-8    Ling   7ap      [83]  879
91a  1-15   LING   7ap       83   887*
69   5-7    Muss   7.1g/f   [79]  1094
68   8-10   Thir   7g/f     [77]  1970
77   4-11   Donc   7g/f      77   2076
76   4-7    Good   7gd      [76]  2374
71   9-18   Catt   7g/f      75   2848
73   6-25   Asco   7g/f      75   3443
76   5-19   Good   8g/f      75   3512
76   4-20   Newm   7g/f      74   3782
73   6-16   Redc   7g/f      74   3809

WHAT A SPREE 2 ch f  £0
3a   12-13  Wolv   8.5af           111

WHATATODO 2 b f  £6028
47   7-19   Kemp   6g/f            1911
63   3-16   Pont   6g/s            2275
46   8-11   Ayr    6g/s            2569
69   1-9    BRIG   7g/f      63   3297*
73   2-11   Newm   7fm       68   3407
48   14-16  Newm   6gd       72   4224
74   4-14   Yarm   7g/s      72   4583
67   12-29  Newm   6gd             5087

WHATS UP DOC 3 b c  £3526
83   1-7    NEWC   10.1gd   [82]  1871*
79   6-9    Kemp   12gd      82   2175

WHATSHEWORTH 2 b g  £0
7    10-10  Newm   5fm             2089
2    6-6    Folk   5g/s            2270

WHAZZAT 2 b f  £27961
91   1-19   NEWB   6g/f            2310*
107  1-11   ASCO   7fm             2578*

WHENWILLITWIN 3 b g  £0
60   6-6    Bath   10.2g/f         2980
56   6-9    Wind   11.6gd          3164
44   7-11   Yarm   10.1gd          3362

WHERE WITH ALL 2 b c  £10810
93   1-10   HAYD   6g/s            2228*
82   7-11   Asco   7fm             2578
107  1-8    BEVE   7.5gd           3311+

WHINHILL HOUSE 4 ch g  £212
0    16-16  Carl   5.9fm     53   2445
2    9-9    Beve   5gd       53   2512
0    18-18  Pont   5g/s      48   3974
47   3-16   Warw   5g/s     [45]  4995
16   12-20  Yarm   6g/s     [45]  5121

WHIPLASH 3 b c  £3536
0    12-13  Wind   8.3g/s   [60]  1058
59   4-7    Folk   7g/s      60   1081
2    18-18  Wind   8.3sft    59   1647
58   1-14   SALI   7g/f     [59]  1720*
21   18-20  Newb   7fm       58   2650
49a  6-12   Ling   8ap      [55]  3286
23a  10-14  Ling   10ap      52   3449
20   12-15  Ling   7.6fm     53   3788
33   6-18   Chep   7.1g/s    53   3900 BL
13   13-15  Bath   8g/s      48   4202 bl
40   9-17   Kemp   7g/f     [45]  4794 bl
```

WHIPPER — column 1

49a	10-11	Wolv	7af	65		363
68a	1-13	LING	6ap	60		471*
67a	2-9	Ling	5ap	[60]		492
70a	1-14	LING	6ap	[65]		516*
71a	3-13	Ling	7ap	70		565
69a	9-14	Ling	7ap	70		604
68	2-20	Wind	6g/s	61		1255
67	1-19	LEIC	6g/s	61		1354*
49	8-15	Brig	5.3g/f	61		1371
67	3-12	Hami	6g/s	[65]		1600
68	2-19	Redc	7g/f	65		1820
68	2-9	Ayr	7.2fm	[65]		1910
58	7-9	Muss	7.1fm	67		2086
46	10-10	Muss	7.1g/f	67		3562
51a	11-14	Ling	7ap	69		3821
64	4-16	Ches	7g/f	66		4051
48	13-15	Epso	7g/f	65		4475
52	13-20	Wind	6g/s	63		4946
46a	6-12	Wolv	6ap	66		4984

WHIPPER 3 b c £276859

116	1-6	MAIS	7sft		1155*
117	5-14	Newm	8g/f		1480
121	2-12	Deau	6.5g/s		3838
122	1-10	DEAU	8sft		4017*
117	5-11	Long	8g/s		4434
112	10-5	Lone	8g/s		5308

WHIRLING 2 ch f £0

37	8-9	Ayr	8sft		5033
28a	11-13	Wolv	8.6ap		5288

WHIRLY BIRD 3 b f £3980

65	3-13	Bath	10.2sft		5173
77a	1-13	WOLV	9.5ap		5290*

WHISPERED PROMISES 3 b c £820

72	12-13	York	10.4sft	82	1664
82	3-6	Kemp	12g/s	82	2681
74	8-15	Newm	12g/f	82	3066
61	5-5	Pont	10gd	80	3459 BL

WHISPERING DEATH 2 br c £0

0	23-23	Newm	6gd		5084
42	11-13	Donc	7hvy		5199
52	11-14	Yarm	7sft		5251

WHISPERING VALLEY 4 ch f £0

52	12-14	Ling	11.5gd		3335
26	9-10	Ling	14fm		3742
42	9-11	Folk	9.7gd		4120
13	15-18	Warw	10.9g/s	50	4669
4	15-16	Bath	8gd	47	4828

WHIST DRIVE 4 ch g £0

60	6-11	Warw	15sft	66	1087

WHISTFUL 3 b f £1495

69	3-20	Nott	6.1gd	67	1239
38	9-10	Folk	6sft	68	1576
70	3-18	Wind	6g/f	68	2268
71	5-9	Wind	6gd	69	2619
33	11-11	Warw	5.5gd	69	3054
63	4-7	Folk	6g/s	[68]	3910
60	8-17	Ling	6g/f	65	4740
41	4-8	Catt	6gd	[63]	4969

WHISTLER 7 ch g £37160

64	12-17	Kemp	5sft	80	944 p
66	17-20	Thir	5g/s	78	1476 p
62	9-20	Thir	5g/f	75	1765 p
77	3-11	Hayd	5g/f	75	1886 p
75	7-15	Muss	5fm	75	2084 p
83	1-10	SAND	5gd	75	2189* p
73	7-11	Ches	5.1gd	78	2286 p
83	3-9	Sali	5fm	81	2420 p
89	1-12	SALI	5gd	81	2698* p
77	7-9	Warw	5.5fm	84	2779 p
95	1-11	SAND	5gd	84	2894* p
93	4-8	Asco	5gd	91	3123 p
83	15-24	Asco	5gd	92	3466 p
93	3-14	Newb	5.2fm	95	3628 p
93	4-20	Hayd	5fm	90	3792 p
59	15-16	Hayd	5fm	90	4382 p
96	4-22	Donc	5.6fm	90	4459 p
96	2-11	Hayd	5sft	90	4780 p
94	6-10	Newm	5g/s	91	5090 p
90	5-13	Muss	5g/s	91	5143 p

WHISTLING ALONG 2 b c £0

60	8-9	Wind	5g/s		1256
30	6-6	Nott	5.1sft		1466
41	10-16	Ripo	6g/f		1780
35	8-10	Wind	5fm		3476

WHITBARROW 5 b g £20276

91	5-11	Newb	5.2gd	93	1207
64	12-14	Ches	5.1gd	92	1594
74	12-20	York	5g/s	92	1683
97	1-11	GOOD	5g/f	90	1845*
91	7-17	Muss	5fm	96	2082
98	7-20	Epso	5fm	97	2253
86	14-29	Asco	6fm	96	2581
89	9-15	Newc	5g/f	97	2727
69	8-8	Asco	5gd	96	3123
94	9-24	Asco	5gd	96	3466 P
72	21-28	Good	6fm	96	3622 p
72	13-14	Epso	5gd	92	4291 bl
88	7-16	Hayd	5fm	92	4382 bl
93	5-22	Donc	5.6fm	92	4459 bl
91	4-8	Yarm	6g/s	[90]	4588 bl
73	9-11	Hayd	5sft	90	4780 bl
81	9-12	Epso	5g/f	89	4908
89	3-13	Muss	5g/s	87	5143
92	2-13	Donc	5sft	87	5218

WHITE HAWK 3 b c £730

74	4-5	Newb	10gd	[100]	1208
67	12-15	Ches	7.6gd	100	1583
77	16-18	Hayd	8.1g/f	95	1919

WHITE LEDGER 5 ch g £9960

23a	12-14	Sout	6af	[65]	2502
39a	11-15	Sout	7af	[60]	2999
47	3-13	Hayd	6gd	[50]	3757 vis
57	1-11	CATT	5sft	[50]	3932* vis
63	1-11	SAND	5sft	54	4070* vis
39	8-9	Yarm	5.2g/s	58	4253
56	6-8	Brig	5.3sft	58	5096 vis
65a	2-13	Wolv	5.1ap	58	5156 vis

WHITE O MORN 4 gr f £2397

12a	12-16	Sout	5af		65
16a	12-12	Wolv	5af		242
12a	11-12	Sout	7af		416
28a	4-11	Wolv	5af	30	508 T
34a	2-11	Sout	5af	[30]	578 t
36a	4-8	Sout	5af	[35]	742 P
39a	1-10	WOLV	5af	[35]	781* t p
24a	9-12	Wolv	5af	[40]	889 t p
39a	2-7	Wolv	5af	[40]	1562 p
0	12-12	Wolv	5af	[40]	1799 p
43	4-20	Beve	5gd	[40]	1948 p
33	10-19	Beve	5g/s	43	2326 p
23	7-11	Nott	5.1gd	42	4038 p

WHITE PARK BAY 3 b f £1708

43a	8-13	Wolv	8.5af	65	40
52a	3-15	Sout	8af	[62]	96
56a	3-10	Wolv	12af	[59]	154
6a	12-14	Ling	13ap	58	264
0	5-6	Sout	11af	[58]	306
57	2-9	Wind	11.6gd	[48]	3164
26a	12-14	Sout	12af	54	3486
38	6-8	Ling	11.5g/s	[54]	4181

WHITE SAIL 3 b f £0

42	11-14	Yarm	7fm		2148

WHITE STAR MAGIC 2 ch c £0

62	7-12	Ayr	7.2hvy		4083
53	9-10	Newc	8hvy		4213
67	6-10	Newc	6g/f		4403
59a	4-12	Wolv	7.1ap	[69]	5158

WHITGIFT ROCK 2 b c £10849

71a	1-11	LING	7ap	[71]	220*
77a	1-7	LING	8ap	71	341*
76a	2-8	Ling	8ap	[72]	934
49	13-16	Beve	7.5g/s	75	1163 VIS
75	7-12	Sand	7.1g/f	75	2098
73	7-13	Sand	8.1gd	75	2365
77	3-9	Leic	8gd	73	2705
73	2-10	Nott	10g/s	[73]	2930
60	10-15	Epso	10.1gd	[73]	3216
66a	7-13	Ling	7ap	75	4318

39	12-13	Epso	8.5gd	73	4469
49a	12-14	Ling	10ap	[73]	4742

WHITKIRK STAR 3 b g £0

0	6-6	Hayd	8.1g/s		3905
0	8-8	Redc	10sft		5306

WHITLAND 2 b c £0

20	14-16	Sali	7gd		3882 T
66	8-14	Sali	7sft		4575 t
52	9-19	Kemp	8g/f		4792 t

WHITSBURY CROSS 3 b c £6262

81	5-19	Newb	8gd		1236
78	5-17	Newb	8g/f		1762
84	1-11	FOLK	9.7g/f	[77]	2274*
88	11-13	Asco	10g/f	[77]	2520
83	4-16	Sand	10g/s	80	2919
84	3-6	Sand	10g/f	80	3358
81	5-14	Newb	10g/f	80	3961

WHITTINGHAMVILLAGE 2 b f £0

42a	4-11	Wolv	6af	[59]	73
21a	8-12	Sout	6af	[50]	200
31a	6-6	Wolv	7af	[44]	283

WHITTLE WARRIOR 4 b g £0

33	14-15	Redc	6fm	65	4562

WHO CARES WINS 8 ch g £0

21	9-14	Yarm	14.1g/s	[45]	5123

WHOLE GRAIN 3 b f £434

75	4-14	Kemp	10g/s		2678

WHOOPSIE 2 b f £0

56	9-11	Donc	5gd		4462
45	16-18	Nott	8.2g/f		4842
0	11-11	Donc	8sft		5205

WHORTLEBERRY 4 ch f £42148

118	1-13	DEAU	10sft		4160* bl
106	9-13	Long	12sft		4567 bl

WHOS WINNING 3 ch g £21178

31	18-19	Newm	6g/s	75	1154
67	8-14	Thir	5g/f	73	1766
61	6-9	Folk	6g/f	70	2271
50	8-13	Newm	7fm	66	2590
69	2-9	Warw	6.1fm	[63]	2778 BL
74	1-7	BRIG	6fm	66	3693*
71	2-15	Sali	5gd	67	4335
79	1-16	GOOD	5g/f	69	4528*
87	1-15	KEMP	6g/f	74	4713+
68a	7-12	Ling	6ap	81	5297

WHY DUBAI 3 br f £689

70	8-9	Kemp	8g/s	[89]	1110
83	6-12	Good	9fm	89	3535
92	6-12	Bath	8g/f	[89]	3965
88	10-15	Donc	7fm	[89]	4479

WHY HARRY 2 b g £3462

69a	3-8	Sout	5ap		1048
56	7-12	Ripo	5g/f		1173
67	1-8	BEVE	5sft		1303*
50	6-11	Thir	5gd		1634
47	6-11	Beve	5g/f		1831

WICKED UNCLE 5 b g £3543

61	10-10	Sand	5gd	76	2189 bl
62	9-11	Ches	5.1gd	76	2286 P
89	1-17	CATT	5g/f	73	2846* vis

WIGGY SMITH 5 ch g £12522

80	5-13	Wind	10gd	[80]	1381
36	17-17	Newb	12g/f	80	1759
90	1-11	EPSO	10.1gd	80	4293+
90	2-10	York	10.1sft	[85]	5255

WIGMO PRINCESS 5 ch m £0

6a	11-12	Wolv	12af	40	634 BL

WIGWAM WILLIE 2 b c £1714

74	4-13	York	5g/s		3431
71	5-15	Nott	5.1gd		3988
79	2-10	Redc	6gd		4244
42	19-21	Donc	6fm	[75]	4490

WILD PITCH 3 ch g £874

58a	7-14	Ling	10ap		473
59	12-20	Wind	10sft		1651
61	3-13	Good	9g/f	60	2024
39	12-16	Wind	11.6g/s	61	2621
49	6-9	Brig	9.9gd	60	2955

WILD POWER 6 b g £1483

57	4-16	Chep	10.2g/s	55	4365
61	2-19	Thir	12g/f	55	4594
57	4-19	Beve	9.9g/f	55	4720

WILD TIDE 5 b m £0

1	16-16	Ripo	8gd		2987
24	7-10	Carl	5.9fm		3545
19	7-13	Hayd	6gd		3757
9	9-12	Hami	8.3g/s		4007
30	10-15	Thir	8fm	[30]	4379

WILD WILD WES 4 ch g £0

2a	15-15	Ling	12ap		521
3a	13-13	Ling	10ap		715

WILDERBROOK LAHRI 4 b g £0

0	13-14	Sout	8af	45	60	bl

WILFORD MAVERICK 2 b c £0

70	7-9	Newm	6g/f		2531
40a	9-9	Sout	6af		3157
41	13-18	Donc	6g/s		3376
43a	10-12	Wolv	5.1ap		4922

WILFRED 3 b g £0

62	7-12	Wind	11.6g/s	72	1260
39	8-9	Wind	11.6g/f	70	1807

WILHEHECKASLIKE 3 b g £0

1a	8-10	Sout	8af	[45]	850	vis
1	8-8	Newc	6sft	[45]	963	vis
7a	9-10	Sout	5af	[40]	1408	vis
0	6-6	Ripo	6g/f	[35]	1975	vis T
1	17-18	Thir	6fm	35	3609	bl
0	6-6	Redc	14.1g/f	[30]	3771	

WILKO 2 ch c £490902

78	3-8	Kemp	5hvy		1510
88	7-11	York	6g/s		1687
90	1-7	YARM	6fm		2144*
103	3-11	Asco	7fm		2578
104	3-12	Newm	7g/f		3060
105	2-10	Good	7fm		3532
103	1-4	YARM	7g/f	[100]	3707*
103	2-5	Newb	7gd	[100]	3919
104	4-10	Donc	7fm	[100]	4493
105	3-8	Asco	8g/f	[100]	4797
120	1-4	LONE	8.5Fast	[100]	5310*

WILL HE WISH 8 b g £12975

91	12-17	Donc	6gd	[92]	952	bl
91a	8-8	Ling	7ap	[92]	1043	bl
100	5-7	Kemp	6gd	[92]	1137	
105	6-11	Leic	7g/s	[92]	1356	
97	7-9	Hayd	7.1g/f	[95]	1486	
69	18-20	Asco	7g/f	95	1926	
57	10-10	York	6gd	92	2357	
81	12-28	Asco	7g/f	92	2558	bl
76	13-15	York	7gd	87	3117	bl
92	1-11	YARM	7gd	84	3364*	bl
94	3-9	Kemp	8g/f	[89]	3689	bl
85	6-8	Sand	7.1g/s	89	3891	bl
94	2-13	Ripo	8gd	89	4279	bl
85	11-15	Donc	8fm	89	4531	bl
77	7-10	Hayd	8.1g/s	89	4767	bl

WILL THE TILL 2 b g £0

0	11-12	Chep	5.1gd		3728
53	9-16	Bath	5.7gd		4823
54	17-19	Leic	7gd		5055

WILLHECONQUERTOO 4 ch g £6015

58a	8-12	Ling	8ap	67	1613	t
38	15-16	Brig	7fm	64	2258	t
66	3-11	Good	6gd	64	2535	t
58	5-9	Epso	6g	63	2871	t
73	1-17	WIND	6fm	63	2975*	t
60	9-15	Wind	5gd	68	3165	t
25	14-16	Wind	6gd	69	3827	t
70	5-10	Wind	6g/f	[69]	3977	t
68	4-18	Bath	5.7g/f	69	4412	t
56a	4-12	Wolv	6ap	69	4984	t
31a	13-13	Wolv	6ap	69	5010	t p
64a	4-13	Wolv	6ap	[65]	5327	t p
66a	2-12	Wolv	5.1ap	[65]	5362	t p

WILLHEGO 3 ch g £4906

50	9-13	Folk	5sft		1575
35	8-14	Carl	7.9fm	52	1954
57a	2-14	Ling	10ap	52	2064
60a	3-14	Ling	10ap	54	3449
65	1-13	LING	10g/s	57	4182*
55a	5-16	Ling	12ap	[60]	4899
31	13-13	Pont	8g/s	[59]	5153
56a	8-16	Ling	12ap	[58]	5296

WILLHEWIZ 4 b c £11945

68	13-20	Donc	5gd	88	927	vis
75	5-9	Thir	5g/s	[85]	1217	vis
76	6-13	Yarm	6g/f	85	1726	
60	7-8	Donc	6g/f	[82]	2074	BL
84	1-8	SAND	5gd	[78]	2361*	vis
81	1-8	NEWM	6fm	[78]	2591*	vis
23	13-16	Wind	6fm	81	2758	vis
64	8-11	Newb	6g/f	81	2878	vis
69	16-22	Good	5fm	79	3537	vis
67	13-16	Newb	7g/f	77	3954	
78	4-11	Bath	6g/f	[77]	4201	
54	17-19	Kemp	6fm	76	4394	
62	10-12	Sand	5gd	[73]	4605	vis
76a	2-13	Wolv	6ap	70	5010	
60a	9-12	Wolv	6ap	73	5291	

WILLIAM JAMES 2 b g £0

58	5-5	Yarm	5.2gd		3993
42	11-11	Epso	7gd		4289 VIS
52a	6-12	Wolv	5.1ap		4922

WILLIAM TELL 2 b c £4766

71	6-8	Newb	7g/f		3267
76	4-11	Sand	8.1g/s		3890
77	5-11	Chep	8.1g/s		4363
83	2-12	Sali	8sft	76	4580
81	2-15	York	7.9gd	[78]	5002
79	2-12	Redc	8g/s	[78]	5107

WILLIAMS WELL 10 ch g £920

42	10-16	Newc	6sft	64	1277	bl
48	12-20	Thir	6gd	63	1638	bl
52	9-12	Newc	6g/f	61	2160	bl
58	5-13	Hayd	6gd	58	2884	bl
44	13-15	Newc	6gd	58	3424	bl
53	6-20	Hayd	6fm	57	3796	bl
57	3-12	Redc	6gd	[55]	4245	bl
60	3-20	Newc	6g/f	55	4408	bl
41	16-26	Ayr	5g/s	55	4618	bl
47	5-14	Catt	6gd	55	4967	bl

WILLJOJO 3 b f £6998

59	3-12	Catt	6gd	[54]	995	
41	5-13	Carl	5.9fm	[57]	1949	vis
43a	4-8	Sout	6af	[55]	2379	
57	1-17	LEIC	7gd	[52]	2704*	vis
60	1-10	CATT	7g/f	53	3016*	vis
58	5-7	Ayr	7.2gd	59	3153	vis

WILLOFCOURSE 3 b g £0

59	9-15	Leic	6g/f		1829

WILLYEVER 10 b g £0

2a	9-9	Sout	7af		661 vis T

WILOM 5 ch g £1046

49a	3-12	Ling	10ap	[42]	272	
48a	2-11	Ling	8ap	[45]	343	
39a	5-10	Ling	8ap	[45]	410	
42a	4-12	Ling	8ap	[45]	538	
39a	5-12	Ling	8ap	[45]	648	
39a	8-14	Ling	10ap	[45]	705	
25a	9-11	Ling	10ap	[40]	970	
0	12-12	Ling	8ap	[40]	1073	BL
0	6-8	Brig	8gd	[40]	1548	

WILSON BLUEBOTTLE 5 ch g £2712

35a	6-13	Wolv	8.5af	[42]	300	bl
47a	1-12	WOLV	9.4af	[46]	668*	bl
30a	8-13	Sout	8af	[46]	776	bl
50a	2-7	Wolv	9.4af	[45]	893	bl
50a	2-15	Sout	8af	45	1028	bl
40a	10-13	Wolv	9.4af	49	1223	bl
36a	8-15	Sout	8af	49	1755	bl
22	12-15	Redc	9g/f	45	2120	bl
30	9-13	Ayr	10gd	43	3325	bl
45a	6-13	Sout	8af	[48]	3482	bl
46a	6-11	Sout	8af	[48]	4090	bl

WILTSHIRE 2 br c £2967

59	12-14	Sand	7.1g/s		4069
25	13-14	Muss	7.1g/f		4171
51	10-14	Thir	8fm		4376
56	8-8	Sand	8.1gd		4608
59	1-8	BRIG	5.3fm		4759*
44	14-19	Ling	6g/f	[60]	4895
63	3-18	Newc	6g/f	59	5013

WIN ALOT 6 b g £0

0	10-10	Catt	13.8sft	45	5322

WIND CHIME 7 ch h £7352

44a	7-14	Ling	10ap	51	498
52a	2-10	Ling	8ap	49	766
26a	11-12	Ling	8ap	51	845
69	1-11	WARW	8.1fm	64	2600*
69	3-13	Kemp	7g/f	66	3034
52	11-12	Good	9fm	66	3625
57	7-12	Good	9g/f	66	4539
43a	7-13	Wolv	8.6ap	51	5365

WINDERMERE 5 b h £21809

116	1-6	LEOP	14g/f	[105]	2138*
51	12-12	Asco	22.2fm		2583

WINDERMERE ISLAND 2 b f £365

76	4-7	Yarm	6g/f		3709

WINDS OF MARCH 3 b f £7116

96	1-10	NEWB	10gd		1209*
95	4-7	Newb	10gd	[95]	1733

WINDS OF TIME 2 b f £8093

88	1-10	NEWM	6g/f		3063*

WINDSCREAMER 2 b f £8173

93	1-13	NEWB	7g/f		3252*
92	6-11	Newm	7g/f		3781
82	7-8	Donc	8fm		4476

WINDSOR BEAUTY 6 b g £0

9	7-9	Folk	15.4sft	52	1271

WINDSOR KNOT 2 ch c £31351

84	4-15	Sand	7.1g/f		3337
94	1-14	NEWM	7g/f		3752*
111	1-8	SAND	7.1g/s		4096*

WINDWOOD 2 b c £0

53	8-9	Sand	5gd		4497
59	7-16	Bath	5.7gd		4823
54a	5-13	Wolv	6ap		4980

WINDY BRITAIN 4 b f £10533

95a	3-14	Ling	10ap	[82]	82
88a	1-10	LING	10ap	[92]	179*
77	12-15	Kemp	10fm	88	2067
91	4-10	Newm	10fm	88	2592
93	2-6	Asco	10gd	87	3072
90	6-15	Good	9.9g/f	88	3506
85	8-20	Hayd	10.5fm	88	3794
80	7-12	Yarm	10.1sft	88	4149
103	7-14	Capa	10g/s	[88]	5244

WINDY PROSPECT 2 ch c £29728

74a	3-10	Ling	5ap		882
78	5-15	Donc	5gd		920
74	2-10	Muss	5gd		1550
85a	1-11	WOLV	6af		2051*
70	7-9	Asco	5g/f		2516
74	3-6	Muss	7.1g/f	80	3560
92	2-6	Hami	6g/f	80	3590
93	2-9	Redc	6g/f	84	3807
95a	1-13	SOUT	7af	84	4040*
102	1-14	HAMI	6sft	89	4692*

WING COLLAR 3 b c £11539

12	11-11	Ripo	12.3gd	66	1174
67	3-11	Redc	10sft	65	1663
70	3-15	Ripo	10g/f	65	1976
70	2-6	Beve	12.1g/s	66	2322
66	8-13	Redc	11g/s	68	2960

69 4-6 Beve 16.2g/s 66 3853
69 3-14 Redc 10fm 65 4342
75 1-12 BEVE 12.1g/f 65 4601*
78 2-12 Redc 14.1g/s 69 5108

WING COMMANDER 5 b g £23087
94 4-24 Donc 8gd 92 951
79 3-9 Pont 10hvy [93] 1068
81 9-11 Newm 7fm 93 2090
87 14-31 Asco 8g/f 93 2489
89 8-21 York 10.4gd 92 3118
101 1-10 PONT 8gd 90 3460*
77 16-21 Good 8fm 96 3565
95 3-10 Asco 8gd 93 3775
86 7-11 York 10.4g/s 95 4021
94 5-11 Epso 10.1gd [94] 4467
90 7-10 Ayr 8sft 93 4685
72 21-32 Newm 9g/f 94 4916 vis

WINGED DARGENT 3 b c £28615
77 1-8 PONT 10hvy 1067*
80 5-9 Sand 10g/s 80 1318
87 1-9 AYR 13.1sft 76 5068*
101 1-8 DONC 14.6sft 82 5204*
99 2-6 Muss 16g/s [96] 5334

WINGMAN 2 b c £13262
67 10-14 Newm 7g/f 3752
82 5-8 York 7gd 4326
101 1-11 GOOD 8g/f 4746*
97 3-4 Long 9hvy 5164

WINGS OF MORNING 2 ch g £4793
64a 8-12 Ling 10ap 116
56a 2-11 Sout 7af 207
69a 1-11 SOUT 7af 488*
56a 5-16 Wolv 7af 70 615
45a 6-8 Sout 7af [68] 744
68 3-16 Beve 7.5g/s 66 1163
31 11-11 Pont 8g/f 67 2040
61a 7-8 Sout 7af 66 2723 BL
43 3-5 Hami 9.2g/s [65] 3876 VIS
62a 4-11 Sout 6af [65] 4041 vis
19 11-15 Yarm 7g/s [63] 4587
39a 12-12 Wolv 7.1ap [60] 5325

WINGSPEED 2 b c £2087
79 5-10 Newb 9sft 3955
79 2-6 Epso 7g/f 4470
64 4-6 Brig 7fm 4760

WINNERS DELIGHT 3 ch g £10665
71 8-9 Kemp 9sft [83] 947
68 9-13 Kemp 9gd 80 1141
81 5-13 Sand 8.1g/s [80] 2126
79 5-11 Good 12gd 80 2538
85 3-16 Sand 10g/s 79 2919
79 7-11 Newm 10g/f 81 3236
74 8-14 Newb 10g/f 79 3961
80 3-13 Yarm 10.1gd 79 4613
65 6-11 Newm 14g/f 80 4919
88a 1-10 LING 12ap 78 5239+

WINNING PLEASURE 5 b g £972
64a 7-13 Wolv 6af 74 113
68a 5-9 Sout 7af 72 193
73a 2-11 Sout 6af 72 198 bl
61a 6-10 Sout 6af 72 390

WINNING VENTURE 7 b g £4301
80 6-20 Newm 6gd 86 1138
69 21-30 Newm 6g/f 86 1481
84 3-13 Donc 8gd [83] 2753
84 2-7 Ayr 7.2gd [82] 3326
81 7-19 Good 8g/f 82 3512
72 7-13 Ches 7.6sft 81 4103
83 2-8 Chep 7.1g/s [81] 4301
78 8-24 Newb 7g/f 81 4642 P
70a 10-12 Wolv 7.1ap 80 5159
50 18-20 Newm 7g/s 79 5286

WINSLOW BOY 2 b c £6905
28a 10-13 Wolv 8.5af 43
57 8-14 Nott 10gd 1241
55 4-13 Beve 12.1g/f 55 1836
51 6-14 Ling 11.5g/f 55 2014
59 1-11 YARM 11.5g/f 53 2346*
60 2-18 Hayd 14gd 58 2905

56 6-13 Sali 14.1gd 60 3454
61 3-9 Sand 14g/s 60 3893
53 6-10 Yarm 14.1g/s 59 4255
54 6-6 Muss 12gd [59] 4805
63 2-11 Ayr 15sft 56 5032

WINSLOW HOMER 3 b c £0
24 10-11 Wind 10gd 4125

WINTER MIST 2 gr f £0
12 17-20 Hayd 6gd 2882
12a 9-10 Ling 6ap 3818
15 11-12 Warw 7.1g/f 4418
13 15-16 Yarm 10.1g/s 5352

WINTER MOON 2 b f £0
48 9-10 Wind 6fm 3290

WINTHORPE 4 b g £7252
55a 10-10 Sout 6af 80 390
58a 10-13 Wolv 6af 77 482
64 12-22 Donc 6gd 80 921
45 10-19 Redc 6sft 78 1145
17 16-17 Donc 6g/s 75 1523
71 4-20 York 6g/f 72 2059
20 17-20 York 6g/f 71 2409
67 3-14 Newc 5g/s 69 2775
74 2-15 Beve 5sft 69 2942
47 16-16 Newm 5g/f 69 3033
69 5-17 Pont 5gd 72 3241
67 4-12 Newc 5gd 71 3427
65 4-10 Beve 5g/f [71] 3503
71 3-15 Redc 6fm 68 4562
47 15-20 Ripo 6gd 68 4785
68 6-19 York 6gd 67 4989 P

WISE DENNIS 2 b c £24564
64 7-7 Good 6g/f 1848
50 10-13 Epso 7g/f 2870
87 3-7 Yarm 6g/f 3709
85a 3-14 Ling 7ap 78 4177
87 3-11 Hayd 8.1fm 79 4387
93 1-12 ASCO 7g/f 80 4810*
104 2-9 Pont 8g/s [89] 5150

WISE OWL 2 b c £7885
87 2-8 York 6gd 2408
86 4-13 Newm 6gd 4223
88 1-10 PONT 6fm 4752*
47 14-15 York 6gd 88 4985

WISE WAGER 2 b f £18187
62a 2-7 Wolv 5af 1652
56 3-6 Carl 5fm 2442
70 3-10 Ripo 5gd 2983
71 3-7 York 5g/f 69 3432
77 1-10 THIR 5fm 66 3607*
79 2-13 Newm 5g/f 73 3943
79 2-10 Ches 5.1g/f 73 4049
76 7-13 Muss 5g/f 77 4551

WISTMAN 3 br c £5308
80 1-14 FOLK 7g/s 1080*
81 3-7 Beve 7.5sft 80 1305

WITCHES BROOM 3 b f £429
31a 8-9 Ling 8ap 1022
59 3-10 Ling 7gd 3446
47 6-8 Sand 8.1g/f 3858
35 16-20 Ling 6g/f 57 4317

WITCHING 3 b f £0
21 6-7 Folk 9.7gd 3385

WITCHRY 2 b c £6709
79 4-13 Newb 6g/f 1760
69 3-10 Newm 5fm 2089
91 1-10 PONT 5gd 3457*
77 7-13 Newm 5g/f 85 3943

WITCHY VIBES 2 ch f £0
11 14-14 Hayd 6sft 4769
16 13-13 Warw 7.1g/s 4996

WITH HONOURS 2 b f £0
34 7-9 Catt 7sft 5316

WITH REASON 6 ch g £23200
98 13-15 Newb 8g/f 1758 T

114 1-8 HAYD 8.1fm [115] 4386* t

WITHERING LADY 2 b f £5984
67 3-11 Warw 5gd 1123
71 4-14 Bath 5gd 1401
72 6-8 Good 5g/f 1816
79 2-11 Sali 5gd 2658
77 7-24 Newb 5.2g/f 3266
79 1-10 BEVE 5g/f 3504*
64 8-12 Wind 6gd 80 3825
63 5-8 Bath 5.7g/s [77] 4198
79 4-18 Wind 5g/f 75 4830

WITHORWITHOUTYOU 3 b f £750
80 6-7 Nott 5.1fm [90] 1004
75 5-5 Ripo 6gd [87] 1175
57 14-14 Bath 5gd [85] 1400
81 10-11 Warw 7.1fm [80] 2574
74 8-9 Newm 7fm 80 3006

WITHOUT CONNEXION 5 b h £0
106 7-9 San 12sft 5168

WITTILY 4 ch f £0
11a 13-16 Sout 5af [40] 374 bl

WITTY GIRL 2 b f £366
56 3-9 Chep 5.1g/f 2625
61 4-5 Brig 6fm 2833
36 11-12 Thir 6g/f 3411

WITWATERSRAND 2 b f £405
75 4-15 Kemp 7g/f 4710

WIZ IN 2 gr g £0
39a 8-12 Ling 6ap 4896
38a 11-12 Ling 8ap 5295

WIZARD LOOKING 2 b c £0
66a 6-11 Ling 8ap 73 54 T
67 6-12 Kemp 8g/f [71] 1915 t
64 10-12 Sand 7.1g/f 69 2098 t
39 16-20 Newb 7g/f 69 2314 t
57 6-10 Newm 8g/f [65] 2732 t
44a 7-12 Ling 8ap [60] 3286 BL t
39 7-14 Leic 8g/f [60] 3344

WIZARD OF EDGE 4 b g £318
52a 6-13 Ling 10ap [70] 338
58 8-19 Chep 12.1gd 70 3398
59 4-9 Newb 9gd 67 3922

WIZARD OF NOZ 4 b g £13730
77 22-31 Asco 8g/f 104 2489
98 5-7 York 7.9g/s 100 3077
97 5-12 Good 7fm [98] 3555
95 5-20 Newm 7g/f 95 3782 VIS
87 5-7 Thir 8g/s [95] 4208 vis
101 1-15 NEWM 7g/f 93 4891* BL
77 11-16 Newm 7sft 97 5101 bl

WIZARD OF THE WEST 4 b g £0
44 9-18 Newm 12fm 56 2088
35 13-16 Folk 12fm 53 2718
32 9-15 Folk 16.4g/s 49 3049

WIZARD OF US 4 b g £4625
62 1-17 AYR 7.2sft 50 5063*
40a 13-13 Wolv 8.6ap [58] 5212
62 2-16 Nott 8.2hvy 58 5347

WIZARDMICKTEE 2 b c £3822
66 8-12 Hayd 6sft 3272
73 2-11 Ches 7fm 3633
74 2-18 Ripo 6g/s 3939
68 4-5 Ches 6.1sft 4105
67 8-12 Muss 5g/f 77 4172
22 16-16 Nott 5.1hvy 74 5343

WIZARDS PRINCESS 4 b f £0
0 5-5 Catt 12sft 3934
38 8-9 Redc 9fm 4336

WIZZSKILAD 2 b c £1004
55a 7-9 Ling 5ap 931
76 4-8 Wind 5g/s 1053
56 6-15 Warw 5g/s 1325
66 3-11 Kemp 5hvy 1640
62 8-13 Nott 5.1gd 1987
60 4-9 Chep 5.1g/f 2625

56	10-15	Nott	5.1gd	[61]	3988
60	3-8	Wind	5g/s	[60]	4218

WODHILL BE 3 b f £865

20a	12-13	Ling	6ap		219
34a	5-5	Wolv	7af		425
58a	6-15	Ling	7ap		814
47a	5-7	Ling	8ap	52	910
42	9-19	Yarm	7g/f	50	1132
0	10-11	Pont	8sft	47	1425
46	3-13	Leic	7g/f	[45]	1827
40	11-12	Yarm	7fm	44	2864
0	13-14	Yarm	8gd	43	3363
30	8-10	Leic	7fm	[40]	3812
38	7-20	Yarm	8gd	40	3996
32	7-18	Chep	8.1gd	[40]	4485
44	2-16	Brig	7gd	[40]	4901
30	8-20	Yarm	6g/s	[40]	5121

WODHILL FOLLY 7 ch m £0

47a	4-12	Wolv	9.4af	45	427 vis
30a	6-9	Wolv	9.4af	[45]	525 vis
13a	8-9	Wolv	9.4af	45	620 vis

WODHILL GOLD 3 ch g £0

47	15-17	Newb	8g/f	1762

WODHILL HOPE 4 b f £849

59	4-10	Nott	14.1sft		1742
47	3-3	Yarm	11.5fm		2867
11	8-12	Newm	12g/f		3783
31	11-11	Yarm	14.1gd	48	3998
17	10-13	Warw	12.6g/s	[45]	4665
37	9-15	Leic	11.8gd	[40]	5060

WOLDS DANCER 2 b f £0

55	6-16	Ripo	6g/f	1780
65	7-12	Redc	6g/f	2119
37	7-8	Beve	7.5gd	2511

WOLF CUB 3 ch g £0

0	16-17	Ling	7g/s	1617

WOLF HAMMER 2 ch c £2709

73	7-10	Redc	7g/s	2959
70	2-4	Ripo	6g/f	3644
75	2-4	Newc	5hvy	4214

WOMAN IN WHITE 3 gr f £2262

62	8-13	Newb	7gd		1210
73	2-8	Good	9gd		2536
71	6-13	Kemp	10g/f		3038
75	3-14	Ling	11.5gd	[73]	3335
61	6-12	Sali	12g/f	73	3868

WON OF A FEW 4 b g £0

52a	9-13	Wolv	9.5ap	5290
37a	7-11	Wolv	5.1ap	5363

WONDER AGAIN 5 b m £86648

118	3-4	Lone	11g/s	5309

WONDER WOLF 3 b f £0

40	7-14	Donc	6g/f		2428
42	5-8	Redc	9g/f		3805
34	9-17	Pont	8g/f	48	4626

WONDERFUL MIND 2 b c £8913

42	8-12	Ripo	5gd		1173
70	5-8	Hayd	5gd		2241
77	2-7	Redc	5gd		2547
76	1-13	BEVE	5gd		2889*
73	5-10	York	5gd	73	3115
74	6-7	York	5gd	75	3432
77	3-10	Ches	5.1g/f	72	4049 BL
74	2-12	Muss	5g/f	71	4172
48	13-13	Muss	5gd	74	4551 bl
73	5-15	Ripo	5gd	73	4784 bl
63	7-11	Epso	5g/f	72	4907 bl

WONKY DONKEY 3 b g £1154

53a	3-9	Wolv	8.5af		751
50a	4-10	Wolv	8.5af		839
56a	3-12	Wolv	6af	53	1374
9	12-12	Leic	6fm	54	2111 T
52a	5-11	Sout	5af	54	2380
1	16-16	Ling	7gd	54	3024

WOOD DALLING 6 b g £3851

53	7-12	Ayr	7.2fm	56	1909
52	7-13	Carl	7.9fm	55	2447
47	6-12	Hami	9.2g/s	53	2832
58	1-14	CARL	6.9g/f	52	3229*
55	6-12	Ayr	8gd	58	3328
45	6-12	Ayr	9.1g/f	56	3766
26	10-15	Ayr	7.2hvy	56	4088
51	6-14	Carl	6.9g/f	55	4345
24	13-13	Muss	8g/f	[54]	4554

WOOD FERN 3 b c £5160

52a	9-13	Ling	10ap		148
53a	14-16	Ling	12ap	70	218
62a	1-15	LING	7ap	[65]	263*
47a	13-14	Ling	7ap	65	499
52	10-13	Kemp	7sft	77	945
17	12-18	Wind	8.3g/s	70	1059
0	11-11	Warw	8.1hvy	65	1536
51	5-12	Sali	7fm	[62]	2288
44	11-13	Ling	7.6g/f	57	2587
26	9-10	Brig	8gd	57	2954
28	15-17	Newb	7g/f	57	3257 VIS
18	13-15	Ling	7.6fm	52	3788
25	6-12	Hami	8.3g/s	[48]	4007
50	1-9	BRIG	7sft	[48]	4164* vis
0	20-20	Chep	7.1g/s	54	4367 vis
30	13-16	Yarm	7gd	49	4616
48	4-16	Chep	7.1hvy	[49]	4707
38	8-19	Kemp	8g/f	[47]	4795
24	10-13	Brig	8g/f	[46]	4902
44	3-19	Yarm	8g/s	[45]	5119

WOOD SPIRIT 2 b f £0

73	6-10	Sali	5g/f	1716
65	6-8	Sali	6sft	4577
66	4-12	Redc	8g/s	5107

WOOD SPRITE 2 b f £0

40	9-11	Donc	8sft	5205

WOOD STREET 5 b g £0

36	9-12	Bath	10.2fm	58	2036

WOODBURY 4 b f £11272

46a	7-14	Ling	6ap	58	121
49a	7-11	Ling	6ap	56	760
53a	4-13	Ling	6ap	53	902
62a	1-11	LING	6ap	53	3333*
41	16-17	Wind	6fm	62	3643
56	4-13	Good	6gd	62	3952
65	1-18	BATH	5.7g/f	58	4412+
64	7-13	Bath	5.7gd	64	4548
62	6-20	Nott	6.1g/s	64	4646
62a	2-12	Wolv	6ap	[57]	5155
56a	5-12	Ling	6ap	57	5241

WOODBURY LANE 2 b r f £0

64	5-12	Redc	8g/s	5107

WOODCOTE 2 b c £7466

93	1-14	WIND	5gd		4121*
98	3-11	York	6gd	[93]	4998

WOODCRACKER 3 ch g £37049

93	1-14	NOTT	10gd		1241*
96	2-13	York	10.4sft	87	1664
77	13-17	Asco	12g/f	90	2519
100	1-11	NEWM	10g/f	90	3029*

WOODFORD CONSULT 2 b f £207

49	8-16	York	7.9gd	4997
49a	10-12	Wolv	7.1ap	5179
62	3-8	Ayr	8sft	5273

WOODFORD WONDER 2 b f £0

21	18-20	York	6g/f	4401
17	14-16	Ripo	5gd	4787
38	10-13	Newc	5g/f	5012

WOODLAND BLAZE 4 b g £2037

79a	1-13	WOLV	5af	73	110*
52a	15-16	Sout	5af	78	171

WOODLAND GLADE 3 b f £3546

76	2-10	Newm	7gd	3921
76	2-10	Sali	8sft	4578
57	5-9	Leic	7gd	5041

WOODSLEY HOUSE 2 b c £7438

89	2-16	Sali	7g/s		3111
89	2-15	Sand	7.1g/f		3337
86	2-13	York	7.9gd		4325
93	5-13	Newb	7sft	[88]	5195

WOODSTOCK EXPRESS 4 b g £0

12	11-14	Bath	18.2fm	28	2417

WOODWIND DOWN 7 b m £3354

50	1-7	MUSS	12gd	45	2966*
41	8-9	Ayr	15gd	49	3327
8	18-19	Thir	12g/f	48	4594

WOODY VALENTINE 3 ch g £22770

77	4-12	Catt	10sft	75	1000
74	2-12	Redc	10sft	73	1144
85	1-10	PONT	10sft	74	1427*
83	6-18	Good	9g/f	80	1813
80	6-12	Sand	9g/f	80	2385
84	1-6	EPSO	10.1g/f	[80]	2874*
85	2-6	Hami	8.3g/f	[82]	3205
78	7-16	Good	9.9fm	82	3553
78	7-16	Redc	8g/f	82	3768
79	5-13	Epso	10.1g/f	81	4473
86	2-12	Good	8gd	[80]	4872
86	4-19	Donc	10.3sft	82	5201

WOOLFALL JOANNA 2 gr f £0

32	19-23	Newm	6gd	5084
33	14-16	Newm	7g/s	5280

WOOLLY BACK 3 b g £3404

79	2-4	Hayd	11.9g/s		1347
79	2-9	Hayd	11.9g/f		1885
61	6-13	Hayd	11.9g/s		2230
17	10-10	Newm	12sft	[80]	5102

WOOLSACK 2 ch c £0

85	5-13	Donc	7hvy	5200
73	6-14	Muss	7.1g/s	5330

WOOLSTONE BOY 3 ch g £0

53	13-18	Bath	10.2gd	5023
66	5-12	Nott	10hvy	5190

WOR KID 2 b r f £0

47	8-9	Carl	5.9gd	2671
39	9-10	Redc	7g/s	2959

WORCESTER LODGE 3 ch g £3549

72	1-17	NEWM	12g/f	62	3618*
45	13-17	Kemp	12sft	68	4033

WORD PERFECT 2 b f £17199

74	3-9	Newc	5sft		962
82	1-12	RIPO	5gd		1173*
96	1-4	DONC	5g/s		3224*
72	5-7	Ripo	6g/s	[93]	3935
73	6-10	Ripo	6gd	90	4306
85	5-10	Ayr	6g/s	85	4655
94	7-24	Redc	6fm	[85]	4928
89	3-15	York	6gd	85	4985
93	2-11	Newm	6sft	[86]	5270

WORLABY DALE 7 b g £0

27a	8-12	Wolv	16.2af	46	7
37a	4-10	Sout	16af	[45]	307
36a	4-12	Sout	16af	35	443
23a	7-10	Sout	16af	35	491
27a	6-9	Sout	16af	35	612

WORLD AT MY FEET 2 b f £8910

72	2-8	Thir	5g/s		1212
87	1-7	THIR	5g/s		1471*
87	3-10	Thir	5g/f		1764
76	9-10	York	5gd	87	3115
87	4-8	Ripo	5gd	[85]	4307
42	9-9	Ayr	6sft	[87]	4684
72	14-24	Redc	6fm	[87]	4928
64	4-7	Catt	5sft	[87]	5124 BL
26	16-21	Donc	6hvy	[85]	5202

WORLD MUSIC 2 b f £641

70	3-11	Bath	5g/s	4200
50a	6-12	Ling	6ap	4896

WORLD REPORT 2 b c £1289

82	4-9	York	6g/s	4026
63	6-15	Chep	7.1gd	4483

82 4-19 Leic 7gd 5055
63 5-14 Newb 6sft 5197

WORTH A GAMBLE 6 ch g £0
31a 8-10 Sout 11af [35] 2499

WORTH A GRAND 2 br g £0
71 7-8 Sali 7gd 2695
66 5-11 Sali 6g/s 3110
47 5-6 Brig 6fm 3671
29 11-12 Sali 8sft 66 4580
57 6-9 Chep 5.1hvy 66 4706
50a 5-12 Wolv 7.1ap [62] 5158

WORTH ABBEY 2 b c £0
68 8-15 Newb 7g/f 2876
53 10-20 Wind 6fm 2970
10 14-17 Wind 8gd 3975
59 8-10 Newb 6g/f 4637

WOTCHALIKE 2 ch c £7826
77 5-14 Newm 7g/f 3752
56 8-17 Ling 6gd 4443
84 2-13 Sali 7sft 4576
84 2-15 Sali 8gd [79] 4851
84 1-12 BATH 8sft [82] 5170*
84 6-9 Newm 10g/s [82] 5281

WOU OODD 3 ch f £1597
78 4-9 Sali 9.9g/f 1719
72 3-8 Ripo 10g/f 2012
75 5-8 Good 9.9gd 79 2377
75 4-8 Ches 12.3g/s 77 2746
47 13-15 Nott 10gd 75 3108

WRENLANE 3 ch g £10392
65 2-7 Pont 6g/f 2042
46 6-6 Redc 6gd 68 2551
64 5-13 Beve 7.5g/s 64 3179
51 9-10 Beve 8.5g/f 64 3501
56 4-9 Thir 8sft 63 3835
57 8-20 York 7.9gd 62 4321
59 3-13 Nott 10g/s [60] 4650
51 4-18 Newc 8g/f [60] 5017
68 1-13 PONT 8g/s [60] 5153*
68a 3-13 Wolv 9.5ap 64 5292
67a 1-13 WOLV 8.6ap [64] 5336*

WUB CUB 4 b f £0
30a 6-15 Sout 6af [45] 773
0 10-10 Sout 6af [40] 907
6a 10-10 Sout 5af [35] 1408

WUJOOD 2 b c £1396
75 7-11 Newm 7g/f 3234
52 10-16 Leic 7fm 3811
71 7-13 Warw 7.1g/f 4416
79 2-12 Bath 8sft 5170

WUNDERBRA 3 b f £21776
58 3-15 Folk 6g/s 1078
44a 4-12 Sout 7af 2339
48a 5-12 Sout 6af 2722
66 1-13 WIND 6fm 55 3479* T
61 3-9 Wind 5fm 60 3804 t
67 1-9 WIND 5g/f 60 3976* t
69a 1-11 SOUT 5af 61 4094* t
77 1-7 BRIG 5.3sft [60] 4169+ t
77 2-7 Good 5sft 73 4236 t
65 5-8 Hami 5g/s [74] 4822 t

WUNDERWOOD 5 b g £52036
81 9-20 Newm 12gd 90 1172
87 9-17 Newb 12g/f 90 1759
98 1-9 NEWM 12g/f [89] 2246*
104 1-13 ASCO 12fm 92 2582*
106 1-7 ASCO 12fm [99] 3464*
104 3-8 Donc 12fm 104 4534

WUXI VENTURE 9 b g £0
57 7-11 Beve 9.9sft 66 1633
65 6-14 Hami 8.3gd 66 1748
47 9-12 Beve 8.5gd 65 2890
38 18-19 Beve 9.9g/f 63 3505
36 12-14 York 10.4g/f 62 4402

WYATT EARP 3 b g £9863
48 12-19 Newm 6g/s 77 1154
78 1-11 NEWB 6gd 74 1734*

52 10-12 Bath 5.7gd 76 3146
77 7-12 Newm 6gd 76 4229
67 9-19 Kemp 6fm 75 4394
81 2-15 Kemp 6g/f 74 4713
79a 3-13 Ling 7ap 74 4897

WYCHBURY 3 ch c £8920
64 5-14 Brig 6fm [79] 1690
72 2-12 Thir 7g/f [77] 1971
75 2-8 Brig 7fm [74] 2259
71 8-13 Sand 8.1gd 74 2365
66 1-9 THIR 7g/f [75] 3413*
73 5-13 Ling 7g/f 75 3604
66 8-12 Sand 10gd 73 4502
64 9-12 Epso 8.5gd 73 4909

WYOMING 3 ch f £1910
62 3-17 Ling 7g/s 1617
58 8-12 Sand 10gd 60 2366
54 8-18 Leic 10gd 59 2706
34 7-10 Folk 12g/s 59 3051
57 3-13 Folk 12gd 56 4119
50 7-12 Good 16g/s 56 4235
57 3-18 Pont 12g/f 55 4938

WYVERN 3 b c £0
47 8-13 Leic 10g/f 4453

XAARA DOON 2 b f £0
48a 9-14 Ling 7ap 5257

XAARIST 2 b c £0
35 12-20 Newc 6sft 2682
31 11-11 Newc 7gd 3429

XALOC BAY 5 br g £6353
28a 10-16 Sout 6af 54 92 bl
54a 2-8 Sout 7af [52] 320
24a 8-11 Wolv 7af [55] 440 p
0 12-13 Sout 6af 55 500 vis
57a 1-8 SOUT 8af [52] 577*
59a 1-12 LING 8ap [52] 675*
58a 2-9 Ling 8ap [53] 717
59a 3-10 Ling 8ap 56 769
54a 6-13 Sout 7af [56] 858
48 7-18 Catt 7gd [56] 996
54a 3-7 Wolv 8.5af [56] 1341
42a 7-15 Sout 8af 54 1755
35a 6-13 Wolv 8.5af [53] 2052
13 12-12 Hayd 6g/s [49] 2186

XANADU 8 ch g £2560
0 13-13 Muss 7.1g/s 50 1463
53 2-15 Hami 6gd 50 1508 p
36 13-14 Muss 7.1gd 53 1794 p
28 9-14 Ayr 6g/f 53 1898 p
41 10-16 Ayr 5g/f 53 2029 p
48 6-13 Hami 6g/f 51 2315 p
55 2-16 Carl 5.9fm 51 2445 p
27 15-19 Beve 5gd 51 2512 p
35 10-14 Hami 6gd 53 3129 p
50 6-18 Carl 6g/f 53 3228 p
51 5-20 Redc 6g/f 51 3767 p
38 7-20 Newc 6g/f 50 4408 p

XEBEC 2 b c £0
55 8-13 York 6gd 4988
37 11-12 Bath 8sft 5170

XEERAN 2 b f £1123
58 5-6 Sand 5g/f 2097
56 5-6 Warw 5fm 2437
63 5-13 Kemp 6g/f 4358
64 4-13 Leic 6gd 62 4697
64 3-18 Pont 6g/f 61 4934
24 13-14 Nott 6.1hvy [61] 5342

XEIGHT EXPRESS 2 b f £0
19 8-10 Thir 6fm 2461
24 13-20 Hayd 6gd 2882
14 9-9 Ches 5.1g/f 3097
37 10-14 Thir 7g/s 4206

XELLANCE 7 b g £0
2 29-29 Asco 20g/f 75 2471

XIXITA 4 ch f £0
26a 6-10 Wolv 12af [45] 315
43a 4-7 Sout 14af [45] 376

12a 8-9 Sout 16af [40] 576

XPRES DIGITAL 3 b c £1318
59 13-15 Sout 7gd 75 1282 t
71 4-14 Ripo 6g/s 75 1360 t
67 8-17 Warw 7.1sft 74 1526 t
68a 3-13 Wolv 6af 73 2053 t
55 11-11 Ripo 6gd 72 2985 t
42a 11-13 Sout 6af 69 4091 t

XPRESSIONS 3 b g £0
46 6-13 Beve 12.1g/f 50 1836
43 6-8 Beve 12.1g/f 50 2164

XSYNNA 7 b g £640
35a 10-16 Ling 7ap [47] 180
36a 9-15 Ling 7ap [47] 216
44a 3-13 Ling 6ap [45] 340 vis
15a 14-15 Ling 7ap [45] 411 vis
30a 6-14 Ling 6ap [45] 709
5a 7-8 Sout 7af [40] 847 P
34 3-10 Warw 6.1g/s [40] 1327 vis
30 10-17 Bath 5g/f 37 2981
43 7-7 Leic 6g/f [34] 3518

XTRA TORRENTIAL 2 b c £10319
91 1-13 YORK 7.9gd 4325*
93 4-9 Newm 8sft 5099

YAAHOMM 3 ch c £5640
80 3-5 Newb 11gd 1211
74 1-12 RIPO 9g/f 1784*
55 8-8 Ches 10.3gd [79] 2283
63 7-7 Pont 10g/f [77] 2994 VIS

YAHESKA 7 b m £0
7 13-14 Yarm 14.1g/s [35] 5123

YAJBILL 2 b c £28781
84 2-13 York 6gd 3120
89 3-4 Newm 6fm 3406
80 2-13 Pont 6gd 3682
83 2-9 Good 6gd [82] 3951
87 1-10 BRIG 6g/s [81] 4139* VIS
100 1-14 EPSO 6g/f 83 4471* vis
103 1-6 SALI 6gd [95] 4854* vis
96 5-11 York 6gd [95] 4998 vis

YAKIMOV 5 ch g £0
83a 11-15 Ling 7ap 85 887
32 26-27 Newb 8gd 92 1231
7 14-14 Kemp 8hvy 89 1512
78 10-13 Kemp 7gd 86 2172

YALLAMBIE 5 b m £0
39 6-7 Warw 10.9g/s [57] 1326 T
0 6-7 Wolv 8.5af [50] 1672 t

YAMATO PINK 2 ch f £2947
42a 4-10 Wolv 8.5af [53] 28
36a 7-15 Sout 7af [49] 87
24a 15-15 Ling 7ap 46 901
48a 1-7 LING 6ap [40] 1453*
54 2-16 Ling 6g/f 50 1985
47 5-18 Sali 7fm 52 2292
52 3-13 Warw 6.1fm 52 2439
45 11-20 Chep 6.1g/s 52 4368
50 4-9 Thir 6g/f 51 4595
34 6-15 Brig 6gd [50] 4905

YANKEEDOODLEDANDY 2 b g £20711
44a 4-10 Sout 8af 50 190
60a 1-9 WOLV 9.4af 45 351*
50a 2-10 Ling 8ap [45] 410
70a 1-6 SOUT 8af 57 506*
72a 2-9 Sout 11af 65 608
75a 1-10 SOUT 12af 65 796*
78 2-12 Catt 12gd 72 1000
75 3-9 Hayd 11.9gd 75 2900
78 2-10 Newm 10fm 75 3404 P
79 3-9 Hayd 14gd 77 3760
82 2-3 Ripo 12.3g/s 77 3940
82 2-8 Hami 13g/s 77 4138 p

YANKEY 2 b c £0
27 14-15 Good 8g/s 4233
3 5-5 Epso 8.5gd 4464
15 10-10 Beve 7.5g/f 4602
0 13-14 Yarm 8g/s 5118

YARDSTICK 2 ch c £0
57	7-8	Epso	7gd		3214
67	6-14	Chep	8.1gd		4484
65a	9-11	Ling	8ap		4744
53	11-15	Pont	10g/f	[65]	4933
44	19-20	Yarm	8g/s	60	5349

YASHIN 3 b g £7776
52	13-16	Ling	7g/f	[65]	1982
22a	10-14	Sout	6af	[60]	2502
66	3-10	Newm	8g/f	[60]	2732
64	2-9	Epso	7gd	59	3218
35	10-12	Yarm	7gd	60	3490
56	4-8	Folk	7g/f	60	3724
0	14-14	Newm	7gd	[59]	4195
50	3-15	Yarm	7g/s	[57]	4587
64	1-18	LEIC	10gd	[53]	5042*
55a	4-11	Wolv	12.2ap	59	5180
69a	2-11	Wolv	7.1ap	[64]	5357

YAWMI 4 ch c £0
| 74 | 11-11 | Sand | 10g/s | [110] | 1350 |
| 0 | 8-8 | Newb | 13.3g/f | [109] | 1757 |

YDRAVLIS 6 ch m £0
| 0 | 11-11 | Ling | 12ap | | 2588 |

YEATS 3 b c £89060
| 120 | 1- | LEOP | 10sft | | 1302* |
| 117 | 1-4 | LEOP | 10g/s | | 1700* |

YEHUDI 2 b c £22134
| 108 | 1-3 | LEOP | 9hvy | | 5314* |

YELDHAM LADY 2 b f £1214
65	7-10	Newm	6g/f		3064
47	13-18	Leic	7g/f		3342
50a	2-8	Ling	6ap		3745
40	7-9	Yarm	6sft	50	4146
46	7-15	Folk	6g/f	[50]	4369
51	3-16	Yarm	8g/s	50	4632 P

YELLOW RIVER 3 b g £0
35a	11-14	Ling	10ap	60	230
49a	4-12	Wolv	9.4af	57	464
3a	10-12	Wolv	9.4af	57	513
19a	8-10	Wolv	7af	53	685
10	12-14	Ling	7sft	40	1625 p
0	14-16	Nott	6.1gd	[40]	1989 BL

YENALED 6 gr g £28154
34a	5-8	Wolv	9.4af	65	157
60a	3-11	Sout	8af	62	457
53a	8-13	Sout	7af	60	556 p
61a	5-11	Sout	7af	60	585 p
9a	9-12	Wolv	9.4af	58	747
50	11-19	Donc	10.3gd	60	924
46a	4-14	Bath	8af	55	1198
56	5-14	Hami	8.3gd	56	1504
64	1-11	BEVE	9.9sft	56	1633*
70a	1-15	SOUT	8af	60	1755*
73	2-14	Ches	12.3gd	63	2285
75	2-15	Ches	10.3g/f	68	3099
70	4-19	Beve	9.9g/f	69	3505
75	2-17	Hami	9.2g/s	69	4008
74	1-8	MUSS	9g/f	[69]	4173+
61	7-11	Muss	9g/f	[72]	4550
69	4-17	Ayr	9.1g/s	[72]	4620
72	1-6	MUSS	12gd	[72]	4805*
82	1-11	CATT	12sft	[70]	5128*

YEOMAN LAD 4 b g £276
53	15-16	Good	7g/f	76	1817
48	11-14	Wind	10g/f	72	2265 VIS
71	4-8	Wind	8.3g/f	72	2448 vis
47	5-5	Sali	9.9gd	69	2694 vis
13a	8-13	Ling	10ap	[69]	3025 vis

YESTERDAY 4 b f £10053
95	5-6	Leop	8g/f		4572
113	4-10	Long	10g/f		4953
112	5-4	Lone	11g/s		5309 VIS

YLANG YLANG 3 ch f £3641
65a	4-12	Sout	8af		460
72a	1-12	WOLV	9.4af		686*
39a	6-10	Sout	12af	72	796

YMLAEN 3 b f £0
| 39a | 7-9 | Wolv | 8.5af | 73 | 2 |

YNYS 2 b c £0
36a	7-12	Ling	8ap	[42]	78
16a	10-16	Sout	8af	[42]	164
0	12-16	Sout	8af	[40]	442
0	11-12	Wolv	9.4af	[35]	668

YOB 4 b c £0
| 11a | 13-16 | Sout | 6af | 40 | 166 t |
| 5a | 8-10 | Wolv | 6af | 33 | 246 vis t |

YOMALO 4 ch f £6777
55	11-20	Ripo	5gd	67	1179
55	8-16	Bath	5.7sft	67	1540
64	5-8	Bath	5.7fm	65	2034
59	6-17	Wind	6g/f	64	2451
66	2-14	Yarm	6g/f	62	2855
61	5-15	Newc	6gd	64	3424
53	6-9	Yarm	6g/f	64	3705
71	2-20	Nott	6.1g/s	64	4646
79	1-19	WIND	6g/f	67	5053*

YORK CLIFF 6 b g £960
63a	12-16	Sout	7af	80	419
73a	5-13	Ling	10ap	75	519
64a	4-7	Wolv	12af	75	642
73a	5-7	Ling	12ap	75	695
60	7-17	Ayr	9.1g/s	[76]	4620
71	4-11	Ayr	10sft	76	5037
54	12-15	Nott	8.2hvy	76	5191

YORKER 5 b g £10052
55a	8-13	Wolv	8.5af	68	44
47a	8-15	Sout	11af	66	196
69a	2-11	Wolv	7af	66	241
46a	8-13	Wolv	8.5af	66	251
70a	2-11	Wolv	7af	68	363
69a	5-13	Wolv	8.5af	69	439
70a	3-11	Sout	7af	68	585
70a	4-12	Wolv	8.5af	68	632
71a	2-12	Wolv	7af	67	704
68a	2-6	Wolv	12af	[67]	752
41a	7-11	Wolv	8.5af	67	806
55a	10-12	Wolv	7af	67	840
57	7-12	Hayd	8.1g/f	65	1485
64a	3-15	Sout	8af	65	2338
53a	6-12	Sout	7af	[65]	2496
44	12-14	Beve	7.5g/s	60	4241
66	1-11	HAMI	6g/s	57	4818* BL
66	3-19	Newc	7g/f	62	5014 bl
42a	10-12	Wolv	7.1ap	62	5112 bl
56a	11-13	Wolv	9.5ap	60	5292 bl
20	14-16	Nott	8.2hvy	62	5347 bl

YORKES FOLLY 3 b f £633
54	7-9	Ripo	6g/f		2485
46	8-11	Carl	6.9gd	56	2936
18	10-10	Hami	6g/f	54	3203
9	12-12	Carl	5.9g/f	50	3655
47	3-9	Thir	6fm	[45]	4380 VIS
44	5-17	Thir	6g/f	45	4595 vis
10	16-19	Redc	6g/s	[45]	5110 vis

YORKIE 5 b g £6072
54a	1-14	LING	6ap	[58]	819*
49a	10-11	Sout	5af	64	859
51a	11-14	Ling	6ap	64	874
46	7-15	Brig	5.3g/f	56	1371
57	2-10	Brig	5.3g/f	53	2044
58	2-12	Brig	5.3g/f	54	2645
51	7-17	Catt	5g/f	54	2846
56	4-15	Bath	5.7g/f	56	3966
57	3-13	Brig	5.3g/f	56	3984
43	8-12	Brig	5.3g/s	56	4140

YORKIES BOY 9 gr g £6571
49	5-14	Kemp	5g/f	56	1914
55	4-14	Wind	5g/f	54	2266
45	7-18	Ling	6gd	54	2396
47	9-13	Warw	5fm	53	2599
36	12-14	Ling	6gd	51	3289
43	8-15	Chep	5.1gd	51	3403 p
50	4-16	Wind	5fm	48	3640 p
25	10-12	Newm	6g/f	48	3751 p
49	3-12	Newm	6g/f	46	3942 p
55	1-20	CHEP	6.1g/s	46	4368* p
56	1-16	FOLK	6g/f	[46]	4370* p
41	12-20	Chep	7.1gd	52	4488 p
28	10-19	Yarm	6g/s	53	4636 p
53	5-19	Ling	5g/f	53	4739 p
43	6-14	Catt	6gd	55	4967 p
45	10-19	Bath	5.7sft	54	5176 p

YORKSHIRE BLUE 5 b g £18457
42	7-13	Muss	7.1g/s	50	1463
39	7-18	Ayr	7.2g/f	48	1897
56	1-10	AYR	7.2g/f	48	2027*
60	1-12	DONC	7gd	52	2235*
54	9-14	Thir	7fm	58	2466
55	5-17	Newb	6g/f	58	3257
64	1-16	REDC	7g/f	57	3809+
48	10-17	York	7g/f	61	4398
28	13-18	Ayr	7.2sft	61	4622

YORKSHIRE LAD 2 b c £0
69	8-15	Donc	5gd		920
57	6-13	Pont	6g/s		3682
59	5-18	Ripo	6g/s		3939

YORKSHIRE SPIRIT 3 b g £0
| 21 | 9-11 | Newc | 8sft | | 1279 |

YOSHKA 3 ch c £16036
78	3-5	Leic	11.8g/s	78	1355
85	1-7	RIPO	12.3g/f	76	2528*
93	1-6	CATT	15.8g/f	81	3015*
95	2-9	Good	14fm	87	3556
80	11-15	Donc	14.6fm	92	4491

YOU FOUND ME 2 b f £550
66	8-19	Newb	6g/f		2310
68	6-14	Folk	7fm		2714
69	3-11	Chep	8.1g/s		4296
66	9-16	Nott	10g/f	67	4848
63	6-19	Pont	8g/s	65	5147

YOUNG ALEX 6 ch g £1182
63	5-16	Sali	8gd	67	4334 p
71	2-16	Sali	7sft	65	4582 VIS
33	19-20	Leic	7gd	68	5046 vis

YOUNG BOLDRIC 2 b g £0
38	13-15	Wind	6gd		3163
38	9-17	Wind	6g/f		3975
29	10-11	Chep	7.1hvy		4703

YOUNG DYNASTY 4 ch g £0
56a	7-12	Ling	8ap		514
44a	5-10	Ling	8ap		785
6a	5-8	Ling	10ap		829
52	10-17	Ling	7g/s	[45]	1617 BL
32a	5-6	Wolv	7af	[45]	1804 bl
2	16-16	Good	9gd	45	2220 bl
0	17-17	Chep	8.1g/s	40	3087 bl

YOUNG KATE 3 b f £0
54	6-19	Redc	6g/f		5110
35a	12-14	Ling	7ap		5240
28a	8-11	Wolv	5.1ap		5363

YOUNG LOVE 3 ch f £300
57	8-20	Wind	10sft		1651
58	6-8	Ling	9g/f		2013
53	4-10	Chep	8.1g/f	55	2624
28	14-16	Ling	9gd	54	3024
37	6-8	Chep	8.1gd	52	3731 VIS
41	4-9	Brig	7sft	[49]	4164
43	4-14	Bath	8g/f	45	4411
41a	4-14	Ling	10ap	[45]	4661

YOUNG MICK 2 br g £928
67	13-15	Newm	7fm		3005
72	3-14	Ling	7.6g/f		3601
73	4-12	Beve	5.8sft		4257
29	13-20	Yarm	8g/s	73	4635

YOUNG MR GRACE 4 b c £37423
58	15-22	Donc	6gd	78	921
75	3-13	Redc	7sft	[75]	1142
74	4-16	Thir	7g/s	75	1474
78	2-12	Hayd	8.1g/f	74	1883
71	5-9	Muss	8fm	[74]	2087
82	1-10	CARL	6.9gd	74	2935*
75	6-9	Donc	8g/s	76	3225
82	2-9	Beve	7.5gd	76	3310

85 1-8 HAYD 8.1fm 78 3797*
84 3-10 Hami 8.3g/s 80 4136
74 9-13 Ripo 8gd 80 4279
89 1-10 AYR 8sft 80 4685*
80 5-10 Hayd 8.1g/s 86 4767
74 16-18 York 7gd 85 5000
82 5-10 Catt 7sft 84 5320

YOUNG OWEN 6 b g £0
22a 5-8 Wolv 12af [70] 347
15a 9-10 Wolv 12af [70] 359

YOUNG PATRIARCH 3 b c £0
56 10-11 Newm 10gd 1148
2 16-16 Brig 11.9fm 63 1693
31 13-17 Hayd 8.1gd 63 2243

YOUNG ROONEY 4 b c £10383
69 4-8 Leic 10g/f 69 3514
38 11-12 Hayd 11.9gd 69 3734
69 3-8 Ayr 10hvy 68 4084
72 2-14 Carl 9.3g/f [68] 4347
75 2-16 Ches 10.3g/f 68 4515 P
73 6-10 Hayd 8.1g/s 70 4767 BL
76 3-11 Redc 10m 70 4931
63 2-13 Ayr 10sft [70] 5066
71 6-17 Redc 10sft 70 5307
98 3-6 Donc 12sft [70] 5369

YOUNG THOMAS 2 ch g £3975
36 13-19 Kemp 6g/f 1911
63 4-7 Muss 7.1g/f 2810
72 4-11 Warw 7.1gd 3053
70 3-9 Ches 7sft 72 4074
68 3-9 Newc 8sft 72 4285
71 5-11 Ayr 8sft 70 4688
0 19-19 Pont 8g/s 69 5147

YOUNG TIGER 3 b c £10282
109 2-4 Sain 10g/s 1696

YOUNG VALENTINO 2 ch g £0
34 12-14 Newb 6sft 5197

YOUNG WARRIOR 3 b g £0
10 16-16 Newc 7sft 966
59 6-7 Muss 8fm 2081
30 6-7 Carl 9.3fm 2443

YOUNGS FORTH 4 b f £0
30a 10-11 Wolv 7af 45 558
23a 8-14 Ling 6ap [45] 709
36a 5-14 Ling 7ap [45] 783 T
32a 5-13 Wolv 8.5af [40] 894
0 P-9 Ling 8ap [40] 1185 VIS

YOUR JUST LOVELY 2 b f £0
49a 10-10 Ling 5ap 13
40a 14-15 Ling 7ap 60 815
0 9-9 Leic 6g/s [60] 1015

YOURS SINCERELY 2 ch c £432
50 4-7 Leic 6g/f 1964

YSOLDINA 2 gr f £7711
102 3-9 Deau 8sft 5243

ZABADANI 2 ch f £0
59a 9-12 Ling 8ap 5293

ZABADOU 3 b g £0
42 9-12 Hayd 8.1sft - 1108
2 6-8 Ripo 10g/s 1363
23a 7-8 Sout 6af [40] 1588

ZABEEL PALACE 2 b c £257
80 7-9 Asco 7gd 3126
74 5-7 Thir 7g/f 3412
83 4-4 Yarm 7g/f 3707

ZACHY BOY 2 b g £0
63a 6-10 Ling 5ap 1071
60 7-9 Yarm 5.2g/f 1133
59 5-15 Warw 5g/s 1325
31 11-11 Kemp 5hvy 1640
26 17-18 Chep 6.1gd 2194
44 6-8 Wind 6ap 2449
57 6-9 Chep 5.1g/f 2625 P
54 5-8 Yarm 6fm 2865 p
60 4-8 Bath 5g/f 2977 BL

54 6-9 Bath 5g/f [58] 3847 bl

ZADALRAKIB 2 ch c £0
77 5-19 Newm 7g/s 5285

ZAFARSHAH 5 b g £12462
63a 1-15 LING 7ap [58] 366*
58a 4-14 Ling 7ap 58 499 vis
65a 1-13 LING 7ap 57 565*
64a 4-15 Ling 7ap 62 698
61a 6-14 Ling 7ap 62 1010
65 2-12 Bath 8g/f 62 1792
58a 8-11 Ling 8ap 62 2018
64 3-7 Good 7gd 63 2223
52 8-11 Warw 8.1fm 63 2600
55 11-20 Chep 7.1g/s 62 3088
60 4-12 Kemp 8g/f 60 3524 vis
25 10-10 Nott 8.2g/f 60 3579 vis
65 1-19 CHEP 8.1g/s [59] 4366*
61 5-17 Nott 8.2gd 64 4862

ZAFFEU 3 ch g £6631
49a 10-13 Ling 10ap 601
71a 6-14 Ling 10ap 759
72a 6-13 Ling 12ap 873
72 2-19 Warw 10.9gd 69 1124
73 4-6 Pont 12sft 70 1429
67 5-9 Donc 10.3g/f 70 2079
72 1-4 BATH 11.7fm [69] 2413*
70 8-10 Sali 12gd 71 2660
24 6-6 Nott 10g/f 70 3578
48 11-12 Bath 11.7g/f 69 3845
55 12-17 Hayd 10.5fm 66 4388 BL
46 9-11 Yarm 11.5g/s [65] 4584 bl
46 11-19 Bath 11.7gd 60 5024
60 2-7 Yarm 11.5g/s [55] 5351

ZAGALA 3 b f £5132
61a 2-10 Wolv 7af [55] 4 T
63a 1-12 WOLV 7af 55 68* t
56a 3-15 Ling 7ap [61] 117 t
64a 2-10 Wolv 6af 61 282 t
47a 9-10 Sout 6af 63 657 t
66a 2-13 Wolv 6af 63 1221 t
44a 7-12 Sout 7af [65] 2496 t
47a 8-15 Sout 7af [64] 2999 t
48a 9-11 Ling 6ap 62 3333 t
50a 6-12 Wolv 6ap [60] 5155 t

ZAGREUS 2 gr g £557
74 3-10 Beve 7.5g/f 4602

ZAHUNDA 4 b f £3385
33a 10-13 Wolv 9.4af 51 38
41a 9-16 Sout 7af [49] 161
21a 9-13 Sout 8af 49 228
27a 6-11 Ling 8ap [45] 408
31a 7-12 Wolv 7af [40] 528 P
43a 2-12 Wolv 8.5af 40 564
11a 7-9 Wolv 9.4af 40 620
44a 4-13 Wolv 8.5af [40] 699
29a 6-12 Wolv 8.5af [40] 777
46a 3-5 Wolv 8.5af 40 861
34a 3-13 Wolv 8.5af [40] 894
22 6-10 Warw 8.1g/s [40] 1328
32 4-14 Hayd 8.1g/s 40 1348
20 9-17 Chep 8.1g/s 38 3087
41 2-14 Ayr 7.2gd [37] 3324
40 4-8 Muss 7.1g/f 37 3528
36 5-9 Ayr 7.2g/f [40] 3764
0 14-15 Ayr 7.2hvy 38 4088
0 10-13 Ayr 8sft [40] 5275

ZAK ATTACK 3 ch g £0
50 19-20 Newm 8g/f 3237

ZAK FACTA 3 b g £1036
52a 5-16 Ling 7ap 57 20 vis
44a 4-14 Sout 8af 56 99 vis
46a 7-15 Ling 7ap 54 151 vis
21a 15-16 Sout 7af 52 208 vis
56a 5-13 Sout 6af [50] 444 vis
54a 5-16 Ling 7ap 50 600 vis T
52a 2-13 Sout 6af [50] 659 vis t
52a 4-13 Ling 7ap 50 761 vis t
53a 6-11 Sout 6af [50] 869 vis t
11a 8-9 Sout 6af 50 1194 vis
37 11-17 Nott 6.1sft 50 1606

32 11-15 Thir 7gd 50 1635 vis
29 7-13 Leic 7g/f [47] 1827 vis
0 11-12 Wolv 9.4af 47 2054 vis
0 11-11 Wolv 6af [45] 2202 vis

ZAKFREE 3 b g £3774
69a 2-8 Ling 10ap [66] 626 bl
68 2-6 Newc 10.1sft [66] 4286 bl
68 2-18 Wind 10g/s [66] 4944 bl
53 6-8 Ayr 10sft [66] 5034 bl

ZALAAL 2 b c £1199
73 6-15 Ling 7gd 3285
82a 2-11 Ling 8ap 3786
0 9-9 Yarm 8sft 4147

ZALAM 4 b g £0
52 15-15 Nott 10gd 74 4860

ZALDA 3 ch f £7820
70 1-8 BEVE 12.1g/f 59 2164*
60 6-7 Ripo 12.3g/f 66 2528
61 5-18 Hayd 14gd 64 2905
7 13-13 Sali 14.1gd 61 3454
70 1-10 SALI 14.1gd 61 3887* VIS

ZALEBE 3 b f £2723
0 12-12 Leic 8fm 2106
60 7-14 Warw 7.1gd 4275
53 1-15 YARM 7g/s 4587*
45 11-17 Leic 7gd 55 5056

ZALKANI 4 ch g £1590
64a 3-14 Ling 10ap [51] 430
57a 3-9 Ling 10ap [67] 476
48a 12-12 Ling 8ap 63 607
14 13-14 Folk 9.7g/s 56 1083
40 9-18 Nott 8.2g/s 53 1778
49 5-16 Yarm 10.1fm 51 2146
27 10-15 Warw 10.9g/f 49 2910
24 11-17 Chep 8.1g/s 49 3087
34 4-14 Chep 10.2g/s 47 3895
43a 11-13 Ling 10ap [61] 4112
30 8-15 Chep 10.2g/s 45 4299
59a 2-14 Ling 10ap [57] 4661

ZALONGO 2 ch c £4193
84 1-14 YARM 7sft 5250*

ZAMBEZI RIVER 5 ch g £0
33 11-11 Bath 8g/s 1101
34a 7-8 Wolv 8.5af 1220
0 17-17 Ling 7g/s 1617
42 6-14 Leic 6g/f 1963
5 12-20 Chep 6.1gd 50 2372
0 8-8 Chep 7.1sft [45] 4055
27 15-15 Chep 5.1gd 40 4489
18 11-19 Kemp 6g/f [40] 4793

ZAMBOOZLE 2 ch c £823
80 4-12 Good 7fm 3568
65 7-14 Sali 8g/s 4078

ZAMEEL 3 b g £0
40 12-13 Thir 12g/f 1768

ZAMEYLA 3 b f £15756
56 8-15 Leic 6g/f 1829
74 2-16 Newm 7fm 2092
77 2-6 Yarm 7g/f 2342
87 1-10 SALI 8sft [74] 4578*
84 1-10 LEIC 8gd [74] 4702*
58 11-14 Hami 8.3g/s 89 4820
58 10-13 Bath 8sft 83 5172

ZAMIR 5 ch g £0
2 11-11 Catt 12sft [30] 5128 VIS

ZAMYATINA 5 br m £0
41 11-15 Sout 7gd 53 1282
27 12-15 Thir 7gd 50 1635
41 7-14 Leic 8g/f 47 2402
23 13-17 Warw 8.1fm 47 2440
39 5-18 Donc 7gd 42 2755
35 9-15 Ches 7.6g/f 41 3102
20 10-18 Thir 6fm 39 3609
19 12-15 Thir 8fm [40] 4379

ZAN LO 4 ch f £3244

19 7-7 Thir 12sft [65] 1226
24 8-9 Newc 10.1sft [60] 1681
52 6-13 Pont 10g/f 58 2038
41 10-11 Thir 12g/f 58 2217
0 7-8 Donc 12g/s 55 3222
47 7-13 Beve 12.1g/f 51 3502
23 9-10 Ripo 12.3g/f 51 3649
46 4-12 Muss 14g/f 44 4170
52 1-13 REDC 14.1fm 45 4340*
20 15-19 Catt 15.8g/f 50 4675
14 11-18 Pont 12g/f 49 4938
23 14-20 York 13.9gd 49 5004
39 11-12 Redc 14.1g/s 49 5108

ZANDEED 6 b g £12109
30 11-12 Ayr 9.1g/f 60 3766
59 3-15 Ayr 7.2hvy 57 4088
62 1-12 REDC 8gd 57 4246*
60 4-13 Newc 10.1g/f 59 4406
48 12-13 Muss 8g/f [59] 4554
57 5-18 Ayr 10.9sft 59 4623
52 7-10 Donc 10.3sft 57 5206

ZANDERIDO 2 b g £338
53 4-5 Beve 5gd 2888
15 12-12 York 6gd 3122
56 6-8 Catt 6g/f 3348
0 16-16 Beve 7.5g/f 50 4597

ZANDO 2 b g £0
24a 8-11 Wolv 6af 2051
56 11-18 York 5g/f 2360
64 6-11 Newc 7gd 3429
54 10-20 Redc 7fm 62 4337

ZANGEAL 3 ch c £2469
75a 4-14 Ling 10ap 759
78 3-12 Sand 10g/f 2193
62 4-8 Pont 12g/f 2608
69 4-15 Wind 10fm [79] 3292 T
77 4-9 Good 8gd 76 3950

ZANJEER 4 b g £10083
30a 8-12 Sout 7af [58] 416
68 1-13 REDC 8gd 50 2552*
67 6-16 Redc 8g/s 66 2958
70 3-14 Carl 6.9g/f 66 3229
73 1-9 BEVE 7.5gd 66 3310*
56 7-12 Ches 7.6fm 70 3634
53 5-5 Ayr 8hvy [70] 4086
21a 12-12 Wolv 7.1ap 69 5289

ZANTERO 2 b c £609
40a 4-11 Wolv 6af 2051
65 6-11 Ches 7fm 3633
51a 4-15 Sout 5af 4089
56 6-19 Carl 5.9g/f 65 4344
43 8-14 Muss 8gd 62 4519
58 6-18 Catt 7g/f 59 4673
57 5-10 Catt 7sft [57] 5127

ZAP ATTACK 4 b g £282
18 16-16 Redc 6g/f 68 1824
63 7-13 Thir 7g/f 66 3571
55 4-9 Redc 8g/f [64] 3806
36 16-17 York 7g/f 62 4398
24 17-19 Nott 6.1g/f [58] 4845

ZAQRAH 3 b f £0
77 10-17 Newm 7gd 1171

ZARA LOUISE 4 b f £0
28a 4-12 Sout 6af [30] 377
0 10-14 Sout 7af [30] 573
15a 8-14 Sout 6af [30] 637

ZARGUS 5 b g £207
58a 5-7 Ling 5ap 69 1011
57 10-16 Bath 5.7g/s [69] 1103
49 10-15 Brig 5.3g/f 65 1371 BL
50 11-12 Sali 5gd 62 2698
37 13-18 Hayd 5gd 57 2951

ZARIANO 4 b g £858
76a 2-12 Ling 8ap [90] 3286
73a 8-13 Ling 7ap 74 3791
54 9-10 Wind 10g/f [72] 3980
56 8-16 Sali 8gd 69 4334
58 12-14 Wind 8.3g/f 65 4832

51a 9-12 Wolv 7.1ap 70 5289

ZARIN 5 b g £4903
39a 10-10 Wolv 8.5af 75 5
69a 2-10 Wolv 7af [69] 152
65a 3-14 Sout 8af 70 195
54a 9-12 Sout 8af 69 530
54a 3-8 Sout 8af [67] 744
15a 13-15 Sout 8af 66 2338
41 9-15 Thir 8g/s [57] 2688
50a 7-15 Sout 7af [63] 2999 BL
36 6-14 Ayr 7.2gd [54] 3324
50 2-17 Thir 8g/s 49 3830
67a 1-11 SOUT 8af [55] 4090*
50 5-12 Redc 8gd 53 4246
53 8-15 Carl 7.9g/f 53 4346
25 20-26 Redc 8fm 52 4926
48a 8-13 Wolv 9.5ap [59] 5338

ZARNEETA 3 b f £690
38 8-8 Ling 7g/f 55 2742
16 12-13 Bath 10.2gd [55] 3144
30 7-10 Redc 10g/f 50 3772
30 7-12 Chep 12.1g/s [45] 4364
44 7-9 Bath 10.2gd [40] 4547
22 8-19 Brig 9.9gd [40] 4903
48 3-18 Wind 10g/s [40] 4944
4 15-15 Yarm 10.1g/s [45] 5122
25a 6-9 Wolv 9.5ap [35] 5360

ZAROVA 2 gr c £0
43 11-14 Donc 6g/f 1874
52 6-13 Beve 5gd 2889
25 15-15 Pont 6gd 3239
31 14-19 Carl 5.9g/f 56 4344

ZARZU 4 b g £19752
79a 5-15 Sout 5af 80 64
72a 4-12 Ling 6ap [80] 106
88a 1-16 SOUT 5af 79 171*
87a 3-12 Wolv 6af 85 361
84a 5-16 Sout 5af 86 461
89a 4-10 Ling 5ap 86 567
91a 3-10 Ling 5ap 86 692
77 4-20 Donc 5af 74 927
75 3-16 Bath 5.7g/s [74] 1103
65 12-19 Kemp 6fm 74 2070
64 9-13 York 5g/f 74 2359
68 13-15 Newc 5g/s 72 2727
84 1-10 MUSS 5g/s 72 2968*
70 6-17 Pont 5gd 75 3241
81 5-20 Hayd 5fm 79 3792
67 12-13 Newb 5.2g/f 78 3960
30 8-8 Kemp 5sft [78] 4031
78 5-20 Donc 5fm 77 4496
30 19-19 Good 6gd 77 4747
84 13-15 Newm 5g/f [77] 4879

ZATHONIA 3 b f £3573
67 2-13 Nott 8.2g/f 2633
67 3-14 Wind 8.3fm 2974
73 2-5 Pont 8gd 3683

ZAVILLE 2 gr f £0
66 10-15 Kemp 7g/f 4710
43 10-14 Leic 8gd 5059

ZAWRAK 4 ch g £5182
60a 3-14 Ling 10ap 60 236
53a 6-13 Ling 13ap 61 342
56a 3-14 Ling 10ap [60] 477
36a 11-14 Ling 10ap 58 520
62 1-14 CARL 7.9fm 55 1954*
8 15-17 Hayd 8.1gd 60 2947
52 5-13 Bath 10.2gd [60] 3144
63 2-18 Pont 8gd 60 3242 VIS
44 8-9 Hami 9.2g/f 62 3593 vis
8 16-16 Yarm 11.5g/s 61 4589
42 13-15 Beve 7.5g/f 61 4719 vis
60a 4-13 Wolv 9.5ap 57 5292 P
49a 7-13 Wolv 9.5ap 56 5361 p

ZAYN ZEN 2 ch f £2397
69 6-10 Newm 7gd 4191
75 4-13 Leic 8g/f 4450
79 2-18 Nott 8.2g/f 4842
63 5-9 Ayr 8sft [80] 5033

ZAZOUS 3 b c £855
60 6-13 Wind 6fm 2756
65 3-6 Donc 7g/f [70] 3595
48 9-10 Chep 7.1gd [70] 3732
45 11-15 Bath 8gd 63 4827
44 11-15 Leic 11.8gd [58] 5060

ZAZZMAN 6 b g £140756
109 3-24 Flem 16g/s 105 5323 bl

ZEENA 2 b f £282
63 5-5 Good 6sft 4234
69 4-13 Sali 7sft 4576
63 5-10 Wind 8.3g/f 4831

ZEIS 4 ch g £6974
64a 9-11 Ling 8ap [78] 800
54a 10-12 Ling 8ap 73 932
44 12-14 Nott 10g/s 68 1776 T
68 1-9 BRIG 9.9g/f [68] 2643* t
68 1-10 LEIC 11.8g/f [68] 3211* t
63 7-8 Leic 10g/f 68 3514 t
52 10-16 Yarm 11.5g/s 67 4589 t
53a 9-12 Wolv 12.2ap 65 4924 t
54a 7-12 Wolv 12.2ap 65 4983 t
29a 9-12 Wolv 13.9ap 60 5160 t

ZEITGEIST 3 b c £26153
77 4-10 Wind 11.6gd 77 1382
84 1-6 REDC 11g/f 77 2103*
90 2-8 Hami 12.1g/f 83 2318
91 5-11 Asco 12gd 87 3070
81 9-16 Good 12fm 87 3534
95 1-7 HAMI 13g/s 87 4819*
95 2-15 Leic 11.8gd 90 5043

ZEITLOS 5 b g £0
0 12-13 Ling 6ap [40] 400 bl

ZELEA 5 br m £0
17a 5-9 Sout 12af [40] 1204 t
28a 4-6 Sout 11af [35] 1409 t
14a 4-6 Sout 12af [35] 1592

ZELOSO 6 b g £864
46a 6-13 Ling 10ap 3288 vis
46a 2-13 Ling 10ap 42 3823 vis

ZENDARO 2 b g £0
56a 4-12 Sout 5af 1439
54 6-19 Kemp 6g/f 1911
54 9-11 Ayr 6g/s 2569
9 18-19 Carl 5.9g/f 57 4344
48 6-12 Pont 6g/s [54] 5152

ZERLINA 3 b f £12784
73 7-9 Kemp 8g/s [86] 1110
54 7-7 Nott 8.2sft [86] 1741
49 8-8 Newm 7gd 80 3928
85a 4-13 Ling 7ap 81 4318
79 2-13 Sand 8.1gd 75 4607
85 1-7 PONT 8g/f 75 4935*
82a 11-12 Ling 8ap [80] 5298

ZERO TOLERANCE 4 ch g £36405
90 1-10 HAYD 10.5sft [85] 1104*
94 4-15 Redc 10g/f 90 2101
77 17-31 Asco 8g/f 90 2489
76 12-21 York 10.4gd 92 3118
1 7-7 Newm 10g/f 90 3474
96 2-11 York 10.4g/s 90 4021
100 2-9 Newm 10gd 90 4227
105 1-13 NEWM 8g/s 94 5284*

ZHITOMIR 5 ch g £9578
50a 8-11 Ling 8ap [52] 145
56 1-18 CATT 7gd [49] 996*
46 6-19 Redc 8sft 51 1661
48 6-18 Ayr 7.2g/f 51 1897
54 1-14 AYR 7.2gd [49] 3324*
46 6-15 Catt 7sft 52 3933
50 4-15 Ayr 7.2hvy 52 4088
42 10-14 Carl 6.9g/f 50 4345
53 2-16 Chep 7.1hvy [48] 4707
60 1-13 WARW 7.1g/s [50] 4994+
42a 6-12 Wolv 7.1ap 50 5112
58a 2-12 Wolv 7.1ap [52] 5358

ZIBELINE 7 b g £4400

```
92  3-13  Epso  12fm      89    2255 bl
87  10-19 Newc  16.1g/s   89    2771 bl
71  14-15 Donc  14.6fm    88    4491 bl

ZIET DALSACE 4 b f £6495
25  14-15 Brig  8fm       55    1691
54  2-10  Brig  7g/f     [52]   1938
32  12-16 Bath  8fm      [52]   2032
41  12-20 Yarm  8fm       52    2149
55  2-11  Brig  7g/f      50    2644
47  10-13 Kemp  7g/f      53    3034
63  1-17  BRIG  7g/f      53    3176*
52  8-11  Yarm  7gd       58    3364
60  4-10  Brig  7fm       60    3672
52  6-6   Brig  7fm      [60]   3696
54  7-19  Nott  6.1g/f   [59]   4845
59a 2-13  Wolv  8.6ap     53    4982
37a 11-12 Ling  8ap      [53]   5077
57a 5-13  Wolv  8.6ap     55    5183
57a 3-12  Wolv  8.6ap    [55]   5337

ZIETORY 4 b f £25700
91  5-8   Newm  9fm      [102]  1491
62  8-8   Good  8g/f     [102]  1863
98  3-12  Bath  8g/f      [99]  3965
99  1-5   SAND  8.1g/s    [99]  4095*
88  11-14 Sali  7gd       99    4331
97a 3-12  Ling  8ap      [95]   5298

ZIETZIG 7 b g £4241
8   14-14 Donc  6g/s     [53]   1522
45  8-15  Thir  7gd       53    1635
22a 11-15 Sout  7af       40    2501
29  13-19 Beve  5gd       51    2657
37  8-20  Nott  6.1gd     45    2928
30  5-19  Nott  6.1gd    [42]   3104
41  6-14  Catt  6g/f     [42]   3459
51  1-18  THIR  6fm       40    3609*
41  10-20 Redc  6g/f      47    3767

ZIGGY DAN 3 b g £0
19a 8-9   Wolv  9.4af            239
11a 7-8   Wolv  8.5af            248
0   5-5   Wolv  12af     [30]    823

ZILCH 5 ch g £56755
68a 7-10  Wolv  8.5af     79       5
78a 3-16  Ling  7ap       75     181
88  1-13  KEMP  7sft      75     945*
89  2-20  Newc  7hvy      83    1035
96  2-20  Kemp  6gd       87    1138
97  1-15  PONT  6hvy      87    1251*
91  4-9   Newm  6fm       92    1490
80  10-18 Newc  7sft      92    2684
102 1-16  WIND  6fm       92    2758*
89  11-19 Newm  7g/f      98    3061
90  7-16  Wind  6gd       98    3827
91  8-24  Ayr   6sft      97    4686
50  20-20 York  6gd       95    5001

ZILMY 3 ch g £0
67  7-10  Good  8g/f            1815

ZIMBALI 2 ch f £4143
49  5-10  Bath  5g/s            1097
62  4-11  Warw  6gd             1123
67  1-15  WARW  5g/s            1325*
64  3-6   Nott  5.1sft          1466
54  4-5   Brig  6g/f            1937
55  2-5   Yarm  6fm             2145
66  2-8   Yarm  6fm             2865

ZINGING 4 b g £2643
49a 3-12  Ling  8ap      [48]    150
54a 1-15  LING  7ap      [48]    216*
48a 7-16  Ling  7ap       52     270
51a 5-14  Ling  6ap       52     328
43a 7-12  Ling  10ap      50     542
52a 6-16  Ling  7ap       50     600
51a 4-11  Ling  8ap       50     732
40a 7-10  Ling  8ap       50     770
43a 7-15  Ling  7ap       48     913
12  6-7   Chep  7.1sft   [40]   1335
20  5-8   Brig  8gd      [40]   1548
36  5-10  Brig  7gd       35    1941
35  6-16  Brig  7fm       35    2258
25  9-11  Brig  7g/f      36    2644
35a 10-12 Ling  8ap      [45]   3286

39  4-10  Brig  7sft      36    4168
31  7-15  Folk  7g/f     [40]   4371
23  6-19  Kemp  6g/f     [40]   4793 vis
41  4-12  Brig  8gd      [40]   4904

ZITHER 3 b f £0
65a 10-11 Ling  8ap       84      80

ZOEANNA 3 b f £0
12a 7-9   Ling  13ap      50      18
21a 12-16 Sout  7af      [50]     61

ZOHAR 2 b c £5720
94  1-14  HAYD  6fm             4385*
37  13-13 Newb  7sft            5195

ZOLASH 2 b c £1598
69  5-13  Nott  5.1gd           1987
42  9-13  Sali  6fm             2287
72  6-8   Ling  6gd             3021
75  7-9   Epso  7fm             3539
57  4-10  Yarm  8g/f            3713
59  4-13  Sali  7g/f            3864
65  3-14  Muss  7.1g/f   [65]   4171
55  6-12  Bath  8g/f     62     4410
35  9-16  Yarm  8g/s     62     4632
47a 9-13  Wolv  8.6ap    [59]   5355

ZOLTANO 6 b g £7264
69  3-12  Newc  16.1sft  65      965
70  1-10  MUSS  16g/f    65     1093*
37  17-17 Ripo  16g/s    69     1361

ZOLUSHKA 2 ch f £364
10a 14-14 Sout  7af      53      158
42a 3-8   Ling  8ap     [45]     326
21a 10-12 Ling  8ap     [45]     538
19a 12-14 Ling  7ap     [45]     783
36a 10-14 Ling  7ap     [45]     804

ZOMERLUST 2 b c £11830
68  3-10  Pont  5gd             3457
76  1-18  RIPO  6g/s            3939*
80  2-10  Ripo  6gd     80      4306
81  4-14  Donc  7fm     80      4535
80  4-12  Newm  6gd     79      4882
88  2-14  Ayr   6sft    79      5035
88  3-20  Donc  7sft    81      5373

ZONERGEM 5 ch g £15493
91a 3-13  Ling  10ap     90     134 bl
86a 7-13  Ling  10ap     91     433 p
87a 6-10  Ling  12ap     90     570 bl
97  3-31  Asco  8g/f      90    2489 p
101 3-11  Epso  10.1gd  [92]    4467 p
52  25-32 Newm  9g/f      92    4916 p

ZONIC 2 b f £882
61  7-13  Wind  6fm             3639
66a 7-8   Ling  7ap             4447
60  3-10  Pont  6fm             4752

ZONIC BOOM 4 b g £1341
57  5-10  Bath  8g/s            1100
63  3-18  Wind  8.3gd    62     1385
51  8-17  Warw  8.1g/s   62     4668
63  3-13  Nott  10gd    [61]    4861
55  9-17  Leic  10gd     62     5062
57a 6-11  Wolv  12.2ap   62     5117

ZONNEBEKE 2 b f £5642
41a 9-10  Wolv  7af               36
48a 4-7   Wolv  7af      [52]     284
36a 5-15  Sout  7af      [47]     462
46a 2-11  Ling  8ap      [45]     535
30a 7-9   Sout  7af      [45]     596 P
40a 3-14  Ling  7ap      [45]     783
26a 14-15 Ling  7ap       45      901
29  10-13 Warw  6.1fm     50     2439
49  3-17  Leic  7gd      [50]    2704 VIS
47  4-11  Yarm  7g/f     [45]    2852 vis
52  1-16  THIR  8g/f      45     3414*
50  2-11  Yarm  8gd       48     3706 vis
36  10-20 Yarm  8gd       48     3996
26  6-9   Brig  8sft      48     4165
29  12-16 Yarm  7gd       46     4616
27  10-20 Yarm  7g/s     [45]    5120
16  15-18 Yarm  6g/s      45     5354

ZONUS 3 b c £39462
93  1-13  DONC  7gd             925*
93  4-15  Newb  8gd     83     1206
89  2-15  Ches  7.6gd   83     1583
93  3-18  Hayd  8.1g/f  87     1919
84  11-27 Asco  8g/f    90     2521
97  3-11  Sand  7.1g/s  90     2918
86  7-13  Newm  8g/f    91     3277
100 1-13  CHES  7.6sft  90     4103+ BL
94  10-14 Newb  7g/f   [100]   4638 bl

ZOOM ZOOM 4 b c £9605
77  1-8   HAYD  6g/s   [70]    1345*
43  10-14 Ayr   6g/f    77     1898
73  5-10  Sand  5gd     76     2189
56  13-26 Ayr   6g/s    75     4652
69  4-10  Newc  7fm    [71]    4869
43  14-19 Ayr   6sft    69     5069
76a 1-12  WOLV  7.1ap  [66]    5340*

ZOOMIEZANDO 3 b g £0
57  7-9   Nott  8.2g/f         3581
24  7-8   Redc  9g/f           3805
1   14-14 Beve  7.5sft         4256

ZORIPP 2 b c £0
65  6-8   York  7g/s           3078
61  10-10 Donc  7g/f           3594
54  12-13 Warw  7.1g/s         4664

ZORN 5 br h £0
8   17-18 Wind  10g/s  [35]    4944
25  10-11 Wind  8.3g/f [35]    5052

ZOSIMA 3 b f £15500
112 3-19  Asco  8g/f    104    2491 T
105 4-6   Good  9.9fm  [107]   3621 t
88  11-15 Donc  7fm    [107]   4479 t

ZOUAVE 3 b c £387
86  7-7   Good  11g/f  [92]    1814
60  12-13 Hayd  11.9gd  92     2238
87  5-5   Sali  14.1fm  87     2418 BL
65  10-10 Asco  16.2g/f [87]   2557 bl

ZOUCHE 4 b g £0
18  11-14 Carl  7.9fm   48     1954
40  10-15 Thir  8g/s   [45]    2688
6   13-15 Warw  10.9g/f 45     2910

ZUCCHERO 8 br g £588
43  12-13 Sali  8gd     80     2662
77  3-10  Nott  8.2gd  [75]    3107 P
65  10-18 Newb  8g/f    75     3265 p

ZUHAIR 11 ch g £0
67  13-20 Thir  5g/s    75     1476
59  10-20 Thir  6gd     72     1638
62  7-16  Redc  6g/f    70     1824
57  11-20 York  6gd     70     2059
52  15-17 Catt  5g/f    67     2846
40  9-10  Hayd  6g/s    66     3136

ZULETA 3 ch f £2737
35  8-8   Chep  10.2g/f 57     2628
39  9-11  Ling  10fm    54     3748
39  6-12  Folk  12g/s   54     3913
50  2-7   Chep  12.1sft 49     4053
40  2-10  Bath  11.7g/s [49]   4199
50  2-11  Catt  13.8g/f [45]   4671
48  4-16  Nott  10gd    47     4857 VIS
50  2-12  Warw  12.6g/s [47]   4991 vis

ZULOAGO 3 b f £1557
49a 5-7   Sout  7af             531
59a 3-12  Wolv  9.4af           686
59a 2-10  Wolv  8.5af           839
9a  12-13 Sout  8af     [60]   1193
2a  11-11 Wolv  8.5af    57    1339
16a 9-11  Sout  8af     [55]   3091

ZUMA 3 b c £3700
76  7-15  Newb  8g/f           1763
76  3-13  Kemp  8fm            2072
78  7-10  Sand  10g/f  [80]    2386
71  5-13  Sali  9.9gd  [79]    2700 VIS
71  5-6   Ches  10.3g/f 76     3084 BL
73  4-7   Newm  12fm   [74]    3405
66a 4-9   Ling  12ap   [73]    4315 P
```

73	2-9	Good	11gd	[72]	5026
70	6-10	Newm	12sft	[72]	5102

ZURI 3 b f £427

51	6-11	Newm	8g/f		2248
59	4-7	Newm	10g/f		2534
54	9-14	Wind	8.3fm		2974
63	9-16	Thir	12g/f	65	3573
55	7-14	Sali	9.9g/f	63	3867
43	9-13	Bath	8gd	62	4546
49a	8-11	Ling	8ap	[58]	4977

ZWADI 3 b f £3909

71	4-13	Kemp	8fm	[75]	2072
58	8-11	Sali	8fm	[75]	2419
66	5-8	Ling	7g/f	73	2742
69	7-13	Wind	6fm	71	3479
73	3-11	Yarm	7g/f	71	3711
70	2-10	Sali	6g/s	[72]	4081
44	4-9	Thir	6fm	[72]	4380
64	3-9	Catt	7g/f	[72]	4674
52	4-11	Wind	8.3g/f	[70]	5052

ZWEIBRUCKEN 3 b f £7124

54	17-18	Good	9g/f	83	1813
78	10-12	Sand	9g/f	83	2385
87	1-5	SALI	8gd	80	3885*
74	11-15	Hayd	8.1g/f	84	4352
78	11-17	Asco	8g/f	83	4777
74	7-13	Bath	8sft	82	5172

Index To Flat Race Meetings By Race Number (contin)

SUPERFORM TOP PRIZE WINNERS 2004

2yo

£490902	2	WILKO
£331203	2	ORATORIO
£269050	2	DIVINE PROPORTIONS
£232726	2	CAESAR BEWARE
£215462	2	DAMSON
£200423	2	OBE GOLD
£198819	2	SHAMARDAL
£167598	2	AFLEET ALEX
£165255	2	PLAYFUL ACT
£152141	2	SALAMANCA
£146891	2	DUBAWI
£134595	2	AD VALOREM
£130880	2	KONIGSTIGER
£129226	2	MAIDS CAUSEWAY
£127017	2	BEAVER PATROL
£126303	2	HELIOS QUERCUS
£124804	2	MOTIVATOR
£121586	2	MAGICAL ROMANCE
£120801	2	CHELSEA ROSE
£104322	2	ICEMAN
£103588	2	RUSSIAN BLUE
£100925	2	ALBERT HALL
£98816	2	SOAR
£94398	2	SLIP DANCE
£94123	2	LAYMAN
£93823	2	SIENA GOLD
£92179	2	SUN KING USA
£89460	2	TONY JAMES
£88217	2	BIBURY FLYER
£86749	2	MONTGOMERYS ARCH
£86391	2	PERFECTPERFORMANC
£82667	2	DISTINCTLY GAME
£82049	2	EARLY MARCH
£78424	2	SILK AND SCARLET
£76268	2	CENTIFOLIA
£75364	2	DEMOCRATIC DEFICIT
£74105	2	ARABIAN DANCER
£74094	2	TOURNEDOS
£71300	2	CAPE COLUMBINE
£71237	2	SUEZ
£70699	2	CHATEAU ISTANA
£68953	2	DUBAI SURPRISE
£68675	2	JEWEL IN THE SAND
£66422	2	ETLAALA
£65414	2	IDEALIST
£61330	2	MYSTICAL LAND
£60275	2	HEARTHSTEAD WINGS
£56880	2	BLUE DAKOTA
£56457	2	CAPTAIN HURRICANE
£56400	2	MERCHANT
£56258	2	REBUTTAL
£53694	2	MOSCOW MUSIC
£53684	2	GALÉOTA
£53675	2	COMIC STRIP
£53538	2	INDESATCHEL
£52882	2	CUPIDS GLORY
£52570	2	SALUT THOMAS
£52236	2	UMNIYA
£52080	2	JAZZ PRINCESS
£51389	2	KESTREL CROSS
£50767	2	BERKHAMSTED
£50473	2	ANDRONIKOS
£50159	2	SHIFTING PLACE
£49138	2	TITIAN TIME

3yo

£1088680	3	NORTH LIGHT
£984241	3	BAGO
£917722	3	OUIJA BOARD
£684087	3	RULE OF LAW
£671000	3	ATTRACTION
£670391	3	LUNDYS LIABILITY
£653338	3	AZAMOUR
£554603	3	GREY SWALLOW
£442634	3	BLUE CANARI
£430124	3	HAAFHD
£427817	3	SHIROCCO
£425662	3	GROOM TESSE
£357542	3	KITTENS JOY
£333793	3	CHERRY MIX
£311533	3	GREY LILAS
£293059	3	MENHOUBAH
£276859	3	WHIPPER
£274959	3	PUNCTILIOUS
£256851	3	QUIFF
£256170	3	ANTONIUS PIUS
£255207	3	ALEXANDER GOLDRUN
£245655	3	DAYANO
£236099	3	PROSPECT PARK
£227009	3	LET THE LION ROAR
£226901	3	LATICE
£223463	3	PETIT PARIS
£221874	3	MAJESTIC DESERT
£220986	3	LUNE DOR
£203542	3	CACIQUE
£203183	3	AMERICAN POST
£202513	3	LITTLE JIM
£199843	3	PRIVY SEAL
£190944	3	VALIXIR
£167987	3	DIAMOND GREEN FR
£156244	3	BACHELOR DUKE
£140838	3	TORRESTRELLA
£138387	3	TYCOON
£135352	3	GATWICK
£133768	3	STEP DANZER
£124702	3	PERCUSSIONIST
£122627	3	VOIX DU NORD
£114576	3	ALL TOO BEAUTIFUL
£111100	3	MISTER MONET
£106183	3	ASK FOR THE MOON
£98592	3	EGERTON
£95405	3	AFRICAN DREAM
£95353	3	BRUNEL
£93655	3	SUNDROP
£92282	3	CATSTAR
£91619	3	HAZARISTA
£89060	3	YEATS
£88028	3	PASTORAL PURSUITS
£87838	3	FIVE DYNASTIES
£87450	3	SAHOOL
£86620	3	MALINAS
£86173	3	BYRON
£86172	3	JACK SULLIVAN
£84396	3	MOSS VALE
£83944	3	DELFOS
£80989	3	SHAPIRA
£80546	3	ELECTROCUTIONIST
£80493	3	MILLIONAIA
£79789	3	LORIANA
£75221	3	HAZYVIEW

4yo+

£2011173	6	PLEASANTLY PERFECT
£1176471	7	MAKYBE DIVA
£778410	5	SULAMANI
£696095	7	POLISH SUMMER
£670391	5	MEDAGLIA DORO
£631612	6	WARRSAN
£581709	5	EPALO
£581006	5	BETTER TALK NOW
£575540	5	RIVER DANCER
£571200	4	DOYEN
£534453	4	SOVIET SONG
£488045	5	SINGLETARY
£446927	7	PAOLINI
£446927	5	RIGHT APPROACH
£432080	6	VINNIE ROE
£431049	4	POWERSCOURT
£418990	4	REFUSE TO BEND
£388463	5	HARD BUCK
£348000	5	RAKTI
£343620	4	NORSE DANCER
£338362	5	CRIMSON PALACE
£335196	4	KICKEN KRIS
£335195	5	VICTORY MOON
£281698	5	WESTERNER
£265066	4	SENEX
£260971	5	SCOTTS VIEW
£247338	5	GAMUT
£236160	5	CHORIST
£231937	7	THE TATLING
£227708	4	SOMNUS
£226749	4	ANCIENT WORLD
£215827	6	ELEGANT FASHION
£213380	6	ALTIERI
£212999	4	PAPINEAU
£212231	6	NAYYIR
£211800	4	SIX PERFECTIONS
£200200	4	FAVOURABLE TERMS
£197368	4	SURVEYOR
£197182	5	ALBANOVA
£196000	4	FRIZZANTE
£194805	4	COMMERCANTE
£192500	7	MILLENARY
£184528	5	MEPHISTO
£176900	4	TANTE ROSE
£169000	4	PIVOTAL POINT
£167597	4	GRAND HOMBRE
£160377	6	BRIAN BORU
£157542	4	FILM MAKER
£156426	4	SWEET STREAM
£148920	9	BAHAMIAN PIRATE
£148807	4	PONGEE
£145505	4	VESPONE
£145495	4	HURRICANE ALAN
£145000	5	FAYR JAG
£144018	7	GATEMAN
£142648	4	POLICY MAKER
£140756	6	ZAZZMAN
£138740	4	KALAMAN
£136950	4	CHIC
£134242	5	MAKTUB
£130567	5	BANDARI
£129870	5	SIMONAS
£127280	5	VORTEX
£122477	4	COURT MASTERPIECE

Superform Top Flat Horses 2004

5f

121	5	c	Var 4952
120	7	g	The Tatling 4952
119	9	g	Bahamian Pirate 4952
118	4	c	Avonbridge 4952
117	5	f	Porlezza 3062
116	6	g	Cape Of Good Hope 3062
114	3	c	Majestic Missile 4678
114	6	c	Orientor 4952
114	5	g	Osterhase 4952
113	3	c	Boogie Street 3551
113	4	c	Steves Champ 4879
112	10	g	Bishops Court 4291
112	6	g	Chookie Heiton 4238
112	7	g	Continent 4952
112	5	f	Ringmoor Down 5088

6f

120	4	f	Tante Rose 4384
119	5	g	Ashdown Express 4384
119	3	c	One Cool Cat 4384
119	6	g	Patavellian 5313
119	4	g	Pivotal Point 4799
117	5	g	Fayr Jag 4060
117	5	f	Frizzante 3838
117	6	g	Royal Millennium 5100
117	5	g	Steenberg 2580
117	4	c	Striking Ambition 5313
116	6	g	Crystal Castle 3508
116	3	f	Dolma 3838
116	6	g	Lucky Strike 4426
116	4	f	Miss Emma 5313
116	3	g	Raffelberger 4426
116	4	c	Star Valley 4313
115	3	c	Moss Vale 5100
115	6	g	The Trader 3838
114	4	c	Key To Pleasure 4426
113	4	c	Arakan 2765
113	3	c	Balmont 5134
113	4	c	Country Reel 5100
112	4	c	Fiepes Shuffle 3009
112	7	r	Quito 5371
112	7	g	Smokin Beau 4098
112	3	c	So Will I 4874
112	4	g	The Kiddykid 3842

7f

121	4	g	Somnus 5070
119	5	c	Firebreak 5134
117	4	c	Monsieur Bond 5070
117	3	c	Pastoral Pursuits 5070
117	3	c	Peak To Creek 2190
117	3	c	Salford City 2916
116	4	c	Trade Fair 3508
115	3	f	Denebola 5070
115	3	c	Leitrim House 1995
115	5	g	Polar Ben 4887
115	5	g	Polar Way 5134
115	4	c	Tout Seul 5283
114	3	c	Kheleyf 4874
114	3	c	Madid 2469
113	4	c	Court Masterpiece 4874
113	6	c	Keltos 5134
113	3	g	Mac Love 4874
113	6	g	Suggestive 4638
112	9	g	Duck Row 1686
112	3	c	Fokine 2486

112	4	g	Polar Bear 5134
112	4	c	Puppeteer 4731

8f

126	3	c	Haafhd 5136
123	4	c	Refuse To Bend 5136
123	4	c	Singletary 5308
123	4	f	Soviet Song 4801
122	3	f	Attraction 4915
122	3	c	Diamond Green Fr 5308
122	3	c	Lucky Story 4801
122	6	g	Nayyir 5070
122	3	c	Snow Ridge 2254
122	3	c	Whipper 5308
121	3	c	American Post 2254
121	3	c	Antonius Pius 5308
121	3	c	Bachelor Duke 2469
121	5	c	Salselon 5136
120	4	f	Chic 4915
120	4	f	Russian Rhythm 1758
120	5	c	Ryono 3168
119	4	g	Ancient World 5074
118	3	c	Ace 4801
118	3	c	Byron 3508
118	3	f	Grey Lilas 4953
118	4	c	Le Vie Dei Colori 5070
118	5	c	Passing Glance 4232
118	3	f	Sundrop 5086
117	3	c	Brunel 4232
117	3	f	Hathrah 1492
117	4	c	Hurricane Alan 5074
117	5	c	My Risk 4017
117	3	f	Torrestrella 1854
116	3	g	African Dream 3886
116	3	c	Art Master 2639
116	4	f	Marbye 3659
116	4	f	Nebraska Tornado 4915
115	3	c	Castleton 2469
115	3	c	Milk It Mick 4495
115	3	c	Mister Sacha 4949
115	3	c	Newton 1995
115	3	c	Pepperstorm 4424
115	8	c	Tillerman 3533
114	3	f	Baqah 3004
114	3	c	Fongs Thong 4801
114	3	f	Illustrious Miss 2005
114	3	f	Majestic Missile 5074
114	3	f	Red Bloom 4735
114	5	g	Shot To Fame 4386
114	4	c	Sublimity 3613
114	6	g	With Reason 4386
113	4	c	Art Moderne 993
113	4	c	Babodana 5283
113	4	c	Eagle Rise 4839
113	3	f	Festive Style 599
113	3	c	Lazio 1860
113	3	f	Secret Charm 4887
113	3	c	Tahreeb 3664
113	3	c	Three Valleys 1188
112	3	c	Assiun 4839
112	5	g	Bowmans Crossing 3124
112	3	f	Carry On Katie 1854
112	5	c	Charming Groom 2826
112	3	c	Fantastic View 4495
112	6	c	Mine 4800
112	3	f	Miss Mambo 2306
112	6	c	Putra Pekan 5283

112	3	f	Zosima 3621

9f

122	4	c	Prince Kirk 2002
119	4	c	Alkaadhem 4748
118	4	c	Autumn Glory 5139
118	3	c	Cacique 4949
118	5	f	Crimson Palace 4013
118	4	f	Favourable Terms 3621
118	7	g	Gateman 4950
118	7	c	Paolini 4434
118	5	c	Right Approach 991
117	3	c	Little Jim 989
117	5	f	Silence Is Golden 3621
117	4	f	Six Perfections 5308
116	4	c	Martillo 3166
116	3	f	Necklace 4013
115	4	c	Checkit 4887
115	5	f	Riskaverse 4013
115	5	c	Sights On Gold 5139
112	3	c	Gatwick 4916
112	3	f	Love And Bubbles 2814
112	5	g	Pentecost 4682

10f

126	5	c	Sulamani 5247
125	5	c	Rakti 4801
124	3	c	Azamour 5136
124	6	h	Pleasantly Perfect 992
123	4	c	Norse Dancer 5136
122	5	c	Medaglia Doro 992
122	3	c	Mister Monet 4158
121	4	c	Powerscourt 5311
121	4	c	Touch Of Land 4950
120	5	c	Epalo 4014
120	3	c	Voix Du Nord 1853
120	3	c	Yeats 1700
119	3	f	Alexander Goldrun 4953
119	6	c	Altieri 1858
119	4	c	Ikhtyar 3306
119	4	c	Kalaman 4002
119	3	c	Millemix 1853
118	4	c	Brian Boru 5247
118	5	f	Bright Sky 991
118	3	c	Bull Run 1294
118	5	f	Chorist 5136
118	7	h	Execute 4956
118	3	c	Intendant 3662
118	4	c	Kicken Kris 4014
118	3	f	Lune Dor 5244
118	7	c	Polish Summer 4568
118	5	c	Special Kaldoun 4950
118	4	f	Whortleberry 4567
117	4	f	Commercante 5246
117	3	c	Into The Dark 4687
117	4	c	Leporello 2252
117	4	c	Muqbil 4812
117	5	g	River Dancer 1438
117	5	g	Scotts View 3662
117	5	c	Vangelis 1061
117	4	c	Vespone 3264
116	3	f	Ask For The Moon 2001
116	3	c	Delfos 4730
116	7	g	Demon Dancer 4016
116	5	c	Nysaean 4568
115	3	f	Asti 2001
115	4	f	Beneventa 3278
115	4	c	Fruhlingssturm 5139

Superform Top Flat Horses 2004

115	3 c	Hazyview 4015
115	4 c	Magistretti 4014
115	4 c	Marshall 4837
115	4 f	Samando 4948
115	5 c	Victory Moon 992
115	4 f	Walkamia 5244
114	3 f	Agata 2460
114	4 c	Big Bad Bob 4492
114	3 c	Greek Sun 4015
114	5 g	Millstreet 4002
114	5 f	Monturani 4735
114	5 c	Parasol 1585
114	3 f	Punctilious 5246
114	4 f	Russian Hill 4948
114	3 f	Super Bobbina 5244
113	4 f	Aubonne 2635
113	6 c	Chancellor 3793
113	4 f	Classic Stamp 5246
113	3 f	Kinnaird 4735
113	3 c	Moscow Ballet 4015
113	4 g	Red Fort 4492
113	4 c	Soldier Hollow 2635
113	4 c	Solskjaer 4002
113	4 f	Yesterday 5309
112	4 f	Actrice 2487
112	3 c	Islero Noir 4158
112	4 c	Look Honey 2635
112	3 c	Meath 2006
112	4 c	Napper Tandy 2004
112	4 c	Nonno Carlo 1858
112	3 f	Quilanga 3836
112	3 c	Simple Exchange 4015
112	3 f	Steel Princess 1850
112	3 f	Super Lina 2001
112	4 g	Surveyor 1859

11f

123	3 f	Ouija Board 5309
119	4 f	Film Maker 5309
119	3 f	Quiff 4532
118	5 m	Wonder Again 5309
114	3 f	Baraka 1619
114	3 c	Go For Gold 4532
113	6 c	Foreign Affairs 5369
112	3 c	Always First 4001

12f

130	4 c	Doyen 5136
128	3 c	Bago 4956
126	3 c	Cherry Mix 4956
125	5 g	Better Talk Now 5311
125	5 c	Hard Buck 3442
124	3 c	Kittens Joy 5311
123	3 c	Grey Swallow 4571
123	3 c	North Light 4956
123	4 c	Policy Maker 4568
122	5 c	Gamut 4428
122	6 c	Warrsan 4956
121	3 c	Acropolis 4956
121	3 c	Valixir 4956
120	5 c	Bandari 4812
120	3 c	Prospect Park 4956
120	5 h	Simonas 5247
120	3 c	Tycoon 4532
119	3 c	Blue Canari 4956
119	3 c	Egerton 4428
119	3 f	Latice 4956
119	3 c	Let The Lion Roar 4532

119	5 h	Olaso 1556
119	3 c	Percussionist 5245
119	4 f	Pride 5165
119	4 c	Senex 4570
119	3 c	Shirocco 5168
118	3 c	Electrocutionist 5168
118	6 c	Fair Mix 5168
118	5 c	First Charter 4733
118	4 c	High Accolade 4812
118	6 c	Imperial Dancer 5168
118	3 c	Lord Du Sud 4947
118	5 c	Mamool 5323
118	4 c	Rotteck 3497
118	4 f	Vallee Enchantee 4956
117	4 c	Alkaased 4391
117	3 c	Day Flight 4639
117	3 c	Dayano 3497
117	3 f	Millionaia 2460
117	4 f	Sweet Stream 5168
116	5 f	Albanova 4841
116	4 c	Bailador 4312
116	5 g	Distinction 5323
116	4 c	Dubai Success 4733
116	3 c	Groom Tesse 2142
116	5 c	Maktub 4570
116	5 c	Martaline 4312
116	4 c	Persian Majesty 3563
115	3 c	Lord Darnley 2824
115	4 f	Royal Fantasy 4567
115	5 c	Short Pause 4568
114	3 f	All Too Beautiful 4735
114	3 g	Orcadian 5224
114	4 c	Phoenix Reach 3442
114	7 g	Self Defense 4812
114	4 c	The Great Gatsby 3958
113	3 c	Ange Gardien 2308
113	3 c	Book Of Kings 2822
113	3 c	Lyonels Glory 4730
113	3 f	Vallera 4567
113	4 f	Visorama 4567
113	7 h	Well Made 1556
112	3 c	Crocodile Dundee 3660
112	3 f	Diamond Tango 4567
112	3 c	Five Dynasties 2822
112	6 g	Razkalla 5323
112	3 f	Saldentigerin 4841
112	3 f	Silverskaya 4956
112	3 c	Simplex 5165

13f

123	7 c	Mubtaker 5247
117	5 c	Systematic 3030
114	8 g	The Whistling Teal 281

14f

122	3 c	Rule Of Law 4532
118	3 c	Maraahel 4532
118	4 c	Orange Touch 4733
117	3 c	Mikado 4959
116	9 g	Alcazar 5334
116	5 c	Windermere 2138
115	3 c	Darsalam 4841
114	5 c	Mkuzi 4162
113	5 g	Barolo 4333
112	3 c	Two Miles West 4733

15f

120	3 c	Reefscape 4947

118	4 c	Forestier 3317
116	4 c	Clear Thinking 4569
116	7 g	Dancing Bay 5138
114	4 g	Gold Medallist 5138
113	4 f	Behkara 5245
113	3 c	Etendard Indien 4565

16f

122	5 c	Mr Dinos 2518
122	6 h	Vinnie Roe 5323
120	7 m	Makybe Diva 5323
120	7 c	Millenary 5138
119	4 c	Risk Seeker 3317
114	4 c	New South Wales 2095
114	5 g	Swing Wing 4312
113	5 g	Defining 5138
113	4 c	Franklins Gardens 5245
112	4 g	Swift Tango 4815

18f

115	5 g	Kasthari 4478

20f

123	4 c	Papineau 2518
122	5 c	Westerner 5245
118	6 g	Darasim 4951
117	7 h	Cut Quartz 4951
116	6 g	Le Carre 4951
113	8 g	Royal Rebel 4000
112	5 c	Highest 2518

Superform's Best 2 Year Olds 2004

122 2 c Shamardal 5137	108 2 f Echelon 4798	103 2 f Cours De La Reine 4954
121 2 c Ad Valorem 4888	108 2 c Footstepsinthesand 524	103 2 c Crimson Sun 4881
121 2 c Dubawi 4734	108 2 c Idealist 5167	103 2 c Dance Night 4651
121 2 c Motivator 5216	108 2 f Lock And Key 4431	103 2 c Doctor Dino 5164
120 2 c Wilko 5310	108 2 c Osidy 4564	103 2 c Grand Marque 4797
119 2 c Oratorio 5137	108 2 c Pike Bishop 2481	103 2 c Harvest Warrior 5217
118 2 c Afleet Alex 5310	108 2 f Portrayal 4954	103 2 c Joseph Henry 5270
118 2 f Divine Proportions 495	108 2 c Scandinavia 4797	103 2 c Kamakiri 3859
118 2 c Rebuttal 4888	108 2 f Shifting Place 3498	103 2 f Kykuit 4430
117 2 f Damson 4880	108 2 f Silk And Scarlet 4432	103 2 f New Largue 4954
117 2 f Early March 4955	108 2 f Toupie 4563	103 2 c Northern Splendour 399
117 2 c Etlaala 4493	108 2 c Vatori 4729	103 2 f Shohrah 4798
117 2 c Iceman 5137	108 2 c Yehudi 5314	103 2 f Soignee 5243
117 2 c Sun King Usa 5310	107 2 g Beckermet 4651	103 2 f Squaw Dance 5282
116 2 c Albert Hall 5216	107 2 c Capable Guest 4729	103 2 c Yajbill 4998
116 2 c Layman 4955	107 2 c Cornus 5132	102 2 c Amsterdam 3494
115 2 c Montgomerys Arch 5137	107 2 f Crossover 4957	102 2 f Ayam Zaman 5281
115 2 c Russian Blue 4888	107 2 c Kay Two 5132	102 2 f Cape Columbine 5087
115 2 c Satchem 4888	107 2 f Mona Lisa 4798	102 2 c Dramaticus 4888
115 2 f Soar 4880	107 2 c Monsoon Rain 4462	102 2 f Faint Heart 4728
114 2 f Centifolia 5312	107 2 c Oude 4493	102 2 c Fox 4096
114 2 c Galeota 4680	107 2 f Pictavia 4432	102 2 c Hills Of Aran 5216
114 2 c Henrik 5216	107 2 c Prince Charming 5312	102 2 c Hypnotic 4429
114 2 c Librettist 5137	107 2 f Queen Of Poland 4954	102 2 c Johnny Jumpup 5195
114 2 f Magical Romance 4880	107 2 c Storm Silk 4393	102 2 f Joint Aspiration 4798
113 2 f Birthstone 4728	107 2 f Whazzat 2578	102 2 f Luas Line 3843
113 2 f Jazz Princess 4958	107 2 f Where With All 3311	102 2 c Mister Genepi 5002
113 2 c Musketier 5164	106 2 c Abraxas Antelope 4280	102 2 f Nanabanana 5267
113 2 f Suez 4880	106 2 f Castelletto 5132	102 2 c Rajwa 4529
112 2 c Berenson 4734	106 2 c Don Pele 3254	102 2 f Royal Copenhagen 4157
112 2 g Caesar Beware 4928	106 2 c Elliots World 4797	102 2 c Sacred Nuts 4022
112 2 c Cupids Glory 5195	106 2 c Elusive Double 4734	102 2 c Safari Sunset 3509
112 2 c Democratic Deficit 495	106 2 c Embossed 5099	102 2 c Stagbury Hill 4390
112 2 c Perfectperformance 513	106 2 f Gorella 4954	102 2 c Turnkey 3319
112 2 f Playful Act 4798	106 2 c Laltro Mondo 2819	102 2 f Virginia Waters 5072
112 2 f Titian Time 4954	106 2 f Penkenna Princess 5133	102 2 c Windy Prospect 4692
111 2 c Afrashad 3196	106 2 f Polly Perkins 2895	102 2 f Ysoldina 5243
111 2 c Beaver Patrol 5216	106 2 c Tournedos 5132	101 2 c Berkhamsted 5167
111 2 c Captain Hurricane 4159	105 2 c Brecon Beacon 5195	101 2 f Daring Love 4427
111 2 g Comic Strip 5150	105 2 c Cape Greko 3126	101 2 c Dario Gee Gee 4928
111 2 f Fraloga 4954	105 2 c Carnegie Hall 4154	101 2 c Destinate 4524
111 2 c Indesatchel 4736	105 2 f Dubai Surprise 4798	101 2 c Forward Move 4722
111 2 c Salut Thomas 5312	105 2 c Hearthstead Wings 5167	101 2 c Gaff 5248
111 2 c Windsor Knot 4096	105 2 c Inhabitant 3658	101 2 c Juantorena 2472
110 2 c Blue Dakota 2516	105 2 c Josh 4888	101 2 c Kappelmann 3169
110 2 c Campo Bueno 5312	105 2 c Obe Gold 5312	101 2 c Liakoura 4328
110 2 c Council Member 4390	105 2 c Propinquity 4328	101 2 c Man O World 2454
110 2 f Golden Legacy 4880	105 2 f Salsa Brava 4680	101 2 c Newsround 4637
110 2 c Helios Quercus 5315	105 2 f Saoire 4958	101 2 f Nufoos 4998
110 2 f Maids Causeway 5133	105 2 f Songerie 5243	101 2 c Omasheriff 4458
110 2 c Merger 5071	105 2 c Space Shuttle 4280	101 2 c Rocamadour 4906
110 2 c Moth Ball 4998	105 2 f Sumora 5132	101 2 c Royal Island 2251
110 2 c Mystical Land 4680	105 2 c Visionist 4390	101 2 c Sant Jordi 5071
110 2 f Something Exciting 528	104 2 f Bibury Flyer 5222	101 2 c Sentiero Rosso 4280
110 2 c Tony James 4955	104 2 c Brahminy Kite 4066	101 2 c Shannon Springs 5167
109 2 f Chelsea Rose 4432	104 2 c Diktatorial 4881	101 2 c Silver Wraith 4096
109 2 f Intrigued 4954	104 2 c Distinctly Game 4458	101 2 f Spirit Of Chester 4059
109 2 f Jewel In The Sand 4432	104 2 f Favourita 5133	101 2 c St Andrews Storm 3028
109 2 c Konigstiger 5167	104 2 c Kings Quay 4881	101 2 c Sundance 4307
109 2 f Slip Dance 4880	104 2 c Merchant 5167	101 2 f Valentin 3440
109 2 f Stop Making Sense 4564	104 2 c Pivotal Flame 5202	101 2 c Wingman 5164
109 2 c Tremar 5137	104 2 f Shanghai Lily 4641	100 2 f Alexander Icequeen 331
108 2 c Andronikos 5217	104 2 c Skywards 3509	100 2 c Blues And Royals 3267
108 2 c Chateau Istana 4888	104 2 g The Crooked Ring 4004	100 2 c Foxhaven 5061
108 2 f Cherokee 5133	104 2 g Wise Dennis 5150	100 2 c Frith 4797
108 2 c Cougar Cat 3319	103 2 f Belle Artiste 4432	100 2 g Imperial Brief 5314
108 2 f Dash To The Top 4798	103 2 g Bond City 5260	100 2 c Joyce 2454

SUPERFORM PROFESSIONAL H'CAP

Superform Professional Handicap analyses all races to come. The horses are printed in-order-of-merit so that the relative chance of any horse can be seen at a glance. The cards are despatched 3 or 4 days in advance of racing so that you can study form at leisure the day or evening before racing. The Professional Handicap makes all the ratings calculations and provides much extra information which greatly speeds up form study - as you can see from the key printed below.

A FREE SAMPLE is available from Furlong Press, High St., Shoreham By Sea, West Sussex. BN43 5DB
Usual subscription rates - Daily for 5 weeks £45   5 Fri/Saturdays only £20
Send cheque or postal order or order by credit card.   **Order Hot-line 01273 452441**   (24 hours)

Labels:
- Adjusted Rating in-order-of-merit
- Last 3 race references
- Last 6 Form Figures
- Extra Edge Ratings adjusted For weight (best in last 18 months)
- Number days since last run
- Trainer plus Wins/places/runs in last 14 days
- Age and Weight
- Three latest ratings plus distance and going
- Official Rating
- Official rise/fall in ratings since last run
- C/D
- Course/Distance Winner or Beaten Favourite
- Indicates Eyecatcher/Spotlight or Fastime horse

Sample:

102 88 1500- 1835* 2347* 2-1211 IN SUPERFORM 21 ATrainer 1/2/23 3-9-0 (R) 6010sft 7012gd 7411fm 70 +7 C/D

With The Extra Edge

Extra Edge: *Many run of the mill handicaps are won by long priced "surprises". They are rarely a surprise to Superform Professional Handicap subscribers who are alert to those horses dropped several pounds below their last winning mark by the BHB handicappers, after a loss of form.*

3.05   8 Decs   1m4f   Gr2 Hardwicke Stakes 4yo+ (A)   6/5 FAV   9/4

- 143	4275}	2209	11124-2	**Doyen** 15 D	Saeed bin Suroor 4-8-9 10/8/36	124 12g/s	122 12sft	118 12.0g/f 121	--	L Dettori
- 137	4489*} 4893}	2209	26212-4	**High Accolade** 15 C/D D BF	M P Tregoning 4-8-9 1/4/13	118 12g/f	118 12.0gd	118 12.0g/f 116	--	W Supple
136	1493	1596* 2209	55-3210	**Systematic** 15 C/D D	M Johnston 5-8-9 7/16/67	116 12fm	117+ 13.4gd	106 12.0g/f 113	--	K Darley

FLAT TRAINERS - Wins/Places/Runners Nov 10 2003 - Nov 6 2004

Trainer	W	P	R
Akehurst J	16	39	252
Alexander H	0	1	25
Allan R	3	0	34
Allen M A	0	2	13
Allen C N	10	11	61
Alston E J	26	59	260
Appleby M	0	4	36
Arbuthnot D W P	6	20	93
Attwater M J	1	6	47
Auvray Jean Rene	0	1	26
Babbage N M	0	0	5
Bailey A	11	31	187
Baker R J	0	0	8
Balding G B	13	40	216
Balding J	16	40	281
Balding A M	47	114	542
Barker D W	13	21	141
Barr R E	4	23	133
Barron T D	61	94	448
Bastiman R	10	21	110
Baugh B P J	9	9	91
Beckett R M	18	39	214
Bell K	3	12	59
Bell M L W	55	98	427
Berry A	36	89	575
Berry N E	13	24	204
Berry John	8	12	66
Best J R	39	62	337
Bethell J D	19	40	190
Bevan E G	1	0	7
Bevis R N	0	0	6
Bishop K	0	0	5
Blanshard M	17	30	231
Blockley P A	46	85	429
Blume H	2	2	4
Booth C B B	0	2	20
Bosley M R	5	15	81
Boutflower Miss K	0	1	21
Bowden Miss R	0	0	3
Bowen P	2	5	17
Bowlby Mrs A J	2	5	50
Bowles Frederick John	0	1	3
Bowring S R	9	34	182
Boyle J R	13	30	152
Bradburne Mrs S C	0	0	2
Bradley J M	39	107	690
Bravery G C	1	4	58
Brennan O	0	0	2
Bridger J J	8	27	232
Bridgwater G F	0	1	6
Bridgwater D G	7	9	70
Brisbourne W M	51	94	592
Brittain C E	29	51	333
Brittain M	6	15	121
Brookshaw S A	1	1	12
Brotherton R	14	27	174
Brown K O Cunningham	0	3	56
Buckley M A	4	16	112
Burchell D	2	6	38
Burgoyne P	4	12	45
Burke K R	60	104	486
Burrough S C	0	1	43
Butler G A	34	74	312
Butler P	0	4	31
Bycroft N	10	27	137
Caldwell T H	0	0	15
Callaghan N A	34	50	282
Camacho Miss J A	4	6	41
Campion Mark	1	1	5
Candlish Mrs J	5	17	69
Candy H	23	43	193
Cantillon D E	4	10	38
Carroll D	16	20	174
Carroll A W	39	98	415
Case B I	1	2	17
Cecil H R A	21	41	149
Chamberlain A J	0	0	11
Chamings P R	9	23	135
Chance Noel T	0	0	2
Channon M R	98	243	1064
Chapman M C	6	39	192
Chapman D W	34	66	395
Chapple-Hyam P W	1	1	3
Charlton A	2	4	40
Charlton R	41	53	233
Chung G C H	8	13	105
Clement N	0	6	6
Clement T T	4	5	80
Clinton P L	0	1	26
Clutterbuck K F	0	0	7
Coakley D J	6	10	57
Cole P F I	39	72	369
Collingridge H J	4	17	106
Collins C	1	1	2
Coogan A B	0	2	11
Cottrell L G	7	14	66
Coupland J F	3	7	34
Cowell R M H	15	37	220
Cox C G	14	20	116
Craggs R	4	8	33
Craig Miss I E	0	0	5
Crook A	0	3	49
Crowley Ms F M	1	4	5
Cumani L M	45	81	298
Cundell P D	8	10	72
Cunningham Michael	1	0	3
Cunningham W S	4	2	18
Curley B J	9	6	52
Curtis R	0	0	18
Cuthbert T A K	0	1	12
Cyzer C A	2	10	82
Cyzer H J	2	8	33
D'Arcy P W	16	29	181
Dace L A	0	0	21
Dalton Mrs H	5	6	42
Daly D J	7	10	81
Dartnall V R A	0	0	2
Davies N A Twiston	0	2	4
Davis D J S ffrench	3	23	98
Davison Miss Z C	2	4	25
Dicken A R	0	3	19
Dickin R	3	5	26
Dickman A	1	12	48
Dods M	31	55	314
Dore C R	7	19	115
Dow S	16	38	268
Doyle Miss Jacqueline S	0	1	16
Drew C	0	0	9
Duffield Mrs A	8	17	118
Duke B W	1	9	93
Dunlop E A L	49	94	407
Dunlop J L	57	115	520
Dunnett Mrs C A	15	21	176
Dutfield Mrs P N	4	24	197
Dwyer C A	14	15	176
Earle Simon	0	0	5
Easterby T D	64	158	740
Easterby M W	32	72	469
Eddy D	6	18	77
Egerton C R	7	9	55
Elliott R P	6	14	114
Ellison B	23	29	237
Elsworth D R C	40	55	313
Embiricos Ms A E	1	1	15
Emmerson Ian	4	14	74
Enright G P	3	10	43
Etherington T J	4	8	100
Eustace J M P	14	27	164
Evans P D	66	124	682
Evans Ms Deborah J	3	15	100
Fahey R A	74	126	620
Fairhurst C W	2	7	66
Fanshawe J R	47	70	291
Featherstone Mrs Lucinda	0	2	50
Feek D B	1	1	27
Feilden Miss J	11	16	129
Felgate P S	2	6	39
Fierro G	0	0	9
Fisher R F	18	29	155
Fitzgerald T J	8	4	46
Flood D	18	24	126
Flower R M	4	9	66
Ford Mrs P	0	3	14
Ford R	1	4	40
Forster Miss S E	0	0	3
Foster B R	0	0	9
Fox J C	1	7	82
Frost J D	0	1	23
Gallagher J	4	9	66
Galpin Mrs Jane	0	0	4
George Miss K M	5	5	59
Gibson R	4	13	18
Gilbert J A	4	14	52
Gilligan P L	8	19	107
Gingell M J	0	0	20
Given J G	32	74	484
Glover J A	11	24	150
Goldie J S	20	44	293
Gollings S	3	15	91
Gordon Rupert Pritchard	0	0	3
Gosden J H M	67	125	461
Graham N A	1	8	28
Grant C	0	8	40
Gray C J	0	2	6
Griffiths S P	0	2	23
Gubby B	4	6	33
Guest R C	2	3	47
Guest R	19	44	218
Haan B De	1	2	13
Haggas W J	46	54	299
Haigh Miss V	3	3	42
Haldane J S	0	2	11
Hales A M	0	3	28
Halford M	0	4	4
Hall Miss S E	0	3	9
Hall L Montague	3	6	51
Ham G A	3	9	63
Hambro Mrs Mary	0	1	13
Hammond M D	11	19	201
Hammond J E	3	8	17
Hanbury B	6	17	92
Hannon R	113	253	1212
Harker G A	1	1	28
Harris John A	9	19	115
Harris M F	2	14	77
Harris P W	45	74	347
Harvey Mrs G	1	0	16
Haslam P C	30	49	293
Hawke N J	0	0	6
Hayes D	0	2	2
Haynes A B	1	1	9
Haynes H E	0	0	7
Haynes M J	0	4	33
Hedger P R	3	3	24
Henderson N J	1	8	20

FLAT TRAINERS - Wins/Places/Runners   Nov 10 2003 - Nov 6 2004

Trainer	W	P	R
Herries Lady	9	14	75
Hetherton J	5	29	155
Hiatt P W	29	47	280
Hills B W	78	137	634
Hills J W	21	57	274
Hoad M R	1	4	33
Hobbs P J	0	2	15
Hodges R J	11	19	135
Hogg K W	0	0	19
Hollinshead R	31	90	428
Horgan C A	11	12	60
Houghton R F Johnson	13	33	177
Howe H S	2	4	52
Howling P	26	39	271
Huffer G A	0	7	26
Hutchinson Ms Caroline	0	1	2
Hyam P W Chapple	29	34	150
Incisa Don Enrico	3	17	122
Ingram R	12	28	138
Ivory D K	24	41	292
James E L	0	0	4
James L R	0	0	9
Jarvis M A	65	99	380
Jarvis A P	13	27	126
Jarvis W	23	31	161
Jay J	13	24	117
Jefferson J M	2	4	36
Jenkins J R	15	57	278
Jenks W	1	0	9
Jewell Mrs L C	0	1	47
Johnson J Howard	8	12	51
Johnson Paul	8	13	102
Johnson B R	7	8	83
Johnston M	122	194	812
Jones Bob	5	6	42
Jones G F H Charles	0	0	3
Jones A E	0	2	7
Jones D Haydn	9	30	153
Jones T M	0	1	25
Jones A P	4	7	86
Jordan F	2	7	48
Juckes A G	3	3	21
Keane D P	0	0	4
Keddy T	5	9	76
Keightley S L	4	19	82
Kellett C N	3	3	42
Kelleway Miss Gay	35	70	370
Kelly G P	0	0	11
King A	4	23	86
King N B	0	2	8
King Mrs A L M	3	9	59
King J S	5	7	40
Kirk S	31	70	374
Kittow W S	7	14	74
Lamyman Mrs S	7	24	133
Lavelle Miss E C	4	15	82
Leavy B D	0	0	16
Lee R	0	1	10
Lewis S T	0	1	10
Lidderdale A J	0	0	8
Liddiard Mrs S A	3	4	24
Liddiard Mrs Stef	19	60	194
Littmoden N P	46	117	543
Llewellyn B J	3	10	57
Lockwood A J	0	0	10
Loder D R	44	74	343
Long J E	3	3	24
Lungo L	3	6	23
Macauley Mrs N	11	22	209
Mackie J	13	21	74
MacLeod D R	2	3	18
Mactaggart B	3	3	26
Madgwick M	4	6	65
Magnusson M A	8	8	45
Makin P J	18	23	152
Manners H J	4	0	18
Margarson G G	21	35	208
Marks Miss K	0	0	11
Marvin R F	4	7	59
McBride P J	4	20	93
McCain D	0	2	11
McCarthy T D	4	11	72
McEntee P S	12	26	172
McGovern T P	1	1	12
McGregor Mrs J C	1	5	22
McHale Miss D A	1	10	66
McInnes I W	11	33	153
McMahon B A	27	38	231
McWilliams H A	0	0	4
Meade M	0	0	8
Meehan B J	59	94	483
Midgley P T	2	7	80
Milligan Miss Kate	0	1	10
Millman B R	21	58	286
Mills T G	20	42	195
Mitchell P	12	20	139
Moffatt James	2	6	57
Mongan Mrs L J	0	0	5
Monteith P	4	8	58
Moore G L	45	85	471
Moore G M	5	12	94
Moore J S	16	43	252
Morgan K A	0	3	50
Morlock C P	0	0	10
Morris D	1	11	83
Morrison H	33	76	330
Morris P	0	1	10
Motion H G	1	1	2
Mountain Miss D	5	9	63
Muggeridge M P	0	0	4
Muir W R	21	58	287
Mulhern J E	2	1	4
Mullarkey D	0	1	9
Mullineaux M	1	24	152
Murphy Ferdy	0	0	3
Murphy P G	0	10	66
Murphy J J	0	2	2
Musson W J	19	49	262
Naughton Mrs A M	0	0	5
Naylor Dr J R J	3	7	60
Newcombe A G	10	25	160
Nicholls D	55	108	701
Nicol J	0	0	3
Niven P D	0	2	17
Nolan D A	1	0	58
Normile Mrs L B	0	0	14
Norton J R	5	13	87
Noseda J	36	60	210
O'Gorman W A	1	3	18
O'Keeffe Jedd	10	22	136
O'Neill E J	4	11	64
O'Neill Jonjo	0	0	9
O'Reilly J	8	23	112
O'Shea J G M	7	20	117
Oertel E R	0	4	18
Old J A B	0	1	11
Osborne J A	36	87	411
Osborne R J	1	3	5
Palling B	10	31	201
Parkes J	7	7	60
Payne J W	4	12	82
Peacock R E	0	1	6
Pearce B A	8	12	57
Pearce J	12	22	130
Pearce Mrs Lydia	2	3	15
Perratt Miss L A	10	27	201
Perrett Mrs A J	48	89	385
Phelan P M	2	6	42
Phillips R T	0	0	8
Pickering J A	0	2	21
Pinder A D W	0	6	42
Pipe M C	3	13	41
Pitman M	2	3	21
Polglase M J	16	42	295
Pollock B N	1	1	5
Portman J G	7	23	134
Poulton Jamie	12	26	166
Poulton Julian	14	51	216
Powell T E	2	5	36
Powell B G	22	41	211
Prescott Sir Mark	75	48	255
Price A E	0	0	3
Price C J	0	1	4
Price R J	12	9	70
Pritchard Dr P	0	0	4
Prodromou G	0	2	18
Quinlan M G	10	16	102
Quinn John A	0	1	5
Quinn J J	30	50	317
Quinn M	12	25	127
Ramsden Mrs J R	17	44	214
Rees Mrs G S	5	12	78
Reid Andrew	21	40	229
Reveley K G	4	4	25
Reveley Mrs M	6	16	95
Richards Mrs L	4	8	27
Ritchens P C	0	1	10
Roberts C	0	3	18
Roberts Miss Victoria	0	0	3
Rogers H	1	3	4
Rolland M	1	2	4
Rothwell B S	1	3	47
Rowe R	0	0	8
Rowland Miss M E	0	0	12
Ryan K A	65	102	470
Ryan M J	6	8	47
Sadik A	0	6	37
Salaman M	0	1	10
Sanders Miss B	18	30	146
Saunders M S	16	16	124
Sayer Mrs Dianne	0	0	6
Scargill Dr J D	2	9	48
Scott Miss V	0	2	3
Scudamore M	0	0	7
Seemar S	0	2	2
Semple I	33	62	309
Senior A	0	0	13
Sharpe Mrs N S	0	0	5
Shaw D	20	45	353
Sheehan J J	1	5	38
Siddall Miss L C	0	3	19
Simcock D M	7	4	62
Sly Mrs P	0	0	17
Smart B	30	68	396
Smith C	3	6	65
Smith A D	1	2	32
Smith R J	0	2	12
Smith Mrs S J	0	1	8
Smith Miss A M Newton	0	2	18
Smith Mrs N	1	1	4
Smith Miss Suzy	0	1	5
Smith V	15	26	125
Southcombe Jane	1	18	79
Sowersby M E	2	3	70
Spearing J L	18	30	207
Stewart A C	9	21	78
Stokell Miss A	3	13	146

FLAT TRAINERS - Wins/Places/Runners   Nov 10 2003 - Nov 6 2004

Storey W	5	21	125
Stoute Sir Michael	86	98	407
Stronge R M	2	4	38
Stubbs Mrs L	10	20	129
Sunderland M P	0	1	3
Supple J A	0	0	19
Suroor Saeed bin	120	124	489
Sweeting Mrs H	7	12	94
Swinbank G A	18	18	118
Tate T P	10	8	78
Taylor Mrs L C	0	0	2
Teague C J	1	2	28
Thompson Ronald	2	3	50
Thompson D W	1	3	41
Thornton C W	2	15	72
Thorpe Mrs A M	0	1	2
Tinkler C	4	20	89
Tinkler N	17	34	262
Tinning W H	6	8	27
Tizzard C L	0	0	6
Todhunter M	4	4	33
Toller J A R	9	33	148
Tompkins M H	35	71	321
Townsley Mrs P	3	2	23
Tregoning M P	27	58	205
Tuck J C	0	0	4
Tuer E W	0	2	16
Turnell Andrew	6	19	98
Turner W de Best	1	3	49
Turner W G M	22	33	190
Tyrrell E	2	1	5
Unett J W	6	23	143
Usher M D I	10	13	86
Vaughan E F	17	17	81
Wainwright J S	17	36	264
Walford T D	0	0	2
Wallace M J	15	35	173
Wall C F	20	46	213
Wall T	3	4	53
Walton Mrs K	0	3	25
Waring Mrs	0	0	12
Watson F	0	1	37
Webber P R	1	2	29
Weeden M J	0	0	7
Weedon C	3	3	13
Weld D K	6	25	50
Wellings M	1	5	40
West Miss S	1	1	26
Weymes J R	7	33	203
Wheeler E A	3	13	88
Whillans A C	2	7	32
Whillans D W	0	0	5
Whitaker R M	14	23	153
White J	0	3	11
Wigham M	6	14	70
Williams S C	33	39	225
Williams Ian	16	11	119
Williams D L	1	2	17
Williams Nick	0	0	3
Williamson Mrs L	0	1	3
Williams Miss Venetia	0	0	8
Wilson N	9	10	57
Wilson C R	0	0	3
Wilton Miss S J	2	6	44
Wingrove K G	0	0	8
Winkworth P	2	5	15
Winters Miss A M	0	0	2
Wintle D J	0	0	24
Wood I A	22	42	323
Woodhouse R D E	0	0	6
Woodman S	3	2	15
Wood P R	0	0	18
Woods Lindsay	1	0	5

Wragg G	26	44	192

Highest Win Percent

Prescott Sir Mark	75	48	255	29%
Suroor Saeed bin	120	124	489	25%
Tinning W H	6	8	27	22%
Stoute Sir Michael	86	98	407	21%
Vaughan E F	17	17	81	21%
Hyam P W Chappl	29	34	150	19%
Charlton R	41	53	233	18%
Mackie J	13	21	74	18%
Horgan C A	11	12	60	18%
Magnusson M A	8	8	45	18%
Jarvis M A	65	99	380	17%
Noseda J	36	60	210	17%
Price R J	12	9	70	17%
Curley B J	9	6	52	17%
Fitzgerald T J	8	4	46	17%
Fanshawe J R	47	70	291	16%
Allen C N	10	11	61	16%
Wilson N	9	10	57	16%
Johnson J Howard	8	12	51	16%
Reveley K G	4	4	25	16%
Johnston M	122	194	812	15%
Gosden J H M	67	125	461	15%
Haggas W J	46	54	299	15%
Cumani L M	45	81	298	15%
Williams S C	33	39	225	15%
Swinbank G A	18	18	118	15%
Richards Mrs L	4	8	27	15%
Ryan K A	65	102	470	14%
Barron T D	61	94	448	14%
Wragg G	26	44	192	14%
Jarvis W	23	31	161	14%
Cecil H R A	21	41	149	14%
Flood D	18	24	126	14%
Pearce B A	8	12	57	14%
Juckes A G	3	3	21	14%
Bell M L W	55	98	427	13%
Harris P W	45	74	347	13%
Loder D R	44	74	343	13%
Elsworth D R C	40	55	313	13%
Tregoning M P	27	58	205	13%
Saunders M S	16	16	124	13%
Williams Ian	16	11	119	13%
Tate T P	10	8	78	13%
Egerton C R	7	9	55	13%
Ryan M J	6	8	47	13%
King J S	5	7	40	13%
Hedger P R	3	3	24	13%
Liddiard Mrs S A	3	4	24	13%
Long J E	3	3	24	13%
Lungo L	3	6	23	13%
Townsley Mrs P	3	2	23	13%
Hills B W	78	137	634	12%
Fahey R A	74	126	620	12%
Burke K R	60	104	486	12%
Meehan B J	59	94	483	12%
Dunlop E A L	49	94	407	12%
Perrett Mrs A J	48	89	385	12%
Best J R	39	62	337	12%
Callaghan N A	34	50	282	12%
McMahon B A	27	38	231	12%
Candy H	23	43	193	12%
Turner W G M	22	33	190	12%
Fisher R F	18	29	155	12%
Makin P J	18	23	152	12%
Sanders Miss B	18	30	146	12%
Smith V	15	26	125	12%
Cox C G	14	20	116	12%
Usher M D I	10	13	86	12%
Herries Lady	9	14	75	12%
Stewart A C	9	21	78	12%
Berry John	8	12	66	12%
Parkes J	7	7	60	12%
Weld D K	6	25	50	12%
Dalton Mrs H	5	6	42	12%
Jones Bob	5	6	42	12%
Craggs R	4	8	33	12%
Gubby B	4	6	33	12%
Todhunter M	4	4	33	12%
Dickin R	3	5	26	12%
Mactaggart B	3	3	26	12%

Top Owners Nov 9 '03 - Nov 6 '04 by Races Won

Owner	Won Most Money	Races Won	Win Money
Godolphin	Sulamani	121	£4371604
Mr Hamdan Al Maktoum	Haafhd	76	£1274499
Mr K Abdulla	Polish Summer	65	£1555367
Cheveley Park Stud	Chorist	57	£822952
Sheikh Mohammed	Privy Seal	55	£486892
Sheikh Ahmed Al Maktoum	Tahreeb	37	£276625
Maktoum Al Maktoum	Favourable Terms	33	£566875
Mr Nigel Shields	Moayed	33	£166268
Mr Paul J Dixon	Ascertain	25	£118686
Mrs John Magnier	Powerscourt	23	£969060
Lucayan Stud	Bahamian Pirate	21	£217316
Mr A S Reid	Bunditten	19	£76295
Elite Racing Club	Dancing Bay	18	£467055
Highclere Thoroughbred Racing	Sentry	17	£249358
Jumeirah Racing	Aleutian	16	£67955
Mr P D Savill	Raccoon	16	£144350
Mrs P W Harris	Cutting Crew	16	£159981
Mr Dennis Deacon	Banningham Blaze	15	£40139
Mr J C Fretwell	Castelletto	15	£127905
Mrs Susan Roy	Wilko	15	£67630
The Queen	Promotion	15	£98131
Waterline Racing Club	Hazewind	15	£51711
Hesmonds Stud	Two Step Kid	14	£153095
Mollers Racing	Autumn Glory	14	£159913
Mrs Ruth M Serrell	Jonny Ebeneezer	14	£108689
Niarchos Family	Bago	13	£1271560
Norcroft Park Stud	Polar Jem	13	£104045
HESheikh Rashid Bin Mohammed	Merchant	12	£71330
Miss K Rausing	Albanova	12	£265092
Mr David W Chapman	Soaked	12	£31319
Great Head House Estates Limit	Beckermet	11	£44872
HRH Sultan Ahmad Shah	Anak Pekan	11	£168935
Miss B Swire	Gold Ring	11	£67187
Mountgrange Stud	Dorothys Friend	11	£107026
Mr Abdulla BuHaleeba	Shamardal	11	£122860
Mr Raymond Tooth	Whistler	11	£98674
HH Aga Khan	Azamour	10	£272395
Mr D J Deer	Avonbridge	10	£44411
Mr M Tabor	Magistretti	10	£73854
Richard Green (Fine Paintings)	Peter Paul Rubens	10	£80707
Steve Jones and Phil McGovern	Sendintank	10	£61076
Favourites Racing	Woody Valentine	9	£57555
Ivy House Racing	H Harrison	9	£27596
Miss Maria McKinney	Realism	9	£33037
Miss Vanessa Church	Salsa Brava	9	£59352
Mr Erik Penser	Compton Bolter	9	£43369
Mr Guy Reed	Alfonso	9	£47405
Mr P Sweeting	Playtime Blue	9	£27508
Mrs Joanna Hughes	Hiawatha	9	£21514
Mrs S J Lawrence	And Toto Too	9	£28234
Diamond Racing Ltd	Diamond Orchid	8	£28756
East Wind Racing Ltd	Kehaar	8	£108505
Ecurie Wildenstein	Westerner	8	£967669
Mr J M Greetham	Forever Phoenix	8	£89208
Mr Khalifa Sultan	Swift Tango	8	£70534
Mr M W Lawrence	Nashaab	8	£43454
Mr R C Bond	Bond City	8	£89560

Top Owners Nov 10 '03 - Nov 6 '04 by Prize Money

Owner	Won Most Money	Races Won	Win Money
Godolphin	Sulamani	121	£4371604
Mr K Abdulla	Polish Summer	67	£1639663
Mr Hamdan Al Maktoum	Haafhd	76	£1274499
Niarchos Family	Bago	13	£1271560
Ecurie Wildenstein	Westerner	9	£1009817
Mrs John Magnier	Powerscourt	23	£969060
Mr Gary A Tanaka	Rakti	6	£948867
Ballymacoll Stud	North Light	7	£921092
Cheveley Park Stud	Chorist	57	£822952
Lord Derby	Ouija Board	4	£788933
Duke of Roxburghe	Attraction	4	£593902
Maktoum Al Maktoum	Favourable Terms	33	£566875
Mrs Rochelle Quinn	Grey Swallow	2	£514679
Sheikh Mohammed	Privy Seal	55	£486892
Elite Racing Club	Dancing Bay	18	£467055
Baron G Von Ullmann	Shirocco	3	£403169
Sheikh Ahmed Al Maktoum	Tahreeb	37	£276625
HH Aga Khan	Azamour	10	£272395
Miss K Rausing	Albanova	12	£265092
Stall Meerbusch	Senex	2	£260841
Highclere Thoroughbred Racing	Sentry	17	£249358
R C Strauss	Whipper	2	£237162
E Ciampi	Latice	2	£226901
Mme P de Moussac	Lune Dor	3	£220986
Lucayan Stud	Bahamian Pirate	21	£217316
Sangster Family	Playful Act	8	£210089
Mrs G Smith	Gamut	3	£202751
Mr Saeed Manana	Menhoubah	7	£196432
Lagardere Family	Cherry Mix	5	£185619
Mr B E Nielsen	Tante Rose	4	£185312
Mill House Partnership	Caesar Beware	3	£184018
Mrs Angie Silver	Mephisto	4	£183778
Baron T de Zuylen de Nyevelt	Voix Du Nord	3	£178283
Mrs N O'Callaghan	Alexander Goldrun	5	£176097
Gestut Ammerland	Grey Lilas	3	£174696
Mrs Jan Hopper & Mrs Elizabeth	Frizzante	2	£174000
HRH Sultan Ahmad Shah	Anak Pekan	11	£168935
Mr Nigel Shields	Moayed	33	£166268
Legard Sidebottom & Sykes	Somnus	2	£160958
Mrs P W Harris	Cutting Crew	16	£159981
Mollers Racing	Autumn Glory	14	£159913
Hesmonds Stud	Two Step Kid	14	£153095
Wood Street Syndicate	Salamanca	2	£151766
Mr P D Savill	Raccoon	16	£144350
Mr W H Ponsonby	Gatwick	5	£134060
Mr F C T Wilson	Magical Romance	6	£133463
Franconson Partners	Montgomerys Arch	6	£129803
Mr J C Fretwell	Castelletto	15	£127905
T Maudet	Helios Quercus	2	£126303
The Royal Ascot Racing Club	Motivator	2	£124804
Mr L Neil Jones	Let The Lion Roar	3	£124687
Mr Richard J Cohen	Spanish Don	6	£124484
Mr Abdulla BuHaleeba	Shamardal	11	£122860
Mrs John Magnier & Mr M Tabor	Damson	2	£121838
Syndicate 2002	Mister Monet	7	£119669
Mr Paul J Dixon	Ascertain	25	£118686
Dab Hand Racing	The Tatling	4	£118331

Top Flat Trainers 2004

Trainer	Won	Placed	Runs	Win %	Win + Plc %	Profit	Prize Money
M Johnston	122	194	812	15%	39%	£-160.5	£2981321
Saeed bin Suroor	120	124	489	25%	50%	£-4.9	£5896663
R Hannon	113	253	1212	9%	30%	£-276.9	£1588129
M R Channon	98	243	1064	9%	32%	£-405.6	£2278680
Sir Michael Stoute	86	98	407	21%	45%	£+22.1	£3304058
B W Hills	78	137	634	12%	34%	£-172.9	£1571682
Sir Mark Prescott	75	48	255	29%	48%	£+30	£864633
R A Fahey	74	126	620	12%	32%	£-42.9	£725572
J H M Gosden	67	125	461	15%	42%	£-98.2	£1590067
P D Evans	66	124	682	10%	28%	£-100.4	£457243
M A Jarvis	65	99	380	17%	43%	£-71.1	£1775101
K A Ryan	65	102	470	14%	36%	£+12.3	£611809
T D Easterby	64	158	740	9%	30%	£-267	£1119812
T D Barron	61	94	448	14%	35%	£-16.6	£483801
K R Burke	60	104	486	12%	34%	£-39.4	£373035
B J Meehan	59	94	483	12%	32%	£-30.9	£892757
J L Dunlop	57	115	520	11%	33%	£-103.4	£1273693
M L W Bell	55	98	427	13%	36%	£-117.1	£655197
D Nicholls	55	108	701	8%	23%	£-235	£876335
W M Brisbourne	51	94	592	9%	24%	£-212.5	£283099
E A L Dunlop	49	94	407	12%	35%	£-132.8	£1514354
Mrs A J Perrett	48	89	385	12%	36%	£-59	£733272
A M Balding	47	114	542	9%	30%	£-178	£677579
J R Fanshawe	47	70	291	16%	40%	£-48.5	£1358366
P A Blockley	46	85	429	11%	31%	£-34.1	£240840
W J Haggas	46	54	299	15%	33%	£+24.4	£773399
N P Littmoden	46	117	543	8%	30%	£-71.2	£572769
L M Cumani	45	81	298	15%	42%	£-65.8	£1911670
P W Harris	45	74	347	13%	34%	£-21	£562185
G L Moore	45	85	471	10%	28%	£-135.4	£324690
D R Loder	44	74	343	13%	34%	£-135.2	£576079
R Charlton	41	53	233	18%	40%	£+16.3	£741674
D R C Elsworth	40	55	313	13%	30%	£+171.9	£969725
J R Best	39	62	337	12%	30%	£+75.7	£216325
J M Bradley	39	107	690	6%	21%	£-222.1	£593573
A W Carroll	39	98	415	9%	33%	£-151.6	£217418
P F I Cole	39	72	369	11%	30%	£-121.4	£654671
A Berry	36	89	575	6%	22%	£-166.7	£338885
J Noseda	36	60	210	17%	46%	£+18.6	£968467
J A Osborne	36	87	411	9%	30%	£-167	£366484
Miss Gay Kelleway	35	70	370	9%	28%	£-78.5	£315429

Top Flat Jockeys 2004

Jockey	Won	Placed	Rides	Win %	Win + Plc %	Profit	Prize Money
L Dettori	208	237	911	23%	49%	£+89.2	£7577763
K Fallon	204	299	1105	18%	46%	£-167.3	£6266844
S Sanders	167	211	1021	16%	37%	£+52.5	£2132599
D Holland	156	275	1186	13%	36%	£-310	£2922728
R L Moore	129	224	970	13%	36%	£+183	£1530526
N Callan	118	214	1001	12%	33%	£-128.6	£951034
R Winston	113	192	959	12%	32%	£-56.1	£1182171
A Culhane	112	229	1036	11%	33%	£-150	£1009623
J Fanning	98	137	747	13%	31%	£-8.1	£1106955
E Ahern	96	189	933	10%	31%	£-178.3	£1170707
S Drowne	92	185	1038	9%	27%	£-211.1	£1347769
P Hanagan	89	141	684	13%	34%	£+92.9	£998364
Dane O'Neill	85	182	1017	8%	26%	£-334.8	£987548
K Darley	83	192	827	10%	33%	£-255.2	£2004681
Martin Dwyer	80	157	808	10%	29%	£-177.9	£1112313
I Mongan	80	158	847	9%	28%	£-198.9	£491996
J Murtagh	79	121	586	13%	34%	£-63.7	£2200177
T Quinn	70	142	633	11%	33%	£-18.7	£1310301
M Fenton	69	142	796	9%	27%	£-188.4	£609209
R Hughes	68	130	604	11%	33%	£-207.7	£1311101
P Robinson	68	129	560	12%	35%	£-157.8	£1997803
R Hills	67	115	457	15%	40%	£-82.9	£1695550
J Quinn	66	185	909	7%	28%	£-247.7	£744206
M Hills	64	102	512	13%	32%	£-111.8	£973882
F Norton	64	133	577	11%	34%	£-18.5	£575353
J Fortune	62	144	555	11%	37%	£-197.4	£1418354
T P Queally	60	106	657	9%	25%	£-220.6	£583328
J F Egan	58	134	696	8%	28%	£-62.1	£1036426
C Catlin	57	136	918	6%	21%	£-335.9	£607920
S W Kelly	57	143	756	8%	26%	£-351.8	£464698
J P Spencer	54	77	237	23%	55%	£-23.4	£2910092
W Supple	53	139	617	9%	31%	£-181.1	£943219
F Lynch	50	85	458	11%	29%	£+52.3	£533911
Darren Williams	50	100	544	9%	28%	£-17.5	£313990
Lisa Jones	49	98	713	7%	21%	£-261.4	£318250
N Mackay	48	67	343	14%	34%	£+72.3	£553687
R Ffrench	47	111	614	8%	26%	£-245.5	£447860
D Sweeney	46	84	544	8%	24%	£-92.7	£340054
K McEvoy	45	63	328	14%	33%	£-43.4	£1810923
T E Durcan	44	110	619	7%	25%	£-265.8	£1279464
D Allan	43	125	548	8%	31%	£-182.1	£435252
J Mackay	43	59	463	9%	22%	£-142	£308069
Dale Gibson	39	91	546	7%	24%	£-87.4	£272075
N Pollard	39	61	453	9%	22%	£-120.2	£207657
W Ryan	39	50	337	12%	26%	£-73.3	£342536

Top Flat Sires 2004

Sire	Won	Placed	Runners	Win %	Win + Plc %	Profit	Prize Money
Danehill	102	100	514	20%	39%	£+150.5	£4464238
Pivotal	91	112	528	17%	38%	£+173.6	£1648093
Sadler's Wells	72	135	530	14%	39%	£-49.2	£4441469
Cadeaux Genereux	67	132	651	10%	31%	£-71.1	£833989
Polar Falcon	66	105	453	15%	38%	£+126.4	£950563
Machiavellian	63	89	426	15%	36%	£-49.4	£1552362
Barathea	62	95	537	12%	29%	£-2.3	£1115569
Grand Lodge	61	114	659	9%	27%	£-253	£845340
Selkirk	60	103	469	13%	35%	£-39.1	£1623473
Efisio	59	101	512	12%	31%	£-28.6	£1326579
Royal Applause	57	112	649	9%	26%	£-202.7	£686416
Tagula	54	81	423	13%	32%	£+23.8	£630212
Inchinor	52	92	533	10%	27%	£-164.2	£898206
Piccolo	52	110	689	8%	24%	£-274.3	£487599
Cape Cross	51	75	332	15%	38%	£+59	£1779198
Green Desert	50	98	473	11%	31%	£-118.3	£985460
Mujadil	50	84	556	9%	24%	£-37.6	£369462
Indian Ridge	48	112	494	10%	32%	£-106.6	£1050398
Marju	48	65	321	15%	35%	£+10.1	£1121660
Danehill Dancer	46	104	477	10%	31%	£-167	£681554
Night Shift	46	131	656	7%	27%	£-153.3	£1147967
Mind Games	45	112	606	7%	26%	£-189.9	£409716
Compton Place	41	84	517	8%	24%	£-97.6	£478385
Dr Fong	41	83	373	11%	33%	£-65.4	£575144
Sri Pekan	41	86	453	9%	28%	£-66.9	£445323
Orpen	39	79	337	12%	35%	£-67.3	£505951
Komaite	38	92	429	9%	30%	£-150.1	£333299
Mark of Esteem	38	53	353	11%	26%	£-104.9	£512753
Pursuit of Love	38	81	453	8%	26%	£-86	£322470
Zafonic	38	94	394	10%	34%	£-64.9	£642358
Atraf	37	57	354	10%	27%	£-50.7	£255573
Groom Dancer	36	68	388	9%	27%	£-82	£850892
Halling	36	52	293	12%	30%	£-81.5	£817818
Kingmambo	35	47	199	18%	41%	£-29.6	£1533003
Magic Ring	35	80	437	8%	26%	£-121.6	£278826
Revoque	35	61	311	11%	31%	£-60.1	£287666
Most Welcome	34	51	238	14%	36%	£-4.8	£283754
Unfuwain	34	67	311	11%	32%	£-63	£496463
Bahamian Bounty	33	53	316	10%	27%	£-36.4	£444162
Daylami	32	50	190	17%	43%	£+1.1	£915056
Desert King	32	59	279	11%	33%	£-66	£1667421
Intikhab	32	60	244	13%	38%	£+15.2	£457144
Spectrum	32	81	450	7%	25%	£-173	£603593
Desert Sun	31	49	261	12%	31%	£-1.9	£315844

Using The Ratings

The ratings in this book are expressed in pounds on a scale of 0-140. To assess any race where the horses are all of the same age, simply subtract the weight each horse is set to carry from 10-0 and add the result to the Superform rating.

E.G. Dunan 4-9-2 rated 61   10-0 minus 9-2 = 12   12 + 61 = 73

Make these calculations for each horse in turn. The horse with the highest adjusted rating is most favoured by the weights.

To assess a race in which there are horses of different ages, consult the scale of age, weight and distance found on the last 3 pages at the back of the book. On consulting the scale, according to the distance of the race, the month in which it is taking place (and time within the month) and the age of the horse, subtract the weight the horse is set to carry from the weight now pin-pointed in the table. Then add the result to the horse's Superform rating.

E.G.   7 furlong race on 11th April

Dunan 4-9-2 rated 61 Table weight 10-0 minus 9-2 =12   12 plus 61=73
Grady 3-8-1   rated 61 Table weight 9-0   minus 8-1 =13   13 plus 61=74
Budge 3-7-10 rated 60 Table weight 9-0   minus 7-10=18   18 plus 60=78
                  Budge has the best chance at the weights

USING THE RATINGS
A considerable time saving method for rating any race meeting is to make calculations only for those horses mentioned in the betting forecast. This applies to the majority of bread and butter racing but valuable handicaps need more detailed treatment. Concentrating only on horses mentioned in the betting forecast should take about twenty minutes per meeting - with practice. Another advantage of working this way is that you can compare the odds on offer with the ratings calculated. It should not take long before you become adept at spotting value for money.

VALUE OF RECENT FORM
Please remember that ratings are not magic figures. Above all, you must take into account whether or not the horse is race-fit. Unless you have a direct stable link the only way to be sure of fitness is to have printed evidence of a good recent run. By recent we mean no more than 40 days ago. Also try to ensure that the rating which you are using was achieved recently. As a general rule form more than 40 days old must be treated with caution. However horses from top stables such as Stoute, Johnston or Saeed bin Suroor can usually be relied upon to be fit whenever they run.

PATTERN OF EVENTS
Don't become so tied up with figures that you miss the broad pattern of events in racehorse performances. Most horses, especially handicappers, need a set of conditions before they are able to produce their best. The distance must be right: their going requirements must be met and for many horses, particularly front running types, the course must be suitable.

Time/Pace/Going Figures

Race times are used to calculate the prevailing going on the day, and also to give an idea of the relative pace at which each race was run.

Firstly we compare the race time with the standard time for the track. When this is calculated on a per furlong basis over 6 races, a fairly accurate picture of the prevailing going emerges.

Take for example a race over 5f that returns a time of 63 seconds. The standard time for the track is 59 seconds. Thus the race was run in 4 seconds slower than standard time. Divide 4 (seconds) by 5 (furlongs) which equals 0.80. Do this for all six races which would typically give figures of .80, 1.00, .65, 1.10, 1.15, 1.05. Add the figures together - total 5.75 for 6 races. Divide 5.75 by 6 (races) and we have an average per furlong figure of .96 (.9583 rounded up).

This would indicate that the going was on the soft side or good since we use the following table as a guide:

1.30 and upwards	HEAVY
0.90 to 1.30	SOFT
0.60 to 0.90	GOOD/SOFT
0.40 to 0.60	GOOD
0.20 to 0.40	GOOD/FIRM
Below 0.20	FIRM

The average figure for each meeting is printed after the going in each race - usually without the decimal point. Thus - Good 60.

The official going report is also printed at the start of each meeting.

Please note that we may omit races from the calculations should these races have been very slow run. There are also days when small fields and/or a succession of slow run races make it impossible to produce any meaningful figure.

PACE FIGURES
We also find this going figure useful in determining the relative **pace** of each race. In the above example the average per furlong figure for the meeting was .96. The third race produced a figure of only .65 and was therefore run at a relatively fast pace. Conversely the fifth race with a figure of 1.15 was a fairly slow run affair.

We indicate in the results whether the race was fast or slow run. This figure is calculated by comparing the figure for each race with the average for the meeting. Thus the first race would be +16 Fast (.96 minus .80) Race five would be -19 slow (.96 - 1.15).

The general conclusions to be drawn from the pace figures are:

Slow pace - Form might be suspect particularly with regard to placed horses (especially in non handicaps).

Fast Pace - Form can be relied on and the form of close up, placed horses should work out well. Easy winners can be followed with some confidence.

Compiling The Ratings

COMPILING THE RATINGS

The ratings published in this book are expressions of opinion, based wherever possible on collateral form. Superform ratings are presented on the same 0-140 scale as used by the official BHB Handicappers and Superform ratings may be compared directly with the official figures.

In studying form and assessing racehorse performance, we are trying to complete a complex jigsaw puzzle. The picture is not complete until the end of the season and sometimes not even then. Many of the "pieces" are definitely shaped and slot into obvious places (the older handicappers), but so many of the pieces have no precise shape and we can only place them tentatively until more of the picture is revealed - and some of the pieces are changing shape as we study them! These non-precise and changing pieces are represented by the late season 2 year olds and those 3 year old maidens that did not run or were lightly raced in their first season.

However experience helps greatly in rating these animals. Collateral form is the basis for our ratings but of course none exists with the early 2 year olds. Experience shows that the early two year old maiden races are won by the same standard of animal each year. Thus we start by giving the early winners "average figures" that one expects for these races and soon the winners or placed horses begin to race against one another and we have the beginnings of collateral form. As results unfold and our handicappers discover that a race has been underrated or overrated, the ratings for the race are revised. **The revision is done on a daily basis throughout the season and all adjustments to the ratings have been incorporated in this annual.**

OFFICIAL RATINGS

At the start of each handicap race, in the right hand margin, the figure in brackets [] represents the official rating of a horse set to carry 10-0 in that race. If the figure is 100, a horse carrying 10-0 is running off an official mark of 100 in that race. A horse carrying 8-8 is rated 80 since it carries 20lb less than 10-0. This has been a feature of Superform since 1985. **However, in handicaps this official figure is now printed in brackets after the horse's weight and also in non-h'caps - where a rating has been allocated.**

GUIDE TO CLASS

The following is a fair guide to class:

130 plus	Top class, cream of the crop, multiple Group 1 winner.
125 - 129	Very high class: a good Group 1 winner.
120 - 125	High class: capable of Group 1/2 success.
115 - 120	Very smart: capable of winning Group 2/3 events.
110 - 115	Smart: capable of Listed/Group 3 success.
100 - 110	Very useful handicapper/ potential Listed/Group 3 winner.
90 - 100	Useful handicapper.
80 - 90	Fair handicapper.
70 - 80	Average handicapper.
60 - 70	Moderate handicapper/Selling class.
50 and below	Moderate/Selling handicapper.

Racecourse Guide

ASCOT A right handed triangular track: quite a stiff course with an uphill finish: 5,6,7f tracks and the straight mile over which the Royal Hunt Cup is run, are undulating with a stiff uphill climb in the last two furlongs. **Round mile**, 10, 12 furlongs and upwards are undulating, the run-in is short, only 2 and a half furlongs, and it is not a good track for coming with a late run: particularly testing track when the ground is soft: on the round course there is little advantage but on soft ground high numbers may have a slight edge.

AYR A left handed, flat galloping track: a very fair course which favours the big and strong galloping types: 5 and 6f tracks are straight and easy and in big fields on soft ground, low numbers are favoured but on fast ground, high numbers have the advantage: races run over 7f and upwards are on the turn, left handed, and low numbers hold an advantage: there is a good run-in of four and a half furlongs.

BATH A left handed, galloping, oval track with quite a steep uphill finish: 5f and 5f170 yards tracks bend to the left and are stiff: low numbers are slightly favoured in races up to 1 mile: the run-in for races over 7f+ is a good half mile and the stiff finish often favours hold up horses: this is the only flat track without a watering system and the ground can be firm or hard in a dry spell.

BEVERLEY A right handed oval course with a stiff uphill finish: the 5f course has a bend to the right and is a particularly tough test for two year olds: the run-in is a short two and a half furlongs: one of the strongest draw bias of any track with high numbers holding a significant advantage at all trips up to 9f.

BRIGHTON A left handed, very undulating track which is against the big long striding animal and favours handy types, front runners, and those who might have lost some of their zest for the game: 5 and 6f tracks are sharp and easy and on the turn, so that a low number and speed from the gate give an advantage: on soft ground, runners tack to the stands side which gives high numbers an edge: the run-in is three and a half furlongs: course stands on chalk and the going is rarely very soft but often firm: a course for specialists.

CARLISLE A right handed, undulating, pear shaped course with a stiff uphill run-in of three and a half furlongs: the undulations are pronounced and the track is a testing one: the subsoil is clay and the going tends to extremes: 5f and 6f tracks are on the turn and high numbers are favoured except on soft ground when low numbers have an edge.

CATTERICK A very sharp, left handed, oval track, only 9f round, and the 5f track is downhill all the way: front runners are at home here with the accent on speed: on fast ground low numbers hold the advantage in sprints but on soft ground the runners can tack to the outside rail: a course for specialists.

CHEPSTOW A left handed oval circuit of 2 miles with undulations but the course is generally galloping: all races up to 1 mile are run on a straight track which provides quite a stiff test and the accent is on stamina: there seems little draw advantage at present: the run-in is 5f.

CHESTER An extremely sharp, left handed track, only 1 mile round: this is a front runner's track where all the racing is done on the turn: it is most definitely a course for specialists: unfortunately form shown here is so often not repeated elsewhere: low numbers have a big advantage in all races up to 7f 122 yards (especially 5f) on fast and soft ground:.

DONCASTER A left handed flat galloping track: ideal for the big, long striding horse, and the powerful galloper: the run-in is 5 furlongs and the accent is on stamina: there is a round mile track where low numbers are slightly favoured: on the straight course there now appears no draw advantage but in big fields when the ground is soft, recently low numbers have done best.

EPSOM A left handed track with pronounced undulations and a fairly short run-in of three and a half furlongs: it is all against the long striding horse: front runners have a good record here and the gradients seem to rekindle enthusiasm in those horses who may have lost some zest: the sprint tracks are fast, downhill nearly all the way: over 5f speed from the gate is essential, high numbers are best: low numbers are favoured from 6f to 1 mile on good or faster ground, however, when it does ride soft the stands rail (high draw) is favoured: not a track for the inexperienced 2 year olds: a course for specialists.

FOLKESTONE A right handed, undulating track with a fairly short run-in of just over two and a half furlongs: easy track, no great demand made on stamina: high numbers hold an edge over 5-6f, however, this is more pronounced on soft or heavy ground.

GOODWOOD A right handed track with severe undulations: totally unsuited to the big long striding animal: small, handy types who can keep good balance galloping downhill, have the advantage: the 5f and 6f track is very fast and speed from the gate is essential: a high draw is generally an advantage on fast ground: the track suits front runners: a course for specialists.

HAMILTON A right handed, undulating course with a run-in of 5 furlongs: the run-in contains a dip 3 furlongs from the winning post and a fairly stiff uphill finish: the course stands on clay and in wet weather it rides very heavy: the 5f and 6f tracks are straight and on the stiff side: on soft ground, high numbers have a definite advantage in the sprints.

HAYDOCK A left handed, flat galloping track, with a run-in of some four and a half furlongs: the home stretch is on the rise and the accent is on stamina and courage: in races up to 1 mile, low numbers have the advantage: however when the going rides soft, runners usually race centre/ stands side and a high draw is favoured over 5-6f.

KEMPTON A right handed track with a three and a half furlong run-in: the bends are quite sharp: a good track for front runners: the separate 5f and 6f track is straight and low numbers have an advantage when the stalls are on the stands' side, especially on soft ground: when the stalls are on the far side, high numbers have the edge: on the round course, in races of 7f - 10f, high numbers are favoured.

LEICESTER A right handed, oval, a stiff galloping track with a run-in of 5 furlongs: all races up to and including one mile are run on a straight track: a low draw has some advantage on the straight course and this increases on soft ground: the track stands on clay and limestone and in wet weather it rides very soft.

LINGFIELD Turf A left handed, undulating track with a short run-in of three and a half furlongs: the gradients and the uphill turn into the straight are similar to Epsom: the track is not for a long striding horse: races from 5f to 7f 140 yards are run on a straight track which is mainly downhill and is therefore, fast and easy: fast starters and front runners do well here: on the straight track, high numbers hold an advantage but on soft or heavy ground, very low numbers are favoured, especially over 7f 140 yards.

LINGFIELD All Weather Left handed, turning track, 10f round, with a run-in of less than 2 furlongs. the 5f track is not straight but turns left throughout the first 3f: the surface is polytrack which seems to provide a faster surface than the fibresand used at Southwell: horses that run well here on polytrack are not certain to reproduce the form on fibresand, and vice versa: polytrack is generally accepted as a very fair surface and as there is very little kick-back hold up horses have a much better record here than at either Southwell or Wolverhampton.

MUSSELBURGH A right handed, oval track, 10 furlongs in circumference: an easy course, on the sharp side and front runners do well here: over the 5f straight track, when the stalls are on the stands side, low numbers are best (especially on soft ground) but high numbers are favoured when the stalls are on the far side: high numbers are best over the round 7f/1m track: the course drains well and has a watering system so that the going is rarely extreme.

NEWBURY A left handed, oval, galloping track with a long run-in of 5 furlongs: the sprint course is quite straight and there are also straight 7f and mile tracks: on the straight course the draw has little advantage, but in big fields and especially on soft going, high numbers are favoured: the course stands on gravel and drains well: the accent is on stamina.

NEWCASTLE A left handed, oval galloping course with a good 4 furlong run-in which rises steadily: the 5f, 6f and 7f tracks are straight and quite stiff: a fair course where stamina is needed and there appears little draw advantage.

NEWMARKET (Rowley Mile Course:) All races from 5f - 10f are run on the straight track with an uphill finish: courage and stamina are needed: races over 12f and upwards are run right handed and the course is stiff and galloping: all meetings, except the summer meetings in June, July and August are held on this course.

NEWMARKET (July Course:) All races up to, and including, one mile are run on a straight track, with the final furlong being uphill: races over 10f turn right into the straight: a stiff galloping track: the meetings in June, July and August are held here.

NOTTINGHAM A left handed, flat, oval track with a long run-in of 5 furlongs: a very fair course with little draw bias.

PONTEFRACT A left handed, undulating track, with a short run-in of 2 furlongs and a stiff uphill finish: the 5f and 6f tracks turn left handed into the straight: the sprint course is stiff, and stamina is important: the going tends to extremes, getting firm or very heavy.

REDCAR   A left handed, flat, galloping track with a long run-in of 5 furlongs: a fair course and is ideal for the big, long striding horse: all races up to and including 9f, are run on a straight track: runners have tended to race towards the centre on the straight course this year.

RIPON   A right handed, oval track with a long run-in of 5f which is slightly on the ascent: the bends are just on the sharp side, the undulations in the straight are more severe than they appear to the eye and the round course favours front runners: a draw close to either rail is a big advantage on the straight course.

SALISBURY   A right handed track, but little racing is done on the turn and there is a long run-in of 7f: the last 4 furlongs of the home straight are uphill: the course is a stiff galloping track where stamina is important: all races up to and including 1 mile are straight and the uphill finish is a stiff test for 2 year olds: a high draw is favoured on fast ground, but low numbers have an advantage on soft ground.

SANDOWN   A right handed, oval, galloping track with an uphill run-in of 4 furlongs - stamina is all important: the 5f track is quite separate, uphill all the way and provides a real test of stamina for a two year old: when the stalls are on the stands side, low numbers are best but high numbers have a big advantage when the stalls are placed on the far side, especially on soft ground.

SOUTHWELL All Weather   A left hand, oval track, 10f around with a run-in of just over 2 furlongs: the 5f track is straight. the surface is fibresand which appears to provide a slower surface than the polytrack used at Lingfield and makes more demands on stamina: the 12f standard time here is 2m 34.3 seconds but at Lingfield it is 2m 29.2 seconds: form on fibresand is often not reproduced on polytrack and vice versa: a handy, front running type of horse, with a low-middle draw fits the bill here in races of 6f to 1m.

THIRSK   A left handed, flat, oval track, 10f round with fairly easy turns: the run-in is 4 furlongs: an easy track with the emphasis on speed: the 5f and 6f track is straight with slight undulations and a draw on either rail is a significant advantage in large fields: over 7f/1m low numbers are favoured.

WARWICK   A left handed, circular track with a short run-in of 3 furlongs: there are undulations on the back straight but all races up to 1 mile are run on flat ground: the 5f and 6f tracks bend left into the short straight: suits front runners and handy types: low numbers are preferred on good or fast ground but on soft or heavy, high numbers hold an advantage up to 1m.

WINDSOR   The track is in the form of a figure of eight: only in races over 12f and upwards do they gallop both right and left handed: only right handed turns are encountered in races up to 1 mile: the 5f and 6f tracks are nearly straight, flat and quite easy: high numbers have a big advantage on fast ground but on soft, low numbers do best: the 5 furlong run-in makes this a fair track despite the turns.

WOLVERHAMPTON All Weather   A left handed oval course of only one mile, with a 380 yards run-in and tight bends: the slower fibresand has been in use since all-weather inception, however, the track has been resurfaced with polytrack for this coming winter season: form on fibresand is often not repeated on polytrack and vice versa.

YARMOUTH   A left handed course with a 5 furlong run-in: races up to and including 1 mile are run on a straight track: suitable course for delivering a late challenge: high numbers are favoured on the straight course except when stalls are on the far side (low).

YORK   A left handed, flat, galloping course: ideal for the big, powerful galloper and stamina and courage are required to win here: the 5f and 6f track is quite straight: over 5/6f low numbers have an advantage on soft ground especially when the stalls are placed on the far side otherwise the draw seems unpredictable.

Abbreviations

abs	= absent or absence	ldrs	= leaders
al	= always	lkd	= looked
appr	= approaching	mdn	= maiden
bhnd	= behind	mid-div	= mid-division
bckd	= backed	mkt	= market (betting)
bl	= blinkers	mod	= 1. moderate
BL	= blinkered first time		= 2. modest
blun	= blundered	mstk	= mistake
blnks	= blinkers	ndd	= needed
btn	= beaten	nrr	= nearer
btr	= better	nrst	= nearest
C/D	= course & distance	nvr	= never
ch	= chance	oh	= see under weights page 6
chall	= challenge	op	= opened
clr	= clear	ow	= see under weights page 6
chse	= chase	plcd	= placed
chsd	= chased	poss	= possibly
cmftbly	= comfortably	press	= pressure
disapp	= disappointing	prev	= previously
dist	= distance i.e 240 yards	prog	= progress
	from winning post	prom	= prominent
drvn	= driven	p.u.	= pulled up
dsptd	= disputed	qcknd	= quickened
eff	= 1. effort	rcd	= raced
	= 2. effective	rdn	= ridden
ent	= entering	rem	= reminder
ev	= every	rnr-up	= runner-up
ex	= penalty for recent win	sev	= several
fav	= 1. After SP = favourite	soft	= soft
	= 2. In text = favoured	sh	= short
fdd	= faded	shld	= should
fin	= finished	shrp	= sharp
fm	= firm going	sn	= soon
gall	= galloping	styd	= stayed
gd	= good	str	= straight
Gr	= Group	swtg	= sweating
hcap	= handicap	t.o.	= tailed off
hd	= head	trk	= track
hdd	= headed	unbtn	= unbeaten
hdle	= hurdle	undul	= undulating
hdwy	= headway	unpl	= unplaced
hmpd	= hampered	vis	= visor
hvy	= heavy	VIS	= visor for first time
impr	= impression/improve	wnr	= winner
ins	= inside	wknd	= weakened
juv	= juvenile	wl	= well
ld	= lead	$	= rating is probably unreliable

Scale Of Age, Weight And Distance

Dist	Age	JAN 1-15	JAN 16-31	FEB 1-15	FEB 16-28	MAR 1-15	MAR 16-31	APR 1-15	APR 16-30
5f	2						6-9	6-12	7-1
	3	8-13	8-13	9-0	9-0	9-1	9-2	9-3	9-4
	4	10-0	10-0	10-0	10-0	10-0	10-0	10-0	10-0
6f	3	8-12	8-12	8-13	8-13	9-0	9-1	9-2	9-3
	4	10-0	10-0	10-0	10-0	10-0	10-0	10-0	10-0
7f	3	8-10	8-10	8-11	8-11	8-12	8-13	9-0	9-1
	4	10-0	10-0	10-0	10-0	10-0	10-0	10-0	10-0
8f	3	8-8	8-8	8-9	8-9	8-10	8-11	8-13	9-0
	4	9-13	9-13	10-0	10-0	10-0	10-0	10-0	10-0
9f	3	8-6	8-6	8-7	8-7	8-8	8-9	8-11	8-13
	4	9-13	9-13	10-0	10-0	10-0	10-0	10-0	10-0
10f	3	8-5	8-5	8-6	8-6	8-7	8-8	8-9	8-11
	4	9-12	9-12	9-13	9-13	10-0	10-0	10-0	10-0
11f	3	8-4	8-4	8-5	8-5	8-6	8-7	8-8	8-9
	4	9-11	9-11	9-12	9-12	9-13	9-13	10-0	10-0
12f	3	8-3	8-3	8-4	8-4	8-5	8-6	8-7	8-8
	4	9-10	9-10	9-11	9-11	9-12	9-12	9-13	9-13
13f	3	8-2	8-2	8-3	8-3	8-4	8-5	8-6	8-7
	4	9-9	9-9	9-10	9-10	9-11	9-11	9-12	9-13
14f	3	8-1	8-1	8-2	8-2	8-3	8-4	8-5	8-6
	4	9-8	9-8	9-9	9-9	9-10	9-10	9-11	9-12
15f	3	8-0	8-0	8-1	8-1	8-2	8-3	8-4	8-5
	4	9-8	9-8	9-9	9-9	9-10	9-10	9-11	9-11
16f	3	7-13	7-13	8-0	8-0	8-1	8-2	8-3	8-4
	4	9-7	9-7	9-8	9-8	9-9	9-9	9-10	9-10
18f	3	7-11	7-11	7-12	7-12	7-13	8-0	8-1	8-2
	4	9-6	9-6	9-7	9-7	9-8	9-8	9-9	9-9
20f	3	7-9	7-9	7-10	7-10	7-11	7-12	7-13	8-0
	4	9-5	9-5	9-6	9-6	9-7	9-7	9-8	9-8

Scale Of Age, Weight And Distance

Dist	Age	MAY 1-15	MAY 16-31	JUNE 1-15	JUNE 16-30	JULY 1-15	JULY 16-31	AUG 1-15	AUG 16-31
5f	2	7-4	7-6	7-8	7-10	7-12	8-0	8-2	8-4
	3	9-5	9-6	9-7	9-8	9-9	9-10	9-11	9-12
	4	10-0	10-0	10-0	10-0	10-0	10-0	10-0	10-0
6f	2	6-12	7-1	7-4	7-6	7-9	7-11	8-0	8-2
	3	9-4	9-5	9-6	9-7	9-8	9-9	9-10	9-11
	4	10-0	10-0	10-0	10-0	10-0	10-0	10-0	10-0
7f	2					7-4	7-7	7-10	7-12
	3	9-2	9-3	9-4	9-5	9-6	9-7	9-8	9-9
	4	10-0	10-0	10-0	10-0	10-0	10-0	10-0	10-0
8f	2							7-5	7-8
	3	9-1	9-2	9-3	9-4	9-5	9-6	9-7	9-8
	4	9-13	9-13	10-0	10-0	10-0	10-0	10-0	10-0
9f	3	9-0	9-1	9-2	9-3	9-4	9-5	9-6	9-7
	4	10-0	10-0	10-0	10-0	10-0	10-0	10-0	10-0
10f	3	8-13	9-0	9-1	9-2	9-3	9-4	9-5	9-6
	4	10-0	10-0	10-0	10-0	10-0	10-0	10-0	10-0
11f	3	8-11	8-13	9-0	9-1	9-2	9-3	9-4	9-5
	4	10-0	10-0	10-0	10-0	10-0	10-0	10-0	10-0
12f	3	8-9	8-11	8-13	9-0	9-1	9-2	9-3	9-4
	4	10-0	10-0	10-0	10-0	10-0	10-0	10-0	10-0
13f	3	8-8	8-9	8-11	8-13	9-0	9-1	9-2	9-3
	4	10-0	10-0	10-0	10-0	10-0	10-0	10-0	10-0
14f	3	8-7	8-8	8-9	8-11	8-13	9-0	9-1	9-2
	4	9-13	10-0	10-0	10-0	10-0	10-0	10-0	10-0
15f	3	8-6	8-7	8-8	8-9	8-11	8-13	9-0	9-1
	4	9-12	9-13	10-0	10-0	10-0	10-0	10-0	10-0
16f	3	8-5	8-6	8-7	8-8	8-9	8-11	8-13	9-0
	4	9-11	9-12	9-13	10-0	10-0	10-0	10-0	10-0
18f	3	8-3	8-4	8-5	8-6	8-7	8-8	8-10	8-12
	4	9-10	9-11	9-12	9-13	10-0	10-0	10-0	10-0
20f	3	8-1	8-2	8-3	8-4	8-5	8-6	8-8	8-10
	4	9-9	9-10	9-11	9-12	9-13	10-0	10-0	10-0

Scale Of Age, Weight And Distance

Dist	Age	SEPT 1-15	SEPT 16-30	OCT 1-15	OCT 16-30	NOV 1-15	NOV 16-30	DEC 1-15	DEC 16-31
5f	2	8-6	8-8	8-9	8-10	8-11	8-11	8-12	8-12
	3	9-13	9-13	10-0	10-0	10-0	10-0	10-0	10-0
	4	10-0	10-0	10-0	10-0	10-0	10-0	10-0	10-0
6f	2	8-4	8-6	8-7	8-8	8-9	8-10	8-11	8-11
	3	9-12	9-12	9-13	9-13	10-0	10-0	10-0	10-0
	4	10-0	10-0	10-0	10-0	10-0	10-0	10-0	10-0
7f	2	8-1	8-2	8-5	8-6	8-7	8-8	8-9	8-9
	3	9-10	9-11	9-12	9-12	9-13	9-13	10-0	10-0
	4	10-0	10-0	10-0	10-0	10-0	10-0	10-0	10-0
8f	2	7-11	8-0	8-2	8-4	8-5	8-6	8-7	8-8
	3	9-9	9-10	9-11	9-11	9-12	9-12	9-13	9-13
	4	9-13	9-13	10-0	10-0	10-0	10-0	10-0	10-0
9f	3	9-8	9-9	9-10	9-10	9-11	9-11	9-12	9-12
	4	10-0	10-0	10-0	10-0	10-0	10-0	10-0	10-0
10f	3	9-7	9-8	9-9	9-9	9-10	9-10	9-11	9-11
	4	10-0	10-0	10-0	10-0	10-0	10-0	10-0	10-0
11f	3	9-6	9-7	9-8	9-8	9-9	9-9	9-10	9-10
	4	10-0	10-0	10-0	10-0	10-0	10-0	10-0	10-0
12f	3	9-5	9-6	9-7	9-7	9-8	9-8	9-9	9-9
	4	10-0	10-0	10-0	10-0	10-0	10-0	10-0	10-0
13f	3	9-4	9-5	9-6	9-6	9-7	9-7	9-8	9-8
	4	10-0	10-0	10-0	10-0	10-0	10-0	10-0	10-0
14f	3	9-3	9-4	9-5	9-5	9-6	9-6	9-7	9-7
	4	10-0	10-0	10-0	10-0	10-0	10-0	10-0	10-0
15f	3	9-2	9-3	9-4	9-5	9-6	9-6	9-7	9-7
	4	10-0	10-0	10-0	10-0	10-0	10-0	10-0	10-0
16f	3	9-1	9-2	9-3	9-4	9-5	9-5	9-6	9-6
	4	10-0	10-0	10-0	10-0	10-0	10-0	10-0	10-0
18f	3	9-0	9-1	9-2	9-3	9-4	9-4	9-5	9-5
	4	10-0	10-0	10-0	10-0	10-0	10-0	10-0	10-0
20f	3	8-12	9-0	9-1	9-2	9-3	9-3	9-4	9-4
	4	10-0	10-0	10-0	10-0	10-0	10-0	10-0	10-0